2019 Canadian
Key Business Directory
Répertoire des principales entreprises Canadiennes 2019

Volume 2

This directory is the property of Mergent Inc.
Ce répertoire est la propriété de Mergent Inc.
Mergent Inc.
444 Madison Ave, Suite 1710
New York, NY 10022

Copyright © 2019

ISBN 978-1-64141-257-5
Printed in the U.S.A.

T0407783

Disclaimer

Any purchaser, reader or user of this directory assumes all responsibility for actions taken as a result of information provided herein. Any purchaser, reader or user agrees that D&B, its employees, subsidiaries and partners hold no liability for the interpretations derived from this directory and any subsequent actions taken as a result of that interpretation including, but not limited to, advertising, direct mailing, telemarketing and business decisions.

Démenti

N'importe quel acheteur, lecteur ou utilisateur de ce répertoire assume toute la responsabilité des mesures prises en raison des informations fournies ci-inclus. N'importe quel acheteur, lecteur ou utilisateur sont en accord que D&B, ses employés, les subsidiaires et les associés ne tiennent aucune responsabilité pour les traductions dérives de ce répertoire et d'aucune mesure subséquent pris en raison de cette interprétation.

Notice concerning use for compilation or dissemination to third parties

Subscribers to D&B Canada publications are not authorized, even on occasion, to use any D&B publication to: compile mailing lists, marketing aids, and other types of data, for sales or otherwise to a third party. Any subscriber doing so will be in direct violation of the contractual agreement under which the Directory is provided to the subscriber. D&B Canada does not permit or acquiesce in such uses of its publications. Any subscriber or other person who does not understand any aspect of this policy, please contact: D&B's Corporate Marketing and Public Affairs office at 1.800.INFO.DNB (1.800.463.6362).

Avis concernant l'utilisation aux fins de dissémination à une tierce partie

Les souscripteurs aux publications de D&B ne sont pas autorisés à utiliser, même occasionnellement, ces publications pour compiler des listes d'adresses, des supports à la commercialisation et d'autres types d'informations, et à les vendre, sinon les offrir à une tierce partie. Tout souscripteur qui agit ainsi est en violation de l'entente contractuelle sous laquelle le répertoire est fourni au souscripteur. D&B ne permet pas et n'accepte pas que ses publications soient utilisées pour les fins précitées. Tout souscripteur ou autre personne qui s'engage dans des actions non autorisées ou qui les encourage doit s'attendre à subir des conséquences d'ordre juridique et financier. Aucun amendement ou renonciation à l'entente n'engage les parties, à moins d'être exprimés par écrit et signés par un fondé de pouvoir de D&B Canada et par le souscripteur. Au cas où un souscripteur, ou toute autre personne, aurait des doutes quant à l'une des dispositions de cette politique, veuillez communiquer avec le Service de commercialisation et des affaires publiques de D&B Canada au 1.800.INFO.DNB (1.800.463.6362).

What's Inside?
Le contenu

Volume 1

Employee Stats, Statistical and County Counts

Section I   Geographic Index

An alphabetical listing of businesses by geographic location.
Business information listed includes all details outlined above.

Inscriptions par région géographique

Une liste des entreprises dans l'ordre alphabétique par région géographique.
Chaque inscription comporte tous les éléments ci-dessus

Volume 2

Section II   Line of Business Index SIC Codes

A numerical listing of businesses by SIC Code.
Business information listed includes all details outlined above.
An SIC Code table is available at the end of this section.

Inscriptions par domaine d'exploitation Codes C.I.S.

Une liste des entreprises dans l'ordre numérique par code C.I.S.
Chaque inscription comporte tous les éléments ci-dessus.
Un tableau des codes C.I.S. figure à la fin de cette section.

Section III   Alphabetic Listing

An alphabetical listing of businesses.
Business information listed includes:
Legal business name and address; reference to parent company; number of employees; sales
volume; space occupied; headquarters, branch, single location indicator; primary line of business
(SIC code) and description; D-U-N-S® Number; officers and management contact names on file.

Source d'information centrale inscriptions dans l'ordre alphabétique

Une liste des entreprises dans l'ordre alphabétique.
Chaque inscription comporte les renseignements suivants :
Raison sociale juridique de l'entreprise et son adresse, une référence à la compagnie mère, la taille
du personnel, le chiffre d'affaires, la surface occupée, un indicateur siège social, succursale,
emplacement unique, le domaine d'exploitation principal (code C.I.S.) et une description, le numéro
D-U-N-S®, les personnes-ressources au sein des membres du bureau de direction et de la direction
disponibles.

Key Business Terms Used by D&B

Branch: A secondary location of a company reporting to a headquarters or subsidiary. Branches carry the same primary name as their headquarters and can only report to a headquarters of subsidiary establishment.

Division: A separate operating unit of a corporation with a division name, performing a specific activity.

Headquarters: An establishment that has a branch or branches operating under the same legal name.

Parent: A business establishment that controls another company through ownership of all or a majority of its shares.

Single Location: A business establishment with no branches reporting to it. A single location may be a parent or subsidiary.

Subsidiary: A corporation which is more than 50% owned by another company. Subsidiary companies are formed for several purposes. The subsidiary may conduct business totally different from that of the parent company, or may be at a different location.

D-U-N-S® Number: The D-U-N-S® Number is proprietary to D&B and helps to distinguish a business and identify it as a unique establishment. Assigned and maintained by D&B, these computer generated numbers provide common identification standards for most business establishments.

Trade Name: A trade name is used by a business for advertising and buying purposes. This should not be confused with a branch or division name. A trade name does not have to be registered.

Glossaire des mots clés de D&B

Compagnie mère : Une compagnie qui contrôle une autre compagnie grâce à la possession de toutes ou d'une tranche majoritaire des actions de cette compagnie.

Division : Une unité particulière d'une compagnie avec sa dénomination et ses propres actvtés. Une division peut comporter des membres du bureau de direction mais n'a pas de capital et n'est pas constituée en compagnie.

Emplacement unique : Un établissement commercial qui n'exploite pas de succursale. Un emplacement unique peut être une compagnie mère et, ou, un filiale.

Filiale : Une compagnie dont plus de 50 % des actions sont détenues par une autre compagnie. Une filiale peut être constituée pour diverses raisons. Les activités d'une filiale peuvent être totalement différentes de celles de la compagnie mère, et elle peut être exploitée d'un emplacement différent.

Numéros D-U-N-S® : Les numéros D-U-N-S® servent à l'identification de chaque établissement unique. Affectés et mis à jour par D&B, ces numéros d'identification informatisés s'avèrent la norme en matière d'identification des établissements commerciaux.

Profil commercial (appellation commerciale) : Une dénomination utilisée par une entreprise aux fins de publicité et, ou, d'achat. À ne pas confondre avec une dénomination de succursale ou de division. Un profil commercial peut être enregistré ou non.

Siège social : Une entreprise qui exploite une ou des succursales sous la même raison sociale reconnue.

Succursale : Un emplacement secondaire d'une compagnie relevant du siège social ou d'une filiale. Une succursale est exploitée sous la même raison sociale principale que le siège social et relève exclusivement du siège social ou d'une filiale.

How to Use a D&B Canadian Directory Listing

The D&B Canadian Directories together, contain more than 140,000 business listings and close to 500,000 contact names. The types of businesses reported on varies between directories.

The Canadian Key Business Directory

This directory contains listings of Canadian businesses with one or more of the following: $5 million in sales, 50 employees at a single or headquarters location, or 250 employees total. Public and private schools are excluded.

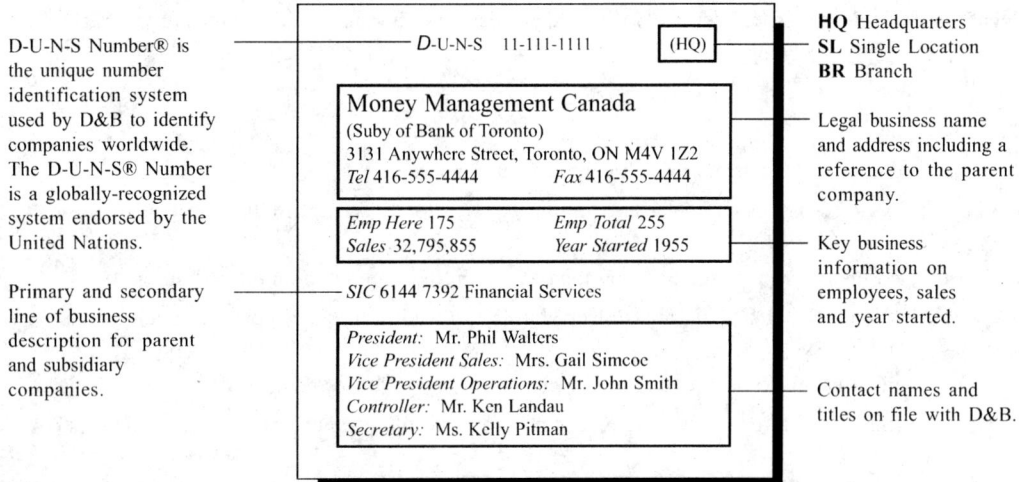

D-U-N-S Number® is the unique number identification system used by D&B to identify companies worldwide. The D-U-N-S® Number is a globally-recognized system endorsed by the United Nations.

Primary and secondary line of business description for parent and subsidiary companies.

HQ Headquarters
SL Single Location
BR Branch

Legal business name and address including a reference to the parent company.

Key business information on employees, sales and year started.

Contact names and titles on file with D&B.

D-U-N-S 11-111-1111 (HQ)

Money Management Canada
(Suby of Bank of Toronto)
3131 Anywhere Street, Toronto, ON M4V 1Z2
Tel 416-555-4444   *Fax* 416-555-4444

Emp Here 175   *Emp Total* 255
Sales 32,795,855   *Year Started* 1955

SIC 6144 7392 Financial Services

President: Mr. Phil Walters
Vice President Sales: Mrs. Gail Simcoe
Vice President Operations: Mr. John Smith
Controller: Mr. Ken Landau
Secretary: Ms. Kelly Pitman

Utilisation des inscriptions dans les répertoires canadiens de D&B

Au total, les répertoires commerciaux canadiens de D&B comportent plus de 140 000 inscriptions d'entreprises et près de 500 000 de personnes-ressources. Les types d'entreprises répertoriées varient d'un répertoire à l'autre.

Le Répertoire des principales entreprises canadiennes

Ce répertoire comporte les inscriptions des entreprises canadiennes qui répondent à un ou plus des critères suivants : chiffre d'affaires de 5 millions de dollars, personnel de 50 au siège social ou à un emplacement unique, ou de 250 au total. Les maisons d'enseignement publiques et privées ne sont pas répertoriées.

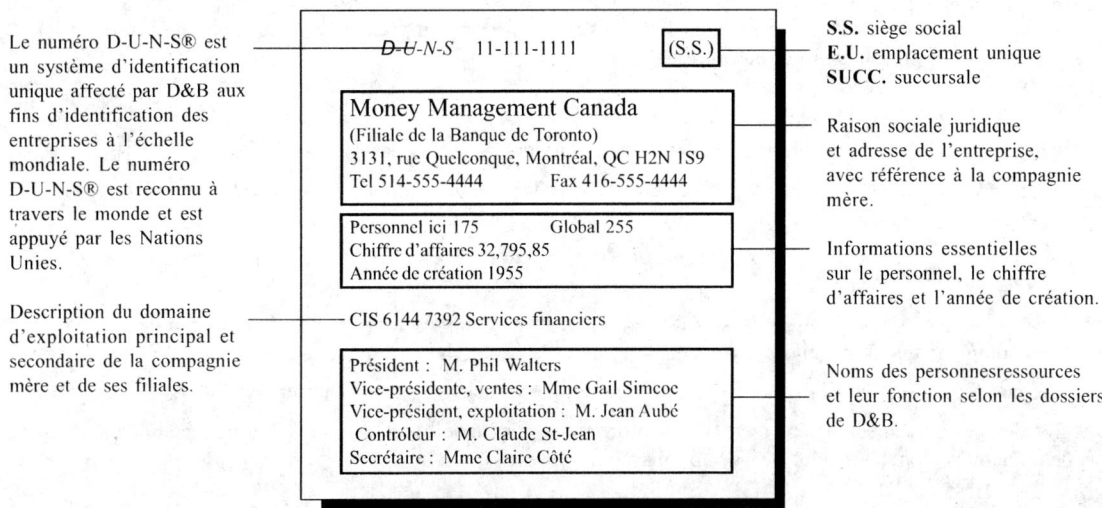

Le numéro D-U-N-S® est un système d'identification unique affecté par D&B aux fins d'identification des entreprises à l'échelle mondiale. Le numéro D-U-N-S® est reconnu à travers le monde et est appuyé par les Nations Unies.

Description du domaine d'exploitation principal et secondaire de la compagnie mère et de ses filiales.

S.S. siège social
E.U. emplacement unique
SUCC. succursale

Raison sociale juridique et adresse de l'entreprise, avec référence à la compagnie mère.

Informations essentielles sur le personnel, le chiffre d'affaires et l'année de création.

Noms des personnesressources et leur fonction selon les dossiers de D&B.

D-U-N-S 11-111-1111 (S.S.)

Money Management Canada
(Filiale de la Banque de Toronto)
3131, rue Quelconque, Montréal, QC H2N 1S9
Tel 514-555-4444   Fax 416-555-4444

Personnel ici 175   Global 255
Chiffre d'affaires 32,795,85
Année de création 1955

CIS 6144 7392 Services financiers

Président : M. Phil Walters
Vice-présidente, ventes : Mme Gail Simcoe
Vice-président, exploitation : M. Jean Aubé
 Contrôleur : M. Claude St-Jean
Secrétaire : Mme Claire Côté

D&B D-U-N-S® Number

In today's global economy, D&B's Data Universal Numbering System, the D&B D-U-N-S® Number, has become the standard for keeping track of more than 97 million businesses and their corporate relationships worldwide. D-U-N-S® Numbers are unique nine-digit identification sequences that act as the nuts and bolts of D&B's database. They provide a secure identification for individual business entities while linking corporate family structures. Used by the world's most influential standards-setting organizations, the D-U-N-S® Number is recognized, recommended or required by more than 50 global associations including the United Nations, the U.S. Federal Government and the European Community.

D&B is the global market leader in the provision of risk management, sales and marketing and supply management information. With the D-U-N-S® Number, D&B can help you gain access to and maintain the information you need to manage your business.

D-U-N-S® Numbers can help you:

- Consolidate, cleanse and eliminate duplicate records within your databases
- Streamline the information held in disparate databases and improve customer service by linking related customer accounts to support a "one customer" view
- Identify risk exposure and highlight cross-selling opportunities within the same corporate family group
- Integrate your internal systems by linking payables/receivables and tracking business documentation to the business entity and location level
- Link interrelated suppliers to enable you to leverage your corporate buying power
- Integrate additional demographic information from D&B to provide a profile of your customers, suppliers and prospects

Le numéro D-U-N-S® D&B

Dans l'économie à l'échelle mondiale d'aujourd'hui, le Système de numérotage universel de données D&B, le numéro D-U-N-S® D&B, est devenu la norme d'identification de plus de 97 millions d'entreprises et de leurs affiliations corporatives à travers le monde. Les numéros D-U-N-S® D&B sont un numéro d'identification unique à neuf chiffres et ils constituent l'élément d'association primordial dans la base de données D&B. Ils permettent l'identification de chaque entreprise et l'association d'entreprises qui sont membres d'une même famille corporative. Utilisés par les organismes mondiaux les plus influents en matière d'établissement de normes, ils sont reconnus, recommandés ou requis par plus de 50 associations mondiales, y compris l'organisation des Nations Unies, le Gouvernement fédéral des É.-U. et la Communauté européenne.

D&B est le premier fournisseur mondial d'information en matière de gestion du risque, de vente, de marketing et de gestion de l'approvisionnement. Le numéro D-U-N-S® D&B vous permet l'accès à et le stockage de l'information dont vous avez besoin pour la gestion de votre entreprise.

Les numéros D-U-N-S® vous permettent :

- De consolider, de nettoyer et d'éliminer les doubles de dossiers dans vos bases de données
- De rationaliser l'information stockée dans diverses bases de données et d'améliorer le service à la clientèle en associant des comptes de clients affiliés pour répondre aux besoins du "client principal"
- D'identifier le niveau du risque et les opportunités de croisement de clientèle au sein d'un groupe de familles corporatives
- D'intégrer vos systèmes internes par l'association des fonctions comptes fournisseurs / comptes clients et de documents commerciaux, à une entité commerciale et au niveau de l'emplacement
- D'associer des fournisseurs affiliés afin d'optimiser le pouvoir d'achat de votre entreprise
- D'intégrer des renseignements supplémentaires d'ordre démographique obtenus de D&B afin d'établir un profil de vos clients actuels et potentiels et de vos fournisseurs

Put the D-U-N-S® Number at the Core of Your Sales and Marketing, Risk Management and Supply Management Operations

- Within enterprise wide solutions, the D-U-N-S® Number ensures accurate data—giving you confidence in the quality of the information you use to manage your business.

- In database marketing applications, D-U-N-S® Numbering allows customers to use D&B's demographic information to profile their best customers and create a model using their characteristics to identify which business are their warmest prospects.

- In risk management, the D-U-N-S® Number can link customer files to respective parent companies to provide a view of your total credit exposure within a single corporate family. This insight into customers' corporate structures means that credit limits can be managed intelligently and collections efforts prioritized.

- The D-U-N-S® Number helps ensure receivables management efforts are carefully managed and properly targeted by pinpointing customer locations and identifying important corporate relationships.

- In supply management, the D-U-N-S® Number enables a better understanding of your supplier base by helping identify duplicate records and providing linkage information on supplier family trees. This understanding allows you to leverage your purchasing power, cut costs out of the purchasing process and reduce the number of redundant suppliers worldwide.

- For companies with an e-commerce strategy, the D-U-N-S® Number can be used as a means of identifying suppliers, trading partners and customers. Companies wishing to be recognized as a credible supplier of online services can use their D-U-N-S® Number as a means of identification allowing potential customers to verify their business credentials before starting a trading relationship.

Intégrez le numéro D-U-N-S® au sein de vos activités de vente et de marketing, de gestion du risque et de gestion de l'approvisionnement

- Peu importe les solutions utilisées au sein de votre entreprise, le numéro D-U-N-S® assure l'exactitude des données - vous pouvez ainsi avoir confiance à la qualité de l'information que vous utilisez dans la gestion de votre entreprise.

- Pour les applications base de données de marketing, le numéro D-U-N-S® permet aux clients d'utiliser l'information d'ordre démographique de D&B afin d'établir un profil de leurs meilleurs clients, et de créer un modèle en se fondant sur leurs caractéristiques pour identifier les entreprises qui s'avèrent les meilleurs clients potentiels.

- En matière de gestion du risque, le numéro D-U-N-S® permet d'associer des dossiers de clients à leur compagnie mère respective afin d'obtenir une vue d'ensemble du risque relatif à toute une famille corporative. Cette vue d'ensemble d'une structure corporative permet une gestion intelligente des plafonds de crédit et l'établissement d'un ordre de priorité en ce qui a trait aux mesures de recouvrement.

- Le numéro D-U-N-S® aide à assurer que la gestion des comptes clients est bien planifiée et bien orientée, par l'identification des emplacements des clients et des liens corporatifs importants.

- En matière de gestion de l'approvisionnement, le numéro D-U-N-S® vous permet de bien connaître votre base de fournisseurs en vous permettant d'identifier les dossiers en double et les liens du réseau filiales de vos fournisseurs. Ainsi, vous êtes en mesure d'optimiser votre pouvoir d'achat, de diminuer vos coûts d'approvisionnement et de réduire le surnombre de fournisseurs à l'échelle internationale.

- En matière de commerce électronique, le numéro D-U-N-S® s'avère une façon d'identifier les fournisseurs, les partenaires d'affaires et les clients. Les entreprises qui souhaitent être reconnues comme un fournisseur fiable de services en ligne, peuvent utiliser leur numéro D-U-N-S® à titre d'élément d'identification ce qui permet aux clients potentiels de vérifier leur situation commerciale avant d'amorcer une relation d'affaires.

How is a D-U-N-S® Number Assigned?

The D-U-N-S® Number is solely maintained by D&B. When a business is first entered into the D&B business information database we assign each location that has its own unique, separate and distinct operation, its own D-U-N-S® Number. For more information call 1.800.INFO.DNB (1.800.463.6362) or visit www.dnb.ca.

Comment un numéro D-U-N-S® est-il affecté?

Seule D&B affecte un numéro D-U-N-S®. Lors de l'intégration d'une entreprise à la base de données commerciale D&B, nous affectons un numéro D-U-N-S® unique à chacun des emplacements avec des activités particulières, indépendantes et distinctes. Pour plus de renseignements, veuillez composer 1.800.INFO.DNB (1.800.463.6362) ou visiter www.dnb.ca/fr.

D&B Ensures Data Accuracy with our Trademarked DUNSRight™ Quality Process

The DUNSRight™Quality Process is D&B's quality assurance program to ensure data quality. Our five quality drivers:

- *Global Data Collection* brings together data from a variety of worldwide sources
- *Entity Matching* is a patented process that produces a single, accurate picture of each business and our next generation of matching technology will help you find more businesses in our database
- *D-U-N-S® Numbers,* unique to each business, are a means of identifying and tracking every activity of a business
- *Corporate Linkage* exposes risk by showing related businesses such as subsidiaries and parent companies
- *Predictive Indicators* use statistical analysis to indicate how companies may perform in the future

L'exactitude des données D&B est assurée par notre processus de qualité breveté DUNSRight™

Le processus de qualité DUNSRight™ est le programme d'assurance de la qualité des données D&B. Voici nos cinq moteurs de la qualité :

- *Collecte de données internationales* auprès de nombreuses sources à travers le monde
- *Assortiment d'entités*, un processus breveté qui donne une image précise de chaque entreprise, notre prochaine génération de technologies vous permettra d'avoir accès à davantage d'entreprises dans notre base de donnée
- *Numéros D-U-N-S®*, un numéro unique affecté à chaque entreprise aux fins d'identification et de suivi de toutes les activités d'une entreprise
- *Association de sociétés,* signale le risque en précisant les entreprises affiliées telles les filiales et les compagnies mères
- *Indicateurs de prévision,* fondés sur une analyste statistique, ils indiquent comment une entreprise est susceptible de se comporter ultérieurement

2019 Canadian Key Business Directory
Répertoire des principales entreprises Canadiennes 2019

Section II

Line of Business Index
SIC Codes

Inscriptions par
domaine d'exploitation
Codes C.I.S.

SIC 0111 Wheat

BENCH HUTTERIAN BRETHREN CORP p1435
HWY 13 W, SHAUNAVON, SK, S0N 2M0
(306) 297-3270 *SIC 0111*

MILFORD COLONY FARMING CO. LTD p153
GD, RAYMOND, AB, T0K 2S0
(403) 752-4478 *SIC 0111*

OAKLANE HUTTERIAN BRETHREN p169
GD STN MAIN, TABER, AB, T1G 2E5
(403) 223-2950 *SIC 0111*

SIC 0119 Cash grains, nec

BERETTA FARMS INC p582
80 GALAXY BLVD UNIT 1, ETOBICOKE, ON, M9W 4Y8
(416) 674-5609 *SIC 0119*

BIG G HOLDINGS LTD p1413
GD, PENNANT STATION, SK, S0N 1X0
(306) 626-3249 *SIC 0119*

BRANTWOOD COLONY FARMS LTD p354
GD, OAKVILLE, MB, R0H 0Y0
(204) 267-2527 *SIC 0119*

BRITESTONE HUTTERIAN BRETHREN p79
GD, CARBON, AB, T0M 0L0
(403) 572-3046 *SIC 0119*

DEERBOINE COLONY FARMS LTD p345
GD, ALEXANDER, MB, R0K 0A0
(204) 728-7383 *SIC 0119*

FAIRVIEW COLONY p81
GD, CROSSFIELD, AB, T0M 0S0
(403) 946-4524 *SIC 0119*

GOLDRIDGE FARMING CO. LTD p170
GD, TURIN, AB, T0K 2H0
(403) 359-5111 *SIC 0119*

HURON COLONY FARMS LTD p349
64082 ROAD 17W, ELIE, MB, R0H 0H0
(204) 353-2704 *SIC 0119*

HUTTERIAN BRETHREN LTD p1427
GD STN MAIN, SASKATOON, SK, S7K 3J4
(306) 242-5652 *SIC 0119*

HUTTERIAN BRETHREN OF ARM RIVER COLONY LTD p1409
PO BOX 570, LUMSDEN, SK, S0G 3C0
(306) 731-2819 *SIC 0119*

HUTTERIAN BRETHREN OF GOLDEN VIEW INC p1404
GD, BIGGAR, SK, S0K 0M0
(306) 948-2716 *SIC 0119*

HUTTERIAN BRETHREN OF RED WILLOW p167
GD, STETTLER, AB, T0C 2L0
(403) 742-3988 *SIC 0119*

HUTTERIAN BRETHREN OF SOUTH BEND p3
1539 12 WEST OF 4TH, ALLIANCE, AB, T0B 0A0
(780) 879-2170 *SIC 0119*

J.R.T. FARM LTD p179
2396 272 ST, ALDERGROVE, BC, V4W 2R1
(604) 856-5552 *SIC 0119*

KIM'S FARM p279
4186 176 ST, SURREY, BC, V3Z 1C3
(604) 649-7938 *SIC 0119*

R ROBITAILLE ET FILS INC p1315
4000 CH BENOIT, SAINT-JEAN-BAPTISTE, QC, J0L 2B0
(450) 795-3915 *SIC 0119*

ROWLAND SEEDS INC p169
6210 64 ST, TABER, AB, T1G 1Z3
(403) 223-8164 *SIC 0119*

SPRING VALLEY COLONY FARMS LTD p347
GD, BRANDON, MB, R7A 5Y4
(204) 728-3830 *SIC 0119*

STAR CITY FARMING CO. LTD p1436
GD, STAR CITY, SK, S0E 1P0
(306) 863-2343 *SIC 0119*

WELLWOOD COLONY FARMS LTD p353
GD, NINETTE, MB, R0K 1R0

(204) 776-2130 *SIC 0119*

SIC 0132 Tobacco

DALTON WHITE FARMS & SUPPLIES LIMITED p564
802 JAMES ST, DELHI, ON, N4B 2E1
(519) 582-2864 *SIC 0132*

PAT POLLOCK FARM p493
10972 TALBOT TRAIL, BLENHEIM, ON, N0P 1A0
(519) 380-5940 *SIC 0132*

SIC 0134 Irish potatoes

CULBERSON, RALPH B & SONS LTD p404
682 ROUTE 560, JACKSONVILLE, NB, E7M 3J8
(506) 328-4366 *SIC 0134*

GERARD BERGERON & FILS INC p1343
1486 RANG BARTHELEMY, SAINT-LEON, QC, J0K 2W0
(819) 228-3936 *SIC 0134*

KROEKER FARMS LIMITED p361
777 CIRCLE K DR, WINKLER, MB, R6W 0K7
(204) 325-4333 *SIC 0134*

L.F.OAKES & SONS LTD. p404
259 MCELROY RD, HOLMESVILLE, NB, E7J 2J4
SIC 0134

ROLLO BAY HOLDINGS LTD p1042
677 2 RTE RR 4, SOURIS, PE, C0A 2B0
(902) 687-3333 *SIC 0134*

SOUTHERN MANITOBA POTATO CO. LTD p361
375 NORTH RAILWAY AVE, WINKLER, MB, R6W 1J4
(204) 325-4318 *SIC 0134*

SIC 0139 Field crops, except cash grain

1019884 ONTARIO INC p596
1913 KINGSDALE AVE, GLOUCESTER, ON, K1T 1H9
SIC 0139

FARMER'S EDGE WEST INC p138
3413 53 AVE, LACOMBE, AB, T4L 0C6
(403) 782-2204 *SIC 0139*

GRAND COLONY FARMS LTD p354
20125 ROAD 57N, OAKVILLE, MB, R0H 0Y0
(204) 267-2292 *SIC 0139*

GV COLONY FARMING CO. LTD p134
723042A RANGE ROAD 74, GRANDE PRAIRIE, AB, T8X 4L1
(780) 539-6513 *SIC 0139*

HUTTERIAN BERTHEREN CHURCH OF QUILL LAKE INC p1415
GD, QUILL LAKE, SK, S0A 3E0
(306) 383-2989 *SIC 0139*

PRAIRIEVIEW SEED POTATOES LTD p170
162035 TOWNSHIP RD 125, VAUXHALL, AB, T0K 2K0
(403) 654-2475 *SIC 0139*

PRODUCTIONS MARAICHERES BOURGET & FRERES INC, LES p1151
410 BOUL SAINTE-MARGUERITE, MERCIER, QC, J6R 2L1
(450) 691-0468 *SIC 0139*

SHOKER FARMS LTD p197
46825 BAILEY RD, CHILLIWACK, BC, V2R 4S8
(604) 824-1541 *SIC 0139*

SONNY NAKASHIMA FARMS LTD p8
GD, BURDETT, AB, T0K 0J0
(403) 655-2270 *SIC 0139*

SIC 0161 Vegetables and melons

132082 CANADA INC p1294
250 CH BELLA-VISTA, SAINT-BASILE-LE-GRAND, QC, J3N 1L1
(450) 461-1988 *SIC 0161*

9329-5558 QUEBEC INC p1357
1596 1ER RANG, SAINTE-CLOTILDE-DE-CHATEAUGUAY, QC, J0L 1W0
(514) 807-0707 *SIC 0161*

BEVO FARMS LTD p226
7170 GLOVER RD, LANGLEY, BC, V2Y 2R1
(604) 888-0420 *SIC 0161*

BRAD, D FARM LTD p836
4939 BRADLEY LINE, PAIN COURT, ON, N0P 1Z0
SIC 0161

CAN-AM PEPPER COMPANY LTD p482
52999 JOHN WISE LINE, AYLMER, ON, N5H 2R5
(519) 773-3250 *SIC 0161*

CENTRE MARAICHER EUGENE GUINOIS JR INC p1357
555 4E RANG, SAINTE-CLOTILDE-DE-CHATEAUGUAY, QC, J0L 1W0
(450) 826-3207 *SIC 0161*

CLOVIS ISABELLE ET FILS INC. p1348
2420 RUE PRINCIPALE, SAINT-MICHEL, QC, J0L 2J0
(450) 454-7200 *SIC 0161*

CULTURES DE CHEZ NOUS INC, LES p1356
1120 9E RANG, SAINTE-BRIGITTE-DES-SAULTS, QC, J0C 1E0
(819) 336-4846 *SIC 0161*

DI CIOCCO FARMS INCORPORATED p644
308 TALBOT RD E, LEAMINGTON, ON, N8H 3V6
(519) 326-2339 *SIC 0161*

FERME E NOTARO ET FILS INC, LES p1376
307 RANG SAINT-FRANCOIS, SHERRINGTON, QC, J0L 2N0
(450) 454-3567 *SIC 0161*

FERME MARAICHERE A. GUINOIS & FILS INC p1314
50 RANG SAINT-PHILIPPE N, SAINT-JACQUES-LE-MINEUR, QC, J0J 1Z0
(450) 515-5212 *SIC 0161*

FERME VERNIER, BENOIT INC p1354
800 RUE PRINCIPALE, SAINT-ZOTIQUE, QC, J0P 1Z0
SIC 0161

FERMES DU SOLEIL INC, LES p1357
800 2E RANG UNITE 2, SAINTE-CLOTILDE-DE-CHATEAUGUAY, QC, J0L 1W0
(450) 826-3401 *SIC 0161*

FERMES HOTTE ET VAN WINDEN INC, LES p1298
316 RANG SAINT-ANDRE, SAINT-CYPRIEN-DE-NAPIERVILLE, QC, J0J 1L0
(450) 245-3433 *SIC 0161*

FERMES J.-F. & C. GAGNON INC., LES p1352
804 RANG DU RUISSEAU-DES-ANGES S, SAINT-ROCH-DE-L'ACHIGAN, QC, J0K 3H0
(450) 588-2226 *SIC 0161*

FERMES PIGEON, ROLAND & FILS INC, LES p1351
1495 RANG NOTRE-DAME, SAINT-REMI, QC, J0L 2L0
(450) 454-3433 *SIC 0161*

FERMES SERBI INC, LES p1301
841 25E AV, SAINT-EUSTACHE, QC, J7R 4K3
(450) 623-2369 *SIC 0161*

GREENWAY FARMS LTD p279
5040 160 ST SUITE 5040, SURREY, BC, V3Z 1E8
(604) 574-1564 *SIC 0161*

GUINOIS R. G. R. INC p1357
522 4E RANG, SAINTE-CLOTILDE-DE-CHATEAUGUAY, QC, J0L 1W0
(450) 826-3140 *SIC 0161*

HACIENDA NORTH FARMS INC p1013
2961 TALBOT TRAIL, WHEATLEY, ON, N0P 2P0
(519) 800-5062 *SIC 0161*

HYDROSERRE INC p1153
9200 RUE DESVOYAUX, MIRABEL, QC, J7N 2H4
(450) 475-7924 *SIC 0161*

JARDINS PAUL COUSINEAU & FILS INC, LES p1298
701 RANG SAINT-PIERRE N, SAINT-CONSTANT, QC, J5A 0R2
(450) 635-9000 *SIC 0161*

KOMIENSKI LIMITED p879
4665 HIGHWAY 24 RR 3, SCOTLAND, ON, N0E 1R0
(519) 446-2315 *SIC 0161*

KOTELES FARMS LIMITED p912
164700 NEW RD SUITE 2, TILLSONBURG, ON, N4G 4G7
(519) 842-5425 *SIC 0161*

LEGUMIERE Y.C. INC, LA p1351
1463 RANG SAINTE-THERESE, SAINT-REMI, QC, J0L 2L0
(450) 454-9437 *SIC 0161*

MILES PRODUCE LTD p1006
1701 OLD HIGHWAY 24, WATERFORD, ON, N0E 1Y0
(519) 443-7227 *SIC 0161*

ORANGELINE FARMS LIMITED p644
627 ESSEX ROAD 14, LEAMINGTON, ON, N8H 3V8
(519) 322-0400 *SIC 0161*

PIHOKKER FARMS INC p1003
58126 CALTON LINE RR 1, VIENNA, ON, N0J 1Z0
(519) 866-5030 *SIC 0161*

POMAS FARMS INC p890
1057 HWY 77, STAPLES, ON, N0P 2J0
(519) 326-4410 *SIC 0161*

PORT KELLS NURSERIES LTD p282
18730 88 AVE, SURREY, BC, V4N 5T1
(604) 882-1344 *SIC 0161*

POTAGER MONTREALAIS LTEE, LE p1357
1803 CH DE LA RIVIERE, SAINTE-CLOTILDE-DE-CHATEAUGUAY, QC, J0L 1W0
(450) 826-3191 *SIC 0161*

POTAGER RIENDEAU INC, LE p1351
1729 RANG SAINT-ANTOINE, SAINT-REMI, QC, J0L 2L0
(450) 454-9091 *SIC 0161*

PROCYK FARMS (1994) LIMITED p1016
GD, WILSONVILLE, ON, N0E 1Z0
(519) 443-4516 *SIC 0161*

RIGA FARMS LTD p756
19810 DUFFERIN ST, NEWMARKET, ON, L3Y 4V9
(905) 775-4217 *SIC 0161*

RIVER VALLEY SPECIALTY FARMS INC p345
GD, BAGOT, MB, R0H 0E0
(204) 274-2467 *SIC 0161*

ROL-LAND FARMS MUSHROOMS INC p3
GD, AIRDRIE, AB, T4B 2A2
(403) 946-4395 *SIC 0161*

ROUGE RIVER FARMS INC p598
24 GORMLEY INDUSTRIAL AVE, GORMLEY, ON, L0H 1G0
(800) 773-9216 *SIC 0161*

SCHONBERGER FAMILY FARMS LIMITED p643
1412 CONCESSION 1 RD ENR, LANGTON, ON, N0E 1G0
(519) 875-2988 *SIC 0161*

SCHRIEMER FAMILY FARM LTD p354
33096 RAT RIVER RD, OTTERBURNE, MB, R0A 1G0
(204) 299-9708 *SIC 0161*

SCOTLYNN SWEETPAC GROWERS INC p1004
1150 VITTORIA RD, VITTORIA, ON, N0E 1W0
(519) 426-2700 *SIC 0161*

SERRES SAVOURA ST-ETIENNE INC, LES p1253

700 RUE LUCIEN-THIBODEAU, PORT-
NEUF, QC, G0A 2Y0
(418) 286-6681   SIC 0161

SIC 0171 Berry crops

ATOCAS DE L'ERABLE INC, LES   p1245
2249 RUE GARNEAU, PLESSISVILLE, QC,
G6L 2Y7
(819) 621-7166   SIC 0171
BERRY FRESH FARMS   p590
1760 BALFOUR ST, FENWICK, ON, L0S
1C0
(905) 892-8231   SIC 0171
BRAGG LUMBER COMPANY LIMITED p442
1536 WYVRN RD, COLLINGWOOD COR-
NER, NS, B0M 1E0
(902) 686-3254   SIC 0171
CANNEBERGES ATOKA INC   p1148
3025 RTE 218, MANSEAU, QC, G0X 1V0
(819) 356-2001   SIC 0171
**FERME MAURICE ET PHILIPPE VAILLAN-
COURT INC**   p1343
6678 CH ROYAL, SAINT-LAURENT-ILE-
D'ORLEANS, QC, G0A 3Z0
(418) 828-9374   SIC 0171
FERME ONESIME POULIOT INC   p1315
5354   CH   ROYAL,   SAINT-JEAN-
D'ORLEANS, QC, G0A 3W0
(418) 829-2801   SIC 0171
FRUITS BLEUS INC, LES   p1296
698 RUE MELANCON, SAINT-BRUNO-
LAC-SAINT-JEAN, QC, G0W 2L0
(418) 343-2206   SIC 0171
LALLY FARMS INC   p178
5327 GLADWIN RD, ABBOTSFORD, BC,
V4X 1X8
(604) 859-6820   SIC 0171
NARANG FARMS & PROCESSORS LTD
p178
351 BRADNER RD, ABBOTSFORD, BC,
V4X 2J5
(604) 856-2020   SIC 0171
**PRODUCTIONS HORTICOLES DEMERS
INC, LES**   p1140
1196 RUE DES CARRIERES, LEVIS, QC,
G7A 0R7
(418) 831-2489   SIC 0171
PUREWAL BLUEBERRY FARMS LTD p244
13753 HALE RD, PITT MEADOWS, BC, V3Y
1Z1
SIC 0171
WESTBERRY FARMS LTD   p176
34488 BATEMAN RD, ABBOTSFORD, BC,
V2S 7Y8
(604) 850-0377   SIC 0171

SIC 0172 Grapes

FERME C.M.J.I. ROBERT INC   p1288
1105 LA PETITE-CAROLINE, ROUGE-
MONT, QC, J0L 1M0
(450) 469-3090   SIC 0172
LJP CORPORATION   p808
793522 MONO 3RD LINE, ORANGEVILLE,
ON, L9W 2Y8
(519) 942-0754   SIC 0172
NK'MIP VINEYARDS LTD   p242
7357 VINEYARD RD, OLIVER, BC, V0H 1T0
(250) 498-3552   SIC 0172
PILLITTERI ESTATES WINERY INC   p761
1696 NIAGARA STONE RD, NIAGARA ON
THE LAKE, ON, L0S 1J0
(905) 468-3147   SIC 0172

SIC 0175 Deciduous tree fruits

CHUDLEIGH'S APPLE FARM LTD   p683
624 MCGEACHIE DR, MILTON, ON, L9T
3Y5
(905) 878-2725   SIC 0175

CIDRERIE MILTON INC   p1356
5 137 RTE N, SAINTE-CECILE-DE-
MILTON, QC, J0E 2C0
(450) 777-2442   SIC 0175
MARTIN'S FAMILY FRUIT FARM LTD p1006
1420 LOBSINGER LINE UNIT 1, WATER-
LOO, ON, N2J 4G8
(519) 664-2750   SIC 0175
VERGERS LEAHY INC   p1102
1772 RTE 209, FRANKLIN, QC, J0S 1E0
(450) 827-2544   SIC 0175
VERGERS PAUL JODOIN INC   p1315
3333 RANG DU CORDON, SAINT-JEAN-
BAPTISTE, QC, J0L 2B0
(450) 467-4744   SIC 0175

SIC 0179 Fruits and tree nuts, nec

CASINO TROPICAL PLANTS LTD.   p271
4148 184TH ST, SURREY, BC, V3S 0R5
(604) 576-1156   SIC 0179
THWAITES FARMS LTD   p761
1984 TOWNLINE RD SUITE 3, NIAGARA
ON THE LAKE, ON, L0S 1J0
(905) 934-3880   SIC 0179

SIC 0181 Ornamental nursery products

ALDERSHOT GREENHOUSES LIMITED
p531
1135 GALLAGHER RD, BURLINGTON, ON,
L7T 2M7
(905) 632-9272   SIC 0181
AVON VALLEY FLORAL INC   p450
285 TOWN RD RR 2, FALMOUTH, NS, B0P
1L0
(902) 798-8381   SIC 0181
BRAUN NURSERY LIMITED   p747
2004 GLANCASTER RD, MOUNT HOPE,
ON, L0R 1W0
(905) 648-1911   SIC 0181
**BROOKDALE TREELAND NURSERIES
LIMITED**   p879
6050 17TH SIDEROAD, SCHOMBERG, ON,
L0G 1T0
(905) 859-4571   SIC 0181
BURNABY LAKE GREENHOUSES LTD p281
17250 80 AVE, SURREY, BC, V4N 6J6
(604) 576-2088   SIC 0181
BYLANDS NURSERIES LTD   p341
1600 BYLAND RD, WEST KELOWNA, BC,
V1Z 1H6
(250) 769-7272   SIC 0181
DARVONDA NURSERIES LTD   p226
6690 216 ST, LANGLEY, BC, V2Y 2N9
(604) 530-6889   SIC 0181
**DAVID OPPENHEIMER & ASSOCIATES
GENERAL PARTNERSHIP**   p200
11 BURBIDGE ST SUITE 101, COQUIT-
LAM, BC, V3K 7B2
(604) 461-6779   SIC 0181
DEGROOT'S NURSERIES   p859
1840 LONDON LINE, SARNIA, ON, N7T
7H2
(519) 542-3436   SIC 0181
DINESEN NURSERIES LTD   p179
2110 272 ST, ALDERGROVE, BC, V4W 2R1
(604) 856-2290   SIC 0181
EAGLE LAKE TURF FARMS LTD   p168
GD STN MAIN, STRATHMORE, AB, T1P
1J5
(403) 934-6808   SIC 0181
ELMSDALE SOD FARMS LIMITED   p449
113 ELMSDALE RD, ELMSDALE, NS, B2S
1K7
(902) 883-2291   SIC 0181
EMMONS GREENHOUSES INC   p1000
1453 DEEBANK RD, UTTERSON, ON, P0B
1M0
(705) 769-3238   SIC 0181
EUROSA FARMS LTD   p180
1304 GREIG AVE, BRENTWOOD BAY, BC,

V8M 1J6
(250) 652-5812   SIC 0181
FAIRFIELD PROPAGATORS LTD   p196
10718 BELL RD, CHILLIWACK, BC, V2P
6H5
(604) 792-9988   SIC 0181
**FEDERATION DE L'UPA DE LA CAPITALE-
NATIONALE-COTE-NORD**   p1277
5185 RUE RIDEAU, QUEBEC, QC, G2E 5S2
(418) 872-0770   SIC 0181
FERNLEA FLOWERS LIMITED   p564
1211 HIGHWAY 3, DELHI, ON, N4B 2W6
(519) 582-3060   SIC 0181
FLOWER GROUP OPERATING LP   p623
2350 4TH AVE, JORDAN STATION, ON,
L0R 1S0
(905) 562-4118   SIC 0181
GAZON SAVARD (SAGUENAY) INC   p1079
3478 RANG SAINT-PAUL, CHICOUTIMI,
QC, G7H 0G6
(418) 543-5739   SIC 0181
GUINOIS & FRERES LTEE   p1314
1365 RUE SAINT-REGIS, SAINT-ISIDORE-
DE-LAPRAIRIE, QC, J0L 2A0
(450) 454-3196   SIC 0181
HAMEL, PLACEMENTS GAETAN INC, LES
p1119
6029   BOUL   WILFRID-HAMEL,
L'ANCIENNE-LORETTE, QC, G2E 2H3
(418) 871-6010   SIC 0181
HARSTER GREENHOUSES INC   p566
250 8 HWY, DUNDAS, ON, L9H 5E1
(905) 628-2430   SIC 0181
**HENDRIKS, ANDREW & SONS GREEN-
HOUSES INC**   p489
5095 NORTH SERVICE RD, BEAMSVILLE,
ON, L0R 1B3
(905) 563-8132   SIC 0181
HERRLE FARMS LTD   p883
1253 ERB'S RD, ST AGATHA, ON, N0B 2L0
(519) 886-7576   SIC 0181
HILLEN NURSERY LTD   p746
23078 ADELAIDE RD, MOUNT BRYDGES,
ON, N0L 1W0
(519) 264-9057   SIC 0181
HOLLANDIA GREENHOUSES LTD   p244
19731 RICHARDSON RD, PITT MEAD-
OWS, BC, V3Y 1Z1
(604) 460-1866   SIC 0181
HORTICO INC   p1005
723 ROBSON RD, WATERDOWN, ON, L8B
1H2
(905) 689-6984   SIC 0181
HOWARD HUY FARMS LTD   p644
932 MERSEA ROAD 7, LEAMINGTON, ON,
N8H 3V8
(519) 324-0631   SIC 0181
JARJA FLORAL INTERNATIONAL CORP
p881
577 CHARLOTTEVILLE ROAD 8, SIMCOE,
ON, N3Y 4K5
(519) 582-3930   SIC 0181
JEFFERY'S GREENHOUSES INC   p886
1036   LAKESHORE   RD   W,   ST
CATHARINES, ON, L2R 6P9
(905) 934-0514   SIC 0181
JOLLY FARMER PRODUCTS INC   p410
56 CRABBE RD, NORTHAMPTON, NB,
E7N 1R6
(506) 325-3850   SIC 0181
KENTUCKY BLUE GRASS LTD   p109
6107 34 ST NW, EDMONTON, AB, T6B 2V6
(780) 415-5201   SIC 0181
MARITIME SOD LTD   p413
1101 BAYSIDE DR, SAINT JOHN, NB, E2J
4Y2
(506) 634-8540   SIC 0181
MARTENS, W. GREENHOUSES INC   p644
1812 MERSEA ROAD 5, LEAMINGTON,
ON, N8H 3V6
SIC 0181
MEADOWVILLE GARDEN CENTRE INC
p604
7767 WELLINGTON ROAD 124, GUELPH,

ON, N1H 6H7
(519) 822-0840   SIC 0181
MEROM FARMS LTD   p178
2244 LEFEUVRE RD, ABBOTSFORD, BC,
V4X 1C6
(604) 856-3511   SIC 0181
MONSANTO CANADA INC   p391
1 RESEARCH RD SUITE 900, WINNIPEG,
MB, R3T 6E3
(204) 985-1000   SIC 0181
NORDIC NURSERIES LTD   p178
29386 HAVERMAN RD, ABBOTSFORD,
BC, V4X 2P3
(604) 607-7074   SIC 0181
PEPINIERE ABBOTSFORD INC   p1350
605 RUE PRINCIPALE E BUREAU 112,
SAINT-PAUL-D'ABBOTSFORD, QC, J0E 1A0
(450) 379-5777   SIC 0181
**PEPINIERE BOUCHER DIVISION PLANTS
FORESTIERS INC**   p1291
94 RANG DES AULNAIES, SAINT-
AMBROISE, QC, G7P 2B4
(418) 672-4779   SIC 0181
PEPINIERE CRAMER INC   p1135
1002 CH SAINT-DOMINIQUE, LES CE-
DRES, QC, J7T 1P4
(450) 452-2121   SIC 0181
PEPINIERE LEMAY INC   p1130
256 RANG SAINT-HENRI, LANORAIE, QC,
J0K 1E0
(450) 887-2761   SIC 0181
PETER THE PLANTMAN INC   p78
250010 MOUNTAIN VIEW TRAIL, CAL-
GARY, AB, T3Z 3S3
(403) 270-8451   SIC 0181
PIONEER HI-BRED PRODUCTION LTD p543
7399 COUNTY RD 2 W, CHATHAM, ON,
N7M 5L1
(519) 352-2700   SIC 0181
PUTZER, M. HORNBY LIMITED   p620
7314 SIXTH LINE, HORNBY, ON, L0P 1E0
(905) 878-7226   SIC 0181
PYRAMID FARMS LIMITED   p645
209 ERIE ST N, LEAMINGTON, ON, N8H
3A5
(519) 326-4989   SIC 0181
QUIK'S FARM LIMITED   p198
8340 PREST RD, CHILLIWACK, BC, V4Z
0A6
(604) 795-4651   SIC 0181
RAINBOW GREENHOUSES INC   p197
43756 SOUTH SUMAS RD, CHILLIWACK,
BC, V2R 4L6
(604) 858-8100   SIC 0181
RIVER'S END FARMS LTD   p204
2046 CORN CREEK RD, CRESTON, BC,
V0B 1G7
(250) 428-3905   SIC 0181
ROSA FLORA LIMITED   p567
717 DILTZ RD SUITE 2, DUNNVILLE, ON,
N1A 2W2
(905) 774-8044   SIC 0181
SERRES DU ST-LAURENT (LES)   p1300
360 BOUL DE LA GABELLE, SAINT-
ETIENNE-DES-GRES, QC, G0X 2P0
(819) 694-6944   SIC 0181
SERRES FRANK ZYRONSKI INC, LES
p1287
1853 CH LALIBERTE, RIVIERE-ROUGE,
QC, J0T 1T0
(819) 275-5156   SIC 0181
SERRES PION, ROSAIRE & FILS INC, LES
p1313
8185 GRAND RANG, SAINT-HYACINTHE,
QC, J2S 9A8
(450) 796-3193   SIC 0181
SHERIDAN NURSERIES LIMITED   p1000
4077 HIGHWAY 7 E, UNIONVILLE, ON, L3R
1L5
(905) 477-2253   SIC 0181
SORENSEN GREENHOUSES INC   p645
3 MILL ST E, LEAMINGTON, ON, N8H 1R6
(519) 322-5024   SIC 0181
SPRING VALLEY GARDENS INC   p886

1846 SEVENTH ST, ST CATHARINES, ON, L2R 6P9
(905) 682-9002   SIC 0181

STEWART BROTHERS NURSERIES LTD   p219
4129 SPIERS RD, KELOWNA, BC, V1W 4B5
(250) 764-2121   SIC 0181

STOKES SEEDS LIMITED   p907
296 COLLIER RD S, THOROLD, ON, L2V 5B6
(905) 688-4300   SIC 0181

SUNSELECT PRODUCE INC   p179
349 264 ST, ALDERGROVE, BC, V4W 2K1
(604) 607-7655   SIC 0181

TOP CROP GARDEN FARM & PET   p204
2101 CRANBROOK ST N, CRANBROOK, BC, V1C 5M6
(250) 489-4555   SIC 0181

WESTBROOK GREENHOUSES LIMITED   p490
4994 NORTH SERVICE RD, BEAMSVILLE, ON, L0R 1B3
(289) 432-1199   SIC 0181

WILLOWBROOK NURSERIES INC   p590
935 VICTORIA AVE, FENWICK, ON, L0S 1C0
(905) 892-5350   SIC 0181

SIC 0182 Food crops grown under cover

1196977 ONTARIO LTD   p643
1002 MERSEA ROAD 7, LEAMINGTON, ON, N8H 3V8
(519) 324-0631   SIC 0182

1266093 ONTARIO LIMITED   p643
614 HIGHWAY 77, LEAMINGTON, ON, N8H 3V8
(519) 326-9878   SIC 0182

4 SEASON KING MUSHROOM LTD   p178
28345 KING RD, ABBOTSFORD, BC, V4X 1C9
(604) 857-2790   SIC 0182

617885 ONTARIO LTD   p858
1581 COUNTY ROAD 34, RUTHVEN, ON, N0P 2G0
(519) 326-4907   SIC 0182

AVINA FRESH PRODUCE LTD   p178
28265 58 AVE, ABBOTSFORD, BC, V4X 2E8
(604) 856-9833   SIC 0182

CARLETON MUSHROOM FARMS LIMITED   p811
6280 DALMENY RD, OSGOODE, ON, K0A 2W0
(613) 826-2868   SIC 0182

CHAMP'S MUSHROOMS INC   p179
3151 260 ST, ALDERGROVE, BC, V4W 2Z6
(604) 607-0789   SIC 0182

CHAMPAG INC   p1395
1156   RTE   MARIE-VICTORIN, VERCHERES, QC, J0L 2R0
(450) 583-3350   SIC 0182

CONTINENTAL MUSHROOM CORPORATION (1989) LTD   p681
2545 NINTH LINE RD, METCALFE, ON, K0A 2P0
SIC 0182

DELTA VIEW FARMS LTD   p210
3330 41B ST, DELTA, BC, V4K 3N2
(604) 946-1776   SIC 0182

DOUBLE DIAMOND ACRES LIMITED   p633
2024 SPINKS DR, KINGSVILLE, ON, N9Y 2E5
(519) 326-1000   SIC 0182

ENNISKILLEN PEPPER CO. LTD   p842
4376 LASALLE LINE RR 3, PETROLIA, ON, N0N 1R0
(519) 882-3423   SIC 0182

ENVIRO MUSHROOM FARM INC   p526
5200 BRITANNIA RD, BURLINGTON, ON, L7M 0S3
(905) 331-8030   SIC 0182

FARMERS' FRESH MUSHROOMS INC   p178
3555 ROSS RD, ABBOTSFORD, BC, V4X 1M6
(604) 857-5610   SIC 0182

GOLDEN ACRE FARMS INC   p633
1451 ROAD 2 E, KINGSVILLE, ON, N9Y 2E4
SIC 0182

GOOD FAMILY FOODS   p849
2899 CROMARTY DR, PUTNAM, ON, N0L 2B0
(519) 269-3700   SIC 0182

GREAT NORTHERN HYDROPONICS   p634
1507 ROAD 3 E, KINGSVILLE, ON, N9Y 2E5
(519) 322-2000   SIC 0182

GREENHOUSE GROWN FOODS INC   p210
3660 41B ST, DELTA, BC, V4K 3N2
(604) 940-7700   SIC 0182

GREENWOOD MUSHROOM FARM   p479
9760 HERON RD, ASHBURN, ON, L0B 1A0
(905) 655-3373   SIC 0182

HIGHLINE MUSHROOMS WEST LIMITED   p81
281090 SERVICE RD, CROSSFIELD, AB, T0M 0S0
(403) 464-4396   SIC 0182

HIGHLINE PRODUCE LIMITED   p493
339 CONLEY RD, BLOOMFIELD, ON, K0K 1G0
(613) 399-3121   SIC 0182

HIGHLINE PRODUCE LIMITED   p644
506 MERSEA ROAD 5, LEAMINGTON, ON, N8H 3V5
(519) 326-8643   SIC 0182

HOUWELING NURSERIES LTD   p211
2776 64 ST, DELTA, BC, V4L 2N7
(604) 946-0844   SIC 0182

LOVEDAY MUSHROOM FARMS LTD   p366
556 MISSION ST, WINNIPEG, MB, R2J 0A2
(204) 233-4378   SIC 0182

M. O. S. ENTERPRISES LIMITED   p858
1475 COUNTY ROAD 34, RUTHVEN, ON, N0P 2G0
(519) 326-9067   SIC 0182

MARAICHER A. BARBEAU & FILS INC, LE   p1349
2430 RUE PRINCIPALE, SAINT-MICHEL, QC, J0L 2J0
(450) 454-2555   SIC 0182

MILLENNIUM PACIFIC GREENHOUSES PARTNERSHIP   p210
3752 ARTHUR DR, DELTA, BC, V4K 3N2
(604) 940-4440   SIC 0182

MONAGHAN MUSHROOMS LTD   p540
7345 GUELPH LINE, CAMPBELLVILLE, ON, L0P 1B0
(905) 878-9375   SIC 0182

MOUNTAIN VIEW MUSHROOMS LTD   p178
38061 ATKINSON RD, ABBOTSFORD, BC, V3G 2G6
SIC 0182

MUCCI FARMS LTD   p634
1876 SEACLIFF DR, KINGSVILLE, ON, N9Y 2N1
(519) 326-8881   SIC 0182

NATURA NATURALS INC   p644
279 TALBOT ST W, LEAMINGTON, ON, N8H 4H3
(877) 786-6286   SIC 0182

NATURE FRESH FARMS INC   p644
634 MERSEA ROAD 7, LEAMINGTON, ON, N8H 3V8
(519) 326-8603   SIC 0182

PEETERS, WIET FARM PRODUCTS LIMITED   p542
LOT 11 CONC 23, CHARING CROSS, ON, N0P 1G0
(519) 351-1945   SIC 0182

PICCIONI BROS MUSHROOM FARM LIMITED   p566
355 ROCK CHAPEL RD, DUNDAS, ON, L9H 5E2
(905) 628-3090   SIC 0182

PLATINUM PRODUCE COMPANY   p493
21037 COMMUNICATION RD, BLENHEIM, ON, N0P 1A0
(519) 676-1772   SIC 0182

RAVINE MUSHROOM (1983) LIMITED   p1028
4101 KING-VAUGHAN RD, WOODBRIDGE, ON, L4H 1E4
(905) 833-5498   SIC 0182

ROL-LAND FARMS MUSHROOMS INC   p493
19002 COMMUNICATION RD RR 4, BLENHEIM, ON, N0P 1A0
(519) 676-8125   SIC 0182

ROSS LAND MUSHROOM FARM LTD   p178
3555 ROSS RD, ABBOTSFORD, BC, V4X 1M6
SIC 0182

SERRES LEFORT INC, LES   p1357
644   3E   RANG,   SAINTE-CLOTILDE-DE-CHATEAUGUAY, QC, J0L 1W0
(450) 826-3117   SIC 0182

SERRES SAVOURA PORTNEUF INC, LES   p1363
2743 BOUL SAINTE-SOPHIE, SAINTE-SOPHIE, QC, J5J 2V3
(450) 431-6343   SIC 0182

SERRES TOUNDRA INC   p1303
4190   RTE   SAINT-EUSEBE,   SAINT-FELICIEN, QC, G8K 2N9
(418) 679-1834   SIC 0182

ST. DAVIDS HYDROPONICS LTD   p761
822 CONCESSION 7 RD RR 4, NIAGARA ON THE LAKE, ON, L0S 1J0
(905) 682-7570   SIC 0182

SUNTASTIC HOTHOUSE INC   p590
40534 THAMES RD E, EXETER, ON, N0M 1S5
(519) 235-3357   SIC 0182

TRUONG'S ENTERPRISES LTD   p179
40 264 ST, ALDERGROVE, BC, V4W 2L6
(604) 856-5674   SIC 0182

TWIN PEAKS HYDROPONICS INC   p634
2237 COUNTY RD 31, KINGSVILLE, ON, N9Y 2E5
(519) 326-1000   SIC 0182

WINDSET FARMS   p211
3660 41B ST, DELTA, BC, V4K 3N2
(604) 940-7700   SIC 0182

WINDSET FARMS (CANADA) LTD   p211
3660 41B ST, DELTA, BC, V4K 3N2
(604) 940-7700   SIC 0182

WINDSET HOLDINGS 2010 LTD   p211
3660 41B ST, DELTA, BC, V4K 3N2
(604) 940-7700   SIC 0182

SIC 0191 General farms, primarily crop

AIRPORT COLONY OF HUTTERIAN BRETHREN TRUST   p354
GD LCD MAIN, PORTAGE LA PRAIRIE, MB, R1N 3A7
(204) 274-2422   SIC 0191

AMCO FARMS INC   p644
523 WILKINSON DR, LEAMINGTON, ON, N8H 1A6
(519) 326-9095   SIC 0191

ARM RIVER FARMING CO. LTD   p1409
GD, LUMSDEN, SK, S0G 3C0
(306) 731-2819   SIC 0191

ARMADA COLONY   p144
GD, LOMOND, AB, T0L 1G0
(403) 792-3388   SIC 0191

ASPENHEIM COLONY FARMS LTD   p345
GD, BAGOT, MB, R0H 0E0
(204) 274-2782   SIC 0191

B. & C. NIGHTINGALE FARMS LTD   p643
1931 WINDHAM RD 19 RR 1, LA SALETTE, ON, N0E 1H0
(519) 582-2461   SIC 0191

BALAMORE FARM LTD   p450
9036 HIGHWAY 2, GREAT VILLAGE, NS, B0M 1L0
(902) 668-2005   SIC 0191

BLUMENGART COLONY FARMS LTD   p354

GD, PLUM COULEE, MB, R0G 1R0
(204) 829-3687   SIC 0191

C & K HAPPY FARMS LTD   p227
22950 16 AVE, LANGLEY, BC, V2Z 1K7
(604) 533-8307   SIC 0191

CALAIS FARMS LTD   p174
33418 DOWNES RD, ABBOTSFORD, BC, V2S 7T4
(604) 852-1660   SIC 0191

CORNIES FARMS LTD   p633
1545 KRATZ RD, KINGSVILLE, ON, N9Y 3K4
(519) 733-5416   SIC 0191

COUNTY LINE FARMS LTD   p158
GD, RIMBEY, AB, T0C 2J0
(403) 843-6275   SIC 0191

DECKER COLONY FARMS LTD   p349
GD, DECKER, MB, R0M 0K0
(204) 764-2481   SIC 0191

FAIRVILLE FARMING CO LTD   p5
GD, BASSANO, AB, T0J 0B0
(403) 641-2404   SIC 0191

FORT PITT FARMS LTD   p1409
GD, LLOYDMINSTER, SK, S9V 0X5
(306) 344-4849   SIC 0191

FRIENDLY FAMILY FARMS LTD   p365
500 DAWSON RD N, WINNIPEG, MB, R2J 0T1
(204) 231-5151   SIC 0191

GEORGE BRAUN & SONS FARMS LIMITED   p564
GD LCD MAIN, DELHI, ON, N4B 2W7
(519) 582-1239   SIC 0191

GOLDEN VALLEY FARMS INC   p479
50 WELLS ST W, ARTHUR, ON, N0G 1A0
(519) 848-3110   SIC 0191

GOOD HOPE COLONY FARMS LTD   p354
GD LCD MAIN, PORTAGE LA PRAIRIE, MB, R1N 3A7
(204) 252-2334   SIC 0191

GOODYEAR FARM LTD   p849
139 RAVENSHOE RD, QUEENSVILLE, ON, L0G 1R0
(905) 478-8388   SIC 0191

GREAT LAKES GREENHOUSES INC   p644
834 MERSEA ROAD 4, LEAMINGTON, ON, N8H 3V6
(519) 326-7589   SIC 0191

GREEN ACRES COLONY LTD   p360
GD, WAWANESA, MB, R0K 2G0
(204) 824-2627   SIC 0191

HAIRY HILL COLONY LTD   p135
GD, HAIRY HILL, AB, T0B 1S0
(780) 768-3770   SIC 0191

HANGAR FARMS INC   p355
RIVERS AIR BASE, RIVERS, MB, R0K 1X0
SIC 0191

HERRLE'S COUNTRY FARM MARKET LTD   p883
1253 ERB'S RD, ST AGATHA, ON, N0B 2L0
(519) 886-7576   SIC 0191

HIGHLINE MUSHROOMS WEST LIMITED   p227
3392 224 ST, LANGLEY, BC, V2Z 2G8
(604) 534-0278   SIC 0191

HILLCREST COLONY INC   p1406
GD, DUNDURN, SK, S0K 1K0
(306) 492-2499   SIC 0191

HODGEVILLE FARMING CO. LTD   p1407
GD, HODGEVILLE, SK, S0H 2B0
(306) 677-2256   SIC 0191

HUTTERIAN BRETHREN CHURCH OF EAGLE CREEK INC   p1404
GD, ASQUITH, SK, S0K 0J0
(306) 329-4476   SIC 0191

HUTTERIAN BRETHREN CHURCH OF EAST CARDSTON (1977)   p79
PO BOX 2520, CARDSTON, AB, T0K 0K0
(403) 653-2451   SIC 0191

HUTTERIAN BRETHREN CHURCH OF ELKWATER   p137
GD, IRVINE, AB, T0J 1V0
(403) 525-4256   SIC 0191

HUTTERIAN   BRETHREN   MANNVILLE

COLONY p145
GD, MANNVILLE, AB, T0B 2W0
(780) 763-3079 SIC 0191

HUTTERIAN BRETHREN OF BRANT, THE p7
GD, BRANT, AB, T0L 0L0
(403) 684-3649 SIC 0191

HUTTERIAN BRETHREN OF ESTUARY CORP p1409
GD, LEADER, SK, S0N 1H0
(306) 628-4116 SIC 0191

HUTTERIAN BRETHREN OF MILTOW p171
GD, WARNER, AB, T0K 2L0
(403) 642-0004 SIC 0191

HUTTERIAN BRETHREN OF PARKLAND, THE p148
GD, NANTON, AB, T0L 1R0
(403) 646-5761 SIC 0191

HUTTERVILLE HUTTERIAN BRETHREN p145
GD, MAGRATH, AB, T0K 1J0
(403) 758-3143 SIC 0191

IBERVILLE FARMS LTD p349
GD, ELIE, MB, R0H 0H0
(204) 864-2058 SIC 0191

INPUT CAPITAL CORP p1418
1914 HAMILTON ST SUITE 300, REGINA, SK, S4P 3N6
(306) 347-3006 SIC 0191

INTERLAKE COLONY FARMS LTD p359
GD, TEULON, MB, R0C 3B0
(204) 886-2107 SIC 0191

JAMES VALLEY COLONY FARMS LTD p349
100 JAMES VALLEY RD, ELIE, MB, R0H 0H0
(204) 353-2827 SIC 0191

JARDINS VEGIBEC INC, LES p1244
171 RANG SAINTE-SOPHIE, OKA, QC, J0N 1E0
(450) 496-0566 SIC 0191

LAPRISE FARMS LTD p836
7359 MAPLE LINE SUITE 1, PAIN COURT, ON, N0P 1Z0
(519) 352-2968 SIC 0191

LIVINGSTONE HUTTERIAN BRETHREN p144
GD, LUNDBRECK, AB, T0K 1H0
(403) 628-2226 SIC 0191

M & M FARMS LTD p644
331 TALBOT ST W, LEAMINGTON, ON, N8H 4H3
(519) 326-2287 SIC 0191

MIAMI COLONY FARMS LTD p352
GD STN MAIN, MORDEN, MB, R6M 1A1
(204) 435-2447 SIC 0191

MURRAY LAKE COLONY FARMING CO. LTD p81
6517 TOWNSHIP RD 110, CYPRESS COUNTY, AB, T1A 7N3
(587) 824-2004 SIC 0191

MURRAY TOWNSHIP FARMS LTD p999
GD LCD MAIN, TRENTON, ON, K8V 5P9
(613) 392-8068 SIC 0191

NEUDORF COLONY EQUIPMENT CO LTD p81
GD, CROSSFIELD, AB, T0M 0S0
(403) 946-4801 SIC 0191

NEW CASTLE FARM LTD p644
414 MERSEA ROAD 3, LEAMINGTON, ON, N8H 3V5
(519) 322-5411 SIC 0191

NEW ROCKPORT HUTTERIAN BRETHREN p148
GD, NEW DAYTON, AB, T0K 1P0
(403) 733-2122 SIC 0191

NEW ROSEDALE COLONY FARMS LTD p355
GD LCD MAIN, PORTAGE LA PRAIRIE, MB, R1N 3B7
(204) 252-2727 SIC 0191

NIGHTINGALE FARMS LIMITED p643
1492 WINDHAM RD 19, LA SALETTE, ON, N0E 1H0
(519) 582-2461 SIC 0191

OAK BLUFF COLONY FARMS LTD p353
GD, MORRIS, MB, R0G 1K0
(204) 746-2122 SIC 0191

PARKS BLUEBERRIES & COUNTRY STORE LTD p496
14815 LONGWOODS RD, BOTHWELL, ON, N0P 1C0
(519) 692-5373 SIC 0191

PINGLE'S FARM MARKET p617
1805 TAUNTON RD, HAMPTON, ON, L0B 1J0
(905) 725-6089 SIC 0191

POPLAR POINT COLONY FARMS LTD p355
94 RIVER RD W, PORTAGE LA PRAIRIE, MB, R1N 3C4
(204) 267-2560 SIC 0191

PRISM FARMS LIMITED p644
731 MERSEA ROAD 6, LEAMINGTON, ON, N8H 3V8
(519) 324-9009 SIC 0191

R. ROBITAILLE & FILS INC p1318
486 RUE DE VERSAILLES, SAINT-JEAN-SUR-RICHELIEU, QC, J3B 4H3
(450) 347-7494 SIC 0191

RANDHAWA FARMS LTD p178
33677 HALLERT RD, ABBOTSFORD, BC, V4X 1W9
(604) 864-8896 SIC 0191

ROBITAILLE R & FILS INC p1081
1051 RANG VICTORIA, CLARENCEVILLE, QC, J0J 1B0
SIC 0191

ROCK LAKE HUTTERIAN BRETHREN p80
GD STN MAIN, COALDALE, AB, T1M 1K8
(403) 345-3892 SIC 0191

ROCKPORT HUTTERIAN BRETHREN CORPORATION p145
GD, MAGRATH, AB, T0K 1J0
(403) 758-3077 SIC 0191

ROSE VALLEY COLONY LTD p350
GD, GRAYSVILLE, MB, R0G 0T0
(204) 828-3338 SIC 0191

ROSEDALE HUTTERIAN BRETHREN p126
GD, ETZIKOM, AB, T0K 0W0
(587) 787-2456 SIC 0191

SIGNATURE MUSHROOMS LTD p4
52557 RANGE ROAD 215, ARDROSSAN, AB, T8E 2H6
(780) 922-2535 SIC 0191

SMOKY LAKE COLONY LTD p164
GD, SMOKY LAKE, AB, T0A 3C0
(780) 656-2372 SIC 0191

SPRUCEWOOD COLONY FARMS LTD p348
GD, BROOKDALE, MB, R0K 0G0
(204) 354-2318 SIC 0191

SUNCREST COLONY FARMS LTD p360
43051 SUNCREST RD, TOUROND, MB, R0A 2G0
(204) 433-7853 SIC 0191

SUNNYSIDE COLONY LTD p353
GD, NEWTON SIDING, MB, R0H 0X0
(204) 267-2812 SIC 0191

SURREY FARMS COMPANY p280
5180 152 ST, SURREY, BC, V3Z 1G9
(604) 574-1390 SIC 0191

TRI-LEAF COLONY OF HUTTERIAN BRETHREN p345
GD, BALDUR, MB, R0K 0B0
(204) 535-2274 SIC 0191

UPPER CANADA GROWERS LTD p761
149 READ RD, NIAGARA ON THE LAKE, ON, L0S 1J0
(289) 646-0737 SIC 0191

VANCO FARMS LTD p1041
280 CROOKED CREEK RD -RTE 251, MONCTON, PE, C1E 0M1
(902) 651-2970 SIC 0191

VERDANT VALLEY FARMING CO LTD p82
GD, DRUMHELLER, AB, T0J 0Y0
(403) 823-4388 SIC 0191

VERMILLION FARMS LTD p356
GD, SANFORD, MB, R0G 2J0
(204) 736-2787 SIC 0191

WIENS FAMILY FARM INC p761

1178 6 RD, NIAGARA ON THE LAKE, ON, L0S 1J0
SIC 0191

WILLOWDALE FARMS INCORPORATED p441
72 CHASE RD RR 1, BERWICK, NS, B0P 1E0
(902) 538-7324 SIC 0191

SIC 0211 Beef cattle feedlots

HIGHWAY 21 FEEDERS LTD p2
GD, ACME, AB, T0M 0A0
(403) 546-2278 SIC 0211

ROSEBURN RANCHES LTD p136
GD STN MAIN, HIGH RIVER, AB, T1V 1M2
(403) 652-3257 SIC 0211

VAN RAAY PASKAL FARMS LTD p152
GD, PICTURE BUTTE, AB, T0K 1V0
(403) 732-5641 SIC 0211

SIC 0212 Beef cattle, except feedlots

AGM BEEF FARMS LTD p278
5175 184 ST, SURREY, BC, V3Z 1B5
(604) 576-8318 SIC 0212

BAGHAI DEVELOPMENT LIMITED p915
678 SHEPPARD AVE E UNIT H, TORONTO, ON, M2K 1B7
(416) 449-5994 SIC 0212

COUNTRY POULTRY p1005
7705 4TH LINE SUITE 2, WALLENSTEIN, ON, N0B 2S0
(519) 698-9930 SIC 0212

DONALDSON FAMILY - BRADNER FARMS p178
28670 58 AVE, ABBOTSFORD, BC, V4X 2E8
(604) 857-1206 SIC 0212

DOUGLAS LAKE CATTLE COMPANY p211
GD, DOUGLAS LAKE, BC, V0E 1S0
(250) 350-3344 SIC 0212

EVERGREEN COLONY LTD p357
GD, SOMERSET, MB, R0G 2L0
(204) 744-2596 SIC 0212

NAMAKA FARMS INC p168
GD STN MAIN, STRATHMORE, AB, T1P 1J5
(403) 934-6122 SIC 0212

NORTHERN BREEZE FARMS LTD p355
GD LCD MAIN, PORTAGE LA PRAIRIE, MB, R1N 3A7
(204) 239-4396 SIC 0212

SIC 0213 Hogs

BIG SKY FARMS INC p1407
10333 8TH AVE E, HUMBOLDT, SK, S0K 2A1
(306) 682-5041 SIC 0213

EXCEL PLAYGREEN GROUP INC p353
18 3 AVE S, NIVERVILLE, MB, R0A 1E0
(204) 388-9250 SIC 0213

F. MENARD INC p1047
251 RTE 235, ANGE-GARDIEN, QC, J0E 1E0
(450) 293-3694 SIC 0213

ISOPORC INC p1310
652 RTE DU MOULIN, SAINT-HUGUES, QC, J0H 1N0
(450) 794-2555 SIC 0213

NETLEY COLONY LTD p354
897 HENRY RD, PETERSFIELD, MB, R0C 2L0
(204) 738-2828 SIC 0213

OAK RIVER COLONY FARMS LTD p354
GD, OAK RIVER, MB, R0K 1T0
(204) 566-2359 SIC 0213

OLYSKY LIMITED PARTNERSHIP p1407
10333 8 AVE, HUMBOLDT, SK, S0K 2A0
(306) 682-5041 SIC 0213

OUTLOOK PORK LTD p150
GD, NOBLEFORD, AB, T0L 1S0
SIC 0213

ROBITAILLE R & FILS INC p1158
522 RANG DE VERSAILLES, MONT-SAINT-GREGOIRE, QC, J0J 1K0
(450) 358-1355 SIC 0213

SOMMERFELD COLONY FARMS LTD p351
GD, HIGH BLUFF, MB, R0H 0K0
(204) 243-2453 SIC 0213

SIC 0241 Dairy farms

AGROPUR COOPERATIVE p181
7650 18TH ST, BURNABY, BC, V3N 4K3
(604) 524-4491 SIC 0241

FOUR STAR DAIRY LIMITED p688
3400 AMERICAN DR, MISSISSAUGA, ON, L4V 1C1
(905) 671-8100 SIC 0241

GRASS RIVER COLONY FARMS LTD p350
GD, GLENELLA, MB, R0J 0V0
(204) 352-4286 SIC 0241

LAITERIE CHAGNON LTEE p1400
550 RUE LEWIS, WATERLOO, QC, J0E 2N0
(450) 539-3535 SIC 0241

SIC 0251 Broiler, fryer, and roaster chickens

BEXEL INC p1225
9001 BOUL DE L'ACADIE BUREAU 200, MONTREAL, QC, H4N 3H7
(514) 858-2222 SIC 0251

BOISJOLI, DORIA LTEE p1402
730 RUE BOISJOLI, WICKHAM, QC, J0C 1S0
(819) 398-6813 SIC 0251

COUVOIR BOIRE & FRERES INC p1402
532 9E RANG, WICKHAM, QC, J0C 1S0
(819) 398-6807 SIC 0251

T&R SARGENT FARMS LTD p712
3410 SEMENYK CRT SUITE 5, MISSISSAUGA, ON, L5C 4P8
(905) 896-1059 SIC 0251

VOLAILLES MARTEL INC, LES p1100
2350 BOUL FOUCAULT, DRUMMONDVILLE, QC, J2E 0E8
(819) 478-7495 SIC 0251

SIC 0252 Chicken eggs

GOLDEN VALLEY FOODS LTD p176
3841 VANDERPOL CRT, ABBOTSFORD, BC, V2T 5W5
(604) 857-0704 SIC 0252

SWEDA FARMS LTD p493
3880 EDGERTON RD SS 101, BLACKSTOCK, ON, L0B 1B0
(905) 986-5747 SIC 0252

SIC 0253 Turkeys and turkey eggs

CUDDY FARMS LIMITED 2008 p897
28429 CENTRE RD, STRATHROY, ON, N7G 3H6
(519) 245-1592 SIC 0253

CUDDY GROUP LIMITED p897
28429 CENTRE RD, STRATHROY, ON, N7G 3H6
(519) 245-1592 SIC 0253

SIC 0254 Poultry hatcheries

BRADNER B.C. ORGANIC FEED LTD p178
28670 58 AVE, ABBOTSFORD, BC, V4X 2E8
(604) 835-3299 SIC 0254

COUVOIR SCOTT LTEE p1366

1798 RTE DU PRESIDENT-KENNEDY, SCOTT, QC, G0S 3G0
(418) 387-2323   SIC 0254

COUVOIR UNIK INC   p1158
222 104 RTE, MONT-SAINT-GREGOIRE, QC, J0J 1K0
(450) 347-0126   SIC 0254

FLEMING CHICKS LIMITED   p489
4412 ONTARIO ST, BEAMSVILLE, ON, L0R 1B0
(905) 563-4914   SIC 0254

GOWANSTOWN POULTRY LIMITED   p896
17 PINE ST, STRATFORD, ON, N5A 1W2
(519) 275-2240   SIC 0254

MAPLE LEAF FOODS INC   p752
70 HERITAGE DR, NEW HAMBURG, ON, N3A 2J4
(519) 662-1501   SIC 0254

PERTH COUNTRY INGREDIENTS INC   p888
20 THAMES RD, ST MARYS, ON, N4X 1C4
(519) 284-3449   SIC 0254

SIERRA CUSTOM FOODS INC   p506
275 WALKER DR, BRAMPTON, ON, L6T 3W5
(905) 595-2260   SIC 0254

WESTERN HATCHERY LTD   p178
505 HAMM ST SUITE 1, ABBOTSFORD, BC, V2T 6B6
(604) 859-7168   SIC 0254

SIC 0259 Poultry and eggs, nec

ATLANTIC POULTRY INCORPORATED p465
791 BELCHER ST SUITE 1, PORT WILLIAMS, NS, B0P 1T0
(902) 678-1335   SIC 0259

BLUE GOOSE CAPITAL CORP   p949
80 RICHMOND ST W SUITE 1502, TORONTO, ON, M5H 2A4
(416) 363-5151   SIC 0259

CANARD IMPERIAL DE BROME LTEE p1306
243 RTE 249, SAINT-GEORGES-DE-WINDSOR, QC, J0A 1J0
(819) 828-2219   SIC 0259

COX BROS. POULTRY FARM LIMITED p462
7520 215 HWY, MAITLAND, NS, B0N 1T0
(902) 261-2823   SIC 0259

HENDRIX GENETICS LIMITED   p640
650 RIVERBEND DR UNIT C, KITCHENER, ON, N2K 3S2
(519) 578-2740   SIC 0259

HUDSON VALLEY FARMS (CA) ULC p1347
228 RUE PRINCIPALE, SAINT-LOUIS-DE-GONZAGUE, QC, J0S 1T0
(450) 377-8766   SIC 0259

HUTTERIAN BRETHREN OF HURON LTD p1404
GD, BROWNLEE, SK, S0H 0M0
(306) 759-2685   SIC 0259

KING COLE DUCKS LIMITED   p894
15351 WARDEN AVE, STOUFFVILLE, ON, L4A 2V5
(905) 836-9461   SIC 0259

L'EQUIPOULE INC   p1149
2010 AV INDUSTRIELLE, MARIEVILLE, QC, J3M 1J5
(450) 730-0336   SIC 0259

NIPISSING GAME FARM INC   p532
367 BIRCHGROVE DR W, CALLANDER, ON, P0H 1H0
(705) 752-2226   SIC 0259

PINE VIEW ALL NATURAL MEATS INC p1413
GD, OSLER, SK, S0K 3A0
(306) 239-4763   SIC 0259

POIRIER-BERARD LTEE   p1303
4401 RUE CREPEAU, SAINT-FELIX-DE-VALOIS, QC, J0K 2M0
(450) 889-5541   SIC 0259

ROSSDOWN FARMS LTD   p178
2325 BRADNER RD, ABBOTSFORD, BC, V4X 1E2

(604) 856-6698   SIC 0259

YAO SUN LOONG KONG CHICKEN LTD p257
2391 VAUXHALL PL, RICHMOND, BC, V6V 1Z5
SIC 0259

SIC 0271 Fur-bearing animals and rabbits

VIKING FUR INC   p421
160 MAIN RD, CAVENDISH, NL, A0B 1J0
(709) 588-2820   SIC 0271

SIC 0272 Horses and other equines

ALPEN HOUSE ULC, THE   p480
14875 BAYVIEW AVE, AURORA, ON, L4G 0K8
(905) 841-0336   SIC 0272

SIC 0273 Animal aquaculture

9356-1405 QUEBEC INC.   p1225
9050, RUE CHARLES-DE LA TOUR, MONTREAL, QC, H4N 1M2
SIC 0273

CANADIAN FISH GUYS   p355
390 REGGIE LEACH DR, RIVERTON, MB, R0C 2R0
(204) 378-5510   SIC 0273

CERMAQ CANADA LTD   p194
919 ISLAND HWY UNIT 203, CAMPBELL RIVER, BC, V9W 2C2
(250) 286-0022   SIC 0273

CREATIVE SALMON COMPANY LTD p283
612 CAMPBELL ST, TOFINO, BC, V0R 2Z0
(250) 725-2884   SIC 0273

MOWI CANADA WEST INC   p195
1334 ISLAND HWY SUITE 124, CAMPBELL RIVER, BC, V9W 8C9
(250) 850-3276   SIC 0273

NICOMEKL ENHANCEMENT SOCIETY p227
5263 232 ST, LANGLEY, BC, V2Z 2P8
(604) 539-2486   SIC 0273

WEST COAST FISHCULTURE (LOIS LAKE) LTD   p248
11060 MORTON RD, POWELL RIVER, BC, V8A 0L9
(604) 487-9200   SIC 0273

SIC 0279 Animal specialties, nec

LABORATOIRES CHARLES RIVER SAINT-CONSTANT S.A.   p1298
324 RANG SAINT-REGIS N, SAINT-CONSTANT, QC, J5A 2E7
(450) 638-1571   SIC 0279

PODOLSKI HONEY FARMS   p349
119 MAIN ST W, ETHELBERT, MB, R0L 0T0
(204) 742-3555   SIC 0279

SIC 0291 General farms, primarily animals

CRITTERS & CROPS LTD   p160
GD, ROSEMARY, AB, T0J 2W0
(403) 378-4934   SIC 0291

CYPRESS COLONY FARMS LTD   p348
GD, CYPRESS RIVER, MB, R0K 0P0
(204) 743-2185   SIC 0291

GREWAL FARMS INC   p175
1088 SUMAS WAY, ABBOTSFORD, BC, V2S 8H2
(604) 832-0083   SIC 0291

HUTTERIAN BRETHERN OF MIXBURN LTD p147
GD, MINBURN, AB, T0B 3B0
(780) 628-5147   SIC 0291

HYLIFE LTD   p351

5 FABAS ST, LA BROQUERIE, MB, R0A 0W0
(204) 424-5359   SIC 0291

KAMSLEY COLONY LTD   p357
GD, SOMERSET, MB, R0G 2L0
(204) 744-2706   SIC 0291

RIDGE VALLEY COLONY LTD   p81
GD, CROOKED CREEK, AB, T0H 0Y0
(780) 957-2607   SIC 0291

ROSETOWN FARMING CO. LTD   p1423
GD, ROSETOWN, SK, S0L 2V0
(306) 882-1991   SIC 0291

WALDHEIM COLONY FARMS LTD   p349
16025 RD 58 NW, ELIE, MB, R0H 0H0
(204) 353-2473   SIC 0291

SIC 0711 Soil preparation services

CONETEC INVESTIGATIONS LTD   p254
12140 VULCAN WAY, RICHMOND, BC, V6V 1J8
(604) 273-4311   SIC 0711

ENGLOBE CORP   p1266
505 BOUL DU PARC-TECHNOLOGIQUE SUITE 200, QUEBEC, QC, G1P 4S9
(418) 781-0191   SIC 0711

SIC 0721 Crop planting and protection

ARBORICULTURE DE BEAUCE INC p1055
364E RTE DU PRESIDENT-KENNEDY, BEAUCEVILLE, QC, G5X 1N9
(418) 774-6217   SIC 0721

ATCO GAS AND PIPELINES LTD   p108
5623 82 AVE NW, EDMONTON, AB, T6B 0E8
(780) 733-2552   SIC 0721

EMONDAGE ST-GERMAIN ET FRERES LTEE   p1174
4032 AV DE LORIMIER, MONTREAL, QC, H2K 3X7
(514) 525-7485   SIC 0721

REVOLUTION VSC ACQUISITION GP INC p524
1100 BURLOAK DR SUITE 200, BURLINGTON, ON, L7L 6B2
(905) 315-6300   SIC 0721

SIC 0722 Crop harvesting

PIER-C PRODUCE INC   p644
7R M C R DR, LEAMINGTON, ON, N8H 3N2
(519) 326-8807   SIC 0722

SIGNALISATION DE MONTREAL INC p1126
15 BOUL SAINT-JOSEPH, LACHINE, QC, H8S 2K9
(514) 821-7668   SIC 0722

SIC 0723 Crop preparation services for market

ADM AGRI-INDUSTRIES COMPANY   p846
1 KING ST SW, PORT COLBORNE, ON, L3K 5W1
(905) 835-4218   SIC 0723

AGT FOOD AND INGREDIENTS INC p1422
6200 E PRIMROSE GREEN DR, REGINA, SK, S4V 3L7
(306) 525-4490   SIC 0723

ALIMENTS BERCY INC, LES   p1169
9210 BOUL PIE-IX, MONTREAL, QC, H1Z 4H7
(514) 528-6262   SIC 0723

BRADFORD CO-OPERATIVE STORAGE LIMITED   p497
61 BRIDGE ST, BRADFORD, ON, L3Z 3H3
(905) 775-3317   SIC 0723

COUTURE, ALFRED LIMITEE   p1291
420 RUE PRINCIPALE, SAINT-ANSELME, QC, G0R 2N0

(418) 885-4425   SIC 0723

FRASER VALLEY PACKERS INC   p174
260 SHORT RD, ABBOTSFORD, BC, V2S 8A7
(604) 852-3525   SIC 0723

GLOBAL CITRUS GROUP, INC   p527
3410 SOUTH SERVICE RD SUITE G3, BURLINGTON, ON, L7N 3T2
(289) 895-8302   SIC 0723

NATURE'S TOUCH FROZEN FOODS (WEST) INC   p177
31122 SOUTH FRASER WAY, ABBOTSFORD, BC, V2T 6L5
(604) 854-1191   SIC 0723

OKANAGAN NORTH GROWERS CO-OPERATIVE   p223
9751 BOTTOM WOOD LAKE RD, KELOWNA, BC, V4V 1S7
SIC 0723

OKANAGAN TREE FRUIT COOPERATIVE p222
880 VAUGHAN AVE, KELOWNA, BC, V1Y 7E4
(250) 763-7003   SIC 0723

OKANAGAN TREE FRUIT COOPERATIVE p224
9751 BOTTOM WOOD LAKE RD, LAKE COUNTRY, BC, V4V 1S7
SIC 0723

PRIDE PAK CANADA LTD   p726
6768 FINANCIAL DR, MISSISSAUGA, ON, L5N 7J6
(905) 828-8280   SIC 0723

SALADE ETCETERA U INC   p1376
147 RANG SAINT-PAUL, SHERRINGTON, QC, J0L 2N0
(450) 454-7712   SIC 0723

SALADEXPRESS INC   p1351
225 RUE SAINT-ANDRE, SAINT-REMI, QC, J0L 2L0
(514) 385-3362   SIC 0723

SLICED FC LTD   p13
4936 52 ST SE, CALGARY, AB, T2B 3R2
(403) 508-6868   SIC 0723

VALLEY SELECT FOODS INC   p178
41212 NO. 3 RD, ABBOTSFORD, BC, V3G 2S1
(604) 823-2341   SIC 0723

SIC 0742 Veterinary services, specialties

534422 B.C. LTD   p286
1988 KOOTENAY ST, VANCOUVER, BC, V5M 4Y3
(604) 294-2629   SIC 0742

698004 ALBERTA LTD   p13
8338 18 ST SE SUITE 100, CALGARY, AB, T2C 4E4
(403) 279-9070   SIC 0742

AFFILIATED ANIMAL SERVICES   p829
900 BOYD AVE, OTTAWA, ON, K2A 2E3
(613) 725-1182   SIC 0742

ASSOCIATE VETERINARY CLINIC (1981) LTD   p33
7140 12 ST SE, CALGARY, AB, T2H 2Y4
(403) 541-0815   SIC 0742

CREDIT VALLEY ANIMAL CENTRE LIMITED   p893
111 HIGHWAY 8, STONEY CREEK, ON, L8G 1C1
(905) 662-6719   SIC 0742

GROUPE DIMENSION MULTI VETERINAIRE INC, LE   p1128
2300 54E AV, LACHINE, QC, H8T 3R2
(514) 633-8888   SIC 0742

GROUPE VETERI MEDIC INC   p1070
7415 BOUL TASCHEREAU, BROSSARD, QC, J4Y 1A2
(450) 656-3660   SIC 0742

HOPITAL VETERINAIRE DAUBIGNY p1267
3349 BOUL WILFRID-HAMEL, QUEBEC, QC, G1P 2J3
(418) 872-5355   SIC 0742

SIC 0751 Livestock services, except veterinary

AMERICAN POULTRY SERVICES LTD p682
63 ELORA ST, MILDMAY, ON, N0G 2J0
(800) 963-3488   *SIC 0751*

BRIANS POULTRY SERVICES LTD p682
GD, MILDMAY, ON, N0G 2J0
(519) 367-2675   *SIC 0751*

KEHO LAKE COLONY p4
GD, BARONS, AB, T0L 0G0
(403) 757-2330   *SIC 0751*

SIC 0762 Farm management services

DEERFIELD HUTTERIAN BRETHERN p145
GD, MAGRATH, AB, T0K 1J0
(403) 758-6461   *SIC 0762*

FAIRHOLME COLONY FARMS LTD p354
E 27-9-8 S, PORTAGE LA PRAIRIE, MB, R1N 3B9
(204) 252-2225   *SIC 0762*

HUTTERIAN BRETHREN OF SPRING POINT COLONY, THE p127
GD, FORT MACLEOD, AB, T0L 0Z0
(403) 553-2284   *SIC 0762*

LAKESIDE COLONY LTD p348
5600 ASSINIBOINE RD, CARTIER, MB, R4K 1C3
(204) 864-2710   *SIC 0762*

SIC 0781 Landscape counseling and planning

ALDERSHOT LANDSCAPE CONTRAC-TORS LP p529
166 FLATT RD, BURLINGTON, ON, L7P 0T3
(905) 689-7321   *SIC 0781*

ARTISTIC LANDSCAPE DESIGNS LIMITED p826
2079 ARTISTIC PL, OTTAWA, ON, K1V 8A8
(613) 733-8220   *SIC 0781*

EDMONTON HORTICULTURAL SOCIETY p100
10746 178 ST NW, EDMONTON, AB, T5S 1J3
(780) 456-3324   *SIC 0781*

EXEL CONTRACTING INC p540
135 WALGREEN RD, CARP, ON, K0A 1L0
(613) 831-3935   *SIC 0781*

GATEMAN-MILLOY INC p637
270 SHOEMAKER ST, KITCHENER, ON, N2E 3E1
(519) 748-6500   *SIC 0781*

LLOYD REFORESTATION LTD p250
13025 WOODLAND RD, PRINCE GEORGE, BC, V2N 5B4
SIC 0781

PRESTIGE LANDSCAPE GROUP p31
105-1212 34 AVE SE, CALGARY, AB, T2G 1V7
(403) 280-5400   *SIC 0781*

ULS MAINTENANCE & LANDSCAPING INC p160
240085 FRONTIER CRES, ROCKY VIEW COUNTY, AB, T1X 0W2
(403) 235-5353   *SIC 0781*

SIC 0782 Lawn and garden services

156560 CANADA INC p1233
1123 NORD LAVAL (A-440) O, MONTREAL, QC, H7L 3W3
(514) 337-1222   *SIC 0782*

ALPHA BETTER LANDSCAPING LTD p70
11800 40 ST SE, CALGARY, AB, T2Z 4T1
(403) 248-3559   *SIC 0782*

BLUE PINE ENTERPRISES LTD p278
18960 34A AVE, SURREY, BC, V3Z 1A7

(604) 535-3026   *SIC 0782*

ELMSDALE LANDSCAPING LIMITED p449
113 ELMSDALE RD, ELMSDALE, NS, B2S 1K7
(902) 883-2291   *SIC 0782*

GREENLAWN, LTD p695
2385 MATHESON BLVD E, MISSISSAUGA, ON, L4W 5B3
(905) 290-1844   *SIC 0782*

TBG ENVIRONMENTAL INC p1016
425 WHITEVALE RD UNIT 5, WHITEVALE, ON, L0H 1M0
(905) 620-1222   *SIC 0782*

TURF OPERATIONS SCARBOROUGH INC p865
80 AUTO MALL DR, SCARBOROUGH, ON, M1B 5N5
(416) 269-8333   *SIC 0782*

SIC 0783 Ornamental shrub and tree services

ARBORCARE TREE SERVICE LTD p77
10100 114 AVE SE, CALGARY, AB, T3S 0A5
(403) 273-6378   *SIC 0783*

ASPLUNDH CANADA ULC p179
26050 31B AVE, ALDERGROVE, BC, V4W 2Z6
(604) 856-2222   *SIC 0783*

ASPLUNDH CANADA ULC p1380
3366 RUE JACOB-JORDAN, TERRE-BONNE, QC, J6X 4J6
(450) 968-1888   *SIC 0783*

DAVEY TREE EXPERT CO. OF CANADA, LIMITED p118
5622 103A ST NW, EDMONTON, AB, T6H 2J5
(780) 428-8733   *SIC 0783*

ENTREPRISES D'EMONDAGE L.D.L. INC, LES p1386
2300 BOUL DES RECOLLETS, TROIS-RIVIERES, QC, G8Z 3X5
(819) 694-0395   *SIC 0783*

ONTARIO LINE CLEARING & TREE EX-PERTS INC p545
7790 TELEPHONE RD, COBOURG, ON, K9A 4J7
(905) 372-6706   *SIC 0783*

REBOITECH INC p1133
112 RUE DE LA PINEDE, LATERRIERE, QC, G7N 1B8
(418) 545-2893   *SIC 0783*

WELLER, W.M. TREE SERVICE LTD p628
18 CIRCLE RIDGE DR, KESWICK, ON, L4P 2G9
(905) 476-4593   *SIC 0783*

SIC 0831 Forest products

103190 ONTARIO INC p567
2452 YORKS CORNERS RD, EDWARDS, ON, K0A 1V0
(613) 821-2751   *SIC 0831*

PF RESOLU CANADA INC p1211
111 BOUL ROBERT-BOURASSA UNITE 5000, MONTREAL, QC, H3C 2M1
(514) 875-2160   *SIC 0831*

TIMBERWEST FOREST COMPANY p316
1055 GEORGIA ST W SUITE 2300, VAN-COUVER, BC, V6E 0B6
(604) 654-4600   *SIC 0831*

SIC 0851 Forestry services

AIRSPRAY (1967) LTD p97
10141 122 ST NW, EDMONTON, AB, T5N 1L7
(780) 453-1737   *SIC 0851*

APOLLO FOREST PRODUCTS LTD p213
2555 TACHIE RD, FORT ST. JAMES, BC,

V0J 1P0
(250) 996-8297   *SIC 0851*

CATHAY FOREST PRODUCTS CORP p851
30 WERTHEIM CRT SUITE 14, RICHMOND HILL, ON, L4B 1B9
SIC 0851

CERVUS AG EQUIPMENT LP p76
333 96 AVE NE SUITE 5201, CALGARY, AB, T3K 0S3
(403) 567-0339   *SIC 0851*

CONAIR GROUP INC p176
1510 TOWER ST, ABBOTSFORD, BC, V2T 6H5
(604) 855-1171   *SIC 0851*

COOP DE TRAVAIL EN AMENAGEMENT FORESTIER DE GRANDE-VALLEE p1112
39C RUE SAINT-FRANCOIS-XAVIER E, GRANDE-VALLEE, QC, G0E 1K0
(418) 393-3339   *SIC 0851*

COOP FORESTIERE DE STE-ROSE p1363
184 RUE DU QUAI, SAINTE-ROSE-DU-NORD, QC, G0V 1T0
SIC 0851

COOPERATIVE DE TRAVAILLEURS FORESTIERS EAUBOIS p1355
48 3E AV O, SAINTE-ANNE-DES-MONTS, QC, G4V 1J5
(418) 763-2255   *SIC 0851*

COOPERATIVE FORESTIERE ST-DOMINIQUE p1299
289 RUE PRINCIPALE, SAINT-DOMINIQUE-DU-ROSAIRE, QC, J0Y 2K0
(819) 732-5723   *SIC 0851*

ENTREPRISES JEAN-MAURICE PAPINEAU LTEE, LES p1102
14 309 RTE N BUREAU 100, FERME-NEUVE, QC, J0W 1C0
(819) 587-3360   *SIC 0851*

FORESTERIE A S L INC, LA p1366
803 14E AV, SENNETERRE, QC, J0Y 2M0
(819) 737-8851   *SIC 0851*

FORESTERIE C. H. B. LTEE p1368
3563 RUE TRUDEL, SHAWINIGAN, QC, G9N 6R4
(819) 731-0477   *SIC 0851*

FOREX INC p1204
1250 BOUL RENE-LEVESQUE O BUREAU 3930, MONTREAL, QC, H3B 4W8
(514) 935-0702   *SIC 0851*

GEO-FOR INC p1347
633 AV GAGNON, SAINT-LUDGER-DE-MILOT, QC, G0W 2B0
SIC 0851

GOLDEN FIRE JUMPERS LTD p215
1717 MOBERLY SCHOOL RD, GOLDEN, BC, V0A 1H1
(250) 344-6464   *SIC 0851*

GROUPEMENT FORESTIER DE KAMOURASKA INC p1291
605 289 RTE, SAINT-ALEXANDRE-DE-KAMOURASKA, QC, G0L 2G0
(418) 495-2054   *SIC 0851*

GROUPEMENT FORESTIER DU HAUT YA-MASKA INC p1088
578 RUE DE LA RIVIERE, COWANSVILLE, QC, J2K 3G6
(450) 263-7120   *SIC 0851*

INDUSTRIAL FORESTRY SERVICE LTD p249
1595 5TH AVE, PRINCE GEORGE, BC, V2L 3L9
(250) 564-4115   *SIC 0851*

M.C. FORET INC p1124
5946 BOUL DU CURE-LABELLE RR 3, LA-BELLE, QC, J0T 1H0
(819) 686-1464   *SIC 0851*

MAG AEROSPACE CANADA CORP p565
1012 HWY 601 UNIT 10, DRYDEN, ON, P8N 0A2
(807) 937-5544   *SIC 0851*

NEXT GENERATION REFORESTATION LTD p5
GD, BEAVERLODGE, AB, T0H 0C0
(780) 532-2220   *SIC 0851*

NORTHERN REFORESTATION INC p163
1312 TAMARACK RD NE, SLAVE LAKE, AB, T0G 2A0
(780) 849-1980   *SIC 0851*

R D I REFORESTATION & DEVELOPMENTS INC p222
534 CHRISTLETON AVE, KELOWNA, BC, V1Y 5J2
(250) 470-1842   *SIC 0851*

REXFORET INC p1148
248 RUE CARTIER, MANIWAKI, QC, J9E 3P5
(819) 449-6088   *SIC 0851*

SEI INDUSTRIES LTD p210
7400 WILSON AVE, DELTA, BC, V4G 1H3
(604) 946-3131   *SIC 0851*

SNJ FORESTERIE p394
4016 ROUTE 480, ACADIEVILLE, NB, E4Y 2B7
(506) 775-2895   *SIC 0851*

SOCIETE D'EXPLOITATION DES RESSOURCES DE LA NEIGETTE INC p1124
1 RUE PRINCIPALE O, LA TRINITE-DES-MONTS, QC, G0K 1B0
(418) 779-2095   *SIC 0851*

SOCIETE D'EXPLOITATION DES RESSOURCES DE LA VALLEE p1124
108 RUE DU NOVICIAT, LAC-AU-SAUMON, QC, G0J 1M0
(418) 778-5877   *SIC 0851*

SOCIETE DE PROTECTION DES FORETS CONTRE LE FEU (SOPFEU) p1151
175 105 RTE, MESSINES, QC, J0X 2J0
(819) 449-4271   *SIC 0851*

SOCIETE DE PROTECTION DES FORETS CONTRE LE FEU (SOPFEU) p1278
715 7E RUE DE L'AEROPORT, QUEBEC, QC, G2G 2S7
(418) 871-3341   *SIC 0851*

SOCIETE DE PROTECTION DES FORETS CONTRE LE FEU (SOPFEU) p1287
1230 RTE DE L'AEROPORT, ROBERVAL, QC, G8H 2M9
(418) 275-6400   *SIC 0851*

SOCIETE DE PROTECTION DES FORETS CONTRE LES INSECTES ET MALADIES p1265
1780 RUE SEMPLE, QUEBEC, QC, G1N 4B8
(418) 681-3381   *SIC 0851*

SOCIETE SYLVICOLE CHAMBORD LTEE p1075
21 RUE DES SOURCES, CHAMBORD, QC, G0W 1G0
(418) 342-6251   *SIC 0851*

SOCIETE SYLVICOLE MISTASSINI LTEE p1090
245 RUE DE QUEN, DOLBEAU-MISTASSINI, QC, G8L 5M3
(418) 276-8080   *SIC 0851*

SPRINGDALE FOREST RESOURCES INC p428
406 LITTLE BAY RD, SPRINGDALE, NL, A0J 1T0
(709) 673-4695   *SIC 0851*

ST. WILLIAMS NURSERY AND ECOLOGY CENTRE INC p890
885 24 HWY E, ST WILLIAMS, ON, N0E 1P0
(519) 586-9116   *SIC 0851*

SIC 0912 Finfish

ARGENT FISHERIES (2007) LIMITED p450
501 MAIN ST, GLACE BAY, NS, B1A 4X5
(902) 849-1005   *SIC 0912*

COOKE AQUACULTURE INC p395
874 MAIN ST, BLACKS HARBOUR, NB, E5H 1E6
(506) 456-6600   *SIC 0912*

COOKE INC p395
669 MAIN ST, BLACKS HARBOUR, NB,

E5H 1K1
(506) 456-6600   *SIC 0912*

F.A.S. SEAFOOD PRODUCERS LTD   *p335*
27 ERIE ST, VICTORIA, BC, V8V 1P8
(250) 383-7764   *SIC 0912*

GRIEG SEAFOOD B.C. LTD   *p195*
1180 IRONWOOD ST SUITE 106, CAMP-
BELL RIVER, BC, V9W 5P7
(250) 286-0838   *SIC 0912*

SIC 0913 Shellfish

M. V. OSPREY LTD   *p464*
P.O. BOX 188 STN MAIN, NORTH SYDNEY,
NS, B2A 3M3
(902) 794-1600   *SIC 0913*

P.E.I. MUSSEL KING (1994) INC   *p1041*
318 RED HEAD RD, MORELL, PE, C0A 1S0
(902) 961-3300   *SIC 0913*

SIC 0921 Fish hatcheries and preserves

**OKANAGAN NATION AQUATIC ENTER-
PRISES LTD**   *p342*
3535 OLD OKANAGAN HWY UNIT 104,
WESTBANK, BC, V4T 3L7
(778) 754-8001   *SIC 0921*

*SIC 0971 Hunting, trapping, game
propagation*

**BRITISH COLUMBIA CONSERVATION
FOUNDATION, THE**   *p271*
17564 56A AVE SUITE 206, SURREY, BC,
V3S 1G3
(604) 576-1433   *SIC 0971*

IGT CANADA SOLUTIONS ULC   *p410*
328 URQUHART AVE, MONCTON, NB,
E1H 2R6
(506) 878-6000   *SIC 0971*

**QUANTUM INTERNATIONAL INCOME
CORP**   *p970*
79 WELLINGTON ST W SUITE 1630,
TORONTO, ON, M5K 1H1
(416) 477-3400   *SIC 0971*

SIC 1011 Iron ores

**ARCELORMITTAL   EXPLOITATION
MINIERE CANADA S.E.N.C.**   *p1144*
1010 RUE DE SERIGNY, LONGUEUIL, QC,
J4K 5G7
(418) 766-2000   *SIC 1011*

ASANKO GOLD INC   *p311*
1066 HASTINGS ST W SUITE 680, VAN-
COUVER, BC, V6E 3X2
(604) 683-8193   *SIC 1011*

ATLANTIC MINERALS LIMITED   *p427*
GD, PORT AU PORT, NL, A0N 1T0
(709) 644-2447   *SIC 1011*

CANADIAN TEST CASE 65   *p720*
6750 CENTURY AVE SUITE 305, MISSIS-
SAUGA, ON, L5N 2V8
(905) 812-5920   *SIC 1011*

COMPAGNIE MINIERE IOC INC   *p425*
2 AVALON DR, LABRADOR CITY, NL, A2V
2Y6
(709) 944-8400   *SIC 1011*

COMPAGNIE MINIERE IOC INC   *p1203*
1190   AV   DES   CANADIENS-DE-
MONTREAL BUREAU 400, MONTREAL,
QC, H3B 0E3
(418) 968-7400   *SIC 1011*

COMPAGNIE MINIERE IOC INC   *p1367*
1 RUE RETTY, SEPT-ILES, QC, G4R 3C7
(418) 968-7400   *SIC 1011*

LION ONE METALS LIMITED   *p240*
311 1ST ST W, NORTH VANCOUVER, BC,
V7M 1B5
(604) 998-1250   *SIC 1011*

MINERAI DE FER QUEBEC INC   *p1102*
556 RTE 389, FERMONT, QC, G0G 1J0
(418) 287-2000   *SIC 1011*

MINERAI DE FER QUEBEC INC   *p1206*
1100 BOUL RENE-LEVESQUE O BUREAU
610, MONTREAL, QC, H3B 4N4
(514) 316-4858   *SIC 1011*

MINES WABUSH   *p1367*
1505 CH POINTE-NOIRE, SEPT-ILES, QC,
G4R 4L4
(418) 962-5131   *SIC 1011*

SPROTT RESOURCE HOLDINGS INC   *p967*
200 BAY ST SUITE 2600, TORONTO, ON,
M5J 2J1
(855) 943-8099   *SIC 1011*

SIC 1021 Copper ores

AFTON OPERATING CORPORATION   *p301*
3300 BURRARD ST, VANCOUVER, BC,
V6C 0B3
(604) 699-4000   *SIC 1021*

AMERIGO RESOURCES LTD   *p302*
355 BURRARD ST SUITE 1260, VANCOU-
VER, BC, V6C 2G8
(604) 681-2802   *SIC 1021*

ATICO MINING CORPORATION   *p302*
543 GRANVILLE ST UNIT 501, VANCOU-
VER, BC, V6C 1X8
(604) 633-9022   *SIC 1021*

AURCANA CORPORATION   *p302*
789 PENDER ST W SUITE 850, VANCOU-
VER, BC, V6C 1H2
(604) 331-9333   *SIC 1021*

AVALON ADVANCED MATERIALS INC *p948*
130   ADELAIDE   ST   W   SUITE   1901,
TORONTO, ON, M5H 3P5
(416) 364-4938   *SIC 1021*

AZARGA METALS CORP   *p343*
15782 MARINE DR UNIT 1, WHITE ROCK,
BC, V4B 1E6
(604) 536-2711   *SIC 1021*

**COPPER MOUNTAIN MINING CORPORA-
TION**   *p303*
700 PENDER ST W SUITE 1700, VANCOU-
VER, BC, V6C 1G8
(604) 682-2992   *SIC 1021*

CORO MINING CORP   *p303*
625 HOWE ST SUITE 1280, VANCOUVER,
BC, V6C 2T6
(604) 682-5546   *SIC 1021*

CUCO RESOURCES LTD   *p950*
155   UNIVERSITY   AVE   SUITE   1230,
TORONTO, ON, M5H 3B7
(647) 247-1381   *SIC 1021*

EQUINOX GOLD CORP   *p304*
700 WEST PENDER ST SUITE 1501, VAN-
COUVER, BC, V6C 1G8
(604) 558-0560   *SIC 1021*

ERO COPPER CORP   *p304*
625 HOWE ST SUITE 1050, VANCOUVER,
BC, V6C 2T6
(604) 449-9244   *SIC 1021*

EXCELSIOR MINING CORP   *p312*
1140 PENDER ST W SUITE 1240, VAN-
COUVER, BC, V6E 4G1
(604) 681-8030   *SIC 1021*

FIRST QUANTUM MINERALS LTD   *p304*
543 GRANVILLE ST 14TH FL, VANCOU-
VER, BC, V6C 1X8
(604) 688-6577   *SIC 1021*

GLENCORE CANADA CORPORATION *p986*
100 KING ST W SUITE 6900, TORONTO,
ON, M5X 2A1
(416) 775-1200   *SIC 1021*

GRID METALS CORP   *p921*
3335 YONGE ST SUITE 304, TORONTO,
ON, M4N 2M1
(416) 955-4773   *SIC 1021*

HIGHLAND COPPER COMPANY INC *p1144*
1111 RUE SAINT-CHARLES O BUREAU
101, LONGUEUIL, QC, J4K 5G4
(450) 677-2455   *SIC 1021*

HUCKLEBERRY MINES LTD   *p215*
GD, HOUSTON, BC, V0J 1Z0
(604) 517-4723   *SIC 1021*

HUDBAY MINERALS INC   *p350*
GD, FLIN FLON, MB, R8A 1N9
(204) 687-2385   *SIC 1021*

KGHM AJAX MINING INC   *p217*
124 SEYMOUR ST SUITE 200, KAM-
LOOPS, BC, V2C 2E1
(250) 374-5446   *SIC 1021*

KGHM AJAX MINING INC   *p306*
800 PENDER ST W SUITE 615, VANCOU-
VER, BC, V6C 2V6
(604) 682-0301   *SIC 1021*

KINCORA COPPER LIMITED   *p314*
1199 WEST HASTINGS ST SUITE 800,
VANCOUVER, BC, V6E 3T5
(604) 283-1722   *SIC 1021*

LOS ANDES COPPER LTD   *p306*
355 BURRARD ST SUITE 1260, VANCOU-
VER, BC, V6C 2G8
(604) 681-2802   *SIC 1021*

LUNDIN MINING CORPORATION   *p954*
150 KING ST W SUITE 1500, TORONTO,
ON, M5H 1J9
(416) 342-5560   *SIC 1021*

MASON RESOURCES CORP   *p315*
1066 HASTINGS ST W SUITE 1650, VAN-
COUVER, BC, V6E 3X1
(604) 673-2001   *SIC 1021*

NEW PACIFIC METALS CORP   *p307*
200 GRANVILLE ST SUITE 1378, VAN-
COUVER, BC, V6C 1S4
(604) 633-1368   *SIC 1021*

NGEX RESOURCES INC   *p307*
885 GEORGIA ST W SUITE 2000, VAN-
COUVER, BC, V6C 3E8
(604) 689-7842   *SIC 1021*

NORTHERN   DYNASTY   MINERALS   LTD
p315
1040 WEST GEORGIA ST 15TH FL, VAN-
COUVER, BC, V6E 4H1
(604) 684-6365   *SIC 1021*

QUATERRA RESOURCES INC   *p316*
1199 HASTINGS ST W SUITE 1100, VAN-
COUVER, BC, V6E 3T5
(855) 681-9059   *SIC 1021*

SIERRA METALS INC   *p966*
161 BAY ST SUITE 4260, TORONTO, ON,
M5J 2S1
(416) 366-7777   *SIC 1021*

**TECK HIGHLAND VALLEY COPPER PART-
NERSHIP**   *p230*
HWY 97C HIGHLAND VALLEY COPPER
MINESITE, LOGAN LAKE, BC, V0K 1W0
(250) 523-2443   *SIC 1021*

TECK RESOURCES LIMITED   *p310*
550 BURRARD ST SUITE 3300, VANCOU-
VER, BC, V6C 0B3
(604) 699-4000   *SIC 1021*

TRILOGY METALS INC   *p330*
609 GRANVILLE ST SUITE 1150, VAN-
COUVER, BC, V7Y 1G5
(604) 638-8088   *SIC 1021*

SIC 1031 Lead and zinc ores

ENERGY FUELS INC   *p938*
82   RICHMOND   ST   E   SUITE   308,
TORONTO, ON, M5C 1P1
(416) 214-2810   *SIC 1031*

GROUP ELEVEN RESOURCES CORP   *p305*
400 BURRARD ST SUITE 1050, VANCOU-
VER, BC, V6C 3A6
(604) 630-8839   *SIC 1031*

NORZINC LTD   *p299*
650 GEORGIA ST W SUITE 1710, VAN-
COUVER, BC, V6B 4N9
(604) 688-2001   *SIC 1031*

PUNA OPERATIONS INC   *p329*
1055 DUNSMUIR ST, VANCOUVER, BC,
V7X 1G4
(604) 689-3846   *SIC 1031*

TINKA RESOURCES LIMITED   *p317*
1090 GEORGIA ST W SUITE 1305, VAN-
COUVER, BC, V6E 3V7
(604) 685-9316   *SIC 1031*

TITAN MINING CORPORATION   *p310*
999 CANADA PL UNIT 555, VANCOUVER,
BC, V6C 3C1
(604) 687-1717   *SIC 1031*

TREVALI MINING CORPORATION   *p317*
1199 HASTINGS ST W UNIT 1400, VAN-
COUVER, BC, V6E 3T5
(604) 488-1661   *SIC 1031*

**ZINC ELECTROLYTIQUE DU CANADA LIM-
ITEE**   *p1366*
860   BOUL   GERARD-CADIEUX,
SALABERRY-DE-VALLEYFIELD, QC, J6T
6L4
(450) 373-9144   *SIC 1031*

ZINCORE METALS INC   *p323*
5626 LARCH ST SUITE 202, VANCOUVER,
BC, V6M 4E1
(604) 669-6611   *SIC 1031*

SIC 1041 Gold ores

AFRICAN GOLD GROUP, INC   *p936*
151 YONGE ST 11TH FL, TORONTO, ON,
M5C 2W7
(647) 775-8538   *SIC 1041*

AGNICO EAGLE MINES LIMITED   *p936*
145 KING ST E SUITE 400, TORONTO, ON,
M5C 2Y7
(416) 947-1212   *SIC 1041*

AGNICO EAGLE MINES LIMITED   *p1288*
10200 RTE DE PREISSAC, ROUYN-
NORANDA, QC, J0Y 1C0
(819) 759-3700   *SIC 1041*

ALACER GOLD CORP   *p1440*
3081 3RD AVE, WHITEHORSE, YT, Y1A
4Z7
(800) 387-0825   *SIC 1041*

ALAMOS GOLD INC   *p680*
259 MATHESON ST, MATACHEWAN, ON,
P0K 1M0
(705) 565-9800   *SIC 1041*

ALAMOS GOLD INC   *p959*
181 BAY ST SUITE 3910, TORONTO, ON,
M5J 2T3
(416) 368-9932   *SIC 1041*

ALDRIDGE MINERALS INC   *p936*
10 KING ST E SUITE 300, TORONTO, ON,
M5C 1C3
SIC 1041

ALEXCO RESOURCE CORP   *p327*
555 BURRARD ST TWO BENTALL CEN-
TRE SUITE 1225, VANCOUVER, BC, V7X
1M9
(604) 633-4888   *SIC 1041*

ALIANZA MINERALS LTD   *p302*
325 HOWE ST SUITE 410, VANCOUVER,
BC, V6C 1Z7
(604) 687-3520   *SIC 1041*

ALIO GOLD INC   *p302*
700 WEST PENDER ST SUITE 507, VAN-
COUVER, BC, V6C 1G8
(604) 682-4002   *SIC 1041*

ANACONDA MINING INC   *p948*
150 YORK ST SUITE 410, TORONTO, ON,
M5H 3S5
(416) 304-6622   *SIC 1041*

ARIZONA SILVER EXPLORATION INC *p302*
750 WEST PENDER ST SUITE 804, VAN-
COUVER, BC, V6C 2T7
(604) 833-4278   *SIC 1041*

ATAC RESOURCES LTD   *p297*
510 HASTINGS ST W SUITE 1016, VAN-
COUVER, BC, V6B 1L8
(604) 687-2522   *SIC 1041*

ATACAMA PACIFIC GOLD CORPORATION
p936
25   ADELAIDE   ST   E   SUITE   1900,
TORONTO, ON, M5C 3A1
(416) 861-8267   *SIC 1041*

▲ Public Company   ■ Public Company Family Member   **HQ** Headquarters   **BR** Branch   **SL** Single Location

ATLANTA GOLD INC *p985*
100 KING ST W SUITE 5600, TORONTO, ON, M5X 1C9
(416) 777-0013 *SIC* 1041

AURA MINERALS INC *p948*
155 UNIVERSITY AVE SUITE 1240, TORONTO, ON, M5H 3B7
(416) 649-1033 *SIC* 1041

AVESORO RESOURCES INC *p971*
199 BAY ST SUITE 5300, TORONTO, ON, M5L 1B9
SIC 1041

B2GOLD CORP *p328*
595 BURRARD ST SUITE 3100, VANCOUVER, BC, V7X 1L7
(604) 681-8371 *SIC* 1041

BANRO CORPORATION *p985*
100 KING ST W SUITE 7070, TORONTO, ON, M5X 2A1
(416) 366-2221 *SIC* 1041

BARKERVILLE GOLD MINES LTD *p948*
155 UNIVERSITY AVE SUITE 1410, TORONTO, ON, M5H 3B7
(416) 775-3671 *SIC* 1041

BARRICK GOLD CORPORATION *p959*
161 BAY ST SUITE 3700, TORONTO, ON, M5J 2S1
(416) 861-9911 *SIC* 1041

BEAUFIELD RESOURCES INC *p1193*
1801 MCGILL COLLEGE AVE BUREAU 950, MONTREAL, QC, H3A 2N4
(514) 842-3443 *SIC* 1041

BELO SUN MINING CORP *p949*
65 QUEEN ST W SUITE 800, TORONTO, ON, M5H 2M5
(416) 309-2137 *SIC* 1041

BLUESTONE RESOURCES INC *p302*
800 PENDER ST W UNIT 1020, VANCOUVER, BC, V6C 2V6
(604) 646-4534 *SIC* 1041

BONTERRA RESOURCES INC *p302*
200 BURRARD ST SUITE 1680, VANCOUVER, BC, V6C 3L6
(604) 678-5308 *SIC* 1041

CACHE EXPLORATION INC *p210*
4770 72ND ST, DELTA, BC, V4K 3N3
(604) 306-5285 *SIC* 1041

CADILLAC VENTURES INC *p941*
65 FRONT ST E SUITE 200, TORONTO, ON, M5E 1B5
(416) 203-7722 *SIC* 1041

CANADIAN MALARTIC GP *p1148*
100 CH DU LAC MOURIER, MALARTIC, QC, J0Y 1Z0
(819) 757-2225 *SIC* 1041

CLAUDE RESOURCES INC *p1408*
1112 FINLAYSON ST, LA RONGE, SK, S0J 1L0
(306) 635-2015 *SIC* 1041

CLAUDE RESOURCES INC *p1408*
GD, LA RONGE, SK, S0J 1L0
(306) 635-2015 *SIC* 1041

CLAUDE RESOURCES INC *p1431*
2100 AIRPORT DR SUITE 202, SASKATOON, SK, S7L 6M6
(306) 668-7505 *SIC* 1041

COLOSSUS MINERALS INC *p986*
100 KING ST W SUITE 5600, TORONTO, ON, M5X 1C9
SIC 1041

COLUMBUS GOLD CORP *p297*
1090 HAMILTON ST, VANCOUVER, BC, V6B 2R9
(604) 634-0970 *SIC* 1041

CONTINENTAL GOLD INC *p979*
155 WELLINGTON ST W SUITE 2920, TORONTO, ON, M5V 3H1
(416) 583-5610 *SIC* 1041

CORE GOLD INC *p312*
1166 ALBERNI ST SUITE 1201, VANCOUVER, BC, V6E 3Z3
(604) 345-4822 *SIC* 1041

DETOUR GOLD CORPORATION *p971*
199 BAY ST SUITE 4100, TORONTO, ON, M5L 1E2
(416) 304-0800 *SIC* 1041

DUNDEE PRECIOUS METALS INC *p938*
1 ADELAIDE ST E SUITE 500, TORONTO, ON, M5C 2V9
(416) 365-5191 *SIC* 1041

EASTWEST GOLD CORPORATION *p962*
25 YORK ST 17 FL, TORONTO, ON, M5J 2V5
(416) 365-5123 *SIC* 1041

ELDORADO GOLD CORPORATION *p303*
550 BURRARD ST 1188 BENTALL 5, VANCOUVER, BC, V6C 2B5
(604) 687-4018 *SIC* 1041

ENDEAVOUR SILVER CORP *p330*
609 GRANVILLE ST SUITE 1130, VANCOUVER, BC, V7Y 1G5
(604) 685-9775 *SIC* 1041

EURO SUN MINING INC *p951*
65 QUEEN ST W SUITE 800, TORONTO, ON, M5H 2M5
(416) 368-7744 *SIC* 1041

FIORE GOLD LTD *p951*
120 ADELAIDE ST W SUITE 1410, TORONTO, ON, M5H 1T1
(416) 639-1426 *SIC* 1041

FORAGE ORBIT GARANT INC *p1390*
3200 BOUL JEAN-JACQUES-COSSETTE, VAL-D'OR, QC, J9P 6Y6
(819) 824-2707 *SIC* 1041

FORTUNE BAY CORP *p453*
1969 UPPER WATER ST SUITE 2001, HALIFAX, NS, B3J 3R7
(902) 442-1421 *SIC* 1041

FRANCO-NEVADA CORPORATION *p971*
199 BAY ST SUITE 2000, TORONTO, ON, M5L 1G9
(416) 306-6300 *SIC* 1041

GABRIEL RESOURCES LTD *p1440*
204 LAMBERT ST SUITE 200, WHITEHORSE, YT, Y1A 1Z4
SIC 1041

GALANE GOLD LTD *p962*
181 BAY ST SUITE 1800, TORONTO, ON, M5J 2T9
(647) 987-7663 *SIC* 1041

GENESIS METALS CORP *p304*
409 GRANVILLE ST SUITE 1500, VANCOUVER, BC, V6C 1T2
(604) 602-1440 *SIC* 1041

GOLD STANDARD VENTURES CORP *p304*
815 HASTINGS ST W SUITE 610, VANCOUVER, BC, V6C 1B4
(604) 687-2766 *SIC* 1041

GOLDCORP CANADA LTD *p304*
666 BURRARD ST SUITE 3400, VANCOUVER, BC, V6C 2X8
(604) 696-3000 *SIC* 1041

GOLDEN QUEEN MINING CO. LTD *p304*
580 HORNBY ST SUITE 880, VANCOUVER, BC, V6C 3B6
(604) 417-7952 *SIC* 1041

GOLDEN STAR RESOURCES LTD *p952*
150 KING ST W SUITE 1200, TORONTO, ON, M5H 1J9
(416) 583-3800 *SIC* 1041

GOLDGROUP MINING INC *p313*
1166 ALBERNI ST SUITE 1502, VANCOUVER, BC, V6E 3Z3
(604) 682-1943 *SIC* 1041

GOLDMINING INC *p313*
1030 W GEORGIA ST SUITE 1830, VANCOUVER, BC, V6E 2Y3
(604) 630-1000 *SIC* 1041

GOLDSTRIKE RESOURCES LTD *p313*
1130 W PENDER ST SUITE 1010, VANCOUVER, BC, V6E 4A4
(604) 681-1820 *SIC* 1041

GUNGNIR RESOURCES INC *p280*
1688 152 ST SUITE 404, SURREY, BC, V4A 4N2
(604) 683-0484 *SIC* 1041

GUYANA GOLDFIELDS INC *p945*
375 UNIVERSITY AV SUITE 802, TORONTO, ON, M5G 2J5
(416) 628-5936 *SIC* 1041

HELIX APPLICATIONS INC *p939*
82 RICHMOND ST SUITE 203 THE CANADIAN VENTURE BUILDING, TORONTO, ON, M5C 1P1
(416) 848-6865 *SIC* 1041

IAMGOLD CORPORATION *p952*
401 BAY ST SUITE 3200, TORONTO, ON, M5H 2Y4
(416) 360-4710 *SIC* 1041

IAMGOLD CORPORATION *p1046*
118 RTE 109 N, AMOS, QC, J9T 3A3
(819) 732-8268 *SIC* 1041

IDM MINING LTD *p328*
555 BURRARD ST SUITE 1800, VANCOUVER, BC, V7X 1M9
(604) 681-5672 *SIC* 1041

IMPERIAL METALS CORPORATION *p305*
580 HORNBY ST SUITE 200, VANCOUVER, BC, V6C 3B6
(604) 669-8959 *SIC* 1041

JAGUAR MINING INC *p987*
100 KING ST W 56TH FL, TORONTO, ON, M5X 1C9
(416) 847-1854 *SIC* 1041

K92 MINING INC *p314*
1090 GEORGIA ST W SUITE 488, VANCOUVER, BC, V6E 3V7
(236) 521-0584 *SIC* 1041

KINROSS GOLD CORPORATION *p882*
4315 GOLDMINE RD, SOUTH PORCUPINE, ON, P0N 1H0
SIC 1041

KIRKLAND LAKE GOLD LTD *p964*
200 BAY ST SUITE 3120, TORONTO, ON, M5J 2J1
(416) 840-7884 *SIC* 1041

LEAGOLD MINING CORPORATION *p328*
595 BURRARD ST SUITE 3043, VANCOUVER, BC, V7X 1J1
(604) 398-4505 *SIC* 1041

LIBERTY GOLD CORP *p314*
1055 HASTINGS ST W SUITE 1900, VANCOUVER, BC, V6E 2E9
(604) 632-4677 *SIC* 1041

LONCOR RESOURCES INC *p987*
100 KING ST W SUITE 7070, TORONTO, ON, M5X 2A1
(416) 361-2510 *SIC* 1041

LUNDIN GOLD INC *p307*
885 GEORGIA ST W SUITE 2000, VANCOUVER, BC, V6C 3E8
(604) 689-7842 *SIC* 1041

MAJESTIC GOLD CORP *p280*
1688 152ND ST SUITE 306, SURREY, BC, V4A 4N2
(604) 560-9060 *SIC* 1041

MANDALAY RESOURCES CORPORATION *p939*
76 RICHMOND ST E SUITE 330, TORONTO, ON, M5C 1P1
(647) 260-1566 *SIC* 1041

MARLIN GOLD MINING LTD *p328*
595 BURRARD ST SUITE 2833, VANCOUVER, BC, V7X 1J1
(604) 646-1580 *SIC* 1041

MAX RESOURCE CORP *p315*
1095 W PENDER ST SUITE 1188, VANCOUVER, BC, V6E 2M6
(604) 365-1522 *SIC* 1041

MCEWEN MINING INC *p954*
150 KING ST W SUITE 2800, TORONTO, ON, M5H 1J9
(647) 258-0395 *SIC* 1041

MIDAS GOLD CORP *p307*
999 HASTINGS ST W SUITE 890, VANCOUVER, BC, V6C 2W2
(778) 724-4700 *SIC* 1041

MINES D'OR DYNACOR INC *p1206*
625 RENE-LEVESQUE BOUL O BUREAU 1105, MONTREAL, QC, H3B 1R2
(514) 393-9000 *SIC* 1041

MOUNT POLLEY MINING CORPORATION *p230*
5720 MOOREHEAD-BOOTJACK RD, LIKELY, BC, V0L 1N0
(250) 790-2215 *SIC* 1041

NEWCASTLE GOLD LTD *p307*
800 PENDER ST W SUITE 730, VANCOUVER, BC, V6C 2V6
(250) 925-2713 *SIC* 1041

NIGHTHAWK GOLD CORP *p955*
141 ADELAIDE ST W SUITE 301, TORONTO, ON, M5H 3L5
(647) 794-4313 *SIC* 1041

NORONT RESOURCES LTD *p955*
212 KING ST W SUITE 501, TORONTO, ON, M5H 1K5
(416) 367-1444 *SIC* 1041

NOVAGOLD RESOURCES INC *p308*
789 W PENDER ST SUITE 720, VANCOUVER, BC, V6C 1H2
(604) 669-6227 *SIC* 1041

ORACLE MINING CORP *p315*
1090 GEORGIA ST W SUITE 250, VANCOUVER, BC, V6E 3V7
(604) 689-9282 *SIC* 1041

ORCA GOLD INC *p308*
885 GEORGIA ST W SUITE 2000, VANCOUVER, BC, V6C 3E8
(604) 689-7842 *SIC* 1041

OREZONE GOLD CORPORATION *p829*
290 PICTON AVE SUITE 201, OTTAWA, ON, K1Z 8P8
(613) 241-3699 *SIC* 1041

PELANGIO EXPLORATION INC *p940*
82 RICHMOND ST E, TORONTO, ON, M5C 1P1
(905) 336-3828 *SIC* 1041

PETAQUILLA MINERALS LTD *p327*
777 HORNBY ST SUITE 1230, VANCOUVER, BC, V6Z 1S4
SIC 1041

PLATINUM GROUP METALS LTD *p308*
550 BURRARD ST SUITE 788, VANCOUVER, BC, V6C 2B5
(604) 899-5450 *SIC* 1041

PORTEX MINERALS INC *p971*
199 BAY ST W SUITE 2901, TORONTO, ON, M5L 1G1
(416) 786-3876 *SIC* 1041

PRETIUM EXPLORATION INC *p329*
1055 DUNSMUIR ST SUITE 2300, VANCOUVER, BC, V7X 1L4
(604) 558-1784 *SIC* 1041

PRETIUM RESOURCES INC *p329*
1055 DUNSMUIR ST SUITE 2300 FOUR BENTALL CTR, VANCOUVER, BC, V7X 1L4
(604) 558-1784 *SIC* 1041

PRIMERO GOLD CANADA INC *p454*
1969 UPPER WATER ST SUITE 2001, HALIFAX, NS, B3J 3R7
(902) 422-1421 *SIC* 1041

PRIMERO MINING CORP *p970*
79 WELLINGTON ST W TD SOUTH TOWER SUITE 2100, TORONTO, ON, M5K 1H1
(416) 814-3160 *SIC* 1041

RED EAGLE MINING CORPORATION *p309*
666 BURRARD ST SUITE 2348, VANCOUVER, BC, V6C 2X8
(604) 638-2545 *SIC* 1041

RESSOURCES METANOR INC *p1391*
2872 CH SULLIVAN BUREAU 2, VAL-D'OR, QC, J9P 0B9
(819) 825-8678 *SIC* 1041

RHYOLITE RESOURCES LTD *p329*
595 BURRARD ST SUITE 1703, VANCOUVER, BC, V7X 1J1
(604) 488-8717 *SIC* 1041

RIO2 LIMITED *p309*
355 BURRARD ST SUITE 1260, VANCOUVER, BC, V6C 2G8
(604) 260-2696 *SIC* 1041

ROCKHAVEN RESOURCES LTD *p300*
510 HASTINGS ST W SUITE 1016, VANCOUVER, BC, V6B 1L8

(604) 688-2568   *SIC* 1041

ROXGOLD INC   p956
360 BAY ST SUITE 500, TORONTO, ON, M5H 2V6
(416) 203-6401   *SIC* 1041

RUSORO MINING LTD   p329
595 BURRARD ST SUITE 3123, VANCOUVER, BC, V7X 1J1
(604) 609-6110   *SIC* 1041

RYE PATCH GOLD CORP   p330
701 WEST GEORGIA ST SUITE 1500, VANCOUVER, BC, V7Y 1C6
(604) 638-1588   *SIC* 1041

SAN GOLD CORPORATION   p386
1661 PORTAGE AVE UNIT 212, WINNIPEG, MB, R3J 3T7
(204) 772-9149   *SIC* 1041

SANDSTORM GOLD LTD   p309
400 BURRARD ST SUITE 1400, VANCOUVER, BC, V6C 3G2
(604) 689-0234   *SIC* 1041

ST ANDREW GOLDFIELDS LTD   p940
20 ADELAIDE ST E SUITE 1500, TORONTO, ON, M5C 2T6
(416) 815-9855   *SIC* 1041

STARCORE INTERNATIONAL MINES LTD p309
580 HORNBY ST SUITE 750, VANCOUVER, BC, V6C 3B6
(604) 602-4935   *SIC* 1041

SUPERIOR GOLD INC   p967
70 UNIVERSITY AVE SUITE 1410, TORONTO, ON, M5J 2M4
(647) 925-1291   *SIC* 1041

TELSON MINING CORPORATION   p316
1111 MELVILLE ST SUITE 1000, VANCOUVER, BC, V6E 3V6
(604) 684-8071   *SIC* 1041

TERANGA GOLD CORPORATION   p970
77 KING ST W SUITE 2110, TORONTO, ON, M5K 2A1
(416) 594-0000   *SIC* 1041

TERRACO GOLD CORP   p316
1055 HASTINGS ST W SUITE 2390, VANCOUVER, BC, V6E 2E9
(604) 443-3830   *SIC* 1041

TMAC RESOURCES INC   p967
95 WELLINGTON ST W SUITE 1010, TORONTO, ON, M5J 2N7
(416) 628-0216   *SIC* 1041

WEALTH MINERALS LTD   p317
1177 HASTINGS ST W SUITE 2300, VANCOUVER, BC, V6E 2K3
(604) 331-0096   *SIC* 1041

WESDOME GOLD MINES LTD   p968
220 BAY ST SUITE 1200, TORONTO, ON, M5J 2W4
(416) 360-3743   *SIC* 1041

WEST KIRKLAND MINING INC   p317
1100 MELVILLE ST SUITE 838, VANCOUVER, BC, V6E 4A6
(604) 685-8311   *SIC* 1041

WHITE GOLD CORP   p941
82 RICHMOND ST E, TORONTO, ON, M5C 1P1
(416) 643-3880   *SIC* 1041

WILLIAMS OPERATING CORPORATION p664
HWY 17, MARATHON, ON, P0T 2E0
(807) 238-1100   *SIC* 1041

YAMANA GOLD INC   p968
200 BAY ST ROYAL BANK PLAZA NORTH TOWER STE 2200, TORONTO, ON, M5J 2J3
(416) 815-0220   *SIC* 1041

SIC 1044 Silver ores

AMERICAN CUMO MINING CORPORATION p292
638 MILLBANK RD, VANCOUVER, BC, V5Z 4B7
(604) 689-7902   *SIC* 1044

AVINO SILVER & GOLD MINES LTD   p302

570 GRANVILLE ST SUITE 900, VANCOUVER, BC, V6C 3P1
(604) 682-3701   *SIC* 1044

CANADIAN TEST CASE 21   p720
6750 CENTURY AVE SUITE 305, MISSISSAUGA, ON, L5N 2V8
(905) 812-5920   *SIC* 1044

FIRST MAJESTIC SILVER CORP   p304
925 GEORGIA ST W SUITE 1800, VANCOUVER, BC, V6C 3L2
(604) 688-3033   *SIC* 1044

FORTUNA SILVER MINES INC   p304
200 BURRARD ST SUITE 650, VANCOUVER, BC, V6C 3L6
(604) 484-4085   *SIC* 1044

GOGOLD RESOURCES INC   p453
2000 BARRINGTON ST SUITE 1301, HALIFAX, NS, B3J 3K1
(902) 482-1998   *SIC* 1044

NICOLA MINING INC   p307
355 BURRARD ST SUITE 1000, VANCOUVER, BC, V6C 2G8
(604) 683-8604   *SIC* 1044

PAN AMERICAN SILVER CORP   p308
625 HOWE ST SUITE 1440, VANCOUVER, BC, V6C 2T6
(604) 684-1175   *SIC* 1044

SANTACRUZ SILVER MINING LTD   p309
580 HORNBY ST SUITE 880, VANCOUVER, BC, V6C 3B6
(604) 569-1609   *SIC* 1044

SILVERCORP METALS INC   p309
200 GRANVILLE ST SUITE 1378, VANCOUVER, BC, V6C 1S4
(604) 669-9397   *SIC* 1044

SSR MINING INC   p329
1055 DUNSMUIR ST SUITE 800, VANCOUVER, BC, V7X 1G4
(604) 689-3846   *SIC* 1044

WHEATON PRECIOUS METALS CORP p317
1021 HASTINGS ST W SUITE 3500, VANCOUVER, BC, V6E 0C3
(604) 684-9648   *SIC* 1044

SIC 1061 Ferroalloy ores, except vanadium

ALLOYCORP MINING INC   p941
67 YONGE ST SUITE 501, TORONTO, ON, M5E 1J8
(416) 847-0376   *SIC* 1061

ALMONTY INDUSTRIES INC   p985
100 KING ST W SUITE 5700, TORONTO, ON, M5X 1C7
(647) 438-9766   *SIC* 1061

ASIAN MINERAL RESOURCES LIMITED p948
120 ADELAIDE ST W SUITE 2500, TORONTO, ON, M5H 1T1
(416) 360-3412   *SIC* 1061

COBALT 27 CAPITAL CORP   p950
4 KING ST W SUITE 401, TORONTO, ON, M5H 1B6
(647) 846-7765   *SIC* 1061

FIRST NICKEL INC   p933
120 FRONT ST E SUITE 206, TORONTO, ON, M5A 4L9
(416) 362-7050   *SIC* 1061

FPX NICKEL CORP   p313
1155 W PENDER ST SUITE 725, VANCOUVER, BC, V6E 2P4
(604) 681-8600   *SIC* 1061

GIYANI METALS CORP   p800
277 LAKESHORE RD E SUITE 403, OAKVILLE, ON, L6J 6J3
(289) 837-0066   *SIC* 1061

IVANHOE MINES LTD   p306
999 CANADA PL SUITE 654, VANCOUVER, BC, V6C 3E1
(604) 688-6630   *SIC* 1061

KOOTENAY SILVER INC   p314
1075 W GEORGIA ST SUITE 1650, VANCOUVER, BC, V6E 3C9
(604) 601-5650   *SIC* 1061

NORTH AMERICAN NICKEL INC   p315
1055 WEST HASTINGS ST SUITE 2200, VANCOUVER, BC, V6E 2E9
(604) 770-4334   *SIC* 1061

ROYAL NICKEL CORPORATION   p956
141 ADELAIDE ST W SUITE 1608, TORONTO, ON, M5H 3L5
(416) 363-0649   *SIC* 1061

TANTALUM MINING CORPORATION OF CANADA LIMITED   p351
BERNIC LAKE, LAC DU BONNET, MB, R0E 1A0
(204) 884-2400   *SIC* 1061

VALE CANADA LIMITED   p360
1 PLANT RD, THOMPSON, MB, R8N 1P3
(204) 778-2211   *SIC* 1061

SIC 1081 Metal mining services

2355291 ONTARIO IN   p912
92 BALSAM ST S SUITE 1, TIMMINS, ON, P4N 2C8
(705) 268-7956   *SIC* 1081

ALEX MACINTYRE & ASSOCIATES LIMITED   p634
1390 GOVERNMENT RD W, KIRKLAND LAKE, ON, P2N 3J5
(705) 567-3266   *SIC* 1081

ALTIUS MINERALS CORPORATION p429
38 DUFFY PL 2ND FL, ST. JOHN'S, NL, A1B 4M5
(709) 576-3440   *SIC* 1081

AMERICAS SILVER CORPORATION p948
145 KING ST W SUITE 2870, TORONTO, ON, M5H 1J8
(416) 848-9503   *SIC* 1081

ANDEANGOLD LTD   p329
701 GEORGIA ST W SUITE 1500, VANCOUVER, BC, V7Y 1K8
(604) 608-6172   *SIC* 1081

ARCHEAN RESOURCES LTD   p431
140 WATER ST SUITE 903, ST. JOHN'S, NL, A1C 6H6
(709) 758-1700   *SIC* 1081

ARCO RESOURCES CORP   p302
570 GRANVILLE ST SUITE 1200, VANCOUVER, BC, V6C 3P1
(604) 689-8336   *SIC* 1081

ARGONAUT GOLD INC   p985
1 FIRST CANADIAN PLACE SUITE 3400, TORONTO, ON, M5X 1A4
SIC 1081

ASCENDANT RESOURCES INC   p968
79 WELLINGTON ST W SUITE 2100, TORONTO, ON, M5K 1H1
(647) 796-0066   *SIC* 1081

ATLATSA RESOURCES CORPORATION p302
666 BURRARD ST SUITE 1700, VANCOUVER, BC, V6C 2X8
(604) 631-1300   *SIC* 1081

AURYN RESOURCES INC   p311
1199 HASTINGS ST W SUITE 600, VANCOUVER, BC, V6E 3T5
(778) 729-0600   *SIC* 1081

AVION GOLD CORPORATION   p948
65 QUEEN ST W SUITE 820, TORONTO, ON, M5H 2M5
(416) 861-9500   *SIC* 1081

AZARGA URANIUM CORP   p343
15782 MARINE DR UNIT 1, WHITE ROCK, BC, V4B 1E6
(604) 536-2711   *SIC* 1081

BESRA GOLD INC   p937
10 KING ST E SUITE 500, TORONTO, ON, M5C 1C3
(416) 572-2525   *SIC* 1081

BREAKWATER RESOURCES LTD   p1134
KM 42 RTE 1000, LEBEL-SUR-QUEVILLON, QC, J0Y 1X0
(819) 755-5550   *SIC* 1081

BREAKWATER RESOURCES LTD   p1288
8900 RANG DES PONTS, ROUYN-

NORANDA, QC, J0Z 1P0
(819) 637-2075   *SIC* 1081

BRIO GOLD INC   p949
22 ADELAIDE ST W UNIT 2020, TORONTO, ON, M5H 4E3
(416) 860-6310   *SIC* 1081

BUL RIVER MINERAL CORPORATION p27
4723 1 ST SW SUITE 350, CALGARY, AB, T2G 4Y8
SIC 1081

CANADIAN ROYALTIES INC   p1202
800 BOUL RENE-LEVESQUE O BUREAU 410, MONTREAL, QC, H3B 1X9
(514) 879-1688   *SIC* 1081

CANICKEL MINING LIMITED   p360
GD, WABOWDEN, MB, R0B 1S0
(204) 689-2972   *SIC* 1081

CAPSTONE MINING CORP   p297
510 GEORGIA ST W SUITE 2100, VANCOUVER, BC, V6B 0M3
(604) 684-8894   *SIC* 1081

CASTLE RESOURCES INC   p969
79 WELLINGTON ST W SUITE 2100, TORONTO, ON, M5K 1H1
(416) 593-8300   *SIC* 1081

CENTERRA GOLD INC   p961
1 UNIVERSITY AVE SUITE 1500, TORONTO, ON, M5J 2P1
(416) 204-1953   *SIC* 1081

CENTRAL SUN MINING INC   p328
595 BURRARD ST SUITE 3100, VANCOUVER, BC, V7X 1L7
(604) 681-8371   *SIC* 1081

CHAMPION IRON MINES LIMITED   p937
20 ADELAIDE ST E SUITE 200, TORONTO, ON, M5C 2T6
(416) 866-2200   *SIC* 1081

CHINA GOLD INTERNATIONAL RESOURCES CORP LTD   p328
505 BURRARD ST SUITE 660, VANCOUVER, BC, V7X 1M4
(604) 609-0598   *SIC* 1081

COLT RESOURCES INC   p1187
500 PLACE D'ARMES BUREAU 1800, MONTREAL, QC, H2Y 2W2
(438) 259-3315   *SIC* 1081

CONTINENTAL MINERALS CORPORATION p303
800 PENDER ST W SUITE 1020, VANCOUVER, BC, V6C 2V6
(604) 684-6365   *SIC* 1081

CORAL GOLD RESOURCES LTD   p303
570 GRANVILLE ST SUITE 900, VANCOUVER, BC, V6C 3P1
(604) 682-3701   *SIC* 1081

CORPORATION AURIFERE MONARQUES p1352
68 AV DE LA GARE UNITE 205, SAINT-SAUVEUR, QC, J0R 1R0
(819) 736-4581   *SIC* 1081

CORSA COAL CORP   p937
110 YONGE ST SUITE 601, TORONTO, ON, M5C 1T4
SIC 1081

CURALEAF HOLDINGS, INC   p303
666 BURRARD ST SUITE 1700, VANCOUVER, BC, V6C 2X8
(604) 218-4766   *SIC* 1081

D.J. DRILLING (2004) LTD   p279
19286 21 AVE UNIT 104, SURREY, BC, V3Z 3M3
(604) 541-1362   *SIC* 1081

DMC MINING SERVICES LTD   p1030
191 CREDITVIEW RD SUITE 400, WOODBRIDGE, ON, L4L 9T1
(905) 780-1980   *SIC* 1081

DUMAS CONTRACTING LTD   p962
200 BAY ST SUITE 2301, TORONTO, ON, M5J 2J1
(416) 594-2525   *SIC* 1081

EASTERN PLATINUM LIMITED   p312
1188 GEORGIA ST W SUITE 1080, VANCOUVER, BC, V6E 4A2
(604) 800-8200   *SIC* 1081

EASTFIELD RESOURCES LTD *p303*
325 HOWE ST SUITE 110, VANCOUVER, BC, V6C 1Z7
(604) 681-7913 *SIC* 1081

ENERGOLD DRILLING CORP *p304*
543 GRANVILLE ST SUITE 1100, VANCOUVER, BC, V6C 1X8
(604) 681-9501 *SIC* 1081

ENTREE GOLD INC *p312*
1066 HASTINGS ST W SUITE 1650, VANCOUVER, BC, V6E 3X1
(604) 687-4777 *SIC* 1081

ERDENE RESOURCE DEVELOPMENT CORPORATION *p444*
99 WYSE RD SUITE 1480, DARTMOUTH, NS, B3A 4S5
(902) 423-6419 *SIC* 1081

EUROMAX RESOURCES LTD *p304*
595 HOWE ST 10 FL, VANCOUVER, BC, V6C 2T5
(604) 669-5999 *SIC* 1081

FIRST BAUXITE CORPORATION *p304*
595 HOWE ST SUITE 206, VANCOUVER, BC, V6C 2T5
SIC 1081

FIRST COBALT CORP *p938*
140 YONGE ST SUITE 201, TORONTO, ON, M5C 1X6
(416) 900-3891 *SIC* 1081

FORAGE LONG TROU CMAC INC *p1390*
185 RUE DES DISTRIBUTEURS, VAL-D'OR, QC, J9P 6Y1
(819) 874-8303 *SIC* 1081

FORAN MINING CORPORATION *p304*
409 GRANVILLE ST SUITE 904, VANCOUVER, BC, V6C 1T2
(604) 488-0008 *SIC* 1081

FREEGOLD VENTURES LIMITED *p330*
700 GEORGIA ST W SUITE 888, VANCOUVER, BC, V7Y 1K8
(604) 662-7307 *SIC* 1081

GEOTECH DRILLING SERVICES LTD *p248*
5052 HARTWAY DR, PRINCE GEORGE, BC, V2K 5B7
(250) 962-9041 *SIC* 1081

GIBRALTAR MINES LTD *p313*
1040 GEORGIA ST W, VANCOUVER, BC, V6E 4H1
(778) 373-4533 *SIC* 1081

GOLDEN ARROW RESOURCES CORPORATION *p304*
837 HASTINGS ST W UNIT 312, VANCOUVER, BC, V6C 3N6
(604) 687-1828 *SIC* 1081

GOLDEN REIGN RESOURCES LTD *p304*
595 HOWE ST SUITE 501, VANCOUVER, BC, V6C 2T5
(604) 685-4655 *SIC* 1081

GRAN COLOMBIA GOLD CORP *p952*
401 BAY ST SUITE 2400, TORONTO, ON, M5H 2Y4
(416) 360-4653 *SIC* 1081

GRANITE OIL CORP *p50*
308 4 AVE SW SUITE 3230, CALGARY, AB, T2P 0H7
SIC 1081

GREAT PANTHER MINING LIMITED *p305*
200 GRANVILLE ST SUITE 1330, VANCOUVER, BC, V6C 1S4
(604) 608-1766 *SIC* 1081

HECLA QUEBEC INC *p305*
800 PENDER ST W SUITE 970, VANCOUVER, BC, V6C 2V6
(604) 682-6201 *SIC* 1081

HECLA QUEBEC INC *p1390*
1010 3E RUE, VAL-D'OR, QC, J9P 4B1
(819) 874-4511 *SIC* 1081

HONEY BADGER EXPLORATION INC *p963*
145 WELLINGTON ST W SUITE 101, TORONTO, ON, M5J 1H8
(416) 364-7029 *SIC* 1081

HUDBAY MINERALS INC *p350*
GD STN MAIN, FLIN FLON, MB, R8A 1N9
(204) 687-2385 *SIC* 1081

HUDBAY MINERALS INC *p963*
25 YORK ST SUITE 800, TORONTO, ON, M5J 2V5
(416) 362-8181 *SIC* 1081

HUNTER DICKINSON INC *p313*
1040 GEORGIA ST W SUITE 1500, VANCOUVER, BC, V6E 4H8
(604) 684-6365 *SIC* 1081

HY-TECH DRILLING LTD *p269*
2715 TATLOW RD, SMITHERS, BC, V0J 2N5
(250) 847-9301 *SIC* 1081

IAMGOLD CORPORATION *p1307*
3400 CH DU COLUMBIUM, SAINT-HONORE-DE-CHICOUTIMI, QC, G0V 1L0
(418) 673-4694 *SIC* 1081

INMET ANATOLIA LIMITED *p953*
330 BAY ST SUITE 1000, TORONTO, ON, M5H 2S8
(416) 361-6400 *SIC* 1081

INTEGRA GOLD CORP *p314*
1055 GEORGIA ST W UNIT 2270, VANCOUVER, BC, V6E 0B6
(604) 629-0891 *SIC* 1081

INTERCONTINENTAL GOLD AND METALS LTD *p953*
365 BAY ST SUITE 400, TORONTO, ON, M5H 2V1
(647) 985-2785 *SIC* 1081

KARMIN EXPLORATION INC *p987*
100 KING ST W SUITE 5700, TORONTO, ON, M5X 1C7
(416) 367-0369 *SIC* 1081

KGHM INTERNATIONAL LTD *p1032*
191 CREDITVIEW RD SUITE 400, WOODBRIDGE, ON, L4L 9T1
(647) 265-9191 *SIC* 1081

KIEWIT-NUVUMIUT, SOCIETE EN COPARTICIPATION *p1062*
4333 BOUL DE LA GRANDE-ALLEE, BOISBRIAND, QC, J7H 1M7
(450) 435-5756 *SIC* 1081

KINROSS GOLD CORPORATION *p964*
25 YORK ST 17TH FL, TORONTO, ON, M5J 2V5
(416) 365-5123 *SIC* 1081

KIRKLAND LAKE GOLD LTD *p634*
1350 GOVERNMENT RD W, KIRKLAND LAKE, ON, P2N 3J1
(705) 567-5208 *SIC* 1081

LARAMIDE RESOURCES LTD *p987*
130 KING ST W SUITE 3680, TORONTO, ON, M5X 2A2
(416) 599-7363 *SIC* 1081

LEADFX INC *p939*
1 ADELAIDE ST E, TORONTO, ON, M5C 2V9
(416) 867-9298 *SIC* 1081

LEVON RESOURCES LTD *p306*
666 BURRARD ST SUITE 500, VANCOUVER, BC, V6C 2X8
(604) 682-2991 *SIC* 1081

LITHIUM AMERIQUE DU NORD INC *p1121*
500 RTE DU LITHIUM, LA CORNE, QC, J0Y 1R0
(819) 734-5000 *SIC* 1081

LITHIUM X ENERGY CORP *p328*
595 BURRARD ST SUITE 3123, VANCOUVER, BC, V7X 1J1
(604) 609-6138 *SIC* 1081

MALAGA INC *p1206*
1 PLACE VILLE-MARIE BUREAU 4000, MONTREAL, QC, H3B 4M4
(514) 393-9000 *SIC* 1081

MARKETING EMS INC *p1070*
7505 BOUL TASCHEREAU BUREAU 100, BROSSARD, QC, J4Y 1A2
(450) 443-0300 *SIC* 1081

MAYA GOLD & SILVER INC *p1206*
1 PLACE VILLE-MARIE BUREAU 2901, MONTREAL, QC, H3B 0E9
(514) 866-2008 *SIC* 1081

MINCORE INC *p954*
80 RICHMOND ST W SUITE 1502,

TORONTO, ON, M5H 2A4
(416) 214-1766 *SIC* 1081

MINDORO RESOURCES LTD *p54*
639 5 AVE SW SUITE 1250, CALGARY, AB, T2P 0M9
(780) 413-8187 *SIC* 1081

MINES ABCOURT INC *p1158*
506 RUE DES FALAISES, MONT-SAINT-HILAIRE, QC, J3H 5R7
(450) 446-5511 *SIC* 1081

MINES DE LA VALLEE DE L'OR LTEE *p1391*
152 CH DE LA MINE-ECOLE, VAL-D'OR, QC, J9P 7B6
(819) 824-2808 *SIC* 1081

MINEWORX TECHNOLOGIES LTD *p182*
8331 EASTLAKE DR UNIT 114, BURNABY, BC, V5A 4W2
(250) 751-3661 *SIC* 1081

MONUMENT MINING LIMITED *p315*
1100 MELVILLE ST SUITE 1580, VANCOUVER, BC, V6E 4A6
(604) 638-1661 *SIC* 1081

MOTION METRICS INTERNATIONAL CORP *p324*
2389 HEALTH SCIENCES MALL UNIT 101, VANCOUVER, BC, V6T 1Z3
(604) 822-5848 *SIC* 1081

NAMIBIA CRITICAL METALS INC *p440*
1550 BEDFORD HWY SUITE 802, BEDFORD, NS, B4A 1E6
(902) 835-8760 *SIC* 1081

NAUTILUS MINERALS INC *p995*
2100 BLOOR ST W SUITE 6125, TORONTO, ON, M6S 5A5
(416) 551-1100 *SIC* 1081

NEVSUN RESOURCES LTD *p315*
1066 HASTINGS ST W SUITE 1750, VANCOUVER, BC, V6E 3X1
(604) 623-4700 *SIC* 1081

NEW GUINEA GOLD CORPORATION *p307*
595 HOWE ST SUITE 900, VANCOUVER, BC, V6C 2T5
(604) 689-1515 *SIC* 1081

NIOBEC INC *p955*
333 BAY ST SUITE 1101, TORONTO, ON, M5H 2R2
(416) 901-9877 *SIC* 1081

NIOBEC INC *p1307*
3400 CH DU COLUMBIUM, SAINT-HONORE-DE-CHICOUTIMI, QC, G0V 1L0
(418) 673-4694 *SIC* 1081

NORTH AMERICAN TUNGSTEN CORPORATION LTD *p307*
400 BURRARD ST SUITE 1680, VANCOUVER, BC, V6C 3A6
(604) 638-7440 *SIC* 1081

NORTHERN VERTEX MINING CORP *p315*
1075 W GEORGIA ST SUITE 1650, VANCOUVER, BC, V6E 3C9
(604) 601-3656 *SIC* 1081

OCEANAGOLD CORPORATION *p326*
777 HORNBY STREET SUITE 1910, VANCOUVER, BC, V6Z 1S4
(604) 235-3360 *SIC* 1081

ORVANA MINERALS CORP *p956*
170 UNIVERSITY AVE SUITE 900, TORONTO, ON, M5H 3B3
(416) 369-1629 *SIC* 1081

OSISKO METALS INCORPORATED *p1207*
1100 AV DES CANADIENS-DE-MONTREAL BUREAU 300, MONTREAL, QC, H3B 2S2
(514) 861-4441 *SIC* 1081

OSISKO MINING INC *p956*
155 UNIVERSITY AVE SUITE 1440, TORONTO, ON, M5H 3B7
(416) 848-9504 *SIC* 1081

PACIFIC WILDCAT RESOURCES CORP *p341*
2300 CARRINGTON RD SUITE 110, WEST KELOWNA, BC, V4T 2N6
(250) 768-0009 *SIC* 1081

PROCON EST DU CANADA LTEE *p1391*
1400 4E AV, VAL-D'OR, QC, J9P 5Z9

(819) 824-2074 *SIC* 1081

PROCON MINING & TUNNELLING LTD *p186*
4664 LOUGHEED HWY UNIT 108, BURNABY, BC, V5C 5T5
(604) 291-8292 *SIC* 1081

QMX GOLD CORPORATION *p956*
65 QUEEN ST W SUITE 800, TORONTO, ON, M5H 2M5
(416) 861-5899 *SIC* 1081

QMX GOLD CORPORATION *p1391*
1900 CH BRADOR, VAL-D'OR, QC, J9P 0A4
(819) 825-3412 *SIC* 1081

RAMBLER METALS AND MINING CANADA LIMITED *p421*
309 410 WILLIAM CHIPP BLDG HWY, BAIE VERTE, NL, A0K 1B0
(709) 800-1929 *SIC* 1081

REDPATH CANADA LIMITED *p763*
101 WORTHINGTON ST E, NORTH BAY, ON, P1B 1G5
(705) 474-2461 *SIC* 1081

REDPATH MINING INC *p763*
101 WORTHINGTON ST E 3RD FL, NORTH BAY, ON, P1B 1G5
(705) 474-2461 *SIC* 1081

REGAL CONSOLIDATED VENTURES LIMITED *p940*
20 ADELAIDE ST E SUITE 1100, TORONTO, ON, M5C 2T6
(416) 642-0602 *SIC* 1081

RESSOURCES ROBEX INC *p1269*
437 GRANDE ALLEE E BUREAU 100, QUEBEC, QC, G1R 2J5
(581) 741-7421 *SIC* 1081

ROCHESTER RESOURCES LTD *p316*
1090 W GEORGIA ST SUITE 1305, VANCOUVER, BC, V6E 3V7
(604) 685-9316 *SIC* 1081

SEMAFO INC *p1324*
100 BOUL ALEXIS-NIHON BUREAU 700, SAINT-LAURENT, QC, H4M 2P3
(514) 744-4408 *SIC* 1081

SERVICES DE FORAGE ORBIT GARANT INC *p1391*
3200 BOUL JEAN-JACQUES-COSSETTE, VAL-D'OR, QC, J9P 6Y6
(819) 824-2707 *SIC* 1081

SHERRITT INTERNATIONAL CORPORATION *p957*
22 ADELAIDE ST W SUITE 4220, TORONTO, ON, M5H 4E3
(416) 924-4551 *SIC* 1081

SOCIETE D'EXPLORATION MINIERE VIO *p1260*
116 RUE SAINT-PIERRE BUREAU 200, QUEBEC, QC, G1K 4A7
(418) 692-2678 *SIC* 1081

SOQUEM INC *p1391*
1740 CH SULLIVAN BUREAU 2000, VAL-D'OR, QC, J9P 7H1
(819) 874-3773 *SIC* 1081

SOUTH AMERICAN GOLD AND COPPER COMPANY LIMITED *p943*
67 YONGE ST SUITE 1201, TORONTO, ON, M5E 1J8
(416) 369-9115 *SIC* 1081

SOUTHGOBI RESOURCES LTD *p309*
250 HOWE ST 20TH FLOOR, VANCOUVER, BC, V6C 3R8
(604) 762-6783 *SIC* 1081

SPANISH MOUNTAIN GOLD LTD *p316*
1095 PENDER ST W SUITE 1120, VANCOUVER, BC, V6E 2M6
(604) 601-3651 *SIC* 1081

SRK CONSULTING (CANADA) INC *p316*
1066 HASTINGS ST W SUITE 2200, VANCOUVER, BC, V6E 3X1
(604) 681-4196 *SIC* 1081

STRATEGIC METALS LTD *p300*
510 HASTINGS ST W SUITE 1016, VANCOUVER, BC, V6B 1L8
(604) 687-2522 *SIC* 1081

SUCCESSION FORAGE GEORGE DOWN-

ING LTEE   *p1112*
410 RUE PRINCIPALE, GRENVILLE-SUR-LA-ROUGE, QC, J0V 1B0
(819) 242-6469   *SIC* 1081

TANGO GOLD MINES INCORPORATED
p987
130 KING ST W, TORONTO, ON, M5X 2A2
(416) 479-4433   *SIC* 1081

TANZANIAN ROYALTY EXPLORATION CORPORATION   *p940*
82 RICHMOND ST W SUITE 208, TORONTO, ON, M5C 1P1
(844) 364-1830   *SIC* 1081

TASEKO MINES LIMITED   *p316*
1040 GEORGIA ST W 15TH FL, VANCOUVER, BC, V6E 4H1
(778) 373-4533   *SIC* 1081

TECHNOLOGIES ORBITE INC   *p1242*
500 BOUL CARTIER O BUREAU 249, MONTREAL-OUEST, QC, H7V 5B7
(450) 680-3341   *SIC* 1081

TECK METALS LTD   *p284*
25 ALDRIDGE AVE, TRAIL, BC, V1R 4L8
(250) 364-4222   *SIC* 1081

TECK METALS LTD   *p957*
11 KING ST W SUITE 1700, TORONTO, ON, M5H 4C7
(647) 788-3000   *SIC* 1081

TECK RESOURCES LIMITED   *p425*
32 RTE 370, MILLERTOWN, NL, A0H 1V0
(709) 852-2195   *SIC* 1081

TERVITA DRILLING AND CORING SERVICES LTD   *p19*
9919 SHEPARD RD SE, CALGARY, AB, T2C 3C5
(855) 837-8482   *SIC* 1081

TOREX GOLD RESOURCES INC   *p987*
130 KING ST W SUITE 740, TORONTO, ON, M5X 2A2
(647) 260-1500   *SIC* 1081

TRIMETALS MINING INC   *p310*
580 HORNBY ST SUITE 880, VANCOUVER, BC, V6C 3B6
(604) 639-4523   *SIC* 1081

TURQUOISE HILL RESOURCES LTD   *p310*
200 GRANVILLE ST SUITE 354, VANCOUVER, BC, V6C 1S4
(604) 688-5755   *SIC* 1081

TVI PACIFIC INC   *p62*
505 2 ST SW SUITE 806, CALGARY, AB, T2P 1N8
(403) 265-4356   *SIC* 1081

U3O8 CORP   *p941*
36 TORONTO ST SUITE 1050, TORONTO, ON, M5C 2C5
(416) 868-1491   *SIC* 1081

UNIGOLD INC   *p941*
44 VICTORIA ST SUITE 504, TORONTO, ON, M5C 1Y2
(416) 866-8157   *SIC* 1081

VERIS GOLD CORP   *p301*
688 HASTINGS ST W SUITE 900, VANCOUVER, BC, V6B 1P1
(604) 688-9427   *SIC* 1081

VMS VENTURES INC   *p240*
200 ESPLANADE W SUITE 500, NORTH VANCOUVER, BC, V7M 1A4
(604) 986-2020   *SIC* 1081

WESTERN COPPER AND GOLD CORPORATION   *p317*
1040 GEORGIA ST W FL 15, VANCOUVER, BC, V6E 4H1
(604) 684-9497   *SIC* 1081

WESTERN RESOURCES CORP   *p317*
1111 GEORGIA ST W SUITE 1400, VANCOUVER, BC, V6E 4M3
(604) 689-9378   *SIC* 1081

ZEPHYR MINERALS LTD   *p454*
1959 UPPER WATER ST SUITE 1300, HALIFAX, NS, B3J 3N2
(902) 446-4189   *SIC* 1081

SIC 1094 Uranium-radium-vanadium ores

CAMECO CORPORATION   *p1432*
2121 11TH ST W, SASKATOON, SK, S7M 1J3
(306) 956-6200   *SIC* 1094

DENISON MINES CORP   *p962*
1100 40 UNIVERSITY AVE, TORONTO, ON, M5J 1T1
(416) 979-1991   *SIC* 1094

FIRST URANIUM CORPORATION   *p969*
77 KING ST W SUITE 400, TORONTO, ON, M5K 0A1
(416) 306-3072   *SIC* 1094

GOVIEX URANIUM INC   *p305*
999 CANADA PL SUITE 654, VANCOUVER, BC, V6C 3E1
(604) 681-5529   *SIC* 1094

LARGO RESOURCES LTD   *p964*
55 UNIVERSITY AVE SUITE 1105, TORONTO, ON, M5J 2H7
(416) 861-9797   *SIC* 1094

MEGA URANIUM LTD   *p935*
211 YONGE ST SUITE 502, TORONTO, ON, M5B 1M4
(416) 643-7630   *SIC* 1094

NEXGEN ENERGY LTD   *p315*
1021 HASTINGS ST W SUITE 3150, VANCOUVER, BC, V6E 0C3
(604) 428-4112   *SIC* 1094

ORANO CANADA INC   *p1431*
817 45TH ST W, SASKATOON, SK, S7L 5X2
(306) 343-4500   *SIC* 1094

UR-ENERGY INC   *p824*
55 METCALFE ST SUITE 1300, OTTAWA, ON, K1P 6L5
(613) 236-3882   *SIC* 1094

URANIUM ONE INC   *p958*
333 BAY ST SUITE 1200, TORONTO, ON, M5H 2R2
(647) 788-8500   *SIC* 1094

VALORE METALS CORP   *p310*
800 PENDER ST W SUITE 1020, VANCOUVER, BC, V6C 2V6
(604) 646-4527   *SIC* 1094

SIC 1099 Metal ores, nec

BEAVER BROOK ANTIMONY MINE INC
p423
GD, GLENWOOD, NL, A0G 2K0
(709) 679-5866   *SIC* 1099

LAC DES ILES MINES LTD   *p953*
130 ADELAIDE ST W SUITE 2116, TORONTO, ON, M5H 3P5
(807) 448-2000   *SIC* 1099

NORTH AMERICAN PALLADIUM LTD *p965*
ONE UNIVERSITY AVE SUITE 1601, TORONTO, ON, M5J 2P1
(416) 360-7590   *SIC* 1099

SIC 1221 Bituminous coal and lignite-surface mining

BUFFALO COAL CORP   *p949*
65 QUEEN ST W, TORONTO, ON, M5H 2M5
(416) 309-2957   *SIC* 1221

CANAF INVESTMENTS INC   *p311*
1111 MELVILLE ST BUREAU 1100, VANCOUVER, BC, V6E 3V6
(604) 283-6110   *SIC* 1221

CARDINAL RIVER COALS LTD   *p136*
GD, HINTON, AB, T7V 1V5
(780) 692-5100   *SIC* 1221

GRANDE CACHE COAL CORPORATION
p50
800 5 AVE SW SUITE 1610, CALGARY, AB, T2P 3T6
(403) 543-7070   *SIC* 1221

GRANDE CACHE COAL CORPORATION
p130

GD, GRANDE CACHE, AB, T0E 0Y0
(780) 827-4646   *SIC* 1221

PEACE RIVER COAL INC   *p315*
1055 HASTINGS ST W SUITE 1900, VANCOUVER, BC, V6E 2E9
SIC 1221

PRAIRIE MINES & ROYALTY ULC   *p126*
GD, EDSON, AB, T7E 1W1
(780) 794-8100   *SIC* 1221

PRAIRIE MINES & ROYALTY ULC   *p127*
GD, FORESTBURG, AB, T0B 1N0
(403) 884-3000   *SIC* 1221

PRAIRIE MINES & ROYALTY ULC   *p135*
GD, HANNA, AB, T0J 1P0
(403) 854-5200   *SIC* 1221

PRAIRIE MINES & ROYALTY ULC   *p171*
GD, WARBURG, AB, T0C 2T0
(780) 848-7786   *SIC* 1221

PRAIRIE MINES & ROYALTY ULC   *p1404*
GD, BIENFAIT, SK, S0C 0M0
(306) 388-2272   *SIC* 1221

PRAIRIE MINES & ROYALTY ULC   *p1405*
GD, CORONACH, SK, S0H 0Z0
(306) 267-4200   *SIC* 1221

PROPHECY DEVELOPMENT CORP   *p308*
409 GRANVILLE ST SUITE 1610, VANCOUVER, BC, V6C 1T2
(604) 569-3661   *SIC* 1221

SUNHILLS MINING LIMITED PARTNERSHIP   *p160*
4419 B SUNDANCE RD, SEBA BEACH, AB, T0E 2B0
(780) 731-5300   *SIC* 1221

TECK COAL LIMITED   *p32*
205 9 AVE SE SUITE 1000, CALGARY, AB, T2G 0R3
(403) 767-8500   *SIC* 1221

TECK COAL LIMITED   *p136*
GD STN MAIN, HINTON, AB, T7V 1T9
(780) 692-5100   *SIC* 1221

TECK COAL LIMITED   *p212*
GD, ELKFORD, BC, V0B 1H0
(250) 865-2271   *SIC* 1221

TECK COAL LIMITED   *p269*
2261 CORBIN RD, SPARWOOD, BC, V0B 2G0
(250) 425-6305   *SIC* 1221

TECK COAL LIMITED   *p269*
GD, SPARWOOD, BC, V0B 2G0
(250) 425-8325   *SIC* 1221

TECK COAL LIMITED   *p269*
GD, SPARWOOD, BC, V0B 2G0
(250) 425-2555   *SIC* 1221

TECK-BULLMOOSE COAL INC   *p310*
550 BURRARD ST SUITE 3300, VANCOUVER, BC, V6C 0B3
(604) 699-4000   *SIC* 1221

SIC 1231 Anthracite mining

GROUPE TRUDO   *p1082*
1999 RTE MARIE-VICTORIN, CONTRECOEUR, QC, J0L 1C0
(450) 587-2098   *SIC* 1231

SIC 1241 Coal mining services

CEMENTATION CANADA INC   *p762*
590 GRAHAM DR, NORTH BAY, ON, P1B 7S1
(705) 472-3381   *SIC* 1241

FRONTIER-KEMPER CONSTRUCTORS ULC   *p239*
4400 LILLOOET RD, NORTH VANCOUVER, BC, V7J 2H9
(604) 988-1665   *SIC* 1241

HCC MINING AND DEMOLITION INC *p1427*
RR 5 LCD MAIN, SASKATOON, SK, S7K 3J8
(306) 652-4168   *SIC* 1241

MINES AGNICO EAGLE LIMITEE   *p1288*
10200 RTE DE PREISSAC, ROUYN-

NORANDA, QC, J0Y 1C0
(819) 759-3644   *SIC* 1241

MINES OPINACA LTEE, LES   *p1077*
333 3E RUE BUREAU 2, CHIBOUGAMAU, QC, G8P 1N4
(418) 748-6449   *SIC* 1241

MORAN MINING & TUNNELLING LTD *p647*
159 FIELDING RD, LIVELY, ON, P3Y 1L7
(705) 682-4070   *SIC* 1241

SERVICES D'ENTRETIEN MINIERS INDUSTRIELS R.N. 2000 INC   *p1290*
155 BOUL INDUSTRIEL, ROUYN-NORANDA, QC, J9X 6P2
(819) 797-4387   *SIC* 1241

SIC 1311 Crude petroleum and natural gas

1986114 ALBERTA INC   *p42*
605 5 AVE SW SUITE 3200, CALGARY, AB, T2P 3H5
(403) 269-4400   *SIC* 1311

ALTAGAS LTD   *p43*
355 4 AVE SW SUITE 1700, CALGARY, AB, T2P 0J1
(403) 691-7575   *SIC* 1311

ALVOPETRO ENERGY LTD   *p43*
525 8 AVE SW SUITE 1700, CALGARY, AB, T2P 1G1
(587) 794-4224   *SIC* 1311

BAYTEX ENERGY CORP   *p44*
520 3 AVE SW SUITE 2800, CALGARY, AB, T2P 0R3
(587) 952-3000   *SIC* 1311

BONAVISTA ENERGY CORPORATION *p44*
525 8 AVE SW SUITE 1500, CALGARY, AB, T2P 1G1
(403) 213-4300   *SIC* 1311

BONTERRA ENERGY CORP   *p64*
1015 4 ST SW SUITE 901, CALGARY, AB, T2R 1J4
(403) 262-5307   *SIC* 1311

BP CANADA ENERGY COMPANY   *p44*
240 4 AVE SW, CALGARY, AB, T2P 4H4
(403) 233-1313   *SIC* 1311

CANACOL ENERGY LTD   *p45*
585 8 AVE SW SUITE 2650, CALGARY, AB, T2P 1G1
(403) 561-1648   *SIC* 1311

CANADIAN COASTAL RESOURCES LTD
p45
202 6 AVE SW SUITE 900, CALGARY, AB, T2P 2R9
SIC 1311

CANADIAN NATURAL RESOURCES LIMITED   *p6*
GD STN MAIN, BONNYVILLE, AB, T9N 2J6
(780) 826-8110   *SIC* 1311

CANADIAN NATURAL RESOURCES LIMITED   *p45*
855 2 ST SW SUITE 2100, CALGARY, AB, T2P 4J8
(403) 517-6700   *SIC* 1311

CANADIAN NATURAL RESOURCES LIMITED   *p45*
324 8 AVE SW SUITE 1800, CALGARY, AB, T2P 2Z2
(403) 517-6700   *SIC* 1311

CANADIAN NATURAL RESOURCES LIMITED   *p131*
9705 97 ST, GRANDE PRAIRIE, AB, T8V 8B9
(780) 831-7475   *SIC* 1311

CANORO RESOURCES LTD   *p45*
717 7 AVE SW SUITE 700, CALGARY, AB, T2P 0Z3
(403) 543-5747   *SIC* 1311

CARDINAL ENERGY LTD   *p46*
400 3 AVE SW SUITE 600, CALGARY, AB, T2P 4H2
(403) 234-8681   *SIC* 1311

CENOVUS FCCL LTD   *p28*
500 CENTRE ST SE SUITE 766, CALGARY, AB, T2G 1A6

---

(403) 766-2000   *SIC* 1311
CHEVRON RESOURCES LTD   p46
500 5 AVE SW SUITE 700, CALGARY, AB,
T2P 0L7
(403) 234-5000   *SIC* 1311
CHIMIE PARACHEM INC   p1238
3500 AV BROADWAY, MONTREAL-EST,
QC, H1B 5B4
(514) 640-2200   *SIC* 1311
CHIMIE PARACHEM S.E.C.   p1238
3500 AV BROADWAY, MONTREAL-EST,
QC, H1B 5B4
(514) 640-2200   *SIC* 1311
CNR (ECHO) RESOURCES INC   p46
855 2 ST SW SUITE 2500, CALGARY, AB,
T2P 4J8
SIC 1311
**CONOCOPHILLIPS CANADA RESOURCES
CORP**   p47
401 9 AVE SW SUITE 1600, CALGARY, AB,
T2P 3C5
(403) 233-4000   *SIC* 1311
**CONOCOPHILLIPS WESTERN CANADA
PARTNERSHIP**   p47
401 9TH AVE SW, CALGARY, AB, T2P 2H7
(403) 233-4000   *SIC* 1311
**CONOCOPHILLIPS WESTERN CANADA
PARTNERSHIP**   p82
GD STN MAIN, DRAYTON VALLEY, AB,
T7A 1T1
SIC 1311
CRESCENT POINT ENERGY CORP   p47
585 8 AVE SW SUITE 2000, CALGARY, AB,
T2P 1G1
(403) 693-0020   *SIC* 1311
CRESCENT POINT ENERGY CORP   p1405
801 RAILWAY AVE, CARLYLE, SK, S0C 0R0
(306) 453-3236   *SIC* 1311
CREW ENERGY INC   p47
250 5 ST SW SUITE 800, CALGARY, AB,
T2P 0R4
(403) 266-2088   *SIC* 1311
DEVON CANADA CORPORATION   p47
400 3 AVE SW SUITE 100, CALGARY, AB,
T2P 4H2
(403) 232-7100   *SIC* 1311
DIRECT ENERGY MARKETING LIMITED
p47
525 8 AVE SW UNIT 1200, CALGARY, AB,
T2P 1G1
(403) 776-2000   *SIC* 1311
DIRECT ENERGY MARKETING LIMITED
p48
111 5 AVE SW SUITE 1000, CALGARY, AB,
T2P 3Y6
(403) 266-6393   *SIC* 1311
ENCANA CORPORATION   p7
2249 COLLEGE DR E, BROOKS, AB, T1R
1G5
(403) 793-4400   *SIC* 1311
ENERPLUS CORPORATION   p48
333 7 AVE SW SUITE 3000, CALGARY, AB,
T2P 2Z1
(403) 298-2200   *SIC* 1311
EPSILON ENERGY LTD   p69
14505 BANNISTER RD SE SUITE 300,
CALGARY, AB, T2X 3J3
SIC 1311
EXXONMOBIL CANADA LTD   p49
237 4 AVE SW SUITE 3000, CALGARY, AB,
T2P 4X7
(403) 232-5300   *SIC* 1311
F. DUFRESNE INC   p1262
455 RUE DES ENTREPRENEURS, QUE-
BEC, QC, G1M 2V2
(418) 688-1820   *SIC* 1311
GRANITE OIL CORP   p50
308 4 AVE SW SUITE 3230, CALGARY, AB,
T2P 0H7
(587) 349-9113   *SIC* 1311
GRIZZLY OIL SANDS ULC   p50
605 5 AVE SW SUITE 2700, CALGARY, AB,
T2P 3H5
(403) 930-6400   *SIC* 1311

HARVEST OPERATIONS CORP   p51
700 2 ST SW SUITE 1500, CALGARY, AB,
T2P 2W1
(403) 265-1178   *SIC* 1311
HUSKY ENERGY INC   p248
2542 PRINCE GEORGE PULPMILL RD,
PRINCE GEORGE, BC, V2K 5P5
SIC 1311
HUSKY ENERGY INC   p1409
HWY 16 E UPGRADER RD, LLOYDMIN-
STER, SK, S9V 1M6
(306) 825-1700   *SIC* 1311
HUSKY ENERGY INC   p1409
4335 44 ST, LLOYDMINSTER, SK, S9V 0Z8
(306) 825-1196   *SIC* 1311
**HUSKY ENERGY INTERNATIONAL SUL-
PHUR CORPORATION**   p51
707 8 AVE SW, CALGARY, AB, T2P 1H5
(403) 298-6111   *SIC* 1311
HUSKY OIL LIMITED   p51
707 8 AVE SW, CALGARY, AB, T2P 1H5
(403) 298-6111   *SIC* 1311
HUSKY OIL OPERATIONS LIMITED   p51
707 8 AVE SW, CALGARY, AB, T2P 1H5
(403) 298-6111   *SIC* 1311
HUSKY OIL OPERATIONS LIMITED   p144
5650 52 ST, LLOYDMINSTER, AB, T9V 0R7
SIC 1311
HUSKY OIL OPERATIONS LIMITED   p153
HWY 58 W, RAINBOW LAKE, AB, T0H 2Y0
(780) 956-8000   *SIC* 1311
HUSKY OIL OPERATIONS LIMITED   p432
351 WATER ST, ST. JOHN'S, NL, A1C 1C2
(709) 724-3900   *SIC* 1311
HUSKY OIL OPERATIONS LIMITED   p1409
4335 44 ST, LLOYDMINSTER, SK, S9V 0Z8
(306) 825-1196   *SIC* 1311
INPLAY OIL CORP   p51
640 5 AVE SW SUITE 920, CALGARY, AB,
T2P 3G4
(587) 955-9570   *SIC* 1311
**INTERNATIONAL PETROLEUM CORPORA-
TION**   p306
885 GEORGIA ST W SUITE 2000, VAN-
COUVER, BC, V6C 3E8
(604) 689-7842   *SIC* 1311
J R & S HOLDINGS LTD   p52
605 5 AVE SW SUITE 1000, CALGARY, AB,
T2P 3H5
(403) 265-5091   *SIC* 1311
KEYERA PARTNERSHIP   p158
44-01 W5 03-05, RIMBEY, AB, T0C 2J0
(403) 843-7100   *SIC* 1311
KMC MINING CORPORATION   p1
28712 114 AVE, ACHESON, AB, T7X 6E6
(780) 454-0664   *SIC* 1311
KOOPMAN RESOURCES, INC   p39
10919 WILLOWGLEN PL SE, CALGARY,
AB, T2J 1R8
(403) 271-4564   *SIC* 1311
LARICINA ENERGY LTD   p52
425 1 ST SW SUITE 800, CALGARY, AB,
T2P 3L8
(403) 750-0810   *SIC* 1311
MADALENA ENERGY INC   p53
333 7 AVE SW, CALGARY, AB, T2P 2Z1
(403) 264-1915   *SIC* 1311
MEG ENERGY CORP   p54
3 AVE SW SUITE 600 25TH FL, CALGARY,
AB, T2P 0G5
(403) 770-0446   *SIC* 1311
MURPHY OIL COMPANY LTD   p54
520 3 AVE SW SUITE 4000, CALGARY, AB,
T2P 0R3
(403) 294-8000   *SIC* 1311
NEXEN HOLDINGS (USA) INC   p54
801 7 AVE SW SUITE 200, CALGARY, AB,
T2P 3P7
(403) 234-6700   *SIC* 1311
NEXEN PETROLEUM INTERNATIONAL LTD
p55
801 7 AVE SW SUITE 2900, CALGARY, AB,
T2P 3P7
(403) 234-6700   *SIC* 1311

NIKO RESOURCES LTD   p55
800 6 AVE SW SUITE 510, CALGARY, AB,
T2P 3G3
(403) 262-1020   *SIC* 1311
OBSIDIAN ENERGY LTD   p55
207 9 AVE SW SUITE 200, CALGARY, AB,
T2P 1K3
(403) 777-2500   *SIC* 1311
PAINTED PONY ENERGY LTD   p55
520 3RD AVE SW SUITE 1200, CALGARY,
AB, T2P 0R3
(403) 475-0440   *SIC* 1311
PAN ORIENT ENERGY CORP   p56
505 3RD ST SW SUITE 1505, CALGARY,
AB, T2P 3E6
(403) 294-1770   *SIC* 1311
PARAMOUNT RESOURCES (ACL) LTD   p79
5018 50 AVE, CASTOR, AB, T0C 0X0
(403) 882-3751   *SIC* 1311
PARAMOUNT RESOURCES (TEC) LTD   p56
332 6 AVE SW SUITE 1400, CALGARY, AB,
T2P 0B2
(403) 290-2900   *SIC* 1311
PARAMOUNT RESOURCES LTD   p56
421-7TH AVE SW SUITE 2800, CALGARY,
AB, T2P 4K9
(403) 290-3600   *SIC* 1311
PENGROWTH ENERGY CORPORATION
p56
222 3 AVE SW SUITE 2100, CALGARY, AB,
T2P 0B4
(403) 233-0224   *SIC* 1311
PENGROWTH ENERGY CORPORATION
p168
GD, SWAN HILLS, AB, T0G 2C0
(780) 333-7100   *SIC* 1311
PERPETUAL ENERGY INC   p56
605 5 AVE SW SUITE 3200, CALGARY, AB,
T2P 3H5
(403) 269-4400   *SIC* 1311
**PETRO-CANADA HIBERNIA PARTNER-
SHIP**   p214
11527 ALASKA RD, FORT ST. JOHN, BC,
V1J 6N2
(250) 787-8200   *SIC* 1311
PETROKAZAKHSTAN INC   p56
140 4 AVE SW SUITE 1460, CALGARY, AB,
T2P 3N3
(403) 221-8435   *SIC* 1311
PETRONAS ENERGY CANADA LTD   p57
215 2 ST SW SUITE 1600, CALGARY, AB,
T2P 1M4
(403) 216-2510   *SIC* 1311
PETRONOVA INC   p57
144 4 AVE SW SUITE 1600, CALGARY, AB,
T2P 3N4
(403) 398-2152   *SIC* 1311
**PEYTO EXPLORATION & DEVELOPMENT
CORP**   p57
600 3 AVE SW SUITE 300, CALGARY, AB,
T2P 0G5
(403) 261-6081   *SIC* 1311
**PRAIRIE PROVIDENT RESOURCES
CANADA LTD**   p57
640 5 AVE SW SUITE 1100, CALGARY, AB,
T2P 3G4
(403) 292-8000   *SIC* 1311
RAZOR ENERGY CORP   p58
500 5 AVE SW SUITE 800, CALGARY, AB,
T2P 3L5
(403) 262-0242   *SIC* 1311
RIFE RESOURCES LTD   p58
144 4 AVE SW SUITE 400, CALGARY, AB,
T2P 3N4
(403) 221-0800   *SIC* 1311
SANLING ENERGY LTD   p58
250 2 ST SW SUITE 1700, CALGARY, AB,
T2P 0C1
(403) 303-8500   *SIC* 1311
SEVEN GENERATIONS ENERGY LTD   p59
525 8 AVE SW UNIT 4400, CALGARY, AB,
T2P 1G1
(403) 718-0700   *SIC* 1311
SHANGHAI ENERGY CORPORATION   p59

605 5 AVE SW UNIT 700, CALGARY, AB,
T2P 3H5
(587) 393-3600   *SIC* 1311
SHELL CANADA LIMITED   p59
400 4 AVE SW, CALGARY, AB, T2P 0J4
(403) 691-3111   *SIC* 1311
SHELL CANADA LIMITED   p152
100 ST, PEACE RIVER, AB, T8S 1V8
(780) 624-6800   *SIC* 1311
SHELL CANADA LIMITED   p152
GD, PINCHER CREEK, AB, T0K 1W0
(403) 627-7200   *SIC* 1311
SIGNALTA RESOURCES LIMITED   p59
840 6 AVE SW SUITE 700, CALGARY, AB,
T2P 3E5
(403) 265-5091   *SIC* 1311
SUNCOR ENERGY INC   p129
512 SNOW EAGLE DR, FORT MCMURRAY,
AB, T9H 0B6
(780) 790-1999   *SIC* 1311
SUNCOR ENERGY INC   p129
GD LCD MAIN, FORT MCMURRAY, AB,
T9H 3E2
(780) 743-6411   *SIC* 1311
**SUNCOR ENERGY OIL SANDS LIMITED
PARTNERSHIP**   p60
150 6 AVE SW UNIT 2, CALGARY, AB, T2P
3Y7
(403) 296-8000   *SIC* 1311
SUNSHINE OILSANDS LTD   p60
903 8 AVE SW UNIT 1020, CALGARY, AB,
T2P 0P7
(403) 984-1450   *SIC* 1311
SYNCRUDE CANADA LTD   p60
525 3 AVE SW SUITE 525, CALGARY, AB,
T2P 0G4
(403) 385-2400   *SIC* 1311
SYNCRUDE CANADA LTD   p129
9911 MACDONALD AVE SUITE 200, FORT
MCMURRAY, AB, T9H 1S7
(780) 790-5911   *SIC* 1311
TAMARACK VALLEY ENERGY LTD   p61
425 1ST ST SW SUITE 600, CALGARY, AB,
T2P 3L8
(403) 263-4440   *SIC* 1311
TAQA NORTH LTD   p61
308 4 AVE SW SUITE 2100, CALGARY, AB,
T2P 0H7
(403) 724-5000   *SIC* 1311
**TOSCANA ENERGY INCOME CORPORA-
TION**   p61
207 9 AVE SW SUITE 900, CALGARY, AB,
T2P 1K3
(403) 410-6790   *SIC* 1311
TOTAL E&P CANADA LTD   p61
240 4 AVE SW SUITE 2900, CALGARY, AB,
T2P 4H4
(403) 571-7599   *SIC* 1311
TUSK ENERGY INC   p62
700 4 AVE SW SUITE 1950, CALGARY, AB,
T2P 3J4
SIC 1311
YANGARRA RESOURCES LTD   p63
715 5 AVE SW SUITE 1530, CALGARY, AB,
T2P 2X6
(403) 262-9558   *SIC* 1311

SIC 1321 Natural gas liquids

CORRIDOR RESOURCES INC   p452
5475 SPRING GARDEN RD SUITE 301,
HALIFAX, NS, B3J 3T2
(902) 429-4511   *SIC* 1321

SIC 1381 Drilling oil and gas wells

1246607 ALBERTA LTD   p155
8080 EDGAR INDUSTRIAL CRES, RED
DEER, AB, T4P 3R3
(403) 347-9727   *SIC* 1381
406421 ALBERTA LTD   p155
8133 EDGAR INDUSTRIAL CLOSE, RED

DEER, AB, T4P 3R4
(403) 340-9825   *SIC* 1381

AKITA DRILLING LTD   *p*148
2302 8 ST, NISKU, AB, T9E 7Z2
(780) 955-6700   *SIC* 1381

ARC RESOURCES LTD   *p*43
308 4 AVE SW SUITE 1200, CALGARY, AB, T2P 0H7
(403) 503-8600   *SIC* 1381

BELLATRIX EXPLORATION LTD   *p*44
800 5 AVE SW UNIT 1920, CALGARY, AB, T2P 3T6
(403) 266-8670   *SIC* 1381

BELLATRIX EXPLORATION LTD   *p*82
5516 INDUSTRIAL RD, DRAYTON VALLEY, AB, T7A 1R1
(403) 266-8670   *SIC* 1381

BEYOND ENERGY SERVICES & TECHNOLOGY CORP   *p*44
444 5 AVE SW, CALGARY, AB, T2P 2T8
(403) 506-1514   *SIC* 1381

BOREAL WELL SERVICES   *p*131
13701 99 ST, GRANDE PRAIRIE, AB, T8V 7N9
(780) 513-3400   *SIC* 1381

CALFRAC WELL SERVICES LTD   *p*155
7310 EDGAR INDUSTRIAL DR, RED DEER, AB, T4P 3R2
(866) 772-3722   *SIC* 1381

CANADIAN ENERGY SERVICES INC   *p*45
700 4 AVE SW SUITE 1400, CALGARY, AB, T2P 3J4
(403) 269-2800   *SIC* 1381

CATHEDRAL ENERGY SERVICES LTD   *p*34
6030 3 ST SE, CALGARY, AB, T2H 1K2
(403) 265-2560   *SIC* 1381

CROSS BORDERS CONSULTING LTD   *p*1413
PO BOX 509, PILOT BUTTE, SK, S0G 3Z0
(306) 781-4484   *SIC* 1381

DIRECT HORIZONTAL DRILLING INC   *p*1
26308 TWP RD 531A SUITE 3, ACHESON, AB, T7X 5A3
(780) 960-6037   *SIC* 1381

ENCANA CORPORATION   *p*6
GD STN MAIN, BONNYVILLE, AB, T9N 2J6
SIC 1381

ENCORE CORING & DRILLING INC   *p*29
1345 HIGHFIELD CRES SE, CALGARY, AB, T2G 5N2
(403) 287-0123   *SIC* 1381

ENHANCED PETROLEUM SERVICES PARTNERSHIP   *p*49
400 5 AVE SW UNIT 900, CALGARY, AB, T2P 0L6
(403) 262-1361   *SIC* 1381

ENSIGN DRILLING INC   *p*49
400 5 AVE SW SUITE 1000, CALGARY, AB, T2P 0L6
(403) 262-1361   *SIC* 1381

ENSIGN ENERGY SERVICES INC   *p*49
400 5 AVE SW SUITE 1000, CALGARY, AB, T2P 0L6
(403) 262-1361   *SIC* 1381

ENSIGN SERVICING PARTNERSHIP   *p*49
400 5 AVE SW SUITE 900, CALGARY, AB, T2P 0L6
(403) 262-1361   *SIC* 1381

EQUINOR CANADA LTD   *p*49
308 4 AVE SW SUITE 3600, CALGARY, AB, T2P 0H7
(403) 234-0123   *SIC* 1381

EXCALIBUR DRILLING LTD   *p*7
490 CANAL ST, BROOKS, AB, T1R 1C8
(403) 793-2092   *SIC* 1381

FORAGES C.C.L. (1993) INC, LES   *p*1089
237 CH SAINT-FRANCOIS-XAVIER, DELSON, QC, J5B 1X8
(450) 632-3995   *SIC* 1381

FRONTERA ENERGY CORPORATION   *p*951
333 BAY ST SUITE 1100, TORONTO, ON, M5H 2R2
(416) 362-7735   *SIC* 1381

GRIMES WELL SERVICING LTD   *p*115

4526 97 ST NW, EDMONTON, AB, T6E 5N9
(780) 437-7871   *SIC* 1381

HAMMERHEAD RESOURCES INC   *p*51
525 8 AVE SW SUITE 2700, CALGARY, AB, T2P 1G1
(403) 930-0560   *SIC* 1381

HIGH ARCTIC ENERGY SERVICES INC   *p*51
700 2ND ST SW SUITE 500, CALGARY, AB, T2P 2W1
(403) 508-7836   *SIC* 1381

JOMAX DRILLING (1988) LTD   *p*52
355 4 AVE SW SUITE 2020, CALGARY, AB, T2P 0J1
(403) 265-5312   *SIC* 1381

KCA DEUTAG DRILLING CANADA INC   *p*428
45 HEBRON WAY SUITE 201, ST. JOHN'S, NL, A1A 0P9
(709) 778-6200   *SIC* 1381

KEANE COMPLETIONS CN CORP   *p*52
435 4 AVE SW SUITE 380, CALGARY, AB, T2P 2S6
(587) 390-0863   *SIC* 1381

MARATHON UNDERGROUND CONSTRUCTOR CORPORATION   *p*599
6847 HIRAM DR, GREELY, ON, K4P 1A2
(613) 821-4800   *SIC* 1381

NABORS DRILLING CANADA LIMITED   *p*54
500 4 AVE SW SUITE 2800, CALGARY, AB, T2P 2V6
(403) 263-6777   *SIC* 1381

NABORS DRILLING CANADA LIMITED   *p*149
902 20 AVE, NISKU, AB, T9E 7Z6
(780) 955-2381   *SIC* 1381

NEWPARK CANADA INC   *p*54
635 6 AVE SW SUITE 300, CALGARY, AB, T2P 0T5
(403) 266-7383   *SIC* 1381

NEWSCO INTERNATIONAL ENERGY SERVICES INC   *p*17
4855 102 AVE SE SUITE 11, CALGARY, AB, T2C 2X7
(403) 243-2331   *SIC* 1381

ORYX PETROLEUM CORPORATION LIMITED   *p*55
350 7 AVE SW SUITE 3400, CALGARY, AB, T2P 3N9
(403) 261-5350   *SIC* 1381

PATTERSON-UTI DRILLING CO. CANADA   *p*56
734 7 AVE SW SUITE 720, CALGARY, AB, T2P 3P8
(403) 269-2858   *SIC* 1381

PETROSHALE INC   *p*57
421 7TH AVE SW SUITE 3230, CALGARY, AB, T2P 4K9
(403) 266-1717   *SIC* 1381

PHOENIX TECHNOLOGY SERVICES INC   *p*57
250 2 ST SW SUITE 1400, CALGARY, AB, T2P 0C1
(403) 543-4466   *SIC* 1381

PHOENIX TECHNOLOGY SERVICES LP   *p*57
250 2 ST SW SUITE 1400, CALGARY, AB, T2P 0C1
(403) 543-4466   *SIC* 1381

PHX ENERGY SERVICES CORP   *p*57
250 2 ST SW SUITE 1400, CALGARY, AB, T2P 0C1
(403) 543-4466   *SIC* 1381

PINE CLIFF ENERGY LTD   *p*65
1015 4 ST SW SUITE 850, CALGARY, AB, T2R 1J4
(403) 269-2289   *SIC* 1381

PRECISION DRILLING CORPORATION   *p*57
525 8 AVE SW SUITE 800, CALGARY, AB, T2P 1G1
(403) 716-4500   *SIC* 1381

PREDATOR DRILLING INC   *p*157
210 CLEARSKYE WAY, RED DEER COUNTY, AB, T4E 0A1
(403) 346-0870   *SIC* 1381

QUESTFIRE ENERGY CORP   *p*57
350 7 AVE SW SUITE 1100, CALGARY, AB, T2P 3N9

(403) 263-6688   *SIC* 1381

REFORM ENERGY SERVICES CORP   *p*58
808 4 AVE SW SUITE 500, CALGARY, AB, T2P 3E8
(403) 262-2181   *SIC* 1381

REZONE WELL OIL AND GAS SERVICE REPAIR   *p*156
8071 EDGAR INDUSTRIAL DR, RED DEER, AB, T4P 3R2
(403) 342-7772   *SIC* 1381

RYAN ENERGY TECHNOLOGIES   *p*58
500 4 AVE SW SUITE 2800, CALGARY, AB, T2P 2V6
(403) 263-6777   *SIC* 1381

SAVANNA ENERGY SERVICES CORP   *p*58
311 6 AVE SW SUITE 800, CALGARY, AB, T2P 3H2
(403) 503-9990   *SIC* 1381

SIMMONS EDECO INC   *p*65
1414 8 ST SW SUITE 500, CALGARY, AB, T2R 1J6
(403) 244-5340   *SIC* 1381

SUREPOINT TECHNOLOGIES GROUP INC   *p*150
1211 8A ST, NISKU, AB, T9E 7R3
(780) 955-3939   *SIC* 1381

TECHNIPFMC PLC   *p*7
380 WELL ST, BROOKS, AB, T1R 1C2
(403) 363-0028   *SIC* 1381

TELEMETRIX DOWNHOLE TECHNOLOGIES INC   *p*76
85 FREEPORT BLVD BE BAY 102, CALGARY, AB, T3J 4X8
(403) 243-2331   *SIC* 1381

TEMPCO DRILLING COMPANY INC   *p*11
720 28 ST NE SUITE 114, CALGARY, AB, T2A 6R3
(403) 259-5533   *SIC* 1381

TORC OIL & GAS LTD   *p*61
525 8 AVE SW SUITE 1800, CALGARY, AB, T2P 1G1
(403) 930-4120   *SIC* 1381

TOUCHSTONE EXPLORATION INC   *p*61
350 7TH AVE SW UNIT 4100, CALGARY, AB, T2P 3N9
(403) 750-4400   *SIC* 1381

TREELINE WELL SERVICES INC   *p*66
333 11 AVE SW SUITE 750, CALGARY, AB, T2R 1L9
(403) 266-2868   *SIC* 1381

TRINIDAD DRILLING LTD   *p*62
400 5TH AVE SW SUITE 1000, CALGARY, AB, T2P 0L6
(403) 262-1361   *SIC* 1381

ULTERRA LP   *p*140
7010 45 ST, LEDUC, AB, T9E 7E7
(780) 980-3500   *SIC* 1381

XTREME DRILLING CORP   *p*63
333 7TH AVE SW SUITE 1000, CALGARY, AB, T2P 2Z1
(403) 292-7979   *SIC* 1381

ZONE DIRECT MWD SERVICES LTD   *p*12
15-2916 5 AVE NE, CALGARY, AB, T2A 6K4
(403) 457-0133   *SIC* 1381

SIC 1382 Oil and gas exploration services

1334130 ALBERTA LTD   *p*42
550 6 AVE SW SUITE 1000, CALGARY, AB, T2P 0S2
(403) 515-2800   *SIC* 1382

988690 ALBERTA INC   *p*146
1771 30 ST SW SUITE 8, MEDICINE HAT, AB, T1B 3N5
(403) 529-6559   *SIC* 1382

ABITIBI GEOPHYSIQUE INC   *p*1390
1746 CH SULLIVAN, VAL-D'OR, QC, J9P 7H1
(819) 874-8800   *SIC* 1382

ADVANTAGE OIL & GAS LTD   *p*42
440 2 AVE SW SUITE 2200, CALGARY, AB, T2P 5E9
(403) 718-8000   *SIC* 1382

AFRICA OIL CORP   *p*301
885 GEORGIA ST W SUITE 2000, VANCOUVER, BC, V6C 3E8
(604) 689-7842   *SIC* 1382

AKITA DRILLING LTD   *p*42
333 7 AVE SW UNIT 1000, CALGARY, AB, T2P 2Z1
(403) 292-7979   *SIC* 1382

ALTURA ENERGY INC   *p*43
640 5 AVE SW SUITE 2500, CALGARY, AB, T2P 3G4
(403) 984-5197   *SIC* 1382

ARCIS SEISMIC SOLUTIONS CORP   *p*43
250 5 ST SW SUITE 2100, CALGARY, AB, T2P 0R4
(403) 781-1700   *SIC* 1382

AUSENCO ENGINEERING CANADA INC   *p*43
401 9 AVE SW STE 1430, CALGARY, AB, T2P 3C5
(403) 705-4100   *SIC* 1382

BANKERS PETROLEUM LTD   *p*44
3700-888 3 ST SW, CALGARY, AB, T2P 5C5
(403) 513-2699   *SIC* 1382

BERTRAM DRILLING CORP   *p*79
347 CARADOC AVE, CARBON, AB, T0M 0L0
(403) 572-3591   *SIC* 1382

BIRCHCLIFF ENERGY LTD   *p*44
600 3RD AVE SW SUITE 1000, CALGARY, AB, T2P 0G5
(403) 261-6401   *SIC* 1382

BJ SERVICES HOLDINGS CANADA ULC   *p*44
215 9 AVE SW UNIT 800, CALGARY, AB, T2P 1K3
(587) 324-2058   *SIC* 1382

BLACKPEARL RESOURCES INC   *p*44
215 9 AVE SW UNIT 900, CALGARY, AB, T2P 1K3
(403) 215-8313   *SIC* 1382

BOW RIVER ENERGY LTD   *p*44
321 6 AVE SW SUITE 500, CALGARY, AB, T2P 3H3
(403) 475-4100   *SIC* 1382

CELTIC EXPLORATION ULC   *p*46
505 3 ST SW SUITE 500, CALGARY, AB, T2P 3E6
(403) 201-5340   *SIC* 1382

CENOVUS ENERGY INC   *p*46
500 CENTRE ST SE, CALGARY, AB, T2P 0M5
(403) 766-2000   *SIC* 1382

CEQUENCE ENERGY LTD   *p*46
215-9TH AVE SW SUITE 1400, CALGARY, AB, T2P 1K3
(403) 229-3050   *SIC* 1382

CES ENERGY SOLUTIONS CORP   *p*46
332 6 AVE SW SUITE 1400, CALGARY, AB, T2P 0B2
(403) 269-2800   *SIC* 1382

CES ENERGY SOLUTIONS CORP   *p*1405
HIGHWAY 9 S, CARLYLE, SK, S0C 0R0
(306) 453-4470   *SIC* 1382

CHINOOK ENERGY INC   *p*46
222 3RD AV SW SUITE 1610, CALGARY, AB, T2P 0B4
(403) 261-6883   *SIC* 1382

CNOOC PETROLEUM NORTH AMERICA ULC   *p*28
500 CENTRE ST SE SUITE 2300, CALGARY, AB, T2G 1A6
(403) 699-4000   *SIC* 1382

CONDOR PETROLEUM INC   *p*47
2400 144 4 AVE SW, CALGARY, AB, T2P 3N4
(403) 201-9694   *SIC* 1382

CONNACHER OIL AND GAS LIMITED   *p*47
640 5 AVE SW SUITE 1040, CALGARY, AB, T2P 3G4
(403) 538-6201   *SIC* 1382

CONOCOPHILLIPS WESTERN CANADA PARTNERSHIP   *p*47
401 9 AVE SW SUITE 1600, CALGARY, AB,

T2P 3C5
(403) 233-4000   *SIC* 1382
CORDY OILFIELD SERVICES INC   *p15*
5366 55 ST SE, CALGARY, AB, T2C 3G9
(403) 262-7667   *SIC* 1382
CROWN POINT ENERGY INC   *p47*
GD, CALGARY, AB, T2P 0T8
(403) 232-1150   *SIC* 1382
CWC ENERGY SERVICES CORP   *p47*
205 5 AVE SW SUITE 610, CALGARY, AB,
T2P 2V7
(403) 264-2177   *SIC* 1382
DALMAC ENERGY INC   *p113*
4934 89 ST NW, EDMONTON, AB, T6E 5K1
(780) 988-8510   ·   *SIC* 1382
DEBEERS CANADA EXPLORATION   *p919*
65 OVERLEA BLVD SUITE 300, TORONTO,
ON, M4H 1P1
(416) 645-1710   *SIC* 1382
DELPHI ENERGY CORP   *p47*
333 7 AVE SW SUITE 2300, CALGARY, AB,
T2P 2Z1
(403) 265-6171   *SIC* 1382
DEVON CANADA CORPORATION   *p126*
10924 92ND AVE, FAIRVIEW, AB, T0H 1L0
SIC 1382
DEVON CANADA CORPORATION   *p131*
9601 116 ST UNIT 101, GRANDE PRAIRIE,
AB, T8V 5W3
(403) 517-6700   *SIC* 1382
DEVON CANADA CORPORATION   *p213*
10514 87 AVE, FORT ST. JOHN, BC, V1J
5K7
SIC 1382
EAGLE CANADA, INC   *p35*
6806 RAILWAY ST SE, CALGARY, AB, T2H
3A8
(403) 781-1192   *SIC* 1382
ECHO SEISMIC LTD   *p22*
4500 8A ST NE, CALGARY, AB, T2E 4J7
(403) 216-0999   *SIC* 1382
EMBER RESOURCES INC   *p48*
400 3 AVE SW SUITE 800, CALGARY, AB,
T2P 4H2
(403) 270-0803   *SIC* 1382
ENCANA CORPORATION   *p29*
500 CENTRE ST SE, CALGARY, AB, T2G
1A6
(403) 645-2000   *SIC* 1382
**ENERCORP SAND SOLUTIONS PARTNER-
SHIP**   *p48*
520 3 AVE SW UNIT 530, CALGARY, AB,
T2P 0R3
(403) 217-1332   *SIC* 1382
**ENGINEERING   SEISMOLOGY   GROUP
CANADA INC**   *p630*
20 HYPERION CRT, KINGSTON, ON, K7K
7K2
(613) 548-8287   *SIC* 1382
ENVIRO-TECH SURVEYS LTD   *p64*
1020 14 AVE SW, CALGARY, AB, T2R 0P1
(403) 345-2901   *SIC* 1382
EXXONMOBIL CANADA ENERGY   *p49*
237 4 AVE SW, CALGARY, AB, T2P 0H6
(403) 260-7910   *SIC* 1382
EXXONMOBIL CANADA PROPERTIES   *p49*
237 4 AVE SW SUITE 4063, CALGARY,
T2P 0H6
(403) 260-7910   *SIC* 1382
FIRST ALERT LOCATING LTD   *p131*
72022B RD 713, GRANDE PRAIRIE, AB,
T8V 3A1
(780) 538-9936   *SIC* 1382
GAIN ENERGY LTD   *p50*
520 3 AVE SW 30TH FL, CALGARY, AB,
T2P 0R3
(403) 294-1336   *SIC* 1382
GASTEM INC   *p1204*
1155 BOUL ROBERT-BOURASSA UNITE
1215, MONTREAL, QC, H3B 3A7
SIC 1382
GEAR ENERGY LTD   *p50*
240 4TH AVE SW SUITE 2600, CALGARY,
AB, T2P 4H4

(403) 538-8435   *SIC* 1382
GENOIL INC   *p67*
1811 4 ST SW SUITE 218, CALGARY, AB,
T2S 1W2
(587) 400-0249   *SIC* 1382
GRAN TIERRA ENERGY INC   *p50*
520 3RD AVE SW SUITE 900, CALGARY,
AB, T2P 0R3
(403) 265-3221   *SIC* 1382
GREENFIRE OIL AND GAS LTD   *p50*
444 5 AVE SW SUITE 1650, CALGARY, AB,
T2P 2T8
(403) 681-7377   *SIC* 1382
GRIFFITHS ENERGY INTERNATIONAL INC
p50
555 4 AVE SW SUITE 2100, CALGARY, AB,
T2P 3E7
(403) 724-7200   *SIC* 1382
HEMISPHERE   ENERGY   CORPORATION
p313
905 W PENDER ST SUITE 501, VANCOU-
VER, BC, V6E 2E9
(604) 685-9255   *SIC* 1382
**HIBERNIA MANAGEMENT AND DEVELOP-
MENT COMPANY LTD**   *p432*
100 NEW GOWER ST SUITE 1000, ST.
JOHN'S, NL, A1C 6K3
SIC 1382
HUSKY ENERGY INC   *p51*
707 8 AVE SW, CALGARY, AB, T2P 1H5
(403) 298-6111   *SIC* 1382
IKKUMA RESOURCES CORP   *p51*
605 5 AVE SW SUITE 2700, CALGARY, AB,
T2P 3H5
(403) 261-5900   *SIC* 1382
IMPERIAL OIL RESOURCES LIMITED   *p51*
237 4 AVE SW, CALGARY, AB, T2P 0H6
(800) 567-3776   *SIC* 1382
INTER PIPELINE LTD   *p52*
215 2 ST SW SUITE 3200, CALGARY, AB,
T2P 1M4
(403) 290-6000   *SIC* 1382
ITHACA ENERGY INC   *p52*
333 7 AVE SW SUITE 1600, CALGARY, AB,
T2P 2Z1
(403) 234-3338   *SIC* 1382
JOURNEY ENERGY INC   *p64*
517 10 AVE SW SUITE 700, CALGARY,
T2R 0A8
(403) 294-1635   *SIC* 1382
JURA ENERGY CORPORATION   *p52*
150-6TH AVE SW SUITE 5100, CALGARY,
AB, T2P 3Y7
(403) 266-6364   *SIC* 1382
KARVE ENERGY INC   *p52*
205 5 AVE SW SUITE 1700, CALGARY, AB,
T2P 2V7
(403) 809-5896   *SIC* 1382
KATALYST DATA MANAGEMENT LP   *p52*
540 5 AVE SW SUITE 1490, CALGARY, AB,
T2P 0M2
(403) 294-5274   *SIC* 1382
KELT EXPLORATION LTD   *p52*
311 SIXTH AVE SW SUITE 300, CALGARY,
AB, T2P 3H2
(403) 294-0154   *SIC* 1382
LAKE SHORE GOLD CORP   *p953*
181 UNIVERSITY AVE, TORONTO, ON,
M5H 3M7
(416) 703-6298   *SIC* 1382
LEGACY OIL + GAS INC   *p53*
525 8 AVE SW SUITE 4400, CALGARY, AB,
T2P 1G1
(403) 206-5035   *SIC* 1382
LEUCROTTA EXPLORATION INC   *p53*
639 5 AVE SW SUITE 700, CALGARY, AB,
T2P 0M9
(403) 705-4525   *SIC* 1382
LONE PINE RESOURCES INC   *p53*
640 5 AVE SW SUITE 1100, CALGARY, AB,
T2P 3G4
(403) 292-8000   *SIC* 1382
LONG RUN EXPLORATION LTD   *p53*
600 3 AVE SW UNIT 600, CALGARY, AB,

T2P 0G5
(403) 261-6012   *SIC* 1382
MARATHON OIL CANADA CORPORATION
p53
440 2 AVE SW SUITE 2400, CALGARY, AB,
T2P 5E9
(403) 233-1700   *SIC* 1382
MARQUEE ENERGY LTD   *p53*
500 4 AVE SW SUITE 1700, CALGARY, AB,
T2P 2V6
(403) 384-0000   *SIC* 1382
NEOS CANADA SERVICES ULC   *p307*
355 BURRARD ST SUITE 1800, VANCOU-
VER, BC, V6C 2G8
(604) 682-7737   *SIC* 1382
NOVUS ENERGY INC.   *p55*
700 4 AVE SW UNIT 1700, CALGARY, AB,
T2P 3J4
(403) 263-4310   *SIC* 1382
NUVISTA ENERGY LTD   *p55*
525 8 AVE SW SUITE 2500, CALGARY, AB,
T2P 1G1
(403) 538-8500   *SIC* 1382
OGI GROUP CORPORATION   *p55*
888 3 ST SW UNIT 1000, CALGARY, AB,
T2P 5C5
(403) 233-7777   *SIC* 1382
PACKERS PLUS ENERGY SERVICES INC
p55
205 5 AVE SW SUITE 2200, CALGARY, AB,
T2P 2V7
(403) 263-7587   *SIC* 1382
PARAMOUNT RESOURCES (ACL) LTD   *p56*
421 7 AVE SW SUITE 2800, CALGARY, AB,
T2P 4K9
(403) 261-1200   *SIC* 1382
PAREX RESOURCES INC   *p56*
2700 EIGHTH AVE PL WEST TOWER 585
8 AVE SW, CALGARY, AB, T2P 1G1
(403) 265-4800   *SIC* 1382
PERSTA RESOURCES INC   *p56*
888 3 ST SW SUITE 3600, CALGARY, AB,
T2P 5C5
(403) 355-6623   *SIC* 1382
PETROCAPITA INCOME TRUST   *p56*
717 7 AVE SW SUITE 1400, CALGARY, AB,
T2P 0Z3
(587) 393-3450   *SIC* 1382
PETROCHINA CANADA LTD   *p56*
707 5 ST SW SUITE 2700, CALGARY, AB,
T2P 1V8
(403) 265-6635   *SIC* 1382
PETROTAL CORP   *p57*
421 7TH AVE SW SUITE 4000, CALGARY,
AB, T2P 4K9
(403) 813-4237   *SIC* 1382
PETROWEST TRANSPORTATION LP   *p134*
9201 163 AVE, GRANDE PRAIRIE, AB, T8X
0B6
(780) 402-0383   *SIC* 1382
PETRUS RESOURCES LTD   *p57*
240 4 AVE SW SUITE 2400, CALGARY, AB,
T2P 4H4
(403) 984-4014   *SIC* 1382
PRAIRIE PROVIDENT RESOURCES INC *p57*
525 8 AVE SW SUITE 1100, CALGARY, AB,
T2P 3G4
(403) 292-8000   *SIC* 1382
PRAIRIESKY ROYALTY LTD   *p57*
350 7TH AVE SW SUITE 1700, CALGARY,
AB, T2P 3N9
(587) 293-4000   *SIC* 1382
QUESTERRE ENERGY CORPORATION *p57*
801 6 AVE SW SUITE 1650, CALGARY, AB,
T2P 3W2
(403) 777-1185   *SIC* 1382
RENAISSANCE OIL CORP   *p329*
595 BURRARD ST SUITE 3123, VANCOU-
VER, BC, V7X 1J1
(604) 536-3637   *SIC* 1382
**REPSOL   CANADA   ENERGY   PARTNER-
SHIP**   *p58*
888 3 ST SW SUITE 2000, CALGARY, AB,
T2P 5C5

(403) 237-1234   *SIC* 1382
REPSOL OIL & GAS CANADA INC   *p58*
888 3 ST SW SUITE 2000, CALGARY, AB,
T2P 5C5
SIC 1382
RIDGEBACK RESOURCES INC   *p58*
525 8 AVE SW UNIT 2800, CALGARY, AB,
T2P 1G1
(403) 268-7800   *SIC* 1382
SAEXPLORATION (CANADA) LTD   *p32*
3333 8 ST SE SUITE 300, CALGARY, AB,
T2G 3A4
(403) 776-1950   *SIC* 1382
SANDER GEOPHYSICS LIMITED   *p827*
260 HUNT CLUB RD, OTTAWA, ON, K1V
1C1
(613) 521-9626   *SIC* 1382
SDX ENERGY INC   *p59*
520 3 AVE SW SUITE 1900, CALGARY, AB,
T2P 0R3
(403) 457-5035   *SIC* 1382
SHAMARAN PETROLEUM CORP   *p309*
885 GEORGIA W SUITE 2000, VAN-
COUVER, BC, V6C 3E8
(604) 689-7842   *SIC* 1382
**SHERRITT INTERNATIONAL OIL AND GAS
LIMITED**   *p59*
425 1 ST SW SUITE 2000, CALGARY, AB,
T2P 3L8
(403) 260-2900   *SIC* 1382
SONORO ENERGY LTD   *p59*
520 5 AVE SW SUITE 900, CALGARY, AB,
T2P 3R7
(403) 262-3252   *SIC* 1382
STORM RESOURCES LTD   *p60*
215 2 ST SW SUITE 600, CALGARY, AB.
T2P 1M4
(403) 817-6145   *SIC* 1382
STRATEGIC OIL & GAS LTD   *p60*
645 7 AVE SW SUITE 1100, CALGARY, AB.
T2P 4G8
(403) 767-9000   *SIC* 1382
STREAM OIL & GAS LTD   *p42*
609 14 ST NW SUITE 300, CALGARY, AB.
T2N 2A1
(403) 531-2358   *SIC* 1382
SURGE ENERGY INC   *p60*
635 8 AVE SW SUITE 2100, CALGARY, AB.
T2P 3M3
(403) 930-1010   *SIC* 1382
SURGE GENERAL PARTNERSHIP   *p60*
635 8 AVE SW SUITE 2100, CALGARY, AB.
T2P 3M3
(403) 930-1010   *SIC* 1382
TAYLOR HILL DEVELOPMENTS   *p492*
106 NORTH FRONT ST, BELLEVILLE, ON.
K8P 3B4
(613) 969-9907   *SIC* 1382
TECHNIPFMC CANADA LTD   *p431*
131 KELSEY DR, ST. JOHN'S, NL, A1B 0L2
(709) 724-1851   *SIC* 1382
TIER 1 ENERGY SOLUTIONS INC   *p117*
453-97 ST EDMONTON AB, EDMONTON,
AB, T6E 5Y7
(780) 476-0099   *SIC* 1382
TOTAL ENERGY SERVICES INC   *p19*
6900 112 AVE SE, CALGARY, AB, T2C 4Z1
(403) 235-5877   *SIC* 1382
TOTAL ENERGY SERVICES INC   *p61*
311 6 AVE SW SUITE 800, CALGARY, AB.
T2P 3H2
(403) 216-3939   *SIC* 1382
TOURMALINE OIL CORP   *p61*
250 6 AVE SW UNIT 3700, CALGARY, AB.
T2P 3H7
(403) 266-5992   *SIC* 1382
TRANSGLOBE   ENERGY   CORPORATION
p62
250 5TH ST SW SUITE 2300, CALGARY,
AB, T2P 0R4
(403) 264-9888   *SIC* 1382
TRIDENT EXPLORATION CORP   *p62*
3100-888 3 ST SW, CALGARY, AB, T2P 5C5
(403) 770-0333   *SIC* 1382

TRIDENT RESOURCES CORP *p62*
888 3 ST SW SUITE 3100, CALGARY, AB, T2P 5C5
(403) 770-0333   *SIC 1382*

TUNDRA OIL & GAS LIMITED *p376*
1 LOMBARD PL SUITE 1700, WINNIPEG, MB, R3B 0X3
(204) 934-5850   *SIC 1382*

UNIVERSAL GEOSYSTEMS *p62*
910 7 AVE SW SUITE 1015, CALGARY, AB, T2P 3N8
(403) 262-1336   *SIC 1382*

VALEURA ENERGY INC *p62*
202 6 AVE SW SUITE 1200, CALGARY, AB, T2P 2R9
(403) 237-7102   *SIC 1382*

VALUE CREATION INC *p62*
635 8 AVE SW UNIT 1100, CALGARY, AB, T2P 3M3
(403) 539-4500   *SIC 1382*

VERMILION ENERGY INC *p62*
520 3RD AVE SW SUITE 3500, CALGARY, AB, T2P 0R3
(403) 269-4884   *SIC 1382*

WEST LAKE ENERGY CORP *p62*
600 3 AVE SW SUITE 700, CALGARY, AB, T2P 0G5
(403) 215-2045   *SIC 1382*

WESTERNZAGROS RESOURCES ULC *p63*
255 5 AVE SW SUITE 1000, CALGARY, AB, T2P 3G6
(403) 693-7001   *SIC 1382*

WSP CANADA INC *p63*
112 4 AVE SW SUITE 1000, CALGARY, AB, T2P 0H3
(403) 266-2800   *SIC 1382*

SIC 1389 Oil and gas field services, nec

1001511 ALBERTA LTD *p153*
GD, PROVOST, AB, T0B 3S0
(780) 753-6404   *SIC 1389*

4 EVERGREEN RESOURCES INC. *p233*
1717 BOUCHER LAKE RD, MOBERLY LAKE, BC, V0C 1X0
(250) 788-7916   *SIC 1389*

747395 ALBERTA LTD *p172*
GD LCD MAIN, WETASKIWIN, AB, T9A 1W7
(780) 352-6041   *SIC 1389*

878175 ALBERTA LTD *p172*
3365 33 ST, WHITECOURT, AB, T7S 0A2
SIC 1389

AECOM CANADA LTD *p1438*
HIGHWAY 1 EAST 3 NORTH SERVICE RD, WHITE CITY, SK, S4L 5B1
(306) 779-2200   *SIC 1389*

AECOM ENERGY SERVICES LTD *p33*
6025 11 ST SE SUITE 240, CALGARY, AB, T2H 2Z2
(403) 218-7100   *SIC 1389*

AECOM ENERGY SERVICES LTD *p126*
10211 98 ST, FAIRVIEW, AB, T0H 1L0
(403) 218-7100   *SIC 1389*

AECOM PRODUCTION SERVICES LTD *p33*
6025 11 ST SE UNIT 240, CALGARY, AB, T2H 2Z2
(403) 386-1000   *SIC 1389*

ALBARRIE GEOCOMPOSITES LIMITED *p486*
85 MORROW RD, BARRIE, ON, L4N 3V7
(705) 737-0551   *SIC 1389*

ALSTAR OILFIELD CONTRACTORS LTD *p136*
310 RIVER RD E, HINTON, AB, T7V 1X5
(780) 865-5938   *SIC 1389*

ALTEX ENERGY LTD *p43*
700 9 AVE SW SUITE 1100, CALGARY, AB, T2P 3V4
(403) 508-7525   *SIC 1389*

ALTUS ENERGY SERVICES LTD *p43*
222 3 AVE SW SUITE 740, CALGARY, AB, T2P 0B4

SIC 1389

ASENIWUCHE DEVELOPEMENT CORPORATION *p130*
10028 99 ST, GRANDE CACHE, AB, T0E 0Y0
(780) 827-5510   *SIC 1389*

AVEDA TRANSPORTATION AND ENERGY SERVICES INC *p43*
435 4 AVE SW SUITE 300, CALGARY, AB, T2P 3A8
(403) 264-4950   *SIC 1389*

AVENTUR ENERGY CORP *p213*
10493 ALDER CRES, FORT ST. JOHN, BC, V1J 4M7
(250) 785-7093   *SIC 1389*

B.& R. ECKEL'S TRANSPORT LTD *p6*
5514B 50 AVE, BONNYVILLE, AB, T9N 2K8
(780) 826-3889   *SIC 1389*

BACKWOODS CONTRACTING LTD *p125*
1259 91 ST SW UNIT 301, EDMONTON, AB, T6X 1E9
(587) 880-2937   *SIC 1389*

BADGER DAYLIGHTING LTD *p64*
919 11TH AVE SW SUITE 400, CALGARY, AB, T2R 1P3
(403) 264-8500   *SIC 1389*

BAKER HUGHES CANADA COMPANY *p13*
4839 90 AVE SE SUITE FRNT, CALGARY, AB, T2C 2S8
(403) 531-5300   *SIC 1389*

BAKER HUGHES CANADA COMPANY *p108*
9010 34 ST NW, EDMONTON, AB, T6B 2V1
(780) 465-9495   *SIC 1389*

BAKER HUGHES CANADA COMPANY *p139*
3905 71 AVE, LEDUC, AB, T9E 0R8
(780) 612-3150   *SIC 1389*

BAKER HUGHES CANADA COMPANY *p155*
7880 EDGAR INDUSTRIAL DR, RED DEER, AB, T4P 3R2
(403) 340-3015   *SIC 1389*

BAKER HUGHES CANADA COMPANY *p155*
4089 77 ST, RED DEER, AB, T4P 2T3
(403) 357-1401   *SIC 1389*

BAKER HUGHES CANADA COMPANY *p158*
1901 BROADWAY AVE E, REDCLIFF, AB, T0J 2P0
SIC 1389

BAXTER, BERT TRANSPORT LTD *p1406*
301 KENSINGTON AVE, ESTEVAN, SK, S4A 2A1
(306) 634-3616   *SIC 1389*

BISSETT RESOURCE CONSULTANTS LTD *p44*
839 5 AVE SW SUITE 250, CALGARY, AB, T2P 3C8
(403) 263-0073   *SIC 1389*

BOHN PETROLEUM SERVICES LTD *p173*
3449 33 ST, WHITECOURT, AB, T7S 1X4
(780) 778-8551   *SIC 1389*

BONNETT'S ENERGY CORP *p134*
65007 HWY 43, GRANDE PRAIRIE, AB, T8W 5E7
(780) 264-3010   *SIC 1389*

BONNETT'S ENERGY SERVICES LP *p134*
65007 HWY 43, GRANDE PRAIRIE, AB, T8W 5E7
(780) 532-5700   *SIC 1389*

BOREK CONSTRUCTION LTD *p204*
9630 RD 223, DAWSON CREEK, BC, V1G 4H8
(250) 782-5561   *SIC 1389*

BRADY OILFIELD SERVICES L.P. *p1407*
1 MERGEN ST, HALBRITE, SK, S0C 1H0
(306) 458-2344   *SIC 1389*

BRANDETTE WELL SERVICING LTD *p82*
3202 63 ST, DRAYTON VALLEY, AB, T7A 1R6
(780) 542-3404   *SIC 1389*

BROCK CANADA INC *p148*
3735 8 ST, NISKU, AB, T9E 8J8
(780) 465-9016   *SIC 1389*

CALFRAC WELL SERVICES LTD *p45*
411 8 AVE SW, CALGARY, AB, T2P 1E3
(866) 770-3722   *SIC 1389*

CANRIG DRILLING TECHNOLOGY LTD *p14*
5250 94 AVE SE, CALGARY, AB, T2C 3Z3
(403) 279-3466   *SIC 1389*

CANYON SERVICES GROUP INC *p46*
645 7 AVE SW SUITE 2900, CALGARY, AB, T2P 4G8
(403) 266-0202   *SIC 1389*

CANYON TECHNICAL SERVICES LTD *p46*
255 5 AVE SW SUITE 2900, CALGARY, AB, T2P 3G6
(403) 355-2300   *SIC 1389*

CANYON TECHNICAL SERVICES LTD *p79*
9102 102 ST SUITE 55, CLAIRMONT, AB, T8X 5G8
(780) 357-2250   *SIC 1389*

CANYON TECHNICAL SERVICES LTD *p153*
28042 HWY 11 UNIT 322, RED DEER, AB, T4N 5H3
SIC 1389

CANYON TECHNICAL SERVICES LTD *p1406*
548 BOURQUIN RD, ESTEVAN, SK, S4A 2A7
(306) 637-3360   *SIC 1389*

CAPSTAN HAULING LTD *p134*
10903 78 AVE, GRANDE PRAIRIE, AB, T8W 2L2
(780) 402-3110   *SIC 1389*

CAPSTONE BLOWOUT RECOVERY, CAPSTONE ABANDONMENTS *p2*
32 EAST LAKE CIR NE, AIRDRIE, AB, T4A 2K1
(403) 437-8587   *SIC 1389*

CASCADE SERVICES LTD *p213*
9619 81 AVE, FORT ST. JOHN, BC, V1J 6P6
(250) 785-0236   *SIC 1389*

CENTERFIRE CONTRACTING LTD *p9*
236 STONY MOUNTAIN RD SUITE 106, ANZAC, AB, T0P 1J0
(780) 334-2277   *SIC 1389*

CERTEK HEAT MACHINES INC *p171*
11101 ST WEMBLEY ST, WEMBLEY, AB, T0H 3S0
(780) 832-3962   *SIC 1389*

CGX ENERGY INC *p950*
333 BAY ST SUITE 1100, TORONTO, ON, M5H 2R2
(416) 364-5569   *SIC 1389*

CHRISTOPHER'S WELDING LTD *p82*
GD, DIDSBURY, AB, T0M 0W0
SIC 1389

CLARK CONSTRUCTION *p136*
GD STN MAIN, HINTON, AB, T7V 1T9
(780) 865-5822   *SIC 1389*

CLEAN HARBORS SURFACE RENTALS PARTNERSHIP *p46*
222 3 AVE SW SUITE 900, CALGARY, AB, T2P 0B4
(403) 543-7325   *SIC 1389*

CLEAN HARBORS SURFACE RENTALS PARTNERSHIP *p139*
3902 77 AVE, LEDUC, AB, T9E 0B6
(780) 980-1868   *SIC 1389*

CLEANTEK INDUSTRIES INC *p160*
261106 WAGON WHEEL CRES SUITE 1, ROCKY VIEW COUNTY, AB, T4A 0E2
(403) 567-8700   *SIC 1389*

CLEARSTREAM ENERGY SERVICES LIMITED PARTNERSHIP *p80*
141 2 AVE E, COCHRANE, AB, T4C 2B9
(403) 932-9565   *SIC 1389*

CLEARSTREAM TRANSPORTATION SERVICES LP *p108*
7809 34 ST NW, EDMONTON, AB, T6B 2V5
(780) 410-1960   *SIC 1389*

COMMAND FISHING AND PIPE RECOVERY LTD *p140*
24521 TOWNSHIP ROAD 510, LEDUC COUNTY, AB, T4X 0T4
(780) 979-2220   *SIC 1389*

CONESTOGA PIPER AND SUPPLY CANADA CORP *p6*
1010 1ST AVE E, BOW ISLAND, AB, T0K 0G0

---

(403) 545-2935   *SIC 1389*

CONTINENTAL LABORATORIES (1985) LTD *p22*
3601 21 ST NE UNIT A, CALGARY, AB, T2E 6T5
(403) 250-3982   *SIC 1389*

CONTROL INNOVATIONS INC *p15*
11222 42 ST SE, CALGARY, AB, T2C 0J9
(403) 720-0277   *SIC 1389*

CONTROL TECHNOLOGY INC *p5*
4305 SOUTH ST, BLACKFALDS, AB, T0C 0B0
(403) 885-2677   *SIC 1389*

CORAL OILFIELD SERVICES INC *p134*
15303 94 ST SUITE 15303, GRANDE PRAIRIE, AB, T8X 0L2
(780) 402-9800   *SIC 1389*

CORE LABORATORIES CANADA LTD *p158*
39139 HIGHWAY 2A UNIT 5409, RED DEER COUNTY, AB, T4S 2A8
(403) 340-1017   *SIC 1389*

CORIX CONTROL SOLUTIONS LIMITED PARTNERSHIP *p113*
8803 58 AVE NW, EDMONTON, AB, T6E 5X1
(780) 468-6950   *SIC 1389*

CORPORATION OF THE CITY OF FREDERICTON *p400*
520 YORK ST, FREDERICTON, NB, E3B 3R2
(506) 460-2020   *SIC 1389*

DALMAC OILFIELD SERVICES INC *p114*
4934 89 ST NW, EDMONTON, AB, T6E 5K1
(780) 988-8510   *SIC 1389*

DATALOG TECHNOLOGY INC *p15*
10707 50 ST SE, CALGARY, AB, T2C 3E5
(403) 243-2024   *SIC 1389*

DECHANT CONSTRUCTION (WESTERN) LTD *p213*
4801 44 AVE, FORT NELSON, BC, V0C 1R0
(250) 775-6064   *SIC 1389*

DEI, CHARLES CONSTRUCTION LTD *p136*
GD, HINES CREEK, AB, T0H 2A0
(780) 494-3838   *SIC 1389*

DEMON OILFIELD SERVICES INC *p81*
812 LAUT AVE, CROSSFIELD, AB, T0M 0S0
(403) 946-4800   *SIC 1389*

DIAL OILFIELD SERVICES 2006 LTD *p82*
5136 54 ST, DRAYTON VALLEY, AB, T7A 1S2
(780) 542-5879   *SIC 1389*

DIAMOND ENERGY SERVICES INC *p1436*
1521 NORTH SERVICE RD W, SWIFT CURRENT, SK, S9H 3S9
(306) 778-6682   *SIC 1389*

DOCKTOR OILFIELD TRANSPORT CORP *p82*
6225 54 AVE, DRAYTON VALLEY, AB, T7A 1S8
SIC 1389

DYNAENERGETICS CANADA HOLDINGS INC *p109*
5911 56 AVE NW, EDMONTON, AB, T6B 3E2
(780) 490-0939   *SIC 1389*

DYNAENERGETICS CANADA INC *p109*
5911 56 AVE NW, EDMONTON, AB, T6B 3E2
(780) 490-0939   *SIC 1389*

DYNAMITAGE CASTONGUAY LTEE *p1375*
5939 RUE JOYAL, SHERBROOKE, QC, J1N 1H1
(819) 864-4201   *SIC 1389*

ECHO NDE INC *p155*
53 BURNT PARK DR, RED DEER, AB, T4P 0J7
(403) 347-7042   *SIC 1389*

ELEMENT TECHNICAL SERVICES INC *p48*
810-530 8 AVE SW, CALGARY, AB, T2P 3S8
(403) 930-0246   *SIC 1389*

EMS CANADA, INC *p40*
5010 4 ST NE SUITE 207, CALGARY, AB,

T2K 5X8
(403) 508-2111   *SIC* 1389
ENERCORP SAND SOLUTIONS INC   *p48*
815 8 AVE SW SUITE 510, CALGARY, AB,
T2P 3P2
(403) 217-1332   *SIC* 1389
ENERGETIC SERVICES INC   *p195*
13366 TOMPKINS FRONTAGE RD, CHAR-
LIE LAKE, BC, V0C 1H0
(250) 785-4761   *SIC* 1389
ENERSUL LIMITED PARTNERSHIP   *p35*
7210 BLACKFOOT TRAIL SE, CALGARY,
AB, T2H 1M5
(403) 253-5969   *SIC* 1389
ESSENTIAL ENERGY SERVICES LTD   *p49*
250 2 ST SW UNIT 1100, CALGARY, AB,
T2P 0C1
(403) 263-6778   *SIC* 1389
EUROPUMP SYSTEMS INC   *p144*
6204 44 ST, LLOYDMINSTER, AB, T9V 1V9
(780) 872-7084   *SIC* 1389
EVOLVED ENERGY SERVICES INC   *p164*
PO BOX 3946 STN MAIN, SPRUCE
GROVE, AB, T7X 3B2
(780) 960-2790   *SIC* 1389
EXACT OILFIELD DEVELOPING LTD   *p163*
1412 TAMARACK RD NE, SLAVE LAKE,
AB, T0G 2A0
(780) 849-2211   *SIC* 1389
EXPLORATION DATA SYSTEMS INC   *p72*
2410 10 AVE SW, CALGARY, AB, T3C 0K6
(403) 249-8931   *SIC* 1389
EXPRO GROUP CANADA INC   *p155*
8130 49 AVE CLOSE, RED DEER, AB, T4P
2V5
(877) 340-0911   *SIC* 1389
F I OILFIELD SERVICES CANADA ULC*p122*
2880 64 AVE NW, EDMONTON, AB, T6P
1W6
(780) 463-3333   *SIC* 1389
FIREMASTER OILFIELD SERVICES INC*p49*
441 5 AVE SW SUITE 570, CALGARY, AB,
T2P 2V1
(403) 266-1811   *SIC* 1389
FJORDS PROCESSING CANADA INC   *p49*
237 4 AVE SW UNIT 2200, CALGARY, AB,
T2P 4K3
(403) 640-4230   *SIC* 1389
**FLINT TUBULAR MANAGEMENT SER-
VICES LTD**   *p148*
950 30 AVE, NISKU, AB, T9E 0S2
(780) 955-3380   *SIC* 1389
FORUM CANADA ULC   *p125*
9503 12 AVE SW, EDMONTON, AB, T6X
0C3
(825) 410-1200   *SIC* 1389
FOURQUEST ENERGY INC   *p114*
9304 39 AVE NW, EDMONTON, AB, T6E
5T9
(780) 485-0690   *SIC* 1389
FRAC SHACK INC   *p1*
25901 114 AVE UNIT 136, ACHESON, AB,
T7X 6E2
(780) 948-9898   *SIC* 1389
FRAC SHACK INTERNATIONAL INC   *p1*
25901 114 AVE UNIT 136, ACHESON, AB,
T7X 6E2
(780) 948-9898   *SIC* 1389
FRACTION ENERGY SERVICES LTD   *p49*
255 5 AVE SW UNIT 2900, CALGARY, AB,
T2P 3G6
(403) 385-4300   *SIC* 1389
FSJ OILFIELD SERVICES   *p213*
8140 ALASKA RD, FORT ST. JOHN, BC,
V1J 0P3
(250) 785-8935   *SIC* 1389
GE OIL & GAS CANADA INC   *p114*
3575 97 ST NW, EDMONTON, AB, T6E 5S7
(780) 450-1031   *SIC* 1389
GENIARP INC   *p1276*
4650 BOUL DE L'AUVERGNE, QUEBEC,
QC, G2C 2B5
(418) 847-3333   *SIC* 1389
GIBSON ENERGY INC   *p50*

440 2 AVE SW SUITE 1700, CALGARY, AB,
T2P 5E9
(403) 206-4000   *SIC* 1389
GLJ PETROLEUM CONSULTANTS LTD *p50*
400 3 AVE SW SUITE 4100, CALGARY, AB,
T2P 4H2
(403) 266-9500   *SIC* 1389
GRANT CORPORATION   *p50*
540 5 AVE SW SUITE 1850, CALGARY, AB,
T2P 0M2
(403) 663-0050   *SIC* 1389
**GRANT PRODUCTION TESTING SERVICES
LTD**   *p50*
505 8 AVE SW SUITE 200, CALGARY, AB,
T2P 1G2
(403) 663-0050   *SIC* 1389
GREYWOLF PRODUCTION SYSTEMS INC
p81
805 LAUT AVE, CROSSFIELD, AB, T0M
0S0
(403) 946-4445   *SIC* 1389
H.F. NODES CONSTRUCTION LTD   *p248*
5102 50 ST, POUCE COUPE, BC, V0C 2C0
(250) 786-5474   *SIC* 1389
HALLIBURTON GROUP CANADA INC   *p50*
645 7 AVE SW SUITE 1600, CALGARY, AB,
T2P 4G8
(403) 231-9300   *SIC* 1389
HALLIBURTON GROUP CANADA INC   *p79*
10202 70 AVE SUITE 780, CLAIRMONT,
AB, T8X 5A7
(780) 513-8888   *SIC* 1389
HALLIBURTON GROUP CANADA INC *p147*
2175 BRIER PARK PL NW, MEDICINE HAT,
AB, T1C 1S7
(403) 527-8895   *SIC* 1389
HALLIBURTON GROUP CANADA INC *p148*
1400 5 ST, NISKU, AB, T9E 7R6
(800) 335-6333   *SIC* 1389
HALLIBURTON GROUP CANADA INC *p155*
8145 EDGAR INDUSTRIAL CLOSE, RED
DEER, AB, T4P 3R4
(800) 335-6333   *SIC* 1389
**HANK'S MAINTENANCE & SERVICE COM-
PANY LTD**   *p1406*
410 MISSISSIPPIAN DR, ESTEVAN, SK,
S4A 2H7
(306) 634-4872   *SIC* 1389
**HARMATTAN GAS PROCESSING LIMITED
PARTNERSHIP**   *p51*
355 4 AVE SW SUITE 1700, CALGARY, AB,
T2P 0J1
(403) 691-7575   *SIC* 1389
HAYDUK PICKER SERVICE LTD   *p82*
GD, DRAYTON VALLEY, AB, T7A 1T1
(780) 542-3217   *SIC* 1389
HOFFMAN, R. J. HOLDINGS LTD   *p1436*
GD, ST WALBURG, SK, S0M 2T0
(306) 248-3466   *SIC* 1389
**HOLLINGWORTH, A B & SON CONSTRUC-
TION LTD**   *p170*
GD, VALLEYVIEW, AB, T0H 3N0
(780) 524-4233   *SIC* 1389
**HUNTING ENERGY SERVICES (CANADA)
LTD**   *p23*
5550 SKYLINE WAY NE, CALGARY, AB,
T2E 7Z7
(403) 543-4477   *SIC* 1389
HYDUKE ENERGY SERVICES INC   *p149*
2107 6 ST, NISKU, AB, T9E 7X8
(780) 955-0360   *SIC* 1389
INDEPENDENT WELL SERVICING LTD
p1406
477 DEVONIAN ST, ESTEVAN, SK, S4A
2A5
(306) 634-2336   *SIC* 1389
IROC ENERGY SERVICES CORP   *p155*
8113 49 AVE CLOSE, RED DEER, AB, T4P
2V5
(403) 346-9710   *SIC* 1389
IRON HORSE COILED TUBING INC   *p158*
1901 DIRKSON DR NE, REDCLIFF, AB, T0J
2P0
(403) 526-4600   *SIC* 1389

**IRONTECH RIG REPAIR & MANUFACTUR-
ING INC**   *p1*
53016 HWY 60 UNIT 11, ACHESON, AB,
T7X 5A7
(780) 960-4881   *SIC* 1389
ISOLATION EQUIPMENT SERVICES INC
p155
8102 49 AVE CLOSE UNIT B, RED DEER,
AB, T4P 2V5
(403) 342-0032   *SIC* 1389
J.D.A. VENTURES LTD   *p134*
713031 RANGE ROAD 64, GRANDE
PRAIRIE, AB, T8W 5E5
(780) 532-5101   *SIC* 1389
KANA OILFIELD SERVICES LTD   *p173*
4107 41 ST, WHITECOURT, AB, T7S 0A9
(780) 778-2385   *SIC* 1389
KEYERA CORP   *p52*
144 4 AVE SW SUITE 200, CALGARY, AB,
T2P 3N4
(403) 205-8300   *SIC* 1389
KONCRETE CONSTRUCTION GROUP
p1409
609 MILLER ST, LEADER, SK, S0N 1H0
(306) 628-3757   *SIC* 1389
**L & L OILFIELD CONSTRUCTION (1990)
LTD**   *p1409*
6107 49 AVE, LLOYDMINSTER, SK, S9V
2G2
(306) 825-6111   *SIC* 1389
LANCO WELL SERVICES LTD   *p65*
525 11 AVE SW SUITE 201, CALGARY, AB,
T2R 0C9
    SIC 1389
LAND AIR CONTRACTORS LTD   *p172*
10011 106 ST SUITE 205, WESTLOCK, AB,
T7P 2K3
    SIC 1389
**LAPRAIRIE WORKS OILFIELDS SERVICES
INC**   *p52*
505 2 ST SW SUITE 702, CALGARY, AB,
T2P 1N8
(403) 767-9942   *SIC* 1389
LEADER ENERGY SERVICES LTD   *p80*
7001 96 ST, CLAIRMONT, AB, T8X 5B3
(780) 402-9876   *SIC* 1389
LEAGUE PROJECTS LTD   *p7*
311 9TH ST E BAY 3, BROOKS, AB, T1R
1C8
(403) 793-2648   *SIC* 1389
LISTER INDUSTRIES LTD   *p110*
7410 68 AVE NW, EDMONTON, AB, T6B
0A1
(780) 468-2040   *SIC* 1389
LOGAN COMPLETION SYSTEMS INC   *p53*
635 8 AVE SW SUITE 850, CALGARY, AB,
T2P 3M3
(403) 930-6810   *SIC* 1389
LOGAN INDUSTRIES LTD   *p7*
6 BOSWELL CRES, BROOKS, AB, T1R 8B8
(403) 362-3736   *SIC* 1389
LONKAR SERVICES LTD   *p7*
BOSWELL CR SUITE 5, BROOKS, AB, T1R
1C2
(403) 362-5300   *SIC* 1389
LONKAR SERVICES LTD   *p156*
8080 EDGAR INDUSTRIAL CRES, RED
DEER, AB, T4P 3R3
(403) 347-9727   *SIC* 1389
M-I DRILLING FLUIDS CANADA, INC   *p53*
700 2 ST SW SUITE 500, CALGARY, AB,
T2P 2W1
(403) 290-5300   *SIC* 1389
MACRO INDUSTRIES INC   *p213*
7904 101 AVE, FORT ST. JOHN, BC, V1J
2A3
(250) 785-0033   *SIC* 1389
MANATOKAN OILFIELD SERVICES INC*p31*
237 8 AVE SE SUITE 222, CALGARY, AB,
T2G 5C3
(403) 718-9842   *SIC* 1389
MAVERICK LAND CONSULTANTS LTD *p36*
6940 FISHER RD SE SUITE 310, CAL-
GARY, AB, T2H 0W3

(403) 243-7833   *SIC* 1389
MAVERICK OILFIELD SERVICES LTD   *p77*
15 ROYAL VISTA PL NW UNIT 320, CAL-
GARY, AB, T3R 0P3
(403) 234-8822   *SIC* 1389
**MCGILLICKY OILFIELD CONSTRUCTION
LTD**   *p1406*
6 HWY 39 E, ESTEVAN, SK, S4A 2A7
(306) 634-8737   *SIC* 1389
MEDALLION ENERGY SERVICES INC *p132*
9516 146 AVE, GRANDE PRAIRIE, AB, T8V
7V9
(780) 357-2164   *SIC* 1389
**MID WESTERN MACHINE WORKS (1987)
INC**   *p17*
7815 46 ST SE, CALGARY, AB, T2C 2Y5
(403) 279-0727   *SIC* 1389
MOUNTAIN WEST SERVICES LTD   *p169*
14 THEVENAZ IND. TRAIL UNIT 3, SYLVAN
LAKE, AB, T4S 2J5
(403) 887-3562   *SIC* 1389
MULLEN GROUP LTD   *p150*
31 SOUTHRIDGE DR SUITE 121A, OKO-
TOKS, AB, T1S 2N3
(403) 995-5200   *SIC* 1389
MULLEN OILFIELD SERVICES LP   *p65*
333 11 AVE SW SUITE 600, CALGARY, AB,
T2R 1L9
(403) 213-4715   *SIC* 1389
NABORS DRILLING CANADA LIMITED   *p7*
GD STN MAIN, BROOKS, AB, T1R 1E4
    SIC 1389
NABORS DRILLING CANADA LIMITED*p132*
HWY 40 W, GRANDE PRAIRIE, AB, T8V
3A1
    SIC 1389
NABORS DRILLING CANADA LIMITED*p156*
8112 EDGAR INDUSTRIAL DR, RED
DEER, AB, T4P 3R2
    SIC 1389
NCS MULTISTAGE INC   *p54*
333 7 AVE SW SUITE 700, CALGARY, AB,
T2P 2Z1
(403) 984-7674   *SIC* 1389
**NELSON BROS. OILFIELD SERVICES 1997
LTD**   *p82*
5399 JUBILEE AVE, DRAYTON VALLEY,
AB, T7A 1R9
(780) 542-5777   *SIC* 1389
NELSON BROS. OILFIELD SERVICES LTD
p82
5399 JUBILEE AVE, DRAYTON VALLEY,
AB, T7A 1R9
(780) 542-5777   *SIC* 1389
NETOOK CONSTRUCTION LTD   *p151*
GD STN MAIN, OLDS, AB, T4H 1R4
(403) 556-2166   *SIC* 1389
NEW WAVE ENERGY SERVICES LTD   *p54*
140 4 AVE SW SUITE 1955, CALGARY, AB,
T2P 3N3
(403) 453-2925   *SIC* 1389
NEW WEST ENERGY SERVICES INC   *p54*
435 4 AVE SW SUITE 500, CALGARY, AB,
T2P 3A8
(403) 984-9798   *SIC* 1389
NINE ENERGY CANADA INC   *p55*
840 7 AVE SW SUITE 1840, CALGARY, AB,
T2P 3G2
(403) 266-0908   *SIC* 1389
NINE ENERGY CANADA INC   *p158*
37337 BURNT LAKE TRAIL UNIT 30, RED
DEER COUNTY, AB, T4S 2K5
(403) 340-4218   *SIC* 1389
NINE ENERGY CANADA INC   *p214*
9404 73 AVE, FORT ST. JOHN, BC, V1J
4H7
(250) 785-4210   *SIC* 1389
NORTHSTAR DRILLSTEM TESTERS INC
p55
440 2 AVE SW UNIT 750, CALGARY, AB,
T2P 5E9
(403) 265-8987   *SIC* 1389
NORTHWELL OILFIELD HAULING (09) INC
p2

26318 TOWNSHIP RD 531A UNIT 3, ACHE-SON, AB, T7X 5A3
(780) 960-4900   *SIC* 1389
NOV ENERFLOW ULC   *p17*
4910 80 AVE SE, CALGARY, AB, T2C 2X3
(403) 569-2222   *SIC* 1389
NOV ENERFLOW ULC   *p149*
2201 9 ST, NISKU, AB, T9E 7Z7
(780) 955-7675   *SIC* 1389
NOV ENERFLOW ULC   *p149*
2201 9 ST, NISKU, AB, T9E 7Z7
(780) 955-7675   *SIC* 1389
NUVISTA ENERGY LTD   *p82*
5219 53 AVE, DRAYTON VALLEY, AB, T7A 1R9
SIC 1389
OIL STATES ENERGY SERVICES (CANADA) INCORPORATED   *p158*
28042 HIGHWAY 11 SUITE 334, RED DEER COUNTY, AB, T4S 2L4
(403) 340-0716   *SIC* 1389
OPSMOBIL INC   *p55*
815 8 AVE SW SUITE 1200, CALGARY, AB, T2P 3P2
(877) 926-5558   *SIC* 1389
PASON SYSTEMS INC   *p37*
6130 3 ST SE, CALGARY, AB, T2H 1K4
(403) 301-3400   *SIC* 1389
PEAK ENERGY SERVICES LTD   *p56*
222 3 AVE SW SUITE 900, CALGARY, AB, T2P 0B4
(403) 543-7325   *SIC* 1389
PERFORMANCE WELL SERVICING LTD *p56*
604 8 AVE SW SUITE 510, CALGARY, AB, T2P 1G4
SIC 1389
PILLAR RESOURCE SERVICES INC   *p65*
550 11 AVE SW, CALGARY, AB, T2R 1M7
(403) 266-7070   *SIC* 1389
PIMEE WELL SERVICING LTD   *p137*
GD, KEHEWIN, AB, T0A 1C0
(780) 826-6392   *SIC* 1389
PIONEER TRUCK LINES LTD   *p122*
8321 1 ST NW, EDMONTON, AB, T6P 1X2
(780) 467-8880   *SIC* 1389
PITBULL ENERGY SERVICES INC   *p122*
2424 91 AVE NW, EDMONTON, AB, T6P 1K9
(780) 757-1688   *SIC* 1389
POINTS NORTH CONTRACTING LTD *p214*
8011 93 ST, FORT ST. JOHN, BC, V1J 6X1
(250) 787-5525   *SIC* 1389
PRAIRIE MOUNTAIN OILFIELD CON-STRUCTION INC   *p82*
4002 62 ST, DRAYTON VALLEY, AB, T7A 1S1
(780) 542-3995   *SIC* 1389
PRAIRIE MUD SERVICE   *p1406*
738 6TH ST, ESTEVAN, SK, S4A 1A4
(306) 634-3411   *SIC* 1389
PRECISION CONTRACTORS LTD   *p144*
5912 50 AVE SUITE 101, LLOYDMINSTER, AB, T9V 0X6
(780) 875-1962   *SIC* 1389
PRECISION LIMITED PARTNERSHIP *p57*
150 6 AVE SW SUITE 4200, CALGARY, AB, T2P 3Y7
(403) 781-5555   *SIC* 1389
PREMIER INTEGRATED TECHNOLOGIES LTD   *p156*
14 BURNT VALLEY AVE UNIT 210, RED DEER, AB, T4P 0M5
(403) 887-1200   *SIC* 1389
PROPIPE GROUP LTD   *p134*
15201 91 ST, GRANDE PRAIRIE, AB, T8X 0B3
(780) 830-0955   *SIC* 1389
Q'MAX SOLUTIONS INC   *p57*
585 8 AVE SW SUITE 1210, CALGARY, AB, T2P 1G1
(403) 269-2242   *SIC* 1389
R E LINE TRUCKING (COLEVILLE) LTD
p1405

4TH AVE, COLEVILLE, SK, S0L 0K0
(306) 965-2472   *SIC* 1389
R.J. HOFFMAN HOLDINGS LTD   *p144*
GD RPO 10, LLOYDMINSTER, AB, T9V 2H2
(780) 871-0723   *SIC* 1389
RECON PETROTECHNOLOGIES LTD *p58*
510 5 ST SW UNIT 410, CALGARY, AB, T2P 3S2
(403) 517-3266   *SIC* 1389
RED FLAME INDUSTRIES INC   *p156*
6736 71 ST, RED DEER, AB, T4P 3Y7
(403) 343-2012   *SIC* 1389
REED HYCALOG CORING SERVICES *p149*
1507 4 ST, NISKU, AB, T9E 7M9
(780) 955-8929   *SIC* 1389
REMEDY ENERGY SERVICES INC   *p11*
720 28 ST NE UNIT 255, CALGARY, AB, T2A 6A5
(403) 272-0703   *SIC* 1389
REWARD OILFIELD SERVICES LTD *p170*
SE 15- 70- 22 W 5, VALLEYVIEW, AB, T0H 3N0
(780) 524-5220   *SIC* 1389
ROAD TRAIN OILFIELD TRANSPORT LTD
p158
39139 HIGHWAY 2A SUITE 4328, RED DEER COUNTY, AB, T4S 2A8
(403) 346-5311   *SIC* 1389
ROCKWELL SERVICING INC   *p4*
440 HWY 28, ARDMORE, AB, T0A 0B0
(780) 826-6464   *SIC* 1389
ROCKWELL SERVICING INC   *p58*
400 5 AVE SW SUITE 1000, CALGARY, AB, T2P 0L6
(403) 265-6361   *SIC* 1389
ROCKWELL SERVICING INC   *p149*
2105 8 ST, NISKU, AB, T9E 7Z1
(780) 955-7066   *SIC* 1389
ROKE TECHNOLOGIES LTD   *p11*
1220 28 ST NE UNIT 100, CALGARY, AB, T2A 6A2
(403) 247-3480   *SIC* 1389
ROSKA DBO INC   *p133*
9715 115 ST, GRANDE PRAIRIE, AB, T8V 5S4
(780) 532-8347   *SIC* 1389
ROSS, SANDY WELL SERVICING LTD
p1408
1004 9TH AVE W, KINDERSLEY, SK, S0L 1S0
(306) 463-3875   *SIC* 1389
RYKER OILFIELD HAULING LTD   *p146*
1779 9 AVE SW, MEDICINE HAT, AB, T1A 8S2
(403) 529-9090   *SIC* 1389
SABRE WELL SERVICING INC   *p58*
435 4 AVE SW SUITE 380, CALGARY, AB, T2P 3A8
(403) 237-0309   *SIC* 1389
SAFETY BOSS INC   *p25*
17-2135 32 AVE NE, CALGARY, AB, T2E 6Z3
(403) 261-5075   *SIC* 1389
SAGE-LINK LTD   *p58*
700 4 AVE SW SUITE 1180, CALGARY, AB, T2P 3J4
(403) 457-1590   *SIC* 1389
SANJEL CANADA LTD   *p18*
10774 42 ST SE, CALGARY, AB, T2C 0L5
(403) 215-4420   *SIC* 1389
SANJEL CANADA LTD   *p58*
505 2 ST SW SUITE 200, CALGARY, AB, T2P 1N8
(403) 269-1420   *SIC* 1389
SANJEL CANADA LTD   *p156*
8051 EDGAR INDUSTRIAL DR, RED DEER, AB, T4P 3R2
(403) 357-1616   *SIC* 1389
SANJEL CANADA LTD   *p158*
1901 DIRKSON DR NE, REDCLIFF, AB, T0J 2P0
SIC 1389
SAVANNA WELL SERVICING INC *p58*

311 6 AVE SW SUITE 800, CALGARY, AB, T2P 3H2
(403) 503-0650   *SIC* 1389
SCHLUMBERGER CANADA LIMITED *p7*
419 AQUADUCT DR, BROOKS, AB, T1R 1C5
(403) 362-3437   *SIC* 1389
SCHLUMBERGER CANADA LIMITED *p18*
8087 54 ST SE, CALGARY, AB, T2C 4R7
(403) 509-4300   *SIC* 1389
SCHLUMBERGER CANADA LIMITED *p32*
125 9 AVE SE SUITE 200, CALGARY, AB, T2G 0P6
(403) 509-4000   *SIC* 1389
SCHLUMBERGER CANADA LIMITED *p65*
322 11 AVE SW SUITE 600, CALGARY, AB, T2R 0C5
SIC 1389
SCHLUMBERGER CANADA LIMITED *p80*
9602 72 AVE, CLAIRMONT, AB, T8X 5B3
(780) 830-4501   *SIC* 1389
SCHLUMBERGER CANADA LIMITED *p147*
2167 BRIER PARK PL NW, MEDICINE HAT, AB, T1C 1S7
(403) 527-8895   *SIC* 1389
SCHLUMBERGER CANADA LIMITED *p149*
1606 8 ST, NISKU, AB, T9E 7S6
(780) 955-2800   *SIC* 1389
SCHLUMBERGER CANADA LIMITED *p149*
406 22 AVE, NISKU, AB, T9E 7W8
(780) 979-0627   *SIC* 1389
SCHLUMBERGER CANADA LIMITED *p156*
6794 65 AVE, RED DEER, AB, T4P 1A5
(403) 356-4398   *SIC* 1389
SCHLUMBERGER CANADA LIMITED *p426*
2 PANTHER PL, MOUNT PEARL, NL, A1N 5B1
(709) 748-7900   *SIC* 1389
SCORE (CANADA) LIMITED   *p123*
9192 14 ST NW, EDMONTON, AB, T6P 0B7
(780) 455-5273   *SIC* 1389
SCORPION OILFIELD SERVICES LTD   *p1409*
406 6TH W, LASHBURN, SK, S0M 1H0
(306) 285-2433   *SIC* 1389
SECURE ENERGY SERVICES INC   *p59*
205 5 AVE SW SUITE 3600, CALGARY, AB, T2P 2V7
(403) 264-1588   *SIC* 1389
SECURE ENERGY SERVICES INC   *p59*
205 5 AVE SW SUITE 3600, CALGARY, AB, T2P 2V7
(403) 984-6100   *SIC* 1389
SECURE ENERGY SERVICES INC   *p133*
9516 146 AVE, GRANDE PRAIRIE, AB, T8V 7V9
(780) 357-5600   *SIC* 1389
SEMCAMS MIDSTREAM ULC   *p59*
520 3 AVE SUITE 700, CALGARY, AB, T2P 0R3
(403) 536-3000   *SIC* 1389
SEMCAMS MIDSTREAM ULC   *p173*
GD, WHITECOURT, AB, T7S 1S1
(780) 778-7800   *SIC* 1389
SERVICE RECREATIFS DEMSIS   *p1077*
75 CH BARNES, CHELSEA, QC, J9B 1H7
SIC 1389
SHELL CANADA LIMITED   *p79*
GD, CAROLINE, AB, T0M 0M0
(403) 722-7000   *SIC* 1389
SITE ENERGY SERVICES LTD   *p163*
120 PEMBINA RD SUITE 170, SHER-WOOD PARK, AB, T8H 0M2
(780) 400-7483   *SIC* 1389
SNUBCO GROUP INC   *p150*
502 23A AVE, NISKU, AB, T9E 8G2
(780) 955-3550   *SIC* 1389
SNUBCO PRESSURE CONTROL LTD *p150*
502 23A AVE, NISKU, AB, T9E 8G2
(780) 955-3550   *SIC* 1389
SOURCE ENERGY SERVICES CANADA LP GP LTD   *p32*
438 11 AVE SE UNIT 500, CALGARY, AB, T2G 0Y4
(403) 262-1312   *SIC* 1389

SPEARING SERVICE (2006) LTD   *p1413*
41 MARION AVE, OXBOW, SK, S0C 2B0
(306) 483-2848   *SIC* 1389
SPECTRA ENERGY MIDSTREAM CORPO-RATION   *p60*
425 1 ST SW SUITE 2200, CALGARY, AB, T2P 3L8
(403) 699-1900   *SIC* 1389
SPM FLOW CONTROL LTD   *p156*
8060 EDGAR INDUSTRIAL CRES UNIT A, RED DEER, AB, T4P 3R3
(403) 341-3410   *SIC* 1389
STEEL VIEW ENERGY & INDUSTRIAL SER-VICES LTD   *p79*
222 MAIN ST, CHAUVIN, AB, T0B 0V0
(780) 858-3820   *SIC* 1389
STREAM FLO INDUSTRIES   *p133*
15501 89 STREET, GRANDE PRAIRIE, AB, T8V 0V7
(780) 532-1433   *SIC* 1389
STRIKE GROUP INC   *p60*
505 3 ST SW SUITE 1300, CALGARY, AB, T2P 3E6
(403) 232-8448   *SIC* 1389
STRIKE GROUP LIMITED PARTNERSHIP *p60*
505 3 ST SW SUITE 1300, CALGARY, AB, T2P 3E6
(403) 232-8448   *SIC* 1389
STRIKE GROUP LIMITED PARTNERSHIP *p135*
10600 94 ST SS 1, HIGH LEVEL, AB, T0H 1Z0
(780) 926-2429   *SIC* 1389
SUMMIT COMPLETIONS LTD   *p5*
4912 50TH ST, BASHAW, AB, T0B 0H0
SIC 1389
SUNCOR ENERGY INC   *p431*
140 KELSEY DR, ST. JOHN'S, NL, A1B 0T2
(709) 778-3500   *SIC* 1389
SUNCOR ENERGY INC   *p715*
2489 NORTH SHERIDAN WAY, MISSIS-SAUGA, ON, L5K 1A8
(905) 804-4500   *SIC* 1389
SURE-FLOW OILFIELD SERVICES INC *p6*
50 AVE BAY SUITE 5506, BONNYVILLE, AB, T9N 2K8
(780) 826-6864   *SIC* 1389
T.J.'S OILFIELD CONTRACTING LTD *p79*
GD, CHARD, AB, T0P 1G0
SIC 1389
TALON ENERGY SERVICES INC   *p432*
215 WATER ST SUITE 301, ST. JOHN'S, NL, A1C 6C9
(709) 739-8450   *SIC* 1389
TARA OILFIELD SERVICES LTD   *p82*
1805 19 ST, DIDSBURY, AB, T0M 0W0
(403) 335-9158   *SIC* 1389
TARPON ENERGY SERVICES LTD *p6*
5001 55 AVE, BONNYVILLE, AB, T9N 0A7
(780) 826-7570   *SIC* 1389
TARPON ENERGY SERVICES LTD *p19*
7020 81 ST SE, CALGARY, AB, T2C 5B8
(403) 234-8647   *SIC* 1389
TARPON ENERGY SERVICES LTD *p133*
11418 91 AVE, GRANDE PRAIRIE, AB, T8V 6K6
(780) 539-9696   *SIC* 1389
TARTAN CANADA CORPORATION   *p61*
401 9TH AVE SW SUITE 960, CALGARY, AB, T2P 2H7
(780) 455-3804   *SIC* 1389
TARTAN INDUSTRIAL LTD   *p158*
5007 48 AVE, REDWATER, AB, T0A 2W0
(780) 942-3802   *SIC* 1389
TECHNIPFMC PLC   *p6*
253 TOWNSHIP RD 394 SUITE 27312, BLACKFALDS, AB, T0M 0J0
(780) 926-2108   *SIC* 1389
TERRACON GEOTECHNIQUE LTD   *p61*
800-734 7 AVE SW, CALGARY, AB, T2P 3P8
(403) 266-1150   *SIC* 1389
TERRAPRO INC   *p161*
53345 RANGE ROAD 232, SHERWOOD

PARK, AB, T8A 4V2
(780) 449-2091   *SIC 1389*
TERROCO INDUSTRIES LTD   *p154*
GD, RED DEER, AB, T4N 5E1
(403) 346-1171   *SIC 1389*
TOMCO PRODUCTION SERVICES LTD*p159*
4227 46TH AVE, ROCKY MOUNTAIN HOUSE, AB, T4T 1A8
(403) 844-2141   *SIC 1389*
TOPCO OILSITE PRODUCTS LTD   *p121*
9519 28 AVE NW, EDMONTON, AB, T6N 0A3
(800) 222-6448   *SIC 1389*
TRACER CANADA COMPANY   *p103*
11004 174 ST NW, EDMONTON, AB, T5S 2P3
(780) 455-8111   *SIC 1389*
TRACER INDUSTRIES CANADA LIMITED *p103*
11004 174 ST NW, EDMONTON, AB, T5S 2P3
(780) 455-8111   *SIC 1389*
TRANSCANADA PIPELINES SERVICES LTD   *p62*
450 1 ST SW, CALGARY, AB, T2P 5H1
(403) 920-2000   *SIC 1389*
TRICAN WELL SERVICE LTD   *p71*
11979 40 ST SE UNIT 418, CALGARY, AB, T2Z 4M3
(403) 723-3688   *SIC 1389*
TRICAN WELL SERVICE LTD   *p80*
9701 99 ST, CLAIRMONT, AB, T8X 5A8
(780) 567-5200   *SIC 1389*
TRICAN WELL SERVICE LTD   *p150*
2305 5A ST, NISKU, AB, T9E 8G6
(780) 955-5675   *SIC 1389*
TRICAN WELL SERVICE LTD   *p347*
59 LIMESTONE RD, BRANDON, MB, R7A 7L5
SIC 1389
TROJAN SAFETY SERVICES LTD   *p214*
11116 TAHLTAN RD, FORT ST. JOHN, BC, V1J 7C4
(250) 785-9557   *SIC 1389*
TUBOSCOPE VETCO CANADA ULC   *p150*
2201 9 ST, NISKU, AB, T9E 7Z7
(780) 955-7675   *SIC 1389*
TUCKER WIRELINE SERVICES CANADA INC   *p62*
444 5 AVE SW SUITE 900, CALGARY, AB, T2P 2T8
(403) 264-7040   *SIC 1389*
TUCKER WIRELINE SERVICES CANADA INC   *p140*
7123 SPARROW DR, LEDUC, AB, T9E 7L1
SIC 1389
UNITED SAFETY LTD   *p3*
104 EAST LAKE RD NE, AIRDRIE, AB, T4A 2J8
(403) 912-3690   *SIC 1389*
VAPERMA INC   *p1352*
2111 4E RUE BUREAU 101, SAINT-ROMUALD, QC, G6W 5M6
SIC 1389
VENOM ENERGY   *p173*
3749 30 ST, WHITECOURT, AB, T7S 0E4
(780) 778-2440   *SIC 1389*
WAYDEX SERVICES LP   *p133*
11420 96 AVE, GRANDE PRAIRIE, AB, T8V 5M4
(780) 538-9101   *SIC 1389*
WAYFINDER CORP   *p26*
4311 12 ST NE SUITE 305, CALGARY, AB, T2E 4P9
SIC 1389
WEATHERFORD ARTIFICIAL LIFT SYSTEMS CANADA LTD   *p144*
4206 59 AVE, LLOYDMINSTER, AB, T9V 2V4
(780) 875-2730   *SIC 1389*
WELL-TECH ENERGY SERVICES INC *p169*
6006 58 ST, TABER, AB, T1G 2B8
(403) 223-4244   *SIC 1389*
WERKLUND CAPITAL CORPORATION *p62*

400 3 AVE SW SUITE 4500, CALGARY, AB, T2P 4H2
(403) 231-6545   *SIC 1389*
WEST OILFIELD HOLDINGS LTD   *p38*
5940 MACLEOD TRAIL SW UNIT 202, CALGARY, AB, T2H 2G4
(403) 452-0844   *SIC 1389*
WESTERN ENERGY SERVICES CORP *p62*
215 9TH AVE SW SUITE 1700, CALGARY, AB, T2P 1K3
(403) 984-5916   *SIC 1389*
WIL-TECH INDUSTRIES LTD   *p1407*
69 ESCANA ST, ESTEVAN, SK, S4A 2H7
(306) 634-6743   *SIC 1389*
X-CALIBUR PIPELINE AND UTILITY LOCATION INC   *p159*
4407 45A AVE, ROCKY MOUNTAIN HOUSE, AB, T4T 1T1
(403) 844-8662   *SIC 1389*
XACT DOWNHOLE TELEMETRY INC   *p26*
906 55 AVE NE, CALGARY, AB, T2E 6Y4
(403) 568-6010   *SIC 1389*
XTREME OILFIELD TECHNOLOGY LTD *p165*
4905 50 AVE, ST PAUL, AB, T0A 3A0
(780) 645-5979   *SIC 1389*
ZEDCOR ENERGY INC   *p63*
330 5 AVE SW SUITE 2400, CALGARY, AB, T2P 0L4
(403) 930-5430   *SIC 1389*

SIC 1411 Dimension stone

A. LACROIX & FILS GRANIT LTEE   *p1352*
450 RUE PRINCIPALE, SAINT-SEBASTIEN-DE-FRONTENAC, QC, G0Y 1M0
(819) 652-2828   *SIC 1411*
ASHCROFT & ASSOCIATES NATURAL STONE LTD   *p594*
381297 CONCESSION 17, GEORGIAN BLUFFS, ON, N0H 2T0
(519) 534-5966   *SIC 1411*
ELRUS INC   *p15*
4409 GLENMORE TRAIL SE, CALGARY, AB, T2C 2R8
(403) 279-7741   *SIC 1411*
GILLIS QUARRIES LIMITED   *p357*
2895 WENZEL ST, SPRINGFIELD, MB, R2E 1H4
(204) 222-2242   *SIC 1411*
TOMLINSON, R. W. LIMITED   *p832*
100 CITIGATE DR, OTTAWA, ON, K2J 6K7
(613) 822-1867   *SIC 1411*
WALKER INDUSTRIES HOLDINGS LIMITED   *p758*
2800 THOROLD TOWN LINE, NIAGARA FALLS, ON, L2E 6S4
(905) 227-4142   *SIC 1411*

SIC 1422 Crushed and broken limestone

9195-7639 QUEBEC INC   *p1302*
780 BOUL HAMEL, SAINT-FELICIEN, QC, G8K 1X9
(418) 679-4533   *SIC 1422*
ATLANTIC MINERALS LIMITED   *p422*
22 COMMERCIAL ST, CORNER BROOK, NL, A2H 2V2
(709) 634-8255   *SIC 1422*
CARRIERE BERNIER LTEE   *p1316*
25 CH DU PETIT-BERNIER, SAINT-JEAN-SUR-RICHELIEU, QC, J2Y 1B8
(514) 875-2841   *SIC 1422*
CARRIERE ST-EUSTACHE LTEE   *p1300*
555 AV MATHERS, SAINT-EUSTACHE, QC, J7P 4C1
(450) 430-9090   *SIC 1422*
CAYUGA MATERIALS & CONSTRUCTION CO. LIMITED   *p541*
4219 HIGHWAY 3 RR 4, CAYUGA, ON, N0A 1E0

(905) 772-3331   *SIC 1422*
COLACEM CANADA INC   *p1086*
2540 BOUL DANIEL-JOHNSON BUREAU 808 8E ETAGE, COTE SAINT-LUC, QC, H7T 2S3
(450)-686-1221   *SIC 1422*
CONCASSAGE T.C.G. INC   *p1078*
111 RUE DES ROUTIERS, CHICOUTIMI, QC, G7H 5B1
(418) 698-4949   *SIC 1422*
CONSTRUCTION DJL INC   *p1295*
580 RANG DES VINGT-CINQ E, SAINT-BRUNO, QC, J3V 0G6
(450) 653-2423   *SIC 1422*
GRAYMONT (NB) INC   *p403*
4634 ROUTE 880, HAVELOCK, NB, E4Z 5K8
(506) 534-2311   *SIC 1422*
GRAYMONT (QC) INC   *p1065*
25 RUE DE LAUZON BUREAU 206, BOUCHERVILLE, QC, J4B 1E7
(450) 449-2262   *SIC 1422*
GRAYMONT (QC) INC   *p1114*
1300 RUE NOTRE-DAME, JOLIETTE, QC, J6E 3Z9
(450) 759-8195   *SIC 1422*
MUNICIPAL CAPITAL INCORPORATED *p468*
19 MACRAE AVE, SYDNEY, NS, B1S 1M1
(902) 564-4541   *SIC 1422*
TEXADA QUARRYING LTD   *p284*
2 AIRPORT RD, VAN ANDA, BC, V0N 3K0
(604) 486-7627   *SIC 1422*
WALKER COMMUNITY DEVELOPMENT CORP   *p758*
2800 THOROLD TOWN LINE, NIAGARA FALLS, ON, L2E 6S4
(905) 227-4142   *SIC 1422*

SIC 1423 Crushed and broken granite

POLYCOR INC   *p1259*
76 RUE SAINT-PAUL BUREAU 100, QUEBEC, QC, G1K 3V9
(418) 692-4695   *SIC 1423*

SIC 1429 Crushed and broken stone, nec

BAU-VAL INC   *p1063*
210 BOUL DE MONTARVILLE BUREAU 2006, BOUCHERVILLE, QC, J4B 6T3
(514) 875-4270   *SIC 1429*
CONCASSES DE LA RIVE-SUD INC *p1135*
333 CH DES SABLES, LEVIS, QC, G6C 1B5
(418) 838-7444   *SIC 1429*
MODERN CONSTRUCTION (1983) LTD*p408*
275 SALISBURY RD, MONCTON, NB, E1E 4N1
(506) 853-8853   *SIC 1429*

SIC 1442 Construction sand and gravel

3887952 CANADA INC   *p1367*
440 HOLIDAY, SEPT-ILES, QC, G4R 4X6
(418) 962-1234   *SIC 1442*
ARTHON INDUSTRIES LIMITED   *p219*
1790 K.L.O. RD UNIT 9, KELOWNA, BC, V1W 3P6
(250) 764-6144   *SIC 1442*
LAFARGE CANADA INC   *p39*
10511 15 ST SE, CALGARY, AB, T2J 7H7
(403) 292-1555   *SIC 1442*
MUSKOKA MINERALS & MINING INC *p620*
1265 ASPDIN RD, HUNTSVILLE, ON, P1H 2J2
(705) 789-4457   *SIC 1442*
NELSON AGGREGATE CO   *p529*
2433 NO 2 SIDE RD, BURLINGTON, ON, L7P 0G8
(905) 335-5250   *SIC 1442*
POLARIS MATERIALS CORPORATION*p315*

1055 GEORGIA ST W SUITE 2740, VANCOUVER, BC, V6E 4N4
(604) 915-5000   *SIC 1442*
SIMARD-BEAUDRY CONSTRUCTION INC *p1302*
699 BOUL INDUSTRIEL, SAINT-EUSTACHE, QC, J7R 6C3
SIC 1442
TBG CONTRACTING LTD   *p124*
12311 17 ST NE, EDMONTON, AB, T6S 1A7
SIC 1442
YOUNG, ROBERT E CONSTRUCTION LTD *p842*
1488 CHEMONG RD, PETERBOROUGH, ON, K9J 6X2
(705) 745-1488   *SIC 1442*

SIC 1446 Industrial sand

SELECT SANDS CORP   *p309*
850 HASTINGS ST W SUITE 310, VANCOUVER, BC, V6C 1E1
(604) 639-4533   *SIC 1446*

SIC 1459 Clay and related minerals, nec

BAYMAG INC   *p68*
10655 SOUTHPORT RD SW SUITE 800, CALGARY, AB, T2W 4Y1
(403) 271-9400   *SIC 1459*
COVIA CANADA LTD   *p577*
10 FOUR SEASONS PL SUITE 600, ETOBICOKE, ON, M9B 6H7
(416) 626-1500   *SIC 1459*

SIC 1474 Potash, soda, and borate minerals

ALLANA POTASH CORP   *p948*
65 QUEEN ST W SUITE 805, TORONTO, ON, M5H 2M5
(416) 861-5800   *SIC 1474*
ASSOCIATED MINING CONSTRUCTION INC   *p1417*
2491 ALBERT ST N, REGINA, SK, S4P 3A2
(306) 206-5000   *SIC 1474*
CANADA GOLDEN FORTUNE POTASH CORP   *p1426*
402 21ST ST E UNIT 200, SASKATOON, SK, S7K 0C3
(306) 668-6877   *SIC 1474*
K+S POTASH CANADA GENERAL PARTNERSHIP   *p1404*
SW 35-19-25-W2, BETHUNE, SK, S0G 0H0
(306) 638-2800   *SIC 1474*
K+S POTASH CANADA GENERAL PARTNERSHIP   *p1428*
220 WALL ST, SASKATOON, SK, S7K 3Y3
(306) 385-8000   *SIC 1474*
MIGAO CORPORATION   *p954*
200 UNIVERSITY AVE SUITE300, TORONTO, ON, M5H 4H1
(416) 869-1108   *SIC 1474*
MOSAIC CANADA ULC   *p1404*
3 KALIUM RD, BELLE PLAINE, SK, S0G 0G0
(306) 345-8067   *SIC 1474*
MOSAIC CANADA ULC   *p1418*
2010 12TH AVE SUITE 1700, REGINA, SK, S4P 0M3
(306) 523-2800   *SIC 1474*
MOSAIC POTASH ESTERHAZY LIMITED PARTNERSHIP   *p1406*
80 PLANT HWY, ESTERHAZY, SK, S0A 0X0
(306) 745-4400   *SIC 1474*
PCS SALES (CANADA) INC   *p1429*
122 1ST AVE S SUITE 500, SASKATOON, SK, S7K 7G3
(306) 933-8500   *SIC 1474*
POTASH CORPORATION OF SASKATCHEWAN INC   *p1404*

GD, ALLAN, SK, S0K 0C0
(306) 257-3312   *SIC 1474*
**POTASH   CORPORATION   OF
SASKATCHEWAN INC**   *p1409*
GD, LANIGAN, SK, S0K 2M0
(306) 365-2030   *SIC 1474*
**POTASH   CORPORATION   OF
SASKATCHEWAN INC**   *p1423*
GD, ROCANVILLE, SK, S0A 3L0
(306) 645-2870   *SIC 1474*
**POTASH   CORPORATION   OF
SASKATCHEWAN INC**   *p1429*
7 MILES WEST ON HWY 7, SASKATOON,
SK, S7K 3N9
(306) 382-0525   *SIC 1474*
**POTASH   CORPORATION   OF
SASKATCHEWAN INC**   *p1429*
122 1ST AVE S SUITE 500, SASKATOON,
SK, S7K 7G3
(306) 933-8500   *SIC 1474*

SIC 1475 Phosphate rock

AECOM CANADIAN OPERATIONS LTD
p627
GD LCD MAIN, KAPUSKASING, ON, P5N
2X9
(705) 335-3800   *SIC 1475*
ARIANNE PHOSPHATE INC   *p1078*
393 RUE RACINE E BUREAU 200,
CHICOUTIMI, QC, G7H 1T2
(418) 549-7316   *SIC 1475*
ITAFOS   *p946*
1 DUNDAS ST W SUITE 2500, TORONTO,
ON, M5G 1Z3
(416) 367-2200   *SIC 1475*

SIC 1479 Chemical and fertilizer mining

ATLANTIC GOLD CORPORATION   *p327*
595 BURRARD ST SUITE 3083, VANCOU-
VER, BC, V7X 1L3
(604) 689-5564   *SIC 1479*
COMPASS MINERALS CANADA CORP *p721*
6700 CENTURY AVE SUITE 202, MISSIS-
SAUGA, ON, L5N 6A4
(905) 567-0231   *SIC 1479*
K+S SEL WINDSOR LTEE   *p126*
GD, ELK POINT, AB, T0A 1A0
(780) 724-4180   *SIC 1479*
K+S SEL WINDSOR LTEE   *p1026*
200 MORTON DR, WINDSOR, ON, N9J
3W9
(519) 972-2201   *SIC 1479*
K+S SEL WINDSOR LTEE   *p1112*
50 CH PRINCIPAL, GROSSE-ILE, QC, G4T
6A6
(418) 985-2931   *SIC 1479*
K+S SEL WINDSOR LTEE   *p1251*
755 BOUL SAINT-JEAN BUREAU 700,
POINTE-CLAIRE, QC, H9R 5M9
(514) 630-0900   *SIC 1479*
NEMASKA LITHIUM INC   *p1259*
450 RUE DE LA GARE-DU-PALAIS, QUE-
BEC, QC, G1K 3X2
(418) 704-6038   *SIC 1479*
NEVADA ENERGY METALS INC   *p307*
789 PENDER ST W SUITE 1220, VANCOU-
VER, BC, V6C 1H2
(604) 428-5690   *SIC 1479*
PURE ENERGY MINERALS LIMITED *p316*
1111 GEORGIA ST SUITE 1400, VANCOU-
VER, BC, V6E 3M3
(604) 608-6611   *SIC 1479*

SIC 1481 NonMetallic mineral services

AECON MATERIALS ENGINEERING CORP
p581
20 CARLSON CRT SUITE 800, ETOBI-
COKE, ON, M9W 7K6

(416) 293-7004   *SIC 1481*
AGNICO EAGLE MINES LIMITED   *p1390*
1953 3RD AV O, VAL-D'OR, QC, J9P 4N9
(819) 874-7822   *SIC 1481*
BODNAR DRILLING LTD   *p358*
23 DELAURIER DR, STE ROSE DU LAC,
MB, R0L 1S0
(204) 447-2755   *SIC 1481*
CAMROVA RESOURCES INC   *p303*
890 W PENDER SUITE 600, VANCOUVER,
BC, V6C 1J9
(604) 685-2323   *SIC 1481*
COMPASS MINERALS CANADA CORP *p597*
300 NORTH HARBOUR RD W, GODERICH,
ON, N7A 3Y9
(519) 524-8351   *SIC 1481*
COVIA CANADA LTEE   *p1153*
11974   RTE   SIR-WILFRID-LAURIER,
MIRABEL, QC, J7N 1P5
(450) 438-1238   *SIC 1481*
CRH CANADA GROUP INC   *p683*
9410 DUBLIN LINE, MILTON, ON, L9T 2X7
(905) 878-6051   *SIC 1481*
EMX ROYALTY CORPORATION   *p304*
543 GRANVILLE ST SUITE 501, VANCOU-
VER, BC, V6C 1X8
(604) 688-6390   *SIC 1481*
FORAGE CHIBOUGAMAU LTEE   *p1289*
180   BOUL   INDUSTRIEL,   ROUYN-
NORANDA, QC, J9X 6T3
(819) 797-9144   *SIC 1481*
GOBIMIN INC   *p952*
120 ADELAIDE ST W SUITE 2110,
TORONTO, ON, M5H 1T1
(416) 915-0133   *SIC 1481*
GRAYMONT (PORTNEUF) INC   *p1348*
595 BOUL BONA-DUSSAULT, SAINT-
MARC-DES-CARRIERES, QC, G0A 4B0
(418) 268-3501   *SIC 1481*
INTER-ROCK MINERALS INC   *p939*
2 TORONTO ST 5TH FL, TORONTO, ON,
M5C 2B6
(416) 367-3003   *SIC 1481*
IOS SERVICES GEOSCIENTIFIQUES INC
p1080
1319 BOUL SAINT-PAUL, CHICOUTIMI,
QC, G7J 3Y2
(418) 698-4498   *SIC 1481*
LEDCOR CMI LTD   *p306*
1067 CORDOVA ST W UNIT 1200, VAN-
COUVER, BC, V6C 1C7
(604) 681-7500   *SIC 1481*
**MAJOR DRILLING GROUP INTERNA-
TIONAL INC**   *p407*
111 ST. GEORGE ST SUITE 100, MONC-
TON, NB, E1C 1T7
(506) 857-8636   *SIC 1481*
NEW GOLD INC   *p965*
181 BAY ST SUITE 3320, TORONTO, ON,
M5J 2T3
(416) 324-6000   *SIC 1481*
NYRSTAR MYRA FALLS LTD.   *p195*
1 BOLIDEN MINE ST, CAMPBELL RIVER,
BC, V9W 5E2
(250) 287-9271   *SIC 1481*
PREMIER GOLD MINES LIMITED   *p909*
1100 RUSSELL ST SUITE 200, THUNDER
BAY, ON, P7B 5N2
(807) 346-1390   *SIC 1481*
UCORE RARE METALS INC   *p440*
210 WATERFRONT DR SUITE 106, BED-
FORD, NS, B4A 0H3
(902) 482-5214   *SIC 1481*

---

*SIC 1499 Miscellaneous nonMetallic
minerals, except fuels*

CGC INC   *p470*
GD, WINDSOR, NS, B0N 2T0
(902) 798-4676   *SIC 1499*
**CONTINENTAL   BUILDING   PRODUCTS
CANADA INC**   *p1074*
8802 BOUL INDUSTRIEL, CHAMBLY, QC,

J3L 4X3
(450) 447-3206   *SIC 1499*
DE BEERS CANADA INC   *p22*
1601 AIRPORT RD NE SUITE 300, CAL-
GARY, AB, T2E 6Z8
(403) 930-0991   *SIC 1499*
DIAVIK DIAMOND MINES (2012) INC *p436*
5201 50 AVE SUITE 300, YELLOWKNIFE,
NT, X1A 3S9
(867) 669-6500   *SIC 1499*
DOMINION DIAMOND EKATI ULC   *p436*
4920 52 ST SUITE 900, YELLOWKNIFE,
NT, X1A 3A3
(867) 669-9292   *SIC 1499*
ELCORA ADVANCED MATERIALS CORP
p439
275 ROCKY LAKE DR SUITE 10, BED-
FORD, NS, B4A 2T3
(902) 802-8847   *SIC 1499*
FURA GEMS INC   *p951*
65 QUEEN ST W SUITE 800, TORONTO,
ON, M5H 2M5
(416) 861-2269   *SIC 1499*
HEVECO LTD   *p418*
4534 ROUTE 11, TABUSINTAC, NB, E9H
1J4
(506) 779-9277   *SIC 1499*
**IMERYS GRAPHITE & CARBON CANADA
INC**   *p1124*
585 CH DU GRAPHITE, LAC-DES-ILES,
QC, J0W 1J0
(819) 597-2911   *SIC 1499*
**IMERYS GRAPHITE & CARBON CANADA
INC**   *p1381*
990 RUE FERNAND-POITRAS, TERRE-
BONNE, QC, J6Y 1V1
(514) 622-9191   *SIC 1499*
IMERYS TALC CANADA INC   *p913*
100 WATER TOWER RD, TIMMINS, ON,
P4N 7J5
(705) 268-2208   *SIC 1499*
LANTECH DRILLING SERVICES INC *p398*
398 DOVER CH, DIEPPE, NB, E1A 7L6
(506) 853-9131   *SIC 1499*
LAYNE CHRISTENSEN CANADA LIMITED
p540
9 REGIONAL RD 84 UNIT 84, CAPREOL,
ON, P0M 1H0
SIC 1499
LUCARA DIAMOND CORP   *p306*
885 GEORGIA ST W SUITE 2000, VAN-
COUVER, BC, V6C 3E8
(604) 689-7842   *SIC 1499*
MASON GRAPHITE INC   *p1087*
3030 BOUL LE CARREFOUR BUREAU
600, COTE SAINT-LUC, QC, H7T 2P5
(514) 289-3580   *SIC 1499*
MAVERIX METALS INC   *p307*
510 BURRARD ST SUITE 575, VANCOU-
VER, BC, V6C 3A8
(604) 449-9290   *SIC 1499*
MOUNTAIN PROVINCE DIAMONDS INC
p965
161 BAY ST SUITE 1410, TORONTO, ON,
M5J 2S1
(416) 361-3562   *SIC 1499*
NATIONAL GYPSUM (CANADA) LTD *p466*
1707 HIGHWAY 2, SPRINGHILL, NS, B0M
1X0
(902) 758-3256   *SIC 1499*
OMYA CANADA INC   *p839*
18595 HWY 7 W, PERTH, ON, K7H 3E4
(613) 267-5367   *SIC 1499*
PREMIER HORTICULTURE LTEE   *p1286*
1 AV PREMIER BUREAU 101, RIVIERE-
DU-LOUP, QC, G5R 6C1
(418) 862-6356   *SIC 1499*
SCOTT CANADA LTD   *p397*
1571 ROUTE 310, COTEAU ROAD, NB,
E8T 3K7
(506) 344-2225   *SIC 1499*
STORNOWAY DIAMOND CORPORATION
p1145
111 RUE SAINT-CHARLES O BUREAU 400,

LONGUEUIL, QC, J4K 5G4
(450) 616-5555   *SIC 1499*
SUN GRO HORTICULTURE CANADA LTD
p349
GD, ELMA, MB, R0E 0Z0
(204) 426-2121   *SIC 1499*
TECHNICA GROUP INC   *p647*
225 FIELDING RD, LIVELY, ON, P3Y 1L8
(705) 692-2204   *SIC 1499*
TIGER CALCIUM SERVICES INC   *p150*
603 15 AVE, NISKU, AB, T9E 7M6
(403) 955-5004   *SIC 1499*
TOURBIERES BERGER LTEE, LES   *p394*
4188 ROUTE 117, BAIE-SAINTE-ANNE,
NB, E9A 1R7
SIC 1499
TOURBIERES LAMBERT INC   *p1287*
106 CH LAMBERT, RIVIERE-OUELLE, QC,
G0L 2C0
(418) 852-2885   *SIC 1499*
USG CANADIAN MINING LTD   *p470*
669 WENTWORTH RD, WINDSOR, NS,
B0N 2T0
(902) 798-4676   *SIC 1499*

SIC 1521 Single-family housing construction

1120919 ONTARIO LTD   *p748*
18 BENTLEY AVE SUITE A, NEPEAN, ON,
K2E 6T8
(613) 723-9227   *SIC 1521*
1266304 ONTARIO INC   *p600*
500 HANLON CREEK BLVD, GUELPH, ON,
N1C 0A1
(519) 826-6700   *SIC 1521*
1356594 ONTARIO LTD   *p682*
1516 CARMEL LINE, MILLBROOK, ON,
L0A 1G0
(705) 932-2996   *SIC 1521*
1428508 ONTARIO LTD   *p547*
407 BASALTIC RD, CONCORD, ON, L4K
4W8
(905) 303-8010   *SIC 1521*
2069718 ONTARIO LTD   *p785*
1140 SHEPPARD AVE W UNIT 13, NORTH
YORK, ON, M3K 2A2
SIC 1521
2313-3606 QUEBEC INC   *p1171*
2251 RUE JEAN-TALON E, MONTREAL,
QC, H2E 1V6
(514) 325-0966   *SIC 1521*
3197786 CANADA INC   *p1106*
13 RUE DUMAS, GATINEAU, QC, J8Y 2M4
(819) 775-9844   *SIC 1521*
3223701 CANADA INC   *p1106*
98 RUE LOIS BUREAU 205, GATINEAU,
QC, J8Y 3R7
(819) 243-7392   *SIC 1521*
6119701 MANITOBA LTD   *p380*
1574 ERIN ST, WINNIPEG, MB, R3E 2T1
(204) 255-5005   *SIC 1521*
6138144 CANADA INC   *p1315*
60 RUE DES GEAIS-BLEUS, SAINT-JEAN-
SUR-RICHELIEU, QC, J2W 3E5
SIC 1521
706017 ONTARIO CORP   *p1029*
101 CASTER AVE, WOODBRIDGE, ON,
L4L 5Z2
(905) 851-3189   *SIC 1521*
745926 ONTARIO LIMITED   *p643*
159 FRASER RD, LEAMINGTON, ON, N8H
4E6
(519) 322-2769   *SIC 1521*
7667965 CANADA INC   *p771*
2942 BAYVIEW AVE, NORTH YORK, ON,
M2N 5K5
(416) 388-2806   *SIC 1521*
782659 ONTARIO LTD   *p1018*
2910 JEFFERSON BLVD, WINDSOR, ON,
N8T 3J2
(519) 944-1212   *SIC 1521*
825209 ALBERTA LTD   *p169*
121 - 17 AVE NE, THREE HILLS, AB, T0M

2A0
(403) 443-2601   *SIC* 1521
871442 ONTARIO INC   p748
18 BENTLEY AVE SUITE A, NEPEAN, ON, K2E 6T8
(613) 723-9227   *SIC* 1521
9105-6705 QUEBEC INC   p1116
2485 RUE ALEXIS-LE-TROTTEUR, JON-QUIERE, QC, G7X 0E4
(418) 820-6647   *SIC* 1521
9130-6381 QUEBEC INC   p1077
971 3E RUE, CHIBOUGAMAU, QC, G8P 1R4
(418) 748-3682   *SIC* 1521
9131-1050 QUEBEC INC   p1355
65 CH DE LA PINERAIE BUREAU 121, SAINTE-ANNE-DES-LACS, QC, J0R 1B0
SIC 1521
9132-8997 QUEBEC INC   p1349
700 RUE NOTRE-DAME, SAINT-NARCISSE, QC, G0X 2Y0
(418) 328-3200   *SIC* 1521
97971 CANADA INC   p1156
5405 AV ROYALMOUNT, MONT-ROYAL, QC, H4P 1H6
(514) 731-7736   *SIC* 1521
ACANA CAPITAL CORP   p275
8338 120 ST SUITE 200, SURREY, BC, V3W 3N4
(604) 592-6881   *SIC* 1521
ACME GLASS LTD   p275
8335 129 ST, SURREY, BC, V3W 0A6
(604) 543-8777   *SIC* 1521
ACTIVA CONSTRUCTION INC   p1006
55 COLUMBIA ST E SUITE 1, WATERLOO, ON, N2J 4N7
(519) 886-9400   *SIC* 1521
ALBERO RIDGE HOMES LTD   p548
29 FLORAL PKY, CONCORD, ON, L4K 5C5
(905) 669-9292   *SIC* 1521
ALBI CORP   p13
4770 110 AVE SE, CALGARY, AB, T2C 2T8
(403) 236-4032   *SIC* 1521
ALMIQ CONTRACTING LTD   p472
1340 ULU LANE, IQALUIT, NU, X0A 0H0
(867) 975-2225   *SIC* 1521
APEX LIMITED PARTNERSHIP   p41
1710 14 AVE NW SUITE 300, CALGARY, AB, T2N 4Y6
(403) 210-3473   *SIC* 1521
ARES VENTURES INC   p1433
668 UNIVERSITY DR, SASKATOON, SK, S7N 0J2
(306) 241-1435   *SIC* 1521
ASHCROFT HOMES - CENTRAL PARK INC   p748
18 ANTARES DR UNIT 102, NEPEAN, ON, K2E 1A9
(613) 226-7266   *SIC* 1521
AVONLEA HOMES LTD   p142
1111 3 AVE S, LETHBRIDGE, AB, T1J 0J5
(403) 320-1989   *SIC* 1521
B.U.I.L.D. BUILDING URBAN INDUSTRIES FOR LOCAL DEVELOPMENT INC   p371
765 MAIN ST UNIT 200, WINNIPEG, MB, R2W 3N5
(204) 943-5981   *SIC* 1521
BALL CONSTRUCTION LTD   p635
5 SHIRLEY AVE, KITCHENER, ON, N2B 2E6
(519) 742-5851   *SIC* 1521
BATITECH LTEE   p1378
578 RUE COMMERCIALE N, TEMISCOUATA-SUR-LE-LAC, QC, G0L 1E0
(418) 854-0854   *SIC* 1521
BEATTIE HOMES LTD   p70
3165 114 AVE SE, CALGARY, AB, T2Z 3X2
SIC 1521
BERT FRENCH & SON LIMITED   p848
126 GREER RD SUITE 1, PORT SYDNEY, ON, P0B 1L0
(705) 385-2311   *SIC* 1521
BETAPLEX INC   p1238

132 RUE PRINCIPALE, MONTREAL, QC, H7X 3V2
(450) 969-3300   *SIC* 1521
BLUETREE HOMES LTD   p328
1055 DUNSMUIR ST SUITE 2000, VAN-COUVER, BC, V7X 1L5
(604) 648-1800   *SIC* 1521
BOLT OFFSITE LTD   p14
7007 84 ST SE, CALGARY, AB, T2C 4T6
(403) 921-5318   *SIC* 1521
BRADON CONSTRUCTION LTD   p78
250031 MOUNTAIN VIEW TRAIL, CAL-GARY, AB, T3Z 3S3
(403) 229-4022   *SIC* 1521
BRAEBURY HOMES CORPORATION   p629
366 KING ST E SUITE 400, KINGSTON, ON, K7K 6Y3
(613) 546-3400   *SIC* 1521
BRAGO CONSTRUCTION INC   p1231
5535 RUE MAURICE-CULLEN, MON-TREAL, QC, H7C 2T8
(450) 661-1121   *SIC* 1521
BRANTHAVEN HOMES 2000 INC   p521
720 OVAL CRT, BURLINGTON, ON, L7L 6A9
(905) 333-8364   *SIC* 1521
BRASS APPLE ENTERPRISES INC   p213
9320 82A AVE, FORT ST. JOHN, BC, V1J 6S2
SIC 1521
BRIGIL CONSTRUCTION INC   p1107
3354 BOUL DES GRIVES BUREAU 3, GATINEAU, QC, J9A 0A6
(819) 243-7392   *SIC* 1521
BURKE'S RESTORATION INC   p755
17705 LESLIE ST UNIT 7, NEWMARKET, ON, L3Y 8C6
(905) 895-2456   *SIC* 1521
BURKE'S RESTORATION INC   p792
98 MILVAN DR, NORTH YORK, ON, M9L 1Z6
(416) 744-2456   *SIC* 1521
C. S. BACHLY BUILDERS LIMITED   p494
27 NIXON RD, BOLTON, ON, L7E 1J7
(905) 951-3100   *SIC* 1521
CALADO AND LIMA HOME IMPROVEMENT INC   p868
15 MANSION AVE, SCARBOROUGH, ON, M1L 1A5
(416) 782-0110   *SIC* 1521
CALSPER DEVELOPMENTS INC   p549
7501 KEELE ST SUITE 100, CONCORD, ON, L4K 1Y2
(905) 761-8200   *SIC* 1521
CANADA BUILDS COMPANY LTD   p645
423 COUNTY RD 36 UNIT 2, LINDSAY, ON, K9V 4R3
(705) 324-8777   *SIC* 1521
CARDEL HOMES LIMITED PARTNERSHIP   p14
180 QUARRY PARK BLVD SE SUITE 200, CALGARY, AB, T2C 3G3
(403) 258-1511   *SIC* 1521
CARLISLE DEVELOPMENTS INC   p8
2891 SUNRIDGE WAY NE UNIT 230, CAL-GARY, AB, T1Y 7K7
(403) 571-8400   *SIC* 1521
CAROLINA HOMES INC   p69
230 EVERSYDE BLVD SW SUITE 2101, CALGARY, AB, T2Y 0J4
(403) 256-5544   *SIC* 1521
CEDARGLEN GROUP INC, THE   p34
550 71 AVE SE SUITE 140, CALGARY, AB, T2H 0S6
(403) 255-2000   *SIC* 1521
CENTRAL HOME IMPROVEMENT WARE-HOUSE   p438
35 MARKET ST, ANTIGONISH, NS, B2G 3B5
(902) 863-6882   *SIC* 1521
CENTRAL HOME IMPROVEMENT WARE-HOUSE   p463
610 RIVER RD E, NEW GLASGOW, NS, B2H 3S1

(902) 755-2555   *SIC* 1521
CGI DEVELOPMENT INC   p426
20 SAGONA AVE, MOUNT PEARL, NL, A1N 4R2
(709) 748-8888   *SIC* 1521
CIVEO STRUCTURES INC   p100
21216 113 AVE NW, EDMONTON, AB, T5S 1Y6
(780) 447-2333   *SIC* 1521
CONSTRUCTION DROLET, MARC INC   p1277
5475 RUE RIDEAU, QUEBEC, QC, G2E 5V9
(418) 871-7574   *SIC* 1521
CONSTRUCTION GARBARINO INC   p1402
4795 RUE SAINTE-CATHERINE O BU-REAU 302, WESTMOUNT, QC, H3Z 1S8
(514) 731-5654   *SIC* 1521
CONSTRUCTION LA-RAY DIVISION ROUYN-NORANDA   p1289
950 RUE SAGUENAY, ROUYN-NORANDA, QC, J9X 7B6
(819) 762-9345   *SIC* 1521
CONSTRUCTION MAURICE BILODEAU INC   p1135
401 RUE DU GRAND-TRONC, LEVIS, QC, G6K 1K8
(418) 831-4024   *SIC* 1521
CONSTRUCTION MICHEL MALTAIS INC   p1244
775 RTE 132 E, NOUVELLE, QC, G0C 2E0
(418) 794-2605   *SIC* 1521
CONSTRUCTION RAYMOND ET FILS INC, LES   p1152
14243 BOUL DU CURE-LABELLE, MIRABEL, QC, J7J 1M2
(450) 979-4847   *SIC* 1521
CONSTRUCTION SOTER INC   p1236
4915 RUE LOUIS-B.-MAYER, MONTREAL, QC, H7P 0E5
(450) 664-2818   *SIC* 1521
CONSTRUCTION VP INC   p1302
1450 RTE 117, SAINT-FAUSTIN-LAC-CARRE, QC, J0T 1J2
SIC 1521
CONSTRUCTIONS JEL BERGERON   p1397
91 RUE MONFETTE, VICTORIAVILLE, QC, G6P 0B7
(819) 795-3030   *SIC* 1521
CONSTRUCTIONS LEO BAROLET INC, LES   p1401
250 2E AV, WEEDON, QC, J0B 3J0
(819) 877-2378   *SIC* 1521
CONVERGE CONSTRUCTION LTD   p233
31413 GILL AVE UNIT 108, MISSION, BC, V4S 0C4
(604) 814-3401   *SIC* 1521
COVENTRY HOMES INC   p100
17615 111 AVE NW, EDMONTON, AB, T5S 0A1
(780) 453-5100   *SIC* 1521
CREE-ASKI SERVICES LTD FIELD OFFICE   p746
196 FERGUSON RD, MOOSONEE, ON, P0L 1Y0
(705) 336-2828   *SIC* 1521
CRH CANADA GROUP INC   p803
585 MICHIGAN DR SUITE 1, OAKVILLE, ON, L6L 0G1
(905) 842-2741   *SIC* 1521
CWP CONSTRUCTORS LTD   p113
8702 48 AVE NW SUITE 210, EDMONTON, AB, T6E 5L1
(780) 757-5834   *SIC* 1521
DALRON CONSTRUCTION LIMITED   p899
130 ELM ST, SUDBURY, ON, P3C 1T6
(705) 560-9770   *SIC* 1521
DEEP CLEAN AUTOMATIC CLEANING & RESTORATION INC   p608
26 BURFORD RD UNIT 200, HAMILTON, ON, L8E 3C7
(905) 578-3445   *SIC* 1521
DELN CONSTRUCTION INC   p1008
550 CONESTOGO RD, WATERLOO, ON, N2L 4E3

(519) 880-9863   *SIC* 1521
DICOCCO CONTRACTORS 2015 INC   p859
550 MCGREGOR SIDE RD, SARNIA, ON, N7T 7H5
(519) 344-8446   *SIC* 1521
DIRHAM CONSTRUCTION LTD   p131
10127 121 AVE UNIT 201, GRANDE PRAIRIE, AB, T8V 7V3
(780) 539-4776   *SIC* 1521
DRAYCOR CONSTRUCTION LTD   p336
GD STN CSC, VICTORIA, BC, V8W 2L9
(250) 391-9899   *SIC* 1521
DREAM RIDGE HOMES CORP   p68
232 WOODPARK BAY SW, CALGARY, AB, T2W 6H2
(403) 616-3542   *SIC* 1521
ECMI LP   p552
125 VILLARBOIT CRES, CONCORD, ON, L4K 4K2
(905) 307-8102   *SIC* 1521
EDENVALE RESTORATION SPECIALISTS LTD   p276
13260 78 AVE UNIT 24, SURREY, BC, V3W 0H6
(604) 590-1440   *SIC* 1521
EL-BRIS LIMITED   p1023
933 GOYEAU ST, WINDSOR, ON, N9A 1H7
SIC 1521
EMPIRE (THE CONTINENTAL) LIMITED PARTNERSHIP   p552
125 VILLARBOIT CRES, CONCORD, ON, L4K 4K2
(905) 307-8102   *SIC* 1521
EMPIRE CONTINENTAL MANAGEMENT INC   p552
125 VILLARBOIT CRES, CONCORD, ON, L4K 4K2
(905) 307-8102   *SIC* 1521
ENTREPRISES DE CONSTRUCTION GI-GARI INC, LES   p1079
766 RUE D'ALMA, CHICOUTIMI, QC, G7H 4E6
(418) 696-1817   *SIC* 1521
ENTREPRISES QMD INC, LES   p1210
990 RUE NOTRE-DAME O BUREAU 200, MONTREAL, QC, H3C 1K1
(514) 875-4356   *SIC* 1521
EON BUILDING SYSTEMS INC   p266
GD, ROBERTS CREEK, BC, V0N 2W0
SIC 1521
ETRO CONSTRUCTION LIMITED   p185
4727 HASTINGS ST, BURNABY, BC, V5C 2K8
(604) 492-0920   *SIC* 1521
EUROHOUSE CONSTRUCTION INC   p327
2474 MARINE DR W, VANCOUVER, BC, V7V 1L1
(604) 354-6325   *SIC* 1521
FALCON HOMES LTD   p169
17 BEJU INDUSTRIAL DR, SYLVAN LAKE, AB, T4S 2J4
(403) 887-7333   *SIC* 1521
FORMCRETE (1994) LTD   p739
7060 PACIFIC CIR, MISSISSAUGA, ON, L5T 2A7
(905) 669-8017   *SIC* 1521
FREETEK CONSTRUCTION LTD   p164
130 YELLOWHEAD RD, SPRUCE GROVE, AB, T7X 3B5
(780) 960-4848   *SIC* 1521
FUSION PROJECT MANAGEMENT LTD   p304
850 HASTINGS ST W SUITE 800, VAN-COUVER, BC, V6C 1E1
(604) 629-0469   *SIC* 1521
GALKO HOMES LTD   p142
407 MAYOR MAGRATH DR S, LETH-BRIDGE, AB, T1J 3L8
(403) 329-3221   *SIC* 1521
GARRISON ESTATES INC   p197
5905 COWICHAN ST, CHILLIWACK, BC, V2R 0G8
(604) 634-3508   *SIC* 1521
GENESIS BUILDERS GROUP INC   p23

7315 8 ST NE, CALGARY, AB, T2E 8A2

(403) 265-9237 *SIC* 1521

GESTION CBCC INC p1081

3 RUE AAHPPISAACH, CHISASIBI, QC, J0M 1E0

(819) 855-2977 *SIC* 1521

GILMAR CONSTRUCTION LTD. p157

129 CLEARWILL AVE, RED DEER COUNTY, AB, T4E 0A1

(403) 343-1028 *SIC* 1521

GOLDEN GLOBE CONSTRUCTION LTD p290

8380 ST. GEORGE ST UNIT 103, VANCOUVER, BC, V5X 3S7

(604) 261-3936 *SIC* 1521

GONTE CONSTRUCTION LTD p503

190 CLARK BLVD, BRAMPTON, ON, L6T 4A8

(905) 456-6488 *SIC* 1521

GORE BROTHERS VINTAGE HOMES INC p196

10805 MCDONALD RD, CHILLIWACK, BC, V2P 6H5

(604) 824-1902 *SIC* 1521

GREAT GULF GROUP OF COMPANIES INC p877

3751 VICTORIA PARK AVE, SCARBOROUGH, ON, M1W 3Z4

(416) 449-1340 *SIC* 1521

GREAT GULF HOMES LIMITED p877

3751 VICTORIA PARK AVE, SCARBOROUGH, ON, M1W 3Z4

(416) 449-1340 *SIC* 1521

GROUP EMPORIO CONSTRUCTION INC p758

4025 DORCHESTER RD SUITE 338, NIAGARA FALLS, ON, L2E 7K8

SIC 1521

GUINDON, REJEAN CONSTRUCTION CORPORATION p810

3809 ST. JOSEPH UNIT 12, ORLEANS, ON, K1C 1T1

SIC 1521

GULFVIEW CONTRACTING LTD p877

3751 VICTORIA PARK AVE, SCARBOROUGH, ON, M1W 3Z4

(416) 449-1340 *SIC* 1521

H & S HOLDINGS INC p1407

101 EAST SERVICE RD, HAGUE, SK, S0K 1X0

(306) 225-2288 *SIC* 1521

H&R DEVELOPMENTS p785

3625 DUFFERIN ST SUITE 503, NORTH YORK, ON, M3K 1N4

(416) 635-7520 *SIC* 1521

H. WILSON INDUSTRIES (2010) LTD p129

1045 MEMORIAL DR, FORT MCMURRAY, AB, T9K 0K4

(780) 743-1881 *SIC* 1521

HABITAT FOR HUMANITY EDMONTON SOCIETY p83

8210 YELLOWHEAD TRAIL NW, EDMONTON, AB, T5B 1G5

(780) 479-3566 *SIC* 1521

HERITAGE DESIGN p636

227 MANITOU DR SUITE 4, KITCHENER, ON, N2C 1L4

SIC 1521

HOME DEPOT OF CANADA INC p93

13360 137 AVE NW, EDMONTON, AB, T5L 5C9

(780) 472-4201 *SIC* 1521

HOME IMPROVEMENT PEOPLE INC, THE p988

1120 CASTLEFIELD AVE, TORONTO, ON, M6B 1E9

(905) 760-7607 *SIC* 1521

HOMES BY AVI (CALGARY) INC p35

245 FORGE RD SE, CALGARY, AB, T2H 0S9

(403) 536-7000 *SIC* 1521

HURLSTONE HOLDINGS CORP p767

245 YORKLAND BLVD SUITE 100, NORTH YORK, ON, M2J 4W9

(416) 490-1400 *SIC* 1521

IMMEUBLES CJS RIVEST INC p1283

96 BOUL INDUSTRIEL, REPENTIGNY, QC, J6A 4X6

(450) 581-4480 *SIC* 1521

ISLAND VIEW CONSTRUCTION LTD p340

2780 VETERANS MEMORIAL PKY SUITE 210, VICTORIA, BC, V9B 3S6

SIC 1521

JAYMAN BUILT LTD p71

3132 118 AVE SE SUITE 200, CALGARY, AB, T2Z 3X1

(403) 258-3772 *SIC* 1521

JPL APRES SINISTRE INC p1106

116 RUE LOIS, GATINEAU, QC, J8Y 3R7

(819) 770-3038 *SIC* 1521

KAITLIN GROUP LTD, THE p894

28 SANDIFORD DR SUITE 201, STOUFFVILLE, ON, L4A 1L8

(905) 642-7050 *SIC* 1521

KING CONSTRUCTION ENR p1243

84 RUE ONTARIO, NOTRE-DAME-DU-NORD, QC, J0Z 3B0

SIC 1521

KLEWCHUK CONSTRUCTION LTD p122

503 69 AVE NW, EDMONTON, AB, T6P 0C2

SIC 1521

LAEBON DEVELOPMENTS LTD p158

289 BURNT PARK DR, RED DEER COUNTY, AB, T4S 2L4

(403) 346-7273 *SIC* 1521

LANDMARK HOMES (EDMONTON) INC p125

1103 95 ST SW UNIT 301, EDMONTON, AB, T6X 0P8

(780) 436-5959 *SIC* 1521

LANDMART BUILDING CORP p478

911 GOLF LINKS RD SUITE 307, ANCASTER, ON, L9K 1H9

(905) 304-6459 *SIC* 1521

LINK-LINE CONSTRUCTION LTD p487

10 CHURCHILL DR, BARRIE, ON, L4N 8Z5

(705) 721-9284 *SIC* 1521

LOCATION RAOUL PELLETIER INC p1138

3650 BOUL GUILLAUME-COUTURE, LEVIS, QC, G6W 7L3

(418) 837-2147 *SIC* 1521

LX CONSTRUCTION INC p349

68132 HIGHWAY 212, DUGALD, MB, R0E 0K0

(204) 898-8453 *SIC* 1521

LYDALE CONSTRUCTION (1983) CO. LTD p1428

859 58TH ST E, SASKATOON, SK, S7K 6X5

(306) 934-6116 *SIC* 1521

MAISON USINEX INC p1151

114 RTE 214, MILAN, QC, G0Y 1E0

(819) 657-4268 *SIC* 1521

MARTIN, BOB CONSTRUCTION CO LTD p632

1473 JOHN COUNTER BLVD SUITE 400, KINGSTON, ON, K7M 8Z6

(613) 548-7136 *SIC* 1521

MELCHERS CONSTRUCTION LIMITED p643

22662 KOMOKA RD, KOMOKA, ON, N0L 1R0

(519) 473-4149 *SIC* 1521

MEYKNECHT-LISCHER CONTRACTORS LTD p541

145 WALGREEN RD, CARP, ON, K0A 1L0

SIC 1521

MID-VALLEY CONSTRUCTION (1997) LIMITED p460

15096 HIGHWAY 1, KINGSTON, NS, B0P 1R0

(902) 765-6312 *SIC* 1521

MINTO GROUP INC p774

4101 YONGE ST UNIT 600, NORTH YORK, ON, M2P 1N6

(416) 977-0777 *SIC* 1521

MISSION GROUP ENTERPRISES LTD p222

1631 DICKSON AVE SUITE 1000, KELOWNA, BC, V1Y 0B5

(250) 448-8810 *SIC* 1521

MORRISON CONSTRUCTION (1983) LTD p17

11158 42 ST SE, CALGARY, AB, T2C 0J9

(403) 279-7600 *SIC* 1521

NEWMARK CONSTRUCTION INC p225

9525 201 ST UNIT 219, LANGLEY, BC, V1M 4A5

(604) 371-3963 *SIC* 1521

NIVTOP HOLDINGS LTD p863

105 BLACK RD, SAULT STE. MARIE, ON, P6B 0A3

(705) 253-3251 *SIC* 1521

NOVA CONSTRUCTION C.P. INC p1255

1259 RUE PAUL-EMILE-GIROUX, QUEBEC, QC, G1C 0K9

(418) 660-8111 *SIC* 1521

NOVA CONSTRUCTION CO. LTD p438

3098 HIGHWAY 104, ANTIGONISH, NS, B2G 2K3

(902) 863-4004 *SIC* 1521

OKE WOODSMITH BUILDING SYSTEMS INC p598

70964 BLUEWATER HWY SUITE 9, GRAND BEND, ON, N0M 1T0

(519) 238-8893 *SIC* 1521

PACIFIC RIM EXTERIORS p337

831 SHAMROCK ST, VICTORIA, BC, V8X 2V1

(250) 686-8738 *SIC* 1521

PARADISE HOMES CORP p915

1 HERONS HILL WAY, TORONTO, ON, M2J 0G2

(416) 756-1972 *SIC* 1521

PAUL'S RESTORATIONS INC p615

1640 UPPER OTTAWA ST, HAMILTON, ON, L8W 3P2

(905) 388-7285 *SIC* 1521

PCL CONSTRUCTORS EASTERN INC p115

9915 56 AVE NW, EDMONTON, AB, T6E 5L7

SIC 1521

PCM POMERY CONSTRUCTION & MAINTENANCE LTD p184

3060 NORLAND AVE SUITE 109, BURNABY, BC, V5B 3A6

(604) 294-6700 *SIC* 1521

PHELPS HOMES LTD p599

166 MAIN ST W, GRIMSBY, ON, L3M 1S3

(905) 945-5451 *SIC* 1521

PIONEER LOG HOMES OF BRITISH COLUMBIA LTD p344

351 HODGSON RD, WILLIAMS LAKE, BC, V2G 3P7

(250) 392-5577 *SIC* 1521

PMC BUILDERS & DEVELOPERS LTD p273

19414 ENTERPRISE WAY, SURREY, BC, V3S 6J9

(604) 534-1822 *SIC* 1521

POTVIN, A. CONSTRUCTION LTD p857

8850 COUNTY ROAD 17, ROCKLAND, ON, K4K 1L6

(613) 446-5181 *SIC* 1521

QUALICO DEVELOPMENTS CALGARY LTD p37

5709 2 ST SE SUITE 200, CALGARY, AB, T2H 2W4

(403) 253-3311 *SIC* 1521

R & F CONSTRUCTION INC p810

73 PATTERSON RD, ORILLIA, ON, L3V 6H1

(705) 325-5746 *SIC* 1521

REID'S HERITAGE HOMES LTD p537

6783 WELLINGTON ROAD 34, CAMBRIDGE, ON, N3C 2V4

(519) 658-6656 *SIC* 1521

REID-BUILT HOMES LTD p102

18140 107 AVE NW, EDMONTON, AB, T5S 1K5

(780) 486-3666 *SIC* 1521

ROBINSON GROUP LIMITED p973

263 DAVENPORT RD, TORONTO, ON, M5R 1J9

(416) 960-2444 *SIC* 1521

ROTERRA PILING LTD p2

25420 114 AVE, ACHESON, AB, T7X 6M4

(780) 948-8556 *SIC* 1521

RUSCO ENTERPRISES LTD p342

2410 MARINE DR, WEST VANCOUVER, BC, V7V 1L1

(604) 925-9095 *SIC* 1521

SANCON CONTRACTING LTD p395

4621 MAIN ST, BELLEDUNE, NB, E8G 2L3

(506) 507-2222 *SIC* 1521

SAVIC HOMES LTD p634

26 IDLE RIDGE CRT, KITCHENER, ON, N2A 3W3

(519) 954-0370 *SIC* 1521

SENATOR HOMES INC p777

250 LESMILL RD, NORTH YORK, ON, M3B 2T5

(416) 445-8552 *SIC* 1521

SHAMROCK BUILDING SERVICES LTD p94

12673 125 ST NW, EDMONTON, AB, T5L 0T6

(780) 472-7351 *SIC* 1521

SHANE HOLDINGS LTD p25

5661 7 ST NE, CALGARY, AB, T2E 8V3

(403) 536-2200 *SIC* 1521

SHANE HOLDINGS LTD p25

5661 7 ST NE, CALGARY, AB, T2E 8V3

(403) 536-2200 *SIC* 1521

SHANE HOMES LIMITED p25

5661 7 ST NE, CALGARY, AB, T2E 8V3

(403) 536-2200 *SIC* 1521

SIMCOE ESTATES LTD p855

24 TANNERY CRT, RICHMOND HILL, ON, L4C 7V4

(705) 259-1344 *SIC* 1521

SINGLA BROS. HOLDINGS LTD p244

567 HEATHER RD SUITE 32860, PENTICTON, BC, V2A 6N8

(250) 490-1700 *SIC* 1521

SMART DESIGN & DEVELOPMENT p37

7130 FISHER RD SE SUITE 10, CALGARY, AB, T2H 0W3

SIC 1521

SOUTHSIDE CONSTRUCTION LONDON p661

3089 WONDERLAND RD S, LONDON, ON, N6L 1R4

(519) 657-6583 *SIC* 1521

SPAR CONSTRUCTION (EDMONTON) LTD p97

14415 114 AVE NW, EDMONTON, AB, T5M 2Y8

(780) 453-3555 *SIC* 1521

STATEVIEW HOMES LTD p1034

410 CHRISLEA RD UNIT 1, WOODBRIDGE, ON, L4L 8B5

(905) 851-1849 *SIC* 1521

STIPSITS HOLDINGS CORP p525

720 OVAL CRT, BURLINGTON, ON, L7L 6A9

(905) 333-8364 *SIC* 1521

SUNDIAL HOMES LIMITED p773

4576 YONGE ST SUITE 500, NORTH YORK, ON, M2N 6N4

(416) 224-1200 *SIC* 1521

SURECAN CONSTRUCTION LTD p112

7707 71 AVE NW, EDMONTON, AB, T6C 0A9

(780) 469-3162 *SIC* 1521

T.G.A. GENERAL CONTRACTING (1980) INC p792

31 DENSLEY AVE, NORTH YORK, ON, M6M 2P5

(416) 247-7471 *SIC* 1521

TAGISH ENTERPRISES LTD p1406

5A SOUTH PLAINS ROAD W, EMERALD PARK, SK, S4L 1A1

(306) 585-8480 *SIC* 1521

TARTAN HOMES CORPORATION p834

233 METCALFE ST SUITE 11, OTTAWA, ON, K2P 2C2

(613) 238-2040 *SIC* 1521

TERRAPAVE CONSTRUCTION LTD p498

12 CADETTA RD UNIT 1, BRAMPTON, ON, L6P 0X4

(905) 761-2865   *SIC 1521*
TLI CHO CONSTRUCTION LTD   *p435*
GD, BEHCHOKO, NT, X0E 0Y0
(867) 766-4909   *SIC 1521*
TOWNE MEADOW DEVELOPMENT COR-PORATION INC   *p676*
80 TIVERTON CRT SUITE 300, MARKHAM, ON, L3R 0G4
(905) 477-7609   *SIC 1521*
TOWNSHIP OF LEEDS AND THE THOU-SAND ISLANDS   *p663*
GD, LYNDHURST, ON, K0E 1N0
(613) 928-3303   *SIC 1521*
TRI-GEN CONSTRUCTION LTD   *p7*
GD, BOYLE, AB, T0A 0M0
(780) 689-3831   *SIC 1521*
TRICO DEVELOPMENTS CORPORATION   *p66*
1005 11 AVE SW, CALGARY, AB, T2R 0G1
(403) 287-9300   *SIC 1521*
TRIPLE CANON CORPORATION   *p786*
1140 SHEPPARD AVE W UNIT 13, NORTH YORK, ON, M3K 2A2
SIC 1521
ULTIMATE CONSTRUCTION INC   *p488*
39 CHURCHILL DR SUITE 1, BARRIE, ON, L4N 8Z5
(705) 726-2300   *SIC 1521*
UNIVERSAL RESTORATION SYSTEMS LTD   *p251*
3675 OPIE CRES, PRINCE GEORGE, BC, V2N 1B9
(250) 612-5177   *SIC 1521*
URBANDALE CONSTRUCTION LIMITED   *p819*
2193 ARCH ST, OTTAWA, ON, K1G 2H5
(613) 731-6331   *SIC 1521*
UTILITY SERVICES LTD.   *p816*
1611 LIVERPOOL CRT, OTTAWA, ON, K1B 4L1
SIC 1521
V.C. RENOVATION   *p396*
103 VANIER ST, CAMPBELLTON, NB, E3N 1T8
(506) 753-6273   *SIC 1521*
VCC ENTREPRENEUR GENERAL INC   *p1401*
42 RTE MAQUATUA, WEMINDJI, QC, J0M 1L0
(819) 978-3335   *SIC 1521*
VIEWMARK HOMES LTD   *p676*
80 TIVERTON CRT SUITE 300, MARKHAM, ON, L3R 0G4
(905) 477-7609   *SIC 1521*
VISION WEST DEVELOPMENT LTD   *p343*
6717 CRABAPPLE DR, WHISTLER, BC, V0N 1B6
(604) 932-5275   *SIC 1521*
VUPOINT SYSTEMS LTD   *p658*
1025 HARGRIEVE RD UNIT 8, LONDON, ON, N6E 1P7
(519) 690-0865   *SIC 1521*
VVI CONSTRUCTION LTD   *p253*
96 CARTIER ST, REVELSTOKE, BC, V0E 2S0
(250) 837-2919   *SIC 1521*
WAHL CONSTRUCTION LTD   *p146*
830 15 ST SW, MEDICINE HAT, AB, T1A 4W7
(403) 526-6235   *SIC 1521*
WINNIPEG BUILDING & DECORATING LTD   *p381*
1586 WALL ST, WINNIPEG, MB, R3E 2S4
(204) 942-6121   *SIC 1521*
ZGEMI INC   *p507*
100 WILKINSON RD UNIT 18, BRAMPTON, ON, L6T 4Y9
(905) 454-0111   *SIC 1521*

SIC 1522 Residential construction, nec

9091-9101 QUEBEC INC   *p1151*
14495 RUE JOSEPH-MARC-VERMETTE, MIRABEL, QC, J7J 1X2
(450) 434-5858   *SIC 1522*
AMAKO CONSTRUCTION LTD   *p241*
1000 3RD ST W SUITE 300, NORTH VAN-COUVER, BC, V7P 3J6
(604) 990-6766   *SIC 1522*
ANTELOPE HILLS CONSTRUCTION LTD   *p666*
80 TIVERTON CRT SUITE 300, MARKHAM, ON, L3R 0G4
(905) 477-7609   *SIC 1522*
ARSENAULT BROS. CONSTRUCTION LTD   *p1042*
5 HILLSIDE AVE, SUMMERSIDE, PE, C1N 4H3
(902) 888-2689   *SIC 1522*
BOSA CONSTRUCTION INC   *p302*
838 HASTINGS ST W UNIT 1100, VAN-COUVER, BC, V6C 0A6
(604) 299-1363   *SIC 1522*
BRODA GROUP HOLDINGS LIMITED PART-NERSHIP   *p1414*
4271 5TH AVE E, PRINCE ALBERT, SK, S6W 0A5
(306) 764-5337   *SIC 1522*
C2 GROUP INC   *p518*
350 WOOLWICH ST S, BRESLAU, ON, N0B 1M0
(519) 648-3118   *SIC 1522*
CAN-DER CONSTRUCTION LTD   *p113*
5410 97 ST NW, EDMONTON, AB, T6E 5C1
(780) 436-2980   *SIC 1522*
CEGERCO INC   *p1078*
255 RUE RACINE E BUREAU 595, CHICOUTIMI, QC, G7H 7L2
(418) 690-3432   *SIC 1522*
CELERITY BUILDERS LTD   *p361*
GD, WINKLER, MB, R6W 4B3
(204) 362-4003   *SIC 1522*
CHAREX INC   *p1153*
14940 RUE LOUIS-M.-TAILLON, MIRABEL, QC, J7N 2K4
(450) 475-1135   *SIC 1522*
CHARLAMARA HOLDINGS INC   *p540*
2962 CARP RD, CARP, ON, K0A 1L0
(613) 831-9039   *SIC 1522*
CLASSIC CONSTRUCTION LTD   *p145*
671 INDUSTRIAL AVE SE, MEDICINE HAT, AB, T1A 3L5
(403) 528-2793   *SIC 1522*
COMPAGNIE DE CONSTRUCTION ET DE DEVELOPPEMENT CRIE LTEE, LA   *p1232*
3983 BOUL LITE, MONTREAL, QC, H7E 1A3
(450) 661-1102   *SIC 1522*
CONCEPTION HABITAT 2015 INC   *p1086*
2400 BOUL DANIEL-JOHNSON, COTE SAINT-LUC, QC, H7T 3A4
(450) 902-2007   *SIC 1522*
CONSTRUCTION BERNARD BORDELEAU INC.   *p1297*
100 RUE ROMEO-GAUDREAULT, SAINT-CHARLES-BORROMEE, QC, J6E 0A1
(450) 752-2660   *SIC 1522*
CONSTRUCTION LANOUE, PASCAL INC   *p1163*
8400 RUE SHERBROOKE E, MONTREAL, QC, H1L 1B2
(514) 544-8999   *SIC 1522*
CONSTRUCTION M.G.P. INC   *p1299*
140 RTE 271 S, SAINT-EPHREM-DE-BEAUCE, QC, G0M 1R0
(418) 484-5740   *SIC 1522*
CONSTRUCTION MANCHAOW INC   *p1081*
2 CLUSTER F7, CHISASIBI, QC, J0M 1E0
(819) 855-2046   *SIC 1522*
CONSTRUCTION PAROX INC   *p1056*
1655 RUE DE L'INDUSTRIE, BELOEIL, QC, J3G 0S5
(450) 813-9655   *SIC 1522*
CONSTRUCTIONS FABMEC INC   *p1078*
1590 BOUL DU ROYAUME O BUREAU 4, CHICOUTIMI, QC, G7H 5B1
(418) 549-3636   *SIC 1522*

CONSTRUCTIONS QUORUM INC   *p1224*
5200 RUE SAINT-PATRICK BUREAU 200, MONTREAL, QC, H4E 4N9
(514) 822-2882   *SIC 1522*
CONSTRUCTIONS RELIANCE INC, LES   *p1127*
3285 BOUL JEAN-BAPTISTE-DESCHAMPS, LACHINE, QC, H8T 3E4
(514) 631-7999   *SIC 1522*
CORSIM CONSTRUCTION INC   *p1172*
2003 RUE GILFORD, MONTREAL, QC, H2H 1H2
(514) 345-9320   *SIC 1522*
COUNTRYWIDE HOMES LTD   *p551*
1500 HIGHWAY 7, CONCORD, ON, L4K 5Y4
(905) 907-1500   *SIC 1522*
COVE PROPERTIES LTD   *p123*
316-14127 23 AVE NW, EDMONTON, AB, T6R 0G4
(780) 469-2683   *SIC 1522*
CRESSEY DEVELOPMENT CORPORATION   *p293*
555 8TH AVE W SUITE 200, VANCOUVER, BC, V5Z 1C6
(604) 683-1256   *SIC 1522*
CUNARD COURT HIGHRISE   *p455*
2065 BRUNSWICK ST SUITE 1706, HALI-FAX, NS, B3K 5T8
(902) 407-8845   *SIC 1522*
D-THIND DEVELOPMENT LTD   *p190*
700-4211 KINGSWAY, BURNABY, BC, V5H 1Z6
(604) 451-7780   *SIC 1522*
DANIELS HR CORPORATION   *p933*
130 QUEENS QUAY E 8 FL, TORONTO, ON, M5A 0P6
(416) 598-2129   *SIC 1522*
DANIELS MIDTOWN CORPORATION   *p933*
130 QUEENS QUAY E 8 FL, TORONTO, ON, M5A 0P6
(416) 598-2129   *SIC 1522*
DAUDET CREEK CONTRACTING LTD   *p224*
495 QUATSINO BLVD, KITIMAT, BC, V8C 2G7
(250) 632-4831   *SIC 1522*
DAVIS INDUSTRIES   *p663*
4855 520 HWY, MAGNETAWAN, ON, P0A 1P0
SIC 1522
DAYTONA CAPITAL CORPORATION   *p100*
11504 170 ST NW SUITE 101, EDMON-TON, AB, T5S 1J7
(780) 452-2288   *SIC 1522*
DEMTEC INC   *p1253*
50 BOUL INDUSTRIEL, PRINCEVILLE, QC, G6L 4P2
(819) 364-2043   *SIC 1522*
EBC-NEILSON, ROMAINE 3 EXCAVATIONS DERIVATION (R3-06-01) S.E.N.C   *p1119*
1095 RUE VALETS, L'ANCIENNE-LORETTE, QC, G2E 4M7
(418) 872-0600   *SIC 1522*
EBC-POMERLEAU, PJCC 62000 S.E.N.C.   *p1119*
1095 RUE VALETS, L'ANCIENNE-LORETTE, QC, G2E 4M7
(418) 872-0600   *SIC 1522*
ELLISDON RESIDENTIAL INC   *p649*
2045 OXFORD ST E, LONDON, ON, N5V 2Z7
(519) 455-6770   *SIC 1522*
FARES CONSTRUCTION LTD   *p456*
3480 JOSEPH HOWE DR SUITE 500, HAL-IFAX, NS, B3L 0B5
(902) 457-6676   *SIC 1522*
FERNBROOK HOMES (LAKE OF DREAMS) LIMITED   *p552*
2220 HIGHWAY 7 UNIT 5, CONCORD, ON, L4K 1W7
(416) 667-0447   *SIC 1522*
FERNBROOK HOMES (WILSON) LTD   *p552*
2220 HIGHWAY 7 UNIT 5, CONCORD, ON, L4K 1W7

(416) 667-0447   *SIC 1522*
FERNBROOK HOMES LIMITED   *p552*
2220 HIGHWAY 7 UNIT 5, CONCORD, ON, L4K 1W7
(416) 667-0447   *SIC 1522*
FOURTH-RITE CONSTRUCTION (1994) LTD   *p176*
2609 PROGRESSIVE WAY SUITE B, AB-BOTSFORD, BC, V2T 6H8
(604) 850-7684   *SIC 1522*
FOXRIDGE HOMES (MANITOBA) LTD   *p365*
30 SPEERS RD, WINNIPEG, MB, R2J 1L9
(204) 488-7578   *SIC 1522*
GORF CONTRACTING LTD   *p846*
6855 HWY 101 E, PORCUPINE, ON, P0N 1C0
(705) 235-3278   *SIC 1522*
GRAPE ARBOR CONSTRUCTION LTD   *p670*
80 TIVERTON CRT SUITE 300, MARKHAM, ON, L3R 0G4
(905) 477-7609   *SIC 1522*
GROUPE MAURICE INC, LE   *p1329*
2400 RUE DES NATIONS BUREAU 137, SAINT-LAURENT, QC, H4R 3G4
(514) 331-2788   *SIC 1522*
HAMILL CREEK TIMBER HOMES INC   *p232*
13440 HWY 31, MEADOW CREEK, BC, V0G 1N0
(250) 366-4320   *SIC 1522*
HIRE HUSBAND   *p568*
200 QUEEN ST W, ELMVALE, ON, L0L 1P0
(705) 733-6355   *SIC 1522*
HOME DEPOT OF CANADA INC   *p120*
2020 101 ST NW, EDMONTON, AB, T6N 1J2
(780) 433-6370   *SIC 1522*
HOMESERVICE CLUB OF CANADA LTD   *p925*
1255 YONGE ST, TORONTO, ON, M4T 1W6
(416) 925-1111   *SIC 1522*
HOPEWELL CAPITAL CORPORATION   *p67*
2020 4 ST SW SUITE 410, CALGARY, AB, T2S 1W3
(403) 232-8821   *SIC 1522*
HUBER DEVELOPMENT LTD   *p222*
516 LAWRENCE AVE, KELOWNA, BC, V1Y 6L7
(250) 860-5858   *SIC 1522*
I CHECK INC   *p696*
1136 MATHESON BLVD E, MISSISSAUGA, ON, L4W 2V4
(905) 625-5156   *SIC 1522*
INDUSTRIES DE FIBRE DE VERRE PRE-MIER INC, LES   *p1240*
3390 RUE DE MONT-JOLI, MONTREAL-NORD, QC, H1H 2X8
(514) 321-6410   *SIC 1522*
LAFARGE CANADA INC   *p1133*
3055 BOUL SAINT-MARTIN O BUREAU 300, LAVAL, QC, H7T 0J3
(438) 265-1010   *SIC 1522*
LAUDERVEST DEVELOPMENTS LTD   *p772*
4576 YONGE ST SUITE 500, NORTH YORK, ON, M2N 6N4
(416) 224-1200   *SIC 1522*
MATTAMY HOMES LIMITED   *p536*
605 SHELDON DR, CAMBRIDGE, ON, N1T 2K1
SIC 1522
MERIDIAN DEVELOPMENT CORP   *p1428*
450 2ND AVE N UNIT 100, SASKATOON, SK, S7K 2C3
(306) 384-0431   *SIC 1522*
METRO-CAN CONSTRUCTION LTD   *p270*
10470 152 ST SUITE 520, SURREY, BC, V3R 0Y3
(604) 583-1174   *SIC 1522*
MORLEY HOPPER LIMITED   *p541*
1818 BRADLEY SIDE RD, CARP, ON, K0A 1L0
(613) 831-5490   *SIC 1522*
MOVELINE INC   *p804*
1317 SPEERS RD, OAKVILLE, ON, L6L 2X5
(905) 814-1700   *SIC 1522*

NORTH RIDGE DEVELOPMENT CORPORATION p1428
3037 FAITHFULL AVE, SASKATOON, SK, S7K 8B3
(306) 242-2434   SIC 1522

OCEAN WEST CONSTRUCTION LTD p291
1083 E KENT AVE NORTH UNIT 113, VANCOUVER, BC, V5X 4V9
(604) 324-3531   SIC 1522

OXVILLE HOMES LTD p557
2220 HIGHWAY 7 UNIT 5, CONCORD, ON, L4K 1W7
(416) 667-0447   SIC 1522

PERRY'S CONSTRUCTION & READY MIX LTD p1043
190 CENTENNIAL DR, TIGNISH, PE, C0B 2B0
(902) 882-3166   SIC 1522

PR POMEROY RESTORATION & CONSTRUCTION LTD p201
2075 BRIGANTINE DR UNIT 18, COQUITLAM, BC, V3K 7B8
(604) 529-9200   SIC 1522

PROVINCIAL READY MIX INC p427
36 PRINCE WILLIAM DR, PLACENTIA, NL, A0B 2Y0
(709) 227-2727   SIC 1522

QUALIFIED CONTRACTORS LTD p275
12788 ROSS PL, SURREY, BC, V3V 6E1
(604) 951-8677   SIC 1522

RESIDENTIAL ENERGY SAVING PRODUCTS INC p893
201 BARTON ST UNIT 3, STONEY CREEK, ON, L8E 2K3
(905) 578-2292   SIC 1522

RIDGE DEVELOPMENT CORPORATION p102
17307 106 AVE NW, EDMONTON, AB, T5S 1E7
(780) 483-7077   SIC 1522

ROCKPORT HOMES LIMITED p780
170 THE DONWAY W SUITE 307, NORTH YORK, ON, M3C 2G3
(416) 447-7391   SIC 1522

ROGER BISSON INC p1309
5450 RUE RAMSAY, SAINT-HUBERT, QC, J3Y 2S4
(514) 990-2519   SIC 1522

ROHIT DEVELOPMENTS LTD p116
9636 51 AVE NW, EDMONTON, AB, T6E 6A5
(780) 436-9015   SIC 1522

ROSS AND ANGLIN LIMITEE p1126
45 BOUL SAINT-JOSEPH, LACHINE, QC, H8S 2K9
(514) 364-4220   SIC 1522

SEYMOUR PACIFIC DEVELOPMENTS LTD p195
100 ST. ANN'S RD, CAMPBELL RIVER, BC, V9W 4C4
(250) 286-8045   SIC 1522

STATESMAN CORPORATION p75
7370 SIERRA MORENA BLVD SW, CALGARY, AB, T3H 4H9
(403) 256-4151   SIC 1522

STEELHEAD CONTRACTING RENOVATION LTD p183
4179 MCCONNELL DR, BURNABY, BC, V5A 3J7
(604) 420-9368   SIC 1522

STERLING HOMES LTD p37
5709 2 ST SE SUITE 200, CALGARY, AB, T2H 2W4
(403) 253-7476   SIC 1522

STREETSIDE DEVELOPMENT CORPORATION p392
1 DR. DAVID FRIESEN DR, WINNIPEG, MB, R3X 0G8
(204) 233-2451   SIC 1522

STUART OLSON BUILDINGS LTD p74
4954 RICHARD RD SW SUITE 400, CALGARY, AB, T3E 6L1
(403) 520-2767   SIC 1522

STUART OLSON BUILDINGS LTD p256

13777 COMMERCE PKY SUITE 300, RICHMOND, BC, V6V 2X3
(604) 273-7765   SIC 1522

STUART OLSON CONSTRUCTION LTD p74
4820 RICHARD RD SW SUITE 600, CALGARY, AB, T3E 6L1
(403) 520-2767   SIC 1522

TOLIN ENTERPRISES LTD p559
400 CREDITSTONE RD, CONCORD, ON, L4K 3Z3
(905) 669-2711   SIC 1522

TORODE RESIDENTIAL LTD p61
209 8 AVE SW SUITE 301, CALGARY, AB, T2P 1B8
(403) 355-6000   SIC 1522

TRICAR DEVELOPMENTS INC p662
3800 COLONEL TALBOT RD, LONDON, ON, N6P 1H5
(519) 652-8900   SIC 1522

TROIKA VENTURES INC p223
1856 AMBROSI RD SUITE 114, KELOWNA, BC, V1Y 4R9
(250) 869-4945   SIC 1522

TWO BLOOR RESIDENCES LIMITED p786
3625 DUFFERIN ST SUITE 500, NORTH YORK, ON, M3K 1Z2
(416) 635-7520   SIC 1522

UPA CONSTRUCTION GROUP LIMITED PARTNERSHIP p69
10655 SOUTHPORT RD SW SUITE 700, CALGARY, AB, T2W 4Y1
(403) 262-4440   SIC 1522

VERTEX RESOURCE GROUP LTD p163
2055 PREMIER WAY SUITE 161, SHERWOOD PARK, AB, T8H 0G2
(780) 464-3295   SIC 1522

WCC CONSTRUCTION CANADA, ULC p775
36 YORK MILLS RD SUITE 302, NORTH YORK, ON, M2P 2E9
(416) 849-9000   SIC 1522

WINDMILL DEVELOPMENT GROUP LTD p825
6 BOOTH ST, OTTAWA, ON, K1R 6K8
(613) 820-5600   SIC 1522

SIC 1531 Operative builders

CAMPUS LIVING CENTRES INC p578
5405 EGLINTON AVE W SUITE 214, ETOBICOKE, ON, M9C 5K6
(416) 620-0635   SIC 1531

CANADIAN CONDOMINIUM MANAGEMENT CORP p108
9440 49 ST NW SUITE 230, EDMONTON, AB, T6B 2M9
(780) 485-0505   SIC 1531

CAPITAL MANAGEMENT LTD p91
9747 104 ST NW SUITE 1604, EDMONTON, AB, T5K 0Y6
(780) 428-6511   SIC 1531

FRANKLIN EMPIRE INC p1262
215 RUE FORTIN, QUEBEC, QC, G1M 3M2
(418) 683-1724   SIC 1531

GIUSTI GROUP LIMITED PARTNERSHIP p77
4 INDUSTRY WAY SE, CALGARY, AB, T3S 0A2
(403) 203-0492   SIC 1531

MUCHALAT CONSTRUCTION LTD p202
3326 DOVE CREEK RD, COURTENAY, BC, V9J 1P3
(250) 338-0995   SIC 1531

NAVELLI DWELLINGS INC p556
1681 LANGSTAFF RD UNIT 1, CONCORD, ON, L4K 5T3
(416) 987-5500   SIC 1531

NEWMARK GROUP INC p226
20780 WILLOUGHBY TOWN CENTRE DR UNIT 300, LANGLEY, BC, V2Y 0M7
(604) 371-3963   SIC 1531

POINTE OF VIEW MARKETING & MANAGEMENT INC p25
1121 CENTRE ST NW SUITE 500, CAL-

GARY, AB, T2E 7K6
(403) 571-8400   SIC 1531

PROPRIETES BELCOURT INC, LES p1341
6500 RTE TRANSCANADIENNE BUREAU 210, SAINT-LAURENT, QC, H4T 1X4
(514) 344-1300   SIC 1531

SAN RUFO HOMES LTD p166
35C RAYBORN CRES, ST. ALBERT, AB, T8N 4A9
(780) 470-4070   SIC 1531

SANT, GEORGE & SONS LTD p642
11831 COLD CREEK RD SUITE 1, KLEINBURG, ON, L0J 1C0
(905) 893-1592   SIC 1531

STATESMAN GROUP OF COMPANIES LTD, THE p75
7370 SIERRA MORENA BLVD SW SUITE 200, CALGARY, AB, T3H 4H9
(403) 256-4151   SIC 1531

STERLING HOMES (EDMONTON) LTD p121
3203 93 ST NW, EDMONTON, AB, T6N 0B2
(780) 461-8369   SIC 1531

TAMARACK DEVELOPMENTS CORPORATION p827
3187 ALBION RD S, OTTAWA, ON, K1V 8Y3
(613) 739-2919   SIC 1531

SIC 1541 Industrial buildings and warehouses

1075177 ONTARIO LTD p858
1129 VANIER RD, SARNIA, ON, N7S 3Y6
SIC 1541

168287 CANADA INC p1284
217 AV LEONIDAS S BUREAU 3B, RIMOUSKI, QC, G5L 2T5
(418) 722-9257   SIC 1541

343315 ONTARIO LTD p898
916 LAPOINTE ST, SUDBURY, ON, P3A 5N8
(705) 521-1575   SIC 1541

4001966 MANITOBA LTD p360
176 HAYES RD, THOMPSON, MB, R8N 1M4
(204) 677-4548   SIC 1541

4089171 CANADA INC p833
207 BANK ST SUITE 405, OTTAWA, ON, K2P 2N2
(613) 235-2126   SIC 1541

723926 ONTARIO LIMITED p812
880 FAREWELL ST SUITE 1, OSHAWA, ON, L1H 6N6
(905) 436-2554   SIC 1541

870892 ALBERTA LTD p38
11435 WILKES RD SE, CALGARY, AB, T2J 2E5
(403) 452-3122   SIC 1541

9075-6602 QUEBEC INC p1276
6275 BOUL DE L'ORMIERE, QUEBEC, QC, G2C 1B9
(418) 842-3232   SIC 1541

9123-1878 QUEBEC INC p1140
1190 CH INDUSTRIEL, LEVIS, QC, G7A 1B1
(418) 831-2245   SIC 1541

9165-2214 QUEBEC INC p1044
130 RUE NOTRE-DAME O, ALMA, QC, G8B 2K1
(819) 964-0057   SIC 1541

A.R.G GROUP INC p548
111 CREDITSTONE RD, CONCORD, ON, L4K 1N3
(905) 669-4133   SIC 1541

ACCIONA INFRASTRUCTURE CANADA INC p327
595 BURRARD ST SUITE 2000, VANCOUVER, BC, V7X 1J1
(604) 622-6550   SIC 1541

ACIER FASTECH INC p1124
652 RUE DU PARC, LAC-DROLET, QC, G0Y 1C0
(819) 549-1010   SIC 1541

AECON CONSTRUCTION GROUP INC p997
20 CARLSON CRT SUITE 800, TORONTO,

ON, M9W 7K6
(416) 293-7004   SIC 1541

AECON GROUP INC p581
20 CARLSON CRT SUITE 800, ETOBICOKE, ON, M9W 7K6
(416) 297-2600   SIC 1541

ARTE GROUP INC p20
4300 5 ST NE, CALGARY, AB, T2E 7C3
(403) 640-4559   SIC 1541

ASTALDI CANADA INC p424
358 HAMILTON RIVER RD, HAPPY VALLEY-GOOSE BAY, NL, A0P 1C0
(709) 896-4470   SIC 1541

ATCO TWO RIVERS LODGING CONSTRUCTION LIMITED PARTNERSHIP p73
4838 RICHARD RD SW SUITE 300, CALGARY, AB, T3E 6L1
(403) 662-8500   SIC 1541

B.L.T. CONSTRUCTION SERVICES INC p918
953A EGLINTON AVE E, TORONTO, ON, M4G 4B5
(416) 755-2505   SIC 1541

BEARSPAW CONTRACTING INC p212
2200 BALMER DR SUITE 2, ELKFORD, BC, V0B 1H0
SIC 1541

BEHLEN INDUSTRIES LP p346
927 DOUGLAS ST, BRANDON, MB, R7A 7B3
(204) 728-1188   SIC 1541

BERTRAM CONSTRUCTION & DESIGN LTD p486
25 GEORGE ST UNIT E, BARRIE, ON, L4N 2G5
(705) 726-0254   SIC 1541

BFI CONSTRUCTORS LTD p112
8404 MCINTYRE RD NW, EDMONTON, AB, T6E 6V3
(780) 485-2703   SIC 1541

BLUNDEN CONSTRUCTION (1995) LIMITED p458
519 HERRING COVE RD, HALIFAX, NS, B3R 1X3
(902) 477-2531   SIC 1541

BOREA CONSTRUCTION ULC p1140
562 RUE OLIVIER, LEVIS, QC, G7A 2N6
(418) 626-2314   SIC 1541

BUTLER BUILDINGS CANADA p492
5 HARVEST CRES, BELLEVILLE, ON, K8P 4M2
SIC 1541

BUTTCON HOLDINGS LIMITED p549
8000 JANE ST SUITE 401, CONCORD, ON, L4K 5B8
(905) 907-4242   SIC 1541

BUTTCON LIMITED p549
8000 JANE ST, CONCORD, ON, L4K 5B8
(905) 907-4242   SIC 1541

C.I.F. CONSTRUCTION LTD p250
6171 OTWAY RD, PRINCE GEORGE, BC, V2M 7B4
(250) 564-8174   SIC 1541

CAN-BEC IMMOBILIER INC p1350
1260 RUE PRINCIPALE E, SAINT-PAUL-D'ABBOTSFORD, QC, J0E 1A0
(450) 379-2088   SIC 1541

CANADIAN AUTOMOBILE ASSOCIATION p1213
1180 RUE DRUMMOND BUREAU 610, MONTREAL, QC, H3G 2S1
(855) 861-5750   SIC 1541

CENTRAL BUILDERS' SUPPLY P.G. LIMITED p250
1501 CENTRAL ST W, PRINCE GEORGE, BC, V2N 1P6
(250) 563-1538   SIC 1541

CH2M HILL CONSTRUCTION CANADA, LTD p28
1100 1 ST SE SUITE 1400, CALGARY, AB, T2G 1B1
(403) 232-9800   SIC 1541

CHEVRON CONSTRUCTION SERVICES LTD p519

4475 COUNTY 15 RD, BROCKVILLE, ON, K6V 5T2

(613) 926-0690   *SIC* 1541

CIMS LIMITED PARTNERSHIP   p246
1610 INDUSTRIAL AVE, PORT COQUIT-LAM, BC, V3C 6N3

(604) 472-4300   *SIC* 1541

CJ OILFIELD CONSTRUCTION LTD   p167
4607 42 ST, STETTLER, AB, T0C 2L0

(403) 742-1102   *SIC* 1541

CLEARWATER ENERGY SERVICES LP   p127
355 MACKENZIE BLVD, FORT MCMURRAY, AB, T9H 5E2

(780) 743-2171   *SIC* 1541

CONCORD PROJECTS LTD   p363
1277 HENDERSON HWY SUITE 200, WINNIPEG, MB, R2G 1M3

(204) 339-1651   *SIC* 1541

CONFORM WORKS INC   p47
GD LCD 1, CALGARY, AB, T2P 2G8

(403) 243-2250   *SIC* 1541

CONSORTIUM M.R. CANADA LTEE   p1152
14243 BOUL DU CURE-LABELLE, MIRABEL, QC, J7J 1M2

(514) 328-6060   *SIC* 1541

CONSTRUCTION DERIC INC   p1277
5145 RUE RIDEAU, QUEBEC, QC, G2E 5H5

(418) 781-2228   *SIC* 1541

CONSTRUCTION DINAMO INC   p1119
6023 BOUL WILFRID-HAMEL, L'ANCIENNE-LORETTE, QC, G2E 2H3

(418) 871-6226   *SIC* 1541

CONSTRUCTION L.F.G. INC   p1349
178 RTE 132 E, SAINT-OMER, QC, G0C 2Z0

(418) 364-7082   *SIC* 1541

CONSTRUCTION TALBON INC   p1289
203 BOUL INDUSTRIEL, ROUYN-NORANDA, QC, J9X 6P2

(819) 797-0122   *SIC* 1541

CONSTRUCTIONS EXCEL S.M. INC, LES   p1360
1083 BOUL VACHON N BUREAU 300, SAINTE-MARIE, QC, G6E 1M8

(418) 386-1442   *SIC* 1541

CONSTRUCTIONS PROCO INC   p1377
516 172 RTE O, ST-NAZAIRE-DU-LAC-ST-JEAN, QC, G0W 2V0

(418) 668-3371   *SIC* 1541

CORMODE & DICKSON CONSTRUCTION (1983) LTD   p95
11450 160 ST NW UNIT 200, EDMONTON, AB, T5M 3Y7

(780) 701-9300   *SIC* 1541

COVER ALL NORTH INC   p131
GD LCD MAIN, GRANDE PRAIRIE, AB, T8V 2Z7

(780) 532-0366   *SIC* 1541

CURRAN & HERRIDGE CONSTRUCTION CO., LIMITED   p859
283 CONFEDERATION ST, SARNIA, ON, N7T 2A3

(519) 332-3610   *SIC* 1541

CURRAN CONTRACTORS LTD   p859
283 CONFEDERATION ST, SARNIA, ON, N7T 2A3

(519) 332-3610   *SIC* 1541

D.A. BUILDING SYSTEMS LTD   p140
2808 2 AVE N, LETHBRIDGE, AB, T1H 0C2

(403) 328-4427   *SIC* 1541

DALTON COMPANY LTD, THE   p988
1140 CASTLEFIELD AVE, TORONTO, ON, M6B 1E9

(416) 789-4195   *SIC* 1541

DEFAVERI GROUP CONTRACTING INC   p891
1259 ARVIN AVE, STONEY CREEK, ON, L8E 0H7

(905) 560-2555   *SIC* 1541

DESHAIES & RAYMOND INC   p1098
650 RUE HAGGERTY, DRUMMONDVILLE, QC, J2C 3G6

(819) 472-5486   *SIC* 1541

DINEEN CONSTRUCTION CORPORATION   p583
70 DISCO RD SUITE 300, ETOBICOKE, ON, M9W 1L9

(416) 675-7676   *SIC* 1541

DIVCO LIMITEE   p1170
8300 BOUL PIE-IX, MONTREAL, QC, H1Z 4E8

(514) 593-8888   *SIC* 1541

E.S. FOX LIMITED   p900
1349 KELLY LAKE RD SUITE 1, SUDBURY, ON, P3E 5P5

(705) 522-3357   *SIC* 1541

EBC INC   p1119
1095 RUE VALETS, L'ANCIENNE-LORETTE, QC, G2E 4M7

(418) 872-0600   *SIC* 1541

ELLISDON CONSTRUCTION LTD   p649
2045 OXFORD ST E, LONDON, ON, N5V 2Z7

(519) 455-6770   *SIC* 1541

ELMARA CONSTRUCTION CO. LIMITED   p807
5365 WALKER RD RR 1, OLDCASTLE, ON, N0R 1L0

(519) 737-1253   *SIC* 1541

ELZEN HOLDINGS LTD   p95
11450 160 ST NW SUITE 200, EDMONTON, AB, T5M 3Y7

(780) 453-6944   *SIC* 1541

EMW INDUSTRIAL LTD   p1423
206 COMMERCIAL ST, SALTCOATS, SK, S0A 3R0

(306) 744-1523   *SIC* 1541

ENTREPOTS E.F.C. INC, LES   p1292
50 RUE DES GRANDS-LACS, SAINT-AUGUSTIN-DE-DESMAURES, QC, G3A 2E6

(418) 878-5660   *SIC* 1541

ENTREPRISE DE CONSTRUCTION T.E.Q. INC   p1223
780 AV BREWSTER BUREAU 3-300, MONTREAL, QC, H4C 2K1

(514) 933-3838   *SIC* 1541

EXECWAY CONSTRUCTION LTD   p864
10157 SHEPPARD AVE E, SCARBOROUGH, ON, M1B 1G1

(416) 286-2019   *SIC* 1541

FCA CANADA INC   p499
2000 WILLIAMS PKY, BRAMPTON, ON, L6S 6B3

(905) 458-2800   *SIC* 1541

FDS PRIME ENERGY SERVICES LTD   p130
11870 88 AVE UNIT 148, FORT SASKATCHEWAN, AB, T8L 0K1
   SIC 1541

FEDERATION CONSTRUCTION SERVICES INC   p80
43220 TOWNSHIP RD 634, COLD LAKE, AB, T9M 1N1

(780) 639-0073   *SIC* 1541

FLUOR CONSTRUCTORS CANADA LTD   p69
60 SUNPARK PLAZA SE, CALGARY, AB, T2X 3Y2

(403) 537-4600   *SIC* 1541

FLYNN BROS. PROJECTS INC   p147
8902 95 ST, MORINVILLE, AB, T8R 1K7

(780) 939-3000   *SIC* 1541

FORTIS CONSTRUCTION GROUP INC   p1018
3070 JEFFERSON BLVD, WINDSOR, ON, N8T 3G9

(519) 419-7828   *SIC* 1541

FOURNIER CONSTRUCTION INDUSTRIELLE INC   p1383
3787 BOUL FRONTENAC O, THETFORD MINES, QC, G6H 2B5

(819) 375-2888   *SIC* 1541

FRARE & GALLANT LTEE   p1100
5530 RUE MAURICE-CULLEN, FABREVILLE, QC, H7C 2T3

(450) 664-4590   *SIC* 1541

FRECON CONSTRUCTION LIMITED   p858

1235 RUSSELL RD S, RUSSELL, ON, K4R 1E1

(613) 445-2944   *SIC* 1541

FWS CONSTRUCTION LTD   p388
275 COMMERCE DR, WINNIPEG, MB, R3P 1B3

(204) 487-2500   *SIC* 1541

GANOTEC INC   p1247
3777 RUE DOLLARD-DESJARDINS, POINTE-AUX-TREMBLES, QC, H1B 5W9

(819) 377-5533   *SIC* 1541

GANOTEC WEST ULC   p1
26230 TWP RD 531A UNIT 131, ACHESON, AB, T7X 5A4

(780) 960-7450   *SIC* 1541

GISBORNE INDUSTRIAL CONSTRUCTION LTD   p148
1201 6 ST, NISKU, AB, T9E 7P1
   SIC 1541

GISBORNE INDUSTRIAL CONSTRUCTION LTD   p187
7476 HEDLEY AVE, BURNABY, BC, V5E 2P9

(604) 520-7300   *SIC* 1541

GRAHAM GROUP LTD   p114
8404 MCINTYRE RD NW, EDMONTON, AB, T6E 6V3

(780) 430-9600   *SIC* 1541

GRAHAM GROUP LTD   p1427
875 57TH ST E, SASKATOON, SK, S7K 5Z2

(306) 934-6644   *SIC* 1541

GRAHAM INCOME TRUST   p70
10840 27 ST SE, CALGARY, AB, T2Z 3R6

(403) 570-5000   *SIC* 1541

GROUPE AECON QUEBEC LTEE   p1196
2015 RUE PEEL BUREAU 600, MONTREAL, QC, H3A 1T8

(514) 388-8928   *SIC* 1541

GROUPE GAGNE CONSTRUCTION INC   p1297
22 RUE DES AFFAIRES, SAINT-CHRISTOPHE-D'ARTHABASK, QC, G6R 0B2

(819) 809-2270   *SIC* 1541

GROUPE HONCO INC   p1140
1190 CH INDUSTRIEL, LEVIS, QC, G7A 1B1

(418) 831-2245   *SIC* 1541

GROUPE MONTONI (1995) DIVISION CONSTRUCTION INC   p1134
4115 DES LAURENTIDES (A-15) E, LAVAL-OUEST, QC, H7L 5W5

(450) 978-7500   *SIC* 1541

GVN STRUCTURES INC   p158
1611 BROADWAY AVE E SUITE 1, REDCLIFF, AB, T0J 2P0

(403) 548-3100   *SIC* 1541

HAYMAN, JOHN AND SONS COMPANY, LIMITED, THE   p653
636 WELLINGTON ST, LONDON, ON, N6A 3R9

(519) 433-3966   *SIC* 1541

HMI CONSTRUCTION INC   p1276
6275 BOUL DE L'ORMIERE, QUEBEC, QC, G2C 1B9

(418) 842-3232   *SIC* 1541

I.C.C. INTEGRATED CONSTRUCTION CONCEPTS LTD   p276
12960 84 AVE SUITE 310, SURREY, BC, V3W 1K7

(604) 599-0706   *SIC* 1541

ICON CONSTRUCTION LTD.   p1416
480 HENDERSON DR, REGINA, SK, S4N 6E3

(306) 584-1991   *SIC* 1541

IDEAL CONTRACT SERVICES LTD   p115
9825 45 AVE NW, EDMONTON, AB, T6E 5C8

(780) 463-2424   *SIC* 1541

INGENUITY DEVELOPMENT INC   p717
3800A LAIRD RD UNIT 1, MISSISSAUGA, ON, L5L 0B2

(905) 569-2624   *SIC* 1541

INNOVA GLOBAL LTD   p30

4000 4 ST SE SUITE 222, CALGARY, AB, T2G 2W3

(403) 292-7804   *SIC* 1541

ITW CANADA INVESTMENTS LIMITED PARTNERSHIP   p678
120 TRAVAIL RD, MARKHAM, ON, L3S 3J1

(905) 471-4250   *SIC* 1541

IYINISIW MANAGEMENT INC   p260
10551 SHELLBRIDGE WAY UNIT 100, RICHMOND, BC, V6X 2W9

(604) 249-3969   *SIC* 1541

J D T CONSTRUCTION LTD   p250
9407 PENN RD, PRINCE GEORGE, BC, V2N 5T6

(250) 561-2027   *SIC* 1541

J. EUCLIDE PERRON LTEE   p1079
41 RUE JACQUES-CARTIER E, CHICOUTIMI, QC, G7H 5G6

(418) 543-0715   *SIC* 1541

J.R. MECANIQUE LTEE   p1366
485A BOUL DES ERABLES, SALABERRY-DE-VALLEYFIELD, QC, J6T 6G3

(450) 377-3615   *SIC* 1541

J.V. DRIVER PROJECTS INC   p149
1205 5 ST, NISKU, AB, T9E 7L6

(780) 980-5837   *SIC* 1541

KAWARTHA CAPITAL CORP   p842
580 ASHBURNHAM DR, PETERBOROUGH, ON, K9L 2A2

(705) 750-0440   *SIC* 1541

KBR INDUSTRIAL CANADA CO.   p126
1302 10 ST NISKU, EDMONTON, AB, T9E 8K2

(780) 468-1341   *SIC* 1541

KEMP, JAMES CONSTRUCTION LIMITED   p609
121 VANSITMART AVE, HAMILTON, ON, L8H 3A6

(905) 547-7715   *SIC* 1541

KIEWIT CONSTRUCTION SERVICES ULC   p68
10333 SOUTHPORT RD SW SUITE 200, CALGARY, AB, T2W 3X6

(403) 693-8701   *SIC* 1541

KINGSTON BYERS INC   p1132
9100 RUE ELMSLIE, LASALLE, QC, H8R 1V6

(514) 365-1642   *SIC* 1541

KITNUNA CORPORATION   p472
10 OMILIK ST, CAMBRIDGE BAY, NU, X0B 0C0

(867) 983-7500   *SIC* 1541

KTC INDUSTRIAL ENGINEERING LTD   p277
12877 76 AVE SUITE 218, SURREY, BC, V3W 1E6

(604) 592-3123   *SIC* 1541

LACROIX CONSTRUCTION CO. (SUDBURY) LTD   p898
861 LAPOINTE ST, SUDBURY, ON, P3A 5N8

(705) 566-1294   *SIC* 1541

LAVAL FORTIN LTEE   p1045
130 RUE NOTRE-DAME O, ALMA, QC, G8B 2K1

(418) 668-3321   *SIC* 1541

LEDCOR INDUSTRIAL LIMITED   p115
9910 39 AVE NW, EDMONTON, AB, T6E 5H8

(780) 462-9616   *SIC* 1541

LEVESQUE & ASSOCIES CONSTRUCTION INC   p1277
475 RUE DES CANETONS, QUEBEC, QC, G2E 5X6

(418) 263-0982   *SIC* 1541

LINDSAY CONSTRUCTION LIMITED   p447
134 EILEEN STUBBS AVE UNIT 105, DARTMOUTH, NS, B3B 0A9

(902) 468-5000   *SIC* 1541

LOCKERBIE & HOLE INC   p106
14940 121A AVE NW, EDMONTON, AB, T5V 1A3
   SIC 1541

M J B ENTERPRISES LTD   p145
601 17 ST SW, MEDICINE HAT, AB, T1A

4X6
(403) 527-3600 *SIC 1541*

M. SULLIVAN & SON LIMITED *p479*
236 MADAWASKA BLVD SUITE 100, ARN-PRIOR, ON, K7S 0A3
(613) 623-6584 *SIC 1541*

MAGAL MANUFACTURING LTD *p106*
14940 121A AVE NW, EDMONTON, AB, T5V 1A3
(780) 452-1250 *SIC 1541*

MAISONNEUVE ALUMINIUM INC *p1172*
5477 RUE CHABOT BUREAU 100, MON-TREAL, QC, H2H 1Z1
(514) 523-1155 *SIC 1541*

MANITOU MECHANICAL LTD *p898*
874 LAPOINTE ST, SUDBURY, ON, P3A 5N8
(705) 566-5702 *SIC 1541*

MASTEC CANADA INC *p53*
333 7 AVE SW UNIT 2000, CALGARY, AB, T2P 2Z1
(403) 770-7365 *SIC 1541*

MATASSA INCORPORATED *p807*
5335 WALKER RD, OLDCASTLE, ON, N0R 1L0
(519) 737-1506 *SIC 1541*

MBG BUILDINGS INC *p272*
17957 55 AVE SUITE 102, SURREY, BC, V3S 6C4
(604) 574-6600 *SIC 1541*

MCF HIGHRISE FORMING INC *p1003*
2900 HIGHWAY 7 W, VAUGHAN, ON, L6A 0K9
(416) 988-9235 *SIC 1541*

MECANIQUE CNC (2002) INC *p1066*
1470 RUE GRAHAM-BELL, BOUCHERVILLE, QC, J4B 6H5
(450) 652-6319 *SIC 1541*

MGN CONSTRUCTORS INC *p85*
11760 109 ST NW UNIT W306, EDMON-TON, AB, T5G 2T8
(780) 471-4840 *SIC 1541*

NASON CONTRACTING GROUP LTD *p102*
18304 105 AVE NW SUITE 205, EDMON-TON, AB, T5S 0C6
(780) 460-7142 *SIC 1541*

NEWMAN BROS. LIMITED *p886*
72 WELLAND AVE, ST CATHARINES, ON, L2R 2M9
(905) 641-8111 *SIC 1541*

NEWTON GROUP LTD *p604*
41 MASSEY RD, GUELPH, ON, N1H 7M6
(519) 822-5281 *SIC 1541*

NOBLE CONSTRUCTION CORP *p1406*
215 SUMNER ST, ESTERHAZY, SK, S0A 0X0
(306) 745-6984 *SIC 1541*

NORPAC CONSTRUCTION INC *p217*
5520 CAMPBELL CREEK RD, KAMLOOPS, BC, V2C 6V4
(778) 696-2434 *SIC 1541*

OMICRON CONSULTING GROUP *p329*
595 BURRARD ST, VANCOUVER, BC, V7X 1L4
(604) 632-3350 *SIC 1541*

ONTARIO HARVESTORE SYSTEMS SERVICES INC *p622*
715647 COUNTY RD NW SUITE 4, IN-NERKIP, ON, N0J 1M0
(519) 469-8200 *SIC 1541*

OPUS ONE DESIGN BUILD & CONSTRUCTION PROJECT MANAGEMENT *p768*
6 LANSING SQ SUITE 237, NORTH YORK, ON, M2J 1T5
SIC 1541

PACIFIC BUILDING SYSTEMS INC *p198*
3730 TRANS CANADA HWY, COBBLE HILL, BC, V0R 1L7
(250) 743-5584 *SIC 1541*

PCL CONSTRUCTION GROUP INC *p115*
9915 56 AVE NW SUITE 1, EDMONTON, AB, T6E 5L7
(780) 733-5000 *SIC 1541*

PCL CONSTRUCTORS INC *p116*

9915 56 AVE NW SUITE 1, EDMONTON, AB, T6E 5L7
(780) 733-5000 *SIC 1541*

PCL INDUSTRIAL CONSTRUCTORS INC *p116*
9915 56 AVE NW, EDMONTON, AB, T6E 5L7
(780) 733-5500 *SIC 1541*

PG4 CONSTRUCTION CORP. *p1247*
3777 RUE DOLLARD-DESJARDINS, POINTE-AUX-TREMBLES, QC, H1B 5W9
(514) 354-5533 *SIC 1541*

PHOENIX INDUSTRIAL MAINTENANCE LTD *p149*
903 9 AVE, NISKU, AB, T9E 1C8
(780) 428-3130 *SIC 1541*

PHOENIX RESTORATION INC *p1015*
1100 BURNS ST E, WHITBY, ON, L1N 6M6
(905) 665-7600 *SIC 1541*

PME INC *p130*
8402 116 ST, FORT SASKATCHEWAN, AB, T8L 0G8
(780) 992-2280 *SIC 1541*

POINTS ATHABASCA CONTRACTING LP *p1433*
401 PACKHAM PL, SASKATOON, SK, S7N 2T7
(306) 242-4927 *SIC 1541*

PRE-CON BUILDERS LTD *p353*
4405 FORT WHYTE WAY SUITE 100, OAK BLUFF, MB, R4G 0B1
(204) 633-2515 *SIC 1541*

PRIORITY RESTORATION SERVICES LTD *p372*
1300 CHURCH AVE, WINNIPEG, MB, R2X 1G4
(204) 786-3344 *SIC 1541*

PRODUITS METALLIQUES POULIOT MACHINERIE INC *p1285*
261 AV DU HAVRE, RIMOUSKI, QC, G5M 0B3
(418) 723-2610 *SIC 1541*

PROFAB ENERGY SERVICES INC *p102*
17303 102 AVE NW SUITE 200, EDMON-TON, AB, T5S 1J8
(780) 236-2450 *SIC 1541*

PRYCON CUSTOM BUILDING & RENOVATIONS INC *p488*
36 MORROW RD SUITE 100, BARRIE, ON, L4N 3V8
(705) 739-0023 *SIC 1541*

PYE CONSTRUCTION LTD *p341*
1647 LITTLE RD, VICTORIA, BC, V9E 2E3
(250) 384-2662 *SIC 1541*

QUINAN CONSTRUCTION LIMITED *p810*
55 PROGRESS DR UNIT 1, ORILLIA, ON, L3V 0T7
(705) 325-7704 *SIC 1541*

QUINN CONTRACTING LTD *p6*
27123 1 HWY, BLACKFALDS, AB, T0M 0J0
(403) 885-4788 *SIC 1541*

QX LTD *p717*
4140 SLADEVIEW CRES UNIT 4, MISSIS-SAUGA, ON, L5L 6A1
(905) 828-9055 *SIC 1541*

RAYONIER A.M. COMPAGNIE DE CONSTRUCTION INC *p1207*
4 PLACE VILLE-MARIE BUREAU 100, MONTREAL, QC, H3B 2E7
(514) 871-0137 *SIC 1541*

REASBECK CONSTRUCTION INC *p901*
1085 KELLY LAKE RD, SUDBURY, ON, P3E 5P5
(705) 222-1800 *SIC 1541*

REID & DELEYE CONTRACTORS LTD *p564*
4926 HIGHWAY 59, COURTLAND, ON, N0J 1E0
(519) 688-2600 *SIC 1541*

RENOVATIONS ET RESTAURATION APRES-SINISTRE RENOVCO INC *p1095*
11355 CH COTE-DE-LIESSE, DORVAL, QC, H9P 1B2
(514) 856-9993 *SIC 1541*

RICE TOOL & MANUFACTURING INC *p529*

2247 HAROLD RD, BURLINGTON, ON, L7P 2J7
(905) 335-0181 *SIC 1541*

ROSATI CONSTRUCTION INC *p1026*
6555 MALDEN RD, WINDSOR, ON, N9H 1T5
(519) 734-6511 *SIC 1541*

ROY, G.R. CONSTRUCTION LTD *p913*
GD LCD MAIN, TIMMINS, ON, P4N 7C4
(705) 266-3585 *SIC 1541*

SCHIEDEL CONSTRUCTION INCORPORATED *p537*
405 QUEEN ST W, CAMBRIDGE, ON, N3C 1G6
(519) 658-9317 *SIC 1541*

SCOTT BUILDERS INC *p156*
8105 49 AVE CLOSE, RED DEER, AB, T4P 2V5
(403) 343-7270 *SIC 1541*

SCOTT STEEL ERECTORS INC *p615*
58 BIGWIN RD, HAMILTON, ON, L8W 3R4
(905) 631-8708 *SIC 1541*

SEPT FRERES CONSTRUCTION INC *p1162*
7910 AV MARCO-POLO, MONTREAL, QC, H1E 2S5
(514) 648-0935 *SIC 1541*

SERVCON INC *p854*
25 WEST BEAVER CREEK RD SUITE 13, RICHMOND HILL, ON, L4B 1K2
(905) 881-4300 *SIC 1541*

SHELTER MODULAR INC *p179*
3294 262 ST, ALDERGROVE, BC, V4W 2X2
(604) 856-1311 *SIC 1541*

SIROIS & SONS GENERAL CONTRACTORS *p828*
38 LYNWOOD AVE, OTTAWA, ON, K1Y 2B3
SIC 1541

SKJODT-BARRETT CONTRACT PACKAGING INC *p500*
5 PRECIDIO CRT, BRAMPTON, ON, L6S 6B7
(905) 671-2884 *SIC 1541*

SMITH BROS. & WILSON (B.C.) LTD *p324*
8729 AISNE ST, VANCOUVER, BC, V6P 3P1
(604) 324-1155 *SIC 1541*

SNC-LAVALIN CONSTRUCTORS (PACIFIC) INC *p262*
7400 RIVER RD SUITE 160, RICHMOND, BC, V6X 1X6
SIC 1541

SPRINGHILL CONSTRUCTION LIMITED *p402*
940 SPRINGHILL RD, FREDERICTON, NB, E3C 1R5
(506) 452-0044 *SIC 1541*

STRABAG INC *p727*
6790 CENTURY AVE SUITE 401, MISSIS-SAUGA, ON, L5N 2V8
(905) 353-5500 *SIC 1541*

STUART OLSON INC *p74*
4820 RICHARD RD SW SUITE 600, CAL-GARY, AB, T3E 6L1
(403) 685-7777 *SIC 1541*

STUART OLSON INDUSTRIAL INC *p126*
2627 ELLWOOD DR SW SUITE 201, ED-MONTON, AB, T6X 0P7
(780) 450-9636 *SIC 1541*

STUART OLSON INDUSTRIAL SERVICES LTD *p156*
8024 EDGAR INDUSTRIAL CRES UNIT 102, RED DEER, AB, T4P 3R3
(780) 481-9600 *SIC 1541*

SUNWEST FOODS PROCESSORS LTD *p1011*
35 NORTHLAND RD, WATERLOO, ON, N2V 1Y8
(519) 747-5546 *SIC 1541*

SYSCOMAX INC *p1060*
1060 BOUL MICHELE-BOHEC BUREAU 106, BLAINVILLE, QC, J7C 5E2
(450) 434-0008 *SIC 1541*

SYSTEMATIC MILL INSTALLATIONS LTD *p223*

1226 ST. PAUL ST, KELOWNA, BC, V1Y 2C8
(236) 420-4041 *SIC 1541*

TERRA GRAIN FUELS INC *p1404*
5 KM N KALIUM RD, BELLE PLAINE, SK, S0G 0G0
(306) 345-2280 *SIC 1541*

TESC CONTRACTING COMPANY LTD *p899*
874 LAPOINTE ST, SUDBURY, ON, P3A 5N8
(705) 566-5702 *SIC 1541*

TRIPLE CROWN ENTERPRISES LTD *p610*
665 PARKDALE AVE N, HAMILTON, ON, L8H 5Z1
(905) 540-1630 *SIC 1541*

TUCKER HI-RISE CONSTRUCTION INC *p878*
3755 VICTORIA PARK AVE, SCARBOR-OUGH, ON, M1W 3Z4
(416) 441-2730 *SIC 1541*

URBACON LIMITED *p921*
750 LAKE SHORE BLVD E, TORONTO, ON, M4M 3M3
(416) 865-9405 *SIC 1541*

URBACON LIMITED *p921*
750 LAKE SHORE BLVD E, TORONTO, ON, M4M 3M3
(416) 865-9405 *SIC 1541*

VERREAULT INC *p1192*
1080 COTE DU BEAVER HALL BUREAU 800, MONTREAL, QC, H2Z 1S8
(514) 845-4104 *SIC 1541*

VIEWORX GEOPHOTO INC *p133*
8716 108 ST UNIT 112, GRANDE PRAIRIE, AB, T8V 4C7
(780) 532-3353 *SIC 1541*

WESTERN INDUSTRIAL CONTRACTORS LTD *p249*
4912 HART HWY, PRINCE GEORGE, BC, V2K 3A1
(250) 962-6011 *SIC 1541*

WESTLAND CONSTRUCTION LTD *p393*
475 DOVERCOURT DR UNIT 1, WIN-NIPEG, MB, R3Y 1G4
(204) 633-6272 *SIC 1541*

WILLOWRIDGE CONSTRUCTION LTD *p130*
11870 88 AVE UNIT 148, FORT SASKATCHEWAN, AB, T8L 0K1
(780) 998-9133 *SIC 1541*

WOODALL CONSTRUCTION CO. LIMITED
p1022
620 NORTH SERVICE RD E, WINDSOR, ON, N8X 3J3
(519) 966-3381 *SIC 1541*

SIC 1542 Nonresidential construction, nec

1148044 ONTARIO LTD *p754*
1250 JOURNEY'S END CIR SUITE 1, NEW-MARKET, ON, L3Y 0B9
(905) 830-6026 *SIC 1542*

1471899 ALBERTA LTD *p92*
13040 148 ST, EDMONTON, AB, T5L 2H8
(780) 460-2399 *SIC 1542*

1514505 ONTARIO INC *p625*
240 TERENCE MATTHEWS CRES SUITE 101, KANATA, ON, K2M 2C4
(613) 592-1114 *SIC 1542*

152610 CANADA INC *p748*
43 AURIGA DR, NEPEAN, ON, K2E 7Y8
(800) 565-2874 *SIC 1542*

176026 CANADA INC *p1001*
134 SAINT PAUL ST UNIT 2A, VANIER, ON, K1L 6A3
(613) 742-7550 *SIC 1542*

2412-8779 QUEBEC INC *p1077*
121 RUE DUBUC, CHIBOUGAMAU, QC, G8P 2H4
(418) 748-4785 *SIC 1542*

305466 B.C. LTD *p191*
8155 NORTH FRASER WAY UNIT 100, BURNABY, BC, V5J 5M8
(604) 435-1220 *SIC 1542*

3469051 CANADA INC p1216
9680 BOUL SAINT-LAURENT, MONTREAL, QC, H3L 2M9
(514) 388-8080   *SIC* 1542

3TWENTY SOLUTIONS INC p1435
36 CAPITAL CIR, SASKATOON, SK, S7R 0H4
(306) 382-3320   *SIC* 1542

416818 ALBERTA LTD p86
10012 JASPER AVE NW, EDMONTON, AB, T5J 1R2
(780) 428-1505   *SIC* 1542

511670 ALBERTA LTD p112
4220 98 ST NW SUITE 201, EDMONTON, AB, T6E 6A1
(780) 466-1262   *SIC* 1542

511670 ALBERTA LTD p1419
845 BROAD ST SUITE 205, REGINA, SK, S4R 8G9
(306) 525-1644   *SIC* 1542

6089585 CANADA LTD p364
500 CAMIEL SYS ST, WINNIPEG, MB, R2J 4K2
(204) 663-2866   *SIC* 1542

9028-7939 QUEBEC INC p1093
117 AV LINDSAY, DORVAL, QC, H9P 2S6
(514) 636-1676   *SIC* 1542

9124-4905 QUEBEC INC p1140
1019 CH INDUSTRIEL, LEVIS, QC, G7A 1B3
(418) 831-1019   *SIC* 1542

9149-8980 QUEBEC INC p1233
1683 RUE TAILLEFER, MONTREAL, QC, H7L 1T9
(514) 467-9555   *SIC* 1542

9275-0181 QUEBEC INC p1284
290 RUE MICHAUD UNITE 101, RIMOUSKI, QC, G5L 6A4
(418) 722-9257   *SIC* 1542

A.P.M. LANDMARK INC p1040
16 MCCARVILLE ST, CHARLOTTETOWN, PE, C1E 2A6
(902) 569-8400   *SIC* 1542

ABCOTT CONSTRUCTION LTD p515
124 GARDEN AVE, BRANTFORD, ON, N3S 7W4
(519) 756-4350   *SIC* 1542

ABOVE BOARD CONSTRUCTION INC p844
1731 ORANGEBROOK CRT, PICKERING, ON, L1W 3G8
(905) 420-0656   *SIC* 1542

ACADIAN CONSTRUCTION (1991) LTD p397
671 BOUL MALENFANT SUITE 2, DIEPPE, NB, E1A 5T8
(506) 857-1909   *SIC* 1542

ACCEL HIGH RISE CONSTRUCTION LTD p978
66 PORTLAND ST SUITE 801, TORONTO, ON, M5V 2M6
SIC 1542

ACROSS CANADA CONSTRUCTION LTD p1029
220 REGINA RD, WOODBRIDGE, ON, L4L 8L6
(905) 264-9500   *SIC* 1542

AECON INDUSTRIAL WESTERN INC p104
14940 121A AVE NW, EDMONTON, AB, T5V 1A3
(780) 452-1250   *SIC* 1542

ALBERICI CONSTRUCTORS, LTD p529
1005 SKYVIEW DR SUITE 300, BURLINGTON, ON, L7P 5B1
(905) 315-3000   *SIC* 1542

ALBERTA CONSTRUCTION GROUP CORP p13
6565 40 ST SE UNIT 11, CALGARY, AB, T2C 2J9
(587) 349-3000   *SIC* 1542

ALFRED HORIE CONSTRUCTION CO. LTD p184
3830 1ST AVE, BURNABY, BC, V5C 3W1
(604) 291-8156   *SIC* 1542

ALLAN CONSTRUCTION p1433
317 103 ST E, SASKATOON, SK, S7N 1Y9

ALLAN CONSTRUCTION CO. LTD p1433
317 103RD ST E, SASKATOON, SK, S7N 1Y9
(306) 477-5520   *SIC* 1542

AMEC CONSTRUCTION INC p1121
312 RUE JOSEPH-GAGNE S, LA BAIE, QC, G7B 3P6
(418) 544-8885   *SIC* 1542

ANDRE, T. A. & SONS (ONTARIO) LIMITED p629
30 RIGNEY ST, KINGSTON, ON, K7K 6Z2
(613) 549-8060   *SIC* 1542

ANJINNOV CONSTRUCTION INC p1246
13550 BOUL HENRI-BOURASSA E, POINTE-AUX-TREMBLES, QC, H1A 0A4
(514) 353-3000   *SIC* 1542

APM CONSTRUCTION SERVICES INC p1040
16 MCCARVILLE ST, CHARLOTTETOWN, PE, C1E 2A6
(902) 569-8400   *SIC* 1542

AQUICON CONSTRUCTION CO. LTD p501
131 DELTA PARK BLVD SUITE 1, BRAMPTON, ON, L6T 5M8
(905) 458-1313   *SIC* 1542

ARCAN GROUP INC p435
112 TALTHEILEI DR, YELLOWKNIFE, NT, X1A 0E9
(867) 873-2520   *SIC* 1542

ARCHEVEQUE & RIVEST LTEE, L' p1282
96 BOUL INDUSTRIEL, REPENTIGNY, QC, J6A 4X6
(450) 581-4480   *SIC* 1542

ARMOUR-CLAD CONTRACTING INC p99
18035 114 AVE NW, EDMONTON, AB, T5S 1T8
SIC 1542

ARTEK GROUP LIMITED, THE p274
12140 103A AVE, SURREY, BC, V3V 7Y9
(604) 584-2131   *SIC* 1542

ARTISTIC STUCCO LTD p81
GD, DE WINTON, AB, T0L 0X0
(403) 888-7412   *SIC* 1542

ASCO CONSTRUCTION LTD p619
1125 TUPPER ST UNIT 1, HAWKESBURY, ON, K6A 3T5
(613) 632-0121   *SIC* 1542

ATEK DEVELOPMENTS INC p153
6320 50 AVE UNIT 405, RED DEER, AB, T4N 4C6
(403) 342-4885   *SIC* 1542

ATLAS CORPORATION, THE p549
111 ORTONA CRT, CONCORD, ON, L4K 3M3
(905) 669-6825   *SIC* 1542

ATLAS PAINTING & RESTORATIONS LTD p253
5020 NO. 7 RD, RICHMOND, BC, V6V 1R7
(604) 244-8244   *SIC* 1542

AVANTAGE PLUS INC p1171
5420 RUE CHAPLEAU, MONTREAL, QC, H2G 2E4
(514) 525-2000   *SIC* 1542

AVONDALE CONSTRUCTION LIMITED p458
49 HOBSONS LAKE DR, HALIFAX, NS, B3S 0E4
(902) 876-1818   *SIC* 1542

AXIM CONSTRUCTION INC p1317
650 RUE BOUCHER BUREAU 106, SAINT-JEAN-SUR-RICHELIEU, QC, J3B 7Z8
(450) 358-3885   *SIC* 1542

AXOR CONSTRUCTION CANADA INC p1193
1555 RUE PEEL BUREAU 1100, MONTREAL, QC, H3A 3L8
(514) 846-4000   *SIC* 1542

B.M.I. CONSTRUCTION CO. LIMITED p844
1058 COPPERSTONE DR SUITE 1, PICKERING, ON, L1W 3V8
(905) 686-4287   *SIC* 1542

BALL CONSTRUCTION INC p635
5 SHIRLEY AVE, KITCHENER, ON, N2B 2E6

(519) 742-5851   *SIC* 1542

BASECRETE INC p1030
396 CHRISLEA RD, WOODBRIDGE, ON, L4L 8A8
(905) 265-9983   *SIC* 1542

BDA INC p570
12 DRUMMOND ST SUITE 1, ETOBICOKE, ON, M8V 1Y8
(416) 251-1757   *SIC* 1542

BEAUVAIS & VERRET INC p1263
2181 RUE LEON-HARMEL, QUEBEC, QC, G1N 4N5
(418) 688-1336   *SIC* 1542

BELANGER, R.M. LIMITED p543
100 RADISSON AVE, CHELMSFORD, ON, P0M 1L0
(705) 855-4555   *SIC* 1542

BELROCK CONSTRUCTION GENERAL CONTRACTOR LIMITED p549
185 ADESSO DR, CONCORD, ON, L4K 3C4
(905) 669-9481   *SIC* 1542

BENCHMARK BUILDING SYSTEMS LTD p200
145 SCHOOLHOUSE ST SUITE 13, COQUITLAM, BC, V3K 4X8
(604) 524-6533   *SIC* 1542

BENOIT JOBIN INC p1284
25 RUE SAINT-GERMAIN E, RIMOUSKI, QC, G5L 1A3
(418) 725-0742   *SIC* 1542

BETCO ENTERPRISES LTD p403
120 MCLEAN AVE, HARTLAND, NB, E7P 2K5
(506) 375-4671   *SIC* 1542

BGL CONTRACTORS CORP p1010
608 COLBY DR, WATERLOO, ON, N2V 1A2
(519) 725-5000   *SIC* 1542

BIASUCCI DEVELOPMENTS INC p863
544 WELLINGTON ST W, SAULT STE. MARIE, ON, P6C 3T6
(705) 946-8701   *SIC* 1542

BINDER CONSTRUCTION LIMITED p95
11635 160 ST NW, EDMONTON, AB, T5M 3Z3
(780) 452-2740   *SIC* 1542

BIRD CONSTRUCTION COMPANY p381
1055 ERIN ST, WINNIPEG, MB, R3G 2X1
(204) 775-7141   *SIC* 1542

BIRD CONSTRUCTION COMPANY LIMITED p257
6900 GRAYBAR RD SUITE 2370, RICHMOND, BC, V6W 0A5
(604) 271-4600   *SIC* 1542

BIRD CONSTRUCTION COMPANY LIMITED p692
5700 EXPLORER DR SUITE 400, MISSISSAUGA, ON, L4W 0C6
(905) 602-4122   *SIC* 1542

BIRD CONSTRUCTION INC p692
5700 EXPLORER DR SUITE 400, MISSISSAUGA, ON, L4W 0C6
(905) 602-4122   *SIC* 1542

BLACKIE CONSTRUCTION INC p713
2133 ROYAL WINDSOR DR UNIT 22, MISSISSAUGA, ON, L5J 1K5
SIC 1542

BLAIS & LANGLOIS INC p1398
345 RUE CARTIER, VICTORIAVILLE, QC, G6R 1E3
(819) 739-2905   *SIC* 1542

BLUEBIRD INVESTMENTS LIMITED p423
12 DUGGAN ST, GRAND FALLS-WINDSOR, NL, A2A 2K6
(709) 489-5403   *SIC* 1542

BOCKSTAEL CONSTRUCTION LIMITED p365
100 PAQUIN RD UNIT 200, WINNIPEG, MB, R2J 3V4
(204) 233-7135   *SIC* 1542

BOLESS INC p1107
15 RUE BUTEAU BUREAU 220, GATINEAU, QC, J8Z 1V4
(819) 770-3028   *SIC* 1542

BOND CONSTRUCTION INC p127
295 MACDONALD CRES, FORT MCMURRAY, AB, T9H 4B7
(780) 743-3448   *SIC* 1542

BONDFIELD CONSTRUCTION COMPANY LIMITED p549
407 BASALTIC RD, CONCORD, ON, L4K 4W8
(416) 667-8422   *SIC* 1542

BORETTA CONSTRUCTION 2002 LTD p365
1383 DUGALD RD, WINNIPEG, MB, R2J 0H3
(204) 237-7375   *SIC* 1542

BRANDT GROUP OF COMPANIES,THE p1423
3710 EASTGATE DR SUITE 1, REGINA, SK, S4Z 1A5
(306) 347-1499   *SIC* 1542

BRENTA CONSTRUCTION INC p183
2810 NORLAND AVE, BURNABY, BC, V5B 3A6
(604) 430-5887   *SIC* 1542

BROCCOLINI CONSTRUCTION (TORONTO) INC p692
2680 MATHESON BLVD E SUITE 104, MISSISSAUGA, ON, L4W 0A5
(416) 242-7772   *SIC* 1542

BROOK RESTORATION LTD p582
11 KELFIELD ST, ETOBICOKE, ON, M9W 5A1
(416) 663-7976   *SIC* 1542

BROUWER CONSTRUCTION (1981) LTD p885
1880 KING ST, ST CATHARINES, ON, L2R 6P7
(905) 984-3060   *SIC* 1542

BUILD IT BY DESIGN (2014) INC p737
1580 TRINITY DR UNIT 12, MISSISSAUGA, ON, L5T 1L6
(905) 696-0468   *SIC* 1542

CAD CONSTRUCTION LTD p421
19 SAWDUST ROAD, BAY ROBERTS, NL, A0A 1G0
SIC 1542

CAMDON CONSTRUCTION LTD p155
6780 76 ST, RED DEER, AB, T4P 4G6
(403) 343-1233   *SIC* 1542

CAMPBELL CONSTRUCTION LTD p338
559 KELVIN RD, VICTORIA, BC, V8Z 1C4
(250) 475-1300   *SIC* 1542

CAN MAR CONTRACTING LIMITED p583
169 CITY VIEW DR, ETOBICOKE, ON, M9W 5B1
(416) 674-8791   *SIC* 1542

CANA CONSTRUCTION CO. LTD p34
5720 4 ST SE SUITE 100, CALGARY, AB, T2H 1K7
(403) 255-5521   *SIC* 1542

CANADIAN TURNER CONSTRUCTION COMPANY LTD p942
48 YONGE ST, TORONTO, ON, M5E 1G6
(416) 607-8300   *SIC* 1542

CANNING CONTRACTING LIMITED p738
525 ABILENE DR, MISSISSAUGA, ON, L5T 2H7
SIC 1542

CANPRO CONSTRUCTION LTD p338
555 DUPPLIN RD, VICTORIA, BC, V8Z 1C2
(250) 475-0975   *SIC* 1542

CANUS CONSTRUCTION INC p93
13030 146 ST NW, EDMONTON, AB, T5L 2H7
SIC 1542

CARBON CONSTRUCTORS INC p28
3915 8 ST SE, CALGARY, AB, T2G 3A5
(403) 203-4900   *SIC* 1542

CARLSON, G. W. CONSTRUCTION LTD p233
78 ESPLANADE, NANAIMO, BC, V9R 4Y8
SIC 1542

CASMAN BUILDING SOLUTIONS INC p127
330 MACKENZIE BLVD, FORT MCMURRAY, AB, T9H 4C4
(780) 791-9283   *SIC* 1542

CASTLE ROCK CONTRACTING LTD *p167*
967 BOULDER BLVD SUITE 101, STONY PLAIN, AB, T7Z 0E7
(780) 968-6828 *SIC* 1542

CAVAN CONTRACTORS LTD *p113*
3722 91 ST NW, EDMONTON, AB, T6E 5M3
(780) 462-5311 *SIC* 1542

CB PARTNERS CORPORATION *p108*
4703 52 AVE NW, EDMONTON, AB, T6B 3R6
(780) 395-3300 *SIC* 1542

CDC CONSTRUCTION LTD *p291*
16 4TH AVE W SUITE 300, VANCOUVER, BC, V5Y 1G3
(604) 873-6656 *SIC* 1542

CENTCOM CONSTRUCTION LTD *p34*
7220 FISHER ST SE SUITE 310, CALGARY, AB, T2H 2H8
(403) 252-5571 *SIC* 1542

CENTRE LEASEHOLD IMPROVEMENTS LIMITED *p843*
1315 PICKERING PKY UNIT 205, PICKERING, ON, L1V 7G5
(905) 492-6131 *SIC* 1542

CENTRON CONSTRUCTION LIMITED *p39*
8826 BLACKFOOT TRAIL SE UNIT 104, CALGARY, AB, T2J 3J1
(403) 252-1120 *SIC* 1542

CENTRON GROUP OF COMPANIES INC *p39*
8826 BLACKFOOT TRAIL SE SUITE 104, CALGARY, AB, T2J 3J1
(403) 252-1120 *SIC* 1542

CERIKO ASSELIN LOMBARDI INC *p1333*
3005 RUE HALPERN, SAINT-LAURENT, QC, H4S 1P5
(514) 956-5511 *SIC* 1542

CGV BUILDERS INC *p545*
56 CONNAUGHT AVE, COCHRANE, ON, P0L 1C0
(705) 272-5404 *SIC* 1542

CHANDOS CONSTRUCTION LTD *p120*
9604 20 AVE NW, EDMONTON, AB, T6N 1G1
(780) 436-8617 *SIC* 1542

CHEYENNE HOLDINGS INC *p185*
3855 HENNING DR SUITE 109, BURNABY, BC, V5C 6N3
(604) 291-9000 *SIC* 1542

CHIMO CONSTRUCTION (2014) LIMITED *p429*
136 CROSBIE RD SUITE 409, ST. JOHN'S, NL, A1B 3K3
(709) 739-5900 *SIC* 1542

CITY PROJECTS LTD *p185*
4483 JUNEAU ST, BURNABY, BC, V5C 4C4
(604) 874-5566 *SIC* 1542

CLARK, RON AND ASSOCIATES (2006) INC *p280*
2195 KING GEORGE BLVD, SURREY, BC, V4A 5A3
SIC 1542

CLIFFORD MASONRY (ONTARIO) LIMITED *p870*
1190 BIRCHMOUNT RD, SCARBOROUGH, ON, M1P 2B8
(416) 691-2341 *SIC* 1542

CLIFFORD RESTORATION LIMITED *p871*
1190 BIRCHMOUNT RD, SCARBOROUGH, ON, M1P 2B8
(416) 691-2341 *SIC* 1542

COAST INDUSTRIAL CONSTRUCTION LTD *p251*
110 1ST AVE W SUITE 260, PRINCE RUPERT, BC, V8J 1A8
(250) 624-4327 *SIC* 1542

COFFRAGE ALLIANCE LTEE *p1083*
2000 RUE DE LIERRE, COTE SAINT-LUC, QC, H7G 4Y4
(514) 326-5200 *SIC* 1542

COLLABORATIVE STRUCTURES LIMITED *p537*
6683 ELLIS RD, CAMBRIDGE, ON, N3C 2V4
(519) 658-2750 *SIC* 1542

COMINAR CONSTRUCTION S.E.C. *p1271*
2820 BOUL LAURIER BUREAU 850, QUEBEC, QC, G1V 0C1
(418) 681-8151 *SIC* 1542

COMPASS CONSTRUCTION RESOURCES LTD *p988*
2700 DUFFERIN ST UNIT 77, TORONTO, ON, M6B 4J3
(416) 789-9819 *SIC* 1542

CON-PRO INDUSTRIES CANADA LTD *p365*
765 MARION ST, WINNIPEG, MB, R2J 0K6
(204) 233-3717 *SIC* 1542

CONCORD ADEX INC *p979*
23 SPADINA AVE, TORONTO, ON, M5V 3M5
(416) 813-0333 *SIC* 1542

CONSTRUCTION ALBERT JEAN LTEE *p1174*
4045 RUE PARTHENAIS, MONTREAL, QC, H2K 3T8
(514) 522-2121 *SIC* 1542

CONSTRUCTION AUBIN, LAVAL LTEE *p1379*
1470 RUE NATIONALE, TERREBONNE, QC, J6W 6M1
(514) 640-0622 *SIC* 1542

CONSTRUCTION BERTRAND DIONNE INC *p1098*
1555 RUE JANELLE, DRUMMONDVILLE, QC, J2C 5S5
(819) 472-2559 *SIC* 1542

CONSTRUCTION BROCCOLINI INC *p1117*
16766 RTE TRANSCANADIENNE UNITE 500, KIRKLAND, QC, H9H 4M7
(514) 737-0076 *SIC* 1542

CONSTRUCTION BSL INC *p1292*
315 RUE DE ROTTERDAM, SAINT-AUGUSTIN-DE-DESMAURES, QC, G3A 2E5
(418) 878-4448 *SIC* 1542

CONSTRUCTION CITADELLE INC *p1254*
419 RUE DES MONTEREGIENNES, QUEBEC, QC, G1C 7J7
(418) 661-9351 *SIC* 1542

CONSTRUCTION CYBCO INC *p1338*
7089 RTE TRANSCANADIENNE, SAINT-LAURENT, QC, H4T 1A2
(514) 284-2228 *SIC* 1542

CONSTRUCTION G. THERRIEN 2010 INC *p1242*
3885 BOUL LOUIS-FRECHETTE, NICOLET, QC, J3T 1T7
(819) 293-6921 *SIC* 1542

CONSTRUCTION GERATEK LTEE *p1373*
535 RUE PEPIN, SHERBROOKE, QC, J1L 1X3
(819) 564-2933 *SIC* 1542

CONSTRUCTION GILLES LANTHIER INC *p1144*
2119 RUE SAINTE-HELENE, LONGUEUIL, QC, J4K 3T5
(450) 670-8238 *SIC* 1542

CONSTRUCTION IDEAL DE GRANBY INC *p1110*
65 RUE SAINT-JUDE S, GRANBY, QC, J2J 2N2
(450) 378-2301 *SIC* 1542

CONSTRUCTION IRENEE PAQUET & FILS INC *p1172*
1300 RUE SAINT-ZOTIQUE E, MONTREAL, QC, H2G 1G5
(514) 273-3910 *SIC* 1542

CONSTRUCTION J.C. LEPAGE LTEE *p1284*
569 RUE DE LAUSANNE, RIMOUSKI, QC, G5L 4A7
(418) 724-4239 *SIC* 1542

CONSTRUCTION JULIEN DALPE INC *p1360*
350 CH DES PRES, SAINTE-MARIE-SALOME, QC, J0K 2Z0
(450) 754-2059 *SIC* 1542

CONSTRUCTION LECLERC & PELLETIER INC *p1367*
475 AV PERREAULT, SEPT-ILES, QC, G4R 1K6

(418) 962-2499 *SIC* 1542

CONSTRUCTION LONGER INC *p1373*
175 RUE LEGER, SHERBROOKE, QC, J1L 1M2
(819) 564-0115 *SIC* 1542

CONSTRUCTION MARIEVILLE INC *p1149*
2010 RUE DU PONT, MARIEVILLE, QC, J3M 1J9
(450) 460-7955 *SIC* 1542

CONSTRUCTION PASCAL *p1051*
8020 BOUL METROPOLITAIN E, ANJOU, QC, H1K 1A1
(514) 493-1054 *SIC* 1542

CONSTRUCTION RENO-GAUTHIER ENTREPRENEUR GENERAL INC *p1073*
1266 RUE DE VIMY, CANTON TREMBLAY, QC, G7G 5H8
(418) 543-8602 *SIC* 1542

CONSTRUCTION SOCAM LTEE *p1233*
3300 AV FRANCIS-HUGHES, MONTREAL, QC, H7L 5A7
(450) 662-9000 *SIC* 1542

CONSTRUCTION VERGO 2011 INC *p1361*
1463 RUE BERLIER, SAINTE-ROSE, QC, H7L 3Z1
(450) 967-2220 *SIC* 1542

CONSTRUCTIONS BE-CON INC, LES *p1279*
1054 BOUL BASTIEN BUREAU 418, QUEBEC, QC, G2K 1E6
(418) 626-3583 *SIC* 1542

CONSTRUCTIONS BELAND & LAPOINTE INC, LES *p1140*
723 CH INDUSTRIEL, LEVIS, QC, G7A 1B5
(418) 831-8638 *SIC* 1542

CONSTRUCTIONS BINET INC, LES *p1294*
227 RTE 271, SAINT-BENOIT-LABRE, QC, G0M 1P0
(418) 228-1578 *SIC* 1542

CONSTRUCTIONS DANIEL LOISELLE INC, LES *p1312*
1350 AV ST-JACQUES, SAINT-HYACINTHE, QC, J2S 6M6
SIC 1542

CONSTRUCTIONS DE CASTEL INC, LES *p1076*
265 BOUL INDUSTRIEL, CHATEAUGUAY, QC, J6J 4Z2
(450) 699-2036 *SIC* 1542

CONSTRUCTIONS DE MAUSOLEES CARRIER INC, LES *p1333*
7575 BOUL THIMENS, SAINT-LAURENT, QC, H4S 2A2
(514) 832-3733 *SIC* 1542

CONSTRUCTIONS E. HUOT INC *p1135*
15 RUE DE L'ARENA BUREAU 400, LEVIS, QC, G6J 0B1
(418) 836-7310 *SIC* 1542

CONSTRUCTIONS FGP INC, LES *p1294*
33 MONTEE ROBERT, SAINT-BASILE-LE-GRAND, QC, J3N 1L7
(450) 441-2727 *SIC* 1542

CONSTRUCTIONS METHODEX INC, LES *p1080*
676 RUE DES ACTIONNAIRES, CHICOUTIMI, QC, G7J 5A8
(418) 545-2280 *SIC* 1542

CONSTRUCTIONS PEPIN ET FORTIN INC, LES *p1398*
371 AV PIE-X, VICTORIAVILLE, QC, G6R 0L6
(819) 357-9274 *SIC* 1542

CONSTRUCTIONS PLACO INC, LES *p1078*
2700 BOUL TALBOT BUREAU 41, CHICOUTIMI, QC, G7H 5B1
(418) 545-3362 *SIC* 1542

CONSTRUCTIONS RICOR INC *p1113*
1214 RUE DE L'ESCALE, HAVRE-SAINT-PIERRE, QC, G0G 1P0
(418) 538-3201 *SIC* 1542

COOPER CONSTRUCTION LIMITED *p796*
2381 BRISTOL CIR SUITE C-200, OAKVILLE, ON, L6H 5S9
(905) 829-0444 *SIC* 1542

COOPER, R J CONSTRUCTION LTD *p250*

1937 OGILVIE ST S, PRINCE GEORGE, BC, V2N 1X2
(250) 563-4649 *SIC* 1542

CORNERSTONE BUILDERS LTD *p491*
195 BELLEVUE DR, BELLEVILLE, ON, K8N 4Z5
(613) 968-3501 *SIC* 1542

CORNERSTONE STRUCTRUAL RESTORATION INC *p639*
85 EDWIN ST, KITCHENER, ON, N2H 4N7
(519) 745-8121 *SIC* 1542

CORPORATE CONTRACTING SERVICES LTD *p473*
575 WESTNEY RD S, AJAX, ON, L1S 4N7
(416) 291-8644 *SIC* 1542

COSOLTEC INC *p1086*
3080 BOUL LE CARREFOUR, COTE SAINT-LUC, QC, H7T 2R5
(450) 682-0000 *SIC* 1542

COWDEN-WOODS DESIGN BUILDERS LTD *p486*
249 SAUNDERS RD UNIT 1, BARRIE, ON, L4N 9A3
(705) 721-8422 *SIC* 1542

CRAWFORD GENERAL CONTRACTING INC *p1017*
507 BIRKDALE CRT, WINDSOR, ON, N8N 4B3
(519) 567-8411 *SIC* 1542

CRT-HAMEL *p1136*
870 RUE ARCHIMEDE, LEVIS, QC, G6V 7M5
(418) 833-8073 *SIC* 1542

CY RHEAULT CONSTRUCTION LTD *p912*
273 THIRD AVE SUITE 404, TIMMINS, ON, P4N 1E2
(705) 268-3445 *SIC* 1542

D. GRANT CONSTRUCTION LIMITED *p662*
9887 LONGWOODS RD, LONDON, ON, N6P 1P2
(519) 652-2949 *SIC* 1542

D.G.S. CONSTRUCTION COMPANY LTD *p270*
13761 116 AVE UNIT A101, SURREY, BC, V3R 0T2
(604) 584-2214 *SIC* 1542

DAKON CONSTRUCTION LTD *p1010*
275 FROBISHER DR UNIT 1, WATERLOO, ON, N2V 2G4
(519) 746-0920 *SIC* 1542

DALCON INC *p1272*
2820 BOUL LAURIER BUREAU 1050, QUEBEC, QC, G1V 0C1
(418) 781-6300 *SIC* 1542

DALREN LIMITED *p545*
8781 DALE RD, COBOURG, ON, K9A 4J9
(905) 377-1080 *SIC* 1542

DAOUST, PAUL CONSTRUCTION GROUP INC *p596*
5424 CANOTEK RD, GLOUCESTER, ON, K1J 1E9
(613) 590-1694 *SIC* 1542

DARWIN CONSTRUCTION (CANADA) LTD *p238*
197 FORESTER ST SUITE 404, NORTH VANCOUVER, BC, V7H 0A6
(604) 929-7944 *SIC* 1542

DAVIAN CONSTRUCTION LTD *p380*
740 LOGAN AVE, WINNIPEG, MB, R3E 1M9
(204) 783-7251 *SIC* 1542

DAWSON WALLACE CONSTRUCTION LTD *p109*
4611 ELENIAK RD NW, EDMONTON, AB, T6B 2N1
(780) 466-8700 *SIC* 1542

DECAREL INC *p1402*
4434 RUE SAINTE-CATHERINE O, WESTMOUNT, QC, H3Z 1R2
(514) 935-6462 *SIC* 1542

DEGELDER CONSTRUCTION CO. (2010) LTD *p318*
1455 GEORGIA ST W SUITE 100, VANCOUVER, BC, V6G 2T3

(604) 688-1515   *SIC* 1542
DELGANT CONSTRUCTION LIMITED *p494*
7 MARCONI CRT, BOLTON, ON, L7E 1H3
(905) 857-7858   *SIC* 1542
DELMAR CONSTRUCTION LIMITED *p471*
77 PARADE ST SUITE 1, YARMOUTH, NS, B5A 3B3
(902) 742-4672   *SIC* 1542
DELNOR CONSTRUCTION LTD *p109*
3609 74 AVE NW, EDMONTON, AB, T6B 2T7
(780) 469-1304   *SIC* 1542
DEMAN CONSTRUCTION CORP *p703*
776 DUNDAS ST E SUITE 201, MISSISSAUGA, ON, L4Y 2B6
(905) 277-0363   *SIC* 1542
DEVITT & FORAND CONTRACTORS INC *p35*
5716 BURBANK CRES SE, CALGARY, AB, T2H 1Z6
(403) 255-8565   *SIC* 1542
DIAMOND PARK BUILDERS (2004) INC *p128*
425 GREGOIRE DR SUITE 600, FORT MCMURRAY, AB, T9H 4K7
SIC 1542
DIASER MANAGEMENT (2006) LTD *p373*
268 ELLEN ST, WINNIPEG, MB, R3A 1A7
(204) 943-8855   *SIC* 1542
DIXON, M.J. CONSTRUCTION LIMITED *p708*
2600 EDENHURST DR SUITE 200, MISSISSAUGA, ON, L5A 3Z8
(905) 270-7770   *SIC* 1542
DOMCO CONSTRUCTION INC *p1415*
860 PARK ST, REGINA, SK, S4N 4Y3
(306) 721-8500   *SIC* 1542
DOMM CONSTRUCTION LTD *p483*
563 LOUISA ST, AYTON, ON, N0G 1C0
(519) 665-7848   *SIC* 1542
DOORNEKAMP, H. R. CONSTRUCTION LTD *p806*
588 SCOTLAND RD, ODESSA, ON, K0H 2H0
(613) 386-3033   *SIC* 1542
DORA CONSTRUCTION LIMITED *p446*
60 DOREY AVE SUITE 101, DARTMOUTH, NS, B3B 0B1
(902) 468-2941   *SIC* 1542
DOUBLE V CONSTRUCTION LTD *p276*
13303 78 AVE SUITE 406, SURREY, BC, V3W 5B9
(604) 590-3131   *SIC* 1542
DOWNS CONSTRUCTION LTD *p339*
870 DEVONSHIRE RD, VICTORIA, BC, V9A 4T6
(250) 384-1390   *SIC* 1542
DUNMAC GENERAL CONTRACTORS LTD *p1427*
3038 FAITHFULL AVE, SASKATOON, SK, S7K 0B1
(306) 934-3044   *SIC* 1542
DURA CONSTRUCTION LTD *p1415*
555 MCDONALD ST, REGINA, SK, S4N 4X1
(306) 721-6866   *SIC* 1542
E.K. CONSTRUCTION 2000 LTD *p371*
11 YARD ST, WINNIPEG, MB, R2W 5J6
(204) 589-8387   *SIC* 1542
EASTERN CONSTRUCTION COMPANY LIMITED *p875*
2075 KENNEDY RD SUITE 1200, SCARBOROUGH, ON, M1T 3V3
(416) 497-7110   *SIC* 1542
EBC-SM (NUNAVUT), S.E.N.C. *p1119*
1095 RUE VALETS, L'ANCIENNE-LORETTE, QC, G2E 4M7
(418) 872-0600   *SIC* 1542
EDENVALE RESTORATION SPECIALISTS LTD *p196*
8465 HARVARD PL SUITE 5, CHILLIWACK, BC, V2P 7Z5
(604) 795-4884   *SIC* 1542
EDWARD COLLINS CONTRACTING LIM-

ITED *p424*
2 GUY ST, JERSEYSIDE, NL, A0B 2G0
(709) 227-5509   *SIC* 1542
ELAN CONSTRUCTION LIMITED *p8*
3639 27 ST NE SUITE 100, CALGARY, AB, T1Y 5E4
(403) 291-1165   *SIC* 1542
ELLIS-DON CONSTRUCTION LTD *p703*
1004 MIDDLEGATE RD SUITE 1000, MISSISSAUGA, ON, L4Y 1M4
(877) 980-4821   *SIC* 1542
ELLISDON CONSTRUCTION SERVICES INC *p649*
2045 OXFORD ST E, LONDON, ON, N5V 2Z7
(519) 455-6770   *SIC* 1542
ELLISDON CORPORATION *p649*
2045 OXFORD ST E, LONDON, ON, N5V 2Z7
(519) 455-6770   *SIC* 1542
ELLISDON FORMING LTD *p649*
2045 OXFORD ST E, LONDON, ON, N5V 2Z7
(519) 455-6770   *SIC* 1542
ELLISDON HOLDINGS INC *p649*
2045 OXFORD ST E, LONDON, ON, N5V 2Z7
(519) 455-6770   *SIC* 1542
ENTREPRISES DE CONSTRUCTION BONNEAU, GUY LTEE, LES *p1090*
100 RUE BOULIANNE, DOLBEAU-MISTASSINI, QC, G8L 5L4
(418) 276-2301   *SIC* 1542
ENTREPRISES J.G GUIMOND INC, LES *p1235*
143 RUE DE LA STATION, MONTREAL, QC, H7M 3W1
(450) 663-7155   *SIC* 1542
ENTREPRISES N.G.A. INC, LES *p1098*
350 RUE ROCHELEAU, DRUMMONDVILLE, QC, J2C 7S7
(819) 477-6891   *SIC* 1542
ERIE GREENHOUSE STRUCTURES INC *p911*
500 HWY 3 UNIT 2, TILLSONBURG, ON, N4G 4G8
(519) 688-6809   *SIC* 1542
ERNST HANSCH CONSTRUCTION LTD *p365*
3 TERRACON PL, WINNIPEG, MB, R2J 4B3
(204) 233-7881   *SIC* 1542
ESTIMATIONS DE CONSTRUCTION DU QUEBEC INC *p1217*
78 RUE DE PORT-ROYAL E, MONTREAL, QC, H3L 1H7
SIC 1542
EURO-TECH CONSTRUCTION INC *p75*
855 ARBOUR LAKE RD NW, CALGARY, AB, T3G 5J2
(403) 457-1277   *SIC* 1542
EVERTRUST DEVELOPMENT GROUP CANADA INC *p670*
3100 STEELES AVE E SUITE 302, MARKHAM, ON, L3R 8T3
(647) 501-2345   *SIC* 1542
FABRICATION BEAUCE-ATLAS INC *p1360*
600 1RE AV DU PARC-INDUSTRIEL, SAINTE-MARIE, QC, G6E 1B5
(418) 387-4872   *SIC* 1542
FARMER CONSTRUCTION LTD *p339*
360 HARBOUR RD, VICTORIA, BC, V9A 3S1
(250) 388-5121   *SIC* 1542
FCNQ CONSTRUCTION INC *p1053*
19400 AV CLARK-GRAHAM, BAIE-D'URFE, QC, H9X 3R8
(514) 457-9375   *SIC* 1542
FILLMORE CONSTRUCTION MANAGEMENT INC *p114*
9114 34A AVE NW, EDMONTON, AB, T6E 5P4
(780) 430-0005   *SIC* 1542
FINN WAY GENERAL CONTRACTOR INC

p910
1301 WALSH ST W, THUNDER BAY, ON, P7E 4X6
(807) 767-2426   *SIC* 1542
FITZGERALD & SNOW (2010) LTD *p1042*
190 GREENWOOD DR, SUMMERSIDE, PE, C1N 4K2
(902) 436-9256   *SIC* 1542
FLATIRON BUILDING GROUP INC *p574*
37 ADVANCE RD UNIT 101, ETOBICOKE, ON, M8Z 2S6
(416) 749-3957   *SIC* 1542
FLOOD, JOHN & SONS (1961) LIMITED *p413*
32 FREDERICK ST, SAINT JOHN, NB, E2J 2A9
(506) 634-1112   *SIC* 1542
FORREC LTD *p991*
219 DUFFERIN ST SUITE 100C, TORONTO, ON, M6K 3J1
(416) 696-8686   *SIC* 1542
FORT MCKAY METIS GROUP LTD *p128*
GD LCD MAIN, FORT MCMURRAY, AB, T9H 3E2
(780) 828-4581   *SIC* 1542
FREY BROTHERS LIMITED *p619*
3435 BROADWAY ST, HAWKESVILLE, ON, N0B 1X0
(519) 699-4641   *SIC* 1542
FRONT CONSTRUCTION INDUSTRIES INC *p1026*
740 MORTON DR UNIT 1, WINDSOR, ON, N9J 3V2
(519) 250-8229   *SIC* 1542
FULLER, THOMAS CONSTRUCTION CO. LIMITED *p830*
2700 QUEENSVIEW DR, OTTAWA, ON, K2B 8H6
(613) 820-6000   *SIC* 1542
FWS COMMERCIAL PROJECTS LTD *p393*
475 DOVERCOURT DR, WINNIPEG, MB, R3Y 1G4
(204) 487-2500   *SIC* 1542
FWS HOLDINGS INC *p388*
275 COMMERCE DR, WINNIPEG, MB, R3P 1B3
(204) 487-2500   *SIC* 1542
G. V. INTERIOR CONTRACTORS LTD *p695*
5446 GORVAN DR, MISSISSAUGA, ON, L4W 3E8
SIC 1542
G.S. WARK LIMITED *p613*
370 YORK BLVD SUITE 101, HAMILTON, ON, L8R 3L1
(905) 529-4717   *SIC* 1542
GABRIEL CONSTRUCTION LTD *p1416*
234 E 11TH AVE, REGINA, SK, S4N 6G8
(306) 757-1399   *SIC* 1542
GABRIEL MILLER INC *p1264*
1850 RUE PROVINCIALE, QUEBEC, QC, G1N 4A2
(418) 628-5550   *SIC* 1542
GAP CONSTRUCTION CO. LTD *p763*
1310 FRANKLIN ST, NORTH BAY, ON, P1B 2M3
(705) 474-3730   *SIC* 1542
GAROY CONSTRUCTION INC *p1256*
4000 BOUL SAINTE-ANNE, QUEBEC, QC, G1E 3M5
(418) 661-1754   *SIC* 1542
GARRITANO BROS. LTD *p812*
881 NELSON ST, OSHAWA, ON, L1H 5N7
(905) 576-8642   *SIC* 1542
GATEWAY CONSTRUCTION & ENGINEERING LTD *p365*
434 ARCHIBALD ST, WINNIPEG, MB, R2J 0X5
(204) 233-8550   *SIC* 1542
GESTION TECHNIQUE D'IMMEUBLES *p1049*
9000 RUE DE L'INNOVATION, ANJOU, QC, H1J 2X9
(514) 354-6666   *SIC* 1542
GGS STRUCTURES INC *p1003*

3559 NORTH SERVICE RD, VINELAND STATION, ON, L0R 2E0
(905) 562-7341   *SIC* 1542
GLOUCESTER CONSTRUCTION LTD *p419*
4260 RUE PRINCIPALE, TRACADIE-SHEILA, NB, E1X 1B9
SIC 1542
GOODON, IRVIN INDUSTRIES LTD *p346*
HWY 10, BOISSEVAIN, MB, R0K 0E0
(204) 534-2468   *SIC* 1542
GRAHAM CONSTRUCTION AND ENGINEERING INC *p70*
10840 27 ST SE, CALGARY, AB, T2Z 3R6
(403) 570-5000   *SIC* 1542
GRAHAM CONSTRUCTION AND ENGINEERING LP *p70*
10840 27 ST SE, CALGARY, AB, T2Z 3R6
(403) 570-5000   *SIC* 1542
GRAHAM GROUP LTD *p70*
10840 27 ST SE, CALGARY, AB, T2Z 3R6
(403) 570-5000   *SIC* 1542
GRAND CONSTRUCTION LTD *p228*
4539 210A ST, LANGLEY, BC, V3A 8Z3
(604) 530-1931   *SIC* 1542
GREENOUGH, L C CONSTRUCTION LTD *p120*
2503 PARSONS RD NW, EDMONTON, AB, T6N 1B8
(780) 463-4977   *SIC* 1542
GREENWOOD READY MIX LIMITED *p808*
HWY 9, ORANGEVILLE, ON, L9W 2Y9
(519) 941-0710   *SIC* 1542
GREER CONTRACTING LTD *p192*
6955 BULLER AVE, BURNABY, BC, V5J 4S1
(604) 438-3550   *SIC* 1542
GREYBACK CONSTRUCTION LTD *p243*
402 WARREN AVE E, PENTICTON, BC, V2A 3M2
(250) 493-7972   *SIC* 1542
GREYFIELD CONSTRUCTION CO LTD *p480*
15185 YONGE ST SUITE 200, AURORA, ON, L4G 1L8
(905) 713-0999   *SIC* 1542
GROSSI, T. & SON CONSTRUCTION LTD *p644*
33 PRINCESS ST UNIT 204, LEAMINGTON, ON, N8H 5C5
(519) 326-9081   *SIC* 1542
GROUPE AXOR INC *p1196*
1555 RUE PEEL BUREAU 1100, MONTREAL, QC, H3A 3L8
(514) 846-4000   *SIC* 1542
GROUPE C. & G. BEAULIEU INC *p1294*
368 BOUL GRAND E, SAINT-BASILE-LE-GRAND, QC, J3N 1M4
(450) 653-9581   *SIC* 1542
GROUPE CIRTECH INC *p1075*
660 RUE NOTRE-DAME BUREAU 100, CHARETTE, QC, G0X 1E0
(819) 221-3400   *SIC* 1542
GROUPE DRUMCO CONSTRUCTION INC, LE *p1096*
4825 RTE 139, DRUMMONDVILLE, QC, J2A 4E5
(819) 474-5035   *SIC* 1542
GROUPE GEYSER INC *p1362*
205 BOUL CURE-LABELLE BUREAU 201, SAINTE-ROSE, QC, H7L 2Z9
(450) 625-2003   *SIC* 1542
GROUPE PICHE CONSTRUCTION INC *p1102*
99 12E RUE BUREAU 204, FERME-NEUVE, QC, J0W 1C0
(819) 587-3193   *SIC* 1542
GROUPE UNIGESCO INC *p1397*
3900 RUE COOL, VERDUN, QC, H4G 1B4
(514) 360-1509   *SIC* 1542
HABITATIONS CONSULTANTS H.L. INC *p1256*
104 RUE SEIGNEURIALE, QUEBEC, QC, G1E 4Y5
(418) 666-1324   *SIC* 1542
HALSE-MARTIN CONSTRUCTION CO. LTD

p241
1636 MCGUIRE AVE, NORTH VANCOUVER, BC, V7P 3B1
(604) 980-4811   *SIC* 1542
HARBRIDGE & CROSS LIMITED   p553
350 CREDITSTONE RD SUITE 202, CONCORD, ON, L4K 3Z2
(905) 738-0051   *SIC* 1542
HEATHERBRAE BUILDERS CO. LTD   p263
12371 HORSESHOE WAY UNIT 140, RICHMOND, BC, V7A 4X6
(604) 277-2315   *SIC* 1542
HELMER, MAX CONSTRUCTION LTD   p216
1000 PANORAMA DR RR 7, INVERMERE, BC, V0A 1K7
(250) 342-6767   *SIC* 1542
HFH INC   p569
6006 HWY 6, ELORA, ON, N0B 1S0
(519) 821-2040   *SIC* 1542
HIGGINS, ROBERT (1984) COMPANY LIMITED   p468
205 MAIN ST, TRENTON, NS, B0K 1X0
(902) 755-5515   *SIC* 1542
HINAN, T.R. CONSTRUCTION LIMITED p885
31 CHURCH ST, ST CATHARINES, ON, L2R 3B7
SIC 1542
HIPPERSON CONSTRUCTION COMPANY (1996) LIMITED   p1418
2161 SCARTH ST UNIT 200, REGINA, SK, S4P 2H8
(306) 359-0303   *SIC* 1542
HODGSON, KING AND MARBLE LIMITED p260
4200 VANGUARD RD, RICHMOND, BC, V6X 2P4
(604) 247-2422   *SIC* 1542
IDL PROJECTS INC   p250
1088 GREAT ST, PRINCE GEORGE, BC, V2N 2K8
(250) 649-0561   *SIC* 1542
INDUSTRIES BLAIS INC, LES   p1289
155 BOUL INDUSTRIEL, ROUYN-NORANDA, QC, J9X 6P2
(819) 764-3284   *SIC* 1542
INSIGHT TECHNOLOGIES CONSTRUCTION CORP   p580
6817 STEELES AVE W, ETOBICOKE, ON, M9V 4R9
(416) 745-8228   *SIC* 1542
IRONCLAD METALS INC   p226
6325 204 ST UNIT 312, LANGLEY, BC, V2Y 3B3
(604) 539-0112   *SIC* 1542
ISLAND WEST COAST DEVELOPMENTS LTD   p234
2214 MCCULLOUGH RD, NANAIMO, BC, V9S 4M8
(250) 756-9665   *SIC* 1542
ITC CONSTRUCTION CANADA INC   p299
564 BEATTY ST SUITE 800, VANCOUVER, BC, V6B 2L3
(604) 685-0111   *SIC* 1542
J. FLORIS CONSTRUCTION LTD   p175
2776 BOURQUIN CRES W SUITE 204, ABBOTSFORD, BC, V2S 6A4
(604) 864-6471   *SIC* 1542
JCB ENTREPRENEURS GENERAUX INC p1070
3875 RUE ISABELLE, BROSSARD, QC, J4Y 2R2
(450) 444-8151   *SIC* 1542
JEN-COL CONSTRUCTION LTD.   p1
9620 266 ST SUITE 100, ACHESON, AB, T7X 6H6
(780) 963-6523   *SIC* 1542
JES CONSTRUCTION LTD   p1277
5145 RUE RIDEAU BUREAU 200, QUEBEC, QC, G2E 5H5
(418) 874-0007   *SIC* 1542
JOHNSTON BUILDERS LTD   p165
265 CARLETON DR UNIT 201, ST. ALBERT, AB, T8N 4J9
(780) 460-0441   *SIC* 1542

JONELJIM CONCRETE CONSTRUCTION (1994) LIMITED   p467
90 RIVERVIEW DR, SYDNEY, NS, B1S 1N5
(902) 567-2400   *SIC* 1542
JONES, TOM CORPORATION   p908
560 SQUIER ST, THUNDER BAY, ON, P7B 4A8
(807) 345-0511   *SIC* 1542
JR CERTUS CONSTRUCTION CO. LTD p1027
81 ZENWAY BLVD UNIT 3, WOODBRIDGE, ON, L4H 0S5
(647) 494-0150   *SIC* 1542
K-RITE CONSTRUCTION LTD   p93
12849 148 ST NW, EDMONTON, AB, T5L 2H9
(780) 452-6291   *SIC* 1542
K.D.S. CONSTRUCTION LTD   p279
16250 20 AVE, SURREY, BC, V3Z 9M8
(604) 535-8152   *SIC* 1542
K.F. CONSTRUCTION INC   p1363
1410 RUE DE JAFFA BUREAU 201, SAINTE-ROSE, QC, H7P 4K9
(450) 681-8338   *SIC* 1542
KAMCO CONSTRUCTION INC   p1122
149 RUE DU PARC-DE-L'INNOVATION, LA POCATIERE, QC, G0R 1Z0
(418) 856-5432   *SIC* 1542
KELLER CONSTRUCTION LTD   p96
11430 160 ST NW, EDMONTON, AB, T5M 3Y7
(780) 484-1010   *SIC* 1542
KENMORE MANAGEMENT INC   p886
151 JAMES ST, ST CATHARINES, ON, L2R 5C4
SIC 1542
KENSTRUCT LTD   p837
24533 PARK RD, PEFFERLAW, ON, L0E 1N0
(416) 505-9737   *SIC* 1542
KERR, WILLIAM J LTD   p405
365 WELLINGTON ST, MIRAMICHI, NB, E1N 1P6
SIC 1542
KETZA CONSTRUCTION CORP   p1440
107 PLATINUM RD, WHITEHORSE, YT, Y1A 5M3
(867) 668-5997   *SIC* 1542
KETZA PACIFIC CONSTRUCTION (1993) LTD   p195
2990 ISLAND HWY, CAMPBELL RIVER, BC, V9W 2H5
(250) 850-2002   *SIC* 1542
KIEWIT/FLATIRON GENERAL PARTNERSHIP   p314
1111 GEORGIA ST W SUITE 1410, VANCOUVER, BC, V6E 4M3
SIC 1542
KINETIC CONSTRUCTION LTD   p337
862 CLOVERDALE AVE SUITE 201, VICTORIA, BC, V8X 2S8
(250) 381-6331   *SIC* 1542
KINGDOM CATS LTD   p81
108 CHRISTINA LAKE DR, CONKLIN, AB, T0P 1H1
(780) 715-4356   *SIC* 1542
KNIGHT, CONTRACTING LTD   p338
37 CADILLAC AVE, VICTORIA, BC, V8Z 1T3
(250) 475-2595   *SIC* 1542
KOCH FARMS/AGRI-SALES INC   p567
LOT 5 CONCESSION 3, EARLTON, ON, P0J 1E0
(705) 563-8325   *SIC* 1542
KOR-ALTA CONSTRUCTION LTD   p122
2461 76 AVE NW, EDMONTON, AB, T6P 1Y8
(780) 440-6661   *SIC* 1542
KRAWFORD CONSTRUCTION INC   p112
8055 ARGYLL RD NW, EDMONTON, AB, T6C 4A9
(780) 436-4381   *SIC* 1542
KUDLIK CONSTRUCTION LTD   p472
1519 FEDERAL RD, IQALUIT, NU, X0A 0H0

(867) 979-1166   *SIC* 1542
L J C CLEANING SERVICES INC   p818
740 BELFAST RD UNIT B, OTTAWA, ON, K1G 0Z5
(613) 244-1997   *SIC* 1542
L.C. ENTREPRENEURS GENERAUX (2000) LTEE   p1062
4045 RUE LAVOISIER, BOISBRIAND, QC, J7H 1N1
(450) 682-1951   *SIC* 1542
L.C. ENTREPRENEURS GENERAUX (2000) LTEE   p1062
4045 RUE LAVOISIER, BOISBRIAND, QC, J7H 1N1
(450) 682-1951   *SIC* 1542
LADSON PROPERTIES LIMITED   p887
235 MARTINDALE RD UNIT 14, ST CATHARINES, ON, L2W 1A5
(905) 684-6542   *SIC* 1542
LARK PROJECTS LTD   p275
13737 96 AVE SUITE 1500, SURREY, BC, V3V 0C6
(604) 576-2935   *SIC* 1542
LCL BUILDS CORPORATION   p776
98 SCARSDALE RD, NORTH YORK, ON, M3B 2R7
(416) 492-0500   *SIC* 1542
LEAR CONSTRUCTION SERVICES INC p24
4200 10 ST NE, CALGARY, AB, T2E 6K3
(403) 250-3818   *SIC* 1542
LEDCOR CONSTRUCTION LIMITED   p306
1067 CORDOVA ST W SUITE 1200, VANCOUVER, BC, V6C 1C7
(604) 681-7500   *SIC* 1542
LEDCOR CONSTRUCTION LIMITED   p314
1055 HASTINGS ST W SUITE 1500, VANCOUVER, BC, V6E 2E9
(604) 646-2493   *SIC* 1542
LEESWOOD DESIGN BUILD LTD   p724
7200 WEST CREDIT AVE, MISSISSAUGA, ON, L5N 5N1
(416) 309-4482   *SIC* 1542
LEEVILLE CONSTRUCTION LTD   p1411
340 8TH AVE NW, MOOSE JAW, SK, S6H 4E7
(306) 692-0677   *SIC* 1542
LEXON PROJECTS INC   p122
2327 91 AVE NW, EDMONTON, AB, T6P 1L1
(780) 435-7476   *SIC* 1542
LIMA'S GARDENS & CONSTRUCTION INC p793
116 TORYORK DR, NORTH YORK, ON, M9L 1X6
(416) 740-9837   *SIC* 1542
LOGAN STEVENS CONSTRUCTION (2000) LTD   p1438
200 YORK RD E, YORKTON, SK, S3N 4E4
(306) 782-2266   *SIC* 1542
LRG CONSTRUCTION LTD   p189
5655 MONARCH ST, BURNABY, BC, V5G 2A2
(604) 291-2135   *SIC* 1542
M. D. STEELE CONSTRUCTION LTD p393
193 HENLOW BAY, WINNIPEG, MB, R3Y 1G4
(204) 488-7070   *SIC* 1542
MAGIL CONSTRUCTION ONTARIO INC p649
1665 OXFORD ST E, LONDON, ON, N5V 2Z5
(519) 451-5270   *SIC* 1542
MAGIL CONSTRUCTION ONTARIO INC p697
5285 SOLAR DR UNIT 102, MISSISSAUGA, ON, L4W 5B8
(905) 890-9193   *SIC* 1542
MALO, GILLES INC   p1243
100 RUE DES ENTREPRISES, NOTRE-DAME-DES-PRAIRIES, QC, J6E 0L9
(450) 757-2424   *SIC* 1542
MAN-SHIELD (ALTA) CONSTRUCTION INC p161
201 KASKA RD UNIT 167, SHERWOOD

PARK, AB, T8A 2J6
(780) 467-2601   *SIC* 1542
MANEL CONTRACTING LTD   p795
41 RIVALDA RD, NORTH YORK, ON, M9M 2M4
(416) 635-0876   *SIC* 1542
MANORCORE CONSTRUCTION INC   p490
4707 CHRISTIE DR, BEAMSVILLE, ON, L0R 1B4
(905) 563-8888   *SIC* 1542
MANORCORE GROUP INC   p490
4707 CHRISTIE DR, BEAMSVILLE, ON, L0R 1B4
(905) 563-8888   *SIC* 1542
MAPLE-REINDERS INC   p724
2660 ARGENTIA RD, MISSISSAUGA, ON, L5N 5V4
(905) 821-4844   *SIC* 1542
MARANT CONSTRUCTION LIMITED   p918
200 WICKSTEED AVE, TORONTO, ON, M4G 2B6
(416) 425-6650   *SIC* 1542
MARCEL CHAREST ET FILS INC   p1349
997 RTE 230 E, SAINT-PASCAL, QC, G0L 3Y0
(418) 492-5911   *SIC* 1542
MARESCO LIMITED   p555
171 BASALTIC RD UNIT 2, CONCORD, ON, L4K 1G4
(905) 669-5700   *SIC* 1542
MARFOGLIA CONSTRUCTION INC   p1049
9031 BOUL PARKWAY, ANJOU, QC, H1J 1N4
(514) 325-8700   *SIC* 1542
MATHESON CONSTRUCTORS LIMITED p481
205 INDUSTRIAL PKWY N UNIT 5, AURORA, ON, L4G 4C4
(905) 669-7999   *SIC* 1542
MAXIM 2000 INC   p414
555 SOMERSET ST UNIT 208, SAINT JOHN, NB, E2K 4X2
(506) 652-9292   *SIC* 1542
MAXIM CONSTRUCTION INC   p414
555 SOMERSET ST UNIT 208, SAINT JOHN, NB, E2K 4X2
(506) 652-9292   *SIC* 1542
MAYLAN CONSTRUCTION SERVICES INC p619
372 BERTHA ST, HAWKESBURY, ON, K6A 2A8
(613) 632-5553   *SIC* 1542
MCGUIRE, J.J. GENERAL CONTRACTORS INC   p813
880 FAREWELL ST SUITE 1, OSHAWA, ON, L1H 6N6
(905) 436-2554   *SIC* 1542
MCMULLEN & WARNOCK INC   p872
70 CROCKFORD BLVD, SCARBOROUGH, ON, M1R 3C3
SIC 1542
MELLOUL-BLAMEY CONSTRUCTION INC p1010
700 RUPERT ST, WATERLOO, ON, N2V 2B5
(519) 886-8850   *SIC* 1542
MERIT CONTRACTORS NIAGARA   p887
235 MARTINDALE RD SUITE 3, ST CATHARINES, ON, L2W 1A5
(905) 641-2374   *SIC* 1542
MERKLEY SUPPLY LIMITED   p828
100 BAYVIEW RD, OTTAWA, ON, K1Y 4L6
(613) 728-2693   *SIC* 1542
METTKO CONSTRUCTION INC   p768
200 YORKLAND BLVD SUITE 610, NORTH YORK, ON, M2J 5C1
(416) 444-9600   *SIC* 1542
MICHANIE CONSTRUCTION INC   p816
2825 SHEFFIELD RD SUITE 201, OTTAWA, ON, K1B 3V8
(613) 737-7717   *SIC* 1542
MID-WEST DESIGN & CONSTRUCTION LTD   p146
1065 30 ST SW, MEDICINE HAT, AB, T1B

3N3

(403) 526-0925 *SIC 1542*

MIDOME CONSTRUCTION SERVICES LTD p555

665 MILLWAY AVE SUITE 65, CONCORD, ON, L4K 3T8

(905) 738-2211 *SIC 1542*

MIELE ENTERPRISES INC p504

87 WENTWORTH CRT, BRAMPTON, ON, L6T 5L4

(416) 740-1096 *SIC 1542*

MIERAU CONSTRUCTION LTD p177

30444 GREAT NORTHERN AVE SUITE 201, ABBOTSFORD, BC, V2T 6Y6

(604) 850-3536 *SIC 1542*

MIHIR INTERNATIONAL p865

531 MEADOWVALE RD, SCARBOROUGH, ON, M1C 1S7

(416) 989-2445 *SIC 1542*

MILNE & NICHOLLS LIMITED p672

7270 WOODBINE AVE SUITE 200, MARKHAM, ON, L3R 4B9

(905) 513-9700 *SIC 1542*

MINERS CONSTRUCTION CO. LTD p1425

440 MELVILLE ST, SASKATOON, SK, S7J 4M2

(306) 934-4703 *SIC 1542*

MIRTREN CONTRACTORS LIMITED p999

18 STOCKDALE RD, TRENTON, ON, K8V 5P6

(613) 392-6511 *SIC 1542*

MODERN GROUNDS MAINTENANCE LTD p225

9702 216 ST, LANGLEY, BC, V1M 3J2

(604) 888-4999 *SIC 1542*

MOORE, MIKE & SONS CONSTRUCTION LTD p863

167 INDUSTRIAL COURT B UNIT A, SAULT STE. MARIE, ON, P6B 5Z9

(705) 759-3173 *SIC 1542*

MOOSE BAND DEVELOPMENT CORPORA-TION p746

22 JONATHAN THETHOO, MOOSE FAC-TORY, ON, P0L 1W0

(705) 658-4335 *SIC 1542*

MORGAN, W. S. CONSTRUCTION LIMITED p837

19 BOWES ST, PARRY SOUND, ON, P2A 2K7

(705) 746-9686 *SIC 1542*

MYTON PROJECT MANAGEMENT LIMITED p455

5555 YOUNG ST, HALIFAX, NS, B3K 1Z7

SIC 1542

NAHANNI CONSTRUCTION LTD p436

100 NAHANNI DR, YELLOWKNIFE, NT, X1A 0E8

(867) 873-2975 *SIC 1542*

NDL CONSTRUCTION LTD p357

83 SYMINGTON LN S, SPRINGFIELD, MB, R2J 3R8

(204) 255-7300 *SIC 1542*

NEW CITY SERVICES GROUP INC. p186

4170 STILL CREEK DR SUITE 200, BURN-ABY, BC, V5C 6C6

(604) 473-7769 *SIC 1542*

NEWCO CONSTRUCTION LTD p409

50 ROONEY CRES, MONCTON, NB, E1E 4M3

(506) 857-8710 *SIC 1542*

NORDMEC CONSTRUCTION INC p1159

390 RUE SIMEON BUREAU 3, MONT-TREMBLANT, QC, J8E 2R2

(819) 429-5555 *SIC 1542*

NORLON BUILDERS LONDON LIMITED p654

151 YORK ST, LONDON, ON, N6A 1A8

(519) 672-7590 *SIC 1542*

NORSON CONSTRUCTION LLP p241

949 3RD ST W SUITE 221, NORTH VAN-COUVER, BC, V7P 3P7

(604) 986-5681 *SIC 1542*

NORTHTOWN STRUCTURAL LTD p495

18 SIMPSON RD, BOLTON, ON, L7E 1G9

(905) 951-6317 *SIC 1542*

NOYE ENTERPRISES INC p1043

87 OTTAWA ST, SUMMERSIDE, PE, C1N 1W2

SIC 1542

OGESCO CONSTRUCTION INC p1274

3070 CH DES QUATRE-BOURGEOIS, QUEBEC, QC, G1W 2K4

(418) 651-8774 *SIC 1542*

OMICRON CONSTRUCTION MANAGE-MENT LTD p329

595 BURRARD ST, VANCOUVER, BC, V7X 1L4

(604) 632-3350 *SIC 1542*

OPUS CORPORATION p68

5119 ELBOW DR SW UNIT 500, CALGARY, AB, T2V 1H2

(403) 209-5555 *SIC 1542*

ORION MANAGEMENT & CONSTRUCTION INC p415

479 ROTHESAY AVE, SAINT JOHN, NB, E2L 4G7

(519) 634-5717 *SIC 1542*

P&C GENERAL CONTRACTING LTD p673

250 SHIELDS CRT SUITE 24, MARKHAM, ON, L3R 9W7

(905) 479-3015 *SIC 1542*

P. & R. DESJARDINS CONSTRUCTION INC p1330

1777 RUE BEGIN, SAINT-LAURENT, QC, H4R 2B5

(514) 748-1234 *SIC 1542*

PARAGON REMEDIATION GROUP LTD p282

8815 HARVIE RD, SURREY, BC, V4N 4B9

(604) 513-1324 *SIC 1542*

PARKWEST PROJECTS LTD p357

1077 OXFORD ST W, SPRINGFIELD, MB, R2C 2Z2

(204) 654-9314 *SIC 1542*

PARKWOOD CONSTRUCTION LTD p199

1404 ROSS AVE, COQUITLAM, BC, V3J 2K1

(604) 936-2792 *SIC 1542*

PAX CONSTRUCTION LTD p186

4452 JUNEAU ST, BURNABY, BC, V5C 4C8

(604) 291-8885 *SIC 1542*

PBL PROJECTS LP p393

405 FORT WHYTE WAY UNIT 100, WIN-NIPEG, MB, R4G 0B1

(204) 633-2515 *SIC 1542*

PCL CONSTRUCTORS CANADA INC p750

49 AURIGA DR, NEPEAN, ON, K2E 8A1

(613) 225-6130 *SIC 1542*

PCL CONSTRUCTORS CANADA INC p798

2201 BRISTOL CIR SUITE 500, OAKVILLE, ON, L6H 0J8

(905) 276-7600 *SIC 1542*

PCL CONSTRUCTORS NORTHERN INC p116

9915 56 AVE NW SUITE 1, EDMONTON, AB, T6E 5L7

(780) 733-5000 *SIC 1542*

PENN-CO CONSTRUCTION CANADA LTD p346

25 PENNER DR, BLUMENORT, MB, R0A 0C0

(204) 326-1341 *SIC 1542*

PENN-CO CONSTRUCTION INT'L LTD p346

16 CENTRE AVE, BLUMENORT, MB, R0A 0C0

(204) 326-1341 *SIC 1542*

PERCON CONSTRUCTION INC p587

20 AIRVIEW RD, ETOBICOKE, ON, M9W 4P2

(416) 744-9967 *SIC 1542*

PERHOL CONSTRUCTION LTD p910

1450 ROSSLYN RD, THUNDER BAY, ON, P7E 6W1

(807) 474-0930 *SIC 1542*

PERMASTEEL PROJECTS LTD p102

17430 103 AVE NW, EDMONTON, AB, T5S 2K8

(780) 452-7281 *SIC 1542*

PETROCOM CONSTRUCTION LTD p102

17505 109A AVE NW, EDMONTON, AB, T5S 2W4

(780) 481-5181 *SIC 1542*

PHOENIX CONSTRUCTION INC p156

7887 50 AVE SUITE 8, RED DEER, AB, T4P 1M8

(403) 342-2225 *SIC 1542*

PHOENIX PETROLEUM LTD p400

400 THOMPSON DR, FREDERICTON, NB, E3A 9X2

(506) 459-6260 *SIC 1542*

POLANE INC p1108

621 RUE DE VERNON, GATINEAU, QC, J9J 3K4

(819) 772-4949 *SIC 1542*

POMERLEAU INC p1305

521 6E AV N, SAINT-GEORGES, QC, G5Y 0H1

(418) 228-6688 *SIC 1542*

POST FARM STRUCTURES INCORPO-RATED p476

80 PEEL ST, ALMA, ON, N0B 1A0

(519) 846-5988 *SIC 1542*

PRISM CONSTRUCTION LTD p207

1525 CLIVEDEN AVE SUITE 201, DELTA, BC, V3M 6L2

(604) 526-3731 *SIC 1542*

PROCAM CONSTRUCTION INC p1067

1220 RUE MARCONI, BOUCHERVILLE, QC, J4B 8G8

(450) 449-5121 *SIC 1542*

PROFESSIONAL GARDENER CO. LTD, THE p31

915 23 AVE SE, CALGARY, AB, T2G 1P1

(403) 263-4200 *SIC 1542*

PROSERVIN INC p1059

1250 BOUL MICHELE-BOHEC UNITE 400, BLAINVILLE, QC, J7C 5S4

(450) 433-1002 *SIC 1542*

QUALITE CONSTRUCTION (CDN) LTEE p1293

155 RUE D'AMSTERDAM, SAINT-AUGUSTIN-DE-DESMAURES, QC, G3A 2V5

(418) 878-4044 *SIC 1542*

QUOREX CONSTRUCTION SERVICES LTD p1421

1630 8TH AVE UNIT A, REGINA, SK, S4R 1E5

(306) 761-2222 *SIC 1542*

QUOREX CONSTRUCTION SERVICES LTD p1432

142 CARDINAL CRES, SASKATOON, SK, S7L 6H6

(306) 244-3717 *SIC 1542*

R-FOUR CONTRACTING LTD p181

7185 11TH AVE, BURNABY, BC, V3N 2M5

(604) 522-4402 *SIC 1542*

RAM CONSTRUCTION INC p210

8369 RIVER WAY SUITE 101, DELTA, BC, V4G 1G2

(604) 501-5265 *SIC 1542*

RCS CONSTRUCTION INCORPORATED p440

26 TOPSAIL CRT, BEDFORD, NS, B4B 1K5

(902) 468-6757 *SIC 1542*

REA INVESTMENTS LIMITED p795

70 DEERHIDE CRES, NORTH YORK, ON, M9M 2Y6

(905) 264-6481 *SIC 1542*

REED ATWOOD BUILDERS (ONTARIO) INC p1000

8693 6TH LINE, UTOPIA, ON, L0M 1T0

(705) 797-0553 *SIC 1542*

REED ATWOOD BUILDERS INC p18

5716 35 ST SE, CALGARY, AB, T2C 2G3

SIC 1542

RELY-EX CONTRACTING INC p1429

516 43RD ST E, SASKATOON, SK, S7K 0V6

(306) 664-2155 *SIC 1542*

RENE ET MARCO DESROCHER CON-STRUCTION INC p1391

1470 4E RUE, VAL-D'OR, QC, J9P 6X2

(819) 825-4279 *SIC 1542*

RENE HENRICHON INC p1381

3160 COTE DE TERREBONNE, TERRE-BONNE, QC, J6Y 1G1

SIC 1542

RENOVATIONS OLYMBEC INC p1327

333 BOUL DECARIE 5E ETAGE, SAINT-LAURENT, QC, H4N 3M9

(514) 344-3334 *SIC 1542*

RESTAURATIONS DYC INC p1089

170 RUE BROSSARD, DELSON, QC, J5B 1X1

(450) 638-5560 *SIC 1542*

RESTORERS GROUP INC, THE p855

344 NEWKIRK RD, RICHMOND HILL, ON, L4C 3G7

(905) 770-1323 *SIC 1542*

RHC DESIGN-BUILD p537

6783 WELLINGTON ROAD 34, CAM-BRIDGE, ON, N3C 2V4

(519) 249-0758 *SIC 1542*

RITE-WAY METALS LTD p225

20058 92A AVE, LANGLEY, BC, V1M 3A4

(604) 882-7557 *SIC 1542*

RMS BUILDERS INC p124

150 WEST RAILWAY ST NW, EDMONTON, AB, T6T 1J1

(780) 414-0330 *SIC 1542*

RNF VENTURES LTD p1414

811 CENTRAL AVE, PRINCE ALBERT, SK, S6V 4V2

(306) 763-3700 *SIC 1542*

ROBINSON, D. CONTRACTING LTD p234

4341 BOBAN DR, NANAIMO, BC, V9T 5V9

SIC 1542

ROCHON BUILDING CORPORATION p993

74 INDUSTRY ST, TORONTO, ON, M6M 4L7

(416) 638-6666 *SIC 1542*

ROCHON NATIONAL SERVICE p784

37 KODIAK CRES, NORTH YORK, ON, M3J 3E5

(416) 398-2888 *SIC 1542*

ROLAND GRENIER CONSTRUCTION LTEE p1050

9150 RUE CLAVEAU, ANJOU, QC, H1J 1Z4

(514) 252-1818 *SIC 1542*

RONAM CONSTRUCTIONS INC p1140

1085 CH INDUSTRIEL, LEVIS, QC, G7A 1B3

(418) 836-5569 *SIC 1542*

ROSCOE CONSTRUCTION LIMITED p441

5765 HIGHWAY 1, CAMBRIDGE, NS, B0P 1G0

(902) 538-8080 *SIC 1542*

ROSSCLAIR CONTRACTORS INC p914

59 COMSTOCK RD SUITE 1, TORONTO, ON, M1L 2G6

(416) 285-0190 *SIC 1542*

RUTHERFORD CONTRACTING LTD p481

224 EARL STEWART DR, AURORA, ON, L4G 6V7

(905) 726-4888 *SIC 1542*

SAJO INC p1155

1320 BOUL GRAHAM BUREAU 129, MONT-ROYAL, QC, H3P 3C8

(514) 385-0333 *SIC 1542*

SALEM CONTRACTING LTD p251

9097 MILWAUKEE WAY, PRINCE GEORGE, BC, V2N 5T3

(250) 564-2244 *SIC 1542*

SALVEX INC p1232

2450 MONTEE SAINT-FRANCOIS BU-REAU 2, MONTREAL, QC, H7E 4P2

(450) 664-4335 *SIC 1542*

SANTE MONTREAL COLLECTIF CJV, S.E.C. p1186

1031 RUE SAINT-DENIS, MONTREAL, QC, H2X 3H9

(514) 394-1440 *SIC 1542*

SAWCHUK DEVELOPMENTS CO. LTD p220

486 ADAMS RD, KELOWNA, BC, V1X 7S1

(250) 765-3838 *SIC 1542*

SAYWELL CONTRACTING LTD p234

2599 MCCULLOUGH RD UNIT B, NANAIMO, BC, V9S 4M9
(250) 729-0197   *SIC* 1542

SCI SITECAST INTERNATIONAL INC *p750*
16 CONCOURSE GATE SUITE 200, NEPEAN, ON, K2E 7S8
(613) 225-8118   *SIC* 1542

SCOTT CONSTRUCTION LTD *p191*
3777 KINGSWAY UNIT 1750, BURNABY, BC, V5H 3Z7
(604) 874-8228   *SIC* 1542

SENTERRE ENTREPRENEUR GENERAL INC *p1142*
550 BOUL GUIMOND, LONGUEUIL, QC, J4G 1P8
(450) 655-9301   *SIC* 1542

SHAW, K. & SONS CONTRACTING LTD *p133*
10424 96 AVE, GRANDE PRAIRIE, AB, T8V 5V2
(780) 539-6960   *SIC* 1542

SHEARWALL TRIFORCE INCORPORATED *p166*
340 CIRCLE DR UNIT 200, ST. ALBERT, AB, T8N 7L5
(780) 459-4777   *SIC* 1542

SHUNDA CONSULTING & CONSTRUCTION MANAGEMENT LTD *p154*
6204 46 AVE, RED DEER, AB, T4N 7A2
(403) 347-6931   *SIC* 1542

SIEMENS CONSTRUCTION INC *p83*
GD, EDBERG, AB, T0B 1J0
(780) 877-2478   *SIC* 1542

SIEMENS, VERNON CONSTRUCTION INC *p83*
GD, EDBERG, AB, T0B 1J0
(780) 877-2478   *SIC* 1542

SIERRA CONSTRUCTION (WOODSTOCK) LIMITED *p1035*
1401 DUNDAS ST, WOODSTOCK, ON, N4S 7V9
(519) 421-9689   *SIC* 1542

SM CONSTRUCTION INC *p1281*
15971 BOUL DE LA COLLINE, QUEBEC, QC, G3G 3A7
(418) 849-7104   *SIC* 1542

SMITH, WAYNE & HAROLD CONSTRUCTION LIMITED *p879*
55 BIRCH ST, SEAFORTH, ON, N0K 1W0
(519) 527-1079   *SIC* 1542

SNC-LAVALIN CONSTRUCTION INC *p1192*
455 BOUL RENE-LEVESQUE O BUREAU 202, MONTREAL, QC, H2Z 1Z3
(514) 393-1000   *SIC* 1542

SOUTHSIDE CONSTRUCTION (LONDON) LIMITED *p659*
75 BLACKFRIARS ST, LONDON, ON, N6H 1K8
(519) 433-0634   *SIC* 1542

SPECIFIED CONSTRUCTION MANAGEMENT INC *p481*
2 VATA CRT UNIT 4, AURORA, ON, L4G 4B6
(905) 726-2902   *SIC* 1542

STEELCORE CONSTRUCTION LTD *p865*
1295 MORNINGSIDE AVE UNIT 27, SCARBOROUGH, ON, M1B 4Z4
(416) 282-4888   *SIC* 1542

STORBURN CONSTRUCTION LTD *p810*
GD, ORILLIA, ON, L3V 6J3
(705) 326-4140   *SIC* 1542

STRUCT-CON CONSTRUCTION LTD *p500*
2051 WILLIAMS PKY UNIT 14, BRAMPTON, ON, L6S 5T3
(905) 791-5445   *SIC* 1542

STRUCTFORM INTERNATIONAL LIMITED *p598*
29 GORMLEY INDUSTRIAL AVE UNIT 6, GORMLEY, ON, L0H 1G0
(416) 291-7576   *SIC* 1542

STRUCTURECRAFT BUILDERS INC *p177*
1929 FOY ST, ABBOTSFORD, BC, V2T 6B1
(604) 940-8889   *SIC* 1542

STUCCOCONTRACTORS.CA *p576*
2 FIELDWAY RD, ETOBICOKE, ON, M8Z 0B9
(416) 900-8715   *SIC* 1542

STUCOR CONSTRUCTION LTD *p623*
2540 SOUTH SERVICE RD, JORDAN STATION, ON, L0R 1S0
(905) 562-1118   *SIC* 1542

SYMCO 2015 INC *p1263*
320 BOUL PIERRE-BERTRAND BUREAU 106, QUEBEC, QC, G1M 2C8
(581) 981-4774   *SIC* 1542

SYNERGY PROJECTS LTD *p166*
110 CARLETON DR SUITE 120, ST. ALBERT, AB, T8N 3Y4
(780) 459-3344   *SIC* 1542

T A F CONSTRUCTION LTD *p284*
2620 HASTINGS ST E, VANCOUVER, BC, V5K 1Z6
(604) 254-1111   *SIC* 1542

T. L. PENNER MANAGEMENT LTD *p351*
HWY 257 E, KOLA, MB, R0M 1B0
(204) 556-2265   *SIC* 1542

TECK CONSTRUCTION INC *p228*
5197 216 ST, LANGLEY, BC, V3A 2N4
(604) 534-7917   *SIC* 1542

TERLIN CONSTRUCTION LTD *p833*
1240 TERON ROAD, OTTAWA, ON, K2K 2B5
(613) 821-0768   *SIC* 1542

THOMAS DESIGN BUILDERS LTD *p393*
2395 MCGILLIVRAY BLVD UNIT C, WINNIPEG, MB, R3Y 1G6
(204) 989-5400   *SIC* 1542

TILT-TECH CONSTRUCTION LTD *p175*
34077 GLADYS AVE UNIT 320, ABBOTSFORD, BC, V2S 2E8
(604) 746-5456   *SIC* 1542

TIMCON CONSTRUCTION (1988) LTD *p156*
7445 45 AVE CLOSE SUITE 100, RED DEER, AB, T4P 4C2
(403) 347-1953   *SIC* 1542

TIMMS, R CONSTRUCTION AND ENGINEERING LIMITED, THE *p1012*
34 EAST MAIN ST SUITE B, WELLAND, ON, L3B 3W3
(905) 734-4513   *SIC* 1542

TONDA CONSTRUCTION LIMITED *p662*
1085 WILTON GROVE RD, LONDON, ON, N6N 1C9
(519) 686-5200   *SIC* 1542

TORQUE BUILDERS INC *p560*
72 CORSTATE AVE, CONCORD, ON, L4K 4X2
(905) 660-3334   *SIC* 1542

TOWER ARCTIC LTD *p1200*
2055 RUE PEEL BUREAU 960, MONTREAL, QC, H3A 1V4
SIC 1542

TRANSPORT MICHEL GASSE ET FILS INC *p1283*
219 RUE DE CAPRI, REPENTIGNY, QC, J6A 5L1
(450) 657-4667   *SIC* 1542

TRAUGOTT BUILDING CONTRACTORS INC *p537*
95 THOMPSON DR, CAMBRIDGE, ON, N1T 2E4
(519) 740-9444   *SIC* 1542

TRI CITY CANADA INC *p218*
150 VICTORIA ST SUITE 102, KAMLOOPS, BC, V2C 1Z7
(250) 372-5576   *SIC* 1542

TRI-COR CONSTRUCTION INC *p1028*
310 VAUGHAN VALLEY BLVD UNIT 1, WOODBRIDGE, ON, L4H 3C3
SIC 1542

TRIBURY CONSTRUCTION (1995) INC *p899*
1549 FAIRBURN ST, SUDBURY, ON, P3A 1N6
(705) 560-8743   *SIC* 1542

TRIGON CONSTRUCTION INC *p1036*
35 RIDGEWAY CIR, WOODSTOCK, ON, N4V 1C9
(519) 602-2222   *SIC* 1542

TRINITY DEVELOPMENT GROUP INC *p834*
359 KENT ST SUITE 400, OTTAWA, ON, K2P 0R6
SIC 1542

TRISAN GENERAL CONTRACTORS INC *p743*
6459 NETHERHART RD, MISSISSAUGA, ON, L5T 1C3
SIC 1542

TROIS-PISTOLES SERVICE *p1384*
289 RUE NOTRE-DAME E, TROIS-PISTOLES, QC, G0L 4K0
(418) 851-2219   *SIC* 1542

TURCON UNITED BUILDING SYSTEMS INC *p133*
99200 100 AVE SUITE B, GRANDE PRAIRIE, AB, T8V 0T9
(780) 532-5533   *SIC* 1542

UNIQUE RESTORATION LTD *p701*
1220 MATHESON BLVD E, MISSISSAUGA, ON, L4W 1R2
(905) 629-9100   *SIC* 1542

UNIVERSAL CONCEPTS *p862*
130 WELLINGTON ST E, SAULT STE. MARIE, ON, P6A 2L5
(705) 575-7521   *SIC* 1542

VAN HORNE CONSTRUCTION LIMITED *p1003*
51A CALDARI RD UNIT 1M, VAUGHAN, ON, L4K 4G3
(905) 677-5150   *SIC* 1542

VANTAGE BUILDERS LTD *p170*
4723 49 AVE, VEGREVILLE, AB, T9C 1L1
(780) 632-3422   *SIC* 1542

VEDDER STEEL LTD *p225*
9663 199A ST UNIT 4, LANGLEY, BC, V1M 2X7
(604) 882-0035   *SIC* 1542

VENTANA CONSTRUCTION CORPORATION *p187*
3875 HENNING DR SUITE 100, BURNABY, BC, V5C 6N5
(604) 291-9000   *SIC* 1542

VERLY CONSTRUCTION GROUP INC *p701*
1650 SISMET RD, MISSISSAUGA, ON, L4W 1R4
(905) 212-9420   *SIC* 1542

VERREAULT INC *p1237*
1200 BOUL SAINT-MARTIN O BUREAU 300, MONTREAL, QC, H7S 2E4
(514) 845-4104   *SIC* 1542

VERTEX RESOURCE SERVICES LTD *p163*
2055 PREMIER WAY SUITE 161, SHERWOOD PARK, AB, T8H 0G2
(780) 464-3295   *SIC* 1542

VESTACON LIMITED *p1003*
3 BRADWICK DR, VAUGHAN, ON, L4K 2T4
(416) 440-7970   *SIC* 1542

VIC VAN ISLE CONSTRUCTION LTD *p253*
96 CARTIER ST, REVELSTOKE, BC, V0E 2S0
(250) 837-2919   *SIC* 1542

VOSKAMP GREENHOUSES INC *p661*
6867 WELLINGTON RD S, LONDON, ON, N6L 1M3
(519) 686-0303   *SIC* 1542

WADE GENERAL CONTRACTING LTD *p839*
56 INDUSTRIAL AVE, PETAWAWA, ON, K8H 2W8
(613) 687-8585   *SIC* 1542

WALES MCLELLAND CONSTRUCTION COMPANY (1988) LIMITED *p259*
6211 FRASERWOOD PL, RICHMOND, BC, V6W 1J2
(604) 638-1212   *SIC* 1542

WARD BROS CONSTRUCTION LTD *p141*
3604 18 AVE N, LETHBRIDGE, AB, T1H 5S7
(403) 328-6698   *SIC* 1542

WATSON, WAYNE CONSTRUCTION LTD *p249*
730 3RD AVE, PRINCE GEORGE, BC, V2L 3C5
(250) 562-8251   *SIC* 1542

WELLINGTON CONSTRUCTION CO LTD *p1043*
1742 124 RTE, WELLINGTON STATION, PE, C0B 2E0
(902) 854-2650   *SIC* 1542

WESCOR CONTRACTING LTD *p339*
3368 TENNYSON AVE, VICTORIA, BC, V8Z 3P6
(250) 475-8882   *SIC* 1542

WESTCOR CONSTRUCTION LTD *p26*
2420 39 AVE NE, CALGARY, AB, T2E 6X1
(403) 663-8677   *SIC* 1542

WESTPRO INFRASTRUCTURE LTD *p278*
8241 129 ST, SURREY, BC, V3W 0A6
(604) 592-9767   *SIC* 1542

WESTRIDGE CONSTRUCTION LTD *p1416*
435 HENDERSON DR, REGINA, SK, S4N 5W8
(306) 352-2434   *SIC* 1542

WHITSON CONTRACTING LTD *p168*
51-26004 TWP RD 544, STURGEON COUNTY, AB, T8T 0B6
(780) 421-4292   *SIC* 1542

WILLOW SPRING CONSTRUCTION (ALTA) LTD *p117*
8616 51 AVE UNIT 250, EDMONTON, AB, T6E 6E6
(780) 438-1990   *SIC* 1542

WINKLER BUILDING SUPPLIES (1981) LTD *p361*
570 CENTENNIAL ST UNIT 300, WINKLER, MB, R6W 1J4
(204) 325-4336   *SIC* 1542

WRIGHT CONSTRUCTION WESTERN INC *p1430*
2919 CLEVELAND AVE, SASKATOON, SK, S7K 8A9
(306) 934-0440   *SIC* 1542

XANA INTERNATIONAL INC *p856*
55 ADMINISTRATION RD UNITS 33 & 34, RICHMOND HILL, ON, L4K 4G9
(416) 477-4770   *SIC* 1542

XDG CONSTRUCTION LIMITED *p518*
250 WOOLWICH ST S, BRESLAU, ON, N0B 1M0
(519) 648-2121   *SIC* 1542

SIC 1611 Highway and street construction

141187 VENTURES LTD *p283*
5720 16 HWY W, TERRACE, BC, V8G 0C6
(250) 638-1881   *SIC* 1611

1468792 ONTARIO INC *p647*
206 FIELDING RD, LIVELY, ON, P3Y 1L6
(705) 682-4471   *SIC* 1611

1652472 ONTARIO INC *p747*
24 ADVANCE AVE, NAPANEE, ON, K7R 3Y6
(613) 354-7653   *SIC* 1611

1835755 ONTARIO LIMITED *p545*
227 HWY 11 S, COCHRANE, ON, P0L 1C0
(705) 272-2090   *SIC* 1611

330558 ALBERTA LTD *p3*
GD, ALTAIRO, AB, T0C 0E0
(403) 552-2477   *SIC* 1611

401 PAVING LTD *p775*
1260 DON MILLS RD, NORTH YORK, ON, M3B 2W6
(416) 441-0401   *SIC* 1611

614128 ONTARIO LTD *p879*
5878 HIGHWAY 9, SCHOMBERG, ON, L0G 1T0
(416) 410-3839   *SIC* 1611

798826 ONTARIO INC *p605*
91 MONARCH RD, GUELPH, ON, N1K 1S4
(519) 767-9628   *SIC* 1611

969774 ONTARIO LIMITED *p889*
140 BURWELL RD, ST THOMAS, ON, N5P 3R8
(519) 631-5041   *SIC* 1611

A S L PAVING LTD *p1425*
1840 ONTARIO AVE, SASKATOON, SK, S7K 1T4
(306) 652-5525   *SIC* 1611

ACADIA PAVING LTD.   p1433
121 105TH ST E, SASKATOON, SK, S7N 1Z2
(306) 374-4738   SIC 1611

ACTION CONSTRUCTION INFRASTRUCTURE ACI INC   p1114
1095 RUE SAMUEL-RACINE, JOLIETTE, QC, J6E 0E8
(450) 755-6887   SIC 1611

AECON TRANSPORTATION WEST LTD   p158
590 HIGHWAY AVE NE, REDCLIFF, AB, T0J 2P0
(403) 548-3961   SIC 1611

ALBERTA HIGHWAY SERVICES LTD   p99
11010 178 ST NW SUITE 200, EDMONTON, AB, T5S 1R7
(780) 701-8668   SIC 1611

ALLEN ENTREPRENEUR GENERAL INC   p1306
118 RUE DE LA GARE, SAINT-HENRI-DE-LEVIS, QC, G0R 3E0
(418) 882-2277   SIC 1611

ALMON ENVIRONMENTAL LTD   p582
45 RACINE RD, ETOBICOKE, ON, M9W 2Z4
(416) 743-1364   SIC 1611

ALMON EQUIPMENT LTD   p582
45 RACINE RD, ETOBICOKE, ON, M9W 2Z4
(416) 743-1771   SIC 1611

ALTA CONSTRUCTION (2011) LTEE   p1225
1655 RUE DE BEAUHARNOIS O, MONTREAL, QC, H4N 1J6
(514) 748-8881   SIC 1611

ANDERSON RENTAL AND PAVING LTD   p1431
3430 IDYLWYLD DR N, SASKATOON, SK, S7L 5Y7
(306) 934-2000   SIC 1611

ARCTIC HOLDINGS & LEASING LTD   p435
135 KAM LAKE RD, YELLOWKNIFE, NT, X1A 0G3
(867) 920-4844   SIC 1611

ARGO ROAD MAINTENANCE (SOUTH OKANAGAN) INC   p243
290 WATERLOO AVE, PENTICTON, BC, V2A 7N3
(250) 493-6969   SIC 1611

ASHLAND PAVING LTD   p548
340 BOWES RD, CONCORD, ON, L4K 1K1
(905) 660-3060   SIC 1611

ASPHALTE DESJARDINS INC   p1381
3030 RUE ANDERSON, TERREBONNE, QC, J6Y 1W1
(450) 430-7160   SIC 1611

ASPHALTE, BETON, CARRIERES RIVE-NORD INC   p1153
5605 RTE ARTHUR-SAUVE, MIRABEL, QC, J7N 2W4
(450) 258-4242   SIC 1611

ASSOCIATED PAVING & MATERIALS LTD   p521
5365 MUNRO CRT, BURLINGTON, ON, L7L 5M7
(905) 637-1966   SIC 1611

AVERY CONSTRUCTION LIMITED   p863
940 SECOND LINE W SUITE B, SAULT STE. MARIE, ON, P6C 2L3
(705) 759-4800   SIC 1611

B L S ASPHALT INC   p1420
711 TORONTO ST, REGINA, SK, S4R 8G1
(306) 775-0080   SIC 1611

B.A. BLACKTOP LTD   p238
111 FORESTER ST SUITE 201, NORTH VANCOUVER, BC, V7H 0A6
(604) 985-0611   SIC 1611

BASIN CONTRACTING LIMITED   p449
100 BEDROCK LANE, ELMSDALE, NS, B2S 2B1
(902) 883-2235   SIC 1611

BAYVIEW CONSTRUCTION LTD   p353
4000 MCGILLIVRAY BLVD, OAK BLUFF, MB, R4G 0B5

(204) 254-7761   SIC 1611

BEAVER ENTERPRISES LIMITED PARTNERSHIP   p435
GD, FORT LIARD, NT, X0G 0A0
(867) 770-2203   SIC 1611

BELANGER CONSTRUCTION (1981) INC   p543
100 RADISSON AVE, CHELMSFORD, ON, P0M 1L0
(705) 855-4555   SIC 1611

BERNT GILBERTSON ENTERPRISES LIMITED   p850
3107 HURON LINE HWY 548, RICHARDS LANDING, ON, P0R 1J0
(705) 246-2076   SIC 1611

BILLABONG ROAD & BRIDGE MAINTENANCE INC   p283
5630 16 HWY W, TERRACE, BC, V8G 0C6
(250) 638-7918   SIC 1611

BIRD ENTREPRENEURS GENERAUX LTEE   p1249
1870 BOUL DES SOURCES BUREAU 200, POINTE-CLAIRE, QC, H9R 5N4
(514) 426-1333   SIC 1611

BLACKNED, JAMES   p1400
9 RUE PONTAX, WASKAGANISH, QC, J0M 1R0
(819) 895-8694   SIC 1611

BORDER PAVING LTD   p155
6711 GOLDEN WEST AVE, RED DEER, AB, T4P 1A7
(403) 343-1177   SIC 1611

BORLAND CONSTRUCTION (1989) LIMITED   p365
751 LAGIMODIERE BLVD, WINNIPEG, MB, R2J 0T8
(204) 255-6444   SIC 1611

BOT CONSTRUCTION LIMITED   p803
1224 SPEERS RD, OAKVILLE, ON, L6L 5B6
(905) 827-4167   SIC 1611

BRENNAN PAVING & CONSTRUCTION LTD   p680
505 MILLER AVE, MARKHAM, ON, L6G 1B2
(905) 475-1440   SIC 1611

BRENNAN PAVING LIMITED   p680
505 MILLER AVE, MARKHAM, ON, L6G 1B2
(905) 475-1440   SIC 1611

BROADWAY PAVING LTD, THE   p1247
3620 39E AV, POINTE-AUX-TREMBLES, QC, H1A 3V1
(514) 642-5811   SIC 1611

BROOKS ASPHALT AND AGGREGATE LTD   p7
PO BOX 686 STN MAIN, BROOKS, AB, T1R 1B6
(403) 362-5597   SIC 1611

BROWN'S PAVING LTD   p418
20 PLANT RD, SUSSEX CORNER, NB, E4E 2W9
(506) 433-4721   SIC 1611

BRUN-WAY HIGHWAYS OPERATIONS INC   p403
1754 ROUTE 640, HANWELL, NB, E3C 2B2
(506) 474-7750   SIC 1611

BRUNO'S CONTRACTING (THUNDER BAY) LIMITED   p907
665 HEWITSON ST, THUNDER BAY, ON, P7B 5V5
(807) 623-1855   SIC 1611

C. VALLEY PAVING LTD   p642
10535 HWY 50, KLEINBURG, ON, L0J 1C0
(416) 736-4220   SIC 1611

CALDWELL & ROSS LIMITED   p402
195 DOAK RD, FREDERICTON, NB, E3C 2E6
(506) 453-1333   SIC 1611

CANADA BETON ET DECORATIONS INC   p1142
777 RUE D'AUVERGNE, LONGUEUIL, QC, J4H 3T9
(450) 463-7084   SIC 1611

CANADIAN ROAD BUILDERS INC   p1

26120 ACHESON RD, ACHESON, AB, T7X 6B3
(780) 962-7800   SIC 1611

CAPILANO HIGHWAY SERVICES COMPANY   p341
118 BRIDGE RD, WEST VANCOUVER, BC, V7P 3R2
(604) 983-2411   SIC 1611

CAPITAL CITY PAVING LTD   p267
6588 BRYN RD, SAANICHTON, BC, V8M 1X6
(250) 652-3626   SIC 1611

CAPITAL PAVING INC   p849
4459 CONCESSION 7, PUSLINCH, ON, N0B 2J0
(519) 822-4511   SIC 1611

CARILLION CANADA INC   p550
7077 KEELE ST, CONCORD, ON, L4K 0B6
(905) 532-5200   SIC 1611

CARMACKS ENTERPRISES LTD   p127
GD LCD MAIN, FORT MCMURRAY, AB, T9H 3E2
(780) 598-1376   SIC 1611

CARMACKS ENTERPRISES LTD   p148
701 25 AVE, NISKU, AB, T9E 0C1
(780) 955-5545   SIC 1611

CASMAN INC   p127
330 MACKENZIE BLVD, FORT MCMURRAY, AB, T9H 4C4
(780) 791-9283   SIC 1611

CEGERCO INC   p1080
1180 RUE BERSIMIS, CHICOUTIMI, QC, G7K 1A5
(418) 543-6159   SIC 1611

CENTRAL CITY ASPHALT LTD   p5
39327 RANGE RD, BLACKFALDS, AB, T0M 0J0
(403) 346-5050   SIC 1611

CENTRAL SERVICE STATION LIMITED   p428
160 FLATBAY JUNCTION RD, ST GEORGES, NL, A0N 1Z0
(709) 647-3500   SIC 1611

CHINOOK INFRASTRUCTURE   p70
3131 114 AVE SE SUITE 100, CALGARY, AB, T2Z 3X2
(403) 355-1655   SIC 1611

COCO PAVING INC   p491
6520 HWY 62, BELLEVILLE, ON, K8N 4Z5
(613) 962-3461   SIC 1611

COCO PAVING INC   p496
3075 MAPLE GROVE RD, BOWMANVILLE, ON, L1C 6N2
(905) 697-0400   SIC 1611

COCO PAVING INC   p599
4139 HWY 34, GREEN VALLEY, ON, K0C 1L0
(613) 525-1750   SIC 1611

COCO PAVING INC   p785
949 WILSON AVE, NORTH YORK, ON, M3K 1G2
(416) 633-9670   SIC 1611

COLAS CANADA INC   p915
4950 YONGE ST SUITE 2400, TORONTO, ON, M2N 6K1
(416) 293-5443   SIC 1611

CON-STRADA CONSTRUCTION INC   p551
30 FLORAL PKY, CONCORD, ON, L4K 4R1
(905) 660-6000   SIC 1611

CONSTRUCTION BAU-VAL INC   p1058
87 RUE EMILIEN-MARCOUX BUREAU 101, BLAINVILLE, QC, J7C 0B4
(514) 788-4660   SIC 1611

CONSTRUCTION DIMCO INC.   p1161
8601 BOUL HENRI-BOURASSA E BUREAU 100, MONTREAL, QC, H1E 1P4
(514) 494-1001   SIC 1611

CONSTRUCTION DJL INC   p1064
1550 RUE AMPERE BUREAU 200, BOUCHERVILLE, QC, J4B 7L4
(450) 641-8000   SIC 1611

CONSTRUCTION DJL INC   p1106
20 RUE EMILE-BOND, GATINEAU, QC, J8Y 3M7
(819) 770-2300   SIC 1611

CONSTRUCTION DJL INC   p1223
6200 RUE SAINT-PATRICK, MONTREAL, QC, H4E 1B3
(514) 766-8256   SIC 1611

CONSTRUCTION DJL INC   p1368
3200 BOUL HUBERT-BIERMANS, SHAWINIGAN, QC, G9N 0A4
(819) 539-2271   SIC 1611

CONSTRUCTION ET PAVAGE PORTNEUF INC   p1348
599 BOUL BONA-DUSSAULT, SAINT-MARC-DES-CARRIERES, QC, G0A 4B0
(418) 268-3558   SIC 1611

CONSTRUCTION GELY INC   p1119
1781 RTE DE L'AEROPORT, L'ANCIENNE-LORETTE, QC, G2G 2P5
(418) 871-3368   SIC 1611

CONSTRUCTION SOTER INC   p1232
4085 RANG SAINT-ELZEAR E, MONTREAL, QC, H7E 4P2
(450) 664-2818   SIC 1611

CONSTRUCTION TAWICH INC   p1401
16 RTE BEAVER, WEMINDJI, QC, J0M 1L0
(819) 978-0264   SIC 1611

CONSTRUCTIONS BOB-SON INC   p1052
2264 AV DU LABRADOR, BAIE-COMEAU, QC, G4Z 3C4
(418) 296-0064   SIC 1611

CORNELL CONSTRUCTION LIMITED   p517
410 HARDY RD, BRANTFORD, ON, N3T 5L8
(519) 753-3125   SIC 1611

CORNWALL GRAVEL COMPANY LTD   p563
390 ELEVENTH ST W, CORNWALL, ON, K6J 3B2
(613) 932-6571   SIC 1611

CORONADO CONTRACTING CORP   p88
TH PO BOX 17 STN MAIN, EDMONTON, AB, T5J 2G9
(780) 449-1654   SIC 1611

CORPORATION OF THE CITY OF KITCHENER   p638
200 KING ST W, KITCHENER, ON, N2G 4V6
(519) 741-2345   SIC 1611

CORPORATION OF THE REGIONAL MUNICIPALITY OF DURHAM, THE   p1016
825 CONLIN RD, WHITBY, ON, L1R 3K3
(905) 655-3344   SIC 1611

COUILLARD CONSTRUCTION LIMITEE   p1081
228 RUE MAIN E, COATICOOK, QC, J1A 1N2
(819) 849-9181   SIC 1611

COUNTY OF FORTY MILE NO 8   p126
GD, ETZIKOM, AB, T0K 0W0
(403) 666-2082   SIC 1611

COX CONSTRUCTION LIMITED   p602
965 YORK RD, GUELPH, ON, N1H 6K5
(519) 824-6570   SIC 1611

CROFT, MICHAEL SAND & GRAVEL INC   p590
400421 GREY RD SUITE 4, FLESHERTON, ON, N0C 1E0
(519) 924-2429   SIC 1611

CUMBERLAND PAVING AND CONTRACTING   p445
8 MOORE RD, DARTMOUTH, NS, B3B 1J2
(902) 832-9062   SIC 1611

CURRAN & BRIGGS LIMITED   p1042
40 ALL WEATHER HWY, SUMMERSIDE, PE, C1N 4J8
(902) 436-2163   SIC 1611

D&G LANDSCAPING INC   p599
1341 COKER ST, GREELY, ON, K4P 1A1
(613) 821-4444   SIC 1611

D. CRUPI & SONS LIMITED   p876
85 PASSMORE AVE, SCARBOROUGH, AB, M1V 4S9
(416) 291-1986   SIC 1611

DAWSON CONSTRUCTION LIMITED   p217
1212 MCGILL RD, KAMLOOPS, BC, V2C 6N6
(250) 374-3657   SIC 1611

▲ Public Company   ■ Public Company Family Member   **HQ** Headquarters   **BR** Branch   **SL** Single Location

DEBLY ENTERPRISES LIMITED p415
170 ASHBURN RD, SAINT JOHN, NB, E2L
3T5
(506) 696-2936 *SIC* 1611

DECHANT CONSTRUCTION LTD p135
11004 97 ST, HIGH LEVEL, AB, T0H 1Z0
(780) 926-4411 *SIC* 1611

DEMERS CONTRACTING SERVICES LTD
p128
240 MACLENNAN CRES, FORT MCMUR-
RAY, AB, T9H 4G1
(780) 799-3222 *SIC* 1611

**DEXTER CONSTRUCTION COMPANY LIM-
ITED** p439
927 ROCKY LAKE DR, BEDFORD, NS, B4A
2T7
(902) 835-3381 *SIC* 1611

**DEXTER CONSTRUCTION COMPANY LIM-
ITED** p468
44 MEADOW DR, TRURO, NS, B2N 5V4
(902) 895-6952 *SIC* 1611

DICRETE CONSTRUCTION LTD p551
71 CREDITSTONE RD, CONCORD, ON,
L4K 1N3
(905) 669-9595 *SIC* 1611

DIMCO DL INC p1162
8601 BOUL HENRI-BOURASSA E, MON-
TREAL, QC, H1E 1P4
(514) 494-1001 *SIC* 1611

DUNCOR ENTERPRISES INC p486
101 BIG BAY POINT RD, BARRIE, ON, L4N
8M5
(705) 730-1999 *SIC* 1611

DUNN PAVING LIMITED p902
485 LITTLE BASELINE RD, TECUMSEH,
ON, N8N 2L9
(519) 727-3838 *SIC* 1611

E CONSTRUCTION LTD p122
10130 21 ST NW, EDMONTON, AB, T6P
1W7
(780) 467-7701 *SIC* 1611

E. & E. SEEGMILLER LIMITED p639
305 ARNOLD ST, KITCHENER, ON, N2H
6G1
(519) 579-6460 *SIC* 1611

EARTHWISE CONSTRUCTION LTD p100
20104 107 AVE NW, EDMONTON, AB, T5S
1W9
(780) 413-4235 *SIC* 1611

EARTHWISE CONTRACTING LTD p100
20104 107 AVE NW, EDMONTON, AB, T5S
1W9
(780) 413-4235 *SIC* 1611

EMCON SERVICES INC p232
1121 MCFARLANE WAY UNIT 105, MER-
RITT, BC, V1K 1B9
(250) 378-4176 *SIC* 1611

**EMIL ANDERSON CONSTRUCTION (EAC)
INC** p221
907 ETHEL ST, KELOWNA, BC, V1Y 2W1
(250) 762-9999 *SIC* 1611

EMIL ANDERSON MAINTENANCE CO. LTD
p266
51160 SACHE ST, ROSEDALE, BC, V0X
1X0
(604) 794-7414 *SIC* 1611

ENTREPRENEURS BLANCHET INC, LES
p1046
722 AV DE L'INDUSTRIE, AMOS, QC, J9T
4L9
(819) 732-5520 *SIC* 1611

ENTREPRISES ALFRED BOIVIN INC, LES
p1079
2205 RUE DE LA FONDERIE,
CHICOUTIMI, QC, G7H 8B9
(418) 549-2457 *SIC* 1611

**ENTREPRISES DE CONSTRUCTION GAS-
TON MORIN (1979) LTEE** p1090
310 RUE DE QUEN, DOLBEAU-
MISTASSINI, QC, G8L 5N1
(418) 276-4166 *SIC* 1611

**ENTREPRISES JACQUES DUFOUR & FILS
INC, LES** p1054
106 RUE SAINTE-ANNE, BAIE-SAINT-

PAUL, QC, G3Z 1P5
(418) 435-2445 *SIC* 1611

ENTREPRISES LEVISIENNES INC, LES
p1135
3104 RTE DES RIVIERES, LEVIS, QC, G6J
0B9
(418) 831-4111 *SIC* 1611

ENVIRONNEMENT ROUTIER NRJ INC
p1125
23 AV MILTON, LACHINE, QC, H8R 1K6
(514) 481-0451 *SIC* 1611

ERIC AUGER & SONS CONTRACTING LTD
p171
61 MAXIM RD, WABASCA, AB, T0G 2K0
(780) 891-3751 *SIC* 1611

ERICKSON CONSTRUCTION (1975) LTD
p355
GD, RIVERTON, MB, R0C 2R0
SIC 1611

EUROVIA QUEBEC CONSTRUCTION INC
p1065
1550 RUE AMPERE BUREAU 200,
BOUCHERVILLE, QC, J4B 7L4
(450) 641-8000 *SIC* 1611

EUROVIA QUEBEC CONSTRUCTION INC
p1224
6200 RUE SAINT-PATRICK, MONTREAL,
QC, H4E 1B3
(514) 766-8256 *SIC* 1611

EUROVIA QUEBEC CONSTRUCTION INC
p1351
104 BOUL SAINT-REMI, SAINT-REMI, QC,
J0L 2L0
(450) 454-0000 *SIC* 1611

**EUROVIA QUEBEC GRANDS PROJETS
INC** p1065
1550 RUE AMPERE BUREAU 200,
BOUCHERVILLE, QC, J4B 7L4
(450) 641-8000 *SIC* 1611

EXCAVATION PARADIS, MICHEL INC p1302
1270 RUE NELLIGAN, SAINT-FELICIEN,
QC, G8K 1N1
(418) 679-4533 *SIC* 1611

FAIRVILLE CONSTRUCTION LTD p416
12 LINTON RD, SAINT JOHN, NB, E2M 5V4
(506) 635-1573 *SIC* 1611

FERMAR PAVING LIMITED p584
1921 ALBION RD, ETOBICOKE, ON, M9W
5S8
(416) 675-3550 *SIC* 1611

**FLATIRON CONSTRUCTORS CANADA
LIMITED** p254
4020 VIKING WAY SUITE 210, RICHMOND,
BC, V6V 2L4
(604) 244-7343 *SIC* 1611

FORAGE ANDRE ROY INC p1314
186 RUE BOYER, SAINT-ISIDORE-DE-
LAPRAIRIE, QC, J0L 2A0
(450) 454-1244 *SIC* 1611

FOUR SEASONS SITE DEVELOPMENT LTD
p503
42 WENTWORTH CRT UNIT 1, BRAMP-
TON, ON, L6T 5K6
(905) 670-7655 *SIC* 1611

**FOWLER CONSTRUCTION COMPANY LIM-
ITED** p497
1218 ROSEWARNE DR, BRACEBRIDGE,
ON, P1L 0A1
(705) 645-2214 *SIC* 1611

FRANCIS POWELL & CO. LIMITED p894
180 RAM FOREST RD, STOUFFVILLE, ON,
L4A 2G8
(905) 727-2518 *SIC* 1611

GAZZOLA PAVING LIMITED p584
529 CARLINGVIEW DR, ETOBICOKE, ON,
M9W 5H2
(416) 675-7007 *SIC* 1611

GEE BEE CONSTRUCTION CO LTD p1408
HIGHWAY 48, KIPLING, SK, S0G 2S0
(306) 736-2332 *SIC* 1611

GIULIANI, G INC p1101
3970 BOUL LEMAN, FABREVILLE, QC,
H7E 1A1
(450) 661-6519 *SIC* 1611

**GOUVERNEMENT DE LA PROVINCE DE
QUEBEC** p1289
80 AV QUEBEC, ROUYN-NORANDA, QC,
J9X 6R1
(819) 763-3237 *SIC* 1611

**GRAHAM BROS. CONSTRUCTION LIM-
ITED** p509
297 RUTHERFORD RD S, BRAMPTON,
ON, L6W 3J8
(905) 453-1200 *SIC* 1611

GREENWOOD PAVING (PEMBROKE) LTD
p838
1495 PEMBROKE ST W, PEMBROKE, ON,
K8A 7A5
(613) 735-4101 *SIC* 1611

**GREY COUNTY TRANSPORTAION AND
PUBLIC SAFETY** p835
595 9TH AVE E, OWEN SOUND, ON, N4K
3E3
(519) 376-2205 *SIC* 1611

GROUPE MULTI-PAVAGE INC. p1161
9855 BOUL HENRI-BOURASSA E, MON-
TREAL, QC, H1C 1G5
(514) 723-3000 *SIC* 1611

GUILBEAULT, R CONSTRUCTION INC
p1099
775 BOUL LEMIRE, DRUMMONDVILLE,
QC, J2C 7X5
(819) 474-6521 *SIC* 1611

GUY J BAILEY LTD p421
6 HIGHWAY 412, BAIE VERTE, NL, A0K
1B0
(709) 532-4642 *SIC* 1611

H.J.R. ASPHALT LP p1432
1605 CHAPPELL DR, SASKATOON, SK,
S7M 3X9
(306) 975-0070 *SIC* 1611

HAMEL-CRT S.E.N.C. p1299
2106 RTE PRINCIPALE, SAINT-EDOUARD-
DE-LOTBINIERE, QC, G0S 1Y0
(418) 796-2074 *SIC* 1611

HARD-CO CONSTRUCTION LTD p1016
625 CONLIN RD, WHITBY, ON, L1R 2W8
(905) 655-2001 *SIC* 1611

HOBAN CONSTRUCTION LTD p268
5121 46 AVE SE, SALMON ARM, BC, V1E
1X2
(250) 832-8831 *SIC* 1611

HOBAN EQUIPMENT LTD p268
2691 13 AVE SW, SALMON ARM, BC, V1E
3K1
(250) 832-8831 *SIC* 1611

HURON CONSTRUCTION CO LIMITED p543
10785 PINEHURST LINE, CHATHAM, ON,
N7M 5J3
(519) 354-0170 *SIC* 1611

INLAND CONTRACTING LTD p243
716 OKANAGAN AVE E, PENTICTON, BC,
V2A 3K6
(250) 492-2626 *SIC* 1611

**INTEGRATED MAINTENANCE & OPERA-
TIONS SERVICES INC** p671
GD, MARKHAM, ON, L3R 9R8
(905) 475-6660 *SIC* 1611

INTER-CITE CONSTRUCTION LTEE p1079
205 BOUL DU ROYAUME E, CHICOUTIMI,
QC, G7H 5H2
(418) 549-0532 *SIC* 1611

INTER-CITE CONSTRUCTION LTEE p1079
209 BOUL DU ROYAUME O, CHICOUTIMI,
QC, G7H 5C2
(418) 549-0532 *SIC* 1611

INTERIOR ROADS LTD p217
1212 MCGILL RD, KAMLOOPS, BC, V2C
6N6
(250) 374-7238 *SIC* 1611

INTEROUTE CONSTRUCTION LTD p213
9503 79TH AVE, FORT ST. JOHN, BC, V1J
4J3
(250) 787-7283 *SIC* 1611

J & D PENNER LTD p393
2560 MCGILLIVRAY BLVD, WINNIPEG, MB,
R3Y 1G5
(204) 895-8602 *SIC* 1611

J. C. PAVING LTD p360
3000 MAIN ST UNIT 7, WEST ST PAUL, MB,
R2V 4Z3
(204) 989-4700 *SIC* 1611

JACOB BROS CONSTRUCTION INC p279
3399 189 ST, SURREY, BC, V3Z 1A7
(604) 541-0303 *SIC* 1611

JACOB BROS. ASSET CO. LTD p279
3399 189 ST, SURREY, BC, V3Z 1A7
(604) 541-0303 *SIC* 1611

JJM CONSTRUCTION LTD p209
8218 RIVER WAY, DELTA, BC, V4G 1C4
(604) 946-0978 *SIC* 1611

JOBERT INC p1357
161 RUE PRINCIPALE, SAINTE-EMELIE-
DE-L'ENERGIE, QC, J0K 2K0
(450) 886-3851 *SIC* 1611

JPW ROAD & BRIDGE INC p179
2310 KIRTON AVE, ARMSTRONG, BC, V0E
1B0
(250) 546-3765 *SIC* 1611

K.J BEAMISH CONSTRUCTION CO. LTD
p629
3300 KING VAUGHAN RD, KING CITY, ON,
L7B 1B2
(905) 833-4666 *SIC* 1611

KASCO CONSTRUCTION ALTA LTD p11
2770 3 AVE NE SUITE 117, CALGARY, AB,
T2A 2L5
SIC 1611

KINGS COUNTY CONSTRUCTION LIMITED
p1041
5284A A MACDONALD HWY, MONTAGUE,
PE, C0A 1R0
(902) 838-2191 *SIC* 1611

KLEDO CONSTRUCTION LTD p213
4301 NAHANNI DR, FORT NELSON, BC,
V0C 1R0
(250) 774-2501 *SIC* 1611

KPM INDUSTRIES LTD p804
555 MICHIGAN DR SUITE 100, OAKVILLE,
ON, L6L 0G4
(905) 639-2993 *SIC* 1611

**LAFARGE PAVING & CONSTRUCTION
(EASTERN) LIMITED** p555
7880 KEELE ST UNIT 5, CONCORD, ON,
L4K 4G7
(905) 738-7070 *SIC* 1611

LAKES DISTRICT MAINTENANCE INC p194
881 16 HWY W, BURNS LAKE, BC, V0J 1E0
(250) 692-7766 *SIC* 1611

LANDRY ASPHALTE LTEE p396
14 RUE DU PORTAGE, CARAQUET, NB,
E1W 1A8
(506) 727-6551 *SIC* 1611

LAPRAIRIE WORKS INC p135
GD, GRIMSHAW, AB, T0H 1W0
(780) 332-4452 *SIC* 1611

LEDCOR CONTRACTORS LTD p109
7008 ROPER RD NW, EDMONTON, AB,
T6B 3H2
(780) 395-5400 *SIC* 1611

LEDCOR HOLDINGS INC p306
1067 CORDOVA ST W SUITE 1200, VAN-
COUVER, BC, V6C 1C7
(604) 681-7500 *SIC* 1611

LEDCOR INDUSTRIES INC p149
3925 8 ST, NISKU, AB, T9E 8M1
(780) 955-1400 *SIC* 1611

LEDCOR INDUSTRIES INC p154
27420 TOWNSHIP RD SUITE 374, RED
DEER, AB, T4N 5H3
(403) 309-7129 *SIC* 1611

LEDCOR INDUSTRIES INC p306
1067 CORDOVA ST W SUITE 1200, VAN-
COUVER, BC, V6C 1C7
(604) 681-7500 *SIC* 1611

LOCATION A.L.R. INC p1045
211 RUE DU MISTRAL, ALMA, QC, G8E
2E2
(418) 347-4665 *SIC* 1611

LOUIS W. BRAY CONSTRUCTION LIMITED
p1002
308 CORDUROY RD, VARS, ON, K0A 3H0

(613) 938-6711   *SIC* 1611
MAINRCAD CONTRACTING LTD   *p272*
17474 56 AVE, SURREY, BC, V3S 1C3
(604) 575-7020   *SIC* 1611

MAINROAD EAST KOOTENAY CONTRACT-ING LTD   *p204*
258 INDUSTRIAL ROAD F, CRANBROOK, BC, V1C 6N8
(250) 417-4624   *SIC* 1611

MAINROAD EAST KOOTENAY CONTRACT-ING LTD   *p272*
17474 56 AVE, SURREY, BC, V3S 1C3
(604) 575-7020   *SIC* 1611

MAINROAD HOWE SOUND CONTRACTING LTD   *p272*
17474 56 AVE, SURREY, BC, V3S 1C3
(604) 575-7020   *SIC* 1611

MAINROAD LOWER MAINLAND CON-TRACTING LTD   *p272*
17474 56 AVE, SURREY, BC, V3S 1C3
(604) 575-7021   *SIC* 1611

MAINROAD MID-ISLAND CONSTRUCTING LTD   *p243*
435 SPRINGHILL RD, PARKSVILLE, BC, V9P 2T2
   SIC 1611

MAPLE LEAF CONSTRUCTION LTD   *p382*
777 ERIN ST, WINNIPEG, MB, R3G 2W2
(204) 783-7091   *SIC* 1611

METRIC CONTRACTING SERVICES COR-PORATION   *p499*
34 BRAMTREE CRT, BRAMPTON, ON, L6S 5Z7
(905) 793-4100   *SIC* 1611

MILLAR, HUGH FAMILY HOLDINGS INC   *p96*
16640 111 AVE NW, EDMONTON, AB, T5M 2S5
(780) 486-8200   *SIC* 1611

MILLER CAPILANO MAINTENANCE COR-PORATION   *p269*
38921 MIDWAY, SQUAMISH, BC, V8B 0J5
(604) 892-1010   *SIC* 1611

MILLER GROUP INC   *p680*
505 MILLER AVE, MARKHAM, ON, L6G 1B2
(905) 475-6660   *SIC* 1611

MILLER MAINTENANCE LIMITED   *p875*
2064 KENNEDY RD, SCARBOROUGH, ON, M1T 3V1
(416) 332-1360   *SIC* 1611

MILLER NORTHWEST LIMITED   *p565*
351 KENNEDY RD, DRYDEN, ON, P8N 2Z2
(807) 223-2844   *SIC* 1611

MILLER PAVING LIMITED   *p395*
2276 ROUTE 128, BERRY MILLS, NB, E1G 4K4
(506) 857-0112   *SIC* 1611

MILLER PAVING LIMITED   *p680*
505 MILLER AVE, MARKHAM, ON, L6G 1B2
(905) 475-6660   *SIC* 1611

MILLER PAVING LIMITED   *p753*
704024 ROCKLEY RD, NEW LISKEARD, ON, P0J 1P0
(705) 647-4331   *SIC* 1611

MILLER PAVING LTD   *p753*
883316 HWY 65, NEW LISKEARD, ON, P0J 1P0
(877) 842-0543   *SIC* 1611

MRDC OPERATIONS CORPORATION   *p410*
203 AV BLACK WATCH, OROMOCTO, NB, E2V 4L7
(506) 357-1240   *SIC* 1611

MSO CONSTRUCTION LIMITED   *p586*
175 BETHRIDGE RD, ETOBICOKE, ON, M9W 1N4
(416) 743-3224   *SIC* 1611

MUNICIPAL CONTRACTING LIMITED   *p470*
927 ROCKY LAKE DR, WAVERLEY, NS, B2R 1S1
(902) 835-3381   *SIC* 1611

MUNICIPAL CONTRACTING LIMITED   *p470*
927 ROCKY LAKE DR, WAVERLEY, NS, B2R 1S1

(902) 835-3381   *SIC* 1611
N.P.A. LTD   *p132*
4201 93 RD ST, GRANDE PRAIRIE, AB, T8V 6T4
(780) 532-4600   *SIC* 1611

NEEGAN DEVELOPMENT CORPORATION LTD   *p128*
GD LCD MAIN, FORT MCMURRAY, AB, T9H 3E2
(780) 791-0654   *SIC* 1611

NELSON RIVER CONSTRUCTION INC   *p366*
101 DAWSON RD N, WINNIPEG, MB, R2J 0S6
(204) 949-8700   *SIC* 1611

NORAMA ENTERPRISES INC   *p2*
53016 HWY 60 SUITE 2, ACHESON, AB, T7X 5A7
(780) 960-7171   *SIC* 1611

NORJOHN CONTRACTING AND PAVING LIMITED   *p760*
9101 BROWN RD, NIAGARA FALLS, ON, L2H 0X1
(905) 371-0809   *SIC* 1611

NORTH WEST PAVING LTD   *p163*
20 TURBO DR, SHERWOOD PARK, AB, T8H 2J6
(780) 468-4144   *SIC* 1611

NORTHERN CONSTRUCTION AND SUP-PLIERS LTD   *p403*
534 WEST RIVER RD, GRAND-SAULT/GRAND FALLS, NB, E3Z 3E7
(506) 473-1822   *SIC* 1611

NORTHERN CONSTRUCTION INC   *p403*
554 WEST RIVER RD, GRAND-SAULT/GRAND FALLS, NB, E3Z 3E7
(506) 473-1822   *SIC* 1611

NOYEN CONSTRUCTION LTD   *p130*
8309 113 ST, FORT SASKATCHEWAN, AB, T8L 4K7
(780) 998-3974   *SIC* 1611

O'HANLON PAVING LTD   *p96*
16511 116 AVE NW, EDMONTON, AB, T5M 3V1
(780) 434-8555   *SIC* 1611

O.K. INDUSTRIES LTD   *p267*
6702 RAJPUR PL, SAANICHTON, BC, V8M 1Z5
(250) 652-9211   *SIC* 1611

OCEAN CONTRACTORS LIMITED   *p444*
204 CONO DR, DARTMOUTH, NS, B2Y 3Y9
(902) 435-1291   *SIC* 1611

P. BAILLARGEON LTEE   *p1318*
800 RUE DES CARRIERES, SAINT-JEAN-SUR-RICHELIEU, QC, J3B 2P2
(514) 866-8333   *SIC* 1611

P.E. PAGEAU INC   *p1262*
460 RUE METIVIER, QUEBEC, QC, G1M 2T8
(418) 681-8080   *SIC* 1611

PALMER CONSTRUCTION GROUP INC   *p862*
845 OLD GOULAIS BAY RD, SAULT STE. MARIE, ON, P6A 0B5
(705) 254-1644   *SIC* 1611

PALMER PAVING   *p863*
1121 PEOPLES RD, SAULT STE. MARIE, ON, P6C 3W4
(705) 254-1644   *SIC* 1611

PARADOX ACCESS SOLUTIONS INC   *p2*
11246 261 ST, ACHESON, AB, T7X 6C7
(587) 461-1500   *SIC* 1611

PAVAGE C.S.F. INC   *p1050*
11101 RUE MIRABEAU, ANJOU, QC, H1J 2S2
(514) 352-7430   *SIC* 1611

PAVAGE SARTIGAN LTEE   *p1305*
2125 98E RUE, SAINT-GEORGES, QC, G5Y 8J5
(418) 228-3875   *SIC* 1611

PAVAGES ABENAKIS LTEE   *p1305*
11380 79E AV, SAINT-GEORGES, QC, G5Y 5B9
(418) 228-8116   *SIC* 1611

PAVAGES D'AMOUR INC   *p1094*
1635 CROIS NEWMAN, DORVAL, QC, H9P 2R6
(514) 631-4570   *SIC* 1611

PAVAGES MASKA INC   *p1313*
3450 BOUL CHOQUETTE, SAINT-HYACINTHE, QC, J2S 8V9
(450) 773-2591   *SIC* 1611

PENSION PLAN - F & L   *p524*
750 APPLEBY LINE, BURLINGTON, ON, L7L 2Y7
(905) 632-2121   *SIC* 1611

PETER KIEWIT INFRASTRUCTURE CO.   *p77*
9500 100 ST SE, CALGARY, AB, T3S 0A2
   SIC 1611

PETER KIEWIT INFRASTRUCTURE CO.   *p102*
11211 WINTERBURN RD NW, EDMON-TON, AB, T5S 2B2
(780) 447-3509   *SIC* 1611

PETER'S BROS. CONSTRUCTION LTD   *p244*
716 OKANAGAN AVE E, PENTICTON, BC, V2A 3K6
(250) 492-2626   *SIC* 1611

PICCOLI, N. CONSTRUCTION LTD   *p651*
1933 GORE RD SUITE 2, LONDON, ON, N5W 6B9
(519) 473-9665   *SIC* 1611

PIONEER CONSTRUCTION INC   *p762*
1975 PROGRESS RD, NORTH BAY, ON, P1A 0B8
(705) 472-0890   *SIC* 1611

PIONEER CONSTRUCTION INC   *p901*
1 CEASAR RD, SUDBURY, ON, P3E 5P3
(705) 560-7200   *SIC* 1611

PIONEER CONSTRUCTION INC   *p910*
1344 OLIVER RD, THUNDER BAY, ON, P7G 1K4
(807) 345-2338   *SIC* 1611

POTZUS PAVING & ROAD MAINTENANCE LTD   *p1438*
16 W HWY, YORKTON, SK, S3N 2X1
(306) 782-7423   *SIC* 1611

POWELL (RICHMOND HILL) CONTRACT-ING LIMITED   *p894*
180 RAM FOREST RD, STOUFFVILLE, ON, L4A 2G8
(905) 727-2518   *SIC* 1611

PRAIRIE NORTH CONST. LTD   *p116*
4936 87 ST NW SUITE 280, EDMONTON, AB, T6E 5W3
(780) 463-3363   *SIC* 1611

PRESTIGE DESIGNS & CONSTRUCTION (OTTAWA) LTD   *p751*
50 CAMELOT DR, NEPEAN, ON, K2G 5X8
(613) 224-9437   *SIC* 1611

RICHARDSON BROS (OLDS) LIMITED   *p151*
GD, OLDS, AB, T4H 1P4
(403) 556-6366   *SIC* 1611

RIDGE NATIONAL INC   *p1023*
100 OUELLETTE AVE SUITE 1004, WIND-SOR, ON, N9A 6T3
(519) 256-2112   *SIC* 1611

ROADSIDE PAVING LIMITED   *p793*
125A TORYORK DR SUITE A, NORTH YORK, ON, M9L 1X9
(416) 740-3876   *SIC* 1611

ROADWAY OPERATIONS & MAINTENANCE CORPORATION OF ONTARIO INC   *p804*
1224 SPEERS RD, OAKVILLE, ON, L6L 5B6
(905) 827-4167   *SIC* 1611

ROCKY ROAD RECYCLING LTD   *p353*
4154 MCGILLIVRAY BLVD, OAK BLUFF, MB, R4G 0B5
(204) 832-7802   *SIC* 1611

ROUGHRIDER CIVIL INFRASTRUCTURE LTD   *p18*
7003 30 ST SE BAY 16, CALGARY, AB, T2C 1N6
(403) 243-1666   *SIC* 1611

RYDER CONTRACTING LTD   *p245*
5700 SHOEMAKER BAY RD, PORT AL-BERNI, BC, V9Y 8X8
(250) 736-1995   *SIC* 1611

RYSEN BOBCAT SERVICES LIMITED   *p2*
107-26230 TOWNSHIP RD 531A, ACHE-SON, AB, T7X 5A4
(780) 470-2085   *SIC* 1611

SINTRA INC   *p1073*
3600 CH DUNANT, CANTON-DE-HATLEY, QC, J0B 2C0
(819) 346-8634   *SIC* 1611

SINTRA INC   *p1118*
3125 BOUL SAINT-CHARLES, KIRKLAND, QC, H9H 3B9
(514) 695-3395   *SIC* 1611

SINTRA INC   *p1140*
678 AV TANIATA UNITE 839, LEVIS, QC, G6Z 2C2
(418) 839-4175   *SIC* 1611

SINTRA INC   *p1228*
4984 PLACE DE LA SAVANE, MONTREAL, QC, H4P 2M9
(514) 341-5331   *SIC* 1611

SINTRA INC   *p1287*
105 RUE LOUIS-PHILIPPE-LEBRUN, RIVIERE-DU-LOUP, QC, G5R 5W5
(418) 862-0000   *SIC* 1611

SINTRA INC   *p1291*
101 RUE DE LA SINTRA, SAINT-ALPHONSE-DE-GRANBY, QC, J0E 2A0
(450) 375-4471   *SIC* 1611

SINTRA INC   *p1314*
7 RANG SAINT-REGIS S, SAINT-ISIDORE-DE-LAPRAIRIE, QC, J0L 2A0
(450) 638-0172   *SIC* 1611

SMITHS CONSTRUCTION COMPANY ARN-PRIOR LIMITED   *p479*
276 MADAWASKA BLVD, ARNPRIOR, ON, K7S 3H4
(613) 623-3144   *SIC* 1611

ST. ISIDORE ASPHALT LTD   *p417*
19 RUE DUCLOS, SAINT-ISIDORE, NB, E8M 1N3
(506) 358-6345   *SIC* 1611

STANDARD GENERAL INC   *p166*
250 CARLETON DR, ST. ALBERT, AB, T8N 6W2
(780) 459-6611   *SIC* 1611

STEED & EVANS LIMITED   *p887*
3000 AMENT LINE, ST CLEMENTS, ON, N0B 2M0
(519) 744-7315   *SIC* 1611

STEVENSVILLE LAWN SERVICE INC   *p890*
2821 STEVENSVILLE RD RR 2, STEVENSVILLE, ON, L0S 1S0
(905) 382-2124   *SIC* 1611

STRILKIWSKI CONTRACTING LTD   *p349*
GD LCD MAIN, DAUPHIN, MB, R7N 2T3
(204) 638-9304   *SIC* 1611

TACKABERRY, G & SONS CONSTRUCTION COMPANY LIMITED   *p479*
109 WASHBURN RD, ATHENS, ON, K0E 1B0
(613) 924-2634   *SIC* 1611

TAHLTAN NATION DEVELOPMENT COR-PORATION   *p205*
HWY 37 N, DEASE LAKE, BC, V0C 1L0
(250) 771-5482   *SIC* 1611

TALON SEBEQ INC   *p1142*
555 BOUL GUIMOND, LONGUEUIL, QC, J4G 1L9
(450) 677-7449   *SIC* 1611

TARANIS CONTRACTING GROUP LTD   *p910*
1473 ROSSLYN RD, THUNDER BAY, ON, P7E 6W1
(807) 475-5443   *SIC* 1611

TAURUS SITE SERVICES INC   *p130*
11401 85 AVE, FORT SASKATCHEWAN, AB, T8L 0A9
(780) 998-5001   *SIC* 1611

TERANORTH CONSTRUCTION & ENGI-NEERING LIMITED   *p901*
799 LUOMA RD, SUDBURY, ON, P3G 1J4
(705) 523-1540   *SIC* 1611

TERCON CONSTRUCTION LTD   *p269*
610 DOUGLAS FIR, SPARWOOD, BC, V0B 2G0

SIC 1611

TERUS CONSTRUCTION LTD p273
15288 54A AVE UNIT 300, SURREY, BC, V3S 6T4
(604) 575-3689   SIC 1611

THOMAS CAVANAGH CONSTRUCTION LIMITED p479
9094A CAVANAGH RD, ASHTON, ON, K0A 1B0
(613) 257-2918   SIC 1611

TOLLESTRUP HOLDINGS LTD p143
806 2 AVE S, LETHBRIDGE, AB, T1J 0C6
(403) 328-8196   SIC 1611

TORBRIDGE CONSTRUCTION LTD p559
3300 HIGHWAY 7 SUITE 803, CONCORD, ON, L4K 4M3
SIC 1611

TRANSIT PAVING INC p147
3047 GERSHAW DR SW, MEDICINE HAT, AB, T1B 3N1
(403) 526-0386   SIC 1611

TWD ROADS MANAGEMENT INC p560
7077 KEELE ST SUITE 100, CONCORD, ON, L4K 0B6
(905) 532-5200   SIC 1611

UNIROC INC p1154
5605 RTE ARTHUR-SAUVE, MIRABEL, QC, J7N 2W4
(450) 258-4242   SIC 1611

VAN ISLE BRICKLOK SURFACING & LANDSCAPE SUPPLIES LTD p340
2717 PEATT RD SUITE 101, VICTORIA, BC, V9B 3V2
(250) 382-5012   SIC 1611

VAN ZUTPHEN, J & T CONSTRUCTION INC p462
10442 HWY 19 SW, MABOU, NS, B0E 1X0
(902) 945-2300   SIC 1611

VAUGHAN PAVING LTD p560
220 BASALTIC RD, CONCORD, ON, L4K 1G6
(905) 669-9579   SIC 1611

VECTOR MANAGEMENT LTD p393
474 DOVERCOURT DR, WINNIPEG, MB, R3Y 1G4
(204) 489-6300   SIC 1611

VILLE DE MONTREAL p1397
1177 RUE DUPUIS, VERDUN, QC, H4G 3L4
(514) 872-7680   SIC 1611

VILLENEUVE, C. CONSTRUCTION CO. LTD p619
1533 HWY 11 W, HEARST, ON, P0L 1N0
(705) 372-1838   SIC 1611

VISTA CONTRACTING LTD. p539
1316 DICKIE SETTLEMENT RD, CAMBRIDGE, ON, N3H 4R8
(519) 650-3481   SIC 1611

VOLKER STEVIN CONTRACTING LTD p38
7175 12 ST SE SUITE 7175, CALGARY, AB, T2H 2S6
(403) 571-5800   SIC 1611

VOLKER STEVIN CONTRACTING LTD p141
4004 6 AVE N, LETHBRIDGE, AB, T1H 6W4
(403) 320-4920   SIC 1611

VSA HIGHWAY MAINTENANCE LTD p180
1504 BLATTNER RD, ARMSTRONG, BC, V0E 1B0
(250) 546-8844   SIC 1611

VSA HIGHWAY MAINTENANCE LTD p232
2925 POOLEY AVE, MERRITT, BC, V1K 1C2
(250) 315-0166   SIC 1611

WEEKS, S.W. CONSTRUCTION LIMITED p463
186 TERRA COTTA DR, NEW GLASGOW, NS, B2H 5W5
(902) 755-3777   SIC 1611

WEINRICH CONTRACTING LTD p123
7212 8 ST NW, EDMONTON, AB, T6P 1V1
(780) 487-6734   SIC 1611

WEST-CAN SEAL COATING INC p7
55501 RR 203, BRUDERHEIM, AB, T0E 0S0

(780) 796-3437   SIC 1611

WINVAN PAVING LTD p237
220 EDWORTHY WAY, NEW WESTMINSTER, BC, V3L 5G5
(604) 522-3921   SIC 1611

YELLOWHEAD ROAD & BRIDGE (KOOTENAY) LTD p236
110 CEDAR ST, NELSON, BC, V1L 6H2
(250) 352-3242   SIC 1611

YRB MANAGEMENT CORP p249
2424 HART HWY, PRINCE GEORGE, BC, V2K 2X8
(250) 614-7604   SIC 1611

SIC 1622 Bridge, tunnel, and elevated highway construction

9051-4076 QUEBEC INC p1307
3500 BOUL SIR-WILFRID-LAURIER, SAINT-HUBERT, QC, J3Y 6T1
(450) 321-2446   SIC 1622

CANAM PONTS CANADA INC p1263
1445 RUE DU GRAND-TRONC, QUEBEC, QC, G1N 4G1
(418) 683-2561   SIC 1622

CHERUBINI METAL WORKS LIMITED p445
570 AV WILKINSON, DARTMOUTH, NS, B3B 0J4
(902) 468-5630   SIC 1622

CONSORTIUM PONT MOHAWK CPM p1116
GD, KAHNAWAKE, QC, J0L 1B0
(450) 635-6063   SIC 1622

CONSTRUCTION DEMATHIEU & BARD (CDB) INC p1319
170 BOUL ROLAND-GODARD, SAINT-JEROME, QC, J7Y 4P7
(450) 569-8043   SIC 1622

CONSTRUCTIONS CONCREATE LTEE p1333
5840 RUE DONAHUE, SAINT-LAURENT, QC, H4S 1C1
(514) 335-0412   SIC 1622

CRT CONSTRUCTION INC p1136
870 RUE ARCHIMEDE, LEVIS, QC, G6V 7M5
(418) 833-8073   SIC 1622

CT CONSTRUCTION LTD p571
55 BROWNS LINE, ETOBICOKE, ON, M8W 3S2
(416) 588-8707   SIC 1622

DB-AECON PONT ST-JACQUES S.E.P p1319
170 BOUL ROLAND-GODARD, SAINT-JEROME, QC, J7Y 4P7
(450) 569-8043   SIC 1622

DIBCO UNDERGROUND LIMITED p494
135 COMMERCIAL RD, BOLTON, ON, L7E 1R6
(905) 857-0458   SIC 1622

E. F. MOON CONSTRUCTION LTD p354
1200 LORNE AVE E, PORTAGE LA PRAIRIE, MB, R1N 4A2
(204) 857-7871   SIC 1622

EARTH BORING CO. LIMITED p713
1576 IFIELD RD, MISSISSAUGA, ON, L5H 3W1
(905) 277-9632   SIC 1622

FACCA INCORPORATED p858
2097 COUNTY RD 31 SUITE 1, RUSCOM STATION, ON, N0R 1R0
(519) 975-0377   SIC 1622

GOLDEN CROSSING CONSTRUCTORS JOINT VENTURE p224
20100 100A AVE, LANGLEY, BC, V1M 3G4
SIC 1622

GROUPE BE-EXC INC p1136
870 RUE ARCHIMEDE BUREAU 92, LEVIS, QC, G6V 7M5
(418) 833-8073   SIC 1622

GROUPE MACADAM INC p1255
4550 BOUL SAINTE-ANNE, QUEBEC, QC, G1C 2H9
(418) 661-2400   SIC 1622

HORSESHOE HILL CONSTRUCTION INC p531
18859 HORSESHOE HILL RD, CALEDON, ON, L7K 2B9
(905) 857-7400   SIC 1622

JACQUES CARTIER AND CHAMPLAIN BRIDGES INCORPORATED, THE p1144
1225 RUE SAINT-CHARLES O UNITE 500, LONGUEUIL, QC, J4K 0B9
(450) 651-8771   SIC 1622

KIEWIT-PARSONS, UN PARTENARIAT p1062
4333 BOUL DE LA GRANDE-ALLEE, BOISBRIAND, QC, J7H 1M7
(450) 435-5756   SIC 1622

MCLEAN TAYLOR CONSTRUCTION LIMITED p888
25 WATER ST N, ST MARYS, ON, N4X 1B1
(519) 284-2580   SIC 1622

NEILSON INC p1140
578 CH OLIVIER, LEVIS, QC, G7A 2N6
(418) 831-2141   SIC 1622

NEILSON-EBC (7) S.E.N.C. p1140
578 CH OLIVIER, LEVIS, QC, G7A 2N6
(418) 831-2141   SIC 1622

NEILSON-EBC (R3-01-02) S.E.N.C p1140
578 CH OLIVIER, LEVIS, QC, G7A 2N6
(418) 831-2141   SIC 1622

NORTHERN LINKWELL CONSTRUCTION LTD p251
2011 PG PULP MILL RD, PRINCE GEORGE, BC, V2N 2K3
(250) 563-2844   SIC 1622

NORTHSTAR SHARP'S FOUNDATION SPECIALISTS LTD p149
1511 SPARROW DR, NISKU, AB, T9E 8H9
(780) 955-2108   SIC 1622

RUSKIN CONSTRUCTION LTD p251
2011 PG PULP MILL RD, PRINCE GEORGE, BC, V2N 2K3
(250) 563-2800   SIC 1622

SIMARD-BEAUDRY CONSTRUCTION INC p1232
4230 RANG SAINT-ELZEAR E, MONTREAL, QC, H7E 4P2
(450) 664-5700   SIC 1622

SUPREME STEEL LP p123
10496 21 ST NW, EDMONTON, AB, T6P 1W4
(780) 467-2266   SIC 1622

SURESPAN CONSTRUCTION LTD p242
38 FELL AVE SUITE 301, NORTH VANCOUVER, BC, V7P 3S2
(604) 998-1133   SIC 1622

SURESPAN INVESTMENTS GROUP INC p242
38 FELL AVE SUITE 301, NORTH VANCOUVER, BC, V7P 3S2
(604) 998-1133   SIC 1622

TECHNICORE UNDERGROUND INC p880
102 BALES DRIVE E, SHARON, ON, L0G 1V0
(905) 898-4889   SIC 1622

TORBRIDGE CONSTRUCTION LTD p589
61 STEINWAY BLVD, ETOBICOKE, ON, M9W 6H6
(905) 669-3909   SIC 1622

TORONTO ZENITH CONTRACTING LIMITED p559
226 BRADWICK DR UNIT 1, CONCORD, ON, L4K 1K8
(905) 738-1500   SIC 1622

SIC 1623 Water, sewer, and utility lines

1254561 ONTARIO INC p479
67 INDUSTRIAL PKY N UNIT 1, AURORA, ON, L4G 4C4
(905) 726-9404   SIC 1623

227835 ALBERTA LTD p107
9211 48 ST NW, EDMONTON, AB, T6B 2R9
(780) 465-9321   SIC 1623

3427951 CANADA INC p1134

180 BOUL BELLEROSE O, LAVAL-OUEST, QC, H7L 6A2
(450) 628-4835   SIC 1623

7190891 CANADA INC p1337
4200 RUE HICKMORE, SAINT-LAURENT, QC, H4T 1K2
(514) 488-2525   SIC 1623

AECOM FACILITY CONSTRUCTION LTD p33
1209 59 AVE SE SUITE 205, CALGARY, AB, T2H 2P6
(403) 218-7113   SIC 1623

AECON UTILITIES INC p597
2495 DEL ZOTTO AVE, GLOUCESTER, ON, K1T 3V6
(613) 822-6193   SIC 1623

ALLIANCE FORMING LTD p494
91 PARR BLVD, BOLTON, ON, L7E 4E3
(416) 749-5030   SIC 1623

ALLTECK LINE CONTRACTORS INC p184
4333 STILL CREEK DR SUITE 300, BURNABY, BC, V5C 6S6
(604) 857-6600   SIC 1623

AMICO INFRASTRUCTURES INC p807
2199 BLACKACRE DR SUITE 100, OLDCASTLE, ON, N0R 1L0
(519) 737-1577   SIC 1623

AQUAREHAB EAU POTABLE INC p1233
2145 RUE MICHELIN, MONTREAL, QC, H7L 5B8
(450) 687-3472   SIC 1623

AQUAREHAB INC p1233
2145 RUE MICHELIN, MONTREAL, QC, H7L 5B8
(450) 687-3472   SIC 1623

ARC LINE CONSTRUCTION LTD p7
GD STN MAIN, BROOKS, AB, T1R 1E4
(403) 362-4315   SIC 1623

ARNASON INDUSTRIES LTD p356
9094 HWY 1, ROSSER, MB, R0H 1E0
(204) 633-2567   SIC 1623

ARNETT & BURGESS OIL FIELD CONSTRUCTION LIMITED p160
4510 50 ST, SEDGEWICK, AB, T0B 4C0
(780) 384-4050   SIC 1623

ARNETT & BURGESS PIPELINERS LTD p161
4510 50 ST S, SEDGEWICK, AB, T0B 4C0
(780) 384-4050   SIC 1623

ARNOTT CONSTRUCTION LIMITED p681
2 BERTRAM INDUSTRIAL PKY SUITE 1, MIDHURST, ON, L0L 1X0
(705) 735-9121   SIC 1623

ARVA LIMITED p773
4120 YONGE ST SUITE 310, NORTH YORK, ON, M2P 2B8
(416) 222-0842   SIC 1623

AVERTEX UTILITY SOLUTIONS INC p863
205235 COUNTY RD 109, SCARBOROUGH, ON, L9W 0T8
(519) 942-3030   SIC 1623

B & B LINE CONSTRUCTION LTD p427
1274 KENMOUNT RD, PARADISE, NL, A1L 1N3
(709) 722-1112   SIC 1623

B-LINE UTILITIES LTD p151
5703 48 AVE, OLDS, AB, T4H 1V1
(403) 556-8563   SIC 1623

BEHAN CONSTRUCTION LIMITED p544
GD LCD MAIN, COBOURG, ON, K9A 4K1
(905) 372-9862   SIC 1623

BELPACIFIC EXCAVATING & SHORING LIMITED PARTNERSHIP p183
3183 NORLAND AVE, BURNABY, BC, V5B 3A9
(604) 291-1255   SIC 1623

BENOIT OILFIELD CONSTRUCTION (1997) LTD p79
302 RUPERT ST, CHAUVIN, AB, T0B 0V0
(780) 858-3794   SIC 1623

BENOIT OILFIELD CONSTRUCTION LTD p79
302 RUPERT ST, CHAUVIN, AB, T0B 0V0
(780) 858-3794   SIC 1623

BERETTA PIPELINE CONSTRUCTION LTD *p1409*
GD, LLOYDMINSTER, SK, S9V 0X5
(780) 875-6522 *SIC* 1623

BIG COUNTRY ENERGY SERVICES LIMITED PARTNERSHIP *p172*
3905 35 ST SUITE 3, WHITECOURT, AB, T7S 0A2
(780) 706-2141 *SIC* 1623

BIRNAM EXCAVATING LTD *p1005*
7046 NAUVOO RD, WARWICK TOWNSHIP, ON, N0N 1J4
(519) 828-3449 *SIC* 1623

BLUE-CON INC *p648*
1915 CRUMLIN, LONDON, ON, N5V 3B8
(519) 659-2400 *SIC* 1623

BLUMETRIC ENVIRONMENTAL INC *p540*
3108 CARP RD, CARP, ON, K0A 1L0
(613) 839-3053 *SIC* 1623

BONNYVILLE WELDING LTD *p6*
PT OF NE 14-616 W 4TH, BONNYVILLE, AB, T9N 2J3
(780) 826-3847 *SIC* 1623

BRANTFORD ENGINEERING AND CONSTRUCTION LIMITED *p515*
54 EWART AVE, BRANTFORD, ON, N3S 0H4
(519) 759-1160 *SIC* 1623

CAN WEST PROJECTS INC *p75*
85 FREEPORT BLVD NE SUITE 202, CALGARY, AB, T3J 4X8
SIC 1623

CANA UTILITIES LTD *p34*
5720 4 ST SE UNIT 100, CALGARY, AB, T2H 1K7
(403) 255-5521 *SIC* 1623

CANADIAN LOCATORS INC *p99*
18215 114 AVE NW UNIT 101, EDMONTON, AB, T5S 2P6
(780) 487-7553 *SIC* 1623

CANADIAN UTILITY CONSTRUCTION CORP *p182*
7950 VENTURE ST, BURNABY, BC, V5A 1V3
SIC 1623

CANADIAN UTILITY CONSTRUCTION CORP *p184*
4333 STILL CREEK DR SUITE 300, BURNABY, BC, V5C 6S6
(604) 574-6640 *SIC* 1623

CANADIAN UTILITY CONSTRUCTION CORP *p271*
6739 176 ST UNIT 1, SURREY, BC, V3S 4G6
(604) 576-9358 *SIC* 1623

CAPTEL INC *p1387*
9395 BOUL PARENT BUREAU 2, TROIS-RIVIERES, QC, G9A 5E1
(819) 373-1454 *SIC* 1623

CARTER BROTHERS LTD *p404*
1797 ROUTE 134, LAKEVILLE-WESTMORLAND, NB, E1H 1A1
(506) 383-9150 *SIC* 1623

CHALLAND PIPELINE LTD *p159*
HWY 11 S, ROCKY MOUNTAIN HOUSE, AB, T4T 1B4
(403) 845-2469 *SIC* 1623

CHERRYFIELD CONTRACTING LTD *p409*
1050 MCLAUGHLIN DR, MONCTON, NB, E1G 3R2
SIC 1623

CHET CONSTRUCTION LTD *p174*
33759 MOREY AVE SUITE 1, ABBOTSFORD, BC, V2S 2W5
(604) 859-1441 *SIC* 1623

CLEAN WATER WORKS INC *p815*
1800 BANTREE ST, OTTAWA, ON, K1B 5L6
(613) 745-2444 *SIC* 1623

CLEARWAY CONSTRUCTION INC *p550*
379 BOWES RD, CONCORD, ON, L4K 1J1
(905) 761-6955 *SIC* 1623

COLAUTTI CONSTRUCTION LTD *p597*
2562 DEL ZOTTO AVE, GLOUCESTER, ON, K1T 3V7

(613) 822-1440 *SIC* 1623

CON-DRAIN COMPANY (1983) LIMITED *p551*
30 FLORAL PKY SUITE 100, CONCORD, ON, L4K 4R1
(905) 669-5400 *SIC* 1623

CON-DRAIN COMPANY LIMITED *p551*
30 FLORAL PKY SUITE 100, CONCORD, ON, L4K 4R1
(416) 798-7153 *SIC* 1623

CON-ELCO LTD *p551*
200 BRADWICK DR, CONCORD, ON, L4K 1K8
(905) 669-4942 *SIC* 1623

CONSTRUCTION ARNO INC *p1386*
2300 BOUL DES RECOLLETS, TROIS-RIVIERES, QC, G8Z 3X5
(819) 379-5222 *SIC* 1623

CONSTRUCTION G-NESIS INC *p1236*
4915 RUE LOUIS-B.-MAYER, MONTREAL, QC, H7P 0E5
(514) 370-8303 *SIC* 1623

CONSTRUCTION GARNIER LTEE *p1101*
3980 BOUL LEMAN, FABREVILLE, QC, H7E 1A1
(450) 661-6470 *SIC* 1623

CONSTRUCTIONS CJRB INC, LES *p1381*
3000 RUE ANDERSON, TERREBONNE, QC, J6Y 1W1
(450) 965-1110 *SIC* 1623

CORIX UTILITIES INC *p312*
1188 GEORGIA ST W SUITE 1160, VANCOUVER, BC, V6E 4A2
(604) 697-6700 *SIC* 1623

CORVET CONSTRUCTION (1977) LTD *p157*
37565 HIGHWAY 2 SUITE 107, RED DEER COUNTY, AB, T4E 1B4
(403) 340-3535 *SIC* 1623

CROSSING COMPANY INCORPORATED, THE *p148*
1807 8 ST, NISKU, AB, T9E 7S8
(780) 955-5051 *SIC* 1623

D.G.C. CONTRACTING INC *p164*
40 DIAMOND AVE, SPRUCE GROVE, AB, T7X 3A8
SIC 1623

DATA WIRING SOLUTIONS INC *p426*
1170 TOPSAIL RD SUITE 3, MOUNT PEARL, NL, A1N 5E8
(709) 747-2150 *SIC* 1623

DISTINCT INFRASTRUCTURE GROUP INC *p583*
77 BELFIELD RD UNIT 102, ETOBICOKE, ON, M9W 1G6
(416) 675-6485 *SIC* 1623

DOLENTE CONCRETE & DRAIN CO. *p792*
52 HIGH MEADOW PL, NORTH YORK, ON, M9L 2Z5
(416) 653-6504 *SIC* 1623

DOM-MERIDIAN CONSTRUCTION LTD *p738*
1021 MEYERSIDE DR UNIT 10, MISSISSAUGA, ON, L5T 1J6
(905) 564-5594 *SIC* 1623

DONCAR CONSTRUCTION INC *p1232*
4085 RANG SAINT-ELZEAR E, MONTREAL, QC, H7E 4P2
SIC 1623

DORAN STEWART OILFIELD SERVICES (1990) LTD *p159*
391043 752 HWY, ROCKY MOUNTAIN HOUSE, AB, T4T 1B3
(403) 845-4044 *SIC* 1623

DREXLER CONSTRUCTION LIMITED *p857*
5274 COUNTY RD 27, ROCKWOOD, ON, N0B 2K0
(519) 856-9526 *SIC* 1623

DUNVEGAN NORTH OILFIELD SERVICES ULC *p126*
GD, FAIRVIEW, AB, T0H 1L0
(780) 835-3511 *SIC* 1623

E.C.S. ENGINEERING & CONSTRUCTION LIMITED *p552*
51 RITIN LANE UNIT 1, CONCORD, ON, L4K 4E1

(905) 761-7009 *SIC* 1623

E.O.S. PIPELINE & FACILITIES INCORPORATED *p48*
736 6 AVE SW SUITE 1205, CALGARY, AB, T2P 3T7
(403) 232-8446 *SIC* 1623

ELECTRO SAGUENAY LTEE *p1045*
245 RUE DES HUARTS, ALMA, QC, G8E 2G1
(418) 347-3371 *SIC* 1623

ENERPOWER UTILITIES INC *p552*
585 APPLEWOOD CRES, CONCORD, ON, L4K 5V7
SIC 1623

ENTREPRISES ELECTRIQUES A. & R. LTEE, LES *p1310*
5655 RUE LAMOUREUX, SAINT-HYACINTHE, QC, J2R 1S3
(450) 253-8690 *SIC* 1623

ENTREPRISES G.N.P. INC *p1399*
750 BOUL PIERRE-ROUX E, VICTORIAVILLE, QC, G6T 1S6
(819) 752-7140 *SIC* 1623

ENTREPRISES LITEL INC, LES *p1261*
465 RUE METIVIER, QUEBEC, QC, G1M 2X2
(418) 527-5643 *SIC* 1623

ENTREPRISES P.E.B. LTEE, LES *p1281*
1190 AV DU LAC-SAINT-CHARLES, QUEBEC, QC, G3G 2S9
(418) 849-2841 *SIC* 1623

EVERGREEN ENERGY LTD *p79*
9416 69 AVE, CLAIRMONT, AB, T8X 5B3
(780) 538-3680 *SIC* 1623

EXCAVATIONS LAFONTAINE INC, LES *p1136*
872 RUE ARCHIMEDE BUREAU 92, LEVIS, QC, G6V 7M5
(418) 838-2121 *SIC* 1623

EXPERTECH NETWORK INSTALLATION INC *p584*
240 ATTWELL DR, ETOBICOKE, ON, M9W 5B2
(866) 553-5539 *SIC* 1623

FABCOR 2001 INC *p79*
10202 74 AVE, CLAIRMONT, AB, T8X 5A7
(780) 532-3350 *SIC* 1623

FER-PAL CONSTRUCTION LTD *p793*
171 FENMAR DR, NORTH YORK, ON, M9L 1M7
(416) 742-3713 *SIC* 1623

FERNVIEW CONSTRUCTION LIMITED *p498*
10605 COLERAINE DR, BRAMPTON, ON, L6P 0V6
(905) 794-0132 *SIC* 1623

FISHER POWERLINE CONSTRUCTION LTD *p129*
230 TAIGANOVA CRES SUITE 2B, FORT MCMURRAY, AB, T9K 0T4
(780) 713-3474 *SIC* 1623

G.L.R. INC *p1119*
1095 RUE VALETS, L'ANCIENNE-LORETTE, QC, G2E 4M7
(418) 872-3365 *SIC* 1623

G.S. HOLDINGS COMPANY LTD *p1*
27060 ACHESON RD, ACHESON, AB, T7X 6B1
(780) 962-3544 *SIC* 1623

GALLOWAY CONSTRUCTION GROUP LTD *p152*
431029 RANGE RD 261, PONOKA, AB, T4J 1R4
(403) 783-2599 *SIC* 1623

GARSON PIPE CONTRACTORS LIMITED *p593*
1191 O'NEIL DR W, GARSON, ON, P3L 1L5
(705) 693-1242 *SIC* 1623

GCS ENERGY SERVICES LTD *p135*
4411 49TH ST, HARDISTY, AB, T0B 1V0
(780) 888-3845 *SIC* 1623

GERVAIS DUBE INC *p1384*
62 2E RANG O, TROIS-PISTOLES, QC, G0L 4K0
(418) 851-2994 *SIC* 1623

GIBBONS, V. CONTRACTING LTD *p890*
1755 STEVENSVILLE RD, STEVENSVILLE, ON, L0S 1S0
(905) 382-2393 *SIC* 1623

GLR - THIRO S.E.N.C. *p1119*
1095 RUE VALETS, L'ANCIENNE-LORETTE, QC, G2E 4M7
(418) 872-3365 *SIC* 1623

GREELY CONSTRUCTION INC *p595*
5689 POWER RD, GLOUCESTER, ON, K1G 3N4
(613) 822-0500 *SIC* 1623

GRIMSBY UTILITY CONSTRUCTION INC *p599*
211 ROBERTS RD, GRIMSBY, ON, L3M 4E8
(905) 945-8878 *SIC* 1623

GROVES, WM. LIMITED *p609*
800 RENNIE ST, HAMILTON, ON, L8H 3R2
(905) 545-1117 *SIC* 1623

HAHN WELDING & OILFIELD SERVICES LTD *p126*
5205 47 ST, ELK POINT, AB, T0A 1A0
(780) 724-3323 *SIC* 1623

HAMM CONSTRUCTION LTD *p1427*
126 ENGLISH CRES, SASKATOON, SK, S7K 8A5
(306) 931-6626 *SIC* 1623

HENRI SICOTTE INC *p1140*
779 RUE DE LA BRIQUETERIE, LEVIS, QC, G7A 2N2
(418) 836-8417 *SIC* 1623

HENUSET PIPELINE CONSTRUCTION INC *p68*
13024 CANSO PL SW, CALGARY, AB, T2W 3A8
(403) 252-5386 *SIC* 1623

HEYINK, HENRY CONSTRUCTION LTD *p543*
275 COLBORNE ST, CHATHAM, ON, N7M 3M3
(519) 354-4593 *SIC* 1623

IGL CANADA (WESTERN) LTD *p101*
17515 106A AVE NW, EDMONTON, AB, T5S 1M7
(780) 489-3245 *SIC* 1623

INLAND PACIFIC RESOURCES INC *p314*
1188 GEORGIA ST W SUITE 1160, VANCOUVER, BC, V6E 4A2
(604) 697-6700 *SIC* 1623

INNOVATIVE PIPELINE CROSSINGS INC *p69*
340 MIDPARK WAY SE SUITE 300, CALGARY, AB, T2X 1P1
(403) 455-0380 *SIC* 1623

INTEGRATED MARKET SOLUTIONS INC *p892*
266 SOUTH SERVICE RD, STONEY CREEK, ON, L8E 2N9
(905) 662-9194 *SIC* 1623

IPAC SERVICES CORPORATION *p79*
8701 102 ST, CLAIRMONT, AB, T8X 5G8
(780) 532-7350 *SIC* 1623

J & T VAN ZUTPHEN CONSTRUCTION INCORPORATED *p465*
10442 SOUTHWEST MABOU, PORT HOOD, NS, B0E 2W0
(902) 945-2300 *SIC* 1623

JOHNSTONE, T. W. COMPANY LIMITED *p660*
284 EXETER RD, LONDON, ON, N6L 1A3
(519) 652-9581 *SIC* 1623

K-LINE MAINTENANCE & CONSTRUCTION LIMITED *p1406*
5 INDUSTRIAL DR, EMERALD PARK, SK, S4L 1B7
(306) 781-2711 *SIC* 1623

KENORA ENTERPRISES LTD *p186*
4638 HASTINGS ST, BURNABY, BC, V5C 2K5
(604) 294-0038 *SIC* 1623

KEVCO PIPELINES LTD *p16*
5050 54 AVE SE, CALGARY, AB, T2C 2Y8
(403) 279-5050 *SIC* 1623

KINECTRICS NCL INC p996
800 KIPLING AVE UNIT 2, TORONTO, ON, M8Z 5G5
(416) 592-2102   SIC 1623

LAKESIDE PERFORMANCE GAS SERVICES LTD p740
6915 DIXIE RD, MISSISSAUGA, ON, L5T 2G2
(289) 562-0054   SIC 1623

LANCORP CONSTRUCTION CO. LTD p555
138 CREDITSTONE RD, CONCORD, ON, L4K 1P2
(905) 660-0778   SIC 1623

LOCATION RAOUL PELLETIER INC p1138
3650 BOUL GUILLAUME-COUTURE, LEVIS, QC, G6W 7L3
(418) 837-2147   SIC 1623

M & N CONSTRUCTION LTD p81
4511 VICTORIA AVE, CORONATION, AB, T0C 1C0
(403) 578-2016   SIC 1623

M.A.P WATER AND SEWER SERVICES LTD p96
14303 116 AVE NW, EDMONTON, AB, T5M 4G2
(780) 453-6996   SIC 1623

MACRO ENTERPRISES INC p213
6807 100 AVE, FORT ST. JOHN, BC, V1J 4J2
(250) 785-0033   SIC 1623

MADYSTA TELECOM LTEE p1389
3600 BOUL L.-P.-NORMAND, TROIS-RIVIERES, QC, G9B 0G2
(819) 373-3336   SIC 1623

MAINIL, JERRY LIMITED p1437
1530 NEW CITY GARDEN RD, WEYBURN, SK, S4H 2L1
(306) 842-5412   SIC 1623

MAINLAND CIVIL SITE SERVICES INC p277
12899 80 AVE UNIT 206, SURREY, BC, V3W 0E6
(604) 591-5599   SIC 1623

MARQUIS CONCEPT INC, LE p1391
180 AV CHAMPLAIN, VAL-D'OR, QC, J9P 2B6
(819) 825-5515   SIC 1623

MASTEC CANADA INC p147
1010 BRIER PARK DR NW, MEDICINE HAT, AB, T1C 1Z7
(403) 529-6444   SIC 1623

MAXX NORTH AMERICA SERVICES LTD p110
5311 72A AVE NW, EDMONTON, AB, T6B 2J1
(780) 482-4144   SIC 1623

MCGREGOR CONSTRUCTION 2000 LTD p115
9925 62 AVE NW, EDMONTON, AB, T6E 0E7
(780) 437-1340   SIC 1623

MEARS CANADA CORP p159
235080 RYAN RD, ROCKY VIEW COUNTY, AB, T1X 0K3
(587) 471-2344   SIC 1623

MEMME EXCAVATION COMPANY LIMITED p697
1315 SHAWSON DR, MISSISSAUGA, ON, L4W 1C4
(905) 564-7972   SIC 1623

MIDLITE CONSTRUCTION LTD p129
135 BOREAL AVE, FORT MCMURRAY, AB, T9K 0T4
(780) 714-6559   SIC 1623

MORGAN CONSTRUCTION AND ENVIRONMENTAL LTD p102
17303 102 AVE NW, EDMONTON, AB, T5S 1J8
(780) 733-9100   SIC 1623

NAVACON CONSTRUCTION INC p517
415 HARDY RD, BRANTFORD, ON, N3T 5L8
(519) 754-4646   SIC 1623

NEWFORCE ENERGY SERVICES LTD p82
5710 - 57 AVE, DRAYTON VALLEY, AB, T7A 1S7
(780) 514-7882   SIC 1623

NORTH STAR CONTRACTING INC p77
64 TECHNOLOGY WAY SE, CALGARY, AB, T3S 0B9
(403) 228-3421   SIC 1623

NPL CANADA LTD p725
7505 DANBRO CRES, MISSISSAUGA, ON, L5N 6P9
(905) 821-8383   SIC 1623

NU EDGE CONSTRUCTION LTD p78
3815A 47 AVE, CAMROSE, AB, T4V 4S4
(780) 679-7825   SIC 1623

O.J. PIPELINES CANADA p149
1409 4 ST, NISKU, AB, T9E 7M9
(780) 955-3900   SIC 1623

OCL GROUP INC p151
325 WOODGATE RD, OKOTOKS, AB, T1S 2A5
(403) 982-9090   SIC 1623

ONTARIO POWER CONTRACTING LIMITED p556
340 BOWES RD, CONCORD, ON, L4K 1K1
SIC 1623

PEDERSEN CONSTRUCTION INC p753
11 & 65 HWY W, NEW LISKEARD, ON, P0J 1P0
(705) 647-6223   SIC 1623

PEDRE CONTRACTORS LTD p229
26620 56 AVE UNIT 101, LANGLEY, BC, V4W 3X5
(604) 881-2411   SIC 1623

PETROCARE SERVICES LIMITED PARTNERSHIP p126
4515 2 AVE, EDSON, AB, T7E 1C1
(780) 723-4237   SIC 1623

PIPE QUEST PROJECTS LTD p4
GD STN MAIN, ATHABASCA, AB, T9S 1A2
(780) 689-9568   SIC 1623

PIPEWORX LTD p2
11122 255 ST, ACHESON, AB, T7X 6C9
(780) 960-2730   SIC 1623

POLLITT, R. OILFIELD CONSTRUCTION LTD p140
GD, LESLIEVILLE, AB, T0M 1H0
(403) 588-1230   SIC 1623

POLY EXCAVATION INC p1084
295 AV DES TERRASSES, COTE SAINT-LUC, QC, H7H 2A7
(450) 622-4100   SIC 1623

PRO CANADA WEST ENERGY INC p1410
HWY 39 S, MIDALE, SK, S0C 1S0
(306) 458-2232   SIC 1623

PRO-LINE BUILDING MATERIALS LTD p31
4910 BUILDERS RD SE, CALGARY, AB, T2G 4C6
(403) 262-1008   SIC 1623

PROGRESSIVE CONTRACTING LTD p261
5591 NO. 3 RD, RICHMOND, BC, V6X 2C7
(604) 273-6655   SIC 1623

PROMARK-TELECON INC p750
203 COLONNADE RD S UNIT 10, NEPEAN, ON, K2E 7K3
(613) 723-9888   SIC 1623

PVS CONTRACTORS INC p883
113 CUSHMAN RD UNIT 5, ST CATHARINES, ON, L2M 6S9
(905) 984-5414   SIC 1623

QUANTA TELECOM CANADA LTD p77
9595 ENTERPRISE WAY SE, CALGARY, AB, T3S 0A1
(587) 620-0201   SIC 1623

RABCON CONTRACTORS LTD p598
9 GORMLEY INDUSTRIAL AVE, GORMLEY, ON, L0H 1G0
(905) 888-6281   SIC 1623

RAMJET CONTRACTING LTD p1416
525 7TH AVE, REGINA, SK, S4N 0G5
(306) 789-6199   SIC 1623

RAYWALT CONSTRUCTION CO. LTD p2
10374 276 ST, ACHESON, AB, T7X 6A5
(780) 962-0030   SIC 1623

REHABILITATION DU O INC p1087
5270 BOUL CLEROUX, COTE SAINT-LUC, QC, H7T 2E8
(450) 682-2733   SIC 1623

REVCON OILFIELD CONSTRUCTORS INCORPORATED p125
625 PARSONS RD SW SUITE 201, EDMONTON, AB, T6X 0N9
(780) 497-8586   SIC 1623

RHYASON CONTRACTING LTD p214
7307 BIPA RD E, FORT ST. JOHN, BC, V1J 4M6
(250) 785-0515   SIC 1623

RIVERSIDE RENTALS INC p149
1807 8 ST, NISKU, AB, T9E 7S8
(780) 955-5051   SIC 1623

RS LINE CONSTRUCTION INC p228
5680 PRODUCTION WAY, LANGLEY, BC, V3A 4N4
(778) 278-7000   SIC 1623

SADE CANADA INC p1267
1564 AV AMPERE, QUEBEC, QC, G1P 4B9
(581) 300-7233   SIC 1623

SANDPIPER CONTRACTING LTD p282
9342 194 ST, SURREY, BC, V4N 4E9
(604) 888-8484   SIC 1623

SCANSA CONSTRUCTION LTD p340
2089 MILLSTREAM RD UNIT 203, VICTORIA, BC, V9B 6H4
(250) 478-5222   SIC 1623

SKOCDOPOLE CONSTRUCTION LTD p83
GD, ECKVILLE, AB, T0M 0X0
(403) 746-5744   SIC 1623

SOMERVILLE, ROBERT B. CO., LIMITED p629
13176 DUFFERIN ST, KING CITY, ON, L7B 1K5
(905) 833-3100   SIC 1623

SOUTHWEST CONTRACTING LTD p282
9426 192 ST, SURREY, BC, V4N 3R9
(604) 888-5221   SIC 1623

STRATUS PIPELINES LTD p80
10828 99 ST SUITE 3, CLAIRMONT, AB, T8X 5B4
(780) 897-0605   SIC 1623

STREAMLINE CONSTRUCTION CO. LTD p103
11030 205 ST NW, EDMONTON, AB, T5S 1Z4
(780) 447-4518   SIC 1623

SUMMIT PIPELINE SERVICES ULC p857
46 COOPER RD SUITE 13, ROSSLYN, ON, P7K 0E3
(807) 939-1100   SIC 1623

SUREWAY CONSTRUCTION LTD p123
9175 14 ST NW, EDMONTON, AB, T6P 0C9
(780) 440-2121   SIC 1623

SUREWAY EQUIPMENT LEASING LTD p123
9175 14 ST NW, EDMONTON, AB, T6P 0C9
(780) 440-2121   SIC 1623

SYSTEMES ET CABLES PRYSMIAN CANADA LTEE p623
137 COMMERCE PL, JOHNSTOWN, ON, K0E 1T1
(613) 925-6008   SIC 1623

TACC CONSTRUCTION CO. LTD p1034
270 CHRISLEA RD, WOODBRIDGE, ON, L4L 8A8
(905) 856-8500   SIC 1623

TACC CONSTRUCTION LTD p1034
270 CHRISLEA RD, WOODBRIDGE, ON, L4L 8A8
(905) 856-8500   SIC 1623

TAG CONSTRUCTION LTD p227
21869 56 AVE UNIT B, LANGLEY, BC, V2Y 2M9
(604) 534-2685   SIC 1623

TAGGART CONSTRUCTION LIMITED p827
3187 ALBION RD S, OTTAWA, ON, K1V 8Y3
(613) 521-3000   SIC 1623

TAHK PROJECTS LTD p161
296 KASKA RD, SHERWOOD PARK, AB, T8A 4G7
(780) 416-7770   SIC 1623

TARGET EXCAVATING INC p153
GD, PROVOST, AB, T0B 3S0
(780) 753-3931   SIC 1623

TESTON PIPELINES LIMITED p559
379 BOWES RD, CONCORD, ON, L4K 1J1
(905) 761-6955   SIC 1623

THIRAU LTEE p1399
489 BOUL PIERRE-ROUX E, VICTORIAVILLE, QC, G6T 1S9
(819) 752-9741   SIC 1623

THOMPSON INFRASTRUCTURE LTD p164
411 SOUTH AVE, SPRUCE GROVE, AB, T7X 3B4
(780) 962-1030   SIC 1623

TRACKER CONTRACTING LTD p214
7648 100 AVE, FORT ST. JOHN, BC, V1J 1V9
SIC 1623

TRANS POWER UTILITY CONTRACTORS INC p560
585 APPLEWOOD CRES, CONCORD, ON, L4K 5V7
(905) 660-9764   SIC 1623

TRANSELEC/COMMON INC p1085
2075 BOUL FORTIN, COTE SAINT-LUC, QC, H7S 1P4
(514) 382-1550   SIC 1623

TRIPLE P POWER SERVICE LTD p145
GD, MA-ME-O BEACH, AB, T0C 1X0
(780) 586-2778   SIC 1623

VALARD CONSTRUCTION LTD p117
4209 99 ST NW SUITE 308, EDMONTON, AB, T6E 5V7
(780) 436-9876   SIC 1623

VALARD CONSTRUCTION LTD p133
14310 97 ST, GRANDE PRAIRIE, AB, T8V 7B7
(780) 539-4750   SIC 1623

VALARD CONSTRUCTION LTD p283
3120 BRAUN ST, TERRACE, BC, V8G 5N9
SIC 1623

VOLTAGE POWER LTD p385
1313 BORDER ST UNIT 26, WINNIPEG, MB, R3H 0X4
(204) 594-1140   SIC 1623

WAIWARD CONSTRUCTION MANAGEMENT INC p106
13015 163 ST NW, EDMONTON, AB, T5V 1M5
(780) 447-1308   SIC 1623

WASCHUK PIPE LINE CONSTRUCTION LTD p158
39015 HIGHWAY 2A SUITE 127, RED DEER COUNTY, AB, T4S 2A3
(403) 346-1114   SIC 1623

WAWASUM ENERGY INC p351
200 ALPINE WAY UNIT 135, HEADINGLEY, MB, R4H 0B7
(204) 299-9400   SIC 1623

WESTOWER COMMUNICATIONS LTD p169
4933 46TH ST, THORSBY, AB, T0C 2P0
(780) 789-2375   SIC 1623

WESTOWER COMMUNICATIONS LTD p273
17886 55 AVE, SURREY, BC, V3S 6C8
(604) 576-4755   SIC 1623

WESTWOOD ELECTRIC LTD p332
887 FAIRWEATHER RD, VERNON, BC, V1T 8T8
(250) 542-5481   SIC 1623

WHISSELL CONTRACTING LTD p71
2500 107 AVE SE SUITE 200, CALGARY, AB, T2Z 3R7
(403) 236-2200   SIC 1623

WILLBROS MINE SERVICES, L.P. p126
1103 95 ST SW, EDMONTON, AB, T6X 0P8
(780) 400-4200   SIC 1623

WILLBROS MINE SERVICES, L.P. p129
1005 MEMORIAL DR, FORT MCMURRAY, AB, T9K 0K4
(780) 743-6247   SIC 1623

WILLBROS PSS MIDSTREAM (CANADA) L.P. p126
1103 95 ST SW, EDMONTON, AB, T6X 0P8
(780) 400-4200   SIC 1623

WORLEYCORD LP p124
2455 130 AVE NE, EDMONTON, AB, T6S

0A4
(780) 440-6942   *SIC* 1623
WPW INC   *p*140
GD, LESLIEVILLE, AB, T0M 1H0
(403) 729-3007   *SIC* 1623
WRD BORGER CONSTRUCTION LTD   *p*160
261046 HIGH PLAINS BLVD, ROCKY VIEW
COUNTY, AB, T4A 3L3
(403) 279-7235   *SIC* 1623

SIC 1629 Heavy construction, nec

115419 ALBERTA LTD   *p*158
28042 HWY 11 UNIT 231, RED DEER
COUNTY, AB, T4S 2L4
(403) 347-6222   *SIC* 1629
1238902 ALBERTA CORP   *p*13
200 RIVERCREST DR SE SUITE 160, CAL-
GARY, AB, T2C 2X5
(403) 203-4747   *SIC* 1629
1685300 ONTARIO INC   *p*680
1835 DIAMOND RD, MATHESON, ON, P0K
1N0
(705) 273-3219   *SIC* 1629
2913097 CANADA INC   *p*1392
650 BOUL LIONEL-BOULET, VARENNES,
QC, J3X 1P7
(450) 652-5400   *SIC* 1629
9015-6472 QUEBEC INC   *p*1290
140 RUE JACQUES-BIBEAU, ROUYN-
NORANDA, QC, J9Y 0A3
(819) 764-4666   *SIC* 1629
A & B RAIL SERVICES LTD   *p*162
50 STRATHMOOR DR SUITE 200, SHER-
WOOD PARK, AB, T8H 2B6
(780) 449-7699   *SIC* 1629
A & B RAIL SERVICES LTD   *p*480
325 INDUSTRIAL PKY S, AURORA, ON,
L4G 3V8
SIC 1629
**ABALONE CONSTRUCTION (WESTERN)
INC**   *p*104
15531 131 AVE NW, EDMONTON, AB, T5V
0A4
(780) 451-3681   *SIC* 1629
**ACE VEGETATION CONTROL SERVICE
LTD**   *p*148
2001 8 ST, NISKU, AB, T9E 7Z1
(780) 955-8980   *SIC* 1629
**AECON CONSTRUCTION AND MATERIALS
LIMITED**   *p*581
20 CARLSON CRT SUITE 800, ETOBI-
COKE, ON, M9W 7K6
(905) 454-1078   *SIC* 1629
ALLIED TRACK SERVICES INC   *p*599
169A SOUTH SERVICE RD, GRIMSBY, ON,
L3M 4H6
(905) 769-1317   *SIC* 1629
ALTO CONSTRUCTION LTD   *p*1433
307 103RD ST E, SASKATOON, SK, S7N
1Y9
(306) 955-0554   *SIC* 1629
ALUMINIUM ANDRE GAGNON INC   *p*1347
1225 RANG DE LA RIVIERE N, SAINT-LIN-
LAURENTIDES, QC, J5M 1Y7
(450) 439-3324   *SIC* 1629
ALUMINIUM J CLEMENT INC   *p*1158
1535 117 RTE, MONT-TREMBLANT, QC,
J8E 2X9
(819) 425-7122   *SIC* 1629
ASI GROUP LTD   *p*891
566 ARVIN AVE, STONEY CREEK, ON, L8E
5P1
(905) 643-3283   *SIC* 1629
BEAR CREEK CONTRACTING LTD   *p*283
3550 16 HWY E, THORNHILL, BC, V8G 5J3
(250) 635-4345   *SIC* 1629
**BENNETT MECHANICAL INSTALLATIONS
(2001) LTD**   *p*682
524 SIXTH CONC W, MILLGROVE, ON,
L0R 1V0
(905) 689-7242   *SIC* 1629
BENNETT MECHANICAL INSTALLATIONS

LTD   *p*682
524 6TH CONCESSION RD W, MILL-
GROVE, ON, L0R 1V0
SIC 1629
**BERMINGHAM FOUNDATION SOLUTIONS
LIMITED**   *p*610
600 FERGUSON AVE N, HAMILTON, ON,
L8L 4Z9
(905) 528-7924   *SIC* 1629
BOB DALE OILFIELD CONSTRUCTION LTD
*p*82
5309 56TH AVE, DRAYTON VALLEY, AB,
T7A 1S7
(780) 542-4834   *SIC* 1629
BOUCHIER CONTRACTING LTD   *p*127
GD LCD MAIN, FORT MCMURRAY, AB,
T9H 3E2
(780) 828-4010   *SIC* 1629
C. B. S. CONSTRUCTION LTD   *p*127
150 MACKAY CRES, FORT MCMURRAY,
AB, T9H 4W8
(780) 743-1810   *SIC* 1629
CANDO RAIL SERVICES LTD   *p*346
740 ROSSER AVE SUITE 400, BRANDON,
MB, R7A 0K9
(204) 725-2627   *SIC* 1629
**CARIBOO CENTRAL RAILROAD CON-
TRACTING LTD**   *p*219
307 BANKS RD UNIT 209, KELOWNA, BC,
V1X 6A1
(778) 478-1745   *SIC* 1629
**CASMAN INDUSTRIAL CONSTRUCTION
INC**   *p*127
330 MACKENZIE BLVD, FORT MCMUR-
RAY, AB, T9H 4C4
(780) 791-9283   *SIC* 1629
CASTONGUAY G.P.   *p*593
640 GARSON CONISTON RD, GARSON,
ON, P3L 1R3
(705) 693-3887   *SIC* 1629
CON-WEST CONTRACTING LTD   *p*284
1311 KOOTENAY ST SUITE 250, VANCOU-
VER, BC, V5K 4Y3
(604) 294-5067   *SIC* 1629
CONSUN CONTRACTING LTD   *p*127
195 MACDONALD CRES, FORT MCMUR-
RAY, AB, T9H 4B3
(780) 743-3163   *SIC* 1629
CONTOUR EARTHMOVING LTD   *p*159
285019 WRANGLER WAY, ROCKY VIEW
COUNTY, AB, T1X 0K3
(403) 275-0154   *SIC* 1629
DBC S.E.P.   *p*1319
170 BOUL ROLAND-GODARD, SAINT-
JEROME, QC, J7Y 4P7
(450) 569-8043   *SIC* 1629
DCM INTEGRATED SOLUTIONS INC   *p*162
56 LIBERTY RD, SHERWOOD PARK, AB,
T8H 2J6
(780) 464-6733   *SIC* 1629
**DEAN CONSTRUCTION COMPANY LIM-
ITED**   *p*1026
2720 FRONT RD, WINDSOR, ON, N9J 2N5
(519) 734-8999   *SIC* 1629
DENE SKY SITE SERVICES LTD   *p*79
351 RICHARD ST, CHARD, AB, T0P 1G0
(780) 559-2202   *SIC* 1629
DETON'CHO / NUNA JOINT VENTURE *p*120
9839 31 AVE NW, EDMONTON, AB, T6N
1C5
(780) 434-9114   *SIC* 1629
DRAGADOS CANADA INC   *p*950
150 KING ST W SUITE 2103, TORONTO,
ON, M5H 1J9
(647) 260-5001   *SIC* 1629
DRAGAGE OCEAN DM INC   *p*1258
105 RUE ABRAHAM-MARTIN UNITE 500,
QUEBEC, QC, G1K 8N1
(418) 694-1414   *SIC* 1629
DRUMMOND, GEORGE W. LIMITED   *p*749
30 RIDEAU HEIGHTS DR, NEPEAN, ON,
K2E 7A6
(613) 226-4440   *SIC* 1629
DYFOTECH INC   *p*1089

120 RUE GOODFELLOW, DELSON, QC,
J5B 1V4
(450) 635-8870   *SIC* 1629
DYNAMITAGE T.C.G. (1993) INC   *p*1079
111 RUE DES ROUTIERS, CHICOUTIMI,
QC, G7H 5B1
(418) 698-5858   *SIC* 1629
EAGLES NEST GOLF CLUB INC   *p*664
10000 DUFFERIN ST, MAPLE, ON, L6A
1S3
(905) 417-2300   *SIC* 1629
ELLISDON INDUSTRIAL SERVICES INC
*p*125
1430 91 ST SW UNIT 101, EDMONTON,
AB, T6X 1M5
(780) 669-8530   *SIC* 1629
**ENTERA UTILITY CONTACTORS CO., LIM-
ITED**   *p*785
1011 WILSON AVE, NORTH YORK, ON,
M3K 1G1
(416) 746-9914   *SIC* 1629
ENTERPRISE GROUP, INC   *p*165
64 RIEL DR SUITE 2, ST. ALBERT, AB, T8N
4A4
(780) 418-4400   *SIC* 1629
ENTREPRISES C. & R. MENARD INC *p*1144
2711 RUE PAPINEAU, LONGUEUIL, QC,
J4K 3M6
(450) 679-3131   *SIC* 1629
**ENTREPRISES CLAUDE CHAGNON INC,
LES**   *p*1308
3500 BOUL SIR-WILFRID-LAURIER,
SAINT-HUBERT, QC, J3Y 6T1
(450) 321-2446   *SIC* 1629
ENTREPRISES D. GAUVREAU ENR   *p*1108
930 CH VANIER, GATINEAU, QC, J9J 3J3
(819) 682-1735   *SIC* 1629
EPCOR WATER SERVICES INC   *p*107
10977 50 ST NW, EDMONTON, AB, T6A
2E9
(780) 969-8496   *SIC* 1629
FILTRUM INC   *p*1262
430 RUE DES ENTREPRENEURS, QUE-
BEC, QC, G1M 1B3
(418) 687-0628   *SIC* 1629
FORACTION INC   *p*1158
270 RUE BRUNET, MONT-SAINT-HILAIRE,
QC, J3H 0M6
(450) 446-8144   *SIC* 1629
FORAGE SAGUENAY INC   *p*1116
2370 RUE DE LA METALLURGIE, JON-
QUIERE, QC, G7X 9H2
(418) 542-5059   *SIC* 1629
FORCE COPPS PILING INC   *p*5
27312 - 213 TWP 394, BLACKFALDS, AB,
T0M 0J0
(403) 341-0030   *SIC* 1629
FRAMATOME CANADA LTD   *p*844
925 BROCK RD SUITE B, PICKERING, ON,
L1W 2X9
(905) 421-2600   *SIC* 1629
FRASER RIVER PILE & DREDGE (GP) INC
*p*237
1830 RIVER DR, NEW WESTMINSTER,
BC, V3M 2A8
(604) 522-7971   *SIC* 1629
**FRPD INVESTMENTS LIMITED PARTNER-
SHIP**   *p*237
1830 RIVER DR, NEW WESTMINSTER,
BC, V3M 2A8
(604) 522-7971   *SIC* 1629
GEMINI FIELD SOLUTIONS LTD   *p*50
839 5 AVE SW SUITE 400, CALGARY, AB,
T2P 3C8
(403) 255-2006   *SIC* 1629
GENSTAR DEVELOPMENT COMPANY *p*69
280 MIDPARK WAY SE SUITE 100, CAL-
GARY, AB, T2X 2B5
(403) 256-4000   *SIC* 1629
GHD CONTRACTORS LIMITED   *p*1008
455 PHILLIP ST, WATERLOO, ON, N2L 3X2
(519) 884-0510   *SIC* 1629
GRASCAN CONSTRUCTION LTD   *p*584
61 STEINWAY BLVD, ETOBICOKE, ON,

M9W 6H6
(416) 644-8858   *SIC* 1629
GREAT PLAINS RAIL CONTRACTORS INC
*p*378
GD, WINNIPEG, MB, R3C 2G1
(204) 633-0135   *SIC* 1629
GROUPE NOKAMIC INC   *p*1090
115 RUE DE LA FALAISE, DOLBEAU-
MISTASSINI, QC, G8L 5A6
(418) 276-0126   *SIC* 1629
GULF OPERATORS LTD   *p*413
633 BAYSIDE DR, SAINT JOHN, NB, E2J
1B4
(506) 633-0116   *SIC* 1629
I.W. KUHN CONSTRUCTION LTD   *p*1
208 RAILWAY AVE E, ACADIA VALLEY, AB,
T0J 0A0
(403) 972-3740   *SIC* 1629
ISLAND COASTAL SERVICES LTD   *p*1039
155 BELVEDERE AVE, CHARLOTTE-
TOWN, PE, C1A 2Y9
(902) 892-1062   *SIC* 1629
J.V. DRIVER CORPORATION INC   *p*149
1205 5 ST, NISKU, AB, T9E 7L6
(780) 980-5837   *SIC* 1629
JEWELL, E & R CONTRACTING LIMITED
*p*590
6 CHESSER ST, FALCONBRIDGE, ON,
P0M 1S0
(705) 693-3761   *SIC* 1629
KENAIDAN GROUP LTD   *p*745
7080 DERRYCREST DR, MISSISSAUGA,
ON, L5W 0G5
(905) 670-2660   *SIC* 1629
KIDCO CONSTRUCTION LTD   *p*16
4949 76 AVE SE, CALGARY, AB, T2C 3C6
(403) 730-2029   *SIC* 1629
KIEWIT ENGINEERING CANADA CO. *p*1062
4333 BOUL DE LA GRANDE-ALLEE, BOIS-
BRIAND, QC, J7H 1M7
(450) 435-5756   *SIC* 1629
LADCO COMPANY LIMITED   *p*366
40 LAKEWOOD BLVD SUITE 200, WIN-
NIPEG, MB, R2J 2M7
(204) 982-5959   *SIC* 1629
LBCO CONTRACTING LTD   *p*24
623 35 AVE NE, CALGARY, AB, T2E 2L2
(403) 277-9555   *SIC* 1629
LMT ENTERPRISES LTD   *p*83
2235 2 AVE, DUNMORE, AB, T1B 0K3
(403) 527-1562   *SIC* 1629
M & M RESOURCES INC   *p*213
4901 44TH AVE, FORT NELSON, BC, V0C
1R0
(250) 774-4862   *SIC* 1629
MABOU MINING INC   *p*544
3493 ERRINGTON AVE, CHELMSFORD,
ON, P0M 1L0
(705) 855-0796   *SIC* 1629
MANROC DEVELOPMENTS INC   *p*663
7 BLACK RD, MANITOUWADGE, ON, P0T
2C0
(807) 826-4564   *SIC* 1629
**MATRIX NORTH AMERICAN CONSTRUC-
TION LTD**   *p*526
3196 MAINWAY SUITE 1, BURLINGTON,
ON, L7M 1A5
(289) 313-1600   *SIC* 1629
MCNALLY CONSTRUCTION INC   *p*609
1855 BARTON ST E SUITE 4, HAMILTON,
ON, L8H 2Y7
(905) 549-6561   *SIC* 1629
MCNALLY INTERNATIONAL INC   *p*609
1855 BARTON ST E, HAMILTON, ON, L8H
2Y7
(905) 549-6561   *SIC* 1629
MIRROR NOVA SCOTIA LIMITED   *p*460
600 OTTER LAKE DR, LAKESIDE, NS, B3T
2E2
(902) 453-3490   *SIC* 1629
NMP GOLF CONSTRUCTION INC   *p*1359
2674 CH PLAMONDON BUREAU 201,
SAINTE-MADELEINE, QC, J0H 1S0
(450) 795-3373   *SIC* 1629

NORTH AMERICA CONSTRUCTION (1993) LTD *p746*
21 QUEEN ST, MORRISTON, ON, N0B 2C0
(519) 821-8000 *SIC 1629*

NORTH AMERICAN CONSTRUCTION GROUP LTD *p2*
27287 100 AVE, ACHESON, AB, T7X 6H8
(780) 960-7171 *SIC 1629*

NORTH AMERICAN CONSTRUCTION GROUP LTD *p2*
100 AVE ACHESON SUITE 27287, ACHESON, AB, T7X 6H8
(780) 960-7171 *SIC 1629*

NORTH AMERICAN CONSTRUCTION MANAGEMENT LTD *p2*
26550 ACHESON RD, ACHESON, AB, T7X 6B2
(780) 960-7171 *SIC 1629*

NORTH AMERICAN CONSTRUCTION MANAGEMENT LTD *p128*
GD, FORT MCMURRAY, AB, T9H 3E2
(780) 791-1997 *SIC 1629*

NORTH AMERICAN KILN SERVICES INC *p910*
960 WALSH ST W, THUNDER BAY, ON, P7E 4X4
(807) 622-7728 *SIC 1629*

NORTH AMERICAN ROCK & DIRT INC *p1414*
4271 5TH AVE E, PRINCE ALBERT, SK, S6W 0A5
(306) 764-5337 *SIC 1629*

NORTHEC CONSTRUCTION INC *p913*
2401 AIRPORT RD, TIMMINS, ON, P4N 7C3
(705) 531-3370 *SIC 1629*

OKANAGAN RESTORATION SERVICES LTD *p331*
6236 PLEASANT VALLEY RD, VERNON, BC, V1B 3R3
(250) 542-3470 *SIC 1629*

OWS RAILROAD CONSTRUCTION & MAINTENANCE LTD *p843*
4320 DISCOVERY LINE, PETROLIA, ON, N0N 1R0
(519) 882-4996 *SIC 1629*

PACIFIC BLASTING & DEMOLITION LTD *p184*
3183 NORLAND AVE, BURNABY, BC, V5B 3A9
(604) 291-1255 *SIC 1629*

PARSEC INTERMODAL OF CANADA LIMITED *p557*
751 BOWES RD SUITE 2, CONCORD, ON, L4K 5C9
(905) 669-7901 *SIC 1629*

PARSEC INTERMODAL OF CANADA LIMITED *p642*
6830 RUTHERFORD RD, KLEINBURG, ON, L0J 1C0
(888) 333-8111 *SIC 1629*

PCL CONSTRUCTORS WESTCOAST INC *p256*
13911 WIRELESS WAY SUITE 310, RICHMOND, BC, V6V 3B9
(604) 241-5200 *SIC 1629*

PEACE RIVER HYDRO PARTNERS CONSTRUCTION LTD *p214*
7007 269 RD, FORT ST. JOHN, BC, V1J 4M7
(250) 263-9920 *SIC 1629*

PEAK ENGINEERING & CONSTRUCTION LTD *p546*
13580 COUNTY ROAD 2, COLBORNE, ON, K0K 1S0
(905) 355-1500 *SIC 1629*

PETER KIEWIT INFRASTRUCTURE CO. *p186*
4350 STILL CREEK DR SUITE 310, BURNABY, BC, V5C 0G5
(604) 629-5419 *SIC 1629*

PIDHERNEY'S INC *p159*
HWY 11 RANGE RD 70, ROCKY MOUNTAIN HOUSE, AB, T4T 1A7

(403) 845-3072 *SIC 1629*

PILLAR RESOURCE SERVICES INC *p110*
4155 84 AVE NW, EDMONTON, AB, T6B 2Z3
(780) 440-2212 *SIC 1629*

PNR RAILWORKS INC *p177*
2595 DEACON ST, ABBOTSFORD, BC, V2T 6L4
(604) 850-9166 *SIC 1629*

PNR RAILWORKS INC *p714*
2380 ROYAL WINDSOR DR UNIT 11, MISSISSAUGA, ON, L5J 1K7
(519) 515-1219 *SIC 1629*

PORT CITY WATER PARTNERS *p413*
380 BAYSIDE DR SUITE 101, SAINT JOHN, NB, E2J 4Y8
(506) 645-9070 *SIC 1629*

QUINN DRILLING INC *p156*
788 ST EDGAR INDUSTRIAL WAY, RED DEER, AB, T4P 3R2
(403) 343-8802 *SIC 1629*

REMCAN PROJECTS LIMITED PARTNERSHIP *p225*
20075 100A AVE SUITE 2, LANGLEY, BC, V1M 3G4
(604) 882-0840 *SIC 1629*

ROWE'S CONSTRUCTION LTD *p435*
25 STUDNEY DR, HAY RIVER, NT, X0E 0R6
(867) 874-3243 *SIC 1629*

S C RESTORATIONS LTD *p223*
1216 ST. PAUL ST SUITE 201, KELOWNA, BC, V1Y 2C8
(250) 832-9818 *SIC 1629*

SAIPEM CANADA INC *p58*
530 8 AVE SW SUITE 2100, CALGARY, AB, T2P 3S8
(403) 441-2793 *SIC 1629*

SCR MINING & TUNNELLING INC *p1001*
2797 WHITE ST, VAL CARON, ON, P3N 1B2
(705) 897-1932 *SIC 1629*

SERVICES ENVIRONNEMENTAUX CLEAN HARBORS QUEBEC, INC *p1356*
6785 RTE 132, SAINTE-CATHERINE, QC, J5C 1B6
(450) 632-6640 *SIC 1629*

SIGFUSSON NORTHERN LTD *p351*
50 SWAN CREEK DR, LUNDAR, MB, R0C 1Y0
(204) 762-5500 *SIC 1629*

SMOOK CONTRACTORS LTD *p360*
101 HAYES RD, THOMPSON, MB, R8N 1M3
(204) 677-1560 *SIC 1629*

SONEX CONSTRUCTION GROUP LTD *p103*
21110 108 AVE NW, EDMONTON, AB, T5S 1X4
(780) 447-4409 *SIC 1629*

STONE TOWN CONSTRUCTION LIMITED *p889*
25 WATER ST N, ST MARYS, ON, N4X 1B1
(519) 284-2580 *SIC 1629*

SUBTERRANEAN (MANITOBA) LTD *p360*
6 ST PAUL BLVD, WEST ST PAUL, MB, R2P 2W5
(204) 775-8291 *SIC 1629*

SUN COUNTRY HOLDINGS LTD *p164*
411 SOUTH AVE, SPRUCE GROVE, AB, T7X 3B5
(780) 962-1030 *SIC 1629*

SUPERPORT MARINE SERVICES LIMITED *p465*
30 WATER ST, PORT HAWKESBURY, NS, B9A 3L1
(902) 625-3375 *SIC 1629*

T.C. BACKHOE & DIRECTIONAL DRILLING LIMITED PARTNERSHIP *p161*
302 CREE RD, SHERWOOD PARK, AB, T8A 4G2
(780) 467-1367 *SIC 1629*

TECTONIC INFRASTRUCTURE INC *p664*
120 RODINEA RD UNIT 1, MAPLE, ON, L6A 1R5

(416) 637-6073 *SIC 1629*

THOMPSON BROS. (CONSTR.) LTD *p164*
411 SOUTH AVE, SPRUCE GROVE, AB, T7X 3B4
(780) 962-1030 *SIC 1629*

THYSSEN MINING CONSTRUCTION OF CANADA LTD *p1419*
2409 ALBERT ST N, REGINA, SK, S4P 3E1
(306) 949-6606 *SIC 1629*

TITAN ENVIRONMENTAL CONTAINMENT LTD *p351*
777 QUEST BLVD, ILE DES CHENES, MB, R0A 0T1
(204) 878-3955 *SIC 1629*

TORNGAIT SERVICES INC *p424*
215 HAMILTON RIVER RD, HAPPY VALLEY-GOOSE BAY, NL, A0P 1E0
(709) 896-5431 *SIC 1629*

TORONTO TERMINALS RAILWAY COMPANY LIMITED, THE *p967*
50 BAY ST SUITE 1400, TORONTO, ON, M5J 3A5
(416) 864-3440 *SIC 1629*

TRANS PEACE CONSTRUCTION (1987) LTD *p80*
9626 69 AVE, CLAIRMONT, AB, T8X 5A1
(780) 539-6855 *SIC 1629*

TRANSCENDENT MINING & MOBILIZATION INC *p212*
4A FRONT ST, ELKFORD, BC, V0B 1H0
(778) 521-5144 *SIC 1629*

TRAVAUX MARITIMES OCEAN INC *p1260*
105 RUE ABRAHAM-MARTIN BUREAU 500, QUEBEC, QC, G1K 8N1
(418) 694-1414 *SIC 1629*

TRITECH GROUP LTD *p230*
5413 271 ST, LANGLEY, BC, V4W 3Y7
(604) 607-8878 *SIC 1629*

URBAN WOOD WASTE RECYCLERS LTD *p291*
110 69TH AVE E, VANCOUVER, BC, V5X 4K6
SIC 1629

VALE CANADA LIMITED *p773*
5 PARK HOME AVE SUITE 300, NORTH YORK, ON, M2N 6L4
SIC 1629

VALE CANADA LIMITED *p968*
200 BAY ST SUITE 1500 ROYAL BANK PLZ, TORONTO, ON, M5J 2K2
(416) 361-7511 *SIC 1629*

VALE NEWFOUNDLAND & LABRADOR LIMITED *p429*
18 HEBRON WAY LEVEL 2 KMK PLACE, ST. JOHN'S, NL, A1A 0L9
(709) 758-8888 *SIC 1629*

VANCOUVER PILE DRIVING LTD *p239*
20 BROOKSBANK AVE, NORTH VANCOUVER, BC, V7J 2B8
(604) 986-5911 *SIC 1629*

VEOLIA EAU TECHNOLOGIES CANADA INC *p1337*
4105 RUE SARTELON, SAINT-LAURENT, QC, H4S 2B3
(514) 334-7230 *SIC 1629*

VEOLIA EAU TECHNOLOGIES CANADA INC *p1337*
3901 RUE SARTELON, SAINT-LAURENT, QC, H4S 2A6
(514) 334-7230 *SIC 1629*

VOICE CONSTRUCTION LTD *p111*
7545 52 ST NW, EDMONTON, AB, T6B 2G2
(780) 469-1351 *SIC 1629*

WESTCON EQUIPMENT & RENTALS LTD *p1419*
HWY 1 E, REGINA, SK, S4P 3B1
(306) 359-7273 *SIC 1629*

WORLEYCORD LP *p38*
8500 MACLEOD TRAIL SE SUITE 400, CALGARY, AB, T2H 2N1
(780) 465-5516 *SIC 1629*

SIC 1711 Plumbing, heating, air-conditioning

1008648 ONTARIO INC *p736*
6243 NETHERHART RD, MISSISSAUGA, ON, L5T 1G5
(905) 564-2800 *SIC 1711*

1022013 ONTARIO LIMITED *p863*
1231 PEOPLES RD, SAULT STE. MARIE, ON, P6C 3W7
(705) 759-5148 *SIC 1711*

1514498 ONTARIO INC *p815*
2445 SHEFFIELD RD, OTTAWA, ON, K1B 3V6
(613) 749-5611 *SIC 1711*

2953-6778 QUEBEC INC *p1063*
549 RUE DE VERRAZANO BUREAU 3000, BOUCHERVILLE, QC, J4B 7W2
(450) 449-1516 *SIC 1711*

2982897 CANADA INC *p1233*
2425 RUE MICHELIN, MONTREAL, QC, H7L 5B9
(514) 332-4830 *SIC 1711*

3075487 MANITOBA LTD *p380*
1124 SANFORD ST, WINNIPEG, MB, R3E 2Z9
(204) 788-4117 *SIC 1711*

49 NORTH MECHANICAL LTD *p324*
3641 29TH AVE W SUITE 201, VANCOUVER, BC, V6S 1T5
(604) 224-7604 *SIC 1711*

9170-7570 QUEBEC INC *p1077*
949 3E RUE, CHIBOUGAMAU, QC, G8P 1R4
(418) 748-2691 *SIC 1711*

995451 ONTARIO INC *p490*
1806 CASEY RD SUITE 6, BELLEVILLE, ON, K8N 4Z6
(613) 969-7403 *SIC 1711*

A.B. MECHANICAL LIMITED *p464*
35 RUDDERHAM RD, POINT EDWARD, NS, B2A 4V4
(902) 567-3897 *SIC 1711*

ABCO SUPPLY & SERVICE LTD *p380*
1346 SPRUCE ST, WINNIPEG, MB, R3E 2V7
(204) 633-8071 *SIC 1711*

ACCESS PLUMBING & HEATING LTD *p165*
215 CARNEGIE DR UNIT 5, ST. ALBERT, AB, T8N 5B1
(780) 459-5999 *SIC 1711*

ADAMSON & DOBBIN LIMITED *p840*
407 PIDO RD, PETERBOROUGH, ON, K9J 6X7
(705) 745-5751 *SIC 1711*

ADVANCE DRAINAGE SYSTEM INC *p1306*
250A BOUL INDUSTRIEL, SAINT-GERMAIN-DE-GRANTHAM, QC, J0C 1K0
(800) 733-7473 *SIC 1711*

ADVANCE SHEET METAL LTD *p205*
1546 DERWENT WAY SUITE 311C, DELTA, BC, V3M 6M4
(604) 540-4955 *SIC 1711*

AERCO INDUSTRIES LTD *p246*
201-1952 KINGSWAY AVE, PORT COQUITLAM, BC, V3C 6C2
(604) 431-6883 *SIC 1711*

AERO MECANIQUE TURCOTTE INC *p1361*
1289 BOUL DAGENAIS O, SAINTE-ROSE, QC, H7L 5Z9
(450) 625-2627 *SIC 1711*

AIRE ONE HEATING AND COOLING INC *p616*
1065 UPPER JAMES ST, HAMILTON, ON, L9C 3A6
(905) 385-2800 *SIC 1711*

ALASKAN TECHNOLOGIES CORP *p104*
11810 152 ST NW, EDMONTON, AB, T5V 1E3
(780) 447-2660 *SIC 1711*

ALCO-TMI INC *p1044*
995 AV BOMBARDIER, ALMA, QC, G8B 6H2
(418) 669-1911 *SIC 1711*

ALLDRITT DEVELOPMENT LIMITED *p95*
15035 114 AVE NW, EDMONTON, AB, T5M

2Z1

(780) 451-2732 *SIC 1711*
ALPINE HEATING LTD p99
10333 174 ST NW, EDMONTON, AB, T5S 1H1

(780) 469-0491 *SIC 1711*
ALSCOTT AIR SYSTEMS LIMITED p663
1127 RIVER RD, MANOTICK, ON, K4M 1B4

(613) 692-9517 *SIC 1711*
AMBASSADOR MECHANICAL L.P. p353
400 FORT WHYTE WAY UNIT 110, OAK BLUFF, MB, R4G 0B1

(204) 231-1094 *SIC 1711*
ANMAR MECHANICAL AND ELECTRICAL CONTRACTORS LTD p647
199 MUMFORD RD, LIVELY, ON, P3Y 0A4

(705) 692-0888 *SIC 1711*
APOLLO SHEET METAL LTD p199
2095 BRIGANTINE DR, COQUITLAM, BC, V3K 7B8

(604) 525-8299 *SIC 1711*
APPLEWOOD AIR-CONDITIONING LIMITED p711
3525 HAWKESTONE RD, MISSISSAUGA, ON, L5C 2V1

(905) 275-4500 *SIC 1711*
ARMAUR PLUMBING LTD p224
20085 100A AVE UNIT 1, LANGLEY, BC, V1M 3G4

(604) 888-1255 *SIC 1711*
ARPI'S INDUSTRIES LTD p13
6815 40 ST SE, CALGARY, AB, T2C 2W7

(403) 236-2444 *SIC 1711*
ARPI'S NORTH INC p92
14445 123 AVE NW, EDMONTON, AB, T5L 2Y1

(780) 452-2096 *SIC 1711*
ATCHISON, S. W. PLUMBING & HEATING LTD p660
4186 RANEY CRES UNIT 4, LONDON, ON, N6L 1C3

(519) 652-0673 *SIC 1711*
ATLANTICA MECHANICAL CONTRACTORS INCORPORATED p445
9 RALSTON AVE, DARTMOUTH, NS, B3B 1H5

(902) 468-2300 *SIC 1711*
ATLAS SERVICE COMPANY INC p796
2590 BRISTOL CIR UNIT 1, OAKVILLE, ON, L6H 6Z7

(905) 279-3440 *SIC 1711*
AV-TECH INC p1263
2300 RUE LEON-HARMEL BUREAU 101, QUEBEC, QC, G1N 4L2

(418) 688-2300 *SIC 1711*
B. D. R. SERVICES LTD p371
11 YARD ST, WINNIPEG, MB, R2W 5J6

(204) 586-8227 *SIC 1711*
B.C. COMFORT AIR CONDITIONING LIMITED p191
7405 LOWLAND DR, BURNABY, BC, V5J 5A8

(604) 439-3344 *SIC 1711*
BARETTE BERNARD - ENERFLAMME INC p1104
36 RUE DE VARENNES BUREAU 1, GATINEAU, QC, J8T 0B6

(819) 243-0143 *SIC 1711*
BARRACUDA HEATING SERVICE LTD p450
152 HOLLAND RD, FLETCHERS LAKE, NS, B2T 1A1

(902) 576-3020 *SIC 1711*
BELISLE, G. HOLDINGS (LONDON) LIMITED p660
4231 BLAKIE RD, LONDON, ON, N6L 1B8

(519) 652-5183 *SIC 1711*
BENNETT MECHANICAL INSTALLATION (2001) LTD p682
524 6TH CONCESSION RD W, MILLGROVE, ON, L0R 1V0

(905) 689-7242 *SIC 1711*
BERWIN LTEE p1169
8651 9E AV BUREAU 1, MONTREAL, QC, H1Z 3A1

(514) 376-0121 *SIC 1711*
BLACK & MCDONALD GROUP LIMITED p928
2 BLOOR ST E SUITE 2100, TORONTO, ON, M4W 1A8

(416) 920-5100 *SIC 1711*
BLACK & MCDONALD LIMITED p380
401 WESTON ST SUITE A, WINNIPEG, MB, R3E 3H4

(204) 774-4403 *SIC 1711*
BLACK & MCDONALD LIMITED p428
29 OTTAWA ST, ST. JOHN'S, NL, A1A 2R9

(709) 896-2639 *SIC 1711*
BLACK & MCDONALD LIMITED p445
60 CUTLER AVE, DARTMOUTH, NS, B3B 0J6

(902) 468-3101 *SIC 1711*
BLACK & MCDONALD LIMITED p878
31 PULLMAN CRT, SCARBOROUGH, ON, M1X 1E4

(416) 298-9977 *SIC 1711*
BLACK & MCDONALD LIMITED p878
35 PULLMAN CRT, SCARBOROUGH, ON, M1X 1E4

(416) 298-9977 *SIC 1711*
BLACK & MCDONALD LIMITED p928
2 BLOOR ST E SUITE 2100, TORONTO, ON, M4W 1A8

(416) 920-5100 *SIC 1711*
BML MULTI TRADES GROUP LTD p515
32 RYAN PL, BRANTFORD, ON, N3S 7S1

(905) 777-7879 *SIC 1711*
BMP MECHANICAL LTD p33
6420 6A ST SE SUITE 110, CALGARY, AB, T2H 2B7

(403) 816-4409 *SIC 1711*
BOUCHER LORTIE INC p1278
850 RUE DES ROCAILLES BUREAU 1124, QUEBEC, QC, G2J 1A5

(418) 623-2323 *SIC 1711*
BRACKNELL CORPORATION p996
195 THE WEST MALL STE 302, TORONTO, ON, M9C 5K1

SIC 1711
BRADLEY AIR-CONDITIONING LIMITED p549
150 CONNIE CRES SUITE 14, CONCORD, ON, L4K 1L9

(905) 660-5400 *SIC 1711*
BRAYER, L. A. INDUSTRIES LTD p113
3811 93 ST NW, EDMONTON, AB, T6E 5K5

(780) 462-4812 *SIC 1711*
BRAZZO CONTRACTORS (CALGARY) LTD p14
2624 54 AVE SE UNIT 1, CALGARY, AB, T2C 1R5

(403) 279-1983 *SIC 1711*
BRENNER MECHANICAL INC p1010
630 SUPERIOR DR, WATERLOO, ON, N2V 2C6

(519) 746-0439 *SIC 1711*
BRICOR MECHANICAL LTD p219
1778 BARON RD, KELOWNA, BC, V1X 7G9

(250) 861-6696 *SIC 1711*
BRIGHTER MECHANICAL LIMITED p188
107-4585 CANADA WAY, BURNABY, BC, V5G 4L6

(604) 279-0901 *SIC 1711*
BROADWAY REFRIGERATION AND AIR CONDITIONING CO. LTD p183
2433 HOLDOM AVE, BURNABY, BC, V5B 5A1

(604) 255-2461 *SIC 1711*
BRUIN'S PLUMBING & HEATING LTD p155
7026 JOHNSTONE DR, RED DEER, AB, T4P 3Y6

(403) 343-6060 *SIC 1711*
BRYMARK INSTALLATIONS GROUP INC p246
1648 BROADWAY ST, PORT COQUITLAM, BC, V3C 2M8

(604) 944-1206 *SIC 1711*
BSM SERVICES (1998) LTD p405
948 CH ROYAL, MEMRAMCOOK, NB, E4K

1Y8

(506) 862-0810 *SIC 1711*
C.M.S. COMMERCIAL MECHANICAL SERVICES LTD p878
2721 MARKHAM RD UNIT 10, SCARBOROUGH, ON, M1X 1L5

(416) 609-9992 *SIC 1711*
CALEDON CREEK MECHANICAL LIMITED p532
18023 HORSESHOE HILL RD, CALEDON VILLAGE, ON, L7K 2B8

(519) 927-0190 *SIC 1711*
CANADIAN STRUCTURAL & MECHANICAL LTD p858
1399 LOUGAR AVE, SARNIA, ON, N7S 5N5

(519) 383-6525 *SIC 1711*
CANYON PLUMBING & HEATING LTD p70
3185 114 AVE SE, CALGARY, AB, T2Z 3X2

(403) 258-1505 *SIC 1711*
CAON SERVICES INC p28
1143 42 AVE SE, CALGARY, AB, T2G 1Z3

(403) 279-6641 *SIC 1711*
CENTRE DE PLOMBERIE ST-JEROME INC p1319
1075 BOUL DU GRAND-HERON, SAINT-JEROME, QC, J7Y 1G2

(450) 436-2318 *SIC 1711*
CENTURION MECHANICAL LTD p73
2509 DIEPPE AVE SW UNIT 301, CALGARY, AB, T3E 7J9

(403) 452-6761 *SIC 1711*
CERVOL SERVICE GROUP INC p716
2295 DUNWIN DR UNIT 4, MISSISSAUGA, ON, L5L 3S4

(905) 569-0557 *SIC 1711*
CHAPMAN MECHANICAL LTD p331
901 WADDINGTON DR, VERNON, BC, V1T 9E2

(250) 545-9040 *SIC 1711*
CHARLTON & HILL LIMITED p140
2620 5 AVE N, LETHBRIDGE, AB, T1H 6J6

(403) 328-2665 *SIC 1711*
CHEMFAB INDUSTRIES INC p563
466 POLYMOORE DR, CORUNNA, ON, N0N 1G0

(519) 862-1433 *SIC 1711*
CLIMAT-CONTROL SB INC p1141
800 RUE JEAN-NEVEU, LONGUEUIL, QC, J4G 2M1

(514) 789-0456 *SIC 1711*
CLIMATISATION VALLEE & FILS INC p1282
83 RUE LAROCHE, REPENTIGNY, QC, J6A 7M3

(450) 581-4360 *SIC 1711*
CLIVENCO INC p1263
1185 RUE PHILIPPE-PARADIS BUREAU 200, QUEBEC, QC, G1N 4E2

(418) 682-6373 *SIC 1711*
COMSTOCK CANADA LTD p652
1200 TRAFALGAR ST, LONDON, ON, N5Z 1H5

SIC 1711
CONESTOGO MECHANICAL INC p640
50 DUMART PL, KITCHENER, ON, N2K 3C7

(519) 579-6740 *SIC 1711*
CONFORT EXPERT INC p1048
9771 BOUL METROPOLITAIN E, ANJOU, QC, H1J 0A4

(514) 640-7711 *SIC 1711*
CONSTRUCTIONS 3P INC p1070
3955 RUE ISABELLE, BROSSARD, QC, J4Y 2R2

(450) 659-6000 *SIC 1711*
COOLTECH AIR SYSTEMS LTD p494
37 NIXON RD, BOLTON, ON, L7E 1K1

(905) 951-0885 *SIC 1711*
CORAL CANADA WIDE LTD p8
2150 29 ST NE UNIT 30, CALGARY, AB, T1Y 7G4

(403) 571-9200 *SIC 1711*
COX MECHANICAL LTD p165
65 CORRIVEAU AVE, ST. ALBERT, AB, T8N 5A3

(780) 459-2530 *SIC 1711*
CTR REFRIGERATION AND FOOD STORE EQUIPMENT LTD p12
4840 52 ST SE, CALGARY, AB, T2B 3R2

(403) 444-2877 *SIC 1711*
CULLITON INC p895
473 DOURO ST, STRATFORD, ON, N5A 3S9

(519) 271-1981 *SIC 1711*
CUSTOM AIR CONDITIONING LTD p246
1835 BROADWAY ST, PORT COQUITLAM, BC, V3C 4Z1

(604) 945-7728 *SIC 1711*
D. PECK PLUMBING p857
15 MYRTLE ST, RIDGETOWN, ON, N0P 2C0

(519) 360-5913 *SIC 1711*
D.C.M. MECHANICAL LTD p35
6335 10 ST SE SUITE 6, CALGARY, AB, T2H 2Z9

(403) 255-9161 *SIC 1711*
D.M.S. MECHANICAL LTD p187
7449 CONWAY AVE UNIT 104, BURNABY, BC, V5E 2P7

(604) 437-8996 *SIC 1711*
DAN-JEN MECHANICAL LTD p260
11786 RIVER RD SUITE 146, RICHMOND, BC, V6X 3Z3

(604) 232-4545 *SIC 1711*
DARYL-EVANS MECHANICAL LTD p200
211 SCHOOLHOUSE ST UNIT 1, COQUITLAM, BC, V3K 4X9

(604) 525-3523 *SIC 1711*
DENIS, MAURICE ET FILS INC p1233
1745 RUE GUILLET, MONTREAL, QC, H7L 5B1

(450) 687-3840 *SIC 1711*
DEVELOPPEMENT EDF RENOUVELABLES INC p1203
1134 RUE SAINTE-CATHERINE O BUREAU 910, MONTREAL, QC, H3B 1H4

(514) 397-9997 *SIC 1711*
DILFO MECHANICAL LIMITED p595
1481 CYRVILLE RD, GLOUCESTER, ON, K1B 3L7

(613) 741-7731 *SIC 1711*
DIXON HEATING & SHEET METAL LTD p271
17741 65A AVE UNIT 101, SURREY, BC, V3S 1Z8

(604) 576-0585 *SIC 1711*
DOUBLE G MECHANICAL LTD p109
8170 50 ST NW UNIT 430, EDMONTON, AB, T6B 1E6

SIC 1711
DOWNSVIEW HEATING & AIR CONDITIONING LTD p502
4299 QUEEN ST E, BRAMPTON, ON, L6T 5V4

(905) 794-1489 *SIC 1711*
DOWNSVIEW PLUMBING LIMITED p502
4299 QUEEN ST E UNIT 1, BRAMPTON, ON, L6T 5V4

(416) 675-6215 *SIC 1711*
E-M AIR SYSTEMS INC p552
69 ROMINA DR, CONCORD, ON, L4K 4Z9

(905) 738-0450 *SIC 1711*
E.S. FOX LIMITED p757
9127 MONTROSE RD, NIAGARA FALLS, ON, L2E 7J9

(905) 354-3700 *SIC 1711*
EAGLE RIDGE MECHANICAL CONTRACTING LTD p246
1515 BROADWAY ST SUITE 116, PORT COQUITLAM, BC, V3C 6M2

(604) 941-1071 *SIC 1711*
EAST SIDE VENTILATION LTD p365
11 DURAND RD, WINNIPEG, MB, R2J 3T1

(204) 667-8700 *SIC 1711*
ELITREX PLUMBING LTD p1031
120 SHARER RD, WOODBRIDGE, ON, L4L 8P4

(905) 264-7418 *SIC 1711*
ENGIE MULTITECH LTD p722
2025 MEADOWVALE BLVD UNIT 2, MIS-

SISSAUGA, ON, L5N 5N1
(905) 812-7900   SIC 1711

ENTREPRISES DE REFRIGERATION L.S. INC, LES   p1234
1610 RUE GUILLET, MONTREAL, QC, H7L 5B2
(450) 682-8105   SIC 1711

ENVIRO 5 INC   p1290
1101 139 RTE, ROXTON POND, QC, J0E 1Z0
(450) 777-2551   SIC 1711

ENVIRONMENTAL DYNAMICS LTD   p105
11810 152 ST NW, EDMONTON, AB, T5V 1E3
(780) 421-0686   SIC 1711

EXCEL CLIMATISATION INC   p1308
4915 BOUL SIR-WILFRID-LAURIER BUREAU 1, SAINT-HUBERT, QC, J3Y 3X5
(450) 676-1944   SIC 1711

FAHRHALL MECHANICAL CONTRACTORS LIMITED   p1025
3822 SANDWICH ST, WINDSOR, ON, N9C 1C1
(519) 969-7822   SIC 1711

FIRENZA PLUMBING & HEATING LTD   p786
1 TORBARRIE RD, NORTH YORK, ON, M3L 1G5
(416) 247-7100   SIC 1711

FOREST CITY FIRE PROTECTION LTD   p652
160 ADELAIDE ST S UNIT A, LONDON, ON, N5Z 3L1
(519) 668-0010   SIC 1711

FRASER VALLEY REFRIGERATION LTD   p179
26121 FRASER HWY, ALDERGROVE, BC, V4W 2W8
(604) 856-8644   SIC 1711

GATEWAY MECHANICAL SERVICES INC   p30
4001 16A ST SE, CALGARY, AB, T2G 3T5
(403) 265-0010   SIC 1711

GATEWAY MECHANICAL SERVICES INC   p93
14605 118 AVE NW, EDMONTON, AB, T5L 2M7
(780) 426-6055   SIC 1711

GENERAL SPRINKLERS INC   p794
315 DEERHIDE CRES SUITE 3, NORTH YORK, ON, M9M 2Z2
(416) 748-1175   SIC 1711

GEO. A. KELSON COMPANY LIMITED   p880
2 BALES DR W, SHARON, ON, L0G 1V0
(905) 898-3400   SIC 1711

GICLEURS ALERTE INC   p1076
1250 RUE DES CASCADES, CHATEAUGUAY, QC, J6J 4Z2
(450) 692-9098   SIC 1711

GISBORNE FIRE PROTECTION ALBERTA LTD   p187
7476 HEDLEY AVE, BURNABY, BC, V5E 2P9
(604) 520-7300   SIC 1711

GLOBAL PLUMBING & HEATING INC   p1031
601 ROWNTREE DAIRY RD SUITE 1, WOODBRIDGE, ON, L4L 5T8
(905) 851-4212   SIC 1711

GML MECHANICAL LTD   p209
7355 72 ST SUITE 13, DELTA, BC, V4G 1L5
(604) 940-9686   SIC 1711

GNR CORBUS INC   p1373
4070 RUE BRODEUR, SHERBROOKE, QC, J1L 1V9
(819) 564-2300   SIC 1711

GOLDBAR CONTRACTORS INC   p122
1415 90 AVE NW SUITE 100, EDMONTON, AB, T6P 0C8
(780) 440-6440   SIC 1711

GORDON LATHAM LIMITED   p319
1060 8TH AVE W SUITE 100, VANCOUVER, BC, V6H 1C4
(604) 683-2321   SIC 1711

GRASSHOPPER SOLAR CORPORATION   p688
5935 AIRPORT RD SUITE 210, MISSIS-

SAUGA, ON, L4V 1W5
(866) 310-1575   SIC 1711

GRAY HAWK (1991) CO. LTD   p619
772 MAIN ST E, HAWKESBURY, ON, K6A 1B4
(613) 632-0921   SIC 1711

GREGG'S PLUMBING & HEATING LTD   p1427
503 51ST ST E, SASKATOON, SK, S7K 6V4
(306) 373-4664   SIC 1711

GRIFFITHS, H. COMPANY LIMITED   p1031
140 REGINA RD SUITE 15, WOODBRIDGE, ON, L4L 8N1
(905) 850-7070   SIC 1711

GRIGG PLUMBING & HEATING LTD   p1358
15739 RUE DE LA CASERNE, SAINTE-GENEVIEVE, QC, H9H 1G3
(514) 631-1148   SIC 1711

GROUPE PAQUETTE MECANIQUE DU BATIMENT INC   p1101
275 BOUL MARC-AURELE-FORTIN, FABREVILLE, QC, H7L 2A2
(450) 625-2297   SIC 1711

GROUPE PGS 2009 INC   p1080
1371 RUE DE LA MANIC, CHICOUTIMI, QC, G7K 1G7
(418) 696-1212   SIC 1711

GROUPE PLOMBACTION INC   p1399
575 BOUL PIERRE-ROUX E, VICTORIAVILLE, QC, G6T 1S7
(819) 752-6064   SIC 1711

GROUPE PRO-B INC   p1389
3535 BOUL L.-P.-NORMAND, TROIS-RIVIERES, QC, G9B 0G8
(819) 377-7218   SIC 1711

GROUPE SCV INC   p1398
435 RUE GAMACHE, VICTORIAVILLE, QC, G6P 3T4
(819) 758-5756   SIC 1711

GTA PLUMBING LTD   p717
3995 SLADEVIEW CRES UNIT 6, MISSISSAUGA, ON, L5L 5Y1
(905) 569-7558   SIC 1711

GUTHRIE INVESTMENTS LTD   p128
9912 MANNING AVE, FORT MCMURRAY, AB, T9H 2B9
(780) 791-1367   SIC 1711

GUTHRIE MECHANICAL SERVICES LTD   p128
9912 MANNING AVE, FORT MCMURRAY, AB, T9H 2B9
(780) 791-1367   SIC 1711

HARDING MECHANICAL CONTRACTORS INC   p540
2210 CAVANMORE RD RR 2, CARP, ON, K0A 1L0
(613) 831-2257   SIC 1711

HIGH LIFE HEATING, AIR CONDITIONING & SECURITY INC   p876
102 PASSMORE AVE, SCARBOROUGH, ON, M1V 4S9
(416) 298-2987   SIC 1711

HOOVER MECHANICAL PLUMBING & HEATING LTD   p16
3640 61 AVE SE SUITE 1, CALGARY, AB, T2C 2J3
(403) 217-5655   SIC 1711

HVAC INC   p1234
2185 RUE LE CHATELIER, MONTREAL, QC, H7L 5B3
(514) 748-4822   SIC 1711

ICON INDUSTRIAL CONTRACTORS LTD   p93
12849 141 ST NW, EDMONTON, AB, T5L 4N1
(780) 455-2299   SIC 1711

INDECK COMBUSTION CORPORATION   p1313
4300 AV BEAUDRY, SAINT-HYACINTHE, QC, J2S 8A5
(450) 774-5326   SIC 1711

INDUSTRIES GARANTIES LIMITEE, LES   p1156
5420 RUE PARE, MONT-ROYAL, QC, H4P

1R3
(514) 342-3400   SIC 1711

INTEGRAL GROUP INC   p306
200 GRANVILLE ST SUITE 180, VANCOUVER, BC, V6C 1S4
(604) 687-1800   SIC 1711

INTEGRITY INSTALLATIONS LTD   p240
705 15TH ST W, NORTH VANCOUVER, BC, V7M 1T2
(604) 988-3700   SIC 1711

INTER WEST MECHANICAL LTD   p1428
1839 SASKATCHEWAN AVE, SASKATOON, SK, S7K 1R1
(306) 955-1800   SIC 1711

INTERIOR PLUMBING AND HEATING LIMITED   p217
782 LAVAL CRES, KAMLOOPS, BC, V2C 5P3
(250) 372-3441   SIC 1711

J.P. LESSARD CANADA INC   p1170
9455 RUE J.-J.-GAGNIER, MONTREAL, QC, H1Z 3C8
(514) 384-0660   SIC 1711

JOHNSON CONTROLS NOVA SCOTIA U.L.C.   p1326
395 AV SAINTE-CROIX BUREAU 100, SAINT-LAURENT, QC, H4N 2L3
(514) 747-2580   SIC 1711

JOHNSON, S.E. MANAGEMENT LTD   p71
4330 122 AVE SE, CALGARY, AB, T2Z 0A6
(403) 291-9600   SIC 1711

JRL HVAC INC   p509
278 RUTHERFORD RD S, BRAMPTON, ON, L6W 3K7
(905) 457-6900   SIC 1711

K.B. HEATING & AIR CONDITIONING LTD   p140
3569 32 AVE N, LETHBRIDGE, AB, T1H 7C2
(403) 328-0337   SIC 1711

KAMTECH SERVICES INC   p1428
3339 FAITHFULL AVE, SASKATOON, SK, S7K 8H5
(306) 931-9655   SIC 1711

KEL-GOR LIMITED   p860
1411 PLANK RD, SARNIA, ON, N7T 7H3
(519) 336-9312   SIC 1711

KENT JB FR COUNCIL 6638   p426
7 GREENWOOD CRES, MOUNT PEARL, NL, A1N 2C1
(709) 781-6638   SIC 1711

KOLOSTAT INC   p1234
2005 RUE LE CHATELIER, MONTREAL, QC, H7L 5B3
(514) 333-7333   SIC 1711

LA-BIL INC   p1262
895 AV GODIN, QUEBEC, QC, G1M 2X5
(418) 842-3216   SIC 1711

LAGRANGE MECHANICAL SERVICES LTD   p167
970 BOULDER BLVD, STONY PLAIN, AB, T7Z 0E6
(780) 968-1782   SIC 1711

LAMSAR INC   p860
608 MCGREGOR RD, SARNIA, ON, N7T 7J2
(519) 332-5010   SIC 1711

LANCASTER GROUP INC   p615
195 HEMPSTEAD DR, HAMILTON, ON, L8W 2E6
(905) 388-3800   SIC 1711

LEADER PLUMBING & HEATING INC   p1032
91 HAIST AVE UNIT 3, WOODBRIDGE, ON, L4L 5V5
(905) 264-1162   SIC 1711

LEHMANN PLUMBING LTD   p110
3645 73 AVE NW, EDMONTON, AB, T6B 2T8
(780) 465-4434   SIC 1711

LEKTER INDUSTRIAL SERVICES INC   p490
500 HARVARD DR RR 1, BELLE RIVER, ON, N0R 1A0
(519) 727-3713   SIC 1711

LEPROHON INC   p1375

6171 BOUL BOURQUE, SHERBROOKE, QC, J1N 1H2
(819) 563-2454   SIC 1711

LESAGE INC   p1085
817 RUE SALABERRY, COTE SAINT-LUC, QC, H7S 1H5
(514) 337-3585   SIC 1711

LIONEL VENNES & FILS INC   p1112
180 32E AV BUREAU 1, GRAND-MERE, QC, G9T 5K5
(819) 538-2308   SIC 1711

LISI MECHANICAL CONTRACTORS LTD   p586
160 DISCO RD, ETOBICOKE, ON, M9W 1M4
(416) 674-8333   SIC 1711

LOCKERBIE & HOLE CONTRACTING LIMITED   p105
14940 121A AVE NW, EDMONTON, AB, T5V 1A3
(780) 452-1250   SIC 1711

LOPES LIMITED   p561
84 SMELTER RD, CONISTON, ON, P0M 1M0
(705) 694-4713   SIC 1711

LOWE MECHANICAL SERVICES LTD   p369
72 PARK LANE AVE, WINNIPEG, MB, R2R 0K2
(204) 233-3292   SIC 1711

LUCIEN CHARBONNEAU LIMITEE   p1224
1955 RUE CABOT, MONTREAL, QC, H4E 1E2
(514) 336-2500   SIC 1711

MACO MECANIQUE INC   p1388
6595 BOUL JEAN-XXIII, TROIS-RIVIERES, QC, G9A 5C9
(819) 378-7070   SIC 1711

MALFAR MECHANICAL INC   p1032
144 WOODSTREAM BLVD SUITE 7, WOODBRIDGE, ON, L4L 7Y3
(905) 850-1242   SIC 1711

MAPLERIDGE MECHANICAL CONTACTING INC   p845
939 DILLINGHAM RD, PICKERING, ON, L1W 1Z7
(905) 831-0524   SIC 1711

MARTIN AIR HEATING & AIR CONDITIONING SERVICES LIMITED   p575
30 FIELDWAY RD, ETOBICOKE, ON, M8Z 0E3
(416) 247-1777   SIC 1711

MARTINO CONTRACTORS LTD   p555
150 CONNIE CRES UNIT 16, CONCORD, ON, L4K 1L9
(905) 760-9894   SIC 1711

MASTER MECHANICAL PLUMBING & HEATING (1986) LTD   p122
2107 87 AVE NW, EDMONTON, AB, T6P 1L5
(780) 449-1400   SIC 1711

MASTER MECHANICAL PLUMBING & HEATING LTD   p36
6025 12 ST SE SUITE 19, CALGARY, AB, T2H 2K1
(403) 243-5880   SIC 1711

MATTINA MECHANICAL LIMITED   p608
211 LANARK ST UNIT A, HAMILTON, ON, L8E 2Z9
(905) 544-6380   SIC 1711

MDF MECHANICAL LIMITED   p504
2100 STEELES AVE E, BRAMPTON, ON, L6T 1A7
(905) 789-9944   SIC 1711

MECANICACTION INC   p1345
6660 RUE P.-E.-LAMARCHE, SAINT-LEONARD, QC, H1P 1J7
(514) 666-9770   SIC 1711

MECANIQUE INDUSTRIELLE FORTIER & FILS INC   p1123
1675 RUE INDUSTRIELLE, LA PRAIRIE, QC, J5R 2E4
(450) 619-9292   SIC 1711

MESSENGER MECHANICAL INCORPORATED   p801

1420 CORNWALL RD UNIT 3, OAKVILLE, ON, L6J 7W5
(905) 844-2949   *SIC* 1711

MIKKELSEN-COWARD & CO LTD   p372
1615 INKSTER BLVD, WINNIPEG, MB, R2X 1R2
(204) 694-8900   *SIC* 1711

MJS MECHANICAL LTD   p77
2401 144 AVE NE, CALGARY, AB, T3P 0T3
(403) 250-1355   *SIC* 1711

MODERN NIAGARA DESIGN SERVICES INC   p626
85 DENZIL DOYLE COURT, KANATA, ON, K2M 2G8
(613) 591-7505   *SIC* 1711

MODERN NIAGARA HVAC SERVICES INC   p626
85 DENZIL DOYLE CRT, KANATA, ON, K2M 2G8
(613) 591-7505   *SIC* 1711

MODERN NIAGARA OTTAWA INC   p626
85 DENZIL DOYLE CRT, KANATA, ON, K2M 2G8
(613) 591-7505   *SIC* 1711

MODERN NIAGARA TORONTO INC   p1028
8125 HIGHWAY 50, WOODBRIDGE, ON, L4H 4S6
(416) 749-6031   *SIC* 1711

MODERN NIAGARA VANCOUVER INC p241
788 HARBOURSIDE DR SUITE 200, NORTH VANCOUVER, BC, V7P 3R7
(604) 980-4891   *SIC* 1711

MODERN/NIAGARA GROUP INC   p1002
8125 HWY 50, VAUGHAN, ON, L4H 4S6
(613) 591-1338   *SIC* 1711

MYSTIQUE MECHANICAL LTD   p9
3605 29 ST NE SUITE 300, CALGARY, AB, T1Y 5W4
SIC 1711

NATIONAL HYDRONICS LTD   p277
12178 86 AVE, SURREY, BC, V3W 3H7
(604) 591-6106   *SIC* 1711

NAVADA LTEE   p1142
675 RUE HERELLE, LONGUEUIL, QC, J4G 2M8
(450) 679-3370   *SIC* 1711

NAYLOR GROUP INCORPORATED   p798
455 NORTH SERVICE RD E, OAKVILLE, ON, L6H 1A5
(905) 338-8000   *SIC* 1711

NEELANDS GROUP LIMITED   p526
4131 PALLADIUM WAY, BURLINGTON, ON, L7M 0V9
(905) 332-4555   *SIC* 1711

NEKISON ENGINEERING & CONTRACTORS LIMITED   p575
17 SAINT LAWRENCE AVE, ETOBICOKE, ON, M8Z 5T8
(416) 259-4631   *SIC* 1711

NELCO MECHANICAL LIMITED   p640
77 EDWIN ST, KITCHENER, ON, N2H 4N7
(519) 744-6511   *SIC* 1711

NETWORK MECHANICAL INC   p556
73 CORSTATE AVE UNIT 1, CONCORD, ON, L4K 4Y2
(905) 761-1417   *SIC* 1711

NEWFOUNDLAND HVAC LIMITED   p426
16 THOMAS BYRNE DR, MOUNT PEARL, NL, A1N 0E1
(709) 738-7700   *SIC* 1711

NORTEK AIR SOLUTIONS CANADA, INC p1347
200 RUE CARTER, SAINT-LEONARD-D'ASTON, QC, J0C 1M0
(819) 399-2175   *SIC* 1711

NORWELD MECHANICAL INSTALLATIONS INC   p251
1416 SANTA FE RD, PRINCE GEORGE, BC, V2N 5T5
(250) 562-6660   *SIC* 1711

NOVEL MECHANICAL INC   p1028
111 ZENWAY BLVD UNIT 23, WOODBRIDGE, ON, L4H 3H9
SIC 1711

O'CONNELL, THOMAS INC   p1223
5700 RUE NOTRE-DAME O, MONTREAL, QC, H4C 1V1
(514) 932-2145   *SIC* 1711

OCEAN PARK MECHANICAL INC   p283
2428 KING GEORGE BLVD SUITE 102, SURREY, BC, V4P 1H5
(604) 536-2363   *SIC* 1711

PAD-CAR MECHANICAL LTD   p147
3271 17 AVE SW, MEDICINE HAT, AB, T1B 4B1
(403) 528-3353   *SIC* 1711

PEAK MECHANICAL LTD   p1429
409 45TH A ST E, SASKATOON, SK, S7K 0W6
(306) 249-4814   *SIC* 1711

PENGUIN POWER SOLAR   p1026
2118 HURON BRUCE RD, WINGHAM, ON, N0G 2W0
(519) 274-2179   *SIC* 1711

PETRIN MECHANICAL LTD   p106
12180 152 ST NW, EDMONTON, AB, T5V 1S1
(780) 451-4943   *SIC* 1711

PIPE-ALL PLUMBING & HEATING LTD p1033
141 STRADA DR, WOODBRIDGE, ON, L4L 5V9
(905) 851-1927   *SIC* 1711

PLOMBERIE & CHAUFFAGE ALAIN DAIGLE INC   p1282
310 RUE CHARLES-MARCHAND, REPENTIGNY, QC, J5Z 4P1
(450) 657-1499   *SIC* 1711

PLOMBERIE DANIEL COTE INC   p1234
3000 MONTEE SAINT-AUBIN, MONTREAL, QC, H7L 3N8
(450) 973-2545   *SIC* 1711

PLOMBERIE DE LA CAPITALE INC   p1119
6345 BOUL WILFRID-HAMEL UNITE 102, L'ANCIENNE-LORETTE, QC, G2E 5W2
(418) 847-2818   *SIC* 1711

PLOMBERIE GOYER INC   p1088
150 RUE DE SHERBROOKE, COWANSVILLE, QC, J2K 3Y9
(450) 263-2226   *SIC* 1711

PLOMBERIE PHCB INC   p1297
4 RUE DES AFFAIRES, SAINT-CHRISTOPHE-D'ARTHABASK, QC, G6R 0B2
(819) 260-4422   *SIC* 1711

PLOMBERIE RICHARD JUBINVILLE INC p1335
5600 CH DU BOIS-FRANC, SAINT-LAURENT, QC, H4S 1A9
(514) 333-0856   *SIC* 1711

POW CITY MECHANICAL PARTNERSHIP p1425
2920 JASPER AVE S, SASKATOON, SK, S7J 4L7
(306) 933-3133   *SIC* 1711

POWERFUL GROUP OF COMPANIES INC p699
5155 SPECTRUM WAY SUITE 8, MISSISSAUGA, ON, L4W 5A1
(416) 674-8046   *SIC* 1711

PRAIRIE METAL INDUSTRIES INC   p106
16420 130 AVE NW, EDMONTON, AB, T5V 1J8
(780) 447-1400   *SIC* 1711

PRICE MECHANICAL LIMITED   p369
404 EGESZ ST, WINNIPEG, MB, R2R 1X5
(204) 633-4808   *SIC* 1711

PRIME BOILER SERVICES LTD   p156
155 QUEENS DR, RED DEER, AB, T4P 0R3
(403) 314-2140   *SIC* 1711

PRIMO MECHANICAL INC   p1033
253 JEVLAN DR UNIT 15, WOODBRIDGE, ON, L4L 7Z6
(905) 851-6718   *SIC* 1711

PRIORITY MECHANICAL INC   p116
9259 35 AVE NW, EDMONTON, AB, T6E 5Y1
(780) 435-3636   *SIC* 1711

PRIORITY MECHANICAL SERVICES LTD p483
3160 ALPS RD, AYR, ON, N0B 1E0
(519) 632-7116   *SIC* 1711

PRODUITS IDEALTFC INC   p1374
4460 RUE HECTOR-BRIEN, SHERBROOKE, QC, J1L 0E2
(819) 566-5696   *SIC* 1711

PROTECTION INCENDIE L.P.G. INC p1355
260 RUE CLEMENT, SAINTE-ANNE-DESPLAINES, QC, J0N 1H0
(514) 915-5913   *SIC* 1711

PYRO-AIR LTEE   p1076
2575 BOUL FORD, CHATEAUGUAY, QC, J6J 4Z2
(450) 691-3460   *SIC* 1711

PYRO-AIR LTEE   p1148
2301 RUE PRINCIPALE O, MAGOG, QC, J1X 0J4
(819) 847-2014   *SIC* 1711

QBD COOLING SYSTEMS INC   p510
31 BRAMSTEELE RD, BRAMPTON, ON, L6W 3K6
(905) 459-0709   *SIC* 1711

QBD MODULAR SYSTEMS INC   p510
31 BRAMSTEELE RD, BRAMPTON, ON, L6W 3K6
(905) 459-0709   *SIC* 1711

QCE CANADA (ONTARIO) LTD   p648
56 R2, LOMBARDY, ON, K0G 1L0
(905) 424-4403   *SIC* 1711

R F CONTRACTING INC   p863
116 INDUSTRIAL PARK CRES, SAULT STE. MARIE, ON, P6B 5P2
(705) 253-1151   *SIC* 1711

R.A.C.E. MECHANICAL SYSTEMS INC p811
9 COBBLEDICK ST, ORONO, ON, L0B 1M0
(905) 983-9800   *SIC* 1711

REFRIGERATION ACTAIR INC   p1067
1370 RUE JOLIOT-CURIE BUREAU 704, BOUCHERVILLE, QC, J4B 7L9
(450) 449-5266   *SIC* 1711

REGGIN TECHNICAL SERVICES LTD   p13
4550 35 ST SE, CALGARY, AB, T2B 3S4
(403) 287-2540   *SIC* 1711

RELIANCE COMFORT LIMITED PARTNERSHIP   p768
2 LANSING SQ, NORTH YORK, ON, M2J 4P8
(416) 499-7600   *SIC* 1711

RIDGEWAY MECHANICAL LTD   p202
925 SHERWOOD AVE UNIT 1, COQUITLAM, BC, V3K 1A9
(604) 525-0238   *SIC* 1711

ROGERS, JOHN C. SHEET METAL LTD p1015
2300 FORBES ST, WHITBY, ON, L1N 8M3
(905) 571-2422   *SIC* 1711

ROSE MECHANICAL INC   p562
18060 GLEN RD, CORNWALL, ON, K6H 5T1
(613) 938-9867   *SIC* 1711

S.A.T SOLAR & ALTERNATIVE TECHNOLOGY   p736
1935 DREW RD SUITE 28, MISSISSAUGA, ON, L5S 1M7
(905) 673-5060   *SIC* 1711

SAINT-AUGUSTIN CANADA ELECTRIQUE INC   p1293
75 RUE D'ANVERS, SAINT-AUGUSTIN-DE-DESMAURES, QC, G3A 1S5
(418) 878-6900   *SIC* 1711

SAYERS & ASSOCIATES LTD.   p545
1000 DEPALMA DR, COBOURG, ON, K9A 5W6
SIC 1711

SCHENDEL MECHANICAL CONTRACTING LTD   p103
20310 107 AVE NW, EDMONTON, AB, T5S 1W9
(780) 447-3400   *SIC* 1711

SCHMIDT, WM. MECHANICAL CONTRACTORS LTD   p25
4603 13 ST NE SUITE D, CALGARY, AB,

T2E 6M3
(403) 250-1157   *SIC* 1711

SERV-ALL MECHANICAL SERVICES LTD p103
18120 107 AVE NW, EDMONTON, AB, T5S 1K5
(780) 484-6681   *SIC* 1711

SIEMENS CANADA LIMITED   p25
1930 MAYNARD RD SE UNIT 24, CALGARY, AB, T2E 6J8
(403) 259-3404   *SIC* 1711

SIEMENS CANADA LIMITED   p827
2435 HOLLY LANE, OTTAWA, ON, K1V 7P2
(613) 733-9781   *SIC* 1711

SIMPLY COMFORT INC.   p768
2225 SHEPPARD AVE E SUITE 1501, NORTH YORK, ON, M2J 5C2
(416) 477-0626   *SIC* 1711

SPERLING INDUSTRIES LTD   p357
51 STATION SR, SPERLING, MB, R0G 2M0
(204) 626-3401   *SIC* 1711

SPRINGBANK MECHANICAL SYSTEMS LIMITED   p717
3615 LAIRD RD UNIT 1, MISSISSAUGA, ON, L5L 5Z8
(905) 569-8990   *SIC* 1711

SPRINT MECHANICAL INC   p588
50 WOODBINE DOWNS BLVD, ETOBICOKE, ON, M9W 5R2
(416) 747-6059   *SIC* 1711

STANDARD MECHANICAL SYSTEMS LIMITED   p703
3055 UNIVERSAL DR, MISSISSAUGA, ON, L4X 2E2
(905) 625-9505   *SIC* 1711

STARKS PLUMBING AND HEATING LTD p147
4850 BOX SPRINGS RD NW, MEDICINE HAT, AB, T1C 0C8
(403) 527-2929   *SIC* 1711

STARTEC REFRIGERATION & COMPRESSION   p25
7664 10 ST NE SUITE 11, CALGARY, AB, T2E 8W1
(403) 347-1131   *SIC* 1711

STERLING PLUMBING & HEATING LTD p1421
1625 8TH AVE, REGINA, SK, S4R 1E6
(306) 586-5050   *SIC* 1711

STRATHCONA MECHANICAL LIMITED p140
6612 44 ST, LEDUC, AB, T9E 7E4
(780) 980-1122   *SIC* 1711

STREAMLINE MECHANICAL L.P.   p161
53113 21 HWY, SHERWOOD PARK, AB, T8A 4T7
(780) 467-6941   *SIC* 1711

STUART OLSON INDUSTRIAL CONSTRUCTORS INC   p899
670 FALCONBRIDGE RD UNIT 1, SUDBURY, ON, P3A 4S4
(705) 222-4848   *SIC* 1711

SUNNY CORNER ENTERPRISES INC p405
259 DALTON AVE, MIRAMICHI, NB, E1V 3C4
(506) 622-5600   *SIC* 1711

SYSTEMES TECHNO-POMPES INC, LES p1279
6055 RUE DES TOURNELLES, QUEBEC, QC, G2J 1P7
(418) 623-2022   *SIC* 1711

TAC MECHANICAL INC   p588
215 CARLINGVIEW DR SUITE 311, ETOBICOKE, ON, M9W 5X8
(416) 798-8400   *SIC* 1711

TBC CONSTRUCTIONS INC   p1263
760 AV GODIN, QUEBEC, QC, G1M 2K4
(418) 681-0671   *SIC* 1711

THERMOGENICS INC   p482
6 SCANLON CRT, AURORA, ON, L4G 7B2
(905) 727-1901   *SIC* 1711

THORPE BROTHERS LIMITED   p1414
HWY 2 S 44TH ST, PRINCE ALBERT, SK, S6V 5R4

(306) 763-8454   *SIC 1711*

TORNADO INSULATION LTD   *p661*
4231 BLAKIE RD, LONDON, ON, N6L 1B8
(519) 652-5183   *SIC 1711*

TOWN & COUNTRY PLUMBING & HEATING (2004) LTD   *p1419*
1450 SOUTH RAILWAY ST, REGINA, SK, S4P 0A2
(306) 352-4328   *SIC 1711*

TROTTER & MORTON FACILITY SERVICES INC   *p38*
5711 1 ST SE, CALGARY, AB, T2H 1H9
(403) 255-7535   *SIC 1711*

TROTTER AND MORTON BUILDING TECH-NOLOGIES INC   *p38*
5711 1 ST SE, CALGARY, AB, T2H 1H9
(403) 255-7535   *SIC 1711*

TROY LIFE & FIRE SAFETY LTD   *p836*
1042 2ND AVE E, OWEN SOUND, ON, N4K 2H7
(519) 371-4747   *SIC 1711*

TRS HEATING & COOLING LTD   *p568*
3520 COON'S RD, ELIZABETHTOWN, ON, K6T 1A6
(613) 342-9733   *SIC 1711*

TU-MEC INC   *p1163*
11700 AV LUCIEN-GENDRON, MON-TREAL, QC, H1E 7J7
(514) 881-1801   *SIC 1711*

UGE INTERNATIONAL LTD   *p958*
56 TEMPERANCE ST 7 FL, TORONTO, ON, M5H 3V5
(416) 789-4655   *SIC 1711*

UNITED THERMO GROUP LTD   *p1034*
261 TROWERS RD, WOODBRIDGE, ON, L4L 5Z8
(905) 851-0500   *SIC 1711*

UNIVERSITY PLUMBING & HEATING LTD   *p785*
3655 KEELE ST, NORTH YORK, ON, M3J 1M8
(416) 630-6010   *SIC 1711*

UNIVERSITY SPRINKLER SYSTEMS IN-CORPORATED   *p211*
1777 56 ST UNIT 500, DELTA, BC, V4L 0A6
(604) 421-4555   *SIC 1711*

URBAN MECHANICAL CONTRACTING LTD   *p589*
254 ATTWELL DR, ETOBICOKE, ON, M9W 5B2
(416) 240-8830   *SIC 1711*

VALLEY REFRIGERATION & AIR CONDI-TIONING LTD   *p404*
35 KINNEY RD, JACKSONVILLE, NB, E7M 3G1
(506) 325-2204   *SIC 1711*

VENSHORE MECHANICAL LTD   *p909*
1019 NORTHERN AVE, THUNDER BAY, ON, P7C 5L6
(807) 623-6414   *SIC 1711*

VENTILABEC INC   *p1357*
1955 BOUL SAINT-ELZEAR O, SAINTE-DOROTHEE, QC, H7L 3N7
(450) 686-7062   *SIC 1711*

VENTILATION G.R. INC   *p1363*
1645 BOUL SAINT-ELZEAR O, SAINTE-ROSE, QC, H7L 3N6
(450) 688-9832   *SIC 1711*

VENTILEX INC   *p1302*
348 BOUL INDUSTRIEL, SAINT-EUSTACHE, QC, J7R 5R4
(450) 473-9843   *SIC 1711*

VERSATECH MECHANICAL LTD   *p869*
50 SKAGWAY AVE SUITE A, SCARBOR-OUGH, ON, M1M 3V1
(416) 292-9220   *SIC 1711*

VET'S SHEET METAL LTD   *p111*
6111 56 AVE NW, EDMONTON, AB, T6B 3E2
(780) 434-7476   *SIC 1711*

VIADUCT SHEET METAL LTD   *p273*
18787 52 AVE, SURREY, BC, V3S 8E5
(604) 575-1600   *SIC 1711*

VICOR MECHANICAL LTD   *p589*

11 HAAS RD, ETOBICOKE, ON, M9W 3A1
SIC 1711

VIKING INSTALLATIONS (CALGARY) LTD   *p32*
4020 4 ST SE, CALGARY, AB, T2G 2W3
(403) 273-7716   *SIC 1711*

VITULLO BROS. PLUMBING CO. LTD   *p560*
121 BRADWICK DR UNIT 3, CONCORD, ON, L4K 1K5
(905) 669-2843   *SIC 1711*

VOLLMER INC   *p1025*
3822 SANDWICH ST, WINDSOR, ON, N9C 1C1
(519) 966-6100   *SIC 1711*

VR MECHANICAL SOLUTIONS INC   *p475*
464 KINGSTON RD W, AJAX, ON, L1T 3A3
(905) 426-7551   *SIC 1711*

WATSON GROUP LTD, THE   *p854*
95 WEST BEAVER CREEK RD UNIT 10, RICHMOND HILL, ON, L4B 1H2
(905) 889-9119   *SIC 1711*

WB MELBACK CORPORATION   *p753*
742252 DAWSON POINT RD, NEW LISKEARD, ON, P0J 1P0
(705) 647-5879   *SIC 1711*

WELSH, FRED LTD   *p202*
94 GLACIER ST UNIT 201, COQUITLAM, BC, V3K 6B2
(604) 942-0012   *SIC 1711*

WEST BAY MECHANICAL LTD   *p341*
584 LEDSHAM RD, VICTORIA, BC, V9C 1J8
(250) 478-8532   *SIC 1711*

WEST KOOTENAY MECHANICAL (2001) LTD   *p284*
8131 OLD WANETA RD, TRAIL, BC, V1R 4X1
(250) 364-1541   *SIC 1711*

WESTCAL INSULATION LTD   *p38*
7005 FAIRMOUNT DR SE UNIT 4165, CAL-GARY, AB, T2H 0J1
(403) 242-1357   *SIC 1711*

X-L-AIR ENERGY SERVICES LTD   *p541*
141 WESCAR LANE, CARP, ON, K0A 1L0
(613) 836-5002   *SIC 1711*

YANCH HEATING AND AIR CONDITIONING (BARRIE) LIMITED   *p489*
89 RAWSON AVE, BARRIE, ON, L4N 6E5
(705) 728-5406   *SIC 1711*

YORKTON PLUMBING & HEATING LTD   *p1439*
HWY 9 N, YORKTON, SK, S3N 4A9
(306) 782-4588   *SIC 1711*

ZENTIL, D. MECHANICAL INC   *p561*
633 EDGELEY BLVD, CONCORD, ON, L4K 4H6
(905) 738-0569   *SIC 1711*

SIC 1721 Painting and paper hanging

3728111 MANITOBA LTD   *p357*
2262 SPRINGFIELD RD BLDG A, SPRING-FIELD, MB, R2C 2Z2
(204) 654-1955   *SIC 1721*

540731 ONTARIO LIMITED   *p736*
7105 PACIFIC CIR, MISSISSAUGA, ON, L5T 2A8
(905) 564-5620   *SIC 1721*

BLASTCO CORPORATION   *p516*
57 OLD ONONDAGA RD W SS 13, BRANT-FORD, ON, N3T 5M1
(519) 756-9050   *SIC 1721*

BRUNELLE, GUY INC   *p1165*
4450 RUE BELANGER, MONTREAL, QC, H1T 1B5
(514) 729-0008   *SIC 1721*

CARNEIL GROUP LTD, THE   *p365*
1035 MISSION ST, WINNIPEG, MB, R2J 0A4
(204) 233-0671   *SIC 1721*

CLARA INDUSTRIAL SERVICES LIMITED   *p910*
1130 COMMERCE ST, THUNDER BAY, ON,

P7E 6E9
(807) 475-4608   *SIC 1721*

FLYING COLOURS CORP   *p840*
901 AIRPORT RD SUITE 120, PETERBOR-OUGH, ON, K9J 0E7
(705) 742-4688   *SIC 1721*

MANZ CONTRACTING SERVICES INC   *p1020*
2680 TEMPLE DR, WINDSOR, ON, N8W 5J5
(519) 974-2899   *SIC 1721*

REVETEMENTS SCELL-TECH INC, LES   *p1085*
1478 RUE CUNARD, COTE SAINT-LUC, QC, H7S 2B7
(514) 990-7886   *SIC 1721*

STANDARD PAINT SYSTEMS LTD   *p1033*
80 ASHBRIDGE CIR UNIT 1-4, WOOD-BRIDGE, ON, L4L 3R5
SIC 1721

TECHNOLOGIES SURFACE PRAXAIR MONTREAL S.E.C.   *p1331*
2300 RUE COHEN, SAINT-LAURENT, QC, H4R 2N8
(514) 333-0030   *SIC 1721*

VALOUR DECORATING (1988) LTD   *p382*
889 WALL ST, WINNIPEG, MB, R3G 2T9
(204) 786-5875   *SIC 1721*

SIC 1731 Electrical work

10365289 CANADA INC   *p1029*
7777 WESTON RD 8TH FL, WOOD-BRIDGE, ON, L4L 0G9
(905) 695-1700   *SIC 1731*

2242974 CANADA INC   *p1288*
1300 RUE SAGUENAY, ROUYN-NORANDA, QC, J9X 7C3
(819) 797-7500   *SIC 1731*

2950-0519 QUEBEC INC   *p1289*
160 BOUL INDUSTRIEL, ROUYN-NORANDA, QC, J9X 6T3
(819) 797-0088   *SIC 1731*

3175120 CANADA INC   *p1379*
1887 CH SAINT-CHARLES, TERRE-BONNE, QC, J6W 5W5
(450) 964-5696   *SIC 1731*

372103 ONTARIO LTD   *p548*
33 CORSTATE AVE, CONCORD, ON, L4K 4Y2
(905) 669-5712   *SIC 1731*

421042 BC LTD   *p331*
887 FAIRWEATHER RD, VERNON, BC, V1T 8T8
(250) 542-5481   *SIC 1731*

567945 ALBERTA LTD   *p4*
116 EAGLE CRES, BANFF, AB, T1L 1A3
(403) 762-3287   *SIC 1731*

593130 BC LTD   *p283*
1200 SECOND AVE, TRAIL, BC, V1R 1L6
(250) 364-2253   *SIC 1731*

9089-3470 QUEBEC INC   *p1280*
290 RUE BERNIER E, QUEBEC, QC, G2M 1K7
(418) 849-6246   *SIC 1731*

9349-6446 QUEBEC INC   *p1068*
6 RUE DE LA PLACE-DU-COMMERCE BU-REAU 100, BROSSARD, QC, J4W 3J9
(450) 923-3000   *SIC 1731*

965591 ALBERTA LTD   *p92*
14721 123 AVE NW, EDMONTON, AB, T5L 2Y6
(780) 455-3000   *SIC 1731*

A A A ALARM SYSTEMS LTD   *p388*
180 NATURE PARK WAY, WINNIPEG, MB, R3P 0X7
(204) 949-0078   *SIC 1731*

A.P.I. ALARM INC   *p770*
700-5775 YONGE ST, NORTH YORK, ON, M2M 4J1
(416) 661-5566   *SIC 1731*

AATEL COMMUNICATIONS INC   *p610*
413 VICTORIA AVE N, HAMILTON, ON, L8L

8G4
(905) 523-5451   *SIC 1731*

ACTION ELECTRIC LTD   *p294*
1277 GEORGIA ST E, VANCOUVER, BC, V6A 2A9
(604) 734-9146   *SIC 1731*

ACTION ELECTRICAL LTD   *p121*
2333 91 AVE, EDMONTON, AB, T6P 1L1
(780) 465-0792   *SIC 1731*

ADT CANADA INC   *p1343*
8481 BOUL LANGELIER, SAINT-LEONARD, QC, H1P 2C3
(514) 323-5000   *SIC 1731*

AECOM PRODUCTION SERVICES LTD   *p79*
10414 84 AVE, CLAIRMONT, AB, T8X 5B2
(780) 539-0069   *SIC 1731*

AINSWORTH INC   *p787*
131 BERMONDSEY RD, NORTH YORK, ON, M4A 1X4
(416) 751-4420   *SIC 1731*

ALLANSON INTERNATIONAL INC   *p678*
83 COMMERCE VALLEY DR E, MARKHAM, ON, L3T 7T3
(416) 755-1191   *SIC 1731*

ALLCO ELECTRICAL LTD   *p383*
930 BRADFORD ST, WINNIPEG, MB, R3H 0N5
(204) 697-1000   *SIC 1731*

ALLIANCE ENERGY LIMITED   *p1415*
504 HENDERSON DR, REGINA, SK, S4N 5X2
(306) 721-6484   *SIC 1731*

ALLIED PROJECTS LTD   *p33*
7017 FARRELL RD SE, CALGARY, AB, T2H 0T3
(403) 543-4530   *SIC 1731*

ALLSTREAM BUSINESS INC   *p666*
7550 BIRCHMOUNT RD, MARKHAM, ON, L3R 6C6
(905) 513-4600   *SIC 1731*

ALLTRADE INDUSTRIAL CONTRACTORS INC   *p532*
1477 BISHOP ST N, CAMBRIDGE, ON, N1R 7J4
(519) 740-1090   *SIC 1731*

ALLWEST ELECTRIC LTD   *p245*
110-2250 FREMONT ST, PORT COQUIT-LAM, BC, V3B 0M3
(604) 464-6200   *SIC 1731*

ALPINE ELECTRIC LTD   *p342*
1085 MILLAR CREEK RD SUITE 3, WHISTLER, BC, V0N 1B1
SIC 1731

ALTA PRO ELECTRIC LTD   *p92*
13415 149 ST NW, EDMONTON, AB, T5L 2T3
(780) 444-6510   *SIC 1731*

AMEC BLACK & MCDONALD LIMITED *p445*
11 FRAZEE AVE, DARTMOUTH, NS, B3B 1Z4
(902) 474-3700   *SIC 1731*

AMELCO ELECTRIC (CALGARY) LTD   *p20*
2230 22 ST NE, CALGARY, AB, T2E 8B7
(403) 250-1270   *SIC 1731*

AMPERE LIMITED   *p786*
15 TORBARRIE RD, NORTH YORK, ON, M3L 1G5
(416) 661-3330   *SIC 1731*

ARCON ELECTRIC LTD   *p648*
1065 CLARKE RD, LONDON, ON, N5V 3B3
(519) 451-6699   *SIC 1731*

ARISS CONTROLS & ELECTRIC INC *p139*
6800 39 ST, LEDUC, AB, T9E 0Z4
(780) 986-1147   *SIC 1731*

ARMATURE ELECTRIC LIMITED   *p191*
3811 NORTH FRASER WAY, BURNABY, BC, V5J 5J2
(604) 879-6141   *SIC 1731*

ARNO ELECTRIQUE LTEE   *p1386*
2300 BOUL DES RECOLLETS, TROIS-RIVIERES, QC, G8Z 3X5
(819) 379-5222   *SIC 1731*

AUTOMATIC SYSTEMES AMERIQUE INC   *p1069*

4005 BOUL MATTE BUREAU D, BROSSARD, QC, J4Y 2P4
(450) 659-0737 *SIC* 1731

AVANTE LOGIXX INC *p775*
1959 LESLIE ST, NORTH YORK, ON, M3B 2M3
(416) 923-6984 *SIC* 1731

AZIMUTH THREE ENTERPRISES INC *p501*
127 DELTA PARK BLVD, BRAMPTON, ON, L6T 5M8
(437) 370-7160 *SIC* 1731

BARTLETT, H J ELECTRIC INC *p425*
51 DUNDEE AVE UNIT 1, MOUNT PEARL, NL, A1N 4R6
(709) 747-2204 *SIC* 1731

BAY HILL CONTRACTING LTD *p278*
19122 21 AVE, SURREY, BC, V3Z 3M3
(604) 536-3306 *SIC* 1731

BELL TECHNICAL SOLUTIONS INC *p1063*
75 RUE J.-A.-BOMBARDIER SUITE 200, BOUCHERVILLE, QC, J4B 8P1
(450) 449-1120 *SIC* 1731

BERT'S ELECTRIC (2001) LTD *p176*
2258 PEARDONVILLE RD, ABBOTSFORD, BC, V2T 6J8
(604) 850-8731 *SIC* 1731

BLACK & MCDONALD LIMITED *p819*
2460 DON REID DR, OTTAWA, ON, K1H 1E1
(613) 526-1226 *SIC* 1731

BOREALIS HOLDINGS TRUST MANAGEMENT INC *p960*
200 BAY ST S SUITE 2100, TORONTO, ON, M5J 2J2
(416) 361-1011 *SIC* 1731

BRIDGE ELECTRIC CORP *p262*
11091 HAMMERSMITH GATE, RICHMOND, BC, V7A 5E6
(604) 273-2744 *SIC* 1731

BRIDGE, P.R. SYSTEMS LTD *p338*
455 BANGA PL SUITE 108, VICTORIA, BC, V8Z 6X5
(250) 475-3766 *SIC* 1731

BRUNEAU ELECTRIQUE INC *p1114*
527 BOUL DOLLARD, JOLIETTE, QC, J6E 4M5
(450) 759-6606 *SIC* 1731

BURMAN & FELLOWS GROUP INC *p678*
170 TRAVAIL RD, MARKHAM, ON, L3S 3J1
(905) 472-1056 *SIC* 1731

C&M ELECTRIC LTD *p540*
3038 CARP RD, CARP, ON, K0A 1L0
(613) 839-3232 *SIC* 1731

C. FRAPPIER ELECTRIQUE INC *p1132*
9607 RUE CLEMENT, LASALLE, QC, H8R 4B4
(514) 363-1712 *SIC* 1731

CABLESHOPPE INC, THE *p870*
1410 BIRCHMOUNT RD, SCARBOROUGH, ON, M1P 2E3
(416) 293-3634 *SIC* 1731

CAMPBELL AND KENNEDY ELECTRIC (1996) LIMITED *p550*
242 APPLEWOOD CRES SUITE 11, CONCORD, ON, L4K 4E5
(905) 761-8550 *SIC* 1731

CANCABLE INC *p612*
100 KING ST W UNIT 700, HAMILTON, ON, L8P 1A2
(905) 769-9705 *SIC* 1731

CANEM SYSTEMS LTD *p95*
11320 151 ST NW, EDMONTON, AB, T5M 4A9
(780) 454-0381 *SIC* 1731

CANEM SYSTEMS LTD *p254*
1600 VALMONT WAY SUITE 100, RICHMOND, BC, V6V 1Y4
(604) 273-1131 *SIC* 1731

CANEM SYSTEMS LTD *p254*
13351 COMMERCE PKY SUITE 1358, RICHMOND, BC, V6V 2X7
(604) 214-8650 *SIC* 1731

CASCADE PROCESS CONTROLS LTD *p7*
420 AQUADUCT DR, BROOKS, AB, T1R

1C8
(403) 362-4722 *SIC* 1731

CATECH SYSTEMS LTD *p667*
201 WHITEHALL DR UNIT 4, MARKHAM, ON, L3R 9Y3
(905) 477-0160 *SIC* 1731

CDN CONTROLS LTD *p131*
10306 118 ST, GRANDE PRAIRIE, AB, T8V 3X9
(780) 532-8151 *SIC* 1731

CEB INVESTMENTS INC *p28*
250 42 AVE SE, CALGARY, AB, T2G 1Y4
(403) 265-4155 *SIC* 1731

CEC SERVICES LIMITED (AURORA) *p629*
16188 BATHURST ST, KING CITY, ON, L7B 1K5
(905) 713-3711 *SIC* 1731

CHAMBERS ELECTRICAL CORP *p200*
204 CAYER ST UNIT 101, COQUITLAM, BC, V3K 5B1
(604) 526-5688 *SIC* 1731

CHEMCO ELECTRICAL CONTRACTORS LTD *p127*
210 MACALPINE CRES SUITE 6, FORT MCMURRAY, AB, T9H 4A6
(780) 714-6206 *SIC* 1731

CHEMCO ELECTRICAL CONTRACTORS LTD *p148*
3135 4 ST, NISKU, AB, T9E 8L1
(780) 436-9570 *SIC* 1731

CHOWN ELECTRICAL CONTRACTORS LTD *p105*
12230 163 ST NW, EDMONTON, AB, T5V 1S2
(780) 447-4525 *SIC* 1731

CIE ELECTRIQUE BRITTON LTEE, LA *p1156*
8555 CH DEVONSHIRE BUREAU 213, MONT-ROYAL, QC, H4P 2L3
(514) 342-5520 *SIC* 1731

CO-PAR ELECTRIC LTD *p124*
1132 156 ST SW, EDMONTON, AB, T6W 1A4
(780) 453-1414 *SIC* 1731

COBRA ELECTRIC LTD *p281*
9688 190 ST, SURREY, BC, V4N 3M9
(604) 594-1633 *SIC* 1731

COLWIN ELECTRIC GROUP *p248*
2829 MURRAY ST, PORT MOODY, BC, V3H 1X3
(604) 461-2181 *SIC* 1731

COM-NET (COMMUNICATION CABLING AND NETWORK SOLUTIONS) INC *p817*
2191 THURSTON DR, OTTAWA, ON, K1G 6C9
(613) 247-7778 *SIC* 1731

COMMUNITY ELECTRIC LTD *p1426*
811 58TH ST E, SASKATOON, SK, S7K 6X5
(306) 477-8822 *SIC* 1731

COMPAGNIE D'APPAREILS ELECTRIQUES PEERLESS LTEE *p1132*
9145 RUE BOIVIN, LASALLE, QC, H8R 2E5
(514) 595-1671 *SIC* 1731

COMPUTER ROOM SERVICES CORPORATION *p475*
75 CHAMBERS DR UNIT 6, AJAX, ON, L1Z 1E1
(905) 686-4000 *SIC* 1731

CONCEPT ELECTRIC LTD *p29*
1260 HIGHFIELD CRES SE, CALGARY, AB, T2G 5M3
(403) 287-8777 *SIC* 1731

CONTI ELECTRIC COMPANY OF CANADA *p1019*
2861 TEMPLE DR, WINDSOR, ON, N8W 5E5
(519) 250-8212 *SIC* 1731

CONTROLS & EQUIPMENT LTD *p408*
185 MILLENNIUM BLVD, MONCTON, NB, E1E 2G7
(506) 857-8836 *SIC* 1731

CORPORATE ELECTRIC LIMITED *p289*
2233 QUEBEC ST, VANCOUVER, BC, V5T 3A1
(604) 879-0551 *SIC* 1731

CRIBTEC INC *p1277*
5145 RUE RIDEAU, QUEBEC, QC, G2E 5H5
(418) 622-5992 *SIC* 1731

CSG SECURITY CORPORATION *p1184*
6680 AV DU PARC, MONTREAL, QC, H2V 4H9
(514) 272-7700 *SIC* 1731

CUSTOM ELECTRIC LTD *p22*
1725 27 AVE NE, CALGARY, AB, T2E 7E1
(403) 736-0205 *SIC* 1731

DELTRO ELECTRIC LTD *p702*
1706 MATTAWA AVE, MISSISSAUGA, ON, L4X 1K1
(905) 566-9816 *SIC* 1731

DIEBOLD COMPANY OF CANADA LIMITED, THE *p721*
6630 CAMPOBELLO RD, MISSISSAUGA, ON, L5N 2L8
(905) 817-7600 *SIC* 1731

DIRCAM ELECTRIC LIMITED *p583*
42 STEINWAY BLVD SUITE 10, ETOBICOKE, ON, M9W 6Y6
(416) 798-1115 *SIC* 1731

DIRECT ENERGY PARTNERSHIP *p48*
525 8 AVE SW SUITE 501, CALGARY, AB, T2P 1G1
(403) 261-9810 *SIC* 1731

DMW ELECTRICAL INSTRUMENTATION INC *p859*
227 CONFEDERATION ST, SARNIA, ON, N7T 1Z9
(519) 336-3003 *SIC* 1731

E-TECH ELECTRICAL SERVICES INC *p552*
30 PENNSYLVANIA AVE, CONCORD, ON, L4K 4A5
(905) 669-4062 *SIC* 1731

E.C.E. ELECTRIQUE INC *p1373*
4345 RUE OUIMET, SHERBROOKE, QC, J1L 1X5
(819) 821-2222 *SIC* 1731

EBI ELECTRIC INC *p1304*
2250 90E RUE, SAINT-GEORGES, QC, G5Y 7J7
(418) 228-5505 *SIC* 1731

ELECTRICITE GRIMARD INC *p1080*
1235 RUE BERSIMIS, CHICOUTIMI, QC, G7K 1A4
(418) 549-6352 *SIC* 1731

ELECTRICITE TRI-TECH INC *p1096*
480 BOUL STRATHMORE, DORVAL, QC, H9S 2J4
(450) 420-0111 *SIC* 1731

ELECTRIQUE PERFECTION INC *p1344*
8685 RUE PASCAL-GAGNON, SAINT-LEONARD, QC, H1P 1Y5
(514) 376-0100 *SIC* 1731

EMC POWER CANADA LTD *p629*
2091 HIGHWAY 21, KINCARDINE, ON, N2Z 2X4
(844) 644-3627 *SIC* 1731

EMERA UTILITY SERVICES INCORPORATED *p460*
31 DOMINION CRES, LAKESIDE, NS, B3T 1M3
(902) 832-7999 *SIC* 1731

ENERGY NETWORK SERVICES INC *p852*
125 WEST BEAVER CREEK RD, RICHMOND HILL, ON, L4B 1C6
(905) 763-2946 *SIC* 1731

ENTREPRISES D'ELECTRICITE E.G. LTEE *p1323*
1753 RUE GRENET, SAINT-LAURENT, QC, H4L 2R6
(514) 748-0505 *SIC* 1731

ENTREPRISES D'ELECTRICITE J.M.N. INC *p1150*
19 RUE DURETTE, MATANE, QC, G4W 0J5
(418) 562-4009 *SIC* 1731

ENTREPRISES DE CONSTRUCTION DAWCO INC *p1156*
8315 CH DEVONSHIRE, MONT-ROYAL, QC, H4P 2L1
(514) 738-3033 *SIC* 1731

ENTREPRISES ELECTRIQUES L.M. INC, LES *p1167*
3006 RUE SAINTE-CATHERINE E, MONTREAL, QC, H1W 2B8
(514) 523-2831 *SIC* 1731

ENTREPRISES LAURENTIEN ELECTRIQUE INC, LES *p1217*
890 BOUL CREMAZIE O, MONTREAL, QC, H3N 1A4
(514) 276-8551 *SIC* 1731

EPSCAN INDUSTRIES LTD *p204*
600 110 AVE, DAWSON CREEK, BC, V1G 2Y6
(250) 782-9656 *SIC* 1731

EXPERTECH BATISSEUR DE RESEAUX INC *p1164*
2555 BOUL DE L'ASSOMPTION, MONTREAL, QC, H1N 2G8
(866) 616-8459 *SIC* 1731

FALCO ELECTRICAL SYSTEMS LTD *p29*
3606 MANCHESTER RD SE, CALGARY, AB, T2G 3Z5
(403) 287-7632 *SIC* 1731

G.J. CAHILL & COMPANY (1979) LIMITED *p433*
240 WATERFORD BRIDGE RD, ST. JOHN'S, NL, A1E 1E2
(709) 368-2125 *SIC* 1731

GARDNER ELECTRIC LTD *p416*
875 BAYSIDE DR, SAINT JOHN, NB, E2R 1A3
(506) 634-3918 *SIC* 1731

GASTIER M.P. INC *p1049*
10400 BOUL DU GOLF, ANJOU, QC, H1J 2Y7
(514) 325-4220 *SIC* 1731

GASTON OUELLETTE & FILS INC *p1240*
9960 BOUL SAINT-VITAL, MONTREAL-NORD, QC, H1H 4S6
(514) 388-3927 *SIC* 1731

GENESIS INTEGRATION INC *p93*
14721 123 AVE NW, EDMONTON, AB, T5L 2Y6
(780) 455-3000 *SIC* 1731

GORDON, AL ELECTRIC LIMITED *p661*
1099 PROGRESS DR, LONDON, ON, N6N 1B7
(519) 672-1273 *SIC* 1731

GRAYWOOD ELECTRIC LIMITED *p593*
10783 SIXTH LINE, GEORGETOWN, ON, L7G 4S6
(905) 877-6070 *SIC* 1731

GRID LINK CORP *p910*
1499 ROSSLYN RD, THUNDER BAY, ON, P7E 6W1
(807) 683-0350 *SIC* 1731

GROUPE LML LTEE, LE *p1318*
360 BOUL DU SEMINAIRE N BUREAU 22, SAINT-JEAN-SUR-RICHELIEU, QC, J3B 5L1
(450) 347-1996 *SIC* 1731

GROUPE PROMEC INC *p1289*
1300 RUE SAGUENAY, ROUYN-NORANDA, QC, J9X 7C3
(819) 797-7500 *SIC* 1731

GUILD ELECTRIC HOLDINGS LIMITED *p871*
470 MIDWEST RD, SCARBOROUGH, ON, M1P 4Y5
(416) 288-8222 *SIC* 1731

GUILD ELECTRIC LIMITED *p871*
470 MIDWEST RD, SCARBOROUGH, ON, M1P 4Y5
(416) 288-8222 *SIC* 1731

HELIX IT INC *p809*
9 ONTARIO ST UNIT 7, ORILLIA, ON, L3V 0T7
(705) 327-6564 *SIC* 1731

HIGH LINE ELECTRICAL CONSTRUCTORS LTD *p124*
2304 119 AVE NE SUITE 200, EDMONTON, AB, T6S 1B3
(780) 452-8900 *SIC* 1731

HOLLAND, E. CONTRACTING INC *p404*
272 ROUTE 105, MAUGERVILLE, NB, E3A 8G2

(506) 472-0649   *SIC* 1731
HONEY ELECTRIC LIMITED   *p543*
400 PARK AVE W, CHATHAM, ON, N7M 1W9
(519) 351-0484   *SIC* 1731

HORIZON CONNEXTIONS INC   *p1049*
9660 BOUL DU GOLF, ANJOU, QC, H1J 2Y7
  SIC 1731

HOULE ELECTRIC LIMITED   *p192*
5050 NORTH FRASER WAY, BURNABY, BC, V5J 0H1
(604) 434-2681   *SIC* 1731

HUMBOLDT ELECTRIC LTD   *p1434*
102 GLADSTONE CRES, SASKATOON, SK, S7P 0C7
(306) 665-6551   *SIC* 1731

ICONIC POWER SYSTEMS INC   *p16*
11090 48 ST SE, CALGARY, AB, T2C 3E1
(403) 910-3823   *SIC* 1731

INDUSTRIAL ELECTRICAL CONTRACTORS LIMITED   *p585*
7 VULCAN ST, ETOBICOKE, ON, M9W 1L3
(416) 749-9782   *SIC* 1731

INLAND AUDIO VISUAL LIMITED   *p378*
422 LUCAS AVE, WINNIPEG, MB, R3C 2E6
(204) 786-6521   *SIC* 1731

INLET ELECTRIC LTD   *p201*
169 GOLDEN DR UNIT 2, COQUITLAM, BC, V3K 6T1
(604) 464-3133   *SIC* 1731

INSTALLATIONS ELECTRIQUES PICHETTE INC, LES   *p1234*
3080 RUE PEUGEOT, MONTREAL, QC, H7L 5C5
(450) 682-4411   *SIC* 1731

INTEGRAL ENERGY SERVICES LTD   *p3*
2890 KINGSVIEW BLVD SE UNIT 101, AIRDRIE, AB, T4A 0E1
(403) 912-1261   *SIC* 1731

ISKUETEU, LIMITED PARTNERSHIP   *p433*
240 WATERFORD BRIDGE RD, ST. JOHN'S, NL, A1E 1E2
(709) 747-4209   *SIC* 1731

J.M.R. ELECTRIC LTD   *p590*
301 THAMES RD, EXETER, ON, N0M 1S3
(519) 235-1516   *SIC* 1731

JANICK ELECTRIC LIMITED   *p786*
1170 SHEPPARD AVE W UNIT 9, NORTH YORK, ON, M3K 2A3
(416) 635-8989   *SIC* 1731

JAY ELECTRIC LIMITED   *p504*
21 KENVIEW BLVD UNIT 2, BRAMPTON, ON, L6T 5G7
(905) 793-4000   *SIC* 1731

JSM ELECTRICAL LTD   *p430*
28 DUFFY PL, ST. JOHN'S, NL, A1B 4M5
(709) 754-3666   *SIC* 1731

K-JAY ELECTRIC LTD   *p101*
10752 178 ST NW, EDMONTON, AB, T5S 1J3
(780) 484-1721   *SIC* 1731

K-LINE MAINTENANCE & CONSTRUCTION LIMITED   *p894*
12731 HIGHWAY 48, STOUFFVILLE, ON, L4A 4A7
(905) 640-2002   *SIC* 1731

KELDON ELECTRIC & DATA LTD   *p222*
1909 BREDIN RD, KELOWNA, BC, V1Y 7S9
(250) 861-4255   *SIC* 1731

KINSEY ENTERPRISES INC   *p1*
26650 116 AVE, ACHESON, AB, T7X 6H2
(780) 452-0467   *SIC* 1731

KONDRO ELECTRIC 1980 LTD   *p144*
6202 50 AVE, LLOYDMINSTER, AB, T9V 2C9
(780) 875-6226   *SIC* 1731

KRUEGER ELECTRICAL LTD   *p222*
1027 TRENCH PL UNIT 100, KELOWNA, BC, V1Y 9Y4
(250) 860-3905   *SIC* 1731

LAIRD ELECTRIC INC   *p109*
6707 59 ST NW, EDMONTON, AB, T6B 3P8
(780) 450-9636   *SIC* 1731

LAMARCHE ELECTRIC INC   *p857*
9374 COUNTY ROAD 17, ROCKLAND, ON, K4K 1K9
(613) 747-8882   *SIC* 1731

LAMBERT SOMEC INC   *p1264*
1505 RUE DES TANNEURS, QUEBEC, QC, G1N 4S7
(418) 687-1640   *SIC* 1731

LAMBTON COMMUNICATIONS LIMITED   *p860*
506 CHRISTINA ST N, SARNIA, ON, N7T 5W4
(519) 332-1234   *SIC* 1731

LAYFIELD GROUP LIMITED   *p263*
11131 HAMMERSMITH GATE, RICHMOND, BC, V7A 5E6
(604) 275-5588   *SIC* 1731

LEXSAN ELECTRICAL INC   *p806*
3328 BURNHAMTHORPE RD W, OAKVILLE, ON, L6M 4H3
(905) 827-1616   *SIC* 1731

MACKENZIE PLUMBING & HEATING (1989) LTD   *p1416*
915 FLEURY ST, REGINA, SK, S4N 4W7
(306) 522-0777   *SIC* 1731

MANCON HOLDINGS LTD   *p1416*
504 HENDERSON DR, REGINA, SK, S4N 5X2
(306) 721-4777   *SIC* 1731

MANN ENGINEERING LTD   *p789*
150 BRIDGELAND AVE SUITE 101, NORTH YORK, ON, M6A 1Z5
(416) 201-9109   *SIC* 1731

MCCAINE ELECTRIC LTD   *p389*
106 LOWSON CRES, WINNIPEG, MB, R3P 2H8
(204) 786-2435   *SIC* 1731

MCL POWER INC   *p98*
16821 107 AVE NW, EDMONTON, AB, T5P 0Y8
(780) 440-8775   *SIC* 1731

MDE ENTERPRISES LTD   *p284*
3947 GRAVELEY ST, VANCOUVER, BC, V5C 3T4
(604) 291-1995   *SIC* 1731

MID SOUTH CONTRACTORS ULC   *p1021*
3110 DEVON DR, WINDSOR, ON, N8X 4L2
(519) 966-6163   *SIC* 1731

MMR CANADA LIMITED   *p17*
11083 48 ST SE, CALGARY, AB, T2C 1G8
(403) 720-9000   *SIC* 1731

MOGO ELECTRICAL SERVICES LTD   *p110*
5663 70 ST NW, EDMONTON, AB, T6B 3P6
(780) 438-3440   *SIC* 1731

MOTT ELECTRIC GENERAL PARTNERSHIP   *p193*
4599 TILLICUM ST SUITE 100, BURNABY, BC, V5J 3J9
(604) 522-5757   *SIC* 1731

MUTH ELECTRICAL MANAGEMENT INC   *p115*
9850 41 AVE NW, EDMONTON, AB, T6E 5L6
(780) 414-0980   *SIC* 1731

NEOLECT INC   *p1073*
104 BOUL MONTCALM N, CANDIAC, QC, J5R 3L8
(514) 382-1550   *SIC* 1731

NET ELECTRIC LIMITED   *p855*
120 NEWKIRK RD UNIT 8, RICHMOND HILL, ON, L4C 9S7
(905) 737-7760   *SIC* 1731

NEW ELECTRIC ENTERPRISES INC   *p806*
3185 DUNDAS ST W, OAKVILLE, ON, L6M 4J4
(905) 827-2555   *SIC* 1731

NEXICOM COMMUNICATIONS INC   *p682*
5 KING ST E, MILLBROOK, ON, L0A 1G0
(888) 639-4266   *SIC* 1731

NIGHTINGALE ELECTRICAL LTD   *p263*
11121 HORSESHOE WAY SUITE 143, RICHMOND, BC, V7A 5G7
(604) 275-0500   *SIC* 1731

NORCAN ELECTRIC INC   *p128*

380 MACKENZIE BLVD SUITE 6B, FORT MCMURRAY, AB, T9H 4C4
(780) 799-3292   *SIC* 1731

NORTOWN ELECTRICAL CONTRACTORS ASSOCIATES   *p781*
3845 BATHURST ST SUITE 102, NORTH YORK, ON, M3H 3N2
(416) 638-6700   *SIC* 1731

NORTOWN ELECTRICAL CONTRACTORS LIMITED   *p781*
3845 BATHURST ST UNIT 102, NORTH YORK, ON, M3H 3N2
(416) 638-6700   *SIC* 1731

O'BRIEN ELECTRIC CO LTD   *p415*
79 MARSH ST, SAINT JOHN, NB, E2L 5R1
  SIC 1731

O'CONNOR ELECTRIC LTD   *p635*
9 CENTENNIAL RD UNIT 2, KITCHENER, ON, N2B 3E9
(519) 745-8886   *SIC* 1731

O'DELL ELECTRIC LTD   *p31*
3827 15A ST SE, CALGARY, AB, T2G 3N7
(403) 266-2935   *SIC* 1731

OCP COMMUNICATIONS INC   *p530*
2319 FAIRVIEW ST UNIT 601, BURLINGTON, ON, L7R 2E3
(289) 337-5994   *SIC* 1731

OZZ ELECTRIC   *p557*
20 FLORAL PKY SUITE A, CONCORD, ON, L4K 4R1
(416) 637-7237   *SIC* 1731

OZZ ELECTRIC INC   *p557*
20 FLORAL PKY SUITE A, CONCORD, ON, L4K 4R1
(416) 637-7237   *SIC* 1731

PAGUI INC   *p1281*
15971 BOUL DE LA COLLINE, QUEBEC, QC, G3G 3A7
(418) 849-1832   *SIC* 1731

PAQUETTE, GERALD ENTREPRENEUR ELECTRICIEN ET ASSOCIES INC   *p1153*
17820 RUE CHARLES, MIRABEL, QC, J7J 1J5
(450) 430-9323   *SIC* 1731

PEERLESS SECURITY LTD   *p1000*
544 GREER RD, UTTERSON, ON, P0B 1M0
(705) 645-4108   *SIC* 1731

PETROCORP GROUP INC   *p123*
14032 23 AVE NW SUITE 166, EDMONTON, AB, T6R 3L6
(780) 910-9436   *SIC* 1731

PIERRE BROSSARD (1981) LTEE   *p1070*
9595 RUE IGNACE, BROSSARD, QC, J4Y 2P3
(450) 659-9641   *SIC* 1731

PLACEMENTS FRANCOIS PICHETTE LTEE, LES   *p1234*
3080 RUE PEUGEOT, MONTREAL, QC, H7L 5C5
(450) 682-4411   *SIC* 1731

PLAN GROUP INC   *p557*
2740 STEELES AVE W, CONCORD, ON, L4K 4T4
(416) 635-9040   *SIC* 1731

PLATINUM ELECTRICAL CONTRACTORS INC   *p557*
270 DRUMLIN CIR UNIT 5, CONCORD, ON, L4K 3E2
(905) 761-7647   *SIC* 1731

PLEXUS CONNECTIVITY SOLUTIONS LTD   *p407*
225 BARKER ST, MONCTON, NB, E1C 0M4
(506) 859-1514   *SIC* 1731

POLAR ELECTRIC INC   *p175*
2236 WEST RAILWAY ST UNIT 1, ABBOTSFORD, BC, V2S 2E2
(604) 850-7522   *SIC* 1731

POLARIS INFRASTRUCTURE INC   *p930*
2 BLOOR ST W SUITE 2700IT, TORONTO, ON, M4W 3E2
(416) 849-2587   *SIC* 1731

POWELL CANADA INC   *p2*
10960 274 ST, ACHESON, AB, T7X 6P7

(780) 948-3300   *SIC* 1731

PP DESLANDES INC   *p1313*
4775 AV TRUDEAU, SAINT-HYACINTHE, QC, J2S 7W9
(450) 778-2426   *SIC* 1731

PRACTICAL ELECTRIC CONTRACTING INC.   *p557*
527 EDGELEY BLVD UNIT 12, CONCORD, ON, L4K 4G6
(416) 663-1500   *SIC* 1731

PRO ELECTRIC INC   *p661*
347 SOVEREIGN RD, LONDON, ON, N6M 1A6
(519) 451-8740   *SIC* 1731

PROCON CONSTRUCTORS INC   *p1012*
401 ENTERPRISE DR, WELLAND, ON, L3B 6H8
(905) 732-0322   *SIC* 1731

PROLUXON INC   *p1169*
5549 BOUL SAINT-MICHEL, MONTREAL, QC, H1Y 2C9
(514) 374-4993   *SIC* 1731

PROTEC INSTALLATIONS GROUP   *p261*
11720 VOYAGEUR WAY SUITE 9, RICHMOND, BC, V6X 3G9
(604) 278-3200   *SIC* 1731

PROVINCIAL ELECTRICAL SERVICES INC   *p110*
7429 72A ST NW, EDMONTON, AB, T6B 1Z3
(780) 490-1183   *SIC* 1731

PROWATT INC   *p1115*
2361 RUE BAUMAN BUREAU 1, JONQUIERE, QC, G7S 5A9
(418) 548-1184   *SIC* 1731

PYRAMID CORPORATION   *p144*
6304 56 ST, LLOYDMINSTER, AB, T9V 3T7
(780) 875-6644   *SIC* 1731

RESIDENTIAL ELECTRICAL CONTRACTOR CORPORATION, THE   *p25*
2616 16 ST NE SUITE 4, CALGARY, AB, T2E 7J8
(403) 735-6120   *SIC* 1731

REVENCO (1991) INC   *p1265*
1755 RUE PROVINCIALE, QUEBEC, QC, G1N 4S9
(418) 682-5993   *SIC* 1731

RIAL ELECTRIQUE INC   *p1377*
2205 RUE LAPRADE, SOREL-TRACY, QC, J3R 2C1
(450) 746-7349   *SIC* 1731

RIVER CITY ELECTRIC LTD   *p102*
11323 174 ST NW, EDMONTON, AB, T5S 0B7
(780) 484-6676   *SIC* 1731

ROBERTS ONSITE INC   *p637*
209 MANITOU DR, KITCHENER, ON, N2C 1L4
(519) 578-2230   *SIC* 1731

ROBERTSON BRIGHT INC   *p726*
2875 ARGENTIA RD UNIT 1, MISSISSAUGA, ON, L5N 8G6
(905) 813-3005   *SIC* 1731

ROSS MORRISON ELECTRICAL LTD   *p186*
3950 1ST AVE, BURNABY, BC, V5C 3W2
(604) 299-0281   *SIC* 1731

RPF LTEE   *p1366*
163 RTE 132 O, SAYABEC, QC, G0J 3K0
(418) 536-5453   *SIC* 1731

RYFAN ELECTRIC LTD   *p436*
9 NAHANNI DR, YELLOWKNIFE, NT, X1A 0E8
(867) 765-6100   *SIC* 1731

S&S/BOLTON ELECTRIC INC   *p596*
5411 CANOTEK RD, GLOUCESTER, ON, K1J 9M3
(613) 748-0432   *SIC* 1731

S. & T. ELECTRICAL CONTRACTORS LIMITED   *p863*
158 SACKVILLE RD SUITE 2, SAULT STE. MARIE, ON, P6B 4T6
(705) 942-3043   *SIC* 1731

SASCO CONTRACTORS LTD   *p184*
3060 NORLAND AVE SUITE 114, BURN-

ABY, BC, V5B 3A6

(604) 299-1640   *SIC* 1731

SCHNEIDER ELECTRIC CANADA INC *p258*

22171 FRASERWOOD WAY, RICHMOND, BC, V6W 1J5

(604) 273-3711   *SIC* 1731

SELECTRA INC   *p896*

750 DOURO ST, STRATFORD, ON, N5A 0E3

(519) 271-0322   *SIC* 1731

SENTREX COMMUNICATIONS INC   *p793*

25 MILVAN DR, NORTH YORK, ON, M9L 1Y8

(416) 749-7400   *SIC* 1731

SENTREX COMMUNICATIONS INC   *p793*

25 MILVAN DR, NORTH YORK, ON, M9L 1Y8

(416) 749-7400   *SIC* 1731

SERVICES ENERGETIQUES ECOSYSTEM INC, LES   *p1273*

2875 BOUL LAURIER BUREAU 950 EDIFICE DELTA 3, QUEBEC, QC, G1V 2M2

(418) 651-1257   *SIC* 1731

SIMMAX CORP   *p116*

8750 58 AVE NW, EDMONTON, AB, T6E 6G6

(780) 437-9315   *SIC* 1731

SITE INTEGRATION PLUS INC   *p1067*

1356 RUE NEWTON, BOUCHERVILLE, QC, J4B 5H2

(450) 449-0094   *SIC* 1731

SKYVIEW ELECTRIC INC   *p106*

12850 149 ST NW, EDMONTON, AB, T5V 1A4

SIC 1731

SMITH AND LONG LIMITED   *p675*

115 IDEMA RD, MARKHAM, ON, L3R 1A9

(416) 391-0443   *SIC* 1731

SPEEDY ELECTRICAL CONTRACTORS LIMITED   *p1033*

114 CASTER AVE SUITE A, WOODBRIDGE, ON, L4L 5Y9

(905) 264-2344   *SIC* 1731

STAMPEDE ELECTRIC INC   *p71*

4300 118 AVE SE, CALGARY, AB, T2Z 4A4

(587) 327-2777   *SIC* 1731

STATE GROUP INC, THE   *p689*

3206 ORLANDO DR, MISSISSAUGA, ON, L4V 1R5

(905) 672-2772   *SIC* 1731

STATUS ELECTRICAL CORPORATIONp177

2669 DEACON ST, ABBOTSFORD, BC, V2T 6L4

(604) 859-1892   *SIC* 1731

STEP ENERGY SERVICES LTD   *p60*

205 5 AVE SW SUITE 1200, CALGARY, AB, T2P 2V7

(403) 457-1772   *SIC* 1731

STUDON ELECTRIC & CONTROLS INC *p156*

8024 EDGAR INDUSTRIAL CRES UNIT 102, RED DEER, AB, T4P 3R3

(403) 342-1666   *SIC* 1731

SUPERIOR HEATING & AIR CONDITIONING/ST. JAMES SHEET METAL LTD   *p373*

1600 CHURCH AVE, WINNIPEG, MB, R2X 1G8

(204) 697-5666   *SIC* 1731

SUTHERLAND-SCHULTZ LTD   *p537*

140 TURNBULL CRT, CAMBRIDGE, ON, N1T 1J2

(519) 653-4123   *SIC* 1731

SYMTECH INNOVATIONS LTD   *p675*

35 RIVIERA DR, MARKHAM, ON, L3R 8N4

(905) 940-8044   *SIC* 1731

SYSTEME DE SECURITE A C DE QUEBEC INC   *p1281*

1394 RUE DE FRONSAC, QUEBEC, QC, G3E 1A3

(418) 842-7440   *SIC* 1731

SYSTEMES URBAINS INC   *p1345*

8345 RUE PASCAL-GAGNON, SAINT-LEONARD, QC, H1P 1Y5

(514) 321-5205   *SIC* 1731

T N L INDUSTRIAL CONTRACTORS LTD *p264*

12391 HORSESHOE WAY SUITE 130, RICHMOND, BC, V7A 4X6

(604) 278-7424   *SIC* 1731

T. & D. ENTERPRISES LTD   *p393*

1546 SASKATCHEWAN AVE, WINNIPEG, MB, S7K 1P7

(204) 786-3384   *SIC* 1731

TAM ELECTRIC LTD   *p794*

456 GARYRAY DR, NORTH YORK, ON, M9L 1P7

(416) 743-6214   *SIC* 1731

TARPON CONSTRUCTION MANAGEMENT LTD   *p111*

3944 53 AVE NW, EDMONTON, AB, T6B 3N7

(780) 468-6333   *SIC* 1731

TEL-E CONNECT SYSTEMS LTD   *p784*

7 KODIAK CRES, NORTH YORK, ON, M3J 3E5

(416) 635-1234   *SIC* 1731

TERRITORIAL ELECTRIC LTD   *p117*

8303 ROPER RD NW, EDMONTON, AB, T6E 6S4

(780) 465-7591   *SIC* 1731

THERMOPOMPES N & R SOL INC   *p1076*

2325 BOUL FORD, CHATEAUGUAY, QC, J6J 4Z2

(450) 699-3232   *SIC* 1731

THIRAU INC   *p1399*

489 BOUL PIERRE-ROUX E BUREAU 200, VICTORIAVILLE, QC, G6T 1S9

(819) 752-9741   *SIC* 1731

TRINITY COMMUNICATION SERVICES LTD *p576*

86 TORLAKE CRES, ETOBICOKE, ON, M8Z 1B8

(416) 503-9796   *SIC* 1731

TRIPLE A ELECTRIC LTD   *p154*

6209 46 AVE SUITE 1, RED DEER, AB, T4N 6Z1

(403) 346-6156   *SIC* 1731

TRISCAP CANADA, INC   *p475*

501 CLEMENTS RD W SUITE 1, AJAX, ON, L1S 7H4

(905) 428-0982   *SIC* 1731

TRYLON TSF INC   *p568*

21 SOUTH FIELD DR, ELMIRA, ON, N3B 0A6

(519) 669-5421   *SIC* 1731

TWIN CITY ALARMS LIMITED   *p456*

6371 LADY HAMMOND RD, HALIFAX, NS, B3K 2S2

(902) 455-0645   *SIC* 1731

TYCO INTEGRATED FIRE & SECURITY CANADA, INC   *p26*

615 18 ST SE, CALGARY, AB, T2E 3L9

(403) 569-4606   *SIC* 1731

TYCO INTEGRATED FIRE & SECURITY CANADA, INC   *p701*

2400 SKYMARK AVE SUITE 1, MISSISSAUGA, ON, L4W 5K5

(905) 212-4400   *SIC* 1731

UNIFIED SYSTEMS GROUP INC   *p38*

1235 64 AVE SE UNIT 4A, CALGARY, AB, T2H 2J7

(403) 240-2280   *SIC* 1731

UNITECH ELECTRICAL CONTRACTING INC   *p38*

700 58 AVE SE SUITE 11, CALGARY, AB, T2H 2E2

(403) 255-2277   *SIC* 1731

VECTOR ELECTRIC AND CONTROLS *p111*

5344 36 ST NW, EDMONTON, AB, T6B 3P3

(780) 469-7900   *SIC* 1731

VOITH HYDRO INC   *p1071*

9955 RUE DE CHATEAUNEUF BUREAU 160, BROSSARD, QC, J4Z 3V5

(450) 766-2100   *SIC* 1731

VULCAN ELECTRICAL LTD   *p103*

18225 107 AVE NW, EDMONTON, AB, T5S 1K4

(780) 483-0036   *SIC* 1731

W.S. NICHOLLS CONSTRUCTION INC *p535*

48 COWANSVIEW RD, CAMBRIDGE, ON, N1R 7N3

(519) 740-3757   *SIC* 1731

WALLWIN ELECTRIC SERVICES LIMITED *p488*

50 INNISFIL ST, BARRIE, ON, L4N 4K5

(705) 726-1859   *SIC* 1731

WEISS-JOHNSON SHEET METAL LTDp111

5803 ROPER RD NW, EDMONTON, AB, T6B 3L6

(780) 463-3096   *SIC* 1731

WESPAC ELECTRICAL CONTRACTORS LTD   *p202*

106 BLUE MOUNTAIN ST, COQUITLAM, BC, V3K 4G8

(604) 522-1322   *SIC* 1731

WESTCANA ELECTRIC INC   *p251*

1643 OGILVIE ST S, PRINCE GEORGE, BC, V2N 1W7

(250) 564-5800   *SIC* 1731

WESTERN PACIFIC ENTERPRISES GPp202

1321 KETCH CRT, COQUITLAM, BC, V3K 6X7

(604) 540-1321   *SIC* 1731

XL ELECTRIC LIMITED   *p449*

118 CUTLER AVE, DARTMOUTH, NS, B3B 0J6

(902) 468-7708   *SIC* 1731

ZEDI INC   *p66*

902 11 AVE SW, CALGARY, AB, T2R 0E7

(403) 444-1100   *SIC* 1731

ZIEBARTH ELECTRICAL CONTRACTORS LIMITED   *p830*

890 BOYD AVE, OTTAWA, ON, K2A 2E3

(613) 798-8020   *SIC* 1731

SIC 1741 Masonry and other stonework

CON-TACT MASONRY LTD   *p807*

2504 BINDER CRES SUITE 1, OLDCASTLE, ON, N0R 1L0

(519) 737-1852   *SIC* 1741

GEORGE AND ASMUSSEN LIMITED   *p518*

5093 FOUNTAIN ST N, BRESLAU, ON, N0B 1M0

(519) 648-2285   *SIC* 1741

J. D. MASONRY   *p603*

5954 WELLINGTON ROAD 7, GUELPH, ON, N1H 6J2

(519) 836-4311   *SIC* 1741

LIMEN GROUP LTD   *p783*

46 LEPAGE CRT SUITE B, NORTH YORK, ON, M3J 1Z9

(416) 638-8880   *SIC* 1741

MEDI GROUP MASONRY LIMITED   *p586*

56 BROCKPORT DR SUITE 3, ETOBICOKE, ON, M9W 5N1

(416) 747-5170   *SIC* 1741

POCKAR MASONRY LTD   *p24*

4632 5 ST NE, CALGARY, AB, T2E 7C3

(403) 276-5591   *SIC* 1741

PRECO-MSE INC   *p1395*

1885 MONTEE LABOSSIERE, VAUDREUIL-DORION, QC, J7V 8P2

(514) 780-1280   *SIC* 1741

RIVER VALLEY MASONRY GROUP LTD *p704*

2444 HAINES RD, MISSISSAUGA, ON, L4Y 1Y6

(905) 270-0599   *SIC* 1741

RJW STONEMASONS LTD   *p816*

2563 EDINBURGH PL, OTTAWA, ON, K1B 5M1

(613) 722-7790   *SIC* 1741

RUMBLE FOUNDATIONS (ONTARIO) LTD *p714*

580 HAZELHURST RD, MISSISSAUGA, ON, L5J 2Z7

(905) 822-3000   *SIC* 1741

SCORPIO MASONRY (NORTHERN) INC *p103*

20203 113 AVE NW, EDMONTON, AB, T5S

2W1

(780) 447-1682   *SIC* 1741

THIBEAULT MASONRY LTD   *p26*

1815 27 AVE NE SUITE 7, CALGARY, AB, T2E 7E1

SIC 1741

VAUGHAN MASONRY INC   *p560*

111 ORTONA CRT, CONCORD, ON, L4K 3M3

(905) 669-6825   *SIC* 1741

VIA-CON MASONRY INC   *p794*

87 IRONDALE DR UNIT 100, NORTH YORK, ON, M9L 2S6

(416) 745-0709   *SIC* 1741

SIC 1742 Plastering, drywall, and insulation

4 STAR DRYWALL (99) LTD   *p1029*

115 SHARER RD UNIT 1, WOODBRIDGE, ON, L4L 8Z3

(905) 660-9676   *SIC* 1742

ALLIED CONTRACTORS INC.   *p13*

7003 30 ST SE BAY 26, CALGARY, AB, T2C 1N6

(403) 243-3311   *SIC* 1742

ALTIMA CONTRACTING LTD   *p290*

8029 FRASER ST, VANCOUVER, BC, V5X 3X5

(604) 327-5977   *SIC* 1742

AT FILMS INC   *p107*

4605 101A AVE NW, EDMONTON, AB, T6A 0L3

(780) 450-7760   *SIC* 1742

ATCO STRUCTURES & LOGISTICS LTDp73

115 PEACEKEEPERS DR, CALGARY, AB, T3E 7X4

(403) 662-8500   *SIC* 1742

BYNG PLASTERING AND TILE LIMITED *p549*

511 EDGELEY BLVD UNIT 2, CONCORD, ON, L4K 4G4

(905) 660-5454   *SIC* 1742

CAPITAL DRYWALL SYSTEMS LTD   *p501*

396 DEERHURST DR, BRAMPTON, ON, L6T 5H9

(905) 458-1112   *SIC* 1742

CONSTRUCTION MICHEL GAGNON LTEE *p1263*

2250 RUE LEON-HARMEL BUREAU 200, QUEBEC, QC, G1N 4L2

(418) 687-3824   *SIC* 1742

DOWNSVIEW DRYWALL CONTRACTING *p552*

160 BASS PRO MILLS DR SUITE 200, CONCORD, ON, L4K 0A7

(905) 660-0048   *SIC* 1742

ELMHURST LATHING AND DRYWALL LTD *p389*

3160 WILKES AVE, WINNIPEG, MB, R3S 1A7

(204) 889-8238   *SIC* 1742

ELTEX ENTERPRISES 2002 LTD   *p271*

18927 62B AVE, SURREY, BC, V3S 8S3

(604) 599-5088   *SIC* 1742

FOUR SEASONS DRYWALL SYSTEMS & ACOUSTICS LIMITED   *p670*

200 KONRAD CRES, MARKHAM, ON, L3R 8T9

(905) 474-9960   *SIC* 1742

FUNDY DRYWALL LTD   *p397*

91 RUE ENGLEHART, DIEPPE, NB, E1A 8K2

(506) 383-6466   *SIC* 1742

GALLAGHER BROS CONTRACTORS LTD *p279*

19140 28 AVE UNIT 114, SURREY, BC, V3Z 6M3

(604) 531-3156   *SIC* 1742

GENROC DRYWALL LTD   *p128*

7307 RAILWAY AVE, FORT MCMURRAY, AB, T9H 1B9

SIC 1742

GUILDFORDS (2005) INC   *p446*

25 GUILDFORD AVE, DARTMOUTH, NS, B3B 0H5
(902) 481-7900   *SIC 1742*

H. T. DRYWALL (CLG) LTD
908 53 AVE NE SUITE F, CALGARY, AB, T2E 6N9
(403) 295-8404   *SIC 1742*

ICON INSULATION INC   *p993*
935 WESTON RD, TORONTO, ON, M6N 3R4
(647) 945-9648   *SIC 1742*

ISOLATION AIR-PLUS INC   *p1262*
560 AV BECHARD, QUEBEC, QC, G1M 2E9
(418) 683-2999   *SIC 1742*

JERTYNE INTERIOR SERVICES LTD   *p78*
60 COMMERCIAL DR, CALGARY, AB, T3Z 2A7
(403) 219-1046   *SIC 1742*

KANDREA INSULATION (1995) LIMITED *p82*
5604B 58 AVE, DRAYTON VALLEY, AB, T7A 0B1
(780) 542-6847   *SIC 1742*

KERR INTERIOR SYSTEMS LTD   *p115*
9335 62 AVE NW, EDMONTON, AB, T6E 0E1
(780) 466-2800   *SIC 1742*

MAXUM DRYWALL INC   *p555*
1681 LANGSTAFF RD UNIT 18, CONCORD, ON, L4K 5T3
(905) 856-4108   *SIC 1742*

MUZZO BROTHERS GROUP INC   *p556*
50 CONFEDERATION PKY, CONCORD, ON, L4K 4T8
(905) 326-4000   *SIC 1742*

NEL-TEKK INDUSTRIAL SPECIALTIES INC *p860*
254 TECUMSEH ST, SARNIA, ON, N7T 2K9
(519) 332-6813   *SIC 1742*

P.J. DALY CONTRACTING LIMITED   *p615*
1320 STONE CHURCH RD E, HAMILTON, ON, L8W 2C8
(905) 575-1525   *SIC 1742*

PACIFIC RIM INDUSTRIAL INSULATION LTD   *p272*
19510 55 AVE UNIT 2, SURREY, BC, V3S 8P7
(604) 543-8178   *SIC 1742*

POWER DRYWALL (2005) LTD   *p225*
19855 98 AVE, LANGLEY, BC, V1M 2X5
(604) 626-4900   *SIC 1742*

QSI INTERIORS LTD   *p102*
10240 180 ST NW, EDMONTON, AB, T5S 1E2
(780) 489-4462   *SIC 1742*

QSI INTERIORS LTD   *p366*
120 TERRACON PL, WINNIPEG, MB, R2J 4G7
(204) 235-0710   *SIC 1742*

QSI INTERIORS LTD   *p368*
975 THOMAS AVE UNIT 1, WINNIPEG, MB, R2L 1P7
(204) 953-1200   *SIC 1742*

R & D DRYWALL INC   *p1429*
211A 47TH ST E, SASKATOON, SK, S7K 5H1
(306) 933-9328   *SIC 1742*

RAICOR CONTRACTING LTD   *p186*
3993 HENNING DR UNIT 101, BURNABY, BC, V5C 6P7
(604) 293-7702   *SIC 1742*

ROBERTSON CONSTRUCTION LTD   *p273*
17802 66 AVE UNIT 101A, SURREY, BC, V3S 7X1
(778) 574-4455   *SIC 1742*

SELECT DRYWALL & ACOUSTICS INC
p1033
75 SHARER RD SUITE 2, WOODBRIDGE, ON, L4L 8Z3
(905) 856-8249   *SIC 1742*

SHOEMAKER DRYWALL SUPPLIES LTD
p25
7012 8 ST NE, CALGARY, AB, T2E 8L8
(403) 291-1013   *SIC 1742*

STEVENSON INSULATION INC   *p635*

260 SHIRLEY AVE, KITCHENER, ON, N2B 2E1
(519) 743-2857   *SIC 1742*

SUNCO DRYWALL LTD   *p38*
7835 FLINT RD SE, CALGARY, AB, T2H 1G3
(403) 250-9701   *SIC 1742*

SUNCO DRYWALL LTD   *p220*
330 HIGHWAY 33 W UNIT 102, KELOWNA, BC, V1X 1X9
(250) 807-2270   *SIC 1742*

SYSTEME INTERIEUR EXCEL + INC *p1060*
735 BOUL INDUSTRIEL BUREAU 107, BLAINVILLE, QC, J7C 3V3
(450) 477-4585   *SIC 1742*

SYSTEMES INTERIEURS BERNARD MNJ & ASSOCIES INC   *p1232*
5000 RUE BERNARD-LEFEBVRE, MONTREAL, QC, H7C 0A5
(450) 665-1335   *SIC 1742*

THERMO DESIGN INSULATION LTD   *p111*
3520 56 AVE NW, EDMONTON, AB, T6B 3S7
(780) 468-2077   *SIC 1742*

THOMAS GROUP INC   *p26*
1115 55 AVE NE, CALGARY, AB, T2E 6W1
(403) 275-3666   *SIC 1742*

TRANS-ONTARIO CEILING & WALL SYSTEMS INC   *p560*
231 MILLWAY AVE UNIT 11, CONCORD, ON, L4K 3W7
(905) 669-0666   *SIC 1742*

UNITED ACOUSTIQUE & PARTITIONS CO INC
645 RUE MCCAFFREY, SAINT-LAURENT, QC, H4T 1N3
(514) 737-8337   *SIC 1742*

SIC 1743 Terrazzo, tile, marble and mossaic work

1249762 ONTARIO INC   *p547*
390 EDGELEY BLVD UNIT 8, CONCORD, ON, L4K 3Z6
(905) 761-9009   *SIC 1743*

STERLING TILE & CARPET   *p1028*
505 CITYVIEW BLVD UNIT 1, WOODBRIDGE, ON, L4H 0L8
(905) 585-4800   *SIC 1743*

TERRAZZO MOSAIC & TILE COMPANY LIMITED   *p994*
900 KEELE ST, TORONTO, ON, M6N 3E7
(416) 653-6111   *SIC 1743*

YORK MARBLE TILE & TERRAZZO INC
p792
2 SHEFFIELD ST, NORTH YORK, ON, M6M 3E6
(416) 235-0161   *SIC 1743*

SIC 1751 Carpentry work

AVENIDA CARPENTRY LTD   *p737*
6801 COLUMBUS RD, MISSISSAUGA, ON, L5T 2G9
(905) 565-0813   *SIC 1751*

BHI INSTALLATIONS INC   *p501*
278 ORENDA RD, BRAMPTON, ON, L6T 4X6
(905) 791-2850   *SIC 1751*

BROFORT INC   *p817*
2161 THURSTON DR, OTTAWA, ON, K1G 6C9
(613) 746-8580   *SIC 1751*

CARPENTER CANADA CO   *p1030*
500 HANLAN RD, WOODBRIDGE, ON, L4L 3P6
(416) 743-5689   *SIC 1751*

CENTENNIAL WINDOWS LTD   *p648*
687 SOVEREIGN RD, LONDON, ON, N5V 4K8
(519) 451-0508   *SIC 1751*

CENTRA CONSTRUCTION GROUP LTD

p224
20178 98 AVE, LANGLEY, BC, V1M 3G1
(604) 882-5010   *SIC 1751*

CORRADO CARPENTER CONTRACTOR LIMITED   *p551*
445 EDGELEY BLVD SUITE 20, CONCORD, ON, L4K 4G1
(905) 660-4411   *SIC 1751*

CREATIVE DOOR SERVICES LTD   *p105*
14904 135 AVE NW, EDMONTON, AB, T5V 1R9
(780) 483-1789   *SIC 1751*

CROSSBY DEWAR INC   *p813*
1143 WENTWORTH ST W SUITE 201, OSHAWA, ON, L1J 8P7
(905) 683-5102   *SIC 1751*

CRYSTAL CONSULTING INC   *p279*
2677 192 ST UNIT 108, SURREY, BC, V3Z 3X1
(778) 294-4425   *SIC 1751*

FUTURE DOORS LTD   *p410*
4009 ROUTE 115, NOTRE-DAME, NB, E4V 2G2
(506) 576-9769   *SIC 1751*

LEVEL IT INSTALLATIONS LTD   *p247*
1515 BROADWAY ST UNIT 804, PORT COQUITLAM, BC, V3C 6M2
(604) 942-2022   *SIC 1751*

MARITIME DOOR & WINDOW LTD   *p407*
118 ALBERT ST, MONCTON, NB, E1C 1B2
(506) 857-8108   *SIC 1751*

MEUBLES D'AUTRAY INC   *p1057*
1180 RUE GREGOIRE, BERTHIERVILLE, QC, J0K 1A0
(450) 836-3187   *SIC 1751*

PENTCO INDUSTRIES INC   *p282*
9274 194 ST, SURREY, BC, V4N 4E9
(604) 888-0508   *SIC 1751*

PORTES JPR INC, LES   *p1087*
4800 SUD LAVAL (A-440) O UNITE 1, COTE SAINT-LUC, QC, H7T 2Z8
(450) 661-5110   *SIC 1751*

PREMONTEX   *p1401*
597 RUE CHEF-MAX-GROS-LOUIS, WENDAKE, QC, G0A 4V0
(418) 847-3630   *SIC 1751*

PUREWOOD INCORPORATED   *p510*
341 HEART LAKE RD, BRAMPTON, ON, L6W 3K8
(905) 874-9797   *SIC 1751*

RIVERSIDE DOOR & TRIM INC   *p1009*
520 CONESTOGO RD, WATERLOO, ON, N2L 4E2
(519) 578-3265   *SIC 1751*

SIMPLE CONCEPT INC   *p1236*
2812 RUE JOSEPH-A.-BOMBARDIER, MONTREAL, QC, H7P 6E2
(450) 978-0602   *SIC 1751*

TARESCO LTD   *p615*
175A NEBO RD, HAMILTON, ON, L8W 2E1
(905) 575-8078   *SIC 1751*

TRIANGLE KITCHEN LTD   *p398*
679 RUE BABIN, DIEPPE, NB, E1A 5M7
(506) 858-5855   *SIC 1751*

VITRERIE VERTECH (2000) INC   *p1062*
4275 BOUL DE LA GRANDE-ALLEE, BOISBRIAND, QC, J7H 1M7
(450) 430-6161   *SIC 1751*

WILCOX DOOR SERVICE INC   *p712*
1045 RANGEVIEW RD, MISSISSAUGA, ON, L5E 1H2
(905) 274-5850   *SIC 1751*

SIC 1752 Floor laying and floor work, nec

2639-1862 QUEBEC INC   *p1402*
1031 7E RANG, WICKHAM, QC, J0C 1S0
(819) 398-6303   *SIC 1752*

3592898 CANADA INC   *p1108*
1706 CH PINK BUREAU F, GATINEAU, QC, J9J 3N7
(819) 771-3969   *SIC 1752*

ANTEX WESTERN LTD   *p371*

1340 CHURCH AVE, WINNIPEG, MB, R2X 1G4
(204) 633-4815   *SIC 1752*

BEATTY FLOORS LTD   *p285*
1840 PANDORA ST, VANCOUVER, BC, V5L 1M7
(604) 254-9571   *SIC 1752*

CENTAUR PRODUCTS INC   *p182*
3145 THUNDERBIRD CRES, BURNABY, BC, V5A 3G1
(604) 357-3510   *SIC 1752*

CLASSIC TILE CONTRACTORS LIMITED
p521
1175 APPLEBY LINE UNIT B2, BURLINGTON, ON, L7L 5H9
(905) 335-1700   *SIC 1752*

FABRIS-MILANO GROUP LTD, THE   *p382*
1035 ERIN ST, WINNIPEG, MB, R3G 2X1
(204) 783-7179   *SIC 1752*

FOURNITURE DE PLANCHERS INNOVATIFS INC   *p1065*
1280 RUE GRAHAM-BELL BUREAU 1, BOUCHERVILLE, QC, J4B 6H5
(450) 641-4566   *SIC 1752*

KBM COMMERCIAL FLOOR COVERINGS INC   *p30*
1260 26 AVE SE, CALGARY, AB, T2G 5S2
(403) 274-5292   *SIC 1752*

KEMBER HARDWOOD FLOORING INC *p598*
246022 COUNTY RD 16, GRAND VALLEY, ON, L9W 6K2
(289) 804-0032   *SIC 1752*

M & A TILE COMPANY LIMITED   *p784*
1155 PETROLIA RD, NORTH YORK, ON, M3J 2X7
(416) 667-8171   *SIC 1752*

STONHARD LTD   *p1015*
95 SUNRAY ST, WHITBY, ON, L1N 9C9
(705) 749-1460   *SIC 1752*

USIHOME INC   *p1148*
1455 BOUL INDUSTRIEL, MAGOG, QC, J1X 4P2
(819) 847-0666   *SIC 1752*

WESTBORO FLOORING & DECOR INC
p750
195 COLONNADE RD S, NEPEAN, ON, K2E 7K3
(613) 226-3830   *SIC 1752*

ZAD HOLDINGS LTD   *p322*
1903 BROADWAY W, VANCOUVER, BC, V6J 1Z3
(604) 739-4477   *SIC 1752*

SIC 1761 Roofing, siding, and sheetMetal work

141517 CANADA LTEE   *p1075*
270 BOUL INDUSTRIEL, CHATEAUGUAY, QC, J6J 4Z2
(450) 692-5527   *SIC 1761*

1702660 ONTARIO INC   *p748*
2013 PRINCE OF WALES DR, NEPEAN, ON, K2C 3J7
(613) 913-5539   *SIC 1761*

944743 ONTARIO INC   *p643*
477 HIGHWAY 77, LEAMINGTON, ON, N8H 3V6
(519) 325-1005   *SIC 1761*

ALLIANCE ROOFING & SHEET METAL LTD
p605
25 COPE CRT, GUELPH, ON, N1K 0A4
(519) 763-1442   *SIC 1761*

ALUMINIUM B. BOUCHARD INC   *p1233*
125 RUE DE LA POINTE-LANGLOIS, MONTREAL, QC, H7L 3J4
(450) 622-9543   *SIC 1761*

ARBUTUS ROOFING & DRAINS (2006) LTD
p259
4260 VANGUARD RD, RICHMOND, BC, V6X 2P5
(604) 272-7277   *SIC 1761*

ATLANTIC ROOFERS LIMITED   *p397*
118 CH COCAGNE CROSS, COCAGNE, NB, E4R 2J2

(506) 576-6683 *SIC* 1761
ATLAS-APEX ROOFING INC *p582*
65 DISCO RD, ETOBICOKE, ON, M9W 1M2
(416) 421-6244 *SIC* 1761
BOTHWELL-ACCURATE CO. INC. *p687*
6675 REXWOOD RD, MISSISSAUGA, ON, L4V 1V1
(905) 673-0615 *SIC* 1761
BOURGAULT INDUSTRIES LTD *p1436*
501 BARBIER DR, ST BRIEUX, SK, S0K 3V0
(306) 275-2300 *SIC* 1761
BRAULT, OMER INC *p1317*
865 RUE AUBRY, SAINT-JEAN-SUR-RICHELIEU, QC, J3B 7R4
(450) 347-3342 *SIC* 1761
CAMBIE ROOFING CONTRACTORS LTD *p290*
1367 E KENT AVE NORTH, VANCOUVER, BC, V5X 4T6
(604) 261-1111 *SIC* 1761
CANTERBURY ROOFING LTD *p28*
3810 16 ST SE, CALGARY, AB, T2G 3R7
(403) 234-8582 *SIC* 1761
CCS CONTRACTING LTD *p100*
18039 114 AVE NW, EDMONTON, AB, T5S 1T8
(780) 481-1776 *SIC* 1761
CENTIMARK LTD *p692*
5597 TIMBERLEA BLVD, MISSISSAUGA, ON, L4W 2S4
(905) 206-0255 *SIC* 1761
CGC INC *p803*
735 FOURTH LINE, OAKVILLE, ON, L6L 5B7
(905) 337-5100 *SIC* 1761
CHANDLER, DEAN ROOFING LIMITED *p868*
275 COMSTOCK RD, SCARBOROUGH, ON, M1L 2H2
(416) 751-7840 *SIC* 1761
COUVERTURE MONTREAL-NORD LTEE *p1344*
8200 RUE LAFRENAIE, SAINT-LEONARD, QC, H1P 2A9
(514) 324-8300 *SIC* 1761
COUVERTURES ST-LEONARD INC, LES *p1162*
11365 55E AV, MONTREAL, QC, H1E 2R2
(514) 648-1118 *SIC* 1761
D.W.S. ROOFING AND WATERPROOFING SERVICES INC *p597*
2562 DEL ZOTTO AVE, GLOUCESTER, ON, K1T 3V7
(613) 260-7700 *SIC* 1761
DESIGN ROOFING & SHEET METAL LTD *p246*
1385 KINGSWAY AVE, PORT COQUITLAM, BC, V3C 1S2
(604) 944-2977 *SIC* 1761
DOMINION SHEET METAL & ROOFING WORKS *p789*
113 CARTWRIGHT AVE SUITE 1, NORTH YORK, ON, M6A 1V4
(416) 789-0601 *SIC* 1761
EMPIRE ROOFING CORPORATION *p1023*
4810 WALKER RD, WINDSOR, ON, N9A 6J3
(519) 969-7101 *SIC* 1761
EXTERIORS BY LEROY & DARCY LTD *p140*
3404 12 AVE N, LETHBRIDGE, AB, T1H 5V1
(403) 327-9113 *SIC* 1761
FABRICATION METELEC LTEE *p1318*
300 RUE CARREAU, SAINT-JEAN-SUR-RICHELIEU, QC, J3B 2G4
(450) 346-6363 *SIC* 1761
FLYNN CANADA LTD *p159*
285221 KLEYSEN WAY, ROCKY VIEW COUNTY, AB, T1X 0K1
(403) 720-8155 *SIC* 1761
FLYNN CANADA LTD *p595*
5661 POWER RD, GLOUCESTER, ON, K1G 3N4
SIC 1761

FLYNN CANADA LTD *p688*
6435 NORTHWEST DR, MISSISSAUGA, ON, L4V 1K2
(905) 671-3971 *SIC* 1761
FLYNN CANADA LTD *p816*
2780 SHEFFIELD RD, OTTAWA, ON, K1B 3V9
(613) 696-0086 *SIC* 1761
FLYNN CANADA LTD *p892*
890 ARVIN AVE, STONEY CREEK, ON, L8E 5Y8
(905) 643-9515 *SIC* 1761
FLYNN CANADA LTD *p1027*
141 ROYAL GROUP CRES, WOOD-BRIDGE, ON, L4H 1X9
(905) 671-3971 *SIC* 1761
FRASER VALLEY ROOFING LTD *p197*
44687 CHALMER PL, CHILLIWACK, BC, V2R 0H8
(604) 795-6620 *SIC* 1761
GENRON ENTERPRISES LTD *p128*
295 MACDONALD CRES, FORT MCMUR-RAY, AB, T9H 4B7
(780) 743-3445 *SIC* 1761
GOODMEN ROOFING LTD *p155*
7700 76 ST CLOSE SUITE 110, RED DEER, AB, T4P 4G6
(403) 343-0380 *SIC* 1761
HAMBLET'S ROOFING & SIDING INC *p760*
7130 KINSMEN CRT, NIAGARA FALLS, ON, L2H 0Y5
(905) 988-6263 *SIC* 1761
HAMILTON, T & SON ROOFING INC *p864*
20 THORNMOUNT DR, SCARBOROUGH, ON, M1B 3J4
(416) 755-5522 *SIC* 1761
IGLOO ERECTORS LTD *p12*
3468 46 AVE SE, CALGARY, AB, T2B 3J2
(403) 253-1121 *SIC* 1761
INDUSTRIES GRC INC, LES *p1115*
2681 RUE DE LA SALLE, JONQUIERE, QC, G7S 2A8
(418) 548-1171 *SIC* 1761
KING KOATING ROOFING INC *p554*
41 PEELAR RD, CONCORD, ON, L4K 1A3
(905) 669-1771 *SIC* 1761
LACASSE & FILS MAITRES COUVREURS INC *p1375*
10230 BOUL BOURQUE, SHERBROOKE, QC, J1N 0G2
(819) 843-2681 *SIC* 1761
LAFLECHE ROOFING (1992) LIMITED *p661*
1100 PROGRESS DR, LONDON, ON, N6N 1B8
(519) 681-7610 *SIC* 1761
M.J. ROOFING & SUPPLY LTD *p372*
909 JARVIS AVE, WINNIPEG, MB, R2X 0A1
(204) 586-8411 *SIC* 1761
MANSEAU & PERRON INC *p1290*
701 AV DAVY, ROUYN-NORANDA, QC, J9Y 0A8
(819) 762-2818 *SIC* 1761
MARINE ROOFING & SHEET METAL LTD *p193*
4909 BYRNE RD SUITE 4, BURNABY, BC, V5J 3H6
(604) 433-4322 *SIC* 1761
MARINE ROOFING LTD *p193*
4909 BYRNE RD SUITE 4, BURNABY, BC, V5J 3H6
(604) 433-4322 *SIC* 1761
MCCARTHY'S ROOFING LIMITED *p443*
850 MAIN ST, DARTMOUTH, NS, B2W 3V1
(902) 469-2260 *SIC* 1761
MILLER BROS. ROOFING & SHEET METAL CO LIMITED *p590*
206 VICTORIA ST W, EXETER, ON, N0M 1S2
(519) 235-3643 *SIC* 1761
MSM CONSTRUCTION SERVICES LTD *p459*
12575 HIGHWAY 4, HAVRE-BOUCHER, NS, B0H 1P0
(902) 234-3202 *SIC* 1761
NEDLAW ROOFING LIMITED *p518*

232 WOOLWICH ST S, BRESLAU, ON, N0B 1M0
(519) 648-2218 *SIC* 1761
NORTEX ROOFING LTD *p586*
40 BETHRIDGE RD, ETOBICOKE, ON, M9W 1N1
(416) 236-6090 *SIC* 1761
NORTHWEST SHEET METAL LTD *p279*
19159 33 AVE, SURREY, BC, V3Z 1A1
(604) 542-9536 *SIC* 1761
OAKWOOD ROOFING AND SHEET METAL CO. LTD *p363*
20 BURNETT AVE, WINNIPEG, MB, R2G 1C1
(204) 237-8361 *SIC* 1761
ORIGINAL ROOF MAINTAINER INC *p255*
16020 RIVER RD, RICHMOND, BC, V6V 1L6
SIC 1761
OVERLANDERS MANUFACTURING LP *p178*
30320 FRASER HWY, ABBOTSFORD, BC, V4X 1G1
(604) 856-6815 *SIC* 1761
PEDDIE ROOFING & WATERPROOFING LTD *p12*
3352 46 AVE SE, CALGARY, AB, T2B 3J2
(403) 273-7000 *SIC* 1761
PENFOLDS ROOFING INC *p295*
1262 VERNON DR, VANCOUVER, BC, V6A 4C9
(604) 254-4663 *SIC* 1761
PROVINCIAL INDUSTRIAL ROOFING AND SHEET METAL COMPANY LIMITED *p557*
166 BOWES RD, CONCORD, ON, L4K 1J6
(905) 669-2569 *SIC* 1761
RAVEN ROOFING LTD *p280*
18988 34A AVE, SURREY, BC, V3Z 1A7
(604) 531-9619 *SIC* 1761
RAYMOND AND ASSOCIATES ROOFING INC *p827*
3091 ALBION RD N SUITE 5B, OTTAWA, ON, K1V 9V9
(613) 274-7508 *SIC* 1761
REVETEMENTS ALNORDICA INC *p1323*
1230 RUE DES ERABLES, SAINT-LAMBERT-DE-LAUZON, QC, G0S 2W0
(418) 889-9761 *SIC* 1761
RIDGE SHEET METAL LTD *p247*
2532 DAVIES AVE, PORT COQUITLAM, BC, V3C 2J9
(604) 942-0244 *SIC* 1761
ROOF TILE MANAGEMENT INC *p742*
360 GIBRALTAR DR, MISSISSAUGA, ON, L5T 2P5
(905) 672-9992 *SIC* 1761
SCHREIBER BROTHERS LIMITED *p608*
50 BROCKLEY DR, HAMILTON, ON, L8E 3P1
(905) 561-7780 *SIC* 1761
SEMPLE GOODER ROOFING CORPORA-TION *p998*
1365 MARTIN GROVE RD, TORONTO, ON, M9W 4X7
(416) 743-5370 *SIC* 1761
SEMPLE-GOODER ROOFING CORPORA-TION *p483*
309 DARRELL DR, AYR, ON, N0B 1E0
(519) 623-3300 *SIC* 1761
SIMLUC CONTRACTORS LIMITED *p816*
2550 BLACKWELL ST, OTTAWA, ON, K1B 5R1
(613) 748-0066 *SIC* 1761
TAM-KAL LIMITED *p598*
34 CARDICO DR UNIT 2, GORMLEY, ON, L4A 2G5
(905) 888-9200 *SIC* 1761
TEK-MOR INCORPORATED *p495*
20 SIMPSON RD, BOLTON, ON, L7E 1G9
(905) 857-6415 *SIC* 1761
THERMAL SYSTEMS KWC LTD *p160*
261185 WAGON WHEEL WAY, ROCKY VIEW COUNTY, AB, T4A 0E2
(403) 250-5507 *SIC* 1761

TITAN METALS LTD *p998*
5982 6TH LINE, TOTTENHAM, ON, L0G 1W0
(905) 729-4347 *SIC* 1761
TOITURES COUTURE & ASSOCIES INC *p1309*
6565 BOUL MARICOURT, SAINT-HUBERT, QC, J3Y 1S8
(450) 678-2562 *SIC* 1761
TOITURES HOGUE INC, LES *p1060*
745 BOUL INDUSTRIEL, BLAINVILLE, QC, J7C 3V3
(450) 435-6336 *SIC* 1761
TOITURES VICK & ASSOCIES INC, LES *p1376*
71 CH GODIN, SHERBROOKE, QC, J1R 0S6
(450) 658-4300 *SIC* 1761
TRANSCONA ROOFING (2000) LTD *p367*
992 DUGALD RD, WINNIPEG, MB, R2J 0G9
(204) 233-3716 *SIC* 1761
WEST AIR SHEET METAL LTD *p26*
1238 45 AVE NE, CALGARY, AB, T2E 2P1
(403) 250-7518 *SIC* 1761

SIC 1771 Concrete work

AMHERST CONCRETE PUMPING LIMITED *p870*
105 NANTUCKET BLVD, SCARBOROUGH, ON, M1P 2N5
(416) 752-2431 *SIC* 1771
ARCHITECTURAL PRECAST STRUC-TURES LTD *p224*
9844 199A ST, LANGLEY, BC, V1M 2X7
(604) 888-1968 *SIC* 1771
BELLAI BROTHERS CONSTRUCTION LTD *p824*
440 LAURIER AVE W SUITE 200, OTTAWA, ON, K1R 7X6
(613) 782-2932 *SIC* 1771
BETONS PREFABRIQUES TRANS-CANADA INC *p1044*
890 RUE DES PINS O, ALMA, QC, G8B 7R3
(418) 668-6161 *SIC* 1771
CAMP FORMING LTD *p794*
105 RIVALDA RD, NORTH YORK, ON, M9M 2M6
(416) 745-8680 *SIC* 1771
COASTAL RESTORATIONS & MASONRY LIMITED *p450*
8 MILLS DR, GOODWOOD, NS, B3T 1P3
(902) 876-8333 *SIC* 1771
CON-WALL CONCRETE INC *p657*
525 EXETER RD, LONDON, ON, N6E 2Z3
(519) 681-6910 *SIC* 1771
CONBORA FORMING INC *p551*
109 EDILCAN DR, CONCORD, ON, L4K 3S6
(905) 738-7979 *SIC* 1771
CONCORD CONCRETE & DRAIN LTD *p551*
109 EDILCAN DR, CONCORD, ON, L4K 3S6
(416) 736-0277 *SIC* 1771
CONSITE CONSTRUCTION LTD *p29*
1802 17 AVE SE, CALGARY, AB, T2G 1K4
(403) 265-0700 *SIC* 1771
CONSTRUCTION BAO INC *p1161*
7875 AV MARCO-POLO, MONTREAL, QC, H1E 1N8
(514) 648-2272 *SIC* 1771
DALMACIJA FORMING LTD *p749*
11 GIFFORD ST SUITE 201, NEPEAN, ON, K2E 7S3
(613) 727-1371 *SIC* 1771
DONALD CONSTRUCTION LIMITED *p584*
333 HUMBERLINE DR, ETOBICOKE, ON, M9W 5X3
(416) 675-4134 *SIC* 1771
DOUBLE STAR DRILLING (1998) LTD *p1*
25180 117 AVE, ACHESON, AB, T7X 6C2
(780) 484-4276 *SIC* 1771
DRANCO CONSTRUCTION LIMITED *p584*

1919 ALBION RD, ETOBICOKE, ON, M9W 5S8

(416) 675-2682 *SIC 1771*

DURON ONTARIO LTD *p694*
1860 SHAWSON DR, MISSISSAUGA, ON, L4W 1R7

(905) 670-1998 *SIC 1771*

DYNAMIC CONCRETE PUMPING INC *p15*
10720 48 ST SE, CALGARY, AB, T2C 3E1

(403) 236-9511 *SIC 1771*

EAST ELGIN CONCRETE FORMING LIMITED
10 ELM ST, TILLSONBURG, ON, N4G 0A7

(519) 842-6667 *SIC 1771*

EKUM-SEKUM INCORPORATED *p533*
1555 BISHOP ST N UNIT 1, CAMBRIDGE, ON, N1R 7J4

(519) 622-1600 *SIC 1771*

EQUIPEMENTS SPM INC *p1149*
1290 AV DE LA GARE, MASCOUCHE, QC, J7K 2Z2

(450) 966-6616 *SIC 1771*

FEMO CONSTRUCTION LTD *p192*
8555 GREENALL AVE SUITE 1, BURNABY, BC, V5J 3M8

(604) 254-3999 *SIC 1771*

GASTALDO CONCRETE LTD *p206*
482 FRASERVIEW PL, DELTA, BC, V3M 6H4

(604) 526-6262 *SIC 1771*

GRAFF COMPANY ULC, THE *p584*
35 PRECISION RD, ETOBICOKE, ON, M9W 5H3

(905) 457-8120 *SIC 1771*

H.P. CONSTRUCTION LTD *p175*
33386 SOUTH FRASER WAY SUITE 202, ABBOTSFORD, BC, V2S 2B5

(604) 850-1288 *SIC 1771*

HALTON FORMING (1992) LTD *p683*
593 MAIN ST E, MILTON, ON, L9T 3J2

(905) 693-4889 *SIC 1771*

INTEGRICON PROPERTY RESTORATION AND CONSTRUCTION GROUP INC *p1031*
219 WESTCREEK DR, WOODBRIDGE, ON, L4L 9T7

(416) 736-0395 *SIC 1771*

J.E. PERRON - INTER-CITE S.E.N.C *p1079*
205 BOUL DU ROYAUME E, CHICOUTIMI, QC, G7H 5K2

(418) 549-0532 *SIC 1771*

LDC PRECISION CONCRETE INC *p1002*
112 CLEMENT ST, VARS, ON, K0A 3H0

(613) 822-2872 *SIC 1771*

MARMOT CONSTRUCTION LTD *p40*
636 BEAVER DAM RD NE, CALGARY, AB, T2K 4W6

(403) 730-8711 *SIC 1771*

MCCANN REDI-MIX INC *p564*
69478 BRONSON LINE, DASHWOOD, ON, N0M 1N0

(519) 237-3647 *SIC 1771*

MIDDLESEX CONCRETE FORMING LTD *p628*
9644 TOWNSEND LINE SUITE 3, KERWOOD, ON, N0M 2B0

(519) 247-3752 *SIC 1771*

PANORAMA BUILDING SYSTEMS LTD *p206*
460 FRASERVIEW PL, DELTA, BC, V3M 6H4

(604) 522-4980 *SIC 1771*

RESFORM CONSTRUCTION LTD *p561*
3761 COUNTY RD 89, COOKSTOWN, ON, L0L 1L0

(705) 458-0600 *SIC 1771*

ROCKY CROSS CONSTRUCTION (NORTH) LTD *p76*
1610 104 AVE NE UNIT 145, CALGARY, AB, T3J 0T5

(403) 252-2550 *SIC 1771*

SOLAR ERECTORS LTD *p893*
332 JONES RD UNIT 1, STONEY CREEK, ON, L8E 5N2

(905) 643-1829 *SIC 1771*

SOLID WALL CONCRETE FORMING LTD

p664
45 RODINEA RD SUITE 8, MAPLE, ON, L6A 1R3

(905) 832-4311 *SIC 1771*

STRUCTURAL FLOOR FINISHING LIMITED *p598*
29 GORMLEY INDUSTRIAL RD, GORMLEY, ON, L0H 1G0

(416) 291-7576 *SIC 1771*

SWARTZ ENTERPRISES INC *p237*
804 WINTHROP ST, NEW WESTMINSTER, BC, V3L 4B1

(778) 859-5040 *SIC 1771*

SYBER CONCRETE FORMING LTD *p282*
18812 96 AVE UNIT 11, SURREY, BC, V4N 3R1

(604) 513-5717 *SIC 1771*

THORNCRETE CONSTRUCTION LIMITED *p559*
381 SPINNAKER WAY, CONCORD, ON, L4K 4N4

(905) 669-6510 *SIC 1771*

TRI-CON CONCRETE FINISHING CO. LTD *p785*
835 SUPERTEST RD SUITE 100, NORTH YORK, ON, M3J 2M9

(416) 736-7700 *SIC 1771*

UCC GROUP INC *p589*
262 GALAXY BLVD, ETOBICOKE, ON, M9W 5R8

(416) 675-7455 *SIC 1771*

VECTOR CONSTRUCTION LTD *p393*
474 DOVERCOURT DR, WINNIPEG, MB, R3Y 1G4

(204) 489-6300 *SIC 1771*

WEATHERTECH RESTORATION SERVICES INC *p650*
553 CLARKE RD, LONDON, ON, N5V 2E1

(519) 258-0535 *SIC 1771*

WEC TOURS QUEBEC INC *p1151*
300 RUE DU PORT, MATANE, QC, G4W 3M6

(514) 363-7266 *SIC 1771*

WEST CARLETON SAND & GRAVEL INC *p541*
3232 CARP RD, CARP, ON, K0A 1L0

(613) 839-2816 *SIC 1771*

YUKON COR CORPORATION *p561*
30 PENNSYLVANIA AVE UNIT 17A, CONCORD, ON, L4K 4A5

SIC 1771

SIC 1781 Water well drilling

ADVANCE DRILLING LTD *p42*
100 4 AVE SW SUITE 706, CALGARY, AB, T2P 3N2

SIC 1781

EAGLE DRILLING SERVICES LTD *p1405*
GD, CARLYLE, SK, S0C 0R0

(306) 453-2506 *SIC 1781*

KLUANE DRILLING LIMITED *p1440*
14 MACDONALD RD, WHITEHORSE, YT, Y1A 4L2

(867) 633-4800 *SIC 1781*

SUEZ CANADA INC *p1095*
1375 RTE TRANSCANADIENNE BUREAU 400, DORVAL, QC, H9P 2W8

(514) 683-1200 *SIC 1781*

SUEZ TREATMENT SOLUTIONS CANADA L.P. *p1228*
5490 BOUL THIMENS BUREAU 100, MONTREAL, QC, H4R 2K9

(514) 683-1200 *SIC 1781*

SIC 1791 Structural steel erection

ACIER AGF INC *p1141*
2270 RUE GARNEAU, LONGUEUIL, QC, J4G 1E7

(450) 442-9494 *SIC 1791*

ACIERS SOLIDER INC, LES *p1398*

300 RUE DE LA JACQUES-CARTIER, VICTORIAVILLE, QC, G6T 1Y3

(819) 758-2897 *SIC 1791*

ADVANCED STEEL STRUCTURES INC *p229*
5250 272 ST, LANGLEY, BC, V4W 1S3

(604) 626-4211 *SIC 1791*

AQUA INDUSTRIAL LTD *p127*
9912 FRANKLIN AVE SUITE 205, FORT MCMURRAY, AB, T9H 2K5

(780) 799-7300 *SIC 1791*

CLEARWATER FABRICATION GP INC *p122*
5710 17 ST NW, EDMONTON, AB, T6P 1S4

(780) 464-4230 *SIC 1791*

DOWCO CONSULTANTS LTD *p184*
2433 HOLDOM AVE, BURNABY, BC, V5B 5A1

(604) 606-5800 *SIC 1791*

DYNAMIC ATTRACTIONS LTD *p246*
1515 KINGSWAY AVE, PORT COQUITLAM, BC, V3C 1S2

(604) 639-8200 *SIC 1791*

DYNAMIC STRUCTURES LTD *p246*
1515 KINGSWAY AVE, PORT COQUITLAM, BC, V3C 1S2

(604) 941-9481 *SIC 1791*

FARR INSTALLATIONS LTD *p248*
4912 HART HWY, PRINCE GEORGE, BC, V2K 3A1

(250) 962-0333 *SIC 1791*

G & M STEEL SERVICE LTD *p271*
5980 ENTERPRISE WAY, SURREY, BC, V3S 6S8

(604) 530-0117 *SIC 1791*

GREATARIO INDUSTRIAL STORAGE SYSTEMS LTD *p622*
715647 COUNTY RD 4, INNERKIP, ON, N0J 1M0

(519) 469-8169 *SIC 1791*

HORTON CBI, LIMITED *p168*
55116 HWY 825, STURGEON COUNTY, AB, T8L 5C1

(780) 998-2800 *SIC 1791*

JANZEN, HENRY STEEL BUILDINGS LTD *p1413*
GD, OSLER, SK, S0K 3A0

(306) 242-7767 *SIC 1791*

LEMIRE, ERIC ENTERPRISES INC *p748*
4815B MCNEELY RD, NAVAN, ON, K4B 0J3

(613) 835-4040 *SIC 1791*

LMS LIMITED PARTNERSHIP *p277*
7452 132 ST, SURREY, BC, V3W 4M7

(604) 598-9930 *SIC 1791*

LMS MANAGEMENT LTD *p272*
6320 148 ST, SURREY, BC, V3S 3C4

(604) 598-9930 *SIC 1791*

MARID INDUSTRIES LIMITED *p470*
99 WINDSOR JUNCTION RD, WINDSOR JUNCTION, NS, B2T 1G7

(902) 860-1138 *SIC 1791*

MATRIX SERVICE CANADA ULC *p139*
7105 39 ST UNIT 102, LEDUC, AB, T9E 0R8

(780) 986-4058 *SIC 1791*

MOMETAL STRUCTURES INC *p1393*
201 CH DE L'ENERGIE, VARENNES, QC, J3X 1P7

(450) 929-3999 *SIC 1791*

MONTAGE SAINT-LAURENT INC *p1237*
807 RUE MARSHALL, MONTREAL, QC, H7S 1J9

(450) 786-1792 *SIC 1791*

MQM QUALITY MANUFACTURING LTD *p419*
2676 COMMERCE ST, TRACADIE-SHEILA, NB, E1X 1G5

(506) 395-7777 *SIC 1791*

NORSEMAN INC *p96*
14545 115 AVE NW, EDMONTON, AB, T5M 3B8

(780) 451-6828 *SIC 1791*

RUSSEL METALS INC *p392*
1510 CLARENCE AVE, WINNIPEG, MB, R3T 1T6

(204) 475-8584 *SIC 1791*

SAMUEL METAL BLANKING *p516*

546 ELGIN ST, BRANTFORD, ON, N3S 7P8

(519) 758-1125 *SIC 1791*

SAMUEL, SON & CO., LIMITED *p537*
133 TROH AVE, CAMBRIDGE, ON, N3C 4B1

(416) 777-9554 *SIC 1791*

SPENCER STEEL LIMITED *p621*
200 KING ST, ILDERTON, ON, N0M 2A0

(519) 471-6888 *SIC 1791*

STRUCTURAL CONTRACTING LTD *p598*
29 GORMLEY INDUSTRIAL AVE UNIT 6, GORMLEY, ON, L0H 1G0

(416) 291-7576 *SIC 1791*

STRUCTURES BRETON INC, LES *p1296*
500 RUE SAGARD, SAINT-BRUNO, QC, J3V 6C2

(450) 653-9999 *SIC 1791*

STRUCTURES DE BEAUCE INC, LES *p1349*
305 RUE DU PARC RR 1, SAINT-ODILON, QC, G0S 3A0

(418) 464-2000 *SIC 1791*

STUBBE'S PRECAST COMMERCIAL INC *p618*
44 MUIR LINE, HARLEY, ON, N0E 1E0

(519) 424-2183 *SIC 1791*

SUPERMETAL QUEBEC INC *p1138*
1955 5E RUE, LEVIS, QC, G6W 5M6

(418) 834-1955 *SIC 1791*

TREPANIER, PHILIPPE INC *p1116*
4573 CH SAINT-ISIDORE, JONQUIERE, QC, G7X 7V5

(418) 547-4734 *SIC 1791*

VENABLES MACHINE WORKS LTD *p1430*
502 50TH ST E, SASKATOON, SK, S7K 6L9

(306) 931-7100 *SIC 1791*

VERTICAL BUILDING SOLUTIONS INC *p133*
64071 HWY 43, GRANDE PRAIRIE, AB, T8V 3A5

(780) 532-0366 *SIC 1791*

WARWICK STRUCTURES GROUP LTD *p160*
285188A FRONTIER RD, ROCKY VIEW COUNTY, AB, T1X 0V9

(403) 695-9999 *SIC 1791*

WESBRIDGE STEELWORKS LIMITED *p210*
7480 WILSON AVE, DELTA, BC, V4G 1H3

(604) 946-8618 *SIC 1791*

WHITEMUD GROUP LTD *p111*
8170 50 ST NW SUITE 300, EDMONTON, AB, T6B 1E6

(780) 701-3295 *SIC 1791*

WHITEMUD IRONWORKS GROUP INC *p111*
8170 50 ST NW SUITE 300, EDMONTON, AB, T6B 1E6

(780) 701-3295 *SIC 1791*

WHITEMUD IRONWORKS LIMITED *p123*
7727 18 ST NW, EDMONTON, AB, T6P 1N9

(780) 465-5888 *SIC 1791*

XL IRONWORKS *p278*
12720 82 AVE, SURREY, BC, V3W 3G1

(604) 596-1747 *SIC 1791*

SIC 1793 Glass and glazing work

ALBERTA GLASS COMPANY INC *p8*
2820 37 AVE NE, CALGARY, AB, T1Y 5T3

(403) 219-7466 *SIC 1793*

BROTHERS COMPANY GLASS CAR CARE LTD *p200*
802 BRUNETTE AVE, COQUITLAM, BC, V3K 1C4

(604) 517-0215 *SIC 1793*

FERGUSON-NEUDORF GLASS INC *p489*
4275 NORTH SERVICE RD, BEAMSVILLE, ON, L0R 1B1

(905) 563-1394 *SIC 1793*

GLASTECH GLAZING CONTRACTORS LTD *p246*
1613 KEBET WAY, PORT COQUITLAM, BC, V3C 5W9

(604) 941-9115 *SIC 1793*

LEPAGE SIGNATURE INC *p1264*
960 RUE RAOUL-JOBIN BUREAU D, QUEBEC, QC, G1N 1S9

---

(418) 476-1678   *SIC* 1793
MERIT GLASS LTD *p606*
61 ARROW RD, GUELPH, ON, N1K 1S8
(519) 822-7416   *SIC* 1793
PRESTIGE GLASS (2002) LTD *p247*
1353 KEBET WAY, PORT COQUITLAM, BC, V3C 6G1
(604) 464-5015   *SIC* 1793
VITRECO INC *p1085*
1860 RUE CUNARD, COTE SAINT-LUC, QC, H7S 2B2
(450) 681-0483   *SIC* 1793
WESTMOUNT STOREFRONT SYSTEMS LTD *p636*
20 RIVERVIEW PL, KITCHENER, ON, N2B 3X8
(519) 570-2850   *SIC* 1793

SIC 1794 Excavation work

1204626 ONTARIO INC *p907*
570 SQUIER PL, THUNDER BAY, ON, P7B 6M2
(807) 935-2792   *SIC* 1794
130395 CANADA INC *p1044*
200 RUE DES PINS O BUREAU 201, ALMA, QC, G8B 6P9
(418) 668-0420   *SIC* 1794
3471250 CANADA INC *p1367*
440 RUE HOLLIDAY, SEPT-ILES, QC, G4R 4X6
(418) 962-1234   *SIC* 1794
561861 ONTARIO LTD *p569*
1482 ST JACQUES RD, EMBRUN, ON, K0A 1W0
(613) 443-2311   *SIC* 1794
9045-1410 QUEBEC INC *p1093*
1620 CROIS NEWMAN, DORVAL, QC, H9P 2R8
(514) 631-1888   *SIC* 1794
9222-0201 QUEBEC INC *p1148*
890 RUE LA SALLE, MALARTIC, QC, J0Y 1Z0
(819) 757-4868   *SIC* 1794
9332-3301 QUEBEC INC *p1392*
84 RUE RIENDEAU, VARENNES, QC, J3X 1P7
(450) 652-9871   *SIC* 1794
A. & J.L. BOURGEOIS LTEE *p1082*
1745 RTE MARIE-VICTORIN, CONTRE-COEUR, QC, J0L 1C0
(450) 587-2724   *SIC* 1794
ALI EXCAVATION INC *p1365*
760 BOUL DES ERABLES, SALABERRY-DE-VALLEYFIELD, QC, J6T 6G4
(450) 373-2010   *SIC* 1794
ALLTERRA CONSTRUCTION LTD *p340*
2158 MILLSTREAM RD, VICTORIA, BC, V9B 6H4
(250) 658-3772   *SIC* 1794
BEDARD, JACQUES EXCAVATION LIMITED *p748*
3006 TENTH LINE RD, NAVAN, ON, K4B 1H8
(613) 824-3208   *SIC* 1794
BOUVET, ANDRE LTEE *p1056*
1840 BOUL DE PORT-ROYAL, BECAN-COUR, QC, G9H 0K7
(819) 233-2357   *SIC* 1794
BYZ CONSTRUCTION INC *p147*
2196 BRIER PARK PL NW, MEDICINE HAT, AB, T1C 1S6
SIC 1794
CHARLES-AUGUSTE FORTIER INC *p1254*
424 BOUL RAYMOND, QUEBEC, QC, G1C 8K9
(418) 661-0043   *SIC* 1794
CHEW EXCAVATING LTD *p334*
575 GORGE RD E, VICTORIA, QC, V8T 2W5
(250) 386-7586   *SIC* 1794
CKB CONSTRUCTION (2004) LTD *p100*
10828 209 ST NW, EDMONTON, AB, T5S

1Z9
(780) 453-6611   *SIC* 1794
CLIPPER CONSTRUCTION LIMITED *p501*
16 MELANIE DR SUITE 200, BRAMPTON, ON, L6T 4K9
(905) 790-2333   *SIC* 1794
CONSTRUCTION ET PAVAGE BOISVERT INC *p1300*
180 BOUL DE LA GABELLE, SAINT-ETIENNE-DES-GRES, QC, G0X 2P0
(819) 374-7277   *SIC* 1794
CONSTRUCTION J. & R. SAVARD LTEE *p1307*
1201 BOUL MARTEL, SAINT-HONORE-DE-CHICOUTIMI, QC, G0V 1L0
(418) 543-5933   *SIC* 1794
CONSTRUCTION LARIVIERE LTEE *p1108*
640 RUE AUGUSTE-MONDOUX, GATINEAU, QC, J9J 3K3
(819) 770-2280   *SIC* 1794
CONSTRUCTION POLARIS INC *p1278*
500 -797 BOUL LEBOURGNEUF, QUEBEC, QC, G2J 0B5
(418) 861-9877   *SIC* 1794
CONSTRUCTION RAOUL PELLETIER (1997) INC *p1137*
3650 BOUL GUILLAUME-COUTURE, LEVIS, QC, G6W 7L3
(418) 837-9833   *SIC* 1794
CONSTRUCTION YVAN BOISVERT INC *p1300*
180 BOUL DE LA GABELLE, SAINT-ETIENNE-DES-GRES, QC, G0X 2P0
(819) 374-7277   *SIC* 1794
CONSTRUCTIONS BRI INC, LES *p1295*
585 RUE SAGARD, SAINT-BRUNO, QC, J3V 6C1
(450) 461-3310   *SIC* 1794
CONSTRUCTIONS EDGUY INC, LES *p1360*
500 1RE AV DU PARC-INDUSTRIEL, SAINTE-MARIE, QC, G6E 1B5
(418) 387-6270   *SIC* 1794
COPCAN CONTRACTING LTD *p235*
1920 BALSAM RD, NANAIMO, BC, V9X 1T5
(250) 754-7260   *SIC* 1794
COTTON INC *p757*
2125 FRUITBELT DR, NIAGARA FALLS, ON, L2E 6S4
(905) 262-2000   *SIC* 1794
COX, G W CONSTRUCTION LTD *p140*
1210 31 ST N, LETHBRIDGE, AB, T1H 5J8
(403) 328-1346   *SIC* 1794
CRAINS' CONSTRUCTION LIMITED *p663*
1800 MAYBERLY 2 ELPHIN RD, MABERLY, ON, K0H 2B0
(613) 268-2308   *SIC* 1794
CUMMING & DOBBIE (1986) LTD *p346*
3000 VICTORIA AVE E, BRANDON, MB, R7A 7L2
(204) 726-0790   *SIC* 1794
DEXTER MINING INC *p425*
1001 LUCE ST, LABRADOR CITY, NL, A2V 2K7
(709) 944-2995   *SIC* 1794
DIVAL DEVELOPMENTS LTD *p615*
90 TRINITY CHURCH RD, HAMILTON, ON, L8W 3S2
(905) 387-8214   *SIC* 1794
DUFRESNE PILING COMPANY (1967) LIMITED *p832*
100 CITIGATE DR, OTTAWA, ON, K2J 6K7
(613) 739-5355   *SIC* 1794
EBI ENERGIE INC *p1057*
670 RUE DE MONTCALM, BERTHIERVILLE, QC, J0K 1A0
(450) 836-8111   *SIC* 1794
ENTREPRISE CLAUDE CHAGNON INC *p1308*
3500 BOUL SIR-WILFRID-LAURIER, SAINT-HUBERT, QC, J3Y 6T1
(450) 321-2446   *SIC* 1794
ENTREPRISES CANBEC CONSTRUCTION INC, LES *p1125*
145 RUE RICHER, LACHINE, QC, H8R 1R4

(514) 481-1226   *SIC* 1794
ENTREPRISES PEP (2000) INC, LES *p1231*
3000 RUE BERNARD-LEFEBVRE, MONTREAL, QC, H7C 0A5
(450) 661-5050   *SIC* 1794
ENTREPRISES R & G ST-LAURENT INC *p1052*
2081 AV DU LABRADOR, BAIE-COMEAU, QC, G4Z 3B9
(418) 589-5453   *SIC* 1794
EQUIPEMENTS GAETAN INC, LES *p1124*
320 CH DU LAC-HURON, LAC-AUX-SABLES, QC, G0X 1M0
(418) 336-2634   *SIC* 1794
EXCAVATION DE CHICOUTIMI INC *p1080*
1201 BOUL SAINT-PAUL, CHICOUTIMI, QC, G7J 3Y2
(418) 549-8343   *SIC* 1794
EXCAVATION NORMAND MAJEAU INC *p1282*
337 RUE CHARLES-MARCHAND, REPENTIGNY, QC, J5Z 4N8
(450) 581-8248   *SIC* 1794
EXCAVATION PARADIS, MICHEL INC *p1302*
780 BOUL HAMEL, SAINT-FELICIEN, QC, G8K 1X9
(418) 679-4533   *SIC* 1794
EXCAVATION R.B. GAUTHIER INC *p1159*
246 RTE 117, MONT-TREMBLANT, QC, J8E 2X1
(819) 425-2074   *SIC* 1794
EXCAVATION RENE ST-PIERRE *p1369*
800 RUE DE L'ARDOISE, SHERBROOKE, QC, J1C 0J6
(819) 565-1494   *SIC* 1794
EXCAVATION ST-PIERRE ET TREMBLAY INC *p1088*
126 RUE DEAN, COWANSVILLE, QC, J2K 3Y3
(450) 266-2100   *SIC* 1794
EXCAVATIONS GILLES ST-ONGE INC, LES *p1307*
1075 CROIS DES HAUTEURS, SAINT-HIPPOLYTE, QC, J8A 0A5
(450) 224-0555   *SIC* 1794
EXCAVATIONS PAYETTE LTEE, LES *p1048*
7900 RUE BOMBARDIER, ANJOU, QC, H1J 1A4
(514) 322-4800   *SIC* 1794
EXCAVATIONS VESPO INC, LES *p1126*
17 BOUL SAINT-JOSEPH, LACHINE, QC, H8S 2K9
(514) 933-5057   *SIC* 1794
FAGA GROUP INC *p904*
137 LANGSTAFF RD E, THORNHILL, ON, L3T 3M6
(905) 881-2552   *SIC* 1794
FARRELLS EXCAVATING LTD *p434*
2700 TRANS-CANADA HWY, ST. JOHN'S, NL, A1N 3C8
(709) 745-5904   *SIC* 1794
FERNAND GILBERT LTEE *p1079*
1700 BOUL TALBOT BUREAU 400, CHICOUTIMI, QC, G7H 7Y1
(418) 549-7705   *SIC* 1794
FISH CREEK EXCAVATING LTD *p15*
7515 84 ST SE, CALGARY, AB, T2C 4Y1
(403) 248-8222   *SIC* 1794
FOUR VALLEYS EXCAVATING & GRADING LIMITED *p553*
137 BOWES RD, CONCORD, ON, L4K 1H3
(905) 669-1588   *SIC* 1794
G.C.L. EQUIPEMENTS INC *p1238*
35 AV LAGANIERE, MONTREAL-EST, QC, H1B 5T1
(514) 640-0840   *SIC* 1794
GESTION PADOMAX INC *p1365*
280 BOUL PIE-XII, SALABERRY-DE-VALLEYFIELD, QC, J6S 6P7
(450) 373-4274   *SIC* 1794
GREGSON HOLDINGS LTD *p235*
1920 BALSAM RD, NANAIMO, BC, V9X 1T5
(250) 754-7260   *SIC* 1794
GROUPE ALLAIREGINCE INFRASTRUC-

TURES INC *p1111*
70 RUE DE GATINEAU, GRANBY, QC, J2J 0P1
(450) 378-1623   *SIC* 1794
GROUPE MINIER CMAC-THYSSEN INC *p1390*
1254 AV 3E E, VAL-D'OR, QC, J9P 0J6
(819) 874-8303   *SIC* 1794
HAMILTON CONSTRUCTION LTD *p546*
7645 POPLAR, COLLINGWOOD, ON, L9Y 3Y9
(705) 445-3220   *SIC* 1794
HCM CONTRACTORS INC *p77*
9777 ENTERPRISE WAY SE, CALGARY, AB, T3S 0A1
(403) 248-4884   *SIC* 1794
HENAULT & GOSSELIN INC *p1166*
4100 RUE NOTRE-DAME E, MONTREAL, QC, H1V 3T5
(514) 522-0909   *SIC* 1794
HEXCEL CONSTRUCTION LTD *p209*
7119 RIVER RD, DELTA, BC, V4G 1A9
(604) 946-8744   *SIC* 1794
ICANDA CORPORATION *p1232*
3131 BOUL DE LA CONCORDE E BUREAU 306, MONTREAL, QC, H7E 4W4
(450) 661-2972   *SIC* 1794
IRON HORSE EARTHWORKS INC *p159*
235090 WRANGLER DR, ROCKY VIEW COUNTY, AB, T1X 0K3
(403) 217-2711   *SIC* 1794
J-AAR EXCAVATING LIMITED *p649*
3003 PAGE ST, LONDON, ON, N5V 4J1
(519) 652-2104   *SIC* 1794
K L S CONTRACTING LTD *p74*
7 GLENBROOK PL SW SUITE 206, CALGARY, AB, T3E 6W4
(403) 240-3030   *SIC* 1794
KEYSTONE EXCAVATING LTD *p12*
4860 35 ST SE, CALGARY, AB, T2B 3M6
(403) 274-5452   *SIC* 1794
KICHTON CONTRACTING LTD *p1*
25296 117 AVE, ACHESON, AB, T7X 6C2
(780) 447-1882   *SIC* 1794
KLS EARTHWORKS INC *p159*
240039 FRONTIER CRES, ROCKY VIEW COUNTY, AB, T1X 0W6
(403) 240-3030   *SIC* 1794
KOWAL CONSTRUCTION ALTA. LTD *p81*
601 MCCOOL ST, CROSSFIELD, AB, T0M 0S0
(403) 946-4450   *SIC* 1794
L. FOURNIER ET FILS INC *p1390*
1095 RUE LEO-FOURNIER, VAL-D'OR, QC, J9P 6X6
(819) 825-4000   *SIC* 1794
L.C.L. EXCAVATION (2006) INC *p396*
214 CRAIG RD, CHARLO, NB, E8E 2J2
(506) 684-3453   *SIC* 1794
LABELLE, M. J. CO. LTD *p545*
109 HIGHWAY 11 W, COCHRANE, ON, P0L 1C0
(705) 272-4201   *SIC* 1794
LAPALME, GERMAIN & FILS INC *p1147*
2972 CH MILLETTA, MAGOG, QC, J1X 0R4
(819) 843-2367   *SIC* 1794
LEE, RON CONSTRUCTION INC *p566*
439 8 HWY, DUNDAS, ON, L9H 5E1
(905) 628-4148   *SIC* 1794
LOISELLE INC *p1103*
1679 RUE JEAN-LOUIS-MALETTE, GATINEAU, QC, J8R 0C1
SIC 1794
LOISELLE INC *p1365*
280 BOUL PIE-XII, SALABERRY-DE-VALLEYFIELD, QC, J6S 6P7
(450) 373-4274   *SIC* 1794
MANN, DON EXCAVATING LTD *p337*
4098 LOCHSIDE DR, VICTORIA, BC, V8X 2C8
(250) 479-8283   *SIC* 1794
MAR-SAN EXCAVATING & GRADING LTD *p495*
21 HOLLAND DR, BOLTON, ON, L7E 4J6

---

(905) 857-1616   *SIC 1794*

MATCON EXCAVATION & SHORING LTD *p201*
2208 HARTLEY AVE, COQUITLAM, BC, V3K 6X3
(604) 520-5909   *SIC 1794*

MCRAE'S ENVIRONMENTAL SERVICES LTD *p209*
7783 PROGRESS WAY, DELTA, BC, V4G 1A3
(604) 434-8313   *SIC 1794*

MENARD CANADA INC *p1066*
1590 RUE AMPERE BUREAU 202, BOUCHERVILLE, QC, J4B 7L4
(450) 449-2633   *SIC 1794*

METRO EXCAVATION INC *p1255*
2144 BOUL LOUIS-XIV, QUEBEC, QC, G1C 1A2
(418) 661-5771   *SIC 1794*

MID-CITY CONSTRUCTION MANAGEMENT INC *p110*
7103 42 ST NW, EDMONTON, AB, T6B 2T1
(780) 463-0385   *SIC 1794*

MUNRO, HUGH CONSTRUCTION LTD *p362*
61053 HWY 207, WINNIPEG, MB, R2C 2Z2
(204) 224-9218   *SIC 1794*

NUNA CONTRACTING LTD *p121*
9839 31 AVE NW, EDMONTON, AB, T6N 1C5
(780) 434-9114   *SIC 1794*

PAVAGE DION INC *p1060*
20855 CH DE LA COTE N, BOISBRIAND, QC, J7E 4H5
(450) 435-0333   *SIC 1794*

PETRIFOND FONDATION COMPAGNIE LIMITEE *p1180*
8320 BOUL SAINT-LAURENT, MONTREAL, QC, H2P 2M3
(514) 387-2838   *SIC 1794*

PROFESSIONAL EXCAVATORS LTD *p17*
10919 84 ST SE, CALGARY, AB, T2C 5A6
(403) 236-5686   *SIC 1794*

R 870 HOLDINGS LTD *p220*
171 COMMERCIAL DR SUITE 203, KELOWNA, BC, V1X 7W2
SIC 1794

R.D.M. ENTERPRISES LTD *p228*
20436 FRASER HWY UNIT 207, LANGLEY, BC, V3A 4G2
(604) 530-6310   *SIC 1794*

RAFAT GENERAL CONTRACTOR INC *p495*
8850 GEORGE BOLTON PKY, BOLTON, ON, L7E 2Y4
(905) 951-1063   *SIC 1794*

RAN DON CRANE & LEASING LTD *p763*
3736 HIGHWAY 11 N SUITE 2, NORTH BAY, ON, P1B 8G3
(705) 474-4374   *SIC 1794*

RANKIN CONSTRUCTION INC *p887*
222 MARTINDALE RD, ST CATHARINES, ON, L2S 0B2
(905) 684-1111   *SIC 1794*

RENALD COTE 2007 INC *p1052*
48 AV WILLIAM-DOBELL, BAIE-COMEAU, QC, G4Z 1T7
(418) 296-2854   *SIC 1794*

ROCCA, LEE FORMING LTD *p802*
488 MORDEN RD UNIT 1, OAKVILLE, ON, L6K 3W4
(905) 842-2543   *SIC 1794*

ROCKWOOD TRANSPORTATION CO. LTD *p410*
909 ROUTE 495, MUNDLEVILLE, NB, E4W 2M8
(506) 523-9813   *SIC 1794*

ROXBORO EXCAVATION INC *p1095*
1620 CROIS NEWMAN, DORVAL, QC, H9P 2R8
(514) 631-1888   *SIC 1794*

ROYER DEVELOPMENTS 2015 LTD. *p94*
14635 134 AVE NW, EDMONTON, AB, T5L 4S9
(780) 454-9677   *SIC 1794*

SKOOKUM ASPHALT LTD *p1440*

1 EAR LAKE RD, WHITEHORSE, YT, Y1A 6L4
(867) 668-6326   *SIC 1794*

SOIL ENGINEER LTD *p854*
90 WEST BEAVER CREEK RD SUITE 100, RICHMOND HILL, ON, L4B 1E7
(416) 754-8515   *SIC 1794*

TESKEY CONSTRUCTION COMPANY LTD *p786*
20 MURRAY RD, NORTH YORK, ON, M3K 1T2
(416) 638-0340   *SIC 1794*

THOMAS BELLEMARE LTEE *p1388*
8750 BOUL INDUSTRIEL, TROIS-RIVIERES, QC, G9A 5E1
(819) 379-2535   *SIC 1794*

TOP NOTCH CONSTRUCTION LTD *p19*
5415 56 AVE SE, CALGARY, AB, T2C 3X6
SIC 1794

TYAM EXCAVATION & SHORING LTD *p208*
6955 120 ST SUITE 202, DELTA, BC, V4E 2A8
(778) 593-2900   *SIC 1794*

UPLAND CONTRACTING LTD *p194*
7295 GOLD RIVER HWY, CAMPBELL RIVER, BC, V9H 1P1
(250) 286-1148   *SIC 1794*

VOICE CONSTRUCTION LTD *p129*
200 MACDONALD CRES, FORT MCMUR-RAY, AB, T9H 4B2
(780) 790-0981   *SIC 1794*

WILLOWS CONSTRUCTION (2001) LTD *p82*
6305 54 AVE, DRAYTON VALLEY, AB, T7A 1R0
(780) 621-0447   *SIC 1794*

ZUTPHEN CONTRACTORS INC *p462*
10442 HIGHWAY 19, MABOU, NS, B0E 1X0
(902) 945-2300   *SIC 1794*

SIC 1795 Wrecking and demolition work

1770918 ONTARIO INC *p748*
92 BENTLEY AVE, NEPEAN, ON, K2E 6T9
(613) 225-9111   *SIC 1795*

DEMOLITION ET EXCAVATION DEMEX INC *p1080*
2253 CH DE LA RESERVE, CHICOUTIMI, QC, G7J 0C9
(418) 698-2222   *SIC 1795*

DEMOSPEC DECONSTRUCTION INC *p1161*
10000 BOUL HENRI-BOURASSA E, MON-TREAL, QC, H1C 1T1
(514) 648-6366   *SIC 1795*

EXCAVATION RENE ST-PIERRE INC *p1369*
800 RUE DE L'ARDOISE, SHERBROOKE, QC, J1C 0J6
(819) 565-1494   *SIC 1795*

GET IT DONE DEMOLITION & DISPOSAL *p278*
12224 BOUNDARY DR N, SURREY, BC, V3X 1Z5
(604) 916-1388   *SIC 1795*

JMX CONTRACTING INC *p894*
130 RAM FOREST RD, STOUFFVILLE, ON, L4A 2G8
(905) 241-2224   *SIC 1795*

LATCON LTD *p818*
3387 HAWTHORNE RD, OTTAWA, ON, K1G 4G2
(613) 738-9061   *SIC 1795*

LITCHFIELD & CO LTD *p247*
3046 WESTWOOD ST, PORT COQUIT-LAM, BC, V3C 3L7
(604) 464-7525   *SIC 1795*

MINI DIG CORP *p31*
2222 ALYTH PL SE, CALGARY, AB, T2G 3K9
(403) 274-0090   *SIC 1795*

MURRAY DEMOLITION CORP *p571*
345 HORNER AVE SUITE 300, ETOBI-COKE, ON, M8W 1Z6
(416) 253-6000   *SIC 1795*

OSC CONSTRUCTORS ULC *p698*

5149 BRADCO BLVD, MISSISSAUGA, ON, L4W 2A6
(905) 458-1005   *SIC 1795*

PICHE, R DYNAMITAGE INC *p1363*
2591 BOUL SAINTE-SOPHIE, SAINTE-SOPHIE, QC, J5J 2V3
(819) 212-0744   *SIC 1795*

PRIESTLY DEMOLITION INC *p629*
3200 LLOYDTOWN-AURORA RD, KING CITY, ON, L7B 0G3
(905) 841-3735   *SIC 1795*

QM LP *p717*
3580 LAIRD RD UNIT 1, MISSISSAUGA, ON, L5L 5Z7
(416) 253-6000   *SIC 1795*

SERVICES ENVIRONNEMENTAUX DELSAN-A.I.M. INC, LES *p1162*
7825 BOUL HENRI-BOURASSA E, MON-TREAL, QC, H1E 1N9
(514) 494-9898   *SIC 1795*

SIC 1796 Installing building equipment

1203130 ONTARIO INC *p490*
391 COLLEGE ST E, BELLEVILLE, ON, K8N 5S7
(613) 962-9003   *SIC 1796*

A.M.I. MECANIQUE INC *p1116*
2455 RUE CANTIN, JONQUIERE, QC, G7X 8S7
(418) 542-3531   *SIC 1796*

ADVANCED MILLWRIGHT SERVICES LTD *p330*
971 HWY 16, VANDERHOOF, BC, V0J 3A1
(250) 567-5756   *SIC 1796*

AIM INDUSTRIAL INC *p538*
29 CHERRY BLOSSOM RD, CAMBRIDGE, ON, N3H 4R7
(519) 747-2255   *SIC 1796*

ALLIED BLOWER & SHEET METAL LTD *p274*
12224 103A AVE, SURREY, BC, V3V 3G9
(604) 930-7000   *SIC 1796*

ASSA ABLOY ENTRANCE SYSTEM CANADA INC *p716*
4020A SLADEVIEW CRES SUITE 4, MIS-SISSAUGA, ON, L5L 6B1
(905) 608-9242   *SIC 1796*

AXIOM MILLWRIGHTING & FABRICATION INC *p535*
55 SAVAGE DR, CAMBRIDGE, ON, N1T 1S5
(519) 620-2000   *SIC 1796*

COPPERLINE EXCAVATING LTD *p164*
375 SASKATCHEWAN AVE, SPRUCE GROVE, AB, T7X 3A1
(780) 968-3805   *SIC 1796*

DIELCO INDUSTRIAL CONTRACTORS LTD *p661*
80 ENTERPRISE DR S, LONDON, ON, N6N 1C2
(519) 685-2224   *SIC 1796*

ENTREPRISES DE CONSTRUCTION RE-FRABEC INC, LES *p1392*
925 BOUL LIONEL-BOULET, VARENNES, QC, J3X 1P7
(450) 652-5391   *SIC 1796*

GROENEVELD LUBRICATION SOLUTIONS INC *p683*
8450 LAWSON RD UNIT 5, MILTON, ON, L9T 0J8
(905) 875-1017   *SIC 1796*

JCB INDUSTRIAL INC *p35*
6031 4 ST SE, CALGARY, AB, T2H 2A5
(587) 349-1071   *SIC 1796*

LIARD CONSTRUCTION INC *p1114*
599 BOUL BASE-DE-ROC, JOLIETTE, QC, J6E 5P3
SIC 1796

LOCATION D'OUTILS SIMPLEX SEC *p1380*
3505 BOUL DES ENTREPRISES, TERRE-BONNE, QC, J6X 4J9
(450) 477-5960   *SIC 1796*

LONESTAR WEST INC *p157*
105 KUUSAMO DR, RED DEER COUNTY, AB, T4E 2J5
(403) 887-2074   *SIC 1796*

PGI HOLDINGS INC *p534*
555 CONESTOGA BLVD, CAMBRIDGE, ON, N1R 7P5
(519) 622-5520   *SIC 1796*

PROCESS GROUP INC *p534*
555 CONESTOGA BLVD, CAMBRIDGE, ON, N1R 7P5
(519) 622-5520   *SIC 1796*

RCI VENTURES INC. *p887*
222 MARTINDALE RD, ST CATHARINES, ON, L2S 0B2
(905) 684-1111   *SIC 1796*

REGULVAR INC *p1277*
2800 RUE JEAN-PERRIN BUREAU 100, QUEBEC, QC, G2C 1T3
(418) 842-5114   *SIC 1796*

RESOURCE INDUSTRIAL GROUP INC *p483*
295 WAYDOM DR SUITE 2, AYR, ON, N0B 1E0
(519) 622-5266   *SIC 1796*

RICHMOND ELEVATOR MAINTENANCE LTD *p264*
12091 NO. 5 RD SUITE 5, RICHMOND, BC, V7A 4E9
(604) 274-8440   *SIC 1796*

RISING EDGE TECHNOLOGIES LTD *p25*
2620 22 ST NE, CALGARY, AB, T2E 7L9
(403) 202-8751   *SIC 1796*

RPC HISTORICAL LIMITED PARTNERSHIP *p202*
80 GOLDEN DR, COQUITLAM, BC, V3K 6T1
(604) 553-1810   *SIC 1796*

SABRE INSTRUMENT SERVICES LTD *p18*
4460 54 AVE SE, CALGARY, AB, T2C 3A8
(403) 258-0566   *SIC 1796*

SAVARIA SALES INSTALLATION AND SER-VICES INC *p657*
85 BESSEMER RD, LONDON, ON, N6E 1P9
(519) 681-3311   *SIC 1796*

SCHINDLER ELEVATOR CORPORATION *p879*
3640 MCNICOLL AVE UNIT A, SCARBOR-OUGH, ON, M1X 1G5
(416) 332-8280   *SIC 1796*

SERVICE D'IMPARTITION INDUSTRIEL INC *p1388*
2300 RUE JULES-VACHON, TROIS-RIVIERES, QC, G9A 5E1
(819) 374-4647   *SIC 1796*

SHERBROOKE O.E.M. LTD *p1374*
3425 BOUL INDUSTRIEL, SHERBROOKE, QC, J1L 2W1
(819) 563-7374   *SIC 1796*

THYSSENKRUPP ELEVATOR (CANADA) LIMITED *p877*
410 PASSMORE AVE UNIT 1, SCARBOR-OUGH, ON, M1V 5C3
(416) 291-2000   *SIC 1796*

TRADE-MARK INDUSTRIAL INC *p538*
250 ROYAL OAK RD, CAMBRIDGE, ON, N3E 0A4
(519) 650-7470   *SIC 1796*

WESTERN MECHANICAL ELECTRICAL MILLWRIGHT SERVICES LTD *p488*
160 BROCK ST, BARRIE, ON, L4N 2M4
(705) 737-4135   *SIC 1796*

SIC 1799 Special trade contractors, nec

6074961 CANADA INC *p748*
20 GURDWARA RD UNIT 16, NEPEAN, ON, K2E 8B3
(613) 225-5500   *SIC 1799*

7648243 CANADA LIMITED *p33*
5730 BURBANK RD SE, CALGARY, AB, T2H 1Z4
(403) 255-0202   *SIC 1799*

8885168 CANADA INC *p1248*
215 RUE VOYAGEUR, POINTE-CLAIRE, QC, H9R 6B2
(819) 294-4484 *SIC 1799*

9144-8720 QUEBEC INC *p1154*
1092 RUE LACHAPELLE, MONT-LAURIER, QC, J9L 3T9
(819) 623-6745 *SIC 1799*

9208-4144 QUEBEC INC *p1369*
561 RUE JOSEPH-LATOUR, SHER-BROOKE, QC, J1C 0W2
(819) 846-3338 *SIC 1799*

961945 ALBERTA LTD *p92*
12240 142 ST NW, EDMONTON, AB, T5L 2G9
(780) 443-4338 *SIC 1799*

ABCO MOVING SERVICES INC *p870*
2480 LAWRENCE AVE E SUITE 1, SCAR-BOROUGH, ON, M1P 2R7
(416) 750-0118 *SIC 1799*

AECOM ENERGY SERVICES LTD *p80*
HWY 55 W, COLD LAKE, AB, T9M 1P7
(780) 639-6034 *SIC 1799*

ALUMA SYSTEMS INC *p127*
GD LCD MAIN, FORT MCMURRAY, AB, T9H 3E2
(780) 790-4852 *SIC 1799*

ALUMITECH ARCHITECTURAL GLASS & METAL LIMITED *p440*
170 BLUEWATER RD, BEDFORD, NS, B4B 1G9
(902) 832-1200 *SIC 1799*

AS DU RANGEMENT RIVE-NORD/ RIVE-SUD INC *p1074*
1635 BOUL LEBEL BUREAU 302, CHAM-BLY, QC, J3L 0R8
(514) 792-4036 *SIC 1799*

ASBEX LTD *p817*
2280 STEVENAGE DR UNIT 200, OTTAWA, ON, K1G 3W3
(613) 228-1080 *SIC 1799*

BAILEY'S WELDING & CONSTRUCTION INC *p82*
6205 56 AVE, DRAYTON VALLEY, AB, T7A 1S5
(780) 542-3578 *SIC 1799*

BELFOR (CANADA) INC *p99*
17408 116 AVE NW, EDMONTON, AB, T5S 2X2
(780) 455-5566 *SIC 1799*

BELFOR (CANADA) INC *p275*
7677D 132 ST, SURREY, BC, V3W 4M8
(604) 599-9980 *SIC 1799*

BELFOR (CANADA) INC *p284*
3300 BRIDGEWAY, VANCOUVER, BC, V5K 1H9
(604) 432-1123 *SIC 1799*

BIGGS AND NARCISO CONSTRUCTION SERVICES INC *p667*
181 BENTLEY ST SUITE 14, MARKHAM, ON, L3R 3Y1
(905) 470-8788 *SIC 1799*

BOART LONGYEAR CANADA *p713*
2442 SOUTH SHERIDAN WAY, MISSIS-SAUGA, ON, L5J 2M7
(905) 822-7922 *SIC 1799*

BRECK CONSTRUCTION *p1426*
6 CORY LANE, SASKATOON, SK, S7K 3J7
(306) 242-5532 *SIC 1799*

BROCK CANADA FIELD SERVICES LTD *p148*
3735 8 ST UNIT 200, NISKU, AB, T9E 8J8
(780) 465-9016 *SIC 1799*

BROCK CANADA INDUSTRIAL LTD *p148*
3735 8 ST, NISKU, AB, T9E 8J8
(780) 465-9016 *SIC 1799*

BROCK CANADA WEST LTD *p200*
1650 BRIGANTINE DR SUITE 100, CO-QUITLAM, BC, V3K 7B5
(604) 519-6788 *SIC 1799*

CABLE CONTROL SYSTEMS INC *p796*
2800 COVENTRY RD, OAKVILLE, ON, L6H 6R1
(905) 829-9910 *SIC 1799*

CABO DRILLING (ONTARIO) CORP *p634*
34 DUNCAN AVE N, KIRKLAND LAKE, ON, P2N 3L3
(705) 567-9311 *SIC 1799*

CANSTAR CONSTRUCTION LTD *p200*
78 FAWCETT RD, COQUITLAM, BC, V3K 6V5
(604) 549-0099 *SIC 1799*

CAPITAL SEWER SERVICES INC *p1027*
401 VAUGHAN VALLEY BLVD, WOOD-BRIDGE, ON, L4H 3B5
(905) 522-0522 *SIC 1799*

CLAYBAR CONTRACTING INC *p566*
424 MACNAB ST, DUNDAS, ON, L9H 2L3
(905) 627-8000 *SIC 1799*

COFFRAGE MAGMA (10 ANS) INC *p1231*
1500 RUE MARCEL-BENOIT, MONTREAL, QC, H7C 0A9
(450) 664-4989 *SIC 1799*

COFFRAGE MEGAFORME INC *p1232*
2500 MONTEE SAINT-FRANCOIS, MON-TREAL, QC, H7E 4P2
SIC 1799

COFFRAGES ATLANTIQUE INC *p1058*
41 RUE GASTON-DUMOULIN, BLAINVILLE, QC, J7C 6B4
(450) 437-5353 *SIC 1799*

COFFRAGES DOMINIC LTEE, LES *p1279*
6921 BOUL PIERRE-BERTRAND, QUE-BEC, QC, G2K 1M1
(418) 626-3271 *SIC 1799*

COFFRAGES L.D. INC *p1139*
2621 AV DE LA ROTONDE, LEVIS, QC, G6X 2M2
(418) 832-7070 *SIC 1799*

COMMISSION DES SERVICES ELEC-TRIQUES DE MONTREAL *p1172*
4305 RUE HOGAN, MONTREAL, QC, H2H 2N2
(514) 868-3111 *SIC 1799*

CONNEXION TECHNIC INC *p1254*
989 AV NORDIQUE BUREAU 100, QUE-BEC, QC, G1C 0C7
(418) 660-6276 *SIC 1799*

CONSBEC INC *p1001*
2736 BELISLE DR, VAL CARON, ON, P3N 1B3
(705) 897-4971 *SIC 1799*

CROSBIE SALAMIS LIMITED *p428*
80 HEBRON WAY, ST. JOHN'S, NL, A1A 0L9
(709) 722-5377 *SIC 1799*

D.M.C. SOUDURE INC *p1147*
1816 RTE 111 E, MACAMIC, QC, J0Z 2S0
(819) 782-2514 *SIC 1799*

DAVCO WELDING LTD *p171*
GD STN MAIN, WAINWRIGHT, AB, T9W 1M3
(780) 842-5559 *SIC 1799*

DNR PRESSURE WELDING LTD *p167*
39123 RANGE RD 19-3, STETTLER, AB, T0C 2L0
(403) 742-2859 *SIC 1799*

DOCK PRODUCTS CANADA INC *p649*
639 SOVEREIGN RD, LONDON, ON, N5V 4K8
(519) 457-7155 *SIC 1799*

DONALCO INC *p864*
20 MELFORD DR UNIT 10, SCARBOR-OUGH, ON, M1B 2X6
(416) 292-7118 *SIC 1799*

DONALCO WESTERN INC *p114*
8218 MCINTYRE RD NW, EDMONTON, AB, T6E 5C4
(780) 448-1660 *SIC 1799*

EASTERN FENCE LIMITED *p408*
80 HENRI DUNANT ST, MONCTON, NB, E1E 1E6
(506) 857-8141 *SIC 1799*

ECHAFAUDAGE PLUS (QUEBEC) INC *p1292*
148 RUE D'AMSTERDAM, SAINT-AUGUSTIN-DE-DESMAURES, QC, G3A 2R1

(418) 878-3885 *SIC 1799*
ECHAFAUDS PLUS (LAVAL) INC *p1362*
2897 AV FRANCIS-HUGHES, SAINTE-ROSE, QC, H7L 4G8
(450) 663-1926 *SIC 1799*

EMPIRE TRANSPORTATION LTD *p599*
263 SOUTH SERVICE RD, GRIMSBY, ON, L3M 1Y6
(905) 945-9654 *SIC 1799*

ENTREPRENEURS ELECTRICIENS SIMP-KIN LTEE *p1221*
5800 RUE SAINT-JACQUES, MONTREAL, QC, H4A 2E9
(514) 481-0125 *SIC 1799*

FIELD AVIATION COMPANY INC *p8*
4300 26 ST NE UNIT 125, CALGARY, AB, T1Y 7H7
(403) 516-8200 *SIC 1799*

FIRST GENERAL ENTERPRISES (ON-TARIO) LTD *p986*
130 KING ST SUITE 1800, TORONTO, ON, M5X 1E3
(905) 665-6680 *SIC 1799*

FIRSTONSITE RESTORATION LIMITED *p739*
60 ADMIRAL BLVD, MISSISSAUGA, ON, L5T 2W1
(905) 696-2900 *SIC 1799*

FORACO CANADA LTD *p762*
1839 SEYMOUR ST, NORTH BAY, ON, P1A 0C7
(705) 495-6363 *SIC 1799*

FORACO CANADA LTD *p762*
1839 SEYMOUR ST, NORTH BAY, ON, P1A 0C7
(705) 495-6363 *SIC 1799*

FORAGES CHIBOUGAMAU LTEE *p1077*
527 RTE 167, CHIBOUGAMAU, QC, G8P 2K5
(418) 748-3977 *SIC 1799*

FULLER AUSTIN INC *p101*
11604 186 ST NW, EDMONTON, AB, T5S 0C4
(780) 452-1701 *SIC 1799*

GDI SERVICES (CANADA) LP *p997*
130 KING ST, TORONTO, ON, M9N 1L5
(416) 364-0643 *SIC 1799*

GROUPE LEFEBVRE M.R.P INC, LE *p1301*
210 RUE ROY, SAINT-EUSTACHE, QC, J7R 5R6
(450) 491-6444 *SIC 1799*

GROUPE TVA INC *p1175*
1475 RUE ALEXANDRE-DESEVE, MON-TREAL, QC, H2L 2V4
(514) 526-9251 *SIC 1799*

HARSCO CANADA CORPORATION *p109*
7030 51 AVE NW, EDMONTON, AB, T6B 2P4
(780) 468-3292 *SIC 1799*

HEAVY INDUSTRIES THEMING CORPORA-TION *p16*
9192 52 ST SE, CALGARY, AB, T2C 5A9
(403) 252-6603 *SIC 1799*

HOLDFAST METALWORKS LTD *p235*
1061 MAUGHAN RD, NANAIMO, BC, V9X 1J2
(250) 591-7400 *SIC 1799*

HOME SOLUTIONS CORPORATION *p70*
11550 40 ST SE, CALGARY, AB, T2Z 4V6
(403) 216-0000 *SIC 1799*

INDUSTRIAL CONSTRUCTION INVEST-MENTS INC *p124*
11850 28 ST NE, EDMONTON, AB, T6S 1G6
(780) 478-4688 *SIC 1799*

INDUSTRIAL SCAFFOLD SERVICES L.P. *p235*
2076 BALSAM RD, NANAIMO, BC, V9X 1T5
(250) 591-3535 *SIC 1799*

INFLIGHT CANADA INC *p1334*
4650 BOUL DE LA COTE-VERTU BUREAU 200, SAINT-LAURENT, QC, H4S 1C7
(514) 331-9771 *SIC 1799*

IP FABRICATIONS LTD *p154*

6835 52 AVE, RED DEER, AB, T4N 4L2
(403) 343-1797 *SIC 1799*

J.Y. MOREAU ELECTRIQUE INC *p1289*
160 BOUL INDUSTRIEL, ROUYN-NORANDA, QC, J9X 6T3
(819) 797-0088 *SIC 1799*

KAEFER INTEGRATED SERVICES LTD *p165*
25 CORRIVEAU AVE, ST. ALBERT, AB, T8N 5A3
(780) 484-4310 *SIC 1799*

KONE INC *p206*
1488 CLIVEDEN AVE, DELTA, BC, V3M 6L9
(604) 777-5663 *SIC 1799*

LABBE-LEECH INTERIORS LTD *p30*
2600 PORTLAND ST SE SUITE 2020, CAL-GARY, AB, T2G 4M6
(403) 252-9991 *SIC 1799*

LEADING EDGE FORMING LTD *p201*
137 GLACIER ST UNIT 107, COQUITLAM, BC, V3K 5Z1
SIC 1799

LINK SCAFFOLD SERVICES INC *p122*
2102 102 AVE NW, EDMONTON, AB, T6P 1W3
(780) 449-6111 *SIC 1799*

LML INDUSTRIAL CONTRACTORS LTD *p1409*
4815 50 ST SUITE 302, LLOYDMINSTER, SK, S9V 0M8
(306) 825-6115 *SIC 1799*

M.P.S. WELDING INC *p81*
GD, COLD LAKE, AB, T9M 1P3
SIC 1799

MADYSTA CONSTRUCTIONS LTEE *p1389*
3600 BOUL L.-P.-NORMAND, TROIS-RIVIERES, QC, G9B 0G2
(819) 377-3336 *SIC 1799*

MARATHON DRILLING CORPORATION *p599*
6847 HIRAM DR, GREELY, ON, K4P 1A2
(613) 821-4800 *SIC 1799*

MATAKANA SCAFFOLDING B.C. INC *p290*
1085 E KENT AVE NORTH SUITE 122, VANCOUVER, BC, V5X 4V9
(604) 873-5140 *SIC 1799*

MATERIAUX ECONOMIQUES INC *p1388*
2900 RUE JULES-VACHON, TROIS-RIVIERES, QC, G9A 5E1
(819) 374-8577 *SIC 1799*

MCGOWAN INSULATIONS LTD *p892*
345 BARTON ST, STONEY CREEK, ON, L8E 2L2
(905) 549-1844 *SIC 1799*

MCINTYRE GROUP OFFICE SERVICES INC *p642*
825 TRILLIUM DR, KITCHENER, ON, N2R 1J9
(519) 740-7636 *SIC 1799*

MCLAREN, P. D. LIMITED *p282*
9725 192 ST UNIT 104, SURREY, BC, V4N 4C7
(604) 371-3732 *SIC 1799*

MEDIA RESOURCES INTERNATIONAL INC *p801*
1387 CORNWALL RD, OAKVILLE, ON, L6J 7T5
(905) 337-0993 *SIC 1799*

METALS CREEK RESOURCES CORP *p908*
945 COBALT CRES, THUNDER BAY, ON, P7B 5Z4
(807) 345-4990 *SIC 1799*

MORE CORE DIAMOND DRILLING SER-VICES LTD *p269*
2511 HWY 37A, STEWART, BC, V0T 1W0
(250) 636-9156 *SIC 1799*

MULTISEAL INC *p997*
4255 WESTON RD, TORONTO, ON, M9L 1W8
(416) 743-6017 *SIC 1799*

NEBB FORMING LTD *p556*
41 RITIN LANE, CONCORD, ON, L4K 4W6
(905) 761-6100 *SIC 1799*

NEWWAY CONCRETE FORMING LTD *p186*
3750 1ST AVE, BURNABY, BC, V5C 3V9

(604) 299-3709   *SIC* 1799
NILEX CONSTRUCTION INC   *p*115
9304 39 AVE NW, EDMONTON, AB, T6E 5T9
(780) 463-9535   *SIC* 1799
NORTHSTAR SCAFFOLD SERVICES INC *p*575
362 OLIVEWOOD RD, ETOBICOKE, ON, M8Z 2Z7
(416) 231-1610   *SIC* 1799
ON SIDE RESTORATION SERVICES LTD *p*287
3157 GRANDVIEW HWY, VANCOUVER, BC, V5M 2E9
(604) 293-1596   *SIC* 1799
PANTHER DRILLING CORPORATION*p*1438
GD LCD MAIN, WEYBURN, SK, S4H 2J7
(306) 842-7370   *SIC* 1799
PARAMOUNT STRUCTURES LTD   *p*495
46 NIXON RD, BOLTON, ON, L7E 1W2
(905) 951-7528   *SIC* 1799
PARK DEROCHIE INC   *p*124
11850 28 ST NE, EDMONTON, AB, T6S 1G6
(780) 478-4688   *SIC* 1799
PARK DEROCHIE INC   *p*124
11850 28 ST NE, EDMONTON, AB, T6S 1G6
(780) 478-4688   *SIC* 1799
PISCINES SOUCY INC   *p*1267
3605 BOUL WILFRID-HAMEL, QUEBEC, QC, G1P 2J4
(418) 872-4440   *SIC* 1799
PRO INSUL LIMITED   *p*893
468 ARVIN AVE, STONEY CREEK, ON, L8E 2M9
(905) 662-6161   *SIC* 1799
RAPID FORMING INC   *p*473
5 MANSEWOOD CRT, ACTON, ON, L7J 0A1
       SIC 1799
REIMAR CONSTRUCTION CORPORATION *p*617
328 TRINITY CHURCH RD, HANNON, ON, L0R 1P0
(905) 692-9900   *SIC* 1799
RELIABLE WINDOW CLEANERS (SUDBURY) LIMITED   *p*913
167 WILSON AVE, TIMMINS, ON, P4N 2T2
(705) 360-1194   *SIC* 1799
RITE-WAY FENCING (2000) INC   *p*18
7710 40 ST SE, CALGARY, AB, T2C 3S4
(403) 243-8733   *SIC* 1799
ROBINS PARKING SERVICES LTD   *p*335
1102 FORT ST SUITE 196, VICTORIA, BC, V8V 3K8
(250) 382-4411   *SIC* 1799
ROCKY CROSS CONSTRUCTION (CALGARY) LIMITED   *p*31
444 42 AVE SE SUITE 4, CALGARY, AB, T2G 1Y4
       SIC 1799
S-A-S PETROLEUM TECHNOLOGIES INC *p*566
432 MACNAB ST, DUNDAS, ON, L9H 2L3
(905) 627-5451   *SIC* 1799
SAFWAY SERVICES CANADA, ULC   *p*129
1005 MEMORIAL DR UNIT 3, FORT MCMURRAY, AB, T9K 0K4
(780) 791-6473   *SIC* 1799
SAFWAY SERVICES CANADA, ULC   *p*130
11237 87 AVE, FORT SASKATCHEWAN, AB, T8L 2S3
(780) 992-1929   *SIC* 1799
SAFWAY SERVICES CANADA, ULC   *p*587
503 CARLINGVIEW DR, ETOBICOKE, ON, M9W 5H2
(416) 675-2449   *SIC* 1799
SERSA TOTAL TRACK LTD   *p*663
68 COUNTY RD 5, MALLORYTOWN, ON, K0E 1R0
(613) 923-5702   *SIC* 1799
SERVICE & CONSTRUCTION MOBILE LTEE   *p*1235

1820 PLACE MARTENOT BUREAU 383, MONTREAL, QC, H7L 5B5
(514) 383-5752   *SIC* 1799
SILVER CONCRETE LTD   *p*6
4901 50 AVE, BONNYVILLE, AB, T9N 2J2
(780) 826-5797   *SIC* 1799
SKY-HI SCAFFOLDING LTD   *p*183
3195 PRODUCTION WAY, BURNABY, BC, V5A 3H2
(604) 291-7245   *SIC* 1799
ST LAWRENCE POOLS (1995) LIMITED *p*632
525 DAYS RD, KINGSTON, ON, K7M 3R8
(613) 389-5510   *SIC* 1799
STEAMATIC METROPOLITAIN INC   *p*1051
8351 BOUL LOUIS-H.-LAFONTAINE, ANJOU, QC, H1J 3B4
(514) 351-7500   *SIC* 1799
STRONE CORPORATION   *p*799
2717 COVENTRY RD, OAKVILLE, ON, L6H 5V9
(905) 829-2766   *SIC* 1799
TARGET EMISSION SERVICES INC   *p*38
1235 64 AVE SE SUITE 12 B, CALGARY, AB, T2H 2J7
(403) 225-8755   *SIC* 1799
TEAM INDUSTRIAL SERVICES (CANADA) INC   *p*680
25 BODRINGTON CRT, MARKHAM, ON, L6G 1B6
(905) 940-9334   *SIC* 1799
TORQUE INDUSTRIAL LTD   *p*213
5100 46 AVE, FORT NELSON, BC, V0C 1R0
(250) 233-8675   *SIC* 1799
TUBE-MAC PIPING TECHNOLOGIES LTD *p*893
853 ARVIN AVE SUITE 1, STONEY CREEK, ON, L8E 5N8
(905) 643-8823   *SIC* 1799
TVE INDUSTRIAL SERVICES LTD   *p*218
60 VICARS RD, KAMLOOPS, BC, V2C 6A4
(250) 377-3533   *SIC* 1799
UNIQUE SCAFFOLD INC   *p*19
4750 104 AVE SE, CALGARY, AB, T2C 2H3
(403) 203-3422   *SIC* 1799
VIC PROGRESSIVE DIAMOND DRILLING INC   *p*411
12992 ROUTE 114 HWY, PENOBSQUIS, NB, E4G 2Z9
(506) 433-6139   *SIC* 1799
VISION COATERS CANADA LTD   *p*794
73 PENN DR, NORTH YORK, ON, M9L 2A6
(416) 746-2988   *SIC* 1799

SIC 2011 Meat packing plants

2993821 CANADA INC   *p*1382
1591 CH SAINTE-CLAIRE, TERREBONNE, QC, J7M 1M2
(450) 478-2055   *SIC* 2011
864773 ONTARIO INC   *p*520
4480 PALETTA CRT, BURLINGTON, ON, L7L 5R2
(905) 825-1856   *SIC* 2011
9067-3385 QUEBEC INC   *p*1101
190 RUE COMEAU, FARNHAM, QC, J2N 2N4
(450) 293-3106   *SIC* 2011
9071-3975 QUEBEC INC   *p*1186
410 RUE SAINT-NICOLAS BUREAU 5, MONTREAL, QC, H2Y 2P5
(514) 286-1754   *SIC* 2011
9071-3975 QUEBEC INC   *p*1403
212 CH DU CANTON S, YAMACHICHE, QC, G0X 3L0
(819) 296-1754   *SIC* 2011
9138-9494 QUEBEC INC   *p*1403
212 CH DU CANTON S, YAMACHICHE, QC, G0X 3L0
(819) 296-1754   *SIC* 2011
ABATTOIR COLBEX INC   *p*1298
455 4E RANG DE SIMPSON, SAINT-

CYRILLE-DE-WENDOVER, QC, J1Z 1T8
       SIC 2011
ABATTOIR DUCHARME INC   *p*1108
110 RUE AUTHIER, GRANBY, QC, J2G 7X2
(450) 375-4620   *SIC* 2011
AGROMEX INC   *p*1047
251 235 RTE, ANGE-GARDIEN, QC, J0E 1E0
(450) 293-3694   *SIC* 2011
ALIMENTS ASTA INC   *p*1291
767 RTE 289, SAINT-ALEXANDRE-DE-KAMOURASKA, QC, G0L 2G0
(418) 495-2728   *SIC* 2011
ALIMENTS LESTERS LIMITEE, LES *p*1084
2105 BOUL INDUSTRIEL, COTE SAINT-LUC, QC, H7S 1P7
(450) 629-1100   *SIC* 2011
ALIMENTS LEVITTS (CANADA) INC, LES *p*1130
7070 RUE SAINT-PATRICK, LASALLE, QC, H8N 1V2
(514) 367-1654   *SIC* 2011
ALIMENTS TRANS GRAS INC, LES *p*1097
2825 RUE POWER, DRUMMONDVILLE, QC, J2C 6Z6
(819) 472-1125   *SIC* 2011
ALIMENTS VERMONT FOODS INC *p*1253
210 RUE SAINT-JEAN-BAPTISTE N, PRINCEVILLE, QC, G6L 5E1
       SIC 2011
ATLANTIC BEEF PRODUCTS INC *p*1038
95 TRAIN STATION RD, ALBANY, PE, C0B 1A0
(902) 437-2727   *SIC* 2011
ATRAHAN TRANSFORMATION INC *p*1403
860 CH DES ACADIENS, YAMACHICHE, QC, G0X 3L0
(819) 296-3791   *SIC* 2011
BEECHGROVE COUNTRY FOODS INC*p*866
20 MINUK ACRES, SCARBOROUGH, ON, M1E 4Y6
(416) 283-8777   *SIC* 2011
BELMONT MEAT PRODUCTS LIMITED*p*792
230 SIGNET DR, NORTH YORK, ON, M9L 1V2
(416) 749-7250   *SIC* 2011
BONTE FOODS LIMITED   *p*397
615 RUE CHAMPLAIN, DIEPPE, NB, E1A 7Z7
(506) 857-0025   *SIC* 2011
BOUVRY EXPORTS CALGARY LTD   *p*33
222 58 AVE SW SUITE 312, CALGARY, AB, T2H 2S3
(403) 253-0717   *SIC* 2011
BOUVRY EXPORTS CALGARY LTD   *p*127
GD, FORT MACLEOD, AB, T0L 0Z0
(403) 553-4431   *SIC* 2011
BRETON TRADITION 1944 INC   *p*1294
1312 RUE SAINT-GEORGES, SAINT-BERNARD, QC, G0S 2G0
(418) 475-6601   *SIC* 2011
C&C PACKING LIMITED PARTNERSHIP *p*1343
6800 BOUL DES GRANDES-PRAIRIES, SAINT-LEONARD, QC, H1P 3P3
(514) 939-2273   *SIC* 2011
CAPITAL PACKERS INC   *p*83
12907 57 ST NW, EDMONTON, AB, T5A 0E7
(780) 476-1391   *SIC* 2011
CARGILL LIMITED   *p*135
472 AVENUE & HWY SUITE 2A, HIGH RIVER, AB, T1V 1P4
(403) 652-4688   *SIC* 2011
CARGILL LIMITED   *p*583
71 REXDALE BLVD, ETOBICOKE, ON, M9W 1P1
       SIC 2011
CARGILL LIMITED   *p*600
781 YORK RD, GUELPH, ON, N1E 6N1
(519) 823-5200   *SIC* 2011
CENTENNIAL 89 CORP   *p*28
4412 MANILLA RD SE SUITE 1, CALGARY, AB, T2G 4B7

(403) 214-0044   *SIC* 2011
CENTENNIAL FOODSERVICE   *p*254
12759 VULCAN WAY UNIT 108, RICHMOND, BC, V6V 3C8
(604) 273-5261   *SIC* 2011
CHARCUTERIE LA TOUR EIFFEL INC*p*1058
1020 BOUL MICHELE-BOHEC, BLAINVILLE, QC, J7C 5E2
(450) 979-0001   *SIC* 2011
CONSCORP INC   *p*1344
6800 BOUL DES GRANDES-PRAIRIES, SAINT-LEONARD, QC, H1P 3P3
(514) 939-2273   *SIC* 2011
COUNTRY PRIME MEATS LTD   *p*224
3171 97 HWY, LAC LA HACHE, BC, V0K 1T1
(250) 396-4111   *SIC* 2011
DELFT BLUE VEAL INC   *p*535
162 SAVAGE DR, CAMBRIDGE, ON, N1T 1S4
(519) 622-2500   *SIC* 2011
DELI-PORC INC   *p*1085
1805 BOUL INDUSTRIEL, COTE SAINT-LUC, QC, H7S 1P5
(450) 629-0294   *SIC* 2011
ERIE MEAT PRODUCTS LIMITED   *p*646
1400 MITCHELL RD S, LISTOWEL, ON, N4W 3G7
(519) 291-6593   *SIC* 2011
ERIE MEAT PRODUCTS LIMITED   *p*702
3240 WHARTON WAY, MISSISSAUGA, ON, L4X 2C1
(905) 624-3811   *SIC* 2011
EXCELDOR COOPERATIVE   *p*1298
125 RUE SAINTE-ANNE GD, SAINT-DAMASE, QC, J0H 1J0
(450) 797-3331   *SIC* 2011
FERNANDIERE INC, LA   *p*1389
12500 BOUL LOUIS-LORANGER, TROIS-RIVIERES, QC, G9B 0L9
(819) 374-6977   *SIC* 2011
FG DELI GROUP LTD   *p*229
27101 56 AVE, LANGLEY, BC, V4W 3Y4
(604) 607-7426   *SIC* 2011
FORGET, JACQUES LTEE   *p*1380
2215 CH COMTOIS, TERREBONNE, QC, J6X 4H4
(450) 477-1002   *SIC* 2011
FRESHOUSE SALES LTD   *p*688
6480 VISCOUNT RD UNIT 2, MISSISSAUGA, ON, L4V 1H3
(905) 671-0220   *SIC* 2011
GENESIS MEAT PACKERS INC   *p*993
70 GLEN SCARLETT RD, TORONTO, ON, M6N 1P4
       SIC 2011
GROBER INC   *p*536
425 DOBBIE DR, CAMBRIDGE, ON, N1T 1S9
(519) 622-2500   *SIC* 2011
HARMONY BEEF COMPANY, LTD   *p*160
260036 RGE RD 291, ROCKY VIEW COUNTY, AB, T4A 0T8
(587) 230-2060   *SIC* 2011
HIGHLAND PACKERS LTD   *p*894
432 HIGHLAND RD E, STONEY CREEK, ON, L8J 3G4
(905) 662-8396   *SIC* 2011
HYLIFE FOODS LP   *p*353
623 MAIN ST E, NEEPAWA, MB, R0J 1H0
(204) 476-3393   *SIC* 2011
HYLIFE LTD   *p*353
623 MAIN ST E, NEEPAWA, MB, R0J 1H0
(204) 476-3624   *SIC* 2011
JADEE MEAT PRODUCTS LIMITED   *p*489
4710 BARTLETT RD, BEAMSVILLE, ON, L0R 1B1
(905) 563-5381   *SIC* 2011
JBS CANADA INC   *p*7
GD STN MAIN, BROOKS, AB, T1R 1E4
(403) 362-3457   *SIC* 2011
JBS CANADA INC   *p*35
5101 11 ST SE, CALGARY, AB, T2H 1M7
       SIC 2011

JOHNSTON PACKERS (1995) LTD p197
5828 PROMONTORY RD, CHILLIWACK, BC, V2R 4M4
(604) 858-4882 SIC 2011

JOHNSTON PACKERS LTD p197
7339 VEDDER RD, CHILLIWACK, BC, V2R 4E4
(604) 824-1985 SIC 2011

JOHNSTON PACKERS LTD p197
5828 PROMONTORY RD, CHILLIWACK, BC, V2R 4M4
(604) 858-4121 SIC 2011

L. G. HEBERT & FILS LTEE p1358
428 RUE HEBERT, SAINTE-HELENE-DE-BAGOT, QC, J0H 1M0
(450) 791-2630 SIC 2011

LEADBETTER FOODS INC p809
255 HUGHES RD, ORILLIA, ON, L3V 2M2
(705) 325-9922 SIC 2011

MACGREGORS MEAT & SEAFOOD LTD p793
265 GARYRAY DR, NORTH YORK, ON, M9L 1P2
(416) 749-5951 SIC 2011

MAPLE LEAF FOODS INC p142
4141 1 AVE S, LETHBRIDGE, AB, T1J 4P8
(403) 328-1756 SIC 2011

MAPLE LEAF FOODS INC p347
6355 RICHMOND AVE E, BRANDON, MB, R7A 7M5
(204) 571-2500 SIC 2011

MAPLE LEAF FOODS INC p366
870 LAGIMODIERE BLVD SUITE 23, WINNIPEG, MB, R2J 0T9
(204) 233-2421 SIC 2011

MAPLE LEAF FOODS INC p575
550 KIPLING AVE, ETOBICOKE, ON, M8Z 5E9
SIC 2011

MAPLE LEAF FOODS INC p608
21 BROCKLEY DR, HAMILTON, ON, L8E 3C3
(800) 268-3708 SIC 2011

MAPLE LEAF FOODS INC p724
6985 FINANCIAL DR, MISSISSAUGA, ON, L5N 0A1
(905) 285-5000 SIC 2011

MAPLE LEAF FOODS INC p724
6985 FINANCIAL DR, MISSISSAUGA, ON, L5N 0A1
(905) 285-5000 SIC 2011

MAPLE LEAF FOODS INC p732
30 EGLINTON AVE W SUITE 500, MISSISSAUGA, ON, L5R 3E7
(905) 501-3076 SIC 2011

MAPLE LEAF FOODS INC p1432
100 MCLEOD AVE, SASKATOON, SK, S7M 5V9
(306) 382-2210 SIC 2011

MONTPAK INTERNATIONAL INC p1342
5730 RUE MAURICE-CULLEN, SAINT-LAURENT, QC, H7C 2V1
(450) 665-9524 SIC 2011

MULTI-PORTIONS INC p1317
815 RUE PLANTE, SAINT-JEAN-SUR-RICHELIEU, QC, J3A 1M8
(450) 347-6152 SIC 2011

NILSSON BROS. INC p166
101 RIEL DR SUITE 100, ST. ALBERT, AB, T8N 3X4
(780) 477-2233 SIC 2011

OLY-ROBI TRANSFORMATION S.E.C. p1403
212 CH DU CANTON S, YAMACHICHE, QC, G0X 3L0
(819) 296-1754 SIC 2011

OLYMEL S.E.C. p505
14 WESTWYN CRT, BRAMPTON, ON, L6T 4T5
(905) 796-6947 SIC 2011

OLYMEL S.E.C. p1050
7770 RUE GRENACHE, ANJOU, QC, H1J 1C3
(514) 353-2830 SIC 2011

OLYMEL S.E.C. p1057
580 RUE LAFERRIERE, BERTHIERVILLE, QC, J0K 1A0
(450) 836-1651 SIC 2011

OLYMEL S.E.C. p1066
1580 RUE EIFFEL, BOUCHERVILLE, QC, J4B 5Y1
(514) 858-9000 SIC 2011

OLYMEL S.E.C. p1099
255 RUE ROCHELEAU, DRUMMONDVILLE, QC, J2C 7G2
(819) 475-3030 SIC 2011

OLYMEL S.E.C. p1254
155 RUE SAINT-JEAN-BAPTISTE N, PRINCEVILLE, QC, G6L 5C9
(819) 364-5501 SIC 2011

OLYMEL S.E.C. p1300
25 RTE 125 E, SAINT-ESPRIT, QC, J0K 2L0
(450) 839-7258 SIC 2011

OLYMEL S.E.C. p1300
125 RUE SAINT-ISIDORE, SAINT-ESPRIT, QC, J0K 2L0
(450) 839-7258 SIC 2011

OLYMEL S.E.C. p1313
2200 AV PRATTE BUREAU 400, SAINT-HYACINTHE, QC, J2S 4B6
(450) 771-0400 SIC 2011

OLYMEL S.E.C. p1318
770 RUE CLAUDE, SAINT-JEAN-SUR-RICHELIEU, QC, J3B 2W5
(450) 347-2241 SIC 2011

OLYMEL S.E.C. p1392
568 CH DE L'ECORE S, VALLEE-JONCTION, QC, G0S 3J0
(418) 253-5437 SIC 2011

PERFECT POULTRY INC p793
239 TORYORK DR, NORTH YORK, ON, M9L 1Y2
(416) 656-9666 SIC 2011

PREMIUM BRANDS OPERATING LIMITED PARTNERSHIP p1438
501 YORK RD W, YORKTON, SK, S3N 2V6
(306) 783-9446 SIC 2011

SJ FINE FOODS LTD p1430
827 56TH ST E, SASKATOON, SK, S7K 5Y9
(306) 653-1702 SIC 2011

SOBEYS WEST INC p18
3440 56 AVE SE, CALGARY, AB, T2C 2C3
(403) 279-2555 SIC 2011

SOFINA FOODS INC p291
8385 FRASER ST, VANCOUVER, BC, V5X 3X8
(604) 668-5800 SIC 2011

SUPRALIMENT S.E.C. p1300
25 125 RTE E, SAINT-ESPRIT, QC, J0K 2L0
(450) 839-7258 SIC 2011

SUPRALIMENT S.E.C. p1306
183 RTE DU PRESIDENT-KENNEDY, SAINT-HENRI-DE-LEVIS, QC, G0R 3E0
(418) 882-2282 SIC 2011

SUPRALIMENT S.E.C. p1313
2200 AV PRATTE BUREAU 400, SAINT-HYACINTHE, QC, J2S 4B6
(450) 771-0400 SIC 2011

SYSCO CANADA, INC p559
1400 CREDITSTONE RD SUITE B, CONCORD, ON, L4K 0E2
(905) 760-7200 SIC 2011

VANTAGE FOODS (MB) INC p367
41 PAQUIN RD, WINNIPEG, MB, R2J 3V9
(204) 667-9903 SIC 2011

VANTAGE FOODS INC p32
4000 4 ST SE SUITE 225, CALGARY, AB, T2G 2W3
(403) 215-2820 SIC 2011

VANTAGE FOODS INC p198
8200 BRANNICK PL, CHILLIWACK, BC, V2R 0E9
(604) 795-4774 SIC 2011

VANTAGE FOODS INC p367
41 PAQUIN RD, WINNIPEG, MB, R2J 3V9
(204) 667-9903 SIC 2011

VAP HOLDINGS L.P. p32
4211 13A ST SE, CALGARY, AB, T2G 3J6

(403) 299-0844 SIC 2011

VIANDE DUBREUIL INC p1358
172 RUE PRINCIPALE, SAINTE-HENEDINE, QC, G0S 2R0
(418) 935-3935 SIC 2011

VIANDE RICHELIEU INC p1150
595 RUE ROYALE, MASSUEVILLE, QC, J0G 1K0
(450) 788-2667 SIC 2011

VIANDES DU BRETON INC, LES p1287
150 CH DES RAYMOND, RIVIERE-DU-LOUP, QC, G5R 5X8
(418) 863-6711 SIC 2011

VIANDES LACROIX INC, LES p1313
4120 BOUL CASAVANT O, SAINT-HYACINTHE, QC, J2S 8E3
(450) 778-0188 SIC 2011

VOLAILLE GIANNONE INC p1298
2320 RUE PRINCIPALE, SAINT-CUTHBERT, QC, J0K 2C0
(450) 836-3063 SIC 2011

SIC 2013 Sausages and other prepared meats

4525663 CANADA INC p1060
87 RUE PREVOST, BOISBRIAND, QC, J7G 3A1
(450) 437-7182 SIC 2013

ALIMENTS EXPRESCO INC p1332
8205 RTE TRANSCANADIENNE, SAINT-LAURENT, QC, H4S 1S4
(514) 344-9499 SIC 2013

ALIMENTS PRINCE, S.E.C. p1097
255 RUE ROCHELEAU, DRUMMONDVILLE, QC, J2C 7G2
(819) 475-3030 SIC 2013

ALIMENTS PRINCE, S.E.C. p1311
2200 AV PRATTE BUREAU 400, SAINT-HYACINTHE, QC, J2S 4B6
(450) 771-7060 SIC 2013

BRANDT, G. MEAT PACKERS LIMITED p702
1878 MATTAWA AVE, MISSISSAUGA, ON, L4X 1K1
(905) 279-4460 SIC 2013

CARDINAL MEAT SPECIALISTS LIMITED p501
155 HEDGEDALE RD, BRAMPTON, ON, L6T 5P3
(905) 459-4436 SIC 2013

CHARCUTERIE L. FORTIN LIMITEE p1045
5371 AV DU PONT N, ALMA, QC, G8E 1T9
(418) 347-3365 SIC 2013

CUISINES GASPESIENNES MATANE LTEE, LES p1150
85 RUE DU PORT BUREAU 1, MATANE, QC, G4W 3M6
(418) 562-5757 SIC 2013

DENNINGER, R. LIMITED p611
284 KING ST E, HAMILTON, ON, L8N 1B7
(905) 528-8468 SIC 2013

MADE-RITE MEAT PRODUCTS INC p229
26656 56 AVE, LANGLEY, BC, V4W 3X5
(604) 607-8844 SIC 2013

MEAT FACTORY LIMITED, THE p892
46 COMMUNITY AVE, STONEY CREEK, ON, L8E 2Y3
(905) 664-2126 SIC 2013

OLYMEL S.E.C. p1059
1020 BOUL MICHELE-BOHEC, BLAINVILLE, QC, J7C 5E2
(450) 979-0001 SIC 2013

PREMIUM BRANDS OPERATING LIMITED PARTNERSHIP p226
8621 201 ST SUITE 120, LANGLEY, BC, V2Y 0G9
(866) 663-4746 SIC 2013

SOFINA FOODS INC p875
170 NUGGET AVE, SCARBOROUGH, ON, M1S 3A7
(416) 297-1062 SIC 2013

SOFINA FOODS INC p905
100 COMMERCE VALLEY DR W SUITE 900, THORNHILL, ON, L3T 0A1

(905) 747-3333 SIC 2013

SPECIALITES M.B. INC p1313
5450 AV TRUDEAU, SAINT-HYACINTHE, QC, J2S 7Y8
(450) 771-1415 SIC 2013

SPECIALITES PRODAL (1975) LTEE, LES p1297
251 AV BOYER, SAINT-CHARLES-DE-BELLECHASSE, QC, G0R 2T0
(418) 887-3301 SIC 2013

SPRING HILL COLONY FARMS LTD p353
30 TOWNSHIP 15 RG SUITE 15, NEEPAWA, MB, R0J 1H0
(204) 476-2715 SIC 2013

WINNIPEG OLD COUNTRY SAUSAGE LTD p371
691 DUFFERIN AVE, WINNIPEG, MB, R2W 2Z3
(204) 589-8331 SIC 2013

WISMER DEVELOPMENTS INC p1008
443 WISMER ST, WATERLOO, ON, N2K 2K6
(519) 743-1412 SIC 2013

ZADI FOODS LIMITED p507
65 DEERHURST DR, BRAMPTON, ON, L6T 5R7
(905) 799-6666 SIC 2013

SIC 2015 Poultry slaughtering and processing

1519694 ONTARIO INC p875
135 SELECT AVE UNIT 8-9, SCARBOROUGH, ON, M1V 4A5
(416) 754-0483 SIC 2015

2308061 ONTARIO LIMITED p792
239 TORYORK DR, NORTH YORK, ON, M9L 1Y2
(416) 640-1790 SIC 2015

9020-2516 QUEBEC INC p1239
5671 BOUL INDUSTRIEL, MONTREAL-NORD, QC, H1G 3Z9
(514) 321-8376 SIC 2015

ALIMENTS EXCEL S.E.C., LES p1295
1081 RUE PARENT, SAINT-BRUNO, QC, J3V 6L7
(450) 441-6111 SIC 2015

ALIMENTS SUNCHEF INC p1047
9750 BOUL DES SCIENCES, ANJOU, QC, H1J 0A1
(514) 272-3238 SIC 2015

AVICOMAX INC p1098
500 RUE LABONTE, DRUMMONDVILLE, QC, J2C 6X9
(819) 471-5000 SIC 2015

BARRON POULTRY LIMITED p477
7470 COUNTY ROAD 18, AMHERSTBURG, ON, N9V 2Y7
(519) 726-5250 SIC 2015

CANARDS DU LAC BROME LTEE p1118
40 CH DU CENTRE, KNOWLTON, QC, J0E 1V0
(450) 242-3825 SIC 2015

CARGILL LIMITED p648
10 CUDDY BLVD, LONDON, ON, N5V 5E3
(519) 453-4996 SIC 2015

COLONIAL FARMS LTD p179
3830 OKANAGAN ST, ARMSTRONG, BC, V0E 1B0
(250) 546-3008 SIC 2015

COOP FEDEREE, LA p1314
3380 RUE PRINCIPALE BUREAU 430, SAINT-JEAN-BAPTISTE, QC, J0L 2B0
(450) 467-2875 SIC 2015

CUDDY INTERNATIONAL CORPORATION p652
1226 TRAFALGAR ST, LONDON, ON, N5Z 1H5
(800) 265-1061 SIC 2015

EMBALLAGE AVICO INC p1264
1460 RUE PROVINCIALE, QUEBEC, QC, G1N 4A2
(418) 682-5024 SIC 2015

EXCELDOR COOPERATIVE *p1136*
5700 RUE J.-B.-MICHAUD SUITE 500, LEVIS, QC, G6V 0B1
(418) 830-5600 *SIC 2015*

EXCELDOR COOPERATIVE *p1136*
5700 RUE J.-B.-MICHAUD BUREAU 500, LEVIS, QC, G6V 0B1
(418) 830-5600 *SIC 2015*

EXCELDOR COOPERATIVE *p1292*
1000 RTE BEGIN, SAINT-ANSELME, QC, G0R 2N0
(418) 885-4451 *SIC 2015*

EXCELDOR FOODS LTD *p617*
478 14TH ST, HANOVER, ON, N4N 1Z9
(519) 364-1770 *SIC 2015*

FERME DES VOLTIGEURS INC *p1100*
2350 BOUL FOUCAULT, DRUM-MONDVILLE, QC, J2E 0E8
(819) 478-7495 *SIC 2015*

FRASER VALLEY DUCK & GOOSE LTD *p197*
4540 SIMMONS RD, CHILLIWACK, BC, V2R 4R7
(604) 823-4435 *SIC 2015*

GLOBAL EGG CORPORATION *p574*
283 HORNER AVE, ETOBICOKE, ON, M8Z 4Y4
(416) 231-2309 *SIC 2015*

GRAND RIVER FOODS LTD *p538*
190 VONDRAU DR, CAMBRIDGE, ON, N3E 1B8
(519) 653-3577 *SIC 2015*

GRAND RIVER FOODS LTD *p538*
685 BOXWOOD DR, CAMBRIDGE, ON, N3E 1B4
(519) 653-3577 *SIC 2015*

GRAND RIVER POULTRY LTD *p538*
190 VONDRAU DR, CAMBRIDGE, ON, N3E 1B8
(519) 653-3577 *SIC 2015*

GRANNY'S POULTRY COOPERATIVE (MANITOBA) LTD *p346*
4 PENNER, BLUMENORT, MB, R0A 0C0
(204) 452-6315 *SIC 2015*

GRANNY'S POULTRY COOPERATIVE (MANITOBA) LTD *p362*
750 PANDORA AVE E, WINNIPEG, MB, R2C 4G5
(204) 488-2230 *SIC 2015*

HALLMARK POULTRY PROCESSORS LTD *p285*
1756 PANDORA ST, VANCOUVER, BC, V5L 1M1
(604) 254-9885 *SIC 2015*

HAYTER'S TURKEY PRODUCTS INC *p564*
37451 DASHWOOD RD, DASHWOOD, ON, N0M 1N0
(519) 237-3561 *SIC 2015*

JD SWEID FOODS (2013) LTD *p225*
9696 199A ST, LANGLEY, BC, V1M 2X7
(800) 665-4355 *SIC 2015*

K & R POULTRY LTD *p177*
31171 PEARDONVILLE RD UNIT 2, AB-BOTSFORD, BC, V2T 6K6
(604) 850-5808 *SIC 2015*

KUTCO INTERNATIONAL INC *p504*
275 WALKER DR, BRAMPTON, ON, L6T 3W5
SIC 2015

LILYDALE INC *p30*
2126 HURST RD SE, CALGARY, AB, T2G 4M5
(403) 265-9010 *SIC 2015*

LILYDALE INC *p177*
31894 MARSHALL PL SUITE 5, ABBOTS-FORD, BC, V2T 5Z9
(604) 850-2633 *SIC 2015*

LILYDALE INC *p247*
1910 KINGSWAY AVE, PORT COQUITLAM, BC, V3C 1S7
(604) 941-4041 *SIC 2015*

LILYDALE INC *p1438*
502 BOSWORTH ST, WYNYARD, SK, S0A 4T0

(306) 554-2555 *SIC 2015*

MAPLE LEAF FOODS INC *p122*
2619 91 AVE NW, EDMONTON, AB, T6P 1S3
(780) 467-6022 *SIC 2015*

MAPLE LEAF FOODS INC *p724*
2626 ARGENTIA RD, MISSISSAUGA, ON, L5N 5N2
(905) 890-0053 *SIC 2015*

MAPLE LEAF FOODS INC *p888*
1865 PERTH ROAD SUITE 139, ST MARYS, ON, N4X 1C8
(519) 229-8900 *SIC 2015*

MAPLE LEAF FOODS INC *p894*
92 HIGHLAND RD E, STONEY CREEK, ON, L8J 2W6
(905) 662-8883 *SIC 2015*

MAPLE LEAF FOODS INC *p993*
100 ETHEL AVE, TORONTO, ON, M6N 4Z7
(416) 767-5151 *SIC 2015*

MAPLE LODGE FARMS LTD *p417*
2222 COMMERCIALE ST, SAINT-FRANCOIS-DE-MADAWASKA, NB, E7A 1B6
(506) 992-2192 *SIC 2015*

MAPLE LODGE FARMS LTD *p511*
8301 WINSTON CHURCHILL BLVD, BRAMPTON, ON, L6Y 0A2
(905) 455-8340 *SIC 2015*

MAXI CANADA INC *p1347*
688 RUE DU PARC, SAINT-LIN-LAURENTIDES, QC, J5M 3B4
(450) 439-2500 *SIC 2015*

MFI FOOD CANADA LTD *p391*
70 IRENE ST, WINNIPEG, MB, R3T 4E1
(204) 453-6613 *SIC 2015*

NORTHERN FREEDOM INC *p359*
PO BOX 510, TEULON, MB, R0C 3B0
(204) 886-2552 *SIC 2015*

OLYMEL S.E.C. *p505*
318 ORENDA RD, BRAMPTON, ON, L6T 1G1
(905) 793-5757 *SIC 2015*

OLYMEL S.E.C. *p1298*
249 RUE PRINCIPALE, SAINT-DAMASE, QC, J0H 1J0
(450) 797-2691 *SIC 2015*

OLYMEL S.E.C. *p1315*
3380 RUE PRINCIPALE, SAINT-JEAN-BAPTISTE, QC, J0L 2B0
(450) 467-2875 *SIC 2015*

PINTY'S DELICIOUS FOODS INC *p524*
5063 NORTH SERVICE RD SUITE 101, BURLINGTON, ON, L7L 5H6
(905) 835-8575 *SIC 2015*

PINTY'S DELICIOUS FOODS INC *p799*
2714 BRISTOL CIR, OAKVILLE, ON, L6H 6A1
(905) 829-1130 *SIC 2015*

PRAIRIE PRIDE NATURAL FOODS LTD *p1434*
3535 MILLAR AVE, SASKATOON, SK, S7P 0A2
(306) 653-1810 *SIC 2015*

PUDDY BROS. LIMITED *p735*
7120 EDWARDS BLVD, MISSISSAUGA, ON, L5S 1Z1
(289) 541-7875 *SIC 2015*

RIVERVIEW POULTRY LIMITED *p541*
1560 KOHLER RD, CAYUGA, ON, N0A 1E0
(905) 957-0300 *SIC 2015*

SERVICE ALIMENTAIRE DESCO INC *p1061*
97 RUE PREVOST, BOISBRIAND, QC, J7G 3A1
(450) 437-7182 *SIC 2015*

SUNRISE POULTRY PROCESSORS LTD *p278*
13558 73 AVE, SURREY, BC, V3W 2R6
(604) 596-9505 *SIC 2015*

THAMES VALLEY PROCESSORS LTD *p634*
15 LINE 155390, KINTORE, ON, N0M 2C0
SIC 2015

TNT FOODS INTERNATIONAL INC *p507*
20 WESTWYN CRT, BRAMPTON, ON, L6T

4T5
(905) 672-1787 *SIC 2015*

VIANDES SEFICLO INC *p1056*
1660 AV LE NEUF, BECANCOUR, QC, G9H 2E4
(819) 233-2653 *SIC 2015*

SIC 2021 Creamery butter

AGRIFOODS INTERNATIONAL COOPERA-TIVE LTD *p153*
5410 50 AVE, RED DEER, AB, T4N 4B5
SIC 2021

FOOTHILLS CREAMERY LTD *p29*
2825 BONNYBROOK RD SE, CALGARY, AB, T2G 4N1
(403) 263-7725 *SIC 2021*

GAY LEA FOODS CO-OPERATIVE LIMITED *p603*
21 SPEEDVALE AVE W, GUELPH, ON, N1H 1J5
(519) 822-5530 *SIC 2021*

GAY LEA FOODS CO-OPERATIVE LIMITED *p609*
20 MORLEY ST, HAMILTON, ON, L8H 3R7
(905) 544-6281 *SIC 2021*

GAY LEA FOODS CO-OPERATIVE LIMITED *p695*
5200 ORBITOR DR, MISSISSAUGA, ON, L4W 5B4
(905) 283-5300 *SIC 2021*

PUNJAB MILK FOODS INC *p273*
6308 146 ST, SURREY, BC, V3S 3A4
(604) 594-9190 *SIC 2021*

WESTERN INVESTMENT COMPANY OF CANADA LIMITED, THE *p136*
1010 24 ST SE, HIGH RIVER, AB, T1V 2A7
(403) 701-7546 *SIC 2021*

SIC 2022 Cheese; natural and processed

1048547 ONTARIO INC *p888*
185 COUNTY RD 10, ST EUGENE, ON, K0B 1P0
(613) 674-3183 *SIC 2022*

9113-0476 QUEBEC INC *p1121*
2152 CH SAINT-JOSEPH, LA BAIE, QC, G7B 3N9
(418) 544-2622 *SIC 2022*

AGRILAIT, COOPERATIVE AGRICOLE *p1306*
83 RANG DE L'EGLISE, SAINT-GUILLAUME, QC, J0C 1L0
(819) 396-2022 *SIC 2022*

AGROPUR COOPERATIVE *p1055*
75 AV LAMBERT, BEAUCEVILLE, QC, G5X 3N5
(418) 774-9848 *SIC 2022*

AGROPUR COOPERATIVE *p1108*
510 RUE PRINCIPALE, GRANBY, QC, J2G 2X2
(450) 375-1991 *SIC 2022*

AGROPUR COOPERATIVE *p1110*
1100 RUE OMER-DESLAURIERS, GRANBY, QC, J2J 0S7
(450) 777-5300 *SIC 2022*

AGROPUR COOPERATIVE *p1244*
1400 CH D'OKA, OKA, QC, J0N 1E0
(450) 479-6396 *SIC 2022*

ALIMENTS SAPUTO LIMITEE *p902*
284 HOPE ST W, TAVISTOCK, ON, N0B 2R0
(519) 655-2337 *SIC 2022*

BOTHWELL CHEESE INC *p353*
61 MAIN ST N, NEW BOTHWELL, MB, R0A 1C0
(204) 388-4666 *SIC 2022*

FINANCIERE BONNET INC *p1298*
54 RUE PRINCIPALE, SAINT-DAMASE, QC, J0H 1J0
(450) 797-3301 *SIC 2022*

FROMAGERIE BERGERON INC *p1292*

3837 RTE MARIE-VICTORIN, SAINT-ANTOINE-DE-TILLY, QC, G0S 2C0
(418) 886-2234 *SIC 2022*

FROMAGERIE L'ANCETRE INC *p1056*
1615 BOUL DE PORT-ROYAL, BECAN-COUR, QC, G9H 1X7
(819) 233-9157 *SIC 2022*

FROMAGERIE VICTORIA INC, LA *p1397*
101 RUE DE L'AQUEDUC, VICTORIAVILLE, QC, G6P 1M2
(819) 752-6821 *SIC 2022*

GRANDE CHEESE COMPANY LIMITED *p1031*
468 JEVLAN DR, WOODBRIDGE, ON, L4L 8L4
(905) 856-6880 *SIC 2022*

IVANHOE CHEESE INC *p663*
11301 HWY 62, MADOC, ON, K0K 2K0
(613) 473-4269 *SIC 2022*

KRAFT HEINZ CANADA ULC *p622*
70 DICKINSON DR, INGLESIDE, ON, K0C 1M0
(613) 537-2226 *SIC 2022*

KRAFT HEINZ CANADA ULC *p1156*
8600 CH DEVONSHIRE, MONT-ROYAL, QC, H4P 2K9
(514) 343-3300 *SIC 2022*

LAITERIE CHALIFOUX INC *p1393*
1625 BOUL LIONEL-BOULET LOCAL 203, VARENNES, QC, J3X 1P7
(450) 809-0211 *SIC 2022*

MARIPOSA DAIRY LTD *p646*
201 ST GEORGE ST, LINDSAY, ON, K9V 5Z9
(705) 324-9306 *SIC 2022*

PARADISE ISLAND FOODS INC *p235*
6451 PORTSMOUTH RD, NANAIMO, BC, V9V 1A3
(800) 889-3370 *SIC 2022*

PARMALAT CANADA INC *p1016*
490 GORDON ST, WINCHESTER, ON, K0C 2K0
(613) 774-2310 *SIC 2022*

PARMALAT CANADA INC *p1149*
2350 RUE SAINT-CESAIRE, MARIEVILLE, QC, J3M 1E1
SIC 2022

SALERNO DAIRY PRODUCTS LIMITED *p609*
20 MORLEY ST, HAMILTON, ON, L8H 3R7
(905) 544-6281 *SIC 2022*

SAPUTO INC *p808*
425 RICHARDSON RD, ORANGEVILLE, ON, L9W 4Z4
(519) 941-9206 *SIC 2022*

SAPUTO INC *p999*
7 RIVERSIDE DRIVE, TRENTON, ON, K8V 5R7
(613) 392-6762 *SIC 2022*

SAPUTO INC *p1345*
6869 BOUL METROPOLITAIN E, SAINT-LEONARD, QC, H1P 1X8
(514) 328-6662 *SIC 2022*

SAPUTO PRODUITS LAITIERS CANADA S.E.N.C. *p1165*
6869 BOUL METROPOLITAIN, MON-TREAL, QC, H1P 1X8
(514) 328-6662 *SIC 2022*

SAPUTO PRODUITS LAITIERS CANADA S.E.N.C. *p1246*
1245 AV FORAND, PLESSISVILLE, QC, G6L 1X5
(819) 362-6378 *SIC 2022*

SAPUTO PRODUITS LAITIERS CANADA S.E.N.C. *p1345*
7750 RUE PASCAL-GAGNON, SAINT-LEONARD, QC, H1P 3L1
(514) 328-6662 *SIC 2022*

SAPUTO PRODUITS LAITIERS CANADA S.E.N.C. *p1351*
71 AV SAINT-JACQUES, SAINT-RAYMOND, QC, G3L 3X9
(418) 337-4287 *SIC 2022*

SILANI SWEET CHEESE LIMITED *p879*

4205 2ND LINE, SCHOMBERG, ON, L0G 1T0

(416) 324-3290   *SIC 2022*

SILANI SWEET CHEESE LIMITED   *p1033*
661 CHRISLEA RD UNIT 14, WOOD-BRIDGE, ON, L4L 0C4

(905) 792-3811   *SIC 2022*

ST-ALBERT CHEESE CO-OPERATIVE INC   *p883*
150 ST PAUL ST, ST ALBERT, ON, K0A 3C0

(613) 987-2872   *SIC 2022*

YOPLAIT LIBERTE CANADA CIE   *p1310*
5000 RUE J.-A.-BOMBARDIER, SAINT-HUBERT, QC, J3Z 1H1

(450) 926-5222   *SIC 2022*

SIC 2023 Dry, condensed and evaporated dairy products

AGROPUR COOPERATIVE   *p1245*
2400 RUE DE LA COOPERATIVE, PLESSISVILLE, QC, G6L 3G8

(819) 362-7338   *SIC 2023*

ATRIUM INNOVATIONS INC   *p1401*
3500 BOUL DE MAISONNEUVE O BU-REAU 2405, WESTMOUNT, QC, H3Z 3C1

(514) 205-6240   *SIC 2023*

BIENA INC   *p1311*
2955 RUE CARTIER, SAINT-HYACINTHE, QC, J2S 1L4

(450) 778-5505   *SIC 2023*

BIOPAK LIMITED   *p113*
7824 51 AVE NW, EDMONTON, AB, T6E 6W2

SIC 2023

CANADIAN MILK MANUFACTURING INC   *p519*
198 PEARL ST E, BROCKVILLE, ON, K6V 1R4

(613) 970-5566   *SIC 2023*

GUY HUBERT ET ASSOCIES INC   *p1143*
80 RUE SAINT-LAURENT O BUREAU 210, LONGUEUIL, QC, J4H 1L8

(579) 721-3252   *SIC 2023*

LABORATOIRES MSP INC   *p1393*
2401 MONTEE DE PICARDIE, VARENNES, QC, J3X 0J1

(450) 652-4295   *SIC 2023*

NATURES FORMULAE HEALTH PROD-UCTS LTD   *p222*
2130 LECKIE PL SUITE 300, KELOWNA, BC, V1Y 7W7

(250) 717-5700   *SIC 2023*

NESTLE CANADA INC   *p662*
980 WILTON GROVE RD, LONDON, ON, N6N 1C7

(519) 686-0182   *SIC 2023*

NEW ROOTS HERBAL INC   *p1395*
3405 RUE F.-X.-TESSIER, VAUDREUIL-DORION, QC, J7V 5V5

(800) 268-9486   *SIC 2023*

PARMALAT CANADA INC   *p579*
405 THE WEST MALL, ETOBICOKE, ON, M9C 5J1

(416) 626-1973   *SIC 2023*

PARMALAT CANADA INC   *p579*
405 THE WEST MALL 10TH FL, ETOBI-COKE, ON, M9C 5J1

(416) 626-1973   *SIC 2023*

PARMALAT CANADA INC   *p1399*
75 BOUL PIERRE-ROUX E, VICTORIAV-ILLE, QC, G6T 1S8

(819) 758-6245   *SIC 2023*

PARMALAT FOOD INC   *p996*
405 THE WEST MALL 10TH FLOOR, TORONTO, ON, M9C 5J1

SIC 2023

PNP PHARMACEUTICALS INC   *p193*
9388 NORTH FRASER CRES, BURNABY, BC, V5J 0E3

(604) 435-6200   *SIC 2023*

SAPUTO INC   *p1435*
122 WAKOOMA ST, SASKATOON, SK, S7R

1A8

(306) 668-6833   *SIC 2023*

SAPUTO PRODUITS LAITIERS CANADA S.E.N.C.   *p183*
6800 LOUGHEED HWY SUITE 3, BURN-ABY, BC, V5A 1W2

(604) 420-6611   *SIC 2023*

SAPUTO PRODUITS LAITIERS CANADA S.E.N.C.   *p1313*
1195 RUE DANIEL-JOHNSON E UNITE 117, SAINT-HYACINTHE, QC, J2S 7Y6

(450) 773-1004   *SIC 2023*

VITALUS NUTRITION INC   *p178*
3911 MT LEHMAN RD, ABBOTSFORD, BC, V2T 5W5

(604) 857-9080   *SIC 2023*

SIC 2024 Ice cream and frozen deserts

329985 ONTARIO LIMITED   *p1026*
50 ROYAL GROUP CRES UNIT 1, WOOD-BRIDGE, ON, L4H 1X9

(905) 652-2363   *SIC 2024*

AGROPUR COOPERATIVE   *p92*
13944 YELLOWHEAD TRAIL NW, EDMON-TON, AB, T5L 3C2

(780) 488-2214   *SIC 2024*

AGROPUR COOPERATIVE   *p1129*
724 RUE PRINCIPALE, LACHUTE, QC, J8H 1Z4

(450) 562-5500   *SIC 2024*

ALIMENTS LEBEL INC, LES   *p1129*
724 RUE PRINCIPALE, LACHUTE, QC, J8H 1Z4

(450) 562-5500   *SIC 2024*

BROOKFIELD ICE CREAM LIMITED   *p432*
314 LEMARCHANT RD, ST. JOHN'S, NL, A1E 1R2

(709) 738-4652   *SIC 2024*

CHAPMAN'S, DAVID ICE CREAM LIMITED   *p664*
100 CHAPMAN'S CRES, MARKDALE, ON, N0C 1H0

(519) 986-3131   *SIC 2024*

JORIKI INC   *p844*
885 SANDY BEACH RD, PICKERING, ON, L1W 3N6

(905) 420-0188   *SIC 2024*

LAITERIE DE COATICOOK LIMITEE   *p1082*
1000 RUE CHILD BUREAU 255, COATI-COOK, QC, J1A 2S5

(819) 849-2272   *SIC 2024*

REID'S DAIRY COMPANY LIMITED, THE   *p492*
222 BELL BLVD, BELLEVILLE, ON, K8P 5L7

(613) 967-1970   *SIC 2024*

RICH PRODUCTS OF CANADA LIMITED   *p1033*
149 ROWNTREE DAIRY RD SUITE 1, WOODBRIDGE, ON, L4L 6E1

(905) 850-3836   *SIC 2024*

STONEY CREEK DISTRIBUTION LTD   *p894*
135 KING ST E, STONEY CREEK, ON, L8G 0B2

SIC 2024

SUBLIME DESSERT INC   *p1336*
7777 BOUL THIMENS, SAINT-LAURENT, QC, H4S 2A2

(514) 333-0338   *SIC 2024*

UNILEVER CANADA INC   *p881*
175 UNION ST, SIMCOE, ON, N3Y 2B1

(519) 426-1673   *SIC 2024*

SIC 2026 Fluid milk

AGRIFOODS INTERNATIONAL COOPERA-TIVE LTD   *p20*
4215 12 ST NE, CALGARY, AB, T2E 4P9

(403) 571-6400   *SIC 2026*

AGROPUR COOPERATIVE   *p1046*
466 132 RTE O BUREAU 1320, AMQUI, QC,

G5J 2G7

(418) 629-3133   *SIC 2026*

AGROPUR COOPERATIVE   *p1260*
2465 1RE AV, QUEBEC, QC, G1L 3M9

(418) 641-0857   *SIC 2026*

ALIMENTS SAPUTO LIMITEE   *p593*
279 GUELPH ST, GEORGETOWN, ON, L7G 4B3

(905) 702-7200   *SIC 2026*

ALIMENTS ULTIMA INC   *p1309*
4600 RUE ARMAND-FRAPPIER, SAINT-HUBERT, QC, J3Z 1G5

(450) 651-3737   *SIC 2026*

AMALGAMATED DAIRIES LIMITED   *p1042*
79 WATER ST SUITE 1, SUMMERSIDE, PE, C1N 1A6

(902) 888-5088   *SIC 2026*

CHOCOLATS FAVORIS INC, LES   *p1276*
4355 RUE JEAN-MARCHAND BUREAU 101, QUEBEC, QC, G2C 0N2

(418) 915-9311   *SIC 2026*

DAIRYTOWN PROCESSING LTD   *p412*
49 MILK BOARD RD, ROACHVILLE, NB, E4G 2G7

(506) 432-1950   *SIC 2026*

DANONE INC   *p1064*
100 RUE DE LAUZON, BOUCHERVILLE, QC, J4B 1E6

(450) 655-7331   *SIC 2026*

NORTHUMBERLAND COOPERATIVE LIM-ITED   *p405*
256 LAWLOR LANE, MIRAMICHI, NB, E1V 3Z9

(506) 627-7720   *SIC 2026*

PARMALAT CANADA INC   *p357*
9 PROVINCIAL RD SUITE 240, ST CLAUDE, MB, R0G 1Z0

(204) 379-2571   *SIC 2026*

PARMALAT CANADA INC   *p366*
330 MAZENOD RD, WINNIPEG, MB, R2J 4L7

(204) 654-6455   *SIC 2026*

PARMALAT CANADA INC   *p505*
16 SHAFTSBURY LANE, BRAMPTON, ON, L6T 4G7

(905) 791-6100   *SIC 2026*

PARMALAT CANADA INC   *p1222*
7470 RUE SAINT-JACQUES, MONTREAL, QC, H4B 1W4

(514) 484-8401   *SIC 2026*

PARMALAT DAIRY & BAKERY INC   *p579*
405 THE WEST MALL 10TH FL, ETOBI-COKE, ON, M9C 5J1

SIC 2026

PARMALAT HOLDINGS LIMITED   *p579*
405 THE WEST MALL 10TH FLOOR, ETO-BICOKE, ON, M9C 5J1

(416) 626-1973   *SIC 2026*

SCOTSBURN CO-OPERATIVE SERVICES LIMITED   *p467*
1120 UPPER PRINCE ST, SYDNEY, NS, B1P 5P6

SIC 2026

YOPLAIT LIBERTE CANADA CIE   *p1069*
1423 BOUL PROVENCHER, BROSSARD, QC, J4W 1Z3

SIC 2026

SIC 2032 Canned specialties

3522920 CANADA INC   *p1242*
80 RUE CAMPBELL RR 2, MORIN-HEIGHTS, QC, J0R 1H0

(450) 226-2314   *SIC 2032*

ALIMENTS BCI INC, LES   *p1311*
4800 AV PINARD, SAINT-HYACINTHE, QC, J2S 8E1

(888) 797-3210   *SIC 2032*

ALIMENTS OUIMET-CORDON BLEU INC   *p1047*
8383 RUE J.-RENE-OUIMET, ANJOU, QC, H1J 2P8

(514) 352-3000   *SIC 2032*

ALIMENTS ROMA LTEE, LES   *p1325*
660 RUE WRIGHT, SAINT-LAURENT, QC, H4N 1M6

(514) 332-0340   *SIC 2032*

CAMPBELL COMPANY OF CANADA   *p570*
60 BIRMINGHAM ST, ETOBICOKE, ON, M8V 2B8

(416) 251-1131   *SIC 2032*

CANYON CREEK SOUP COMPANY LTD   *p74*
60 CROWFOOT CRES NW SUITE 204, CALGARY, AB, T3G 3J9

SIC 2032

CONAGRA FOODS CANADA INC   *p565*
759 WELLINGTON ST, DRESDEN, ON, N0P 1M0

(519) 683-4422   *SIC 2032*

CONAGRA FOODS CANADA INC   *p693*
5055 SATELLITE DR UNIT 1-2, MISSIS-SAUGA, ON, L4W 5K7

(416) 679-4200   *SIC 2032*

DEL MONTE CANADA INC   *p565*
GD, DRESDEN, ON, N0P 1M0

(519) 683-4422   *SIC 2032*

FLORA MANUFACTURING AND DIS-TRIBUTING LTD   *p192*
7400 FRASER PARK DR, BURNABY, BC, V5J 5B9

(604) 436-6000   *SIC 2032*

FRESH HEMP FOODS LTD   *p369*
69 EAGLE DR, WINNIPEG, MB, R2R 1V4

(204) 953-0233   *SIC 2032*

GINGER BEEF EXPRESS LTD   *p35*
5521 3 ST SE, CALGARY, AB, T2H 1K1

(403) 272-8088   *SIC 2032*

GROUPE COMMENSAL INC   *p1062*
3737 BOUL DE LA GRANDE-ALLEE, BOIS-BRIAND, QC, J7H 1M6

(450) 979-5772   *SIC 2032*

GROUPE RAMACIERI INC   *p1326*
660 RUE WRIGHT, SAINT-LAURENT, QC, H4N 1M6

(514) 332-0340   *SIC 2032*

INDIANLIFE FOOD CORPORATION   *p186*
3835 2ND AVE, BURNABY, BC, V5C 3W7

(604) 205-9176   *SIC 2032*

INTERNATIONAL VINEYARD INC   *p260*
4631 SHELL RD SUITE 165, RICHMOND, BC, V6X 3M4

(604) 303-5778   *SIC 2032*

MONDELEZ CANADA INC   *p572*
3300 BLOOR ST W SUITE 1801, ETOBI-COKE, ON, M8X 2X2

SIC 2032

MONDELEZ CANADA INC   *p614*
45 EWEN RD, HAMILTON, ON, L8S 3C3

(905) 526-7212   *SIC 2032*

NUTRI-NATION FUNCTIONAL FOODS INC   *p247*
1560 BROADWAY ST SUITE 1110, PORT COQUITLAM, BC, V3C 2M8

(604) 552-5549   *SIC 2032*

PRO-AMINO INTERNATIONAL INC   *p1153*
12700 BOUL HENRI-FABRE E, MIRABEL, QC, J7N 0A6

(800) 555-2170   *SIC 2032*

PROSNACK NATURAL FOODS INC   *p244*
19100 AIRPORT WAY UNIT 108, PITT MEADOWS, BC, V3Y 0E2

(604) 465-0548   *SIC 2032*

PROTENERGY NATURAL FOODS CORP   *p853*
125 EAST BEAVER CREEK RD, RICH-MOND HILL, ON, L4B 4R3

(905) 707-6223   *SIC 2032*

QUE PASA MEXICAN FOODS LTD   *p261*
9100 VAN HORNE WAY, RICHMOND, BC, V6X 1W3

(866) 880-7284   *SIC 2032*

RIVERSIDE NATURAL FOODS LTD   *p558*
2720 STEELES AVE W, CONCORD, ON, L4K 4S3

(416) 360-8200   *SIC 2032*

SPRAGUE FOODS LIMITED   *p492*
385 COLLEGE ST E, BELLEVILLE, ON,

K8N 5S7

(613) 966-1200   *SIC 2032*

SIC 2033 Canned fruits and specialties

2469447 ONTARIO LIMITED   *p782*
14 ASHWARREN RD, NORTH YORK, ON, M3J 1Z5
(416) 636-7772   *SIC 2033*

A & P FRUIT GROWERS LTD   *p178*
1794 PEARDONVILLE RD, ABBOTSFORD, BC, V4X 2M4
(604) 864-4900   *SIC 2033*

A. LASSONDE INC   *p1288*
170 5E AV, ROUGEMONT, QC, J0L 1M0
(450) 469-4926   *SIC 2033*

ALIMENTS ORIGINAL, DIVISION CANTIN INC   *p1255*
1910 AV DU SANCTUAIRE, QUEBEC, QC, G1E 3L2
(418) 663-3523   *SIC 2033*

ARIANA HOLDINGS INC   *p692*
4544 EASTGATE PKY, MISSISSAUGA, ON, L4W 3W6
(905) 238-6300   *SIC 2033*

BONDUELLE CANADA INC   *p1299*
540 CH DES PATRIOTES, SAINT-DENIS-SUR-RICHELIEU, QC, J0H 1K0
(450) 787-3411   *SIC 2033*

BONDUELLE CANADA INC   *p1360*
316 RUE SAINT-JOSEPH RR 2, SAINTE-MARTINE, QC, J0S 1V0
(450) 427-2130   *SIC 2033*

CROFTERS FOOD LTD   *p837*
7 GREAT NORTH RD, PARRY SOUND, ON, P2A 2X8
(705) 746-6301   *SIC 2033*

E.D. SMITH FOODS, LTD   *p892*
944 HIGHWAY 8, STONEY CREEK, ON, L8E 5S3
(905) 643-1211   *SIC 2033*

INDUSTRIES LASSONDE INC   *p1288*
705 RUE PRINCIPALE, ROUGEMONT, QC, J0L 1M0
(450) 469-4926   *SIC 2033*

JORIKI INC   *p876*
3431 MCNICOLL AVE, SCARBOROUGH, ON, M1V 2V3
(416) 754-2747   *SIC 2033*

LIQUID NUTRITION GROUP INC   *p1401*
60 CH BELVEDERE, WESTMOUNT, QC, H3Y 1P8
(514) 932-7555   *SIC 2033*

OLIVER OLIVES INC   *p495*
99 PILLSWORTH RD, BOLTON, ON, L7E 4E4
(905) 951-9096   *SIC 2033*

PIED-MONT DORA INC   *p1355*
176 RUE SAINT-JOSEPH, SAINTE-ANNE-DES-PLAINES, QC, J0N 1H0
(450) 478-0801   *SIC 2033*

SKJODT-BARRETT FOODS INC   *p500*
5 PRECIDIO CRT, BRAMPTON, ON, L6S 6B7
(905) 671-2884   *SIC 2033*

SMUCKER FOODS OF CANADA CORP   *p675*
80 WHITEHALL DR, MARKHAM, ON, L3R 0P3
(905) 940-9600   *SIC 2033*

SPECIALITES LASSONDE INC   *p1062*
3810 RUE ALFRED-LALIBERTE, BOISBRIAND, QC, J7H 1P8
(450) 979-0717   *SIC 2033*

SPECIALITES LASSONDE INC   *p1288*
170 5E AV, ROUGEMONT, QC, J0L 1M0
(450) 469-0856   *SIC 2033*

SUN RICH FRESH FOODS INC   *p258*
22151 FRASERWOOD WAY, RICHMOND, BC, V6W 1J5
(604) 244-8800   *SIC 2033*

SUN RICH FRESH FOODS INC   *p500*
35 BRAMTREE CRT UNIT 1, BRAMPTON,

ON, L6S 6G2
(905) 789-0200   *SIC 2033*

SUN-BRITE FOODS INC   *p858*
1532 COUNTY ROAD 34, RUTHVEN, ON, N0P 2G0
(519) 326-9033   *SIC 2033*

SUN-RYPE PRODUCTS LTD   *p223*
1165 ETHEL ST, KELOWNA, BC, V1Y 2W4
(250) 860-7973   *SIC 2033*

SIC 2034 Dried and dehydrated fruits, vegetables and soup mixes

2188652 ONTARIO INC   *p760*
337 FOUR MILE CREEK RD, NIAGARA ON THE LAKE, ON, L0S 1J0
(905) 262-8200   *SIC 2034*

AFD PROCESSING LTD   *p229*
5292 272 ST, LANGLEY, BC, V4W 1S3
(604) 856-3886   *SIC 2034*

AGRAWEST INVESTMENTS LIMITED *p1042*
30 HOPE ST, SOURIS, PE, C0A 2B0
(902) 687-1400   *SIC 2034*

ALIMENTS LUDA FOODS INC   *p1249*
6200 RTE TRANSCANADIENNE, POINTE-CLAIRE, QC, H9R 1B9
(514) 695-3333   *SIC 2034*

ALIMENTS TRIOVA INC, LES   *p1114*
696 RUE MARION, JOLIETTE, QC, J6E 8S2
(450) 756-6322   *SIC 2034*

HILLATON FOODS LIMITED   *p465*
1853 SAXON ST, PORT WILLIAMS, NS, B0P 1T0
(902) 582-3343   *SIC 2034*

PRODUITS ALIMENTAIRES BERTHELET INC   *p1234*
1805 RUE BERLIER, MONTREAL, QC, H7L 3S4
(514) 334-5503   *SIC 2034*

SIC 2035 Pickles, sauces, and salad dressings

768308 ONTARIO INC   *p903*
30043 JANE RD, THAMESVILLE, ON, N0P 2K0
(519) 692-4416   *SIC 2035*

CELTRADE CANADA INC   *p685*
7566 BATH RD, MISSISSAUGA, ON, L4T 1L2
(905) 678-1322   *SIC 2035*

CORAL BEACH FARMS LTD   *p224*
16351 CARRS LANDING RD, LAKE COUNTRY, BC, V4V 1A9
(250) 766-5393   *SIC 2035*

E.D. SMITH & SONS, LP   *p879*
151 MAIN ST S, SEAFORTH, ON, N0K 1W0
(800) 263-9246   *SIC 2035*

FEATURE FOODS INTERNATIONAL INC *p503*
30 FINLEY RD, BRAMPTON, ON, L6T 1A9
(905) 452-7741   *SIC 2035*

SEENERGY FOODS LIMITED   *p558*
475 NORTH RIVERMEDE RD, CONCORD, ON, L4K 3N1
(905) 660-0041   *SIC 2035*

SOYLUTIONS INC   *p1281*
1629 AV DES AFFAIRES, QUEBEC, QC, G3J 1Y7
(418) 845-9888   *SIC 2035*

SIC 2037 Frozen fruits and vegetables

BONDUELLE CANADA INC   *p1217*
600 RUE HENRI BOURASSA O BUREAU 630, MONTREAL, QC, H3M 3E2
(514) 384-4281   *SIC 2037*

FIRST CHOICE BEVERAGE INC   *p739*
265 COURTNEYPARK DR E, MISSISSAUGA, ON, L5T 2T6
(905) 565-7288   *SIC 2037*

MAISON RUSSET INC   *p1113*
142 RTE 202 BUREAU 103, HUNTINGDON, QC, J0S 1H0
(450) 264-9449   *SIC 2037*

MCCAIN FOODS GROUP INC   *p399*
8800 MAIN ST, FLORENCEVILLE-BRISTOL, NB, E7L 1B2
(506) 392-5541   *SIC 2037*

MCCAIN FOODS LIMITED   *p981*
439 KING ST W SUITE 500, TORONTO, ON, M5V 1K4
(416) 955-1700   *SIC 2037*

MCCAIN INTERNATIONAL INC   *p399*
8734 MAIN ST UNIT 3, FLORENCEVILLE-BRISTOL, NB, E7L 3G6
(506) 392-5541   *SIC 2037*

MICHEL ST-ARNEAULT INC   *p1308*
4605 AV THIBAULT, SAINT-HUBERT, QC, J3Y 3S8
(450) 445-0550   *SIC 2037*

MINUTE MAID COMPANY CANADA INC, THE   *p841*
781 LANSDOWNE ST W, PETERBOROUGH, ON, K9J 1Z2
(705) 742-8011   *SIC 2037*

NESTLE CANADA INC   *p999*
1 DOUGLAS RD, TRENTON, ON, K8V 5S7
(613) 394-4712   *SIC 2037*

NOR CLIFF FARMS INC   *p847*
888 BARRICK RD, PORT COLBORNE, ON, L3K 6H2
(905) 835-0808   *SIC 2037*

OXFORD FROZEN FOODS LIMITED   *p464*
4881 MAIN ST, OXFORD, NS, B0M 1P0
(902) 447-2320   *SIC 2037*

PACIFIC COAST FRUIT PRODUCTS LTD *p175*
34352 INDUSTRIAL WAY, ABBOTSFORD, BC, V2S 7M6
(604) 850-3505   *SIC 2037*

PENNISULA FOODS   *p418*
514 ROUTE 365, TILLEY ROAD, NB, E8M 1P4
(506) 358-6366   *SIC 2037*

TREGUNNO FRUIT FARMS INC   *p761*
15176 NIAGARA RIVER PKY, NIAGARA ON THE LAKE, ON, L0S 1J0
(905) 262-4755   *SIC 2037*

SIC 2038 Frozen specialties, nec

9223-4202 QUEBEC INC   *p1281*
15369 RUE DU PETIT-VALLON, QUEBEC, QC, G3K 0E6
(418) 840-2406   *SIC 2038*

ALIYA'S FOODS LIMITED   *p108*
6364 ROPER RD NW, EDMONTON, AB, T6B 3P9
(780) 467-4600   *SIC 2038*

APETITO CANADA LIMITED   *p501*
12 INDELL LANE, BRAMPTON, ON, L6T 3Y3
(905) 799-1022   *SIC 2038*

BOSTON PIZZA   *p1394*
52 BOUL DE LA CITE-DES-JEUNES, VAUDREUIL-DORION, QC, J7V 9L5
(450) 455-4464   *SIC 2038*

DR. OETKER CANADA LTD   *p735*
2229 DREW RD, MISSISSAUGA, ON, L5S 1E5
(905) 678-1311   *SIC 2038*

FOOD ROLL SALES (NIAGARA) LTD *p759*
8464 EARL THOMAS AVE, NIAGARA FALLS, ON, L2G 0B6
(905) 358-5747   *SIC 2038*

FREYBE GOURMET CHEF LTD   *p282*
19405 94 AVE, SURREY, BC, V4N 4E6
(604) 856-5221   *SIC 2038*

HAMEL INC   *p1138*
436 AV TANIATA, LEVIS, QC, G6W 5M6
(418) 839-4193   *SIC 2038*

MAPLE LEAF FOODS INC   *p848*
15350 OLD SIMCOE RD, PORT PERRY,

ON, L9L 1L8
(905) 985-7373   *SIC 2038*

MARSAN FOODS LIMITED   *p869*
160 THERMOS RD, SCARBOROUGH, ON, M1L 4W2
(416) 755-9262   *SIC 2038*

MOLINARO'S FINE ITALIAN FOODS LTD *p704*
2345 STANFIELD RD UNIT 50, MISSISSAUGA, ON, L4Y 3Y3
(905) 281-0352   *SIC 2038*

MORRISON LAMOTHE INC   *p878*
141 FINCHDENE SQ, SCARBOROUGH, ON, M1X 1A7
(416) 291-9121   *SIC 2038*

MORRISON LAMOTHE INC   *p914*
825 MIDDLEFIELD RD UNIT 1, TORONTO, ON, M1V 4Z7
(416) 291-6762   *SIC 2038*

MORRISON LAMOTHE INC   *p996*
399 EVANS AVE, TORONTO, ON, M8Z 1K9
(416) 255-7731   *SIC 2038*

NALEWAY FOODS LTD.   *p372*
233 HUTCHINGS ST, WINNIPEG, MB, R2X 2R4
(204) 633-6535   *SIC 2038*

PETER THE CHEF FINE FOOD LIMITED *p587*
401 HUMBERLINE DR SUITE 4, ETOBICOKE, ON, M9W 6Y4
(416) 674-5800   *SIC 2038*

PLATS DU CHEF ULC, LES   *p1091*
51 RUE KESMARK, DOLLARD-DES-ORMEAUX, QC, H9B 3J1
(514) 685-9955   *SIC 2038*

PRIVATE RECIPES LIMITED   *p505*
12 INDELL LANE, BRAMPTON, ON, L6T 3Y3
(905) 799-1022   *SIC 2038*

R.F.G. CANADA INC   *p587*
50A CLAIREPORT CRES, ETOBICOKE, ON, M9W 6P4
(416) 798-9900   *SIC 2038*

SERVICES ALIMENTAIRES DELTA DAILY-FOOD (CANADA) INC, LES   *p1284*
26 RUE J.-MARC-SEGUIN, RIGAUD, QC, J0P 1P0
(450) 451-6761   *SIC 2038*

SOFINA FOODS INC   *p689*
3340 ORLANDO DR, MISSISSAUGA, ON, L4V 1C7
(905) 673-7145   *SIC 2038*

VLR FOOD CORPORATION   *p560*
575 OSTER LANE, CONCORD, ON, L4K 2B9
(905) 669-0700   *SIC 2038*

WESTERN WAFFLES CORP   *p207*
529 ANNANCE CRT, DELTA, BC, V3M 6Y7
(604) 524-2540   *SIC 2038*

WESTERN WAFFLES CORP   *p518*
175 SAVANNAH OAKS DR, BRANTFORD, ON, N3V 1E8
(519) 759-2025   *SIC 2038*

ZINETTI FOOD PRODUCTS LTD   *p273*
17760 66 AVE, SURREY, BC, V3S 7X1
(604) 574-2028   *SIC 2038*

SIC 2041 Flour and other grain mill products

AGRI-MARCHE INC   *p1314*
236 RUE SAINTE-GENEVIEVE, SAINT-ISIDORE, QC, G0S 2S0
(418) 882-5656   *SIC 2041*

ARDENT MILLS ULC   *p1215*
2110 RUE NOTRE-DAME O, MONTREAL, QC, H3J 1N2
(514) 939-8051   *SIC 2041*

GENERAL MILLS CANADA CORPORATION *p681*
111 PILLSBURY DR, MIDLAND, ON, L4R 4L4
(705) 526-6311   *SIC 2041*

GENERAL MILLS CANADA CORPORATION

---

p695
5825 EXPLORER DR, MISSISSAUGA, ON, L4W 5P6
(905) 212-4000 *SIC 2041*

GRAIN PROCESS ENTERPRISES LIMITED *p874*
105 COMMANDER BLVD, SCARBOROUGH, ON, M1S 3M7
(416) 291-3226 *SIC 2041*

HOWSON & HOWSON LIMITED *p493*
232 WESTMORELAND ST, BLYTH, ON, N0M 1H0
(519) 523-4241 *SIC 2041*

MAPLE LEAF BREAD LTD *p555*
144 VICEROY RD, CONCORD, ON, L4K 2L8
(905) 738-1242 *SIC 2041*

NUTRASUN FOODS LIMITED PARTNERSHIP *p1422*
6201 E PRIMROSE GREEN DR, REGINA, SK, S4V 3L7
(306) 751-2040 *SIC 2041*

PRODUITS ZINDA CANADA INC *p1073*
104 AV LIBERTE, CANDIAC, QC, J5R 6X1
(450) 635-6664 *SIC 2041*

ROGERS FOODS LTD *p180*
4420 LARKIN CROSS RD, ARMSTRONG, BC, V0E 1B6
(250) 546-8744 *SIC 2041*

SOCIETE COOPERATIVE AGRICOLE LA SEIGNEURIE *p1349*
404 RUE SAINT-FRANCOIS, SAINT-NARCISSE-DE-BEAURIVAGE, QC, G0S 1W0
(418) 475-6645 *SIC 2041*

SIC 2043 Cereal breakfast foods

1661899 ONTARIO LIMITED *p719*
6980 CREDITVIEW RD, MISSISSAUGA, ON, L5N 8E2
(905) 812-7300 *SIC 2043*

CALDIC CANADA INC *p720*
6980 CREDITVIEW RD, MISSISSAUGA, ON, L5N 8E2
(905) 812-7300 *SIC 2043*

GRAIN MILLERS CANADA CORP *p1438*
1 GRAIN MILLERS DR, YORKTON, SK, S3N 3Z4
(306) 783-2931 *SIC 2043*

KELLOGG CANADA INC *p696*
5350 CREEKBANK RD, MISSISSAUGA, ON, L4W 5S1
(905) 290-5200 *SIC 2043*

KRAFT HEINZ CANADA ULC *p776*
95 MOATFIELD DR SUITE 316, NORTH YORK, ON, M3B 3L6
(416) 441-5000 *SIC 2043*

NORTHERN GOLD FOODS LTD *p247*
1725 COAST MERIDIAN RD, PORT COQUITLAM, BC, V3C 3T7
(604) 941-0731 *SIC 2043*

PEPSICO CANADA ULC *p841*
14 HUNTER ST E, PETERBOROUGH, ON, K9J 7B2
(705) 743-6330 *SIC 2043*

POST FOODS CANADA INC *p759*
5651 LEWIS AVE, NIAGARA FALLS, ON, L2G 3R8
(905) 374-7111 *SIC 2043*

RICHARDSON MILLING LIMITED *p5*
PO BOX 4615 STN MAIN, BARRHEAD, AB, T7N 1A5
(780) 674-4669 *SIC 2043*

SUNNY CRUNCH FOODS HOLDINGS LTD *p675*
200 SHIELDS CRT, MARKHAM, ON, L3R 9T5
(905) 475-0422 *SIC 2043*

WEETABIX OF CANADA LIMITED *p545*
751 D'ARCY ST, COBOURG, ON, K9A 4B1
(905) 372-5441 *SIC 2043*

SIC 2044 Rice milling

ARDENT MILLS ULC *p1426*
95 33RD ST E, SASKATOON, SK, S7K 0R8
(306) 665-7200 *SIC 2044*

SHASHI FOODS INC *p918*
55 ESANDAR DR, TORONTO, ON, M4G 4H2
(416) 645-0611 *SIC 2044*

SIC 2045 Prepared flour mixes and doughs

2104225 ONTARIO LTD *p1417*
GD LCD MAIN, REGINA, SK, S4P 2Z4
(306) 359-7400 *SIC 2045*

ADM AGRI-INDUSTRIES COMPANY *p27*
4002 BONNYBROOK RD SE, CALGARY, AB, T2G 4M9
(403) 267-5600 *SIC 2045*

ALIMENTS DA VINCI LTEE, LES *p1223*
5655 RUE BEAULIEU, MONTREAL, QC, H4E 3E4
(514) 769-1234 *SIC 2045*

ENGLISH BAY BATTER L.P. *p205*
904 CLIVEDEN AVE, DELTA, BC, V3M 5R5
(604) 540-0622 *SIC 2045*

NOVALI GOURMET INC *p1066*
14 RUE DE MONTGOLFIER, BOUCHERVILLE, QC, J4B 7Y4
(450) 655-7790 *SIC 2045*

SIC 2046 Wet corn milling

ADM AGRI-INDUSTRIES COMPANY *p1072*
155 AV D'IBERIA, CANDIAC, QC, J5R 3H1
(450) 659-1911 *SIC 2046*

INGREDION CANADA CORPORATION *p710*
90 BURNHAMTHORPE RD W UNIT 1600, MISSISSAUGA, ON, L5B 0H9
(905) 281-7950 *SIC 2046*

SIC 2047 Dog and cat food

BIO BISCUIT INC *p1311*
5505 AV TRUDEAU BUREAU 15, SAINT-HYACINTHE, QC, J2S 1H5
(450) 778-1349 *SIC 2047*

BIO BISCUIT INC *p1311*
5505 AV TRUDEAU BUREAU 15, SAINT-HYACINTHE, QC, J2S 1H5
(450) 778-1349 *SIC 2047*

GESTION J. M. BRASSEUR INC *p1065*
1361 RUE GRAHAM-BELL, BOUCHERVILLE, QC, J4B 6A1
(450) 655-3155 *SIC 2047*

NESTLE CANADA INC *p137*
5128 54 ST, INNISFAIL, AB, T4G 1S1
(403) 227-3777 *SIC 2047*

NESTLE CANADA INC *p714*
2500 ROYAL WINDSOR DR, MISSISSAUGA, ON, L5J 1K8
(905) 822-1611 *SIC 2047*

PLB INTERNATIONAL INC *p1067*
1361 RUE GRAHAM-BELL, BOUCHERVILLE, QC, J4B 6A1
(450) 655-3155 *SIC 2047*

ROLLOVER PREMIUM PET FOOD LTD *p136*
12 11 AVE SE, HIGH RIVER, AB, T1V 1E6
SIC 2047

SIMMONS PET FOOD ON, INC *p727*
8 FALCONER DR, MISSISSAUGA, ON, L5N 1B1
(905) 826-3870 *SIC 2047*

SIC 2048 Prepared feeds, nec

ABSORBENT PRODUCTS LTD *p218*
724 SARCEE ST E, KAMLOOPS, BC, V2H 1E7
(250) 372-1600 *SIC 2048*

ALL TREAT FARMS LIMITED *p479*
7963 WELLINGTON ROAD 109 RR 4, ARTHUR, ON, N0G 1A0
(519) 848-3145 *SIC 2048*

ARMSTRONG MILLING CO. LTD *p607*
1021 HALDIMAND RD UNIT 20, HAGERSVILLE, ON, N0A 1H0
(905) 779-2473 *SIC 2048*

BARTELSE HOLDINGS LIMITED *p535*
162 SAVAGE DR, CAMBRIDGE, ON, N1T 1S4
(519) 622-2500 *SIC 2048*

BELISLE SOLUTION-NUTRITION INC *p1348*
196 CH DES PATRIOTES, SAINT-MATHIAS-SUR-RICHELIEU, QC, J3L 6A7
(450) 658-8733 *SIC 2048*

CARGILL LIMITED *p1035*
404 MAIN ST, WOODSTOCK, ON, N4S 7X5
(519) 539-8561 *SIC 2048*

CERMAQ CANADA LTD *p283*
61 4TH ST, TOFINO, BC, V0R 2Z0
(250) 725-1255 *SIC 2048*

CLARENCE FARM SERVICES LIMITED *p468*
70 INDUSTRIAL AVE, TRURO, NS, B2N 6V2
(902) 895-5434 *SIC 2048*

CLEARBROOK GRAIN & MILLING COMPANY LIMITED *p176*
2425 TOWNLINE RD, ABBOTSFORD, BC, V2T 6L6
(604) 850-1108 *SIC 2048*

COMAX, COOPERATIVE AGRICOLE *p1310*
4880 RUE DES SEIGNEURS E, SAINT-HYACINTHE, QC, J2R 1Z5
(450) 799-3211 *SIC 2048*

COOPERATIVE AGRICOLE DES APPALACHES *p1133*
303 CH DE LA GROSSE-?LE, LAURIERVILLE, QC, G0S 1P0
(819) 385-4272 *SIC 2048*

COREY NUTRITION COMPANY INC *p402*
136 HODGSON RD, FREDERICTON, NB, E3C 2G4
(506) 444-7744 *SIC 2048*

ELMIRA PET PRODUCTS LTD *p568*
35 MARTIN'S LANE, ELMIRA, ON, N3B 2Z5
(519) 669-3330 *SIC 2048*

ESSEX TOPCROP SALES LIMITED *p570*
904 COUNTY RD 8, ESSEX, ON, N8M 2Y1
(519) 776-6411 *SIC 2048*

EWOS CANADA LTD *p276*
7721 132 ST, SURREY, BC, V3W 4M8
(604) 591-6368 *SIC 2048*

GRAND VALLEY FORTIFIERS LIMITED *p533*
486 MAIN ST, CAMBRIDGE, ON, N1R 5S7
(519) 621-5204 *SIC 2048*

GROBER INC *p536*
162 SAVAGE DR, CAMBRIDGE, ON, N1T 1S4
(519) 622-2500 *SIC 2048*

JAKE FRIESEN INC *p177*
2425 TOWNLINE RD, ABBOTSFORD, BC, V2T 6L6
(604) 850-1108 *SIC 2048*

KENPAL FARM PRODUCTS INC *p541*
69819 LONDON RD SUITE 1, CENTRALIA, ON, N0M 1K0
(519) 228-6444 *SIC 2048*

MAPLE LEAF FOODS INC *p366*
607 DAWSON RD N SUITE 555, WINNIPEG, MB, R2J 0T2
(204) 233-7347 *SIC 2048*

MARBRO CAPITAL LIMITED *p568*
35 EARL MARTIN DR, ELMIRA, ON, N3B 3L4
(519) 669-5171 *SIC 2048*

MASTERFEEDS INC *p657*
1020 HARGRIEVE RD SUITE 1, LONDON, ON, N6E 1P5
(519) 685-4300 *SIC 2048*

MONDOU, REAL INC *p1153*

12429 RTE ARTHUR-SAUVE, MIRABEL, QC, J7N 2C2
(450) 258-2817 *SIC 2048*

NORTHEAST NUTRITION INC *p469*
494 WILLOW ST, TRURO, NS, B2N 6X8
(902) 893-9449 *SIC 2048*

RIDLEY INC *p366*
34 TERRACON PL, WINNIPEG, MB, R2J 4G7
(204) 956-1717 *SIC 2048*

RIDLEY MF INC *p366*
715 MARION ST, WINNIPEG, MB, R2J 0K6
(204) 233-1112 *SIC 2048*

RITCHIE-SMITH FEEDS INC *p175*
33777 ENTERPRISE AVE, ABBOTSFORD, BC, V2S 7T9
(604) 859-7128 *SIC 2048*

SKRETTING CANADA INC *p291*
1370 E KENT AVE SOUTH, VANCOUVER, BC, V5X 2Y2
(604) 325-0302 *SIC 2048*

SKRETTING CANADA INC *p291*
1370 E KENT AVE SOUTH, VANCOUVER, BC, V5X 2Y2
(604) 325-0302 *SIC 2048*

SPB SOLUTIONS INC *p1067*
1350 RUE NEWTON, BOUCHERVILLE, QC, J4B 5H2
(450) 655-3505 *SIC 2048*

TROUW NUTRITION CANADA INC *p197*
46255 CHILLIWACK CENTRAL RD, CHILLIWACK, BC, V2P 1J7
(604) 702-4500 *SIC 2048*

TROUW NUTRITION CANADA INC *p602*
150 RESEARCH LANE SUITE 200, GUELPH, ON, N1G 4T2
(519) 823-7000 *SIC 2048*

TROUW NUTRITION CANADA INC *p1310*
4780 RUE MARTINEAU, SAINT-HYACINTHE, QC, J2R 1V1
(450) 799-5011 *SIC 2048*

W-S FEED & SUPPLIES LIMITED *p902*
45 MARIA ST, TAVISTOCK, ON, N0B 2R0
(519) 664-2237 *SIC 2048*

WETASKIWIN CO-OPERATIVE ASSOCIATION LIMITED *p172*
4707 40 AVE, WETASKIWIN, AB, T9A 2B8
(780) 352-9121 *SIC 2048*

SIC 2051 Bread, cake, and related products

138984 CANADA LTEE *p1217*
6744 RUE HUTCHISON, MONTREAL, QC, H3N 1Y4
(514) 270-3024 *SIC 2051*

1721502 ONTARIO INC *p729*
5880 FALBOURNE ST, MISSISSAUGA, ON, L5R 0E6
(905) 238-8328 *SIC 2051*

1726837 ONTARIO INC *p577*
10 FOUR SEASONS PL SUITE 601, ETOBICOKE, ON, M9B 6H7
(416) 695-8900 *SIC 2051*

176061 CANADA INC *p1217*
6915 AV QUERBES, MONTREAL, QC, H3N 2B3
(514) 270-5567 *SIC 2051*

2104225 ONTARIO LTD *p389*
1485 CHEVRIER BLVD, WINNIPEG, MB, R3T 1Y7
(416) 252-7323 *SIC 2051*

2104225 ONTARIO LTD *p573*
1425 THE QUEENSWAY, ETOBICOKE, ON, M8Z 1T3
(416) 252-7323 *SIC 2051*

2104225 ONTARIO LTD *p629*
83 RAILWAY ST, KINGSTON, ON, K7K 2L7
(613) 548-4434 *SIC 2051*

2104225 ONTARIO LTD *p1145*
2700 BOUL JACQUES-CARTIER E BUREAU 67, LONGUEUIL, QC, J4N 1L5
(450) 448-7246 *SIC 2051*

2104225 ONTARIO LTD *p1242*

150 BOUL INDUSTRIEL, NAPIERVILLE, QC, J0J 1L0

(450) 245-7542 *SIC* 2051

2104225 ONTARIO LTD *p1419*
1310 OTTAWA ST, REGINA, SK, S4R 1P4

(306) 359-3096 *SIC* 2051

312407 ALBERTA LTD *p92*
14728 119 AVE NW, EDMONTON, AB, T5L 2P2

(780) 454-5797 *SIC* 2051

7979134 CANADA INC *p1182*
7075 AV CASGRAIN, MONTREAL, QC, H2S 3A3

SIC 2051

838116 ONTARIO INC *p548*
35 ADESSO DR SUITE 18, CONCORD, ON, L4K 3C7

(905) 760-0850 *SIC* 2051

8956642 CANADA CORP *p868*
757 WARDEN AVE UNIT 4, SCARBOROUGH, ON, M1L 4B5

(416) 759-2000 *SIC* 2051

ANNETTE'S DONUTS LIMITED *p997*
1965 LAWRENCE AVE W, TORONTO, ON, M9N 1H5

(416) 656-3444 *SIC* 2051

APPLE VALLEY FOODS INCORPORATED *p459*
14 CALKIN DR, KENTVILLE, NS, B4N 1J5

(902) 679-4701 *SIC* 2051

BAGOS BUN BAKERY LTD *p33*
303 58 AVE SE SUITE 3, CALGARY, AB, T2H 0P3

(403) 252-3660 *SIC* 2051

BAKERY DELUXE COMPANY *p794*
50 MARMORA ST, NORTH YORK, ON, M9M 2X5

(416) 746-1010 *SIC* 2051

BENEVITO FOODS INC *p577*
17 VICKERS RD, ETOBICOKE, ON, M9B 1C1

SIC 2051

BOULANGERIE ANDALOS INC *p1325*
350 BOUL LEBEAU, SAINT-LAURENT, QC, H4N 1R5

(514) 856-0983 *SIC* 2051

BOULANGERIE ET FROMENT ET DE SEVE INC *p1171*
2355 RUE BEAUBIEN E, MONTREAL, QC, H2G 1N3

(514) 722-4301 *SIC* 2051

BOULANGERIE GADOUA LTEE *p1122*
170 BOUL TASCHEREAU BUREAU 220, LA PRAIRIE, QC, J5R 5H6

(450) 245-3326 *SIC* 2051

BOULANGERIE LES MOULINS LA FAYETTE INC *p1352*
7 AV DE L'EGLISE, SAINT-SAUVEUR, QC, J0R 1R0

(450) 227-2632 *SIC* 2051

BOULANGERIE PATISSERIE DUMAS INC *p1266*
2391 AV WATT, QUEBEC, QC, G1P 3X2

(418) 658-2037 *SIC* 2051

BOULANGERIES RENE ULC, LES *p1053*
375 AV LEE, BAIE-D'URFE, QC, H9X 3S3

(514) 457-4500 *SIC* 2051

BOULANGERIES WESTON QUEBEC LIMITEE *p1145*
2700 BOUL JACQUES-CARTIER E, LONGUEUIL, QC, J4N 1L5

(450) 448-7246 *SIC* 2051

BOULART INC *p1127*
1355 32E AV, LACHINE, QC, H8T 3H2

(514) 631-4040 *SIC* 2051

BOWNESS BAKERY (ALBERTA) INC *p21*
4280 23 ST NE SUITE 1, CALGARY, AB, T2E 6X7

(403) 250-9760 *SIC* 2051

BYBLOS BAKERY LTD *p21*
2479 23 ST NE, CALGARY, AB, T2E 8J8

(403) 250-3711 *SIC* 2051

C.B. INVESTMENTS LTD *p158*
28042 HWY 11 SUITE 207, RED DEER

COUNTY, AB, T4S 2L4

(403) 346-2948 *SIC* 2051

CALGARY ITALIAN BAKERY LTD *p34*
5310 5 ST SE, CALGARY, AB, T2H 1L2

(403) 255-3515 *SIC* 2051

CANADA BREAD COMPANY, LIMITED *p14*
4320 80 AVE SE, CALGARY, AB, T2C 4N6

(403) 203-1675 *SIC* 2051

CANADA BREAD COMPANY, LIMITED *p105*
12151 160 ST NW, EDMONTON, AB, T5V 1M4

(780) 451-4663 *SIC* 2051

CANADA BREAD COMPANY, LIMITED *p226*
6350 203 ST, LANGLEY, BC, V2Y 1L9

(604) 532-8200 *SIC* 2051

CANADA BREAD COMPANY, LIMITED *p406*
235 BOTSFORD ST, MONCTON, NB, E1C 4X9

(506) 857-9158 *SIC* 2051

CANADA BREAD COMPANY, LIMITED *p550*
711 RIVERMEDE RD, CONCORD, ON, L4K 2G9

(905) 660-3034 *SIC* 2051

CANADA BREAD COMPANY, LIMITED *p577*
10 FOUR SEASONS PL SUITE 1200, ETOBICOKE, ON, M9B 6H7

(416) 622-2040 *SIC* 2051

CANADA BREAD COMPANY, LIMITED *p578*
35 RAKELY CRT SUITE 1, ETOBICOKE, ON, M9C 5A5

(416) 622-2040 *SIC* 2051

CANADA BREAD COMPANY, LIMITED *p993*
130 CAWTHRA AVE, TORONTO, ON, M6N 3C2

(416) 626-4382 *SIC* 2051

CHEZ PIGGY RESTAURANT LIMITED *p630*
68R PRINCESS ST, KINGSTON, ON, K7L 1A5

(613) 549-7673 *SIC* 2051

CINNAGARD INC *p533*
120 MAIN ST UNIT 3, CAMBRIDGE, ON, N1R 1V7

(519) 622-3188 *SIC* 2051

CITY BREAD CO. LTD, THE *p371*
238 DUFFERIN AVE, WINNIPEG, MB, R2W 2X6

(204) 586-8409 *SIC* 2051

CITY BREAD CO. LTD, THE *p371*
232 JARVIS AVE, WINNIPEG, MB, R2W 3A1

(204) 586-8409 *SIC* 2051

COMMISSO BROS. & RACCO ITALIAN BAKERY INC *p992*
8 KINCORT ST, TORONTO, ON, M6M 3E1

(416) 651-7671 *SIC* 2051

CROISSANTS D' OLIVIER LTD, LES *p200*
12 KING EDWARD ST UNIT 101, COQUITLAM, BC, V3K 0E7

(778) 285-8662 *SIC* 2051

DARE FOODS LIMITED *p265*
6751 ELMBRIDGE WAY, RICHMOND, BC, V7C 4N1

(604) 233-1117 *SIC* 2051

DARE FOODS LIMITED *p538*
25 CHERRY BLOSSOM RD, CAMBRIDGE, ON, N3H 4R7

(519) 893-5500 *SIC* 2051

DARE FOODS LIMITED *p1322*
845 AV SAINT-CHARLES, SAINT-LAMBERT, QC, J4P 2A2

(450) 671-6121 *SIC* 2051

DARE FOODS LIMITED *p1360*
15 RANG DUBUC, SAINTE-MARTINE, QC, J0S 1V0

(450) 427-8410 *SIC* 2051

DEL'S PASTRY LIMITED *p574*
344 BERING AVE, ETOBICOKE, ON, M8Z 3A7

(416) 231-4383 *SIC* 2051

DIMPFLMEIER BAKERY LIMITED *p574*
26 ADVANCE RD, ETOBICOKE, ON, M8Z 2T4

(416) 236-2701 *SIC* 2051

DOUGH DELIGHT LTD *p1002*

144 VICEROY RD, VAUGHAN, ON, L4K 2L8

SIC 2051

ENGEL'S BAKERIES LTD *p22*
4709 14 ST NE UNIT 6, CALGARY, AB, T2E 6S4

(403) 250-9560 *SIC* 2051

FGF BRANDS INC *p997*
2071 ORMONT DR, TORONTO, ON, M9L 2W6

(905) 761-3333 *SIC* 2051

FRANCE DELICES INC *p1166*
5065 RUE ONTARIO E, MONTREAL, QC, H1V 3V2

(514) 259-2291 *SIC* 2051

FURLANI'S FOOD CORPORATION *p695*
1730 AIMCO BLVD, MISSISSAUGA, ON, L4W 1V1

(905) 602-6102 *SIC* 2051

FUTURE BAKERY LIMITED *p574*
106 NORTH QUEEN ST, ETOBICOKE, ON, M8Z 2E2

(416) 231-1491 *SIC* 2051

GIVE AND GO PREPARED FOODS CORP *p584*
15 MARMAC DR UNIT 200, ETOBICOKE, ON, M9W 1E7

(416) 675-0114 *SIC* 2051

GIZELLA PASTRY ULC *p286*
3436 LOUGHEED HWY, VANCOUVER, BC, V5M 2A4

(604) 253-5220 *SIC* 2051

GROUPE PREMIERE MOISSON INC *p1394*
189 BOUL HARWOOD, VAUDREUIL-DORION, QC, J7V 1Y3

(450) 455-2827 *SIC* 2051

HANDI FOODS LTD *p793*
190 NORELCO DR, NORTH YORK, ON, M9L 1S4

(416) 743-6634 *SIC* 2051

ISLAND CITY BAKING COMPANY INC *p255*
12753 VULCAN WAY SUITE 105, RICHMOND, BC, V6V 3C8

(604) 278-6979 *SIC* 2051

ITALIAN HOME BAKERY LIMITED *p585*
271 ATTWELL DR, ETOBICOKE, ON, M9W 5B9

(416) 674-4555 *SIC* 2051

KRAFT HEINZ CANADA ULC *p570*
2150 LAKE SHORE BLVD W, ETOBICOKE, ON, M8V 1A3

(416) 506-6000 *SIC* 2051

KRAFT HEINZ CANADA ULC *p871*
370 PROGRESS AVE, SCARBOROUGH, ON, M1P 2Z4

(416) 291-3713 *SIC* 2051

KRAFT HEINZ CANADA ULC *p1166*
3055 RUE VIAU BUREAU 4, MONTREAL, QC, H1V 3J5

(514) 259-6921 *SIC* 2051

LANTHIER BAKERY LTD *p476*
58 DOMINION ST, ALEXANDRIA, ON, K0C 1A0

(613) 525-2435 *SIC* 2051

LOBLAWS INC *p1025*
2950 DOUGALL AVE SUITE 18, WINDSOR, ON, N9E 1S2

(519) 969-3087 *SIC* 2051

MANOUCHER FINE FOODS INC *p795*
703 CLAYSON RD, NORTH YORK, ON, M9M 2H4

(416) 747-1234 *SIC* 2051

MAPLEHURST BAKERIES INC *p504*
379 ORENDA RD, BRAMPTON, ON, L6T 1G6

(905) 791-7400 *SIC* 2051

MAPLEHURST BAKERIES INC *p1416*
1700 PARK ST, REGINA, SK, S4N 6B2

(306) 359-7400 *SIC* 2051

MARTIN DESSERT INC *p1279*
665 RUE DES ROCAILLES, QUEBEC, QC, G2J 1A9

(418) 622-0220 *SIC* 2051

MCBUNS BAKERY *p405*
122 SHEDIAC RD, MONCTON, NB, E1A

2R9

(506) 858-1700 *SIC* 2051

MRS. DUNSTER'S (1996) INC *p418*
30 LEONARD DR, SUSSEX, NB, E4E 5T5

(506) 433-9333 *SIC* 2051

MRS. WILLMAN'S BAKING LIMITED *p24*
4826 11 ST NE UNIT 4, CALGARY, AB, T2E 2W7

SIC 2051

MULTI-MARQUES INC *p1166*
3265 RUE VIAU, MONTREAL, QC, H1V 3J5

(514) 255-9492 *SIC* 2051

MULTI-MARQUES INC *p1256*
553 AV ROYALE, QUEBEC, QC, G1E 1Y4

(418) 661-4400 *SIC* 2051

MULTI-MARQUES INC *p1297*
1295 1E AV O, SAINT-COME-LINIERE, QC, G0M 1J0

(418) 685-3351 *SIC* 2051

NONUTS BAKING CO INC *p793*
1295 ORMONT DR, NORTH YORK, ON, M9L 2W6

(905) 532-9517 *SIC* 2051

NUSTEF FOODS LIMITED *p708*
2440 CAWTHRA RD, MISSISSAUGA, ON, L5A 2X1

(905) 896-3060 *SIC* 2051

ORANGE PASTRIES INC *p1028*
39 TURNING LEAF DR, WOODBRIDGE, ON, L4H 2J5

(289) 236-0270 *SIC* 2051

ORIGINAL BAKED QUALITY PITA DIPS INC, L' *p1106*
320 BOUL SAINT-JOSEPH, GATINEAU, QC, J8Y 3Y8

(819) 525-6555 *SIC* 2051

ORIGINAL CHIMNEYS INC *p871*
300 BOROUGH DR, SCARBOROUGH, ON, M1P 4P5

(416) 697-8884 *SIC* 2051

PATISSERIE CHEVALIER INC *p1368*
155 RUE DU PARC-INDUSTRIEL, SHAWINIGAN, QC, G9N 6T5

(819) 537-8807 *SIC* 2051

PATISSERIE GAUDET INC *p1044*
1048 RUE MACDONALD, ACTON VALE, QC, J0H 1A0

(450) 546-3221 *SIC* 2051

PBF PITA BREAD FACTORY LTD *p182*
8000 WINSTON ST, BURNABY, BC, V5A 2H5

(604) 528-6111 *SIC* 2051

PETITE BRETONNE INC, LA *p1059*
1210 BOUL MICHELE-BOHEC, BLAINVILLE, QC, J7C 5S4

(450) 435-3381 *SIC* 2051

PURITY FACTORIES LIMITED *p433*
96 BLACKMARSH RD, ST. JOHN'S, NL, A1E 1S8

(709) 579-2035 *SIC* 2051

QUALI DESSERTS INC *p1166*
5067 RUE ONTARIO E, MONTREAL, QC, H1V 3V2

(514) 259-2415 *SIC* 2051

SAGINAW ENTERPRISES LTD *p280*
2520 190 ST SUITE 102, SURREY, BC, V3Z 3W6

(604) 385-2520 *SIC* 2051

SILVERSTEIN'S BAKERY LIMITED *p977*
195 MCCAUL ST, TORONTO, ON, M5T 1W6

(416) 598-3478 *SIC* 2051

SILVERSTEIN'S HOLDINGS INC *p977*
195 MCCAUL ST, TORONTO, ON, M5T 1W6

(416) 598-3478 *SIC* 2051

SOBEYS WEST INC *p381*
1525 ERIN ST, WINNIPEG, MB, R3E 2T2

(204) 775-0344 *SIC* 2051

STUYVER'S BAKESTUDIO *p230*
27353 58 CRES UNIT 101, LANGLEY, BC, V4W 3W7

(604) 607-7760 *SIC* 2051

SUNRISE BAKERY LTD *p94*
14728 119 AVE NW, EDMONTON, AB, T5L 2P2

▲ Public Company   ■ Public Company Family Member   **HQ** Headquarters   **BR** Branch   **SL** Single Location

(780) 454-5797   SIC 2051
SURATI SWEET MART LIMITED   p875
300 MIDDLEFIELD RD, SCARBOROUGH,
ON, M1S 5B1
(416) 752-3366   SIC 2051
TWI FOODS INC   p589
40 SHAFT RD SUITE 20, ETOBICOKE, ON,
M9W 4M2
(647) 775-1400   SIC 2051
VIBRANT HEALTH PRODUCTS INC   p175
34494 MCLARY AVE, ABBOTSFORD, BC,
V2S 4N8
(604) 850-5600   SIC 2051
VILLA DI MANNO BAKERY LTD   p560
22 BUTTERMILL AVE, CONCORD, ON, L4K
3X4
(905) 761-9191   SIC 2051
WESTON BAKERIES LIMITED   p901
695 MARTINDALE RD, SUDBURY, ON, P3E
4H6
(705) 673-4185   SIC 2051
WESTON FOODS (CANADA) INC   p576
1425 THE QUEENSWAY, ETOBICOKE, ON,
M8Z 1T3
(416) 252-7323   SIC 2051
WHOLESOME HARVEST BAKING LTD   p19
4320 80 AVE SE, CALGARY, AB, T2C 4N6
(403) 203-1675   SIC 2051
WHOLESOME HARVEST BAKING LTDp561
144 VICEROY RD, CONCORD, ON, L4K
2L8
(905) 738-1242   SIC 2051

SIC 2052 Cookies and crackers

BISCUITS LECLERC LTEE   p1292
91 RUE DE ROTTERDAM, SAINT-
AUGUSTIN-DE-DESMAURES, QC, G3A
1T1
(418) 878-2601   SIC 2052
BISCUITS LECLERC LTEE   p1292
70 RUE DE ROTTERDAM, SAINT-
AUGUSTIN-DE-DESMAURES, QC, G3A
1S9
(418) 878-2601   SIC 2052
COMMERCIAL BAKERIES CORP   p786
45 TORBARRIE RD, NORTH YORK, ON,
M3L 1G5
(416) 247-5478   SIC 2052
ELITE SWEETS BRANDS INC   p499
9 EDVAC DR, BRAMPTON, ON, L6S 5X8
(905) 790-9428   SIC 2052
ENGLISH BAY BATTER (TORONTO) INC
p739
6925 INVADER CRES, MISSISSAUGA, ON,
L5T 2B7
(905) 670-1110   SIC 2052
FAR EAST FOOD PRODUCTS LIMITEDp855
273 ENFORD RD, RICHMOND HILL, ON,
L4C 3E9
(905) 883-8717   SIC 2052
PURATOS CANADA INC   p742
520 SLATE DR, MISSISSAUGA, ON, L5T
0A1
(905) 362-3668   SIC 2052
SELECTION DU PATISSIER INC   p1253
450 2E AV, PORTNEUF, QC, G0A 2Y0
(418) 286-3400   SIC 2052
SOLIS FOODS CORPORATION INC   p513
79 EASTON RD, BRANTFORD, ON, N3P
1J4
(519) 349-2020   SIC 2052
TERRA COTTA FOODS LTD   p594
36 ARMSTRONG AVE UNIT 9, GEORGE-
TOWN, ON, L7G 4R9
(905) 877-4216   SIC 2052
THINADDICTIVES INC   p1327
258 BOUL LEBEAU, SAINT-LAURENT, QC,
H4N 1R4
(514) 484-4321   SIC 2052
VOORTMAN COOKIES LIMITED   p525
4475 NORTH SERVICE RD SUITE 600,
BURLINGTON, ON, L7L 4X7

(905) 335-9500   SIC 2052

---

*SIC 2053 Frozen bakery products, except
bread*

2168587 ONTARIO LTD   p781
55 CANARCTIC DR SUITE UPPER,
NORTH YORK, ON, M3J 2N7
(416) 661-9455   SIC 2053
2168587 ONTARIO LTD   p794
50 MARMORA ST, NORTH YORK, ON,
M9M 2X5
(416) 661-7744   SIC 2053
8561567 CANADA INC   p1114
585 RUE SAINT-PIERRE S, JOLIETTE, QC,
J6E 8R8
(450) 759-6361   SIC 2053
BACKERHAUS VEIT LTD   p737
6745 INVADER CRES, MISSISSAUGA, ON,
L5T 2B6
(905) 850-9229   SIC 2053
BRIDOR INC   p1064
1370 RUE GRAHAM-BELL,
BOUCHERVILLE, QC, J4B 6H5
(450) 641-1265   SIC 2053
FIERA FOODS COMPANY   p794
50 MARMORA ST, NORTH YORK, ON,
M9M 2X5
(416) 746-1010   SIC 2053
ICE CREAM UNLIMITED INC   p372
55 PLYMOUTH ST, WINNIPEG, MB, R2X
2V5
SIC 2053
MAPLEHURST BAKERIES INC   p724
2095 MEADOWVALE BLVD, MISSIS-
SAUGA, ON, L5N 5N1
(905) 567-0660   SIC 2053
RICH PRODUCTS OF CANADA LIMITED
p592
12 HAGEY AVE, FORT ERIE, ON, L2A 1W3
(905) 871-2605   SIC 2053
TRADITION FINE FOODS LTD   p869
663 WARDEN AVE, SCARBOROUGH, ON,
M1L 3Z5
(416) 444-4777   SIC 2053
WOWU FACTOR DESSERTS LTD   p161
152 CREE RD, SHERWOOD PARK, AB,
T8A 3X8
(780) 464-0303   SIC 2053

SIC 2061 Raw cane sugar

REDPATH SUGAR LTD   p943
95 QUEENS QUAY E, TORONTO, ON, M5E
1A3
(416) 366-3561   SIC 2061
STREAMLINE FOODS INC.   p492
315 UNIVERSITY AVE, BELLEVILLE, ON,
K8N 5T7
(613) 961-1265   SIC 2061

SIC 2062 Cane sugar refining

LANTIC INC   p295
123 ROGERS ST, VANCOUVER, BC, V6A
3N2
(604) 253-1131   SIC 2062
LANTIC INC   p1167
4026 RUE NOTRE-DAME E, MONTREAL,
QC, H1W 2K3
(514) 527-8686   SIC 2062

---

*SIC 2064 Candy and other confectionery
products*

2121361 ONTARIO INC   p847
6829 DALE RD, PORT HOPE, ON, L1A 3V6
(905) 885-9237   SIC 2064
ALIMENTS JARDI INC, LES   p1372
4650 BOUL DE PORTLAND, SHER-

BROOKE, QC, J1L 0H6
(819) 820-1003   SIC 2064
ALIMENTS NOBLE INC   p1249
250 AV AVRO, POINTE-CLAIRE, QC, H9R
6B1
(514) 426-0680   SIC 2064
ALLAN CANDY COMPANY LIMITED, THE
p704
3 ROBERT SPECK PKY SUITE 250, MIS-
SISSAUGA, ON, L4Z 2G5
(905) 270-2221   SIC 2064
ALLAN CANDY COMPANY LIMITED, THE
p1110
850 BOUL INDUSTRIEL, GRANBY, QC, J2J
1B8
(450) 372-1080   SIC 2064
BONBONS OINK OINK INC, LES   p1227
4810 RUE JEAN-TALON O, MONTREAL,
QC, H4P 2N5
(514) 731-4555   SIC 2064
CAVALIER CANDIES LTD   p374
185 BANNATYNE AVE, WINNIPEG, MB,
R3B 0R4
(204) 957-8777   SIC 2064
CE DE CANDY COMPANY LIMITED   p755
150 HARRY WALKER PKY N, NEWMAR-
KET, ON, L3Y 7B2
(905) 853-7171   SIC 2064
CHOCOLATERIE LA CABOSSE D'OR INC
p1244
973 CH OZIAS-LEDUC, OTTERBURN
PARK, QC, J3G 4S6
(450) 464-6937   SIC 2064
COLLINS CONCESSIONS LIMITED   p758
8621 EARL THOMAS AVE, NIAGARA
FALLS, ON, L2G 0B5
SIC 2064
DARE FOODS LIMITED   p683
725 STEELES AVE E, MILTON, ON, L9T
5H1
(905) 875-1223   SIC 2064
FERRERO CANADA LIMITED   p771
100 SHEPPARD AVE E SUITE 900, NORTH
YORK, ON, M2N 6N5
(416) 590-0775   SIC 2064
GANONG BROS., LIMITED   p418
1 CHOCOLATE DR, ST STEPHEN, NB, E3L
2X5
(506) 465-5600   SIC 2064
HERSHEY CANADA INC   p443
375 PLEASANT ST, DARTMOUTH, NS, B2Y
4N4
SIC 2064
HERSHEY CANADA INC   p696
5750 EXPLORER DR SUITE 400, MISSIS-
SAUGA, ON, L4W 0A9
(905) 602-9200   SIC 2064
KARMA CANDY INC   p611
356 EMERALD ST N, HAMILTON, ON, L8L
8K6
(905) 527-6222   SIC 2064
KERR BROS. LIMITED   p575
956 ISLINGTON AVE, ETOBICOKE, ON,
M8Z 4P6
(416) 252-7341   SIC 2064
KRAFT HEINZ CANADA ULC   p991
277 GLADSTONE AVE, TORONTO, ON,
M6J 3L9
(416) 667-6224   SIC 2064
MARS CANADA INC   p495
12315 COLERAINE DR, BOLTON, ON, L7E
3B4
(905) 857-5620   SIC 2064
MARS CANADA INC   p495
37 HOLLAND DR, BOLTON, ON, L7E 5S4
(905) 857-5700   SIC 2064
MARS CANADA INC   p755
285 HARRY WALKER PKY N, NEWMAR-
KET, ON, L3Y 7B3
(905) 853-6000   SIC 2064
**NELLSON NUTRACEUTIQUE CANADA,
INC**   p1128
1125 50E AV, LACHINE, QC, H8T 3P3
(514) 380-8383   SIC 2064

NESTLE CANADA INC   p995
72 STERLING RD, TORONTO, ON, M6R
2B6
(416) 535-2181   SIC 2064
OAK LEAF CONFECTIONS CO.   p869
440 COMSTOCK RD, SCARBOROUGH,
ON, M1L 2H6
(416) 751-0740   SIC 2064
ROGERS' CHOCOLATES LTD   p338
4253 COMMERCE CIR, VICTORIA, BC,
V8Z 4M2
(250) 384-7021   SIC 2064
TOOTSIE ROLL OF CANADA ULC   p559
519 NORTH RIVERMEDE RD, CONCORD,
ON, L4K 3N1
(905) 738-9108   SIC 2064

SIC 2066 Chocolate and cocoa products

BARRY CALLEBAUT CANADA INC   p1311
2950 RUE NELSON, SAINT-HYACINTHE,
QC, J2S 1Y7
(450) 774-9131   SIC 2066
**BLOMMER CHOCOLATE COMPANY OF
CANADA INC**   p539
103 SECOND AVE, CAMPBELLFORD, ON,
K0L 1L0
(705) 653-5821   SIC 2066
BROCKMANN CHOCOLATE INC   p208
7863 PROGRESS WAY, DELTA, BC, V4G
1A3
(604) 946-4111   SIC 2066
CHEWTERS CHOCOLATES (1992) INCp205
1648 DERWENT WAY, DELTA, BC, V3M
6R9
(888) 515-7117   SIC 2066
CHOCOLAT LAMONTAGNE INC   p1373
4045 RUE DE LA GARLOCK, SHER-
BROOKE, QC, J1L 1W9
(819) 564-1014   SIC 2066
COCOCO CHOCOLATIERS INC   p22
2320 2 AVE SE, CALGARY, AB, T2E 6J9
(403) 265-5777   SIC 2066
HERSHEY CANADA INC   p881
1 HERSHEY DR, SMITHS FALLS, ON, K7A
4T8
SIC 2066
NUTRIART INC   p1262
550 AV GODIN, QUEBEC, QC, G1M 2K2
(418) 687-5320   SIC 2066
PURDY, R.C. CHOCOLATES LTD   p291
8330 CHESTER ST, VANCOUVER, BC,
V5X 3Y7
(604) 454-2777   SIC 2066

SIC 2067 Chewing gum

WRIGLEY CANADA INC   p766
3389 STEELES AVE E, NORTH YORK, ON,
M2H 3S8
(416) 449-8600   SIC 2067

---

*SIC 2068 Salted and roasted nuts and
seeds*

**ENTREPRISE COMMERCIALE SHAH LIMI-
TEE, L'**   p1333
3401 RUE DOUGLAS-B.-FLOREANI,
SAINT-LAURENT, QC, H4S 1Y6
(514) 336-2462   SIC 2068
GOLDEN BOY FOODS LTD   p182
7725 LOUGHEED HWY, BURNABY, BC,
V5A 4V8
(604) 433-2200   SIC 2068
PRT GROWING SERVICES LTD   p335
1006 FORT ST UNIT 101, VICTORIA, BC,
V8V 3K4
(250) 381-1404   SIC 2068

SIC 2075 Soybean oil mills

HAIN-CELESTIAL CANADA, ULC *p584*
180 ATTWELL DR SUITE 410, ETOBI-COKE, ON, M9W 6A9
(416) 849-6210   *SIC* 2075

SIC 2076 Vegetable oil mills, nec

BUNGE OF CANADA LTD   *p610*
515 VICTORIA AVE N, HAMILTON, ON, L8L 8G7
(905) 527-9121   *SIC* 2076

FERONIA INC   *p962*
181 BAY ST SUITE 1800, TORONTO, ON, M5J 2T9
(647) 987-7663   *SIC* 2076

SIC 2077 Animal and marine fats and oils

ALTA PROCESSING CO   *p13*
7030 OGDEN DALE PL SE, CALGARY, AB, T2C 2A3
(403) 279-4441   *SIC* 2077

DSM NUTRITIONAL PRODUCTS CANADA INC   *p463*
39 ENGLAND DR, MULGRAVE, NS, B0E 2G0
(902) 747-3500   *SIC* 2077

SANIMAX ACI INC   *p1139*
2001 AV DE LA ROTONDE, LEVIS, QC, G6X 2L8
(418) 832-4645   *SIC* 2077

SANIMAX LOM INC   *p1161*
9900 BOUL MAURICE-DUPLESSIS, MON-TREAL, QC, H1C 1G1
(514) 648-3000   *SIC* 2077

SANIMAX SAN INC   *p1161*
9900 BOUL MAURICE-DUPLESSIS, MON-TREAL, QC, H1C 1G1
(514) 648-6001   *SIC* 2077

WEST COAST REDUCTION LTD   *p19*
7030 OGDEN DALE PL SE, CALGARY, AB, T2C 2A3
(403) 279-4441   *SIC* 2077

WEST COAST REDUCTION LTD   *p296*
1292 VENABLES ST, VANCOUVER, BC, V6A 4B4
(604) 255-9301   *SIC* 2077

SIC 2079 Edible fats and oils

ADM AGRI-INDUSTRIES COMPANY *p1024*
5550 MAPLEWOOD DR, WINDSOR, ON, N9C 0B9
(519) 972-8100   *SIC* 2079

ALIMENTS SARDO INC., LES   *p494*
99 PILLSWORTH RD, BOLTON, ON, L7E 4E4
(905) 951-9096   *SIC* 2079

BUNGE CANADA HOLDINGS 1 ULC *p803*
2190 SOUTH SERVICE RD W, OAKVILLE, ON, L6L 5N1
(905) 825-7900   *SIC* 2079

BUNGE OF CANADA LTD   *p803*
2190 SOUTH SERVICE RD W, OAKVILLE, ON, L6L 5N1
(905) 825-7900   *SIC* 2079

HUBBERT'S PROCESSING AND SALES LIMITED   *p503*
109 EAST DR, BRAMPTON, ON, L6T 1B6
(905) 791-0101   *SIC* 2079

MARGARINE THIBAULT INC   *p1388*
3000 RUE JULES-VACHON, TROIS-RIVIERES, QC, G9A 5E1
(819) 373-3333   *SIC* 2079

PRODUITS ALIMENTAIRES SA-GER INC, LES   *p1330*
6755 BOUL HENRI-BOURASSA O, SAINT-LAURENT, QC, H4R 1E1
(514) 643-4887   *SIC* 2079

RICHARDSON INTERNATIONAL LIMITED
p799
2835 BRISTOL CIR, OAKVILLE, ON, L6H 6X5
(905) 829-2942   *SIC* 2079

RICHARDSON OILSEED LIMITED   *p141*
2415 2A AVE N, LETHBRIDGE, AB, T1H 6P5
(403) 329-5500   *SIC* 2079

RICHARDSON OILSEED LIMITED   *p375*
1 LOMBARD PL SUITE 2800, WINNIPEG, MB, R3B 0X3
(204) 934-5961   *SIC* 2079

RICHARDSON OILSEED LIMITED   *p1438*
HWY 16 3 MILES W, YORKTON, SK, S3N 2W1
(306) 828-2200   *SIC* 2079

SUNORA FOODS INC   *p72*
4616 VALIANT DR NW SUITE 205, CAL-GARY, AB, T3A 0X9
(403) 247-8300   *SIC* 2079

UPFIELD CANADA INC   *p947*
480 UNIVERSITY AVE SUITE 803, TORONTO, ON, M5G 1V2
(416) 595-5300   *SIC* 2079

SIC 2082 Malt beverages

AMSTERDAM BREWING CO. LIMITED *p917*
45 ESANDAR DR UNIT 2, TORONTO, ON, M4G 4C5
(416) 504-1040   *SIC* 2082

BIG ROCK BREWERY INC   *p14*
5555 76 AVE SE SUITE 1, CALGARY, AB, T2C 4L8
(403) 720-3239   *SIC* 2082

BIGRIDGE BREWING CORPORATION *p271*
5580 152 ST, SURREY, BC, V3S 5J9
(604) 574-2739   *SIC* 2082

BRASSERIE MCAUSLAN INC, LA *p1222*
5080 RUE SAINT-AMBROISE, MONTREAL, QC, H4C 2G1
(514) 939-3060   *SIC* 2082

BRASSEURS DU NORD INC, LES *p1058*
875 BOUL MICHELE-BOHEC BUREAU 221, BLAINVILLE, QC, J7C 5J6
(450) 979-8400   *SIC* 2082

BRASSEURS GMT INC, LES   *p1173*
5585 RUE DE LA ROCHE, MONTREAL, QC, H2J 3K3
(514) 274-4941   *SIC* 2082

BRASSEURS RJ INC, LES   *p1173*
5585 RUE DE LA ROCHE, MONTREAL, QC, H2J 3K3
(514) 274-4941   *SIC* 2082

BROUE-ALLIANCE INC   *p1101*
3838 BOUL LEMAN, FABREVILLE, QC, H7E 1A1
(450) 661-0281   *SIC* 2082

BUSHWAKKER BREWING COMPANY LTD
p1420
2206 DEWDNEY AVE, REGINA, SK, S4R 1H3
(306) 359-7276   *SIC* 2082

CHURCH BREWING COMPANY LTD, THE
p471
329 MAIN ST, WOLFVILLE, NS, B4P 1C8
(902) 818-8277   *SIC* 2082

CRAIG STREET BREWING COMPANY *p211*
25 CRAIG ST, DUNCAN, BC, V9L 1V7
(250) 737-2337   *SIC* 2082

CREEMORE SPRINGS BREWERY LIMITED
p564
139 MILL ST SUITE 369, CREEMORE, ON, L0M 1G0
(705) 466-2240   *SIC* 2082

GP BREWING CO. LTD   *p132*
8812 111A ST, GRANDE PRAIRIE, AB, T8V 5L3
(780) 533-4677   *SIC* 2082

GREAT WESTERN BREWING COMPANY LIMITED   *p1427*
519 2ND AVE N, SASKATOON, SK, S7K 2C6

(306) 653-4653   *SIC* 2082

JOHN LABATT LIMITED   *p654*
150 SIMCOE ST, LONDON, ON, N6A 8M3
(519) 663-5050   *SIC* 2082

LABATT BREWING COMPANY LIMITED
p115
10119 45 AVE NW, EDMONTON, AB, T6E 0G8
(780) 436-6060   *SIC* 2082

LABATT BREWING COMPANY LIMITED
p433
60 LESLIE ST, ST. JOHN'S, NL, A1E 2V8
(709) 579-0121   *SIC* 2082

LABATT BREWING COMPANY LIMITED
p964
207 QUEENS QUAY W SUITE 299, TORONTO, ON, M5J 1A7
(416) 361-5050   *SIC* 2082

LABATT BREWING COMPANY LIMITED
p1132
50 AV LABATT BUREAU 42, LASALLE, QC, H8R 3E7
(514) 366-5050   *SIC* 2082

MOLSON BREWERIES OF CANADA LIM-ITED   *p321*
1550 BURRARD ST, VANCOUVER, BC, V6J 3G5
(604) 664-1786   *SIC* 2082

MOLSON CANADA 2005   *p321*
1550 BURRARD ST, VANCOUVER, BC, V6J 3G5
(604) 664-1786   *SIC* 2082

MOLSON CANADA 2005   *p432*
131 CIRCULAR RD, ST. JOHN'S, NL, A1C 2Z9
(709) 726-1786   *SIC* 2082

MOLSON CANADA 2005   *p586*
1 CARLINGVIEW DR, ETOBICOKE, ON, M9W 5E5
(416) 675-1786   *SIC* 2082

MOLSON CANADA 2005   *p586*
33 CARLINGVIEW DR SUITE 2005, ETOBI-COKE, ON, M9W 5E4
(416) 679-1786   *SIC* 2082

MOLSON COORS CANADA INC   *p586*
33 CARLINGVIEW DR, ETOBICOKE, ON, M9W 5E4
(416) 679-1786   *SIC* 2082

MOLSON SASKATCHEWAN BREWERY LTD   *p1416*
395 PARK ST SUITE 2, REGINA, SK, S4N 5B2
(306) 359-1786   *SIC* 2082

MOOSEHEAD BREWERIES LIMITED *p416*
89 MAIN ST W, SAINT JOHN, NB, E2M 3H2
(506) 635-7000   *SIC* 2082

PACIFIC WESTERN BREWING COMPANY LTD   *p189*
3876 NORLAND AVE, BURNABY, BC, V5G 4T9
(604) 421-2119   *SIC* 2082

PRODUITS JUPITER INC, LES   *p1321*
338 RUE SAINT-GEORGES, SAINT-JEROME, QC, J7Z 5A5
(450) 436-7500   *SIC* 2082

PUMP HOUSE BREWERY LTD   *p406*
131 MILL RD, MONCTON, NB, E1A 6R1
(506) 854-2537   *SIC* 2082

SLEEMAN BREWERIES LTD   *p332*
2808 27 AVE, VERNON, BC, V1T 9K4
(250) 542-2337   *SIC* 2082

SLEEMAN BREWERIES LTD   *p602*
505 SOUTHGATE DR, GUELPH, ON, N1G 3W6
(519) 822-1834   *SIC* 2082

SLEEMAN BREWING & MALTING COM-PANY LTD, THE   *p606*
551 CLAIR RD W, GUELPH, ON, N1L 1E9
(519) 822-1834   *SIC* 2082

STEAM WHISTLE BREWING INC   *p983*
255 BREMNER BLVD, TORONTO, ON, M5V 3M9
(416) 362-2337   *SIC* 2082

TRILLIUM BEVERAGE INC   *p787*

125 BERMONDSEY RD, NORTH YORK, ON, M4A 1X3
(416) 759-6565   *SIC* 2082

WELLINGTON COUNTY BREWERY INC
p606
950 WOODLAWN RD W, GUELPH, ON, N1K 1G2
(519) 837-2337   *SIC* 2082

SIC 2083 Malt

CANADA MALTING CO. LIMITED   *p28*
3316 BONNYBROOK RD SE, CALGARY, AB, T2G 4M9
(403) 571-7000   *SIC* 2083

RAHR MALTING CANADA LTD   *p3*
HWY 12 E, ALIX, AB, T0C 0B0
(403) 747-2777   *SIC* 2083

SIC 2084 Wines, brandy, and brandy spirits

984379 ONTARIO INC   *p1003*
3620 MOYER RD, VINELAND, ON, L0R 2C0
(905) 562-7088   *SIC* 2084

ANDREW PELLER LIMITED   *p599*
697 SOUTH SERVICE RD, GRIMSBY, ON, L3M 4E8
(905) 643-4131   *SIC* 2084

ANDREW PELLER LIMITED   *p599*
697 SOUTH SERVICE RD, GRIMSBY, ON, L3M 4E8
(905) 643-4131   *SIC* 2084

ANDREW PELLER LIMITED   *p760*
1249 NIAGARA STONE RD, NIAGARA ON THE LAKE, ON, L0S 1J0
(905) 468-7123   *SIC* 2084

ARTERRA WINES CANADA, INC   *p737*
441 COURTNEYPARK DR E, MISSIS-SAUGA, ON, L5T 2V3
(905) 564-6900   *SIC* 2084

BURROWING OWL VINEYARDS LTD *p242*
100 BURROWING OWL PL, OLIVER, BC, V0H 1T0
(250) 498-0620   *SIC* 2084

DOMAINE DE CHABERTON ESTATES LTD
p227
1064 216 ST, LANGLEY, BC, V2Z 1R3
(604) 530-1736   *SIC* 2084

LAKEVIEW CELLARS ESTATE WINERY LIMITED   *p761*
1067 NIAGARA STONE RD, NIAGARA ON THE LAKE, ON, L0S 1J0
(905) 641-1042   *SIC* 2084

MAGNOTTA WINERY CORPORATION *p1003*
271 CHRISLEA RD, VAUGHAN, ON, L4L 8N6
(905) 738-9463   *SIC* 2084

MAISON DES FUTAILLES, S.E.C. *p1164*
2021 RUE DES FUTAILLES, MONTREAL, QC, H1N 3M7
(450) 645-9777   *SIC* 2084

MARK ANTHONY GROUP INC   *p206*
465 FRASERVIEW PL, DELTA, BC, V3M 6H4
(604) 519-5370   *SIC* 2084

MARK ANTHONY GROUP INC   *p289*
887 GREAT NORTHERN WAY SUITE 500, VANCOUVER, BC, V5T 4T5
(888) 394-1122   *SIC* 2084

PELEE ISLAND WINERY & VINEYARDS INC
p634
455 SEACLIFF DR, KINGSVILLE, ON, N9Y 2K5
(519) 733-6551   *SIC* 2084

TWO SISTERS VINEYARD CORP   *p761*
240 JOHN ST E, NIAGARA ON THE LAKE, ON, L0S 1J0
(905) 468-0592   *SIC* 2084

VINS ARTERRA CANADA, DIVISION QUE-BEC, INC   *p1288*
175 CH DE MARIEVILLE, ROUGEMONT, QC, J0L 1M0

---

(514) 861-2404   *SIC 2084*

SIC 2085 Distilled and blended liquors

ALBERTA DISTILLERS LIMITED   *p27*
1521 34 AVE SE, CALGARY, AB, T2G 1V9
(403) 265-2541   *SIC 2085*

BACARDI CANADA INC   *p572*
3250 BLOOR ST W SUITE 1050, ETOBI-COKE, ON, M8X 2X9
(905) 451-6100   *SIC 2085*

CANADIAN MIST DISTILLERS LIMITED
p546
202 MACDONALD RD, COLLINGWOOD, ON, L9Y 4J2
(705) 445-4690   *SIC 2085*

CANRIM PACKAGING LTD   *p221*
1125 RICHTER ST, KELOWNA, BC, V1Y 2K6
(250) 762-3332   *SIC 2085*

CONSTELLATION BRANDS SCHENLEY ULC   *p140*
2925 9 AVE N, LETHBRIDGE, AB, T1H 5E3
(403) 317-2100   *SIC 2085*

CORBY SPIRIT AND WINE LIMITED   *p979*
225 KING ST W SUITE 1100, TORONTO, ON, M5V 3M2
(416) 479-2400   *SIC 2085*

DIAGEO CANADA INC   *p477*
110 ST. ARNAUD ST, AMHERSTBURG, ON, N9V 2N8
(519) 736-2161   *SIC 2085*

DIAGEO CANADA INC   *p996*
401 THE WEST MALL SUITE 800, TORONTO, ON, M9C 5P8
(416) 626-2000   *SIC 2085*

FORTY CREEK DISTILLERY LTD   *p599*
297 SOUTH SERVICE RD, GRIMSBY, ON, L3M 1Y6
(905) 945-9225   *SIC 2085*

FORTY CREEK DISTILLERY LTD   *p991*
1 PARDEE AVE SUITE 102, TORONTO, ON, M6K 3H1
(905) 945-9225   *SIC 2085*

HIRAM WALKER & SONS LIMITED   *p1022*
2072 RIVERSIDE DR E, WINDSOR, ON, N8Y 4S5
(519) 254-5171   *SIC 2085*

NORTHAM BEVERAGES LTD   *p217*
965 MCGILL PL, KAMLOOPS, BC, V2C 6N9
(250) 851-2543   *SIC 2085*

NORTHAM BEVERAGES LTD   *p299*
68 WATER ST UNIT 501, VANCOUVER, BC, V6B 1A4
(604) 731-2900   *SIC 2085*

SIC 2086 Bottled and canned soft drinks

2156775 ONTARIO INC   *p691*
4544 EASTGATE PKY, MISSISSAUGA, ON, L4W 3W6
(905) 238-6300   *SIC 2086*

A. LASSONDE INC   *p581*
95 VULCAN ST, ETOBICOKE, ON, M9W 1L4
(416) 244-4224   *SIC 2086*

ALL 4 WATER CORP   *p108*
7115 GIRARD RD NW, EDMONTON, AB, T6B 2C5
SIC 2086

BIG 8 BEVERAGES LIMITED   *p466*
120 NORTH FOORD ST, STELLARTON, NS, B0K 0A2
(902) 755-6333   *SIC 2086*

BROWNING HARVEY LIMITED   *p432*
15 ROPEWALK LANE, ST. JOHN'S, NL, A1E 4P1
(709) 579-4116   *SIC 2086*

CANADA DRY MOTT'S INC   *p730*
30 EGLINTON AVE W SUITE 600, MISSIS-SAUGA, ON, L5R 3E7
(905) 712-4121   *SIC 2086*

CANADA YOUTH ORANGE NETWORK INC
p285
1638 PANDORA ST, VANCOUVER, BC, V5L 1L6
(604) 254-7733   *SIC 2086*

CAPE BRETON BEVERAGES LIMITED *p449*
65 HARBOUR DR, EDWARDSVILLE, NS, B2A 4T7
(902) 564-4536   *SIC 2086*

COCA-COLA CANADA BOTTLING LIMITED
p22
3851 23 ST NE, CALGARY, AB, T2E 6T2
(403) 291-3111   *SIC 2086*

COCA-COLA CANADA BOTTLING LIMITED
p120
9621 27 AVE NW, EDMONTON, AB, T6N 1E7
(780) 450-2653   *SIC 2086*

COCA-COLA CANADA BOTTLING LIMITED
p372
1331 INKSTER BLVD, WINNIPEG, MB, R2X 1P6
(204) 633-2590   *SIC 2086*

COCA-COLA CANADA BOTTLING LIMITED
p460
20 LAKESIDE PARK DR, LAKESIDE, NS, B3T 1L8
(902) 876-8661   *SIC 2086*

COCA-COLA CANADA BOTTLING LIMITED
p501
15 WESTCREEK BLVD, BRAMPTON, ON, L6T 5T4
(905) 874-7202   *SIC 2086*

COCA-COLA CANADA BOTTLING LIMITED
p661
950 GREEN VALLEY RD, LONDON, ON, N6N 1E3
(800) 241-2653   *SIC 2086*

COCA-COLA CANADA BOTTLING LIMITED
p792
24 FENMAR DR, NORTH YORK, ON, M9L 1L8
(416) 741-0440   *SIC 2086*

COCA-COLA CANADA BOTTLING LIMITED
p933
335 KING ST E, TORONTO, ON, M5A 1L1
(416) 424-6000   *SIC 2086*

COCA-COLA LTD   *p1387*
8500 BOUL INDUSTRIEL, TROIS-RIVIERES, QC, G9A 5E1
(819) 694-4000   *SIC 2086*

COCA-COLA REFRESHMENTS CANADA COMPANY   *p219*
406 OLD VERNON RD SUITE 100, KELOWNA, BC, V1X 4R2
(250) 491-3414   *SIC 2086*

COCA-COLA REFRESHMENTS CANADA COMPANY   *p609*
1575 BARTON ST E, HAMILTON, ON, L8H 7K6
(905) 548-3206   *SIC 2086*

COCA-COLA REFRESHMENTS CANADA COMPANY   *p933*
335 KING ST E, TORONTO, ON, M5A 1L1
(416) 424-6000   *SIC 2086*

COCA-COLA REFRESHMENTS CANADA COMPANY   *p1164*
2750 BOUL DE L'ASSOMPTION, MON-TREAL, QC, H1N 2G9
(514) 254-9411   *SIC 2086*

COTT CORPORATION   *p687*
6525 VISCOUNT RD, MISSISSAUGA, ON, L4V 1H6
(905) 672-1900   *SIC 2086*

COULOMBE QUEBEC LIMITEE   *p1263*
2300 RUE CYRILLE-DUQUET, QUEBEC, QC, G1N 2G5
(418) 687-2700   *SIC 2086*

DELTA BEVERAGES INC   *p1030*
21 MARYCROFT AVE, WOODBRIDGE, ON, L4L 5Y6
(905) 850-8077   *SIC 2086*

LEADING BRANDS OF CANADA, INC *p292*
33 8TH AVE W UNIT 101, VANCOUVER,

BC, V5Y 1M8
(604) 685-5200   *SIC 2086*

MINUTE MAID COMPANY CANADA INC, THE   *p841*
781 LANSDOWNE ST W, PETERBOR-OUGH, ON, K9J 1Z2
(705) 742-8011   *SIC 2086*

NORTHERN BOTTLING LTD   *p134*
15415 91 ST, GRANDE PRAIRIE, AB, T8X 0B4
(780) 532-4222   *SIC 2086*

P A BOTTLERS LTD   *p1414*
85 11TH ST NW, PRINCE ALBERT, SK, S6V 5T2
(306) 922-7777   *SIC 2086*

PEPSI BOTTLING GROUP (CANADA), ULC, THE   *p17*
4815 78 AVE SE, CALGARY, AB, T2C 2Y9
(403) 279-1500   *SIC 2086*

PEPSI BOTTLING GROUP (CANADA), ULC, THE   *p102*
11315 182 ST NW, EDMONTON, AB, T5S 1R3
(780) 930-7700   *SIC 2086*

PEPSI BOTTLING GROUP (CANADA), ULC, THE   *p206*
747 CHESTER RD, DELTA, BC, V3M 6E7
(604) 520-8000   *SIC 2086*

PEPSI BOTTLING GROUP (CANADA), ULC, THE   *p384*
1850 ELLICE AVE, WINNIPEG, MB, R3H 0B8
(204) 784-0600   *SIC 2086*

PEPSI BOTTLING GROUP (CANADA), ULC, THE   *p409*
220 HENRI DUNANT ST, MONCTON, NB, E1E 1E6
(506) 853-4010   *SIC 2086*

PEPSI BOTTLING GROUP (CANADA), ULC, THE   *p608*
2799 BARTON ST E, HAMILTON, ON, L8E 2J8
(905) 560-7774   *SIC 2086*

PEPSI BOTTLING GROUP (CANADA), ULC, THE   *p699*
5205 SATELLITE DR, MISSISSAUGA, ON, L4W 5J7
(905) 212-7377   *SIC 2086*

PEPSI BOTTLING GROUP (CANADA), ULC, THE   *p732*
5900 FALBOURNE ST, MISSISSAUGA, ON, L5R 3M2
(905) 568-8787   *SIC 2086*

PEPSI BOTTLING GROUP (CANADA), ULC, THE   *p898*
801 LAPOINTE ST, SUDBURY, ON, P3A 5N8
(705) 525-4000   *SIC 2086*

PEPSI BOTTLING GROUP (CANADA), ULC, THE   *p1330*
3700 BOUL THIMENS, SAINT-LAURENT, QC, H4R 1T8
(514) 332-3770   *SIC 2086*

PEPSICO CANADA ULC   *p1111*
855 RUE J.-A.-BOMBARDIER, GRANBY, QC, J2J 1E9
(450) 375-5555   *SIC 2086*

RED BULL CANADA LTD   *p983*
381 QUEEN ST W SUITE 200, TORONTO, ON, M5V 2A5
(416) 593-1629   *SIC 2086*

REFRESCO CANADA INC   *p689*
6525 VISCOUNT RD, MISSISSAUGA, ON, L4V 1H6
(905) 672-1900   *SIC 2086*

UNILEVER CANADA INC   *p1157*
5430 CH DE LA COTE-DE-LIESSE, MONT-ROYAL, QC, H4P 1A5
SIC 2086

SIC 2087 Flavoring extracts and syrups, nec

BELL FLAVORS & FRAGRANCES

(CANADA) CO   *p1069*
3800 RUE ISABELLE BUREAU H, BROSSARD, QC, J4Y 2R3
(450) 444-3819   *SIC 2087*

EMBASSY INGREDIENTS LTD   *p502*
5 INTERMODAL DR UNIT 1, BRAMPTON, ON, L6T 5V9
(905) 789-3200   *SIC 2087*

FIT FOODS LTD   *p246*
1589 KEBET WAY, PORT COQUITLAM, BC, V3C 6L5
(604) 464-3524   *SIC 2087*

IMPERIAL FLAVOURS INC   *p685*
7550 TORBRAM RD, MISSISSAUGA, ON, L4T 3L8
(905) 678-6680   *SIC 2087*

WILD FLAVORS (CANADA) INC   *p744*
7315 PACIFIC CIR, MISSISSAUGA, ON, L5T 1V1
(905) 670-1108   *SIC 2087*

SIC 2091 Canned and cured fish and seafoods

BAIE STE-ANNE SEAFOODS (2014) INC
p399
143 CH ESCUMINAC POINT, ESCUMINAC, NB, E9A 1V6
(506) 228-4444   *SIC 2091*

BARRY GROUP INC   *p423*
GD, DOVER, NL, A0G 1X0
(709) 537-5888   *SIC 2091*

BCF INVESTMENTS INC   *p208*
9829 RIVER RD, DELTA, BC, V4G 1B4
(604) 583-3474   *SIC 2091*

BEACH POINT PROCESSING COMPANY
p1042
75 WHARF LANE, MURRAY HARBOUR, PE, C0A 1V0
(902) 962-4340   *SIC 2091*

BOLERO SHELLFISH PROCESSING INC
p417
1324 ROUTE 335, SAINT-SIMON, NB, E8P 2B2
(506) 727-5217   *SIC 2091*

CRABIERS DU NORD INC, LES   *p1253*
428 RUE PRINCIPALE, PORTNEUF-SUR-MER, QC, G0T 1P0
(418) 238-2132   *SIC 2091*

E. GAGNON ET FILS LTEE   *p1364*
405 RTE 132, SAINTE-THERESE-DE-GASPE, QC, G0C 3B0
(418) 385-3011   *SIC 2091*

FJORD PACIFIC MARINE INDUSTRIES LTD.
p260
2400 SIMPSON RD, RICHMOND, BC, V6X 2P9
(604) 270-3393   *SIC 2091*

FUMOIR GRIZZLY INC   *p1293*
159 RUE D'AMSTERDAM, SAINT-AUGUSTIN-DE-DESMAURES, QC, G3A 2V5
(418) 878-8941   *SIC 2091*

FUMOIRS GASPE CURED INC, LES *p1074*
65 RUE DE LA STATION, CAP-D'ESPOIR, QC, G0C 1G0
(418) 782-5920   *SIC 2091*

GREEN ISLAND DISTRIBUTORS PART-NERSHIP   *p439*
616 LOWER RD, ARICHAT, NS, B0E 1A0
(902) 226-2633   *SIC 2091*

GROUPE ALIMENTAIRE NORDIQUE INC, LE   *p1172*
6569 AV PAPINEAU BUREAU 100, MON-TREAL, QC, H2G 2X3
(514) 419-3510   *SIC 2091*

ICEWATER SEAFOODS INC   *p421*
24 HIGH LINER AVE, ARNOLDS COVE, NL, A0B 1A0
(709) 463-2445   *SIC 2091*

IMO FOODS LIMITED   *p471*
26 WATER ST, YARMOUTH, NS, B5A 1K9
(902) 742-3519   *SIC 2091*

INNOVATIVE FISHERY PRODUCTS INCOR-

PORATED   p440
3569 1 HWY, BELLIVEAU COVE, NS, B0W
1J0
(902) 837-5163   SIC 2091

KING'S, ERIC FISHERIES LIMITED   p421
17 PLANT RD SUITE 15, BURNT ISLANDS
BLP, NL, A0M 1B0
(709) 698-3421   SIC 2091

LAHAVE SEAFOODS LIMITED   p460
3371 HWY 331, LAHAVE, NS, B0R 1C0
(902) 688-2773   SIC 2091

LELIEVRE, LELIEVRE & LEMOIGNAN LTEE
p1364
52 RUE DES VIGNEAUX, SAINTE-
THERESE-DE-GASPE, QC, G0C 3B0
(418) 385-3310   SIC 2091

LOCHIEL ENTERPRISES LIMITED   p466
8000 HIGHWAY 7, SHERBROOKE, NS, B0J
3C0
(902) 522-2005   SIC 2091

LOUISBOURG SEAFOODS LTD   p461
3 COMMERCIAL ST, LOUISBOURG, NS,
B1C 1B5
(902) 733-2079   SIC 2091

MARINE HARVEST CANADA INC   p247
7200 COHOE RD, PORT HARDY, BC, V0N
2P0
(250) 949-9448   SIC 2091

NU SEA PRODUCTS INC   p427
MAIN RD, PORT DE GRAVE, NL, A0A 3J0
(709) 786-6302   SIC 2091

**O'NEILL, RAYMOND & SON FISHERIES
LTD**
221 CH ESCUMINAC POINT, ESCUMINAC,
NB, E9A 1V6
(506) 228-4794   SIC 2091

ORCA SPECIALTY FOODS LTD   p272
17350 56 AVE SUITE 4, SURREY, BC, V3S
1C3
(604) 574-6722   SIC 2091

PACK FRESH FOODS LTD   p272
17350 56 AVE SUITE 3, SURREY, BC, V3S
1C3
(604) 574-6720   SIC 2091

PETIT DE GRAT PACKERS LIMITED   p464
24 HWY 206, PETIT DE GRAT, NS, B0E 2L0
(902) 226-0029   SIC 2091

POISSON SALE GASPESIEN LTEE   p1112
39 RUE DU PARC, GRANDE-RIVIERE, QC,
G0C 1V0
(418) 385-2424   SIC 2091

RICHARD, B. A. LTEE   p417
374 CH COTE SAINTE-ANNE, SAINTE-
ANNE-DE-KENT, NB, E4S 1M6
(506) 743-6198   SIC 2091

SABLE FISH PACKERS (1988) LIMITED
p442
377 DANIELS HEAD RD, CLARKS HAR-
BOUR, NS, B0W 1P0
(902) 745-2500   SIC 2091

SCHOONER SEAFOODS LIMITED   p470
51 DOUCET WHARF RD, WEDGEPORT,
NS, B0W 3P0
(902) 663-2521   SIC 2091

WALCAN SEAFOOD LTD   p215
GD, HERIOT BAY, BC, V0P 1H0
(250) 285-3361   SIC 2091

WESTMORLAND FISHERIES LTD   p396
64 GAUTREAU ST, CAP-PELE, NB, E4N
1V3
(506) 577-4325   SIC 2091

WM.R.MURPHY FISHERIES LTD   p439
52 WHARF RD LITTLE RIVER HARBOUR,
ARCADIA, NS, B0W 1B0
(902) 663-4301   SIC 2091

SIC 2092 Fresh or frozen packaged fish

434870 B.C. LTD   p233
262 SOUTHSIDE DR, NANAIMO, BC, V9R
6Z5
(250) 753-4135   SIC 2092

ALLEN'S FISHERIES LIMITED   p421

151 MAIN RD, BENOITS COVE, NL, A0L
1A0
(709) 789-3139   SIC 2092

ALLIANCE SEAFOOD INCORPORATED
p397
621 CH GAUVIN, DIEPPE, NB, E1A 1M7
(506) 854-5800   SIC 2092

AQUASHELL HOLDINGS INC   p470
13915 ROUTE 6, WALLACE, NS, B0K 1Y0
(902) 257-2920   SIC 2092

ASSELS SEAFOOD INC   p1376
11 132 RTE, SHIGAWAKE, QC, G0C 3E0
SIC 2092

BARRY GROUP INC   p421
1 MASONIC TERRACE, CLARENVILLE,
NL, A5A 1N2
(709) 466-7186   SIC 2092

BELLE BAY PRODUCTS LTD   p396
10 RUE DU QUAI, CARAQUET, NB, E1W
1B6
(506) 727-4414   SIC 2092

BELLE RIVER ENTERPRISES LTD   p1038
GD, BELLE RIVER, PE, C0A 1B0
(902) 962-2248   SIC 2092

BREAKWATER FISHERIES LIMITED   p423
23 HILL VIEW DR, COTTLESVILLE, NL,
A0G 1S0
SIC 2092

CALKINS & BURKE HOLDINGS LTD   p318
1500 GEORGIA ST W SUITE 800, VAN-
COUVER, BC, V6G 2Z6
(604) 669-3741   SIC 2092

CAPE BREEZE SEAFOODS LIMITED   p465
3203 MAIN RD, PORT LA TOUR, NS, B0W
2T0
(902) 768-2550   SIC 2092

CAPE BROYLE SEA PRODUCTS LIMITED
p421
GD, CAPE BROYLE, NL, A0A 1P0
(709) 432-2400   SIC 2092

CAPTAIN DAN'S INC   p397
463 CHAMPLAIN ST, DIEPPE, NB, E1A 1P2
(506) 872-7621   SIC 2092

CLEARWATER SEAFOODS HOLDINGS INC
p439
757 BEDFORD HWY, BEDFORD, NS, B4A
3Z7
(902) 443-0550   SIC 2092

**CLEARWATER SEAFOODS LIMITED PART-
NERSHIP**   p439
757 BEDFORD HWY, BEDFORD, NS, B4A
3Z7
(902) 443-0550   SIC 2092

COLD NORTH SEAFOODS LIMITED   p425
2 WATER ST, LA SCIE, NL, A0K 3M0
SIC 2092

COMEAU'S SEA FOODS LIMITED   p465
60 SAULNIERVILLE RD, SAULNIERVILLE,
NS, B0W 2Z0
(902) 769-2101   SIC 2092

COMEAU'S SEA FOODS LIMITED   p465
GD, PUBNICO, NS, B0W 2W0
(902) 762-3333   SIC 2092

CRUSTACES DES MONTS INC, LES   p1355
1 RUE DU PARC-INDUSTRIEL, SAINTE-
ANNE-DES-MONTS, QC, G4V 2V9
(418) 763-5561   SIC 2092

DELTA PACIFIC SEAFOODS LTD   p210
6001 60 AVE, DELTA, BC, V4K 0B2
(604) 946-5160   SIC 2092

EASTERN QUEBEC SEAFOODS (1998) LTD
p1150
1600 RUE DE MATANE-SUR-MER,
MATANE, QC, G4W 3M6
(418) 562-1273   SIC 2092

**FINEST AT SEA OCEAN PRODUCTS LIM-
ITED**
27 ERIE ST, VICTORIA, BC, V8V 1P8
(250) 383-7760   SIC 2092

**FOGO ISLAND CO-OPERATIVE SOCIETY
LIMITED**   p423
22-24 GARRISON RD, FOGO, NL, A0G 2B0
(709) 266-2448   SIC 2092

FRESHWATER FISH MARKETING CORPO-

RATION   p362
1199 PLESSIS RD, WINNIPEG, MB, R2C
3L4
(204) 983-6600   SIC 2092

FRUITS DE MER BLUEWATER INC   p1127
1640 CROIS BRANDON BUREAU 201, LA-
CHINE, QC, H8T 2N1
(514) 637-1171   SIC 2092

FURLONG BROTHERS LIMITED   p427
GD, PLATE COVE WEST, NL, A0C 2E0
(709) 545-2251   SIC 2092

GREEN, E J & COMPANY LTD   p434
287 MAIN ST, WINTERTON, NL, A0B 3M0
(709) 583-2670   SIC 2092

**HAPPY ADVENTURE SEA PRODUCTS
(1991) LIMITED**   p423
PLANT RD, EASTPORT, NL, A0G 1Z0
(709) 677-2612   SIC 2092

HIGH LINER FOODS INCORPORATEDp461
100 BATTERY PT, LUNENBURG, NS, B0J
2C0
(902) 634-8811   SIC 2092

ICHIBOSHI L.P.C LTD   p396
24 RUE DU QUAI, CARAQUET, NB, E1W
1B6
(506) 727-0807   SIC 2092

INSHORE FISHERIES LIMITED   p461
95 DENNIS POINT RD, LOWER WEST
PUBNICO, NS, B0W 2C0
(902) 762-2522   SIC 2092

KA'LE BAY SEAFOODS LTD   p443
501 MAIN ST, DARTMOUTH, NS, B2W 4K1
(902) 842-9454   SIC 2092

KAWAKI (CANADA) LTD   p255
2500 VISCOUNT WAY, RICHMOND, BC,
V6V 1N1
(604) 277-7158   SIC 2092

KELLY COVE SALMON LTD   p395
874 MAIN ST, BLACKS HARBOUR, NB,
E5H 1E6
(506) 456-6600   SIC 2092

**L.J. ROBICHEAU & SON FISHERIES LIM-
ITED**   p460
219 SHORE RD, LITTLE RIVER, NS, B0V
1C0
(902) 834-2792   SIC 2092

LA CREVETTE DU NORD ATLANTIQUE INC
p1102
139 RUE DE LA REINE, GASPE, QC, G4X
1T5
(418) 368-1414   SIC 2092

**LABRADOR FISHERMEN'S UNION
SHRIMP COMPANY LIMITED**   p425
46 WATERFRONT RD, L'ANSE AU LOUP,
NL, A0K 3L0
(709) 927-5816   SIC 2092

**LOWER NORTH SHORE COMMUNITY
SEAFOOD COOPERATIVE**   p1113
2 DOCKSIDE DR, HARRINGTON HAR-
BOUR, QC, G0G 1N0
(418) 795-3244   SIC 2092

MCMILLAN, J.S. FISHERIES LTD   p239
12 ORWELL ST, NORTH VANCOUVER, BC,
V7J 2G1
(604) 982-9207   SIC 2092

MCMILLAN, J.S. FISHERIES LTD   p251
GD STN MAIN, PRINCE RUPERT, BC, V8J
3P3
(250) 624-2146   SIC 2092

MILLS SEA FOOD LTD   p395
5 RUE MILLS, BOUCTOUCHE, NB, E4S
3S3
SIC 2092

**NORTHERN HARVEST SEA FARMS NEW-
FOUNDLAND LTD**   p428
183 MAIN ST, ST ALBANS, NL, A0H 2E0
(709) 538-3231   SIC 2092

NORTHERN SHRIMP COMPANY LTD   p424
GD, JACKSONS ARM, NL, A0K 3H0
SIC 2092

NOTRE DAME SEAFOODS INC   p430
88 KENMOUNT RD, ST. JOHN'S, NL, A1B
3R1
(709) 758-0034   SIC 2092

OCEAN CHOICE INTERNATIONAL   p427
7476 FISHER ST, PORT AU CHOIX, NL,
A0K 4C0
(709) 861-3506   SIC 2092

OCEAN CHOICE INTERNATIONAL   p428
69 WATER ST W, ST LAWRENCE, NL, A0E
2V0
(709) 873-2798   SIC 2092

OCEAN LEADER FISHERIES LIMITED   p461
138 JACQUARD RD, LOWER WEDGE-
PORT, NS, B0W 2B0
(902) 663-4579   SIC 2092

OCEAN PIER INC   p417
20 PATTISON ST, SCOUDOUC, NB, E4P
3R4
(506) 532-3010   SIC 2092

OMEGA PACKING COMPANY LIMITEDp231
2040 HARRISON, MASSET, BC, V0T 1M0
(250) 626-3391   SIC 2092

PATUREL INTERNATIONAL COMPANY
p410
349 NORTHERN HARBOUR RD, NORTH-
ERN HARBOUR, NB, E5V 1G6
(506) 747-1888   SIC 2092

**PECHERIES BAS-CARAQUET FISHERIES
INC**   p394
2270 INDUSTRIELLE ST, BAS-CARAQUET,
NB, E1W 5Z2
(506) 727-3632   SIC 2092

PECHERIES F.N. FISHERIES LTD   p418
99 15E RUE, SHIPPAGAN, NB, E8S 1E2
SIC 2092

PECHERIES MARINARD LTEE, LES   p1102
41 RUE DE L'ENTREPOT, GASPE, QC, G4X
5L3
(418) 269-3381   SIC 2092

PRINCE EDWARD AQUA FARMS INCp1041
GD, KENSINGTON, PE, C0B 1M0
(902) 886-2220   SIC 2092

QUINLAN BROTHERS LIMITED   p432
215 WATER ST SUITE 302, ST. JOHN'S,
NL, A1C 6C9
(709) 739-6960   SIC 2092

RENAISSANCE DES ILES INC, LA   p1120
521 CH DU GROS-CAP, L'ETANG-DU-
NORD, QC, G4T 3M1
(418) 986-2710   SIC 2092

RIVER SEAFOODS INC   p237
522 SEVENTH ST UNIT 320, NEW WEST-
MINSTER, BC, V3M 5T5
SIC 2092

**RIVERSIDE LOBSTER INTERNATIONAL
INC**   p462
11 JOHN THIBODEAU RD, METEGHAN
CENTRE, NS, B0W 2K0
(902) 645-3433   SIC 2092

**RIVERSIDE LOBSTER INTERNATIONAL
INC**   p462
11 JOHN THIBODEAU RD, METEGHAN
CENTRE, NS, B0W 2K0
(902) 645-3455   SIC 2092

SCANNER ENTERPRISES (1982) INC   p277
8305 128 ST, SURREY, BC, V3W 4G1
(604) 591-2908   SIC 2092

SEA TIDE IMPORT & EXPORT LTD   p396
45 RUE CORMIER, CAP-PELE, NB, E4N
1N8
(506) 577-4070   SIC 2092

THAI UNION CANADA INC   p419
78 RUE DU QUAI, VAL-COMEAU, NB, E1X
4L1
(506) 395-3292   SIC 2092

THORNVALE HOLDINGS LIMITED   p461
68 WATER ST, LOCKEPORT, NS, B0T 1L0
(902) 656-2413   SIC 2092

THORNVALE HOLDINGS LIMITED   p462
240 MONTAGUE ST, LUNENBURG, NS,
B0J 2C0
(902) 634-8049   SIC 2092

TRUE NORTH SALMON CO. LTD   p395
669 MAIN ST, BLACKS HARBOUR, NB,
E5H 1K1
(506) 456-6600   SIC 2092

TRUE NORTH SALMON LIMITED PART-

NERSHIP *p395*
669 MAIN ST, BLACKS HARBOUR, NB, E5H 1K1
(506) 456-6610 *SIC 2092*

UNIPECHE M.D.M. LTEE *p1245*
66 AV DU QUAI, PASPEBIAC, QC, G0C 2K0
(418) 752-6700 *SIC 2092*

SIC 2095 Roasted coffee

FRATELLO GROUP INC *p29*
4021 9 ST SE, CALGARY, AB, T2G 3C7
(403) 265-2112 *SIC 2095*

GESTION MARC NADEAU INC *p1262*
625 RUE DU MARAIS, QUEBEC, QC, G1M 2Y2
(418) 681-0696 *SIC 2095*

KEURIG CANADA INC *p1170*
3700 RUE JEAN-RIVARD BUREAU 1, MONTREAL, QC, H1Z 4K3
(514) 593-7711 *SIC 2095*

MOTHER PARKER'S TEA & COFFEE INC *p704*
2530 STANFIELD RD, MISSISSAUGA, ON, L4Y 1S4
(905) 279-9100 *SIC 2095*

MOTHER PARKER'S TEA & COFFEE INC *p704*
2531 STANFIELD RD, MISSISSAUGA, ON, L4Y 1S4
(905) 279-9100 *SIC 2095*

NESTLE CANADA INC *p544*
171 MAIN ST N, CHESTERVILLE, ON, K0C 1H0
(613) 448-2338 *SIC 2095*

NESTLE CANADA INC *p772*
25 SHEPPARD AVE W SUITE 1700, NORTH YORK, ON, M2N 6S6
(416) 512-9000 *SIC 2095*

SIC 2096 Potato chips and similar snacks

ALIMENTS KRISPY KERNELS INC *p1400*
40 RUE DU MOULIN, WARWICK, QC, J0A 1M0
(819) 358-3600 *SIC 2096*

HOSTESS FOOD PRODUCTS *p440*
230 BLUEWATER RD, BEDFORD, NS, B4B 1G9
(902) 832-2865 *SIC 2096*

OL' GRANDAD'S SNACKS (1992) INC *p534*
1680 BISHOP ST N, CAMBRIDGE, ON, N1R 7J3
(519) 624-9992 *SIC 2096*

OLD DUTCH FOODS LTD *p3*
215 EAST LAKE BLVD NE, AIRDRIE, AB, T4A 2G1
(403) 948-3339 *SIC 2096*

OLD DUTCH FOODS LTD *p17*
3103 54 AVE SE, CALGARY, AB, T2C 0A9
(403) 279-2771 *SIC 2096*

OLD DUTCH FOODS LTD *p372*
100 BENTALL ST, WINNIPEG, MB, R2X 2Y5
(204) 632-0249 *SIC 2096*

OLD DUTCH FOODS LTD *p1043*
4 SLEMON PARK DR, SUMMERSIDE, PE, C1N 4K4
(902) 888-5160 *SIC 2096*

OLD DUTCH FOODS LTD *p1335*
6525 RUE ABRAMS, SAINT-LAURENT, QC, H4S 1X9
(514) 745-4449 *SIC 2096*

PEPSICO CANADA ULC *p13*
2867 45 AVE SE, CALGARY, AB, T2B 3L8
(403) 571-9530 *SIC 2096*

PEPSICO CANADA ULC *p141*
2200 31 ST N, LETHBRIDGE, AB, T1H 5K8
(403) 380-5775 *SIC 2096*

PEPSICO CANADA ULC *p169*
5904 54 AVE, TABER, AB, T1G 1X3
(403) 223-3574 *SIC 2096*

PEPSICO CANADA ULC *p460*

---

59 WAREHOUSE RD, KENTVILLE, NS, B4N 3W9
(902) 681-2923 *SIC 2096*

PEPSICO CANADA ULC *p460*
GD, KENTVILLE, NS, B4N 3W9
(902) 681-6183 *SIC 2096*

PEPSICO CANADA ULC *p539*
1001 BISHOP ST N, CAMBRIDGE, ON, N3H 4V8
(519) 653-5721 *SIC 2096*

PEPSICO CANADA ULC *p699*
5550 EXPLORER DR, MISSISSAUGA, ON, L4W 0C3
(289) 374-5000 *SIC 2096*

PEPSICO CANADA ULC *p732*
55 STANDISH CRT SUITE 700, MISSISSAUGA, ON, L5R 4B2
SIC 2096

PEPSICO CANADA ULC *p1137*
8450 BOUL GUILLAUME-COUTURE, LEVIS, QC, G6V 7L7
(418) 833-2121 *SIC 2096*

PEPSICO CANADA ULC *p1231*
6755 RUE ERNEST-CORMIER, MONTREAL, QC, H7C 2T4
(450) 664-5800 *SIC 2096*

SARATOGA POTATO CHIP COMPANY INC *p506*
230 DEERHURST DR, BRAMPTON, ON, L6T 5R8
(905) 458-4100 *SIC 2096*

SHEARER'S FOODS CANADA, INC *p602*
745 SOUTHGATE DR, GUELPH, ON, N1G 3R3
(519) 746-0045 *SIC 2096*

SUPER-PUFFT SNACKS CORP *p736*
880 GANA CRT, MISSISSAUGA, ON, L5S 1N8
(905) 564-1180 *SIC 2096*

SIC 2097 Manufactured ice

AGI CCAA INC *p373*
625 HENRY AVE, WINNIPEG, MB, R3A 0V1
(204) 772-2473 *SIC 2097*

ICECULTURE INC *p620*
81 BROCK ST, HENSALL, ON, N0M 1X0
(519) 262-3500 *SIC 2097*

SIC 2098 Macaroni and spaghetti

2319793 ONTARIO INC *p547*
350 CREDITSTONE RD UNIT 103, CONCORD, ON, L4K 3Z2
(905) 760-0000 *SIC 2098*

ALIMENTS O SOLE MIO INC, LES *p1061*
4600 RUE AMBROISE-LAFORTUNE, BOISBRIAND, QC, J7H 0G1
(450) 435-4111 *SIC 2098*

ALIMENTS PASTA ROMANA INC *p1239*
11430 BOUL ALBERT-HUDON, MONTREAL-NORD, QC, H1G 3J8
(514) 494-4767 *SIC 2098*

CATELLI FOODS CORPORATION *p205*
1631 DERWENT WAY, DELTA, BC, V3M 6K8
(604) 525-2278 *SIC 2098*

CATELLI FOODS CORPORATION *p607*
80 BROCKLEY DR, HAMILTON, ON, L8E 3C5
(905) 560-6200 *SIC 2098*

CATELLI FOODS CORPORATION *p1164*
6890 RUE NOTRE-DAME E, MONTREAL, QC, H1N 2E5
(514) 256-1601 *SIC 2098*

FOOD DIRECTIONS INC *p864*
120 MELFORD DR UNIT 8, SCARBOROUGH, ON, M1B 2X5
(416) 609-0016 *SIC 2098*

ITALPASTA LIMITED *p504*
199 SUMMERLEA RD, BRAMPTON, ON, L6T 4E5

---

(905) 792-9928 *SIC 2098*

ITALPASTA LIMITED *p504*
116 NUGGETT CRT, BRAMPTON, ON, L6T 5A9
(416) 798-7154 *SIC 2098*

PASTA KITCHEN LP *p557*
350 CREDITSTONE RD UNIT 103, CONCORD, ON, L4K 3Z2
(905) 760-0000 *SIC 2098*

PATES A TOUT INC *p1273*
2500 CH DES QUATRE-BOURGEOIS, QUEBEC, QC, G1V 4P9
(418) 651-8284 *SIC 2098*

PRIMO FOODS INC *p795*
56 HUXLEY RD, NORTH YORK, ON, M9M 1H2
(416) 741-9300 *SIC 2098*

PRODUITS GRISSPASTA LTEE *p1142*
805 BOUL GUIMOND, LONGUEUIL, QC, J4G 1M1
(450) 651-4150 *SIC 2098*

WING HING LUNG LIMITED *p996*
550 KIPLING AVE, TORONTO, ON, M8Z 5E9
(416) 531-5768 *SIC 2098*

SIC 2099 Food preparations, nec

9020-2292 QUEBEC INC *p1140*
1060 CH OLIVIER, LEVIS, QC, G7A 2M7
(418) 853-6265 *SIC 2099*

9030-5418 QUEBEC INC *p1319*
801 MONTEE SAINT-NICOLAS, SAINT-JEROME, QC, J7Y 4C7
(450) 569-8001 *SIC 2099*

AB MAURI (CANADA) LIMITEE *p1131*
31 RUE AIRLIE, LASALLE, QC, H8R 1Z8
(514) 366-1053 *SIC 2099*

ALIMENTS BARI INC, LES *p1347*
297 155 RTE, SAINT-LEONARD-D'ASTON, QC, J0C 1M0
(819) 399-2277 *SIC 2099*

ALIMENTS FONTAINE SANTE INC *p1325*
450 RUE DESLAURIERS, SAINT-LAURENT, QC, H4N 1V8
(514) 745-3085 *SIC 2099*

ALIMENTS MARTEL INC *p1125*
2387 RUE REMEMBRANCE, LACHINE, QC, H8S 1X4
SIC 2099

ALIMENTS MARTEL INC *p1381*
460 RUE FERNAND-POITRAS, TERREBONNE, QC, J6Y 1Y4
(514) 493-9423 *SIC 2099*

ALTIUS EPICES ET ASSAISONNEMENTS INC *p1052*
19000 AUT TRANSCANADIENNE, BAIE D URFE, QC, H9X 3S4
(514) 457-2200 *SIC 2099*

ASSOCIATED BRANDS INC *p891*
944 HIGHWAY 8, STONEY CREEK, ON, L8E 5S3
(905) 643-1211 *SIC 2099*

BFG CANADA LTD *p593*
88 TODD RD, GEORGETOWN, ON, L7G 4R7
(905) 873-8744 *SIC 2099*

CABANE A SUCRE CONSTANTIN (1992) INC *p1301*
1054 BOUL ARTHUR-SAUVE, SAINT-EUSTACHE, QC, J7R 4K3
(450) 473-2374 *SIC 2099*

CATELLI FOODS CORPORATION *p578*
401 THE WEST MALL SUITE 11, ETOBICOKE, ON, M9C 5J5
(416) 626-3500 *SIC 2099*

CIE MCCORMICK CANADA CO., LA *p648*
600 CLARKE RD, LONDON, ON, N5V 3K5
(519) 432-7311 *SIC 2099*

CITADELLE COOPERATIVE DE PRODUCTEURS DE SIROP D'ERABLE *p1246*
2100 AV SAINT-LAURENT, PLESSISVILLE, QC, G6L 2R3

---

(819) 362-3241 *SIC 2099*

FINE CHOICE FOODS LTD *p254*
23111 FRASERWOOD WAY, RICHMOND, BC, V6V 3B3
(604) 522-3110 *SIC 2099*

FRESH DIRECT FOODS LTD *p70*
11505 35 ST SE UNIT 103, CALGARY, AB, T2Z 4B1
(403) 508-6868 *SIC 2099*

FRESH MIX LIMITED *p487*
530 WELHAM RD, BARRIE, ON, L4N 8Z7
(705) 734-1580 *SIC 2099*

G. E. BARBOUR INC *p418*
165 STEWART AVE, SUSSEX, NB, E4E 3H1
(506) 432-2300 *SIC 2099*

GENERAL MILLS CANADA CORPORATION *p391*
1555 CHEVRIER BLVD SUITE B, WINNIPEG, MB, R3T 1Y7
(204) 477-8338 *SIC 2099*

GOLDEN BOY FOODS GP (2007) INC *p182*
7725 LOUGHEED HWY, BURNABY, BC, V5A 4V8
(778) 373-3800 *SIC 2099*

GRIFFITH FOODS LIMITED *p868*
757 PHARMACY AVE, SCARBOROUGH, ON, M1L 3J8
(416) 288-3050 *SIC 2099*

HEALTHCARE FOOD SERVICES INC *p811*
1010 DAIRY DR, ORLEANS, ON, K4A 3N3
(613) 841-7786 *SIC 2099*

HERITAGE FROZEN FOODS LTD *p93*
14615 124 AVE NW, EDMONTON, AB, T5L 3B2
(780) 454-7383 *SIC 2099*

HIGHBURY CANCO CORPORATION *p644*
148 ERIE ST S, LEAMINGTON, ON, N8H 0C3
(519) 322-1288 *SIC 2099*

HSF FOODS LTD *p396*
741 CENTRAL ST SUITE 501, CENTREVILLE, NB, E7K 2M4
(506) 276-3621 *SIC 2099*

INGREDIENTS ALIMENTAIRES BSA INC, LES *p1344*
6005 BOUL COUTURE, SAINT-LEONARD, QC, H1P 3E1
(514) 852-2719 *SIC 2099*

INOVATA FOODS CORP *p93*
12803 149 ST NW, EDMONTON, AB, T5L 2J7
(780) 454-8665 *SIC 2099*

INOVATA FOODS CORP *p911*
98 SPRUCE ST, TILLSONBURG, ON, N4G 5V3
SIC 2099

KERRY (CANADA) INC *p1036*
615 JACK ROSS AVE, WOODSTOCK, ON, N4V 1B7
(519) 537-3461 *SIC 2099*

KRAFT HEINZ CANADA ULC *p871*
1440 BIRCHMOUNT RD, SCARBOROUGH, ON, M1P 2E3
SIC 2099

LALLEMAND INC *p1164*
5494 RUE NOTRE-DAME E, MONTREAL, QC, H1N 2C4
(514) 255-4887 *SIC 2099*

LALLEMAND INC *p1167*
1620 RUE PREFONTAINE, MONTREAL, QC, H1W 2N8
(514) 522-2131 *SIC 2099*

LAMB WESTON CANADA ULC *p169*
102017 RIDGE RD, TABER, AB, T1G 2E5
(403) 223-3088 *SIC 2099*

LINSEY FOODS LTD *p672*
121 MCPHERSON ST, MARKHAM, ON, L3R 3L3
(905) 940-3850 *SIC 2099*

LYNCH, W. T. FOODS LIMITED *p775*
72 RAILSIDE RD, NORTH YORK, ON, M3A 1A3
(416) 449-5464 *SIC 2099*

MAITRE SALADIER INC p1062
1755 BOUL LIONEL-BERTRAND, BOIS-BRIAND, QC, J7H 1N8
(450) 435-0674   *SIC* 2099

MAPLE TREAT CORPORATION, THE p1111
1037 BOUL INDUSTRIEL, GRANBY, QC, J2J 2B8
(450) 777-4464   *SIC* 2099

MONTOUR LTEE p1059
1080 BOUL MICHELE-BOHEC, BLAINVILLE, QC, J7C 5N5
(450) 433-1312   *SIC* 2099

NEWLY WEDS FOODS CO. p121
9110 23 AVE NW, EDMONTON, AB, T6N 1H9
(780) 414-9500   *SIC* 2099

NEWLY WEDS FOODS CO. p741
450 SUPERIOR BLVD, MISSISSAUGA, ON, L5T 2R9
(905) 670-7776   *SIC* 2099

NEWLY WEDS FOODS CO. p1066
1381 RUE AMPERE, BOUCHERVILLE, QC, J4B 5Z5
(450) 641-2200   *SIC* 2099

NOSSACK DISTRIBUTION CENTRE p156
7240 JOHNSTONE DR SUITE 100, RED DEER, AB, T4P 3Y6
(403) 346-5006   *SIC* 2099

NOSSACK GOURMET FOODS LTD p137
5804 37 ST, INNISFAIL, AB, T4G 1S8
(403) 227-2121   *SIC* 2099

PEPES MEXICAN FOODS INC p587
122 CARRIER DR, ETOBICOKE, ON, M9W 5R1
(416) 674-0882   *SIC* 2099

PLACEMENTS LALLEMAND INC p1168
1620 RUE PREFONTAINE, MONTREAL, QC, H1W 2N8
(514) 522-2133   *SIC* 2099

PLAISIRS GASTRONOMIQUES INC p1062
3740 RUE LA VERENDRYE, BOISBRIAND, QC, J7H 1R5
(450) 433-1970   *SIC* 2099

PREMIUM BRANDS HOLDINGS CORPO-RATION p84
12251 WILLIAM SHORT RD NW, EDMON-TON, AB, T5B 2B7
(780) 474-5201   *SIC* 2099

PREMIUM BRANDS HOLDINGS CORPO-RATION p261
10991 SHELLBRIDGE WAY UNIT 100, RICHMOND, BC, V6X 3C6
(604) 656-3100   *SIC* 2099

PREMIUM BRANDS OPERATING LIMITED PARTNERSHIP p261
10991 SHELLBRIDGE WAY SUITE 100, RICHMOND, BC, V6X 3C6
(604) 656-3100   *SIC* 2099

RECTOR FOODS LIMITED p500
2280 NORTH PARK DR, BRAMPTON, ON, L6S 6C6
(905) 789-9691   *SIC* 2099

REINHART FOODS LIMITED p768
235 YORKLAND BLVD SUITE 1101, NORTH YORK, ON, M2J 4Y8
(416) 645-4910   *SIC* 2099

REINHART FOODS LIMITED p890
7449 HWY 26, STAYNER, ON, L0M 1S0
(705) 428-2422   *SIC* 2099

SANDRA TEA & COFFEE LIMITED p474
144 MILLS RD, AJAX, ON, L1S 2H1
(905) 683-5080   *SIC* 2099

SELECT FOOD PRODUCTS LIMITED p916
120 SUNRISE AVE, TORONTO, ON, M4A 1B4
(416) 759-9316   *SIC* 2099

SIMPLOT CANADA (II) LIMITED p355
HWY 1 W & SIMPLOT RD, PORTAGE LA PRAIRIE, MB, R1N 3A4
(204) 857-1400   *SIC* 2099

SKOR CULINARY CONCEPTS INC p700
1330 CRESTLAWN DR, MISSISSAUGA, ON, L4W 1P8
(905) 625-4447   *SIC* 2099

SUNRISE MARKETS INC p296
729 POWELL ST, VANCOUVER, BC, V6A 1H5
(604) 253-2326   *SIC* 2099

TRANS-HERB E INC p1296
1090 RUE PARENT, SAINT-BRUNO, QC, J3V 6L8
(450) 441-0779   *SIC* 2099

UNILEVER CANADA INC p589
195 BELFIELD RD, ETOBICOKE, ON, M9W 1G8
(416) 246-1650   *SIC* 2099

UNILEVER CANADA INC p931
160 BLOOR ST E SUITE 1400, TORONTO, ON, M4W 3R2
(416) 415-3000   *SIC* 2099

WIBERG CORPORATION p805
931 EQUESTRIAN CRT, OAKVILLE, ON, L6L 6L7
(905) 825-9900   *SIC* 2099

SIC 2111 Cigarettes

ALLAN RAMSAY ET COMPAGNIE LIMITEE p1222
3711 RUE SAINT-ANTOINE O, MON-TREAL, QC, H4C 3P6
(514) 932-6161   *SIC* 2111

DU MAURIER LTEE p1222
3711 RUE SAINT-ANTOINE O, MON-TREAL, QC, H4C 3P6
(514) 932-6161   *SIC* 2111

GRAND RIVER ENTERPRISES SIX NA-TIONS LIMITED p806
2176 CHIEFSWOOD RD, OHSWEKEN, ON, N0A 1M0
(519) 445-0919   *SIC* 2111

IMPERIAL TOBACCO CANADA LIMITEE p1223
3711 RUE SAINT-ANTOINE O, MON-TREAL, QC, H4C 3P6
(514) 932-6161   *SIC* 2111

IMPERIAL TOBACCO COMPAGNIE LIMI-TEE p603
107 WOODLAWN RD W, GUELPH, ON, N1H 1B4
    SIC 2111

JTI-MACDONALD CORP p706
1 ROBERT SPECK PKY SUITE 1601, MIS-SISSAUGA, ON, L4Z 0A2
(905) 804-7300   *SIC* 2111

JTI-MACDONALD CORP p1174
2455 RUE ONTARIO E BUREAU 4, MON-TREAL, QC, H2K 1W3
(514) 598-2525   *SIC* 2111

ROTHMANS, BENSON & HEDGES INC p777
1500 DON MILLS RD SUITE 900, NORTH YORK, ON, M3B 3L1
(416) 449-5525   *SIC* 2111

SIC 2131 Chewing and smoking tobacco

GESTION A.D.L. SENC p1150
1665 RUE NISHK, MASHTEUIATSH, QC, G0W 2H0
(418) 275-6161   *SIC* 2131

SIC 2211 Broadwoven fabric mills, cotton

ANTEX DESIGNS INC p704
330 BRITANNIA RD E, MISSISSAUGA, ON, L4Z 1X9
(905) 507-8778   *SIC* 2211

BUFFALO INTERNATIONAL INC p1216
400 RUE SAUVE O, MONTREAL, QC, H3L 1Z8
(514) 388-3551   *SIC* 2211

CAMTX CORPORATION p972
106 AVENUE RD, TORONTO, ON, M5R 2H3
(416) 920-0500   *SIC* 2211

DOUBLETEX p980

352 ADELAIDE ST W, TORONTO, ON, M5V 1R8
(416) 593-0320   *SIC* 2211

DOUBLETEX p1217
9785 RUE JEANNE-MANCE, MONTREAL, QC, H3L 3B6
(514) 382-1770   *SIC* 2211

TEKNION LS INC p1133
359 RUE SAINT-JOSETH, LAURIER-STATION, QC, G0S 1N0
(418) 830-0855   *SIC* 2211

TRIMONT MFG. INC p875
115 MILNER AVE SUITE 2, SCARBOR-OUGH, ON, M1S 4L7
(416) 640-2045   *SIC* 2211

XERIUM CANADA INC p460
650 PARK ST, KENTVILLE, NS, B4N 3W6
(902) 678-7311   *SIC* 2211

SIC 2221 Broadwoven fabric mills, manmade

ASTENJOHNSON, INC p623
48 RICHARDSON SIDE RD, KANATA, ON, K2K 1X2
(613) 592-5851   *SIC* 2221

DUVALTEX (CANADA) INC p1305
2805 90E RUE, SAINT-GEORGES, QC, G6A 1K1
(418) 227-9897   *SIC* 2221

FABRENE INC p763
240 DUPONT RD, NORTH BAY, ON, P1B 9B4
(705) 476-7057   *SIC* 2221

HOLIDAY HOME FASHIONS INC p554
2740 STEELES AVE W SUITE 2, CON-CORD, ON, L4K 4T4
    SIC 2221

INTERTAPE POLYMER INC p469
50 ABBEY AVE, TRURO, NS, B2N 6W4
    SIC 2221

NORTHERN FEATHER CANADA LTD p209
8088 RIVER WAY, DELTA, BC, V4G 1K9
(604) 940-8283   *SIC* 2221

PRODUITS KRUGER SHERBROOKE INC p1218
3285 CH DE BEDFORD, MONTREAL, QC, H3S 1G5
(514) 737-1131   *SIC* 2221

RAYONESE TEXTILE INC p1320
500 BOUL MONSEIGNEUR-DUBOIS, SAINT-JEROME, QC, J7Y 3L8
(450) 476-1991   *SIC* 2221

TEXTILES MONTEREY (1996) INC p1097
2575 BOUL SAINT-JOSEPH, DRUM-MONDVILLE, QC, J2B 7V4
(819) 475-4333   *SIC* 2221

VOITH CANADA INC p619
925 TUPPER ST, HAWKESBURY, ON, K6A 3T5
(613) 632-4163   *SIC* 2221

SIC 2231 Broadwoven fabric mills, wool

ALBANY INTERNATIONAL CANADA CORP p839
2947 RIDEAU FERRY RD, PERTH, ON, K7H 3E3
(613) 267-6600   *SIC* 2231

ALBANY INTERNATIONAL CANADA CORP p1088
300 RUE DE WESTMOUNT, COW-ANSVILLE, QC, J2K 1S9
(450) 263-2880   *SIC* 2231

BRAND FELT OF CANADA LIMITED p702
2559 WHARTON GLEN AVE, MISSIS-SAUGA, ON, L4X 2A8
(905) 279-6680   *SIC* 2231

LAINAGES VICTOR LTEE, LES p1353
260 RTE DE LA STATION BUREAU 218, SAINT-VICTOR, QC, G0M 2B0
(418) 588-6827   *SIC* 2231

SIC 2241 Narrow fabric mills

INDUSTRIES COVER INC p1049
9300 BOUL RAY-LAWSON, ANJOU, QC, H1J 1Y6
(514) 353-3880   *SIC* 2241

NARROFLEX INC p892
590 SOUTH SERVICE RD, STONEY CREEK, ON, L8E 2W1
(905) 643-6066   *SIC* 2241

VOA CANADA INC p547
190 MACDONALD RD, COLLINGWOOD, ON, L9Y 4N6
(705) 444-2561   *SIC* 2241

WAH LUNG LABELS (CANADA) INC p677
150 TELSON RD, MARKHAM, ON, L3R 1E5
(905) 948-8877   *SIC* 2241

WENTWORTH TEXTILES INC p893
590 SOUTH SERVICE RD, STONEY CREEK, ON, L8E 2W1
(905) 643-6066   *SIC* 2241

SIC 2251 Women's hosiery, except socks

BONNETERIE BELLA INC. p972
1191 BATHURST ST, TORONTO, ON, M5R 3H4
(416) 537-2137   *SIC* 2251

BONNETERIE BELLA INC. p1225
1401 RUE LEGENDRE O, MONTREAL, QC, H4N 2R9
(514) 381-8519   *SIC* 2251

MANUFACTURE DE BAS CULOTTES LAM-OUR INC p1179
55 RUE DE LOUVAIN O BUREAU 200, MONTREAL, QC, H2N 1A4
(514) 381-7687   *SIC* 2251

PHANTOM INDUSTRIES INC p994
207 WESTON RD, TORONTO, ON, M6N 4Z3
(416) 762-7177   *SIC* 2251

SIC 2252 Hosiery, nec

BAS A.Y.K. INC, LES p1345
5505 BOUL DES GRANDES-PRAIRIES, SAINT-LEONARD, QC, H1R 1B3
(514) 279-4648   *SIC* 2252

GILDAN APPAREL (CANADA) LP p1170
3701 RUE JARRY E, MONTREAL, QC, H1Z 2G1
(514) 376-3000   *SIC* 2252

MCGREGOR INDUSTRIES INC p871
1360 BIRCHMOUNT RD, SCARBOROUGH, ON, M1P 2E3
    SIC 2252

TRICOTS DUVAL & RAYMOND LTEE, LES p1254
11 RUE SAINT-JACQUES O, PRINCEVILLE, QC, G6L 5E6
(819) 364-2927   *SIC* 2252

SIC 2253 Knit outerwear mills

ARTEX SPORTSWEAR INC p876
40 TIFFIELD RD UNIT 9, SCARBOROUGH, ON, M1V 5B6
(416) 755-3382   *SIC* 2253

DOROTHEA KNITTING MILLS LIMITED p919
51 BETH NEALSON DR, TORONTO, ON, M4H 0A4
(416) 421-3773   *SIC* 2253

INDUSTRIES SPLEND'OR LTEE, LES p1170
8660 8E AV, MONTREAL, QC, H1Z 2W8
    SIC 2253

QUALITY KNITTING LIMITED p914
1210 BIRCHMOUNT RD, TORONTO, ON, M1P 2C3
(416) 598-2422   *SIC* 2253

SOLIDWEAR ENTERPRISES LIMITED p875

---

59 MILNER AVE, SCARBOROUGH, ON, M1S 3P6
(416) 298-2667   *SIC 2253*

TRICOT IDEAL INC   *p1179*
9494 BOUL SAINT-LAURENT BUREAU 400, MONTREAL, QC, H2N 1P4
(514) 381-4496   *SIC 2253*

SIC 2257 Weft knit fabric mills

AJAX TEXTILE CORPORATION   *p473*
170 COMMERCIAL AVE, AJAX, ON, L1S 2H5
(905) 683-6800   *SIC 2257*

TRICOTS LIESSE (1983) INC   *p1222*
2125 RUE LILY-SIMON, MONTREAL, QC, H4B 3A1
(514) 342-0685   *SIC 2257*

SIC 2258 Lace and warp knit fabric mills

8756074 CANADA INC   *p1325*
828 RUE DESLAURIERS, SAINT-LAURENT, QC, H4N 1X1
(514) 336-0445   *SIC 2258*

PRESCOTT FINISHING INC   *p848*
823 WALKERS ST, PRESCOTT, ON, K0E 1T0
(613) 925-2859   *SIC 2258*

THAI OCCIDENTAL LTD   *p773*
5334 YONGE ST SUITE 907, NORTH YORK, ON, M2N 6V1
SIC 2258

TISSUS RENTEX INC., LES   *p1158*
8650 CH DELMEADE, MONT-ROYAL, QC, H4T 1L6
(514) 735-2641   *SIC 2258*

TRICOTS MAXIME INC, LES   *p1054*
19500 AV CLARK-GRAHAM, BAIE-D'URFE, QC, H9X 3R8
(514) 336-0445   *SIC 2258*

SIC 2259 Knitting mills, nec

GILDAN ACTIVEWEAR INC   *p1196*
600 BOUL DE MAISONNEUVE O 33EME ETAGE, MONTREAL, QC, H3A 3J2
(514) 735-2023   *SIC 2259*

SIC 2261 Finishing plants, cotton

ANNABEL CANADA INC   *p1098*
1645 RUE HAGGERTY, DRUM-MONDVILLE, QC, J2C 5P7
(819) 472-1367   *SIC 2261*

SIC 2269 Finishing plants, nec

DI-TECH INC   *p1222*
2125 RUE LILY-SIMON, MONTREAL, QC, H4B 3A1
SIC 2269

SIC 2273 Carpets and rugs

ANI-MAT INC   *p1375*
395 RUE RODOLPHE-RACINE, SHER-BROOKE, QC, J1R 0S7
(819) 821-2091   *SIC 2273*

COMPAGNIE BEAULIEU CANADA   *p1044*
335 RUE DE ROXTON, ACTON VALE, QC, J0H 1A0
(450) 546-5000   *SIC 2273*

COMPAGNIE BEAULIEU CANADA   *p1101*
1144 BOUL MAGENTA E, FARNHAM, QC, J2N 1C1
SIC 2273

KORHANI OF CANADA INC   *p554*
7500 KEELE ST, CONCORD, ON, L4K 1Z9
(905) 660-0863   *SIC 2273*

KRAUS CARPET LP   *p1008*
65 NORTHFIELD DR W, WATERLOO, ON, N2L 0A8
(519) 884-2310   *SIC 2273*

TANDUS CENTIVA LIMITED   *p469*
435 WILLOW ST SUITE 30, TRURO, NS, B2N 6T2
(902) 895-5491   *SIC 2273*

TANDUS FLOORING LIMITED   *p469*
GD RPO PRINCE, TRURO, NS, B2N 5B5
(902) 895-5491   *SIC 2273*

TAPIS VENTURE INC   *p1305*
700 120E RUE, SAINT-GEORGES, QC, G5Y 6R6
(418) 227-5955   *SIC 2273*

SIC 2281 Yarn spinning mills

FILATURE LEMIEUX INC   *p1299*
125 108 RTE E, SAINT-EPHREM-DE-BEAUCE, QC, G0M 1R0
(418) 484-2169   *SIC 2281*

FILSPEC INC   *p1373*
85 RUE DE LA BURLINGTON, SHER-BROOKE, QC, J1L 1G9
(819) 573-8700   *SIC 2281*

SPINRITE CORP   *p647*
320 LIVINGSTONE AVE S, LISTOWEL, ON, N4W 0C9
(519) 291-3780   *SIC 2281*

SPINRITE LIMITED PARTNERSHIP   *p647*
320 LIVINGSTONE AVE S, LISTOWEL, ON, N4W 3H3
(519) 291-3780   *SIC 2281*

SIC 2282 Throwing and winding mills

COMPAGNIE BEAULIEU CANADA   *p1402*
1003 RUE PRINCIPALE RR 21, WICKHAM, QC, J0C 1S0
SIC 2282

REGITEX INC   *p1322*
745 AV GUY-POULIN, SAINT-JOSEPH-DE-BEAUCE, QC, G0S 2V0
(418) 397-5775   *SIC 2282*

SIC 2284 Thread mills

AMERICAN & EFIRD CANADA INCOR-POREE   *p1047*
8301 BOUL RAY-LAWSON, ANJOU, QC, H1J 1X9
(514) 352-4800   *SIC 2284*

CANSEW INC   *p1178*
111 RUE CHABANEL O BUREAU 101, MONTREAL, QC, H2N 1C9
(514) 382-2807   *SIC 2284*

SIC 2295 Coated fabrics, not rubberized

COPAP INC   *p1249*
755 BOUL SAINT-JEAN BUREAU 305, POINTE-CLAIRE, QC, H9R 5M9
(514) 693-9150   *SIC 2295*

INTERTAPE POLYMER INC.   *p1229*
800 RUE DU SQUARE-VICTORIA, MON-TREAL, QC, H4Z 1A1
SIC 2295

MORBERN INC   *p562*
80 BOUNDARY RD, CORNWALL, ON, K6H 6M1
(613) 932-8811   *SIC 2295*

STEDFAST INC   *p1110*
230 RUE SAINT-CHARLES S, GRANBY, QC, J2G 3Y3
(450) 378-8441   *SIC 2295*

SURTECO CANADA LTD   *p506*
230 ORENDA RD, BRAMPTON, ON, L6T 1E9
(905) 759-1074   *SIC 2295*

SIC 2296 Tire cord and fabrics

BRIDGESTONE CANADA INC   *p1035*
1200 DUNDAS ST, WOODSTOCK, ON, N4S 7V9
(519) 537-6231   *SIC 2296*

SIC 2297 Nonwoven fabrics

190712 CANADA INC   *p1177*
270 RUE DE LOUVAIN O, MONTREAL, QC, H2N 1B6
(514) 389-8221   *SIC 2297*

ALBARRIE CANADA LIMITED   *p486*
85 MORROW RD, BARRIE, ON, L4N 3V7
(705) 737-0551   *SIC 2297*

FYBON INDUSTRIES LIMITED   *p503*
5 TILBURY CRT, BRAMPTON, ON, L6T 3T4
(905) 291-1090   *SIC 2297*

JASZTEX FIBRES INC   *p1251*
61 BOUL HYMUS, POINTE-CLAIRE, QC, H9R 1E2
(514) 697-3096   *SIC 2297*

TEXEL MATERIAUX TECHNIQUES INC   *p1299*
485 RUE DES ERABLES, SAINT-ELZEAR, QC, G0S 2J0
(418) 387-5910   *SIC 2297*

TEXEL MATERIAUX TECHNIQUES INC   *p1360*
1300 2E RUE DU PARC-INDUSTRIEL, SAINTE-MARIE, QC, G6E 1G8
(418) 658-0200   *SIC 2297*

SIC 2298 Cordage and twine

DANA CANADA CORPORATION   *p542*
1010 RICHMOND ST, CHATHAM, ON, N7M 5J5
(519) 351-1221   *SIC 2298*

WINCHESTER AUBURN MILLS INC   *p565*
70 DUNDAS ST, DESERONTO, ON, K0K 1X0
(877) 224-2673   *SIC 2298*

SIC 2299 Textile goods, nec

ASTENJOHNSON, INC   *p623*
1243 TERON RD, KANATA, ON, K2K 1X2
(613) 592-5851   *SIC 2299*

ASTENJOHNSON, INC   *p1365*
213 BOUL DU HAVRE, SALABERRY-DE-VALLEYFIELD, QC, J6S 1R9
(450) 373-2425   *SIC 2299*

AUTONEUM CANADA LTD   *p648*
1800 HURON ST, LONDON, ON, N5V 3A6
(519) 659-0560   *SIC 2299*

AUTONEUM CANADA LTD   *p911*
1451 BELL MILL SIDEROAD, TILLSON-BURG, ON, N4G 4H8
(519) 842-6411   *SIC 2299*

BARRDAY, INC   *p537*
260 HOLIDAY INN DR, CAMBRIDGE, ON, N3C 4E8
(519) 621-3620   *SIC 2299*

CONSOLTEX INC   *p1088*
400 RUE WILLARD, COWANSVILLE, QC, J2K 3A2
(514) 333-8800   *SIC 2299*

CONSOLTEX INC   *p1216*
560 BOUL HENRI-BOURASSA O BUREAU 302, MONTREAL, QC, H3L 1P4
(514) 333-8800   *SIC 2299*

DIFCO, TISSUS DE PERFORMANCE INC

p1147
160 RUE PRINCIPALE E, MAGOG, QC, J1X 4X5
SIC 2299

DIFCO, TISSUS DE PERFORMANCE INC   *p1195*
1411 RUE PEEL BUREAU 505, MON-TREAL, QC, H3A 1S5
(819) 434-2159   *SIC 2299*

GARLOCK OF CANADA LTD   *p1373*
4100 RUE DE LA GARLOCK, SHER-BROOKE, QC, J1L 1W5
(819) 563-8080   *SIC 2299*

INVISTA (CANADA) COMPANY   *p489*
GD, BATH, ON, K0H 1G0
(613) 634-5124   *SIC 2299*

INVISTA (CANADA) COMPANY   *p630*
455 FRONT RD, KINGSTON, ON, K7L 4Z6
(613) 544-6000   *SIC 2299*

LINCOLN FABRICS HOLDINGS LIMITED
p884
63 LAKEPORT RD, ST CATHARINES, ON, L2N 4P6
SIC 2299

SEAWAY YARNS LIMITED   *p562*
3320 LOYALIST ST, CORNWALL, ON, K6H 6C8
(613) 933-2770   *SIC 2299*

SIC 2311 Men's and boy's suits and coats

FREED & FREED INTERNATIONAL LTD
p372
1309 MOUNTAIN AVE, WINNIPEG, MB, R2X 2Y1
(204) 786-6081   *SIC 2311*

INNOTEX INC   *p1283*
275 RUE GOUIN BUREAU 1010, RICH-MOND, QC, J0B 2H0
(819) 826-5971   *SIC 2311*

JACK VICTOR LIMITED   *p1205*
1250 RUE SAINT-ALEXANDRE BUREAU 100, MONTREAL, QC, H3B 3H6
(514) 866-4891   *SIC 2311*

KANUK INC   *p1173*
485 RUE RACHEL E, MONTREAL, QC, H2J 2H1
(514) 284-4494   *SIC 2311*

MANUFACTURE DE VETEMENTS EMPIRE INC   *p1182*
5800 RUE SAINT-DENIS BUREAU 302, MONTREAL, QC, H2S 3L5
(514) 279-7341   *SIC 2311*

SAMUELSOHN LIMITEE   *p1218*
6930 AV DU PARC, MONTREAL, QC, H3N 1W9
(514) 273-7741   *SIC 2311*

UNIFORMES F.O.B. (1991) LTEE   *p1122*
645 14E AV, LA GUADELOUPE, QC, G0M 1G0
SIC 2311

VETEMENTS PEERLESS INC   *p1171*
8888 BOUL PIE-IX, MONTREAL, QC, H1Z 4J5
(514) 593-9300   *SIC 2311*

VETEMENTS S & F (CANADA) LTEE   *p1062*
3720 RUE LA VERENDRYE, BOISBRIAND, QC, J7H 1R5
SIC 2311

SIC 2321 Men's and boy's furnishings

CHEMISE EMPIRE LTEE   *p1146*
451 AV SAINT-LAURENT, LOUISEVILLE, QC, J5V 1K4
(819) 228-2821   *SIC 2321*

MWG APPAREL CORP   *p381*
1147 NOTRE DAME AVE, WINNIPEG, MB, R3E 3G1
(204) 774-2561   *SIC 2321*

NISE N KOSY INCORPORATED   *p781*
120 OVERBROOK PL SUITE 100, NORTH

YORK, ON, M3H 4P8
(416) 665-8802   *SIC 2321*
SOUS-VETEMENTS U.M. INC, LES   p1179
9200 BOUL SAINT-LAURENT, MONTREAL, QC, H2N 1M9
(514) 387-3791   *SIC 2321*
TDI-DYNAMIC CANADA ULC   p872
1870 BIRCHMOUNT RD, SCARBOROUGH, ON, M1P 2J7
(877) 722-2003   *SIC 2321*

SIC 2322 Men's and boy's underwear and nightwear

JIMMISS CANADA INC   p1183
5425 AV CASGRAIN BUREAU 502, MONTREAL, QC, H2T 1X6
(514) 271-3133   *SIC 2322*
STANFIELD'S LIMITED   p469
1 LOGAN ST, TRURO, NS, B2N 5C2
(902) 895-5406   *SIC 2322*
TEXTILES WIN-SIR INC, LES   p1076
295 BOUL INDUSTRIEL BUREAU A, CHATEAUGUAY, QC, J6J 4Z2
(450) 691-2747   *SIC 2322*

SIC 2325 Men's and boys' trousers and slacks

BALLIN INC   p1332
2825 RUE BRABANT-MARINEAU, SAINT-LAURENT, QC, H4S 1R8
(514) 333-5501   *SIC 2325*
CANADAY'S APPAREL LTD   p1410
115 CORONATION DR, MOOSE JAW, SK, S6H 4P3
(306) 692-6406   *SIC 2325*
CONFECTION ST METHODE INC   p1044
228 RUE NOTRE-DAME N, ADSTOCK, QC, G0N 1S0
(418) 422-2206   *SIC 2325*
PEERLESS GARMENTS LTD   p375
515 NOTRE DAME AVE, WINNIPEG, MB, R3B 1R9
SIC 2325

SIC 2326 Men's and boy's work clothing

CODET INC   p1081
49 RUE MAPLE, COATICOOK, QC, J1A 1C3
(819) 849-4819   *SIC 2326*
FUNDY TEXTILE & DESIGN LIMITED   p468
189 INDUSTRIAL AVE, TRURO, NS, B2N 6V3
(902) 897-0010   *SIC 2326*
G&K SERVICES CANADA INC   p868
940 WARDEN AVE SUITE 1, SCARBOROUGH, ON, M1L 4C9
(647) 933-2627   *SIC 2326*
GESTION JEAN LAFRAMBOISE INC   p1239
11450 BOUL ALBERT-HUDON, MONTREAL-NORD, QC, H1G 3J9
SIC 2326
GROUPE DE LA COTE INC   p1053
332 RUE DE PUYJALON, BAIE-COMEAU, QC, G5C 1M5
(418) 589-8397   *SIC 2326*
S. COHEN INC   p1341
153 RUE GRAVELINE, SAINT-LAURENT, QC, H4T 1R4
(514) 342-6700   *SIC 2326*
WILLIAMSON-DICKIE CANADA COMPANY   p537
415 THOMPSON DR, CAMBRIDGE, ON, N1T 2K7
(888) 664-6636   *SIC 2326*
WINNIPEG PANTS & SPORTSWEAR MFG. LTD   p374
85 ADELAIDE ST, WINNIPEG, MB, R3A 0V9

(204) 942-3494   *SIC 2326*

SIC 2329 Men's and boy's clothing, nec

ACCOLADE GROUP INC   p850
66 WEST BEAVER CREEK RD, RICHMOND HILL, ON, L4B 1G5
(416) 465-7211   *SIC 2329*
BARBARIAN SPORTSWEAR INC   p642
575 TRILLIUM DR, KITCHENER, ON, N2R 1J9
(519) 895-1932   *SIC 2329*
C&O APPAREL INC   p192
3788 NORTH FRASER WAY, BURNABY, BC, V5J 5G1
(604) 451-9799   *SIC 2329*
DUVET COMFORT INC   p874
130 COMMANDER BLVD, SCARBOROUGH, ON, M1S 3H7
(416) 754-1455   *SIC 2329*
INVESTISSEURS 3 B INC   p1314
15855 AV HUBERT, SAINT-HYACINTHE, QC, J2T 4C9
(450) 773-5258   *SIC 2329*
LOUIS GARNEAU SPORTS INC   p1293
30 RUE DES GRANDS-LACS, SAINT-AUGUSTIN-DE-DESMAURES, QC, G3A 2E6
(418) 878-4135   *SIC 2329*
MAC MOR OF CANADA LTD   p791
21 BENTON RD, NORTH YORK, ON, M6M 3G2
(416) 596-8237   *SIC 2329*
REGENCY APPAREL CO LTD   p777
255 DUNCAN MILL RD SUITE 303, NORTH YORK, ON, M3B 3H9
SIC 2329
RICHLU SPORTSWEAR MFG. LTD   p373
85 ADELAIDE ST, WINNIPEG, MB, R3A 0V9
(204) 942-3494   *SIC 2329*
SPORT MASKA INC   p1314
15855 AV HUBERT, SAINT-HYACINTHE, QC, J2T 4C9
(450) 773-5258   *SIC 2329*
SPORTS INTERNATIONAL CSTS INC   p576
221 EVANS AVE, ETOBICOKE, ON, M8Z 1J5
(416) 251-2132   *SIC 2329*
SUGOI PERFORMANCE APPAREL LIMITED PARTNERSHIP   p289
144 7TH AVE E, VANCOUVER, BC, V5T 1M6
(604) 875-0887   *SIC 2329*
VETEMENTS S P INC, LES   p1111
1237 BOUL INDUSTRIEL, GRANBY, QC, J2J 2B8
(450) 776-6111   *SIC 2329*

SIC 2331 Women's and misses' blouses and shirts

CANADA GOOSE HOLDINGS INC   p989
250 BOWIE AVE, TORONTO, ON, M6E 4Y2
(416) 780-9850   *SIC 2331*
JOSEPH RIBKOFF INC   p1094
2375 RUE DE L'AVIATION, DORVAL, QC, H9P 2X6
(514) 685-9191   *SIC 2331*

SIC 2335 Women's, junior's, and misses' dresses

CONFECTION B L INC   p397
681 RUE PRINCIPALE, CLAIR, NB, E7A 2H3
(506) 992-3602   *SIC 2335*
DESIGN FRANK LYMAN INC   p1250
2500 BOUL DES SOURCES, POINTE-CLAIRE, QC, H9R 0B3
(514) 695-1719   *SIC 2335*
GROUPE ALGO INC   p1178
225 RUE CHABANEL O, MONTREAL, QC,

H2N 2C9
(514) 384-3551   *SIC 2335*
GROUPE ALGO INC   p1334
5555 RUE CYPIHOT, SAINT-LAURENT, QC, H4S 1R3
(514) 388-8888   *SIC 2335*
IMPORTATIONS JEREMY D. LIMITED   p1179
9333 BOUL SAINT-LAURENT BUREAU 200, MONTREAL, QC, H2N 1P6
(514) 385-3898   *SIC 2335*
JAMEI COMPANY LTD   p874
180 COMMANDER BLVD, SCARBOROUGH, ON, M1S 3C8
(416) 293-8385   *SIC 2335*

SIC 2337 Women's and misses' suits and coats

COLLECTION CONRAD C INC   p1178
9320 BOUL SAINT-LAURENT BUREAU 200, MONTREAL, QC, H2N 1N7
(514) 385-9599   *SIC 2337*
CONFECTION 4E DIMENSION LTEE   p417
11 RUE INDUSTRIELLE, SAINT-LEONARD, NB, E7E 2A9
(506) 423-7660   *SIC 2337*
SATISFASHION INC   p874
33 COMMANDER BLVD SUITE 1, SCARBOROUGH, ON, M1S 3E7
SIC 2337
TANG APPAREL CO. LIMITED   p917
50 NORTHLINE RD, TORONTO, ON, M4B 3E2
(416) 603-0021   *SIC 2337*
UNISYNC GROUP LIMITED   p743
6375 DIXIE RD UNIT 6, MISSISSAUGA, ON, L5T 2E7
(905) 361-8989   *SIC 2337*
VETEMENTS COOKSHIRE INC   p1082
725 RUE POPE, COOKSHIRE-EATON, QC, J0B 1M0
(819) 875-5538   *SIC 2337*

SIC 2339 Women's and misses' outerwear, nec

BALLIN INC   p1297
2100 AV DE L'UNION, SAINT-CESAIRE, QC, J0L 1T0
(450) 469-4957   *SIC 2339*
BENTLEYS OF LONDON SLACKS LTD   p371
1309 MOUNTAIN AVE, WINNIPEG, MB, R2X 2Y1
(204) 786-6081   *SIC 2339*
BLACK FEATHER HOLDINGS INCORPORATED   p989
250 BOWIE AVE, TORONTO, ON, M6E 4Y2
(416) 780-9850   *SIC 2339*
COALISION INC   p1187
700 RUE SAINT-ANTOINE E BUREAU 110, MONTREAL, QC, H2Y 1A6
(514) 798-3534   *SIC 2339*
COLLECTIONS SHAN INC, LES   p1400
4390 SUD LAVAL (A-440) O, VIMONT, QC, H7T 2P7
(450) 687-7101   *SIC 2339*
COUTURE C G H INC   p1298
12 RUE BELANGER, SAINT-DAMASE-DES-AULNAIES, QC, G0R 2X0
(418) 598-3208   *SIC 2339*
JERICO SPORTSWEAR LTD   p874
120 COMMANDER BLVD, SCARBOROUGH, ON, M1S 3H7
(416) 288-0822   *SIC 2339*
JONES APPAREL GROUP CANADA ULC   p554
388 APPLEWOOD CRES, CONCORD, ON, L4K 4B4
(905) 760-6000   *SIC 2339*
LULULEMON ATHLETICA CANADA INC   p321
1818 CORNWALL AVE SUITE 400, VANCOUVER, BC, V6J 1C7

(604) 732-6124   *SIC 2339*
MONDOR LTEE   p1316
785 RUE HONORE-MERCIER, SAINT-JEAN-SUR-RICHELIEU, QC, J2X 3S2
(450) 347-5321   *SIC 2339*
UNISYNC CORP   p310
885 WEST GEORGIA ST SUITE 1328, VANCOUVER, BC, V6C 3E8
(778) 370-1725   *SIC 2339*

SIC 2341 Women's and children's underwear

COLLECTION ARIANNE INC   p1225
1655 RUE DE LOUVAIN O, MONTREAL, QC, H4N 1G6
(514) 385-9393   *SIC 2341*
HAMILTON LINGERIE (1978) LTD   p1170
3565 RUE JARRY E BUREAU 600, MONTREAL, QC, H1Z 4K6
(514) 721-2151   *SIC 2341*
MANUFACTURE UNIVERSELLE S.B. INC   p1183
5555 AV CASGRAIN BUREAU 300, MONTREAL, QC, H2T 1Y1
(514) 271-1177   *SIC 2341*

SIC 2342 Bras, girdles, and allied garments

COCONUT GROVE PADS INC   p668
525 DENISON ST UNIT 1, MARKHAM, ON, L3R 1B8
(905) 752-0566   *SIC 2342*

SIC 2353 Hats, caps, and millinery

CROWN CAP (1987) LTD   p380
1130 WALL ST, WINNIPEG, MB, R3E 2R9
(204) 775-7740   *SIC 2353*
DOMINION REGALIA LIMITED   p919
4 OVERLEA BLVD, TORONTO, ON, M4H 1A4
(416) 752-9987   *SIC 2353*
FERSTEN WORLDWIDE INC   p1329
4600 BOUL POIRIER, SAINT-LAURENT, QC, H4R 2C5
(514) 739-1644   *SIC 2353*

SIC 2369 Girl's and children's outerwear, nec

PEEKABOO BEANS INC   p325
11120 BRIDGEPORT RD UNIT 170, VANCOUVER, BC, V6X 1T2
(604) 279-2326   *SIC 2369*

SIC 2381 Fabric dress and work gloves

SUPERIOR GLOVE WORKS LIMITED   p473
36 VIMY ST, ACTON, ON, L7J 1S1
(519) 853-1920   *SIC 2381*

SIC 2386 Leather and sheep-lined clothing

RUDSAK INC   p1179
9160 BOUL SAINT-LAURENT BUREAU 400, MONTREAL, QC, H2N 1M9
(514) 389-9661   *SIC 2386*

SIC 2387 Apparel belts

APPAREL TRIMMINGS INC   p873
20 COMMANDER BLVD, SCARBOROUGH, ON, M1S 3L9
(416) 298-8836   *SIC 2387*
CUSTOM LEATHER CANADA LIMITED   p635
460 BINGEMANS CENTRE DR, KITCH-

ENER, ON, N2B 3X9
(519) 741-2070 *SIC* 2387
GESTION SUMMIT STEPS INC *p1172*
5700 RUE FULLUM, MONTREAL, QC, H2G 2H7
(514) 271-2358 *SIC* 2387

SIC 2389 Apparel and accessories, nec

FRANCIS INTERNATIONAL TRADING (CANADA) INC *p1225*
1605 RUE CHABANEL O BUREAU 300, MONTREAL, QC, H4N 2T7
(514) 858-1088 *SIC* 2389
GASPARD & SONS (1963) LIMITED *p372*
1266 FIFE ST, WINNIPEG, MB, R2X 2N6
(204) 949-5700 *SIC* 2389
GASPARD LP *p372*
1266 FIFE ST, WINNIPEG, MB, R2X 2N6
(204) 949-5700 *SIC* 2389
GRUVEN INC *p878*
19 NEWGALE GATE, SCARBOROUGH, ON, M1X 1B6
(416) 292-7331 *SIC* 2389
JEAN-FRANCOIS ROCHEFORT INC *p1182*
6600 RUE SAINT-URBAIN BUREAU 440, MONTREAL, QC, H2S 3G8
(514) 273-7256 *SIC* 2389
MODE RVING INC *p1179*
555 RUE CHABANEL O BUREAU M42B, MONTREAL, QC, H2N 2J2
(514) 577-2172 *SIC* 2389

SIC 2391 Curtains and draperies

WESTPORT MANUFACTURING CO LTD *p324*
1122 MARINE DR SW, VANCOUVER, BC, V6P 5Z3
(604) 261-9326 *SIC* 2391

SIC 2392 Household furnishings, nec

MARIMAC INC *p1340*
6395 CH DE LA COTE-DE-LIESSE, SAINT-LAURENT, QC, H4T 1E5
(514) 725-7600 *SIC* 2392
MIP INC *p1049*
9100 BOUL RAY-LAWSON, ANJOU, QC, H1J 1K8
(514) 356-1224 *SIC* 2392

SIC 2394 Canvas and related products

AUTOLIV CANADA INC *p666*
7455 BIRCHMOUNT RD, MARKHAM, ON, L3R 5C2
(905) 475-1468 *SIC* 2394
AUTOLIV CANADA INC *p911*
20 AUTOLIV DR, TILBURY, ON, N0P 2L0
(519) 682-1083 *SIC* 2394
INLAND PLASTICS LTD *p160*
201 CENTRE ST, ROSEDALE STATION, AB, T0J 2V0
(403) 823-6252 *SIC* 2394
INTERNATIONAL TENTNOLOGY CORP *p272*
15427 66 AVE, SURREY, BC, V3S 2A1
(604) 597-8368 *SIC* 2394
NORSEMAN GROUP LTD *p96*
14545 115 AVE NW, EDMONTON, AB, T5M 3B8
(780) 451-6939 *SIC* 2394
SSH BEDDING CANADA CO *p32*
3636 11A ST SE, CALGARY, AB, T2G 3H3
(403) 287-0600 *SIC* 2394
SSH BEDDING CANADA CO *p1118*
17400 RTE TRANSCANADIENNE, KIRKLAND, QC, H9J 2M5

(514) 694-3030 *SIC* 2394

SIC 2399 Fabricated textile products, nec

CREATIONS MORIN INC, LES *p1096*
2575 BOUL SAINT-JOSEPH, DRUMMONDVILLE, QC, J2B 7V4
(819) 474-4664 *SIC* 2399
FELLFAB LIMITED *p608*
2343 BARTON ST E, HAMILTON, ON, L8E 5V8
(905) 560-9230 *SIC* 2399
GREEN BELTING INDUSTRIES LIMITED *p739*
381 AMBASSADOR DR, MISSISSAUGA, ON, L5T 2J3
(905) 564-6712 *SIC* 2399
HINSPERGERS POLY INDUSTRIES LTD *p708*
645 NEEDHAM LANE, MISSISSAUGA, ON, L5A 1T9
(905) 272-0144 *SIC* 2399
PRODUITS BELT-TECH INC *p1109*
386 RUE DORCHESTER, GRANBY, QC, J2G 3Z7
(450) 372-5826 *SIC* 2399
TRIPLEWELL ENTERPRISES LTD *p878*
3440 PHARMACY AVE UNIT 9, SCARBOROUGH, ON, M1W 2P8
(416) 498-5637 *SIC* 2399
TRQSS, INC *p902*
255 PATILLO RD, TECUMSEH, ON, N8N 2L9
(519) 973-7400 *SIC* 2399
VINTEX INC *p746*
1 MOUNT FOREST DR SS 2, MOUNT FOREST, ON, N0G 2L2
(519) 323-0100 *SIC* 2399

SIC 2411 Logging

1260261 ONTARIO INC *p541*
GD, CHAPLEAU, ON, P0M 1K0
(705) 864-1974 *SIC* 2411
1383791 ONTARIO INC *p621*
952 HUMPHREY RD, IGNACE, ON, P0T 1T0
(807) 934-6500 *SIC* 2411
9196-5905 QUEBEC INC *p1154*
395 BOUL DES RUISSEAUX, MONT-LAURIER, QC, J9L 0H6
(819) 623-4422 *SIC* 2411
CANADIAN AIR-CRANE LTD *p208*
7293 WILSON AVE, DELTA, BC, V4G 1E5
(604) 940-1715 *SIC* 2411
COOPERATIVE DE GESTION FORESTIERE DES APPALACHES *p1356*
519 RTE PRINCIPALE, SAINTE-APOLLINE-DE-PATTON, QC, G0R 2P0
(418) 469-3033 *SIC* 2411
COOPERATIVE FORESTIERE DE FERLAND-BOILLEAU *p1102*
445 381 RTE, FERLAND-ET-BOILLEAU, QC, G0V 1H0
(418) 676-2626 *SIC* 2411
COOPERATIVE FORESTIERE DE PETIT-PARIS *p1347*
576 RUE GAUDREAULT, SAINT-LUDGER-DE-MILOT, QC, G0W 2B0
(418) 373-2575 *SIC* 2411
COOPERATIVE FORESTIERE DU HAUT ST-MAURICE *p1124*
50 RUE BOSTONNAIS, LA TUQUE, QC, G9X 2E8
(819) 523-2737 *SIC* 2411
COOPERATIVE FORESTIERE HAUT PLAN VERT LAC-DES-AIGLES *p1124*
109 RUE PRINCIPALE, LAC-DES-AIGLES, QC, G0K 1V0
(418) 779-2612 *SIC* 2411
COULSON FOREST PRODUCTS LIMITED *p245*

4890 CHERRY CREEK RD, PORT ALBERNI, BC, V9Y 8E9
(250) 723-8118 *SIC* 2411
D & J ISLEY & SONS CONTRACTING LTD *p131*
11517 89 AVE, GRANDE PRAIRIE, AB, T8V 5Z2
(780) 539-7580 *SIC* 2411
ENTREPRISES AGRICOLES & FORESTIERES DE PERCE INC, LES *p1073*
884 RUE PRINCIPALE, CAP-D'ESPOIR, QC, G0C 1G0
(418) 782-2621 *SIC* 2411
GROOT BROS. CONTRACTING LTD *p215*
3377 THIRTEENTH ST UNIT 3, HOUSTON, BC, V0J 1Z0
(250) 845-0093 *SIC* 2411
GROUPEMENT FORESTIER DE L'EST DU LAC TEMISCOUATA INC *p1052*
710 RUE DU CLOCHER, AUCLAIR, QC, G0L 1A0
(418) 899-6673 *SIC* 2411
HELIFOR CANADA CORP *p326*
815 HORNBY ST SUITE 406, VANCOUVER, BC, V6Z 2E6
SIC 2411
HELIFOR INDUSTRIES LIMITED *p323*
1200 73RD AVE W SUITE 828, VANCOUVER, BC, V6P 6G5
(604) 269-2000 *SIC* 2411
ISLAND PACIFIC LOGGING LTD *p196*
3473 SMILEY RD RR 4, CHEMAINUS, BC, V0R 1K4
(250) 246-1414 *SIC* 2411
J V LOGGING LTD *p250*
9453 ROCK ISLAND RD, PRINCE GEORGE, BC, V2N 5T4
(250) 561-2220 *SIC* 2411
LAUZON-RESSOURCES FORESTIERES INC *p1148*
77 RUE COMMERCIALE, MANIWAKI, QC, J9E 1N8
(819) 449-3636 *SIC* 2411
LEMARE LAKE LOGGING LTD *p247*
3341 MINE RD, PORT MCNEILL, BC, V0N 2R0
(250) 956-3123 *SIC* 2411
LO-BAR LOG TRANSPORT CO. LTD *p248*
8377 HART HWY, PRINCE GEORGE, BC, V2K 3B8
(250) 962-8644 *SIC* 2411
MCRAE LUMBER COMPANY LIMITED *p1016*
384 HAY CREEK RD, WHITNEY, ON, K0J 2M0
(613) 637-2190 *SIC* 2411
MOUNT SICKER LUMBER COMPANY LTD *p212*
7795 MAYS RD, DUNCAN, BC, V9L 6A8
(250) 746-4121 *SIC* 2411
REDROCK CAMPS INC *p65*
322 11 AVENUE SW STE 302, CALGARY, AB, T2R 0C5
(403) 264-7610 *SIC* 2411
SAN FORESTRY LTD *p152*
9925 100 ST, PLAMONDON, AB, T0A 2T0
SIC 2411
TAMARACK CANADA INC *p1353*
381 153 RTE, SAINT-TITE, QC, G0X 3H0
(819) 694-0395 *SIC* 2411
WESTERN CANADIAN TIMBER PRODUCTS LTD *p215*
14250 MORRIS VALLEY RD, HARRISON MILLS, BC, V0M 1L0
(604) 796-0314 *SIC* 2411

SIC 2421 Sawmills and planing mills, general

'HORISOL', COOPERATIVE DE TRAVAILLEURS *p1315*
18 RUE DES SOCIETAIRES, SAINT-JEAN-PORT-JOLI, QC, G0R 3G0

(418) 598-3048 *SIC* 2421
6929818 CANADA INC *p729*
10 KINGSBRIDGE GARDEN CIR SUITE 704, MISSISSAUGA, ON, L5R 3K6
SIC 2421
ARBEC, BOIS D'OEUVRE INC *p1124*
1053 BOUL DUCHARME, LA TUQUE, QC, G9X 3C3
(819) 523-2765 *SIC* 2421
ASPEN PLANERS LTD *p232*
1375 HOUSTON ST, MERRITT, BC, V1K 1B8
(250) 378-9266 *SIC* 2421
ASPEN PLANERS LTD *p274*
12745 116 AVE, SURREY, BC, V3V 7H9
(604) 580-2781 *SIC* 2421
ASSOCIATION COOPERATIVE FORESTIERE DE ST-ELZEAR *p1299*
215 RTE DE L'EGLISE, SAINT-ELZEAR-DE-BONAVENTURE, QC, G0C 2W0
(418) 534-2596 *SIC* 2421
BABINE FOREST PRODUCTS LIMITED *p194*
19479 16 HWY E RR 3, BURNS LAKE, BC, V0J 1E3
(250) 692-7177 *SIC* 2421
BARRETTE-CHAPAIS LTEE *p1317*
583 CH DU GRAND-BERNIER N, SAINT-JEAN-SUR-RICHELIEU, QC, J3B 8K1
(450) 357-7000 *SIC* 2421
BLANCHETTE & BLANCHETTE INC *p1400*
520 2E AV, WEEDON, QC, J0B 3J0
(819) 877-2622 *SIC* 2421
BOIS DAAQUAM INC *p1271*
2590 BOUL LAURIER BUREAU 740, QUEBEC, QC, G1V 4M6
SIC 2421
BOIS DAAQUAM INC *p1322*
370 RTE 204, SAINT-JUST-DE-BRETENIERES, QC, G0R 3H0
(418) 244-3601 *SIC* 2421
BOIS DE SCIAGE LAFONTAINE INC *p1361*
144 RANG LAFONTAINE, SAINTE-PERPETUE-DE-L'ISLET, QC, G0R 3Z0
(418) 359-2500 *SIC* 2421
BOIS MARSOUI G.D.S. INC *p1149*
2 RTE DE LA MINE CANDEGO, MARSOUI, QC, G0E 1S0
(418) 288-5635 *SIC* 2421
BOIS NOBLES KA'N'ENDA LTEE *p1154*
701 RUE IBERVILLE, MONT-LAURIER, QC, J9L 3W7
(819) 623-2445 *SIC* 2421
BOIS POULIN INC, LES *p1124*
658 RUE POULIN, LAC-DROLET, QC, G0Y 1C0
(819) 549-2090 *SIC* 2421
BOISACO INC *p1290*
648 CH DU MOULIN BUREAU 15, SACRE-COEUR-SAGUENAY, QC, G0T 1Y0
(418) 236-4633 *SIC* 2421
BRINK FOREST PRODUCTS LTD *p249*
2023 RIVER RD, PRINCE GEORGE, BC, V2L 5S8
(250) 564-0412 *SIC* 2421
BUCHANAN, GORDON ENTERPRISES LTD *p84*
34 AIRPORT RD NW, EDMONTON, AB, T5G 0W7
(780) 424-2202 *SIC* 2421
BUCHANAN, GORDON ENTERPRISES LTD *p135*
1 RAILWAY AVE, HIGH PRAIRIE, AB, T0G 1E0
(780) 523-4544 *SIC* 2421
CANA LIMITED *p34*
5720 4 ST SE SUITE 100, CALGARY, AB, T2H 1K7
(403) 255-5521 *SIC* 2421
CANADIAN FOREST PRODUCTS LTD *p180*
36654 HART HWY, BEAR LAKE, BC, V0J 3G0
(250) 972-4700 *SIC* 2421
CANADIAN FOREST PRODUCTS LTD *p215*

1397 MORICE RIVER FOREST SERVICE RD RR 1, HOUSTON, BC, V0J 1Z1

(250) 845-5200   *SIC* 2421

CANADIAN FOREST PRODUCTS LTD *p230*
MILL RD, MACKENZIE, BC, V0J 2C0

(250) 997-3271   *SIC* 2421

CANADIAN FOREST PRODUCTS LTD *p236*
430 CANFOR AVE, NEW WESTMINSTER, BC, V3L 5G2

SIC 2421

CANADIAN FOREST PRODUCTS LTD *p249*
5162 NORTHWOOD PULP MILL RD, PRINCE GEORGE, BC, V2L 4W2

(250) 962-3500   *SIC* 2421

CANADIAN FOREST PRODUCTS LTD *p250*
2789 PULP MILL RD, PRINCE GEORGE, BC, V2N 2K3

(250) 563-0161   *SIC* 2421

CANADIAN FOREST PRODUCTS LTD *p250*
2533 PRINCE GEORGE PULPMILL RD, PRINCE GEORGE, BC, V2N 2K3

(250) 563-0161   *SIC* 2421

CANADIAN FOREST PRODUCTS LTD *p283*
8300 CHERRY AVE E, TAYLOR, BC, V0C 2K0

(250) 789-9300   *SIC* 2421

CANADIAN FOREST PRODUCTS LTD *p323*
1700 75TH AVE W UNIT 100, VANCOUVER, BC, V6P 6G2

(604) 661-5241   *SIC* 2421

CANADIAN FOREST PRODUCTS LTD *p330*
1399 BEARHEAD RD, VANDERHOOF, BC, V0J 3A2

(250) 567-4725   *SIC* 2421

CANADIAN FOREST PRODUCTS LTD *p344*
GD, WOSS, BC, V0N 3P0

(250) 281-2300   *SIC* 2421

CANADIAN TEST CASE 165   *p730*
5770 HURONTARIO ST, MISSISSAUGA, ON, L5R 3G5

SIC 2421

CANADIAN TEST CASE 56   *p708*
5770 HURONTARIO ST, MISSISSAUGA, ON, L5A 4G4

SIC 2421

CANFOR CORPORATION   *p323*
1700 75TH AVE W SUITE 100, VANCOUVER, BC, V6P 6G2

(604) 661-5241   *SIC* 2421

CARRIER LUMBER LTD   *p250*
4722 CONTINENTAL WAY, PRINCE GEORGE, BC, V2N 5S5

(250) 563-9271   *SIC* 2421

CLERMOND HAMEL LTEE   *p1299*
25 7E RANG S, SAINT-EPHREM-DE-BEAUCE, QC, G0M 1R0

(418) 484-2888   *SIC* 2421

CONIFEX INC   *p213*
300 TAKLA RD, FORT ST. JAMES, BC, V0J 1P0

(250) 996-8241   *SIC* 2421

CONIFEX TIMBER INC   *p330*
700 WEST GEORGIA ST SUITE 980, VANCOUVER, BC, V7Y 1B6

(604) 216-2949   *SIC* 2421

DECKER LAKE FOREST PRODUCTS LTD *p194*
GD, BURNS LAKE, BC, V0J 1E0

(250) 698-7304   *SIC* 2421

DELTA CEDAR PRODUCTS LTD   *p207*
10104 RIVER RD, DELTA, BC, V4C 2R3

(604) 583-4159   *SIC* 2421

DOMTAR INC   *p217*
2005 MISSION FLATS RD, KAMLOOPS, BC, V2C 5M7

(250) 434-6000   *SIC* 2421

DOMTAR INC   *p565*
1 DUKE ST, DRYDEN, ON, P8N 2Z7

(807) 223-2323   *SIC* 2421

DOWNIE TIMBER LTD   *p253*
1621 MILL ST, REVELSTOKE, BC, V0E 2S0

(250) 837-2222   *SIC* 2421

EACOM TIMBER CORPORATION   *p747*
100 OLD NAIRN RD, NAIRN CENTRE, ON,

P0M 2L0

(705) 869-4020   *SIC* 2421

EAST FRASER FIBER CO LTD   *p230*
1000 SHEPPARD RD, MACKENZIE, BC, V0J 2C0

(250) 997-6360   *SIC* 2421

FAWCETT, H. A. & SON LIMITED   *p411*
2 KING ST SUITE 2, PETITCODIAC, NB, E4Z 4L2

(506) 756-3366   *SIC* 2421

FLAVELLE SAWMILL COMPANY LTD *p248*
2400 MURRAY ST, PORT MOODY, BC, V3H 4H6

(604) 939-1141   *SIC* 2421

FORNEBU LUMBER COMPANY INC *p396*
5060 ROUTE 430, BRUNSWICK MINES, NB, E2A 6W6

(506) 547-8690   *SIC* 2421

GALLOWAY LUMBER COMPANY LTD *p214*
7325 GALLOWAY MILL RD, GALLOWAY, BC, V0B 1T2

(250) 429-3496   *SIC* 2421

GESTION VALBEC INC   *p1129*
389 CH DU MOULIN, LANDRIENNE, QC, J0Y 1V0

(819) 732-6404   *SIC* 2421

GESTOFOR INC   *p1351*
592 RUE GUYON, SAINT-RAYMOND, QC, G3L 0A5

(418) 337-4621   *SIC* 2421

GORMAN BROS. LUMBER LTD   *p341*
3900 DUNFIELD RD, WEST KELOWNA, BC, V4T 1W4

(250) 768-5131   *SIC* 2421

GRANULES COMBUSTIBLES ENERGEX INC   *p1125*
3891 RUE DU PRESIDENT-KENNEDY, LAC-MEGANTIC, QC, G6B 3B8

(819) 583-5131   *SIC* 2421

GROUPE CRETE CHERTSEY INC   *p1077*
8227 RTE 125, CHERTSEY, QC, J0K 3K0

(450) 882-2555   *SIC* 2421

GROUPE DE SCIERIES G.D.S. INC *p1089*
207 RTE 295, DEGELIS, QC, G5T 1R1

(418) 853-2566   *SIC* 2421

GROUPE LEBEL INC   *p1286*
54 RUE AMYOT, RIVIERE-DU-LOUP, QC, G5R 3E9

(877) 567-5910   *SIC* 2421

GROUPE SAVOIE INC   *p417*
251 ROUTE 180, SAINT-QUENTIN, NB, E8A 2K9

(506) 235-2228   *SIC* 2421

HALO SAWMILL LIMITED PARTNERSHIP *p244*
17700 FRASER DYKE RD, PITT MEADOWS, BC, V3Y 0A7

(604) 465-0682   *SIC* 2421

HOKUM, BEN AND SON LIMITED   *p598*
206 BLACK POINT RD, GOLDEN LAKE, ON, K0J 1X0

(613) 757-2399   *SIC* 2421

HOWE SOUND PULP & PAPER CORPORATION   *p290*
8501 ONTARIO ST, VANCOUVER, BC, V5X 4W2

(604) 301-3300   *SIC* 2421

INDUSTRIE T.L.T. INC   *p1361*
144 RUE LAROUCHE, SAINTE-MONIQUE-LAC-SAINT-JEA, QC, G0W 2T0

(418) 347-3355   *SIC* 2421

INTERFOR CORPORATION   *p195*
9200 HOLDING RD SUITE 2, CHASE, BC, V0E 1M2

(250) 679-3234   *SIC* 2421

INTERFOR CORPORATION   *p328*
1055 DUNSMUIR ST SUITE 3500, VANCOUVER, BC, V7X 1H7

(604) 689-6800   *SIC* 2421

IRVING, J. D. LIMITED   *p396*
290 MAIN ST, CHIPMAN, NB, E4A 2M7

(506) 339-7910   *SIC* 2421

IRVING, J. D. LIMITED   *p398*
120 SOUTH RD, DOAKTOWN, NB, E9C

1H2

(506) 365-1020   *SIC* 2421

IRVING, J. D. LIMITED   *p415*
300 UNION ST SUITE 5, SAINT JOHN, NB, E2L 4Z2

(506) 632-7777   *SIC* 2421

J.M. CHAMPEAU INC   *p1347*
491 RTE 253, SAINT-MALO, QC, J0B 2Y0

(819) 658-2245   *SIC* 2421

KALESNIKOFF LUMBER CO. LTD   *p195*
2090 3A HWY, CASTLEGAR, BC, V1N 4N1

(250) 399-4211   *SIC* 2421

KENORA FOREST PRODUCTS LTD   *p369*
165 RYAN ST, WINNIPEG, MB, R2R 0N9

(204) 989-9600   *SIC* 2421

KENORA FOREST PRODUCTS LTD   *p628*
1060 LAKEVIEW DR, KENORA, ON, P9N 3X8

(807) 468-1550   *SIC* 2421

KRUGER IPI INC   *p1218*
3285 CH DE BEDFORD, MONTREAL, QC, H3S 1G5

(514) 343-3100   *SIC* 2421

LA CRETE SAWMILLS LTD   *p137*
GD, LA CRETE, AB, T0H 2H0

(780) 928-2292   *SIC* 2421

LAKELAND MILLS LTD   *p249*
GD, PRINCE GEORGE, BC, V2L 4V4

(250) 564-7976   *SIC* 2421

LAREAU, FRANK INC   *p1047*
150 RUE LAGUE, ANGE-GARDIEN, QC, J0E 1E0

(450) 293-2602   *SIC* 2421

LECOURS LUMBER CO. LIMITED   *p532*
HWY 663 N, CALSTOCK, ON, P0L 1B0

(705) 362-4368   *SIC* 2421

LEDWIDGE LUMBER COMPANY LIMITED *p464*
195 OLD POST RD, OLDHAM, NS, B2T 1E2

(902) 883-9889   *SIC* 2421

LONGLAC LUMBER INC   *p663*
101 BLUEBERRY RD, LONGLAC, ON, P0T 2A0

(807) 876-2626   *SIC* 2421

LULUMCO INC   *p1359*
79 RUE SAINT-ALPHONSE, SAINTE-LUCE, QC, G0K 1P0

(418) 739-4881   *SIC* 2421

MACKENZIE SAWMILL LTD   *p270*
11732 130 ST, SURREY, BC, V3R 2Y3

(604) 580-4500   *SIC* 2421

MAIBEC INC   *p1138*
1984 5E RUE BUREAU 202, LEVIS, QC, G6W 5M6

(418) 830-8855   *SIC* 2421

MAIBEC INC   *p1349*
24 6E RANG BUREAU 6, SAINT-PAMPHILE, QC, G0R 3X0

(418) 356-3531   *SIC* 2421

MANNING FOREST PRODUCTS LTD   *p145*
GD, MANNING, AB, T0H 2M0

(780) 836-3111   *SIC* 2421

MANUFACTURIERS WARWICK LTEE, LES   *p1400*
235 RUE SAINT-LOUIS, WARWICK, QC, J0A 1M0

(819) 358-4100   *SIC* 2421

MARWOOD LTD   *p459*
1948 HAMMONDS PLAINS RD, HAMMONDS PLAINS, NS, B4B 1P4

(902) 835-9629   *SIC* 2421

MATERIAUX BLANCHET INC   *p1046*
2771 RTE DE L'AEROPORT, AMOS, QC, J9T 3A8

(819) 732-6581   *SIC* 2421

MATERIAUX BLANCHET INC   *p1119*
6019 BOUL WILFRID-HAMEL BUREAU 200, L'ANCIENNE-LORETTE, QC, G2E 2H3

(418) 871-2626   *SIC* 2421

MATERIAUX BLANCHET INC   *p1349*
1030 RTE ELGIN S, SAINT-PAMPHILE, QC, G0R 3X0

(418) 356-3344   *SIC* 2421

MEADOW CREEK CEDAR LTD   *p218*

GD, KASLO, BC, V0G 1M0

(250) 366-4434   *SIC* 2421

MILLAR WESTERN INDUSTRIES LTD *p173*
5004 52 ST, WHITECOURT, AB, T7S 1N2

(780) 778-2221   *SIC* 2421

MURRAY BROS. LUMBER COMPANY LIMITED   *p663*
24749 HWY 60, MADAWASKA, ON, K0J 2C0

(613) 637-2840   *SIC* 2421

NECHAKO LUMBER CO. LTD   *p331*
1241 HWY 16 W, VANDERHOOF, BC, V0J 3A0

(250) 567-4701   *SIC* 2421

NORSASK FOREST PRODUCTS INC *p1410*
HWY 55 E, MEADOW LAKE, SK, S9X 1V7

(306) 236-5601   *SIC* 2421

NORTH AMERICAN FOREST PRODUCTS LTD   *p417*
40 LABRIE CH, SAINT-QUENTIN, NB, E8A 2E1

(506) 235-2873   *SIC* 2421

NORTH ENDERBY TIMBER LTD   *p212*
6261 HWY 97A RR 3, ENDERBY, BC, V0E 1V3

(250) 838-9668   *SIC* 2421

PALLISER LUMBER SALES LTD   *p81*
16 MCCOOL CRES, CROSSFIELD, AB, T0M 0S0

(403) 946-5494   *SIC* 2421

PANNEAUX MASKI INC   *p1146*
50 10E AV, LOUISEVILLE, QC, J5V 0A5

(819) 228-8461   *SIC* 2421

PASTWAY PLANING LIMITED   *p547*
2916 ROCKINGHAM RD, COMBERMERE, ON, K0J 1L0

(613) 756-2742   *SIC* 2421

PF RESOLU CANADA INC   *p910*
2001 NEEBING AVE, THUNDER BAY, ON, P7E 6S3

(807) 475-2110   *SIC* 2421

PF RESOLU CANADA INC   *p1075*
7499 BOUL SAINTE-ANNE, CHATEAU-RICHER, QC, G0A 1N0

(418) 824-4233   *SIC* 2421

PF RESOLU CANADA INC   *p1108*
2250 RANG SAINT-JOSEPH N, GIRARDVILLE, QC, G0W 1R0

(418) 630-3433   *SIC* 2421

PF RESOLU CANADA INC   *p1121*
5850 AV DES JARDINS, LA DORE, QC, G8J 1B4

(418) 256-3816   *SIC* 2421

PF RESOLU CANADA INC   *p1148*
200 CH DE MONTCERF, MANIWAKI, QC, J9E 1A1

(819) 449-2100   *SIC* 2421

PF RESOLU CANADA INC   *p1303*
900 BOUL HAMEL, SAINT-FELICIEN, QC, G8K 2X4

(418) 679-0552   *SIC* 2421

PF RESOLU CANADA INC   *p1353*
300 AV DU MOULIN, SAINT-THOMAS-DIDYME, QC, G0W 1P0

(418) 274-3340   *SIC* 2421

PRODUITS FORESTIERS ARBEC S.E.N.C. *p1119*
5005 RTE UNIFORET, L'ASCENSION-DE-NOTRE-SEIGNEUR, QC, G0W 1Y0

(418) 347-4900   *SIC* 2421

PRODUITS FORESTIERS ARBEC S.E.N.C. *p1253*
175 BOUL PORTAGE DES MOUSSES, PORT-CARTIER, QC, G5B 2V9

(418) 766-2299   *SIC* 2421

PRODUITS FORESTIERS ARBEC S.E.N.C. *p1345*
8770 BOUL LANGELIER BUREAU 216, SAINT-LEONARD, QC, H1P 3C6

(514) 327-3350   *SIC* 2421

PRODUITS FORESTIERS ARBEC S.E.N.C. *p1369*
775 CH DE TURCOTTE, SHAWINIGAN, QC, G9T 5K7

---

(819) 538-0735   *SIC 2421*
PRODUITS FORESTIERS D&G LTEE, LES
p1273
2590 BOUL LAURIER BUREAU 500, QUE-
BEC, QC, G1V 4M6
(418) 657-6505   *SIC 2421*
PRODUITS FORESTIERS MAURICIE S.E.C.
p1124
2419 155 RTE S, LA TUQUE, QC, G9X 3N8
(819) 523-5626   *SIC 2421*
**PRODUITS FORESTIERS TEMREX, SOCI-
ETE EN COMMANDITE**   *p1244*
521 RTE 132 O, NOUVELLE-OUEST, QC,
G0C 2G0
(418) 794-2211   *SIC 2421*
RAINTREE LUMBER SPECIALTIES LTD
p273
5390 192 ST, SURREY, BC, V3S 8E5
(604) 574-0444   *SIC 2421*
RAYONIER A.M. CANADA G.P.   *p546*
70 17TH AVE, COCHRANE, ON, P0L 1C0
(705) 272-4321   *SIC 2421*
RAYONIER A.M. CANADA G.P.   *p1054*
67 RUE PRINCIPALE S, BEARN, QC, J0Z
1G0
(819) 726-3551   *SIC 2421*
RAYONIER A.M. CANADA INDUSTRIES INC
p1207
4 PLACE VILLE-MARIE BUREAU 100,
MONTREAL, QC, H3B 2E7
(514) 871-0137   *SIC 2421*
ROCKY WOOD PRESERVERS LTD   *p159*
GD STN MAIN, ROCKY MOUNTAIN
HOUSE, AB, T4T 1T1
(403) 845-2212   *SIC 2421*
SAWARNE LUMBER CO. LTD   *p321*
1770 BURRARD ST SUITE 280, VANCOU-
VER, BC, V6J 3G7
(604) 324-4666   *SIC 2421*
SCIERIE ST-ELZEAR INC   *p1299*
215 RTE DE L'EGLISE, SAINT-ELZEAR-DE-
BONAVENTURE, QC, G0C 2W0
(418) 534-2596   *SIC 2421*
SCOTSBURN LUMBER LTD   *p465*
65 CONDON RD, SCOTSBURN, NS, B0K
1R0
(902) 485-8041   *SIC 2421*
SKEENA SAWMILLS LTD   *p316*
1030 WEST GEORGIA ST SUITE 1518,
VANCOUVER, BC, V6E 2Y3
(604) 800-5990   *SIC 2421*
**SOCIETE EN COMMANDITE SCIERIE OPIT-
CIWAN**   *p1244*
DE LA POINTE, OBEDJIWAN, QC, G0W
3B0
(819) 974-1116   *SIC 2421*
**SOCIETE EN COMMANDITE STADACONA
WB**   *p1257*
10 BOUL DES CAPUCINS, QUEBEC, QC,
G1J 0G9
(418) 842-8405   *SIC 2421*
**SOCIETE EN COMMANDITE STADACONA
WB**   *p1281*
1092 AV LAPIERRE BUREAU 220, QUE-
BEC, QC, G3E 1Z3
    SIC 2421
**STAGEM   DIVISION   ENTREPRISE
D'INSERTION INC**   *p1287*
150 RTE DE SAINTE-HEDWIDGE, ROBER-
VAL, QC, G8H 2M9
(418) 275-7241   *SIC 2421*
SUNDRE FOREST PRODUCTS INC   *p168*
5541 HWY 584 W, SUNDRE, AB, T0M 1X0
(403) 638-4093   *SIC 2421*
TEMBEC INC   *p542*
175 PLANER RD, CHAPLEAU, ON, P0M
1K0
(705) 864-3014   *SIC 2421*
TERMINAL FOREST PRODUCTS LTD *p256*
12180 MITCHELL RD, RICHMOND, BC,
V6V 1M8
(604) 717-1200   *SIC 2421*
TERMINAL FOREST PRODUCTS LTD *p291*
8708 YUKON ST, VANCOUVER, BC, V5X

2Y9
(604) 327-6344   *SIC 2421*
TOLKO FOREST PRODUCTS LTD   *p332*
3000 28 ST, VERNON, BC, V1T 9W9
(250) 545-4411   *SIC 2421*
TOLKO INDUSTRIES LTD   *p135*
11401 92 ST SS 1 SUITE 1, HIGH LEVEL,
AB, T0H 1Z0
(780) 926-3781   *SIC 2421*
TOLKO INDUSTRIES LTD   *p180*
844 OTTER LAKE CROSS RD, ARM-
STRONG, BC, V0E 1B6
(250) 546-3171   *SIC 2421*
TOLKO INDUSTRIES LTD   *p198*
6200 JEFFERS DR, COLDSTREAM, BC,
V1B 3G4
(250) 545-4992   *SIC 2421*
TOLKO INDUSTRIES LTD   *p232*
1750 LINDLEY CREEK RD, MERRITT, BC,
V1K 0A2
(250) 378-2224   *SIC 2421*
TOLKO INDUSTRIES LTD   *p252*
1879 BROWNMILLER RD, QUESNEL, BC,
V2J 6R9
(250) 992-1700   *SIC 2421*
TOLKO INDUSTRIES LTD   *p332*
3000 28 ST, VERNON, BC, V1T 1W1
(250) 545-4411   *SIC 2421*
TOLKO INDUSTRIES LTD   *p344*
5000 SODA CREEK RD, WILLIAMS LAKE,
BC, V2G 5E4
(250) 398-3600   *SIC 2421*
TWIN RIVERS PAPER COMPANY INC *p411*
31 RENOUS RD SUITE 36, PLASTER
ROCK, NB, E7G 4B5
(506) 356-4132   *SIC 2421*
USINE SARTIGAN INC   *p1307*
888   RTE   269,   SAINT-HONORE-DE-
SHENLEY, QC, G0M 1V0
(418) 485-6797   *SIC 2421*
VANDERWELL CONTRACTORS (1971) LTD
p164
695 WEST MITSUE IND RD, SLAVE LAKE,
AB, T0G 2A0
(780) 849-3824   *SIC 2421*
WEST FRASER MILLS LTD   *p6*
GD, BLUE RIDGE, AB, T0E 0B0
(780) 648-6333   *SIC 2421*
WEST FRASER MILLS LTD   *p164*
GD, SLAVE LAKE, AB, T0G 2A0
(780) 849-4145   *SIC 2421*
WEST FRASER MILLS LTD   *p174*
1020 CHASM RD, 70 MILE HOUSE, BC,
V0K 2K0
(250) 459-2229   *SIC 2421*
WEST FRASER MILLS LTD   *p196*
3598 FRASER ST W, CHETWYND, BC,
V0C 1J0
(250) 788-2686   *SIC 2421*
WEST FRASER MILLS LTD   *p252*
1000 PLYWOOD RD, QUESNEL, BC, V2J
3J5
(250) 991-7619   *SIC 2421*
WEST FRASER MILLS LTD   *p269*
2375 TATLOW RD, SMITHERS, BC, V0J
2N5
(250) 847-2656   *SIC 2421*
WEST FRASER MILLS LTD   *p301*
858 BEATTY ST SUITE 501, VANCOUVER,
BC, V6B 1C1
(604) 895-2700   *SIC 2421*
WEST FRASER MILLS LTD   *p344*
4255 ROTTACKER RD, WILLIAMS LAKE,
BC, V2G 5E4
(250) 392-7784   *SIC 2421*
WEST FRASER MILLS LTD   *p344*
4200 MACKENZIE AVE N, WILLIAMS
LAKE, BC, V2G 1N4
(250) 392-7731   *SIC 2421*
WESTERN FOREST PRODUCTS INC *p330*
700 GEORGIA ST W SUITE 510, VANCOU-
VER, BC, V7Y 1K8
    SIC 2421
WEYERHAEUSER COMPANY LIMITED *p131*

GD, GRANDE CACHE, AB, T0E 0Y0
    SIC 2421
WEYERHAEUSER COMPANY LIMITED *p207*
1272 DERWENT WAY, DELTA, BC, V3M
5R1
(604) 526-4665   *SIC 2421*
WEYERHAEUSER COMPANY LIMITED *p245*
GD LCD MAIN, PORT ALBERNI, BC, V9Y
7M3
(250) 724-6511   *SIC 2421*
WEYERHAEUSER COMPANY LIMITED *p252*
201 OLD HEDLEY RD, PRINCETON, BC,
V0X 1W0
(250) 295-3281   *SIC 2421*
WEYERHAEUSER COMPANY LIMITED *p288*
3650 E KENT AVE S, VANCOUVER, BC,
V5S 2J2
    SIC 2421
WEYERHAEUSER COMPANY LIMITED *p317*
1140 PENDER ST W SUITE 440, VANCOU-
VER, BC, V6E 4G1
(604) 661-8000   *SIC 2421*
WEYERHAEUSER   COMPANY   LIMITED
p1407
HIWAY 9 S, HUDSON BAY, SK, S0E 0Y0
(306) 865-1700   *SIC 2421*
WHITE RIVER FOREST PRODUCTS GP INC
p1016
315 HWY 17, WHITE RIVER, ON, P0M 3G0
(807) 822-1818   *SIC 2421*
WOODLAND IMPROVEMENTS CORP *p415*
300 UNION ST, SAINT JOHN, NB, E2L 4Z2
(506) 632-7777   *SIC 2421*
WYNNDEL BOX & LUMBER COMPANY LTD
p344
1140 WINLAW RD, WYNNDEL, BC, V0B
2N1
(250) 866-5231   *SIC 2421*

---

*SIC 2426 Hardwood dimension and flooring
mills*

8008655 CANADA INC.   *p573*
409 EVANS AVE, ETOBICOKE, ON, M8Z
1K8
(416) 521-6100   *SIC 2426*
BARCO MATERIALS HANDLING LIMITED
p848
24 KERR CRES SUITE 3, PUSLINCH, ON,
N0B 2J0
(519) 763-1037   *SIC 2426*
BOA-FRANC INC   *p1304*
1255 98E RUE, SAINT-GEORGES, QC,
G5Y 8J5
(418) 227-1181   *SIC 2426*
BOA-FRANC, S.E.N.C.   *p1304*
1255 98E RUE, SAINT-GEORGES, QC,
G5Y 8J5
(418) 227-1181   *SIC 2426*
BOIS DE PLANCHER P.G. INC, LES *p1299*
2424 RUE PRINCIPALE, SAINT-EDOUARD-
DE-LOTBINIERE, QC, G0S 1Y0
(418) 796-2328   *SIC 2426*
BREEZE DRIED INC   *p911*
1300 JACKSON SUITE 2, TILLSONBURG,
ON, N4G 4G7
(519) 688-0224   *SIC 2426*
EACOM TIMBER CORPORATION   *p1203*
1100 BOUL RENE-LEVESQUE O BUREAU
2110, MONTREAL, QC, H3B 4N4
(514) 848-6815   *SIC 2426*
EASTWOOD   WOOD   SPECIALTIES   LTD
p883
6 PEACOCK BAY, ST CATHARINES, ON,
L2M 7N8
(905) 937-3030   *SIC 2426*
ENTREPRISES DAVID LAUZON, LES *p1349*
1680 RUE PRINCIPALE RR 5, SAINT-
NORBERT, QC, J0K 3C0
(450) 427-5144   *SIC 2426*
**ERIE FLOORING & WOOD PRODUCTS LIM-
ITED**   *p1013*
1191 JANE ST, WEST LORNE, ON, N0L
2P0

(519) 768-1200   *SIC 2426*
ERRION GROUP INC   *p593*
42 ARMSTRONG AVE, GEORGETOWN,
ON, L7G 4R9
(905) 877-7300   *SIC 2426*
FOOTHILLS FOREST PRODUCTS INC *p130*
HIGHWAY 40 S, GRANDE CACHE, AB, T0E
0Y0
(780) 827-2225   *SIC 2426*
GIGUERE & MORIN INC   *p1303*
1175 RTE 243, SAINT-FELIX-DE-KINGSEY,
QC, J0B 2T0
(819) 848-2525   *SIC 2426*
GOODFELLOW INC   *p1098*
1750   RUE   HAGGERTY,   DRUM-
MONDVILLE, QC, J2C 5P8
(819) 477-6898   *SIC 2426*
IRVING, J. D. LIMITED   *p397*
632 RUE PRINCIPALE, CLAIR, NB, E7A
2H2
(506) 992-9068   *SIC 2426*
**LAUZON - PLANCHERS DE BOIS EX-
CLUSIFS INC**   *p1349*
1680 RUE PRINCIPALE RR 5, SAINT-
NORBERT, QC, J0K 3C0
(450) 836-4405   *SIC 2426*
PANELS.CA ONTARIO INC   *p1012*
123 CENTRE ST, WELLAND, ON, L3B 0E1
(905) 734-6060   *SIC 2426*
PLANCHERS DES APPALACHES LTEE
p1088
454 RUE DE LA RIVIERE, COWANSVILLE,
QC, J2K 3G6
(450) 266-3999   *SIC 2426*
**PLANCHERS   MERCIER   (DRUM-
MONDVILLE) INC, LES**   *p1099*
1125   RUE   ROCHELEAU,   DRUM-
MONDVILLE, QC, J2C 6L8
(819) 472-1670   *SIC 2426*
PLANCHERS MERCIER INC, LES   *p1160*
330 RUE DES ENTREPRENEURS, MONT-
MAGNY, QC, G5V 4T1
(418) 248-1785   *SIC 2426*
PREVERCO INC   *p1293*
285   RUE   DE   ROTTERDAM,   SAINT-
AUGUSTIN-DE-DESMAURES,   QC,   G3A
2E5
(800) 667-2725   *SIC 2426*
PRODUITS SEATPLY INC   *p1340*
150 RUE MERIZZI, SAINT-LAURENT, QC,
H4T 1S4
(514) 340-1513   *SIC 2426*
RENYCO INC   *p1384*
425 GALIPEAU RANG 5 RR 1, THURSO,
QC, J0X 3B0
    SIC 2426
**SATIN FINISH HARDWOOD FLOORING,
LIMITED**   *p793*
15 FENMAR DR, NORTH YORK, ON, M9L
1L4
(416) 747-9924   *SIC 2426*
SOCIETE   EN   COMMANDITE   PROLAM
p1074
439   CH   VINCELOTTE,   CAP-SAINT-
IGNACE, QC, G0R 1H0
(418) 246-5101   *SIC 2426*
STARWOOD MANUFACTURING INC *p714*
2370 SOUTH SHERIDAN WAY, MISSIS-
SAUGA, ON, L5J 2M4
    SIC 2426
UNIBOARD CANADA INC   *p1232*
5555 RUE ERNEST-CORMIER, MON-
TREAL, QC, H7C 2S9
(450) 661-7122   *SIC 2426*
WHITE RIVER FOREST PRODUCTS LTD
p1016
315 HWY 17, WHITE RIVER, ON, P0M 3G0
(807) 822-1818   *SIC 2426*

SIC 2429 Special product sawmills, nec

**CIE MATERIAUX DE CONSTRUCTION BP
CANADA, LA**   *p1114*

351 RUE ALICE, JOLIETTE, QC, J6E 8P2
(450) 682-4428   *SIC* 2429
CIE MATERIAUX DE CONSTRUCTION BP CANADA, LA   *p*1132
9500 RUE SAINT-PATRICK, LASALLE, QC, H8R 1R8
(514) 364-0161   *SIC* 2429
CLAIR INDUSTRIAL DEVELOPMENT CORPORATION LTD   *p*397
14 AV 2 IEME INDUSTRIEL, CLAIR, NB, E7A 2B1
(506) 992-2152   *SIC* 2429
FRASER CEDAR PRODUCTS LTD   *p*230
27400 LOUGHEED HWY, MAPLE RIDGE, BC, V2W 1L1
(604) 462-7335   *SIC* 2429
MAIBEC INC   *p*1353
340 RTE DU PRESIDENT-KENNEDY, SAINT-THEOPHILE, QC, G0M 2A0
(418) 597-3388   *SIC* 2429
SPECIALISTE DU BARDEAU DE CEDRE INC, LE   *p*1350
754 8E RUE, SAINT-PROSPER-DE-DORCHESTER, QC, G0M 1Y0
(418) 594-6201   *SIC* 2429
TEAL CEDAR PRODUCTS LTD   *p*282
17897 TRIGGS RD, SURREY, BC, V4N 4M8
(604) 587-8700   *SIC* 2429
WALDUN FOREST PRODUCTS LTD   *p*231
9393 287 ST, MAPLE RIDGE, BC, V2W 1L1
(604) 462-8266   *SIC* 2429
WHEATLAND HUTTERIAN BRETHREN OF CABRI INC   *p*1405
GD, CABRI, SK, S0N 0J0
(306) 587-2458   *SIC* 2429

SIC 2431 Millwork

2843-5816 QUEBEC INC   *p*1129
235 2E AV, LAMBTON, QC, G0M 1H0
(418) 486-7401   *SIC* 2431
ALL-FAB BUILDING COMPONENTS INC   *p*364
1755 DUGALD RD, WINNIPEG, MB, R2J 0H3
(204) 661-8880   *SIC* 2431
ALLWOOD INDUSTRIES LTD   *p*573
33 ATOMIC AVE UNIT 1, ETOBICOKE, ON, M8Z 5K8
(416) 398-1460   *SIC* 2431
ALPA STAIRS & RAILINGS INC.   *p*687
3770 NASHUA DR UNIT 3, MISSISSAUGA, ON, L4V 1M5
(905) 694-9556   *SIC* 2431
ARTISTIC STAIRS LTD   *p*13
3504 80 AVE SE, CALGARY, AB, T2C 1J3
(403) 279-5898   *SIC* 2431
ATIS PORTES ET FENETRES CORP.   *p*1381
2175 BOUL DES ENTREPRISES, TERREBONNE, QC, J6Y 1W9
(450) 492-0404   *SIC* 2431
ATIS S.E.C.   *p*1144
1111 RUE SAINT-CHARLES O, LONGUEUIL, QC, J4K 5G4
(450) 928-0101   *SIC* 2431
BEAUBOIS GROUP INC   *p*1304
521 6E AV N, SAINT-GEORGES, QC, G5Y 0H1
(418) 228-5104   *SIC* 2431
BOIS D'OEUVRE CEDRICO INC   *p*1253
39 RUE SAINT-JEAN-BAPTISTE, PRICE, QC, G0J 1Z0
(418) 775-7516   *SIC* 2431
BOIS KENNEBEC LTEE   *p*1305
8475 25E AV, SAINT-GEORGES, QC, G6A 1M8
(418) 228-1414   *SIC* 2431
BOIS OUVRE DE BEAUCEVILLE (1992) INC   *p*1055
201 134E RUE, BEAUCEVILLE, QC, G5X 3H9
(418) 774-3606   *SIC* 2431
BOISERIES RAYMOND INC   *p*1161

11880 56E AV, MONTREAL, QC, H1E 2L6
(514) 494-1141   *SIC* 2431
BOLZANO HOLDINGS LTD   *p*338
477 BOLESKINE RD, VICTORIA, BC, V8Z 1E7
(250) 475-1441   *SIC* 2431
BRENLO LTD   *p*582
41 RACINE RD, ETOBICOKE, ON, M9W 2Z4
(416) 749-6857   *SIC* 2431
C. & C. WOOD PRODUCTS LTD   *p*252
1751 QUESNEL-HIXON RD, QUESNEL, BC, V2J 5Z5
(250) 992-7471   *SIC* 2431
CASA BELLA WINDOWS INC   *p*786
124 NORFINCH DR, NORTH YORK, ON, M3N 1X1
(416) 650-1033   *SIC* 2431
CENTRAP INC   *p*1154
1111 RUE INDUSTRIELLE, MONT-JOLI, QC, G5H 3T9
(418) 775-7202   *SIC* 2431
CENTRE DE L'ESCALIER INC   *p*1380
3535 BOUL DES ENTREPRISES, TERREBONNE, QC, J6X 4J9
(514) 592-0241   *SIC* 2431
CONTINENTAL CABINET COMPANY INCORPORATED   *p*648
547 CLARKE RD, LONDON, ON, N5V 2E1
(519) 455-3830   *SIC* 2431
CORPORATION INTERNATIONALE MASONITE   *p*1194
1501 AV MCGILL COLLEGE SUITE 26E, MONTREAL, QC, H3A 3N9
(514) 841-6400   *SIC* 2431
DESA HOLDINGS LTD   *p*159
285079 BLUEGRASS DR, ROCKY VIEW COUNTY, AB, T1X 0P5
(403) 230-5011   *SIC* 2431
EBENISTERIE ST-URBAIN LTEE   *p*1347
226 RUE PRINCIPALE, SAINT-LOUIS-DE-GONZAGUE, QC, J0S 1T0
(450) 427-2687   *SIC* 2431
ELEGANCE COLONIAL INC   *p*1160
3800 BOUL DU TRICENTENAIRE, MONTREAL, QC, H1B 5T8
(514) 640-1212   *SIC* 2431
ELIAS WOODWORKING AND MANUFACTURING LTD   *p*361
275 BADGER RD, WINKLER, MB, R6W 0K5
(204) 325-9962   *SIC* 2431
ELL-ROD HOLDINGS INC   *p*811
19 TAMBLYN RD RR 1, ORONO, ON, L0B 1M0
(905) 983-5456   *SIC* 2431
ESCALIERS GRENIER, GILLES INC   *p*1299
586 AV TEXEL, SAINT-ELZEAR, QC, G0S 2J2
(418) 387-6317   *SIC* 2431
G & P MILLWORK LTD   *p*878
191 FINCHDENE SQ, SCARBOROUGH, ON, M1X 1E3
(416) 298-4204   *SIC* 2431
GIENOW CANADA INC   *p*16
7140 40 ST SE, CALGARY, AB, T2C 2B6
(403) 203-8200   *SIC* 2431
INDUSTRIES J SUSS INC, LES   *p*1397
3865 RUE LESAGE, VERDUN, QC, H4G 1A3
(514) 769-5666   *SIC* 2431
INDUSTRIES SEFINA LTEE, LES   *p*1340
750 RUE MCARTHUR, SAINT-LAURENT, QC, H4T 1W2
(514) 735-5911   *SIC* 2431
JELD-WEN OF CANADA LTD   *p*367
485 WATT ST, WINNIPEG, MB, R2K 2R9
(204) 694-6012   *SIC* 2431
JELD-WEN OF CANADA LTD   *p*1292
90 RUE INDUSTRIELLE BUREAU 200, SAINT-APOLLINAIRE, QC, G0S 2E0
(418) 881-3974   *SIC* 2431
JELD-WEN OF CANADA LTD   *p*1306
115 RUE DE LA GARE, SAINT-HENRI-DE-LEVIS, QC, G0R 3E0

(418) 882-2223   *SIC* 2431
KOHLTECH INTERNATIONAL LIMITED*p*449
583 MACELMON RD, DEBERT, NS, B0M 1G0
(902) 662-3100   *SIC* 2431
LAFLAMME PORTES ET FENETRES CORP   *p*1292
39 RUE INDUSTRIELLE, SAINT-APOLLINAIRE, QC, G0S 2E0
(418) 881-3950   *SIC* 2431
LANDMARK HOME SOLUTIONS INC   *p*907
3430 SCHMON PKY, THOROLD, ON, L2V 4Y6
(905) 646-8995   *SIC* 2431
LEWIS MOULDINGS & WOOD SPECIALTIES LIMITED   *p*470
134 FORT POINT RD, WEYMOUTH, NS, B0W 3T0
(902) 837-7393   *SIC* 2431
LOUISIANA-PACIFIC CANADA LTD   *p*213
8220 259 RD SITE 13 COMP 14, FORT ST. JOHN, BC, V1J 4M6
(250) 263-6600   *SIC* 2431
LOUISIANA-PACIFIC CANADA LTD   *p*1060
1012 CH DU PARC-INDUSTRIEL, BOIS-FRANC, QC, J9E 3A9
(819) 449-7030   *SIC* 2431
LOUISIANA-PACIFIC CANADA LTD   *p*1189
507 PLACE D'ARMES BUREAU 400, MONTREAL, QC, H2Y 2W8
(514) 861-4724   *SIC* 2431
LUX WINDOWS AND GLASS LTD   *p*24
6875 9 ST NE, CALGARY, AB, T2E 8R9
(403) 276-7770   *SIC* 2431
M AND J WOODCRAFTS LTD   *p*209
7338 PROGRESS WAY UNIT 1, DELTA, BC, V4G 1L4
(604) 946-4767   *SIC* 2431
MADSEN'S CUSTOM CABINETS (1983) LTD   *p*94
14504 123 AVE NW, EDMONTON, AB, T5L 2Y3
(780) 454-6790   *SIC* 2431
MANTEI HOLDINGS LTD   *p*40
5935 6 ST NE, CALGARY, AB, T2K 5R5
(403) 295-0028   *SIC* 2431
MASON WINDOWS LIMITED   *p*845
913 BROCK RD, PICKERING, ON, L1W 2X9
(905) 839-1171   *SIC* 2431
MASONITE INTERNATIONAL CORPORATION   *p*1299
430 RTE 108 O BUREAU 489, SAINT-EPHREM-DE-BEAUCE, QC, G0M 1R0
(418) 484-5666   *SIC* 2431
MENUISERIE DES PINS LTEE   *p*1243
3150 CH ROYAL, NOTRE-DAME-DES-PINS, QC, G0M 1K0
(418) 774-3324   *SIC* 2431
MENUISEROX INC   *p*1055
159 181E RUE, BEAUCEVILLE, QC, G5X 2S9
(418) 774-9019   *SIC* 2431
METRIE CANADA LTD   *p*17
5367 50 ST SE, CALGARY, AB, T2C 3W1
(403) 543-3260   *SIC* 2431
METRIE CANADA LTD   *p*328
1055 DUNSMUIR ST SUITE 3500, VANCOUVER, QC, V7X 1H3
(604) 691-9100   *SIC* 2431
MILLWORKS CUSTOM MANUFACTURING (2001) INC   *p*993
25 BERTAL RD UNIT 9, TORONTO, ON, M6M 4M7
(416) 760-0222   *SIC* 2431
MOULURE ALEXANDRIA MOULDING INC   *p*476
20352 POWER DAM RD, ALEXANDRIA, ON, K0C 1A0
(613) 525-2784   *SIC* 2431
NORBORD INDUSTRIES INC   *p*404
137 JUNIPER RD, JUNIPER, NB, E7L 1G8
(506) 246-1125   *SIC* 2431
NORBORD INDUSTRIES INC   *p*940
1 TORONTO ST UNIT 600, TORONTO, ON,

M5C 2W4
(416) 365-0705   *SIC* 2431
NOSE CREEK FOREST PRODUCTS CORP   *p*68
184 MALIBOU RD SW, CALGARY, AB, T2V 1X9
    SIC 2431
PLACEMENTS JACQUES GOULET LTEE, LES   *p*1322
830 AV BELAND, SAINT-JOSEPH-DE-BEAUCE, QC, G0S 2V0
    SIC 2431
PLAINTREE SYSTEMS INC   *p*489
14 CONWAY ST, BARRYS BAY, ON, K0J 1B0
(613) 756-7066   *SIC* 2431
POLLARD WINDOWS INC   *p*531
1217 KING RD, BURLINGTON, ON, L7T 0B7
(905) 634-2365   *SIC* 2431
PORTES MILETTE INC   *p*1295
100 AV INDUSTRIELLE, SAINT-BONIFACE-DE-SHAWINIGAN, QC, G0X 2L0
(819) 535-5588   *SIC* 2431
PORTES SAINT-GEORGES INC, LES*p*1356
2 RUE DES CERISIERS, SAINTE-AURELIE, QC, G0M 1M0
(418) 593-3784   *SIC* 2431
PRENDIVILLE INDUSTRIES LTD   *p*389
986 LORIMER BLVD UNIT 5, WINNIPEG, MB, R3P 0Z8
(204) 989-9600   *SIC* 2431
PRODUITS FORESTIERS D&G LTEE, LES*p*1356
313 RANG SAINT-JOSEPH, SAINTE-AURELIE, QC, G0M 1M0
(418) 593-3516   *SIC* 2431
PRODUITS MATRA INC   *p*1348
21 11E RUE O, SAINT-MARTIN, QC, G0M 1B0
(418) 382-5151   *SIC* 2431
PROVINCIAL STORE FIXTURES LTD   *p*712
910 CENTRAL PKY W, MISSISSAUGA, ON, L5C 2V5
(905) 564-6700   *SIC* 2431
R S CABINET DOORS LTD   *p*1433
1102 17TH ST W, SASKATOON, SK, S7M 3Y3
    SIC 2431
RENIN CANADA CORP   *p*505
110 WALKER DR, BRAMPTON, ON, L6T 4H6
(905) 791-7930   *SIC* 2431
ROLAND BOULANGER & CIE, LTEE   *p*1400
235 RUE SAINT-LOUIS, WARWICK, QC, J0A 1M0
(819) 358-4100   *SIC* 2431
SECHOIRS DE BEAUCE INC   *p*1055
201 134E RUE, BEAUCEVILLE, QC, G5X 3H9
(418) 774-3606   *SIC* 2431
SHIPWAY STAIRS LIMITED   *p*524
1820 IRONSTONE DR, BURLINGTON, ON, L7L 5V3
(905) 336-1296   *SIC* 2431
SOUTHCOAST MILLWORK LTD   *p*230
23347 MCKAY AVE, MAPLE RIDGE, BC, V2W 1B9
(604) 467-0111   *SIC* 2431
SPINDLE FACTORY LTD, THE   *p*103
11319 199 ST NW, EDMONTON, AB, T5S 2C6
(780) 453-5973   *SIC* 2431
STAIRFAB AND RAILINGS INC   *p*756
450 KENT DR, NEWMARKET, ON, L3Y 4Y9
(905) 895-1050   *SIC* 2431
THEO MINEAULT INC   *p*1103
2135 CH DE MONTREAL O, GATINEAU, QC, J8M 1P3
(819) 986-3190   *SIC* 2431
TRADEWOOD INDUSTRIES LIMITED   *p*885
7 WRIGHT ST, ST CATHARINES, ON, L2P 3J2
(905) 641-4949   *SIC* 2431

▲ Public Company   ■ Public Company Family Member   **HQ** Headquarters   **BR** Branch   **SL** Single Location

TURKSTRA INDUSTRIES INC p616
1050 UPPER WELLINGTON ST, HAMILTON, ON, L9A 3S6
(905) 388-8220 *SIC 2431*

VINYLBILT GROUP INC p560
3333 LANGSTAFF RD SUITE 1, CONCORD, ON, L4K 5A8
(905) 669-1200 *SIC 2431*

VISTA RAILING SYSTEMS INC p231
23282 RIVER RD, MAPLE RIDGE, BC, V2W 1B6
(604) 467-5147 *SIC 2431*

WOODLAND SUPPLY & MFG. CO. p364
867 MCLEOD AVE, WINNIPEG, MB, R2G 0Y4
(204) 668-0079 *SIC 2431*

WOODTONE SPECIALTIES INC p180
4175 CROZIER RD, ARMSTRONG, BC, V0E 1B6
(250) 546-6808 *SIC 2431*

SIC 2434 Wood kitchen cabinets

1118741 ONTARIO LTD p855
278 NEWKIRK RD, RICHMOND HILL, ON, L4C 3G7
(905) 780-7722 *SIC 2434*

1376302 ONTARIO INC p661
329 SOVEREIGN RD, LONDON, ON, N6M 1A6
(519) 859-5056 *SIC 2434*

2757-5158 QUEBEC INC p1316
1050 BOUL DU SEMINAIRE N BUREAU 210, SAINT-JEAN-SUR-RICHELIEU, QC, J3A 1S7
(450) 359-7980 *SIC 2434*

ARMOIRES CONTESSA INC p1394
370 RUE JOSEPH-CARRIER, VAUDREUIL-DORION, QC, J7V 5V5
(450) 455-6682 *SIC 2434*

ARMOIRES DE CUISINE BERNIER INC p1137
1955 3E RUE BUREAU 70, LEVIS, QC, G6W 5M6
(418) 839-8142 *SIC 2434*

ARMOIRES FABRITEC LTEE p1068
80 BOUL DE L'AEROPORT, BROMONT, QC, J2L 1S9
(450) 534-1659 *SIC 2434*

ARMOIRES FABRITEC LTEE p1154
1230 RUE INDUSTRIELLE, MONT-JOLI, QC, G5H 3S2
(418) 775-7010 *SIC 2434*

AYA KITCHENS AND BATHS LTD p702
1551 CATERPILLAR RD, MISSISSAUGA, ON, L4X 2Z6
(905) 848-1999 *SIC 2434*

BENSON INDUSTRIES LIMITED p267
2201 KEATING CROSS RD, SAANICHTON, BC, V8M 2A5
(250) 652-4417 *SIC 2434*

CARTIER KITCHENS INC p501
8 CHELSEA LANE, BRAMPTON, ON, L6T 3Y4
(905) 793-0063 *SIC 2434*

CLASSIC KITCHENS & CABINETS LIMITED p22
1122 40 AVE NE, CALGARY, AB, T2E 5T8
(403) 250-9470 *SIC 2434*

COLUMBIA KITCHEN CABINETS LTD p176
2221 TOWNLINE RD, ABBOTSFORD, BC, V2T 6H1
(604) 850-3538 *SIC 2434*

CORTINA KITCHENS INC p1030
70 REGINA RD, WOODBRIDGE, ON, L4L 8L6
(905) 264-6464 *SIC 2434*

CUISINE CROTONE INC p1161
9800 BOUL MAURICE-DUPLESSIS, MONTREAL, QC, H1C 1G1
(514) 648-3553 *SIC 2434*

CUISINE IDEALE INC p1372
980 RUE PANNETON, SHERBROOKE, QC,

J1K 2B2
(819) 566-2401 *SIC 2434*

CUISINES LAURIER INC p1133
266 RUE DE LA STATION, LAURIER-STATION, QC, G0S 1N0
(418) 728-3630 *SIC 2434*

DECOR CABINETS LTD p352
200 ROUTE 100, MORDEN, MB, R6M 1Y4
(204) 822-6151 *SIC 2434*

DOWNSVIEW WOODWORKING LIMITED p685
2635 RENA RD, MISSISSAUGA, ON, L4T 1G6
(905) 677-9354 *SIC 2434*

EBENISTERIE A. BEAUCAGE INC p1120
188 CH DES COMMISSAIRES, L'ASSOMPTION, QC, J5W 2T7
(450) 589-6412 *SIC 2434*

ELMWOOD GROUP LIMITED, THE p883
570 WELLAND AVE, ST CATHARINES, ON, L2M 5V6
(905) 688-5205 *SIC 2434*

GLENWOOD KITCHENS LTD p417
191 MAIN ST, SHEDIAC, NB, E4P 2A5
(506) 532-4491 *SIC 2434*

GROUPE CABICO INC p1082
677 RUE AKHURST, COATICOOK, QC, J1A 0B4
(819) 849-7969 *SIC 2434*

INDUSTRIES CARON (MEUBLES) INC, LES p1160
45 4E RUE, MONTMAGNY, QC, G5V 3K8
(418) 248-0255 *SIC 2434*

KITCHEN CRAFT OF CANADA p362
1180 SPRINGFIELD RD, WINNIPEG, MB, R2C 2Z2
(204) 224-3211 *SIC 2434*

LAURYSEN KITCHENS LTD p891
2415 CARP RD, STITTSVILLE, ON, K2S 1B3
(613) 836-5353 *SIC 2434*

MIRALIS INC p1291
200 RUE DES FABRICANTS, SAINT-ANACLET, QC, G0K 1H0
(418) 723-6686 *SIC 2434*

NEFF KITCHEN MANUFACTURERS LIMITED p505
151 EAST DR, BRAMPTON, ON, L6T 1B5
(905) 791-7770 *SIC 2434*

NORELCO CABINETS LTD p220
677 WILLOW PARK RD UNIT 2, KELOWNA, BC, V1X 5H9
(250) 765-2121 *SIC 2434*

NORMAC KITCHENS LIMITED p905
59 GLEN CAMERON RD, THORNHILL, ON, L3T 5W2
(905) 889-1342 *SIC 2434*

PREMOULE INC p1267
2375 AV DALTON UNITE 200, QUEBEC, QC, G1P 3S3
(418) 652-1422 *SIC 2434*

RAYWAL LIMITED PARTNERSHIP, THE p905
68 GREEN LANE, THORNHILL, ON, L3T 6K8
(905) 889-6243 *SIC 2434*

SANDERSON-HAROLD COMPANY LIMITED, THE p854
245 WEST BEAVER CREEK RD UNIT 2, RICHMOND HILL, ON, L4B 1L1
(519) 442-6311 *SIC 2434*

SELBA INDUSTRIES INC p558
3231 LANGSTAFF RD, CONCORD, ON, L4K 4L2
(905) 660-1614 *SIC 2434*

SIGNAL HILL EQUITY PARTNERS INC p936
2 CARLTON ST SUITE 1700, TORONTO, ON, M5B 1J3
(416) 847-1502 *SIC 2434*

SUPERIOR MILLWORK LTD p1432
747 46TH ST W, SASKATOON, SK, S7L 6A1
(306) 667-6600 *SIC 2434*

VANICO-MARONYX INC p1382

1151 BOUL DE LA PINIERE, TERREBONNE, QC, J6Y 0P3
(450) 471-4447 *SIC 2434*

WESTRIDGE CABINETS (1993) LTD p157
412 LIBERTY AVE, RED DEER COUNTY, AB, T4E 1B9
(403) 342-6671 *SIC 2434*

WESTWOOD FINE CABINETRY INC p223
2140 LECKIE PL, KELOWNA, BC, V1Y 7W7
(250) 860-3900 *SIC 2434*

SIC 2435 Hardwood veneer and plywood

BIRCHLAND PLYWOOD - VENEER LIMITED p903
50 GENELLE ST, THESSALON, ON, P0R 1L0
(705) 842-2430 *SIC 2435*

COMPAGNIE COMMONWEALTH PLYWOOD LTEE, LA p1364
15 BOUL DU CURE-LABELLE, SAINTE-THERESE, QC, J7E 2X1
(450) 435-6541 *SIC 2435*

COMPAGNIE COMMONWEALTH PLYWOOD LTEE, LA p1368
1155 AV DE LA FONDERIE, SHAWINIGAN, QC, G9N 1W9
(819) 537-6621 *SIC 2435*

CONTRE-PLAQUE ST-CASIMIR INC p1296
420 RTE GUILBAULT, SAINT-CASIMIR, QC, G0A 3L0
(418) 339-2313 *SIC 2435*

LEVESQUE PLYWOOD LIMITED p619
225 PRINCE ST, HEARST, ON, P0L 1N0
(705) 362-4242 *SIC 2435*

MASONITE INTERNATIONAL CORPORATION p1125
6184 RUE NOTRE-DAME, LAC-MEGANTIC, QC, G6B 3B5
(819) 583-1550 *SIC 2435*

NORBORD INC p174
995 EXETER STN RD, 100 MILE HOUSE, BC, V0K 2E0
(250) 395-6246 *SIC 2435*

NORBORD INC p940
1 TORONTO ST SUITE 600, TORONTO, ON, M5C 2W4
(416) 365-0705 *SIC 2435*

NORBORD INDUSTRIES INC p546
4 BOISVERT CRES, COCHRANE, ON, P0L 1C0
(705) 272-4210 *SIC 2435*

PLACAGES ST-RAYMOND INC p1351
595 RUE GUYON, SAINT-RAYMOND, QC, G3L 1Z1
(418) 337-4607 *SIC 2435*

PRO-PLY CUSTOM PLYWOOD INC p505
1195 CLARK BLVD SUITE 905, BRAMPTON, ON, L6T 3W4
(905) 564-2327 *SIC 2435*

TOLKO INDUSTRIES LTD p218
6275 OLD HWY 5, KAMLOOPS, BC, V2H 1T8
(250) 578-7212 *SIC 2435*

WEST FRASER MILLS LTD p252
2000 PLYWOOD RD, QUESNEL, BC, V2J 5W1
(250) 992-5511 *SIC 2435*

WESTLAM INDUSTRIES LTD p226
19755 98 AVE, LANGLEY, BC, V1M 2X5
(604) 888-2894 *SIC 2435*

SIC 2436 Softwood veneer and plywood

CIPA LUMBER CO. LTD p205
797 CARLISLE RD, DELTA, BC, V3M 5P4
(604) 523-2250 *SIC 2436*

COAL ISLAND LTD p259
10991 SHELLBRIDGE WAY SUITE 310, RICHMOND, BC, V6X 3C6
(604) 873-4312 *SIC 2436*

COASTLAND WOOD INDUSTRIES LTD p233

84 ROBARTS ST SUITE 2, NANAIMO, BC, V9R 2S5
(250) 754-1962 *SIC 2436*

FEDERATED CO-OPERATIVES LIMITED p267
8160 TRANS CAN HWY NE, SALMON ARM, BC, V1E 2S6
(250) 833-1200 *SIC 2436*

LOUISIANA-PACIFIC CANADA LTD p215
800 9TH ST N, GOLDEN, BC, V0A 1H0
(250) 344-8800 *SIC 2436*

LP ENGINEERED WOOD PRODUCTS LTD p215
1221 10TH AVE N, GOLDEN, BC, V0A 1H2
(250) 344-8800 *SIC 2436*

PANOLAM INDUSTRIES LTD p621
61 DOMTAR RD, HUNTSVILLE, ON, P1H 2J7
(705) 789-9683 *SIC 2436*

RICHMOND PLYWOOD CORPORATION LIMITED p256
13911 VULCAN WAY, RICHMOND, BC, V6V 1K7
(604) 278-9111 *SIC 2436*

THOMPSON RIVER VENEER PRODUCTS LIMITED p218
8405 DALLAS DR, KAMLOOPS, BC, V2C 6X2
(250) 573-6002 *SIC 2436*

SIC 2439 Structural wood members, nec

1312983 ONTARIO INC p648
2016 OXFORD ST E, LONDON, ON, N5V 2Z8
(519) 659-2711 *SIC 2439*

316291 ALBERTA LTD p107
4315 92 AVE NW, EDMONTON, AB, T6B 3M7
(780) 465-9771 *SIC 2439*

ACUTRUSS INDUSTRIES (1996) LTD p331
2003 43 ST, VERNON, BC, V1T 6K7
(250) 545-3215 *SIC 2439*

ALL SPAN BUILDING SYSTEMS LTD p80
424 GRIFFIN RD W, COCHRANE, AB, T4C 2E1
(403) 932-7878 *SIC 2439*

ALPA ROOF TRUSSES INC p664
10311 KEELE ST, MAPLE, ON, L6A 3Y9
(905) 832-2250 *SIC 2439*

ALPA ROOF TRUSSES INC p894
5532 SLATERS RD, STOUFFVILLE, ON, L4A 2G7
(905) 713-6616 *SIC 2439*

CHANTIERS DE CHIBOUGAMAU LTEE, LES p1077
521 CH MERRILL, CHIBOUGAMAU, QC, G8P 2K7
(418) 748-6481 *SIC 2439*

CLYVANOR LTEE p1304
2125 95E RUE BUREAU 1, SAINT-GEORGES, QC, G5Y 8J1
(418) 228-7690 *SIC 2439*

DAVIDSON ENMAN LUMBER LIMITED p15
9515 44 ST SE, CALGARY, AB, T2C 2P7
(403) 279-5525 *SIC 2439*

FRENECO LTEE p1253
261 RUE SAINT-CHARLES, PORTNEUF, QC, G0A 2Y0
(418) 286-3341 *SIC 2439*

KEFOR LTEE p1314
175 RUE BOYER, SAINT-ISIDORE-DE-LAPRAIRIE, QC, J0L 2A0
(450) 454-4636 *SIC 2439*

KENT TRUSSES LIMITED p902
204 FOREST LAKE RD, SUNDRIDGE, ON, P0A 1Z0
(705) 384-5326 *SIC 2439*

LEDUC TRUSS INC p139
4507 61 AVE, LEDUC, AB, T9E 7B5
(780) 986-0334 *SIC 2439*

PF RESOLU CANADA INC p1134
2050 RTE 805 N, LEBEL-SUR-

QUEVILLON, QC, J0Y 1X0
(819) 755-2500　*SIC 2439*

PHOENIX BUILDING COMPONENTS INC *p882*
93 OTTAWA AVE, SOUTH RIVER, ON, P0A 1X0
(705) 386-0007　*SIC 2439*

PHOENIX BUILDING COMPONENTS INC *p1000*
5650 SIDEROAD 30, UTOPIA, ON, L0M 1T0
(705) 733-3843　*SIC 2439*

PRODUITS PBM LTEE, LES *p1350*
130 RUE DU MOULIN, SAINT-PIERRE-DE-LAMY, QC, G0L 4B0
(418) 497-3927　*SIC 2439*

RIVERBEND COLONY LTD *p348*
GD, CARBERRY, MB, R0K 0H0
(204) 834-3141　*SIC 2439*

STRUCTURE LAFERTE INC *p1097*
2300 BOUL LEMIRE, DRUMMONDVILLE, QC, J2B 6X9
(819) 477-7723　*SIC 2439*

STRUCTURES ST-JOSEPH LTEE *p1322*
200 RUE DU PARC, SAINT-JOSEPH-DE-BEAUCE, QC, G0S 2V0
(418) 397-5712　*SIC 2439*

STRUCTURLAM MASS TIMBER CORPORATION *p244*
2176 GOVERNMENT ST, PENTICTON, BC, V2A 8B5
(250) 492-8912　*SIC 2439*

SUPERIOR TRUSS CO LTD *p353*
165 INDUSTRIAL RD, OAK BLUFF, MB, R4G 0A5
(204) 888-7663　*SIC 2439*

TIMBER INVESTMENT HOLDINGS INC *p4*
262029 BALZAC BLVD, BALZAC, AB, T4B 2T3
(403) 226-8617　*SIC 2439*

TIMBER-TECH TRUSS INC *p141*
1405 31 ST N, LETHBRIDGE, AB, T1H 5G8
(403) 328-5499　*SIC 2439*

TOITURES FECTEAU INC *p1294*
320 RTE 271, SAINT-BENOIT-LABRE, QC, G0M 1P0
(418) 228-9651　*SIC 2439*

TOITURES P.L.C. INC, LES *p1133*
235 RUE DE LA STATION, LAURIER-STATION, QC, G0S 1N0
(418) 682-2033　*SIC 2439*

WATFORD ROOF TRUSS LIMITED *p1011*
330 FRONT ST, WATFORD, ON, N0M 2S0
(519) 876-2612　*SIC 2439*

WEYERHAEUSER COMPANY LIMITED *p628*
1000 JONES RD, KENORA, ON, P9N 3X8
(807) 548-8000　*SIC 2439*

SIC 2441 Nailed wood boxes and shook

MILLETTE & FILS LTEE *p1134*
2105 RUE DE L'EGLISE, LAWRENCEVILLE, QC, J0E 1W0
(450) 535-6305　*SIC 2441*

NEFAB INC *p841*
211 JAMESON DR, PETERBOROUGH, ON, K9J 6X6
(705) 748-4888　*SIC 2441*

SIC 2448 Wood pallets and skids

4117638 MANITOBA LTD *p346*
94 PENNER DR S, BLUMENORT, MB, R0A 0C0
(204) 346-9314　*SIC 2448*

ADVANCE PALLET & CRATE LTD *p274*
12184 OLD YALE RD, SURREY, BC, V3V 3X5
(888) 791-2323　*SIC 2448*

BERSACO, INC *p1112*
717 RUE DE LA MONTAGNE, GRANDES-BERGERONNES, QC, G0T 1G0
(418) 232-1100　*SIC 2448*

BOIS D'INGENIERIE RESOLU-LP LAROUCHE INC *p1130*
900 CH DU LAC-HIPPOLYTE, LAROUCHE, QC, G0W 1Z0
(418) 547-2828　*SIC 2448*

CANADA PALLET CORP *p544*
755 DIVISION ST, COBOURG, ON, K9A 3T1
(905) 373-0761　*SIC 2448*

CETAL *p1133*
179 BOUL LAURIER, LAURIER-STATION, QC, G0S 1N0
(418) 728-3119　*SIC 2448*

CHRISTINA RIVER ENTERPRISES LIMITED PARTNERSHIP *p127*
GD LCD MAIN, FORT MCMURRAY, AB, T9H 3E2
(780) 334-2446　*SIC 2448*

PALLETSOURCE INC *p545*
755 DIVISION ST, COBOURG, ON, K9A 3T1
(905) 373-0761　*SIC 2448*

PARAMOUNT PALLET LP *p587*
1330 MARTIN GROVE RD, ETOBICOKE, ON, M9W 4X3
(416) 742-6006　*SIC 2448*

PINNACLE RENEWABLE ENERGY INC *p265*
3600 LYSANDER LN SUITE 350, RICHMOND, BC, V7B 1C3
(604) 270-9613　*SIC 2448*

POUTRELLES INTERNATIONALES INC *p1246*
480 RUE JOCELYN-BASTILLE, POHENEGAMOOK, QC, G0L 1J0
(418) 893-1515　*SIC 2448*

SIC 2451 Mobile homes

533438 ONTARIO LIMITED *p589*
165 THAMES RD W SS 3 SUITE 83, EXETER, ON, N0M 1S3
(519) 235-1530　*SIC 2451*

TRIPLE M HOUSING LTD *p141*
3501 GIFFEN RD N, LETHBRIDGE, AB, T1H 0E8
(403) 320-8588　*SIC 2451*

SIC 2452 Prefabricated wood buildings

ALTA-FAB STRUCTURES LTD *p148*
1205 5 ST, NISKU, AB, T9E 7L6
(780) 955-7733　*SIC 2452*

BARRCANA HOMES INC *p4*
59504 RANGE RD 32, BARRHEAD, AB, T7N 1A4
(780) 305-0505　*SIC 2452*

BRITCO LP *p178*
1825 TOWER DR, AGASSIZ, BC, V0M 1A2
(604) 796-2257　*SIC 2452*

BRITCO MANAGEMENT INC *p224*
20091 91A AVE UNIT 100, LANGLEY, BC, V1M 3A2
(604) 455-8000　*SIC 2452*

GROUPE PRO-FAB INC *p1292*
294 RUE LAURIER BUREAU 881, SAINT-APOLLINAIRE, QC, G0S 2E0
(418) 881-2288　*SIC 2452*

GUILDCREST BUILDING CORPORATION *p746*
20 MILL ST, MOREWOOD, ON, K0A 2R0
(613) 448-2349　*SIC 2452*

HORIZON NORTH MODULAR MANUFACTURING INC *p51*
240 4 AVE SW SUITE 900, CALGARY, AB, T2P 4H4
(403) 517-4654　*SIC 2452*

INDUSTRIES BONNEVILLE LTEE, LES *p1057*
601 RUE DE L'INDUSTRIE, BELOEIL, QC, J3G 0S5
(450) 464-1001　*SIC 2452*

INDUSTRIES BONNEVILLE LTEE, LES *p1355*
316 RUE PRINCIPALE O, SAINTE-ANNE-DE-LA-ROCHELLE, QC, J0E 2B0
(450) 539-3100　*SIC 2452*

IRVING, J. D. LIMITED *p395*
28 CH DU COUVENT, BOUCTOUCHE, NB, E4S 3B9
(506) 743-2481　*SIC 2452*

LINWOOD HOMES LTD *p209*
8250 RIVER RD, DELTA, BC, V4G 1B5
(604) 946-5421　*SIC 2452*

M.M.H. PRESTIGE HOMES INC *p418*
14 INDUSTRIAL DR, SUSSEX, NB, E4E 2R8
(506) 433-9130　*SIC 2452*

MAISONS LAPRISE INC *p1160*
166 4E RUE, MONTMAGNY, QC, G5V 3L5
(418) 248-0401　*SIC 2452*

MAISONS LAPRISE INC *p1273*
2700 BOUL LAURIER UNITE 2540, QUEBEC, QC, G1V 2L8
(418) 683-3343　*SIC 2452*

MAISONS USINEES COTE INC *p1347*
388 RUE SAINT-ISIDORE, SAINT-LIN-LAURENTIDES, QC, J5M 2V1
(450) 439-8737　*SIC 2452*

MAPLE LEAF HOMES INC *p401*
655 WILSEY RD, FREDERICTON, NB, E3B 7K3
(506) 459-1335　*SIC 2452*

MOUNTAIN VIEW LEASING INC *p119*
4916 WHITEMUD RD NW, EDMONTON, AB, T6H 5M3
(780) 462-9600　*SIC 2452*

NORTHGATE INDUSTRIES LTD *p94*
12345 121 ST NW, EDMONTON, AB, T5L 4Y7
(780) 448-9222　*SIC 2452*

PACIFIC BUILDERS SUPPLIES *p198*
3730 TRANS CANADA HWY, COBBLE HILL, BC, V0R 1L7
(250) 743-5584　*SIC 2452*

QUALITY ENGINEERED HOMES LTD *p628*
7307 HWY 6, KENILWORTH, ON, N0G 2E0
(519) 323-4208　*SIC 2452*

R.C.M. MODULAIRE INC *p1294*
28 RUE INDUSTRIELLE, SAINT-BENOIT-LABRE, QC, G0M 1P0
(418) 227-4044　*SIC 2452*

ROYAL HOMES LIMITED *p1026*
213 ARTHUR ST, WINGHAM, ON, N0G 2W0
(519) 357-2606　*SIC 2452*

STRUCTURES ULTRATEC INC, LES *p1133*
235 RUE DE LA STATION, LAURIER-STATION, QC, G0S 1N0
(418) 682-2033　*SIC 2452*

SIC 2491 Wood preserving

2161-1298 QUEBEC INC *p1402*
1031 7E RANG, WICKHAM, QC, J0C 1S0
(819) 398-6303　*SIC 2491*

2621-9634 QUEBEC INC *p1291*
37 204 RTE E, SAINT-ADALBERT, QC, G0R 2M0
(418) 356-5591　*SIC 2491*

GENICS INC *p1*
27717 ACHESON RD, ACHESON, AB, T7X 6B1
SIC 2491

GROUPE CEDRICO INC *p1124*
50 RANG DIDIER, LAC-AU-SAUMON, QC, G0J 1M0
SIC 2491

NORTHERN SAWMILLS INC *p909*
490 MAUREEN ST, THUNDER BAY, ON, P7B 6T2
SIC 2491

PRODUITS FORESTIERS PETIT PARIS INC *p1347*
75 CH DE CHUTES-DES-PASSES, SAINT-

LUDGER-DE-MILOT, QC, G0W 2B0
(418) 373-2801　*SIC 2491*

RAM FOREST PRODUCTS INC *p598*
1 RAM FOREST RD, GORMLEY, ON, L0H 1G0
SIC 2491

SPRAY LAKE SAWMILLS (1980) LTD *p80*
305 GRIFFIN RD W, COCHRANE, AB, T4C 2C4
(403) 932-2234　*SIC 2491*

STELLA-JONES INC *p1331*
3100 BOUL DE LA COTE-VERTU BUREAU 300, SAINT-LAURENT, QC, H4R 2J8
(514) 934-8666　*SIC 2491*

SIC 2493 Reconstituted wood products

ARAUCO CANADA LIMITED *p861*
657 BASE LINE, SAULT STE. MARIE, ON, P6A 5K6
(705) 253-0770　*SIC 2493*

CIE MATERIAUX DE CONSTRUCTION BP CANADA, LA *p1132*
9510 RUE SAINT-PATRICK, LASALLE, QC, H8R 1R9
(514) 364-0161　*SIC 2493*

FOOTNER FOREST PRODUCTS LTD *p135*
GD, HIGH LEVEL, AB, T0H 1Z0
(780) 841-0008　*SIC 2493*

GROUPE ISOLOFOAM INC *p1360*
1346 BOUL VACHON N, SAINTE-MARIE, QC, G6E 1N4
(800) 463-8886　*SIC 2493*

LOUISIANA-PACIFIC CANADA LTD *p442*
2005 HIGHWAY 14, CHESTER, NS, B0J 1J0
(902) 275-3556　*SIC 2493*

MEADOW LAKE OSB LIMITED PARTNERSHIP *p1410*
12 KM SOUTH OF HWY 55, MEADOW LAKE, SK, S9X 1Y2
(306) 236-6565　*SIC 2493*

NORBORD INC *p133*
6700 HWY 40 S, GRANDE PRAIRIE, AB, T8V 6Y9
(780) 831-2500　*SIC 2493*

SPECIALTY LAMINATE MANUFACTURING LTD *p18*
2624 54 AVE SE BAY SUITE B, CALGARY, AB, T2C 1R5
(403) 273-3800　*SIC 2493*

UNIBOARD CANADA INC *p1155*
845 RUE JEAN-BAPTISTE-REID, MONT-LAURIER, QC, J9L 3W3
(819) 623-7133　*SIC 2493*

UNIBOARD CANADA INC *p1232*
5555 RUE ERNEST-CORMIER, MONTREAL, QC, H7C 2S9
(450) 664-6000　*SIC 2493*

UNIBOARD CANADA INC *p1366*
152 RTE POULIOT, SAYABEC, QC, G0J 3K0
(418) 536-5465　*SIC 2493*

UNIBOARD CANADA INC *p1391*
2700 BOUL JEAN-JACQUES-COSSETTE, VAL-D'OR, QC, J9P 6Y5
(819) 825-6550　*SIC 2493*

WEYERHAEUSER COMPANY LIMITED *p82*
GD STN MAIN, DRAYTON VALLEY, AB, T7A 1T1
(780) 542-8000　*SIC 2493*

SIC 2499 Wood products, nec

ACIER AGF INC *p1265*
595 AV NEWTON, QUEBEC, QC, G1P 4C4
(418) 877-7715　*SIC 2499*

BFCO INC *p1054*
5 RUE PAUL-RENE-TREMBLAY, BAIE-SAINT-PAUL, QC, G3Z 3E4
(418) 435-3682　*SIC 2499*

BOISE ALLJOIST LTD *p417*

70 RUE INDUSTRIELLE, SAINT-JACQUES, NB, E7B 1T1
(506) 735-3561   SIC 2499
CADRES COLUMBIA INC   p1164
6251 RUE NOTRE-DAME E, MONTREAL, QC, H1N 2E9
(514) 253-2999   SIC 2499
CENTOCO PLASTICS LIMITED   p1019
2450 CENTRAL AVE, WINDSOR, ON, N8W 4J3
(519) 948-2300   SIC 2499
CONGO CORPORATE WOODS INCORPO-RATED   p687
5935 AIRPORT RD, MISSISSAUGA, ON, L4V 1W5
(647) 388-6615   SIC 2499
CONROS CORPORATION   p776
41 LESMILL RD, NORTH YORK, ON, M3B 2T3
(416) 751-4343   SIC 2499
DELTA CEDAR SPECIALTIES LTD   p207
10104 RIVER RD, DELTA, BC, V4C 2R3
(604) 589-9006   SIC 2499
DH MANUFACTURING INC   p215
1250 HOLS RD, HOUSTON, BC, V0J 1Z1
(250) 845-3390   SIC 2499
FRASERVIEW CEDAR PRODUCTS LTD   p276
6630 144 ST, SURREY, BC, V3W 5R5
(604) 590-9355   SIC 2499
IMAGES 2000 INC   p570
33 DRUMMOND ST, ETOBICOKE, ON, M8V 1Y7
(416) 252-9693   SIC 2499
INDUSTRIES JOHN LEWIS LTEE   p1049
8545 RUE JULES-LEGER, ANJOU, QC, H1J 1A8
(514) 352-2950   SIC 2499
INDUSTRIES JOHN LEWIS LTEE   p1124
1101 BOUL DUCHARME, LA TUQUE, QC, G9X 3C3
(819) 523-7636   SIC 2499
KINGSWAY COLLEGE   p814
1200 LELAND RD, OSHAWA, ON, L1K 2H4
(905) 433-1144   SIC 2499
LE GRENIER D'ART (1987) INC   p1070
9205 BOUL TASCHEREAU, BROSSARD, QC, J4Y 3B8
(450) 659-6999   SIC 2499
MARWOOD LTD   p419
3307 ROUTE 101, TRACYVILLE, NB, E5L 1N7
(506) 459-7777   SIC 2499
NORBORD INDUSTRIES INC   p1123
210 9E AV E, LA SARRE, QC, J9Z 2L2
(819) 333-5464   SIC 2499
NOVA POLE INTERNATIONAL INC   p279
2579 188 ST, SURREY, BC, V3Z 2A1
(604) 881-0090   SIC 2499
PINKWOOD LTD   p40
5929 6 ST NE, CALGARY, AB, T2K 5R5
(403) 279-3700   SIC 2499
REN-WIL INC   p1132
9181 RUE BOIVIN, LASALLE, QC, H8R 2E8
(514) 367-1741   SIC 2499
ROMA MOULDING INC   p1033
360 HANLAN RD, WOODBRIDGE, ON, L4L 3P6
(905) 850-1500   SIC 2499
RS TECHNOLOGIES INC   p40
3553 31 ST NW, CALGARY, AB, T2L 2K7
(403) 219-8000   SIC 2499
RS TECHNOLOGIES INC   p911
22 INDUSTRIAL PARK RD, TILBURY, ON, N0P 2L0
(519) 682-1110   SIC 2499
TAFISA CANADA INC   p1125
4660 RUE VILLENEUVE, LAC-MEGANTIC, QC, G6B 2C3
(819) 583-2930   SIC 2499
TOLKO INDUSTRIES LTD   p360
HWY 10 N, THE PAS, MB, R9A 1S1
(204) 623-7411   SIC 2499
UFP CANADA INC   p1294

110 MONTEE GUAY, SAINT-BERNARD-DE-LACOLLE, QC, J0J 1V0
(450) 246-3829   SIC 2499

SIC 2511 Wood household furniture

BARONET INC   p1359
234 AV BARONET, SAINTE-MARIE, QC, G6E 2R1
(418) 209-1009   SIC 2511
BARRETTEBOIS INC   p1317
583 CH DU GRAND-BERNIER N, SAINT-JEAN-SUR-RICHELIEU, QC, J3B 8K1
(450) 357-7000   SIC 2511
BERMEX INTERNATIONAL INC   p1150
215 BOUL OUEST, MASKINONGE, QC, J0K 1N0
(819) 601-8702   SIC 2511
BESTAR INC   p1125
4220 RUE VILLENEUVE, LAC-MEGANTIC, QC, G6B 2C3
(819) 583-1017   SIC 2511
BUHLER FURNITURE INC   p383
700 KING EDWARD ST, WINNIPEG, MB, R3H 1B4
(204) 775-7799   SIC 2511
CANADEL INC   p1146
700 RUE CANADEL, LOUISEVILLE, QC, J5V 3A4
(819) 228-8471   SIC 2511
CANADEL INC   p1146
700 RUE CANADEL, LOUISEVILLE, QC, J5V 3A4
(819) 228-8471   SIC 2511
CHERVIN INC   p1010
20 BENJAMIN RD, WATERLOO, ON, N2V 2J9
(519) 885-3542   SIC 2511
DEFEHR FURNITURE (2009) LTD   p363
125 FURNITURE PARK, WINNIPEG, MB, R2G 1B9
(204) 988-5630   SIC 2511
DURHAM FURNITURE INC   p567
450 LAMBTON ST W, DURHAM, ON, N0G 1R0
(519) 369-2345   SIC 2511
DYNAMIC FURNITURE CORP   p15
5300 61 AVE SE, CALGARY, AB, T2C 4N1
(403) 236-3220   SIC 2511
INDUSTRIES DOREL INC, LES   p562
3305 LOYALIST ST, CORNWALL, ON, K6H 6W6
(613) 937-0711   SIC 2511
INDUSTRIES DOREL INC, LES   p1239
12345 BOUL ALBERT-HUDON BUREAU 100, MONTREAL-NORD, QC, H1G 3L1
(514) 323-1247   SIC 2511
INDUSTRIES STEMA-PRO INC, LES   p1369
2699 5E AV BUREAU 26, SHAWINIGAN, QC, G9T 2P7
(819) 533-4756   SIC 2511
MEUBLE IDEAL LTEE   p1297
6 RUE SAINT-THOMAS, SAINT-CHARLES-DE-BELLECHASSE, QC, G0R 2T0
(418) 887-3331   SIC 2511
MEUBLES BDM + INC   p1150
215 BOUL OUEST, MASKINONGE, QC, J0K 1N0
(819) 227-2284   SIC 2511
MEUBLES CATHEDRA INC   p1398
34 RUE DE L'ARTISAN, VICTORIAVILLE, QC, G6P 7E3
(819) 752-1641   SIC 2511
MOBILIER M.E.Q. LTEE   p1122
22 RUE OLIVIER-MOREL, LA DURAN-TAYE, QC, G0R 1W0
(418) 884-3050   SIC 2511
MOBILIER RUSTIQUE (BEAUCE) INCp1348
50 1E RUE O, SAINT-MARTIN, QC, G0M 1B0
(418) 382-5987   SIC 2511
SHERMAG IMPORT INC   p1057
10 RUE BISHOP, BISHOPTON, QC, J0B

1G0
(819) 884-1145   SIC 2511
SHERMAG IMPORT INC   p1111
825 BOUL INDUSTRIEL, GRANBY, QC, J2J 1A5
(450) 776-6361   SIC 2511
SOUTH SHORE INDUSTRIES LTD   p1357
6168 RUE PRINCIPALE, SAINTE-CROIX, QC, G0S 2H0
(418) 926-3291   SIC 2511
WEST FURNITURE CO INC   p618
582 14TH ST, HANOVER, ON, N4N 2A1
(519) 364-7770   SIC 2511

SIC 2512 Upholstered household furniture

AMEUBLEMENTS EL RAN LTEE   p1249
2751 RTE TRANSCANADIENNE, POINTE-CLAIRE, QC, H9R 1B4
(514) 630-5656   SIC 2512
BARRYMORE FURNITURE CO. LTD   p788
1168 CALEDONIA RD, NORTH YORK, ON, M6A 2W5
(416) 532-2891   SIC 2512
BIRCHWOOD FURNITURE CO INC   p12
4770 46 AVE SE, CALGARY, AB, T2B 3T7
(403) 252-5111   SIC 2512
BRENTWOOD CLASSICS LIMITED   p549
57 ADESSO DR, CONCORD, ON, L4K 3C7
(905) 761-0195   SIC 2512
CAMPIO FURNITURE LIMITED   p1030
5770 HIGHWAY 7 UNIT 1, WOODBRIDGE, ON, L4L 1T8
(905) 850-6636   SIC 2512
DECOR-REST FURNITURE LTD   p1030
511 CHRISLEA RD SUITE 8, WOOD-BRIDGE, ON, L4L 8N6
(905) 856-5956   SIC 2512
DYNASTY FURNITURE MANUFACTURING INC   p15
3344 54 AVE SE, CALGARY, AB, T2C 0A8
(403) 279-2958   SIC 2512
GROUPE DUTAILIER INC   p1350
299 RUE CHAPUT, SAINT-PIE, QC, J0H 1W0
(450) 772-2403   SIC 2512
HOLSAG CANADA INC   p646
164 NEEDHAM ST, LINDSAY, ON, K9V 5R7
(888) 745-0721   SIC 2512
INDUSTRIES DOREL INC, LES   p1402
1255 AV GREENE BUREAU 300, WEST-MOUNT, QC, H3Z 2A4
(514) 934-3034   SIC 2512
MARZILLI INTERNATIONAL INC   p1032
511 CHRISLEA RD, WOODBRIDGE, ON, L4L 8N6
(289) 268-2040   SIC 2512
MEUBLES JAYMAR CORP   p1379
75 RUE JAYMAR, TERREBONNE, QC, J6W 1M5
(450) 471-4172   SIC 2512
PALLISER FURNITURE UPHOLSTERY HOLDINGS LTD   p363
70 LEXINGTON PK, WINNIPEG, MB, R2G 4H2
(204) 988-5600   SIC 2512
PALLISER FURNITURE UPHOLSTERY LTD   p364
70 LEXINGTON PK, WINNIPEG, MB, R2G 4H2
(204) 988-5600   SIC 2512
RODI DESIGN INC   p1142
1100 BOUL MARIE-VICTORIN, LONGUEUIL, QC, J4G 2H9
(450) 679-7755   SIC 2512
STATUM DESIGNS INC   p793
180 NORELCO DR, NORTH YORK, ON, M9L 1S4
(416) 740-4010   SIC 2512
STYLUS SOFAS INC   p193
7885 RIVERFRONT GATE, BURNABY, BC, V5J 5L6
(604) 436-4100   SIC 2512

SUPERSTYLE FURNITURE LTD   p1034
123 ASHBRIDGE CIR, WOODBRIDGE, ON, L4L 3R5
(905) 850-6060   SIC 2512
TREND-LINE FURNITURE LTD   p787
166 NORFINCH DR, NORTH YORK, ON, M3N 1Y4
(416) 650-0504   SIC 2512
VAN GOGH DESIGNS FURNITURE LTD   p280
19178 34A AVE, SURREY, BC, V3Z 1A7
(604) 372-3001   SIC 2512

SIC 2514 Metal household furniture

2757-5158 QUEBEC INC   p1363
2854 RTE 235, SAINTE-SABINE, QC, J0J 2B0
(450) 293-5037   SIC 2514
AMYLIOR INC   p1394
3190 RUE F.-X.-TESSIER, VAUDREUIL-DORION, QC, J7V 5V5
(450) 424-0288   SIC 2514
HAUSER INDUSTRIES INC   p1006
330 WEBER ST N, WATERLOO, ON, N2J 3H6
(519) 747-1138   SIC 2514
INDUSTRIES AMISCO LTEE, LES   p1121
33 5E RUE, L'ISLET, QC, G0R 2C0
(418) 247-5025   SIC 2514
JULIEN BEAUDOIN LTEE   p1089
320 6E RUE, DAVELUYVILLE, QC, G0Z 1C0
(819) 367-2344   SIC 2514
KI CANADA CORPORATION   p838
1000 OLYMPIC DR, PEMBROKE, ON, K8A 0E1
(613) 735-5566   SIC 2514
KNOLL NORTH AMERICA CORP   p1032
600 ROWNTREE DAIRY RD, WOOD-BRIDGE, ON, L4L 5T8
(416) 741-5453   SIC 2514
SANI METAL LTEE   p1277
5170 RUE RIDEAU, QUEBEC, QC, G2E 5S4
(418) 872-5170   SIC 2514

SIC 2515 Mattresses and bedsprings

GESTION CENTURION INC   p1349
555 RUE PANNETON, SAINT-NARCISSE, QC, G0X 2Y0
(418) 328-3361   SIC 2515
MAJOLI FURNITURE (1983) LIMITED   p697
5510 AMBLER DR UNIT 2, MISSISSAUGA, ON, L4W 2V1
(905) 542-0481   SIC 2515
MATELAS DAUPHIN INC   p1139
8124 RUE DU BLIZZARD, LEVIS, QC, G6X 1C9
(418) 832-2951   SIC 2515
OWEN & COMPANY LIMITED   p1028
51 STONE RIDGE RD SUITE LBBY, WOODBRIDGE, ON, L4H 0A5
(905) 265-9203   SIC 2515
REST-WELL MATTRESS COMPANY LTD   p273
14922 54A AVE, SURREY, BC, V3S 5X7
(604) 576-2339   SIC 2515
SEALY CANADA LTD   p97
14550 112 AVE NW, EDMONTON, AB, T5M 2T9
(780) 452-3070   SIC 2515
SEALY CANADA LTD   p875
145 MILNER AVE, SCARBOROUGH, ON, M1S 3R1
(416) 699-7170   SIC 2515
SPRINGWALL SLEEP PRODUCTS INCp417
211 PARKER RD, SCOUDOUC, NB, E4P 3P7
(506) 532-4481   SIC 2515
WATERLOO BEDDING COMPANY, LIMITED   p642

---

825 TRILLIUM DR, KITCHENER, ON, N2R 1J9

SIC 2515

SIC 2517 Wood television and radio cabinets

MYLEX LIMITED *p575*
1460 THE QUEENSWAY, ETOBICOKE, ON, M8Z 1S7
(416) 259-5595   *SIC 2517*
MYLEX LIMITED *p586*
37 BETHRIDGE RD, ETOBICOKE, ON, M9W 1M8
(416) 745-1733   *SIC 2517*

SIC 2519 Household furniture, nec

C. R. PLASTIC PRODUCTS INC *p895*
1172 ERIE ST, STRATFORD, ON, N4Z 0A1
(519) 271-1283   *SIC 2519*
ROYAL GROUP, INC *p1028*
30 ROYAL GROUP CRES, WOODBRIDGE, ON, L4H 1X9
(905) 264-0701   *SIC 2519*
TRICA INC *p1321*
800 RUE PASTEUR, SAINT-JEROME, QC, J7Z 7K9
(450) 431-4897   *SIC 2519*

SIC 2521 Wood office furniture

10393266 CANADA INC *p1192*
925 BOUL DE MAISONNEUVE O BUREAU 247, MONTREAL, QC, H3A 0A5
SIC 2521
135770 CANADA LTEE *p1084*
2037 AV FRANCIS-HUGHES, COTE SAINT-LUC, QC, H7S 2G2
(450) 669-3002   *SIC 2521*
BURO DESIGN INTERNATIONAL A.Q. INC *p1343*
5715 BOUL METROPOLITAIN E, SAINT-LEONARD, QC, H1P 1X3
(514) 955-6644   *SIC 2521*
BURO DESIGN INTERNATIONAL A.Q. INC *p1347*
125 RUE QUINTAL, SAINT-LIN-LAURENTIDES, QC, J5M 2S8
(450) 439-8554   *SIC 2521*
DESCOR INDUSTRIES INC *p669*
15 RIVIERA DR, MARKHAM, ON, L3R 8N4
(905) 470-0010   *SIC 2521*
DSI UPHOLSTERY INC *p552*
452 MILLWAY AVE, CONCORD, ON, L4K 3V7
(905) 669-1357   *SIC 2521*
EGAN TEAMBOARD INC *p1031*
300 HANLAN RD, WOODBRIDGE, ON, L4L 3P6
(905) 851-2826   *SIC 2521*
EVANS CONSOLES CORPORATION *p23*
1616 27 AVE NE, CALGARY, AB, T2E 8W4
(403) 291-4444   *SIC 2521*
GLOBAL WOOD CONCEPTS LTD *p783*
1300 FLINT RD, NORTH YORK, ON, M3J 2J7
(416) 663-4191   *SIC 2521*
GROUPE LACASSE INC *p1350*
99 RUE SAINT-PIERRE, SAINT-PIE, QC, J0H 1W0
(450) 772-2495   *SIC 2521*
HEARTWOOD MANUFACTURING LTD *p220*
251 ADAMS RD, KELOWNA, BC, V1X 7R1
(250) 765-4145   *SIC 2521*
KEILHAUER LTD *p914*
1450 BIRCHMOUNT RD, TORONTO, ON, M1P 2E3
(416) 759-5665   *SIC 2521*
KNOLL NORTH AMERICA CORP *p795*
1000 ARROW RD, NORTH YORK, ON, M9M 2Y7
(416) 741-5453   *SIC 2521*
KRUG INC *p636*
421 MANITOU DR, KITCHENER, ON, N2C 1L5
(519) 748-5100   *SIC 2521*
MOBILIER DE BUREAU LOGIFLEX INC *p1375*
1235 CH SAINT-ROCH N, SHERBROOKE, QC, J1N 0H2
(877) 864-9323   *SIC 2521*
OFIS SYSTEMS INC *p556*
452 MILLWAY AVE SUITE 2, CONCORD, ON, L4K 3V7
SIC 2521
PRO-MEUBLES INC *p1111*
800 RUE VADNAIS BUREAU 450, GRANBY, QC, J2J 1A7
(450) 378-0189   *SIC 2521*
ROY & BRETON, INC *p1353*
577 RTE DE SAINT-VALLIER, SAINT-VALLIER, QC, G0R 4J0
(418) 833-0047   *SIC 2521*
ROY & BRETON, INC *p1353*
577 RTE DE SAINT-VALLIER, SAINT-VALLIER, QC, G0R 4J0
(418) 884-4041   *SIC 2521*
TAYCO PANELINK LTD *p580*
400 NORRIS GLEN RD, ETOBICOKE, ON, M9C 1H5
(416) 252-8000   *SIC 2521*
TEKNION (ALBERTA) LTD *p19*
6403 48 ST SE SUITE 60, CALGARY, AB, T2C 3J7
(403) 264-4210   *SIC 2521*
THREE H FURNITURE SYSTEMS LIMITED *p753*
156462 CLOVER VALLEY RD, NEW LISKEARD, ON, P0J 1P0
(705) 647-4323   *SIC 2521*
WOODLORE INTERNATIONAL INC *p507*
160 DELTA PARK BLVD, BRAMPTON, ON, L6T 5T6
(905) 791-9555   *SIC 2521*

SIC 2522 Office furniture, except wood

ALLSEATING CORPORATION *p729*
5800 AVEBURY RD UNIT 3, MISSISSAUGA, ON, L5R 3M3
(905) 502-7200   *SIC 2522*
ARTOPEX INC *p1110*
800 RUE VADNAIS, GRANBY, QC, J2J 1A7
(450) 378-0189   *SIC 2522*
ARTOPEX INC *p1233*
2129 RUE BERLIER, MONTREAL, QC, H7L 3M9
(450) 973-9655   *SIC 2522*
DIRTT ENVIRONMENTAL SOLUTIONS LTD *p15*
7303 30 ST SE, CALGARY, AB, T2C 1N6
(403) 723-5000   *SIC 2522*
ERGOCENTRIC INC *p739*
275 SUPERIOR BLVD UNIT 2, MISSISSAUGA, ON, L5T 2L6
(905) 696-6800   *SIC 2522*
EXPERT MANUFACTURING INC *p552*
180 VICEROY RD, CONCORD, ON, L4K 2L8
(905) 738-7575   *SIC 2522*
GLOBAL CONTRACT INC *p783*
565 PETROLIA RD, NORTH YORK, ON, M3J 2X8
(416) 739-5000   *SIC 2522*
GLOBAL FILE INC *p553*
7939 KEELE ST, CONCORD, ON, L4K 1Y6
(905) 761-3284   *SIC 2522*
GLOBAL UPHOLSTERY CO. INC *p783*
565 PETROLIA RD, NORTH YORK, ON, M3J 2X8
(416) 739-5000   *SIC 2522*
GLOBAL UPHOLSTERY CO. INC *p783*
560 SUPERTEST RD, NORTH YORK, ON, M3J 2M6
(416) 661-3660   *SIC 2522*
INSCAPE CORPORATION *p620*
67 TOLL RD, HOLLAND LANDING, ON, L9N 1H2
(905) 836-7676   *SIC 2522*
KRUEGER PEMBROKE LP *p838*
1000 OLYMPIC DR, PEMBROKE, ON, K8A 0E1
SIC 2522
KRUG INC *p636*
421 MANITOU DR, KITCHENER, ON, N2C 1L5
(519) 748-5100   *SIC 2522*
MURAFLEX INC *p1165*
5502 RUE NOTRE-DAME E, MONTREAL, QC, H1N 2C4
(450) 462-3632   *SIC 2522*
NIENKAMPER FURNITURE & ACCES-SORIES INC *p914*
257 FINCHDENE SQUARE, TORONTO, ON, M1X 1B9
(416) 298-5700   *SIC 2522*
NOVA-LINK LIMITED *p606*
935A SOUTHGATE DR UNIT 5, GUELPH, ON, N1L 0B9
(905) 858-3500   *SIC 2522*
PERFIX INC *p1061*
645 BOUL DU CURE-BOIVIN, BOIS-BRIAND, QC, J7G 2J2
(450) 435-0540   *SIC 2522*
PROFILE INDUSTRIES LIMITED *p793*
201 GARYRAY DR, NORTH YORK, ON, M9L 2T2
(416) 748-2505   *SIC 2522*
SPEC FURNITURE INC *p588*
165 CITY VIEW DR, ETOBICOKE, ON, M9W 5B1
(416) 246-5550   *SIC 2522*
TEKNION CORPORATION *p784*
1150 FLINT RD, NORTH YORK, ON, M3J 2J5
(416) 661-1577   *SIC 2522*
TEKNION LIMITED *p559*
1400 ALNESS ST UNIT 12, CONCORD, ON, L4K 2W6
(416) 669-2035   *SIC 2522*
TEKNION LIMITED *p784*
1150 FLINT RD, NORTH YORK, ON, M3J 2J5
(416) 661-1577   *SIC 2522*
TEKNION LIMITED *p1139*
975 RUE DES CALFATS BUREAU 45, LEVIS, QC, G6Y 9E8
(418) 833-0047   *SIC 2522*
TEKNION LIMITED *p1160*
45 CH DES CASCADES, MONTMAGNY, QC, G5V 3M6
(418) 248-5711   *SIC 2522*

SIC 2531 Public building and related furniture

ARCONAS CORPORATION *p729*
5700 KEATON CRES UNIT 1, MISSISSAUGA, ON, L5R 3H5
(905) 272-0727   *SIC 2531*
ARCONAS INVESTMENTS LTD *p729*
5700 KEATON CRES UNIT 1, MISSISSAUGA, ON, L5R 3H5
(905) 272-0727   *SIC 2531*
BRODART CANADA COMPANY *p514*
109 ROY BLVD, BRANTFORD, ON, N3R 7K1
SIC 2531
FABRICATIONS DOR-VAL LTEE, LES *p1323*
11800 BOUL LAURENTIEN, SAINT-LAURENT, QC, H4K 2E1
(514) 336-7780   *SIC 2531*
JOHNSON CONTROLS NOVA SCOTIA U.L.C. *p808*
120 C LINE, ORANGEVILLE, ON, L9W 3Z8
SIC 2531
JOHNSON CONTROLS NOVA SCOTIA U.L.C. *p852*
56 LEEK CRES, RICHMOND HILL, ON, L4B 1H1
(866) 468-1484   *SIC 2531*
JOHNSON CONTROLS NOVA SCOTIA U.L.C. *p912*
100 TOWNLINE RD, TILLSONBURG, ON, N4G 2R7
(519) 842-5971   *SIC 2531*
MEUBLES FOLIOT INC *p1320*
721 BOUL ROLAND-GODARD, SAINT-JEROME, QC, J7Y 4C1
(450) 565-9166   *SIC 2531*
PPD SOLUTION DE MOUSSE INC *p1099*
1275 RUE JANELLE, DRUMMONDVILLE, QC, J2C 3E4
(819) 850-0159   *SIC 2531*
PPD SOLUTION DE MOUSSE INC *p1400*
325 RUE PRINCIPALE N, WATERVILLE, QC, J0B 3H0
(819) 837-2491   *SIC 2531*
TS TECH CANADA INC *p757*
17855 LESLIE ST, NEWMARKET, ON, L3Y 3E3
(905) 953-0098   *SIC 2531*
VEN-REZ PRODUCTS LIMITED *p466*
380 SANDY POINT RD, SHELBURNE, NS, B0T 1W0
(902) 875-3178   *SIC 2531*

SIC 2541 Wood partitions and fixtures

BELANGER LAMINES INC *p1063*
1435 RUE JOLIOT-CURIE, BOUCHERVILLE, QC, J4B 7M4
(450) 449-3447   *SIC 2541*
BUILDERS FURNITURE LTD *p367*
695 WASHINGTON AVE, WINNIPEG, MB, R2K 1M4
(204) 668-0783   *SIC 2541*
CAMBRIA FABSHOP-TORONTO INC *p494*
41 SIMPSON RD, BOLTON, ON, L7E 2R6
(905) 951-1011   *SIC 2541*
CAYUGA DISPLAYS INC *p541*
88 TALBOT ST E, CAYUGA, ON, N0A 1E0
(905) 772-5214   *SIC 2541*
CDA INDUSTRIES INC *p844*
1055 SQUIRES BEACH RD, PICKERING, ON, L1W 4A6
(905) 686-7000   *SIC 2541*
DESLAURIER CUSTOM CABINETS INC *p849*
550 HALL AVE E, RENFREW, ON, K7V 2S9
(613) 432-5431   *SIC 2541*
EURO-RITE CABINETS LTD *p244*
19100 AIRPORT WAY SUITE 212, PITT MEADOWS, BC, V3Y 0E2
(604) 464-5060   *SIC 2541*
FLOFORM INDUSTRIES LTD *p390*
125 HAMELIN ST, WINNIPEG, MB, R3T 3Z1
(204) 474-2334   *SIC 2541*
FLOFORM INDUSTRIES LTD *p1431*
2209 SPEERS AVE, SASKATOON, SK, S7L 5X6
(306) 665-7733   *SIC 2541*
I.S.P.A. WOODWORKING LIMITED *p593*
114 ARMSTRONG AVE, GEORGETOWN, ON, L7G 4S2
(905) 702-2727   *SIC 2541*
LT CUSTOM FURNISHINGS INC *p664*
10899 KEELE ST, MAPLE, ON, L6A 0K6
(905) 303-0005   *SIC 2541*
PF CUSTOM COUNTERTOPS LTD *p102*
10417 174 ST NW, EDMONTON, AB, T5S 1H1
(780) 484-0831   *SIC 2541*
PINEHURST GROUP, INC *p808*
120 C LINE, ORANGEVILLE, ON, L9W 3Z8
(519) 943-0100   *SIC 2541*
PREPAC MANUFACTURING LTD *p209*
6705 DENNETT PL, DELTA, BC, V4G 1N4
(604) 940-2300   *SIC 2541*
PRESTOLAM INC *p1306*

2766 RTE DU PRESIDENT-KENNEDY, SAINT-HENRI-DE-LEVIS, QC, G0R 3E0
(418) 882-2242   *SIC 2541*

SUNRISE KITCHENS LTD   p278
13375 COMBER WAY, SURREY, BC, V3W 5V8
(604) 597-0364   *SIC 2541*

UNIQUE STORE FIXTURES LTD   p560
554 MILLWAY AVE, CONCORD, ON, L4K 3V5
(905) 738-6588   *SIC 2541*

VISUAL ELEMENTS MANUFACTURING INC   p1034
21 REGINA RD, WOODBRIDGE, ON, L4L 8L9
(905) 761-5222   *SIC 2541*

WAM INDUSTRIES LTD   p794
375 FENMAR DR, NORTH YORK, ON, M9L 2X4
(416) 741-0660   *SIC 2541*

WILDWOOD CABINETS LTD   p407
400 COLLISHAW ST, MONCTON, NB, E1C 0B4
(506) 858-9219   *SIC 2541*

SIC 2542 Partitions and fixtures, except wood

2072223 ONTARIO LIMITED   p473
274 MACKENZIE AVE SUITE 2, AJAX, ON, L1S 2E9
(905) 686-7000   *SIC 2542*

ACRYLIC FABRICATORS LIMITED   p548
89A CONNIE CRES UNIT 4, CONCORD, ON, L4K 1L3
(905) 660-6666   *SIC 2542*

ALLIANCE STORE FIXTURES INC   p1027
370 NEW HUNTINGTON RD, WOOD-BRIDGE, ON, L4H 0R4
(905) 660-5944   *SIC 2542*

AMEUBLEMENTS GILBERT LTEE, LES   p1332
8855 BOUL HENRI-BOURASSA O, SAINT-LAURENT, QC, H4S 1P7
SIC 2542

ARPAC STORAGE SYSTEMS CORPORATION   p208
7663 PROGRESS WAY, DELTA, BC, V4G 1A2
(604) 940-4000   *SIC 2542*

CONCORD METAL MANUFACTURING INC   p551
121 SPINNAKER WAY, CONCORD, ON, L4K 2T2
(905) 738-2127   *SIC 2542*

ECONO-RACK GROUP (2015) INC, THE   p515
132 ADAMS BLVD, BRANTFORD, ON, N3S 7V2
(519) 753-2227   *SIC 2542*

EQUIPEMENT BONI INC   p1295
1299 RUE MARIE-VICTORIN, SAINT-BRUNO, QC, J3V 6B7
(450) 653-1299   *SIC 2542*

ETALEX INC   p1048
8501 RUE JARRY, ANJOU, QC, H1J 1H7
(514) 351-2000   *SIC 2542*

GESTION CARRIER, ROBERT INC   p1117
73 RUE DU CHAMBERTIN, KIRKLAND, QC, H9H 5E3
SIC 2542

GROUPE ARTITALIA INC   p1162
11755 BOUL RODOLPHE-FORGET, MON-TREAL, QC, H1E 7J8
(514) 643-0114   *SIC 2542*

HADRIAN MANUFACTURING INC   p522
965 SYSCON RD, BURLINGTON, ON, L7L 5S3
(905) 333-0300   *SIC 2542*

HAWORTH, LTD   p585
110 CARRIER DR, ETOBICOKE, ON, M9W 5R1
SIC 2542

INTERIOR MANUFACTURING GROUP INC

p712
974 LAKESHORE RD E, MISSISSAUGA, ON, L5E 1E4
(905) 278-9510   *SIC 2542*

JPMA GLOBAL INC   p1162
7335 BOUL HENRI-BOURASSA E, MON-TREAL, QC, H1E 3T5
(514) 648-1042   *SIC 2542*

M & P TOOL PRODUCTS INC   p513
43 REGAN RD, BRAMPTON, ON, L7A 1B2
(905) 840-5550   *SIC 2542*

MATRICES CARRITEC INC, LES   p1053
575 BOUL MORGAN, BAIE-D'URFE, QC, H9X 3T6
(514) 457-7779   *SIC 2542*

MODERCO INC   p1066
115 RUE DE LAUZON, BOUCHERVILLE, QC, J4B 1E7
(450) 641-3150   *SIC 2542*

MONTEL INC   p1160
225 4E AV, MONTMAGNY, QC, G5V 4N9
(418) 248-0235   *SIC 2542*

NORTH AMERICAN STEEL EQUIPMENT INC   p1014
300 HOPKINS ST, WHITBY, ON, L1N 2B9
(905) 668-3300   *SIC 2542*

PAN-OSTON LTD   p841
660 NEAL DR, PETERBOROUGH, ON, K9J 6X7
(705) 748-4811   *SIC 2542*

PATHER PLASTICS CANADA INC   p673
7400 VICTORIA PARK AVE SUITE 1, MARKHAM, ON, L3R 2V4
(905) 475-6549   *SIC 2542*

PINEHURST STORE FIXTURES INC   p808
120 C LINE, ORANGEVILLE, ON, L9W 3Z8
(519) 943-0100   *SIC 2542*

PRO-SYSTEMES APX INC   p1111
1050 BOUL INDUSTRIEL, GRANBY, QC, J2J 1A4
(450) 378-0189   *SIC 2542*

PRODUITS METALLIQUES ROY INC, LES   p1377
52 CH DE MORIGEAU, ST-FRANCOIS-DE-LA-RIVIERE-DU-S, QC, G0R 3A0
(418) 259-2711   *SIC 2542*

VIC MOBILIER DE MAGASINS INC   p1398
1440 RUE NOTRE-DAME O, VICTORIAV-ILLE, QC, G6P 7L7
(819) 758-0626   *SIC 2542*

WILSON, J. A. DISPLAY LTD   p702
1610 SISMET RD, MISSISSAUGA, ON, L4W 1R4
(905) 625-6778   *SIC 2542*

WILSON, J. A. DISPLAY LTD   p702
1645 AIMCO BLVD, MISSISSAUGA, ON, L4W 1H8
(905) 625-9200   *SIC 2542*

SIC 2591 Drapery hardware and window blinds and shades

7912854 CANADA INC   p1380
3530 BOUL DES ENTREPRISES, TERRE-BONNE, QC, J6X 4J8
(450) 968-0880   *SIC 2591*

BLINDS TO GO INC   p1163
3100 BOUL DE L'ASSOMPTION, MON-TREAL, QC, H1N 3S4
(514) 259-9955   *SIC 2591*

GROUPE ATIS INC   p1144
1111 RUE SAINT-CHARLES O BUREAU 952, LONGUEUIL, QC, J4K 5G4
(450) 928-0101   *SIC 2591*

HUNTER DOUGLAS CANADA HOLDINGS INC   p96
15508 114 AVE NW, EDMONTON, AB, T5M 3S8
(800) 265-1363   *SIC 2591*

MW CANADA LTD   p534
291 ELGIN ST N, CAMBRIDGE, ON, N1R 7H9
(519) 621-5460   *SIC 2591*

SIC 2599 Furniture and fixtures, nec

ADVANCE WIRE PRODUCTS LTD   p278
19095 24 AVE SUITE 19095, SURREY, BC, V3Z 3S9
(604) 541-4666   *SIC 2599*

DURHAM CUSTOM MILLWORK INC   p811
19 TAMBLYN RD, ORONO, ON, L0B 1M0
(905) 683-8444   *SIC 2599*

EGAN VISUAL INC   p1031
300 HANLAN RD, WOODBRIDGE, ON, L4L 3P6
(905) 851-2826   *SIC 2599*

FRANK DEFEHR HOLDINGS LTD   p363
125 FURNITURE PARK, WINNIPEG, MB, R2G 1B9
(204) 988-5630   *SIC 2599*

PETER ANTHONY DESIGNS INC   p1021
2700 OUELLETTE AVE, WINDSOR, ON, N8X 1L7
(519) 969-7332   *SIC 2599*

QUALITY & COMPANY INC   p557
67 JACOB KEFFER PKY, CONCORD, ON, L4K 5N8
(905) 660-6996   *SIC 2599*

SUPERIOR SEATING HOSPITALITY INC   p559
9000 KEELE ST UNIT 11, CONCORD, ON, L4K 0B3
(905) 738-7900   *SIC 2599*

SUPERIOR SEATING HOSPITALITY INC   p559
9000 KEELE ST UNIT 11, CONCORD, ON, L4K 0B3
(905) 738-7900   *SIC 2599*

VERY JAZZROO ENTERPRISES INCORPORATED   p264
11720 HORSESHOE WAY, RICHMOND, BC, V7A 4V5
(604) 248-1806   *SIC 2599*

SIC 2611 Pulp mills

ALBERTA-PACIFIC FOREST INDUSTRIES INC   p7
P.O. BOX 8000, BOYLE, AB, T0A 0M0
(780) 525-8000   *SIC 2611*

AV GROUP NB INC   p410
103 PINDER RD, NACKAWIC, NB, E6G 1W4
(506) 575-3314   *SIC 2611*

AV TERRACE BAY INC   p902
21 MILL RD, TERRACE BAY, ON, P0T 2W0
(807) 825-1075   *SIC 2611*

CANFOR PULP LTD   p250
5353 NORTHWOOD PULP MILL RD, PRINCE GEORGE, BC, V2N 2K3
(250) 962-3666   *SIC 2611*

CARIBOO PULP & PAPER COMPANY   p252
50 NORTH STAR RD, QUESNEL, BC, V2J 3J6
(250) 992-0200   *SIC 2611*

CASCADES CANADA ULC   p574
66 SHORNCLIFFE RD, ETOBICOKE, ON, M8Z 5K1
(416) 231-2525   *SIC 2611*

COSMOPOLITAN INDUSTRIES LTD   p1427
28 34TH ST E, SASKATOON, SK, S7K 3Y2
(306) 664-3158   *SIC 2611*

DOMTAR CORPORATION   p1195
395 BOUL DE MAISONNEUVE O BUREAU 200, MONTREAL, QC, H3A 1L6
(514) 848-5555   *SIC 2611*

DOMTAR INC   p569
1 STATION RD, ESPANOLA, ON, P5E 1R6
(705) 869-2020   *SIC 2611*

DOMTAR INC   p1195
395 BOUL DE MAISONNEUVE O BUREAU 200, MONTREAL, QC, H3A 1L6
(514) 848-5555   *SIC 2611*

DOMTAR INC   p1403
609 RANG 12, WINDSOR, QC, J1S 2L9

(800) 263-8366   *SIC 2611*

FIBREK S.E.N.C.   p1303
4000 CH SAINT EUSEBE, SAINT-FELICIEN, QC, G8K 2R6
(418) 679-8585   *SIC 2611*

FORTRESS GLOBAL ENTERPRISES INC   p240
157 CHADWICK CRT FL 2, NORTH VAN-COUVER, BC, V7M 3K2
(888) 820-3888   *SIC 2611*

FORTRESS SPECIALTY CELLULOSE INC   p1384
451 RUE VICTORIA, THURSO, QC, J0X 3B0
(819) 985-2233   *SIC 2611*

GRAND FOREST HOLDINGS INCORPORATED   p415
300 UNION ST, SAINT JOHN, NB, E2L 4Z2
(506) 635-6666   *SIC 2611*

HOWE SOUND PULP & PAPER CORPORATION   p248
3838 PORT MELLON HWY, PORT MEL-LON, BC, V0N 2S0
(604) 884-5223   *SIC 2611*

INTERNATIONAL PAPER CANADA PULP HOLDINGS ULC   p132
GD, GRANDE PRAIRIE, AB, T8V 6V4
(780) 539-8500   *SIC 2611*

LOUISIANA-PACIFIC CANADA LTD   p1075
572 155 RTE, CHAMBORD, QC, G0W 1G0
(418) 342-6212   *SIC 2611*

MEADOW LAKE MECHANICAL PULP INC   p1410
HWY 55 903, MEADOW LAKE, SK, S9X 1V7
(306) 236-2444   *SIC 2611*

MERCER CELGAR PULP LTD   p195
1921 ARROW LAKES DR, CASTLEGAR, BC, V1N 3H9
(250) 365-7211   *SIC 2611*

MERCER INTERNATIONAL INC   p307
700 PENDER ST W SUITE 1120, VANCOU-VER, BC, V6C 1G8
(604) 684-1099   *SIC 2611*

MERCER PEACE RIVER PULP LTD   p307
510 BURRARD ST SUITE 700, VANCOU-VER, BC, V6C 3A8
(604) 684-4326   *SIC 2611*

MILLAR WESTERN FOREST PRODUCTS LTD   p96
16640 111 AVE NW, EDMONTON, AB, T5M 2S5
(780) 486-8200   *SIC 2611*

MILLAR WESTERN FOREST PRODUCTS LTD   p173
5501 50 AVE, WHITECOURT, AB, T7S 1N9
(780) 778-2036   *SIC 2611*

NANAIMO FOREST PRODUCTS LTD   p235
1000 WAVE PL, NANAIMO, BC, V9X 1J2
(250) 722-3211   *SIC 2611*

NORTHERN FIBRE TERMINAL INCORPORATED   p453
1869 UPPER WATER ST, HALIFAX, NS, B3J 1S9
(902) 422-3030   *SIC 2611*

PAPER EXCELLENCE CANADA HOLDINGS CORPORATION   p261
10551 SHELLBRIDGE WAY SUITE 95, RICHMOND, BC, V6X 2W9
(604) 232-2453   *SIC 2611*

PAPIER DOMTAR (CANADA) INC   p1198
395 BOUL DE MAISONNEUVE O BUREAU 200, MONTREAL, QC, H3A 1L6
(514) 848-5555   *SIC 2611*

PAPIERS DE PUBLICATION KRUGER INC   p1218
3285 CH DE BEDFORD, MONTREAL, QC, H3S 1G5
(514) 737-1131   *SIC 2611*

PAPIERS DE PUBLICATION KRUGER INC   p1388
3735 BOUL GENE-H.-KRUGER, TROIS-RIVIERES, QC, G9A 6B1
(819) 375-1691   *SIC 2611*

▲ Public Company   ■ Public Company Family Member   **HQ** Headquarters   **BR** Branch   **SL** Single Location

PF RESOLU CANADA INC p592
427 MOWAT AVE, FORT FRANCES, ON, P9A 1Y8
(807) 274-5311   *SIC* 2611

PORT ALICE SPECIALTY CELLULOSE INC p245
PO BOX 2000, PORT ALICE, BC, V0N 2N0
SIC 2611

RAYONIER A.M. CANADA ENTERPRISES INC p1207
4 PLACE VILLE-MARIE BUREAU 100, MONTREAL, QC, H3B 2E7
(514) 871-0137   *SIC* 2611

RAYONIER A.M. CANADA G.P. p542
175 PLANER RD, CHAPLEAU, ON, P0M 1K0
(705) 864-1060   *SIC* 2611

RAYONIER A.M. CANADA G.P. p1151
400 RUE DU PORT, MATANE, QC, G4W 3M6
(418) 794-2001   *SIC* 2611

RAYONIER A.M. CANADA G.P. p1207
4 PLACE VILLE-MARIE BUREAU 100, MONTREAL, QC, H3B 2E7
(514) 871-0137   *SIC* 2611

RAYONIER A.M. CANADA G.P. p1378
10 CH GATINEAU, TEMISCAMING, QC, J0Z 3R0
(819) 627-4387   *SIC* 2611

SKOOKUMCHUCK PULP INC p269
4501 FARSTAD WAY, SKOOKUMCHUCK, BC, V0B 2E0
(250) 422-3261   *SIC* 2611

SLAVE LAKE PULP CORPORATION p163
GD, SLAVE LAKE, AB, T0G 2A0
(780) 849-7777   *SIC* 2611

SLAVE LAKE PULP CORPORATION p300
858 BEATTY ST SUITE 501, VANCOUVER, BC, V6B 1C1
(604) 895-2700   *SIC* 2611

TEMBEC INC p913
5310 HWY 101 W, TIMMINS, ON, P4N 7J3
(705) 268-1462   *SIC* 2611

TERRACE BAY PULP INC p903
21 MILL RD, TERRACE BAY, ON, P0T 2W0
SIC 2611

WEST FRASER TIMBER CO. LTD p253
1000 FINNING RD, QUESNEL, BC, V2J 6A1
(250) 992-8919   *SIC* 2611

WESTERN FOREST PRODUCTS INC p196
9469 TRANS CANADA HWY, CHEMAINUS, BC, V0R 1K4
(250) 246-1566   *SIC* 2611

WESTERN FOREST PRODUCTS INC p196
2860 VICTORIA ST, CHEMAINUS, BC, V0R 1K0
(250) 246-3221   *SIC* 2611

WESTERN FOREST PRODUCTS INC p215
300 WESTERN DR, GOLD RIVER, BC, V0P 1G0
(250) 283-2961   *SIC* 2611

WESTERN FOREST PRODUCTS INC p234
31 PORT WAY, NANAIMO, BC, V9R 5L5
(250) 755-4600   *SIC* 2611

WESTERN FOREST PRODUCTS INC p234
500 DUKE PT RD, NANAIMO, BC, V9R 1K1
(250) 722-2533   *SIC* 2611

WESTERN FOREST PRODUCTS INC p245
2500 1ST AVE, PORT ALBERNI, BC, V9Y 8H7
(250) 724-7438   *SIC* 2611

WESTERN FOREST PRODUCTS INC p317
800-1055 GEORGIA ST W, VANCOUVER, BC, V6E 0B6
(604) 648-4500   *SIC* 2611

ZELLSTOFF CELGAR LIMITED PARTNERSHIP p195
1921 ARROW LAKES DR, CASTLEGAR, BC, V1N 3H9
(250) 365-7211   *SIC* 2611

SIC 2621 Paper mills

3120772 NOVA SCOTIA COMPANY p1103
2 CH DE MONTREAL E, GATINEAU, QC, J8M 1E9
(819) 986-4300   *SIC* 2621

ATLANTIC PACKAGING PRODUCTS LTD p1013
1900 THICKSON RD S, WHITBY, ON, L1N 9E1
(905) 686-5944   *SIC* 2621

BOWATER CANADIAN LIMITED p1210
111 BOUL ROBERT-BOURASSA UNITE 5000, MONTREAL, QC, H3C 2M1
(514) 875-2160   *SIC* 2621

BOWATER PRODUITS FORESTIERS DU CANADA ULC p1202
1155 METCALFE RUE BUREAU 800, MONTREAL, QC, H3B 5H2
SIC 2621

BUCKEYE CANADA CO. p208
7979 VANTAGE WAY, DELTA, BC, V4G 1A6
SIC 2621

CAN-CELL INDUSTRIES INC p93
14735 124 AVE NW, EDMONTON, AB, T5L 3B2
(780) 447-1255   *SIC* 2621

CANADIAN KRAFT PAPER INDUSTRIES LIMITED p359
HWY 10 N, THE PAS, MB, R9A 1L4
(204) 623-7411   *SIC* 2621

CANFOR PULP PRODUCTS INC p323
1700 75TH AVE W UNIT 230, VANCOUVER, BC, V6P 6G2
(604) 661-5241   *SIC* 2621

CASCADES CANADA ULC p1072
75 BOUL MARIE-VICTORIN, CANDIAC, QC, J5R 1C2
(450) 444-6500   *SIC* 2621

CASCADES GROUPE PAPIERS FINS INC p720
7280 WEST CREDIT AVE, MISSISSAUGA, ON, L5N 5N1
(905) 813-9400   *SIC* 2621

CASCADES INC p1117
404 BOUL MARIE-VICTORIN, KINGSEY FALLS, QC, J0A 1B0
(819) 363-5100   *SIC* 2621

CATALYST PAPER CORPORATION p204
8541 HAY ROAD N, CROFTON, BC, V0R 1R0
(250) 246-6100   *SIC* 2621

CATALYST PAPER CORPORATION p245
4000 STAMP AVE, PORT ALBERNI, BC, V9Y 5J7
(250) 723-2161   *SIC* 2621

CATALYST PAPER CORPORATION p248
5775 ASH AVE, POWELL RIVER, BC, V8A 4R3
(604) 483-3722   *SIC* 2621

CATALYST PAPER CORPORATION p264
3600 LYSANDER LANE SUITE 200 FL 2, RICHMOND, BC, V7B 1C3
(604) 247-4400   *SIC* 2621

CATALYST PAPER CORPORATION p274
10555 TIMBERLAND RD, SURREY, BC, V3V 3T3
(604) 953-0373   *SIC* 2621

COMMANDITE KRUGER BROMPTON INC p1218
3285 CH DE BEDFORD, MONTREAL, QC, H3S 1G5
(514) 737-1131   *SIC* 2621

COMPAGNIE DE PAPIERS WHITE BIRCH CANADA p1257
10 BOUL DES CAPUCINS, QUEBEC, QC, G1J 0G9
(418) 525-2500   *SIC* 2621

CORNER BROOK PULP AND PAPER LIMITED p422
1 MILLS RD, CORNER BROOK, NL, A2H 6B9
(709) 637-3104   *SIC* 2621

DOMTAR INC p1392
609 12E RANG, VAL-JOLI, QC, J1S 0H1
(819) 845-2771   *SIC* 2621

DONOHUE MALBAIE INC p1210
111 BOUL ROBERT-BOURASSA UNITE 5000, MONTREAL, QC, H3C 2M1
(514) 875-2160   *SIC* 2621

ENTREPRISES ROLLAND INC, LES p1319
256 BOUL JEAN-BAPTISTE-ROLLAND O, SAINT-JEROME, QC, J7Y 0L6
(450) 569-3951   *SIC* 2621

FELXIA CORPORATION p224
19680 94A AVE, LANGLEY, BC, V1M 3B7
(604) 513-1266   *SIC* 2621

GLASSINE CANADA INC p1257
1245 BOUL MONTMORENCY, QUEBEC, QC, G1J 5L6
(418) 522-8262   *SIC* 2621

GLATFELTER GATINEAU LTEE p1103
1680 RUE ATMEC, GATINEAU, QC, J8R 7G7
(819) 669-8100   *SIC* 2621

GRAPHIC PACKAGING INTERNATIONAL CANADA, ULC p1100
2 RUE ANGUS N, EAST ANGUS, QC, J0B 1R0
(819) 832-5300   *SIC* 2621

INTERLAKE ACQUISITION CORPORATION LIMITED p887
45 MERRITT ST, ST CATHARINES, ON, L2T 1J4
(905) 680-3000   *SIC* 2621

IRVING PULP & PAPER, LIMITED p415
300 UNION ST, SAINT JOHN, NB, E2L 4Z2
(506) 632-7777   *SIC* 2621

IRVING, J. D. LIMITED p398
102 RUE DAWSON, DIEPPE, NB, E1A 0C1
(506) 859-5018   *SIC* 2621

KIMBERLY-CLARK INC p620
570 RAVENSCLIFFE RD, HUNTSVILLE, ON, P1H 2A1
(705) 788-5200   *SIC* 2621

KRUGER BROMPTON S.E.C p1218
3285 CH DE BEDFORD, MONTREAL, QC, H3S 1G5
(819) 846-2721   *SIC* 2621

KRUGER BROMPTON S.E.C p1369
220 RTE DE WINDSOR, SHERBROOKE, QC, J1C 0E6
(819) 846-2721   *SIC* 2621

KRUGER PRODUCTS L.P. p237
1625 FIFTH AVE, NEW WESTMINSTER, BC, V3M 1Z7
(604) 522-7893   *SIC* 2621

KRUGER PRODUCTS L.P. p723
1900 MINNESOTA CRT SUITE 200, MISSISSAUGA, ON, L5N 5R5
(905) 812-6900   *SIC* 2621

KRUGER PRODUCTS L.P. p1105
20 RUE LAURIER, GATINEAU, QC, J8X 4H3
(819) 595-5302   *SIC* 2621

KRUGER TROIS-RIVIERES S.E.C. p1388
3735 BOUL GENE-H.-KRUGER, TROIS-RIVIERES, QC, G9A 6B1
(819) 375-1691   *SIC* 2621

KRUGER WAYAGAMACK S.E.C. p1218
3285 CH DE BEDFORD, MONTREAL, QC, H3S 1G5
(514) 343-3100   *SIC* 2621

MARTIN-PRODUITS DE BUREAU INC p1114
576 RUE SAINT-VIATEUR, JOLIETTE, QC, J6E 3B6
(450) 757-7587   *SIC* 2621

PEMBROKE MDF INC p838
777 FIBREBOARD DR, PEMBROKE, ON, K8A 6W4
(613) 732-3939   *SIC* 2621

PF RESOLU CANADA INC p887
2 ALLANBURG RD S, ST CATHARINES, ON, L2T 3W9
(905) 227-5000   *SIC* 2621

PF RESOLU CANADA INC p910
2001 NEEBING AVE, THUNDER BAY, ON, P7E 6S3
(807) 475-2400   *SIC* 2621

PF RESOLU CANADA INC p1045
1100 RUE MELANCON O, ALMA, QC, G8B 7G2
(418) 668-9400   *SIC* 2621

PF RESOLU CANADA INC p1046
801 RUE DES PAPETIERS, AMOS, QC, J9T 3X5
(819) 727-1515   *SIC* 2621

PF RESOLU CANADA INC p1081
100 RUE DE LA DONOHUE, CLERMONT, QC, G4A 1A7
(418) 439-5300   *SIC* 2621

PF RESOLU CANADA INC p1090
1 4E AV, DOLBEAU-MISTASSINI, QC, G8L 2R4
(418) 239-2350   *SIC* 2621

PF RESOLU CANADA INC p1090
200 RUE DE QUEN, DOLBEAU-MISTASSINI, QC, G8L 5M8
(418) 679-1010   *SIC* 2621

PF RESOLU CANADA INC p1116
3750 RUE DE CHAMPLAIN, JONQUIERE, QC, G7X 1M1
(418) 695-9100   *SIC* 2621

PF RESOLU CANADA INC p1366
40 CH SAINT-PIERRE, SENNETERRE, QC, J0Y 2M0
(819) 737-2300   *SIC* 2621

PORT HAWKESBURY PAPER LIMITED PARTNERSHIP p464
120 PULP MILL RD POINT TUPPER INDUSTRIAL PARK, PORT HAWKESBURY, NS, B9A 1A1
(902) 625-2460   *SIC* 2621

RESOLUTE FOREST PRODUCTS INC p1212
111 BOUL ROBERT-BOURASSA BUREAU 5000, MONTREAL, QC, H3C 2M1
(514) 875-2160   *SIC* 2621

SCHWEITZER-MAUDUIT CANADA, INC p361
340 AIRPORT DR, WINKLER, MB, R6W 0J9
(204) 325-7986   *SIC* 2621

SOCIETE EN COMMANDITE FF SOUCY WB p1287
191 RUE DELAGE, RIVIERE-DU-LOUP, QC, G5R 6E2
(418) 862-6941   *SIC* 2621

SOCIETE EN COMMANDITE PAPIER MASSON WB p1103
2 CH DE MONTREAL E, GATINEAU, QC, J8M 1E9
(819) 986-4300   *SIC* 2621

SYMCOR INC p1216
650 RUE BRIDGE, MONTREAL, QC, H3K 3K9
(514) 787-4325   *SIC* 2621

TANN PAPER LIMITED p420
149 HELLER RD, WOODSTOCK, NB, E7M 1X3
(506) 325-9100   *SIC* 2621

TECHNOCELL INC p1099
3075 RUE KUNZ, DRUMMONDVILLE, QC, J2C 6Y4
(819) 475-0066   *SIC* 2621

TEMBEC INC p627
1 GOVERNMENT RD W, KAPUSKASING, ON, P5N 2X8
(705) 337-9784   *SIC* 2621

TWIN RIVERS PAPER COMPANY INC p399
27 RUE RICE, EDMUNDSTON, NB, E3V 1S9
(506) 735-5551   *SIC* 2621

UMOE SOLAR NEW BRUNSWICK INC p405
345 CURTIS RD, MIRAMICHI, NB, E1V 3R7
SIC 2621

WEST FRASER MILLS LTD p214
6626 HIGHWAY 16 E, FRASER LAKE, BC, V0J 1S0
(250) 699-6235   *SIC* 2621

WEST FRASER TIMBER CO. LTD p173
9 KM W OF WHITECOURT HWY SUITE 43, WHITECOURT, AB, T7S 1P9
(780) 778-7000   *SIC* 2621

WESTERN FOREST PRODUCTS INC p234
495 DUNSMUIR ST UNIT 201, NANAIMO, BC, V9R 6B9

---

(250) 734-4700   *SIC 2621*

SIC 2631 Paperboard mills

1359470 ONTARIO INC.   *p679*
138 ANDERSON AVE UNIT 6, MARKHAM, ON, L6E 1A4
(905) 472-7773   *SIC 2631*

ARAUCO CANADA LIMITED   *p666*
80 TIVERTON CRT SUITE 701, MARKHAM, ON, L3R 0G4
(905) 475-9686   *SIC 2631*

ASTRA TRADE FINISHING LIMITED   *p864*
390 TAPSCOTT RD SUITE 1, SCARBOROUGH, ON, M1B 2Y9
(416) 291-2272   *SIC 2631*

CASCADES CANADA ULC   *p734*
7447 BRAMALEA RD, MISSISSAUGA, ON, L5S 1C4
(905) 671-2940   *SIC 2631*

CASCADES CANADA ULC   *p920*
495 COMMISSIONERS ST, TORONTO, ON, M4M 1A5
(416) 461-8261   *SIC 2631*

CASCADES CANADA ULC   *p1100*
248 RUE WARNER, EAST ANGUS, QC, J0B 1R0
(819) 832-5300   *SIC 2631*

CASCADES CANADA ULC   *p1116*
4010 CH SAINT-ANDRE, JONQUIERE, QC, G7Z 0A5
SIC 2631

CASCADES CANADA ULC   *p1166*
2755 RUE VIAU, MONTREAL, QC, H1V 3J4
(514) 251-3800   *SIC 2631*

CASCADES CANADA ULC   *p1295*
1061 RUE PARENT, SAINT-BRUNO, QC, J3V 6R7
(450) 461-8600   *SIC 2631*

CASCADES CANADA ULC   *p1378*
520 RUE COMMERCIALE N, TEMISCOUATA-SUR-LE-LAC, QC, G0L 1E0
(418) 854-2803   *SIC 2631*

CASCADES CANADA ULC   *p1394*
400 RUE FORBES, VAUDREUIL-DORION, QC, J7V 6N8
(450) 455-5731   *SIC 2631*

CASCADES CS+ INC   *p1117*
465 BOUL MARIE-VICTORIN, KINGSEY FALLS, QC, J0A 1B0
(819) 363-5920   *SIC 2631*

EMBALLAGES SXP INC   *p1250*
269 BOUL SAINT JEAN STE 211B, POINTE-CLAIRE, QC, H9R 3J1
(514) 364-3269   *SIC 2631*

GRAPHIC PACKAGING INTERNATIONAL CANADA ULC   *p367*
531 GOLSPIE ST, WINNIPEG, MB, R2K 2T9
(204) 667-6600   *SIC 2631*

GRAPHIC PACKAGING INTERNATIONAL CANADA ULC   *p545*
740 DIVISION ST, COBOURG, ON, K9A 0H6
(905) 372-5199   *SIC 2631*

GRAPHIC PACKAGING INTERNATIONAL CANADA ULC   *p735*
7830 TRANMERE DR, MISSISSAUGA, ON, L5S 1L9
(905) 678-8211   *SIC 2631*

KRUGER INC   *p1223*
5845 PLACE TURCOT, MONTREAL, QC, H4C 1V9
(514) 934-0600   *SIC 2631*

MINAS BASIN PULP AND POWER COMPANY LIMITED   *p440*
3 BEDFORD HILLS RD, BEDFORD, NS, B4A 1J5
(902) 835-7100   *SIC 2631*

SONOCO CANADA CORPORATION   *p999*
5 BERNARD LONG RD, TRENTON, ON, K8V 5P6

(613) 394-6903   *SIC 2631*

STRATHCONA PAPER LP   *p748*
77 COUNTY RD 16, NAPANEE, ON, K7R 3L2
(613) 378-6676   *SIC 2631*

STRATHCONA PAPER LP   *p748*
77 COUNTY RD 16, NAPANEE, ON, K7R 3L2
(613) 378-6672   *SIC 2631*

TOLKO INDUSTRIES LTD   *p135*
HWY 2 W, HIGH PRAIRIE, AB, T0G 1E0
(780) 523-2101   *SIC 2631*

SIC 2652 Setup paperboard boxes

BOEHMER BOX LP   *p637*
120 TRILLIUM DR, KITCHENER, ON, N2E 2C4
(519) 576-2480   *SIC 2652*

BOEHMER BOX LP   *p642*
1560 BATTLER RD, KITCHENER, ON, N2R 1J6
(519) 576-2480   *SIC 2652*

CASCADES CANADA ULC   *p1166*
2755 RUE VIAU, MONTREAL, QC, H1V 3J4
(514) 251-3800   *SIC 2652*

SIC 2653 Corrugated and solid fiber boxes

2014767 ONTARIO LIMITED   *p547*
96 PLANCHET RD, CONCORD, ON, L4K 2C7
(905) 738-0583   *SIC 2653*

AL-PACK ENTERPRISES LTD   *p409*
60 COMMERCE ST, MONCTON, NB, E1H 0A5
(506) 852-4262   *SIC 2653*

ATLANTIC PACKAGING PRODUCTS LTD   *p621*
45 CHISHOLM DR, INGERSOLL, ON, N5C 2C7
(800) 268-5620   *SIC 2653*

ATLANTIC PACKAGING PRODUCTS LTD   *p692*
5711 ATLANTIC DR, MISSISSAUGA, ON, L4W 1H3
(800) 268-5620   *SIC 2653*

ATLANTIC PACKAGING PRODUCTS LTD   *p876*
55 MILLIKEN BLVD, SCARBOROUGH, ON, M1V 1V3
(416) 298-5508   *SIC 2653*

ATLANTIC PACKAGING PRODUCTS LTD   *p876*
118 TIFFIELD RD, SCARBOROUGH, ON, M1V 5N2
(800) 268-5620   *SIC 2653*

BOXES NEXT DAY INC   *p573*
54 ATOMIC AVE, ETOBICOKE, ON, M8Z 5L1
(416) 253-7350   *SIC 2653*

C & B DISPLAY PACKAGING INC   *p713*
2560 SOUTH SHERIDAN WAY, MISSISSAUGA, ON, L5J 2M4
(905) 823-7770   *SIC 2653*

CASCADES CANADA ULC   *p34*
416 58 AVE SE, CALGARY, AB, T2H 0P4
(403) 531-3800   *SIC 2653*

CASCADES CANADA ULC   *p254*
3300 VIKING WAY, RICHMOND, BC, V6V 1N6
(604) 273-7321   *SIC 2653*

CASCADES CANADA ULC   *p382*
680 WALL ST, WINNIPEG, MB, R3G 2T8
(204) 786-5761   *SIC 2653*

CASCADES CANADA ULC   *p408*
232 BAIG BLVD, MONCTON, NB, E1E 1C8
(506) 869-2200   *SIC 2653*

CASCADES CANADA ULC   *p550*
655 CREDITSTONE RD SUITE 41, CONCORD, ON, L4K 5P9
(905) 760-3900   *SIC 2653*

CASCADES CANADA ULC   *p888*
304 JAMES ST S, ST MARYS, ON, N4X 1B7
(519) 284-1840   *SIC 2653*

CASCADES CANADA ULC   *p1399*
400 BOUL DE LA BONAVENTURE, VICTORIAVILLE, QC, G6T 1V8
(819) 758-3177   *SIC 2653*

CENTRAL GRAPHICS AND CONTAINER GROUP LTD   *p692*
5526 TIMBERLEA BLVD, MISSISSAUGA, ON, L4W 2T7
(905) 238-8400   *SIC 2653*

COLEMAN CONTAINERS LIMITED   *p574*
54 ATOMIC AVE, ETOBICOKE, ON, M8Z 5L1
(416) 253-7441   *SIC 2653*

CORRPAR INDUSTRIES LTD   *p755*
17775 LESLIE ST, NEWMARKET, ON, L3Y 3E3
(905) 836-4599   *SIC 2653*

CRAIG PACKAGING LIMITED   *p623*
5911 CARMEN RD S, IROQUOIS, ON, K0E 1K0
(613) 652-4856   *SIC 2653*

CROWN CORRUGATED COMPANY   *p263*
13911 GARDEN CITY RD, RICHMOND, BC, V7A 2S5
(604) 277-7111   *SIC 2653*

EMBALLAGES MONTCORR LTEE, LES   *p1088*
40 RUE INDUSTRIELLE, COTEAU-DU-LAC, QC, J0P 1B0
(450) 763-0920   *SIC 2653*

FLINT PACKAGING PRODUCTS LTD   *p552*
311 CALDARI RD, CONCORD, ON, L4K 4S9
(905) 738-7205   *SIC 2653*

GERRITY CORRUGATED PAPER PRODUCTS LTD   *p553*
75 DONEY CRES SUITE 1, CONCORD, ON, L4K 1P6
(416) 798-7758   *SIC 2653*

GREAT LITTLE BOX COMPANY LTD, THE   *p254*
11300 TWIGG PL, RICHMOND, BC, V6V 3C1
(604) 301-3700   *SIC 2653*

GROUPE APTAS INC   *p1360*
1332 BOUL VACHON N, SAINTE-MARIE, QC, G6E 1N3
(418) 387-4003   *SIC 2653*

IBOX PACKAGING LTD   *p206*
620 AUDLEY BLVD, DELTA, BC, V3M 5P2
(604) 522-4269   *SIC 2653*

IDEON PACKAGING   *p263*
11251 DYKE RD, RICHMOND, BC, V7A 0A1
(604) 524-0524   *SIC 2653*

INDEPENDENT CORRUGATOR INC   *p696*
1177 AEROWOOD DR, MISSISSAUGA, ON, L4W 1Y6
(905) 629-2702   *SIC 2653*

INSTABOX (ALBERTA) INC   *p23*
1139 40 AVE NE, CALGARY, AB, T2E 6M9
(403) 250-9217   *SIC 2653*

JDC #10 LIMITED   *p585*
274 HUMBERLINE DR, ETOBICOKE, ON, M9W 5S2
(416) 675-1123   *SIC 2653*

KRUGER INC   *p504*
10 PEDIGREE CRT, BRAMPTON, ON, L6T 5T8
(905) 759-1012   *SIC 2653*

KRUGER INC   *p1131*
7474 RUE CORDNER, LASALLE, QC, H8N 2W3
(514) 366-8050   *SIC 2653*

LOEB PACKAGING LTD   *p595*
1475 STAR TOP RD SUITE 8, GLOUCESTER, ON, K1B 3W5
(613) 746-8171   *SIC 2653*

MARITIME PAPER PRODUCTS LIMITED PARTNERSHIP   *p447*
25 BORDEN AVE, DARTMOUTH, NS, B3B 1C7

(902) 468-5353   *SIC 2653*

MASTER PACKAGING INC   *p398*
333 BOUL ADELARD-SAVOIE, DIEPPE, NB, E1A 7G9
(506) 389-3737   *SIC 2653*

MASTER PACKAGING INC   *p1039*
60 BELVEDERE AVE, CHARLOTTETOWN, PE, C1A 6B1
(902) 368-3737   *SIC 2653*

MENASHA PACKAGING CANADA L.P.   *p499*
35 PRECIDIO CRT, BRAMPTON, ON, L6S 6B7
(905) 792-7092   *SIC 2653*

MENASHA PACKAGING CANADA L.P.   *p732*
5875 CHEDWORTH WAY, MISSISSAUGA, ON, L5R 3L9
(905) 507-3042   *SIC 2653*

MITCHEL-LINCOLN PACKAGING LTD *p1099*
925 RUE ROCHELEAU, DRUMMONDVILLE, QC, J2C 6L8
(819) 477-9700   *SIC 2653*

MITCHEL-LINCOLN PACKAGING LTD *p1330*
3737 BOUL THIMENS, SAINT-LAURENT, QC, H4R 1V1
(514) 332-3480   *SIC 2653*

MOORE PACKAGING CORPORATION *p487*
191 JOHN ST, BARRIE, ON, L4N 2L4
(705) 737-1023   *SIC 2653*

PACKAGING TECHNOLOGIES INC   *p557*
310A COURTLAND AVE, CONCORD, ON, L4K 4Y6
(905) 738-8226   *SIC 2653*

PERIMETER INDUSTRIES LTD   *p357*
2262 SPRINGFIELD RD SUITE 5, SPRINGFIELD, MB, R2C 2Z2
(204) 988-2140   *SIC 2653*

PINTO-PACKAGING LTD   *p649*
148 STRONACH CRES, LONDON, ON, N5V 3A1
(519) 455-5790   *SIC 2653*

PLANET PAPER BOX INC   *p557*
2841 LANGSTAFF RD UNIT 1, CONCORD, ON, L4K 4W7
(905) 669-9363   *SIC 2653*

PRESENTOIRS POINT 1 INC   *p1157*
8479 PLACE DEVONSHIRE BUREAU 100, MONT-ROYAL, QC, H4P 2K1
(514) 344-4888   *SIC 2653*

PROTAGON DISPLAY INC   *p878*
719 TAPSCOTT RD, SCARBOROUGH, ON, M1X 1A2
(416) 293-9500   *SIC 2653*

ROYAL CONTAINERS LTD   *p506*
80 MIDAIR CRT, BRAMPTON, ON, L6T 5V1
(905) 789-8787   *SIC 2653*

SHIPMASTER CONTAINERS LIMITED *p675*
380 ESNA PARK DR, MARKHAM, ON, L3R 1G5
(416) 493-9193   *SIC 2653*

WESTROCK COMPANY OF CANADA CORP *p33*
1115 34 AVE SE, CALGARY, AB, T2G 1V5
(403) 214-5200   *SIC 2653*

WESTROCK COMPANY OF CANADA CORP *p576*
730 ISLINGTON AVE, ETOBICOKE, ON, M8Z 4N8
(416) 259-8421   *SIC 2653*

WESTROCK COMPANY OF CANADA CORP *p605*
390 WOODLAWN RD W, GUELPH, ON, N1H 7K3
(519) 821-4930   *SIC 2653*

WESTROCK COMPANY OF CANADA CORP *p1421*
1400 1ST AVE, REGINA, SK, S4R 8G5
(306) 525-7700   *SIC 2653*

SIC 2655 Fiber cans, drums, and similar products

ABZAC CANADA INC   *p1096*
2945 BOUL LEMIRE, DRUMMONDVILLE,

QC, J2B 6Y8
(514) 866-3488   *SIC 2655*

CANDUCT INDUSTRIES LIMITED   *p660*
4575 BLAKIE RD, LONDON, ON, N6L 1P8
(519) 652-9014   *SIC 2655*

COMPETITION COMPOSITES INC   *p479*
251 FIFTH AVE, ARNPRIOR, ON, K7S 3M3
(613) 599-6951   *SIC 2655*

EMBALLAGE CANFAB INC   *p1216*
2740 RUE SAINT-PATRICK, MONTREAL, QC, H3K 1B8
(514) 935-5265   *SIC 2655*

INVESTISSEMENTS CANFAB INC., LES   *p1216*
2740 RUE SAINT-PATRICK, MONTREAL, QC, H3K 1B8
(514) 935-5265   *SIC 2655*

JIFFY PRODUCTS (N.B.) LTD   *p418*
125 RUE PARC INDUSTRIEL, SHIPPAGAN, NB, E8S 1X9
(506) 336-2284   *SIC 2655*

SONOCO CANADA CORPORATION   *p516*
33 PARK AVE E, BRANTFORD, ON, N3S 7R9
(905) 823-7910   *SIC 2655*

SONOCO CANADA CORPORATION   *p543*
674 RICHMOND ST, CHATHAM, ON, N7M 5K4
(519) 352-8201   *SIC 2655*

SONOCO CANADA CORPORATION   *p1385*
530 RUE DES ERABLES, TROIS-RIVIERES, QC, G8T 8N6
(819) 374-5222   *SIC 2655*

VAN NELLE CANADA LIMITED   *p420*
147 HELLER RD, WOODSTOCK, NB, E7M 1X4
(506) 325-1930   *SIC 2655*

SIC 2656 Sanitary food containers

DART CANADA INC   *p864*
2121 MARKHAM RD, SCARBOROUGH, ON, M1B 2W3
(416) 293-2877   *SIC 2656*

STONE STRAW LIMITED   *p516*
72 PLANT FARM BLVD, BRANTFORD, ON, N3S 7W3
(519) 756-1974   *SIC 2656*

SIC 2657 Folding paperboard boxes

ALCAN PACKAGING CANADA LIMITED   *p794*
130 ARROW RD, NORTH YORK, ON, M9M 2M1
   SIC 2657

AMCOR PACKAGING CANADA, INC   *p508*
95 BISCAYNE CRES, BRAMPTON, ON, L6W 4R2
(905) 450-5579   *SIC 2657*

AMCOR PACKAGING CANADA, INC   *p1127*
2150 RUE ONESIME-GAGNON, LACHINE, QC, H8T 3M8
   SIC 2657

BELLWYCK PACKAGING INC   *p835*
GD, OWEN SOUND, ON, N4K 5N9
(800) 265-3708   *SIC 2657*

BELLWYCK PACKAGING INC   *p914*
21 FINCHDENE SQ, TORONTO, ON, M1X 1A7
(416) 752-1210   *SIC 2657*

BEMIS FLEXIBLE PACKAGING CANADA LIMITED   *p794*
130 ARROW RD, NORTH YORK, ON, M9M 2M1
(416) 742-8910   *SIC 2657*

CASCADES CANADA ULC   *p367*
531 GOLSPIE ST, WINNIPEG, MB, R2K 2T9
(204) 667-6600   *SIC 2657*

CASCADES CANADA ULC   *p571*
450 EVANS AVE, ETOBICOKE, ON, M8W

2T5
(416) 255-8541   *SIC 2657*

ELLIS PACKAGING LIMITED   *p844*
1830 SANDSTONE MANOR, PICKERING, ON, L1W 3Y1
(905) 831-5777   *SIC 2657*

ELLIS PACKAGING WEST INC   *p600*
136 VICTORIA RD S, GUELPH, ON, N1E 5P6
(519) 822-7060   *SIC 2657*

ELLIS PAPER BOX INC   *p694*
2345 MATHESON BLVD E, MISSISSAUGA, ON, L4W 5B3
(905) 212-9177   *SIC 2657*

EMBALLAGES GAB LTEE, LES   *p1072*
140 BOUL DE L'INDUSTRIE, CANDIAC, QC, J5R 1J2
(450) 444-4884   *SIC 2657*

EMBALLAGES STUART INC   *p1156*
5454 CH DE LA COTE-DE-LIESSE, MONT-ROYAL, QC, H4P 1A5
(514) 344-5000   *SIC 2657*

GOLDRICH PRINTPAK INC   *p992*
100 INDUSTRY ST, TORONTO, ON, M6M 4L8
(416) 769-9000   *SIC 2657*

GUNTHER MELE LIMITED   *p514*
30 CRAIG ST, BRANTFORD, ON, N3R 7J1
(519) 756-4330   *SIC 2657*

INGERSOLL PAPER BOX CO. LIMITED *p621*
327 KING ST W, INGERSOLL, ON, N5C 2K9
(519) 485-1830   *SIC 2657*

J. J. MARSHALL INC   *p1217*
9780 RUE WAVERLY, MONTREAL, QC, H3L 2V5
(514) 381-5647   *SIC 2657*

JONES PACKAGING INC   *p605*
271 MASSEY RD, GUELPH, ON, N1K 1B2
   SIC 2657

JONES PACKAGING INC   *p649*
3000 PAGE ST SUITE 1, LONDON, ON, N5V 5H3
(519) 451-2100   *SIC 2657*

PAPIERS ATLAS INC, LES   *p1162*
9000 RUE PIERRE-BONNE, MONTREAL, QC, H1E 6W5
(514) 494-1931   *SIC 2657*

SHEEN LEGEND PACKAGING CORP   *p736*
2280 DREW RD SUITE B, MISSISSAUGA, ON, L5S 1B8
(905) 677-2888   *SIC 2657*

SHOREWOOD CARTON CORPORATION LIMITED   *p873*
44 ROLARK DR, SCARBOROUGH, ON, M1R 4G2
(416) 940-2436   *SIC 2657*

SHOREWOOD PACKAGING CORP. OF CANADA LIMITED   *p872*
2220 MIDLAND AVE UNIT 50, SCARBOR-OUGH, ON, M1P 3E6
(416) 940-2400   *SIC 2657*

WESTROCK COMPANY OF CANADA CORP   *p1124*
1000 CH DE L'USINE BUREAU 2632, LA TUQUE, QC, G9X 3P8
(819) 676-8100   *SIC 2657*

WESTROCK COMPANY OF CANADA CORP   *p1247*
15400 RUE SHERBROOKE E BUREAU A-15, POINTE-AUX-TREMBLES, QC, H1A 3S2
(514) 642-9251   *SIC 2657*

WESTROCK COMPANY OF CANADA CORP   *p1360*
433 2E AV DU PARC-INDUSTRIEL, SAINTE-MARIE, QC, G6E 3H2
(418) 387-5438   *SIC 2657*

WESTROCK PACKAGING SYSTEMS LP   *p475*
281 FAIRALL ST, AJAX, ON, L1S 1R7
(905) 683-2330   *SIC 2657*

SIC 2671 Paper; coated and laminated packaging

CULINARY PAPERS INC   *p1014*
125 CONSUMERS DR, WHITBY, ON, L1N 1C4
(905) 668-7533   *SIC 2671*

DE LUXE PRODUITS DE PAPIER INC *p1238*
200 AV MARIEN, MONTREAL-EST, QC, H1B 4V2
(514) 645-4571   *SIC 2671*

ECP L.P.   *p468*
50 ABBEY AVE, TRURO, NS, B2N 6W4
(902) 895-1686   *SIC 2671*

EMBALLAGE WORKMAN INC   *p1339*
345 MONTEE DE LIESSE, SAINT-LAURENT, QC, H4T 1P5
(514) 344-7227   *SIC 2671*

EMBALLAGES KRUGER S.E.C.   *p1218*
3285 CH DE BEDFORD, MONTREAL, QC, H3S 1G5
(514) 737-1131   *SIC 2671*

FPC FLEXIBLE PACKAGING CORPORA-TION   *p868*
1891 EGLINTON AVE E, SCARBOROUGH, ON, M1L 2L7
(416) 288-3060   *SIC 2671*

GREAT PACIFIC ENTERPRISES LIMITED PARTNERSHIP   *p480*
285 INDUSTRIAL PKY S, AURORA, ON, L4G 3V8
(905) 727-0121   *SIC 2671*

HC CANADA OPERATING COMPANY, LTD, THE   *p514*
325 WEST ST UNIT B200, BRANTFORD, ON, N3R 3V6
(519) 753-2666   *SIC 2671*

INTERWRAP ULC   *p314*
1177 HASTINGS ST W SUITE 1818, VAN-COUVER, BC, V6E 2K3
(800) 567-9727   *SIC 2671*

J. H. MCNAIRN LIMITED   *p1014*
125 CONSUMERS DR, WHITBY, ON, L1N 1C4
(905) 668-7533   *SIC 2671*

TEMPO FLEXO LTD   *p622*
2237 INDUSTRIAL PARK RD, INNISFIL, ON, L9S 3V9
(705) 436-4442   *SIC 2671*

TRANSCONTINENTAL FLEXSTAR INC *p257*
13320 RIVER RD, RICHMOND, BC, V6V 1W7
(604) 273-9277   *SIC 2671*

TRANSCONTINENTAL PACKAGING WHITBY ULC   *p1015*
201 SOUTH BLAIR ST, WHITBY, ON, L1N 5S6
(905) 668-5811   *SIC 2671*

SIC 2672 Paper; coated and laminated, nec

3M CANADA COMPANY   *p518*
60 CALIFORNIA AVE, BROCKVILLE, ON, K6V 7N5
(613) 498-5900   *SIC 2672*

3M CANADA COMPANY   *p839*
2 CRAIG ST, PERTH, ON, K7H 3E2
(613) 267-5300   *SIC 2672*

ATLANTIC COATED PAPERS LTD   *p1013*
1605 MCEWEN DR, WHITBY, ON, L1N 7L4
(416) 299-1675   *SIC 2672*

AVERY DENNISON CANADA CORPORA-TION   *p844*
1840 CLEMENTS RD, PICKERING, ON, L1W 3Y2
(905) 837-4700   *SIC 2672*

B & R HOLDINGS INC   *p916*
32 CRANFIELD RD, TORONTO, ON, M4B 3H3
(416) 701-9800   *SIC 2672*

CAMERON INDUSTRIES INC   *p600*
309 ELIZABETH ST, GUELPH, ON, N1E 2X8
(519) 824-3561   *SIC 2672*

CCL INDUSTRIES INC   *p914*

---

111 GORDON BAKER RD SUITE 801, TORONTO, ON, M2H 3R1
(416) 756-8500   *SIC 2672*

COMPAGNIE CANADIAN TECHNICAL TAPE LTEE   *p563*
1400 ROSEMOUNT AVE, CORNWALL, ON, K6J 3E6
(613) 932-3105   *SIC 2672*

COMPAGNIE CANADIAN TECHNICAL TAPE LTEE   *p1325*
455 BOUL DE LA COTE-VERTU, SAINT-LAURENT, QC, H4N 1E8
(514) 334-1510   *SIC 2672*

COMPOUNDS FELIX INC, LES   *p1308*
3455 RUE RICHELIEU, SAINT-HUBERT, QC, J3Y 7P9
(450) 443-6888   *SIC 2672*

DESIGN LABEL SYSTEMS INC   *p738*
150 CAPITAL CRT, MISSISSAUGA, ON, L5T 2R8
(905) 405-1121   *SIC 2672*

ELLWORTH INDUSTRIES LTD   *p200*
61 CLIPPER ST SUITE 61, COQUITLAM, BC, V3K 6X2
(604) 525-4764   *SIC 2672*

ETIQUETTES PROFECTA INC   *p1309*
5050 RUE ARMAND-FRAPPIER, SAINT-HUBERT, QC, J3Z 1G5
(450) 676-0000   *SIC 2672*

GROUPE INTERTAPE POLYMER INC, LE *p1324*
9999 BOUL CAVENDISH BUREAU 200, SAINT-LAURENT, QC, H4M 2X5
(514) 731-7591   *SIC 2672*

IMPRIMERIE STE-JULIE INC   *p1359*
1851 RUE NOBEL, SAINTE-JULIE, QC, J3E 1Z6
(450) 649-5479   *SIC 2672*

INGENIOUS PACKAGING, INC   *p865*
999 PROGRESS AVE, SCARBOROUGH, ON, M1B 6J1
(416) 292-6600   *SIC 2672*

SCAPA TAPES NORTH AMERICA LTD *p849*
609 BARNET BLVD, RENFREW, ON, K7V 0A9
(613) 432-8545   *SIC 2672*

VIBAC CANADA INC   *p1248*
12250 BOUL INDUSTRIEL, POINTE-AUX-TREMBLES, QC, H1B 5M5
(514) 640-0250   *SIC 2672*

SIC 2673 Bags: plastic, laminated, and coated

191609 CANADA INC   *p1337*
4125 RUE GRIFFITH, SAINT-LAURENT, QC, H4T 1A9
(514) 731-9466   *SIC 2673*

9330-4855 QUEBEC INC   *p1047*
7900 RUE JARRY, ANJOU, QC, H1J 1H1
(514) 353-1710   *SIC 2673*

ALLIED-HALO INDUSTRIES INC   *p870*
345 NANTUCKET BLVD, SCARBOROUGH, ON, M1P 2P2
(416) 751-2042   *SIC 2673*

ALPHA POLY CORPORATION   *p501*
296 WALKER DR, BRAMPTON, ON, L6T 4B3
(905) 789-6770   *SIC 2673*

BELLE-PAK PACKAGING INC   *p667*
7465 BIRCHMOUNT RD, MARKHAM, ON, L3R 5X9
(905) 475-5151   *SIC 2673*

CLOROX COMPANY OF CANADA, LTD, THE   *p808*
101 JOHN ST, ORANGEVILLE, ON, L9W 2R1
(519) 941-0720   *SIC 2673*

DIRECT PLASTICS LTD   *p808*
20 STEWART CRT, ORANGEVILLE, ON, L9W 3Z9
(519) 942-8511   *SIC 2673*

ECO II MANUFACTURING INC   *p876*
3391 MCNICOLL AVE UNIT 6, SCARBOR-

OUGH, ON, M1V 2V4
(416) 292-0220　SIC 2673
EMBALLAGE ST-JEAN LTEE　p1315
80 RUE MOREAU, SAINT-JEAN-SUR-RICHELIEU, QC, J2W 2M4
(450) 349-5871　SIC 2673
EMBALLAGES POLIPLASTIC INC　p1109
415 RUE SAINT-VALLIER, GRANBY, QC, J2G 7Y3
(450) 378-8417　SIC 2673
EMBALLAGES SALERNO CANADA INC p1076
2275 BOUL FORD, CHATEAUGUAY, QC, J6J 4Z2
(450) 692-8642　SIC 2673
EMBALLAGES TRANSCONTINENTAL FLEXIPAK INC　p1329
5020 BOUL THIMENS, SAINT-LAURENT, QC, H4R 2B2
(514) 335-0001　SIC 2673
ENDURAPAK INC　p372
55 PLYMOUTH ST, WINNIPEG, MB, R2X 2V5
(204) 947-1383　SIC 2673
FARNELL PACKAGING LIMITED　p446
30 ILSLEY AVE, DARTMOUTH, NS, B3B 1L3
(902) 468-9378　SIC 2673
HOOD PACKAGING CORPORATION p1345
4755 BOUL DES GRANDES-PRAIRIES, SAINT-LEONARD, QC, H1R 1A6
(514) 323-4517　SIC 2673
HYMOPACK LTD　p574
41 MEDULLA AVE, ETOBICOKE, ON, M8Z 5L6
(416) 232-1733　SIC 2673
HYMOPACK LTD　p1326
1225 RUE HODGE, SAINT-LAURENT, QC, H4N 2B5
SIC 2673
INDUSTRIES POLYKAR INC, LES　p1334
5637 RUE KIERAN, SAINT-LAURENT, QC, H4S 0A3
(514) 335-0059　SIC 2673
INTEPLAST BAGS AND FILMS CORPORATION　p209
7503 VANTAGE PL, DELTA, BC, V4G 1A5
(604) 946-5431　SIC 2673
INTERPAC CORPORATION INC　p1340
6855 CH DE LA COTE-DE-LIESSE, SAINT-LAURENT, QC, H4T 1E5
(514) 340-9440　SIC 2673
LICAPLAST INDUSTRIES EMBALLAGES INC　p1330
2835 RUE DUCHESNE, SAINT-LAURENT, QC, H4R 1J2
(514) 335-4091　SIC 2673
M'PLAST INC　p1128
2530 RUE ALPHONSE-GARIEPY, LACHINE, QC, H8T 3M2
(514) 633-8181　SIC 2673
MALPACK LTD　p474
120 FULLER RD, AJAX, ON, L1S 3R2
(888) 678-0707　SIC 2673
MALPACK LTD　p474
510 FINLEY AVE, AJAX, ON, L1S 2E3
(905) 428-3751　SIC 2673
OMNIPLAST INC　p1308
5350 RUE RAMSAY, SAINT-HUBERT, QC, J3Y 2S4
(450) 656-9272　SIC 2673
PEEL PLASTIC PRODUCTS LIMITED p510
49 RUTHERFORD RD S, BRAMPTON, ON, L6W 3J3
(905) 456-3660　SIC 2673
PLACEMENTS LUC CHAMBERLAND INC, LES　p1096
2540 139 RTE, DRUMMONDVILLE, QC, J2A 2P9
(819) 478-4967　SIC 2673
POP ENVIRO BAGS & PRODUCTS　p708
615 ORWELL ST, MISSISSAUGA, ON, L5A 2W4
(905) 272-2247　SIC 2673

PRODUITS POLYWRAP DU CANADA LTEE, LES　p1223
5590 BOUL MONK, MONTREAL, QC, H4C 3R8
(514) 933-2121　SIC 2673
SALERNO PELLICULE ET SACS DE PLASTIQUE (CANADA) INC　p1076
2275 BOUL FORD, CHATEAUGUAY, QC, J6J 4Z2
(450) 692-8642　SIC 2673
SCHOLLE IPN CANADA LTD　p1054
22000 AV CLARK-GRAHAM, BAIE-D'URFE, QC, H9X 4B6
(514) 457-1569　SIC 2673
SIGNODE PACKAGING GROUP CANADA ULC　p675
241 GOUGH RD, MARKHAM, ON, L3R 5B3
(905) 479-9754　SIC 2673
SYSTEMES D'EMBALLAGE SECURITAIRE NELMAR INC　p1382
3100 RUE DES BATISSEURS, TERREBONNE, QC, J6Y 0A2
(450) 477-0001　SIC 2673
T.FLEXO CORPORATION　p665
528 RAYMERVILLE DR, MARKHAM, ON, L3P 6G4
(647) 477-8482　SIC 2673
TRIPLE THREE TRADING LTD　p32
908 34 AVE SE, CALGARY, AB, T2G 1V3
(403) 240-2540　SIC 2673
UNITREND PLASTICS MANUFACTURING LTD　p210
7351 PROGRESS PL, DELTA, BC, V4G 1A1
(604) 940-8900　SIC 2673
W. RALSTON (CANADA) INC　p1331
3300 BOUL DE LA COTE-VERTU BUREAU 200, SAINT-LAURENT, QC, H4R 2B7
(514) 334-5656　SIC 2673

SIC 2674 Bags: uncoated paper and multiwall

APC FILTRATION INC　p515
10C ABBOTT CRT UNIT 303, BRANTFORD, ON, N3S 0E7
(888) 689-1235　SIC 2674
ATLAS PAPER BAG COMPANY LIMITED p876
90 DYNAMIC DR, SCARBOROUGH, ON, M1V 2V1
(416) 293-2125　SIC 2674
BULLDOG BAG LTD　p253
13631 VULCAN WAY, RICHMOND, BC, V6V 1K4
(604) 273-8021　SIC 2674
EMBALLAGE CODERRE PACKAGING INC p1306
413 RTE 122, SAINT-GERMAIN-DE-GRANTHAM, QC, J0C 1K0
(819) 395-4223　SIC 2674
GELPAC ROUVILLE SOLUTIONS EMBALLAGE INC　p1149
400 RUE HENRI-BOURASSA, MARIEVILLE, QC, J3M 1R9
(450) 460-4466　SIC 2674
HOOD PACKAGING CORPORATION　p16
5615 44 ST SE, CALGARY, AB, T2C 1V2
(403) 279-4000　SIC 2674
HOOD PACKAGING CORPORATION　p530
2380 MCDOWELL RD, BURLINGTON, ON, L7R 4A1
(905) 637-5611　SIC 2674
HOOD PACKAGING CORPORATION p1100
15 RUE DAVID-SWAN, EAST ANGUS, QC, J0B 1R0
(819) 832-4971　SIC 2674
SENECHAL, EMILE ET FILS LTEE　p403
190 CH INDUSTRIEL, GRANDSAULT/GRAND FALLS, NB, E3Y 3V3
(506) 473-2392　SIC 2674
TOLKO INDUSTRIES LTD　p360
HWY 10 N, THE PAS, MB, R9A 1L4
(204) 623-7411　SIC 2674
WEDLOCK PAPER CONVERTERS LIMITED

p704
2327 STANFIELD RD, MISSISSAUGA, ON, L4Y 1R6
(905) 277-9461　SIC 2674

SIC 2675 Die-cut paper and board

CPI CARD GROUP-CANADA INC　p551
460 APPLEWOOD CRES, CONCORD, ON, L4K 4Z3
(905) 761-8222　SIC 2675
HARTMANN CANADA INC　p517
58 FRANK ST, BRANTFORD, ON, N3T 5E2
(519) 756-8500　SIC 2675
STANPAC INC　p882
2790 THOMPSON RD, SMITHVILLE, ON, L0R 2A0
(905) 957-3326　SIC 2675
TERDUN MATERIAL MANAGEMENT INC p701
5130 CREEKBANK RD, MISSISSAUGA, ON, L4W 2G2
(905) 602-4567　SIC 2675

SIC 2676 Sanitary paper products

ATLANTIC PACKAGING PRODUCTS LTD p876
45 MILLIKEN BLVD, SCARBOROUGH, ON, M1V 1V3
(416) 298-5566　SIC 2676
CASCADES CANADA ULC　p1072
77 BOUL MARIE-VICTORIN, CANDIAC, QC, J5R 1C2
(450) 444-6400　SIC 2676
CASCADES CANADA ULC　p1117
467 BOUL MARIE-VICTORIN, KINGSEY FALLS, QC, J0A 1B0
(819) 363-5600　SIC 2676
CASCADES CANADA ULC　p1129
115 RUE DE LA PRINCESSE, LACHUTE, QC, J8H 4M3
(450) 562-8585　SIC 2676
CASCADES CANADA ULC　p1236
2345 DES LAURENTIDES (A-15) E, MONTREAL, QC, H7S 1Z7
(450) 688-1152　SIC 2676
FEMPRO CONSUMER PRODUCTS ULC p1098
1330 RUE JEAN-BERCHMANS-MICHAUD, DRUMMONDVILLE, QC, J2C 2Z5
(819) 475-8900　SIC 2676
IRVING CONSUMER PRODUCTS LIMITED p992
1551 WESTON RD, TORONTO, ON, M6M 4Y4
(416) 246-6666　SIC 2676
IRVING CONSUMER PRODUCTS LIMITED p993
1551 WESTON RD, TORONTO, ON, M6M 4Y4
(416) 246-6666　SIC 2676
KIMBERLY-CLARK INC　p710
50 BURNHAMTHORPE RD W SUITE 1402, MISSISSAUGA, ON, L5B 3C2
(905) 277-6500　SIC 2676
KRUGER PRODUCTS L.P.　p1089
100 1E AV, CRABTREE, QC, J0K 1B0
(450) 754-2855　SIC 2676
METRO PAPER INDUSTRIES INC　p869
111 MANVILLE RD, SCARBOROUGH, ON, M1L 4J2
(416) 757-2737　SIC 2676
PROCTER & GAMBLE INC　p491
355 UNIVERSITY AVE, BELLEVILLE, ON, K8N 5T8
(613) 966-5130　SIC 2676

SIC 2677 Envelopes

ROYAL ENVELOPE LTD　p558

111 JACOB KEFFER PKY, CONCORD, ON, L4K 4V1
(905) 879-0000　SIC 2677
SUPREMEX INC　p588
400 HUMBERLINE DR, ETOBICOKE, ON, M9W 5T3
(416) 675-9370　SIC 2677
SUPREMEX INC　p700
5300 TOMKEN RD, MISSISSAUGA, ON, L4W 1P2
(905) 624-4973　SIC 2677
SUPREMEX INC　p1131
7213 RUE CORDNER, LASALLE, QC, H8N 2J7
(514) 595-0555　SIC 2677
SUPREMEX INC　p1327
645 RUE STINSON, SAINT-LAURENT, QC, H4N 2E6
(514) 331-7110　SIC 2677

SIC 2678 Stationery products

ACCO BRANDS CANADA LP　p733
7381 BRAMALEA RD, MISSISSAUGA, ON, L5S 1C4
(905) 364-2600　SIC 2678
INTERNATIONAL GRAPHICS ULC　p896
505 DOURO ST, STRATFORD, ON, N5A 3S9
(519) 271-3010　SIC 2678
INTERNATIONAL GRAPHICS ULC　p1084
2135A BOUL DES LAURENTIDES, COTE SAINT-LUC, QC, H7M 4M2
SIC 2678

SIC 2679 Converted paper products, nec

011810 N.B. LIMITED　p412
435 BAYSIDE DR, SAINT JOHN, NB, E2J 1B2
(506) 633-3333　SIC 2679
APOLLO HEALTH AND BEAUTY CARE INC p782
1 APOLLO PL, NORTH YORK, ON, M3J 0H2
(416) 758-3700　SIC 2679
ASSOCIATED LABELS & PRINTING LTD p199
61 CLIPPER ST, COQUITLAM, BC, V3K 6X2
(604) 525-4764　SIC 2679
ATLANTIC PACKAGING PRODUCTS LTD p870
111 PROGRESS AVE, SCARBOROUGH, ON, M1P 2Y9
(416) 298-5456　SIC 2679
ATLANTIC PACKAGING PRODUCTS LTD p870
111 PROGRESS AVE, SCARBOROUGH, ON, M1P 2Y9
(416) 298-8101　SIC 2679
BRITISH CONFECTIONERY COMPANY LIMITED　p429
187 KENMOUNT RD SUITE 2, ST. JOHN'S, NL, A1B 3P9
(709) 747-2377　SIC 2679
CASCADES CANADA ULC　p864
5910 FINCH AVE E, SCARBOROUGH, ON, M1B 5P8
(416) 412-3500　SIC 2679
CASCADES CANADA ULC　p998
300 MARMORA ST, TRENTON, ON, K8V 5R8
SIC 2679
CASCADES SONOCO INC　p1117
457 BOUL MARIE-VICTORIN, KINGSEY FALLS, QC, J0A 1B0
(819) 363-5400　SIC 2679
CCL INDUSTRIES INC　p1295
1315 RUE RENE-DESCARTES, SAINT-BRUNO, QC, J3V 0B7
(450) 653-3071　SIC 2679

CCL INTERNATIONAL INC p764
105 GORDON BAKER RD SUITE 800, NORTH YORK, ON, M2H 3P8
(416) 756-8500 *SIC 2679*

CKF INC p583
30 IRON ST, ETOBICOKE, ON, M9W 5E1
(416) 249-2207 *SIC 2679*

CRISTINI AMERIQUE DU NORD INC p1129
700 BOUL CRISTINI, LACHUTE, QC, J8H 4N3
(450) 562-5511 *SIC 2679*

FD ALPHA CANADA ACQUISITION INC p1085
2277 DESSTE DES LAURENTIDES (A-15) E, COTE SAINT-LUC, QC, H7S 1Z6
(450) 680-5000 *SIC 2679*

GEORGIA-PACIFIC CANADA LP p907
319 ALLANBURG RD, THOROLD, ON, L2V 5C3
(905) 451-0620 *SIC 2679*

GLENWOOD LABEL & BOX MFG. LTD p236
15 BRAID ST SUITE 117, NEW WESTMINSTER, BC, V3L 5N7
(604) 522-6001 *SIC 2679*

HANWEI ENERGY SERVICES CORP p305
595 HOWE ST SUITE 902, VANCOUVER, BC, V6C 2T5
(604) 685-2239 *SIC 2679*

HONEYWELL LIMITED p239
500 BROOKSBANK AVE, NORTH VANCOUVER, BC, V7J 3S4
(604) 980-3421 *SIC 2679*

INDUSTRIES PAULYMARK INC p1288
340 LA GRANDE-CAROLINE, ROUGEMONT, QC, J0L 1M0
(514) 861-0180 *SIC 2679*

INTERPLAST PACKAGING INC p1381
955 BOUL INDUSTRIEL, TERREBONNE, QC, J6Y 1V7
(450) 971-0500 *SIC 2679*

IRVING CONSUMER PRODUCTS LIMITED p397
100 PROM MIDLAND, DIEPPE, NB, E1A 6X4
(506) 858-7777 *SIC 2679*

IRVING, J. D. LIMITED p398
100 PROM MIDLAND, DIEPPE, NB, E1A 6X4
(506) 859-5757 *SIC 2679*

IRVING, J. D. LIMITED p419
600 ROUTE 785, UTOPIA, NB, E5C 2K4
(506) 755-3384 *SIC 2679*

JET LABEL AND PACKAGING LTD p109
9445 49 ST NW, EDMONTON, AB, T6B 2L8
(780) 440-5135 *SIC 2679*

LABELS UNLIMITED INC p366
67 ARCHIBALD ST, WINNIPEG, MB, R2J 0V7
(204) 233-4444 *SIC 2679*

MABEL'S LABELS INC p613
150 CHATHAM ST UNIT 1, HAMILTON, ON, L8P 2B6
(905) 667-0306 *SIC 2679*

NORTH AMERICAN PAPER INCORPORATED p499
16 AUTOMATIC RD, BRAMPTON, ON, L6S 5N3
(905) 793-8202 *SIC 2679*

PAPIERS SOLIDERR INC, LES p1045
525 AV DU PONT S, ALMA, QC, G8B 2T9
(418) 668-5377 *SIC 2679*

PF RESOLU CANADA INC p1052
20 AV MARQUETTE, BAIE-COMEAU, QC, G4Z 1K6
(418) 296-3371 *SIC 2679*

POLLARD BANKNOTE LIMITED p391
140 OTTER ST, WINNIPEG, MB, R3T 0M8
(204) 474-2323 *SIC 2679*

PRODUITS DE PAPIER LAPACO LTEE, LES p1309
5200 RUE J.-A.-BOMBARDIER, SAINT-HUBERT, QC, J3Z 1H1
(450) 632-5140 *SIC 2679*

QUINCO & CIE INC p1148

2035 RUE RENE-PATENAUDE, MAGOG, QC, J1X 7J2
(819) 847-4001 *SIC 2679*

SEASIDE PAPER PRODUCTS LTD p210
9999 RIVER WAY, DELTA, BC, V4G 1M8
(604) 930-2700 *SIC 2679*

SLEEVER INTERNATIONAL INC p743
6815 COLUMBUS RD, MISSISSAUGA, ON, L5T 2G9
(905) 565-0952 *SIC 2679*

SPECIALIZED PACKAGING (LONDON) COMPANY ULC p650
5 CUDDY BLVD, LONDON, ON, N5V 3Y3
(519) 659-7011 *SIC 2679*

TENCORR PACKAGING INC p507
6 SHAFTSBURY LANE, BRAMPTON, ON, L6T 3X7
(905) 799-9955 *SIC 2679*

UFR URBAN FOREST RECYCLERS INC p1437
201 INDUSTRIAL DR, SWIFT CURRENT, SK, S9H 5R4
(306) 777-0600 *SIC 2679*

WALLCROWN LIMITED p589
88 RONSON DR, ETOBICOKE, ON, M9W 1B9
(416) 245-2900 *SIC 2679*

WESTROCK PACKAGING COMPANY p690
3270 AMERICAN DR, MISSISSAUGA, ON, L4V 1B5
(416) 683-1270 *SIC 2679*

SIC 2711 Newspapers

1032451 B.C. LTD p20
2615 12 ST NE SUITE 1, CALGARY, AB, T2E 7W9
(403) 250-4192 *SIC 2711*

1032451 B.C. LTD p107
9300 47 ST NW, EDMONTON, AB, T6B 2P6
(780) 468-0506 *SIC 2711*

1032451 B.C. LTD p107
4990 92 AVE NW SUITE 350, EDMONTON, AB, T6B 3A1
(780) 468-0100 *SIC 2711*

1032451 B.C. LTD p131
10604 100 ST, GRANDE PRAIRIE, AB, T8V 2M5
(780) 532-1110 *SIC 2711*

1032451 B.C. LTD p139
4504 61 AVE, LEDUC, AB, T9E 3Z1
(780) 986-2271 *SIC 2711*

1032451 B.C. LTD p518
1600 CALIFORNIA AVE, BROCKVILLE, ON, K6V 5T6
(613) 342-4441 *SIC 2711*

1032451 B.C. LTD p655
369 YORK ST SUITE 2A, LONDON, ON, N6B 3R4
(519) 679-1111 *SIC 2711*

1032451 B.C. LTD p748
6 ANTARES DR SUITE 3, NEPEAN, ON, K2E 8A9
SIC 2711

1032451 B.C. LTD p895
16 PACKHAM RD, STRATFORD, ON, N5A 6T6
(519) 271-2220 *SIC 2711*

1032451 B.C. LTD p911
25 TOWNLINE RD SUITE 190, TILLSONBURG, ON, N4G 2R5
(519) 688-6397 *SIC 2711*

1032451 B.C. LTD p932
333 KING ST E UNIT 1, TORONTO, ON, M5A 0E1
(416) 947-2222 *SIC 2711*

3834310 CANADA INC p1077
1051 BOUL TALBOT, CHICOUTIMI, QC, G7H 5C1
(418) 545-4474 *SIC 2711*

3834310 CANADA INC p1257
410 BOUL CHAREST E BUREAU 300, QUEBEC, QC, G1K 8G3

9069-5057 QUEBEC INC p1209
1000 RUE SAINT-ANTOINE O STE 509, MONTREAL, QC, H3C 3R7
SIC 2711

B A S P BUY & SELL PRESS LTD, THE p184
4664 LOUGHEED HWY SUITE 202, BURNABY, BC, V5C 5T5
(604) 540-4455 *SIC 2711*

B I V PUBLICATIONS LTD p288
102 4TH AVE E, VANCOUVER, BC, V5T 1G2
(604) 669-8500 *SIC 2711*

BLACK PRESS GROUP LTD p156
2950 BREMNER AVE, RED DEER, AB, T4R 1M9
(403) 343-2400 *SIC 2711*

BLACK PRESS GROUP LTD p174
34375 GLADYS AVE, ABBOTSFORD, BC, V2S 2H5
(604) 853-1144 *SIC 2711*

BLACK PRESS GROUP LTD p219
2495 ENTERPRISE WAY, KELOWNA, BC, V1X 7K2
(250) 766-4688 *SIC 2711*

BLACK PRESS GROUP LTD p333
3175 BEACH DR, VICTORIA, BC, V8R 6L7
(250) 480-3220 *SIC 2711*

BRUNSWICK NEWS INC p406
939 MAIN ST, MONCTON, NB, E1C 8P3
(506) 859-4900 *SIC 2711*

CHRONICLE JOURNAL, THE p908
75 CUMBERLAND ST S, THUNDER BAY, ON, P7B 1A3
(807) 343-6200 *SIC 2711*

COMPAGNIE D'EDITION ANDRE PAQUETTE INC, LA p619
1100 ABERDEEN ST, HAWKESBURY, ON, K6A 1K7
(613) 632-4155 *SIC 2711*

CONTINENTAL NEWSPAPERS (CANADA) LTD p221
550 DOYLE AVE, KELOWNA, BC, V1Y 7V1
(250) 763-4000 *SIC 2711*

DEVOIR INC, LE p1195
2050 RUE DE BLEURY, MONTREAL, QC, H3A 2J5
(514) 985-3333 *SIC 2711*

EDITIONS BLAINVILLE-DEUX-MONTAGNES INC, LES p1301
53 RUE SAINT-EUSTACHE, SAINT-EUSTACHE, QC, J7R 2L2
(450) 473-1700 *SIC 2711*

EDITIONS DE L'ACADIE NOUVELLE (1984) LTEE, LES p396
476 BOUL ST-PIERRE O, CARAQUET, NB, E1W 1A3
(800) 561-2255 *SIC 2711*

FP CANADIAN NEWSPAPERS LIMITED PARTNERSHIP p372
1355 MOUNTAIN AVE, WINNIPEG, MB, R2X 3B6
(204) 697-7000 *SIC 2711*

GESCA LTEE p821
47 CLARENCE ST SUITE 222, OTTAWA, ON, K1N 9K1
(613) 562-0111 *SIC 2711*

GESCA LTEE p1188
750 BOUL SAINT-LAURENT, MONTREAL, QC, H2Y 2Z4
(514) 285-7000 *SIC 2711*

GLACIER MEDIA INC p249
150 BRUNSWICK ST, PRINCE GEORGE, BC, V2L 2B3
(250) 562-6666 *SIC 2711*

GLACIER MEDIA INC p334
2621 DOUGLAS ST, VICTORIA, BC, V8T 4M2
(250) 380-5211 *SIC 2711*

GLACIER MEDIA INC p1427
2310 MILLAR AVE, SASKATOON, SK, S7K 2Y2
(306) 665-3500 *SIC 2711*

GLACIER PUBLICATIONS LIMITED PART-

NERSHIP p292
1970 ALBERTA ST, VANCOUVER, BC, V5Y 3X4
(604) 708-3291 *SIC 2711*

GREAT WEST NEWSPAPERS LIMITED PARTNERSHIP p165
340 CARLETON DR, ST. ALBERT, AB, T8N 7L3
(780) 460-5500 *SIC 2711*

GROUPE LEXIS MEDIA INC p1309
7750 BOUL COUSINEAU BUREAU 103, SAINT-HUBERT, QC, J3Z 0C8
(514) 394-7156 *SIC 2711*

HALIFAX HERALD LIMITED, THE p440
311 BLUEWATER RD, BEDFORD, NS, B4B 1Z9
(902) 426-2811 *SIC 2711*

HALIFAX HERALD LIMITED, THE p457
2717 JOSEPH HOWE DR SUITE 101, HALIFAX, NS, B3L 4T9
(902) 426-2811 *SIC 2711*

IMPRIMERIE D'ARTHABASKA INC, L' p1398
370 RUE GIROUARD, VICTORIAVILLE, QC, G6P 5V2
SIC 2711

IMPRIMERIES TRANSCONTINENTAL INC p1027
100 ROYAL GROUP CRES UNIT B, WOODBRIDGE, ON, L4H 1X9
(905) 663-1216 *SIC 2711*

IMPRIMERIES TRANSCONTINENTAL INC p1049
10807 RUE MIRABEAU, ANJOU, QC, H1J 1T7
(514) 355-4134 *SIC 2711*

ISLAND PUBLISHERS LTD p336
818 BROUGHTON ST, VICTORIA, BC, V8W 1E4
(250) 480-0755 *SIC 2711*

ISLAND PUBLISHERS LTD p336
818 BROUGHTON ST, VICTORIA, BC, V8W 1E4
(250) 480-0755 *SIC 2711*

LANGLEY TIMES PUBLISHING CO p228
20258 FRASER HWY, LANGLEY, BC, V3A 4E6
(604) 533-4157 *SIC 2711*

LAURENTIAN PUBLISHING LIMITED p901
158 ELGIN ST, SUDBURY, ON, P3E 3N5
(705) 673-5120 *SIC 2711*

MEDIAQMI INC p1211
612 RUE SAINT-JACQUES, MONTREAL, QC, H3C 4M8
(514) 380-6400 *SIC 2711*

MEDIAS TRANSCONTINENTAL INC p433
430 TOPSAIL RD SUITE 86, ST. JOHN'S, NL, A1E 4N1
(709) 364-6300 *SIC 2711*

MEDIAS TRANSCONTINENTAL INC p1039
165 PRINCE ST, CHARLOTTETOWN, PE, C1A 4R7
(902) 629-6000 *SIC 2711*

MEDIAS TRANSCONTINENTAL S.E.N.C. p467
255 GEORGE ST, SYDNEY, NS, B1P 1J7
(902) 564-5451 *SIC 2711*

METROLAND MEDIA GROUP LTD p523
5046 MAINWAY UNIT 2, BURLINGTON, ON, L7L 5Z1
(905) 632-4444 *SIC 2711*

METROLAND MEDIA GROUP LTD p612
44 FRID ST, HAMILTON, ON, L8N 3G3
(905) 526-3333 *SIC 2711*

METROLAND MEDIA GROUP LTD p711
3145 WOLFEDALE RD, MISSISSAUGA, ON, L5C 3A9
(905) 281-5656 *SIC 2711*

METROLAND MEDIA GROUP LTD p717
3715 LAIRD RD UNIT 6, MISSISSAUGA, ON, L5L 0A3
(905) 281-5656 *SIC 2711*

METROLAND MEDIA GROUP LTD p802
467 SPEERS RD SUITE 1, OAKVILLE, ON, L6K 3S4

(905) 845-3824   *SIC 2711*
METROLAND MEDIA GROUP LTD   *p813*
865 FAREWELL ST, OSHAWA, ON, L1H 6N8
(905) 579-4400   *SIC 2711*
METROLAND MEDIA GROUP LTD   *p841*
884 FORD ST, PETERBOROUGH, ON, K9J 5V3
(705) 749-3383   *SIC 2711*
METROLAND MEDIA GROUP LTD   *p882*
65 LORNE ST, SMITHS FALLS, ON, K7A 3K8
(800) 267-7936   *SIC 2711*
MING PAO NEWSPAPERS (CANADA) LIMITED   *p255*
5368 PARKWOOD PL, RICHMOND, BC, V6V 2N1
(604) 231-8998   *SIC 2711*
MING PAO NEWSPAPERS (CANADA) LIMITED   *p982*
23 SPADINA AVE, TORONTO, ON, M5V 3M5
(416) 321-0088   *SIC 2711*
NORTHERN NEWS SERVICES LTD   *p436*
5108 50 ST, YELLOWKNIFE, NT, X1A 1S2
(867) 873-4031   *SIC 2711*
OSPREY MEDIA PUBLISHING INC   *p517*
53 DALHOUSIE ST SUITE 306, BRANTFORD, ON, N3T 2H9
(519) 756-2020   *SIC 2711*
OSPREY MEDIA PUBLISHING INC   *p630*
6 CATARAQUI ST SUITE 427, KINGSTON, ON, K7K 1Z7
(613) 544-5000   *SIC 2711*
OSPREY MEDIA PUBLISHING INC   *p673*
100 RENFREW DR SUITE 110, MARKHAM, ON, L3R 9R6
(905) 752-1132   *SIC 2711*
OSPREY MEDIA PUBLISHING INC   *p763*
259 WORTHINGTON ST W, NORTH BAY, ON, P1B 3B5
(705) 472-3200   *SIC 2711*
OSPREY MEDIA PUBLISHING INC   *p860*
140 FRONT ST S, SARNIA, ON, N7T 7M8
(519) 344-3641   *SIC 2711*
OSPREY MEDIA PUBLISHING INC   *p860*
140 FRONT ST S SUITE FRONT, SARNIA, ON, N7T 7M8
(519) 344-3641   *SIC 2711*
OSPREY MEDIA PUBLISHING INC   *p886*
17 QUEEN ST, ST CATHARINES, ON, L2R 5G4
(905) 684-7251   *SIC 2711*
PERFORMANCE PRINTING LIMITED   *p882*
65 LORNE ST, SMITHS FALLS, ON, K7A 3K8
(613) 283-5650   *SIC 2711*
POSTMEDIA NETWORK CANADA CORP   *p930*
365 BLOOR ST E, TORONTO, ON, M4W 3L4
(416) 383-2300   *SIC 2711*
POSTMEDIA NETWORK INC   *p25*
215 16 ST SE, CALGARY, AB, T2E 7P5
(403) 235-7168   *SIC 2711*
POSTMEDIA NETWORK INC   *p90*
10006 101 ST NW, EDMONTON, AB, T5J 0S1
(780) 429-5100   *SIC 2711*
POSTMEDIA NETWORK INC   *p217*
393 SEYMOUR ST, KAMLOOPS, BC, V2C 6P6
SIC 2711
POSTMEDIA NETWORK INC   *p234*
2575 MCCULLOUGH RD SUITE B1, NANAIMO, BC, V9S 4M9
SIC 2711
POSTMEDIA NETWORK INC   *p308*
200 GRANVILLE ST SUITE 1, VANCOUVER, BC, V6C 3N3
(604) 605-2000   *SIC 2711*
POSTMEDIA NETWORK INC   *p308*
200 GRANVILLE ST SUITE 1, VANCOUVER, BC, V6C 3N3

(604) 605-2000   *SIC 2711*
POSTMEDIA NETWORK INC   *p831*
1101 BAXTER RD, OTTAWA, ON, K2C 3M4
(613) 829-9100   *SIC 2711*
POSTMEDIA NETWORK INC   *p930*
365 BLOOR ST E SUITE 1601, TORONTO, ON, M4W 3L4
(416) 383-2300   *SIC 2711*
POSTMEDIA NETWORK INC   *p1023*
167 FERRY ST, WINDSOR, ON, N9A 0C5
(519) 255-5720   *SIC 2711*
POSTMEDIA NETWORK INC   *p1207*
1010 RUE SAINTE-CATHERINE O BUREAU 200, MONTREAL, QC, H3B 5L1
(514) 284-0040   *SIC 2711*
POSTMEDIA NETWORK INC   *p1416*
1964 PARK ST, REGINA, SK, S4N 7M5
(306) 781-5211   *SIC 2711*
POSTMEDIA NETWORK INC   *p1429*
204 5TH AVE N, SASKATOON, SK, S7K 2P1
(306) 657-6206   *SIC 2711*
PRESSE (2018) INC, LA   *p1190*
750 BOUL SAINT-LAURENT, MONTREAL, QC, H2Y 2Z4
(514) 285-7000   *SIC 2711*
PRINTERON INC   *p642*
221 MCINTYRE DR, KITCHENER, ON, N2R 1G1
(519) 748-2848   *SIC 2711*
QUEBECOR MEDIA INC   *p1212*
612 RUE SAINT-JACQUES, MONTREAL, QC, H3C 4M8
(514) 380-1999   *SIC 2711*
SING TAO (CANADA) LIMITED   *p324*
8508 ASH ST, VANCOUVER, BC, V6P 3M2
(604) 321-1111   *SIC 2711*
SING TAO NEWSPAPERS (CANADA 1988) LIMITED   *p675*
221 WHITEHALL DR, MARKHAM, ON, L3R 9T1
(416) 596-8140   *SIC 2711*
ST. CATHARINES STANDARD GROUP INC   *p886*
1 ST. PAUL ST SUITE 10, ST CATHARINES, ON, L2R 7L4
(905) 684-7251   *SIC 2711*
ST. JOSEPH PRINTING LIMITED   *p777*
236 LESMILL RD, NORTH YORK, ON, M3B 2T5
(416) 449-4579   *SIC 2711*
SUN DISTRIBUTION   *p111*
4990 92 AVE NW, EDMONTON, AB, T6B 3A1
SIC 2711
TORONTO STAR NEWSPAPERS LIMITED   *p943*
1 YONGE ST SUITE 400, TORONTO, ON, M5E 1E6
(416) 869-4000   *SIC 2711*
TORONTO STAR NEWSPAPERS LIMITED   *p1034*
1 CENTURY PL, WOODBRIDGE, ON, L4L 8R2
(416) 502-8273   *SIC 2711*
TORSTAR CORPORATION   *p639*
160 KING ST E, KITCHENER, ON, N2G 4E5
(519) 821-2022   *SIC 2711*
TORSTAR CORPORATION   *p813*
865 FAREWELL ST, OSHAWA, ON, L1H 6N8
(905) 579-4400   *SIC 2711*
TRANSCONTINENTAL INC   *p464*
9185 COMMERCIAL ST SUITE 2, NEW MINAS, NS, B4N 3G1
(902) 681-2121   *SIC 2711*
UNIVERSITY PRESS OF NEW BRUNSWICK   *p402*
984 PROSPECT ST, FREDERICTON, NB, E3B 2T8
(506) 452-6671   *SIC 2711*

SIC 2721 Periodicals

10684210 CANADA INC   *p1224*
101 BOUL MARCEL-LAURIN BUREAU 320, MONTREAL, QC, H4N 2M3
(514) 286-1066   *SIC 2721*
1772887 ONTARIO LIMITED   *p791*
15 BENTON RD, NORTH YORK, ON, M6M 3G2
(416) 364-3333   *SIC 2721*
ANNEX PUBLISHING & PRINTING INC *p880*
105 DONLY DR S, SIMCOE, ON, N3Y 4N5
(519) 428-3471   *SIC 2721*
ANNEX-NEWCOM LIMITED PARTNERSHIP   *p775*
80 VALLEYBROOK DR, NORTH YORK, ON, M3B 2S9
(416) 442-5600   *SIC 2721*
B. & C. LIST (1982) LTD   *p290*
8278 MANITOBA ST, VANCOUVER, BC, V5X 3A2
(604) 482-3100   *SIC 2721*
BRUNICO COMMUNICATIONS LTD   *p979*
366 ADELAIDE ST W SUITE 100, TORONTO, ON, M5V 1R9
(416) 408-2300   *SIC 2721*
C.B.U. PUBLICATIONS LTD   *p833*
420 O'CONNOR ST SUITE 1600, OTTAWA, ON, K2P 1W4
(613) 230-0721   *SIC 2721*
CANADA WIDE MEDIA LIMITED   *p184*
4180 LOUGHEED HWY SUITE 102, BURNABY, BC, V5C 6A7
(604) 299-7311   *SIC 2721*
CLB MEDIA INC   *p480*
240 EDWARD ST SUITE 1, AURORA, ON, L4G 3S9
SIC 2721
EDITIONS NOVALIS INC, LES   *p1172*
4475 RUE FRONTENAC, MONTREAL, QC, H2H 2S2
SIC 2721
EDITIONS PRATICO-PRATIQUES INC *p1280*
1685 BOUL TALBOT, QUEBEC, QC, G2N 0C6
(418) 877-0259   *SIC 2721*
GLACIER MEDIA INC   *p291*
2188 YUKON ST, VANCOUVER, BC, V5Y 3P1
(604) 872-8565   *SIC 2721*
GOUVERNEMENT DE LA PROVINCE DE QUEBEC   *p1269*
200 CH SAINTE-FOY 3E ETAGE BUREAU 300, QUEBEC, QC, G1R 5T4
(418) 691-2401   *SIC 2721*
HACHETTE DISTRIBUTION SERVICES (CANADA) INC   *p1049*
8155 RUE LARREY, ANJOU, QC, H1J 2L5
(514) 355-3334   *SIC 2721*
JWP PUBLISHING LIMITED PARTNERSHIP   *p23*
816 55 AVE NE 2ND FL, CALGARY, AB, T2E 6Y4
(403) 265-3700   *SIC 2721*
MEDIAS TRANSCONTINENTAL INC   *p1206*
1 PLACE VILLE MARIE BUREAU 3240, MONTREAL, QC, H3B 0G1
(514) 954-4000   *SIC 2721*
MEDIAS TRANSCONTINENTAL S.E.N.C.   *p1206*
1 PLACE VILLE-MARIE BUREAU 3315, MONTREAL, QC, H3B 3N2
(514) 392-9000   *SIC 2721*
NATIONAL COMMITTEE FOR THE NATIONAL PILGRIM VIRGIN OF CANADA, THE   *p591*
452 KRAFT RD, FORT ERIE, ON, L2A 4M7
(905) 871-7607   *SIC 2721*
NAYLOR (CANADA), INC   *p382*
1200 PORTAGE AVE SUITE 200, WINNIPEG, MB, R3G 0T5
(204) 975-0415   *SIC 2721*
NEWCOM MEDIA INC   *p996*
5353 DUNDAS ST W SUITE 400, TORONTO, ON, M9B 6H8

(416) 614-2200   *SIC 2721*
NOW COMMUNICATIONS INC   *p935*
189 CHURCH ST, TORONTO, ON, M5B 1Y7
(416) 364-1300   *SIC 2721*
RENAISSANCE PRINTING INC   *p845*
1800 IRONSTONE MANOR, PICKERING, ON, L1W 3J9
(905) 831-3000   *SIC 2721*
RICARDO MEDIA INC   *p1323*
300 RUE D'ARRAN, SAINT-LAMBERT, QC, J4R 1K5
(450) 465-4500   *SIC 2721*
ROGERS MEDIA INC   *p930*
333 BLOOR ST E, TORONTO, ON, M4W 1G9
(416) 935-8200   *SIC 2721*
STP PUBLICATIONS LIMITED PARTNERSHIP   *p292*
2188 YUKON ST, VANCOUVER, BC, V5Y 3P1
(604) 983-3434   *SIC 2721*
TRADER CORPORATION   *p189*
3555 GILMORE WAY 1 WEST, BURNABY, BC, V5G 0B3
(604) 540-4455   *SIC 2721*
TRADER CORPORATION   *p580*
405 THE WEST MALL SUITE 110, ETOBICOKE, ON, M9C 5J1
(416) 784-5200   *SIC 2721*
TRADER CORPORATION   *p1215*
1600 BOUL RENE-LEVESQUE O BUREAU 140, MONTREAL, QC, H3H 1P9
(514) 764-4000   *SIC 2721*
TRANSCONTINENTAL INC   *p1200*
2001 BOUL ROBERT-BOURASSA UNITE 900, MONTREAL, QC, H3A 2A6
(514) 499-0491   *SIC 2721*
WOLTERS KLUWER CANADA LIMITED *p773*
90 SHEPPARD AVE E SUITE 300, NORTH YORK, ON, M2N 6X1
(416) 224-2224   *SIC 2721*

SIC 2731 Book publishing

ADVOCATE PRINTING AND PUBLISHING COMPANY LIMITED   *p464*
GD, PICTOU, NS, B0K 1H0
(902) 485-1990   *SIC 2731*
CASTLE ROCK RESEARCH CORPORATION   *p87*
10180 101 ST NW SUITE 2410, EDMONTON, AB, T5J 3S4
(780) 448-9619   *SIC 2731*
COMPANY'S COMING PUBLISHING LIMITED   *p120*
2311 96 ST NW, EDMONTON, AB, T6N 1G3
(780) 450-6223   *SIC 2731*
EDITEUR GUERIN LTEE   *p1183*
4501 RUE DROLET, MONTREAL, QC, H2T 2G2
(514) 842-3481   *SIC 2731*
EDITIONS DU RENOUVEAU PEDAGOGIQUE INC   *p1176*
1611 BOUL CREMAZIE E ETAGE 10, MONTREAL, QC, H2M 2P2
(514) 334-2690   *SIC 2731*
GROUPE EDUCALIVRES INC   *p1234*
955 RUE BERGAR, MONTREAL, QC, H7L 4Z6
(514) 334-8466   *SIC 2731*
GROUPE SOGIDES INC   *p1141*
2315 RUE DE LA PROVINCE, LONGUEUIL, QC, J4G 1G4
(450) 640-1237   *SIC 2731*
GROUPE SOGIDES INC   *p1175*
955 RUE AMHERST, MONTREAL, QC, H2L 3K4
(514) 523-1182   *SIC 2731*
HARLEQUIN ENTERPRISES LIMITED *p952*
22 ADELAIDE STREET W 41ST FL, TORONTO, ON, M5H 4E3
(416) 445-5860   *SIC 2731*

▲ Public Company   ■ Public Company Family Member   **HQ** Headquarters   **BR** Branch   **SL** Single Location

IMPRIMERIE NORECOB INC   p1322
340 RUE PRINCIPALE, SAINT-JULES, QC, G0N 1R0
(418) 397-2233   *SIC 2731*

IMPRIMERIE QUEBECOR MEDIA (2015) INC   p1152
12800 RUE BRAULT, MIRABEL, QC, J7J 0W4
(514) 380-3600   *SIC 2731*

INTERINFORMA INC   p611
400 WELLINGTON ST N UNIT 1, HAMILTON, ON, L8L 5B1
(905) 526-0701   *SIC 2731*

JOHN WILEY & SONS CANADA LIMITED   p922
90 EGLINTON AVE E SUITE 300, TORONTO, ON, M4P 2Y3
(416) 236-4433   *SIC 2731*

LEXISNEXIS CANADA INC   p765
111 GORDON BAKER RD SUITE 900, NORTH YORK, ON, M2H 3R1
(905) 479-2665   *SIC 2731*

MCGRAW-HILL RYERSON LIMITED   p954
145 KING ST WEST SUITE 1501, TORONTO, ON, M5H 1J8
(800) 245-2914   *SIC 2731*

MOORE CANADA CORPORATION   p1326
395 AV SAINTE-CROIX BUREAU 100, SAINT-LAURENT, QC, H4N 2L3
SIC 2731

NELSON EDUCATION LTD   p914
1120 BIRCHMOUNT RD, TORONTO, ON, M1K 5G4
(416) 752-9100   *SIC 2731*

PEARSON CANADA HOLDINGS INC   p756
195 HARRY WALKER PKY N SUITE A, NEWMARKET, ON, L3Y 7B3
(905) 853-7888   *SIC 2731*

PEARSON CANADA HOLDINGS INC   p780
26 PRINCE ANDREW PL, NORTH YORK, ON, M3C 2C4
(416) 447-5101   *SIC 2731*

PEARSON CANADA INC   p756
195 HARRY WALKER PKY N SUITE A, NEWMARKET, ON, L3Y 7B3
(905) 853-7888   *SIC 2731*

PEARSON CANADA INC   p780
26 PRINCE ANDREW PL, NORTH YORK, ON, M3C 2H4
(416) 447-5101   *SIC 2731*

PENGUIN RANDOM HOUSE CANADA LIMITED   p982
320 FRONT ST W SUITE 1400, TORONTO, ON, M5V 3B6
(416) 364-4449   *SIC 2731*

REED ELSEVIER CANADA LTD   p983
555 RICHMOND ST W SUITE 1100, TORONTO, ON, M5V 3B1
(416) 253-3640   *SIC 2731*

RICOH DOCUMENT MANAGEMENT LIMITED PARTNERSHIP   p481
205 INDUSTRIAL PKY N UNIT 2, AURORA, ON, L4G 4C4
(905) 841-8433   *SIC 2731*

THOMSON COMPANY INC, THE   p957
65 QUEEN ST W SUITE 2400, TORONTO, ON, M5H 2M8
(416) 364-8700   *SIC 2731*

UNIVERSITY OF TORONTO PRESS   p781
5201 DUFFERIN ST, NORTH YORK, ON, M3H 5T8
(416) 667-7791   *SIC 2731*

UNIVERSITY OF TORONTO PRESS   p781
5201 DUFFERIN ST, NORTH YORK, ON, M3H 5T8
(416) 667-7791   *SIC 2731*

UNIVERSITY OF TORONTO PRESS   p932
10 ST MARY ST SUITE 700, TORONTO, ON, M4Y 2W8
(416) 978-2239   *SIC 2731*

SIC 2732 Book printing

CANADIAN MARKETING TEST CASE 206 LIMITED   p730
5770 HURONTARIO ST, MISSISSAUGA, ON, L5R 3G5
(905) 555-5555   *SIC 2732*

FRIESENS CORPORATION   p345
1 PRINTERS WAY, ALTONA, MB, R0G 0B0
(204) 324-6401   *SIC 2732*

GROUPE SCABRINI INC   p1172
2700 RUE RACHEL E, MONTREAL, QC, H2H 1S7
SIC 2732

IMPRESSION ALLIANCE 9000 INC   p1046
142 RUE DU PONT, AMQUI, QC, G5J 2R3
(418) 629-5256   *SIC 2732*

IMPRIMERIES TRANSCONTINENTAL 2005 S.E.N.C.   p835
2049 20TH ST E, OWEN SOUND, ON, N4K 5R2
(519) 376-8330   *SIC 2732*

MARQUIS IMPRIMEUR INC   p1146
750 RUE DEVEAULT, LOUISEVILLE, QC, J5V 3C2
(819) 228-2766   *SIC 2732*

MARQUIS IMPRIMEUR INC   p1160
350 RUE DES ENTREPRENEURS, MONTMAGNY, QC, G5V 4T1
(418) 246-5666   *SIC 2732*

UNIGRAPHICS LIMITED   p382
488 BURNELL ST, WINNIPEG, MB, R3G 2B4
(204) 784-1030   *SIC 2732*

WEBCOM INC   p878
3480 PHARMACY AVE, SCARBOROUGH, ON, M1W 2S7
(416) 496-1000   *SIC 2732*

SIC 2741 Miscellaneous publishing

EDITIONS QUEBEC-AMERIQUE INC, LES   p1181
7240 RUE SAINT-HUBERT, MONTREAL, QC, H2R 2N1
(514) 499-3000   *SIC 2741*

GROUPE PAGES JAUNES CORP   p864
325 MILNER AVE SUITE 4, SCARBOROUGH, ON, M1B 5N1
(416) 412-5000   *SIC 2741*

HANSON PUBLICATIONS INC.   p981
111 PETER ST,STE 406, TORONTO, ON, M5V 2H1
SIC 2741

NET-LINX AMERICAS, INC   p97
12431 STONY PLAIN RD NW SUITE 200, EDMONTON, AB, T5N 3N3
SIC 2741

OLE MEDIA MANAGEMENT (GP) L.P.   p965
120 BREMNER BLVD SUITE 2900, TORONTO, ON, M5J 0A8
(416) 850-1163   *SIC 2741*

PAGES JAUNES LIMITEE   p1216
1751 RUE RICHARDSON BUREAU 2300, MONTREAL, QC, H3K 1G6
(514) 934-2611   *SIC 2741*

PATIENT NEWS PUBLISHING LTD   p607
5152 COUNTY RD 121, HALIBURTON, ON, K0M 1S0
(705) 457-4030   *SIC 2741*

SONOVISION CANADA INC   p1155
4480 CH DE LA COTE-DE-LIESSE BUREAU 215, MONT-ROYAL, QC, H4N 2R1
(514) 344-5008   *SIC 2741*

TAMEC INC   p1212
980 RUE SAINT-ANTOINE O BUREAU 400, MONTREAL, QC, H3C 1A8
SIC 2741

TRENDS INTERNATIONAL PUBLISHING CORPORATION   p718
3500 LAIRD RD UNIT 2, MISSISSAUGA, ON, L5L 5Y4
(905) 569-8500   *SIC 2741*

WINDSOR PENNYSAVER   p1020
4525 RHODES DR UNIT 400, WINDSOR, ON, N8W 5R8
SIC 2741

SIC 2752 Commercial printing, lithographic

1627880 ONTARIO INC   p500
100 PARKSHORE DR, BRAMPTON, ON, L6T 5M1
SIC 2752

1637136 ONTARIO INC   p485
82 WELHAM RD, BARRIE, ON, L4N 8Y4
(705) 733-1349   *SIC 2752*

1959197 ONTARIO INC   p527
875 LAURENTIAN DR SUITE 12, BURLINGTON, ON, L7N 3W7
(905) 634-1900   *SIC 2752*

2214264 ONTARIO INC   p702
1550 CATERPILLAR RD, MISSISSAUGA, ON, L4X 1E7
(905) 848-1550   *SIC 2752*

746746 ONTARIO LIMITED   p826
400 HUNT CLUB RD, OTTAWA, ON, K1V 1C1
(613) 741-0962   *SIC 2752*

8388059 CANADA INC   p679
210 DUFFIELD DR, MARKHAM, ON, L6G 1C9
(416) 848-8500   *SIC 2752*

9049-3347 QUEBEC INC   p1398
383 BOUL DE LA BONAVENTURE, VICTORIAVILLE, QC, G6T 1V5
(819) 758-0667   *SIC 2752*

AGFA INC   p729
5975 FALBOURNE ST SUITE 2, MISSISSAUGA, ON, L5R 3V8
(905) 361-6982   *SIC 2752*

AVANT IMAGING & INTEGRATED MEDIA INC   p480
205 INDUSTRIAL PKY N UNIT 1, AURORA, ON, L4G 4C4
(905) 841-6444   *SIC 2752*

BATTLEFIELD GRAPHICS INC   p521
5355 HARVESTER RD, BURLINGTON, ON, L7L 5K4
(905) 333-4114   *SIC 2752*

C.J. GRAPHICS INC   p708
560 HENSALL CIR, MISSISSAUGA, ON, L5A 1Y1
(416) 588-0808   *SIC 2752*

COBER PRINTING LIMITED   p642
1351 STRASBURG RD, KITCHENER, ON, N2R 1H2
(519) 745-7136   *SIC 2752*

CONTINU-GRAPH INC   p1325
409 BOUL LEBEAU, SAINT-LAURENT, QC, H4N 1S2
(514) 331-0741   *SIC 2752*

COPIES DE LA CAPITALE INC, LES   p1258
235 BOUL CHAREST E, QUEBEC, QC, G1K 3G8
(418) 648-1911   *SIC 2752*

CORPORATION MULTI-COLOR MONTREAL CANADA   p1127
1925 32E AV, LACHINE, QC, H8T 3J1
(514) 341-4850   *SIC 2752*

DUHA COLOR SERVICES LIMITED   p384
750 BRADFORD ST, WINNIPEG, MB, R3H 0N3
(204) 786-8961   *SIC 2752*

EASTERN SIGN-PRINT LIMITED   p466
125 NORTH FOORD ST, STELLARTON, NS, B0K 0A2
(902) 752-2722   *SIC 2752*

FOND SRS DE L'ETABLISSEMENT DE DETENTION DE QUEBEC, LE   p1256
500 RUE DE LA FAUNE, QUEBEC, QC, G1G 0G9
(418) 622-7100   *SIC 2752*

FORMULES D'AFFAIRES SUPRATECH INC   p1111
960 RUE ANDRE-LINE, GRANBY, QC, J2J 1E2
(450) 777-1041   *SIC 2752*

GILMORE PRINTING SERVICES INC   p624
110 HERZBERG RD, KANATA, ON, K2K 3B7
(613) 599-3776   *SIC 2752*

HURONWEB OFFSET PRINTING INC   p1037
395 BROADWAY ST, WYOMING, ON, N0N 1T0
(519) 845-0821   *SIC 2752*

IMPRESSION PARAGRAPH INC   p1334
8150 RTE TRANSCANADIENNE BUREAU 100, SAINT-LAURENT, QC, H4S 1M5
(514) 735-7770   *SIC 2752*

IMPRIMERIE DUMAINE INC   p1313
5350 AV TRUDEAU, SAINT-HYACINTHE, QC, J2S 7Y8
(450) 774-3536   *SIC 2752*

IMPRIMERIE L'EMPREINTE INC   p1234
4177 BOUL INDUSTRIEL, MONTREAL, QC, H7L 0G7
(514) 331-0741   *SIC 2752*

IMPRIMERIE SOLISCO INC   p1366
120 10E RUE, SCOTT, QC, G0S 3G0
(418) 387-8908   *SIC 2752*

IMPRIMERIES TRANSCONTINENTAL 2005 S.E.N.C   p1162
8000 AV BLAISE-PASCAL, MONTREAL, QC, H1E 2S7
SIC 2752

IMPRIMERIES TRANSCONTINENTAL 2005 S.E.N.C.   p1105
1 PLACE VILLE-MARIE BUREAU 3240, MONTREAL, QC, H3B 0G1
(514) 954-4000   *SIC 2752*

IMPRIMERIES TRANSCONTINENTAL INC   p35
5516 5 ST SE, CALGARY, AB, T2H 1L3
(403) 258-3788   *SIC 2752*

IMPRIMERIES TRANSCONTINENTAL INC   p206
725 HAMPSTEAD CLOSE, DELTA, BC, V3M 6R6
(604) 540-2333   *SIC 2752*

IMPRIMERIES TRANSCONTINENTAL INC   p372
1615 INKSTER BLVD, WINNIPEG, MB, R2X 1R2
(204) 988-9476   *SIC 2752*

IMPRIMERIES TRANSCONTINENTAL INC   p481
275 WELLINGTON ST E, AURORA, ON, L4G 6J9
(905) 841-4400   *SIC 2752*

IMPRIMERIES TRANSCONTINENTAL INC   p835
1590 20TH ST E, OWEN SOUND, ON, N4K 5R2
(519) 371-5171   *SIC 2752*

IMPRIMERIES TRANSCONTINENTAL INC   p1055
150 181E RUE, BEAUCEVILLE, QC, G5X 3P3
(418) 774-3367   *SIC 2752*

IMPRIMERIES TRANSCONTINENTAL INC   p1065
1603 BOUL DE MONTARVILLE, BOUCHERVILLE, QC, J4B 5Y2
(450) 655-2801   *SIC 2752*

IMPRIMERIES TRANSCONTINENTAL INC   p1132
999 AV 90E, LASALLE, QC, H8R 3A4
(514) 861-2411   *SIC 2752*

IMPRIMERIES TRANSCONTINENTAL INC   p1205
1 PLACE VILLE-MARIE UNITE 3240, MONTREAL, QC, H3B 3Y2
(514) 954-4000   *SIC 2752*

IMPRIMERIES TRANSCONTINENTAL INC   p1313
2700 BOUL CASAVANT O, SAINT-HYACINTHE, QC, J2S 7S4
(450) 773-0289   *SIC 2752*

IMPRIMERIES TRANSCONTINENTAL INC   p1373
4001 BOUL DE PORTLAND, SHER-

BROOKE, QC, J1L 1X9
(819) 563-4001   *SIC 2752*
KROMAR PRINTING LTD   *p382*
725 PORTAGE AVE, WINNIPEG, MB, R3G
0M8
(204) 775-8721   *SIC 2752*
LOWE-MARTIN COMPANY INC   *p732*
5990 FALBOURNE ST, MISSISSAUGA, ON,
L5R 3S7
(905) 507-8782   *SIC 2752*
LOWE-MARTIN COMPANY INC   *p827*
400 HUNT CLUB RD, OTTAWA, ON, K1V
1C1
(613) 741-0962   *SIC 2752*
M & T INSTA-PRINT LIMITED   *p635*
907 FREDERICK ST SUITE 4, KITCH-
ENER, ON, N2B 2B9
(519) 571-0101   *SIC 2752*
M & T INSTA-PRINT LIMITED   *p661*
318 NEPTUNE CRES SUITE 1, LONDON,
ON, N6M 1A1
(519) 455-6667   *SIC 2752*
MARACLE PRESS LIMITED   *p813*
1156 KING ST E, OSHAWA, ON, L1H 1H8
(905) 723-3438   *SIC 2752*
MEDIAS TRANSCONTINENTAL S.E.N.C.
p1276
2850 RUE JEAN-PERRIN, QUEBEC, QC,
G2C 2C8
    SIC 2752
MERRILL CORPORATION CANADA   *p939*
3000-1 ADELAIDE ST E, TORONTO, ON,
M5C 2V9
(416) 214-2448   *SIC 2752*
MI5 DIGITAL COMMUNICATIONS INC   *p703*
1550 CATERPILLAR RD, MISSISSAUGA,
ON, L4X 1E7
(905) 848-1550   *SIC 2752*
MILLENIUM PRINTING INC   *p556*
139 BASALTIC RD, CONCORD, ON, L4K
1G4
(905) 760-5522   *SIC 2752*
MITCHELL PRESS LIMITED   *p181*
8328 RIVERBEND CRT, BURNABY, BC,
V3N 5C9
(604) 528-9882   *SIC 2752*
MM&T PACKAGING COMPANY   *p697*
5485 TOMKEN RD, MISSISSAUGA, ON,
L4W 3Y3
(800) 651-5951   *SIC 2752*
MOORE CANADA CORPORATION   *p777*
180 BOND AVE, NORTH YORK, ON, M3B
3P3
(416) 445-8800   *SIC 2752*
PARKER PAD AND PRINTING LIMITED *p678*
208 TRAVAIL RD, MARKHAM, ON, L3S 3J1
(905) 294-7997   *SIC 2752*
PENTAGON GRAPHICS LTD   *p1252*
271 AV LABROSSE, POINTE-CLAIRE, QC,
H9R 1A3
(514) 339-5995   *SIC 2752*
PHIPPS DICKSON INTEGRIA (PDI) INC
p1118
18103 RTE TRANSCANADIENNE, KIRK-
LAND, QC, H9J 3Z4
(514) 695-1333   *SIC 2752*
POINTONE GRAPHICS INC   *p575*
14 VANSCO RD, ETOBICOKE, ON, M8Z
5J4
(416) 255-8202   *SIC 2752*
PREMIER PRINTING LTD   *p366*
1 BEGHIN AVE, WINNIPEG, MB, R2J 3X5
(204) 663-9000   *SIC 2752*
PRINTING HOUSE LIMITED, THE   *p973*
1403 BATHURST ST, TORONTO, ON, M5R
3H8
(416) 536-6113   *SIC 2752*
PRINTWORKS LTD   *p116*
3850 98 ST NW, EDMONTON, AB, T6E 3L2
(780) 452-8921   *SIC 2752*
PROLIFIC GRAPHICS INC   *p372*
150 WYATT RD, WINNIPEG, MB, R2X 2X6
(204) 694-2300   *SIC 2752*
ROS-MAR INC   *p1054*

19500 AV CLARK-GRAHAM, BAIE-
D'URFE, QC, H9X 3R8
(514) 694-2178   *SIC 2752*
ROS-MAR LITHO INC   *p1054*
19500 AV CLARK-GRAHAM, BAIE-
D'URFE, QC, H9X 3R8
(514) 694-2178   *SIC 2752*
**RR DONELLEY CANADA FINANCIAL COM-
PANY**   *p780*
60 GERVAIS DR, NORTH YORK, ON, M3C
1Z3
(416) 445-8800   *SIC 2752*
SENTON INCORPORATED   *p650*
1669 OXFORD ST E, LONDON, ON, N5V
2Z5
(519) 455-5500   *SIC 2752*
ST JOSEPH PRINT GROUP INC   *p595*
1165 KENASTON ST, GLOUCESTER, ON,
K1B 3N9
(613) 729-4303   *SIC 2752*
ST. JOSEPH CORPORATION   *p558*
50 MACINTOSH BLVD, CONCORD, ON,
L4K 4P3
(905) 660-3111   *SIC 2752*
ST. JOSEPH PRINT GROUP INC   *p775*
135 RAILSIDE RD, NORTH YORK, ON,
M3A 1B7
(613) 746-4005   *SIC 2752*
ST. JOSEPH PRINTING LIMITED   *p559*
50 MACINTOSH BLVD, CONCORD, ON,
L4K 4P3
(905) 660-3111   *SIC 2752*
ST. JOSEPH PRINTING LIMITED   *p791*
15 BENTON RD, NORTH YORK, ON, M6M
3G2
(416) 248-4868   *SIC 2752*
STRUCTO NORTH AMERICA INC   *p996*
200 EVANS AVE UNIT 11, TORONTO, ON,
M8Z 1J7
(877) 787-8286   *SIC 2752*
SYMCOR INC   *p700*
1625 TECH AVE, MISSISSAUGA, ON, L4W
5P5
(289) 360-2000   *SIC 2752*
TELDON MEDIA GROUP INC   *p256*
12751 VULCAN WAY SUITE 100, RICH-
MOND, BC, V6V 3C8
(604) 231-3454   *SIC 2752*
THISTLE PRINTING LIMITED   *p916*
35 MOBILE DR, TORONTO, ON, M4A 2P6
(416) 288-1288   *SIC 2752*
TI GROUP INC   *p919*
115 THORNCLIFFE PARK DR, TORONTO,
ON, M4H 1M1
(416) 696-2853   *SIC 2752*
TORSTAR CORPORATION   *p943*
1 YONGE ST, TORONTO, ON, M5E 1E5
(416) 869-4010   *SIC 2752*
TORSTAR CORPORATION   *p984*
590 KING ST W SUITE 400, TORONTO,
ON, M5V 1M3
    SIC 2752
TRADE SECRET PRINTING INC   *p576*
40 HORNER AVE, ETOBICOKE, ON, M8Z
4X3
(416) 231-9660   *SIC 2752*
TRANSCONTINENTAL INC   *p459*
11 RAGGED LAKE BLVD, HALIFAX, NS,
B3S 1R3
(902) 450-5611   *SIC 2752*
TRI-CO GROUP INC, THE   *p831*
47-B ANTARES DR, OTTAWA, ON, K2E
7W6
(613) 736-7777   *SIC 2752*
UNICOM GRAPHICS LIMITED   *p32*
4501 MANITOBA RD SE, CALGARY, AB,
T2G 4B9
(403) 287-2020   *SIC 2752*
WEST CANADIAN DIGITAL IMAGING INC
p32
1601 9 AVE SE SUITE 200, CALGARY, AB,
T2G 0H4
(403) 245-2555   *SIC 2752*
WEST STAR PRINTING LIMITED   *p576*

10 NORTH QUEEN ST, ETOBICOKE, ON,
M8Z 2C4
(416) 201-0881   *SIC 2752*
WESTROCK PACKAGING COMPANY   *p690*
3270 AMERICAN DR, MISSISSAUGA, ON,
L4V 1B5
(905) 677-3592   *SIC 2752*

SIC 2754 Commercial printing, gravure

407994 ONTARIO LIMITED   *p885*
417 LAKESHORE RD, ST CATHARINES,
ON, L2R 7K6
(905) 646-6247   *SIC 2754*
BOMBARDIER INC   *p631*
1059 TAYLOR-KIDD BLVD, KINGSTON, ON,
K7M 6J9
(613) 384-3100   *SIC 2754*
ELOPAK CANADA INC   *p1061*
3720 AV DES GRANDES TOURELLES,
BOISBRIAND, QC, J7H 0A1
(450) 970-2846   *SIC 2754*
SAULT STAR, LIMITED   *p862*
145 OLD GARDEN RIVER RD, SAULT STE.
MARIE, ON, P6A 5M5
(705) 759-3030   *SIC 2754*

SIC 2759 Commercial printing, nec

9220-9147 QUEBEC INC   *p1381*
355 RUE GEORGE-VI, TERREBONNE, QC,
J6Y 1N9
(450) 621-4856   *SIC 2759*
ACORN PACKAGING INC   *p708*
563 QUEENSWAY E UNIT B, MISSIS-
SAUGA, ON, L5A 3X6
(905) 279-5256   *SIC 2759*
AMPCO MANUFACTURERS INC   *p199*
9 BURBIDGE ST UNIT 101, COQUITLAM,
BC, V3K 7B2
    SIC 2759
AMPCO MANUFACTURERS INC   *p199*
9 BURBIDGE ST SUITE 101, COQUITLAM,
BC, V3K 7B2
(604) 472-3800   *SIC 2759*
ASL PRINT FX LTD   *p1029*
1 ROYAL GATE BLVD UNIT A, WOOD-
BRIDGE, ON, L4L 8Z7
(416) 798-7310   *SIC 2759*
ASTLEY GILBERT LIMITED   *p787*
42 CARNFORTH RD, NORTH YORK, ON,
M4A 2K7
(416) 288-8666   *SIC 2759*
BRANT INSTORE CORPORATION   *p515*
254 HENRY ST, BRANTFORD, ON, N3S
7R5
(800) 265-8480   *SIC 2759*
BRANT INSTORE CORPORATION   *p516*
555 GREENWICH ST, BRANTFORD, ON,
N3T 5T3
(519) 759-4361   *SIC 2759*
BRAR CAPITAL CORP   *p796*
2320 BRISTOL CIR UNIT 3, OAKVILLE, ON,
L6H 5S3
(905) 844-1291   *SIC 2759*
**BROADRIDGE CUSTOMER COMMUNICA-
TIONS CANADA, ULC**   *p667*
2601 14TH AVE, MARKHAM, ON, L3R 0H9
(905) 470-2000   *SIC 2759*
C2 MEDIA CANADA ULC   *p253*
14291 BURROWS RD, RICHMOND, BC,
V6V 1K9
(604) 270-4000   *SIC 2759*
**CANADIAN BANK NOTE COMPANY, LIM-
ITED**   *p828*
145 RICHMOND RD, OTTAWA, ON, K1Z
1A1
(613) 722-3421   *SIC 2759*
**CANADIAN BANK NOTE COMPANY, LIM-
ITED**   *p828*
975 GLADSTONE AVE, OTTAWA, ON, K1Y
4W5

(613) 722-3421   *SIC 2759*
COWAN GRAPHICS INC   *p109*
4864 93 AVE NW, EDMONTON, AB, T6B
2P8
(780) 577-5700   *SIC 2759*
**DATA COMMUNICATIONS MANAGEMENT
CORP**   *p72*
1311 9 AVE SW SUITE 300, CALGARY, AB,
T3C 0H9
(403) 272-7440   *SIC 2759*
**DATA COMMUNICATIONS MANAGEMENT
CORP**   *p738*
80 AMBASSADOR DR, MISSISSAUGA,
ON, L5T 2Y9
(905) 696-8884   *SIC 2759*
DESCHAMPS IMPRESSION INC   *p1255*
755 BOUL DES CHUTES, QUEBEC, QC,
G1E 2C2
(418) 667-3322   *SIC 2759*
EPC INDUSTRIES LIMITED   *p438*
12 TUPPER BLVD, AMHERST, NS, B4H
4S7
(902) 667-7241   *SIC 2759*
FD ALPHA CANADA ACQUISITION INC
p644
128 OAK ST W, LEAMINGTON, ON, N8H
2B6
(519) 326-3173   *SIC 2759*
GILMORE, R. E. INVESTMENTS CORP *p624*
120 HERZBERG RD, KANATA, ON, K2K
3B7
(613) 592-2944   *SIC 2759*
GROUPE LELYS INC   *p1362*
3275 AV FRANCIS-HUGHES, SAINTE-
ROSE, QC, H7L 5A5
(450) 662-7161   *SIC 2759*
IDEE PRO INC   *p1259*
54 RUE DE LA POINTE-AUX-LIEVRES,
QUEBEC, QC, G1K 5Y3
(418) 522-4455   *SIC 2759*
INSTIMAX CORPORATION   *p23*
901 CENTRE ST NW UNIT 303, CALGARY,
AB, T2E 2P6
(403) 398-8911   *SIC 2759*
INTERGRAPHICS DECAL LIMITED   *p365*
180 DE BAETS ST, WINNIPEG, MB, R2J
3W6
(204) 958-9570   *SIC 2759*
MCCALLUM PRINTING GROUP INC   *p86*
11755 108 AVE NW, EDMONTON, AB, T5H
1B8
(780) 455-8885   *SIC 2759*
MIDDLETON GROUP INC   *p672*
75 DENISON ST SUITE 6, MARKHAM, ON,
L3R 1B5
(905) 475-6556   *SIC 2759*
MIRAZED INC   *p1308*
3715 BOUL LOSCH, SAINT-HUBERT, QC,
J3Y 5T7
(450) 656-6320   *SIC 2759*
MOORE CANADA CORPORATION   *p1216*
1500 RUE SAINT-PATRICK, MONTREAL,
QC, H3K 0A3
(514) 415-7300   *SIC 2759*
MULTIPAK LTEE   *p689*
6417 VISCOUNT RD, MISSISSAUGA, ON,
L4V 1K8
    SIC 2759
POLLARD EQUITIES LIMITED   *p5*
GD STN MAIN, BARRHEAD, AB, T7N 1B8
(780) 674-4750   *SIC 2759*
PRIME GRAPHIC RESOURCES LTD   *p186*
3988 STILL CREEK AVE, BURNABY, BC,
V5C 6N9
(604) 437-5800   *SIC 2759*
PRODUITS LABELINK INC, LES   *p1050*
9201 RUE CLAVEAU, ANJOU, QC, H1J 2C8
(514) 328-1887   *SIC 2759*
QSG INC   *p1335*
8102 RTE TRANSCANADIENNE, SAINT-
LAURENT, QC, H4S 1M5
(514) 744-1000   *SIC 2759*
SERIGRAPHIE RICHFORD INC   *p1252*
2001 BOUL DES SOURCES BUREAU 101,

POINTE-CLAIRE, QC, H9R 5Z4
(514) 426-8700   SIC 2759

SMART ENTERPRISES CORPORATION
p506
7956 TORBRAM RD UNIT 25, BRAMPTON, ON, L6T 5A2
(416) 798-0168   SIC 2759

SOCIETE QUEBECOISE D'INFORMATION JURIDIQUE   *p1190*
715 RUE DU SQUARE-VICTORIA BUREAU 600, MONTREAL, QC, H2Y 2H7
(514) 842-8741   SIC 2759

SONOCO FLEXIBLE PACKAGING CANADA CORPORATION   *p392*
1664 SEEL AVE, WINNIPEG, MB, R3T 4X5
SIC 2759

SOUTHERN ALBERTA WEB PRINTERS
p147
3257 DUNMORE RD SE, MEDICINE HAT, AB, T1B 3R2
(403) 528-5674   SIC 2759

SUNWEST SCREEN GRAPHICS LTD   *p386*
277 CREE CRES, WINNIPEG, MB, R3J 3X4
(204) 888-0003   SIC 2759

TASUS CANADA CORPORATION   *p608*
41A BROCKLEY DR UNIT 1, HAMILTON, ON, L8E 3C3
(905) 560-1337   SIC 2759

TLTC HOLDINGS INC   *p227*
6270 205 ST, LANGLEY, BC, V2Y 1N7
(604) 533-3294   SIC 2759

TRANS-SOL AVIATION SERVICE INC *p1278*
230 2E AV DE L'AEROPORT, QUEBEC, QC, G2G 2T2
(418) 877-6708   SIC 2759

TVA PUBLICATIONS INC   *p1244*
7 CH BATES, OUTREMONT, QC, H2V 4V7
(514) 848-7000   SIC 2759

WINDSOR STAR PRINT PLANT   *p1020*
3000 STARWAY AVE, WINDSOR, ON, N8W 5P1
(519) 255-5730   SIC 2759

SIC 2761 Manifold business forms

2619473 ONTARIO INC   *p758*
8481 EARL THOMAS AVE, NIAGARA FALLS, ON, L2G 0B5
(905) 358-0699   SIC 2761

ALL TRADE COMPUTER FORMS INC *p737*
60 ADMIRAL BLVD, MISSISSAUGA, ON, L5T 2W1
SIC 2761

DATA COMMUNICATIONS MANAGEMENT CORP   *p499*
9195 TORBRAM RD, BRAMPTON, ON, L6S 6H2
(905) 791-3151   SIC 2761

DATA COMMUNICATIONS MANAGEMENT CORP   *p1098*
1750 RUE JEAN-BERCHMANS-MICHAUD, DRUMMONDVILLE, QC, J2C 7S2
(819) 472-1111   SIC 2761

DATA COMMUNICATIONS MANAGEMENT CORP   *p1110*
855 BOUL INDUSTRIEL, GRANBY, QC, J2J 1A6
SIC 2761

MOORE CANADA CORPORATION   *p102*
18330 102 AVE NW, EDMONTON, AB, T5S 2J9
(780) 452-5592   SIC 2761

MOORE CANADA CORPORATION   *p590*
650 VICTORIA TERR, FERGUS, ON, N1M 1G7
(519) 843-2510   SIC 2761

MOORE CANADA CORPORATION   *p999*
8 DOUGLAS RD, TRENTON, ON, K8V 5R4
(613) 392-1205   SIC 2761

NEBS BUSINESS PRODUCTS LIMITED
p681
330 CRANSTON CRES, MIDLAND, ON, L4R 4V9

(705) 526-4233   SIC 2761

SIC 2771 Greeting cards

COUTTS, WILLIAM E. COMPANY, LIMITED
p668
3762 14TH AVE UNIT 100, MARKHAM, ON, L3R 0G7
(416) 492-1300   SIC 2771

FOREST CITY GRAPHICS LIMITED   *p661*
982 HUBREY RD, LONDON, ON, N6N 1B5
(519) 668-2191   SIC 2771

SIC 2782 Blankbooks and looseleaf binders

COMPAGNIE D'ECHANTILLONS NATIONAL LIMITEE   *p1161*
11500 BOUL ARMAND-BOMBARDIER, MONTREAL, QC, H1E 2W9
(514) 648-4000   SIC 2782

DAVIS GROUP OF COMPANIES CORP *p669*
25 RIVIERA DR SUITE 7, MARKHAM, ON, L3R 8N4
(905) 477-7440   SIC 2782

GROSNOR INDUSTRIES INC   *p584*
375 REXDALE BLVD, ETOBICOKE, ON, M9W 1R9
(416) 744-2011   SIC 2782

MOORE CANADA CORPORATION   *p732*
333 FOSTER CRES SUITE 2, MISSISSAUGA, ON, L5R 3Z9
(905) 890-1080   SIC 2782

MOORE CANADA CORPORATION   *p1050*
11150 AV L.-J.-FORGET, ANJOU, QC, H1J 2K9
(514) 353-9090   SIC 2782

PRODESIGN LIMITED   *p587*
375 REXDALE BLVD, ETOBICOKE, ON, M9W 1R9
(416) 744-2011   SIC 2782

TRIMSEAL PLASTICS LTD   *p257*
3511 JACOMBS RD, RICHMOND, BC, V6V 1Z8
(604) 278-3803   SIC 2782

VENTES ALLAJOY LTEE   *p1051*
8301 RUE J.-RENE-OUIMET, ANJOU, QC, H1J 2H7
(514) 374-9010   SIC 2782

SIC 2789 Bookbinding and related work

EDICIBLE LTEE   *p1333*
2825 RUE BRABANT-MARINEAU, SAINT-LAURENT, QC, H4S 1R8
(514) 336-0710   SIC 2789

HOLMES PLASTIC BINDINGS LTD   *p671*
200 FERRIER ST, MARKHAM, ON, L3R 2Z5
(905) 513-6211   SIC 2789

MARWICK MANUFACTURING INC   *p688*
6325 NORTHWEST DR, MISSISSAUGA, ON, L4V 1P6
(905) 677-0677   SIC 2789

MULTI-RELIURE S.F. INC   *p1368*
2112 AV DE LA TRANSMISSION, SHAWINIGAN, QC, G9N 8N8
(819) 537-6008   SIC 2789

PACIFIC BINDERY SERVICES LTD   *p324*
870 KENT AVE SOUTH W, VANCOUVER, BC, V6P 6Y6
(604) 873-4291   SIC 2789

SPECIALTIES GRAPHIC FINISHERS LTD
p869
946 WARDEN AVE, SCARBOROUGH, ON, M1L 4C9
(416) 701-0111   SIC 2789

STORESUPPORT CANADA INC   *p727*
2000 ARGENTIA RD SUITE 440, MISSISSAUGA, ON, L5N 1P7
(905) 847-6513   SIC 2789

TIP TOP BINDERY LTD   *p877*
335 PASSMORE AVE, SCARBOROUGH,

ON, M1V 4B5
(416) 609-3281   SIC 2789

USINE TAC TIC INC, L'   *p1305*
2030 127E RUE, SAINT-GEORGES, QC, G5Y 2W8
(418) 227-4279   SIC 2789

SIC 2791 Typesetting

SAJY COMMUNICATIONS INC   *p1052*
7070 RUE BEAUBIEN E, ANJOU, QC, H1M 1B2
(514) 521-4301   SIC 2791

SIC 2796 Platemaking services

CANADIAN BANK NOTE COMPANY, LIMITED   *p748*
18 AURIGA DR, NEPEAN, ON, K2E 7T9
(613) 722-3421   SIC 2796

SIC 2812 Alkalies and chlorine

CHEMTRADE ELECTROCHEM INC   *p46*
144 4 AVE SW SUITE 2100, CALGARY, AB, T2P 3N4
SIC 2812

CHEMTRADE ELECTROCHEM INC   *p238*
100 AMHERST AVE, NORTH VANCOUVER, BC, V7H 1S4
(604) 929-1107   SIC 2812

SIC 2813 Industrial gases

AIR LIQUIDE CANADA INC   *p112*
10020 56 AVE NW, EDMONTON, AB, T6E 5Z2
(780) 434-2060   SIC 2813

AIR LIQUIDE CANADA INC   *p1201*
1250 BOUL RENE-LEVESQUE O BUREAU 1700, MONTREAL, QC, H3B 5E6
(514) 933-0303   SIC 2813

CARBON ENGINEERING LTD   *p269*
37321 GALBRAITH RD, SQUAMISH, BC, V8B 0A2
(778) 386-1457   SIC 2813

INVENTYS THERMAL TECHNOLOGIES INC   *p192*
8528 GLENLYON PKY UNIT 143, BURNABY, BC, V5J 0B6
(604) 456-0504   SIC 2813

K-G SPRAY-PAK INC   *p554*
8001 KEELE ST, CONCORD, ON, L4K 1Y8
(905) 669-9855   SIC 2813

PRAXAIR CANADA INC   *p505*
80 WESTCREEK BLVD UNIT 1, BRAMPTON, ON, L6T 0B8
(905) 595-3788   SIC 2813

PRAXAIR CANADA INC   *p710*
1 CITY CENTRE DR SUITE 1200, MISSISSAUGA, ON, L5B 1M2
(905) 803-1600   SIC 2813

PRAXAIR CANADA INC   *p1429*
834 51ST ST E SUITE 5, SASKATOON, SK, S7K 5C7
(306) 242-3325   SIC 2813

SIC 2816 Inorganic pigments

2946-4617 QUEBEC INC   *p1324*
393A AV SAINTE-CROIX, SAINT-LAURENT, QC, H4N 2L3
SIC 2816

AMPACET CANADA COMPANY   *p636*
101 SASAGA DR, KITCHENER, ON, N2C 2G8
(519) 748-5576   SIC 2816

CHEMOURS CANADA COMPANY, THE*p721*

2233 ARGENTIA RD UNIT 402, MISSISSAUGA, ON, L5N 2X7
(905) 816-2310   SIC 2816

DOMINION COLOUR CORPORATION *p474*
445 FINLEY AVE, AJAX, ON, L1S 2E2
(905) 683-0231   SIC 2816

DOMINION COLOUR CORPORATION *p570*
199 NEW TORONTO ST, ETOBICOKE, ON, M8V 3X4
(416) 253-4260   SIC 2816

DOMINION COLOUR CORPORATION *p767*
515 CONSUMERS RD UNIT 700, NORTH YORK, ON, M2J 4Z2
(416) 791-4200   SIC 2816

KRONOS CANADA INC   *p1205*
1255 BOUL ROBERT-BOURASSA BUREAU 1102, MONTREAL, QC, H3B 3W7
(514) 397-3501   SIC 2816

KRONOS CANADA INC   *p1393*
3390 RTE MARIE-VICTORIN, VARENNES, QC, J3X 1P7
(450) 929-5000   SIC 2816

PRODUITS CHIMIQUES G.H. LTEE   *p1314*
1550 RUE BROUILLETTE, SAINT-HYACINTHE, QC, J2T 2G8
(450) 774-9151   SIC 2816

RIO TINTO GESTION CANADA INC   *p1208*
1190 AV DES CANADIENS-DE-MONTREAL BUREAU 400, MONTREAL, QC, H3B 0E3
(514) 288-8400   SIC 2816

ZOCHEM ULC   *p507*
1 TILBURY CRT, BRAMPTON, ON, L6T 3T4
(905) 453-4100   SIC 2816

SIC 2819 Industrial inorganic chemicals, nec

ARKEMA CANADA INC   *p1055*
655 BOUL ALPHONSE-DESHAIES, BECANCOUR, QC, G9H 2Y8
(819) 294-9965   SIC 2819

ATOMIC ENERGY OF CANADA LIMITED
p354
GD, PINAWA, MB, R0E 1L0
(204) 753-2311   SIC 2819

ATOMIC ENERGY OF CANADA LIMITED
p913
GD, TIVERTON, ON, N0G 2T0
SIC 2819

AXENS CANADA SPECIALTY ALUMINAS INC   *p519*
4000 DEVELOPMENT DR, BROCKVILLE, ON, K6V 5V5
(613) 342-7462   SIC 2819

BORDER CHEMICAL COMPANY LIMITED
p385
2147 PORTAGE AVE, WINNIPEG, MB, R3J 0L4
(204) 837-1383   SIC 2819

BWXT NUCLEAR ENERGY CANADA INC
p840
1160 MONAGHAN RD, PETERBOROUGH, ON, K9J 0A8
(855) 696-9588   SIC 2819

CANADIAN NUCLEAR LABORATORIES LTD   *p541*
286 PLANT RD, CHALK RIVER, ON, K0J 1J0
(613) 584-3311   SIC 2819

CEDA INTERNATIONAL CORPORATION
p39
11012 MACLEOD TRAIL SE SUITE 625, CALGARY, AB, T2J 6A5
(403) 253-3233   SIC 2819

CELANESE CANADA ULC   *p1064*
50 BOUL MARIE-VICTORIN BUREAU 100, BOUCHERVILLE, QC, J4B 1V5
(450) 655-0396   SIC 2819

CEPSA CHIMIE BECANCOUR INC   *p1056*
5250 BOUL BECANCOUR, BECANCOUR, QC, G9H 3X3
(819) 294-1414   SIC 2819

CHEMTRADE LOGISTICS INC   *p764*

155 GORDON BAKER RD UNIT 300, NORTH YORK, ON, M2H 3N5
(416) 496-5856   *SIC 2819*
CHEMTRADE LOGISTICS INCOME FUND   *p765*
155 GORDON BAKER RD SUITE 300, NORTH YORK, ON, M2H 3N5
(416) 496-5856   *SIC 2819*
CLEARTECH INDUSTRIES INC   *p105*
12720 INLAND WAY NW, EDMONTON, AB, T5V 1K2
(800) 387-7503   *SIC 2819*
CLEARTECH INDUSTRIES INC   *p1426*
1500 QUEBEC AVE, SASKATOON, SK, S7K 1V7
(306) 664-2522   *SIC 2819*
CRITERION CATALYSTS & TECHNOLO-GIES CANADA, INC   *p118*
5241 CALGARY TRAIL NW UNIT 810, ED-MONTON, AB, T6H 5G8
(780) 438-4188   *SIC 2819*
CYTEC CANADA INC   *p760*
9061 GARNER RD, NIAGARA FALLS, ON, L2H 0Y2
(905) 356-9000   *SIC 2819*
DIGITAL SPECIALTY CHEMICALS LIMITED   *p866*
470 CORONATION DR, SCARBOROUGH, ON, M1E 4Y4
(416) 231-2991   *SIC 2819*
DOW CHEMICAL CANADA ULC   *p859*
GD LCD MAIN, SARNIA, ON, N7T 7H7
SIC 2819
EAGLEPICHER ENERGY PRODUCTS ULC   *p276*
13136 82A AVE, SURREY, BC, V3W 9Y6
(604) 543-4350   *SIC 2819*
ENERSUL INC   *p35*
7210 BLACKFOOT TRAIL SE, CALGARY, AB, T2H 1M5
(403) 253-5969   *SIC 2819*
ETHYL CANADA INC   *p522*
5045 SOUTH SERVICE RD SUITE 101, BURLINGTON, ON, L7L 5Y7
(905) 631-5470   *SIC 2819*
GCP CANADA INC   *p474*
294 CLEMENTS RD W, AJAX, ON, L1S 3C6
(905) 683-8561   *SIC 2819*
GCP CANADA INC   *p1132*
255 AV LAFLEUR, LASALLE, QC, H8R 3H4
(514) 366-3362   *SIC 2819*
GCP CANADA INC   *p1365*
42 RUE FABRE, SALABERRY-DE-VALLEYFIELD, QC, J6S 4K7
(450) 373-4224   *SIC 2819*
GUARDIAN CHEMICALS INC   *p168*
55202 825 HWY SUITE 155, STURGEON COUNTY, AB, T8L 5C1
(780) 998-3771   *SIC 2819*
INDUSTRIES HAGEN LTEE   *p1334*
3235 RUE GUENETTE, SAINT-LAURENT, QC, H4S 1N2
(514) 331-2818   *SIC 2819*
INNOPHOS CANADA, INC   *p711*
3265 WOLFEDALE RD, MISSISSAUGA, ON, L5C 1V8
(905) 270-9328   *SIC 2819*
LITHION POWER GROUP LTD   *p53*
333 7 AVE SW UNIT 970, CALGARY, AB, T2P 2Z1
(587) 349-5468   *SIC 2819*
MEGLOBAL CANADA ULC   *p130*
HWY 15 BAG 16, FORT SASKATCHEWAN, AB, T8L 2P4
(877) 885-7237   *SIC 2819*
MEGLOBAL CANADA ULC   *p154*
HWY 597 & PRENTISS RD, RED DEER, AB, T4N 6N1
SIC 2819
METALLURGIE SYCA INC   *p1299*
500 RUE PRINCIPALE, SAINT-DOMINIQUE, QC, J0H 1L0
(450) 261-0853   *SIC 2819*
MILLAR WESTERN INDUSTRIES LTD   *p96*

16640 111 AVE NW, EDMONTON, AB, T5M 2S5
(780) 486-8200   *SIC 2819*
NALCO CANADA CO.   *p530*
1055 TRUMAN ST, BURLINGTON, ON, L7R 3V7
(905) 633-1000   *SIC 2819*
NATIONAL SILICATES PARTNERSHIP *p575*
429 KIPLING AVE, ETOBICOKE, ON, M8Z 5C7
(416) 255-7771   *SIC 2819*
NEO PERFORMANCE MATERIALS ULC *p955*
121 KING ST W SUITE 1740, TORONTO, ON, M5H 3T9
(416) 367-8588   *SIC 2819*
NORCAN ALUMINUM INC   *p1066*
61 CH DU TREMBLAY, BOUCHERVILLE, QC, J4B 7L6
(450) 449-6207   *SIC 2819*
NORDION (CANADA) INC   *p625*
447 MARCH RD, KANATA, ON, K2K 1X8
(613) 592-2790   *SIC 2819*
OLIN CANADA ULC   *p1056*
675 BOUL ALPHONSE-DESHAIES, BE-CANCOUR, QC, G9H 2Y8
(819) 294-6633   *SIC 2819*
OLIN CANADA ULC   *p1198*
2020 BOUL ROBERT-BOURASSA BU-REAU 2190, MONTREAL, QC, H3A 2A5
(514) 397-6100   *SIC 2819*
PEROXYCHEM CANADA LTD   *p249*
2147 PRINCE GEORGE PULPMILL RD, PRINCE GEORGE, BC, V2K 5P5
(250) 561-4200   *SIC 2819*
SEKISUI DIAGNOSTICS P.E.I. INC   *p1041*
70 WATTS AVE SUITE 24, CHARLOTTE-TOWN, PE, C1E 2B9
(902) 566-1396   *SIC 2819*
SHAWINIGAN ALUMINIUM INC   *p1368*
1250 BOUL SAINT-SACREMENT, SHAW-INIGAN, QC, G9N 0E3
(819) 731-0644   *SIC 2819*
SHRADER CANADA LIMITED   *p805*
830 PROGRESS CRT, OAKVILLE, ON, L6L 6K1
(905) 847-0222   *SIC 2819*
SILICYCLE INC   *p1268*
2500 BOUL DU PARC-TECHNOLOGIQUE, QUEBEC, QC, G1P 4S6
(418) 874-0054   *SIC 2819*
SUPERIOR PLUS CORP   *p984*
200 WELLINGTON ST W SUITE 401, TORONTO, ON, M5V 3C7
(416) 345-8050   *SIC 2819*
SUPERIOR PLUS LP   *p578*
302 THE EAST MALL SUITE 200, ETOBI-COKE, ON, M9B 6C7
(416) 239-7111   *SIC 2819*
SUPERIOR PLUS LP   *p1102*
101 CH DONALDSON, GATINEAU, QC, J8L 3X3
(819) 986-1135   *SIC 2819*
SUPERIOR PLUS LP   *p1430*
GD STN MAIN, SASKATOON, SK, S7K 3J4
(306) 931-7767   *SIC 2819*
TECHNAKORD CHEMICAL INDUSTRIES INC   *p588*
5 MCLACHLAN DR, ETOBICOKE, ON, M9W 1E3
(416) 798-9898   *SIC 2819*
TERRA INTERNATIONAL (CANADA) INC *p564*
161 BICKFORD LINE, COURTRIGHT, ON, N0N 1H0
(519) 867-2739   *SIC 2819*
TORONTO RESEARCH CHEMICALS INC *p785*
2 BRISBANE RD, NORTH YORK, ON, M3J 2J8
(416) 665-9696   *SIC 2819*
UMICORE AUTOCAT CANADA CORP *p525*
4261 MAINWAY, BURLINGTON, ON, L7L 5N9

(905) 336-3424   *SIC 2819*
W. R. GRACE CANADA CORP   *p1365*
42 RUE FABRE, SALABERRY-DE-VALLEYFIELD, QC, J6S 4K7
(450) 373-4224   *SIC 2819*

SIC 2821 Plastics materials and resins

2525-7577 QUEBEC INC.   *p1233*
3050 BOUL INDUSTRIEL, MONTREAL, QC, H7L 4P7
SIC 2821
3M CANADA COMPANY   *p352*
400 ROUTE 100, MORDEN, MB, R6M 1Z9
(204) 822-6284   *SIC 2821*
ACR CANADA CORPORATION   *p364*
122 PAQUIN RD, WINNIPEG, MB, R2J 3V4
(204) 669-2345   *SIC 2821*
ALTE-REGO CORPORATION   *p582*
36 TIDEMORE AVE, ETOBICOKE, ON, M9W 5H4
(416) 740-3397   *SIC 2821*
AOC RESINS AND COATINGS COMPANY *p602*
38 ROYAL RD, GUELPH, ON, N1H 1G3
(519) 821-5180   *SIC 2821*
ARCHITECTURAL ORNAMENT INC   *p548*
55 BRADWICK DR, CONCORD, ON, L4K 1K5
SIC 2821
ARCLIN CANADA LTD   *p544*
56 WILLMOTT ST, COBOURG, ON, K9A 4S3
(905) 372-1896   *SIC 2821*
ATELIER DE TRI DES MATIERES PLAS-TIQUES RECYCLABLES DU QUEBEC INC *p1233*
3405 BOUL INDUSTRIEL, MONTREAL, QC, H7L 4S3
(450) 667-5347   *SIC 2821*
BASF CANADA INC   *p729*
100 MILVERTON DR UNIT 500, MISSIS-SAUGA, ON, L5R 4H1
(289) 360-1300   *SIC 2821*
BASF CANADA INC   *p729*
100 MILVERTON DR FLOOR 5, MISSIS-SAUGA, ON, L5R 4H1
(289) 360-1300   *SIC 2821*
CANAM PLASTICS 2000 INC   *p494*
30 HOLLAND DR, BOLTON, ON, L7E 1G6
(905) 951-6166   *SIC 2821*
CANPLEX PROFILES INC   *p848*
1 EASY ST, PORT PERRY, ON, L9L 1B2
(905) 985-2759   *SIC 2821*
CANUCK COMPOUNDERS INC   *p533*
180 SHELDON DR UNIT 12, CAMBRIDGE, ON, N1R 6V1
(519) 621-6521   *SIC 2821*
CELANESE CANADA ULC   *p87*
4405 101 AVE, EDMONTON, AB, T5J 2K1
(780) 468-0800   *SIC 2821*
CKF INC   *p227*
19978 57A AVE, LANGLEY, BC, V3A 6G6
(604) 530-9121   *SIC 2821*
CYRO CANADA INC   *p758*
6515 BARKER ST, NIAGARA FALLS, ON, L2G 1Y6
(905) 677-1388   *SIC 2821*
DIE-MOLD TOOL LIMITED   *p593*
82 TODD RD, GEORGETOWN, ON, L7G 4R7
(905) 877-3071   *SIC 2821*
DUREZ CANADA COMPANY LTD   *p591*
100 DUNLOP ST, FORT ERIE, ON, L2A 5M6
(905) 346-8700   *SIC 2821*
ENTREPRISE INDORAMA PTA MONTREAL S.E.C   *p1238*
10200 RUE SHERBROOKE E, MONTREAL-EST, QC, H1B 1B4
(514) 645-7887   *SIC 2821*
EURAMAX CANADA, INC   *p486*
26 LORENA ST, BARRIE, ON, L4N 4P4

(705) 728-7141   *SIC 2821*
EXO-S INC   *p1371*
2100 RUE KING O BUREAU 240, SHER-BROOKE, QC, J1J 2E8
(819) 346-3967   *SIC 2821*
FOAMEX CANADA INC   *p995*
415 EVANS AVE, TORONTO, ON, M8W 2T2
SIC 2821
GROTE INDUSTRIES CO.   *p1010*
95 BATHURST DR, WATERLOO, ON, N2V 1N2
(519) 884-4991   *SIC 2821*
GROUPE HAMELIN INC   *p1213*
1328 REDPATH CRES, MONTREAL, QC, H3G 2K2
(514) 934-5577   *SIC 2821*
HEXION CANADA INC   *p105*
12621 156 ST NW, EDMONTON, AB, T5V 1E1
(780) 447-1270   *SIC 2821*
HNA ACQUISITION ULC   *p1065*
50 BOUL MARIE-VICTORIN, BOUCHERVILLE, QC, J4B 1V5
(450) 655-0396   *SIC 2821*
ICON TECHNOLOGIES LTD   *p361*
925 ROBLIN BLVD E, WINKLER, MB, R6W 0N2
(204) 325-1081   *SIC 2821*
INDUSTRIES DE MOULAGE POLYCELL INC, LES   *p1109*
448 RUE EDOUARD, GRANBY, QC, J2G 3Z3
(450) 378-9093   *SIC 2821*
INDUSTRIES LECO INC   *p1329*
3235 RUE SARTELON, SAINT-LAURENT, QC, H4R 1E9
(514) 332-0535   *SIC 2821*
INGENIA POLYMERS CORP   *p517*
565 GREENWICH ST, BRANTFORD, ON, N3T 5M2
(519) 758-8941   *SIC 2821*
INGENIA POLYMERS CORP   *p767*
200 YORKLAND BLVD SUITE 605, NORTH YORK, ON, M2J 5C1
(416) 920-8100   *SIC 2821*
LEFKO PRODUITS DE PLASTIQUE INC *p1147*
1700 BOUL INDUSTRIEL, MAGOG, QC, J1X 4V9
(819) 843-9237   *SIC 2821*
MANSONVILLE PLASTICS (B.C.) LIMITED *p272*
19402 56 AVE, SURREY, BC, V3S 6K4
(604) 534-8626   *SIC 2821*
NOVA CHEMICALS (CANADA) LTD   *p154*
GD, RED DEER, AB, T4N 5E6
(403) 314-8611   *SIC 2821*
NOVA CHEMICALS (CANADA) LTD   *p563*
785 PETROLIA LINE RR 2, CORUNNA, ON, N0N 1G0
(519) 862-2911   *SIC 2821*
NOVA CHEMICALS CORPORATION   *p55*
1000 7 AVE SW SUITE 1000, CALGARY, AB, T2P 5L5
(403) 750-3600   *SIC 2821*
NOVA CHEMICALS CORPORATION   *p745*
510 MOORE LINE, MOORETOWN, ON, N0N 1M0
(519) 862-2961   *SIC 2821*
NYACK TECHNOLOGY INC   *p1318*
160 RUE VANIER, SAINT-JEAN-SUR-RICHELIEU, QC, J3B 3R4
(450) 245-0373   *SIC 2821*
OXY VINYLS CANADA CO   *p758*
8800 THOROLD TOWN LINE, NIAGARA FALLS, ON, L2E 6V9
(905) 357-3131   *SIC 2821*
PAPIERS C.C.T. INC   *p1057*
830 RUE SAINT-VIATEUR, BERTHIERVILLE, QC, J0K 1A0
(450) 836-3846   *SIC 2821*
PERFORMANCE SCIENCE MATERIALS COMPANY   *p563*
291 ALBERT ST, CORUNNA, ON, N0N 1G0

(519) 862-5700   *SIC 2821*
PLASTECH INC   *p1374*
370 RUE LEGER, SHERBROOKE, QC, J1L 1Y5
(819) 822-1590   *SIC 2821*
PLASTI-FAB LTD   *p9*
300-2891 SUNRIDGE WAY NE, CALGARY, AB, T1Y 7K7
(403) 569-4300   *SIC 2821*
PLASTI-FAB LTD   *p81*
802 MCCOOL ST, CROSSFIELD, AB, T0M 0S0
(403) 946-4576   *SIC 2821*
PLASTIQUES JOLIETTE   *p1134*
190 CH DES INDUSTRIES, LAVALTRIE, QC, J5T 3R2
SIC 2821
PLASTIQUES MULTICAP INC, LES   *p1234*
3232 RUE DELAUNAY, MONTREAL, QC, H7L 5E1
(450) 681-1661   *SIC 2821*
PLASTUBE INC   *p1111*
590 RUE SIMONDS S, GRANBY, QC, J2J 1E1
(450) 378-2633   *SIC 2821*
POLYONE CANADA INC   *p758*
940 CHIPPAWA CREEK RD, NIAGARA FALLS, ON, L2E 6S5
(905) 353-4200   *SIC 2821*
PORTOLA PACKAGING CANADA LTD.   *p263*
12431 HORSESHOE WAY, RICHMOND, BC, V7A 4X6
(604) 272-5000   *SIC 2821*
RBI PLASTIQUE INC   *p399*
6 AV CRABTREE, EDMUNDSTON, NB, E3V 3K5
(506) 739-9180   *SIC 2821*
REICHHOLD INDUSTRIES LIMITED   *p248*
50 DOUGLAS ST, PORT MOODY, BC, V3H 3L9
(604) 939-1181   *SIC 2821*
SILCOTECH NORTH AMERICA INC   *p495*
54 NIXON RD, BOLTON, ON, L7E 1W2
(905) 857-9998   *SIC 2821*
SPECTIS MOULDERS INC   *p353*
100 CEDAR DR, NIVERVILLE, MB, R0A 1E0
(204) 388-6700   *SIC 2821*
SPRINGFIELD INDUSTRIES LTD   *p364*
125 FURNITURE PARK, WINNIPEG, MB, R2G 1B9
SIC 2821
STYROCHEM CANADA LTEE   *p1054*
19250 AV CLARK-GRAHAM, BAIE-D'URFE, QC, H9X 3R8
(514) 457-3226   *SIC 2821*
TECHNOLOGIES GSC INC   *p1318*
160 RUE VANIER, SAINT-JEAN-SUR-RICHELIEU, QC, J3B 3R4
(450) 245-0373   *SIC 2821*
VALSPAR INC   *p562*
1915 SECOND ST W, CORNWALL, ON, K6H 5R6
(613) 932-8960   *SIC 2821*
WEGU MANUFACTURING INC   *p1015*
1707 HARBOUR ST, WHITBY, ON, L1N 9G6
(905) 668-2359   *SIC 2821*
WENTWORTH MOLD LTD   *p516*
156 ADAMS BLVD, BRANTFORD, ON, N3S 7V5
(519) 754-5400   *SIC 2821*
WILSONART CANADA ULC   *p1133*
385 AV LAFLEUR, LASALLE, QC, H8R 3H7
(514) 366-2710   *SIC 2821*

SIC 2822 Synthetic rubber

ABC CANADA TECHNOLOGY GROUP LTD *p1425*
1802 QUEBEC AVE, SASKATOON, SK, S7K 1W2
(306) 653-4303   *SIC 2822*
ARLANXEO CANADA INC   *p859*

1265 VIDAL ST S, SARNIA, ON, N7T 7M2
(519) 337-8251   *SIC 2822*
BAYER INC   *p859*
1265 VIDAL ST S, SARNIA, ON, N7T 7M2
(519) 337-8251   *SIC 2822*
ECOSYNTHETIX INC   *p526*
3365 MAINWAY SUITE 1, BURLINGTON, ON, L7M 1A6
(905) 335-5669   *SIC 2822*
INDUSTRIAL RUBBER SUPPLY (1995) LTD *p372*
55 DUNLOP AVE, WINNIPEG, MB, R2X 2V2
(204) 694-4444   *SIC 2822*
INVISTA COMPANY CANADA   *p563*
291 ALBERT ST, CORUNNA, ON, N0N 1G0
(519) 862-6881   *SIC 2822*
MULTIRIM INC   *p556*
226 JARDIN DR SUITE 7, CONCORD, ON, L4K 1Y1
(905) 669-3566   *SIC 2822*
NATIONAL RUBBER TECHNOLOGIES CORP   *p993*
394 SYMINGTON AVE, TORONTO, ON, M6N 2W3
(416) 657-1111   *SIC 2822*
NATIONAL RUBBER TECHNOLOGIES CORP   *p993*
35 CAWTHRA AVE, TORONTO, ON, M6N 5B3
(416) 657-1111   *SIC 2822*
NOVA CHEMICALS CORPORATION   *p9*
3620 32 ST NE, CALGARY, AB, T1Y 6G7
(403) 291-8444   *SIC 2822*
OLDCASTLE BUILDING PRODUCTS CANADA, INC *p1073*
2 AV D'INVERNESS, CANDIAC, QC, J5R 4W5
(450) 444-5214   *SIC 2822*
PPD HOLDING INC   *p1400*
400 RUE RAYMOND, WATERVILLE, QC, J0B 3H0
SIC 2822
PRODUITS DE CONSTRUCTION DERBY INC   *p1293*
160 RUE DES GRANDS-LACS, SAINT-AUGUSTIN-DE-DESMAURES, QC, G3A 2K1
(418) 878-6161   *SIC 2822*
SALFLEX POLYMERS LTD   *p795*
1925 WILSON AVE, NORTH YORK, ON, M9M 1A9
(416) 741-0273   *SIC 2822*

SIC 2824 Organic fibers, noncellulosic

NYLENE CANADA INC   *p479*
200 MCNAB ST, ARNPRIOR, ON, K7S 2C7
(613) 623-3191   *SIC 2824*
PIONEER HI-BRED LIMITED   *p726*
1919 MINNESOTA CRT, MISSISSAUGA, ON, L5N 0C9
(905) 821-3300   *SIC 2824*
VPC GROUP INC   *p785*
150 TORO RD, NORTH YORK, ON, M3J 2A9
(416) 630-6633   *SIC 2824*

SIC 2833 Medicinals and botanicals

AURORA CANNABIS INC   *p311*
1199 HASTINGS ST W SUITE 1500, VANCOUVER, BC, V6E 3T5
SIC 2833
DELMAR CHEMICALS INC   *p1132*
9321 RUE AIRLIE, LASALLE, QC, H8R 2B2
(514) 366-7950   *SIC 2833*
FACTORS GROUP OF NUTRITIONAL COMPANIES INC *p200*
1550 UNITED BLVD, COQUITLAM, BC, V3K 6Y2
(604) 777-1757   *SIC 2833*
FLOWR CORPORATION, THE   *p670*

100 ALLSTATE PKY SUITE 201, MARKHAM, ON, L3R 6H3
(905) 940-3993   *SIC 2833*
GFR PHARMA LTD   *p200*
65 NORTH BEND ST UNIT 65, COQUITLAM, BC, V3K 6N9
(604) 460-8440   *SIC 2833*
IOVATE HEALTH SCIENCES INTERNATIONAL INC *p806*
381 NORTH SERVICE RD W, OAKVILLE, ON, L6M 0H4
(905) 678-3119   *SIC 2833*
JAMIESON LABORATORIES LTD   *p927*
2 ST CLAIR AVE W, TORONTO, ON, M4V 1L5
(416) 960-0052   *SIC 2833*
JAMIESON WELLNESS INC   *p939*
1 ADELAIDE ST E SUITE 2200, TORONTO, ON, M5C 2V9
(833) 223-2666   *SIC 2833*
LIFE SCIENCE NUTRITIONALS INC   *p1044*
1190 RUE LEMAY, ACTON VALE, QC, J0H 1A0
(450) 546-0101   *SIC 2833*
MUSKOKA GROWN LIMITED   *p497*
50 KEITH RD UNIT A, BRACEBRIDGE, ON, P1L 0A1
(705) 645-2295   *SIC 2833*
RB HEALTH (CANADA) INC   *p699*
1680 TECH AVE UNIT 2, MISSISSAUGA, ON, L4W 5S9
(905) 283-7000   *SIC 2833*
RHEMA HEALTH PRODUCTS LIMITED *p244*
19055 AIRPORT WAY UNIT 601, PITT MEADOWS, BC, V3Y 0G4
(604) 516-0199   *SIC 2833*
SANTE NATURELLE A.G. LTEE   *p1070*
3555 BOUL MATTE, BROSSARD, QC, J4Y 2P4
(450) 659-7723   *SIC 2833*
SUPPLEMENTS AROMATIK INC   *p1393*
2334 RTE MARIE-VICTORIN BUREAU 87, VARENNES, QC, J3X 1R4
(450) 929-1933   *SIC 2833*
TILRAY CANADA LTD   *p235*
1100 MAUGHAN RD, NANAIMO, BC, V9X 1J2
(250) 722-3991   *SIC 2833*
UNITED NATURALS INC   *p289*
2416 MAIN ST UNIT 132, VANCOUVER, BC, V5T 3E2
(604) 999-9999   *SIC 2833*
VITA HEALTH PRODUCTS INC   *p367*
150 BEGHIN AVE, WINNIPEG, MB, R2J 3W2
(204) 661-8386   *SIC 2833*

SIC 2834 Pharmaceutical preparations

ACTAVIS PHARMA COMPANY   *p719*
6500 KITIMAT RD, MISSISSAUGA, ON, L5N 2B8
(905) 814-1820   *SIC 2834*
ADARE PHARMACEUTICALS, ULC   *p1158*
597 BOUL SIR-WILFRID-LAURIER, MONT-SAINT-HILAIRE, QC, J3H 6C4
(514) 774-2973   *SIC 2834*
ANI PHARMACEUTICALS CANADA INC *p796*
400 IROQUOIS SHORE RD, OAKVILLE, ON, L6H 1M5
(905) 337-4500   *SIC 2834*
APOPHARMA INC   *p792*
200 BARMAC DR, NORTH YORK, ON, M9L 2Z7
(416) 749-9300   *SIC 2834*
APOTEX FERMENTATION INC   *p393*
50 SCURFIELD BLVD, WINNIPEG, MB, R3Y 1G4
(204) 989-6830   *SIC 2834*
APOTEX INC   *p582*
50 STEINWAY BLVD SUITE 3, ETOBICOKE, ON, M9W 6Y3

(416) 675-0338   *SIC 2834*
APOTEX INC   *p792*
200 BARMAC DR, NORTH YORK, ON, M9L 2Z7
(800) 268-4623   *SIC 2834*
APOTEX INC   *p792*
285 GARYRAY DR, NORTH YORK, ON, M9L 1P2
(416) 749-9300   *SIC 2834*
APOTEX INC   *p855*
380 ELGIN MILLS RD E, RICHMOND HILL, ON, L4C 5H2
(905) 884-2050   *SIC 2834*
APOTEX INC   *p996*
150 SIGNET DR, TORONTO, ON, M9L 1T9
(416) 401-7328   *SIC 2834*
APOTEX PHARMACHEM INC   *p516*
11 SPALDING DR, BRANTFORD, ON, N3T 6B7
(519) 756-8942   *SIC 2834*
APOTEX PHARMACHEM INC   *p516*
34 SPALDING DR, BRANTFORD, ON, N3T 6B8
(519) 756-8942   *SIC 2834*
ARBUTUS BIOPHARMA CORPORATION *p191*
8900 GLENLYON PKY SUITE 100, BURNABY, BC, V5J 5J8
(604) 419-3200   *SIC 2834*
ASTRAZENECA CANADA INC   *p703*
1004 MIDDLEGATE RD SUITE 5000, MISSISSAUGA, ON, L4Y 1M4
(905) 277-7111   *SIC 2834*
BAUSCH HEALTH COMPANIES INC *p1361*
2150 BOUL SAINT-ELZEAR O, SAINTE-ROSE, QC, H7L 4A8
(514) 744-6792   *SIC 2834*
BAXTER CORPORATION   *p720*
7125 MISSISSAUGA RD, MISSISSAUGA, ON, L5N 0C2
(905) 369-6000   *SIC 2834*
BIMEDA-MTC ANIMAL HEALTH INC   *p537*
420 BEAVERDALE RD, CAMBRIDGE, ON, N3C 2W4
(519) 654-8000   *SIC 2834*
BIO AGRI MIX LP   *p745*
11 ELLENS ST, MITCHELL, ON, N0K 1N0
(519) 348-9865   *SIC 2834*
BIOSYENT INC   *p582*
170 ATTWELL DR SUITE 520, ETOBICOKE, ON, M9W 5Z5
(905) 206-0013   *SIC 2834*
BIOVECTRA INC   *p1040*
29 MCCARVILLE ST, CHARLOTTETOWN, PE, C1E 2A7
(902) 566-9116   *SIC 2834*
BIOVECTRA INC   *p1040*
11 AVIATION AVE, CHARLOTTETOWN, PE, C1E 0A1
(902) 566-9116   *SIC 2834*
BWXT ITG CANADA, INC   *p532*
581 CORONATION BLVD, CAMBRIDGE, ON, N1R 5V3
(613) 592-3400   *SIC 2834*
BWXT ITG CANADA, INC   *p832*
447 MARCH RD, OTTAWA, ON, K2K 1X8
(613) 592-3400   *SIC 2834*
C H R CENTRAL PRODUCTION PHARMACY   *p21*
1119 55 AVE NE, CALGARY, AB, T2E 6W1
SIC 2834
CANADIAN TEST CASE 145   *p730*
5770 HURONTARIO ST, MISSISSAUGA, ON, L5R 3G5
SIC 2834
CANNIMED LTD   *p1426*
RR 5 LCD MAIN, SASKATOON, SK, S7K 3J8
(306) 975-1207   *SIC 2834*
CANPEPTIDE INC   *p1249*
265 BOUL HYMUS BUREAU 1500, POINTE-CLAIRE, QC, H9R 1G6
(514) 697-2168   *SIC 2834*
CAPRION BIOSCIENCES INC   *p1185*

---

201 AV DU PRESIDENT-KENNEDY BUREAU 3900, MONTREAL, QC, H2X 3Y7
(514) 360-3600   SIC 2834
CHIEF MEDICAL SUPPLIES LTD p22
411 19 ST SE, CALGARY, AB, T2E 6J7
(403) 207-6034   SIC 2834
CHURCH & DWIGHT CANADA CORP p734
635 SECRETARIAT CRT, MISSISSAUGA, ON, L5S 0A5
(905) 696-6570   SIC 2834
CIPHER PHARMACEUTICALS INC p796
209 OAK PARK BLVD SUITE 501, OAKVILLE, ON, L6H 0M2
(905) 602-5840   SIC 2834
CONTRACT PHARMACEUTICALS LIMITED CANADA p721
7600 EAST DANBRO CRES, MISSISSAUGA, ON, L5N 6L6
(905) 821-7600   SIC 2834
CONTRACT PHARMACEUTICALS LIMITED CANADA p721
2145 MEADOWPINE BLVD 1ST FL, MISSISSAUGA, ON, L5N 6R8
(905) 821-7600   SIC 2834
CORPORATION ABBVIE p1333
8401 RTE TRANSCANADIENNE, SAINT-LAURENT, QC, H4S 1Z1
(514) 906-9700   SIC 2834
COVIDIEN CANADA ULC p1333
8455 RTE TRANSCANADIENNE, SAINT-LAURENT, QC, H4S 1Z1
(514) 332-1220   SIC 2834
DALTON CHEMICAL LABORATORIES INC p916
349 WILDCAT RD, TORONTO, ON, M3J 2S3
(416) 661-2102   SIC 2834
DERMA SCIENCES CANADA INC p873
104 SHORTING RD, SCARBOROUGH, ON, M1S 3S4
(416) 299-4003   SIC 2834
DERMOLAB PHARMA LTEE p1358
1421 RUE NOBEL, SAINTE-JULIE, QC, J3E 1Z4
(450) 649-8886   SIC 2834
DUCHESNAY INC p1059
950 BOUL MICHELE-BOHEC, BLAINVILLE, QC, J7C 5E2
(450) 433-7734   SIC 2834
ELI LILLY CANADA INC p870
3650 DANFORTH AVE, SCARBOROUGH, ON, M1N 2E8
(416) 694-3221   SIC 2834
ENTREPRISES IMPORTFAB INC p1250
50 BOUL HYMUS, POINTE-CLAIRE, QC, H9R 1C9
(514) 694-0721   SIC 2834
FAMAR MONTREAL INC p1250
3535 RTE TRANSCANADIENNE, POINTE-CLAIRE, QC, H9R 1B4
(514) 428-7488   SIC 2834
G PRODUCTION INC p1053
19400 AUT TRANSCANADIENNE, BAIE-D'URFE, QC, H9X 3S4
(514) 457-3366   SIC 2834
GILEAD ALBERTA ULC p124
1021 HAYTER RD NW, EDMONTON, AB, T6S 1A1
(780) 701-6400   SIC 2834
GLAXOSMITHKLINE INC p722
7333 MISSISSAUGA RD, MISSISSAUGA, ON, L5N 6L4
(905) 819-3000   SIC 2834
GLAXOSMITHKLINE INC p722
7333 MISSISSAUGA RD, MISSISSAUGA, ON, L5N 6L4
(905) 819-3000   SIC 2834
GLAXOSMITHKLINE INC p797
2030 BRISTOL CIR, OAKVILLE, ON, L6H 0H2
SIC 2834
GREEN CROSS BIOTHERAPEUTIQUES INC p1334
2911 AV MARIE-CURIE, SAINT-LAURENT,

QC, H4S 0B7
(514) 375-5800   SIC 2834
GROUPE PARIMA INC p1334
4450 RUE COUSENS, SAINT-LAURENT, QC, H4S 1X6
(514) 338-3780   SIC 2834
HALO PHARMACEUTICAL CANADA INC p1152
17800 RUE LAPOINTE, MIRABEL, QC, J7J 0W8
(450) 433-7673   SIC 2834
HERBALAND NATURALS INC p255
13330 MAYCREST WAY, RICHMOND, BC, V6V 2J7
(604) 284-5050   SIC 2834
HLS THERAPEUTICS INC p585
10 CARLSON CRT UNIT 701, ETOBICOKE, ON, M9W 6L2
(647) 495-9000   SIC 2834
HLS THERAPEUTICS INC p814
940 THORNTON RD S, OSHAWA, ON, L1J 7E2
(905) 725-5445   SIC 2834
HOFFMANN-LA ROCHE LIMITED p723
7070 MISSISSAUGA RD, MISSISSAUGA, ON, L5N 5M8
(800) 561-1759   SIC 2834
HOMEOCAN INC p1164
3025 BOUL DE L'ASSOMPTION, MONTREAL, QC, H1N 2H2
(514) 256-6303   SIC 2834
HYDRX FARMS LTD p1014
209 DUNDAS ST E, WHITBY, ON, L1N 5R7
(844) 493-7922   SIC 2834
JANSSEN INC p779
19 GREEN BELT DR, NORTH YORK, ON, M3C 1L9
(416) 449-9444   SIC 2834
JOHNSON & JOHNSON INC p605
890 WOODLAWN RD W, GUELPH, ON, N1K 1A5
SIC 2834
JOHNSON & JOHNSON INC p605
890 WOODLAWN RD W, GUELPH, ON, N1K 1A5
(519) 826-6226   SIC 2834
JUBILANT DRAXIMAGE INC p1117
16751 RTE TRANSCANADIENNE, KIRKLAND, QC, H9H 4J4
(514) 694-8220   SIC 2834
JUBILANT HOLLISTERSTIER GENERAL PARTNERSHIP p1117
16751 RTE TRANSCANADIENNE, KIRKLAND, QC, H9H 4J4
(514) 694-8220   SIC 2834
LABORATOIRE ATLAS INC p1049
9600 BOUL DES SCIENCES, ANJOU, QC, H1J 3B6
(514) 254-7188   SIC 2834
LABORATOIRE RIVA INC p1059
660 BOUL INDUSTRIEL, BLAINVILLE, QC, J7C 3V4
(450) 434-7482   SIC 2834
LABORATOIRES ABBOTT, LIMITEE p723
7115 MILLCREEK DR, MISSISSAUGA, ON, L5N 3R3
(905) 858-2450   SIC 2834
LABORATOIRES ABBOTT, LIMITEE p1335
8625 RTE TRANSCANADIENNE, SAINT-LAURENT, QC, H4S 1Z6
(514) 832-7000   SIC 2834
LABORATOIRES CONFAB INC p1308
4355 BOUL SIR-WILFRID-LAURIER, SAINT-HUBERT, QC, J3Y 3X3
(450) 443-6666   SIC 2834
LABORATOIRES ODAN LTEE, LES p1251
325 AV STILLVIEW, POINTE-CLAIRE, QC, H9R 2Y6
(514) 428-1628   SIC 2834
LABORATOIRES OMEGA LIMITEE p1217
11177 RUE HAMON, MONTREAL, QC, H3M 3E4
(514) 335-0310   SIC 2834
MCNEIL PDI INC p606

890 WOODLAWN RD W, GUELPH, ON, N1K 1A5
SIC 2834
MEDICURE INC p391
1250 WAVERLEY ST SUITE 2, WINNIPEG, MB, R3T 6C6
(204) 487-7412   SIC 2834
MERIAL CANADA INC p1053
20000 AV CLARK-GRAHAM, BAIE-D'URFE, QC, H9X 4B6
(514) 457-1555   SIC 2834
MERUS LABS INTERNATIONAL INC p970
100 WELLINGTON ST W SUITE 2110, TORONTO, ON, M5K 1H1
(905) 726-0995   SIC 2834
MYLAN PHARMACEUTICALS ULC p575
85 ADVANCE RD, ETOBICOKE, ON, M8Z 2S6
(416) 236-2631   SIC 2834
NOVELION THERAPEUTICS INC p299
510 WEST GEORGIA ST SUITE 1800, VANCOUVER, BC, V6B 0M3
(877) 764-3131   SIC 2834
NOVOCOL PHARMACEUTICAL OF CANADA, INC p534
25 WOLSELEY CRT, CAMBRIDGE, ON, N1R 6X3
(519) 623-4800   SIC 2834
NUGALE PHARMACEUTICAL INC p914
41 PULLMAN CRT, TORONTO, ON, M1X 1E4
(416) 298-7275   SIC 2834
NUTRALAB CANADA CORP p878
980 TAPSCOTT RD, SCARBOROUGH, ON, M1X 1C3
(905) 752-1823   SIC 2834
NUVO PHARMACEUTICALS INC p725
6733 MISSISSAUGA RD UNIT 610, MISSISSAUGA, ON, L5N 6J5
(905) 673-6980   SIC 2834
OMEGACHEM INC p1138
480 RUE PERREAULT, LEVIS, QC, G6W 7V6
(418) 837-4444   SIC 2834
PALADIN LABS INC p1324
100 BOUL ALEXIS-NIHON BUREAU 600, SAINT-LAURENT, QC, H4M 2P2
(514) 340-1112   SIC 2834
PANCAP PHARMA INC p673
50 VALLEYWOOD DR SUITE 6, MARKHAM, ON, L3R 6E9
(905) 470-6844   SIC 2834
PATHEON INC p524
977 CENTURY DR, BURLINGTON, ON, L7L 5J8
(905) 639-5254   SIC 2834
PATHEON INC p725
2100 SYNTEX CRT, MISSISSAUGA, ON, L5N 7K9
(905) 821-4001   SIC 2834
PATHEON INC p1015
111 CONSUMERS DR, WHITBY, ON, L1N 5Z5
(905) 668-3368   SIC 2834
PF CONSUMER HEALTHCARE CANADA ULC p732
55 STANDISH CRT SUITE 450, MISSISSAUGA, ON, L5R 4B2
(905) 507-7000   SIC 2834
PF CONSUMER HEALTHCARE CANADA ULC p1330
1025 BOUL MARCEL-LAURIN, SAINT-LAURENT, QC, H4R 1J6
(514) 695-0500   SIC 2834
PFIZER CANADA SRI p347
720 17TH ST E, BRANDON, MB, R7A 7H2
(204) 728-1511   SIC 2834
PFIZER CANADA SRI p1118
17300 RTE TRANSCANADIENNE, KIRKLAND, QC, H9J 2M5
(514) 695-0500   SIC 2834
PFIZER CANADA SRI p1330
1025 BOUL MARCEL-LAURIN, SAINT-LAURENT, QC, H4R 1J6

(514) 744-6771   SIC 2834
PHARMALAB INC p1137
8750 BOUL GUILLAUME-COUTURE, LEVIS, QC, G6V 9G9
(418) 833-7603   SIC 2834
PHARMASCIENCE INC p1073
100 BOUL DE L'INDUSTRIE, CANDIAC, QC, J5R 1J1
(450) 444-9989   SIC 2834
PHARMASCIENCE INC p1180
8580 AV DE L'ESPLANADE, MONTREAL, QC, H2P 2R8
(514) 384-6516   SIC 2834
PHARMASCIENCE INC p1228
6111 AV ROYALMOUNT BUREAU 100, MONTREAL, QC, H4P 2T4
(514) 340-1114   SIC 2834
PIC CANADA LTD p393
99 SCURFIELD BLVD UNIT 161, WINNIPEG, MB, R3Y 1Y1
(204) 927-7120   SIC 2834
PILLAR5 PHARMA INC p479
365 MADAWASKA BLVD, ARNPRIOR, ON, K7S 0C9
(613) 623-4221   SIC 2834
PROMETIC BIOSCIENCES INC p1241
500 BOUL CARTIER O BUREAU 150, MONTREAL-OUEST, QC, H7V 5B7
(450) 781-0115   SIC 2834
PROMETIC SCIENCES DE LA VIE INC p1241
440 BOUL ARMAND-FRAPPIER BUREAU 300, MONTREAL-OUEST, QC, H7V 4B4
(450) 781-0115   SIC 2834
PURDUE PHARMA p845
575 GRANITE CRT, PICKERING, ON, L1W 3W8
(905) 420-6400   SIC 2834
ROPACK INC p1163
10801 RUE MIRABEAU, MONTREAL, QC, H1J 1T7
(514) 353-7000   SIC 2834
RW CONSUMER PRODUCTS LTD p369
200 OMANDS CREEK BLVD, WINNIPEG, MB, R2R 1V7
(204) 786-6873   SIC 2834
SANDOZ CANADA INC p1067
145 RUE JULES-LEGER, BOUCHERVILLE, QC, J4B 7K8
(450) 641-4903   SIC 2834
SANTE BAUSCH, CANADA INC p1362
2150 BOUL SAINT-ELZEAR O, SAINTE-ROSE, QC, H7L 4A8
(514) 744-6792   SIC 2834
SCHERING-PLOUGH CANADA INC p1118
16750 RTE TRANSCANADIENNE, KIRKLAND, QC, H9H 4M7
(514) 426-7300   SIC 2834
SERVICES PHARMACEUTIQUES AVARA BOUCHERVILLE INC p1067
145 RUE JULES-LEGER, BOUCHERVILLE, QC, J4B 7K8
(450) 650-3050   SIC 2834
SOCIETE BRISTOL-MYERS SQUIBB CANADA, LA p1336
2344 BOUL ALFRED-NOBEL BUREAU 300, SAINT-LAURENT, QC, H4S 0A4
(514) 333-3200   SIC 2834
STERINOVA INC p1313
3005 AV JOSE-MARIA-ROSELL, SAINT-HYACINTHE, QC, J2S 0J9
(450) 252-2520   SIC 2834
SUMMIT VETERINARY PHARMACY INC p482
25 FURBACHER LANE SUITE 1, AURORA, ON, L4G 6W3
(905) 713-2040   SIC 2834
SUNOVION PHARMACEUTICALS CANADA INC p727
6790 CENTURY AVE SUITE 100, MISSISSAUGA, ON, L5N 2V8
(905) 814-9145   SIC 2834
TARO PHARMACEUTICALS INC p506
130 EAST DR, BRAMPTON, ON, L6T 1C1

(905) 791-8276   *SIC 2834*

TELESTA THERAPEUTICS INC   *p1336*
2600 BOUL ALFRED-NOBEL BUREAU 301, SAINT-LAURENT, QC, H4S 0A9
(514) 697-6636   *SIC 2834*

TEVA CANADA LIMITED   *p676*
575 HOOD RD, MARKHAM, ON, L3R 4E1
(905) 475-3370   *SIC 2834*

TEVA CANADA LIMITED   *p865*
30 NOVOPHARM CRT, SCARBOROUGH, ON, M1B 2K9
(416) 291-8876   *SIC 2834*

TEVA CANADA LIMITED   *p895*
5691 MAIN ST, STOUFFVILLE, ON, L4A 1H5
(416) 291-8888   *SIC 2834*

TEVA CANADA LIMITED   *p1153*
17800 RUE LAPOINTE BUREAU 123, MIRABEL, QC, J7J 0W8
(450) 433-7673   *SIC 2834*

THERAPEUTIQUE KNIGHT INC   *p1221*
3400 BOUL DE MAISONNEUVE O BUREAU 1055, MONTREAL, QC, H3Z 3B8
(514) 484-4483   *SIC 2834*

THERAPURE BIOPHARMA INC   *p727*
2585 MEADOWPINE BLVD, MISSISSAUGA, ON, L5N 8H9
(905) 286-6200   *SIC 2834*

TRILLIUM HEALTH CARE PRODUCTS INC   *p520*
2337 PARKDALE AVE E, BROCKVILLE, ON, K6V 5W5
(613) 342-4436   *SIC 2834*

UNIPRIX LAURENT TETREAULT & ASSOCIATE (AFFILIATED PHARMACY)   *p1184*
5647 AV DU PARC, MONTREAL, QC, H2V 4H2
(514) 276-9353   *SIC 2834*

UPGI PHARMA INC   *p1123*
100 BOUL DE L'INDUSTRIE, LA PRAIRIE, QC, J5R 1J1
(514) 998-9059   *SIC 2834*

VALEANT CANADA LIMITEE   *p1363*
2150 BOUL SAINT-ELZEAR O, SAINTE-ROSE, QC, H7L 4A8
(514) 744-6792   *SIC 2834*

VIVIER PHARMA INC   *p1395*
288 RUE ADRIEN-PATENAUDE, VAUDREUIL-DORION, QC, J7V 5V5
(450) 455-9779   *SIC 2834*

WELLSPRING PHARMACEUTICAL CANADA CORP   *p799*
400 IROQUOIS SHORE RD, OAKVILLE, ON, L6H 1M5
(905) 337-4500   *SIC 2834*

WN PHARMACEUTICALS LTD   *p202*
2000 BRIGANTINE DR, COQUITLAM, BC, V3K 7B5
(778) 284-7400   *SIC 2834*

SIC 2835 Diagnostic substances

BTNX INC   *p667*
570 HOOD RD UNIT 23, MARKHAM, ON, L3R 4G7
(905) 944-9565   *SIC 2835*

GENEOHM SCIENCES CANADA INC   *p1266*
2555 BOUL DU PARC-TECHNOLOGIQUE, QUEBEC, QC, G1P 4S5
(418) 780-5800   *SIC 2835*

GENEPOC INC   *p1266*
360 RUE FRANQUET BUREAU 100, QUEBEC, QC, G1P 4N3
(418) 650-3535   *SIC 2835*

OXOID INC   *p750*
1926 MERIVALE RD SUITE 100, NEPEAN, ON, K2G 1E8
(613) 226-1318   *SIC 2835*

SIC 2836 Biological products, except diagnostic

CEDARLANE CORPORATION   *p521*
4410 PALETTA CRT, BURLINGTON, ON, L7L 5R2
(289) 288-0001   *SIC 2836*

DOMINION BIOLOGICALS LIMITED   *p446*
5 ISNOR DR, DARTMOUTH, NS, B3B 1M1
(902) 468-3992   *SIC 2836*

KEMIRA WATER SOLUTIONS CANADA INC   *p1393*
3405 RTE MARIE-VICTORIN, VARENNES, QC, J3X 1P7
(450) 652-0665   *SIC 2836*

LALLEMAND SOLUTIONS SANTE INC   *p1152*
17975 RUE DES GOUVERNEURS, MIRABEL, QC, J7J 2K7
(450) 433-9139   *SIC 2836*

SANOFI PASTEUR LIMITED   *p775*
1755 STEELES AVE W, NORTH YORK, ON, M2R 3T4
(416) 667-2700   *SIC 2836*

STEMCELL TECHNOLOGIES CANADA INC   *p296*
1618 STATION ST, VANCOUVER, BC, V6A 1B6
(604) 877-0713   *SIC 2836*

SIC 2841 Soap and other detergents

ESCENTS BODY PRODUCTS INC   *p200*
18 FAWCETT RD, COQUITLAM, BC, V3K 6X9
(604) 298-9298   *SIC 2841*

GEMINI PACKAGING LTD   *p258*
12071 JACOBSON WAY UNIT 150, RICHMOND, BC, V6W 1L5
(604) 278-3455   *SIC 2841*

HUNTER AMENITIES INTERNATIONAL LTD   *p569*
37 YORK ST E, ELORA, ON, N0B 1S0
(519) 846-2489   *SIC 2841*

JEMPAK GK INC   *p804*
1485 SPEERS RD, OAKVILLE, ON, L6L 2X5
(905) 827-1123   *SIC 2841*

KOREX CANADA COMPANY   *p575*
78 TITAN RD, ETOBICOKE, ON, M8Z 2J8
(416) 231-7800   *SIC 2841*

PERTH SOAP MANUFACTURING INC   *p839*
5 HERRIOTT ST, PERTH, ON, K7H 3E5
(613) 267-1881   *SIC 2841*

PROCTER & GAMBLE INC   *p520*
1475 CALIFORNIA AVE, BROCKVILLE, ON, K6V 6K4
(613) 342-9592   *SIC 2841*

PROCTER & GAMBLE INC   *p773*
4711 YONGE ST, NORTH YORK, ON, M2N 6K8
(416) 730-4711   *SIC 2841*

PROCTER & GAMBLE INVESTMENT CORPORATION   *p520*
1475 CALIFORNIA AVE, BROCKVILLE, ON, K6V 6K4
(613) 342-9592   *SIC 2841*

RGM CHEMTECH INTERNATIONAL INC   *p256*
14351 BURROWS RD SUITE 100, RICHMOND, BC, V6V 1K9
(604) 270-3320   *SIC 2841*

SANI-MARC INC   *p1398*
42 RUE DE L'ARTISAN, VICTORIAVILLE, QC, G6P 7E3
(819) 758-1541   *SIC 2841*

SC JOHNSON PROFESSIONAL CA INC   *p518*
1 WEBSTER ST, BRANTFORD, ON, N3T 5R1
(519) 443-8697   *SIC 2841*

SHANDEX PERSONAL CARE MANUFACTURING INC   *p839*
5 HERRIOTT ST, PERTH, ON, K7H 3E5
(613) 267-1881   *SIC 2841*

ULLMAN, KEN ENTERPRISES INC   *p482*
92 KENNEDY ST W, AURORA, ON, L4G 2L7
(905) 727-5677   *SIC 2841*

V I P SOAP PRODUCTS LTD   *p233*
32859 MISSION WAY, MISSION, BC, V2V 6E4
(604) 820-8665   *SIC 2841*

VOYAGEUR SOAP & CANDLE COMPANY LTD   *p273*
19257 ENTERPRISE WAY SUITE 14, SURREY, BC, V3S 6J8
(604) 530-8979   *SIC 2841*

SIC 2842 Polishes and sanitation goods

AVMOR LTEE   *p1233*
950 RUE MICHELIN, MONTREAL, QC, H7L 5C1
(450) 629-8074   *SIC 2842*

BASIC PACKAGING INDUSTRIES INC   *p704*
5591 MCADAM RD, MISSISSAUGA, ON, L4Z 1N4
(905) 890-0922   *SIC 2842*

CANTOL CORP   *p667*
199 STEELCASE RD W, MARKHAM, ON, L3R 2M4
(905) 475-6141   *SIC 2842*

CHARLOTTE PRODUCTS LTD   *p840*
2060 FISHER DR, PETERBOROUGH, ON, K9J 6X6
(705) 740-2880   *SIC 2842*

DIVERSEY CANADA, INC   *p716*
3755 LAIRD RD UNIT 10, MISSISSAUGA, ON, L5L 0B3
(905) 829-1200   *SIC 2842*

DUSTBANE PRODUCTS LIMITED   *p817*
25 PICKERING PL, OTTAWA, ON, K1G 5P4
(800) 387-8226   *SIC 2842*

ECOLAB CO.   *p694*
5105 TOMKEN RD SUITE 1, MISSISSAUGA, ON, L4W 2X5
(905) 238-0171   *SIC 2842*

GESTION BRINEKY INC   *p1219*
5035 CH MIRA, MONTREAL, QC, H3W 2B9
(514) 282-3300   *SIC 2842*

KIK HOLDCO COMPANY INC   *p585*
2000 KIPLING AVE, ETOBICOKE, ON, M9W 4J6
(416) 743-6255   *SIC 2842*

KIK HOLDCO COMPANY INC   *p585*
13 BETHRIDGE RD, ETOBICOKE, ON, M9W 1M6
(416) 740-7400   *SIC 2842*

KOREX CANADA COMPANY   *p575*
104 JUTLAND RD, ETOBICOKE, ON, M8Z 2H1
(416) 259-9214   *SIC 2842*

LABORATOIRES CHOISY LTEE   *p1146*
390 BOUL SAINT-LAURENT E, LOUISEVILLE, QC, J5V 2L7
(819) 228-5564   *SIC 2842*

LAROSE & FILS LTEE   *p1085*
2255 BOUL INDUSTRIEL, COTE SAINT-LUC, QC, H7S 1P8
(514) 382-7000   *SIC 2842*

MICRO-CLAIR INTERNATIONAL INC   *p1308*
3050 2E RUE, SAINT-HUBERT, QC, J3Y 8Y7
(438) 796-5712   *SIC 2842*

MONDO PRODUCTS COMPANY LIMITED   *p474*
695 WESTNEY RD S UNIT 1, AJAX, ON, L1S 6M9
(800) 465-5676   *SIC 2842*

OSTREM CHEMICAL COMPANY LTD   *p122*
2310 80 AVE NW, EDMONTON, AB, T6P 1N2
(780) 440-1911   *SIC 2842*

PRO-BEL THE SAFETY ROOF ANCHOR CO   *p474*
765 WESTNEY RD S, AJAX, ON, L1S 6W1
(905) 427-0616   *SIC 2842*

RECKITT BENCKISER (CANADA) INC   *p699*
1680 TECH AVE UNIT 2, MISSISSAUGA, ON, L4W 5S9
(905) 283-7000   *SIC 2842*

S.C. JOHNSON AND SON, LIMITED   *p517*
1 WEBSTER ST, BRANTFORD, ON, N3T 5A3
(519) 756-7900   *SIC 2842*

VIROX TECHNOLOGIES INC   *p799*
2770 COVENTRY RD, OAKVILLE, ON, L6H 6R1
(905) 813-0110   *SIC 2842*

WEST PENETONE INC   *p1051*
10900 RUE SECANT, ANJOU, QC, H1J 1S5
(514) 355-4660   *SIC 2842*

WGI MANUFACTURING INC   *p342*
1455 BELLEVUE AVE SUITE 300, WEST VANCOUVER, BC, V7T 1C3
(604) 922-6563   *SIC 2842*

WOOD WYANT CANADA INC   *p1398*
42 RUE DE L'ARTISAN, VICTORIAVILLE, QC, G6P 7E3
(819) 758-1541   *SIC 2842*

SIC 2844 Toilet preparations

A.G. PROFESSIONAL HAIR CARE PRODUCTS LTD   *p199*
14 KING EDWARD ST, COQUITLAM, BC, V3K 0E7
(604) 294-8870   *SIC 2844*

ACUITY HOLDINGS, INC   *p99*
11627 178 ST NW, EDMONTON, AB, T5S 1N6
(780) 453-5800   *SIC 2844*

AG HAIR LTD   *p199*
14 KING EDWARD ST, COQUITLAM, BC, V3K 0E7
(604) 294-8870   *SIC 2844*

AVON CANADA INC   *p143*
10 PURDUE CRT W, LETHBRIDGE, AB, T1K 4R8
SIC 2844

BRANDS INTERNATIONAL CORPORATION   *p754*
594 NEWPARK BLVD, NEWMARKET, ON, L3X 2S2
(905) 830-4404   *SIC 2844*

COLGATE-PALMOLIVE CANADA INC   *p687*
6400 NORTHWEST DR, MISSISSAUGA, ON, L4V 1K1
SIC 2844

COLGATE-PALMOLIVE CANADA INC   *p779*
895 DON MILLS RD, NORTH YORK, ON, M3C 1W3
(416) 421-6000   *SIC 2844*

COSMACEUTICAL RESEARCH LAB INC   *p276*
12920 84 AVE, SURREY, BC, V3W 1K7
(604) 590-1373   *SIC 2844*

COSMETICA LABORATORIES INC   *p868*
1960 EGLINTON AVE E, SCARBOROUGH, ON, M1L 2M5
(416) 615-2400   *SIC 2844*

CRYSTAL CLAIRE COSMETICS INC   *p873*
165 MILNER AVE, SCARBOROUGH, ON, M1S 4G7
(416) 421-1882   *SIC 2844*

CRYSTAL INTERNATIONAL (GROUP) INC.   *p873*
165 MILNER AVE, SCARBOROUGH, ON, M1S 4G7
(416) 421-9299   *SIC 2844*

CSR COSMETIC SOLUTIONS INC   *p486*
149 VICTORIA ST, BARRIE, ON, L4N 2J6
(705) 728-5917   *SIC 2844*

ESTEE LAUDER COSMETICS LTD   *p874*
161 COMMANDER BLVD, SCARBOROUGH, ON, M1S 3K9
(416) 292-1111   *SIC 2844*

GROUPE MARCELLE INC   *p1128*
9200 CH DE LA COTE-DE-LIESSE, LACHINE, QC, H8T 1A1
(514) 631-7710   *SIC 2844*

GROUPE MARCELLE INC   *p1157*

5600 CH DE LA COTE-DE-LIESSE, MONT-ROYAL, QC, H4T 4L1
(514) 735-2309 *SIC 2844*

HUNTER AMENITIES INTERNATIONAL LTD *p522*
1205 CORPORATE DR, BURLINGTON, ON, L7L 5V5
(905) 331-2855 *SIC 2844*

L'OREAL CANADA INC *p1197*
1500 BOUL ROBERT-BOURASSA BUREAU 600, MONTREAL, QC, H3A 3S7
(514) 287-4800 *SIC 2844*

LABORATOIRE DU-VAR INC *p1066*
1460 RUE GRAHAM-BELL, BOUCHERVILLE, QC, J4B 6H5
(450) 641-4740 *SIC 2844*

LABORATOIRES DELON (1990) INC *p1091*
69 BOUL BRUNSWICK, DOLLARD-DES-ORMEAUX, QC, H9B 2N4
(514) 685-9966 *SIC 2844*

LABORATOIRES DERMO-COSMETIK INC *p1326*
68 RUE STINSON, SAINT-LAURENT, QC, H4N 2E7
(514) 735-1531 *SIC 2844*

LUSH HANDMADE COSMETICS LTD *p323*
8688 CAMBIE ST, VANCOUVER, BC, V6P 6M6
(604) 638-3632 *SIC 2844*

LUSH MANUFACTURING LTD *p323*
8680 CAMBIE ST, VANCOUVER, BC, V6P 6M9
(888) 733-5874 *SIC 2844*

NETTLEWOODS INC *p717*
4060 RIDGEWAY DR UNIT 16, MISSISSAUGA, ON, L5L 5X9
(905) 608-1919 *SIC 2844*

NORWOOD MANUFACTURING CANADA INC *p277*
8519 132 ST, SURREY, BC, V3W 4N8
SIC 2844

PEARLON PRODUCTS INC *p741*
6290 SHAWSON DR, MISSISSAUGA, ON, L5T 1H5
(905) 670-1040 *SIC 2844*

PRODUITS DE BEAUTE IRIS INC *p1091*
69 BOUL BRUNSWICK, DOLLARD-DES-ORMEAUX, QC, H9B 2N4
(514) 685-9966 *SIC 2844*

REVLON CANADA INC *p700*
1590 SOUTH GATEWAY RD, MISSISSAUGA, ON, L4W 0A8
(905) 276-4500 *SIC 2844*

REVOLUTION LANDFILL LP *p524*
1100 BURLOAK DR, BURLINGTON, ON, L7L 6B2
(905) 315-6304 *SIC 2844*

SIGAN INDUSTRIES INC *p506*
296 ORENDA RD, BRAMPTON, ON, L6T 4X6
(905) 456-8888 *SIC 2844*

SUSANNE LANG FRAGRANCE INC *p989*
670 CALEDONIA RD UNIT 100, TORONTO, ON, M6E 4V9
(416) 961-1234 *SIC 2844*

VEGEWAX CANDLEWORX LTD *p560*
300 NORTH RIVERMEDE RD, CONCORD, ON, L4K 3N6
(905) 760-7944 *SIC 2844*

WILLARD MANUFACTURING INC *p525*
5295 JOHN LUCAS DR SUITE 1, BURLINGTON, ON, L7L 6A8
(905) 633-6905 *SIC 2844*

SIC 2851 Paints and allied products

AKZO NOBEL COATINGS LTD *p582*
110 WOODBINE DOWNS BLVD UNIT 4, ETOBICOKE, ON, M9W 5S6
(416) 674-6633 *SIC 2851*

AKZO NOBEL COATINGS LTD *p1319*
1001 BOUL ROLAND-GODARD, SAINT-JEROME, QC, J7Y 4C2

SIC 2851

AKZO NOBEL WOOD COATINGS LTD *p847*
155 ROSE GLEN RD, PORT HOPE, ON, L1A 3V6
(905) 885-6388 *SIC 2851*

ALLCOLOUR PAINT LIMITED *p803*
1257 SPEERS RD, OAKVILLE, ON, L6L 2X5
(905) 827-4173 *SIC 2851*

BASF CANADA INC *p1023*
845 WYANDOTTE ST W, WINDSOR, ON, N9A 5Y1
(519) 256-3155 *SIC 2851*

CANLAK INC *p1089*
674 RUE PRINCIPALE BUREAU 309, DAVELUYVILLE, QC, G0Z 1C0
(819) 367-3264 *SIC 2851*

CLOVERDALE PAINT INC *p279*
2630 CROYDON DR UNIT 400, SURREY, BC, V3Z 6T3
(604) 596-6261 *SIC 2851*

ENDURA MANUFACTURING COMPANY LIMITED *p93*
12425 149 ST NW, EDMONTON, AB, T5L 2J6
(780) 451-4242 *SIC 2851*

ENNIS PAINT CANADA ULC *p844*
850 MCKAY RD, PICKERING, ON, L1W 2Y4
(905) 686-2770 *SIC 2851*

ENVIRO-COATINGS CANADA LTD *p713*
2359 ROYAL WINDSOR DR UNIT 10, MISSISSAUGA, ON, L5J 4S9
SIC 2851

GENERAL PAINT CORP *p1368*
5230 BOUL ROYAL, SHAWINIGAN, QC, G9N 4R6
(819) 537-5925 *SIC 2851*

GUERTIN COATINGS, SEALANTS AND POLYMERS LTD *p365*
50 PANET RD, WINNIPEG, MB, R2J 0R9
(204) 237-0241 *SIC 2851*

HENRY COMPANY CANADA INC *p866*
15 WALLSEND DR, SCARBOROUGH, ON, M1E 3X6
(416) 724-2000 *SIC 2851*

KORZITE COATINGS INC *p603*
7134 WELLINGTON RD W, GUELPH, ON, N1H 6J3
(519) 821-1250 *SIC 2851*

MOORE, BENJAMIN & CO., LIMITED *p556*
8775 KEELE ST, CONCORD, ON, L4K 2N1
(905) 761-4800 *SIC 2851*

PEINTURE UCP INC *p1054*
19500 AUT TRANSCANADIENNE, BAIE-D'URFE, QC, H9X 3S4
(514) 457-1512 *SIC 2851*

PEINTURES M.F. INC *p1234*
1605 BOUL DAGENAIS O, MONTREAL, QC, H7L 5A3
(450) 628-3831 *SIC 2851*

PPG ARCHITECTURAL COATINGS CANADA INC *p1067*
500 - 1550 RUE AMPERE, BOUCHERVILLE, QC, J4B 7L4
(450) 655-3121 *SIC 2851*

PPG CANADA INC *p557*
8200 KEELE ST, CONCORD, ON, L4K 2A5
(905) 669-1020 *SIC 2851*

PPG CANADA INC *p714*
2301 ROYAL WINDSOR DR, MISSISSAUGA, ON, L5J 1K5
SIC 2851

PRISM POWDER COATINGS LTD *p557*
321 EDGELEY BLVD, CONCORD, ON, L4K 3Y2
(905) 660-5361 *SIC 2851*

PROTECH CHIMIE LTEE *p1335*
7600 BOUL HENRI-BOURASSA O, SAINT-LAURENT, QC, H4S 1W3
(514) 745-0200 *SIC 2851*

RPM CANADA *p919*
220 WICKSTEED AVE, TORONTO, ON, M4H 1G7
(416) 421-3300 *SIC 2851*

RPM CANADA COMPANY FINANCE ULC

p1015
95 SUNRAY ST, WHITBY, ON, L1N 9C9
(905) 430-3333 *SIC 2851*

SHERWIN-WILLIAMS CANADA INC *p592*
224 CATHERINE ST, FORT ERIE, ON, L2A 0B1
(905) 871-2724 *SIC 2851*

SHERWIN-WILLIAMS CANADA INC *p600*
13 IROQUOIS TRAIL, GRIMSBY, ON, L3M 5E6
(905) 945-3802 *SIC 2851*

SOCIETE LAURENTIDE INC *p1368*
4660 BOUL DE SHAWINIGAN-SUD, SHAWINIGAN, QC, G9N 6T5
(819) 537-6636 *SIC 2851*

SPECIALTY POLYMER COATINGS INC *p228*
20529 62 AVE SUITE 104, LANGLEY, BC, V3A 8R4
(604) 514-9711 *SIC 2851*

SYNERVEST HOLDINGS INC *p684*
490 MCGEACHIE DR, MILTON, ON, L9T 3Y5
SIC 2851

TARKETT INC *p1101*
1001 RUE YAMASKA E, FARNHAM, QC, J2N 1J7
(450) 293-3173 *SIC 2851*

TIGER DRYLAC CANADA INC *p602*
110 SOUTHGATE DR, GUELPH, ON, N1G 4P5
(519) 766-4781 *SIC 2851*

SIC 2861 Gum and wood chemicals

NATURAL RESOURCES CANADA *p613*
183 LONGWOOD RD S, HAMILTON, ON, L8P 0A5
(905) 645-0683 *SIC 2861*

SIC 2865 Cyclic crudes and intermediates

2417821 CANADA INC *p592*
210 JAMES A. BRENNAN RD, GANANOQUE, ON, K7G 1N7
(613) 549-3221 *SIC 2865*

COLORTECH INC *p502*
8027 DIXIE RD, BRAMPTON, ON, L6T 3V1
(888) 257-8324 *SIC 2865*

INEOS STYRENICS LTD *p860*
872 TASHMOO AVE, SARNIA, ON, N7T 7H5
(519) 339-7339 *SIC 2865*

RUETGERS CANADA INC *p609*
725 STRATHEARNE AVE, HAMILTON, ON, L8H 5L3
(905) 544-2891 *SIC 2865*

TRI-TEXCO INC *p1302*
1001 BOUL INDUSTRIEL, SAINT-EUSTACHE, QC, J7R 6C3
(450) 974-1001 *SIC 2865*

SIC 2869 Industrial organic chemicals, nec

9343-8919 QUEBEC INC *p1072*
300 AV LIBERTE, CANDIAC, QC, J5R 6X1
(450) 633-9303 *SIC 2869*

ANAERGIA INC *p521*
4210 SOUTH SERVICE RD, BURLINGTON, ON, L7L 4X5
(905) 766-3333 *SIC 2869*

BARTEK INGREDIENTS INC *p891*
421 SEAMAN ST, STONEY CREEK, ON, L8E 3J4
(905) 662-1127 *SIC 2869*

CHARLES TENNANT & COMPANY (CANADA) LIMITED *p794*
34 CLAYSON RD, NORTH YORK, ON, M9M 2G8
(416) 741-9264 *SIC 2869*

ENERKEM ALBERTA BIOFUELS LP *p124*
250 AURUM RD NE SUITE 460, EDMON-

TON, AB, T6S 1G9
(780) 473-2896 *SIC 2869*

ENERKEM INC *p1195*
1130 RUE SHERBROOKE O BUREAU 1500, MONTREAL, QC, H3A 2M8
(514) 875-0284 *SIC 2869*

GREENFIELD GLOBAL QUEBEC INC *p503*
2 CHELSEA LN, BRAMPTON, ON, L6T 3Y4
(905) 790-7500 *SIC 2869*

GREENFIELD GLOBAL, INC *p939*
20 TORONTO ST SUITE 1400, TORONTO, ON, M5C 2B8
(416) 304-1700 *SIC 2869*

INEOS CANADA PARTNERSHIP *p154*
GD, RED DEER, AB, T4N 6A1
(403) 314-4500 *SIC 2869*

INEOS STYROLUTION CANADA LTD *p860*
872 TASHMOO AVE, SARNIA, ON, N7T 8A3
(226) 784-2872 *SIC 2869*

IOGEN BIO-PRODUCTS CORPORATION *p827*
300 HUNT CLUB RD, OTTAWA, ON, K1V 1C1
(613) 733-9830 *SIC 2869*

IOGEN CORPORATION *p827*
310 HUNT CLUB RD, OTTAWA, ON, K1V 1C1
(613) 733-9830 *SIC 2869*

LABORATOIRES BUCKMAN DU CANADA, LTEE *p1395*
351 RUE JOSEPH-CARRIER, VAUDREUIL-DORION, QC, J7V 5V5
(450) 424-4404 *SIC 2869*

LE HAVRE DES CANTONS *p1147*
231 DOLLARD, MAGOG, QC, J1X 2M5
(819) 868-1010 *SIC 2869*

METHANEX CORPORATION *p307*
200 BURRARD ST SUITE 1800, VANCOUVER, BC, V6C 3M1
(604) 661-2600 *SIC 2869*

NOVA CHEMICALS (CANADA) LTD *p24*
2928 16 ST NE, CALGARY, AB, T2E 7K7
SIC 2869

NOVA CHEMICALS (CANADA) LTD *p55*
1000 7 AVE SW SUITE 1000, CALGARY, AB, T2P 5L5
(403) 750-3600 *SIC 2869*

NOVA CHEMICALS (CANADA) LTD *p156*
4940 81 ST SUITE 6, RED DEER, AB, T4P 3V3
(403) 314-8611 *SIC 2869*

NOVA CHEMICALS (CANADA) LTD *p745*
510 MOORE LINE, MOORETOWN, ON, N0N 1M0
(519) 862-2961 *SIC 2869*

NOVA CHEMICALS (CANADA) LTD *p860*
872 TASHMOO AVE, SARNIA, ON, N7T 7H5
(519) 332-1212 *SIC 2869*

RUETGERS POLYMERES LTEE *p1073*
120 BOUL DE L'INDUSTRIE, CANDIAC, QC, J5R 1J2
(450) 659-9693 *SIC 2869*

SILTECH CORPORATION *p919*
225 WICKSTEED AVE, TORONTO, ON, M4H 1G5
(416) 424-4567 *SIC 2869*

STEPAN CANADA INC *p662*
3800 LONGFORD MILLS RD, LONGFORD MILLS, ON, L0K 1L0
(705) 326-7329 *SIC 2869*

SIC 2873 Nitrogenous fertilizers

ADVANCED NUTRIENTS LTD *p176*
32526 GEORGE FERGUSON WAY SUITE 102, ABBOTSFORD, BC, V2T 4Y1
(604) 854-6793 *SIC 2873*

AGRIUM INC *p39*
13131 LAKE FRASER DR SE, CALGARY, AB, T2J 7E8
(403) 225-7000 *SIC 2873*

CANADIAN FERTILIZERS LIMITED   p145
1250 52 ST NW, MEDICINE HAT, AB, T1A 7R9
(403) 527-8887   *SIC 2873*
KOCH FERTILIZER CANADA, ULC   p347
1400 17TH ST E, BRANDON, MB, R7A 7C4
(204) 729-2900   *SIC 2873*
NUTRIEN LTD   p1428
122 1ST AVE S SUITE 500, SASKATOON, SK, S7K 7G3
(306) 933-8500   *SIC 2873*
PARKLAND FUEL CORPORATION   p77
333 96 AVE NE SUITE 6302, CALGARY, AB, T3K 0S3
(403) 567-2500   *SIC 2873*

SIC 2874 Phosphatic fertilizers

AGROCENTRE BELCAN INC   p1360
180 MONT E SAINTE-MARIE, SAINTE-MARTHE, QC, J0P 1W0
(450) 459-4288   *SIC 2874*
AGROCENTRE LANAUDIERE INC   p1353
531 RANG SUD, SAINT-THOMAS, QC, J0K 3L0
(450) 759-1520   *SIC 2874*
CENTRE ENGRAIS MINERAUX   p1352
390 263 RTE, SAINT-SEBASTIEN-DE-FRONTENAC, QC, G0Y 1M0
(819) 652-2266   *SIC 2874*
FERTI TECHNOLOGIES INC   p1348
560 CH RHEAUME, SAINT-MICHEL, QC, J0L 2J0
(450) 454-5367   *SIC 2874*
GREEN DROP LTD   p11
1230 MERIDIAN RD NE, CALGARY, AB, T2A 2N9
(403) 273-9845   *SIC 2874*
HOUDE, WILLIAM LTEE   p1352
8 3E RANG O, SAINT-SIMON-DE-BAGOT, QC, J0H 1Y0
(450) 798-2002   *SIC 2874*
NUTRIAG LTD   p997
62 ARROW RD, TORONTO, ON, M9M 2L8
(416) 636-1555   *SIC 2874*
SYNAGRI S.E.C.   p1353
80 RUE DES ERABLES, SAINT-THOMAS, QC, J0K 3L0
(450) 759-8070   *SIC 2874*
YARA BELLE PLAINE INC   p1404
2 KALIUM RD, BELLE PLAINE, SK, S0G 0G0
(306) 345-4200   *SIC 2874*
YARA BELLE PLAINE INC   p1419
1874 SCARTH ST SUITE 1800, REGINA, SK, S4P 4B3
(306) 525-7600   *SIC 2874*

SIC 2875 Fertilizers, mixing only

9310-6607 QUEBEC INC   p1294
771 RUE PRINCIPALE BUREAU 396, SAINT-BONAVENTURE, QC, J0C 1C0
(819) 396-2293   *SIC 2875*
ACADIAN SEAPLANTS LIMITED   p444
30 BROWN AVE, DARTMOUTH, NS, B3B 1X8
(902) 468-2840   *SIC 2875*
ENVIREM ORGANICS INC   p404
274 ROUTE 148, KILLARNEY ROAD, NB, E3G 9E2
(506) 459-3464   *SIC 2875*
GRO-BARK (ONTARIO) LTD   p531
816 MAYFIELD RD, CALEDON, ON, L7C 0Y6
(905) 846-1515   *SIC 2875*
GROUPE SOMAVRAC INC   p1387
3450 BOUL GENE-H.-KRUGER, TROIS-RIVIERES, QC, G9A 4M3
(819) 379-3311   *SIC 2875*
GSI ENVIRONNEMENT INC   p1393
100 RUE JEAN-COUTU BUREAU 101,

VARENNES, QC, J3X 0E1
(418) 882-2736   *SIC 2875*
S. BOUDRIAS HORTICOLE INC   p1342
29 RUE SAULNIER, SAINT-LAURENT, QC, H7M 1S7
(450) 663-4245   *SIC 2875*
SUEZ CANADA WASTE SERIVCES INC   p116
9426 51 AVE NW SUITE 307, EDMONTON, AB, T6E 5A6
(780) 391-7303   *SIC 2875*

SIC 2879 Agricultural chemicals, nec

9264 0085 QUEBEC INC   p1221
6080 RUE SHERBROOKE O, MONTREAL, QC, H4A 1Y1
    SIC 2879
BAYER CROPSCIENCE INC   p13
160 QUARRY PARK BLVD SE SUITE 200, CALGARY, AB, T2C 3G3
(403) 723-7400   *SIC 2879*
DOW AGROSCIENCES CANADA INC.   p48
215 2 ST SW SUITE 2400, CALGARY, AB, T2P 1M4
(403) 735-8800   *SIC 2879*
DOW AGROSCIENCES CANADA INC.p1433
421 DOWNEY RD SUITE 101, SASKATOON, SK, S7N 4L8
(800) 352-6776   *SIC 2879*
ELEVEURS DE PORCS DU QUEBEC LES   p1143
555 BOUL ROLAND-THERRIEN BUREAU 120, LONGUEUIL, QC, J4H 4E9
(450) 679-0540   *SIC 2879*
NUFARM AGRICULTURE INC   p77
333 96 AVE NE SUITE 5101, CALGARY, AB, T3K 0S3
(403) 692-2500   *SIC 2879*
PLANTBEST, INC   p680
170 DUFFIELD DR UNIT 200, MARKHAM, ON, L6G 1B5
(905) 470-0724   *SIC 2879*

SIC 2891 Adhesives and sealants

3M CANADA COMPANY   p518
1360 CALIFORNIA AVE, BROCKVILLE, ON, K6V 5V8
(613) 345-0111   *SIC 2891*
3M CANADA COMPANY   p648
300 TARTAN DR, LONDON, ON, N5V 4M9
(519) 451-2500   *SIC 2891*
CIMENT MCINNIS INC   p1213
1350 BOUL RENE-LEVESQUE O BUREAU 205, MONTREAL, QC, H3G 2W2
(438) 382-3331   *SIC 2891*
COOPER-STANDARD AUTOMOTIVE CANADA LIMITED   p593
346 GUELPH ST, GEORGETOWN, ON, L7G 4B5
(905) 873-6921   *SIC 2891*
COOPER-STANDARD AUTOMOTIVE CANADA LIMITED   p895
703 DOURO ST, STRATFORD, ON, N5A 3T1
(519) 271-3360   *SIC 2891*
DOMINION SURE SEAL LIMITED   p738
6175 DANVILLE RD, MISSISSAUGA, ON, L5T 2H7
(905) 670-5411   *SIC 2891*
DURABOND PRODUCTS LIMITED   p872
55 UNDERWRITERS RD, SCARBOROUGH, ON, M1R 3B4
(416) 759-4133   *SIC 2891*
HALLTECH INC   p866
465 CORONATION DR, SCARBOROUGH, ON, M1E 2K2
(416) 284-6111   *SIC 2891*
LAFARGE CANADA INC   p441
87 CEMENT PLANT RD, BROOKFIELD, NS, B0N 1C0

(902) 673-2281   *SIC 2891*
LAFARGE CANADA INC   p688
6509 AIRPORT RD, MISSISSAUGA, ON, L4V 1S7
(905) 738-7070   *SIC 2891*
MAPEI INC   p504
95 WALKER DR, BRAMPTON, ON, L6T 5K5
(905) 799-2663   *SIC 2891*
MAPEI INC   p1362
2900 AV FRANCIS-HUGHES, SAINTE-ROSE, QC, H7L 3J5
(450) 662-1212   *SIC 2891*
MULTIBOND INC   p1094
550 AV MARSHALL, DORVAL, QC, H9P 1C9
(514) 636-6230   *SIC 2891*
ROBERTS COMPANY CANADA LIMITED   p510
34 HANSEN RD S, BRAMPTON, ON, L6W 3H4
(905) 791-4444   *SIC 2891*
SCOTT BADER ATC INC   p1099
2400 RUE CANADIEN BUREAU 303, DRUMMONDVILLE, QC, J2C 7W3
(819) 477-1752   *SIC 2891*
SIKA CANADA INC   p106
16910 129 AVE NW SUITE 1, EDMONTON, AB, T5V 1L1
(780) 453-3060   *SIC 2891*
SIKA CANADA INC   p1252
601 AV DELMAR, POINTE-CLAIRE, QC, H9R 4A9
(514) 697-2610   *SIC 2891*
TECHNICAL ADHESIVES LIMITED   p703
3035 JARROW AVE, MISSISSAUGA, ON, L4X 2C6
(905) 625-1284   *SIC 2891*
WATERVILLE TG INC   p1400
10 RUE DU DEPOT, WATERVILLE, QC, J0B 3H0
(819) 837-2421   *SIC 2891*

SIC 2892 Explosives

DYNO NOBEL CANADA INC   p15
48 QUARRY PARK BLVD SE SUITE 210, CALGARY, AB, T2C 5P2
(403) 726-7500   *SIC 2892*
EPC CANADA EXPLOSIVES LTD   p634
22 GOVERNMENT RD E, KIRKLAND LAKE, ON, P2N 1A3
(705) 642-3265   *SIC 2892*
ORICA CANADA INC   p1072
301 RUE DE L'HOTEL-DE-VILLE, BROWNSBURG-CHATHAM, QC, J8G 3B5
(450) 533-4201   *SIC 2892*
ORICA CANADA INC   p1072
342 RUE MCMASTER, BROWNSBURG-CHATHAM, QC, J8G 3A8
(450) 533-4201   *SIC 2892*
WHITSON MANUFACTURING INC   p1001
2725 BELISLE DR, VAL CARON, ON, P3N 1B3
(705) 897-4971   *SIC 2892*
ZOOK CANADA INC   p526
4400 SOUTH SERVICE RD, BURLINGTON, ON, L7L 5R8
(905) 681-2885   *SIC 2892*

SIC 2893 Printing ink

HUBERGROUP CANADA LIMITED   p735
2150A DREW RD, MISSISSAUGA, ON, L5S 1B1
(905) 671-0750   *SIC 2893*
SIEGWERK CANADA INC   p506
40 WESTWYN CRT, BRAMPTON, ON, L6T 4T5
    SIC 2893
SUN CHEMICAL LIMITED   p506
10 WEST DR, BRAMPTON, ON, L6T 4Y4
(905) 796-2222   *SIC 2893*

WIKOFF COLOR CORPORATION - CANADA INC   p561
475 BOWES RD, CONCORD, ON, L4K 1J5
(905) 669-1311   *SIC 2893*

SIC 2895 Carbon black

BIRLA CARBON CANADA LTD   p609
755 PARKDALE AVE N, HAMILTON, ON, L8H 7N5
(905) 544-3343   *SIC 2895*
CABOT CANADA LTD   p859
800 TASHAMOO AVE, SARNIA, ON, N7T 7N4
(519) 336-2261   *SIC 2895*
CANCARB LIMITED   p147
1702 BRIER PARK CRES NW, MEDICINE HAT, AB, T1C 1T9
(403) 527-1121   *SIC 2895*

SIC 2899 Chemical preparations, nec

4270797 CANADA INC   p1063
1270 RUE NOBEL, BOUCHERVILLE, QC, J4B 5H1
(450) 645-0296   *SIC 2899*
BLACKBROOK CHEMICAL LTD   p754
1245 MAPLE HILL CRT SUITE 1, NEWMARKET, ON, L3Y 9E8
    SIC 2899
BRI-CHEM CORP   p1
27075 ACHESON RD, ACHESON, AB, T7X 6B1
(780) 962-9490   *SIC 2899*
CANADIAN TEST CASE 101 LTD   p730
5770 HURONTARIO ST, MISSISSAUGA, ON, L5R 3G5
    SIC 2899
CAPO INDUSTRIES LIMITED   p521
1200 CORPORATE DR, BURLINGTON, ON, L7L 5R6
(905) 332-6626   *SIC 2899*
CATALENT ONTARIO LIMITED   p1024
2125 AMBASSADOR DR, WINDSOR, ON, N9C 3R5
(519) 969-5404   *SIC 2899*
CHEMICAL LIME COMPANY OF CANADA INC   p224
102 B AVENUE SUITE 20303, LANGLEY, BC, V1M 4B4
(604) 888-2575   *SIC 2899*
CHEMTRADE ELECTROCHEM INC   p238
100 AMHERST AVE, NORTH VANCOUVER, BC, V7H 1S4
(604) 929-1107   *SIC 2899*
COMPASS MINERALS CANADA CORPp597
245 REGENT ST, GODERICH, ON, N7A 3Y5
(519) 524-8351   *SIC 2899*
DEMILEC INC   p1060
870 BOUL DU CURE-BOIVIN, BOISBRIAND, QC, J7G 2A7
(866) 345-3916   *SIC 2899*
DOW CHEMICAL CANADA ULC   p48
215 2 ST SW SUITE 2400, CALGARY, AB, T2P 1M4
(403) 267-3500   *SIC 2899*
DOW CHEMICAL CANADA ULC   p130
HIGHWAY 15, FORT SASKATCHEWAN, AB, T8L 2P4
(780) 998-8000   *SIC 2899*
DOW CHEMICAL CANADA ULC   p153
GD, RED DEER, AB, T4N 6N1
(403) 885-7000   *SIC 2899*
ENCRES INTERNATIONALE INX CORP   p1379
1247 RUE NATIONALE, TERREBONNE, QC, J6W 6H8
(450) 477-8606   *SIC 2899*
FLOW WATER INC   p821
110 CLARENCE ST SUITE 202, OTTAWA, ON, K1N 5P6

(613) 680-3569 *SIC* 2899
GENERAL DYNAMICS PRODUITS DE DEFENSE ET SYSTEMES TACTIQUES-CANADA VALLEYFIELD INC *p1365*
55 RUE MASSON, SALABERRY-DE-VALLEYFIELD, QC, J6S 4V9
(450) 371-5520 *SIC* 2899

GURIT AMERICAS INC *p1147*
555 BOUL POIRIER, MAGOG, QC, J1X 7L1
(819) 847-2182 *SIC* 2899

K+S SEL WINDSOR LTEE *p1025*
30 PROSPECT AVE, WINDSOR, ON, N9C 3G3
(519) 255-5400 *SIC* 2899

KENNEY & ROSS LIMITED *p465*
6493 SHORE RD RR 3, SHELBURNE, NS, B0T 1W0
(902) 637-2616 *SIC* 2899

KLENZOID CANADA INC *p706*
245 MATHESON BLVD E SUITE 2, MISSISSAUGA, ON, L4Z 3C9
(905) 712-4000 *SIC* 2899

MACCO ORGANIQUES INC *p1365*
100 RUE MCARTHUR, SALABERRY-DE-VALLEYFIELD, QC, J6S 4M5
(450) 371-1066 *SIC* 2899

MANCUSO CHEMICALS LIMITED *p759*
5725 PROGRESS ST, NIAGARA FALLS, ON, L2G 0C1
(905) 357-3626 *SIC* 2899

MYE CANADA INC *p110*
7115 GIRARD RD NW, EDMONTON, AB, T6B 2C5
(780) 486-6663 *SIC* 2899

NATURAL GLACIAL WATERS INC *p212*
8430 BERRAY RD RR 1, FANNY BAY, BC, V0R 1W0
(250) 335-9119 *SIC* 2899

NEOVA TECHNOLOGIES INC *p177*
31212 PEARDONVILLE RD, ABBOTSFORD, BC, V2T 6K8
(604) 504-0695 *SIC* 2899

NITROCHEM CORP *p725*
6733 MISSISSAUGA RD SUITE 306, MISSISSAUGA, ON, L5N 6J5
(905) 814-6665 *SIC* 2899

NITTA GELATIN CANADA, INC *p990*
60 PATON RD, TORONTO, ON, M6H 1R8
(416) 532-5111 *SIC* 2899

NOURYON PATE ET PERFORMANCE CANADA INC *p1148*
1900 RUE SAINT-PATRICE E BUREAU 25, MAGOG, QC, J1X 3W5
(819) 843-8942 *SIC* 2899

PCAS CANADA INC *p1318*
725 RUE TROTTER, SAINT-JEAN-SUR-RICHELIEU, QC, J3B 8J8
(450) 348-0901 *SIC* 2899

PIRAMAL HEALTHCARE (CANADA) LIMITED *p481*
110 INDUSTRIAL PKY N, AURORA, ON, L4G 4C3
(905) 727-9417 *SIC* 2899

PRODUITS CHIMIQUES MAGNUS LIMITEE *p1067*
1271 RUE AMPERE, BOUCHERVILLE, QC, J4B 5Z5
(450) 655-1344 *SIC* 2899

RECOCHEM INC *p1341*
850 MONTEE DE LIESSE, SAINT-LAURENT, QC, H4T 1P4
(514) 341-3550 *SIC* 2899

ROCHESTER MIDLAND LIMITED *p804*
851 PROGRESS CRT SUITE 1, OAKVILLE, ON, L6L 6K1
(905) 847-3000 *SIC* 2899

ROHM AND HAAS CANADA LP *p866*
2 MANSE RD, SCARBOROUGH, ON, M1E 3T9
(416) 284-4711 *SIC* 2899

ROYAL ADHESIVES & SEALANTS CANADA LTD *p587*
266 HUMBERLINE DR, ETOBICOKE, ON, M9W 5X1

(416) 679-5676 *SIC* 2899
SAINT-GOBAIN SOLAR GUARD, INC *p804*
760 PACIFIC RD UNIT 1, OAKVILLE, ON, L6L 6M5
(905) 847-2790 *SIC* 2899

TERGEL INC *p1382*
895 RUE ITALIA, TERREBONNE, QC, J6Y 2C8
(450) 621-2345 *SIC* 2899

VIQUA HOLDINGS *p607*
425 CLAIR RD W, GUELPH, ON, N1L 1R1
(519) 763-1032 *SIC* 2899

XYNYTH MANUFACTURING CORP *p187*
3989 HENNING DR UNIT 122, BURNABY, BC, V5C 6P8
(604) 473-9343 *SIC* 2899

SIC 2911 Petroleum refining

ALBERTA ENVIROFUELS INC *p121*
9511 17 ST NW, EDMONTON, AB, T6P 1Y3
(780) 449-7800 *SIC* 2911

BITUMAR INC *p1238*
11155 RUE SAINTE-CATHERINE E, MONTREAL-EST, QC, H1B 0A4
(514) 645-4561 *SIC* 2911

CHEVRON CANADA LIMITED *p185*
355 WILLINGDON AVE N, BURNABY, BC, V5C 1X4
(604) 257-4040 *SIC* 2911

CHEVRON CANADA LIMITED *p311*
1050 PENDER ST W SUITE 1200, VANCOUVER, BC, V6E 3T4
(604) 668-5300 *SIC* 2911

CONA RESOURCES LTD *p47*
421 7 AVE SW SUITE 1900, CALGARY, AB, T2P 4K9
(403) 930-3000 *SIC* 2911

CONDOR CHIMIQUES INC *p1298*
2645 BOUL TERRA-JET BUREAU B, SAINT-CYRILLE-DE-WENDOVER, QC, J1Z 1B3
(819) 474-6661 *SIC* 2911

CONSUMERS' CO-OPERATIVE REFINERIES LIMITED *p1415*
580 PARK ST, REGINA, SK, S4N 5A9
(306) 719-4353 *SIC* 2911

CONSUMERS' CO-OPERATIVE REFINERIES LIMITED *p1415*
550E E 9TH AVE N, REGINA, SK, S4N 7B3
(306) 721-5353 *SIC* 2911

ENERGIE VALERO INC *p1136*
165 CH DES ILES, LEVIS, QC, G6V 7M5
(418) 837-3641 *SIC* 2911

ENGENIUM CHEMICALS CORP *p12*
4333 46 AVE SE, CALGARY, AB, T2B 3N5
(403) 279-8545 *SIC* 2911

FREEHOLD ROYALTIES PARTNERSHIP *p49*
144 4 AVE SW SUITE 400, CALGARY, AB, T2P 3N4
(403) 221-0802 *SIC* 2911

HUSKY OIL OPERATIONS LIMITED *p249*
2542 PG PULPMILL RD, PRINCE GEORGE, BC, V2L 4V4
SIC 2911

IMPERIAL OIL LIMITED *p16*
505 QUARRY PARK BLVD SE, CALGARY, AB, T2C 5N1
(800) 567-3776 *SIC* 2911

IMPERIAL OIL LIMITED *p860*
453 CHRISTINA ST N, SARNIA, ON, N7T 5W3
(519) 339-2712 *SIC* 2911

IMPERIAL OIL LIMITED *p860*
PO BOX 3004 STN MAIN, SARNIA, ON, N7T 7M5
(519) 339-4015 *SIC* 2911

INTERNATIONAL GROUP, INC, THE *p874*
50 SALOME DR, SCARBOROUGH, ON, M1S 2A8
(416) 293-4151 *SIC* 2911

IOGEN CORPORATION *p827*
310 HUNT CLUB RD, OTTAWA, ON, K1V

1C1
(613) 733-9830 *SIC* 2911
IRVING OIL LIMITED *p415*
10 SYDNEY ST, SAINT JOHN, NB, E2L 5E6
(506) 202-2000 *SIC* 2911

NORTH ATLANTIC REFINING LIMITED *p430*
29 PIPPY PL, ST. JOHN'S, NL, A1B 3X2
(709) 463-8811 *SIC* 2911

NORTH WEST REDWATER PARTNERSHIP *p55*
140 4 AVE SW SUITE 2800, CALGARY, AB, T2P 3N3
(403) 398-0900 *SIC* 2911

OBSIDIAN ENERGY LTD *p127*
GD, FALHER, AB, T0H 1M0
(780) 837-2929 *SIC* 2911

PARKLAND INDUSTRIES LIMITED PARTNERSHIP *p154*
4919 59 ST SUITE 236, RED DEER, AB, T4N 6C9
(403) 343-1515 *SIC* 2911

PLACEMENTS BITUMAR INC, LES *p1238*
11155 RUE SAINTE-CATHERINE E, MONTREAL-EST, QC, H1B 0A4
(514) 645-4561 *SIC* 2911

SHELL CANADA LIMITED *p130*
55522 RANGE ROAD 214, FORT SASKATCHEWAN, AB, T8L 4A4
(780) 992-3600 *SIC* 2911

SHELL CANADA LIMITED *p563*
150 ST CLAIR PKY, CORUNNA, ON, N0N 1G0
(519) 481-1245 *SIC* 2911

SHELL CANADA LIMITED *p1238*
10501 RUE SHERBROOKE E, MONTREAL-EST, QC, H1B 1B3
(514) 645-1661 *SIC* 2911

SINOPEC DAYLIGHT ENERGY LTD *p59*
112 4 AVE SW SUITE 2700, CALGARY, AB, T2P 0H3
(403) 266-6900 *SIC* 2911

SUNCOR ENERGY INC *p60*
6 AVE SW SUITE 150, CALGARY, AB, T2P 3Y7
(403) 296-8000 *SIC* 2911

SUNCOR ENERGY INC *p91*
GD STN MAIN, EDMONTON, AB, T5J 2G8
(780) 410-5610 *SIC* 2911

SUNCOR ENERGY INC *p124*
801 PETROLEUM WAY NW, EDMONTON, AB, T6S 1H5
(780) 410-5681 *SIC* 2911

SUNCOR ENERGY INC *p214*
11527 ALASKA RD, FORT ST. JOHN, BC, V1J 6N2
(250) 787-8200 *SIC* 2911

SUNCOR ENERGY INC *p746*
535 ROKEBY LINE RR 1, MOORETOWN, ON, N0N 1M0
(519) 481-0454 *SIC* 2911

SUNCOR ENERGY INC *p805*
3275 REBECCA ST, OAKVILLE, ON, L6L 6N5
(905) 804-7152 *SIC* 2911

SUNCOR ENERGY INC *p1248*
11701 RUE SHERBROOKE E, POINTE-AUX-TREMBLES, QC, H1B 1C3
(514) 640-8000 *SIC* 2911

SUNCOR ENERGY PRODUCTS INC *p715*
2489 NORTH SHERIDAN WAY, MISSISSAUGA, ON, L5K 1A8
(905) 804-4500 *SIC* 2911

SUNCOR ENERGY PRODUCTS INC *p774*
36 YORK MILLS RD SUITE 110, NORTH YORK, ON, M2P 2E9
(416) 498-7751 *SIC* 2911

SUNCOR ENERGY PRODUCTS PARTNERSHIP *p60*
150 6 AVE SW, CALGARY, AB, T2P 3Y7
(403) 296-8000 *SIC* 2911

TOTAL CANADA INC *p1132*
220 AV LAFLEUR, LASALLE, QC, H8R 4C9
(514) 595-7579 *SIC* 2911

TRANSMONTAIGNE MARKETING CANADA

INC *p844*
1305 PICKERING PKY SUITE 101, PICKERING, ON, L1V 3P2
SIC 2911
WEST LORNE BIOOIL CO-GENERATION LIMITED PARTNERSHIP *p1013*
191 JANE ST, WEST LORNE, ON, N0L 2P0
SIC 2911

SIC 2951 Asphalt paving mixtures and blocks

FERMAR ASPHALT LIMITED *p584*
1921 ALBION RD, ETOBICOKE, ON, M9W 5S8
(416) 675-3550 *SIC* 2951

MUNICIPAL ENTERPRISES LIMITED *p440*
927 ROCKY LAKE DR, BEDFORD, NS, B4A 2T3
(902) 835-3381 *SIC* 2951

PAVAGE BOISVERT INC *p1300*
180 BOUL DE LA GABELLE, SAINT-ETIENNE-DES-GRES, QC, G0X 2P0
(819) 374-8277 *SIC* 2951

STANDARD GENERAL ASPHALT PLANT INC *p106*
12230 170 ST NW, EDMONTON, AB, T5V 1L7
(780) 447-1666 *SIC* 2951

SIC 2952 Asphalt felts and coatings

2595385 ONTARIO INC *p542*
650 RIVERVIEW DR, CHATHAM, ON, N7M 0N2
(519) 380-9265 *SIC* 2952

IKO INDUSTRIES LTD *p509*
80 STAFFORD DR, BRAMPTON, ON, L6W 1L4
(905) 457-2880 *SIC* 2952

IKO INDUSTRIES LTD *p619*
1451 SPENCE AVE, HAWKESBURY, ON, K6A 3T4
(613) 632-8581 *SIC* 2952

IKO INDUSTRIES LTD *p663*
105084 HWY 7, MADOC, ON, K0K 2K0
(613) 473-0430 *SIC* 2952

SOPREMA INC *p1099*
1688 RUE JEAN-BERCHMANS-MICHAUD, DRUMMONDVILLE, QC, J2C 8E9
(819) 478-8163 *SIC* 2952

SIC 2992 Lubricating oils and greases

CANADIAN TEST CASE 27 LTD *p730*
5770 HURONTARIO ST, MISSISSAUGA, ON, L5R 3G5
SIC 2992

ENVIROSYSTEMS INCORPORATED *p446*
11 BROWN AVE, DARTMOUTH, NS, B3B 1Z7
(902) 481-8008 *SIC* 2992

H.L. BLACHFORD, LTD *p713*
2323 ROYAL WINDSOR DR, MISSISSAUGA, ON, L5J 1K5
(905) 823-3200 *SIC* 2992

HIGHLANDS BLENDING & PACKAGING G.P. *p415*
555 COURTENAY CAUSEWAY, SAINT JOHN, NB, E2L 4E6
(506) 632-7000 *SIC* 2992

KLEEN-FLO TUMBLER INDUSTRIES LIMITED *p504*
75 ADVANCE BLVD, BRAMPTON, ON, L6T 4N1
(905) 793-4311 *SIC* 2992

LANXESS CANADA CO./CIE *p568*
25 ERB ST, ELMIRA, ON, N3B 3A3
(519) 669-1671 *SIC* 2992

LUBRIZOL CANADA LIMITED *p1032*
3700 STEELES AVE W SUITE 201, WOOD-

BRIDGE, ON, L4L 8K8
(905) 264-4646 *SIC 2992*
SAFETY-KLEEN CANADA INC *p518*
300 WOOLWICH ST S, BRESLAU, ON, N0B 1M0
(519) 648-2291 *SIC 2992*
SHELL CANADA LIMITED *p563*
339 LASALLE LINE RR 1, CORUNNA, ON, N0N 1G0
(519) 481-1369 *SIC 2992*

SIC 3011 Tires and inner tubes

AVANCEZ ASSEMBLY CANADA, ULC *p1024*
599 SPRUCEWOOD AVE, WINDSOR, ON, N9C 0B3
(226) 221-8800 *SIC 3011*
BRIDGESTONE CANADA INC *p1114*
1200 BOUL FIRESTONE, JOLIETTE, QC, J6E 2W5
(450) 756-1061 *SIC 3011*
CAMSO INC *p1147*
2633 RUE MACPHERSON, MAGOG, QC, J1X 0E6
(819) 868-1500 *SIC 3011*
DENRAY TIRE LTD *p369*
344 OAK POINT HWY, WINNIPEG, MB, R2R 1V1
(204) 632-7339 *SIC 3011*
GOODYEAR CANADA INC *p147*
1271 12 ST NW, MEDICINE HAT, AB, T1C 1W8
(403) 527-3353 *SIC 3011*
GOODYEAR CANADA INC *p574*
450 KIPLING AVE, ETOBICOKE, ON, M8Z 5E1
(416) 201-4300 *SIC 3011*
GOODYEAR CANADA INC *p747*
388 GOODYEAR RD, NAPANEE, ON, K7R 3L2
(613) 354-7411 *SIC 3011*
GOODYEAR CANADA INC *p1365*
2600 BOUL MONSEIGNEUR-LANGLOIS, SALABERRY-DE-VALLEYFIELD, QC, J6S 5G6
(450) 377-6800 *SIC 3011*
MICHELIN AMERIQUE DU NORD (CANADA) INC *p441*
233 LOGAN RD, BRIDGEWATER, NS, B4V 3T3
(902) 543-8141 *SIC 3011*

SIC 3021 Rubber and plastics footwear

CHAUSSURES RALLYE INC *p1048*
10001 BOUL RAY-LAWSON, ANJOU, QC, H1J 1L6
(514) 353-5888 *SIC 3021*
CROCS CANADA INC *p851*
1455 16TH AVE UNIT 7, RICHMOND HILL, ON, L4B 4W5
(905) 747-3366 *SIC 3021*

SIC 3052 Rubber and plastics hose and beltings

ACCUFLEX INDUSTRIAL HOSE LTD *p605*
760 IMPERIAL RD N, GUELPH, ON, N1K 1Z3
(519) 836-5460 *SIC 3052*
BREMO INC *p1292*
214 138 RTE, SAINT-AUGUSTIN-DE-DESMAURES, QC, G3A 2X9
(418) 878-4070 *SIC 3052*
KURIYAMA CANADA, INC *p514*
140 ROY BLVD, BRANTFORD, ON, N3R 7K2
(519) 753-6717 *SIC 3052*

SIC 3053 Gaskets; packing and sealing devices

A.R. THOMSON GROUP *p120*
10030 31 AVE NW, EDMONTON, AB, T6N 1G4
(780) 450-8080 *SIC 3053*
A.R. THOMSON GROUP *p278*
3420 189 ST, SURREY, BC, V3Z 1A7
(604) 507-6050 *SIC 3053*
ELRINGKLINGER CANADA, INC *p644*
1 SENECA RD, LEAMINGTON, ON, N8H 5P2
(519) 326-6113 *SIC 3053*
FLEXITALLIC CANADA LTD *p109*
4340 78 AVE NW, EDMONTON, AB, T6B 3J5
(780) 466-5050 *SIC 3053*
FREUDENBERG-NOK, INC *p911*
65 SPRUCE ST, TILLSONBURG, ON, N4G 5C4
(519) 842-6451 *SIC 3053*
HAMILTON KENT INC *p997*
77 CARLINGVIEW DR, TORONTO, ON, M9W 5E6
(416) 675-9873 *SIC 3053*
INDUSTRIES PRO-TAC INC, LES *p1296*
445 RUE JEAN-CLERMONT, SAINT-CELESTIN, QC, J0C 1G0
(819) 229-1288 *SIC 3053*
JACOBS & THOMPSON INC *p793*
89 KENHAR DR, NORTH YORK, ON, M9L 2R3
(416) 749-0600 *SIC 3053*
MULTI X INC *p1082*
60 RUE SHEARD, COATICOOK, QC, J1A 0B2
(819) 849-7036 *SIC 3053*
ROBCO INC *p1131*
7200 RUE SAINT-PATRICK, LASALLE, QC, H8N 2W7
(514) 367-2252 *SIC 3053*

SIC 3061 Mechanical rubber goods

CRANE, JOHN CANADA INC *p891*
423 GREEN RD, STONEY CREEK, ON, L8E 3A1
(905) 662-6191 *SIC 3061*

SIC 3069 Fabricated rubber products, nec

3011933 CANADA INC *p1082*
80 CH DES ETANGS, COOKSHIRE-EATON, QC, J0B 1M0
(819) 875-5559 *SIC 3069*
3101-2883 QUEBEC INC *p1370*
760 RUE CHALIFOUX, SHERBROOKE, QC, J1G 1R6
(819) 820-0808 *SIC 3069*
ABCO STC INC *p1377*
75 RUE PRINCIPALE, STANSTEAD, QC, J0B 3E5
(819) 876-7281 *SIC 3069*
ACR FULLER GROUP *p148*
511 12 AVE, NISKU, AB, T9E 7N8
(780) 955-2802 *SIC 3069*
ADVANCE ENGINEERED PRODUCTS LTD *p1415*
144 HENDERSON DR, REGINA, SK, S4N 5P7
(306) 721-5678 *SIC 3069*
AIRBOSS ENGINEERED PRODUCTS INC *p1044*
970 RUE LANDRY, ACTON VALE, QC, J0H 1A0
(450) 546-2776 *SIC 3069*
AIRBOSS OF AMERICA CORP *p638*
101 GLASGOW ST, KITCHENER, ON, N2G 4X8
(519) 576-5565 *SIC 3069*
AIRBOSS OF AMERICA CORP *p753*

16441 YONGE ST, NEWMARKET, ON, L3X 2G8
(905) 751-1188 *SIC 3069*
BARE SPORTS CANADA LTD *p191*
3711 NORTH FRASER WAY SUITE 50, BURNABY, BC, V5J 5J2
(604) 235-2630 *SIC 3069*
C.M. BRAKE INC *p546*
118 COUNTY ROAD 31, COLBORNE, ON, K0K 1S0
(905) 265-0265 *SIC 3069*
CG CANADIAN GLOVE CORP *p972*
67 KIMBARK BLVD, TORONTO, ON, M5N 2X9
(416) 939-5066 *SIC 3069*
CHAMPAGNE EDITION INC *p140*
57425 RGE RD 253, LEGAL, AB, T0G 1L0
(780) 961-3229 *SIC 3069*
CLARKE ROLLER & RUBBER LIMITED *p738*
6225 KENNEDY RD, MISSISSAUGA, ON, L5T 2S8
(905) 564-3215 *SIC 3069*
CONTITECH CANADA, INC *p721*
6711 MISSISSAUGA RD SUITE 01, MISSISSAUGA, ON, L5N 2W3
(905) 366-2010 *SIC 3069*
CONTITECH CANADA, INC *p1291*
127 RANG PARENT, SAINT-ALPHONSE-DE-GRANBY, QC, J0E 2A0
(450) 375-5050 *SIC 3069*
COOPER-STANDARD AUTOMOTIVE CANADA LIMITED *p895*
703 DOURO ST, STRATFORD, ON, N5A 3T1
(519) 271-3360 *SIC 3069*
FARLEY MANUFACTURING INC *p849*
6 KERR CRES, PUSLINCH, ON, N0B 2J0
(519) 821-5422 *SIC 3069*
GROUPE SOLMAX INC *p1392*
2801 RTE MARIE-VICTORIN, VARENNES, QC, J3X 1P7
(450) 929-1234 *SIC 3069*
INFINITY RUBBER TECHNOLOGY GROUP INC *p1011*
100 KENNEDY ST, WELLAND, ON, L3B 0B4
(905) 735-6366 *SIC 3069*
INTERWRAP ULC *p246*
1650 BROADWAY ST SUITE 101, PORT COQUITLAM, BC, V3C 2M8
SIC 3069
LOGIX ITS INC *p1132*
992 RUE D'UPTON, LASALLE, QC, H8R 2T9
(514) 448-9660 *SIC 3069*
MUSTANG SURVIVAL ULC *p193*
7525 LOWLAND DR, BURNABY, BC, V5J 5L1
(604) 270-8631 *SIC 3069*
PIONEER BALLOON CANADA LIMITED *p608*
333 KENORA AVE, HAMILTON, ON, L8E 2W3
(905) 560-6534 *SIC 3069*
POLY-NOVA TECHNOLOGIES INC *p601*
125 SOUTHGATE DR, GUELPH, ON, N1G 3M5
(519) 822-2109 *SIC 3069*
POLY-NOVA TECHNOLOGIES LIMITED PARTNERSHIP *p601*
125 SOUTHGATE DR, GUELPH, ON, N1G 3M5
(519) 822-2109 *SIC 3069*
POLYCORP LTD *p569*
33 YORK ST W, ELORA, ON, N0B 1S0
(519) 846-2075 *SIC 3069*
POLYCORP LTD *p965*
123 FRONT ST W SUITE 905, TORONTO, ON, M5J 2M2
(416) 364-2241 *SIC 3069*
PRODUCTIONS ATLAN INC., LES *p1293*
120 RUE DE ROTTERDAM, SAINT-AUGUSTIN-DE-DESMAURES, QC, G3A 1T3

(418) 878-5881 *SIC 3069*
PRODUITS AMERICAN BILTRITE (CANADA) LTEE *p1371*
200 RUE BANK, SHERBROOKE, QC, J1H 4K3
(819) 829-3300 *SIC 3069*
PRODUITS AMERICAN BILTRITE (CANADA) LTEE *p1374*
635 RUE PEPIN, SHERBROOKE, QC, J1L 2P8
(819) 823-3300 *SIC 3069*
RCR INTERNATIONAL INC *p793*
89 KENHAR DR, NORTH YORK, ON, M9L 2R3
(416) 749-0600 *SIC 3069*
ROYAL MAT INC *p1055*
132 181E RUE, BEAUCEVILLE, QC, G5X 2S8
(418) 774-3694 *SIC 3069*
SOCIETE MONDO AMERICA INC *p1362*
2655 AV FRANCIS-HUGHES, SAINTE-ROSE, QC, H7L 3S8
(450) 967-5800 *SIC 3069*
SOUCY BARON INC *p1320*
851 RUE BARON, SAINT-JEROME, QC, J7Y 4E1
(450) 436-2433 *SIC 3069*
SOUCY TECHNO INC *p1375*
2550 CH SAINT-ROCH S, SHERBROOKE, QC, J1N 2R6
(819) 864-4284 *SIC 3069*
TULMAR SAFETY SYSTEMS INC *p619*
1123 CAMERON ST, HAWKESBURY, ON, K6A 2B8
(613) 632-1282 *SIC 3069*
WATERVILLE TG INC *p843*
4491 DISCOVERY LINE, PETROLIA, ON, N0N 1R0
(519) 882-4366 *SIC 3069*
WATERVILLE TG INC *p1082*
500 RUE DIONNE, COATICOOK, QC, J1A 2E8
(819) 849-7031 *SIC 3069*

SIC 3081 Unsupported plastics film and sheet

6894658 CANADA INC *p1160*
10660 BOUL HENRI-BOURASSA E, MONTREAL, QC, H1C 1G9
(514) 881-1234 *SIC 3081*
ALROS PRODUCTS LIMITED *p782*
350 WILDCAT RD, NORTH YORK, ON, M3J 2N5
(416) 661-1750 *SIC 3081*
ATELIER POLY-TECK INC *p1373*
151 RUE LEGER, SHERBROOKE, QC, J1L 2G8
(819) 563-6636 *SIC 3081*
BERRY PLASTICS CANADA INC *p866*
595 CORONATION DR, SCARBOROUGH, ON, M1E 2K4
(416) 281-6000 *SIC 3081*
CANADIAN GENERAL-TOWER LIMITED *p533*
52 MIDDLETON ST, CAMBRIDGE, ON, N1R 5T6
(519) 623-1633 *SIC 3081*
CASCADES INC *p1117*
455 BOUL MARIE-VICTORIN, KINGSEY FALLS, QC, J0A 1B0
(819) 363-5300 *SIC 3081*
COPOL INTERNATIONAL LTD.-PACKAGING FILMS *p464*
69 HARTIGAN DR, NORTH SYDNEY, NS, B0A 1H0
(902) 794-9685 *SIC 3081*
DOW CHEMICAL CANADA ULC *p794*
122 ARROW RD, NORTH YORK, ON, M9M 2M1
SIC 3081
EMBALLAGE PERFORMANT INC *p1088*
301 BOUL GRAND N, COWANSVILLE, QC, J2K 1A8

(450) 263-6363   *SIC 3081*
EMBALLAGES POLYSTAR INC   *p1162*
7975 AV MARCO-POLO, MONTREAL, QC, H1E 1N8
(514) 648-8171   *SIC 3081*
ENTREPOSEURS DE FIBRES R & F LTEE   *p1162*
7975 AV MARCO-POLO, MONTREAL, QC, H1E 1N8
(514) 648-8171   *SIC 3081*
EPAK INC   *p372*
55 PLYMOUTH ST, WINNIPEG, MB, R2X 2V5
(204) 947-1383   *SIC 3081*
GREAT PACIFIC ENTERPRISES INC   *p305*
1067 CORDOVA ST W UNIT 1800, VANCOUVER, BC, V6C 1C7
(604) 688-6764   *SIC 3081*
GREAT PACIFIC ENTERPRISES INC   *p1085*
1890 BOUL FORTIN, COTE SAINT-LUC, QC, H7S 1N8
(450) 662-1030   *SIC 3081*
GREAT PACIFIC ENTERPRISES INC   *p1111*
700 RUE VADNAIS, GRANBY, QC, J2J 1A7
(450) 378-3995   *SIC 3081*
GREAT PACIFIC ENTERPRISES LIMITED PARTNERSHIP   *p480*
325 INDUSTRIAL PKY S, AURORA, ON, L4G 3V8
(905) 727-0121   *SIC 3081*
HAREMAR PLASTIC MANUFACTURING LIMITED   *p553*
200 GREAT GULF DR, CONCORD, ON, L4K 5W1
(905) 761-7552   *SIC 3081*
IMAFLEX INC   *p1223*
5710 RUE NOTRE-DAME O, MONTREAL, QC, H4C 1V2
(514) 935-5710   *SIC 3081*
INDUSTRIES D'EMBALLAGES STARPAC LTEE, LES   *p1247*
12105 BOUL INDUSTRIEL, POINTE-AUX-TREMBLES, QC, H1B 5W4
(514) 645-5895   *SIC 3081*
INDUSTRIES DE MOULAGE POLYTECH INC, LES   *p1109*
454 RUE EDOUARD, GRANBY, QC, J2G 3Z3
(450) 378-9093   *SIC 3081*
INDUSTRIES DE PLASTIQUE TRANSCO LTEE, LES   *p1156*
8096 CH MONTVIEW, MONT-ROYAL, QC, H4P 2L7
(514) 733-9951   *SIC 3081*
INTEPLAST BAGS AND FILMS CORPORATION   *p1130*
1 RUE VIFAN, LANORAIE, QC, J0K 1E0
(450) 887-7711   *SIC 3081*
IRIDIAN SPECTRAL TECHNOLOGIES LIMITED   *p818*
2700 SWANSEA CRES, OTTAWA, ON, K1G 6R8
(613) 741-4513   *SIC 3081*
LAYFIELD CANADA LTD   *p263*
11131 HAMMERSMITH GATE, RICHMOND, BC, V7A 5E6
(604) 275-5588   *SIC 3081*
MERCURY PLASTICS OF CANADA INC   *p206*
880 CLIVEDEN AVE, DELTA, BC, V3M 5R5
(604) 525-1061   *SIC 3081*
NEUCEL SPECIALTY CELLULOSE LTD   *p245*
300 MARINE DRIVE, PORT ALICE, BC, V0N 2N0
(250) 284-3331   *SIC 3081*
NEUCEL SPECIALTY CELLULOSE LTD   *p263*
11331 COPPERSMITH WAY SUITE 305, RICHMOND, BC, V7A 5J9
SIC 3081
PACKALL CONSULTANTS (1981) LIMITED   *p505*
2 SHAFTSBURY LANE, BRAMPTON, ON,

L6T 3X7
(905) 793-0177   *SIC 3081*
PACKALL PACKAGING INC   *p505*
2 SHAFTSBURY LANE, BRAMPTON, ON, L6T 3X7
(905) 793-0177   *SIC 3081*
PLASSEIN INTERNATIONAL OF NEWMARKET INC   *p756*
175 DEERFIELD RD, NEWMARKET, ON, L3Y 2L8
(905) 895-2308   *SIC 3081*
PLASTIQUES BALCAN LIMITEE, LES *p1345*
9340 RUE DE MEAUX, SAINT-LEONARD, QC, H1R 3H2
(514) 326-0200   *SIC 3081*
PLASTIQUES BERRY CANADA INC   *p810*
301 FOREST AVE, ORILLIA, ON, L3V 3Y7
(705) 326-8921   *SIC 3081*
POLYEXPERT INC   *p1342*
850 AV MUNCK, SAINT-LAURENT, QC, H7S 1B1
(514) 384-5060   *SIC 3081*
POLYFORM A.G.P. INC   *p1111*
870 BOUL INDUSTRIEL, GRANBY, QC, J2J 1A4
(450) 378-9093   *SIC 3081*
PROPAK PLASTICS (1979) LTD   *p1118*
16817 BOUL HYMUS, KIRKLAND, QC, H9H 3L4
(514) 695-9520   *SIC 3081*
REGENCY PLASTICS COMPANY LIMITED *p784*
50 BRISBANE RD, NORTH YORK, ON, M3J 2K2
(416) 661-3000   *SIC 3081*
SOLMAX INTERNATIONAL INC   *p1393*
2801 RTE MARIE-VICTORIN, VARENNES, QC, J3X 1P7
(450) 929-1234   *SIC 3081*
UTHANE RESEARCH LTD   *p676*
140 BENTLEY ST UNIT 2, MARKHAM, ON, L3R 3L2
(905) 940-2356   *SIC 3081*
VINS PLASTICS LTD   *p498*
12 INDUSTRIAL CRT, BRADFORD, ON, L3Z 3G6
(905) 775-7901   *SIC 3081*
WINPAK LTD   *p386*
100 SAULTEAUX CRES, WINNIPEG, MB, R3J 3T3
(204) 889-1015   *SIC 3081*

SIC 3083 Laminated plastics plate and sheet

DOMFOAM INC   *p1344*
8785 BOUL LANGELIER, SAINT-LEONARD, QC, H1P 2C9
(514) 325-8120   *SIC 3083*
GROUPE ERA INC   *p1329*
2500 RUE GUENETTE, SAINT-LAURENT, QC, H4R 2H2
(514) 335-0550   *SIC 3083*
PREMOULE INC   *p1267*
2375 AV DALTON BUREAU 200, QUEBEC, QC, G1P 3S3
(418) 652-7777   *SIC 3083*
PREMOULE INC   *p1293*
270 RUE DES GRANDS-LACS, SAINT-AUGUSTIN-DE-DESMAURES, QC, G3A 2K1
(418) 878-5384   *SIC 3083*
PRODUITS THERMOVISION INC   *p1318*
680 BOUL INDUSTRIEL, SAINT-JEAN-SUR-RICHELIEU, QC, J3B 7X4
(450) 348-4970   *SIC 3083*
PUBCO PRODUITS INTERNATIONALS INC *p1059*
32 BOUL DE LA SEIGNEURIE E, BLAINVILLE, QC, J7C 3V5
(450) 433-4272   *SIC 3083*
ROCHLING ENGINEERING PLASTICS LTD *p808*
21 TIDEMAN DR, ORANGEVILLE, ON, L9W 3K3

(519) 941-5300   *SIC 3083*
VIVA HEALTHCARE PACKAGING (CANADA) LTD   *p879*
1663 NEILSON RD SUITE 13, SCARBOROUGH, ON, M1X 1T1
(416) 321-0622   *SIC 3083*

SIC 3084 Plastics pipe

POLYTUBES 2009 INC   *p106*
16221 123 AVE NW, EDMONTON, AB, T5V 1N9
(780) 453-2211   *SIC 3084*
POLYTUBES 2009 INC   *p841*
416 PIDO RD, PETERBOROUGH, ON, K9J 6X7
(705) 740-2872   *SIC 3084*
ROYAL GROUP, INC   *p1033*
131 REGALCREST CRT, WOODBRIDGE, ON, L4L 8P3
(905) 652-0461   *SIC 3084*
ST. SHREDDIES CELLO CO. LTD   *p743*
6141 ATLANTIC DR UNIT 1, MISSISSAUGA, ON, L5T 1L9
(905) 670-2414   *SIC 3084*

SIC 3085 Plastics bottles

CONTAINER CORPORATION OF CANADA LTD   *p851*
68 LEEK CRES, RICHMOND HILL, ON, L4B 1H1
(905) 764-3777   *SIC 3085*
MPI PACKAGING INC   *p735*
7400B BRAMALEA RD, MISSISSAUGA, ON, L5S 1W9
(905) 673-6447   *SIC 3085*
WEBER INTERNATIONAL PACKAGING CORPORATION   *p1395*
269 RUE ADRIEN-PATENAUDE, VAUDREUIL-DORION, QC, J7V 5V5
(450) 455-0169   *SIC 3085*

SIC 3086 Plastics foam products

10013340 CANADA INC   *p1088*
75 BOUL DUPONT, COTEAU-DU-LAC, QC, J0P 1B0
(450) 455-0961   *SIC 3086*
643487 ONTARIO LIMITED   *p1001*
1 PARRATT RD, UXBRIDGE, ON, L9P 1R1
(905) 862-0830   *SIC 3086*
A-Z FOAM LTD   *p205*
811 CUNDY AVE, DELTA, BC, V3M 5P6
(604) 525-1665   *SIC 3086*
CKF INC   *p459*
48 PRINCE ST, HANTSPORT, NS, B0P 1P0
(902) 684-3231   *SIC 3086*
CKF INC   *p583*
218 BELFIELD RD, ETOBICOKE, ON, M9W 1H3
(416) 249-4612   *SIC 3086*
COLOR AD PACKAGING LTD   *p365*
200 BEGHIN AVE, WINNIPEG, MB, R2J 3W2
(204) 777-7770   *SIC 3086*
CUSTOM FOAM SYSTEMS LTD   *p637*
360 TRILLIUM DR, KITCHENER, ON, N2E 2K6
(519) 748-1700   *SIC 3086*
DOMFOAM INC   *p1344*
6675 RUE BOMBARDIER, SAINT-LEONARD, QC, H1P 2W2
(514) 852-3959   *SIC 3086*
DOMFOAM INTERNATIONAL INC   *p1344*
8785 BOUL LANGELIER, SAINT-LEONARD, QC, H1P 2C9
(514) 325-8120   *SIC 3086*
FOAMCO INDUSTRIES CORPORATION *p552*
8400 KEELE ST UNIT 2, CONCORD, ON,

L4K 2A6
(416) 784-9777   *SIC 3086*
GREAT PACIFIC ENTERPRISES LIMITED PARTNERSHIP   *p716*
3185 PEPPER MILL CRT, MISSISSAUGA, ON, L5L 4X3
(905) 569-3660   *SIC 3086*
GROUPE EMBALLAGE SPECIALISE S.E.C. *p890*
140 IBER RD, STITTSVILLE, ON, K2S 1E9
(613) 742-6766   *SIC 3086*
HARTMANN DOMINION INC   *p517*
58 FRANK ST, BRANTFORD, ON, N3T 5E2
(519) 756-8500   *SIC 3086*
ICYNENE INC   *p723*
6747 CAMPOBELLO RD, MISSISSAUGA, ON, L5N 2L7
(905) 363-4040   *SIC 3086*
INDUSTRIES DE MOULAGE POLYMAX INC, LES   *p1109*
454 RUE EDOUARD, GRANBY, QC, J2G 3Z3
(450) 378-9093   *SIC 3086*
KOOLATRON CORPORATION   *p513*
139 COPERNICUS BLVD, BRANTFORD, ON, N3P 1N4
(519) 756-3950   *SIC 3086*
KRISTOFOAM INDUSTRIES INC   *p554*
160 PLANCHET RD, CONCORD, ON, L4K 2C7
(905) 669-6616   *SIC 3086*
KRISTOFOAM INDUSTRIES INC   *p555*
120 PLANCHET RD, CONCORD, ON, L4K 2C7
(905) 669-6616   *SIC 3086*
LEPAGES 2000 INC   *p776*
41 LESMILL RD, NORTH YORK, ON, M3B 2T3
(416) 751-4343   *SIC 3086*
PFB CORPORATION   *p9*
2891 SUNRIDGE WAY NE SUITE 300, CALGARY, AB, T1Y 7K7
(403) 569-4300   *SIC 3086*
POLYMOS INC   *p1378*
150 5E BOUL, TERRASSE-VAUDREUIL, QC, J7V 5M3
(514) 453-1920   *SIC 3086*
POLYNOVA INDUSTRIES INC   *p263*
11480 BLACKSMITH PL UNIT 101, RICHMOND, BC, V7A 4X1
(604) 277-1274   *SIC 3086*
SONOCO FLEXIBLE PACKAGING CANADA CORPORATION   *p516*
33 PARK AVE E, BRANTFORD, ON, N3S 7R9
(519) 752-6591   *SIC 3086*
THERMALITE PRODUCTS INC   *p396*
2598 CH ACADIE, CAP-PELE, NB, E4N 1E3
(506) 577-4351   *SIC 3086*
WESTERN CONCORD MANUFACTURING (NEW WEST) LTD   *p207*
880 CLIVEDEN AVE, DELTA, BC, V3M 5R5
(604) 525-1061   *SIC 3086*
WOODBRIDGE FOAM CORPORATION *p708*
4240 SHERWOODTOWNE BLVD SUITE 300, MISSISSAUGA, ON, L4Z 2G6
(905) 896-3626   *SIC 3086*

SIC 3087 Custom compound purchased resins

LAVERGNE GROUPE INC   *p1049*
8800 1ER CROISSANT, ANJOU, QC, H1J 1C8
(514) 354-5757   *SIC 3087*
POLYNT COMPOSITES CANADA INC *p513*
29 REGAN RD, BRAMPTON, ON, L7A 1B2
(905) 495-0606   *SIC 3087*

SIC 3088 Plastics plumbing fixtures

130355 CANADA INC   *p1301*

225 RUE ROY, SAINT-EUSTACHE, QC, J7R 5R5
(450) 472-0024   *SIC 3088*

BROOKFIELD CAPITAL PARTNERS II L.P. *p960*
181 BAY ST SUITE 300, TORONTO, ON, M5J 2T3
(416) 363-9491   *SIC 3088*

CANPLAS INDUSTRIES LTD *p486*
500 VETERANS DR, BARRIE, ON, L4N 9J5
(705) 726-3361   *SIC 3088*

GROHE CANADA INC *p731*
5900 AVEBURY RD, MISSISSAUGA, ON, L5R 3M3
(905) 271-2929   *SIC 3088*

IPEX INC *p228*
20460 DUNCAN WAY, LANGLEY, BC, V3A 7A3
(604) 534-8631   *SIC 3088*

IPEX INC *p868*
807 PHARMACY AVE, SCARBOROUGH, ON, M1L 3K2
(416) 445-3400   *SIC 3088*

IPEX INC *p1314*
247 RUE PRINCIPALE, SAINT-JACQUES, QC, J0K 2R0
(450) 839-2655   *SIC 3088*

MAAX BATH INC *p1126*
160 BOUL SAINT-JOSEPH, LACHINE, QC, H8S 2L3
(514) 844-4155   *SIC 3088*

MCCAFFERY GROUP INC *p106*
12160 160 ST NW, EDMONTON, AB, T5V 1H5
(780) 452-8375   *SIC 3088*

POLYTUBES INC *p106*
12160 160 ST NW, EDMONTON, AB, T5V 1H5
(780) 453-2211   *SIC 3088*

UPONOR INFRA LTD *p621*
37 CENTRE ST N, HUNTSVILLE, ON, P1H 1X4
(705) 789-2396   *SIC 3088*

SIC 3089 Plastics products, nec

1147048 ONTARIO LIMITED *p807*
5000 REGAL DR, OLDCASTLE, ON, N0R 1L0
(519) 737-7535   *SIC 3089*

119678 CANADA INC *p1239*
11600 BOUL ALBERT-HUDON, MONTREAL-NORD, QC, H1G 3K2
(514) 328-4230   *SIC 3089*

1216037 ONTARIO INC *p870*
170 MIDWEST RD, SCARBOROUGH, ON, M1P 3A9
(416) 751-9445   *SIC 3089*

1939243 ONTARIO LTD *p500*
316 ORENDA RD, BRAMPTON, ON, L6T 1G3
(905) 793-7100   *SIC 3089*

600956 ONTARIO LTD *p609*
469 WOODWARD AVE, HAMILTON, ON, L8H 6N6
(905) 549-4572   *SIC 3089*

682770 ONTARIO INC *p915*
49 RAILSIDE RD, TORONTO, ON, M3A 1B3
(416) 289-2344   *SIC 3089*

A.P. PLASMAN INC *p1017*
418 SILVER CREEK INDUSTRIAL DR, WINDSOR, ON, N8N 4Y3
(519) 727-4545   *SIC 3089*

A.P. PLASMAN INC *p1022*
5245 BURKE ST, WINDSOR, ON, N9A 6J3
(519) 737-6984   *SIC 3089*

A.P. PLASMAN INC *p1022*
5265 OUTER DR, WINDSOR, ON, N9A 6J3
(519) 737-9602   *SIC 3089*

A.P. PLASMAN INC *p1022*
5265 OUTER DR SUITE 2, WINDSOR, ON, N9A 6J3
(519) 737-9602   *SIC 3089*

A.P. PLASMAN INC *p1024*
635 SPRUCEWOOD AVE, WINDSOR, ON, N9C 0B3
(519) 791-9119   *SIC 3089*

ABC AIR MANAGEMENT SYSTEMS INC *p581*
110 RONSON DR, ETOBICOKE, ON, M9W 1B6
(416) 744-3113   *SIC 3089*

ABC CLIMATE CONTROL SYSTEMS INC *p581*
54 BETHRIDGE RD, ETOBICOKE, ON, M9W 1N1
(416) 744-3113   *SIC 3089*

ABC INOAC EXTERIOR SYSTEMS INC *p581*
220 BROCKPORT DR, ETOBICOKE, ON, M9W 5S1
(416) 675-7480   *SIC 3089*

ABC INTERIOR SYSTEMS INC *p581*
10 DISCO RD, ETOBICOKE, ON, M9W 1L7
(416) 675-2220   *SIC 3089*

ABC TECHNOLOGIES INC *p500*
303 ORENDA RD SUITE B, BRAMPTON, ON, L6T 5C3
(905) 450-3600   *SIC 3089*

ABC TECHNOLOGIES INC *p581*
20 BRYDON DR, ETOBICOKE, ON, M9W 5R6
SIC 3089

ABC TECHNOLOGIES INC *p687*
3325 ORLANDO DR, MISSISSAUGA, ON, L4V 1C5
(905) 671-0310   *SIC 3089*

ABC TECHNOLOGIES INC *p792*
2 NORELCO DR, NORTH YORK, ON, M9L 2X6
(416) 246-1782   *SIC 3089*

ABCORP CA LTD *p870*
15 GOLDEN GATE CRT, SCARBOROUGH, ON, M1P 3A4
(416) 293-3842   *SIC 3089*

ACAN WINDOWS INC *p427*
1641 TOPSAIL RD, PARADISE, NL, A1L 1V1
SIC 3089

ACCORD PLASTICS CORP *p548*
60 COURTLAND AVE, CONCORD, ON, L4K 5B3
SIC 3089

ACRYLIQUE WEEDON (1995) INC *p1383*
591 RUE DES ENTREPRISES, THETFORD MINES, QC, G6H 4B2
(418) 332-4224   *SIC 3089*

ACRYLON PLASTICS INC *p357*
2954 DAY ST, SPRINGFIELD, MB, R2C 2Z2
(204) 669-2224   *SIC 3089*

ACRYLON PLASTICS MB (1983) INC *p361*
355 AIRPORT DR, WINKLER, MB, R6W 0J9
(204) 325-9569   *SIC 3089*

ADVANTAGE ENGINEERING INC *p807*
5000 REGAL DR, OLDCASTLE, ON, N0R 1L0
(519) 737-7535   *SIC 3089*

ADVANTAGE ENGINEERING INC *p1023*
2030 NORTH TALBOT RD, WINDSOR, ON, N9A 6J3
(519) 737-7535   *SIC 3089*

ADVENTEC MANUFACTURING INC *p566*
55 INNOVATION DR, DUNDAS, ON, L9H 7L8
(289) 895-7909   *SIC 3089*

ALLCARD LIMITED *p537*
765 BOXWOOD DR SUITE 650, CAMBRIDGE, ON, N3E 1A4
(519) 650-9515   *SIC 3089*

AMCOR RIGID PLASTICS ATLANTIC, INC *p508*
95 BISCAYNE CRES, BRAMPTON, ON, L6W 4R2
(905) 450-5579   *SIC 3089*

AMHIL ENTERPRISES *p704*
400 TRADERS BLVD E, MISSISSAUGA, ON, L4Z 1W7
(905) 890-5261   *SIC 3089*

AMHIL ENTERPRISES LTD *p704*
400 TRADERS BLVD E, MISSISSAUGA, ON, L4Z 1W7
(905) 890-5261   *SIC 3089*

ARMADA TOOLWORKS LIMITED *p645*
6 LOF DR, LINDSAY, ON, K9V 4S5
(705) 328-9599   *SIC 3089*

ATLANTIC ALL-WEATHER WINDOWS LTD *p411*
49 EAST MAIN ST, PORT ELGIN, NB, E4M 2X9
(506) 538-2361   *SIC 3089*

AVENEX COATING TECHNOLOGIES INC *p259*
11938 BRIDGEPORT RD UNIT 260, RICHMOND, BC, V6X 1T2
(604) 716-4599   *SIC 3089*

AXIOM PLASTICS INC *p480*
115 MARY ST, AURORA, ON, L4G 1G3
(905) 727-2878   *SIC 3089*

B.T.E. ASSEMBLY LTD *p646*
801 TREMAINE AVE S, LISTOWEL, ON, N4W 3G9
(519) 291-5322   *SIC 3089*

BAINS ULTRA INC *p1140*
956 CH OLIVIER, LEVIS, QC, G7A 2N1
(418) 831-4344   *SIC 3089*

BAYTECH PLASTICS INC *p681*
16403 HWY 12, MIDLAND, ON, L4R 4L6
(705) 526-7801   *SIC 3089*

BAYTECH PLASTICS INC *p681*
320 ELIZABETH ST, MIDLAND, ON, L4R 1Y9
(705) 526-7801   *SIC 3089*

BEAVER PLASTICS LTD *p1*
11581 272 ST, ACHESON, AB, T7X 6E9
(780) 962-4433   *SIC 3089*

BOCK NORTH AMERICA LTD *p538*
18 CHERRY BLOSSOM RD, CAMBRIDGE, ON, N3H 4R7
(519) 653-3334   *SIC 3089*

BOW GROUPE DE PLOMBERIE INC *p1108*
15 RUE VITTIE, GRANBY, QC, J2G 6N8
(450) 372-5481   *SIC 3089*

BOW GROUPE DE PLOMBERIE INC *p1157*
5700 CH DE LA COTE-DE-LIESSE, MONTROYAL, QC, H4T 1B1
(514) 735-5551   *SIC 3089*

CARON & GUAY INC *p1055*
95 RUE INDUSTRIELLE, BEAUPRE, QC, G0A 1E0
(418) 827-2459   *SIC 3089*

CARPENTER CANADA CO *p14*
5800 36 ST SE, CALGARY, AB, T2C 2A9
(403) 279-2466   *SIC 3089*

CASA BELLA WINDOWS INC *p685*
7630 AIRPORT RD, MISSISSAUGA, ON, L4T 4G6
(416) 650-1033   *SIC 3089*

CASCADES CANADA ULC *p1096*
500 RUE LAUZON, DRUMMONDVILLE, QC, J2B 2Z3
(819) 472-5757   *SIC 3089*

COLOURFAST SECURE CARD TECHNOLOGY INC *p693*
5380 TIMBERLEA BLVD, MISSISSAUGA, ON, L4W 2S6
(905) 206-9477   *SIC 3089*

COLUMBIA PLASTICS LTD *p271*
19320 60 AVE, SURREY, BC, V3S 3M2
(604) 530-9990   *SIC 3089*

CONCEPT PLASTICS LIMITED *p517*
27 CATHARINE AVE, BRANTFORD, ON, N3T 1X5
(519) 759-1900   *SIC 3089*

CONTENANTS I.M.L. D'AMERIQUE DU NORD INC, LES *p1350*
2625 344 RTE, SAINT-PLACIDE, QC, J0V 2B0
(450) 258-3130   *SIC 3089*

COVERTECH FABRICATING INC *p583*
279 HUMBERLINE DR SUITE 1, ETOBICOKE, ON, M9W 5T6
(416) 798-1340   *SIC 3089*

CREST MOLD TECHNOLOGY INC *p807*
2055 BLACKACRE DR RR 1, OLDCASTLE, ON, N0R 1L0
(519) 737-1546   *SIC 3089*

CUBE PACKAGING SOLUTIONS INC *p480*
200 INDUSTRIAL PKY N, AURORA, ON, L4G 4C3
(905) 750-2823   *SIC 3089*

CUSTOM PLASTICS INTERNATIONAL LIMITED *p545*
887 D'ARCY ST, COBOURG, ON, K9A 4B4
(905) 372-2281   *SIC 3089*

DEL WINDOWS & DOORS INC *p891*
241 ARVIN AVE, STONEY CREEK, ON, L8E 2L9
(905) 561-4335   *SIC 3089*

DOLLKEN WOODTAPE *p502*
230 ORENDA RD, BRAMPTON, ON, L6T 1E9
(905) 673-5156   *SIC 3089*

DRADER MANUFACTURING INDUSTRIES LTD *p109*
5750 50 ST NW, EDMONTON, AB, T6B 2Z8
(780) 440-2231   *SIC 3089*

DURON PLASTICS LIMITED *p636*
965 WILSON AVE, KITCHENER, ON, N2C 1J1
(519) 884-8011   *SIC 3089*

DYNE-A-PAK INC *p1362*
3375 AV FRANCIS-HUGHES, SAINTEROSE, QC, H7L 5A5
(450) 667-3626   *SIC 3089*

EASY PLASTIC CONTAINERS CORPORATION *p552*
101 JARDIN DR UNIT 10, CONCORD, ON, L4K 1X6
(905) 669-4466   *SIC 3089*

EG INDUSTRIES CANADA, ULC *p896*
291 GRIFFITH RD UNIT 2, STRATFORD, ON, N5A 6S4
(519) 273-3733   *SIC 3089*

ENTREPRISES DERO INC *p1240*
9960 AV PLAZA, MONTREAL-NORD, QC, H1H 4L6
(514) 327-1108   *SIC 3089*

EUROLINE WINDOWS INC *p208*
7620 MACDONALD RD, DELTA, BC, V4G 1N2
(604) 940-8485   *SIC 3089*

EXCO TECHNOLOGIES LIMITED *p446*
35 AKERLEY BLVD, DARTMOUTH, NS, B3B 1J7
(902) 468-6663   *SIC 3089*

EXO-S INC *p1283*
425 10E AV, RICHMOND, QC, J0B 2H0
(819) 826-5911   *SIC 3089*

EXTREME WINDOW AND ENTRANCE SYSTEMS INC *p408*
80 LOFTUS ST, MONCTON, NB, E1E 2N2
(506) 384-3667   *SIC 3089*

FENE-TECH INC *p1046*
264 BOUL SAINT-BENOIT E, AMQUI, QC, G5J 2C5
(418) 629-4675   *SIC 3089*

FENETRES MAGISTRAL WINDOWS INC *p1059*
705 BOUL INDUSTRIEL, BLAINVILLE, QC, J7C 3V3
(450) 433-8733   *SIC 3089*

FORMICA CANADA INC *p1318*
25 RUE MERCIER, SAINT-JEAN-SUR-RICHELIEU, QC, J3B 6E9
(450) 347-7541   *SIC 3089*

FOURMARK MANUFACTURING INC *p797*
2690 PLYMOUTH DR, OAKVILLE, ON, L6H 6W3
(905) 855-8777   *SIC 3089*

FUTURA MANUFACTURIER DE PORTES ET FENETRES INC *p1264*
1451 RUE FRANK-CARREL, QUEBEC, QC, G1N 4N7
(418) 681-7272   *SIC 3089*

G-SPEK INC *p1147*
2039 RUE RENE-PATENAUDE, MAGOG,

QC, J1X 7J2
(819) 868-7655   *SIC* 3089
GESTION BC-A INC   *p*1348
38 AV DU PONT O, SAINT-MARTIN, QC, G0M 1B0
(418) 382-3930   *SIC* 3089
GESTION SOLUTIONS PLASTIK INC *p*1147
2123 BOUL INDUSTRIEL, MAGOG, QC, J1X 7J7
(819) 847-2466   *SIC* 3089
GIESECKE+DEVRIENT MOBILE SECURITY CANADA, INC   *p*679
316 MARKLAND ST, MARKHAM, ON, L6C 0C1
(905) 475-1333   *SIC* 3089
GLOBAL PLAS INC   *p*553
120 SPINNAKER WAY, CONCORD, ON, L4K 2P6
(905) 760-2800   *SIC* 3089
GLOBAL PLASTICS   *p*271
19440 ENTERPRISE WAY, SURREY, BC, V3S 6J9
(604) 514-0600   *SIC* 3089
GLOBAL WINDOW SOLUTIONS INC *p*411
128 RUE INDUSTRIAL, RICHIBUCTO, NB, E4W 4A4
(506) 523-4900   *SIC* 3089
GOLDEN WINDOWS LIMITED   *p*639
888 GUELPH ST, KITCHENER, ON, N2H 5Z6
(519) 579-3810   *SIC* 3089
GRACIOUS LIVING CORPORATION *p*1031
7200 MARTIN GROVE RD, WOODBRIDGE, ON, L4L 9J3
(905) 264-5660   *SIC* 3089
GRACIOUS LIVING INNOVATIONS INC*p*744
151 COURTNEYPARK DR W SUITE 201, MISSISSAUGA, ON, L5W 1Y5
(905) 795-5505   *SIC* 3089
GRAHAM PACKAGING CANADA LIMITED *p*711
3174 MAVIS RD, MISSISSAUGA, ON, L5C 1T8
(905) 277-1486   *SIC* 3089
GROUPE EMBALLAGE SPECIALISE S.E.C. *p*1250
3300 RTE TRANSCANADIENNE, POINTE-CLAIRE, QC, H9R 1B1
(514) 636-7951   *SIC* 3089
GROUPE G.L.P. HI-TECH INC   *p*1318
440 RUE SAINT-MICHEL, SAINT-JEAN-SUR-RICHELIEU, QC, J3B 1T4
(450) 348-4918   *SIC* 3089
GROUPE POLYALTO INC   *p*1276
3825 RUE JEAN-MARCHAND, QUEBEC, QC, G2C 2J2
(418) 847-8311   *SIC* 3089
GROUPE PPD INC   *p*1400
325 RUE PRINCIPALE N, WATERVILLE, QC, J0B 3H0
(819) 837-2491   *SIC* 3089
H.S.T. SYNTHETICS LTD   *p*739
6630 EDWARDS BLVD, MISSISSAUGA, ON, L5T 2V6
(905) 670-3432   *SIC* 3089
HAWK PLASTICS LTD   *p*1023
5295 BURKE ST, WINDSOR, ON, N9A 6J3
(519) 737-1452   *SIC* 3089
HOFMANN, E. PLASTICS, INC   *p*808
51 CENTENNIAL RD, ORANGEVILLE, ON, L9W 3R1
(519) 943-5050   *SIC* 3089
HORIZON PLASTICS INTERNATIONAL INC *p*545
BLDG 3 NORTHAM INDUSTRIAL PARK, COBOURG, ON, K9A 4L1
(905) 372-2291   *SIC* 3089
HUTCHINSON AERONAUTIQUE & INDUSTRIE LIMITEE   *p*1160
3650 BOUL DU TRICENTENAIRE, MONTREAL, QC, H1B 5M8
(514) 640-9006   *SIC* 3089
IAC AUTOMOTIVE COMPONENTS ALBERTA ULC   *p*554

375 BASALTIC RD, CONCORD, ON, L4K 4W8
(905) 879-0292   *SIC* 3089
INDUSTRIES REHAU INC   *p*1053
625 AV LEE, BAIE-D'URFE, QC, H9X 3S3
(514) 905-0345   *SIC* 3089
INDUSTRIES RONDI INC, LES   *p*1247
12425 BOUL INDUSTRIEL, POINTE-AUX-TREMBLES, QC, H1B 5M7
(514) 640-0888   *SIC* 3089
INDUSTRIES UNICOR INC   *p*1049
9151 RUE CLAVEAU, ANJOU, QC, H1J 2C8
(514) 353-0857   *SIC* 3089
INOAC CANADA LIMITED   *p*888
575 JAMES ST S, ST MARYS, ON, N4X 1C6
(519) 349-2170   *SIC* 3089
INOAC INTERIOR SYSTEMS LP   *p*888
575 JAMES ST S, ST MARYS, ON, N4X 1C6
(519) 349-2170   *SIC* 3089
INTEGRITY TOOL & MOLD INC   *p*807
5015 O'NEIL DR, OLDCASTLE, ON, N0R 1L0
(519) 737-2650   *SIC* 3089
IPEX INC   *p*109
4225 92 AVE NW, EDMONTON, AB, T6B 3M7
(780) 415-5300   *SIC* 3089
IPEX INC   *p*661
1055 WILTON GROVE RD, LONDON, ON, N6N 1C9
(519) 681-2140   *SIC* 3089
IPEX INC   *p*917
11 BERMONDSEY RD, TORONTO, ON, M4B 1Z3
(416) 751-3820   *SIC* 3089
IPEX INC   *p*1334
6665 CH SAINT-FRANCOIS, SAINT-LAURENT, QC, H4S 1B6
(514) 337-2624   *SIC* 3089
IPL INC   *p*399
20 RUE BOYD, EDMUNDSTON, NB, E3V 4H4
(506) 739-9559   *SIC* 3089
IPL INC   *p*1299
140 RUE COMMERCIALE, SAINT-DAMIEN-DE-BUCKLAND, QC, G0R 2Y0
(418) 789-2880   *SIC* 3089
KANWAL INC   *p*1147
1426 BOUL INDUSTRIEL, MAGOG, QC, J1X 4V9
(819) 868-5152   *SIC* 3089
KAYTEC VINYL INC   *p*1088
105 RUE DES INDUSTRIES, COWANSVILLE, QC, J2K 3Y4
(450) 263-5368   *SIC* 3089
KUMI CANADA CORPORATION   *p*497
55 REAGEN'S INDUSTRIAL PKY, BRADFORD, ON, L3Z 0Z9
(905) 778-1464   *SIC* 3089
LAKESIDE PLASTICS LIMITED   *p*807
5186 O'NEIL DR RR 1, OLDCASTLE, ON, N0R 1L0
(519) 737-1271   *SIC* 3089
LAKESIDE PLASTICS LIMITED   *p*807
3786 NORTH TALBOT RD SUITE 1, OLD-CASTLE, ON, N0R 1L0
(519) 737-1271   *SIC* 3089
LEPAGE, ALPHONSE INC   *p*1286
141 CH DES RAYMOND, RIVIERE-DU-LOUP, QC, G5R 5X9
(418) 862-2611   *SIC* 3089
LISTOWEL TECHNOLOGY INC   *p*647
1700 MITCHELL RD S, LISTOWEL, ON, N4W 3H4
(519) 291-9900   *SIC* 3089
LITELINE CORPORATION   *p*852
90 WEST BEAVER CREEK RD, RICH-MOND HILL, ON, L4B 1E7
(416) 996-1856   *SIC* 3089
MACHINERIE WEBER MONTREAL HOLDING INC   *p*1395
269 RUE ADRIEN-PATENAUDE, VAUDREUIL-DORION, QC, J7V 5V5
(450) 455-0169   *SIC* 3089

MADIX ENGINEERING INC   *p*891
139 IBER RD, STITTSVILLE, ON, K2S 1E7
(613) 591-1474   *SIC* 3089
MAHLE FILTER SYSTEMS CANADA, ULC *p*911
16 INDUSTRIAL PARK RD, TILBURY, ON, N0P 2L0
(519) 682-0444   *SIC* 3089
MARKDOM PLASTIC PRODUCTS LIMITED *p*914
1220 BIRCHMOUNT RD, TORONTO, ON, M1P 2C3
(416) 752-4290   *SIC* 3089
MASTERNET LTD   *p*735
690 GANA CRT, MISSISSAUGA, ON, L5S 1P2
(905) 795-0005   *SIC* 3089
MATERIAUX DE CONSTRUCTION KP LTEE *p*1251
3075 AUT TRANSCANADIENNE, POINTE-CLAIRE, QC, H9R 1B4
(514) 694-5855   *SIC* 3089
MATRA PLAST INDUSTRIES INC   *p*1057
420 RUE NOTRE-DAME, BERTHIERVILLE, QC, J0K 1A0
(450) 836-7071   *SIC* 3089
MATRIX MOTORSPORTS   *p*76
20 FREEPORT LANDNG NE, CALGARY, AB, T3J 5H6
(403) 265-5000   *SIC* 3089
MBI PLASTIQUE INC   *p*1322
1335 AV DU PALAIS, SAINT-JOSEPH-DE-BEAUCE, QC, G0S 2V0
(418) 397-8088   *SIC* 3089
MELET PLASTICS INC   *p*366
34 DE BAETS ST, WINNIPEG, MB, R2J 3S9
(204) 667-6635   *SIC* 3089
MERIT PRECISION MOULDING LIMITED *p*841
2035 FISHER DR, PETERBOROUGH, ON, K9J 6X6
(705) 742-4209   *SIC* 3089
MICHELIN AMERIQUE DU NORD (CANADA) INC   *p*470
866 RANDOLPH RD, WATERVILLE, NS, B0P 1V0
(902) 535-3675   *SIC* 3089
MIROLIN INDUSTRIES CORP   *p*575
60 SHORNCLIFFE RD, ETOBICOKE, ON, M8Z 5K1
(416) 231-5790   *SIC* 3089
MITTEN INC   *p*516
225 HENRY ST UNIT 5A, BRANTFORD, ON, N3S 7R4
(519) 805-4701   *SIC* 3089
MONARCH PLASTICS LIMITED   *p*804
2335 SPEERS RD, OAKVILLE, ON, L6L 2X9
(905) 791-8805   *SIC* 3089
MPI MOULIN A PAPIER DE PORTNEUF, INC *p*1253
200 RUE DU MOULIN, PORTNEUF, QC, G0A 2Y0
(418) 286-3461   *SIC* 3089
MVA STRATFORD INC   *p*896
753 ONTARIO ST, STRATFORD, ON, N5A 7Y2
(519) 275-2203   *SIC* 3089
N.A.P. WINDOWS & DOORS LTD   *p*223
8775 JIM BAILEY CRES UNIT B1, KELOWNA, BC, V4V 2L7
(250) 762-5343   *SIC* 3089
NEATFREAK GROUP INC   *p*698
5320 TIMBERLEA BLVD, MISSISSAUGA, ON, L4W 2S6
(905) 624-6262   *SIC* 3089
NEWMAR WINDOW MANUFACTURING INC *p*686
7630 AIRPORT RD, MISSISSAUGA, ON, L4T 4G6
(905) 672-1233   *SIC* 3089
NEXTRUSION INC   *p*1050
10500 RUE COLBERT, ANJOU, QC, H1J 2H8
(514) 355-6868   *SIC* 3089

NMC DYNAPLAS LTD   *p*876
380 PASSMORE AVE, SCARBOROUGH, ON, M1V 4B4
(416) 293-3855   *SIC* 3089
NORSPEX LTD   *p*673
290 FERRIER ST SUITE 1, MARKHAM, ON, L3R 2Z5
(905) 513-8889   *SIC* 3089
NORTH STAR MANUFACTURING (LONDON) LTD   *p*889
40684 TALBOT LINE, ST THOMAS, ON, N5P 3T2
(519) 637-7899   *SIC* 3089
NOVA CHEMICALS CORPORATION *p*563
285 ALBERT ST, CORUNNA, ON, N0N 1G0
(519) 862-1445   *SIC* 3089
NOVO PLASTICS INC   *p*679
388 MARKLAND ST, MARKHAM, ON, L6C 1Z6
(905) 887-8818   *SIC* 3089
NUFORM BUILDING TECHNOLOGIES INC. *p*1032
100 GALCAT DR UNIT 2, WOODBRIDGE, ON, L4L 0B9
(905) 652-0001   *SIC* 3089
ONTARIO DOOR SALES LTD   *p*684
8400 LAWSON RD UNIT 2, MILTON, ON, L9T 0J8
(905) 876-1290   *SIC* 3089
OPPLAST INC   *p*490
4743 CHRISTIE DR, BEAMSVILLE, ON, L0R 1B4
(905) 563-1462   *SIC* 3089
ORBIS CANADA LIMITED   *p*580
39 WESTMORE DR, ETOBICOKE, ON, M9V 3Y6
(416) 745-6980   *SIC* 3089
ORION PLASTICS INC   *p*166
35 CALDER PL, ST. ALBERT, AB, T8N 5A6
(780) 431-2112   *SIC* 3089
OSTACO 2000 WINDOORS INC   *p*557
248 BOWES RD, CONCORD, ON, L4K 1J9
(905) 660-5021   *SIC* 3089
OTTAWA MOULD CRAFT LIMITED   *p*819
2510 DON REID DR, OTTAWA, ON, K1H 1E1
(613) 521-6402   *SIC* 3089
P.H. TECH INC   *p*1137
8650 BOUL GUILLAUME-COUTURE BUREAU 220, LEVIS, QC, G6V 9G9
(418) 833-3231   *SIC* 3089
PACKALL PACKAGING INC   *p*1087
3470 BOUL DE CHENONCEAU, COTE SAINT-LUC, QC, H7T 3B6
SIC 3089
PACTIV CANADA INC   *p*901
6870 RICHMOND RD, SUMMERSTOWN, ON, K0C 2E0
(613) 931-1439   *SIC* 3089
PANO CAP (CANADA) LIMITED   *p*637
55 WEBSTER RD, KITCHENER, ON, N2C 2E7
(519) 893-6055   *SIC* 3089
PAPP PLASTICS AND DISTRIBUTING LIMITED   *p*643
6110 MORTON INDUSTRIAL PKY, LASALLE, ON, N9J 3W3
(519) 734-0700   *SIC* 3089
PAPP PLASTICS AND DISTRIBUTING LIMITED   *p*1026
6110 MORTON INDUSTRIAL PKY, WINDSOR, ON, N9J 3W3
(519) 734-1112   *SIC* 3089
PARAMOUNT WINDOWS INC   *p*366
105 PANET RD, WINNIPEG, MB, R2J 0S1
(204) 233-4966   *SIC* 3089
PATHWAY DESIGN & MANUFACTURING INC   *p*193
7400 MACPHERSON AVE SUITE 111, BURNABY, BC, V5J 5B6
(604) 603-1053   *SIC* 3089
PEARL RIVER HOLDINGS LIMITED   *p*654
383 RICHMOND ST SUITE 502, LONDON, ON, N6A 3C4

(519) 679-1200   *SIC 3089*

PENINSULA PLASTICS LIMITED   p592
620 INDUSTRIAL DR, FORT ERIE, ON, L2A 5M4
(905) 871-4766   *SIC 3089*

PLASTICASE INC   p1381
1059 BOUL DES ENTREPRISES, TERRE-BONNE, QC, J6Y 1V2
(450) 628-1006   *SIC 3089*

PLASTIPAK INDUSTRIES INC   p587
260 REXDALE BLVD, ETOBICOKE, ON, M9W 1R2
(416) 744-4220   *SIC 3089*

PLASTIPAK INDUSTRIES INC   p1067
150 BOUL INDUSTRIEL, BOUCHERVILLE, QC, J4B 2X3
(450) 650-2200   *SIC 3089*

PLASTIPAK INDUSTRIES INC   p1082
345 RUE BIBEAU, COOKSHIRE-EATON, QC, J0B 1M0
(819) 875-3355   *SIC 3089*

PLASTIQUE CADUNA INC   p1223
5655 RUE PHILIPPE-TURCOT, MON-TREAL, QC, H4C 3K8
(514) 932-7821   *SIC 3089*

PLASTIQUE D.C.N. INC   p1400
250 RUE SAINT-LOUIS, WARWICK, QC, J0A 1M0
(819) 358-3700   *SIC 3089*

PLASTIQUE MICRON INC   p1356
21 BOUL BEGIN BUREAU 190, SAINTE-CLAIRE, QC, G0R 2V0
(418) 883-3333   *SIC 3089*

PLASTIQUES ANCHOR LTEE   p1120
730 RUE SAINT-ETIENNE, L'ASSOMPTION, QC, J5W 1Z1
(450) 589-5627   *SIC 3089*

PLASTIQUES BERRY CANADA INC   p1400
33 RUE TAYLOR, WATERLOO, QC, J0E 2N0
(450) 539-2772   *SIC 3089*

PLASTIQUES G PLUS INC   p1288
180 RUE D'EVAIN, ROUYN-NORANDA, QC, J0Z 1Y0
(819) 768-8888   *SIC 3089*

PLASTIQUES G.P.R. INC   p1303
5200 CH DE SAINT-GABRIEL, SAINT-FELIX-DE-VALOIS, QC, J0K 2M0
(450) 889-7277   *SIC 3089*

PLASTIQUES GAGNON INC   p1315
117 AV DE GASPE O, SAINT-JEAN-PORT-JOLI, QC, G0R 3G0
(418) 598-3361   *SIC 3089*

PLASTIQUES IPL INC   p1199
1000 SHERBROOKE W ST SUITE 700, MONTREAL, QC, H3A 3G4
(438) 320-6188   *SIC 3089*

PLEXTRON HOLDINGS INC   p871
2045 MIDLAND AVE, SCARBOROUGH, ON, M1P 3E2
(416) 293-1156   *SIC 3089*

POLAR RAY-O-MAX WINDOWS LTD   p367
672 KIMBERLY AVE, WINNIPEG, MB, R2K 0Y2
(204) 956-6555   *SIC 3089*

POLYONE DSS CANADA INC   p1109
440 RUE ROBINSON S, GRANBY, QC, J2G 9R3
(450) 378-8433   *SIC 3089*

POLYTAINERS INC   p575
197 NORSEMAN ST, ETOBICOKE, ON, M8Z 2R5
(416) 239-7311   *SIC 3089*

POLYWHEELS MANUFACTURING LTDp799
1455 NORTH SERVICE RD E, OAKVILLE, ON, L6H 1A7
SIC 3089

PORTES & FENETRES ABRITEK INCp1305
5195 127E RUE, SAINT-GEORGES, QC, G5Y 5B9
(418) 228-3293   *SIC 3089*

PPD HOLDING INC   p1371
1649 RUE BELVEDERE S, SHERBROOKE, QC, J1H 4E4

(819) 837-2491   *SIC 3089*

PPD HOLDING INC   p1400
325 RUE PRINCIPALE N, WATERVILLE, QC, J0B 3H0
(819) 837-2491   *SIC 3089*

PRETIUM CANADA COMPANY   p1252
3300 RTE TRANSCANADIENNE, POINTE-CLAIRE, QC, H9R 1B1
(514) 428-0002   *SIC 3089*

PRETIUM CANADA COMPANY   p1335
2800 RUE HALPERN, SAINT-LAURENT, QC, H4S 1R2
(514) 336-8210   *SIC 3089*

PRIMEX MANUFACTURING LTD   p225
20160 92A AVE, LANGLEY, BC, V1M 3A4
(604) 881-7875   *SIC 3089*

PRO-WESTERN PLASTICS LTD   p166
30 RIEL DR, ST. ALBERT, AB, T8N 3Z7
(780) 459-4491   *SIC 3089*

PRODUITS AUTOMOBILES LAURENTIDE INC   p1162
9355 BOUL HENRI-BOURASSA E, MON-TREAL, QC, H1E 1P4
(514) 643-1917   *SIC 3089*

PRODUITS DE PLASTIQUE AGE INC, LES   p1165
7295 RUE TELLIER, MONTREAL, QC, H1N 3S9
(514) 251-9550   *SIC 3089*

PRODUITS PLASTIQUES JAY INC   p1345
8875 BOUL LANGELIER, SAINT-LEONARD, QC, H1P 2C8
(514) 321-7272   *SIC 3089*

PRODUITS PLASTITEL INC, LES   p1237
2604 RUE DEBRAY, MONTREAL, QC, H7S 2J8
(450) 687-0060   *SIC 3089*

PROTOPLAST INC   p545
210 WILLMOTT ST UNIT 2, COBOURG, ON, K9A 0E9
(905) 372-6451   *SIC 3089*

QUALITY MODELS LIMITED   p1017
478 SILVER CREEK INDUSTRIAL DR SUITE 1, WINDSOR, ON, N8N 4Y3
(519) 727-4255   *SIC 3089*

R.T. RECYCLING TECHNOLOGY INC   p784
801 FLINT RD, NORTH YORK, ON, M3J 2J6
(416) 650-1498   *SIC 3089*

RELIANCE PRODUCTS LTD   p385
1093 SHERWIN RD, WINNIPEG, MB, R3H 1A4
(204) 633-4403   *SIC 3089*

RITZ PLASTICS INC   p842
435 PIDO RD, PETERBOROUGH, ON, K9J 6X7
(705) 748-6776   *SIC 3089*

ROPAK CANADA INC   p230
5850 272 ST, LANGLEY, BC, V4W 3Z1
(604) 857-1177   *SIC 3089*

ROPAK CANADA INC   p466
29 MEMORIAL CRES, SPRINGHILL, NS, B0M 1X0
(902) 597-3787   *SIC 3089*

ROPAK CANADA INC   p804
2240 WYECROFT RD, OAKVILLE, ON, L6L 6M1
(905) 827-9340   *SIC 3089*

ROYAL GROUP, INC   p1028
10 ROYBRIDGE GATE SUITE 201, WOOD-BRIDGE, ON, L4H 3M8
(905) 264-1660   *SIC 3089*

ROYAL GROUP, INC   p1028
111 ROYAL GROUP CRES, WOOD-BRIDGE, ON, L4H 1X9
SIC 3089

ROYAL GROUP, INC   p1323
1401 RUE BELLEVUE, SAINT-LAMBERT-DE-LAUZON, QC, G0S 2W0
SIC 3089

ROYPLAST LIMITED   p1002
91 ROYAL GROUP CRT, VAUGHAN, ON, L4H 1X9
SIC 3089

SCEPTER CANADA INC   p872

170 MIDWEST RD, SCARBOROUGH, ON, M1P 3A9
(416) 751-9445   *SIC 3089*

SCOTT-DOUGLAS PLASTICS LIMITEDp622
50 JANES RD, INGERSOLL, ON, N5C 0A9
(519) 485-1943   *SIC 3089*

SEALED AIR (CANADA) CO./CIE   p717
3755 LAIRD RD UNIT 10, MISSISSAUGA, ON, L5L 0B3
(905) 829-1200   *SIC 3089*

SHIRLON PLASTIC COMPANY INC   p534
100 PINEBUSH RD, CAMBRIDGE, ON, N1R 8J8
(519) 620-1333   *SIC 3089*

SIGMA INDUSTRIES INC   p1300
55 RTE 271 S, SAINT-EPHREM-DE-BEAUCE, QC, G0M 1R0
(418) 484-5282   *SIC 3089*

SIGMA MOULDERS   p865
150 MCLEVIN AVE, SCARBOROUGH, ON, M1B 4Z7
(416) 297-0088   *SIC 3089*

SILGAN PLASTICS CANADA INC   p736
1575 DREW RD, MISSISSAUGA, ON, L5S 1S5
(905) 677-2324   *SIC 3089*

SILGAN PLASTICS CANADA INC   p872
1200 ELLESMERE RD, SCARBOROUGH, ON, M1P 2X4
(416) 293-8233   *SIC 3089*

SILGAN PLASTICS CANADA INC   p1033
400 ROWNTREE DAIRY RD, WOOD-BRIDGE, ON, L4L 8H2
(416) 746-8300   *SIC 3089*

SIMPORT SCIENTIFIQUE INC   p1348
2588 RUE BERNARD-PILON BUREAU 1, SAINT-MATHIEU-DE-BELOEIL, QC, J3G 4S5
(450) 464-1723   *SIC 3089*

SLE-CO PLASTICS INC   p650
1425 CREAMERY RD, LONDON, ON, N5V 5B3
(519) 451-3748   *SIC 3089*

SOLARIS QUEBEC PORTES ET FENETRES INC   p1119
6150 BOUL SAINTE-ANNE, L'ANGE GAR-DIEN, QC, G0A 2K0
(418) 822-0643   *SIC 3089*

SONIPLASTICS INC   p1067
1610 RUE EIFFEL, BOUCHERVILLE, QC, J4B 5Y1
(450) 449-6000   *SIC 3089*

SONOCO PLASTICS CANADA ULC   p707
245 BRITANNIA RD E, MISSISSAUGA, ON, L4Z 4J3
(905) 624-2337   *SIC 3089*

SOUCY PLASTIQUES INC   p1097
5755 PLACE KUBOTA, DRUMMONDVILLE, QC, J2B 6V4
(819) 474-5151   *SIC 3089*

SPIRAL OF CANADA INC   p743
6155 TOMKEN RD UNIT 10, MISSIS-SAUGA, ON, L5T 1X3
(905) 564-8990   *SIC 3089*

SPONGEZZ INC   p784
79 SAINT REGIS CRES N, NORTH YORK, ON, M3J 1Y9
(416) 636-6611   *SIC 3089*

STAR PLASTICS INC   p736
1930 DREW RD UNIT 1, MISSISSAUGA, ON, L5S 1J6
(905) 672-0298   *SIC 3089*

STOREX INDUSTRIES CORPORATION
p1132
9440 RUE CLEMENT, LASALLE, QC, H8R 3W1
(514) 745-1234   *SIC 3089*

SUDBURY WINDOW MANUFACTURING LTD   p899
902 NEWGATE AVE, SUDBURY, ON, P3A 5J9
(705) 560-5700   *SIC 3089*

SUPREME WINDOWS (CALGARY) INC   p18
4705 102 AVE SE, CALGARY, AB, T2C 2X7
(403) 279-2797   *SIC 3089*

SWISSPLAS LIMITED   p506
735 INTERMODAL DR, BRAMPTON, ON, L6T 5W2
(905) 789-9300   *SIC 3089*

TECHSTAR PLASTICS INC   p848
15400 OLD SIMCOE RD, PORT PERRY, ON, L9L 1L8
(905) 985-8479   *SIC 3089*

TG MINTO CORPORATION   p836
300 TORONTO ST, PALMERSTON, ON, N0G 2P0
(519) 343-2800   *SIC 3089*

THERMOFORME D'AMERIQUE INC   p1242
970 RUE THEOPHILE-SAINT-LAURENT, NICOLET, QC, J3T 1B4
(819) 293-8899   *SIC 3089*

THK RHYTHM AUTOMOTIVE CANADA LIM-ITED   p912
1417 BELL MILL SIDEROAD, TILLSON-BURG, ON, N4G 4G9
(519) 688-4200   *SIC 3089*

TOOLPLAS SYSTEMS INC   p807
1905 BLACKACRE DR, OLDCASTLE, ON, N0R 1L0
(519) 737-9948   *SIC 3089*

TOYOTA BOSHOKU CANADA, INC   p568
45 SOUTH FIELD DR SUITE 1, ELMIRA, ON, N3B 3L6
(519) 669-8883   *SIC 3089*

TOYOTA BOSHOKU CANADA, INC   p1036
230 UNIVERSAL RD, WOODSTOCK, ON, N4S 7W3
(519) 421-7556   *SIC 3089*

TRIUMPH GEAR SYSTEMS-TORONTO ULC
p794
11 FENMAR DR, NORTH YORK, ON, M9L 1L5
(416) 743-4417   *SIC 3089*

TWINPAK ATLANTIC INC   p409
66 ENGLISH DR, MONCTON, NB, E1E 4G1
(506) 857-8116   *SIC 3089*

ULTRA MANUFACTURING LIMITED   p642
60 WASHBURN DR, KITCHENER, ON, N2R 1S2
(519) 893-3831   *SIC 3089*

VAILLANCOURT INC   p1306
252 BOUL INDUSTRIEL, SAINT-GERMAIN-DE-GRANTHAM, QC, J0C 1K0
(819) 395-4484   *SIC 3089*

VALIANT TOOL & MOLD INC   p1019
6775 HAWTHORNE DR, WINDSOR, ON, N8T 3B8
(519) 251-4800   *SIC 3089*

VANGA PRODUCTS (PLASTICS) INC   p280
2330 190 ST SUITE 102, SURREY, BC, V3Z 3W7
(604) 538-4088   *SIC 3089*

VENTRA GROUP CO   p1019
2800 KEW DR, WINDSOR, ON, N8T 3C6
(519) 944-1102   *SIC 3089*

VISION EXTRUSIONS GROUP LIMITED
p1029
201 ZENWAY BLVD, WOODBRIDGE, ON, L4H 3H9
(905) 265-9970   *SIC 3089*

VISION PLASTICS INC   p228
5800 PRODUCTION WAY, LANGLEY, BC, V3A 4N4
(604) 530-1882   *SIC 3089*

VIVA MEDIA PACKAGING (CANADA) LTD
p879
1663 NEILSON RD SUITE 13, SCARBOR-OUGH, ON, M1X 1T1
(416) 321-0622   *SIC 3089*

VUTEQ CANADA INC   p1036
920 KEYES DR, WOODSTOCK, ON, N4V 1C2
(519) 421-0011   *SIC 3089*

W. RALSTON (CANADA) INC   p82
1100 RAILWAY AVE S, DRUMHELLER, AB, T0J 0Y0
(403) 823-3468   *SIC 3089*

WESTBRIDGE PET CONTAINERS LIMITED
p19

3838E 80 AVE SE, CALGARY, AB, T2C 2J7
(403) 248-1513   SIC 3089
WESTECH BUILDING PRODUCTS ULC p19
5201 64 AVE SE, CALGARY, AB, T2C 4Z9
(403) 279-4497   SIC 3089
WESTLAND PLASTICS LTD   p389
12 ROTHWELL RD, WINNIPEG, MB, R3P
2H7
(204) 488-6075   SIC 3089
WINDSOR MOLD INC   p477
95 VICTORIA ST N, AMHERSTBURG, ON,
N9V 3L1
(519) 736-5466   SIC 3089
WINDSOR MOLD INC   p1022
310 ELLIS ST E, WINDSOR, ON, N8X 2H2
(519) 258-3211   SIC 3089
WINPAK PORTION PACKAGING LTD p589
26 TIDEMORE AVE, ETOBICOKE, ON,
M9W 7A7
(416) 741-6182   SIC 3089

SIC 3111 Leather tanning and finishing

RABER GLOVE MFG. CO. LTD   p373
560 MCDERMOT AVE, WINNIPEG, MB,
R3A 0C1
(204) 786-2469   SIC 3111

SIC 3131 Footwear cut stock

CLOUTIER, EUGENE INC   p1281
1659 RUE DES ROSELINS, QUEBEC, QC,
G3E 1G2
(418) 842-2087   SIC 3131
EQUIPEMENTS ADRIEN PHANEUF (LES)
p1122
23 RUE OLIVIER-MOREL, LA DURAN-
TAYE, QC, G0R 1W0
(418) 884-2841   SIC 3131

SIC 3143 Men's footwear, except athletic

BLUE MOOSE CLOTHING COMPANY LTD
p371
90 SUTHERLAND AVE UNIT 100, WIN-
NIPEG, MB, R2W 3C7
(204) 783-2557   SIC 3143
DON MICHAEL HOLDINGS INC   p988
1400 CASTLEFIELD AVE SUITE 2,
TORONTO, ON, M6B 4N4
(416) 781-3574   SIC 3143
ENTREPRISES LA CANADIENNE INCp1156
5745 RUE PARE, MONT-ROYAL, QC, H4P
1S1
(514) 731-2112   SIC 3143
GENFOOT INC   p1082
4945 RUE LEGENDRE, CONTRECOEUR,
QC, J0L 1C0
(450) 587-2051   SIC 3143
L.P. ROYER INC   p1124
712 RUE PRINCIPALE, LAC-DROLET, QC,
G0Y 1C0
(819) 549-2100   SIC 3143
MELLOW WALK FOOTWEAR INC   p791
17 MILFORD AVE, NORTH YORK, ON,
M6M 2W1
(416) 241-1312   SIC 3143
ROOTS CORPORATION   p988
1400 CASTLEFIELD AVE SUITE 2,
TORONTO, ON, M6B 4N4
(416) 781-3574   SIC 3143

SIC 3144 Women's footwear, except athletic

ALFRED CLOUTIER LIMITEE   p1280
1737 RUE WILLIAM-MARSH, QUEBEC,
QC, G3E 1K9
(418) 842-4390   SIC 3144
AUCLAIR & MARTINEAU INC   p1280

2277 RUE DE LA FAUNE, QUEBEC, QC,
G3E 1S9
(418) 842-1943   SIC 3144
BOULET, G.A. INC   p1353
501 RUE SAINT-GABRIEL, SAINT-TITE,
QC, G0X 3H0
(418) 365-5174   SIC 3144
CHAUSSURES DE LUCA MONTREAL INC
p1240
9999 BOUL SAINT-MICHEL, MONTREAL-
NORD, QC, H1H 5G7
(514) 279-4541   SIC 3144
CHAUSSURES REGENCE INC   p1280
655 RUE DE L'ARGON, QUEBEC, QC, G2N
2G7
(418) 849-7997   SIC 3144

SIC 3149 Footwear, except rubber, nec

HICHAUD INC   p1267
2485 BOUL NEUVIALLE, QUEBEC, QC,
G1P 3A6
(418) 682-0782   SIC 3149
MATH SPORT INC   p1265
1130 BOUL CHAREST O BUREAU 7, QUE-
BEC, QC, G1N 2E2
(581) 999-7707   SIC 3149

SIC 3161 Luggage

**ENGINEERED CASE MANUFACTURERS
INC**   p694
5191 CREEKBANK RD, MISSISSAUGA,
ON, L4W 1R3
(905) 366-2273   SIC 3161
ETUIS BOBLEN CASES INC   p1172
4455 RUE FRONTENAC, MONTREAL, QC,
H2H 2S2
(514) 523-8163   SIC 3161
PRESENTATION ULTIMA INC   p1067
55 RUE DE MONTGOLFIER,
BOUCHERVILLE, QC, J4B 8C4
(450) 641-0670   SIC 3161

SIC 3171 Women's handbags and purses

HB CONNECTIONS INC   p1156
8190 CH ROYDEN, MONT-ROYAL, QC, H4P
2T2
(514) 340-4414   SIC 3171

SIC 3172 Personal leather goods, nec

IMPENCO LTEE   p1180
240 RUE GUIZOT O, MONTREAL, QC, H2P
1L5
(514) 383-1200   SIC 3172

SIC 3199 Leather goods, nec

CARISTRAP INTERNATIONAL INC   p1085
1760 BOUL FORTIN, COTE SAINT-LUC,
QC, H7S 1N8
(450) 667-4700   SIC 3199
LANDES CANADA INC   p1109
400 RUE SAINT-VALLIER, GRANBY, QC,
J2G 7Y4
(450) 378-9853   SIC 3199
MEDIKE BRANDING SOLUTIONS INC p665
216 MAIN ST W, MARKDALE, ON, N0C 1H0
(519) 986-2072   SIC 3199
PERRI'S LEATHERS LTD   p557
45 CASMIR CRT UNIT 11 & 15, CONCORD,
ON, L4K 4H5
(905) 761-8549   SIC 3199

SIC 3211 Flat glass

AGC FLAT GLASS NORTH AMERICA LTD
p1253
250 RUE DE COPENHAGUE, PORTNEUF,
QC, G0A 2Y0
SIC 3211
BRONCO INDUSTRIES INC   p208
7988 82 ST, DELTA, BC, V4G 1L8
(604) 940-8821   SIC 3211
C.R. LAURENCE OF CANADA LIMITED
p549
65 TIGI CRT, CONCORD, ON, L4K 5E4
(905) 303-7966   SIC 3211
GOLDRAY INDUSTRIES LTD   p16
4605 52 AVE SE, CALGARY, AB, T2C 4N7
(403) 236-1333   SIC 3211
GROUPE NOVATECH INC   p1358
160 RUE DE MURANO, SAINTE-JULIE,
QC, J3E 0C6
(450) 922-1045   SIC 3211
GUARDIAN INDUSTRIES CANADA CORP
p584
355 ATTWELL DR, ETOBICOKE, ON, M9W
5C2
(416) 674-6945   SIC 3211
GUARDIAN INDUSTRIES CANADA CORP
p911
10 ROUSE ST, TILLSONBURG, ON, N4G
5W8
(416) 674-6945   SIC 3211
MULTIVER LTEE   p1265
1950 RUE LEON-HARMEL, QUEBEC, QC,
G1N 4K3
(418) 687-0770   SIC 3211
NOVATECH CANADA INC   p1359
160 RUE DE MURANO, SAINTE-JULIE,
QC, J3E 0C6
(450) 922-1045   SIC 3211
**OLDCASTLE BUILDING PRODUCTS
CANADA, INC**   p229
5075 275 ST, LANGLEY, BC, V4W 0A8
(604) 607-1300   SIC 3211
**OLDCASTLE BUILDINGENVELOPE
CANADA INC**   p556
210 GREAT GULF DR, CONCORD, ON,
L4K 5W1
(905) 660-4520   SIC 3211
PPG CANADA INC   p836
1799 20TH ST E, OWEN SOUND, ON, N4K
2C3
SIC 3211
PRELCO INC   p1286
94 BOUL CARTIER, RIVIERE-DU-LOUP,
QC, G5R 2M9
(418) 862-2274   SIC 3211
PRELSECUR INC   p1286
94 BOUL CARTIER, RIVIERE-DU-LOUP,
QC, G5R 2M9
(418) 862-2274   SIC 3211
PROTEMP GLASS INC   p557
360 APPLEWOOD CRES, CONCORD, ON,
L4K 4V2
(905) 760-0701   SIC 3211
THERMAFIX A. J. INC   p1377
1396 RTE DU RONDIN, ST-NAZAIRE-DU-
LAC-ST-JEAN, QC, G0W 2V0
(418) 668-6131   SIC 3211
**TRULITE GLASS & ALUMINUM SOLU-
TIONS CANADA, ULC**   p1028
20 ROYAL GROUP CRES, WOODBRIDGE,
ON, L4H 1X9
(905) 605-7040   SIC 3211
VERRE SELECT INC   p1381
3816 RUE GEORGES-CORBEIL, TERRE-
BONNE, QC, J6X 4J4
(450) 968-0112   SIC 3211

SIC 3221 Glass containers

ESKA INC   p938
25 ADELAIDE ST E SUITE 1000,
TORONTO, ON, M5C 3A1
(416) 504-2222   SIC 3221

O-I CANADA CORP   p505
100 WEST DR, BRAMPTON, ON, L6T 2J5
(905) 457-2423   SIC 3221
RECOCHEM INC   p684
8725 HOLGATE CRES, MILTON, ON, L9T
5G7
(905) 878-5544   SIC 3221
RICHARDS PACKAGING INC   p742
6095 ORDAN DR, MISSISSAUGA, ON, L5T
2M7
(905) 670-7760   SIC 3221

SIC 3229 Pressed and blown glass, nec

ACCURATE DORWIN INC   p390
1535 SEEL AVE, WINNIPEG, MB, R3T 1C6
(204) 982-4640   SIC 3229
**FYI EYE CARE SERVICES AND PRODUCTS
INC**   p67
2424 4 ST SW SUITE 300, CALGARY, AB,
T2S 2T4
(403) 234-2020   SIC 3229
RAYTHEON CANADA LIMITED   p825
360 ALBERT ST SUITE 1640, OTTAWA,
ON, K1R 7X7
(613) 233-4121   SIC 3229

SIC 3231 Products of purchased glass

AGC AUTOMOTIVE CANADA, INC   p497
120 ARTESIAN INDUSTRIAL PKY, BRAD-
FORD, ON, L3Z 3G3
(905) 778-8224   SIC 3231
ALL TEAM GLASS & MIRROR LTD   p1029
281 HANLAN RD, WOODBRIDGE, ON, L4L
3R7
(905) 851-7711   SIC 3231
GARIBALDI GLASS INDUSTRIES INC p181
8183 WIGGINS ST, BURNABY, BC, V3N
0C4
(604) 420-4527   SIC 3231
GENERAL GLASS INDUSTRIES LTD p176
2146 QUEEN ST, ABBOTSFORD, BC, V2T
6J4
(604) 854-5757   SIC 3231
GROUPE LCI CANADA, INC   p1111
850 RUE MOELLER, GRANBY, QC, J2J 1K7
(450) 378-6722   SIC 3231
INDUSTRIES APRIL INC, LES   p1247
12755 BOUL INDUSTRIEL, POINTE-AUX-
TREMBLES, QC, H1A 4Z6
(514) 640-5355   SIC 3231
INTERSTYLE CERAMIC & GLASS LTDp182
3625 BRIGHTON AVE, BURNABY, BC, V5A
3H5
(604) 421-7229   SIC 3231
LAMI GLASS PRODUCTS, LLC   p182
7344 WINSTON ST, BURNABY, BC, V5A
2G9
(604) 420-3600   SIC 3231
MIROIRS LAURIER LTEE   p1133
153 BOUL LAURIER BUREAU 300,
LAURIER-STATION, QC, G0S 1N0
(418) 728-2023   SIC 3231
MULTIVER LTEE   p1262
436 RUE BERUBE, QUEBEC, QC, G1M
1C8
(418) 687-0770   SIC 3231
NATIONAL GLASS LTD   p228
5744 198 ST, LANGLEY, BC, V3A 7J2
(604) 530-2311   SIC 3231
PILKINGTON GLASS OF CANADA LTDp547
1000 26 HWY, COLLINGWOOD, ON, L9Y
4V8
(705) 445-4780   SIC 3231
PORTES DECKO INC   p1381
2375 RUE EDOUARD-MICHELIN, TERRE-
BONNE, QC, J6Y 4P2
(450) 477-0199   SIC 3231
PORTES DUSCO LTEE, LES   p1162
11825 AV J.-J.-JOUBERT, MONTREAL, QC,
H1E 7J5

---

(514) 355-4877 *SIC 3231*

PORTES PATIO NOVATECH INC p1055
100 181E RUE, BEAUCEVILLE, QC, G5X
2T1
(418) 774-2949 *SIC 3231*

ROBOVER INC p1265
1595 BOUL WILFRID-HAMEL, QUEBEC,
QC, G1N 3Y7
(418) 682-3580 *SIC 3231*

SAAND LONDON INC p651
14 FIRESTONE BLVD, LONDON, ON, N5W
5L4
(519) 659-0819 *SIC 3231*

SAAND TORONTO INC p587
250 BROCKPORT DR SUITE 3, ETOBI-
COKE, ON, M9W 5S1
(416) 798-2345 *SIC 3231*

**SCHOTT GEMTRON (CANADA) CORPORA-
TION** p682
125 ALBERT ST, MIDLAND, ON, L4R 4L3
(705) 526-3771 *SIC 3231*

VERRERIE WALKER LTEE, LA p1051
9551 BOUL RAY-LAWSON, ANJOU, QC,
H1J 1L5
(514) 352-3030 *SIC 3231*

VITRUM INDUSTRIES LTD p226
9739 201 ST, LANGLEY, BC, V1M 3E7
(604) 882-3513 *SIC 3231*

WINDOW CITY INDUSTRIES INC p1034
5690 STEELES AVE W, WOODBRIDGE,
ON, L4L 9T4
(905) 265-9975 *SIC 3231*

WINDOWCITY MFRS. INC p1034
5690 STEELES AVE W, WOODBRIDGE,
ON, L4L 9T4
(905) 265-9975 *SIC 3231*

Z. & R. HOLDINGS LTD p229
5744 198 ST, LANGLEY, BC, V3A 7J2
(604) 530-2311 *SIC 3231*

SIC 3241 Cement, hydraulic

BRIQUE & PAVE DONAT FORTIER p1314
2036 RANG DE LA RIVIERE, SAINT-
ISIDORE, QC, G0S 2S0
(418) 882-5879 *SIC 3241*

CIMENT QUEBEC INC p1294
145 BOUL DU CENTENAIRE, SAINT-
BASILE, QC, G0A 3G0
(418) 329-2100 *SIC 3241*

CRH CANADA GROUP INC p713
2391 LAKESHORE RD W, MISSISSAUGA,
ON, L5J 1K1
(905) 822-1653 *SIC 3241*

CRH CANADA GROUP INC p1114
966 CH DES PRAIRIES, JOLIETTE, QC,
J6E 0L4
(450) 756-1076 *SIC 3241*

CRH CANADA GROUP INC p1141
435 RUE JEAN-NEVEU, LONGUEUIL, QC,
J4G 2P9
(450) 651-1117 *SIC 3241*

FEDERAL WHITE CEMENT LTD p569
355151 35TH LINE, EMBRO, ON, N0J 1J0
(519) 485-5410 *SIC 3241*

GROUPE CIMENT QUEBEC INC p1294
145 BOUL DU CENTENAIRE, SAINT-
BASILE, QC, G0A 3G0
(418) 329-2100 *SIC 3241*

LEHIGH HANSON MATERIALS LIMITED
p105
12640 INLAND WAY NW, EDMONTON, AB,
T5V 1K2
(780) 420-2500 *SIC 3241*

ST. MARYS CEMENT INC. (CANADA) p496
400 BOWMANVILLE AVE, BOWMANVILLE,
ON, L1C 7B5
(905) 623-3341 *SIC 3241*

ST. MARYS CEMENT INC. (CANADA) p889
585 WATER ST S, ST MARYS, ON, N4X
1B6
(519) 284-1020 *SIC 3241*

ST. MARYS CEMENT INC. (CANADA) p918

---

55 INDUSTRIAL ST, TORONTO, ON, M4G
3W9
(416) 423-1300 *SIC 3241*

SIC 3251 Brick and structural clay tile

1442503 ONTARIO INC p581
18 NAMCO RD, ETOBICOKE, ON, M9W
1M5
(416) 741-4498 *SIC 3251*

BRAMPTON BRICK LIMITED p513
225 WANLESS DR, BRAMPTON, ON, L7A
1E9
(905) 840-1011 *SIC 3251*

I-XL LTD p145
525 2 ST SE, MEDICINE HAT, AB, T1A 0C5
(403) 526-5501 *SIC 3251*

I.XL INDUSTRIES LTD p145
612 PORCELAIN AVE SE, MEDICINE HAT,
AB, T1A 8S4
(403) 526-5901 *SIC 3251*

MERIDIAN BRICK CANADA LTD p530
5155 DUNDAS ST W, BURLINGTON, ON,
L7R 3Y2
(905) 335-3401 *SIC 3251*

MERIDIAN BRICK CANADA LTD p530
5155 DUNDAS ST RR 1, BURLINGTON,
ON, L7R 3X4
(800) 263-6229 *SIC 3251*

PRODUITS ALBA INC p1121
300 BOUL DE LA GRANDE-BAIE N BU-
REAU 3, LA BAIE, QC, G7B 3K3
(418) 544-3361 *SIC 3251*

SHAW GROUP LIMITED, THE p457
255 LACEWOOD DR SUITE 100C, HALI-
FAX, NS, B3M 4G2
(902) 457-0689 *SIC 3251*

SHAW GROUP LIMITED, THE p460
1101 HIGHWAY 2, LANTZ, NS, B2S 1M9
(902) 883-2201 *SIC 3251*

SIC 3253 Ceramic wall and floor tile

FLEXTILE LTD p571
121 THIRTIETH ST, ETOBICOKE, ON,
M8W 3C1
(416) 255-1111 *SIC 3253*

SIC 3255 Clay refractories

CLAYBURN INDUSTRIES LTD p174
33765 PINE ST, ABBOTSFORD, BC, V2S
5C1
(604) 859-5288 *SIC 3255*

**COORSTEK ADVANCED MATERIALS
HAMILTON ULC** p836
45 CURTIS AVE N, PARIS, ON, N3L 3W1
(519) 442-6395 *SIC 3255*

SIC 3259 Structural clay products, nec

SELKIRK CANADA CORPORATION p520
1400 CALIFORNIA AVE, BROCKVILLE,
ON, K6V 5V3
(888) 693-9563 *SIC 3259*

SELKIRK CANADA CORPORATION p762
21 WOODS RD, NOBEL, ON, P0G 1G0
(705) 342-5236 *SIC 3259*

SELKIRK CANADA CORPORATION p893
375 GREEN RD SUITE 1, STONEY
CREEK, ON, L8E 4A5
(905) 662-6600 *SIC 3259*

---

*SIC 3262 Vitreous china table and
kitchenware*

BROWNE & CO p667
505 APPLE CREEK BLVD UNIT 2,
MARKHAM, ON, L3R 5B1

---

(905) 475-6104 *SIC 3262*

SIC 3271 Concrete block and brick

**ABBOTSFORD CONCRETE PRODUCTS
LTD** p174
3422 MCCALLUM RD, ABBOTSFORD, BC,
V2S 7W6
(604) 852-4967 *SIC 3271*

ALUFORME LTEE p1083
2000 RUE DE LIERRE, COTE SAINT-LUC,
QC, H7G 4Y4
(450) 669-6690 *SIC 3271*

AMVIC INC p764
501 MCNICOLL AVE, NORTH YORK, ON,
M2H 2E2
(416) 410-5674 *SIC 3271*

CINDERCRETE PRODUCTS LIMITED p1417
HWY 1 E, REGINA, SK, S4P 3A1
(306) 789-2636 *SIC 3271*

ONTARIO REDIMIX LTD p586
21 GOODMARK PL UNIT 3, ETOBICOKE,
ON, M9W 6P9
(416) 674-8237 *SIC 3271*

**RAINBOW CONCRETE INDUSTRIES LIM-
ITED** p899
2477 MALEY DR, SUDBURY, ON, P3A 4R7
(705) 566-1740 *SIC 3271*

RICHVALE YORK BLOCK INC p895
5 CARDICO DR, STOUFFVILLE, ON, L4A
2G5
(416) 213-7444 *SIC 3271*

SHOULDICE DESIGNER STONE LTD p879
281227 SHOULDICE BLOCK RD SUITE
281, SHALLOW LAKE, ON, N0H 2K0
(800) 265-3174 *SIC 3271*

SIMCOE BLOCK (1979) LIMITED p488
140 FERNDALE DR N, BARRIE, ON, L4N
9W1
(705) 728-1773 *SIC 3271*

SIC 3272 Concrete products, nec

9090-5092 QUEBEC INC p1134
56 CH DE LAVALTRIE, LAVALTRIE, QC, J5T
2H1
(450) 586-1400 *SIC 3272*

9098-0145 QUEBEC INC p1375
4701 BOUL BOURQUE, SHERBROOKE,
QC, J1N 2G6
(819) 564-2257 *SIC 3272*

A C PRODUCTS LTD p174
3422 MCCALLUM RD, ABBOTSFORD, BC,
V2S 7W6
(604) 852-4967 *SIC 3272*

ADVANCED PRECAST INC p494
6 NIXON RD, BOLTON, ON, L7E 1K3
(905) 857-6111 *SIC 3272*

AE CONCRETE PRODUCTS INC p271
19060 54 AVE, SURREY, BC, V3S 8E5
(604) 576-1808 *SIC 3272*

ANCHOR CONCRETE PRODUCTS LIMITED
p630
1645 SYDENHAM RD, KINGSTON, ON,
K7L 4V4
(613) 546-6683 *SIC 3272*

AP INFRASTRUCTURE SOLUTIONS LP p1
26229 TWP RD 531A, ACHESON, AB, T7X
5A4
(780) 444-1560 *SIC 3272*

AP INFRASTRUCTURE SOLUTIONS LP p12
4300 50 AVE SE SUITE 217, CALGARY, AB,
T2B 2T7
(403) 248-3171 *SIC 3272*

ARMTEC HOLDINGS LIMITED p602
370 SPEEDVALE AVE W SUITE 101,
GUELPH, ON, N1H 7M7
(519) 822-0210 *SIC 3272*

BAINS OCEANIA INC. p1383
591 RUE DES ENTREPRISES, THETFORD
MINES, QC, G6H 4B2
(418) 332-4224 *SIC 3272*

**BASALITE CONCRETE PRODUCTS-
VANCOUVER ULC** p275
8650 130 ST, SURREY, BC, V3W 1G1
(604) 596-3844 *SIC 3272*

BEST WAY STONE LIMITED p1030
8821 WESTON RD, WOODBRIDGE, ON,
L4L 1A6
(416) 747-0988 *SIC 3272*

BETON BOLDUC INC p1359
1358 2E RUE DU PARC-INDUSTRIEL,
SAINTE-MARIE, QC, G6E 1G8
(418) 387-2634 *SIC 3272*

BETONS PREFABRIQUES DU LAC INC
p1044
890 RUE DES PINS O, ALMA, QC, G8B 7R3
(418) 668-6161 *SIC 3272*

CAST-STONE PRECAST INC p494
487 PIERCEY RD, BOLTON, ON, L7E 5B8
(905) 857-6111 *SIC 3272*

CEMATRIX CORPORATION p14
5440 53 ST SE, CALGARY, AB, T2C 4B6
(403) 219-0484 *SIC 3272*

CENTRAL PRECAST INC p749
25 BONGARD AVE, NEPEAN, ON, K2E 6V2
(613) 225-9510 *SIC 3272*

COLDSTREAM CONCRETE LIMITED p621
402 QUAKER LANE, ILDERTON, ON, N0M
2A0
(519) 666-0604 *SIC 3272*

CON-CAST PIPE INC p849
299 BROCK RD S, PUSLINCH, ON, N0B
2J0
(519) 763-8655 *SIC 3272*

CORESLAB STRUCTURES (ONT) INC p566
205 CORESLAB DR, DUNDAS, ON, L9H
0B3
(905) 689-3993 *SIC 3272*

DECAST LTD p1000
8807 COUNTY ROAD 56, UTOPIA, ON,
L0M 1T0
(800) 461-5632 *SIC 3272*

FORTERRA PIPE & PRECAST BC, ULC
p1149
1331 AV DE LA GARE, MASCOUCHE, QC,
J7K 3G6
SIC 3272

FORTERRA PIPE & PRECAST, LTD p533
2099 ROSEVILLE RD SUITE 2, CAM-
BRIDGE, ON, N1R 5S3
(519) 622-7574 *SIC 3272*

FORTERRA PRESSURE PIPE, ULC p1000
102 PROUSE RD, UXBRIDGE, ON, L4A
7X4
(905) 642-4383 *SIC 3272*

FORTERRA PRESSURE PIPE, ULC p1301
699 BOUL INDUSTRIEL, SAINT-
EUSTACHE, QC, J7R 6C3
(450) 623-2200 *SIC 3272*

GLOBAL PRECAST INC p664
2101 TESTON RD, MAPLE, ON, L6A 1R3
(905) 832-4307 *SIC 3272*

GROUPE CARON & CARON INC p1316
800 BOUL PIERRE-TREMBLAY, SAINT-
JEAN-SUR-RICHELIEU, QC, J2X 4W8
(450) 545-7174 *SIC 3272*

**INDUSTRIES DE CIMENT LA GUADE-
LOUPE INC, LES** p1122
238 14E AV, LA GUADELOUPE, QC, G0M
1G0
(418) 459-3542 *SIC 3272*

LECUYER & FILS LTEE p1351
17 RUE DU MOULIN, SAINT-REMI, QC, J0L
2L0
(514) 861-5623 *SIC 3272*

M-CON PRODUCTS INC p541
2150 RICHARDSON SIDE RD RR 3, CARP,
ON, K0A 1L0
(613) 831-1736 *SIC 3272*

**NATIONAL CONCRETE ACCESSORIES
COMPANY INC** p586
172 BETHRIDGE RD, ETOBICOKE, ON,
M9W 1N3
(416) 245-4720 *SIC 3272*

OLDCASTLE BUILDING PRODUCTS

CANADA, INC _p892_
682 ARVIN AVE, STONEY CREEK, ON, L8E 5R4
SIC 3272

OSHAWA YOUNG WOMEN CHRISTIAN ASSOCIATION, THE _p813_
33 MCGRIGOR ST, OSHAWA, ON, L1H 1X8
(905) 576-6356   _SIC 3272_

P.C. OILFIELD SUPPLIES LTD _p205_
501 ROLLA RD, DAWSON CREEK, BC, V1G 4E9
(250) 782-5134   _SIC 3272_

PATIO DRUMMOND LTEE _p1096_
8435 BOUL SAINT-JOSEPH, DRUMONDVILLE, QC, J2A 3W8
(819) 394-2505   _SIC 3272_

PRE-CON INC _p510_
35 RUTHERFORD RD S, BRAMPTON, ON, L6W 3J4
(905) 457-4140   _SIC 3272_

PRESTRESSED SYSTEMS INCORPORATED _p1023_
4955 WALKER RD, WINDSOR, ON, N9A 6J3
(519) 737-1216   _SIC 3272_

PRESTRESSED SYSTEMS INCORPORATED _p1023_
4955 WALKER RD, WINDSOR, ON, N9A 6J3
(519) 737-1216   _SIC 3272_

PRODUITS DE BETON CASAUBON INC, LES _p1357_
2145 RANG DE LA RIVIERE S, SAINTE-ELISABETH, QC, J0K 2J0
(450) 753-3565   _SIC 3272_

RES PRECAST INC _p622_
3450 THOMAS ST, INNISFIL, ON, L9S 3W6
(705) 436-7383   _SIC 3272_

RINOX INC _p1381_
3155 BOUL DES ENTREPRISES, TERREBONNE, QC, J6X 4J9
(450) 477-7888   _SIC 3272_

SCHOKBETON QUEBEC INC _p1302_
430 BOUL ARTHUR-SAUVE BUREAU 6030, SAINT-EUSTACHE, QC, J7R 6V7
(450) 473-6831   _SIC 3272_

SILO SUPERIEUR (1993) INC _p1138_
520 2E AV, LEVIS, QC, G6W 5M6
(418) 839-8808   _SIC 3272_

STRESCON LIMITED _p414_
400 CHESLEY DR SUITE 3, SAINT JOHN, NB, E2K 5L6
(506) 633-8877   _SIC 3272_

STRESS-CRETE LIMITED _p528_
840 WALKER'S LINE SUITE 7, BURLINGTON, ON, L7N 2G2
(905) 827-6901   _SIC 3272_

STUBBE'S REDI-MIX INC _p618_
30 MUIR LINE, HARLEY, ON, N0E 1E0
(519) 424-2183   _SIC 3272_

T.A.C. CORROSION-RESISTANT TECHNOLOGY INC _p1155_
1255 BOUL LAIRD BUREAU 240, MONTROYAL, QC, H3P 2T1
(514) 737-8566   _SIC 3272_

T.M.S. SYSTEME INC _p1306_
170 RTE DU PRESIDENT-KENNEDY, SAINT-HENRI-DE-LEVIS, QC, G0R 3E0
(418) 895-6877   _SIC 3272_

TARGET PRODUCTS LTD _p183_
8535 EASTLAKE DR, BURNABY, BC, V5A 4T7
(604) 444-3620   _SIC 3272_

TECHO-BLOC INC _p1309_
5255 RUE ALBERT-MILLICHAMP, SAINT-HUBERT, QC, J3Y 8Z8
(877) 832-4625   _SIC 3272_

TRI-KRETE LIMITED _p794_
152 TORYORK DR, NORTH YORK, ON, M9L 1X6
(416) 746-2479   _SIC 3272_

UNILOCK LTD _p580_
401 THE WEST MALL SUITE 610, ETOBICOKE, ON, M9C 5J5

(416) 646-5180   _SIC 3272_

WESTCON PRECAST INC _p166_
19 RIEL DR, ST. ALBERT, AB, T8N 3Z2
(780) 459-6695   _SIC 3272_

ZENCO ALBERTA LTD _p166_
19 RIEL DR, ST. ALBERT, AB, T8N 3Z2
(780) 459-6695   _SIC 3272_

SIC 3273 Ready-mixed concrete

9338-4337 QUEBEC INC _p1307_
6600 GRANDE ALLEE, SAINT-HUBERT, QC, J3Y 1B7
(450) 656-5121   _SIC 3273_

ALEXANDER CENTRE INDUSTRIES LIMITED _p900_
1297 KELLY LAKE RD, SUDBURY, ON, P3E 5P5
(705) 674-4291   _SIC 3273_

BETON AMIX LTEE _p1108_
600B RUE DE VERNON, GATINEAU, QC, J9J 3K5
(819) 770-5092   _SIC 3273_

BETON PREFABRIQUE DU RICHELIEU INC, _p1044_
890 RUE DES PINS O, ALMA, QC, G8B 7R3
(418) 668-6161   _SIC 3273_

BURNCO ROCK PRODUCTS LTD _p34_
155 GLENDEER CIR SE SUITE 200, CALGARY, AB, T2H 2S8
(403) 255-2600   _SIC 3273_

BUTLER BROTHERS SUPPLIES LTD _p267_
1851 KEATING CROSS RD UNIT 101, SAANICHTON, BC, V8M 1W9
(250) 652-1680   _SIC 3273_

CAPITAL READY MIX LIMITED _p429_
TRANS CANADA HWY, ST. JOHN'S, NL, A1B 3N4
(709) 364-5008   _SIC 3273_

CARRIERE D'ACTON VALE LTEE _p1044_
525 116 RTE, ACTON VALE, QC, J0H 1A0
(450) 546-3201   _SIC 3273_

CARRIERES DE ST-DOMINIQUE LTEE, LES _p1299_
700 RUE PRINCIPALE, SAINT-DOMINIQUE, QC, J0H 1L0
(450) 774-2591   _SIC 3273_

CASEY CONCRETE LIMITED _p438_
96 PARK ST, AMHERST, NS, B4H 2R7
(902) 667-3395   _SIC 3273_

CASEY CONCRETE LIMITED _p468_
69 GLENWOOD DR, TRURO, NS, B2N 1E9
(902) 895-1618   _SIC 3273_

CIMENT QUEBEC INC _p1123_
1250 CH SAINT-JOSE, LA PRAIRIE, QC, J5R 6A9
(450) 444-7942   _SIC 3273_

CLOTURES ARBOIT INC, LES _p1120_
230 RUE ARBOIT, L'ASSOMPTION, QC, J5W 4P5
(450) 589-8484   _SIC 3273_

CO-FO CONCRETE FORMING CONSTRUCTION LIMITED _p653_
72 ANN ST, LONDON, ON, N6A 1P9
(519) 432-2391   _SIC 3273_

CONCRETE PRODUCTS LIMITED _p428_
260 EAST WHITE HILLS RD, ST. JOHN'S, NL, A1A 5J7
(709) 368-3171   _SIC 3273_

CRH CANADA GROUP INC _p666_
7655 WOODBINE AVE, MARKHAM, ON, L3R 2N4
(905) 475-6631   _SIC 3273_

CRH CANADA GROUP INC _p1141_
435 RUE JEAN-NEVEU, LONGUEUIL, QC, J4G 2P9
(450) 651-1117   _SIC 3273_

DANIS CONSTRUCTION INC _p1377_
13000 RTE MARIE-VICTORIN, SOREL-TRACY, QC, J3R 0J9
SIC 3273

FISHER WAVY INC _p910_
1344 OLIVER RD, THUNDER BAY, ON, P7G

1K4
(807) 345-5925   _SIC 3273_

FLESHERTON CONCRETE PRODUCTS INC _p590_
GD, FLESHERTON, ON, N0C 1E0
(519) 924-2429   _SIC 3273_

FORTIER 2000 LTEE _p1306_
146 RUE COMMERCIALE, SAINT-HENRI-DE-LEVIS, QC, G0R 3E0
(418) 882-2205   _SIC 3273_

GREENWOOD CONSTRUCTION COMPANY LIMITED _p808_
HWY 9, ORANGEVILLE, ON, L9W 2Y9
(519) 941-0732   _SIC 3273_

INNOCON INC _p855_
50 NEWKIRK RD, RICHMOND HILL, ON, L4C 3G3
(905) 508-7676   _SIC 3273_

MCCANN REDI-MIX INC _p590_
140 THAMES RD W SS 3, EXETER, ON, N0M 1S3
(519) 235-0338   _SIC 3273_

MSA INFRASTRUCTURES INC _p1318_
800 RUE DES CARRIERES, SAINT-JEAN-SUR-RICHELIEU, QC, J3B 2P2
(450) 346-4441   _SIC 3273_

MUNICIPAL READY-MIX LIMITED _p468_
19 MACRAE AVE, SYDNEY, NS, B1S 1M1
(902) 564-4541   _SIC 3273_

PAVAGES DES MONTS INC, LES _p1150_
2245 RUE DU PHARE O, MATANE, QC, G4W 3N1
(418) 562-4343   _SIC 3273_

QUALITY CONCRETE INC _p448_
20 MACDONALD AVE, DARTMOUTH, NS, B3B 1C5
(902) 468-8040   _SIC 3273_

REMPEL BROS. CONCRETE LTD _p227_
20353 64 AVE UNIT 203, LANGLEY, BC, V2Y 1N5
(604) 525-9344   _SIC 3273_

RMC READY-MIX LTD _p273_
19275 54 AVE, SURREY, BC, V3S 8E5
(604) 574-1164   _SIC 3273_

ROLLING MIX CONCRETE (B.C.) LTD _p251_
105 FOOTHILL BLVD, PRINCE GEORGE, BC, V2N 2J8
(250) 563-9213   _SIC 3273_

ROLLING MIX CONCRETE (EDMONTON) LTD _p102_
22235 115 AVE NW, EDMONTON, AB, T5S 2N6
(780) 434-3736   _SIC 3273_

ROLLING MIX MANAGEMENT LTD _p37_
7209 RAILWAY ST SE, CALGARY, AB, T2H 2V6
(403) 253-6426   _SIC 3273_

SARJEANT COMPANY LIMITED, THE _p488_
15 SARJEANT DR, BARRIE, ON, L4N 4V9
(705) 728-2460   _SIC 3273_

SOUTH SHORE READY MIX LIMITED _p441_
1896 KING ST, BRIDGEWATER, NS, B4V 2W9
(902) 543-4639   _SIC 3273_

SPIVAK, N-J LIMITED _p661_
3334 WONDERLAND RD S SUITE 2, LONDON, ON, N6L 1A6
(519) 652-3276   _SIC 3273_

ST. MARYS CEMENT INC. (CANADA) _p918_
55 INDUSTRIAL ST, TORONTO, ON, M4G 3W9
(416) 423-1300   _SIC 3273_

TESKEY CONCRETE COMPANY CORP _p786_
20 MURRAY RD, NORTH YORK, ON, M3K 1T2
(416) 638-0340   _SIC 3273_

TORONTO REDI MIX LIMITED _p559_
401 BOWES RD, CONCORD, ON, L4K 1J4
(416) 798-7060   _SIC 3273_

WARREN READY-MIX LTD _p411_
58 CALIFORNIA RD, REXTON, NB, E4W 1W8
(506) 523-4240   _SIC 3273_

WETASKIWIN READY MIX LTD _p172_
5410 50 ST, WETASKIWIN, AB, T9A 2G9
(780) 352-4301   _SIC 3273_

WHEAT CITY CONCRETE PRODUCTS LTD _p347_
4801 VICTORIA AVE E, BRANDON, MB, R7A 7L2
(204) 725-5600   _SIC 3273_

SIC 3274 Lime

CARMEUSE LIME (CANADA) LIMITED _p621_
374681 COUNTY RD 6, INGERSOLL, ON, N5C 3K5
(519) 423-6283   _SIC 3274_

GRAYMONT WESTERN CANADA INC _p23_
3025 12 ST NE SUITE 190, CALGARY, AB, T2E 7J2
(403) 250-9100   _SIC 3274_

SIC 3275 Gypsum products

CABOT MANUFACTURING ULC _p397_
521 BOUL FERDINAND, DIEPPE, NB, E1A 7G1
(506) 386-2868   _SIC 3275_

CERTAINTEED GYPSUM CANADA, INC _p205_
1070 DERWENT WAY, DELTA, BC, V3M 5R1
(604) 527-1405   _SIC 3275_

CERTAINTEED GYPSUM CANADA, INC _p1356_
700 1RE AV, SAINTE-CATHERINE, QC, J5C 1C5
(450) 632-5440   _SIC 3275_

CGC INC _p607_
55 THIRD LINE RD, HAGERSVILLE, ON, N0A 1H0
(905) 768-3331   _SIC 3275_

CGC INC _p709_
350 BURNHAMTHORPE RD W SUITE 500, MISSISSAUGA, ON, L5B 3J1
(905) 803-5600   _SIC 3275_

CGC INC _p1164_
7200 RUE NOTRE-DAME E, MONTREAL, QC, H1N 3L6
(514) 255-4061   _SIC 3275_

GEORGIA-PACIFIC CANADA LP _p274_
12509 116 AVE, SURREY, BC, V3V 3S6
(604) 209-6588   _SIC 3275_

PLASTER FORM INC _p712_
1180 LAKESHORE RD E, MISSISSAUGA, ON, L5E 1E9
(905) 891-9500   _SIC 3275_

PSL PARTITION SYSTEMS LTD _p123_
1105 70 AVE NW, EDMONTON, AB, T6P 1N5
(780) 465-0001   _SIC 3275_

SIC 3281 Cut stone and stone products

ARRISCRAFT CANADA INC _p538_
875 SPEEDSVILLE RD, CAMBRIDGE, ON, N3H 4R6
(519) 653-3275   _SIC 3281_

CARRIERES DUCHARME INC, LES _p1113_
564 CH DE COVEY HILL, HAVELOCK, QC, J0S 2C0
(450) 247-2787   _SIC 3281_

CONRAD BROTHERS LIMITED _p443_
31 CONO DR, DARTMOUTH, NS, B2W 3Y2
(902) 435-3233   _SIC 3281_

GLENDYNE INC _p1348_
396 RUE PRINCIPALE, SAINT-MARC-DU-LAC-LONG, QC, G0L 1T0
(418) 893-7221   _SIC 3281_

GRANICOR INC _p1293_
300 RUE DE ROTTERDAM BUREAU 21, SAINT-AUGUSTIN-DE-DESMAURES, QC, G3A 1T4

(418) 878-3530   *SIC 3281*
GRANIT C. ROULEAU INC   *p1378*
140 CH DES URSULINES, STANSTEAD, QC, J0B 3E0
(819) 876-7171   *SIC 3281*
HURLEY SLATE WORKS COMPANY INC *p422*
250 MINERALS RD, CONCEPTION BAY SOUTH, NL, A1W 5A2
(709) 834-2320   *SIC 3281*
ITALBEC INTERNATIONAL INC   *p1180*
375 RUE DE LIEGE O, MONTREAL, QC, H2P 1H6
(514) 383-0668   *SIC 3281*
JADE STONE LTD   *p16*
6429 79 AVE SE, CALGARY, AB, T2C 5P1
(403) 287-0398   *SIC 3281*
K.J. BEAMISH HOLDINGS LIMITED   *p629*
3300 KING VAUGHAN RD, KING CITY, ON, L7B 1B2
(905) 833-4666   *SIC 3281*
MAPLE TERRAZZO MARBLE & TILE INCORPORATED   *p495*
16 NIXON RD, BOLTON, ON, L7E 1K3
(905) 850-3006   *SIC 3281*
OWEN SOUND LEDGEROCK LIMITED *p836*
138436 LEDGEROCK RD, OWEN SOUND, ON, N4K 5P7
(519) 376-0366   *SIC 3281*
PIERCON LTEE   *p1063*
387 RUE NOTRE-DAME, BON-CONSEIL, QC, J0C 1A0
(819) 336-3777   *SIC 3281*
ROCK OF AGES CANADA INC   *p1378*
4 RUE ROCK OF AGES, STANSTEAD, QC, J0B 3E2
(819) 876-2745   *SIC 3281*
SANDERSON MONUMENT COMPANY LIMITED   *p810*
33 PETER ST S, ORILLIA, ON, L3V 5A8
(705) 326-6131   *SIC 3281*
SUMMUM GRANIT INC   *p1352*
460 RUE PRINCIPALE, SAINT-SEBASTIEN-DE-FRONTENAC, QC, G0Y 1M0
(819) 652-2333   *SIC 3281*
TORNGAIT UJAGANNIAVINGIT CORPORATION   *p427*
2 MORHDT RD, NAIN, NL, A0P 1L0
(709) 922-2143   *SIC 3281*
WHOLESALE STONE INDUSTRIES INC *p91*
10180 101 ST NW SUITE 3400, EDMONTON, AB, T5J 3S4
(587) 523-1127   *SIC 3281*

SIC 3291 Abrasive products

BARTONAIR FABRICATIONS INC   *p610*
394 SHERMAN AVE N, HAMILTON, ON, L8L 6P1
(905) 524-2234   *SIC 3291*
FORGES DE SOREL CIE, LES   *p1322*
100 RUE MCCARTHY, SAINT-JOSEPH-DE-SOREL, QC, J3R 3M8
(450) 746-4030   *SIC 3291*
MATALCO INC   *p504*
850 INTERMODAL DR, BRAMPTON, ON, L6T 0B5
(905) 790-2511   *SIC 3291*
OPTA MINERALS INC   *p1005*
407 PARKSIDE DR, WATERDOWN, ON, L0R 2H0
(905) 689-7361   *SIC 3291*
SAINT-GOBAIN CANADA INC   *p846*
28 ALBERT ST W, PLATTSVILLE, ON, N0J 1S0
(519) 684-7441   *SIC 3291*
WASHINGTON MILLS ELECTRO MINERALS CORPORATION   *p758*
7780 STANLEY AVE, NIAGARA FALLS, ON, L2E 6X8
(905) 357-5500   *SIC 3291*
WINOA CANADA INC   *p1012*

650 RUSHOLME RD, WELLAND, ON, L3B 5N7
(905) 735-4691   *SIC 3291*

SIC 3295 Minerals, ground or treated

E-Z-EM CANADA INC   *p1048*
11065 BOUL LOUIS-H.-LAFONTAINE, ANJOU, QC, H1J 2Z4
(514) 353-5820   *SIC 3295*
GROUPE INTERSAND CANADA INC, LE *p1065*
125 RUE DE LA BARRE, BOUCHERVILLE, QC, J4B 2X6
(450) 449-7070   *SIC 3295*
HARSCO CANADA CORPORATION   *p614*
151 YORK BLVD, HAMILTON, ON, L8R 3M2
(905) 522-8123   *SIC 3295*
NORMERICA INC   *p713*
1599 HURONTARIO ST SUITE 300, MISSISSAUGA, ON, L5G 4S1
(416) 626-0556   *SIC 3295*

SIC 3296 Mineral wool

CERTAINTEED CANADA, INC   *p1027*
61 ROYAL GROUP CRES, WOODBRIDGE, ON, L4H 1X9
(905) 652-5200   *SIC 3296*
DIMENSION COMPOSITE INC   *p1305*
2530 95E RUE, SAINT-GEORGES, QC, G6A 1E3
(418) 228-0212   *SIC 3296*
MECART INC   *p1293*
110 RUE DE ROTTERDAM, SAINT-AUGUSTIN-DE-DESMAURES, QC, G3A 1T3
(418) 880-7000   *SIC 3296*
OC CANADA HOLDINGS COMPANY   *p517*
11 SPALDING DR, BRANTFORD, ON, N3T 6B7
(519) 752-5436   *SIC 3296*
OC CANADA HOLDINGS COMPANY   *p876*
3450 MCNICOLL AVE, SCARBOROUGH, ON, M1V 1Z5
(416) 292-4000   *SIC 3296*
OC CANADA HOLDINGS COMPANY *p1073*
131 BOUL MONTCALM N, CANDIAC, QC, J5R 3L6
(450) 619-2000   *SIC 3296*
OFI L.P.   *p595*
3985 BELGREEN DR, GLOUCESTER, ON, K1G 3N2
(613) 736-1215   *SIC 3296*
OTTAWA FIBRE L.P.   *p827*
1365 JOHNSTON RD, OTTAWA, ON, K1V 8Z1
(613) 247-7116   *SIC 3296*
ROXUL INC   *p215*
6526 INDUSTRIAL PKWY, GRAND FORKS, BC, V0H 1H0
(250) 442-5253   *SIC 3296*
ROXUL INC   *p684*
8024 ESQUESING LINE, MILTON, ON, L9T 6W3
(905) 878-8474   *SIC 3296*

SIC 3297 Nonclay refractories

GROUPE REFRACO INC   *p1080*
1207 RUE ANTONIO-LEMAIRE, CHICOUTIMI, QC, G7K 1J2
(418) 545-4200   *SIC 3297*
HARBISONWALKER INTERNATIONAL CORP   *p882*
2689 INDUSTRIAL PARK RD, SMITHVILLE, ON, L0R 2A0
(905) 957-3311   *SIC 3297*
JAYNE INDUSTRIES INC   *p892*
550 SEAMAN ST, STONEY CREEK, ON, L8E 3X7

(905) 643-9200   *SIC 3297*
RHI CANADA INC   *p524*
4355 FAIRVIEW ST, BURLINGTON, ON, L7L 2A4
(905) 633-4500   *SIC 3297*
VESUVIUS CANADA INC   *p1012*
333 PRINCE CHARLES DR, WELLAND, ON, L3C 5A6
(905) 732-4441   *SIC 3297*

SIC 3299 NonMetallic mineral products,

CARFAIR COMPOSITES INC   *p365*
692 MISSION ST, WINNIPEG, MB, R2J 0A3
(204) 233-0671   *SIC 3299*
E. I. DUPONT CANADA - THETFORD INC *p1382*
1045 RUE MONFETTE E, THETFORD MINES, QC, G6G 7K7
(418) 338-8567   *SIC 3299*
EQUINOX INDUSTRIES LTD   *p362*
401 CHRISLIND ST, WINNIPEG, MB, R2C 5G4
(204) 633-7564   *SIC 3299*
FABRICATED PLASTICS LIMITED   *p664*
2175 TESTON RD, MAPLE, ON, L6A 1R3
(905) 832-8161   *SIC 3299*
FAROEX LTD   *p350*
123 ANSON ST, GIMLI, MB, R0C 1B1
(204) 642-6400   *SIC 3299*
FIBRE LAMINATIONS LTD   *p610*
651 BURLINGTON ST E, HAMILTON, ON, L8L 4J5
(905) 312-9152   *SIC 3299*
FILAMAT COMPOSITES INC   *p712*
880 RANGEVIEW RD, MISSISSAUGA, ON, L5E 1G9
(905) 891-3993   *SIC 3299*
FORMGLAS PRODUCTS LTD   *p1003*
181 REGINA RD, VAUGHAN, ON, L4L 8M3
(416) 635-8030   *SIC 3299*
IMASCO MINERALS INC   *p282*
19287 98A AVE, SURREY, BC, V4N 4C8
(604) 888-3848   *SIC 3299*
INLINE FIBERGLASS LTD   *p585*
30 CONSTELLATION CRT, ETOBICOKE, ON, M9W 1K1
(416) 679-1171   *SIC 3299*
INTERTEC INSTRUMENTATION LTD   *p860*
255 HENRY DR, SARNIA, ON, N7T 7H5
(519) 337-2773   *SIC 3299*
JOHNS MANVILLE CANADA INC   *p137*
5301 42 AVE, INNISFAIL, AB, T4G 1A2
(403) 227-7100   *SIC 3299*
MONTECO LTD   *p927*
55 ST CLAIR AVE W SUITE 408, TORONTO, ON, M4V 2Y7
(416) 960-9968   *SIC 3299*
NEMATO CORP   *p1014*
1605 MCEWEN DR, WHITBY, ON, L1N 7L4
SIC 3299
PIONEER HI-BRED LIMITED   *p1383*
1045 RUE MONFETTE E, THETFORD MINES, QC, G6G 7K7
SIC 3299
PLASTICON CANADA INC   *p1135*
1395 MONTEE CHENIER, LES CEDRES, QC, J7T 1L9
(450) 452-1104   *SIC 3299*
RPS COMPOSITES INC   *p462*
740 MAIN ST S, MAHONE BAY, NS, B0J 2E0
(902) 624-8383   *SIC 3299*
STRUCTURAL COMPOSITE TECHNOLOGIES LTD   *p363*
100 HOKA ST UNIT 200, WINNIPEG, MB, R2C 3N2
(204) 668-9320   *SIC 3299*
SYSTEMES ADEX INC, LES   *p1113*
67 RUE SAINT-PAUL RR 1, HEBERTVILLE-STATION, QC, G0W 1T0
(418) 343-2640   *SIC 3299*
WHITEWATER COMPOSITES LTD   *p223*

9505 HALDANE RD, KELOWNA, BC, V4V 2K5
(250) 766-5152   *SIC 3299*
WINGENBACK INC   *p26*
707 BARLOW TRAIL SE, CALGARY, AB, T2E 8C2
(403) 221-8120   *SIC 3299*
ZCL COMPOSITES INC   *p126*
1420 PARSONS RD SW, EDMONTON, AB, T6X 1M5
SIC 3299

SIC 3312 Blast furnaces and steel mills

1045761 ONTARIO LIMITED   *p573*
289 HORNER AVE, ETOBICOKE, ON, M8Z 4Y4
(416) 259-1113   *SIC 3312*
1627198 ONTARIO INC   *p633*
1956 SETTERINGTON DR, KINGSVILLE, ON, N9Y 2E5
(519) 326-1333   *SIC 3312*
3680215 CANADA INC   *p1343*
6660 RUE P.-E.-LAMARCHE, SAINT-LEONARD, QC, H1P 1J7
(514) 325-4488   *SIC 3312*
ABILITY FABRICATORS INC   *p548*
187 ROMINA DR, CONCORD, ON, L4K 4V3
(905) 761-1401   *SIC 3312*
ACIER INOXYDABLE FAFARD INC   *p1063*
21 RUE DE MONTGOLFIER, BOUCHERVILLE, QC, J4B 8C4
(450) 641-4349   *SIC 3312*
ACIER NOVA INC   *p891*
830 SOUTH SERVICE RD, STONEY CREEK, ON, L8E 5M7
(905) 643-3300   *SIC 3312*
ACIER NOVA INC   *p1034*
807 PATTULLO AVE, WOODSTOCK, ON, N4S 7W3
(519) 537-6639   *SIC 3312*
ACIER OUELLETTE INC   *p1364*
935 BOUL DU HAVRE, SALABERRY-DE-VALLEYFIELD, QC, J6S 5L1
(450) 377-4248   *SIC 3312*
ACIERS TECHFORM MONTAL INC   *p1380*
3139 BOUL DES ENTREPRISES, TERREBONNE, QC, J6X 4J9
(450) 477-5705   *SIC 3312*
ALGOMA STEEL INC   *p861*
105 WEST ST, SAULT STE. MARIE, ON, P6A 7B4
(705) 945-2351   *SIC 3312*
ALMITA PILING INC   *p125*
1603 91 ST SW SUITE 200, EDMONTON, AB, T6X 0W8
(800) 363-4868   *SIC 3312*
AP INFRASTRUCTURE SOLUTIONS LP *p13*
8916 48 ST SE, CALGARY, AB, T2C 2P9
(403) 204-8500   *SIC 3312*
AP INFRASTRUCTURE SOLUTIONS LP *p257*
7900 NELSON RD, RICHMOND, BC, V6W 1G4
(604) 278-9766   *SIC 3312*
AP INFRASTRUCTURE SOLUTIONS LP *p548*
3300 HIGHWAY 7 SUITE 500, CONCORD, ON, L4K 4M3
(647) 795-9250   *SIC 3312*
AP INFRASTRUCTURE SOLUTIONS LP *p1316*
800 BOUL PIERRE-TREMBLAY, SAINT-JEAN-SUR-RICHELIEU, QC, J2X 4W8
(450) 346-4481   *SIC 3312*
ARCELORMITTAL PRODUITS LONGS CANADA S.E.N.C.   *p1082*
3900 RTE DES ACIERIES, CONTRE-COEUR, QC, J0L 1C0
(450) 587-8600   *SIC 3312*
ARCELORMITTAL PRODUITS LONGS CANADA S.E.N.C.   *p1082*
2050 RTE DES ACIERIES, CONTRE-

COEUR, QC, J0L 1C0

(450) 587-2012   SIC 3312

ARCELORMITTAL PRODUITS LONGS CANADA S.E.N.C.   p1082
4000 RTE DES ACIERIES, CONTRE-COEUR, QC, J0L 1C0

(450) 587-8600   SIC 3312

ARCELORMITTAL PRODUITS LONGS CANADA S.E.N.C.   p1223
5900 RUE SAINT-PATRICK, MONTREAL, QC, H4E 1B3

(514) 762-5260   SIC 3312

ARMTEC INC   p370
2500 FERRIER ST, WINNIPEG, MB, R2V 4P6

(204) 338-9311   SIC 3312

AUSTIN STEEL GROUP INC   p498
39 PROGRESS CRT, BRAMPTON, ON, L6S 5X2

(905) 799-3324   SIC 3312

AUTOTUBE LIMITED   p897
300 HIGH ST E, STRATHROY, ON, N7G 4C5

(519) 245-1742   SIC 3312

BAILEY METAL PRODUCTS LIMITED   p549
1 CALDARI RD, CONCORD, ON, L4K 3Z9

(905) 738-9267   SIC 3312

BAILEY-HUNT LIMITED   p549
1 CALDARI RD, CONCORD, ON, L4K 3Z9

(905) 738-9267   SIC 3312

BOLTON STEEL TUBE CO. LTD   p494
455A PIERCEY RD, BOLTON, ON, L7E 5B8

(905) 857-6830   SIC 3312

BRASS WORKS LTD   p371
511 JARVIS AVE, WINNIPEG, MB, R2W 3A8

(204) 582-3737   SIC 3312

BULL MOOSE TUBE LIMITED   p529
2170 QUEENSWAY DR, BURLINGTON, ON, L7R 3T1

(905) 637-8261   SIC 3312

CANADA PIPE COMPANY ULC   p1357
6200 RUE PRINCIPALE, SAINTE-CROIX, QC, G0S 2H0

(418) 926-3262   SIC 3312

CANADIAN NATIONAL STEEL CORPORATION   p78
5302 39 ST, CAMROSE, AB, T4V 2N8

(780) 672-3116   SIC 3312

CANADIAN SOLAR INC   p605
545 SPEEDVALE AVE W, GUELPH, ON, N1K 1E6

(519) 837-1881   SIC 3312

CAPITAL TOOL & DESIGN LTD.   p550
270 SPINNAKER WAY SUITE 13, CONCORD, ON, L4K 4W1

(905) 760-8088   SIC 3312

CENTRAL WIRE INDUSTRIES LTD   p839
1 NORTH ST, PERTH, ON, K7H 2S2

(613) 267-3752   SIC 3312

D.F. BARNES SERVICES LIMITED   p433
22 SUDBURY ST, ST. JOHN'S, NL, A1E 2V1

(709) 579-5041   SIC 3312

DFI CORPORATION   p122
2404 51 AVE NW, EDMONTON, AB, T6P 0E4

(780) 466-5237   SIC 3312

EAST COAST METAL FABRICATION (2015) INC   p449
10 MARINE DR, EDWARDSVILLE, NS, B2A 4S6

(902) 564-5600   SIC 3312

EDMONTON EXCHANGER & MANUFACTURING LTD   p114
5545 89 ST NW, EDMONTON, AB, T6E 5W9

(780) 468-6722   SIC 3312

EVRAZ INC. NA CANADA   p15
7201 OGDEN DALE RD SE, CALGARY, AB, T2C 2A4

(403) 279-3351   SIC 3312

EVRAZ INC. NA CANADA   p1417
100 ARMOUR RD, REGINA, SK, S4P 3C7

(306) 924-7700   SIC 3312

FORGES DE SOREL CIE, LES   p1322

100 RUE MCCARTHY, SAINT-JOSEPH-DE-SOREL, QC, J3R 3M8

(450) 746-4030   SIC 3312

GERDAU AMERISTEEL CORPORATION   p356
27 MAIN ST, SELKIRK, MB, R1A 1P6

(204) 482-3241   SIC 3312

GERDAU AMERISTEEL CORPORATION   p536
160 ORION PL, CAMBRIDGE, ON, N1T 1R9

(519) 740-2488   SIC 3312

GERDAU AMERISTEEL CORPORATION   p1014
1 GERDAU CRT, WHITBY, ON, L1N 7G8

(905) 668-8811   SIC 3312

GESTION STRUCTURES XL INC   p1381
3005 RUE DES BATISSEURS, TERREBONNE, QC, J6Y 0A2

(450) 968-0800   SIC 3312

HARRIS STEEL ULC   p522
5400 HARVESTER RD, BURLINGTON, ON, L7L 5N5

(905) 681-6811   SIC 3312

HELICAL PIER SYSTEMS LTD   p162
180 STRATHMOOR DR, SHERWOOD PARK, AB, T8H 2B7

(780) 400-3700   SIC 3312

HIGH STRENGTH PLATES & PROFILES INC   p735
7464 TRANMERE DR, MISSISSAUGA, ON, L5S 1K4

(905) 673-5770   SIC 3312

HOOVER ENTERPRISES INC   p911
81 LINCOLN ST, TILLSONBURG, ON, N4G 5Y4

(519) 842-2890   SIC 3312

INDUSTRIES D'ACIER INOXYDABLE LIMITEE   p1066
1440 RUE GRAHAM-BELL, BOUCHERVILLE, QC, J4B 6H5

(450) 449-4000   SIC 3312

INOX INDUSTRIES INC   p504
60 SUMMERLEA RD, BRAMPTON, ON, L6T 4X3

(905) 799-9996   SIC 3312

IVACO ROLLING MILLS 2004 L.P.   p643
1040 HWY 17, L'ORIGNAL, ON, K0B 1K0

(613) 675-4671   SIC 3312

J.V. DRIVER FABRICATORS INC   p149
706 25 AVE, NISKU, AB, T9E 0G6

(780) 955-4282   SIC 3312

LEGGETT & PLATT CANADA CO   p1010
195 BATHURST DR, WATERLOO, ON, N2V 2B2

(519) 884-1860   SIC 3312

LEHNER WOOD PRESERVERS LTD   p1414
2690 4TH AVE W, PRINCE ALBERT, SK, S6V 5Y9

(306) 763-4232   SIC 3312

MAX AICHER (NORTH AMERICA) LIMITED   p611
855 INDUSTRIAL DR, HAMILTON, ON, L8L 0B2

(289) 426-5670   SIC 3312

MAX AICHER (NORTH AMERICA) REALTY INC   p611
855 INDUSTRIAL DR, HAMILTON, ON, L8L 0B2

(289) 426-5670   SIC 3312

MOLY-COP ALTASTEEL LTD   p110
9401 34 ST NW, EDMONTON, AB, T6B 2X6

(780) 468-1133   SIC 3312

MULTICHAIR INC   p741
6900 DAVAND DR, MISSISSAUGA, ON, L5T 1J5

SIC 3312

NEXANS CANADA INC   p590
670 GZOWSKI ST, FERGUS, ON, N1M 2W9

(519) 843-3000   SIC 3312

NEXANS CANADA INC   p673
140 ALLSTATE PKY SUITE 300, MARKHAM, ON, L3R 0Z7

(905) 944-4300   SIC 3312

NEXANS CANADA INC   p1438
1770 EAST AVE, WEYBURN, SK, S4H 0B8

(306) 842-7451   SIC 3312

OLD STEELCO INC   p862
GD, SAULT STE. MARIE, ON, P6A 5P2

(705) 945-3301   SIC 3312

OLD STEELCO INC   p862
105 WEST ST, SAULT STE. MARIE, ON, P6A 7B4

(705) 945-2351   SIC 3312

OLD STEELCO INC   p862
GD, SAULT STE. MARIE, ON, P6A 5P2

(705) 945-3172   SIC 3312

ORPHAN INDUSTRIES LIMITED   p428
45 PEPPERRELL RD, ST. JOHN'S, NL, A1A 5N8

(709) 726-6820   SIC 3312

PRUDENTIAL STEEL ULC   p18
8919 BARLOW TRAIL SE, CALGARY, AB, T2C 2N7

(403) 279-4401   SIC 3312

PYRAMID PROCESS FABRICATORS CORPORATION   p149
2308 8 ST, NISKU, AB, T9E 7Z2

(780) 955-2708   SIC 3312

RESCO CANADA, INC   p1112
1330 RTE 148, GRENVILLE-SUR-LA-ROUGE, QC, J0V 1B0

(819) 242-2721   SIC 3312

RUSSEL METALS INC   p18
5724 40 ST SE, CALGARY, AB, T2C 2A1

(403) 279-6600   SIC 3312

SANDVIK CANADA, INC   p479
425 MCCARTNEY, ARNPRIOR, ON, K7S 3P3

(613) 623-6501   SIC 3312

SANDVIK CANADA, INC   p727
2550 MEADOWVALE BLVD UNIT 3, MISSISSAUGA, ON, L5N 8C2

(905) 826-8900   SIC 3312

SOUDURES J.M. TREMBLAY (1987) INC, LES   p1291
1303 RTE 132, SAINT-ANICET, QC, J0S 1M0

(450) 264-5690   SIC 3312

STELCO INC   p611
386 WILCOX ST, HAMILTON, ON, L8L 8K5

(905) 528-2511   SIC 3312

STELCO INC   p747
2330 HALDIMAND RD 3, NANTICOKE, ON, N0A 1L0

(905) 587-4541   SIC 3312

STRUCTURES G.B. LTEE, LES   p1285
105 MONTEE INDUSTRIELLE-ET-COMMERCIALE, RIMOUSKI, QC, G5M 1A8

(418) 724-9433   SIC 3312

TECFAB INTERNATIONAL INC   p1305
11535 1RE AV BUREAU 500, SAINT-GEORGES, QC, G5Y 7H5

(418) 228-8031   SIC 3312

TECFAB INTERNATIONAL INC   p1367
5190 RANG SAINT-MATHIEU, SHAWINIGAN, QC, G0X 1L0

(819) 536-4445   SIC 3312

TENARIS GLOBAL SERVICES (CANADA) INC   p61
530 8 AVE SW SUITE 400, CALGARY, AB, T2P 3S8

(403) 767-0100   SIC 3312

TRIANGLE STEEL LTD   p19
2915 54 AVE SE, CALGARY, AB, T2C 0A9

(403) 279-2622   SIC 3312

VOESTALPINE NORTRAK LTD   p257
5500 PARKWOOD WAY, RICHMOND, BC, V6V 2M4

(604) 273-3030   SIC 3312

VULCRAFT CANADA, INC   p478
1362 OSPREY DR, ANCASTER, ON, L9G 4V5

(289) 443-2000   SIC 3312

WALLACE INTERNATIONAL LTD   p389
115 LOWSON CRES, WINNIPEG, MB, R3P 1A6

(204) 452-2700   SIC 3312

WELDED TUBE OF CANADA CORP   p561
111 RAYETTE RD, CONCORD, ON, L4K 2E9

(905) 669-1111   SIC 3312

WESTMAN STEEL INDUSTRIES   p357
2976 DAY ST, SPRINGFIELD, MB, R2C 2Z2

(204) 777-5345   SIC 3312

WINDSOR MACHINE & STAMPING (2009) LTD   p1026
1555 TALBOT RD SUITE 401, WINDSOR, ON, N9H 2N2

(519) 737-7155   SIC 3312

SIC 3313 ElectroMetallurgical products

ELKEM METAL CANADA INC   p1080
2020 CH DE LA RESERVE, CHICOUTIMI, QC, G7J 0E1

(418) 549-4171   SIC 3313

SIC 3315 Steel wire and related products

BELDEN CANADA INC   p1332
2310 BOUL ALFRED-NOBEL, SAINT-LAURENT, QC, H4S 2B4

(514) 822-2345   SIC 3315

DUCHESNE ET FILS LTEE   p1403
871 BOUL DUCHESNE, YAMACHICHE, QC, G0X 3L0

(819) 296-3737   SIC 3315

GENERAL CABLE COMPANY LTD   p503
156 PARKSHORE DR, BRAMPTON, ON, L6T 5M1

(905) 791-6886   SIC 3315

HARBOUR INDUSTRIES (CANADA) LTD   p1101
1365 BOUL INDUSTRIEL, FARNHAM, QC, J2N 2X3

(450) 293-5304   SIC 3315

NVENT THERMAL CANADA LTD   p999
250 WEST ST, TRENTON, ON, K8V 5S2

(613) 392-6571   SIC 3315

PHOENIX FENCE CORP   p106
12816 156 ST NW, EDMONTON, AB, T5V 1E9

(780) 447-1919   SIC 3315

SIC 3316 Cold finishing of steel shapes

ARCELORMITTAL PRODUITS LONGS CANADA S.E.N.C.   p1145
2555 CH DU LAC, LONGUEUIL, QC, J4N 1C1

(450) 442-7700   SIC 3316

COMMERCIAL ROLL FORMED PRODUCTS LIMITED   p502
225 PARKHURST SQ, BRAMPTON, ON, L6T 5H5

(905) 790-5665   SIC 3316

REPUBLIC CANADIAN DRAWN, INC   p613
155 CHATHAM ST, HAMILTON, ON, L8P 2B7

(905) 546-5656   SIC 3316

STELLARC PRECISION BAR INC   p516
101 WAYNE GRETZKY PKY, BRANTFORD, ON, N3S 7N9

SIC 3316

UNION DRAWN STEEL II LIMITED   p610
1350 BURLINGTON ST E, HAMILTON, ON, L8H 3L3

(905) 547-4480   SIC 3316

UNION DRAWN STEEL II LIMITED PARTNERSHIP   p610
1350 BURLINGTON ST E, HAMILTON, ON, L8H 3L3

(905) 547-4480   SIC 3316

SIC 3317 Steel pipe and tubes

▲ Public Company   ■ Public Company Family Member   **HQ** Headquarters   **BR** Branch   **SL** Single Location

2008788 ONTARIO LIMITED   p888
580 JAMES ST S, ST MARYS, ON, N4X 1B3
(519) 349-2850   *SIC 3317*

ALGOMA TUBES INC   p863
547 WALLACE TERR, SAULT STE. MARIE, ON, P6C 1L9
(705) 946-8130   *SIC 3317*

ATLAS TUBE CANADA ULC   p618
200 CLARK ST, HARROW, ON, N0R 1G0
(519) 738-5000   *SIC 3317*

ATLAS TUBE CANADA ULC   p1011
160 DAIN AVE, WELLAND, ON, L3B 5Y6
(905) 735-7473   *SIC 3317*

CHEMINEES SECURITE INTERNATIONAL LTEE   p1233
2125 RUE MONTEREY, MONTREAL, QC, H7L 3T6
(450) 973-9999   *SIC 3317*

CS AUTOMOTIVE TUBING INC   p661
2400 INNOVATION DR, LONDON, ON, N6M 0C5
(519) 453-0123   *SIC 3317*

KUBOTA MATERIALS CANADA CORPORATION   p809
25 COMMERCE RD, ORILLIA, ON, L3V 6L6
(705) 325-2781   *SIC 3317*

WELDED TUBE OF CANADA CORP   p561
541 BOWES RD, CONCORD, ON, L4K 1J5
(905) 669-1111   *SIC 3317*

SIC 3321 Gray and ductile iron foundries

ARCHIE MCCOY (HAMILTON) LIMITED p999
1890 HIGHWAY 5 W, TROY, ON, L0R 2B0
(519) 647-3411   *SIC 3321*

BRADKEN CANADA MANUFACTURED PRODUCTS LTD   p1154
105 AV DE LA FONDERIE, MONT-JOLI, QC, G5H 1W2
(418) 775-4358   *SIC 3321*

CROWE FOUNDRY LIMITED   p537
95 SHEFFIELD ST, CAMBRIDGE, ON, N3C 1C4

SIC 3321

DELANEY HOLDINGS INC   p361
200 PACIFIC ST, WINKLER, MB, R6W 0K2
(204) 325-7376   *SIC 3321*

FONDERIE POITRAS LTEE   p1121
168 BOUL NILUS-LECLERC, L'ISLET, QC, G0R 2C0
(418) 247-5041   *SIC 3321*

INTEGRA CASTINGS INC   p361
200 PACIFIC ST, WINKLER, MB, R6W 0K2
(204) 325-7376   *SIC 3321*

LAKE FOUNDRY LTD   p599
287 SOUTH SERVICE RD, GRIMSBY, ON, L3M 1Y6
(905) 643-1248   *SIC 3321*

LETHBRIDGE IRON WORKS COMPANY LIMITED   p141
720 32 ST N, LETHBRIDGE, AB, T1H 5K5
(403) 329-4242   *SIC 3321*

MONARCH INDUSTRIES LIMITED   p361
280 MONARCH DR, WINKLER, MB, R6W 0J6
(204) 325-4393   *SIC 3321*

ROBAR INDUSTRIES LTD   p277
12945 78 AVE, SURREY, BC, V3W 2X8
(604) 591-8811   *SIC 3321*

SOUCY BELGEN INC   p1097
4475 BOUL SAINT-JOSEPH, DRUMMONDVILLE, QC, J2B 1T8
(819) 477-2434   *SIC 3321*

TIFFANY METAL CASTING LTD   p864
286075 COUNTY RD 10, SCARBOROUGH, ON, L9W 6P5
(519) 941-7026   *SIC 3321*

WABTEC CANADA INC   p1005
40 MASON ST, WALLACEBURG, ON, N8A 4M1
(519) 627-1244   *SIC 3321*

SIC 3322 Malleable iron foundries

3135772 CANADA INC   p412
73 LORNE ST, SACKVILLE, NB, E4L 4A2
SIC 3322

ANCAST INDUSTRIES LTD   p380
1350 SASKATCHEWAN AVE, WINNIPEG, MB, R3E 0L2
(204) 786-7911   *SIC 3322*

CANADA PIPE COMPANY ULC   p1349
106 MONTEE BASSE, SAINT-OURS, QC, J0G 1P0
(450) 785-2205   *SIC 3322*

FORD MOTOR COMPANY OF CANADA, LIMITED   p1023
2900 TRENTON ST, WINDSOR, ON, N9A 7B2
(519) 257-2000   *SIC 3322*

PENTICTON FOUNDRY LTD   p244
568 DAWSON AVE, PENTICTON, BC, V2A 3N8
(250) 492-7043   *SIC 3322*

SIC 3324 Steel investment foundries

ALPHACASTING INC   p1325
391 AV SAINTE-CROIX, SAINT-LAURENT, QC, H4N 2L3
(514) 748-7511   *SIC 3324*

ELIMETAL INC   p1333
1515 BOUL PITFIELD, SAINT-LAURENT, QC, H4S 1G3
(514) 956-7400   *SIC 3324*

VESTSHELL INC   p1240
10378 AV PELLETIER, MONTREAL-NORD, QC, H1H 3R3
(514) 326-1280   *SIC 3324*

SIC 3325 Steel foundries, nec

ALLOY CASTING INDUSTRIES LIMITED p752
374 HAMILTON RD UNIT 1, NEW HAMBURG, ON, N3A 2K2
(519) 662-3111   *SIC 3325*

AMSCO CAST PRODUCTS (CANADA) INC p356
35 MERCY ST, SELKIRK, MB, R1A 1N5
(204) 482-4442   *SIC 3325*

AMSCO CAST PRODUCTS (CANADA) INC p356
35 MERCY ST, SELKIRK, MB, R1A 1N5
(204) 482-4442   *SIC 3325*

BRADKEN CANADA MANUFACTURED PRODUCTS LTD   p937
90 RICHMOND ST E SUITE 4000, TORONTO, ON, M5C 1P1
(416) 975-8251   *SIC 3325*

CENTURY PACIFIC FOUNDRY LTD   p276
8239 128 ST, SURREY, BC, V3W 4G1
(604) 596-7451   *SIC 3325*

DIEMAX MANUFACTURING LTD   p473
729 FINLEY AVE, AJAX, ON, L1S 3T1
(905) 619-9380   *SIC 3325*

ESCO LIMITED   p246
1855 KINGSWAY AVE, PORT COQUITLAM, BC, V3C 1T1
(604) 942-7261   *SIC 3325*

ESCO LIMITED   p434
21 SECOND AVE, WABUSH, NL, A0R 1B0
(709) 282-3660   *SIC 3325*

ESCO LIMITED   p847
185 HOPE ST S, PORT HOPE, ON, L1A 4C2
(905) 885-6301   *SIC 3325*

GAMMA FOUNDRIES INC   p855
115 NEWKIRK RD, RICHMOND HILL, ON, L4C 3G4
(905) 884-9091   *SIC 3325*

GESTION METALLURGIE CASTECH INC
p1382

500 BOUL FRONTENAC E, THETFORD MINES, QC, G6G 7M8
(418) 338-3171   *SIC 3325*

HIGHLAND FOUNDRY LTD   p282
9670 187 ST, SURREY, BC, V4N 3N6
(604) 888-8444   *SIC 3325*

MAGOTTEAUX LTEE   p1148
601 RUE CHAMPLAIN, MAGOG, QC, J1X 2N1
(819) 843-0443   *SIC 3325*

MARITIME STEEL AND FOUNDRIES LIMITED   p463
379 GLASGOW ST, NEW GLASGOW, NS, B2H 5C3
SIC 3325

METALLURGIE CASTECH INC   p1383
500 BOUL FRONTENAC E, THETFORD MINES, QC, G6G 7M8
(418) 338-3171   *SIC 3325*

TURPOL TECH INDUSTRIES INC   p615
100 LANCING DR UNIT 3, HAMILTON, ON, L8W 3L6
(905) 512-9881   *SIC 3325*

WABI IRON & STEEL CORP   p753
330 BROADWOOD AVE, NEW LISKEARD, ON, P0J 1P0
(705) 647-4383   *SIC 3325*

SIC 3334 Primary aluminum

ALCOA CANADA CIE   p1090
1 BOUL DES SOURCES, DESCHAMBAULT, QC, G0A 1S0
(418) 286-5287   *SIC 3334*

ALCOA CANADA CIE   p1201
1 PLACE VILLE-MARIE BUREAU 2310, MONTREAL, QC, H3B 3M5
(514) 904-5030   *SIC 3334*

ALCOA CANADA CIE   p1233
4001 DES LAURENTIDES (A-15) E, MONTREAL, QC, H7L 3H7
(450) 680-2500   *SIC 3334*

ALCOA DESCHAMBAULT LTEE   p1090
1 BOUL DES SOURCES, DESCHAMBAULT, QC, G0A 1S0
(418) 286-5287   *SIC 3334*

ALCOA-ALUMINERIE DE DESCHAMBAULT S.E.C.   p1090
1 BOUL DES SOURCES, DESCHAMBAULT, QC, G0A 1S0
(418) 286-5287   *SIC 3334*

ALUMINERIE ALOUETTE INC   p1367
400 CH DE LA POINTE-NOIRE, SEPT-ILES, QC, G4R 5M9
(418) 964-7000   *SIC 3334*

GESTION ALCOA CANADA CIE   p1204
1 PLACE VILLE-MARIE BUREAU 2310, MONTREAL, QC, H3B 3M5
(514) 904-5030   *SIC 3334*

HYDRO ALUMINIUM CANADA INC   p1197
2000 AV MCGILL COLLEGE BUREAU 2310, MONTREAL, QC, H3A 3H3
(514) 840-9110   *SIC 3334*

NEMOF OF CANADA CORPORATION p1025
4600 G N BOOTH DR, WINDSOR, ON, N9C 4G8
(519) 250-2500   *SIC 3334*

RIO TINTO ALCAN INC   p224
1 SMELTER SITE RD, KITIMAT, BC, V8C 2H2
(250) 639-8000   *SIC 3334*

RIO TINTO ALCAN INC   p1115
1955 BOUL MELLON, JONQUIERE, QC, G7S 0L4
(418) 699-2002   *SIC 3334*

RIO TINTO ALCAN INC   p1121
5000 RTE DU PETIT PARC, LA BAIE, QC, G7B 4G9
(418) 697-9600   *SIC 3334*

RIO TINTO ALCAN INC   p1208
1190 AV DES CANADIENS-DE-MONTREAL BUREAU 400, MONTREAL, QC, H3B 0E3

(514) 848-8000   *SIC 3334*

RIO TINTO ALCAN INC   p1368
1100 BOUL SAINT-SACREMENT, SHAWINIGAN, QC, G9N 0E3
(819) 539-0765   *SIC 3334*

SOCIETE D'ELECTROLYSE ET DE CHIMIE ALCAN LIMITEE   p1199
1188 RUE SHERBROOKE O, MONTREAL, QC, H3A 3G2
SIC 3334

SIC 3339 Primary nonferrous Metals, nec

5N PLUS INC   p1328
4385 RUE GARAND, SAINT-LAURENT, QC, H4R 2B4
(514) 856-0644   *SIC 3339*

ASAHI REFINING CANADA LTD   p508
130 GLIDDEN RD, BRAMPTON, ON, L6W 3M8
(905) 453-6120   *SIC 3339*

HMZ METALS INC   p939
2 TORONTO ST SUITE 500, TORONTO, ON, M5C 2B6
SIC 3339

INCA ONE GOLD CORP   p314
1140 WEST PENDER SUITE 850, VANCOUVER, BC, V6E 4G1
(604) 568-4877   *SIC 3339*

PMR INC   p1062
4640 BOUL DE LA GRANDE-ALLEE, BOISBRIAND, QC, J7H 1S7
(450) 420-7361   *SIC 3339*

PRODUITS MICROZINC INC, LES   p1314
1375 RUE BROUILLETTE, SAINT-HYACINTHE, QC, J2T 2G7
(450) 774-9151   *SIC 3339*

SHERRITT INTERNATIONAL CORPORATION   p130
10101 114 ST, FORT SASKATCHEWAN, AB, T8L 2T3
(780) 992-7000   *SIC 3339*

SOCIETE EN COMMANDITE REVENU NORANDA   p1366
860 BOUL GERARD-CADIEUX, SALABERRY-DE-VALLEYFIELD, QC, J6T 6L4
(450) 373-9144   *SIC 3339*

TIMMINCO LIMITED   p958
150 KING ST W SUITE 2401, TORONTO, ON, M5H 1J9
(416) 364-5171   *SIC 3339*

SIC 3341 Secondary nonferrous Metals

9462287 CANADA INC   p1232
2000 RUE LEOPOLD-HAMELIN, MONTREAL, QC, H7E 4P2
(450) 720-1331   *SIC 3341*

BALL TECHNOLOGIES AVANCEES D'ALUMINIUM CANADA S.E.C.   p1372
2205 RUE ROY, SHERBROOKE, QC, J1K 1B8
(819) 563-3589   *SIC 3341*

COMPAGNIE AMERICAINE DE FER & METAUX INC, LA   p1238
9100 BOUL HENRI-BOURASSA E, MONTREAL-EST, QC, H1E 2S4
(514) 494-2000   *SIC 3341*

COMPAGNIE AMERICAINE DE FER & METAUX INC, LA   p1257
999 BOUL MONTMORENCY, QUEBEC, QC, G1J 3W1
(418) 649-1000   *SIC 3341*

NEUMAN HOLDING CANADA INC   p1372
2205 RUE ROY, SHERBROOKE, QC, J1K 1B8
(819) 563-3589   *SIC 3341*

REAL ALLOY CANADA LTD   p686
7496 TORBRAM RD, MISSISSAUGA, ON, L4T 1G9
(905) 672-5569   *SIC 3341*

REVOLUTION VSC LP   p524
1100 BURLOAK DR SUITE 500, BURLINGTON, ON, L7L 6B2
(905) 279-9555   SIC 3341

ROBERT FER ET METEAUX S.E.C.   p1368
3206 CH DES BUISSONS, SHAWINIGAN, QC, G9N 6T5
(819) 539-7318   SIC 3341

TOCAN HOLDING CORP   p704
1333 TONOLLI RD, MISSISSAUGA, ON, L4Y 4C2
(905) 279-9555   SIC 3341

TOTAL METAL RECUPERATION (TMR) INC p1232
2000 RUE LEOPOLD-HAMELIN, MONTREAL, QC, H7E 4P2
(450) 720-1331   SIC 3341

TRIPLE M METAL LP   p507
471 INTERMODAL DR, BRAMPTON, ON, L6T 5G4
(905) 793-7083   SIC 3341

UMICORE PRECIOUS METALS CANADA INC   p676
451 DENISON ST, MARKHAM, ON, L3R 1B7
(905) 475-9566   SIC 3341

SIC 3351 Copper rolling and drawing

BRAWO BRASSWORKING LIMITED   p520
500 ONTARIO ST N, BURKS FALLS, ON, P0A 1C0
(705) 382-3637   SIC 3351

ESSEX GROUP CANADA INC   p880
20 GILBERTSON DR SUITE 20, SIMCOE, ON, N3Y 4L5
(519) 428-3900   SIC 3351

GREAT LAKES COPPER LTD   p649
1010 CLARKE RD, LONDON, ON, N5V 3B2
(519) 455-0770   SIC 3351

IBC ADVANCED ALLOYS CORP   p305
570 GRANVILLE ST UNIT 1200, VANCOUVER, BC, V6C 3P1
(604) 685-6263   SIC 3351

RATCLIFFS/SEVERN LTD   p855
10537 YONGE ST, RICHMOND HILL, ON, L4C 3C5
SIC 3351

SIC 3353 Aluminum sheet, plate, and foil

ARZON LIMITED   p521
4485 MAINWAY, BURLINGTON, ON, L7L 7P3
(905) 332-5600   SIC 3353

SURAL LAMINATED PRODUCTS OF CANADA INC   p1056
6900 BOUL RAOUL-DUCHESNE, BECANCOUR, QC, G9H 2V2
(819) 294-2900   SIC 3353

SIC 3354 Aluminum extruded products

6482066 CANADA INC   p1121
905 RUE DE L'INNOVATION, LA BAIE, QC, G7B 3N8
(418) 677-3939   SIC 3354

9283-9034 QUEBEC INC   p1045
2185 BOUL EUGENE-ROBITAILLE, ALMA, QC, G8C 0H5
(418) 769-3113   SIC 3354

ALCOA CANADA CIE   p1052
100 RTE MARITIME, BAIE-COMEAU, QC, G4Z 2L6
(418) 296-3311   SIC 3354

ALFINITI INC   p1080
1152 RUE DE LA MANIC, CHICOUTIMI, QC, G7K 1A2
(418) 696-2545   SIC 3354

ALMAG ALUMINUM INC   p501
22 FINLEY RD, BRAMPTON, ON, L6T 1A9

(905) 457-9000   SIC 3354

APEL EXTRUSIONS LIMITED   p13
7929 30 ST SE, CALGARY, AB, T2C 1H7
(403) 279-3321   SIC 3354

APEX ALUMINUM EXTRUSIONS LTD p224
9767 201 ST, LANGLEY, BC, V1M 3E7
(604) 882-3542   SIC 3354

CAN ART ALUMINUM EXTRUSION INC p501
85 PARKSHORE DR, BRAMPTON, ON, L6T 5M1
(905) 791-1464   SIC 3354

COMPAGNIE DE GESTION ALCOA-LAURALCO   p1090
1 BOUL DES SOURCES, DESCHAMBAULT, QC, G0A 1S0
(418) 286-5287   SIC 3354

DAJCOR ALUMINUM LTD   p542
155 IRWIN ST, CHATHAM, ON, N7M 0N5
(519) 351-2424   SIC 3354

EXTRUDEX ALUMINUM LIMITED   p1031
411 CHRISLEA RD, WOODBRIDGE, ON, L4L 8N4
(416) 745-4444   SIC 3354

HYDRO EXTRUSION CANADA INC   p706
5675 KENNEDY RD, MISSISSAUGA, ON, L4Z 2H9
(905) 890-8821   SIC 3354

HYDRO EXTRUSION CANADA INC   p1250
325 AV AVRO, POINTE-CLAIRE, QC, H9R 5W3
(514) 697-5120   SIC 3354

K.L.S (2009) INC   p1080
1615 BOUL SAINT-PAUL, CHICOUTIMI, QC, G7J 3Y3
(418) 543-1515   SIC 3354

KAISER ALUMINUM CANADA LIMITED
p649
3021 GORE RD, LONDON, ON, N5V 5A9
(519) 457-3610   SIC 3354

PRO-ROD INC   p123
3201 84 AVE NW SUITE 3201, EDMONTON, AB, T6P 1K1
(780) 449-7101   SIC 3354

SIGNATURE ALUMINUM CANADA INC p845
1850 CLEMENTS RD, PICKERING, ON, L1W 3R8
(905) 427-6550   SIC 3354

SPECTRA ALUMINUM PRODUCTS LTD
p497
95 REAGEN'S INDUSTRIAL PKY, BRADFORD, ON, L3Z 0Z9
(905) 778-8093   SIC 3354

SPECTUBE INC   p1081
1152 RUE DE LA MANIC, CHICOUTIMI, QC, G7K 1A2
(418) 696-2545   SIC 3354

SIC 3355 Aluminum rolling and drawing, nec

METRA ALUMINIUM INC   p1237
2000 BOUL FORTIN, MONTREAL, QC, H7S 1P3
(450) 629-4260   SIC 3355

MOULAGE D'ALUMINIUM HOWMET LTEE
p1234
4001 DESSTE DES LAURENTIDES (A-15) E, MONTREAL, QC, H7L 3H7
(450) 680-2500   SIC 3355

SIC 3356 Nonferrous rolling and drawing, nec

CALL2RECYCLE CANADA, INC   p995
5140 YONGE ST UNIT 1570, TORONTO, ON, M7A 2K2
(888) 224-9764   SIC 3356

MAGINDUSTRIES CORP   p767
235 YORKLAND BLVD UNIT 409, NORTH YORK, ON, M2J 4Y8
(416) 491-6088   SIC 3356

PRODUITS NON FERREUX GAUTHIER INC,

LES   p1248
12355 RUE APRIL, POINTE-AUX-TREMBLES, QC, H1B 5L8
(514) 642-4090   SIC 3356

SIC 3357 Nonferrous wiredrawing and insulating

DOMTECH INC   p998
40 DAVIS ST E, TRENTON, ON, K8V 6S4
(613) 394-4884   SIC 3357

ELECTRO CABLES INC   p998
9 RIVERSIDE DR, TRENTON, ON, K8V 5P8
(613) 394-4896   SIC 3357

GENERAL CABLE COMPANY LTD   p1122
2600 BOUL DE COMPORTE, LA MALBAIE, QC, G5A 1N4
SIC 3357

GENERAL CABLE COMPANY LTD   p1320
800 CH DE LA RIVIERE-DU-NORD, SAINT-JEROME, QC, J7Y 5G2
(450) 436-1450   SIC 3357

NORTHERN CABLES INC   p519
50 CALIFORNIA AVE, BROCKVILLE, ON, K6V 6E6
(613) 345-1594   SIC 3357

SOUTHWIRE CANADA COMPANY   p733
5705 CANCROSS CRT SUITE 100, MISSISSAUGA, ON, L5R 3E9
(800) 668-0303   SIC 3357

SIC 3364 Nonferrous die-castings except aluminum

INDUSTRIES CAPITOL INC, LES   p1182
5795 AV DE GASPE, MONTREAL, QC, H2S 2X3
(514) 273-0451   SIC 3364

MERIDIAN LIGHTWEIGHT TECHNOLOGIES HOLDINGS INC   p897
25 MCNAB ST, STRATHROY, ON, N7G 4H6
(519) 246-9600   SIC 3364

MERIDIAN LIGHTWEIGHT TECHNOLOGIES INC   p897
25 MCNAB ST, STRATHROY, ON, N7G 4H6
(519) 246-9600   SIC 3364

MERIDIAN LIGHTWEIGHT TECHNOLOGIES INC   p897
155 HIGH ST E, STRATHROY, ON, N7G 1H4
(519) 245-4040   SIC 3364

ROTO FASCO CANADA INC.   p742
6625 ORDAN DR UNIT 1, MISSISSAUGA, ON, L5T 1X2
(905) 670-8559   SIC 3364

SIC 3365 Aluminum foundries

ACCURCAST INC   p1004
333 ARNOLD ST, WALLACEBURG, ON, N8A 3P3
(519) 627-2227   SIC 3365

AMG METALS INC   p880
21 BALES DR W, SHARON, ON, L0G 1V0
(905) 953-4111   SIC 3365

C.I.F. METAL LTEE   p1382
1900 RUE SETLAKWE, THETFORD MINES, QC, G6G 8B2
(418) 338-6250   SIC 3365

CAM-TAG INDUSTRIES INC   p597
2783 FENTON RD, GLOUCESTER, ON, K1T 3T8
(613) 822-1921   SIC 3365

COMMDOOR ALUMINUM   p1030
471 CHRISLEA RD SUITE 1, WOODBRIDGE, ON, L4L 8N6
(416) 743-3667   SIC 3365

CUSTOM CASTINGS LIMITED   p365
2015 DUGALD RD, WINNIPEG, MB, R2J 0H3
(204) 663-9142   SIC 3365

FCA CANADA INC   p995
15 BROWNS LINE, TORONTO, ON, M8W 3S3
(416) 253-2300   SIC 3365

FONDERIE LEMOLTECH INC   p1253
30 RUE SAINT-PIERRE, PRINCEVILLE, QC, G6L 5A9
(819) 364-7616   SIC 3365

FONDERIES SHELLCAST INC   p1239
10645 AV LAMOUREUX, MONTREAL-NORD, QC, H1G 5L4
(514) 322-3760   SIC 3365

FONDREC INC   p1152
14078 RUE DE LA CHAPELLE, MIRABEL, QC, J7J 2C8
(450) 432-2688   SIC 3365

FONDREMY INC   p1074
1465 BOUL INDUSTRIEL BUREAU 100, CHAMBLY, QC, J3L 4C4
(450) 658-7111   SIC 3365

FOREST CITY CASTINGS INC   p889
10 HIGHBURY AVE, ST THOMAS, ON, N5P 4C7
(519) 633-2999   SIC 3365

HOWMET CANADA COMPANY   p593
93 MOUNTAINVIEW RD N, GEORGETOWN, ON, L7G 4J6
(905) 877-6936   SIC 3365

HOWMET CANADA COMPANY   p1234
4001 DES LAURENTIDES (A-15) E, MONTREAL, QC, H7L 3H7
(450) 680-2500   SIC 3365

HOWMET LAVAL CASTING LTD   p1133
4001 AUT DES LAURENTIDES, LAVAL, QC, H7L 3H7
(450) 680-2500   SIC 3365

MAGELLAN AEROSPACE LIMITED   p607
634 MAGNESIUM RD, HALEY STATION, ON, K0J 1Y0
(613) 432-8841   SIC 3365

METEOR FOUNDRY COMPANY LIMITED
p741
1730 BONHILL RD, MISSISSAUGA, ON, L5T 1C8
(905) 670-2890   SIC 3365

MOULAGE SOUS PRESSION A.M.T. INC
p1298
106 RUE COTE, SAINT-CYPRIEN, QC, G0L 2P0
(418) 963-3227   SIC 3365

NORWOOD FOUNDRY LIMITED   p149
605 18 AVE, NISKU, AB, T9E 7T7
(780) 955-8844   SIC 3365

ORLICK INDUSTRIES LIMITED   p609
411 PARKDALE AVE N, HAMILTON, ON, L8H 5Y4
(905) 544-1997   SIC 3365

ORLICK INDUSTRIES LIMITED   p893
500 SEAMAN ST, STONEY CREEK, ON, L8E 2V9
(905) 662-5954   SIC 3365

PABER ALUMINIUM INC   p1074
296 CH VINCELOTTE, CAP-SAINT-IGNACE, QC, G0R 1H0
(418) 246-5626   SIC 3365

POWERCAST INC   p1302
540 BOUL INDUSTRIEL, SAINT-EUSTACHE, QC, J7R 5V3
(450) 473-1517   SIC 3365

RAMSDEN INDUSTRIES LIMITED   p651
128 OAKLAND AVE, LONDON, ON, N5W 4H6
(519) 451-6720   SIC 3365

VERBOM INC   p1392
5066 RTE 222, VALCOURT, QC, J0E 2L0
(819) 566-4200   SIC 3365

SIC 3366 Copper foundries

NEXANS CANADA INC   p1238
460 AV DUROCHER, MONTREAL-EST, QC, H1B 5H6
(514) 645-2301   SIC 3366

SIC 3369 Nonferrous foundries, nec

CENTRA INDUSTRIES INC p538
24 CHERRY BLOSSOM RD, CAMBRIDGE, ON, N3H 4R7
(519) 650-2828 *SIC 3369*

DYNACAST LTD p840
710 NEAL DR, PETERBOROUGH, ON, K9J 6X7
(705) 748-9522 *SIC 3369*

INDUSTRIES LYSTER INC p1147
2555 RUE BECANCOUR, LYSTER, QC, G0S 1V0
SIC 3369

J & K DIE CASTING LIMITED p871
18 GOLDEN GATE CRT, SCARBOROUGH, ON, M1P 3A5
(416) 293-8229 *SIC 3369*

KENNAMETAL STELLITE, INC p491
471 DUNDAS ST E, BELLEVILLE, ON, K8N 1G2
(613) 968-3481 *SIC 3369*

MERIDIAN LIGHTWEIGHT TECHNOLOGIES INC p897
800 WRIGHT ST, STRATHROY, ON, N7G 4H7
(519) 246-9620 *SIC 3369*

MONARCH INVESTMENTS LTD p366
51 BURMAC RD, WINNIPEG, MB, R2J 4J3
(204) 786-7921 *SIC 3369*

PLOMBCO INC p1365
66 RUE EDMOND, SALABERRY-DE-VALLEYFIELD, QC, J6S 3E8
(450) 371-8800 *SIC 3369*

RIVERSIDE BRASS & ALUMINUM FOUNDRY LIMITED p753
55 HAMILTON RD, NEW HAMBURG, ON, N3A 2H1
(800) 265-2197 *SIC 3369*

SCHAEFFLER AEROSPACE CANADA INC p895
151 WRIGHT BLVD, STRATFORD, ON, N4Z 1H3
(519) 271-3230 *SIC 3369*

SIC 3398 Metal heat treating

METEX HEAT TREATING LTD p504
225 WILKINSON RD, BRAMPTON, ON, L6T 4M2
(905) 453-9700 *SIC 3398*

NITEK LASER INC p1242
305 RTE DU PORT, NICOLET, QC, J3T 1R7
(819) 293-4887 *SIC 3398*

SOTREM (1993) INC p1081
1685 RUE DE LA MANIC, CHICOUTIMI, QC, G7K 1G8
(418) 696-2019 *SIC 3398*

T. A. BRANNON STEEL LIMITED p506
14 TILBURY CRT, BRAMPTON, ON, L6T 3T4
(905) 453-4730 *SIC 3398*

TISI CANADA INC p805
781 WESTGATE RD, OAKVILLE, ON, L6L 6R7
(905) 845-9542 *SIC 3398*

SIC 3399 Primary Metal products

AIM METAUX & ALLIAGES S.E.C. p1238
9100 BOUL HENRI-BOURASSA E, MONTREAL-EST, QC, H1E 2S4
(514) 494-2000 *SIC 3399*

ATELIERS B.G. INC, LES p1370
2980 RUE KING E, SHERBROOKE, QC, J1G 5J2
(819) 346-2195 *SIC 3399*

AXTON INCORPORATED p205
441 DERWENT PL, DELTA, BC, V3M 5Y9
(604) 522-2731 *SIC 3399*

BRIDGES, DAVID INC p365
360 DAWSON RD N, WINNIPEG, MB, R2J 0S7
(204) 233-0500 *SIC 3399*

CORBEC INC p1126
1 RUE PROVOST BUREAU 201, LACHINE, QC, H8S 4H2
(514) 364-4000 *SIC 3399*

GKN SINTER METALS - ST THOMAS LTD p889
7 MICHIGAN BLVD, ST THOMAS, ON, N5P 1H1
(519) 631-4880 *SIC 3399*

LASER AMP INC p1111
770 RUE GEORGES-CROS, GRANBY, QC, J2J 1N2
(450) 776-6982 *SIC 3399*

MECANO-SOUDURE DRUMMOND INC p1142
700 RUE TALON, LONGUEUIL, QC, J4G 1P7
(514) 526-4411 *SIC 3399*

OERLIKON METCO (CANADA) INC p130
10108 114 ST, FORT SASKATCHEWAN, AB, T8L 4R1
(780) 992-5100 *SIC 3399*

RIO TINTO ALCAN INC p1045
3000 RUE DES PINS O, ALMA, QC, G8B 5W2
(418) 480-6000 *SIC 3399*

RIO TINTO FER ET TITANE INC p1377
1625 RTE MARIE-VICTORIN, SOREL-TRACY, QC, J3R 1M6
(450) 746-3000 *SIC 3399*

SHAPE INDUSTRIES INC p372
255 HUTCHINS ST, WINNIPEG, MB, R2X 2R4
(204) 947-0409 *SIC 3399*

SOCIETE EN COMMANDITE BROSPEC 2001 p1113
13 RUE MILL, HOWICK, QC, J0S 1G0
SIC 3399

VIDIR MACHINE INC p345
8126 RD 138 NORTH, ARBORG, MB, R0C 0A0
(204) 364-2442 *SIC 3399*

SIC 3411 Metal cans

BALL PACKAGING PRODUCTS CANADA CORP p1013
1506 WENTWORTH ST, WHITBY, ON, L1N 7C1
(905) 666-3600 *SIC 3411*

CROWN METAL PACKAGING CANADA LP p15
4455 75 AVE SE, CALGARY, AB, T2C 2K8
(403) 236-0241 *SIC 3411*

CROWN METAL PACKAGING CANADA LP p997
21 FENMAR DR, TORONTO, ON, M9L 2Y9
(416) 741-6002 *SIC 3411*

CROWN METAL PACKAGING CANADA LP p1333
5789 RUE CYPIHOT, SAINT-LAURENT, QC, H4S 1R3
(514) 956-8900 *SIC 3411*

SIC 3412 Metal barrels, drums, and pails

1942675 ALBERTA LTD p13
7905 46 ST SE, CALGARY, AB, T2C 2Y6
(403) 279-2090 *SIC 3412*

MAUSER CANADA LTD p526
1121 PIONEER RD, BURLINGTON, ON, L7M 1K5
(905) 332-4800 *SIC 3412*

SIC 3423 Hand and edge tools, nec

GALA SYSTEMES INC p1308
3185 1RE RUE, SAINT-HUBERT, QC, J3Y 8Y6
(450) 678-7226 *SIC 3423*

GARANT GP p1377
375 CH SAINT-FRANCOIS O, ST-FRANCOIS-DE-LA-RIVIERE-DU-S, QC, G0R 3A0
(418) 259-7711 *SIC 3423*

GESTION D'ACTIFS GLADU INC p1149
2115 RUE SAINT-CESAIRE, MARIEVILLE, QC, J3M 1E5
(450) 460-4481 *SIC 3423*

GRAY TOOLS CANADA INC p503
299 ORENDA RD, BRAMPTON, ON, L6T 1E8
(800) 567-0518 *SIC 3423*

LEE VALLEY HOLDINGS LIMITED p832
1090 MORRISON DR, OTTAWA, ON, K2H 1C2
(613) 596-0350 *SIC 3423*

ONTARIO DIE COMPANY LIMITED p1006
119 ROGER ST, WATERLOO, ON, N2J 1A4
(519) 576-8950 *SIC 3423*

VERITAS TOOLS INC p832
1090 MORRISON DR, OTTAWA, ON, K2H 1C2
(613) 596-1922 *SIC 3423*

SIC 3425 Saw blades and handsaws

BLOUNT HOLDINGS LTD p602
505 EDINBURGH RD N, GUELPH, ON, N1H 6L4
(519) 822-6870 *SIC 3425*

HUSQVARNA CANADA CORP p744
850 MATHESON BLVD W SUITE 4, MISSISSAUGA, ON, L5V 0B4
(905) 817-1510 *SIC 3425*

WOOD FIBER CANADA INC p1139
2341 AV DE LA ROTONDE, LEVIS, QC, G6X 2M2
(418) 832-2918 *SIC 3425*

SIC 3429 Hardware, nec

2119485 ALBERTA LTD p547
301 MILLWAY AVE, CONCORD, ON, L4K 4T3
(905) 761-0808 *SIC 3429*

A. RAYMOND TINNERMAN MANUFACTURING HAMILTON, INC p609
686 PARKDALE AVE N, HAMILTON, ON, L8H 5Z4
(905) 549-4661 *SIC 3429*

ASCO AEROSPACE CANADA LTD p208
8510 RIVER RD, DELTA, BC, V4G 1B5
(604) 946-4900 *SIC 3429*

ATLAS HOLDINGS COMPANY LIMITED p501
8043 DIXIE RD, BRAMPTON, ON, L6T 3V1
(905) 791-3888 *SIC 3429*

CANADIAN HEATING PRODUCTS INC p229
27342 GLOUCESTER WAY, LANGLEY, BC, V4W 4A1
(604) 607-6422 *SIC 3429*

CANIMEX INC p1098
285 RUE SAINT-GEORGES, DRUMMONDVILLE, QC, J2C 4H3
(819) 477-1335 *SIC 3429*

CLOUD-RIDER DESIGNS INC p1420
1260 8TH AVE, REGINA, SK, S4R 1C9
(306) 761-2119 *SIC 3429*

ELMWOOD GROUP LIMITED, THE p883
570 WELLAND AVE, ST CATHARINES, ON, L2M 5V6
(905) 688-5205 *SIC 3429*

FLEXIFORCE CANADA INC p176
30840 PEARDONVILLE RD, ABBOTSFORD, BC, V2T 6K2
(604) 854-3660 *SIC 3429*

GAL AVIATION INC p1394
264 RUE ADRIEN-PATENAUDE, VAUDREUIL-DORION, QC, J7V 5V5

(514) 418-0033 *SIC 3429*

GUNN METAL STAMPINGS COMPANY p606
32 AIRPARK PL, GUELPH, ON, N1L 1B2
SIC 3429

KS CENTOCO WHEEL CORPORATION p1020
2450 CENTRAL AVE, WINDSOR, ON, N8W 4J3
(519) 974-2727 *SIC 3429*

LARSEN & SHAW LIMITED p1004
575 DURHAM ST W, WALKERTON, ON, N0G 2V0
(519) 881-1320 *SIC 3429*

LELAND INDUSTRIES INC p874
95 COMMANDER BLVD, SCARBOROUGH, ON, M1S 3S9
(416) 291-5308 *SIC 3429*

LITENS AUTOMOTIVE PARTNERSHIP p1032
730 ROWNTREE DAIRY RD, WOODBRIDGE, ON, L4L 5T7
(905) 856-0200 *SIC 3429*

MERCEDES TEXTILES LIMITED p1335
5838 RUE CYPIHOT, SAINT-LAURENT, QC, H4S 1Y5
(514) 335-4337 *SIC 3429*

MILES INDUSTRIES LTD p238
2255 DOLLARTON HWY SUITE 190, NORTH VANCOUVER, BC, V7H 3B1
(604) 983-3496 *SIC 3429*

MTO METAL PRODUCTS LTD p1035
1205 WELFORD PL SUITE 54, WOODSTOCK, ON, N4S 7W3
(519) 537-8257 *SIC 3429*

MULTIMATIC INC p556
300 BASALTIC RD SUITE 1, CONCORD, ON, L4K 4Y9
(905) 879-0500 *SIC 3429*

MULTIMATIC INC p567
125 CORCORAN CRT, EAST GWILLIMBURY, ON, L9N 0M8
(905) 853-8820 *SIC 3429*

MULTIMATIC INC p672
8688 WOODBINE AVE SUITE 200, MARKHAM, ON, L3R 8B9
(905) 470-9149 *SIC 3429*

MULTIMATIC INC p853
35 WEST WILMOT ST, RICHMOND HILL, ON, L4B 1L7
(905) 764-5120 *SIC 3429*

MULTIMATIC NICHE VEHICLES INC p672
8688 WOODBINE AVE, MARKHAM, ON, L3R 8B9
(905) 470-9149 *SIC 3429*

NORCRAFT CANADA CORPORATION p363
1980 SPRINGFIELD RD, WINNIPEG, MB, R2C 2Z2
(204) 222-9888 *SIC 3429*

OCEANWORKS INTERNATIONAL CORPORATION p315
100-535 THURLOW ST, VANCOUVER, BC, V6E 0C8
(604) 398-4998 *SIC 3429*

OETIKER LIMITED p476
203 DUFFERIN ST S, ALLISTON, ON, L9R 1E9
(705) 435-4394 *SIC 3429*

PRECISION PULLEY & IDLER INC p280
3388 190 ST, SURREY, BC, V3Z 1A7
(604) 560-8188 *SIC 3429*

SCOTT PLASTICS LTD p268
2065 HENRY AVE W, SIDNEY, BC, V8L 5Z6
(250) 656-8102 *SIC 3429*

SPIROL INDUSTRIES LIMITED p1020
3103 ST ETIENNE BLVD, WINDSOR, ON, N8W 5B1
(519) 974-3334 *SIC 3429*

STANLEY BLACK & DECKER CANADA CORPORATION p727
6275 MILLCREEK DR, MISSISSAUGA, ON, L5N 7K6
(289) 290-4638 *SIC 3429*

WESKO LOCKS LTD p702
4570 EASTGATE PKY, MISSISSAUGA, ON,

L4W 3W6
(905) 629-3227   *SIC 3429*

SIC 3431 Metal sanitary ware

BOBRICK WASHROOM EQUIPMENT COMPANY   *p872*
45 ROLARK DR, SCARBOROUGH, ON, M1R 3B1
(416) 298-1611   *SIC 3431*

CRANE PLUMBING CANADA CORP   *p895*
15 CRANE AVE, STRATFORD, ON, N5A 6S4
   SIC 3431

LIXIL CANADA INC   *p732*
5900 AVEBURY RD, MISSISSAUGA, ON, L5R 3M3
(905) 949-4800   *SIC 3431*

MIROLIN INDUSTRIES CORP   *p575*
200 NORSEMAN ST, ETOBICOKE, ON, M8Z 2R4
(416) 231-9030   *SIC 3431*

PRODUITS NEPTUNE INC, LES   *p1313*
6835 RUE PICARD, SAINT-HYACINTHE, QC, J2S 1H3
(450) 773-7058   *SIC 3431*

ROYAL GROUP, INC   *p1101*
3035 BOUL LE CORBUSIER BUREAU 7, FABREVILLE, QC, H7L 4C3
(450) 687-5115   *SIC 3431*

STERIS CANADA ULC   *p1255*
490 BOUL ARMAND-PARIS, QUEBEC, QC, G1C 8A3
(418) 664-1549   *SIC 3431*

SIC 3432 Plumbing fixture fittings and trim

CAMBRIDGE BRASS, INC   *p535*
140 ORION PL, CAMBRIDGE, ON, N1T 1R9
(519) 621-5520   *SIC 3432*

CELLO PRODUCTS INC   *p533*
210 AVENUE RD, CAMBRIDGE, ON, N1R 8H5
(519) 621-9150   *SIC 3432*

MASCO CANADA LIMITED   *p889*
350 SOUTH EDGEWARE RD, ST THOMAS, ON, N5P 4L1
(519) 633-5050   *SIC 3432*

MASCO CANADA LIMITED   *p889*
35 CURRAH RD, ST THOMAS, ON, N5P 3R2
   SIC 3432

SIC 3433 Heating equipment, except electric

AIRTEX MANUFACTURING PARTNERSHIP   *p27*
1401 HASTINGS CRES SE SUITE 1421, CALGARY, AB, T2G 4C8
(403) 287-2590   *SIC 3433*

BOUSQUET TECHNOLOGIES INC   *p1358*
2121 RUE NOBEL BUREAU 101, SAINTE-JULIE, QC, J3E 1Z9
(514) 874-9050   *SIC 3433*

COPPER CORE LIMITED   *p583*
275 CARRIER DR, ETOBICOKE, ON, M9W 5Y8
(416) 675-1177   *SIC 3433*

DUNDAS JAFINE INC   *p502*
80 WEST DR, BRAMPTON, ON, L6T 3T6
(905) 450-7200   *SIC 3433*

ECCO HEATING PRODUCTS LTD   *p95*
14310 111 AVE NW SUITE 300, EDMONTON, AB, T5M 3Z7
(780) 452-7350   *SIC 3433*

FABRICANT DE POELES INTERNATIONAL INC   *p1293*
250 RUE DE COPENHAGUE BUREAU 1, SAINT-AUGUSTIN-DE-DESMAURES, QC,

G3A 2H3
(418) 878-3040   *SIC 3433*

FPI FIREPLACE PRODUCTS INTERNATIONAL LTD   *p209*
6988 VENTURE ST, DELTA, BC, V4G 1H4
(604) 946-5155   *SIC 3433*

GRIT INDUSTRIES INC   *p144*
10-50-1-4 AIRPORT RD NW, LLOYDMINSTER, AB, T9V 3A5
(780) 875-5577   *SIC 3433*

INDUSTRIES SPECTRA PREMIUM INC, LES   *p1066*
1421 RUE AMPERE, BOUCHERVILLE, QC, J4B 5Z5
(450) 641-3090   *SIC 3433*

INDUSTRIES SPECTRA PREMIUM INC, LES   *p1363*
1313 CHOMEDEY (A-13) E, SAINTE-ROSE, QC, H7W 5L7
(450) 681-1313   *SIC 3433*

MESTEK CANADA INC   *p735*
7555 TRANMERE DR, MISSISSAUGA, ON, L5S 1L4
(905) 670-5888   *SIC 3433*

NAPOLEON SYSTEMS & DEVELOPMENTS LTD   *p484*
24 NAPOLEON RD, BARRIE, ON, L4M 0G8
(705) 721-1212   *SIC 3433*

PACIFIC ENERGY FIREPLACE PRODUCTS LTD   *p212*
2975 ALLENBY RD, DUNCAN, BC, V9L 6V8
(250) 748-1184   *SIC 3433*

RIELLO CANADA, INC   *p726*
2165 MEADOWPINE BLVD, MISSISSAUGA, ON, L5N 6H6
(905) 542-0303   *SIC 3433*

SCOTT SPRINGFIELD MFG. INC   *p32*
2234 PORTLAND ST SE, CALGARY, AB, T2G 4M6
(403) 236-1212   *SIC 3433*

SHERWOOD INDUSTRIES LTD   *p267*
6782 OLDFIELD RD, SAANICHTON, BC, V8M 2A3
(250) 652-6080   *SIC 3433*

STELPRO DESIGN INC   *p1296*
1041 RUE PARENT, SAINT-BRUNO, QC, J3V 6L7
(450) 441-0101   *SIC 3433*

TIW WESTERN INC   *p19*
7770 44 ST SE, CALGARY, AB, T2C 2L5
(403) 279-8310   *SIC 3433*

VALLEY COMFORT SYSTEMS INC   *p244*
1290 COMMERCIAL WAY, PENTICTON, BC, V2A 3H5
(250) 493-7444   *SIC 3433*

VIESSMANN MANUFACTURING COMPANY INC   *p1011*
750 MCMURRAY RD, WATERLOO, ON, N2V 2G5
(519) 885-6300   *SIC 3433*

WOLF STEEL LTD   *p485*
24 NAPOLEON RD, BARRIE, ON, L4M 0G8
(705) 721-1212   *SIC 3433*

WOLF STEEL LTD   *p485*
9 NAPOLEON RD, BARRIE, ON, L4M 0G8
(705) 721-1212   *SIC 3433*

SIC 3441 Fabricated structural Metal

331265 ONTARIO LIMITED   *p762*
1872 SEYMOUR ST SUITE 3, NORTH BAY, ON, P1A 0E2
(705) 472-5454   *SIC 3441*

3539491 CANADA INC   *p1125*
500 RUE NOTRE-DAME, LACHINE, QC, H8S 2B2
(514) 634-2287   *SIC 3441*

401919 ALBERTA LTD   *p107*
3740 73 AVE NW, EDMONTON, AB, T6B 2Z2
(780) 440-1414   *SIC 3441*

462673 ONTARIO INC   *p567*
3315 67 HWY, EARLTON, ON, P0J 1E0

(705) 563-2656   *SIC 3441*

9121-2936 QUEBEC INC   *p1092*
167 RUE ARMAND-BOMBARDIER, DONNACONA, QC, G3M 1V4
(418) 285-4499   *SIC 3441*

A & H STEEL LTD   *p108*
4710 82 AVE NW, EDMONTON, AB, T6B 0E4
(780) 465-6425   *SIC 3441*

A I INDUSTRIES   *p274*
12349 104 AVE, SURREY, BC, V3V 3H2
(604) 583-2171   *SIC 3441*

A. & R. METAL INDUSTRIES LTD   *p253*
2020 NO. 6 RD, RICHMOND, BC, V6V 1P1
(604) 276-2838   *SIC 3441*

ACIER TRIMAX INC   *p1359*
1440 3E AV DU PARC-INDUSTRIEL, SAINTE-MARIE, QC, G6E 3T9
(418) 387-7798   *SIC 3441*

ACIERS SOFATEC INC, LES   *p1355*
867 5E AV BUREAU A, SAINTE-ANNE-DES-PLAINES, QC, J0N 1H0
(450) 478-3365   *SIC 3441*

ACL STEEL LTD   *p635*
2255 SHIRLEY DR, KITCHENER, ON, N2B 3X4
(519) 568-8822   *SIC 3441*

ADJ INDUSTRIES INC   *p648*
2068 PIPER LANE, LONDON, ON, N5V 3N6
(519) 455-4065   *SIC 3441*

ADVANCED TOWER SERVICES (2007) LTD   *p685*
54 MILL ST W, MILVERTON, ON, N0K 1M0
(519) 595-3500   *SIC 3441*

AGI-METAL FAB   *p388*
198 COMMERCE DR, WINNIPEG, MB, R3P 0Z6
(204) 489-1855   *SIC 3441*

B. K. FER OUVRE INC   *p1295*
1800 RUE MARIE-VICTORIN, SAINT-BRUNO, QC, J3V 6B9
(514) 820-7423   *SIC 3441*

B.F.L. ENERGY SERVICES LTD   *p6*
5610 54 AVE, BONNYVILLE, AB, T9N 2N3
   SIC 3441

BARNES, D.F. LIMITED   *p432*
22 SUDBURY ST, ST. JOHN'S, NL, A1E 2V1
(709) 579-5041   *SIC 3441*

BELLEVUE FABRICATING LTD   *p490*
525 BELLEVUE DR, BELLEVILLE, ON, K8N 4Z5
(613) 968-6721   *SIC 3441*

BID GROUP TECHNOLOGIES LTD   *p330*
3446 MOUNTAIN VIEW RD, VANDERHOOF, BC, V0J 3A2
(250) 567-2578   *SIC 3441*

BRADLEY STEEL PROCESSORS INC   *p362*
1201 REGENT AVE W, WINNIPEG, MB, R2C 3B2
(204) 987-2080   *SIC 3441*

BRENCO INDUSTRIES LTD   *p208*
10030 RIVER WAY, DELTA, BC, V4G 1M9
(604) 584-2700   *SIC 3441*

CANADIAN GUIDE RAIL CORPORATION   *p349*
2840 WENZEL ST, EAST ST PAUL, MB, R2E 1E7
(204) 222-2142   *SIC 3441*

CANAM BATIMENTS ET STRUCTURES INC   *p734*
1739 DREW RD, MISSISSAUGA, ON, L5S 1J5
(905) 671-3460   *SIC 3441*

CANAM BATIMENTS ET STRUCTURES INC   *p1304*
11505 1RE AV BUREAU 500, SAINT-GEORGES, QC, G5Y 7X3
(418) 582-3331   *SIC 3441*

CANERECTOR INC   *p885*
23 SMITH ST, ST CATHARINES, ON, L2R 6Y6
(905) 684-2022   *SIC 3441*

CAPITOL STEEL CORPORATION   *p380*
1355 SASKATCHEWAN AVE, WINNIPEG,

MB, R3E 3K4
(204) 889-9980   *SIC 3441*

COLLINS INDUSTRIES LTD   *p108*
3740 73 AVE NW, EDMONTON, AB, T6B 2Z2
(780) 440-1796   *SIC 3441*

COOKSVILLE STEEL LIMITED   *p708*
510 HENSALL CIR, MISSISSAUGA, ON, L5A 1Y1
(905) 277-9538   *SIC 3441*

CRAIG MANUFACTURING LTD   *p403*
96 MCLEAN AVE, HARTLAND, NB, E7P 2K5
(506) 375-4493   *SIC 3441*

DESIGN BUILT MECHANICAL INC   *p396*
168 CRAIG RD, CHARLO, NB, E8E 2J6
(506) 684-2765   *SIC 3441*

DSME TRENTON LTD   *p468*
34 POWERPLANT RD, TRENTON, NS, B0K 1X0
(902) 753-7777   *SIC 3441*

EASTERN FABRICATORS INC   *p1041*
341 GEORGETOWN RD, GEORGETOWN, PE, C0A 1L0
(902) 283-3229   *SIC 3441*

EMPIRE INDUSTRIES LTD   *p371*
717 JARVIS AVE, WINNIPEG, MB, R2W 3B4
(204) 589-9300   *SIC 3441*

ESKIMO STEEL LTD   *p162*
526 STREAMBANK AVE, SHERWOOD PARK, AB, T8H 1N1
(780) 417-9200   *SIC 3441*

FABRIMET INC   *p1096*
4375 BOUL SAINT-JOSEPH, DRUMMONDVILLE, QC, J2B 1T8
(819) 472-1164   *SIC 3441*

FRAZIER INDUSTRIAL CO., LTD   *p999*
163 NORTH MURRAY ST, TRENTON, ON, K8V 6R7
(613) 394-6621   *SIC 3441*

FUTURE SALES CORPORATION   *p670*
1405 DENISON ST, MARKHAM, ON, L3R 5V2
(905) 477-1894   *SIC 3441*

GILBERT STEEL LIMITED   *p695*
1650 BRITANNIA RD E, MISSISSAUGA, ON, L4W 1J2
(905) 670-5771   *SIC 3441*

GROUPE CANAM INC   *p1065*
270 CH DU TREMBLAY, BOUCHERVILLE, QC, J4B 5X9
(866) 506-4000   *SIC 3441*

GROUPE CANAM INC   *p1065*
200 BOUL INDUSTRIEL, BOUCHERVILLE, QC, J4B 2X4
(450) 641-8770   *SIC 3441*

GROUPE CANAM INC   *p1303*
115 BOUL CANAM N, SAINT-GEDEON-DE-BEAUCE, QC, G0M 1T0
(418) 582-3331   *SIC 3441*

GROUPE CANAM INC   *p1304*
11505 1RE AV BUREAU 500, SAINT-GEORGES, QC, G5Y 7H5
(418) 228-8031   *SIC 3441*

HARRIS STEEL ULC   *p12*
3208 52 ST SE, CALGARY, AB, T2B 1N2
(403) 272-8801   *SIC 3441*

INDUSTRIES CANATAL INC   *p1383*
2885 BOUL FRONTENAC E, THETFORD MINES, QC, G6G 6P6
(418) 338-6044   *SIC 3441*

ISM INDUSTRIAL STEEL & MANUFACTURING INC   *p209*
7690 VANTAGE WAY, DELTA, BC, V4G 1A7
(604) 940-4769   *SIC 3441*

J. OSKAM STEEL FABRICATORS LIMITED   *p846*
70 ROSEDALE AVE, PORT COLBORNE, ON, L3K 6G5
(905) 834-7321   *SIC 3441*

JNE WELDING LIMITED PARTNERSHIP   *p1435*
3915 THATCHER AVE, SASKATOON, SK,

S7R 1A3
(306) 242-0884   *SIC 3441*
LAINCO INC   *p1381*
1010 RUE FERNAND-POITRAS, TERRE-
BONNE, QC, J6Y 1V1
(450) 965-6010   *SIC 3441*
LOCWELD INC   *p1073*
50 AV IBERVILLE, CANDIAC, QC, J5R 1J5
(450) 659-9661   *SIC 3441*
LOR-DON LIMITED   *p651*
485 MCCORMICK BLVD, LONDON, ON,
N5W 5N1
(519) 679-2322   *SIC 3441*
M & G STEEL LTD   *p804*
2285 SPEERS RD, OAKVILLE, ON, L6L 2X9
(905) 469-6442   *SIC 3441*
MACDOUGALL STEEL ERECTORS INC
p1038
168   INDUSTRIAL   DR,   BORDEN-
CARLETON, PE, C0B 1X0
(902) 855-2100   *SIC 3441*
MANSTEEL LTD   *p855*
105 INDUSTRIAL RD SUITE 200, RICH-
MOND HILL, ON, L4C 2Y4
(905) 780-1488   *SIC 3441*
MARSHALL-BARWICK INC   *p772*
100 SHEPPARD AVE E UNIT 930, NORTH
YORK, ON, M2N 6N5
(416) 225-6240   *SIC 3441*
METAL NORGATE 2012 INC   *p1122*
791 8E RUE E, LA GUADELOUPE, QC,
G0M 1G0
(418) 459-6988   *SIC 3441*
METAL PERREAULT INC   *p1092*
167 RUE ARMAND-BOMBARDIER, DON-
NACONA, QC, G3M 1V4
(418) 285-4499   *SIC 3441*
NICO METAL INC   *p1388*
1005 RUE DU PERE-DANIEL, TROIS-
RIVIERES, QC, G9A 2W9
(819) 375-6426   *SIC 3441*
NORFAB MFG. (1993) INC   *p106*
16425 130 AVE NW, EDMONTON, AB, T5V
1K5
(780) 447-5454   *SIC 3441*
NORTHERN WELD ARC LTD   *p163*
141 STRATHMOOR WAY, SHERWOOD
PARK, AB, T8H 1Z7
(780) 467-1522   *SIC 3441*
NOVA TUBE INC   *p1224*
5870 RUE SAINT-PATRICK, MONTREAL,
QC, H4E 1B3
(514) 762-5220   *SIC 3441*
OCEAN STEEL & CONSTRUCTION LTD
p414
400 CHESLEY DR, SAINT JOHN, NB, E2K
5L6
(506) 632-2600   *SIC 3441*
PREBILT STRUCTURES LTD   *p1040*
423 MOUNT EDWARD RD, CHARLOTTE-
TOWN, PE, C1E 2A1
(902) 892-8577   *SIC 3441*
PREMSTEEL FABRICATORS INC   *p57*
GD LCD 1, CALGARY, AB, T2P 2G8
(403) 720-6907   *SIC 3441*
**PRODUITS DE BATIMENT FUSION BUILD-
ING PRODUCTS INC**   *p1231*
4500 RUE BERNARD-LEFEBVRE, MON-
TREAL, QC, H7C 0A5
(514) 381-7456   *SIC 3441*
PROMETEK INC   *p1255*
1005 AV NORDIQUE, QUEBEC, QC, G1C
0C7
(418) 527-4445   *SIC 3441*
RASSAUN SERVICES INC   *p881*
22 BOSWELL DR, SIMCOE, ON, N3Y 4N5
(519) 426-0150   *SIC 3441*
RKO STEEL LIMITED   *p448*
85 MACDONALD AVE, DARTMOUTH, NS,
B3B 1T8
(902) 468-1322   *SIC 3441*
RLP MACHINE & STEEL FABRICATION INC
p913
259 RELIABLE LANE, TIMMINS, ON, P4N

7W7
(705) 267-1445   *SIC 3441*
RMW HOLDINGS LTD   *p268*
2066 HENRY AVE W, SIDNEY, BC, V8L 5Y1
(250) 656-5314   *SIC 3441*
**SLEEGERS ENGINEERED PRODUCTS
INC.**   *p650*
5 CUDDY BLVD, LONDON, ON, N5V 3Y3
(519) 451-5480   *SIC 3441*
STANDARD WEST STEEL LTD   *p156*
6749 65 AVE, RED DEER, AB, T4P 1X5
(403) 358-4227   *SIC 3441*
STRUCTURES CPI INC   *p1377*
516 RTE 172 O, ST-NAZAIRE-DU-LAC-ST-
JEAN, QC, G0W 2V0
(418) 668-3371   *SIC 3441*
STURO METAL INC   *p1139*
600 RUE JEAN-MARCHAND, LEVIS, QC,
G6Y 9G6
(418) 833-2107   *SIC 3441*
SUPERMETAL SHERBROOKE INC   *p1371*
375 RUE DE COURCELETTE, SHER-
BROOKE, QC, J1H 3X4
(819) 566-2965   *SIC 3441*
SUPERMETAL STRUCTURES INC   *p1138*
1955 5E RUE, LEVIS, QC, G6W 5M6
(418) 834-1955   *SIC 3441*
SUPREME STEEL LP   *p2*
28169 96 AVE, ACHESON, AB, T7X 6J7
(780) 483-3278   *SIC 3441*
TIW STEEL PLATEWORK INC   *p885*
23 SMITH ST, ST CATHARINES, ON, L2P
3J7
(905) 684-9421   *SIC 3441*
TRAPP AVE INDUSTRIES   *p181*
6010 TRAPP AVE APP AVE, BURNABY,
BC, V3N 2V4
(604) 526-2333   *SIC 3441*
TRESMAN STEEL INDUSTRIES LTD   *p736*
286 STATESMAN DR, MISSISSAUGA, ON,
L5S 1X7
(905) 795-8757   *SIC 3441*
TRIODETIC LTD   *p479*
10 DIDAK DR, ARNPRIOR, ON, K7S 0C3
(613) 623-3434   *SIC 3441*
TSE STEEL LTD   *p19*
4436 90 AVE SE, CALGARY, AB, T2C 2S7
(403) 279-6060   *SIC 3441*
WARD EMPIRE GROUP INC, THE   *p941*
2 LOMBARD ST SUITE 203, TORONTO,
ON, M5C 1M1
(416) 366-7227   *SIC 3441*
WGI WESTMAN GROUP INC   *p357*
2976 DAY ST, SPRINGFIELD, MB, R2C 2Z2
(204) 777-5345   *SIC 3441*
WHITE, GLEN INDUSTRIES LTD   *p482*
7825 SPRINGWATER RD, AYLMER, ON,
N5H 2R4
(519) 765-2244   *SIC 3441*
XCEL FABRICATION & DESIGN LTD   *p912*
24 CLEARVIEW DR, TILLSONBURG, ON,
N4G 4G8
(519) 688-3193   *SIC 3441*

SIC 3442 Metal doors, sash, and trim

2972-6924 QUEBEC INC   *p1263*
2150 RUE LEON-HARMEL, QUEBEC, QC,
G1N 4L2
(418) 683-2431   *SIC 3442*
A.K. DRAFT SEAL LTD   *p229*
100-4825 275 ST, LANGLEY, BC, V4W 0C7
(604) 451-1080   *SIC 3442*
ALL WEATHER WINDOWS LTD   *p99*
18550 118A AVE NW, EDMONTON, AB,
T5S 2K7
(780) 468-2989   *SIC 3442*
ALMETCO BUILDING PRODUCTS LTD *p205*
620 AUDLEY BLVD, DELTA, BC, V3M 5P2
   SIC 3442
ALUMINART PRODUCTS LIMITED   *p501*
1 SUMMERLEA RD, BRAMPTON, ON, L6T
4V2

(905) 791-7521   *SIC 3442*
ALUMINIUM CARUSO & FILS INC   *p1239*
5528 RUE DE CASTILLE, MONTREAL-
NORD, QC, H1G 3E5
(514) 326-2274   *SIC 3442*
AMBICO LIMITED   *p595*
1120 CUMMINGS AVE, GLOUCESTER,
ON, K1J 7R8
(613) 746-4663   *SIC 3442*
APEX INDUSTRIES INC   *p407*
100 MILLENNIUM BLVD, MONCTON, NB,
E1E 2G8
(506) 867-1600   *SIC 3442*
ASSA ABLOY DOOR GROUP INC   *p1029*
101 ASHBRIDGE CIR, WOODBRIDGE, ON,
L4L 3R5
(416) 749-2111   *SIC 3442*
**BORDER GROUP OF COMPANIES INC,
THE**   *p374*
53 HIGGINS AVE, WINNIPEG, MB, R3B
0A8
(204) 957-7200   *SIC 3442*
CANADIAN THERMO WINDOWS INC *p1030*
75 ROWNTREE DAIRY RD, WOOD-
BRIDGE, ON, L4L 6C8
(905) 856-8805   *SIC 3442*
CAPE-MAN HOLDINGS LTD   *p165*
11 ESTATE CRES, ST. ALBERT, AB, T8N
5X2
(780) 459-0510   *SIC 3442*
CLEARVIEW INDUSTRIES LTD   *p792*
45 FENMAR DR, NORTH YORK, ON, M9L
1M1
(416) 745-6666   *SIC 3442*
DAYBAR INDUSTRIES LIMITED   *p502*
50 WEST DR, BRAMPTON, ON, L6T 2J4
(905) 625-8000   *SIC 3442*
DELAFONTAINE INC   *p1373*
4115 RUE BRODEUR, SHERBROOKE, QC,
J1L 1K4
(819) 348-1219   *SIC 3442*
DORPLEX INDUSTRIES LIMITED   *p792*
50 IRONDALE DR, NORTH YORK, ON, M9L
1R8
(416) 739-7794   *SIC 3442*
DURABUILT WINDOWS & DOORS INC *p100*
10920 178 ST NW, EDMONTON, AB, T5S
1R7
(780) 455-0440   *SIC 3442*
ENERGI FENESTRATION SOLUTIONS, LTD
p1027
30 ROYAL GROUP CRES, WOODBRIDGE,
ON, L4H 1X9
(905) 851-6637   *SIC 3442*
ERIE ARCHITECTURAL PRODUCTS INC
p1017
477 JUTRAS DR S, WINDSOR, ON, N8N
5C4
(519) 727-0372   *SIC 3442*
FENPLAST INC   *p1072*
160 BOUL DE L'INDUSTRIE, CANDIAC,
QC, J5R 1J3
(514) 990-0012   *SIC 3442*
GARAGA INC   *p1305*
8500 25E AV, SAINT-GEORGES, QC, G6A
1K5
(418) 227-2828   *SIC 3442*
GESTION JUSTERO INC   *p1049*
11001 RUE COLBERT, ANJOU, QC, H1J
2S1
(514) 355-7484   *SIC 3442*
GROUPE LESSARD INC   *p1362*
2025 BOUL DAGENAIS O, SAINTE-ROSE,
QC, H7L 5V1
(514) 636-3999   *SIC 3442*
GROUPE LMT INC   *p1141*
2025   RUE   DE   LA   METROPOLE,
LONGUEUIL, QC, J4G 1S9
(450) 640-8700   *SIC 3442*
HIGHRISE WINDOW TECHNOLOGIES INC
p554
131 CALDARI RD UNIT 1, CONCORD, ON,
L4K 3Z9
(905) 738-8600   *SIC 3442*

INDUSTRIES CENDREX INC, LES   *p1162*
11303 26E AV, MONTREAL, QC, H1E 6N6
(514) 493-1489   *SIC 3442*
INDUSTRIES LYNX INC   *p1323*
175   RUE   UPPER   EDISON,   SAINT-
LAMBERT, QC, J4R 2R3
(514) 866-1068   *SIC 3442*
INNOMOTIVE SOLUTIONS GROUP INC
p528
3435 SOUTH SERVICE RD, BURLINGTON,
ON, L7N 3W6
(877) 845-3816   *SIC 3442*
KAWNEER COMPANY CANADA LIMITED
p141
4000 18 AVE N SUITE SIDE, LETHBRIDGE,
AB, T1H 5S8
(403) 320-7755   *SIC 3442*
KML WINDOWS INC   *p897*
71 SECOND ST, STRATHROY, ON, N7G
3H8
(519) 245-2270   *SIC 3442*
LOXCREEN CANADA LTD   *p697*
5720 AMBLER DR, MISSISSAUGA, ON,
L4W 2B1
(905) 625-3210   *SIC 3442*
NORSTAR WINDOWS & DOORS LTD *p892*
944 SOUTH SERVICE RD, STONEY
CREEK, ON, L8E 6A2
(905) 643-9333   *SIC 3442*
**PORTES & FENETRES NOUVEL HORIZON
INC**   *p1388*
1135 RUE LA VERENDRYE, TROIS-
RIVIERES, QC, G9A 2T1
(819) 694-0783   *SIC 3442*
PORTES ET CHASSIS BOULET, EDDY INC
p1377
10700 RTE MARIE-VICTORIN, SOREL-
TRACY, QC, J3R 0K2
(450) 742-9424   *SIC 3442*
PORTES GENSTEEL INC   *p1340*
4950 RUE HICKMORE, SAINT-LAURENT,
QC, H4T 1K6
(514) 733-3562   *SIC 3442*
PORTES STANDARD INC   *p1085*
2300 AV FRANCIS-HUGHES, COTE SAINT-
LUC, QC, H7S 2C1
(514) 634-8911   *SIC 3442*
PRODUITS DALMEN PRODUCTS LTD *p888*
5630 ST CATHERINE ST, ST ISIDORE, ON,
K0C 2B0
(613) 524-2268   *SIC 3442*
QUEST WINDOW SYSTEMS INC   *p689*
6811 GOREWAY DR UNIT 1, MISSIS-
SAUGA, ON, L4V 1L9
(905) 851-8588   *SIC 3442*
RAYNOR CANADA CORP   *p699*
5100 TIMBERLEA BLVD SUITE A, MISSIS-
SAUGA, ON, L4W 2S5
(905) 625-0037   *SIC 3442*
ROBERGE ET FILS INC   *p1123*
45 7E AV E, LA SARRE, QC, J9Z 1M5
(819) 333-5405   *SIC 3442*
SKY WINDOW TECHNOLOGIES INC   *p784*
40 SAINT REGIS CRES N, NORTH YORK,
ON, M3J 1Z2
(416) 633-1881   *SIC 3442*
STARLINE WINDOWS LTD   *p280*
19091 36 AVE, SURREY, BC, V3Z 0P6
(604) 882-5100   *SIC 3442*
STATE WINDOW CORPORATION   *p1002*
220 HUNTER'S VALLEY RD, VAUGHAN,
ON, L4H 3V9
(416) 646-1421   *SIC 3442*
STEEL - CRAFT DOOR PRODUCTS LTD *p94*
13504 ST ALBERT TRAIL NW, EDMON-
TON, AB, T5L 4P4
(780) 453-3761   *SIC 3442*
TNR INDUSTRIAL DOORS INC   *p488*
200 FAIRVIEW RD UNIT 2, BARRIE, ON,
L4N 8X8
(705) 792-9968   *SIC 3442*
TORO ALUMINUM   *p559*
330 APPLEWOOD CRES, CONCORD, ON,
L4K 4V2

▲ Public Company   ■ Public Company Family Member   **HQ** Headquarters   **BR** Branch   **SL** Single Location

(905) 738-5220   *SIC* 3442
TRU TECH CORPORATION   *p*1028
20 VAUGHAN VALLEY BLVD, WOODBRIDGE, ON, L4H 0B1
(905) 856-0096   *SIC* 3442
WEST FOUR GROUP OF COMPANIES INC
*p*1430
2505 WENTZ AVE, SASKATOON, SK, S7K 2K9
(306) 934-5147   *SIC* 3442
WHITING GROUP OF CANADA INC   *p*528
3435 SOUTH SERVICE RD, BURLINGTON, ON, L7N 3W6
(905) 333-6745   *SIC* 3442
WILLIAMS BROTHERS CORPORATION, THE   *p*879
777 TAPSCOTT RD, SCARBOROUGH, ON, M1X 1A2
(416) 299-7767   *SIC* 3442

SIC 3443 Fabricated plate work (boiler shop)

3075109 CANADA INC   *p*1072
47 BOUL MARIE-VICTORIN, CANDIAC, QC, J5R 1B6
(450) 444-4405   *SIC* 3443
AG GROWTH INTERNATIONAL INC   *p*364
450 RUE DESAUTELS, WINNIPEG, MB, R2H 3E6
(204) 233-7133   *SIC* 3443
AGI ENVIROTANK LTD   *p*1404
401 HWY 4, BIGGAR, SK, S0K 0M0
(306) 948-5262   *SIC* 3443
ALTEX INDUSTRIES INC   *p*108
6831 42 ST NW, EDMONTON, AB, T6B 2X1
(780) 468-6862   *SIC* 3443
ARGO SALES INC   *p*43
717 7 AVE SW SUITE 1300, CALGARY, AB, T2P 0Z3
(403) 265-6633   *SIC* 3443
ARGO SALES INC   *p*145
925 23 ST SW, MEDICINE HAT, AB, T1A 8R1
(403) 526-3142   *SIC* 3443
ARMATURES BOIS-FRANCS INC   *p*1399
249 BOUL DE LA BONAVENTURE, VICTORIAVILLE, QC, G6T 1V5
(819) 758-7501   *SIC* 3443
ATELIER GERARD BEAULIEU INC   *p*417
164 RUE MGR-MARTIN E, SAINT-QUENTIN, NB, E8A 1W1
(506) 235-2243   *SIC* 3443
BOUILLOIRE FALMEC INC   *p*1044
200 RUE DES PINS O BUREAU 109, ALMA, QC, G8B 6P9
(418) 668-0788   *SIC* 3443
CALHEX INDUSTRIES LTD   *p*14
9515 48 ST SE, CALGARY, AB, T2C 2R1
(403) 225-4395   *SIC* 3443
CANERECTOR INC   *p*764
1 SPARKS AVE, NORTH YORK, ON, M2H 2W1
(416) 225-6240   *SIC* 3443
CITERNES BEDARD INC   *p*1222
5785 PLACE TURCOT, MONTREAL, QC, H4C 1V9
(514) 937-1670   *SIC* 3443
CLEAVER-BROOKS OF CANADA LIMITED
*p*895
161 LORNE AVE W, STRATFORD, ON, N5A 6S4
(519) 271-9220   *SIC* 3443
CONTENANTS DURABAC INC, LES   *p*1110
22 CH MILTON, GRANBY, QC, J2J 0P2
(450) 378-1723   *SIC* 3443
DACRO INDUSTRIES INC   *p*113
9325 51 AVE NW, EDMONTON, AB, T6E 4W8
(780) 434-8900   *SIC* 3443
DANA CANADA CORPORATION   *p*746
205 INDUSTRIAL DR, MOUNT FOREST, ON, N0G 2L1

(519) 323-9494   *SIC* 3443
DANA CANADA CORPORATION   *p*803
1400 ADVANCE RD, OAKVILLE, ON, L6L 6L6
(905) 825-8856   *SIC* 3443
DEPENDABLE TRUCK AND TANK LIMITED
*p*509
275 CLARENCE ST, BRAMPTON, ON, L6W 3R3
(905) 453-6724   *SIC* 3443
DEVELOPPEMENTS ANGELCARE INC, LES
*p*1072
201 BOUL DE L'INDUSTRIE BUREAU 104, CANDIAC, QC, J5R 6A6
(514) 761-0511   *SIC* 3443
ELLETT INDUSTRIES LTD   *p*246
1575 KINGSWAY AVE, PORT COQUITLAM, BC, V3C 1S2
(604) 941-8211   *SIC* 3443
EXCHANGER INDUSTRIES LIMITED   *p*15
5811 46 ST SE SUITE 200, CALGARY, AB, T2C 4Y5
(403) 236-0166   *SIC* 3443
FABSPEC INC   *p*1376
160 RUE DU ROI, SOREL-TRACY, QC, J3P 4N5
(450) 742-0451   *SIC* 3443
FLINT FABRICATION AND MODULARIZATION LTD
*p*162
180 STRATHMOOR DR, SHERWOOD PARK, AB, T8H 2B7
(780) 416-3501   *SIC* 3443
G & L SLOTCO OILFIELD SERVICES LTD
*p*50
700 4 AVE SW SUITE 1110, CALGARY, AB, T2P 3J4
(403) 261-1717   *SIC* 3443
G.T. MACHINING & FABRICATING LTD *p*747
7 KELLWOOD CRES, NAPANEE, ON, K7R 4A1
(613) 354-6621   *SIC* 3443
GOLDEC HAMMS MANUFACTURING LTD
*p*155
6760 65 AVE, RED DEER, AB, T4P 1A5
(403) 343-6607   *SIC* 3443
GRANBY INDUSTRIES LIMITED PARTNERSHIP
*p*1111
1020 RUE ANDRE-LINE, GRANBY, QC, J2J 1J9
(450) 378-2334   *SIC* 3443
GROUPE CANAM INC   *p*1264
1445 RUE DU GRAND-TRONC, QUEBEC, QC, G1N 4G1
(418) 683-2561   *SIC* 3443
HEROUX-DEVTEK INC   *p*871
1480 BIRCHMOUNT RD, SCARBOROUGH, ON, M1P 2E3
(416) 757-2366   *SIC* 3443
HOOPER WELDING ENTERPRISES LIMITED
*p*804
1390 ADVANCE RD, OAKVILLE, ON, L6L 6L6
(905) 827-2600   *SIC* 3443
HT INDUSTRIAL LTD   *p*514
36 CRAIG ST, BRANTFORD, ON, N3R 7J1
(519) 759-3010   *SIC* 3443
I.C.C. COMPAGNIE DE CHEMINEES INDUSTRIELLES INC
*p*1320
400 RUE JOHN-F.-KENNEDY, SAINT-JEROME, QC, J7Y 4B7
(450) 565-6336   *SIC* 3443
KLASSEN, P CUSTOM FAB INC   *p*807
5140 URE ST, OLDCASTLE, ON, N0R 1L0
(519) 737-6631   *SIC* 3443
LANDMARK ONTARIO LTD   *p*526
3091 HARRISON CRT, BURLINGTON, ON, L7M 0W4
(905) 319-7700   *SIC* 3443
LEADING MANUFACTURING GROUP HOLDINGS INC
*p*149
801 25 AVE, NISKU, AB, T9E 7Z4
(780) 955-8895   *SIC* 3443
LEADING MANUFACTURING GROUP HOLDINGS INC
*p*171

3801 48 AVE, VERMILION, AB, T9X 1G9
(780) 854-0004   *SIC* 3443
LEADING MANUFACTURING GROUP INC
*p*149
2313 8 ST, NISKU, AB, T9E 7Z3
(780) 955-8895   *SIC* 3443
M & M OFFSHORE LTD   *p*428
456 LOGY BAY RD, ST. JOHN'S, NL, A1A 5C6
(709) 726-9112   *SIC* 3443
MANUFACTURE FRAMECO LTEE   *p*1322
230 RUE DU PARC, SAINT-JOSEPH-DE-BEAUCE, QC, G0S 2V0
(418) 397-6895   *SIC* 3443
MILEPOST OILFIELD SERVICES LTD   *p*168
26004 TWP RD 544 UNIT 43, STURGEON COUNTY, AB, T8T 0B6
(780) 459-1030   *SIC* 3443
NATCO CANADA, LTD   *p*17
9423 SHEPARD RD SE, CALGARY, AB, T2C 4R6
(403) 203-2119   *SIC* 3443
NWP INDUSTRIES LP   *p*137
4017 60 AVE, INNISFAIL, AB, T4G 1S9
(403) 227-4100   *SIC* 3443
POLYCORE TUBULAR LININGS CORPORATION
*p*65
1011 1 ST SW SUITE 510, CALGARY, AB, T2R 1J2
(403) 444-5554   *SIC* 3443
PRESVAC SYSTEMS (BURLINGTON) LIMITED
*p*524
4131 MORRIS DR, BURLINGTON, ON, L7L 5L5
(905) 637-2353   *SIC* 3443
PRO-PAR INC   *p*1374
65 RUE WINDER, SHERBROOKE, QC, J1M 1L5
(819) 566-8211   *SIC* 3443
PRODUITS D'ACIER HASON INC, LES
*p*1130
7 RUE PINAT, LANORAIE, QC, J0K 1E0
(450) 887-0800   *SIC* 3443
REMTECH INC   *p*1075
933 AV SIMARD, CHAMBLY, QC, J3L 4B7
(450) 658-6671   *SIC* 3443
RESERVOIRS GIL-FAB INTERNATIONAL INC, LES
*p*1149
1429 AV DE LA GARE, MASCOUCHE, QC, J7K 3G6
(450) 474-7400   *SIC* 3443
RITZ MACHINE WORKS INC   *p*349
507 1ST AVE SE, DAUPHIN, MB, R7N 2Z8
(204) 638-1633   *SIC* 3443
ROSE CORPORATION, THE   *p*777
156 DUNCAN MILL RD SUITE 12, NORTH YORK, ON, M3B 3N2
(416) 449-3535   *SIC* 3443
SASKATOON BOILER MFG CO LTD   *p*1429
2011 QUEBEC AVE, SASKATOON, SK, S7K 1W5
(306) 652-7022   *SIC* 3443
SMARDT INC   *p*1095
1800 RTE TRANSCANADIENNE, DORVAL, QC, H9P 1H7
(514) 426-8989   *SIC* 3443
SOCIETE DE CHAUDIERES INDECK   *p*1313
4300 AV BEAUDRY, SAINT-HYACINTHE, QC, J2S 8A5
(450) 774-5326   *SIC* 3443
STEELCRAFT INC   *p*896
904 DOWNIE RD, STRATFORD, ON, N5A 6T3
(519) 271-4750   *SIC* 3443
STEELCRAFT INC   *p*1009
446 ALBERT ST, WATERLOO, ON, N2L 3V3
(519) 884-4320   *SIC* 3443
THERMON HEATING SYSTEMS, INC   *p*111
5918 ROPER RD NW, EDMONTON, AB, T6B 3E1
(780) 466-3178   *SIC* 3443
THERMON HEATING SYSTEMS, INC   *p*810
1 HUNTER VALLEY RD, ORILLIA, ON, L3V 0Y7

(705) 325-3473   *SIC* 3443
TI TITANIUM LTEE   *p*1331
5055 RUE LEVY, SAINT-LAURENT, QC, H4R 2N9
(514) 334-5781   *SIC* 3443
TREMCAR DRUMMOND INC   *p*1099
1450 RUE HEBERT, DRUMMONDVILLE, QC, J2C 0C7
(450) 469-4840   *SIC* 3443
TREMCAR INC   *p*1316
790 AV MONTRICHARD, SAINT-JEAN-SUR-RICHELIEU, QC, J2X 5G4
(450) 347-7822   *SIC* 3443
TRENERGY INC   *p*885
87 GRANTHAM AVE, ST CATHARINES, ON, L2P 2Y8
(905) 687-8736   *SIC* 3443
UNIVERSAL INDUSTRIES (FOREMOST) CORP
*p*144
5014 65 ST, LLOYDMINSTER, AB, T9V 2K2
(780) 875-6161   *SIC* 3443
VALTECH FABRICATION INC   *p*1366
730 BOUL DES ERABLES, SALABERRY-DE-VALLEYFIELD, QC, J6T 6G4
(450) 371-0033   *SIC* 3443
VESTAS-CANADIAN WIND TECHNOLOGY, INC
*p*958
65 QUEEN ST W SUITE 2000, TORONTO, ON, M5H 2M5
(647) 837-6101   *SIC* 3443
WABASH MFG. INC   *p*172
9312 110A ST, WESTLOCK, AB, T7P 2M4
(780) 349-4282   *SIC* 3443

SIC 3444 Sheet Metalwork

1343080 ALBERTA LTD   *p*1438
2 RAMM AVE, WHITE CITY, SK, S4L 5B1
(306) 757-2403   *SIC* 3444
9099-7768 QUEBEC INC   *p*1292
109 RUE DES GRANDS-LACS, SAINT-AUGUSTIN-DE-DESMAURES, QC, G3A 1V9
(418) 878-3616   *SIC* 3444
A.P.S. METAL INDUSTRIES INC   *p*844
895 SANDY BEACH RD UNIT 4, PICKERING, ON, L1W 3N7
(905) 831-7698   *SIC* 3444
ALGGIN METAL INDUSTRIES LTD   *p*12
4540 46 AVE SE, CALGARY, AB, T2B 3N7
(403) 252-0132   *SIC* 3444
AMAZING KOBOTIC INDUSTRIES INC *p*704
5671 KENNEDY RD, MISSISSAUGA, ON, L4Z 3E1
(905) 712-1000   *SIC* 3444
ARTMETCO INC   *p*1328
2375 RUE COHEN, SAINT-LAURENT, QC, H4R 2N5
(514) 339-2707   *SIC* 3444
ASSOCIATED MATERIALS CANADA LIMITED
*p*13
4069 112 AVE SE SUITE 7, CALGARY, AB, T2C 0J4
(403) 640-0906   *SIC* 3444
ASSOCIATED MATERIALS CANADA LIMITED
*p*521
1001 CORPORATE DR, BURLINGTON, ON, L7L 5V5
(905) 319-5561   *SIC* 3444
ASSOCIATED MATERIALS CANADA LIMITED
*p*1249
2501 AUT TRANSCANADIENNE, POINTE-CLAIRE, QC, H9R 1B3
(514) 426-7801   *SIC* 3444
AUVENTS MULTIPLES INC   *p*1056
1505A RUE DE L'INDUSTRIE, BELOEIL, QC, J3G 0S5
(450) 446-4182   *SIC* 3444
BAILEY WEST INC   *p*275
7715 129A ST, SURREY, BC, V3W 6A2
(604) 590-5100   *SIC* 3444
BUCHNER MANUFACTURING INC   *p*837
30004 HWY 48, PEFFERLAW, ON, L0E 1N0
(705) 437-1734   *SIC* 3444

C.L. MALACH COMPANY (1997) LTD *p353*
3501 MCGILLIVRAY BLVD, OAK BLUFF, MB, R4G 0B5
(204) 895-8002   *SIC* 3444

C.P. LOEWEN ENTERPRISES LTD *p358*
77 PTH 52 W, STEINBACH, MB, R5G 1B2
(204) 326-6446   *SIC* 3444

CROSSTOWN METAL INDUSTRIES LTD *p270*
13133 115 AVE SUITE 100, SURREY, BC, V3R 2V8
(604) 589-3133   *SIC* 3444

DAYTON SUPERIOR CANADA LTD *p738*
6650 PACIFIC CIR, MISSISSAUGA, ON, L5T 1V6
(416) 798-2000   *SIC* 3444

DEFLECTO CANADA LTD *p883*
221 BUNTING RD, ST CATHARINES, ON, L2M 3Y2
(905) 641-8872   *SIC* 3444

EFCO CANADA CO *p593*
30 TODD RD, GEORGETOWN, ON, L7G 4R7
(905) 877-6957   *SIC* 3444

ENTREPRISES BERNARD SORNIN INC, LES *p1288*
325 LA GRANDE-CAROLINE, ROUGE-MONT, QC, J0L 1M0
(450) 469-4934   *SIC* 3444

FONDATIONS ROY-LAROUCHE INC *p1403*
1695 RUE SKIROULE RR 21, WICKHAM, QC, J0C 1S0
(819) 398-7333   *SIC* 3444

FORMNET INC *p584*
326 HUMBER COLLEGE BLVD, ETOBICOKE, ON, M9W 5P4
(416) 675-3404   *SIC* 3444

G.T.C.A. MET-ALL INC *p1333*
1215 MONTEE DE LIESSE, SAINT-LAURENT, QC, H4S 1J7
(514) 334-2801   *SIC* 3444

I.G. MACHINE & FIBERS LTD *p509*
87 ORENDA RD, BRAMPTON, ON, L6W 1V8
(905) 457-0745   *SIC* 3444

IDEAL ROOFING COMPANY LIMITED *p816*
1418 MICHAEL ST, OTTAWA, ON, K1B 3R2
(613) 746-3206   *SIC* 3444

IMPERIAL MANUFACTURING GROUP INC *p411*
40 INDUSTRIAL PARK ST, RICHIBUCTO, NB, E4W 4A4
(506) 523-9117   *SIC* 3444

IMT PARTNERSHIP *p636*
530 MANITOU DR, KITCHENER, ON, N2C 1L3
(519) 748-0848   *SIC* 3444

IMT PARTNERSHIP *p846*
837 REUTER RD, PORT COLBORNE, ON, L3K 5V7
(905) 834-7211   *SIC* 3444

INDUSTRIE LEMIEUX INC *p1065*
1401 RUE GRAHAM-BELL, BOUCHERVILLE, QC, J4B 6A1
(450) 655-7910   *SIC* 3444

INDUSTRIES GRC INC, LES *p1259*
10C COTE DE LA CANOTERIE BUREAU 7, QUEBEC, QC, G1K 3X4
(418) 692-1112   *SIC* 3444

MATERIEL INDUSTRIEL LTEE, LE *p1288*
325 LA GRANDE-CAROLINE RR 5, ROUGEMONT, QC, J0L 1M0
(450) 469-4934   *SIC* 3444

MATICAIR SUPPLY AND MANUFACTURING (1996) LTD *p555*
99 MCCLEARY CRT, CONCORD, ON, L4K 3Z1
(905) 738-5888   *SIC* 3444

MEP TECHNOLOGIES INC *p1234*
3100 RUE PEUGEOT, MONTREAL, QC, H7L 5C6
(450) 682-0804   *SIC* 3444

METAL ARTECH INC *p1170*
9455 RUE J.-J.-GAGNIER, MONTREAL, QC, H1Z 3C8
(514) 384-0660   *SIC* 3444

METAL LEETWO INC *p1118*
18025 RTE TRANSCANADIENNE, KIRKLAND, QC, H9J 3Z4
(514) 695-5911   *SIC* 3444

QUALIFIED METAL FABRICATORS LTD *p587*
55 STEINWAY BLVD, ETOBICOKE, ON, M9W 6H6
(416) 675-7777   *SIC* 3444

QUEST-TECH PRECISION INC *p491*
193 JAMIESON BONE RD, BELLEVILLE, ON, K8N 5T4
(613) 966-7551   *SIC* 3444

TATE ASP ACCESS FLOORS INC *p805*
880 EQUESTRIAN CRT, OAKVILLE, ON, L6L 6L7
(905) 847-0138   *SIC* 3444

TERMACO LTEE *p1318*
325 BOUL INDUSTRIEL, SAINT-JEAN-SUR-RICHELIEU, QC, J3B 7M3
(450) 346-6871   *SIC* 3444

TRIMASTER MANUFACTURING INC *p606*
95 CURTIS DR, GUELPH, ON, N1K 1E1
(519) 823-2661   *SIC* 3444

VICWEST INC *p525*
200-5050 SOUTH SERVICE RD, BURLINGTON, ON, L7L 5Y7
(905) 825-2252   *SIC* 3444

VICWEST INC *p897*
362 LORNE AVE E, STRATFORD, ON, N5A 6S4
(519) 271-5553   *SIC* 3444

VICWEST INC *p1399*
707 BOUL PIERRE-ROUX E, VICTORIAVILLE, QC, G6T 1S7
(819) 758-0661   *SIC* 3444

WESGAR INC *p247*
1634 KEBET WAY UNIT 1, PORT COQUITLAM, BC, V3C 5W9
(604) 942-9558   *SIC* 3444

WESTFORM METALS INC *p198*
6435 LICKMAN RD, CHILLIWACK, BC, V2R 4A9
(604) 858-7134   *SIC* 3444

WESTMAN STEEL INC *p357*
2976 DAY ST, SPRINGFIELD, MB, R2C 2Z2
(204) 777-5345   *SIC* 3444

WINDSPEC INC *p561*
1310 CREDITSTONE RD, CONCORD, ON, L4K 5T7
(905) 738-8311   *SIC* 3444

YORK SHEET METAL LIMITED *p1034*
227 WESTCREEK DR, WOODBRIDGE, ON, L4L 9T7
(416) 742-8242   *SIC* 3444

SIC 3446 Architectural Metalwork

BORDEN METAL PRODUCTS (CANADA) LIMITED *p490*
50 DAYFOOT ST, BEETON, ON, L0G 1A0
(905) 729-2229   *SIC* 3446

C/S CONSTRUCTION SPECIALTIES COMPANY *p720*
2240 ARGENTIA RD, MISSISSAUGA, ON, L5N 2K7
(905) 274-3611   *SIC* 3446

CANADA SCAFFOLD SUPPLY CO. LTD *p253*
11331 TWIGG PL, RICHMOND, BC, V6V 3C9
(604) 324-7691   *SIC* 3446

DECOR GRATES INCORPORATED *p473*
4 CHISHOLM CRT, AJAX, ON, L1S 4N8
(647) 777-3544   *SIC* 3446

DUROSE MANUFACTURING LIMITED *p600*
460 ELIZABETH ST, GUELPH, ON, N1E 6C1
(519) 822-5251   *SIC* 3446

EAST & WEST ALUM CRAFT LTD *p187*
7465 CONWAY AVE, BURNABY, BC, V5E 2P7
(604) 438-6261   *SIC* 3446

ETOBICOKE IRONWORKS LIMITED *p794*
141 RIVALDA RD, NORTH YORK, ON, M9M 2M6
(416) 742-7111   *SIC* 3446

FABRICATION RAMPES ET ESCALIERS PRESTIGE INC *p1162*
11750 AV J.-J.-JOUBERT, MONTREAL, QC, H1E 7E7
(514) 324-2107   *SIC* 3446

GRECO ALUMINUM RAILINGS LTD *p1022*
3255 WYANDOTTE ST E, WINDSOR, ON, N8Y 1E9
(905) 966-4210   *SIC* 3446

HARRIS STEEL ULC *p522*
750 APPLEBY LINE, BURLINGTON, ON, L7L 2Y7
(905) 632-2121   *SIC* 3446

METALTECH-OMEGA INC *p1362*
1735 BOUL SAINT-ELZEAR O, SAINTE-ROSE, QC, H7L 3N6
(450) 681-6440   *SIC* 3446

MULTI-METAL G. BOUTIN INC *p1276*
6500 RUE ROLAND-BEDARD, QUEBEC, QC, G2C 0J2
(418) 842-5888   *SIC* 3446

NORBEC ARCHITECTURAL INC *p1066*
97 RUE DE VAUDREUIL, BOUCHERVILLE, QC, J4B 1K7
(450) 449-1499   *SIC* 3446

OMEGA II INC *p1362*
1735 BOUL SAINT-ELZEAR O, SAINTE-ROSE, QC, H7L 3N6
(450) 681-6440   *SIC* 3446

OPENAIRE SALES INC *p801*
2360 CORNWALL RD UNIT B, OAKVILLE, ON, L6J 7T9
(905) 901-8535   *SIC* 3446

PRODUITS DE FIL ET DE METAL COGAN LTEE *p1380*
2460 BOUL DES ENTREPRISES, TERREBONNE, QC, J6X 4J8
(514) 353-9141   *SIC* 3446

PRODUITS FRACO LTEE, LES *p1348*
91 CH DES PATRIOTES, SAINT-MATHIAS-SUR-RICHELIEU, QC, J3L 6B6
(514) 990-7750   *SIC* 3446

QUALI-T-GROUP ULC *p1068*
22 BOUL DE L'AEROPORT, BROMONT, QC, J2L 1S6
(450) 534-2032   *SIC* 3446

RAILCRAFT (2010) INTERNATIONAL INC *p277*
13272 COMBER WAY, SURREY, BC, V3W 5V9
(604) 543-7245   *SIC* 3446

SOUDURE M. COUTURE & FILS INC *p1310*
8020 AV DUPLESSIS, SAINT-HYACINTHE, QC, J2R 1S6
(450) 796-1617   *SIC* 3446

TRACTEL LTD *p873*
1615 WARDEN AVE, SCARBOROUGH, ON, M1R 2T3
(416) 298-8822   *SIC* 3446

TRACTEL NORTH AMERICA INC *p873*
1615 WARDEN AVE, SCARBOROUGH, ON, M1R 2T3
(416) 298-8822   *SIC* 3446

WALLACE PERIMETER SECURITY *p389*
115 LOWSON CRES, WINNIPEG, MB, R3P 1A6
(866) 300-1110   *SIC* 3446

SIC 3448 Prefabricated Metal buildings and components

ALUM-TEK INDUSTRIES LTD *p179*
26221 30A AVE, ALDERGROVE, BC, V4W 2W6
SIC 3448

BRYTEX BUILDING SYSTEMS INC *p113*
5610 97 ST NW, EDMONTON, AB, T6E 3J1
(780) 437-7970   *SIC* 3448

CRAVO EQUIPMENT LTD *p517*
30 WHITE SWAN RD, BRANTFORD, ON, N3T 5L4
(519) 759-8226   *SIC* 3448

DYNAMIC AIR SHELTERS LTD *p15*
200 RIVERCREST DR SE SUITE 170, CALGARY, AB, T2C 2X5
(403) 203-9311   *SIC* 3448

DYNAMIC SHELTERS INC *p68*
10333 SOUTHPORT RD SW SUITE 523, CALGARY, AB, T2W 3X6
(403) 203-9311   *SIC* 3448

ECONOSPAN STRUCTURES CORP *p195*
472 AYLMER RD, CHASE, BC, V0E 1M1
(250) 679-3400   *SIC* 3448

ENSEICOM INC *p1125*
225 RUE NORMAN, LACHINE, QC, H8R 1A3
(514) 486-2626   *SIC* 3448

FUTURE STEEL BUILDINGS INTL. CORP *p499*
220 CHRYSLER DR, BRAMPTON, ON, L6S 6B6
(905) 790-8500   *SIC* 3448

INDUSTRIES HARNOIS INC, LES *p1353*
1044 RUE PRINCIPALE, SAINT-THOMAS, QC, J0K 3L0
(450) 756-1041   *SIC* 3448

KINGSPAN INSULATED PANELS LTD *p495*
12557 COLERAINE DR, BOLTON, ON, L7E 3B5
(905) 951-5600   *SIC* 3448

KROPF INDUSTRIAL INC *p879*
1 QUEBEC DR, SEGUIN, ON, P2A 0B2
(705) 378-2453   *SIC* 3448

MAKLOC BUILDINGS INC *p149*
706 17 AVE, NISKU, AB, T9E 7T1
(780) 955-2951   *SIC* 3448

MITEK CANADA, INC *p497*
100 INDUSTRIAL RD, BRADFORD, ON, L3Z 3G7
(905) 952-2900   *SIC* 3448

MODUS STRUCTURES INC *p81*
34 MCCOOL CRES, CROSSFIELD, AB, T0M 0S0
(403) 274-2422   *SIC* 3448

NOBLE ACCEPTANCE LTD *p102*
21216 113 AVE NW, EDMONTON, AB, T5S 1Y6
SIC 3448

NORSEMAN INC *p1434*
3815 WANUSKEWIN RD, SASKATOON, SK, S7P 1A4
(306) 385-2888   *SIC* 3448

NRB INC *p599*
183 SOUTH SERVICE RD BUREAU 1, GRIMSBY, ON, L3M 4H6
(905) 945-9622   *SIC* 3448

PRO FAB SUNROOMS LTD *p368*
342 NAIRN AVE, WINNIPEG, MB, R2L 0W9
(204) 668-3544   *SIC* 3448

ROBERTSON BUILDING SYSTEMS LIMITED *p478*
1343 SANDHILL DR, ANCASTER, ON, L9G 4V5
(905) 304-1111   *SIC* 3448

ROYAL GROUP, INC *p1028*
100 ROYAL GROUP CRES UNIT B, WOODBRIDGE, ON, L4H 1X9
(905) 264-2989   *SIC* 3448

SPACEMAKER LIMITED *p712*
3069 WOLFEDALE RD, MISSISSAUGA, ON, L5C 1V9
(905) 279-2632   *SIC* 3448

SUNSPACE MODULAR ENCLOSURES INC *p753*
300 TORONTO ST, NEWCASTLE, ON, L1B 1C2
(905) 987-4111   *SIC* 3448

TREVLUC HOLDINGS LTD *p357*
2976 DAY ST, SPRINGFIELD, MB, R2C 2Z2
(204) 777-5345   *SIC* 3448

▲ Public Company   ■ Public Company Family Member   **HQ** Headquarters   **BR** Branch   **SL** Single Location

SIC 3449 Miscellaneous Metalwork

A. & D. PREVOST INC *p1283*
305 12E AV, RICHELIEU, QC, J3L 3T2
(450) 658-8771   *SIC 3449*

AGF - REBAR INC *p666*
2800 14TH AVE SUITE 204, MARKHAM, ON, L3R 0E4
(416) 862-5015   *SIC 3449*

ALUMINUM CURTAINWALL SYSTEMS INC *p216*
1820 KRYCZKA PL, KAMLOOPS, BC, V1S 1S4
(250) 372-3600   *SIC 3449*

ENNOVA FACADES INC *p1025*
620 SPRUCEWOOD AVE, WINDSOR, ON, N9C 0B2
(519) 969-1740   *SIC 3449*

EPSYLON CONCEPT INC *p1255*
1010 AV NORDIQUE, QUEBEC, QC, G1C 0H9
(418) 661-6262   *SIC 3449*

GESTION ROBERT M. HARVEY INC *p1322*
210 BOUL DESAULNIERS, SAINT-LAMBERT, QC, J4P 1M6
(450) 658-8771   *SIC 3449*

HARRIS STEEL ULC *p892*
318 ARVIN AVE, STONEY CREEK, ON, L8E 2M2
(905) 662-0611   *SIC 3449*

HODGSON CUSTOM ROLLING INC *p760*
5580 KALAR RD, NIAGARA FALLS, ON, L2H 3L1
(905) 356-8132   *SIC 3449*

JASWALL INC *p513*
70 VAN KIRK DR, BRAMPTON, ON, L7A 1B1
(905) 846-3177   *SIC 3449*

SKYFOLD INC *p1054*
325 AV LEE, BAIE-D'URFE, QC, H9X 3S3
(514) 457-4767   *SIC 3449*

SIC 3451 Screw machine products

A. BERGER PRECISION LTD *p512*
28 REGAN RD SUITE 1, BRAMPTON, ON, L7A 1A7
(905) 840-4207   *SIC 3451*

L & M PRECISION PRODUCTS INC *p793*
150 MILVAN DR, NORTH YORK, ON, M9L 1Z9
(416) 741-0700   *SIC 3451*

LEMIRE PRECISION INC *p1099*
3000 RUE POWER, DRUMMONDVILLE, QC, J2C 6H9
(819) 475-5121   *SIC 3451*

SIC 3452 Bolts, nuts, rivets, and washers

HILLMAN GROUP CANADA ULC, THE *p868*
55 MILNE AVE, SCARBOROUGH, ON, M1L 4N3
(416) 694-3351   *SIC 3452*

IFASTGROUPE 2004 L.P. *p1149*
700 RUE OUELLETTE, MARIEVILLE, QC, J3M 1P6
(450) 658-8741   *SIC 3452*

R B & W CORPORATION OF CANADA *p500*
10 SUN PAC BLVD, BRAMPTON, ON, L6S 4R5
(905) 595-9700   *SIC 3452*

SIMPSON STRONG-TIE CANADA LIMITED *p506*
5 KENVIEW BLVD, BRAMPTON, ON, L6T 5G5
(800) 999-5099   *SIC 3452*

SIC 3462 Iron and steel forgings

AMSTED CANADA INC *p362*

2500 DAY ST, WINNIPEG, MB, R2C 3A4
(204) 222-4252   *SIC 3462*

AMSTED CANADA INC *p362*
104 REGENT AVE E, WINNIPEG, MB, R2C 0C1
(204) 222-4252   *SIC 3462*

CAM CHAIN CO. LTD *p276*
8355 128 ST, SURREY, BC, V3W 4G1
(604) 599-1522   *SIC 3462*

CANADA FORGINGS INC *p1011*
130 HAGAR WELLAND, WELLAND, ON, L3B 5P8
(905) 735-1220   *SIC 3462*

CANADOIL FORGE LTEE *p1056*
805 BOUL ALPHONSE-DESHAIES, BECANCOUR, QC, G9H 2Y8
(819) 294-6600   *SIC 3462*

CONTINENTAL CHAIN & RIGGING LTD *p108*
7011 GIRARD RD NW, EDMONTON, AB, T6B 2C4
(780) 437-2701   *SIC 3462*

DYNAMIC INSTALLATIONS INC *p246*
1556 KEBET WAY, PORT COQUITLAM, BC, V3C 5M5
(604) 464-7695   *SIC 3462*

EODC ENGINEERING, DEVELOPING AND LICENSING, INC *p815*
1377 TRIOLE ST, OTTAWA, ON, K1B 4T4
(613) 748-5549   *SIC 3462*

PROGRESS RAIL TRANSCANADA CORPORATION *p372*
478 MCPHILLIPS ST SUITE 300, WINNIPEG, MB, R2X 2G8
(204) 934-4307   *SIC 3462*

TRI-LAD FLANGE AND FITTINGS INC *p837*
30 WOODSLEE AVE, PARIS, ON, N3L 3N6
(519) 442-6520   *SIC 3462*

SIC 3463 Nonferrous forgings

ALUMINERIE DE BECANCOUR INC *p1055*
5555 RUE PIERRE-THIBAULT BUREAU 217, BECANCOUR, QC, G9H 2T7
(819) 294-6101   *SIC 3463*

EWING INTERNATIONAL INC *p1014*
1445 HOPKINS ST, WHITBY, ON, L1N 2C2
(416) 291-1675   *SIC 3463*

SIC 3465 Automotive stampings

9205-2976 QUEBEC INC *p1075*
1200 RUE DES CASCADES, CHATEAU-GUAY, QC, J6J 4Z2
(450) 699-9300   *SIC 3465*

A.G. SIMPSON AUTOMOTIVE INC *p532*
560 CONESTOGA BLVD, CAMBRIDGE, ON, N1R 7P7
(519) 621-7953   *SIC 3465*

A.G. SIMPSON AUTOMOTIVE INC *p812*
901 SIMCOE ST S, OSHAWA, ON, L1H 4L1
(905) 571-2121   *SIC 3465*

ABC PLASTICS LIMITED *p792*
2 NORELCO DR, NORTH YORK, ON, M9L 2X6
(416) 742-9600   *SIC 3465*

AISIN CANADA INC *p895*
180 WRIGHT BLVD, STRATFORD, ON, N4Z 1H3
(519) 271-1575   *SIC 3465*

BD ENGINE BRAKE INC *p174*
33541 MACLURE RD, ABBOTSFORD, BC, V2S 7W2
(604) 853-6096   *SIC 3465*

CANADA TUBEFORM INC *p661*
2879 INNOVATION DR, LONDON, ON, N6M 0B6
(519) 451-9995   *SIC 3465*

COOPER-STANDARD AUTOMOTIVE CANADA LIMITED *p1373*
4045 RUE BRODEUR, SHERBROOKE, QC, J1L 1K4
(819) 562-4440   *SIC 3465*

COOPER-STANDARD AUTOMOTIVE CANADA LIMITED *p1373*
3995 BOUL INDUSTRIEL, SHERBROOKE, QC, J1L 2S7
(819) 562-4440   *SIC 3465*

COOPER-STANDARD AUTOMOTIVE CANADA LIMITED *p1375*
4870 RUE ROBERT BOYD, SHER-BROOKE, QC, J1R 0W8
(819) 562-4440   *SIC 3465*

EXCO TECHNOLOGIES LIMITED *p670*
130 SPY CRT, MARKHAM, ON, L3R 5H6
(905) 477-3065   *SIC 3465*

FIO AUTOMOTIVE CANADA CORPORATION *p895*
220 DUNN RD, STRATFORD, ON, N4Z 0A7
(519) 275-6070   *SIC 3465*

FLEX-N-GATE CANADA COMPANY *p902*
538 BLANCHARD PK, TECUMSEH, ON, N8N 2L9
(519) 727-3931   *SIC 3465*

GENERAL MOTORS OF CANADA COMPANY *p885*
570 GLENDALE AVE, ST CATHARINES, ON, L2R 7B3
(905) 641-6424   *SIC 3465*

GUELPH MANUFACTURING GROUP INC *p603*
20 MASSEY RD, GUELPH, ON, N1H 7X8
(519) 822-5401   *SIC 3465*

GUELPH MANUFACTURING GROUP INC *p603*
39 ROYAL RD, GUELPH, ON, N1H 1G2
(519) 822-5401   *SIC 3465*

HAYASHI CANADA INC *p895*
300 DUNN RD, STRATFORD, ON, N4Z 0A7
(519) 271-5600   *SIC 3465*

HENNIGES AUTOMOTIVE SCHLEGEL CANADA INC *p522*
4445 FAIRVIEW ST, BURLINGTON, ON, L7L 2A4
(289) 636-4461   *SIC 3465*

JEFFERSON ELORA CORPORATION *p569*
60 1ST LINE, ELORA, ON, N0B 1S0
(519) 846-2728   *SIC 3465*

KIRCHHOFF AUTOMOTIVE CANADA INC *p850*
25 MURAL ST, RICHMOND, ON, L4B 1J4
(905) 727-8585   *SIC 3465*

MARTINREA METALLIC CANADA INC *p1002*
3210 LANGSTAFF RD, VAUGHAN, ON, L4K 5B2
(416) 749-0314   *SIC 3465*

MATCOR AUTOMOTIVE INC *p724*
7299 EAST DANBRO CRES, MISSISSAUGA, ON, L5N 6P8
(905) 819-9900   *SIC 3465*

MATSU MANUFACTURING INC *p504*
7657 BRAMALEA RD, BRAMPTON, ON, L6T 5V3
(905) 291-5000   *SIC 3465*

MCBRIDE METAL FABRICATING CORPORATION *p902*
305 PATILLO RD, TECUMSEH, ON, N8N 2L9
(519) 727-6640   *SIC 3465*

MULTIMATIC INC *p556*
301 JACOB KEFFER PKY, CONCORD, ON, L4K 4V6
(905) 879-0200   *SIC 3465*

STAHLSCHMIDT LTD *p700*
5208 EVEREST DR, MISSISSAUGA, ON, L4W 2R4
(905) 629-4568   *SIC 3465*

TAKUMI STAMPING CANADA INC *p890*
100 DENNIS RD, ST THOMAS, ON, N5P 0B6
(519) 633-6070   *SIC 3465*

THI CANADA INC *p525*
5230 HARVESTER RD UNIT 3, BURLINGTON, ON, L7L 4X4
(905) 849-3633   *SIC 3465*

TI AUTOMOTIVE CANADA INC *p507*

316 ORENDA RD, BRAMPTON, ON, L6T 1G3
(905) 793-7100   *SIC 3465*

TOYOTETSU CANADA, INC *p881*
88 PARK RD, SIMCOE, ON, N3Y 4J9
(519) 428-6500   *SIC 3465*

VENTRA GROUP CO *p498*
75 REAGEN'S INDUSTRIAL PKY, BRADFORD, ON, L3Z 0Z9
(705) 778-7900   *SIC 3465*

VENTRA GROUP CO *p998*
65 INDUSTRIAL RD, TOTTENHAM, ON, L0G 1W0
(905) 936-4245   *SIC 3465*

VENTRA GROUP CO *p1022*
1425 HOWARD AVE, WINDSOR, ON, N8X 5C9
(519) 258-3509   *SIC 3465*

VUTEQ CANADA INC *p1036*
885 KEYES DR, WOODSTOCK, ON, N4V 1C3
(519) 421-0011   *SIC 3465*

WARREN INDUSTRIES LTD *p561*
401 SPINNAKER WAY, CONCORD, ON, L4K 4N4
(905) 669-1260   *SIC 3465*

SIC 3466 Crowns and closures

CAPSULES AMCOR FLEXIBLES CANADA INC *p1297*
2301 RTE 112, SAINT-CESAIRE, QC, J0L 1T0
(450) 469-0777   *SIC 3466*

SIC 3469 Metal stampings, nec

1443190 ONTARIO INC *p643*
605 COUNTY RD 18, LEAMINGTON, ON, N8H 3V5
(519) 322-2264   *SIC 3469*

506165 ONTARIO LIMITED *p637*
50 STECKLE PL, KITCHENER, ON, N2E 2C3
(519) 748-5295   *SIC 3469*

ABF CUSTOM MFG. LTD *p687*
6750 PROFESSIONAL CRT, MISSISSAUGA, ON, L4V 1X6
(905) 612-0743   *SIC 3469*

ACCURATE MACHINE & TOOL LIMITED *p794*
1844 WILSON AVE, NORTH YORK, ON, M9M 1A1
(416) 742-8301   *SIC 3469*

ARCON METAL PROCESSING INC *p855*
105 INDUSTRIAL RD, RICHMOND HILL, ON, L4C 2Y4
SIC 3469

CANADA STAMPINGS LTD *p1036*
1299 COMMERCE WAY, WOODSTOCK, ON, N4V 0A2
(519) 537-6245   *SIC 3469*

CANADIAN TOOL & DIE LTD *p390*
1331 CHEVRIER BLVD, WINNIPEG, MB, R3T 1Y4
(204) 453-6833   *SIC 3469*

CENTRAL STAMPINGS LIMITED *p1019*
2525 CENTRAL AVE, WINDSOR, ON, N8W 4J6
(519) 945-1111   *SIC 3469*

CLOVER TOOL MANUFACTURING LTD *p550*
8271 KEELE ST SUITE 3, CONCORD, ON, L4K 1Z1
(905) 669-1999   *SIC 3469*

COMP-TECH MFG. INC *p776*
58 SCARSDALE RD, NORTH YORK, ON, M3B 2R7
(416) 510-1035   *SIC 3469*

CUSTOM DIAMOND INTERNATIONAL INC *p1342*
895 AV MUNCK, SAINT-LAURENT, QC,

H7S 1A9

(450) 668-0330   *SIC 3469*

DBG CANADA LIMITED *p1036*
980 JULIANA DR, WOODSTOCK, ON, N4V 1B9

SIC 3469

EGAR TOOL AND DIE LTD *p535*
336 PINEBUSH RD, CAMBRIDGE, ON, N1T 1Z6

(519) 623-3023   *SIC 3469*

EL-MET-PARTS INC *p566*
47 HEAD ST, DUNDAS, ON, L9H 3H6

(905) 628-6366   *SIC 3469*

ELECTROMAC GROUP INC, THE *p1024*
1965 AMBASSADOR DR, WINDSOR, ON, N9C 3R5

(519) 969-4632   *SIC 3469*

ENCLOSURES DIRECT INC *p817*
2120 THURSTON DR, OTTAWA, ON, K1G 6E1

(613) 723-4477   *SIC 3469*

FAB 3R INC *p1387*
227 BOUL DU SAINT-MAURICE, TROIS-RIVIERES, QC, G9A 3N8

(819) 371-8227   *SIC 3469*

FLEETWOOD METAL INDUSTRIES INC *p807*
1885 BLACKACRE DR, OLDCASTLE, ON, N0R 1L0

(519) 737-1919   *SIC 3469*

FLEETWOOD METAL INDUSTRIES INC *p835*
71 DOVER ST, OTTERVILLE, ON, N0J 1R0

(519) 879-6577   *SIC 3469*

FLEETWOOD METAL INDUSTRIES INC *p911*
21 CLEARVIEW DR, TILLSONBURG, ON, N4G 4G8

(519) 737-1919   *SIC 3469*

GESTION GUYTA INC *p1097*
4275 BOUL SAINT-JOSEPH, DRUMMONDVILLE, QC, J2B 1T8

(819) 477-1596   *SIC 3469*

HALKIN TOOL LTD *p272*
17819 66 AVE, SURREY, BC, V3S 7X1

(604) 574-9799   *SIC 3469*

HAMMOND MANUFACTURING COMPANY LIMITED *p603*
394 EDINBURGH RD N, GUELPH, ON, N1H 1E5

(519) 822-2960   *SIC 3469*

HANSEN INDUSTRIES LTD *p260*
2871 OLAFSEN AVE, RICHMOND, BC, V6X 2R4

(604) 278-2223   *SIC 3469*

ISE METAL INC *p1369*
20 RTE DE WINDSOR, SHERBROOKE, QC, J1C 0E5

(819) 846-1044   *SIC 3469*

KINGSVILLE STAMPING LIMITED *p634*
1931 SETTERINGTON DR, KINGSVILLE, ON, N9Y 2E5

(519) 326-6331   *SIC 3469*

KIRCHHOFF AUTOMOTIVE CANADA INC *p795*
114 CLAYSON RD, NORTH YORK, ON, M9M 2H2

(416) 740-2656   *SIC 3469*

KOBAY ENSTEL LIMITED *p876*
125 NASHDENE RD UNIT 5, SCARBOROUGH, ON, M1V 2W3

(416) 292-7088   *SIC 3469*

KOZMA'S MANUFACTURING CO. LTD *p798*
2751 PLYMOUTH DR, OAKVILLE, ON, L6H 5R5

(905) 829-3660   *SIC 3469*

KROMET INTERNATIONAL INC *p534*
200 SHELDON DR, CAMBRIDGE, ON, N1R 7K1

(519) 623-2511   *SIC 3469*

KROMET INTERNATIONAL INC *p608*
20 MILBURN RD, HAMILTON, ON, L8E 3L9

(905) 561-7773   *SIC 3469*

MANUFACTURE D'EQUIPMENT HARDT

INC *p1128*
1400 50E AV, LACHINE, QC, H8T 2V3

(514) 631-7271   *SIC 3469*

METOSAK INC *p1369*
570 RUE JOSEPH-LATOUR, SHERBROOKE, QC, J1C 0W2

(819) 846-0608   *SIC 3469*

METRICAN STAMPING CO. INC *p523*
1380 ARTISANS CRT, BURLINGTON, ON, L7L 5Y2

(905) 332-3200   *SIC 3469*

NAHANNI STEEL PRODUCTS INC *p505*
38 DEERHURST DR, BRAMPTON, ON, L6T 5R8

(905) 791-2100   *SIC 3469*

NASG CANADA INC *p1035*
975 PATTULO AVE E, WOODSTOCK, ON, N4S 7W3

(519) 539-7491   *SIC 3469*

NORTH AMERICAN METALS OF CANADA LTD *p756*
130 HARRY WALKER PKY N, NEWMARKET, ON, L3Y 7B2

(905) 898-2291   *SIC 3469*

NOVANNI STAINLESS INC *p546*
2978 SOUTHORN RD, COLDWATER, ON, L0K 1E0

(705) 686-3301   *SIC 3469*

PLIMETAL INC *p1238*
8555 PLACE MARIEN, MONTREAL-EST, QC, H1B 5W6

(514) 648-2260   *SIC 3469*

PRECISION RESOURCE CANADA LTD *p539*
4 CHERRY BLOSSOM RD, CAMBRIDGE, ON, N3H 4R7

(519) 653-7777   *SIC 3469*

PRODUITS DE METAL VULCAIN INC *p1320*
31 RUE JOHN-F.-KENNEDY, SAINT-JEROME, QC, J7Y 4B4

(450) 436-5355   *SIC 3469*

PRYOR METALS LIMITED *p597*
2683 FENTON RD, GLOUCESTER, ON, K1T 3T8

(613) 822-0953   *SIC 3469*

PWO CANADA INCORPORATED *p642*
255 MCBRINE PL, KITCHENER, ON, N2R 1G7

(519) 893-6880   *SIC 3469*

RALSTON METAL PRODUCTS LIMITED *p606*
50 WATSON RD S, GUELPH, ON, N1L 1E2

(519) 836-2998   *SIC 3469*

SNAP-ON TOOLS OF CANADA LTD *p756*
145 HARRY WALKER PKY N, NEWMARKET, ON, L3Y 7B3

(905) 812-5774   *SIC 3469*

TEMPEL CANADA COMPANY *p525*
5045 NORTH SERVICE RD, BURLINGTON, ON, L7L 5H6

(905) 335-2530   *SIC 3469*

THETA INDUSTRIES LIMITED *p488*
8 TRUMAN RD, BARRIE, ON, L4N 8Y8

(705) 726-2620   *SIC 3469*

THETA TTS INC *p488*
8 TRUMAN RD, BARRIE, ON, L4N 8Y8

(705) 726-2620   *SIC 3469*

THUNDER TOOL & MANUFACTURING LTD *p588*
975 MARTIN GROVE RD, ETOBICOKE, ON, M9W 4V6

(416) 742-1936   *SIC 3469*

TITAN TOOL & DIE LIMITED *p1021*
2801 HOWARD AVE, WINDSOR, ON, N8X 3Y1

(519) 966-1234   *SIC 3469*

TRIPAR INC *p1161*
9750 BOUL MAURICE-DUPLESSIS, MONTREAL, QC, H1C 1G1

(514) 648-7471   *SIC 3469*

TUBE-FAB LTD *p701*
1020 BREVIK PL UNIT 11, MISSISSAUGA, ON, L4W 4N7

(905) 206-0311   *SIC 3469*

UTIL CANADA LIMITED *p560*

270 SPINNAKER WAY SUITE 13, CONCORD, ON, L4K 4W1

(905) 760-8088   *SIC 3469*

VARI-FORM MANUFACTURING INC *p897*
233 LOTHIAN AVE, STRATHROY, ON, N7G 4J1

(519) 245-5200   *SIC 3469*

WALDALE MANUFACTURING LIMITED *p438*
17 TANTRAMAR CRES, AMHERST, NS, B4H 4J6

(902) 667-3307   *SIC 3469*

WOODBINE TOOL & DIE MANUFACTURING LTD *p677*
3300 14TH AVE, MARKHAM, ON, L3R 0H3

(905) 475-5223   *SIC 3469*

SIC 3471 Plating and polishing

105675 ONTARIO LIMITED *p686*
6577 NORTHWEST DR, MISSISSAUGA, ON, L4V 1L1

(905) 293-9900   *SIC 3471*

1544982 ONTARIO INC *p643*
50 VICTORIA AVE N, LEAMINGTON, ON, N8H 2W1

(519) 776-9153   *SIC 3471*

A I M QUEBEC *p1238*
9100 BOUL HENRI-BOURASSA E, MONTREAL-EST, QC, H1E 2S4

(514) 648-3883   *SIC 3471*

ALUMICO METAL & OXIDATION INC *p1166*
4343 RUE HOCHELAGA BUREAU 100, MONTREAL, QC, H1V 1C2

(514) 255-4343   *SIC 3471*

ANM INDUSTRIES (2005) INC *p1019*
2500 CENTRAL AVE, WINDSOR, ON, N8W 4J5

(519) 258-2550   *SIC 3471*

ANODIZING & PAINT T.N.M INC *p1249*
211 CH DE L'AVIATION, POINTE-CLAIRE, QC, H9R 4Z2

(514) 335-7001   *SIC 3471*

AUTOTEK ELECTROPLATING LTD *p582*
20 HUDDERSFIELD RD, ETOBICOKE, ON, M9W 5Z6

(416) 674-0063   *SIC 3471*

COATINGS 85 LTD *p738*
6995 DAVAND DR, MISSISSAUGA, ON, L5T 1L5

(905) 564-1711   *SIC 3471*

DAOUST, JACQUES COATINGS MANAGEMENT INC *p533*
32 MCKENZIE ST, CAMBRIDGE, ON, N1R 4E1

(519) 624-1515   *SIC 3471*

DEPENDABLE ANODIZING LIMITED *p669*
268 DON PARK RD SUITE 1, MARKHAM, ON, L3R 1C3

(905) 475-1229   *SIC 3471*

DURAPAINT INDUSTRIES LIMITED *p878*
247 FINCHDENE SQ SUITE 1, SCARBOROUGH, ON, M1X 1B9

(416) 754-3664   *SIC 3471*

FOUR STAR PLATING INDUSTRIES LIMITED *p793*
1162 BARMAC DR, NORTH YORK, ON, M9L 1X5

(416) 745-1742   *SIC 3471*

KUNTZ ELECTROPLATING INC *p636*
851 WILSON AVE, KITCHENER, ON, N2C 1J1

(519) 893-7680   *SIC 3471*

LATEM INDUSTRIES LIMITED *p534*
90 STRUCK CRT, CAMBRIDGE, ON, N1R 8L2

(519) 740-0292   *SIC 3471*

MILITEX COATINGS INC *p649*
1881 HURON ST, LONDON, ON, N5V 3A5

(519) 659-0528   *SIC 3471*

PLACAGE JAY GE LTEE *p1085*
1800 BOUL FORTIN, COTE SAINT-LUC, QC, H7S 1N8

(450) 663-7070   *SIC 3471*

PROGRESSIVE ANODIZERS INC *p873*
41 CROCKFORD BLVD, SCARBOROUGH, ON, M1R 3B7

(416) 751-5487   *SIC 3471*

SPECTRA ANODIZING LTD *p1033*
201 HANLAN RD, WOODBRIDGE, ON, L4L 3R7

(905) 851-1141   *SIC 3471*

TECNICKROME AERONAUTIQUE INC *p1248*
12264 RUE APRIL BUREAU 1, POINTE-AUX-TREMBLES, QC, H1B 5N5

(514) 640-0333   *SIC 3471*

TORCAD LIMITED *p576*
275 NORSEMAN ST, ETOBICOKE, ON, M8Z 2R5

(416) 239-3928   *SIC 3471*

VAUGHAN METAL POLISHING LIMITED *p794*
206 MILVAN DR, NORTH YORK, ON, M9L 1Z9

(416) 743-7500   *SIC 3471*

SIC 3479 Metal coating and allied services

1528593 ONTARIO INC *p1004*
6941 BASE LINE, WALLACEBURG, ON, N8A 4L3

(519) 627-7885   *SIC 3479*

3323501 CANADA INC *p1238*
8201 PLACE MARIEN, MONTREAL-EST, QC, H1B 5W6

(514) 322-9120   *SIC 3479*

A/D FIRE PROTECTION SYSTEMS INC *p864*
420 TAPSCOTT RD UNIT 5, SCARBOROUGH, ON, M1B 1Y4

(416) 292-2361   *SIC 3479*

ALUMICOR INTERNATIONAL INC *p582*
290 HUMBERLINE DR, ETOBICOKE, ON, M9W 5S2

(416) 745-4222   *SIC 3479*

ALUMICOR LIMITED *p582*
290 HUMBERLINE DR SUITE 1, ETOBICOKE, ON, M9W 5S2

(416) 745-4222   *SIC 3479*

AP&C REVETEMENTS & POUDRES AVANCEES INC *p1061*
3765 RUE LA VERENDRYE BUREAU 110, BOISBRIAND, QC, J7H 1R8

(450) 434-1004   *SIC 3479*

ARCELORMITTAL COTEAU-DU-LAC INC *p1088*
25 RUE DE L'ACIER, COTEAU-DU-LAC, QC, J0P 1B0

(450) 763-0915   *SIC 3479*

ARCELORMITTAL COTEAU-DU-LAC LIMITED PARTNERSHIP *p1088*
25 RUE DE L'ACIER, COTEAU-DU-LAC, QC, J0P 1B0

(450) 763-0915   *SIC 3479*

ARCELORMITTAL DOFASCO G.P. *p611*
1330 BURLINGTON ST E, HAMILTON, ON, L8N 3J5

(905) 548-7200   *SIC 3479*

AUTOMATIC COATING LIMITED *p873*
211 NUGGET AVE, SCARBOROUGH, ON, M1S 3B1

(416) 335-7500   *SIC 3479*

BAYCOAT LIMITED *p607*
244 LANARK ST, HAMILTON, ON, L8E 4B3

(905) 561-0965   *SIC 3479*

CANADIAN ELECTROCOATING LTD *p1024*
945 PRINCE RD, WINDSOR, ON, N9C 2Z4

(519) 977-7523   *SIC 3479*

CATELECTRIC INC *p873*
125 COMMANDER BLVD, SCARBOROUGH, ON, M1S 3M7

(416) 299-4864   *SIC 3479*

CONTINUOUS COLOUR COAT LIMITED *p583*
1430 MARTIN GROVE RD, ETOBICOKE, ON, M9W 4Y1

(416) 743-7980   *SIC* 3479
CP TECH CORPORATION   *p*1328
2300 RUE COHEN, SAINT-LAURENT, QC, H4R 2N8
(514) 333-0030   *SIC* 3479
DAAM GALVANIZING CO. LTD   *p*109
9390 48 ST NW, EDMONTON, AB, T6B 2R3
(780) 468-6868   *SIC* 3479
DIVACCO LIMITED   *p*694
5191 CREEKBANK RD, MISSISSAUGA, ON, L4W 1R3
(905) 564-1711   *SIC* 3479
DJ GALVANIZING CORPORATION   *p*1024
300 SPRUCEWOOD AVE, WINDSOR, ON, N9C 0B7
(519) 250-2120   *SIC* 3479
DURABLE RELEASE COATERS LIMITED *p*502
4 FINLEY RD, BRAMPTON, ON, L6T 1A9
(905) 457-2000   *SIC* 3479
DURO-COTE COMPANY LIMITED   *p*502
29 MELANIE DR, BRAMPTON, ON, L6T 4K8
SIC 3479
EBCO METAL FINISHING LIMITED PARTNERSHIP   *p*254
15200 KNOX WAY, RICHMOND, BC, V6V 3A6
(604) 244-1500   *SIC* 3479
G3 GALVANIZING LIMITED   *p*446
160 JOSEPH ZATZMAN DR, DARTMOUTH, NS, B3B 1P1
(902) 468-1040   *SIC* 3479
GALVANISATION QUEBEC INC   *p*1254
225   RUE   JEREMIE-PACAUD, PRINCEVILLE, QC, G6L 0A1
(819) 505-4440   *SIC* 3479
GALVCAST MANUFACTURING INC   *p*473
49 COMMERCE CRES, ACTON, ON, L7J 2X2
(519) 853-3540   *SIC* 3479
HUDSON PLATING AND COATING CO. LTD *p*192
3750 NORTH FRASER WAY UNIT 102, BURNABY, BC, V5J 5E9
(604) 430-8384   *SIC* 3479
INTEGRATED PROTECTIVE COATINGS INC *p*162
500 STREAMBANK AVE, SHERWOOD PARK, AB, T8H 1N1
(780) 467-3299   *SIC* 3479
JEMS COATING LIMITED   *p*554
210 JACOB KEFFER PKY, CONCORD, ON, L4K 4W3
(905) 303-7433   *SIC* 3479
K.G. ENTERPRISES INC   *p*660
2126 JACK NASH DR, LONDON, ON, N6K 5R1
(519) 473-4111   *SIC* 3479
MDS COATING TECHNOLOGIES CORPORATION   *p*1042
60 AEROSPACE BLVD, SLEMON PARK, PE, C0B 2A0
(902) 888-3900   *SIC* 3479
METAL 7 INC   *p*1367
285 RUE DES PIONNIERS, SEPT-ILES, QC, G4R 4X9
(418) 968-5822   *SIC* 3479
METOKOTE CANADA LIMITED   *p*536
50 RAGLIN RD, CAMBRIDGE, ON, N1T 1Z5
(519) 621-2884   *SIC* 3479
METOPOXY INC   *p*1162
7335 BOUL HENRI-BOURASSA E, MONTREAL, QC, H1E 3T5
(514) 648-1042   *SIC* 3479
METROPOLITAN RUST PROOFING INC *p*1375
4232 BOUL BOURQUE, SHERBROOKE, QC, J1N 1W7
(819) 829-2888   *SIC* 3479
ONBELAY AUTOMOTIVE INC   *p*543
540 PARK AVE E, CHATHAM, ON, N7M 5J4
(519) 354-6515   *SIC* 3479
PMT INDUSTRIES LIMITED   *p*515

32 BODINE DR, BRANTFORD, ON, N3R 7M4
(519) 758-5505   *SIC* 3479
PMT INDUSTRIES LIMITED   *p*587
369 ATTWELL DR, ETOBICOKE, ON, M9W 5C2
(416) 675-3352   *SIC* 3479
POLYCOTE INC   *p*557
8120 KEELE ST, CONCORD, ON, L4K 2A3
(905) 660-7552   *SIC* 3479
POWDER TECH LIMITED   *p*488
699 BAYVIEW DR, BARRIE, ON, L4N 9A5
(705) 726-4580   *SIC* 3479
SAMUEL, SON & CO., LIMITED   *p*893
400 GLOVER RD, STONEY CREEK, ON, L8E 5X1
(905) 662-1404   *SIC* 3479
SHAWCOR LTD   *p*123
10275 21 ST NW, EDMONTON, AB, T6P 1P3
(780) 467-5501   *SIC* 3479
SIXPRO INC   *p*1063
1576 10E RANG DE SIMPSON, BON-CONSEIL, QC, J0C 1A0
(819) 336-2117   *SIC* 3479
TECHNOLOGIES SURFACE PRAXAIR MONTREAL S.E.C.   *p*1095
10300 AV RYAN, DORVAL, QC, H9P 2T7
(514) 631-2240   *SIC* 3479
ULTRASPEC FINISHING INC   *p*1337
2600 RUE DE MINIAC, SAINT-LAURENT, QC, H4S 1L7
(514) 337-1782   *SIC* 3479
VERSATILE SPRAY PAINTING LTD   *p*495
102 HEALEY RD, BOLTON, ON, L7E 5A7
(905) 857-4915   *SIC* 3479
Z.M.C. METAL COATING INC   *p*1034
40 GAUDAUR RD SUITE 3, WOOD-BRIDGE, ON, L4L 4S6
(905) 856-3838   *SIC* 3479

SIC 3483 Ammunition, except for small arms, nec

GENERAL DYNAMICS PRODUITS DE DEFENSE ET SYSTEMES TACTIQUES-CANADA INC   *p*1282
5 MONTEE DES ARSENAUX, RE-PENTIGNY, QC, J5Z 2P4
(450) 581-3080   *SIC* 3483

SIC 3484 Small arms

COLT CANADA CORPORATION   *p*636
1036 WILSON AVE, KITCHENER, ON, N2C 1J3
(519) 893-6840   *SIC* 3484
SAVAGE ARMS (CANADA) INC   *p*643
248 WATER ST, LAKEFIELD, ON, K0L 2H0
(705) 652-8000   *SIC* 3484

SIC 3491 Industrial valves

AINSWORTH ENGINEERED CANADA LIMITED PARTNERSHIP   *p*327
1055 DUNSMUIR ST SUITE 3194, VAN-COUVER, BC, V7X 1L3
(604) 661-3200   *SIC* 3491
BROCK SOLUTIONS INC   *p*636
90 ARDELT AVE, KITCHENER, ON, N2C 2C9
(519) 571-1522   *SIC* 3491
COMPASS ENERGY SYSTEMS LTD   *p*159
285028 FRONTIER RD, ROCKY VIEW COUNTY, AB, T1X 0V9
(403) 262-2487   *SIC* 3491
CVS CONTROLS LTD   *p*113
3900 101 ST NW, EDMONTON, AB, T6E 0A5
(780) 437-3055   *SIC* 3491
HI-KALIBRE EQUIPMENT LIMITED   *p*109

7321 68 AVE NW, EDMONTON, AB, T6B 3T6
(780) 435-1111   *SIC* 3491
IMW INDUSTRIES LTD   *p*197
44688 SOUTH SUMAS RD UNIT 610, CHILLIWACK, BC, V2R 5M3
(604) 795-9491   *SIC* 3491
RODA DEACO VALVE INC   *p*121
3230 97 ST NW, EDMONTON, AB, T6N 1K4
(780) 465-4429   *SIC* 3491

SIC 3492 Fluid power valves and hose fittings

ATLAS HYDRAULICS INC   *p*515
369 ELGIN ST, BRANTFORD, ON, N3S 7P5
(519) 756-8210   *SIC* 3492
EMERSON ELECTRIC CANADA LIMITED *p*517
17 AIRPORT RD, BRANTFORD, ON, N3T 5M8
(519) 758-2700   *SIC* 3492
HEBDRAULIQUE INC   *p*1344
8410 RUE CHAMP D'EAU, SAINT-LEONARD, QC, H1P 1Y3
(514) 327-5966   *SIC* 3492
LYNCH FLUID CONTROLS INC   *p*724
1799 ARGENTIA RD, MISSISSAUGA, ON, L5N 3A2
(905) 363-2400   *SIC* 3492
MARINE CANADA ACQUISITION LIMITED PARTNERSHIP   *p*255
3831 NO. 6 RD, RICHMOND, BC, V6V 1P6
(604) 270-6899   *SIC* 3492
MSSC CANADA INC   *p*543
201 PARK AVE E, CHATHAM, ON, N7M 3V7
(905) 878-2395   *SIC* 3492
NORWESCO INDUSTRIES (1983) LTD   *p*36
6908 6 ST SE BAY SUITE L, CALGARY, AB, T2H 2K4
(403) 258-3883   *SIC* 3492
PETERSON SPRING OF CANADA LIMITED *p*634
208 WIGLE AVE, KINGSVILLE, ON, N9Y 2J9
(519) 733-2358   *SIC* 3492

SIC 3493 Steel springs, except wire

HENDRICKSON CANADA ULC   *p*896
532 ROMEO ST S, STRATFORD, ON, N5A 4V4
(519) 271-4840   *SIC* 3493
HS SPRING OF CANADA INC   *p*585
25 WORCESTER RD, ETOBICOKE, ON, M9W 1K9
(416) 675-9072   *SIC* 3493
IMT STANDEN'S LIMITED PARTNERSHIP *p*35
1222 58 AVE SE, CALGARY, AB, T2H 2E9
(403) 258-7800   *SIC* 3493
MSSC CANADA INC   *p*543
105 ST GEORGE ST, CHATHAM, ON, N7M 4P3
(519) 354-1100   *SIC* 3493

SIC 3494 Valves and pipe fittings, nec

AECOM PRODUCTION SERVICES LTD   *p*13
9727 40 ST SE, CALGARY, AB, T2C 2P4
(403) 236-5611   *SIC* 3494
ARGUS MACHINE CO. LTD   *p*112
5820 97 ST NW, EDMONTON, AB, T6E 3J1
(780) 434-9451   *SIC* 3494
CURTISS-WRIGHT FLOW CONTROL COMPANY CANADA   *p*517
15 SHAVER RD, BRANTFORD, ON, N3T 5M1
(519) 756-4800   *SIC* 3494
DAHL VALVE LIMITED   *p*713
2600 SOUTH SHERIDAN WAY, MISSIS-

SAUGA, ON, L5J 2M4
(905) 822-2330   *SIC* 3494
HOERBIGER (CANADA) LTD   *p*706
330 BRUNEL RD, MISSISSAUGA, ON, L4Z 2C2
(905) 568-3013   *SIC* 3494
IPEX INC   *p*713
2441 ROYAL WINDSOR DR, MISSIS-SAUGA, ON, L5J 4C7
(905) 403-8133   *SIC* 3494
IPEX INC   *p*1396
3 PLACE DU COMMERCE BUREAU 101, VERDUN, QC, H3E 1H7
(514) 769-2200   *SIC* 3494
MANLUK INDUSTRIES (2008) INC   *p*172
4815 42 AVE, WETASKIWIN, AB, T9A 2P6
(780) 352-5522   *SIC* 3494
MASTER FLO VALVE INC.   *p*110
4611 74 AVE NW, EDMONTON, AB, T6B 2H5
(780) 468-4433   *SIC* 3494
SOCIETE HOLDING VELAN LTEE   *p*1341
7007 CH DE LA COTE-DE-LIESSE, SAINT-LAURENT, QC, H4T 1G2
(514) 748-7743   *SIC* 3494
SOUTHAMPTON INDUSTRIAL MANUFACTURING INC   *p*18
5605 48 ST SE, CALGARY, AB, T2C 4X8
(403) 930-9299   *SIC* 3494
SURE FLOW EQUIPMENT INC   *p*525
5010 NORTH SERVICE RD, BURLINGTON, ON, L7L 5R5
(905) 335-1350   *SIC* 3494
UNIVERSE MACHINE CORPORATION *p*117
5545 91 ST NW, EDMONTON, AB, T6E 6K4
(780) 468-5211   *SIC* 3494
VELAN INC   *p*1111
1010 RUE COWIE, GRANBY, QC, J2J 1E7
(450) 378-2305   *SIC* 3494
VELAN INC   *p*1324
2125 RUE WARD, SAINT-LAURENT, QC, H4M 1T6
(514) 748-7743   *SIC* 3494
VELAN INC   *p*1342
550 RUE MCARTHUR, SAINT-LAURENT, QC, H4T 1X8
(514) 748-7743   *SIC* 3494
VELAN INC   *p*1342
7007 CH DE LA COTE-DE-LIESSE, SAINT-LAURENT, QC, H4T 1G2
(514) 748-7743   *SIC* 3494
VICTAULIC COMPANY OF CANADA ULC *p*856
123 NEWKIRK RD, RICHMOND HILL, ON, L4C 3G5
(905) 884-7444   *SIC* 3494

SIC 3495 Wire springs

COMMERCIAL SPRING AND TOOL COMPANY LIMITED   *p*705
160 WATLINE AVE, MISSISSAUGA, ON, L4Z 1R1
(905) 568-3899   *SIC* 3495
NORSWAY INVESTMENTS & CONSULTANTS INC   *p*324
8563 SELKIRK ST, VANCOUVER, BC, V6P 4J1
(604) 267-1307   *SIC* 3495
RESSORTS LIBERTE INC   *p*1160
173 RUE DES INDUSTRIES, MONT-MAGNY, QC, G5V 4G2
(418) 248-8871   *SIC* 3495

SIC 3496 Miscellaneous fabricated wire products

AG GROWTH INTERNATIONAL INC   *p*388
198 COMMERCE DR, WINNIPEG, MB, R3P 0Z6
(204) 489-1855   *SIC* 3496
ALLIANCE HANGER INC   *p*1328

2500 RUE GUENETTE, SAINT-LAURENT, QC, H4R 2H2

(514) 339-9600   *SIC 3496*

DECA CABLES INC   *p998*
150 NORTH MURRAY ST, TRENTON, ON, K8V 6R8

(613) 392-3585   *SIC 3496*

ENTREPRISES BARRETTE LTEE, LES   *p1317*
583 CH DU GRAND-BERNIER N, SAINT-JEAN-SUR-RICHELIEU, QC, J3B 8K1

(450) 357-7000   *SIC 3496*

FEDERAL SCREEN PRODUCTS INC   *p685*
7524 BATH RD, MISSISSAUGA, ON, L4T 1L2

(905) 677-4171   *SIC 3496*

FILOCHROME INC   *p1114*
1355 RUE LEPINE, JOLIETTE, QC, J6E 4B7

(450) 759-1826   *SIC 3496*

INDUSTRIES DE CABLES D'ACIER LTEE   *p1251*
5501 RTE TRANSCANADIENNE, POINTE-CLAIRE, QC, H9R 1B7

(800) 565-5501   *SIC 3496*

NATIONAL-STANDARD COMPANY OF CANADA, LTD   *p604*
20 CAMPBELL RD, GUELPH, ON, N1H 1C1
SIC 3496

NORTH WEST RUBBER LTD   *p175*
33850 INDUSTRIAL AVE, ABBOTSFORD, BC, V2S 7T9

(604) 859-2002   *SIC 3496*

NUMESH INC   *p1362*
3000 AV FRANCIS-HUGHES, SAINTE-ROSE, QC, H7L 3J5

(450) 663-8700   *SIC 3496*

PRICE INDUSTRIES LIMITED   *p367*
638 RALEIGH ST, WINNIPEG, MB, R2K 3Z9

(204) 669-4220   *SIC 3496*

PROMAT INC   *p1035*
594711 COUNTY RD 59 S, WOODSTOCK, ON, N4S 7V8

(519) 456-2284   *SIC 3496*

SCP 89 INC   *p1133*
3641 RUE DES FORGES, LATERRIERE, QC, G7N 1N4

(418) 678-1506   *SIC 3496*

SIVACO WIRE GROUP 2004 L.P.   *p622*
330 THOMAS ST, INGERSOLL, ON, N5C 3K5

(800) 265-0418   *SIC 3496*

SIVACO WIRE GROUP 2004 L.P.   *p1149*
800 RUE OUELLETTE, MARIEVILLE, QC, J3M 1P5

(450) 658-8741   *SIC 3496*

TREE ISLAND INDUSTRIES LTD   *p257*
3933 BOUNDARY RD, RICHMOND, BC, V6V 1T8

(604) 524-3744   *SIC 3496*

TREE ISLAND STEEL LTD   *p257*
3933 BOUNDARY RD, RICHMOND, BC, V6V 1T8

(604) 524-3744   *SIC 3496*

W. S. TYLER CANADA LTD   *p886*
225 ONTARIO ST, ST CATHARINES, ON, L2R 7J2

(905) 688-2644   *SIC 3496*

WIRCO PRODUCTS LIMITED   *p658*
1011 ADELAIDE ST S, LONDON, ON, N6E 1R4

(519) 681-2100   *SIC 3496*

X-ACT TECHNOLOGIES LTD   *p13*
4447 46 AVE SE SUITE 151, CALGARY, AB, T2B 3N6

(403) 291-9175   *SIC 3496*

SIC 3497 Metal foil and leaf

COMPAGNIE DIVERSIFIEE DE L'EST LTEE   *p1249*
131 BOUL HYMUS, POINTE-CLAIRE, QC, H9R 1E7

(514) 694-5353   *SIC 3497*

EMBALLAGES WINPAK HEAT SEAL INC, LES   *p1394*
21919 CH DUMBERRY, VAUDREUIL-DORION, QC, J7V 8P7

(450) 424-0191   *SIC 3497*

SIC 3498 Fabricated pipe and fittings

ACADEMY CONSTRUCTION & MAINTE-NANCE LIMITED PARTNERSHIP   *p108*
4066 78 AVE NW, EDMONTON, AB, T6B 3M8

(780) 395-4914   *SIC 3498*

ACADEMY CONSTRUCTION & MAINTE-NANCE LTD   *p108*
4066 78 AVE NW, EDMONTON, AB, T6B 3M8

(780) 466-6360   *SIC 3498*

ACADEMY FABRICATORS LIMITED PART-NERSHIP   *p151*
5208 LAC STE ANNE TR N, ONOWAY, AB, T0E 1V0

(780) 967-3111   *SIC 3498*

AGGRESSIVE TUBE BENDING INC   *p281*
9750 188 ST, SURREY, BC, V4N 3M2

(604) 882-4872   *SIC 3498*

ARMTEC INC   *p99*
10423 178 ST NW UNIT 201, EDMONTON, AB, T5S 1R5

(780) 487-3404   *SIC 3498*

CINTUBE LTEE   *p1074*
1577 RUE WATTS, CHAMBLY, QC, J3L 2Z3

(450) 658-5140   *SIC 3498*

CINTUBE LTEE   *p1126*
333 BOUL SAINT-JOSEPH BUREAU 105, LACHINE, QC, H8S 2K9

(514) 634-3592   *SIC 3498*

DOUGLAS BARWICK INC   *p1061*
599 BOUL DU CURE-BOIVIN, BOIS-BRIAND, QC, J7G 2A8

(450) 435-3643   *SIC 3498*

EPFC CORP   *p64*
999 8 ST SW SUITE 555, CALGARY, AB, T2R 1J5

(403) 541-9400   *SIC 3498*

EZEFLOW INC   *p1110*
985 RUE ANDRE-LINE, GRANBY, QC, J2J 1J6

(450) 375-3575   *SIC 3498*

FISCHER CANADA STAINLESS STEEL TUBING INC   *p1010*
190 FROBISHER DR SUITE 2, WATER-LOO, ON, N2V 2A2

(519) 746-0088   *SIC 3498*

GESTION SOLENO INC   *p1316*
1160 RTE 133, SAINT-JEAN-SUR-RICHELIEU, QC, J2X 4J5

(450) 347-7855   *SIC 3498*

IDEAL PIPE   *p903*
1100 IDEAL DR, THORNDALE, ON, N0M 2P0

(519) 473-2669   *SIC 3498*

IDEAL WELDERS LTD   *p206*
660 CALDEW ST, DELTA, BC, V3M 5S2

(604) 525-5558   *SIC 3498*

INFRA PIPE SOLUTIONS LTD   *p723*
6507 MISSISSAUGA RD UNIT A, MISSIS-SAUGA, ON, L5N 1A6

(905) 858-0206   *SIC 3498*

INFRA PIPE SOLUTIONS LTD   *p1425*
348 EDSON ST, SASKATOON, SK, S7J 0P9

(306) 242-0755   *SIC 3498*

JETCO MANUFACTURING LIMITED   *p793*
36 MILVAN DR, NORTH YORK, ON, M9L 1Z4

(416) 741-1800   *SIC 3498*

NARDEI FABRICATORS LTD   *p17*
8915 44 ST SE, CALGARY, AB, T2C 2P5

(403) 279-3301   *SIC 3498*

QUALIFAB INC   *p1139*
2256 AV DE LA ROTONDE, LEVIS, QC, G6X 2L8

(418) 832-9193   *SIC 3498*

ROBERT MITCHELL INC   *p1323*
350 BOUL DECARIE, SAINT-LAURENT, QC, H4L 3K5

(514) 747-2471   *SIC 3498*

ST. CLAIR MECHANICAL INC   *p518*
2963 BRIGDEN RD SUITE 1, BRIGDEN, ON, N0N 1B0

(519) 864-0927   *SIC 3498*

SUPERHEAT FGH TECHNOLOGIES INC   *p629*
1463 HIGHWAY 21, KINCARDINE, ON, N2Z 2X3

(519) 396-1324   *SIC 3498*

ULTRA-FIT MANUFACTURING INCORPO-RATED   *p743*
1840 COURTNEYPARK DR E, MISSIS-SAUGA, ON, L5T 1W1

(905) 795-0344   *SIC 3498*

UPONOR INFRA LTD   *p1425*
348 EDSON ST, SASKATOON, SK, S7J 0P9

(306) 242-0755   *SIC 3498*

SIC 3499 Fabricated Metal products, nec

A7 INTEGRATION INC   *p1110*
884 RUE COWIE, GRANBY, QC, J2J 1A8

(450) 305-6218   *SIC 3499*

ABS MACHINING   *p702*
1495 SEDLESCOMB DR, MISSISSAUGA, ON, L4X 1M4

(905) 625-5941   *SIC 3499*

ACIERS RICHELIEU INC, LES   *p1376*
190 RUE DU ROI, SOREL-TRACY, QC, J3P 4N5

(450) 743-1265   *SIC 3499*

ADVANCED DESIGN SOLUTIONS INC   *p895*
533 ROMEO ST S SUITE 1, STRATFORD, ON, N5A 4V3

(519) 271-7810   *SIC 3499*

AGORA MANUFACTURING INC   *p734*
7770 TRANMERE DR, MISSISSAUGA, ON, L5S 1L9

(905) 362-1700   *SIC 3499*

ALL-WELD COMPANY LIMITED   *p875*
49 PASSMORE AVE, SCARBOROUGH, ON, M1V 4T1

(416) 299-3311   *SIC 3499*

ALLIANCE FABRICATING LTD   *p858*
763 CHESTER ST, SARNIA, ON, N7S 5N2

(519) 336-4328   *SIC 3499*

AMICO CANADA INC   *p520*
1080 CORPORATE DR, BURLINGTON, ON, L7L 5R6

(905) 335-4474   *SIC 3499*

ATLANTIC INDUSTRIES LIMITED   *p412*
32 YORK ST, SACKVILLE, NB, E4L 4R4

(506) 364-4600   *SIC 3499*

AWC MANUFACTURING LP   *p605*
163 CURTIS DR, GUELPH, ON, N1K 1S9

(519) 822-0577   *SIC 3499*

BEDCO, DIVISION DE GERODON INC   *p1084*
2305 AV FRANCIS-HUGHES, COTE SAINT-LUC, QC, H7S 1N5

(514) 384-2820   *SIC 3499*

BELL-CAMP MANUFACTURING INC   *p621*
543925 CLARKE RD E, INGERSOLL, ON, N5C 3J8

(519) 485-3120   *SIC 3499*

BEN MACHINE PRODUCTS COMPANY IN-CORPORATED   *p1027*
8065 HUNTINGTON RD SUITE 1, WOOD-BRIDGE, ON, L4H 3T9

(905) 856-7707   *SIC 3499*

BEND ALL AUTOMOTIVE ULC   *p483*
575 WAYDOM DR, AYR, ON, N0B 1E0

(519) 623-2001   *SIC 3499*

BEND ALL AUTOMOTIVE ULC   *p535*
445 DOBBIE DR, CAMBRIDGE, ON, N1T 1S9

(519) 623-2001   *SIC 3499*

BERNARDO METAL PRODUCTS LIMITED   *p737*

170 CAPITAL CRT, MISSISSAUGA, ON, L5T 2R8

(905) 362-1252   *SIC 3499*

BMP METALS INC   *p501*
18 CHELSEA LANE, BRAMPTON, ON, L6T 3Y4

(905) 799-2002   *SIC 3499*

BOURQUE INDUSTRIAL LTD   *p416*
85 INDUSTRIAL DR, SAINT JOHN, NB, E2R 1A4

(506) 633-7740   *SIC 3499*

CAMALOR MFG. INC   *p519*
100 CENTRAL AVE W, BROCKVILLE, ON, K6V 4N8

(613) 342-2259   *SIC 3499*

CANADIAN BUSINESS MACHINES LIM-ITED   *p683*
8750 HOLGATE CRES, MILTON, ON, L9T 0K3

(905) 878-0648   *SIC 3499*

CAPPRODUCTS, LTD   *p544*
25 WINNIPEG RD RR 5, CLINTON, ON, N0M 1L0

(519) 482-5000   *SIC 3499*

CESSCO FABRICATION & ENGINEERING LIMITED   *p113*
7310 99 ST NW, EDMONTON, AB, T6E 3R8

(780) 433-9531   *SIC 3499*

CHRIMA IRON WORK LIMITED   *p895*
559 DOURO ST, STRATFORD, ON, N5A 0E3

(519) 271-5399   *SIC 3499*

CMP SOLUTIONS MECANIQUES AVANCEES LTEE   *p1075*
1241 RUE DES CASCADES, CHATEAU-GUAY, QC, J6J 4Z2

(450) 691-5510   *SIC 3499*

COLSON GROUP CANADA, INC   *p533*
1600 BISHOP ST N SUITE 300, CAM-BRIDGE, ON, N1R 7N6

(519) 623-9420   *SIC 3499*

CRANE, JOHN CANADA INC   *p891*
423 GREEN RD, STONEY CREEK, ON, L8E 3A1

(905) 662-6191   *SIC 3499*

CRYSTAL FOUNTAINS HOLDINGS INC   *p551*
60 SNOW BLVD SUITE 3, CONCORD, ON, L4K 4B3

(905) 660-6674   *SIC 3499*

DBG CANADA LIMITED   *p738*
110 AMBASSADOR DR, MISSISSAUGA, ON, L5T 2X8

(905) 362-2311   *SIC 3499*

DBG GROUP LTD   *p738*
110 AMBASSADOR DR, MISSISSAUGA, ON, L5T 2X8

(905) 670-1555   *SIC 3499*

DIETER'S METAL FABRICATING LIMITED   *p538*
275 INDUSTRIAL RD, CAMBRIDGE, ON, N3H 4R7

(519) 884-8555   *SIC 3499*

DINGWELL'S MACHINERY AND SUPPLY LIMITED   *p908*
963 ALLOY DR, THUNDER BAY, ON, P7B 5Z8

(807) 623-4477   *SIC 3499*

DOMINO MACHINE INC   *p114*
4040 98 ST NW, EDMONTON, AB, T6E 3L3

(780) 809-1787   *SIC 3499*

ELECTRONIC METALFORM INDUSTRIES LIMITED   *p669*
435 STEELCASE RD E, MARKHAM, ON, L3R 2M2

(905) 475-1217   *SIC 3499*

EM DYNAMICS INC   *p874*
160 COMMANDER BLVD, SCARBOR-OUGH, ON, M1S 3C8

(416) 293-8385   *SIC 3499*

ENDURON INC   *p385*
150 CREE CRES, WINNIPEG, MB, R3J 3W1

(204) 885-2580   *SIC 3499*

ESSEX WELD SOLUTIONS LTD   *p570*

340 ALLEN AVE, ESSEX, ON, N8M 3G6
(519) 776-9153   *SIC* 3499
EWS INC   *p570*
340 ALLEN AVE, ESSEX, ON, N8M 3G6
(519) 776-9153   *SIC* 3499
FEATHERLITE INDUSTRIES LIMITED *p480*
100 ENGELHARD DR, AURORA, ON, L4G
3V2
(905) 727-0031   *SIC* 3499
FRANKE KINDRED CANADA LIMITED *p681*
1000 KINDRED RD, MIDLAND, ON, L4R
4K9
(705) 526-5427   *SIC* 3499
G.W. ANGLIN MANUFACTURING INC *p902*
220 PATILLO RD SUITE 1, TECUMSEH,
ON, N8N 2L9
(519) 727-4398   *SIC* 3499
**GARDEL METAL PRODUCTS INCORPO-
RATED**   *p852*
140 WEST BEAVER CREEK RD UNIT 1,
RICHMOND HILL, ON, L4B 1C2
(905) 881-7992   *SIC* 3499
GARNEAU MANUFACTURING INC   *p147*
8806 98 ST, MORINVILLE, AB, T8R 1K7
(780) 939-2129   *SIC* 3499
GEMINI FABRICATION LTD   *p152*
4100 67 ST, PONOKA, AB, T4J 1J8
SIC 3499
GLUECKLER METAL INC   *p568*
13 WILLIAM ST, ELMVALE, ON, L0L 1P0
(705) 737-9486   *SIC* 3499
GROUPE DE SECURITE MGM INC *p1099*
975 RUE CORMIER, DRUMMONDVILLE,
QC, J2C 2N5
(819) 478-4558   *SIC* 3499
HANDY & HARMAN OF CANADA, LIMITED
p584
290 CARLINGVIEW DR, ETOBICOKE, ON,
M9W 5G1
(416) 675-1600   *SIC* 3499
HARRIS STEEL GROUP INC   *p892*
318 ARVIN AVE, STONEY CREEK, ON, L8E
2M2
(905) 662-0611   *SIC* 3499
HARRIS STEEL ULC   *p130*
11215 87 AVE, FORT SASKATCHEWAN,
AB, T8L 2S3
(780) 992-0777   *SIC* 3499
HAYTON GROUP INC   *p605*
163 CURTIS DR, GUELPH, ON, N1K 1S9
(519) 822-0577   *SIC* 3499
HI-TECH GEARS CANADA INC, THE *p603*
361 SPEEDVALE AVE W SUITE 29,
GUELPH, ON, N1H 1C7
(519) 836-3180   *SIC* 3499
HIGHLAND EQUIPMENT INC   *p574*
136 THE EAST MALL, ETOBICOKE, ON,
M8Z 5V5
(416) 236-9610   *SIC* 3499
HILLMAR INDUSTRIES LIMITED   *p209*
7371 VANTAGE WAY, DELTA, BC, V4G 1C9
(604) 946-7115   *SIC* 3499
IAFRATE MACHINE WORKS LIMITED *p907*
1150 BEAVERDAMS RD, THOROLD, ON,
L2V 4T3
(905) 227-6141   *SIC* 3499
INDUSTRIES CRESSWELL INC   *p1109*
424 RUE SAINT-VALLIER, GRANBY, QC,
J2G 7Y4
(450) 378-4611   *SIC* 3499
JEBCO INDUSTRIES INC   *p487*
111 ELLIS DR, BARRIE, ON, L4N 8Z3
(705) 797-8888   *SIC* 3499
KENROD STEEL FABRICATING LIMITED
p836
6 ADAMS ST SUITE A, PARIS, ON, N3L 3X4
(519) 865-7921   *SIC* 3499
KOCH STAINLESS PRODUCTS LTD *p371*
511 JARVIS AVE, WINNIPEG, MB, R2W
3A8
(204) 586-8364   *SIC* 3499
KUBES STEEL INC   *p892*
930 ARVIN AVE, STONEY CREEK, ON, L8E
5Y8

(905) 643-1229   *SIC* 3499
L & A METALWORKS INC   *p401*
1968 LINCOLN RD, FREDERICTON, NB,
E3B 8M7
(506) 458-1100   *SIC* 3499
LENWORTH METAL PRODUCTS LIMITED
p998
275 CARRIER DR, TORONTO, ON, M9W
5Y8
SIC 3499
LEON'S MFG. COMPANY INC   *p1438*
135 YORK RD E, YORKTON, SK, S3N 3Z4
(306) 786-2600   *SIC* 3499
LIFT RITE INC   *p732*
5975 FALBOURNE ST UNIT 3, MISSIS-
SAUGA, ON, L5R 3L8
(905) 456-2603   *SIC* 3499
LIMPACT INTERNATIONAL LIMITED *p545*
569 D'ARCY ST, COBOURG, ON, K9A 4B1
(905) 373-4100   *SIC* 3499
LOUISVILLE LADDER CORP   *p481*
100 ENGELHARD DR, AURORA, ON, L4G
3V2
(905) 727-0031   *SIC* 3499
MACDONALD STEEL LIMITED   *p534*
200 AVENUE RD, CAMBRIDGE, ON, N1R
8H5
(519) 620-0400   *SIC* 3499
MACKOW INDUSTRIES   *p381*
1395 WHYTE AVE, WINNIPEG, MB, R3E
1V7
(204) 774-8323   *SIC* 3499
MANCOR CANADA INC   *p804*
2485 SPEERS RD, OAKVILLE, ON, L6L 2X9
(905) 827-3737   *SIC* 3499
MARTINREA AUTOMOTIVE INC   *p1002*
3210 LANGSTAFF RD, VAUGHAN, ON, L4K
5B2
(289) 982-3000   *SIC* 3499
MARTINREA INTERNATIONAL INC *p1002*
3210 LANGSTAFF RD, VAUGHAN, ON, L4K
5B2
(416) 749-0314   *SIC* 3499
MARTINREA INTERNATIONAL INC *p1032*
30 AVIVA PARK DR, WOODBRIDGE, ON,
L4L 9C7
(905) 264-0149   *SIC* 3499
MELITRON CORPORATION   *p604*
404 SILVERCREEK PKWY N, GUELPH,
ON, N1H 1E8
(519) 763-6660   *SIC* 3499
METAL SIGMA INC   *p1316*
750 RUE LUCIEN-BEAUDIN, SAINT-JEAN-
SUR-RICHELIEU, QC, J2X 5M3
(450) 348-7333   *SIC* 3499
METAL U.P. INC   *p1380*
3745 RUE PASCAL-GAGNON, TERRE-
BONNE, QC, J6X 4J3
(450) 477-1122   *SIC* 3499
METATUBE (1993) INC   *p1121*
2713 AV DU PORT, LA BAIE, QC, G7B 4S8
(418) 544-3303   *SIC* 3499
MIDWEST FABRICATORS LTD   *p101*
18073 107 AVE NW SUITE 235, EDMON-
TON, AB, T5S 1K3
(780) 447-0747   *SIC* 3499
NELSON INDUSTRIAL INC   *p845*
1155 SQUIRES BEACH RD, PICKERING,
ON, L1W 3T9
(905) 428-2240   *SIC* 3499
NEO PERFORMANCE MATERIALS INC
p955
121 KING ST W SUITE 1740, TORONTO,
ON, M5H 3T9
(416) 367-8588   *SIC* 3499
NMT MACHINING GROUP INC   *p637*
290 SHOEMAKER ST, KITCHENER, ON,
N2E 3E1
(519) 748-5459   *SIC* 3499
NORANCO INC   *p1032*
710 ROWNTREE DAIRY RD, WOOD-
BRIDGE, ON, L4L 5T7
(905) 264-2050   *SIC* 3499
NORTHWESTERN SYSTEMS CORPORA-

TION   *p209*
7601 MACDONALD RD, DELTA, BC, V4G
1N3
(604) 952-0925   *SIC* 3499
NORWEST PRECISION LIMITED   *p793*
460 SIGNET DR, NORTH YORK, ON, M9L
2T6
(416) 742-8082   *SIC* 3499
**OUTILLAGE DE PRECISION DRUMMOND
INC**   *p1097*
5250 RUE SAINT-ROCH S, DRUM-
MONDVILLE, QC, J2B 6V4
(819) 474-2622   *SIC* 3499
PATRIOT FORGE CO.   *p516*
280 HENRY ST, BRANTFORD, ON, N3S
7R5
(519) 758-8100   *SIC* 3499
PATRIOT FORGE OF PARIS INC   *p837*
100 CONSOLIDATED DR, PARIS, ON, N3L
3T6
(519) 720-1033   *SIC* 3499
PRECISION FAB INC   *p482*
259 ELM ST, AYLMER, ON, N5H 3H3
(519) 773-5244   *SIC* 3499
PRITCHARD METALFAB INC   *p389*
110 LOWSON CRES, WINNIPEG, MB, R3P
2H8
(204) 784-7600   *SIC* 3499
**PRODUITS DE FIL DE FER LAURENTIEN
LTEE**
10500 RUE SECANT, ANJOU, QC, H1J 1S3
(514) 351-8814   *SIC* 3499
PROTOCASE INCORPORATED   *p467*
46 WABANA CRT, SYDNEY, NS, B1P 0B9
(866) 849-3911   *SIC* 3499
QUADRANT INDUSTRIES INC   *p557*
1800 STEELES AVE W, CONCORD, ON,
L4K 2P3
(905) 761-9110   *SIC* 3499
ROBADAIR LTD   *p816*
2400 LANCASTER RD, OTTAWA, ON, K1B
3W9
(613) 731-6019   *SIC* 3499
ROUSSEAU METAL INC   *p1315*
105 AV DE GASPE O, SAINT-JEAN-PORT-
JOLI, QC, G0R 3G0
(418) 598-3381   *SIC* 3499
ROYAL LASER MFG INC   *p587*
25 CLAIREVILLE DR, ETOBICOKE, ON,
M9W 5Z7
(416) 679-9474   *SIC* 3499
SECURIFORT INC   *p1384*
45 RUE CAYOUETTE, TINGWICK, QC, J0A
1L0
(819) 359-2226   *SIC* 3499
SENTRY PRECISION SHEET METAL LTD
p751
20 ENTERPRISE AVE, NEPEAN, ON, K2G
0A6
(613) 224-4341   *SIC* 3499
SHANAHAN'S LIMITED PARTNERSHIP *p18*
2731 57 AVE SE SUITE 1, CALGARY, AB,
T2C 0B2
(403) 279-2890   *SIC* 3499
SOBOTEC LTD   *p608*
67 BURFORD RD, HAMILTON, ON, L8E
3C6
(905) 578-1278   *SIC* 3499
SOUCY RIVALAIR INC   *p1099*
650   RUE   ROCHELEAU,   DRUM-
MONDVILLE, QC, J2C 7R8
(819) 474-2908   *SIC* 3499
SOUTHWESTERN MANUFACTURING INC
p1025
3710 PETER ST, WINDSOR, ON, N9C 1J9
(519) 985-6161   *SIC* 3499
SPG INTERNATIONAL LTEE   *p1097*
4275   BOUL   SAINT-JOSEPH,   DRUM-
MONDVILLE, QC, J2B 1T8
(819) 477-1596   *SIC* 3499
SPINNAKER INDUSTRIES INC   *p756*
1171 GORHAM ST, NEWMARKET, ON, L3Y
8Y2
(416) 742-0598   *SIC* 3499

SUREWAY METAL SYSTEMS LIMITED *p159*
285120 DUFF DR, ROCKY VIEW COUNTY,
AB, T1X 0K1
(403) 287-2742   *SIC* 3499
SURROUND TECHNOLOGIES INC   *p230*
27222 LOUGHEED HWY, MAPLE RIDGE,
BC, V2W 1M4
(604) 462-8223   *SIC* 3499
TERMEL INDUSTRIES LTD   *p239*
1667 RAILWAY ST, NORTH VANCOUVER,
BC, V7J 1B5
(604) 984-9652   *SIC* 3499
TRI-METAL FABRICATORS   *p280*
19150 21 AVE, SURREY, BC, V3Z 3M3
(604) 531-5518   *SIC* 3499
**WAIWARD INDUSTRIAL LIMITED PART-
NERSHIP**   *p111*
10030 34 ST NW, EDMONTON, AB, T6B
2Y5
(780) 469-1258   *SIC* 3499
WALTER'S GROUP INC   *p615*
1318 RYMAL RD E, HAMILTON, ON, L8W
3N1
(905) 388-7111   *SIC* 3499
WALTER'S INC   *p615*
1318 RYMAL RD E, HAMILTON, ON, L8W
3N1
(905) 388-7111   *SIC* 3499
WILSON, DAVID W. MANUFACTURING LTD
p541
193 HWY 53, CATHCART, ON, N0E 1B0
(519) 458-8911   *SIC* 3499
YARMOUTH GROUP INC, THE   *p890*
9462 TOWER RD, ST THOMAS, ON, N5P
3S7
(519) 631-2663   *SIC* 3499

---

*SIC 3511 Turbines and turbine generator
sets*

ALSTOM CANADA INC   *p1193*
1010 RUE SHERBROOKE O BUREAU
2320, MONTREAL, QC, H3A 2R7
(514) 281-6200   *SIC* 3511
**GE   ENERGIES   RENOUVELABLES
CANADA INC**   *p1071*
5005 BOUL LAPINIERE BUREAU 6000,
BROSSARD, QC, J4Z 0N5
(450) 746-6500   *SIC* 3511
LIBURDI ENGINEERING LIMITED   *p566*
400 6 HWY, DUNDAS, ON, L9H 7K4
(905) 689-0734   *SIC* 3511
**SIEMENS GAMESA RENEWABLE ENERGY
LIMITED**   *p799*
1577 NORTH SERVICE RD E 4TH FL,
OAKVILLE, ON, L6H 0H6
(905) 465-8000   *SIC* 3511

SIC 3519 Internal combustion engines, nec

A.P.M. DIESEL (1992) INC.   *p1088*
135 RUE MINER, COWANSVILLE, QC, J2K
3Y5
(450) 260-1999   *SIC* 3519
**FORD MOTOR COMPANY OF CANADA,
LIMITED**   *p1023*
1000 HENRY FORD CENTRE DR, WIND-
SOR, ON, N9A 7E8
(519) 257-2020   *SIC* 3519
MRC GLOBAL (CANADA) LTD   *p54*
255 5 AVE SW SUITE 910, CALGARY, AB,
T2P 3G6
(403) 233-7166   *SIC* 3519
PRATT & WHITNEY CANADA CIE   *p141*
4045 26 AVE N, LETHBRIDGE, AB, T1H
6G2
(403) 380-5100   *SIC* 3519
PRATT & WHITNEY CANADA CIE   *p742*
1801 COURTNEYPARK DR E, MISSIS-
SAUGA, ON, L5T 1J3
(905) 564-7500   *SIC* 3519
PRATT & WHITNEY CANADA CIE   *p1142*

1000 BOUL MARIE-VICTORIN, LONGUEUIL, QC, J4G 1A1
(450) 677-9411   SIC 3519

PRATT & WHITNEY CANADA CIE   p1153
11155 RUE JULIEN-AUDETTE, MIRABEL, QC, J7N 0G6
(450) 476-0049   SIC 3519

WESTPORT FUEL SYSTEMS INC   p324
1750 75TH AVE W SUITE 101, VANCOUVER, BC, V6P 6G2
(604) 718-2000   SIC 3519

WESTPORT LIGHT DUTY INC   p324
1750 75TH AVE W SUITE 101, VANCOUVER, BC, V6P 6G2
(604) 718-2000   SIC 3519

SIC 3523 Farm machinery and equipment

1708828 ONTARIO LIMITED   p646
8082 ROAD 129, LISTOWEL, ON, N4W 3G8
(519) 291-4162   SIC 3523

1742009 ALBERTA INC   p167
28007 HIGHWAY 16, STONY PLAIN, AB, T7Z 1S5
(780) 963-2251   SIC 3523

AG GROWTH INTERNATIONAL INC   p150
215 BARONS ST, NOBLEFORD, AB, T0L 1S0
(403) 320-5585   SIC 3523

ALLIANCE AGRI-TURF INC   p494
8112 KING ST, BOLTON, ON, L7E 0T8
(905) 857-2000   SIC 3523

BATCO-REM   p1436
201 INDUSTRIAL DR, SWIFT CURRENT, SK, S9H 5R4
SIC 3523

BERCOMAC LIMITEE   p1044
92 RUE FORTIN N, ADSTOCK, QC, G0N 1S0
(418) 422-2252   SIC 3523

BOURGAULT INDUSTRIES LTD   p1436
500 HWY UNIT 368 N, ST BRIEUX, SK, S0K 3V0
(306) 275-2300   SIC 3523

BRANDT INDUSTRIES CANADA LTD p1417
13 AVE & PINKIE RD, REGINA, SK, S4P 3A1
(306) 791-7777   SIC 3523

BUHLER EZEE-ON, INC   p170
5110 62 ST, VEGREVILLE, AB, T9C 1N6
(780) 632-2126   SIC 3523

BUHLER INDUSTRIES INC   p352
301 MOUNTAIN ST S, MORDEN, MB, R6M 1X7
(204) 822-4467   SIC 3523

BUHLER INDUSTRIES INC   p390
1260 CLARENCE AVE SUITE 112, WINNIPEG, MB, R3T 1T2
(204) 661-8711   SIC 3523

BUHLER INDUSTRIES INC   p390
1260 CLARENCE AVE, WINNIPEG, MB, R3T 1T2
(204) 661-8711   SIC 3523

BUHLER VERSATILE INC   p390
1260 CLARENCE AVE, WINNIPEG, MB, R3T 1T2
(204) 284-6100   SIC 3523

BUNGE DU CANADA LTEE   p1258
300 RUE DALHOUSIE, QUEBEC, QC, G1K 8M8
(418) 692-3761   SIC 3523

CANCADE COMPANY LIMITED   p346
1651 12TH ST, BRANDON, MB, R7A 7L1
(204) 728-4450   SIC 3523

CNH INDUSTRIAL CANADA, LTD   p1434
1000 71ST ST E, SASKATOON, SK, S7P 0B5
(306) 934-3500   SIC 3523

CONVEY-ALL INDUSTRIES INC   p361
130 CANADA ST, WINKLER, MB, R6W 0J3
(204) 325-4195   SIC 3523

CS WIND CANADA INC   p1017
9355 ANCHOR DR, WINDSOR, ON, N8N

5A8
(519) 735-0973   SIC 3523

DEGELMAN INDUSTRIES LTD   p1417
272 INDUSTRIAL DR, REGINA, SK, S4P 3B1
(306) 543-4447   SIC 3523

DIEMO MACHINE WORKS INC   p345
HWY 326 N, ARBORG, MB, R0C 0A0
(204) 364-2404   SIC 3523

DMI CANADA INC   p890
2677 WINGER RD, STEVENSVILLE, ON, L0S 1S0
(905) 382-5793   SIC 3523

DUTCH INDUSTRIES LTD   p1413
500 PORTICO DRIVE, PILOT BUTTE, SK, S0G 3Z0
(306) 781-4820   SIC 3523

EQUIPEMENTS DE FERME JAMESWAY INC   p1377
12 RTE 249, ST-FRANCOIS-XAVIER-DE-BROMPTON, QC, J0B 2V0
(819) 845-7824   SIC 3523

F.P. BOURGAULT TILLAGE TOOLS LTD   p1436
200 5 AVE S, ST BRIEUX, SK, S0K 3V0
(306) 275-4500   SIC 3523

GEA FARM TECHNOLOGIES CANADA INC   p1096
4591 BOUL SAINT-JOSEPH, DRUMMONDVILLE, QC, J2A 0C6
(819) 477-7444   SIC 3523

GURIT OUTILLAGE (AMERICAS) INC p1339
7562 CH DE LA COTE-DE-LIESSE, SAINT-LAURENT, QC, H4T 1E7
(514) 522-6329   SIC 3523

HARMON INTERNATIONAL INDUSTRIES INC   p1427
2401 MILLAR AVE, SASKATOON, SK, S7K 2Y4
(306) 931-1161   SIC 3523

HI-TEC INDUSTRIES INC   p355
1000 6TH AVE NE, PORTAGE LA PRAIRIE, MB, R1N 0B4
(204) 239-4270   SIC 3523

HIGHLINE MANUFACTURING LTD   p1437
HWY 27, VONDA, SK, S0K 4N0
(306) 258-2233   SIC 3523

HONEY BEE MANUFACTURING LTD p1407
GD, FRONTIER, SK, S0N 0W0
(306) 296-2297   SIC 3523

HUNCO HOLDINGS LTD   p172
6010 47 ST, WETASKIWIN, AB, T9A 2R3
(780) 352-6061   SIC 3523

INDUSTRIES ET EQUIPEMENTS LALIBERTE LTEE, LES   p1356
550 RTE BEGIN, SAINTE-CLAIRE, QC, G0R 2V0
(418) 883-3338   SIC 3523

J. BOND & SONS LTD   p233
31413 GILL AVE UNIT 103, MISSION, BC, V4S 0C4
(604) 826-5391   SIC 3523

JAMESWAY INCUBATOR COMPANY INC   p533
30 HIGH RIDGE CRT, CAMBRIDGE, ON, N1R 7L3
(519) 624-4646   SIC 3523

JOHN BUHLER INC   p391
1260 CLARENCE AVE, WINNIPEG, MB, R3T 1T2
(204) 661-8711   SIC 3523

JOHN DEERE CANADA ULC   p599
295 HUNTER RD, GRIMSBY, ON, L3M 4H5
(905) 945-9281   SIC 3523

KESMAC INC   p628
23324 WOODBINE AVE, KESWICK, ON, L4P 3E9
(888) 341-5113   SIC 3523

LAURIN CONTENEURS INC   p1363
487 RUE PRINCIPALE, SAINTE-ROSE, QC, H7X 1C4
(450) 689-1962   SIC 3523

LINKLETTER'S WELDING LTD   p1042
26 AV LINKLETTER SUITE 3, SUMMER-

SIDE, PE, C1N 4J9
(902) 887-2652   SIC 3523

MACDON INDUSTRIES LTD   p386
680 MORAY ST, WINNIPEG, MB, R3J 3S3
(204) 885-5590   SIC 3523

MICHEL'S INDUSTRIES LTD   p1436
3 ENTRANCE RD, ST GREGOR, SK, S0K 3X0
(306) 366-2184   SIC 3523

MORRIS INDUSTRIES LTD   p352
284 6TH AVE NW, MINNEDOSA, MB, R0J 1E0
(204) 867-2713   SIC 3523

MORRIS INDUSTRIES LTD   p1423
85 YORK RD W, ROKEBY, SK, S0A 3N0
(306) 783-8585   SIC 3523

MORRIS INDUSTRIES LTD   p1431
2131 AIRPORT DR, SASKATOON, SK, S7L 7E1
(306) 933-8585   SIC 3523

NATT TOOLS GROUP INC   p611
460 SHERMAN AVE N, HAMILTON, ON, L8L 8J6
(905) 549-7433   SIC 3523

PALES D'EOLIENNE LM (CANADA) INC p1102
7 RUE DES CERISIERS, GASPE, QC, G4X 2M1
(418) 361-3486   SIC 3523

RALPH MCKAY INDUSTRIES INC   p1416
130 HODSMAN RD, REGINA, SK, S4N 5X4
(306) 721-9292   SIC 3523

RED MOUNTAIN HOLDINGS LTD   p1418
2800 PASQUA ST N, REGINA, SK, S4P 3E1
(306) 545-4044   SIC 3523

SNOWBEAR LIMITED   p604
155 DAWSON RD, GUELPH, ON, N1H 1A4
SIC 3523

TARKETT SPORTS CANADA INC   p1341
7445 CH DE LA COTE-DE-LIESSE BUREAU 200, SAINT-LAURENT, QC, H4T 1G2
(514) 340-9311   SIC 3523

TUBE-LINE MANUFACTURING LTD   p568
6455 REID WOODS DR SUITE 4, ELMIRA, ON, N3B 2Z3
(519) 669-9488   SIC 3523

TURF CARE PRODUCTS CANADA LIMITED p757
200 PONY DR, NEWMARKET, ON, L3Y 7B6
(905) 836-0988   SIC 3523

VADERSTAD INDUSTRIES INC   p1409
HWY 9, LANGBANK, SK, S0G 2X0
(306) 538-2221   SIC 3523

VALMETAL INC   p1306
230 BOUL INDUSTRIEL, SAINT-GERMAIN-DE-GRANTHAM, QC, J0C 1K0
(819) 395-4282   SIC 3523

WESTFIELD INDUSTRIES LTD   p355
74 HWY 200, E, ROSENORT, MB, R0G 1W0
(204) 746-2396   SIC 3523

WHEATHEART MANUFACTURING LTD p1432
3455 IDYLWYLD DR N, SASKATOON, SK, S7L 6B5
(306) 934-0611   SIC 3523

SIC 3524 Lawn and garden equipment

COMPAGNIE NORMAND LTEE, LA   p1349
340 RUE TACHE, SAINT-PASCAL, QC, G0L 3Y0
(418) 492-2712   SIC 3524

RAD TECHNOLOGIES INC   p1383
2835 CH DE L'AEROPORT BUREAU 3, THETFORD MINES, QC, G6G 5R7
(418) 338-4499   SIC 3524

SPECTRUM BRANDS CANADA, INC   p745
255 LONGSIDE DR UNIT 101, MISSISSAUGA, ON, L5W 0G7
(800) 566-7899   SIC 3524

SIC 3531 Construction machinery

BLACK CAT WEAR PARTS LTD   p108
5720 59 ST NW, EDMONTON, AB, T6B 3L4
(780) 465-6666   SIC 3531

BLACK CAT WEAR PARTS LTD   p108
5604 59 ST NW, EDMONTON, AB, T6B 3C3
(780) 465-6666   SIC 3531

BLACK CAT WEAR PARTS LTD   p356
71 RAILWAY ST, SELKIRK, MB, R1A 4L4
(204) 482-9046   SIC 3531

COH PROJETS ET SERVICES INC   p1060
801 BOUL DU CURE-BOIVIN, BOISBRIAND, QC, J7G 2J2
(450) 430-6500   SIC 3531

CRH CANADA GROUP INC   p551
2300 STEELES AVE W SUITE 400, CONCORD, ON, L4K 5X6
(905) 532-3000   SIC 3531

CRS CRANESYSTEMS INC   p162
333 STRATHMOOR WAY, SHERWOOD PARK, AB, T8H 2K2
(780) 416-8800   SIC 3531

CWS INDUSTRIES (MFG) CORP   p281
19490 92 AVE, SURREY, BC, V4N 4G7
(604) 888-9008   SIC 3531

CWS VENTURES INC   p281
19490 92 AVE, SURREY, BC, V4N 4G7
(604) 888-9008   SIC 3531

FOREMOST INDUSTRIES LP   p23
1225 64 AVE NE, CALGARY, AB, T2E 8P9
(403) 295-5800   SIC 3531

GROUPE CANAM INC   p1065
270 CH DU TREMBLAY, BOUCHERVILLE, QC, J4B 5X9
(418) 251-3152   SIC 3531

GROUPE ENVIRONNEMENTAL LABRIE INC   p1140
175 RTE MARIE-VICTORIN BUREAU B, LEVIS, QC, G7A 2T3
(418) 831-8250   SIC 3531

GROUPE R.Y. BEAUDOIN INC   p1399
1400 BOUL PIERRE-ROUX E, VICTORIAVILLE, QC, G6T 2T7
(819) 604-1396   SIC 3531

JEAMAR WINCHES CORPORATION p1036
125 BYSHAM PARK DR, WOODSTOCK, ON, N4T 1R2
(519) 537-8855   SIC 3531

LINAMAR CORPORATION   p478
GD, ARISS, ON, N0B 1B0
(519) 822-4080   SIC 3531

LONDON MACHINERY INC   p649
15790 ROBIN'S HILL RD, LONDON, ON, N5V 0A4
(519) 963-2500   SIC 3531

LOVSUNS TUNNELING CANADA LIMITED p998
441 CARLINGVIEW DR, TORONTO, ON, M9W 5G7
(647) 255-0018   SIC 3531

MCCLOSKEY INTERNATIONAL LIMITED p627
1 MCCLOSKEY RD, KEENE, ON, K9J 0G6
(705) 295-4925   SIC 3531

PROALL INTERNATIONAL MFG. INC   p151
5810 47 AVE, OLDS, AB, T4H 1V1
(403) 335-9500   SIC 3531

REEL COH INC   p1061
801 BOUL DU CURE-BOIVIN, BOISBRIAND, QC, J7G 2J2
(450) 430-6500   SIC 3531

RISLEY MANUFACTURING LTD   p133
9024 108 ST, GRANDE PRAIRIE, AB, T8V 4C8
(780) 532-3282   SIC 3531

ROBERTS WELDING & FABRICATING LTD p1035
873 DEVONSHIRE AVE, WOODSTOCK, ON, N4S 8Z4
(519) 421-0036   SIC 3531

ROTOBEC INC   p1359
200 RUE INDUSTRIELLE BUREAU 383, SAINTE-JUSTINE, QC, G0R 1Y0
(418) 383-3002   SIC 3531

▲ Public Company   ■ Public Company Family Member   **HQ** Headquarters   **BR** Branch   **SL** Single Location

SAF-T-CAB, INC   p621
7 CANADA AVE, HURON PARK, ON, N0M
1Y0
(519) 228-6538   *SIC* 3531

SKYJACK INC   p604
55 CAMPBELL RD SUITE 1, GUELPH, ON,
N1H 1B9
(519) 837-0888   *SIC* 3531

SKYJACK INC   p604
55 CAMPBELL RD, GUELPH, ON, N1H 1B9
(519) 837-0888   *SIC* 3531

TC INDUSTRIES OF CANADA COMPANY
p604
249 SPEEDVALE AVE W, GUELPH, ON,
N1H 1C5
(519) 836-7100   *SIC* 3531

TIGERCAT INDUSTRIES INC   p515
54 MORTON AVE E, BRANTFORD, ON,
N3R 7J7
(519) 753-2000   *SIC* 3531

TIGERCAT INDUSTRIES INC   p515
54 MORTON AVE E, BRANTFORD, ON,
N3R 7J7
(519) 753-2000   *SIC* 3531

TIGERCAT INDUSTRIES INC   p515
54 MORTON AVE E, BRANTFORD, ON,
N3R 7J7
(519) 753-2000   *SIC* 3531

TIGERCAT INDUSTRIES INC   p1035
1403 DUNDAS ST, WOODSTOCK, ON, N4S
7V9
(519) 537-3000   *SIC* 3531

TIMBERLAND EQUIPMENT LIMITED p1036
459 INDUSTRIAL AVE, WOODSTOCK, ON,
N4S 7L1
(519) 537-6262   *SIC* 3531

TLD (CANADA) INC   p1372
800 RUE CABANA, SHERBROOKE, QC,
J1K 3C3
(819) 566-8118   *SIC* 3531

TORNADO GLOBAL HYDROVACS LTD p38
7015 MACLEOD TRAIL SW SUITE 510,
CALGARY, AB, T2H 2K6
(403) 204-6363   *SIC* 3531

TWG CANADA CONSOLIDATED INC p280
19350 22 AVE, SURREY, BC, V3Z 3S6
(604) 547-2100   *SIC* 3531

VALLEY BLADES LIMITED   p1009
435 PHILLIP ST, WATERLOO, ON, N2L 3X2
(519) 885-5500   *SIC* 3531

WELDCO-BEALES MFG. ALBERTA LTD
p106
12155 154 ST NW, EDMONTON, AB, T5V
1J3
(780) 454-5244   *SIC* 3531

WELDCO-BEALES MFG. ALBERTA LTD
p228
5770 PRODUCTION WAY, LANGLEY, BC,
V3A 4N4
(604) 533-8933   *SIC* 3531

WELDCO-BEALES MFG. ONTARIO LTD
p488
515 WELHAM RD SUITE 1, BARRIE, ON,
L4N 8Z6
(705) 733-2668   *SIC* 3531

SIC 3532 Mining machinery

BREAKER TECHNOLOGY LTD   p903
35 ELGIN ST, THORNBURY, ON, N0H 2P0
(519) 599-2015   *SIC* 3532

CANROS GRP INC   p856
30 VIA RENZO DR SUITE 255, RICHMOND
HILL, ON, L4S 0B8
(905) 918-0640   *SIC* 3532

DSI UNDERGROUND CANADA LTD   p898
15 TOULOUSE CRES, STURGEON FALLS,
ON, P2B 0A5
(705) 753-4872   *SIC* 3532

DSI UNDERGROUND CANADA LTD   p1434
3919 MILLAR AVE, SASKATOON, SK, S7P
0C1
(306) 244-6244   *SIC* 3532

DYNAINDUSTRIAL INC   p1427
3326 FAITHFULL AVE, SASKATOON, SK,
S7K 8H1
(306) 933-4303   *SIC* 3532

FLSMIDTH LTD   p809
174 WEST ST S, ORILLIA, ON, L3V 6L4
(705) 325-6181   *SIC* 3532

HAYDEN DIAMOND BIT INDUSTRIES LTD
p263
12020 NO. 5 RD, RICHMOND, BC, V7A 4G1
(604) 341-6941   *SIC* 3532

HITACHI CONSTRUCTION TRUCK MANU-
FACTURING LTD   p603
200 WOODLAWN RD W, GUELPH, ON,
N1H 1B6
(519) 823-2000   *SIC* 3532

INDUSTRIAL FABRICATION INC   p647
240 FIELDING RD, LIVELY, ON, P3Y 1L6
(705) 523-1621   *SIC* 3532

JOY GLOBAL (CANADA) LTD   p9
90-2150 29 ST NE, CALGARY, AB, T1Y 7G4
(403) 730-9851   *SIC* 3532

JOY GLOBAL (CANADA) LTD   p269
749 DOUGLAS FIR RD SUITE 618, SPAR-
WOOD, BC, V0B 2G0
(250) 433-4100   *SIC* 3532

LONGYEAR CANADA, ULC   p713
2442 SOUTH SHERIDAN WAY, MISSIS-
SAUGA, ON, L5J 2M7
(905) 822-7922   *SIC* 3532

MACLEAN ENGINEERING & MARKETING
CO. LIMITED   p835
1000 6TH ST E, OWEN SOUND, ON, N4K
1H1
(705) 445-5707   *SIC* 3532

MANLUK INDUSTRIES INC   p172
4815 42 AVE, WETASKIWIN, AB, T9A 2P6
(780) 352-5522   *SIC* 3532

NORDIC MINESTEEL TECHNOLOGIES INC
p763
373 MAIN ST W UNIT 1, NORTH BAY, ON,
P1B 2T9
(705) 474-2777   *SIC* 3532

NORSTAR INDUSTRIES LTD   p352
27157 HWY 422, MORRIS, MB, R0G 1K0
(204) 746-8200   *SIC* 3532

NUTANA MACHINE LTD   p1428
2615 1ST AVE N, SASKATOON, SK, S7K
6E9
(306) 242-3822   *SIC* 3532

PRAIRIE MACHINE & PARTS MFG. - PART-
NERSHIP   p1429
3311 MILLAR AVE, SASKATOON, SK, S7K
5Y5
(306) 933-4812   *SIC* 3532

RCR INDUSTRIAL INC   p647
145 MAGILL ST, LIVELY, ON, P3Y 1K6
(705) 692-3661   *SIC* 3532

RDH MINING EQUIPMENT LTD   p475
904 HWY 64, ALBAN, ON, P0M 1A0
(705) 857-2154   *SIC* 3532

SANDVIK CANADA, INC   p524
4445 FAIRVIEW ST, BURLINGTON, ON,
L7L 2A4
    SIC 3532

SEPRO MINERAL SYSTEMS CORP   p225
9850 201 ST UNIT 101A, LANGLEY, BC,
V1M 4A3
(604) 888-5568   *SIC* 3532

SOURCE ENERGY SERVICES LTD   p32
438 11 AVE SE SUITE 500, CALGARY, AB,
T2G 0Y4
(403) 262-1312   *SIC* 3532

SIC 3533 Oil and gas field machinery

1089243 ALBERTA LTD   p131
9625 144 AVE, GRANDE PRAIRIE, AB, T8V
7V4
(780) 830-0955   *SIC* 3533

ALCO GAS & OIL PRODUCTION EQUIP-
MENT LTD   p112
5203 75 ST NW, EDMONTON, AB, T6E 5S5

---

(780) 465-9061   *SIC* 3533

APOLLO MACHINE & WELDING LTD p112
4141 93 ST NW, EDMONTON, AB, T6E 5Y3
(780) 463-3600   *SIC* 3533

BAKER HUGHES INC   p44
401 9 AVE SW SUITE 1000, CALGARY, AB,
T2P 3C5
(403) 537-3400   *SIC* 3533

BILTON WELDING AND MANUFACTURING
LTD   p136
5815 37 ST, INNISFAIL, AB, T4G 1S8
(403) 227-7799   *SIC* 3533

BVL CONSTRUCTION SERVICES INC p171
GD, WABASCA, AB, T0G 2K0
    SIC 3533

DNOW CANADA ULC   p10
1616 MERIDIAN RD NE, CALGARY, AB,
T2A 2P1
(403) 569-2222   *SIC* 3533

DNOW CANADA ULC   p109
7127 56 AVE NW, EDMONTON, AB, T6B
3L2
(780) 465-0999   *SIC* 3533

DNOW CANADA ULC   p114
6415 75 ST NW, EDMONTON, AB, T6E 0T3
    SIC 3533

DNOW CANADA ULC   p114
3550 93 ST NW, EDMONTON, AB, T6E 5N3
(780) 465-9500   *SIC* 3533

DRECO ENERGY SERVICES ULC   p15
6771 84 ST SE, CALGARY, AB, T2C 4T6
(403) 319-2333   *SIC* 3533

DRECO ENERGY SERVICES ULC   p148
1704 5 ST, NISKU, AB, T9E 8P8
(780) 944-3800   *SIC* 3533

DRECO ENERGY SERVICES ULC   p148
506 17 AVE, NISKU, AB, T9E 7T1
(780) 955-5451   *SIC* 3533

DRECO INTERNATIONAL HOLDINGS ULC
p114
6415 75 ST NW, EDMONTON, AB, T6E 0T3
(780) 944-3800   *SIC* 3533

EMERSON ELECTRIC CANADA LIMITED
p114
4112 91A ST NW, EDMONTON, AB, T6E
5V2
(780) 450-3600   *SIC* 3533

GN CORPORATIONS INC   p3
2873 KINGSVIEW BLVD SE, AIRDRIE, AB,
T4A 0E1
(403) 948-6464   *SIC* 3533

GRENCO INDUSTRIES INC   p109
3710 78 AVE NW, EDMONTON, AB, T6B
3E5
(780) 468-2000   *SIC* 3533

ISOLATION EQUIPMENT SERVICES INC
p132
12925 97B ST, GRANDE PRAIRIE, AB, T8V
6K1
(780) 402-3060   *SIC* 3533

LEE SPECIALTIES INC   p5
27312-68 TWP RD 394, BLACKFALDS, AB,
T0M 0J0
(403) 346-4487   *SIC* 3533

MAR-QUINN INDUSTRIES LTD   p139
7115 SPARROW DR, LEDUC, AB, T9E 7L1
(780) 986-7805   *SIC* 3533

MAXFIELD INC   p81
1026 WESTERN DR, CROSSFIELD, AB,
T0M 0S0
(403) 946-5678   *SIC* 3533

MCCOY GLOBAL INC   p156
7911 EDGAR INDUSTRIAL DR, RED
DEER, AB, T4P 3R2
(780) 453-3277   *SIC* 3533

MCPIKE INVESTMENTS LTD   p3
440 EAST LAKE RD NE, AIRDRIE, AB, T4A
2J8
(403) 912-7200   *SIC* 3533

NOV ENERFLOW ULC   p12
4800 27 ST SE, CALGARY, AB, T2B 3M4
(403) 279-9696   *SIC* 3533

NOV ENERFLOW ULC   p17
8625 68 ST SE, CALGARY, AB, T2C 2R6

---

(403) 695-3189   *SIC* 3533

OIL LIFT TECHNOLOGY INC   p24
950 64 AVE NE, CALGARY, AB, T2E 8S8
(403) 291-5300   *SIC* 3533

PETROFIELD INDUSTRIES INC   p167
4102 44TH AVE, STETTLER, AB, T0C 2L0
(403) 883-2400   *SIC* 3533

PLAINSMAN MFG. INC   p116
8305 MCINTYRE RD NW, EDMONTON, AB,
T6E 5J7
(780) 496-9800   *SIC* 3533

PROPAK SYSTEMS LTD   p3
440 EAST LAKE RD NE, AIRDRIE, AB, T4A
2J8
(403) 912-7000   *SIC* 3533

QUINN'S PRODUCTION SERVICES INC
p154
6798 52 AVE, RED DEER, AB, T4N 4K9
(780) 499-0299   *SIC* 3533

RED DEER IRONWORKS INC   p156
6430 GOLDEN WEST AVE, RED DEER,
AB, T4P 1A6
(403) 343-1141   *SIC* 3533

RIG SHOP LIMITED, THE   p123
1704 66 AVE NW, EDMONTON, AB, T6P
1M4
(780) 440-4202   *SIC* 3533

SCHLUMBERGER CANADA LIMITED p116
5003 93 ST NW, EDMONTON, AB, T6E 5S9
(780) 434-3476   *SIC* 3533

SCHLUMBERGER CANADA LIMITED p126
9803 12 AVE SW, EDMONTON, AB, T6X
0E3
    SIC 3533

SERVA GROUP (CANADA) ULC   p18
7345 110 AVE SE, CALGARY, AB, T2C 3B8
(403) 269-7847   *SIC* 3533

SHAWCOR LTD   p588
25 BETHRIDGE RD, ETOBICOKE, ON,
M9W 1M7
(416) 743-7111   *SIC* 3533

STEWART & STEVENSON CANADA INC
p18
3111 SHEPARD PL SE SUITE 403, CAL-
GARY, AB, T2C 4P1
(403) 215-5300   *SIC* 3533

STIMLINE SERVICES INC   p18
7475 51 ST SE, CALGARY, AB, T2C 4L6
(403) 720-0874   *SIC* 3533

STREAM-FLO INDUSTRIES LTD   p111
4505 74 AVE NW, EDMONTON, AB, T6B
2H5
(780) 468-6789   *SIC* 3533

TERRAVEST INDUSTRIES LIMITED PART-
NERSHIP   p170
4901 BRUCE RD, VEGREVILLE, AB, T9C
1C3
(780) 632-2040   *SIC* 3533

TORNADO COMBUSTION TECHNOLOGIES
INC   p160
261200 WAGON WHEEL WAY SUITE 200,
ROCKY VIEW COUNTY, AB, T4A 0E3
(403) 244-3333   *SIC* 3533

TRYTON TOOL SERVICES LTD   p144
6702 56 ST, LLOYDMINSTER, AB, T9V 3T7
(780) 875-0800   *SIC* 3533

VOLANT PRODUCTS INC   p111
4110 56 AVE NW, EDMONTON, AB, T6B
3R8
(780) 490-5185   *SIC* 3533

WARRIOR RIG TECHNOLOGIES LIMITED
p12
1515 28 ST NE, CALGARY, AB, T2A 3T1
(403) 291-6444   *SIC* 3533

WATERFLOOD SERVICE & SALES LTD
p1407
130 PERKINS ST, ESTEVAN, SK, S4A 2K1
(306) 634-7212   *SIC* 3533

WEATHERFORD CANADA LTD   p6
4816 56 AVE, BONNYVILLE, AB, T9N 2N8
(780) 826-7878   *SIC* 3533

WEATHERFORD CANADA LTD   p80
8001 102 ST, CLAIRMONT, AB, T8X 5A7
(780) 539-6400   *SIC* 3533

WEATHERFORD CANADA LTD   p123
1917A 84 AVE NW, EDMONTON, AB, T6P 1K1
(780) 449-3266   *SIC 3533*

WEATHERFORD CANADA LTD   p123
2004 64 AVE NW, EDMONTON, AB, T6P 1Z3
(780) 465-9311   *SIC 3533*

WEATHERFORD CANADA LTD   p133
9601 156 AVE, GRANDE PRAIRIE, AB, T8V 2P3
(780) 567-6250   *SIC 3533*

WEATHERFORD CANADA LTD   p144
4604 62 AVE, LLOYDMINSTER, AB, T9V 2G2
(780) 875-6123   *SIC 3533*

WEATHERFORD CANADA LTD   p150
2603 5 ST, NISKU, AB, T9E 0C2
(780) 979-4500   *SIC 3533*

WELLMASTER PIPE AND SUPPLY INC p912
1494 BELL MILL SIDEROAD, TILLSONBURG, ON, N4G 5Y1
(519) 688-0500   *SIC 3533*

WENZEL DOWNHOLE TOOLS LTD   p38
5920 MACLEOD TRAIL SW SUITE 504, CALGARY, AB, T2H 0K2
(403) 205-6696   *SIC 3533*

WENZEL DOWNHOLE TOOLS LTD   p121
3115 93 ST NW, EDMONTON, AB, T6N 1L7
(780) 440-4220   *SIC 3533*

SIC 3534 Elevators and moving stairways

CNIM CANADA INC   p1210
1499 RUE WILLIAM, MONTREAL, QC, H3C 1R4
(514) 932-1220   *SIC 3534*

EHC CANADA, INC   p813
1287 BOUNDARY RD, OSHAWA, ON, L1J 6Z7
(905) 432-3200   *SIC 3534*

GROUPE TARDIF GLF INC, LE   p1293
120 RUE DE NAPLES, SAINT-AUGUSTIN-DE-DESMAURES, QC, G3A 2Y2
(418) 878-4116   *SIC 3534*

MAD ELEVATOR INC   p740
6635 ORDAN DR, MISSISSAUGA, ON, L5T 1K6
(416) 245-8500   *SIC 3534*

OTIS CANADA, INC   p287
2788 RUPERT ST, VANCOUVER, BC, V5M 3T7
(604) 412-3400   *SIC 3534*

SAVARIA CONCORD LIFTS INC   p506
2 WALKER DR, BRAMPTON, ON, L6T 5E1
(905) 791-5555   *SIC 3534*

SCHINDLER ELEVATOR CORPORATION p1158
8577 CH DALTON, MONT-ROYAL, QC, H4T 1V5
(514) 737-5507   *SIC 3534*

THYSSENKRUPP NORTHERN ELEVATOR CORPORATION   p877
410 PASSMORE AVE UNIT 1, SCARBOROUGH, ON, M1V 5C3
(416) 291-2000   *SIC 3534*

SIC 3535 Conveyors and conveying equipment

BRANDT AGRICULTURAL PRODUCTS p1417
302 MILL ST, REGINA, SK, S4P 3E1
(306) 791-7557   *SIC 3535*

COMPAGNIE DE DYNAMIQUE AVANCEE LTEE, LA   p1295
1700 RUE MARIE-VICTORIN, SAINT-BRUNO, QC, J3V 6B9
(450) 653-7220   *SIC 3535*

DELTA WIRE & MFG   p618
29 DELTA DR, HARROW, ON, N0R 1G0
(519) 738-3514   *SIC 3535*

INDUSTRIAL EQUIPMENT MANUFACTURING LTD   p282
19433 96 AVE UNIT 109, SURREY, BC, V4N 4C4
(604) 513-9930   *SIC 3535*

INTERROLL CANADA LIMITED   p755
1201 GORHAM ST, NEWMARKET, ON, L3Y 8Y2
(905) 953-8510   *SIC 3535*

LAMBTON CONVEYOR LIMITED   p1004
102 ARNOLD ST, WALLACEBURG, ON, N8A 3P4
(519) 627-8228   *SIC 3535*

LAW-MAROT-MILPRO INC   p1314
1150 RUE BROUILLETTE, SAINT-HYACINTHE, QC, J2T 2G8
(450) 771-6262   *SIC 3535*

LUFF INDUSTRIES LTD   p159
235010 WRANGLER RD, ROCKY VIEW COUNTY, AB, T1X 0K3
(403) 279-3555   *SIC 3535*

PRECISION INDUSTRIAL LTD   p1414
1020 1ST AVE NW, PRINCE ALBERT, SK, S6V 6J9
SIC 3535

RULMECA CANADA LIMITED   p1005
75 MASON ST, WALLACEBURG, ON, N8A 4L7
(519) 627-2277   *SIC 3535*

S. HUOT INC   p1265
1000 RUE RAOUL-JOBIN, QUEBEC, QC, G1N 4N3
(418) 681-0291   *SIC 3535*

SHAW ALMEX INDUSTRIES LIMITED p837
17 SHAW ALMEX DR, PARRY SOUND, ON, P2A 2X4
(705) 746-5884   *SIC 3535*

SHAW-ALMEX INDUSTRIES LIMITED p893
323 GLOVER RD, STONEY CREEK, ON, L8E 5M2
(905) 643-7750   *SIC 3535*

SIDEL CANADA INC   p1238
1045 CHOMEDEY (A-13) E, MONTREAL, QC, H7W 4V3
(450) 973-3337   *SIC 3535*

WEBB, JERVIS B. COMPANY OF CANADA, LTD   p610
1647 BURLINGTON ST E, HAMILTON, ON, L8H 3L2
(905) 547-0411   *SIC 3535*

SIC 3536 Hoists, cranes, and monorails

O'BRIEN LIFTING SOLUTIONS INC   p523
4435 CORPORATE DR, BURLINGTON, ON, L7L 5T9
(905) 336-8245   *SIC 3536*

SLING-CHOKER MFG. (HAMILTON) LTD p610
605 RENNIE ST, HAMILTON, ON, L8H 3P8
(905) 545-5025   *SIC 3536*

SNAP-ON TOOLS OF CANADA LTD   p727
6500A MILLCREEK DR, MISSISSAUGA, ON, L5N 2W6
(905) 826-8600   *SIC 3536*

SIC 3537 Industrial trucks and tractors

CASCADE (CANADA) LTD   p692
5570 TIMBERLEA BLVD, MISSISSAUGA, ON, L4W 4M6
(905) 629-7777   *SIC 3537*

CASCADE (CANADA) LTD   p849
4 NICHOLAS BEAVER RD, PUSLINCH, ON, N0B 2J0
(519) 763-3675   *SIC 3537*

EXPRESS CUSTOM TRAILERS MFG. INC p243
1365 ALBERNI HWY, PARKSVILLE, BC, V9P 2B9
SIC 3537

G.N. JOHNSTON EQUIPMENT CO. LTD.

p670
181 WHITEHALL DR SUITE 2, MARKHAM, ON, L3R 9T1
(416) 798-7195   *SIC 3537*

LIFTKING MANUFACTURING CORP p1032
7135 ISLINGTON AVE, WOODBRIDGE, ON, L4L 1V9
(905) 851-3988   *SIC 3537*

MAMMOET CRANE (ASSETS) INC   p604
7504 MCLEAN RD E, GUELPH, ON, N1H 6H9
(519) 740-0550   *SIC 3537*

PENTALIFT EQUIPMENT CORPORATION p849
21 NICHOLAS BEAVER RD, PUSLINCH, ON, N0B 2J0
(519) 763-3625   *SIC 3537*

SELLICK EQUIPMENT LIMITED   p618
2131 ROSEBOROUGH RD, HARROW, ON, N0R 1G0
(519) 738-2255   *SIC 3537*

TRAILTECH INC   p1407
GD, GRAVELBOURG, SK, S0H 1X0
(306) 648-3158   *SIC 3537*

WILLOW CREEK COLONY FARMS LTD p348
GD, CARTWRIGHT, MB, R0K 0L0
(204) 529-2178   *SIC 3537*

SIC 3541 Machine tools, Metal cutting type

ADVANTAGE MACHINE & TOOL INC p745
155 HURON RD SS 1, MITCHELL, ON, N0K 1N0
(519) 348-4414   *SIC 3541*

ALCO INC   p118
6925 104 ST NW, EDMONTON, AB, T6H 2L5
(780) 435-3502   *SIC 3541*

AXIOM GROUP INC   p480
115 MARY ST, AURORA, ON, L4G 1G3
(905) 727-2878   *SIC 3541*

BURLINGTON AUTOMATION CORPORATION   p566
63 INNOVATION DR, DUNDAS, ON, L9H 7L8
(905) 689-7771   *SIC 3541*

COLONIAL TOOL GROUP INC   p1019
1691 WALKER RD, WINDSOR, ON, N8W 3P1
(519) 253-2461   *SIC 3541*

ETBO TOOL & DIE   p482
7288 RICHMOND RD, AYLMER, ON, N5H 2R5
(519) 773-5117   *SIC 3541*

FBT INC   p885
413 LAKESHORE RD, ST CATHARINES, ON, L2R 7K6
(905) 937-3333   *SIC 3541*

FIVES LINE MACHINES INC   p1110
1000 RUE ANDRE-LINE, GRANBY, QC, J2J 1E2
(450) 372-6480   *SIC 3541*

J.M. DIE LIMITED   p696
909 PANTERA DR, MISSISSAUGA, ON, L4W 2R9
(905) 625-9571   *SIC 3541*

L.H.M. TECHNOLOGIES INC   p1032
446 ROWNTREE DAIRY RD, WOODBRIDGE, ON, L4L 8H2
(905) 856-2466   *SIC 3541*

QUADRO ENGINEERING CORP   p1011
613 COLBY DR, WATERLOO, ON, N2V 1A1
(226) 270-6017   *SIC 3541*

ROYCE-AYR CUTTING TOOLS INC   p536
405 SHELDON DR, CAMBRIDGE, ON, N1T 2B7
(519) 623-0580   *SIC 3541*

STRONGCO ENGINEERED SYSTEMS INC p700
1640 ENTERPRISE RD, MISSISSAUGA, ON, L4W 4L4
(905) 670-5100   *SIC 3541*

TRI-MACH GROUP INC   p568
23 DONWAY CRT, ELMIRA, ON, N3B 0B1
(519) 744-6565   *SIC 3541*

VALCO MANUFACTURING INC   p1022
1235 ST LUKE RD, WINDSOR, ON, N8Y 4W7
(519) 971-9666   *SIC 3541*

VALIANT MACHINE & TOOL INC   p1017
9355 ANCHOR DR, WINDSOR, ON, N8N 5A8
(519) 974-5200   *SIC 3541*

VIBRA FINISH LIMITED   p701
5329 MAINGATE DR, MISSISSAUGA, ON, L4W 1G6
(905) 625-9955   *SIC 3541*

WEBER MANUFACTURING TECHNOLOGIES INC   p682
16566 HWY 12, MIDLAND, ON, L4R 4L1
(705) 526-7896   *SIC 3541*

WOODBINE TOOL & DIE MANUFACTURING LTD   p677
190 ROYAL CREST CRT, MARKHAM, ON, L3R 9X6
(905) 475-5223   *SIC 3541*

SIC 3542 Machine tools, Metal forming type

1923921 ONTARIO INC   p547
200 SPINNAKER WAY, CONCORD, ON, L4K 5E5
(905) 738-3682   *SIC 3542*

ARCELORMITTAL TAILORED BLANKS AMERICAS LIMITED   p548
55 CONFEDERATION PKY, CONCORD, ON, L4K 4Y7
(905) 761-1525   *SIC 3542*

DIEFFENBACHER NORTH AMERICA INC p1017
9495 TWIN OAKS DR, WINDSOR, ON, N8N 5B8
(519) 979-6937   *SIC 3542*

F.& K. MFG., CO., LIMITED   p793
155 TURBINE DR, NORTH YORK, ON, M9L 2S7
(416) 749-3980   *SIC 3542*

SAMCO MACHINERY LIMITED   p914
351 PASSMORE AVE, TORONTO, ON, M1V 3N8
(416) 285-0619   *SIC 3542*

SATURN TOOL & DIE (WINDSOR) INC p807
5175 HENNIN DR, OLDCASTLE, ON, N0R 1L0
SIC 3542

SIC 3544 Special dies, tools, jigs, and fixtures

1589711 ONTARIO INC   p515
156 ADAMS BLVD, BRANTFORD, ON, N3S 7V5
(905) 643-9044   *SIC 3544*

1589711 ONTARIO INC   p891
566 ARVIN AVE UNIT 3, STONEY CREEK, ON, L8E 5P1
SIC 3544

9184-2518 QUEBEC INC   p1265
2511 BOUL DU PARC-TECHNOLOGIQUE, QUEBEC, QC, G1P 4S5
(418) 656-9917   *SIC 3544*

A V GAUGE & FIXTURE INC   p807
4000 DELDUCA DR, OLDCASTLE, ON, N0R 1L0
(519) 737-7677   *SIC 3544*

A.B.M. TOOL & DIE CO. LTD   p500
80 WALKER DR, BRAMPTON, ON, L6T 4H6
(905) 458-2203   *SIC 3544*

AALBERS TOOL & MOLD INC   p807
5390 BRENDAN LANE, OLDCASTLE, ON, N0R 1L0
(519) 737-1369   *SIC 3544*

AARKEL TOOL AND DIE INC   p1004
17 ELM DR S, WALLACEBURG, ON, N8A

5E8
(519) 627-6078   *SIC* 3544
AARKEL TOOL AND DIE INC   *p*1004
740 LOWE AVE, WALLACEBURG, ON, N8A
5H5
(519) 627-9601   *SIC* 3544
AARKEL TOOL AND DIE INC   *p*1004
760 LOWE AVE, WALLACEBURG, ON, N8A
5H5
(519) 627-9601   *SIC* 3544
ABSOLUTE TOOL TECHNOLOGIES INC
*p*1022
5455 OUTER DR, WINDSOR, ON, N9A 6J3
(519) 737-9428   *SIC* 3544
ACTIVE INDUSTRIAL SOLUTIONS INC
*p*1023
5250 PULLEYBLANK ST, WINDSOR, ON,
N9A 6J3
SIC 3544
ACTIVE INDUSTRIAL SOLUTIONS INC
*p*1023
2155 NORTH TALBOT RD SUITE 3, WIND-
SOR, ON, N9A 6J3
(519) 737-1341   *SIC* 3544
ALUMINUM MOLD & PATTERN LTD *p*782
15 VANLEY CRES, NORTH YORK, ON, M3J
2B7
(416) 749-3000   *SIC* 3544
ANCHOR DANLY INC   *p*1021
2590 OUELLETTE AVE, WINDSOR, ON,
N8X 1L7
(519) 966-4431   *SIC* 3544
ARMO-TOOL LIMITED   *p*662
9827 LONGWOODS RD, LONDON, ON,
N6P 1P2
(519) 652-3700   *SIC* 3544
BETA-TECH INC   *p*486
318 SAUNDERS RD, BARRIE, ON, L4N 9Y2
(705) 797-0119   *SIC* 3544
BRIADCO TOOL & MOULD INC   *p*807
5605 ROSCON INDUSTRIAL DR, OLD-
CASTLE, ON, N0R 1L0
(519) 737-1760   *SIC* 3544
CANA-DATUM MOULDS LTD   *p*573
55 GOLDTHORNE AVE, ETOBICOKE, ON,
M8Z 5S7
(416) 252-1212   *SIC* 3544
**CANADIAN ENGINEERING AND TOOL
COMPANY LIMITED, THE**   *p*1024
2265 SOUTH CAMERON BLVD, WINDSOR,
ON, N9B 3P6
(519) 969-1618   *SIC* 3544
CAVALIER TOOL & MANUFACTURING LTD
*p*1019
3450 WHEELTON DR, WINDSOR, ON,
N8W 5A7
(519) 944-2144   *SIC* 3544
COMPACT MOULD LIMITED   *p*1030
120 HAIST AVE, WOODBRIDGE, ON, L4L
5V4
(905) 851-7724   *SIC* 3544
COMPES INTERNATIONAL LIMITED *p*502
25 DEVON RD, BRAMPTON, ON, L6T 5B6
(905) 458-5994   *SIC* 3544
CONCORDE PRECISION MACHINING INC
*p*1017
469 SILVER CREEK INDUSTRIAL DR,
WINDSOR, ON, N8N 4W2
(519) 727-3287   *SIC* 3544
CONCOURS MOLD INC   *p*1017
465 JUTRAS DR S, WINDSOR, ON, N8N
5C4
(519) 727-9949   *SIC* 3544
DIE-MAX TOOL AND DIE LTD   *p*473
23 BARR RD, AJAX, ON, L1S 3Y1
(905) 619-6554   *SIC* 3544
DIETRON TOOL & DIE INC   *p*864
64 MELFORD DR, SCARBOROUGH, ON,
M1B 6B7
(416) 297-5858   *SIC* 3544
ELECTROMAC GROUP INC, THE   *p*1024
600 SPRUCEWOOD AVE, WINDSOR, ON,
N9C 0B2
(519) 969-4632   *SIC* 3544

ENTREPRISES DBM REFLEX INC, LES
*p*1362
1620 BOUL DAGENAIS O, SAINTE-ROSE,
QC, H7L 5C7
(450) 622-3100   *SIC* 3544
EXCO TECHNOLOGIES LIMITED   *p*670
130 SPY CRT UNIT 1, MARKHAM, ON, L3R
5H6
(905) 477-3065   *SIC* 3544
EXCO TECHNOLOGIES LIMITED   *p*755
1314 RINGWELL DR, NEWMARKET, ON,
L3Y 9C6
(905) 853-8568   *SIC* 3544
GARRTECH INC   *p*892
910 ARVIN AVE, STONEY CREEK, ON, L8E
5Y8
(905) 643-6414   *SIC* 3544
GLIDER GUARD TOOL & DIE INC   *p*807
5135 URE ST SUITE 1, OLDCASTLE, ON,
N0R 1L0
(519) 737-7313   *SIC* 3544
I. THIBAULT INC   *p*1299
26 RUE DE L'ENTREPRISE, SAINT-
DAMIEN-DE-BUCKLAND, QC, G0R 2Y0
(418) 789-2891   *SIC* 3544
J.F.K. SYSTEMS INC   *p*807
3160 MOYNAHAN ST, OLDCASTLE, ON,
N0R 1L0
(519) 737-1361   *SIC* 3544
KAPCO TOOL & DIE LIMITED   *p*1021
3200 DEVON DR, WINDSOR, ON, N8X 4L4
(519) 966-0320   *SIC* 3544
LAMKO TOOL & MOLD INCORPORATED
*p*657
105 TOWERLINE PL, LONDON, ON, N6E
2T3
(519) 686-2643   *SIC* 3544
LJ WELDING AUTOMATION LTD   *p*110
4747 76 AVE NW, EDMONTON, AB, T6B
0A3
(780) 466-6658   *SIC* 3544
MANOR TOOL AND DIE LTD   *p*807
5264 PULLEYBANK ST, OLDCASTLE, ON,
N0R 1L0
(519) 737-6537   *SIC* 3544
MOULES INDUSTRIELS (C.H.F.G.) INC
*p*1374
3100 BOUL INDUSTRIEL, SHERBROOKE,
QC, J1L 1V8
(819) 822-3697   *SIC* 3544
OMEGA TOOL CORP   *p*807
2045 SOLAR CRES, OLDCASTLE, ON,
N0R 1L0
(519) 737-1201   *SIC* 3544
PROG-DIE TOOL & STAMPING LTD   *p*712
3161 WOLFEDALE RD, MISSISSAUGA,
ON, L5C 1V8
(905) 277-4651   *SIC* 3544
RE-DOE MOLD COMPANY LIMITED   *p*1026
665 MORTON DR, WINDSOR, ON, N9J 3T9
(519) 734-6161   *SIC* 3544
REKO INTERNATIONAL GROUP INC *p*1017
469 SILVER CREEK INDUSTRIAL DR,
WINDSOR, ON, N8N 4W2
(519) 727-3287   *SIC* 3544
REKO MANUFACTURING GROUP INC
*p*1017
469 SILVER CREEK INDUSTRIAL DR,
WINDSOR, ON, N8N 4W2
(519) 727-3287   *SIC* 3544
REMATEK INC   *p*1335
8975 BOUL HENRI-BOURASSA O, SAINT-
LAURENT, QC, H4S 1P7
(514) 333-6414   *SIC* 3544
REVSTONE PLASTICS CANADA INC *p*807
2045 SOLAR CRES RR 1, OLDCASTLE,
ON, N0R 1L0
(519) 737-1201   *SIC* 3544
**RHO-CAN MACHINE & TOOL COMPANY
LTD**   *p*650
770 INDUSTRIAL RD, LONDON, ON, N5V
3N7
(519) 451-9100   *SIC* 3544
RUSSELL TOOL & DIE LIMITED   *p*543

381 PARK AVE W, CHATHAM, ON, N7M
1W6
(519) 352-8168   *SIC* 3544
SACOPAN INC   *p*1290
652 CH DU MOULIN, SACRE-COEUR-
SAGUENAY, QC, G0T 1Y0
(418) 236-1414   *SIC* 3544
SELECT TOOL INC   *p*807
3015 NORTH TALBOT RD, OLDCASTLE,
ON, N0R 1L0
(519) 737-6406   *SIC* 3544
SERVICE MOLD + AEROSPACE INC *p*1020
2711 ST ETIENNE BLVD, WINDSOR, ON,
N8W 5B1
(519) 945-3344   *SIC* 3544
STACKTECK SYSTEMS LIMITED   *p*506
1 PAGET RD, BRAMPTON, ON, L6T 5S2
(416) 749-0880   *SIC* 3544
STANDARD TOOL & MOLD INC   *p*1024
5110 HALFORD DR, WINDSOR, ON, N9A
6J3
(519) 737-1778   *SIC* 3544
STAR-TECH ENTERPRISES INC   *p*657
25 INVICTA CRT, LONDON, ON, N6E 2T4
(519) 681-8672   *SIC* 3544
THERMOPLAST INC   *p*1101
3035 BOUL LE CORBUSIER BUREAU 7,
FABREVILLE, QC, H7L 4C3
(450) 687-5115   *SIC* 3544
TIPCO INC   *p*507
1 COVENTRY RD, BRAMPTON, ON, L6T
4B1
(905) 791-9811   *SIC* 3544
TOP GRADE MOLDS LTD   *p*701
929 PANTERA DR, MISSISSAUGA, ON,
L4W 2R9
(905) 625-9865   *SIC* 3544
UNIQUE TOOL & GAUGE INC   *p*1024
1505 MORO DR, WINDSOR, ON, N9A 6J3
(519) 737-1159   *SIC* 3544
WINDSOR METAL TECHNOLOGIES INC
*p*807
3900 DELDUCA DR, OLDCASTLE, ON,
N0R 1L0
(519) 737-7611   *SIC* 3544
WINDSOR MOLD INC   *p*1020
1628 DURHAM PL, WINDSOR, ON, N8W
2Z8
(519) 258-7300   *SIC* 3544
WINDSOR MOLD INC   *p*1025
4035 MALDEN RD, WINDSOR, ON, N9C
2G4
(519) 972-9032   *SIC* 3544
WINDSOR MOLD INC   *p*1025
4035 MALDEN RD, WINDSOR, ON, N9C
2G4
(519) 972-9032   *SIC* 3544
ZF AUTOMOTIVE CANADA LIMITED *p*682
16643 HWY 12, MIDLAND, ON, L4R 4L5
(705) 526-8791   *SIC* 3544

SIC 3545 Machine tool accessories

ABS EQUIPMENT LEASING LTD   *p*702
1495 SEDLESCOMB DR, MISSISSAUGA,
ON, L4X 1M4
(905) 625-5941   *SIC* 3545
ABSOLUTE ENERGY SOLUTIONS INC*p*108
5710 36 ST NW, EDMONTON, AB, T6B 3T2
(780) 440-9058   *SIC* 3545
B.C. PRECISION INC   *p*879
41 PROCTOR RD, SCHOMBERG, ON, L0G
1T0
(905) 939-7323   *SIC* 3545
CAMECO FUEL MANUFACTURING INC
*p*544
2C ST NORTHAM INDUSTRIAL PK,
COBOURG, ON, K9A 4K5
(905) 372-0147   *SIC* 3545
CWS INDUSTRIES (MFG) CORP   *p*122
7622 18 ST NW, EDMONTON, AB, T6P 1Y6
(780) 469-9185   *SIC* 3545
DISHON LIMITED   *p*551

40 CITATION DR, CONCORD, ON, L4K 2W9
(416) 638-8900   *SIC* 3545
EXCO TECHNOLOGIES LIMITED   *p*1001
2 PARRATT RD, UXBRIDGE, ON, L9P 1R1
(905) 852-0121   *SIC* 3545
INTEGRITY HD INC   *p*1021
3126 DEVON DR, WINDSOR, ON, N8X 4L2
(519) 946-1400   *SIC* 3545
LIKRO PRECISION LIMITED   *p*717
3150 PEPPER MILL CRT, MISSISSAUGA,
ON, L5L 4X4
(905) 828-9191   *SIC* 3545
LMI TECHNOLOGIES INC   *p*193
9200 GLENLYON PKY UNIT 1, BURNABY,
BC, V5J 5J8
(604) 636-1011   *SIC* 3545
MARMEN INC   *p*1385
845 RUE BERLINGUET, TROIS-RIVIERES,
QC, G8T 8N9
(819) 379-0453   *SIC* 3545
MARMEN INC   *p*1385
557 RUE DES ERABLES, TROIS-
RIVIERES, QC, G8T 8Y8
(819) 379-0453   *SIC* 3545
MERIDIAN MANUFACTURING INC   *p*78
4232 38 ST, CAMROSE, AB, T4V 4B2
(780) 672-4516   *SIC* 3545
MERIDIAN MANUFACTURING INC   *p*141
3125 24 AVE N, LETHBRIDGE, AB, T1H
5G2
(403) 320-7070   *SIC* 3545
MERIDIAN MANUFACTURING INC   *p*1418
2800 PASQUA ST, REGINA, SK, S4P 2Z4
(306) 545-4044   *SIC* 3545
METRICAN MFG. CO. INC   *p*804
2100 WYECROFT RD, OAKVILLE, ON, L6L
5V6
(905) 332-3200   *SIC* 3545
NSE AUTOMATECH INC   *p*1109
520 RUE RUTHERFORD, GRANBY, QC,
J2G 0B2
(450) 378-7207   *SIC* 3545
PILOT DIAMOND TOOLS LIMITED   *p*762
1851 SEYMOUR ST, NORTH BAY, ON, P1A
0C7
(705) 497-3715   *SIC* 3545
TECHNOLOGIES ITF INC   *p*1327
400 BOUL MONTPELLIER, SAINT-
LAURENT, QC, H4N 2G7
(514) 748-4848   *SIC* 3545
TRU-DIE LIMITED   *p*890
236 EDWARD ST, ST THOMAS, ON, N5P
1Z5
(519) 633-1040   *SIC* 3545
ULTRA-FORM MFG. CO. LTD   *p*581
73 BAYWOOD RD, ETOBICOKE, ON, M9V
3Y8
(416) 749-9323   *SIC* 3545

SIC 3546 Power-driven handtools

INNOVAK GROUP INC, THE   *p*1251
62 BOUL HYMUS, POINTE-CLAIRE, QC,
H9R 1E1
(514) 695-7221   *SIC* 3546

SIC 3547 Rolling mill machinery

THURSTON MACHINE COMPANY LIMITED
*p*847
45 INVERTOSE DR, PORT COLBORNE,
ON, L3K 5V8
(905) 834-3606   *SIC* 3547

SIC 3548 Welding apparatus

9089-8131 QUEBEC INC   *p*1389
2888 CH SULLIVAN BUREAU 3, VAL-D'OR,
QC, J9P 0B9
(819) 874-3435   *SIC* 3548
AMH CANADA LTEE   *p*1284

391 RUE SAINT-JEAN-BAPTISTE E, RI-MOUSKI, QC, G5L 1Z2
(418) 724-4105 *SIC* 3548

CENTERLINE (WINDSOR) LIMITED *p*643
595 MORTON DR, LASALLE, ON, N9J 3T8
(519) 734-6886 *SIC* 3548

CENTERLINE (WINDSOR) LIMITED *p*643
655 MORTON DR, LASALLE, ON, N9J 3T9
(519) 734-8330 *SIC* 3548

GROUPE MECANITEC INC *p*1358
2091 RUE LEONARD-DE VINCI, SAINTE-JULIE, QC, J3E 1Z2
SIC 3548

JORDAHL CANADA INC *p*504
35 DEVON RD, BRAMPTON, ON, L6T 5B6
(905) 458-5855 *SIC* 3548

LIBURDI AUTOMATION INC *p*566
400 6 HWY, DUNDAS, ON, L9H 7K4
(905) 689-0734 *SIC* 3548

LINCOLN ELECTRIC COMPANY OF CANADA LP *p*735
939 GANA CRT, MISSISSAUGA, ON, L5S 1N9
(905) 564-1151 *SIC* 3548

LINCOLN ELECTRIC COMPANY OF CANADA LP *p*918
179 WICKSTEED AVE, TORONTO, ON, M4G 2B9
(416) 421-2600 *SIC* 3548

VALIANT MACHINE & TOOL INC *p*1019
6555 HAWTHORNE DR, WINDSOR, ON, N8T 3G6
(519) 974-5200 *SIC* 3548

SIC 3549 Metalworking machinery, nec

KINOVA INC *p*1062
4333 BOUL DE LA GRANDE-ALLEE, BOIS-BRIAND, QC, J7H 1M7
(514) 277-3777 *SIC* 3549

SCHULTE INDUSTRIES LTD *p*1406
1 RAILWAY AVE, ENGLEFELD, SK, S0K 1N0
(306) 287-3715 *SIC* 3549

TRAVAIL ADAPTE DE LANAUDIERE *p*1281
3131 5E AV, RAWDON, QC, J0K 1S0
(450) 834-7678 *SIC* 3549

SIC 3552 Textile machinery

BELFAST MINI MILLS LTD *p*1038
1820 GARFIELD RD, BELFAST, PE, C0A 1A0
(902) 659-2430 *SIC* 3552

MYANT INC *p*586
100 RONSON DR, ETOBICOKE, ON, M9W 1B6
(416) 423-7906 *SIC* 3552

SIC 3553 Woodworking machinery

381572 ONTARIO LIMITED *p*645
2 FLEETWOOD RD, LINDSAY, ON, K9V 6H4
(705) 324-3762 *SIC* 3553

4170083 CANADA INC *p*1245
2250 RUE SAINT-JEAN, PLESSISVILLE, QC, G6L 2Y4
(819) 362-6317 *SIC* 3553

AXYZ INTERNATIONAL INC *p*521
5330 SOUTH SERVICE RD, BURLINGTON, ON, L7L 5L1
(905) 634-4940 *SIC* 3553

BID GROUP TECHNOLOGIES LTD *p*1152
18095 RUE LAPOINTE, MIRABEL, QC, J7J 1E3
(450) 435-2121 *SIC* 3553

BID GROUP TECHNOLOGIES LTD *p*1304
4000 40E RUE, SAINT-GEORGES, QC, G5Y 8G4
(418) 228-8911 *SIC* 3553

DOUCET MACHINERIES INC *p*1089
340 6E RUE, DAVELUYVILLE, QC, G0Z 1C0
(819) 367-2633 *SIC* 3553

GENFOR MACHINERY INC *p*209
8320 RIVER RD, DELTA, BC, V4G 1B5
(604) 946-6911 *SIC* 3553

INDUSTRIES J. HAMELIN INC, LES *p*1320
690 BOUL ROLAND-GODARD, SAINT-JEROME, QC, J7Y 4C5
(450) 431-3221 *SIC* 3553

L. & M. LUMBER LTD *p*331
1241 HWY 16 W, VANDERHOOF, BC, V0J 3A0
(250) 567-4701 *SIC* 3553

MACHINAGE PICHE INC *p*1089
414 RUE INDUSTRIELLE, DAVELUYVILLE, QC, G0Z 1C0
(819) 367-3233 *SIC* 3553

NICHOLSON MANUFACTURING LTD *p*268
9896 GALARAN RD, SIDNEY, BC, V8L 4K4
(250) 656-3131 *SIC* 3553

O.S.I. MACHINERIE INC *p*1305
2510 98E RUE, SAINT-GEORGES, QC, G6A 1E4
(418) 228-6868 *SIC* 3553

OPTIMIL MACHINERY INC *p*209
8320 RIVER RD, DELTA, BC, V4G 1B5
(604) 946-6911 *SIC* 3553

PRODUITS GILBERT INC, LES *p*1287
1840 BOUL MARCOTTE, ROBERVAL, QC, G8H 2P2
(418) 275-5041 *SIC* 3553

USNR/KOCKUMS CANCAR COMPANY *p*1246
1600 RUE SAINT-PAUL, PLESSISVILLE, QC, G6L 1C1
(819) 362-7362 *SIC* 3553

SIC 3554 Paper industries machinery

AIKAWA FIBER TECHNOLOGIES INC*p*1374
72 RUE QUEEN, SHERBROOKE, QC, J1M 2C3
(819) 562-4754 *SIC* 3554

CONSTRUCTIONS E.D.B. INC *p*1392
545 RTE 249, VAL-JOLI, QC, J1S 0E6
(819) 845-5436 *SIC* 3554

DEACRO INDUSTRIES LTD *p*738
135 CAPITAL CRT, MISSISSAUGA, ON, L5T 2R8
(905) 564-6566 *SIC* 3554

MASTER PACKAGING INC *p*1038
23784 TRANS CANADA HIGHWAY, BORDEN-CARLETON, PE, C0B 1X0
(902) 437-3737 *SIC* 3554

VALMET LTEE *p*1331
4900 BOUL THIMENS, SAINT-LAURENT, QC, H4R 2B2
(514) 335-5424 *SIC* 3554

SIC 3555 Printing trades machinery

HCH LAZERMAN INC *p*977
278 BATHURST ST, TORONTO, ON, M5T 2S3
(416) 504-2154 *SIC* 3555

SOUTHERN GRAPHIC SYSTEMS-CANADA LTD *p*576
2 DORCHESTER AVE, ETOBICOKE, ON, M8Z 4W3
(416) 252-9331 *SIC* 3555

SIC 3556 Food products machinery

ABCO INDUSTRIES LIMITED *p*461
81 TANNERY RD, LUNENBURG, NS, B0J 2C0
(902) 634-8821 *SIC* 3556

AGROPUR COOPERATIVE *p*1325
333 BOUL LEBEAU, SAINT-LAURENT, QC, H4N 1S3
(800) 501-1150 *SIC* 3556

AMF AUTOMATION TECHNOLOGIES COMPANY OF CANADA *p*1372
1025 RUE CABANA BUREAU 1, SHERBROOKE, QC, J1K 2M4
(819) 563-3111 *SIC* 3556

GESTION MCNALLY INC *p*1134
2030 BOUL DAGENAIS O, LAVAL-OUEST, QC, H7L 5W2
(450) 625-4662 *SIC* 3556

GRAPHIC PACKAGING INTERNATIONAL CANADA CORPORATION *p*695
1355 AEROWOOD DR, MISSISSAUGA, ON, L4W 1C2
(905) 602-7877 *SIC* 3556

GROUPE SINOX INC *p*1292
16 RUE TURGEON, SAINT-ANSELME, QC, G0R 2N0
(418) 885-8276 *SIC* 3556

INOX-TECH CANADA INC *p*1356
1905 RUE PASTEUR, SAINTE-CATHERINE, QC, J5C 1B7
(450) 638-5441 *SIC* 3556

NUTRABLEND FOODS INC *p*536
415 DOBBIE DR, CAMBRIDGE, ON, N1T 1S8
(519) 622-4178 *SIC* 3556

PT ENTERPRISES INC *p*1040
54 HILLSTROM AVE, CHARLOTTETOWN, PE, C1E 2C6
(902) 628-6900 *SIC* 3556

SCHNEIDER ELECTRIC SYSTEMS CANADA INC *p*1091
4 RUE LAKE, DOLLARD-DES-ORMEAUX, QC, H9B 3H9
(514) 421-4210 *SIC* 3556

SPECIFIC MECHANICAL SYSTEMS LTD *p*267
6848 KIRKPATRICK CRES, SAANICHTON, BC, V8M 1Z9
(250) 652-2111 *SIC* 3556

WEXXAR PACKAGING INC *p*257
13471 VULCAN WAY, RICHMOND, BC, V6V 1K4
(604) 930-9300 *SIC* 3556

SIC 3559 Special industry machinery, nec

BRAMPTON ENGINEERING INC *p*501
8031 DIXIE RD, BRAMPTON, ON, L6T 3V1
(905) 793-3000 *SIC* 3559

CANADIAN CAPSULE EQUIPMENT LIMITED *p*1021
2510 OUELLETTE AVE SUITE 102, WINDSOR, ON, N8X 1L4
(519) 966-1122 *SIC* 3559

CONCEPTROMEC INC *p*1147
1782 BOUL INDUSTRIEL, MAGOG, QC, J1X 4V9
(819) 847-3627 *SIC* 3559

CONTITECH CANADA, INC *p*745
79 ARTHUR ST, MITCHELL, ON, N0K 1N0
SIC 3559

CORMA INC *p*551
10 MCCLEARY CRT, CONCORD, ON, L4K 2Z3
(905) 669-9397 *SIC* 3559

ECO-TEC INC *p*844
1145 SQUIRES BEACH RD, PICKERING, ON, L1W 3T9
(905) 427-0077 *SIC* 3559

FLIR INTEGRATED IMAGING SOLUTIONS, INC *p*258
12051 RIVERSIDE WAY, RICHMOND, BC, V6W 1K7
(604) 242-9937 *SIC* 3559

G.N. PLASTICS COMPANY LIMITED *p*442
345 OLD TRUNK 3, CHESTER, NS, B0J 1J0
(902) 275-3571 *SIC* 3559

INDUSTRIES MACHINEX INC *p*1246
2121 RUE OLIVIER, PLESSISVILLE, QC, G6L 3G9
(819) 362-3281 *SIC* 3559

KOCH-GLITSCH CANADA LP *p*1001
18 DALLAS ST, UXBRIDGE, ON, L9P 1C6
(905) 852-3381 *SIC* 3559

MACRO ENGINEERING & TECHNOLOGY INC *p*706
199 TRADERS BLVD E, MISSISSAUGA, ON, L4Z 2E5
(905) 507-9000 *SIC* 3559

MOLD-MASTERS (2007) LIMITED *p*594
233 ARMSTRONG AVE, GEORGETOWN, ON, L7G 4X5
(905) 877-0185 *SIC* 3559

O'HARA TECHNOLOGIES INC *p*853
20 KINNEAR CRT, RICHMOND HILL, ON, L4B 1K8
(905) 707-3286 *SIC* 3559

SYSTEMES B.M.H. INC, LES *p*1296
1395 RUE RENE-DESCARTES, SAINT-BRUNO, QC, J3V 0B7
(450) 441-1770 *SIC* 3559

TOMLINSON ENVIRONMENTAL SERVICES LTD *p*752
970 MOODIE DR, NEPEAN, ON, K2R 1H3
(613) 820-2332 *SIC* 3559

TOP-CO INC *p*123
7720 17 ST NW, EDMONTON, AB, T6P 1S7
(780) 440-4440 *SIC* 3559

TURNKEY MODULAR SYSTEMS INC *p*801
2590 SHERIDAN GARDEN DR, OAKVILLE, ON, L6J 7R2
(905) 608-8006 *SIC* 3559

VANRX PHARMASYSTEMS INC *p*194
3811 NORTH FRASER WAY SUITE 200, BURNABY, BC, V5J 5J2
(604) 453-8660 *SIC* 3559

VTR FEEDER SOLUTIONS INC *p*600
623 SOUTH SERVICE RD UNIT 6, GRIMSBY, ON, L3M 4E8
(905) 643-7300 *SIC* 3559

WHITING EQUIPMENT CANADA INC *p*1012
350 ALEXANDER ST, WELLAND, ON, L3B 2R3
(905) 732-7585 *SIC* 3559

SIC 3561 Pumps and pumping equipment

ALLIANCE CONCRETE PUMPS INC *p*179
26162 30A AVE, ALDERGROVE, BC, V4W 2W5
(604) 607-0908 *SIC* 3561

CLYDE UNION CANADA LIMITED *p*521
4151 NORTH SERVICE RD UNIT 1, BURLINGTON, ON, L7L 4X6
(905) 315-3800 *SIC* 3561

CPC PUMPS INTERNATIONAL INC *p*522
5200 MAINWAY, BURLINGTON, ON, L7L 5Z1
(289) 288-4753 *SIC* 3561

FLOWSERVE CANADA CORP *p*603
225 SPEEDVALE AVE W, GUELPH, ON, N1H 1C5
(519) 824-4600 *SIC* 3561

LUFKIN INDUSTRIES CANADA ULC *p*149
1107 8A ST, NISKU, AB, T9E 7R3
(780) 955-7566 *SIC* 3561

NATIONAL PROCESS EQUIPMENT INC*p*17
5409 74 AVE SE, CALGARY, AB, T2C 3C9
(403) 724-4300 *SIC* 3561

PLAD EQUIPEMENT LTEE *p*1060
680 RUE DE LA SABLIERE, BOIS-DES-FILION, QC, J6Z 4T7
(450) 965-0224 *SIC* 3561

RAYMOND-CBE MACHINERY INC *p*261
11788 RIVER RD SUITE 118, RICHMOND, BC, V6X 1Z7
SIC 3561

S. A. ARMSTRONG LIMITED *p*869
23 BERTRAND AVE, SCARBOROUGH, ON, M1L 2P3
(416) 755-2291 *SIC* 3561

SULZER PUMPS (CANADA) INC *p*183
4129 LOZELLS AVE, BURNABY, BC, V5A

2Z5
(604) 415-7800   *SIC 3561*
TOYO PUMPS NORTH AMERICA CORP   *p202*
1550 BRIGANTINE DR, COQUITLAM, BC, V3K 7C1
(604) 298-1213   *SIC 3561*
WESTRON PUMPS & COMPRESSORS LTD   *p26*
3600 21 ST NE UNIT 3, CALGARY, AB, T2E 6V6
(403) 291-6777   *SIC 3561*

SIC 3562 Ball and roller bearings

DARCOR LIMITED   *p571*
7 STAFFORDSHIRE PL, ETOBICOKE, ON, M8W 1T1
(416) 255-8563   *SIC 3562*
NTN BEARING CORPORATION OF CANADA LIMITED   *p725*
6740 KITIMAT RD, MISSISSAUGA, ON, L5N 1M6
(905) 826-5500   *SIC 3562*
SCHAEFFLER CANADA INC   *p896*
801 ONTARIO ST, STRATFORD, ON, N5A 7Y2
(519) 271-3231   *SIC 3562*
TIMKEN CANADA LP   *p690*
5955 AIRPORT RD SUITE 100, MISSISSAUGA, ON, L4V 1R9
(905) 826-9520   *SIC 3562*

SIC 3563 Air and gas compressors

BIDELL EQUIPMENT LIMITED PARTNERSHIP   *p14*
6900 112 AVE SE, CALGARY, AB, T2C 4Z1
(403) 235-5877   *SIC 3563*
COMPRESSION TECHNOLOGY INC   *p213*
10911 89 AVE, FORT ST. JOHN, BC, V1J 6V2
(250) 787-8655   *SIC 3563*
DV SYSTEMS INC   *p486*
490 WELHAM RD, BARRIE, ON, L4N 8Z4
(705) 728-5657   *SIC 3563*
ENERFLEX LTD   *p29*
1331 MACLEOD TRL SE SUITE 904, CALGARY, AB, T2G 0K3
(403) 387-6377   *SIC 3563*
STARTEC REFRIGERATION SERVICES LTD   *p18*
9423 SHEPARD RD SE, CALGARY, AB, T2C 4R6
(403) 295-5855   *SIC 3563*
VMAC GLOBAL TECHNOLOGY INC   *p235*
1333 KIPP RD, NANAIMO, BC, V9X 1R3
(250) 740-3200   *SIC 3563*

SIC 3564 Blowers and fans

9228-5329 QUEBEC INC   *p1346*
100 RUE CARTER, SAINT-LEONARD-D'ASTON, QC, J0C 1M0
(819) 399-3400   *SIC 3564*
AIREX INDUSTRIES INC   *p1231*
2500 RUE BERNARD-LEFEBVRE, MONTREAL, QC, H7C 0A5
(514) 351-2303   *SIC 3564*
ANNEXAIR INC   *p1098*
1125 RUE BERGERON, DRUMMONDVILLE, QC, J2C 7V5
(819) 475-3302   *SIC 3564*
APGN INC   *p1058*
1270 BOUL MICHELE-BOHEC, BLAINVILLE, QC, J7C 5S4
(450) 939-0799   *SIC 3564*
CAFRAMO LIMITED   *p594*
501273 GREY ROAD 1, GEORGIAN BLUFFS, ON, N0H 2T0
(519) 534-1080   *SIC 3564*

CIRCUL-AIRE INC   *p1328*
3999 BOUL DE LA COTE-VERTU, SAINT-LAURENT, QC, H4R 1R2
(514) 337-3331   *SIC 3564*
DELHI INDUSTRIES INC   *p519*
2157 PARKEDALE AVE, BROCKVILLE, ON, K6V 0B4
(613) 342-5424   *SIC 3564*
DIVERSITECH EQUIPMENT AND SALES 1984 LTD   *p1127*
1200 55E AV, LACHINE, QC, H8T 3J8
(514) 631-7300   *SIC 3564*
FILTRATION L.A.B. INC   *p1347*
193 RANG DE L'EGLISE, SAINT-LIGUORI, QC, J0K 2X0
(450) 754-4222   *SIC 3564*
FIVE SEASONS COMFORT LIMITED   *p552*
351 NORTH RIVERMEDE RD, CONCORD, ON, L4K 3N2
(905) 669-5620   *SIC 3564*
GESTION R.M.L. RODRIGUE INC   *p1138*
1890 1RE RUE, LEVIS, QC, G6W 5M6
(418) 839-0671   *SIC 3564*
GROUPE AVIATION ET PUISSANCE INC   *p1059*
1270 BOUL MICHELE-BOHEC, BLAINVILLE, QC, J7C 5S4
(450) 939-0799   *SIC 3564*
HALTON INDOOR CLIMATE SYSTEMS, LTD   *p695*
1021 BREVIK PL, MISSISSAUGA, ON, L4W 3R7
(905) 624-0301   *SIC 3564*
HAUL-ALL EQUIPMENT LTD   *p140*
4115 18 AVE N, LETHBRIDGE, AB, T1H 5G1
(403) 328-5353   *SIC 3564*
NORTEK AIR SOLUTIONS CANADA, INC   *p1428*
1502D QUEBEC AVE, SASKATOON, SK, S7K 1V7
(306) 242-3663   *SIC 3564*
REVERSOMATIC MANUFACTURING LTD   *p1033*
790 ROWNTREE DAIRY RD, WOODBRIDGE, ON, L4L 5V3
(905) 851-6701   *SIC 3564*
SYSTEMAIR INC   *p395*
50 KANALFLAKT WAY ROUTE, BOUCTOUCHE, NB, E4S 3M5
(506) 743-9500   *SIC 3564*
VENTILATION MAXIMUM LTEE   *p1163*
9229 RUE PIERRE-BONNE, MONTREAL, QC, H1E 7J6
(514) 648-8011   *SIC 3564*

SIC 3565 Packaging machinery

AFA SYSTEMS LTD   *p500*
8 TILBURY CRT, BRAMPTON, ON, L6T 3T4
(905) 456-8700   *SIC 3565*
CAPMATIC LTEE   *p1239*
12180 BOUL ALBERT-HUDON, MONTREAL-NORD, QC, H1G 3K7
(514) 322-0062   *SIC 3565*
EDSON PACKAGING MACHINERY LIMITED   *p615*
215 HEMPSTEAD DR, HAMILTON, ON, L8W 2E6
(905) 385-3201   *SIC 3565*
EMBALLAGES CRE-O-PACK CANADA INC   *p1157*
8420 CH DARNLEY, MONT-ROYAL, QC, H4T 1M4
(514) 343-9666   *SIC 3565*
HIBAR SYSTEMS LIMITED   *p852*
35 POLLARD ST, RICHMOND HILL, ON, L4B 1A8
(905) 731-2400   *SIC 3565*
LONGFORD INTERNATIONAL LTD   *p874*
41 LAMONT AVE, SCARBOROUGH, ON, M1S 1A8
(416) 298-6622   *SIC 3565*

PREMIER TECH TECHNOLOGIES LIMITEE   *p1286*
1 AV PREMIER, RIVIERE-DU-LOUP, QC, G5R 6C1
(418) 867-8883   *SIC 3565*
SEPTIMATECH GROUP INC   *p1011*
106 RANDALL DR, WATERLOO, ON, N2V 1K5
(519) 746-7463   *SIC 3565*
SYSTEMES D'EMBALLAGE AESUS INC   *p1252*
188 AV ONEIDA, POINTE-CLAIRE, QC, H9R 1A8
(514) 694-3439   *SIC 3565*

SIC 3566 Speed changers, drives, and gears

CVTECH INC   *p1098*
300 RUE LABONTE, DRUMMONDVILLE, QC, J2C 6X9
(819) 477-3232   *SIC 3566*
DAVID BROWN SYSTEM (CANADA) INC   *p1053*
20375 AV CLARK-GRAHAM, BAIE-D'URFE, QC, H9X 3T5
(514) 457-7700   *SIC 3566*
RAPID PRECISION MACHINING & GEARING INC   *p642*
1596 STRASBURG RD, KITCHENER, ON, N2R 1E9
(519) 748-4828   *SIC 3566*
SEW-EURODRIVE COMPANY OF CANADA LTD   *p506*
210 WALKER DR, BRAMPTON, ON, L6T 3W1
(905) 791-1553   *SIC 3566*

SIC 3567 Industrial furnaces and ovens

9183-7252 QUEBEC INC   *p1058*
730 BOUL INDUSTRIEL, BLAINVILLE, QC, J7C 3V4
(450) 979-8700   *SIC 3567*
AUREUS ENERGY SERVICES INC   *p79*
9510 78 AVE, CLAIRMONT, AB, T8X 0M2
(780) 567-3009   *SIC 3567*
CAN-ENG FURNACES INTERNATIONAL LTD   *p757*
6800 MONTROSE RD, NIAGARA FALLS, ON, L2E 6V5
(905) 356-1327   *SIC 3567*
CAN-ENG PARTNERS LTD   *p757*
6800 MONTROSE RD, NIAGARA FALLS, ON, L2E 6V5
(905) 356-1327   *SIC 3567*
COMAINTEL INC   *p1369*
121 AV CHAHOON BUREAU 100, SHAWINIGAN, QC, G9T 7G1
(819) 538-6583   *SIC 3567*
ECCO HEATING PRODUCTS LTD   *p228*
19860 FRASER HWY, LANGLEY, BC, V3A 4C9
(604) 530-4151   *SIC 3567*
ELEMENTS CHAUFFANTS TEMPORA INC., LES   *p1130*
2501 AV DOLLARD, LASALLE, QC, H8N 1S2
(514) 933-1649   *SIC 3567*
ELTHERM CANADA INC   *p530*
1440 GRAHAMS LN UNIT 5, BURLINGTON, ON, L7R 2J2
(289) 812-6631   *SIC 3567*
ESYS ENERGIE SYSTEME INC   *p1362*
3404 BOUL INDUSTRIEL, SAINTE-ROSE, QC, H7L 4R9
(450) 641-1344   *SIC 3567*
NUHEAT INDUSTRIES LIMITED   *p258*
6900 GRAYBAR RD SUITE 3105, RICHMOND, BC, V6W 0A5
(800) 778-9276   *SIC 3567*
OUELLET CANADA INC   *p1121*

180 3E AV, L'ISLET, QC, G0R 2C0
(418) 247-3947   *SIC 3567*
SIGMA CONVECTOR ENCLOSURE CORP   *p689*
3325A ORLANDO DR, MISSISSAUGA, ON, L4V 1C5
(905) 670-3200   *SIC 3567*
SILEX INNOVATIONS INC   *p743*
6659 ORDAN DR, MISSISSAUGA, ON, L5T 1K6
(905) 612-4000   *SIC 3567*
TRENT METALS (2012) LIMITED   *p842*
2040 FISHER DR, PETERBOROUGH, ON, K9J 6X6
(705) 745-4736   *SIC 3567*
VAC AERO INTERNATIONAL INC   *p525*
5420 NORTH SERVICE RD SUITE 205, BURLINGTON, ON, L7L 6C7
(905) 827-4171   *SIC 3567*
WELLONS CANADA CORP   *p282*
19087 96 AVE, SURREY, BC, V4N 3P2
(604) 888-0122   *SIC 3567*
XEBEC ADSORPTION INC   *p1060*
730 BOUL INDUSTRIEL, BLAINVILLE, QC, J7C 3V4
(450) 979-8700   *SIC 3567*

SIC 3568 Power transmission equipment, nec

BLOUNT CANADA LTD   *p602*
505 EDINBURGH RD N, GUELPH, ON, N1H 6L4
(519) 822-6870   *SIC 3568*
GATES CANADA INC   *p1019*
3303 ST ETIENNE BLVD, WINDSOR, ON, N8W 5B1
(519) 945-4200   *SIC 3568*
SCHAEFFLER AEROSPACE CANADA INC   *p896*
801 ONTARIO ST, STRATFORD, ON, N5A 6T2
(519) 271-3230   *SIC 3568*
VAN DER GRAAF INC   *p507*
2 VAN DER GRAAF CRT UNIT 1, BRAMPTON, ON, L6T 5R6
(905) 793-8100   *SIC 3568*

SIC 3569 General industrial machinery, nec

1894359 ONTARIO INC   *p485*
455 WELHAM RD, BARRIE, ON, L4N 8Z6
(705) 726-5841   *SIC 3569*
ABCO INDUSTRIES INC   *p461*
81 TANNERY RD, LUNENBURG, NS, B0J 2C0
(902) 634-8821   *SIC 3569*
ABS MANUFACTURING AND DISTRIBUTING LIMITED   *p647*
185 MAGILL ST, LIVELY, ON, P3Y 1K6
(705) 692-5445   *SIC 3569*
ADVANCED FLOW SYSTEMS INC   *p230*
27222 LOUGHEED HWY, MAPLE RIDGE, BC, V2W 1M4
(604) 462-1514   *SIC 3569*
AMICO CORPORATION   *p850*
85 FULTON WAY, RICHMOND HILL, ON, L4B 2N4
(905) 764-0800   *SIC 3569*
ATS AUTOMATION TOOLING SYSTEMS INC   *p538*
730 FOUNTAIN ST SUITE 2B, CAMBRIDGE, ON, N3H 4R7
(519) 653-6500   *SIC 3569*
BLUE GIANT EQUIPMENT CORPORATION   *p508*
85 HEART LAKE RD, BRAMPTON, ON, L6W 3K2
(905) 457-3900   *SIC 3569*
BOS INNOVATIONS INC   *p565*
500 HUDSON DR, DORCHESTER, ON, N0L 1G5

(519) 268-8563 *SIC* 3569
BURNCO MANUFACTURING INC *p*549
40 CITRON CRT, CONCORD, ON, L4K 2P5
(905) 761-6155 *SIC* 3569
CAMFIL CANADA INC *p*550
2700 STEELES AVE W, CONCORD, ON, L4K 3C8
(905) 660-0688 *SIC* 3569
CANMEC INDUSTRIEL INC *p*1080
1750 RUE LA GRANDE, CHICOUTIMI, QC, G7K 1H7
(418) 543-9151 *SIC* 3569
CHARL-POL INC *p*1121
4653 CH SAINT-ANICET, LA BAIE, QC, G7B 0J4
(418) 544-7355 *SIC* 3569
CHARL-POL INC *p*1121
805 RUE DE L'INNOVATION, LA BAIE, QC, G7B 3N8
(418) 677-1518 *SIC* 3569
CHARL-POL INC *p*1253
440 RUE LUCIEN-THIBODEAU, PORT-NEUF, QC, G0A 2Y0
(418) 286-4881 *SIC* 3569
CIMCORP AUTOMATION LTD *p*599
635 SOUTH SERVICE RD, GRIMSBY, ON, L3M 4E8
(905) 643-9700 *SIC* 3569
CUSCO FABRICATORS LLC *p*855
305 ENFORD RD, RICHMOND HILL, ON, L4C 3E9
(905) 883-1214 *SIC* 3569
DAFCO FILTRATION GROUP CORPORATION *p*693
5390 AMBLER DR, MISSISSAUGA, ON, L4W 1G9
(905) 624-9165 *SIC* 3569
DCSR INVESTMENT CORP *p*486
455 WELHAM RD, BARRIE, ON, L4N 8Z6
(705) 726-5841 *SIC* 3569
ENWAVE CORPORATION *p*205
1668 DERWENT WAY UNIT 1, DELTA, BC, V3M 6R9
(604) 806-6110 *SIC* 3569
EQUIPEMENTS FRONTMATEC INC *p*1291
51 RTE MORISSETTE, SAINT-ANSELME, QC, G0R 2N0
(418) 885-4493 *SIC* 3569
EQUIPEMENTS LAPIERRE INC, LES *p*1347
99 RUE DE L'ESCALE, SAINT-LUDGER, QC, G0M 1W0
(819) 548-5454 *SIC* 3569
FILTERFAB COMPANY *p*883
16 SEAPARK DR, ST CATHARINES, ON, L2M 6S6
(905) 684-8363 *SIC* 3569
FILTRATION GROUP CANADA CORPORATION *p*739
6190 KESTREL RD, MISSISSAUGA, ON, L5T 1Z1
(905) 795-9559 *SIC* 3569
GARIER INC *p*1152
13050 RUE BRAULT UNITE 123, MIRABEL, QC, J7J 0W4
(450) 437-7852 *SIC* 3569
GARRY MACHINE MFG INC *p*735
165 STATESMAN DR, MISSISSAUGA, ON, L5S 1X4
(905) 564-5340 *SIC* 3569
HAYLEY INDUSTRIAL ELECTRONICS LTD *p*16
7071 112 AVE SE, CALGARY, AB, T2C 5A5
(403) 259-5575 *SIC* 3569
HOWARD MARTEN COMPANY LIMITED *p*844
902 DILLINGHAM RD, PICKERING, ON, L1W 1Z6
(905) 831-2901 *SIC* 3569
HYD-MECH GROUP LIMITED *p*1035
1079 PARKINSON RD, WOODSTOCK, ON, N4S 7W3
(519) 539-6341 *SIC* 3569
I-CUBED INDUSTRY INNOVATORS INC *p*892
999 BARTON ST, STONEY CREEK, ON,

L8E 5H4
(905) 643-8685 *SIC* 3569
INDUSTRIES MAILHOT INC *p*1314
2721 RANG SAINT-JACQUES, SAINT-JACQUES, QC, J0K 2R0
(450) 477-6222 *SIC* 3569
INDUSTRIES MAILHOT INC *p*1314
2721 RANG SAINT-JACQUES, SAINT-JACQUES, QC, J0K 2R0
(450) 839-3663 *SIC* 3569
INNOVATIVE AUTOMATION INC *p*487
625 WELHAM RD, BARRIE, ON, L4N 0B7
(705) 733-0555 *SIC* 3569
INNOVATIVE STEAM TECHNOLOGIES INC *p*533
549 CONESTOGA BLVD, CAMBRIDGE, ON, N1R 7P5
(519) 740-0036 *SIC* 3569
INUKTUN SERVICES LTD *p*234
2569 KENWORTH RD SUITE C, NANAIMO, BC, V9T 3M4
(250) 729-8080 *SIC* 3569
J.A. LARUE INC *p*1275
3003 AV WATT, QUEBEC, QC, G1X 3W2
(418) 658-3003 *SIC* 3569
JTL INTEGRATED MACHINE LTD. *p*846
857 REUTER RD, PORT COLBORNE, ON, L3K 5W1
(905) 834-3992 *SIC* 3569
KADANT CANADA CORP *p*272
15050 54A AVE UNIT 8, SURREY, BC, V3S 5X7
(604) 299-3431 *SIC* 3569
LAKER ENERGY PRODUCTS LTD *p*804
835 FOURTH LINE, OAKVILLE, ON, L6L 5B8
(905) 332-3231 *SIC* 3569
LINEAR TRANSFER AUTOMATION INC *p*487
61 RAWSON AVE, BARRIE, ON, L4N 6E5
(705) 735-0000 *SIC* 3569
LINERGY MANUFACTURING INC *p*603
87 CAMPBELL RD, GUELPH, ON, N1H 1B9
(519) 341-5996 *SIC* 3569
MAIN FILTER INC *p*863
188 INDUSTRIAL PARK CRES, SAULT STE. MARIE, ON, P6B 5P2
(705) 256-6622 *SIC* 3569
MAINLAND MACHINERY LTD *p*177
2255 TOWNLINE RD, ABBOTSFORD, BC, V2T 6H1
(604) 854-4244 *SIC* 3569
MARMEN ENERGIE INC *p*1150
1905 AV DU PHARE O, MATANE, QC, G4W 3M6
(418) 562-4569 *SIC* 3569
MATISS INC *p*1305
8800 25E AV, SAINT-GEORGES, QC, G6A 1K5
(418) 227-9141 *SIC* 3569
MECFOR INC *p*1081
1788 RUE MITIS, CHICOUTIMI, QC, G7K 1H5
(418) 543-1632 *SIC* 3569
MELLOY INDUSTRIAL SERVICES INC *p*149
2305 5 ST, NISKU, AB, T9E 7X1
(780) 955-8500 *SIC* 3569
METSO MINERALS CANADA INC *p*492
161 BRIDGE ST W UNIT 6, BELLEVILLE, ON, K8P 1K2
(613) 962-3411 *SIC* 3569
MURRAY LATTA PROGRESSIVE MACHINE INC *p*277
8717 132 ST, SURREY, BC, V3W 4P1
(604) 599-9598 *SIC* 3569
NIEDNER INC *p*1082
675 RUE MERRILL, COATICOOK, QC, J1A 2S2
(819) 849-2751 *SIC* 3569
NIIGON MACHINES LTD *p*1028
372 NEW ENTERPRISE WAY, WOOD-BRIDGE, ON, L4H 0S8
(905) 265-0277 *SIC* 3569
OUTOTEC (CANADA) LTD *p*524

1551 CORPORATE DR, BURLINGTON, ON, L7L 6M3
(905) 335-0002 *SIC* 3569
OVIVO INC *p*1198
1010 RUE SHERBROOKE O BUREAU 1700, MONTREAL, QC, H3A 2R7
(514) 284-2224 *SIC* 3569
PARKER HANNIFIN CANADA *p*1234
2785 AV FRANCIS-HUGHES, MONTREAL, QC, H7L 3J6
(450) 629-3030 *SIC* 3569
PHIL MAUER & ASSOCIATES INC *p*567
56954 EDEN LINE, EDEN, ON, N0J 1H0
(519) 866-5677 *SIC* 3569
PHILLIPS ENGINEERING TECHNOLOGIES CORP *p*557
385 CONNIE CRES, CONCORD, ON, L4K 5R2
  SIC 3569
PROCECO LTEE *p*1165
7300 RUE TELLIER, MONTREAL, QC, H1N 3T7
(514) 254-8494 *SIC* 3569
PRODUITS D'ACIER ROGER INC, LES *p*1379
1350 GRANDE ALLEE, TERREBONNE, QC, J6W 4M4
(450) 471-2000 *SIC* 3569
PRODUITS INDUSTRIELS DE HAUTE TEMPERATURE PYROTEK INC *p*1097
2400 BOUL LEMIRE, DRUMMONDVILLE, QC, J2B 6X9
(819) 477-0734 *SIC* 3569
PROMATION ENGINEERING LTD *p*799
2767 BRIGHTON RD, OAKVILLE, ON, L6H 6J4
(905) 625-6093 *SIC* 3569
PROTECTOLITE COMPOSITES INC *p*775
84 RAILSIDE RD, NORTH YORK, ON, M3A 1A3
(416) 444-4484 *SIC* 3569
RESEAU SOLUTIONS CANADA ULC *p*1123
1400 RUE INDUSTRIELLE BUREAU 100, LA PRAIRIE, QC, J5R 2E5
(450) 659-8921 *SIC* 3569
RLM MANUFACTURING INC *p*1015
701 ROSSLAND RD E UNIT 370, WHITBY, ON, L1N 8Y9
(905) 434-4567 *SIC* 3569
RODRIGUE METAL LTEE *p*1138
1890 1RE RUE, LEVIS, QC, G6W 5M6
(418) 839-0400 *SIC* 3569
SANYO CANADIAN MACHINE WORKS INCORPORATED *p*568
33 INDUSTRIAL DR, ELMIRA, ON, N3B 3B1
(519) 669-1591 *SIC* 3569
SPM AUTOMATION (CANADA) INC *p*1023
5445 OUTER DR, WINDSOR, ON, N9A 6J3
(519) 737-0320 *SIC* 3569
STAS INC *p*1080
622 RUE DES ACTIONNAIRES, CHICOUTIMI, QC, G7J 5A9
(418) 696-0074 *SIC* 3569
SYSTEMES DE LIGNES D'EXTRUSION FABE INC *p*1129
1930 52E AV, LACHINE, QC, H8T 2Y3
(514) 633-5933 *SIC* 3569
TEKNA SYSTEMES PLASMA INC *p*1374
2935 BOUL INDUSTRIEL, SHERBROOKE, QC, J1L 2T9
(819) 820-2204 *SIC* 3569
THERMO DESIGN ENGINEERING LTD *p*123
1424 70 AVE NW, EDMONTON, AB, T6P 1P5
(780) 440-6064 *SIC* 3569
TRANSFORMIX ENGINEERING INC *p*633
1150 GARDINERS RD, KINGSTON, ON, K7P 1R7
(613) 544-5970 *SIC* 3569
VIPOND INC *p*744
6380 VIPOND DR, MISSISSAUGA, ON, L5T 1A1
(905) 564-7060 *SIC* 3569

WEIR CANADA, INC *p*728
2360 MILLRACE CRT, MISSISSAUGA, ON, L5N 1W2
(905) 812-7100 *SIC* 3569
ZETON INC *p*525
740 OVAL CRT, BURLINGTON, ON, L7L 6A9
(905) 632-3123 *SIC* 3569

SIC 3571 Electronic computers

CIENA CANADA, INC *p*832
385 TERRY FOX DR, OTTAWA, ON, K2K 0L1
(613) 670-2000 *SIC* 3571
HYPERTEC SYSTEMS INC *p*1334
9300 RTE TRANSCANADIENNE, SAINT-LAURENT, QC, H4S 1K5
(514) 745-4540 *SIC* 3571
IBM CANADA LIMITED *p*89
10044 108 ST NW SUITE 401, EDMONTON, AB, T5J 3S7
(780) 642-4100 *SIC* 3571
IBM CANADA LIMITED *p*671
3600 STEELES AVE E, MARKHAM, ON, L3R 9Z7
(905) 316-5000 *SIC* 3571
INFODEV ELECTRONIC DESIGNERS INTERNATIONAL *p*1264
1995 RUE FRANK-CARREL BUREAU 202, QUEBEC, QC, G1N 4H9
(418) 681-3539 *SIC* 3571
LENOVO (CANADA) INC *p*774
10 YORK MILLS RD SUITE 400, NORTH YORK, ON, M2P 2G4
(855) 253-6686 *SIC* 3571
NORTHERN MICRO INC *p*818
3155 SWANSEA CRES, OTTAWA, ON, K1G 3J3
(613) 226-1117 *SIC* 3571
PROSYS TECH CORPORATION *p*1050
7751 RUE JARRY, ANJOU, QC, H1J 1H3
(450) 681-7744 *SIC* 3571
PSION INC *p*1341
7575 RTE TRANSCANADIENNE BUREAU 500, SAINT-LAURENT, QC, H4T 1V6
  SIC 3571
RTDS TECHNOLOGIES INC *p*392
100-150 INNOVATION DR, WINNIPEG, MB, R3T 2E1
(204) 989-9700 *SIC* 3571
SIMEX INC *p*934
600-210 KING ST E, TORONTO, ON, M5A 1J7
(416) 597-1585 *SIC* 3571

SIC 3577 Computer peripheral equipment, nec

ATI TECHNOLOGIES ULC *p*678
1 COMMERCE VALLEY DR E, MARKHAM, ON, L3T 7X6
(905) 882-2600 *SIC* 3577
BUSKRO INTERNATIONAL LTD *p*844
1738 ORANGEBROOK CRT UNIT 1, PICKERING, ON, L1W 3G8
(905) 839-6018 *SIC* 3577
EMC CORPORATION OF CANADA *p*951
120 ADELAIDE ST W SUITE 1400, TORONTO, ON, M5H 1T1
(416) 628-5973 *SIC* 3577
GUESTLOGIX INC *p*980
111 PETER ST SUITE 407, TORONTO, ON, M5V 2H1
(647) 317-1517 *SIC* 3577
PROMAG DISPLAYCORR CANADA INC *p*1050
11150 AV L.-J.-FORGET, ANJOU, QC, H1J 2K9
(514) 352-9511 *SIC* 3577
SLI MANUFACTURING INC *p*765
550 MCNICOLL AVE, NORTH YORK, ON,

M2H 2E1
(416) 493-8900   *SIC 3577*

SIC 3578 Calculating and accounting equipment

INGENICO CANADA LTD   *p696*
5180 ORBITOR DR 2ND FL, MISSISSAUGA, ON, L4W 5L9
(905) 212-9464   *SIC 3578*
INTERNATIONAL TRANSACTION SYSTEMS (CANADA) LTD   *p685*
7415 TORBRAM RD, MISSISSAUGA, ON, L4T 1G8
(905) 677-2088   *SIC 3578*
LEMIEUX NOLET COMPTABLES AGREES S.E.N.C.R.L.   *p1160*
25 BOUL TACHE O BUREAU 205, MONT-MAGNY, QC, G5V 2Z9
(418) 248-1910   *SIC 3578*
LLOYD DOUGLAS SOLUTIONS INC   *p891*
130 IBER RD, STITTSVILLE, ON, K2S 1E9
(613) 369-5189   *SIC 3578*
NCR CANADA CORP   *p640*
580 WEBER ST E, KITCHENER, ON, N2H 1G8
SIC 3578
PAYTECH LTD   *p777*
1500 DON MILLS RD SUITE 400, NORTH YORK, ON, M3B 3K4
(888) 263-1938   *SIC 3578*

SIC 3579 Office machines, nec

ACCO BRANDS CANADA INC   *p733*
7381 BRAMALEA RD, MISSISSAUGA, ON, L5S 1C4
(905) 364-2600   *SIC 3579*

SIC 3581 Automatic vending machines

BEAVER MACHINE CORPORATION   *p754*
250 HARRY WALKER PKY N UNIT 1, NEWMARKET, ON, L3Y 7B4
(905) 836-4700   *SIC 3581*

SIC 3585 Refrigeration and heating equipment

A.C. DISPENSING EQUIPMENT INCORPORATED   *p461*
100 DISPENSING WAY, LOWER SACKVILLE, NS, B4C 4H2
(902) 865-9602   *SIC 3585*
AIRTEX MANUFACTURING PARTNERSHIP   *p754*
1175 TWINNEY DR, NEWMARKET, ON, L3Y 9C8
(905) 898-1114   *SIC 3585*
ARNEG CANADA INC   *p1129*
18 RUE RICHELIEU, LACOLLE, QC, J0J 1J0
(450) 246-3837   *SIC 3585*
BERG CHILLING SYSTEMS INC   *p870*
51 NANTUCKET BLVD, SCARBOROUGH, ON, M1P 2N5
(416) 755-2221   *SIC 3585*
CANADIAN CURTIS REFRIGERATION INC   *p891*
881 ARVIN AVE, STONEY CREEK, ON, L8E 5N8
(905) 643-1977   *SIC 3585*
CANCOIL THERMAL CORPORATION   *p630*
991 JOHN F. SCOTT RD, KINGSTON, ON, K7L 4V3
(613) 541-1235   *SIC 3585*
CONDAIR HUMIDITY LTD   *p597*
2740 FENTON RD, GLOUCESTER, ON, K1T 3T7
(613) 822-0335   *SIC 3585*

DECTRON INC   *p1329*
3999 BOUL DE LA COTE-VERTU, SAINT-LAURENT, QC, H4R 1R2
(514) 336-3330   *SIC 3585*
DECTRON INTERNATIONALE INC   *p1329*
3999 BOUL DE LA COTE-VERTU, SAINT-LAURENT, QC, H4R 1R2
(514) 336-3330   *SIC 3585*
DSI DISPENSING SYSTEMS INTERNATIONAL INC   *p1333*
5800 BOUL THIMENS, SAINT-LAURENT, QC, H4S 1S5
(514) 433-4562   *SIC 3585*
ECR INTERNATIONAL LTD   *p1004*
6800 BASE LINE, WALLACEBURG, ON, N8A 2K6
(519) 627-0791   *SIC 3585*
EPSILON INDUSTRIES INC   *p632*
751 DALTON AVE, KINGSTON, ON, K7M 8N6
(613) 544-1133   *SIC 3585*
HAAKON INDUSTRIES (CANADA) LTD   *p263*
11851 DYKE RD, RICHMOND, BC, V7A 4X8
(604) 273-0161   *SIC 3585*
HABCO MANUFACTURING INC   *p765*
501 GORDON BAKER RD, NORTH YORK, ON, M2H 2S6
(416) 491-6008   *SIC 3585*
INGENIA TECHNOLOGIES INC   *p1152*
18101 RUE J.A.BOMBARDIER, MIRABEL, QC, J7J 2H8
(450) 979-1212   *SIC 3585*
MECAR METAL INC   *p1296*
1560 RUE MARIE-VICTORIN, SAINT-BRUNO, QC, J3V 6B9
(450) 653-1002   *SIC 3585*
MINUS FORTY TECHNOLOGIES CORP   *p594*
30 ARMSTRONG AVE, GEORGETOWN, ON, L7G 4R9
(905) 702-1441   *SIC 3585*
NATIONAL ENVIRONMENTAL PRODUCTS LTD   *p1326*
400 BOUL LEBEAU, SAINT-LAURENT, QC, H4N 1R6
(514) 333-1433   *SIC 3585*
NATIONAL REFRIGERATION & AIR CONDITIONING CANADA CORP   *p514*
159 ROY BLVD, BRANTFORD, ON, N3R 7K1
(519) 751-0444   *SIC 3585*
NEWPORT CUSTOM METAL FABRICATIONS INC   *p449*
114 LANCASTER CRES LOT 208, DEBERT, NS, B0M 1G0
(902) 662-3840   *SIC 3585*
RAPID REFRIGERATION MANUFACTURING COMPANY LIMITED   *p871*
1550 BIRCHMOUNT RD, SCARBOROUGH, ON, M1P 2H1
(416) 285-8282   *SIC 3585*
REFPLUS INC   *p1310*
2777 GRANDE ALLEE, SAINT-HUBERT, QC, J4T 2R4
(450) 641-2665   *SIC 3585*
SILENT AIRE MANUFACTURING INC   *p123*
7107 8 ST NW, EDMONTON, AB, T6P 1T9
(780) 456-1061   *SIC 3585*
SILENT-AIRE LIMITED PARTNERSHIP   *p123*
7107 8 ST NW, EDMONTON, AB, T6P 1T9
(780) 456-1061   *SIC 3585*
SOLUTIONS D'AIR NORTEK QUEBEC, INC   *p1050*
9100 RUE DU PARCOURS, ANJOU, QC, H1J 2Z1
(514) 354-7776   *SIC 3585*
SYSTEMES NORBEC INC   *p1067*
97 RUE DE VAUDREUIL, BOUCHERVILLE, QC, J4B 1K7
(450) 449-1499   *SIC 3585*
TOROMONT INDUSTRIES LTD   *p934*
65 VILLIERS ST, TORONTO, ON, M5A 3S1
(416) 465-7581   *SIC 3585*
TRANE CANADA ULC   *p676*

---

525 COCHRANE DR SUITE 101, MARKHAM, ON, L3R 8E3
(416) 499-3600   *SIC 3585*
WATERCO CANADA INC   *p1068*
1380 RUE NEWTON BUREAU 208, BOUCHERVILLE, QC, J4B 5H2
(450) 748-1421   *SIC 3585*

SIC 3589 Service industry machinery, nec

242408 STEEL FABRICATION LIMITED   *p844*
1625 FELDSPAR CRT, PICKERING, ON, L1W 3R7
(905) 831-6172   *SIC 3589*
BE PRESSURE SUPPLY INC   *p176*
30585 PROGRESSIVE WAY, ABBOTSFORD, BC, V2T 6W3
(604) 850-6662   *SIC 3589*
BUNN-O-MATIC CORPORATION OF CANADA   *p480*
280 INDUSTRIAL PKY S, AURORA, ON, L4G 3T9
(905) 841-2866   *SIC 3589*
CELESTICA INC   *p916*
844 DON MILLS RD, TORONTO, ON, M3C 1V7
(416) 448-5800   *SIC 3589*
CLEVELAND RANGE LTD   *p550*
8251 KEELE ST, CONCORD, ON, L4K 1Z1
(905) 660-4747   *SIC 3589*
CORIX WATER SYSTEMS INC   *p254*
1128 BURDETTE ST, RICHMOND, BC, V6V 2Z3
(604) 273-4987   *SIC 3589*
CROWN FOOD SERVICE EQUIPMENT LTD   *p786*
70 OAKDALE RD, NORTH YORK, ON, M3N 1V9
(416) 746-2358   *SIC 3589*
DYNABLAST INC   *p721*
2625 MEADOWPINE BLVD, MISSISSAUGA, ON, L5N 7K5
(888) 881-6667   *SIC 3589*
ECODYNE LIMITED   *p522*
4475 CORPORATE DR, BURLINGTON, ON, L7L 5T9
(905) 332-1404   *SIC 3589*
ENTREPRISES CAFECTION INC   *p1266*
2355 AV DALTON, QUEBEC, QC, G1P 3S3
(418) 650-6162   *SIC 3589*
EVOQUA WATER TECHNOLOGIES LTD   *p735*
2045 DREW RD, MISSISSAUGA, ON, L5S 1S4
(905) 890-2803   *SIC 3589*
FALCO TECHNOLOGIES INC   *p1123*
1245 RUE INDUSTRIELLE, LA PRAIRIE, QC, J5R 2E4
(450) 444-0566   *SIC 3589*
GARLAND COMMERCIAL RANGES LIMITED   *p695*
1177 KAMATO RD, MISSISSAUGA, ON, L4W 1X4
(905) 624-0260   *SIC 3589*
H2O INNOVATION INC   *p1259*
330 RUE DE SAINT-VALLIER E BUREAU 340, QUEBEC, QC, G1K 9C5
(418) 688-0170   *SIC 3589*
INDUSTRIES M.K.E. (1984) INC, LES   *p1072*
183 BOUL MONTCALM N, CANDIAC, QC, J5R 3L6
(450) 659-6531   *SIC 3589*
MEQUIPCO INC   *p71*
5126 126 AVE SE UNIT 101, CALGARY, AB, T2Z 0H2
(403) 259-8333   *SIC 3589*
MOYER DIEBEL LIMITED   *p623*
2674 NORTH SERVICE RD, JORDAN STATION, ON, L0R 1S0
(905) 562-4195   *SIC 3589*
NEWTERRA LTD   *p519*
1291 CALIFORNIA AVE, BROCKVILLE, ON, K6V 7N5

---

(613) 498-1876   *SIC 3589*
QUEST METAL PRODUCTS LTD   *p382*
889 ERIN ST, WINNIPEG, MB, R3G 2W6
(204) 786-2403   *SIC 3589*
SHRED-TECH CORPORATION   *p536*
295 PINEBUSH RD, CAMBRIDGE, ON, N1T 1B2
(519) 621-3560   *SIC 3589*
STILMAS AMERICAS INC   *p528*
3250 HARVESTER RD UNIT 6, BURLINGTON, ON, L7N 3W9
(905) 639-7025   *SIC 3589*
SUEZ TREATMENT SOLUTIONS CANADA L.P.   *p478*
1295 CORMORANT RD SUITE 200, ANCASTER, ON, L9G 4V5
(289) 346-1000   *SIC 3589*
TROJAN TECHNOLOGIES GROUP ULC   *p650*
3020 GORE RD, LONDON, ON, N5V 4T7
(519) 457-3400   *SIC 3589*
TRUE ROCK FINANCIAL INC   *p794*
1240 ORMONT DR, NORTH YORK, ON, M9L 2V4
(905) 669-8333   *SIC 3589*
WATERITE, INC   *p370*
200 DISCOVERY PLACE UNIT 5, WINNIPEG, MB, R2R 0P7
(204) 786-1604   *SIC 3589*

SIC 3592 Carburetors, pistons, piston rings and valves

AUTOLINE PRODUCTS LTD   *p367*
675 GOLSPIE ST, WINNIPEG, MB, R2K 2V2
(204) 668-8242   *SIC 3592*

SIC 3593 Fluid power cylinders and actuators

HEROUX-DEVTEK INC   *p1144*
1111 RUE SAINT-CHARLES O BUREAU 600, LONGUEUIL, QC, J4K 5G4
(450) 679-3330   *SIC 3593*
HYCO CANADA LIMITED   *p1354*
1025 RUE PRINCIPALE, SAINT-WENCESLAS, QC, G0Z 1J0
(819) 224-4000   *SIC 3593*
HYDRA DYNE TECHNOLOGY INC   *p621*
55 SAMNAH CRES, INGERSOLL, ON, N5C 3J7
(519) 485-2200   *SIC 3593*
INDUSTRIES TOURNEBO INC, LES   *p1359*
3611 346 RTE, SAINTE-JULIENNE, QC, J0K 2T0
(450) 831-3229   *SIC 3593*
LHD EQUIPMENT LIMITED   *p763*
21 EXETER ST, NORTH BAY, ON, P1B 8G5
(705) 472-5207   *SIC 3593*
MAGNUM INTEGRATED TECHNOLOGIES INC   *p509*
200 FIRST GULF BLVD, BRAMPTON, ON, L6W 4T5
(905) 595-1998   *SIC 3593*
MONARCH INDUSTRIES LIMITED   *p366*
51 BURMAC RD, WINNIPEG, MB, R2J 4J3
(204) 786-7921   *SIC 3593*
PARKER HANNIFIN CANADA   *p684*
160 CHISHOLM DR SUITE 1, MILTON, ON, L9T 3G9
(905) 693-3000   *SIC 3593*
PARKER HANNIFIN CANADA   *p893*
1100 SOUTH SERVICE RD UNIT 318, STONEY CREEK, ON, L8E 0C5
(905) 309-8230   *SIC 3593*

SIC 3596 Scales and balances, except laboratory

WEIGH-TRONIX CANADA, ULC   *p1228*
6429 RUE ABRAMS, MONTREAL, QC, H4S

1X9

(514) 695-0380   *SIC* 3596

WESTERN SCALE CO LTD   p247
1670 KINGSWAY AVE, PORT COQUITLAM, BC, V3C 3Y9

(604) 941-3474   *SIC* 3596

SIC 3599 Industrial machinery, nec

383565 ONTARIO INC   p719
2660 MEADOWVALE BLVD UNIT 17, MISSISSAUGA, ON, L5N 6M6

(905) 670-8700   *SIC* 3599

742906 ONTARIO INC   p535
300 SHELDON DR, CAMBRIDGE, ON, N1T 1A8

(519) 740-7797   *SIC* 3599

9091-4532 QUEBEC INC   p1121
89 RUE VILLERAY, L'ISLE-VERTE, QC, G0L 1L0

(418) 898-3330   *SIC* 3599

ADRICO MACHINE WORKS LTD   p27
1165J 44 AVE SE, CALGARY, AB, T2G 4X4

(403) 243-7930   *SIC* 3599

ADVANCED PRECISION MACHINING AND FABRICATION LIMITED   p445
70 THORNHILL DR, DARTMOUTH, NS, B3B 1S3

(902) 468-5653   *SIC* 3599

ALLAIN EQUIPMENT MANUFACTURING LTD   p410
577 ROUTE 535, NOTRE-DAME, NB, E4V 2K4

(506) 576-6436   *SIC* 3599

ALTA PRECISION INC   p1047
11120 RUE COLBERT, ANJOU, QC, H1J 2X4

(514) 353-0919   *SIC* 3599

AMEC USINAGE INC   p1292
110 RUE DES GRANDS-LACS, SAINT-AUGUSTIN-DE-DESMAURES, QC, G3A 2K1

(418) 878-4133   *SIC* 3599

ARMOR MACHINE & MANUFACTURING LIMITED   p120
9962 29 AVE NW, EDMONTON, AB, T6N 1A2

(780) 465-6152   *SIC* 3599

ARVA INDUSTRIES INC   p889
43 GAYLORD RD, ST THOMAS, ON, N5P 3R9

(519) 637-1855   *SIC* 3599

ATOM-JET INDUSTRIES (2002) LTD   p347
2110 PARK AVE, BRANDON, MB, R7B 0R9

(204) 728-8590   *SIC* 3599

BARRIE WELDING & MACHINE (1974) LIMITED   p486
39 ANNE ST S, BARRIE, ON, L4N 2C7

(705) 726-1444   *SIC* 3599

BAUMEIER CORPORATION   p538
1050 FOUNTAIN ST N, CAMBRIDGE, ON, N3H 4R7

(519) 650-5553   *SIC* 3599

BRISTOL MACHINE WORKS LIMITED   p900
2100 ALGONQUIN RD, SUDBURY, ON, P3E 4Z6

(705) 522-1550   *SIC* 3599

CAMERON STEEL INC   p645
52 WALSH RD SUITE 3, LINDSAY, ON, K9V 4R3

(705) 878-0544   *SIC* 3599

CANADIAN MARITIME ENGINEERING LIMITED   p445
90 THORNHILL DR, DARTMOUTH, NS, B3B 1S3

(902) 468-1888   *SIC* 3599

CARRIER FOREST PRODUCTS LTD   p250
4722 CONTINENTAL WAY, PRINCE GEORGE, BC, V2N 5S5

(250) 963-9664   *SIC* 3599

CENTERLINE (WINDSOR) LIMITED   p1026
415 MORTON DR, WINDSOR, ON, N9J 3T8

(519) 734-8464   *SIC* 3599

CENTRAL MACHINE & MARINE INC   p859

649 MCGREGOR SIDE RD, SARNIA, ON, N7T 7H5

(519) 337-3722   *SIC* 3599

CGL MANUFACTURING INC   p605
151 ARROW RD, GUELPH, ON, N1K 1S8

(519) 836-0322   *SIC* 3599

CMP AUTOMATION INC   p483
229 BOIDA AVE SUITE 1, AYR, ON, N0B 1E0

(519) 740-6035   *SIC* 3599

CONVOYEUR CONTINENTAL & USINAGE LTEE   p1382
470 RUE SAINT-ALPHONSE S, THETFORD MINES, QC, G6G 3V8

(418) 338-4682   *SIC* 3599

CUSTOM FABRICATORS & MACHINISTS LIMITED   p416
45 GIFFORD RD, SAINT JOHN, NB, E2M 5K7

(506) 648-2226   *SIC* 3599

DEVTEK AEROSPACE INC   p1233
3675 BOUL INDUSTRIEL, MONTREAL, QC, H7L 4S3

(450) 629-3454   *SIC* 3599

DYNAMIC MACHINE CORPORATION   p365
1407 DUGALD RD, WINNIPEG, MB, R2J 0H3

(204) 982-4900   *SIC* 3599

EBCO INDUSTRIES LTD   p260
7851 ALDERBRIDGE WAY, RICHMOND, BC, V6X 2A4

(604) 278-5578   *SIC* 3599

ECLIPSE AUTOMATION INC   p535
130 THOMPSON DR, CAMBRIDGE, ON, N1T 2E5

(519) 620-1906   *SIC* 3599

ESTAMPRO INC   p1302
104 RUE DU PARC-INDUSTRIEL, SAINT-EVARISTE-DE-FORSYTH, QC, G0M 1S0

(418) 459-3423   *SIC* 3599

ETSM TECHNICAL SERVICES LTD   p602
407 SILVERCREEK PKY N, GUELPH, ON, N1H 8G8

(519) 827-1500   *SIC* 3599

EXPLOITS WELDING & MACHINE SHOP LTD   p424
2 QUEENSWAY, GRAND FALLS-WINDSOR, NL, A2B 1J3

(709) 489-5618   *SIC* 3599

FABRIS INC.   p892
1216 SOUTH SERVICE RD, STONEY CREEK, ON, L8E 5C4

(905) 643-4111   *SIC* 3599

FLEXMASTER CANADA LIMITED   p852
20 EAST PEARCE ST SUITE 1, RICHMOND HILL, ON, L4B 1B7

(905) 731-9411   *SIC* 3599

G.T. MACHINING & FABRICATING LTD   p747
101 RICHMOND BLVD, NAPANEE, ON, K7R 3Z8

(613) 354-6621   *SIC* 3599

GEORGE A. WRIGHT & SON LIMITED   p630
146 HICKSON AVE, KINGSTON, ON, K7K 2N9

(613) 542-4913   *SIC* 3599

GESTION M.E.W. INC   p1246
2255 AV VALLEE, PLESSISVILLE, QC, G6L 3P8

(819) 362-6315   *SIC* 3599

GIVENS ENGINEERING INC   p661
327 SOVEREIGN RD, LONDON, ON, N6M 1A6

(519) 453-9008   *SIC* 3599 ·

GROUPE J.L. LECLERC INC   p1292
4919 RTE MARIE-VICTORIN, SAINT-ANTOINE-DE-TILLY, QC, G0S 2C0

(418) 886-2474   *SIC* 3599

GROUPE LEV-FAB INC   p1320
640 BOUL MONSEIGNEUR-DUBOIS, SAINT-JEROME, QC, J7Y 3L8

(450) 438-7164   *SIC* 3599

GROUPE MELOCHE INC   p1366
491 BOUL DES ERABLES, SALABERRY-DE-VALLEYFIELD, QC, J6T 6G3

(450) 371-4646   *SIC* 3599

GYPSUM TECHNOLOGIES INC   p529
578 KING FOREST CRT, BURLINGTON, ON, L7P 5C1

(905) 567-2000   *SIC* 3599

H & O CENTERLESS GRINDING COMPANY LTD   p1010
45 BATHURST DR, WATERLOO, ON, N2V 1N2

(519) 884-0322   *SIC* 3599

HANDLING SPECIALTY MANUFACTURING LIMITED   p599
219 SOUTH SERVICE RD, GRIMSBY, ON, L3M 1Y6

(905) 945-9661   *SIC* 3599

HARMONIC MACHINE INC   p197
44365 PROGRESS WAY, CHILLIWACK, BC, V2R 0L1

(604) 823-4479   *SIC* 3599

INDUSTRIAL MACHINE & MFG. INC   p1428
3315 MINERS AVE, SASKATOON, SK, S7K 7K9

(306) 242-8400   *SIC* 3599

INGADALE INDUSTRIES INC   p872
48 CROCKFORD BLVD, SCARBOROUGH, ON, M1R 3C3

(416) 752-6266   *SIC* 3599

J.M.Y. INC   p1121
480 RUE JOSEPH-GAGNE S, LA BAIE, QC, G7B 3P6

(418) 544-8442   *SIC* 3599

JEBCO MANUFACTURING INC   p546
188 KING ST E RR 2, COLBORNE, ON, K0K 1S0

(905) 355-3757   *SIC* 3599

KK PRECISION INC   p787
104 OAKDALE RD, NORTH YORK, ON, M3N 1V9

(416) 742-5911   *SIC* 3599

KONAL ENGINEERING AND EQUIPMENT INC   p493
1 GRAHAM ST, BLENHEIM, ON, N0P 1A0

(519) 676-8133   *SIC* 3599

L. & G. CLOUTIER INC   p1121
303 BOUL NILUS-LECLERC, L'ISLET, QC, G0R 2C0

(418) 247-5071   *SIC* 3599

L.P. CUSTOM MACHINING LTD   p892
211 BARTON ST, STONEY CREEK, ON, L8E 2K3

SIC 3599

LAKELAND MULTI-TRADE INC   p545
566 D'ARCY ST, COBOURG, ON, K9A 4A9

(905) 372-7413   *SIC* 3599

LAR MACHINERIE INC   p1151
1760 169 RTE, METABETCHOUAN-LAC-A-LA-CROIX, QC, G8G 1B1

(418) 349-2875   *SIC* 3599

MAC-WELD MACHINING LTD   p858
1324 LOUGAR AVE, SARNIA, ON, N7S 5N7

(519) 332-1388   *SIC* 3599

MACHINERIE P.W. INC   p1280
1501 BOUL LOUIS-XIV, QUEBEC, QC, G2K 1W6

(418) 622-5155   *SIC* 3599

MAKSTEEL CORP   p686
7615 TORBRAM RD, MISSISSAUGA, ON, L4T 4A8

(905) 671-9000   *SIC* 3599

MEIKLE AUTOMATION INC   p637
975 BLEAMS RD UNIT 5-10, KITCHENER, ON, N2E 3Z5

(519) 896-0800   *SIC* 3599

MERCIER, INDUSTRIES EN MECANIQUE LTEE   p1115
2035 RUE FAY, JONQUIERE, QC, G7S 2N5

(418) 548-7141   *SIC* 3599

MONASHEE MANUFACTURING CORPORATION LTD   p222
1247 ELLIS ST, KELOWNA, BC, V1Y 1Z6

(250) 762-2646   *SIC* 3599

NORQUEST INDUSTRIES INC   p110
3911 74 AVE NW, EDMONTON, AB, T6B 2Z7

(780) 434-3322   *SIC* 3599

ODCO, INC   p1011
45 BATHURST DR, WATERLOO, ON, N2V 1N2

(519) 884-0322   *SIC* 3599

OPTIMA MANUFACTURING INC   p24
2480 PEGASUS RD NE, CALGARY, AB, T2E 8G8

(403) 291-2007   *SIC* 3599

PAZMAC ENTERPRISES LTD   p229
26777 GLOUCESTER WAY, LANGLEY, BC, V4W 3X6

(604) 857-8838   *SIC* 3599

PHOTON DYNAMICS CANADA INC   p674
221 WHITEHALL DR, MARKHAM, ON, L3R 9T1

SIC 3599

POCZO MANUFACTURING COMPANY LIMITED   p505
215 WILKINSON RD, BRAMPTON, ON, L6T 4M2

(905) 452-0567   *SIC* 3599

PRO-METAL PLUS INC   p1090
12 BOUL DES SOURCES, DESCHAMBAULT, QC, G0A 1S0

(418) 286-4949   *SIC* 3599

QUEENSWAY MACHINE PRODUCTS LIMITED, THE   p576
8 RANGEMORE RD, ETOBICOKE, ON, M8Z 5H7

(416) 259-4261   *SIC* 3599

R M H INDUSTRIE INC   p1293
130 RUE DE ROTTERDAM, SAINT-AUGUSTIN-DE-DESMAURES, QC, G3A 1T3

(418) 878-0875   *SIC* 3599

R.P.M. TECH INC   p1377
1318 RUE PRINCIPALE, ST-VALERIEN, QC, J0H 2B0

(418) 285-1811   *SIC* 3599

RTI-CLARO INC   p1232
5515 RUE ERNEST-CORMIER, MONTREAL, QC, H7C 2S9

(450) 786-2001   *SIC* 3599

RUSSEL METALS INC   p1429
503 50TH ST E, SASKATOON, SK, S7K 6H3

(306) 244-7511   *SIC* 3599

SICOM INDUSTRIES LTD   p230
27385 GLOUCESTER WAY, LANGLEY, BC, V4W 3Z8

(604) 856-3455   *SIC* 3599

SOCIETE D'OUTILLAGE M.R. LTEE   p1336
8500 BOUL HENRI-BOURASSA O, SAINT-LAURENT, QC, H4S 1P4

(514) 336-5182   *SIC* 3599

SOGEFI AIR & COOLING CANADA CORP   p1165
1500 RUE DE BOUCHERVILLE, MONTREAL, QC, H1N 3V3

(514) 764-8806   *SIC* 3599

STAMCO SPECIALTY TOOL & MFG. CO. (1979) LTD   p116
6048 97 ST NW, EDMONTON, AB, T6E 3J4

(780) 436-2647   *SIC* 3599

TECH-CON AUTOMATION ULC   p525
1219 CORPORATE DR, BURLINGTON, ON, L7L 5V5

(905) 639-4989   *SIC* 3599

TECHNOLOGIES K.K. INC, LES   p1243
64 RUE HUOT, NOTRE-DAME-DE-L'ILE-PERROT, QC, J7V 7Z8

(514) 453-6732   *SIC* 3599

TIMKEN CANADA LP   p1430
868 60TH ST E, SASKATOON, SK, S7K 8G8

(306) 931-3343   *SIC* 3599

TREL OF SARNIA LIMITED   p859
1165 CONFEDERATION ST, SARNIA, ON, N7S 3Y5

(519) 344-7025   *SIC* 3599

USINATECH INC   p1151
1099 CH D'ELY, MELBOURNE, QC, J0B 2B0

(819) 826-3774   *SIC* 3599

W S MACHINING & FABRICATION INC p359
49 LIFE SCIENCES PKY, STEINBACH, MB,
R5G 2G7
(204) 326-5444   SIC 3599
WRIGHT, GEORGE A. & SON (TORONTO)
LIMITED   p877
21 STATE CROWN BLVD, SCARBOR-
OUGH, ON, M1V 4B1
(416) 261-6499   SIC 3599

SIC 3612 Transformers, except electric

3680258 CANADA INC   p1108
795 BOUL INDUSTRIEL, GRANBY, QC,
J2G 9A1
(450) 378-3617   SIC 3612
9215-5936 QUEBEC INC   p1315
860 RUE LUCIEN-BEAUDIN, SAINT-JEAN-
SUR-RICHELIEU, QC, J2X 5V5
(450) 346-6363   SIC 3612
ABB INC   p1332
800 BOUL HYMUS, SAINT-LAURENT, QC,
H4S 0B5
(514) 710-1203   SIC 3612
ABB INC   p1392
1600 BOUL LIONEL-BOULET, VARENNES,
QC, J3X 1P7
(450) 652-1500   SIC 3612
ALLANSON INTERNATIONAL INC   p678
83 COMMERCE VALLEY DR E,
MARKHAM, ON, L3T 7T3
(800) 668-9162   SIC 3612
CAM TRAN CO. LTD   p546
203 PURDY RD, COLBORNE, ON, K0K 1S0
(905) 355-3224   SIC 3612
CARTE INTERNATIONAL INC   p369
1995 LOGAN AVE, WINNIPEG, MB, R2R
0H8
(204) 633-7220   SIC 3612
DEMYSH GROUP INC   p713
2568 ROYAL WINDSOR DR, MISSIS-
SAUGA, ON, L5J 1K7
SIC 3612
ELECTPOGROUPE PIONEER CANADA INC
p1110
612 CH BERNARD, GRANBY, QC, J2J 0H6
(450) 378-9018   SIC 3612
HAMMOND MUSEUM OF RADIO   p1004
15 INDUSTRIAL RD, WALKERTON, ON,
N0G 2V0
(519) 881-3552   SIC 3612
HAMMOND POWER SOLUTIONS INC p601
595 SOUTHGATE DR, GUELPH, ON, N1G
3W6
(519) 822-2441   SIC 3612
KINECTRICS INC   p575
800 KIPLING AVE SUITE 2, ETOBICOKE,
ON, M8Z 5G5
(416) 207-6000   SIC 3612
NORTHERN TRANSFORMER CORPORA-
TION   p664
245 MCNAUGHTON RD E, MAPLE, ON,
L6A 4P5
(905) 669-1853   SIC 3612
PARTNER TECHNOLOGIES INCORPO-
RATED   p1416
1155 PARK ST, REGINA, SK, S4N 4Y8
(306) 721-3114   SIC 3612
TRANSFACTOR INDUSTRIES INC   p560
65 BASALTIC RD, CONCORD, ON, L4K
1G4
(905) 695-8844   SIC 3612
TRANSFORMATEURS DELTA STAR INC
p1316
860 RUE LUCIEN-BEAUDIN, SAINT-JEAN-
SUR-RICHELIEU, QC, J2X 5V5
(450) 346-6622   SIC 3612
TRENCH LIMITED   p872
390 MIDWEST RD, SCARBOROUGH, ON,
M1P 3B5
(416) 751-8570   SIC 3612

---

*SIC 3613 Switchgear and switchboard
apparatus*

AUTOMATISATION JRT INC   p1266
405 AV GALILEE, QUEBEC, QC, G1P 4M6
(418) 871-6016   SIC 3613
CELCO CONTROLS LTD   p371
78 HUTCHINGS ST, WINNIPEG, MB, R2X
3B1
(204) 788-1677   SIC 3613
COMMERCIAL SWITCHGEAR LIMITED
p906
175 RACCO PKWY, THORNHILL, ON, L4J
8X9
(905) 669-9270   SIC 3613
CONNECTEURS ELECTRIQUES WECO
INC   p1118
18050 RTE TRANSCANADIENNE, KIRK-
LAND, QC, H9J 4A1
(514) 694-9136   SIC 3613
DELTA CONTROLS INC   p271
17850 56 AVE, SURREY, BC, V3S 1C7
(604) 574-9444   SIC 3613
ENGINEERED ELECTRIC CONTROLS LIM-
ITED   p536
230 SHELDON DR, CAMBRIDGE, ON, N1T
1A8
(519) 621-5370   SIC 3613
G&W CANADA CORPORATION   p511
7965 HERITAGE RD, BRAMPTON, ON, L6Y
5X5
(905) 542-2000   SIC 3613
KELTOUR CONTROLS INC   p523
4375 MAINWAY, BURLINGTON, ON, L7L
5N9
(905) 335-6000   SIC 3613
MANUFACTURE EXM LTEE   p1059
870 BOUL MICHELE-BOHEC, BLAINVILLE,
QC, J7C 5E2
(450) 979-4373   SIC 3613
MEMTRONIK INNOVATIONS INC   p1170
8648 BOUL PIE-IX, MONTREAL, QC, H1Z
4G2
(514) 374-1010   SIC 3613
ROCKWELL AUTOMATION CANADA CON-
TROL SYSTEMS   p534
12 RAGLIN PL, CAMBRIDGE, ON, N1R 7J2
(519) 740-5500   SIC 3613
S & C ELECTRIC CANADA LTD   p998
90 BELFIELD RD, TORONTO, ON, M9W
1G4
(416) 249-9171   SIC 3613
TECHNOLOGIES DUAL-ADE INC   p1374
4025 RUE LETELLIER, SHERBROOKE,
QC, J1L 1Z3
(819) 829-2100   SIC 3613
THEATRIXX TECHNOLOGIES INC   p1216
1655 RUE RICHARDSON, MONTREAL,
QC, H3K 3J7
(514) 939-3077   SIC 3613
UNIT ELECTRICAL ENGINEERING LTD
p242
1406 MAPLE ST, OKANAGAN FALLS, BC,
V0H 1R2
(250) 497-5254   SIC 3613

SIC 3621 Motors and generators

ABB INC   p77
9800 ENDEAVOR DR SE, CALGARY, AB,
T3S 0A1
(403) 252-7551   SIC 3621
ABB INC   p1332
800 BOUL HYMUS, SAINT-LAURENT, QC,
H4S 0B5
(438) 843-6000   SIC 3621
BWXT CANADA LTD   p532
581 CORONATION BLVD, CAMBRIDGE,
ON, N1R 5V3
(519) 621-2130   SIC 3621
BWXT CANADA LTD   p532
581 CORONATION BLVD, CAMBRIDGE,
ON, N1R 3E9

---

(519) 621-2130   SIC 3621
CAMBRIDGE PRO FAB INC   p517
84 SHAVER RD, BRANTFORD, ON, N3T
5M1
(519) 751-4351   SIC 3621
CONSTRUCTION ENERGIE RENOUVE-
LABLE S.E.N.C.   p1349
178 132 RTE E, SAINT-OMER, QC, G0C
2Z0
(418) 364-6027   SIC 3621
FABRICATION DELTA INC   p1242
154 CH SAINT-EDGAR, NEW RICHMOND,
QC, G0C 2B0
(418) 392-2624   SIC 3621
FOCAL TECHNOLOGIES CORPORATION
p446
77 FRAZEE AVE, DARTMOUTH, NS, B3B
1Z4
(902) 468-2263   SIC 3621
FRONTIER POWER PRODUCTS LTD   p209
7983 PROGRESS WAY, DELTA, BC, V4G
1A3
(604) 946-5531   SIC 3621
IEC HOLDEN INC   p1339
8180 CH DE LA COTE-DE-LIESSE, SAINT-
LAURENT, QC, H4T 1G8
(514) 735-4371   SIC 3621
JET POWER AND CONTROLS SYSTEMS
LTD   p109
7730 34 ST NW, EDMONTON, AB, T6B 3J6
(780) 485-1438   SIC 3621
MOTOR COILS MFG. LTD   p519
1879 PARKEDALE AVE E, BROCKVILLE,
ON, K6V 5T2
(613) 345-3580   SIC 3621
PIVOTAL POWER INC   p440
150 BLUEWATER RD, BEDFORD, NS, B4B
1G9
(902) 835-7268   SIC 3621
SMP MOTOR PRODUCTS LTD   p889
33 GAYLORD RD, ST THOMAS, ON, N5P
3R9
(519) 633-8422   SIC 3621
TM4 INC   p1067
135 RUE J.-A.-BOMBARDIER BUREAU 25,
BOUCHERVILLE, QC, J4B 8P1
(450) 645-1444   SIC 3621
TOTAL POWER LIMITED   p743
6450 KESTREL RD UNIT 3, MISSIS-
SAUGA, ON, L5T 1Z7
(905) 670-1535   SIC 3621
VENT DE L'EST INC   p1149
711 BOUL PERRON, MARIA, QC, G0C 1Y0
(418) 759-3054   SIC 3621
VON WEISE OF CANADA COMPANY   p535
505 CONESTOGA BLVD, CAMBRIDGE,
ON, N1R 7P4
SIC 3621
WIND WORKS POWER CORP   p518
14 LAKECREST CIR, BRIGHTON, ON, K0K
1H0
(613) 226-7883   SIC 3621

SIC 3624 Carbon and graphite products

MERSEN CANADA DN LTD   p571
496 EVANS AVE, ETOBICOKE, ON, M8W
2T7
(416) 251-2334   SIC 3624

SIC 3625 Relays and industrial controls

156861 CANADA INC   p1091
64 BOUL BRUNSWICK, DOLLARD-DES-
ORMEAUX, QC, H9B 2L3
(514) 421-4445   SIC 3625
ARMATURE DNS 2000 INC   p1239
11001 AV JEAN-MEUNIER, MONTREAL-
NORD, QC, H1G 4S7
(514) 324-1141   SIC 3625
ARP AUTOMATION CONTROLS INC   p135
80042 475 AVE E UNIT 200, HIGH RIVER,

AB, T1V 1M3
(403) 652-7130   SIC 3625
ARROW SPEED CONTROLS LIMITED   p253
13851 BRIDGEPORT RD, RICHMOND, BC,
V6V 1J6
(604) 321-4033   SIC 3625
BIONX INTERNATIONAL CORPORATION
p480
455 MAGNA DR, AURORA, ON, L4G 7A9
(905) 726-9105   SIC 3625
D-BOX TECHNOLOGIES INC   p1141
2172 RUE DE LA PROVINCE, LONGUEUIL,
QC, J4G 1R7
(450) 442-3003   SIC 3625
DELCO AUTOMATION INC   p1435
3735 THATCHER AVE, SASKATOON, SK,
S7R 1B8
(306) 244-6449   SIC 3625
DOUGLAS LIGHTING CONTROLS INC p188
3605 GILMORE WAY SUITE 280, BURN-
ABY, BC, V5G 4X5
(604) 873-2797   SIC 3625
EATON INDUSTRIES (CANADA) COMPANY
p683
610 INDUSTRIAL DR, MILTON, ON, L9T
5C3
(905) 875-4379   SIC 3625
ECKEL INDUSTRIES OF CANADA LIMITED
p746
35 ALLISON AVE, MORRISBURG, ON, K0C
1X0
(613) 543-2967   SIC 3625
ELECTRIC POWER EQUIPMENT LIMITED
p298
1285 HOMER ST, VANCOUVER, BC, V6B
2Z2
(604) 682-4221   SIC 3625
EQUIPEMENTS POWER SURVEY LTEE,
LES   p1339
7880 RTE TRANSCANADIENNE, SAINT-
LAURENT, QC, H4T 1A5
(514) 333-8392   SIC 3625
ETRATECH ENTERPRISES INC   p531
1047 COOKE BLVD, BURLINGTON, ON,
L7T 4A8
(905) 681-7544   SIC 3625
FJORD-TECH INDUSTRIE INC   p1121
2760 BOUL DE LA GRANDE-BAIE N, LA
BAIE, QC, G7B 3N8
(418) 544-7091   SIC 3625
GE MULTILIN   p679
650 MARKLAND ST, MARKHAM, ON, L6C
0M1
(905) 927-7070   SIC 3625
GECKO ALLIANCE GROUP INC   p1277
450 AV SAINT-JEAN-BAPTISTE BUREAU
200, QUEBEC, QC, G2E 6H5
(418) 872-4411   SIC 3625
GECKO ALLIANCE GROUP INC   p1277
450 RUE DES CANETONS, QUEBEC, QC,
G2E 5W6
(418) 872-4411   SIC 3625
GENERAL ELECTRIC CANADA COMPANY
p526
1150 WALKER'S LINE, BURLINGTON, ON,
L7M 1V2
(905) 335-6301   SIC 3625
GENERAL ELECTRIC CANADA COMPANY
p722
1919 MINNESOTA CRT, MISSISSAUGA,
ON, L5N 0C9
(905) 858-5100   SIC 3625
GENERAL ELECTRIC CANADA COMPANY
p803
1290 SOUTH SERVICE RD W, OAKVILLE,
ON, L6L 5T7
(905) 849-5048   SIC 3625
GENERAL ELECTRIC CANADA COMPANY
p841
107 PARK ST N SUITE 2, PETERBOR-
OUGH, ON, K9J 7B5
(705) 748-8486   SIC 3625
GENERAL ELECTRIC CANADA COMPANY
p1068

---

2 BOUL DE L'AEROPORT, BROMONT, QC, J2L 1S6
(450) 534-0917   *SIC 3625*

GENERAL ELECTRIC CANADA COMPANY *p1264*
1130 BOUL CHAREST O, QUEBEC, QC, G1N 2E2
(418) 682-8500   *SIC 3625*

GENTEC INC *p1266*
2625 AV DALTON, QUEBEC, QC, G1P 3S9
(418) 651-8000   *SIC 3625*

JCA INDUSTRIES INC *p384*
118 KING EDWARD ST E, WINNIPEG, MB, R3H 0N8
(204) 415-1104   *SIC 3625*

LOAD SYSTEMS INTERNATIONAL INC *p1267*
2666 BOUL DU PARC-TECHNOLOGIQUE BUREAU 190, QUEBEC, QC, G1P 4S6
(418) 650-2330   *SIC 3625*

LOCKHEED MARTIN CANADA INC *p823*
45 O'CONNOR ST SUITE 870, OTTAWA, ON, K1P 1A4
(613) 688-0698   *SIC 3625*

NITREX METAL INC *p1330*
3474 BOUL POIRIER, SAINT-LAURENT, QC, H4R 2J5
(514) 335-7191   *SIC 3625*

NORAC SYSTEMS INTERNATIONAL INC *p1434*
3702 KINNEAR PL, SASKATOON, SK, S7P 0A6
(306) 664-6711   *SIC 3625*

OES INC *p660*
4056 BLAKIE RD, LONDON, ON, N6L 1P7
(519) 652-5833   *SIC 3625*

PARKER HANNIFIN CANADA *p391*
1305 CLARENCE AVE, WINNIPEG, MB, R3T 1T4
(204) 452-6776   *SIC 3625*

REGAL BELOIT CANADA ULC *p229*
4916 275 ST, LANGLEY, BC, V4W 0A3
(604) 888-0110   *SIC 3625*

RELIABLE CONTROLS CORPORATION *p339*
120 HALLOWELL RD, VICTORIA, BC, V9A 7K2
(250) 475-2036   *SIC 3625*

ROCKWELL AUTOMATION CANADA CONTROL SYSTEMS *p534*
135 DUNDAS ST, CAMBRIDGE, ON, N1R 5N9
(519) 623-1810   *SIC 3625*

ROCKWELL AUTOMATION CANADA INC *p534*
135 DUNDAS ST N, CAMBRIDGE, ON, N1R 5X1
(519) 623-1810   *SIC 3625*

SIEMENS CANADA LIMITED *p524*
1550 APPLEBY LINE, BURLINGTON, ON, L7L 6X7
(905) 319-3600   *SIC 3625*

SIEMENS CANADA LIMITED *p558*
300 APPLEWOOD CRES SUITE 1, CONCORD, ON, L4K 5C7
(905) 856-5288   *SIC 3625*

SIEMENS CANADA LIMITED *p799*
1577 NORTH SERVICE RD E, OAKVILLE, ON, L6H 0H6
(905) 465-8000   *SIC 3625*

SIEMENS CANADA LIMITED *p1095*
1425 RTE TRANSCANADIENNE UNITE 400, DORVAL, QC, H9P 2W9
SIC 3625

SIEMENS CANADA LIMITED *p1095*
9505 CH COTE-DE-LIESSE BUREAU 9501, DORVAL, QC, H9P 2N9
(514) 828-3400   *SIC 3625*

SIEMENS CANADA LIMITED *p1277*
2800 AV SAINT-JEAN-BAPTISTE BUREAU 190, QUEBEC, QC, G2E 6J5
(418) 687-4524   *SIC 3625*

SWEGON NORTH AMERICA INC *p675*
355 APPLE CREEK BLVD, MARKHAM, ON,

L3R 9X7
(416) 291-7371   *SIC 3625*

TECHSOL MARINE INC *p1268*
4800 RUE RIDEAU, QUEBEC, QC, G1P 4P4
(418) 688-2230   *SIC 3625*

TORNATECH INC *p1087*
4100 DESSTE SUD LAVAL (A-440) O, LAVAL, QC, H7T 0H3
(514) 334-2503   *SIC 3625*

TRAC RAIL INC *p662*
955 GREEN VALLEY RD, LONDON, ON, N6N 1E4
(519) 452-1233   *SIC 3625*

TULSAR CANADA LTD *p516*
15 WORTHINGTON DR, BRANTFORD, ON, N3S 0H4
(519) 748-5055   *SIC 3625*

VAW SYSTEMS LTD *p373*
1300 INKSTER BLVD, WINNIPEG, MB, R2X 1P5
(204) 697-7770   *SIC 3625*

ZABER TECHNOLOGIES INC *p324*
605 KENT AVE NORTH W UNIT 2, VANCOUVER, BC, V6P 6T7
(604) 569-3780   *SIC 3625*

SIC 3629 Electrical industrial apparatus, nec

ADDENERGIE TECHNOLOGIES INC *p1266*
2800 RUE LOUIS-LUMIERE STE 100, QUEBEC, QC, G1P 0A4
(877) 505-2674   *SIC 3629*

DELTA-Q TECHNOLOGIES CORP *p188*
3755 WILLINGDON AVE, BURNABY, BC, V5G 3H3
(604) 327-8244   *SIC 3629*

GENTHERM GLOBAL POWER TECHNOLOGIES INC *p16*
7875 57 ST SE UNIT 16, CALGARY, AB, T2C 5K7
(403) 236-5556   *SIC 3629*

SIC 3631 Household cooking equipment

ONWARD MANUFACTURING COMPANY LIMITED *p1011*
585 KUMPF DR, WATERLOO, ON, N2V 1K3
(519) 885-4540   *SIC 3631*

ONWARD MULTI-CORP INC *p1011*
585 KUMPF DR, WATERLOO, ON, N2V 1K3
(519) 885-4540   *SIC 3631*

PADINOX INC *p1038*
489 BRACKLEY POINT RD RTE 15, BRACKLEY, PE, C1E 1Z3
(902) 629-1500   *SIC 3631*

SIC 3633 Household laundry equipment

WHIRLPOOL CANADA LP *p728*
6750 CENTURY AVE UNIT 200, MISSISSAUGA, ON, L5N 0B7
(905) 821-6400   *SIC 3633*

SIC 3634 Electric housewares and fans

ELECTROLUX CANADA CORP *p1120*
802 BOUL DE L'ANGE-GARDIEN, L'ASSOMPTION, QC, J5W 1T6
(450) 589-5701   *SIC 3634*

GLENGARRY INDUSTRIES LTD *p538*
1040 FOUNTAIN ST N SUITE 6, CAMBRIDGE, ON, N3E 1A3
(519) 653-1098   *SIC 3634*

INDUSTRIES DETTSON INC *p1374*
3400 BOUL INDUSTRIEL, SHERBROOKE, QC, J1L 1V8
(819) 346-8493   *SIC 3634*

LENNOX INDUSTRIES (CANADA) LTD *p579*
400 NORRIS GLEN RD, ETOBICOKE, ON,

M9C 1H5
(416) 621-9302   *SIC 3634*

NESTLE CANADA INC *p1214*
2060 RUE DE LA MONTAGNE BUREAU 304, MONTREAL, QC, H3G 1Z7
(514) 350-5754   *SIC 3634*

TOPVIEW TECHNOLOGY CORP *p257*
14488 KNOX WAY UNIT 123, RICHMOND, BC, V6V 2Z5
(604) 231-5858   *SIC 3634*

TWA PANEL SYSTEMS INC *p150*
1201 4 ST, NISKU, AB, T9E 7L3
(780) 955-8757   *SIC 3634*

VENMAR VENTILATION ULC *p1100*
550 BOUL LEMIRE, DRUMMONDVILLE, QC, J2C 7W9
(819) 477-6226   *SIC 3634*

SIC 3635 Household vacuum cleaners

INDUSTRIES TROVAC LIMITEE, LES *p1059*
3 RUE MARCEL-AYOTTE, BLAINVILLE, QC, J7C 5L7
(450) 434-2233   *SIC 3635*

SIC 3639 Household appliances, nec

A.O. SMITH ENTERPRISES LTD *p590*
599 HILL ST W, FERGUS, ON, N1M 2X1
(519) 843-1610   *SIC 3639*

ITW CANADA INC *p835*
2875 EAST BAY SHORE ROAD, OWEN SOUND, ON, N4K 5P5
(519) 376-8886   *SIC 3639*

USINES GIANT INC *p1238*
11021 RUE NOTRE-DAME E, MONTREAL-EST, QC, H1B 2V5
(514) 645-8893   *SIC 3639*

SIC 3641 Electric lamps

ARTIKA FOR LIVING INC *p1127*
1756 50E AV, LACHINE, QC, H8T 2V5
(514) 249-4557   *SIC 3641*

LEDVANCE LTD *p696*
5450 EXPLORER DR SUITE 100, MISSISSAUGA, ON, L4W 5N1
(905) 361-9333   *SIC 3641*

LEDVANCE LTD *p1099*
1 RUE SYLVAN, DRUMMONDVILLE, QC, J2C 2S8
(819) 478-6500   *SIC 3641*

SIGNIFY CANADA LTD *p562*
525 EDUCATION RD, CORNWALL, ON, K6H 6C7
SIC 3641

SIC 3643 Current-carrying wiring devices

BURNDY CANADA INC *p844*
870 BROCK RD, PICKERING, ON, L1W 1Z8
(905) 752-5400   *SIC 3643*

CICAME ENERGIE INC *p1309*
5400 RUE J.-A.-BOMBARDIER, SAINT-HUBERT, QC, J3Z 1G8
(450) 679-7778   *SIC 3643*

CIRCA ENTERPRISES INC *p68*
10333 SOUTHPORT RD SW SUITE 535, CALGARY, AB, T2W 3X6
(403) 258-2011   *SIC 3643*

ELECTRICAL CONTACTS LIMITED *p617*
519 22ND AVE, HANOVER, ON, N4N 3T6
(519) 364-1878   *SIC 3643*

ILSCO OF CANADA COMPANY *p708*
615 ORWELL ST, MISSISSAUGA, ON, L5A 2W4
(905) 274-2341   *SIC 3643*

LEGRAND CANADA INC *p1002*
9024 KEELE ST, VAUGHAN, ON, L4K 2N2

(905) 738-9195   *SIC 3643*

NEXANS CANADA INC *p1262*
1081 BOUL PIERRE-BERTRAND, QUEBEC, QC, G1M 2E8
SIC 3643

TECHSPAN INDUSTRIES INC *p718*
3131 PEPPER MILL CRT UNIT 1, MISSISSAUGA, ON, L5L 4X6
(905) 820-6150   *SIC 3643*

TYCO ELECTRONICS CANADA ULC *p676*
20 ESNA PARK DR, MARKHAM, ON, L3R 1E1
(905) 475-6222   *SIC 3643*

SIC 3644 Noncurrent-carrying wiring devices

ABB PRODUITS D'INSTALLATION LTEE *p1317*
100 RUE LONGTIN, SAINT-JEAN-SUR-RICHELIEU, QC, J3B 3G5
(450) 347-2304   *SIC 3644*

ACE MANUFACTURING METALS LTD *p5*
GD, BITTERN LAKE, AB, T0C 0L0
(780) 352-7145   *SIC 3644*

APPLETON GROUP CANADA, LTD *p568*
99 UNION ST, ELMIRA, ON, N3B 3L7
(519) 669-9222   *SIC 3644*

APPLIED WIRING (GEORGETOWN) INC. *p593*
2 ROSETTA ST, GEORGETOWN, ON, L7G 3P2
(905) 873-1717   *SIC 3644*

BRAND ENERGY SOLUTION (CANADA) LTD *p27*
601 34 AVE SE, CALGARY, AB, T2G 1V2
(403) 243-0283   *SIC 3644*

ELECTRO COMPOSITES (2008) ULC *p1321*
325 RUE SCOTT, SAINT-JEROME, QC, J7Z 1H3
(450) 431-2777   *SIC 3644*

K-LINE INSULATORS LIMITED *p876*
50 PASSMORE AVE, SCARBOROUGH, ON, M1V 4T1
(416) 292-2008   *SIC 3644*

PREFORMED LINE PRODUCTS (CANADA) LIMITED *p536*
1711 BISHOP ST N, CAMBRIDGE, ON, N1T 1N5
(519) 740-6666   *SIC 3644*

PRODUITS BEL INC *p1240*
6868 BOUL MAURICE-DUPLESSIS, MONTREAL-NORD, QC, H1G 1Z6
(514) 327-2800   *SIC 3644*

SLACAN INDUSTRIES INC *p515*
145 ROY BLVD, BRANTFORD, ON, N3R 7K1
(519) 758-8888   *SIC 3644*

SIC 3645 Residential lighting fixtures

4453760 CANADA INC *p1179*
225 RUE DE LIEGE O BUREAU 200, MONTREAL, QC, H2P 1H4
(514) 385-3515   *SIC 3645*

ARTCRAFT ELECTRIC LIMITED *p501*
8050 TORBRAM RD, BRAMPTON, ON, L6T 3T2
(905) 791-1551   *SIC 3645*

BETA-CALCO INC *p782*
25 KODIAK CRES, NORTH YORK, ON, M3J 3E5
(416) 531-9942   *SIC 3645*

ECLAIRAGE UNILIGHT LIMITEE *p1339*
4400 RUE HICKMORE, SAINT-LAURENT, QC, H4T 1K2
(514) 769-1533   *SIC 3645*

INDUSTRIES CENTURY INC, LES *p1156*
5645 AV ROYALMOUNT, MONT-ROYAL, QC, H4P 2P9
(514) 842-3933   *SIC 3645*

LUMENWERX ULC *p1326*

B-393 RUE SAINTE-CROIX, SAINT-LAURENT, QC, H4N 2L3
(514) 225-4304 *SIC 3645*

LUSTRE ARTCRAFT DE MONTREAL LTEE *p1049*
8525 RUE JULES-LEGER, ANJOU, QC, H1J 1A8
(514) 353-7200 *SIC 3645*

MODER, JAMES R. CRYSTAL CHANDE-LIER (CANADA) LTD *p289*
106 7TH AVE E, VANCOUVER, BC, V5T 1M6
(604) 879-0934 *SIC 3645*

SOLOTECH INC *p1167*
5200 RUE HOCHELAGA BUREAU 100, MONTREAL, QC, H1V 1G3
(514) 526-3094 *SIC 3645*

SOLOTECH INC *p1268*
935 RUE LACHANCE BUREAU 200, QUEBEC, QC, G1P 2H3
(418) 683-5553 *SIC 3645*

SIC 3646 Commercial lighting fixtures

1909203 ONTARIO INC *p795*
35 OAK ST, NORTH YORK, ON, M9N 1A1
(416) 245-7991 *SIC 3646*

BEGHELLI CANADA INC *p667*
3900 14TH AVE SUITE 1, MARKHAM, ON, L3R 4R3
(905) 948-9500 *SIC 3646*

BJ TAKE INC *p567*
220 RAMSEY DR, DUNNVILLE, ON, N1A 0A7
(905) 774-5988 *SIC 3646*

DELVIRO INC *p997*
94 BROCKPORT DR, TORONTO, ON, M9W 7J8
(416) 502-3434 *SIC 3646*

GROUPE LUMENPULSE INC *p1141*
1220 BOUL MARIE-VICTORIN, LONGUEUIL, QC, J4G 2H9
(514) 937-3003 *SIC 3646*

GROUPE LUMENPULSE INC *p1277*
445 AV SAINT-JEAN-BAPTISTE BUREAU 120, QUEBEC, QC, G2E 5N7
(418) 871-8039 *SIC 3646*

GVA LIGHTING, INC *p797*
2771 BRISTOL CIR, OAKVILLE, ON, L6H 6X5
(905) 569-6044 *SIC 3646*

LIGHTHEADED LIGHTING LTD *p246*
572 NICOLA PL SUITE 1150, PORT COQUITLAM, BC, V3B 0K4
(604) 464-5644 *SIC 3646*

LITE-TECH INDUSTRIES LIMITED *p787*
161 BARTLEY DR, NORTH YORK, ON, M4A 1E6
(416) 751-5644 *SIC 3646*

METALUMEN MANUFACTURING INC *p601*
570 SOUTHGATE DR, GUELPH, ON, N1G 4P6
(519) 822-4381 *SIC 3646*

SIGNIFY CANADA LTD *p679*
281 HILLMOUNT RD, MARKHAM, ON, L6C 2S3
(905) 927-4900 *SIC 3646*

SIGNIFY CANADA LTD *p1061*
640 BOUL DU CURE-BOIVIN, BOIS-BRIAND, QC, J7G 2A7
(450) 430-7040 *SIC 3646*

SIGNIFY CANADA LTD *p1129*
3015 RUE LOUIS-A.-AMOS, LACHINE, QC, H8T 1C4
(514) 636-0670 *SIC 3646*

VISCOR INC *p795*
35 OAK ST, NORTH YORK, ON, M9N 1A1
(416) 245-7991 *SIC 3646*

SIC 3647 Vehicular lighting equipment

MARBLE ELECTRONICS INC *p606*

650 WOODLAWN RD W SUITE 16A, GUELPH, ON, N1K 1B8
(519) 767-2863 *SIC 3647*

SWS STAR WARNING SYSTEMS INC *p760*
7695 BLACKBURN PKY, NIAGARA FALLS, ON, L2H 0A6
(905) 357-0222 *SIC 3647*

SIC 3648 Lighting equipment, nec

ABB PRODUITS D'INSTALLATION LTEE *p1093*
1811 BOUL HYMUS, DORVAL, QC, H9P 1J5
(514) 685-2277 *SIC 3648*

CARMANAH TECHNOLOGIES CORPORA-TION *p339*
250 BAY ST, VICTORIA, BC, V9A 3K5
(250) 380-0052 *SIC 3648*

CONGLOM FUTURCHEM INC *p685*
7385 BREN RD SUITE 3, MISSISSAUGA, ON, L4T 1H3
SIC 3648

CONXCORP LTD *p738*
6350 NETHERHART RD UNIT 2, MISSISSAUGA, ON, L5T 1K3
(866) 815-2669 *SIC 3648*

ECLAIRAGE AXIS INC *p1130*
2505 RUE SENKUS, LASALLE, QC, H8N 2X8
(514) 948-6272 *SIC 3648*

FLUXWERX ILLUMINATION INC *p281*
9255 194 ST, SURREY, BC, V4N 4G1
(604) 549-9379 *SIC 3648*

GROUPE LUMINAIRES INC, LE *p1180*
225 RUE DE LIEGE O BUREAU 200, MONTREAL, QC, H2P 1H4
(514) 385-3515 *SIC 3648*

LAMPADAIRES FERALUX INC *p1359*
2250 RUE BOMBARDIER, SAINTE-JULIE, QC, J3E 2J9
(450) 649-4114 *SIC 3648*

LED ROADWAY LIGHTING LTD *p458*
115 CHAIN LAKE DR SUITE 201, HALIFAX, NS, B3S 1B3
(902) 450-2222 *SIC 3648*

LUMIFY INC *p672*
2700 JOHN ST, MARKHAM, ON, L3R 2W4
(905) 474-0555 *SIC 3648*

METALUMEN HOLDINGS INC *p601*
570 SOUTHGATE DR, GUELPH, ON, N1G 4P6
(519) 822-4381 *SIC 3648*

MP DESIGN INC *p292*
16 4TH AVE W, VANCOUVER, BC, V5Y 1G3
(604) 708-1184 *SIC 3648*

SMAEA HOLDINGS INC *p602*
570 SOUTHGATE DR, GUELPH, ON, N1G 4P6
(519) 822-4381 *SIC 3648*

SNOC INC *p1314*
17200 AV CENTRALE, SAINT-HYACINTHE, QC, J2T 4J7
(450) 774-5238 *SIC 3648*

SIC 3651 Household audio and video equipment

1508235 ONTARIO INC *p992*
1 WOODBOROUGH AVE, TORONTO, ON, M6M 5A1
(416) 654-8008 *SIC 3651*

ADAMSON SYSTEMS ENGINEERING INC *p848*
1401 SCUGOG LINE 6, PORT PERRY, ON, L9L 1B2
(905) 982-0520 *SIC 3651*

AVIGILON CORPORATION *p297*
555 ROBSON ST 3RD FL, VANCOUVER, BC, V6B 3K9
(604) 629-5182 *SIC 3651*

BRYSTON LTD *p840*

677 NEAL DR, PETERBOROUGH, ON, K9J 6X7
(705) 742-5325 *SIC 3651*

CIRCUS WORLD DISPLAYS LIMITED *p760*
4080 MONTROSE RD, NIAGARA FALLS, ON, L2H 1J9
(905) 353-0732 *SIC 3651*

CITY WIRELESS *p8*
2150 29 ST NE SUITE 10, CALGARY, AB, T1Y 7G4
SIC 3651

DWS DATA WIRING SOLUTIONS INC *p458*
127 CHAIN LAKE DR UNIT 1, HALIFAX, NS, B3S 1B3
(902) 445-9473 *SIC 3651*

KONGSBERG INC *p1112*
2801 3E RUE, GRAND-MERE, QC, G9T 5K5
(819) 533-3202 *SIC 3651*

LENBROOK INDUSTRIES LIMITED *p845*
633 GRANITE CRT, PICKERING, ON, L1W 3K1
(905) 831-6333 *SIC 3651*

PARADIGM ELECTRONICS INC *p741*
205 ANNAGEM BLVD, MISSISSAUGA, ON, L5T 2V1
(905) 564-1994 *SIC 3651*

TAMAGGO INC *p1200*
2001 AV MCGILL COLLEGE BUREAU 700, MONTREAL, QC, H3A 1G1
SIC 3651

VIQ SOLUTIONS INC *p690*
5915 AIRPORT RD SUITE 700, MISSISSAUGA, ON, L4V 1T1
(905) 948-8266 *SIC 3651*

SIC 3652 Prerecorded records and tapes

CINRAM CANADA OPERATIONS ULC *p873*
400 NUGGET AVE, SCARBOROUGH, ON, M1S 4A4
(416) 332-9000 *SIC 3652*

WARNER MUSIC CANADA CO. *p766*
155 GORDON BAKER RD UNIT 401, NORTH YORK, ON, M2H 3N5
(416) 491-5005 *SIC 3652*

SIC 3661 Telephone and telegraph apparatus

BAYLIN TECHNOLOGIES INC *p667*
60 COLUMBIA WAY SUITE 205, MARKHAM, ON, L3R 0C9
(416) 805-9127 *SIC 3661*

MITEL NETWORKS CORPORATION *p624*
350 LEGGET DR, KANATA, ON, K2K 2W7
(613) 592-2122 *SIC 3661*

POSITRON INC *p1228*
5101 RUE BUCHAN SUITE 220, MONTREAL, QC, H4P 2R9
(514) 345-2220 *SIC 3661*

REDLINE COMMUNICATIONS INC *p674*
302 TOWN CENTRE BLVD SUITE 100, MARKHAM, ON, L3R 0E8
(905) 479-8344 *SIC 3661*

SCI BROCKVILLE CORP *p625*
500 MARCH RD, KANATA, ON, K2K 0J9
(613) 886-6148 *SIC 3661*

TERAXION INC *p1268*
2716 RUE EINSTEIN, QUEBEC, QC, G1P 4S8
(418) 658-9500 *SIC 3661*

SIC 3663 Radio and t.v. communications equipment

BIOSCRYPT INC *p667*
50 ACADIA AVE UNIT 200, MARKHAM, ON, L3R 0B3
(905) 624-7700 *SIC 3663*

BLACKLINE SAFETY CORP *p27*

803 24 AVE SE UNIT 100, CALGARY, AB, T2G 1P5
(403) 451-0327 *SIC 3663*

C-COM SATELLITE SYSTEMS INC *p815*
2574 SHEFFIELD RD, OTTAWA, ON, K1B 3V7
(613) 745-4110 *SIC 3663*

CHELTON TECHNOLOGIES CANADA LIMITED *p221*
1925 KIRSCHNER RD SUITE 14, KELOWNA, BC, V1Y 4N7
(250) 763-2232 *SIC 3663*

COMMUNICATIONS & POWER INDUSTRIES CANADA INC *p593*
45 RIVER DR UPPER LEVEL, GEORGETOWN, ON, L7G 2J4
(905) 877-0161 *SIC 3663*

COMMUNICATIONS & POWER INDUSTRIES CANADA INC *p593*
LOWER LEVEL 45 RIVER DR, GEORGETOWN, ON, L7G 2J4
(905) 877-0161 *SIC 3663*

DDS WIRELESS INTERNATIONAL INC *p263*
11920 FORGE PL, RICHMOND, BC, V7A 4V9
(604) 241-1441 *SIC 3663*

EVERTZ MICROSYSTEMS LTD *p522*
5292 JOHN LUCAS DR, BURLINGTON, ON, L7L 5Z9
(905) 335-3700 *SIC 3663*

HLS HARD-LINE SOLUTIONS INC *p565*
53 MAIN ST W, DOWLING, ON, P0M 1R0
(705) 855-1310 *SIC 3663*

ICC IMAGINE COMMUNICATIONS CANADA LTD *p776*
25 DYAS RD, NORTH YORK, ON, M3B 1V7
(416) 445-9640 *SIC 3663*

INNOVATIVE BIOMETRIC TECHNOLOGIES CORP *p772*
5000 YONGE ST SUITE 1901, NORTH YORK, ON, M2N 7E9
(416) 222-5000 *SIC 3663*

ITS ELECTRONICS INC *p1002*
3280 LANGSTAFF RD UNIT B, VAUGHAN, ON, L4K 5B6
(905) 660-0405 *SIC 3663*

LAIRD CONTROLS CANADA LIMITED *p1340*
3950 RUE HICKMORE, SAINT-LAURENT, QC, H4T 1K2
(514) 908-1659 *SIC 3663*

MACDONALD, DETTWILER AND ASSOCIATES CORPORATION *p1355*
21025 AUT TRANSCANADIENNE, SAINTE-ANNE-DE-BELLEVUE, QC, H9X 3R2
(514) 457-2150 *SIC 3663*

MICRO-ONDES APOLLO LTEE *p1094*
1650 RTE TRANSCANADIENNE, DORVAL, QC, H9P 1H7
(514) 421-2211 *SIC 3663*

NAUTEL LIMITED *p451*
10089 PEGGYS COVE RD HWY 333, HACKETTS COVE, NS, B3Z 3J4
(902) 823-3900 *SIC 3663*

RESEAU SANS FIL OTODATA INC *p1226*
9280 BOUL DE L'ACADIE, MONTREAL, QC, H4N 3C5
(514) 673-0244 *SIC 3663*

ROSS VIDEO LIMITED *p623*
8 JOHN ST, IROQUOIS, ON, K0E 1K0
(613) 652-4886 *SIC 3663*

ROSS VIDEO LIMITED *p750*
64 AURIGA DR SUITE 1, NEPEAN, ON, K2E 1B8
(613) 228-0688 *SIC 3663*

SDP TELECOM ULC *p1095*
1725 RTE TRANSCANADIENNE, DORVAL, QC, H9P 1J1
(514) 421-5959 *SIC 3663*

SINCLAIR TECHNOLOGIES INC *p481*
85 MARY ST, AURORA, ON, L4G 6X5
(905) 727-0165 *SIC 3663*

UTSTARCOM CANADA COMPANY *p257*

4600 JACOMBS RD SUITE 120, RICH-
MOND, BC, V6V 3B1
(604) 276-0055   SIC 3663
VECIMA NETWORKS INC   p339
771 VANALMAN AVE SUITE 201, VICTO-
RIA, BC, V8Z 3B8
(250) 881-1982   SIC 3663
WESCAM INC.   p529
649 NORTH SERVICE RD, BURLINGTON,
ON, L7P 5B9
(905) 633-4000   SIC 3663
ZEBRA TECHNOLGIES CANADA, ULC p728
2100 MEADOWVALE BLVD, MISSIS-
SAUGA, ON, L5N 7J9
(905) 813-9900   SIC 3663

SIC 3669 Communications equipment, nec

ALPHA TECHNOLOGIES LTD   p191
7700 RIVERFRONT GATE, BURNABY, BC,
V5J 5M4
(604) 436-5900   SIC 3669
ATS TRAFFIC-BRITISH COLUMBIA LTD
p122
7798 16 ST NW, EDMONTON, AB, T6P 1L9
(780) 440-4114   SIC 3669
COM DEV INTERNATIONAL LTD   p533
155 SHELDON DR, CAMBRIDGE, ON, N1R
7H6
(519) 622-2300   SIC 3669
COM DEV LTD   p533
155 SHELDON DR, CAMBRIDGE, ON, N1R
7H6
(519) 622-2300   SIC 3669
CORINEX COMMUNICATIONS CORP p312
1090 PENDER ST W SUITE 1000, VAN-
COUVER, BC, V6E 2N7
(604) 692-0520   SIC 3669
D. & R. ELECTRONICS CO. LTD   p494
8820 GEORGE BOLTON PKY, BOLTON,
ON, L7E 2Y4
(905) 951-9997   SIC 3669
DANIELS ELECTRONICS LTD   p335
43 ERIE ST, VICTORIA, BC, V8V 1P8
(250) 382-8268   SIC 3669
EVERTZ TECHNOLOGIES LIMITED   p522
5292 JOHN LUCAS DR, BURLINGTON,
ON, L7L 5Z9
(905) 335-3700   SIC 3669
FORTRAN TRAFFIC SYSTEMS LIMITED
p871
470 MIDWEST RD, SCARBOROUGH, ON,
M1P 4Y5
(416) 288-1320   SIC 3669
**FTS FOREST TECHNOLOGY SYSTEMS
LTD**   p340
1065 HENRY ENG PL, VICTORIA, BC, V9B
6B2
(250) 478-5561   SIC 3669
**INNOVASEA MARINE SYSTEMS CANADA
INC**   p440
20 ANGUS MORTON DR, BEDFORD, NS,
B4B 0L9
(902) 450-1700   SIC 3669
**INTERNATIONAL DATACASTING CORPO-
RATION**   p624
10 BREWER HUNT WAY, KANATA, ON, K2K
2B5
(613) 596-4120   SIC 3669
KAPSCH TRAFFICCOM CANADA INC p696
6020 AMBLER DR, MISSISSAUGA, ON,
L4W 2P1
(905) 624-3020   SIC 3669
LUMENTUM OTTAWA INC   p752
61 BILL LEATHEM DR, NEPEAN, ON, K2J
0P7
(613) 843-3000   SIC 3669
M2S ELECTRONIQUE LTEE   p1276
2855 RUE DE CELLES, QUEBEC, QC, G2C
1K7
(418) 842-1717   SIC 3669
MACPHERSON, PAUL & ASSOCIATES LTD
p342

1010 DUCHESS AVE, WEST VANCOU-
VER, BC, V7T 1G9
(604) 925-0609   SIC 3669
MENTOR ENGINEERING INC   p9
2175 29 ST NE SUITE 10, CALGARY, AB,
T1Y 7H8
(403) 777-3760   SIC 3669
MGC SYSTEMS INTERNATIONAL LTD p555
25 INTERCHANGE WAY, CONCORD, ON,
L4K 5W3
(905) 660-4655   SIC 3669
MICROHARD SYSTEMS INC   p76
150 COUNTRY HILLS LANDNG NW SUITE
101, CALGARY, AB, T3K 5P3
(403) 248-0028   SIC 3669
MIRCOM GROUP HOLDINGS INC   p556
25 INTERCHANGE WAY, CONCORD, ON,
L4K 5W3
(905) 660-4655   SIC 3669
MIRCOM TECHNOLOGIES LTD   p556
25 INTERCHANGE WAY UNIT 1, CON-
CORD, ON, L4K 5W3
(905) 660-4655   SIC 3669
NORSAT INTERNATIONAL INC   p255
4020 VIKING WAY UNIT 110, RICHMOND,
BC, V6V 2N2
(604) 821-2800   SIC 3669
RAYTHEON CANADA LIMITED   p1009
400 PHILLIP ST, WATERLOO, ON, N2L 6R7
(519) 885-0110   SIC 3669
RHEINMETALL CANADA INC   p1318
225 BOUL DU SEMINAIRE S, SAINT-JEAN-
SUR-RICHELIEU, QC, J3B 8E9
(450) 358-2000   SIC 3669
SAFETY FIRST CONTRACTING (1995) LTD
p448
116 THORNE AVE, DARTMOUTH, NS, B3B
1Z2
(902) 464-0889   SIC 3669
SIGNALISATION VER-MAC INC   p1278
1781 RUE BRESSE, QUEBEC, QC, G2G
2V2
(418) 654-1303   SIC 3669
SIMPLER NETWORKS INC   p1095
1840 RTE TRANSCANADIENNE UNITE
100, DORVAL, QC, H9P 1H7
(514) 684-2112   SIC 3669
**SPIRENT COMMUNICATIONS OF OTTAWA
LTD**   p627
750 PALLADIUM DR UNIT 310, KANATA,
ON, K2V 1C7
(613) 592-2661   SIC 3669
SYSTEMES DE SECURITE PARADOX LTEE
p1302
780 BOUL INDUSTRIEL, SAINT-
EUSTACHE, QC, J7R 5V3
(450) 491-7444   SIC 3669
SYSTEMES HAIVISION INC   p1228
2600 BOUL ALFRED-NOBEL 5EME
ETAGE, MONTREAL, QC, H4S 0A9
(514) 334-5445   SIC 3669
TECHNOLOGIES HUMANWARE INC p1099
1800 RUE JEAN-BERCHMANS-MICHAUD,
DRUMMONDVILLE, QC, J2C 7G7
(819) 471-4818   SIC 3669
TIMES FIBER CANADA LIMITED   p850
580 O'BRIEN RD, RENFREW, ON, K7V 3Z2
(613) 432-8566   SIC 3669
UTC FIRE & SECURITY CANADA INC p701
5201 EXPLORER DR, MISSISSAUGA, ON,
L4W 4H1
(905) 629-2600   SIC 3669
**VESTA SOLUTIONS COMMUNICATIONS
CORP**   p1107
200 BOUL DE LA TECHNOLOGIE BUREAU
300, GATINEAU, QC, J8Z 3H6
(819) 778-2053   SIC 3669

SIC 3671 Electron tubes

BEND ALL AUTOMOTIVE ULC   p483
115 WANLESS CRT, AYR, ON, N0B 1E0
(519) 623-2003   SIC 3671

SIC 3672 Printed circuit boards

656706 ONTARIO INC   p665
2701 JOHN ST, MARKHAM, ON, L3R 2W5
(905) 479-9515   SIC 3672
AIRBORN FLEXIBLE CIRCUITS INC p916
11 DOHME AVE, TORONTO, ON, M4B 1Y7
(416) 752-2224   SIC 3672
C-VISION LIMITED   p438
21 TANTRAMAR CRES, AMHERST, NS,
B4H 4S8
(902) 667-1228   SIC 3672
CAMPTECH II CIRCUITS INC   p667
81 BENTLEY ST, MARKHAM, ON, L3R 3L1
(905) 477-8790   SIC 3672
CELESTICA INTERNATIONAL LP   p755
213 HARRY WALKER PKY S, NEWMAR-
KET, ON, L3Y 8T3
(416) 448-2559   SIC 3672
CELESTICA INTERNATIONAL LP   p916
844 DON MILLS RD, TORONTO, ON, M3C
1V7
(416) 448-2559   SIC 3672
CIRCUIT CENTER INC   p870
175 MIDWEST RD, SCARBOROUGH, ON,
M1P 3A6
(416) 285-5550   SIC 3672
CIRCUIT TECH INC   p668
399 DENISON ST, MARKHAM, ON, L3R
1B7
(905) 474-9227   SIC 3672
CRIMP CIRCUITS INC   p783
675 PETROLIA RD, NORTH YORK, ON,
M3J 2N6
(416) 665-2466   SIC 3672
DICA ELECTRONICS LTD   p540
160 INDUSTRIAL AVE, CARLETON
PLACE, ON, K7C 3T2
(613) 257-5379   SIC 3672
DY 4 SYSTEMS INC   p626
333 PALLADIUM DR, KANATA, ON, K2V
1A6
(613) 599-9199   SIC 3672
DYNAMIC & PROTO CIRCUITS INC p891
869 BARTON ST, STONEY CREEK, ON,
L8E 5G6
SIC 3672
**FIRAN TECHNOLOGY GROUP CORPORA-
TION**   p878
250 FINCHDENE SQ, SCARBOROUGH,
ON, M1X 1A5
(416) 299-4000   SIC 3672
INTEGRATED TECHNOLOGY LIMITED p671
90 DON PARK RD, MARKHAM, ON, L3R
1C4
(905) 475-6658   SIC 3672
MARA TECHNOLOGIES INC   p678
5680 14TH AVE, MARKHAM, ON, L3S 3K8
(905) 201-1787   SIC 3672
METAPLAST CIRCUITS LIMITED   p914
180 HYMUS RD, TORONTO, ON, M1L 2E1
(416) 285-5000   SIC 3672
MILPLEX CIRCUIT (CANADA) INC   p876
70 MAYBROOK DR, SCARBOROUGH, ON,
M1V 4B6
(416) 292-8645   SIC 3672
NEW CIRCUITS LIMITED   p673
399 DENISON ST, MARKHAM, ON, L3R
1B7
(905) 474-9227   SIC 3672
QTA CIRCUITS LTD   p674
144 GIBSON DR, MARKHAM, ON, L3R 2Z3
(905) 477-4400   SIC 3672
SIGMAPOINT TECHNOLOGIES INC p562
2880 MARLEAU AVE, CORNWALL, ON,
K6H 6B5
(613) 937-4462   SIC 3672
SMTC CORPORATION   p675
7050 WOODBINE AVE SUITE 300,
MARKHAM, ON, L3R 4G8
(905) 479-1810   SIC 3672
**SMTC MANUFACTURING CORPORATION
OF CANADA**   p675

7050 WOODBINE AVE SUITE 300,
MARKHAM, ON, L3R 4G8
(905) 479-1810   SIC 3672
SMTC NOVA SCOTIA COMPANY   p675
7050 WOODBINE AVE SUITE 300,
MARKHAM, ON, L3R 4G8
(905) 479-1810   SIC 3672
VIASYSTEMS TORONTO INC   p914
8150 SHEPPARD AVE E, TORONTO, ON,
M1B 5K2
(416) 208-2100   SIC 3672

---

*SIC 3674 Semiconductors and related
devices*

2142064 ONTARIO INC   p704
5570 KENNEDY RD, MISSISSAUGA, ON,
L4Z 2A9
(905) 238-1777   SIC 3674
AMIRIX SYSTEMS INC   p440
20 ANGUS MORTON DR, BEDFORD, NS,
B4B 0L9
(902) 450-1700   SIC 3674
BALLARD POWER SYSTEMS INC   p191
9000 GLENLYON PKY, BURNABY, BC, V5J
5J8
(604) 454-0900   SIC 3674
DAVIS, W.R. ENGINEERING LIMITED p815
1260 OLD INNES RD SUITE 606, OTTAWA,
ON, K1B 3V3
(613) 748-5500   SIC 3674
DRS TECHNOLOGIES CANADA LTD p626
700 PALLADIUM DR, KANATA, ON, K2V
1C6
(613) 591-6000   SIC 3674
DRS TECHNOLOGIES CANADA LTD p626
500 PALLADIUM DR SUITE 1100, KANATA,
ON, K2V 1C2
(613) 591-5800   SIC 3674
IBM CANADA LIMITED   p1068
23 BOUL DE L'AEROPORT, BROMONT,
QC, J2L 1A3
(450) 534-6000   SIC 3674
LUMENIX CORPORATION   p571
15 AKRON RD, ETOBICOKE, ON, M8W 1T3
(855) 586-3649   SIC 3674
MICRALYNE INC   p121
1911 94 ST NW, EDMONTON, AB, T6N 1E6
(780) 431-4400   SIC 3674
MICROSEMI SEMICONDUCTOR ULC p624
400 MARCH RD, KANATA, ON, K2K 3H4
(613) 592-0200   SIC 3674
REDLEN TECHNOLOGIES INC   p267
1763 SEAN HTS UNIT 123, SAANICHTON,
BC, V8M 0A5
(250) 656-5411   SIC 3674
SIDENSE CORP   p625
84 HINES RD SUITE 260, KANATA, ON,
K2K 3G3
(613) 287-0292   SIC 3674
SILFAB SOLAR INC   p743
240 COURTNEYPARK DR E, MISSIS-
SAUGA, ON, L5T 2S5
(905) 255-2501   SIC 3674
SILICIUM BECANCOUR INC   p1056
6500 RUE YVON-TRUDEAU, BECAN-
COUR, QC, G9H 2V8
(819) 294-6000   SIC 3674
**SILICIUM QUEBEC SOCIETE EN COMMAN-
DITE**   p1056
6500 RUE YVON-TRUDEAU, BECAN-
COUR, QC, G9H 2V8
(819) 294-6000   SIC 3674
SILONEX INC   p1324
2150 RUE WARD, SAINT-LAURENT, QC,
H4M 1T7
SIC 3674
SMART TECHNOLOGIES INC   p40
3636 RESEARCH RD NW, CALGARY, AB,
T2L 1Y1
(403) 245-0333   SIC 3674
SMART TECHNOLOGIES ULC   p40
3636 RESEARCH RD NW, CALGARY, AB,
T2L 1Y1

(403) 245-0333   *SIC 3674*
SMART TECHNOLOGIES ULC   *p627*
501 PALLADIUM DR, KANATA, ON, K2V 0A2

(403) 245-0333   *SIC 3674*
SYSTEMES ELECTRONIQUES MATROX LTEE   *p1095*
1055 BOUL SAINT-REGIS, DORVAL, QC, H9P 2T4

(514) 822-6000   *SIC 3674*
TELEDYNE DALSA SEMICONDUCTEUR INC   *p1068*
18 BOUL DE L'AEROPORT, BROMONT, QC, J2L 1S7

(450) 534-2321   *SIC 3674*
TERADICI CORPORATION   *p189*
4601 CANADA WAY SUITE 300, BURNABY, BC, V5G 4X8

(604) 451-5800   *SIC 3674*
VIXS SYSTEMS INC   *p769*
1210 SHEPPARD AVE E SUITE 800, NORTH YORK, ON, M2K 1E3

(416) 646-2000   *SIC 3674*

SIC 3675 Electronic capacitors

NESSCAP ENERGY INC   *p955*
40 KING ST W SUITE 5800, TORONTO, ON, M5H 3S1

(416) 596-2127   *SIC 3675*

SIC 3677 Electronic coils and transformers

AIRCRAFT APPLIANCES AND EQUIPMENT LIMITED   *p501*
150 EAST DR, BRAMPTON, ON, L6T 1C1

(905) 791-1666   *SIC 3677*
ATC-FROST MAGNETICS INC   *p796*
1130 EIGHTH LINE, OAKVILLE, ON, L6H 2R4

(905) 844-6681   *SIC 3677*
ATC-FROST MAGNETICS INC   *p1008*
550 PARKSIDE DR UNIT D6, WATERLOO, ON, N2L 5V4

(905) 844-6681   *SIC 3677*
BROWNSBURG ELECTRONIK INC   *p1129*
741 RUE LOWE, LACHUTE, QC, J8H 4N9

(450) 562-5211   *SIC 3677*
FILTRAN LIMITED   *p624*
360 TERRY FOX DR SUITE 100, KANATA, ON, K2K 2P5

(613) 270-9009   *SIC 3677*
POLYCAST INDUSTRIAL PRODUCTS LTD   *p372*
486 SHEPPARD ST, WINNIPEG, MB, R2X 2P8

(204) 632-5428   *SIC 3677*
POWERSMITHS INTERNATIONAL CORP   *p505*
8985 AIRPORT RD, BRAMPTON, ON, L6T 5T2

(905) 791-1493   *SIC 3677*

SIC 3678 Electronic connectors

DNA DATA NETWORKING AND ASSEMBLIES LTD   *p192*
8057 NORTH FRASER WAY, BURNABY, BC, V5J 5M8

(604) 439-1099   *SIC 3678*
JITE TECHNOLOGIES INC   *p871*
11 PROGRESS AVE UNIT 25, SCARBOROUGH, ON, M1P 4S7

(416) 298-6447   *SIC 3678*

SIC 3679 Electronic components, nec

1150018 ONTARIO INC   *p831*
15 CAPELLA CRT UNIT 115, OTTAWA, ON, K2E 7X1

(613) 225-5044   *SIC 3679*
3330389 CANADA INC   *p1248*
125 BOUL HYMUS, POINTE-CLAIRE, QC, H9R 1E6

(514) 428-8898   *SIC 3679*
3GMETALWORX INC   *p548*
90 SNOW BLVD UNIT 2, CONCORD, ON, L4K 4A2

(905) 738-7973   *SIC 3679*
6094376 CANADA LTD   *p162*
117 PEMBINA RD SUITE 109, SHERWOOD PARK, AB, T8H 0J4

(780) 467-4118   *SIC 3679*
ABSOPULSE ELECTRONICS LTD   *p540*
110 WALGREEN RD, CARP, ON, K0A 1L0

(613) 836-3511   *SIC 3679*
ADVANTECH WIRELESS TECHNOLOGIES INC   *p1117*
16715 BOUL HYMUS, KIRKLAND, QC, H9H 5M8

(514) 694-8666   *SIC 3679*
AMPHENOL TECHNICAL PRODUCTS INTERNATIONAL CO   *p383*
2110 NOTRE DAME AVE, WINNIPEG, MB, R3H 0K1

(204) 697-2222   *SIC 3679*
ARTAFLEX INC   *p850*
174 WEST BEAVER CREEK RD, RICHMOND HILL, ON, L4B 1B4

(905) 470-0109   *SIC 3679*
ASCS CANADIAN SIGNAL CORPORATION   *p1013*
606 BEECH ST W, WHITBY, ON, L1N 7T8

(905) 665-4300   *SIC 3679*
AXIOMATIC TECHNOLOGIES CORPORATION   *p704*
5915 WALLACE ST, MISSISSAUGA, ON, L4Z 1Z8

(905) 602-9270   *SIC 3679*
BROSE CANADA INC   *p661*
1500 MAX BROSE DR, LONDON, ON, N6N 1P7

(519) 644-5200   *SIC 3679*
CANTWELL CULLEN & COMPANY INC *p803*
1131 SOUTH SERVICE RD W, OAKVILLE, ON, L6L 6K4

(905) 825-3255   *SIC 3679*
CELESTICA INTERNATIONAL INC   *p779*
844 DON MILLS RD, NORTH YORK, ON, M3C 1V7

(416) 448-5800   *SIC 3679*
CHINA KELI ELECTRIC COMPANY LTD *p328*
555 BURRARD ST SUITE 900, VANCOUVER, BC, V7X 1M8

SIC 3679
CREATION TECHNOLOGIES INC   *p192*
8999 FRASERTON CRT, BURNABY, BC, V5J 5H8

(604) 430-4336   *SIC 3679*
CREATION TECHNOLOGIES LP   *p192*
8999 FRASERTON CRT, BURNABY, BC, V5J 5H8

(604) 430-4336   *SIC 3679*
CREATION TECHNOLOGIES LP   *p192*
8997 FRASERTON CRT SUITE 102, BURNABY, BC, V5J 5H8

(604) 430-4336   *SIC 3679*
CREATION TECHNOLOGIES LP   *p680*
110 CLEGG RD, MARKHAM, ON, L6G 1E1

(866) 754-5004   *SIC 3679*
CREATION TECHNOLOGIES LP   *p721*
6820 CREDITVIEW RD, MISSISSAUGA, ON, L5N 0A9

(877) 812-4212   *SIC 3679*
CTI INDUSTRIES INC   *p864*
5621 FINCH AVE E UNIT 3, SCARBOROUGH, ON, M1B 2T9

(416) 297-8738   *SIC 3679*
CTS OF CANADA CO   *p718*
80 THOMAS ST, MISSISSAUGA, ON, L5M 1Y9

(905) 826-1141   *SIC 3679*

DATA CABLE COMPANY INC, THE   *p808*
31 ROBB BLVD, ORANGEVILLE, ON, L9W 3L1

(519) 941-7020   *SIC 3679*
DIGICO RESEAU GLOBAL INC   *p1101*
950 RUE BERGAR, FABREVILLE, QC, H7L 5A1

(450) 967-7100   *SIC 3679*
DORIGO SYSTEMS LTD   *p185*
3885 HENNING DR, BURNABY, BC, V5C 6N5

(604) 294-4600   *SIC 3679*
DYNAMIC SOURCE MANUFACTURING INC *p75*
2765 48 AVE NE UNIT 117, CALGARY, AB, T3J 5M9

(403) 516-1888   *SIC 3679*
E.D. PRODUCTS LTD   *p1011*
90 ATLAS AVE, WELLAND, ON, L3B 6H5

(905) 732-9473   *SIC 3679*
EATON INDUSTRIES (CANADA) COMPANY *p3*
403 EAST LAKE BLVD NE, AIRDRIE, AB, T4A 2G1

(403) 948-7955   *SIC 3679*
EATON INDUSTRIES (CANADA) COMPANY *p584*
380 CARLINGVIEW DR, ETOBICOKE, ON, M9W 5X9

(416) 798-0112   *SIC 3679*
ECI TECHNOLOGY GROUP INC   *p876*
815 MIDDLEFIELD RD UNIT 1-2, SCARBOROUGH, ON, M1V 2P9

(416) 291-2220   *SIC 3679*
ECOTEMP MANUFACTURING INC   *p1017*
8400 TWIN OAKS DR, WINDSOR, ON, N8N 5C2

SIC 3679
ELECTRICAL COMPONENTS CANADA, INC   *p911*
91 LINCOLN ST, TILLSONBURG, ON, N4G 2P9

(519) 842-9063   *SIC 3679*
ELECTROMEC INC   *p8*
4300 26 ST NE SUITE 125, CALGARY, AB, T1Y 7H7

SIC 3679
ELECTRONIQUES PROMARK INC   *p1250*
215 RUE VOYAGEUR, POINTE-CLAIRE, QC, H9R 6B2

(514) 426-4104   *SIC 3679*
EPM GLOBAL SERVICES INC   *p669*
195 ROYAL CREST CRT, MARKHAM, ON, L3R 9X6

(905) 479-6203   *SIC 3679*
EXCELITAS CANADA INC   *p1394*
22001 CH DUMBERRY, VAUDREUIL-DORION, QC, J7V 8P7

(450) 424-3300   *SIC 3679*
FIBER CONNECTIONS INC   *p998*
80 QUEEN ST S, TOTTENHAM, ON, L0G 1W0

(800) 353-1127   *SIC 3679*
GRAKON HAMSAR HOLDINGS LTD   *p522*
5320 DOWNEY ST, BURLINGTON, ON, L7L 6M2

(905) 332-4094   *SIC 3679*
GRASS VALLEY CANADA   *p1334*
3499 RUE DOUGLAS-B.-FLOREANI, SAINT-LAURENT, QC, H4S 2C6

(514) 333-1772   *SIC 3679*
HARRIS CANADA SYSTEMS, INC   *p723*
2895 ARGENTIA RD UNIT 5, MISSISSAUGA, ON, L5N 8G6

(905) 817-8300   *SIC 3679*
HDI TECHNOLOGIES INC   *p1112*
200 RUE DES BATISSEURS, GRANDMERE, QC, G9T 5K5

(819) 538-3398   *SIC 3679*
IMS INNOVATIVE MANUFACTURING SOURCE INC   *p16*
3855 64 AVE SE SUITE 3, CALGARY, AB, T2C 2V5

(403) 279-7702   *SIC 3679*

KONGSBERG INC   *p1369*
2699 5E AV, SHAWINIGAN, QC, G9T 2P7

(819) 533-4757   *SIC 3679*
KONGSBERG INC   *p1369*
90 28E RUE, SHAWINIGAN, QC, G9T 5K7

(819) 533-3201   *SIC 3679*
LOGICAN TECHNOLOGIES INC   *p121*
150 KARL CLARK RD NW, EDMONTON, AB, T6N 1E2

(780) 450-4400   *SIC 3679*
M.P.I.Q.C. INC   *p562*
550 CAMPBELL ST, CORNWALL, ON, K6H 6T7

(613) 936-2000   *SIC 3679*
MERSEN CANADA TORONTO INC   *p741*
6220 KESTREL RD, MISSISSAUGA, ON, L5T 1Y9

(647) 846-8684   *SIC 3679*
MERSEN CANADA TORONTO INC   *p741*
6200 KESTREL RD, MISSISSAUGA, ON, L5T 1Z1

(416) 252-9371   *SIC 3679*
METOCEAN TELEMATICS LIMITED   *p447*
21 THORNHILL DR, DARTMOUTH, NS, B3B 1R9

(902) 468-2505   *SIC 3679*
MICROART SERVICES INC   *p680*
190 DUFFIELD DR, MARKHAM, ON, L6G 1B5

(905) 752-0800   *SIC 3679*
NURAN WIRELESS INC   *p1265*
2150 CYRILLE-DUQUET, QUEBEC, QC, G1N 2G3

(418) 914-7484   *SIC 3679*
OCTASIC INC   *p1168*
2901 RUE RACHEL E BUREAU 30, MONTREAL, QC, H1W 4A4

(514) 282-8858   *SIC 3679*
PFC FLEXIBLE CIRCUITS LIMITED   *p873*
11 CANADIAN RD SUITE 7, SCARBOROUGH, ON, M1R 5G1

(416) 750-8433   *SIC 3679*
POWERSONIC INDUSTRIES INC   *p495*
13 SIMPSON RD, BOLTON, ON, L7E 1E4

(905) 951-6399   *SIC 3679*
PRECISION ELECTRONIC CORPORATION *p997*
70 BARTOR RD, TORONTO, ON, M9M 2G5

(416) 744-8840   *SIC 3679*
PRECISION ELECTRONICS CORPORATION   *p795*
70 BARTOR RD, NORTH YORK, ON, M9M 2G5

(416) 744-8840   *SIC 3679*
SAE POWER COMPANY   *p872*
1810 BIRCHMOUNT RD, SCARBOROUGH, ON, M1P 2H7

(416) 298-0560   *SIC 3679*
SEMTECH CANADA CORPORATION *p524*
4281 HARVESTER RD, BURLINGTON, ON, L7L 5M4

(905) 632-2996   *SIC 3679*
SEMTECH CANADA CORPORATION *p524*
4281 HARVESTER RD, BURLINGTON, ON, L7L 5M4

(905) 632-2996   *SIC 3679*
SIEMENS CANADA LIMITED   *p25*
1930 MAYNARD RD SE UNIT 24, CALGARY, AB, T2E 6J8

(403) 259-3404   *SIC 3679*
SPACEBRIDGE INC   *p1095*
657 AV ORLY, DORVAL, QC, H9P 1G1

(514) 420-0045   *SIC 3679*
SURTEK INDUSTRIES INC   *p278*
13018 84 AVE UNIT 4, SURREY, BC, V3W 1L2

(604) 590-2235   *SIC 3679*
TECH DIGITAL MANUFACTURING LTD *p675*
350 STEELCASE RD W, MARKHAM, ON, L3R 1B3

(905) 513-9004   *SIC 3679*
TURNKEY SOLUTIONS INC   *p9*
4300 26 ST NE BAY SUITE 105, CALGARY, AB, T1Y 7H7

▲ Public Company   ■ Public Company Family Member   **HQ** Headquarters   **BR** Branch   **SL** Single Location

SIC 3679

ULTRA ELECTRONICS MARITIME SYSTEMS INC   *p444*
40 ATLANTIC ST, DARTMOUTH, NS, B2Y 4N2
(902) 466-7491   *SIC 3679*

ULTRA ELECTRONICS MARITIME SYSTEMS INC   *p444*
40 ATLANTIC ST, DARTMOUTH, NS, B2Y 4N2
(902) 466-7491   *SIC 3679*

ULTRA ELECTRONICS TCS INC   *p1158*
5990 CH DE LA COTE-DE-LIESSE, MONT-ROYAL, QC, H4T 1V7
(514) 855-6363   *SIC 3679*

VARISYSTEMS CORP   *p13*
5304 HUBALTA RD SE, CALGARY, AB, T2B 1T6
(403) 272-0318   *SIC 3679*

VEONEER CANADA, INC   *p676*
7455 BIRCHMOUNT RD, MARKHAM, ON, L3R 5C2
(905) 475-4150   *SIC 3679*

WENZEL INTERNATIONAL INC   *p1015*
500 BEECH ST W, WHITBY, ON, L1N 7T8
(905) 668-3324   *SIC 3679*

XMARK CORPORATION   *p625*
309 LEGGET DR SUITE 100, KANATA, ON, K2K 3A3
(613) 592-6997   *SIC 3679*

SIC 3691 Storage batteries

E-ONE MOLI ENERGY (CANADA) LIMITED   *p231*
20000 STEWART CRES, MAPLE RIDGE, BC, V2X 9E7
(604) 466-6654   *SIC 3691*

EBERSPAECHER VECTURE INC.   *p552*
8900 KEELE STREET UNIT 3, CONCORD, ON, L4K 2N2
(905) 761-0331   *SIC 3691*

ENERGIZER CANADA INC   *p722*
6733 MISSISSAUGA RD SUITE 800, MISSISSAUGA, ON, L5N 6J5
(800) 383-7323   *SIC 3691*

SURRETTE BATTERY COMPANY LIMITED   *p466*
1 STATION RD, SPRINGHILL, NS, B0M 1X0
(902) 597-3767   *SIC 3691*

SIC 3692 Primary batteries, dry and wet

ENGINEERED POWER GP LTD   *p11*
3103 14 AVE NE SUITE 20, CALGARY, AB, T2A 7N6
(403) 235-2584   *SIC 3692*

ENGINEERED POWER LIMITED PARTNERSHIP   *p11*
3103 14 AVE NE UNIT 20, CALGARY, AB, T2A 7N6
(403) 235-2584   *SIC 3692*

SIC 3694 Engine electrical equipment

1100378 ONTARIO LIMITED   *p792*
805 FENMAR DR, NORTH YORK, ON, M9L 1C8
SIC 3694

ANDROID - BRAMPTON, L.L.C.   *p498*
14 PRECIDIO CRT, BRAMPTON, ON, L6S 6E3
(905) 458-4774   *SIC 3694*

BLUE STREAK ELECTRONICS INC   *p549*
30 MOYAL CRT, CONCORD, ON, L4K 4R8
(905) 669-4812   *SIC 3694*

COURT HOLDINGS LIMITED   *p489*
5071 KING ST, BEAMSVILLE, ON, L0R 1B0
(905) 563-0782   *SIC 3694*

D & V ELECTRONICS LTD   *p1027*
130 ZENWAY BLVD, WOODBRIDGE, ON,

L4H 2Y7
(905) 264-7646   *SIC 3694*

PACIFIC INSIGHT ELECTRONICS CORP   *p236*
1155 INSIGHT DR, NELSON, BC, V1L 5P5
(250) 354-1155   *SIC 3694*

SIC 3699 Electrical equipment and supplies, nec

9138-4529 QUEBEC INC   *p1398*
330 RUE DE LA JACQUES-CARTIER, VICTORIAVILLE, QC, G6T 1Y3
(514) 868-1811   *SIC 3699*

ABB PRODUITS D'INSTALLATION LTEE   *p1248*
180 AV LABROSSE, POINTE-CLAIRE, QC, H9R 1A1
(514) 630-4877   *SIC 3699*

ABB PRODUITS D'INSTALLATION LTEE   *p1248*
4025 RTE TRANSCANADIENNE, POINTE-CLAIRE, QC, H9R 1B4
(514) 694-6800   *SIC 3699*

ABB PRODUITS D'INSTALLATION LTEE   *p1316*
700 AV THOMAS, SAINT-JEAN-SUR-RICHELIEU, QC, J2X 2M9
(450) 347-5318   *SIC 3699*

AUGUST ELECTRONICS INC   *p20*
1810 CENTRE AVE NE, CALGARY, AB, T2E 0A6
(403) 273-3131   *SIC 3699*

BLUEDROP PERFORMANCE LEARNING INC   *p431*
18 PRESCOTT ST, ST. JOHN'S, NL, A1C 3S4
(709) 739-9000   *SIC 3699*

BSM TECHNOLOGIES LTD   *p188*
4299 CANADA WAY SUITE 215, BURNABY, BC, V5G 1H3
(604) 434-7337   *SIC 3699*

BSM TECHNOLOGIES LTD   *p583*
75 INTERNATIONAL BLVD SUITE 100, ETOBICOKE, ON, M9W 6L9
(416) 675-1201   *SIC 3699*

CAE INC   *p1338*
8585 CH DE LA COTE-DE-LIESSE, SAINT-LAURENT, QC, H4T 1G6
(514) 341-6780   *SIC 3699*

CAE SANTE CANADA INC   *p1338*
8585 CH DE LA COTE-DE-LIESSE, SAINT-LAURENT, QC, H4T 1G6
(514) 341-6780   *SIC 3699*

CANTEGA TECHNOLOGIES INC   *p95*
11603 165 ST NW, EDMONTON, AB, T5M 3Z1
(780) 448-9700   *SIC 3699*

CDN TECHNOLOGY   *p1013*
901 BURNS ST E, WHITBY, ON, L1N 0E6
(905) 430-7295   *SIC 3699*

CGC GYPSUM   *p155*
7550 40 AVE, RED DEER, AB, T4P 2H8
(403) 277-0586   *SIC 3699*

CLASSE AUDIO INC   *p1127*
5070 RUE FRANCOIS-CUSSON, LACHINE, QC, H8T 1B3
(514) 636-6384   *SIC 3699*

COHERENT CANADA INC   *p713*
1222 APRIL RD, MISSISSAUGA, ON, L5J 3J7
(905) 823-5808   *SIC 3699*

COMPOSITES VCI INC   *p1347*
830 12E AV BUREAU 915, SAINT-LIN-LAURENTIDES, QC, J5M 2V9
(450) 302-4646   *SIC 3699*

CSG SECURITY CORPORATION   *p693*
5201 EXPLORER DR, MISSISSAUGA, ON, L4W 4H1
(905) 629-1446   *SIC 3699*

DELUXE ALARMS INC   *p551*
9000 KEELE ST UNIT 12, CONCORD, ON, L4K 0B3

(416) 410-3020   *SIC 3699*

DORMAKABA CANADA INC   *p1227*
7301 BOUL DECARIE, MONTREAL, QC, H4P 2G7
(514) 735-5410   *SIC 3699*

FLEETMIND SEON SOLUTIONS INC   *p200*
3B BURBIDGE ST SUITE 111, COQUITLAM, BC, V3K 7B2
(604) 941-0880   *SIC 3699*

I3 INTERNATIONAL INC   *p868*
780 BIRCHMOUNT RD UNIT 16, SCARBOROUGH, ON, M1K 5H4
(416) 261-2266   *SIC 3699*

IDEAL INDUSTRIES (CANADA), CORP   *p474*
33 FULLER RD, AJAX, ON, L1S 2E1
(905) 683-3400   *SIC 3699*

ISC APPLIED SYSTEMS CORP   *p1251*
290 AV LABROSSE, POINTE-CLAIRE, QC, H9R 5L8
(514) 782-1400   *SIC 3699*

LOCKWOOD INDUSTRIES INC   *p523*
1100 CORPORATE DR, BURLINGTON, ON, L7L 5R6
(905) 336-0300   *SIC 3699*

MARCH NETWORKS CORPORATION   *p624*
303 TERRY FOX DR SUITE 200, KANATA, ON, K2K 3J1
(613) 591-8181   *SIC 3699*

MATCOR METAL FABRICATION INC   *p724*
7275 EAST DANBRO CRES, MISSISSAUGA, ON, L5N 6P8
(905) 814-7479   *SIC 3699*

MITSUBISHI HITACHI POWER SYSTEMS CANADA, LTD   *p1434*
3903 BRODSKY AVE SUITE 100, SASKATOON, SK, S7P 0C9
(306) 242-9222   *SIC 3699*

MONITEURS ANGELCARE INC   *p1073*
201 BOUL DE L'INDUSTRIE LOCAL 104, CANDIAC, QC, J5R 6A6
(450) 462-2000   *SIC 3699*

PASON SYSTEMS CORP   *p36*
6130 3 ST SE, CALGARY, AB, T2H 1K4
(403) 301-3400   *SIC 3699*

SAFENET CANADA INC   *p750*
20 COLONNADE RD SUITE 200, NEPEAN, ON, K2E 7M6
(613) 723-5077   *SIC 3699*

SCHNEIDER ELECTRIC CANADA INC   *p733*
5985 MCLAUGHLIN RD, MISSISSAUGA, ON, L5R 1B8
(905) 366-3999   *SIC 3699*

SCHNEIDER ELECTRIC CANADA INC   *p1070*
4100 PLACE JAVA, BROSSARD, QC, J4Y 0C4
(450) 444-0143   *SIC 3699*

SCHNEIDER ELECTRIC CANADA INC   *p1252*
825 AV BANCROFT, POINTE-CLAIRE, QC, H9R 4L6
(514) 341-6780   *SIC 3699*

SECURE 724 LTD   *p777*
1959 LESLIE ST, NORTH YORK, ON, M3B 2M3
(416) 923-6984   *SIC 3699*

SECUREKEY TECHNOLOGIES INC   *p774*
4101 YONGE ST SUITE 501, NORTH YORK, ON, M2P 1N6
(416) 477-5625   *SIC 3699*

SENSTAR CORPORATION   *p541*
119 JOHN CAVANAUGH DR, CARP, ON, K0A 1L0
(613) 839-5572   *SIC 3699*

STARTCO ENGINEERING LTD   *p1434*
3714 KINNEAR PL, SASKATOON, SK, S7P 0A6
(306) 373-5505   *SIC 3699*

STOCKERYALE CANADA INC   *p1091*
275 RUE KESMARK, DOLLARD-DES-ORMEAUX, QC, H9B 3J1
SIC 3699

SYSTEMES D'ENTRAINEMENT MEGGITT (QUEBEC) INC   *p1331*

6140 BOUL HENRI-BOURASSA O, SAINT-LAURENT, QC, H4R 3A6
(514) 339-9938   *SIC 3699*

TRENCH LIMITED   *p877*
71 MAYBROOK DR, SCARBOROUGH, ON, M1V 4B6
(416) 298-8108   *SIC 3699*

TRU SIMULATION + TRAINING CANADA INC   *p1341*
6767 CH DE LA COTE-DE-LIESSE, SAINT-LAURENT, QC, H4T 1E5
(514) 342-0800   *SIC 3699*

TYCO SAFETY PRODUCTS CANADA LTD   *p560*
3301 LANGSTAFF RD, CONCORD, ON, L4K 4L2
(905) 760-3000   *SIC 3699*

TYCO SAFETY PRODUCTS CANADA LTD   *p790*
95 BRIDGELAND AVE, NORTH YORK, ON, M6A 1Y7
(905) 760-3000   *SIC 3699*

TYCO SAFETY PRODUCTS CANADA LTD   *p1071*
9995 RUE DE CHATEAUNEUF UNITE L, BROSSARD, QC, J4Z 3V7
(450) 444-2040   *SIC 3699*

VIRTEK VISION INTERNATIONAL INC   *p1011*
785 BRIDGE ST W SUITE 8, WATERLOO, ON, N2V 2K1
(519) 746-7190   *SIC 3699*

SIC 3711 Motor vehicles and car bodies

2000007 ONTARIO INC   *p792*
3605 WESTON RD, NORTH YORK, ON, M9L 1V7
(416) 744-3322   *SIC 3711*

AFTERMARKET PARTS COMPANY LLC, THE   *p362*
630 KERNAGHAN AVE DOOR 76, WINNIPEG, MB, R2C 5G1
(800) 665-2637   *SIC 3711*

CRESTLINE COACH LTD   *p1434*
126 WHEELER ST, SASKATOON, SK, S7P 0A9
(306) 934-8844   *SIC 3711*

FCA CANADA INC   *p1023*
2199 CHRYSLER CTR, WINDSOR, ON, N9A 4H6
(519) 973-2000   *SIC 3711*

FCA CANADA INC   *p1023*
1 RIVERSIDE DR W, WINDSOR, ON, N9A 5K3
(519) 973-2000   *SIC 3711*

FORD MOTOR COMPANY OF CANADA, LIMITED   *p800*
1 CANADIAN RD, OAKVILLE, ON, L6J 5E4
(905) 845-2511   *SIC 3711*

FORD MOTOR COMPANY OF CANADA, LIMITED   *p1018*
6500 CANTELON DR, WINDSOR, ON, N8T 0A6
(519) 251-4401   *SIC 3711*

FORT GARRY FIRE TRUCKS LTD   *p378*
53 BERGEN CUTOFF RD, WINNIPEG, MB, R3C 2E6
(204) 594-3473   *SIC 3711*

GENERAL DYNAMICS LAND SYSTEMS - CANADA CORPORATION   *p649*
1991 OXFORD ST E BLDG 15, LONDON, ON, N5V 2Z7
(519) 964-5900   *SIC 3711*

GENERAL DYNAMICS LAND SYSTEMS - CANADA CORPORATION   *p649*
2035 OXFORD ST E, LONDON, ON, N5V 2Z7
(519) 964-5900   *SIC 3711*

GENERAL DYNAMICS LAND SYSTEMS - CANADA CORPORATION   *p751*
1941 ROBERTSON RD, NEPEAN, ON, K2H 5B7

---

(613) 596-7000 *SIC 3711*

GENERAL MOTORS OF CANADA COMPANY *p621*
300 INGERSOLL ST, INGERSOLL, ON, N5C 3J7
(519) 485-6400 *SIC 3711*

GENERAL MOTORS OF CANADA COMPANY *p812*
1908 COLONEL SAM DR, OSHAWA, ON, L1H 8P7
(905) 644-5000 *SIC 3711*

GENERAL MOTORS OF CANADA COMPANY *p812*
1908 COLONEL SAM DR, OSHAWA, ON, L1H 8P7
(289) 676-0530 *SIC 3711*

GENERAL MOTORS OF CANADA COMPANY *p814*
461 PARK RD S, OSHAWA, ON, L1J 8R3
(905) 845-5456 *SIC 3711*

GRANDE WEST TRANSPORTATION GROUP INC *p179*
3168 262 ST, ALDERGROVE, BC, V4W 2Z6
(604) 607-4000 *SIC 3711*

GROUPE VOLVO CANADA INC *p1303*
155 RTE MARIE-VICTORIN, SAINT-FRANCOIS-DU-LAC, QC, J0G 1M0
(450) 568-3335 *SIC 3711*

GROUPE VOLVO CANADA INC *p1356*
35 BOUL GAGNON, SAINTE-CLAIRE, QC, G0R 2V0
(418) 883-3391 *SIC 3711*

HBPO CANADA INC *p1020*
2570 CENTRAL AVE, WINDSOR, ON, N8W 4J5
(519) 251-4300 *SIC 3711*

HONDA CANADA INC *p476*
4700 TOTTENHAM RD, ALLISTON, ON, L9R 1A2
(705) 435-5561 *SIC 3711*

HONDA CANADA INC *p679*
180 HONDA BLVD SUITE 200, MARKHAM, ON, L6C 0H9
(905) 888-8110 *SIC 3711*

MARTINREA AUTOMOTIVE SYSTEMS CANADA LTD *p474*
650 FINLEY AVE, AJAX, ON, L1S 6N1
(905) 428-3737 *SIC 3711*

MARTINREA AUTOMOTIVE SYSTEMS CANADA LTD *p662*
3820 COMMERCE RD, LONDON, ON, N6N 1P6
(519) 644-1567 *SIC 3711*

MOTOR COACH INDUSTRIES LIMITED *p391*
1475 CLARENCE AVE, WINNIPEG, MB, R3T 1T5
(204) 284-5360 *SIC 3711*

NAVISTAR CANADA, INC *p627*
405 VAN BUREN ST, KEMPTVILLE, ON, K0G 1J0
(613) 258-1126 *SIC 3711*

NEW FLYER INDUSTRIES CANADA ULC *p362*
711 KERNAGHAN AVE SUITE 3, WINNIPEG, MB, R2C 3T4
(204) 224-1251 *SIC 3711*

NEW FLYER INDUSTRIES CANADA ULC *p366*
25 DE BAETS ST, WINNIPEG, MB, R2J 4G5
(204) 982-8400 *SIC 3711*

NFI GROUP INC *p363*
711 KERNAGHAN AVE, WINNIPEG, MB, R2C 3T4
(204) 224-1251 *SIC 3711*

ONTARIO DRIVE & GEAR LIMITED *p752*
3551 BLEAMS RD, NEW HAMBURG, ON, N3A 2J1
(519) 662-2840 *SIC 3711*

PACCAR OF CANADA LTD *p1364*
10 RUE SICARD, SAINTE-THERESE, QC, J7E 4K9
(450) 435-6171 *SIC 3711*

STREIT MANUFACTURING INC *p682*
111 PILLSBURY DR, MIDLAND, ON, L4R 4L4
(705) 526-6557 *SIC 3711*

TENCO INC *p1377*
1318 RUE PRINCIPALE, ST-VALERIEN, QC, J0H 2B0
(800) 318-3626 *SIC 3711*

TOYOTA MOTOR MANUFACTURING CANADA INC *p539*
1055 FOUNTAIN ST N, CAMBRIDGE, ON, N3H 4R7
(519) 653-1111 *SIC 3711*

TOYOTA MOTOR MANUFACTURING CANADA INC *p1036*
1717 DUNDAS ST, WOODSTOCK, ON, N4S 0A4
(519) 653-1111 *SIC 3711*

TOYOTA MOTOR MANUFACTURING CANADA INC *p1036*
715106 OXFORD RD SUITE 4, WOODSTOCK, ON, N4S 7V9
SIC 3711

TRACKLESS VEHICLES LIMITED *p564*
55 THUNDERBIRD DR, COURTLAND, ON, N0J 1E0
(519) 688-0370 *SIC 3711*

TRI-STAR INDUSTRIES LIMITED *p471*
88 FOREST ST, YARMOUTH, NS, B5A 4G6
(902) 742-2355 *SIC 3711*

TRIPLE E CANADA LTD *p361*
301 ROBLIN BLVD, WINKLER, MB, R6W 4C4
(204) 325-4361 *SIC 3711*

VIKING-CIVES LTD *p746*
42626 GREY RD 109, MOUNT FOREST, ON, N0G 2L0
(519) 323-4433 *SIC 3711*

WALLACEBURG PREFERRED PARTNERS CORP *p543*
203 KEIL DR S, CHATHAM, ON, N7M 6J5
(519) 351-5558 *SIC 3711*

SIC 3713 Truck and bus bodies

2967-3183 QUEBEC INC *p1002*
300 RUE UNIVERSELLE SS 4, VARS, ON, K0A 3H0
(613) 443-0044 *SIC 3713*

ALUMI-BUNK CORPORATION *p566*
5 KEPPEL ST, DUNDALK, ON, N0C 1B0
(800) 700-2865 *SIC 3713*

ATELIERS BEAU-ROC INC, LES *p1002*
300 RUE UNIVERSELLE, VARS, ON, K0A 3H0
(613) 443-0044 *SIC 3713*

CBI MANUFACTURING LTD *p143*
702 1 AVE NW, LINDEN, AB, T0M 1J0
(403) 546-3851 *SIC 3713*

COLLINS MANUFACTURING CO. LTD *p224*
9835 199A ST SUITE 5, LANGLEY, BC, V1M 2X7
(604) 888-2812 *SIC 3713*

CORPORATION MICRO BIRD INC *p1100*
3000 RUE GIRARDIN, DRUMMONDVILLE, QC, J2E 0A1
(819) 477-8222 *SIC 3713*

DEMERS BRAUN MANUFACTURIER D'AMBULANCES INC *p1057*
28 RUE RICHELIEU, BELOEIL, QC, J3G 4N5
(450) 467-4683 *SIC 3713*

DEMERS, AMBULANCE MANUFACTURER INC *p1057*
28 RUE RICHELIEU, BELOEIL, QC, J3G 4N5
(450) 467-4683 *SIC 3713*

DIESEL EQUIPMENT LIMITED *p755*
210 HARRY WALKER PKY N, NEWMARKET, ON, L3Y 7B4
(416) 421-5851 *SIC 3713*

DYNAMIC ATTRACTIONS LTD *p167*
4102 44 AVE, STETTLER, AB, T0C 2L0
SIC 3713

EVEREST EQUIPMENT CO *p1052*
1077 RUE WESTMOUNT, AYER'S CLIFF, QC, J0B 1C0
(819) 838-4257 *SIC 3713*

FANOTECH ENVIRO INC *p620*
220 OLD NORTH RD, HUNTSVILLE, ON, P1H 2J4
(705) 788-3046 *SIC 3713*

FIBROCAP INC *p1057*
201 RUE SAINT-GEORGES, BELOEIL, QC, J3G 4N4
(450) 467-8611 *SIC 3713*

FOURGONS TRANSIT INC, LES *p1362*
3600 BOUL INDUSTRIEL, SAINTE-ROSE, QC, H7L 4R9
(514) 382-0104 *SIC 3713*

FRANK FAIR INDUSTRIES LTD *p365*
400 ARCHIBALD ST, WINNIPEG, MB, R2J 0W9
(204) 237-7987 *SIC 3713*

GENERAL BODY & EQUIPMENT LTD *p114*
8124 DAVIES RD NW, EDMONTON, AB, T6E 4N2
(780) 468-5359 *SIC 3713*

GROUPE BIBEAU INC *p1303*
4581 RANG CASTLE-D'AUTRAY, SAINT-FELIX-DE-VALOIS, QC, J0K 2M0
(450) 889-5505 *SIC 3713*

INTERCONTINENTAL TRUCK BODY (B.C.) INC *p272*
5285 192 ST, SURREY, BC, V3S 8E5
(604) 576-2971 *SIC 3713*

INTERCONTINENTAL TRUCK BODY LTD *p80*
1806 11 ST, COALDALE, AB, T1M 1N1
(403) 345-4427 *SIC 3713*

MAXI-METAL INC *p1305*
9345 25E AV, SAINT-GEORGES, QC, G6A 1L1
(418) 228-6637 *SIC 3713*

MICRO BIRD HOLDINGS, INC *p1100*
3000 RUE GIRARDIN, DRUMMONDVILLE, QC, J2E 0A1
(819) 477-2012 *SIC 3713*

MIDLAND MANUFACTURING LIMITED *p355*
36 MAIN ST E, ROSENORT, MB, R0G 1W0
(204) 746-2348 *SIC 3713*

MILNER-RIGSBY CO. LIMITED, THE *p1013*
139 ELM ST, WEST LORNE, ON, N0L 2P0
(519) 768-1250 *SIC 3713*

MORGAN CANADA CORPORATION *p504*
12 CHELSEA LANE, BRAMPTON, ON, L6T 3Y4
(905) 791-8130 *SIC 3713*

SYSTEM ONE MFG INC *p111*
4420 76 AVE NW, EDMONTON, AB, T6B 0A5
(780) 485-6006 *SIC 3713*

THERMO KING WESTERN INC *p106*
15825 118 AVE NW, EDMONTON, AB, T5V 1B7
(780) 447-1578 *SIC 3713*

UNICELL LIMITED *p918*
50 INDUSTRIAL ST, TORONTO, ON, M4G 1Y9
(416) 421-6845 *SIC 3713*

WALINGA INC *p604*
5656 HIGHWAY 6, GUELPH, ON, N1H 6J2
(519) 824-8520 *SIC 3713*

WILCOX BODIES LIMITED *p685*
550 MCGEACHIE DR, MILTON, ON, L9T 3Y5
(905) 203-9995 *SIC 3713*

SIC 3714 Motor vehicle parts and accessories

1334869 ONTARIO LIMITED *p736*
6575 KESTREL RD, MISSISSAUGA, ON, L5T 1P4
(905) 670-9100 *SIC 3714*

2027844 ONTARIO INC *p493*
325 CHATHAM ST N, BLENHEIM, ON, N0P 1A0
(519) 676-8161 *SIC 3714*

792716 ONTARIO LTD *p1024*
735 PRINCE RD, WINDSOR, ON, N9C 2Z2
(519) 256-6700 *SIC 3714*

A.G. SIMPSON AUTOMOTIVE INC *p915*
200 YORKLAND BLVD SUITE 800, TORONTO, ON, M2J 5C1
(416) 438-6650 *SIC 3714*

ABCOR FILTERS INC *p581*
41 CITY VIEW DR, ETOBICOKE, ON, M9W 5A5
(416) 245-6886 *SIC 3714*

ABS FRICTION INC *p606*
55 TAGGART ST, GUELPH, ON, N1L 1M6
(519) 763-9000 *SIC 3714*

ACCURIDE CANADA INC *p650*
31 FIRESTONE BLVD, LONDON, ON, N5W 6E6
(519) 453-0880 *SIC 3714*

ALI ARC INDUSTRIES LP *p364*
155 ELAN BLVD, WINNIPEG, MB, R2J 4H1
(204) 253-6080 *SIC 3714*

ARCELORMITTAL TUBULAR PRODUCTS CANADA G.P. *p510*
14 HOLTBY AVE, BRAMPTON, ON, L6X 2M3
(905) 451-2400 *SIC 3714*

ARCELORMITTAL TUBULAR PRODUCTS CANADA G.P. *p1034*
193 GIVINS ST, WOODSTOCK, ON, N4S 5Y8
(519) 537-6671 *SIC 3714*

ARCELORMITTAL TUBULAR PRODUCTS CANADA G.P. *p1034*
193 GIVINS ST, WOODSTOCK, ON, N4S 5Y8
(519) 537-6671 *SIC 3714*

CANADIAN AUTOPARTS TOYOTA INC *p208*
7233 PROGRESS WAY, DELTA, BC, V4G 1E7
(604) 946-5636 *SIC 3714*

CANADIAN TEST CASE 168 INC. *p730*
5770 HURONTARIO ST, MISSISSAUGA, ON, L5R 3G5
SIC 3714

CANADIAN TEST CASE 168 INC. *p1085*
1450 RUE CUNARD, COTE SAINT-LUC, QC, H7S 2B7
SIC 3714

CANADIAN TEST CASE 185 *p720*
6750 CENTURY AVE SUITE 300, MISSISSAUGA, ON, L5N 0B7
(905) 812-5920 *SIC 3714*

CANADIAN TEST CASE 192 *p21*
1110 CENTRE ST NE SUITE 204, CALGARY, AB, T2E 2R2
(403) 276-5546 *SIC 3714*

CONTITECH CANADA, INC *p835*
3225 3RD AVE E, OWEN SOUND, ON, N4K 5N3
SIC 3714

COOPER-STANDARD AUTOMOTIVE CANADA LIMITED *p594*
268 APPIN RD RR 4, GLENCOE, ON, N0L 1M0
(519) 287-2450 *SIC 3714*

COSMA INTERNATIONAL (CANADA) INC *p502*
2550 STEELES AVE, BRAMPTON, ON, L6T 5R3
SIC 3714

CPK INTERIOR PRODUCTS INC *p847*
128 PETER ST, PORT HOPE, ON, L1A 1C4
(905) 885-7231 *SIC 3714*

CULASSES DU FUTUR L. R. INC, LES *p1149*
1390 AV DE LA GARE, MASCOUCHE, QC, J7K 2Z2
(514) 966-3450 *SIC 3714*

DANA CANADA CORPORATION *p486*
120 WELHAM RD, BARRIE, ON, L4N 8Y4
(705) 737-2300 *SIC 3714*

DANA CANADA CORPORATION *p533*
401 FRANKLIN BLVD, CAMBRIDGE, ON, N1R 8G8
(519) 621-1303 *SIC 3714*

▲ Public Company   ■ Public Company Family Member   **HQ** Headquarters   **BR** Branch   **SL** Single Location

DANA CANADA CORPORATION   p802
656 KERR ST, OAKVILLE, ON, L6K 3E4
(905) 849-1200   *SIC* 3714

DANA CANADA CORPORATION   p888
500 JAMES ST S, ST MARYS, ON, N4X 1B4
SIC 3714

DCL INTERNATIONAL INC   p551
241 BRADWICK DR, CONCORD, ON, L4K 1K5
(905) 660-6450   *SIC* 3714

DURA-LITE HEAT TRANSFER PRODUCTS LTD   p70
12012 44 ST SE, CALGARY, AB, T2Z 4A2
(403) 259-2691   *SIC* 3714

ELECTRO CANADA LIMITED   p988
30 TYCOS DR, TORONTO, ON, M6B 1V9
SIC 3714

ELITE COMPOSITE INC   p1357
1036 RUE PRINCIPALE, SAINTE-CLOTILDE-DE-BEAUCE, QC, G0N 1C0
(418) 427-2622   *SIC* 3714

ELRINGKLINGER CANADA, INC   p644
1 SENECA RD SUITE 4, LEAMINGTON, ON, N8H 5P2
(519) 326-6113   *SIC* 3714

ENVIROMECH INDUSTRIES INC   p221
2092 ENTERPRISE WAY SUITE 100, KELOWNA, BC, V1Y 6H7
(250) 765-1777   *SIC* 3714

F&P MFG INC   p896
275 WRIGHT BLVD, STRATFORD, ON, N5A 7Y1
SIC 3714

F&P MFG INC   p998
1 NOLAN RD, TOTTENHAM, ON, L0G 1W0
(905) 936-3435   *SIC* 3714

FAURECIA EMISSIONS CONTROL TECHNOLOGIES CANADA, LTD   p503
40 SUMMERLEA RD, BRAMPTON, ON, L6T 4X3
(905) 595-5668   *SIC* 3714

FEDERAL-MOGUL CANADA LIMITED   p722
6860 CENTURY AVE, MISSISSAUGA, ON, L5N 2W5
(905) 761-5400   *SIC* 3714

FLEX-N-GATE CANADA COMPANY   p840
775 TECHNOLOGY DR, PETERBOROUGH, ON, K9J 6X7
(705) 742-3534   *SIC* 3714

FORD MOTOR COMPANY OF CANADA, LIMITED   p1018
7654 TECUMSEH RD E, WINDSOR, ON, N8T 1E9
(519) 944-8564   *SIC* 3714

GENERAL KINETICS ENGINEERING CORPORATION   p503
110 EAST DR, BRAMPTON, ON, L6T 1C1
(905) 458-0888   *SIC* 3714

GENERAL MOTORS OF CANADA COMPANY   p1019
1550 KILDARE RD, WINDSOR, ON, N8W 2W4
(519) 255-4161   *SIC* 3714

GENTHERM CANADA ULC   p1020
3445 WHEELTON DR, WINDSOR, ON, N8W 5A6
(519) 948-4808   *SIC* 3714

GMA COVER CORP   p600
965 YORK RD, GUELPH, ON, N1E 6Y9
SIC 3714

GNUTTI CARLO CANADA LTD   p621
404 CANADA AVE, HURON PARK, ON, N0M 1Y0
(519) 228-6685   *SIC* 3714

GROUND EFFECTS LTD   p1020
2775 ST ETIENNE BLVD, WINDSOR, ON, N8W 5B1
(519) 944-3800   *SIC* 3714

GROUND EFFECTS LTD   p1020
4505 RHODES DR, WINDSOR, ON, N8W 5R8
(519) 944-3800   *SIC* 3714

HANON SYSTEMS CANADA INC   p491
360 UNIVERSITY AVE SUITE 2,

BELLEVILLE, ON, K8N 5T6
(613) 969-1460   *SIC* 3714

HANON SYSTEMS EFP CANADA LTD   p553
800 TESMA WAY, CONCORD, ON, L4K 5C2
(905) 303-1689   *SIC* 3714

HEARN AUTOMOTIVE INC   p1018
6630 TECUMSEH RD E, WINDSOR, ON, N8T 1E6
SIC 3714

HERD NORTH AMERICA INC   p362
2168 SPRINGFIELD RD, WINNIPEG, MB, R2C 2Z2
(204) 222-0880   *SIC* 3714

HOPKINS CANADA, INC   p493
281 CHATHAM ST S, BLENHEIM, ON, N0P 1A0
(519) 676-5441   *SIC* 3714

IGB AUTOMOTIVE LTD   p1021
3090 MARENTETTE AVE, WINDSOR, ON, N8X 4G2
(519) 250-5777   *SIC* 3714

INDUSTRIES SPECTRA PREMIUM INC, LES   p896
533 ROMEO ST S, STRATFORD, ON, N5A 4V3
(519) 275-3802   *SIC* 3714

KAUTEX CORPORATION   p1020
2701 KAUTEX DR, WINDSOR, ON, N8W 5B1
(519) 974-6656   *SIC* 3714

KINETICS DRIVE SOLUTIONS INC   p229
27489 56 AVE, LANGLEY, BC, V4W 3X1
(604) 607-8877   *SIC* 3714

KSR INTERNATIONAL INC   p857
172 CENTRE ST, RODNEY, ON, N0L 2C0
(519) 785-0121   *SIC* 3714

KSR INTERNATIONAL INC   p857
95 ERIE ST S, RIDGETOWN, ON, N0P 2C0
(519) 674-5413   *SIC* 3714

KTH SHELBURNE MFG. INC   p880
300 2ND LINE, SHELBURNE, ON, L9V 3N4
(519) 925-3030   *SIC* 3714

LINAMAR CORPORATION   p603
287 SPEEDVALE AVE W, GUELPH, ON, N1H 1C5
(519) 836-7550   *SIC* 3714

LINAMAR CORPORATION   p603
74 CAMPBELL RD, GUELPH, ON, N1H 1C1
(519) 821-1650   *SIC* 3714

LINAMAR CORPORATION   p603
347 SILVERCREEK PKY N, GUELPH, ON, N1H 1E6
(519) 837-3055   *SIC* 3714

LINAMAR CORPORATION   p603
280 SPEEDVALE AVE W, GUELPH, ON, N1H 1C4
(519) 824-8899   *SIC* 3714

LINAMAR CORPORATION   p603
355 SILVERCREEK PKY N, GUELPH, ON, N1H 1E6
(519) 821-7576   *SIC* 3714

LINAMAR CORPORATION   p603
277 SILVERCREEK PKY N, GUELPH, ON, N1H 1E6
(519) 763-0063   *SIC* 3714

LINAMAR CORPORATION   p605
30 MINTO RD, GUELPH, ON, N1K 1H5
(519) 821-1429   *SIC* 3714

LINAMAR CORPORATION   p605
148 ARROW RD, GUELPH, ON, N1K 1T4
(519) 780-2270   *SIC* 3714

LINAMAR CORPORATION   p605
381 MASSEY RD, GUELPH, ON, N1K 1B2
(519) 767-9711   *SIC* 3714

LINAMAR CORPORATION   p605
301 MASSEY RD, GUELPH, ON, N1K 1B2
(519) 767-9711   *SIC* 3714

LINAMAR CORPORATION   p605
12 INDEPENDENCE PL, GUELPH, ON, N1K 1H8
(519) 827-9423   *SIC* 3714

LINAMAR CORPORATION   p605
415 ELMIRA RD N, GUELPH, ON, N1K 1H3
(519) 763-5369   *SIC* 3714

LINAMAR CORPORATION   p605
150 ARROW RD, GUELPH, ON, N1K 1T4
(519) 822-6627   *SIC* 3714

LINAMAR CORPORATION   p605
30 MALCOLM RD, GUELPH, ON, N1K 1A9
(519) 767-0219   *SIC* 3714

LINAMAR CORPORATION   p605
285 MASSEY RD, GUELPH, ON, N1K 1B2
(519) 763-0704   *SIC* 3714

LINAMAR CORPORATION   p605
355 MASSEY RD, GUELPH, ON, N1K 1B2
(519) 837-0880   *SIC* 3714

LINAMAR CORPORATION   p605
375 MASSEY RD, GUELPH, ON, N1K 1B2
(519) 822-9008   *SIC* 3714

LINAMAR CORPORATION   p605
32 INDEPENDENCE PL, GUELPH, ON, N1K 1H8
(519) 827-9423   *SIC* 3714

LINAMAR CORPORATION   p1017
3590 VALTEC CRT, WINDSOR, ON, N8N 5E6
(519) 739-3465   *SIC* 3714

LINAMAR HOLDINGS INC.   p603
287 SPEEDVALE AVE W, GUELPH, ON, N1H 1C5
(519) 836-7550   *SIC* 3714

M.B.R.P. INC   p620
315 OLD FERGUSON RD SUITE 1, HUNTSVILLE, ON, P1H 2J2
(705) 788-2845   *SIC* 3714

MADDOCKS ENGINEERING LTD   p604
84 ROYAL RD, GUELPH, ON, N1H 1G3
(519) 823-1092   *SIC* 3714

MAGNA EXTERIORS INC   p555
50 CASMIR CRT, CONCORD, ON, L4K 4J5
(905) 669-2888   *SIC* 3714

MAGNA INTERNATIONAL INC   p481
337 MAGNA DR, AURORA, ON, L4G 7K1
(905) 726-2462   *SIC* 3714

MAGNA INTERNATIONAL INC   p555
90 SNIDERCROFT RD, CONCORD, ON, L4K 2K1
(905) 738-3700   *SIC* 3714

MAGNA INTERNATIONAL INC   p606
65 INDEPENDENCE PL, GUELPH, ON, N1K 1H8
(519) 763-6042   *SIC* 3714

MAGNA INTERNATIONAL INC   p889
1 COSMA CRT, ST THOMAS, ON, N5P 4J5
(519) 633-8400   *SIC* 3714

MAGNA MECHANICAL INC   p464
65 MEMORIAL DR, NORTH SYDNEY, NS, B2A 0B9
SIC 3714

MAGNA POWERTRAIN INC   p481
245 EDWARD ST, AURORA, ON, L4G 3M7
(905) 713-0746   *SIC* 3714

MAGNA POWERTRAIN INC   p555
50 CASMIR CRT, CONCORD, ON, L4K 4J5
(905) 532-2100   *SIC* 3714

MAGNA POWERTRAIN INC   p1032
390 HANLAN RD, WOODBRIDGE, ON, L4L 3P6
(905) 851-6791   *SIC* 3714

MAGNA SEATING INC   p481
337 MAGNA DR, AURORA, ON, L4G 7K1
(905) 726-2462   *SIC* 3714

MAGNA SEATING INC   p662
3915 COMMERCE RD, LONDON, ON, N6N 1P4
(519) 808-9035   *SIC* 3714

MAGNA SEATING INC   p754
564 NEWPARK BLVD, NEWMARKET, ON, L3X 2S2
(905) 853-3604   *SIC* 3714

MAGNA SEATING INC   p754
550 NEWPARK BLVD, NEWMARKET, ON, L3X 2S2
(905) 895-4701   *SIC* 3714

MARWOOD INTERNATIONAL INC   p912
35 TOWNLINE RD, TILLSONBURG, ON, N4G 2R5
(519) 688-1144   *SIC* 3714

MERITOR AFTERMARKET CANADA INC   p511
60 GILLINGHAM DR SUITE 501, BRAMPTON, ON, L6X 0Z9
(905) 454-7070   *SIC* 3714

METARIS INC   p784
101 CANARCTIC DR, NORTH YORK, ON, M3J 2N7
(416) 638-6000   *SIC* 3714

MOBILE CLIMATE CONTROL, INC   p556
7540 JANE ST, CONCORD, ON, L4K 0A6
(905) 482-2750   *SIC* 3714

MUSASHI AUTO PARTS CANADA INC   p479
500 DOMVILLE ST, ARTHUR, ON, N0G 1A0
(519) 848-2800   *SIC* 3714

MUSASHI AUTO PARTS CANADA INC   p479
333 DOMVILLE ST, ARTHUR, ON, N0G 1A0
(519) 848-2800   *SIC* 3714

NEW WORLD FRICTION CORP   p534
539 COLLIER MACMILLAN DR UNIT B, CAMBRIDGE, ON, N1R 7P3
(519) 623-0011   *SIC* 3714

NIAGARA PISTON INC   p490
4708 ONTARIO ST, BEAMSVILLE, ON, L0R 1B4
(905) 563-4981   *SIC* 3714

NORTHSHORE SUDBURY LTD   p115
8113 CORONET RD NW, EDMONTON, AB, T6E 4N7
(780) 455-5177   *SIC* 3714

NUCAP INDUSTRIES INC   p877
3370 PHARMACY AVE, SCARBOROUGH, ON, M1W 3K4
(416) 494-1444   *SIC* 3714

NUCAP INDUSTRIES INC   p877
3370 PHARMACY AVE, SCARBOROUGH, ON, M1W 3K4
(416) 494-1444   *SIC* 3714

PACBRAKE COMPANY   p282
19594 96 AVE, SURREY, BC, V4N 4C3
(604) 882-0183   *SIC* 3714

PACIFIC RADIATOR MFG. LTD   p228
20579 LANGLEY BYPASS SUITE 203, LANGLEY, BC, V3A 5E8
(604) 534-7555   *SIC* 3714

PARKER HANNIFIN CANADA   p490
4635 DURHAM RD RR 3, BEAMSVILLE, ON, L0R 1B3
SIC 3714

PAT'S DRIVE LINE SPECIALTY & MACHINE EDMONTON LTD   p96
14715 116 AVE NW, EDMONTON, AB, T5M 3E8
(780) 453-5105   *SIC* 3714

PAVACO PLASTICS INC   p606
659 SPEEDVALE AVE W, GUELPH, ON, N1K 1E6
(519) 823-1383   *SIC* 3714

PRINCE METAL PRODUCTS LTD   p1025
945 PRINCE RD, WINDSOR, ON, N9C 2Z4
(519) 977-5333   *SIC* 3714

RADIATEURS MONTREAL INC   p1184
270 RUE BEAUBIEN O, MONTREAL, QC, H2V 1C4
(514) 276-8521   *SIC* 3714

RAUFOSS AUTOMOTIVE COMPONENTS CANADA INC   p1062
4050 RUE LAVOISIER, BOISBRIAND, QC, J7H 1R4
(450) 419-4911   *SIC* 3714

RENE MATERIAUX COMPOSITES LTEE   p1300
55 RTE 271 S, SAINT-EPHREM-DE-BEAUCE, QC, G0M 1R0
(418) 484-5282   *SIC* 3714

RESSORTS LIBERTE MEXIQUE INC   p1160
173 RUE DES INDUSTRIES, MONTMAGNY, QC, G5V 4G2
(418) 248-8871   *SIC* 3714

RIMEX SUPPLY LTD   p230
5929 274 ST, LANGLEY, BC, V4W 0B8
(604) 888-0025   *SIC* 3714

ROYAL AUTOMOTIVE GROUP LTD   p1033
30 AVIVA PARK DR, WOODBRIDGE, ON,

L4L 9C7
(416) 749-0314   *SIC* 3714
S.I.F. SUPERIOR INDUSTRIAL FRICTIONS LTD   *p96*
11570 154 ST NW, EDMONTON, AB, T5M 3N8
(780) 451-6894   *SIC* 3714
SAF-HOLLAND CANADA LIMITED   *p796*
20 PHOEBE ST, NORWICH, ON, N0J 1P0
(519) 863-3414   *SIC* 3714
SAF-HOLLAND CANADA LIMITED   *p1035*
595 ATHLONE AVE, WOODSTOCK, ON, N4S 7V8
(519) 537-2366   *SIC* 3714
SHOWA CANADA INC   *p879*
1 SHOWA CRT, SCHOMBERG, ON, L0G 1T0
(905) 939-0575   *SIC* 3714
SOUCY INTERNATIONAL INC   *p1097*
5450 RUE SAINT-ROCH S, DRUM-MONDVILLE, QC, J2B 6V4
(819) 474-6666   *SIC* 3714
ST. CLAIR TECHNOLOGIES INC   *p1005*
827 DUFFERIN AVE, WALLACEBURG, ON, N8A 2V5
(519) 627-1673   *SIC* 3714
STACKPOLE INTERNATIONAL POWDER METAL, LTD.   *p478*
1325 CORMORANT RD 1ST FL, AN-CASTER, ON, L9G 4V5
(905) 304-9455   *SIC* 3714
STACKPOLE INTERNATIONAL POWDER METAL, LTD.   *p478*
1325 CORMORANT RD 2ND FL, AN-CASTER, ON, L9G 4V5
(905) 304-9455   *SIC* 3714
STACKPOLE INTERNATIONAL POWDER METAL, LTD.   *p896*
128 MONTEITH AVE, STRATFORD, ON, N5A 2P5
(519) 271-6060   *SIC* 3714
STACKPOLE INTERNATIONAL ULC   *p478*
1325 CORMORANT RD FL 2, ANCASTER, ON, L9G 4V5
(905) 304-9455   *SIC* 3714
STANDEN'S MANAGEMENT INC   *p37*
1222 58 AVE SE, CALGARY, AB, T2H 2E9
(403) 258-7800   *SIC* 3714
SYNCREON CANADA INC   *p1362*
1340 BOUL DAGENAIS O, SAINTE-ROSE, QC, H7L 5C7
(450) 625-0400   *SIC* 3714
TERMINAL & CABLE TC INC   *p1074*
1930 CH BELLERIVE, CARIGNAN, QC, J3L 4Z4
(450) 658-1742   *SIC* 3714
TERRAVEST INDUSTRIES INC   *p170*
4901 BRUCE RD, VEGREVILLE, AB, T9C 1C3
(780) 632-2040   *SIC* 3714
TIERCON CORP   *p893*
591 ARVIN AVE, STONEY CREEK, ON, L8E 5N7
(905) 643-4176   *SIC* 3714
TIERCON CORP   *p893*
352 ARVIN AVE, STONEY CREEK, ON, L8E 2M4
(905) 662-1097   *SIC* 3714
TRANSFORM AUTOMOTIVE CANADA LIMITED   *p662*
3745 COMMERCE RD, LONDON, ON, N6N 1R1
(519) 644-2434   *SIC* 3714
UVIEW ULTRAVIOLET SYSTEMS INC   *p704*
1324 BLUNDELL RD, MISSISSAUGA, ON, L4Y 1M5
(905) 615-8620   *SIC* 3714
VENTRA GROUP CO   *p642*
675 TRILLIUM DR, KITCHENER, ON, N2R 1G6
(519) 895-0290   *SIC* 3714
VENTRA GROUP CO   *p902*
538 BLANCHARD PK, TECUMSEH, ON, N8N 2L9

(519) 727-3931   *SIC* 3714
VENTRA GROUP CO   *p1015*
200 MONTECORTE ST, WHITBY, ON, L1N 9V8
SIC 3714
VINELAND MANUFACTURING LTD   *p1003*
4937 VICTORIA AVE SUITE 1, VINELAND STATION, ON, L0R 2E0
(905) 562-7308   *SIC* 3714
VOESTALPINE ROTEC SUMMO CORP *p525*
4041 NORTH SERVICE RD, BURLINGTON, ON, L7L 4X6
(905) 336-0014   *SIC* 3714
WES-T-RANS COMPANY   *p370*
515 OAK POINT HWY, WINNIPEG, MB, R2R 1V2
(204) 633-9282   *SIC* 3714
WESCAST INDUSTRIES INC   *p518*
150 SAVANNAH OAKS DR, BRANTFORD, ON, N3V 1E7
(519) 750-0000   *SIC* 3714
WESCAST INDUSTRIES INC   *p1026*
200 WATER ST, WINGHAM, ON, N0G 2W0
(519) 357-3450   *SIC* 3714
WESCAST INDUSTRIES INC   *p1026*
100 WATER ST, WINGHAM, ON, N0G 2W0
(519) 357-3450   *SIC* 3714
WESTPORT POWER INC   *p640*
100 HOLLINGER CRES, KITCHENER, ON, N2K 2Z3
(519) 576-4270   *SIC* 3714
ZF AUTOMOTIVE CANADA LIMITED   *p912*
101 SPRUCE ST, TILLSONBURG, ON, N4G 5C4
(519) 688-4200   *SIC* 3714
ZF AUTOMOTIVE CANADA LIMITED *p1036*
155 BEARDS LANE, WOODSTOCK, ON, N4S 7W3
(519) 537-2331   *SIC* 3714

SIC 3715 Truck trailers

5274398 MANITOBA LTD   *p352*
418 SOUTH RAILWAY ST SUITE 2, MOR-DEN, MB, R6M 2G2
(204) 822-9509   *SIC* 3715
ARNE'S WELDING LTD   *p365*
835 MISSION ST, WINNIPEG, MB, R2J 0A4
(204) 233-7111   *SIC* 3715
B.W.S. MANUFACTURING LTD   *p396*
29 HAWKINS RD, CENTREVILLE, NB, E7K 1A4
(506) 276-4567   *SIC* 3715
CHALMERS SUSPENSION INTERNA-TIONAL INC   *p687*
6400 NORTHAM DR, MISSISSAUGA, ON, L4V 1J1
(905) 362-6400   *SIC* 3715
DELOUPE INC   *p1302*
102 RUE DU PARC-INDUSTRIEL, SAINT-EVARISTE-DE-FORSYTH, QC, G0M 1S0
(418) 459-6443   *SIC* 3715
DOEPKER INDUSTRIES LTD   *p267*
5301 40 AVE SE, SALMON ARM, BC, V1E 1X1
SIC 3715
DOEPKER INDUSTRIES LTD   *p1404*
300 DOEPKER AVE, ANNAHEIM, SK, S0K 0G0
(306) 598-2171   *SIC* 3715
DOEPKER INDUSTRIES LTD   *p1411*
1955 CARIBOU ST, MOOSE JAW, SK, S6H 4P2
(306) 693-2525   *SIC* 3715
FERICAR INC   *p1075*
112 RTE 155, CHAMBORD, QC, G0W 1G0
(418) 342-6221   *SIC* 3715
GROUPE ST-HENRI INC   *p1130*
8000 RUE SAINT-PATRICK, LASALLE, QC, H8N 1V1
(514) 363-0000   *SIC* 3715
INNOVATIVE TRAILER DESIGN INDUS-TRIES INC   *p996*

161 THE WEST MALL, TORONTO, ON, M9C 4V8
(416) 620-7755   *SIC* 3715
K-LINE TRAILERS LTD   *p229*
27360 58 CRES, LANGLEY, BC, V4W 3W7
(604) 856-7899   *SIC* 3715
LOAD LINE INCORPORATED   *p361*
9081 HWY 32, WINKLER, MB, R6W 4B7
(204) 325-4798   *SIC* 3715
MAGNUM TRAILER AND EQUIPMENT INC   *p175*
660 RIVERSIDE RD, ABBOTSFORD, BC, V2S 7M6
(604) 855-7544   *SIC* 3715
MANAC INC   *p1305*
2275 107E RUE, SAINT-GEORGES, QC, G5Y 8G6
(418) 228-2018   *SIC* 3715
PEERLESS LIMITED   *p244*
575 PAGE AVE, PENTICTON, BC, V2A 6P3
(250) 492-0408   *SIC* 3715
RAGLAN INDUSTRIES INC   *p813*
5151 SIMCOE ST N, OSHAWA, ON, L1H 0S4
(905) 655-3355   *SIC* 3715
REMEQ INC   *p1254*
391 RUE SAINT-JEAN-BAPTISTE N, PRINCEVILLE, QC, G6L 5G3
(819) 364-5400   *SIC* 3715
SOUTHLAND TRAILER CORP   *p141*
1405 41 ST N, LETHBRIDGE, AB, T1H 6G3
(403) 327-8212   *SIC* 3715
TEMISKO (1983) INC   *p1243*
91 RUE ONTARIO, NOTRE-DAME-DU-NORD, QC, J0Z 3B0
(819) 723-2416   *SIC* 3715
TITAN TRAILERS INC   *p564*
1129 HIGHWAY 3, DELHI, ON, N4B 2W6
(519) 688-4826   *SIC* 3715

SIC 3716 Motor homes

PLEASURE-WAY INDUSTRIES LTD *p1425*
302 PORTAGE AVE, SASKATOON, SK, S7J 4C6
(306) 934-6578   *SIC* 3716
VALID MANUFACTURING LTD   *p268*
5320 48 AVE SE, SALMON ARM, BC, V1E 1X2
(250) 832-6477   *SIC* 3716
VAN ACTION (2005) INC   *p1342*
4870 RUE COURVAL, SAINT-LAURENT, QC, H4T 1L1
(514) 342-5000   *SIC* 3716

SIC 3721 Aircraft

ABIPA CANADA INC   *p1061*
3700 AV DES GRANDES TOURELLES, BOISBRIAND, QC, J7H 0A1
(450) 963-6888   *SIC* 3721
AIRBUS HELICOPTERS CANADA LIMITED *p591*
1100 GILMORE RD, FORT ERIE, ON, L2A 5M4
(905) 871-7772   *SIC* 3721
BELL HELICOPTER TEXTRON CANADA LIMITEE   *p1152*
12800 RUE DE L'AVENIR, MIRABEL, QC, J7J 1R4
(450) 971-6500   *SIC* 3721
BOMBARDIER INC   *p785*
123 GARRATT BLVD, NORTH YORK, ON, M3K 1Y5
(416) 633-7310   *SIC* 3721
BOMBARDIER INC   *p1092*
200 CH DE LA COTE-VERTU BUREAU 1110, DORVAL, QC, H4S 2A3
(514) 420-4000   *SIC* 3721
DE HAVILLAND AIRCRAFT OF CANADA LIMITED   *p916*
123 GARRATT BLVD, TORONTO, ON, M3K

1Y5
(416) 633-7310   *SIC* 3721
DIAMOND AIRCRAFT INDUSTRIES INC *p649*
1560 CRUMLIN, LONDON, ON, N5V 1S2
(519) 457-4000   *SIC* 3721
LISI AEROSPACE CANADA CORP   *p1094*
2000 PLACE TRANSCANADIENNE, DOR-VAL, QC, H9P 2X5
(514) 421-4567   *SIC* 3721
PROVINCIAL AEROSPACE LTD   *p428*
HANGAR NO 1 ST JOHN'S INTERNA-TIONAL AIRPORT, ST. JOHN'S, NL, A1A 5B5
(709) 576-1800   *SIC* 3721
SOCIETE EN COMMANDITE AIRBUS CANADA   *p1153*
13100 BOUL HENRI-FABRE E, MIRABEL, QC, J7N 3C6
(514) 855-7110   *SIC* 3721
STELIA AERONAUTIQUE CANADA INC *p1153*
12000 RUE HENRY-GIFFARD, MIRABEL, QC, J7N 1H4
(450) 595-8300   *SIC* 3721

SIC 3724 Aircraft engines and engine parts

MDS AEROSPACE CORPORATION   *p816*
200-1220 OLD INNES RD, OTTAWA, ON, K1B 3V3
(613) 744-7257   *SIC* 3724
PRATT & WHITNEY CANADA CIE   *p450*
189 PRATT WHITNEY PK, ENFIELD, NS, B2T 1L1
(902) 873-4241   *SIC* 3724
RBC BEARINGS CANADA, INC   *p1050*
8121 RUE JARRY, ANJOU, QC, H1J 1H6
(514) 352-9425   *SIC* 3724

SIC 3728 Aircraft parts and equipment, nec

333111 ONTARIO LIMITED   *p733*
7805 TRANMERE DR, MISSISSAUGA, ON, L5S 1V5
(905) 364-5000   *SIC* 3728
AERO MAG 2000 (YUL) INC   *p1332*
8181 RUE HERVE-SAINT-MARTIN, SAINT-LAURENT, QC, H4S 2A5
(514) 636-1930   *SIC* 3728
AEROSPATIALE HEMMINGFORD INC*p1113*
447 RTE 202 O, HEMMINGFORD, QC, J0L 1H0
(450) 247-2722   *SIC* 3728
ARNPRIOR AEROSPACE INC   *p478*
107 BASKIN DR, ARNPRIOR, ON, K7S 3M1
(613) 623-4267   *SIC* 3728
AVCORP INDUSTRIES INC   *p208*
10025 RIVER WAY, DELTA, BC, V4G 1M7
(604) 582-1137   *SIC* 3728
AVIANOR INC   *p1153*
12405 RUE SERVICE A-2, MIRABEL, QC, J7N 1E4
SIC 3728
BLUEDROP SIMULATION SERVICES INC *p458*
36 SOLUTIONS DR SUITE 300, HALIFAX, NS, B3S 1N2
(800) 563-3638   *SIC* 3728
BLUEDROP TRAINING & SIMULATION INC *p458*
36 SOLUTIONS DR SUITE 300, HALIFAX, NS, B3S 1N2
(800) 563-3638   *SIC* 3728
BOEING CANADA OPERATIONS LTD *p385*
99 MURRAY PARK RD, WINNIPEG, MB, R3J 3M6
(204) 888-2300   *SIC* 3728
BRISTOL AEROSPACE LIMITED   *p383*
660 BERRY ST, WINNIPEG, MB, R3H 0S5
(204) 775-8331   *SIC* 3728
CADORATH AEROSPACE INC   *p369*
2070 LOGAN AVE, WINNIPEG, MB, R2R

0H9
(204) 633-2707   *SIC 3728*
COLUMBIA INDUSTRIES LTD   *p14*
7150 112 AVE SE, CALGARY, AB, T2C 4Z1
(403) 236-3420   *SIC 3728*
COORDINATE INDUSTRIES LTD   *p797*
2251 WINSTON PARK DR, OAKVILLE, ON, L6H 5R1
(905) 829-0099   *SIC 3728*
CORMER GROUP INDUSTRIES INC   *p372*
33 BENTALL ST, WINNIPEG, MB, R2X 2Z7
(204) 987-6400   *SIC 3728*
CYCLONE MANUFACTURING INCORPO-RATED   *p721*
7300 RAPISTAN CRT, MISSISSAUGA, ON, L5N 5S1
(905) 567-5601   *SIC 3728*
DEVTEK AEROSPACE INC   *p641*
1665 HIGHLAND RD W, KITCHENER, ON, N2N 3K5
(519) 576-8910   *SIC 3728*
DEVTEK AEROSPACE INC   *p641*
1665 HIGHLAND RD W, KITCHENER, ON, N2N 3K5
(519) 576-8910   *SIC 3728*
EXCENTROTECH PRECISION INC   *p1031*
55 WESTCREEK DR, WOODBRIDGE, ON, L4L 9N6
(905) 856-1801   *SIC 3728*
FIELD AVIATION WEST LTD   *p8*
4300 26 ST NE UNIT 125, CALGARY, AB, T1Y 7H7
(403) 516-8200   *SIC 3728*
FLEET CANADA INC   *p591*
1011 GILMORE RD, FORT ERIE, ON, L2A 5M4
(905) 871-2100   *SIC 3728*
GOODRICH AEROSPACE CANADA LTD   *p803*
1400 SOUTH SERVICE RD W, OAKVILLE, ON, L6L 5Y7
(905) 827-7777   *SIC 3728*
HELIGEAR CANADA ACQUISITION COR-PORATION   *p683*
180 MARKET DR, MILTON, ON, L9T 3H5
(905) 875-4000   *SIC 3728*
HEROUX-DEVTEK INC   *p1143*
755 RUE THURBER, LONGUEUIL, QC, J4H 3N2
(450) 679-5450   *SIC 3728*
HPG INC   *p804*
2240 SPEERS RD, OAKVILLE, ON, L6L 2X8
(905) 825-1218   *SIC 3728*
HPG INC   *p804*
2250 SPEERS RD, OAKVILLE, ON, L6L 2X8
(905) 825-1218   *SIC 3728*
INDAL TECHNOLOGIES INC   *p711*
3570 HAWKESTONE RD, MISSISSAUGA, ON, L5C 2V8
(905) 275-5300   *SIC 3728*
INDUSTRIES C.P.S. INC, LES   *p1251*
30 CH DE L'AVIATION, POINTE-CLAIRE, QC, H9R 5M6
(514) 695-0400   *SIC 3728*
INDUSTRIES LEESTA LTEE, LES   *p1251*
6 AV DU PLATEAU, POINTE-CLAIRE, QC, H9R 5W2
(514) 694-3930   *SIC 3728*
KRAUS GLOBAL LTD   *p366*
25 PAQUIN RD, WINNIPEG, MB, R2J 3V9
(204) 663-3601   *SIC 3728*
MAGELLAN AEROSPACE LIMITED   *p384*
660 BERRY ST, WINNIPEG, MB, R3H 0S5
(204) 775-8331   *SIC 3728*
MAGELLAN AEROSPACE LIMITED   *p686*
3160 DERRY RD E, MISSISSAUGA, ON, L4T 1A9
(905) 677-1889   *SIC 3728*
MECACHROME CANADA INC   *p1153*
11100 RUE JULIEN-AUDETTE, MIRABEL, QC, J7N 3L3
(450) 476-3939   *SIC 3728*
MECAER AMERIQUE INC   *p1357*
5555 RUE WILLIAM-PRICE, SAINTE-

DOROTHEE, QC, H7L 6C4
(450) 682-7117   *SIC 3728*
MESOTEC INC   *p1374*
4705 BOUL DE PORTLAND, SHER-BROOKE, QC, J1L 0H3
(819) 822-2777   *SIC 3728*
MHI CANADA AEROSPACE INC   *p688*
6390 NORTHWEST DR, MISSISSAUGA, ON, L4V 1S1
(905) 612-6781   *SIC 3728*
NWI PRECISION TUBE ULC   *p997*
9 FENMAR DR, TORONTO, ON, M9L 1L5
(416) 743-4417   *SIC 3728*
PCC AEROSTRUCTURES DORVAL INC   *p1094*
123 AV AVRO, DORVAL, QC, H9P 2Y9
(514) 421-0344   *SIC 3728*
PLACETECO INC   *p1368*
3763 RUE BURRILL BUREAU 2, SHAWINI-GAN, QC, G9N 0C4
(819) 539-8808   *SIC 3728*
PRODUITS INTEGRES AVIOR INC   *p1235*
1001 NORD LAVAL (A-440) O BUREAU 200, MONTREAL, QC, H7L 3W3
(450) 629-6200   *SIC 3728*
QINETIQ GROUP CANADA INC   *p147*
1735 BRIER PARK RD NW UNIT 3, MEDICINE HAT, AB, T1C 1V5
(403) 528-8782   *SIC 3728*
RAMPF COMPOSITE SOLUTIONS INC *p524*
5322 JOHN LUCAS DR, BURLINGTON, ON, L7L 6A6
(905) 331-8042   *SIC 3728*
SAFRAN LANDING SYSTEMS CANADA INC   *p474*
574 MONARCH AVE, AJAX, ON, L1S 2G8
(905) 683-3100   *SIC 3728*
SAFRAN LANDING SYSTEMS CANADA INC   *p1153*
13000 RUE DU PARC, MIRABEL, QC, J7J 0W6
(450) 434-3400   *SIC 3728*
SONACA MONTREAL INC   *p1153*
13075 RUE BRAULT, MIRABEL, QC, J7J 0W2
(450) 434-6114   *SIC 3728*
SPP CANADA AIRCRAFT, INC   *p727*
2025 MEADOWVALE BLVD UNIT 1, MIS-SISSAUGA, ON, L5N 5N1
(905) 821-9339   *SIC 3728*
STELIA AEROSPACE NORTH AMERICA INC   *p462*
71 HALL ST, LUNENBURG, NS, B0J 2C0
(902) 634-8448   *SIC 3728*
TECHNIPRODEC LTEE   *p1162*
11865 AV ADOLPHE-CARON, MONTREAL, QC, H1E 6J8
(514) 648-5423   *SIC 3728*
TRIDENT INDUSTRIES INC, LES   *p1163*
8277 BOUL HENRI-BOURASSA E, MON-TREAL, QC, H1E 1P4
(514) 648-0285   *SIC 3728*
TRIUMPH GEAR SYSTEMS-TORONTO ULC *p997*
9 FENMAR DR, TORONTO, ON, M9L 1L5
(416) 743-4417   *SIC 3728*
VIKING AIR LIMITED   *p269*
1959 DE HAVILLAND WAY, SIDNEY, BC, V8L 5V5
(250) 656-7227   *SIC 3728*

SIC 3731 Shipbuilding and repairing

6318703 CANADA INC   *p1150*
1460 RUE DE MATANE-SUR-MER, MATANE, QC, G4W 3M6
(418) 562-0911   *SIC 3731*
ALGOMA CENTRAL CORPORATION   *p846*
1 CHESTNUT ST, PORT COLBORNE, ON, L3K 1R3
(905) 834-4549   *SIC 3731*
ALLIED SHIPBUILDERS LTD   *p238*
1870 HARBOUR RD, NORTH VANCOU-

VER, BC, V7H 1A1
(604) 929-2365   *SIC 3731*
GROUPE OCEAN INC, LE   *p1259*
105 RUE ABRAHAM-MARTIN BUREAU 500, QUEBEC, QC, G1K 8N1
(418) 694-1414   *SIC 3731*
HEDDLE MARINE SERVICE INC   *p610*
208 HILLYARD ST, HAMILTON, ON, L8L 6B6
(905) 528-2635   *SIC 3731*
INDUSTRIES OCEAN INC   *p1259*
105 RUE ABRAHAM-MARTIN BUREAU 500, QUEBEC, QC, G1K 8N1
(418) 438-2745   *SIC 3731*
IRVING SHIPBUILDING INC   *p455*
3099 BARRINGTON ST, HALIFAX, NS, B3K 5M7
(902) 423-9271   *SIC 3731*
IRVING SHIPBUILDING INC   *p455*
3099 BARRINGTON ST, HALIFAX, NS, B3K 2X6
(902) 423-9271   *SIC 3731*
IRVING SHIPBUILDING INC   *p1041*
115 WATER ST, GEORGETOWN, PE, C0A 1L0
SIC 3731
LUNENBURG FOUNDRY & ENGINEERING LIMITED   *p462*
53 FALKLAND ST, LUNENBURG, NS, B0J 2C0
(902) 634-8827   *SIC 3731*
NEPTUNUS YACHTS INTERNATIONAL INC *p883*
8 KEEFER RD, ST CATHARINES, ON, L2M 7N9
(905) 937-3737   *SIC 3731*
ST. JOHN'S DOCKYARD LIMITED   *p433*
475 WATER ST, ST. JOHN'S, NL, A1E 6B5
(709) 758-6800   *SIC 3731*
THERIAULT, A. F. & SON LTD   *p462*
9027 MAIN HWY, METEGHAN RIVER, NS, B0W 2L0
(902) 645-2327   *SIC 3731*
VANCOUVER SHIPYARDS CO. LTD   *p242*
10 PEMBERTON AVENUE, NORTH VAN-COUVER, BC, V7P 2R1
(604) 988-6361   *SIC 3731*
VICTORIA SHIPYARDS CO. LTD   *p340*
825 ADMIRALS RD, VICTORIA, BC, V9A 2P1
(250) 380-1602   *SIC 3731*
WARTSILA CANADA, INCORPORATED   *p257*
1771 SAVAGE RD, RICHMOND, BC, V6V 1R1
(604) 244-8181   *SIC 3731*

SIC 3732 Boatbuilding and repairing

BATEAUX PRINCECRAFT INC   *p1253*
725 RUE SAINT-HENRI, PRINCEVILLE, QC, G6L 5C2
(819) 364-5581   *SIC 3732*
CAMPION MARINE INC   *p219*
200 CAMPION ST, KELOWNA, BC, V1X 7S8
(250) 765-7795   *SIC 3732*
CANADIAN TEST CASE 173   *p720*
6750 CENTURY AVE, SUITE 305, MISSIS-SAUGA, ON, L5N 0B7
(905) 812-5920   *SIC 3732*
DBC MARINE SAFETY SYSTEMS LTD *p205*
1689 CLIVEDEN AVE, DELTA, BC, V3M 6V5
(604) 278-3221   *SIC 3732*
HICAT CORPORATION INC   *p1283*
640 14E AV BUREAU 102, RICHELIEU, QC, J3L 5R5
(450) 982-1494   *SIC 3732*
KINGFISHER BOATS INC   *p331*
8160 HIGHLAND RD, VERNON, BC, V1B 3W6
(250) 545-9171   *SIC 3732*
KOBELT MANUFACTURING CO. LTD   *p277*

8238 129 ST, SURREY, BC, V3W 0A6
(604) 572-3935   *SIC 3732*
METAL CRAFT MARINE INCORPORATED *p630*
347 WELLINGTON ST, KINGSTON, ON, K7K 6N7
(613) 549-7747   *SIC 3732*
PELICAN INTERNATIONAL INC   *p1231*
1000 PLACE PAUL-KANE, MONTREAL, QC, H7C 2T2
(450) 664-1222   *SIC 3732*
PHILBROOK'S BOATYARD LTD   *p268*
2324 HARBOUR RD, SIDNEY, BC, V8L 2P6
(250) 656-1157   *SIC 3732*
PRODUITS RECREATIFS FUTURE BEACH INC   *p1318*
160 RUE VANIER, SAINT-JEAN-SUR-RICHELIEU, QC, J3B 3R4
(450) 245-0373   *SIC 3732*
REMBOURRAGE ANP INC   *p1254*
105 RUE BEAUDET, PRINCEVILLE, QC, G6L 4L3
(819) 364-2645   *SIC 3732*
VERREAULT NAVIGATION INC   *p1135*
108 RUE DU COLLEGE, LES MECHINS, QC, G0J 1T0
(418) 729-3733   *SIC 3732*
ZODIAC HURRICANE TECHNOLOGIES INC *p210*
7830 VANTAGE WAY, DELTA, BC, V4G 1A7
(604) 940-2999   *SIC 3732*

SIC 3743 Railroad equipment

510172 ONTARIO LTD   *p898*
100 FOUNDRY ST, SUDBURY, ON, P3A 4R7
(705) 674-5626   *SIC 3743*
ALSTOM TRANSPORT CANADA INC *p1191*
1050 COTE DU BEAVER HALL BUREAU 1840, MONTREAL, QC, H2Z 0A5
(514) 333-0888   *SIC 3743*
BOMBARDIER INC   *p1202*
800 BOUL RENE-LEVESQUE O 29E ETAGE, MONTREAL, QC, H3B 1Y8
(514) 861-9481   *SIC 3743*
BOMBARDIER TRANSPORTATION CANADA INC   *p909*
1001 MONTREAL ST, THUNDER BAY, ON, P7C 4V6
(807) 475-2810   *SIC 3743*
JOHNSTON EQUIPMENT ENGINEERED *p731*
5990 AVEBURY RD, MISSISSAUGA, ON, L5R 3R2
(905) 712-6000   *SIC 3743*
KELSO TECHNOLOGIES INC   *p280*
13966 18B AVE, SURREY, BC, V4A 8J1
(250) 764-3618   *SIC 3743*
KNORR BRAKE LIMITED   *p919*
101 CONDOR AVE, TORONTO, ON, M4J 3N2
(416) 461-4343   *SIC 3743*
METROLINX   *p712*
3500 WOLFEDALE RD, MISSISSAUGA, ON, L5C 2V6
SIC 3743
NATIONAL STEEL CAR LIMITED   *p612*
600 KENILWORTH AVE N, HAMILTON, ON, L8N 3J4
(905) 544-3311   *SIC 3743*
WABTEC CANADA INC   *p893*
475 SEAMAN ST, STONEY CREEK, ON, L8E 2R2
(905) 561-8700   *SIC 3743*
WABTEC CANADA INC   *p1337*
10655 BOUL HENRI-BOURASSA O, SAINT-LAURENT, QC, H4S 1A1
(514) 335-4200   *SIC 3743*

SIC 3751 Motorcycles, bicycles and parts

▲ Public Company   ■ Public Company Family Member   **HQ** Headquarters   **BR** Branch   **SL** Single Location

CERVELO CYCLES INC   p788
15 LESWYN RD UNIT 1, NORTH YORK, ON, M6A 1J8
(416) 782-6789   *SIC 3751*

CYCLE DEVINCI INC   p1080
1555 RUE DE LA MANIC, CHICOUTIMI, QC, G7K 1G8
(418) 549-6218   *SIC 3751*

INDUSTRIES RAD INC   p1344
6363 BOUL DES GRANDES-PRAIRIES, SAINT-LEONARD, QC, H1P 1A5
(418) 228-8934   *SIC 3751*

LTP SPORTS GROUP INC   p247
1465 KEBET WAY SUITE B, PORT CO-QUITLAM, BC, V3C 6L3
(604) 552-2930   *SIC 3751*

NORCO MANAGEMENT LTD   p247
1465 KEBET WAY SUITE B, PORT CO-QUITLAM, BC, V3C 6L3
(604) 552-2930   *SIC 3751*

RALEIGH CANADA LIMITED   p799
2124 LONDON LANE, OAKVILLE, ON, L6H 5V8
(905) 829-5555   *SIC 3751*

SIC 3769 Space vehicle equipment, nec

MACDONALD, DETTWILER AND ASSO-CIATES INC   p499
9445 AIRPORT RD SUITE 100, BRAMP-TON, ON, L6S 4J3
(905) 790-2800   *SIC 3769*

SIC 3792 Travel trailers and campers

CITAIR, INC   p620
73 MILL RD, HENSALL, ON, N0M 1X0
(519) 262-2600   *SIC 3792*

TRIPLE E CANADA LTD   p361
135 CANADA ST, WINKLER, MB, R6W 0J3
(204) 325-4345   *SIC 3792*

SIC 3795 Tanks and tank components

ARMATEC SURVIVABILITY CORP   p565
1 NEWTON AVE, DORCHESTER, ON, N0L 1G4
(519) 268-2999   *SIC 3795*

DEW ENGINEERING AND DEVELOPMENT ULC   p405
99 GENERAL MANSON WAY, MIRAMICHI, NB, E1N 6K6
(506) 778-8000   *SIC 3795*

DEW ENGINEERING AND DEVELOPMENT ULC   p817
3429 HAWTHORNE RD, OTTAWA, ON, K1G 4G2
(613) 736-5100   *SIC 3795*

PORTEFEUILLE SOUCY INC   p1097
5450 RUE SAINT-ROCH S, DRUM-MONDVILLE, QC, J2B 6V4
(819) 474-6666   *SIC 3795*

SOUCY INTERNATIONAL INC   p1100
5195 RUE RICHARD, DRUMMONDVILLE, QC, J2E 1A7
(819) 474-4522   *SIC 3795*

TECMOTIV CORPORATION   p559
131 SARAMIA CRES 2ND FL, CONCORD, ON, L4K 4P7
(905) 669-5911   *SIC 3795*

SIC 3799 Transportation equipment, nec

611421 ONTARIO INC.   p762
119 PROGRESS CRT, NORTH BAY, ON, P1A 0C1
(705) 476-4222   *SIC 3799*

BOMBARDIER PRODUITS RECREATIFS INC   p1392

726 RUE SAINT-JOSEPH, VALCOURT, QC, J0E 2L0
(450) 532-2211   *SIC 3799*

BOMBARDIER PRODUITS RECREATIFS INC   p1392
565 RUE DE LA MONTAGNE BUREAU 210, VALCOURT, QC, J0E 2L0
(450) 532-2211   *SIC 3799*

DOPPELMAYR CANADA LTD   p220
567 ADAMS RD, KELOWNA, BC, V1X 7R9
(250) 765-3000   *SIC 3799*

DOPPELMAYR CANADA LTEE   p1319
800 MONTEE SAINT-NICOLAS, SAINT-JEROME, QC, J7Y 4C8
(450) 432-1128   *SIC 3799*

INDUSTRIES N.R.C. INC   p1350
2430 RUE PRINCIPALE E BUREAU 160, SAINT-PAUL-D'ABBOTSFORD, QC, J0E 1A0
(450) 379-5796   *SIC 3799*

PAR NADO INC   p1303
821 RUE DU PARC, SAINT-FREDERIC, QC, G0N 1P0
(418) 426-3666   *SIC 3799*

SIC 3812 Search and navigation equipment

ADACEL INC   p1201
895 RUE DE LA GAUCHETIERE O BU-REAU 300, MONTREAL, QC, H3B 4G1
(450) 444-2687   *SIC 3812*

AKTELUX CORPORATION   p719
2145 MEADOWPINE BLVD, MISSIS-SAUGA, ON, L5N 6R8
SIC 3812

ATS TRAFFIC GROUP LTD   p121
9015 14 ST NW, EDMONTON, AB, T6P 0C9
(780) 440-4114   *SIC 3812*

BOMBARDIER INC   p1328
1800 BOUL MARCEL-LAURIN, SAINT-LAURENT, QC, H4R 1K2
(514) 855-5000   *SIC 3812*

CELESTICA INTERNATIONAL LP   p716
3333 UNITY DR SUITE A, MISSISSAUGA, ON, L5L 3S6
(416) 448-2559   *SIC 3812*

CFN PRECISION LTD   p550
1000 CREDITSTONE RD, CONCORD, ON, L4K 4P8
(905) 669-8191   *SIC 3812*

EMS TECHNOLOGIES CANADA, LTD   p626
400 MAPLE GROVE RD, KANATA, ON, K2V 1B8
(613) 591-6040   *SIC 3812*

FLYHT AEROSPACE SOLUTIONS LTD   p23
1144 29 AVE NE SUITE 300E, CALGARY, AB, T2E 7P1
(403) 250-9956   *SIC 3812*

FORTRESS TECHNOLOGY INC   p864
51 GRAND MARSHALL DR, SCARBOR-OUGH, ON, M1B 5N6
(416) 754-2898   *SIC 3812*

GEOTAB INC   p797
2440 WINSTON PARK DR, OAKVILLE, ON, L6H 7V2
(416) 434-4309   *SIC 3812*

INTELCAN TECHNOSYSTEMS INC   p749
69 AURIGA DR, NEPEAN, ON, K2E 7Z2
(613) 228-1150   *SIC 3812*

KONGSBERG MESOTECH LTD   p247
1598 KEBET WAY, PORT COQUITLAM, BC, V3C 5M5
(604) 464-8144   *SIC 3812*

L-3 COMMUNICATIONS ELECTRONIC SYS-TEMS INC   p450
249 AEROTECH DR, GOFFS, NS, B2T 1K3
(902) 873-2000   *SIC 3812*

LYNCH DYNAMICS INC   p724
1799 ARGENTIA RD, MISSISSAUGA, ON, L5N 3A2
(905) 363-2400   *SIC 3812*

MCLEOD SAFETY SERVICES LTD   p469
30 UPHAM DR, TRURO, NS, B2N 6W5
(902) 897-7233   *SIC 3812*

NANOWAVE TECHNOLOGIES INC   p571
425 HORNER AVE SUITE 1, ETOBICOKE, ON, M8W 4W3
(416) 252-5602   *SIC 3812*

NAV CANADA   p386
777 MORAY ST, WINNIPEG, MB, R3J 3W8
(204) 983-8566   *SIC 3812*

NOVATEL INC   p76
10921 14 ST NE, CALGARY, AB, T3K 2L5
(403) 295-4500   *SIC 3812*

NOVATRONICS INC   p895
789 ERIE ST, STRATFORD, ON, N4Z 1A2
(519) 271-3880   *SIC 3812*

OSI MARITIME SYSTEMS LTD   p189
4585 CANADA WAY SUITE 400, BURNABY, BC, V5G 4L6
(778) 373-4600   *SIC 3812*

RASAKTI INC   p1306
148 RUE SYLVESTRE, SAINT-GERMAIN-DE-GRANTHAM, QC, J0C 1K0
(819) 395-1111   *SIC 3812*

RAYTHEON CANADA LIMITED   p25
919 72 AVE NE, CALGARY, AB, T2E 8N9
(403) 295-6900   *SIC 3812*

SAFRAN ELECTRONICS & DEFENSE CANADA INC   p842
2000 FISHER DR, PETERBOROUGH, ON, K9J 6X6
(705) 743-6903   *SIC 3812*

SMITHS DETECTION MONTREAL INC p727
6865 CENTURY AVE SUITE 3002, MISSIS-SAUGA, ON, L5N 7K2
(905) 817-5990   *SIC 3812*

SOLACOM TECHNOLOGIES INC   p1107
80 RUE JEAN-PROULX, GATINEAU, QC, J8Z 1W1
(819) 205-8100   *SIC 3812*

ULTRA ELECTRONICS CANADA INC   p444
40 ATLANTIC ST, DARTMOUTH, NS, B2Y 4N2
(902) 466-7491   *SIC 3812*

SIC 3821 Laboratory apparatus and furniture

ACUREN GROUP INC   p262
12271 HORSESHOE WAY, RICHMOND, BC, V7A 4V4
(604) 275-3800   *SIC 3821*

AURORA INSTRUMENTS LTD   p294
1001 PENDER ST E, VANCOUVER, BC, V6A 1W2
(604) 215-8700   *SIC 3821*

CADEX INC   p1316
755 AV MONTRICHARD, SAINT-JEAN-SUR-RICHELIEU, QC, J2X 5K8
(450) 348-6774   *SIC 3821*

CIF LAB CASEWORK SOLUTIONS INC p550
56 EDILCAN DR, CONCORD, ON, L4K 3S6
(905) 738-5821   *SIC 3821*

CIF LAB SOLUTIONS LP   p550
53 COURTLAND AVE SUITE 1, CONCORD, ON, L4K 3T2
(905) 738-5821   *SIC 3821*

CONTROLLED ENVIRONMENTS LIMITED p384
590 BERRY ST, WINNIPEG, MB, R3H 0R9
(204) 786-6451   *SIC 3821*

GREENLIGHT INNOVATION CORPORA-TION   p182
3430 BRIGHTON AVE UNIT 104A, BURN-ABY, BC, V5A 3H4
(604) 676-4000   *SIC 3821*

I.C.T.C. HOLDINGS CORPORATION   p206
720 EATON WAY, DELTA, BC, V3M 6J9
(604) 522-6543   *SIC 3821*

MANTECH INC.   p601
2 ADMIRAL PL, GUELPH, ON, N1G 4N4
(519) 763-4245   *SIC 3821*

PHASE ANALYZER COMPANY LTD   p263
11168 HAMMERSMITH GATE, RICH-MOND, BC, V7A 5H8
(604) 241-9568   *SIC 3821*

QUANSER CONSULTING INC   p674

---

119 SPY CRT, MARKHAM, ON, L3R 5H6
(905) 940-3575   *SIC 3821*

SCHLUMBERGER CANADA LIMITED   p121
9450 17 AVE NW, EDMONTON, AB, T6N 1M9
SIC 3821

TEKRAN INSTRUMENTS CORPORATION
p872
330 NANTUCKET BLVD, SCARBOROUGH, ON, M1P 2P4
(416) 449-3084   *SIC 3821*

TRYTON INVESTMENT COMPANY LIMITED
p385
590 BERRY ST, WINNIPEG, MB, R3H 0R9
(204) 772-7110   *SIC 3821*

ULTRA ELECTRONICS FORENSIC TECH-NOLOGY INC   p1083
5757 BOUL CAVENDISH BUREAU 200, COTE SAINT-LUC, QC, H4W 2W8
(514) 489-4247   *SIC 3821*

Z-SC1 CORP   p1221
4148A RUE SAINTE-CATHERINE O BU-REAU 337, MONTREAL, QC, H3Z 0A2
(877) 381-5500   *SIC 3821*

SIC 3822 Environmental controls

AMI AIR MANAGEMENT INC   p687
3223 ORLANDO DR, MISSISSAUGA, ON, L4V 1C5
(905) 694-9676   *SIC 3822*

BIOREM INC   p848
7496 WELLINGTON RD 34, PUSLINCH, ON, N0B 2J0
(519) 767-9100   *SIC 3822*

CRYOPAK INDUSTRIES (2007) ULC   p205
1081 CLIVEDEN AVE SUITE 110, DELTA, BC, V3M 5V1
(604) 515-7977   *SIC 3822*

DISTECH CONTROLES INC   p1070
4205 PLACE JAVA, BROSSARD, QC, J4Y 0C4
(450) 444-9898   *SIC 3822*

FPS FOOD PROCESS SOLUTIONS COR-PORATION   p258
7431 NELSON RD UNIT 130, RICHMOND, BC, V6W 1G3
(604) 232-4145   *SIC 3822*

GREYSTONE ENERGY SYSTEMS INC p408
150 ENGLISH DR, MONCTON, NB, E1E 4G7
(506) 853-3057   *SIC 3822*

GREYSTONE INDUSTRIES LTD   p408
150 ENGLISH DR, MONCTON, NB, E1E 4G7
(506) 853-3057   *SIC 3822*

HONEYWELL LIMITED   p717
3333 UNITY DR, MISSISSAUGA, ON, L5L 3S6
(905) 608-6000   *SIC 3822*

HONEYWELL LIMITED   p1128
2100 52E AV, LACHINE, QC, H8T 2Y5
(514) 422-3400   *SIC 3822*

HONEYWELL LIMITED   p1264
2366 RUE GALVANI BUREAU 4, QUEBEC, QC, G1N 4G4
(418) 688-8320   *SIC 3822*

JOHNSON CONTROLS NOVA SCOTIA U.L.C.   p684
8205 PARKHILL DR, MILTON, ON, L9T 5G8
(905) 875-2128   *SIC 3822*

NAILOR INDUSTRIES INC   p793
98 TORYORK DR, NORTH YORK, ON, M9L 1X6
(416) 744-3300   *SIC 3822*

SYNAPSE ELECTRONIQUE INC   p1369
1010 7E AV, SHAWINIGAN, QC, G9T 2B8
(819) 533-3553   *SIC 3822*

T.A. MORRISON & CO. INC   p891
27 IBER RD, STITTSVILLE, ON, K2S 1E6
(613) 831-7000   *SIC 3822*

TARGETED MICROWAVE SOLUTIONS INC
p316

1066 HASTINGS ST W SUITE 2300, VAN-COUVER, BC, V6E 3X2

(778) 995-5833   SIC 3822

THEVCO ELECTRONIQUE INC   p1309
5200 RUE ARMAND-FRAPPIER, SAINT-HUBERT, QC, J3Z 1G5

(450) 926-2777   SIC 3822

VICONICS TECHNOLOGIES INC   p1181
7262 RUE MARCONI, MONTREAL, QC, H2R 2Z5

(514) 321-5660   SIC 3822

SIC 3823 Process control instruments

ABB INC   p527
3450 HARVESTER RD, BURLINGTON, ON, L7N 3W5

(905) 639-8840   SIC 3823

ABB INC   p1257
585 BOUL CHAREST E BUREAU 300, QUEBEC, QC, G1K 9H4

(418) 877-2944   SIC 3823

ATLANTIC CATCH DATA LIMITED   p452
1801 HOLLIS ST SUITE 1220, HALIFAX, NS, B3J 3N4

(902) 422-4745   SIC 3823

ATS TEST INC   p1029
600 CHRISLEA RD, WOODBRIDGE, ON, L4L 8K9

(905) 850-8600   SIC 3823

EXPEDIA CANADA CORP   p1188
63 RUE DE BRESOLES BUREAU 100, MONTREAL, QC, H2Y 1V7

(514) 286-8180   SIC 3823

FJORDS PROCESSING CANADA INC   p15
115 QUARRY PARK RD SE SUITE 110, CALGARY, AB, T2C 5G9

(403) 640-4230   SIC 3823

GROUPE SIMONEAU INC, LE   p1065
1541   RUE   DE   COULOMB, BOUCHERVILLE, QC, J4B 8C5

(450) 641-9140   SIC 3823

HOWE PRECISION INDUSTRIAL INC p244
11718 HARRIS RD, PITT MEADOWS, BC, V3Y 1Y6

(604) 460-2892   SIC 3823

INSTRUMENTS ISAAC INC   p1074
240 BOUL FRECHETTE, CHAMBLY, QC, J3L 2Z5

(450) 658-7520   SIC 3823

LTG RAIL CANADA LTEE   p1122
151 RUE DU PARC-DE-L'INNOVATION, LA POCATIERE, QC, G0R 1Z0

(418) 856-1454   SIC 3823

ORUS INTEGRATION INC   p1238
1109 CHOMEDEY (A-13) E, MONTREAL, QC, H7W 5J8

SIC 3823

PRIVA NORTH AMERICA INC   p1003
3468   SOUTH   SERVICE   RD   SS   1, VINELAND STATION, ON, L0R 2E0

(905) 562-7351   SIC 3823

RDC CONTROLE LTEE   p1059
1100   BOUL   MICHELE-BOHEC, BLAINVILLE, QC, J7C 5N5

(450) 434-0216   SIC 3823

SCIEMETRIC INSTRUMENTS INC   p625
359 TERRY FOX DR SUITE 100, KANATA, ON, K2K 2E7

(613) 254-7054   SIC 3823

SHOWA DENKO CARBONE CANADA INC
p1129
505   AV   BETHANY   BUREAU   202, LACHUTE, QC, J8H 4A6

(450) 409-0727   SIC 3823

SIEMENS CANADA LIMITED   p842
1954 TECHNOLOGY DR, PETERBOR-OUGH, ON, K9J 6X7

(705) 745-2431   SIC 3823

SOLINST CANADA LTD   p594
35 TODD RD, GEORGETOWN, ON, L7G 4R8

(905) 873-2255   SIC 3823

TENOVA GOODFELLOW INC   p727
6711 MISSISSAUGA RD SUITE 200, MIS-SISSAUGA, ON, L5N 2W3

(905) 567-3030   SIC 3823

VIBROSYSTM INC   p1146
2727   BOUL   JACQUES-CARTIER   E, LONGUEUIL, QC, J4N 1L7

(450) 646-2157   SIC 3823

VISHAY PRECISION GROUP CANADA ULC
p778
48 LESMILL RD, NORTH YORK, ON, M3B 2T5

(416) 445-5850   SIC 3823

WIKA INSTRUMENTS LTD   p121
3103 PARSONS RD NW, EDMONTON, AB, T6N 1C8

(780) 438-6662   SIC 3823

SIC 3824 Fluid meters and counting devices

DIGITAL PAYMENT TECHNOLOGIES CORP
p185
4260 STILL CREEK DR SUITE 330, BURN-ABY, BC, V5C 6C6

(604) 317-4055   SIC 3824

MACKAY, J. J. CANADA LIMITED   p463
1342 ABERCROMBIE ROAD, NEW GLAS-GOW, NS, B2H 5C6

(902) 752-5124   SIC 3824

NEPTUNE   TECHNOLOGY   GROUP (CANADA) LIMITED   p725
7275 WEST CREDIT AVE, MISSISSAUGA, ON, L5N 5M9

(905) 858-4211   SIC 3824

ROMET LIMITED   p700
5030 TIMBERLEA BLVD, MISSISSAUGA, ON, L4W 2S5

(905) 624-1591   SIC 3824

WINTERS INSTRUMENTS LTD   p775
121 RAILSIDE RD, NORTH YORK, ON, M3A 1B2

(416) 444-2345   SIC 3824

SIC 3825 Instruments to measure electricity

AMERESCO CANADA INC   p850
30 LEEK CRES SUITE 301, RICHMOND HILL, ON, L4B 4N4

(888) 483-7627   SIC 3825

AVERNA TECHNOLOGIES INC   p1210
87 RUE PRINCE BUREAU 510, MON-TREAL, QC, H3C 2M7

(514) 842-7577   SIC 3825

CADEX ELECTRONICS INC   p258
22000 FRASERWOOD WAY, RICHMOND, BC, V6W 1J6

(604) 231-7777   SIC 3825

CAMERON FLOW SYSTEMS LTD   p21
7944 10 ST NE, CALGARY, AB, T2E 8W1

(403) 291-4814   SIC 3825

CONVERSANT   INTELLECTUAL   PROP-ERTY MANAGEMENT INC   p832
515 LEGGET DR SUITE 704, OTTAWA, ON, K2K 3G4

(613) 576-3000   SIC 3825

GALVANIC APPLIED SCIENCES INC   p35
7000 FISHER RD SE, CALGARY, AB, T2H 0W3

(403) 252-8470   SIC 3825

GLOBE STAR SYSTEMS INC   p783
7 KODIAK CRES SUITE 100, NORTH YORK, ON, M3J 3E5

(416) 636-2282   SIC 3825

GUILDLINE INSTRUMENTS LIMITED   p881
21 GILROY ST, SMITHS FALLS, ON, K7A 5B7

(613) 283-3000   SIC 3825

INSPECTIONAIR GAUGE LIMITED   p1020
3298 RIBERDY RD, WINDSOR, ON, N8W 3T9

(519) 966-1232   SIC 3825

NDT TECHNOLOGIES INC   p1054

20275   AV   CLARK-GRAHAM,   BAIE-D'URFE, QC, H9X 3T5

(514) 457-7650   SIC 3825

POWER MEASUREMENT LTD   p267
2195 KEATING CROSS RD, SAANICHTON, BC, V8M 2A5

(250) 652-7100   SIC 3825

POWER MEASUREMENT, INC   p267
2195 KEATING CROSS RD, SAANICHTON, BC, V8M 2A5

(250) 652-7100   SIC 3825

RMC INTERNATIONAL INC   p592
505 CENTRAL AVE, FORT ERIE, ON, L2A 3T9

(905) 991-0431   SIC 3825

SANDVINE INCORPORATED ULC   p1009
408 ALBERT ST, WATERLOO, ON, N2L 3V3

(519) 880-2600   SIC 3825

SANDVINE LTD   p1009
408 ALBERT ST, WATERLOO, ON, N2L 3V3

(519) 880-2600   SIC 3825

SOLACE CORPORATION   p625
535 LEGGET DR FL 3, KANATA, ON, K2K 3B8

(613) 271-1010   SIC 3825

TERRAN NETWORKS CORP.   p451
5503 ATLANTIC ST, HALIFAX, NS, B3H 1G5

(902) 497-1191   SIC 3825

TRILLIANT ENERGY SERVICES INC   p560
20 FLORAL PKY, CONCORD, ON, L4K 4R1

(905) 669-6223   SIC 3825

TRILLIANT HOLDINGS (ONTARIO) INCp560
20 FLORAL PKY, CONCORD, ON, L4K 4R1

(905) 669-6223   SIC 3825

TRILLIANT   NETWORKS   (CANADA)   INC
p1111
610 RUE DU LUXEMBOURG, GRANBY, QC, J2J 2V2

(450) 375-0556   SIC 3825

SIC 3826 Analytical instruments

GENTEC ELECTRO-OPTIQUE INC   p1277
445 AV SAINT-JEAN-BAPTISTE BUREAU 160, QUEBEC, QC, G2E 5N7

(418) 651-8003   SIC 3826

PERKINELMER   HEALTH   SCIENCES CANADA, INC   p495
32 NIXON RD UNIT 1, BOLTON, ON, L7E 1W2

(905) 857-5665   SIC 3826

R.S.T. INSTRUMENTS LTD   p231
11545 KINGSTON ST, MAPLE RIDGE, BC, V2X 0Z5

(604) 540-1100   SIC 3826

SPARTAN BIOSCIENCE INC   p751
2934 BASELINE RD SUITE 500, NEPEAN, ON, K2H 1B2

(613) 228-7756   SIC 3826

SIC 3827 Optical instruments and lenses

DBM OPTIX INC   p1361
1630 BLVD DAGENAIS O, SAINTE-ROSE, QC, H7L 5C7

(450) 622-3100   SIC 3827

EXFO INC   p1262
436 RUE NOLIN, QUEBEC, QC, G1M 1E7

(418) 683-0211   SIC 3827

EXFO INC   p1262
400 AV GODIN, QUEBEC, QC, G1M 2K2

(418) 683-0211   SIC 3827

FISO TECHNOLOGIES INC   p1277
500 AV SAINT-JEAN-BAPTISTE BUREAU 195, QUEBEC, QC, G2E 5R9

(418) 688-8065   SIC 3827

LUMEN DYNAMICS GROUP INC   p724
2260 ARGENTIA RD, MISSISSAUGA, ON, L5N 6H7

(905) 821-2600   SIC 3827

LUMENTUM CANADA LTD   p752
61 BILL LEATHEM DR, NEPEAN, ON, K2J

0P7

(613) 843-3000   SIC 3827

MEASURAND INC   p403
2111 ROUTE 640, HANWELL, NB, E3C 1M7

(506) 462-9119   SIC 3827

OPSENS INC   p1267
750 BOUL DU PARC-TECHNOLOGIQUE, QUEBEC, QC, G1P 4S3

(418) 781-0333   SIC 3827

OZ OPTICS LIMITED   p815
219 WESTBROOK RD, OTTAWA, ON, K0A 1L0

(613) 831-0981   SIC 3827

RAYTHEON CANADA LIMITED   p681
450 LEITZ RD SUITE 2, MIDLAND, ON, L4R 5B8

(705) 526-5401   SIC 3827

TELEDYNE DALSA, INC   p1011
605 MCMURRAY RD, WATERLOO, ON, N2V 2E9

(519) 886-6000   SIC 3827

THALES OPTRONIQUE CANADA INCp1331
4868 RUE LEVY, SAINT-LAURENT, QC, H4R 2P1

(514) 337-7878   SIC 3827

UTMC CANADA INC   p718
2390 DUNWIN DR, MISSISSAUGA, ON, L5L 1J9

(905) 828-9300   SIC 3827

SIC 3829 Measuring and controlling devices, nec

3089554 NOVA SCOTIA ULC   p1263
875 BOUL CHAREST O BUREAU 100, QUEBEC, QC, G1N 2C9

(418) 266-3020   SIC 3829

ALCOHOL COUNTERMEASURE SYSTEMS CORP   p582
60 INTERNATIONAL BLVD, ETOBICOKE, ON, M9W 6J2

(416) 619-3500   SIC 3829

APPLANIX CORPORATION   p850
85 LEEK CRES, RICHMOND HILL, ON, L4B 3B3

(289) 695-6000   SIC 3829

ARMSTRONG MONITORING CORPORA-TION, THE   p831
215 COLONNADE RD S, OTTAWA, ON, K2E 7K3

(613) 225-9531   SIC 3829

AVCOM SYSTEMS INC   p199
1312 KETCH CRT UNIT 101, COQUITLAM, BC, V3K 6W1

(604) 944-8650   SIC 3829

BW TECHNOLOGIES LTD   p10
2840 2 AVE SE, CALGARY, AB, T2A 7X9

(403) 248-9226   SIC 3829

BW TECHNOLOGIES PARTNERSHIP   p27
4411 6 ST SE SUITE 110, CALGARY, AB, T2G 4E8

(403) 248-9226   SIC 3829

CLARIUS MOBILE HEALTH CORP   p188
3605 GILMORE WAY SUITE 350, BURN-ABY, BC, V5G 4X5

(778) 800-9975   SIC 3829

CRONE GEOPHYSICS & EXPLORATION LTD   p721
2135   MEADOWPINE   BLVD,   MISSIS-SAUGA, ON, L5N 6L5

(905) 814-0100   SIC 3829

DNA GENOTEK INC   p835
500 PALLADIUM DR UNIT 3000, OTTAWA, ON, K2V 1C2

(613) 723-5757   SIC 3829

FUJIFILM VISUALSONICS INC   p921
3080 YONGE ST SUITE 6100, TORONTO, ON, M4N 3N1

(416) 484-5000   SIC 3829

GROUPE BARBE & ROBIDOUX.SAT INC
p1159
991 RUE DE SAINT-JOVITE RM 201, MONT-TREMBLANT, QC, J8E 3J8

(819) 425-2777   *SIC 3829*
INOVA SYSTEMS CORPORATION   p76
1769 120 AVE NE, CALGARY, AB, T3K 0S5
(403) 537-2100   *SIC 3829*
MARSH INSTRUMENTATION LTD   p523
1016C SUTTON DR UNIT 1, BURLINGTON, ON, L7L 6B8
(905) 332-1172   *SIC 3829*
MIRION TECHNOLOGIES (IST CANADA) INC   p536
465 DOBBIE DR, CAMBRIDGE, ON, N1T 1T1
(519) 623-4880   *SIC 3829*
NANOMETRICS INC   p624
250 HERZBERG RD, KANATA, ON, K2K 2A1
(613) 592-6776   *SIC 3829*
NET SAFETY MONITORING INC   p9
2721 HOPEWELL PL NE, CALGARY, AB, T1Y 7J7
(403) 219-0688   *SIC 3829*
OLYMPUS NDT CANADA INC   p1267
3415 RUE PIERRE-ARDOUIN, QUEBEC, QC, G1P 0B3
(418) 872-1155   *SIC 3829*
PATRICK PLASTICS INC   p673
1495 DENISON ST, MARKHAM, ON, L3R 5H1
(905) 660-9066   *SIC 3829*
PHOENIX GEOPHYSICS LIMITED   p877
3781 VICTORIA PARK AVE UNIT 3, SCARBOROUGH, ON, M1W 3K5
(416) 491-7340   *SIC 3829*
RADIATION SOLUTIONS INC   p706
5875 WHITTLE RD, MISSISSAUGA, ON, L4Z 2H4
(905) 890-1111   *SIC 3829*
SARTREX POWER CONTROL SYSTEMS INC   p558
222 SNIDERCROFT RD SUITE 2, CONCORD, ON, L4K 2K1
(905) 669-2278   *SIC 3829*
SCINTREX LIMITED   p558
222 SNIDERCROFT RD SUITE 2, CONCORD, ON, L4K 2K1
(905) 669-2280   *SIC 3829*
SEASON TECHNOLOGY INC   p558
18 BASALTIC RD SUITE 1, CONCORD, ON, L4K 1G6
(905) 660-9066   *SIC 3829*
SENSORS & SOFTWARE INC   p700
1040 STACEY CRT, MISSISSAUGA, ON, L4W 2X8
(905) 614-1789   *SIC 3829*
SPARTEK SYSTEMS INC   p169
1 THEVENAZ IND. TRAIL, SYLVAN LAKE, AB, T4S 2J6
(403) 887-2443   *SIC 3829*
THERMO-KINETICS COMPANY LIMITED   p743
6740 INVADER CRES, MISSISSAUGA, ON, L5T 2B6
(905) 670-2266   *SIC 3829*
TTC TECHNOLOGY CORP   p257
13151 VANIER PL SUITE 150, RICHMOND, BC, V6V 2J1
(604) 276-9884   *SIC 3829*

SIC 3841 Surgical and medical instruments

1073849 ONTARIO LIMITED   p485
75 DYMENT RD, BARRIE, ON, L4N 3H6
(705) 733-0022   *SIC 3841*
2437090 ONTARIO LTD   p485
75 DYMENT RD, BARRIE, ON, L4N 3H6
(705) 733-0022   *SIC 3841*
2941881 CANADA INC   p686
6415 NORTHWEST DR UNIT 11, MISSISSAUGA, ON, L4V 1X1
(905) 612-1170   *SIC 3841*
ABBOTT POINT OF CARE CANADA LIMITED   p751
185 CORKSTOWN RD, NEPEAN, ON, K2H

8V4
(613) 688-5949   *SIC 3841*
ALDACO INDUSTRIES INC   p850
25B EAST PEARCE ST SUITE 1, RICHMOND HILL, ON, L4B 2M9
(905) 764-7736   *SIC 3841*
AMICO CLINICAL SOLUTIONS CORP   p850
85 FULTON WAY, RICHMOND HILL, ON, L4B 2N4
(905) 764-0800   *SIC 3841*
ARJOHUNTLEIGH MAGOG INC   p1147
2001 RUE TANGUAY, MAGOG, QC, J1X 5Y5
(819) 868-0441   *SIC 3841*
ARTRON LABORATORIES INC   p191
3938 NORTH FRASER WAY, BURNABY, BC, V5J 5H6
(604) 415-9757   *SIC 3841*
BARD CANADA INC   p796
2715 BRISTOL CIR UNIT 1, OAKVILLE, ON, L6H 6X5
(289) 291-8000   *SIC 3841*
BEST THERATRONICS LTD   p623
413 MARCH RD SUITE 25, KANATA, ON, K2K 0E4
(613) 591-2100   *SIC 3841*
BOSTON SCIENTIFIC LTD   p737
6430 VIPOND DR, MISSISSAUGA, ON, L5T 1W8
(705) 291-6900   *SIC 3841*
CLASS 1 INCORPORATED   p538
565 BOXWOOD DR, CAMBRIDGE, ON, N3E 1A5
(519) 650-2355   *SIC 3841*
CRH MEDICAL CORPORATION   p303
999 CANADA PL SUITE 578, VANCOUVER, BC, V6C 3E1
(604) 633-1440   *SIC 3841*
EXCEL-TECH LTD   p797
2568 BRISTOL CIR, OAKVILLE, ON, L6H 5S1
(905) 829-5300   *SIC 3841*
GLOBALMED INC   p999
155 MURRAY ST N, TRENTON, ON, K8V 5R5
(613) 394-9844   *SIC 3841*
IND DIAGNOSTIC INC   p206
1629 FOSTER'S WAY, DELTA, BC, V3M 6S7
   SIC 3841
LIVANOVA CANADA CORP   p193
5005 NORTH FRASER WAY, BURNABY, BC, V5J 5M1
(604) 412-5650   *SIC 3841*
LIVANOVA CANADA CORP   p679
280 HILLMOUNT RD UNIT 8, MARKHAM, ON, L6C 3A1
(905) 284-4245   *SIC 3841*
MEDICAL PLASTIC DEVICES M.P.D. INC   p1251
161 AV ONEIDA, POINTE-CLAIRE, QC, H9R 1A9
(514) 694-9835   *SIC 3841*
NORTHERN DIGITAL INC   p1010
103 RANDALL DR, WATERLOO, ON, N2V 1C5
(519) 884-5142   *SIC 3841*
NUMED CANADA INC   p563
45 SECOND ST W, CORNWALL, ON, K6J 1G3
(613) 936-2592   *SIC 3841*
OSELA INC   p1128
1869 32E AV, LACHINE, QC, H8T 3J1
(514) 631-2227   *SIC 3841*
PHOTON CONTROL INC   p256
13500 VERDUN PL SUITE 130, RICHMOND, BC, V6V 1V2
(604) 900-3150   *SIC 3841*
PROLLENIUM MEDICAL TECHNOLOGIES INC   p481
138 INDUSTRIAL PKY N, AURORA, ON, L4G 4C3
(905) 508-1469   *SIC 3841*
SCIENTEK MEDICAL EQUIPMENT   p261
11151 BRIDGEPORT RD, RICHMOND, BC,

V6X 1T3
   SIC 3841
SHOEBOX LTD   p826
80 ABERDEEN ST SUITE 301, OTTAWA, ON, K1S 5R5
(877) 349-9934   *SIC 3841*
SIEMENS HEALTHCARE DIAGNOSTICS LTD   p799
1577 NORTH SERVICE RD E 2FL, OAKVILLE, ON, L6H 0H6
(905) 564-7333   *SIC 3841*
SOUTHMEDIC INCORPORATED   p485
50 ALLIANCE BLVD, BARRIE, ON, L4M 5K3
(705) 726-9383   *SIC 3841*
STARFISH PRODUCT ENGINEERING INC   p339
455 BOLESKINE RD, VICTORIA, BC, V8Z 1E7
(250) 388-3537   *SIC 3841*
STARPLEX SCIENTIFIC INC   p588
50A STEINWAY BLVD, ETOBICOKE, ON, M9W 6Y3
(416) 674-7474   *SIC 3841*
TECHNOLOGIE DE PENSEE LTEE   p1228
5250 RUE FERRIER BUREAU 812, MONTREAL, QC, H4P 1L4
(514) 489-8251   *SIC 3841*
TRUDELL MEDICAL INTERNATIONAL   p650
725 BARANSWAY DR, LONDON, ON, N5V 5G4
(519) 455-7060   *SIC 3841*
UMANO MEDICAL INC   p1121
230 BOUL NILUS-LECLERC, L'ISLET, QC, G0R 2C0
(418) 247-3986   *SIC 3841*
VISTA MEDICAL LTD   p393
55 HENLOW BAY UNIT 3, WINNIPEG, MB, R3Y 1G4
(204) 949-7678   *SIC 3841*

SIC 3842 Surgical appliances and supplies

9137-0080 QUEBEC INC   p1135
5500 BOUL GUILLAUME-COUTURE BUREAU 140, LEVIS, QC, G6V 4Z2
(418) 830-8800   *SIC 3842*
ACTIONWEAR SASKATOON INC   p1424
114 MELVILLE ST, SASKATOON, SK, S7J 0R1
(306) 933-3088   *SIC 3842*
AGO INDUSTRIES INC   p661
500 SOVEREIGN RD, LONDON, ON, N6M 1A4
(519) 452-3780   *SIC 3842*
AIRWAY SURGICAL APPLIANCES LTD   p831
189 COLONNADE RD, OTTAWA, ON, K2E 7J4
(613) 723-4790   *SIC 3842*
ALLEN VANGUARD CORP   p837
421 UPPER VALLEY DR, PEMBROKE, ON, K8A 6W5
(613) 735-3996   *SIC 3842*
ALPHA PRO TECH, LTD   p666
60 CENTURIAN DR SUITE 112, MARKHAM, ON, L3R 9R2
(800) 749-1363   *SIC 3842*
AMD MEDICOM INC   p1248
2555 CH DE L'AVIATION, POINTE-CLAIRE, QC, H9P 2Z2
(514) 633-1111   *SIC 3842*
AUDMET CANADA LTD   p719
6950 CREDITVIEW RD, MISSISSAUGA, ON, L5N 0A6
(905) 677-3231   *SIC 3842*
BELLA HOSIERY MILLS INC   p1225
1401 RUE LEGENDRE O BUREAU 200, MONTREAL, QC, H4N 2R9
(514) 274-6500   *SIC 3842*
BRODA ENTERPRISES INC   p635
560 BINGEMANS CENTRE DR, KITCHENER, ON, N2B 3X9
(519) 746-8080   *SIC 3842*
C.G. AIR SYSTEMES INC   p1378

207 RUE INDUSTRIELLE, STE-MARGUERITE-DE-DORCHESTER, QC, G0S 2X0
(418) 935-7075   *SIC 3842*
CAPITAL SAFETY GROUP CANADA ULC   p734
260 EXPORT BLVD, MISSISSAUGA, ON, L5S 1Y9
(905) 795-9333   *SIC 3842*
COMPAGNIE U.S. COTON (CANADA), LA   p1127
2100 52E AV BUREAU 100, LACHINE, QC, H8T 2Y5
   SIC 3842
ENTREPRISES CLOUTIER, ALBERT LTEE, LES   p1351
149 RUE ALBERT-EDOUARD, SAINT-RAYMOND, QC, G3L 2C5
(418) 337-2766   *SIC 3842*
EQUIPEMENTS ADAPTES PHYSIPRO INC, LES   p1370
370 10E AV S, SHERBROOKE, QC, J1G 2R7
(819) 823-2252   *SIC 3842*
ERGORECHERCHE LTEE   p1237
2101 BOUL LE CARREFOUR BUREAU 200, MONTREAL, QC, H7S 2J7
(450) 973-6700   *SIC 3842*
F.A.S.T. FIRST AID & SURVIVAL TECHNOLOGIES INC   p209
8850 RIVER RD, DELTA, BC, V4G 1B5
(604) 940-3222   *SIC 3842*
FORMEDICA LTEE   p1082
4859 RUE DES ORMES, CONTRECOEUR, QC, J0L 1C0
(450) 587-2821   *SIC 3842*
HANGER, J. E. OF MONTREAL INC   p1221
5545 RUE SAINT-JACQUES, MONTREAL, QC, H4A 2E3
(514) 489-8213   *SIC 3842*
INFECTIO DIAGNOSTIC INC   p1267
2555 BOUL DU PARC-TECHNOLOGIQUE, QUEBEC, QC, G1P 4S5
(418) 681-4343   *SIC 3842*
JOHNSON & JOHNSON INC   p671
88 MCNABB ST, MARKHAM, ON, L3R 5L2
(905) 968-2000   *SIC 3842*
JOHNSON & JOHNSON INC   p671
200 WHITEHALL DR, MARKHAM, ON, L3R 0T5
(905) 946-8999   *SIC 3842*
KINETIC HEALTH INC   p939
140 YONGE ST, TORONTO, ON, M5C 1X6
(416) 302-4724   *SIC 3842*
LINK SUSPENSIONS OF CANADA, LIMITED PARTNERSHIP   p149
601 18 AVE, NISKU, AB, T9E 7T7
(780) 955-2859   *SIC 3842*
MAPLE LEAF WHEELCHAIR MANUFACTURING INC   p740
6540 TOMKEN RD, MISSISSAUGA, ON, L5T 2E9
(905) 564-2250   *SIC 3842*
MED-ENG HOLDINGS ULC   p818
2400 ST. LAURENT BLVD, OTTAWA, ON, K1G 6C4
(613) 482-8835   *SIC 3842*
O-TWO SYSTEMS INTERNATIONAL INC   p735
7575 KIMBEL ST UNIT 5, MISSISSAUGA, ON, L5S 1C8
   SIC 3842
ORTHOFAB INC   p1276
2160 RUE DE CELLES, QUEBEC, QC, G2C 1X8
(418) 847-5225   *SIC 3842*
ORTHOTIC GROUP INC, THE   p679
160 MARKLAND ST, MARKHAM, ON, L6C 0C6
(800) 551-3008   *SIC 3842*
OSSUR CANADA INC   p258
6900 GRAYBAR RD UNIT 2150, RICHMOND, BC, V6W 0A5
(604) 241-8152   *SIC 3842*

OTTO BOCK HEALTHCARE CANADA LTD
p845
901 DILLINGHAM RD, PICKERING, ON,
L1W 2Y5
SIC 3842

PACIFIC SAFETY PRODUCTS INC *p479*
124 FOURTH AVE, ARNPRIOR, ON, K7S
0A9
(613) 623-6001 *SIC 3842*

PARIS ORTHOTICS LTD *p287*
3630 1ST AVE E, VANCOUVER, BC, V5M
1C3
(604) 301-2150 *SIC 3842*

PERFORMANCE ORTHOTICS INC *p474*
291 CLEMENTS RD W, AJAX, ON, L1S
3W7
(905) 428-2692 *SIC 3842*

PRODUITS DE SECURITE NORTH LTEE
p1050
10550 BOUL PARKWAY, ANJOU, QC, H1J
2K4
(514) 351-7233 *SIC 3842*

RAPID AID CORP *p717*
4120A SLADEVIEW CRES UNIT 1-4, MIS-
SISSAUGA, ON, L5L 5Z3
(905) 820-4788 *SIC 3842*

SONOVA CANADA INC *p745*
80 COURTNEYPARK DR W SUITE 1, MIS-
SISSAUGA, ON, L5W 0B3
(905) 677-1167 *SIC 3842*

SOUND DESIGN TECHNOLOGIES LTD*p525*
970 FRASER DR, BURLINGTON, ON, L7L
5P5
(905) 635-0800 *SIC 3842*

**SPERIAN VETEMENTS DE PROTECTION
LTEE** *p1184*
4200 BOUL SAINT-LAURENT, MONTREAL,
QC, H2W 2R2
SIC 3842

SPI SECURITE INC *p1060*
60 RUE GASTON-DUMOULIN,
BLAINVILLE, QC, J7C 0A3
(450) 967-0911 *SIC 3842*

STARFIELD LION COMPANY INC *p791*
22 BENTON RD, NORTH YORK, ON, M6M
3G4
(416) 789-4354 *SIC 3842*

STARKEY LABS-CANADA CO *p727*
2476 ARGENTIA RD SUITE 301, MISSIS-
SAUGA, ON, L5N 6M1
(905) 542-7555 *SIC 3842*

TRULIFE LIMITED *p999*
39 DAVIS ST E, TRENTON, ON, K8V 4K8
(613) 392-6528 *SIC 3842*

TSO3 INC *p1268*
2505 AV DALTON, QUEBEC, QC, G1P 3S5
(418) 651-0003 *SIC 3842*

UNITRON HEARING LTD *p639*
20 BEASLEY DR, KITCHENER, ON, N2G
4X1
(519) 895-0100 *SIC 3842*

WIDEX CANADA LTD *p525*
5041 MAINWAY SUITE 1, BURLINGTON,
ON, L7L 5H9
(905) 315-8303 *SIC 3842*

SIC 3843 Dental equipment and supplies

**CALEY ORTHODONTIC LABORATORY
LIMITED** *p1008*
151 PARK ST, WATERLOO, ON, N2L 1Y5
(519) 742-1467 *SIC 3843*

**CARESTREAM HEALTH CANADA COM-
PANY** *p550*
8800 DUFFERIN ST SUITE 201, CON-
CORD, ON, L4K 0C5
(905) 532-0877 *SIC 3843*

GERMIPHENE CORPORATION *p517*
1379 COLBORNE ST E, BRANTFORD, ON,
N3T 5M1
(519) 759-7100 *SIC 3843*

LED MEDICAL DIAGNOSTICS INC *p306*
580 HORNBY ST SUITE 810, VANCOU-

VER, BC, V6C 3B6
(604) 434-4614 *SIC 3843*

MEDICOM GROUP INC *p1248*
2555 CH DE L'AVIATION, POINTE-CLAIRE,
QC, H9P 2Z2
(514) 636-6262 *SIC 3843*

MODULAR & CUSTOM CABINETS LIMITED
p664
10721 KEELE ST, MAPLE, ON, L6A 3Y9
(905) 832-8311 *SIC 3843*

OTHODENT LTD *p813*
311 VIOLA AVE, OSHAWA, ON, L1H 3A7
(905) 436-3731 *SIC 3843*

PANTHERA DENTAL INC *p1265*
2035 RUE DU HAUT-BORD, QUEBEC, QC,
G1N 4R7
(418) 527-0388 *SIC 3843*

SCICAN LTD *p916*
1440 DON MILLS RD, TORONTO, ON, M3B
3P9
(416) 445-1600 *SIC 3843*

STRITE INDUSTRIES LIMITED *p537*
298 SHEPHERD AVE, CAMBRIDGE, ON,
N3C 1V1
(519) 658-9361 *SIC 3843*

SYBRON CANADA LP *p746*
55 LAURIER DR, MORRISBURG, ON, K0C
1X0
(613) 543-3791 *SIC 3843*

SIC 3844 X-ray apparatus and tubes

EMD TECHNOLOGIES INCORPORATED
p1301
400 RUE DU PARC, SAINT-EUSTACHE,
QC, J7R 0A1
(450) 491-2100 *SIC 3844*

TECHNOLOGIES GREAT NORTH INC*p1118*
3551 BOUL SAINT-CHARLES BUREAU
363, KIRKLAND, QC, H9H 3C4
(514) 620-3724 *SIC 3844*

SIC 3845 Electromedical equipment

ARXIUM INC *p388*
96 NATURE PARK WAY, WINNIPEG, MB,
R3P 0X8
(204) 943-0066 *SIC 3845*

**CANON MEDICAL SYSTEMS CANADA LIM-
ITED** *p667*
75 TIVERTON CT, MARKHAM, ON, L3R
4M8
(800) 668-9729 *SIC 3845*

KARL STORZ ENDOSCOPY CANADA LTD
p723
7171 MILLCREEK DR, MISSISSAUGA, ON,
L5N 3R3
(905) 816-8100 *SIC 3845*

LANTHEUS MI CANADA INC *p1324*
1111 BOUL DR.-FREDERIK-PHILIPS BU-
REAU 100, SAINT-LAURENT, QC, H4M 2X6
(514) 333-1003 *SIC 3845*

**LUDLOW TECHNICAL PRODUCTS
CANADA, LTD** *p593*
215 HERBERT ST, GANANOQUE, ON, K7G
2Y7
(613) 382-4733 *SIC 3845*

MEDTRONIC OF CANADA LTD *p512*
99 HEREFORD ST, BRAMPTON, ON, L6Y
0R3
(905) 460-3800 *SIC 3845*

NU BODY EQUIPMENT SALES LTD *p245*
5211 COMPTON RD, PORT ALBERNI, BC,
V9Y 7B5
(778) 552-4540 *SIC 3845*

PROTECH HOME MEDICAL CORP *p322*
5626 LARCH ST SUITE 202, VANCOUVER,
BC, V6M 4E1
(877) 811-9690 *SIC 3845*

VOTI INC *p1324*
790 RUE BEGIN, SAINT-LAURENT, QC,
H4M 2N5

(514) 782-1566 *SIC 3845*

SIC 3851 Ophthalmic goods

ESSILOR GROUPE CANADA INC *p187*
7541 CONWAY AVE SUITE 5, BURNABY,
BC, V5E 2P7
(604) 437-5300 *SIC 3851*

OPTIQUE NIKON CANADA INC *p1172*
5075 RUE FULLUM BUREAU 100, MON-
TREAL, QC, H2H 2K3
(514) 521-6565 *SIC 3851*

PLASTIC PLUS LIMITED *p789*
14 LESWYN RD, NORTH YORK, ON, M6A
1K2
(416) 789-4307 *SIC 3851*

REVISION MILITAIRE INC *p1224*
3800 RUE SAINT-PATRICK BUREAU 200,
MONTREAL, QC, H4E 1A4
(514) 739-4444 *SIC 3851*

RIVERSIDE OPTICALAB LIMITED *p816*
2485 LANCASTER RD UNIT 10, OTTAWA,
ON, K1B 5L1
(613) 523-5765 *SIC 3851*

UNIVERSITE LAVAL *p1274*
2375 RUE DE LA TERRASSE, QUEBEC,
QC, G1V 0A6
(418) 656-2454 *SIC 3851*

VISIONS ONE HOUR OPTICAL LTD *p175*
2030 SUMAS WAY UNIT 100, ABBOTS-
FORD, BC, V2S 2C7
(604) 854-3266 *SIC 3851*

ZEISS, CARL VISION CANADA INC *p778*
45 VALLEYBROOK DR, NORTH YORK, ON,
M3B 2S6
(416) 449-4523 *SIC 3851*

---

*SIC 3861 Photographic equipment and
supplies*

111616 OPERATIONS (CANADA) INC*p1200*
1 PLACE VILLE-MARIE UNITE 3900, MON-
TREAL, QC, H3B 4M7
(800) 465-6325 *SIC 3861*

AERYON LABS INC *p1010*
575 KUMPF DR, WATERLOO, ON, N2V 1K3
(519) 489-6726 *SIC 3861*

**ALLIED VISION TECHNOLOGIES CANADA
INC** *p187*
4621 CANADA WAY SUITE 300, BURNABY,
BC, V5G 4X8
(604) 875-8855 *SIC 3861*

CHRISTIE DIGITAL SYSTEMS CANADA INC
p638
809 WELLINGTON ST N, KITCHENER, ON,
N2G 4Y7
(519) 744-8005 *SIC 3861*

DANZER CANADA INC *p567*
402725 HWY 4, DURHAM, ON, N0G 1R0
(519) 369-3310 *SIC 3861*

KODAK CANADA ULC *p189*
4225 KINCAID ST, BURNABY, BC, V5G 4P5
(604) 451-2700 *SIC 3861*

LUCID VISION LABS, INC *p255*
13200 DELF PL UNIT 130, RICHMOND, BC,
V6V 2A2
(833) 465-8243 *SIC 3861*

LUMENERA CORPORATION *p749*
7 CAPELLA CRT, NEPEAN, ON, K2E 8A7
(613) 736-4077 *SIC 3861*

METAFIX INC *p1128*
1925 46E AV, LACHINE, QC, H8T 2P1
(514) 633-8663 *SIC 3861*

MUSIQUE SELECT INC *p1211*
612 RUE SAINT-JACQUES, MONTREAL,
QC, H3C 4M8
(514) 380-1999 *SIC 3861*

RADIAL ENGINEERING LTD *p247*
1588 KEBET WAY, PORT COQUITLAM, BC,
V3C 5M5
(604) 942-1001 *SIC 3861*

SOLARFECTIVE PRODUCTS LIMITED *p869*

55 HYMUS RD, SCARBOROUGH, ON, M1L
2C6
(416) 421-3800 *SIC 3861*

**SYSTEMES D'ECRAN STRONG/MDI INC,
LES** *p1115*
1440 RUE RAOUL-CHARETTE, JOLIETTE,
QC, J6E 8S7
(450) 755-3795 *SIC 3861*

**TELEDYNE QUANTITATIVE IMAGING COR-
PORATION** *p273*
19535 56 AVE SUITE 101, SURREY, BC,
V3S 6K3
(604) 530-5800 *SIC 3861*

**TELEDYNE QUANTITATIVE IMAGING COR-
PORATION** *p273*
19535 56 AVE SUITE 101, SURREY, BC,
V3S 6K3
(604) 530-5800 *SIC 3861*

TORONTO MICROELECTRONICS INC *p743*
6185 DANVILLE RD, MISSISSAUGA, ON,
L5T 2H7
(905) 362-8090 *SIC 3861*

SIC 3911 Jewelry, precious Metal

CORONA JEWELLERY COMPANY LTD*p995*
16 RIPLEY AVE, TORONTO, ON, M6S 3P1
(416) 762-2222 *SIC 3911*

CREATIONS MALO INC *p1241*
750 BOUL CURE-LABELLE BUREAU 200,
MONTREAL-OUEST, QC, H7V 2T9
(450) 682-6561 *SIC 3911*

**O.C. TANNER RECOGNITION COMPANY
LIMITED** *p523*
4200 FAIRVIEW ST, BURLINGTON, ON,
L7L 4Y8
(905) 632-7255 *SIC 3911*

SILVER STAR MANUFACTURING CO INC
p1241
750 BOUL CURE-LABELLE BUREAU 205,
MONTREAL-OUEST, QC, H7V 2T9
(450) 682-3381 *SIC 3911*

SIC 3914 Silverware and plated ware

JULIEN INC *p1267*
955 RUE LACHANCE, QUEBEC, QC, G1P
2H3
(418) 687-3630 *SIC 3914*

---

*SIC 3915 Jewelers' materials and lapidary
work*

ARSLANIAN CUTTING WORKS NWT LTD
p435
106 ARCHIBALD ST, YELLOWKNIFE, NT,
X1A 2P4
(867) 873-0138 *SIC 3915*

DEEPAK INTERNATIONAL LTD *p986*
1 FIRST CANADIAN PL UNIT 6000,
TORONTO, ON, M5X 1B5
SIC 3915

SIC 3931 Musical instruments

CASAVANT FRERES S.E.C *p1311*
900 RUE GIROUARD E, SAINT-
HYACINTHE, QC, J2S 2Y2
(450) 773-5001 *SIC 3931*

GUITABEC INC *p1053*
19420 AV CLARK-GRAHAM, BAIE-
D'URFE, QC, H9X 3R8
(514) 457-7977 *SIC 3931*

LARRIVEE, JEAN GUITARS LTD *p295*
780 CORDOVA ST E, VANCOUVER, BC,
V6A 1M3
SIC 3931

SABIAN LTD *p405*
219 MAIN ST, MEDUCTIC, NB, E6H 2L5
(506) 272-2019 *SIC 3931*

TOUCHTUNES DIGITAL JUKEBOX INC p1181
7250 RUE DU MILE END BUREAU 202, MONTREAL, QC, H2R 3A4
(514) 762-6244   *SIC* 3931

SIC 3942 Dolls and stuffed toys

BEST MADE TOYS INTERNATIONAL, ULC p782
120 SAINT REGIS CRES N, NORTH YORK, ON, M3J 1Z3
(416) 630-6665   *SIC* 3942

SIC 3944 Games, toys, and children's vehicles

800743 ALBERTA LTD p20
1225 34 AVE NE, CALGARY, AB, T2E 6N4
(403) 291-4239   *SIC* 3944

BASIC FUN, LTD p692
1200 AEROWOOD DR UNIT 27-28, MISSISSAUGA, ON, L4W 2S7
(905) 629-3836   *SIC* 3944

DOMINET CORPORATION p874
10 COMPASS CRT, SCARBOROUGH, ON, M1S 5R3
(416) 646-5232   *SIC* 3944

GLOBAL-SKY LOGISTICS INC p1250
81 BOUL HYMUS, POINTE-CLAIRE, QC, H9R 1E2
(514) 223-3399   *SIC* 3944

JAKKS PACIFIC (CANADA), INC p511
125 EDGEWARE RD SUITE 15, BRAMPTON, ON, L6Y 0P5
(905) 452-6279   *SIC* 3944

MEGA BRANDS INC p1340
4505 RUE HICKMORE, SAINT-LAURENT, QC, H4T 1K4
(514) 333-5555   *SIC* 3944

NEXT LEVEL GAMES INC p299
208 ROBSON ST, VANCOUVER, BC, V6B 6A1
(604) 484-6111   *SIC* 3944

NRT TECHNOLOGY CORP p874
10 COMPASS CRT, SCARBOROUGH, ON, M1S 5R3
(416) 646-5232   *SIC* 3944

SPIN MASTER LTD p983
225 KING ST W SUITE 200, TORONTO, ON, M5V 1B6
(416) 364-6002   *SIC* 3944

STARS GROUP INC, THE p967
200 BAY ST SUITE 3205, TORONTO, ON, M5J 2J3
(437) 371-5742   *SIC* 3944

UBISOFT DIVERTISSEMENTS INC p1260
390 BOUL CHAREST E BUREAU 600, QUEBEC, QC, G1K 3H4
(418) 524-1222   *SIC* 3944

SIC 3949 Sporting and athletic goods, nec

1794342 ONTARIO INC p1372
2745 RUE DE LA SHERWOOD, SHERBROOKE, QC, J1K 1E1
(819) 563-2202   *SIC* 3949

AMER SPORTS CANADA INC p187
4250 MANOR ST, BURNABY, BC, V5G 1B2
(604) 454-9900   *SIC* 3949

AMER SPORTS CANADA INC p286
2770 BENTALL ST, VANCOUVER, BC, V5M 4H4
(604) 960-3001   *SIC* 3949

ATHLETICA SPORT SYSTEMS INC p1008
554 PARKSIDE DR, WATERLOO, ON, N2L 5Z4
(519) 747-1856   *SIC* 3949

BAUER HOCKEY LTD p720
6925 CENTURY AVE UNIT 600, MISSISSAUGA, ON, L5N 7K2

(905) 363-3200   *SIC* 3949

CANADIAN MARKETING TEST CASE 200 LIMITED p730
5770 HURONTARIO ST, MISSISSAUGA, ON, L5R 3G5
(800) 986-5569   *SIC* 3949

CANADIAN TEST CASE 110 p730
5770 HURONTARIO ST, MISSISSAUGA, ON, L5R 3G5
SIC 3949

CANADIAN TEST CASE 111 p730
5770 HURONTARIO ST, MISSISSAUGA, ON, L5R 3G5
SIC 3949

CANADIAN TEST CASE 52 p730
5770 HURONTARIO ST, MISSISSAUGA, ON, L5R 3G5
SIC 3949

CENTRE DE CONDITIONNEMENT PHYSIQUE ATLANTIS INC p1399
1201 BOUL DES LAURENTIDES, VIMONT, QC, H7M 2X9
(450) 629-1500   *SIC* 3949

CENTRE DE CONDITIONNEMENT PHYSIQUE ATLANTIS INC. p1231
4745 AV DES INDUSTRIES, MONTREAL, QC, H7C 1A1
(450) 664-2285   *SIC* 3949

CIVIC POWER SPORTS p171
10111 107 ST, WESTLOCK, AB, T7P 1W9
(780) 349-5277   *SIC* 3949

COMBAT p819
5390 CANOTEK RD UNIT 20, OTTAWA, ON, K1J 1H8
SIC 3949

CRYSTAL WATER INVESTMENTS COMPANY p1130
7050 RUE SAINT-PATRICK, LASALLE, QC, H8N 1V2
(514) 363-3232   *SIC* 3949

FLEXIBLE SOLUTIONS INTERNATIONAL INC p169
6001 54 AVE, TABER, AB, T1G 1X4
(403) 223-2995   *SIC* 3949

FLITE HOCKEY INC p705
705 MATHESON BLVD E, MISSISSAUGA, ON, L4Z 3X9
(905) 828-6030   *SIC* 3949

FOX 40 INTERNATIONAL INC p608
340 GRAYS RD, HAMILTON, ON, L8E 2Z2
(905) 561-4040   *SIC* 3949

GRAF CANADA LTD p30
2308 PORTLAND ST SE, CALGARY, AB, T2G 4M6
(403) 287-8585   *SIC* 3949

GYM FABRIK INC p1378
281 RUE EDWARD-ASSH, STE-CATHERINE-DE-LA-J-CARTIE, QC, G3N 1A3
(418) 875-2600   *SIC* 3949

HAYWARD POOL PRODUCTS CANADA, INC p797
2880 PLYMOUTH DR, OAKVILLE, ON, L6H 5R4
(905) 829-2880   *SIC* 3949

HENDERSON RECREATION EQUIPMENT LIMITED p881
11 GILBERTSON DR, SIMCOE, ON, N3Y 4K8
(519) 426-9380   *SIC* 3949

INGLASCO INC p1372
2745 RUE DE LA SHERWOOD, SHERBROOKE, QC, J1K 1E1
(819) 563-2205   *SIC* 3949

INTERNATIONAL PLAY COMPANY INC p229
27353 58 CRES UNIT 215, LANGLEY, BC, V4W 3W7
(604) 607-1111   *SIC* 3949

IPLAYCO CORPORATION LTD p229
27353 58 CRES UNIT 215, LANGLEY, BC, V4W 3W7
(604) 607-1111   *SIC* 3949

JUNGLE JAC'S PLAY CENTRE p244
19800 LOUGHEED HWY SUITE 115, PITT

MEADOWS, BC, V3Y 2W1
(604) 460-1654   *SIC* 3949

LATHAM POOL PRODUCTS INC p474
430 FINLEY AVE, AJAX, ON, L1S 2E3
(905) 428-6990   *SIC* 3949

LATHAM POOL PRODUCTS INC p516
383 ELGIN ST, BRANTFORD, ON, N3S 7P5
(800) 638-7422   *SIC* 3949

LUMI-O INTERNATIONAL INC p1320
370 BOUL LAJEUNESSE O, SAINT-JEROME, QC, J7Y 4E5
(450) 565-5544   *SIC* 3949

MUSTANG DRINKWARE INC p889
35 CURRAH RD, ST THOMAS, ON, N5P 3R2
(519) 631-3030   *SIC* 3949

NANCY LOPEZ GOLF p1006
185 WEBER ST S, WATERLOO, ON, N2J 2B1
(866) 649-1759   *SIC* 3949

NORTHERN LIGHTS FITNESS PRODUCTS INCORPORATED p563
700 WALLRICH AVE, CORNWALL, ON, K6J 5X4
(613) 938-8196   *SIC* 3949

PHOENIX PERFORMANCE PRODUCTS INC p557
100 BASS PRO MILLS DR UNIT 32, CONCORD, ON, L4K 5X1
(905) 539-0370   *SIC* 3949

PRODUITS DE PISCINE TRENDIUM INC p1131
2673 BOUL ANGRIGNON, LASALLE, QC, H8N 3J3
(514) 363-7001   *SIC* 3949

PRODUITS DE PISCINE TRENDIUM INC p1131
7050 RUE SAINT-PATRICK, LASALLE, QC, H8N 1V2
(514) 363-3232   *SIC* 3949

SCOTT, S.F. MANUFACTURING CO. LIMITED p146
724 14 ST SW, MEDICINE HAT, AB, T1A 4V7
(403) 526-9170   *SIC* 3949

SOLOWAVE DESIGN INC p746
375 SLIGO RD W SS 1 SUITE 1, MOUNT FOREST, ON, N0G 2L0
(519) 323-3833   *SIC* 3949

SOLOWAVE DESIGN INC p1009
103 BAUER PL SUITE 5, WATERLOO, ON, N2L 6B5
(519) 323-3833   *SIC* 3949

SOLOWAVE INVESTMENTS LIMITED p1009
103 BAUER PL SUITE 5, WATERLOO, ON, N2L 6B5
(519) 725-5379   *SIC* 3949

SPIETH-ANDERSON INTERNATIONAL INC p811
135 FORESTVIEW RD, ORO-MEDONTE, ON, L3V 0R4
(705) 325-2274   *SIC* 3949

SPIVO CANADA INC p1220
3150 PLACE DE RAMEZAY BUREAU 202, MONTREAL, QC, H3Y 0A3
(514) 726-1749   *SIC* 3949

SPORT MASKA INC p1331
3400 RUE RAYMOND-LASNIER, SAINT-LAURENT, QC, H4R 3L3
(514) 461-8000   *SIC* 3949

SPORT MASKA INC p1331
3400 RUE RAYMOND-LASNIER, SAINT-LAURENT, QC, H4R 3L3
(514) 461-8000   *SIC* 3949

SPRINGFREE TRAMPOLINE INC p675
151 WHITEHALL DR UNIT 2, MARKHAM, ON, L3R 9T1
(905) 948-0124   *SIC* 3949

TRAK SPORT INC p1089
135 RUE DEAN BUREAU 4, COWANSVILLE, QC, J2K 3Y2
SIC 3949

TREVI FABRICATION INC p1153
12775 RUE BRAULT, MIRABEL, QC, J7J

0C4
(514) 228-7384   *SIC* 3949

VAUGHN CUSTOM SPORTS CANADA LTD p651
455 HIGHBURY AVE N, LONDON, ON, N5W 5K7
(519) 453-4229   *SIC* 3949

VBALLS TARGET SYSTEMS INC p387
51 ALLARD AVE, WINNIPEG, MB, R3K 0S8
SIC 3949

VORTEX STRUCTURES AQUATIQUES INTERNATIONALES INC p1252
328 AV AVRO, POINTE-CLAIRE, QC, H9R 5W5
(514) 694-3868   *SIC* 3949

WMI MANUFACTURING CORP p223
1451 ELLIS ST, KELOWNA, BC, V1Y 2A3
(250) 712-3393   *SIC* 3949

YORK BARBELL CO. LTD p805
1450 SOUTH SERVICE RD W, OAKVILLE, ON, L6L 5T7
(905) 827-6362   *SIC* 3949

SIC 3953 Marking devices

STERLING MARKING PRODUCTS INC p659
1147 GAINSBOROUGH RD, LONDON, ON, N6H 5L5
(519) 434-5785   *SIC* 3953

SIC 3955 Carbon paper and inked ribbons

DENSI CORPORATION p1295
1100 RUE PARENT, SAINT-BRUNO, QC, J3V 6L8
(450) 441-1300   *SIC* 3955

LASERNETWORKS INC p688
6300 VISCOUNT RD UNIT 2, MISSISSAUGA, ON, L4V 1H3
(800) 461-4879   *SIC* 3955

SIC 3961 Costume jewelry

A. T. DESIGNS INSIGNIA LTD p866
70 PRODUCTION DR, SCARBOROUGH, ON, M1H 2X8
(800) 288-0111   *SIC* 3961

JOSTENS CANADA LTD p384
1643 DUBLIN AVE, WINNIPEG, MB, R3H 0G9
(204) 783-1310   *SIC* 3961

NERON INC p1218
550 AV BEAUMONT BUREAU 500, MONTREAL, QC, H3N 1V1
(514) 759-8672   *SIC* 3961

SIC 3965 Fasteners, buttons, needles, and pins

COBRA FIXATIONS CIE LTEE p1048
8051 BOUL METROPOLITAIN E, ANJOU, QC, H1J 1J8
(514) 354-2240   *SIC* 3965

EXELTOR INC p1056
110 RUE DE LA RIVIERE, BEDFORD, QC, J0J 1A0
(450) 248-4343   *SIC* 3965

INDUSTRIES CANZIP (2000) INC, LES p1226
1615 RUE CHABANEL O, MONTREAL, QC, H4N 2T7
(514) 934-0331   *SIC* 3965

KIDD, H.A. AND COMPANY LIMITED p917
5 NORTHLINE RD, TORONTO, ON, M4B 3P2
(416) 364-6451   *SIC* 3965

VELCRO CANADA INC p507
114 EAST DR, BRAMPTON, ON, L6T 1C1
(905) 791-1630   *SIC* 3965

YKK CANADA INC p1331
3939 BOUL THIMENS, SAINT-LAURENT,

QC, H4R 1X3

(514) 332-3350   *SIC* 3965

SIC 3991 Brooms and brushes

ATLAS GRAHAM FURGALE LTD   *p*383
1725 SARGENT AVE, WINNIPEG, MB, R3H 0C5
(204) 775-4451   *SIC* 3991
JOSEPH & COMPANY LTD   *p*384
1725 SARGENT AVE, WINNIPEG, MB, R3H 0C5
(204) 775-4451   *SIC* 3991
T. S. SIMMS & CO. LIMITED   *p*414
560 MAIN ST SUITE 320, SAINT JOHN, NB, E2K 1J5
(506) 635-6330   *SIC* 3991
T.S. SIMMS & CO   *p*569
300 MAIN ST, ERIN, ON, N0B 1T0
(905) 362-1470   *SIC* 3991

SIC 3993 Signs and advertising specialties

109578 CANADA LTEE   *p*1156
5790 RUE FERRIER, MONT-ROYAL, QC, H4P 1M7
(514) 937-0044   *SIC* 3993
3093-6975 QUEBEC INC   *p*1233
1780 PLACE MARTENOT BUREAU 17, MONTREAL, QC, H7L 5B5
(450) 668-4888   *SIC* 3993
4355768 CANADA INC   *p*1257
410 BOUL CHAREST E BUREAU 500, QUEBEC, QC, G1K 8G3
(418) 977-3169   *SIC* 3993
9132-1604 QUEBEC INC   *p*1125
1600 CROIS CLAIRE, LACHINE, QC, H8S 1A2
(514) 485-1121   *SIC* 3993
ARRAY CANADA INC   *p*870
45 PROGRESS AVE, SCARBOROUGH, ON, M1P 2Y6
(416) 299-4865   *SIC* 3993
ATS TRAFFIC - ALBERTA LTD   *p*121
9015 14 ST NW, EDMONTON, AB, T6P 0C9
(780) 440-4114   *SIC* 3993
BLANCHETT NEON LIMITED   *p*93
12850 ST ALBERT TRAIL NW, EDMONTON, AB, T5L 4H6
(780) 453-2441   *SIC* 3993
CLAUDE NEON LIMITEE   *p*1249
1868 BOUL DES SOURCES BUREAU 200, POINTE-CLAIRE, QC, H9R 5R2
(514) 693-9436   *SIC* 3993
DECO SIGNALISATION INC   *p*1048
9225 RUE DU PARCOURS, ANJOU, QC, H1J 3A8
(514) 494-1004   *SIC* 3993
DESIGN FRANC ART INC   *p*1348
29 7E RUE O, SAINT-MARTIN, QC, G0M 1B0
(418) 382-3122   *SIC* 3993
DIAMOND DIVERSIFIED INDUSTRIES LTD *p*442
55 BREN ST, CORNWALLIS, NS, B0S 1H0
(902) 638-8616   *SIC* 3993
E. E. C. INDUSTRIES LIMITED   *p*241
1237 WELCH ST, NORTH VANCOUVER, BC, V7P 1B3
(604) 986-5633   *SIC* 3993
ENSEIGNES MONTREAL NEON INC *p*1086
4130 SUD LAVAL (A-440) O, COTE SAINT-LUC, QC, H7T 0H3
(450) 668-4888   *SIC* 3993
ENSEIGNES TRANSWORLD CIE   *p*1048
9310 BOUL PARKWAY, ANJOU, QC, H1J 1N7
(514) 352-8030   *SIC* 3993
ENSEIGNES VISION DEK-OR INC   *p*1048
9225 RUE DU PARCOURS, ANJOU, QC, H1J 3A8
(514) 354-8383   *SIC* 3993

ENTRO COMMUNICATIONS INC   *p*962
33 HARBOUR SQ SUITE 202, TORONTO, ON, M5J 2G2
(416) 368-1095   *SIC* 3993
FORWARD SIGNS INC   *p*874
60 EMBLEM CRT, SCARBOROUGH, ON, M1S 1B1
(416) 291-4477   *SIC* 3993
H.A.S. NOVELTIES LIMITED   *p*990
300 GEARY AVE, TORONTO, ON, M6H 2C5
(416) 593-1101   *SIC* 3993
HARDING DISPLAY CORP   *p*876
150 DYNAMIC DR, SCARBOROUGH, ON, M1V 5A5
(416) 754-3215   *SIC* 3993
HI SIGNS THE FATH GROUP LTD   *p*115
9570 58 AVE NW, EDMONTON, AB, T6E 0B6
(780) 468-6181   *SIC* 3993
HOLMAN EXHIBITS LIMITED   *p*776
160 LESMILL RD, NORTH YORK, ON, M3B 2T5
SIC 3993
INSTACHANGE DISPLAYS LIMITED   *p*755
360 HARRY WALKER PKY S UNIT 1-3, NEWMARKET, ON, L3Y 9E9
(289) 279-1100   *SIC* 3993
INTERNATIONAL NAME PLATE SUPPLIES LIMITED   *p*649
1420 CRUMLIN, LONDON, ON, N5V 1S1
(519) 455-7647   *SIC* 3993
KLASSEN BRONZE LIMITED   *p*752
30 MARVIN ST, NEW HAMBURG, ON, N3A 4H8
(519) 662-1010   *SIC* 3993
KOST KLIP MANUFACTURING LTD   *p*247
1611 BROADWAY ST UNIT 119, PORT CO-QUITLAM, BC, V3C 2M7
(604) 468-1117   *SIC* 3993
KOST KLIP MANUFACTURING LTD   *p*247
1611 BROADWAY ST UNIT 119, PORT CO-QUITLAM, BC, V3C 2M7
(604) 468-7917   *SIC* 3993
KUBIK INC   *p*703
1680 MATTAWA AVE, MISSISSAUGA, ON, L4X 3A5
(905) 272-2818   *SIC* 3993
MEDIA RESOURCES INC   *p*801
1387 CORNWALL RD, OAKVILLE, ON, L6J 7T5
(905) 337-0993   *SIC* 3993
MODULEX AMERICAS INC   *p*11
3200 14 AVE NE SUITE 1, CALGARY, AB, T2A 6J4
(403) 272-0597   *SIC* 3993
NATIONAL SIGNCORP INVESTMENTS LTD *p*206
1471 DERWENT WAY, DELTA, BC, V3M 6N2
(604) 525-4300   *SIC* 3993
PACIFIC SIGN GROUP INC   *p*209
7462 PROGRESS WAY, DELTA, BC, V4G 1E1
(604) 940-2211   *SIC* 3993
PATTISON, JIM INDUSTRIES LTD   *p*872
555 ELLESMERE RD, SCARBOROUGH, ON, M1R 4E8
(416) 759-1111   *SIC* 3993
PORTABLES EXHIBIT SYSTEMS LIMITED, THE   *p*256
3551 VIKING WAY SUITE 109, RICHMOND, BC, V6V 1W1
(604) 276-2366   *SIC* 3993
POSIMAGE INC   *p*1119
6285 BOUL WILFRID-HAMEL, L'ANCIENNE-LORETTE, QC, G2E 5W2
(418) 877-2775   *SIC* 3993
PRESENTOIR FILOTECH INC   *p*1321
234 RUE DE SAINTE-PAULE, SAINT-JEROME, QC, J7Z 1A8
(450) 432-2266   *SIC* 3993
PRIDE SIGNS LIMITED   *p*536
255 PINEBUSH RD UNIT I, CAMBRIDGE, ON, N1T 1B9

(519) 622-4040   *SIC* 3993
PROVINCIAL SIGN SERVICE LIMITED *p*845
1655 FELDSPAR CRT, PICKERING, ON, L1W 3R7
(905) 837-1791   *SIC* 3993
SELKIRK SIGNS & SERVICES LTD   *p*204
421 PATTERSON ST W, CRANBROOK, BC, V1C 6T3
(250) 489-3321   *SIC* 3993
SIGNEL SERVICES INC   *p*1348
700 MONTEE MONETTE, SAINT-MATHIEU-DE-LAPRAIRIE, QC, J0L 2H0
(450) 444-0006   *SIC* 3993
SOCIETE EN COMMANDITE LES PROMENADES DU PARC   *p*1146
1910 RUE ADONCOUR BUREAU 500, LONGUEUIL, QC, J4N 1T3
(450) 448-3448   *SIC* 3993
SOMERVILLE MERCHANDISING INC   *p*865
5760 FINCH AVE E, SCARBOROUGH, ON, M1B 5J9
(416) 754-7228   *SIC* 3993
SOUVENIRS AVANTI INC   *p*1252
116 AV LEACOCK, POINTE-CLAIRE, QC, H9R 1H1
(514) 694-0707   *SIC* 3993
SRB TECHNOLOGIES (CANADA) INC *p*838
320 BOUNDARY RD E SUITE 140, PEMBROKE, ON, K8A 6W5
(613) 732-0055   *SIC* 3993
STEEL ART SIGNS CORP   *p*675
37 ESNA PARK DR, MARKHAM, ON, L3R 1C9
(905) 474-1678   *SIC* 3993
TAYLOR MANUFACTURING INDUSTRIES INC   *p*510
255 BISCAYNE CRES, BRAMPTON, ON, L6W 4R2
(905) 451-5800   *SIC* 3993
TEKSIGN INC   *p*516
86 PLANT FARM BLVD, BRANTFORD, ON, N3S 7W3
(519) 756-1089   *SIC* 3993
WSI SIGN SYSTEMS LTD   *p*496
31 SIMPSON RD, BOLTON, ON, L7E 2R6
(905) 857-8044   *SIC* 3993
ZIP SIGNS LTD   *p*526
5040 NORTH SERVICE RD, BURLINGTON, ON, L7L 5R5
(905) 332-8332   *SIC* 3993

SIC 3995 Burial caskets

CERCUEILS ALLIANCE CASKETS INC *p*398
355 DU POUVOIR CH, EDMUNDSTON, NB, E3V 4K1
(506) 739-6226   *SIC* 3995
NORTHERN CASKET (1976) LIMITED *p*646
165 ST PETER ST, LINDSAY, ON, K9V 5A7
(705) 324-6164   *SIC* 3995
VICTORIAVILLE & CO INC   *p*1399
333 RUE DE LA JACQUES-CARTIER, VIC-TORIAVILLE, QC, G6T 1Y1
(819) 752-3388   *SIC* 3995

SIC 3996 Hard surface floor coverings, nec

INDUSTRIES MONDIALES ARMSTRONG CANADA LTEE, LES   *p*1241
1595 BOUL DANIEL-JOHNSON BUREAU 300, MONTREAL-OUEST, QC, H7V 4C2
(450) 902-3900   *SIC* 3996
PLANCHERS GROLEAU INC   *p*1147
541 AV DALCOURT, LOUISEVILLE, QC, J5V 2Z7
(819) 228-4446   *SIC* 3996

SIC 3999 Manufacturing industries, nec

133876 CANADA INC   *p*1075
800 BOUL FORD BUREAU 104, CHATEAU-

GUAY, QC, J6J 4Z2
(450) 692-5570   *SIC* 3999
ARTIFACT LOGICIEL INC   *p*1187
300 RUE DU SAINT-SACREMENT BUREAU 223, MONTREAL, QC, H2Y 1X4
(514) 286-6665   *SIC* 3999
ASPASIE INC   *p*1387
2106 RUE BELLEFEUILLE, TROIS-RIVIERES, QC, G9A 3Y9
(819) 379-2157   *SIC* 3999
BEACHCOMBER HOT TUBS GROUP   *p*275
13245 COMBER WAY, SURREY, BC, V3W 5V8
(604) 502-4733   *SIC* 3999
BLUE FALLS MANUFACTURING LTD   *p*169
4549 52 ST, THORSBY, AB, T0C 2P0
(780) 789-2626   *SIC* 3999
BOLD EVENT CREATIVE INC   *p*182
7570 CONRAD ST, BURNABY, BC, V5A 2H7
(604) 437-7677   *SIC* 3999
COAST SPAS MANUFACTURING INC   *p*226
6315 202 ST, LANGLEY, BC, V2Y 1N1
(604) 514-8111   *SIC* 3999
COLORIDE INC   *p*1146
80 AV SAINT-MARTIN, LOUISEVILLE, QC, J5V 1B4
(819) 228-5553   *SIC* 3999
COMPAGNIE TOP TUBES   *p*1060
870 RUE INDUSTRIEL, BOIS-DES-FILION, QC, J6Z 4V7
(450) 621-9600   *SIC* 3999
CORPORATION SAVARIA   *p*1342
4350 DESSTE CHOMEDEY (A-13) O, SAINT-LAURENT, QC, H7R 6E9
(450) 681-5655   *SIC* 3999
COURONNES PLUS.COM INC, LES   *p*1102
9 RUE DES CERISIERS, GASPE, QC, G4X 2M1
(418) 368-3670   *SIC* 3999
DECTRONIQUE (1984) INC   *p*1266
1000 BOUL DU PARC-TECHNOLOGIQUE, QUEBEC, QC, G1P 4S3
(418) 650-0303   *SIC* 3999
F & D SCENE CHANGES LTD   *p*29
803 24 AVE SE SUITE 2B, CALGARY, AB, T2G 1P5
(403) 233-7633   *SIC* 3999
FESTO DIDACTIQUE LTEE   *p*1280
675 RUE DU CARBONE, QUEBEC, QC, G2N 2K7
(418) 849-1000   *SIC* 3999
GARAVENTA (CANADA) LTD   *p*279
18920 36 AVE, SURREY, BC, V3Z 0P6
(604) 594-0422   *SIC* 3999
IGT CANADA SOLUTIONS ULC   *p*410
328 URQUHART AVE, MONCTON, NB, E1H 2R6
(506) 878-6000   *SIC* 3999
KETCHUM MANUFACTURING INC   *p*519
1245 CALIFORNIA AVE, BROCKVILLE, ON, K6V 7N5
(613) 342-8455   *SIC* 3999
LEVEL-RITE SYSTEMS COMPANY   *p*513
29 REGAN RD, BRAMPTON, ON, L7A 1B2
SIC 3999
LUMI-O INNOVAPLAS INC   *p*1096
2257 139 RTE, DRUMMONDVILLE, QC, J2A 2G2
(819) 850-2935   *SIC* 3999
MAILLOUX BAILLARGEON INC   *p*1298
222 RUE SAINT-PIERRE, SAINT-CONSTANT, QC, J5A 2A2
(514) 861-8417   *SIC* 3999
MEDICAL TECHNOLOGY (W.B.) INC   *p*662
1015 GREEN VALLEY RD, LONDON, ON, N6N 1E4
(519) 686-0028   *SIC* 3999
MEDICAL TECHNOLOGY (W.B.) INC   *p*662
1040 WILTON GROVE RD, LONDON, ON, N6N 1C7
(519) 686-0028   *SIC* 3999
NORMERICA INC   *p*515
46 MORTON AVE E, BRANTFORD, ON,

N3R 7J7
(519) 756-8414   *SIC 3999*

POLLARD BANKNOTE INCOME FUND p391
140 OTTER ST, WINNIPEG, MB, R3T 0M8
(204) 474-2323   *SIC 3999*

PREMIER CANDLE CORP p699
960 BRITANNIA RD E, MISSISSAUGA, ON,
L4W 5M7
(905) 795-8833   *SIC 3999*

SEMENCES PROGRAIN INC p1297
145 RANG DU BAS-DE-LA-RIVIERE N,
SAINT-CESAIRE, QC, J0L 1T0
(450) 469-5744   *SIC 3999*

SEVEN CONTINENTS CORPORATION p786
945 WILSON AVE SUITE 1, NORTH YORK,
ON, M3K 1E8
(416) 784-3717   *SIC 3999*

SILHOUET-TONE CORPORATION p1235
1985 RUE MONTEREY, MONTREAL, QC,
H7L 3T6
(450) 688-0123   *SIC 3999*

STAGELINE SCENE MOBILE INC p1120
700 RUE MARSOLAIS, L'ASSOMPTION,
QC, J5W 2G9
(450) 589-1063   *SIC 3999*

STAGELINE SCENE MOBILE INC p1120
827 BOUL DE L'ANGE-GARDIEN,
L'ASSOMPTION, QC, J5W 1T3
(450) 589-1063   *SIC 3999*

SYNAGRI S.E.C. p1310
5175 BOUL LAURIER E, SAINT-
HYACINTHE, QC, J2R 2B4
(450) 799-3225   *SIC 3999*

TRIOTECH AMUSEMENT INC p1115
780 RUE MARION, JOLIETTE, QC, J6E 8S2
(450) 760-9082   *SIC 3999*

WALTER'S SHOE CARE INC p795
180 BARTOR RD, NORTH YORK, ON, M9M
2W6
(416) 782-4492   *SIC 3999*

WILSON WREATH CO LTD p412
11 SQUIRE ST, SACKVILLE, NB, E4L 4K8
SIC 3999

SIC 4011 Railroads, line-haul operating

ALGOMA CENTRAL RAILWAY INC p861
129 BAY ST, SAULT STE. MARIE, ON, P6A
1W7
(705) 541-2900   *SIC 4011*

**BESSEMER AND LAKE ERIE RAILROAD
COMPANY** p1202
935 RUE DE LA GAUCHETIERE O BU-
REAU 11, MONTREAL, QC, H3B 2M9
(514) 399-4536   *SIC 4011*

CANADIAN PACIFIC RAILWAY COMPANY p253
420 VICTORIA RD, REVELSTOKE, BC, V0E
2S0
(250) 837-8229   *SIC 4011*

CANADIAN PACIFIC RAILWAY COMPANY p1083
5901 AV WESTMINSTER, COTE SAINT-
LUC, QC, H4W 2J9
(514) 483-7102   *SIC 4011*

CANADIAN PACIFIC RAILWAY COMPANY p1410
3 MANITOBA ST W, MOOSE JAW, SK, S6H
1P8
(306) 693-5421   *SIC 4011*

CANADIAN PACIFIC RAILWAY LIMITED p14
7550 OGDEN DALE RD SE, CALGARY, AB,
T2C 4X9
(888) 333-6370   *SIC 4011*

**CHICAGO, CENTRAL & PACIFIC RAIL-
ROAD COMPANY** p1202
935 RUE DE LA GAUCHETIERE O, MON-
TREAL, QC, H3B 2M9
(514) 399-4536   *SIC 4011*

**COMPAGNIE DE CHEMIN DE FER DU
LITTORAL NORD DE QUEBEC ET DU
LABRADOR INC** p1367
1 RUE RETTY, SEPT-ILES, QC, G4R 3C7

(418) 968-7400   *SIC 4011*

**COMPAGNIE DE CHEMIN DE FER
ROBERVAL-SAGUENAY INC, LA** p1115
1955 BOUL MELLON EDIFICE 1001, JON-
QUIERE, QC, G7S 4L2
(418) 699-2714   *SIC 4011*

**COMPAGNIE DES CHEMINS DE FER NA-
TIONAUX DU CANADA** p84
10229 127 AVE NW, EDMONTON, AB, T5E
0B9
(780) 472-3452   *SIC 4011*

**COMPAGNIE DES CHEMINS DE FER NA-
TIONAUX DU CANADA** p84
11703 127 AVE NW, EDMONTON, AB, T5E
0C9
(780) 472-3486   *SIC 4011*

**COMPAGNIE DES CHEMINS DE FER NA-
TIONAUX DU CANADA** p93
12103 127 AVE NW, EDMONTON, AB, T5L
4X7
(780) 472-3261   *SIC 4011*

**COMPAGNIE DES CHEMINS DE FER NA-
TIONAUX DU CANADA** p398
194 RUE ST-FRANCOIS, EDMUNDSTON,
NB, E3V 1E9
(506) 735-1201   *SIC 4011*

**COMPAGNIE DES CHEMINS DE FER NA-
TIONAUX DU CANADA** p491
257 AIRPORT PKY, BELLEVILLE, ON, K8N
4Z6
(613) 969-2247   *SIC 4011*

**COMPAGNIE DES CHEMINS DE FER NA-
TIONAUX DU CANADA** p550
73 DIESEL DR UNIT 1B, CONCORD, ON,
L4K 1B9
SIC 4011

**COMPAGNIE DES CHEMINS DE FER NA-
TIONAUX DU CANADA** p551
GD, CONCORD, ON, L4K 1B9
(905) 669-3302   *SIC 4011*

**COMPAGNIE DES CHEMINS DE FER NA-
TIONAUX DU CANADA** p574
123 JUDSON ST, ETOBICOKE, ON, M8Z
1A4
(416) 253-6395   *SIC 4011*

**COMPAGNIE DES CHEMINS DE FER NA-
TIONAUX DU CANADA** p859
699 MACGREGOR RD, SARNIA, ON, N7T
7H8
(519) 339-1253   *SIC 4011*

**COMPAGNIE DES CHEMINS DE FER NA-
TIONAUX DU CANADA** p911
1825 BROADWAY AVE, THUNDER BAY,
ON, P7K 1M8
SIC 4011

**COMPAGNIE DES CHEMINS DE FER NA-
TIONAUX DU CANADA** p1002
1 ADMINISTRATION RD, VAUGHAN, ON,
L4K 1B9
(905) 669-3128   *SIC 4011*

**COMPAGNIE DES CHEMINS DE FER NA-
TIONAUX DU CANADA** p1139
2600 AV DE LA ROTONDE, LEVIS, QC,
G6X 2M1
SIC 4011

**COMPAGNIE DES CHEMINS DE FER NA-
TIONAUX DU CANADA** p1203
935 RUE DE LA GAUCHETIERE 16E
ETAGE O, MONTREAL, QC, H3B 2M9
(514) 399-5430   *SIC 4011*

**COMPAGNIE DES CHEMINS DE FER NA-
TIONAUX DU CANADA** p1203
5 PLACE VILLE-MARIE BUREAU 1100,
MONTREAL, QC, H3B 2G2
(514) 399-4811   *SIC 4011*

**DULUTH, MISSABE AND IRON RANGE
RAILWAY COMPANY** p1203
935 RUE DE LA GAUCHETIERE O BU-
REAU 4E, MONTREAL, QC, H3B 2M9
(514) 399-4536   *SIC 4011*

GENESEE & WYOMING CANADA INC p1226
9001 BOUL DE L'ACADIE BUREAU 904,
MONTREAL, QC, H4N 3H5
(514) 948-6999   *SIC 4011*

**GODERICH-EXETER RAILWAY COMPANY
LIMITED** p896
101 SHAKESPEARE ST SUITE 2, STRAT-
FORD, ON, N5A 3W5
(519) 271-4441   *SIC 4011*

ILLINOIS CENTRAL RAILROAD COMPANY p1205
935 RUE DE LA GAUCHETIERE O BU-
REAU 11, MONTREAL, QC, H3B 2M9
(514) 399-4536   *SIC 4011*

METROLINX p784
200 STEEPROCK DR, NORTH YORK, ON,
M3J 2T4
SIC 4011

METROLINX p965
20 BAY ST SUITE 600, TORONTO, ON, M5J
2W3
(416) 869-3200   *SIC 4011*

METROLINX p965
97 FRONT ST W SUITE 200, TORONTO,
ON, M5J 1E6
(416) 874-5900   *SIC 4011*

**NEW BRUNSWICK SOUTHERN RAILWAY
COMPANY LIMITED** p416
11 GIFFORD RD, SAINT JOHN, NB, E2M
4X8
(506) 632-6314   *SIC 4011*

OMNITRAX CANADA INC p379
155 CARLTON ST SUITE 300, WINNIPEG,
MB, R3C 3H8
(204) 947-0033   *SIC 4011*

ON-TRACK RAILWAY OPERATIONS LTD p168
55024 RGE RD 234, STURGEON COUNTY,
AB, T8T 2A7
(780) 973-6003   *SIC 4011*

RAILINK CANADA LTD p763
445 OAK ST E, NORTH BAY, ON, P1B 1A3
(705) 472-6200   *SIC 4011*

**SOUTHERN RAILWAY OF BRITISH
COLUMBIA LIMITED** p238
2102 RIVER DR, NEW WESTMINSTER,
BC, V3M 6S3
(604) 521-1851   *SIC 4011*

**TRANSPORT FERROVIAIRE TSHIUETIN
INC** p1389
148 BOUL DES MONTAGNAIS, UASHAT,
QC, G4R 5R2
(418) 960-0982   *SIC 4011*

SIC 4013 Switching and terminal services

**COMPAGNIE DES CHEMINS DE FER NA-
TIONAUX DU CANADA** p1338
4500 RUE HICKMORE, SAINT-LAURENT,
QC, H4T 1K2
(514) 734-2288   *SIC 4013*

**ESSEX TERMINAL RAILWAY COMPANY,
THE** p1022
1601 LINCOLN RD, WINDSOR, ON, N8Y
2J3
(519) 973-8222   *SIC 4013*

RAIL-TERM INC p1095
10765 CH COTE-DE-LIESSE SUITE 201,
DORVAL, QC, H9P 2R9
(514) 420-1200   *SIC 4013*

WWL VEHICLE SERVICES CANADA LTD p207
820 DOCK RD UNIT 100, DELTA, BC, V3M
6A3
(604) 521-6681   *SIC 4013*

SIC 4111 Local and suburban transit

464290 ONTARIO LIMITED p548
3300 STEELES AVE W SUITE 202, CON-
CORD, ON, L4K 2Y4
(416) 445-1999   *SIC 4111*

A C TAXI LTD p233
835 OLD VICTORIA RD, NANAIMO, BC,
V9R 5Z9
(250) 754-9555   *SIC 4111*

ATLANTIC AMBASSATOURS LIMITED p454
6575 BAYNE ST, HALIFAX, NS, B3K 0H1
(902) 423-6242   *SIC 4111*

AUTOBUS AUGER METROPOLITAIN INC p1076
147 RUE PRINCIPALE, CHATEAUGUAY,
QC, J6K 1G2
(450) 691-1654   *SIC 4111*

AUTOLUX LTD p844
970 BROCK RD, PICKERING, ON, L1W 2A1
(416) 266-1500   *SIC 4111*

BOMBARDIER INC p737
6291 ORDAN DR, MISSISSAUGA, ON, L5T
1G9
(905) 795-7869   *SIC 4111*

BOMBARDIER INC p1295
1101 RUE PARENT, SAINT-BRUNO, QC,
J3V 6E6
(450) 441-2020   *SIC 4111*

**BRITISH COLUMBIA RAPID TRANSIT
COMPANY LTD** p181
6800 14TH AVE, BURNABY, BC, V3N 4S7
(604) 520-3641   *SIC 4111*

CANADIAN PACIFIC RAILWAY COMPANY p1210
1100 RUE DE LA GAUCHETIERE, MON-
TREAL, QC, H3C 3E4
(514) 395-5151   *SIC 4111*

CHEMINS DE FER QUEBEC-GATINEAU INC p1225
9001 BOUL DE L'ACADIE BUREAU 600,
MONTREAL, QC, H4N 3H5
(514) 948-6999   *SIC 4111*

CITY OF GREATER SUDBURY, THE p900
1700 KINGSWAY RD, SUDBURY, ON, P3E
3L7
(705) 675-3333   *SIC 4111*

CITY OF OTTAWA p817
1500 ST. LAURENT BLVD, OTTAWA, ON,
K1G 0Z8
(613) 741-6440   *SIC 4111*

CITY OF REGINA, THE p1420
333 WINNIPEG ST, REGINA, SK, S4R 8P2
(306) 777-7726   *SIC 4111*

COAST MOUNTAIN BUS COMPANY LTD p185
3855 KITCHENER ST SUITE 420, BURN-
ABY, BC, V5C 3L8
(604) 205-6111   *SIC 4111*

COAST MOUNTAIN BUS COMPANY LTD p236
287 NELSON'S CRT SUITE 700, NEW
WESTMINSTER, BC, V3L 0E7
(778) 375-6400   *SIC 4111*

**COMPAGNIE DES CHEMINS DE FER NA-
TIONAUX DU CANADA** p93
12646 124 ST NW, EDMONTON, AB, T5L
0N9
(780) 472-3078   *SIC 4111*

**COMPAGNIE DES CHEMINS DE FER NA-
TIONAUX DU CANADA** p218
309 CN RD, KAMLOOPS, BC, V2H 1K3
(250) 828-6331   *SIC 4111*

**COMPAGNIE DES CHEMINS DE FER NA-
TIONAUX DU CANADA** p250
1108 INDUSTRIAL WAY, PRINCE
GEORGE, BC, V2N 5S1
(250) 561-4190   *SIC 4111*

**COMPAGNIE DES CHEMINS DE FER NA-
TIONAUX DU CANADA** p270
13477 116 AVE, SURREY, BC, V3R 6W4
(604) 589-6552   *SIC 4111*

**COMPAGNIE DES CHEMINS DE FER NA-
TIONAUX DU CANADA** p979
277 FRONT ST W, TORONTO, ON, M5V
2X4
(888) 888-5909   *SIC 4111*

**COMPAGNIE DES CHEMINS DE FER NA-
TIONAUX DU CANADA** p1366
171 4E RUE O, SENNETERRE, QC, J0Y
2M0
(819) 737-8121   *SIC 4111*

**COMPAGNIE DES CHEMINS DE FER NA-
TIONAUX DU CANADA** p1410

GD, MELVILLE, SK, S0A 2P0
SIC 4111

CORPORATION OF THE DISTRICT OF WEST VANCOUVER, THE *p241*
221 LLOYD AVE, NORTH VANCOUVER, BC, V7P 3M2
(604) 985-7777   *SIC* 4111

DETROIT & CANADA TUNNEL *p1023*
555 GOYEAU ST, WINDSOR, ON, N9A 1H1
(519) 258-7424   *SIC* 4111

DIGNITY TRANSPORTATION INC *p669*
50 MCINTOSH DR SUITE 110, MARKHAM, ON, L3R 9T3
(905) 470-2399   *SIC* 4111

DIVERSIFIED TRANSPORTATION LTD *p128*
8030 GOLOSKY AVE, FORT MCMURRAY, AB, T9H 1V5
(780) 790-3960   *SIC* 4111

ELGIE BUS LINES LIMITED *p661*
400 SOVEREIGN RD, LONDON, ON, N6M 1A5
(519) 451-4440   *SIC* 4111

HALIFAX REGIONAL MUNICIPALITY *p446*
200 ILSLEY AVE, DARTMOUTH, NS, B3B 1V1
(902) 490-6614   *SIC* 4111

HALLCON CREW TRANSPORT INC *p770*
5775 YONGE ST SUITE 1010, NORTH YORK, ON, M2M 4J1
(416) 964-9191   *SIC* 4111

HAMILTON STREET RAILWAY COMPANY, THE *p747*
2200 UPPER JAMES ST, MOUNT HOPE, ON, L0R 1W0
(905) 528-4200   *SIC* 4111

HUDSON BAY RAILWAY COMPANY *p359*
728 BIGNEL AVE, THE PAS, MB, R9A 1L8
(204) 627-2007   *SIC* 4111

KUNKEL BUS LINES LTD *p617*
301205 KNAPVILLE RD, HANOVER, ON, N4N 3T1
(519) 364-2530   *SIC* 4111

LANAU BUS S.E.C. *p1380*
2450 BOUL DES ENTREPRISES, TERREBONNE, QC, J6X 4J8
(450) 968-2450   *SIC* 4111

LETHBRIDGE, CITY OF *p141*
619 4 AVE N, LETHBRIDGE, AB, T1H 0K4
(403) 320-3885   *SIC* 4111

LONDON TRANSIT COMMISSION, THE *p651*
450 HIGHBURY AVE N, LONDON, ON, N5W 5L2
(519) 451-1340   *SIC* 4111

MEDI-VAN TRANSPORTATION SPECIALISTS INC *p386*
284 ROUGE RD, WINNIPEG, MB, R3K 1K2
(204) 982-0790   *SIC* 4111

MENZIES AVIATION (CANADA) LTD *p24*
175 AERO WAY NE UNIT 130, CALGARY, AB, T2E 6K2
(403) 250-2033   *SIC* 4111

MILLER TRANSIT LIMITED *p672*
8050 WOODBINE AVE, MARKHAM, ON, L3R 2N8
(905) 475-1367   *SIC* 4111

NIAGARA AIR BUS INC *p760*
8626 LUNDY'S LANE, NIAGARA FALLS, ON, L2H 1H4
(905) 374-8111   *SIC* 4111

ONTARIO NORTHLAND TRANSPORTATION COMMISSION *p569*
3RD ST, ENGLEHART, ON, P0J 1H0
(705) 544-2292   *SIC* 4111

PACIFIC WESTERN TRANSPORTATION LTD *p24*
1857 CENTRE AVE SE, CALGARY, AB, T2E 6L3
(403) 248-4300   *SIC* 4111

PROTRANS BC OPERATIONS LTD *p261*
9851 VAN HORNE WAY, RICHMOND, BC, V6X 1W4
(604) 247-5757   *SIC* 4111

RESEAU DE TRANSPORT DE LONGUEUIL

p1142
1150 BOUL MARIE-VICTORIN, LONGUEUIL, QC, J4G 2M4
(450) 442-8600   *SIC* 4111

RIIDE HOLDINGS INC *p1432*
225 AVENUE B N, SASKATOON, SK, S7L 1E1
(306) 244-3767   *SIC* 4111

SAINT JOHN TRANSIT COMMISSION *p413*
55 MCDONALD ST, SAINT JOHN, NB, E2J 0C7
(506) 658-4710   *SIC* 4111

SERVICES INTERNATIONALS SKYPORT INC *p1095*
400 AV MICHEL-JASMIN BUREAU 200, DORVAL, QC, H9P 1C1
(514) 631-1155   *SIC* 4111

SOCIETE DE TRANSPORT DE MONTREAL *p1050*
8150 RUE LARREY, ANJOU, QC, H1J 2J5
(514) 280-5913   *SIC* 4111

SOCIETE DE TRANSPORT DE MONTREAL *p1131*
7770 RUE SAINT-PATRICK, LASALLE, QC, H8N 1V1
(514) 280-6382   *SIC* 4111

SOCIETE DE TRANSPORT DE MONTREAL *p1176*
2000 RUE BERRI, MONTREAL, QC, H2L 4V7
(514) 786-6876   *SIC* 4111

SOCIETE DE TRANSPORT DE MONTREAL *p1230*
800 RUE DE LA GAUCHETIERE O BUREAU 8420, MONTREAL, QC, H5A 1J6
(514) 786-4636   *SIC* 4111

SOCIETE DE TRANSPORT DE SHERBROOKE *p1372*
895 RUE CABANA, SHERBROOKE, QC, J1K 2M3
(819) 564-2687   *SIC* 4111

SOCIETE DES TRAVERSIERS DU QUEBEC *p1376*
9 RUE ELIZABETH, SOREL-TRACY, QC, J3P 4G1
(450) 742-3313   *SIC* 4111

SOUTH COAST BRITISH COLUMBIA TRANSPORTATION AUTHORITY *p237*
287 NELSON'S CRT SUITE 400, NEW WESTMINSTER, BC, V3L 0E7
(778) 375-7500   *SIC* 4111

SOUTH COAST BRITISH COLUMBIA TRANSPORTATION AUTHORITY *p237*
287 NELSON'S CRT SUITE 300, NEW WESTMINSTER, BC, V3L 0E7
(604) 515-8300   *SIC* 4111

ST. JOHN'S TRANSPORTATION COMMISSION *p431*
25 MESSENGER DR, ST. JOHN'S, NL, A1B 0H6
(709) 570-2020   *SIC* 4111

STOCK TRANSPORTATION LTD *p895*
24 CARDICO DR, STOUFFVILLE, ON, L4A 2G5
SIC 4111

SYNDICAT DES INSPECTEURS ET DES REPARTITEURS DU RESEAU DE TRANSPORT DE LA CAPITALE (FISA) *p1279*
720 RUE DES ROCAILLES, QUEBEC, QC, G2J 1A5
(418) 627-2351   *SIC* 4111

TORONTO TRANSIT COMMISSION *p919*
400 GREENWOOD AVE, TORONTO, ON, M4J 4Y5
(416) 393-3176   *SIC* 4111

TORONTO TRANSIT COMMISSION *p924*
1900 YONGE ST SUITE 400, TORONTO, ON, M4S 1Z2
(416) 393-4000   *SIC* 4111

TRANSPORT CANADA *p1168*
3400 RUE NOTRE-DAME E, MONTREAL, QC, H1W 2J2
(514) 283-7020   *SIC* 4111

TRANSPORT EN COMMUN LA QUEBE-

COISE INC *p1123*
300 RUE DES CONSEILLERS, LA PRAIRIE, QC, J5R 2E6
SIC 4111

TRENTWAY-WAGAR INC *p758*
4555 ERIE AVE, NIAGARA FALLS, ON, L2E 7G9
(905) 358-7230   *SIC* 4111

TST SOLUTIONS L.P. *p701*
5200 MAINGATE DR, MISSISSAUGA, ON, L4W 1G5
SIC 4111

VALLEY BUS LINES LTD *p627*
782 VAN BUREN ST, KEMPTVILLE, ON, K0G 1J0
(613) 258-4022   *SIC* 4111

VIA RAIL CANADA INC *p451*
1161 HOLLIS ST, HALIFAX, NS, B3H 2P6
(902) 494-7900   *SIC* 4111

VIA RAIL CANADA INC *p531*
1199 WATERDOWN RD, BURLINGTON, ON, L7T 4A8
SIC 4111

VIA RAIL CANADA INC *p968*
65 FRONT ST W SUITE 222, TORONTO, ON, M5J 1E6
(888) 842-7245   *SIC* 4111

VIA RAIL CANADA INC *p1209*
3 PLACE VILLE-MARIE BUREAU 500, MONTREAL, QC, H3B 2C9
(514) 871-6000   *SIC* 4111

VIA RAIL CANADA INC *p1209*
895 RUE DE LA GAUCHETIERE O BUREAU 429, MONTREAL, QC, H3B 4G1
(514) 989-2626   *SIC* 4111

VIA RAIL CANADA INC *p1245*
44 132 RTE O BUREAU LB1, PERCE, QC, G0C 2L0
(418) 782-2747   *SIC* 4111

VOYAGEUR PATIENT TRANSFER SERVICES INC *p650*
573 ADMIRAL CRT, LONDON, ON, N5V 4L3
(519) 455-4579   *SIC* 4111

SIC 4119 Local passenger transportation, nec

AIR CAB LIMOUSINE (1985) LIMITED *p548*
7733 KEELE ST, CONCORD, ON, L4K 1Y5
(416) 225-1555   *SIC* 4119

ALAGASH INVESTMENTS LIMITED *p861*
73 BROCK ST, SAULT STE. MARIE, ON, P6A 3B4
SIC 4119

ALMONTE GENERAL HOSPITAL *p540*
37 NEELIN ST, CARLETON PLACE, ON, K7C 2J6
(613) 205-1021   *SIC* 4119

AMBULANCE CHICOUTIMI INC *p1080*
784 BOUL BARRETTE, CHICOUTIMI, QC, G7J 3Z7
(418) 543-5045   *SIC* 4119

AMBULANCE NEW BRUNSWICK INC *p406*
210 JOHN ST SUITE 101, MONCTON, NB, E1C 0B8
(506) 872-6500   *SIC* 4119

COOPERATIVE DES PARAMEDICS DE L'OUTAOUAIS *p1103*
505 BOUL DES AFFAIRES, GATINEAU, QC, J8R 0B2
(819) 643-5005   *SIC* 4119

CORPORATION OF THE COUNTY OF LAMBTON *p842*
3958 PETROLIA LINE RR 4, PETROLIA, ON, N0N 1R0
(519) 882-3797   *SIC* 4119

CORPORATION OF THE COUNTY OF LAMBTON *p859*
6362 TELFER RD, SARNIA, ON, N7T 7H4
(519) 882-2442   *SIC* 4119

DESSERCOM INC *p1312*
592 AV SAINTE-MARIE, SAINT-HYACINTHE, QC, J2S 4R5
(450) 773-5223   *SIC* 4119

EMC EMERGENCY MEDICAL CARE INCORPORATED *p446*
239 BROWNLOW AVE SUITE 300, DARTMOUTH, NS, B3B 2B2
(902) 832-8320   *SIC* 4119

EMERGENCY AND HEALTH SERVICES COMMISSION *p267*
2261 KEATING CROSS RD, SAANICHTON, BC, V8M 2A5
(250) 953-3298   *SIC* 4119

EMERGENCY MEDICAL SERVICES *p8*
3705 35 ST NE SUITE 100, CALGARY, AB, T1Y 6C2
(403) 955-9550   *SIC* 4119

GRIFFIN TRANSPORTATION SERVICES INC *p295*
873 HASTINGS ST E, VANCOUVER, BC, V6A 1R8
(604) 628-4474   *SIC* 4119

ISLAND EMS INC *p1040*
229 SHERWOOD RD, CHARLOTTETOWN, PE, C1E 0E5
(902) 892-9995   *SIC* 4119

M.D. AMBULANCE CARE LTD *p1425*
430 MELVILLE ST, SASKATOON, SK, S7J 4M2
(306) 975-8808   *SIC* 4119

ROYAL CITY AMBULANCE SERVICE LTD *p606*
355 ELMIRA RD N SUITE 134, GUELPH, ON, N1K 1S5
(519) 824-1510   *SIC* 4119

SUN COUNTRY REGIONAL HEALTH AUTHORITY *p1415*
18 EICHORST ST, REDVERS, SK, S0C 2H0
(306) 452-3553   *SIC* 4119

TAXELCO INC *p1209*
355 RUE SAINTE-CATHERINE O BUREAU 500, MONTREAL, QC, H3B 1A5
(514) 504-8293   *SIC* 4119

THAMES EMERGENCY MEDICAL SERVICES INC *p656*
340 WATERLOO ST, LONDON, ON, N6B 2N6
(519) 679-5466   *SIC* 4119

UNITED COUNTIES OF LEEDS AND GRENVILLE *p520*
25 CENTRAL AVE W SUITE 100, BROCKVILLE, ON, K6V 4N6
(613) 342-3840   *SIC* 4119

URGENCES-SANTE *p1165*
6700 RUE JARRY E, MONTREAL, QC, H1P 0A4
(514) 723-5600   *SIC* 4119

SIC 4121 Taxicabs

1210670 ONTARIO INC *p866*
1940 ELLESMERE RD UNIT 18, SCARBOROUGH, ON, M1H 2V7
(416) 438-5151   *SIC* 4121

341-7777 TAXI LTD *p153*
4819 48 AVE UNIT 280, RED DEER, AB, T4N 3T2
(403) 341-7777   *SIC* 4121

BLUE BIRD CABS LTD *p334*
2612 QUADRA ST, VICTORIA, BC, V8T 4E4
(250) 382-2222   *SIC* 4121

BLUE LINE TRANSPORTATION LTD *p611*
160 JOHN ST S, HAMILTON, ON, L8N 2C4
(905) 525-2583   *SIC* 4121

BONNY'S TAXI LTD *p192*
5759 SIDLEY ST, BURNABY, BC, V5J 5E6
(604) 435-8233   *SIC* 4121

CHILLIWACK TAXI LTD *p196*
45877 HOCKING AVE, CHILLIWACK, BC, V2P 1B5
(604) 795-9111   *SIC* 4121

CITY CAB (BRANTFORD-DARLING STREET) LIMITED *p517*
40 DALHOUSIE ST, BRANTFORD, ON, N3T 2H8
(519) 759-7800   *SIC* 4121

▲ Public Company   ■ Public Company Family Member   **HQ** Headquarters   **BR** Branch   **SL** Single Location

CITY CAB INC   *p1038*
168 PRINCE ST, CHARLOTTETOWN, PE,
C1A 4R6
(902) 892-6567   *SIC 4121*

DELTA SUNSHINE TAXI (1972) LTD   *p276*
12837 76 AVE UNIT 203, SURREY, BC,
V3W 2V3
(604) 594-5444   *SIC 4121*

DUFFY'S TAXI (1996) LTD   *p380*
1100 NOTRE DAME AVE, WINNIPEG, MB,
R3E 0N8
(204) 925-0101   *SIC 4121*

GUILDFORD CAB (1993) LTD   *p276*
8299 129 ST UNIT 101, SURREY, BC, V3W
0A6
(604) 585-8888   *SIC 4121*

LOCATION RADIO TAXI UNION LTEE *p1144*
1605 RUE VERCHERES, LONGUEUIL, QC,
J4K 2Z6
(450) 679-6262   *SIC 4121*

MACLURES CABS (1984) LTD   *p323*
1275 75TH AVE W, VANCOUVER, BC, V6P
3G4
(604) 683-6666   *SIC 4121*

MAPLE LEAF TAXI-CAB LIMITED   *p919*
1245 DANFORTH AVE SUITE 203,
TORONTO, ON, M4J 5B5
(416) 465-2445   *SIC 4121*

RIZZUTO BROS. LIMITED   *p612*
160 JOHN ST S, HAMILTON, ON, L8N 2C4
(905) 522-2525   *SIC 4121*

ROACH'S TAXI (1988) LTD   *p907*
216 CAMELOT ST, THUNDER BAY, ON,
P7A 4B1
(807) 344-8481   *SIC 4121*

SUNSHINE CABS LIMITED   *p239*
1465 RUPERT ST, NORTH VANCOUVER,
BC, V7J 1G1
(604) 988-8888   *SIC 4121*

VANCOUVER TAXI LTD   *p286*
790 CLARK DR, VANCOUVER, BC, V5L
3J2
(604) 871-1111   *SIC 4121*

WHISTLER TAXI LTD   *p343*
1080 MILLAR CREEK RD SUITE 201,
WHISTLER, BC, V8E 0S7
(604) 932-4430   *SIC 4121*

---

*SIC 4131 Intercity and rural bus
transportation*

2755-4609 QUEBEC INC   *p1061*
4243 RUE MARCEL-LACASSE, BOIS-
BRIAND, QC, J7H 1N4
(450) 435-8899   *SIC 4131*

AIRWAYS TRANSIT SERVICE LIMITED*p566*
35 5 HWY W, DUNDAS, ON, L9H 7L5
(905) 333-3113   *SIC 4131*

AIRWAYS TRANSIT SERVICE LIMITED
p1010
99 NORTHLAND RD UNIT A, WATERLOO,
ON, N2V 1Y8
(519) 658-5521   *SIC 4131*

AUTOCARS ORLEANS EXPRESS INC
p1210
740 RUE NOTRE-DAME O BUREAU 1000,
MONTREAL, QC, H3C 3X6
(514) 395-4000   *SIC 4131*

CITY OF REGINA, THE   *p1420*
333 WINNIPEG ST, REGINA, SK, S4R 8P2
(306) 777-7780   *SIC 4131*

FAIRWAY COACHLINES INC   *p365*
339 ARCHIBALD ST, WINNIPEG, MB, R2J
0W6
(204) 989-7007   *SIC 4131*

FIRSTCANADA ULC   *p1415*
140 E 4TH AVE, REGINA, SK, S4N 4Z4
(306) 721-4499   *SIC 4131*

**GREYHOUND CANADA TRANSPORTA-
TION ULC**   *p72*
877 GREYHOUND WAY SW, CALGARY,
AB, T3C 3V8
(403) 218-3000   *SIC 4131*

**GREYHOUND CANADA TRANSPORTA-
TION ULC**   *p295*
1150 STATION ST UNIT 200, VANCOUVER,
BC, V6A 4C7
(604) 683-8133   *SIC 4131*

**GREYHOUND CANADA TRANSPORTA-
TION ULC**   *p487*
24 MAPLE AVE UNIT 205, BARRIE, ON,
L4N 7W4
    SIC 4131

METROLINX   *p920*
580 COMMISSIONERS ST, TORONTO, ON,
M4M 1A7
(416) 393-4111   *SIC 4131*

MONCTON, CITY OF   *p408*
140 MILLENNIUM BLVD, MONCTON, NB,
E1E 2G8
(506) 857-2008   *SIC 4131*

PIONEER TRANSPORT INC   *p404*
208 ROUTE 590, JACKSONVILLE, NB,
E7M 3R7
(506) 325-2211   *SIC 4131*

RED CAR SERVICE INC   *p600*
530 ELIZABETH ST, GUELPH, ON, N1E
6C3
(519) 824-9344   *SIC 4131*

ROBERT Q'S AIRBUS INC   *p659*
105 WHARNCLIFFE RD S, LONDON, ON,
N6J 2K2
(519) 673-6804   *SIC 4131*

SOCIETE DE TRANSPORT DU SAGUENAY
p1081
1330 RUE BERSIMIS, CHICOUTIMI, QC,
G7K 1A5
(418) 545-3683   *SIC 4131*

TRANSDEV QUEBEC INC   *p1057*
1500 RUE LOUIS-MARCHAND, BELOEIL,
QC, J3G 6S3
(450) 446-8899   *SIC 4131*

TRENTWAY-WAGAR INC   *p842*
2015 FISHER DR UNIT 101, PETERBOR-
OUGH, ON, K9J 6X6
(705) 748-6411   *SIC 4131*

WESTCAN BULK TRANSPORT LTD   *p19*
3780 76 AVE SE, CALGARY, AB, T2C 1J8
(403) 279-5505   *SIC 4131*

SIC 4141 Local bus charter service

564242 ONTARIO LIMITED   *p840*
728 RYE ST, PETERBOROUGH, ON, K9J
6W9
(705) 745-1666   *SIC 4141*

**ATTRIDGE TRANSPORTATION INCORPO-
RATED**   *p1005*
27 MILL ST S, WATERDOWN, ON, L0R 2H0
(905) 690-2632   *SIC 4141*

WEST COAST SIGHTSEEING LTD   *p301*
200-110 CAMBIE ST, VANCOUVER, BC,
V6B 2M8
(604) 451-1600   *SIC 4141*

SIC 4142 Bus charter service, except local

ACADIAN COACH LINES LP   *p406*
300 MAIN ST UNIT B2-2, MONCTON, NB,
E1C 1B9
    SIC 4142

AUTOBUS GRANBY INC   *p1110*
1254 RUE PRINCIPALE, GRANBY, QC, J2J
0M2
(450) 378-9951   *SIC 4142*

AUTOBUS LASALLE INC   *p1369*
149 RUE WEST, SHAWVILLE, QC, J0X 2Y0
(819) 647-5696   *SIC 4142*

BEAVER BUS LINES LIMITED   *p365*
339 ARCHIBALD ST, WINNIPEG, MB, R2J
0W6
(204) 989-7007   *SIC 4142*

COAST MOUNTAIN BUS COMPANY LTD
p263
11133 COPPERSMITH WAY, RICHMOND,

BC, V7A 5E8
(604) 277-7787   *SIC 4142*

DIVERSIFIED TRANSPORTATION LTD   *p88*
10014 104 ST NW UNIT 20, EDMONTON,
AB, T5J 0Z1
(780) 425-0820   *SIC 4142*

DIVERSIFIED TRANSPORTATION LTD *p114*
8351 MCINTYRE RD NW, EDMONTON, AB,
T6E 5J7
(780) 468-6771   *SIC 4142*

DIVERSIFIED TRANSPORTATION LTD *p128*
120 MACLENNAN CRES, FORT MCMUR-
RAY, AB, T9H 4E8
(780) 743-2244   *SIC 4142*

DIVERSIFIED TRANSPORTATION LTD *p248*
391 NORTH NECHAKO RD, PRINCE
GEORGE, BC, V2K 4K8
(250) 563-5431   *SIC 4142*

FIRSTCANADA ULC   *p836*
829 REST ACRES RD, PARIS, ON, N3L 3E3
    SIC 4142

GREAT CANADIAN COACHES INC   *p636*
353 MANITOU DR, KITCHENER, ON, N2C
1L5
(519) 896-8687   *SIC 4142*

INTERNATIONAL STAGE LINES INC   *p260*
4171 VANGUARD RD, RICHMOND, BC,
V6X 2P6
(604) 270-6135   *SIC 4142*

IRON RANGE BUS LINES INC   *p908*
1141 GOLF LINKS RD, THUNDER BAY, ON,
P7B 7A3
(807) 345-7387   *SIC 4142*

TOKMAKJIAN INC   *p559*
221 CALDARI RD, CONCORD, ON, L4K
3Z9
(905) 669-2850   *SIC 4142*

TRENTWAY-WAGAR INC   *p690*
6020 INDIAN LINE, MISSISSAUGA, ON,
L4V 1G5
(905) 677-3841   *SIC 4142*

TROTT TRANSIT LTD   *p719*
15 JAMES ST, MISSISSAUGA, ON, L5M
1R4
    SIC 4142

VANCOUVER TOURS AND TRANSIT LTD
p210
8730 RIVER RD, DELTA, BC, V4G 1B5
(604) 940-1707   *SIC 4142*

WILSON'S TRANSPORTATION LTD   *p339*
4196 GLANFORD AVE, VICTORIA, BC, V8Z
4B6
(250) 475-3235   *SIC 4142*

SIC 4151 School buses

1429634 ONTARIO LIMITED   *p496*
51 PORT DARLINGTON RD SUITE 1, BOW-
MANVILLE, ON, L1C 3K3
(905) 697-0503   *SIC 4151*

417 BUS LINE LIMITED   *p541*
50 INDUSTRIAL ST, CASSELMAN, ON,
K0A 1M0
(613) 764-2192   *SIC 4151*

473980 ONTARIO LTD   *p812*
485 WATERLOO CRT, OSHAWA, ON, L1H
3X2
(905) 433-1392   *SIC 4151*

944622 ONTARIO LIMITED   *p617*
175 SWAYZE RD, HANNON, ON, L0R 1P0
(905) 692-4488   *SIC 4151*

947465 ONTARIO LTD   *p648*
573 ADMIRAL CRT, LONDON, ON, N5V 4L3
(519) 455-1390   *SIC 4151*

A. GIRARDIN INC   *p1100*
4000 RUE GIRARDIN, DRUMMONDVILLE,
QC, J2E 0A1
(819) 477-3222   *SIC 4151*

ALLANDALE SCHOOL TRANSIT LIMITED
p486
137 BROCK ST, BARRIE, ON, L4N 2M3
(705) 728-1100   *SIC 4151*

ALOUETTE BUS LINES LTD   *p898*

194 FRONT ST SUITE FRONT, STUR-
GEON FALLS, ON, P2B 2J3
(705) 753-3911   *SIC 4151*

**ATTRIDGE TRANSPORTATION INCORPO-
RATED**   *p521*
5439 HARVESTER RD, BURLINGTON, ON,
L7L 5J7
(905) 333-4047   *SIC 4151*

AUTOBUS AUGER INC   *p1137*
880 RUE DE SAINT-ROMUALD, LEVIS, QC,
G6W 5M6
(418) 833-2181   *SIC 4151*

AUTOBUS BRUNET INC, LES   *p1319*
986 RUE DES LACS, SAINT-JEROME, QC,
J5L 1T4
(450) 438-8363   *SIC 4151*

AUTOBUS DU VILLAGE INC, LES   *p1102*
65 RUE THIBAULT, GATINEAU, QC, J8L
3Z1
(819) 281-9235   *SIC 4151*

AUTOBUS IDEAL INC   *p1239*
5101 BOUL INDUSTRIEL, MONTREAL-
NORD, QC, H1G 3H1
(514) 323-2355   *SIC 4151*

AUTOBUS LA QUEBECOISE INC   *p1108*
545 RUE DE VERNON, GATINEAU, QC, J9J
3K4
(819) 770-1070   *SIC 4151*

AUTOBUS LA QUEBECOISE INC   *p1278*
607 6E AVENUE DE L'AEROPORT, QUE-
BEC, QC, G2G 2T4
(418) 872-5525   *SIC 4151*

AUTOBUS LAVAL LTEE   *p1254*
445 RUE DES ALLEGHANYS BUREAU
201, QUEBEC, QC, G1C 4N4
(418) 667-3265   *SIC 4151*

AUTOBUS MAHEUX LTEE, LES   *p1123*
156 393 RTE S, LA SARRE, QC, J9Z 2X2
(819) 333-2217   *SIC 4151*

AUTOBUS MAHEUX LTEE, LES   *p1390*
855 BOUL BARRETTE, VAL-D'OR, QC, J9P
0J8
(819) 825-4767   *SIC 4151*

AUTOBUS RIVE-NORD LTEE   *p1232*
1325 MONTEE MASSON, MONTREAL,
QC, H7E 4P2
(450) 661-7140   *SIC 4151*

AUTOBUS TERREMONT LTEE   *p1150*
343 CH DES ANGLAIS, MASCOUCHE, QC,
J7L 3P8
(450) 477-1500   *SIC 4151*

AUTOBUS TRANSCO (1988) INC   *p1130*
8201 RUE ELMSLIE, LASALLE, QC, H8N
2W6
(514) 363-4315   *SIC 4151*

AUTOBUS TRANSCO (1988) INC   *p1161*
7975 BOUL HENRI-BOURASSA E, MON-
TREAL, QC, H1E 1N9
(514) 648-8625   *SIC 4151*

AUTOBUS TRANSCOBEC (1987) INC, LES
p1319
21 RUE JOHN-F-KENNEDY, SAINT-
JEROME, QC, J7Y 4B4
(450) 432-9748   *SIC 4151*

AUTOBUS YVES SEGUIN & FILS INC *p1381*
1730 RUE EFFINGHAM, TERREBONNE,
QC, J6Y 1R7
(450) 433-6958   *SIC 4151*

AUTOCAR HELIE INC.   *p1055*
3505 BOUL DE PORT-ROYAL, BECAN-
COUR, QC, G9H 1Y2
(819) 371-1177   *SIC 4151*

BERLINES TRANSIT INC   *p1058*
719 BOUL INDUSTRIEL BUREAU 102B,
BLAINVILLE, QC, J7C 3V3
(450) 437-3589   *SIC 4151*

BLONDEAU TAXI LIMITEE   *p815*
2161 BANTREE ST, OTTAWA, ON, K1B 4X3
    SIC 4151

**CASEY TRANSPORTATION COMPANY
LIMITED**   *p629*
1312 WELLINGTON ST W SUITE 1, KING
CITY, ON, L7B 1K5
    SIC 4151

DAN NEL COACH LINES COMPANY LIMITED p883
12 KEEFER RD SUITE 10, ST CATHARINES, ON, L2M 7N9
(905) 934-1124   *SIC* 4151

DENNY BUS LINES LTD p473
5414 ERIN FOURTH LINE, ACTON, ON, L7J 2L8
(519) 833-9117   *SIC* 4151

ELLIOTT COACH LINES (FERGUS) LTD p590
680 GLEN GARRY CRES, FERGUS, ON, N1M 2W8
SIC 4151

ELLIOTT, FRED COACH LINES LIMITED p606
760 VICTORIA RD S, GUELPH, ON, N1L 1C6
(519) 822-5225   *SIC* 4151

FIRSTCANADA ULC p169
6304B 52 ST, TABER, AB, T1G 1J7
(403) 223-5670   *SIC* 4151

FIRSTCANADA ULC p274
12079 103A AVE, SURREY, BC, V3V 3G7
(604) 583-7060   *SIC* 4151

FIRSTCANADA ULC p477
1185 SMITH RD, ANCASTER, ON, L9G 3L1
(905) 648-1386   *SIC* 4151

FIRSTCANADA ULC p497
23 GRAY RD, BRACEBRIDGE, ON, P1L 1P8
SIC 4151

FIRSTCANADA ULC p522
1111 INTERNATIONAL BLVD, BURLINGTON, ON, L7L 6W1
(289) 288-4359   *SIC* 4151

FIRSTCANADA ULC p526
5401 DUNDAS ST, BURLINGTON, ON, L7M 0Y8
(905) 335-7010   *SIC* 4151

FIRSTCANADA ULC p543
100 CURRIE ST, CHATHAM, ON, N7M 6L9
(519) 352-1920   *SIC* 4151

FIRSTCANADA ULC p608
50 COVINGTON ST, HAMILTON, ON, L8E 2Y5
(905) 522-3232   *SIC* 4151

FIRSTCANADA ULC p642
40 MCBRINE DR, KITCHENER, ON, N2R 1E7
(519) 748-4777   *SIC* 4151

FIRSTCANADA ULC p711
3599 WOLFEDALE RD, MISSISSAUGA, ON, L5C 1V8
(905) 270-0561   *SIC* 4151

FIRSTCANADA ULC p752
1027 MOODIE DR, NEPEAN, ON, K2R 1H4
SIC 4151

FIRSTCANADA ULC p761
349 AIRPORT RD, NIAGARA ON THE LAKE, ON, L0S 1J0
(905) 688-9600   *SIC* 4151

FIRSTCANADA ULC p775
103 RAILSIDE RD, NORTH YORK, ON, M3A 1B2
(905) 294-5104   *SIC* 4151

FIRSTCANADA ULC p809
445 LACLIE ST, ORILLIA, ON, L3V 4P7
(705) 326-7376   *SIC* 4151

FIRSTCANADA ULC p835
2180 20TH ST E, OWEN SOUND, ON, N4K 5P7
(519) 376-5712   *SIC* 4151

FIRSTCANADA ULC p862
70 INDUSTRIAL COURT A, SAULT STE. MARIE, ON, P6B 5W6
(705) 759-2192   *SIC* 4151

FIRSTCANADA ULC p883
4598 SIXTEEN RD, ST ANNS, ON, L0R 1Y0
SIC 4151

FIRSTCANADA ULC p896
4321 LINE 34, STRATFORD, ON, N5A 6S7
(519) 393-6727   *SIC* 4151

FIRSTCANADA ULC p904

120 DONCASTER AVE, THORNHILL, ON, L3T 1L3
(905) 764-6662   *SIC* 4151

FIRSTCANADA ULC p1012
1049 NIAGARA ST, WELLAND, ON, L3C 1M5
(905) 735-5944   *SIC* 4151

GLENGARRY BUS LINE INC p476
104 VIAU ST, ALEXANDRIA, ON, K0C 1A0
(613) 525-1443   *SIC* 4151

GOLDEN ARROW SCHOOLBUSES LTD p101
20204 111 AVE NW, EDMONTON, AB, T5S 2G6
(780) 447-1538   *SIC* 4151

HAMILTON, ELLWOOD ENTERPRISES LTD p643
1325 OLD YOUNG'S POINT RD, LAKEFIELD, ON, K0L 2H0
(705) 652-6090   *SIC* 4151

HAMMOND TRANSPORTATION LIMITED p497
450 ECCLESTONE DR, BRACEBRIDGE, ON, P1L 1R1
(705) 645-5431   *SIC* 4151

HERTZ NORTHERN BUS (2006) LTD p1433
330 103RD ST E, SASKATOON, SK, S7N 1Z1
(306) 374-5161   *SIC* 4151

HOWARD, R. A. BUS SERVICE LIMITED p479
31 HENRY ST, ATHENS, ON, K0E 1B0
(613) 924-2720   *SIC* 4151

JEAN JACQUES CAMPEAU INC p1072
60 RUE RENAUD, BROWNSBURG-CHATHAM, QC, J8G 2E6
(450) 562-2838   *SIC* 4151

LAFLEUR SCHOOL TRANSPORTATION LTD p544
1546 BASELINE RD, CLARENCE CREEK, ON, K0A 1N0
(613) 488-2337   *SIC* 4151

LANGS BUS LINES LIMITED p897
66 ZIMMERMAN AVE, STRATHROY, ON, N7G 2G7
(519) 245-2350   *SIC* 4151

LYNCH BUS LINES LTD p193
4687 BYRNE RD, BURNABY, BC, V5J 3H6
(604) 439-0842   *SIC* 4151

MARTIN, C. BUS SERVICE LIMITED p747
106 ADVANCE AVE, NAPANEE, ON, K7R 3Y6
(613) 354-7545   *SIC* 4151

MCCLUSKEY TRANSPORTATION SERVICES LIMITED p586
514 CARLINGVIEW DR UNIT 200, ETOBICOKE, ON, M9W 5R3
(416) 246-1422   *SIC* 4151

MURPHY, J & T LIMITED p479
21588 RICHMOND ST, ARVA, ON, N0M 1C0
(519) 660-8200   *SIC* 4151

PAQUETTE, ROBERT AUTOBUS & FILS INC p1301
222 25E AV, SAINT-EUSTACHE, QC, J7P 4Z8
(450) 473-4526   *SIC* 4151

PARKHURST, AL TRANSPORTATION LTD p492
125 COLLEGE ST E, BELLEVILLE, ON, K8P 5A2
(613) 969-0606   *SIC* 4151

PARKINSON COACH LINES 2000 INC p508
10 KENNEDY RD N, BRAMPTON, ON, L6V 1X4
(416) 451-4776   *SIC* 4151

PARKVIEW TRANSIT INC p619
5 SMALL CRES, HAWKESTONE, ON, L0L 1T0
(705) 327-7100   *SIC* 4151

PRAIRIE BUS LINES LTD p154
5310 54 ST, RED DEER, AB, T4N 6M1
(403) 342-6390   *SIC* 4151

RILLING BUS LTD p1438

GD STN MAIN, YORKTON, SK, S3N 2V5
(306) 782-2955   *SIC* 4151

ROXBOROUGH BUS LINES LIMITED p680
17504 DYER RD, MAXVILLE, ON, K0C 1T0
(613) 538-2461   *SIC* 4151

SABEM, SEC p1282
1500 RUE RAYMOND-GAUDREAULT, REPENTIGNY, QC, J5Y 4E3
(450) 585-1210   *SIC* 4151

SHARP BUS LINES LIMITED p518
567 OAK PARK RD, BRANTFORD, ON, N3T 5L8
(519) 751-3434   *SIC* 4151

SHARP BUS LINES LIMITED p622
6 SCOTT ST, INNERKIP, ON, N0J 1M0
SIC 4151

SOUTHLAND TRANSPORTATION LTD p32
823 HIGHFIELD AVE SE, CALGARY, AB, T2G 4C7
(403) 287-1395   *SIC* 4151

SOUTHLAND TRANSPORTATION LTD p80
216 GRIFFIN RD E, COCHRANE, AB, T4C 2B9
(403) 932-7100   *SIC* 4151

STEVENSON, G & L TRANSPORT LIMITED p569
1244 COUNTY ROAD 22, EMERYVILLE, ON, N0R 1C0
(519) 727-3478   *SIC* 4151

STOCK TRANSPORTATION LTD p103
11454 WINTERBURN RD NW, EDMONTON, AB, T5S 2Y3
(780) 451-9536   *SIC* 4151

STOCK TRANSPORTATION LTD p448
51 FRAZEE AVE, DARTMOUTH, NS, B3B 1Z4
(902) 481-8400   *SIC* 4151

STOCK TRANSPORTATION LTD p588
60 MCCULLOCH AVE, ETOBICOKE, ON, M9W 4M6
(416) 244-5341   *SIC* 4151

STOCK TRANSPORTATION LTD p762
59 COMMERCE CRES, NORTH BAY, ON, P1A 0B3
(705) 474-4370   *SIC* 4151

STOCK TRANSPORTATION LTD p856
550 EDWARD AVE, RICHMOND HILL, ON, L4C 3K4
(905) 883-6665   *SIC* 4151

STOCK TRANSPORTATION LTD p869
17 UPTON RD, SCARBOROUGH, ON, M1L 2C1
(416) 754-4949   *SIC* 4151

STOCK TRANSPORTATION LTD p901
36 12 HWY, SUNDERLAND, ON, L0C 1H0
(705) 357-3187   *SIC* 4151

STUDENT TRANSPORTATION INC p488
160 SAUNDERS RD UNIT 6, BARRIE, ON, L4N 9A4
(705) 721-2626   *SIC* 4151

STUDENT TRANSPORTATION OF CANADA INC p488
160 SAUNDERS RD UNIT 6, BARRIE, ON, L4N 9A4
(705) 721-2626   *SIC* 4151

TRANSCOBEC (1987) INC p1320
21 RUE JOHN-F.-KENNEDY, SAINT-JEROME, QC, J7Y 4B4
(450) 432-9748   *SIC* 4151

TRANSDEV INC p1318
720 RUE TROTTER, SAINT-JEAN-SUR-RICHELIEU, QC, J3B 8T2
(514) 787-1998   *SIC* 4151

SIC 4173 Bus terminal and service facilities

REGIONAL MUNICIPALITY OF WATERLOO, THE p638
250 STRASBURG RD, KITCHENER, ON, N2E 3M6
(519) 585-7597   *SIC* 4173

SCHOOL DISTRICT 73 (KAMLOOPS/THOMPSON) p217

710 MCGILL RD, KAMLOOPS, BC, V2C 0A2
(250) 372-5853   *SIC* 4173

SCHOOL DISTRICT NO. 36 (SURREY) p277
6700 144 ST, SURREY, BC, V3W 5R5
(604) 572-0500   *SIC* 4173

SIC 4212 Local trucking, without storage

11198173 CANADA INC p850
155 EAST BEAVER CREEK RD UNIT 24, RICHMOND HILL, ON, L4B 2N1
(905) 904-0612   *SIC* 4212

112792 CANADA INC p208
9924 RIVER RD, DELTA, BC, V4G 1B5
(604) 940-4208   *SIC* 4212

1266192 ONTARIO LTD p902
302 PATILLO RD SUITE 1, TECUMSEH, ON, N8N 2L9
(519) 727-4578   *SIC* 4212

1329481 ONTARIO INC p564
2930 FRENCH HILL RD, CUMBERLAND, ON, K4C 1K7
(613) 833-1917   *SIC* 4212

1456661 ONTARIO INCORPORATED p903
300 JOHN ST SUITE 87552, THORNHILL, ON, L3T 5W4
(905) 669-1103   *SIC* 4212

175784 CANADA INC p1295
585 RUE SAGARD, SAINT-BRUNO, QC, J3V 6C1
(450) 461-3310   *SIC* 4212

1840807 ALBERTA LTD p27
1208 3 ST SE UNIT 11, CALGARY, AB, T2G 2S9
(403) 460-1401   *SIC* 4212

2851262 MANITOBA INC p364
393 DAWSON RD N, WINNIPEG, MB, R2J 0S8
(204) 988-3278   *SIC* 4212

3580768 CANADA INC p736
6505 VIPOND DR, MISSISSAUGA, ON, L5T 1J9
(905) 670-6613   *SIC* 4212

3618358 CANADA INC p13
2680 61 AVE SE, CALGARY, AB, T2C 4V2
(403) 279-5208   *SIC* 4212

4211677 CANADA INC p1093
10315 CH COTE-DE-LIESSE, DORVAL, QC, H9P 1A6
(514) 636-8033   *SIC* 4212

4TRACKS LTD p356
374 EAGLE DR, ROSSER, MB, R0H 1E0
SIC 4212

591182 ONTARIO LIMITED p1019
2500 AIRPORT RD, WINDSOR, ON, N8W 5E7
(519) 966-8970   *SIC* 4212

662117 ONTARIO INC p807
17 SHANNON CRT, ORANGEVILLE, ON, L9W 5L8
(519) 941-2950   *SIC* 4212

7062001 CANADA LIMITED p371
1180 FIFE ST, WINNIPEG, MB, R2X 2N6
(204) 633-8161   *SIC* 4212

777603 ONTARIO INC p621
952 HUMPHREY RD, IGNACE, ON, P0T 1T0
(807) 934-6500   *SIC* 4212

9055-5749 QUEBEC INC p1110
1060 RUE ANDRE-LINE, GRANBY, QC, J2J 1J9
(450) 772-1112   *SIC* 4212

9064-4287 QUEBEC INC p1289
543 BOUL TEMISCAMINGUE, ROUYN-NORANDA, QC, J9X 7C8
(819) 762-2620   *SIC* 4212

9342-7490 QUEBEC INC p1101
3980 BOUL LEMAN, FABREVILLE, QC, H7E 1A1
(514) 209-1750   *SIC* 4212

A LA CARTE EXPRESS INC p1222
4700 RUE SAINT-AMBROISE BUREAU 44,

MONTREAL, QC, H4C 2C7
(514) 933-7000   *SIC 4212*
ACTIVE TRANSPORT INC   *p682*
245 BRONTE ST N, MILTON, ON, L9T 3N7
(905) 878-8167   *SIC 4212*
AERODROME INTERNATIONAL MAINTE-NANCE INC   *p593*
330 GUELPH ST UNIT 4, GEORGETOWN, ON, L7G 4B5
(905) 873-8777   *SIC 4212*
AGRIFOODS INTERNATIONAL COOPERATIVE LTD   *p95*
11671 160 ST NW, EDMONTON, AB, T5M 3Z3
(780) 962-5787   *SIC 4212*
ALL-CAN EXPRESS LTD   *p183*
2830 NORLAND AVE, BURNABY, BC, V5B 3A7
(604) 294-8631   *SIC 4212*
ALTERNATIVE PROCESSING SYSTEMS INC   *p790*
60 WINGOLD AVE, NORTH YORK, ON, M6B 1P5
(416) 256-2010   *SIC 4212*
APPS CARTAGE INC   *p737*
6495 TOMKEN RD, MISSISSAUGA, ON, L5T 2X7
(905) 451-2720   *SIC 4212*
ARGUS CARRIERS LTD   *p184*
3839 MYRTLE ST, BURNABY, BC, V5C 4G1
(604) 433-2066   *SIC 4212*
ARROW TRANSPORTATION SYSTEMS INC *p216*
1805 MISSION FLATS RD, KAMLOOPS, BC, V2C 1A9
(250) 374-6715   *SIC 4212*
AUTOLINX EXPRESS INC   *p494*
12673 COLERAINE DR, BOLTON, ON, L7E 3B5
(905) 951-1900   *SIC 4212*
B & B CONTRACTING LTD   *p278*
3077 188 ST SUITE 100, SURREY, BC, V3Z 9V5
(604) 539-7200   *SIC 4212*
BATTIST, GERALD TRUCKING LIMITED *p463*
2559 GRANTON RD SUITE 3, NEW GLASGOW, NS, B2H 5C6
(902) 396-1398   *SIC 4212*
BESSETTE ET BOUDREAU INC   *p1392*
680 RTE 143, VAL-JOLI, QC, J1S 0G6
(819) 845-7722   *SIC 4212*
BESTWAY CARTAGE LIMITED   *p737*
6505 VIPOND DR, MISSISSAUGA, ON, L5T 1J9
(905) 565-8877   *SIC 4212*
BRUCE R. SMITH LIMITED   *p880*
51 PARK RD, SIMCOE, ON, N3Y 4J9
(519) 426-0904   *SIC 4212*
BULK TRANSFER SYSTEMS INC   *p642*
11339 ALBION VAUGHAN RD, KLEINBURG, ON, L0J 1C0
(905) 893-2626   *SIC 4212*
CALIFORNIA L.I.N.E. INC   *p1297*
701 RANG SAINT-PIERRE N UNIT? 1, SAINT-CONSTANT, QC, J5A 0R2
(450) 632-9000   *SIC 4212*
CAM-SCOTT TRANSPORT LTD   *p1013*
1900 BOUNDARY RD, WHITBY, ON, L1N 8P8
(905) 438-9555   *SIC 4212*
CANADA CARTAGE DIVERSIFIED ULC *p734*
1115 CARDIFF BLVD, MISSISSAUGA, ON, L5S 1L8
(905) 564-2115   *SIC 4212*
CANADA CLEAN FUELS INC   *p782*
4425 CHESSWOOD DR, NORTH YORK, ON, M3J 2C2
(416) 521-9533   *SIC 4212*
CANADA DRAYAGE INC   *p1127*
4415 RUE FAIRWAY, LACHINE, QC, H8T 1B5
(514) 639-7878   *SIC 4212*

CARDINAL MOVERS KINGSTON INC *p633*
921 WOODBINE RD, KINGSTON, ON, K7P 2X4
(289) 395-0003   *SIC 4212*
CASSENS TRANSPORT LTD   *p661*
1237 GREEN VALLEY RD, LONDON, ON, N6N 1E4
(519) 690-2603   *SIC 4212*
CEVA LOGISTICS CANADA, ULC   *p499*
2600 NORTH PARK DR, BRAMPTON, ON, L6S 6E2
(905) 789-2904   *SIC 4212*
CHAPPLE FUELS LIMITED   *p542*
175 BOTHWELL ST, CHATHAM, ON, N7M 5J5
(519) 351-7194   *SIC 4212*
CHARGER LOGISTICS INC   *p501*
25 PRODUCTION RD, BRAMPTON, ON, L6T 4N8
(905) 793-3525   *SIC 4212*
CHARRON TRANSPORT LIMITED   *p542*
123 BYNG AVE, CHATHAM, ON, N7M 6C6
(519) 352-8970   *SIC 4212*
CHECKER CABS LTD   *p10*
316 MERIDIAN RD SE, CALGARY, AB, T2A 1X2
(403) 299-9999   *SIC 4212*
CHESTER CARTAGE & MOVERS LTD *p864*
1995 MARKHAM RD, SCARBOROUGH, ON, M1B 2W3
(416) 754-7716   *SIC 4212*
CHIEF HAULING CONTRACTORS INC *p14*
5654 55 ST SE, CALGARY, AB, T2C 3G9
(403) 215-4312   *SIC 4212*
COLDSTAR SOLUTIONS INC   *p340*
937 DUNFORD AVE UNIT 1, VICTORIA, BC, V9B 2S4
(250) 391-7425   *SIC 4212*
COLE CARRIERS CORP   *p609*
89 GLOW AVE, HAMILTON, ON, L8H 3V7
(905) 548-0979   *SIC 4212*
COLEMAN, DOUG TRUCKING LTD   *p648*
540 FIRST ST, LONDON, ON, N5V 1Z3
(519) 451-4349   *SIC 4212*
COONEY BULK SALES LIMITED   *p491*
77 BELLEVUE DR, BELLEVILLE, ON, K8N 4Z5
(613) 962-6666   *SIC 4212*
CULP, J. E. TRANSPORT LTD   *p489*
4815 MERRITT RD, BEAMSVILLE, ON, L0R 1B1
(905) 563-5055   *SIC 4212*
CURTIS CONSTRUCTION LTD   *p1417*
2930 PASQUA ST N, REGINA, SK, S4P 3H1
(306) 543-3944   *SIC 4212*
CWH DISTRIBUTION SERVICES INC *p583*
1245 MARTIN GROVE RD, ETOBICOKE, ON, M9W 4X2
(416) 674-5826   *SIC 4212*
DANACA TRANSPORT MONTREAL LTEE *p1141*
2555 RUE JEAN-DESY, LONGUEUIL, QC, J4G 1G6
(450) 463-0020   *SIC 4212*
DAVID CORDINGLEY TRANSPORT CORP *p515*
148 MOHAWK ST, BRANTFORD, ON, N3S 7G5
(519) 752-7810   *SIC 4212*
DAY & ROSS DEDICATED LOGISTICS *p721*
6711 MISSISSAUGA RD SUITE 410, MISSISSAUGA, ON, L5N 2W3
(905) 285-2355   *SIC 4212*
DCT CHAMBERS TRUCKING LTD   *p269*
4631 FARSTAD WAY RR 1, SKOOKUMCHUCK, BC, V0B 2E0
(250) 422-3535   *SIC 4212*
DCT CHAMBERS TRUCKING LTD   *p331*
600 WADDINGTON DR, VERNON, BC, V1T 8T6
(250) 549-2157   *SIC 4212*
DELLELCE CONSTRUCTION & EQUIPMENT LTD   *p900*
1375 REGENT ST SUITE 2, SUDBURY, ON,

P3E 6K4
SIC 4212
DELTA ROCK & SAND LTD   *p1436*
1910 SOUTH RAILWAY ST E, SWIFT CURRENT, SK, S9H 4G6
(306) 773-9808   *SIC 4212*
DHL EXPRESS (CANADA) LTD   *p502*
18 PARKSHORE DR, BRAMPTON, ON, L6T 0G7
(905) 861-3400   *SIC 4212*
DIRECT LIMITED PARTNERSHIP   *p15*
5555 69 AVE SE SUITE 121, CALGARY, AB, T2C 4Y7
(403) 296-0291   *SIC 4212*
DIRECT LIMITED PARTNERSHIP   *p734*
1115 CARDIFF BLVD, MISSISSAUGA, ON, L5S 1L8
(905) 564-2115   *SIC 4212*
DOLPHIN DELIVERY LTD   *p182*
4201 LOZELLS AVE, BURNABY, BC, V5A 2Z4
(604) 421-1115   *SIC 4212*
DRURY'S TRANSFER REG'D   *p418*
160 STEWART AVE, SUSSEX, NB, E4E 2G2
SIC 4212
DUNLOP STERLING TRUCK CENTRE LTD *p140*
4110 9 AVE N, LETHBRIDGE, AB, T1H 6L9
(403) 317-2450   *SIC 4212*
DYER ROAD LEASING LTD   *p562*
850 EDUCATION RD, CORNWALL, ON, K6H 6B8
(613) 932-8038   *SIC 4212*
ENTREPRISE SANITAIRE F.A. LTEE *p1231*
4799 RUE BERNARD-LEFEBVRE, MONTREAL, QC, H7C 0A5
(450) 661-5080   *SIC 4212*
ENTREPRISES DUPONT 1972 INC, LES *p1295*
601 RUE SAGARD, SAINT-BRUNO, QC, J3V 6C1
(450) 653-9362   *SIC 4212*
ENTREPRISES JULIEN BERNIER INC, LES *p1253*
46 CH DE LA SCIERIE RR 1, POINTE-LEBEL, QC, G0H 1N0
SIC 4212
EQUIPEMENT MAX-ATLAS INTERNATIONAL INC   *p1317*
371 CH DU GRAND-BERNIER N, SAINT-JEAN-SUR-RICHELIEU, QC, J3B 4S2
(450) 346-8848   *SIC 4212*
ERB TRANSPORT LIMITED   *p752*
290 HAMILTON RD, NEW HAMBURG, ON, N3A 1A2
(519) 662-2710   *SIC 4212*
ERB TRANSPORT LIMITED   *p998*
4 RIVERSIDE DR, TRENTON, ON, K8V 5P8
(613) 965-6633   *SIC 4212*
EXCEL TRANSPORTATION ALBERTA INC *p248*
333 ONGMAN RD, PRINCE GEORGE, BC, V2K 4K9
(250) 563-7356   *SIC 4212*
EXCEL TRANSPORTATION INC   *p248*
333 ONGMAN RD, PRINCE GEORGE, BC, V2K 4K9
(250) 563-7356   *SIC 4212*
FALCON MOTOR XPRESS LTD   *p498*
8 WALLABY WAY BLDG 8, BRAMPTON, ON, L6R 3C7
(866) 383-9100   *SIC 4212*
FAST TRUCKING SERVICE LTD   *p1405*
1 FAST LANE, CARNDUFF, SK, S0C 0S0
(306) 482-3244   *SIC 4212*
FCA CANADA INC   *p1019*
2410 WALKER RD, WINDSOR, ON, N8W 3P6
(519) 973-2000   *SIC 4212*
FEDEX FREIGHT CANADA, CORP   *p785*
1011 WILSON AVE, NORTH YORK, ON, M3K 1G1
(800) 463-3339   *SIC 4212*

FIRST TEAM TRANSPORT INC   *p739*
6141 VIPOND DR, MISSISSAUGA, ON, L5T 2B2
(416) 500-8541   *SIC 4212*
FLINT FLUID HAUL SERVICES LTD   *p7*
10 INDUSTRIAL RD, BROOKS, AB, T1R 1B5
(403) 793-8384   *SIC 4212*
FREGEAU, B. & FILS INC   *p1291*
402 RUE SAINT-DENIS, SAINT-ALEXANDRE-D'IBERVILLE, QC, J0J 1S0
(450) 346-3487   *SIC 4212*
G4S CASH SOLUTIONS (CANADA) LTD *p595*
1303 MICHAEL ST, GLOUCESTER, ON, K1B 3M9
SIC 4212
GANGSTER ENTERPRISES LTD   *p75*
600 CROWFOOT CRES NW SUITE 230, CALGARY, AB, T3G 0B4
(403) 241-9494   *SIC 4212*
GENERAL CARTAGE & EXPRESS COMPANY LIMITED   *p574*
48 NORTH QUEEN ST, ETOBICOKE, ON, M8Z 2C4
(416) 236-2460   *SIC 4212*
GEO A. HALL INC   *p1049*
8800 6E CROISSANT, ANJOU, QC, H1J 1A1
(514) 352-5550   *SIC 4212*
GIGG EXPRESS INC   *p695*
5355 CREEKBANK RD, MISSISSAUGA, ON, L4W 5L5
(905) 614-0544   *SIC 4212*
GLOVIS CANADA, INC   *p731*
5770 HURONTARIO ST SUITE 700, MISSISSAUGA, ON, L5R 3G5
(905) 361-1642   *SIC 4212*
GLS LOGISTICS SYSTEMS CANADA LTD *p1094*
10755 CH COTE-DE-LIESSE, DORVAL, QC, H9P 1A7
(888) 463-4266   *SIC 4212*
GO SMOOTH TRANSPORT LTD   *p723*
7 RIMINI MEWS, MISSISSAUGA, ON, L5N 4K1
(905) 696-7023   *SIC 4212*
GRIMSHAW TRUCKING LP   *p96*
11510 151 ST NW, EDMONTON, AB, T5M 3N6
(780) 414-2850   *SIC 4212*
GROUPE ROBERT INC   *p1065*
20 BOUL MARIE-VICTORIN, BOUCHERVILLE, QC, J4B 1V5
(514) 521-1011   *SIC 4212*
GUARDIAN VAN LINES LIMITED   *p844*
1051 TOY AVE, PICKERING, ON, L1W 3N9
(905) 686-0002   *SIC 4212*
GUNTER TRANSPORTATION LTD   *p1034*
445 SPRINGBANK AVE S, WOODSTOCK, ON, N0J 1E4
(519) 539-9222   *SIC 4212*
HI-WAY 13 TRANSPORT INC   *p78*
4621 39 ST, CAMROSE, AB, T4V 0Z4
(780) 672-1695   *SIC 4212*
HI-WAY 9 EXPRESS LTD   *p82*
711 ELGIN CLOSE, DRUMHELLER, AB, T0J 0Y0
(403) 823-4242   *SIC 4212*
HI-WAY 9 EXPRESS LTD   *p155*
4120 78 ST CRES SUITE 4120, RED DEER, AB, T4P 3E3
(403) 342-4266   *SIC 4212*
HUSBY FOREST PRODUCTS LTD   *p210*
6425 RIVER RD, DELTA, BC, V4K 5B9
(604) 940-1234   *SIC 4212*
HUTTERIAN BRETHREN OF WINNIFRED *p145*
GD LCD 1, MEDICINE HAT, AB, T1A 7E4
SIC 4212
HUTTON TRANSPORT LIMITED   *p643*
962979 19TH LINE, LAKESIDE, ON, N0M 2G0
(519) 349-2233   *SIC 4212*

INFORMATION COMMUNICATION SERVICES (ICS) INC   p585
96 DISCO RD, ETOBICOKE, ON, M9W 0A3
(416) 642-2477   *SIC* 4212

INFORMATION COMMUNICATION SERVICES (ICS) INC   p1094
81 AV LINDSAY, DORVAL, QC, H9P 2S6
(514) 636-9744   *SIC* 4212

INTERLINE MOTOR FREIGHT INC   p255
13562 MAYCREST WAY SUITE 5108, RICHMOND, BC, V6V 2J7
SIC 4212

IRL INTERNATIONAL TRUCK CENTRES LTD   p216
1495 IRON MASK RD, KAMLOOPS, BC, V1S 1C8
(250) 372-1445   *SIC* 4212

J.M.F. TRANSPORT (1992) LTEE   p1392
5609 CH DE L'AEROPORT, VALCOURT, QC, J0E 2L0
(450) 532-2285   *SIC* 4212

JADE TRANSPORT LTD   p366
963 DUGALD RD, WINNIPEG, MB, R2J 0G8
(204) 233-3566   *SIC* 4212

JMB CRUSHING SYSTEMS ULC   p6
660 RANGE RD 455 1 MILE N AND 1 MILE E, BONNYVILLE, AB, T9N 2H4
(780) 826-1774   *SIC* 4212

JUTRAS, PHIL & SON LIMITED   p899
2042 KINGSWAY, SUDBURY, ON, P3B 4J8
(705) 525-5560   *SIC* 4212

KIM-TAM LOGISTICS INC   p704
2360 DIXIE RD, MISSISSAUGA, ON, L4Y 1Z7
(905) 335-9195   *SIC* 4212

KING'S TRANSFER VAN LINES INC   p1211
287 RUE ELEANOR, MONTREAL, QC, H3C 2C1
(514) 932-2957   *SIC* 4212

KMC OILFIELD MAINTENANCE LTD   p168
4728 WATSON CRES, SWAN HILLS, AB, T0G 2C0
(780) 333-4300   *SIC* 4212

L. BILODEAU ET FILS LTEE   p1113
366 RUE SAINT-JEAN, HONFLEUR, QC, G0R 1N0
(418) 885-4495   *SIC* 4212

L. SIMARD TRANSPORT LIMITEE   p1128
3500 RUE FAIRWAY, LACHINE, QC, H8T 1B4
(514) 636-0852   *SIC* 4212

L. SIMARD TRANSPORT LIMITEE   p1128
1212 32E AV, LACHINE, QC, H8T 3K7
(514) 636-9411   *SIC* 4212

L.M.B. TRANSPORT INC   p540
209 PUTMAN INDUSTRIAL RD, CANNIFTON, ON, K0K 1K0
(613) 968-7524   *SIC* 4212

LAC LA BICHE TRANSPORT LTD   p137
66569 RR 143, ISLAY, AB, T0A 2C0
(780) 623-4711   *SIC* 4212

LAC LA BICHE TRANSPORT LTD   p138
555 TOWER RD, LAC LA BICHE, AB, T0A 2C0
(780) 623-4711   *SIC* 4212

LANDTRAN SYSTEMS INC   p109
9011 50 ST NW, EDMONTON, AB, T6B 2Y2
(780) 468-4300   *SIC* 4212

LAROCQUE, CHRISTIAN SERVICES LTEE   p403
5106 ROUTE 113, HAUT-LAMEQUE, NB, E8T 3L4
(506) 344-7077   *SIC* 4212

LIQUID CARGO LINES LIMITED   p713
452 SOUTHDOWN RD, MISSISSAUGA, ON, L5J 2Y4
SIC 4212

LUCKHART TRANSPORT LTD   p879
4049 PERTH COUNTY RD 135, SEBRINGVILLE, ON, N0K 1X0
(519) 393-6108   *SIC* 4212

MAMMOET CANADA EASTERN LTD   p849
7504 MCLEAN RD E, PUSLINCH, ON, N0B 2J0

(519) 740-0550   *SIC* 4212

MAMMOET CRANE INC   p124
12920 33 ST NE, EDMONTON, AB, T6S 1H6
(780) 449-0552   *SIC* 4212

MANITOULIN TRANSPORTATION   p251
9499 MILWAUKEE WAY, PRINCE GEORGE, BC, V2N 5T3
(250) 563-9138   *SIC* 4212

MANTEI'S TRANSPORT LTD   p17
8715 44 ST SE, CALGARY, AB, T2C 2P5
(403) 531-1600   *SIC* 4212

MARITIME-ONTARIO FREIGHT LINES LIMITED   p499
1 MARITIME ONTARIO BLVD SUITE 100, BRAMPTON, ON, L6S 6G4
(905) 792-6100   *SIC* 4212

MCCLAY GROUP LTD   p622
132 INGERSOLL ST S, INGERSOLL, ON, N5C 3K1
(519) 485-3088   *SIC* 4212

MERCHANT'S EXPRESS LIMITED   p244
19981 RICHARDSON RD, PITT MEADOWS, BC, V3Y 1Z1
(604) 460-1971   *SIC* 4212

MIDLAND TRANSPORT LIMITED   p447
31 SIMMONDS DR, DARTMOUTH, NS, B3B 1R4
(902) 494-5555   *SIC* 4212

MIDLAND TRANSPORT LIMITED   p504
102 GLIDDEN RD, BRAMPTON, ON, L6T 5N4
(905) 456-5555   *SIC* 4212

MIDLAND TRANSPORT LIMITED   p1094
1560 BOUL HYMUS, DORVAL, QC, H9P 1J6
(888) 643-5263   *SIC* 4212

MINTO TRUCK CENTRE LIMITED   p618
5196 HWY 23 N, HARRISTON, ON, N0G 2P0
(519) 510-2120   *SIC* 4212

MITRI, S HAULAGE LTD   p741
6855 INVADER CRES, MISSISSAUGA, ON, L5T 2B7
(905) 564-1200   *SIC* 4212

MULTI RECYCLAGE S.D. INC   p1232
3030 MONTEE SAINT-FRANCOIS, MONTREAL, QC, H7E 4P2
(450) 625-9191   *SIC* 4212

MUSKOKA DELIVERY SERVICES INC   p497
581 ECCLESTONE DR, BRACEBRIDGE, ON, P1L 1W2
(705) 645-1258   *SIC* 4212

NCSG CRANE & HEAVY HAUL TRANS TECH INC   p1
28765 ACHESON RD, ACHESON, AB, T7X 6A8
(780) 960-6300   *SIC* 4212

NEW HORIZONS CAR & TRUCK RENTALS LTD   p795
720 ARROW RD, NORTH YORK, ON, M9M 2M1
(416) 744-0123   *SIC* 4212

OLYMEL S.E.C.   p1300
57 125 RTE, SAINT-ESPRIT, QC, J0K 2L0
(450) 839-7258   *SIC* 4212

OTTAWAY MOTOR EXPRESS (2010) INC   p1035
520 BEARDS LANE UNIT B, WOODSTOCK, ON, N4S 7W3
(519) 602-3026   *SIC* 4212

P. & R. REPAIRS LTD   p267
2005 KEATING CROSS RD, SAANICHTON, BC, V8M 2A5
(250) 652-9139   *SIC* 4212

PAPIERS SOLIDERR INC, LES   p1045
1025 RUE DES PINS O, ALMA, QC, G8B 7V7
(418) 668-1234   *SIC* 4212

PARIAN LOGISTICS INC   p391
530 GAMBLE PL, WINNIPEG, MB, R3T 1N6
(204) 885-4200   *SIC* 4212

PARSONS TRUCKING LIMITED   p427

1 MAIN ST, SOUTHERN HARBOUR PB, NL, A0B 3H0
(709) 463-8540   *SIC* 4212

PATRIK'S WATER HAULING LTD   p149
504 19 AVE, NISKU, AB, T9E 7W1
(780) 955-8878   *SIC* 4212

PETRELLA TRANSPORT LIMITED   p531
12404 AIRPORT RD, CALEDON, ON, L7C 2W1
(905) 951-0584   *SIC* 4212

PRIDE GROUP LOGISTICS LTD   p742
6050 DIXIE RD, MISSISSAUGA, ON, L5T 1A6
(905) 564-7458   *SIC* 4212

PRUDENTIAL TRANSPORTATION LTDp277
8138 128 ST UNIT 239, SURREY, BC, V3W 1R1
(604) 543-2147   *SIC* 4212

QUICK AS A WINK COURIER SERVICE LTD   p261
9300 VAN HORNE WAY, RICHMOND, BC, V6X 1W3
(604) 276-8686   *SIC* 4212

RIG LOGISTICS INC   p159
10 WRANGLER PL UNIT 4, ROCKY VIEW COUNTY, AB, T1X 0L7
(403) 285-1111   *SIC* 4212

ROADSTAR TRANSPORT COMPANY LTD   p207
10064 RIVER RD, DELTA, BC, V4C 2R3
(604) 882-7623   *SIC* 4212

ROGUE TRANSPORTATION SERVICES INC   p745
255 COURTNEYPARK DR W UNIT 102, MISSISSAUGA, ON, L5W 0A5
(905) 362-9401   *SIC* 4212

ROSEDALE TRANSPORT LIMITED   p742
6845 INVADER CRES, MISSISSAUGA, ON, L5T 2B7
(905) 670-0057   *SIC* 4212

ROSENAU TRANSPORT LTD   p159
234180 WRANGLER RD, ROCKY VIEW COUNTY, AB, T1X 0K2
(403) 279-4800   *SIC* 4212

ROYAL CITY TAXI LTD   p237
436 ROUSSEAU ST, NEW WESTMINSTER, BC, V3L 3R3
(604) 526-6666   *SIC* 4212

RSB LOGISTIC INC   p1432
219 CARDINAL CRES, SASKATOON, SK, S7L 7K8
(306) 242-8300   *SIC* 4212

SANIMAX EEI INC   p1161
9900 BOUL MAURICE-DUPLESSIS, MONTREAL, QC, H1C 1G1
(514) 648-3000   *SIC* 4212

SASKATOON HOT SHOT TRANSPORTER SERVICES (1995) LTD   p1432
2342B HANSELMAN AVE, SASKATOON, SK, S7L 5Z3
(306) 653-5255   *SIC* 4212

SCAMP INDUSTRIES LTD   p230
26988 GLOUCESTER WAY, LANGLEY, BC, V4W 3Y5
(604) 856-8211   *SIC* 4212

SEABOARD LIQUID CARRIERS LIMITED   p448
721 WILKINSON AVE, DARTMOUTH, NS, B3B 0H4
(902) 468-4447   *SIC* 4212

SKYLARK LOGISTICS INC   p537
7295 MASON RD, CAMBRIDGE, ON, N3C 2V4
(519) 821-7999   *SIC* 4212

SLH TRANSPORT INC   p97
14525 112 AVE NW, EDMONTON, AB, T5M 2V5
(780) 451-7543   *SIC* 4212

SOLUTION MORNEAU INC   p1050
9601 BOUL DES SCIENCES, ANJOU, QC, H1J 0A6
(514) 325-2727   *SIC* 4212

SPEEDY TRANSPORT GROUP INC   p510
265 RUTHERFORD RD S, BRAMPTON,

ON, L6W 1V9
(416) 510-2035   *SIC* 4212

SPILAK TANK TRUCK SERVICE LTD   p164
911 6 AVE NW, SLAVE LAKE, AB, T0G 2A1
(780) 849-2757   *SIC* 4212

STEVE'S LIVESTOCK TRANSPORTATION (BLUMENORT) LTD   p346
214 CENTER AVE SS 10, BLUMENORT, MB, R0A 0C1
(204) 326-6380   *SIC* 4212

SUTCO CONTRACTING LTD   p267
8561 HWY 6, SALMO, BC, V0G 1Z0
(250) 357-2612   *SIC* 4212

TANDET MANAGEMENT INC   p880
2510 DAVIS DR, SHARON, ON, L0G 1V0
(905) 953-5457   *SIC* 4212

TEDI TRANSLOGIC EXPRESS DEDICATED INC   p510
241 CLARENCE ST UNIT 21-24, BRAMPTON, ON, L6W 4P2
(905) 451-3033   *SIC* 4212

TOPAC ENTERPRISES INC   p495
9 SIMPSON RD, BOLTON, ON, L7E 1E4
(905) 857-2209   *SIC* 4212

TRAILERMASTER FREIGHT CARRIERS LTD   p576
34 CANMOTOR AVE, ETOBICOKE, ON, M8Z 4E5
(416) 252-7725   *SIC* 4212

TRANSBOIS (CANADA) LTEE   p1349
631 RUE PRINCIPALE N, SAINT-PAMPHILE, QC, G0R 3X0
(418) 356-3371   *SIC* 4212

TRANSPORT A. LABERGE ET FILS INC   p1158
255 104 RTE, MONT-SAINT-GREGOIRE, QC, J0J 1N0
(450) 347-4336   *SIC* 4212

TRANSPORT BOURASSA INC   p1318
800 RUE DE DIJON, SAINT-JEAN-SUR-RICHELIEU, QC, J3B 8G3
(450) 346-5313   *SIC* 4212

TRANSPORT BOURRET INC   p1099
375 BOUL LEMIRE, DRUMMONDVILLE, QC, J2C 0C6
(819) 477-2202   *SIC* 4212

TRANSPORT DEMARK INC   p1132
9235 RUE BOIVIN, LASALLE, QC, H8R 2E8
(514) 365-5666   *SIC* 4212

TRANSPORT ECOLE-BEC MONTREAL (EBM) INC   p1336
8835 BOUL HENRI-BOURASSA O, SAINT-LAURENT, QC, H4S 1P7
(514) 595-5609   *SIC* 4212

TRANSPORT EXPRESS MINIMAX INC p562
605 EDUCATION RD, CORNWALL, ON, K6H 6C7
(613) 936-0660   *SIC* 4212

TRANSPORT JACQUES AUGER INC p1137
860 RUE ARCHIMEDE, LEVIS, QC, G6V 7M5
(418) 835-9266   *SIC* 4212

TRANSPORT JACQUES AUGER INC p1248
12305 BOUL METROPOLITAIN E, POINTE-AUX-TREMBLES, QC, H1B 5R3
(514) 493-3835   *SIC* 4212

TRANSPORT LAURENTIEN LTEE   p1060
926 RUE JACQUES PASCHINI BUREAU 300, BOIS-DES-FILION, QC, J6Z 4W4
(450) 628-2372   *SIC* 4212

TRANSPORT LEMIEUX, HERVE (1975) INC   p1336
6500 CH SAINT-FRANCOIS, SAINT-LAURENT, QC, H4S 1B7
(514) 337-2203   *SIC* 4212

TRANSPORT TFI 22 S.E.C.   p1337
8801 RTE TRANSCANADIENNE BUREAU 500, SAINT-LAURENT, QC, H4S 1Z6
(514) 331-4000   *SIC* 4212

TRANSPORT TFI 23 S.E.C.   p1046
200 RUE DES ROUTIERS, AMOS, QC, J9T 3A6
(819) 727-1304   *SIC* 4212

TRANSPORT TRANSBO INC   p1353

170 RUE SAINT-EDOUARD, SAINT-SIMON-DE-BAGOT, QC, J0H 1Y0
(450) 798-2155   *SIC 4212*

TRANSPORT YN.-GONTHIER INC   *p1139*
2170 3E RUE, LEVIS, QC, G6W 6V4
(418) 839-7311   *SIC 4212*

TRANSPORTS DELSON LTEE, LES   *p1089*
121 RUE PRINCIPALE N, DELSON, QC, J5B 1Z2
(450) 632-2960   *SIC 4212*

TRANSPORTS INTER-NORD INC, LES
p1319
455 BOUL LAJEUNESSE O, SAINT-JEROME, QC, J5L 2P7
(450) 438-7133   *SIC 4212*

TRANSPORTS LACOMBE INC, LES   *p1165*
5644 RUE HOCHELAGA, MONTREAL, QC, H1N 3L7
(514) 256-0050   *SIC 4212*

TRANSPORTS M. CHARETTE INC   *p1115*
635 RUE NAZAIRE-LAURIN, JOLIETTE, QC, J6E 0L6
(450) 760-9600   *SIC 4212*

TRANSPORTS R.M.T. INC   *p1283*
400 BOUL RICHELIEU, RICHELIEU, QC, J3L 3R8
(450) 658-1795   *SIC 4212*

TRIANGLE FREIGHT SERVICES LTD   *p701*
5355 CREEKBANK RD, MISSISSAUGA, ON, L4W 5L5
(905) 624-1614   *SIC 4212*

TUC'S CONTRACTING LTD   *p129*
283 MACALPINE CRES SUITE C, FORT MCMURRAY, AB, T9H 4Y4
(780) 743-8110   *SIC 4212*

ULCH TRANSPORT LIMITED   *p889*
100 SOUTH SERVICE RD, ST MARYS, ON, N4X 1A9
(519) 349-2340   *SIC 4212*

UNITED PARCEL SERVICE CANADA LTD
p407
77 FOUNDRY ST, MONCTON, NB, E1C 5H7
(506) 877-6657   *SIC 4212*

UNITED PARCEL SERVICE CANADA LTD
p560
2900 STEELES AVE W, CONCORD, ON, L4K 3S2
(800) 742-5877   *SIC 4212*

UNITED PARCEL SERVICE CANADA LTD
p736
1930 DERRY RD E, MISSISSAUGA, ON, L5S 1E2
(800) 742-5877   *SIC 4212*

UNITED PARCEL SERVICE CANADA LTD
p1060
71 RUE OMER-DESERRES, BLAINVILLE, QC, J7C 5N3
(450) 979-9390   *SIC 4212*

UNITED VAN LINES (CANADA) LTD   *p743*
7229 PACIFIC CIR, MISSISSAUGA, ON, L5T 1S9
(905) 564-6400   *SIC 4212*

UPS SCS INC   *p525*
4156 MAINWAY, BURLINGTON, ON, L7L 0A7
(905) 315-5500   *SIC 4212*

URGEL CHARETTE TRANSPORT LIMITEE
p1360
555 BOUL SAINT-JEAN-BAPTISTE E RR 3, SAINTE-MARTINE, QC, J0S 1V0
(450) 691-5151   *SIC 4212*

VACUUM TRUCKS OF CANADA ULC   *p495*
180 HEALEY RD, BOLTON, ON, L7E 5B1
(905) 857-7474   *SIC 4212*

VAIL, MIKE TRUCKING LTD   *p13*
4531 32 ST SE, CALGARY, AB, T2B 3P8
(403) 272-5487   *SIC 4212*

VIP SITTERS INC   *p943*
22 LEADER LANE SUITE 540, TORONTO, ON, M5E 0B2
(416) 999-6666   *SIC 4212*

VOLUME TANK TRANSPORT INC   *p702*
1230 SHAWSON DR, MISSISSAUGA, ON,

L4W 1C3
(905) 670-7090   *SIC 4212*

WAL-MART CANADA CORP   *p562*
6227 BOUNDARY RD, CORNWALL, ON, K6H 5R5
(613) 932-7879   *SIC 4212*

WASTE MANAGEMENT OF CANADA CORPORATION   *p1363*
2535 1RE RUE, SAINTE-SOPHIE, QC, J5J 2R7
(450) 431-2313   *SIC 4212*

WESTCAN BULK TRANSPORT LTD   *p124*
12110 17 ST NE, EDMONTON, AB, T6S 1A5
(780) 472-6951   *SIC 4212*

WHITE GLOVE TRANSPORTATION SYSTEMS LTD   *p744*
215 COURTNEYPARK DR E, MISSISSAUGA, ON, L5T 2T6
(905) 565-1053   *SIC 4212*

WHITE GLOVE TRANSPORTATION SYSTEMS LTD   *p744*
6141 VIPOND DR, MISSISSAUGA, ON, L5T 2B2
(905) 565-1053   *SIC 4212*

WILF BRANDT TRUCKING LTD   *p171*
48176 HWY 770, WARBURG, AB, T0C 2T0
(780) 848-7668   *SIC 4212*

WILSON'S TRUCK LINES INC   *p580*
111 THE WEST MALL, ETOBICOKE, ON, M9C 1C1
(416) 621-9020   *SIC 4212*

SIC 4213 Trucking, except local

1175648 ONTARIO LIMITED   *p736*
1190 MEYERSIDE DR, MISSISSAUGA, ON, L5T 1R7
(905) 564-8784   *SIC 4213*

1957444 ONTARIO INC   *p498*
40 MARBLESEED CRES, BRAMPTON, ON, L6R 2J7
(905) 795-1101   *SIC 4213*

2350936 ONTARIO INC   *p691*
1080 FEWSTER DR UNIT 10, MISSISSAUGA, ON, L4W 2T2
(905) 282-6000   *SIC 4213*

2635-8762 QUEBEC INC   *p1129*
922 GRANDE COTE O, LANORAIE, QC, J0K 1E0
(450) 887-7446   *SIC 4213*

2701545 CANADA INC   *p1125*
300 RUE DE LA BERGE-DU-CANAL BUREAU 312, LACHINE, QC, H8R 1H3
(514) 367-0000   *SIC 4213*

3394603 CANADA INC   *p531*
34 PERDUE CRT, CALEDON, ON, L7C 3M6
(905) 840-4300   *SIC 4213*

374872 ONTARIO INC   *p532*
21 INDUSTRIAL DR SUITE 6, CALEDONIA, ON, N3W 1H8
(905) 765-5424   *SIC 4213*

410648 ONTARIO LIMITED   *p879*
225 HURON RD, SEBRINGVILLE, ON, N0K 1X0
(519) 393-6194   *SIC 4213*

425480 B.C. LTD   *p224*
9440 202 ST UNIT 117, LANGLEY, BC, V1M 4A6
(604) 882-2550   *SIC 4213*

4345240 CANADA INC   *p1076*
147 RUE PRINCIPALE, CHATEAUGUAY, QC, J6K 1G2
(450) 691-1654   *SIC 4213*

441861 ONTARIO LTD   *p479*
8035 LINE 2 W, ARTHUR, ON, N0G 1A0
(519) 848-2575   *SIC 4213*

452056 ONTARIO LTD   *p618*
3191 COUNTY ROAD 11, HARROW, ON, N0R 1G0
(519) 738-6885   *SIC 4213*

553562 ONTARIO LIMITED   *p640*
7 GRAND AVE, KITCHENER, ON, N2K 1B2

(519) 744-3597   *SIC 4213*

601861 SASKATCHEWAN LTD   *p1425*
855 60TH ST E, SASKATOON, SK, S7K 5Z7
(306) 934-3383   *SIC 4213*

615315 SASKATCHEWAN LTD   *p1425*
875 58TH ST E, SASKATOON, SK, S7K 6X5
(306) 653-5400   *SIC 4213*

618717 ONTARIO INC   *p762*
348 BIRCHS RD, NORTH BAY, ON, P1A 4A9
(705) 476-4411   *SIC 4213*

621189 ONTARIO INC   *p485*
85 ELLIS DR, BARRIE, ON, L4N 8Z3
(705) 739-1551   *SIC 4213*

669779 ONTARIO LTD   *p571*
355 HORNER AVE SUITE 416, ETOBICOKE, ON, M8W 1Z7
(416) 754-0999   *SIC 4213*

682439 ONTARIO INC   *p762*
348 BIRCHS RD SUITE 824, NORTH BAY, ON, P1A 4A9
(705) 476-0444   *SIC 4213*

689803 ALBERTA LTD   *p1*
25245 111 AVE, ACHESON, AB, T7X 6C8
(780) 452-9414   *SIC 4213*

7013990 CANADA INC   *p602*
367 SPEEDVALE AVE W, GUELPH, ON, N1H 1C7
(519) 265-5161   *SIC 4213*

7853807 CANADA INC   *p1348*
3126 RUE BERNARD-PILON, SAINT-MATHIEU-DE-BELOEIL, QC, J3G 4S5
(450) 467-7352   *SIC 4213*

882819 ONTARIO LTD   *p1021*
3049 DEVON DR, WINDSOR, ON, N8X 4L3
(519) 250-8008   *SIC 4213*

9007-6720 QUEBEC INC   *p1116*
3495 RUE DE LA RECHERCHE, JONQUIERE, QC, G7X 0H5
(418) 695-4181   *SIC 4213*

9048-9493 QUEBEC INC   *p1294*
27 RUE INDUSTRIELLE, SAINT-BENOIT-LABRE, QC, G0M 1P0
(418) 228-6979   *SIC 4213*

9052-9025 QUEBEC INC   *p1337*
700 MONTEE DE LIESSE, SAINT-LAURENT, QC, H4T 1N8
(514) 631-6669   *SIC 4213*

9138-7472 QUEBEC INC   *p1381*
1060 RUE ARMAND-BOMBARDIER, TERREBONNE, QC, J6Y 1R9
(450) 477-9996   *SIC 4213*

9327-0197 QUEBEC INC   *p1247*
12321 BOUL METROPOLITAIN E, POINTE-AUX-TREMBLES, QC, H1B 5R3
(514) 645-7184   *SIC 4213*

9327-0197 QUEBEC INC   *p1331*
8801 RTE TRANSCANADIENNE BUREAU 500, SAINT-LAURENT, QC, H4S 1Z6
(514) 331-4000   *SIC 4213*

A. BEAUMONT TRANSPORT INC   *p1292*
280 RTE DE FOSSAMBAULT, SAINT-AUGUSTIN-DE-DESMAURES, QC, G3A 2P9
(418) 878-4888   *SIC 4213*

ABBEYWOOD MOVING & STORAGE INC
p878
480 FINCHDENE SQ, SCARBOROUGH, ON, M1X 1C2
(416) 292-1107   *SIC 4213*

ACCORD TRANSPORTATION LTD   *p271*
17665 66A AVE SUITE 801, SURREY, BC, V3S 2A7
(604) 575-7500   *SIC 4213*

ACTTON TRANSPORT LTD   *p271*
19395 LANGLEY BYPASS, SURREY, BC, V3S 6K1
(604) 533-4423   *SIC 4213*

AGGRESSIVE TRANSPORT LTD   *p229*
5111 272 ST, LANGLEY, BC, V4W 3Z2
(604) 626-4511   *SIC 4213*

ALLIED SYSTEMS (CANADA) COMPANY
p498
2000 WILLIAMS PKY, BRAMPTON, ON, L6S 6B3

(905) 458-0900   *SIC 4213*

ALLIED SYSTEMS (CANADA) COMPANY
p662
6151 COLONEL TALBOT RD, LONDON, ON, N6P 1J2
SIC 4213

ALLIED SYSTEMS (CANADA) COMPANY
p1019
1790 PROVINCIAL RD, WINDSOR, ON, N8W 5W3
SIC 4213

ALLIED SYSTEMS (CANADA) COMPANY
p1083
5901 AV WESTMINSTER, COTE SAINT-LUC, QC, H4W 2J9
SIC 4213

AMAN ENTERPRISES 1989 LTD   *p224*
20255 102 AVE, LANGLEY, BC, V1M 4B4
(604) 513-0462   *SIC 4213*

ANDERSON, DON HAULAGE LIMITED *p598*
36 GORDON COLLINS DR, GORMLEY, ON, L0H 1G0
(416) 798-7737   *SIC 4213*

ANDY TRANSPORT INC   *p1364*
4225 BOUL HEBERT, SALABERRY-DE-VALLEYFIELD, QC, J6S 6J2
(514) 667-8500   *SIC 4213*

APEX MOTOR EXPRESS LTD   *p498*
60 WARD RD, BRAMPTON, ON, L6S 4L5
(905) 789-5000   *SIC 4213*

APPLIED SYSTEMS CANADA ULC   *p719*
6865 CENTURY AVENUE SUITE 3000, MISSISSAUGA, ON, L5N 2E2
(905) 363-6500   *SIC 4213*

ARMOUR TRANSPORT INC   *p408*
689 EDINBURGH DR, MONCTON, NB, E1E 2L4
(506) 857-0205   *SIC 4213*

ARMOUR TRANSPORT INC   *p445*
80 GUILDFORD AVE, DARTMOUTH, NS, B3B 0G3
(902) 468-8855   *SIC 4213*

ARNOLD BROS. TRANSPORT LTD   *p365*
739 LAGIMODIERE BLVD, WINNIPEG, MB, R2J 0T8
(204) 257-6666   *SIC 4213*

ARNONE TRANSPORT LIMITED   *p907*
300 WATER ST S, THUNDER BAY, ON, P7B 6P6
(807) 345-1478   *SIC 4213*

ARROW TRANSPORTATION SYSTEMS INC
p302
999 HASTINGS ST W SUITE 1300, VANCOUVER, BC, V6C 2W2
(604) 324-1333   *SIC 4213*

ATLANTICA DIVERSIFIED TRANSPORTATION SYSTEMS   *p421*
5 MYERS AVE, CLARENVILLE, NL, A5A 1T5
(709) 466-7052   *SIC 4213*

ATLANTIS TRANSPORTATION SERVICES INC   *p728*
6500 SILVER DART DR, MISSISSAUGA, ON, L5P 1C4
(905) 672-5171   *SIC 4213*

AYR MOTOR EXPRESS INC   *p419*
46 POPLAR ST, WOODSTOCK, NB, E7M 4G2
(506) 325-2205   *SIC 4213*

B.S.D. LOGISTICS INC   *p508*
350 RUTHERFORD RD S SUITE 202, BRAMPTON, ON, L6W 3M2
(289) 801-4045   *SIC 4213*

BANDSTRA TRANSPORTATION SYSTEMS LTD   *p269*
3394 HWY 16 E, SMITHERS, BC, V0J 2N0
(250) 847-2057   *SIC 4213*

BARTEL BULK FREIGHT INC   *p352*
405 STAMPEDE DR, MORRIS, MB, R0G 1K0
(204) 746-2053   *SIC 4213*

BAYRIDGE TRANSPORT LTD   *p259*
9900 RIVER DR, RICHMOND, BC, V6X 3S3
(604) 278-6622   *SIC 4213*

BERRY & SMITH TRUCKING LTD   p243
301 WARREN AVE E, PENTICTON, BC,
V2A 3M1
(250) 492-4042   *SIC* 4213
BIG FREIGHT SYSTEMS INC   p371
10 HUTCHINGS ST, WINNIPEG, MB, R2X
2X1
(204) 772-3434   *SIC* 4213
BISON TRANSPORT INC   p162
80 LIBERTY RD, SHERWOOD PARK, AB,
T8H 2J6
(780) 416-7736   *SIC* 4213
BISON TRANSPORT INC   p383
1001 SHERWIN RD, WINNIPEG, MB, R3H
0T8
(204) 833-0000   *SIC* 4213
BISON TRANSPORT INC   p692
5850 SHAWSON DR, MISSISSAUGA, ON,
L4W 3W5
(905) 364-4401   *SIC* 4213
BLM GROUP INC, THE   p642
120 MCBRINE DR, KITCHENER, ON, N2R
1E7
(519) 748-9880   *SIC* 4213
BLUE LINE DISTRIBUTION LIMITED   p683
8175 LAWSON RD, MILTON, ON, L9T 5E5
(905) 875-4630   *SIC* 4213
BOUTIN, V. EXPRESS INC   p1246
1397 RUE SAVOIE, PLESSISVILLE, QC,
G6L 1J8
(819) 362-7333   *SIC* 4213
BRANDT, PAUL TRUCKING LTD   p352
226 STATION ST S, MORRIS, MB, R0G 1K0
(204) 746-2555   *SIC* 4213
BRASSEUR TRANSPORT INC   p1123
1250 RUE INDUSTRIELLE, LA PRAIRIE,
QC, J5R 5G4
(450) 444-7079   *SIC* 4213
BRIAN KURTZ TRUCKING LTD   p518
6960 SPEEDVALE RD W RR 2, BRESLAU,
ON, N0B 1M0
(519) 836-5821   *SIC* 4213
**BROOKVILLE CARRIERS VAN LIMITED
PARTNERSHIP**   p416
65 ALLOY DR, SAINT JOHN, NB, E2M 7S9
(506) 633-7555   *SIC* 4213
BROWN, DAVID UNITED LTD   p441
761 CAMBRIDGE RD, CAMBRIDGE, NS,
B0P 1G0
(902) 538-8088   *SIC* 4213
BSL PROPERTY GROUP INC   p45
335 8 AVE SW, CALGARY, AB, T2P 1C9
(403) 253-1100   *SIC* 4213
BUCKHAM TRANSPORT LIMITED   p484
HWY 28, BAILIEBORO, ON, K0L 1B0
(705) 939-6311   *SIC* 4213
BUCKLEY CARTAGE LIMITED   p692
1905 SHAWSON DR, MISSISSAUGA, ON,
L4W 1T9
(905) 564-3211   *SIC* 4213
BULK CARRIERS (P.E.I) LIMITED   p1041
779 BANNOCKBURN RD, CORNWALL, PE,
C0A 1H0
(902) 675-2600   *SIC* 4213
**BURGESS TRANSPORTATION SERVICES
INC**   p411
20 SMITH ST, PETITCODIAC, NB, E4Z 4W1
(506) 756-2250   *SIC* 4213
C.A.T. INC   p1088
4 RUE DU TRANSPORT, COTEAU-DU-
LAC, QC, J0P 1B0
(450) 763-6363   *SIC* 4213
CALNASH TRUCKING LTD   p138
1 PARKER RD, LAC LA BICHE, AB, T0A
2C0
SIC 4213
CAN-AM WEST CARRIERS INC   p174
400 RIVERSIDE RD, ABBOTSFORD, BC,
V2S 7M4
(604) 857-1375   *SIC* 4213
**CANADA CARTAGE SYSTEM LIMITED
PARTNERSHIP**   p14
4700 102 AVE SE, CALGARY, AB, T2C 2X8
(403) 296-0290   *SIC* 4213

CANADIAN LYNDEN TRANSPORT LTD p1
27340 ACHESON RD, ACHESON, AB, T7X
6B1
(780) 960-9444   *SIC* 4213
**CANAMEX-CARBRA   TRANSPORTATION
SERVICES INC**   p685
7415 TORBRAM RD, MISSISSAUGA, ON,
L4T 1G8
(905) 458-5363   *SIC* 4213
CANEDA TRANSPORT LTD   p12
4330 46 AVE SE, CALGARY, AB, T2B 3N7
(403) 236-7900   *SIC* 4213
CANPAR TRANSPORT L.P.   p570
205 NEW TORONTO ST, ETOBICOKE, ON,
M8V 0A1
(416) 869-1332   *SIC* 4213
CANXPRESS LTD   p70
11400 27 ST SE, CALGARY, AB, T2Z 3R6
(403) 236-9088   *SIC* 4213
CARAVAN LOGISTICS INC   p803
2284 WYECROFT RD, OAKVILLE, ON, L6L
6M1
(905) 338-5885   *SIC* 4213
CASCADES TRANSPORT INC   p1117
2 RUE PARENTEAU, KINGSEY FALLS, QC,
J0A 1B0
(819) 363-5800   *SIC* 4213
**CASSIDY'S TRANSFER & STORAGE LIM-
ITED**   p838
1001 MCKAY ST, PEMBROKE, ON, K8A
6X7
(613) 735-6881   *SIC* 4213
CHALLENGER INVESTMENTS INC   p538
300 MAPLE GROVE RD, CAMBRIDGE, ON,
N3E 1B7
(519) 653-6226   *SIC* 4213
CHALLENGER MOTOR FREIGHT INC p538
300 MAPLE GROVE RD, CAMBRIDGE, ON,
N3E 1B7
(519) 653-6226   *SIC* 4213
CHALLENGER MOTOR FREIGHT INCp1093
2770 AV ANDRE, DORVAL, QC, H9P 1K6
(514) 684-2025   *SIC* 4213
CHANTLER TRANSPORT INC   p622
3235 CLIFFORD CRT, INNISFIL, ON, L9S
3V8
(705) 431-4022   *SIC* 4213
CHEBOGUE FISHERIES LIMITED   p471
98 CLIFF ST, YARMOUTH, NS, B5A 3J9
(902) 742-9157   *SIC* 4213
CHOHAN CARRIERS LTD   p281
15760 110 AVE, SURREY, BC, V4N 4Z1
(604) 888-1855   *SIC* 4213
CLARKE TRANSPORT INC   p550
751 BOWES RD SUITE 2, CONCORD, ON,
L4K 5C9
(416) 665-5585   *SIC* 4213
**CLASSIC FREIGHT SYSTEMS (2011) LIM-
ITED**   p445
50 JOSEPH ZATZMAN DR, DARTMOUTH,
NS, B3B 1N8
(902) 481-3701   *SIC* 4213
COASTAL PACIFIC XPRESS INC   p271
5355 152 ST SUITE 105, SURREY, BC, V3S
5A5
(604) 575-4200   *SIC* 4213
COHEN, JERRY FORWARDERS LTD p1127
5203 RUE FAIRWAY, LACHINE, QC, H8T
3K8
(514) 635-1033   *SIC* 4213
**COMMERCIAL TRANSPORT (NORTHERN)
LIMITED**   p647
70 MAGILL ST, LIVELY, ON, P3Y 1K7
(705) 692-4727   *SIC* 4213
COMOX VALLEY DISTRIBUTION LTD p233
140 TENTH ST, NANAIMO, BC, V9R 6Z5
(250) 754-7773   *SIC* 4213
CONCORD CONCRETE GROUP INC   p551
125 EDILCAN DR, CONCORD, ON, L4K
3S6
(905) 738-7979   *SIC* 4213
CONCORD TRANSPORTATION INC   p583
96 DISCO RD, ETOBICOKE, ON, M9W 0A3
(416) 679-7400   *SIC* 4213

CONNORS TRANSFER LIMITED   p466
39 CONNORS LN, STELLARTON, NS, B0K
0A2
(902) 752-1142   *SIC* 4213
CONSOLIDATED FASTFRATE INC   p1027
9701 HIGHWAY 50, WOODBRIDGE, ON,
L4H 2G4
(905) 893-2600   *SIC* 4213
CONTINENTAL CARTAGE INC   p1
26215 TWP RD 531A UNIT 412, ACHE-
SON, AB, T7X 5A4
(780) 452-9414   *SIC* 4213
CONTRANS FLATBED GROUP GP INCp607
80 THIRD LINE RD, HAGERSVILLE, ON,
N0A 1H0
(905) 768-3375   *SIC* 4213
COONEY TRANSPORT LTD   p491
77 BELLEVUE DR, BELLEVILLE, ON, K8N
4Z5
(613) 962-6666   *SIC* 4213
**COOPERATIVE DE TRANSPORT MAR-
ITIME AERIEN ASSOCIATION COOPERA-
TIVE**   p1073
435 CH AVILA-ARSENEAU, CAP-AUX-
MEULES, QC, G4T 1J3
(418) 986-6600   *SIC* 4213
CORPORATION   TRANSPORT   VITESSE
p1127
1111 46E AV, LACHINE, QC, H8T 3C5
(514) 631-2777   *SIC* 4213
D & D ENERGY SERVICES LTD   p134
9201 163 AVE, GRANDE PRAIRIE, AB, T8X
0B6
(780) 402-0383   *SIC* 4213
D & W FORWARDERS INC   p509
81 ORENDA RD, BRAMPTON, ON, L6W
1V7
(905) 459-3560   *SIC* 4213
D.J. KNOLL TRANSPORT LTD   p1406
4 GREAT PLAINS INDUSTRIAL DR, EMER-
ALD PARK, SK, S4L 1B6
(306) 789-4824   *SIC* 4213
DANFREIGHT SYSTEMS INC   p1114
1400 CH LASALLE, JOLIETTE, QC, J6E
0L8
(450) 755-6190   *SIC* 4213
DAY & NIGHT CARRIERS LTD   p693
1270 AEROWOOD DR, MISSISSAUGA,
ON, L4W 1B7
SIC 4213
DAY & ROSS INC   p403
398 MAIN ST, HARTLAND, NB, E7P 1C6
(506) 375-4401   *SIC* 4213
DAY & ROSS INC   p409
623 MAPLETON RD, MONCTON, NB, E1G
2K5
(866) 329-7677   *SIC* 4213
DAY & ROSS INC   p513
170 VAN KIRK DR, BRAMPTON, ON, L7A
1K9
(905) 846-6300   *SIC* 4213
DAYTONA FREIGHT SYSTEMS INC   p494
124 COMMERCIAL RD, BOLTON, ON, L7E
1K4
(416) 744-2020   *SIC* 4213
DE JONG, WM ENTERPRISES INC   p796
773451 59 HWY RR 3, NORWICH, ON, N0J
1P0
(519) 424-9007   *SIC* 4213
**DEMENAGEMENT KING'S TRANSFER IN-
TERNATIONAL INC**   p1210
287 RUE ELEANOR, MONTREAL, QC, H3C
2C1
(514) 932-2957   *SIC* 4213
**DEMENAGEMENT   MONT-
BRUNO/LAKESHORE INC**   p1295
1900 RUE MARIE-VICTORIN, SAINT-
BRUNO, QC, J3V 6B9
(450) 653-7891   *SIC* 4213
**DISTRIBUTIONS BEAULAC, CARL INC,
LES**   p1138
15 RUE DES EMERAUDES, LEVIS, QC,
G6W 6Y7
(418) 835-1414   *SIC* 4213

DONNELLY FARMS LTD   p404
40 STOCKFORD RD, LANSDOWNE, NB,
E7L 4K4
(506) 375-4564   *SIC* 4213
DRIVE STAR SHUTTLE SYSTEMS LTDp615
1625 STONE CHURCH RD E, HAMILTON,
ON, L8W 3Y5
(866) 378-7827   *SIC* 4213
DRIVING FORCE DECKS INT'L LTD   p176
30691 SIMPSON RD, ABBOTSFORD, BC,
V2T 6C7
(604) 514-1191   *SIC* 4213
DUCKERING'S TRANSPORT LTD   p155
7794 47 AVENUE CLOSE, RED DEER, AB,
T4P 2J9
(403) 346-8855   *SIC* 4213
DYNEVOR EXPRESS LTD   p584
24 BETHRIDGE RD, ETOBICOKE, ON,
M9W 1N1
(416) 749-2010   *SIC* 4213
EARL PADDOCK TRANSPORTATION INC
p892
199 ARVIN AVE, STONEY CREEK, ON, L8E
2L9
(905) 667-8755   *SIC* 4213
EASSONS TRANSPORT LIMITED   p442
1505 HARRINGTON RD, COLDBROOK,
NS, B4N 3V7
(902) 679-1153   *SIC* 4213
EBD ENTERPRISES INC   p377
29 ROY ROCHE DR, WINNIPEG, MB, R3C
2E6
(204) 633-1657   *SIC* 4213
ECLIPSE TRANSPORT LTD   p179
3120 CEMETERY RD, AGASSIZ, BC, V0M
1A1
(604) 796-8972   *SIC* 4213
EDMONTON TRANSFER LTD   p83
8830 126 AVE NW, EDMONTON, AB, T5B
1G9
(780) 477-1111   *SIC* 4213
ELGIN MOTOR FREIGHT INC   p661
1497 WILTON GROVE RD, LONDON, ON,
N6N 1M3
(519) 644-9090   *SIC* 4213
ENTREC CORPORATION   p6
6708 50 AVE, BONNYVILLE, AB, T9N 0B7
(780) 826-4565   *SIC* 4213
ENTREC CORPORATION   p6
4902 66 ST, BONNYVILLE, AB, T9N 2R5
(780) 826-4565   *SIC* 4213
EQUIPMENT EXPRESS INC   p483
60 WANLESS CRT, AYR, ON, N0B 1E0
(519) 740-8008   *SIC* 4213
ERB GROUP OF COMPANIES, THE   p752
290 HAMILTON RD, NEW HAMBURG, ON,
N3A 1A2
(519) 662-2710   *SIC* 4213
ERB TRANSPORT INC   p1394
3001 RUE HENRY-FORD, VAUDREUIL-
DORION, QC, J7V 8K2
(450) 510-2538   *SIC* 4213
ERB TRANSPORT LIMITED   p694
1889 BRITANNIA RD E, MISSISSAUGA,
ON, L4W 1S6
(905) 670-8490   *SIC* 4213
ESKIMO EXPRESS INC   p1277
5055 RUE RIDEAU BUREAU 500, QUE-
BEC, QC, G2E 5H5
(418) 681-1212   *SIC* 4213
EV LOGISTICS   p229
5111 272 ST, LANGLEY, BC, V4W 3Z2
(604) 857-6750   *SIC* 4213
EXPRESS DU MIDI INC, L'   p1356
1425 1RE AV, SAINTE-CATHERINE, QC,
J5C 1C5
(450) 638-0654   *SIC* 4213
FLEETWAY TRANSPORT INC   p517
31 GARNET RD, BRANTFORD, ON, N3T
5M1
(519) 753-5223   *SIC* 4213
FLORADALE FEED MILL LIMITED   p591
2131 FLORADALE RD, FLORADALE, ON,
N0B 1V0

(519) 669-5478   *SIC* 4213
FORBES HEWLETT TRANSPORT INC *p509*
156 GLIDDEN RD, BRAMPTON, ON, L6W 3L2
(905) 455-2211   *SIC* 4213
FORTIN, J E INC *p1294*
116 BOUL FORTIN, SAINT-BERNARD-DE-LACOLLE, QC, J0J 1V0
(450) 246-3867   *SIC* 4213
FREIGHTCOM INC *p494*
77 PILLSWORTH RD UNIT 1, BOLTON, ON, L7E 4G4
(877) 335-8740   *SIC* 4213
GESTION JEAN-PIERRE ROBIDOUX INC *p1353*
320 201 RTE, SAINT-STANISLAS-DE-KOSTKA, QC, J0S 1W0
(450) 377-2535   *SIC* 4213
GESTION TFI, SOCIETE EN COMMANDITE *p1138*
1950 3E RUE, LEVIS, QC, G6W 5M6
SIC 4213
GILMYR TRANSPORT INC *p1159*
315 CH DU COTEAU, MONTMAGNY, QC, G5V 3R8
(418) 241-5747   *SIC* 4213
GLOBCO INTERNATIONAL INC *p1138*
1660 BOUL GUILLAUME-COUTURE, LEVIS, QC, G6W 5M6
(418) 834-1844   *SIC* 4213
GOLD STAR TRANSPORT (1975) LTD *p132*
11002 89 AVE, GRANDE PRAIRIE, AB, T8V 4W4
(780) 532-0773   *SIC* 4213
GOLIATH TRACTOR SERVICE LTD *p8*
10 WRANGLER PLACE S.E. SUITE 4, CAL-GARY, AB, T1X 0L7
(403) 203-7352   *SIC* 4213
GORSKI BULK TRANSPORT INC *p807*
5400 WALKER RD, OLDCASTLE, ON, N0R 1L0
(519) 737-1275   *SIC* 4213
GRANT'S TRANSPORT LIMITED *p753*
251 GRAY RD, NEW LISKEARD, ON, P0J 1P0
(705) 647-8171   *SIC* 4213
GREAT WEST DISTRIBUTION LTD *p1425*
201 EDSON ST, SASKATOON, SK, S7J 4C8
(306) 933-0027   *SIC* 4213
GROUPE BOUTIN INC *p1065*
128 CH DU TREMBLAY, BOUCHERVILLE, QC, J4B 6Z6
(450) 449-7373   *SIC* 4213
GROUPE G3 INC, LE *p1162*
9135 BOUL HENRI-BOURASSA E, MON-TREAL, QC, H1E 1P4
(514) 648-8522   *SIC* 4213
GROUPE GUILBAULT LTEE *p1264*
435 RUE FARADAY, QUEBEC, QC, G1N 4G6
(418) 681-0575   *SIC* 4213
GROUPE J.F. NADEAU INC, LE *p1360*
850 RTE PRINCIPALE, SAINTE-MELANIE, QC, J0K 3A0
(450) 889-7237   *SIC* 4213
GROUPE LEVASSE INC *p1138*
1660 BOUL GUILLAUME-COUTURE, LEVIS, QC, G6W 0R5
(418) 834-1844   *SIC* 4213
GROUPE ROBERT INC *p1065*
20 BOUL MARIE-VICTORIN, BOUCHERVILLE, QC, J4B 1V5
(514) 521-1011   *SIC* 4213
GROUPE ROBERT INC *p1288*
500 RTE 112, ROUGEMONT, QC, J0L 1M0
(450) 460-1112   *SIC* 4213
GROUPE TRANSTECK INC *p1267*
2797 AV WATT, QUEBEC, QC, G1P 3X3
(418) 651-9595   *SIC* 4213
GROUPE TYT INC *p1097*
675 BOUL LEMIRE O, DRUMMONDVILLE, QC, J2B 8A9
(819) 474-4884   *SIC* 4213
GROUPE TYT INC *p1141*

454 RUE JEAN-NEVEU, LONGUEUIL, QC, J4G 1N8
(819) 474-4884   *SIC* 4213
GTL TRANSPORTATION INC *p446*
115 TRIDER CRES, DARTMOUTH, NS, B3B 1V6
(902) 468-3100   *SIC* 4213
GUSGO TRANSPORT LP *p642*
7050 MAJOR MACKENZIE DR, KLEIN-BURG, ON, L0J 1C0
(905) 893-9930   *SIC* 4213
HALL, KEITH & SONS TRANSPORT LIMITED *p520*
297 BISHOPSGATE RD, BURFORD, ON, N0E 1A0
(519) 449-2401   *SIC* 4213
HARBOUR LINK CONTAINER SERVICES INC *p209*
7420 HOPCOTT RD, DELTA, BC, V4G 1B6
(604) 940-5522   *SIC* 4213
HARMAC TRANSPORTATION INC *p795*
55 ARROW RD, NORTH YORK, ON, M9M 2L4
(416) 642-0515   *SIC* 4213
HBC TRANSPORTATION INC *p509*
100 KENNEDY RD S, BRAMPTON, ON, L6W 3E7
(416) 639-6764   *SIC* 4213
HEALTH TRANS SERVICES INC *p870*
104 BLANTYRE AVE, SCARBOROUGH, ON, M1N 2R5
SIC 4213
HEAVY CRUDE HAULING L.P. *p144*
6601 62 ST, LLOYDMINSTER, AB, T9V 3T6
(780) 875-5358   *SIC* 4213
HERITAGE TRUCK LINES INC *p483*
105 GUTHRIE ST, AYR, ON, N0B 1E0
(519) 632-9052   *SIC* 4213
HIGHLIGHT MOTOR FREIGHT INC *p554*
391 CREDITSTONE RD, CONCORD, ON, L4K 1N8
(905) 761-1400   *SIC* 4213
HILLMAN'S TRANSFER LIMITED *p467*
1159 UPPER PRINCE ST, SYDNEY, NS, B1P 5P8
(902) 564-8113   *SIC* 4213
HOLDING CANADIAN AMERICAN TRANS-PORTATION C.A.T. INC *p1088*
4 RUE DU TRANSPORT, COTEAU-DU-LAC, QC, J0P 1B0
(450) 763-6363   *SIC* 4213
HOLMES FREIGHT LINES INC *p499*
70 WARD RD, BRAMPTON, ON, L6S 4L5
(905) 458-1155   *SIC* 4213
HOYT'S MOVING & STORAGE LIMITED *p446*
320 WRIGHT AVE UNIT 12, DARTMOUTH, NS, B3B 0B3
(902) 876-8202   *SIC* 4213
HUNT'S TRANSPORT LIMITED *p428*
168 MAJOR'S PATH, ST. JOHN'S, NL, A1A 5A1
(709) 747-4868   *SIC* 4213
HYNDMAN TRANSPORT (1972) LIMITED *p1036*
1001 BELMORE LINE, WROXETER, ON, N0G 2X0
(519) 335-3575   *SIC* 4213
IFS INTERNATIONAL FREIGHT SYSTEMS INC *p911*
18900 COUNTY ROAD 42 RR 5, TILBURY, ON, N0P 2L0
(519) 682-3544   *SIC* 4213
INTEGRATED DEALER SYSTEMS CANADA LTD *p844*
1730 MCPHERSON CRT UNIT 7, PICKER-ING, ON, L1W 3E6
(800) 769-7425   *SIC* 4213
INTERNATIONAL TRUCKLOAD SERVICES INC *p491*
107 BELLEVUE DR, BELLEVILLE, ON, K8N 4Z5
(613) 961-5144   *SIC* 4213
IPPOLITO TRANSPORTATION INC *p529*

201 NORTH SERVICE RD SUITE 1, BURLINGTON, ON, L7P 5C4
(905) 639-7700   *SIC* 4213
J-LINE TRANSPORT LIMITED *p489*
4751 CHRISTIE DR, BEAMSVILLE, ON, L0R 1B4
(905) 945-3122   *SIC* 4213
J. & R. HALL TRANSPORT INC *p483*
552 PIPER ST, AYR, ON, N0B 1E0
(519) 632-7429   *SIC* 4213
J.& F. TRUCKING CORPORATION *p474*
610 FINLEY AVE, AJAX, ON, L1S 2E3
(905) 683-7111   *SIC* 4213
JACK COOPER CANADA 2 LIMITED PART-NERSHIP *p1340*
8050 BOUL CAVENDISH, SAINT-LAURENT, QC, H4T 1T1
(514) 731-3016   *SIC* 4213
JAY'S TRANSPORTATION GROUP LTD *p1416*
555 PARK ST, REGINA, SK, S4N 5B2
(306) 569-9369   *SIC* 4213
JBT TRANSPORT INC *p483*
235 WAYDOM DR SUITE 1, AYR, ON, N0B 1E0
(519) 622-3604   *SIC* 4213
JET TRANSPORT LTD *p598*
154 540B HWY RR 1, GORE BAY, ON, P0P 1H0
(705) 282-2640   *SIC* 4213
JTI TRUCKING *p358*
33 CLEAR SPRINGS RD E, STEINBACH, MB, R5G 1V2
(866) 346-1673   *SIC* 4213
JTL GROUP CORP *p998*
37 ADVANCE RD, TORONTO, ON, T5K 1P2
SIC 4213
K-DAC ENTERPRISES INC *p483*
3025 SANDHILLS RD, BADEN, ON, N3A 3B8
(519) 634-8223   *SIC* 4213
KEE WEST AUTO CARRIERS INC *p378*
12-15-2 EPM, WINNIPEG, MB, R3C 2E6
(204) 774-2937   *SIC* 4213
KEENA TRUCK LEASING AND TRANS-PORT LIMITED *p495*
27 SIMPSON RD, BOLTON, ON, L7E 1E4
(905) 857-1189   *SIC* 4213
KELTIC TRANSPORTATION INC *p410*
90 MACNAUGHTON AVE, MONCTON, NB, E1H 3L9
(506) 854-1233   *SIC* 4213
KEPA TRANSPORT INC *p1390*
12 RUE FINLAY, VAL-D'OR, QC, J9P 0K9
(819) 874-0262   *SIC* 4213
KEYSTONE WESTERN INC *p350*
594 BERNAT RD, GRANDE POINTE, MB, R5A 1H5
(204) 256-0800   *SIC* 4213
KHANNA TRANSPORT INC *p580*
100 WESTMORE DR SUITE 12B, ETOBI-COKE, ON, M9V 5C3
(416) 675-9388   *SIC* 4213
KINDERSLEY TRANSPORT LTD *p16*
5515 98 AVE SE, CALGARY, AB, T2C 4L1
(403) 279-8721   *SIC* 4213
KINDERSLEY TRANSPORT LTD *p1428*
2411 WENTZ AVE, SASKATOON, SK, S7K 3V6
(306) 975-9367   *SIC* 4213
KINDERSLEY TRANSPORT LTD *p1428*
2411 WENTZ AVE, SASKATOON, SK, S7K 3V6
(306) 242-3355   *SIC* 4213
KING FREIGHT LINES LIMITED *p464*
131 HARRIS RD, PICTOU, NS, B0K 1H0
(902) 485-8077   *SIC* 4213
KLEYSEN GROUP LTD *p353*
2800 MCGILLIVRAY BLVD, OAK BLUFF, MB, R4G 0B4
(204) 488-5550   *SIC* 4213
KOCH TRANSPORT INC *p536*
151 SAVAGE DR UNIT B, CAMBRIDGE, ON, N1T 1S6

SIC 4213
KOCSIS TRANSPORT LTD *p1433*
401 PACKHAM PL, SASKATOON, SK, S7N 2T7
(306) 664-0025   *SIC* 4213
KRISKA HOLDINGS LIMITED *p740*
6424A DANVILLE RD, MISSISSAUGA, ON, L5T 2S6
(905) 795-2770   *SIC* 4213
KRISKA HOLDINGS LIMITED *p848*
850 SOPHIA ST, PRESCOTT, ON, K0E 1T0
(613) 925-5903   *SIC* 4213
KVAERNER PROCESS SYSTEMS CANADA INC *p36*
1209 59 AVE SE SUITE 100, CALGARY, AB, T2H 2P6
(403) 640-4230   *SIC* 4213
L. HANSEN'S FORWARDING LTD *p876*
105 NASHDENE RD, SCARBOROUGH, ON, M1V 2W3
(416) 293-9135   *SIC* 4213
LAIDLAW CARRIERS BULK LP *p1035*
240 UNIVERSAL RD, WOODSTOCK, ON, N4S 7W3
(519) 539-0471   *SIC* 4213
LAIDLAW CARRIERS FLATBED LP *p607*
11 6 HWY N, HAGERSVILLE, ON, N0A 1H0
(905) 768-3375   *SIC* 4213
LAIDLAW CARRIERS VAN LP *p416*
65 ALLOY DR, SAINT JOHN, NB, E2M 7S9
(506) 648-0499   *SIC* 4213
LAIDLAW CARRIERS VAN LP *p849*
21 KERR CRES, PUSLINCH, ON, N0B 2J0
(519) 766-0660   *SIC* 4213
LANDTRAN LOGISTICS INC *p109*
4819 90A AVE NW, EDMONTON, AB, T6B 2Y3
(780) 486-8607   *SIC* 4213
LASER TRANSPORT INC *p1020*
3380 WHEELTON DR, WINDSOR, ON, N8W 5A7
(519) 974-3435   *SIC* 4213
LIBERTY LINEHAUL INC *p483*
214 BOIDA AVE SS 2, AYR, ON, N0B 1E0
(519) 740-8181   *SIC* 4213
LIGHT SPEED LOGISTICS INC *p17*
5720 84 AVE SE, CALGARY, AB, T2C 4T6
(403) 208-5441   *SIC* 4213
LINAMAR TRANSPORTATION INC *p605*
32 INDEPENDENCE PL, GUELPH, ON, N1K 1H8
(519) 837-2056   *SIC* 4213
LINEAR LOGISTICS LTD *p36*
7015 MACLEOD TRAIL SW UNIT 603, CAL-GARY, AB, T2H 2K6
(587) 353-5454   *SIC* 4213
LOGISTIQUES TRANS-WEST INC *p1128*
1900 52E AV BUREAU 100, LACHINE, QC, H8T 2X9
(514) 345-1090   *SIC* 4213
LOTUS TERMINALS LTD *p272*
18833 52 AVE, SURREY, BC, V3S 8E5
(604) 534-1119   *SIC* 4213
M.D. TRANSPORT CO. LTD *p177*
1683 MT LEHMAN RD, ABBOTSFORD, BC, V2T 6H6
(604) 850-1818   *SIC* 4213
MACKIE MOVING SYSTEMS *p447*
30 GURHOLT DR, DARTMOUTH, NS, B3B 1J9
(902) 481-2041   *SIC* 4213
MACKIE TRANSPORTATION INC *p1014*
1900 BOUNDARY RD UNIT 2, WHITBY, ON, L1N 8P8
(905) 728-1000   *SIC* 4213
MACKINNON TRANSPORT INC *p601*
405 LAIRD RD, GUELPH, ON, N1G 4P7
(519) 821-2311   *SIC* 4213
MALO TRANSPORT (1971) INC *p1350*
23 CH SAINT-JACQUES, SAINT-PAUL, QC, J6E 3H2
(450) 756-8008   *SIC* 4213
MAMMOET CANADA WESTERN LTD *p124*
12920 33 ST NE, EDMONTON, AB, T6S

1H6
(780) 449-0552 *SIC* 4213

MANITOULIN TRANSPORT INC *p*598
154 540B HWY, GORE BAY, ON, P0P 1H0
(705) 282-2640 *SIC* 4213

MANITOULIN TRANSPORTATION *p*1
53114 RGE RD 262 UNIT 402, ACHESON,
AB, T7X 5A1
(780) 490-1112 *SIC* 4213

MARCUS, HAROLD LIMITED *p*496
15124 LONGWOODS RD SUITE 2, BOTH-
WELL, ON, N0P 1C0
(519) 695-3734 *SIC* 4213

**MARITIME-ONTARIO FREIGHT LINES LIM-
ITED** *p*499
1 MARITIME ONTARIO BLVD, BRAMPTON,
ON, L6S 6G4
(905) 792-6101 *SIC* 4213

MARNOR HOLDINGS LTD *p*179
3243 264 ST, ALDERGROVE, BC, V4W 2X3
(604) 857-8853 *SIC* 4213

MARPOLE TRANSPORT LIMITED *p*209
7086 BROWN ST, DELTA, BC, V4G 1G8
(604) 940-7000 *SIC* 4213

MAVRON TRANSPORT INC *p*697
5758 DIXIE RD, MISSISSAUGA, ON, L4W
1E7
(905) 670-9455 *SIC* 4213

MCCONNELL TRANSPORT LIMITED *p*404
208 ROUTE 590, JACKSONVILLE, NB,
E7M 3R7
(506) 325-2211 *SIC* 4213

MCKEVITT TRUCKING LIMITED *p*908
1200 CARRICK ST, THUNDER BAY, ON,
P7B 5P9
(807) 623-0054 *SIC* 4213

MCWILLIAMS CARTAGE LIMITED *p*841
712 THE KINGSWAY, PETERBOROUGH,
ON, K9J 6W6
(800) 461-6464 *SIC* 4213

MELBURN TRUCK LINES CORP *p*714
2215 ROYAL WINDSOR DR, MISSIS-
SAUGA, ON, L5J 1K5
(905) 823-7800 *SIC* 4213

MELDRUM THE MOVER INC *p*1222
6645 RUE SHERBROOKE O, MONTREAL,
QC, H4B 1N4
(514) 400-0182 *SIC* 4213

MERCER, GARRY TRUCKING INC *p*741
1140 MID-WAY BLVD, MISSISSAUGA, ON,
L5T 2C1
(905) 670-4721 *SIC* 4213

MERKS FARMS LIMITED *p*439
2250 GASPEREAU RIVER RD, AVON-
PORT, NS, B0P 1B0
(902) 542-4200 *SIC* 4213

MEYERS TRANSPORT LIMITED *p*491
53 GRILLS RD, BELLEVILLE, ON, K8N 4Z5
(613) 967-8440 *SIC* 4213

MID WEST COAST CANADA INC *p*892
400 JONES RD SUITE 106, STONEY
CREEK, ON, L8E 5P4
(905) 578-9993 *SIC* 4213

MID-ARCTIC TRANSPORTATION CO. LTD
*p*101
18151 107 AVE NW, EDMONTON, AB, T5S
1K4
(780) 484-8800 *SIC* 4213

MID-NITE SUN TRANSPORTATION LTD
*p*115
5805 98 ST NW, EDMONTON, AB, T6E 3L4
(780) 431-2877 *SIC* 4213

MIDLAND TRANSPORT LIMITED *p*398
100 MIDLAND DR, DIEPPE, NB, E1A 6X4
(506) 858-5555 *SIC* 4213

MIDLAND TRANSPORT LIMITED *p*504
102 GLIDDEN RD, BRAMPTON, ON, L6T
5N4
(905) 456-5555 *SIC* 4213

MIDNIGHT EXPRESS & CARTAGE LTD *p*697
5355 CREEKBANK RD, MISSISSAUGA,
ON, L4W 5L5
(905) 629-0712 *SIC* 4213

MILL CREEK MOTOR FREIGHT L.P. *p*483

101 EARL THOMPSON RD SS 2, AYR, ON,
N0B 1E0
(519) 623-6632 *SIC* 4213

MIQ LOGISTICS, LLC *p*725
6580 MILLCREEK DR SUITE 905, MISSIS-
SAUGA, ON, L5N 8B3
(905) 542-7525 *SIC* 4213

MITRUX SERVICES LTD *p*177
2160 PEARDONVILLE RD, ABBOTSFORD,
BC, V2T 6J8
(604) 746-1008 *SIC* 4213

MOE'S TRANSPORT TRUCKING INC *p*1024
1333 COLLEGE AVE, WINDSOR, ON, N9B
1M8
(519) 253-8442 *SIC* 4213

MULLEN TRUCKING CORP *p*3
80079 MAPLE LEAF RD E UNIT 100,
ALDERSYDE, AB, T0L 0A0
(403) 652-8888 *SIC* 4213

MUNICIPAL TANK LINES LIMITED *p*54
800 5 AVE SW SUITE 1700, CALGARY, AB,
T2P 3T6
(403) 298-5100 *SIC* 4213

MURRAY'S TRUCKING INC *p*110
6211 76 AVE NW, EDMONTON, AB, T6B
0A7
(780) 439-2222 *SIC* 4213

MUSKET EQUIPMENT LEASING LTD *p*714
2215 ROYAL WINDSOR DR, MISSIS-
SAUGA, ON, L5J 1K5
(905) 823-7800 *SIC* 4213

MUSKET TRANSPORT LTD, THE *p*714
2215 ROYAL WINDSOR DR, MISSIS-
SAUGA, ON, L5J 1K5
(905) 823-7800 *SIC* 4213

MUSKOKA TRANSPORT LIMITED *p*497
456 ECCLESTONE DR, BRACEBRIDGE,
ON, P1L 1R1
(705) 645-4481 *SIC* 4213

MUSKOKA TRANSPORT LIMITED *p*497
456 ECCLESTONE DR, BRACEBRIDGE,
ON, P1L 1R1
(705) 645-4481 *SIC* 4213

N. YANKE TRANSFER LTD *p*1432
1359 FLETCHER RD, SASKATOON, SK,
S7M 5H5
SIC 4213

NESEL FAST FREIGHT INCORPORATED
*p*495
20 HOLLAND DR, BOLTON, ON, L7E 1G6
(905) 951-7770 *SIC* 4213

NESEL FAST FREIGHT INCORPORATED
*p*901
19216 HAY RD, SUMMERSTOWN, ON,
K0C 2E0
SIC 4213

NEW HOPE TRANSPORT LTD *p*353
170 AGRI PARK RD, OAK BLUFF, MB, R4G
0A5
SIC 4213

NORMANDIN TRANSIT INC *p*1242
151 BOUL INDUSTRIEL, NAPIERVILLE,
QC, J0J 1L0
(450) 245-0445 *SIC* 4213

NORTHERN CARTAGE LIMITED *p*369
60 EAGLE DR SUITE 204, WINNIPEG, MB,
R2R 1V5
(204) 633-5795 *SIC* 4213

NORTHERN INDUSTRIAL CARRIERS LTD
*p*110
7823 34 ST NW, EDMONTON, AB, T6B 2V5
(780) 465-0341 *SIC* 4213

**NORTHERN RESOURCE TRUCKING LIM-
ITED PARTNERSHIP** *p*1428
2945 MILLAR AVE, SASKATOON, SK, S7K
6P6
(306) 933-3010 *SIC* 4213

NORTHWEST TANK LINES INC *p*229
7025 272 ST, LANGLEY, BC, V4W 1R3
(604) 856-6666 *SIC* 4213

NTP/STAG CANADA INC *p*1296
1545 RUE MARIE-VICTORIN, SAINT-
BRUNO, QC, J3V 6B7
(450) 441-2707 *SIC* 4213

OCULUS TRANSPORT LTD. *p*55
444 5 AVE SW SUITE 650, CALGARY, AB,
T2P 2T8
(403) 262-0006 *SIC* 4213

ONE WORLD LOGISTICS OF AMERICA INC
*p*543
400 NATIONAL RD, CHATHAM, ON, N7M
5J5
(519) 380-0800 *SIC* 4213

ONTARIO NEW ENGLAND EXPRESS INC
*p*684
8450 LAWSON RD UNIT 2, MILTON, ON,
L9T 0J8
(905) 876-3996 *SIC* 4213

OVERLAND WEST FREIGHT LINES LTD
*p*270
11398 BRIDGEVIEW DR, SURREY, BC,
V3R 0C2
(604) 888-6300 *SIC* 4213

PACIFIC COAST EXPRESS LIMITED *p*275
10299 GRACE RD, SURREY, BC, V3V 3V7
(604) 582-3230 *SIC* 4213

PANNU BROS. TRUCKING LTD *p*178
30260 FRASER HWY, ABBOTSFORD, BC,
V4X 1G2
(604) 857-2213 *SIC* 4213

PAPINEAU INT, S.E.C. *p*1320
851 BOUL ROLAND-GODARD, SAINT-
JEROME, QC, J7Y 4C2
(450) 432-7555 *SIC* 4213

PAUL'S HAULING LTD *p*347
1515 RICHMOND AVE E, BRANDON, MB,
R7A 7A3
(204) 728-5785 *SIC* 4213

PAUL'S HAULING LTD *p*369
250 OAK POINT HWY, WINNIPEG, MB,
R2R 1V1
(204) 633-4330 *SIC* 4213

PENNER INTERNATIONAL INC *p*358
20 PTH 12 N, STEINBACH, MB, R5G 1B7
(204) 326-3487 *SIC* 4213

PENSKE LOGISTICS CANADA LTD *p*634
3065 KING ST E, KITCHENER, ON, N2A
1B1
(519) 650-0123 *SIC* 4213

PETROWEST CORPORATION *p*57
407 2 ST SW SUITE 800, CALGARY, AB,
T2P 2Y3
(403) 237-0881 *SIC* 4213

POLE STAR TRANSPORT INCORPORATED
*p*409
689 EDINBURGH DR, MONCTON, NB, E1E
2L4
(506) 859-7025 *SIC* 4213

POLE STAR TRANSPORT INCORPORATED
*p*448
80 GUILDFORD AVE, DARTMOUTH, NS,
B3B 0G3
(902) 468-8855 *SIC* 4213

PRECISION TRUCK LINES INC *p*1028
8111 HUNTINGTON RD, WOODBRIDGE,
ON, L4H 0S6
(905) 851-1996 *SIC* 4213

Q-LINE TRUCKING LTD *p*1429
101 WURTZ AVE, SASKATOON, SK, S7K
3J7
(306) 651-3540 *SIC* 4213

QUIK X TRANSPORTATION INC *p*699
5425 DIXIE RD BLDG B, MISSISSAUGA,
ON, L4W 1E6
(905) 238-8584 *SIC* 4213

R & G TRANSPORT LTD *p*412
16 MILK BOARD RD, ROACHVILLE, NB,
E4G 2G8
(506) 432-9128 *SIC* 4213

R. R. PLETT TRUCKING LTD *p*225
19675 98 AVE, LANGLEY, BC, V1M 2X5
(604) 513-9920 *SIC* 4213

R.E.M. TRANSPORT LTD *p*410
4 HALL RD, OLD RIDGE, NB, E3L 5E1
(506) 466-2918 *SIC* 4213

R.S. HARRIS TRANSPORT LTD *p*391
555 HERVO ST UNIT 15, WINNIPEG, MB,
R3T 3L6

(204) 255-2700 *SIC* 4213

RAZIR TRANSPORT SERVICES LTD *p*391
1460 CLARENCE AVE SUITE 204, WIN-
NIPEG, MB, R3T 1T6
(204) 489-2258 *SIC* 4213

RBS BULK SYSTEMS INC *p*18
9910 48 ST SE, CALGARY, AB, T2C 2R2
(403) 248-1530 *SIC* 4213

RICK NICKELL TRUCKING INC *p*179
4280 SPALLUMCHEEN DR, ARMSTRONG,
BC, V0E 1B6
(250) 546-2566 *SIC* 4213

RIDSDALE TRANSPORT LTD *p*1435
210 APEX ST, SASKATOON, SK, S7R 0A2
(306) 668-9200 *SIC* 4213

RIGEL SHIPPING CANADA INC *p*417
3521 ROUTE 134, SHEDIAC CAPE, NB,
E4P 3G6
(506) 533-9000 *SIC* 4213

ROBERGE TRANSPORT INC *p*1411
1750 STADACONA ST W, MOOSE JAW, SK,
S6H 4P4
(800) 667-5190 *SIC* 4213

**ROBYN'S TRANSPORTATION & DISTRIBU-
TION SERVICES LTD** *p*37
6404 BURBANK RD SE, CALGARY, AB,
T2H 2C2
(403) 292-9260 *SIC* 4213

ROSENAU TRANSPORT LTD *p*116
5805 98 ST NW, EDMONTON, AB, T6E 3L4
(780) 431-2065 *SIC* 4213

ROSENAU TRANSPORT LTD *p*123
3300 76 AVE NW, EDMONTON, AB, T6P
1J4
(780) 431-2877 *SIC* 4213

RST INDUSTRIES LIMITED *p*413
485 MCALLISTER DR, SAINT JOHN, NB,
E2J 2S8
(506) 634-8800 *SIC* 4213

RTL- ROBINSON ENTERPRISES LTD *p*103
10821 209 ST NW, EDMONTON, AB, T5S
1Z7
(780) 447-4900 *SIC* 4213

RTL- ROBINSON ENTERPRISES LTD *p*436
350 OLD AIRPORT RD, YELLOWKNIFE,
NT, X1A 3T4
(867) 873-6271 *SIC* 4213

S.G.T. 2000 INC *p*1306
354 CH YAMASKA, SAINT-GERMAIN-DE-
GRANTHAM, QC, J0C 1K0
(819) 395-4213 *SIC* 4213

SCI GROUP INC *p*588
180 ATTWELL DR SUITE 600, ETOBI-
COKE, ON, M9W 6A9
(416) 401-3011 *SIC* 4213

SEABOARD LIQUID CARRIERS LIMITED
*p*414
120 ASHBURN RD, SAINT JOHN, NB, E2K
5J5
(506) 652-7070 *SIC* 4213

SEARCY TRUCKING LTD *p*392
1470 CHEVRIER BLVD, WINNIPEG, MB,
R3T 1Y6
(204) 475-8411 *SIC* 4213

SELECT CLASSIC CARRIERS INC *p*1425
226A PORTAGE AVE, SASKATOON, SK,
S7J 4C6
(306) 374-2733 *SIC* 4213

SERVICE TRANS-WEST INC *p*1128
1900 52E AV BUREAU 100, LACHINE, QC,
H8T 2X9
(514) 345-1090 *SIC* 4213

SERVICES DE CAMIONNAGE VITESSE INC
*p*1128
1111 46E AV, LACHINE, QC, H8T 3C5
(514) 631-2777 *SIC* 4213

SERVICES JAG INC, LES *p*1357
425 RUE LAURIER, SAINTE-CROIX, QC,
G0S 2H0
(418) 926-2412 *SIC* 4213

SEVEN STAR EXPRESS LINE LTD *p*608
36 COVINGTON ST, HAMILTON, ON, L8E
2Y5
SIC 4213

SLH TRANSPORT INC *p440*
347 BLUEWATER RD, BEDFORD, NS, B4B 1Y3
(902) 832-4900   *SIC 4213*

SLH TRANSPORT INC *p633*
1585 CENTENNIAL DR, KINGSTON, ON, K7P 0K4
(613) 384-9515   *SIC 4213*

SLH TRANSPORT INC *p700*
905 SHAWSON DR, MISSISSAUGA, ON, L4W 1T9
(905) 893-5170   *SIC 4213*

SLH TRANSPORT INC *p1330*
3075 BOUL THIMENS, SAINT-LAURENT, QC, H4R 1Y3
(514) 335-4990   *SIC 4213*

SM FREIGHT INC *p493*
25 GRAHAM ST, BLENHEIM, ON, N0P 1A0
(519) 676-5198   *SIC 4213*

SOKIL EXPRESS LINES LTD *p84*
8830 126 AVE NW, EDMONTON, AB, T5B 1G9
(780) 479-1955   *SIC 4213*

SOMAVRAC INC *p1386*
2550 RUE DE LA SIDBEC S, TROIS-RIVIERES, QC, G8Z 4H1
(819) 374-7551   *SIC 4213*

STERLING PACKERS LIMITED *p506*
250 SUMMERLEA RD, BRAMPTON, ON, L6T 3V6
(905) 595-4300   *SIC 4213*

SUBURBAN CENTRE & AUTO SERVICE LTD *p363*
130 TRANSPORT RD, WINNIPEG, MB, R2C 2Z2
(204) 953-6200   *SIC 4213*

SUNBURY TRANSPORT LIMITED *p413*
485 MCALLISTER DR, SAINT JOHN, NB, E2J 2S8
(800) 786-2878   *SIC 4213*

SYSTEMES LUMINESCENT CANADA INC *p1095*
55 AV LINDSAY, DORVAL, QC, H9P 2S6
(514) 636-9921   *SIC 4213*

T & T TRUCKING LTD *p1430*
855 60TH ST E, SASKATOON, SK, S7K 5Z7
(306) 934-3383   *SIC 4213*

T BELL TRANSPORT INC *p747*
231 HWY 17, NAIRN CENTRE, ON, P0M 2L0
(705) 869-5959   *SIC 4213*

T.E.A.M. LOGISTICS SYSTEMS INC *p483*
118 EARL THOMPSON RD, AYR, ON, N0B 1E0
(519) 622-2473   *SIC 4213*

TALLMAN TRANSPORTS LIMITED *p1012*
1003 NIAGARA ST, WELLAND, ON, L3C 1M5
(416) 735-1410   *SIC 4213*

TANDET LOGISTICS INC *p805*
1351 SPEERS RD, OAKVILLE, ON, L6L 2X5
(905) 827-4200   *SIC 4213*

TANDET MANAGEMENT INC *p805*
1351 SPEERS RD, OAKVILLE, ON, L6L 2X5
(905) 827-0501   *SIC 4213*

TANK TRUCK TRANSPORT INC *p642*
11339 ALBION VAUGHAN RD, KLEINBURG, ON, L0J 1C0
(905) 893-3447   *SIC 4213*

TFI INTERNATIONAL *p1336*
8801 RTE TRANSCANADIENNE BUREAU 500, SAINT-LAURENT, QC, H4S 1Z6
(514) 331-4113   *SIC 4213*

TFI TRANSPORT 12 L.P. / TRANSPORT TFI 12, S.E.C. *p1336*
8801 RTE TRANSCANADIENNE UNIT? 500, SAINT-LAURENT, QC, H4S 1Z6
(514) 331-4000   *SIC 4213*

THOMSON TERMINALS LIMITED *p588*
102 IRON ST, ETOBICOKE, ON, M9W 5L9
(416) 240-0897   *SIC 4213*

TITANIUM TRUCKING SERVICES INC *p495*
32 SIMPSON RD, BOLTON, ON, L7E 1G9
(905) 851-1688   *SIC 4213*

TMG LOGISTICS INC *p273*
14722 64 AVE UNIT 9, SURREY, BC, V3S 1X7
(604) 598-3680   *SIC 4213*

TOTRAN TRANSPORTATION SERVICES LTD *p78*
9350 VENTURE AVE SE, CALGARY, AB, T3S 0A2
(403) 723-0025   *SIC 4213*

TRA ATLANTIC *p431*
63 GLENCOE DR, ST. JOHN'S, NL, A1B 4A5
(709) 364-7771   *SIC 4213*

TRAILWOOD TRANSPORT LTD *p476*
4925 C.W. LEACH RD, ALLISTON, ON, L9R 2B1
(705) 435-4362   *SIC 4213*

TRANS4 LOGISTICS *p701*
1575 SOUTH GATEWAY RD UNIT A&B, MISSISSAUGA, ON, L4W 5J1
(905) 212-9001   *SIC 4213*

TRANSAM CARRIERS INC *p560*
205 DONEY CRES, CONCORD, ON, L4K 1P6
(416) 907-8101   *SIC 4213*

TRANSIT LOGISTICS SOLUTIONS INC *p1024*
4455 COUNTY RD 42, WINDSOR, ON, N9A 6J3
(519) 967-0911   *SIC 4213*

TRANSNAT EXPRESS INC *p1246*
1397 RUE SAVOIE, PLESSISVILLE, QC, G6L 1J8
(819) 362-7333   *SIC 4213*

TRANSOURCE FREIGHTWAYS LTD *p19*
19-6991 48 ST SE, CALGARY, AB, T2C 5A4
(403) 726-4366   *SIC 4213*

TRANSOURCE FREIGHTWAYS LTD *p207*
1659 FOSTER'S WAY, DELTA, BC, V3M 6S7
(604) 525-0527   *SIC 4213*

TRANSPORT ALFRED BOIVIN INC *p1080*
2205 RUE DE LA FONDERIE, CHICOUTIMI, QC, G7H 8B9
(418) 693-8681   *SIC 4213*

TRANSPORT BAIE-COMEAU INC *p1052*
62 AV WILLIAM-DOBELL, BAIE-COMEAU, QC, G4Z 1T7
(418) 296-5229   *SIC 4213*

TRANSPORT BELLEMARE INTERNATIONAL INC *p1389*
8750 BOUL INDUSTRIEL, TROIS-RIVIERES, QC, G9A 5E1
(819) 379-4546   *SIC 4213*

TRANSPORT BERNIERES INC *p1265*
1721 RUE A.-R.-DECARY, QUEBEC, QC, G1N 3Z7
(418) 684-2421   *SIC 4213*

TRANSPORT COUTURE & FILS LTEE *p1300*
99 RTE 271 S, SAINT-EPHREM-DE-BEAUCE, QC, G0M 1R0
(418) 484-2104   *SIC 4213*

TRANSPORT DOUCET & FILS MISTASSINI INC *p1090*
124 RUE LAVOIE, DOLBEAU-MISTASSINI, QC, G8L 4M8
(418) 276-7395   *SIC 4213*

TRANSPORT GILMYR INC *p1160*
315 CH DU COTEAU, MONTMAGNY, QC, G5V 3R8
(418) 241-5747   *SIC 4213*

TRANSPORT GUILBAULT CANADA INC *p1265*
435 RUE FARADAY, QUEBEC, QC, G1N 4G6
(418) 681-5272   *SIC 4213*

TRANSPORT GUILBAULT INC *p1265*
435 RUE FARADAY, QUEBEC, QC, G1N 4G6
(418) 681-0575   *SIC 4213*

TRANSPORT GUILBAULT INTERNATIONAL INC *p1265*
435 RUE FARADAY, QUEBEC, QC, G1N 4G6
(418) 681-0575   *SIC 4213*

TRANSPORT GUY LEVASSEUR INC *p1246*
876 RUE PRINCIPALE, POHENEGAMOOK, QC, G0L 1J0
(418) 859-2294   *SIC 4213*

TRANSPORT JAGUAR INTERNATIONAL INC *p1062*
3777 RUE LA FAYETTE O, BOISBRIAND, QC, J7H 1N5
(450) 433-8000   *SIC 4213*

TRANSPORT L.F.L. INC *p1392*
431 CH DE L'ECORE N, VALLEE-JONCTION, QC, G0S 3J0
(418) 253-5423   *SIC 4213*

TRANSPORT MATTE LTEE *p1092*
487 RUE PAGE, DONNACONA, QC, G3M 1W6
(418) 285-0777   *SIC 4213*

TRANSPORT MORNEAU INC *p1051*
9601 BOUL DES SCIENCES, ANJOU, QC, H1J 0A6
(514) 325-2727   *SIC 4213*

TRANSPORT MORNEAU INC *p1292*
40 RUE PRINCIPALE, SAINT-ARSENE, QC, G0L 2K0
(418) 862-2727   *SIC 4213*

TRANSPORT N SERVICE INC *p604*
5075 WHITELAW RD, GUELPH, ON, N1H 6J4
(519) 821-0400   *SIC 4213*

TRANSPORT NORD-OUEST INC *p1391*
1355B CH SULLIVAN, VAL-D'OR, QC, J9P 1M2
(819) 874-2003   *SIC 4213*

TRANSPORT ROBERT (1973) LTEE *p1068*
65 RUE DE VAUDREUIL, BOUCHERVILLE, QC, J4B 1K7
(514) 521-1416   *SIC 4213*

TRANSPORT ROBERT (1973) LTEE *p1125*
4075 RUE VILLENEUVE, LAC-MEGANTIC, QC, G6B 2C2
(819) 583-2230   *SIC 4213*

TRANSPORT ROBERT (1973) LTEE *p1288*
500 RTE 112, ROUGEMONT, QC, J0L 1M0
(450) 469-3153   *SIC 4213*

TRANSPORT ROBERT (1973) LTEE *p1360*
1199 2E RUE DU PARC-INDUSTRIEL, SAINTE-MARIE, QC, G6E 1G7
(514) 521-1416   *SIC 4213*

TRANSPORT S A S DRUMMONDVILLE INC *p1099*
850 RUE LABONTE, DRUMMONDVILLE, QC, J2C 5Y4
(819) 477-6599   *SIC 4213*

TRANSPORT SYLVESTER & FORGET INC *p1353*
320 RTE 201, SAINT-STANISLAS-DE-KOSTKA, QC, J0S 1W0
(450) 377-2535   *SIC 4213*

TRANSPORT TFI 1, S.E.C. *p1389*
1200 RUE DU PERE-DANIEL, TROIS-RIVIERES, QC, G9A 5R6
(819) 370-3422   *SIC 4213*

TRANSPORT TFI 11 S.E.C. *p1139*
1956B 3E RUE, LEVIS, QC, G6W 5M6
(418) 839-6655   *SIC 4213*

TRANSPORT TFI 14 S.E.C. *p1337*
8801 RTE TRANSCANADIENNE BUREAU 500, SAINT-LAURENT, QC, H4S 1Z6
(514) 331-4000   *SIC 4213*

TRANSPORT TFI 15 S.E.C. *p1337*
8801 RTE TRANSCANADIENNE BUREAU 500, SAINT-LAURENT, QC, H4S 1Z6
(514) 331-4000   *SIC 4213*

TRANSPORT TFI 19, S.E.C. *p1303*
1214 RTE 255, SAINT-FELIX-DE-KINGSEY, QC, J0B 2T0
(819) 848-2042   *SIC 4213*

TRANSPORT TFI 2, S.E.C. *p1337*
8801 RTE TRANSCANADIENNE BUREAU 500, SAINT-LAURENT, QC, H4S 1Z6
(514) 331-4000   *SIC 4213*

TRANSPORT TFI 3 L.P. *p676*
2815 14TH AVE, MARKHAM, ON, L3R 0H9
(800) 268-6231   *SIC 4213*

TRANSPORT TFI 4, S.E.C. *p1293*
140 RUE DES GRANDS-LACS, SAINT-AUGUSTIN-DE-DESMAURES, QC, G3A 2K1
(418) 870-5454   *SIC 4213*

TRANSPORT TFI 5, S.E.C. *p701*
1100 HAULTAIN CRT, MISSISSAUGA, ON, L4W 2T1
(905) 624-4050   *SIC 4213*

TRANSPORT TFI 5, S.E.C. *p1337*
6700 CH SAINT-FRANCOIS, SAINT-LAURENT, QC, H4S 1B7
(514) 856-5559   *SIC 4213*

TRANSPORT TFI 6 S.E.C. *p1139*
1950 3E RUE, LEVIS, QC, G6W 5M6
(418) 834-9891   *SIC 4213*

TRANSPORT TFI 6 S.E.C. *p1359*
100A RUE SAINT-ALPHONSE, SAINTE-LUCE, QC, G0K 1P0
(418) 731-2327   *SIC 4213*

TRANSPORT TFI 7 S.E.C. *p183*
7867 EXPRESS ST, BURNABY, BC, V5A 1S7
(604) 420-2030   *SIC 4213*

TRANSPORT TFI 7 S.E.C *p1337*
8801 RTE TRANSCANADIENNE BUREAU 500, SAINT-LAURENT, QC, H4S 1Z6
(514) 331-4000   *SIC 4213*

TRANSPORTS DUCAMPRO INC *p1298*
229 RTE 204, SAINT-DAMASE-DES-AULNAIES, QC, G0R 2X0
(418) 598-9319   *SIC 4213*

TRANSPORTS DUCAMPRO INC *p1316*
1200 BOUL SAINT-LUC, SAINT-JEAN-SUR-RICHELIEU, QC, J2Y 1A5
(450) 348-4400   *SIC 4213*

TRANSPORTS J.M. BERNIER INC *p1151*
75 RUE DES ERABLES, METABETCHOUAN-LAC-A-LA-CROIX, QC, G8G 1P9
(418) 349-3496   *SIC 4213*

TRANSPORTS YVON TURCOTTE LTEE, LES *p1097*
675 BOUL LEMIRE O, DRUMMONDVILLE, QC, J2B 8A9
(819) 474-4884   *SIC 4213*

TRANSX LTD *p159*
285115 61 AVE SE, ROCKY VIEW COUNTY, AB, T1X 0K3
(403) 236-9300   *SIC 4213*

TRANSX LTD *p379*
2595 INKSTER BLVD, WINNIPEG, MB, R3C 2E6
(204) 632-6694   *SIC 4213*

TRANSX TRANSPORT INC *p380*
2595 INKSTER BLVD SUITE 2, WINNIPEG, MB, R3C 2E6
(204) 632-6694   *SIC 4213*

TRAPPERS TRANSPORT LTD *p363*
1300 REDONDA ST, WINNIPEG, MB, R2C 2Z2
(204) 697-7647   *SIC 4213*

TRAVELERS TRANSPORTATION SERVICES INC *p510*
195 HEART LAKE RD, BRAMPTON, ON, L6W 3N6
(905) 457-8789   *SIC 4213*

TRAVELERS TRANSPORTATION SERVICES INC *p1005*
735 GILLARD ST, WALLACEBURG, ON, N8A 5G7
(519) 627-5848   *SIC 4213*

TRI-LINE CARRIERS LP *p160*
235185 RYAN RD, ROCKY VIEW COUNTY, AB, T1X 0K1
(403) 279-7070   *SIC 4213*

TRIANGLE FREIGHT SERVICES LTD *p1432*
3550 IDYLWYLD DR N, SASKATOON, SK, S7L 6G3
(306) 373-7744   *SIC 4213*

TRIANGLE LOGISTICS SOLUTIONS INC *p905*
8500 LESLIE ST SUITE 320, THORNHILL, ON, L3T 7M8
(416) 747-6474   *SIC 4213*

▲ Public Company   ■ Public Company Family Member   **HQ** Headquarters   **BR** Branch   **SL** Single Location

TRIPLE EIGHT TRANSPORT INC *p177*
2548 CLEARBROOK RD 1ST FL, ABBOTS-FORD, BC, V2T 2Y4
(604) 755-2285   *SIC* 4213

TRIPLE K TRANSPORT LTD *p891*
6640 HAZELDEAN RD, STITTSVILLE, ON, K2S 1B9
(613) 836-7333   *SIC* 4213

TST SOLUTIONS L.P. *p701*
5200 MAINGATE DR, MISSISSAUGA, ON, L4W 1G5
(905) 625-7601   *SIC* 4213

TUDHOPE CARTAGE LIMITED *p448*
4 VIDITO DR, DARTMOUTH, NS, B3B 1P9
(902) 468-4447   *SIC* 4213

URSUS TRANSPORT INC *p589*
85 VULCAN ST, ETOBICOKE, ON, M9W 1L4
(416) 243-8780   *SIC* 4213

V.D.M. TRUCKING SERVICE LTD *p123*
2010 76 AVE NW, EDMONTON, AB, T6P 1J5
(780) 467-9897   *SIC* 4213

VALLEY CARRIERS LTD *p178*
4491 GLADWIN RD, ABBOTSFORD, BC, V4X 1W6
(604) 853-1075   *SIC* 4213

VAN-KAM FREIGHTWAYS LTD *p275*
10155 GRACE RD, SURREY, BC, V3V 3V7
(604) 582-7451   *SIC* 4213

VANDERMAREL TRUCKING LIMITED *p590*
655 DICKSON DR, FERGUS, ON, N1M 2W7
(519) 787-1563   *SIC* 4213

VEDDER TRANSPORT LTD *p175*
400 RIVERSIDE RD, ABBOTSFORD, BC, V2S 7M4
(604) 853-3341   *SIC* 4213

VENTURES WEST TRANSPORT INC *p130*
182 STURGEON WAY, FORT SASKATCHEWAN, AB, T8L 2N9
(780) 449-5542   *SIC* 4213

VERSPEETEN CARTAGE LIMITED *p622*
274129 WALLACE LINE RR 4, INGER-SOLL, ON, N5C 3J7
(519) 425-7881   *SIC* 4213

VITRAN EXPRESS CANADA INC *p275*
10077 GRACE RD, SURREY, BC, V3V 3V7
(604) 582-4500   *SIC* 4213

VITRAN EXPRESS CANADA INC *p560*
1201 CREDITSTONE RD, CONCORD, ON, L4K 0C2
(416) 798-4965   *SIC* 4213

W.J. DEANS TRANSPORTATION INC *p1089*
196 RUE SUTTON, DELSON, QC, J5B 1X3
(450) 638-5933   *SIC* 4213

WALTER, B & D TRUCKING LTD *p141*
1435 31 ST N, LETHBRIDGE, AB, T1H 5G8
SIC 4213

WARREN GIBSON LIMITED *p476*
206 CHURCH ST S, ALLISTON, ON, L9R 2B7
(705) 435-4342   *SIC* 4213

WARREN TRANSPORT LTD *p411*
58 CALIFORNIA RD, REXTON, NB, E4W 1W8
SIC 4213

WATT & STEWART COMMODITIES INC *p80*
4134 3 ST E, CLARESHOLM, AB, T0L 0T0
(403) 625-4436   *SIC* 4213

WEST ARM TRUCK LINES LTD *p195*
1077 COLUMBIA RD, CASTLEGAR, BC, V1N 4K5
(250) 365-2127   *SIC* 4213

WESTCAN BULK TRANSPORT LTD *p1411*
850 MANITOBA ST E, MOOSE JAW, SK, S6H 4P1
(306) 692-6478   *SIC* 4213

WESTCAN BULK TRANSPORT LTD *p1435*
110 71ST ST W, SASKATOON, SK, S7R 1A1
(306) 242-5899   *SIC* 4213

WHITE OAK TRANSPORT LIMITED *p893*
365 LEWIS RD, STONEY CREEK, ON, L8E 5N4
(905) 643-9500   *SIC* 4213

WILKENING, HARV TRANSPORT LTD *p111*
4205 76 AVE NW, EDMONTON, AB, T6B 2H7
(780) 466-9155   *SIC* 4213

WILLIAMS PHARMALOGISTICS INC *p1129*
2165 RUE ONESIME-GAGNON, LACHINE, QC, H8T 3M7
(514) 526-5901   *SIC* 4213

WINNIPEG MOTOR EXPRESS INC *p373*
1180 FIFE ST, WINNIPEG, MB, R2X 2N6
SIC 4213

WITHERS L.P. *p168*
3602 93 ST, STURGEON COUNTY, AB, T8W 5A8
(780) 539-5347   *SIC* 4213

WORLD WIDE CARRIERS LTD *p496*
124 COMMERCIAL RD, BOLTON, ON, L7E 1K4
(416) 213-1334   *SIC* 4213

XPO LOGISTICS FREIGHT CANADA INC *p702*
5425 DIXIE RD ROOM 202, MISSISSAUGA, ON, L4W 1E6
(905) 602-9477   *SIC* 4213

XTL TRANSPORT INC *p589*
75 REXDALE BLVD, ETOBICOKE, ON, M9W 1P1
(416) 742-0610   *SIC* 4213

YRC FREIGHT CANADA COMPANY *p106*
16060 128 AVE NW, EDMONTON, AB, T5V 1B6
(780) 447-2434   *SIC* 4213

YRC FREIGHT CANADA COMPANY *p187*
3985 STILL CREEK AVE, BURNABY, BC, V5C 4E2
(604) 433-3321   *SIC* 4213

YRC FREIGHT CANADA COMPANY *p373*
1400 INKSTER BLVD, WINNIPEG, MB, R2X 1R1
(204) 958-5000   *SIC* 4213

YRC FREIGHT CANADA COMPANY *p702*
5919 SHAWSON DR, MISSISSAUGA, ON, L4W 3Y2
(905) 670-9366   *SIC* 4213

ZAVCOR TRUCKING LIMITED *p890*
3650 EAGLE ST, STEVENSVILLE, ON, L0S 1S0
(905) 382-3444   *SIC* 4213

ZAVCOR TRUCKING LIMITED *p890*
3650 EAGLE ST, STEVENSVILLE, ON, L0S 1S0
(905) 382-3444   *SIC* 4213

ZAVITZ, G. LIMITED *p760*
5795 THOROLD STONE RD, NIAGARA FALLS, ON, L2J 1A1
(905) 356-4945   *SIC* 4213

SIC 4214 Local trucking with storage

1149318 ONTARIO INC *p733*
6900 TRANMERE DR, MISSISSAUGA, ON, L5S 1L9
(866) 576-4228   *SIC* 4214

1300323 ONTARIO INC *p678*
176 HILLMOUNT RD, MARKHAM, ON, L6C 1Z9
(905) 887-5557   *SIC* 4214

3705391 CANADA LIMITED *p595*
5370 CANOTEK RD UNIT 1, GLOUCES-TER, ON, K1J 9E6
(613) 742-7555   *SIC* 4214

465439 ONTARIO INC *p530*
1200 PLAINS RD E, BURLINGTON, ON, L7S 1W6
(905) 632-8010   *SIC* 4214

AMJ CAMPBELL INC *p734*
7075 TOMKEN RD, MISSISSAUGA, ON, L5S 1R7
(905) 795-3785   *SIC* 4214

BEDWELL VAN LINES LIMITED *p844*
1051 TOY AVE, PICKERING, ON, L1W 3N9
(905) 686-0002   *SIC* 4214

BEKINS MOVING AND STORAGE (CANADA) LTD *p278*
3779 190 ST, SURREY, BC, V3Z 0P6
(604) 270-1120   *SIC* 4214

BEST CHOICE OCEAN CONTAINER TERMINAL INC *p642*
11339 ALBION VAUGHAN RD, KLEIN-BURG, ON, L0J 1C0
SIC 4214

BOYD MOVING & STORAGE LTD *p815*
1255 LEEDS AVE UNIT 1, OTTAWA, ON, K1B 3W2
(613) 244-4444   *SIC* 4214

CAMPBELL BROS. MOVERS LIMITED *p661*
55 MIDPARK CRES, LONDON, ON, N6N 1A9
(519) 681-5710   *SIC* 4214

CLAN PANNETON (1993) INC, LE *p1216*
2660 RUE MULLINS, MONTREAL, QC, H3K 1P4
(514) 937-0707   *SIC* 4214

DEMENAGEMENT OUTAOUAIS INC *p1107*
150 RUE JEAN-PROULX, GATINEAU, QC, J8Z 1V3
(819) 771-1634   *SIC* 4214

EXC HOLDINGS LTD. *p221*
1631 DICKSON AVE 10TH FL, KELOWNA, BC, V1Y 0B5
(250) 448-0030   *SIC* 4214

FLUKE TRANSPORT LIMITED *p610*
450 SHERMAN AVE N 2ND FL, HAMILTON, ON, L8L 8J6
(905) 578-0677   *SIC* 4214

FRED GUY MOVING & STORAGE LTD *p816*
1199 NEWMARKET ST, OTTAWA, ON, K1B 3V1
(613) 744-8632   *SIC* 4214

HIGHLAND MOVING & STORAGE LTD *p124*
14490 157 AVE NW, EDMONTON, AB, T6V 0K8
(780) 453-6777   *SIC* 4214

QUICK TRANSFER LTD *p363*
766 PANDORA AVE E UNIT 200, WIN-NIPEG, MB, R2C 3A6
(204) 786-6011   *SIC* 4214

QUICK TRANSFER LTD *p385*
1680 SARGENT AVE, WINNIPEG, MB, R3H 0C2
(204) 786-6011   *SIC* 4214

ROCKBRUNE BROTHERS LIMITED *p474*
725 FINLEY AVE, AJAX, ON, L1S 3T1
(905) 683-4321   *SIC* 4214

SHEFFIELD MOVING AND STORAGE INC *p596*
5499 CANOTEK RD, GLOUCESTER, ON, K1J 9J5
(613) 741-3015   *SIC* 4214

SHEFFIELD MOVING AND STORAGE INC *p877*
4069 GORDON BAKER RD, SCARBOR-OUGH, ON, M1W 2P3
(416) 291-1200   *SIC* 4214

SIMPLEX INDUSTRIES INC *p816*
2762 SHEFFIELD RD, OTTAWA, ON, K1B 3V9
(613) 244-0586   *SIC* 4214

SIRVA CANADA LP *p103*
10403 172 ST NW SUITE 310, EDMON-TON, AB, T5S 1K9
(780) 443-6800   *SIC* 4214

TAYLOR MOVING & STORAGE LIMITED *p531*
1200 PLAINS RD E, BURLINGTON, ON, L7S 1W6
(905) 632-8010   *SIC* 4214

TR WESTCAN INC *p194*
8035 NORTH FRASER WAY, BURNABY, BC, V5J 5M8
(604) 324-5015   *SIC* 4214

TRANSPORT LYON INC *p1239*
9999 RUE NOTRE-DAME E, MONTREAL-EST, QC, H1L 3R5
(514) 322-4422   *SIC* 4214

TRANSPORT TFI 16, S.E.C. *p1060*
801 BOUL INDUSTRIEL BUREAU 228, BOIS-DES-FILION, QC, J6Z 4T3
(450) 628-8000   *SIC* 4214

TWO SMALL MEN WITH BIG HEARTS MOVING (B.C.) CORPORATION *p275*
11180 SCOTT RD, SURREY, BC, V3V 8B8
(604) 581-1616   *SIC* 4214

WILLIAMS MOVING & STORAGE (B.C.) LTD *p202*
2401 UNITED BLVD, COQUITLAM, BC, V3K 5X9
SIC 4214

SIC 4215 Courier services, except by air

FEDERAL EXPRESS CANADA CORPORATION *p735*
6895 BRAMALEA RD SUITE 1, MISSIS-SAUGA, ON, L5S 1Z7
(800) 463-3339   *SIC* 4215

OVATION LOGISTIQUE INC *p1374*
531 RUE PEPIN, SHERBROOKE, QC, J1L 1X3
(819) 569-9923   *SIC* 4215

PENGUIN PICK-UP LIMITED PARTNER-SHIP *p1002*
700 APPLEWOOD CRES UNIT 1, VAUGHAN, ON, L4K 5X3
(905) 760-6200   *SIC* 4215

UNITED PARCEL SERVICE CANADA LTD *p819*
2281 STEVENAGE DR, OTTAWA, ON, K1G 3W1
(613) 670-6061   *SIC* 4215

SIC 4221 Farm product warehousing and storage

ALLIANCE GRAIN TERMINAL LTD *p294*
1155 STEWART ST, VANCOUVER, BC, V6A 4H4
(604) 254-4414   *SIC* 4221

G3 CANADA LIMITED *p374*
423 MAIN ST SUITE 800, WINNIPEG, MB, R3B 1B3
(204) 983-0239   *SIC* 4221

PRINCE RUPERT GRAIN LTD *p251*
GD STN MAIN, PRINCE RUPERT, BC, V8J 3P3
(250) 627-8777   *SIC* 4221

SOUTH WEST TERMINAL LTD *p1407*
GD, GULL LAKE, SK, S0N 1A0
(306) 672-4112   *SIC* 4221

VITERRA INC *p1422*
2625 VICTORIA AVE, REGINA, SK, S4T 1Z8
(306) 569-4411   *SIC* 4221

SIC 4222 Refrigerated warehousing and storage

ARGENTIA FREEZERS & TERMINALS LIMITED *p423*
GD, FRESHWATER PB, NL, A0B 1W0
(709) 227-5603   *SIC* 4222

CONESTOGA COLD STORAGE LIMITED *p637*
299 TRILLIUM DR, KITCHENER, ON, N2E 1W9
(519) 748-5415   *SIC* 4222

CONGEBEC INC *p1261*
810 AV GODIN, QUEBEC, QC, G1M 2X9
(418) 683-3491   *SIC* 4222

CONGEBEC LOGISTIQUE INC *p390*
1555 CHEVRIER BLVD UNIT A, WIN-NIPEG, MB, R3T 1Y7
(204) 475-5570   *SIC* 4222

NOVA COLD LOGISTICS ULC *p505*
745 INTERMODAL DR, BRAMPTON, ON, L6T 5W2

OMSTEAD FOODS LIMITED p1013
303 MILO RD, WHEATLEY, ON, N0P 2P0
(519) 825-4611 *SIC* 4222

SAPUTO INC p76
5434 44 ST NE, CALGARY, AB, T3J 3Z3
(403) 568-3800 *SIC* 4222

THORNVALE HOLDINGS LIMITED p439
441 CAPE AUGET RD, ARICHAT, NS, B0E 1A0
(902) 226-3510 *SIC* 4222

TRENTON COLD STORAGE INC p999
21 ALBERT ST, TRENTON, ON, K8V 4S4
(613) 394-3317 *SIC* 4222

USINE DE CONGELATION DE ST-BRUNO INC p1296
698 RUE MELANCON, SAINT-BRUNO-LAC-SAINT-JEAN, QC, G0W 2L0
(418) 343-2206 *SIC* 4222

VERSACOLD CANADA CORPORATION p286
2115 COMMISSIONER ST SUITE 1, VANCOUVER, BC, V5L 1A6
(604) 255-4656 *SIC* 4222

VERSACOLD GROUP LIMITED PARTNERSHIP p19
5600 76 AVE SE, CALGARY, AB, T2C 4N4
(403) 216-5600 *SIC* 4222

VERSACOLD GROUP LIMITED PARTNERSHIP p207
1188 DERWENT WAY, DELTA, BC, V3M 5R1
(604) 216-6238 *SIC* 4222

VERSACOLD GROUP LIMITED PARTNERSHIP p507
107 WALKER DR, BRAMPTON, ON, L6T 5K5
(905) 793-2653 *SIC* 4222

VERSACOLD INTERNATIONAL CORPORATION p286
2115 COMMISSIONER ST SUITE 1, VANCOUVER, BC, V5L 1A6
(604) 255-4656 *SIC* 4222

VERSACOLD LOGISTICS SERVICES p257
3371 NO. 6 RD, RICHMOND, BC, V6V 1P6
(604) 258-0350 *SIC* 4222

SIC 4225 General warehousing and storage

3M CANADA COMPANY p682
2751 PEDDIE RD, MILTON, ON, L9T 0K1
(905) 875-2568 *SIC* 4225

500323 (N.B.) LTD p412
406 GRANDVIEW AVE, SAINT JOHN, NB, E2J 4N1
(506) 642-6683 *SIC* 4225

A 52 WAREHOUSE INC p224
20146 100A AVE SUITE 2, LANGLEY, BC, V1M 3G2
(604) 881-0251 *SIC* 4225

ACCURISTIX p1026
122 STONE RIDGE RD, WOODBRIDGE, ON, L4H 0A5
(905) 829-9927 *SIC* 4225

ASCO CANADA LIMITED p425
10 CORISANDE DR, MOUNT PEARL, NL, A1N 5A4
(709) 748-7800 *SIC* 4225

ASL DISTRIBUTION SERVICES LIMITED p796
2160 BUCKINGHAM RD, OAKVILLE, ON, L6H 6M7
(905) 829-5141 *SIC* 4225

ASPECT RETAIL LOGISTICS INC p844
1400 CHURCH ST, PICKERING, ON, L1W 4C1
(905) 428-9947 *SIC* 4225

BREWERS' DISTRIBUTOR LTD p70
11500 29 ST SE SUITE 101, CALGARY, AB, T2Z 3W9
(800) 661-2337 *SIC* 4225

CANADIAN MINI-WAREHOUSE PROPERTIES COMPANY p720

1740 ARGENTIA RD, MISSISSAUGA, ON, L5N 3K3
(905) 677-0363 *SIC* 4225

CARQUEST CANADA LTD p583
35 WORCESTER RD SUITE 1, ETOBICOKE, ON, M9W 1K9
(416) 679-3045 *SIC* 4225

CARQUEST CANADA LTD p1064
1670 RUE EIFFEL BUREAU 100, BOUCHERVILLE, QC, J4B 7W1
(450) 641-5757 *SIC* 4225

CN WORLDWIDE DISTRIBUTION SERVICES (CANADA) INC p761
303 TOWNLINE RD SUITE 200, NIAGARA ON THE LAKE, ON, L0S 1J0
(905) 641-3139 *SIC* 4225

COCA-COLA REFRESHMENTS CANADA COMPANY p258
7200 NELSON RD, RICHMOND, BC, V6W 1G4
(416) 424-6000 *SIC* 4225

COMPAGNIE KATOEN NATIE CANADA p100
18210 109 AVE NW, EDMONTON, AB, T5S 2K2
(780) 489-9040 *SIC* 4225

CONESTOGA COLD STORAGE (QUEBEC) LIMITED p1093
10000 AV RYAN, DORVAL, QC, H9P 3A1
(514) 631-5040 *SIC* 4225

COVERED BRIDGE POTATO CHIP COMPANY INC p418
149 ST THOMAS RD, ST THOMAS, NB, E7P 2X6
(506) 375-2447 *SIC* 4225

CWS LOGISTICS LTD p390
1664 SEEL AVE, WINNIPEG, MB, R3T 4X5
(204) 474-2278 *SIC* 4225

DGN MARKETING SERVICES LTD p738
1633 MEYERSIDE DR, MISSISSAUGA, ON, L5T 1B9
(905) 670-4070 *SIC* 4225

DYMON STORAGE CORPORATION p819
1830 WALKLEY RD UNIT 1, OTTAWA, ON, K1H 8K3
(613) 247-9908 *SIC* 4225

ENTREPOSAGE MASKA LTEE p1312
2825 BOUL CASAVANT O, SAINT-HYACINTHE, QC, J2S 7Y4
(450) 773-9615 *SIC* 4225

ENTREPOTS LAFRANCE INC p1164
7055 RUE NOTRE-DAME E, MONTREAL, QC, H1N 3R8
(514) 254-6688 *SIC* 4225

ENTREPOTS P C G INC, LES p1089
121 RUE PRINCIPALE N, DELSON, QC, J5B 1Z2
(450) 635-8053 *SIC* 4225

ENTREPOTS SIMARD INC, LES p1127
2737 RUE LOUIS-A.-AMOS, LACHINE, QC, H8T 1C3
(514) 636-9411 *SIC* 4225

EV LOGISTICS p229
5111 272 ST, LANGLEY, BC, V4W 3Z2
(604) 857-6750 *SIC* 4225

EXEL CANADA LTD p513
100 SANDALWOOD PKY W, BRAMPTON, ON, L7A 1A8
(905) 840-7540 *SIC* 4225

EXEL CANADA LTD p731
90 MATHESON BLVD W SUITE 111, MISSISSAUGA, ON, L5R 3R3
(905) 366-7700 *SIC* 4225

FEDERATED CO-OPERATIVES LIMITED p1427
604 45TH ST E, SASKATOON, SK, S7K 3T3
(306) 242-1505 *SIC* 4225

FEDERATED CO-OPERATIVES LIMITED p1427
401 22ND ST E, SASKATOON, SK, S7K 0H2
(306) 244-3311 *SIC* 4225

FORT MCKAY SERVICES LIMITED PARTNERSHIP p128
GD LCD MAIN, FORT MCMURRAY, AB, T9H 3E2
(780) 828-2400 *SIC* 4225

FOURNIER VAN & STORAGE, LIMITED p844
1051 TOY AVE, PICKERING, ON, L1W 3N9
(905) 686-0002 *SIC* 4225

GREGG DISTRIBUTORS CO LTD p109
3611 76 AVE NW, EDMONTON, AB, T6B 2S8
(780) 450-2233 *SIC* 4225

GROUPE ROBERT INC p1065
65 RUE DE VAUDREUIL, BOUCHERVILLE, QC, J4B 1K7
(514) 521-1416 *SIC* 4225

HCL LOGISTICS INC p649
2021 OXFORD ST E, LONDON, ON, N5V 2Z7
(519) 681-4254 *SIC* 4225

HEARN INDUSTRIAL SERVICES INC p804
2189 SPEERS RD, OAKVILLE, ON, L6L 2X9
(866) 297-6914 *SIC* 4225

HEARN INDUSTRIAL SERVICES INC p1022
2480 SEMINOLE ST, WINDSOR, ON, N8Y 1X3
(226) 674-3200 *SIC* 4225

HOME DEPOT OF CANADA INC p1027
8966 HUNTINGTON RD, WOODBRIDGE, ON, L4H 3V1
(905) 265-4400 *SIC* 4225

HOPEWELL LOGISTICS INC p499
255 CHRYSLER DR SUITE 3A, BRAMPTON, ON, L6S 6C8
(905) 458-8860 *SIC* 4225

HOPEWELL LOGISTICS INC p499
9050 AIRPORT RD SUITE 201, BRAMPTON, ON, L6S 6G6
(905) 458-1041 *SIC* 4225

HUDSON'S BAY COMPANY p258
18111 BLUNDELL RD, RICHMOND, BC, V6W 1L8
(604) 249-3000 *SIC* 4225

I & S WAREHOUSING INC p554
21 STAFFERN DR, CONCORD, ON, L4K 2X2
(905) 761-0250 *SIC* 4225

IMMEUBLES RB LTEE p1288
500 RTE 112, ROUGEMONT, QC, J0L 1M0
(450) 469-3153 *SIC* 4225

LIQUOR CONTROL BOARD OF ONTARIO, THE p1014
2000 BOUNDARY RD, WHITBY, ON, L1N 7G4
(905) 723-3417 *SIC* 4225

LOCHER EVERS INTERNATIONAL INC p206
456 HUMBER PL, DELTA, BC, V3M 6A5
(604) 525-0577 *SIC* 4225

MACCOSHAM INC p110
7220 68 AVE NW, EDMONTON, AB, T6B 0A1
(780) 448-1910 *SIC* 4225

MATRIX LOGISTICS SERVICES LIMITED p9
2525 29 ST NE, CALGARY, AB, T1Y 7B5
(403) 291-9292 *SIC* 4225

MATRIX LOGISTICS SERVICES LIMITED p410
10 DEWARE DR SUITE 1, MONCTON, NB, E1H 2S6
(506) 863-1300 *SIC* 4225

MATRIX LOGISTICS SERVICES LIMITED p511
2675 STEELES AVE W, BRAMPTON, ON, L6Y 5X3
(905) 451-6792 *SIC* 4225

MATRIX LOGISTICS SERVICES LIMITED p740
6941 KENNEDY RD, MISSISSAUGA, ON, L5T 2R6
(905) 795-2200 *SIC* 4225

METRO LOGISTIQUE INC p686
7380 BREN RD UNIT 2, MISSISSAUGA, ON, L4T 1H3
(905) 461-0006 *SIC* 4225

METRO ONTARIO INC p579
170 THE WEST MALL, ETOBICOKE, ON, M9C 5L6
(416) 626-4910 *SIC* 4225

METRO RICHELIEU INC p1161
11555 BOUL MAURICE-DUPLESSIS BUREAU 1, MONTREAL, QC, H1C 2A1
(514) 643-1000 *SIC* 4225

MTD METRO TOOL & DIE LIMITED p697
1065 PANTERA DR, MISSISSAUGA, ON, L4W 2X4
(905) 625-8464 *SIC* 4225

MTE LOGISTIX EDMONTON INC p94
14627 128 AVE NW, EDMONTON, AB, T5L 3H3
(780) 944-9009 *SIC* 4225

MTE LOGISTIX EDMONTON INC p102
11250 189 ST NW, EDMONTON, AB, T5S 2V6
(780) 944-9009 *SIC* 4225

NFI DOMINION CANADA, ULC p586
1920 ALBION RD, ETOBICOKE, ON, M9W 5T2
(416) 744-2438 *SIC* 4225

OLD DUTCH FOODS LTD p102
18027 114 AVE NW, EDMONTON, AB, T5S 1T8
(780) 453-2341 *SIC* 4225

PIC GROUP LTD, THE p1015
202 SOUTH BLAIR ST UNIT 12, WHITBY, ON, L1N 8X9
(416) 676-5659 *SIC* 4225

POLYMER DISTRIBUTION INC p600
256 VICTORIA RD S, GUELPH, ON, N1E 5R1
(519) 837-4535 *SIC* 4225

PROVIGO DISTRIBUTION INC p1237
2700 AV FRANCIS-HUGHES BUREAU 2172, MONTREAL, QC, H7S 2B9
(514) 383-8800 *SIC* 4225

QUAD LOGISTIX INC p505
5 PAGET RD, BRAMPTON, ON, L6T 5S2
(905) 789-6225 *SIC* 4225

SCI LOGISTICS LTD p588
180 ATTWELL DR SUITE 600, ETOBICOKE, ON, M9W 6A9
(416) 401-3011 *SIC* 4225

SENTINEL SELF-STORAGE CORPORATION p90
10123 99 ST NW SUITE 1970, EDMONTON, AB, T5J 3H1
(780) 424-8945 *SIC* 4225

SERVICES NOLITREX INC p1116
3462 RUE DE L'ENERGIE, JONQUIERE, QC, G7X 9H3
(418) 542-0386 *SIC* 4225

SHERWAY WAREHOUSING INC p743
325A ANNAGEM BLVD SUITE 2, MISSISSAUGA, ON, L5T 3A7
(905) 364-3300 *SIC* 4225

SMITH, J.D. & SONS LIMITED p558
180 BASALTIC RD, CONCORD, ON, L4K 1G6
(905) 669-8980 *SIC* 4225

SOBEYS WEST INC p32
203 42 AVE SE, CALGARY, AB, T2G 1Y3
(403) 287-4048 *SIC* 4225

SOBEYS WEST INC p40
215 42 AVE NW, CALGARY, AB, T2K 0H3
(403) 730-3500 *SIC* 4225

STAVSTAN INC p1071
3955 RUE DE LONGFORD, BROSSARD, QC, J4Y 3J6
(450) 445-7390 *SIC* 4225

STORAGEVAULT CANADA INC p1416
6050 DIEFENBAKER AVE, REGINA, SK, S4N 7L2
(306) 546-5999 *SIC* 4225

TAYLOR STEEL INC p893
395 GREEN RD, STONEY CREEK, ON, L8E 5V4
(905) 662-5555 *SIC* 4225

TFT GLOBAL INC p912
25 TOWNLINE RD SUITE 200, TILLSONBURG, ON, N4G 2R5
(519) 842-4540 *SIC* 4225

▲ Public Company ■ Public Company Family Member **HQ** Headquarters **BR** Branch **SL** Single Location

THOMSON TERMINALS LIMITED   p588
55 CITY VIEW DR, ETOBICOKE, ON, M9W 5A5
(416) 240-0897   *SIC* 4225
THYSSENKRUPP SUPPLY CHAIN SERVICES CA, INC   p1021
2491 OUELLETTE AVE, WINDSOR, ON, N8X 1L5
(519) 977-8420   *SIC* 4225
TRENTON COLD STORAGE INC   p999
17489 TELEPHONE RD, TRENTON, ON, K8V 5P4
(613) 394-3317   *SIC* 4225
TST SOLUTIONS L.P.   p1015
1601 TRICONT AVE, WHITBY, ON, L1N 7N5
SIC 4225
UNIVAR CANADA LTD   p785
777 SUPERTEST RD, NORTH YORK, ON, M3J 2M9
(416) 740-5300   *SIC* 4225
VAN-WHOLE PRODUCE LTD   p296
830 MALKIN AVE, VANCOUVER, BC, V6A 2K2
(604) 251-3330   *SIC* 4225
W.D.I. SERVICES LTD   p324
1588 RAND AVE, VANCOUVER, BC, V6P 3G2
(604) 263-2739   *SIC* 4225
WALLSA HOLDINGS LTD   p210
8188 RIVER WAY, DELTA, BC, V4G 1K5
(604) 940-8891   *SIC* 4225
WALMART CANADA LOGISTICS ULC p10
3400 39 AVE NE, CALGARY, AB, T1Y 7J4
(403) 250-3648   *SIC* 4225
WALMART CANADA LOGISTICS ULC p160
261039 WAGON WHEEL CRES, ROCKY VIEW COUNTY, AB, T4A 0E2
(403) 295-8364   *SIC* 4225
WALMART CANADA LOGISTICS ULC p745
200 COURTNEYPARK DR W, MISSISSAUGA, ON, L5W 1Y6
(905) 564-1484   *SIC* 4225
WALMART CANADA LOGISTICS ULC p745
6800 MARITZ DR, MISSISSAUGA, ON, L5W 1W2
(905) 670-9966   *SIC* 4225
WESTROCK COMPANY OF CANADA CORP p1157
5550 AV ROYALMOUNT, MONT-ROYAL, QC, H4P 1H7
(514) 736-6889   *SIC* 4225
WILLS TRANSFER LIMITED   p882
146 HWY 15, SMITHS FALLS, ON, K7A 4S7
(613) 283-0225   *SIC* 4225

SIC 4226 Special warehousing and storage, nec

115161 CANADA INC   p1126
5203 RUE FAIRWAY, LACHINE, QC, H8T 3K8
(514) 635-1088   *SIC* 4226
9517154 CANADA LTD   p691
5300 SATELLITE DR, MISSISSAUGA, ON, L4W 5J2
(905) 602-1225   *SIC* 4226
AUTOPORT LIMITED   p449
1180 MAIN RD, EASTERN PASSAGE, NS, B3G 0B5
(902) 465-6050   *SIC* 4226
CONNECT LOGISTICS SERVICES INC p165
50 CORRIVEAU AVE, ST. ALBERT, AB, T8N 3T5
(780) 458-4492   *SIC* 4226
FRASER WHARVES LTD   p258
13800 STEVESTON HWY, RICHMOND, BC, V6W 1A8
(604) 277-1141   *SIC* 4226
GENERAL MOTORS OF CANADA COMPANY   p1035
1401 PARKINSON RD, WOODSTOCK, ON, N4S 7W3
(519) 539-6136   *SIC* 4226

GEORGETOWN TERMINAL WAREHOUSES LIMITED   p593
34 ARMSTRONG AVE, GEORGETOWN, ON, L7G 4R9
(905) 873-2750   *SIC* 4226
GOLDEN BOY FOODS LTD   p182
3151 LAKE CITY WAY, BURNABY, BC, V5A 3A3
(604) 421-4500   *SIC* 4226
IRON MOUNTAIN CANADA OPERATIONS ULC   p504
195 SUMMERLEA RD, BRAMPTON, ON, L6T 4P6
(905) 792-7099   *SIC* 4226
IRON MOUNTAIN CANADA OPERATIONS ULC   p554
70 TALMAN CRT SUITE 415, CONCORD, ON, L4K 4L5
(905) 695-0564   *SIC* 4226
IRON MOUNTAIN CANADA OPERATIONS ULC   p1241
1655 RUE FLEETWOOD, MONTREAL-OUEST, QC, H7N 4B2
(450) 667-5960   *SIC* 4226
PIVAL INTERNATIONAL INC   p1094
1600 RTE TRANSCANADIENNE BUREAU 100, DORVAL, QC, H9P 1H7
(514) 684-1600   *SIC* 4226
SCHENKER OF CANADA LIMITED   p587
1920 ALBION RD, ETOBICOKE, ON, M9W 5T2
(416) 798-8070   *SIC* 4226
SERVICES DOCUMENTAIRES MULTIMEDIA (S.D.M) INC   p1172
5650 RUE D'IBERVILLE BUREAU 620, MONTREAL, QC, H2G 2B3
(514) 382-0895   *SIC* 4226
SERVITANK INC   p1388
3450 BOUL GENE-H.-KRUGER, TROIS-RIVIERES, QC, G9A 4M3
(819) 379-4081   *SIC* 4226
SYMCOR INC   p454
1580 GRAFTON ST, HALIFAX, NS, B3J 2C2
(902) 404-4606   *SIC* 4226

SIC 4231 Trucking terminal facilities

CENTRAL CARRIERS (EDMONTON) LTD p105
13008 163 ST NW, EDMONTON, AB, T5V 1L6
(780) 447-1610   *SIC* 4231
COAST 2000 TERMINALS LTD   p258
16080 PORTSIDE RD SUITE 100, RICHMOND, BC, V6W 1M1
(604) 270-3625   *SIC* 4231
COMPAGNIE DES CHEMINS DE FER NATIONAUX DU CANADA   p408
255 HUMP YARD RD, MONCTON, NB, E1E 4S3
(506) 853-2866   *SIC* 4231
COURTESY FREIGHT SYSTEMS LTD p909
340 SIMPSON ST, THUNDER BAY, ON, P7C 3H7
(807) 623-3278   *SIC* 4231
FEDEX TRADE NETWORKS TRANSPORT & BROKERAGE (CANADA), INC   p739
7075 ORDAN DR, MISSISSAUGA, ON, L5T 1K6
(905) 677-7371   *SIC* 4231
MACKIE MOVING SYSTEMS CORPORATION   p814
933 BLOOR ST W, OSHAWA, ON, L1J 5Y7
(905) 728-2400   *SIC* 4231
TITANIUM TRANSPORTATION GROUP INC p495
32 SIMPSON RD, BOLTON, ON, L7E 1G9
(905) 851-1688   *SIC* 4231
TRANSFRT MCNAMARA INC   p483
1126 INDUSTRIAL RD, AYR, ON, N0B 1E0
(519) 740-6500   *SIC* 4231
TST SOLUTIONS L.P.   p370
1987 BROOKSIDE BLVD, WINNIPEG, MB,

R2R 2Y3
(204) 697-5795   *SIC* 4231
YRC FREIGHT CANADA COMPANY p1096
1725 CH SAINT-FRANCOIS, DORVAL, QC, H9P 2S1
(514) 684-9970   *SIC* 4231

SIC 4311 U.s. postal service

CANADA POST CORPORATION   p236
24 OVENS AVE, NEW WESTMINSTER, BC, V3L 1Z2
(604) 516-7802   *SIC* 4311
CANADA POST CORPORATION   p637
70 TRILLIUM DR, KITCHENER, ON, N2E 0E2
(519) 748-3056   *SIC* 4311
CANADA POST CORPORATION   p815
2701 RIVERSIDE DR, OTTAWA, ON, K1A 1M2
(613) 734-8440   *SIC* 4311
CANADA POST CORPORATION   p815
2701 RIVERSIDE DR, OTTAWA, ON, K1A 0B1
(613) 734-8440   *SIC* 4311
CANADA POST CORPORATION   p815
2701 RIVERSIDE DR, OTTAWA, ON, K1A 1L5
(613) 734-8440   *SIC* 4311
CANADA POST CORPORATION   p870
280 PROGRESS AVE, SCARBOROUGH, ON, M1P 5H8
(416) 299-4577   *SIC* 4311
CANADA POST CORPORATION   p884
163 SCOTT ST, ST CATHARINES, ON, L2N 1H3
(905) 934-9792   *SIC* 4311
CANADA POST CORPORATION   p1030
21 HAIST AVE SUITE 1, WOODBRIDGE, ON, L4L 5V5
(905) 851-1237   *SIC* 4311
CANADA POST CORPORATION   p1056
595 BOUL SIR-WILFRID-LAURIER, BELOEIL, QC, J3G 4J1
SIC 4311
CANADA POST CORPORATION   p1061
4570 RUE AMBROISE-LAFORTUNE, BOISBRIAND, QC, J7H 0E5
(450) 435-4527   *SIC* 4311
CANADA POST CORPORATION   p1078
1939 RUE DES SAPINS UNITE 1, CHICOUTIMI, QC, G7H 0H7
(418) 690-0350   *SIC* 4311
CANADA POST CORPORATION   p1164
6700 RUE SHERBROOKE E, MONTREAL, QC, H1N 1C9
(514) 259-3233   *SIC* 4311
CANADA POST CORPORATION   p1263
600 RUE GRAHAM-BELL, QUEBEC, QC, G1N 0B2
(418) 847-2160   *SIC* 4311
CANADA POST CORPORATION   p1278
6700 BOUL PIERRE-BERTRAND BUREAU 200, QUEBEC, QC, G2J 0B6
SIC 4311
CANADA POST CORPORATION   p1338
555 RUE MCARTHUR BUREAU 1506, SAINT-LAURENT, QC, H4T 1T4
(514) 345-4571   *SIC* 4311
CANADA POST CORPORATION   p1384
1285 RUE NOTRE-DAME E, TROIS-RIVIERES, QC, G8T 4J9
(819) 691-4215   *SIC* 4311
CGI POSTES CANADA   p1263
1940 RUE LEON-HARMEL, QUEBEC, QC, G1N 4K3
(418) 682-8663   *SIC* 4311

SIC 4412 Deep sea foreign transportation of freight

CMA CGM (CANADA) INC   p1210

740 RUE NOTRE-DAME O BUREAU 1330, MONTREAL, QC, H3C 3X6
(514) 908-7001   *SIC* 4412
DESGAGNES MARINE CARGO INC p1258
21 RUE DU MARCHE-CHAMPLAIN BUREAU 100, QUEBEC, QC, G1K 8Z8
(418) 692-1000   *SIC* 4412
DESGAGNES MARINE PETRO INC p1258
21 RUE DU MARCHE-CHAMPLAIN BUREAU 100, QUEBEC, QC, G1K 8Z8
(418) 692-1000   *SIC* 4412
FEDNAV INTERNATIONAL LTEE   p1204
1000 RUE DE LA GAUCHETIERE O BUREAU 3500, MONTREAL, QC, H3B 4W5
(514) 878-6500   *SIC* 4412
FEDNAV LIMITEE   p1204
1000 RUE DE LA GAUCHETIERE O BUREAU 3500, MONTREAL, QC, H3B 4W5
(514) 878-6500   *SIC* 4412
FLOWRIDER SURF LTD   p258
6700 MCMILLAN WAY, RICHMOND, BC, V6W 1J7
(604) 273-1068   *SIC* 4412
MCASPHALT MARINE TRANSPORTATION LTD   p609
180 PIER 24 GATEWAY, HAMILTON, ON, L8H 0A3
(905) 549-9408   *SIC* 4412
SERVICES DE TRANSPORT TRAC-WORLD INC   p1356
6565 BOUL HEBERT, SAINTE-CATHERINE, QC, J5C 1B5
(450) 635-8271   *SIC* 4412
TEEKAY (ATLANTIC) MANAGEMENT ULC p434
5 SPRINGDALE ST SUITE 105, ST. JOHN'S, NL, A1E 0E4
(855) 485-9351   *SIC* 4412
TEEKAY SHIPPING (CANADA) LTD   p310
550 BURRARD ST SUITE 2000, VANCOUVER, BC, V6C 2K2
(604) 683-3529   *SIC* 4412

SIC 4424 Deep sea domestic transportation of freight

C.T.M.A. TRAVERSIER LTEE   p1073
435 CH AVILA-ARSENEAU, CAP-AUX-MEULES, QC, G4T 1J3
(418) 986-6600   *SIC* 4424
CANSHIP UGLAND LTD   p429
1315 TOPSAIL RD, ST. JOHN'S, NL, A1B 3N4
(709) 782-3333   *SIC* 4424
COASTAL SHIPPING LIMITED   p425
128 MAIN ST, LEWISPORTE, NL, A0G 3A0
(709) 535-6944   *SIC* 4424
CROISIERES AML INC   p1258
124 RUE SAINT-PIERRE, QUEBEC, QC, G1K 4A7
(866) 856-6668   *SIC* 4424
GROUPE CSL INC   p1188
759 RUE DU SQUARE-VICTORIA BUREAU 600, MONTREAL, QC, H2Y 2K3
(514) 982-3800   *SIC* 4424
OCEANEX INC   p432
10 FORT WILLIAM PL SUITE 701, ST. JOHN'S, NL, A1C 1K4
(709) 758-0382   *SIC* 4424
OCEANEX INC   p432
701 KENT FORT WILLIAM PLACE, ST. JOHN'S, NL, A1C 1K4
(709) 722-6280   *SIC* 4424
OCEANEX INC   p1206
630 BOUL RENE-LEVESQUE O BUREAU 2550, MONTREAL, QC, H3B 1S6
SIC 4424
PUDDISTER TRADING COMPANY LIMITED p433
23 SPRINGDALE ST, ST. JOHN'S, NL, A1E 2P9
(709) 722-4000   *SIC* 4424
RELAIS NORDIK INC   p1259

---

21 RUE DU MARCHE-CHAMPLAIN BUREAU 100, QUEBEC, QC, G1K 8Z8
(418) 692-1000   *SIC 4424*
SEAWAY SELF UNLOADERS   *p886*
63 CHURCH ST SUITE 503, ST CATHARINES, ON, L2R 3C4
(905) 988-2600   *SIC 4424*

SIC 4432 Freight transportation on the great lakes

ALGOMA CENTRAL CORPORATION   *p885*
63 CHURCH ST SUITE 600, ST CATHARINES, ON, L2R 3C4
SIC 4432
ALGOMA CENTRAL CORPORATION   *p885*
63 CHURCH ST SUITE 600, ST CATHARINES, ON, L2R 3C4
(905) 687-7888   *SIC 4432*
NAVIGATION MADELEINE INC   *p1073*
435 CH AVILA-ARSENEAU, CAP-AUX-MEULES, QC, G4T 1J3
(418) 986-6600   *SIC 4432*
ST. LAWRENCE SEAWAY MANAGEMENT CORPORATION, THE   *p886*
508 GLENDALE AVE, ST CATHARINES, ON, L2R 6V8
(905) 641-1932   *SIC 4432*

SIC 4449 Water transportation of freight

BAY FERRIES LIMITED   *p1038*
94 WATER ST, CHARLOTTETOWN, PE, C1A 1A6
(902) 566-3838   *SIC 4449*
CONTRANS GROUP INC   *p683*
100 MARKET DR, MILTON, ON, L9T 3H5
(905) 693-8088   *SIC 4449*
COOPER BARGING SERVICE LTD   *p212*
GD, FORT NELSON, BC, V0C 1R0
(250) 774-3359   *SIC 4449*
FRASER RIVER MARINE TRANSPORTATION LTD   *p230*
23888 RIVER RD, MAPLE RIDGE, BC, V2W 1B7
(604) 463-3044   *SIC 4449*
LOWER LAKES TOWING LTD   *p847*
517 MAIN ST, PORT DOVER, ON, N0A 1N0
(519) 583-0982   *SIC 4449*
NORTHUMBERLAND FERRIES LIMITED   *p1039*
94 WATER ST, CHARLOTTETOWN, PE, C1A 1A6
(902) 566-3838   *SIC 4449*
ST. LAWRENCE SEAWAY MANAGEMENT CORPORATION, THE   *p563*
202 PITT ST, CORNWALL, ON, K6J 3P7
(613) 932-5170   *SIC 4449*

SIC 4482 Ferries

BRITISH COLUMBIA FERRY SERVICES INC   *p336*
1321 BLANSHARD ST SUITE 500, VICTORIA, BC, V8W 0B7
(250) 381-1401   *SIC 4482*
COASTAL TRANSPORT LIMITED   *p415*
22 GERMAIN ST SUITE 104, SAINT JOHN, NB, E2L 2E5
(506) 642-0520   *SIC 4482*
CONTRANS GROUP INC   *p839*
42 LANARK RD, PERTH, ON, K7H 3K5
(613) 267-2007   *SIC 4482*
MARINE ATLANTIC INC   *p421*
GD, CHANNEL-PORT-AUX-BASQUES, NL, A0M 1C0
(709) 695-4200   *SIC 4482*
MARINE ATLANTIC INC   *p432*
10 FORT WILLIAM PL SUITE 302, ST. JOHN'S, NL, A1C 1K4
(709) 772-8957   *SIC 4482*

MARINE ATLANTIC INC   *p464*
355 PURVES ST, NORTH SYDNEY, NS, B2A 3V2
(902) 794-5200   *SIC 4482*
SEASPAN FERRIES CORPORATION   *p210*
7700 HOPCOTT RD, DELTA, BC, V4G 1B6
(604) 940-7228   *SIC 4482*
SOCIETE DES TRAVERSIERS DU QUEBEC   *p1260*
250 RUE SAINT-PAUL, QUEBEC, QC, G1K 9K9
(418) 643-2019   *SIC 4482*
SOCIETE FERROVIAIRE ET PORTUAIRE DE POINTE-NOIRE S.E.C.   *p1367*
1505 CH POINTE-NOIRE, SEPT-ILES, QC, G4R 4L4
(418) 962-5131   *SIC 4482*
WESTERN PACIFIC MARINE LTD   *p319*
501 DENMAN ST, VANCOUVER, BC, V6G 2W9
(604) 681-5199   *SIC 4482*

SIC 4489 Water passenger transportation

GANANOQUE BOAT LINE LIMITED   *p592*
280 MAIN ST, GANANOQUE, ON, K7G 2M2
(613) 382-2144   *SIC 4489*
GREAT LAKES SCHOONER COMPANY LIMITED   *p963*
249 QUEENS QUAY W SUITE 111, TORONTO, ON, M5J 2N5
(416) 260-6355   *SIC 4489*
ROCKPORT BOAT LINE (1994) LIMITED   *p857*
23 FRONT ST, ROCKPORT, ON, K0E 1V0
(613) 659-3402   *SIC 4489*

SIC 4491 Marine cargo handling

(T.P.Q.) TERMINAUX PORTUAIRES DU QUEBEC INC   *p1257*
961 BOUL CHAMPLAIN, QUEBEC, QC, G1K 4J9
(418) 529-6521   *SIC 4491*
ADMINISTRATION PORTUAIRE DU QUEBEC   *p1257*
150 RUE DALHOUSIE BUREAU 2268, QUEBEC, QC, G1K 4C4
(418) 648-3640   *SIC 4491*
COSCO SHIPPING LINES (CANADA) INC   *p328*
1055 DUNSMUIR ST SUITE 2288, VANCOUVER, BC, V7X 1K8
(604) 689-8989   *SIC 4491*
DP WORLD (CANADA) INC   *p294*
777 CENTENNIAL RD, VANCOUVER, BC, V6A 1A3
(604) 255-5151   *SIC 4491*
FUNDY STEVEDORING INC   *p395*
140 CHAMPLAIN PROM, BAYSIDE, NB, E5B 2Y2
(506) 529-8821   *SIC 4491*
GCT CANADA LIMITED PARTNERSHIP   *p295*
1285 FRANKLIN ST, VANCOUVER, BC, V6A 1J9
(604) 267-5200   *SIC 4491*
HALIFAX PORT AUTHORITY   *p451*
1215 MARGINAL RD, HALIFAX, NS, B3H 4P8
(902) 426-8222   *SIC 4491*
HALTERM LIMITED   *p451*
577 MARGINAL RD, HALIFAX, NS, B3H 4P6
(902) 421-1778   *SIC 4491*
HARVEY, A. & COMPANY LIMITED   *p432*
60 WATER ST, ST JOHN'S, NL, A1C 1A3
(709) 576-4761   *SIC 4491*
HUDSON BAY PORT COMPANY   *p348*
1 AXWORTHY WAY, CHURCHILL, MB, R0B 0E0
(204) 675-8823   *SIC 4491*

I.H. MATHERS & SON LIMITED   *p453*
1525 BIRMINGHAM ST, HALIFAX, NS, B3J 2J6
(902) 429-5680   *SIC 4491*
LOGISTEC ARRIMAGE INC   *p1189*
360 RUE SAINT-JACQUES BUREAU 1500, MONTREAL, QC, H2Y 3X1
(514) 844-9381   *SIC 4491*
LOGISTEC CORPORATION   *p1189*
360 RUE SAINT-JACQUES BUREAU 1500, MONTREAL, QC, H2Y 3X1
(514) 844-9381   *SIC 4491*
LOGISTEC STEVEDORING (NOVA SCOTIA) INC.   *p451*
1096 MARGINAL RD SUITE 208, HALIFAX, NS, B3H 4N4
(902) 422-7483   *SIC 4491*
MONTREAL GATEWAY TERMINALS PARTNERSHIP   *p1163*
305 RUE CURATTEAU, MONTREAL, QC, H1L 6R6
(514) 257-3040   *SIC 4491*
MONTREAL PORT ADMINISTRATION   *p1211*
2100 AV PIERRE-DUPUY BUREAU 1, MONTREAL, QC, H3C 3R5
(514) 283-7011   *SIC 4491*
MORTERM LIMITED   *p1022*
1601 LINCOLN RD, WINDSOR, ON, N8Y 2J3
(519) 973-8200   *SIC 4491*
NEPTUNE BULK TERMINALS (CANADA) LTD   *p239*
1001 LOW LEVEL RD, NORTH VANCOUVER, BC, V7L 1A7
(604) 985-7461   *SIC 4491*
PACIFIC COAST TERMINALS CO. LTD   *p248*
2300 COLUMBIA ST, PORT MOODY, BC, V3H 5J9
(604) 939-7371   *SIC 4491*
PENNECON ENERGY MARINE BASE LTD   *p433*
650 WATER ST, ST. JOHN'S, NL, A1E 1B9
(709) 334-2820   *SIC 4491*
QSL CANADA INC   *p1259*
961 BOUL CHAMPLAIN, QUEBEC, QC, G1K 4J9
(418) 522-4701   *SIC 4491*
QUEBEC STEVEDORING COMPANY LTD   *p1259*
961 BOUL CHAMPLAIN, QUEBEC, QC, G1K 4J9
(418) 522-4701   *SIC 4491*
RIDLEY TERMINALS INC   *p252*
2110 RIDLEY RD, PRINCE RUPERT, BC, V8J 4H3
(250) 624-9511   *SIC 4491*
SHORE TO SEA SERVICES LLS   *p309*
999 CANADA PL, VANCOUVER, BC, V6C 3C1
(604) 775-7200   *SIC 4491*
SOMAVRAC INC   *p1388*
3450 BOUL GENE-H.-KRUGER, TROIS-RIVIERES, QC, G9A 4M3
(819) 379-3311   *SIC 4491*
SQUAMISH TERMINALS LTD   *p269*
37500 THIRD AVE, SQUAMISH, BC, V8B 0B1
(604) 892-3511   *SIC 4491*
VANCOUVER FRASER PORT AUTHORITY   *p310*
999 CANADA PL SUITE 100, VANCOUVER, BC, V6C 3T4
(604) 665-9000   *SIC 4491*
WESTERN STEVEDORING COMPANY LIMITED   *p239*
15 MOUNTAIN HWY, NORTH VANCOUVER, BC, V7J 2J9
(604) 904-2800   *SIC 4491*
WESTSHORE TERMINALS LTD   *p211*
1 ROBERTS BANK RD, DELTA, BC, V4M 4G5
(604) 946-4491   *SIC 4491*
ZIM CIE DE SERVICES DE NAVIGATION INTEGREE (CANADA) LTEE   *p1209*

1155 BOUL RENE-LEVESQUE O BUREAU 400, MONTREAL, QC, H3B 4R1
(844) 454-5072   *SIC 4491*

SIC 4492 Towing and tugboat service

ATLANTIC TOWING LIMITED   *p414*
300 UNION ST SUITE 2, SAINT JOHN, NB, E2L 4Z2
(506) 648-2750   *SIC 4492*
CATHERWOOD TOWING LTD   *p232*
32885 MISSION WAY SUITE 101, MISSION, BC, V2V 6E4
(604) 826-9221   *SIC 4492*
HODDER TUGBOAT CO. LTD   *p260*
11171 RIVER RD, RICHMOND, BC, V6X 1Z6
(604) 273-2821   *SIC 4492*
ISLAND TUG AND BARGE LTD   *p186*
800 GLASGOW AVE, BURNABY, BC, V5C 0C9
(604) 873-4312   *SIC 4492*
JONES MARINE GROUP LTD   *p196*
9871 ESPLANADE ST, CHEMAINUS, BC, V0R 1K1
(250) 246-1100   *SIC 4492*
LOCATION OCEAN INC   *p1259*
105 RUE ABRAHAM-MARTIN BUREAU 500, QUEBEC, QC, G1K 8N1
(418) 694-1414   *SIC 4492*
PACIFIC TOWING SERVICES LTD   *p239*
14 ORWELL ST, NORTH VANCOUVER, BC, V7J 2G1
(604) 990-0591   *SIC 4492*
SAAM SMIT CANADA INC   *p285*
2285 COMMISSIONER ST, VANCOUVER, BC, V5L 1A8
(604) 255-1133   *SIC 4492*
SEASPAN ULC   *p242*
10 PEMBERTON AVE, NORTH VANCOUVER, BC, V7P 2R1
(604) 988-3111   *SIC 4492*
SEASPAN ULC   *p242*
10 PEMBERTON AVE, NORTH VANCOUVER, BC, V7P 2R1
(604) 988-3111   *SIC 4492*
SMIT MARINE CANADA INC   *p285*
2285 COMMISSIONER ST, VANCOUVER, BC, V5L 1A8
(604) 255-1133   *SIC 4492*
WESTRAN PORTSIDE TERMINAL LIMITED   *p259*
16060 PORTSIDE RD, RICHMOND, BC, V6W 1M1
(604) 244-1975   *SIC 4492*

SIC 4493 Marinas

2437-0223 QUEBEC INC   *p1282*
364 RUE NOTRE-DAME, REPENTIGNY, QC, J6A 2S5
(450) 581-7071   *SIC 4493*
ASSOCIATION SOGERIVE INC   *p1142*
101 CH DE LA RIVE, LONGUEUIL, QC, J4H 4C9
(450) 442-9575   *SIC 4493*
CHANTIER DAVIE CANADA INC   *p1136*
22 RUE GEORGE-D.-DAVIE, LEVIS, QC, G6V 0K4
(418) 837-5841   *SIC 4493*
OAK BAY MARINA LTD   *p333*
1327 BEACH DR, VICTORIA, BC, V8S 2N4
(250) 370-6509   *SIC 4493*
TOTEM COVE HOLDINGS INC   *p342*
5776 MARINE DR, WEST VANCOUVER, BC, V7W 2S2
(604) 921-7434   *SIC 4493*
VANISLE MARINA CO. LTD   *p268*
2320 HARBOUR RD, SIDNEY, BC, V8L 2P6
(250) 656-1138   *SIC 4493*

SIC 4499 Water transportation services,

AMIX MARINE PROJECTS LTD p237
625 AGNES ST UNIT 425, NEW WESTMINSTER, BC, V3M 5Y4
(604) 516-0857   *SIC 4499*

ATLANTIC PILOTAGE AUTHORITY p452
1791 BARRINGTON ST SUITE 1801, HALIFAX, NS, B3J 3K9
(902) 426-2550   *SIC 4499*

CORPORATION DES PILOTES DU BAS SAINT-LAURENT INC p1258
240 RUE DALHOUSIE, QUEBEC, QC, G1K 8M8
(418) 692-0444   *SIC 4499*

CORPORATION DES PILOTES DU SAINT-LAURENT CENTRAL INC p1387
1350 RUE ROYALE BUREAU 800, TROIS-RIVIERES, QC, G9A 4J4
(819) 379-8882   *SIC 4499*

DND HMCS HURON p336
GD STN CSC, VICTORIA, BC, V8W 2L9
(250) 363-5482   *SIC 4499*

GREAT LAKES PILOTAGE AUTHORITY p563
202 PITT ST 2ND FL, CORNWALL, ON, K6J 3P7
(613) 933-2991   *SIC 4499*

LAURENTIAN PILOTAGE AUTHORITY p1135
40 RUE DES PILOTES, LES ESCOUMINS, QC, G0T 1K0
(418) 233-2995   *SIC 4499*

MARINE RECYCLING CORPORATION p846
17 INVERTOSE DR, PORT COLBORNE, ON, L3K 5V5
(905) 835-1203   *SIC 4499*

MCKEIL MARINE LIMITED p523
1001 CHAMPLAIN AVE SUITE 401, BURLINGTON, ON, L7L 5Z4
(905) 528-4780   *SIC 4499*

ST. LAWRENCE SEAWAY MANAGEMENT CORPORATION, THE p1069
9200 BOUL MARIE-VICTORIN, BROSSARD, QC, J4X 1A3
(450) 672-4115   *SIC 4499*

SIC 4512 Air transportation, scheduled

148274 CANADA INC p1092
100 AV JENKINS BUREAU 100, DORVAL, QC, H9P 2R1
(514) 631-5058   *SIC 4512*

2553-4330 QUEBEC INC p1277
714 7E AVENUE DE L'AEROPORT, QUEBEC, QC, G2G 2T6
(418) 877-2808   *SIC 4512*

2553-4330 QUEBEC INC p1367
18 AVIATION GENERAL E, SEPT-ILES, QC, G4R 4K2
(418) 961-2808   *SIC 4512*

3611981 CANADA INC p1307
6200 RTE DE L'A?ROPORT, SAINT-HUBERT, QC, J3Y 8Y9
(450) 443-0500   *SIC 4512*

420877 B.C. LTD p264
5200 MILLER RD UNIT 2170, RICHMOND, BC, V7B 1L1
(604) 233-1377   *SIC 4512*

9736140 CANADA INC p1307
6200 RTE DE L'AEROPORT, SAINT-HUBERT, QC, J3Y 8Y9
(450) 443-0500   *SIC 4512*

AIR BOREALIS LIMITED PARTNERSHIP p424
1 CENTRALIA DR, HAPPY VALLEY-GOOSE BAY, NL, A0P 1C0
(709) 576-1800   *SIC 4512*

AIR CANADA p374
355 PORTAGE AVE SUITE 3850, WINNIPEG, MB, R3B 0J6
(204) 941-2684   *SIC 4512*

AIR CANADA p1229

735 STUART GRAHAM N, MONTREAL, QC, H4Y 1C3
SIC 4512

AIR CANADA p1332
7373 BOUL DE LA COTE-VERTU BUREAU 1290, SAINT-LAURENT, QC, H4S 1Z3
(514) 393-3333   *SIC 4512*

AIR CREEBEC INC p912
GD LCD MAIN, TIMMINS, ON, P4N 7C4
(705) 264-9521   *SIC 4512*

AIR CREEBEC INC p1400
18 RUE WASKAGANISH, WASKAGANISH, QC, J0M 1R0
(819) 895-8355   *SIC 4512*

AIR INUIT LTEE p1332
6005 BOUL DE LA COTE-VERTU, SAINT-LAURENT, QC, H4S 0B1
(514) 905-9445   *SIC 4512*

AIR NORTH PARTNERSHIP p264
1 3RD SUITE 3135, RICHMOND, BC, V7B 1Y7
(604) 207-1165   *SIC 4512*

AIR NORTH PARTNERSHIP p1440
150 CONDOR RD, WHITEHORSE, YT, Y1A 6E6
(867) 668-2228   *SIC 4512*

AIR TRANSAT A.T. INC p1332
5959 BOUL DE LA COTE-VERTU, SAINT-LAURENT, QC, H4S 2E6
(514) 906-0330   *SIC 4512*

AIT WORLDWIDE LOGISTICS (CANADA), INC p450
588 BARNES DR, GOFFS, NS, B2T 1K3
(902) 873-5285   *SIC 4512*

BEARSKIN LAKE AIR SERVICE LP p910
216 ROUND BLVD SUITE 2, THUNDER BAY, ON, P7E 3N9
(807) 475-0006   *SIC 4512*

BEARSKIN LAKE AIR SERVICE LP p910
1475 WALSH ST W, THUNDER BAY, ON, P7E 4X6
(807) 577-1141   *SIC 4512*

BEAVER AIR SERVICES LIMITED PARTNERSHIP p359
2 GRACE LAKE RD, THE PAS, MB, R9A 1M3
(204) 623-7160   *SIC 4512*

BUFFALO AIRWAYS LTD p435
25 INDUSTRIAL DR, HAY RIVER, NT, X0E 0R6
(867) 874-3333   *SIC 4512*

C.A.S.A.R.A YUKON p1440
25 PILGRIM PL UNIT 2, WHITEHORSE, YT, Y1A 0M7
(867) 668-6431   *SIC 4512*

CALM AIR INTERNATIONAL LP p383
930 FERRY RD, WINNIPEG, MB, R3H 0Y8
(204) 778-6471   *SIC 4512*

CANADIAN NORTH INC p21
580 PALMER RD NE SUITE 200, CALGARY, AB, T2E 7R3
(403) 503-2310   *SIC 4512*

CARGOJET AIRWAYS LTD p714
2281 NORTH SHERIDAN WAY, MISSISSAUGA, ON, L5K 2S3
(905) 501-7373   *SIC 4512*

CARGOJET INC p714
2281 NORTH SHERIDAN WAY, MISSISSAUGA, ON, L5K 2S3
(905) 501-7373   *SIC 4512*

CARGOJET INC p747
9300 AIRPORT RD SUITE 320, MOUNT HOPE, ON, L0R 1W0
(905) 679-9127   *SIC 4512*

CARGOJET PARTNERSHIP p705
350 BRITANNIA RD E UNIT 5 6, MISSISSAUGA, ON, L4Z 1X9
(905) 501-7373   *SIC 4512*

CENTRAL MOUNTAIN AIR LTD p264
4180 AGAR DR, RICHMOND, BC, V7B 1A3
(604) 207-0130   *SIC 4512*

CENTRAL MOUNTAIN AIR LTD p269
6431 AIRPORT RD, SMITHERS, BC, V0J 2N2

(250) 877-5000   *SIC 4512*

CHORUS AVIATION INC p445
3 SPECTACLE LAKE DR, DARTMOUTH, NS, B3B 1W8
(902) 873-5000   *SIC 4512*

ELS MARKETING LIMITED PARTNERSHIP p688
3133 ORLANDO DR, MISSISSAUGA, ON, L4V 1C5
(905) 612-1259   *SIC 4512*

FAST AIR LTD p385
80 HANGAR LINE RD, WINNIPEG, MB, R3J 3Y7
(204) 982-7240   *SIC 4512*

FEDERAL EXPRESS CANADA CORPORATION p694
5985 EXPLORER DR, MISSISSAUGA, ON, L4W 5K6
(800) 463-3339   *SIC 4512*

GLOBEX COURRIER EXPRESS INTERNATIONAL INC p1329
2267 RUE GUENETTE, SAINT-LAURENT, QC, H4R 2E9
(514) 739-7977   *SIC 4512*

HARBOUR AIR LTD p264
4760 INGLIS DR, RICHMOND, BC, V7B 1W4
(604) 278-3478   *SIC 4512*

HARBOUR AIR LTD p305
1055 CANADA PL UNIT 1, VANCOUVER, BC, V6C 0C3
(604) 233-3501   *SIC 4512*

INNU MIKUN INC p424
GD STN, HAPPY VALLEY-GOOSE BAY, NL, A0P 1C0
(709) 896-5521   *SIC 4512*

INVESTISSEMENTS NOLINOR INC, LES p1153
11600 RUE LOUIS-BISSON, MIRABEL, QC, J7N 1G9
(450) 476-0018   *SIC 4512*

JAZZ AVIATION LP p447
3 SPECTACLE LAKE DR SUITE 100, DARTMOUTH, NS, B3B 1W8
(902) 873-5000   *SIC 4512*

JETPORT INC p747
9300 AIRPORT RD SUITE 520, MOUNT HOPE, ON, L0R 1W0
(905) 679-2400   *SIC 4512*

KELOWNA FLIGHTCRAFT AIR CHARTER LTD p218
5655 AIRPORT WAY SUITE 1, KELOWNA, BC, V1V 1S1
(250) 491-5500   *SIC 4512*

LONDON AIR SERVICES LIMITED p265
4580 COWLEY CRES, RICHMOND, BC, V7B 1B8
(604) 272-8123   *SIC 4512*

MAX AVIATION INC p1308
6100 RTE DE L'AEROPORT, SAINT-HUBERT, QC, J3Y 8Y9
(450) 462-8511   *SIC 4512*

MUSTANG HELICOPTERS INC p5
237-27312 TOWNSHIP RD 394, BLACKFALDS, AB, T0M 0J0
(403) 885-5500   *SIC 4512*

NAKINA OUTPOST CAMPS & AIR SERVICE LTD p747
GD, NAKINA, ON, P0T 2H0
(807) 329-5341   *SIC 4512*

NORTH CARIBOO FLYING SERVICE LTD p214
9945 CARIBOU WAY, FORT ST. JOHN, BC, V1J 4J2
(250) 787-0311   *SIC 4512*

NORTHWESTERN AIR LEASE LTD p435
HANGAR 1, FORT SMITH, NT, X0E 0P0
(867) 872-2216   *SIC 4512*

ONNI AIRWAYS LTD p299
550 ROBSON ST UNIT 300, VANCOUVER, BC, V6B 2B7
(604) 602-7711   *SIC 4512*

PACIFIC COASTAL AIRLINES LIMITED p265
4440 COWLEY CRES SUITE 204, RICH-

MOND, BC, V7B 1B8
(604) 273-8666   *SIC 4512*

PAL AIRLINES LTD. p428
ST JOHNS INTERNATIONAL AIRPORT, ST. JOHN'S, NL, A1A 5B5
(709) 576-1800   *SIC 4512*

PROPAIR INC p1290
20 RUE PRONOVOST, ROUYN-NORANDA, QC, J9Y 0G1
(819) 762-0811   *SIC 4512*

PROVINCIAL AIRLINES LIMITED p429
HANGAR NO 4 ST JOHN'S INTERNATIONAL AIRPORT, ST. JOHN'S, NL, A1A 5B5
(709) 576-1800   *SIC 4512*

RIO TINTO ALCAN INC p1121
262 1RE RUE, LA BAIE, QC, G7B 3R1
(418) 544-9660   *SIC 4512*

SKY REGIONAL AIRLINES INC p729
6120 MIDFIELD RD, MISSISSAUGA, ON, L5P 1B1
(905) 362-5941   *SIC 4512*

SKY SERVICE F.B.O. INC. p1095
9785 AV RYAN, DORVAL, QC, H9P 1A2
(514) 636-3300   *SIC 4512*

SKYLINK AVIATION INC p914
100 SHEPPARD AVE E SUITE 760, TORONTO, ON, M1T 3L3
(416) 924-9000   *SIC 4512*

SKYLINK EXPRESS INC p727
2000 ARGENTIA RD PLAZA 4 SUITE 101, MISSISSAUGA, ON, L5N 1W1
(416) 925-4530   *SIC 4512*

SOCIETE AIR FRANCE p729
6500 SILVER DART DR VISTA, MISSISSAUGA, ON, L5P 1A2
(905) 676-2782   *SIC 4512*

SOCIETE MAKIVIK p1324
1111 BOUL DR.-FREDERIK-PHILIPS 3E ETAGE, SAINT-LAURENT, QC, H4M 2X6
(514) 745-8880   *SIC 4512*

UPS SCS INC p736
1930 DERRY RD E, MISSISSAUGA, ON, L5S 1E2
(800) 742-5877   *SIC 4512*

VCC CARGO SERVICE INC p729
6500 SILVER DART DR, MISSISSAUGA, ON, L5P 1B1
(905) 676-4047   *SIC 4512*

VOYAGEUR AIRWAYS LIMITED p764
1500 AIRPORT RD, NORTH BAY, ON, P1B 8G2
(705) 476-1750   *SIC 4512*

WASAYA AIRWAYS LIMITED PARTNERSHIP p592
300 ANEMKI PL UNIT B, FORT WILLIAM FIRST NATION, ON, P7J 1H9
(807) 473-1200   *SIC 4512*

WEST COAST AIR LTD p265
4760 INGLIS DR, RICHMOND, BC, V7B 1W4
(604) 278-3478   *SIC 4512*

WEST COAST AIR LTD p265
5220 AIRPORT RD S, RICHMOND, BC, V7B 1B4
SIC 4512

WESTJET AIRLINES LTD p26
22 AERIAL PL NE, CALGARY, AB, T2E 3J1
(888) 937-8538   *SIC 4512*

WESTJET AIRLINES LTD p265
3880 GRANT MCCONACHIE WAY SUITE 4130, RICHMOND, BC, V7B 0A5
(604) 249-1165   *SIC 4512*

SIC 4513 Air courier services

UNITED PARCEL SERVICE CANADA LTD p401
900 HANWELL RD, FREDERICTON, NB, E3B 6A2
(506) 447-3601   *SIC 4513*

UNITED PARCEL SERVICE CANADA LTD p662
60 MIDPARK RD, LONDON, ON, N6N 1B3

(519) 686-8200   *SIC 4513*
UNITED PARCEL SERVICE CANADA LTD   *p984*
12 MERCER ST, TORONTO, ON, M5V 1H3
SIC 4513

SIC 4522 Air transportation, nonscheduled

7506406 CANADA INC   *p691*
5310 EXPLORER DR, MISSISSAUGA, ON, L4W 5H8
(647) 428-2005   *SIC 4522*
947786 ALBERTA LTD   *p1404*
BUFFALO NARROWS AIRPORT, BUFFALO NARROWS, SK, S0M 0J0
(306) 235-4373   *SIC 4522*
AIR GEORGIAN LIMITED   *p734*
2450 DERRY RD E SUITE 3, MISSISSAUGA, ON, L5S 1B2
(905) 676-1221   *SIC 4522*
AIR TINDI LTD   *p435*
28 MITCHELL DR, YELLOWKNIFE, NT, X1A 2H5
(867) 669-8200   *SIC 4522*
AIRMEDIC INC   *p1307*
4980 RTE DE L'AEROPORT, SAINT-HUBERT, QC, J3Y 8Y9
(450) 766-0770   *SIC 4522*
AIRSPRINT INC   *p20*
1910 MCCALL LANDNG NE, CALGARY, AB, T2E 9B5
(403) 730-2344   *SIC 4522*
ALPINE HELICOPTERS LTD   *p341*
1295 INDUSTRIAL RD, WEST KELOWNA, BC, V1Z 1G4
(250) 769-4111   *SIC 4522*
ATLANTIC SKY SERVICE   *p450*
647 BARNES DR, GOFFS, NS, B2T 1K3
(902) 873-3575   *SIC 4522*
AURORA HELICOPTERS LTD   *p127*
410 SNOW EAGLE DR, FORT MCMURRAY, AB, T9H 0H7
(780) 743-5588   *SIC 4522*
AVIATION STARLINK INC   *p1093*
9025 AV RYAN, DORVAL, QC, H9P 1A2
(514) 631-7500   *SIC 4522*
BAILEY HELICOPTERS LTD   *p21*
600 PALMER RD NE, CALGARY, AB, T2E 7R3
(403) 219-2770   *SIC 4522*
BEARSKIN LAKE AIR SERVICE LP   *p881*
7 AIRPORT RD, SIOUX LOOKOUT, ON, P8T 1J6
(807) 737-3473   *SIC 4522*
BRADLEY AIR SERVICES LIMITED   *p626*
20 COPE DR, KANATA, ON, K2M 2V8
(613) 254-6200   *SIC 4522*
CAMPBELL HELICOPTERS LTD   *p176*
30740 THRESHOLD DR, ABBOTSFORD, BC, V2T 6H5
(604) 852-1122   *SIC 4522*
CANADIAN HELICOPTERS LIMITED   *p134*
1000 AIRPORT RD SUITE 4500, GRANDE PRAIRIE, AB, T9E 0V3
(780) 429-6900   *SIC 4522*
CARGAIR LTEE   *p1307*
6100 RTE DE L'AEROPORT, SAINT-HUBERT, QC, J3Y 8Y9
(450) 656-4783   *SIC 4522*
CARSON AIR LTD   *p218*
00-6197 AIRPORT WAY, KELOWNA, BC, V1V 2S2
(250) 765-7776   *SIC 4522*
CHC HELICOPTER HOLDING S.A.R.L.   *p264*
4740 AGAR DR, RICHMOND, BC, V7B 1A3
(604) 276-7500   *SIC 4522*
CHC HELICOPTERS CANADA INC   *p264*
4740 AGAR DR, RICHMOND, BC, V7B 1A3
(604) 276-7500   *SIC 4522*
CHRONO AVIATION INC   *p1278*
706A 7E AV DE L'AEROPORT, QUEBEC, QC, G2J 2T6
(418) 529-4444   *SIC 4522*

COAST TO COAST HELICOPTERS INC   *p5*
27312 TOWNSHIP RD 394 UNIT 237, BLACKFALDS, AB, T0M 0J0
(403) 885-5220   *SIC 4522*
COUGAR HELICOPTERS INC   *p428*
10 AV JETSTREAM, ST. JOHN'S, NL, A1A 0R7
(709) 758-4800   *SIC 4522*
COULSON AIRCRANE LTD   *p245*
4890 CHERRY CREEK RD, PORT ALBERNI, BC, V9Y 8E9
(250) 723-8118   *SIC 4522*
CUSTOM HELICOPTERS LTD   *p357*
706 SOUTH GATE RD, ST ANDREWS, MB, R1A 3P8
(204) 338-7953   *SIC 4522*
DELTA HELICOPTERS LTD   *p168*
26004 TWP RD 544 UNIT 13, STURGEON COUNTY, AB, T8T 0B6
(780) 458-3564   *SIC 4522*
DISCOVERY AIR INC   *p436*
126 CRYSTAL AVE, YELLOWKNIFE, NT, X1A 2P3
(867) 873-5350   *SIC 4522*
EXPEDITION HELICOPTERS INC   *p545*
190 HWY 11 W, COCHRANE, ON, P0L 1C0
(705) 272-5755   *SIC 4522*
FLAIR AIRLINES LTD   *p218*
5795 AIRPORT WAY, KELOWNA, BC, V1V 1S1
(250) 491-5513   *SIC 4522*
GREAT SLAVE HELICOPTERS LTD   *p436*
106 DICKENS ST, YELLOWKNIFE, NT, X1A 3T2
(867) 873-2081   *SIC 4522*
HELICOPTER TRANSPORT SERVICES (CANADA) INC   *p541*
5 HUISSON RD, CARP, ON, K0A 1L0
(613) 839-5868   *SIC 4522*
HELIJET INTERNATIONAL INC   *p265*
5911 AIRPORT RD S, RICHMOND, BC, V7B 1B5
(604) 273-4688   *SIC 4522*
HELIQWEST AVIATION INC   *p168*
27018 SH 633 UNIT 37, STURGEON COUNTY, AB, T8T 0E3
(780) 458-3005   *SIC 4522*
HIGHLAND HELICOPTERS LTD   *p265*
4240 AGAR DR, RICHMOND, BC, V7B 1A3
(604) 273-6161   *SIC 4522*
KENN BOREK AIR LTD   *p24*
290 MCTAVISH RD NE SUITE 4, CALGARY, AB, T2E 7G5
(403) 291-3300   *SIC 4522*
MORNINGSTAR AIR EXPRESS INC   *p134*
3759 60 AVE E, GRANDE PRAIRIE, AB, T9E 0V4
(780) 453-3022   *SIC 4522*
NAV CANADA   *p1094*
1750 CH SAINT-FRANCOIS, DORVAL, QC, H9P 2P6
(514) 633-2884   *SIC 4522*
NORTHERN THUNDERBIRD AIR INC   *p251*
4245 HANGER RD UNIT 100, PRINCE GEORGE, BC, V2N 4M6
(250) 963-9611   *SIC 4522*
NORTHWAY AVIATION LTD   *p357*
501 AIRLINE RD, ST ANDREWS, MB, R1A 3P4
(204) 339-2310   *SIC 4522*
ORNGE   *p698*
5310 EXPLORER DR, MISSISSAUGA, ON, L4W 5H8
(647) 428-2005   *SIC 4522*
PERIMETER AVIATION LP   *p384*
626 FERRY RD, WINNIPEG, MB, R3H 0T7
(204) 786-7031   *SIC 4522*
SEA TO SKY HELI RIGGING LTD   *p269*
GD, SQUAMISH, BC, V8B 0J2
SIC 4522
SHOCK TRAUMA AIR RESCUE SERVICE   *p25*
1441 AVIATION PK NE UNIT 570, CALGARY, AB, T2E 8M7

(403) 295-1811   *SIC 4522*
SHOCK TRAUMA AIR RESCUE SERVICE   *p134*
1519 35 AVE E SUITE 100; GRANDE PRAIRIE, AB, T9E 0V6
(780) 890-3131   *SIC 4522*
SKYCARE AIR AMBULANCE   *p881*
17 AIRPORT RD, SIOUX LOOKOUT, ON, P8T 1A3
(807) 737-0038   *SIC 4522*
SKYSERVICE BUSINESS AVIATION INC   *p729*
6120 MIDFIELD RD, MISSISSAUGA, ON, L5P 1B1
(905) 677-3300   *SIC 4522*
SKYSERVICE BUSINESS AVIATION INC   *p1095*
9785 AV RYAN, DORVAL, QC, H9P 1A2
(514) 636-3300   *SIC 4522*
STARS AVIATION CANADA INC   *p25*
1441 AVIATION PK NE, CALGARY, AB, T2E 8M7
(403) 295-1811   *SIC 4522*
SUMMIT AIR LTD   *p436*
100 DICKENS ST, YELLOWKNIFE, NT, X1A 3T2
(867) 873-4464   *SIC 4522*
SUMMIT HELICOPTERS LTD   *p436*
27 YELLOWKNIFE AIRPORT 100 DICKINS ST, YELLOWKNIFE, NT, X1A 3T2
(867) 765-5969   *SIC 4522*
SUNWING AIRLINES INC   *p588*
27 FASKEN DR, ETOBICOKE, ON, M9W 1K6
(416) 620-4955   *SIC 4522*
SUNWING CANADA INC   *p588*
27 FASKEN DR, ETOBICOKE, ON, M9W 1K6
(416) 695-0500   *SIC 4522*
THUNDER AIRLINES LIMITED   *p910*
310 HECTOR DOUGALL WAY, THUNDER BAY, ON, P7E 6M6
(807) 475-4211   *SIC 4522*
TRANSWEST AIR LIMITED PARTNERSHIP   *p1414*
GD, PRINCE ALBERT, SK, S6V 5R4
(306) 764-1404   *SIC 4522*
UNIVERSAL HELICOPTERS (NFLD) LIMITED   *p424*
82 WINNIPEG ST, HAPPY VALLEY-GOOSE BAY, NL, A0P 1C0
(709) 896-2444   *SIC 4522*
VIH HELICOPTERS LTD   *p238*
1962 CANSO RD, NORTH SAANICH, BC, V8L 5V5
(250) 656-3987   *SIC 4522*
WEST COAST HELICOPTERS MAINTENANCE AND CONTRACTING LTD   *p248*
1011 AIRPORT RD, PORT MCNEILL, BC, V0N 2R0
(250) 956-2244   *SIC 4522*
WEST WIND AVIATION LIMITED PARTNERSHIP   *p1432*
3 HANGAR RD, SASKATOON, SK, S7L 5X4
(306) 652-9121   *SIC 4522*
YELLOWHEAD HELICOPTERS LTD   *p284*
3010 SELWYN RD, VALEMOUNT, BC, V0E 2Z0
(250) 566-4401   *SIC 4522*

SIC 4581 Airports, flying fields, and services

3552047 CANADA INC   *p1092*
545 BOUL STUART-GRAHAM N BUREAU 201, DORVAL, QC, H4Y 1E2
(514) 633-1118   *SIC 4581*
765865 ONTARIO INC   *p511*
8501 MISSISSAUGA RD SUITE 302, BRAMPTON, ON, L6Y 5G8
(905) 497-4114   *SIC 4581*
AAA CANADA INC   *p1222*
780 AV BREWSTER BUREAU 03-200, MONTREAL, QC, H4C 2K1

(514) 733-6655   *SIC 4581*
AAR AIRCRAFT SERVICES - TROIS RIVIERES ULC   *p1387*
3750 RUE DE L'AEROPORT, TROIS-RIVIERES, QC, G9A 5E1
(819) 377-4500   *SIC 4581*
AAS CO OF NFLD ULC   *p423*
1000 JAMES BLVD, GANDER, NL, A1V 2V4
(709) 256-8043   *SIC 4581*
AERO AVIATION INC   *p20*
2139 PEGASUS WAY NE SUITE 13, CALGARY, AB, T2E 8T2
(403) 250-7553   *SIC 4581*
AERO AVIATION INC   *p20*
393 PALMER RD NE SUITE 59, CALGARY, AB, T2E 7G4
(403) 250-3663   *SIC 4581*
AERO MAG 2000 (YEG) INC   *p134*
4123 39 ST E, GRANDE PRAIRIE, AB, T9E 0V4
(780) 890-7273   *SIC 4581*
AERO RECIP. (CANADA) LTD   *p383*
540 MARJORIE ST, WINNIPEG, MB, R3H 0S9
(204) 788-4765   *SIC 4581*
AEROPORT DE QUEBEC INC   *p1278*
505 RUE PRINCIPALE, QUEBEC, QC, G2G 0J4
(418) 640-2700   *SIC 4581*
AEROPORT REGIONAL DE ROUYN NORANDA   *p1290*
80 AV DE L'AEROPORT BUREAU 82, ROUYN-NORANDA, QC, J9Y 0G1
(819) 762-8171   *SIC 4581*
AEROPORTS DE MONTREAL   *p1092*
800 PLACE LEIGH-CAPREOL BUREAU 1000, DORVAL, QC, H4Y 0A5
(514) 394-7200   *SIC 4581*
AEROPORTS DE MONTREAL   *p1092*
580 BOUL STUART-GRAHAM S, DORVAL, QC, H4Y 1G4
(514) 633-2811   *SIC 4581*
AEROPORTS DE MONTREAL   *p1153*
12655 BOUL HENRI-FABRE O UNITE A4, MIRABEL, QC, J7N 1E1
(514) 394-7377   *SIC 4581*
AIR CANADA   *p383*
2020 SARGENT AVE, WINNIPEG, MB, R3H 0E1
(204) 788-7871   *SIC 4581*
AIR CANADA   *p383*
2000 WELLINGTON AVE RM 222, WINNIPEG, MB, R3H 1C1
(204) 788-6953   *SIC 4581*
AIR CANADA   *p450*
1 BELL BLVD SUITE 7, ENFIELD, NS, B2T 1K2
(902) 873-2350   *SIC 4581*
AIRPORT TERMINAL SERVICE INC CANADIAN   *p728*
6500 SILVER DART DR UNIT 211, MISSISSAUGA, ON, L5P 1B1
(905) 405-9550   *SIC 4581*
AIRPORT TERMINAL SERVICES CANADIAN COMPANY   *p20*
8075 22 ST NE, CALGARY, AB, T2E 7Z6
(403) 291-0965   *SIC 4581*
AIRPORT TERMINAL SERVICES CANADIAN COMPANY   *p383*
2000 WELLINGTON AVE SUITE 221, WINNIPEG, MB, R3H 1C1
SIC 4581
AJW TECHNIQUE INC   *p1332*
7055 RUE ALEXANDER-FLEMING BUREAU 100, SAINT-LAURENT, QC, H4S 2B7
(514) 339-5100   *SIC 4581*
ALPINE AEROTECH LIMITED PARTNERSHIP   *p341*
1260 INDUSTRIAL RD, WEST KELOWNA, BC, V1Z 1G5
(250) 769-6344   *SIC 4581*
AVMAX AVIATION SERVICES INC   *p1394*
264 RUE ADRIEN-PATENAUDE, VAUDREUIL-DORION, QC, J7V 5V5

▲ Public Company   ■ Public Company Family Member   **HQ** Headquarters   **BR** Branch   **SL** Single Location

AVMAX GROUP INC   *p21*
2055 PEGASUS RD NE, CALGARY, AB,
T2E 8C3
(403) 291-2464   *SIC 4581*

AVMAX GROUP INC   *p21*
380 MCTAVISH RD NE, CALGARY, AB, T2E
7G5
(403) 735-3299   *SIC 4581*

CALGARY AIRPORT AUTHORITY, THE *p21*
2000 AIRPORT RD NE, CALGARY, AB, T2E
6W5
(403) 735-1200   *SIC 4581*

CARGOJET HOLDINGS LTD   *p714*
2281 NORTH SHERIDAN WAY, MISSIS-
SAUGA, ON, L5K 2S3
(905) 501-7373   *SIC 4581*

CASCADE AEROSPACE INC   *p176*
1337 TOWNLINE RD, ABBOTSFORD, BC,
V2T 6E1
(604) 850-7372   *SIC 4581*

**CONSEIL INTERNATIONAL DES AERO-
PORTS**   *p1229*
800 RUE SQ VICTORIA BUREAU 1810,
MONTREAL, QC, H4Z 1G8
(514) 373-1224   *SIC 4581*

CORE LOGISTICS INTERNATIONAL INC
p687
3133 ORLANDO DR, MISSISSAUGA, ON,
L4V 1C5
(905) 670-2000   *SIC 4581*

**CORPORATION OF THE CITY OF
KINGSTON, THE**   *p632*
1114 LEN BIRCHALL WAY, KINGSTON,
ON, K7M 9A1
(613) 389-6404   *SIC 4581*

DAC AVIATION INTERNATIONAL LTEE
p1132
9371 RUE WANKLYN, LASALLE, QC, H8R
1Z2
(514) 876-0135   *SIC 4581*

EAGLE COPTERS MAINTENANCE LTD *p22*
823 MCTAVISH RD NE, CALGARY, AB, T2E
7G9
(403) 250-7370   *SIC 4581*

**EDMONTON REGIONAL AIRPORTS AU-
THORITY**   *p134*
1000 AIRPORT RD TERMINAL 1, GRANDE
PRAIRIE, AB, T9E 0V3
(780) 890-8900   *SIC 4581*

FIELD AVIATION COMPANY INC   *p735*
2450 DERRY RD E, MISSISSAUGA, ON,
L5S 1B2
(905) 676-1540   *SIC 4581*

**FREDERICTON INTERNATIONAL AIRPORT
AUTHORITY INC**   *p404*
2570 ROUTE 102 UNIT 22, LINCOLN, NB,
E3B 9G1
(506) 460-0920   *SIC 4581*

G.T.A. WORLD CARGO LTD   *p695*
2710 BRITANNIA RD E (CARGO 2 TOWER
7), MISSISSAUGA, ON, L4W 2P7
(905) 671-4443   *SIC 4581*

GENAIRE LIMITED   *p761*
468 NIAGARA STONE RD UNIT D, NIA-
GARA ON THE LAKE, ON, L0S 1J0
(905) 684-1165   *SIC 4581*

GLOBAL AEROSPACE CORPORATION
p735
7075 FIR TREE DR, MISSISSAUGA, ON,
L5S 1J7
(905) 678-6311   *SIC 4581*

**GOUVERNEMENT DE LA PROVINCE DE
QUEBEC**   *p1257*
700 RUE 7E, QUEBEC, QC, G1J 2S1
(418) 528-8350   *SIC 4581*

GRANDE PRAIRIE AIRPORT COMMISSION
p132
10610 AIRPORT DR SUITE 220, GRANDE
PRAIRIE, AB, T8V 7Z5
(780) 539-5270   *SIC 4581*

**GREATER MONCTON INTERNATIONAL
AIRPORT AUTHORITY INC**   *p397*
777 AV AVIATION UNIT 12, DIEPPE, NB,

E1A 7Z5
(506) 856-5444   *SIC 4581*

**GREATER TORONTO AIRPORTS AUTHOR-
ITY**   *p729*
3111 CONVAIR DR, MISSISSAUGA, ON,
L5P 1B2
(416) 776-3000   *SIC 4581*

H-S TOOL & PARTS INC   *p260*
2560 SIMPSON RD SUITE 140, RICH-
MOND, BC, V6X 2P9
(604) 273-4743   *SIC 4581*

**HALIFAX INTERNATIONAL AIRPORT AU-
THORITY**   *p450*
1 BELL BLVD FL 3, ENFIELD, NS, B2T 1K2
(902) 873-4422   *SIC 4581*

**HAMILTON INTERNATIONAL AIRPORT
LIMITED**   *p747*
9300 AIRPORT RD SUITE 2206, MOUNT
HOPE, ON, L0R 1W0
(905) 679-1999   *SIC 4581*

HSS HELITECH SUPPORT SERVICES LTD
p176
1640 THRESHOLD DR, ABBOTSFORD,
BC, V2T 6H5
(604) 557-9690   *SIC 4581*

**I.M.P. GROUP INTERNATIONAL INCORPO-
RATED**   *p457*
2651 JOSEPH HOWE DR, HALIFAX, NS,
B3L 4T1
(902) 453-2400   *SIC 4581*

I.M.P. GROUP LIMITED   *p457*
2651 JOSEPH HOWE DR SUITE 400, HAL-
IFAX, NS, B3L 4T1
(902) 453-2400   *SIC 4581*

I.M.P. GROUP LIMITED   *p459*
3101 HAMMONDS PLAINS RD, HAM-
MONDS PLAINS, NS, B3Z 1H7
(902) 835-4433   *SIC 4581*

I.M.P. GROUP LIMITED   *p1094*
10225 AV RYAN, DORVAL, QC, H9P 1A2
(514) 636-7070   *SIC 4581*

**INLAND TECHNOLOGIES CANADA INCOR-
PORATED**   *p469*
14 QUEEN ST, TRURO, NS, B2N 2A8
(902) 895-6346   *SIC 4581*

INTEC INVESTMENT HOLDINGS INC *p469*
9 COMMERCIAL ST, TRURO, NS, B2N 3H8
(902) 895-6346   *SIC 4581*

**KELOWNA FLIGHTCRAFT AIR CHARTER
LTD**   *p747*
9300 AIRPORT RD, MOUNT HOPE, ON,
L0R 1W0
   SIC 4581

KELOWNA FLIGHTCRAFT LTD   *p218*
5655 AIRPORT WAY UNIT 1, KELOWNA,
BC, V1V 1S1
(250) 491-5500   *SIC 4581*

KELOWNA FLIGHTCRAFT LTD   *p747*
9500 AIRPORT RD, MOUNT HOPE, ON,
L0R 1W0
(905) 679-3313   *SIC 4581*

KELOWNA INTERNATIONAL AIRPORT
p219
5533 AIRPORT WAY SUITE 1, KELOWNA,
BC, V1V 1S1
(250) 807-4300   *SIC 4581*

L3 TECHNOLOGIES MAS INC   *p735*
7785 TRANMERE DR, MISSISSAUGA, ON,
L5S 1W5
(905) 671-5879   *SIC 4581*

LIBURDI TURBINE SERVICES INC   *p566*
400 6 HWY, DUNDAS, ON, L9H 7K4
(905) 689-0734   *SIC 4581*

LOCKHEED MARTIN CANADA INC *p1335*
7171 BOUL DE LA COTE-VERTU, SAINT-
LAURENT, QC, H4S 1Z3
(514) 340-8400   *SIC 4581*

NAV CANADA   *p134*
4396 34 ST E, GRANDE PRAIRIE, AB, T9E
0V4
(780) 890-8360   *SIC 4581*

NAVSTAR AVIATION INC   *p729*
6500 SILVER DART DR SUITE 205, MIS-
SISSAUGA, ON, L5P 1A5

(905) 673-7827   *SIC 4581*

NEW UNITED GODERICH INC   *p621*
403 CANADA AVE, HURON PARK, ON,
N0M 1Y0
(519) 228-6052   *SIC 4581*

**OTTAWA MACDONALD-CARTIER INTER-
NATIONAL AIRPORT AUTHORITY**   *p827*
1000 AIRPORT PARKWAY PVT SUITE
2500, OTTAWA, ON, K1V 9B4
(613) 248-2000   *SIC 4581*

PAL AEROSPACE LTD   *p428*
ST. JOHNS INTERNATIONAL AIRPORT,
HANGAR 1, ST. JOHN'S, NL, A1A 5B5
(709) 576-1800   *SIC 4581*

PORTER AIRLINES INC   *p983*
4 TORONTO ISLAND AIRPORT,
TORONTO, ON, M5V 1A1
(416) 203-8100   *SIC 4581*

PREMIER AVIATION QUEBEC INC   *p1276*
800 8E RUE DE L'AEROPORT, QUEBEC,
QC, G2C 2S6
(418) 800-1325   *SIC 4581*

REGINA AIRPORT AUTHORITY INC *p1422*
5201 REGINA AVE UNIT 1, REGINA, SK,
S4W 1B3
(306) 761-7555   *SIC 4581*

ROLLS-ROYCE CANADA LIMITEE   *p1095*
9545 CH COTE-DE-LIESSE BUREAU 100,
DORVAL, QC, H9P 1A5
(514) 636-0964   *SIC 4581*

ROLLS-ROYCE CANADA LIMITEE   *p1128*
9500 CH DE LA COTE-DE-LIESSE, LA-
CHINE, QC, H8T 1A2
(514) 631-3541   *SIC 4581*

SASKATOON AIRPORT AUTHORITY *p1432*
2625 AIRPORT DR SUITE 1, SASKATOON,
SK, S7L 7L1
(306) 975-4274   *SIC 4581*

SKY SERVICE F.B.O. INC.   *p729*
6120 MIDFIELD RD, MISSISSAUGA, ON,
L5P 1B1
(905) 677-3300   *SIC 4581*

**ST. JOHN'S INTERNATIONAL AIRPORT
AUTHORITY**   *p429*
100 WORLD PARKWAY SUITE 1, ST.
JOHN'S, NL, A1A 5T2
(709) 758-8500   *SIC 4581*

STANDARD AERO LIMITED   *p227*
21330 56 AVE UNIT 48, LANGLEY, BC, V2Y
0E5
(604) 514-0388   *SIC 4581*

STANDARD AERO LIMITED   *p256*
20699 WESTMINSTER HWY, RICHMOND,
BC, V6V 1B3
(604) 273-6040   *SIC 4581*

STANDARD AERO LIMITED   *p265*
4551 AGAR DR, RICHMOND, BC, V7B 1A4
(604) 276-7600   *SIC 4581*

SWISSPORT CANADA HANDLING INC*p729*
6500 SILVER DART DR, MISSISSAUGA,
ON, L5P 1A2
(905) 676-2888   *SIC 4581*

SWISSPORT CANADA INC   *p25*
1601 AIRPORT RD NE SUITE 810, CAL-
GARY, AB, T2E 6Z8
(403) 221-1660   *SIC 4581*

SWISSPORT CANADA INC   *p265*
GD, RICHMOND, BC, V7B 1Y4
(604) 303-4550   *SIC 4581*

SWISSPORT CANADA INC   *p827*
130 THAD JOHNSON PVT, OTTAWA, ON,
K1V 0X1
(613) 521-4730   *SIC 4581*

SWISSPORT CANADA INC   *p1324*
100 BOUL ALEXIS-NIHON UNITE 400,
SAINT-LAURENT, QC, H4M 2N8
(514) 748-2277   *SIC 4581*

TORONTO AIRWAYS LIMITED   *p676*
2833 16TH AVE SUITE 100, MARKHAM,
ON, L3R 0P8
(905) 477-8100   *SIC 4581*

TORONTO PORT AUTHORITY   *p967*
60 HARBOUR ST, TORONTO, ON, M5J 1B7
(416) 863-2000   *SIC 4581*

TORONTO SKY AVIATION INC   *p559*
30 RAYETTE RD, CONCORD, ON, L4K 2G3
(905) 760-0731   *SIC 4581*

VANCOUVER AIRPORT AUTHORITY   *p265*
3211 GRANT MCCONACHIE WAY, RICH-
MOND, BC, V7B 0A4
(604) 207-7077   *SIC 4581*

**VECTOR AEROSPACE ENGINE SERVICES-
ATLANTIC INC**   *p1043*
800 AEROSPACE BLVD, SUMMERSIDE,
PE, C1N 4P6
(902) 436-1333   *SIC 4581*

VICTORIA AIRPORT AUTHORITY   *p238*
1640 ELECTRA BLVD SUITE 201, NORTH
SAANICH, BC, V8L 5V4
(250) 953-7500   *SIC 4581*

VIH AEROSPACE INC   *p238*
1962 CANSO RD, NORTH SAANICH, BC,
V8L 5V5
(250) 656-3987   *SIC 4581*

VOYAGEUR AEROTECH INC   *p764*
1500 AIRPORT RD, NORTH BAY, ON, P1B
8G2
(705) 476-1750   *SIC 4581*

WINNIPEG AIRPORTS AUTHORITY INC
p385
2000 WELLINGTON AVE RM 249, WIN-
NIPEG, MB, R3H 1C2
(204) 987-9400   *SIC 4581*

WOODWARD'S LIMITED   *p424*
16 LORING DR, HAPPY VALLEY-GOOSE
BAY, NL, A0P 1C0
(709) 896-2421   *SIC 4581*

**WRIGHT INTERNATIONAL AIRCRAFT
MAINTENANCE SERVICES INC**   *p690*
3182 ORLANDO DR SUITE 14, MISSIS-
SAUGA, ON, L4V 1R5
(905) 677-6393   *SIC 4581*

SIC 4612 Crude petroleum pipelines

ENBRIDGE INC   *p48*
425 1 ST SW SUITE 200, CALGARY, AB,
T2P 3L8
(403) 231-3900   *SIC 4612*

ENBRIDGE PIPELINES (NW) INC   *p48*
425 1 ST SW SUITE 3000, CALGARY, AB,
T2P 3L8
   SIC 4612

ENBRIDGE PIPELINES INC   *p48*
425 1 ST SW SUITE 200, CALGARY, AB,
T2P 3L8
(403) 231-3900   *SIC 4612*

PEMBINA PIPELINE CORPORATION   *p56*
585 8 AVE SW UNIT 4000, CALGARY, AB,
T2P 1G1
(403) 231-7500   *SIC 4612*

PIPE-LINES MONTREAL LIMITEE, LES
p1238
10803 RUE SHERBROOKE E,
MONTREAL-EST, QC, H1B 1B3
(514) 645-8797   *SIC 4612*

PLAINS MIDSTREAM CANADA ULC   *p57*
607 8 AVE SW SUITE 1400, CALGARY, AB,
T2P 0A7
(403) 298-2100   *SIC 4612*

**TEML SASKATCHEWAN PIPELINES LIM-
ITED**   *p1406*
402 KENSINGTON AVE, ESTEVAN, SK,
S4A 2K9
(306) 634-2681   *SIC 4612*

TRANS MOUNTAIN CANADA INC   *p61*
300 5 AVE SW SUITE 2700, CALGARY, AB,
T2P 5J2
(403) 514-6400   *SIC 4612*

SIC 4613 Refined petroleum pipelines

SUNCOR ENERGY INC   *p161*
241 KASKA RD, SHERWOOD PARK, AB,
T8A 4E8
(780) 449-2100   *SIC 4613*

TRANS-NORTHERN PIPELINES INC   *p854*
45 VOGELL RD SUITE 310, RICHMOND HILL, ON, L4B 3P6
(905) 770-3353   *SIC 4613*

SIC 4619 Pipelines, nec

ACCESS PIPELINE INC   *p42*
520 3 AVE SW SUITE 1500, CALGARY, AB, T2P 0R3
(403) 264-6514   *SIC 4619*

BANDIT ENERGY SERVICES   *p143*
500018 RR21 & HWY 16 WEST, LLOYD-MINSTER, AB, T9V 3C5
(780) 875-8764   *SIC 4619*

COCHRANE/EMPRESS V PARTNERSHIP   *p80*
262145 RANGE ROAD 43, COCHRANE, AB, T4C 2J8
(403) 932-8555   *SIC 4619*

DUZ CHO CONSTRUCTION LIMITED PARTNERSHIP   *p196*
4821 ACCESS RD S, CHETWYND, BC, V0C 1J0
(250) 788-3120   *SIC 4619*

KELSEY PIPELINES LTD   *p1428*
107-3239 FAITHFULL AVE, SASKATOON, SK, S7K 8H4
(306) 385-6285   *SIC 4619*

MACRO PIPELINES INC   *p214*
6807 100 AVE, FORT ST. JOHN, BC, V1J 4J2
(250) 785-0033   *SIC 4619*

PEMBINA PIPELINE   *p56*
585 8 AVE SW UNIT 4000, CALGARY, AB, T2P 1G1
(403) 231-7500   *SIC 4619*

SPIRIT PIPELINES LTD   *p172*
GD LCD MAIN, WETASKIWIN, AB, T9A 1W7
(780) 352-7305   *SIC 4619*

WEAVER WELDING LTD   *p152*
7501 107 AVE, PEACE RIVER, AB, T8S 1M6
(780) 618-7522   *SIC 4619*

SIC 4724 Travel agencies

1437782 ONTARIO INC   *p690*
2810 MATHESON BLVD E SUITE 300, MISSISSAUGA, ON, L4W 4X7
(905) 694-2650   *SIC 4724*

1529295 ONTARIO INC   *p770*
386 SHEPPARD AVE E UNIT 2, NORTH YORK, ON, M2N 3B7
(416) 226-6667   *SIC 4724*

1572900 ONTARIO INC   *p728*
6301 SILVER DART DR, MISSISSAUGA, ON, L5P 1B2
(416) 776-2247   *SIC 4724*

1987 THE TRAVEL GROUP LTD   *p301*
890 PENDER ST W SUITE 330, VANCOUVER, BC, V6C 1J9
(604) 681-6345   *SIC 4724*

2759-9687 QUEBEC INC.   *p1143*
1516 CH DE CHAMBLY, LONGUEUIL, QC, J4J 3X5
(450) 670-1235   *SIC 4724*

320114 ALBERTA INC   *p27*
328 CENTRE ST SE SUITE 202, CALGARY, AB, T2G 4X6
(403) 777-0777   *SIC 4724*

320114 ALBERTA INC   *p42*
400 4 AVE SW SUITE 230, CALGARY, AB, T2P 0J4
SIC 4724

3225518 CANADA INC   *p1171*
2590 RUE JEAN-TALON E, MONTREAL, QC, H2A 1T9
(514) 847-1287   *SIC 4724*

375645 ONTARIO LIMITED   *p548*
8800 DUFFERIN ST UNIT 101, CONCORD,
ON, L4K 0C5
(416) 736-6010   *SIC 4724*

4358376 CANADA INC   *p691*
400-5450 EXPLORER DR, MISSISSAUGA, ON, L4W 5N1
(905) 238-3399   *SIC 4724*

679475 ONTARIO INC   *p665*
4440 STEELES AVE E UNIT 3, MARKHAM, ON, L3R 0L4
SIC 4724

734758 ONTARIO LIMITED   *p716*
3100 RIDGEWAY DR UNIT 16, MISSISSAUGA, ON, L5L 5M5
(905) 820-2266   *SIC 4724*

9064-6795 QUEBEC INC   *p1300*
497 CH DE LA GRANDE-COTE, SAINT-EUSTACHE, QC, J7P 1K3
(450) 473-2934   *SIC 4724*

9277-8091 QUEBEC INC   *p1257*
105 COTE DE LA MONTAGNE SUITE 105, QUEBEC, QC, G1K 4E4
(418) 692-3621   *SIC 4724*

9368-7952 QUEBEC INC   *p1300*
497 CH DE LA GRANDE-COTE, SAINT-EUSTACHE, QC, J7P 1K3
(450) 473-2934   *SIC 4724*

AGENCE DE VOYAGES DE L'AUTOMOBILE ET TOURING CLUB DU QUEBEC INC *p1278*
444 RUE BOUVIER, QUEBEC, QC, G2J 1E3
(418) 624-2424   *SIC 4724*

ALBERTA MOTOR ASSOCIATION   *p73*
4700 17 AVE SW, CALGARY, AB, T3E 0E3
(403) 240-5300   *SIC 4724*

ALBERTA MOTOR ASSOCIATION TRAVEL AGENCY LTD   *p118*
10310 39A AVE, EDMONTON, AB, T6H 5X9
(780) 430-5555   *SIC 4724*

BAINS TRAVEL LIMITED   *p290*
6550 FRASER ST, VANCOUVER, BC, V5X 3T3
(604) 324-2277   *SIC 4724*

BILODEAU, L. & FILS LTEE   *p1064*
1405 RUE GRAHAM-BELL BUREAU 101, BOUCHERVILLE, QC, J4B 6A1
(450) 449-6542   *SIC 4724*

BLYTH & COMPANY TRAVEL LIMITED *p972*
13 HAZELTON AVE, TORONTO, ON, M5R 2E1
(416) 964-2569   *SIC 4724*

BUSINESS TRAVEL NETWORK INC   *p928*
1027 YONGE ST SUITE 103, TORONTO, ON, M4W 2K9
(416) 924-6000   *SIC 4724*

CAA TRAVEL (SOUTH CENTRAL ONTARIO) INC.   *p903*
60 COMMERCE VALLEY DR E, THORN-HILL, ON, L3T 7P9
(905) 771-3000   *SIC 4724*

CAMPBELL TRAVEL LTD   *p297*
181 KEEFER PL SUITE 201, VANCOUVER, BC, V6B 6C1
(604) 688-2913   *SIC 4724*

CANAD CORPORATION LTD   *p369*
930 JEFFERSON AVE SUITE 3, WINNIPEG, MB, R2P 1W1
(204) 697-1495   *SIC 4724*

CANADA INTERNATIONAL TRAVEL SERVICE INC   *p1009*
794 PARIS BLVD, WATERLOO, ON, N2T 2Z2
(519) 746-0579   *SIC 4724*

CANADA TOUR SYSTEM INC   *p297*
510 HASTINGS ST W SUITE 1308, VANCOUVER, BC, V6B 1L8
(604) 681-9747   *SIC 4724*

CAPILANO SUSPENSION BRIDGE LTD *p242*
3735 CAPILANO RD SUITE 1889, NORTH VANCOUVER, BC, V7R 4J1
(604) 985-7474   *SIC 4724*

CARLSON WAGONLIT CANADA   *p428*
92 ELIZABETH AVE, ST. JOHN'S, NL, A1A 1W7
(709) 726-2900   *SIC 4724*

CARLSON WAGONLIT CANADA   *p692*
2425 MATHESON BLVD E SUITE 600, MISSISSAUGA, ON, L4W 5K4
(905) 740-3500   *SIC 4724*

CARLSON WAGONLIT CANADA   *p830*
885 MEADOWLANDS DR SUITE 401, OTTAWA, ON, K2C 3N2
(613) 274-6969   *SIC 4724*

CARTER   *p511*
72 LINKS LANE, BRAMPTON, ON, L6Y 5H1
(416) 574-3770   *SIC 4724*

CASCADIA MOTIVATION INC   *p153*
4646 RIVERSIDE DR SUITE 14A, RED DEER, AB, T4N 6Y5
(403) 340-8687   *SIC 4724*

CLINIQUE SANTE VOYAGE SAINT-LUC *p1175*
1560 RUE SHERBROOKE E, MONTREAL, QC, H2L 4M1
(514) 890-8332   *SIC 4724*

CONFERENCE WORLD TOURS   *p769*
1200 SHEPPARD AVE E SUITE 201, NORTH YORK, ON, M2K 2S5
(416) 221-6411   *SIC 4724*

CONTINENTAL TRAVEL BUREAU LTD *p377*
222 OSBORNE ST N, WINNIPEG, MB, R3C 1V4
(204) 989-8575   *SIC 4724*

COQUITLAM CRUISESHIPCENTERS   *p200*
1021 AUSTIN AVE, COQUITLAM, BC, V3K 3N9
(604) 937-7125   *SIC 4724*

CORPORATE TRAVEL MANAGEMENT SOLUTIONS INC   *p781*
5000 DUFFERIN ST SUITE 219B, NORTH YORK, ON, M3H 5T5
(416) 665-2867   *SIC 4724*

CREATIVE TRAVEL SOLUTIONS INC *p923*
118 EGLINTON AVE W SUITE 500, TORONTO, ON, M4R 2G4
(416) 485-6387   *SIC 4724*

CRUISEPLUS MANAGEMENT LTD   *p230*
7143 CAILLET RD, LANTZVILLE, BC, V0R 2H0
(250) 390-0220   *SIC 4724*

CUSTOM TRAVEL SOLUTIONS INC   *p66*
2424 4 ST SW SUITE 800, CALGARY, AB, T2S 2T4
(403) 272-1000   *SIC 4724*

CWT CONCIERGE   *p1054*
53 MAPLE CRES, BEACONSFIELD, QC, H9W 4T3
(514) 695-7215   *SIC 4724*

DAVE'S CRUISES   *p235*
6490 PTARMIGAN WAY, NANAIMO, BC, V9V 1V7
(250) 390-1115   *SIC 4724*

DAVID'S VACATION CLUB RENTALS   *p657*
4-1106 DEARNESS DR, LONDON, ON, N6E 1N9
(519) 686-7694   *SIC 4724*

DELTA TOUR AND TRAVEL SERVICES (CANADA) INC   *p260*
5611 COONEY RD SUITE 160, RICHMOND, BC, V6X 3J6
(604) 233-0081   *SIC 4724*

DESTINATIONS ESCAPA INC   *p1061*
362 CH DE LA GRANDE-COTE, BOIS-BRIAND, QC, J7G 1B1
(514) 338-1160   *SIC 4724*

DESTINATIONS ETC INC   *p1195*
1470 RUE PEEL BUREAU 110, MONTREAL, QC, H3A 1T1
(514) 849-0707   *SIC 4724*

E F VOYAGES CULTURELS   *p1188*
407 RUE MCGILL BUREAU 400, MONTREAL, QC, H2Y 2G3
(800) 387-7708   *SIC 4724*

EF EDUCATION   *p1188*
407 RUE MCGILL BUREAU 400, MONTREAL, QC, H2Y 2G3
(514) 904-0180   *SIC 4724*

EXPEDIA CRUISE SHIP CENTRE MONC-

TON   *p409*
1633 MOUNTAIN RD SUITE 13, MONCTON, NB, E1G 1A5
(506) 386-7447   *SIC 4724*

EXPEDIA CRUISE SHIP CENTRES, TERWILLEGAR   *p123*
14256 23 AVE NW, EDMONTON, AB, T6R 3B9
(780) 822-9283   *SIC 4724*

EXPEDIA CRUISESHIPCENTERS   *p221*
1980 COOPER RD UNIT 106, KELOWNA, BC, V1Y 8K5
(250) 763-2900   *SIC 4724*

FLIGHT CENTRE TRAVEL GROUP (CANADA) INC   *p326*
980 HOWE ST SUITE 700, VANCOUVER, BC, V6Z 0C8
(604) 682-5202   *SIC 4724*

FLIGHT NETWORK LTD   *p951*
145 KING ST W SUITE 1401, TORONTO, ON, M5H 1J8
(905) 829-8699   *SIC 4724*

FORFAITERIE INC, LA   *p1378*
107 1RE AV, STONEHAM-ET-TEWKESBURY, QC, G3C 0L3
(418) 848-1518   *SIC 4724*

FREEWHEELING ADVENTURES INCORPORATED   *p459*
2070 HIGHWAY 329, HUBBARDS, NS, B0J 1T0
(902) 857-3600   *SIC 4724*

GLOBESPAN TRAVEL LTD   *p293*
660 LEG IN BOOT SQ UNIT C, VANCOUVER, BC, V5Z 4B3
(604) 879-6466   *SIC 4724*

GRAND PACIFIC TRAVEL & TRADE (CANADA) CORP   *p260*
8877 ODLIN CRES SUITE 100, RICHMOND, BC, V6X 3Z7
(604) 276-2616   *SIC 4724*

GROUP VOYAGES VP INC   *p1175*
1259 RUE BERRI BUREAU 600, MONTREAL, QC, H2L 4C7
(514) 939-9999   *SIC 4724*

GROUPE INCURSION INC   *p1278*
815 BOUL LEBOURGNEUF BUREAU 202, QUEBEC, QC, G2J 0C1
(418) 687-2400   *SIC 4724*

H.I.S. CANADA INC   *p305*
636 HORNBY ST, VANCOUVER, BC, V6C 2G2
(604) 685-3524   *SIC 4724*

HAGENS TRAVEL (1957 OPERATIONS) LTD *p270*
13606 KELLY AVE, SUMMERLAND, BC, V0H 1Z0
(250) 494-5202   *SIC 4724*

HANDA TRAVEL SERVICES LTD   *p819*
2269 RIVERSIDE DR SUITE 135, OTTAWA, ON, K1H 8K2
(613) 731-1111   *SIC 4724*

HARVEY'S TRAVEL LTD   *p428*
92 ELIZABETH AVE, ST. JOHN'S, NL, A1A 1W7
(709) 726-2900   *SIC 4724*

HIS INTERNATIONAL TOURS BC INC *p305*
636 HORNBY ST, VANCOUVER, BC, V6C 2G2
(604) 685-3524   *SIC 4724*

HOLLAND AMERICA LINE   *p305*
999 CANADA PL SUITE 200, VANCOUVER, BC, V6C 3C1
(604) 683-5776   *SIC 4724*

ISYARI CANADA INC   *p696*
5045 ORBITOR DR BUILDING 12 SUITE 400, MISSISSAUGA, ON, L4W 4Y4
(905) 212-2515   *SIC 4724*

JACCO TOURS (ONTARIO) INC   *p876*
633 SILVER STAR BLVD UNIT 122, SCARBOROUGH, ON, M1V 5N1
(416) 332-0808   *SIC 4724*

JACCO TOURS ONTARIO INC   *p671*
7828 KENNEDY RD SUITE 203, MARKHAM, ON, L3R 5P1

(905) 305-3888 *SIC* 4724
JEMCO VENTURES INC p68
11440 BRAESIDE DR SW SUITE 25, CAL-
GARY, AB, T2W 3N4
(403) 278-7447 *SIC* 4724
JONVIEW CANADA TRANSAT p579
800-191 THE WEST MALL, ETOBICOKE,
ON, M9C 5K8
(416) 323-9090 *SIC* 4724
JUBILEE TOURS & TRAVEL LTD p182
3011 UNDERHILL AVE SUITE 201, BURN-
ABY, BC, V5A 3C2
(604) 669-6607 *SIC* 4724
JUST VACATIONS INC p658
101 CHERRYHILL BLVD, LONDON, ON,
N6H 4S4
(519) 472-2700 *SIC* 4724
**KINTETSU INTERNATIONAL EXPRESS
(CANADA) INC** p314
1140 PENDER ST W SUITE 910, VANCOU-
VER, BC, V6E 4G1
(778) 328-9754 *SIC* 4724
LEXUS TRAVEL INC p1197
1411 RUE PEEL BUREAU 403, MON-
TREAL, QC, H3A 1S5
(514) 397-9221 *SIC* 4724
LGV QUEBEC INC p1326
400 AV SAINTE-CROIX BUREAU 110,
SAINT-LAURENT, QC, H4N 3L4
(514) 748-2522 *SIC* 4724
LGV QUEBEC INC p1326
400 AV SAINTE-CROIX BUREAU 100,
SAINT-LAURENT, QC, H4N 3L4
(514) 748-2522 *SIC* 4724
**LION INTERNATIONAL TRAVEL SERVICE
CO LTD** p260
110-4140 NO. 3 RD, RICHMOND, BC, V6X
2C2
(604) 231-8256 *SIC* 4724
LONTOURS CANADA LIMITED p996
3280 BLOOR ST W 4 FL SUITE 400,
TORONTO, ON, M8X 2X3
(800) 268-3636 *SIC* 4724
MAGELLAN VACATION INC p387
730 TAYLOR AVE, WINNIPEG, MB, R3M
2K8
(204) 992-5215 *SIC* 4724
MAPLE FUN TOURS LTD p299
997 SEYMOUR ST W SUITE 610, VANCOU-
VER, BC, V6B 3M1
(604) 683-5244 *SIC* 4724
MARITIME TRAVEL INC p453
2000 BARRINGTON ST SUITE 202, HALI-
FAX, NS, B3J 3K1
(902) 420-1554 *SIC* 4724
MARSHALL ANDERSON TOURS LTD p65
1117 1 ST SW SUITE 303, CALGARY, AB,
T2R 0T9
(780) 417-2642 *SIC* 4724
MCCOY TOURS p633
566 CATARAQUI WOODS DR, KINGSTON,
ON, K7P 2Y5
(613) 384-0347 *SIC* 4724
ME TO WE TRIPS INC p934
145 BERKELEY ST, TORONTO, ON, M5A
2X1
(416) 964-8942 *SIC* 4724
MENNO TRAVEL SERVICE CANADA LTD
p177
GD, ABBOTSFORD, BC, V2T 0A1
(604) 853-0751 *SIC* 4724
MERIDICAN TRAVEL INC p672
16 ESNA PARK DR SUITE 103, MARKHAM,
ON, L3R 5X1
(905) 477-7700 *SIC* 4724
MERIT TRAVEL GROUP INC p982
111 PETER ST SUITE 200, TORONTO, ON,
M5V 2H1
(416) 364-3775 *SIC* 4724
MISSISSAUGA CRUISE SHIP CENTREp725
6465 MILLCREEK DR SUITE 170, MISSIS-
SAUGA, ON, L5N 5R3
(905) 821-7447 *SIC* 4724
MML CLUB SERVICES LTD p382

870 EMPRESS ST, WINNIPEG, MB, R3G
3H3
(204) 262-6131 *SIC* 4724
NEW WAVE CRUISE SHIP CENTRES p282
15957 84 AVE SUITE 102, SURREY, BC,
V4N 0W7
(604) 572-9500 *SIC* 4724
NIAGARA GORGE JET BOATING LTD p761
61 MELVILLE ST, NIAGARA ON THE LAKE,
ON, L0S 1J0
(905) 468-4800 *SIC* 4724
NORTH-WRIGHT AIRWAYS LTD p435
2200, NORMAN WELLS, NT, X0E 0V0
(867) 587-2288 *SIC* 4724
ODENZA MARKETING GROUP INC p189
4370 DOMINION ST SUITE 600, BURN-
ABY, BC, V5G 4L7
(604) 451-1414 *SIC* 4724
ORBITOUR LTEE p1259
105 COTE DE LA MONTAGNE BUREAU
601, QUEBEC, QC, G1K 4E4
(418) 692-1223 *SIC* 4724
PACESETTER TRAVEL LIMITED p921
3284 YONGE ST SUITE 300, TORONTO,
ON, M4N 3M7
(416) 322-1031 *SIC* 4724
PARTENAIRES EN VOYAGES INC p1324
100 BOUL ALEXIS-NIHON, STE 110,
SAINT-LAURENT, QC, H4M 2N6
SIC 4724
RAYLINK LTD p1039
134 KENT ST, CHARLOTTETOWN, PE,
C1A 8R8
(902) 629-8400 *SIC* 4724
RED LABEL VACATIONS INC p699
5450 EXPLORER DR SUITE 400, MISSIS-
SAUGA, ON, L4W 5N1
(905) 283-6020 *SIC* 4724
RENSHAW TRAVEL LTD p322
2175 4TH AVE W, VANCOUVER, BC, V6K
1N7
(604) 838-1008 *SIC* 4724
ROBERT Q'S TRAVEL MART INC p659
105 WHARNCLIFFE RD S, LONDON, ON,
N6J 2K2
(519) 672-9020 *SIC* 4724
**SERVICES DE VOYAGES YVES BORDE-
LEAU INC, LES** p1385
765 BOUL THIBEAU BUREAU 100, TROIS-
RIVIERES, QC, G8T 7A4
(819) 374-0747 *SIC* 4724
SILK HOLIDAYS INC p293
4012 CAMBIE ST, VANCOUVER, BC, V5Z
2X8
SIC 4724
SINORAMA CORPORATION p1192
998 BLVD SAINT-LAURENT OFFICE 518,
MONTREAL, QC, H2Z 9Y9
(514) 866-6888 *SIC* 4724
SKYLAND TRAVEL INC p292
445 6TH AVE W SUITE 100, VANCOUVER,
BC, V5Y 1L3
(604) 685-6885 *SIC* 4724
SUNWING TRAVEL GROUP INC p588
27 FASKEN DR, ETOBICOKE, ON, M9W
1K6
(416) 620-4955 *SIC* 4724
TAI PAN VACATIONS INC p794
3668 WESTON RD UNIT A, NORTH YORK,
ON, M9L 1W2
(416) 646-8828 *SIC* 4724
TARGET VACATIONS p559
3175 RUTHERFORD RD UNIT 55, CON-
CORD, ON, L4K 5Y6
(416) 687-5925 *SIC* 4724
TIAN BAO TRAVEL CO INC p875
4002 SHEPPARD AVE E UNIT 106A,
SCARBOROUGH, ON, M1S 4R5
(416) 292-9990 *SIC* 4724
TIAN BAO TRAVEL LTD p854
60 WEST WILMOT ST UNIT 1, RICHMOND
HILL, ON, L4B 1M6
(905) 695-2229 *SIC* 4724
TOUR EAST HOLIDAYS (CANADA) INCp778

15 KERN RD SUITE 9, NORTH YORK, ON,
M3B 1S9
(416) 250-1098 *SIC* 4724
TOURAM LIMITED PARTNERSHIP p690
5925 AIRPORT RD SUITE 700, MISSIS-
SAUGA, ON, L4V 1W1
(905) 615-8020 *SIC* 4724
TOURAM LIMITED PARTNERSHIP p1214
1440 RUE SAINTE-CATHERINE O BU-
REAU 600, MONTREAL, QC, H3G 1R8
(514) 876-0700 *SIC* 4724
TOURS JUMPSTREET TOURS INC, LES
p1223
780 AV BREWSTER SUITE 02-300, MON-
TREAL, QC, H4C 2K1
(514) 843-3311 *SIC* 4724
TRANSAT DISTRIBUTION CANADA INC
p580
191 THE WEST MALL SUITE 700, ETOBI-
COKE, ON, M9C 5K8
SIC 4724
TRAVEL ALBERTA IN-PROVINCE p86
10949 120 ST NW, EDMONTON, AB, T5H
3R2
SIC 4724
TRAVEL EDGE (CANADA) INC p941
2 QUEEN ST E SUITE 200, TORONTO, ON,
M5C 3G7
(416) 649-9093 *SIC* 4724
TRAVEL GALLERY, THE p1422
1230 BLACKFOOT DR SUITE 110,
REGINA, SK, S4S 7G4
SIC 4724
TRAVEL MASTERS INC p322
2678 BROADWAY W SUITE 200, VANCOU-
VER, BC, V6K 2G3
(604) 659-4150 *SIC* 4724
TRAVEL SUPERSTORE INC p614
77 JAMES ST N SUITE 230, HAMILTON,
ON, L8R 2K3
(905) 570-9999 *SIC* 4724
UNIGLOBE BEACON TRAVEL LTD p42
1400 KENSINGTON RD NW SUITE 200,
CALGARY, AB, T2N 3P9
(877) 596-6860 *SIC* 4724
UNIGLOBE ONE TRAVEL INC p318
1444 ALBERNI ST SUITE 300, VANCOU-
VER, BC, V6G 2Z4
(604) 688-3551 *SIC* 4724
**UNIGLOBE PREMIERE TRAVEL PLAN-
NERS INC** p1001
24 SELKIRK ST SUITE 100, VANIER, ON,
K1L 0A4
(613) 230-7411 *SIC* 4724
**UNIGLOBE TRAVEL INTERNATIONAL LIM-
ITED** p317
1199 PENDER ST W SUITE 900, VANCOU-
VER, BC, V6E 2R1
(604) 718-2600 *SIC* 4724
UNIGLOBE VISION TRAVEL GROUP INC
p319
1444 ALBERNI ST SUITE 300, VANCOU-
VER, BC, V6G 2Z4
(604) 688-3551 *SIC* 4724
UNIKTOUR INC p1192
555 BOUL RENE-LEVESQUE O BUREAU
3, MONTREAL, QC, H2Z 1B1
(514) 722-0909 *SIC* 4724
UNIWORLD TRAVEL & TOURS INC p768
235 YORKLAND BLVD SUITE 300, NORTH
YORK, ON, M2J 4Y8
(416) 493-3322 *SIC* 4724
VISION 2000 TRAVEL MANAGEMENT INC
p769
1200 SHEPPARD AVE E SUITE 201,
NORTH YORK, ON, M2K 2S5
(416) 487-5385 *SIC* 4724
VISION NEW WAVE TRAVEL INC p976
1075 BAY ST, TORONTO, ON, M5S 2B1
(416) 928-3113 *SIC* 4724
VISION TRAVEL DT ONTARIO-WEST INC
p915
251 CONSUMERS RD SUITE 700,
TORONTO, ON, M2J 4R3

(416) 487-5385 *SIC* 4724
VOS VACATION p1181
8060 RUE SAINT-HUBERT, MONTREAL,
QC, H2R 2P3
(514) 270-3186 *SIC* 4724
VOYAGE GARTH ALLEN MARKSTED INC
p1157
8260 CH DEVONSHIRE BUREAU 210,
MONT-ROYAL, QC, H4P 2P7
(514) 344-8888 *SIC* 4724
VOYAGES BERGERON INC p1181
7725 RUE SAINT-DENIS, MONTREAL, QC,
H2R 2E9
(514) 273-3301 *SIC* 4724
VOYAGES BERNARD GENDRON INCp1365
1465 BOUL MONSEIGNEUR-LANGLOIS,
SALABERRY-DE-VALLEYFIELD, QC, J6S
1C2
(450) 373-8747 *SIC* 4724
VOYAGES ENCORE TRAVEL INC p1327
1285 RUE HODGE BUREAU 101, SAINT-
LAURENT, QC, H4N 2B6
(514) 738-7171 *SIC* 4724
VOYAGES ESCAPADE INC p1374
2855 RUE KING O, SHERBROOKE, QC,
J1L 1C6
(819) 563-5344 *SIC* 4724
VOYAGES LAURIER DU VALLON INC, LES
p1274
2450 BOUL LAURIER BUREAU 10, QUE-
BEC, QC, G1V 2L1
(418) 653-1882 *SIC* 4724
VOYAGES MALAVOY INC p1168
3425 RUE BEAUBIEN E, MONTREAL, QC,
H1X 1G8
(514) 286-7559 *SIC* 4724
VOYAGES TRADITUORS INC p1237
1575 BOUL DE L'AVENIR BUREAU 100,
MONTREAL, QC, H7S 2N5
(514) 907-7712 *SIC* 4724
VOYAGES VISION DT QUEBEC-EST INC
p1226
400 AV SAINTE-CROIX 100 O, MON-
TREAL, QC, H4N 3L4
(514) 748-2522 *SIC* 4724
VOYAGESARABAIS INC p1385
699 BOUL THIBEAU BUREAU 100, TROIS-
RIVIERES, QC, G8T 7A2
(819) 693-8937 *SIC* 4724
VOYZANT INC p677
7100 WOODBINE AVE UNIT 102,
MARKHAM, ON, L3R 5J2
(647) 783-3371 *SIC* 4724
VR TRAVEL LTD p931
2 BLOOR ST W SUITE 2120, TORONTO,
ON, M4W 3E2
SIC 4724
WESTCAN TRAVEL LTD p118
8412 109 ST NW, EDMONTON, AB, T6G
1E2
(780) 439-9118 *SIC* 4724
WESTWOOD CRUISESHIPCENTERS p246
2748 LOUGHEED HWY SUITE 304, PORT
COQUITLAM, BC, V3B 6P2
(604) 464-7447 *SIC* 4724
**WORKING ENTERPRISES TRAVEL SER-
VICES LTD** p240
233 1ST ST W SUITE 430, NORTH VAN-
COUVER, BC, V7M 1B3
(604) 969-5585 *SIC* 4724
WYNFORD GROUP INC, THE p778
101 DUNCAN MILL RD SUITE 500, NORTH
YORK, ON, M3B 1Z3
(416) 443-9696 *SIC* 4724

SIC 4725 Tour operators

492632 BC LTD p341
1412 SANDHURST PL, WEST VANCOU-
VER, BC, V7S 2P3
(604) 451-1600 *SIC* 4725
ACCENT CRUISES.CA p319
1676 DURANLEAU ST SUITE 100, VAN-

COUVER, BC, V6H 3S4
(604) 688-8072   *SIC 4725*

ACP MARKETING CANADA INC   *p1227*
8375 RUE BOUGAINVILLE BUREAU 100, MONTREAL, QC, H4P 2G5
(514) 733-5247   *SIC 4725*

ALBERTA PRAIRIE STEAM TOURS LTD   *p167*
4611 47TH AVE, STETTLER, AB, T0C 2L0
(403) 742-2811   *SIC 4725*

AMBASSATOURS LIMITED   *p454*
6575 BAYNE ST, HALIFAX, NS, B3K 0H1
(902) 423-6242   *SIC 4725*

ATLANTIC TOURS LIMITED   *p455*
2631 KING ST, HALIFAX, NS, B3K 4T7
(902) 423-6242   *SIC 4725*

AVONLEA VILLAGE   *p1042*
GD, NORTH RUSTICO, PE, C0A 1X0
(902) 963-3050   *SIC 4725*

BIG RED DOG INC   *p342*
4122 VILLAGE GREEN SUITE 5, WHISTLER, BC, V0N 1B4
(604) 938-9656   *SIC 4725*

BREWSTER INC   *p4*
100 GOPHER ST, BANFF, AB, T1L 1J3
(403) 762-6700   *SIC 4725*

CANADIAN CO CO TOURS, INC   *p4*
220 BEAR ST SUITE 306, BANFF, AB, T1L 1A2
(403) 762-5600   *SIC 4725*

CANADIAN TRAVEL TEAM   *p241*
935 MARINE DR SUITE 304, NORTH VANCOUVER, BC, V7P 1S3
(604) 990-7370   *SIC 4725*

CLUB MED VENTES CANADA INC   *p1401*
3500 BOUL DE MAISONNEUVE O BUREAU 1500, WESTMOUNT, QC, H3Z 3C1
(514) 937-1428   *SIC 4725*

CVS CRUISE VICTORIA LTD   *p335*
185 DALLAS RD, VICTORIA, BC, V8V 1A1
(250) 386-8652   *SIC 4725*

DARGAL INTERLINE CRUISE & TOURS LTD   *p221*
1632 DICKSON AVE SUITE 200, KELOWNA, BC, V1Y 7T2
(250) 861-3223   *SIC 4725*

DENURE TOURS LTD   *p645*
71 MOUNT HOPE ST, LINDSAY, ON, K9V 5N5
(705) 324-9161   *SIC 4725*

DUFFERIN TRAVEL INC   *p942*
35 THE ESPLANADE SUITE 200, TORONTO, ON, M5E 1Z4
(416) 369-1750   *SIC 4725*

EAST COAST OUTFITTERS   *p461*
2017 LOWER PROSPECT RD, LOWER PROSPECT, NS, B3T 1Y8
(902) 624-0334   *SIC 4725*

EDUCATOURS LTD   *p995*
3280 BLOOR ST W SUITE 901, TORONTO, ON, M8X 2X3
(416) 251-3390   *SIC 4725*

ELLISON TRAVEL & TOURS LTD   *p589*
311 MAIN ST N, EXETER, ON, N0M 1S3
(519) 235-2000   *SIC 4725*

EMPIRE SANDY INC   *p933*
151 QUEENS QUAY E, TORONTO, ON, M5A 1B6
(416) 364-3244   *SIC 4725*

G ADVENTURES INC   *p980*
19 CHARLOTTE ST SUITE 200, TORONTO, ON, M5V 2H5
(416) 260-0999   *SIC 4725*

GATEWAYS INTERNATIONAL INC   *p852*
30 WERTHEIM CRT UNIT 20, RICHMOND HILL, ON, L4B 1B9
(905) 889-0483   *SIC 4725*

GOTREKKERS INC   *p71*
4625 VARSITY DR NW SUITE 305, CALGARY, AB, T3A 0Z9
(403) 289-6938   *SIC 4725*

GOWAY TRAVEL LIMITED   *p921*
3284 YONGE ST SUITE 500, TORONTO, ON, M4N 3M7

(416) 322-1034   *SIC 4725*

GREAT CANADIAN HOLIDAYS INC   *p636*
353 MANITOU DR, KITCHENER, ON, N2C 1L5
(519) 896-8687   *SIC 4725*

GREAT CANADIAN RAILTOUR COMPANY LTD   *p218*
525 CN RD, KAMLOOPS, BC, V2H 1K3
(250) 314-0576   *SIC 4725*

GREAT CANADIAN RAILTOUR COMPANY LTD   *p326*
980 HOWE ST, VANCOUVER, BC, V6Z 1N9
(604) 606-7200   *SIC 4725*

GROUPE VOYAGES QUEBEC INC   *p1269*
174 GRANDE ALLEE O, QUEBEC, QC, G1R 2G9
(418) 525-4585   *SIC 4725*

HOGG ROBINSON CANADA INC   *p1197*
1550 RUE METCALFE BUREAU 700, MONTREAL, QC, H3A 1X6
(514) 286-6300   *SIC 4725*

JADE TRAVEL LTD   *p857*
1650 ELGIN MILLS RD E UNIT 403, RICHMOND HILL, ON, L4S 0B2
(905) 787-9288   *SIC 4725*

JAPAN OTTAWA TRAVEL INC   *p750*
139 CRAIG HENRY DR, NEPEAN, ON, K2G 3Z8
(613) 820-8800   *SIC 4725*

JONVIEW CANADA INC   *p579*
191 THE WEST MALL SUITE 800, ETOBICOKE, ON, M9C 5K8
(416) 323-9090   *SIC 4725*

JOY OF TRAVEL LTD, THE   *p852*
30 WERTHEIM CRT UNIT 20, RICHMOND HILL, ON, L4B 1B9
(905) 889-1681   *SIC 4725*

JTB INTERNATIONAL (CANADA) LTD   *p260*
8899 ODLIN CRES, RICHMOND, BC, V6X 3Z7
(604) 276-0300   *SIC 4725*

NIAGARA KANKO TOURS INC   *p759*
5719 STANLEY AVE, NIAGARA FALLS, ON, L2G 3X6
(905) 356-2025   *SIC 4725*

NIPPON TRAVEL AGENCY CANADA LTD   *p315*
1199 PENDER ST W SUITE 370, VANCOUVER, BC, V6E 2R1
(604) 685-4663   *SIC 4725*

NITE TOURS INTERNATIONAL   *p85*
67 AIRPORT RD NW, EDMONTON, AB, T5G 0W6
SIC 4725

NORDIC EQUITY LIMITED   *p698*
2800 SKYMARK AVE, MISSISSAUGA, ON, L4W 5A6
(905) 629-8530   *SIC 4725*

PROMOTION SAGUENAY INC   *p1079*
295 RUE RACINE E, CHICOUTIMI, QC, G7H 1S7
(418) 698-3157   *SIC 4725*

SENIOR DISCOVERY TOURS INC   *p923*
225 EGLINTON AVE W, TORONTO, ON, M4R 1A9
(416) 322-1500   *SIC 4725*

SILKWAY TRAVEL & DESTINATION MANAGEMENT INC   *p293*
4018 CAMBIE ST SUITE 4012, VANCOUVER, BC, V5Z 2X8
SIC 4725

SKICAN LIMITED   *p924*
745 MOUNT PLEASANT RD SUITE 300, TORONTO, ON, M4S 2N4
(416) 488-1169   *SIC 4725*

ST TOURING CANADA LTD   *p309*
900 GEORGIA ST W, VANCOUVER, BC, V6C 2W6
(604) 689-1553   *SIC 4725*

SUNWING VACATIONS INC   *p588*
27 FASKEN DR, ETOBICOKE, ON, M9W 1K6
(416) 620-5999   *SIC 4725*

TEMPLE AND TEMPLE TOURS INC   *p930*

819 YONGE ST 2ND FL, TORONTO, ON, M4W 2G9
(416) 928-3227   *SIC 4725*

TORONTO TOURS LTD   *p934*
259 LAKE SHORE BLVD E, TORONTO, ON, M5A 3T7
(416) 868-0400   *SIC 4725*

TOURLAND TRAVEL LTD   *p262*
8899 ODLIN CRES, RICHMOND, BC, V6X 3Z7
(604) 276-9592   *SIC 4725*

TOURNEES CLUB SELECT INC, LES   *p1137*
874 RUE ARCHIMEDE, LEVIS, QC, G6V 7M5
(418) 835-3336   *SIC 4725*

TOURS CHANTECLERC INC   *p1191*
152 RUE NOTRE-DAME E, MONTREAL, QC, H2Y 3P6
(514) 398-9535   *SIC 4725*

TOURS NEW YORK INC   *p1200*
1410 RUE STANLEY BUREAU 1015, MONTREAL, QC, H3A 1P8
(514) 287-1066   *SIC 4725*

TRANSAT DISTRIBUTION CANADA INC   *p1186*
300 RUE LEO-PARISEAU BUREAU 600, MONTREAL, QC, H2X 4C2
(514) 987-1616   *SIC 4725*

TRANSAT TOURS CANADA INC   *p1186*
300 RUE LEO-PARISEAU BUREAU 500, MONTREAL, QC, H2X 4B3
(514) 987-1616   *SIC 4725*

TRAVEL CORPORATION (CANADA), THE   *p778*
33 KERN RD, NORTH YORK, ON, M3B 1S9
(416) 322-8468   *SIC 4725*

TRAVELBRANDS INC   *p701*
5450 EXPLORER DR UNIT 300, MISSISSAUGA, ON, L4W 5M1
(416) 649-3939   *SIC 4725*

TRAVELBRANDS INC   *p943*
26 WELLINGTON ST E, TORONTO, ON, M5E 1S2
(416) 364-5100   *SIC 4725*

ULTIMATE TRAVEL GROUP INC   *p799*
1660 NORTH SERVICE RD E SUITE 101, OAKVILLE, ON, L6H 7G3
(905) 755-0999   *SIC 4725*

VISION GROUP OF COMPANIES LTD, THE   *p984*
99 BLUE JAYS WAY SUITE 300, TORONTO, ON, M5V 9G9
(416) 341-2474   *SIC 4725*

WHISTLER CONNECTION TOUR & TRAVEL SERVICES LTD   *p343*
8056 NESTERS RD, WHISTLER, BC, V8E 0G4
(604) 938-9711   *SIC 4725*

WHISTLER PLATINUM RESERVATIONS   *p343*
204 4230 GATEWAY DR, WHISTLER, BC, V8E 0Z8
(604) 932-0100   *SIC 4725*

X O TOURS CANADA LTD   *p322*
1788 BROADWAY W UNIT 600, VANCOUVER, BC, V6J 1Y1
(604) 738-6188   *SIC 4725*

YYZ TRAVEL SERVICES (INT'L) INC   *p906*
7851 DUFFERIN ST SUITE 100, THORNHILL, ON, L4J 3M4
(905) 660-7000   *SIC 4725*

SIC 4729 Passenger transportation arrangement

CANADIAN NORTH INC   *p21*
150 PALMER RD NE, CALGARY, AB, T2E 7R3
(780) 890-8600   *SIC 4729*

GESTION TERMICO INC   *p1144*
120 PLACE CHARLES-LE MOYNE BUREAU 300, LONGUEUIL, QC, J4K 2T4
(450) 670-3422   *SIC 4729*

OVERSEAS AIR CARGO   *p261*
10451 SHELLBRIDGE WAY SUITE 100, RICHMOND, BC, V6X 2W8
(604) 734-8155   *SIC 4729*

SKYLINK VOYAGES INC   *p1199*
1450 RUE CITY COUNCILLORS BUREAU 110, MONTREAL, QC, H3A 2E6
(514) 842-6344   *SIC 4729*

UNITED AIRLINES   *p729*
PO BOX 247 STN TORONTO AMF, MISSISSAUGA, ON, L5P 1B1
SIC 4729

SIC 4731 Freight transportation arrangement

1092072 ONTARIO INC   *p1331*
2520 AV MARIE-CURIE, SAINT-LAURENT, QC, H4S 1N1
(800) 511-1100   *SIC 4731*

1341611 ONTARIO INC   *p736*
6975 PACIFIC CIR UNIT D, MISSISSAUGA, ON, L5T 2H3
(905) 362-1111   *SIC 4731*

1476482 ONTARIO INC   *p618*
323 FRONT RD, HAWKESBURY, ON, K6A 2T1
(613) 632-1816   *SIC 4731*

150147 CANADA INC   *p1173*
4284 RUE DE LA ROCHE BUREAU 220, MONTREAL, QC, H2J 3H9
(438) 380-3516   *SIC 4731*

1519418 ONTARIO INC   *p733*
265 EXPORT BLVD, MISSISSAUGA, ON, L5S 1Y4
(905) 670-9300   *SIC 4731*

1579901 ONTARIO INC   *p498*
27 AUTOMATIC RD, BRAMPTON, ON, L6S 5N8
(416) 741-5454   *SIC 4731*

1625443 ONTARIO INC   *p535*
75 LINGARD RD, CAMBRIDGE, ON, N1T 2A8
(519) 624-9914   *SIC 4731*

1787930 ONTARIO INC   *p889*
150 DENNIS RD, ST THOMAS, ON, N5P 0B6
(519) 631-9604   *SIC 4731*

18 WHEELS LOGISTICS LTD   *p180*
7185 11TH AVE, BURNABY, BC, V3N 2M5
(604) 439-8938   *SIC 4731*

2088847 ONTARIO INC   *p547*
155 DRUMLIN CIR UNIT 2, CONCORD, ON, L4K 3E7
(905) 761-9999   *SIC 4731*

2136284 ONTARIO INC   *p535*
55 FLEMING DR UNIT 2, CAMBRIDGE, ON, N1T 2A9
(905) 696-1977   *SIC 4731*

2326236 ONTARIO INC   *p508*
31 SELBY RD, BRAMPTON, ON, L6W 1K5
(905) 455-9100   *SIC 4731*

2809664 CANADA INC   *p1117*
16711 RTE TRANSCANADIENNE, KIRKLAND, QC, H9H 3L1
(514) 343-0044   *SIC 4731*

3235149 CANADA INC   *p1393*
1033 RUE VALOIS, VAUDREUIL-DORION, QC, J7V 8P2
(450) 455-4545   *SIC 4731*

3307862 NOVA SCOTIA LIMITED   *p444*
132 TRIDER CRES SUITE 2, DARTMOUTH, NS, B3B 1R6
(800) 371-8022   *SIC 4731*

3618358 CANADA INC   *p581*
96 DISCO RD, ETOBICOKE, ON, M9W 0A3
(416) 679-7979   *SIC 4731*

4513380 CANADA INC   *p686*
6725 AIRPORT RD SUITE 400, MISSISSAUGA, ON, L4V 1V2
(905) 676-3700   *SIC 4731*

4513380 CANADA INC   *p686*
6725 AIRPORT RD UNIT 500, MISSIS-

SAUGA, ON, L4V 1V2
(905) 676-3700   SIC 4731
531442 ONTARIO INC   p591
1031 HELENA ST, FORT ERIE, ON, L2A
4K3
(905) 871-3358   SIC 4731
575636 ONTARIO LIMITED   p498
1 LASCELLES BLVD, BRAMPTON, ON, L6S
3T1
SIC 4731
594827 SASKATCHEWAN LTD   p1431
715 46TH ST W SUITE E, SASKATOON,
SK, S7L 6A1
(306) 249-3515   SIC 4731
673753 ONTARIO LIMITED   p682
375 WHEELABRATOR WAY SUITE 1, MIL-
TON, ON, L9T 3C1
(905) 875-0708   SIC 4731
673753 ONTARIO LIMITED   p800
104-610 CHARTWELL RD, OAKVILLE, ON,
L6J 4A5
(905) 875-0708   SIC 4731
8027722 CANADA INC   p1093
9500 AV RYAN, DORVAL, QC, H9P 3A1
(514) 634-7655   SIC 4731
9108-1950 QUEBEC INC   p1179
8355 RUE JEANNE-MANCE, MONTREAL,
QC, H2P 2Y1
SIC 4731
9162-7331 QUEBEC INC   p1331
7420 RUE VERITE, SAINT-LAURENT, QC,
H4S 1C5
(877) 353-7683   SIC 4731
979861 ONTARIO INC   p687
3220 CARAVELLE DR, MISSISSAUGA, ON,
L4V 1K9
(905) 362-8877   SIC 4731
**A & A CONTRACT CUSTOMS BROKERS
LTD**   p278
120 176 ST SUITE 101, SURREY, BC, V3Z
9S2
(604) 538-1042   SIC 4731
A.D. RUTHERFORD INTERNATIONAL INC
p371
1355 MOUNTAIN AVE SUITE 301, WIN-
NIPEG, MB, R2X 3B6
(204) 633-7207   SIC 4731
ABCO INTERNATIONAL FREIGHT INC p687
5945 AIRPORT RD SUITE 338, MISSIS-
SAUGA, ON, L4V 1R9
(905) 405-8088   SIC 4731
ACCORD LOGISTICS LTD   p271
17660 65A AVE UNIT 207, SURREY, BC,
V3S 5N4
(604) 331-9515   SIC 4731
ACGI SHIPPING INC   p301
900 HASTINGS ST W SUITE 1100, VAN-
COUVER, BC, V6C 1E5
(604) 683-4221   SIC 4731
**ADVANCE DISTRIBUTION LOGISTICS IN-
TERNATIONAL INC**   p737
7391 PACIFIC CIR, MISSISSAUGA, ON,
L5T 2A4
(905) 362-0548   SIC 4731
ADVANTEX EXPRESS INC   p687
6725 AIRPORT RD SUITE 101, MISSIS-
SAUGA, ON, L4V 1V2
(905) 677-0340   SIC 4731
**AGENCE INTERNATIONALE TRADE-
BRIDGE INC**   p1209
620 RUE SAINT-JACQUES BUREAU 500,
MONTREAL, QC, H3C 1C7
(514) 393-9100   SIC 4731
AGILITY LOGISTICS, CO   p737
185 COURTNEYPARK DR E SUITE B, MIS-
SISSAUGA, ON, L5T 2T6
(905) 612-7500   SIC 4731
AGRI TRANS SERVICES INC   p179
2200 KIRTON AVE, ARMSTRONG, BC, V0E
1B0
(250) 546-8898   SIC 4731
AIRLINE EXPRESS SERVICES INC   p687
3133 ORLANDO DR, MISSISSAUGA, ON,
L4V 1C5

(905) 670-2000   SIC 4731
**ALL-CONNECT LOGISTICAL SERVICES
INC**   p803
2070 WYECROFT RD, OAKVILLE, ON, L6L
5V6
(905) 847-6555   SIC 4731
**ALLIANCE OCCIDENTALE LOGISTIQUES
INC**   p1117
16766 RTE TRANSCANADIENNE BUREAU
400, KIRKLAND, QC, H9H 4M7
(514) 534-0114   SIC 4731
ALPINE INT'L TRANSPORTATION INC p482
480 WAYDOM DR, AYR, ON, N0B 1E0
(519) 624-6776   SIC 4731
**AMERICAN TRANSPORTATION & LOGIS-
TICS (AT&L) CANADA INC**   p1084
400 BOUL SAINT-MARTIN O BUREAU 206,
COTE SAINT-LUC, QC, H7M 3Y8
(514) 316-6496   SIC 4731
AMEX FREIGHT INC   p477
7066 SMITH INDUSTRIAL DR, AMHERST-
BURG, ON, N0R 1J0
(519) 726-4444   SIC 4731
ANDY LOGISTIQUE INC   p1364
4225 BOUL HEBERT, SALABERRY-DE-
VALLEYFIELD, QC, J6S 6J2
(514) 667-8494   SIC 4731
ARMBRO TRANSPORT INC   p737
6050 DIXIE RD, MISSISSAUGA, ON, L5T
1A6
(416) 213-7299   SIC 4731
ATLANTIC CUSTOM BROKERS   p431
233 DUCKWORTH ST SUITE 301, ST.
JOHN'S, NL, A1C 1G8
(709) 745-8700   SIC 4731
**ATLANTICA DIVERSIFIED TRANSPORTA-
TION SYSTEMS INC**   p445
10 MORRIS DR UNIT 19, DARTMOUTH,
NS, B3B 1K8
SIC 4731
**ATLAS INTERNATIONAL FREIGHT FOR-
WARDING INC**   p687
6365 NORTHWEST DR SUITE 18, MISSIS-
SAUGA, ON, L4V 1J8
(905) 673-5000   SIC 4731
ATLAS VAN LINES (CANADA) LTD   p796
485 NORTH SERVICE RD E, OAKVILLE,
ON, L6H 1A5
(905) 844-0701   SIC 4731
**ATS ANDLAUER TRANSPORTATION SER-
VICES INC**   p99
11264 186 ST NW, EDMONTON, AB, T5S
2W2
(780) 440-4005   SIC 4731
AXSUN INC   p1309
4900 RUE ARMAND-FRAPPIER BUREAU
450, SAINT-HUBERT, QC, J3Z 1G5
(450) 445-3003   SIC 4731
**AXXESS INTERNATIONAL COURTIERS EN
DOUANES INC**   p734
1804 ALSTEP DR UNIT 1, MISSISSAUGA,
ON, L5S 1W1
(905) 672-0270   SIC 4731
**AXXESS INTERNATIONAL COURTIERS EN
DOUANES INC**   p1187
360 RUE SAINT-JACQUES BUREAU 1200,
MONTREAL, QC, H2Y 1P5
(514) 849-9377   SIC 4731
BBE EXPEDITING LTD   p134
1759 35 AVE E, GRANDE PRAIRIE, AB,
T9E 0V6
(780) 890-8611   SIC 4731
BBT TRANSPORT LTD   p419
1999 CH VAL-DOUCET, VAL-DOUCET, NB,
E8R 1Z5
(506) 764-8004   SIC 4731
BCG LOGISTICS (2000) INC   p803
1300 SOUTH SERVICE RD W, OAKVILLE,
ON, L6L 5T7
(905) 238-3444   SIC 4731
BDP CANADA, ULC   p582
10 CARLSON CRT SUITE 801, ETOBI-
COKE, ON, M9W 6L2
(905) 602-0200   SIC 4731

**BEACON INTERNATIONAL DESPATCH
LIMITED**   p687
2-6300 NORTHWEST DR, MISSISSAUGA,
ON, L4V 1J7
(416) 640-0434   SIC 4731
**BEACON INTERNATIONAL WAREHOUS-
ING LTD**   p514
325 WEST ST SUITE B110, BRANTFORD,
ON, N3R 3V6
SIC 4731
BISON TRANSPORT INC   p8
234090 WRANGLER RD, CALGARY, AB,
P1X 0K2
(403) 444-0555   SIC 4731
BLM DECK DIVISION INC   p642
120 MCBRINE DR, KITCHENER, ON, N2R
1E7
(519) 894-0008   SIC 4731
BOLLORE LOGISTIQUES CANADA INC
p1332
3400 RUE DOUGLAS-B.-FLOREANI,
SAINT-LAURENT, QC, H4S 1V2
(514) 956-7870   SIC 4731
**BREMNER, GORDON C. INTERNATIONAL
INC**   p878
420 FINCHDENE SQ, SCARBOROUGH,
ON, M1X 1C2
(416) 321-6943   SIC 4731
BRIDGEPOINT LOGISTICS INC   p549
20 BARNES CRT UNIT 2, CONCORD, ON,
L4K 4L4
(416) 307-2100   SIC 4731
BUCKLAND CUSTOMS BROKERS LIMITED
p889
73 GAYLORD RD, ST THOMAS, ON, N5P
3R9
(519) 631-4944   SIC 4731
**BULK PLUS LOGISTICS LIMITED PART-
NERSHIP**   p713
452 SOUTHDOWN RD, MISSISSAUGA,
ON, L5J 2Y4
(905) 403-7854   SIC 4731
**BUSY BEE EXPRESS LINES INCORPO-
RATED**   p27
4127 16 ST SE, CALGARY, AB, T2G 3R9
(403) 233-2353   SIC 4731
BYEXPRESS CORPORATION   p826
2471 HOLLY LN, OTTAWA, ON, K1V 7P2
(613) 739-3000   SIC 4731
C.H. ROBINSON COMPANY (CANADA) LTD
p549
610 APPLEWOOD CRES UNIT 601, CON-
CORD, ON, L4K 0E3
(905) 851-8865   SIC 4731
C.H. ROBINSON MONDIAL CANADA, LTEE
p1210
645 RUE WELLINGTON BUREAU 400,
MONTREAL, QC, H3C 0L1
(514) 288-2161   SIC 4731
C.H. ROBINSON PROJECT LOGISTICS LTD
p21
6715 8 ST NE SUITE 102, CALGARY, AB,
T2E 7H7
(403) 295-1505   SIC 4731
CANADA ADMINISTRATION   p1258
271 RUE DE L'ESTUAIRE, QUEBEC, QC,
G1K 8S8
(418) 648-3645   SIC 4731
**CANADA CARTAGE SYSTEM LIMITED
PARTNERSHIP**   p734
1115 CARDIFF BLVD, MISSISSAUGA, ON,
L5S 1L8
(905) 564-2115   SIC 4731
CANADIAN COURIER LTD   p423
20 AV ROE, GANDER, NL, A1V 0H5
(709) 256-3528   SIC 4731
**CANADIAN INTERNATIONAL FREIGHT
FORWARDERS ASSOCIATION INC**   p583
170 ATTWELL DR UNIT 480, ETOBICOKE,
ON, M9W 5Z5
(416) 234-5100   SIC 4731
CANPAR TRANSPORT L.P.   p182
8399 EASTLAKE DR, BURNABY, BC, V5A
4W2

(604) 421-3452   SIC 4731
CANPAR TRANSPORT L.P.   p1004
18 INDUSTRIAL RD, WALKERTON, ON,
N0G 2V0
(519) 881-2770   SIC 4731
CARGOLUTION INC   p1092
800 BOUL STUART-GRAHAM S BUREAU
360, DORVAL, QC, H4Y 1J6
(514) 636-2576   SIC 4731
CARNBRO LTD   p598
HWY 540 B, GORE BAY, ON, P0P 1H0
(705) 282-2723   SIC 4731
CARSON CUSTOM BROKERS LIMITED
p278
17735 1 AVE SUITE 260, SURREY, BC, V3Z
9S1
(604) 538-4966   SIC 4731
**CAVALIER TRANSPORTATION SERVICES
INC**   p494
14091 HUMBER STATION RD, BOLTON,
ON, L7E 0Z9
(905) 857-6981   SIC 4731
CCT CANADA INC   p734
6900 TRANMERE DR, MISSISSAUGA, ON,
L5S 1L9
(905) 362-9198   SIC 4731
CENTRE DE MAINTENANCE ANDY INC, LE
p1365
4225 BOUL HEBERT, SALABERRY-DE-
VALLEYFIELD, QC, J6S 6J2
(514) 667-8500   SIC 4731
CEVA FREIGHT CANADA CORP   p693
1880 MATHESON BLVD E, MISSISSAUGA,
ON, L4W 5K9
(905) 672-3456   SIC 4731
CEVA LOGISTICS CANADA, ULC   p648
15745 ROBIN'S HILL RD, LONDON, ON,
N5V 0A5
(519) 659-2382   SIC 4731
CHALLENGER LOGISTICS INC   p538
300 MAPLE GROVE RD, CAMBRIDGE, ON,
N3E 1B7
(519) 653-6226   SIC 4731
CLARKE TRANSPORT INC   p501
201 WESTCREEK BLVD SUITE 200,
BRAMPTON, ON, L6T 5S6
(905) 291-3000   SIC 4731
COLE INTERNATIONAL INC   p22
1111 49 AVE NE, CALGARY, AB, T2E 8V2
(403) 262-2771   SIC 4731
COMMERCIAL LOGISTICS INC   p258
16133 BLUNDELL RD, RICHMOND, BC,
V6W 0A3
(604) 276-1300   SIC 4731
COMPAGNIE D'ARRIMAGE EMPIRE LTEE
p1187
500 PLACE D'ARMES BUREAU 2800,
MONTREAL, QC, H2Y 2W2
(514) 288-2221   SIC 4731
CONSOLIDATED FASTFRATE INC   p15
11440 54 ST SE, CALGARY, AB, T2C 4Y6
(403) 264-1687   SIC 4731
CONSOLIDATED FASTFRATE INC   p88
7725 101 ST, EDMONTON, AB, T5J 2M1
(780) 439-0061   SIC 4731
CONSOLIDATED FASTFRATE INC   p1127
4415 RUE FAIRWAY, LACHINE, QC, H8T
1B5
(514) 639-7747   SIC 4731
**CONTAINERWORLD FORWARDING SER-
VICES INC**   p258
16133 BLUNDELL RD, RICHMOND, BC,
V6W 0A3
(604) 276-1300   SIC 4731
CONTINENTAL CARGO SYSTEMS INC p734
7175 TRANMERE DR UNIT 1B, MISSIS-
SAUGA, ON, L5S 1N4
(905) 405-0096   SIC 4731
CONTROLE TOTAL LOGISTIQUE INC p1394
200 AV LOYOLA-SCHMIDT, VAUDREUIL-
DORION, QC, J7V 8P2
(450) 424-1700   SIC 4731
CORNERSTONE LOGISTICS LP   p797
2180 BUCKINGHAM RD SUITE 204,

OAKVILLE, ON, L6H 6H1

(905) 339-1456   *SIC* 4731

COSTCO WHOLESALE CANADA LTD   *p2*
1003 HAMILTON BLVD NE, AIRDRIE, AB, T4A 0G2

(403) 945-4267   *SIC* 4731

COURTAGE BGL LTEE   *p1187*
300 RUE DU SAINT-SACREMENT BUREAU 123, MONTREAL, QC, H2Y 1X4

(514) 288-8111   *SIC* 4731

COURTIER DOUANES INTERNATIONAL SKYWAY LTEE   *p1127*
9230 CH DE LA COTE-DE-LIESSE, LA-CHINE, QC, H8T 1A1

(514) 636-0250   *SIC* 4731

COURTIERS EN DOUANES GENERAL INC, LES   *p1187*
112 RUE MCGILL BUREAU 200, MON-TREAL, QC, H2Y 2E5

(514) 876-1704   *SIC* 4731

COURTIERS EN TRANSPORT G.M.R. INC, LES   *p1138*
2111 4E RUE BUREAU 100, LEVIS, QC, G6W 5M6

(418) 839-5768   *SIC* 4731

CRAILIN LOGISTICS SERVICES INC   *p622*
14722 HEART LAKE RD, INGLEWOOD, ON, L7C 2J7

(905) 838-3215   *SIC* 4731

CVC SLING SHOT TRANSPORTATION INC   *p205*
1345 DERWENT WAY, DELTA, BC, V3M 5V9

(604) 515-9462   *SIC* 4731

DACOTA FREIGHT SERVICE LTD   *p203*
1474 THEATRE RD, CRANBROOK, BC, V1C 7G1

(250) 426-3808   *SIC* 4731

DAHNAY LOGISTICS CANADA LTD   *p703*
2501 STANFIELD RD, MISSISSAUGA, ON, L4Y 1R6

(289) 803-1982   *SIC* 4731

DAMCO CANADA INC   *p693*
5700 EXPLORER DR UNIT 101, MISSIS-SAUGA, ON, L4W 0C6

(866) 361-3073   *SIC* 4731

DAMCO DISTRIBUTION CANADA INC   *p208*
8400 RIVER RD, DELTA, BC, V4G 1B5

(604) 940-1357   *SIC* 4731

DATA PARCEL EXPRESS INCORPORATED   *p738*
6500 VAN DEEMTER CRT, MISSISSAUGA, ON, L5T 1S1

(905) 564-5555   *SIC* 4731

DAVIDSON & SONS CUSTOMS BROKERS LTD   *p312*
1188 GEORGIA ST W SUITE 1220, VAN-COUVER, BC, V6E 4A2

(604) 681-5313   *SIC* 4731

DAVIS, PERCY H. LIMITED   *p1413*
4 ABBOTT AVE, NORTH PORTAL, SK, S0C 1W0

(306) 927-2165   *SIC* 4731

DCR LOGISTICS INC   *p1289*
150 AV MARCEL-BARIL, ROUYN-NORANDA, QC, J9X 7C1

(819) 764-4944   *SIC* 4731

DEDICATED FREIGHT CARRIERS INC   *p419*
634 ROUTE 590, WATERVILLE CARLETON CO, NB, E7P 1B7

(506) 375-1010   *SIC* 4731

DELMAR INTERNATIONAL INC   *p1127*
10636 CH DE LA COTE-DE-LIESSE, LA-CHINE, QC, H8T 1A5

(514) 636-8800   *SIC* 4731

DHL GLOBAL FORWARDING (CANADA) INC   *p734*
1825 ALSTEP DR, MISSISSAUGA, ON, L5S 1Y5

SIC 4731

DHL GLOBAL FORWARDING (CANADA) INC   *p738*
6200 EDWARDS BLVD SUITE 100, MISSIS-SAUGA, ON, L5T 2V7

(289) 562-6500   *SIC* 4731

DHL GLOBAL FORWARDING (CANADA) INC   *p1339*
555 MONTEE DE LIESSE, SAINT-LAURENT, QC, H4T 1P5

(514) 344-3447   *SIC* 4731

DIMERCO EXPRESS (CANADA) CORPO-RATION   *p694*
5100 ORBITOR DR SUITE 201, MISSIS-SAUGA, ON, L4W 4Z4

(905) 282-8118   *SIC* 4731

DOLBEC Y. LOGISTIQUE/LOGISTICS IN-TERNATIONAL INC.   *p1261*
361 RUE DES ENTREPRENEURS, QUE-BEC, QC, G1M 1B4

(418) 688-9115   *SIC* 4731

DSV AIR & SEA INC   *p502*
70 DRIVER RD UNIT 4, BRAMPTON, ON, L6T 5V2

(905) 629-0055   *SIC* 4731

E. & J. GALLO WINERY CANADA, LTD   *p722*
6711 MISSISSAUGA RD SUITE 202, MIS-SISSAUGA, ON, L5N 2W3

(905) 819-9600   *SIC* 4731

ECCO TRANSPORT SERVICES LTD   *p93*
12841 141 ST NW, EDMONTON, AB, T5L 4N1

(780) 454-4495   *SIC* 4731

ECONOFAST SHIPPING SYSTEMS INC   *p114*
9742 54 AVE NW, EDMONTON, AB, T6E 0A9

(780) 461-0578   *SIC* 4731

ECU LINE CANADA INC   *p735*
1804 ALSTEP DR SUITE 2, MISSISSAUGA, ON, L5S 1W1

(905) 677-8334   *SIC* 4731

ENERGY LOGISTICS INC   *p1130*
2555 AV DOLLARD EDIFICE 8, LASALLE, QC, H8N 3A9

(514) 363-9555   *SIC* 4731

EUROFRET CANADA INC   *p1059*
1140 BOUL MICHELE-BOHEC, BLAINVILLE, QC, J7C 5N5

(450) 430-1313   *SIC* 4731

EVERLAST GROUP LTD   *p510*
40 HOLTBY AVE SUITE 1, BRAMPTON, ON, L6X 2M1

(905) 846-9944   *SIC* 4731

EXPEDITORS CANADA INC   *p731*
55 STANDISH CRT SUITE 1100, MISSIS-SAUGA, ON, L5R 4A1

(905) 290-6000   *SIC* 4731

EXPERT CUSTOMS BROKERS   *p377*
2595 INKSTER BLVD, WINNIPEG, MB, R3C 2E6

(204) 633-1200   *SIC* 4731

FAIRMONT SHIPPING (CANADA) LIMITED   *p313*
1112 PENDER ST W SUITE 300, VANCOU-VER, BC, V6E 2S1

(604) 685-3318   *SIC* 4731

FARROW, RUSSELL A. LIMITED   *p483*
106 EARL THOMPSON RD, AYR, ON, N0B 1E0

(519) 740-9866   *SIC* 4731

FARROW, RUSSELL A. LIMITED   *p1025*
2001 HURON CHURCH RD, WINDSOR, ON, N9C 2L6

(519) 966-3003   *SIC* 4731

FEDEX SUPPLY CHAIN DISTRIBUTION SYSTEM OF CANADA, INC   *p15*
6336 114 AVE SE, CALGARY, AB, T2C 4T9

(800) 463-3339   *SIC* 4731

FEDEX SUPPLY CHAIN DISTRIBUTION SYSTEM OF CANADA, INC   *p1088*
50 BOUL DUPONT, COTEAU-DU-LAC, QC, J0P 1B0

(450) 763-6400   *SIC* 4731

FEDEX TRADE NETWORKS TRANSPORT & BROKERAGE (CANADA), INC   *p739*
7075 ORDAN DR, MISSISSAUGA, ON, L5T 1K6

(905) 677-7371   *SIC* 4731

FEDEX TRADE NETWORKS TRANSPORT & BROKERAGE (CANADA), INC   *p1324*
9800 CAVENDISH BLVD 3RD FL, SAINT-LAURENT, QC, H4M 2V9

(514) 845-3171   *SIC* 4731

FLS TRANSPORTATION SERVICES LIM-ITED   *p1326*
50 AV SAINTE-CROIX, SAINT-LAURENT, QC, H4N 3L4

(514) 739-0939   *SIC* 4731

FMI LOGISTICS INC   *p16*
7151 44 ST SE UNIT 111, CALGARY, AB, T2C 4E8

(866) 723-6660   *SIC* 4731

FORTIGO FREIGHT INC   *p584*
50 BELFIELD RD SUITE 5, ETOBICOKE, ON, M9W 1G1

(416) 367-8446   *SIC* 4731

FORTIGO FREIGHT SERVICES INC   *p584*
50 BELFIELD RD SUITE 4, ETOBICOKE, ON, M9W 1G1

(416) 367-8446   *SIC* 4731

FRASER DIRECT DISTRIBUTION SER-VICES LTD   *p683*
8300 LAWSON RD, MILTON, ON, L9T 0A4

(905) 877-4411   *SIC* 4731

FREEWAY TRANSPORTATION INC   *p503*
15 STRATHEARN AVE, BRAMPTON, ON, L6T 4P1

(905) 790-0446   *SIC* 4731

FRONTIER SUPPLY CHAIN SOLUTIONS INC   *p391*
555 HERVO ST STE 10, WINNIPEG, MB, R3T 3L6

(204) 784-4800   *SIC* 4731

G.E. FORWARDERS LTD   *p685*
2797 THAMESGATE DR, MISSISSAUGA, ON, L4T 1G5

(905) 676-9555   *SIC* 4731

G2 LOGISTICS INC   *p380*
944 HENRY AVE, WINNIPEG, MB, R3E 3L2

(204) 633-8989   *SIC* 4731

G2 OCEAN SHIPPING (CANADA) LTD   *p313*
1111 HASTINGS ST W SUITE 900, VAN-COUVER, BC, V6E 2J3

(604) 661-2020   *SIC* 4731

GARDEN CITY CUSTOMS SERVICES INC   *p759*
6045 PROGRESS ST, NIAGARA FALLS, ON, L2G 7X1

(905) 353-8735   *SIC* 4731

GARDEWINE GROUP INC   *p369*
60 EAGLE DR, WINNIPEG, MB, R2R 1V5

(204) 633-5795   *SIC* 4731

GENERAL NOLI CANADA INC   *p1344*
8000 BOUL LANGELIER BUREAU 514, SAINT-LEONARD, QC, H1P 3K2

(514) 852-6262   *SIC* 4731

GEODIS FF CANADA LTD   *p688*
3061 ORLANDO DR, MISSISSAUGA, ON, L4V 1R4

(905) 677-5266   *SIC* 4731

GILLESPIE-MUNRO INC   *p1210*
740 RUE NOTRE-DAME O BUREAU 1120, MONTREAL, QC, H3C 3X6

(514) 871-1033   *SIC* 4731

GLOBETROTTER LOGISTICS INC   *p578*
35 RAKELY CRT, ETOBICOKE, ON, M9C 5A5

(416) 742-2232   *SIC* 4731

GLS LOGISTICS SYSTEMS CANADA LTD   *p1094*
10500 AV RYAN, DORVAL, QC, H9P 2T7

(514) 636-8033   *SIC* 4731

GOLD FREIGHT   *p642*
11339 ALBION VAUGHAN LINE, KLEIN-BURG, ON, L0J 1C0

(905) 893-0700   *SIC* 4731

GRAB 2 HOLDINGS LTD   *p1431*
2405B WHEATON AVE, SASKATOON, SK, S7L 5Y3

(306) 633-2137   *SIC* 4731

GRAND POWER LOGISTICS GROUP INC   *p50*

505 6 ST SW SUITE 2806, CALGARY, AB, T2P 1X5

(403) 237-8211   *SIC* 4731

GRAND TRUNK WESTERN RAILROAD IN-CORPORATED   *p1205*
935 RUE DE LA GAUCHETIERE O BU-REAU 14, MONTREAL, QC, H3B 2M9

(514) 399-4536   *SIC* 4731

GUILBAULT LOGISTIQUE INC   *p1276*
8000 RUE ARMAND-VIAU BUREAU 300, QUEBEC, QC, G2C 2E2

(418) 843-5587   *SIC* 4731

H & R TRANSPORT LIMITED   *p16*
4540 54 AVE SE, CALGARY, AB, T2C 2Y8

(403) 720-8344   *SIC* 4731

HAPAG-LLOYD (CANADA) INC   *p1220*
3400 BOUL DE MAISONNEUVE O BU-REAU 1200, MONTREAL, QC, H3Z 3E7

(514) 934-5133   *SIC* 4731

HARCUT ENTERPRISES INC   *p1128*
10636 CH DE LA COTE-DE-LIESSE, LA-CHINE, QC, H8T 1A5

(514) 636-8800   *SIC* 4731

HARMONY LOGISTICS CANADA INC   *p76*
1724 115 AVE NE, CALGARY, AB, T3K 0P9

(403) 537-8996   *SIC* 4731

HARTWICK O'SHEA & CARTWRIGHT LIM-ITED   *p688*
3245 AMERICAN DR, MISSISSAUGA, ON, L4V 1B8

(905) 672-5100   *SIC* 4731

HEART LOGISTICS INC   *p740*
6975 PACIFIC CIR UNIT D, MISSISSAUGA, ON, L5T 2H3

(905) 362-1100   *SIC* 4731

HELLMANN WORLDWIDE LOGISTICS INC   *p735*
1375 CARDIFF BLVD UNIT 1, MISSIS-SAUGA, ON, L5S 1R1

(905) 564-6620   *SIC* 4731

HERCULES FORWARDING ULC   *p236*
151 SPRUCE ST, NEW WESTMINSTER, BC, V3L 5E6

(604) 517-1331   *SIC* 4731

HORIZON NORTH LOGISTICS INC   *p51*
240 4 AVE SW SUITE 900, CALGARY, AB, T2P 4H4

(403) 517-4654   *SIC* 4731

HORIZON NORTH LOGISTICS INC   *p132*
10320 140 AVE SUITE 102, GRANDE PRAIRIE, AB, T8V 8A4

(780) 830-5333   *SIC* 4731

HURON CENTRAL RAILWAY INC   *p861*
30 OAKLAND AVE, SAULT STE. MARIE, ON, P6A 2T3

(705) 254-4511   *SIC* 4731

HYNDMAN TRANSPORT LIMITED   *p1036*
1001 BELMORE LINE, WROXETER, ON, N0G 2X0

(519) 335-3575   *SIC* 4731

HYPHEN TRANSPORTATION MANAGE-MENT INC   *p585*
96 DISCO RD, ETOBICOKE, ON, M9W 0A3

(877) 549-7436   *SIC* 4731

IHAUL FREIGHT LTD   *p226*
105-8047 199 ST, LANGLEY, BC, V2Y 0E2

(604) 594-4100   *SIC* 4731

INTEGRAL TRANSPORTATION NET-WORKS CORP   *p740*
6975 PACIFIC CIR UNIT D, MISSISSAUGA, ON, L5T 2H3

(905) 362-1111   *SIC* 4731

INTERNATIONAL FASTLINE FORWARDING INC   *p265*
5200 MILLER RD SUITE 106, RICHMOND, BC, V7B 1K5

(604) 278-0191   *SIC* 4731

INTRALEC ELECTRICAL PRODUCTS LTD   *p735*
1200 CARDIFF BLVD UNIT 1, MISSIS-SAUGA, ON, L5S 1P6

(905) 670-0970   *SIC* 4731

ISG TRANSPORTATION INC   *p504*
7965 GOREWAY DR SUITE 2, BRAMPTON,

ON, L6T 5T5
(905) 799-1300   *SIC* 4731

ITN INTERNATIONAL CORP   *p23*
2915 21 ST NE SUITE 201, CALGARY, AB,
T2E 7T1
(403) 219-8440   *SIC* 4731

ITN TRANSBORDER SERVICES INC *p740*
6975 PACIFIC CIR UNIT D, MISSISSAUGA,
ON, L5T 2H3
(905) 362-1122   *SIC* 4731

J. RENE HEBERT LTEE   *p1188*
300 RUE DU SAINT-SACREMENT BUREAU
28, MONTREAL, QC, H2Y 1X4
(514) 281-0112   *SIC* 4731

JAS CANADA INC   *p686*
7685 BATH RD, MISSISSAUGA, ON, L4T
3T1
(905) 677-3497   *SIC* 4731

JOURNEY FREIGHT INTERNATIONAL INC
p1118
18100 RTE TRANSCANADIENNE, KIRK-
LAND, QC, H9J 4A1
(514) 344-2202   *SIC* 4731

JUST ON TIME FREIGHT SYSTEMS INC
p504
95 HEDGEDALE RD UNIT 3-4, BRAMP-
TON, ON, L6T 5P3
(905) 846-9552   *SIC* 4731

K N CUSTOMS BROKERS   *p23*
2415 PEGASUS RD NE UNIT 210, CAL-
GARY, AB, T2E 8C3
(403) 250-3075   *SIC* 4731

KEE TRANSPORT GROUP INC   *p740*
6760 DAVAND DR SUITE 9, MISSIS-
SAUGA, ON, L5T 2L9
(905) 670-0835   *SIC* 4731

**KINTETSU WORLD EXPRESS (CANADA)
INC**   *p688*
6405 NORTHAM DR, MISSISSAUGA, ON,
L4V 1J2
(905) 677-8830   *SIC* 4731

KRG LOGISTICS INC   *p706*
170 TRADERS BLVD E, MISSISSAUGA,
ON, L4Z 1W7
(905) 501-7277   *SIC* 4731

KUEHNE + NAGEL LOGISTICS INC *p1335*
2500 AV MARIE-CURIE, SAINT-LAURENT,
QC, H4S 1N1
(514) 683-9630   *SIC* 4731

KUEHNE + NAGEL LTD   *p723*
2300 HOGAN DR, MISSISSAUGA, ON, L5N
0C8
(905) 567-4168   *SIC* 4731

KUEHNE + NAGEL LTD   *p731*
77 FOSTER CRES, MISSISSAUGA, ON,
L5R 0K1
(905) 502-7776   *SIC* 4731

KUEHNE + NAGEL LTD   *p740*
6335 EDWARDS BLVD, MISSISSAUGA,
ON, L5T 2W7
(905) 670-6901   *SIC* 4731

KUEHNE + NAGEL LTD   *p1185*
3510 BOUL SAINT-LAURENT BUREAU
400, MONTREAL, QC, H2X 2V2
(514) 397-9900   *SIC* 4731

LABRADOR MARINE INC   *p425*
111 MAIN ST SUITE 502, LEWISPORTE,
NL, A0G 3A0
(709) 535-0810   *SIC* 4731

LAIDLAW CARRIERS BULK GP INC *p1035*
240 UNIVERSAL RD, WOODSTOCK, ON,
N4S 7W3
(519) 539-0471   *SIC* 4731

LANTRAX LOGISTICS LTD   *p282*
19272 96 AVE SUITE 10, SURREY, BC,
V4N 4C1
(604) 526-8729   *SIC* 4731

LCL CANADA LIMITED   *p523*
1016B SUTTON DR UNIT 205, BURLING-
TON, ON, L7L 6B8
(416) 639-1889   *SIC* 4731

**LEGACY TRANSPORTATION SOLUTIONS
INC**   *p504*
1 KENVIEW BLVD UNIT 210, BRAMPTON,

ON, L6T 5E6
(416) 798-4940   *SIC* 4731

LINK + CORPORATION   *p660*
4151 PERKINS RD, LONDON, ON, N6L
1G8
(519) 681-4002   *SIC* 4731

LIVINGSTON INTERNATIONAL INC   *p579*
405 THE WEST MALL SUITE 400, ETOBI-
COKE, ON, M9C 5K7
(416) 626-2800   *SIC* 4731

LIVINGSTON INTERNATIONAL INC   *p591*
36 QUEEN ST, FORT ERIE, ON, L2A 0B5
(905) 871-6500   *SIC* 4731

LOCHER EVERS INTERNATIONAL INC
p206
456 HUMBER PL, DELTA, BC, V3M 6A5
(604) 523-5100   *SIC* 4731

LOGIKOR INC   *p536*
290 PINEBUSH RD, CAMBRIDGE, ON, N1T
1Z6
(519) 622-8400   *SIC* 4731

LOGISTICS IN MOTION INC   *p475*
500 BAYLY ST E, AJAX, ON, L1Z 0B2
(905) 427-5880   *SIC* 4731

LOGISTIQUE CANAMEX INC   *p1062*
1933 BOUL LIONEL-BERTRAND, BOIS-
BRIAND, QC, J7H 1N8
(450) 434-1939   *SIC* 4731

LOGISTIQUE KERRY (CANADA) INC *p1094*
1425 RTE TRANSCANADIENNE BUREAU
150, DORVAL, QC, H9P 2W9
(514) 420-0282   *SIC* 4731

LOGISTIQUE TRANS-PRO INC   *p1189*
407 RUE MCGILL BUREAU 910, MON-
TREAL, QC, H2Y 2G3
(514) 858-6482   *SIC* 4731

LOGITRANS INC   *p1302*
440 RUE DU PARC, SAINT-EUSTACHE,
QC, J7R 7G6
(450) 565-8900   *SIC* 4731

LYNDEN CANADA CO   *p684*
8300 PARKHILL DR UNIT 3, MILTON, ON,
L9T 5V7
(905) 636-2970   *SIC* 4731

M CONSOLIDATION LINES LTD   *p688*
6300 NORTHWEST DR UNIT 2, MISSIS-
SAUGA, ON, L4V 1J7
(905) 362-0249   *SIC* 4731

MACTRANS LOGISTICS INC   *p1027*
81 ZENWAY BLVD UNIT 16, WOOD-
BRIDGE, ON, L4H 0S5
(905) 856-6800   *SIC* 4731

MAERSK CANADA INC   *p697*
2576 MATHESON BLVD E SUITE 101, MIS-
SISSAUGA, ON, L4W 5H1
(905) 624-5585   *SIC* 4731

MALTACOURT (CANADA) LTD   *p534*
150 WATER ST S SUITE 201, CAM-
BRIDGE, ON, N1R 3E2
(519) 756-6463   *SIC* 4731

MANITOULIN GLOBAL FORWARDING INC
p740
7035 ORDAN, MISSISSAUGA, ON, L5T 1T1
(905) 283-1600   *SIC* 4731

MANTORIA INCORPOREE   *p1402*
4492 RUE SAINTE-CATHERINE O, WEST-
MOUNT, QC, H3Z 1R7
(514) 488-4004   *SIC* 4731

MAPLE FREIGHT PARTNERSHIP   *p265*
4871 MILLER RD UNIT 1162, RICHMOND,
BC, V7B 1K8
(604) 279-2525   *SIC* 4731

MARBLE RIDGE FARMS LTD   *p351*
GD, HODGSON, MB, R0C 1M0
(204) 372-6438   *SIC* 4731

MARTEL BROS LTD   *p362*
359 PANDORA AVE W, WINNIPEG, MB,
R2C 1M6
(204) 233-2022   *SIC* 4731

MCGILL LOGISTICS INC   *p809*
GD LCD MAIN, ORILLIA, ON, L3V 6H8
(705) 329-5891   *SIC* 4731

MCKAY, W. G. LIMITED   *p964*
40 UNIVERSITY AVE SUITE 602,

TORONTO, ON, M5J 1J9
(416) 593-1380   *SIC* 4731

MCLEAN KENNEDY INC   *p1189*
368 RUE NOTRE-DAME O BUREAU 100,
MONTREAL, QC, H2Y 1T9
(514) 849-6111   *SIC* 4731

**MEDITERRANEAN SHIPPING COMPANY
(CANADA) INC**   *p1189*
7 RUE SAINT-JACQUES, MONTREAL, QC,
H2Y 1K9
(514) 844-3711   *SIC* 4731

MEEST CORPORATION INC   *p575*
97 SIX POINT RD, ETOBICOKE, ON, M8Z
2X3
(416) 236-2032   *SIC* 4731

METRO FREIGHTLINER BRANTFORD *p517*
31 GARNET RD, BRANTFORD, ON, N3T
5M1
(519) 750-0055   *SIC* 4731

MI GROUP LTD, THE   *p697*
2425 MATHESON BLVD E, MISSISSAUGA,
ON, L4W 5K4
(905) 812-8900   *SIC* 4731

MILL CREEK MOTOR FREIGHT LTD   *p483*
101 EARL THOMPSON RD, AYR, ON, N0B
1E0
(519) 623-6632   *SIC* 4731

**MITSUBISHI MOTOR SALES OF CANADA,
INC**   *p697*
2090 MATHESON BLVD E, MISSISSAUGA,
ON, L4W 5P8
(905) 214-9000   *SIC* 4731

MITSUI HOME CANADA INC   *p225*
19680 94A AVE, LANGLEY, BC, V1M 3B7
(604) 882-8415   *SIC* 4731

MONTSHIP INC   *p1189*
360 RUE SAINT-JACQUES BUREAU 1000,
MONTREAL, QC, H2Y 1R2
(514) 286-4646   *SIC* 4731

NATIONAL SHIPPERS & RECEIVERS INC
p366
45 BEGHIN AVE SUITE 7, WINNIPEG, MB,
R2J 4B9
(204) 222-6289   *SIC* 4731

NAVIGATION CP LIMITEE   *p1220*
3400 BOUL DE MAISONNEUVE O BU-
REAU 1200, MONTREAL, QC, H3Z 3E7
(514) 934-5133   *SIC* 4731

**NAVIGATION DES ETATS INDEPENDANTS
DU COMMONWEALTH INC**   *p1189*
478 RUE MCGILL, MONTREAL, QC, H2Y
2H2
(514) 499-1999   *SIC* 4731

NEAR NORTH CUSTOMS BROKERS INC
p487
20 ELLIOTT AVE, BARRIE, ON, L4N 4V7
(705) 739-0024   *SIC* 4731

NEWFOUND TRADING LIMITED   *p447*
11 MORRIS DR SUITE 206, DARTMOUTH,
NS, B3B 1M2
(902) 468-7100   *SIC* 4731

NFI IPD, LLC   *p698*
200 SKYMARK AVE SUITE 501, MISSIS-
SAUGA, ON, L4W 5A6
(905) 625-2300   *SIC* 4731

NIPPON EXPRESS CANADA LTD   *p741*
6250 EDWARDS BLVD, MISSISSAUGA,
ON, L5T 2X3
(905) 565-7525   *SIC* 4731

NIPPON EXPRESS CANADA LTD   *p741*
6250 EDWARDS BLVD, MISSISSAUGA,
ON, L5T 2X3
(905) 565-7525   *SIC* 4731

NOLAN LOGISTICS GROUP INC   *p499*
9150 AIRPORT RD UNIT 10, BRAMPTON,
ON, L6S 6G1
(800) 387-5148   *SIC* 4731

NORTEC MARINE AGENCIES INC   *p1190*
465 RUE SAINT-JEAN BUREAU 708, MON-
TREAL, QC, H2Y 2R6
(514) 985-2329   *SIC* 4731

**NORTH ATLANTIC INTERNATIONAL LO-
GISTICS INC**   *p620*
22 DAIRY LANE SUITE 291, HUNTSVILLE,

ON, P1H 1T4
(416) 291-2688   *SIC* 4731

OAK MARITIME (CANADA) INC   *p315*
1111 GEORGIA ST W SUITE 1500, VAN-
COUVER, BC, V6E 4M3
(604) 689-8083   *SIC* 4731

**OEC GROUPAGE OUTREMER EXPRESS
(MONTREAL) INC**   *p1340*
725 MONTEE DE LIESSE, SAINT-
LAURENT, QC, H4T 1P5
(514) 633-1246   *SIC* 4731

OMNITRANS INC   *p1228*
4300 RUE JEAN-TALON O, MONTREAL,
QC, H4P 1W3
(514) 288-6664   *SIC* 4731

OMTRANS LOGISTICS INC   *p1028*
111 ZENWAY BLVD UNIT 5, WOOD-
BRIDGE, ON, L4H 3H9
(416) 921-2255   *SIC* 4731

**ONTARIO NORTHLAND TRANSPORTA-
TION COMMISSION**   *p763*
555 OAK ST E, NORTH BAY, ON, P1B 8E3
(705) 472-4500   *SIC* 4731

OOCL (CANADA) INC   *p579*
703 EVANS AVE SUITE 300, ETOBICOKE,
ON, M9C 5E9
(416) 620-4040   *SIC* 4731

**OVERSEAS CONTAINER FORWARDING,
INC**   *p261*
10451 SHELLBRIDGE WAY UNIT 100,
RICHMOND, BC, V6X 2W8
(604) 734-8155   *SIC* 4731

**OVERSEAS EXPRESS CONSOLIDATORS
(CANADA) INC**   *p1340*
725 MONTEE DE LIESSE, SAINT-
LAURENT, QC, H4T 1P5
(514) 905-1246   *SIC* 4731

OZBURN-HESSEY LOGISTICS   *p509*
300 KENNEDY RD S UNIT B, BRAMPTON,
ON, L6W 4V2
(905) 450-1151   *SIC* 4731

P.F. COLLINS CUSTOMS BROKER LIMITED
p428
251 EAST WHITE HILLS RD UNIT 100, ST.
JOHN'S, NL, A1A 5X7
(709) 726-7596   *SIC* 4731

PACIFIC COAST DISTRIBUTION LTD   *p229*
27433 52 AVE, LANGLEY, BC, V4W 4B2
(604) 888-8489   *SIC* 4731

PACIFIC CUSTOMS BROKERS LTD   *p279*
17637 1 AVE SUITE 101, SURREY, BC, V3Z
9S1
(604) 538-1566   *SIC* 4731

**PACIFIC NORTHWEST MOVING (YUKON)
LIMITED**   *p1440*
3 BURNS RD, WHITEHORSE, YT, Y1A 4Z3
(867) 668-2511   *SIC* 4731

PANALPINA INC   *p732*
6350 CANTAY RD, MISSISSAUGA, ON, L5R
4E2
(905) 755-4500   *SIC* 4731

PANALPINA INC   *p1335*
2520 AV MARIE-CURIE, SAINT-LAURENT,
QC, H4S 1N1
(514) 421-7444   *SIC* 4731

PEACE TRANSPORTATION   *p735*
7370 BRAMALEA RD SUITE 22, MISSIS-
SAUGA, ON, L5S 1N6
(905) 405-1002   *SIC* 4731

PERMICOM PERMITS SERVICES INC *p557*
161 PENNSYLVANIA AVE UNIT 5, CON-
CORD, ON, L4K 1C3
    SIC 4731

POLARIS INTERNATIONAL CARRIERS INC
p686
7099 TORBRAM RD, MISSISSAUGA, ON,
L4T 1G7
(905) 672-7952   *SIC* 4731

POLARIS TRANSPORT CARRIERS INC
p686
7099 TORBRAM RD, MISSISSAUGA, ON,
L4T 1G7
(905) 671-3100   *SIC* 4731

POWER EXPRESS   *p122*

303 69 AVE NW, EDMONTON, AB, T6P 0C2
(780) 461-4000   SIC 4731

PREFERRED SERVICE CUSTOM BRO-KERS INC   p265
5980 MILLER RD UNIT 115, RICHMOND, BC, V7B 1K2
(604) 270-6607   SIC 4731

PREMIUM LINE TRANSPORT INC   p505
11 WEST DR, BRAMPTON, ON, L6T 4T2
(905) 454-2222   SIC 4731

PROACTIVE SUPPLY CHAIN SOLUTIONS INC   p689
3909 NASHUA DRIVE UNIT 4-9, MISSIS-SAUGA, ON, L4V 1R3
(416) 798-3303   SIC 4731

PROCAM INTERNATIONAL INC   p1362
2035 BOUL DAGENAIS O BUREAU 200, SAINTE-ROSE, QC, H7L 5V1
(450) 963-4442   SIC 4731

PROMAX TRANSPORT LTD   p137
4215 52 STREET CLOSE, INNISFAIL, AB, T4G 1P9
(403) 227-2852   SIC 4731

PROTOS SHIPPING LTD   p579
701 EVANS AVE SUITE 700, ETOBICOKE, ON, M9C 1A3
(416) 621-4381   SIC 4731

PROVIDER TRANSPORTATION & LOGIS-TICS INC   p483
3184 ALPS RD, AYR, ON, N0B 1E0
SIC 4731

PUROLATOR HOLDINGS LTD   p732
5995 AVEBURY RD SUITE 100, MISSIS-SAUGA, ON, L5R 3T8
(905) 712-1251   SIC 4731

PUROLATOR INC   p25
30 AERO DR NE, CALGARY, AB, T2E 8Z9
(403) 516-6200   SIC 4731

PUROLATOR INC   p431
16 DUFFY PL, ST. JOHN'S, NL, A1B 4M5
(709) 579-5671   SIC 4731

PUROLATOR INC   p526
3455 MAINWAY, BURLINGTON, ON, L7M 1A9
(905) 336-3230   SIC 4731

PUROLATOR INC   p587
62 VULCAN ST, ETOBICOKE, ON, M9W 1L2
(416) 241-4496   SIC 4731

PUROLATOR INC   p587
1151 MARTIN GROVE RD SUITE 7, ETOBI-COKE, ON, M9W 0C1
(416) 614-0300   SIC 4731

PUROLATOR INC   p606
147 MASSEY RD, GUELPH, ON, N1K 1B2
(905) 660-6007   SIC 4731

PUROLATOR INC   p732
5995 AVEBURY RD, MISSISSAUGA, ON, L5R 3P9
(905) 712-1084   SIC 4731

PUROLATOR INC   p795
1100 ARROW RD, NORTH YORK, ON, M9M 2Z1
(416) 241-4496   SIC 4731

PUROLATOR INC   p845
1075 SQUIRES BEACH RD, PICKERING, ON, L1W 3S3
(888) 744-7123   SIC 4731

PUROLATOR INC   p876
90 SILVER STAR BLVD, SCARBOROUGH, ON, M1V 4V8
(888) 744-7123   SIC 4731

PUROLATOR INC   p921
20 MORSE ST, TORONTO, ON, M4M 2P6
(416) 461-9031   SIC 4731

PUROLATOR INC   p1067
1330   RUE   GRAHAM-BELL, BOUCHERVILLE, QC, J4B 6H5
(450) 641-2430   SIC 4731

PUROLATOR INC   p1277
7000 RUE ARMAND-VIAU, QUEBEC, QC, G2C 2C4
(888) 744-7123   SIC 4731

PUROLATOR INC   p1330

1305 RUE TEES, SAINT-LAURENT, QC, H4R 2A7
(514) 337-6710   SIC 4731

QUARTERBACK TRANSPORTATION INC   p769
1210 SHEPPARD AVE E SUITE 114, NORTH YORK, ON, M2K 1E3
(416) 385-2713   SIC 4731

QUICKLOAD CEF INC   p252
1220 RIDLEY ISLAND, PRINCE RUPERT, BC, V8J 4P8
(250) 627-5623   SIC 4731

R. DIAMOND GROUP OF COMPANIES LTD, THE   p277
13350 COMBER WAY, SURREY, BC, V3W 5V9
(604) 591-8641   SIC 4731

R.O.E. LOGISTICS INC   p1252
195 RUE VOYAGEUR, POINTE-CLAIRE, QC, H9R 6B2
(514) 396-0000   SIC 4731

RADIANT GLOBAL LOGISTICS (CANADA) INC   p742
1280 COURTNEYPARK DR E, MISSIS-SAUGA, ON, L5T 1N6
(905) 602-2700   SIC 4731

RADIUS GLOBAL SOLUTIONS INC   p280
2455 192 ST SUITE 108, SURREY, BC, V3Z 3X1
(604) 541-1910   SIC 4731

RANGER EXPRESS FORWARDING INC   p686
7685 BATH RD, MISSISSAUGA, ON, L4T 3T1
(905) 672-3434   SIC 4731

RAY-MONT LOGISTIQUES CANADA INC   p1216
1751 RUE RICHARDSON BUREAU 4504, MONTREAL, QC, H3K 1G6
(514) 933-4449   SIC 4731

RIGHT AT HOME REALTY, INC   p780
895 DON MILLS RD SUITE 202, NORTH YORK, ON, M3C 1W3
(416) 391-3232   SIC 4731

RIOUX, GILBERT M & FILS LTEE   p416
855 ROUTE 108, SAINT-ANDRE, NB, E3Y 4A5
(506) 473-1764   SIC 4731

RIVERBEND FREIGHT SERVICES LIMITED   p426
26 KYLE AVE, MOUNT PEARL, NL, A1N 4R5
(709) 368-1773   SIC 4731

ROBERT TRANSPORT SPECIALIZED INC   p1288
500 RTE 112, ROUGEMONT, QC, J0L 1M0
(450) 460-1112   SIC 4731

RODAIR INTERNATIONAL LTD   p742
350 PENDANT DR, MISSISSAUGA, ON, L5T 2W6
(905) 671-4655   SIC 4731

ROHDE & LIESENFELD CANADA INC   p58
144 4 AVE SW SUITE 1600, CALGARY, AB, T2P 3N4
(403) 514-6907   SIC 4731

ROME TRANSPORTATION INC   p640
100 CAMPBELL AVE UNIT 2, KITCHENER, ON, N2H 4X8
(519) 883-4105   SIC 4731

ROYAL SUPPLY CHAIN INC   p988
65A WINGOLD AVE, TORONTO, ON, M6B 1P8
(647) 344-8142   SIC 4731

RUTHERFORD, WILLIAM L (BC) LTD   p265
6086 RUSS BAKER WAY SUITE 125, RICH-MOND, BC, V7B 1B4
(604) 273-8611   SIC 4731

RUTHERFORD, WILLIAM L. LIMITED   p689
3350 AIRWAY DR, MISSISSAUGA, ON, L4V 1T3
(905) 673-2222   SIC 4731

S. M. HEWITT (SARNIA) LIMITED   p846
1555 VENETIAN BLVD SUITE 11 3RD FL, POINT EDWARD, ON, N7T 0A9

(519) 332-4411   SIC 4731

SAFESEA-AMI SHIPPING INC   p700
1030 KAMATO RD SUITE 210, MISSIS-SAUGA, ON, L4W 4B6
SIC 4731

SAHIB FREIGHT SERVICES INC   p700
1665 ENTERPRISE RD, MISSISSAUGA, ON, L4W 4L4
(905) 696-8050   SIC 4731

SCHENKER OF CANADA LIMITED   p210
8181 CHURCHILL ST, DELTA, BC, V4K 0C2
(604) 688-8511   SIC 4731

SCHENKER OF CANADA LIMITED   p316
1030 GEORGIA ST W SUITE 3A, VANCOU-VER, BC, V6E 2Y3
(604) 688-8511   SIC 4731

SCHENKER OF CANADA LIMITED   p495
12315 COLERAINE DR, BOLTON, ON, L7E 3B4
(905) 857-5620   SIC 4731

SCHENKER OF CANADA LIMITED   p689
5935 AIRPORT RD SUITE 9, MISSIS-SAUGA, ON, L4V 1W5
(905) 676-0676   SIC 4731

SCHENKER OF CANADA LIMITED   p1095
1200 AV REVERCHON BUREAU 257, DORVAL, QC, H9P 2S7
(514) 636-6350   SIC 4731

SCOUT LOGISTICS CORPORATION   p994
3351 DUNDAS ST W, TORONTO, ON, M6P 2A6
(416) 630-7268   SIC 4731

SEA AIR INTERNATIONAL FORWARDERS LIMITED   p742
1720 MEYERSIDE DR, MISSISSAUGA, ON, L5T 1A3
(905) 677-7701   SIC 4731

SEAWAY MARINE TRANSPORT   p886
63 CHURCH ST SUITE 600, ST CATHARINES, ON, L2R 3C4
(905) 988-2600   SIC 4731

SECURE FREIGHT SYSTEMS INC   p265
4871 MILLER RD SUITE 1160, RICHMOND, BC, V7B 1K8
(604) 276-2369   SIC 4731

SERVICES DE FRET PATRIOT INC   p1336
6800 CH SAINT-FRANCOIS, SAINT-LAURENT, QC, H4S 1B7
(514) 631-2900   SIC 4731

SERVICES EN TRANSPORT S.T.C.H. INC   p1076
248 BOUL INDUSTRIEL, CHATEAUGUAY, QC, J6J 4Z2
(450) 699-2357   SIC 4731

SILVER PACIFIC INVESTMENTS INC   p208
7337 120 ST SUITE 245, DELTA, BC, V4C 6P5
(604) 588-0227   SIC 4731

SIMARD WESTLINK INC   p258
16062 PORTSIDE RD, RICHMOND, BC, V6W 1M1
(604) 231-8756   SIC 4731

SOCIETE TRANSPORT TROIS-RIVIERES   p1388
2000 RUE BELLEFEUILLE, TROIS-RIVIERES, QC, G9A 3Y2
(819) 373-4533   SIC 4731

SOTECH-NITRAM INC   p1062
3975 BOUL DE LA GRANDE-ALLEE, BOIS-BRIAND, QC, J7H 1M6
(450) 975-2100   SIC 4731

STARSHIP LOGISTICS INC   p594
36 ARMSTRONG AVE SUITE 200, GEORGETOWN, ON, L7G 4R9
(905) 702-1800   SIC 4731

STATION PARK LOGISTICS   p890
28 MAJESTIC CRT, ST THOMAS, ON, N5R 0B9
(519) 207-3399   SIC 4731

STEELHORSE FREIGHT SERVICES INC   p136
82054 466 AVE, HIGH RIVER, AB, T1V 1P3
SIC 4731

SUMMIT INTERNATIONAL TRADE SER-

VICES INC   p265
5200 MILLER RD SUITE 2060, RICHMOND, BC, V7B 1L1
(604) 278-3551   SIC 4731

SUPERFREIGHT TRANSPORTATION INC   p536
445 DOBBIE DR, CAMBRIDGE, ON, N1T 1S9
(519) 650-5555   SIC 4731

SUPREME CHAIN LOGISTICS LTD   p278
8277 129 ST UNIT.201, SURREY, BC, V3W 0A6
(604) 585-1415   SIC 4731

SYNERGIE CANADA INC   p1060
60 RUE EMILIEN-MARCOUX, BLAINVILLE, QC, J7C 0B5
(450) 939-5757   SIC 4731

SYNERGY TRUCKING LTD   p278
7184 120 ST SUITE 190, SURREY, BC, V3W 0M6
(604) 598-3498   SIC 4731

TFI TRANSPORT 17 LP   p588
96 DISCO RD, ETOBICOKE, ON, M9W 0A3
(416) 679-7979   SIC 4731

THOMPSON, AHERN & CO. LIMITED   p690
6299 AIRPORT RD SUITE 506, MISSIS-SAUGA, ON, L4V 1N3
(905) 677-3471   SIC 4731

TIANJIN AUTO PARTS INC   p754
431 WOODSPRING AVE, NEWMARKET, ON, L3X 3H5
(647) 999-9612   SIC 4731

TITANIUM LOGISTICS INC   p495
32 SIMPSON RD, BOLTON, ON, L7E 1G9
(905) 851-1688   SIC 4731

TOTAL RETURN SOLUTIONS CORP   p560
51 GRANITERIDGE RD, CONCORD, ON, L4K 5M9
(905) 761-6835   SIC 4731

TRADESPAN CARGO LTD   p743
6305 DANVILLE RD UNIT 2, MISSIS-SAUGA, ON, L5T 2H7
(416) 410-1009   SIC 4731

TRAFFIC TECH INC   p1118
16711 RTE TRANSCANADIENNE, KIRK-LAND, QC, H9H 3L1
(514) 343-0044   SIC 4731

TRAFFIC TECH INTERNATIONAL INCp1118
16711 RTE TRANSCANADIENNE, KIRK-LAND, QC, H9H 3L1
(514) 343-0044   SIC 4731

TRANS-PLUS V.M. INC   p1336
2400 RUE HALPERN, SAINT-LAURENT, QC, H4S 1S8
(514) 332-5020   SIC 4731

TRANSCORE LINK LOGISTICS CORPORA-TION   p707
2 ROBERT SPECK PKY SUITE 900, MIS-SISSAUGA, ON, L4Z 1H8
(905) 795-0580   SIC 4731

TRANSITAIRES DAVID KIRSCH LTEEp1096
455 BOUL FENELON BUREAU 130, DOR-VAL, QC, H9S 5T8
(514) 636-0233   SIC 4731

TRANSITAIRES INTERNATIONAUX SKY-WAY LTEE   p1129
9262 CH DE LA COTE-DE-LIESSE, LA-CHINE, QC, H8T 1A1
(514) 636-0250   SIC 4731

TRANSNET FREIGHT LTD   p507
247 SUMMERLEA RD, BRAMPTON, ON, L6T 4E1
(647) 868-2762   SIC 4731

TRANSPECT INVESTMENT INC   p707
4 ROBERT SPECK PKY SUITE 1500, MIS-SISSAUGA, ON, L4Z 1S1
(905) 366-7320   SIC 4731

TRANSPLACE CANADA LTD   p854
45A WEST WILMOT ST UNIT 213, RICH-MOND HILL, ON, L4B 2P2
(800) 443-3107   SIC 4731

TRANSPORT F. GILBERT LTEE   p1080
150 RUE DES ROUTIERS, CHICOUTIMI, QC, G7H 5B1

▲ Public Company   ■ Public Company Family Member   **HQ** Headquarters   **BR** Branch   **SL** Single Location

(418) 698-4848   *SIC 4731*
TRANSPORT GUILBAULT LONGUE DISTANCE INC   *p1265*
435 RUE FARADAY, QUEBEC, QC, G1N 4G6
(418) 681-0575   *SIC 4731*
TRANSPORT REMCO LIMITEE   *p1129*
5203 RUE FAIRWAY, LACHINE, QC, H8T 3K8
(514) 737-1900   *SIC 4731*
TRANSPORT SAF (1994) INC   *p1296*
1227 RANG SAINT-JOSEPH, SAINT-CELESTIN, QC, J0C 1G0
(819) 229-3638   *SIC 4731*
TRANSPORT TFI 7 S.E.C   *p94*
14520 130 AVE NW, EDMONTON, AB, T5L 3M6
(780) 482-9483   *SIC 4731*
TRANSPORTEURS EN VRAC SHEFFORD INC, LES   *p1110*
438 RUE DE LA PROVIDENCE, GRANBY, QC, J2H 1H1
(450) 375-2331   *SIC 4731*
TRANSPORTS FUEL INC, LES   *p1131*
2480 RUE SENKUS, LASALLE, QC, H8N 2X9
(514) 948-2225   *SIC 4731*
TRANSX TRANSPORT INC   *p1395*
2351 RUE HENRY-FORD, VAUDREUIL-DORION, QC, J7V 0J1
(450) 424-0114   *SIC 4731*
TRENDWOOD LIMITED   *p124*
2431 121 AVE NE, EDMONTON, AB, T6S 1B2
(780) 472-6606   *SIC 4731*
TRI-AD INTERNATIONAL FREIGHT FORWARDING LTD   *p743*
375 ANNAGEM BLVD UNIT 100, MISSISSAUGA, ON, L5T 3A7
(905) 624-8214   *SIC 4731*
TRIPAR TRANSPORTATION LP   *p799*
2180 BUCKINGHAM RD, OAKVILLE, ON, L6H 6H1
(905) 829-8500   *SIC 4731*
TRIUMPH EXPRESS SERVICE CANADA INC   *p690*
3030 ORLANDO DR SUITE 509, MISSISSAUGA, ON, L4V 1S8
(905) 673-9300   *SIC 4731*
TRUCK TRANSFER INC   *p701*
5939 SHAWSON DR, MISSISSAUGA, ON, L4W 3Y2
(416) 717-1000   *SIC 4731*
TST SOLUTIONS L.P.   *p701*
5200 MAINGATE DR, MISSISSAUGA, ON, L4W 1G5
(905) 624-7058   *SIC 4731*
U.S. TRAFFIC LIMITED   *p728*
6645 KITIMAT RD SUITE 18, MISSISSAUGA, ON, L5N 6J3
(905) 858-2222   *SIC 4731*
UNITED PARCEL SERVICE CANADA LTD   *p26*
3650 12 ST NE SUITE D, CALGARY, AB, T2E 6N1
SIC 4731
UNIVERSAL LOGISTICS INC   *p905*
125 COMMERCE VALLEY DR W SUITE 750, THORNHILL, ON, L3T 7W4
(905) 882-4880   *SIC 4731*
UPS CARTAGE SERVICES INC   *p1092*
750 BOUL STUART-GRAHAM S, DORVAL, QC, H4Y 1G2
(514) 636-1333   *SIC 4731*
UPS SCS INC   *p258*
7451 NELSON RD, RICHMOND, BC, V6W 1L7
(604) 270-9449   *SIC 4731*
UPS SCS INC   *p525*
4156 MAINWAY, BURLINGTON, ON, L7L 0A7
(905) 315-5500   *SIC 4731*
UPS SCS INC   *p690*
6655 AIRPORT RD, MISSISSAUGA, ON,

L4V 1V8
(905) 677-6735   *SIC 4731*
UPS SCS INC   *p1327*
101 BOUL MARCEL-LAURIN, SAINT-LAURENT, QC, H4N 2M3
(514) 285-1500   *SIC 4731*
UPS SCS, INC   *p1092*
800 BOUL STUART-GRAHAM S BUREAU 351, DORVAL, QC, H4Y 1J6
SIC 4731
US CUSTOMS & BORDER PROTECTION   *p26*
2016D AIRPORT ROAD NE UNIT 172A, CALGARY, AB, T2E 3B9
(403) 221-1641   *SIC 4731*
UTI, CANADA, INC   *p507*
70 DRIVER RD UNIT 4, BRAMPTON, ON, L6T 5V2
(905) 790-1616   *SIC 4731*
UTI, CANADA, INC   *p701*
2540 MATHESON BLVD E, MISSISSAUGA, ON, L4W 4Z2
SIC 4731
UTILITY INTERNATIONAL INC   *p475*
610 FINLEY AVE SUITE 6, AJAX, ON, L1S 2E3
(905) 686-3512   *SIC 4731*
V K DELIVERY & MOVING SERVICES LTD   *p207*
588 ANNANCE CRT UNIT 2, DELTA, BC, V3M 6Y8
(604) 540-0384   *SIC 4731*
VANDEGRIFT CANADA ULC   *p589*
63 GALAXY BLVD UNIT 1-2, ETOBICOKE, ON, M9W 5R7
(416) 213-9093   *SIC 4731*
VINPAC LINES (TORONTO) INC   *p701*
2601 MATHESON BLVD E UNIT 202, MISSISSAUGA, ON, L4W 5A8
SIC 4731
VISION TRANSPORTATION SYSTEMS INC   *p507*
7659 BRAMALEA RD, BRAMPTON, ON, L6T 5V3
(905) 858-7333   *SIC 4731*
VORTEX FREIGHT SYSTEMS INC   *p744*
6615 ORDAN DR UNIT 14-15, MISSISSAUGA, ON, L5T 1X2
(905) 499-3000   *SIC 4731*
WATSON & ASH TRANSPORTATION COMPANY LTD   *p195*
1050 9TH AVE, CAMPBELL RIVER, BC, V9W 4C2
(250) 287-7433   *SIC 4731*
WESTCON TERMINALS (ONTARIO) LIMITED   *p507*
30 MIDAIR CRT, BRAMPTON, ON, L6T 5V1
(905) 494-0880   *SIC 4731*
WESTERN CANADA EXPRESS INC   *p561*
62 ADMINISTRATION RD, CONCORD, ON, L4K 2R7
(905) 738-2106   *SIC 4731*
WESTERN LOGISTICS INC   *p202*
1555 BRIGANTINE DR, COQUITLAM, BC, V3K 7C2
(604) 525-7211   *SIC 4731*
WIDE RANGE TRANSPORTATION SERVICES INC   *p600*
689 SOUTH SERVICE RD, GRIMSBY, ON, L3M 4E8
(905) 643-5100   *SIC 4731*
WILLSON INTERNATIONAL LIMITED   *p728*
2345 ARGENTIA RD SUITE 201, MISSISSAUGA, ON, L5N 8K4
(905) 363-1133   *SIC 4731*
WING TAT GAME BIRD PACKERS INC   *p264*
11951 FORGE PL, RICHMOND, BC, V7A 4V9
(604) 278-4450   *SIC 4731*
WOODCOCK TRANSPORTATION SERVICES INC   *p879*
225 HERON RD, SEBRINGVILLE, ON, N0K 1X0
(519) 393-5353   *SIC 4731*

WORLD WIDE CUSTOMS BROKERS LTD   *p63*
GD LCD 1, CALGARY, AB, T2P 2G8
(403) 538-3199   *SIC 4731*
WORLD WIDE CUSTOMS BROKERS LTD   *p77*
10710 25 ST NE UNIT 133, CALGARY, AB, T3N 0A1
(403) 291-2543   *SIC 4731*
WORLD WIDE LOGISTICS INC   *p1002*
330 NEW HUNTINGTON RD SUITE 101, VAUGHAN, ON, L4H 4C9
(416) 213-9522   *SIC 4731*
WORLDWIDE FLIGHT SERVICES LTD   *p1154*
11955 RUE HENRY-GIFFARD SUITE 200, MIRABEL, QC, J7N 1G3
(450) 476-9248   *SIC 4731*
XTRUX INC   *p744*
6175 KENWAY DR, MISSISSAUGA, ON, L5T 2L3
(905) 362-1277   *SIC 4731*
YOUNG, GEO H & CO LTD   *p376*
167 LOMBARD AVE UNIT 809, WINNIPEG, MB, R3B 3H8
(204) 947-6851   *SIC 4731*
YUSEN LOGISTICS (CANADA) INC   *p507*
261 PARKHURST SQ, BRAMPTON, ON, L6T 5H5
(905) 458-9622   *SIC 4731*

SIC 4741 Rental of railroad cars

HALLCON CORPORATION   *p995*
5775 YONGE ST SUITE 1010, TORONTO, ON, M7A 2E5
(416) 964-9191   *SIC 4741*
PROCOR LIMITED   *p804*
585 MICHIGAN DR UNIT 2, OAKVILLE, ON, L6L 0G1
(905) 827-4111   *SIC 4741*

SIC 4783 Packing and crating

3174891 CANADA INC   *p1093*
2945 AV ANDRE, DORVAL, QC, H9P 1K7
(514) 685-9505   *SIC 4783*
473464 ONTARIO LIMITED   *p548*
380 SPINNAKER WAY, CONCORD, ON, L4K 4W1
(905) 669-6464   *SIC 4783*
ATELIER DES VIEILLES FORGES INC   *p1386*
1000 PLACE BOLAND, TROIS-RIVIERES, QC, G8Z 4H2
(819) 376-1834   *SIC 4783*
BUTCHER ENGINEERING ENTERPRISES LIMITED, THE   *p1018*
2755 LAUZON PKY, WINDSOR, ON, N8T 3H5
(519) 944-9200   *SIC 4783*
CRATEX INDUSTRIES (CALGARY) LTD   *p15*
3347 57 AVE SE, CALGARY, AB, T2C 0B2
(403) 203-0880   *SIC 4783*
CRATEX INDUSTRIES LTD   *p109*
4735 82 AVE NW, EDMONTON, AB, T6B 0E5
(780) 468-4769   *SIC 4783*
CROWN WORLDWIDE LTD   *p522*
1375 ARTISANS CRT, BURLINGTON, ON, L7L 5Y2
(905) 827-4899   *SIC 4783*
JOHNVINCE FOODS   *p1066*
1630 RUE EIFFEL BUREAU 1, BOUCHERVILLE, QC, J4B 7W1
(450) 645-1999   *SIC 4783*
MOORE PACKAGING CORPORATION   *p487*
191 JOHN ST SUITE 12, BARRIE, ON, L4N 2L4
(705) 737-1023   *SIC 4783*
SERLAN LIMITED   *p1115*
957 RUE RAOUL-CHARETTE, JOLIETTE, QC, J6E 8S4

(450) 752-0030   *SIC 4783*
STALCO INC   *p916*
64 BAKERSFIELD ST, TORONTO, ON, M3J 2W7
(647) 367-2459   *SIC 4783*

SIC 4785 Inspection and fixed facilities

407 ETR CONCESSION COMPANY LIMITED   *p1026*
6300 STEELES AVE W, WOODBRIDGE, ON, L4H 1J1
(905) 265-4070   *SIC 4785*
407 INTERNATIONAL INC   *p1026*
6300 STEELES AVE W, WOODBRIDGE, ON, L4H 1J1
(905) 265-4070   *SIC 4785*
ATLANTIC HIGHWAYS MANAGEMENT CORPORATION LIMITED   *p450*
209 COBEQUID PASS, GREAT VILLAGE, NS, B0M 1L0
(902) 668-2211   *SIC 4785*
BLUE WATER BRIDGE CANADA   *p846*
1555 VENETIAN BLVD SUITE 436, POINT EDWARD, ON, N7T 0A9
(519) 336-2720   *SIC 4785*
BUFFALO AND FORT ERIE PUBLIC BRIDGE COMPANY   *p591*
100 QUEEN ST, FORT ERIE, ON, L2A 3S6
(905) 871-1608   *SIC 4785*
CANADIAN LOGISTICS SYSTEMS LIMITED   *p324*
3433 BROADWAY W SUITE 201, VANCOUVER, BC, V6R 2B4
(604) 731-8001   *SIC 4785*
CANADIAN TOLLING COMPANY INTERNATIONAL INC   *p1027*
6300 STEELES AVE W, WOODBRIDGE, ON, L4H 1J1
(905) 265-4070   *SIC 4785*
HALIFAX-DARTMOUTH BRIDGE COMMISSION   *p444*
125 WYSE RD, DARTMOUTH, NS, B3A 4K9
(902) 463-2800   *SIC 4785*
INTERNATIONAL BRIDGE ADMINISTRATION   *p861*
125 HURON ST, SAULT STE. MARIE, ON, P6A 1R3
(705) 942-4345   *SIC 4785*
INTERNATIONAL ROAD DYNAMICS INC   *p1428*
702 43RD ST E, SASKATOON, SK, S7K 3T9
(306) 653-6600   *SIC 4785*
MANASTE INSPECTION QUALITY QUANTITY (CANADA) INC   *p1239*
9756 RUE NOTRE-DAME E, MONTREAL-EST, QC, H1L 3R4
(514) 645-5554   *SIC 4785*
NIAGARA FALLS BRIDGE COMMISSION   *p759*
5781 RIVER RD, NIAGARA FALLS, ON, L2G 3K9
(905) 354-5641   *SIC 4785*
NORTHWEST LOGISTICS INC   *p322*
2906 BROADWAY W SUITE 260, VANCOUVER, BC, V6K 2G8
(604) 731-8001   *SIC 4785*
SASK HIGHWAYS MAINTENANCE   *p1436*
1200 SOUTH SERVICE RD W, SWIFT CURRENT, SK, S9H 5G7
(306) 778-8364   *SIC 4785*
SEAWAY INTERNATIONAL BRIDGE CORPORATION LTD, THE   *p475*
200 AKWESASNE INTERNATIONAL RD, AKWESASNE, ON, K6H 5R7
(613) 932-6601   *SIC 4785*
STRAIT CROSSING BRIDGE LIMITED   *p1038*
104 ABEGWEIT BLVD SUITE 2032, BORDEN-CARLETON, PE, C0B 1X0
(902) 437-7300   *SIC 4785*
STRAIT CROSSING DEVELOPMENT INC   *p1038*
104 ABEGWEIT BLVD, BORDEN-

CARLETON, PE, C0B 1X0
(902) 437-7300   *SIC 4785*
STRATOSPHERE QUALITY, INC   *p805*
1515 REBECCA ST, OAKVILLE, ON, L6L 1Z8
(877) 224-8584   *SIC 4785*
THOUSAND ISLANDS BRIDGE CO   *p643*
379 HWY 137, LANSDOWNE, ON, K0E 1L0
(613) 659-2308   *SIC 4785*

SIC 4789 Transportation services, nec

9088-3570 QUEBEC INC   *p1058*
40 RUE EMILIEN-MARCOUX BUREAU 109, BLAINVILLE, QC, J7C 0B5
(450) 420-9814   *SIC 4789*
ALSTOM CANADA INC   *p13*
7550 OGDEN DALE RD SE SUITE 200, CALGARY, AB, T2C 4X9
SIC 4789
ARI FLEET SERVICES OF CANADA INC   *p859*
1000 DEGURSE RD, SARNIA, ON, N7T 7H5
(519) 332-3739   *SIC 4789*
ARROW RELOAD SYSTEMS INC   *p161*
53309 RANGE ROAD 232 UNIT 38, SHERWOOD PARK, AB, T8A 4V2
(780) 464-4640   *SIC 4789*
AUTO WAREHOUSING COMPANY CANADA LIMITED   *p813*
1150 STEVENSON RD S SUITE 1, OSHAWA, ON, L1J 0B3
(905) 725-6549   *SIC 4789*
C & E EXPRESS INC   *p512*
1B CONESTOGA DR SUITE 101, BRAMPTON, ON, L6Z 4N5
(905) 495-7934   *SIC 4789*
CAD INDUSTRIES FERROVIAIRES LTEE   *p1126*
155 BOUL MONTREAL-TORONTO, LACHINE, QC, H8S 1B4
(514) 634-3131   *SIC 4789*
CALTRAX INC   *p28*
1805 30 AVE SE, CALGARY, AB, T2G 4X8
(403) 234-0585   *SIC 4789*
COMPAGNIE DES CHEMINS DE FER NATIONAUX DU CANADA   *p362*
150 PANDORA AVE W, WINNIPEG, MB, R2C 4H5
(204) 235-2626   *SIC 4789*
COMPAGNIE DES CHEMINS DE FER NATIONAUX DU CANADA   *p551*
GD, CONCORD, ON, L4K 1B9
(905) 669-3009   *SIC 4789*
D W I SERVICE LIMITED   *p423*
738 MAIN RD, GOULDS, NL, A1S 1J2
(709) 745-7054   *SIC 4789*
EASTERN RAILWAY SERVICES   *p396*
205 ROSEBERRY ST, CAMPBELLTON, NB, E3N 2H4
(506) 753-0462   *SIC 4789*
GLOBAL AGRICULTURE TRANS-LOADING INC   *p270*
11678 130 ST, SURREY, BC, V3R 2Y3
(604) 580-1786   *SIC 4789*
GROUPE SEMA STRUCTURE FERROVIAIRES INC   *p1358*
125 RUE DE L'EXPANSION, SAINTE-FLAVIE, QC, G0J 2L0
(418) 775-7141   *SIC 4789*
IDC DISTRIBUTION SERVICES LTD   *p274*
10550 TIMBERLAND RD, SURREY, BC, V3V 7Z1
(604) 812-5048   *SIC 4789*
MANUTENTIONS MARSOLAIS BRENDON INC   *p1298*
7255 CH DE SAINTE-?M?LIE, SAINT-DAMIEN, QC, J0K 2E0
SIC 4789
MOUNTAIN VIEW RELOAD INC   *p175*
419 SUMAS WAY, ABBOTSFORD, BC, V2S 8E5

SIC 4789
PNR RAILWORKS QUEBEC INC   *p1089*
100 RUE GOODFELLOW, DELSON, QC, J5B 1V4
(450) 632-6241   *SIC 4789*
RANDON ENTERPRISES LTD   *p180*
11953 241 RD, ARRAS, BC, V0C 1B0
(250) 843-7394   *SIC 4789*
RED RIVER AIR BRAKE INC   *p363*
171 GUNN RD, WINNIPEG, MB, R2C 2Z8
(204) 231-4111   *SIC 4789*
SERVICES DE CALECHES & TRAINEAUX LUCKY LUC ENR, LES   *p1215*
1810 RUE BASIN, MONTREAL, QC, H3J 1S3
(514) 934-6105   *SIC 4789*
WATTS PROJECTS INC   *p156*
82 QUEENS DR, RED DEER, AB, T4P 0R4
(403) 358-5555   *SIC 4789*

SIC 4812 Radiotelephone communication

BEYOND WIRELESS INC   *p898*
444 BARRYDOWNE RD UNIT 3, SUDBURY, ON, P3A 3T3
(705) 525-7091   *SIC 4812*
CELLMART COMMUNICATIONS INC   *p259*
5300 NO. 3 RD SUITE 432, RICHMOND, BC, V6X 2X9
(604) 247-2355   *SIC 4812*
INTERDIGITAL CANADA LTEE   *p1197*
1000 RUE SHERBROOKE O BUREAU 1000, MONTREAL, QC, H3A 3G4
(514) 904-6300   *SIC 4812*
MOBILE SERVICE CENTER CANADA LIMITED   *p1105*
169 BOUL GREBER, GATINEAU, QC, J8T 3R1
(819) 568-3846   *SIC 4812*
PRIME COMMUNICATIONS CANADA INC   *p665*
9275 HIGHWAY 48 UNIT 1B3, MARKHAM, ON, L3P 3J3
(647) 848-1388   *SIC 4812*

SIC 4813 Telephone communication, except radio

1359238 ONTARIO INC.   *p1029*
643 CHRISLEA RD UNIT 3, WOODBRIDGE, ON, L4L 8A3
(905) 669-3882   *SIC 4813*
2931028 CANADA INC   *p1331*
6405 RUE VANDEN-ABEELE, SAINT-LAURENT, QC, H4S 1S1
(514) 335-6161   *SIC 4813*
500PX, INC   *p948*
20 DUNCAN ST UNIT 100, TORONTO, ON, M5H 3G8
(647) 465-1033   *SIC 4813*
7513283 CANADA INC   *p1328*
3333 BOUL DE LA COTE-VERTU BUREAU 600, SAINT-LAURENT, QC, H4R 2N1
(514) 570-7741   *SIC 4813*
ACCESS COMMUNICATIONS CO-OPERATIVE LIMITED   *p1415*
2250 PARK ST, REGINA, SK, S4N 7K7
(306) 569-2225   *SIC 4813*
ALERT SERVICES INC   *p1227*
8255 AV MOUNTAIN SIGHTS BUREAU 100, MONTREAL, QC, H4P 2B5
SIC 4813
AVI-SPL CANADA LTD   *p851*
35 EAST BEAVER CREEK RD SUITE 1, RICHMOND HILL, ON, L4B 1B3
(866) 797-5635   *SIC 4813*
AXIA NETMEDIA CORPORATION   *p63*
220 12 AVE SW SUITE 110, CALGARY, AB, T2R 0E9
(403) 538-4000   *SIC 4813*
AXIA SUPERNET LTD   *p63*
220 12 AVE SW SUITE 110, CALGARY, AB, T2R 0E9

(403) 538-4000   *SIC 4813*
BELAIR NETWORKS INC   *p623*
603 MARCH RD, KANATA, ON, K2K 2M5
(613) 254-7070   *SIC 4813*
BLUEGENESIS.COM CORP   *p687*
5915 AIRPORT RD SUITE 800, MISSISSAUGA, ON, L4V 1T1
(905) 673-3232   *SIC 4813*
CACTUS (ISP) INTERNET INC   *p1106*
490 BOUL SAINT-JOSEPH BUREAU 300, GATINEAU, QC, J8Y 3Y7
(819) 778-0313   *SIC 4813*
CANOE INC   *p932*
333 KING ST E SUITE 1, TORONTO, ON, M5A 0E1
(416) 947-2154   *SIC 4813*
COMPAGNIE DE TELEPHONE BELL DU CANADA OU BELL CANADA, LA   *p969*
100 WELLINGTON ST W, TORONTO, ON, M5K 1J3
(416) 365-7200   *SIC 4813*
COMPAGNIE DE TELEPHONE BELL DU CANADA OU BELL CANADA, LA   *p979*
21 CANNIFF ST, TORONTO, ON, M5V 3G1
(647) 393-3039   *SIC 4813*
COOPTEL COOP DE TELECOMMUNICATION   *p1392*
5521 CH DE L'AEROPORT, VALCOURT, QC, J0E 2L0
(450) 532-2667   *SIC 4813*
CORPORATION STELLAR CANADA INC   *p1176*
255 BOUL CREMAZIE E BUREAU 400, MONTREAL, QC, H2M 1L5
(514) 850-6900   *SIC 4813*
CORRIDOR COMMUNICATIONS, INC   *p22*
465 AVIATION RD NE SUITE 137, CALGARY, AB, T2E 7H8
(888) 240-2224   *SIC 4813*
CROSSWINDS INTERNET COMMUNICATIONS INC   *p942*
1 YONGE ST, TORONTO, ON, M5E 1E5
(416) 364-2202   *SIC 4813*
CUSTOMER EXPRESSIONS CORP   *p830*
2255 CARLING AVE SUITE 500, OTTAWA, ON, K2B 7Z5
(613) 244-5111   *SIC 4813*
DATA ACCESS SOLUTIONS INC   *p851*
15 WERTHEIM CRT UNIT 107, RICHMOND HILL, ON, L4B 3H7
(905) 370-9960   *SIC 4813*
DATAWAVE SYSTEMS INC   *p254*
13575 COMMERCE PKY SUITE 110, RICHMOND, BC, V6V 2L1
(604) 295-1800   *SIC 4813*
DATAWIND INC   *p734*
7895 TRANMERE DR SUITE 207, MISSISSAUGA, ON, L5S 1V9
(905) 671-0202   *SIC 4813*
EPALS CLASSROOM EXCHANGE INC   *p834*
331 COOPER ST SUITE 500, OTTAWA, ON, K2P 0G5
(613) 562-9847   *SIC 4813*
EXECULINK TELECOM INC   *p1036*
1127 RIDGEWAY RD, WOODSTOCK, ON, N4V 1E3
(877) 393-2854   *SIC 4813*
FIBRENOIRE INC   *p1217*
550 AV BEAUMONT BUREAU 320, MONTREAL, QC, H3N 1V1
(514) 907-3002   *SIC 4813*
GLENTEL INC   *p182*
8501 COMMERCE CRT, BURNABY, BC, V5A 4N3
(604) 415-6500   *SIC 4813*
GUEST-TEK INTERACTIVE ENTERTAINMENT LTD   *p50*
777 8 AVE SW SUITE 600, CALGARY, AB, T2P 3R5
(403) 509-1010   *SIC 4813*
GVIC COMMUNICATIONS CORP   *p292*
303 5TH AVE W, VANCOUVER, BC, V5Y 1J6

(604) 638-2451   *SIC 4813*
INQUENT TECHNOLOGIES INC   *p953*
150 YORK ST, TORONTO, ON, M5H 3S5
(416) 645-4600   *SIC 4813*
INTER.NET CANADA LTEE   *p1221*
5252 BOUL DE MAISONNEUVE O BUREAU 200, MONTREAL, QC, H4A 3S5
(514) 481-2585   *SIC 4813*
MUNICIPALITY OF KINCARDINE, THE   *p913*
3145 HWY 21 N, TIVERTON, ON, N0G 2T0
(519) 368-2000   *SIC 4813*
ORICOM INTERNET INC   *p1262*
400 RUE NOLIN BUREAU 150, QUEBEC, QC, G1M 1E7
(418) 683-4557   *SIC 4813*
PRIMUS MANAGEMENT ULC   *p699*
2680 SKYMARK AVE UNIT 100, MISSISSAUGA, ON, L4W 5L6
(416) 236-3636   *SIC 4813*
QUICKPLAY MEDIA CO   *p983*
901 KING ST W UNIT 200, TORONTO, ON, M5V 3H5
(416) 586-6200   *SIC 4813*
QUNARA INC   *p375*
136 MARKET AVE SUITE 8, WINNIPEG, MB, R3B 0P4
(204) 925-0050   *SIC 4813*
RADIANT COMMUNICATIONS CORP   *p316*
1050 PENDER ST W SUITE 1600, VANCOUVER, BC, V6E 4T3
(604) 257-0500   *SIC 4813*
ROGERS COMMUNICATIONS CANADA INC   *p930*
333 BLOOR ST E FL 8, TORONTO, ON, M4W 1G9
(800) 485-9745   *SIC 4813*
RPSC HOLDINGS LTD   *p1199*
2050 RUE DE BLEURY BUREAU 300, MONTREAL, QC, H3A 2J5
(514) 286-2636   *SIC 4813*
SEARCH ENGINE PEOPLE INC   *p843*
1305 PICKERING PKY SUITE 500, PICKERING, ON, L1V 3P2
(905) 421-9340   *SIC 4813*
SHAW COMMUNICATIONS INC   *p59*
630 3 AVE SW SUITE 900, CALGARY, AB, T2P 4L4
(403) 750-4500   *SIC 4813*
SHERWEB INC   *p1372*
95 BOUL JACQUES-CARTIER S BUREAU 400, SHERBROOKE, QC, J1J 2Z3
(819) 562-6610   *SIC 4813*
SOFTCOM INC   *p967*
88 QUEENS QUAY W SUITE 2610, TORONTO, ON, M5J 0B8
(416) 957-7400   *SIC 4813*
SOGETEL   *p1054*
37 RUE VERVILLE, BAIE-DU-FEBVRE, QC, J0G 1A0
(450) 783-1005   *SIC 4813*
SOGETEL INC   *p1242*
111 RUE DU 12-NOVEMBRE, NICOLET, QC, J3T 1S3
(819) 293-6125   *SIC 4813*
SYMANTEC (CANADA) CORPORATION   *p60*
100 4 AVE SW SUITE 1000, CALGARY, AB, T2P 3N2
SIC 4813
TECHNOLOGIES IWEB INC   *p1396*
20 PLACE DU COMMERCE, VERDUN, QC, H3E 1Z6
(514) 286-4242   *SIC 4813*
TEKSAVVY SOLUTIONS INC   *p543*
800 RICHMOND ST, CHATHAM, ON, N7M 5J5
(519) 360-1575   *SIC 4813*
TEL-PAL COMM INC   *p228*
20316 56 AVE SUITE 225, LANGLEY, BC, V3A 3Y7
(250) 202-8770   *SIC 4813*
TELEBEC, SOCIETE EN COMMANDITE   *p1056*
625 AV GODEFROY, BECANCOUR, QC, G9H 1S3

SIC 4813

TELEBEC, SOCIETE EN COMMANDITE
p1186
87 RUE ONTARIO O 200, MONTREAL, QC,
H2X 0A7
(514) 493-5300   *SIC 4813*

TELEBEC, SOCIETE EN COMMANDITE
p1391
100 RUE DES DISTRIBUTEURS, VAL-
D'OR, QC, J9P 6Y1
(819) 824-7451   *SIC 4813*

TERAGO INC   *p905*
55 COMMERCE VALLEY DR W SUITE 800,
THORNHILL, ON, L3T 7V9
(866) 837-2465   *SIC 4813*

TERAGO NETWORKS INC   *p905*
55 COMMERCE VALLEY DR W SUITE 800,
THORNHILL, ON, L3T 7V9
(866) 837-2465   *SIC 4813*

TUCOWS INC   *p992*
96 MOWAT AVE, TORONTO, ON, M6K 3M1
(416) 535-0123   *SIC 4813*

TUCOWS.COM CO   *p992*
96 MOWAT AVE, TORONTO, ON, M6K 3M1
(416) 535-0123   *SIC 4813*

UNIQUE BROADBAND SYSTEMS LTD *p560*
400 SPINNAKER WAY SUITE 1, CON-
CORD, ON, L4K 5Y9
(905) 669-8533   *SIC 4813*

XPLORNET COMMUNICATIONS INC *p347*
5 GRANITE RD, BRANDON, MB, R7A 7V2
(204) 578-7840   *SIC 4813*

XPLORNET COMMUNICATIONS INC *p347*
5 GRANITE RD, BRANDON, MB, R7A 7V2
(204) 578-7840   *SIC 4813*

XPLORNET COMMUNICATIONS INC *p367*
275 DE BAETS ST SUITE 4, WINNIPEG,
MB, R2J 4A8
(204) 669-7007   *SIC 4813*

XPLORNET COMMUNICATIONS INC *p420*
300 LOCKHART MILL RD, WOODSTOCK,
NB, E7M 6B5
(506) 328-8853   *SIC 4813*

XPLORNET LIMITED   *p404*
300 LOCKHART MILL RD, JACKSONVILLE,
NB, E7M 5C3
(506) 328-1274   *SIC 4813*

ZEUGMA SYSTEMS INC   *p257*
13571 COMMERCE PKY SUITE 250, RICH-
MOND, BC, V6V 2R2
(604) 247-3250   *SIC 4813*

SIC 4832 Radio broadcasting stations

0781337 B.C. LTD   *p291*
380 2ND AVE W SUITE 300, VANCOUVER,
BC, V5Y 1C8
(604) 699-2328   *SIC 4832*

629112 SASKATCHEWAN LTD   *p1425*
366 3RD AVE S, SASKATOON, SK, S7K
1M5
(306) 244-1975   *SIC 4832*

ASTRAL MEDIA RADIO ATLANTIC INC *p*
206 ROOKWOOD AVE, FREDERICTON,
NB, E3B 2M2
(506) 451-9111   *SIC 4832*

ASTRAL MEDIA RADIO INC   *p926*
2 ST CLAIR AVE W SUITE 200, TORONTO,
ON, M4V 1L6
(416) 323-5200   *SIC 4832*

ASTRAL MEDIA RADIO INC   *p1214*
2100 RUE SAINTE-CATHERINE O BU-
REAU 1000, MONTREAL, QC, H3H 2T3
(514) 529-3200   *SIC 4832*

**BAYSHORE BROADCASTING CORPORA-
TION**   *p835*
270 9 ST E, OWEN SOUND, ON, N4K 5P5
(519) 376-2030   *SIC 4832*

BELL MEDIA INC   *p326*
969 ROBSON ST UNIT 500, VANCOUVER,
BC, V6Z 1X5
(604) 871-9000   *SIC 4832*

BELL MEDIA INC   *p659*

1 COMMUNICATIONS RD, LONDON, ON,
N6J 4Z1
(519) 686-8810   *SIC 4832*

BELL MEDIA INC   *p1175*
1717 BOUL RENE-LEVESQUE E BUREAU
120, MONTREAL, QC, H2L 4T9
(514) 529-3200   *SIC 4832*

BELL MEDIA INC   *p1175*
1717 BOUL RENE-LEVESQUE E, MON-
TREAL, QC, H2L 4T9
(514) 529-3200   *SIC 4832*

BELL MEDIA RADIO S.E.N.C.   *p1193*
1800 AV MCGILL COLLEGE UNITE 1600,
MONTREAL, QC, H3A 3K9
(514) 939-5000   *SIC 4832*

BLACKBURN RADIO INC   *p653*
700 RICHMOND ST UNIT 102, LONDON,
ON, N6A 5C7
(519) 679-8680   *SIC 4832*

**CANADIAN BROADCASTING CORPORA-
TION**   *p41*
1724 WESTMOUNT BLVD NW, CALGARY,
AB, T2N 3G7
(403) 521-6000   *SIC 4832*

**CANADIAN BROADCASTING CORPORA-
TION**   *p297*
700 HAMILTON ST, VANCOUVER, BC, V6B
2R5
(604) 662-6000   *SIC 4832*

**CANADIAN BROADCASTING CORPORA-
TION**   *p406*
250 ARCHIBALD ST, MONCTON, NB, E1C
8N8
SIC 4832

**CANADIAN BROADCASTING CORPORA-
TION**   *p452*
5600 SACKVILLE ST, HALIFAX, NS, B3J
1L2
(902) 420-4483   *SIC 4832*

**CANADIAN BROADCASTING CORPORA-
TION**   *p979*
250 FRONT ST W, TORONTO, ON, M5V
3G5
(416) 205-3311   *SIC 4832*

**CANADIAN BROADCASTING CORPORA-
TION**   *p1268*
888 RUE SAINT-JEAN UNITE 224, QUE-
BEC, QC, G1R 5H6
(418) 656-8206   *SIC 4832*

**CANADIAN BROADCASTING CORPORA-
TION**   *p1417*
2440 BROAD ST, REGINA, SK, S4P 0A5
(306) 347-9540   *SIC 4832*

CKMS-FM 100.3   *p1008*
200 UNIVERSITY AVE W, WATERLOO, ON,
N2L 3G1
SIC 4832

COGECO INC   *p1202*
5 PLACE VILLE-MARIE BUREAU 1700,
MONTREAL, QC, H3B 0B3
(514) 764-4700   *SIC 4832*

**CORUS AUDIO & ADVERTISING SERVICES
LTD**   *p47*
630 3 AVE SW SUITE 501, CALGARY, AB,
T2P 4L4
(403) 716-6500   *SIC 4832*

CORUS ENTERTAINMENT INC   *p330*
700 GEORGIA ST W SUITE 2000, VAN-
COUVER, BC, V7Y 1K8
(604) 687-5177   *SIC 4832*

CORUS ENTERTAINMENT INC   *p330*
700 GEORGIA ST W SUITE 2000, VAN-
COUVER, BC, V7Y 1K8
(604) 687-5177   *SIC 4832*

CORUS ENTERTAINMENT INC   *p330*
700 GEORGIA ST W SUITE 2000, VAN-
COUVER, BC, V7Y 1K8
(604) 687-5177   *SIC 4832*

CORUS ENTERTAINMENT INC   *p933*
25 DOCKSIDE DR, TORONTO, ON, M5A
0B5
(416) 479-7000   *SIC 4832*

GENEX COMMUNICATIONS INC   *p1259*
410 BOUL CHAREST E, QUEBEC, QC,

G1K 8G3
(418) 266-6166   *SIC 4832*

GOLDEN WEST BROADCASTING   *p345*
125 CENTRE AVE W SUITE 201, ALTONA,
MB, R0G 0B0
(204) 324-6464   *SIC 4832*

HARVARD BROADCASTING INC   *p1418*
1900 ROSE ST, REGINA, SK, S4P 0A9
(306) 546-6200   *SIC 4832*

**MARITIME BROADCASTING SYSTEM LIM-
ITED**   *p458*
90 LOVETT LAKE CRT SUITE 101, HALI-
FAX, NS, B3S 0H6
(902) 425-1225   *SIC 4832*

MY BROADCASTING CORPORATION *p849*
321B RAGLAN ST S SUITE B, RENFREW,
ON, K7V 1R6
(613) 432-6936   *SIC 4832*

NEWCAP INC   *p104*
8882 170 ST NW SUITE 2394, EDMON-
TON, AB, T5T 4M2
(780) 451-8097   *SIC 4832*

NEWCAP INC   *p104*
2394 WEST EDMONTON MALL, EDMON-
TON, AB, T5T 4M2
(780) 432-3165   *SIC 4832*

NEWCAP INC   *p447*
8 BASINVIEW DR, DARTMOUTH, NS, B3B
1G4
(902) 468-7557   *SIC 4832*

NEWCAP RADIO OTTAWA   *p749*
6 ANTARES DR SUITE 100, NEPEAN, ON,
K2E 8A9
(613) 723-8990   *SIC 4832*

**NEWFOUNDLAND CAPITAL CORPORA-
TION LIMITED**   *p430*
391 KENMOUNT RD, ST. JOHN'S, NL, A1B
3P9
(709) 726-5590   *SIC 4832*

**NEWFOUNDLAND CAPITAL CORPORA-
TION LIMITED**   *p447*
8 BASINVIEW DR, DARTMOUTH, NS, B3B
1G4
(902) 468-7557   *SIC 4832*

O/L ENTERPRISES INC   *p425*
GD, LA SCIE, NL, A0K 3M0
(709) 675-2085   *SIC 4832*

PATTISON, JIM BROADCAST GROUP LTD
p158
10 BOUNDARY RD SE, REDCLIFF, AB, T0J
2P0
(403) 548-8282   *SIC 4832*

PATTISON, JIM BROADCAST GROUP LTD
p217
460 PEMBERTON TER, KAMLOOPS, BC,
V2C 1T5
(250) 372-3322   *SIC 4832*

**QUINTE BROADCASTING COMPANY LIM-
ITED**   *p491*
10 SOUTH FRONT ST, BELLEVILLE, ON,
K8N 2Y3
(613) 969-5555   *SIC 4832*

RADIO 1540 LIMITED   *p990*
622 COLLEGE ST SUITE 2, TORONTO,
ON, M6G 1B6
(416) 531-9991   *SIC 4832*

RAWLCO CAPITAL LTD   *p37*
6807 RAILWAY ST SE SUITE 140, CAL-
GARY, AB, T2H 2V6
(403) 451-9893   *SIC 4832*

RAWLCO CAPITAL LTD   *p1418*
2401 SASKATCHEWAN DR SUITE 210,
REGINA, SK, S4P 4H8
(306) 525-0000   *SIC 4832*

RAWLCO RADIO LTD   *p1433*
715 SASKATCHEWAN CRES W, SASKA-
TOON, SK, S7M 5V7
(306) 934-2222   *SIC 4832*

RNC MEDIA INC   *p1289*
380 AV MURDOCH, ROUYN-NORANDA,
QC, J9X 1G5
(819) 762-0741   *SIC 4832*

RNC MEDIA INC   *p1402*
1 PL WESTMOUNT SQUARE BUREAU

1405, WESTMOUNT, QC, H3Z 2P9
(514) 866-8686   *SIC 4832*

ROGERS MEDIA INC   *p58*
535 7 AVE SW, CALGARY, AB, T2P 0Y4
(403) 250-9797   *SIC 4832*

ROGERS MEDIA INC   *p293*
2440 ASH ST, VANCOUVER, BC, V5Z 4J6
(604) 872-2557   *SIC 4832*

ROGERS SPORTS GROUP INC   *p930*
333 BLOOR ST E, TORONTO, ON, M4W
1G9
(416) 935-8200   *SIC 4832*

SIRIUS XM CANADA HOLDINGS INC *p992*
135 LIBERTY ST 4TH FLOOR, TORONTO,
ON, M6K 1A7
(416) 408-6000   *SIC 4832*

SIRIUS XM CANADA INC   *p992*
135 LIBERTY ST SUITE 400, TORONTO,
ON, M6K 1A7
(416) 513-7470   *SIC 4832*

**STANDARD BROADCAST PRODUCTIONS
LTD**   *p1215*
1411 RUE DU FORT UNITE 300, MON-
TREAL, QC, H3H 2N7
(514) 989-2523   *SIC 4832*

TOUCH CANADA BROADCASTING INC
p119
5316 CALGARY TRAIL NW, EDMONTON,
AB, T6H 4J8
(780) 469-5200   *SIC 4832*

VISTA RADIO LTD   *p203*
910 FITZGERALD AVE UNIT 201,
COURTENAY, BC, V9N 2R5
(250) 334-2421   *SIC 4832*

SIC 4833 Television broadcasting stations

0859291 B.C. LTD   *p334*
780 KINGS RD, VICTORIA, BC, V8T 5A2
(250) 480-3732   *SIC 4833*

**ABORIGINAL PEOPLE'S TELEVISION NET-
WORK INCORPORATED**   *p374*
339 PORTAGE AVE, WINNIPEG, MB, R3B
2C3
(204) 947-9331   *SIC 4833*

ANTHEM MEDIA GROUP INC   *p991*
171 EAST LIBERTY ST SUITE 230,
TORONTO, ON, M6K 3P6
(416) 987-7841   *SIC 4833*

**ASIAN TELEVISION NETWORK INTERNA-
TIONAL LIMITED**   *p666*
330 COCHRANE DR, MARKHAM, ON, L3R
8E4
(905) 948-8199   *SIC 4833*

ASTRAL BROADCASTING GROUP INC
p1214
1616 BOUL RENE-LEVESQUE O BUREAU
300, MONTREAL, QC, H3H 1P8
(514) 939-3150   *SIC 4833*

BELL EXPRESSVU INC   *p1096*
200 BOUL BOUCHARD BUREAU 72, DOR-
VAL, QC, H9S 1A8
(514) 828-6600   *SIC 4833*

BELL MEDIA INC   *p75*
80 PATINA RISE SW, CALGARY, AB, T3H
2W4
(403) 240-5600   *SIC 4833*

BELL MEDIA INC   *p99*
18520 STONY PLAIN RD NW SUITE 100,
EDMONTON, AB, T5S 1A8
(780) 486-2800   *SIC 4833*

BELL MEDIA INC   *p326*
750 BURRARD ST SUITE 300, VANCOU-
VER, BC, V6Z 2V6
(604) 608-2868   *SIC 4833*

BELL MEDIA INC   *p377*
345 GRAHAM AVE SUITE 400, WINNIPEG,
MB, R3C 5S6
(204) 788-3300   *SIC 4833*

BELL MEDIA INC   *p455*
2885 ROBIE ST, HALIFAX, NS, B3K 5Z4
(902) 453-4000   *SIC 4833*

BELL MEDIA INC   *p638*

864 KING ST W, KITCHENER, ON, N2G
1E8
(519) 578-1313 *SIC 4833*
BELL MEDIA INC p821
87 GEORGE ST, OTTAWA, ON, K1N 9H7
(613) 224-1313 *SIC 4833*
BELL MEDIA INC p873
9 CHANNEL NINE CRT, SCARBOROUGH,
ON, M1S 4B5
(416) 332-5000 *SIC 4833*
BELL MEDIA INC p922
50 EGLINTON AVE E SUITE 1, TORONTO,
ON, M4P 1A6
(416) 924-6664 *SIC 4833*
BELL MEDIA INC p978
299 QUEEN ST W, TORONTO, ON, M5V
2Z5
(416) 591-5757 *SIC 4833*
BELL MEDIA INC p1174
1205 AV PAPINEAU, MONTREAL, QC, H2K
4R2
(514) 273-6311 *SIC 4833*
BELL MEDIA INC p1426
216 1ST AVE N, SASKATOON, SK, S7K
3W3
(306) 665-8600 *SIC 4833*
**CANADIAN BROADCASTING CORPORA-
TION** p87
123 EDMONTON CITY CENTRE NW, ED-
MONTON, AB, T5J 2Y8
(780) 468-7777 *SIC 4833*
**CANADIAN BROADCASTING CORPORA-
TION** p429
95 UNIVERSITY AVE, ST. JOHN'S, NL, A1B
1Z4
(709) 576-5000 *SIC 4833*
**CANADIAN BROADCASTING CORPORA-
TION** p822
181 QUEEN ST, OTTAWA, ON, K1P 1K9
(613) 288-6000 *SIC 4833*
**CANADIAN BROADCASTING CORPORA-
TION** p979
205 WELLINGTON ST W UNIT 9A211,
TORONTO, ON, M5V 3G7
(416) 205-3072 *SIC 4833*
**CANADIAN BROADCASTING CORPORA-
TION** p979
205 WELLINGTON ST W RM 4E301 B,
TORONTO, ON, M5V 3G7
(416) 205-5807 *SIC 4833*
**CANADIAN BROADCASTING CORPORA-
TION** p1175
1400 BOUL RENE-LEVESQUE E, MON-
TREAL, QC, H2L 2M2
(514) 597-6000 *SIC 4833*
CHCH TV p612
163 JACKSON ST W, HAMILTON, ON, L8P
0A8
(905) 522-1101 *SIC 4833*
CORUS MEDIA HOLDINGS INC p22
222 23 ST NE, CALGARY, AB, T2E 7N2
(403) 235-7777 *SIC 4833*
CORUS MEDIA HOLDINGS INC p445
14 AKERLEY BLVD, DARTMOUTH, NS,
B3B 1J3
(902) 481-7400 *SIC 4833*
CORUS MEDIA HOLDINGS INC p779
81 BARBER GREENE RD, NORTH YORK,
ON, M3C 2A2
(416) 446-5311 *SIC 4833*
CORUS MEDIA HOLDINGS INC p933
25 DOCKSIDE DR, TORONTO, ON, M5A
0B5
(416) 479-7000 *SIC 4833*
**CROSSROADS CHRISTIAN COMMUNICA-
TIONS INCORPORATED** p530
1295 NORTH SERVICE RD, BURLINGTON,
ON, L7R 4M2
(905) 845-5100 *SIC 4833*
CTV SPECIALTY TELEVISION INC p638
864 KING ST W, KITCHENER, ON, N2G
1E8
SIC 4833
CTV SPECIALTY TELEVISION INC p899

699 FROOD RD, SUDBURY, ON, P3C 5A3
(705) 674-8301 *SIC 4833*
GESTION AUDEM INC p1204
5 PLACE VILLE-MARIE BUREAU 915,
MONTREAL, QC, H3B 2G2
(514) 874-2600 *SIC 4833*
**GOUVERNEMENT DE LA PROVINCE DE
QUEBEC** p1174
1000 RUE FULLUM, MONTREAL, QC, H2K
3L7
(514) 521-2424 *SIC 4833*
GROUPE TVA INC p1175
1600 BOUL DE MAISONNEUVE E, MON-
TREAL, QC, H2L 4P2
(514) 526-9251 *SIC 4833*
GROUPE TVA INC p1262
450 AV BECHARD, QUEBEC, QC, G1M 2E9
(418) 688-9330 *SIC 4833*
GROUPE TVA INC p1373
3330 RUE KING O, SHERBROOKE, QC,
J1L 1C9
(819) 565-7777 *SIC 4833*
INSIGHT SPORTS LTD p953
184 PEARL ST SUITE 302, TORONTO, ON,
M5H 1L5
(416) 593-0915 *SIC 4833*
MUSIQUEPLUS INC p1206
355 RUE SAINTE-CATHERINE O, MON-
TREAL, QC, H3B 1A5
(514) 284-7587 *SIC 4833*
OUAT MEDIA INC p994
2844 DUNDAS ST W, TORONTO, ON, M6P
1Y7
(416) 492-1595 *SIC 4833*
OWN INC p965
181 BAY ST SUITE 1630, TORONTO, ON,
M5J 2T3
(416) 642-3770 *SIC 4833*
**PELMOREX WEATHER NETWORKS (TELE-
VISION) INC** p798
2655 BRISTOL CIR, OAKVILLE, ON, L6H
7W1
(905) 829-1159 *SIC 4833*
**PELMOREX WEATHER NETWORKS (TELE-
VISION) INC** p1174
1755 BOUL RENE-LEVESQUE E BUREAU
251, MONTREAL, QC, H2K 4P6
(514) 597-1700 *SIC 4833*
PELMOREX WEATHER NETWORKS INC
p798
2655 BRISTOL CIR, OAKVILLE, ON, L6H
7W1
(905) 829-1159 *SIC 4833*
POSTMEDIA NETWORK INC p335
780 KINGS RD, VICTORIA, ON, V8T 5A2
(250) 383-2435 *SIC 4833*
RNC MEDIA INC p1107
171A RUE JEAN-PROULX BUREAU 5,
GATINEAU, QC, J8Z 1W5
(819) 503-9711 *SIC 4833*
ROGERS SPORTSNET INC p874
9 CHANNEL NINE CRT, SCARBOROUGH,
ON, M1S 4B5
(416) 764-6000 *SIC 4833*
SHAW CABLESYSTEMS LIMITED p25
2400 32 AVE NE, CALGARY, AB, T2E 9A7
(403) 750-4500 *SIC 4833*
SNAP TOGETHER PRODUCTIONS p454
5091 TERMINAL RD, HALIFAX, NS, B3J
3Y1
(902) 422-6287 *SIC 4833*
THUNDER BAY ELECTRONICS LIMITED
p907
87 HILL ST N, THUNDER BAY, ON, P7A
5V6
(807) 346-2600 *SIC 4833*
V INTERACTIONS INC p1209
355 RUE SAINTE-CATHERINE O, MON-
TREAL, QC, H3B 1A5
(514) 390-6100 *SIC 4833*
YTV CANADA, INC p935
25 DOCKSIDE DR, TORONTO, ON, M5A
0B5
(416) 479-7000 *SIC 4833*

---

*SIC 4841 Cable and other pay television
services*

9084-2733 QUEBEC INC p1254
2650 CH DU PETIT-VILLAGE, QUEBEC,
QC, G1C 1V9
(418) 624-1301 *SIC 4841*
BELL EXPRESSVU INC p778
100 WYNFORD DR SUITE 300, NORTH
YORK, ON, M3C 4B4
(416) 383-6600 *SIC 4841*
BELL MTS INC p346
517 18TH ST, BRANDON, MB, R7A 5Y9
(204) 727-4500 *SIC 4841*
BELL MTS INC p377
333 MAIN ST, WINNIPEG, MB, R3C 4E2
(204) 225-5687 *SIC 4841*
**BRAGG COMMUNICATIONS INCORPO-
RATED** p455
6080 YOUNG ST SUITE 800, HALIFAX, NS,
B3K 5L2
(902) 453-2800 *SIC 4841*
CABLE PUBLIC AFFAIRS CHANNEL INC
p822
45 O'CONNOR ST SUITE 1750, OTTAWA,
ON, K1P 1A4
SIC 4841
COGECO COMMUNICATIONS INC p1202
5 PLACE VILLE-MARIE BUREAU 1700,
MONTREAL, QC, H3B 0B3
(514) 874-2600 *SIC 4841*
COGECO CONNEXION INC p1202
5 PLACE VILLE-MARIE BUREAU 1700,
MONTREAL, QC, H3B 0B3
(514) 764-4700 *SIC 4841*
DERY TELECOM INC p1121
1013 RUE BAGOT, LA BAIE, QC, G7B 2N6
(418) 544-3358 *SIC 4841*
DTS COMM INC p486
324 SAUNDERS RD UNIT 6, BARRIE, ON,
L4N 9Y2
(647) 428-8838 *SIC 4841*
FAIRCHILD TELEVISION LTD p852
35 EAST BEAVER CREEK RD UNIT 8,
RICHMOND HILL, ON, L4B 1B3
(905) 889-8090 *SIC 4841*
K-RIGHT COMMUNICATIONS LIMITEDp455
6080 YOUNG ST, HALIFAX, NS, B3K 5L2
(902) 484-2800 *SIC 4841*
PERSONA COMMUNICATIONS INC p431
17 DUFFY PL, ST. JOHN'S, NL, A1B 4M7
(709) 754-3775 *SIC 4841*
PERSONA COMMUNICATIONS INC p899
500 BARRYDOWNE RD UNIT 15, SUD-
BURY, ON, P3A 3T3
(705) 560-1560 *SIC 4841*
RESEAU DES SPORTS (RDS) INC, LEp1174
1755 BOUL RENE-LEVESQUE E BUREAU
300, MONTREAL, QC, H2K 4P6
(514) 599-2244 *SIC 4841*
ROGERS COMMUNICATIONS CANADA INC
p930
333 BLOOR ST E 9TH FL, TORONTO, ON,
M4W 1G9
(416) 935-7777 *SIC 4841*
SCORE TELEVISION NETWORK LTD, THE
p983
370 KING ST W SUITE 435, TORONTO,
ON, M5V 1J9
(416) 977-6787 *SIC 4841*
SHAW CABLESYSTEMS G.P. p59
630 3 AVE SW, CALGARY, AB, T2P 4L4
(403) 750-4500 *SIC 4841*
SHAW CABLESYSTEMS G.P. p103
10450 178 ST NW, EDMONTON, AB, T5S
1S2
(780) 490-3555 *SIC 4841*
SHAW CABLESYSTEMS G.P. p592
1037 FIRST ST E, FORT FRANCES, ON,
P9A 1L8
(807) 274-5522 *SIC 4841*
SHAW COMMUNICATIONS INC p103
10450 178 ST NW, EDMONTON, AB, T5S
1S2

(780) 490-3555 *SIC 4841*
SHAW COMMUNICATIONS INC p337
861 CLOVERDALE AVE, VICTORIA, BC,
V8X 4S7
(250) 475-5655 *SIC 4841*
**STAR CHOICE TELEVISION NETWORK IN-
CORPORATED** p25
2924 11 ST NE, CALGARY, AB, T2E 7L7
(403) 538-4672 *SIC 4841*
TELESAT CANADA p834
160 ELGIN ST SUITE 2100, OTTAWA, ON,
K2P 2P7
(613) 748-0123 *SIC 4841*
VIDEON CABLESYSTEMS INC p62
630 3 AVE SW SUITE 900, CALGARY, AB,
T2P 4L4
(403) 750-4500 *SIC 4841*
VIDEOTRON LTEE p1212
612 RUE SAINT-JACQUES BUREAU 700,
MONTREAL, QC, H3C 4M8
(514) 281-1232 *SIC 4841*
WESTMAN MEDIA COOPERATIVE LTD
p348
1906 PARK AVE, BRANDON, MB, R7B 0R9
(204) 725-4300 *SIC 4841*

SIC 4899 Communication services, nec

1043133 ONTARIO INC p830
1825 WOODWARD DR, OTTAWA, ON, K2C
0P9
(613) 228-6557 *SIC 4899*
1357000 ALBERTA ULC p1126
2409 46E AV, LACHINE, QC, H8T 3C9
SIC 4899
7660715 CANADA INC p1212
2100 DRUMMOND ST, MONTREAL, QC,
H3G 1X1
(514) 845-2727 *SIC 4899*
7868774 CANADA INC p616
762 UPPER JAMES ST UNIT 287, HAMIL-
TON, ON, L9C 3A2
(866) 635-6918 *SIC 4899*
9273743 CANADA INC p1235
4141 NORD LAVAL (A-440) O BUREAU
200, MONTREAL, QC, H7P 4W6
(450) 973-8808 *SIC 4899*
ACCELERATED CONNECTIONS INC p978
155 WELLINGTON ST W SUITE 3740,
TORONTO, ON, M5V 3H1
(416) 637-3432 *SIC 4899*
ACE COM CANADA CORPORATION p1193
1981 AV MCGILL COLLEGE BUREAU 500,
MONTREAL, QC, H3A 2X1
SIC 4899
ADVANTAGE COMMUNICATIONS INC
p1040
265 BRACKLEY POINT RD, CHARLOTTE-
TOWN, PE, C1E 2A3
(902) 892-1585 *SIC 4899*
AIC GLOBAL COMMUNICATIONS INC p187
3707 WAYBURNE DR, BURNABY, BC, V5G
3L1
(604) 708-3899 *SIC 4899*
ALCATEL-LUCENT CANADA INC p832
600 MARCH RD, OTTAWA, ON, K2K 2T6
(613) 591-3600 *SIC 4899*
ALGO COMMUNICATION PRODUCTS LTD
p191
4500 BEEDIE ST, BURNABY, BC, V5J 5L2
(604) 438-3333 *SIC 4899*
**ALLIANCE ATLANTIS COMMUNICATIONS
INC** p928
121 BLOOR ST E SUITE 1500, TORONTO,
ON, M4W 3M5
(416) 967-1174 *SIC 4899*
ALLIED INTERNATIONAL CREDIT CORP
p753
16635 YONGE ST SUITE 26, NEWMAR-
KET, ON, L3X 1V6
(905) 470-8181 *SIC 4899*
ALLSTREAM BUSINESS INC p346
517 18TH ST, BRANDON, MB, R7A 5Y9

(204) 225-5687   *SIC* 4899
ALLSTREAM BUSINESS INC   *p*691
5160 ORBITOR DR, MISSISSAUGA, ON,
L4W 5H2
(888) 288-2273   *SIC* 4899
AMERICA ONLINE CANADA INC   *p*406
11 OCEAN LIMITED WAY, MONCTON, NB,
E1C 0H1
    SIC 4899
ASRJ COMMUNICATIONS INC   *p*532
179 MORRISON DR, CALEDONIA, ON,
N3W 1A8
    SIC 4899
ASURION CANADA, INC   *p*406
11 OCEAN LIMITED WAY, MONCTON, NB,
E1C 0H1
(506) 386-9200   *SIC* 4899
AT&T ENTERPRISES CANADA CO   *p*903
55 COMMERCE VALLEY DR W SUITE 700,
THORNHILL, ON, L3T 7V9
(905) 762-7390   *SIC* 4899
AT&T GLOBAL SERVICES CANADA CO
*p*903
55 COMMERCE VALLEY DR W SUITE 700,
THORNHILL, ON, L3T 7V9
(905) 762-7390   *SIC* 4899
ATCO MIDSTREAM LTD   *p*43
240 4 AVE SW SUITE 900, CALGARY, AB,
T2P 4H4
(403) 513-3700   *SIC* 4899
**ATI TELECOM INTERNATIONAL, COM-
PANY**   *p*112
4336 97 ST NW, EDMONTON, AB, T6E 5R9
(780) 424-9100   *SIC* 4899
ATRIA NETWORKS LP   *p*639
301 VICTORIA ST N, KITCHENER, ON,
N2H 5E1
(888) 623-0623   *SIC* 4899
ATS SERVICES LTD   *p*748
35 AURIGA DR SUITE 213, NEPEAN, ON,
K2E 8B7
(613) 288-9139   *SIC* 4899
AVAYA CANADA CORP   *p*666
11 ALLSTATE PKY SUITE 300, MARKHAM,
ON, L3R 9T8
(905) 474-6000   *SIC* 4899
AVOTUS CORPORATION   *p*729
110 MATHESON BLVD W SUITE 300, MIS-
SISSAUGA, ON, L5R 4G7
(905) 890-9199   *SIC* 4899
B3CG INTERCONNECT INC   *p*1301
310 BOUL INDUSTRIEL, SAINT-
EUSTACHE, QC, J7R 5R4
(450) 491-4040   *SIC* 4899
BAYCADD SOLUTIONS INC   *p*828
1296 CARLING AVE, OTTAWA, ON, K1Z
7K8
(613) 298-4918   *SIC* 4899
BCE INC   *p*1395
1 CARREFOUR ALEXANDER-GRAHAM-
BELL BUREAU A-8-1, VERDUN, QC, H3E
3B3
(888) 932-6666   *SIC* 4899
**BELL ALIANT REGIONAL COMMUNICA-
TIONS INC**   *p*406
27 ALMA ST, MONCTON, NB, E1C 4Y2
(506) 860-8655   *SIC* 4899
**BELL ALIANT REGIONAL COMMUNICA-
TIONS INC**   *p*413
1 BRUNSWICK PL SUITE 1800, SAINT
JOHN, NB, E2K 1B5
(800) 665-6000   *SIC* 4899
**BELL ALIANT REGIONAL COMMUNICA-
TIONS INC**   *p*414
GD, SAINT JOHN, NB, E2L 4K2
(506) 658-7169   *SIC* 4899
**BELL ALIANT REGIONAL COMMUNICA-
TIONS INC**   *p*425
760 TOPSAIL RD SUITE 2110, MOUNT
PEARL, NL, A1N 3J5
(709) 739-2122   *SIC* 4899
**BELL ALIANT REGIONAL COMMUNICA-
TIONS INC**   *p*452
1505 BARRINGTON ST SUITE 1102, HALI-

FAX, NS, B3J 3K5
(902) 487-4609   *SIC* 4899
**BELL ALIANT REGIONAL COMMUNICA-
TIONS, LIMITED PARTNERSHIP**   *p*452
1505 BARRINGTON ST, HALIFAX, NS, B3J
3K5
(888) 214-7896   *SIC* 4899
BELL EXPRESSVU INC   *p*775
115 SCARSDALE RD, NORTH YORK, ON,
M3B 2R2
(416) 383-6299   *SIC* 4899
BELL MOBILITE INC   *p*286
2925 VIRTUAL WAY SUITE 400, VANCOU-
VER, BC, V5M 4X5
(604) 678-4160   *SIC* 4899
BELL MOBILITE INC   *p*1396
1 CARREFOUR ALEXANDER-GRAHAM-
BELL BUREAU A-7, VERDUN, QC, H3E 3B3
(514) 870-6550   *SIC* 4899
BELL TECHNICAL SOLUTIONS INC   *p*750
1740 WOODROFFE AVE, NEPEAN, ON,
K2G 3R8
(613) 746-4465   *SIC* 4899
BELL TECHNICAL SOLUTIONS INC   *p*1307
6396 GRANDE ALLEE, SAINT-HUBERT,
QC, J3Y 8J8
(450) 678-0100   *SIC* 4899
BPONOVO INC   *p*914
3660 MIDLAND AVE UNIT V3022,
TORONTO, ON, M1V 0B8
(416) 479-0416   *SIC* 4899
BROADSTREET DATA SOLUTIONS INC
*p*773
10 YORK MILLS RD SUITE 214, NORTH
YORK, ON, M2P 2G4
(416) 792-2000   *SIC* 4899
CALIAN LTD   *p*835
4-770 PALLADIUM DR, OTTAWA, ON, K2V
1C8
(613) 599-8600   *SIC* 4899
CALIAN LTD   *p*1433
18 INNOVATION BLVD, SASKATOON, SK,
S7N 3R1
(306) 931-3425   *SIC* 4899
**CANADIAN NETWORK INSTALLATIONS
LTD**   *p*667
1351 RODICK RD UNIT 6, MARKHAM, ON,
L3R 5K4
(905) 946-2188   *SIC* 4899
CAPELLA TELECOMMUNICATIONS INC
*p*1101
2065 RUE MICHELIN, FABREVILLE, QC,
H7L 5B7
(450) 686-0033   *SIC* 4899
CBCI TELECOM CANADA INC   *p*1127
2260 46E AV, LACHINE, QC, H8T 2P3
(514) 422-9333   *SIC* 4899
CEDROM-SNI INC   *p*1244
825 AV QUERBES BUREAU 200, OUT-
REMONT, QC, H2V 3X1
(514) 278-6060   *SIC* 4899
CELLCOM WIRELESS INC   *p*271
17650 66A AVE, SURREY, BC, V3S 4S4
(604) 575-1700   *SIC* 4899
CIK TELECOM INC   *p*766
282 CONSUMERS RD, NORTH YORK, ON,
M2J 1P8
(416) 800-4111   *SIC* 4899
CITOYEN OPTIMUM S.E.C.   *p*1258
300 RUE SAINT-PAUL BUREAU 300, QUE-
BEC, QC, G1K 7R1
(418) 647-2727   *SIC* 4899
CITOYEN RELATIONS INC   *p*1258
300 RUE SAINT-PAUL BUREAU 300, QUE-
BEC, QC, G1K 7R1
(418) 521-3744   *SIC* 4899
CITY WEST CABLE & TELEPHONE CORP
*p*251
248 3RD AVE W, PRINCE RUPERT, BC,
V8J 1L1
(250) 624-2111   *SIC* 4899
CNW GROUP LTD   *p*961
88 QUEENS QUAY W SUITE 3000,
TORONTO, ON, M5J 0B8

(416) 863-9350   *SIC* 4899
COMMUNICATIONS FORMEDIC INC   *p*668
20 TORBAY RD, MARKHAM, ON, L3R 1G6
(905) 415-1940   *SIC* 4899
**COMMUNICATIONS GROUP RED DEER
LTD**   *p*155
7434 50 AVE, RED DEER, AB, T4P 1X7
(403) 347-0777   *SIC* 4899
COMMUNICATIONS POMERLEAU INC
*p*1046
111 BOUL MERCIER, AMOS, QC, J9T 2P2
(819) 732-5571   *SIC* 4899
**COMPAGNIE DE TELEPHONE BELL DU
CANADA OU BELL CANADA, LA**   *p*88
10104 103 AVE NW SUITE 2800, EDMON-
TON, AB, T5J 0H8
(780) 409-6800   *SIC* 4899
**COMPAGNIE DE TELEPHONE BELL DU
CANADA OU BELL CANADA, LA**   *p*312
1066 HASTINGS ST W SUITE 1500, VAN-
COUVER, BC, V6E 3X2
(604) 484-1010   *SIC* 4899
**COMPAGNIE DE TELEPHONE BELL DU
CANADA OU BELL CANADA, LA**   *p*721
7111 SYNTEX DR, MISSISSAUGA, ON,
L5N 8C3
    SIC 4899
**COMPAGNIE DE TELEPHONE BELL DU
CANADA OU BELL CANADA, LA**   *p*1272
2715 BOUL DU VERSANT-NORD, QUE-
BEC, QC, G1V 1A3
(418) 691-1080   *SIC* 4899
**COMPAGNIE DE TELEPHONE BELL DU
CANADA OU BELL CANADA, LA**   *p*1396
1 CARREF ALEXANDER-GRAHAM-BELL
TOWER A-7-1, VERDUN, QC, H3E 3B3
(514) 786-8424   *SIC* 4899
**COMPAGNIE DE TELEPHONE BELL DU
CANADA OU BELL CANADA, LA**   *p*1396
1 CARREF ALEXANDER-GRAHAM-BELL,
VERDUN, QC, H3E 3B3
    SIC 4899
COMPROD INC   *p*1064
88 BOUL INDUSTRIEL, BOUCHERVILLE,
QC, J4B 2X2
(450) 641-1454   *SIC* 4899
COMWAVE NETWORKS INC   *p*782
61 WILDCAT RD, NORTH YORK, ON, M3J
2P5
(866) 288-5779   *SIC* 4899
**CONCENTRIX TECHNOLOGIES SERVICES
(CANADA) LIMITED**   *p*411
720 COVERDALE RD, RIVERVIEW, NB,
E1B 3L8
(506) 860-5900   *SIC* 4899
**CONCENTRIX TECHNOLOGIES SERVICES
(CANADA) LIMITED**   *p*443
375 PLEASANT ST SUITE 103, DART-
MOUTH, NS, B2Y 4N4
(902) 428-9999   *SIC* 4899
**CONCENTRIX TECHNOLOGIES SERVICES
(CANADA) LIMITED**   *p*812
1189 COLONEL SAM DR, OSHAWA, ON,
L1H 8W8
(416) 380-3800   *SIC* 4899
CONCORD IDEA CORP   *p*668
3993 14TH AVE, MARKHAM, ON, L3R 4Z6
(905) 513-7686   *SIC* 4899
CONNEX TELECOMMUNICATIONS INC
*p*851
44 EAST BEAVER CREEK RD UNIT 16,
RICHMOND HILL, ON, L4B 1G8
(905) 944-6500   *SIC* 4899
**CONSEILLERS EN GESTION ET INFORMA-
TIQUE CGI INC**   *p*1176
9555 AV CHRISTOPHE-COLOMB, MON-
TREAL, QC, H2M 2E3
(514) 374-7777   *SIC* 4899
**CORPORATION OF THE CITY OF THUN-
DER BAY, THE**   *p*908
1046 LITHIUM DR, THUNDER BAY, ON,
P7B 6G3
(807) 623-4400   *SIC* 4899
COSSETTE COMMUNICATION INC   *p*991

32 ATLANTIC AVE, TORONTO, ON, M6K
1X8
(416) 922-2727   *SIC* 4899
COSSETTE DIGITAL INC   *p*1258
300 RUE SAINT-PAUL BUREAU 300, QUE-
BEC, QC, G1K 7R1
(418) 647-2727   *SIC* 4899
CRAIG EVAN CORPORATION, THE   *p*648
2480 HURON ST UNIT 3, LONDON, ON,
N5V 0B1
(519) 455-6760   *SIC* 4899
**CYBERLINK PACIFIC TELECOMMUNICA-
TIONS LIMITED**   *p*303
888 DUNSMUIR ST SUITE 868, VANCOU-
VER, BC, V6C 3K4
(604) 708-9688   *SIC* 4899
DBC COMMUNICATIONS INC   *p*1312
655 AV SAINTE-ANNE, SAINT-
HYACINTHE, QC, J2S 5G4
(450) 773-3190   *SIC* 4899
**DISTRIBUTEL COMMUNICATIONS LIM-
ITED**   *p*833
177 NEPEAN ST UNIT 300, OTTAWA, ON,
K2P 0B4
(613) 237-7055   *SIC* 4899
**DISTRIBUTEL COMMUNICATIONS LIM-
ITED**   *p*995
3300 BLOOR ST W SUITE 800, TORONTO,
ON, M8X 2X2
(416) 324-2861   *SIC* 4899
**E-COMM EMERGENCY COMMUNICA-
TIONS FOR SOUTHWEST BRITISH
COLUMBIA INCORPORATED**   *p*284
3301 PENDER ST E, VANCOUVER, BC,
V5K 5J3
(604) 215-5000   *SIC* 4899
ELECTRO SAGUENAY LTEE   *p*1237
1555 BOUL DE L'AVENIR BUREAU 306,
MONTREAL, QC, H7S 2N5
    SIC 4899
ELECTRONIQUES ARBELL INC   *p*1091
3633 BOUL DES SOURCES BUREAU 208,
DOLLARD-DES-ORMEAUX, QC, H9B 2K4
(514) 685-5603   *SIC* 4899
ELITE COMMUNICATIONS INC   *p*384
585 CENTURY ST, WINNIPEG, MB, R3H
0W1
(204) 989-2995   *SIC* 4899
ERICSSON CANADA INC   *p*694
5255 SATELLITE DR, MISSISSAUGA, ON,
L4W 5E3
(905) 629-6700   *SIC* 4899
EXACTEARTH LTD   *p*537
260 HOLIDAY INN DR UNIT 30, CAM-
BRIDGE, ON, N3C 4E8
(519) 622-4445   *SIC* 4899
**FEDERATION DES CAISSES DESJARDINS
DU QUEBEC**   *p*1164
3155 BOUL DE L'ASSOMPTION, MON-
TREAL, QC, H1N 3S8
(514) 253-7300   *SIC* 4899
FEEL LIKE TALKING CONNECTIONS LTD
*p*120
9848 33 AVE NW, EDMONTON, AB, T6N
1C6
(780) 465-6055   *SIC* 4899
FIBERNETICS CORPORATION   *p*538
605 BOXWOOD DR SUITE 2972, CAM-
BRIDGE, ON, N3E 1A5
(519) 489-6700   *SIC* 4899
FIDO SOLUTIONS INC   *p*1230
800 RUE DE LA GAUCHETIERE O BU-
REAU 4000, MONTREAL, QC, H5A 1K3
(514) 937-2121   *SIC* 4899
FRIENDLY TELECOM INC   *p*76
44 BERKSHIRE CRT NW, CALGARY, AB,
T3K 1Z5
(403) 243-6688   *SIC* 4899
G.B.S. COMMUNICATIONS INC   *p*456
3480 JOSEPH HOWE DR UNIT 200, HALI-
FAX, NS, B3L 0B5
(902) 431-1100   *SIC* 4899
GESTION GRATIEN PAQUIN INC   *p*1369
1173 AV DE GRAND-MERE, SHAWINIGAN,

QC, G9T 2J4

(819) 538-1707   SIC 4899

GEXEL TELECOM INTERNATIONAL INC   p1220

5250 BOUL DECARIE BUREAU 100, MONTREAL, QC, H3X 2H9

(514) 935-9300   SIC 4899

GILL TECHNOLOGIES GLOBAL COMMUNICATIONS INC   p841

150 KING ST, PETERBOROUGH, ON, K9J 2R9

(877) 507-6988   SIC 4899

GLOBALIVE COMMUNICATIONS CORP   p942

48 YONGE ST SUITE 1200, TORONTO, ON, M5E 1G6

(416) 640-1088   SIC 4899

GLYNSKAR ENTERPRISES LTD   p491

260 ADAM ST, BELLEVILLE, ON, K8N 5S4

(613) 962-5100   SIC 4899

GOLD LINE TELEMANAGEMENT INC p670

300 ALLSTATE PKY, MARKHAM, ON, L3R 0P2

(905) 709-3570   SIC 4899

GROUPE CLR INC   p1387

7200 BOUL JEAN-XXIII, TROIS-RIVIERES, QC, G9A 5C9

(819) 377-2424   SIC 4899

GROUPE PAGES JAUNES CORP   p1396

16 PLACE DU COMMERCE, VERDUN, QC, H3E 2A5

(514) 934-2000   SIC 4899

GROUPE SOMITEL INC   p1269

1026 RUE SAINT-JEAN BUREAU 400, QUEBEC, QC, G1R 1R7

(418) 692-5892   SIC 4899

GROUPE TELTECH INC   p1282

345D RUE MARION, REPENTIGNY, QC, J5Z 4W8

(450) 657-2000   SIC 4899

HOLDING BELL MOBILITE INC   p1396

1 CARREF ALEXANDER-GRAHAM-BELL BUREAU A-7, VERDUN, QC, H3E 3B3

(514) 420-7700   SIC 4899

HUAWEI TECHNOLOGIES CANADA CO., LTD   p671

19 ALLSTATE PKY, MARKHAM, ON, L3R 5A4

(905) 944-5000   SIC 4899

ICT CANADA MARKETING INC   p407

1234 MAIN ST SUITE 2001, MONCTON, NB, E1C 1H7

SIC 4899

INBOX MARKETER CORPORATION   p603

2 WYNDHAM ST N, GUELPH, ON, N1H 4E3

(519) 824-6664   SIC 4899

INMARSAT SOLUTIONS (CANADA) INC   p426

34 GLENCOE DR, MOUNT PEARL, NL, A1N 4P6

(709) 724-5400   SIC 4899

INNOVATIVE VISION MARKETING INC p915

515 CONSUMERS RD 6TH FLOOR, TORONTO, ON, M2J 4Z2

(416) 321-8189   SIC 4899

INTEGRATED MESSAGING INC   p384

550 BERRY ST, WINNIPEG, MB, R3H 0R9

SIC 4899

INTEK COMMUNICATIONS INC   p665

9 HERITAGE RD, MARKHAM, ON, L3P 1M3

(905) 294-0400   SIC 4899

INTELLIGENT MECHATRONICS SYSTEMS INC.   p1006

435 KING ST N, WATERLOO, ON, N2J 2Z5

(519) 745-8887   SIC 4899

INTERNATIONAL CUSTOMER CARE SERVICES INC   p1031

3800 STEELES AVE W UNIT 100E, WOODBRIDGE, ON, L4L 4G9

(905) 850-4760   SIC 4899

IRIS TECHNOLOGIES INC   p671

675 COCHRANE DR SUITE 6, MARKHAM, ON, L3R 0B8

(416) 800-4747   SIC 4899

J2 GLOBAL CANADA, INC   p749

2 GURDWARA RD, NEPEAN, ON, K2E 1A2

(613) 733-0000   SIC 4899

JAN KELLEY MARKETING   p529

1005 SKYVIEW DR SUITE 322, BURLINGTON, ON, L7P 5B1

(905) 631-7934   SIC 4899

JUMP.CA WIRELESS SUPPLY CORP p1416

1845 E VICTORIA AVE UNIT B, REGINA, SK, S4N 6E6

(306) 545-5867   SIC 4899

JUNIPER NETWORKS CANADA INC   p624

340 TERRY FOX DR, KANATA, ON, K2K 3A2

(613) 591-2700   SIC 4899

KIMCOT INC   p779

29 GERVAIS DR UNIT 203, NORTH YORK, ON, M3C 1Y9

(416) 854-2772   SIC 4899

KNOWROAMING LTD.   p922

90 EGLINTON AVE E SUITE 701, TORONTO, ON, M4P 2Y3

(416) 482-8193   SIC 4899

KONTRON CANADA INC   p1340

600 RUE MCCAFFREY, SAINT-LAURENT, QC, H4T 1N1

(450) 437-4661   SIC 4899

KORE WIRELES CANADA INC   p375

93 LOMBARD AVE SUITE 412, WINNIPEG, MB, R3B 3B1

(204) 954-2888   SIC 4899

LEMIEUX BEDARD COMMUNICATIONS INC   p1374

2665 RUE KING O BUREAU 315, SHERBROOKE, QC, J1L 2G5

(819) 823-0850   SIC 4899

LORAC COMMUNICATIONS INC   p546

115 FIRST ST SUITE 107, COLLINGWOOD, ON, L9Y 4W3

(905) 457-5350   SIC 4899

MACNO TELECOM INC   p1247

12655 BOUL INDUSTRIEL, POINTE-AUX-TREMBLES, QC, H1A 4Z6

(514) 498-1555   SIC 4899

MEMOTEC INC   p1335

7755 BOUL HENRI-BOURASSA O, SAINT-LAURENT, QC, H4S 1P7

(514) 738-4781   SIC 4899

MOBIA TECHNOLOGY INNOVATIONS INCORPORATED   p447

340 WRIGHT AVE UNIT 13, DARTMOUTH, NS, B3B 0B3

(902) 468-8000   SIC 4899

MOHAWK INTERNET TECHNOLOGIES   p1206

1250 BOUL RENE-LEVESQUE O BUREAU 4100, MONTREAL, QC, H3B 4W8

(450) 638-4007   SIC 4899

NAV CANADA   p277

7421 135 ST, SURREY, BC, V3W 0M8

(604) 775-9534   SIC 4899

NAV CANADA   p597

1600 TOM ROBERTS AVE, GLOUCESTER, ON, K1V 1E6

(800) 876-4693   SIC 4899

NAV CANADA   p698

6055 MIDFIELD RD, MISSISSAUGA, ON, L4W 2P7

(905) 676-5045   SIC 4899

NAV CANADA   p824

77 METCALFE ST, OTTAWA, ON, K1P 5L6

(613) 563-5588   SIC 4899

NAV CANADA   p1278

515 RUE PRINCIPALE, QUEBEC, QC, G2G 2T8

(418) 871-7032   SIC 4899

NAVIGATA COMMUNICATIONS 2009, INC   p241

949 3RD ST W SUITE 121, NORTH VANCOUVER, BC, V7P 3P7

(604) 998-4490   SIC 4899

NAVIGATA COMMUNICATIONS LIMITED   p318

1550 ALBERNI ST SUITE 300, VANCOUVER, BC, V6G 1A5

(604) 990-2000   SIC 4899

NETNATION COMMUNICATIONS INC p307

550 BURRARD ST SUITE 200, VANCOUVER, BC, V6C 2B5

(604) 688-8946   SIC 4899

NEXICOM TELECOMMUNICATIONS INC   p682

9 BANK ST N, MILLBROOK, ON, L0A 1G0

(705) 775-6394   SIC 4899

NOKIA CANADA INC   p832

600 MARCH RD, OTTAWA, ON, K2K 2T6

(613) 591-3600   SIC 4899

NORDIA INC   p638

160 KING ST E SUITE 400, KITCHENER, ON, N2G 4L3

(519) 579-8906   SIC 4899

NORDIA INC   p1267

5200 BOUL DE L'ORMIERE, QUEBEC, QC, G1P 1K7

(418) 864-7359   SIC 4899

NORTEL NETWORKS LIMITED   p492

250 SIDNEY ST, BELLEVILLE, ON, K8P 3Z3

SIC 4899

NORTHWESTEL INC   p436

5201 50 AVE SUITE 300, YELLOWKNIFE, NT, X1A 3S9

(867) 920-3500   SIC 4899

NORTHWESTEL INC   p1440

301 LAMBERT ST SUITE 2727, WHITEHORSE, YT, Y1A 1Z5

(867) 668-5300   SIC 4899

NORTHWESTEL INC   p1440

301 LAMBERT ST SUITE 2727, WHITEHORSE, YT, Y1A 1Z5

(888) 423-2333   SIC 4899

NORTHWESTEL INC   p1440

183 RANGE RD, WHITEHORSE, YT, Y1A 3E5

(867) 668-5475   SIC 4899

NOVATEL WIRELESS TECHNOLOGIES LTD   p24

6715 8 ST NE SUITE 200, CALGARY, AB, T2E 7H7

SIC 4899

NUMERIQ INC   p1211

612 RUE SAINT-JACQUES, MONTREAL, QC, H3C 4M8

(514) 380-1827   SIC 4899

OATH (CANADA) CORP   p982

99 SPADINA AVE SUITE 200, TORONTO, ON, M5V 3P8

(416) 263-8100   SIC 4899

ON PATH BUSINESS SOLUTIONS INC p595

1165 KENASTON ST, GLOUCESTER, ON, K1B 3N9

(613) 564-6565   SIC 4899

OPEN CALL CENTRE INC   p75

600 CROWFOOT CRES NW SUITE 340, CALGARY, AB, T3G 0B4

(888) 582-4515   SIC 4899

OPTIMA COMMUNICATIONS INTERNATIONAL INC   p965

144 FRONT ST W SUITE 200, TORONTO, ON, M5J 2L7

(416) 581-1236   SIC 4899

PAGES JAUNES SOLUTIONS NUMERIQUES ET MEDIAS LIMITEE   p1396

16 PLACE DU COMMERCE, VERDUN, QC, H3E 2A5

(514) 934-2611   SIC 4899

PHEROMONE INTERACTIF INC   p1211

75 RUE QUEEN BUREAU 3100, MONTREAL, QC, H3C 2N6

SIC 4899

PHONE EXPERTS COMMUNICATIONS LTD, THE   p154

4724 60 ST, RED DEER, AB, T4N 7C7

(403) 343-1122   SIC 4899

PLEASE HOLD CANADA INC   p860

775 EXMOUTH ST, SARNIA, ON, N7T 5P7

(519) 339-8842   SIC 4899

PREMIERE CONFERENCING (CANADA) LIMITED   p983

225 KING ST W SUITE 900, TORONTO, ON, M5V 3M2

(416) 516-5170   SIC 4899

PROMARK-TELECON INC   p1181

7450 RUE DU MILE END, MONTREAL, QC, H2R 2Z6

(514) 644-2214   SIC 4899

QUARTERHILL INC   p640

30 DUKE ST W SUITE 604, KITCHENER, ON, N2H 3W5

(613) 688-1693   SIC 4899

RADIO-ONDE INC   p1280

6655 BOUL PIERRE-BERTRAND BUREAU 643, QUEBEC, QC, G2K 1M1

(418) 527-1602   SIC 4899

RADISYS CANADA INC   p186

4190 STILL CREEK DR SUITE 300, BURNABY, BC, V5C 6C6

(604) 918-6300   SIC 4899

RAMKEY COMMUNICATIONS INC   p515

20 ROY BLVD UNIT 2, BRANTFORD, ON, N3R 7K2

(519) 759-0643   SIC 4899

RAREMETHOD INTERACTIVE STUDIOS INC   p67

1812 4 ST SW SUITE 601, CALGARY, AB, T2S 1W1

SIC 4899

REDLINE COMMUNICATIONS GROUP INC   p674

302 TOWN CENTRE BLVD 4TH FL, MARKHAM, ON, L3R 0E8

(905) 479-8344   SIC 4899

RETHINK COMMUNICATIONS INC   p309

470 GRANVILLE ST SUITE 700, VANCOUVER, BC, V6C 1V5

(604) 685-8911   SIC 4899

ROADWAY SYSTEMS LIMITED   p409

64 ROONEY CRES, MONCTON, NB, E1E 4M3

(506) 384-3069   SIC 4899

ROAM MOBILITY HOLDINGS, INC   p992

96 MOWAT AVE, TORONTO, ON, M6K 3M1

(416) 535-0123   SIC 4899

ROGERS COMMUNICATIONS INC   p190

4710 KINGSWAY SUITE 1900, BURNABY, BC, V5H 4W4

(604) 431-1400   SIC 4899

ROGERS COMMUNICATIONS INC   p930

333 BLOOR ST E, TORONTO, ON, M4W 1G9

(416) 935-7777   SIC 4899

RSCOM LTD   p481

238 WELLINGTON ST E SUITE 210, AURORA, ON, L4G 1J5

(647) 989-8603   SIC 4899

SASKATCHEWAN TELECOMMUNICATIONS HOLDING CORPORATION   p1419

2121 SASKATCHEWAN DR, REGINA, SK, S4P 3Y2

(800) 992-9912   SIC 4899

SASKATCHEWAN TELECOMMUNICATIONS INTERNATIONAL, INC   p1419

2121 SASKATCHEWAN DR, REGINA, SK, S4P 3Y2

(306) 777-2201   SIC 4899

SHAW SATELLITE SERVICES INC   p715

2055 FLAVELLE BLVD, MISSISSAUGA, ON, L5K 1Z8

(905) 403-2020   SIC 4899

SIERRA WIRELESS, INC   p256

13811 WIRELESS WAY, RICHMOND, BC, V6V 3A4

(604) 231-1100   SIC 4899

SPACEBRIDGE INC   p1095

657 AV ORLY, DORVAL, QC, H9P 1G1

(514) 420-0045   SIC 4899

STERICYCLE COMMUNICATION SOLUTIONS, LLC   p777

2 DUNCAN MILL RD, NORTH YORK, ON, M3B 1Z4

SIC 4899

STRIDE MANAGEMENT CORP *p25*
3950 12 ST NE, CALGARY, AB, T2E 8H9
(403) 508-7313   *SIC 4899*

SURECALL CONTACT CENTERS LTD *p11*
3030 3 AVE NE SUITE 240, CALGARY, AB,
T2A 6T7
(403) 291-5400   *SIC 4899*

SYDNEY CALL CENTRE INC, THE *p467*
90 INGLIS ST UNIT A005, SYDNEY, NS,
B1P 1W8
(877) 707-0365   *SIC 4899*

TANTALUS SYSTEMS CORP *p189*
3555 GILMORE WAY SUITE 200, BURN-
ABY, BC, V5G 0B3
(604) 299-0458   *SIC 4899*

TATA COMMUNICATIONS (CANADA) LTD
p1212
1441 RUE CARRIE-DERICK, MONTREAL,
QC, H3C 4S9
(514) 868-7272   *SIC 4899*

TEKTELIC COMMUNICATIONS INC *p26*
7657 10 ST NE, CALGARY, AB, T2E 8X2
(403) 338-6900   *SIC 4899*

TELE-MOBILE COMPANY *p867*
200 CONSILIUM PL SUITE 1600, SCAR-
BOROUGH, ON, M1H 3J3
(800) 308-5992   *SIC 4899*

TELE-MOBILE COMPANY *p1336*
8851 RTE TRANSCANADIENNE BUREAU
1, SAINT-LAURENT, QC, H4S 1Z6
(514) 832-2000   *SIC 4899*

**TELECOMMUNICATIONS DENIS GIGNAC
INC** *p1151*
143 BOUL DION, MATANE, QC, G4W 3L8
(418) 562-9000   *SIC 4899*

**TELECOMMUNICATIONS GLOBAL
CROSSING-CANADA LTEE** *p1200*
1140 BOUL DE MAISONNEUVE O, MON-
TREAL, QC, H3A 1M8
(800) 668-4210   *SIC 4899*

TELECON INC *p1240*
6789 BOUL LEGER, MONTREAL-NORD,
QC, H1G 6H8
SIC 4899

TELECON INC *p1293*
104 RUE D'ANVERS, SAINT-AUGUSTIN-
DE-DESMAURES, QC, G3A 1S4
(418) 878-9595   *SIC 4899*

**TELECONFERENCE GLOBAL CROSSING-
CANADA LTEE** *p1200*
1140 BOUL DE MAISONNEUVE O, MON-
TREAL, QC, H3A 1M8
SIC 4899

TELESAT CANADA *p618*
GD, HANOVER, ON, N4N 3C2
(519) 364-1221   *SIC 4899*

TELIPHONE CORP *p318*
1550 ALBERNI ST 3RD FL, VANCOUVER,
BC, V6G 1A5
(604) 990-2000   *SIC 4899*

TELLZA INC *p914*
190 BOROUGH DR SUITE 3302,
TORONTO, ON, M1P 0B6
SIC 4899

TELUS COMMUNICATIONS (QUEBEC) INC
p1209
630 BOUL RENE-LEVESQUE O BUREAU
2200, MONTREAL, QC, H3B 1S6
(514) 242-8870   *SIC 4899*

TELUS COMMUNICATIONS COMPANY *p191*
3777 KINGSWAY SUITE 501, BURNABY,
BC, V5H 3Z7
(604) 432-2151   *SIC 4899*

TELUS COMMUNICATIONS INC *p191*
3777 KINGSWAY, BURNABY, BC, V5H 3Z7
(604) 432-5010   *SIC 4899*

TELUS COMMUNICATIONS INC *p300*
510 WEST GEORGIA ST 7TH FL, VAN-
COUVER, BC, V6B 0M3
(888) 493-2007   *SIC 4899*

TELUS COMMUNICATIONS INC *p1212*
111 BOUL ROBERT-BOURASSA UNITE
4200, MONTREAL, QC, H3C 2M1
(514) 392-0373   *SIC 4899*

TELUS COMMUNICATIONS INC *p1285*
6 RUE JULES-A.-BRILLANT BUREAU
20602, RIMOUSKI, QC, G5L 1W8
(418) 310-1212   *SIC 4899*

TELUS CORPORATION *p300*
510 WEST GEORGIA ST FL 8, VANCOU-
VER, BC, V6B 0M3
(604) 697-8044   *SIC 4899*

**TRANSCOM WORLDWIDE (NORTH AMER-
ICA) INC** *p884*
300 BUNTING RD 4, ST CATHARINES, ON,
L2M 3Y3
(905) 323-3939   *SIC 4899*

TRITON DIGITAL CANADA INC *p1214*
1440 RUE SAINTE-CATHERINE O BU-
REAU 1200, MONTREAL, QC, H3G 1R8
(514) 448-4037   *SIC 4899*

TRJ TELECOM INC *p1115*
1355 RUE LEPINE, JOLIETTE, QC, J6E
4B7
(450) 499-1017   *SIC 4899*

UNIGLOBE GEO TRAVEL LTD *p91*
10237 109 ST NW, EDMONTON, AB, T5J
1N2
(780) 424-8310   *SIC 4899*

UPSOURCE CANADA CORP *p464*
116 KING ST UNIT 9A, NORTH SYDNEY,
NS, B2A 3R7
SIC 4899

VERIZON CANADA LTD *p941*
1 ADELAIDE ST E SUITE 2400, TORONTO,
ON, M5C 2V9
(416) 933-6500   *SIC 4899*

VIIZ COMMUNICATIONS CANADA INC *p38*
6420 6A ST SE UNIT 200, CALGARY, AB,
T2H 2B7
(403) 476-9400   *SIC 4899*

VISION 7 COMMUNICATIONS INC *p992*
32 ATLANTIC AVE, TORONTO, ON, M6K
1X8
(647) 253-0570   *SIC 4899*

VISION 7 COMMUNICATIONS INC *p1214*
2100 RUE DRUMMOND, MONTREAL, QC,
H3G 1X1
(514) 282-4709   *SIC 4899*

**VISTACARE COMMUNICATIONS SER-
VICES OF CANADA INC** *p440*
200 BLUEWATER RD UNIT 201, BED-
FORD, NS, B4B 1G9
(902) 444-7404   *SIC 4899*

VOIS INC *p66*
628 12 AVE SW UNIT 201, CALGARY, AB,
T2R 0H6
(403) 775-2000   *SIC 4899*

VONAGE CANADA CORP *p702*
2660 MATHESON BLVD E SUITE 301, MIS-
SISSAUGA, ON, L4W 5M2
(416) 907-6100   *SIC 4899*

VOXDATA SOLUTIONS INC *p774*
20 YORK MILLS RD SUITE 201, NORTH
YORK, ON, M2P 2C2
SIC 4899

VOXDATA SOLUTIONS INC *p1209*
1155 RUE METCALFE BUREAU 1860,
MONTREAL, QC, H3B 2V6
(514) 871-1920   *SIC 4899*

**WESBELL GROUP OF COMPANIES INC,
THE** *p744*
6300 ORDAN DR, MISSISSAUGA, ON, L5T
1W6
(905) 595-8000   *SIC 4899*

WEST SAFETY SERVICES CANADA INC
p1337
7150 RUE ALEXANDER-FLEMING, SAINT-
LAURENT, QC, H4S 2C8
(514) 340-3300   *SIC 4899*

WESTCAN WIRELESS *p94*
12540 129 ST NW, EDMONTON, AB, T5L
4R4
(780) 451-2355   *SIC 4899*

WESTWORLD COMPUTERS LTD *p98*
10333 170 ST NW, EDMONTON, AB, T5P
4V4
(780) 454-5190   *SIC 4899*

WIRECOMM SYSTEMS (2008), INC *p489*
122 SAUNDERS RD SUITE 10, BARRIE,
ON, L4N 9A8
(905) 405-8018   *SIC 4899*

WYNDHAM WORLDWIDE CANADA INC
p416
180 CROWN ST SUITE 200, SAINT JOHN,
NB, E2L 2X7
(506) 646-2700   *SIC 4899*

YAK COMMUNICATIONS INC *p944*
48 YONGE ST SUITE 1202, TORONTO,
ON, M5E 1G6
(800) 490-7235   *SIC 4899*

ZAYO CANADA INC *p824*
45 O'CONNOR ST SUITE 1400, OTTAWA,
ON, K1P 1A4
(613) 688-4688   *SIC 4899*

ZAYO CANADA INC *p985*
200 WELLINGTON ST W SUITE 800,
TORONTO, ON, M5V 3C7
(416) 363-4444   *SIC 4899*

SIC 4911 Electric services

4318200 CANADA INC *p1377*
3295 RUE JOSEPH-SIMARD, SOREL-
TRACY, QC, J3R 0E4
(450) 742-5663   *SIC 4911*

701671 ALBERTA LTD *p42*
450 1 ST SW, CALGARY, AB, T2P 5H1
(403) 920-2000   *SIC 4911*

**ABB SOLUTIONS INDUSTRIELLES
(CANADA) INC** *p1332*
800 BOUL HYMUS, SAINT-LAURENT, QC,
H4S 0B5
(450) 688-8690   *SIC 4911*

ALBERTA ELECTRIC SYSTEM OPERATOR
p42
330 5 AVE SW SUITE 2500, CALGARY, AB,
T2P 0L4
(403) 539-2450   *SIC 4911*

ALBERTA POWER (2000) LTD *p63*
919 11 AVE SW SUITE 400, CALGARY, AB,
T2R 1P3
(403) 209-6900   *SIC 4911*

ALECTRA INC *p719*
2185 DERRY RD W, MISSISSAUGA, ON,
L5N 7A6
(905) 273-7425   *SIC 4911*

ALECTRA UTILITIES CORPORATION *p613*
55 JOHN ST N, HAMILTON, ON, L8R 3M8
(905) 522-6611   *SIC 4911*

ALECTRA UTILITIES CORPORATION *p613*
55 JOHN ST N, HAMILTON, ON, L8R 3M8
(905) 522-9200   *SIC 4911*

ALGOMA POWER INC *p862*
2 SACKVILLE RD SUITE A, SAULT STE.
MARIE, ON, P6B 6J6
(705) 256-3850   *SIC 4911*

**ALGONQUIN POWER SERVICES CANADA
INC** *p796*
2845 BRISTOL CIR, OAKVILLE, ON, L6H
6X5
(905) 465-4500   *SIC 4911*

ALGONQUIN POWER SYSTEMS INC *p800*
354 DAVIS RD, OAKVILLE, ON, L6J 0C5
(905) 465-4500   *SIC 4911*

ALSTOM CANADA INC *p1377*
1350 CH SAINT-ROCH, SOREL-TRACY,
QC, J3R 5P9
(450) 746-6500   *SIC 4911*

ALTALINK MANAGEMENT LTD *p10*
2611 3 AVE SE, CALGARY, AB, T2A 7W7
(403) 267-3400   *SIC 4911*

ALTALINK, L.P. *p10*
2611 3 AVE SE, CALGARY, AB, T2A 7W7
(403) 267-3400   *SIC 4911*

AMP SOLAR GROUP INC *p712*
55 PORT ST E UNIT A, MISSISSAUGA, ON,
L5G 4P3
(905) 271-7800   *SIC 4911*

ATCO ELECTRIC LTD *p87*
10035 105 ST NW, EDMONTON, AB, T5J
2V6
(780) 420-7310   *SIC 4911*

ATCO ELECTRIC LTD *p131*
9717 97 AVE, GRANDE PRAIRIE, AB, T8V
6L9
(780) 538-7032   *SIC 4911*

ATCO ELECTRIC LTD *p135*
GD, HANNA, AB, T0J 1P0
(403) 854-5141   *SIC 4911*

ATCO ENERGY SOLUTIONS LTD *p63*
909 11 AVE SW SUITE 800, CALGARY, AB,
T2R 1L7
(403) 292-7500   *SIC 4911*

ATCO LTD *p73*
5302 FORAND ST SW, CALGARY, AB, T3E
8B4
(403) 292-7500   *SIC 4911*

ATCO POWER (2010) LTD *p63*
919 11 AVE SW SUITE 400, CALGARY, AB,
T2R 1P3
(403) 209-6900   *SIC 4911*

ATCO POWER CANADA LTD *p63*
919 11 AVE SW SUITE 400, CALGARY, AB,
T2R 1P3
(403) 209-6900   *SIC 4911*

ATCO TECHNOLOGY MANAGEMENT LTD
p87
10035 105 ST, EDMONTON, AB, T5J 2V6
(403) 292-7500   *SIC 4911*

ATLANTIC POWER (WILLIAMS LAKE) LTD
p343
4455 MACKENZIE AVE N, WILLIAMS
LAKE, BC, V2G 5E8
(250) 392-6394   *SIC 4911*

ATOMIC ENERGY OF CANADA LIMITED
p541
286 PLANT RD STN 508A, CHALK RIVER,
ON, K0J 1J0
(613) 584-3311   *SIC 4911*

BAYSIDE POWER L.P. *p412*
509 BAYSIDE DR, SAINT JOHN, NB, E2J
1B4
(506) 694-1400   *SIC 4911*

BLUEARTH RENEWABLES INC *p64*
214 11 AVE SW SUITE 400, CALGARY, AB,
T2R 0K1
(403) 668-1575   *SIC 4911*

BLUEWATER POWER CORPORATION *p859*
855 CONFEDERATION ST SUITE 716,
SARNIA, ON, N7T 2E4
(519) 337-8201   *SIC 4911*

**BLUEWATER POWER DISTRIBUTION COR-
PORATION** *p859*
855 CONFEDERATION ST, SARNIA, ON,
N7T 2E4
(519) 337-8201   *SIC 4911*

BORALEX INC *p1117*
36 RUE LAJEUNESSE, KINGSEY FALLS,
QC, J0A 1B0
(819) 363-6363   *SIC 4911*

**BRITISH COLUMBIA HYDRO AND POWER
AUTHORITY** *p297*
333 DUNSMUIR ST, VANCOUVER, BC,
V6B 5R3
(604) 224-9376   *SIC 4911*

**BROOKFIELD RENEWABLE ENERGY
MARKETING LP** *p1105*
41 RUE VICTORIA, GATINEAU, QC, J8X
2A1
(819) 561-2722   *SIC 4911*

**BROOKFIELD RENEWABLE PARTNERS
L.P.** *p960*
181 BAY ST SUITE 300, TORONTO, ON,
M5J 2T3
(416) 363-9491   *SIC 4911*

**BROOKFIELD RENEWABLE TRADING
AND MARKETING LP** *p1105*
41 RUE VICTORIA, GATINEAU, QC, J8X
2A1
(819) 561-2722   *SIC 4911*

BROOKLYN POWER CORPORATION *p441*
65 BOWATER MERSEY HAULING RD,
BROOKLYN, NS, B0J 1H0
(902) 354-2299   *SIC 4911*

BRUCE POWER L.P. p913
177 TIE RD MUNICIPAL KINCARDINE RR 2, TIVERTON, ON, N0G 2T0
(519) 361-2673 *SIC* 4911

BRUCE POWER L.P. p944
700 UNIVERSITY AVE SUITE 200, TORONTO, ON, M5G 1X6
(519) 361-2673 *SIC* 4911

BULLFROG POWER INC p979
366 ADELAIDE ST W SUITE 701, TORONTO, ON, M5V 1R9
(416) 360-3464 *SIC* 4911

BURLINGTON HYDRO ELECTRIC INC p530
1340 BRANT ST, BURLINGTON, ON, L7R 3Z7
(905) 332-1851 *SIC* 4911

BURLINGTON HYDRO INC p530
1340 BRANT ST, BURLINGTON, ON, L7R 3Z7
(905) 332-1851 *SIC* 4911

CALGARY ENERGY CENTRE NO. 2 INC p78
14417 68 ST NE, CALGARY, AB, T4B 2T4
(403) 567-5135 *SIC* 4911

CAMBRIDGE AND NORTH DUMFRIES ENERGY PLUS INC p532
1500 BISHOP ST N, CAMBRIDGE, ON, N1R 7N6
(519) 621-3530 *SIC* 4911

CANADIAN GAS & ELECTRIC INC p67
1324 17 AVE SW SUITE 500, CALGARY, AB, T2T 5S8
(403) 269-9379 *SIC* 4911

CANADIAN HYDRO DEVELOPERS, INC p64
110 12 AVE SW, CALGARY, AB, T2R 0G7
(403) 267-7110 *SIC* 4911

CANADIAN NIAGARA POWER INC p591
1130 BERTIE ST, FORT ERIE, ON, L2A 5Y2
(905) 871-0330 *SIC* 4911

CANADIAN RENEWABLE ENERGY CORPORATION p1026
4 LINE RD SUITE 209, WOLFE ISLAND, ON, K0H 2Y0
(613) 385-2045 *SIC* 4911

CANADIAN UTILITIES LIMITED p87
10035 105 ST NW, EDMONTON, AB, T5J 1C8
(780) 420-7209 *SIC* 4911

CAPITAL POWER CORPORATION p85
10423 101 ST NW SUITE 1200, EDMONTON, AB, T5H 0E9
(780) 392-5100 *SIC* 4911

CAPSTONE INFRASTRUCTURE CORPORATION p979
155 WELLINGTON ST W SUITE 2930, TORONTO, ON, M5V 3H1
(416) 649-1300 *SIC* 4911

CARTIER ENERGIE EOLIENNE INC p1144
1111 RUE SAINT-CHARLES O BUREAU 1155E, LONGUEUIL, QC, J4K 5G4
(450) 928-0426 *SIC* 4911

CHAPAIS ENERGIE, SOCIETE EN COMMANDITE p942
67 YONGE ST SUITE 810, TORONTO, ON, M5E 1J8
SIC 4911

CHURCHILL FALL LABRADOR CORPORATION p421
GD, CHURCHILL FALLS, NL, A0R 1A0
(709) 925-8298 *SIC* 4911

CHURCHILL FALLS (LABRADOR) CORPORATION LIMITED p430
500 COLUMBUS DR, ST. JOHN'S, NL, A1B 4K7
(709) 737-1450 *SIC* 4911

CNOOC MARKETING CANADA p46
801 7 AVE SW SUITE 1700, CALGARY, AB, T2P 3P7
(403) 699-4000 *SIC* 4911

COENTREPRISE TRANSELEC-ARNO p1085
2075 BOUL FORTIN, COTE SAINT-LUC, QC, H7S 1P4
(514) 382-1550 *SIC* 4911

COGENT POWER INC p527

845 LAURENTIAN DR, BURLINGTON, ON, L7N 3W7
(905) 637-3033 *SIC* 4911

COLLUS POWERSTREAM CORP p546
43 STEWART RD, COLLINGWOOD, ON, L9Y 4M7
(705) 445-1800 *SIC* 4911

COOPER INDUSTRIES (ELECTRICAL) INC p730
5925 MCLAUGHLIN RD, MISSISSAUGA, ON, L5R 1B8
(905) 507-4000 *SIC* 4911

COOPERATIVE REGIONALE D'ELECTRICITE DE ST-JEAN-BAPTISTE-DE-ROUVILLE p1315
3113 RUE PRINCIPALE, SAINT-JEAN-BAPTISTE, QC, J0L 2B0
(450) 467-5583 *SIC* 4911

CORNWALL STREET RAILWAY LIGHT AND POWER COMPANY LIMITED p562
1001 SYDNEY ST, CORNWALL, ON, K6H 3K1
(613) 932-0123 *SIC* 4911

CP ENERGY MARKETING L.P. p85
2000-10423 101 ST NW, EDMONTON, AB, T5H 0E8
(403) 717-4600 *SIC* 4911

CROWN INVESTMENTS CORPORATION OF SASKATCHEWAN p1417
2400 COLLEGE AVE SUITE 400, REGINA, SK, S4P 1C8
(306) 787-6851 *SIC* 4911

DAPP POWER L.P. p172
RR 1, WESTLOCK, AB, T7P 2N9
(780) 954-2089 *SIC* 4911

DYNASTY POWER INC p48
638 6 AVE SW UNIT 200, CALGARY, AB, T2P 0S4
(403) 613-6882 *SIC* 4911

E.L.K. ENERGY INC p569
172 FOREST AVE, ESSEX, ON, N8M 3E4
(519) 776-5291 *SIC* 4911

EASTERN POWER DEVELOPERS p664
7 EAGLET CRT, MAPLE, ON, L6A 4E2
SIC 4911

EASTERN POWER LIMITED p570
2275 LAKE SHORE BLVD W SUITE 401, ETOBICOKE, ON, M8V 3Y3
(416) 234-1301 *SIC* 4911

ECHO POWER GENERATION INC p944
777 BAY ST SUITE 1910, TORONTO, ON, M5G 2C8
(416) 364-6513 *SIC* 4911

EL CON p803
861 REDWOOD SQ SUITE 1900, OAKVILLE, ON, L6L 6R6
(905) 825-9400 *SIC* 4911

EMERA ENERGY INCORPORATED p452
1223 LOWER WATER ST, HALIFAX, NS, B3J 3S8
(902) 474-7800 *SIC* 4911

EMERA INCORPORATED p453
1223 LOWER WATER ST, HALIFAX, NS, B3J 3S8
(902) 450-0507 *SIC* 4911

ENEL GREEN POWER CANADA INC p1302
1250 RUE DE L'ENERGIE, SAINT-FELICIEN, QC, G8K 3J2
(418) 630-3800 *SIC* 4911

ENERGIE EOLIENNE DU MONT COPPER INC p1242
1500 198 RTE, MURDOCHVILLE, QC, G0E 1W0
(418) 784-2800 *SIC* 4911

ENERSOURCE CORPORATION p722
2185 DERRY RD W, MISSISSAUGA, ON, L5N 7A6
(905) 273-9050 *SIC* 4911

ENMAX CORPORATION p15
8820 52 ST SE SUITE 1940, CALGARY, AB, T2C 4E7
(403) 514-3700 *SIC* 4911

ENMAX CORPORATION p29
141 50 AVE SE SUITE 2708, CALGARY, AB,

T2G 4S7
(403) 514-3000 *SIC* 4911

ENMAX ENERGY CORPORATION p29
141 50 AVE SE SUITE 2708, CALGARY, AB, T2G 4S7
(403) 514-3000 *SIC* 4911

ENMAX ENERGY MARKETING INC p29
141 50 AVE SE, CALGARY, AB, T2G 4S7
(403) 514-3000 *SIC* 4911

ENMAX POWER SERVICES CORP p23
239 MAYLAND PL NE, CALGARY, AB, T2E 7Z8
(403) 514-3000 *SIC* 4911

ENWIN UTILITIES LTD p1023
787 OUELLETTE AVE SUITE 517, WINDSOR, ON, N9A 4J4
(519) 255-2727 *SIC* 4911

EPCOR DISTRIBUTION & TRANSMISSION INC p86
10423 101 ST NW SUITE 2000, EDMONTON, AB, T5H 0E8
(780) 412-3414 *SIC* 4911

EQUS REA LTD p137
5803 42 ST, INNISFAIL, AB, T4G 1S8
(403) 227-4011 *SIC* 4911

ESI ENERGY SERVICES INC p49
727 7 AVE SW SUITE 500, CALGARY, AB, T2P 0Z5
(403) 262-9344 *SIC* 4911

ESPANOLA REGIONAL HYDRO p569
598 SECOND AVE, ESPANOLA, ON, P5E 1C4
(705) 869-2771 *SIC* 4911

ESSEX POWER CORPORATION p570
360 FAIRVIEW AVE W SUITE 218, ESSEX, ON, N8M 3G4
(519) 946-2002 *SIC* 4911

ESSEX POWER CORPORATION p807
2199 BLACKACRE DR SUITE 2, OLDCASTLE, ON, N0R 1L0
(519) 946-2002 *SIC* 4911

ESSEX POWERLINES CORPORATION p570
360 FAIRVIEW AVE W SUITE 218, ESSEX, ON, N8M 3G4
(519) 946-2002 *SIC* 4911

FORBES BROS. LTD p125
1290 91 ST SW SUITE 200, EDMONTON, AB, T6X 0P2
(780) 960-1950 *SIC* 4911

FORTIS INC p433
5 SPRINGDALE ST SUITE 1100, ST. JOHN'S, NL, A1E 0E4
(709) 737-2800 *SIC* 4911

FORTISALBERTA INC p66
320 17 AVE SW, CALGARY, AB, T2S 2V1
(403) 514-4000 *SIC* 4911

FORTISBC INC p221
1975 SPRINGFIELD RD SUITE 100, KELOWNA, BC, V1Y 7V7
(604) 576-7000 *SIC* 4911

FORTISBC PACIFIC HOLDINGS INC p222
1975 SPRINGFIELD RD SUITE 100, KELOWNA, BC, V1Y 7V7
(250) 469-8000 *SIC* 4911

FORTISONTARIO INC p591
1130 BERTIE ST, FORT ERIE, ON, L2A 5Y2
(905) 871-0330 *SIC* 4911

GOREWAY STATION PARTNERSHIP p503
8600 GOREWAY DR, BRAMPTON, ON, L6T 0A8
(905) 595-4700 *SIC* 4911

GREAT LAKES POWER LIMITED p862
243 INDUSTRIAL PARK CRES, SAULT STE. MARIE, ON, P6B 5P3
(705) 256-7575 *SIC* 4911

GREATER SUDBURY HYDRO INC p901
500 REGENT ST, SUDBURY, ON, P3E 3Y2
(705) 675-7536 *SIC* 4911

GREATER SUDBURY UTILITIES INC p901
500 REGENT ST SUITE 250, SUDBURY, ON, P3E 3Y2
(705) 675-7536 *SIC* 4911

GREENFIELD ENERGY CENTRE LP p998
66 WELLINGTON ST W SUITE 3515,

TORONTO, ON, N5K 1H1
(416) 362-0978 *SIC* 4911

GUELPH HYDRO ELECTRIC SYSTEMS INC p601
395 SOUTHGATE DR, GUELPH, ON, N1G 4Y1
(519) 822-3010 *SIC* 4911

H2O POWER LIMITED PARTNERSHIP p814
560 KING ST W UNIT 2, OSHAWA, ON, L1J 7J1
(905) 438-8539 *SIC* 4911

HALDIMAND COUNTY HYDRO INC p532
1 GREENDALE DR SUITE 1, CALEDONIA, ON, N3W 2J3
(905) 765-5211 *SIC* 4911

HALTON HILLS HYDRO INC p473
43 ALICE ST, ACTON, ON, L7J 2A9
(519) 853-3700 *SIC* 4911

HAMILTON UTILITIES CORPORATION p614
55 JOHN ST N, HAMILTON, ON, L8R 3M8
(905) 317-4595 *SIC* 4911

HUDSON ENERGY CANADA CORP p740
6345 DIXIE RD SUITE 200, MISSISSAUGA, ON, L5T 2E6
(905) 670-4440 *SIC* 4911

HYDRO DISTRIBUTION INC p684
8069 LAWSON RD, MILTON, ON, L9T 5C4
(905) 876-4611 *SIC* 4911

HYDRO ONE INC p531
1225 KING RD, BURLINGTON, ON, L7T 0B7
(905) 681-4421 *SIC* 4911

HYDRO ONE INC p945
483 BAY ST SUITE 1000, TORONTO, ON, M5G 2P5
(416) 345-5000 *SIC* 4911

HYDRO ONE LIMITED p945
483 BAY ST 8TH FL SOUTH TOWER, TORONTO, ON, M5G 2P5
(416) 345-5000 *SIC* 4911

HYDRO ONE NETWORKS INC p657
727 EXETER RD, LONDON, ON, N6E 1L3
(519) 668-5800 *SIC* 4911

HYDRO ONE NETWORKS INC p839
99 DRUMMOND ST W, PERTH, ON, K7H 3E7
(613) 267-6473 *SIC* 4911

HYDRO ONE NETWORKS INC p898
957 FALCONBRIDGE RD, SUDBURY, ON, P3A 5K8
(705) 566-8955 *SIC* 4911

HYDRO ONE NETWORKS INC p945
483 BAY ST SUITE 1000, TORONTO, ON, M5G 2P5
(416) 345-5000 *SIC* 4911

HYDRO ONE REMOTE COMMUNITIES INC p945
483 BAY ST SUITE 1000, TORONTO, ON, M5G 2P5
SIC 4911

HYDRO ONE SAULT STE. MARIE LP p863
2B SACKVILLE RD, SAULT STE. MARIE, ON, P6B 6J6
(705) 254-7444 *SIC* 4911

HYDRO OTTAWA HOLDING INC p827
3025 ALBION RD N, OTTAWA, ON, K1V 9V9
(613) 738-5499 *SIC* 4911

HYDRO-QUEBEC p1045
GD, ALMA, QC, G8B 5V5
(418) 668-1400 *SIC* 4911

HYDRO-QUEBEC p1053
1161 RUE MCCORMICK, BAIE-COMEAU, QC, G5C 2S7
(418) 295-1507 *SIC* 4911

HYDRO-QUEBEC p1077
128 CH MILL, CHELSEA, QC, J9B 1K8
(819) 827-7137 *SIC* 4911

HYDRO-QUEBEC p1124
90 RUE BEAUMONT, LA TUQUE, QC, G9X 3P7
(819) 676-4280 *SIC* 4911

HYDRO-QUEBEC p1175
888 BOUL DE MAISONNEUVE E, MON-

TREAL, QC, H2L 4S8
(514) 286-2020   SIC 4911
HYDRO-QUEBEC   p1276
2625 BOUL LEBOURGNEUF BUREAU 14, QUEBEC, QC, G2C 1P1
(888) 385-7252   SIC 4911
HYDRO-QUEBEC   p1390
1600 RUE DE L'HYDRO, VAL-D'OR, QC, J9P 6Z1
(819) 825-4880   SIC 4911
HYDRO-QUEBEC   p1390
1600 RUE DE L'HYDRO, VAL-D'OR, QC, J9P 6Z1
(819) 825-3320   SIC 4911
INDEPENDENT ELECTRICITY SYSTEM OPERATOR   p953
120 ADELAIDE ST W SUITE 1600, TORONTO, ON, M5H 1P9
(905) 855-6100   SIC 4911
INDEPENDENT SYSTEM OPERATOR   p51
2500-330 5 AVE SW, CALGARY, AB, T2P 0L4
(403) 539-2450   SIC 4911
INNERGEX RENEWABLE ENERGY INC   p305
888 DUNSMUIR ST SUITE 1100, VANCOUVER, BC, V6C 3K4
(604) 669-4999   SIC 4911
INNISFIL ENERGY SERVICES LIMITED   p622
7251 YONGE ST, INNISFIL, ON, L9S 0J3
(705) 431-4321   SIC 4911
INNPOWER CORPORATION   p622
7251 YONGE ST, INNISFIL, ON, L9S 0J3
(705) 431-4321   SIC 4911
JUST ENERGY GROUP INC   p740
6345 DIXIE RD SUITE 400, MISSISSAUGA, ON, L5T 2E6
(905) 670-4440   SIC 4911
JUST ENERGY ONTARIO L.P   p740
6345 DIXIE RD SUITE 200, MISSISSAUGA, ON, L5T 2E6
(905) 670-4440   SIC 4911
K2 WIND ONTARIO LIMITED PARTNERSHIP   p597
46 VICTORIA ST N, GODERICH, ON, N7A 2R6
(519) 441-1067   SIC 4911
KANATA HYDRO ELECTRIC COMMISSION   p626
100 MAPLE GROVE RD, KANATA, ON, K2V 1B8
SIC 4911
KIRKLAND LAKE POWER CORP   p634
505 ARCHER DR, KIRKLAND LAKE, ON, P2N 3M7
(705) 567-9501   SIC 4911
KITCHENER-WILMOT HYDRO INC   p638
301 VICTORIA ST S, KITCHENER, ON, N2G 4L2
(519) 745-4771   SIC 4911
LABRADOR-ISLAND LINK LIMITED PARTNERSHIP   p430
500 COLUMBUS DR, ST. JOHN'S, NL, A1B 0C9
(709) 737-4860   SIC 4911
LANGLEY UTILITIES CONTRACTING LTD   p496
71 MEARNS CRT UNIT 1, BOWMANVILLE, ON, L1C 4N4
(905) 623-5798   SIC 4911
LONDON HYDRO INC   p656
111 HORTON ST E, LONDON, ON, N6B 3N9
(519) 661-5503   SIC 4911
MANITOBA HYDRO-ELECTRIC BOARD, THE   p378
360 PORTAGE AVE SUITE 6, WINNIPEG, MB, R3C 0G8
(204) 360-3311   SIC 4911
MARITIME ELECTRIC COMPANY, LIMITED   p1039
180 KENT ST, CHARLOTTETOWN, PE, C1A 1N9

(800) 670-1012   SIC 4911
MAXIM POWER CORP   p53
715 5 AVE SW SUITE 1210, CALGARY, AB, T2P 2X6
(403) 263-3021   SIC 4911
MIDLAND POWER UTILITY CORPORATION   p681
16984 12 HWY, MIDLAND, ON, L4R 4P4
(705) 526-9361   SIC 4911
MILNER POWER INC   p54
715 5 AVE SW SUITE 1220, CALGARY, AB, T2P 2X6
(403) 750-9300   SIC 4911
MILNER POWER LIMITED PARTNERHSIP   p54
715 5 AVE SW SUITE 1210, CALGARY, AB, T2P 2X6
(403) 263-3021   SIC 4911
MILTON HYDRO DISTRIBUTION INC   p684
200 CHISHOLM DR, MILTON, ON, L9T 3G9
(905) 876-4611   SIC 4911
MISSISSAGI POWER TRUST   p903
4917 129 HWY, THESSALON, ON, P0R 1L0
(705) 842-3377   SIC 4911
NALCOR ENERGY   p430
500 COLUMBUS DR, ST. JOHN'S, NL, A1B 4K7
(709) 737-1440   SIC 4911
NALCOR ENERGY MARKETING CORPORATION   p430
500 COLUMBUS DR, ST. JOHN'S, NL, A1B 0P5
(709) 737-1491   SIC 4911
NEW BRUNSWICK POWER CORPORATION   p399
239 GILBERT ST, FREDERICTON, NB, E3A 0J6
(506) 458-4308   SIC 4911
NEW BRUNSWICK POWER CORPORATION   p401
515 KING ST, FREDERICTON, NB, E3B 1E7
(506) 458-4444   SIC 4911
NEW BRUNSWICK POWER CORPORATION   p404
451 ROUTE 105, KESWICK RIDGE, NB, E6L 1B2
(506) 462-3800   SIC 4911
NEWFOUNDLAND & LABRADOR HYDRO   p424
1 THERMAL PLANT RD, HOLYROOD, NL, A0A 2R0
(709) 229-7441   SIC 4911
NEWFOUNDLAND & LABRADOR HYDRO   p425
1 KEMP BOGGY ROAD, MILLTOWN, NL, A0H 1W0
(709) 882-2551   SIC 4911
NEWFOUNDLAND & LABRADOR HYDRO   p430
500 COLUMBUS DR, ST. JOHN'S, NL, A1B 4K7
(709) 737-1400   SIC 4911
NEWFOUNDLAND POWER INC   p430
55 KENMOUNT RD, ST. JOHN'S, NL, A1B 3P8
(709) 737-5600   SIC 4911
NEWMARKET HYDRO HOLDINGS INC p756
590 STEVEN CRT, NEWMARKET, ON, L3Y 6Z2
(905) 895-2309   SIC 4911
NEWMARKET-TAY POWER DISTRIBUTION LTD   p756
590 STEVEN CRT, NEWMARKET, ON, L3Y 6Z2
(905) 895-2309   SIC 4911
NEXSOURCE POWER INC   p169
40 INDUSTRIAL DR, SYLVAN LAKE, AB, T4S 1P4
(403) 887-3654   SIC 4911
NIAGARA PENINSULA ENERGY INC   p758
7447 PIN OAK DR, NIAGARA FALLS, ON, L2E 6S9
(905) 356-2681   SIC 4911

NIAGARA-ON-THE-LAKE HYDRO INC p1004
8 HENEGAN RD, VIRGIL, ON, L0S 1T0
(905) 468-4235   SIC 4911
NORFOLK POWER DISTRIBUTION INC p881
70 VICTORIA ST, SIMCOE, ON, N3Y 1L5
(519) 426-4440   SIC 4911
NORTH BAY HYDRO DISTRIBUTION LIMITED   p762
74 COMMERCE CRES, NORTH BAY, ON, P1A 0B4
(705) 474-8100   SIC 4911
NORTHLAND POWER INC   p927
30 ST CLAIR AVE W 12 FL, TORONTO, ON, M4V 3A1
(416) 962-6262   SIC 4911
NORTHLAND UTILITIES (YELLOWKNIFE) LTD   p436
481 RANGE LAKE RD, YELLOWKNIFE, NT, X1A 3R9
(867) 873-4865   SIC 4911
NORTHPOINT ENERGY SOLUTIONS INC p1418
2025 VICTORIA AVE, REGINA, SK, S4P 0S1
(306) 566-2103   SIC 4911
NORTHWEST TERRITORIES HYDRO CORPORATION   p435
4 CAPITAL DR SS 98 SUITE 98, HAY RIVER, NT, X0E 1G2
(867) 874-5200   SIC 4911
NORTHWEST TERRITORIES POWER CORPORATION   p435
4 CAPITAL DR SS 98 SUITE 98, HAY RIVER, NT, X0E 1G2
(867) 874-5200   SIC 4911
NOVA SCOTIA POWER INCORPORATED p453
1223 LOWER WATER ST, HALIFAX, NS, B3J 3S8
(902) 428-6221   SIC 4911
NOVA SCOTIA POWER INCORPORATED p468
108 POWER PLANT RD, TRENTON, NS, B0K 1X0
(902) 755-5811   SIC 4911
NS POWER ENERGY MARKETING INCORPORATED   p454
1223 LOWER WATER ST, HALIFAX, NS, B3J 3S8
(902) 428-6496   SIC 4911
NUNAVUT POWER CORPORATION   p472
2ND FLOOR GN BUILDING, BAKER LAKE, NU, X0C 0A0
(867) 793-4200   SIC 4911
OAKVILLE ENTERPRISES CORPORATION p804
861 REDWOOD SQ SUITE 1900, OAKVILLE, ON, L6L 6R6
(905) 825-9400   SIC 4911
OAKVILLE HYDRO ELECTRICITY DISTRIBUTION INC   p804
861 REDWOOD SQ SUITE 1900, OAKVILLE, ON, L6L 6R6
(905) 825-9400   SIC 4911
ONTARIO POWER GENERATION INC p489
7263 HWY 33, BATH, ON, K0H 1G0
(613) 352-3525   SIC 4911
ONTARIO POWER GENERATION INC p843
1675 MONTGOMERY PARK RD, PICKERING, ON, L1V 2R5
(905) 839-1151   SIC 4911
ONTARIO POWER GENERATION INC p947
700 UNIVERSITY AVE, TORONTO, ON, M5G 1X6
(416) 592-2555   SIC 4911
ORILLIA POWER CORPORATION   p809
360 WEST ST S, ORILLIA, ON, L3V 5G8
(705) 326-7315   SIC 4911
ORILLIA POWER DISTRIBUTION CORPORATION   p809
360 WEST ST S, ORILLIA, ON, L3V 5G8
(705) 326-7315   SIC 4911

OSHAWA PUC NETWORKS INC   p813
100 SIMCOE ST S, OSHAWA, ON, L1H 7M7
(905) 723-4623   SIC 4911
OTTAWA RIVER POWER CORPORATION p838
283 PEMBROKE ST E, PEMBROKE, ON, K8A 3K2
(613) 732-3687   SIC 4911
PEAK POWER INC   p956
214 KING ST W SUITE 414, TORONTO, ON, M5H 3S6
(647) 226-1834   SIC 4911
PF RESOLU CANADA INC   p1103
79 RUE MAIN, GATINEAU, QC, J8P 4X6
(819) 643-7500   SIC 4911
POWER COMMISSION OF THE CITY OF SAINT JOHN   p416
325 SIMMS ST, SAINT JOHN, NB, E2M 3L6
(506) 658-5252   SIC 4911
POWER SUPPLY GRAND RAPIDS GS p350
GD, GRAND RAPIDS, MB, R0C 1E0
(204) 639-4138   SIC 4911
PUBLIC UTILITIES COMMISSION FOR THE MUNICIPALITY OF CHATHAM-KENT p543
320 QUEEN ST, CHATHAM, ON, N7M 2H6
(519) 352-6300   SIC 4911
PURNELL ENERGY SERVICES LTD   p133
10502 123 ST, GRANDE PRAIRIE, AB, T8V 8B8
(587) 259-9600   SIC 4911
QULLIQ ENERGY CORPORATION   p472
GD, BAKER LAKE, NU, X0C 0A0
(866) 710-4200   SIC 4911
REGIONAL POWER INC   p726
6755 MISSISSAUGA RD SUITE 308, MISSISSAUGA, ON, L5N 7Y2
(905) 363-4200   SIC 4911
REGIONAL POWER OPCO INC   p726
6755 MISSISSAUGA RD SUITE 308, MISSISSAUGA, ON, L5N 7Y2
(905) 363-4200   SIC 4911
RIDEAU ST LAWRENCE DISTRIBUTION INC   p848
985 INDUSTRIAL RD, PRESCOTT, ON, K0E 1T0
(613) 925-3851   SIC 4911
RIO TINTO ALCAN INC   p1115
1954 RUE DAVIS, JONQUIERE, QC, G7S 3B6
SIC 4911
RMSENERGY DALHOUSIE MOUNTAIN GP INC   p465
1383 MOUNT THOM RD, SALT SPRINGS, NS, B0K 1P0
(902) 925-9463   SIC 4911
ROTATING ENERGY SERVICES CA CORP p158
39139 HIGHWAY 2A SUITE 4016, RED DEER COUNTY, AB, T4S 2A8
(403) 358-5577   SIC 4911
SAMSUNG RENEWABLE ENERGY INC p727
2050 DERRY RD W 2FL, MISSISSAUGA, ON, L5N 0B9
(905) 501-4934   SIC 4911
SASKATCHEWAN POWER CORPORATION p1405
GD, CORONACH, SK, S0H 0Z0
(306) 267-5200   SIC 4911
SASKATCHEWAN POWER CORPORATION p1406
GD LCD MAIN, ESTEVAN, SK, S4A 2A1
(306) 634-1700   SIC 4911
SASKATCHEWAN POWER CORPORATION p1406
18 BOUNDARY DAM HWY W, ESTEVAN, SK, S4A 2A6
(306) 634-1300   SIC 4911
SASKATCHEWAN POWER CORPORATION p1419
2025 VICTORIA AVE, REGINA, SK, S4P 0S1
(306) 566-2121   SIC 4911
SASKATOON, CITY OF   p1425

322 BRAND RD, SASKATOON, SK, S7J 5J3
(306) 975-2414   *SIC 4911*

SCONA ELECTRIC INC   p116
10003 69 AVE NW, EDMONTON, AB, T6E 0T1
(780) 433-4247   *SIC 4911*

SFE ENERGY MARYLAND, INC   p733
100 MILVERTON DR SUITE 608, MISSISSAUGA, ON, L5R 4H1
(905) 366-7037   *SIC 4911*

SHELL ENERGY NORTH AMERICA (CANADA) INC   p59
400 4 AVE SW SUITE 212, CALGARY, AB, T2P 0J4
(403) 216-3600   *SIC 4911*

SITHE GLOBAL CANADIAN POWER SERVICES LTD   p506
8600 GOREWAY DR, BRAMPTON, ON, L6T 0A8
(905) 595-4700   *SIC 4911*

SOCIETE EN COMMANDITE COULONGE ENERGIE   p1400
GD, WALTHAM, QC, J0X 3H0
(819) 689-5226   *SIC 4911*

SOLACE POWER INC.   p426
1118 TOPSAIL RD SUITE 201, MOUNT PEARL, NL, A1N 5E7
(709) 745-6099   *SIC 4911*

ST THOMAS ENERGY INC   p889
135 EDWARD ST, ST THOMAS, ON, N5P 4A8
(519) 631-5550   *SIC 4911*

STRAD MANUFACTURING INC   p150
602 25 AVE, NISKU, AB, T9E 0G6
(780) 955-9393   *SIC 4911*

SUMMITT ENERGY MANAGEMENT INC   p733
100 MILVERTON DR SUITE 608, MISSISSAUGA, ON, L5R 4H1
(905) 366-7000   *SIC 4911*

SWIFT POWER CORP   p300
55 WATER ST SUITE 608, VANCOUVER, BC, V6B 1A1
(604) 637-6393   *SIC 4911*

SYSTEMES D'ENERGIE RENOUVELABLE CANADA INC   p1186
300 RUE LEO-PARISEAU BUREAU 2516, MONTREAL, QC, H2X 4B3
(514) 525-2113   *SIC 4911*

THUNDER BAY HYDRO ELECTRICITY DISTRIBUTION INC   p907
34 CUMBERLAND ST N SUITE 101, THUNDER BAY, ON, P7A 4L4
(807) 343-1111   *SIC 4911*

TOROMONT ENERGY LTD   p559
3131 HIGHWAY 7 SUITE A, CONCORD, ON, L4K 5E1
(416) 667-5758   *SIC 4911*

TORONTO HYDRO CORPORATION   p936
14 CARLTON ST SUITE 6, TORONTO, ON, M5B 1K5
(416) 542-8000   *SIC 4911*

TORONTO HYDRO-ELECTRIC SYSTEM LIMITED   p770
5800 YONGE ST, NORTH YORK, ON, M2M 3T3
(416) 542-3564   *SIC 4911*

TORONTO HYDRO-ELECTRIC SYSTEM LIMITED   p936
14 CARLTON ST, TORONTO, ON, M5B 1K5
(416) 542-3100   *SIC 4911*

TORQ INSTRUMENT SUPPLY INC   p133
11436 97 AVE, GRANDE PRAIRIE, AB, T8V 5Z5
(780) 532-1115   *SIC 4911*

TRANSALTA CORPORATION   p65
110 12 AVE SW, CALGARY, AB, T2R 0G7
(403) 267-7110   *SIC 4911*

TRANSALTA RENEWABLES INC   p61
110 12TH AVE SW, CALGARY, AB, T2P 2M1
(403) 267-2520   *SIC 4911*

TRANSCANADA QUEBEC INC   p1056
7005 BOUL RAOUL-DUCHESNE, BECAN-COUR, QC, G9H 4X6
(819) 294-1282   *SIC 4911*

TRINITY POWER CORPORATION   p202
1301 KETCH CRT UNIT 8B, COQUITLAM, BC, V3K 6X7
(604) 529-1134   *SIC 4911*

VERIDIAN CONNECTIONS INC   p475
55 TAUNTON RD E, AJAX, ON, L1T 3V3
(905) 427-9870   *SIC 4911*

VERIDIAN CORPORATION   p475
55 TAUNTON RD E, AJAX, ON, L1T 3V3
(905) 427-9870   *SIC 4911*

VILLE DE SHERBROOKE   p1372
1800 RUE ROY, SHERBROOKE, QC, J1K 1B6
(819) 821-5727   *SIC 4911*

WATERLOO NORTH HYDRO INC   p1007
526 COUNTRY SQUIRE RD, WATERLOO, ON, N2J 4G8
(519) 886-5090   *SIC 4911*

WELLAND HYDRO-ELECTRIC SYSTEMS CORP   p1012
950 EAST MAIN ST, WELLAND, ON, L3B 3Y9
SIC 4911

WESTARIO POWER INC   p1004
24 EASTRIDGE RD, WALKERTON, ON, N0G 2V0
(519) 507-6937   *SIC 4911*

WHITBY HYDRO ENERGY SERVICES CORPORATION   p812
100 TAUNTON RD E, OSHAWA, ON, L1G 7N1
(905) 668-5878   *SIC 4911*

WINDSOR CANADA UTILITIES LTD   p1024
787 OUELLETTE AVE, WINDSOR, ON, N9A 4J4
(519) 255-2727   *SIC 4911*

WOODSTOCK HYDRO SERVICES INC   p1036
16 GRAHAM ST SUITE 1598, WOODSTOCK, ON, N4S 6J6
(519) 537-7172   *SIC 4911*

YUKON ENERGY CORPORATION   p1440
2 MILES CANYON RD, WHITEHORSE, YT, Y1A 6S7
(867) 393-5300   *SIC 4911*

SIC 4922 Natural gas transmission

AECO GAS STORAGE PARTNERSHIP   p42
607 8 AVE SW SUITE 400, CALGARY, AB, T2P 0A7
(403) 513-8600   *SIC 4922*

ALLIANCE PIPELINE LIMITED PARTNERSHIP   p42
605 5 AVE SW SUITE 800, CALGARY, AB, T2P 3H5
(403) 266-4464   *SIC 4922*

BURSTALL NGL STORAGE L.P.   p45
222 3 AVE SW SUITE 900, CALGARY, AB, T2P 0B4
(403) 296-0140   *SIC 4922*

CAMPUS ENERGY PARTNERS LP   p45
355 4 AVE SW SUITE 1700, CALGARY, AB, T2P 0J1
(403) 691-7575   *SIC 4922*

CISTEK SOLUTIONS INC.   p46
SUITE 1000 605 5 AVE SW, CALGARY, AB, T2P 3H5
(403) 264-0018   *SIC 4922*

CORPORATION CHAMPION PIPE LINE LIMITEE   p1174
1717 RUE DU HAVRE, MONTREAL, QC, H2K 2X3
(514) 598-3444   *SIC 4922*

CROSSALTA GAS STORAGE & SERVICES LTD   p47
700 2 ST SW SUITE 1600, CALGARY, AB, T2P 2W1
(403) 298-3575   *SIC 4922*

EMERA BRUNSWICK PIPELINE COMPANY LTD   p415
1 GERMAIN ST SUITE 1102, SAINT JOHN, NB, E2L 4V1
(506) 693-4214   *SIC 4922*

ENBRIDGE GAS NEW BRUNSWICK LIMITED PARTNERSHIP   p400
440 WILSEY RD SUITE 101, FREDERICTON, NB, E3B 7G5
(506) 444-7773   *SIC 4922*

ENBRIDGE INCOME FUND   p48
425 1 ST SW SUITE 3000, CALGARY, AB, T2P 3L8
(403) 767-3642   *SIC 4922*

ENBRIDGE PIPELINES (ATHABASCA) INC   p48
425 1 ST SW SUITE 3000, CALGARY, AB, T2P 3L8
(780) 392-4179   *SIC 4922*

ENBRIDGE PIPELINES (WOODLAND) INC   p48
425 1 ST SW SUITE 3000, CALGARY, AB, T2P 3L8
(780) 392-4179   *SIC 4922*

ENERGY FUNDAMENTALS GROUP LIMITED PARTNERSHIP   p662
2324 MAIN ST, LONDON, ON, N6P 1A9
(519) 652-3196   *SIC 4922*

FOOTHILLS PIPE LINES (SOUTH B.C.) LTD   p49
112 4 AVE SW SUITE 300, CALGARY, AB, T2P 0H3
(403) 920-2000   *SIC 4922*

FOOTHILLS PIPE LINES LTD   p49
450 1 ST SW, CALGARY, AB, T2P 5H1
(403) 920-2000   *SIC 4922*

GAZ METRO INC   p1174
1717 RUE DU HAVRE, MONTREAL, QC, H2K 2X3
(514) 598-3444   *SIC 4922*

GREAT LAKES PIPELINE CANADA LTD   p50
450 1 ST SW, CALGARY, AB, T2P 5H1
(403) 920-6852   *SIC 4922*

IBERDROLA CANADA ENERGY SERVICES LTD   p73
5 RICHARD WAY SW SUITE 208, CALGARY, AB, T3E 7M8
(403) 206-3160   *SIC 4922*

INFRASOURCE SERVICES   p598
21 CARDICO DR, GORMLEY, ON, L0H 1G0
SIC 4922

KEYERA ENERGY LTD   p52
144 4 AVE SW SUITE 600, CALGARY, AB, T2P 3N4
(403) 205-8300   *SIC 4922*

MANY ISLANDS PIPELINES (CANADA) LIMITED   p1418
1777 VICTORIA AVE SUITE 500, REGINA, SK, S4P 4K5
(306) 777-9500   *SIC 4922*

MECHANOVA INC   p77
2501 BEARSPAW SUMMIT PL, CALGARY, AB, T3R 1B5
SIC 4922

PEMBINA NGL CORPORATION   p56
525 8 AVE SW SUITE 3800, CALGARY, AB, T2P 1G1
(403) 231-7500   *SIC 4922*

PETROLEUM TANK MANAGEMENT ASSOCIATION OF ALBERTA   p90
10303 JASPER AVE NW SUITE 980, EDMONTON, AB, T5J 3N6
(780) 425-8265   *SIC 4922*

TC ENERGY CORPORATION   p61
450 1 ST SW, CALGARY, AB, T2P 5H1
(403) 920-2000   *SIC 4922*

TERREAU BIOGAS, LIMITED PARTNERSHIP   p1271
1327 AV MAGUIRE BUREAU 100, QUEBEC, QC, G1T 1Z2
(418) 476-1686   *SIC 4922*

TIDEWATER MIDSTREAM AND INFRASTRUCTURE LTD   p61
222 3 AVE SW SUITE 900, CALGARY, AB, T2P 0B4
(587) 475-0210   *SIC 4922*

TRANSCANADA PIPELINES LIMITED   p62
450 1 ST SW, CALGARY, AB, T2P 5H1
(403) 920-2000   *SIC 4922*

TRANSCANADA PIPELINES LIMITED   p676
675 COCHRANE DR SUITE 701, MARKHAM, ON, L3R 0B8
(905) 946-7800   *SIC 4922*

TRANSCANADA PIPELINES LTD   p163
2301 PREMIER WAY UNIT 112, SHERWOOD PARK, AB, T8H 2K8
SIC 4922

TRANSCANADA PIPELINES LTD   p623
11235 ZERON RD, IROQUOIS, ON, K0E 1K0
(613) 652-4287   *SIC 4922*

VAULT PIPELINES LTD   p129
142 DICKINS DR BAY 4, FORT MCMURRAY, AB, T9K 1X4
(587) 537-5520   *SIC 4922*

VERESEN MIDSTREAM LIMITED PARTNERSHIP   p62
222 3 AVE SW SUITE 900, CALGARY, AB, T2P 0B4
(403) 296-0140   *SIC 4922*

WILD GOOSE STORAGE INC. & DESIGN   p63
607 8 AVE SW SUITE 400, CALGARY, AB, T2P 0A7
(403) 513-8616   *SIC 4922*

SIC 4923 Gas transmission and distribution

ALTAGAS EXTRACTION AND TRANSMISSION LIMITED PARTNERSHIP   p43
355 4 AVE SW UNIT 1700, CALGARY, AB, T2P 0J1
(403) 691-7575   *SIC 4923*

ALTAGAS UTILITIES INC   p139
5509 45 ST, LEDUC, AB, T9E 6T6
(780) 986-5215   *SIC 4923*

ATCO GAS AND PIPELINES LTD   p20
4415 12 ST NE, CALGARY, AB, T2E 4R1
(403) 245-7857   *SIC 4923*

ATCO GAS AND PIPELINES LTD   p63
1040 11 AVE SW, CALGARY, AB, T2R 0G3
(403) 245-7551   *SIC 4923*

ATCO GAS AND PIPELINES LTD   p63
909 11 AVE SW SUITE 1200, CALGARY, AB, T2R 1L7
(403) 245-7060   *SIC 4923*

B. C. GAS UTILITY LTD.   p203
110 SLATER RD NW, CRANBROOK, BC, V1C 5C8
(250) 426-6388   *SIC 4923*

CHANGFENG ENERGY INC   p668
32 SOUTH UNIONVILLE AVENUE, MARKHAM, ON, L3R 9S6
(647) 313-0066   *SIC 4923*

CHANGFENG ENERGY INC   p668
32 SOUTH UNIONVILLE AVE SUITE 2036-2038, MARKHAM, ON, L3R 9S6
(647) 313-0066   *SIC 4923*

CHANGFENG ENERGY INC.   p961
55 UNIVERSITY AVE, TORONTO, ON, M5J 2H7
SIC 4923

CHEVRON CORP.   p312
1050 PENDER ST W SUITE 1200, VANCOUVER, BC, V6E 3T4
(604) 668-5671   *SIC 4923*

CHINOOK GAS CO-OP LTD   p147
125 8 AVE NW, MILK RIVER, AB, T0K 1M0
(403) 647-3588   *SIC 4923*

CSV MIDSTREAM SOLUTIONS CORP   p47
355 4 AVE SW SUITE 700, CALGARY, AB, T2P 0J1
(587) 316-6900   *SIC 4923*

ENBRIDGE OPERATIONAL SERVICES INC   p88
10201 JASPER AVE NW, EDMONTON, AB, T5J 3N7
(780) 420-8850   *SIC 4923*

ENERSHARE TECHNOLOGY CORP   p783

87 BAKERSFIELD ST, NORTH YORK, ON, M3J 1Z4
SIC 4923

EUREST-TERASEN GAS-633　　*p281*
16705 FRASER HWY, SURREY, BC, V4N 0E7
SIC 4923

FORTISBC ENERGY INC　　*p281*
16705 FRASER HWY, SURREY, BC, V4N 0E8
(604) 576-7000　*SIC 4923*

FORTISBC HOLDINGS INC　　*p313*
1111 GEORGIA ST W SUITE 1000, VANCOUVER, BC, V6E 4M3
(604) 443-6525　*SIC 4923*

HUSKY GAS MARKETING INC　　*p51*
707 8 AVE SW, CALGARY, AB, T2P 1H5
SIC 4923

MINCO GAS CO-OP LTD　　*p137*
4907 51 ST, INNISFREE, AB, T0B 2G0
(780) 592-3911　*SIC 4923*

NORTHERN LIGHTS GAS CO-OP LTD　*p138*
10205 101 ST, LA CRETE, AB, T0H 2H0
(780) 928-3881　*SIC 4923*

NORTHRIVER MIDSTREAM INC　　*p55*
425 1 ST SW SUITE 2200, CALGARY, AB, T2P 3L8
(403) 699-1955　*SIC 4923*

NOVA GAS TRANSMISSION LTD　　*p55*
450 1 ST SW, CALGARY, AB, T2P 5H1
(403) 920-2000　*SIC 4923*

PACIFIC NORTHERN CARRIERS LTD　*p282*
15760 110 AVE, SURREY, BC, V4N 4Z1
(604) 592-9630　*SIC 4923*

PACIFIC NORTHERN GAS LTD　　*p315*
SUITE 2550 1066 HASTINGS ST W, VANCOUVER, BC, V6E 3X2
(604) 697-9221　*SIC 4923*

PACIFIC NORTHERN RAIL CONTRACTORS CORP　　*p497*
251 HOLLAND STREET W, BRADFORD, ON, L3Z 1H9
(905) 775-6564　*SIC 4923*

PLAINS MIDSTREAM CANADA ULC　*p860*
1182 PLANK RD, SARNIA, ON, N7T 7H9
(519) 336-4270　*SIC 4923*

PROGAS USA INC　　*p57*
240 4 AVE SW SUITE 2400, CALGARY, AB, T2P 4H4
(403) 233-1301　*SIC 4923*

ROCKY GAS CO-OP LTD　　*p159*
4920 43 ST, ROCKY MOUNTAIN HOUSE, AB, T4T 1A5
(403) 845-2766　*SIC 4923*

SASKENERGY INCORPORATED　　*p1419*
1777 VICTORIA AVE SUITE 1000, REGINA, SK, S4P 4K5
(306) 777-9225　*SIC 4923*

TERASEN GAS LTD　　*p281*
2310 KING GEORGE BOULEVARD, SURREY, BC, V4A 5A5
(604) 536-2956　*SIC 4923*

TERASEN PIPELINES PETROLEUM　*p61*
300 5 AVE SW SUITE 2700, CALGARY, AB, T2P 5J2
(403) 514-6400　*SIC 4923*

TERASEN WESTERN REGION　　*p183*
7815 SHELLMONT ST, BURNABY, BC, V5A 4S9
SIC 4923

TERMINAL BRIGHAM INC　　*p1110*
280 RUE SAINT-CHARLES S, GRANBY, QC, J2G 7A9
(450) 378-4108　*SIC 4923*

TRANSGAS LIMITED　　*p1419*
1777 VICTORIA AVE SUITE 500, REGINA, SK, S4P 4K5
(306) 777-9500　*SIC 4923*

UNION GAS　　*p482*
9924 SPRINGER HILL RD, AYLMER, ON, N5H 2R3
(519) 765-1487　*SIC 4923*

UNION GAS　　*p565*
PO BOX 280 STN MAIN, DRYDEN, ON,

P8N 2Y8
SIC 4923

UNION GAS　　*p662*
1151 GREEN VALLEY RD, LONDON, ON, N6N 1E4
SIC 4923

UNION GAS LIMITED　　*p660*
109 COMMISSIONERS RD W, LONDON, ON, N6J 1X7
(519) 667-4100　*SIC 4923*

SIC 4924 Natural gas distribution

9180-2710 QUEBEC INC　　*p1161*
7364 BOUL HENRI-BOURASSA E, MONTREAL, QC, H1E 1P2
(514) 351-4000　*SIC 4924*

ACTIVE ENERGY CORP　　*p529*
390 BRANT ST SUITE 402, BURLINGTON, ON, L7R 4J4
(416) 238-5540　*SIC 4924*

AFFORDABLE FUELS　　*p468*
362 WILLOW ST, TRURO, NS, B2N 5A5
(902) 895-4328　*SIC 4924*

AG ENERGY CO-OPERATIVE LTD　*p602*
45 SPEEDVALE AVE E SUITE 2, GUELPH, ON, N1H 1J2
(519) 763-3026　*SIC 4924*

ALTAGAS LPG LIMITED PARTNERSHIP　*p43*
355 4 AVE SW SUITE 1700, CALGARY, AB, T2P 0J1
(403) 691-7196　*SIC 4924*

ALTAGAS NORTHWEST PROCESSING LIMITED PARTNERSHIP　　*p43*
55 4 AVE SW SUITE 1700, CALGARY, AB, T2P 0J1
(403) 691-7196　*SIC 4924*

ATCO GAS　　*p291*
115 3RD AVE W, VANCOUVER, BC, V5Y 1E6
SIC 4924

ATLANTIC SPEEDY PROPANE　　*p419*
668 MAIN ST, WOODSTOCK, NB, E7M 2C8
SIC 4924

ATLANTIC SPEEDY PROPANE　　*p467*
546 GEORGE ST, SYDNEY, NS, B1P 1K7
SIC 4924

ATLANTIC SPEEDY PROPANE　　*p471*
65A STARRS RD, YARMOUTH, NS, B5A 2T2
(902) 742-8305　*SIC 4924*

ATLANTIC WALLBOARD LIMITED PARTNERSHIP　　*p412*
30 JERVIS LANE, SAINT JOHN, NB, E2J 0A9
(506) 633-3311　*SIC 4924*

AVENIR TRADING CORP　　*p43*
808 1 ST SW SUITE 300, CALGARY, AB, T2P 1M9
(403) 237-9949　*SIC 4924*

B. C. GAS INC.　　*p216*
910 COLUMBIA ST W, KAMLOOPS, BC, V2C 1L2
SIC 4924

BEYOND ENERGY & TRADE INC　*p44*
205 5 AVE SW SUITE 1870, CALGARY, AB, T2P 2V7
(403) 531-2699　*SIC 4924*

BLACKBURN + H.P.　　*p1281*
21 RUE ROLLET, REPENTIGNY, QC, J5Y 3R3
SIC 4924

CANADIAN RENEWABLE ENERGY ACADEMY　　*p1002*
445 EDGELEY BOULEVARD, VAUGHAN, ON, L4K 4G1
(647) 832-0553　*SIC 4924*

CANADIAN UTILITIES LIMITED　　*p73*
5302 FORAND ST, CALGARY, AB, T3E 8B4
(403) 292-7500　*SIC 4924*

CANGAS SOLUTIONS INC　　*p45*
555 4 AVE SW SUITE 1250, CALGARY, AB, T2P 3E7

(403) 930-0123　*SIC 4924*

CASATI NATURAL GAS　　*p498*
7 ADRIATIC CRES, BRAMPTON, ON, L6P 1W7
(905) 460-4023　*SIC 4924*

CENTRA GAS MANITOBA INC.　　*p358*
175 NORTH FRONT DR, STEINBACH, MB, R5G 1X3
(204) 326-9805　*SIC 4924*

CENTRE FOR MARINE CNG INC　*p433*
130 SOUTHSIDE RD, ST. JOHN'S, NL, A1E 0A2
SIC 4924

CESIDIO ALTERNATE ENERGY　　*p855*
298 DEMAINE CRES, RICHMOND HILL, ON, L4C 2W5
(416) 822-6750　*SIC 4924*

COAST ENERGY CANADA INC　　*p46*
530 8 AVE SW SUITE 920, CALGARY, AB, T2P 3S8
(403) 508-6700　*SIC 4924*

COLUMBIA ENERGY INC　　*p334*
2659 DOUGLAS ST SUITE 200, VICTORIA, BC, V8T 4M3
(250) 474-3533　*SIC 4924*

COMSATEC INC　　*p532*
61 HIGH ST N, CALLANDER, ON, P0H 1H0
(705) 752-4342　*SIC 4924*

COUNTY OF TWO HILLS NATURAL GAS　　*p170*
5606 51 ST, TWO HILLS, AB, T0B 4K0
(780) 657-2800　*SIC 4924*

CRIUS ENERGY TRUST　　*p986*
100 KING ST W SUITE 3400, TORONTO, ON, M5X 1A4
(416) 644-1753　*SIC 4924*

CROSSROADS GAS CO-OP LTD　　*p137*
36060 RANGE ROAD 282, INNISFAIL, AB, T4G 1T5
(403) 227-4861　*SIC 4924*

ENBRIDGE ENERGY DISTRIBUTION INC　　*p767*
500 CONSUMERS RD, NORTH YORK, ON, M2J 1P8
(416) 492-5000　*SIC 4924*

ENBRIDGE GAS NEW BRUNSWICK INC　　*p400*
440 WILSEY RD SUITE 101, FREDERICTON, NB, E3B 7G5
(506) 444-7773　*SIC 4924*

ENERGIR INC　　*p1048*
11401 AV L.-J.-FORGET, ANJOU, QC, H1J 2Z8
(514) 356-8777　*SIC 4924*

ENERGIR INC　　*p1130*
2200 RUE DE CANNES-BRULEES, LASALLE, QC, H8N 2Z2
(514) 367-2525　*SIC 4924*

ENERGIR INC　　*p1174*
1717 RUE DU HAVRE, MONTREAL, QC, H2K 2X3
(514) 598-3444　*SIC 4924*

ENERGIR, S.E.C.　　*p1174*
1717 RUE DU HAVRE, MONTREAL, QC, H2K 2X3
(514) 598-3444　*SIC 4924*

ENERGY HEALING VANCOUVER - KIM U-MING　　*p293*
900 8TH AVE W, VANCOUVER, BC, V5Z 1E5
(604) 790-6400　*SIC 4924*

ENERGY MASTER　　*p1178*
9150 RUE MEILLEUR, MONTREAL, QC, H2N 2A5
(514) 433-6487　*SIC 4924*

ENERGY SOURCE CANADA INC　　*p605*
415 MICHENER RD, GUELPH, ON, N1K 1E8
(519) 826-0777　*SIC 4924*

ENERGY SOURCE NATURAL GAS INC　*p605*
415 MICHENER RD UNIT 1, GUELPH, ON, N1K 1E8
(519) 826-0777　*SIC 4924*

ENERGY WORKS CREATIVE HEALING

ARTS　　*p231*
23085 118 AVENUE, MAPLE RIDGE, BC, V2X 3J7
(604) 817-9956　*SIC 4924*

EXXONMOBIL　　*p459*
GD, ISAACS HARBOUR, NS, B0H 1S0
(902) 387-3000　*SIC 4924*

FEDERATION-ALBERTA GAS COOPS *p107*
9945 50 ST NW SUITE 400, EDMONTON, AB, T6A 0L4
(780) 469-3200　*SIC 4924*

FULL CIRCLE ENERGY HEALING　*p338*
994 ABBEY RD, VICTORIA, BC, V8Y 1L2
(778) 350-3260　*SIC 4924*

GAS ALBERTA INC　　*p8*
2618 HOPEWELL PLACE NE SUITE 350, CALGARY, AB, T1Y 7J7
(403) 509-2600　*SIC 4924*

GAZ METROPOLITAIN　　*p1059*
1230 BOUL MICHELE-BOHEC, BLAINVILLE, QC, J7C 5S4
(450) 419-5000　*SIC 4924*

GAZ NATUREL WESTMOUNT　　*p1223*
325 RUE SAINT-AUGUSTIN, MONTREAL, QC, H4C 2N7
(514) 564-1189　*SIC 4924*

GAZIFERE INC　　*p1105*
706 BOUL GREBER, GATINEAU, QC, J8V 3P8
(819) 771-8321　*SIC 4924*

GLOBAL PETROLEUM MARKETING INC *p50*
600 6 AVE SW SUITE 600, CALGARY, AB, T2P 0S5
(403) 237-7828　*SIC 4924*

HERITAGE GAS LIMITED　　*p446*
238 BROWNLOW AVE SUITE 200, DARTMOUTH, NS, B3B 1Y2
(902) 466-2003　*SIC 4924*

HIGHLANDS FUEL DELIVERY G.P.　*p415*
10 SYDNEY ST, SAINT JOHN, NB, E2L 5E6
(506) 202-2000　*SIC 4924*

HIGHLANDS FUEL DELIVERY G.P.　*p415*
201 CROWN ST, SAINT JOHN, NB, E2L 5E5
(506) 202-2000　*SIC 4924*

I C G PROPANE　　*p152*
9504 94 ST, PEACE RIVER, AB, T8S 1J2
SIC 4924

I C G PROPANE　　*p783*
3993 KEELE ST, NORTH YORK, ON, M3J 2X6
SIC 4924

ICG PROPANE　　*p136*
430 8 ST SW, HIGH RIVER, AB, T1V 1B9
SIC 4924

ICG PROPANE　　*p411*
63 GOLDSBORO AVE, RIVERVIEW, NB, E1B 4E9
SIC 4924

ICG PROPANE INC.　　*p204*
10117 17 ST, DAWSON CREEK, BC, V1G 4C1
SIC 4924

ICG PROPANE INC.　　*p282*
19433 96 AVE SUITE 200, SURREY, BC, V4N 4C4
SIC 4924

ICG PROPANE LTD.　　*p749*
71 BONGARD AVE, NEPEAN, ON, K2E 6V2
(613) 723-5823　*SIC 4924*

INTERNATIONAL BULK SERVICES　*p130*
21423 TOWNSHIP ROAD 554, FORT SASKATCHEWAN, AB, T8L 4A4
(780) 220-9264　*SIC 4924*

INTRA ENERGY BC INC　　*p288*
3665 KINGSWAY SUITE 300, VANCOUVER, BC, V5R 5W2
SIC 4924

INUVIK GAS LTD　　*p435*
107 MACKENZIE RD SUITE 102, INUVIK, NT, X0E 0T0
(867) 777-3422　*SIC 4924*

IRVING ENERGY SERVICES LIMITED *p415*

10 SYDNEY ST, SAINT JOHN, NB, E2L 5E6
(506) 202-2000   SIC 4924

KO ENERGY p436
4902 45 ST, YELLOWKNIFE, NT, X1A 1K5
(867) 447-3457   SIC 4924

LITTLE BOW GAS CO-OP LTD p4
108 MAIN ST, BARONS, AB, T0L 0G0
(403) 757-3888   SIC 4924

MANA ENERGY CONNECTION p239
431 MOUNTAIN HIGHWAY, NORTH VANCOUVER, BC, V7J 2L1
SIC 4924

MAURICE FOUCAULT INC p1320
260 BOUL ROLAND-GODARD, SAINT-JEROME, QC, J7Y 4P7
(450) 530-3420   SIC 4924

MOMENTIS CANADA CORP p741
6345 DIXIE RD SUITE 200, MISSISSAUGA, ON, L5T 2E6
(905) 670-4440   SIC 4924

NEW BRUNSWICK OIL BURNER TECH p408
555 EDINBURGH DR SUITE 4, MONCTON, NB, E1E 4E3
SIC 4924

NORTH PEACE GAS CO-OPERATIVE LTD p126
10908 92 AVE, FAIRVIEW, AB, T0H 1L0
(780) 835-5444   SIC 4924

O.L.E.G. ENERGY CORPORATION p915
1319 STEELES AVENUE W, TORONTO, ON, M2R 3N2
(416) 886-4798   SIC 4924

PACIFIC NORTHERN GAS (N.E.) LTD p315
1185 GEORGIA ST W SUITE 950, VANCOUVER, BC, V6E 4E6
(604) 691-5680   SIC 4924

PETROCHINA INTERNATIONAL (CANADA) TRADING LTD p56
111 5 AVE SW SUITE 1800, CALGARY, AB, T2P 3Y6
(587) 233-1200   SIC 4924

POSTE DE LIVRAISON VAUDREUIL p1395
972 AV SAINT-CHARLES, VAUDREUIL-DORION, QC, J7V 8P5
(450) 455-8325   SIC 4924

PROGAS ENTERPRISES LIMITED p57
240 4 AVE SW SUITE 2400, CALGARY, AB, T2P 4H4
(403) 233-1301   SIC 4924

PURE ENERGY REIKI p81
16 WILD HAY DR, DEVON, AB, T9G 1S4
(780) 405-7606   SIC 4924

RENEWABLE ENERGY SOLUTIONS THESSALON p903
48 FELTHAM RD, THESSALON, ON, P0R 1L0
(705) 842-6911   SIC 4924

SASKENERGY INCORPORATED p1430
408 36TH ST E, SASKATOON, SK, S7K 4J9
(306) 975-8561   SIC 4924

SIX NATIONS NATURAL GAS LIMITED PARTNERSHIP p806
1953 FOURTH LINE, OHSWEKEN, ON, N0A 1M0
(519) 445-4213   SIC 4924

SNOWSHOE MOUNTAIN RESOURCES CORP p230
GD, MACKENZIE, BC, V0J 2C0
(250) 988-1325   SIC 4924

SPECTRA ENERGY p283
4716 LAZELLE AVE SUITE 210, TERRACE, BC, V8G 1T2
SIC 4924

SPECTRA ENERGY p592
410 MOWAT AVE, FORT FRANCES, ON, P9A 1Y7
(807) 274-3924   SIC 4924

SUPERIOR PROPANE INC. p60
425 1 ST SW SUITE 1400, CALGARY, AB, T2P 3L8
SIC 4924

SWAN SOURCE p1016
47 BUTTERFIELD CRES, WHITBY, ON,

L1R 1K5
(647) 967-6723   SIC 4924

TD ENERGY TRADING INC p61
421 7 AVE SW SUITE 36, CALGARY, AB, T2P 4K9
(403) 299-8572   SIC 4924

ULTRAMAR BUSINESS & HOME ENERGY p410
335 MACNAUGHTON AVE, MONCTON, NB, E1H 2J9
(506) 855-2424   SIC 4924

VECTOR ENERGY INC p62
855 2 ST SW SUITE 1760, CALGARY, AB, T2P 4J7
(403) 265-9500   SIC 4924

WESTCOAST ENERGY INC p62
425 1 ST SW SUITE 2600, CALGARY, AB, T2P 3L8
(403) 699-1999   SIC 4924

WESTCOAST ENERGY VENTURES INC p245
4529 MELROSE ST, PORT ALBERNI, BC, V9Y 1K7
SIC 4924

WESTCOAST GREEN ENERGY SYSTEMS LTD. p265
6880 MILLER RD, RICHMOND, BC, V7B 1L3
(604) 244-0421   SIC 4924

SIC 4925 Gas production and/or distribution

ALBERNI DISTRICT CO-OPERATIVE ASSOCIATION p245
4006 JOHNSTON RD, PORT ALBERNI, BC, V9Y 5N3
(250) 724-0008   SIC 4925

ALL-CAN MEDICAL INC p734
7575 KIMBEL ST UNIT 5, MISSISSAUGA, ON, L5S 1C8
(905) 677-9410   SIC 4925

AVALANT INTERNATIONAL LTD p43
315 8 AVE SW, CALGARY, AB, T2P 4K1
SIC 4925

CALTEST ENERGY SERVICES LTD p64
602 12 AVE SW SUITE 610, CALGARY, AB, T2R 1J3
SIC 4925

CHATHAM, W. T ASSOCIATES LTD p880
83 MAPLE ST, SIMCOE, ON, N3Y 2G1
(519) 426-0379   SIC 4925

CORAL ENERGY p665
30 AVONDALE CRES, MARKHAM, ON, L3P 2K1
SIC 4925

DOUBLE G GAS SERVICES p844
962 ALLIANCE RD, PICKERING, ON, L1W 3M9
SIC 4925

EVASION STREET ENERGY LTD p12
3412 33A AVE SE, CALGARY, AB, T2B 0K4
SIC 4925

FACTOR GAS LIQUIDS INC p64
611 10 AVE SW SUITE 180, CALGARY, AB, T2R 0B2
(403) 266-8778   SIC 4925

FERUS INC p49
401 9 AVE SW SUITE 1220, CALGARY, AB, T2P 3C5
(403) 517-8777   SIC 4925

FERUS NATURAL GAS FUELS INC p49
401 9 AVE SW SUITE 1220, CALGARY, AB, T2P 3C5
(403) 517-8777   SIC 4925

FOOTHILLS INDUSTRIAL PRODUCTS p35
15-6143 4 ST SE, CALGARY, AB, T2H 2H9
(403) 255-3250   SIC 4925

FREW ENERGY LIMITED p531
1380 GRAHAMS LANE, BURLINGTON, ON, L7S 1W3
(905) 637-0033   SIC 4925

GAZ COMPRIME INTERNATIONAL p1072
1705 RTE DU NORD, BROWNSBURG-

CHATHAM, QC, J8G 1E4
(450) 533-5911   SIC 4925

IRVING OIL COMMERCIAL G.P. p415
10 SYDNEY ST, SAINT JOHN, NB, E2L 5E6
(506) 202-2000   SIC 4925

KEYERA PARTNERSHIP p52
144 4 AVE SW 2ND FL SUITE 600, CALGARY, AB, T2P 3N4
(403) 205-8414   SIC 4925

MEDICINE HAT, CITY OF p146
364 KIPLING ST SE, MEDICINE HAT, AB, T1A 1Y4
(403) 529-8190   SIC 4925

NATURAL GAS CUSTOM PIPING p1014
244 BROCK ST S, WHITBY, ON, L1N 4K1
SIC 4925

PADDLE PRAIRIE GAS CO-OP LTD p151
GD, PADDLE PRAIRIE, AB, T0H 2W0
(780) 981-2467   SIC 4925

PETRO-CANADA p747
4663 6 HWY S, MOUNT HOPE, ON, L0R 1W0
(905) 679-1445   SIC 4925

RAMESH ESSO p679
550 BUR OAK AVE, MARKHAM, ON, L6C 0C4
(905) 927-0920   SIC 4925

ROBERT TRANS GAZ ENR p1151
15 RUE GIROUX, MERCIER, QC, J6R 2P3
SIC 4925

SALMEER ENTERPRISES p104
17046 90 AVE NW, EDMONTON, AB, T5T 1L6
(780) 486-6466   SIC 4925

SPORTSMANS CORNER GAS 2002 p223
3162 10TH AVE SS 1, KEREMEOS, BC, V0X 1N1
(250) 499-7192   SIC 4925

STOODLEY BRIAN p65
1014 12 AVE SW UNIT A, CALGARY, AB, T2R 0J6
(403) 262-9402   SIC 4925

WARM WITH CORN INC p537
55 FLEMING DR UNIT 6, CAMBRIDGE, ON, N1T 2A9
(519) 624-5974   SIC 4925

SIC 4931 Electric and other services combined

CU INC p73
5302 FORAND ST SW 4TH FL, CALGARY, AB, T3E 8B4
(403) 292-7500   SIC 4931

GRAND WEST ELECTRIC LTD p16
2408 91 AVE SE, CALGARY, AB, T2C 5H2
(403) 291-2688   SIC 4931

INNERGEX INC p1144
1225 RUE SAINT-CHARLES O 10E ETAGE, LONGUEUIL, QC, J4K 0B9
(450) 928-2550   SIC 4931

INNERGEX RENEWABLE ENERGY INC p1144
1225 RUE SAINT-CHARLES O BUREAU 10, LONGUEUIL, QC, J4K 0B9
(450) 928-2550   SIC 4931

PROMARK UTILITY LOCATORS INC p31
4538 MANILLA RD SE, CALGARY, AB, T2G 4B7
(403) 243-1993   SIC 4931

SOCIETE DE COGENERATION DE ST-FELICIEN, SOCIETE EN COMMANDITE p1303
1250 RUE DE L'ENERGIE, SAINT-FELICIEN, QC, G8K 3J2
(418) 630-3800   SIC 4931

TRANSALTA GENERATION PARTNERSHIP p66
110 12 AVE SW, CALGARY, AB, T2R 0G7
(403) 267-7110   SIC 4931

SIC 4941 Water supply

AQUA 7 REGIONAL WATER COMMISSION p169
GD, THREE HILLS, AB, T0M 2A0
(403) 443-5541   SIC 4941

AQUATECH CANADIAN WATER SERVICES INC. p80
BAY 5 41070 COOK RD, COCHRANE, AB, T4C 1A1
(403) 932-4507   SIC 4941

AQUATECH SOCIETE DE GESTION DE L'EAU INC p1141
2099 BOUL FERNAND-LAFONTAINE, LONGUEUIL, QC, J4G 2J4
(450) 646-5270   SIC 4941

CORPORATION OF THE REGIONAL MUNICIPALITY OF DURHAM, THE p1013
105 CONSUMERS DR, WHITBY, ON, L1N 6A3
(905) 668-7721   SIC 4941

EPCOR UTILITIES INC p86
10423 101 ST NW SUITE 2000, EDMONTON, AB, T5H 0E8
(780) 412-3414   SIC 4941

GREATER VANCOUVER WATER DISTRICT p190
4330 KINGSWAY SUITE 505, BURNABY, BC, V5H 4G8
(604) 432-6200   SIC 4941

HALIFAX REGIONAL WATER COMMISSION p458
450 COWIE HILL RD, HALIFAX, NS, B3P 2V3
(902) 490-4840   SIC 4941

ICONIX WATERWORKS LIMITED PARTNERSHIP p255
1128 BURDETTE ST, RICHMOND, BC, V6V 2Z3
(604) 273-4987   SIC 4941

LOU ROMANO WATER RECLAMATION PLANT p1025
4155 OJIBWAY PKY, WINDSOR, ON, N9C 4A5
(519) 253-7217   SIC 4941

ONTARIO CLEAN WATER AGENCY p943
1 YONGE ST SUITE 1700, TORONTO, ON, M5E 1E5
(416) 314-5600   SIC 4941

PETERBOROUGH UTILITIES SERVICES INC p842
1867 ASHBURNHAM DR, PETERBOROUGH, ON, K9L 1P8
(705) 748-9300   SIC 4941

SASKATCHEWAN WATER CORPORATION p1411
111 FAIRFORD ST E SUITE 400, MOOSE JAW, SK, S6H 7X9
(306) 694-3098   SIC 4941

SASKWATER p1411
111 FAIRFORD ST E SUITE 200, MOOSE JAW, SK, S6H 1C8
SIC 4941

VEOLIA WATER CANADA, INC p757
150 PONY DR UNIT 2, NEWMARKET, ON, L3Y 7B6
(905) 868-9683   SIC 4941

WATER SECURITY AGENCY p1411
111 FAIRFORD ST E SUITE 400, MOOSE JAW, SK, S6H 7X9
(306) 694-3900   SIC 4941

WATERPLAY SOLUTIONS CORP p223
1451 ELLIS ST UNIT B, KELOWNA, BC, V1Y 2A3
(250) 712-3393   SIC 4941

SIC 4953 Refuse systems

1416720 ONTARIO LIMITED p570
260 NEW TORONTO ST, ETOBICOKE, ON, M8V 2E8
(416) 243-7000   SIC 4953

ABSOLUTE PALLET & CRATE INC p884
104 DUNKIRK RD, ST CATHARINES, ON,

L2P 3H5
SIC 4953
AEVITAS INC *p482*
75 WANLESS CRT, AYR, ON, N0B 1E0
(519) 740-1333   *SIC* 4953
ALBERTA BEVERAGE CONTAINER RECY-CLING CORPORATION *p20*
901 57 AVE NE, CALGARY, AB, T2E 8X9
(403) 264-0170   *SIC* 4953
ALBERTA ENVIRONMENTAL RUBBER PRODUCTS INC *p104*
13520 170 ST NW, EDMONTON, AB, T5V 1M7
(780) 447-1994   *SIC* 4953
ALGONQUIN POWER ENERGY FROM WASTE INC *p501*
7656 BRAMALEA RD, BRAMPTON, ON, L6T 5M5
(905) 791-2777   *SIC* 4953
ALLIANCE ENVIRONMENTAL & ABATE-MENT CONTRACTORS INC *p876*
589 MIDDLEFIELD RD UNIT 14, SCAR-BOROUGH, ON, M1V 4Y6
(416) 298-4500   *SIC* 4953
AMERICAN IRON & METAL LP *p609*
75 STEEL CITY CRT, HAMILTON, ON, L8H 3Y2
(905) 547-5533   *SIC* 4953
AMHERST, TOWN OF *p438*
98 VICTORIA ST E, AMHERST, NS, B4H 1X6
(902) 667-7743   *SIC* 4953
AQUATERA UTILITIES INC *p131*
11101 104 AVE, GRANDE PRAIRIE, AB, T8V 8H6
(780) 532-9725   *SIC* 4953
ASDR CANADA INC *p1390*
1462 RUE DE LA QUEBECOISE, VAL-D'OR, QC, J9P 5H4
(819) 757-3039   *SIC* 4953
ATELIERS ACTIBEC 2000 INC, LES *p1112*
508 GRANDE ALLEE O, GRANDE-RIVIERE-OUEST, QC, G0C 1W0
(418) 385-1414   *SIC* 4953
BLUE MOUNTAIN PLASTICS INC *p880*
400 SECOND LINE, SHELBURNE, ON, L0N 1S5
(519) 925-3550   *SIC* 4953
BLUEWATER RECYCLING ASSOCIATION *p621*
415 CANADA AVE, HURON PARK, ON, N0M 1Y0
(519) 228-6678   *SIC* 4953
BOUFFARD SANITAIRE INC *p1150*
75 RUE SAVARD, MATANE, QC, G4W 0H9
(418) 562-5116   *SIC* 4953
CALGARY AGGREGATE RECYCLING LTD *p14*
6020 94 AVE SE, CALGARY, AB, T2C 3Z3
(403) 279-8330   *SIC* 4953
CAMPOR ENVIRONNEMENT INC *p1286*
98 RUE DES EQUIPEMENTS, RIVIERE-DU-LOUP, QC, G5R 5W9
(418) 867-8577   *SIC* 4953
CANADA FIBERS LTD *p782*
35 VANLEY CRES SUITE 500, NORTH YORK, ON, M3J 2B7
SIC 4953
CANADIAN LIQUIDS PROCESSORS LIMITED *p610*
15 BIGGAR AVE, HAMILTON, ON, L8L 3Z3
(888) 312-1000   *SIC* 4953
CASCADES CANADA ULC *p235*
800 MAUGHAN RD, NANAIMO, BC, V9X 1J2
(250) 722-3396   *SIC* 4953
CASCADES CANADA ULC *p515*
434 HENRY ST, BRANTFORD, ON, N3S 7W1
(519) 756-5264   *SIC* 4953
CASCADES CANADA ULC *p1126*
63 BOUL SAINT-JOSEPH, LACHINE, QC, H8S 2K9
(514) 595-2870   *SIC* 4953

CERTEX-CENTRE DE RECUPERATION ET DE RECYCLAGE DU TEXTILE INC *p1307*
7500 GRANDE ALLEE, SAINT-HUBERT, QC, J3Y 0V7
(450) 926-1733   *SIC* 4953
CLEAN HARBORS CANADA INC *p563*
4090 TELFER RD, CORUNNA, ON, N0N 1G0
(519) 864-1021   *SIC* 4953
CLEANRIVER RECYCLING SOLUTIONS INC *p480*
189 EARL STEWART DR UNIT 1, AURORA, ON, L4G 6V5
(905) 717-4984   *SIC* 4953
COMPAGNIE DE RECYCLAGE DE PAPIERS MD INC, LA *p1076*
235 BOUL INDUSTRIEL, CHATEAUGUAY, QC, J6J 4Z2
(450) 699-3425   *SIC* 4953
COVANTA SOLUTIONS ENVIRONNEMEN-TALES INC *p1074*
7860 RUE SAMUEL-HATT, CHAMBLY, QC, J3L 6W4
(450) 447-1212   *SIC* 4953
CROWN SHRED & RECYCLING INC *p1415*
225 E 6TH AVE, REGINA, SK, S4N 6A6
(306) 545-5454   *SIC* 4953
DARLING INTERNATIONAL CANADA INC *p468*
169 LOWER TRURO RD, TRURO, NS, B2N 5C1
(902) 895-2801   *SIC* 4953
DARLING INTERNATIONAL CANADA INC *p535*
485 PINEBUSH RD, CAMBRIDGE, ON, N1T 0A6
(519) 780-3342   *SIC* 4953
DARLING INTERNATIONAL CANADA INC *p566*
880 5 HWY W, DUNDAS, ON, L9H 5E2
(905) 628-2258   *SIC* 4953
DARLING INTERNATIONAL CANADA INC *p745*
8406 WELLINGTON COUNTY RR, MOOREFIELD, ON, N0G 2K0
(519) 638-3081   *SIC* 4953
DARLING INTERNATIONAL CANADA INC *p1356*
605 1RE AV, SAINTE-CATHERINE, QC, J5C 1C5
(450) 632-3250   *SIC* 4953
DETOX ENVIRONMENTAL LTD *p496*
322 BENNETT RD, BOWMANVILLE, ON, L1C 3Z2
(905) 623-1367   *SIC* 4953
DEUCE DISPOSAL LTD *p163*
240 BALSOM RD NE, SLAVE LAKE, AB, T0G 2A0
(780) 849-3334   *SIC* 4953
DIVERSIFIED ROYALTY CORP *p303*
510 BURRARD ST SUITE 902, VANCOU-VER, BC, V6C 3A8
(604) 235-3146   *SIC* 4953
DIVISION 2 CONTRACTING LTD *p274*
10553 120 ST, SURREY, BC, V3V 4G4
(604) 589-4663   *SIC* 4953
DRAIN-ALL LTD *p815*
1611 LIVERPOOL CRT, OTTAWA, ON, K1B 4L1
(613) 739-1070   *SIC* 4953
E-CYCLE SOLUTIONS INC *p685*
7510 BREN RD, MISSISSAUGA, ON, L4T 4H1
(905) 671-2900   *SIC* 4953
EBI ENVIRONNEMENT INC *p1057*
670 RUE DE MONTCALM, BERTHIERVILLE, QC, J0K 1A0
(450) 836-8111   *SIC* 4953
ELECTRONIC RECYCLING ASSOCIATION OF ALBERTA, THE *p29*
1301 34 AVE SE, CALGARY, AB, T2G 1V8
(403) 262-4488   *SIC* 4953
EMTERRA ENVIRONMENTAL *p694*
1611 BRITANNIA ROAD E, MISSISSAUGA,

ON, L4W 1S5
(289) 562-0091   *SIC* 4953
ENCORP PACIFIC (CANADA) *p188*
4259 CANADA WAY SUITE 100, BURNABY, BC, V5G 4Y2
(604) 473-2400   *SIC* 4953
ENVIROPLAST INC *p1048*
11060 BOUL PARKWAY, ANJOU, QC, H1J 1R6
(514) 352-6060   *SIC* 4953
ESSEX WINDSOR SOLID WASTE AUTHOR-ITY *p570*
360 FAIRVIEW AVE W SUITE 211, ESSEX, ON, N8M 3G4
(519) 776-6441   *SIC* 4953
EVER GREEN ECOLOGICAL SERVICES INC *p100*
20204 113 AVE NW, EDMONTON, AB, T5S 0G3
(780) 239-9419   *SIC* 4953
EVER GREEN ECOLOGICAL SERVICES INC *p109*
6105 76 AVE NW, EDMONTON, AB, T6B 0A7
(780) 417-2282   *SIC* 4953
EVERGREEN INDUSTRIES LTD *p340*
1045 DUNFORD AVE, VICTORIA, BC, V9B 2S4
(250) 474-5145   *SIC* 4953
FCM RECYCLING INC *p1134*
91 CH BOISJOLY, LAVALTRIE, QC, J5T 3L7
(450) 586-5185   *SIC* 4953
FERO WASTE & RECYCLING INC *p408*
203 DESBRISAY AVE, MONCTON, NB, E1E 0G7
(506) 855-3376   *SIC* 4953
FREDERICTON REGION SOLID WASTE COMMISSION *p401*
1775 WILSEY RD, FREDERICTON, NB, E3B 7K4
(506) 453-9930   *SIC* 4953
GEEP ALBERTA INC *p124*
250 AURUM RD NE SUITE 700, EDMON-TON, AB, T6S 1G9
(780) 475-6545   *SIC* 4953
GEEP CANADA INC *p487*
220 JOHN ST, BARRIE, ON, L4N 2L2
(705) 725-1919   *SIC* 4953
GFL ENVIRONMENTAL INC *p1002*
100 NEW PARK PL SUITE 500, VAUGHAN, ON, L4K 0H9
(905) 326-0101   *SIC* 4953
GREATER VANCOUVER REGIONAL DIS-TRICT *p206*
1299 DERWENT WAY, DELTA, BC, V3M 5V9
(604) 525-5681   *SIC* 4953
GREEN CIRCLE SALONS INC *p980*
401 RICHMOND ST W SUITE 371, TORONTO, ON, M5V 3A8
(647) 341-6812   *SIC* 4953
GREENISLE ENVIRONMENTAL INC *p1040*
7 SUPERIOR CRES, CHARLOTTETOWN, PE, C1E 2A1
(902) 892-1333   *SIC* 4953
GREENTEC INTERNATIONAL INC *p533*
95 STRUCK CRT, CAMBRIDGE, ON, N1R 8L2
(519) 624-3300   *SIC* 4953
H.R.D.A. ENTERPRISES LIMITED *p456*
7071 BAYERS RD SUITE 5009, HALIFAX, NS, B3L 2C2
(902) 454-2851   *SIC* 4953
HALTON RECYCLING LTD *p381*
1029 HENRY AVE, WINNIPEG, MB, R3E 1V6
(204) 772-0770   *SIC* 4953
HALTON RECYCLING LTD *p526*
1122 PIONEER RD SUITE 1, BURLING-TON, ON, L7M 1K4
(905) 336-9084   *SIC* 4953
HANNA PAPER FIBRES LIMITED *p680*
70 ADDISCOTT CRT, MARKHAM, ON, L6G 1A6

(905) 475-9844   *SIC* 4953
HARVEY, AUREL & FILS INC *p1122*
555 RUE SAINT-ETIENNE, LA MALBAIE, QC, G5A 1J3
(418) 665-4461   *SIC* 4953
HEBERT'S RECYCLING INC *p405*
53 WALSH AVE, MIRAMICHI, NB, E1N 3A5
(506) 773-1880   *SIC* 4953
HEMATITE MANUFACTURING INC *p516*
46 PLANT FARM BLVD, BRANTFORD, ON, N3S 7W3
(519) 752-8402   *SIC* 4953
HGC MANAGEMENT INC *p517*
50 SHAVER ST, BRANTFORD, ON, N3T 5M1
(519) 754-4732   *SIC* 4953
INLAND AND MARINE SALVAGE LIMITED *p902*
4408 YORK RD SUITE 32, SUTTON WEST, ON, L0E 1R0
(905) 473-2600   *SIC* 4953
INTERNATIONAL MARINE SALVAGE INC *p846*
17 INVERTOSE DR, PORT COLBORNE, ON, L3K 5V5
(905) 835-1203   *SIC* 4953
J & F WASTE SYSTEMS INC *p474*
610 FINLEY AVE, AJAX, ON, L1S 2E3
(905) 427-8064   *SIC* 4953
KASH VENTURES LTD *p101*
11403 199 ST NW, EDMONTON, AB, T5S 2C6
(780) 428-3867   *SIC* 4953
KBL ENVIRONMENTAL LTD *p436*
17 CAMERON RD, YELLOWKNIFE, NT, X1A 0E8
(867) 873-5263   *SIC* 4953
KITNUNA PROJECTS INC *p472*
10 OMILIK ST, CAMBRIDGE BAY, NU, X0B 0C0
(867) 983-7500   *SIC* 4953
LIBERTY TIRE RECYCLING CANADA LTD *p168*
57425 RGE RD 253, STURGEON COUNTY, AB, T0G 1L1
(780) 961-2090   *SIC* 4953
LIBERTY TIRE RECYCLING CANADA LTD *p516*
300 HENRY ST, BRANTFORD, ON, N3S 7R5
(519) 752-7696   *SIC* 4953
LOOP INDUSTRIES, INC *p1381*
480 RUE FERNAND-POITRAS, TERRE-BONNE, QC, J6Y 1Y4
(450) 951-8555   *SIC* 4953
LORAAS DISPOSAL SERVICES LTD *p1428*
805 47TH ST E, SASKATOON, SK, S7K 8G7
(306) 242-2300   *SIC* 4953
MAPLE LEAF DISPOSAL LTD *p228*
20380 LANGLEY BYPASS, LANGLEY, BC, V3A 5E7
(604) 533-4993   *SIC* 4953
MERLIN PLASTICS ALBERTA INC *p36*
616 58 AVE SE, CALGARY, AB, T2H 0P8
(403) 259-6637   *SIC* 4953
METRO WASTE RECYCLING INC *p816*
2811 SHEFFIELD RD, OTTAWA, ON, K1B 3V8
(613) 742-1222   *SIC* 4953
METROBEC INC *p1308*
5055 RUE RAMSAY, SAINT-HUBERT, QC, J3Y 2S3
(450) 656-6666   *SIC* 4953
MILL LANE ENTERPRISES *p433*
807 WATER ST, ST. JOHN'S, NL, A1E 1C4
SIC 4953
MILLER ENVIRONMENTAL CORPORATION *p369*
1803 HEKLA AVE, WINNIPEG, MB, R2R 0K3
(204) 925-9600   *SIC* 4953
MILLER PAVING LIMITED *p816*
1815 BANTREE ST, OTTAWA, ON, K1B 4L6

(613) 749-2222   *SIC* 4953
MILLER WASTE SYSTEMS INC   *p395*
2276 ROUTE 128, BERRY MILLS, NB, E1G
4K4
(506) 855-9783   *SIC* 4953
MILLER WASTE SYSTEMS INC   *p672*
8050 WOODBINE AVE, MARKHAM, ON,
L3R 2N8
(905) 475-6356   *SIC* 4953
MULTI RECYCLAGE S.D. INC   *p1342*
140 RUE SAULNIER, SAINT-LAURENT, QC,
H7M 1S8
(450) 975-9952   *SIC* 4953
NEXCYCLE CANADA LTD   *p505*
235 WILKINSON RD, BRAMPTON, ON, L6T
4M2
(905) 454-2666   *SIC* 4953
NEXCYCLE PLASTICS INC   *p505*
235 WILKINSON RD, BRAMPTON, ON, L6T
4M2
(905) 454-2666   *SIC* 4953
NEXCYCLE PLASTICS INC   *p505*
235 WILKINSON RD, BRAMPTON, ON, L6T
4M2
(905) 454-2666   *SIC* 4953
NIAGARA EMPLOYMENT AGENCY INC
p760
4935 KENT AVE, NIAGARA FALLS, ON,
L2H 1J5
(905) 356-4141   *SIC* 4953
NORTHWEST WASTE SYSTEMS INC   *p272*
19500 56 AVE, SURREY, BC, V3S 6K4
(604) 539-1900   *SIC* 4953
P. G. DISPOSAL SERVICE LTD   *p921*
9 DIBBLE ST SUITE 1, TORONTO, ON,
M4M 2E7
(416) 467-8717   *SIC* 4953
P.E.T. PROCESSING INC   *p206*
917 CLIVEDEN AVE UNIT 105, DELTA, BC,
V3M 5R6
(604) 522-6727   *SIC* 4953
PLASTREC INC   *p1115*
1461 RUE LEPINE, JOLIETTE, QC, J6E
4B7
(450) 760-3830   *SIC* 4953
PWS ONTARIO LTD   *p793*
155 FENMAR DR, NORTH YORK, ON, M9L
1M7
(416) 665-8377   *SIC* 4953
RAM IRON & METAL INC   *p784*
60 ASHWARREN RD, NORTH YORK, ON,
M3J 1Z5
(416) 630-4545   *SIC* 4953
RAW MATERIALS COMPANY INC   *p847*
17 INVERTOSE DR, PORT COLBORNE,
ON, L3K 5V5
(905) 835-1203   *SIC* 4953
RAYAN INVESTMENTS LTD   *p409*
1635 BERRY MILLS RD, MONCTON, NB,
E1E 4R7
(506) 858-1600   *SIC* 4953
**RBDS RUBBISH BOYS DISPOSAL SER-
VICE INC**   *p289*
887 GREAT NORTHERN WAY SUITE 301,
VANCOUVER, BC, V5T 4T5
(604) 731-5782   *SIC* 4953
REBUTS SOLIDES CANADIENS INC *p1215*
1635 RUE SHERBROOKE O BUREAU 300,
MONTREAL, QC, H3H 1E2
(514) 987-5151   *SIC* 4953
**RECUPERACTION CENTRE DU QUEBEC
INC**   *p1097*
5620 RUE SAINT-ROCH S, DRUM-
MONDVILLE, QC, J2B 6V4
(819) 477-1312   *SIC* 4953
RECUPERATION FRONTENAC INC *p1383*
217 RUE MONFETTE O, THETFORD
MINES, QC, G6G 7Y3
(418) 338-8551   *SIC* 4953
**RECUPERATION MAURICIE, SOCIETE EN
NOM COLLECTIF**   *p1300*
400 BOUL LA GABELLE BUREAU 23,
SAINT-ETIENNE-DES-GRES, QC, G0X 2P0
(819) 372-5125   *SIC* 4953

RECYCAN INC   *p1054*
20500 AV CLARK-GRAHAM, BAIE-
D'URFE, QC, H9X 4B6
(514) 457-0322   *SIC* 4953
RECYCAN INC   *p1330*
3555 RUE ASHBY, SAINT-LAURENT, QC,
H4R 2K3
(514) 379-1006   *SIC* 4953
REGENS DISPOSAL LTD   *p1406*
500 BOURQUIN RD, ESTEVAN, SK, S4A
2H8
(306) 634-7209   *SIC* 4953
REMPLE DISPOSAL INC   *p178*
35321 DELAIR RD, ABBOTSFORD, BC,
V3G 2C8
(604) 866-9020   *SIC* 4953
**RESOURCE RECOVERY FUND BOARD, IN-
CORPORATED**   *p469*
35 COMMERCIAL ST SUITE 400, TRURO,
NS, B2N 3H9
(902) 895-7732   *SIC* 4953
REVITAL POLYMERS INC   *p858*
1271 LOUGAR AVE, SARNIA, ON, N7S 5N5
(519) 332-0430   *SIC* 4953
**REVOLUTION ENVIRONMENTAL SOLU-
TIONS ACQUISITION GP INC**   *p524*
1100 BURLOAK DR UNIT 500, BURLING-
TON, ON, L7L 6B2
(800) 263-8602   *SIC* 4953
**REVOLUTION ENVIRONMENTAL SOLU-
TIONS LP**   *p524*
1100 BURLOAK DR SUITE 500, BURLING-
TON, ON, L7L 6B2
(905) 315-6300   *SIC* 4953
RICHMOND STEEL RECYCLING LIMITED
p256
11760 MITCHELL RD, RICHMOND, BC,
V6V 1V8
(604) 324-4656   *SIC* 4953
RIDGE MEADOWS RECYCLING SOCIETY
p231
10092 236 ST, MAPLE RIDGE, BC, V2X
7G2
(604) 463-5545   *SIC* 4953
RPM ENVIRONNEMENT LTEE   *p1060*
100 RUE MARIUS-WARNET, BLAINVILLE,
QC, J7C 5P9
(450) 435-0777   *SIC* 4953
S W C RECYCLING   *p401*
760 WILSEY RD, FREDERICTON, NB, E3B
7K4
(506) 453-9931   *SIC* 4953
SANI-ECO INC   *p1109*
530 RUE EDOUARD, GRANBY, QC, J2G
3Z6
(450) 777-4977   *SIC* 4953
SANIMAX ABP INC   *p1161*
9900 6E RUE, MONTREAL, QC, H1C 1G2
(514) 643-3391   *SIC* 4953
SANIMAX LTD   *p604*
5068 WHITELAW RD SUITE 6, GUELPH,
ON, N1H 6J3
(519) 824-2381   *SIC* 4953
**SASKATCHEWAN ASSOCIATION OF RE-
HABILITATION CENTRES**   *p1432*
111 CARDINAL CRES, SASKATOON, SK,
S7L 6H5
(306) 933-0616   *SIC* 4953
SASKATOON, CITY OF   *p1433*
1030 AVENUE H S, SASKATOON, SK, S7M
1X5
(306) 975-2534   *SIC* 4953
SCOTIA RECYCLING (NL) LIMITED   *p429*
55 ELIZABETH AVE STE 49, ST. JOHN'S,
NL, A1A 1W9
(709) 579-7466   *SIC* 4953
**SERVICES DE RECYCLAGE GLOBE
METAL, GMR INC**   *p1356*
1545 1RE AV, SAINTE-CATHERINE, QC,
J5C 1C5
(450) 635-9397   *SIC* 4953
SERVICES RICOVA INC   *p1309*
5000 RUE ARMAND-FRAPPIER, SAINT-
HUBERT, QC, J3Z 1G5

(450) 466-6688   *SIC* 4953
SERVICES SANITAIRES MAJ INC   *p1077*
225 AV DU PROGRES, CHERTSEY, QC,
J0K 3K0
(450) 882-9186   *SIC* 4953
SHELDRICK, J. W. SANITATION LTD   *p882*
4278 LONDON RD, SMITHVILLE, ON, L0R
2A0
(905) 957-3165   *SIC* 4953
SHIFT RECYCLING INC   *p793*
700 ORMONT DR, NORTH YORK, ON, M9L
2V4
(416) 995-4202   *SIC* 4953
SLM-LOGISTICS CORPORATION   *p506*
15 BRAMALEA RD SUITE 101, BRAMP-
TON, ON, L6T 2W4
(416) 743-8866   *SIC* 4953
SMITHRITE DISPOSAL LTD   *p202*
70 GOLDEN DR, COQUITLAM, BC, V3K
6B5
(604) 529-4030   *SIC* 4953
SOCIETE VIA ENVIRONNEMENT   *p1139*
1200 RUE DES RIVEURS, LEVIS, QC, G6Y
9G2
(418) 833-0421   *SIC* 4953
SOUTHERN SANITATION INC   *p790*
161 BRIDGELAND AVE, NORTH YORK,
ON, M6A 1Z1
(416) 787-5000   *SIC* 4953
STABLEX CANADA INC   *p1060*
760 BOUL INDUSTRIEL, BLAINVILLE, QC,
J7C 3V4
(450) 430-9230   *SIC* 4953
STERICYCLE ULC   *p506*
95 DEERHURST DR SUITE 1, BRAMP-
TON, ON, L6T 5R7
(905) 789-6660   *SIC* 4953
STERICYCLE ULC   *p506*
19 ARMTHORPE RD, BRAMPTON, ON,
L6T 5M4
(905) 595-2651   *SIC* 4953
SUEZ CANADA WASTE SERIVCES INC
p117
9426 51 AVE NW SUITE 307, EDMONTON,
AB, T6E 5A6
(780) 989-5212   *SIC* 4953
SUEZ CANADA WASTE SERIVCES INC
p168
10000 CHRYSTINA LAKE RD, SWAN
HILLS, AB, T0G 2C0
(780) 333-4197   *SIC* 4953
SUMAS ENVIRONMENTAL SERVICES INC
p193
4623 BYRNE RD, BURNABY, BC, V5J 3H6
(604) 682-6678   *SIC* 4953
SUPERIOR SANITATION SERVICES LTD
p1041
7 SUPERIOR CRES, CHARLOTTETOWN,
PE, C1E 2A1
(902) 892-1333   *SIC* 4953
TERRATEC ENVIRONMENTAL LTD   *p610*
200 EASTPORT BLVD, HAMILTON, ON,
L8H 7S4
(905) 544-0444   *SIC* 4953
THOMSON METALS AND DISPOSAL LP
p525
961 ZELCO DR, BURLINGTON, ON, L7L
4Y2
(905) 681-8832   *SIC* 4953
TIRU (CANADA) INC   *p1257*
1210 BOUL MONTMORENCY, QUEBEC,
QC, G1J 3V9
(418) 648-8818   *SIC* 4953
**TRANS CONTINENTAL TEXTILE RECY-
CLING LTD**   *p278*
13120 78A AVE, SURREY, BC, V3W 1P4
(604) 592-2845   *SIC* 4953
TRANSPORT M. J. LAVOIE INC   *p1351*
800 RUE NOTRE-DAME, SAINT-REMI, QC,
J0L 2L0
(450) 454-5333   *SIC* 4953
TRANSPORT ROLLEX LTEE   *p1393*
910 BOUL LIONEL-BOULET, VARENNES,
QC, J3X 1P7

(450) 652-4282   *SIC* 4953
TRY RECYCLING INC   *p564*
11110 LONGWOODS RD, DELAWARE,
ON, N0L 1E0
(519) 858-2199   *SIC* 4953
U-PAK DISPOSALS (1989) LTD   *p589*
15 TIDEMORE AVE, ETOBICOKE, ON,
M9W 7E9
(416) 675-3700   *SIC* 4953
URBAN IMPACT RECYCLING LTD   *p257*
15360 KNOX WAY, RICHMOND, BC, V6V
3A6
(604) 273-0089   *SIC* 4953
**VEOLIA ES CANADA SERVICES INDUS-
TRIELS INC**   *p1248*
1705 3E AV, POINTE-AUX-TREMBLES, QC,
H1B 5M9
(514) 645-1621   *SIC* 4953
**VEOLIA ES CANADA SERVICES INDUS-
TRIELS INC**   *p1310*
7950 AV PION, SAINT-HYACINTHE, QC,
J2R 1R9
(450) 796-6060   *SIC* 4953
VERSATECH INDUSTRIES INC   *p385*
500 MADISON ST, WINNIPEG, MB, R3H
0L4
(204) 956-9700   *SIC* 4953
VILLE DE LAVAL   *p1237*
2550 BOUL INDUSTRIEL, MONTREAL,
QC, H7S 2G7
(450) 662-4600   *SIC* 4953
WASTE CONNECTIONS OF CANADA INC
p160
285122 BLUEGRASS DR, ROCKY VIEW
COUNTY, AB, T1X 0P5
(403) 236-3883   *SIC* 4953
WASTE CONNECTIONS OF CANADA INC
p176
34321 INDUSTRIAL WAY, ABBOTSFORD,
BC, V2S 7M6
(604) 517-2617   *SIC* 4953
WASTE CONNECTIONS OF CANADA INC
p497
580 ECCLESTONE DR, BRACEBRIDGE,
ON, P1L 1R2
(705) 645-4453   *SIC* 4953
WASTE CONNECTIONS OF CANADA INC
p561
610 APPLEWOOD CRES, CONCORD, ON,
L4K 0E3
(905) 532-7510   *SIC* 4953
WASTE CONNECTIONS OF CANADA INC
p595
1152 KENASTON ST, GLOUCESTER, ON,
K1B 3P5
(613) 749-8000   *SIC* 4953
WASTE CONNECTIONS OF CANADA INC
p1062
4141 BOUL DE LA GRANDE-ALLEE, BOIS-
BRIAND, QC, J7H 1M7
(450) 435-2627   *SIC* 4953
WASTE CONNECTIONS, INC   *p1003*
610 APPLEWOOD CRES, VAUGHAN, ON,
L4K 0C3
(905) 532-7510   *SIC* 4953
**WASTE MANAGEMENT OF CANADA COR-
PORATION**   *p13*
4668 25 ST SE, CALGARY, AB, T2B 3M2
SIC 4953
**WASTE MANAGEMENT OF CANADA COR-
PORATION**   *p223*
350 BEAVER LAKE RD, KELOWNA, BC,
V4V 1S5
(250) 766-9100   *SIC* 4953
**WASTE MANAGEMENT OF CANADA COR-
PORATION**   *p507*
117 WENTWORTH CRT, BRAMPTON, ON,
L6T 5L4
(905) 595-3360   *SIC* 4953
**WASTE MANAGEMENT OF CANADA COR-
PORATION**   *p541*
254 WESTBROOK RD, CARP, ON, K0A 1L0
(613) 831-1281   *SIC* 4953
WASTE MANAGEMENT OF CANADA COR-

PORATION p561
550 BOWES RD, CONCORD, ON, L4K 1K2
(905) 669-7196   *SIC 4953*
WASTE MANAGEMENT OF CANADA CORPORATION p884
124 CUSHMAN RD, ST CATHARINES, ON, L2M 6T6
(905) 687-9605   *SIC 4953*
WASTE MANAGEMENT OF CANADA CORPORATION p1008
219 LABRADOR DR SUITE 100, WATERLOO, ON, N2K 4M8
(519) 886-3974   *SIC 4953*
WASTE MANAGEMENT OF CANADA CORPORATION p1011
645 CONRAD PL, WATERLOO, ON, N2V 1C4
(519) 886-6932   *SIC 4953*
WASTE-NOT RECYCLING AND DISPOSAL INC p264
12171 HORSESHOE WAY, RICHMOND, BC, V7A 4V4
(604) 273-0089   *SIC 4953*
WESTMORLAND-ALBERT SOLID WASTE CORPORATION p395
2024 ROUTE 128, BERRY MILLS, NB, E1G 4K6
(506) 877-1050   *SIC 4953*
WM QUEBEC INC p1051
9501 BOUL RAY-LAWSON BUREAU 114, ANJOU, QC, H1J 1L4
(514) 352-1596   *SIC 4953*
WM QUEBEC INC p1146
2457 CH DU LAC, LONGUEUIL, QC, J4N 1P1
(450) 646-7870   *SIC 4953*
YORK DISPOSAL SERVICE LIMITED p561
650 CREDITSTONE RD, CONCORD, ON, L4K 5C8
(905) 669-1900   *SIC 4953*

SIC 4959 Sanitary services, nec

ATLAS POWER SWEEPING LTD p183
2796 NORLAND AVE, BURNABY, BC, V5B 3A6
(604) 294-6333   *SIC 4959*
BEARSTONE ENVIRONMENTAL SOLUTIONS INC p44
435 4 AVE SW SUITE 500, CALGARY, AB, T2P 3A8
(403) 984-9798   *SIC 4959*
CICCARELLI, OTTAVIO & SON CONTRACTING LTD p477
807 GARNER RD E SUITE 1, ANCASTER, ON, L9G 3K9
(905) 648-5178   *SIC 4959*
CORPORATION OF THE CITY OF WINDSOR p1019
3540 NORTH SERVICE RD E, WINDSOR, ON, N8W 5X2
(519) 974-2277   *SIC 4959*
DP ENVIRONMENTAL SERVICE INC p512
39 SHADYWOOD RD, BRAMPTON, ON, L6Z 4M1
(905) 840-4480   *SIC 4959*
EASTERN CANADA RESPONSE CORPORATION LTD p823
275 SLATER ST SUITE 1201, OTTAWA, ON, K1P 5H9
(613) 230-7369   *SIC 4959*
EDMONDS LANDSCAPE & CONSTRUCTION SERVICES LIMITED p455
2675 CLIFTON ST, HALIFAX, NS, B3K 4V4
(902) 453-5500   *SIC 4959*
ENTREPRISES ANTONIO BARRETTE INC, LES p1254
437 RUE DES MONTEREGIENNES, QUEBEC, QC, G1C 7J7
(418) 686-6455   *SIC 4959*
ENTREPRISES L.T. LTEE, LES p1254
1209 RUE WILBROD-ROBERT, QUEBEC, QC, G1C 0L1

(418) 663-0555   *SIC 4959*
ENVIROBATE INC p458
93 SUSIE LAKE CRES, HALIFAX, NS, B3S 1C3
(902) 832-0820   *SIC 4959*
GFL ENVIRONMENTAL CORP p844
1070 TOY AVE, PICKERING, ON, L1W 3P1
(905) 428-8992   *SIC 4959*
GREEN EARTH NANO SCIENCE INC p952
181 UNIVERSITY AVE SUITE 2200, TORONTO, ON, M5H 3M7
(416) 800-0969   *SIC 4959*
LASFAM INVESTMENTS INC p193
3751 NORTH FRASER WAY SUITE 12, BURNABY, BC, V5J 5G4
(604) 327-7264   *SIC 4959*
NELSON ENVIRONMENTAL REMEDIATION LTD p2
30541 100 AVE, ACHESON, AB, T7X 6L8
(780) 960-3660   *SIC 4959*
PARADIS AMENAGEMENT URBAIN INC p1255
436 RUE DES ADIRONDACKS, QUEBEC, QC, G1C 7E8
(418) 660-4060   *SIC 4959*
PESTALTO ENVIRONMENTAL HEALTH SERVICES INC p600
400 ELIZABETH ST UNIT I, GUELPH, ON, N1E 2Y1
SIC 4959
QUANTUM MURRAY-NWDD PARTNERSHIP p256
3600 VIKING WAY SUITE 100, RICHMOND, BC, V6V 1N6
(604) 270-7388   *SIC 4959*
REVOLUTION ENVIRONMENTAL SOLUTIONS LP p524
1100 BURLOAK DR SUITE 500, BURLINGTON, ON, L7L 6B2
(800) 263-8602   *SIC 4959*
SANEXEN SERVICES ENVIRONNEMENTAUX INC p1071
9935 RUE DE CHATEAUNEUF UNITE 200, BROSSARD, QC, J4Z 3V4
(450) 466-2123   *SIC 4959*
TERRAPURE ENVIRONMENTAL LTD p525
1100 BURLOAK DR SUITE 500, BURLINGTON, ON, L7L 6B2
(800) 263-8602   *SIC 4959*
WALCO INDUSTRIES LTD p245
6113 BEAVER CREEK RD, PORT ALBERNI, BC, V9Y 8X4
(250) 723-6919   *SIC 4959*
YOUNG, PETER LIMITED p679
9693 KENNEDY RD, MARKHAM, ON, L6C 1A4
(905) 887-9122   *SIC 4959*

SIC 4961 Steam and air-conditioning supply

BARETTE BERNARD - ENERFLAMME INC p1104
37 RUE DE VALCOURT, GATINEAU, QC, J8T 8G9
(819) 243-0143   *SIC 4961*
COVANTA BURNABY RENEWABLE ENERGY, INC / ENERGIE RENOUVELABLE COVANTA BURNABY, INC p181
5150 RIVERBEND DR, BURNABY, BC, V3N 4V3
(604) 521-1025   *SIC 4961*
ENWAVE ENERGY CORPORATION p951
333 BAY ST SUITE 710, TORONTO, ON, M5H 2R2
(416) 392-6838   *SIC 4961*
J C INDOOR CLEAN AIR SERVICES INC p611
18 LINDEN ST, HAMILTON, ON, L8L 3H6
(905) 383-7855   *SIC 4961*

SIC 4971 Irrigation systems

EASTERN IRRIGATION DISTRICT p7
550 INDUSTRIAL RD W, BROOKS, AB, T0J 2A0
(403) 362-1400   *SIC 4971*
EPCOR WATER SERVICES INC p86
10423 101 ST NW SUITE 2000, EDMONTON, AB, T5H 0E8
(780) 412-3850   *SIC 4971*
MANAGEMENT SIMO INC p1142
2099 BOUL FERNAND-LAFONTAINE, LONGUEUIL, QC, J4G 2J4
(514) 281-6525   *SIC 4971*
METROPOLITAN TORONTO WATERWORKS SYSTEM p982
55 JOHN ST, TORONTO, ON, M5V 3C6
(416) 392-8211   *SIC 4971*
PUC SERVICES INC p862
765 QUEEN ST E, SAULT STE. MARIE, ON, P6A 2A8
(705) 759-6500   *SIC 4971*
ST. MARY RIVER IRRIGATION DISTRICT p141
1210 36 ST N, LETHBRIDGE, AB, T1H 5H8
(403) 380-6152   *SIC 4971*
VILLE DE MONTREAL p1161
12001 BOUL MAURICE-DUPLESSIS, MONTREAL, QC, H1C 1V3
(514) 280-4400   *SIC 4971*

SIC 5012 Automobiles and other motor vehicles

3025052 NOVA SCOTIA LIMITED p454
3363 KEMPT RD, HALIFAX, NS, B3K 4X5
(902) 453-2110   *SIC 5012*
401 AUTO DEALERS EXCHANGE p629
60 RIGNEY ST, KINGSTON, ON, K7K 6Z2
(613) 536-0401   *SIC 5012*
4488601 CANADA INC p1261
120 RUE DU MARAIS, QUEBEC, QC, G1M 3G2
(418) 683-6565   *SIC 5012*
9155-8593 QUEBEC INC p1226
5015 RUE BUCHAN, MONTREAL, QC, H4P 1S4
SIC 5012
923416 ALBERTA LTD p73
25 RICHARD WAY SW, CALGARY, AB, T3E 7M8
(403) 568-2834   *SIC 5012*
9306609 CANADA INC p511
2 BERKWOOD HOLLOW, BRAMPTON, ON, L6Y 0X6
(647) 993-1968   *SIC 5012*
ACTION TRAILER SALES INC p734
2332 DREW RD, MISSISSAUGA, ON, L5S 1B8
(905) 678-1444   *SIC 5012*
ADESA AUCTIONS CANADA CORPORATION p2
1621 VETERANS BLVD NW, AIRDRIE, AB, T4A 2G7
(403) 912-4400   *SIC 5012*
ADESA AUCTIONS CANADA CORPORATION p148
1701 9 ST, NISKU, AB, T9E 8M8
(780) 955-4400   *SIC 5012*
ADESA AUCTIONS CANADA CORPORATION p257
7111 NO. 8 RD, RICHMOND, BC, V6W 1L9
(604) 232-4403   *SIC 5012*
ADESA AUCTIONS CANADA CORPORATION p376
HWY 7 N, WINNIPEG, MB, R3C 2E6
(204) 697-4400   *SIC 5012*
ADESA AUCTIONS CANADA CORPORATION p482
55 WAYDOM DR SUITE 1, AYR, ON, N0B 1E0
(519) 622-9500   *SIC 5012*
ADESA AUCTIONS CANADA CORPORATION p500
55 AUCTION LANE 2ND FLOOR, BRAMPTON, ON, L6T 5P4

(905) 790-7653   *SIC 5012*
ADESA AUCTIONS CANADA CORPORATION p500
55 AUCTION LANE, BRAMPTON, ON, L6T 5P4
(905) 790-7653   *SIC 5012*
ADESA AUCTIONS CANADA CORPORATION p1002
1717 BURTON RD, VARS, ON, K0A 3H0
(613) 443-4400   *SIC 5012*
ADESA AUCTIONS CANADA CORPORATION p1425
37507 HWY 12, SASKATOON, SK, S7K 3J7
(306) 242-8771   *SIC 5012*
ANTRIM TRUCK CENTER LTD p478
580 WHITE LAKE RD, ARNPRIOR, ON, K7S 3G9
(613) 623-9618   *SIC 5012*
ATELIER DE MECANIQUE PREMONT INC p1266
2495 BOUL WILFRID-HAMEL, QUEBEC, QC, G1P 2H9
(418) 683-0563   *SIC 5012*
AUTO MODENA INC. p1227
3980 RUE JEAN-TALON O, MONTREAL, QC, H4P 1V6
(514) 337-7274   *SIC 5012*
BARRIE AUTO AUCTION LTD p486
434 TIFFIN ST, BARRIE, ON, L4N 9W8
(705) 725-8183   *SIC 5012*
BMW CANADA INC p856
50 ULTIMATE DR, RICHMOND HILL, ON, L4S 0C8
(905) 770-1758   *SIC 5012*
BRP INC p1392
726 RUE SAINT-JOSEPH, VALCOURT, QC, J0E 2L0
(450) 532-2211   *SIC 5012*
CALGARY PETERBILT LTD p70
11550 44 ST SE, CALGARY, AB, T2Z 4A2
(403) 235-2550   *SIC 5012*
CAMIONS FREIGHTLINER RIVIERE-DU-LOUP INC p1286
100 BOUL INDUSTRIEL, RIVIERE-DU-LOUP, QC, G5R 0K5
(418) 862-3192   *SIC 5012*
CAMIONS INTER-ANJOU INC p1047
8300 RUE EDISON, ANJOU, QC, H1J 1S8
(514) 353-9720   *SIC 5012*
CAMIONS LUSSIER-LUSSICAM INC p1358
1341 RUE PRINCIPALE, SAINTE-JULIE, QC, J3E 0C4
(450) 649-1265   *SIC 5012*
CAMIONS MASKA INC p1348
690 MONT?E MONETTE, SAINT-MATHIEU-DE-LAPRAIRIE, QC, J0L 2H0
(450) 444-5600   *SIC 5012*
CANADA WEST TRUCK CENTRE p1431
3750 IDYLWYLD DR N SUITE 107, SASKATOON, SK, S7L 6G3
(306) 934-1110   *SIC 5012*
CANADIAN KAWASAKI MOTORS INC p868
101 THERMOS RD, SCARBOROUGH, ON, M1L 4W8
(416) 445-7775   *SIC 5012*
CENTRE DU CAMION (BEAUCE) INC, LE p1305
8900 25E AV, SAINT-GEORGES, QC, G6A 1K5
(418) 228-8005   *SIC 5012*
DEELEY, FRED IMPORTS LTD. p551
830 EDGELEY BLVD, CONCORD, ON, L4K 4X1
(905) 660-3500   *SIC 5012*
DUECK CHEVROLET BUICK CADILLAC GMC LIMITED p290
400 MARINE DR SE, VANCOUVER, BC, V5X 4X2
(604) 324-7222   *SIC 5012*
EAST COAST INTERNATIONAL TRUCKS INC p410
100 URQUHART AVE, MONCTON, NB, E1H 2R5
(506) 857-2857   *SIC 5012*

ENCHERES D'AUTOMOBILES ST-PIERRE (ESP) LTEE, LES   p1126
1600 RUE NORMAN, LACHINE, QC, H8S 1A9
(514) 489-3131   SIC 5012

FCA CANADA INC   p1250
3000 RTE TRANSCANADIENNE, POINTE-CLAIRE, QC, H9R 1B1
(514) 630-2500   SIC 5012

FIRST TRUCK CENTRE INC   p281
18688 96 AVE, SURREY, BC, V4N 3P9
(604) 888-1424   SIC 5012

FORD MOTOR COMPANY OF CANADA, LIMITED   p1339
6505 RTE TRANSCANADIENNE BUREAU 200, SAINT-LAURENT, QC, H4T 1S3
(514) 744-1800   SIC 5012

G. J. BELL ENTERPISES LTD   p1427
2030 1ST AVE N, SASKATOON, SK, S7K 2A1
(306) 242-1251   SIC 5012

GENERAL MOTORS OF CANADA COMPANY   p1250
5000 RTE TRANSCANADIENNE, POINTE-CLAIRE, QC, H9R 1B6
(514) 630-6209   SIC 5012

GIN-COR INDUSTRIES INC   p763
255A FISHER ST, NORTH BAY, ON, P1B 2C8
(705) 744-5543   SIC 5012

GLASVAN TRAILERS INC   p695
1201 AIMCO BLVD SUITE 625, MISSISSAUGA, ON, L4W 1B3
(905) 625-8441   SIC 5012

GROUPE VOLVO CANADA INC   p1301
1000 BOUL INDUSTRIEL BUREAU 1160, SAINT-EUSTACHE, QC, J7R 5A5
(450) 472-6410   SIC 5012

HINO MOTORS CANADA, LTD   p723
6975 CREDITVIEW RD UNIT 2, MISSISSAUGA, ON, L5N 8E9
(905) 670-3352   SIC 5012

HONDA CANADA INC   p1065
1750 RUE EIFFEL, BOUCHERVILLE, QC, J4B 7W1
(450) 641-9062   SIC 5012

HYUNDAI AUTO CANADA CORP   p671
75 FRONTENAC DR, MARKHAM, ON, L3R 6H2
(905) 477-0202   SIC 5012

KENWORTH TORONTO LTD   p554
500 CREDITSTONE RD, CONCORD, ON, L4K 3Z3
(905) 695-0740   SIC 5012

KIA CANADA INC   p731
180 FOSTER CRES, MISSISSAUGA, ON, L5R 4J5
(905) 755-6250   SIC 5012

LAKESIDE AUTOMOTIVE GROUP LTD p362
950 REGENT AVE W, WINNIPEG, MB, R2C 3A8
(204) 667-9200   SIC 5012

LEEDS TRANSIT INC   p568
542 MAIN ST, ELGIN, ON, K0G 1E0
(613) 359-5344   SIC 5012

LEGGAT CHEVROLET BUICK GMC LTD p585
360 REXDALE BLVD, ETOBICOKE, ON, M9W 1R7
(416) 743-1810   SIC 5012

LOGAN, JOHN CHEVROLET OLDSMOBILE INC   p509
241 QUEEN ST E, BRAMPTON, ON, L6W 2B5
(905) 451-2030   SIC 5012

MACK STE-FOY INC   p1267
2550 AV WATT, QUEBEC, QC, G1P 3T4
(418) 651-9397   SIC 5012

MACKAY'S TRUCK & TRAILER CENTER LIMITED   p469
124 LOWER TRURO RD, TRURO, NS, B2N 5E8
(902) 895-0511   SIC 5012

MARLIN CHEVROLET BUICK GMC INC

p1265
2145 RUE FRANK-CARREL, QUEBEC, QC, G1N 2G2
(418) 688-1212   SIC 5012

MAZDA CANADA INC   p853
55 VOGELL RD, RICHMOND HILL, ON, L4B 3K5
(905) 787-7000   SIC 5012

MERCEDES-BENZ CANADA INC   p918
98 VANDERHOOF AVE, TORONTO, ON, M4G 4C9
(416) 425-3550   SIC 5012

MOBIS PART CANADA CORPORATION p679
10 MOBIS DR, MARKHAM, ON, L6C 0Y3
(905) 927-3350   SIC 5012

NISSAN CANADA INC   p698
5290 ORBITOR DR, MISSISSAUGA, ON, L4W 4Z5
(905) 602-0792   SIC 5012

NORTRUX INC   p102
18110 118 AVE NW, EDMONTON, AB, T5S 2G2
(780) 452-6225   SIC 5012

OBI PARTS INC   p714
350 HAZELHURST RD, MISSISSAUGA, ON, L5J 4T8
(905) 403-7800   SIC 5012

OPENLANE CANADA INC   p943
11 CHURCH ST SUITE 200, TORONTO, ON, M5E 1W1
(416) 861-1366   SIC 5012

PACCAR OF CANADA LTD   p725
6711 MISSISSAUGA RD SUITE 500, MISSISSAUGA, ON, L5N 4J8
(905) 858-7000   SIC 5012

POLARIS INDUSTRIES LTD   p366
50 PRAIRIE WAY, WINNIPEG, MB, R2J 3J8
(204) 925-7100   SIC 5012

QUICK LANE TIRE AND AUTO CENTRE p1413
2222 100TH ST, NORTH BATTLEFORD, SK, S9A 0X6
(306) 445-4495   SIC 5012

RM SOTHEBY'S   p493
1 CLASSIC CAR DR, BLENHEIM, ON, N0P 1A0
(519) 352-4575   SIC 5012

ROY, ROB TRADING & SAMCO HOLDINGS p1435
105 71ST ST W, SASKATOON, SK, S7R 1B4
(306) 931-7666   SIC 5012

SARNIA FINE CARS 2019 INC   p860
799 CONFEDERATION ST, SARNIA, ON, N7T 2E4
(519) 332-2886   SIC 5012

STERLING TRUCK & TRAILER SALES LTD p1416
762 MCDONALD ST, REGINA, SK, S4N 7M7
(306) 525-0466   SIC 5012

SUBARU CANADA, INC   p733
560 SUFFOLK CRT, MISSISSAUGA, ON, L5R 4J7
(905) 568-4959   SIC 5012

SUMMIT MOTORS LTD   p169
4801 46 AVE, TABER, AB, T1G 2A4
(403) 223-3563   SIC 5012

SUZUKI CANADA INC.   p488
360 SAUNDERS RD, BARRIE, ON, L4N 9Y2
(705) 999-8600   SIC 5012

TATRO TRUCKS LTD   p543
7744 SEVENTH LINE E, CHATHAM, ON, N7M 5J6
(519) 354-4352   SIC 5012

THUNDER BAY TRUCK CENTRE INC p910
1145 COMMERCE ST, THUNDER BAY, ON, P7E 6E8
(807) 577-5793   SIC 5012

TIREKICKER INSPECTIONS INC   p622
3230 THOMAS ST, INNISFIL, ON, L9S 3W5
(705) 436-4111   SIC 5012

TOYOTA CANADA INC   p867

1 TOYOTA PL, SCARBOROUGH, ON, M1H 1H9
(416) 438-6320   SIC 5012

TRANSIT TRAILER LIMITED   p543
22217 BLOOMFIELD RD SUITE 3, CHATHAM, ON, N7M 5J3
(519) 354-9944   SIC 5012

TYCORRA INVESTMENTS INC   p635
10 FORWELL RD, KITCHENER, ON, N2B 3E7
(519) 576-9290   SIC 5012

V T L LOCATION INC   p1347
CP 99, SAINT-LOUIS-DU-HA-HA, QC, G0L 3S0
(418) 854-7383   SIC 5012

VOLKSWAGEN GROUP CANADA INC p475
777 BAYLY ST W, AJAX, ON, L1S 7G7
(905) 428-6700   SIC 5012

VOLVO CARS OF CANADA CORP   p854
9130 LESLIE ST SUITE 101, RICHMOND HILL, ON, L4B 0B9
(905) 695-9626   SIC 5012

WARNER BUS INDUSTRIES LTD   p1416
330 E 4TH AVE, REGINA, SK, S4N 4Z6
(306) 359-1930   SIC 5012

WINNIPEG EQUIPMENT SALES LTD p370
33 OAK POINT HWY, WINNIPEG, MB, R2R 0T8
(204) 632-9100   SIC 5012

SIC 5013 Motor vehicle supplies and new parts

1551121 ONTARIO INC   p815
1427 MICHAEL ST, OTTAWA, ON, K1B 3R3
(613) 749-4858   SIC 5013

168406 CANADA INC   p1393
135 RUE DU CHEMINOT, VAUDREUIL-DORION, QC, J7V 5V5
(450) 455-9877   SIC 5013

3225537 NOVA SCOTIA LIMITED   p371
90 HUTCHINGS ST UNIT B, WINNIPEG, MB, R2X 2X1
(204) 272-2880   SIC 5013

3600106 MANITOBA INC   p381
660 WALL ST SUITE 843, WINNIPEG, MB, R3G 2T3
(204) 783-0816   SIC 5013

370071 ALBERTA LTD   p80
5609 55 ST, COLD LAKE, AB, T9M 1R6
(780) 594-4666   SIC 5013

389259 ONTARIO LIMITED   p508
236 RUTHERFORD RD S, BRAMPTON, ON, L6W 3J6
(905) 451-6470   SIC 5013

4213424 CANADA INC   p733
7885 TRANMERE DR UNIT 1, MISSISSAUGA, ON, L5S 1V8
(905) 677-7299   SIC 5013

4475470 CANADA INC   p131
12803 100 ST SUITE 100, GRANDE PRAIRIE, AB, T8V 4H3
(780) 532-4488   SIC 5013

612337 ALBERTA LTD.   p140
3042 2 AVE N, LETHBRIDGE, AB, T1H 0C6
(403) 328-9621   SIC 5013

A.P.M. LIMITED   p406
96 KING ST, MONCTON, NB, E1C 4M6
(506) 857-3838   SIC 5013

ACCESSOIRES D'AUTO LEBLANC LTEE p1387
3125 BOUL GENE-H.-KRUGER BUREAU 1624, TROIS-RIVIERES, QC, G9A 4M2
(819) 378-2871   SIC 5013

ACTION CAR AND TRUCK ACCESSORIES INC   p407
200 HORSMAN RD, MONCTON, NB, E1E 0E8
(506) 857-8786   SIC 5013

ACTIVE GEAR COMPANY OF CANADA LIMITED   p548
201R SNIDERCROFT RD SUITE 1, CONCORD, ON, L4K 2J9

(905) 669-2292   SIC 5013

ALL PARTS AUTOMOTIVE LIMITED   p582
66 RONSON DR, ETOBICOKE, ON, M9W 1B6
(416) 743-1200   SIC 5013

AMIOT, MARIUS INC   p1284
350 2E RUE E, RIMOUSKI, QC, G5L 7J4
(418) 723-1155   SIC 5013

ANSWER PRECISION TOOL INC   p636
146 OTONABEE DR, KITCHENER, ON, N2C 1L6
(519) 748-0079   SIC 5013

ASSEMBLY INTERNATIONAL INC   p1021
3233 DEVON DR, WINDSOR, ON, N8X 4L5
  SIC 5013

ATLAS TRAILER COACH PRODUCTS LTD p20
2530 21 ST NE, CALGARY, AB, T2E 7L3
(403) 291-1225   SIC 5013

ATPAC INC   p1160
10700 BOUL HENRI-BOURASSA E, MONTREAL, QC, H1C 1G9
(514) 881-8888   SIC 5013

AUTO ELECTRIC SERVICE LTD   p1420
1360 BROAD ST, REGINA, SK, S4R 1Y5
(306) 525-2551   SIC 5013

AUTO MACHINERY AND GENERAL SUPPLY COMPANY, LIMITED   p400
50 WHITING RD, FREDERICTON, NB, E3B 5V5
(506) 453-1600   SIC 5013

AUTO PARTS PLUS   p118
10341 58 AVE NW, EDMONTON, AB, T6H 5E4
(780) 437-4917   SIC 5013

AUTOMANN HEAVY DUTY CANADA ULC p508
350 FIRST GULF BLVD, BRAMPTON, ON, L6W 4T5
(905) 654-6500   SIC 5013

AVENUE MOTOR WORKS INC   p1029
681 ROWNTREE DAIRY RD, WOODBRIDGE, ON, L4L 5T9
(905) 850-2268   SIC 5013

AVG (OEM) INC   p876
50 TIFFIELD RD UNIT 1, SCARBOROUGH, ON, M1V 5B7
(416) 321-2978   SIC 5013

AXALTA COATING SYSTEMS CANADA COMPANY   p473
408 FAIRALL ST, AJAX, ON, L1S 1R6
(905) 683-5500   SIC 5013

B & B DIXON AUTOMOTIVE INC   p754
395 HARRY WALKER PKY N UNIT 3, NEWMARKET, ON, L3Y 7B3
(905) 895-5184   SIC 5013

BAKER SUPPLY LTD   p233
33 CLIFF ST, NANAIMO, BC, V9R 5E6
(250) 754-6315   SIC 5013

BARTON AUTO PARTS LIMITED   p610
367 CANNON ST E UNIT 361, HAMILTON, ON, L8L 2C3
(905) 522-5124   SIC 5013

BASQUE, GILLES SALES LTD   p404
878 ROUTE 113, INKERMAN, NB, E8P 1C9
(506) 336-4738   SIC 5013

BAUMAN, T & W ENTERPRISES INC p1030
7835 HIGHWAY 50 UNIT 14 & 15, WOODBRIDGE, ON, L4L 1A5
(905) 264-0080   SIC 5013

BENSON GROUP INC   p561
700 EDUCATION RD, CORNWALL, ON, K6H 6B8
(613) 933-1700   SIC 5013

BENSON GROUP INC   p1104
95 BOUL GREBER, GATINEAU, QC, J8T 3P9
(819) 669-6555   SIC 5013

BESTBUY DISTRIBUTORS LIMITED   p687
3355 AMERICAN DR, MISSISSAUGA, ON, L4V 1Y7
(905) 673-0444   SIC 5013

BRANDON CHRYSLER DODGE (1987) LTD p347

3250 VICTORIA AVE, BRANDON, MB, R7B 3Y4

(204) 728-3396 *SIC* 5013

BUY SELL TRADE *p*895
945 ERIE ST, STRATFORD, ON, N5A 6S4

(519) 271-6824 *SIC* 5013

C & S AUTO PARTS LIMITED *p*873
151 NUGGET AVE, SCARBOROUGH, ON, M1S 3B1

(416) 754-8500 *SIC* 5013

CANADIAN TIRE MAGASIN ASSOCIATES *p*1368
1555 RUE TRUDEL, SHAWINIGAN, QC, G9N 8K8

(819) 537-3888 *SIC* 5013

CARCONE'S AUTO RECYCLING LIMITED *p*480
1030 BLOOMINGTON RD SUITE 2, AURORA, ON, L4G 0L7

(905) 773-5778 *SIC* 5013

CARDONE INDUSTRIES ULC *p*99
17803 111 AVE NW, EDMONTON, AB, T5S 2X3

(780) 444-5033 *SIC* 5013

CARLSON BODY SHOP SUPPLY LTD *p*113
5308 97 ST NW, EDMONTON, AB, T6E 5W5

(780) 438-0808 *SIC* 5013

CBS PARTS LTD *p*281
9505 189 ST SUITE 9505, SURREY, BC, V4N 5L8

(604) 888-1944 *SIC* 5013

CENTRAL AUTO PARTS DISTRIBUTORS LTD *p*28
34 HIGHFIELD CIR SE, CALGARY, AB, T2G 5N5

(403) 259-8655 *SIC* 5013

CENTRILIFT A BAKER HUGHES COMPANY *p*46
401 9 AVE SW SUITE 1000, CALGARY, AB, T2P 3C5

(403) 537-3400 *SIC* 5013

CHIEFTAIN AUTO PARTS (1987) INC *p*249
555 3RD AVE, PRINCE GEORGE, BC, V2L 3C2

(250) 562-1258 *SIC* 5013

CHUCK'S AUTO SUPPLY LTD *p*344
861 MACKENZIE AVE S, WILLIAMS LAKE, BC, V2G 3X8

(250) 398-7012 *SIC* 5013

COLONIAL GARAGE & DISTRIBUTORS LIMITED *p*433
355 HAMILTON AVE, ST. JOHN'S, NL, A1E 1K1

(709) 579-4011 *SIC* 5013

CONSOLIDATED DEALERS CO-OPERATIVE INC *p*1030
441 HANLAN RD, WOODBRIDGE, ON, L4L 3T1

(905) 264-7022 *SIC* 5013

CRANE CARRIER (CANADA) LIMITED *p*100
11523 186 ST NW, EDMONTON, AB, T5S 2W6

(780) 443-2493 *SIC* 5013

CRESTWOOD ENGINEERING COMPANY LTD *p*226
6217 205 ST, LANGLEY, BC, V2Y 1N7

(604) 533-8675 *SIC* 5013

CTP DISTRIBUTORS CUSTOM TRUCK PARTS INC *p*131
13313 100 ST, GRANDE PRAIRIE, AB, T8V 4H4

(780) 538-2211 *SIC* 5013

DANA CANADA CORPORATION *p*489
5095 SOUTH SERVICE RD, BEAMSVILLE, ON, L0R 1B0

  SIC 5013

DELVED LTD *p*851
88A E BEAVER CREEK RD UNIT A, RICHMOND HILL, ON, L4B 4A8

(289) 597-5140 *SIC* 5013

DENSO MANUFACTURING CANADA, INC *p*606
900 SOUTHGATE DR, GUELPH, ON, N1L 1K1

(519) 837-6600 *SIC* 5013

DENSO SALES CANADA, INC *p*705
195 BRUNEL RD, MISSISSAUGA, ON, L4Z 1X3

(905) 890-0890 *SIC* 5013

DISCOVER ENERGY CORP *p*254
13511 CRESTWOOD PL UNIT 4, RICHMOND, BC, V6V 2E9

(778) 776-3288 *SIC* 5013

DIX PERFORMANCE NORTH LTD *p*100
11670 170 ST NW, EDMONTON, AB, T5S 1J7

(780) 465-9266 *SIC* 5013

DU-SO / JAC-SIL INC *p*1260
377 RUE DUPUY, QUEBEC, QC, G1L 1P2

(418) 626-5276 *SIC* 5013

EBERSPAECHER CLIMATE CONTROL SYSTEMS CANADA INC *p*738
6099A VIPOND DR, MISSISSAUGA, ON, L5T 2B2

(905) 670-0960 *SIC* 5013

EDMONTON GEAR CENTRE LTD *p*95
14811 116 AVE NW, EDMONTON, AB, T5M 3E8

(780) 452-6933 *SIC* 5013

ENTREPOT DE MONTREAL 1470 INC*p*1170
3455 RUE JARRY E, MONTREAL, QC, H1Z 2G1

(514) 374-9880 *SIC* 5013

ENTREPRISE ROBERT THIBERT INC*p*1151
200 BOUL SAINT-JEAN-BAPTISTE BUREAU 212, MERCIER, QC, J6R 2L2

(450) 699-0560 *SIC* 5013

ENTREPRISES R.E.R. INC *p*1077
1530 BOUL SAINTE-GENEVIEVE, CHICOUTIMI, QC, G7G 2H1

  SIC 5013

EQUIPEMENTS TWIN INC *p*1048
10401 BOUL PARKWAY, ANJOU, QC, H1J 1R4

(514) 353-1190 *SIC* 5013

EXHAUST MASTERS INC *p*153
GD STN POSTAL BOX CTR BOX, RED DEER, AB, T4N 5E6

(403) 885-5800 *SIC* 5013

FORD MOTOR COMPANY OF CANADA, LIMITED *p*100
11604 181 ST NW, EDMONTON, AB, T5S 1M6

(780) 454-9621 *SIC* 5013

FORD MOTOR COMPANY OF CANADA, LIMITED *p*503
8000 DIXIE RD, BRAMPTON, ON, L6T 2J7

(905) 459-2210 *SIC* 5013

FORT GARRY INDUSTRIES LTD *p*369
2525 INKSTER BLVD UNIT 2, WINNIPEG, MB, R2R 2Y4

(204) 632-8261 *SIC* 5013

FORTIN'S SUPPLY LTD *p*196
45750 AIRPORT RD, CHILLIWACK, BC, V2P 1A2

(604) 795-9739 *SIC* 5013

G2S EQUIPEMENT DE FABRICATION ET D'ENTRETIEN INC *p*1094
1895 CH SAINT-FRANCOIS, DORVAL, QC, H9P 1P3

(514) 683-8665 *SIC* 5013

GAMMA SALES INC *p*809
100 HUNTER VALLEY RD, ORILLIA, ON, L3V 0Y7

(705) 325-3088 *SIC* 5013

GENERAL MOTORS OF CANADA COMPANY *p*229
27475 58 CRES, LANGLEY, BC, V4W 3W3

(604) 857-5277 *SIC* 5013

GESTION MARC-ANDRE LORD INC *p*1123
91 2E RUE E BUREAU 233, LA SARRE, QC, J9Z 3J9

  SIC 5013

GLOBAL POINT DESIGN INC *p*800
2861 SHERWOOD HEIGHTS DR UNIT 27, OAKVILLE, ON, L6J 7K1

(905) 829-4424 *SIC* 5013

GORD DAVENPORT AUTOMOTIVE INC *p*808
74 FIRST ST, ORANGEVILLE, ON, L9W 2E4

(519) 941-1233 *SIC* 5013

GRAND PRIX IMPORT INC *p*1170
8275 17E AV, MONTREAL, QC, H1Z 4J9

(514) 328-2300 *SIC* 5013

GRAND VALLEY DISTRIBUTORS INC *p*533
1595 BISHOP ST N, CAMBRIDGE, ON, N1R 7J4

(519) 621-2260 *SIC* 5013

GREGG DISTRIBUTORS LIMITED PARTNERSHIP *p*105
16215 118 AVE NW, EDMONTON, AB, T5V 1C7

(780) 447-3447 *SIC* 5013

GROTE INDUSTRIES CO. *p*678
230 TRAVAIL RD, MARKHAM, ON, L3S 3J1

(905) 209-9744 *SIC* 5013

HARMAN HEAVY VEHICLE SPECIALISTS LTD *p*639
8 SEREDA RD, KITCHENER, ON, N2H 4X7

(519) 743-4378 *SIC* 5013

HEISSIG IMPORT & EXPORT LTD *p*717
3100 RIDGEWAY DR UNIT 30, MISSISSAUGA, ON, L5L 5M5

  SIC 5013

HERNICK, J. LIMITED *p*585
63 GALAXY BLVD SUITE 5, ETOBICOKE, ON, M9W 5R7

(416) 213-9913 *SIC* 5013

HOSIE & BROWN AUTO ELECTRIC LTD *p*595
1352 GOSSET ST, GLOUCESTER, ON, K1B 3P7

(613) 741-8112 *SIC* 5013

IMPORTATIONS THIBAULT LTEE *p*1373
165 RUE SAUVE, SHERBROOKE, QC, J1L 1L6

(819) 569-6212 *SIC* 5013

INTER-CONTINENTAL GEAR & BRAKE INC *p*696
1415 SHAWSON DR SUITE 1, MISSISSAUGA, ON, L4W 1C4

(905) 564-5633 *SIC* 5013

ISN CANADA GROUP HOLDINGS INC*p*1066
88 CH DU TREMBLAY, BOUCHERVILLE, QC, J4B 6Z6

(514) 327-0222 *SIC* 5013

JASSUN HOLDINGS LTD *p*217
874 NOTRE DAME DR, KAMLOOPS, BC, V2C 6L5

(250) 372-1991 *SIC* 5013

K. C.'S AUTOMOTIVE INC *p*835
222R 14TH ST W, OWEN SOUND, ON, N4K 3X8

(519) 376-2501 *SIC* 5013

KEYSTONE AUTOMOTIVE INDUSTRIES ON INC *p*816
1230 OLD INNES RD SUITE 401, OTTAWA, ON, K1B 3V3

(613) 745-4088 *SIC* 5013

KEYSTONE AUTOMOTIVE INDUSTRIES ON INC *p*1348
2095 RUE DE L'INDUSTRIE, SAINT-MATHIEU-DE-BELOEIL, QC, J3G 4S5

(450) 464-2511 *SIC* 5013

KEYSTONE AUTOMOTIVE OPERATIONS OF CANADA INC *p*688
3770 NASHUA DR UNIT 4, MISSISSAUGA, ON, L4V 1M5

(905) 405-0999 *SIC* 5013

KILDONAN VENTURES LTD *p*357
2850 DAY ST, SPRINGFIELD, MB, R2C 2Z2

  SIC 5013

KOOLIAN ENTREPRISES INC, LES *p*1128
2295 52E AV, LACHINE, QC, H8T 3C3

(514) 633-9292 *SIC* 5013

LONESTAR AUTOMOTIVE *p*1414
1125 2ND AVE W, PRINCE ALBERT, SK, S6V 5A9

(306) 763-4777 *SIC* 5013

MACPEK INC *p*1275
2970 AV WATT, QUEBEC, QC, G1X 4P7

(418) 659-1144 *SIC* 5013

MAGNA CLOSURES INC *p*754
521 NEWPARK BLVD, NEWMARKET, ON, L3X 2S2

(905) 898-2665 *SIC* 5013

MAGNA CLOSURES INC *p*838
11 CENTENNIAL DR SUITE 1, PENETANGUISHENE, ON, L9M 1G8

(705) 549-7406 *SIC* 5013

MANN+HUMMEL FILTRATION TECHNOLOGY CANADA ULC *p*483
1035 INDUSTRIAL RD, AYR, ON, N0B 1E0

(519) 622-4545 *SIC* 5013

MARCOR AUTOMOTIVE INC *p*526
1164 WALKER'S LINE, BURLINGTON, ON, L7M 1V2

(905) 549-6445 *SIC* 5013

MASS ELECTRONICS LTD *p*853
45 WEST WILMOT ST UNIT 16-17, RICHMOND HILL, ON, L4B 1K1

(905) 764-9533 *SIC* 5013

MATECH B.T.A. INC *p*1099
1570 BOUL SAINT-CHARLES, DRUMMONDVILLE, QC, J2C 4Z5

(819) 478-4015 *SIC* 5013

MCCOY GLOBAL INC *p*110
9910 39TH AVE NW SUITE 201, EDMONTON, AB, T6B 3H2

(780) 453-8451 *SIC* 5013

MEVOTECH LP *p*988
240 BRIDGELAND AVE, TORONTO, ON, M6A 1Z4

(416) 783-7800 *SIC* 5013

MODERN SALES CO-OP *p*487
87 CAPLAN AVE, BARRIE, ON, L4N 9J3

(705) 733-1771 *SIC* 5013

MONIDEX DISTRIBUTION INTERNATIONAL INC *p*1050
10700 RUE COLBERT, ANJOU, QC, H1J 2H8

(514) 323-9932 *SIC* 5013

MOTORCADE INDUSTRIES INC *p*993
90 KINCORT ST, TORONTO, ON, M6M 5G1

(416) 614-6118 *SIC* 5013

MOTOVAN CORPORATION *p*1066
1391 RUE GAY-LUSSAC BUREAU 100, BOUCHERVILLE, QC, J4B 7K1

(450) 449-3903 *SIC* 5013

NATIONAL EXHAUST SYSTEMS INC *p*509
38 HANSEN RD S, BRAMPTON, ON, L6W 3H4

(905) 453-4111 *SIC* 5013

NGK SPARK PLUGS CANADA LIMITED *p*673
275 RENFREW DR SUITE 101, MARKHAM, ON, L3R 0C8

(905) 477-7780 *SIC* 5013

P.B.E. DISTRIBUTORS INC *p*115
5308 97 ST NW, EDMONTON, AB, T6E 5W5

(780) 438-0303 *SIC* 5013

P.H. VITRES D'AUTOS INC *p*1361
2635 RANG SAINT-JOSEPH, SAINTE-PERPETUE, QC, J0C 1R0

(819) 336-6660 *SIC* 5013

PACIFIC PARTS LTD *p*292
110 5TH AVE W, VANCOUVER, BC, V5Y 1H7

(604) 879-1481 *SIC* 5013

PANGEO CORPORATION *p*1020
3000 TEMPLE DR, WINDSOR, ON, N8W 5J6

(519) 737-1678 *SIC* 5013

PARRY AUTOMOTIVE LIMITED *p*809
84 DUNEDIN ST, ORILLIA, ON, L3V 5T6

(705) 325-1345 *SIC* 5013

PARTS CANADA DEVELOPMENT CO. *p*24
2916 21 ST NE, CALGARY, AB, T2E 6Z2

(403) 250-6611 *SIC* 5013

PARTS FOR TRUCKS, INC *p*447
15 MACDONALD AVE, DARTMOUTH, NS, B3B 1C6

(902) 468-6100 *SIC* 5013

PETERBOROUGH AUTOMOTIVE & MACHINE LTD *p*841

898 FORD ST, PETERBOROUGH, ON, K9J 5V3

(705) 742-2446 *SIC 5013*

PICO OF CANADA LTD p183
7590 CONRAD ST, BURNABY, BC, V5A 2H7

(604) 438-7571 *SIC 5013*

PIECES D'AUTO AT-PAC INC p1161
10700 BOUL HENRI-BOURASSA E, MONTREAL, QC, H1C 1G9

(514) 881-8888 *SIC 5013*

PIECES D'AUTO LACROIX INC p1302
825 BOUL ARTHUR-SAUVE, SAINT-EUSTACHE, QC, J7R 4K3

(450) 473-0661 *SIC 5013*

PIECES D'AUTO LEON GRENIER (1987) INC, LES p1155
1260 BOUL ALBINY-PAQUETTE, MONTLAURIER, QC, J9L 1M7

(819) 623-3740 *SIC 5013*

PIECES D'AUTO PINCOURT INC, LES p1245
35 CH DUHAMEL, PINCOURT, QC, J7W 4C6

(514) 453-5610 *SIC 5013*

PIECES D'AUTO ST-JEAN INC p1318
650 RUE DE DIJON, SAINT-JEAN-SUR-RICHELIEU, QC, J3B 8G3

(450) 348-3871 *SIC 5013*

PIECES D'AUTO TRANSIT INC, LES p1139
1100 RUE JEAN-MARCHAND, LEVIS, QC, G6Y 9G8

(866) 937-8916 *SIC 5013*

PIECES D'AUTOS G. M. INC p1124
1564 277 RTE, LAC-ETCHEMIN, QC, G0R 1S0

(418) 625-3132 *SIC 5013*

PIECES D'AUTOS LE PORTAGE LTEE p1120
1059 BOUL DE L'ANGE-GARDIEN N, L'ASSOMPTION, QC, J5W 1N7

(450) 589-5735 *SIC 5013*

PIECES D'AUTOS O. FONTAINE INC p1359
415 CH DE TOURAINE, SAINTE-JULIE, QC, J3E 1Y2

(450) 649-1489 *SIC 5013*

PIECES D'AUTOS PAUL LAVIGNE INC, LES p1163
3087 RUE DES ORMEAUX, MONTREAL, QC, H1L 4Y1

(514) 351-4210 *SIC 5013*

PIECES DE TRANSMISSION UNITRANS LTEE, LES p1380
3795 RUE GEORGES-CORBEIL, TERREBONNE, QC, J6X 4J5

(450) 968-2000 *SIC 5013*

PIECES POUR AUTOMOBILE JEAN-TALON (1993) LTEE p1346
7655 BOUL VIAU, SAINT-LEONARD, QC, H1S 2P4

(514) 374-2113 *SIC 5013*

POWER BATTERY SALES LTD p475
165 HARWOOD AVE N, AJAX, ON, L1Z 1L9
(905) 427-2718 *SIC 5013*

POWER BATTERY SALES LTD p475
165 HARWOOD AVE N, AJAX, ON, L1Z 1L9
(905) 427-3035 *SIC 5013*

PRINOTH LTD p1111
1001 RUE J.-A.-BOMBARDIER, GRANBY, QC, J2J 1E9

(450) 776-3600 *SIC 5013*

PRO AUTO LTD p391
1761 PEMBINA HWY UNIT 3, WINNIPEG, MB, R3T 2G6

(204) 982-3020 *SIC 5013*

R.T.A. HOLDINGS LTD p84
12029 75 ST NW, EDMONTON, AB, T5B 0X3

(780) 436-9949 *SIC 5013*

RALPH'S RADIO LTD p289
220 1ST AVE E, VANCOUVER, BC, V5T 1A5

(604) 879-4281 *SIC 5013*

RECYCLAGE AUTOMOBILES GRAVEL INC p1060
677 BOUL DU CURE-LABELLE,

BLAINVILLE, QC, J7C 2J5

(450) 435-8335 *SIC 5013*

ROWMONT HOLDINGS LIMITED p479
5445 MADAWASKA BLVD, ARNPRIOR, ON, K7S 3H4

(613) 623-7361 *SIC 5013*

RPG SUPPLY INC p1015
40 SUNRAY ST, WHITBY, ON, L1N 8Y3

(905) 430-8170 *SIC 5013*

S & S TRUCK PARTS CANADA INC p742
6460 KESTREL RD, MISSISSAUGA, ON, L5T 1Z7

(905) 564-7100 *SIC 5013*

SANOH CANADA, LTD p808
300 C LINE, ORANGEVILLE, ON, L9W 3Z8

(519) 941-2229 *SIC 5013*

SERVICE DE FREINS MONTREAL LTEE p1162
11650 6E AV BUREAU 151, MONTREAL, QC, H1E 1S1

(514) 648-7403 *SIC 5013*

SERVICE REMTEC INC p1247
3560 39E AV, POINTE-AUX-TREMBLES, QC, H1A 3V1

(514) 642-6020 *SIC 5013*

SHERWOOD INNOVATIONS INC p588
125 BETHRIDGE RD, ETOBICOKE, ON, M9W 1N4

(416) 740-2777 *SIC 5013*

SILVER AUTOMOTIVE (LETHBRIDGE) LTD p141
3042 2 AVE N, LETHBRIDGE, AB, T1H 0C6

(403) 328-9621 *SIC 5013*

SIMCOE PARTS SERVICE INC p476
6795 INDUSTRIAL PKY, ALLISTON, ON, L9R 1V4

(705) 435-7814 *SIC 5013*

SNAP-ON TOOLS OF CANADA LTD p756
195 HARRY WALKER PKY N UNIT A, NEWMARKET, ON, L3Y 7B3

(905) 836-8121 *SIC 5013*

SPARK AUTO ELECTRIC CO LTD p868
401 BIRCHMOUNT RD, SCARBOROUGH, ON, M1K 1N3

(416) 690-3133 *SIC 5013*

SPECIALTY SALES & MARKETING INC p727
6725 MILLCREEK DR UNIT 5, MISSISSAUGA, ON, L5N 5V3

(905) 816-0011 *SIC 5013*

SPEEDY AUTOMOTIVE LIMITED p422
92 BROADWAY, CORNER BROOK, NL, A2H 4C8

(709) 639-8929 *SIC 5013*

STACKPOLE INTERNATIONAL ENGINEERED PRODUCTS, LTD p478
1310 CORMORANT RD, ANCASTER, ON, L9G 4V5

(905) 304-8533 *SIC 5013*

STACKPOLE INTERNATIONAL ENGINEERED PRODUCTS, LTD p478
1325 CORMORANT RD, ANCASTER, ON, L9G 4V5

(905) 304-9455 *SIC 5013*

STACKPOLE INTERNATIONAL ENGINEERED PRODUCTS, LTD p714
2400 ROYAL WINDSOR DR, MISSISSAUGA, ON, L5J 1K7

(905) 403-0550 *SIC 5013*

SUNFORCE PRODUCTS INC p1241
9015 CH AVON BUREAU 2017, MONTREAL-OUEST, QC, H4X 2G8

(514) 989-2100 *SIC 5013*

TAS AVIATION INC p559
30 MOYAL CRT, CONCORD, ON, L4K 4R8

(905) 669-4812 *SIC 5013*

TCED INTL INC p1315
700 CH DU GRAND-BERNIER N, SAINT-JEAN-SUR-RICHELIEU, QC, J2W 2H1

(450) 348-8720 *SIC 5013*

TOOLQUIP AGENCY LTD p571
270 BROWNS LINE, ETOBICOKE, ON, M8W 3T5

SIC 5013

TOYOTA TSUSHO CANADA INC p538
1080 FOUNTAIN ST N UNIT 2, CAMBRIDGE, ON, N3E 1A3

(519) 653-6600 *SIC 5013*

TOYOTA TSUSHO CANADA INC p1036
270 BEARDS LANE, WOODSTOCK, ON, N4S 7W3

(519) 533-5577 *SIC 5013*

TRANSAXLE PARTS HAMILTON INC p893
730 SOUTH SERVICE RD UNIT 1, STONEY CREEK, ON, L8E 5S7

(905) 643-0700 *SIC 5013*

TTM TECHNOLOGIES INC p914
8150 SHEPPARD AVE E SUITE 1, TORONTO, ON, M1B 5K2

(416) 208-2159 *SIC 5013*

TVH CANADA LTD p736
1039 CARDIFF BLVD, MISSISSAUGA, ON, L5S 1P4

(905) 564-0003 *SIC 5013*

TY-CROP MANUFACTURING LTD p266
9880 MCGRATH RD, ROSEDALE, BC, V0X 1X0

(604) 794-7078 *SIC 5013*

UAP INC p38
5530 3 ST SE SUITE 489, CALGARY, AB, T2H 1J9

(403) 212-4600 *SIC 5013*

UAP INC p225
9325 200 ST UNIT 100, LANGLEY, BC, V1M 3A7

(604) 513-9458 *SIC 5013*

UAP INC p1165
2095 AV HAIG, MONTREAL, QC, H1N 3E2

(514) 251-7638 *SIC 5013*

UAP INC p1165
7025 RUE ONTARIO E, MONTREAL, QC, H1N 2B3

(514) 251-6565 *SIC 5013*

UNI-SELECT EASTERN INC p103
11754 170 ST NW, EDMONTON, AB, T5S 1J7

(780) 452-2440 *SIC 5013*

UNI-SELECT EASTERN INC p1068
170 BOUL INDUSTRIEL, BOUCHERVILLE, QC, J4B 2X3

(450) 641-2440 *SIC 5013*

UNI-SELECT INC p507
145 WALKER DR SUITE 1, BRAMPTON, ON, L6T 5P5

(905) 789-0115 *SIC 5013*

UNI-SELECT INC p1068
170 BOUL INDUSTRIEL, BOUCHERVILLE, QC, J4B 2X3

(450) 641-2440 *SIC 5013*

UNI-SELECT PACIFIC INC p202
91 GLACIER ST, COQUITLAM, BC, V3K 5Z1

(604) 472-4900 *SIC 5013*

UNIFIED AUTO PARTS INC p1414
365 36TH ST W, PRINCE ALBERT, SK, S6V 7L4

(306) 764-4220 *SIC 5013*

UNIVERSAL INDUSTRIAL SUPPLY GROUP INC p633
505 O'CONNOR DR, KINGSTON, ON, K7P 1J9

(613) 634-6272 *SIC 5013*

VAST-AUTO DISTRIBUTION LTEE p1346
4840 BOUL DES GRANDES-PRAIRIES, SAINT-LEONARD, QC, H1R 1A1

(514) 955-3188 *SIC 5013*

VAST-AUTO DISTRIBUTION ONTARIO LTD p507
10 DRIVER RD, BRAMPTON, ON, L6T 5V2

(905) 595-2886 *SIC 5013*

VICTORY FORD LINCOLN SALES LTD p543
301 RICHMOND ST, CHATHAM, ON, N7M 1P5

(519) 436-1430 *SIC 5013*

WAGONMASTER ENTERPRISES (BC) INC p257
12671 BATHGATE WAY SUITE 3, RICHMOND, BC, V6V 1Y5

---

(604) 270-2033 *SIC 5013*

WAKEFIELD-SPERLING AUTO PARTS LTD p175
33406 SOUTH FRASER WAY, ABBOTSFORD, BC, V2S 2B5

(604) 853-8179 *SIC 5013*

WAREHOUSE SERVICES INC p117
9815 42 AVE NW, EDMONTON, AB, T6E 0A3

(780) 437-4917 *SIC 5013*

WHITE & PETERS LTD p202
1368 UNITED BLVD UNIT 101, COQUITLAM, BC, V3K 6Y2

(604) 540-6585 *SIC 5013*

WINACOTT SPRING TRACTOR TRAILER REPAIR CENTRE LTD p1430
3002 FAITHFULL AVE SUITE 1, SASKATOON, SK, S7K 0B1

(306) 931-4448 *SIC 5013*

WORLDPAC CANADA INC p744
6956 COLUMBUS RD, MISSISSAUGA, ON, L5T 2G1

(905) 238-9390 *SIC 5013*

ZF AUTOMOTIVE CANADA LIMITED p1017
3355 MUNICH CRT, WINDSOR, ON, N8N 5G2

(519) 739-9861 *SIC 5013*

SIC 5014 Tires and tubes

9022-9097 QUEBEC INC p1260
103 3E AV, QUEBEC, QC, G1L 2V3
(418) 529-5378 *SIC 5014*

ACHESON, ALAN J. LIMITED p444
30 LAMONT TERR, DARTMOUTH, NS, B3B 0B5

(902) 434-2823 *SIC 5014*

ADRA SALES INC p412
400 WESTMORLAND RD SUITE 254, SAINT JOHN, NB, E2J 2G4

(506) 634-2606 *SIC 5014*

AL BARNIM INC p621
90 SAMNAH CRES, INGERSOLL, ON, N5C 3J7

(519) 424-3402 *SIC 5014*

ANNISONS LTD p880
140 QUEENSWAY E, SIMCOE, ON, N3Y 4Y7

(519) 426-1513 *SIC 5014*

ATLAS TIRE WHOLESALE INC p737
6200 TOMKEN RD, MISSISSAUGA, ON, L5T 1X7

(905) 670-7354 *SIC 5014*

B-LINE TIRE & AUTO SUPPLY LTD p165
32 RAYBORN CRES, ST. ALBERT, AB, T8N 4B1

(780) 458-7619 *SIC 5014*

BARNIM HOLDINGS INC p520
593771 HWY 59, BURGESSVILLE, ON, N0J 1C0

(519) 424-9865 *SIC 5014*

BRIDGESTONE CANADA INC p729
5770 HURONTARIO ST SUITE 400, MISSISSAUGA, ON, L5R 3G5

(877) 468-6270 *SIC 5014*

CAMSO DISTRIBUTION CANADA INC p692
5485 TOMKEN RD, MISSISSAUGA, ON, L4W 3Y3

(416) 674-5441 *SIC 5014*

CANADIAN TIRE p69
250 SHAWVILLE WAY SE, CALGARY, AB, T2Y 3J1

(403) 201-2002 *SIC 5014*

CANADIAN TIRE p79
1110 GATEWAY AVE, CANMORE, AB, T1W 0J1

(403) 678-3295 *SIC 5014*

CANADIAN TIRE p234
4585 UPLANDS DR, NANAIMO, BC, V9T 6M8

(250) 585-5485 *SIC 5014*

CANADIAN TIRE p242
34017 97TH ST, OLIVER, BC, V0H 1T0

---

(250) 498-8473   *SIC 5014*
CANADIAN TIRE   *p425*
500 VANIER AVE, LABRADOR CITY, NL, A2V 2W7
(709) 944-7740   *SIC 5014*
CANADIAN TIRE   *p449*
269 HIGHWAY 214, ELMSDALE, NS, B2S 1K1
(902) 883-1771   *SIC 5014*
CANADIAN TIRE   *p597*
4792 BANK ST, GLOUCESTER, ON, K1T 3W7
(613) 822-2163   *SIC 5014*
CANADIAN TIRE   *p839*
1050 CHEMONG RD, PETERBOROUGH, ON, K9H 7S2
(705) 745-1388   *SIC 5014*
CANADIAN TIRE   *p1011*
158 PRIMEWAY DRIVE, WELLAND, ON, L3B 0A1
(905) 732-1371   *SIC 5014*
CANADIAN TIRE   *p1074*
3400 BOUL FRECHETTE, CHAMBLY, QC, J3L 6Z6
(450) 447-8393   *SIC 5014*
CANADIAN TIRE   *p1081*
85 RUE WELLINGTON, COATICOOK, QC, J1A 2H6
SIC 5014
CANADIAN TIRE   *p1150*
145 RUE PIUZE, MATANE, QC, G4W 0H7
(418) 562-5144   *SIC 5014*
CIE CANADA TIRE INC, LA   *p1053*
21500 AUT TRANSCANADIENNE, BAIE-D'URFE, QC, H9X 4B7
(514) 457-0155   *SIC 5014*
CONTINENTAL TIRE CANADA, INC   *p542*
700 PARK AVENUE E, CHATHAM, ON, N7M 5M7
(519) 352-6700   *SIC 5014*
DISTRIBUTION STOX INC   *p1064*
235 RUE J.-A.-BOMBARDIER, BOUCHERVILLE, QC, J4B 8P1
(450) 449-0362   *SIC 5014*
DUBREUIL, GILLES LTEE   *p1064*
1055 BOUL DE MONTARVILLE BUREAU 332, BOUCHERVILLE, QC, J4B 6P5
(450) 655-6950   *SIC 5014*
DUMAIS, ALBERT INC   *p1390*
1806 3E AV, VAL-D'OR, QC, J9P 7A9
(819) 825-9999   *SIC 5014*
DYNAMIC TIRE INC   *p1027*
211 HUNTER'S VALLEY RD, WOOD-BRIDGE, ON, L4H 3V9
(905) 595-5558   *SIC 5014*
ENTREPRISES DE VENTE LEWIS, R. INC, LES   *p1354*
50 BOUL NORBERT-MORIN, SAINTE-AGATHE-DES-MONTS, QC, J8C 2V6
(819) 326-8900   *SIC 5014*
ENTREPRISES J.C. LEVESQUE INC, LES   *p1304*
500 107E RUE, SAINT-GEORGES, QC, G5Y 8K1
(418) 228-8843   *SIC 5014*
ENTREPRISES PIERRE L BOULOS INC, LES   *p1310*
5930 RUE MARTINEAU, SAINT-HYACINTHE, QC, J2R 2H6
(450) 796-4226   *SIC 5014*
ENTREPRISES SYLVIE DROLET INC   *p1368*
1555 RUE TRUDEL BUREAU 131, SHAW-INIGAN, QC, G9N 8K8
(819) 537-3888   *SIC 5014*
EQUIPEMENTS QUE-MONT INC, LES   *p1061*
3685 AV DES GRANDES TOURELLES, BOISBRIAND, QC, J7H 0E2
(514) 331-0302   *SIC 5014*
FEIST ENTERPRISES LTD   *p104*
9909 178 ST NW SUITE 288, EDMONTON, AB, T5T 6H6
(780) 444-1816   *SIC 5014*
FORMULA DISTRIBUTORS LTD   *p209*
7205 BROWN ST, DELTA, BC, V4G 1G5

(604) 946-0146   *SIC 5014*
GARAGE VILLEMAIRE & FILS INC   *p1300*
55 RUE GREGOIRE, SAINT-ESPRIT, QC, J0K 2L0
(450) 839-7777   *SIC 5014*
GESTION FSTG INC   *p541*
95 LAFLECHE BLVD, CASSELMAN, ON, K0A 1M0
(613) 764-0401   *SIC 5014*
GESTION MARCEL G GAGNE INC   *p1368*
1555 RUE TRUDEL BUREAU 131, SHAW-INIGAN, QC, G9N 8K8
(819) 537-8999   *SIC 5014*
GESTIONS JEAN-MARC GAGNE LTEE   *p1130*
2221 BOUL ANGRIGNON, LASALLE, QC, H8N 3E3
SIC 5014
GROUPE TOUCHETTE INC   *p1179*
9000 BOUL SAINT-LAURENT, MONTREAL, QC, H2N 1M7
(514) 381-1888   *SIC 5014*
GUITARD, CHARLES MERCHANDISING LTD   *p401*
1110 SMYTHE ST, FREDERICTON, NB, E3B 3H6
(506) 450-8920   *SIC 5014*
HERCULES TIRE INTERNATIONAL INC   *p636*
155 ARDELT AVE, KITCHENER, ON, N2C 2E1
(519) 885-3100   *SIC 5014*
INVESTISSEMENTS JEAN C. LAPIERRE LTEE   *p1147*
2135 RUE SHERBROOKE, MAGOG, QC, J1X 2T5
(819) 843-3939   *SIC 5014*
J & M TIRE INTERNATIONAL INC   *p812*
717 DRAKE ST, OSHAWA, ON, L1H 7R3
(905) 723-3323   *SIC 5014*
KAL TIRE LTD   *p332*
1540 KALAMALKA LAKE RD, VERNON, BC, V1T 6V2
(250) 542-2366   *SIC 5014*
KAVCO SALES LTD   *p798*
2510 HYDE PARK GATE, OAKVILLE, ON, L6H 6M2
(905) 829-5552   *SIC 5014*
LONDON TIRE SALES LIMITED   *p897*
290 ELLOR ST, STRATHROY, ON, N7G 2L4
(519) 245-1133   *SIC 5014*
M. & A. WRIGHT CO. LIMITED   *p481*
14700 YONGE ST SUITE 189, AURORA, ON, L4G 7H8
(905) 727-9484   *SIC 5014*
M. & P. VARLEY ENTERPRISES LTD   *p119*
2331 66 ST NW UNIT 200, EDMONTON, AB, T6K 4B4
(780) 450-1800   *SIC 5014*
MAGASIN POULIN INC   *p1320*
700 BOUL MONSEIGNEUR-DUBOIS, SAINT-JEROME, QC, J7Y 4Y9
(450) 438-3506   *SIC 5014*
MAGASIN RENE VEILLEUX INC   *p544*
3595 144 HWY, CHELMSFORD, ON, P0M 1L0
(705) 855-9011   *SIC 5014*
MICHELIN AMERIQUE DU NORD (CANADA) INC   *p463*
2863 GRANTON RD, NEW GLASGOW, NS, B2H 5C6
(888) 871-4444   *SIC 5014*
MICHELIN AMERIQUE DU NORD (CANADA) INC   *p470*
866 RANDOLPH RD, WATERVILLE, NS, B0P 1V0
(902) 538-8021   *SIC 5014*
MILLER FAMILY SALES AND SERVICE LTD   *p3*
202 VETERANS BLVD NE SUITE 300, AIR-DRIE, AB, T4B 3P2
(403) 948-3993   *SIC 5014*
MILLER TIRE SERVICES LTD   *p447*
16 GLORIA MCCLUSKEY AVE, DART-

MOUTH, NS, B3B 2C2
(902) 431-7733   *SIC 5014*
NATIONAL TIRE DISTRIBUTORS INC   *p523*
5035 SOUTH SERVICE RD 4TH FL, BURLINGTON, ON, L7L 6M9
(877) 676-0007   *SIC 5014*
PNEUS CHARTRAND DISTRIBUTION INC   *p1145*
1060 BOUL LA FAYETTE, LONGUEUIL, QC, J4K 3B1
(450) 670-1585   *SIC 5014*
PNEUS G.B.M., S.E.N.C.   *p1289*
1000 RUE SAGUENAY, ROUYN-NORANDA, QC, J9X 7B6
(819) 762-0854   *SIC 5014*
PNEUS ROBERT BERNARD LTEE, LES   *p1350*
765 RUE PRINCIPALE E, SAINT-PAUL-D'ABBOTSFORD, QC, J0E 1A0
(450) 379-5757   *SIC 5014*
PNEUS UNIMAX LTEE   *p1067*
235 RUE J.-A.-BOMBARDIER, BOUCHERVILLE, QC, J4B 8P1
(450) 449-0362   *SIC 5014*
PNEUS UNIMAX LTEE   *p1080*
255 RUE SAINTE-ANNE, CHICOUTIMI, QC, G7J 2M2
(418) 549-1210   *SIC 5014*
PROVINCIAL TIRE DISTRIBUTORS INC   *p488*
466 WELHAM RD, BARRIE, ON, L4N 8Z4
(705) 726-5510   *SIC 5014*
RANGER TIRE INC   *p31*
4020 9 ST SE UNIT 2, CALGARY, AB, T2G 3C4
(403) 723-0777   *SIC 5014*
ROB WILLITTS SALES LTD   *p356*
1041 MANITOBA AVE SUITE 447, SELKIRK, MB, R1A 3T7
(204) 482-8473   *SIC 5014*
SERVICE DE PNEUS LAVOIE OUTAOUAIS INC   *p1107*
27 RUE MANGIN, GATINEAU, QC, J8Y 3L8
(819) 771-2392   *SIC 5014*
STURGEON TIRE (1993) LTD   *p367*
791 MARION ST, WINNIPEG, MB, R2J 0K6
(204) 987-9566   *SIC 5014*
T MACRAE FAMILY SALES LTD   *p239*
1350 MAIN ST SUITE 601, NORTH VAN-COUVER, BC, V7J 1C6
(604) 982-9101   *SIC 5014*
TELFER, S & T MERCHANDISING LTD   *p746*
525 QUEEN ST W, MOUNT FOREST, ON, N0G 2L1
(519) 323-1080   *SIC 5014*
TIRE DISCOUNTER GROUP INC   *p864*
65379 COUNTY RD 3, SCARBOROUGH, ON, L9W 7J8
(519) 941-4136   *SIC 5014*
TIREMASTER LIMITED   *p510*
145 ORENDA RD, BRAMPTON, ON, L6W 1W3
(905) 453-4300   *SIC 5014*
TYSACH HIGGINS LTD   *p283*
3059 152 ST SUITE 485, SURREY, BC, V4P 3K1
(604) 542-4326   *SIC 5014*
WHITE, BART SALES LTD   *p753*
997431 HWY 11, NEW LISKEARD, ON, P0J 1P0
(705) 647-7331   *SIC 5014*
WHOLESALE TIRE DISTRIBUTORS INC   *p561*
35 CITRON CRT, CONCORD, ON, L4K 2S7
(905) 882-6797   *SIC 5014*

SIC 5015 Motor vehicle parts, used

A. BISSON ET FILS LTEE   *p1382*
410 BOUL FRONTENAC O, THETFORD MINES, QC, G6G 6N7
(418) 335-2928   *SIC 5015*
ALTROM AUTO GROUP LTD   *p182*

4242 PHILLIPS AVE UNIT C, BURNABY, BC, V5A 2X2
(604) 294-2311   *SIC 5015*
BEND ALL AUTOMOTIVE ULC   *p483*
655 WAYDOM DR, AYR, ON, N0B 1E0
(519) 623-2002   *SIC 5015*
GPS PRODUCTS INC   *p1009*
622 FRIEBURG DR, WATERLOO, ON, N2T 2Y4
(519) 885-7235   *SIC 5015*
NEARING, ROBERT C. HOLDINGS INC   *p908*
939 FORT WILLIAM RD SUITE 83, THUN-DER BAY, ON, P7B 3A6
(807) 623-1999   *SIC 5015*
PIECES D'AUTO VALLEYFIELD INC   *p1365*
940 BOUL MONSEIGNEUR-LANGLOIS, SALABERRY-DE-VALLEYFIELD, QC, J6S 1C3
(450) 373-9505   *SIC 5015*
UAP INC   *p538*
525 BOXWOOD DR, CAMBRIDGE, ON, N3E 1A5
(519) 650-4444   *SIC 5015*
VAST-AUTO DISTRIBUTION ATLANTIC LTD   *p402*
50 WHITING RD, FREDERICTON, NB, E3B 5V5
(506) 453-1600   *SIC 5015*
WARREN AUTOMOTIVE DE MEXICO   *p561*
401 SPINNAKER WAY, CONCORD, ON, L4K 4N4
SIC 5015

SIC 5021 Furniture

10033618 CANADA INC   *p1337*
4930 RUE COURVAL, SAINT-LAURENT, QC, H4T 1L1
(514) 343-0220   *SIC 5021*
1092072 ONTARIO INC   *p1327*
4500 BOUL THIMENS, SAINT-LAURENT, QC, H4R 2P2
(514) 344-3533   *SIC 5021*
2865-8169 QUEBEC INC   *p1222*
4700 RUE SAINT-AMBROISE BUREAU 100, MONTREAL, QC, H4C 2C7
(514) 937-1117   *SIC 5021*
3496252 CANADA INC   *p1282*
340 RUE SAINT-PAUL, REPENTIGNY, QC, J5Z 4H9
(450) 585-0308   *SIC 5021*
3609022 CANADA INC   *p1235*
4155 CHOMEDEY (A-13) E, MONTREAL, QC, H7P 0A8
(450) 628-4488   *SIC 5021*
4 ON THE FLOOR SEATING COMPANY LIMITED   *p932*
13 POLSON ST, TORONTO, ON, M5A 1A4
(416) 466-3376   *SIC 5021*
9391134 CANADA LTD   *p199*
91 GOLDEN DR UNIT 18, COQUITLAM, BC, V3K 6R2
(604) 428-9644   *SIC 5021*
ALLWEST FURNISHINGS LTD   *p95*
14325 112 AVE NW, EDMONTON, AB, T5M 2V3
(780) 452-8212   *SIC 5021*
ALTERNATE CHOICE INC   *p527*
3325 NORTH SERVICE RD UNIT 1, BURLINGTON, ON, L7N 3G2
(905) 336-8818   *SIC 5021*
AMEUBLEMENT BRANCHAUD INC   *p1100*
52 RTE 105, EGAN, QC, J9E 3A9
(819) 449-2610   *SIC 5021*
ARTICLES MENAGERS DURA INC   *p1361*
2105 BOUL DAGENAIS O, SAINTE-ROSE, QC, H7L 5W9
(450) 622-3872   *SIC 5021*
ATLANTIC BUSINESS INTERIORS LIMITED   *p445*
30 TROOP AVE, DARTMOUTH, NS, B3B 1Z1
(902) 468-3200   *SIC 5021*

BEACHCOMBER HOME & LEISURE LTD *p331*
5309 26 ST, VERNON, BC, V1T 7G4
(250) 542-3399 *SIC 5021*

BRIGHOLME INC *p667*
4118 14TH AVE, MARKHAM, ON, L3R 0J3
(905) 475-0043 *SIC 5021*

CAPITAL OFFICE INTERIORS LIMITED *p749*
16 ANTARES DR, NEPEAN, ON, K2E 7Y7
(613) 723-2000 *SIC 5021*

CASANA FURNITURE COMPANY LTD *p363*
90 LEXINGTON PK, WINNIPEG, MB, R2G 4H2
(204) 988-3189 *SIC 5021*

CIME DECOR INC *p1187*
420 RUE MCGILL BUREAU 100, MON-TREAL, QC, H2Y 2G1
(514) 842-2463 *SIC 5021*

CONTEMPORARY OFFICE INTERIORS LTD *p29*
2206 PORTLAND ST SE, CALGARY, AB, T2G 4M6
(403) 265-1133 *SIC 5021*

CORLIVING DISTRIBUTION LTD *p279*
2252 190 ST, SURREY, BC, V3Z 3W7
(604) 542-7650 *SIC 5021*

CORPORATION ZEDBED INTERNATIONAL INC *p1368*
5352 RUE BURRILL, SHAWINIGAN, QC, G9N 0C3
(819) 539-1112 *SIC 5021*

COSMOS FURNITURE LTD *p502*
1055 CLARK BLVD, BRAMPTON, ON, L6T 3W4
(905) 790-2676 *SIC 5021*

COUNTRY FURNITURE LTD *p241*
1365 PEMBERTON AVE, NORTH VAN-COUVER, BC, V7P 2R6
(604) 985-9700 *SIC 5021*

DUFRESNE GROUP INC, THE *p388*
116 NATURE PARK WAY, WINNIPEG, MB, R3P 0X8
(204) 989-9898 *SIC 5021*

FLAIR ENTERPRISES INC *p16*
3916 72 AVE SE, CALGARY, AB, T2C 2E2
(403) 219-1006 *SIC 5021*

FRENDEL KITCHENS LIMITED *p695*
1350 SHAWSON DR, MISSISSAUGA, ON, L4W 1C5
(905) 670-7898 *SIC 5021*

G.H. JOHNSONS FURNITURE INC *p990*
950 DUPONT ST, TORONTO, ON, M6H 1Z2
(613) 736-7000 *SIC 5021*

GALAXY HOME FURNISHING INC *p739*
455 GIBRALTAR DR, MISSISSAUGA, ON, L5T 2S9
(905) 670-5555 *SIC 5021*

GRAND & TOY LIMITED *p23*
37 AERO DR NE, CALGARY, AB, T2E 8Z9
(866) 391-8111 *SIC 5021*

GROUPE AMEUBLEMENT FOCUS INC *p1392*
1567 BOUL LIONEL-BOULET, VARENNES, QC, J3X 1P7
(514) 644-5551 *SIC 5021*

HARKEL OFFICE FURNITURE LIMITED *p553*
1743 CREDITSTONE RD, CONCORD, ON, L4K 5X7
(905) 417-5335 *SIC 5021*

HERMAN MILLER CANADA, INC *p981*
462 WELLINGTON ST W SUITE 200, TORONTO, ON, M5V 1E3
(416) 366-3300 *SIC 5021*

IRVING, J. D. LIMITED *p413*
225 THORNE AVE, SAINT JOHN, NB, E2J 1W8
(506) 658-8000 *SIC 5021*

ISA INTERNATIONAL INC *p789*
46 DUFFLAW RD, NORTH YORK, ON, M6A 2W1
(416) 782-9100 *SIC 5021*

JANSEN INTERNATIONAL CANADA LTD *p489*

4700 SOUTH SERVICE RD, BEAMSVILLE, ON, L0R 1B1
(905) 563-1822 *SIC 5021*

K-WOOD KITCHENS INC *p872*
32 CONTINENTAL PL, SCARBOROUGH, ON, M1R 2T4
(416) 335-4027 *SIC 5021*

KORSON FURNITURE IMPORTS LTD *p1027*
7933 HUNTINGTON RD UNIT 1, WOOD-BRIDGE, ON, L4H 0S9
(905) 850-1530 *SIC 5021*

LEGACY KITCHEN DESIGN GROUP INC *p9*
2980 SUNRIDGE WAY NE, CALGARY, AB, T1Y 7H9
(403) 291-6868 *SIC 5021*

LITERIE PRIMO INC *p1164*
7000 RUE HOCHELAGA, MONTREAL, QC, H1N 1Y7
(514) 256-7543 *SIC 5021*

LOVER (1996) LTD *p652*
200 ADELAIDE ST S, LONDON, ON, N5Z 3L1
(519) 681-2254 *SIC 5021*

MAB PROFIL INC *p1276*
2800 RUE JEAN-PERRIN BUREAU 200, QUEBEC, QC, G2C 1T3
(418) 842-4100 *SIC 5021*

MAGNUSSEN HOME FURNISHINGS LTD *p752*
66 HINCKS ST SUITE 1, NEW HAMBURG, ON, N3A 2A3
(519) 662-3040 *SIC 5021*

MAYHEW INC *p853*
28 SIMS CRES, RICHMOND HILL, ON, L4B 2N9
(905) 707-4747 *SIC 5021*

MOBILIER DE BUREAU MBH INC *p1259*
25 RUE SAINT-JOSEPH E, QUEBEC, QC, G1K 3A6
(418) 647-1332 *SIC 5021*

NATART JUVENILE INC *p1254*
289 BOUL BARIL O, PRINCEVILLE, QC, G6L 3V8
SIC 5021

OFFICE SOURCE INCORPORATED, THE *p698*
4800 EASTGATE PKY UNIT 1, MISSIS-SAUGA, ON, L4W 3W6
(905) 602-7090 *SIC 5021*

OLD HIPPY WOOD PRODUCTS INC *p122*
2415 80 AVE NW, EDMONTON, AB, T6P 1N3
(780) 448-1163 *SIC 5021*

POI BUSINESS INTERIORS INC *p674*
120 VALLEYWOOD DR, MARKHAM, ON, L3R 6A7
(905) 479-1123 *SIC 5021*

RAPIDO EQUIPEMENT INC *p1262*
735 AV PRUNEAU BUREAU 100, QUEBEC, QC, G1M 2J9
(418) 684-9000 *SIC 5021*

RATANA INTERNATIONAL LTD *p291*
8310 MANITOBA ST, VANCOUVER, BC, V5X 3A5
(604) 321-6776 *SIC 5021*

RENAUD FURNITURE LTD *p416*
4327 ROUTE 115, SAINT-ANTOINE SUD, NB, E4V 2Z4
(506) 525-2493 *SIC 5021*

RGO PRODUCTS LTD *p11*
229 33 ST NE SUITE 100, CALGARY, AB, T2A 4Y6
(403) 569-4400 *SIC 5021*

ROSEDALE SEATING INC *p791*
920 CALEDONIA RD UNIT 3, NORTH YORK, ON, M6B 3Y1
(647) 348-6666 *SIC 5021*

SCI INTERIORS LIMITED *p674*
11 ALLSTATE PKY SUITE 204, MARKHAM, ON, L3R 9T8
(905) 479-7007 *SIC 5021*

SITCONF LIMITED *p665*
160 BULLOCK DR, MARKHAM, ON, L3P 1W2

(905) 554-6029 *SIC 5021*

SPECIALITES MONARCH INC, LES *p1236*
4155 CHOMEDEY (A-13) E, MONTREAL, QC, H7P 0A8
(450) 628-4488 *SIC 5021*

STORK CRAFT MANUFACTURING INC *p258*
12033 RIVERSIDE WAY SUITE 200, RICH-MOND, BC, V6W 1K6
(604) 274-5121 *SIC 5021*

SUSTEMA INC *p1341*
3590 RUE GRIFFITH, SAINT-LAURENT, QC, H4T 1A7
(514) 744-5499 *SIC 5021*

TEKNION FURNITURE SYSTEMS CO. LIM-ITED *p784*
1150 FLINT RD, NORTH YORK, ON, M3J 2J5
(416) 661-3370 *SIC 5021*

TEKNION ROY & BRETON INC *p1139*
975 RUE DES CALFATS, LEVIS, QC, G6Y 9E8
(418) 884-4041 *SIC 5021*

TRANSPORT TFI 21, S.E.C. *p1337*
8801 RTE TRANSCANADIENNE BUREAU 500, SAINT-LAURENT, QC, H4S 1Z6
(514) 856-7500 *SIC 5021*

TRIUM MOBILIER DE BUREAU INC *p1216*
3200 RUE SAINT-PATRICK, MONTREAL, QC, H3K 3H5
(514) 878-8000 *SIC 5021*

WORKPLACE ESSENTIALS LTD *p460*
59 WEBSTER ST, KENTVILLE, NS, B4N 1H6
(902) 678-6106 *SIC 5021*

XENALI INC *p104*
11430 170 ST NW, EDMONTON, AB, T5S 1L7
(780) 487-6669 *SIC 5021*

SIC 5023 Homefurnishings

191017 CANADA INC *p1331*
4747 BOUL DE LA COTE-VERTU, SAINT-LAURENT, QC, H4S 1C9
(514) 336-8780 *SIC 5023*

9076-5223 QUEBEC INC *p1177*
9200 RUE MEILLEUR STE 501, MON-TREAL, QC, H2N 2A5
(514) 274-5677 *SIC 5023*

ALLIANCE MERCANTILE INC *p187*
3451 WAYBURNE DR, BURNABY, BC, V5G 3L1
(604) 299-3566 *SIC 5023*

ALTEX INC *p1380*
3530 BOUL DES ENTREPRISES, TERRE-BONNE, QC, J6X 4J8
(450) 968-0880 *SIC 5023*

ALUMET MFG., INC *p198*
2660 BARNET HWY, COQUITLAM, BC, V3B 1B7
(604) 464-5451 *SIC 5023*

ANGLO ORIENTAL LIMITED *p666*
255 SHIELDS CRT, MARKHAM, ON, L3R 8V2
(905) 752-0612 *SIC 5023*

ARGOS CARPETS LTD *p750*
1914 MERIVALE RD, NEPEAN, ON, K2G 1E8
(613) 226-6573 *SIC 5023*

ATLANTIC PROMOTIONS INC *p1141*
770 BOUL GUIMOND, LONGUEUIL, QC, J4G 1V6
(514) 871-1671 *SIC 5023*

BIG D PRODUCTS LTD *p331*
7861 HWY 97 SUITE 1, VERNON, BC, V1B 3R9
SIC 5023

BOIS BSL INC *p1154*
1081 BOUL INDUSTRIEL, MONT-JOLI, QC, G5H 3K8
(418) 775-5360 *SIC 5023*

BONAVISTA BOVI HOME/MAISON INC *p1156*

8515 PLACE DEVONSHIRE BUREAU 100, MONT-ROYAL, QC, H4P 2K1
(514) 273-6300 *SIC 5023*

BORDER TRENDS INC *p692*
5496 GORVAN DR, MISSISSAUGA, ON, L4W 3E8
(905) 238-1807 *SIC 5023*

BUCKWOLD WESTERN LTD *p1426*
3239 FAITHFULL AVE UNIT 70, SASKA-TOON, SK, S7K 8H4
(306) 652-1660 *SIC 5023*

CANADIAN DRAPERY HARDWARE LTD *p782*
150 STEEPROCK DR, NORTH YORK, ON, M3J 2T4
(416) 630-6900 *SIC 5023*

CARPETTE MULTI DESIGN C.M.D. INC *p1227*
8134 BOUL DECARIE BUREAU A, MON-TREAL, QC, H4P 2S8
(514) 344-8877 *SIC 5023*

CARPETTES LANART INC *p1317*
300 RUE SAINT-LOUIS, SAINT-JEAN-SUR-RICHELIEU, QC, J3B 1Y4
(450) 348-4843 *SIC 5023*

CELADON IMPORTS INC *p527*
3345 NORTH SERVICE RD UNIT 107, BURLINGTON, ON, L7N 3G2
(905) 335-6444 *SIC 5023*

CENTURA (HAMILTON) LIMITED *p615*
140 NEBO RD, HAMILTON, ON, L8W 2E4
(905) 383-5100 *SIC 5023*

CENTURA (OTTAWA) LIMITED *p988*
950 LAWRENCE AVE W, TORONTO, ON, M6A 1C4
(416) 785-5151 *SIC 5023*

CENTURA LIMITED *p788*
950 LAWRENCE AVE W, NORTH YORK, ON, M6A 1C4
(416) 785-5165 *SIC 5023*

COUREY, GEORGE INC *p1231*
6620 RUE ERNEST-CORMIER, MON-TREAL, QC, H7C 2T5
(450) 661-6620 *SIC 5023*

COUVRE-PLANCHER HAUTE VILLE INC *p1124*
14 CH DU BOISE, LAC-BEAUPORT, QC, G3B 2A2
(418) 841-0440 *SIC 5023*

DANESCO INC *p1118*
18111 RTE TRANSCANADIENNE, KIRK-LAND, QC, H9J 3K1
(514) 694-9111 *SIC 5023*

DANICA IMPORTS LTD *p291*
348 7TH AVE W, VANCOUVER, BC, V5Y 1M4
(604) 255-6150 *SIC 5023*

DECOLIN INC *p1178*
9150 AV DU PARC, MONTREAL, QC, H2N 1Z2
(514) 384-2910 *SIC 5023*

DELCO FIREPLACES LTD *p227*
20679 LANGLEY BYPASS, LANGLEY, BC, V3A 5E8
(604) 530-2166 *SIC 5023*

DIAMOND FIREPLACE DISTRIBUTORS LTD *p75*
10221 15 ST NE SUITE 4, CALGARY, AB, T3J 0T1
(403) 273-0000 *SIC 5023*

DIVINE HARDWOOD FLOORING LTD *p159*
235075 RYAN RD, ROCKY VIEW COUNTY, AB, T1X 0K3
(403) 285-2188 *SIC 5023*

EDGEWOOD MATTING LTD *p100*
18120 109 AVE NW, EDMONTON, AB, T5S 2K2
(780) 466-2084 *SIC 5023*

ENESCO CANADA CORPORATION *p739*
989 DERRY RD E SUITE 303, MISSIS-SAUGA, ON, L5T 2J8
(905) 673-9200 *SIC 5023*

ENTREPRISES LEZNOFF LTEE, LES *p1184*
6525 RUE WAVERLY, MONTREAL, QC.

H2V 4M2
(514) 273-7207   *SIC 5023*
FHE GROUP INC, THE   *p552*
260 SPINNAKER WAY UNITS 2-5, CON-
CORD, ON, L4K 4P9
(416) 749-1505   *SIC 5023*
FORBO FLOORING SYSTEMS   *p580*
111 WESTMORE DR, ETOBICOKE, ON,
M9V 3Y6
(416) 745-4200   *SIC 5023*
FOTIOU FRAMES LIMITED   *p1027*
135 RAINBOW CREEK DR, WOOD-
BRIDGE, ON, L4H 0A4
(800) 668-8420   *SIC 5023*
FOX RUN CANADA CORP   *p553*
460 APPLEWOOD CRES SUITE 2, CON-
CORD, ON, L4K 4Z3
(905) 669-4145   *SIC 5023*
FRAMERS CHOICE   *p321*
1695 2ND AVE W, VANCOUVER, BC, V6J
1H3
(604) 732-8477   *SIC 5023*
GESCO INDUSTRIES INC   *p503*
50 KENVIEW BLVD, BRAMPTON, ON, L6T
5S8
(905) 789-3755   *SIC 5023*
GESCO LIMITED PARTNERSHIP   *p503*
50 KENVIEW BLVD, BRAMPTON, ON, L6T
5S8
(905) 789-3755   *SIC 5023*
GLEN DIMPLEX AMERICAS LIMITED   *p539*
1367 INDUSTRIAL RD SUITE 768, CAM-
BRIDGE, ON, N3H 4W3
(519) 650-3630   *SIC 5023*
GOLDEN TRIM ENTERPRISES INC   *p182*
8411 LOUGHEED HWY, BURNABY, BC,
V5A 1X3
(604) 421-3998   *SIC 5023*
GROUPE ACCENT-FAIRCHILD INC   *p1329*
5151 BOUL THIMENS, SAINT-LAURENT,
QC, H4R 2C8
(514) 748-6721   *SIC 5023*
GROUPE LINENCORP INC   *p1339*
6435 CH DE LA COTE-DE-LIESSE, SAINT-
LAURENT, QC, H4T 1E5
(514) 335-2120   *SIC 5023*
HARMAN INVESTMENTS LTD   *p739*
310 ANNAGEM BLVD, MISSISSAUGA, ON,
L5T 2V5
(905) 670-0801   *SIC 5023*
HAYWARD & WARWICK LIMITED   *p415*
85 PRINCESS ST, SAINT JOHN, NB, E2L
1K5
(506) 653-9066   *SIC 5023*
HEARTHLAND FIREPLACES LIMITED   *p522*
5450 MAINWAY, BURLINGTON, ON, L7L
6A4
(905) 319-0474   *SIC 5023*
**HIGHLAND FEATHER MANUFACTURING
INC**   *p874*
171 NUGGET AVE, SCARBOROUGH, ON,
M1S 3B1
(416) 754-7443   *SIC 5023*
HOME TEXTILES INC   *p503*
35 COVENTRY RD, BRAMPTON, ON, L6T
4V7
(905) 792-1551   *SIC 5023*
**HUNTER DOUGLAS CANADA HOLDINGS
INC**   *p509*
132 FIRST GULF BLVD, BRAMPTON, ON,
L6W 4T7
(905) 796-7883   *SIC 5023*
INTERBEST HOUSEWARES INC   *p182*
7588 WINSTON ST, BURNABY, BC, V5A
4X5
(604) 216-3333   *SIC 5023*
IRVINE, G. ERNEST LIMITED   *p484*
514 BAYFIELD ST, BARRIE, ON, L4M 5A2
(705) 728-5566   *SIC 5023*
JETRICH CANADA LIMITED   *p688*
3270 ORLANDO DR SUITE A, MISSIS-
SAUGA, ON, L4V 1C6
(905) 673-3110   *SIC 5023*
JHL INTERNATIONAL TRADING CO. LTD

p181
8168 GLENWOOD DR, BURNABY, BC, V3N
5E9
(604) 421-5520   *SIC 5023*
KEY FOOD EQUIPMENT SERVICES LTD
p193
8528 GLENLYON PKY SUITE 145, BURN-
ABY, BC, V5J 0B6
(800) 665-2655   *SIC 5023*
KRAUS CANADA LP   *p372*
1551 CHURCH AVE SUITE 167, WIN-
NIPEG, MB, R2X 1G7
(204) 633-1020   *SIC 5023*
LAMWOOD PRODUCTS (1990) LIMITED
p585
44 WOODBINE DOWNS BLVD, ETOBI-
COKE, ON, M9W 5R2
SIC 5023
LARSON-JUHL CANADA LTD   *p706*
416 WATLINE AVE, MISSISSAUGA, ON,
L4Z 1X2
(905) 890-1234   *SIC 5023*
LENNOX INDUSTRIES (CANADA) LTD   *p71*
11500 35 ST SE SUITE 8002, CALGARY,
AB, T2Z 3W4
(403) 279-4448   *SIC 5023*
LIEBERMAN-TRANCHEMONTAGNE   INC
p1326
653 RUE HODGE, SAINT-LAURENT, QC,
H4N 2A3
(514) 747-5510   *SIC 5023*
M. BLOCK CANADA, ULC   *p998*
134 BETHRIDGE RD, TORONTO, ON, M9W
1N3
(705) 252-6471   *SIC 5023*
MAISON LIANG   *p1076*
177A   BOUL   SAINT-JEAN-BAPTISTE,
CHATEAUGUAY, QC, J6K 3B4
(450) 692-1160   *SIC 5023*
MARKETING MANN, ALBERT INC   *p1157*
8191 CH MONTVIEW, MONT-ROYAL, QC,
H4P 2P2
(514) 800-6266   *SIC 5023*
MAXWELL FABRICS LTD   *p323*
8811 LAUREL ST UNIT 113, VANCOUVER,
BC, V6P 3V9
(604) 253-7744   *SIC 5023*
MAZIN FURNITURE INDUSTRIES LIMITED
p555
8080 KEELE ST, CONCORD, ON, L4K 2A3
(905) 761-1594   *SIC 5023*
MELMART DISTRIBUTORS INC   *p688*
6100 INDIAN LINE, MISSISSAUGA, ON,
L4V 1G5
(905) 677-7600   *SIC 5023*
MERCANA FURNITURE & DECOR LTD   *p279*
3250 189 ST, SURREY, BC, V3Z 1A7
(604) 596-1668   *SIC 5023*
**METROPOLITAN HARDWOOD FLOORS,
INC**   *p206*
811 CLIVEDEN AVE, DELTA, BC, V3M 5R6
(604) 395-2000   *SIC 5023*
MODERN HOUSEWARE IMPORTS INC   *p186*
2300 MADISON AVE, BURNABY, BC, V5C
4Y9
(604) 299-5132   *SIC 5023*
MODES MAISON HERITAGE INC   *p1227*
5000 RUE JEAN-TALON O BUREAU 150,
MONTREAL, QC, H4P 1W9
(514) 341-1311   *SIC 5023*
MULTY HOME LP   *p556*
7900 KEELE ST UNIT 100, CONCORD, ON,
L4K 2A3
(905) 760-3737   *SIC 5023*
NELLA CUTLERY (HAMILTON) INC   *p608*
2775 BARTON ST E, HAMILTON, ON, L8E
2J8
(905) 561-3456   *SIC 5023*
NORAM ENTERPRISES INC   *p698*
1325 AIMCO BLVD, MISSISSAUGA, ON,
L4W 1B4
(905) 238-0470   *SIC 5023*
**NORTH WOOD CARPET & TILE COMPANY
LTD**   *p495*

16 NIXON RD, BOLTON, ON, L7E 1K3
(905) 790-0085   *SIC 5023*
OMNI FLOORCOVERINGS LTD   *p741*
6310 KESTREL RD, MISSISSAUGA, ON,
L5T 1Z3
SIC 5023
PACIFIC RIM FLOORING LTD   *p277*
13375 76 AVE SUITE 101, SURREY, BC,
V3W 6J3
(604) 591-3431   *SIC 5023*
PANABO SALES LTD   *p239*
233 1ST ST E, NORTH VANCOUVER, BC,
V7L 1B4
(604) 988-5051   *SIC 5023*
PHOENIX A.M.D. INTERNATIONAL INC *p496*
41 BUTLER CRT, BOWMANVILLE, ON, L1C
4P8
(905) 427-7440   *SIC 5023*
PHOENIX FLOOR & WALL PRODUCTS INC
p580
111 WESTMORE DR, ETOBICOKE, ON,
M9V 3Y6
(416) 745-4200   *SIC 5023*
PICTURE PICTURE COMPANY LTD., THE
p789
122 CARTWRIGHT AVE, NORTH YORK,
ON, M6A 1V2
(416) 787-9827   *SIC 5023*
PLANCHERS DAVA INC, LES   *p1388*
3400 BOUL GENE-H.-KRUGER, TROIS-
RIVIERES, QC, G9A 4M3
(418) 338-0888   *SIC 5023*
PSP USA LLC   *p853*
35 EAST BEAVER CREEK UNIT 6,
RICHMOND HILL, ON, L4B 1B3
(905) 764-1121   *SIC 5023*
PUDDIFOOT, W. H. LTD   *p324*
1566 RAND AVE, VANCOUVER, BC, V6P
3G2
(604) 263-0971   *SIC 5023*
QUALITY CRAFT LTD   *p273*
17750 65A AVE UNIT 301, SURREY, BC,
V3S 5N4
(604) 575-5550   *SIC 5023*
QUICKSTYLE INDUSTRIES INC   *p1335*
4505 RUE COUSENS, SAINT-LAURENT,
QC, H4S 1X5
(514) 956-9711   *SIC 5023*
RAM DISTRIBUTORS LIMITED   *p657*
993 ADELAIDE ST S, LONDON, ON, N6E
1R5
(519) 681-1961   *SIC 5023*
REAL DEALS ENTERPRISES INC   *p587*
18 HUDDERSFIELD RD SUITE 1, ETOBI-
COKE, ON, M9W 5Z6
(416) 248-2020   *SIC 5023*
ROBELY TRADING INC   *p558*
20 BARNES CRT SUITE H, CONCORD,
ON, L4K 4L4
(905) 881-2222   *SIC 5023*
**SANDS COMMERCIAL FLOOR COVER-
INGS INC**   *p674*
180 BENTLEY ST, MARKHAM, ON, L3R
3L2
(905) 475-6380   *SIC 5023*
SCANTRADE INTERNATIONAL LIMITED
p742
6685 KENNEDY RD SUITE 7, MISSIS-
SAUGA, ON, L5T 3A5
(905) 795-9380   *SIC 5023*
SERVICE DE COUPAGE DOMINION INC
p1179
99 RUE CHABANEL O BUREAU 104, MON-
TREAL, QC, H2N 1C3
(514) 270-4118   *SIC 5023*
**SHAMROCK FLOORING ACCESSORIES
LTD**   *p37*
7510 5 ST SE UNIT D, CALGARY, AB, T2H
2L9
(403) 253-5330   *SIC 5023*
SOL-R PRODUITS DE FENETRES   *p1327*
50 RUE BENJAMIN-HUDON, SAINT-
LAURENT, QC, H4N 1H8
SIC 5023

ST. GENEVE FINE BEDLINENS LTD   *p264*
11160 SILVERSMITH PL, RICHMOND, BC,
V7A 5E4
(604) 272-3004   *SIC 5023*
**STEELITE INTERNATIONAL CANADA LIM-
ITED**   *p675*
26 RIVIERA DR UNIT 2, MARKHAM, ON,
L3R 5M1
(905) 752-1074   *SIC 5023*
STEINER & ALEXANDERS INC   *p1244*
45 CH BATES BUREAU 200, OUTREMONT,
QC, H2V 1A6
(514) 271-1101   *SIC 5023*
SWISSMAR LTD   *p854*
35 EAST BEAVER CREEK RD UNIT 6,
RICHMOND HILL, ON, L4B 1B3
(905) 764-6068   *SIC 5023*
THANE DIRECT CANADA INC   *p701*
5255 ORBITOR DR SUITE 501, MISSIS-
SAUGA, ON, L4W 5M6
(905) 625-3800   *SIC 5023*
THANE DIRECT COMPANY   *p701*
5255 ORBITOR DR SUITE 501, MISSIS-
SAUGA, ON, L4W 5M6
(905) 625-3800   *SIC 5023*
TIMBER REALIZATION COMPANY LIMITED
p26
3420 12 ST NE UNIT 108, CALGARY, AB,
T2E 6N1
(403) 219-3303   *SIC 5023*
TORLYS INC   *p736*
1900 DERRY RD E, MISSISSAUGA, ON,
L5S 1Y6
(905) 612-8772   *SIC 5023*
TRICIFIC ENTERPRISES INC   *p877*
155 DYNAMIC DR, SCARBOROUGH, ON,
M1V 5L8
(905) 470-8811   *SIC 5023*
TRUDEAU CORPORATION 1889 INC *p1068*
1600 RUE EIFFEL, BOUCHERVILLE, QC,
J4B 5Y1
(450) 655-7441   *SIC 5023*
UMBRA LTD   *p875*
40 EMBLEM CRT, SCARBOROUGH, ON,
M1S 1B1
(416) 299-0088   *SIC 5023*
VESTATE (CANADA) LTD   *p97*
16602 114 AVE NW, EDMONTON, AB, T5M
3R8
(780) 433-1695   *SIC 5023*
VILLEROY & BOCH TABLEWARE LTD *p757*
1100 GORHAM ST UNIT 22, NEWMARKET,
ON, L3Y 8Y8
(705) 458-0435   *SIC 5023*
WEBER-STEPHEN (CANADA) COMPANY
p1029
1 ROYBRIDGE GATE, WOODBRIDGE, ON,
L4H 4E6
(905) 850-8999   *SIC 5023*
WILTON INDUSTRIES CANADA COMPANY
p589
98 CARRIER DR, ETOBICOKE, ON, M9W
5R1
(416) 679-0790   *SIC 5023*
WINSHAM FABRIK CANADA LTD   *p905*
25 MINTHORN BLVD, THORNHILL, ON,
L3T 7N5
(905) 882-1827   *SIC 5023*
ZWILLING J.A. HENCKELS CANADA LTD
p677
435 COCHRANE DR SUITE 4, MARKHAM,
ON, L3R 9R5
(905) 475-2555   *SIC 5023*

SIC 5031 Lumber, plywood, and millwork

113514 CANADA INC   *p1303*
262 RUE MARCEL RR 2, SAINT-GABRIEL-
DE-BRANDON, QC, J0K 2N0
(450) 835-2066   *SIC 5031*
2365927 ONTARIO LIMITED   *p657*
90 BESSEMER RD UNIT 2, LONDON, ON,
N6E 1R1

(519) 668-7331   *SIC* 5031
2730-8303 QUEBEC INC   p1350
239 RTE 230 O, SAINT-PHILIPPE-DE-NERI, QC, G0L 4A0
(418) 498-2100   *SIC* 5031
3235 ONTARIO INC   p540
9184 TWISS RD RR 2, CAMPBELLVILLE, ON, L0P 1B0
(416) 233-1227   *SIC* 5031
804652 ALBERTA LTD   p155
7703 EDGAR INDUSTRIAL DR SUITE 1, RED DEER, AB, T4P 3R2
(403) 343-1316   *SIC* 5031
9190-5730 QUEBEC INC   p1263
1175 RUE LOMER-GOUIN, QUEBEC, QC, G1N 1T3
(418) 687-4711   *SIC* 5031
ADVANCE DOOR SYSTEMS LTD   p1417
GD, REGINA, SK, S4P 2Z4
(306) 781-0207   *SIC* 5031
ALBERTA TRUSS LTD   p121
2140 RAILWAY ST NW, EDMONTON, AB, T6P 1X3
(780) 464-5551   *SIC* 5031
ALPA LUMBER INC   p685
7630 AIRPORT RD, MISSISSAUGA, ON, L4T 4G6
(905) 612-1222   *SIC* 5031
ALUMICO ARCHITECTURAL INC   p1166
4343 RUE HOCHELAGA BUREAU 100, MONTREAL, QC, H1V 1C2
(514) 255-4343   *SIC* 5031
ANGLO AMERICAN CEDAR PRODUCTS LTD   p232
7160 BEATTY DR, MISSION, BC, V2V 6B4
(604) 826-7185   *SIC* 5031
AQUILA CEDAR PRODUCTS LTD   p242
1282 ALBERNI HWY, PARKSVILLE, BC, V9P 2C9
(250) 248-5922   *SIC* 5031
ARGO LUMBER INC   p664
10275 KEELE ST, MAPLE, ON, L6A 3Y9
(905) 832-2251   *SIC* 5031
AT LIMITED PARTNERSHIP   p398
365 CH CANADA, EDMUNDSTON, NB, E3V 1W2
(506) 737-2345   *SIC* 5031
BLUE RIDGE LUMBER INC   p173
GD STN MAIN, WHITECOURT, AB, T7S 1S1
(780) 648-6200   *SIC* 5031
BOIS AISE DE MONTREAL INC   p1137
1190A RUE DE COURCHEVEL BUREAU 420, LEVIS, QC, G6W 0M5
(418) 832-4200   *SIC* 5031
BOIS EXPANSION INC   p1216
9750 BOUL SAINT-LAURENT, MONTREAL, QC, H3L 2N3
(514) 381-5626   *SIC* 5031
BOIS FRANCS D.V. INC, LES   p1102
131 RUE PRINCIPALE, FASSETT, QC, J0V 1H0
(819) 423-2338   *SIC* 5031
BOIS INDIFOR INC, LES   p1271
2590 BOUL LAURIER BUREAU 1040, QUEBEC, QC, G1V 4M6
(418) 877-2294   *SIC* 5031
BOSCUS CANADA INC   p1249
900 AV SELKIRK, POINTE-CLAIRE, QC, H9R 3S3
(514) 694-9805   *SIC* 5031
BPWOOD LTD   p243
186 NANAIMO AVE W UNIT 102, PENTICTON, BC, V2A 1N4
(250) 493-9339   *SIC* 5031
BRAMWOOD FOREST INC   p582
38 TABER RD, ETOBICOKE, ON, M9W 3A8
(416) 747-7244   *SIC* 5031
BRUNSWICK VALLEY LUMBER INC   p399
367 MAIN ST SUITE 1, FREDERICTON, NB, E3A 1E6
(506) 457-1900   *SIC* 5031
C.A. SPENCER INC   p1235
2930 BOUL DAGENAIS O, MONTREAL,

QC, H7P 1T1
(450) 622-2420   *SIC* 5031
CADRES VERBEC INC   p1395
101   MONTEE   CALIXA-LAVALLEE, VERCHERES, QC, J0L 2R0
(450) 583-3378   *SIC* 5031
CANADIAN ENGINEERED WOOD PRODUCTS LTD   p169
1 ERICKSON DR, SYLVAN LAKE, AB, T4S 1P5
(403) 887-6677   *SIC* 5031
CANADIAN FOREST PRODUCTS LTD p213
9312 259 RD LCD MAIN, FORT ST. JOHN, BC, V1J 4M6
(250) 787-3600   *SIC* 5031
CENTRAL LUMBER LIMITED   p550
1900 STEELES AVE W, CONCORD, ON, L4K 1A1
(416) 736-6263   *SIC* 5031
CENTURY LANE KITCHENS INC.   p219
800 MCCURDY RD, KELOWNA, BC, V1X 2P7
(250) 765-2366   *SIC* 5031
COAST FRASER ENTERPRISES LTD p312
1177 WEST HASTINGS ST SUITE 2101, VANCOUVER, BC, V6E 2K3
(604) 498-1110   *SIC* 5031
COLUMBIA FOREST PRODUCTS LTD p858
HWY 17 E, RUTHERGLEN, ON, P0H 2E0
(705) 776-7622   *SIC* 5031
COLUMBIA MANUFACTURING CO. LTD p192
4575 TILLICUM ST, BURNABY, BC, V5J 5K9
(604) 437-3377   *SIC* 5031
COMPAGNIE DU BOIS FRANC DZD INC, LA p1319
450 BOUL ROLAND-GODARD, SAINT-JEROME, QC, J7Y 4G8
(450) 431-1643   *SIC* 5031
CONCEPT MAT INC   p1150
41 RUE BRILLANT, MATANE, QC, G4W 0J7
(418) 562-6680   *SIC* 5031
CONTREPLAQUE & PLACAGE CANADA INC   p1364
15 BOUL DU CURE-LABELLE, SAINTE-THERESE, QC, J7E 2X1
(450) 435-6541   *SIC* 5031
CONVENIENCE GROUP INC   p571
10 BUTTERICK RD, ETOBICOKE, ON, M8W 3Z8
(416) 233-6900   *SIC* 5031
CUTLER FOREST PRODUCTS INC   p1027
81 ROYAL GROUP CRES UNIT A, WOODBRIDGE, ON, L4H 1X9
(905) 212-1414   *SIC* 5031
CWP INDUSTRIEL INC   p1187
407 RUE MCGILL BUREAU 315, MONTREAL, QC, H2Y 2G3
(514) 871-2120   *SIC* 5031
DAKERYN INDUSTRIES LTD   p240
233 1ST ST W SUITE 210, NORTH VANCOUVER, BC, V7M 1B3
(604) 986-0323   *SIC* 5031
DE LA FONTAINE & ASSOCIES INC p1380
3700 RUE PASCAL-GAGNON, TERREBONNE, QC, J6X 4J2
(450) 471-2982   *SIC* 5031
DEVON LUMBER CO. LTD   p399
200 GIBSON ST, FREDERICTON, NB, E3A 4E3
(506) 457-7123   *SIC* 5031
DIMENSIONS PORTES ET FENETRES INC p1061
4065 RUE ALFRED-LALIBERTE, BOISBRIAND, QC, J7H 1P7
(450) 430-4486   *SIC* 5031
DIRECT TIMBER INC   p813
1181 THORNTON RD S SUITE 1, OSHAWA, ON, L1J 8P4
(905) 571-4441   *SIC* 5031
DOMINION CROWN MOULDING INC p174
34450 VYE RD, ABBOTSFORD, BC, V2S 7P6

(604) 852-4224   *SIC* 5031
DOORTECH MFG. AND DISTRIBUTION LTD p372
530 SHEPPARD ST, WINNIPEG, MB, R2X 2P8
(204) 633-7133   *SIC* 5031
DUNBAR LUMBER SUPPLY   p210
4989 BRIDGE ST, DELTA, BC, V4K 2K3
(604) 946-7322   *SIC* 5031
DURAGUARD WHOLESALE FENCE LTD p100
10624 214 ST NW, EDMONTON, AB, T5S 2A5
(780) 447-5465   *SIC* 5031
EASTWOOD FOREST PRODUCTS INC p428
112 TRANS CANADA HWY, ST JUDES, NL, A8A 3A1
(709) 635-7280   *SIC* 5031
EDWARDS DOORS SYSTEMS LIMITED p846
124 KENDALL ST, POINT EDWARD, ON, N7V 4G5
(519) 336-4990   *SIC* 5031
ELK TRADING CO. LTD   p185
4664 LOUGHEED HWY SUITE 174, BURNABY, BC, V5C 5T5
(604) 684-6688   *SIC* 5031
EUROLINE WINDOWS INC   p338
3352 TENNYSON AVE, VICTORIA, BC, V8Z 3P6
(250) 383-8465   *SIC* 5031
FABELTA ALUMINIUM INC   p1380
3840 RUE GEORGES-CORBEIL, TERREBONNE, QC, J6X 4J4
(450) 477-7611   *SIC* 5031
FAMA INDUSTRIES CORPORATION   p209
7480 MACDONALD RD, DELTA, BC, V4G 1N2
(604) 952-0880   *SIC* 5031
FINMAC LUMBER LIMITED   p380
945 ELGIN AVE, WINNIPEG, MB, R3E 1B3
(204) 786-7694   *SIC* 5031
FREEMAN, HARRY AND SON LIMITED p450
4804 MEEDWAY RIVER RD, GREENFIELD, NS, B0T 1E0
(902) 685-2792   *SIC* 5031
GILLIES LUMBER INC   p539
777 INDUSTRIAL RD, CAMBRIDGE, ON, N3H 4W2
(519) 653-3219   *SIC* 5031
GLASSMASTERS AUTOGLASS LTD   p35
6221 CENTRE ST SW, CALGARY, AB, T2H 0C7
(403) 692-0934   *SIC* 5031
GLENORA LUMBER & BUILDING SUPPLIES LTD   p96
14505 116 AVE NW, EDMONTON, AB, T5M 3E8
(780) 453-5691   *SIC* 5031
GLOBAL LUMBER RESOURCES INC p705
48 VILLAGE CENTRE PL UNIT 100, MISSISSAUGA, ON, L4Z 1V9
(905) 306-7874   *SIC* 5031
GOODFELLOW INC   p540
9184 TWISS RD, CAMPBELLVILLE, ON, L0P 1B0
(416) 233-1227   *SIC* 5031
GOODFELLOW INC   p1089
225 RUE GOODFELLOW, DELSON, QC, J5B 1V5
(450) 635-6511   *SIC* 5031
GRIFF BUILDING SUPPLIES LTD   p237
340 EWEN AVE, NEW WESTMINSTER, BC, V3M 5B1
(877) 934-7433   *SIC* 5031
GROUPE CRETE DIVISION ST-FAUSTIN INC   p1302
1617   RTE   117,   SAINT-FAUSTIN-LAC-CARRE, QC, J0T 1J2
(819) 688-5550   *SIC* 5031
GROUPE CRETE INC   p1302
1617   RTE   117,   SAINT-FAUSTIN-LAC-CARRE, QC, J0T 1J2
(418) 365-4457   *SIC* 5031

GULICK FOREST PRODUCTS LIMITED
p836
6216 PALMER RD, PALMER RAPIDS, ON, K0J 2E0
(613) 758-2369   *SIC* 5031
H. J. CRABBE & SONS, LTD   p399
6   LOCKHARTS   MILL   RD, FLORENCEVILLE-BRISTOL, NB, E7L 2R2
(506) 392-5563   *SIC* 5031
HANFORD LUMBER LIMITED   p584
45 BETHRIDGE RD SUITE 1, ETOBICOKE, ON, M9W 1M9
(416) 743-5384   *SIC* 5031
HARDWOOD FOREST PRODUCTS CO LTD p391
1213 CHEVRIER BLVD, WINNIPEG, MB, R3T 1Y4
(204) 981-1490   *SIC* 5031
HARDWOODS DISTRIBUTION INC   p225
9440 202 ST UNIT 306, LANGLEY, BC, V1M 4A6
(604) 881-1988   *SIC* 5031
HARDWOODS SPECIALTY PRODUCTS LP
p225
9440 202 ST SUITE 306, LANGLEY, BC, V1M 4A6
(604) 881-1988   *SIC* 5031
HURON WINDOW CORPORATION   p352
345 MOUNTAIN ST S, MORDEN, MB, R6M 1J5
(204) 822-6281   *SIC* 5031
HUTTON FOREST PRODUCTS INC   p536
320 PINEBUSH ROAD UNIT 8, CAMBRIDGE, ON, N1T 1Z6
(519) 620-4374   *SIC* 5031
IMAC ENTERPRISES CORP   p255
11488 EBURNE WAY, RICHMOND, BC, V6V 3E1
(604) 324-8288   *SIC* 5031
INTERNATIONAL LUMBER INC   p875
3410 SHEPPARD AVE E SUITE 400, SCARBOROUGH, ON, M1T 3K4
(416) 754-1020   *SIC* 5031
IRVING FOREST PRODUCTS LIMITED p415
300 UNION ST SUITE 5777, SAINT JOHN, NB, E2L 4Z2
(506) 632-7777   *SIC* 5031
KAYCAN LTEE   p473
323 MAIN ST N, ACTON, ON, L7J 2L9
(519) 853-1230   *SIC* 5031
KINNEAR INDUSTRIES CORPORATION LIMITED   p706
254 MATHESON BLVD E, MISSISSAUGA, ON, L4Z 1P5
(905) 890-1402   *SIC* 5031
KITCHENER FOREST PRODUCTS INC p912
1300 JACKSON, TILLSONBURG, ON, N4G 4G7
(519) 842-7381   *SIC* 5031
KOTT INC   p752
3228 MOODIE DR, NEPEAN, ON, K2J 4S8
(613) 838-2775   *SIC* 5031
KOTT LUMBER   p894
14 ANDERSON BLVD, STOUFFVILLE, ON, L4A 7X4
(905) 642-4400   *SIC* 5031
KWP INC   p1379
1367 RUE NATIONALE, TERREBONNE, QC, J6W 6H8
(450) 964-5786   *SIC* 5031
LAMBTON LUMBER INC   p585
170 BROCKPORT DR UNIT 14, ETOBICOKE, ON, M9W 5C8
(416) 798-1994   *SIC* 5031
LAUZON - PLANCHERS DE BOIS EXCLUSIFS INC   p1244
2101 COTE DES CASCADES, PAPINEAUVILLE, QC, J0V 1R0
(819) 427-5144   *SIC* 5031
LUSSIER, SIMON LTEE   p1059
16 BOUL DE LA SEIGNEURIE E, BLAINVILLE, QC, J7C 3V5
(450) 435-6591   *SIC* 5031
MAPLE LEAF FOREST PRODUCTS INC

*p*861
418 FOURTH LINE W, SAULT STE. MARIE, ON, P6A 0B5

(705) 450-2696   *SIC 5031*

MATERIAUX DE CONSTRUCTION R OLIGNY LTEE, LES   *p*1073
101 BOUL TASCHEREAU, CANDIAC, QC, J5R 1X4

(450) 659-5444   *SIC 5031*

MCGILL ST-LAURENT INC   *p*1189
407 RUE MCGILL BUREAU 315, MONTREAL, QC, H2Y 2G3

(514) 871-2120   *SIC 5031*

MCILVEEN LUMBER INDUSTRIES (ALTA.)(2012) LTD   *p*17
9440 48 ST SE, CALGARY, AB, T2C 2R2

(403) 273-5333   *SIC 5031*

MEDBRIDGE INVESTMENTS LTD   *p*141
2835 12 AVE N, LETHBRIDGE, AB, T1H 5K9

(403) 328-0922   *SIC 5031*

MERITCO INDUSTRIES LTD   *p*540
2675 REID SIDE RD, CAMPBELLVILLE, ON, L0P 1B0

(905) 854-2228   *SIC 5031*

METEO FENETRES ET PORTES INC *p*1323
132C RUE LEON-VACHON, SAINT-LAMBERT-DE-LAUZON, QC, G0S 2W0
SIC 5031

MOUNTAIN VIEW SPECIALTY PRODUCTS INC   *p*175
3013 TURNER ST, ABBOTSFORD, BC, V2S 7T9

(604) 850-2070   *SIC 5031*

NEUMAN, THOMAS J LIMITED   *p*836
6421 PALMER RD, PALMER RAPIDS, ON, K0J 2E0

(613) 758-2555   *SIC 5031*

NICHOLSON AND CATES LIMITED   *p*526
3060 MAINWAY SUITE 300, BURLINGTON, ON, L7M 1A3

(905) 335-3366   *SIC 5031*

NORTHERN BUILDING SUPPLY LTD   *p*288
1640 E KENT AVE SOUTH, VANCOUVER, BC, V5P 2S7

(604) 321-6141   *SIC 5031*

OASIS WINDOWS LTD   *p*277
7677 134 ST, SURREY, BC, V3W 9E9

(604) 597-5033   *SIC 5031*

OLYMPIC INDUSTRIES ULC   *p*240
221 ESPLANADE W SUITE 402, NORTH VANCOUVER, BC, V7M 3J8

(604) 985-2115   *SIC 5031*

OWL DISTRIBUTION INC   *p*1035
220 UNIVERSAL RD, WOODSTOCK, ON, N4S 7W3

(519) 539-8115   *SIC 5031*

PARQUET DE LUXE LASALLE INC *p*1132
8801 RUE ELMSLIE, LASALLE, QC, H8R 1V4

(514) 364-9760   *SIC 5031*

PEELLE COMPANY LIMITED, THE   *p*513
195 SANDALWOOD PKY W, BRAMPTON, ON, L7A 1J6

(905) 846-4545   *SIC 5031*

PELLETIER, RICHARD & FILS INC   *p*1377
4 RUE SAINT-MARC, SQUATEC, QC, G0L 4H0

(418) 855-2951   *SIC 5031*

PHOENIX GLASS INC   *p*209
8166 92 ST, DELTA, BC, V4G 0A4

(604) 525-2800   *SIC 5031*

PIERRE ET MAURICE DE LA FONTAINE INC   *p*1102
1000 RUE DOLLARD, GATINEAU, QC, J8L 3H3

(819) 986-8601   *SIC 5031*

PORTES A R D INC, LES   *p*1129
755 BOUL CRISTINI, LACHUTE, QC, J8H 4N6

(450) 562-2624   *SIC 5031*

PORTES ET FENETRES M.P.M. INC *p*1293
167 RUE D'AMSTERDAM, SAINT-AUGUSTIN-DE-DESMAURES, QC, G3A

2V5

(418) 870-1544   *SIC 5031*

PRODUITS DE BOIS CANADIENS - MONTREAL INC   *p*1190
407 RUE MCGILL BUREAU 315, MONTREAL, QC, H2Y 2G3

(514) 871-2120   *SIC 5031*

PRODUITS FORESTIERS AMPRO INC *p*1313
3025 RUE CARTIER, SAINT-HYACINTHE, QC, J2S 1L4

(450) 250-7888   *SIC 5031*

PRODUITS FORESTIERS M.E.S. INC, LES *p*1296
590 RUE SAGARD, SAINT-BRUNO, QC, J3V 6C2

(450) 461-1767   *SIC 5031*

QUADRA WOOD PRODUCTS LTD   *p*175
34371 INDUSTRIAL WAY, ABBOTSFORD, BC, V2S 7M6

(604) 854-1835   *SIC 5031*

QUALITY HARDWOODS LTD   *p*848
196 LATOUR CRES RR 3, POWASSAN, ON, P0H 1Z0

(705) 724-2424   *SIC 5031*

REGIONAL DOORS & HARDWARE (NIAGARA) LIMITED   *p*886
44 SCOTT ST W, ST CATHARINES, ON, L2R 1C9

(905) 684-8161   *SIC 5031*

REIMER HARDWOODS LTD   *p*177
31135 PEARDONVILLE RD, ABBOTSFORD, BC, V2T 6K6

(604) 850-9281   *SIC 5031*

REMBOS INC   *p*517
60 OLD ONONDAGA RD E, BRANTFORD, ON, N3T 5L4

(519) 770-1207   *SIC 5031*

RENE BERNARD INC   *p*1055
88 AV LAMBERT, BEAUCEVILLE, QC, G5X 3N4

(418) 774-3382   *SIC 5031*

RENE ST-CYR (1996) INC   *p*1243
3330 RTE 157, NOTRE-DAME-DU-MONT-CARMEL, QC, G0X 3J0

(819) 379-2202   *SIC 5031*

RIVERSIDE MILLWORK GROUP INC   *p*662
1275 HUBREY RD SUITE 7, LONDON, ON, N6N 1E2

(519) 686-7573   *SIC 5031*

ROBLIN FOREST PRODUCTS LTD   *p*355
83 N HWY, ROBLIN, MB, R0L 1P0

(204) 937-2103   *SIC 5031*

ROJAC ENTREPRISES INC   *p*417
1671 CH NICHOLAS-DENYS, SAINTE-ROSETTE, NB, E8K 3J9
SIC 5031

ROYAL GROUP, INC   *p*1380
1085 RUE DES CHEMINOTS BUREAU 10, TERREBONNE, QC, J6W 0A1

(450) 668-5549   *SIC 5031*

SAVONA SPECIALTY PLYWOOD CO. LTD *p*268
7273 KAMLOOPS LAKE DR, SAVONA, BC, V0K 2J0

(250) 373-5600   *SIC 5031*

SCIERIES ADRIEN ARSENEAULT LTEE *p*394
47 DU MOULIN ST, BALMORAL, NB, E8E 1H6
SIC 5031

SERVICES J. SONIC INC   *p*1330
6869 BOUL HENRI-BOURASSA O, SAINT-LAURENT, QC, H4R 1E1

(514) 341-5789   *SIC 5031*

SHAW, HERB AND SONS LIMITED   *p*838
31 SHARON ST, PEMBROKE, ON, K8A 7J5

(613) 732-9989   *SIC 5031*

SKANA FOREST PRODUCTS LTD   *p*256
20800 WESTMINSTER HWY SUITE 1303, RICHMOND, BC, V6V 2W3

(604) 273-5441   *SIC 5031*

SLEGG DEVELOPMENTS LTD   *p*341
2901 SOOKE RD, VICTORIA, BC, V9C 3W7

(250) 386-3667   *SIC 5031*

SLEGG LIMITED PARTNERSHIP   *p*235
4950 JORDAN AVE, NANAIMO, BC, V9T 2H8

(250) 758-8329   *SIC 5031*

SLEGG LIMITED PARTNERSHIP   *p*268
2030 MALAVIEW AVE W, SIDNEY, BC, V8L 5X6

(250) 656-1125   *SIC 5031*

SPRUCE TOP LUMBER SALES LTD   *p*359
11 TONY'S TRAIL, STONEWALL, MB, R0C 2Z0

(204) 467-1915   *SIC 5031*

STANDARD BUILDING SUPPLIES LTD *p*187
4925 STILL CREEK AVE, BURNABY, BC, V5C 5V1

(604) 294-4411   *SIC 5031*

STARLINE WINDOWS (2001) LTD   *p*280
19091 36 AVE, SURREY, BC, V3Z 0P6

(604) 882-5100   *SIC 5031*

STEADFAST CEDAR PRODUCTS LTD *p*230
27400 LOUGHEED HWY, MAPLE RIDGE, BC, V2W 1L1

(604) 462-7335   *SIC 5031*

STRUCTURES BARRETTE INC   *p*1385
545 RANG SAINT-MALO, TROIS-RIVIERES, QC, G8V 0A8

(819) 374-8784   *SIC 5031*

SUNAC WOODWORK INC   *p*94
13030 146 ST NW, EDMONTON, AB, T5L 2H7
SIC 5031

T.B.T. WINDOWS & DOORS EXTRUSION INC.   *p*786
27 TORBARRIE RD UNIT 25, NORTH YORK, ON, M3L 1G5

(416) 244-0000   *SIC 5031*

TAIGA BUILDING PRODUCTS LTD   *p*191
4710 KINGSWAY SUITE 800, BURNABY, BC, V5H 4M2

(604) 438-1471   *SIC 5031*

THOMSON, PETER & SONS INC   *p*476
256 VICTORIA ST W, ALLISTON, ON, L9R 1L9
SIC 5031

TOLKO MARKETING AND SALES LTD *p*332
3000 28 ST, VERNON, BC, V1T 9W9

(250) 545-4411   *SIC 5031*

TOWNE MILLWORK LTD   *p*177
2690 PROGRESSIVE WAY SUITE A, ABBOTSFORD, BC, V2T 6H9

(604) 850-7738   *SIC 5031*

TOWNSEND LUMBER INC   *p*912
1300 JACKSON SUITE 2, TILLSONBURG, ON, N4G 4G7

(519) 842-7381   *SIC 5031*

TRANS-PACIFIC TRADING LTD   *p*257
13091 VANIER PL UNIT 368, RICHMOND, BC, V6V 2J1

(604) 232-5400   *SIC 5031*

TRIDENT MILLWORK AND DISPLAY INDUSTRIES LTD   *p*262
11140 RIVER RD, RICHMOND, BC, V6X 1Z5

(604) 276-2855   *SIC 5031*

TVC HOLDINGS LIMITED   *p*801
2740 SHERWOOD HEIGHTS DR, OAKVILLE, ON, L6J 7V5

(905) 829-0280   *SIC 5031*

ULTRA-LITE OVERHEAD DOORS LTD *p*19
7307 40 ST SE, CALGARY, AB, T2C 2K4

(403) 280-2000   *SIC 5031*

UPPER CANADA - SIERRA GROUP SERVICE   *p*728
7088 FINANCIAL DR, MISSISSAUGA, ON, L5N 7H5

(905) 814-8800   *SIC 5031*

UPPER CANADA FOREST PRODUCTS LTD *p*728
7088 FINANCIAL DR, MISSISSAUGA, ON, L5N 7H5

(905) 814-8000   *SIC 5031*

VELCAN FOREST PRODUCTS INC   *p*814
1240 SKAE DR, OSHAWA, ON, L1J 7A1

(905) 571-2477   *SIC 5031*

VELUX CANADA INC   *p*801
2740 SHERWOOD HEIGHTS DR, OAKVILLE, ON, L6J 7V5

(905) 829-0280   *SIC 5031*

VISSCHER LUMBER INC   *p*198
6545 LICKMAN RD, CHILLIWACK, BC, V2R 4A9

(604) 858-3375   *SIC 5031*

VITRERIE LEVIS INC   *p*1137
12 RUE DU TERROIR, LEVIS, QC, G6V 9J3

(418) 833-2161   *SIC 5031*

W. I. WOODTONE INDUSTRIES INC   *p*198
8007 AITKEN RD, CHILLIWACK, BC, V2R 4H5

(604) 792-3680   *SIC 5031*

WANDEROSA WOOD PRODUCTS LIMITED PARTNERSHIP   *p*496
150 PARR BLVD, BOLTON, ON, L7E 4E6

(905) 857-6227   *SIC 5031*

WELCO LUMBER CORP   *p*187
4445 LOUGHEED HWY SUITE 1001, BURNABY, BC, V5C 0E4

(604) 732-1411   *SIC 5031*

WEST CHILCOTIN FOREST PRODUCTS LTD   *p*179
21841 CHILCOTIN HWY SUITE 20, ANAHIM LAKE, BC, V0L 1C0
SIC 5031

WEST FRASER MILLS LTD   *p*173
53115 HWY 47, YELLOWHEAD COUNTY, AB, T7E 3E9

(780) 723-3977   *SIC 5031*

WEST FRASER MILLS LTD   *p*252
1250 BROWNMILLER RD, QUESNEL, BC, V2J 6P5

(250) 992-9244   *SIC 5031*

WEST FRASER TIMBER CO. LTD   *p*159
GD STN MAIN, ROCKY MOUNTAIN HOUSE, AB, T4T 1T1

(403) 845-5522   *SIC 5031*

WEST FRASER TIMBER CO. LTD   *p*174
910 EXETER RD, 100 MILE HOUSE, BC, V0K 2E0

(250) 395-8200   *SIC 5031*

WEST FRASER TIMBER CO. LTD   *p*253
1250 BROWNMILLER RD, QUESNEL, BC, V2J 6P5

(250) 992-9244   *SIC 5031*

WEST FRASER TIMBER CO. LTD   *p*301
858 BEATTY ST SUITE 501, VANCOUVER, BC, V6B 1C1

(604) 895-2700   *SIC 5031*

WESTON FOREST PRODUCTS INC   *p*686
7600 TORBRAM RD, MISSISSAUGA, ON, L4T 3L8

(905) 677-9364   *SIC 5031*

WESTON WOOD SOLUTIONS INC   *p*507
300 ORENDA RD, BRAMPTON, ON, L6T 1G2

(905) 677-9120   *SIC 5031*

WEYERHAEUSER COMPANY LIMITED*p*133
GD STN MAIN, GRANDE PRAIRIE, AB, T8V 3A9

(780) 539-8500   *SIC 5031*

WEYERHAEUSER COMPANY LIMITED*p*592
40 DUNLOP ST, FORT ERIE, ON, L2A 4H8
SIC 5031

WIPTEC INC   *p*1374
3160 BOUL INDUSTRIEL, SHERBROOKE, QC, J1L 1V8

(819) 564-7117   *SIC 5031*

WOLF CREEK BUILDING SUPPLIES LTD *p*138
5645 WOLF CREEK DR SUITE 5808, LACOMBE, AB, T4L 2H8

(403) 782-1780   *SIC 5031*

WOODBRIDGE LUMBER INC   *p*1034
8100 KIPLING AVE, WOODBRIDGE, ON, L4L 2A1

(905) 581-2804   *SIC 5031*

___

SIC 5032 Brick, stone, and related material

___

059884 N.B. INC   p412
1360 ROTHESAY RD, SAINT JOHN, NB, E2H 2J1
(506) 633-1200   *SIC 5032*

1759800 ONTARIO INC   p590
804 COUNTY ROAD 8, FENELON FALLS, ON, K0M 1N0
(705) 887-9458   *SIC 5032*

543077 ALBERTA LTD   p124
305 116 AVE NW, EDMONTON, AB, T6S 1G3
(780) 440-2121   *SIC 5032*

853569 ONTARIO LIMITED   p480
33 ERIC T SMITH WAY, AURORA, ON, L4G 0Z6
(905) 726-9669   *SIC 5032*

9173-1307 QUEBEC INC   p1152
13448 BOUL DU CURE-LABELLE, MIRABEL, QC, J7J 1G9
(450) 939-3255   *SIC 5032*

A - 1 BUILDING SUPPLIES LTD   p275
8683 132 ST, SURREY, BC, V3W 4P1
(604) 599-3822   *SIC 5032*

ACADIA DRYWALL SUPPLIES LTD   p397
521 BOUL FERDINAND, DIEPPE, NB, E1A 7G1
(506) 858-1319   *SIC 5032*

ALBERTA WILBERT SALES LTD   p104
16910 129 AVE NW SUITE 1, EDMONTON, AB, T5V 1L1
(780) 447-2222   *SIC 5032*

ALLARD CONTRACTORS LTD   p199
1520 PIPELINE RD, COQUITLAM, BC, V3E 3P6
(604) 944-2556   *SIC 5032*

ALLSTONE QUARRY PRODUCTS INC p879
16105 HIGHWAY 27 RR 1, SCHOMBERG, ON, L0G 1T0
(905) 939-8491   *SIC 5032*

AMES TILE & STONE LTD   p237
415 BOYNE ST SUITE 301, NEW WEST-MINSTER, BC, V3M 5K2
(604) 515-3486   *SIC 5032*

ANATOLIA GROUP INC   p1029
8300 HUNTINGTON RD, WOODBRIDGE, ON, L4L 1A5
(905) 771-3800   *SIC 5032*

ANCO CONTRACTING INC   p1029
140 REGINA RD UNIT 15, WOODBRIDGE, ON, L4L 8N1
(905) 652-2353   *SIC 5032*

ARTEX SYSTEMS INC   p548
523 BOWES RD, CONCORD, ON, L4K 1J5
(905) 669-1425   *SIC 5032*

ATLANTIC READY MIX   p422
280 HUMBER RD, CORNER BROOK, NL, A2H 7H1
(709) 634-1885   *SIC 5032*

BARKMAN CONCRETE LTD   p358
152 BRANDT ST, STEINBACH, MB, R5G 0R2
(204) 326-3445   *SIC 5032*

BELL & MACKENZIE CO. LTD   p610
500 SHERMAN AVE N, HAMILTON, ON, L8L 8J6
(905) 527-6000   *SIC 5032*

BETON BARRETTE INC   p1390
1000 BOUL BARRETTE, VAL-D'OR, QC, J9P 0J8
(819) 825-8112   *SIC 5032*

BETON CHEVALIER INC   p1378
50 CH ROURKE, STONEHAM-ET-TEWKESBURY, QC, G3C 0W3
(418) 848-1966   *SIC 5032*

BRIQUE ET PIERRE MONTREAL INCp1231
1070 MONTEE MASSON, MONTREAL, QC, H7C 2R2
(514) 321-8402   *SIC 5032*

C&S GROUP OPERATIONS LTD   p184
2820 INGLETON AVE, BURNABY, BC, V5C 6G7
(604) 435-4431   *SIC 5032*

C. D. R. YOUNG'S AGGREGATES INC p846

31 HWY 35, PONTYPOOL, ON, L0A 1K0
(705) 277-3972   *SIC 5032*

CAMPBELL'S CONCRETE LTD   p1040
420 MOUNT EDWARD RD, CHARLOTTE-TOWN, PE, C1E 2A1
(902) 368-3442   *SIC 5032*

CENTURA (TORONTO) LIMITED   p788
950 LAWRENCE AVE W, NORTH YORK, ON, M6A 1C4
(416) 785-5165   *SIC 5032*

CENTURA (VANCOUVER) LIMITED   p188
4616 CANADA WAY, BURNABY, BC, V5G 1K5
(604) 298-8453   *SIC 5032*

CENTURA QUEBEC LTEE   p1338
5885 CH DE LA COTE-DE-LIESSE, SAINT-LAURENT, QC, H4T 1C3
(514) 336-4311   *SIC 5032*

CERAGRES TILE GROUP   p790
170 TYCOS DR, NORTH YORK, ON, M6B 1W8
(416) 286-3553   *SIC 5032*

CERAMIQUE ITAL-NORD LTEE   p1245
569 BOUL DES LAURENTIDES BUREAU 117, PIEDMONT, QC, J0R 1K0
(450) 227-8866   *SIC 5032*

CERAMIQUES ROYAL LTEE, LES   p1343
8845 RUE PASCAL-GAGNON, SAINT-LEONARD, QC, H1P 1Z4
(514) 324-0002   *SIC 5032*

CERATEC INC   p1263
414 AV SAINT-SACREMENT, QUEBEC, QC, G1N 3Y3
(418) 681-0101   *SIC 5032*

CERATEC INC   p1325
1620 BOUL JULES-POITRAS, SAINT-LAURENT, QC, H4N 1Z3
(514) 956-0341   *SIC 5032*

CIOT INC   p1178
9151 BOUL SAINT-LAURENT, MONTREAL, QC, H2N 1N2
(514) 382-5180   *SIC 5032*

COAST BUILDING SUPPLIES LTD   p276
8484 128 ST UNIT 100, SURREY, BC, V3W 4G3
(604) 590-0055   *SIC 5032*

COAST RANGE CONCRETE LTD   p230
1011 HWY 99 N, LILLOOET, BC, V0K 1V0
(250) 256-7803   *SIC 5032*

DAL-TILE OF CANADA ULC   p551
40 GRANITERIDGE RD UNIT 1, CONCORD, ON, L4K 5M8
(905) 738-2099   *SIC 5032*

DAUBOIS INC   p1344
6155 BOUL DES GRANDES-PRAIRIES, SAINT-LEONARD, QC, H1P 1A5
(514) 328-1253   *SIC 5032*

DELTA AGGREGATES LTD   p208
7469 HUME AVE, DELTA, BC, V4G 1C3
(604) 940-1300   *SIC 5032*

DEMERS, ROBERT & GILLES INC   p1381
3055 RUE DES BATISSEURS, TERREBONNE, QC, J6Y 0A2
(450) 477-2727   *SIC 5032*

DIAMOND READY MIX CONCRETE LTD p358
399 PTH 12 N, STEINBACH, MB, R5G 1V1
(204) 326-3456   *SIC 5032*

DICK, JAMES CONSTRUCTION LIMITED p494
14442 REGIONAL ROAD 50, BOLTON, ON, L7E 3E2
(905) 857-3500   *SIC 5032*

DOLAN'S CONCRETE LTD   p245
4779 ROGER ST, PORT ALBERNI, BC, V9Y 3Z3
(250) 723-6442   *SIC 5032*

DRYCO DRYWALL SUPPLIES LTD   p182
7027 WINSTON ST, BURNABY, BC, V5A 2G7
(604) 253-4121   *SIC 5032*

EURO CERAMIC TILE DISTRIBUTORS LTD p188
4288 MANOR ST, BURNABY, BC, V5G 1B2

(604) 437-3876   *SIC 5032*

EURO TILE & STONE INC   p817
3103 HAWTHORNE RD, OTTAWA, ON, K1G 3V8
(613) 244-4315   *SIC 5032*

FON-TILE CORPORATION LIMITED   p294
270 TERMINAL AVE, VANCOUVER, BC, V6A 2L6
(604) 683-9358   *SIC 5032*

GESTION CERATEC INC   p1264
414 AV SAINT-SACREMENT, QUEBEC, QC, G1N 3Y3
(418) 681-0101   *SIC 5032*

GESTION GUY GERVAIS INC   p1226
1370 RUE CHABANEL O, MONTREAL, QC, H4N 1H4
(514) 384-5590   *SIC 5032*

GRANIREX   p1382
1045 RUE MONFETTE E, THETFORD MINES, QC, G6G 7K7
SIC 5032

GRANIT PLUS INC   p1352
386 RUE PRINCIPALE, SAINT-SEBASTIEN-DE-FRONTENAC, QC, G0Y 1M0
(819) 652-2514   *SIC 5032*

GRAYMONT LIMITED   p260
10991 SHELLBRIDGE WAY SUITE 200, RICHMOND, BC, V6X 3C6
(604) 207-4292   *SIC 5032*

GROUPE CARREAUX CERAGRES INC p1326
825 RUE DESLAURIERS, SAINT-LAURENT, QC, H4N 1X3
(514) 384-5590   *SIC 5032*

GROUPE GIROUX MACONNEX INC p1080
2223 BOUL SAINT-PAUL, CHICOUTIMI, QC, G7K 1E5
(418) 549-7345   *SIC 5032*

HALOW, B. J. & SON CONSTRUCTORS LTD p857
22 WING RD, ROSSLYN, ON, P7K 0L2
(807) 939-2533   *SIC 5032*

I-XL MASONRY SUPPLIES LTD   p16
4900 102 AVE SE, CALGARY, AB, T2C 2X8
(403) 243-6031   *SIC 5032*

ICAN CONTRACTING LTD   p182
3131 THUNDERBIRD CRES, BURNABY, BC, V5A 3G1
(604) 299-0146   *SIC 5032*

ICON STONE & TILE INC   p30
521 36 AVE SE, CALGARY, AB, T2G 1W5
(403) 532-3383   *SIC 5032*

JAMER MATERIALS LIMITED   p395
3019 ROUTE 127, BAYSIDE, NB, E5B 2S4
(506) 529-1117   *SIC 5032*

K AND L CONTRACTING   p266
10704 HWY 9, ROSEDALE, BC, V0X 1X1
(604) 794-0107   *SIC 5032*

KEETHILLS AGGREGATE CO LTD   p96
11428 168 ST NW SUITE 100, EDMONTON, AB, T5M 3T9
SIC 5032

KNELSEN SAND & GRAVEL LTD   p137
10005 100 ST, LA CRETE, AB, T0H 2H0
(780) 928-3935   *SIC 5032*

L & D PETCH CONTRACTING LTD   p220
204 CAMBRO RD, KELOWNA, BC, V1X 7T3
(250) 491-0405   *SIC 5032*

LAFARGE CANADA INC   p555
7880 KEELE ST UNIT 5, CONCORD, ON, L4K 4G7
(905) 738-7070   *SIC 5032*

LAFARGE CANADA INC   p1340
4000 RUE HICKMORE, SAINT-LAURENT, QC, H4T 1K2
(514) 344-1788   *SIC 5032*

LEHIGH HANSON MATERIALS LIMITED p323
8955 SHAUGHNESSY ST, VANCOUVER, BC, V6P 3Y7
(604) 261-6225   *SIC 5032*

MAGNUM CONCRETE INC   p179
26162 30A AVE SUITE 201, ALDER-

GROVE, BC, V4W 2W5
(604) 607-6576   *SIC 5032*

MARTIN MARIETTA MATERIALS CANADA LIMITED   p463
266 LOWER QUARRIE RD, MULGRAVE, NS, B0E 2G0
(902) 747-2882   *SIC 5032*

MASKIMO CONSTRUCTION INC   p1388
2500 RUE LEON-TREPANIER, TROIS-RIVIERES, QC, G9A 5E1
(819) 601-2999   *SIC 5032*

MASON'S MASONRY SUPPLY LIMITED p740
6291 NETHERHART RD, MISSISSAUGA, ON, L5T 1A2
(905) 670-1233   *SIC 5032*

MAYCO MIX LTD   p235
1125 CEDAR RD, NANAIMO, BC, V9X 1K9
(250) 722-0064   *SIC 5032*

METRIX READY MIX LTD   p793
777 FENMAR DR, NORTH YORK, ON, M9L 1C8
(416) 746-4600   *SIC 5032*

MOOSE JAW REFINERY ULC   p54
440 2 AVE SW SUITE 1700, CALGARY, AB, T2P 5E9
(403) 206-4000   *SIC 5032*

MSI STONE ULC   p725
2140 MEADOWPINE BLVD, MISSISSAUGA, ON, L5N 6H6
(905) 812-6100   *SIC 5032*

NATIONAL CONCRETE ACCESSORIES CANADA INC   p96
14760 116 AVE NW, EDMONTON, AB, T5M 3G1
(780) 451-1212   *SIC 5032*

O.C.P. CONSTRUCTION SUPPLIES INC p900
1072 WEBBWOOD DR, SUDBURY, ON, P3C 3B7
(705) 674-7073   *SIC 5032*

OLYMPIA TILE INTERNATIONAL INC p988
1000 LAWRENCE AVE W, TORONTO, ON, M6A 1C6
(416) 785-6666   *SIC 5032*

PARSONS PRECAST INC   p615
1315 RYMAL RD E, HAMILTON, ON, L8W 3N1
(905) 387-0810   *SIC 5032*

PIPEFLO CONTRACTING CORP   p613
111 FRID ST, HAMILTON, ON, L8P 4M3
(905) 572-7767   *SIC 5032*

REDA ENTERPRISES LTD   p6
GD STN MAIN, BONNYVILLE, AB, T9N 2J6
(780) 826-2737   *SIC 5032*

RINTALA CONSTRUCTION COMPANY LIMITED   p647
377 BLACK LAKE RD, LIVELY, ON, P3Y 1H8
(705) 692-3648   *SIC 5032*

SABLES OLIMAG INC, LES   p1383
2899 BOUL FRONTENAC E, THETFORD MINES, QC, G6G 6P6
(418) 338-3562   *SIC 5032*

SABLIERE DRAPEAU (1986) INC   p1079
205 BOUL DU ROYAUME E, CHICOUTIMI, QC, G7H 5H2
(450) 549-0532   *SIC 5032*

ST-GERMAIN EGOUTS & AQUEDUCS INC p1309
3800 BOUL SIR-WILFRID-LAURIER, SAINT-HUBERT, QC, J3Y 6T1
(450) 671-6171   *SIC 5032*

STEEP ROCK LTD   p81
11524 RANGE ROAD 52 UNIT 1, CYPRESS COUNTY, AB, T1B 0K7
(403) 529-9668   *SIC 5032*

STONE TILE INTERNATIONAL INC   p791
834 CALEDONIA RD SUITE 1, NORTH YORK, ON, M6B 3X9
(416) 515-9000   *SIC 5032*

STONY VALLEY CONTRACTING LTD p129
245 TAIGANOVA CRES, FORT MCMURRAY, AB, T9K 0T4
(780) 743-0527   *SIC 5032*

▲ Public Company   ■ Public Company Family Member   **HQ** Headquarters   **BR** Branch   **SL** Single Location

STRADA AGGREGATES INC p559
30 FLORAL PKY SUITE 400, CONCORD, ON, L4K 4R1
(905) 738-2200   *SIC 5032*

STRADA CRUSH LIMITED p559
69 CONNIE CRES SUITE 1, CONCORD, ON, L4K 1L3
(905) 303-6200   *SIC 5032*

SUTHERLAND, HAROLD CONSTRUCTION LTD p627
323545 E LINTON W, KEMBLE, ON, N0H 1S0
(519) 376-5698   *SIC 5032*

TANGRAM SURFACES INC p448
66 WRIGHT AVE, DARTMOUTH, NS, B3B 1H3
(902) 468-7679   *SIC 5032*

TIERRA SOL CERAMIC TILE LTD p183
4084 MCCONNELL CRT UNIT 100, BURNABY, BC, V5A 3L8
(604) 435-5400   *SIC 5032*

UNITED CONCRETE & GRAVEL LTD p252
1077 CARSON PIT RD, QUESNEL, BC, V2J 7H2
(250) 992-7281   *SIC 5032*

VALLEY GRAVEL SALES LTD p178
700 LEFEUVRE RD, ABBOTSFORD, BC, V4X 1H7
(604) 856-4461   *SIC 5032*

WEBSTER & FILS LIMITEE p1327
2585 CH DE LA COTE-DE-LIESSE, SAINT-LAURENT, QC, H4N 2M8
(514) 332-4541   *SIC 5032*

SIC 5033 Roofing, siding, and insulation

518162 ALBERTA INC p98
11104 180 ST NW, EDMONTON, AB, T5S 2X5
(780) 452-7410   *SIC 5033*

ACOUSTIQUE ISOLATION QUATRE SAISONS INC p1282
525 RUE LANAUDIERE, REPENTIGNY, QC, J6A 7N1
(450) 657-5000   *SIC 5033*

ALL THERM SERVICES INC p191
8528 GLENLYON PKY UNIT 141, BURNABY, BC, V5J 0B6
(604) 559-4331   *SIC 5033*

ALL WEATHER PRODUCTS LTD p275
12510 82 AVE, SURREY, BC, V3W 3E9
(604) 572-8088   *SIC 5033*

BUHLER VERSATILE INDUSTRIES p1426
NORTH CORMAN INDUSTRIAL PARK, SASKATOON, SK, S7K 0A1
(306) 931-3000   *SIC 5033*

CANAM BUILDING ENVELOPE SPECIALISTS INC p919
50 BETH NEALSON DR, TORONTO, ON, M4H 1M6
(416) 467-3485   *SIC 5033*

DISPRO INC p1048
10280 BOUL RAY-LAWSON, ANJOU, QC, H1J 1L8
(514) 354-5251   *SIC 5033*

ENERCON PRODUCTS LTD p114
9610 54 AVE NW, EDMONTON, AB, T6E 5V1
(780) 437-7003   *SIC 5033*

ENTREPRISES POL R INC p1277
5085 RUE RIDEAU, QUEBEC, QC, G2E 5H5
(418) 872-0000   *SIC 5033*

GLASSCELL ISOFAB INC p584
1000 MARTIN GROVE RD SUITE 1, ETOBICOKE, ON, M9W 4V8
(416) 241-8663   *SIC 5033*

HUSKY ENERGY INC p144
5650 52 ST, LLOYDMINSTER, AB, T9V 0R7
(780) 871-6571   *SIC 5033*

KAYCAN LTEE p1251
3075 RTE TRANSCANADIENNE, POINTE-CLAIRE, QC, H9R 1B4

(514) 694-5855   *SIC 5033*

MULTI-GLASS INSULATION LTD p504
3925 STEELES AVE E UNIT 1 & 2, BRAMPTON, ON, L6T 5W5
(416) 798-3900   *SIC 5033*

OC CANADA HOLDINGS COMPANY p124
831 HAYTER RD NW, EDMONTON, AB, T6S 1A1
(780) 472-6644   *SIC 5033*

PRO-LINE CONSTRUCTION MATERIALS LTD p228
20109 LOGAN AVE, LANGLEY, BC, V3A 4L5
(604) 534-2060   *SIC 5033*

PRODUITS MURPHCO LTEE, LES p1223
5363 RUE NOTRE-DAME O BUREAU 117, MONTREAL, QC, H4C 1T7
(514) 937-3275   *SIC 5033*

PRODUITS POUR ANIMAUX YAMAS INC p1313
3175 BOUL CHOQUETTE, SAINT-HYACINTHE, QC, J2S 7Z8
(418) 771-4622   *SIC 5033*

PRODUITS POUR TOITURES FRANSYL LTEE p1379
671 RUE LEVEILLE, TERREBONNE, QC, J6W 1Z9
(450) 492-2392   *SIC 5033*

PRODUITS POUR TOITURES FRANSYL LTEE p1381
1845 RUE JEAN-MONNET, TERREBONNE, QC, J6X 4L7
(450) 477-4423   *SIC 5033*

ROOFMART ALBERTA INC p37
6125 11 ST SE SUITE 250, CALGARY, AB, T2H 2L6
(403) 233-8030   *SIC 5033*

ROOFMART HOLDINGS LIMITED p510
305 RUTHERFORD RD S, BRAMPTON, ON, L6W 3R5
(905) 453-9689   *SIC 5033*

ROOFMART PACIFIC LTD p37
6125 11 ST SE SUITE 250, CALGARY, AB, T2H 2L6
(403) 233-8030   *SIC 5033*

ROOFMART WESTERN LTD p37
6125 11 ST SE SUITE 250, CALGARY, AB, T2H 2L6
(403) 233-8030   *SIC 5033*

SAKO MATERIALS LIMITED p510
71 ORENDA RD, BRAMPTON, ON, L6W 1V8
(905) 457-5321   *SIC 5033*

STYRO RAIL INC p1400
65 RTE 105, WAKEFIELD, QC, J0X 3G0
(819) 643-4456   *SIC 5033*

TREMBLAY, RODRIGUE (SHERBROOKE) INC p1372
2540 RUE ROY, SHERBROOKE, QC, J1K 1C1
(819) 346-4527   *SIC 5033*

SIC 5039 Construction materials, nec

1146898 ONTARIO INC p1029
101 WESTCREEK DR, WOODBRIDGE, ON, L4L 9N6
(905) 850-2212   *SIC 5039*

1719108 ONTARIO INC p547
368 FOUR VALLEY DR, CONCORD, ON, L4K 5Z1
(416) 749-5665   *SIC 5039*

24 HOUR THERMAL GLASS INSULATION LTD p547
250 BOWES RD, CONCORD, ON, L4K 1J9
(905) 738-7585   *SIC 5039*

2732-3930 QUEBEC INC p1315
950 RUE BERNIER, SAINT-JEAN-SUR-RICHELIEU, QC, J2W 2H1
(450) 359-1311   *SIC 5039*

4577 NUNAVUT LIMITED p748
69 JAMIE AVE, NEPEAN, ON, K2E 7Y6
SIC 5039

45TH STREET LIMITED PARTNERSHIP p1431
701 45TH ST W, SASKATOON, SK, S7L 5W5
(306) 934-0600   *SIC 5039*

9050-7641 QUEBEC INC p1137
4457 BOUL GUILLAUME-COUTURE, LEVIS, QC, G6W 6M9
(418) 838-4464   *SIC 5039*

9168-1924 QUEBEC INC p1154
1351 BOUL ALBINY-PAQUETTE, MONT-LAURIER, QC, J9L 1M8
(819) 623-1767   *SIC 5039*

9223-3196 QUEBEC INC p1150
9 RUE NOTTAWAY, MATAGAMI, QC, J0Y 2A0
SIC 5039

ACME AWNINGS PRESTIGE p1163
5598 RUE HOCHELAGA BUREAU 101, MONTREAL, QC, H1N 3L7
(514) 252-1998   *SIC 5039*

AFA FOREST PRODUCTS INC p494
244 ELLWOOD DR W, BOLTON, ON, L7E 4W4
(905) 857-6423   *SIC 5039*

ALL-FAB BUILDING COMPONENTS INC p1415
610 HENDERSON DR, REGINA, SK, S4N 5X3
(306) 721-8131   *SIC 5039*

ALLMAR INC p368
287 RIVERTON AVE, WINNIPEG, MB, R2L 0N2
(204) 668-1000   *SIC 5039*

ALSIP'S INDUSTRIAL PRODUCTS LTD p368
1 COLE AVE, WINNIPEG, MB, R2L 1J3
(204) 667-3330   *SIC 5039*

ARAUCO CANADA LIMITED p418
151 CHURCH ST, ST STEPHEN, NB, E3L 5H1
(506) 466-2370   *SIC 5039*

ARROW CONSTRUCTION PRODUCTS LIMITED p402
50 GERVAIS CRT, FREDERICTON, NB, E3C 1L4
(506) 458-9610   *SIC 5039*

ATIS LP p408
70 RIDEOUT ST, MONCTON, NB, E1E 1E2
(506) 853-8080   *SIC 5039*

BARBER GROUP INVESTMENTS INC p601
485 SOUTHGATE DR, GUELPH, ON, N1G 3W6
SIC 5039

BEACON ROOFING SUPPLY CANADA COMPANY p1247
13145 RUE PRINCE-ARTHUR, POINTE-AUX-TREMBLES, QC, H1A 1A9
(514) 642-8998   *SIC 5039*

BEAUCHESNE, EDOUARD (1985) INC p1348
3211 RUE DE L'INDUSTRIE, SAINT-MATHIEU-DE-BELOEIL, QC, J3G 4S5
(450) 467-8776   *SIC 5039*

BERNARDI BUILDING SUPPLY LTD p792
469 GARYRAY DR, NORTH YORK, ON, M9L 1P9
(416) 741-0941   *SIC 5039*

BIRD, J.W. AND COMPANY LIMITED p400
670 WILSEY RD, FREDERICTON, NB, E3B 7K4
(506) 453-9915   *SIC 5039*

BOIS TURCOTTE LTEE p1390
1338 3E AV, VAL-D'OR, QC, J9P 1V5
(819) 824-3661   *SIC 5039*

BROCK WHITE CANADA ULC p371
879 KEEWATIN ST, WINNIPEG, MB, R2X 2S7
(204) 694-3600   *SIC 5039*

BUILDDIRECT.COM TECHNOLOGIES INC p297
401 GEORGIA ST W SUITE 2200, VANCOUVER, BC, V6B 5A1
(604) 662-8100   *SIC 5039*

CAN-SAVE SUPPLY AND DISTRIBUTION p486
411 BAYVIEW DR, BARRIE, ON, L4N 8Y2
(705) 722-7283   *SIC 5039*

CANAC IMMOBILIER INC p1255
947 AV ROYALE, QUEBEC, QC, G1E 1Z9
(418) 667-1729   *SIC 5039*

CANAC IMMOBILIER INC p1278
5355 BOUL DES GRADINS, QUEBEC, QC, G2J 1C8
(418) 667-1313   *SIC 5039*

CANADA WATERWORKS INC p583
35 SHAFT RD, ETOBICOKE, ON, M9W 4M3
(416) 244-4848   *SIC 5039*

CANADIAN TRADE INTERNATIONAL, INC p1431
2241 HANSELMAN AVE SUITE 8, SASKATOON, SK, S7L 6A7
(306) 931-4111   *SIC 5039*

CANEX BUILDING SUPPLIES LTD p197
46070 KNIGHT RD, CHILLIWACK, BC, V2R 1B7
(604) 858-8188   *SIC 5039*

CANWEL BUILDING MATERIALS GROUP LTD p311
1055 GEORGIA ST W SUITE 1100, VANCOUVER, BC, V6E 0B6
(604) 432-1400   *SIC 5039*

CANWEL BUILDING MATERIALS LTD p311
1055 WEST GEORGIA ST SUITE 1100, VANCOUVER, BC, V6E 3P3
(604) 432-1400   *SIC 5039*

CAPITAL BUILDING SUPPLIES LTD p250
4150 COWART RD, PRINCE GEORGE, BC, V2N 6H9
(250) 562-1125   *SIC 5039*

CATLEN HOLDINGS LIMITED p738
7361 PACIFIC CIR, MISSISSAUGA, ON, L5T 2A4
(905) 362-1161   *SIC 5039*

CENTRAL CANADIAN GLASS LTD p550
60 SNOW BLVD UNIT 1, CONCORD, ON, L4K 4B3
(905) 660-1676   *SIC 5039*

CENTRE DU BRICOLEUR LACHINE LTEE p1126
650 RUE NOTRE-DAME BUREAU 1849, LACHINE, QC, H8S 2B3
(514) 637-3767   *SIC 5039*

CHALLENGER BUILDING SUPPLIES LTD p140
3304 8 AVE N, LETHBRIDGE, AB, T1H 5C9
(403) 327-8501   *SIC 5039*

CHETICAMP COOP LTD. p442
15081 CABOT TRAIL RD, CHETICAMP, NS, B0E 1H0
(902) 224-2066   *SIC 5039*

CITY LUMBER CORPORATION p105
15711 128 AVE NW, EDMONTON, AB, T5V 1K4
(780) 447-1344   *SIC 5039*

CLOTURE SPEC-II INC p1064
65 RUE DE MONTGOLFIER, BOUCHERVILLE, QC, J4B 8C4
(450) 449-7732   *SIC 5039*

CLOTURES JERMAR INC. p1394
877 RTE HARWOOD, VAUDREUIL-DORION, QC, J7V 8P2
(450) 732-1121   *SIC 5039*

COASTAL DOOR & FRAME INC p445
40 RADDALL AVE, DARTMOUTH, NS, B3B 1T2
(902) 468-2333   *SIC 5039*

COMPTOIRS MOULES RIVE-NORD INC, LES p1254
414 BOUL RAYMOND, QUEBEC, QC, G1C 0L6
(418) 667-8814   *SIC 5039*

CONSOLIDATED GYPSUM SUPPLY LTD p100
11660 170 ST NW, EDMONTON, AB, T5S 1J7
(780) 452-7786   *SIC 5039*

CONVOY SUPPLY LTD p276
8183 130 ST, SURREY, BC, V3W 7X4

(604) 591-5381 *SIC 5039*
COPP BUILDING MATERIALS LIMITED
p653
45 YORK ST, LONDON, ON, N6A 1A4
(519) 679-9000 *SIC 5039*
CP DISTRIBUTORS LTD *p1434*
3719 KOCHAR AVE, SASKATOON, SK, S7P 0B8
(306) 242-3315 *SIC 5039*
CROWN BUILDING SUPPLIES LTD *p276*
7550 132 ST UNIT 10, SURREY, BC, V3W 4M7
(604) 591-5555 *SIC 5039*
DIACO INTERNATIONAL INC *p29*
3620 BLACKBURN RD SE, CALGARY, AB, T2G 4A5
(403) 287-4494 *SIC 5039*
DISTRIBUTION STE-FOY (1982) LTEE *p1266*
685 AV NEWTON, QUEBEC, QC, G1P 4C4
(418) 871-8133 *SIC 5039*
DISTRIBUTIONS B.M.B. (1985) S.E.C. , LES
p1231
4500 RUE BERNARD-LEFEBVRE, MONTREAL, QC, H7C 0A5
(514) 382-6520 *SIC 5039*
DOKA CANADA LTD./LTEE *p15*
5404 36 ST SE, CALGARY, AB, T2C 1P1
(403) 243-6629 *SIC 5039*
DOMTEK INC *p351*
GD STN LOCKPORT, LOCKPORT, MB, R1A 3R9
(204) 981-1266 *SIC 5039*
DORKEN SYSTEMS INC *p489*
4655 DELTA WAY, BEAMSVILLE, ON, L0R 1B4
(905) 563-3255 *SIC 5039*
DOUBLE R BUILDING PRODUCTS LTD *p15*
8209 30 ST SE, CALGARY, AB, T2C 1H7
(403) 236-8322 *SIC 5039*
DRYCO BUILDING SUPPLIES INC *p227*
5955 205A ST, LANGLEY, BC, V3A 8C4
(604) 533-2313 *SIC 5039*
DSI CANADA CIVIL, LTD *p281*
19433 96 AVE SUITE 103, SURREY, BC, V4N 4C4
(604) 888-8818 *SIC 5039*
DURADEK CANADA LIMITED *p276*
8288 129 ST, SURREY, BC, V3W 0A6
(604) 591-5594 *SIC 5039*
ENGINEERED ASSEMBLIES INC *p722*
6535 MILLCREEK DR UNIT 75, MISSISSAUGA, ON, L5N 2M2
(905) 816-2218 *SIC 5039*
ENTREPRISES LISE LAVOIE INC, LES
p1149
1407 AV DE LA GARE, MASCOUCHE, QC, J7K 3G6
(450) 474-0404 *SIC 5039*
ERNEWEIN, JOHN LIMITED *p1004*
18 INDUSTRIAL RD, WALKERTON, ON, N0G 2V0
(519) 881-0187 *SIC 5039*
EROSIONCONTROLBLANKET.COM INC
p355
1 BROADWAY AVE, RIVERTON, MB, R0C 2R0
(204) 378-5610 *SIC 5039*
FBM CANADA GSD, INC *p12*
5155 48 AVE SE, CALGARY, AB, T2B 3S8
(403) 255-8157 *SIC 5039*
FORM & BUILD SUPPLY INC *p651*
1175 FRANCES ST, LONDON, ON, N5W 2L9
(519) 453-4300 *SIC 5039*
FORMATIONS INC *p93*
12220 142 ST NW, EDMONTON, AB, T5L 2G9
(780) 451-6400 *SIC 5039*
FRASER VALLEY BUILDING SUPPLIES INC *p232*
7072 WREN ST, MISSION, BC, V2V 2V9
(604) 820-1134 *SIC 5039*
GEROQUIP INC *p1236*
4795 RUE LOUIS-B.-MAYER, MONTREAL,

QC, H7P 6G5
(450) 978-0200 *SIC 5039*
GIVESCO INC *p1344*
9495 RUE PASCAL-GAGNON, SAINT-LEONARD, QC, H1P 1Z4
(514) 327-7175 *SIC 5039*
GRANT FARMS CORP *p753*
863169 UNO PARK RD, NEW LISKEARD, ON, P0J 1P0
(705) 647-3129 *SIC 5039*
GROUPE ADF INC *p1344*
8788 RUE AETERNA, SAINT-LEONARD, QC, H1P 2R9
(514) 327-5383 *SIC 5039*
GROUPE BMR INC *p1065*
1501 RUE AMPERE BUREAU 200, BOUCHERVILLE, QC, J4B 5Z5
(450) 655-2441 *SIC 5039*
GROUPE PATRICK MORIN INC *p1350*
620 BOUL DE L'INDUSTRIE, SAINT-PAUL, QC, J0K 3E0
(450) 752-4774 *SIC 5039*
GROUPE ROYAL INC *p1379*
1085 RUE DES CHEMINOTS, TERRE-BONNE, QC, J6W 0A1
(450) 492-5080 *SIC 5039*
GUARDIAN BUILDING PRODUCTS DISTRIBUTION CANADA, INC *p569*
300 MAIN ST SS 1, ERIN, ON, N0B 1T0
(519) 833-9645 *SIC 5039*
GYM-CON LTD *p487*
93 RAWSON AVE, BARRIE, ON, L4N 6E5
(705) 728-2222 *SIC 5039*
H & S BUILDING SUPPLIES LIMITED *p553*
96 MAPLECRETE RD UNIT 4 5, CONCORD, ON, L4K 2B5
(905) 738-6003 *SIC 5039*
HALIBURTON LUMBER & ENTERPRISES LIMITED *p607*
GD, HALIBURTON, ON, K0M 1S0
(705) 457-2510 *SIC 5039*
HOME DEPOT OF CANADA INC *p1223*
4625 RUE SAINT-ANTOINE O, MONTREAL, QC, H4C 1E2
(514) 846-4770 *SIC 5039*
IGLOO BUILDING SUPPLIES GROUP LTD
p101
21421 111 AVE NW, EDMONTON, AB, T5S 1Y1
(780) 451-0600 *SIC 5039*
IGLOO MANUFACTURING LTD *p101*
21421 111 AVE NW, EDMONTON, AB, T5S 1Y1
(780) 451-0600 *SIC 5039*
INMARCA HOLDING INC *p706*
51 VILLAGE CENTRE PL UNIT 7, MISSISSAUGA, ON, L4W 1V9
(416) 471-1914 *SIC 5039*
INSUL-WEST BUILDING MATERIALS LTD
p220
860 MCCURDY RD, KELOWNA, BC, V1X 2P7
(250) 807-2551 *SIC 5039*
JAMAC SALES LIMITED *p671*
141 DON PARK RD, MARKHAM, ON, L3R 1C2
(905) 947-9824 *SIC 5039*
KASA SUPPLY LTD *p274*
13237 KING GEORGE BLVD, SURREY, BC, V3T 2T3
(604) 581-5815 *SIC 5039*
KAYCAN LTEE *p1251*
160 AV ONEIDA, POINTE-CLAIRE, QC, H9R 1A8
(514) 694-7200 *SIC 5039*
KENROC BUILDING MATERIALS CO. LTD
p1420
1275 BROAD ST UNIT 200, REGINA, SK, S4R 1Y2
(306) 525-1415 *SIC 5039*
KRYTON CANADA CORPORATION *p287*
1645 E KENT AVE NORTH, VANCOUVER, BC, V5P 2S8
(604) 324-8280 *SIC 5039*

LAURENT LAPOINTE LTEE *p1080*
1150 BOUL SAINT-PAUL BUREAU 400, CHICOUTIMI, QC, G7J 3C5
SIC 5039
LEFEBVRE & BENOIT S.E.C. *p1231*
4500 RUE BERNARD-LEFEBVRE, MONTREAL, QC, H7C 0A5
(450) 667-6000 *SIC 5039*
LUMBER MART LIMITED *p459*
751 HERRING COVE RD, HERRING COVE, NS, B3R 1Y9
(902) 477-6500 *SIC 5039*
MANUGYPSE INC *p1277*
5385 RUE RIDEAU BUREAU 871, QUEBEC, QC, G2E 5V9
(418) 871-8088 *SIC 5039*
MARQUIS BUILDING MAINTENANCE SUPPLIES LIMITED *p703*
1786 MATTAWA AVE UNIT 2, MISSISSAUGA, ON, L4X 1K1
(905) 275-0985 *SIC 5039*
MATERIAUX AUDET INC *p1348*
294 BOUL BONA-DUSSAULT, SAINT-MARC-DES-CARRIERES, QC, G0A 4B0
(418) 268-3525 *SIC 5039*
MATERIAUX BOMAT INC *p1140*
1212 CH INDUSTRIEL, LEVIS, QC, G7A 1B1
(418) 831-4848 *SIC 5039*
MATERIAUX DE CONSTRUCTION D L INC
p1108
760 RUE DE VERNON, GATINEAU, QC, J9J 3K5
(819) 770-9974 *SIC 5039*
MCKILLICAN CANADIAN INC *p106*
16420 118 AVE NW, EDMONTON, AB, T5V 1C8
(780) 453-3841 *SIC 5039*
MCKILLICAN INTERNATIONAL, INC *p106*
16420 118 AVE NW, EDMONTON, AB, T5V 1C8
(780) 453-3841 *SIC 5039*
MENARD, J. R. LIMITED *p888*
5 RANGER ST, ST ISIDORE, ON, K0C 2B0
(613) 524-2885 *SIC 5039*
MME MULTIURETHANES LTD *p697*
5245 CREEKBANK RD, MISSISSAUGA, ON, L4W 1N3
(905) 564-7650 *SIC 5039*
NEW BRUNSWICK WIRE FENCE COMPANY LIMITED *p409*
80 HENRI DUNANT ST, MONCTON, NB, E1E 1E6
(506) 857-8141 *SIC 5039*
NORTHCOAST BUILDING PRODUCTS LTD
p272
14682 66 AVE, SURREY, BC, V3S 1Z9
(604) 597-8884 *SIC 5039*
NORTHWEST WOOD TREATERS LP *p251*
10553 WILLOW CALE FOREST, PRINCE GEORGE, BC, V2N 4T7
(250) 963-9628 *SIC 5039*
NOVA SCOTIA BUILDING SUPPLIES (1982) LIMITED *p441*
459 HWY 3, BLOCKHOUSE, NS, B0J 1E0
(902) 624-8328 *SIC 5039*
OLDCASTLE BUILDING PRODUCTS CANADA, INC *p2*
28234 ACHESON RD, ACHESON, AB, T7X 6A9
(780) 962-4010 *SIC 5039*
OLDCASTLE BUILDING PRODUCTS CANADA, INC *p684*
8375 NO 5 SIDE RD, MILTON, ON, L9T 2X7
(905) 875-4215 *SIC 5039*
OLDCASTLE BUILDING PRODUCTS CANADA, INC *p1073*
2 AV D'INVERNESS, CANDIAC, QC, J5R 4W5
(450) 444-5214 *SIC 5039*
OLYMPIC BUILDING SYSTEMS LTD *p366*
1783 DUGALD RD, WINNIPEG, MB, R2J 0H3
(204) 661-8600 *SIC 5039*

OSTIGUY ET FRERES INC *p1075*
1000 BOUL INDUSTRIEL, CHAMBLY, QC, J3L 6Z7
(450) 658-4371 *SIC 5039*
PACIFIC WEST SYSTEMS SUPPLY LTD *p228*
20109 LOGAN AVE, LANGLEY, BC, V3A 4L5
(604) 530-7489 *SIC 5039*
PARKLAND BUILDING SUPPLIES (1998) LTD *p268*
1125 EAGLE PA WAY RR 2, SICAMOUS, BC, V0E 2V2
(250) 836-2514 *SIC 5039*
PATENE BUILDING SUPPLIES LTD *p606*
641 SPEEDVALE AVE W, GUELPH, ON, N1K 1E6
(519) 824-4030 *SIC 5039*
PEAK INNOVATIONS INC *p263*
11782 HAMMERSMITH WAY UNIT 203, RICHMOND, BC, V7A 5E2
(604) 448-8000 *SIC 5039*
PEAK PRODUCTS MANUFACTURING INC
p263
11782 HAMMERSMITH WAY UNIT 203, RICHMOND, BC, V7A 5E2
(604) 448-8000 *SIC 5039*
PILON LTEE *p1106*
5 BOUL MONTCLAIR, GATINEAU, QC, J8Y 2E3
(819) 771-5841 *SIC 5039*
PORT COQUITLAM BUILDING SUPPLIES LTD *p247*
2650 MARY HILL RD, PORT COQUITLAM, BC, V3C 3B3
(604) 942-7282 *SIC 5039*
PORTES ET FENETRES VERDUN LTEE
p1296
1305 RUE MARIE-VICTORIN BUREAU 300, SAINT-BRUNO, QC, J3V 6B7
(450) 441-0472 *SIC 5039*
PRODUITS & SERVICES DE LA CONSTRUCTION (MONTREAL) INC *p1050*
9711 RUE COLBERT, ANJOU, QC, H1J 1Z9
(514) 355-9650 *SIC 5039*
PRODUITS DESIGNER ALLIANCE INC
p1362
225 BOUL BELLEROSE O, SAINTE-ROSE, QC, H7L 6A1
(450) 624-1611 *SIC 5039*
PROULX, G. INC *p1076*
2800 BOUL FORD, CHATEAUGUAY, QC, J6J 4Z2
(450) 691-7110 *SIC 5039*
PROULX, GRATIEN BUILDING MATERIALS LTD *p595*
1499 STAR TOP RD SUITE A, GLOUCESTER, ON, K1B 3W5
(613) 749-3344 *SIC 5039*
RICHMOND BUILDING SUPPLIES CO. LTD
p256
12231 BRIDGEPORT RD, RICHMOND, BC, V6V 1J4
(604) 278-9865 *SIC 5039*
ROMA FENCE LIMITED *p495*
10 HOLLAND DR, BOLTON, ON, L7E 1G6
(905) 951-9063 *SIC 5039*
ROYAL GROUP, INC *p1028*
71 ROYAL GROUP CRES SUITE 2, WOODBRIDGE, ON, L4H 1X9
(905) 264-5500 *SIC 5039*
SAAND INC *p587*
250 BROCKPORT DR SUITE 3, ETOBICOKE, ON, M9W 5S1
(416) 798-2345 *SIC 5039*
SAAND INC *p587*
355 ATTWELL DR, ETOBICOKE, ON, M9W 5C2
(416) 674-6945 *SIC 5039*
SDS INDUSTRIAL BUILDING SUPPLIES LTD *p121*
2920 101 ST NW, EDMONTON, AB, T6N 1A6
(780) 224-8058 *SIC 5039*

SHANAHAN'S BUILDING SPECIALTIES LIMITED *p18*
2808 58 AVE SE SUITE 2, CALGARY, AB, T2C 0B3
(403) 279-2782 *SIC 5039*

SHANAHAN'S LIMITED PARTNERSHIP *p277*
13139 80 AVE, SURREY, BC, V3W 3B1
(604) 591-5111 *SIC 5039*

SHEARS, W BRYANT LIMITED *p423*
201 NICHOLSVILLE RD, DEER LAKE, NL, A8A 1W5
(709) 635-2186 *SIC 5039*

SIMPSON'S FENCE LTD *p543*
1030 RICHMOND ST, CHATHAM, ON, N7M 5J5
(519) 354-0540 *SIC 5039*

SOUTHRIDGE BUILDING SUPPLIES LTD *p273*
17444 56 AVE, SURREY, BC, V3S 1C3
(604) 576-2113 *SIC 5039*

SPRINGHILL LUMBER WHOLESALE LTD *p364*
1820 DE VRIES AVE, WINNIPEG, MB, R2G 3S8
(204) 661-1055 *SIC 5039*

SUNVIEW PATIO DOORS LTD *p1028*
500 ZENWAY BLVD, WOODBRIDGE, ON, L4H 0S7
(905) 851-1006 *SIC 5039*

TAMAR BUILDING PRODUCTS (1981) LTD *p1020*
3957 WALKER RD, WINDSOR, ON, N8W 3T4
(519) 969-7060 *SIC 5039*

TECHNOLOGIES BIONEST INC *p1369*
55 12E RUE, SHAWINIGAN, QC, G9T 5K7
(819) 538-5662 *SIC 5039*

U.P. INC *p1381*
3745 RUE PASCAL-GAGNON, TERRE-BONNE, QC, J6X 4J3
(450) 477-1122 *SIC 5039*

VINYL WINDOW DESIGNS LTD *p787*
550 OAKDALE RD, NORTH YORK, ON, M3N 1W6
(416) 741-7820 *SIC 5039*

VITRERIE LONGUEUIL INC *p1144*
241 BOUL SAINTE-FOY, LONGUEUIL, QC, J4J 1X1
(450) 651-0900 *SIC 5039*

WALLACE CONSTRUCTION SPECIALTIES LTD *p1430*
1940 ONTARIO AVE, SASKATOON, SK, S7K 1T6
(306) 653-2020 *SIC 5039*

WATSON BUILDING SUPPLIES INC *p1029*
50 ROYAL GROUP CRES UNIT 2, WOODBRIDGE, ON, L4H 1X9
(905) 669-1898 *SIC 5039*

WAYNE BUILDING PRODUCTS LTD *p94*
12603 123 ST NW, EDMONTON, AB, T5L 0H9
(780) 455-8929 *SIC 5039*

WEST-WOOD INDUSTRIES LTD *p417*
249 PARKER RD, SCOUDOUC, NB, E4P 3P8
(506) 532-0908 *SIC 5039*

WILLIS SUPPLY COMPANY LIMITED, THE *p527*
1149 PIONEER RD, BURLINGTON, ON, L7M 1K5
(905) 639-8584 *SIC 5039*

SIC 5043 Photographic equipment and supplies

901089 ONTARIO LIMITED *p665*
90 ROYAL CREST CRT SUITE 1, MARKHAM, ON, L3R 9X6
(905) 513-7733 *SIC 5043*

FRAMOS TECHNOLOGIES INC *p816*
2733 LANCASTER DR SUITE 210, OTTAWA, ON, K1B 0A9

(613) 208-1082 *SIC 5043*

FUJIFILM CANADA INC *p731*
600 SUFFOLK CRT, MISSISSAUGA, ON, L5R 4G4
(800) 461-0416 *SIC 5043*

NIKON CANADA INC *p698*
1366 AEROWOOD DR, MISSISSAUGA, ON, L4W 1C1
(905) 625-9910 *SIC 5043*

PENTAX CANADA INC *p725*
6715 MILLCREEK DR UNIT 1, MISSISSAUGA, ON, L5N 5V2
(905) 286-5570 *SIC 5043*

PHOTO SERVICE LTEE *p1190*
222 RUE NOTRE-DAME O, MONTREAL, QC, H2Y 1T3
(514) 849-2291 *SIC 5043*

PROFLASH TECHNOLOGIES INTERNATIONAL INC *p1123*
904 CH SAINT-JOSE, LA PRAIRIE, QC, J5R 6A9
(450) 444-1384 *SIC 5043*

REKAM IMPORT EXPORT INTERNATIONAL INC *p781*
222 FAYWOOD BLVD, NORTH YORK, ON, M3H 6A9
(416) 630-2892 *SIC 5043*

ROYAL PHOTO INC *p1172*
2106 BOUL ROSEMONT, MONTREAL, QC, H2G 1T4
(514) 273-1723 *SIC 5043*

SMARTEYES DIRECT INC *p675*
7755 WARDEN AVE UNIT 1, MARKHAM, ON, L3R 0N3
(905) 946-8998 *SIC 5043*

STENEK CORPORATION *p438*
40 TANTRAMAR CRES, AMHERST, NS, B4H 0A1
SIC 5043

SIC 5044 Office equipment

1021076 ONTARIO INC *p1393*
434 RUE AIME-VINCENT, VAUDREUIL-DORION, QC, J7V 5V5
(450) 510-0560 *SIC 5044*

4 OFFICE AUTOMATION LTD *p736*
425 SUPERIOR BLVD UNIT 1, MISSISSAUGA, ON, L5T 2W5
(905) 564-0522 *SIC 5044*

406106 ALBERTA INC *p180*
6741 CARIBOO RD SUITE 101, BURNABY, BC, V3N 4A3
(604) 421-5677 *SIC 5044*

702856 ALBERTA LTD *p63*
940A 11 AVE SW, CALGARY, AB, T2R 0E7
(403) 262-7224 *SIC 5044*

AHEARN & SOPER INC *p581*
100 WOODBINE DOWNS BLVD, ETOBICOKE, ON, M9W 5S6
(416) 675-3999 *SIC 5044*

AKINAI CANADA INC *p27*
2600 PORTLAND ST SE SUITE 1010, CALGARY, AB, T2G 4M6
(403) 280-6482 *SIC 5044*

AMS IMAGING INC *p748*
77 AURIGA DR UNIT 17, NEPEAN, ON, K2E 7Z7
(613) 723-1668 *SIC 5044*

ANATOME INC *p729*
5800 AVEBURY RD UNIT 3, MISSISSAUGA, ON, L5R 3M3
(905) 502-7200 *SIC 5044*

AUTOMATION ONE BUSINESS SYSTEMS INC *p284*
1365 BOUNDARY RD, VANCOUVER, BC, V5K 4T9
(604) 233-7702 *SIC 5044*

BASICS OFFICE PRODUCTS LTD *p538*
1040 FOUNTAIN ST N SUITE 1, CAMBRIDGE, ON, N3E 1A3
(519) 653-8984 *SIC 5044*

BLACKBURN & BLACKBURN INC *p1078*

980 BOUL DE L'UNIVERSITE E, CHICOUTIMI, QC, G7H 6H1
(418) 549-4900 *SIC 5044*

CANADIAN AUTOMATED BANK MACHINES INC *p278*
17637 1 AVE SUITE 101, SURREY, BC, V3Z 9S1
(866) 538-2982 *SIC 5044*

CANON CANADA INC *p511*
8000 MISSISSAUGA RD, BRAMPTON, ON, L6Y 5Z7
(905) 863-8000 *SIC 5044*

CAPITAL PAPER RECYCLING LTD *p14*
10595 50 ST SE, CALGARY, AB, T2C 3E3
(403) 543-3322 *SIC 5044*

CAXTON MARK INC *p644*
10 IROQUOIS RD, LEAMINGTON, ON, N8H 3V7
(519) 322-1002 *SIC 5044*

COPICOM INC *p1317*
50 RUE SAINT-JACQUES, SAINT-JEAN-SUR-RICHELIEU, QC, J3B 2J9
(450) 347-8252 *SIC 5044*

CORBETT OFFICE EQUIPMENT LTD *p331*
3306 30 AVE, VERNON, BC, V1T 2C8
(250) 549-2236 *SIC 5044*

COST LESS EXPRESS LTD *p200*
11 BURBIDGE ST SUITE 204, COQUITLAM, BC, V3K 7B2
(604) 444-4467 *SIC 5044*

DANKA MDS *p1328*
5924 BOUL HENRI-BOURASSA O, SAINT-LAURENT, QC, H4R 1V9
(514) 339-5000 *SIC 5044*

DASCO STORAGE SOLUTIONS LTD *p502*
346 ORENDA RD, BRAMPTON, ON, L6T 1G1
(905) 792-7080 *SIC 5044*

DIGITEX CANADA INC *p157*
130 LEVA AVE, RED DEER COUNTY, AB, T4E 1B9
(403) 309-3341 *SIC 5044*

DOCUMENT DIRECTION LIMITED *p774*
4100 YONGE ST SUITE 600, NORTH YORK, ON, M2P 2B5
(416) 218-4360 *SIC 5044*

DOCUSYSTEMS INTEGRATIONS INC *p188*
3920 NORLAND AVE SUITE 101, BURNABY, BC, V5G 4K7
SIC 5044

E MADILL OFFICE CO *p233*
100 ROCKY CREEK WAY, NANAIMO, BC, V9R 5C8
(250) 754-1611 *SIC 5044*

E.O.E. GROUP INC *p694*
5484 TOMKEN RD UNIT 4, MISSISSAUGA, ON, L4W 2Z6
(905) 602-6400 *SIC 5044*

EQUIPEMENT DE BUREAU ROBERT LEGARE LTEE *p1319*
411 RUE JOHN-F.-KENNEDY, SAINT-JEROME, QC, J7Y 4B5
(450) 438-3894 *SIC 5044*

EXPERTS EN MEMOIRE INTERNATIONALE INC, LES *p1329*
2321 RUE COHEN, SAINT-LAURENT, QC, H4R 2N7
(514) 333-5010 *SIC 5044*

FRANCOTYP-POSTALIA CANADA INC *p553*
82 CORSTATE AVE SUITE 2000, CONCORD, ON, L4K 4X2
(905) 761-6554 *SIC 5044*

GLORY GLOBAL SOLUTIONS (CANADA) INC *p1237*
1111 CHOMEDEY (A-13) E UNITE 200, MONTREAL, QC, H7W 5J8
(450) 686-8800 *SIC 5044*

GROUPE A&A SPECIALISTE DU DOCUMENT (MONTREAL) INC, LE *p1049*
10985 BOUL LOUIS-H.-LAFONTAINE BUREAU 101, ANJOU, QC, H1J 2E8
(514) 325-7700 *SIC 5044*

GROUPE CT INC *p1231*
5545 RUE MAURICE-CULLEN, MONTREAL, QC, H7C 2T8
(450) 967-3142 *SIC 5044*

HI-TECH BUSINESS SYSTEMS LTD *p132*
10115 100 AVE, GRANDE PRAIRIE, AB, T8V 0V4
(780) 538-4128 *SIC 5044*

HOWELL DATA SYSTEMS INC *p554*
160 PENNSYLVANIA AVE UNIT 4, CONCORD, ON, L4K 4A9
(905) 761-1712 *SIC 5044*

IKON OFFICE SOLUTIONS, ULC *p503*
100 WESTCREEK BLVD, BRAMPTON, ON, L6T 5V7
SIC 5044

KONICA MINOLTA BUSINESS SOLUTIONS (CANADA) LTD *p120*
9651 25 AVE NW, EDMONTON, AB, T6N 1H7
(780) 465-6232 *SIC 5044*

KONICA MINOLTA BUSINESS SOLUTIONS (CANADA) LTD *p255*
21500 WESTMINSTER HWY, RICHMOND, BC, V6V 2V1
(604) 276-1611 *SIC 5044*

KONICA MINOLTA BUSINESS SOLUTIONS (CANADA) LTD *p696*
5875 EXPLORER DR, MISSISSAUGA, ON, L4W 0E1
(905) 890-6600 *SIC 5044*

KONICA MINOLTA BUSINESS SOLUTIONS (CANADA) LTD *p1334*
8555 RTE TRANSCANADIENNE, SAINT-LAURENT, QC, H4S 1Z6
(514) 335-2157 *SIC 5044*

KYOCERA DOCUMENT SOLUTIONS CANADA, LTD *p740*
6120 KESTREL RD, MISSISSAUGA, ON, L5T 1S8
(905) 670-4425 *SIC 5044*

LANIEL (CANADA) INC *p1340*
7101 RTE TRANSCANADIENNE, SAINT-LAURENT, QC, H4T 1A2
(514) 331-3031 *SIC 5044*

MAXWELL PAPER CANADA INC *p491*
270 FRONT ST, BELLEVILLE, ON, K8N 2Z2
(613) 962-7846 *SIC 5044*

MCCOPIER (CANADA) INC *p1330*
4430 RUE GARAND, SAINT-LAURENT, QC, H4R 2A3
(514) 344-1515 *SIC 5044*

MEGAPOL CANADA *p708*
833 MISSISSAUGA VALLEY BLVD, MISSISSAUGA, ON, L5A 1Z7
(416) 346-1554 *SIC 5044*

NCR CANADA CORP *p1010*
50 NORTHLAND RD, WATERLOO, ON, N2V 1N3
(519) 880-7700 *SIC 5044*

NEOPOST CANADA LIMITED *p673*
150 STEELCASE RD W, MARKHAM, ON, L3R 3J9
(905) 475-3722 *SIC 5044*

NOVEXCO INC *p1231*
950 PLACE PAUL-KANE, MONTREAL, QC, H7C 2T2
(450) 686-1212 *SIC 5044*

OFFICE INTERIORS *p447*
656 WINDMILL RD, DARTMOUTH, NS, B3B 1B8
(902) 422-4011 *SIC 5044*

OPTEL VISION INC *p1267*
2680 BOUL DU PARC-TECHNOLOGIQUE, QUEBEC, QC, G1P 4S6
(418) 688-0334 *SIC 5044*

PALASAD BILLIARDS LIMITED *p660*
141 PINE VALLEY BLVD, LONDON, ON, N6K 3T6
(519) 685-1390 *SIC 5044*

PAYSTATION INC *p741*
6345 DIXIE RD UNIT 4, MISSISSAUGA, ON, L5T 2E6
(905) 364-0700 *SIC 5044*

PHILIP BUSINESS DEVELOPMENT & INVESTMENT LTD. *p742*

▲ Public Company ■ Public Company Family Member **HQ** Headquarters **BR** Branch **SL** Single Location

1680 COURTNEYPARK DR E UNIT 5, MISSISSAUGA, ON, L5T 1R4
(905) 366-8999   SIC 5044
PITNEY BOWES OF CANADA LTD   p189
3001 WAYBURNE DR SUITE 125, BURNABY, BC, V5G 4W3
(778) 328-8900   SIC 5044
PITNEY BOWES OF CANADA LTD   p431
31 PIPPY PL, ST. JOHN'S, NL, A1B 3X2
SIC 5044
PITNEY BOWES OF CANADA LTD   p699
5500 EXPLORER DR SUITE 1, MISSISSAUGA, ON, L4W 5C7
(905) 219-3000   SIC 5044
PITNEY BOWES OF CANADA LTD   p699
5500 EXPLORER DR UNIT 2, MISSISSAUGA, ON, L4W 5C7
(800) 672-6937   SIC 5044
PITNEY BOWES OF CANADA LTD   p769
1200 SHEPPARD AVE E SUITE 400, NORTH YORK, ON, M2K 2S5
SIC 5044
QUICKSERVICE TECHNOLOGIES INC p883
610 WELLAND AVE, ST CATHARINES, ON, L2M 5V6
(905) 687-8440   SIC 5044
RICOH CANADA INC   p700
5560 EXPLORER DR SUITE 100, MISSISSAUGA, ON, L4W 5M3
(905) 795-9659   SIC 5044
RICOH CANADA INC   p774
4100 YONGE ST SUITE 600, NORTH YORK, ON, M2P 2B5
(416) 218-4360   SIC 5044
SEGUE SYSTEMS INC   p116
4504 101 ST NW, EDMONTON, AB, T6E 5G9
(780) 442-2340   SIC 5044
SHADDY INTERNATIONAL MARKETING LTD   p820
373 COVENTRY RD, OTTAWA, ON, K1K 2C5
(613) 749-2053   SIC 5044
SPECIALISTE DU BUREAU FREDAL INC, LE   p1107
186 RUE JEAN-PROULX, GATINEAU, QC, J8Z 1V8
(819) 205-9555   SIC 5044
TAB PRODUCTS OF CANADA, CO.   p765
136 SPARKS AVE, NORTH YORK, ON, M2H 2S4
(416) 497-1552   SIC 5044
TOSHIBA TEC CANADA BUSINESS SOLUTIONS INC   p676
75 TIVERTON CRT, MARKHAM, ON, L3R 4M8
(905) 470-3500   SIC 5044
TOSHIBA TEC CANADA INC   p676
75 TIVERTON CRT, MARKHAM, ON, L3R 4M8
(905) 470-3500   SIC 5044
VENTREX VENDING SERVICES INC p816
1550 LIVERPOOL CRT UNIT 6, OTTAWA, ON, K1B 4L2
(613) 747-0455   SIC 5044
XEROX CANADA INC   p91
10180 101 ST NW SUITE 1350, EDMONTON, AB, T5J 3S4
(780) 493-7800   SIC 5044
XEROX CANADA INC   p775
20 YORK MILLS RD 5TH FLR, NORTH YORK, ON, M2P 2C2
(416) 229-3769   SIC 5044
XEROX CANADA LTD   p74
37 RICHARD WAY SW SUITE 200, CALGARY, AB, T3E 7M8
(403) 260-8800   SIC 5044
XEROX CANADA LTD   p317
1055 GEORGIA ST W, VANCOUVER, BC, V6E 0B6
(604) 668-2300   SIC 5044
XEROX CANADA LTD   p392
895 WAVERLEY ST, WINNIPEG, MB, R3T 5P4

(204) 488-5100   SIC 5044
XEROX CANADA LTD   p449
215-237 BROWNLOW AVE, DARTMOUTH, NS, B3B 2C6
(902) 470-3000   SIC 5044
XEROX CANADA LTD   p690
6800 NORTHWEST DR, MISSISSAUGA, ON, L4V 1Z1
(905) 672-4700   SIC 5044
XEROX CANADA LTD   p690
6800 NORTHWEST DR, MISSISSAUGA, ON, L4V 1Z1
(905) 672-4709   SIC 5044
XEROX CANADA LTD   p690
5925 AIRPORT RD, MISSISSAUGA, ON, L4V 1W1
SIC 5044
XEROX CANADA LTD   p826
333 PRESTON ST SUITE 1000, OTTAWA, ON, K1S 5N4
(613) 230-1002   SIC 5044
XEROX CANADA LTD   p931
33 BLOOR ST E, TORONTO, ON, M4W 3H1
(416) 921-0210   SIC 5044
XEROX CANADA LTD   p1221
3400 BOUL DE MAISONNEUVE O BUREAU 900, MONTREAL, QC, H3Z 3G1
(514) 939-3769   SIC 5044

SIC 5045 Computers, peripherals, and software

1371185 ONTARIO INC   p665
4011 14TH AVE, MARKHAM, ON, L3R 0Z9
(905) 415-1166   SIC 5045
2213802 ONTARIO INC   p736
964 WESTPORT CRES SUITE 6, MISSISSAUGA, ON, L5T 1S3
(905) 696-6932   SIC 5045
3081354 CANADA INC   p1091
2001 RUE SAINT-REGIS, DOLLARD-DES-ORMEAUX, QC, H9B 2M9
SIC 5045
3096-3227 QUEBEC INC   p1226
8270 RUE MAYRAND, MONTREAL, QC, H4P 2C5
(514) 288-6000   SIC 5045
887804 ONTARIO INC   p691
5580 AMBLER DR, MISSISSAUGA, ON, L4W 2K9
(905) 629-2990   SIC 5045
9015-0178 QUEBEC INC   p1093
1405 RTE TRANS-CANADA BUREAU 100, DORVAL, QC, H9P 2V9
SIC 5045
9136-3283 QUEBEC INC   p1307
5335 RUE ALBERT-MILLICHAMP BUREAU 1, SAINT-HUBERT, QC, J3Y 8Z8
(450) 350-0420   SIC 5045
9144-1923 QUEBEC INC   p1284
192 RUE SAINT-GERMAIN E, RIMOUSKI, QC, G5L 1A8
(418) 723-0606   SIC 5045
9156-4302 QUEBEC INC   p1226
7881 BOUL DECARIE BUREAU 300, MONTREAL, QC, H4P 2H2
(514) 733-5828   SIC 5045
ABLE-ONE SYSTEMS INC   p638
127 VICTORIA ST S SUITE 101, KITCHENER, ON, N2G 2B4
(519) 570-9100   SIC 5045
ACI WORLDWIDE (CANADA) INC   p978
200 WELLINGTON ST W SUITE 700, TORONTO, ON, M5V 3C7
(416) 813-3000   SIC 5045
ALTA E-SOLUTIONS   p737
1145 WESTPORT CRES, MISSISSAUGA, ON, L5T 1E8
(905) 564-5539   SIC 5045
ALTHON INC   p666
140 SHIELDS CRT, MARKHAM, ON, L3R 9T5
(905) 513-1221   SIC 5045
APPLE CANADA INC   p959

120 BREMNER BLVD SUITE 1600, TORONTO, ON, M5J 0A8
(647) 943-4400   SIC 5045
ASD SOLUTIONS LTD   p734
190 STATESMAN DR, MISSISSAUGA, ON, L5S 1X7
(519) 271-4900   SIC 5045
ASI COMPUTER TECHNOLOGIES (CANADA) CORP   p666
3930 14TH AVE UNIT 1, MARKHAM, ON, L3R 0A8
(905) 470-1000   SIC 5045
ASIA LINK COMPUTER INC   p850
45A WEST WILMOT ST UNIT 5 7, RICHMOND HILL, ON, L4B 2P2
(905) 731-1928   SIC 5045
ATLANTIA HOLDINGS INCORPORATED p241
949 3RD ST W SUITE 121, NORTH VANCOUVER, BC, V7P 3P7
(604) 985-7257   SIC 5045
BLUEWATER OFFICE EQUIPMENT LTD p597
223 HURON RD, GODERICH, ON, N7A 2Z8
(519) 524-9863   SIC 5045
BRAINS II SOLUTIONS, INC   p667
165 KONRAD CRES, MARKHAM, ON, L3R 9T9
(905) 946-8700   SIC 5045
C.P.U. DESIGN INC   p1263
2323 BOUL DU VERSANT-NORD BUREAU 100, QUEBEC, QC, G1N 4P4
(418) 681-6974   SIC 5045
CDI COMPUTER DEALERS INC   p680
130 SOUTH TOWN CENTRE BLVD, MARKHAM, ON, L6G 1B8
(905) 946-1119   SIC 5045
CDW CANADA CORP   p687
5925 AIRPORT RD UNIT 800, MISSISSAUGA, ON, L4V 1W1
(647) 259-1034   SIC 5045
CDW CANADA CORP   p996
185 THE WEST MALL SUITE 1700, TORONTO, ON, M9C 1B8
(647) 288-5700   SIC 5045
CENTRE INFORMATIQUE DNB LIMITEE p1229
800 PLACE VICTORIA BUREAU 2700, MONTREAL, QC, H4Z 1B7
SIC 5045
CINCOM SYSTEMS OF CANADA LTD p708
2085 HURONTARIO ST SUITE 500, MISSISSAUGA, ON, L5A 4G1
(905) 279-4220   SIC 5045
CINRAM CANADA OPERATIONS ULC p864
2255 MARKHAM RD, SCARBOROUGH, ON, M1B 2W3
(416) 298-8190   SIC 5045
CNB COMPUTERS INC   p687
6400 NORTHWEST DR, MISSISSAUGA, ON, L4V 1K1
(905) 501-0099   SIC 5045
COASTAL RANGE SYSTEMS INC   p188
6400 ROBERTS ST SUITE 200, BURNABY, BC, V5G 4C9
(604) 473-2100   SIC 5045
COMPUCOM CANADA CO.   p693
1830 MATHESON BLVD UNIT 1, MISSISSAUGA, ON, L4W 0B3
(289) 261-3000   SIC 5045
COMPUTER BOULEVARD INC   p383
1250 ST JAMES ST UNIT B, WINNIPEG, MB, R3H 0L1
(204) 775-3202   SIC 5045
COMPUTER ENHANCEMENT CORPORATION   p693
5112 TIMBERLEA BLVD SUITE 2, MISSISSAUGA, ON, L4W 2S5
(905) 625-9100   SIC 5045
COMPUTER MEDIA PRODUCTS LTD p817
250 TREMBLAY RD SUITE 520, OTTAWA, ON, K1G 3J8
(613) 226-7071   SIC 5045
COMSALE COMPUTER INC   p551

111 SNIDERCROFT RD, CONCORD, ON, L4K 2J8
(905) 761-6466   SIC 5045
COMSALE COMPUTER INC   p664
158 WALLENBERG DR, MAPLE, ON, L6A 4M2
(647) 648-2323   SIC 5045
COMTRONIC COMPUTER INC   p851
30 KINNEAR CRT UNIT 1, RICHMOND HILL, ON, L4B 1K8
(905) 881-3606   SIC 5045
COREIO INC   p1030
55 DIRECTOR CRT, WOODBRIDGE, ON, L4L 4S5
(905) 264-8520   SIC 5045
COREWORX INC   p639
22 FREDERICK ST SUITE 800, KITCHENER, ON, N2H 6M6
(519) 772-3181   SIC 5045
CORPORATION COMPUWARE DU CANADA   p1187
500 PLACE D'ARMES BUREAU 1800, MONTREAL, QC, H2Y 2W2
(438) 259-3300   SIC 5045
CRISTOMEL INC   p1324
100 BOUL ALEXIS-NIHON BUREAU 105, SAINT-LAURENT, QC, H4M 2N6
(514) 747-1575   SIC 5045
DAIWA DISTRIBUTION (ONTARIO) INC p668
361 ALDEN RD, MARKHAM, ON, L3R 3L4
(905) 940-2889   SIC 5045
DATA INTEGRITY INC   p856
30 VIA RENZO DR UNIT 3, RICHMOND HILL, ON, L4S 0B8
(416) 638-0111   SIC 5045
DISTRIBUTION HARTCO SOCIETE EN COMMANDITE   p1048
9393 BOUL LOUIS-H.-LAFONTAINE, ANJOU, QC, H1J 1Z1
(514) 354-3810   SIC 5045
DYADEM INTERNATIONAL LTD   p765
155 GORDON BAKER RD SUITE 401, NORTH YORK, ON, M2H 3N5
(416) 649-9200   SIC 5045
ELCO SYSTEMS INC   p669
215 SHIELDS CRT UNIT 4-6, MARKHAM, ON, L3R 8V2
(905) 470-0082   SIC 5045
ENTERTAINMENT LIQUIDATORS OF CANADA INC   p702
1550 CATERPILLAR RD, MISSISSAUGA, ON, L4X 1E7
(905) 629-7283   SIC 5045
EPIC INFORMATION SOLUTIONS INC p393
1730 MCGILLIVRAY BLVD, WINNIPEG, MB, R3Y 1A1
(204) 453-2300   SIC 5045
EPROM INC   p669
100 SHIELDS CRT, MARKHAM, ON, L3R 9T5
(905) 944-9000   SIC 5045
EPSON CANADA LIMITED EPSON CANADA LIMITEE   p669
185 RENFREW DR, MARKHAM, ON, L3R 6G3
(416) 498-4574   SIC 5045
ESIT CANADA ENTERPRISE SERVICES CO p624
100 HERZBERG RD, KANATA, ON, K2K 3B7
(613) 592-5111   SIC 5045
FAMIC TECHNOLOGIES INC   p1324
9999 BOUL CAVENDISH BUREAU 350, SAINT-LAURENT, QC, H4M 2X5
(514) 748-8050   SIC 5045
FIELDPOINT SERVICE APPLICATIONS INC p800
2660 SHERWOOD HEIGHTS DR SUITE 103, OAKVILLE, ON, L6J 7Y8
(905) 855-2111   SIC 5045
FILBITRON SYSTEMS GROUP INC   p670
178 TORBAY RD, MARKHAM, ON, L3R 1G6
(905) 477-0450   SIC 5045
FLEET INFORMATIQUE INC   p1057

---

750 RUE NOTRE-DAME BUREAU D, BERTHIERVILLE, QC, J0K 1A0

(450) 836-4877   *SIC* 5045

FLEMING COMMUNICATIONS INC   *p817*
920 BELFAST RD SUITE 101, OTTAWA, ON, K1G 0Z6

(613) 244-6770   *SIC* 5045

FUJITSU CANADA, INC   *p951*
155 UNIVERSITY AVE SUITE 1600, TORONTO, ON, M5H 3B7

(905) 286-9666   *SIC* 5045

GEEP ECOSYS INC   *p1234*
2995 BOUL LE CORBUSIER, MONTREAL, QC, H7L 3M3

(450) 506-0220   *SIC* 5045

GENATEC INC   *p1339*
5929 RTE TRANSCANADIENNE BUREAU 240, SAINT-LAURENT, QC, H4T 1Z6

(514) 855-1223   *SIC* 5045

GLASSHOUSE SYSTEMS INC   *p779*
885 DON MILLS ROAD, NORTH YORK, ON, M3C 1V9

(416) 229-2950   *SIC* 5045

GOGO GEEK ENTERPRISES INC   *p254*
13988 CAMBIE RD SUITE 373, RICHMOND, BC, V6V 2K4

(604) 248-0782   *SIC* 5045

GROUPE STINGRAY INC   *p1211*
730 RUE WELLINGTON, MONTREAL, QC, H3C 1T4

(514) 664-1244   *SIC* 5045

HERJAVEC GROUP INC, THE   *p624*
555 LEGGET DR SUITE 530, KANATA, ON, K2K 2X3

(613) 271-2400   *SIC* 5045

HIGHVAIL SYSTEMS INC   *p926*
1 ST CLAIR AVE W SUITE 1201, TORONTO, ON, M4V 1K6

(416) 867-3000   *SIC* 5045

HUBIO SOLUTIONS INC   *p939*
20 VICTORIA ST, TORONTO, ON, M5C 2N8

(416) 364-6306   *SIC* 5045

IN-HOUSE SOLUTIONS INC   *p537*
240 HOLIDAY INN DR UNIT A, CAMBRIDGE, ON, N3C 3X4

(519) 658-1471   *SIC* 5045

INETCO SYSTEMS LTD   *p186*
4664 LOUGHEED HWY SUITE 295, BURNABY, BC, V5C 5T5

(604) 451-1567   *SIC* 5045

INFINITE CABLES INC   *p671*
3993 14TH AVE, MARKHAM, ON, L3R 4Z6

(905) 477-4433   *SIC* 5045

INFORMATION BUILDERS (CANADA) INC   *p953*
150 YORK ST SUITE 1000, TORONTO, ON, M5H 3S5

(416) 364-0349   *SIC* 5045

INFORMATIQUE PRO-CONTACT INC *p1277*
1000 AV SAINT-JEAN-BAPTISTE BUREAU 111, QUEBEC, QC, G2E 5G5

(418) 871-1622   *SIC* 5045

INGRAM MICRO INC   *p258*
7451 NELSON RD, RICHMOND, BC, V6W 1L7

(604) 276-8357   *SIC* 5045

INGRAM MICRO INC   *p731*
55 STANDISH CRT SUITE 1, MISSISSAUGA, ON, L5R 4A1

(905) 755-5000   *SIC* 5045

INTEC BILLING CANADA LTD   *p904*
123 COMMERCE VALLEY DR E, THORNHILL, ON, L3T 7W8

SIC 5045

INTEL OF CANADA, LTD   *p585*
200 RONSON DR SUITE 201, ETOBICOKE, ON, M9W 5Z9

(647) 259-0101   *SIC* 5045

INTELLICO - IDS INC   *p1340*
6830 CH DE LA COTE-DE-LIESSE, SAINT-LAURENT, QC, H4T 2A1

(800) 317-2323   *SIC* 5045

INTERGRAPH CANADA LTD   *p76*
10921 14 ST NE, CALGARY, AB, T3K 2L5

(877) 569-5500   *SIC* 5045

INTERMEC TECHNOLOGIES CANADA ULC *p717*
3333 UNITY DR, MISSISSAUGA, ON, L5L 3S6

(905) 608-3167   *SIC* 5045

INTERNATIONAL COMPUTER BROKERS INC   *p510*
9052 CREDITVIEW RD, BRAMPTON, ON, L6X 0E3

(905) 459-2100   *SIC* 5045

IT XCHANGE (ONTARIO) CORP   *p717*
3500 RIDGEWAY DR UNIT 4, MISSISSAUGA, ON, L5L 0B4

(888) 829-5333   *SIC* 5045

KNOWLEDGE MANAGEMENT INNOVATIONS LTD   *p801*
586 ARGUS RD SUITE 201, OAKVILLE, ON, L6J 3J3

(416) 410-4817   *SIC* 5045

LASER VALLEY TECHNOLOGIES CORP *p282*
9761 192 ST UNIT 1, SURREY, BC, V4N 4C7

(604) 888-7085   *SIC* 5045

LEI TECHNOLOGY CANADA LTD   *p688*
3160 ORLANDO DR UNIT A, MISSISSAUGA, ON, L4V 1R5

(877) 813-2132   *SIC* 5045

LEXMARK CANADA INC   *p904*
125 COMMERCE VALLEY DR W UNIT 600, THORNHILL, ON, L3T 7W4

(905) 763-0560   *SIC* 5045

MASTER MERCHANT SYSTEMS SOFTWARE LIMITED   *p447*
202 BROWNLOW AVE SUITE 700, DARTMOUTH, NS, B3B 1T5

(902) 496-9500   *SIC* 5045

MDG COMPUTERS CANADA INC   *p798*
2940 BRISTOL CIR, OAKVILLE, ON, L6H 6G4

(905) 829-3538   *SIC* 5045

MEDISOLUTION (2009) INC   *p1180*
110 BOUL CREMAZIE O BUREAU 1200, MONTREAL, QC, H2P 1B9

(514) 850-5000   *SIC* 5045

MEDISOLUTIONS INC   *p688*
5935 AIRPORT RD SUITE 500, MISSISSAUGA, ON, L4V 1W5

(905) 673-7715   *SIC* 5045

MICRO ELECTRONIQUES G.B. INC *p1335*
6620 RUE ABRAMS, SAINT-LAURENT, QC, H4S 1Y1

(514) 333-7373   *SIC* 5045

MICRO LOGIC SAINTE-FOY LTEE   *p1273*
2786 CH SAINTE-FOY, QUEBEC, QC, G1V 1V8

(418) 658-6624   *SIC* 5045

MICROSOFT CANADA INC   *p724*
1950 MEADOWVALE BLVD, MISSISSAUGA, ON, L5N 8L9

(905) 568-0434   *SIC* 5045

MINI-MICRO SUPPLY INC. CANADA   *p915*
524 GORDON BAKER RD, TORONTO, ON, M2H 3B4

(905) 305-7671   *SIC* 5045

MULTIFORCE TECHNOLOGIES INC *p1273*
2954 BOUL LAURIER UNITE 320, QUEBEC, QC, G1V 4T2

(418) 780-8020   *SIC* 5045

NWD SYSTEMS (MONTREAL) INC *p1134*
4209 DES LAURENTIDES (A-15) E, LAVAL-OUEST, QC, H7L 5W5

(450) 973-6678   *SIC* 5045

ONX ENTERPRISE SOLUTIONS LTD   *p905*
165 COMMERCE VALLEY DR W SUITE 300, THORNHILL, ON, L3T 7V8

(905) 881-4414   *SIC* 5045

ORDINATEURS EN GROS MICROBYTES INC, LES   *p1251*
940 BOUL SAINT-JEAN BUREAU 15, POINTE-CLAIRE, QC, H9R 5N8

(514) 426-2586   *SIC* 5045

PC CORP INC   *p92*

9947 109 ST NW, EDMONTON, AB, T5K 1H6

(780) 428-3000   *SIC* 5045

PC MEDIC INCORPORATED   *p447*
50 AKERLEY BLVD SUITE 12, DARTMOUTH, NS, B3B 1R8

(902) 468-7237   *SIC* 5045

PC OUTLET INC   *p853*
45A WEST WILMOT ST SUITE 17, RICHMOND HILL, ON, L4B 2P2

SIC 5045

PM CANADA INC   *p391*
135 INNOVATION DR UNIT 300, WINNIPEG, MB, R3T 6A8

(905) 889-5320   *SIC* 5045

POWERNODE COMPUTER INC   *p674*
35 RIVIERA DR SUITE 11-12, MARKHAM, ON, L3R 8N4

(905) 474-1040   *SIC* 5045

PRESAGIS CANADA INC   *p1228*
4700 RUE DE LA SAVANE BUREAU 300, MONTREAL, QC, H4P 1T7

(514) 341-3874   *SIC* 5045

PRO IT PLUS INC.   *p571*
16 BROOKERS LANE SUITE 2908, ETOBICOKE, ON, M8V 0A5

(905) 977-8168   *SIC* 5045

PRO-DATA INC   *p385*
1560 ST JAMES ST, WINNIPEG, MB, R3H 0L2

(204) 779-9960   *SIC* 5045

PSI PERIPHERAL SOLUTIONS INC   *p717*
3535 LAIRD RD UNIT 9, MISSISSAUGA, ON, L5L 5Z4

(905) 858-3600   *SIC* 5045

PURKINJE INC   *p1211*
614 RUE SAINT-JACQUES BUREAU 200, MONTREAL, QC, H3C 1E2

(514) 355-0888   *SIC* 5045

QUANTUM CAPITAL CORPORATION *p1207*
615 BOUL RENE LEVESQUE, STE 460, MONTREAL, QC, H3B 1P5

SIC 5045

REYNOLDS AND REYNOLDS (CANADA) LIMITED   *p707*
3 ROBERT SPECK PKY UNIT 600, MISSISSAUGA, ON, L4Z 2G5

(905) 267-6000   *SIC* 5045

REYNOLDS AND REYNOLDS (CANADA) LIMITED   *p1050*
11075 BOUL LOUIS-H.-LAFONTAINE, ANJOU, QC, H1J 3A3

(514) 355-7550   *SIC* 5045

RINAX SYSTEMS LTD   *p37*
5542 1A ST SW, CALGARY, AB, T2H 0E7

(403) 243-4074   *SIC* 5045

S.T.R. ELECTRONIQUE INC   *p1255*
610 RUE ARDOUIN, QUEBEC, QC, G1C 7J8

(418) 660-8899   *SIC* 5045

SAMTACK INC   *p674*
1100 RODICK RD, MARKHAM, ON, L3R 8C3

(905) 940-1880   *SIC* 5045

SERTI INFORMATIQUE INC   *p1050*
7555 RUE BECLARD, ANJOU, QC, H1J 2S5

(514) 493-1909   *SIC* 5045

SERTI INFORMATIQUE INC   *p1050*
10975 BOUL LOUIS-H.-LAFONTAINE UNITE 201, ANJOU, QC, H1J 2E8

(514) 493-1909   *SIC* 5045

SEYDACO PACKAGING CORP   *p742*
215 COURTNEYPARK DR E, MISSISSAUGA, ON, L5T 2T6

(905) 565-8030   *SIC* 5045

SIS STRATEGIC INFORMATION SYSTEMS INC   *p103*
11432 WINTERBURN RD NW, EDMONTON, AB, T5S 2Y3

(780) 701-4050   *SIC* 5045

SOFTVOYAGE INC   *p1183*
201 AV LAURIER E BUREAU 630, MONTREAL, QC, H2T 3E6

(514) 273-0008   *SIC* 5045

SOLID CADDGROUP INC   *p854*
25B EAST PEARCE ST, RICHMOND HILL, ON, L4B 2M9

(905) 474-1499   *SIC* 5045

SOLUTION Q INC   *p777*
222 LESMILL RD, NORTH YORK, ON, M3B 2T5

(416) 385-0774   *SIC* 5045

SOROC TECHNOLOGY INC   *p1033*
607 CHRISLEA RD, WOODBRIDGE, ON, L4L 8A3

(905) 265-8000   *SIC* 5045

STARTECH.COM LTD   *p650*
45 ARTISANS CRES, LONDON, ON, N5V 5E9

(800) 265-1844   *SIC* 5045

STORAGE APPLIANCE CORPORATION *p854*
30 WEST BEAVER CREEK RD UNIT 115, RICHMOND HILL, ON, L4B 3K1

(416) 484-0009   *SIC* 5045

SUDDEN SERVICE TECHNOLOGIES CORPORATION   *p193*
7635 NORTH FRASER WAY UNIT 103, BURNABY, BC, V5J 0B8

(604) 873-3910   *SIC* 5045

SYMBILITY SOLUTIONS INC   *p984*
111 PETER ST SUITE 900, TORONTO, ON, M5V 2H1

(647) 775-8601   *SIC* 5045

SYNERGEX CORPORATION   *p743*
1280 COURTNEYPARK DR E, MISSISSAUGA, ON, L5T 1N6

(905) 565-1212   *SIC* 5045

SYNNEX CANADA LIMITED   *p588*
200 RONSON DR SUITE 104, ETOBICOKE, ON, M9W 5Z9

(416) 240-7012   *SIC* 5045

SYNNEX CANADA LIMITED   *p604*
107 WOODLAWN RD W, GUELPH, ON, N1H 1B4

(519) 837-2444   *SIC* 5045

SYSTEMES INFORMATIQUES O.G.C. INC, LES   *p1341*
7575 RTE TRANSCANADIENNE BUREAU 403, SAINT-LAURENT, QC, H4T 1V6

(514) 331-7873   *SIC* 5045

TAKNOLOGY (CANADA) INC   *p854*
50 EAST PEARCE ST, RICHMOND HILL, ON, L4B 1B7

(905) 882-2299   *SIC* 5045

TAO SOLUTIONS INC   *p957*
11 KING ST W SUITE 1600, TORONTO, ON, M5H 4C7

(416) 309-7557   *SIC* 5045

TASKTOP TECHNOLOGIES INCORPORATED   *p318*
1500 GEORGIA ST W SUITE 1100, VANCOUVER, BC, V6G 2Z6

(778) 588-6896   *SIC* 5045

TECH DATA CANADA CORPORATION *p727*
6911 CREDITVIEW RD, MISSISSAUGA, ON, L5N 8G1

(905) 286-6800   *SIC* 5045

TELECOM COMPUTER INC   *p525*
5245 HARVESTER RD, BURLINGTON, ON, L7L 5L4

(905) 333-9621   *SIC* 5045

THINQ TECHNOLOGIES LTD   *p655*
572 WELLINGTON ST, LONDON, ON, N6A 3R3

(519) 659-4900   *SIC* 5045

TRIWARE TECHNOLOGIES INC   *p434*
76 BROOKFIELD RD, ST. JOHN'S, NL, A1E 3T9

(709) 579-5000   *SIC* 5045

WBM TECHNOLOGIES INC   *p1435*
3718 KINNEAR PL UNIT 104, SASKATOON, SK, S7P 0A6

(306) 664-2686   *SIC* 5045

YAMATECH SCIENTIFIC LTD   *p1083*
5568 AV KING-EDWARD, COTE SAINT-LUC, QC, H4V 2K4

(514) 737-5434   *SIC* 5045

ZYCOM TECHNOLOGY INC p630
271 CONCESSION ST, KINGSTON, ON, K7K 2B7
(613) 549-6558 SIC 5045

SIC 5046 Commercial equipment, nec

A. D. WELDING & FABRICATION INC p500
21 MELANIE DR, BRAMPTON, ON, L6T 4K8
(905) 791-2914 SIC 5046

ADVANTAGE RESTAURANT SUPPLY INC p759
4529 KENT AVE, NIAGARA FALLS, ON, L2H 1J1
(905) 356-1152 SIC 5046

ALIMEX INC p1172
4425 RUE D'IBERVILLE, MONTREAL, QC, H2H 2L7
(514) 522-5700 SIC 5046

AUTHENTIQUE POSE CAFE INC, L' p1304
9555 10E AV, SAINT-GEORGES, QC, G5Y 8J8
(418) 228-3191 SIC 5046

CARIBBEAN INTERNATIONAL SUPPLY LIMITED p550
160 APPLEWOOD CRES SUITE 21, CONCORD, ON, L4K 4H2
SIC 5046

DESPRES, LAPORTE INC p1373
185 RUE DE LA BURLINGTON, SHERBROOKE, QC, J1L 1G9
(819) 566-2620 SIC 5046

DIGI CANADA INCORPORATED p551
87 MOYAL CRT, CONCORD, ON, L4K 4R8
(905) 879-0833 SIC 5046

DISTRIBUTION GROUP INCORPORATED p433
99 BLACKMARSH RD, ST. JOHN'S, NL, A1E 1S6
(709) 579-2151 SIC 5046

DISTRIBUTIONS BELLUCCI LTEE, LES p1180
8145 BOUL SAINT-LAURENT, MONTREAL, QC, H2P 2M1
(514) 388-1555 SIC 5046

DOMINION NEON INC p1048
9225 RUE DU PARCOURS, ANJOU, QC, H1J 3A8
(514) 354-6366 SIC 5046

ELITE CONCEPTS INC p867
1079 MIDLAND AVE, SCARBOROUGH, ON, M1K 4G7
(416) 827-3007 SIC 5046

ENTREPRISES TZANET INC, LES p1225
1375 RUE DE LOUVAIN O BUREAU 71, MONTREAL, QC, H4N 1G6
(514) 383-0030 SIC 5046

EVO MERCHANT SERVICES CORP. CANADA p1195
505 BOUL DE MAISONNEUVE O BUREAU 150, MONTREAL, QC, H3A 3C2
SIC 5046

FOOD SERVICE SOLUTIONS INC p722
6599 KITIMAT RD UNIT 2, MISSISSAUGA, ON, L5N 4J4
(905) 363-0309 SIC 5046

H & K CANADA INC p553
50 MCCLEARY CRT, CONCORD, ON, L4K 3L5
(905) 695-0440 SIC 5046

HARRCO DESIGN AND MANUFACTURING LIMITED p503
50 DEVON RD, BRAMPTON, ON, L6T 5B5
(905) 564-0577 SIC 5046

HI-CUBE STORAGE PRODUCTS LTD p209
7363 WILSON AVE, DELTA, BC, V4G 1E5
(604) 946-4838 SIC 5046

IMPACT XM INC p798
1303 NORTH SERVICE RD E UNIT 1, OAKVILLE, ON, L6H 1A7
(905) 287-4862 SIC 5046

IMPERIAL COFFEE AND SERVICES INC p783
12 KODIAK CRES, NORTH YORK, ON, M3J 3G5
(416) 638-7404 SIC 5046

ITIF INC p993
25 BERTAL RD UNIT 9, TORONTO, ON, M6M 4M7
SIC 5046

J.R.S. AMENITIES LTD p263
11151 HORSESHOE WAY UNIT 25, RICHMOND, BC, V7A 4S5
(604) 244-7627 SIC 5046

LAUER'S RESTAURANT EQUIPMENT LIMITED p809
3823 CAMPBELL RD, ORILLIA, ON, L3V 6H3
(705) 325-9938 SIC 5046

LEGRAND AV CANADA ULC p891
113 IBER RD, STITTSVILLE, ON, K2S 1E7
(613) 836-2501 SIC 5046

LOCATION MONTFE p1102
7 RUE DU CAMP, FERMONT, QC, G0G 1J0
(418) 287-9402 SIC 5046

MAXI CRISP INC p1142
2066 RUE DE LA PROVINCE, LONGUEUIL, QC, J4G 1R7
(450) 670-4256 SIC 5046

MCCALL'S SCHOOL OF CAKE DECORATION (1987) INC p577
3810 BLOOR ST W, ETOBICOKE, ON, M9B 6C2
(416) 231-8040 SIC 5046

MIDDLE ATLANTIC PRODUCTS-CANADA, INC p891
113 IBER RD, STITTSVILLE, ON, K2S 1E7
(613) 836-2501 SIC 5046

MONAS & CIE LTEE p1184
4575 AV DU PARC, MONTREAL, QC, H2V 4E4
(514) 842-1421 SIC 5046

NELLA CUTLERY & FOOD EQUIPMENT INC p698
1255 FEWSTER DR, MISSISSAUGA, ON, L4W 1A2
(905) 823-1110 SIC 5046

NIVEL INC p1340
4850 RUE BOURG, SAINT-LAURENT, QC, H4T 1J2
(514) 735-4251 SIC 5046

OFFICE COFFEE SOLUTIONS LTD p993
82 INDUSTRY ST, TORONTO, ON, M6M 4L7
(416) 516-9333 SIC 5046

ORANGE TRAFFIC INC p1152
18195 RUE J.A.BOMBARDIER, MIRABEL, QC, J7J 0E7
(800) 363-5913 SIC 5046

OZAWA CANADA INC p853
100 EAST BEAVER CREEK RD UNIT 2, RICHMOND HILL, ON, L4B 1J6
(905) 731-5088 SIC 5046

PACIFIC RESTAURANT SUPPLY, INC p295
1020 CORDOVA ST E, VANCOUVER, BC, V6A 4A3
(604) 216-2566 SIC 5046

PRECISION GIANT SYSTEMS INC p110
7217 GIRARD RD NW, EDMONTON, AB, T6B 2C5
(780) 463-0026 SIC 5046

PRODUITS D'ENTREPOSAGE PEDLEX LTEE, LES p1050
10000 BOUL DU GOLF, ANJOU, QC, H1J 2Y7
(514) 324-5310 SIC 5046

RUSSELL FOOD EQUIPMENT (CALGARY) LIMITED p37
5707 4 ST SE, CALGARY, AB, T2H 1K8
(403) 253-1383 SIC 5046

RUSSELL FOOD EQUIPMENT LIMITED p295
1255 VENABLES ST, VANCOUVER, BC, V6A 3X6
(604) 253-6611 SIC 5046

S.T.O.P. RESTAURANT SUPPLY LTD p635
206 CENTENNIAL CRT, KITCHENER, ON, N2B 3X2
(519) 749-2710 SIC 5046

SANI PRO INC p433
99 BLACKMARSH RD, ST. JOHN'S, NL, A1E 1S6
(709) 579-2151 SIC 5046

SERVICES DE CAFE VAN HOUTTE INC p1170
3700 RUE JEAN-RIVARD, MONTREAL, QC, H1Z 4K3
(514) 593-7711 SIC 5046

STAINLESS PROCESS EQUIPMENT INC p736
1317 CARDIFF BLVD, MISSISSAUGA, ON, L5S 1R1
(905) 670-1163 SIC 5046

STELLAR METAL PRODUCTS INC p1034
609 HANLAN RD, WOODBRIDGE, ON, L4L 4R8
(289) 371-0218 SIC 5046

SYSCO GUEST SUPPLY CANADA INC p707
570 MATHESON BLVD E SUITE 8, MISSISSAUGA, ON, L4Z 4G4
(905) 896-1060 SIC 5046

SYSTEMES CALE INC p1071
9005 BOUL DU QUARTIER, BROSSARD, QC, J4Y 0A8
(450) 444-4484 SIC 5046

TARRISON PRODUCTS LTD p799
2780 COVENTRY RD, OAKVILLE, ON, L6H 6R1
(905) 825-9665 SIC 5046

TAYLOR FREEZERS INC p507
52 ARMTHORPE RD, BRAMPTON, ON, L6T 5M4
(905) 790-2211 SIC 5046

W.D. COLLEDGE COMPANY LIMITED p690
3220 ORLANDO DR UNIT 3, MISSISSAUGA, ON, L4V 1R5
(905) 677-4428 SIC 5046

WAYMARC INDUSTRIES LTD p97
16304 117 AVE NW, EDMONTON, AB, T5M 3W2
(780) 453-2358 SIC 5046

SIC 5047 Medical and hospital equipment

1127770 B.C. LTD p292
777 BROADWAY W, VANCOUVER, BC, V5Z 4J7
SIC 5047

1207273 ALBERTA ULC p704
570 MATHESON BLVD E UNIT 8, MISSISSAUGA, ON, L4Z 4G4
(905) 890-8300 SIC 5047

1363199 ONTARIO LIMITED p1018
5923 TECUMSEH RD E SUITE 1, WINDSOR, ON, N8T 1E4
(519) 252-2011 SIC 5047

1767388 ONTARIO INC p657
1020 ADELAIDE ST S, LONDON, ON, N6E 1R6
(519) 963-4010 SIC 5047

2188262 ONTARIO LTD p921
586 EGLINTON AVE E UNIT 208, TORONTO, ON, M4P 1P2
(416) 802-2382 SIC 5047

2946-5440 QUEBEC INC p1331
4850 CH DU BOIS-FRANC BUREAU 100, SAINT-LAURENT, QC, H4S 1A7
(514) 335-3433 SIC 5047

301776 ALBERTA LTD p84
10611 KINGSWAY NW SUITE 114, EDMONTON, AB, T5G 3C8
(780) 424-6094 SIC 5047

443696 B.C. LTD p334
1856 QUADRA ST, VICTORIA, BC, V8T 4B9
(250) 384-8000 SIC 5047

A.M.G. MEDICALE INC p1157
8505 CH DALTON, MONT-ROYAL, QC, H4T 1V5
(514) 737-5251 SIC 5047

ADVANCED MEDICAL SOLUTIONS INC p435
233 UTSINGI DR, YELLOWKNIFE, NT, X1A 0E7
(866) 578-9111 SIC 5047

AGFA HEALTHCARE INC p729
5975 FALBOURNE ST SUITE 2, MISSISSAUGA, ON, L5R 3V8
(416) 241-1110 SIC 5047

AMAX HEALTH INC p883
27 SEAPARK DR UNIT 1, ST CATHARINES, ON, L2M 6S5
(905) 682-8070 SIC 5047

AMAX HEALTH INC p883
27 SEAPARK DR UNIT 1, ST CATHARINES, ON, L2M 6S5
(905) 682-8070 SIC 5047

AMICO PATIENT CARE CORPORATION p850
85 FULTON WAY, RICHMOND HILL, ON, L4B 2N4
(905) 764-0800 SIC 5047

AMT ELECTROSURGERY INC p637
20 STECKLE PL UNIT 16, KITCHENER, ON, N2E 2C3
(519) 895-0452 SIC 5047

APOLLO MEDICAL LTD p413
379 SOMERSET ST, SAINT JOHN, NB, E2K 2Y5
(506) 693-3300 SIC 5047

ARJO CANADA INC p729
90 MATHESON BLVD W SUITE 350, MISSISSAUGA, ON, L5R 3R3
(905) 238-7880 SIC 5047

ASSOCIATED HEALTH SYSTEMS INC p275
8145 130 ST UNIT 6, SURREY, BC, V3W 7X4
(604) 591-8012 SIC 5047

AUTO CONTROL MEDICAL INC p719
6695 MILLCREEK DR UNIT 6, MISSISSAUGA, ON, L5N 5R8
(905) 814-6350 SIC 5047

B. BRAUN OF CANADA, LTD p720
6711 MISSISSAUGA RD SUITE 504, MISSISSAUGA, ON, L5N 2W3
(905) 363-4335 SIC 5047

BAYLIS MEDICALE CIE INC p692
2645 MATHESON BLVD E, MISSISSAUGA, ON, L4W 5S4
(905) 602-4875 SIC 5047

BAYLIS MEDICALE CIE INC p1338
5959 RTE TRANSCANADIENNE, SAINT-LAURENT, QC, H4T 1A1
(514) 488-9801 SIC 5047

BC STEVENS COMPANY p208
8188 SWENSON WAY, DELTA, BC, V4G 1J6
(604) 634-3088 SIC 5047

BD BIOSCIENCES p720
2280 ARGENTIA RD, MISSISSAUGA, ON, L5N 6H8
SIC 5047

BECKMAN COULTER CANADA INC p720
7075 FINANCIAL DR, MISSISSAUGA, ON, L5N 6V8
(905) 819-1234 SIC 5047

BECTON DICKINSON CANADA INC p720
2100 DERRY RD W SUITE 100, MISSISSAUGA, ON, L5N 0B3
(905) 288-6000 SIC 5047

BECTON DICKINSON CANADA INC p796
2771 BRISTOL CIR, OAKVILLE, ON, L6H 6R5
SIC 5047

BEST BUY MEDICAL SUPPLIES INC p406
211 BROMLEY AVE SUITE 7, MONCTON, NB, E1C 5V5
(506) 851-1644 SIC 5047

BIOMEDICAL INDUSTRY GROUP INC p820
532 MONTREAL RD SUITE 362, OTTAWA, ON, K1K 4R4
(613) 745-4139 SIC 5047

BIOMERIEUX CANADA, INC p1332
7815 BOUL HENRI-BOURASSA O, SAINT-LAURENT, QC, H4S 1P7

BIOTRONIK CANADA INC p578
185 THE WEST MALL SUITE 1000, ETOBI-
COKE, ON, M9C 5L5
(416) 620-0069 *SIC* 5047

BRASSELER CANADA INC p1256
4500 BOUL HENRI-BOURASSA BUREAU
230, QUEBEC, QC, G1H 3A5
(418) 622-1195 *SIC* 5047

BSN MEDICAL INC p1235
4455 NORD LAVAL (A-440) O UNITE 255,
MONTREAL, QC, H7P 4W6
(450) 978-0738 *SIC* 5047

C.D.M.V. INC p1311
2999 BOUL CHOQUETTE, SAINT-
HYACINTHE, QC, J2S 6H5
(450) 771-2368 *SIC* 5047

**CANADIAN HOSPITAL SPECIALTIES LIM-
ITED** p796
2810 COVENTRY RD, OAKVILLE, ON, L6H
6R1
(905) 825-9300 *SIC* 5047

CARDINAL HEALTH CANADA INC p550
1000 TESMA WAY, CONCORD, ON, L4K
5R8
(905) 417-2900 *SIC* 5047

CARDINAL HEALTH CANADA INC p738
1330 MEYERSIDE DR, MISSISSAUGA,
ON, L5T 1C2
(905) 761-0068 *SIC* 5047

CARDIOMED SUPPLIES INC p645
199 ST DAVID ST, LINDSAY, ON, K9V 5K7
(705) 328-2518 *SIC* 5047

CARLOU MARKETING INC p1431
820 45TH ST W, SASKATOON, SK, S7L
6A5
(306) 664-1188 *SIC* 5047

**CENTRE DE READAPTATION INTERNA-
TIONAL** p1386
3450 RUE SAINTE-MARGUERITE, TROIS-
RIVIERES, QC, G8Z 1X3
(819) 691-7536 *SIC* 5047

**CENTRE OPTOMETRIQUE DE GRANBY
INC** p1110
220 RUE SAINT-JUDE N, GRANBY, QC, J2J
0C2
(450) 372-1031 *SIC* 5047

CERUM DENTAL SUPPLIES LTD p66
115 17 AVE SW, CALGARY, AB, T2S 0A1
(403) 228-5199 *SIC* 5047

CHRISTIE INNOMED INC p1301
516 RUE DUFOUR, SAINT-EUSTACHE,
QC, J7R 0C3
(450) 472-9120 *SIC* 5047

CLARION MEDICAL TECHNOLOGIES INC
p535
125 FLEMING DR, CAMBRIDGE, ON, N1T
2B8
(519) 620-3900 *SIC* 5047

**CLINICAL RESEARCH DENTAL SUPPLIES
& SERVICES INC** p653
167 CENTRAL AVE SUITE 200, LONDON,
ON, N6A 1M6
(519) 641-3066 *SIC* 5047

COLOPLAST CANADA CORPORATION
p796
2401 BRISTOL CIR SUITE 205A,
OAKVILLE, ON, L6H 6P1
(877) 820-7008 *SIC* 5047

CONFI-DENT INC p668
90 NOLAN CRT UNIT 14, MARKHAM, ON,
L3R 4L9
(905) 474-4444 *SIC* 5047

CONVATEC CANADA LTEE p1093
1425 RTE TRANSCANADIENNE BUREAU
250, DORVAL, QC, H9P 2W9
(514) 822-5985 *SIC* 5047

COOK (CANADA) INC p894
165 MOSTAR ST, STOUFFVILLE, ON, L4A
0Y2
(905) 640-7110 *SIC* 5047

**COOPERATIVE DES PARAMEDICS DU
TEMISCOUATA** p1378
148 RUE DE L'EGLISE, TEMISCOUATA-

SUR-LE-LAC, QC, G0L 1X0
(418) 899-2047 *SIC* 5047

COVIDIEN CANADA ULC p1333
8455 RTE TRANSCANADIENNE, SAINT-
LAURENT, QC, H4S 1Z1
(877) 664-8926 *SIC* 5047

**D.S.L. DIAGNOSTIC PRODUCTS INCORPO-
RATED** p668
50 VALLEYWOOD DR SUITE 1,
MARKHAM, ON, L3R 6E9
(905) 470-0431 *SIC* 5047

**DANIELS SHARPSMART CANADA LIM-
ITED** p509
52 BRAMSTEELE RD SUITE 8, BRAMP-
TON, ON, L6W 3M5
(905) 793-2966 *SIC* 5047

DENTAL BRANDS FOR LESS INC p669
61 AMBER ST, MARKHAM, ON, L3R 3J7
(905) 669-9329 *SIC* 5047

DENTSPLY CANADA LTD p1030
161 VINYL CRT, WOODBRIDGE, ON, L4L
4A3
(905) 851-6060 *SIC* 5047

**DIAMOND ATHLETIC MEDICAL SUPPLIES
INC** p387
75 POSEIDON BAY UNIT 185, WINNIPEG,
MB, R3M 3E4
(204) 488-7820 *SIC* 5047

DRAEGER MEDICAL CANADA INC p694
2425 SKYMARK AVE UNIT 1, MISSIS-
SAUGA, ON, L4W 4Y6
(905) 212-6600 *SIC* 5047

DUFORT ET LAVIGNE LTEE p1238
8581 PLACE MARIEN, MONTREAL-EST,
QC, H1B 5W6
(514) 527-9381 *SIC* 5047

**ECO ENVIRONMENT PRODUCTS (1989)
LTD** p100
18303 107 AVE NW SUITE 1989, EDMON-
TON, AB, T5S 1K4
(780) 483-6232 *SIC* 5047

EDMONTON DENTAL SUPPLIES LTD p85
10578 109 ST NW, EDMONTON, AB, T5H
3B2
(780) 429-2567 *SIC* 5047

EDWARDS LIFESCIENCES (CANADA) INC
p711
1290 CENTRAL PKY W SUITE 300, MIS-
SISSAUGA, ON, L5C 4R3
(905) 273-7138 *SIC* 5047

ELEKTA LTEE p1195
2050 RUE DE BLEURY BUREAU 200,
MONTREAL, QC, H3A 2J5
(514) 840-9600 *SIC* 5047

ESSITY CANADA INC p805
1275 NORTH SERVICE RD W SUITE 800,
OAKVILLE, ON, L6M 3G4
(905) 339-3539 *SIC* 5047

ESSITY CANADA INC p1098
999 RUE FARRELL, DRUMMONDVILLE,
QC, J2C 5P6
(819) 475-4500 *SIC* 5047

FRESENIUS MEDICAL CARE CANADA INC
p852
45 STAPLES AVE SUITE 110, RICHMOND
HILL, ON, L4B 4W6
(905) 770-0855 *SIC* 5047

GENIE AUDIO INC p1326
125 RUE GAGNON BUREAU 102, SAINT-
LAURENT, QC, H4N 1T1
(514) 856-9212 *SIC* 5047

GENSCI OCF INC p1237
1105 CHOMEDEY (A-13) E, MONTREAL,
QC, H7W 5J8
(450) 688-8699 *SIC* 5047

GETINGE CANADA LIMITED p731
90 MATHESON BLVD W SUITE 300, MIS-
SISSAUGA, ON, L5R 3R3
(905) 629-8777 *SIC* 5047

HENRY SCHEIN CANADA, INC p206
1619 FOSTER'S WAY, DELTA, BC, V3M 6S7
(604) 527-8888 *SIC* 5047

HENRY SCHEIN CANADA, INC p761
345 TOWNLINE RD, NIAGARA ON THE

LAKE, ON, L0S 1J0
(905) 646-1711 *SIC* 5047

HENRY SCHEIN CANADA, INC p1339
3403 RUE GRIFFITH, SAINT-LAURENT,
QC, H4T 1W5
(800) 668-5558 *SIC* 5047

HIGHGATE RETIREMENT HOMES INC p477
325 FIDDLER'S GREEN RD SUITE 215,
ANCASTER, ON, L9G 1W9
(905) 648-8399 *SIC* 5047

HILL-ROM CANADA LTD p723
6950 CREDITVIEW RD UNIT 4, MISSIS-
SAUGA, ON, L5N 0A6
(905) 206-1355 *SIC* 5047

HOLLISTER LIMITED p480
95 MARY ST, AURORA, ON, L4G 1G3
(905) 727-4344 *SIC* 5047

HOME HEALTH CARE SOLUTIONS INC
p115
5405 99 ST NW, EDMONTON, AB, T6E 3N8
(780) 434-3131 *SIC* 5047

HOSPITAL LOGISTICS INC p945
1 DUNDAS ST W SUITE 1700, TORONTO,
ON, M5G 1Z3
(416) 673-5600 *SIC* 5047

ICU MEDICAL CANADA INC p1334
2600 BOUL ALFRED-NOBEL BUREAU 100,
SAINT-LAURENT, QC, H4S 0A9
(514) 905-2600 *SIC* 5047

IMPERIAL SURGICAL LTD p1094
850 AV HALPERN, DORVAL, QC, H9P 1G6
(514) 631-7988 *SIC* 5047

INTEGRA CANADA ULC p798
2590 BRISTOL CIR UNIT 1, OAKVILLE, ON,
L6H 6Z7
(905) 618-1603 *SIC* 5047

INVACARE CANADA L.P. p706
570 MATHESON BLVD E SUITE 8, MISSIS-
SAUGA, ON, L4Z 4G4
(905) 890-8300 *SIC* 5047

K-DENTAL INC p671
750 COCHRANE DR, MARKHAM, ON, L3R
8E1
(416) 293-8365 *SIC* 5047

KANE VETERINARY SUPPLIES LTD p101
11204 186 ST NW, EDMONTON, AB, T5S
2W2
(780) 453-1516 *SIC* 5047

KCI MEDICAL CANADA INC p745
75 COURTNEYPARK DR W SUITE 2, MIS-
SISSAUGA, ON, L5W 0E3
(905) 565-7187 *SIC* 5047

KEIR SURGICAL LTD p290
408 E KENT AVE SOUTH SUITE 126, VAN-
COUVER, BC, V5X 2X7
(604) 261-9596 *SIC* 5047

LINVATEC CANADA ULC p724
2330 MILLRACE CRT UNIT 5, MISSIS-
SAUGA, ON, L5N 1W2
(905) 814-8900 *SIC* 5047

**LUMINEX MOLECULAR DIAGNOSTICS,
INC** p946
439 UNIVERSITY AVE SUITE 900,
TORONTO, ON, M5G 1Y8
(416) 593-4323 *SIC* 5047

M-HEALTH SOLUTIONS INC p528
3190 HARVESTER RD SUITE 203,
BURLINGTON, ON, L7N 3T1
(289) 636-0102 *SIC* 5047

MEDELA CANADA INC p717
4160 SLADEVIEW CRES UNIT 8, MISSIS-
SAUGA, ON, L5L 0A1
(905) 608-7272 *SIC* 5047

MEDICAL MART SUPPLIES LIMITED p732
6200 CANTAY RD, MISSISSAUGA, ON, L5R
3Y9
(905) 624-6200 *SIC* 5047

MEDICALE ABBOTT CANADA, INC p724
6975 CREDITVIEW RD UNIT 1, MISSIS-
SAUGA, ON, L5N 8E9
(905) 812-8600 *SIC* 5047

MEDICANA INC p1330
2261 RUE GUENETTE, SAINT-LAURENT,
QC, H4R 2E9

MEDLINE CANADA, CORPORATION p684
8690 ESCARPMENT WAY UNIT 3, MILTON,
ON, L9T 0M1
(905) 636-2100 *SIC* 5047

MEDTRONIC CRYOCATH LP p1251
9000 RTE TRANSCANADIENNE, POINTE-
CLAIRE, QC, H9R 5Z8
(514) 694-1212 *SIC* 5047

MEDXL INC p1251
285 AV LABROSSE, POINTE-CLAIRE, QC,
H9R 1A3
(514) 695-7474 *SIC* 5047

NATIONAL SHOE SPECIALTIES LIMITED
p876
3015 KENNEDY RD UNIT 8-18, SCARBOR-
OUGH, ON, M1V 1E7
(416) 292-7181 *SIC* 5047

NOBEL BIOCARE CANADA INC p853
9133 LESLIE ST UNIT 100, RICHMOND
HILL, ON, L4B 4N1
(905) 762-3500 *SIC* 5047

OLYMPUS CANADA INC p853
25 LEEK CRES, RICHMOND HILL, ON, L4B
4B3
(289) 269-0100 *SIC* 5047

**ONTARIO HOME OXYGEN AND RESPIRA-
TORY SERVICES INC** p896
29 MONTEITH AVE, STRATFORD, ON, N5A
7J9
(519) 273-1744 *SIC* 5047

ONTARIO MEDICAL SUPPLY INC p595
1100 ALGOMA RD, GLOUCESTER, ON,
K1B 0A3
(613) 244-8620 *SIC* 5047

OTTO BOCK HEALTHCARE CANADA LTD
p798
2897 BRIGHTON RD, OAKVILLE, ON, L6H
6C9
SIC 5047

PACIFIC SURGICAL HOLDINGS LTD p291
408 E KENT AVE SOUTH SUITE 126, VAN-
COUVER, BC, V5X 2X7
(604) 261-9596 *SIC* 5047

PATTERSON DENTAIRE CANADA INC
p1217
1205 BOUL HENRI-BOURASSA O, MON-
TREAL, QC, H3M 3E6
(514) 745-4040 *SIC* 5047

PHYSIO CONTROL CANADA SALES LTD
p745
45 INNOVATION DR, MISSISSAUGA, ON,
L9H 7L8
(800) 895-5896 *SIC* 5047

RADION LABORATORIES LTD p210
7198 PROGRESS WAY, DELTA, BC, V4G
1J2
(604) 946-7712 *SIC* 5047

RELAXUS PRODUCTS LTD p285
1590 POWELL ST, VANCOUVER, BC, V5L
1H3
(604) 879-3895 *SIC* 5047

RESPONSE BIOMEDICAL CORP p324
1781 75TH AVE W, VANCOUVER, BC, V6P
6P2
(604) 456-6010 *SIC* 5047

ROXON MEDI-TECH LTEE p1345
9400 RUE PASCAL-GAGNON, SAINT-
LEONARD, QC, H1P 1Z7
(514) 326-7780 *SIC* 5047

SENSE INC p596
2339 OGILVIE RD SUITE 46095,
GLOUCESTER, ON, K1J 8M6
(877) 556-5268 *SIC* 5047

SENTIMED MEDICAL CORPORATION
p1067
135 BOUL DE MORTAGNE UNIT E,
BOUCHERVILLE, QC, J4B 6G4
SIC 5047

SIGVARIS CORPORATION p1158
8423 CH DALTON, MONT-ROYAL, QC, H4T
1V5
(514) 336-2362 *SIC* 5047

SINCLAIR DENTAL CO. LTD p242

900 HARBOURSIDE DR, NORTH VAN-
COUVER, BC, V7P 3T8
(604) 986-1544   *SIC* 5047
SLEEP MANAGEMENT GROUP LIMITED
p802
466 SPEERS RD UNIT 4, OAKVILLE, ON,
L6K 3W9
(905) 337-0699   *SIC* 5047
SMITH & NEPHEW INC   *p1336*
2250 BOUL ALFRED-NOBEL BUREAU 300,
SAINT-LAURENT, QC, H4S 2C9
(514) 956-1010   *SIC* 5047
SMITHS MEDICAL CANADA LTD   *p675*
301 GOUGH RD, MARKHAM, ON, L3R 4Y8
(905) 477-2000   *SIC* 5047
STANCE HEALTHCARE INC   *p637*
45 GOODRICH DR, KITCHENER, ON, N2C
0B8
(519) 896-2400   *SIC* 5047
STARKMAN SURGICAL SUPPLY INC *p974*
1243 BATHURST ST, TORONTO, ON, M5R
3H3
(416) 534-8411   *SIC* 5047
STERIS CANADA INC   *p707*
375 BRITANNIA RD E UNIT 2, MISSIS-
SAUGA, ON, L4Z 3E2
(905) 677-0863   *SIC* 5047
STEVENS COMPANY LIMITED, THE *p513*
425 RAILSIDE DR, BRAMPTON, ON, L7A
0N8
(905) 791-8600   *SIC* 5047
STRYKER CANADA LP   *p1005*
2 MEDICORUM PLACE, WATERDOWN,
ON, L8B 1W2
(905) 690-5700   *SIC* 5047
SUNRISE MEDICAL CANADA INC   *p559*
237 ROMINA DR UNIT 3, CONCORD, ON,
L4K 4V3
(905) 660-2459   *SIC* 5047
SUNSTAR AMERICAS, INC   *p606*
515 GOVERNORS RD, GUELPH, ON, N1K
1C7
(519) 837-2500   *SIC* 5047
SUPERIOR MEDICAL LIMITED   *p784*
520 CHAMPAGNE DR, NORTH YORK, ON,
M3J 2T9
(416) 635-9797   *SIC* 5047
SYNCA MARKETING INC   *p1282*
337 RUE MARION, REPENTIGNY, QC, J5Z
4W8
(450) 582-1093   *SIC* 5047
**SYSTEMES DE DIFFUSION SPRAYLOGIK
INC, LES**   *p1314*
17420 AV CENTRALE, SAINT-HYACINTHE,
QC, J2T 3L7
(450) 778-1850   *SIC* 5047
TELEFLEX MEDICAL CANADA INC   *p676*
500 HOOD RD SUITE 310, MARKHAM, ON,
L3R 9Z3
(800) 387-9699   *SIC* 5047
TELEFLEX MEDICAL L.P   *p676*
165 GIBSON DR SUITE 1, MARKHAM, ON,
L3R 3K7
(905) 943-9000   *SIC* 5047
THERMOR LTD   *p756*
16975 LESLIE ST, NEWMARKET, ON, L3Y
9A1
(905) 952-3737   *SIC* 5047
TRIBE MEDICAL GROUP INC   *p650*
580 SOVEREIGN RD, LONDON, ON, N5V
4K7
(519) 680-0707   *SIC* 5047
**TRUDELL MEDICAL INTERNATIONAL EU-
ROPE LIMITED**   *p650*
725 BARANSWAY DR, LONDON, ON, N5V
5G4
(519) 455-7060   *SIC* 5047
TRUDELL MEDICAL MARKETING LIMITED
p650
758 BARANSWAY DR, LONDON, ON, N5V
5J7
(519) 685-8800   *SIC* 5047
UNIVERSAL HEALTH PRODUCTS   *p1021*
635 TECUMSEH RD W, WINDSOR, ON,

N8X 1H4
(519) 258-6717   *SIC* 5047
VANTAGE ENDOSCOPY INC   *p638*
20 STECKLE PL UNIT 16, KITCHENER,
ON, N2E 2C3
(866) 677-4121   *SIC* 5047
**VETERINARY PURCHASING COMPANY
LIMITED**   *p889*
485 QUEEN ST W, ST MARYS, ON, N4X
1B7
(519) 284-1371   *SIC* 5047
**WESTERN DRUG DISTRIBUTION CENTER
LIMITED**   *p103*
17611 109A AVE NW, EDMONTON, AB,
T5S 2W4
(780) 413-2508   *SIC* 5047
ZIMMER OF CANADA LIMITED   *p728*
2323 ARGENTIA RD, MISSISSAUGA, ON,
L5N 5N3
(905) 858-8588   *SIC* 5047

SIC 5048 Ophthalmic goods

CIBA VISION CANADA INC   *p721*
7 RIMINI MEWS, MISSISSAUGA, ON, L5N
4K1
    SIC 5048
IRIS, GROUPE VISUEL (1990) INC, LE *p1086*
3030 BOUL LE CARREFOUR BUREAU
1200, COTE SAINT-LUC, QC, H7T 2P5
(450) 688-9060   *SIC* 5048
MARCHON CANADA INC   *p1094*
1975 BOUL HYMUS BUREAU 250, DOR-
VAL, QC, H9P 1J8
(800) 956-9290   *SIC* 5048
NOVARTIS PHARMA CANADA INC   *p725*
2150 TORQUAY MEWS, MISSISSAUGA,
ON, L5N 2M6
    SIC 5048
THEA PHARMA INC   *p799*
2150 WINSTON PARK DR UNIT 4,
OAKVILLE, ON, L6H 5V1
(905) 829-5283   *SIC* 5048

SIC 5049 Professional equipment, nec

108786 CANADA INC   *p1331*
4775 RUE COUSENS, SAINT-LAURENT,
QC, H4S 1X5
(514) 383-0042   *SIC* 5049
1936100 ONTARIO INC   *p483*
1457 GINGERICH RD, BADEN, ON, N3A
3J7
(519) 634-5708   *SIC* 5049
966850 ONTARIO INC   *p571*
100 CARSON ST UNIT A, ETOBICOKE,
ON, M8W 3R9
(416) 259-0282   *SIC* 5049
ACTIVE OPTICAL SUPPLY   *p485*
125 ANNE ST S SUITE 207, BARRIE, ON,
L4N 7B6
(705) 812-2602   *SIC* 5049
ANACHEMIA CANADA CO   *p1125*
255 RUE NORMAN, LACHINE, QC, H8R
1A3
(514) 489-5711   *SIC* 5049
BEDCOLAB LTEE   *p1084*
2305 AV FRANCIS-HUGHES, COTE SAINT-
LUC, QC, H7S 1N5
(514) 384-2820   *SIC* 5049
**BIO-RAD LABORATORIES (CANADA) LIM-
ITED**   *p737*
1329 MEYERSIDE DR, MISSISSAUGA,
ON, L5T 1C9
(905) 364-3435   *SIC* 5049
BRAULT & BOUTHILLIER LTEE   *p1217*
700 AV BEAUMONT, MONTREAL, QC, H3N
1V5
(514) 273-9186   *SIC* 5049
BRUKER LTD   *p683*
2800 HIGHPOINT DR, MILTON, ON, L9T
6P4

(905) 876-4641   *SIC* 5049
CANADAWIDE SCIENTIFIC LIMITED   *p817*
2300 WALKLEY RD SUITE 4, OTTAWA, ON,
K1G 6B1
(613) 736-8811   *SIC* 5049
CANSEL SURVEY EQUIPMENT INC   *p192*
3900 NORTH FRASER WAY, BURNABY,
BC, V5J 5H6
(604) 299-5766   *SIC* 5049
CENTENNIAL OPTICAL LIMITED   *p786*
158 NORFINCH DR, NORTH YORK, ON,
M3N 1X6
(416) 739-8539   *SIC* 5049
CHRISTIE LITES TORONTO LTD   *p571*
100 CARSON ST UNIT A, ETOBICOKE,
ON, M8W 3R9
(416) 644-1010   *SIC* 5049
CHROMATOGRAPHIC SPECIALTIES INC
p519
300 LAURIER BLVD, BROCKVILLE, ON,
K6V 5W1
(613) 342-4678   *SIC* 5049
**CIE CANADIENNE DE PRODUITS OP-
TIQUES LTEE, LA**   *p1227*
8360 RUE MAYRAND, MONTREAL, QC,
H4P 2C9
(514) 737-6777   *SIC* 5049
**COMMISSION SCOLAIRE DE LA CAPI-
TALE, LA**   *p1258*
125 RUE DES COMMISSAIRES O BUREAU
210, QUEBEC, QC, G1K 1M7
(418) 686-4040   *SIC* 5049
COX, FRANK J SALES LIMITED   *p502*
40 WEST DR, BRAMPTON, ON, L6T 3T6
(905) 457-9190   *SIC* 5049
DRAEGER SAFETY CANADA LIMITED *p694*
2425 SKYMARK AVE UNIT 1, MISSIS-
SAUGA, ON, L4W 4Y6
(905) 212-6600   *SIC* 5049
DRAFTING CLINIC CANADA LIMITED, THE
p738
1500 TRINITY DR SUITE 16, MISSIS-
SAUGA, ON, L5T 1L6
(905) 564-1300   *SIC* 5049
**DYNAMIX PROFESSIONAL VIDEO SYS-
TEMS INC**   *p851*
100 LEEK CRES SUITE 1, RICHMOND
HILL, ON, L4B 3E6
(905) 882-4000   *SIC* 5049
EDUCATOR SUPPLIES LIMITED   *p651*
2323 TRAFALGAR ST, LONDON, ON, N5Y
5S7
(519) 453-7470   *SIC* 5049
EPPENDORF CANADA LTD   *p722*
2810 ARGENTIA RD UNIT 2, MISSIS-
SAUGA, ON, L5N 8L2
(905) 826-5525   *SIC* 5049
ESBE SCIENTIFIC INDUSTRIES INC   *p670*
80 MCPHERSON ST, MARKHAM, ON, L3R
3V6
(905) 475-8232   *SIC* 5049
ESSILOR GROUPE CANADA INC   *p187*
7541 CONWAY AVE SUITE 5, BURNABY,
BC, V5E 2P7
(604) 437-5333   *SIC* 5049
ESSILOR GROUPE CANADA INC   *p574*
347 EVANS AVE, ETOBICOKE, ON, M8Z
1K2
(416) 252-5458   *SIC* 5049
ESSILOR GROUPE CANADA INC   *p1325*
371 RUE DESLAURIERS, SAINT-
LAURENT, QC, H4N 1W2
(514) 337-2211   *SIC* 5049
FISHER SCIENTIFIC COMPANY   *p749*
112 COLONNADE RD S, NEPEAN, ON,
K2E 7L6
(613) 226-8874   *SIC* 5049
FISHER SCIENTIFIC COMPANY   *p1014*
111 SCOTIA CRT, WHITBY, ON, L1N 6J6
(905) 725-7341   *SIC* 5049
FOUNDATION DISTRIBUTING INC   *p811*
9 COBBLEDICK ST, ORONO, ON, L0B 1M0
(905) 983-1188   *SIC* 5049
GENEQ INC   *p1049*

10700 RUE SECANT, ANJOU, QC, H1J 1S5
(514) 354-2511   *SIC* 5049
GEOCALM INC   *p681*
478 BAY ST SUITE 216, MIDLAND, ON,
L4R 1K9
(705) 528-6888   *SIC* 5049
GROUPE ASPEX INC   *p1156*
5440 RUE PARE, MONT-ROYAL, QC, H4P
1R3
(514) 938-2020   *SIC* 5049
HOSKIN SCIENTIFIC LIMITED   *p185*
3735 MYRTLE ST, BURNABY, BC, V5C 4E7
(604) 872-7894   *SIC* 5049
HOYA LENS CANADA INC   *p717*
3330 RIDGEWAY DR UNIT 21, MISSIS-
SAUGA, ON, L5L 5Z9
(905) 828-3477   *SIC* 5049
IMAX CORPORATION   *p715*
2525 SPEAKMAN DR, MISSISSAUGA, ON,
L5K 1B1
(905) 403-6500   *SIC* 5049
INNOVA MEDICAL OPHTHALMICS INC *p787*
48 CARNFORTH RD, NORTH YORK, ON,
M4A 2K7
(416) 615-0185   *SIC* 5049
KHEOPS VERRE D'ART INC   *p1113*
541 8E RANG, HAM-NORD, QC, G0P 1A0
(819) 344-2152   *SIC* 5049
LEICA GEOSYSTEMS LTD   *p877*
3761 VICTORIA PARK AVE UNIT 1, SCAR-
BOROUGH, ON, M1W 3S2
(416) 497-2460   *SIC* 5049
LYNUM MANAGEMENT RESOURCES INC
p277
8456 129A ST UNIT 17, SURREY, BC, V3W
1A2
(604) 594-0100   *SIC* 5049
M.D. CHARLTON CO. LTD   *p267*
2200 KEATING CROSS RD SUITE E,
SAANICHTON, BC, V8M 2A6
(250) 652-5266   *SIC* 5049
MANDEL SCIENTIFIC COMPANY INC *p601*
2 ADMIRAL PL, GUELPH, ON, N1G 4N4
(888) 883-3636   *SIC* 5049
MOTTLAB INC   *p523*
5230 SOUTH SERVICE RD, BURLINGTON,
ON, L7L 5K2
(905) 331-1877   *SIC* 5049
NEWCON INTERNATIONAL LTD   *p765*
105 SPARKS AVE, NORTH YORK, ON,
M2H 2S5
(416) 663-6963   *SIC* 5049
OPAL OPTICAL LTD   *p725*
10 FALCONER DR UNIT 11, MISSIS-
SAUGA, ON, L5N 3L8
    SIC 5049
**OPTELIAN ACCESS NETWORKS CORPO-
RATION**   *p625*
1 BREWER HUNT WAY, KANATA, ON, K2K
2B5
(613) 287-2000   *SIC* 5049
OPTICASET INC   *p1157*
5440 RUE PARE BUREAU 101, MONT-
ROYAL, QC, H4P 1R3
(514) 739-6993   *SIC* 5049
OPTIQ LTD   *p556*
344 NORTH RIVERMEDE RD UNIT 2,
CONCORD, ON, L4K 3N2
(905) 669-6251   *SIC* 5049
OPTIQUE PERFECT INC   *p1244*
1265 AV DUCHARME, OUTREMONT, QC,
H2V 1E6
(514) 274-9407   *SIC* 5049
OPTO-PLUS INC   *p1396*
4 PLACE DU COMMERCE BUREAU 460,
VERDUN, QC, H3E 1J4
(514) 762-2020   *SIC* 5049
PERFECT OPTICAL HOLDINGS LTD *p1244*
1265 AV DUCHARME, OUTREMONT, QC,
H2V 1E6
(514) 274-9407   *SIC* 5049
**PERKINELMER HEALTH SCIENCES
CANADA, INC**   *p1032*
501 ROWNTREE DAIRY RD UNIT 6,

WOODBRIDGE, ON, L4L 8H1
(905) 851-4585   *SIC 5049*
PRECISION BIOLOGIC INC   *p448*
140 EILEEN STUBBS AVE, DARTMOUTH, NS, B3B 0A9
(800) 267-2796   *SIC 5049*
PROSCAFF NORTH AMERICA INC   *p988*
148 DEWBOURNE AVE, TORONTO, ON, M6C 1Z2
(416) 783-7500   *SIC 5049*
QUALITY EDGE CONVERTING LTD   *p366*
94 DURAND RD, WINNIPEG, MB, R2J 3T2
(204) 256-4115   *SIC 5049*
S I METRIC MANIFACTURING LTD   *p756*
150 PONY DR, NEWMARKET, ON, L3Y 7B6
(905) 898-6322   *SIC 5049*
SAFILO CANADA INC   *p1169*
4800 RUE MOLSON, MONTREAL, QC, H1Y 3J8
(514) 521-2555   *SIC 5049*
SEIGNIORY CHEMICAL PRODUCTS LTD
p1052
21800 AV CLARK-GRAHAM, BAIE D URFE, QC, H9X 4B6
(514) 457-0701   *SIC 5049*
SERVICES OPTOMETRIQUES (OPT) INC
p1396
4 PLACE DU COMMERCE BUREAU 460, VERDUN, QC, H3E 1J4
(514) 762-2020   *SIC 5049*
SOMAGEN DIAGNOSTICS INC   *p121*
9220 25 AVE NW, EDMONTON, AB, T6N 1E1
(780) 702-9500   *SIC 5049*
SOWA TOOL AND MACHINE COMPANY LIMITED   *p637*
500 MANITOU DR, KITCHENER, ON, N2C 1L3
(519) 748-5750   *SIC 5049*
SPECTRIS CANADA INC   *p1268*
350 RUE FRANQUET BUREAU 45, QUEBEC, QC, G1P 4P3
(418) 656-6453   *SIC 5049*
SPECTRIS CANADA INC   *p1331*
4921 PLACE OLIVIA, SAINT-LAURENT, QC, H4R 2V6
(514) 956-2132   *SIC 5049*
THERMO FISHER SCIENTIFIC (MISSISSAUGA) INC   *p728*
2845 ARGENTIA RD UNIT 4, MISSISSAUGA, ON, L5N 8G6
(905) 890-1034   *SIC 5049*
UKE 2000 HOLDINGS LIMITED   *p267*
2200 KEATING CROSS RD UNIT E, SAANICHTON, BC, V8M 2A6
(250) 652-5266   *SIC 5049*
VWR INTERNATIONAL CO.   *p728*
2360 ARGENTIA RD, MISSISSAUGA, ON, L5N 5Z7
(905) 813-7377   *SIC 5049*
WATERS LIMITED   *p690*
6427 NORTHAM DR, MISSISSAUGA, ON, L4V 1J2
(905) 678-2162   *SIC 5049*
WINTERGREEN LEARNING MATERIALS LIMITED   *p498*
3075 LINE 8, BRADFORD, ON, L3Z 3R5
(905) 778-8584   *SIC 5049*

SIC 5051 Metals service centers and offices

1083211 ONTARIO LTD   *p591*
19 WARREN ST, FORT ERIE, ON, L2A 2N4
(905) 994-0800   *SIC 5051*
1124178 ONTARIO INC   *p809*
351 WEST ST S, ORILLIA, ON, L3V 5H1
(705) 327-1300   *SIC 5051*
1373744 ONTARIO INC   *p500*
155 HEDGEDALE RD, BRAMPTON, ON, L6T 5P3
(905) 672-1300   *SIC 5051*
1520940 ONTARIO LTD   *p747*
9196 DICKENSON RD, MOUNT HOPE, ON,

L0R 1W0
(905) 679-6066   *SIC 5051*
2023225 ONTARIO LTD   *p766*
259 YORKLAND RD SUITE 300, NORTH YORK, ON, M2J 5B2
(416) 733-9500   *SIC 5051*
2261079 ONTARIO LTD   *p1029*
100 HAIST AVE UNIT B, WOODBRIDGE, ON, L4L 5V4
(905) 851-0173   *SIC 5051*
2529-0032 QUEBEC INC   *p1122*
3005 BOUL TASCHEREAU, LA PRAIRIE, QC, J5R 5S6
(450) 444-3112   *SIC 5051*
2969-9477 QUEBEC INC   *p1319*
11 RUE JOHN-F.-KENNEDY BUREAU 2, SAINT-JEROME, QC, J7Y 4B4
(450) 436-9390   *SIC 5051*
360 STEEL INC   *p117*
11050 UNIVERSITY AVE NW, EDMONTON, AB, T6G 1Y3
(780) 429-0360   *SIC 5051*
570026 ONTARIO LIMITED   *p994*
26 ERNEST AVE, TORONTO, ON, M6P 3M7
(416) 531-1131   *SIC 5051*
612031-376964 ONTARIO LTD   *p859*
1275 PLANK RD, SARNIA, ON, N7T 7H3
(519) 344-5532   *SIC 5051*
6368425 CANADA LTD   *p1104*
47 RUE LE BARON, GATINEAU, QC, J8T 4C3
SIC 5051
6648215 CANADA LTD   *p566*
115 5 HWY W, DUNDAS, ON, L9H 7L6
(905) 689-4774   *SIC 5051*
701466 ONTARIO LIMITED   *p733*
7195 TRANMERE DR SUITE 4, MISSISSAUGA, ON, L5S 1N4
(905) 672-6370   *SIC 5051*
A. M. CASTLE & CO. (CANADA) INC   *p719*
2150 ARGENTIA RD, MISSISSAUGA, ON, L5N 2K7
(905) 858-3888   *SIC 5051*
ACCESS METAL SERVICE INC   *p737*
1035 MID-WAY BLVD, MISSISSAUGA, ON, L5T 2C1
(905) 670-3151   *SIC 5051*
ACCUCUT PROFILE & GRINDING LIMITED
p548
300 CONNIE CRES, CONCORD, ON, L4K 5W6
(416) 798-7716   *SIC 5051*
ACCURATE SCREEN LTD   *p13*
7571 57 ST SE, CALGARY, AB, T2C 5M2
(403) 723-0323   *SIC 5051*
ACIER DRUMMOND INC   *p1097*
1750 RUE JANELLE, DRUMMONDVILLE, QC, J2C 3E5
(819) 477-4418   *SIC 5051*
ACIER GENDRON LTEE   *p1141*
2270 RUE GARNEAU, LONGUEUIL, QC, J4G 1E7
(450) 442-9494   *SIC 5051*
ACIER HYDRAULIQUE INC   *p1292*
173 RUE DE LIVERPOOL, SAINT-AUGUSTIN-DE-DESMAURES, QC, G3A 2C8
(418) 878-5711   *SIC 5051*
ACIER INOXYDABLE PINACLE INC   *p737*
455 AMBASSADOR DR, MISSISSAUGA, ON, L5T 2J3
(905) 795-2882   *SIC 5051*
ACIER LACHINE INC   *p1125*
1520 CROIS CLAIRE, LACHINE, QC, H8S 4E6
(514) 634-2252   *SIC 5051*
ACIER NOVA INC   *p1130*
6001 RUE IRWIN, LASALLE, QC, H8N 1A1
(514) 789-0511   *SIC 5051*
ACIER OUELLETTE INC   *p1319*
22 RUE JOHN-F.-KENNEDY, SAINT-JEROME, QC, J7Y 4B6
(514) 876-1414   *SIC 5051*

ACIER PACIFIQUE INC   *p1342*
845 AV MUNCK, SAINT-LAURENT, QC, H7S 1A9
(514) 384-4690   *SIC 5051*
ACIER PICARD INC   *p1137*
3000 RUE DE L'ETCHEMIN, LEVIS, QC, G6W 7X6
(418) 834-8300   *SIC 5051*
ACIER PICARD INC   *p1392*
1951 CH DE L'ENERGIE, VARENNES, QC, J3X 1P7
(450) 652-7000   *SIC 5051*
ACIER QUEBEC-MARITIMES INC   *p1285*
396 RUE TEMISCOUATA, RIVIERE-DU-LOUP, QC, G5R 2Z2
(418) 862-1320   *SIC 5051*
ACIER VALLEYFIELD INC   *p1365*
480 BOUL DES ERABLES, SALABERRY-DE-VALLEYFIELD, QC, J6T 6G4
(450) 373-4350   *SIC 5051*
ACIER VICTORIA LTEE   *p1398*
900 RUE DE L'ACADIE, VICTORIAVILLE, QC, G6T 1V1
(819) 758-7575   *SIC 5051*
ACIERS H & H INC, LES   *p1317*
920 RUE PIERRE-CAISSE, SAINT-JEAN-SUR-RICHELIEU, QC, J3B 7Y5
(450) 349-5801   *SIC 5051*
ACM PANELWORX INC   *p1017*
357 CROFT DR, WINDSOR, ON, N8N 2L9
(519) 739-2380   *SIC 5051*
ACTION STEEL SALES (OKANAGAN) LTD
p243
2365 BARNES ST, PENTICTON, BC, V2A 7K6
(250) 492-7822   *SIC 5051*
ADVANCED BENDING TECHNOLOGIES INC   *p229*
27372 GLOUCESTER WAY, LANGLEY, BC, V4W 4A1
(604) 856-6220   *SIC 5051*
ADVANCED COPPER FOIL INC   *p737*
1116 MID-WAY BLVD UNIT 5, MISSISSAUGA, ON, L5T 2H2
(905) 362-8404   *SIC 5051*
AIRPORT STEEL & TUBING LTD   *p501*
155 HEDGEDALE RD, BRAMPTON, ON, L6T 5P3
SIC 5051
ALASKAN COPPER & BRASS CANADA INC   *p199*
225 NORTH RD, COQUITLAM, BC, V3K 3V7
(604) 937-6620   *SIC 5051*
ALBERTA TUBULAR PRODUCTS LTD   *p42*
500 4 AVE SW SUITE 1100, CALGARY, AB, T2P 2V6
(403) 264-2136   *SIC 5051*
ALLIAGES ZABO INC   *p1322*
201 RUE MONTCALM BUREAU 213, SAINT-JOSEPH-DE-SOREL, QC, J3R 1B9
(450) 746-1126   *SIC 5051*
ALLIANCE SUPPLY LTD   *p246*
1585 BROADWAY ST SUITE 104, PORT COQUITLAM, BC, V3C 2M7
(604) 944-4081   *SIC 5051*
ARMOUR STEEL SUPPLY LIMITED   *p891*
540 SEAMAN ST, STONEY CREEK, ON, L8E 3X7
(905) 388-7751   *SIC 5051*
ASBURY WILKINSON INC   *p521*
1115 SUTTON DR, BURLINGTON, ON, L7L 5Z8
(905) 332-0862   *SIC 5051*
AVENTECH INTERNATIONAL INC   *p1261*
850 BOUL PIERRE-BERTRAND BUREAU 185, QUEBEC, QC, G1M 3K8
(418) 843-8966   *SIC 5051*
BAILEY WEST PROCESSING INC   *p549*
1 CALDARI RD, CONCORD, ON, L4K 3Z9
(905) 738-9267   *SIC 5051*
BANBRICO LIMITED   *p532*
480 COLLIER MACMILLAN DR, CAMBRIDGE, ON, N1R 6R5

(905) 668-9174   *SIC 5051*
BARTIN PIPE & PILING SUPPLY LTD.   *p13*
6835 GLENMORE TRAIL SE, CALGARY, AB, T2C 2S2
(403) 279-7473   *SIC 5051*
BASTILLE, MARTIN INC   *p1285*
227 RTE DE L'ANSE-AU-PERSIL, RIVIERE-DU-LOUP, QC, G5R 5Z5
(418) 862-1705   *SIC 5051*
BEAUCE METAL INC   *p1304*
11855 35E AV, SAINT-GEORGES, QC, G5Y 5B9
(418) 228-5566   *SIC 5051*
BELLEVILLE METAL SALES LIMITED   *p490*
222 UNIVERSITY AVE, BELLEVILLE, ON, K8N 5S5
(613) 968-2188   *SIC 5051*
BERGA RECYCLING INC   *p1133*
3055 BOUL SAINT-MARTIN O BUREAU T500, LAVAL, QC, H7T 0J3
(514) 949-7244   *SIC 5051*
BHD TUBULAR LIMITED   *p108*
6903 72 AVE NW, EDMONTON, AB, T6B 3A5
(780) 434-6824   *SIC 5051*
BORDER STEEL LIMITED   *p1021*
3209 DEVON DR, WINDSOR, ON, N8X 4L5
(519) 966-0760   *SIC 5051*
BOSS STEEL LIMITED   *p855*
320 NEWKIRK RD, RICHMOND HILL, ON, L4C 3G7
(888) 301-6403   *SIC 5051*
BRONZART CASTING LTD   *p14*
4315 64 AVE SE SUITE 1, CALGARY, AB, T2C 2C8
(403) 279-6584   *SIC 5051*
BRUNSWICK ENTERPRISES LIMITED *p362*
125 BISMARCK ST, WINNIPEG, MB, R2C 2Z2
(204) 224-1472   *SIC 5051*
C.F.F. HOLDINGS INC   *p609*
1840 BURLINGTON ST E, HAMILTON, ON, L8H 3L4
(905) 549-2603   *SIC 5051*
C.F.F. STAINLESS STEELS INC   *p609*
1840 BURLINGTON ST E, HAMILTON, ON, L8H 3L4
(905) 549-2603   *SIC 5051*
C.W. CARRY LTD   *p113*
5815 75 ST NW, EDMONTON, AB, T6E 0T3
(780) 465-0381   *SIC 5051*
CABLES BEN-MOR INC, LES   *p1313*
1105 RUE LEMIRE, SAINT-HYACINTHE, QC, J2T 1L8
(450) 778-0022   *SIC 5051*
CAC ENTERPRISES GROUP INC   *p190*
4538 KINGSWAY UNIT 619, BURNABY, BC, V5H 4T9
(604) 430-8835   *SIC 5051*
CAD TEK INC   *p583*
321 HUMBERLINE DR, ETOBICOKE, ON, M9W 5T6
(416) 679-9780   *SIC 5051*
CANADA STEEL SERVICE CENTRE INC
p648
25 CUDDY BLVD, LONDON, ON, N5V 3Y3
(519) 453-5600   *SIC 5051*
CANADIAN BRASS & COPPER CO   *p550*
225 DONEY CRES SUITE 1, CONCORD, ON, L4K 1P6
(416) 736-0797   *SIC 5051*
CANADIAN SPECIALTY METALS ULC *p583*
81 STEINWAY BLVD, ETOBICOKE, ON, M9W 6H6
(416) 213-0000   *SIC 5051*
CANADIAN STEEL NETWORK INC   *p738*
6445 KENNEDY RD UNIT A, MISSISSAUGA, ON, L5T 2W4
(905) 670-2900   *SIC 5051*
CANADIAN TUBULARS (1997) LTD   *p45*
825 8 AVE SW SUITE 4100, CALGARY, AB, T2P 2T4
(403) 266-2218   *SIC 5051*
CANTAK CORPORATION   *p45*

355 4 AVE SW SUITE 1050, CALGARY, AB, T2P 0J1
(403) 269-5536 *SIC 5051*

CANTECH TUBULAR SERVICES LTD p155
7983 EDGAR INDUSTRIAL DR SUITE A, RED DEER, AB, T4P 3R2
SIC 5051

CANWEST WIRE ROPE INC p281
9323 194 ST SUITE 200, SURREY, BC, V4N 4G1
SIC 5051

CASCADIA METALS LTD p208
7630 BERG RD, DELTA, BC, V4G 1G4
(604) 946-3890 *SIC 5051*

CHRISTIANSON PIPE INC p135
GD STN MAIN, HIGH RIVER, AB, T1V 1M2
(403) 652-4336 *SIC 5051*

CMP GROUP LTD p208
7733 PROGRESS WAY, DELTA, BC, V4G 1A3
(604) 940-2010 *SIC 5051*

COILPLUS CANADA INC p621
18 UNDERWOOD RD, INGERSOLL, ON, N5C 3V6
(519) 485-6393 *SIC 5051*

COLOR STEELS INC p906
251 RACCO PKY, THORNHILL, ON, L4J 8X9
(905) 879-0300 *SIC 5051*

COMPAGNIE D'ACIER ARCHIDROME DU CANADA LTEE, LA p1308
3100 BOUL LOSCH, SAINT-HUBERT, QC, J3Y 3V8
(450) 678-4444 *SIC 5051*

CONCORD STEEL CENTRE LIMITED p1030
147 ASHBRIDGE CIR, WOODBRIDGE, ON, L4L 3R5
(905) 856-1717 *SIC 5051*

CONESTOGA PIPE & SUPPLY CANADA CORPORATION p47
736 8 AVE SW SUITE 430, CALGARY, AB, T2P 1H4
(403) 444-5554 *SIC 5051*

CONSTRUCTIONS BEAUCE-ATLAS INC, LES p1360
600 1RE AV DU PARC-INDUSTRIEL, SAINTE-MARIE, QC, G6E 1B5
(418) 387-4872 *SIC 5051*

CORPORATION D'ACIER ALLIANCE, LA p1083
1060 BOUL DES LAURENTIDES, COTE SAINT-LUC, QC, H7G 2W1
(514) 382-5780 *SIC 5051*

CRAWFORD METAL CORPORATION p771
132 SHEPPARD AVE W SUITE 200, NORTH YORK, ON, M2N 1M5
(416) 224-1515 *SIC 5051*

DATCOM p873
1361 HUNTINGWOOD DR UNIT 13, SCARBOROUGH, ON, M1S 3J1
(416) 293-2866 *SIC 5051*

DEAN INDUSTRIES, INC p153
4915 54 ST 3RD FLR, RED DEER, AB, T4N 2G7
SIC 5051

DEL INDUSTRIAL METALS INC p502
7653 BRAMALEA RD, BRAMPTON, ON, L6T 5V3
(905) 595-1222 *SIC 5051*

DISTRIBUTIONS D'ACIER ANICA INC, LES p1053
540 AV FIRING, BAIE-D'URFE, QC, H9X 3T2
(514) 457-3071 *SIC 5051*

DIVERSIFIED ULBRICH OF CANADA p1027
150 NEW HUNTINGTON RD UNIT 1, WOODBRIDGE, ON, L4H 4N4
(416) 663-7130 *SIC 5051*

DOLBEAU OXYGENE INC p1090
303 8E AV BUREAU 11, DOLBEAU-MISTASSINI, QC, G8L 1Z6
(418) 276-0555 *SIC 5051*

DOMINION PIPE & PILING LTD p208
6845 TILBURY RD, DELTA, BC, V4G 0A3

(604) 946-2655 *SIC 5051*

DRAKA ELEVATOR PRODUCTS INCORPORATED p514
17 WOODYATT DR UNIT 13, BRANTFORD, ON, N3R 7K3
(519) 758-0605 *SIC 5051*

EASTERN FOUNDRY LIMITED p422
3 WHARF RD SUITE 147, CLARENVILLE, NL, A5A 2B2
(709) 466-3814 *SIC 5051*

EDGEN MURRAY CANADA INC p125
1253 91 ST SW SUITE 302E, EDMONTON, AB, T6X 1E9
(780) 440-1475 *SIC 5051*

EDMONTON STEEL PLATE LTD p114
5545 89 ST NW, EDMONTON, AB, T6E 5W9
(780) 468-6722 *SIC 5051*

EII LIMITED p526
1124 NORTHSIDE RD, BURLINGTON, ON, L7M 1H4
(905) 635-3111 *SIC 5051*

ELECTRO-WIND SUPPLY INC p606
2 TAGGART ST, GUELPH, ON, N1L 1M5
(519) 836-2280 *SIC 5051*

ELECTROMART (ONTARIO) INC p609
1701 BRAMPTON ST, HAMILTON, ON, L8H 3S2
(905) 524-1555 *SIC 5051*

ELLWOOD SPECIALTY METALS COMPANY p1019
3282 ST ETIENNE BLVD, WINDSOR, ON, N8W 5E1
(519) 944-4411 *SIC 5051*

ELMA STEEL & EQUIPMENT LTD p646
515 TREMAINE AVE S, LISTOWEL, ON, N4W 3G9
(519) 291-1388 *SIC 5051*

EPS LANTRIC INC p1339
7750 RTE TRANSCANADIENNE, SAINT-LAURENT, QC, H4T 1A5
(514) 735-4561 *SIC 5051*

EQUIPEMENTS MARQUIS INC p1375
1155 CH SAINT-ROCH N, SHERBROOKE, QC, J1N 0H2
(819) 822-3382 *SIC 5051*

ETHEREAL NAIL & BEAUTY p280
1688 152 ST UNIT 107, SURREY, BC, V4A 4N2
(604) 531-6889 *SIC 5051*

EVEREST STEEL LTD p739
6445 KENNEDY RD UNIT C, MISSISSAUGA, ON, L5T 2W4
(905) 670-7373 *SIC 5051*

EXTRUDE-A-TRIM INC p584
360 CARLINGVIEW DR, ETOBICOKE, ON, M9W 5X9
(416) 798-1277 *SIC 5051*

F.X. LANGE INC p1248
10550 BOUL HENRI-BOURASSA E, POINTE-AUX-TREMBLES, QC, H1C 1G6
(514) 648-7445 *SIC 5051*

FASTEEL INDUSTRIES LTD p279
19176 21 AVE, SURREY, BC, V3Z 3M3
(604) 542-8881 *SIC 5051*

FORTIS ENGINEERING & MANUFACTURING INC p1427
802 57TH ST E, SASKATOON, SK, S7K 5Z2
(306) 242-4427 *SIC 5051*

FRASER VALLEY STEEL & WIRE LTD p178
3174 MT LEHMAN RD, ABBOTSFORD, BC, V4X 2M9
(604) 856-3391 *SIC 5051*

GANTREX CANADA INC p474
12 BARR RD, AJAX, ON, L1S 3X9
(905) 686-0560 *SIC 5051*

GATEWAY TUBULARS LTD p50
144 4 AVE SW SUITE 2800, CALGARY, AB, T2P 3N4
(403) 457-2288 *SIC 5051*

GATSTEEL INDUSTRIES INC p584
361 ATTWELL DR, ETOBICOKE, ON, M9W 5C2
(416) 675-2370 *SIC 5051*

GESTION BEAUCE-ATLAS INC p1360

600 1RE AV DU PARC-INDUSTRIEL, SAINTE-MARIE, QC, G6E 1B5
(418) 387-4872 *SIC 5051*

GESTION YVON GUILLOTTE INC p1318
920 RUE PIERRE-CAISSE, SAINT-JEAN-SUR-RICHELIEU, QC, J3B 7Y5
(450) 349-5801 *SIC 5051*

GLOBAL ALLOY PIPE AND SUPPLY, INC p122
2125 64 AVE NW, EDMONTON, AB, T6P 1Z4
(780) 469-6603 *SIC 5051*

GREENER STEEL INC p913
352 RAILWAY ST, TIMMINS, ON, P4N 2P6
(705) 268-7197 *SIC 5051*

HALLMARK TUBULARS LTD p50
308 4 AVE SW SUITE 400, CALGARY, AB, T2P 0H7
(403) 266-3807 *SIC 5051*

HAMILTON METALS CANADA, LLC p122
3215 76 AVE NW, EDMONTON, AB, T6P 1T4
(587) 881-3921 *SIC 5051*

HERCULES SLR INC p446
520 WINDMILL RD, DARTMOUTH, NS, B3B 1B3
(902) 482-3125 *SIC 5051*

HERCULES SLR INC p522
737 OVAL CRT, BURLINGTON, ON, L7L 6A9
SIC 5051

HOME-RAIL (CALGARY) LTD p35
5520 4 ST SE, CALGARY, AB, T2H 1K7
(403) 202-5493 *SIC 5051*

HONDA TRADING CANADA INC p476
4700 INDUSTRIAL PKWY, ALLISTON, ON, L9R 1W7
(705) 435-0172 *SIC 5051*

HOUSE OF METALS COMPANY LIMITED p918
45 COMMERCIAL RD, TORONTO, ON, M4G 1Z3
(416) 421-1572 *SIC 5051*

HUBERT SABOURIN HOLDINGS LTD p476
135 SANDFIELD AVE, ALEXANDRIA, ON, K0C 1A0
(613) 525-1032 *SIC 5051*

HUNTER STEEL SALES LTD p896
500 LORNE AVE E, STRATFORD, ON, N5A 6S4
(519) 273-3151 *SIC 5051*

HYUNDAI CANADA INC p772
5160 YONGE ST SUITE 1003, NORTH YORK, ON, M2N 6L9
(416) 229-6668 *SIC 5051*

IMPACT STEEL CANADA COMPANY p523
1100 BURLOAK DR SUITE 300, BURLINGTON, ON, L7L 6B2
(905) 336-8939 *SIC 5051*

IMPULSE TECHNOLOGIES LTD p735
920 GANA CRT, MISSISSAUGA, ON, L5S 1Z4
(905) 564-9266 *SIC 5051*

INNOVATIVE STEEL GROUP INC p517
85 MORRELL ST, BRANTFORD, ON, N3T 4J6
(519) 720-9797 *SIC 5051*

INOX DISTRIBUTION INC p1066
1440 RUE GRAHAM-BELL BUREAU A, BOUCHERVILLE, QC, J4B 6H5
(450) 449-9200 *SIC 5051*

INPROHEAT INDUSTRIES LIMITED p295
680 RAYMUR AVE, VANCOUVER, BC, V6A 2R1
(604) 254-0461 *SIC 5051*

INTERNATIONAL CASTINGS & SUPPLIES LTD p276
12383 83A AVE, SURREY, BC, V3W 9Y7
(604) 596-4961 *SIC 5051*

J. M. LAHMAN MFG. INC p646
3617 LICHTY RD, LINWOOD, ON, N0B 2A0
(519) 698-2440 *SIC 5051*

JANCO STEEL LTD p892
925 ARVIN AVE, STONEY CREEK, ON, L8E

5N9
(905) 643-3535 *SIC 5051*

K.P. BRONZE LIMITED p481
16 ALLAURA BLVD SUITE 20, AURORA, ON, L4G 3S5
(905) 727-8706 *SIC 5051*

KANAS HOLDINGS CORPORATION p36
5312 3 ST SE, CALGARY, AB, T2H 1J8
(403) 283-2566 *SIC 5051*

KAWARTHA METALS CORP p841
1-1961 FISHER DR, PETERBOROUGH, ON, K9J 6X6
(705) 748-6993 *SIC 5051*

KENWAL CANADA INC p892
1100 SOUTH SERVICE RD SUITE 317, STONEY CREEK, ON, L8E 0C5
(905) 643-8930 *SIC 5051*

KOTYCK BROS. LIMITED p509
80 HALE RD SUITE 7, BRAMPTON, ON, L6W 3N9
(905) 595-1127 *SIC 5051*

KP BUILDING PRODUCTS LTD p473
323 MAIN ST N SUITE 3, ACTON, ON, L7J 2L9
(519) 853-1230 *SIC 5051*

LA SALLE STEEL CORPORATION p1186
180 BOUL RENE-LEVESQUE E BUREAU 500, MONTREAL, QC, H2X 1N6
(514) 933-8899 *SIC 5051*

LAVAL CABLE ET GRANULATIONS INC p1234
270 BOUL SAINT-ELZEAR O, MONTREAL, QC, H7L 3P2
(450) 668-8100 *SIC 5051*

LIFTING SOLUTIONS INC p110
3710 78 AVE NW, EDMONTON, AB, T6B 3E5
(780) 784-7725 *SIC 5051*

LOUCON METAL LIMITED p750
39 GRENFELL CRES SUITE 37, NEPEAN, ON, K2G 0G3
(613) 226-1102 *SIC 5051*

MAC INDUSTRIES LTD p282
9445 193A ST, SURREY, BC, V4N 4N5
(604) 513-4536 *SIC 5051*

MAGNUM STEEL & TUBE INC p523
4380 CORPORATE DR, BURLINGTON, ON, L7L 5R3
(905) 319-9852 *SIC 5051*

MANUFACTURIERS D'ALUMINIUM OTTAWA INC, LES p1302
439 BOUL INDUSTRIEL, SAINT-EUSTACHE, QC, J7R 5R3
(450) 983-3766 *SIC 5051*

MARMON/KEYSTONE CANADA INC p523
1220 HERITAGE RD, BURLINGTON, ON, L7L 4X9
(905) 319-4646 *SIC 5051*

MEGANTIC METAL LTEE p1383
1400 BOUL FRONTENAC E, THETFORD MINES, QC, G6G 6Z2
(418) 338-3188 *SIC 5051*

METAL CORE ATLANTIC INC p408
180 EDINBURGH DR SUITE 1, MONCTON, NB, E1E 2K7
(506) 854-2673 *SIC 5051*

METAL GOSSELIN LTEE p1154
1591 BOUL ALBINY-PAQUETTE, MONT-LAURIER, QC, J9L 1M8
(819) 623-3369 *SIC 5051*

METAL SUPERMARKETS SERVICE COMPANY INC p741
520 ABILENE DR 2ND FL, MISSISSAUGA, ON, L5T 2H7
(905) 362-8226 *SIC 5051*

METALIUM INC p1234
4020 RUE GARAND, MONTREAL, QC, H7L 5C9
(450) 963-0411 *SIC 5051*

METALS PLUS LTD p1014
1610 MCEWEN DR UNIT 1-3, WHITBY, ON, L1N 8V7
(905) 721-0050 *SIC 5051*

METAUX ABSOLUS INC p1152

17550 RUE CHARLES, MIRABEL, QC, J7J 1X9
(450) 437-1777   *SIC* 5051

METAUX M.P.I. INC   *p1152*
12695 RUE DU PARC, MIRABEL, QC, J7J 0W5
(450) 420-0858   *SIC* 5051

METAUX PROFUSION INC   *p1094*
2000 BOUL HYMUS, DORVAL, QC, H9P 1J7
(514) 822-0922   *SIC* 5051

MIDLAND METALS INTERNATIONAL INC *p768*
259 YORKLAND RD SUITE 300, NORTH YORK, ON, M2J 5B2
(416) 733-9500   *SIC* 5051

MINERAUX MART INC   *p1322*
201 RUE MONTCALM BUREAU 213, SAINT-JOSEPH-DE-SOREL, QC, J3R 1B9
(450) 746-1126   *SIC* 5051

MISTEELCO INC   *p651*
850 DUNDAS ST, LONDON, ON, N5W 2Z7
(519) 679-1939   *SIC* 5051

MITSUBISHI CANADA LIMITED   *p307*
200 GRANVILLE ST SUITE 2800, VAN-COUVER, BC, V6C 1G6
(604) 654-8000   *SIC* 5051

MITSUI & CO. (CANADA) LTD   *p970*
66 WELLINGTON ST W SUITE 3510, TORONTO, ON, M5K 1K2
(416) 365-3800   *SIC* 5051

MNZ GLOBAL INC   *p904*
300 JOHN ST SUITE 503, THORNHILL, ON, L3T 5W4
(905) 597-0207   *SIC* 5051

MYER SALIT LIMITED   *p759*
7771 STANLEY AVE, NIAGARA FALLS, ON, L2G 0C7
(905) 354-5691   *SIC* 5051

NEW WEST METALS INC   *p375*
13 HIGGINS AVE, WINNIPEG, MB, R3B 0A3
(204) 949-0967   *SIC* 5051

NOLRAD INTERNATIONAL INC   *p556*
1380 CREDITSTONE RD UNIT 5, CON-CORD, ON, L4K 0J1
(905) 738-4646   *SIC* 5051

NORTH AMERICAN PIPE & STEEL LTD *p209*
7449 RIVER RD, DELTA, BC, V4G 1B9
(604) 946-0916   *SIC* 5051

NORTH YORK IRON CORPORATION *p784*
1100 FLINT RD, NORTH YORK, ON, M3J 2J5
(416) 661-2888   *SIC* 5051

NORTH-EAST TUBES INC   *p505*
29 NUGGETT CRT, BRAMPTON, ON, L6T 5A9
(905) 792-1200   *SIC* 5051

NORTHERN ALLIED SUPPLY COMPANY LIMITED   *p913*
352 RAILWAY ST, TIMMINS, ON, P4N 2P6
(705) 264-5291   *SIC* 5051

NORTHERN STRANDS CO. LTD   *p1428*
3235 MILLAR AVE, SASKATOON, SK, S7K 5Y3
(306) 242-7073   *SIC* 5051

NUCOR CANADA INC   *p531*
1455 LAKESHORE RD SUITE 204N, BURLINGTON, ON, L7S 2J1
(905) 634-6868   *SIC* 5051

NUVU CORPORATION   *p756*
450 HARRY WALKER PKY S, NEWMAR-KET, ON, L3Y 8E3
(905) 952-2288   *SIC* 5051

PACIFIC TUBULARS LTD   *p55*
734 7 AVE SW SUITE 600, CALGARY, AB, T2P 3P8
(403) 269-7600   *SIC* 5051

PACRIM PIPES (CANADA) ULC   *p55*
505 4 AVE SW SUITE 1610, CALGARY, AB, T2P 0J8
(403) 234-8228   *SIC* 5051

PHOENIX/PMA INC   *p742*

1080 MEYERSIDE DR, MISSISSAUGA, ON, L5T 1J4
(905) 678-9400   *SIC* 5051

PIONEER STEEL LIMITED   *p706*
355 TRADERS BLVD E, MISSISSAUGA, ON, L4Z 2E5
(905) 890-0209   *SIC* 5051

PIPE & PILING SUPPLIES (WESTERN) LTD *p17*
5515 40 ST SE, CALGARY, AB, T2C 2A8
(403) 236-1332   *SIC* 5051

POINTE-CLAIRE STEEL INC   *p611*
408 WENTWORTH ST N, HAMILTON, ON, L8L 5W3
(905) 544-5604   *SIC* 5051

POINTE-CLAIRE/GREEN VALLEY STEEL GROUP INC   *p611*
408 WENTWORTH ST N, HAMILTON, ON, L8L 5W3
(905) 544-5604   *SIC* 5051

PRICE STEEL LTD   *p106*
13500 156 ST NW, EDMONTON, AB, T5V 1L3
(780) 447-9999   *SIC* 5051

PROVO LTD   *p1033*
620 ROWNTREE DAIRY RD, WOOD-BRIDGE, ON, L4L 5T8
(905) 851-8520   *SIC* 5051

QUALITY TUBING CANADA INC   *p154*
4610 49 AVE SUITE 103, RED DEER, AB, T4N 6M5
(403) 342-1000   *SIC* 5051

R & R TRADING CO. LTD   *p209*
7449 RIVER RD, DELTA, BC, V4G 1B9
(604) 946-0916   *SIC* 5051

RELIABLE TUBE (EDMONTON) LTD   *p2*
26936 ACHESON RD, ACHESON, AB, T7X 6B2
(780) 962-0130   *SIC* 5051

RELIABLE TUBE INC   *p230*
26867 GLOUCESTER WAY, LANGLEY, BC, V4W 3Y3
(604) 857-9861   *SIC* 5051

RELIANCE FOUNDRY CO. LTD   *p273*
6450 148 ST UNIT 207, SURREY, BC, V3S 7G7
(604) 547-0460   *SIC* 5051

RELIANCE METALS CANADA LIMITED *p123*
6925 8 ST NW, EDMONTON, AB, T6P 1T9
(780) 801-4114   *SIC* 5051

RICHFORM CONSTRUCTION SUPPLY CO LTD   *p202*
35 LEEDER ST UNIT A, COQUITLAM, BC, V3K 3V5
(604) 777-9974   *SIC* 5051

RIVER CABLE LTD   *p270*
11406 132A ST, SURREY, BC, V3R 7S2
(604) 580-4636   *SIC* 5051

RIVERVIEW STEEL CO. LTD   *p1017*
8165 ANCHOR DR, WINDSOR, ON, N8N 5B7
(519) 979-5576   *SIC* 5051

ROLARK STAINLESS STEEL INC   *p1028*
71 CONAIR PKWY, WOODBRIDGE, ON, L4H 0S4
(416) 798-7770   *SIC* 5051

ROLLED ALLOYS-CANADA, INC   *p726*
7111 SYNTEX DR SUITE 120, MISSIS-SAUGA, ON, L5N 8C3
(905) 363-0277   *SIC* 5051

ROYAL CANADIAN STEEL INC   *p506*
70 TITAN RD, BRAMPTON, ON, L6T 4A3
(905) 454-7274   *SIC* 5051

RUNNALLS INDUSTRIES INC   *p736*
1275 CARDIFF BLVD, MISSISSAUGA, ON, L5S 1R1
(905) 453-4220   *SIC* 5051

RUSKCAST INC   *p907*
110 ORMOND ST S, THOROLD, ON, L2V 4J6
(905) 227-4011   *SIC* 5051

RUSSEL METALS INC   *p116*
7016 99 ST NW, EDMONTON, AB, T6E 3R3

SIC 5051
RUSSEL METALS INC   *p207*
830 CARLISLE RD, DELTA, BC, V3M 5P4
(604) 525-0544   *SIC* 5051

RUSSEL METALS INC   *p385*
1359 ST JAMES ST, WINNIPEG, MB, R3H 0K9
SIC 5051

RUSSEL METALS INC   *p460*
28 LAKESIDE PARK DR, LAKESIDE, NS, B3T 1A3
(902) 876-7861   *SIC* 5051

RUSSEL METALS INC   *p726*
6600 FINANCIAL DR, MISSISSAUGA, ON, L5N 7J6
(905) 819-7777   *SIC* 5051

RUSSEL METALS INC   *p726*
1900 MINNESOTA CRT SUITE 210, MIS-SISSAUGA, ON, L5N 3C9
(905) 567-8500   *SIC* 5051

RYERSON CANADA, INC   *p524*
1219 CORPORATE DR SUITE 2, BURLING-TON, ON, L7L 5V5
(416) 622-3100   *SIC* 5051

RYERSON CANADA, INC   *p1362*
3399 AV FRANCIS-HUGHES, SAINTE-ROSE, QC, H7L 5A5
(450) 975-7171   *SIC* 5051

S.M.P SPECIALTY METAL PRODUCTS LTD *p707*
326 WATLINE AVE, MISSISSAUGA, ON, L4Z 1X2
SIC 5051

SAMUEL, SON & CO., LIMITED   *p149*
1709 8 ST, NISKU, AB, T9E 7S8
(780) 955-7516   *SIC* 5051

SAMUEL, SON & CO., LIMITED   *p516*
546 ELGIN ST, BRANTFORD, ON, N3S 7P8
(519) 758-2710   *SIC* 5051

SAMUEL, SON & CO., LIMITED   *p609*
410 NASH RD N, HAMILTON, ON, L8H 7R9
(800) 263-6553   *SIC* 5051

SAMUEL, SON & CO., LIMITED   *p674*
7455 WOODBINE AVE, MARKHAM, ON, L3R 1A7
(905) 475-6464   *SIC* 5051

SAMUEL, SON & CO., LIMITED   *p893*
12 TEAL AVE, STONEY CREEK, ON, L8E 3Y5
(800) 263-1316   *SIC* 5051

SAMUEL, SON & CO., LIMITED   *p1054*
21525 AV CLARK-GRAHAM, BAIE-D'URFE, QC, H9X 3T5
(800) 361-3483   *SIC* 5051

SAMUEL, SON & CO., LIMITED   *p1085*
2225 AV FRANCIS-HUGHES, COTE SAINT-LUC, QC, H7S 1N5
(514) 384-5220   *SIC* 5051

SANDVIK CANADA, INC   *p647*
100 MAGILL ST, LIVELY, ON, P3Y 1K7
(705) 692-5881   *SIC* 5051

SAPUNJIS ENTERPRISES INC   *p18*
7520 114 AVE SE, CALGARY, AB, T2C 4T3
(403) 216-5150   *SIC* 5051

SB NAVITAS TUBULAR INC   *p58*
435 4 AVE SW SUITE 480, CALGARY, AB, T2P 3A8
(403) 984-9548   *SIC* 5051

SCHMOLZ + BICKENBACH CANADA, INC. *p742*
6350 VIPOND DR, MISSISSAUGA, ON, L5T 1G2
(416) 675-5941   *SIC* 5051

SHERWOOD STEEL LTD   *p123*
3303 84 AVE NW, EDMONTON, AB, T6P 1K1
(780) 449-6548   *SIC* 5051

SKYLINE (PHP) CANADA ULC   *p1069*
2220 BOUL LAPINIERE BUREAU 205, BROSSARD, QC, J4W 1M2
(450) 461-6366   *SIC* 5051

SMP SPECIALTY METAL PRODUCTS INC *p707*
326 WATLINE AVE, MISSISSAUGA, ON,

L4Z 1X2
(905) 568-4459   *SIC* 5051

SNAP TIGHT ALUMINUM RAILING SYS-TEM INTERNATIONAL LTD   *p187*
7465 CONWAY AVE, BURNABY, BC, V5E 2P7
(604) 438-6261   *SIC* 5051

SSAB SWEDISH STEEL LTD   *p207*
1031 CLIVEDEN AVE, DELTA, BC, V3M 5V1
(604) 526-3700   *SIC* 5051

STAR ALUMINUM RAILING SYSTEMS INC *p18*
3511 64 AVE SE UNIT 1, CALGARY, AB, T2C 1N3
(403) 640-7878   *SIC* 5051

STEEL CANADA LIMITED   *p707*
355 TRADERS BLVD E, MISSISSAUGA, ON, L4Z 2E5
(905) 890-0209   *SIC* 5051

SUMITOMO CANADA LIMITED   *p60*
350 7 AVE SW SUITE 2400, CALGARY, AB, T2P 3N9
(403) 264-7021   *SIC* 5051

T & C STEEL LTD   *p1424*
4032 TAYLOR ST E, SASKATOON, SK, S7H 5J5
(306) 373-5191   *SIC* 5051

TAYLOR STEEL INC   *p893*
477 ARVIN AVE, STONEY CREEK, ON, L8E 2N1
(905) 662-4925   *SIC* 5051

TEMPCO HEATING & SHEET METAL INC *p588*
180 BELFIELD RD, ETOBICOKE, ON, M9W 1H1
(416) 766-1237   *SIC* 5051

TERRA NOVA STEEL & IRON (ONTARIO) INC   *p712*
3595 HAWKESTONE RD, MISSISSAUGA, ON, L5C 2V1
(905) 273-3872   *SIC* 5051

TERRA NOVA STEEL INC   *p210*
7812 PROGRESS WAY, DELTA, BC, V4G 1A4
(604) 946-5383   *SIC* 5051

TEVELEC LIMITED   *p701*
5350 TIMBERLEA BLVD SUITE 1, MISSIS-SAUGA, ON, L4W 2S6
(905) 624-5241   *SIC* 5051

TIGES QUATRE SAISONS (2009) INC, LES *p1352*
192 6E RANG, SAINT-ROSAIRE, QC, G0Z 1K0
(819) 758-1155   *SIC* 5051

TITAN TUBULAR SOLUTIONS LTD   *p150*
606 22 AVE, NISKU, AB, T9E 7X6
(780) 955-7002   *SIC* 5051

TRI PROVINCE ENTERPRISES (1984) LTD *p406*
158 TOOMBS ST, MONCTON, NB, E1A 3A5
(506) 858-8110   *SIC* 5051

TRIMAR STEEL   *p1005*
3595 AMENT LINE RR 3, WALLENSTEIN, ON, N0B 2S0
(519) 699-5444   *SIC* 5051

TROJAN INDUSTRIES INC   *p19*
4900 54 AVE SE, CALGARY, AB, T2C 2Y8
(403) 269-6525   *SIC* 5051

TUBULAR STEEL INC   *p868*
285 RALEIGH AVE, SCARBOROUGH, ON, M1K 1A5
(416) 261-2089   *SIC* 5051

TUYAUX ET MATERIEL DE FONDATION LTEE   *p1309*
5025 RUE RAMSAY, SAINT-HUBERT, QC, J3Y 2S3
(450) 445-0050   *SIC* 5051

UCC INDUSTRIES INTERNATIONAL INC *p845*
895 SANDY BEACH RD UNIT 12, PICKER-ING, ON, L1W 3N7
(905) 831-7724   *SIC* 5051

ULBRICH OF CANADA INC   *p1028*
150 NEW HUNTINGTON RD UNIT 1,

WOODBRIDGE, ON, L4H 4N4
(416) 663-7130   SIC 5051
UNIFIED ALLOYS (BRITISH COLUMBIA) LTD   p230
26835 GLOUCESTER WAY, LANGLEY, BC, V4W 3Y3
(604) 607-6750   SIC 5051
UNIFIED ALLOYS (EDMONTON) LTD   p117
8835 50 AVE NW, EDMONTON, AB, T6E 5H4
(780) 468-5656   SIC 5051
UNITED WIRE & CABLE (CANADA) INC   p854
1 WEST PEARCE ST UNIT 303, RICHMOND HILL, ON, L4B 3K3
(905) 771-0099   SIC 5051
VAN LEEUWEN PIPE AND TUBE (CANADA) INC   p123
2875 64 AVE NW, EDMONTON, AB, T6P 1R1
(780) 469-7410   SIC 5051
VANGUARD STEEL LTD   p728
2160 MEADOWPINE BLVD, MISSISSAUGA, ON, L5N 6H6
(905) 821-1100   SIC 5051
VARSTEEL LTD   p141
2900 5 AVE N, LETHBRIDGE, AB, T1H 6K3
(403) 329-0233   SIC 5051
VARSTEEL LTD   p143
220 4 ST S SUITE 330, LETHBRIDGE, AB, T1J 4J7
(403) 320-1953   SIC 5051
VARZARI TRADING LTD   p143
220 4 ST S UNIT 330, LETHBRIDGE, AB, T1J 4J7
(403) 320-1953   SIC 5051
VCS VALLEY CUT STEEL CORP   p282
9515 190 ST SUITE 4, SURREY, BC, V4N 3S1
(604) 513-8866   SIC 5051
VENTURE STEEL INC   p589
60 DISCO RD, ETOBICOKE, ON, M9W 1L8
(416) 798-9396   SIC 5051
VERBOM INC   p1392
5066 RTE 222, VALCOURT, QC, J0E 2L0
(450) 532-3672   SIC 5051
VIMETAL INC   p1337
4700 CH DU BOIS-FRANC, SAINT-LAURENT, QC, H4S 1A7
(514) 336-6824   SIC 5051
VITRERIE NORCRISTAL (1982) INC   p1367
360 AV PERREAULT, SEPT-ILES, QC, G4R 1K3
(418) 968-8796   SIC 5051
VOESTALPINE HIGH PERFORMANCE METALS LTD   p728
2595 MEADOWVALE BLVD, MISSISSAUGA, ON, L5N 7Y3
(905) 812-9440   SIC 5051
VOESTALPINE ROTEC SUMMO CORP p525
1200 BURLOAK DR, BURLINGTON, ON, L7L 6B4
(905) 336-0014   SIC 5051
WABTEC CANADA INC   p1324
10000 BOUL CAVENDISH, SAINT-LAURENT, QC, H4M 2V1
(514) 335-4200   SIC 5051
WESTERN CANADA STEEL & TECHNOLOGIES INC   p262
5811 NO. 3 RD UNIT 1807, RICHMOND, BC, V6X 4L7
(604) 247-1442   SIC 5051
WESTVIEW SALES LTD   p208
7251 120 ST, DELTA, BC, V4C 6P5
(604) 591-7747   SIC 5051
WINSTON STEEL INC   p736
7496 TRANMERE DR, MISSISSAUGA, ON, L5S 1K4
(905) 747-7579   SIC 5051

SIC 5052 Coal and other minerals and ores

ASLCHEM INTERNATIONAL INC   p259

4871 SHELL RD SUITE 1260, RICHMOND, BC, V6X 3Z6
(604) 270-8824   SIC 5052
RUSTAN METALS LTD   p295
630 RAYMUR AVE, VANCOUVER, BC, V6A 3L2
SIC 5052
SVAH TRADERS INC   p208
11322 77 AVE, DELTA, BC, V4C 1L9
(604) 897-8272   SIC 5052

SIC 5063 Electrical apparatus and equipment

141793 CANADA INC   p1144
869 BOUL CURE-POIRIER O, LONGUEUIL, QC, J4K 2C3
(450) 674-1521   SIC 5063
152429 CANADA INC   p1319
298 RUE DE MARTIGNY O BUREAU 10, SAINT-JEROME, QC, J7Y 4C9
(450) 438-1263   SIC 5063
3100-7669 QUEBEC INC   p1101
1989 RUE MICHELIN, FABREVILLE, QC, H7L 5B7
(450) 973-7765   SIC 5063
381611 ONTARIO LTD   p490
60 DUNDAS ST E, BELLEVILLE, ON, K8N 1B8
SIC 5063
4499034 CANADA INC   p278
19275 25 AVE, SURREY, BC, V3Z 3X1
(604) 542-4773   SIC 5063
ABB INC   p13
2 SMED LANE SE SUITE 110, CALGARY, AB, T2C 4T5
(403) 806-1700   SIC 5063
ACIER PROFILE S.B.B. INC   p1058
10 RUE EMILIEN-MARCOUX, BLAINVILLE, QC, J7C 0B5
(450) 970-3055   SIC 5063
ADT SECURITY SERVICES CANADA, INC p691
2815 MATHESON BLVD E, MISSISSAUGA, ON, L4W 5J8
(416) 218-1000   SIC 5063
ANIXTER CANADA INC   p729
200 FOSTER CRES, MISSISSAUGA, ON, L5R 3Y5
(905) 568-8999   SIC 5063
ANIXTER CANADA INC   p1127
3000 RUE LOUIS-A.-AMOS, LACHINE, QC, H8T 3P8
(514) 636-3636   SIC 5063
AZTEC ELECTRICAL SUPPLY INC   p549
25 NORTH RIVERMEDE RD UNIT 4-10, CONCORD, ON, L4K 5V4
(905) 761-7762   SIC 5063
B J ELECTRIC SUPPLIES LTD   p112
4143 97 ST NW, EDMONTON, AB, T6E 6E9
(780) 461-2334   SIC 5063
BEAULIEU & LAMOUREUX INC   p1294
283 BOUL SIR-WILFRID-LAURIER, SAINT-BASILE-LE-GRAND, QC, J3N 1M2
(450) 653-1752   SIC 5063
BECTROL INC   p1311
4550 AV BEAUDRY, SAINT-HYACINTHE, QC, J2S 8A5
(450) 774-1330   SIC 5063
BEL VOLT SALES LIMITED   p870
1350 BIRCHMOUNT RD, SCARBOROUGH, ON, M1P 2E4
(416) 757-2277   SIC 5063
BELIMO AIRCONTROLS (CAN.) INC p704
5845 KENNEDY RD, MISSISSAUGA, ON, L4Z 2G3
(905) 712-3118   SIC 5063
BELL MOBILITE INC   p595
1420 BLAIR PL SUITE 700, GLOUCESTER, ON, K1J 9L8
SIC 5063
BIRD-STAIRS LTD   p400
670 WILSEY RD, FREDERICTON, NB, E3B

7K4
(506) 453-9915   SIC 5063
BREWS SUPPLY LTD   p70
12203 40 ST SE, CALGARY, AB, T2Z 4E6
(403) 243-1144   SIC 5063
BRITE-LITE INC   p12
2880 45 AVE SE UNIT 252, CALGARY, AB, T2B 3M1
(403) 720-6877   SIC 5063
BROOK CROMPTON LTD   p582
264 ATTWELL DR, ETOBICOKE, ON, M9W 5B2
(416) 675-3844   SIC 5063
CALALTA SUPPLY LTD   p21
3800 19 ST NE UNIT 8, CALGARY, AB, T2E 6V2
(403) 250-3195   SIC 5063
CANARM LTD   p519
2157 PARKEDALE AVE, BROCKVILLE, ON, K6V 0B4
(613) 342-5424   SIC 5063
CAPITAL POWER (K3) LIMITED PARTNERSHIP   p87
10065 JASPER AVE NW, EDMONTON, AB, T5J 3B1
(780) 392-5305   SIC 5063
CATHELLE INC   p1355
19925 CH SAINTE-MARIE, SAINTE-ANNE-DE-BELLEVUE, QC, H9X 3Y3
(514) 428-8888   SIC 5063
CDN ENERGY AND POWER CORP   p14
10550 42 ST SE SUITE 107, CALGARY, AB, T2C 5C7
(403) 236-0333   SIC 5063
CENTRE DE DISTRIBUTION ELECTRIQUE LIMITEE   p1319
298 RUE DE MARTIGNY O, SAINT-JEROME, QC, J7Y 4C9
(450) 438-1263   SIC 5063
CIE D'ECLAIRAGE UNION LTEE, LA p1227
8150 BOUL DECARIE, MONTREAL, QC, H4P 2S8
(514) 340-5000   SIC 5063
CITY ELECTRIC SUPPLY CORPORATION p531
10 PERDUE CRT UNIT 6, CALEDON, ON, L7C 3M6
(905) 495-0535   SIC 5063
COLLICUTT ENERGY SERVICES CORP p155
8133 EDGAR INDUSTRIAL CLOSE, RED DEER, AB, T4P 3R4
(403) 309-9250   SIC 5063
COMMERCIAL LIGHTING PRODUCTS LTD p205
1535 CLIVEDEN AVE, DELTA, BC, V3M 6P7
(604) 540-4999   SIC 5063
CONGLOM INC   p1333
2600 AV MARIE-CURIE, SAINT-LAURENT, QC, H4S 2C3
(514) 333-6666   SIC 5063
CONVECTAIR-NMT INC   p1364
30 CAR SICARD, SAINTE-THERESE, QC, J7E 3X6
(450) 951-4367   SIC 5063
CORPORATION D'ECLAIRAGE GREEN-LITE, LA   p1249
115 BOUL BRUNSWICK BUREAU 102, POINTE-CLAIRE, QC, H9R 5N2
(514) 695-9090   SIC 5063
CREE CANADA CORP   p687
6889 REXWOOD RD UNIT 3, MISSISSAUGA, ON, L4V 1R2
(905) 671-1991   SIC 5063
CUMMINS EST DU CANADA SEC   p1378
3614 RTE TEWKESBURY, STONEHAM-ET-TEWKESBURY, QC, G3C 2L8
(418) 848-6464   SIC 5063
DAINOLITE LIMITED   p738
1401 COURTNEYPARK DR E UNIT 2, MISSISSAUGA, ON, L5T 2E4
(905) 564-1262   SIC 5063
DANIELS, ETLIN   p794
1850 WILSON AVE, NORTH YORK, ON,

M9M 1A1
(416) 741-7336   SIC 5063
DIAMONDGEAR INDUSTRIAL MANUFACTURING LTD   p1
26229 TWP RD 531A SUITE 206, ACHESON, AB, T7X 5A4
(780) 451-3912   SIC 5063
DUBO ELECTRIQUE LTEE   p1164
5780 RUE ONTARIO E, MONTREAL, QC, H1N 0A2
(514) 255-7711   SIC 5063
DUKE ELECTRIC (1977) LIMITED   p610
986 BARTON ST E, HAMILTON, ON, L8L 3C7
(905) 547-9171   SIC 5063
DVI LIGHTING INC   p552
120 GREAT GULF DR, CONCORD, ON, L4K 5W1
(905) 660-2381   SIC 5063
E.B. HORSMAN & SON LTD   p279
19295 25 AVE, SURREY, BC, V3Z 3X1
(778) 545-9916   SIC 5063
E.C.S. ELECTRICAL CABLE SUPPLY LTD p258
6900 GRAYBAR RD UNIT 3135, RICHMOND, BC, V6W 0A5
(604) 207-1500   SIC 5063
ECLAIRAGE CONTRASTE M.L. INC p1139
1009 RUE DU PARC-INDUSTRIEL, LEVIS, QC, G6Z 1C5
(418) 839-4624   SIC 5063
ECLAIRAGE DIMENSION PLUS INC p1182
6666 RUE SAINT-URBAIN BUREAU 320, MONTREAL, QC, H2S 3H1
(514) 332-9966   SIC 5063
EECOL ELECTRIC CORP   p15
11004 48 ST SE, CALGARY, AB, T2C 3E1
(403) 243-5594   SIC 5063
EECOL ELECTRIC CORP   p69
63 SUNPARK DR SE, CALGARY, AB, T2X 3V4
(403) 253-1952   SIC 5063
EECOL ELECTRIC ULC   p69
63 SUNPARK DR SE, CALGARY, AB, T2X 3V4
SIC 5063
EECOL HOLDINGS LTD   p69
63 SUNPARK DR SE, CALGARY, AB, T2X 3V4
(403) 571-8400   SIC 5063
ELECTRICAL WHOLESALERS (CALGARY) LTD   p22
1323 36 AVE NE, CALGARY, AB, T2E 6T6
(403) 250-7060   SIC 5063
ELECTRIMAT LTEE   p1068
2180 BOUL LAPINIERE, BROSSARD, QC, J4W 1M2
(450) 462-2116   SIC 5063
ELECTROZAD SUPPLY CO. (SARNIA) LIMITED   p860
625 SCOTT RD, SARNIA, ON, N7T 8G3
(519) 336-8550   SIC 5063
ELECTROZAD SUPPLY COMPANY LIMITED   p1018
2900 JEFFERSON BLVD, WINDSOR, ON, N8T 3J2
(519) 944-2900   SIC 5063
EM PLASTIC & ELECTRIC PRODUCTS LIMITED   p502
14 BREWSTER RD, BRAMPTON, ON, L6T 5B7
(905) 913-3000   SIC 5063
EMERSON ELECTRIC CANADA LIMITED p15
110 QUARRY PARK BLVD SE SUITE 200, CALGARY, AB, T2C 3G3
(403) 258-6200   SIC 5063
EMERSON ELECTRIC CANADA LIMITED p852
66 LEEK CRES 2ND FL, RICHMOND HILL, ON, L4B 1H1
(905) 762-1010   SIC 5063
EMSPEC INC   p1060
904 RUE JACQUES PASCHINI, BOIS-DES-

▲ Public Company   ■ Public Company Family Member   **HQ** Headquarters   **BR** Branch   **SL** Single Location

FILION, QC, J6Z 4W4
(450) 430-5522   *SIC* 5063
ENER-RIG SUPPLY INC   p148
2104 7 ST SUITE 2, NISKU, AB, T9E 7Y2
(780) 955-2067   *SIC* 5063
ENERSYS CANADA INC   p494
61 PARR BLVD UNIT 3, BOLTON, ON, L7E 4E3
(905) 951-2228   *SIC* 5063
ENTREPRISES MICROTEC INC, LES p1048
8125 BOUL DU GOLF, ANJOU, QC, H1J 0B2
(514) 388-8177   *SIC* 5063
ENTREPRISES MICROTEC INC, LES p1293
4780 RUE SAINT-FELIX, SAINT-AUGUSTIN-DE-DESMAURES, QC, G3A 2J9
(418) 864-7924   *SIC* 5063
EPCOR POWER DEVELOPMENT CORPORATION   p89
10065 JASPER AVE NW, EDMONTON, AB, T5J 3B1
(780) 412-3191   *SIC* 5063
EPITRON INC   p912
841 PINE ST S, TIMMINS, ON, P4N 8S3
(705) 267-7382   *SIC* 5063
EUROFASE INC   p852
33 WEST BEAVER CREEK RD, RICHMOND HILL, ON, L4B 1L8
(905) 695-2055   *SIC* 5063
EXCELL BATTERY COMPANY   p271
18525 53 AVE SUITE 133, SURREY, BC, V3S 7A4
(604) 575-5011   *SIC* 5063
EXIDE TECHNOLOGIES CANADA CORPORATION   p722
6950 CREDITVIEW RD SUITE 3, MISSISSAUGA, ON, L5N 0A6
(905) 817-1773   *SIC* 5063
FAVA INVESTMENTS INC   p552
25 INTERCHANGE WAY, CONCORD, ON, L4K 5W3
(905) 660-4111   *SIC* 5063
FLUKE ELECTRONICS CANADA INC. p705
400 BRITANNIA RD E UNIT 1, MISSISSAUGA, ON, L4Z 1X9
(800) 363-5853   *SIC* 5063
FRANKLIN EMPIRE INC   p1157
8421 CH DARNLEY, MONT-ROYAL, QC, H4T 2B2
(514) 341-3720   *SIC* 5063
FUTECH HITECH INC   p1339
352 RUE MCARTHUR, SAINT-LAURENT, QC, H4T 1X8
(514) 351-1495   *SIC* 5063
G.A.L. POWER SYSTEMS INC   p540
2558 CARP RD, CARP, ON, K0A 1L0
(613) 831-3188   *SIC* 5063
GERRIE ELECTRIC WHOLESALE LIMITED p522
4104 SOUTH SERVICE RD, BURLINGTON, ON, L7L 4X5
(905) 681-3660   *SIC* 5063
GESTION H. LEVESQUE LTEE   p1068
2180 BOUL LAPINIERE, BROSSARD, QC, J4W 1M2
(450) 462-2116   *SIC* 5063
GLC CONTROLS INC   p11
3300 14 AVE NE SUITE 2, CALGARY, AB, T2A 6J4
SIC 5063
GLOBE ELECTRIC COMPANY INC   p1250
150 AV ONEIDA, POINTE-CLAIRE, QC, H9R 1A8
(888) 543-1388   *SIC* 5063
GRAYBAR CANADA LIMITED   p456
3600 JOSEPH HOWE DR, HALIFAX, NS, B3L 4H7
(902) 457-8787   *SIC* 5063
GRAYBAR ELECTRIC CANADA LIMITED p456
3600 JOSEPH HOWE DR, HALIFAX, NS, B3L 4H7
(902) 443-8311   *SIC* 5063

GROUPE COTE-HUOT INC   p1260
165 BOUL DES CEDRES, QUEBEC, QC, G1L 1M8
(418) 626-1142   *SIC* 5063
GUILLEVIN INTERNATIONAL CIE   p1344
6555 BOUL METROPOLITAIN E BUREAU 301, SAINT-LEONARD, QC, H1P 3H3
(514) 329-2100   *SIC* 5063
HAMPTON POWER SYSTEMS LTD   p8
3415 29 ST NE SUITE 200, CALGARY, AB, T1Y 5W4
SIC 5063
HARWELL ELECTRIC SUPPLY CO. LIMITED   p503
2 WILKINSON RD, BRAMPTON, ON, L6T 4M3
(905) 848-0060   *SIC* 5063
HORIZON NORTH POWER SYTEMS   p51
900-240 4 AVE SW, CALGARY, AB, T2P 4H4
(780) 955-2992   *SIC* 5063
HOUSE OF ELECTRICAL SUPPLIES LIMITED   p671
115 SHIELDS CRT UNIT B, MARKHAM, ON, L3R 9T5
(905) 752-2323   *SIC* 5063
HYDROGENICS CORPORATION   p740
220 ADMIRAL BLVD, MISSISSAUGA, ON, L5T 2N6
(905) 361-3660   *SIC* 5063
IDEAL SUPPLY INC   p647
1045 WALLACE AVE N SUITE PH519, LISTOWEL, ON, N4W 1M6
(519) 291-1060   *SIC* 5063
IEM INDUSTRIAL ELECTRIC MFG. (CANADA) INC   p229
27353 58 CRES UNIT 201, LANGLEY, BC, V4W 3W7
(866) 302-9836   *SIC* 5063
ILLUMINATIONS LIGHTING SOLUTIONS LTD   p334
2885 QUESNEL ST, VICTORIA, BC, V8T 4K2
(250) 382-5483   *SIC* 5063
IMAGE HOME PRODUCTS INC, L'   p1205
1175 PLACE DU FRERE-ANDRE, MONTREAL, QC, H3B 3X9
(514) 383-4720   *SIC* 5063
INCOSPEC COMMUNICATIONS INC p1101
2065 RUE MICHELIN, FABREVILLE, QC, H7L 5B7
(450) 686-0033   *SIC* 5063
INDEPENDENT ELECTRIC SUPPLY INC p874
48 MILNER AVE, SCARBOROUGH, ON, M1S 3P8
(416) 291-0048   *SIC* 5063
INFOSAT COMMUNICATIONS LP   p70
3130 114 AVE SE, CALGARY, AB, T2Z 3V6
(403) 543-8188   *SIC* 5063
INTEGRATED DISTRIBUTION SYSTEMS LIMITED PARTNERSHIP   p1306
243 RUE DES ARTISANS, SAINT-GERMAIN-DE-GRANTHAM, QC, J0C 1K0
(819) 472-4076   *SIC* 5063
KODICOM CANADA   p867
2811 EGLINTON AVE E, SCARBOROUGH, ON, M1J 2E1
(416) 261-2266   *SIC* 5063
KUZCO LIGHTING INC   p279
19054 28 AVE SUITE 19054, SURREY, BC, V3Z 6M3
(604) 538-7162   *SIC* 5063
LIGHTFORM CANADA INC   p97
10545 124 ST NW, EDMONTON, AB, T5N 1R8
(780) 413-9898   *SIC* 5063
LORD'STACE INC   p1206
1155 BOUL RENE-LEVESQUE O UNITE 4000, MONTREAL, QC, H3B 3V2
(418) 575-4942   *SIC* 5063
LUMIPRO INC   p1094
640 AV LEPINE, DORVAL, QC, H9P 1G2
(514) 633-9320   *SIC* 5063

LUMISOLUTION INC   p1264
162 AV DU SACRE-COEUR, QUEBEC, QC, G1N 2W2
(418) 522-5693   *SIC* 5063
M & P DIRECTED ELECTRONICS INCp1089
188 CH SAINT-FRANCOIS-XAVIER, DELSON, QC, J5B 1X9
(450) 635-7777   *SIC* 5063
MAC'S II AGENCIES LTD   p201
1851 BRIGANTINE DR UNIT 100, COQUITLAM, BC, V3K 7B4
(604) 540-6646   *SIC* 5063
MANUFACTURE LEVITON DU CANADA LTEE   p1251
165 BOUL HYMUS, POINTE-CLAIRE, QC, H9R 1E9
(514) 954-1840   *SIC* 5063
MARCHAND ELECTRICAL COMPANY LIMITED   p595
1283 ALGOMA RD, GLOUCESTER, ON, K1B 3W7
(613) 749-2279   *SIC* 5063
MCLOUGHLAN SUPPLIES LIMITED   p433
24 BLACKMARSH RD SUITE 22, ST. JOHN'S, NL, A1E 1S3
(709) 576-4091   *SIC* 5063
MERCOR LIGHTING GROUP INC, THEp555
71 ORTONA CRT UNIT 1, CONCORD, ON, L4K 3M2
(905) 738-6161   *SIC* 5063
MERCURY LIGHTING LIMITED   p555
71 ORTONA CRT UNIT 1, CONCORD, ON, L4K 3M2
(905) 738-6161   *SIC* 5063
METRO NORAMCO INC   p1335
5855 RUE KIERAN, SAINT-LAURENT, QC, H4S 0A3
(514) 595-9595   *SIC* 5063
MGM ELECTRIC LIMITED   p908
724 MACDONELL ST, THUNDER BAY, ON, P7B 4A6
(807) 345-7767   *SIC* 5063
MONITROL R & D INC   p1066
1291 RUE AMPERE, BOUCHERVILLE, QC, J4B 5Z5
(450) 641-4810   *SIC* 5063
NCS INTERNATIONAL CO   p201
70 GLACIER ST, COQUITLAM, BC, V3K 5Y9
(604) 472-6980   *SIC* 5063
NCS INTERNATIONAL CO   p735
7635 TRANMERE DR, MISSISSAUGA, ON, L5S 1L4
(905) 673-0660   *SIC* 5063
NCS INTERNATIONAL CO   p735
7635 TRANMERE DR, MISSISSAUGA, ON, L5S 1L4
(905) 673-0660   *SIC* 5063
NII NORTHERN INTERNATIONAL INC p201
1 BURBIDGE ST SUITE 101, COQUITLAM, BC, V3K 7B2
(604) 464-8606   *SIC* 5063
NORLITE INC   p495
5 SIMPSON RD, BOLTON, ON, L7E 1E4
(905) 857-5955   *SIC* 5063
NORTHERN MARKETING & SALES INC p652
11 BUCHANAN CRT, LONDON, ON, N5Z 4P9
(519) 680-0385   *SIC* 5063
O'NEIL, EARL ELECTRIC SUPPLY LIMITED p1032
150 CREDITVIEW RD, WOODBRIDGE, ON, L4L 9N4
(416) 798-7722   *SIC* 5063
OSCAN ELECTRICAL SUPPLIES LTD p813
209 BLOOR ST E, OSHAWA, ON, L1H 3M3
(905) 728-3800   *SIC* 5063
OSSO HOLDINGS LTD   p814
725 BLOOR ST W, OSHAWA, ON, L1J 5Y6
(905) 576-1700   *SIC* 5063
PAISLEY PRODUCTS OF CANADA INCORPORATED   p869
40 UPTON RD, SCARBOROUGH, ON, M1L

2B9
(416) 751-3700   *SIC* 5063
PAMENSKY, V.J. CANADA INC   p789
64 SAMOR RD, NORTH YORK, ON, M6A 1J6
(416) 781-4617   *SIC* 5063
POWERTRADE ELECTRIC LTD   p871
255 MIDWEST RD, SCARBOROUGH, ON, M1P 3A6
(416) 757-3008   *SIC* 5063
PRISTINE LED INC   p1018
3215 JEFFERSON BLVD SUITE 100, WINDSOR, ON, N8T 2W7
SIC 5063
PRODUITS STANDARD INC   p1341
5905 CH DE LA COTE-DE-LIESSE, SAINT-LAURENT, QC, H4T 1C3
(514) 342-1199   *SIC* 5063
PROTECTION INCENDIE VIKING INCp1062
1935 BOUL LIONEL-BERTRAND, BOISBRIAND, QC, J7H 1N8
(450) 430-7516   *SIC* 5063
PROTECTION INCENDIE VIKING INCp1335
3005 BOUL PITFIELD, SAINT-LAURENT, QC, H4S 1H4
(514) 332-5110   *SIC* 5063
PROVINCE ELECTRIC SUPPLY LTD   p742
425 SUPERIOR BLVD UNIT 6, MISSISSAUGA, ON, L5T 2W5
(905) 795-1795   *SIC* 5063
REGAL BELOIT CANADA   p742
320 SUPERIOR BLVD SUITE 1, MISSISSAUGA, ON, L5T 2N7
(905) 670-4770   *SIC* 5063
REXEL CANADA ELECTRICAL INC   p184
5700 KINGSLAND DR, BURNABY, BC, V5B 4W6
(604) 205-2700   *SIC* 5063
REXEL CANADA ELECTRICAL INC   p385
1650 NOTRE DAME AVE UNIT 1, WINNIPEG, MB, R3H 0Y7
(204) 954-9900   *SIC* 5063
REXEL CANADA ELECTRICAL INC   p732
5600 KEATON CRES, MISSISSAUGA, ON, L5R 3G3
(905) 712-4004   *SIC* 5063
REXEL CANADA ELECTRICAL INC   p733
5600 KEATON CRES, MISSISSAUGA, ON, L5R 3G3
(905) 712-4004   *SIC* 5063
REXEL CANADA ELECTRICAL INC   p742
301 AMBASSADOR DR, MISSISSAUGA, ON, L5T 2J3
(905) 565-2985   *SIC* 5063
REXEL CANADA ELECTRICAL INC   p742
1180 COURTNEYPARK DR E, MISSISSAUGA, ON, L5T 1P2
(905) 670-2800   *SIC* 5063
RICHARDSON HOUSE OF FIXTURES AND SUPPLIES LTD   p1421
2101 7TH AVE, REGINA, SK, S4R 1C3
(306) 525-8301   *SIC* 5063
RICHMOND INTERNATIONAL TECHNOLOGY CORP   p256
4460 JACOMBS RD SUITE 102, RICHMOND, BC, V6V 2C5
(604) 273-8248   *SIC* 5063
RITTAL SYSTEMS LTD   p742
6485 ORDAN DR, MISSISSAUGA, ON, L5T 1X2
(905) 795-0777   *SIC* 5063
ROBERTSON ELECTRIC WHOLESALE 2008 LIMITED   p1028
180 NEW HUNTINGTON RD UNIT 2, WOODBRIDGE, ON, L4H 0P5
(905) 856-9311   *SIC* 5063
ROLAN INC   p568
63 UNION ST, ELMIRA, ON, N3B 2Y3
(519) 669-1842   *SIC* 5063
RUSSELL INDUSTRIES LTD   p183
4062 MCCONNELL DR, BURNABY, BC, V5A 3A8
(604) 420-2440   *SIC* 5063
SCHNEIDER ELECTRIC CANADA INC p94

12825 144 ST NW, EDMONTON, AB, T5L 4N7

(780) 453-3561   *SIC 5063*

SECURITY ONE ALARM SYSTEMS LTD *p645*

200 SHERK ST, LEAMINGTON, ON, N8H 0A8

(519) 326-2020   *SIC 5063*

SIEMENS CANADA LIMITED *p1171*

8455 19E AV, MONTREAL, QC, H1Z 4J2   *SIC 5063*

SIGNALISATION SIGNA PRO INC *p1348*

700 MONTEE MONETTE, SAINT-MATHIEU-DE-LAPRAIRIE, QC, J0L 2H0

(450) 444-0006   *SIC 5063*

SIMPLY BOSS INC *p116*

4529 97 ST NW, EDMONTON, AB, T6E 5Y8   *SIC 5063*

SISTEMALUX INC *p1179*

9320 BOUL SAINT-LAURENT BUREAU 100, MONTREAL, QC, H2N 1N7

(514) 523-1339   *SIC 5063*

SLS GROUP INDUSTRIES INC *p292*

22 2ND AVE W SUITE 2, VANCOUVER, BC, V5Y 1B3

(604) 874-2226   *SIC 5063*

SOLUTIONS MAGNETIQUES TRANSFAB INC *p1142*

2315 RUE DE LA METROPOLE, LONGUEUIL, QC, J4G 1E5

(450) 449-0412   *SIC 5063*

SOMMERS MOTOR-GENERATOR SALES LIMITED *p895*

70 PACKHAM AVE, STRATFORD, ON, N4Z 0A6

(519) 655-2396   *SIC 5063*

SONEPAR CANADA INC *p103*

11330 189 ST NW, EDMONTON, AB, T5S 2V6

(780) 944-9331   *SIC 5063*

SONEPAR CANADA INC *p275*

10449 120 ST, SURREY, BC, V3V 4G4

(604) 528-3700   *SIC 5063*

SONEPAR CANADA INC *p500*

250 CHRYSLER DR UNIT 4, BRAMPTON, ON, L6S 6B6

(905) 696-2838   *SIC 5063*

SONEPAR CANADA INC *p1236*

4655 NORD LAVAL (A-440) O, MONTREAL, QC, H7P 5P9

(450) 688-9249   *SIC 5063*

SONEPAR CANADA INC *p1252*

117 BOUL HYMUS BUREAU 17, POINTE-CLAIRE, QC, H9R 1E5

(514) 426-0629   *SIC 5063*

SONEPAR CANADA INC *p1398*

415 BOUL LABBE N, VICTORIAVILLE, QC, G6P 9J4

(819) 758-6205   *SIC 5063*

SOPER'S SUPPLY LTD *p86*

10519 114 ST NW, EDMONTON, AB, T5H 3J6

(780) 423-4066   *SIC 5063*

STANPRO LIGHTING SYSTEMS INC *p1095*

2233 RUE DE L'AVIATION, DORVAL, QC, H9P 2X6

(514) 739-9984   *SIC 5063*

STOCKDALES ELECTRIC MOTOR CORP *p1416*

1441 FLEURY ST, REGINA, SK, S4N 7N5

(306) 352-4505   *SIC 5063*

SUPER-LITE LIGHTING LTD *p392*

1040 WAVERLEY ST, WINNIPEG, MB, R3T 0P3

(204) 989-7277   *SIC 5063*

SUPREME LIGHTING & ELECTRIC SUPPLY LTD *p665*

9 LAIDLAW BLVD, MARKHAM, ON, L3P 1W5

(905) 477-3113   *SIC 5063*

SUREWAY INTERNATIONAL ELECTRIC INC *p703*

3151 WHARTON WAY, MISSISSAUGA, ON, L4X 2B6

(905) 624-0077   *SIC 5063*

SURPLEC INC *p1376*

149 CH GODIN, SHERBROOKE, QC, J1R 0S6

(819) 821-3636   *SIC 5063*

TARGRAY TECHNOLOGIE INTERNATIONALE INC *p1118*

18105 RTE TRANSCANADIENNE, KIRKLAND, QC, H9J 3Z4

(514) 695-8095   *SIC 5063*

TECO-WESTINGHOUSE MOTORS (CANADA) INC *p103*

18060 109 AVE NW, EDMONTON, AB, T5S 2K2

(780) 444-8933   *SIC 5063*

THERMON CANADA INC *p26*

1806 CENTRE AVE NE, CALGARY, AB, T2E 0A6

(403) 273-5558   *SIC 5063*

TORBRAM ELECTRIC SUPPLY CORPORATION *p227*

6360 202 ST SUITE 103, LANGLEY, BC, V2Y 1N2

(604) 539-9331   *SIC 5063*

TRENTON DISTRIBUTORS LIMITED *p999*

75 HUFF AVE, TRENTON, ON, K8V 0H3

(613) 392-3875   *SIC 5063*

UNIVERSAL CHINA LAMP & GLASS COMPANY LIMITED *p790*

121 CARTWRIGHT AVE, NORTH YORK, ON, M6A 1V4

(416) 787-8900   *SIC 5063*

UNIWELL INTERNATIONAL ENTERPRISES CORP *p294*

999 BROADWAY W SUITE 880, VANCOUVER, BC, V5Z 1K5

(604) 730-2877   *SIC 5063*

VERTIV CANADA ULC *p718*

3800B LAIRD RD UNIT 7, MISSISSAUGA, ON, L5L 0B2

(905) 569-8282   *SIC 5063*

WEG ELECTRIC MOTORS *p988*

64 SAMOR RD, TORONTO, ON, M6A 1J6

(416) 781-4617   *SIC 5063*

WESCO DISTRIBUTION CANADA LP *p103*

18207 111 AVE NW, EDMONTON, AB, T5S 2P2

(780) 452-7920   *SIC 5063*

WESCO DISTRIBUTION CANADA LP *p677*

500 HOOD RD, MARKHAM, ON, L3R 9Z3

(905) 475-7400   *SIC 5063*

WESCO DISTRIBUTION CANADA LP *p733*

6170 BELGRAVE RD, MISSISSAUGA, ON, L5R 4G8

(905) 890-3344   *SIC 5063*

WESTERN EQUIPMENT LIMITED *p542*

97 ST CLAIR ST, CHATHAM, ON, N7L 3J2

(519) 352-0530   *SIC 5063*

WIDE LOYAL DEVELOPMENT LTD *p257*

13160 VANIER PL SUITE 160, RICHMOND, BC, V6V 2J2

(604) 303-0931   *SIC 5063*

WIELAND ELECTRIC INC *p799*

2889 BRIGHTON RD, OAKVILLE, ON, L6H 6C9

(905) 829-8414   *SIC 5063*

WOLF, PAUL LIGHTING & ELECTRIC SUPPLY LIMITED *p994*

425 ALLIANCE AVE, TORONTO, ON, M6N 2J1

(416) 504-8195   *SIC 5063*

ZANEEN GROUP INC *p791*

30 TYCOS DR, NORTH YORK, ON, M6B 1V9

(416) 247-9221   *SIC 5063*

SIC 5064 Electrical appliances, television and radio

AIR-KING LIMITED *p498*

8 EDVAC DR, BRAMPTON, ON, L6S 5P2

(905) 456-2033   *SIC 5064*

AMRE SUPPLY COMPANY LIMITED *p125*

1259 91 ST SW STE 201, EDMONTON, AB,

T6X 1E9

(780) 461-2929   *SIC 5064*

BRADFORD WHITE - CANADA INC *p593*

9 BRIGDEN GATE, GEORGETOWN, ON, L7G 0A3

(905) 203-0600   *SIC 5064*

BREVILLE CANADA S.E.C. *p1324*

9800 CAVENDISH BLVD STE 250, SAINT-LAURENT, QC, H4M 2V9

(514) 683-3535   *SIC 5064*

CENTRE DE PIECES ET SERVICES EXPERT INC *p1169*

8260 BOUL PIE-IX, MONTREAL, QC, H1Z 3T6

(514) 943-5755   *SIC 5064*

CLARION CANADA INC *p796*

2239 WINSTON PARK DR, OAKVILLE, ON, L6H 5R1

(905) 829-4600   *SIC 5064*

CONAIR CONSUMER PRODUCTS ULC *p1027*

100 CONAIR PKY, WOODBRIDGE, ON, L4H 0L2

(905) 851-5162   *SIC 5064*

DANBY PRODUCTS LIMITED *p602*

5070 WHITELAW RD, GUELPH, ON, N1H 6Z9

(519) 837-0920   *SIC 5064*

DE'LONGHI CANADA INC *p731*

6150 MCLAUGHLIN RD SUITE 2, MISSISSAUGA, ON, L5R 4E1

(905) 362-2340   *SIC 5064*

DISTINCTIVE APPLIANCES INC *p1237*

2025 RUE CUNARD, MONTREAL, QC, H7S 2N1

(450) 687-6311   *SIC 5064*

DISTRIBUTIONS MAROLINE INC *p1216*

751 RUE RICHARDSON BUREAU 4600, MONTREAL, QC, H3K 1G6

(514) 343-0448   *SIC 5064*

ECHELON HOME PRODUCTS LTD *p263*

11120 HORSESHOE WAY UNIT 120, RICHMOND, BC, V7A 5H7

(604) 275-2210   *SIC 5064*

ELECTROLUX CANADA CORP *p744*

5855 TERRY FOX WAY, MISSISSAUGA, ON, L5V 3E4

(905) 813-7700   *SIC 5064*

ELITE GROUP INC *p1203*

1175 PLACE DU FRERE-ANDRE, MONTREAL, QC, H3B 3X9

(514) 383-4720   *SIC 5064*

GROUPE SEB CANADA INC *p876*

36 NEWMILL GATE, SCARBOROUGH, ON, M1V 0E2

(416) 297-4131   *SIC 5064*

H.J. SUTTON INDUSTRIES LIMITED *p553*

8701 JANE ST UNIT C, CONCORD, ON, L4K 2M6

(905) 660-4311   *SIC 5064*

HAMILTON BEACH BRANDS CANADA, INC *p670*

7300 WARDEN AVE SUITE 201, MARKHAM, ON, L3R 9Z6

(905) 513-6222   *SIC 5064*

KEYESBURY DISTRIBUTORS LIMITED *p540*

99 BRUCE CRES, CARLETON PLACE, ON, K7C 3T3

(613) 257-8100   *SIC 5064*

LG ELECTRONICS CANADA, INC *p793*

20 NORELCO DR SUITE, NORTH YORK, ON, M9L 2X6

(647) 253-6300   *SIC 5064*

MC COMMERCIAL INC *p523*

5420 NORTH SERVICE RD SUITE 300, BURLINGTON, ON, L7L 6C7

(905) 315-2300   *SIC 5064*

MEGA GROUP INC *p1428*

720 1ST AVE N, SASKATOON, MB, S7K 6R9

(306) 242-7366   *SIC 5064*

MIDBEC LTEE *p1099*

1725 BOUL LEMIRE, DRUMMONDVILLE,

QC, J2C 5A5

(819) 477-1070   *SIC 5064*

MIELE LIMITED *p556*

161 FOUR VALLEY DR, CONCORD, ON, L4K 4V8

(905) 532-2270   *SIC 5064*

PACIFIC SPECIALTY BRANDS CO. ULC *p193*

7595 LOWLAND DR, BURNABY, BC, V5J 5L1

(604) 430-5253   *SIC 5064*

PANASONIC CANADA INC *p698*

5770 AMBLER DR SUITE 70, MISSISSAUGA, ON, L4W 2T3

(905) 624-5010   *SIC 5064*

PHILIPS ELECTRONICS LTD *p679*

281 HILLMOUNT RD, MARKHAM, ON, L6C 2S3

(905) 201-4100   *SIC 5064*

PIONEER ELECTRONICS OF CANADA, INC *p495*

2 MARCONI CRT UNIT 15, BOLTON, ON, L7E 1E5

(905) 479-4411   *SIC 5064*

PROVENT HCE INC *p1345*

6150 BOUL DES GRANDES-PRAIRIES, SAINT-LEONARD, QC, H1P 1A2

(514) 643-0642   *SIC 5064*

SAMSUNG ELECTRONICS CANADA INC *p726*

2050 DERRY RD W SUITE 1, MISSISSAUGA, ON, L5N 0B9

(905) 542-3535   *SIC 5064*

SANYO CANADA INC *p1033*

201 CREDITVIEW RD, WOODBRIDGE, ON, L4L 9T1

(905) 760-9944   *SIC 5064*

SHARP ELECTRONICS OF CANADA LTD *p707*

335 BRITANNIA RD E, MISSISSAUGA, ON, L4Z 1W9

(905) 890-2100   *SIC 5064*

SONY OF CANADA LTD *p768*

2235 SHEPPARD AVE E SUITE 700, NORTH YORK, ON, M2J 5B5

(416) 499-1414   *SIC 5064*

SUNBEAM CORPORATION (CANADA) LIMITED *p512*

20 HEREFORD ST SUITE B, BRAMPTON, ON, L6Y 0M1

(905) 593-6255   *SIC 5064*

T N T GROUP INC *p790*

65 DUFFLAW RD, NORTH YORK, ON, M6A 2W2

(416) 781-9156   *SIC 5064*

TOSHIBA OF CANADA LIMITED *p676*

75 TIVERTON CRT, MARKHAM, ON, L3R 4M8

(905) 470-3500   *SIC 5064*

UVALUX INTERNATIONAL INC *p1036*

470 INDUSTRIAL AVE, WOODSTOCK, ON, N4S 7L1

(519) 421-1212   *SIC 5064*

SIC 5065 Electronic parts and equipment, nec

0962358 B.C. LTD *p178*

29898 MACLURE RD, ABBOTSFORD, BC, V4X 1G5

(604) 825-5060   *SIC 5065*

1542053 ONTARIO LIMITED *p520*

1175 CORPORATE DR UNIT 8, BURLINGTON, ON, L7L 5V5

(905) 332-7755   *SIC 5065*

1588545 ALBERTA LTD *p8*

3825 34 ST NE SUITE 113B, CALGARY, AB, T1Y 6Z8

(403) 272-3032   *SIC 5065*

1642852 ONTARIO LIMITED *p547*

30 MACINTOSH BLVD UNIT 7, CONCORD, ON, L4K 4P1

(416) 252-5907   *SIC 5065*

569398 ALBERTA LTD *p98*

17311 103 AVE NW UNIT 100, EDMONTON, AB, T5S 1J4

(780) 454-5864   *SIC* 5065

828324 ONTARIO LIMITED   *p757*
6913 OAKWOOD DR, NIAGARA FALLS, ON, L2E 6S5

(905) 646-3333   *SIC* 5065

9117-4227 QUEBEC INC   *p1169*
8018 20E AV, MONTREAL, QC, H1Z 3S7

(514) 376-1740   *SIC* 5065

9156-0763,QUEBEC INC   *p1248*
6500 RTE TRANSCANADIENNE UNITE 400, POINTE-CLAIRE, QC, H9R 0A5

(514) 695-9192   *SIC* 5065

ABB INC   *p500*
201 WESTCREEK BLVD, BRAMPTON, ON, L6T 0G8

(905) 460-3000   *SIC* 5065

ACA TMETRIX INC   *p716*
3585 LAIRD RD UNIT 15-16, MISSISSAUGA, ON, L5L 5Y4

(905) 890-2010   *SIC* 5065

ACER AMERICA CORPORATION CANADA   *p704*
5540 MCADAM RD, MISSISSAUGA, ON, L4Z 1P1

(905) 755-7570   *SIC* 5065

ACHAT SURPLUS MONTREAL INC   *p1332*
2800 RUE DE MINIAC, SAINT-LAURENT, QC, H4S 1K9

(438) 995-2650   *SIC* 5065

ADVANCED MOTION & CONTROLS LTD   *p485*
26 SAUNDERS RD, BARRIE, ON, L4N 9A8

(705) 726-2260   *SIC* 5065

ALBERTA COMPUTER CABLE INC   *p20*
1816 25 AVE NE, CALGARY, AB, T2E 7K1

(403) 291-5560   *SIC* 5065

ALLEN-VANGUARD CORPORATION   *p817*
2405 ST. LAURENT BLVD, OTTAWA, ON, K1G 5B4

(613) 739-9646   *SIC* 5065

ALLIANCE CORPORATION   *p719*
2395 MEADOWPINE BLVD, MISSISSAUGA, ON, L5N 7W6

(905) 821-4797   *SIC* 5065

AMPHENOL CANADA CORP   *p864*
605 MILNER AVE, SCARBOROUGH, ON, M1B 5X6

(416) 291-4401   *SIC* 5065

ANODYNE ELECTRONICS HOLDING CORP   *p221*
1925 KIRSCHNER RD UNIT 15, KELOWNA, BC, V1Y 4N7

(250) 763-1088   *SIC* 5065

ANODYNE ELECTRONICS MANUFACTURING CORP   *p221*
1925 KIRSCHNER RD UNIT 15, KELOWNA, BC, V1Y 4N7

(250) 763-1088   *SIC* 5065

ARGUS TELECOM INTERNATIONAL INC   *p1328*
2505 RUE GUENETTE, SAINT-LAURENT, QC, H4R 2E9

(514) 331-0840   *SIC* 5065

ARROW ELECTRONICS CANADA LTD *p737*
171 SUPERIOR BLVD SUITE 2, MISSISSAUGA, ON, L5T 2L6

(905) 565-4405   *SIC* 5065

ATLANTIC MOBILITY PRODUCTS LIMITED PARTNERSHIP   *p440*
200 BLUEWATER RD UNIT 1, BEDFORD, NS, B4B 1G9

(902) 481-6699   *SIC* 5065

AUSTCO MARKETING & SERVICE (CANADA) LIMITED   *p577*
940 THE EAST MALL SUITE 101, ETOBICOKE, ON, M9B 6J7

(888) 670-9997   *SIC* 5065

AUTO MOTION LIMITED   *p468*
568 PRINCE ST, TRURO, NS, B2N 1G3

(902) 893-2288   *SIC* 5065

AVNET INTERNATIONAL (CANADA) LTD
p719

6950 CREDITVIEW RD UNIT 2, MISSISSAUGA, ON, L5N 0A6

(905) 812-4400   *SIC* 5065

B K A OFFICE INC   *p782*
675 PETROLIA RD, NORTH YORK, ON, M3J 2N6

(416) 665-2466   *SIC* 5065

BEST BUY CANADA LTD   *p498*
9200 AIRPORT RD, BRAMPTON, ON, L6S 6G6

(905) 494-7000   *SIC* 5065

BOSE LIMITED   *p678*
280 HILLMOUNT RD SUITE 5, MARKHAM, ON, L6C 3A1

(905) 887-5950   *SIC* 5065

BRUNET-GOULARD AGENCIES INC   *p596*
5370 CANOTEK RD UNIT 21, GLOUCESTER, ON, K1J 9E8

(613) 748-7377   *SIC* 5065

BTI BLUETOOTH TECHNOLOGIES INC
p800
169 ROBINSON ST, OAKVILLE, ON, L6J 5W7

SIC 5065

C.E.V. INC   *p1167*
3055 RUE ADAM, MONTREAL, QC, H1W 3Y7

(514) 521-8253   *SIC* 5065

CAMACC SYSTEMS INC   *p267*
2261 KEATING CROSS RD UNIT 200B, SAANICHTON, BC, V8M 2A5

(250) 652-3406   *SIC* 5065

CARTE INTERNATIONAL INC   *p1074*
2032 AV BOURGOGNE BUREAU 107, CHAMBLY, QC, J3L 1Z6

(450) 447-5815   *SIC* 5065

CENTURY CELLULAR (RICHMOND HILL) CORPORATION   *p855*
10520 YONGE ST SUITE 26, RICHMOND HILL, ON, L4C 3C7

(905) 884-0000   *SIC* 5065

CESIUM TELECOM INCORPORATED *p1156*
5798 RUE FERRIER, MONT-ROYAL, QC, H4P 1M7

(514) 798-8686   *SIC* 5065

CIMTEL (QUEBEC) INC   *p1240*
71 AV WESTMINSTER N, MONTREAL-OUEST, QC, H4X 1Y8

(514) 481-4344   *SIC* 5065

CISCO SYSTEMS CANADA CO   *p961*
88 QUEENS QUAY W SUITE 2700, TORONTO, ON, M5J 0B8

(416) 306-7000   *SIC* 5065

CISCO SYSTEMS CO.   *p873*
100 MIDDLEFIELD RD UNIT 1, SCARBOROUGH, ON, M1S 4M6

(416) 299-6888   *SIC* 5065

COBRA INTEGRATED SYSTEMS LTD *p185*
4427 DAWSON ST, BURNABY, BC, V5C 4B8

(604) 664-7671   *SIC* 5065

COMMUNICATIONS INTERVOX INC, LES
p1375
6420 CH DE SAINT-ELIE, SHERBROOKE, QC, J1R 0P6

(819) 563-3222   *SIC* 5065

COMMUNICATIONS LMT INC   *p1194*
1500 AV MCGILL COLLEGE, MONTREAL, QC, H3A 3J5

(514) 285-9263   *SIC* 5065

COMMUNICATIONS TRISPEC INC, LES
p1344
8500 RUE PASCAL-GAGNON, SAINT-LEONARD, QC, H1P 1Y4

(514) 328-2025   *SIC* 5065

COPISCOPE INC   *p1325*
460 BOUL MONTPELLIER BUREAU 267, SAINT-LAURENT, QC, H4N 2G7

(514) 744-3610   *SIC* 5065

COSMO COMMUNICATIONS CANADA INC
p678
55 TRAVAIL RD UNIT 2, MARKHAM, ON, L3S 3J1

(905) 209-0488   *SIC* 5065

CRAWFORD, ALLAN ASSOCIATES LIMITED   *p705*
5805 KENNEDY RD, MISSISSAUGA, ON, L4Z 2G3

(905) 890-2010   *SIC* 5065

CSG SECURITY CORPORATION   *p693*
2740 MATHESON BLVD E UNIT 1, MISSISSAUGA, ON, L4W 4X3

(905) 629-2600   *SIC* 5065

CURTIS INTERNATIONAL LTD   *p734*
7045 BECKETT DR UNIT 15, MISSISSAUGA, ON, L5S 2A3

(416) 674-2123   *SIC* 5065

D & H CANADA ULC   *p511*
7975 HERITAGE RD SUITE 20, BRAMPTON, ON, L6Y 5X5

(905) 796-0030   *SIC* 5065

DALTCO ELECTRIC & SUPPLY (1979) LTD
p630
26 LAPPANS LANE, KINGSTON, ON, K7K 6Z4

(613) 546-3677   *SIC* 5065

DIGITAL CONCEPT INC   *p942*
1 YONGE ST SUITE 1801, TORONTO, ON, M5E 1W7

SIC 5065

DISPLAY-VU CORP   *p735*
7045 BECKETT DR UNIT 15, MISSISSAUGA, ON, L5S 2A3

(416) 674-2123   *SIC* 5065

DOMINION PROTECTION SERVICES LTD
p22
1935 32 AVE NE SUITE 124, CALGARY, AB, T2E 3R1

(403) 717-1732   *SIC* 5065

DSL LOGIC   *p1260*
75 RUE DES EPINETTES, QUEBEC, QC, G1L 1N6

SIC 5065

DYNEX POWER INC   *p624*
515 LEGGET DR SUITE 800, KANATA, ON, K2K 3G4

(613) 822-2500   *SIC* 5065

EASTERN INDEPENDENT TELECOMMUNICATIONS LTD   *p519*
100 STROWGER BLVD SUITE 112, BROCKVILLE, ON, K6V 5J9

(613) 342-9652   *SIC* 5065

EATON INDUSTRIES (CANADA) COMPANY
p522
5050 MAINWAY, BURLINGTON, ON, L7L 5Z1

(905) 333-6442   *SIC* 5065

ELECTRO SONIC GROUP INC   *p669*
60 RENFREW DR SUITE 110, MARKHAM, ON, L3R 0E1

(905) 470-3015   *SIC* 5065

ELECTRO-5 INC   *p1373*
4135 BOUL INDUSTRIEL, SHERBROOKE, QC, J1L 2S7

(819) 823-5355   *SIC* 5065

ELECTROMIKE INC   *p1264*
1375 RUE FRANK-CARREL BUREAU 2, QUEBEC, QC, G1N 2E7

(418) 681-4138   *SIC* 5065

ELECTRONIQUE ABRA CORPORATION
p1327
5465 CH DE LA COTE-DE-LIESSE, SAINT-LAURENT, QC, H4P 1A1

(514) 731-0117   *SIC* 5065

EMX ENTERPRISES LIMITED   *p852*
250 GRANTON DR, RICHMOND HILL, ON, L4B 1H7

(905) 764-0040   *SIC* 5065

ERICSSON CANADA INC   *p1156*
8400 BOUL DECARIE, MONT-ROYAL, QC, H4P 2N2

(514) 345-7900   *SIC* 5065

ERICSSON CANADA INC   *p1333*
8275 RTE TRANSCANADIENNE, SAINT-LAURENT, QC, H4S 0B6

(514) 738-8300   *SIC* 5065

ETHOCA TECHNOLOGIES INC   *p771*
100 SHEPPARD AVE E SUITE 605, NORTH

YORK, ON, M2N 6N5

(416) 849-6091   *SIC* 5065

EVOLUTION MOBILE   *p1258*
305 BOUL CHAREST E, QUEBEC, QC, G1K 3H3

(418) 524-3436   *SIC* 5065

EXPERT MOBILE COMMUNICATIONS LTD
p131
8701 112 ST, GRANDE PRAIRIE, AB, T8V 6A4

(780) 539-3962   *SIC* 5065

FUSION CINE SALES & RENTALS INC *p285*
1469 VENABLES ST, VANCOUVER, BC, V5L 2G1

(604) 879-0003   *SIC* 5065

FUTURE ELECTRONICS (CDA) LTD *p1250*
237 BOUL HYMUS, POINTE-CLAIRE, QC, H9R 5C7

(514) 694-7710   *SIC* 5065

FUTURE ELECTRONIQUE INC   *p1250*
237 BOUL HYMUS, POINTE-CLAIRE, QC, H9R 5C7

(514) 694-7710   *SIC* 5065

GAP WIRELESS INC   *p722*
2880 ARGENTIA RD UNIT 8-9, MISSISSAUGA, ON, L5N 7X8

(905) 826-3781   *SIC* 5065

GIDDEN MORTON ASSOCIATES INC *p735*
7050A BRAMALEA RD UNIT 27A, MISSISSAUGA, ON, L5S 1T1

(905) 671-8111   *SIC* 5065

GRAND ALARMS LTD   *p553*
9000 KEELE ST UNIT 12, CONCORD, ON, L4K 0B3

(416) 657-2100   *SIC* 5065

GREENVISION TECHNOLOGIES CORPORATION   *p1334*
7809 RTE TRANSCANADIENNE, SAINT-LAURENT, QC, H4S 1L3

(514) 745-0310   *SIC* 5065

GROUPE VARITRON INC   *p1308*
4811 CH DE LA SAVANE, SAINT-HUBERT, QC, J3Y 9G1

(450) 926-1778   *SIC* 5065

GTA ADANAC CUSTOM SYSTEMS INC *p553*
467 EDGELEY BLVD SUITE 4, CONCORD, ON, L4K 4E9

SIC 5065

GUARD RFID SOLUTIONS INC   *p206*
766 CLIVEDEN PL UNIT 140, DELTA, BC, V3M 6C7

(604) 998-4018   *SIC* 5065

GUNNEBO CANADA INC   *p503*
9 VAN DER GRAAF CRT, BRAMPTON, ON, L6T 5E5

(905) 595-4140   *SIC* 5065

HALO METRICS INC   *p258*
21320 GORDON WAY UNIT 230, RICHMOND, BC, V6W 1J8

(604) 273-4456   *SIC* 5065

HEINEMANN ELECTRIC CANADA LIMITEE
p1326
343 RUE DESLAURIERS, SAINT-LAURENT, QC, H4N 1W2

(514) 332-1163   *SIC* 5065

HITFAR CONCEPTS LTD   *p182*
2999 UNDERHILL AVE SUITE 109, BURNABY, BC, V5A 3C2

(604) 873-8364   *SIC* 5065

HUB PARKING TECHNOLOGY CANADA LTD   *p723*
2900 ARGENTIA RD SUITE 1, MISSISSAUGA, ON, L5N 7X9

(905) 813-1966   *SIC* 5065

I B S INTEGRATED BUSINESS SERVICES
p321
1632 6TH AVE W, VANCOUVER, BC, V6J 1R3

(604) 714-1100   *SIC* 5065

I.D.C. WHOLESALE INC   *p365*
1385 NIAKWA RD E, WINNIPEG, MB, R2J 3T3

(204) 254-8282   *SIC* 5065

INMARSAT SOLUTIONS (CANADA) INC

p426
34 GLENCOE DR, MOUNT PEARL, NL, A1N 4S8
SIC 5065

INSTANT BRANDS INC *p624*
495 MARCH RD SUITE 200, KANATA, ON, K2K 3G1
(800) 828-7280 *SIC 5065*

INTERNATIONAL ELECTRONIC COMPONENTS INC *p793*
352 SIGNET DR, NORTH YORK, ON, M9L 1V2
(416) 293-2961 *SIC 5065*

INTROTEL COMMUNICATIONS INC *p696*
5170 TIMBERLEA BLVD UNIT B, MISSISSAUGA, ON, L4W 2S5
(905) 625-8700 *SIC 5065*

J-SQUARED TECHNOLOGIES INC *p624*
4015 CARLING AVE SUITE 101, KANATA, ON, K2K 2A3
(613) 592-9540 *SIC 5065*

KOPEL INC *p1308*
3360 2E RUE, SAINT-HUBERT, QC, J3Y 8Y7
(514) 398-9595 *SIC 5065*

LENBROOK CORP *p845*
633 GRANITE CRT, PICKERING, ON, L1W 3K1
(905) 831-6333 *SIC 5065*

LIGHTNING CIRCUITS INC *p883*
12 SEAPARK DR, ST CATHARINES, ON, L2M 6S6
(905) 984-4006 *SIC 5065*

LOCKHEED MARTIN CANADA INC *p447*
1000 WINDMILL RD, DARTMOUTH, NS, B3B 1L7
(902) 468-3399 *SIC 5065*

LOGIC-CONTROLE INC *p1264*
2300 RUE LEON-HARMEL BUREAU 101, QUEBEC, QC, G1N 4L2
(418) 686-2300 *SIC 5065*

M.G. CHEMICALS LTD *p282*
9347 193 ST, SURREY, BC, V4N 4E7
(604) 888-3084 *SIC 5065*

MAGOR COMMUNICATIONS CORP *p749*
400-1 ANTARES DR, NEPEAN, ON, K2E 8C4
(613) 686-1731 *SIC 5065*

MARANTZ CANADA INC *p672*
505 APPLE CREEK BLVD UNIT 5, MARKHAM, ON, L3R 5B1
(905) 415-9292 *SIC 5065*

MATRIX ELECTRONICS LIMITED *p740*
1124 MID-WAY BLVD, MISSISSAUGA, ON, L5T 2C1
(905) 670-8400 *SIC 5065*

MATRIX TECHNOLOGY LTD *p679*
280 HILLMOUNT RD UNIT 6, MARKHAM, ON, L6C 3A1
(905) 477-4442 *SIC 5065*

MATRIX VIDEO COMMUNICATIONS CORP *p76*
1626 115 AVE NE UNIT 103, CALGARY, AB, T3K 2E4
(403) 640-4490 *SIC 5065*

MAZIN INVESTMENTS LTD *p624*
4015 CARLING AVE SUITE 102, KANATA, ON, K2K 2A3
(613) 831-9943 *SIC 5065*

MEGASTAR ELECTRONICS INC. *p1239*
5061 RUE D'AMIENS, MONTREAL-NORD, QC, H1G 3G2
(514) 329-0042 *SIC 5065*

MICROCEL CORPORATION *p756*
1274 RINGWELL DR UNIT 2, NEWMARKET, ON, L3Y 9C7
(905) 853-2568 *SIC 5065*

MITEC TECHNOLOGIES INC *p715*
2333 NORTH SHERIDAN WAY SUITE 200, MISSISSAUGA, ON, L5K 1A7
(905) 822-8170 *SIC 5065*

MOTOROLA SOLUTIONS CANADA INC *p680*
8133 WARDEN AVE, MARKHAM, ON, L6G 1B3
(905) 948-5200 *SIC 5065*

MRO ELECTRONIC SUPPLY LTD *p24*
2240 PEGASUS RD NE, CALGARY, AB, T2E 8G8
(403) 291-0501 *SIC 5065*

NEC CANADA, INC. *p36*
7260 12 ST SE UNIT 110, CALGARY, AB, T2H 2S5
(403) 640-6400 *SIC 5065*

NEXT SUCCESS INC *p1335*
8086 RTE TRANSCANADIENNE, SAINT-LAURENT, QC, H4S 1M5
(514) 343-5544 *SIC 5065*

NOOELEC INC *p756*
250 HARRY WALKER PKY N UNIT 3, NEWMARKET, ON, L3Y 7B4
(888) 653-3532 *SIC 5065*

NORSTAN CANADA LTD *p768*
2225 SHEPPARD AVE E SUITE 1600, NORTH YORK, ON, M2J 5C2
(416) 490-9500 *SIC 5065*

NORTHERN VOICE & DATA INC *p901*
174 DOUGLAS ST, SUDBURY, ON, P3E 1G1
(705) 674-2729 *SIC 5065*

OMRON CANADA INC *p867*
100 CONSILIUM PL SUITE 802, SCARBOROUGH, ON, M1H 3E3
(416) 986-6766 *SIC 5065*

OMRON ELECTRONIC COMPONENTS CANADA, INC *p867*
100 CONSILIUM PL SUITE 802, SCARBOROUGH, ON, M1H 3E3
(416) 286-6465 *SIC 5065*

OPTIMONT INC *p1071*
9995 RUE DE CHATEAUNEUF, BROSSARD, QC, J4Z 3V7
(450) 465-1818 *SIC 5065*

PAGING NETWORK OF CANADA INC *p698*
1685 TECH AVE SUITE 1, MISSISSAUGA, ON, L4W 0A7
(905) 614-3100 *SIC 5065*

PALADIN SECURITY SYSTEMS LTD *p186*
4664 LOUGHEED HWY SUITE 295, BURNABY, BC, V5C 5T5
(416) 591-1745 *SIC 5065*

PANASONIC CANADA INC *p698*
5810 AMBLER DR UNIT 4, MISSISSAUGA, ON, L4W 4J5
SIC 5065

PEERLESS SECURITY INC *p621*
21 HIGH ST, HUNTSVILLE, ON, P1H 1N9
(705) 789-6253 *SIC 5065*

PHASON INC *p366*
2 TERRACON PL, WINNIPEG, MB, R2J 4G7
(204) 233-1400 *SIC 5065*

PHOENIX CONTACT LTD *p684*
8240 PARKHILL DR, MILTON, ON, L9T 5V7
(905) 864-8700 *SIC 5065*

PINDER'S LOCK & SECURITY INC *p884*
25 NIHAN DR, ST CATHARINES, ON, L2N 1L2
(905) 934-6333 *SIC 5065*

PIONEER STANDARD CANADA INC *p689*
3415 AMERICAN DR, MISSISSAUGA, ON, L4V 1T4
SIC 5065

POLYCOM CANADA LTD *p189*
3605 GILMORE WAY SUITE 200, BURNABY, BC, V5G 4X5
(604) 453-9400 *SIC 5065*

POSSCAN SYSTEMS INC *p338*
4243 GLANFORD AVE SUITE 100, VICTORIA, BC, V8Z 4B9
(250) 380-5020 *SIC 5065*

POWER & TELEPHONE SUPPLY OF CANADA LTD *p531*
1141 KING RD UNIT 1, BURLINGTON, ON, L7T 0B4
(289) 288-3260 *SIC 5065*

PRIORITY ELECTRONICS LTD *p391*
55 TROTTIER BAY, WINNIPEG, MB, R3T 3R3
(204) 284-0164 *SIC 5065*

QUESTZONE.NET INC *p1364*
8 RUE ROUX BUREAU 200, SAINTE-THERESE, QC, J7E 1L3
(450) 979-3339 *SIC 5065*

RADIOCO LTD *p1025*
1983 AMBASSADOR DR, WINDSOR, ON, N9C 3R5
(519) 250-9100 *SIC 5065*

REPERAGE BOOMERANG INC *p1226*
9280 BOUL DE L'ACADIE, MONTREAL, QC, H4N 3C5
(514) 234-8722 *SIC 5065*

RF-MTL ELECTRONIQUE INC *p1336*
1415 RUE SAINT-AMOUR, SAINT-LAURENT, QC, H4S 1T4
(514) 332-9998 *SIC 5065*

ROTALEC INTERNATIONAL INC *p1341*
900 RUE MCCAFFREY, SAINT-LAURENT, QC, H4T 2C7
(514) 341-3685 *SIC 5065*

ROVA PRODUCTS CANADA INC *p500*
30 AUTOMATIC RD, BRAMPTON, ON, L6S 5N8
(905) 793-1955 *SIC 5065*

RUSH ELECTRONICS LTD *p686*
2738 SLOUGH ST, MISSISSAUGA, ON, L4T 1G3
SIC 5065

RUSSELL SECURITY SERVICES INC *p488*
80 BRADFORD ST SUITE 826, BARRIE, ON, L4N 6S7
(705) 721-1480 *SIC 5065*

RYCOM INC *p1028*
6201 7 HWY UNIT 8, WOODBRIDGE, ON, L4H 0K7
(905) 264-4800 *SIC 5065*

S.F. MARKETING INC *p1096*
325 BOUL BOUCHARD, DORVAL, QC, H9S 1A9
(514) 780-2070 *SIC 5065*

SAFETY NET SECURITY LTD *p909*
857 MAY ST N, THUNDER BAY, ON, P7C 3S2
(807) 623-1844 *SIC 5065*

SALMON CAPITAL CORPORATION *p651*
100 KELLOGG LANE, LONDON, ON, N5W 0B4
(519) 266-3400 *SIC 5065*

SANDTRON AUTOMATION LIMITED *p526*
1221 DILLON RD, BURLINGTON, ON, L7M 1K6
(905) 827-8230 *SIC 5065*

SAYAL PURCHASING SERVICES INC *p877*
3791 VICTORIA PARK AVE UNIT 1, SCARBOROUGH, ON, M1W 3K6
(416) 494-8999 *SIC 5065*

SECURITE KOLOSSAL INC *p1212*
1390 RUE BARRE, MONTREAL, QC, H3C 1N4
(514) 253-4021 *SIC 5065*

SELTECH ELECTRONICS INC *p684*
342 BRONTE ST S UNIT 5-6, MILTON, ON, L9T 5B7
(905) 875-2985 *SIC 5065*

SENNHEISER (CANADA) INC *p1091*
275 RUE KESMARK, DOLLARD-DES-ORMEAUX, QC, H9B 3J1
(514) 426-3013 *SIC 5065*

SENSUS COMMUNICATION SOLUTIONS INC *p193*
5589 BYRNE RD SUITE 124, BURNABY, BC, V5J 3J1
(604) 263-9399 *SIC 5065*

SERVICES ET SOLUTIONS PROFESSIONNELS EN TELECOMMUNICATIONS S.S.P. INC *p1386*
2535 RUE DE LA SIDBEC S, TROIS-RIVIERES, QC, G8Z 4M6

(819) 693-2535 *SIC 5065*
SIMCONA ELECTRONICS OF CANADA INC *p660*
3422 WONDERLAND RD S, LONDON, ON, N6L 1A7
(519) 652-1130 *SIC 5065*

SKYWAVE MOBILE COMMUNICATIONS INC *p627*
750 PALLADIUM DR SUITE 368, KANATA, ON, K2V 1C7
(613) 836-4844 *SIC 5065*

SPECTRUM COMMUNICATIONS LTD *p656*
79 WELLINGTON ST, LONDON, ON, N6B 2K4
(519) 663-2109 *SIC 5065*

STANEX INC *p1331*
2437 RUE GUENETTE, SAINT-LAURENT, QC, H4R 2E9
(514) 333-5280 *SIC 5065*

STANLEY SECURITY SOLUTIONS CANADA INC *p1341*
160 RUE GRAVELINE, SAINT-LAURENT, QC, H4T 1R7
SIC 5065

SUMMA ENGINEERING LIMITED *p689*
6423 NORTHAM DR, MISSISSAUGA, ON, L4V 1J2
(905) 678-3388 *SIC 5065*

SYMBOL TECHNOLOGIES CANADA, ULC *p700*
5180 ORBITOR DR, MISSISSAUGA, ON, L4W 5L9
(905) 629-7226 *SIC 5065*

SYSTEMES FONEX DATA INC, LES *p1336*
5400 CH SAINT-FRANCOIS, SAINT-LAURENT, QC, H4S 1P6
(514) 333-6639 *SIC 5065*

SYSTEMES TESTFORCE INC *p1336*
9450 RTE TRANSCANADIENNE, SAINT-LAURENT, QC, H4S 1R7
(514) 856-0970 *SIC 5065*

SYSTEMES VERINT CANADA, INC *p1362*
1800 RUE BERLIER, SAINTE-ROSE, QC, H7L 4S4
(450) 686-9000 *SIC 5065*

SYSTEMES WESTCON CANADA (WCSI) INC, LES *p799*
1383 JOSHUAS CREEK DR, OAKVILLE, ON, L6H 7G4
(888) 307-7218 *SIC 5065*

T.F. LYNN AND ASSOCIATES INC *p40*
5512 4 ST NW SUITE 224, CALGARY, AB, T2K 1A9
(403) 215-6880 *SIC 5065*

TASK MICRO-ELECTRONICS INC *p1118*
16700 RTE TRANSCANADIENNE, KIRKLAND, QC, H9H 4M7
(514) 697-6616 *SIC 5065*

TECH-TREK LTD *p700*
1015 MATHESON BLVD E SUITE 6, MISSISSAUGA, ON, L4W 3A4
(905) 238-0319 *SIC 5065*

TELSCO SECURITY SYSTEMS INC *p94*
12750 127 ST NW, EDMONTON, AB, T5L 1A5
(780) 424-6971 *SIC 5065*

TEXAS INSTRUMENTS CANADA LIMITED *p625*
505 MARCH RD SUITE 200, KANATA, ON, K2K 3A4
(613) 271-8649 *SIC 5065*

TRENDS ELECTRONICS INTERNATIONAL INC *p183*
2999 UNDERHILL AVE SUITE 202, BURNABY, BC, V5A 3C2
(604) 988-2966 *SIC 5065*

TRI-ED LTD *p690*
3688 NASHUA DR UNIT A-F, MISSISSAUGA, ON, L4V 1M5
(905) 677-8664 *SIC 5065*

UNITY CONNECTED SOLUTIONS INC *p757*
450 HARRY WALKER PKY S, NEWMARKET, ON, L3Y 8E3
(905) 952-2475 *SIC 5065*

UTECH ELECTRONICS *p1001*
25 ANDERSON BLVD, UXBRIDGE, ON, L9P 0C7
(416) 609-2900   *SIC 5065*

VENATOR ELECTRONICS SALES & SERVICE LTD *p701*
4500 DIXIE RD UNIT 10, MISSISSAUGA, ON, L4W 1V7
SIC 5065

VENTURER ELECTRONICS INC *p676*
725 DENISON ST, MARKHAM, ON, L3R 1B8
(905) 477-7878   *SIC 5065*

VIDEOGLOBE 1 INC *p1192*
455 RUE SAINT-ANTOINE O BUREAU 300, MONTREAL, QC, H2Z 1J1
(514) 738-6665   *SIC 5065*

VIZIMAX INC *p1142*
2284 RUE DE LA PROVINCE, LONGUEUIL, QC, J4G 1G1
(450) 679-0003   *SIC 5065*

VOLTAM INC *p1116*
3455 RUE DU TRANSPORT, JONQUIERE, QC, G7X 0B6
(418) 548-0002   *SIC 5065*

W INTERCONNECTIONS CANADA INC *p677*
10 SPY CRT, MARKHAM, ON, L3R 5H6
(905) 475-1507   *SIC 5065*

WILLIAMS TELECOMMUNICATIONS CORP *p708*
5610 KENNEDY RD, MISSISSAUGA, ON, L4Z 2A9
(905) 712-4242   *SIC 5065*

YORK ELECTRONICS (2010) LTD *p12*
1430 28 ST NE UNIT 8, CALGARY, AB, T2A 7W6
(403) 207-0202   *SIC 5065*

SIC 5072 Hardware

1095086 ONTARIO INC *p921*
3080 YONGE ST SUITE 4054, TORONTO, ON, M4N 3N1
SIC 5072

1254613 ONTARIO LIMITED *p645*
207 KENT ST W, LINDSAY, ON, K9V 2Y9
(705) 324-4611   *SIC 5072*

4361806 CANADA INC *p1147*
205 RUE DU CENTRE, MAGOG, QC, J1X 5B6
(819) 843-4441   *SIC 5072*

ALLEGION CANADA INC *p712*
1076 LAKESHORE RD E, MISSISSAUGA, ON, L5E 1E4
(905) 403-1800   *SIC 5072*

ALLEN, A.W. HOMES LIMITED *p462*
166 COMMERCIAL ST, MIDDLETON, NS, B0S 1P0
(902) 825-4854   *SIC 5072*

ANCHOR CONSTRUCTION INDUSTRIAL PRODUCTS LTD *p383*
1810 DUBLIN AVE, WINNIPEG, MB, R3H 0H3
(204) 633-0064   *SIC 5072*

ASSA ABLOY OF CANADA LTD *p548*
160 FOUR VALLEY DR, CONCORD, ON, L4K 4T9
(905) 738-2466   *SIC 5072*

BLUM CANADA LIMITED *p737*
7135 PACIFIC CIR, MISSISSAUGA, ON, L5T 2A8
(905) 670-7920   *SIC 5072*

BOLTS PLUS INCORPORATED *p685*
7100 TORBRAM RD, MISSISSAUGA, ON, L4T 4B5
(905) 673-5554   *SIC 5072*

BRELCOR HOLDINGS LTD *p113*
8635 63 AVE NW, EDMONTON, AB, T6E 0E8
(780) 465-1466   *SIC 5072*

BUYERS GROUP OF MISSISSAUGA INC *p667*
205 TORBAY RD SUITE 12, MARKHAM, ON, L3R 3W4
(905) 948-1911   *SIC 5072*

CADIEUX & ASSOCIES S.E.N.C. *p1129*
225 RUE PRINCIPALE, LACHUTE, QC, J8H 2Z7
(450) 562-5285   *SIC 5072*

CANAROPA (1954) INC *p1127*
1725 50E AV, LACHINE, QC, H8T 3C8
(514) 636-6466   *SIC 5072*

CAPLAN INDUSTRIES INC *p208*
6800 DENNETT PL, DELTA, BC, V4G 1N4
(604) 946-3100   *SIC 5072*

CAYER, JEAN-CLAUDE ENTERPRISES LTD *p645*
708 LIMOGES RD, LIMOGES, ON, K0A 2M0
(613) 443-2293   *SIC 5072*

CHAINES DE TRACTION QUEBEC LTEE *p1048*
9401 BOUL PARKWAY, ANJOU, QC, H1J 1N4
(514) 353-9210   *SIC 5072*

CID BISSETT FASTENERS LIMITED *p499*
175 SUN PAC BLVD UNIT 2A, BRAMPTON, ON, L6S 5Z6
(905) 595-0411   *SIC 5072*

CITYWIDE DOOR & HARDWARE INC *p1030*
80 VINYL CRT, WOODBRIDGE, ON, L4L 4A3
(905) 265-2444   *SIC 5072*

COOP FEDEREE, LA *p1386*
4225 RUE SAINT-JOSEPH BUREAU 379, TROIS-RIVIERES, QC, G8Z 4G3
(819) 379-8551   *SIC 5072*

COOPERATIVE D'APPROVISIONNEMENTS DE STE-JULIE *p1358*
1590 RUE PRINCIPALE, SAINTE-JULIE, QC, J3E 1W6
(450) 922-5555   *SIC 5072*

DE LA FONTAINE & ASSOCIES INC *p1070*
7503 BOUL TASCHEREAU BUREAU B, BROSSARD, QC, J4Y 1A2
(450) 676-8335   *SIC 5072*

DISTRIBUTIONS GYPCO (1988) INC *p1048*
9550 BOUL RAY-LAWSON, ANJOU, QC, H1J 1L3
(514) 352-0150   *SIC 5072*

DONALD CHOI CANADA LIMITED *p1010*
147 BATHURST DR, WATERLOO, ON, N2V 1Z4
(519) 886-5010   *SIC 5072*

E. ROKO DISTRIBUTORS LTD *p338*
646 ALPHA ST, VICTORIA, BC, V8Z 1B2
(250) 381-2552   *SIC 5072*

ENTREPRISES Z-TECH INC., LES *p1061*
4230 RUE MARCEL-LACASSE, BOISBRIAND, QC, J7H 1N3
SIC 5072

EQUIPEMENTS INDUSTRIELS JOLIETTE INC *p1114*
1295 RUE DE LANAUDIERE, JOLIETTE, QC, J6E 3N9
(450) 756-0564   *SIC 5072*

EQUIPEMENTS RAPCO INC, LES *p1333*
5510 RUE VANDEN-ABEELE, SAINT-LAURENT, QC, H4S 1P9
(514) 332-6562   *SIC 5072*

FABORY CANADA INC *p1101*
1220 RUE MICHELIN, FABREVILLE, QC, H7L 4R3
(450) 629-6900   *SIC 5072*

FAIRWAY PRODUCTS INC *p254*
13611 MAYCREST WAY, RICHMOND, BC, V6V 2J4
(604) 278-1919   *SIC 5072*

FERCO FERRURES DE BATIMENTS INC *p1362*
2000 RUE BERLIER, SAINTE-ROSE, QC, H7L 4S4
(450) 973-1437   *SIC 5072*

FOURNITURES DE MEUBLES ET DE LITERIE SINCA INC *p1250*
870 AV ELLINGHAM, POINTE-CLAIRE, QC, H9R 3S4
(514) 697-0101   *SIC 5072*

GRAY HAND TOOL SALES LIMITED *p503*
299 ORENDA RD, BRAMPTON, ON, L6T 1E8
(905) 457-3014   *SIC 5072*

GROUPE BMR INC *p1065*
1660 RUE EIFFEL, BOUCHERVILLE, QC, J4B 7W1
(450) 655-2441   *SIC 5072*

H. DAGENAIS & FILS INC *p1352*
304 RUE PRINCIPALE, SAINT-SAUVEUR, QC, J0R 1R0
(450) 227-2649   *SIC 5072*

HAEFELE CANADA INC *p522*
5323 JOHN LUCAS DR, BURLINGTON, ON, L7L 6A8
(905) 336-6608   *SIC 5072*

HDS CANADA, INC *p1031*
100 GALCAT DR, WOODBRIDGE, ON, L4L 0B9
(905) 850-8085   *SIC 5072*

HETTICH CANADA LIMITED PARTNERSHIP *p1339*
140 RUE BARR, SAINT-LAURENT, QC, H4T 1Y4
(514) 333-3952   *SIC 5072*

HOLLAND IMPORTS INC *p185*
2306 MADISON AVE, BURNABY, BC, V5C 4Y9
(604) 299-5741   *SIC 5072*

INDUSTRIES DESORMEAU INC *p1344*
8195 RUE PASCAL-GAGNON, SAINT-LEONARD, QC, H1P 1Y5
(514) 321-2432   *SIC 5072*

INTENSITY SECURITY INC *p823*
45 O'CONNOR ST SUITE 1150, OTTAWA, ON, K1P 1A4
(613) 755-4094   *SIC 5072*

INTERFAST INC *p997*
22 WORCESTER RD, TORONTO, ON, M9W 5X2
(416) 674-0770   *SIC 5072*

INTERNATIONAL DISTRIBUTION NETWORK CANADA LTD *p791*
70 FLORAL PKY, NORTH YORK, ON, M6L 2B9
(416) 248-5625   *SIC 5072*

INVESTMENTS HARDWARE LIMITED *p1031*
250 ROWNTREE DAIRY RD, WOODBRIDGE, ON, L4L 9J7
(905) 851-8974   *SIC 5072*

J & R HOME PRODUCTS LTD *p181*
5628 RIVERBEND DR UNIT 1, BURNABY, BC, V3N 0C1
(604) 525-8333   *SIC 5072*

JIMEXS INC *p1057*
1360 RUE LOUIS-MARCHAND, BELOEIL, QC, J3G 6S3
SIC 5072

JPW SYSTEMS INC *p643*
30 DOAN DR, KOMOKA, ON, N0L 1R0
(519) 474-9797   *SIC 5072*

KALA'S HARDWARE LIMITED *p887*
1380 FOURTH AVE SUITE 3, ST CATHARINES, ON, L2S 0B8
(905) 688-5520   *SIC 5072*

KNELL INVESTMENTS INC *p635*
2090 SHIRLEY DR, KITCHENER, ON, N2B 0A3
(519) 578-1000   *SIC 5072*

KNELL, WILLIAM AND COMPANY LIMITED *p635*
2090 SHIRLEY DR, KITCHENER, ON, N2B 0A3
(519) 578-1000   *SIC 5072*

LAFLAMME, GEORGES INC *p1297*
2609 AV ROYALE O RR 1, SAINT-CHARLES-DE-BELLECHASSE, QC, G0R 2T0
(418) 887-3347   *SIC 5072*

LASER SALES INC *p649*
1717 OXFORD ST E, LONDON, ON, N5V 2Z5
(519) 452-0501   *SIC 5072*

LOYOLA SCHMIDT LTEE *p1395*
243 BOUL HARWOOD, VAUDREUIL-DORION, QC, J7V 1Y3
SIC 5072

MACMOR INDUSTRIES LTD *p384*
1175 SHERWIN RD, WINNIPEG, MB, R3H 0V1
(204) 786-5891   *SIC 5072*

MAKITA CANADA INC *p1014*
1950 FORBES ST, WHITBY, ON, L1N 7B7
(905) 571-2200   *SIC 5072*

MANTO, MARK BUILDING MATERIALS LTD *p132*
10921 100 ST, GRANDE PRAIRIE, AB, T8V 2M9
(780) 532-2092   *SIC 5072*

MANUFACTURIERS D'ACCESSOIRES MORTUAIRES LTEE *p1101*
211 RUE BERARD, FARNHAM, QC, J2N 2L4
(450) 293-1712   *SIC 5072*

MARATHON FASTENERS & HARDWARE INC *p717*
4170 SLADEVIEW CRES UNIT 7, MISSISSAUGA, ON, L5L 0A1
(905) 607-8665   *SIC 5072*

MCFADDEN'S HARDWOOD & HARDWARE INC *p798*
2323 WINSTON PARK DR SUITE 1, OAKVILLE, ON, L6H 6R7
(416) 674-3333   *SIC 5072*

MCGREGOR & THOMPSON HARDWARE LTD *p295*
1250 GEORGIA ST E, VANCOUVER, BC, V6A 2B1
(604) 253-8252   *SIC 5072*

MCGREGOR AND THOMPSON HARDWARE LTD *p234*
1920 BOXWOOD RD, NANAIMO, BC, V9S 5Y2
(604) 729-7888   *SIC 5072*

MIBRO PARTNERS *p869*
111 SINNOTT RD, SCARBOROUGH, ON, M1L 4S6
(416) 285-9000   *SIC 5072*

NORTHERN HARDWARE LTD *p31*
549 CLEVELAND CRES SE, CALGARY, AB, T2G 4R8
(403) 243-5401   *SIC 5072*

ORGANIZED INTERIORS INC *p1003*
201 CHRISLEA RD, VAUGHAN, ON, L4L 8N6
(905) 264-5678   *SIC 5072*

OTTAWA FASTENER SUPPLY LTD *p751*
2205 ROBERTSON RD, NEPEAN, ON, K2H 5Z2
(613) 828-5311   *SIC 5072*

OUTILLAGE SUMMIT *p1321*
803 RUE SAINT-GEORGES, SAINT-JEROME, QC, J7Z 5E1
(450) 592-0747   *SIC 5072*

OUTILLEURS, S.E.C., L' *p1323*
1325 RUE DU PONT, SAINT-LAMBERT-DE-LAUZON, QC, G0S 2W0
(418) 889-9521   *SIC 5072*

P.R. NISSEN & CIE LTEE *p1395*
102B BOUL DE LA CITE-DES-JEUNES UNITE 54, VAUDREUIL-DORION, QC, J7V 8B9
(514) 694-0250   *SIC 5072*

PREMIER QUEBEC INC *p1280*
6655 BOUL PIERRE-BERTRAND BUREAU 101, QUEBEC, QC, G2K 1M1
(418) 681-4733   *SIC 5072*

PRIME FASTENERS LTD *p17*
5940 30 ST SE SUITE 6, CALGARY, AB, T2C 1X8
(403) 279-1043   *SIC 5072*

QUINCAILLERIE BEAUBIEN INC *p1169*
3194 RUE BEAUBIEN E, MONTREAL, QC, H1Y 1H4
(514) 727-0525   *SIC 5072*

QUINCAILLERIE RICHELIEU LTEE *p1142*
800 RUE BERIAULT, LONGUEUIL, QC, J4G

1R8
(514) 259-3737   *SIC 5072*
QUINCAILLERIE RICHELIEU LTEE   *p1335*
7900 BOUL HENRI-BOURASSA O BU-REAU 200, SAINT-LAURENT, QC, H4S 1V4
(514) 336-4144   *SIC 5072*
RENO-DIRECT INC   *p1362*
1329 BOUL DAGENAIS O, SAINTE-ROSE, QC, H7L 5Z9
(450) 625-2660   *SIC 5072*
RICHELIEU CANADA LTD   *p256*
2600 VIKING WAY, RICHMOND, BC, V6V 1N2
(604) 273-3108   *SIC 5072*
RICHELIEU HARDWARE CANADA LTD
p1228
7900 BOUL HENRI-BOURASSA O, MON-TREAL, QC, H4S 1V4
(514) 336-4144   *SIC 5072*
RIVETT ARCHITECTURAL HARDWARE LTD   *p1015*
111 INDUSTRIAL DR UNIT 1, WHITBY, ON, L1N 5Z9
(905) 668-4455   *SIC 5072*
ROCHELEAU, PAUL INC   *p1399*
760 BOUL PIERRE-ROUX E, VICTORIAV-ILLE, QC, G6T 1S6
(819) 758-7525   *SIC 5072*
RONA INC   *p566*
52 DUNDAS ST E, DUNDAS, ON, L9H 0C2
(905) 689-8700   *SIC 5072*
RONA INC   *p632*
2342 PRINCESS ST, KINGSTON, ON, K7M 3G4
(613) 531-6225   *SIC 5072*
RONA INC   *p659*
820 BLYTHWOOD RD, LONDON, ON, N6H 5T8
(519) 471-6621   *SIC 5072*
RONA INC   *p1067*
220 CH DU TREMBLAY, BOUCHERVILLE, QC, J4B 8H7
(514) 599-5900   *SIC 5072*
RONA INC   *p1074*
1458 CH DE CHAMBLY, CARIGNAN, QC, J3L 0J4
(450) 658-8774   *SIC 5072*
RONA INC   *p1076*
99 RUE PRINCIPALE, CHATEAUGUAY, QC, J6K 1G2
(450) 692-9992   *SIC 5072*
RONA INC   *p1099*
875 RUE HAINS, DRUMMONDVILLE, QC, J2C 7Y8
SIC 5072
RONA INC   *p1107*
95 RUE ATAWE, GATINEAU, QC, J8Y 6W7
(819) 770-7366   *SIC 5072*
RONA INC   *p1245*
3933 BOUL SAINT-CHARLES, PIERRE-FONDS, QC, H9H 3C7
(514) 624-2332   *SIC 5072*
RONA INC   *p1352*
180 RUE PRINCIPALE, SAINT-SAUVEUR, QC, J0R 1R0
(450) 227-2627   *SIC 5072*
RONA INC   *p1395*
3010 BOUL DE LA GARE, VAUDREUIL-DORION, QC, J7V 0H1
(450) 455-3067   *SIC 5072*
SATURN INDUSTRIES LTD   *p369*
37 SYLVAN WAY, WINNIPEG, MB, R2R 2B9
(204) 633-1529   *SIC 5072*
SOLUTIONS 2 GO INC   *p506*
15 PRODUCTION DR, BRAMPTON, ON, L6T 4N8
(905) 564-1140   *SIC 5072*
SPALDING HARDWARE LTD   *p73*
1616 10 AVE SW, CALGARY, AB, T3C 0J5
(403) 244-5531   *SIC 5072*
SPALDING HARDWARE SYSTEMS INC *p73*
1616 10 AVE SW, CALGARY, AB, T3C 0J5
(403) 244-5531   *SIC 5072*
TAYMOR INDUSTRIES LTD   *p207*

1655 DERWENT WAY, DELTA, BC, V3M 6K8
(604) 540-9525   *SIC 5072*
TEAM CID INC   *p500*
175 SUN PAC BLVD SUITE 2A, BRAMP-TON, ON, L6S 5Z6
(905) 595-0411   *SIC 5072*
TECHTRONIC INDUSTRIES CANADA INC *p675*
7303 WARDEN AVE SUITE 202, MARKHAM, ON, L3R 5Y6
(905) 479-4355   *SIC 5072*
TRADEMARK INDUSTRIES INC   *p679*
380 MARKLAND ST, MARKHAM, ON, L6C 1T6
(905) 532-0442   *SIC 5072*
TRADEMARK TOOLS INC   *p560*
21 STAFFERN DR, CONCORD, ON, L4K 2X2
(905) 532-0442   *SIC 5072*
TRILLIUM ARCHITECTURAL PRODUCTS LTD   *p780*
52 PRINCE ANDREW PL, NORTH YORK, ON, M3C 2H4
(416) 391-5555   *SIC 5072*
TS MACHINES AND SERVICE CORP   *p701*
5940 SHAWSON DR, MISSISSAUGA, ON, L4W 3W5
(905) 670-5785   *SIC 5072*
UPPER CANADA SPECIALTY HARDWARE LIMITED   *p676*
7100 WARDEN AVE UNIT 1, MARKHAM, ON, L3R 8B5
(905) 940-8358   *SIC 5072*
VIBRANT POWER INC   *p744*
310 COURTNEYPARK DR E, MISSIS-SAUGA, ON, L5T 2S5
(905) 564-8644   *SIC 5072*
VIKING CHAINS INC   *p210*
7392 PROGRESS PL, DELTA, BC, V4G 1A1
(604) 952-4146   *SIC 5072*

SIC 5074 Plumbing and heating equipment and supplies (hydronics)

13876 ENTERPRISES LTD   *p213*
10020 93 AVE, FORT ST. JOHN, BC, V1J 1E2
(250) 785-6679   *SIC 5074*
150157 CANADA INC   *p1327*
2320 RUE COHEN, SAINT-LAURENT, QC, H4R 2N8
(514) 745-1080   *SIC 5074*
2179321 ONTARIO LIMITED   *p775*
27 LARABEE CRES, NORTH YORK, ON, M3A 3E6
(416) 219-1050   *SIC 5074*
4131827 MANITOBA LTD   *p369*
75 MERIDIAN DR UNIT 3, WINNIPEG, MB, R2R 2V9
(204) 786-1604   *SIC 5074*
9323-7055 QUEBEC INC   *p1058*
1190 BOUL MICHELE-BOHEC, BLAINVILLE, QC, J7C 5S4
(450) 433-2210   *SIC 5074*
ANDERSON PUMP HOUSE LTD   *p1412*
9802 THATCHER AVE, NORTH BATTLE-FORD, SK, S9A 3W2
(306) 937-7741   *SIC 5074*
ANTHRATECH WESTERN INC   *p12*
4450 46 AVE SE, CALGARY, AB, T2B 3N7
(403) 255-7377   *SIC 5074*
AQUACLEAR FILTRATION   *p99*
10518 180 ST NW UNIT 101, EDMONTON, AB, T5S 2P1
(780) 809-3146   *SIC 5074*
AQUIFER DISTRIBUTION LTD   *p1426*
227 VENTURE CRES, SASKATOON, SK, S7K 6N8
(306) 242-1567   *SIC 5074*
BARCLAY SALES LTD   *p246*
1441 KEBET WAY, PORT COQUITLAM, BC, V3C 6L3

(604) 945-1010   *SIC 5074*
BARDON SUPPLIES LIMITED   *p490*
405 COLLEGE ST E, BELLEVILLE, ON, K8N 4Z6
(613) 966-5643   *SIC 5074*
BARIL MANUFACTURIER INC   *p1384*
579 BOUL SAINTE-MADELEINE, TROIS-RIVIERES, QC, G8T 9J8
(819) 693-3871   *SIC 5074*
BARTLE & GIBSON CO LTD   *p83*
13475 FORT RD NW, EDMONTON, AB, T5A 1C6
(780) 472-2850   *SIC 5074*
BMI CANADA INC   *p1061*
3437 BOUL DE LA GRANDE-ALLEE, BOIS-BRIAND, QC, J7H 1H5
(450) 434-1313   *SIC 5074*
BOONE PLUMBING AND HEATING SUP-PLY INC   *p594*
1282 ALGOMA RD SUITE 613, GLOUCES-TER, ON, K1B 3W8
(613) 746-8560   *SIC 5074*
BRITA CANADA CORPORATION   *p508*
150 BISCAYNE CRES, BRAMPTON, ON, L6W 4V3
(905) 789-2465   *SIC 5074*
CAN-AQUA INTERNATIONAL LTEE   *p1233*
2250 BOUL DAGENAIS O, MONTREAL, QC, H7L 5Y2
(450) 625-3088   *SIC 5074*
CANTU BATHROOMS & HARDWARE LTD *p290*
8351 ONTARIO ST, VANCOUVER, BC, V5X 3E8
(604) 688-1252   *SIC 5074*
CARMANAH TECHNOLOGIES CORPORA-TION   *p339*
203 HARBOUR RD SUITE 4, VICTORIA, BC, V9A 3S2
(250) 380-0052   *SIC 5074*
CB SUPPLIES LTD   *p278*
3325 190 ST, SURREY, BC, V3Z 1A7
(604) 535-5088   *SIC 5074*
CONTRACTEURS ARMSERV INC   *p1333*
6400 RUE VANDEN-ABEELE, SAINT-LAURENT, QC, H4S 1R9
(514) 333-5340   *SIC 5074*
CULLIGAN WATER CONDITIONING (BAR-RIE) LIMITED   *p486*
15 MORROW RD, BARRIE, ON, L4N 3V7
(705) 728-4782   *SIC 5074*
DESCHENES & FILS LTEE   *p1170*
3901 RUE JARRY E BUREAU 100, MON-TREAL, QC, H1Z 2G1
(514) 374-3110   *SIC 5074*
DESCHENES & FILS LTEE   *p1279*
1105 RUE DES ROCAILLES, QUEBEC, QC, G2K 2K6
(418) 627-4711   *SIC 5074*
DESCO PLUMBING AND HEATING SUPPLY INC   *p734*
7550 TRANMERE DR, MISSISSAUGA, ON, L5S 1S6
(416) 293-8219   *SIC 5074*
DICKINSON MARINE (1997) LTD   *p200*
204 CAYER ST UNIT 407, COQUITLAM, BC, V3K 5B1
(604) 525-4444   *SIC 5074*
DISTRIBUTION AD WATERS (CAN) INC *p1217*
9805 RUE CLARK, MONTREAL, QC, H3L 2R5
(514) 381-4141   *SIC 5074*
DOBBIN SALES LIMITED   *p1030*
51 TERECAR DR UNIT 2, WOODBRIDGE, ON, L4L 0B5
(905) 264-5465   *SIC 5074*
DSI RECYCLING SYSTEMS INC   *p1006*
1595 LOBSINGER LINE SUITE 1, WATER-LOO, ON, N2J 4G8
(905) 664-3586   *SIC 5074*
ECO-LOGIXX - GROSSISTE ALIMENTAIRE ET PRODUITS D'EMBALLAGES INC *p1344*
9209 BOUL LANGELIER, SAINT-

LEONARD, QC, H1P 3K9
(514) 351-3031   *SIC 5074*
EDDY GROUP LIMITED   *p394*
660 ST. ANNE ST, BATHURST, NB, E2A 2N6
(506) 546-6631   *SIC 5074*
EMCO CORPORATION   *p122*
3011 101 AVE NW, EDMONTON, AB, T6P 1X7
(780) 440-7333   *SIC 5074*
EMCO CORPORATION   *p446*
111 WRIGHT AVE, DARTMOUTH, NS, B3B 1K6
(902) 555-7744   *SIC 5074*
EMCO CORPORATION   *p649*
2124 OXFORD ST E, LONDON, ON, N5V 0B7
(519) 453-9600   *SIC 5074*
FAIRVIEW FITTINGS & MANUFACTURING LIMITED   *p797*
1170 INVICTA DR UNIT C, OAKVILLE, ON, L6H 6G1
(905) 338-0800   *SIC 5074*
FAIRVIEW LTD   *p797*
1170 INVICTA DR UNIT C, OAKVILLE, ON, L6H 6G1
(905) 338-0800   *SIC 5074*
FLOCOR INC   *p892*
470 SEAMAN ST, STONEY CREEK, ON, L8E 2V9
(905) 664-9230   *SIC 5074*
FOREMOST INTERNATIONAL LTD   *p731*
5970 CHEDWORTH WAY SUITE B, MISSIS-SAUGA, ON, L5R 4G5
(905) 507-2005   *SIC 5074*
FOURNITURES DE PLOMBERIE ET CHAUFFAGE SUTTON LTEE   *p1221*
2174 AV DE CLIFTON, MONTREAL, QC, H4A 2N6
(514) 488-2581   *SIC 5074*
FUNDY ENERGY LIMITED   *p407*
132 BEAVERBROOK ST, MONCTON, NB, E1C 9S8
(506) 857-3283   *SIC 5074*
G & G GENERAL SUPPLY LTD   *p553*
511 MILLWAY AVE, CONCORD, ON, L4K 3V4
(905) 669-9556   *SIC 5074*
GHP GROUP ULC   *p605*
271 MASSEY RD, GUELPH, ON, N1K 1B2
(519) 837-9724   *SIC 5074*
GLOBE UNION (CANADA) INC   *p1334*
4610 CH DU BOIS-FRANC, SAINT-LAURENT, QC, H4S 1A7
(514) 907-8000   *SIC 5074*
GRO-MEC INC   *p1080*
1911 RUE DES OUTARDES, CHICOUTIMI, QC, G7K 1C3
(418) 549-5961   *SIC 5074*
HONEYCOMB HILL HOLDINGS OF MUL-MUR INC   *p808*
410 RICHARDSON RD, ORANGEVILLE, ON, L9W 4W8
(519) 942-9999   *SIC 5074*
HOULE, J.U. LTEE   *p1399*
20 RUE FRANCOIS-BOURGEOIS, VICTO-RIAVILLE, QC, G6T 2G8
(819) 758-5235   *SIC 5074*
HTH HEATECH INC   *p77*
61 INDUSTRY WAY SE, CALGARY, AB, T3S 0A2
(403) 279-1990   *SIC 5074*
INDEPENDENT MECHANICAL SUPPLY INC *p585*
310 CARLINGVIEW DR, ETOBICOKE, ON, M9W 5G1
(416) 679-1048   *SIC 5074*
INTERLINE BRANDS INC   *p723*
6990 CREDITVIEW RD SUITE 4, MISSIS-SAUGA, ON, L5N 8R9
(905) 821-8292   *SIC 5074*
JBW PIPE & SUPPLY LTD   *p30*
1320 HIGHFIELD CRES SE, CALGARY, AB, T2G 5M3

(403) 259-6671   *SIC 5074*
JETCO MECHANICAL LIMITED   *p*96
15035 114 AVE NW, EDMONTON, AB, T5M 2Z1
(780) 451-2732   *SIC 5074*
JOHNSON PATERSON INC   *p*481
360 INDUSTRIAL PKY S SUITE 7, AURORA, ON, L4G 3V7
(905) 727-0084   *SIC 5074*
KATHDEN SERVICES INC   *p*504
239 ADVANCE BLVD, BRAMPTON, ON, L6T 4J2
   SIC 5074
KLEIN INTERNATIONAL LTD   *p*852
66 WEST WILMOT ST, RICHMOND HILL, ON, L4B 1H8
(905) 889-4881   *SIC 5074*
M.I. VIAU & FILS LIMITEE   *p*1152
14311   RTE   SIR-WILFRID-LAURIER, MIRABEL, QC, J7J 2G4
(450) 436-8221   *SIC 5074*
MARCEL BARIL LTEE   *p*1289
101   AV   MARCEL-BARIL,   ROUYN-NORANDA, QC, J9X 5P5
(819) 764-3211   *SIC 5074*
MARKS SUPPLY INC   *p*640
300 ARNOLD ST, KITCHENER, ON, N2H 6E9
(519) 578-5560   *SIC 5074*
MOEN INC   *p*798
2816 BRISTOL CIR, OAKVILLE, ON, L6H 5S7
(905) 829-3400   *SIC 5074*
NALCO CANADA CO.   *p*530
1055 TRUMAN ST, BURLINGTON, ON, L7R 3V7
(905) 632-8791   *SIC 5074*
NELCO INC   *p*1221
5510 RUE SAINT-JACQUES, MONTREAL, QC, H4A 2E2
(514) 481-5614   *SIC 5074*
NEXT PLUMBING & HYDRONICS SUPPLY INC   *p*1032
300 GALCAT DR, WOODBRIDGE, ON, L4L 0B9
(289) 304-2000   *SIC 5074*
NORTH ATLANTIC PETROLEUM LIMITED   *p*430
29 PIPPY PL, ST. JOHN'S, NL, A1B 3X2
(709) 579-5831   *SIC 5074*
NORTHEAST EQUIPMENT LIMITED   *p*447
135 JOSEPH ZATZMAN DR, DARTMOUTH, NS, B3B 1W1
(902) 468-7473   *SIC 5074*
POLYTUBES (MAN) INC   *p*369
1803 HEKLA AVE, WINNIPEG, MB, R2R 0K3
   SIC 5074
PRESTON PHIPPS INC   *p*1335
6400   RUE   VANDEN-ABEELE,   SAINT-LAURENT, QC, H4S 1R9
(514) 333-5340   *SIC 5074*
PRODUITS SANITAIRES LEPINE INC, LES   *p*1081
1105 RUE BERSIMIS, CHICOUTIMI, QC, G7K 1A4
(418) 545-0794   *SIC 5074*
PROMINENT FLUID CONTROLS LTD   *p*601
490 SOUTHGATE DR, GUELPH, ON, N1G 4P5
(519) 836-5692   *SIC 5074*
PURIBEC INC   *p*1285
177 RUE DE L'EVECHE O, RIMOUSKI, QC, G5L 4H8
(418) 722-7326   *SIC 5074*
RHEEM CANADA LTD   *p*512
125 EDGEWARE RD UNIT 1, BRAMPTON, ON, L6Y 0P5
(905) 450-4460   *SIC 5074*
ROBINSON, B.A. CO. LTD   *p*385
619 BERRY ST, WINNIPEG, MB, R3H 0S2
(204) 784-0150   *SIC 5074*
SEXAUER LTD   *p*727
6990 CREDITVIEW RD UNIT 3, MISSIS-

SAUGA, ON, L5N 8R9
(905) 821-8292   *SIC 5074*
SHERET, ANDREW HOLDINGS LIMITED   *p*335
721 KINGS RD, VICTORIA, BC, V8T 1W4
(250) 386-7744   *SIC 5074*
SHERET, ANDREW LIMITED   *p*335
740 HILLSIDE AVE SUITE 401, VICTORIA, BC, V8T 1Z4
(250) 386-7744   *SIC 5074*
SIMO MANAGEMENT   *p*1061
150 RUE CHAUVIN, BOISBRIAND, QC, J7G 2N5
   SIC 5074
TRU-WAY ENTERPRISES LTD   *p*252
135 KEIS AVE, QUESNEL, BC, V2J 3S1
(250) 992-8512   *SIC 5074*
UNIVCO INVESTMENTS LTD   *p*287
2835 12TH AVE E, VANCOUVER, BC, V5M 4P9
(604) 253-4000   *SIC 5074*
VERSA FITTINGS INC   *p*744
290 COURTNEYPARK DR E, MISSIS-SAUGA, ON, L5T 2S5
(905) 564-2600   *SIC 5074*
WATER PIK TECHNOLOGIES CANADA INC   *p*677
625 COCHRANE DR, MARKHAM, ON, L3R 9R9
   SIC 5074
WATERLOO MANUFACTURING COMPANY LIMITED   *p*1009
505 DOTZERT CRT UNIT 1, WATERLOO, ON, N2L 6A7
(519) 884-0600   *SIC 5074*
WOLSELEY CANADA INC   *p*528
880 LAURENTIAN DR SUITE 1, BURLINGTON, ON, L7N 3V6
(905) 335-7373   *SIC 5074*
WOLSELEY CANADA INC   *p*1342
4200 RUE HICKMORE, SAINT-LAURENT, QC, H4T 1K2
(514) 344-9378   *SIC 5074*
YORKLAND CONTROLS LIMITED   *p*785
2693 STEELES AVE W SUITE 661, NORTH YORK, ON, M3J 2Z8
(416) 661-3306   *SIC 5074*
YORKWEST PLUMBING SUPPLY INC   *p*1034
201 AVIVA PARK DR, WOODBRIDGE, ON, L4L 9C1
(905) 856-9466   *SIC 5074*

SIC 5075 Warm air heating and air conditioning

1503647 ONTARIO LIMITED   *p*690
1173 MATHESON BLVD E, MISSISSAUGA, ON, L4W 1B6
(416) 255-7370   *SIC 5075*
1630389 ONTARIO LTD   *p*485
11 KING ST UNIT 4, BARRIE, ON, L4N 6B5
(705) 721-1600   *SIC 5075*
3099-3562 QUEBEC INC   *p*1081
1021 RUE CHILD, COATICOOK, QC, J1A 2S5
(819) 849-0532   *SIC 5075*
AAF CANADA INC   *p*1328
3233 RUE SARTELON, SAINT-LAURENT, QC, H4R 1E6
(514) 333-9048   *SIC 5075*
AIREAU QUALITE CONTROLE INC   *p*1060
660 RUE DE LA SABLIERE, BOIS-DES-FILION, QC, J6Z 4T7
(450) 621-6661   *SIC 5075*
AIREX INC   *p*501
5 SANDHILL CRT UNIT C, BRAMPTON, ON, L6T 5J5
(905) 790-8667   *SIC 5075*
ALLTEMP PRODUCTS COMPANY LIMITED   *p*844
827 BROCK RD, PICKERING, ON, L1W 3J2
(905) 831-3311   *SIC 5075*
AQUA AIR SYSTEMS LTD   *p*108

8703 50 ST NW, EDMONTON, AB, T6B 1E7
(780) 465-8011   *SIC 5075*
BOUTETTE & BARNETT INC   *p*648
1950 OXFORD ST E, LONDON, ON, N5V 2Z8
(519) 679-1770   *SIC 5075*
CANADIAN ENGINEERED PRODUCTS AND SALES LTD   *p*208
7449 HUME AVE SUITE 6, DELTA, BC, V4G 1C3
(604) 940-8188   *SIC 5075*
CARBONMASTERS INNOVATION LTD   *p*200
35 LEEDER ST, COQUITLAM, BC, V3K 3V5
(778) 684-2096   *SIC 5075*
CARRIER ENTERPRISE CANADA, L.P.   *p*734
195 STATESMAN DR, MISSISSAUGA, ON, L5S 1X4
(905) 672-0606   *SIC 5075*
CARRIER   ENTERPRISE   CANADA, L.P.   *p*1361
2025 BOUL DAGENAIS O, SAINTE-ROSE, QC, H7L 5V1
(514) 324-5050   *SIC 5075*
COMETAL INC   *p*1137
2965   BOUL   GUILLAUME-COUTURE, LEVIS, QC, G6W 6N6
(418) 839-8831   *SIC 5075*
COMFORT SYSTEM SOLUTIONS INC   *p*705
150 BRITANNIA RD E UNIT 1, MISSIS-SAUGA, ON, L4Z 2A4
(905) 568-1661   *SIC 5075*
CONTROLES A.C. INC, LES   *p*1137
2185 5E RUE, LEVIS, QC, G6W 5M6
(418) 834-2777   *SIC 5075*
CWI CLIMATEWORX INTERNATIONAL INC   *p*502
18 CHELSEA LANE, BRAMPTON, ON, L6T 3Y4
(905) 405-0800   *SIC 5075*
DAIKIN APPLIED CANADA INC   *p*1141
603 RUE BERIAULT, LONGUEUIL, QC, J4G 1Z1
(450) 674-2442   *SIC 5075*
EASTERN REFRIGERATION SUPPLY CO. LIMITED   *p*851
30 VOGELL RD UNIT 5, RICHMOND HILL, ON, L4B 3K6
(905) 787-8383   *SIC 5075*
ECOBEE INC   *p*962
207 QUEENS QUAY W SUITE 600, TORONTO, ON, M5J 1A7
(877) 932-6233   *SIC 5075*
EFI CONCEPTS   *p*584
315 HUMBERLINE DR SUITE A, ETOBICOKE, ON, M9W 5T6
(416) 674-6744   *SIC 5075*
ENERGIE CONVEX ENERGY INC   *p*831
1771 WOODWARD DR, OTTAWA, ON, K2C 0P9
(613) 723-3141   *SIC 5075*
ENERTRAK INC   *p*1363
2875   RUE   JULES-BRILLANT, SAINTE-ROSE, QC, H7P 6B2
(450) 973-2000   *SIC 5075*
FORTRESS GROUP INC   *p*1010
85 BAFFIN PL, WATERLOO, ON, N2V 2C1
(519) 747-4604   *SIC 5075*
FROST FIGHTER INC   *p*380
1500 NOTRE DAME AVE UNIT 100, WINNIPEG, MB, R3E 0P9
(204) 775-8252   *SIC 5075*
GOODMAN COMPANY CANADA   *p*553
8305 JANE ST UNIT 3, CONCORD, ON, L4K 5Y3
(905) 760-2737   *SIC 5075*
GROUPE MASTER INC, LE   *p*1065
1675   BOUL   DE   MONTARVILLE, BOUCHERVILLE, QC, J4B 7W4
(514) 527-2301   *SIC 5075*
HTS ENGINEERING LTD   *p*787
115 NORFINCH DR, NORTH YORK, ON, M3N 1W8
(416) 661-3400   *SIC 5075*
INDUSTRIES THERMOPLUS AIR INC, LES

*p*1321
262 RUE SCOTT, SAINT-JEROME, QC, J7Z 1H1
(450) 436-7555   *SIC 5075*
KERR CONTROLS LIMITED   *p*469
125 POLYMER RD, TRURO, NS, B2N 7A7
(902) 895-9285   *SIC 5075*
L-K METAL PRODUCTS CO. LIMITED   *p*1022
1595 LINCOLN RD, WINDSOR, ON, N8Y 2J3
(519) 256-1861   *SIC 5075*
MDS INVESTMENTS LTD   *p*86
10914 120 ST NW, EDMONTON, AB, T5H 3P7
(780) 452-3110   *SIC 5075*
MITSUBISHI ELECTRIC SALES CANADA INC   *p*672
4299 14TH AVE, MARKHAM, ON, L3R 0J2
(905) 475-7728   *SIC 5075*
OLYMPIC INTEGRATED SERVICES INC   *p*31
2226 PORTLAND ST SE, CALGARY, AB, T2G 4M6
(587) 955-9977   *SIC 5075*
OLYMPIC INTERNATIONAL AGENCIES LTD   *p*239
344 HARBOUR AVE, NORTH VANCOUVER, BC, V7J 2E9
(604) 986-1400   *SIC 5075*
ONTOR LIMITED   *p*789
12 LESWYN RD, NORTH YORK, ON, M6A 1K3
(416) 781-5286   *SIC 5075*
PERRY MECHANICAL INC   *p*814
285 BLOOR ST W, OSHAWA, ON, L1J 1R1
(905) 725-3582   *SIC 5075*
POLAR MOBILITY RESEARCH LTD   *p*17
7860 62 ST SE, CALGARY, AB, T2C 5K2
(403) 279-3633   *SIC 5075*
POWRMATIC DU CANADA LTEE   *p*1050
9530 BOUL RAY-LAWSON, ANJOU, QC, H1J 1L1
(514) 493-6400   *SIC 5075*
QUALITY HVAC PRODUCTS LTD   *p*110
3904 53 AVE NW, EDMONTON, AB, T6B 3N7
(780) 643-3215   *SIC 5075*
RANDEBAR ENTERPRISES INC   *p*750
24 GURDWARA RD, NEPEAN, ON, K2E 8B5
(613) 225-9774   *SIC 5075*
REDMOND/WILLIAMS   DISTRIBUTIONS INC   *p*699
5605 TIMBERLEA BLVD, MISSISSAUGA, ON, L4W 2S4
(905) 238-8208   *SIC 5075*
REFRIGERATIVE SUPPLY   *p*193
8028 NORTH FRASER WAY, BURNABY, BC, V5J 0E1
(604) 435-7151   *SIC 5075*
SINCLAIR SUPPLY LTD   *p*86
10914 120 ST NW, EDMONTON, AB, T5H 3P7
(780) 452-3110   *SIC 5075*
SOUTHERN SUPPLIES LIMITED   *p*814
323 BLOOR ST W, OSHAWA, ON, L1J 6X4
(905) 728-6216   *SIC 5075*
SPIRAX SARCO CANADA LIMITED   *p*558
383 APPLEWOOD CRES, CONCORD, ON, L4K 4J3
(905) 660-5510   *SIC 5075*
SPIRO MEGA INC   *p*1362
1225 RUE MICHELIN, SAINTE-ROSE, QC, H7L 4S2
(450) 663-4457   *SIC 5075*
SUNRISE TRADEX CORP   *p*1082
271 RUE SAINT-JACQUES S, COATICOOK, QC, J1A 2P3
(819) 804-0551   *SIC 5075*
SUNRISE TRADEX CORPORATION   *p*1348
3122 RUE BERNARD-PILON, SAINT-MATHIEU-DE-BELOEIL, QC, J3G 4S5
(450) 536-2175   *SIC 5075*
SYSTEMS VIC INC   *p*1309
5200 RUE ARMAND-FRAPPIER, SAINT-

HUBERT, QC, J3Z 1G5
(450) 926-3164 *SIC 5075*
THERMON CANADA INC *p111*
5607 67 ST NW, EDMONTON, AB, T6B 3H5
(780) 437-6326 *SIC 5075*
TRANE CANADA ULC *p220*
2260 HUNTER RD SUITE 3, KELOWNA, BC, V1X 7J8
(250) 491-4600 *SIC 5075*
UPONOR LTD *p1416*
662 E 1ST AVE SUITE 200, REGINA, SK, S4N 5T6
(306) 721-2449 *SIC 5075*
WOLSELEY CANADA INC *p1236*
4200 RUE LOUIS-B.-MAYER, MONTREAL, QC, H7P 0G1
(450) 680-4040 *SIC 5075*
ZESTA ENGINEERING LIMITED *p708*
212 WATLINE AVE, MISSISSAUGA, ON, L4Z 1P4
(905) 568-3112 *SIC 5075*

SIC 5078 Refrigeration equipment and supplies

9272-8781 QUEBEC INC *p1047*
11020 BOUL PARKWAY, ANJOU, QC, H1J 1R6
(514) 270-7181 *SIC 5078*
C.T. CONTROL TEMP LTD *p184*
4340 DAWSON ST, BURNABY, BC, V5C 4B6
(604) 298-2000 *SIC 5078*
CALIFORNIA INNOVATIONS INC *p788*
36 DUFFLAW RD, NORTH YORK, ON, M6A 2W1
(416) 590-7700 *SIC 5078*
CENTRAL TRANSPORT REFRIGERATION (MAN.) LTD *p382*
986 WALL ST SUITE 480, WINNIPEG, MB, R3G 2V3
(204) 772-2481 *SIC 5078*
DESCAIR INC *p1170*
8335 BOUL SAINT-MICHEL, MONTREAL, QC, H1Z 3E6
(514) 744-6751 *SIC 5078*
DSL LTD *p93*
14520 128 AVE NW, EDMONTON, AB, T5L 3H6
(780) 452-7580 *SIC 5078*
EQUIPEMENTS DE SUPERMARCHES CONCEPT INTERNATIONAL INC *p1282*
429 RUE DES INDUSTRIES, REPENTIGNY, QC, J5Z 4Y8
(450) 582-3017 *SIC 5078*
ESKIMO REFRIGERATION LTD *p15*
4705 61 AVE SE, CALGARY, AB, T2C 4W1
(403) 279-8091 *SIC 5078*
GEA REFRIGERATION CANADA INC *p254*
2551 VIKING WAY SUITE 150, RICHMOND, BC, V6V 1N4
(604) 278-4118 *SIC 5078*
HUSSMANN CANADA INC *p539*
5 CHERRY BLOSSOM RD SUITE 3, CAMBRIDGE, ON, N3H 4R7
(519) 653-9980 *SIC 5078*
INDEPENDENT SUPPLY COMPANY INC *p272*
19505 56 AVE UNIT 104, SURREY, BC, V3S 6K3
(604) 298-4472 *SIC 5078*
JONES FOOD STORE EQUIPMENT LTD *p184*
2896 NORLAND AVE, BURNABY, BC, V5B 3A6
(604) 294-6321 *SIC 5078*
MANUFACT LOGISTICS LTD *p793*
3655 WESTON RD SUITE 1, NORTH YORK, ON, M9L 1V8
(416) 739-8411 *SIC 5078*
SOLUTIONS D'AIR DESHUMIDIFIE INC *p1228*
5685 RUE CYPIHOT, MONTREAL, QC, H4S

1R3
(514) 336-3330 *SIC 5078*
UNITED REFRIGERATION OF CANADA LTD *p676*
130 RIVIERA DR, MARKHAM, ON, L3R 5M1
(905) 479-1212 *SIC 5078*

SIC 5082 Construction and mining machinery

353903 ONTARIO LTD. *p444*
161 JOSEPH ZATZMAN DR, DARTMOUTH, NS, B3B 1M7
(902) 463-0101 *SIC 5082*
8782601 CANADA INC *p1172*
4293 RUE HOGAN, MONTREAL, QC, H2H 2N2
(514) 931-7228 *SIC 5082*
9231-4897 QUEBEC INC *p1280*
625 RUE DE L'ARGON, QUEBEC, QC, G2N 2G7
(418) 841-2001 *SIC 5082*
ACADIAN TIMBER CORP *p311*
1055 GEORGIA ST W SUITE 1800, VANCOUVER, BC, V6E 0B6
(604) 661-9143 *SIC 5082*
ACCESSOIRES OUTILLAGE LIMITEE *p1177*
8755 BOUL SAINT-LAURENT, MONTREAL, QC, H2N 1M2
(514) 387-6466 *SIC 5082*
ALBERTA PETROLEUM INDUSTRIES LTD *p108*
6607 59 ST NW, EDMONTON, AB, T6B 3P8
(780) 436-9693 *SIC 5082*
ALO CANADA INC *p760*
8485 MONTROSE RD, NIAGARA FALLS, ON, L2H 3L7
(800) 361-7563 *SIC 5082*
ALPA EQUIPMENT COMPANY LIMITED *p394*
258 DRAPEAU ST, BALMORAL, NB, E8E 1H3
(506) 826-2717 *SIC 5082*
ARROW-WEST EQUIPMENT LTD *p1*
53016 HWY 60 UNIT 109, ACHESON, AB, T7X 5A7
(780) 962-4490 *SIC 5082*
ASPHALTE, BETON, CARRIERES RIVE-NORD INC *p1291*
134 RTE DU LONG-SAULT, SAINT-ANDRE-D'ARGENTEUIL, QC, J0V 1X0
(450) 258-4242 *SIC 5082*
ATLAS COPCO CANADA INC *p647*
200 MUMFORD RD SUITE A, LIVELY, ON, P3Y 1L2
(705) 673-6711 *SIC 5082*
ATLAS COPCO CANADA INC *p737*
1025 TRISTAR DR, MISSISSAUGA, ON, L5T 1W5
(289) 562-0100 *SIC 5082*
ATLAS COPCO CANADA INC *p737*
1025 TRISTAR DR, MISSISSAUGA, ON, L5T 1W5
(289) 562-0100 *SIC 5082*
BLACK SUN RISING INC *p113*
10548 82 AVE NW SUITE G, EDMONTON, AB, T6E 2A4
SIC 5082
C & T RENTALS & SALES LTD *p377*
116 WHEATFIELD RD, WINNIPEG, MB, R3C 2E6
(204) 594-7368 *SIC 5082*
CALROC INDUSTRIES INC *p143*
6847 66 ST, LLOYDMINSTER, AB, T9V 3R7
(780) 875-8802 *SIC 5082*
CARIBOU ROAD SERVICES LTD *p248*
5201 52ND AVE, POUCE COUPE, BC, V0C 2C0
(250) 786-5440 *SIC 5082*
CARRIERE INDUSTRIAL SUPPLY LIMITED *p647*
190 MAGILL ST, LIVELY, ON, P3Y 1K7

(705) 692-4784 *SIC 5082*
CATERPILLAR OF CANADA CORPORATION *p1030*
3700 STEELES AVE W SUITE 902, WOODBRIDGE, ON, L4L 8K8
(905) 265-5802 *SIC 5082*
CERVUS CONTRACTORS EQUIPMENT LTD *p76*
333 96 AVE NE SUITE 5201, CALGARY, AB, T3K 0S3
(877) 567-0339 *SIC 5082*
CERVUS EQUIPMENT CORP *p76*
333 96 AVE NE UNIT 5201, CALGARY, AB, T3K 0S3
(403) 567-0339 *SIC 5082*
CFO RENTALS INC *p1437*
GD LCD MAIN, WEYBURN, SK, S4H 2J7
(306) 842-3454 *SIC 5082*
COMMERCIAL EQUIPMENT CORP *p205*
591 CHESTER RD, DELTA, BC, V3M 6G7
(604) 526-6126 *SIC 5082*
CREIGHTON ROCK DRILL LIMITED *p734*
2222 DREW RD, MISSISSAUGA, ON, L5S 1B1
(905) 673-8200 *SIC 5082*
CUBEX LIMITED *p369*
42 ST PAUL BLVD, WINNIPEG, MB, R2P 2W5
(204) 336-0008 *SIC 5082*
CUSTOM ENERGIZED AIR LTD *p113*
9555 62 AVE NW, EDMONTON, AB, T6E 0E1
(780) 465-2247 *SIC 5082*
DE RIGUEUR INC *p622*
2521 BOWMAN ST, INNISFIL, ON, L9S 0E9
(705) 733-7700 *SIC 5082*
DENDROTIK INC *p1274*
3083 CH DES QUATRE-BOURGEOIS BUREAU 100, QUEBEC, QC, G1W 2K6
(418) 653-7066 *SIC 5082*
DIRECT EQUIPMENT LTD *p800*
1363 CORNWALL RD, OAKVILLE, ON, L6J 7T5
(905) 844-7831 *SIC 5082*
DORSON LTEE *p1048*
8551 BOUL PARKWAY, ANJOU, QC, H1J 1N1
(514) 351-0160 *SIC 5082*
EPIROC CANADA INC *p739*
1025 TRISTAR DR, MISSISSAUGA, ON, L5T 1W5
(289) 562-0100 *SIC 5082*
EQUIPMENT CORPS INC *p892*
1256 ARVIN AVE, STONEY CREEK, ON, L8E 0H7
(905) 545-1234 *SIC 5082*
EQUIPMENT SALES & SERVICE LIMITED *p584*
1030 MARTIN GROVE RD, ETOBICOKE, ON, M9W 4W3
(416) 249-8141 *SIC 5082*
FGI SUPPLY LTD *p1435*
3914 THATCHER AVE SUITE LBBY, SASKATOON, SK, S7R 1A4
(306) 931-7880 *SIC 5082*
FINNING INTERNATIONAL INC *p79*
7601 99 ST, CLAIRMONT, AB, T8X 5B1
(780) 831-2600 *SIC 5082*
FRONTLINE MACHINERY LTD *p197*
43779 PROGRESS WAY, CHILLIWACK, BC, V2R 0E6
(604) 625-2009 *SIC 5082*
GEKKO SYSTEMS INC *p313*
1112 PENDER ST W SUITE 908, VANCOUVER, BC, V6E 2S1
(604) 681-2288 *SIC 5082*
GROUPE PROCAN EQUIPEMENT INC *p1152*
11700 RUE DE L'AVENIR BUREAU 204, MIRABEL, QC, J7J 0G7
(450) 420-1119 *SIC 5082*
HOOD LOGGING EQUIPMENT CANADA INCORPORATED *p908*
GD STN CSC, THUNDER BAY, ON, P7B

5E6
(807) 939-2641 *SIC 5082*
HURLEY MINING EQUIPMENT & SERVICES INC *p647*
10 NELSON RD, LIVELY, ON, P3Y 1M1
(705) 682-0681 *SIC 5082*
INLAND KENWORTH LTD *p186*
2482 DOUGLAS RD, BURNABY, BC, V5C 6C9
(604) 291-6021 *SIC 5082*
INTEGRATED DISTRIBUTION SYSTEMS LIMITED PARTNERSHIP *p703*
1865 SHARLYN RD, MISSISSAUGA, ON, L4X 1R1
(905) 624-5611 *SIC 5082*
J & L SUPPLY CO. LTD *p30*
4511 MANITOBA RD SE, CALGARY, AB, T2G 4B9
(403) 287-3300 *SIC 5082*
J. R. BRISSON EQUIPMENT LTD *p1002*
121 ST PIERRE RD, VARS, ON, K0A 3H0
(613) 443-3300 *SIC 5082*
JASCO SALES INC *p740*
1680 BONHILL RD, MISSISSAUGA, ON, L5T 1C8
(905) 677-4032 *SIC 5082*
LEGAULT METAL INC *p1384*
2 CH BOURGEOIS O, TRECESSON, QC, J0Y 2S0
(819) 732-8818 *SIC 5082*
LIEBHERR-CANADA LTD *p523*
1015 SUTTON DR, BURLINGTON, ON, L7L 5Z8
(905) 319-9222 *SIC 5082*
LOCATION BLAIS INC *p1289*
792 AV QUEBEC, ROUYN-NORANDA, QC, J9X 7B1
(819) 797-9292 *SIC 5082*
MACHINES ROGER INTERNATIONAL INC *p1390*
1161 RUE DES MANUFACTURIERS, VAL-D'OR, QC, J9P 6Y7
(819) 825-4657 *SIC 5082*
MALMBERG TRUCK TRAILER EQUIPMENT LTD *p816*
1621 MICHAEL ST, OTTAWA, ON, K1B 3T3
(613) 741-3360 *SIC 5082*
MANSOUR MINING TECHNOLOGIES INC *p901*
2502 ELM, SUDBURY, ON, P3E 4R8
(705) 682-0671 *SIC 5082*
MASLACK SUPPLY LIMITED *p898*
488 FALCONBRIDGE RD, SUDBURY, ON, P3A 4S4
(705) 566-1270 *SIC 5082*
MOBILE PARTS INC *p1001*
2472 EVANS RD, VAL CARON, ON, P3N 1P5
(705) 897-4955 *SIC 5082*
NORTHERN DOCK SYSTEMS INC *p741*
415 AMBASSADOR DR, MISSISSAUGA, ON, L5T 2J3
(905) 625-1758 *SIC 5082*
NORTRAX CANADA INC *p698*
1655 BRITANNIA RD E SUITE 155, MISSISSAUGA, ON, L4W 1S5
(905) 670-1655 *SIC 5082*
NOVA INTERNATIONAL LIMITED *p470*
4449 HIGHWAY 1 RR 2, WINDSOR, NS, B0N 2T0
(902) 798-9544 *SIC 5082*
OAKEN HOLDINGS INC *p505*
241 DEERHURST DR, BRAMPTON, ON, L6T 5K3
(416) 679-4172 *SIC 5082*
PHQ GLOBAL INC *p524*
1175 APPLEBY LINE UNIT C2, BURLINGTON, ON, L7L 5H9
(905) 332-3271 *SIC 5082*
PLATE 2000 INC *p1292*
1239 RTE BEGIN, SAINT-ANSELME, QC, G0R 2N0
(418) 885-0085 *SIC 5082*
Q2 ARTIFICIAL LIFT SERVICES ULC *p156*

7883 EDGAR INDUSTRIAL WAY, RED DEER, AB, T4P 3R2

(403) 343-8802   *SIC 5082*

QUADCO INC   *p1302*
30 BOUL INDUSTRIEL, SAINT-EUSTACHE, QC, J7R 5C1

(450) 623-3340   *SIC 5082*

R.C. MOFFATT SUPPLY LIMITED   *p909*
1135 RUSSELL ST, THUNDER BAY, ON, P7B 5M6

(807) 626-0040   *SIC 5082*

RAPTOR MINING PRODUCTS INC   *p102*
18131 AVE NW SUITE 118, EDMONTON, AB, T5S 1M8

(780) 444-1284   *SIC 5082*

ROCKY MOUNTAIN DEALERSHIPS INC *p31*
3345 8 ST SE SUITE 301, CALGARY, AB, T2G 3A4

(403) 265-7364   *SIC 5082*

ROCKY MOUNTAIN DEALERSHIPS INC *p142*
3939 1 AVE S, LETHBRIDGE, AB, T1J 4P8

(403) 327-3154   *SIC 5082*

ROCKY MOUNTAIN DEALERSHIPS INC *p160*
260180 WRITING CREEK CRES, ROCKY VIEW COUNTY, AB, T4A 0M9

(403) 513-7000   *SIC 5082*

SANDVIK CANADA, INC   *p764*
400 KIRKPATRICK ST SUITE B, NORTH BAY, ON, P1B 8G5

SIC 5082

SERVICE D'EQUIPEMENT G.D. INC   *p1293*
104 RUE D'ANVERS, SAINT-AUGUSTIN-DE-DESMAURES, QC, G3A 1S4

(418) 681-0080   *SIC 5082*

SHEARFORCE EQUIPMENT   *p177*
2707 PROGRESSIVE WAY SUITE 107, ABBOTSFORD, BC, V2T 0A7

(604) 855-5101   *SIC 5082*

SKYWAY CANADA LIMITED   *p588*
170 CLAIREVILLE DR, ETOBICOKE, ON, M9W 5Y3

(416) 744-6000   *SIC 5082*

SMS CONSTRUCTION AND MINING SYSTEMS INC   *p2*
53113 RANGE ROAD 263A, ACHESON, AB, T7X 5A5

(780) 948-2200   *SIC 5082*

SMS EQUIPMENT INC   *p2*
11285 274 ST, ACHESON, AB, T7X 6P9

(780) 454-0101   *SIC 5082*

SMS EQUIPMENT INC   *p97*
16116 111 AVE NW, EDMONTON, AB, T5M 2S1

(780) 451-2630   *SIC 5082*

SMS EQUIPMENT INC   *p129*
22K HIGHWAY 63 NORTH, FORT MCMURRAY, AB, T9H 3G2

(780) 714-5300   *SIC 5082*

SOUTHSTAR EQUIPMENT LTD   *p218*
728 TAGISH ST, KAMLOOPS, BC, V2H 1B7

(250) 828-7820   *SIC 5082*

STANMORE EQUIPMENT LIMITED   *p895*
3 ANDERSON BLVD, STOUFFVILLE, ON, L4A 7X4

(416) 291-1928   *SIC 5082*

STRONGCO LIMITED PARTNERSHIP *p700*
1640 ENTERPRISE RD, MISSISSAUGA, ON, L4W 4L4

(905) 670-5100   *SIC 5082*

SUREWAY LOGGING LTD   *p138*
GD, LA CRETE, AB, T0H 2H0

(780) 539-0388   *SIC 5082*

TECHNOLOGIES ELEMENT PSW INC *p1391*
1117 RUE DES MANUFACTURIERS, VAL-D'OR, QC, J9P 6Y7

(819) 825-1117   *SIC 5082*

THIESSEN EQUIPMENT LTD   *p228*
20131 LOGAN AVE, LANGLEY, BC, V3A 4L5

(604) 532-8611   *SIC 5082*

TOROMONT INDUSTRIES LTD   *p401*
165 URQUHART CRES, FREDERICTON,

NB, E3B 8K4

(506) 452-6651   *SIC 5082*

TOROMONT INDUSTRIES LTD   *p427*
24 THIRD ST, MOUNT PEARL, NL, A1N 2A5

(709) 282-5537   *SIC 5082*

TOROMONT INDUSTRIES LTD   *p448*
175 AKERLEY BLVD, DARTMOUTH, NS, B3B 3Z6

(902) 468-0581   *SIC 5082*

TOROMONT INDUSTRIES LTD   *p559*
3131 HIGHWAY 7 SUITE A, CONCORD, ON, L4K 5E1

(416) 667-5511   *SIC 5082*

TOROMONT INDUSTRIES LTD   *p559*
548 EDGELEY BLVD, CONCORD, ON, L4K 4G4

(416) 667-5900   *SIC 5082*

TOROMONT INDUSTRIES LTD   *p625*
5 EDGEWATER ST, KANATA, ON, K2L 1V7

(613) 836-5171   *SIC 5082*

TOROMONT INDUSTRIES LTD   *p647*
25 MUMFORD RD, LIVELY, ON, P3Y 1K9

(705) 692-4764   *SIC 5082*

TOROMONT INDUSTRIES LTD   *p1073*
350 AV LIBERTE, CANDIAC, QC, J5R 6X1

(450) 638-6091   *SIC 5082*

TOROMONT INDUSTRIES LTD   *p1252*
4000 AUT TRANSCANADIENNE, POINTE-CLAIRE, QC, H9R 1B2

(514) 426-6700   *SIC 5082*

TOROMONT INDUSTRIES LTD   *p1293*
100 RUE DE ROTTERDAM, SAINT-AUGUSTIN-DE-DESMAURES, QC, G3A 1T2

(418) 878-3000   *SIC 5082*

TOROMONT INDUSTRIES LTD   *p1391*
1200 3E AV E, VAL-D'OR, QC, J9P 0J6

(819) 825-5494   *SIC 5082*

TRACKS & WHEELS EQUIPMENT BROKERS INC   *p899*
400 HWY 69 N, SUDBURY, ON, P3A 4S9

(705) 566-5438   *SIC 5082*

TWD ROADS MANAGEMENT INC   *p631*
1010 MIDDLE RD, KINGSTON, ON, K7L 4V3

SIC 5082

TWIN EQUIPMENT LTD   *p827*
3091 ALBION RD N, OTTAWA, ON, K1V 9V9

(613) 745-7095   *SIC 5082*

VARIPERM (CANADA) LIMITED   *p10*
3424 26 ST NE SUITE 10, CALGARY, AB, T1Y 4T7

(403) 250-7263   *SIC 5082*

WEST COAST MACHINERY LTD   *p230*
27050 GLOUCESTER WAY, LANGLEY, BC, V4W 3Y5

(604) 855-5101   *SIC 5082*

WEST KOOTENAY DISTRICT OFFICE *p236*
310 WARD ST SUITE 400, NELSON, BC, V1L 5S4

(250) 354-6521   *SIC 5082*

WIG'S PUMPS AND WATERWORKS LTD *p1430*
227B VENTURE CRES, SASKATOON, SK, S7K 6N8

(306) 652-4276   *SIC 5082*

WILSON EQUIPMENT LIMITED   *p449*
66 ATLANTIC CENTRAL DR, EAST MOUNTAIN, NS, B6L 2A3

(902) 895-1611   *SIC 5082*

SIC 5083 Farm and garden machinery

125668 CANADA INC   *p1389*
292 RUE PRINCIPALE, UPTON, QC, J0H 2E0

(450) 549-5811   *SIC 5083*

1777621 ONTARIO INC   *p594*
73 MAIN ST, GLENCOE, ON, N0L 1M0

(519) 913-5420   *SIC 5083*

609905 SASKATCHEWAN LTD   *p1408*

30 HIGHWAY 3, KINISTINO, SK, S0J 1H0

(306) 864-2200   *SIC 5083*

AESTHETICS LANDSCAPE CONTRACTORS   *p891*
1092 HIGHWAY 8, STONEY CREEK, ON, L8E 5H8

(905) 643-9933   *SIC 5083*

AGCO CANADA, LTD   *p1415*
515 DEWDNEY AVE, REGINA, SK, S4N 6S1

(306) 757-2681   *SIC 5083*

AGLAND CORP   *p143*
HWY 16, LLOYDMINSTER, AB, T9V 3A2

(780) 874-4154   *SIC 5083*

AGRITIBI R.H. INC   *p1045*
2711 RTE 111 E BUREAU 2, AMOS, QC, J9T 3A1

(819) 732-6296   *SIC 5083*

ATLANTIC TRAILER & EQUIPMENT LTD *p425*
8 LINTROS PL, MOUNT PEARL, NL, A1N 5K2

(709) 745-3260   *SIC 5083*

AUBIN & ST-PIERRE INC   *p1123*
350 RUE RAYGO, LA PRESENTATION, QC, J0H 1B0

(450) 796-2966   *SIC 5083*

AVENUE MACHINERY CORP   *p174*
1521 SUMAS WAY, ABBOTSFORD, BC, V2S 8M9

(604) 792-4111   *SIC 5083*

BRABER EQUIPMENT LTD   *p174*
34425 MCCONNELL RD SUITE 117, ABBOTSFORD, BC, V2S 7P1

(604) 850-7770   *SIC 5083*

BRINDLEY AUCTION SERVICE LTD   *p567*
37110 DUNGANNON RD, DUNGANNON, ON, N0M 1R0

(519) 529-7625   *SIC 5083*

BRYAN'S FARM & INDUSTRIAL SUPPLY LTD   *p849*
4062 HIGHWAY 6 RR 2, PUSLINCH, ON, N0B 2J0

(519) 837-0710   *SIC 5083*

BURNABY LAKE GREENHOUSES LTD *p281*
17250 80 AVE, SURREY, BC, V4N 6J6

(604) 576-2088   *SIC 5083*

CANADA WEST HARVEST CENTRE INC *p1406*
8 INDUSTRIAL DR, EMERALD PARK, SK, S4L 1B6

(306) 525-2300   *SIC 5083*

CANADIAN TEST CASE 120-TEST   *p720*
6750 CENTURY AVE SUITE 305, MISSISSAUGA, ON, L5N 0B7

(905) 812-5920   *SIC 5083*

CANAGRO EXPORTS INC   *p361*
24084 HWY 3 E, WINKLER, MB, R6W 4B1

(204) 325-5090   *SIC 5083*

CATONS LTD   *p138*
3806 53 AVE, LACOMBE, AB, T4L 0A9

(403) 786-9999   *SIC 5083*

CENTRAL IRRIGATION SUPPLY OF CANADA INC   *p550*
272 BRADWICK DR, CONCORD, ON, L4K 1K8

(905) 532-0977   *SIC 5083*

CENTRE AGRICOLE COATICOOK INC *p1081*
525 RUE MAIN O, COATICOOK, QC, J1A 1R2

(819) 849-2663   *SIC 5083*

CENTRE AGRICOLE J.L.D. INC   *p1232*
3900 SUD LAVAL (A-440) E, MONTREAL, QC, H7E 5N2

(514) 373-4899   *SIC 5083*

CENTRE AGRICOLE NICOLET-YAMASKA INC   *p1242*
2025 BOUL LOUIS-FRECHETTE, NICOLET, QC, J3T 1M4

(819) 293-4441   *SIC 5083*

CLARK AG SYSTEMS LTD   *p532*
186 GREENS RD, CALEDONIA, ON, N3W 1X2

(905) 765-4401   *SIC 5083*

COMPAGNIE D'ENTRETIEN BRITE-LITE LTEE   *p1361*
940 RUE BERGAR, SAINTE-ROSE, QC, H7L 4Z8

(450) 669-3803   *SIC 5083*

COMPTOIR AGRICOLE DE ST-HYACINTHE *p1313*
4420 RUE SAINT-PIERRE O, SAINT-HYACINTHE, QC, J2T 5G8

SIC 5083

CONESTOGO AGRI SYSTEMS INC   *p476*
7506 WELLINGTON ROAD 11, ALMA, ON, N0B 1A0

(519) 638-3022   *SIC 5083*

CONSOLIDATED TURF EQUIPMENT (1965) LTD   *p383*
986 POWELL AVE, WINNIPEG, MB, R3H 0H6

(204) 633-7276   *SIC 5083*

COOP PURDEL, LA   *p1284*
155 RUE SAINT-JEAN-BAPTISTE E, RIMOUSKI, QC, G5L 1Y7

(418) 736-4363   *SIC 5083*

DAIRYLAND AGRO SUPPLY LTD   *p1435*
4030 THATCHER AVE, SASKATOON, SK, S7R 1A2

(306) 242-5850   *SIC 5083*

DEERLAND FARM EQUIPMENT (1985) LTD *p130*
8599 112 ST, FORT SASKATCHEWAN, AB, T8L 3V3

(780) 998-3249   *SIC 5083*

DEMUTH STEEL PRODUCTS INC   *p1008*
419 ALBERT ST, WATERLOO, ON, N2L 3V2

(519) 884-2980   *SIC 5083*

DISTRIBUTION JEAN BLANCHARD INC *p1375*
1686 CH LALIBERTE, SHERBROOKE, QC, J1R 0C5

(819) 820-9777   *SIC 5083*

DORTMANS BROS. BARN EQUIP. INC *p897*
2234 EGREMONT DR SUITE 5, STRATHROY, ON, N7G 3H6

(519) 247-3435   *SIC 5083*

DOUGLAS LAKE EQUIPMENT LIMITED PARTNERSHIP   *p211*
111 DOUGLAS LAKE RD, DOUGLAS LAKE, BC, V0E 1S0

(250) 851-2044   *SIC 5083*

DU-RITE MOTORS LIMITED   *p346*
237 MILL RD, BOISSEVAIN, MB, R0K 0E0

(204) 534-2929   *SIC 5083*

DYTERRA CORPORATION   *p351*
7501 WILKES AVE, HEADINGLEY, MB, R4H 1B8

(204) 885-8260   *SIC 5083*

E. BOURASSA & SONS PARTNERSHIP *p1415*
HWY 28 S, RADVILLE, SK, S0C 2G0

(306) 869-2277   *SIC 5083*

EARTH POWER TRACTORS AND EQUIPMENT INC   *p681*
206005 HWY 26 W, MEAFORD, ON, N4L 1A5

(519) 538-1660   *SIC 5083*

EDMONTON KUBOTA LTD   *p105*
15550 128 AVE NW, EDMONTON, AB, T5V 1S7

(780) 443-3800   *SIC 5083*

ELJAY IRRIGATION LTD   *p15*
3700 78 AVE SE SUITE 3, CALGARY, AB, T2C 2L8

(403) 279-2425   *SIC 5083*

ENNS BROTHERS LTD   *p353*
400 FORT WHYTE WAY UNIT 310, OAK BLUFF, MB, R4G 0B1

(204) 895-0212   *SIC 5083*

ENNS BROTHERS LTD   *p388*
55 ROTHWELL RD, WINNIPEG, MB, R3P 2M5

(204) 475-3667   *SIC 5083*

ENTREPRISES ANTONIO LAPORTE & FILS INC, LES   *p1243*

---

501 RTE 131, NOTRE-DAME-DES-PRAIRIES, QC, J6E 0M1
(450) 756-1779 *SIC 5083*

EQUIPEMENTS A. PROVENCHER & FILS INC, LES *p1246*
2175 RUE SAINT-JEAN, PLESSISVILLE, QC, G6L 2Y4
(819) 225-0225 *SIC 5083*

EQUIPEMENTS ADRIEN PHANEUF INC, LES *p1389*
292 RUE PRINCIPALE, UPTON, QC, J0H 2E0
(450) 549-5811 *SIC 5083*

EQUIPEMENTS LAGUE & MARTIN INC *p1392*
555 BOUL LIONEL-BOULET, VARENNES, QC, J3X 1P7
(450) 929-2382 *SIC 5083*

EQUIPEMENTS LAPLANTE & LEVESQUE LTEE, LES *p1244*
780 RTE 201, ORMSTOWN, QC, J0S 1K0
(450) 829-3516 *SIC 5083*

FARM-FLEET INC *p888*
23703 WELLBURN RD RR 3, ST MARYS, ON, N4X 1C6
(519) 461-1499 *SIC 5083*

FAWCETT TRACTOR SUPPLY LTD *p888*
2126 ROAD 120, ST MARYS, ON, N4X 1C5
(519) 284-2379 *SIC 5083*

FRIESEN EQUIPMENT LTD *p175*
339 SUMAS WAY, ABBOTSFORD, BC, V2S 8E5
(604) 864-9844 *SIC 5083*

FULLINE FARM & GARDEN EQUIPMENT LTD *p594*
21911 SIMPSON RD, GLENCOE, ON, N0L 1M0
(519) 287-2840 *SIC 5083*

FUTURE AG INC *p157*
69 BELICH CRES, RED DEER, AB, T4S 2K5
(403) 343-6101 *SIC 5083*

G. C. DUKE EQUIPMENT LTD *p531*
1184 PLAINS RD E, BURLINGTON, ON, L7S 1W6
(905) 637-5216 *SIC 5083*

GIROUARD, ANDRE & FILS INC *p1399*
650 BOUL PIERRE-ROUX E, VICTORIAVILLE, QC, G6T 1T2
(819) 758-0643 *SIC 5083*

GREEN DIAMOND EQUIPMENT *p410*
70 COMMERCE ST, MONCTON, NB, E1H 0A5
(506) 388-3337 *SIC 5083*

GREEN LEA AG CENTER INC *p746*
324055 MOUNT ELGIN RD, MOUNT ELGIN, ON, N0J 1N0
(519) 485-6861 *SIC 5083*

GUERTIN EQUIPMENT LTD *p392*
35 MELNICK RD, WINNIPEG, MB, R3X 1V5
(204) 255-0260 *SIC 5083*

HANLON AG CENTRE LTD *p140*
3005 18 AVE N, LETHBRIDGE, AB, T1H 5V2
(403) 329-8686 *SIC 5083*

HARKNESS, JIM EQUIPMENT LTD *p618*
5808 HIGHWAY 9 RR 4, HARRISTON, ON, N0G 1Z0
(519) 338-3946 *SIC 5083*

HI LINE FARM EQUIPMENT LTD *p172*
4723 39 AVE, WETASKIWIN, AB, T9A 2J4
(780) 352-9244 *SIC 5083*

HURON TRACTOR LTD *p590*
39995 HARVEST RD, EXETER, ON, N0M 1S3
(519) 235-1115 *SIC 5083*

J.R. CAZA & FRERE INC *p1291*
3755 RTE 132, SAINT-ANICET, QC, J0S 1M0
(450) 264-2300 *SIC 5083*

JOHN BOB FARM EQUIPMENT LTD *p1437*
HWY 3 W, TISDALE, SK, S0E 1T0
(306) 873-4588 *SIC 5083*

JONKMAN EQUIPMENT LTD *p178*

28355 FRASER HWY, ABBOTSFORD, BC, V4X 1K9
(604) 857-2000 *SIC 5083*

JOYAL, CLAUDE INC *p1306*
1 RUE PRINCIPALE, SAINT-GUILLAUME, QC, J0C 1L0
(819) 396-2161 *SIC 5083*

KEARNEY, B. R. ENTERPRISES LTD *p903*
14232 TURIN LINE, THAMESVILLE, ON, N0P 2K0
(519) 678-3206 *SIC 5083*

KENSINGTON AGRICULTURAL SERVICES LTD *p1041*
15 PARK RD, KENSINGTON, PE, C0B 1M0
(902) 836-3212 *SIC 5083*

KUCERA FARM SUPPLY LIMITED *p477*
3212 NAUVOO RD, ALVINSTON, ON, N0N 1A0
(519) 898-2961 *SIC 5083*

LAFOND, J.-RENE INC *p1153*
3203 CH CHARLES-LEONARD, MIRABEL, QC, J7N 2Y7
(450) 258-2448 *SIC 5083*

LASALLE, RAYMOND INC *p1353*
1561 RTE 158, SAINT-THOMAS, QC, J0K 3L0
(450) 756-2121 *SIC 5083*

LELY CANADA INC *p1036*
1015 RIDGEWAY RD, WOODSTOCK, ON, N4V 1E2
(519) 602-6737 *SIC 5083*

LEO'S SALES & SERVICE LTD *p378*
STURGEON RD & HWY 101, WINNIPEG, MB, R3C 2E6
(204) 694-4978 *SIC 5083*

MACHINERIE C. & H. INC *p1306*
12 RTE 122, SAINT-GUILLAUME, QC, J0C 1L0
(819) 396-2185 *SIC 5083*

MACHINERIES NORDTRAC LTEE *p1294*
1060 MONTEE SAINT-LAURENT, SAINT-BARTHELEMY, QC, J0K 1X0
(450) 885-3202 *SIC 5083*

MACLEOD'S FARM MACHINERY LIMITED *p461*
12412 HWY 2, LOWER ONSLOW, NS, B6L 5E3
(902) 662-2516 *SIC 5083*

MCGAVIN FARM EQUIPMENT LTD *p1005*
83145 BRUSSELS LINE, WALTON, ON, N0K 1Z0
(519) 887-6365 *SIC 5083*

MELBOURNE FARM AUTOMATION LTD *p681*
6687 LONGWOODS RD, MELBOURNE, ON, N0L 1T0
(519) 289-5256 *SIC 5083*

MILLER EQUIPMENT LTD *p1411*
1604 PARK AVE, MOOSOMIN, SK, S0G 3N0
(306) 435-3866 *SIC 5083*

MILLER FARM EQUIPMENT 2005 INC *p1411*
GD, MOOSOMIN, SK, S0G 3N0
(306) 435-3866 *SIC 5083*

MMD SALES LTD *p101*
17104 118 AVE NW, EDMONTON, AB, T5S 2L7
(780) 452-2790 *SIC 5083*

MOODY'S EQUIPMENT LP *p1428*
71ST ST HWY 16, SASKATOON, SK, S7K 3K1
(306) 934-4686 *SIC 5083*

MOODY'S EQUIPMENT LTD *p1428*
71 ST & HWY SUITE 16, SASKATOON, SK, S7K 3K1
(306) 934-4686 *SIC 5083*

MTD PRODUCTS LIMITED *p638*
97 KENT AVE, KITCHENER, ON, N2G 3R2
(519) 579-5500 *SIC 5083*

MTD PRODUCTS LIMITED *p638*
97 KANT AVE, KITCHENER, ON, N2G 4J1
(519) 579-5500 *SIC 5083*

MTI CANADA INC *p1138*
1720 BOUL GUILLAUME-COUTURE,

LEVIS, QC, G6W 5M6
(418) 839-4127 *SIC 5083*

NEW-WAY IRRIGATION LTD *p169*
6003 54 AVE, TABER, AB, T1G 1X4
(403) 223-3591 *SIC 5083*

NIEBOER FARM SUPPLIES (1977) LTD *p150*
233016 HWY 519, NOBLEFORD, AB, T0L 1S0
(403) 824-3404 *SIC 5083*

NORDSTRONG EQUIPMENT LIMITED *p368*
5 CHESTER ST, WINNIPEG, MB, R2L 1W5
(204) 667-1553 *SIC 5083*

NORMAC EQUIPMENT SALES LTD *p198*
8409 KALAVISTA DR, COLDSTREAM, BC, V1B 1K4
(250) 542-4726 *SIC 5083*

NORSASK FARM EQUIPMENT LTD *p1412*
HWY 16 EAST, NORTH BATTLEFORD, SK, S9A 2M4
(306) 445-8128 *SIC 5083*

NORTHERN ACREAGE SUPPLY LTD *p251*
4870 CONTINENTAL WAY, PRINCE GEORGE, BC, V2N 5S5
(250) 596-2273 *SIC 5083*

NORTHQUIP INC *p393*
141 RAILWAY AVE, WOODLANDS, MB, R0C 3H0
(866) 383-7827 *SIC 5083*

NORWELL DAIRY SYSTEMS LTD *p565*
37 DRAYTON INDUSTRIAL DR, DRAYTON, ON, N0G 1P0
(519) 638-3535 *SIC 5083*

NOVLAN BROS SALES INC *p1413*
GD, PARADISE HILL, SK, S0M 2G0
(877) 344-4433 *SIC 5083*

NOVLAN BROTHERS SALES PARTNERSHIP *p1413*
47 FIRST AVE, PARADISE HILL, SK, S0M 2G0
(306) 344-4448 *SIC 5083*

NUCOR SYSTEMS INC *p41*
918 16 AVE NW SUITE 349, CALGARY, AB, T2M 0K3
(403) 236-2824 *SIC 5083*

O'NEIL'S FARM EQUIPMENT (1971) LIMITED *p493*
2461 HWY 56, BINBROOK, ON, L0R 1C0
(905) 572-6714 *SIC 5083*

PACIFIC DAIRY CENTRE LTD *p197*
8558 CHILLIWACK MOUNTAIN RD, CHILLIWACK, BC, V2R 3W8
(604) 852-9020 *SIC 5083*

PARTNER AG SERVICES LTD *p902*
3694 BRUCE RD 10, TARA, ON, N0H 2N0
(519) 934-2343 *SIC 5083*

PATTISON AGRICULTURE LIMITED *p1438*
580 YORK RD W HWY 16, YORKTON, SK, S3N 2V7
(306) 783-9459 *SIC 5083*

PENNER FARM SERVICES (AVONBANK) LTD *p598*
15456 ELGINFIELD RD RR 3, GRANTON, ON, N0M 1V0
(519) 225-2507 *SIC 5083*

PENTA EQUIPMENT INC *p843*
4480 PROGRESS DR, PETROLIA, ON, N0N 1R0
(519) 882-3350 *SIC 5083*

PRAIRIECOAST EQUIPMENT INC *p133*
15102 101 ST, GRANDE PRAIRIE, AB, T8V 0P7
(780) 532-8402 *SIC 5083*

PRAIRIECOAST EQUIPMENT INC *p197*
44158 PROGRESS WAY, CHILLIWACK, BC, V2R 0W3
(604) 792-1516 *SIC 5083*

RANCHERS SUPPLY INC *p152*
1165 MAIN ST, PINCHER CREEK, AB, T0K 1W0
(403) 627-4451 *SIC 5083*

RAYNARD FARM EQUIPMENT LTD *p1436*
2524 SOUTH SERVICE RD W, SWIFT CURRENT, SK, S9H 5J9
(306) 773-3030 *SIC 5083*

REDDIN FARM EQUIPMENT LTD *p1042*
237 MASON RD, STRATFORD, PE, C1B 2G1
(902) 569-2500 *SIC 5083*

REIMER FARM SUPPLIES LTD *p358*
340 PTH 12 N, STEINBACH, MB, R5G 1T6
(204) 326-1305 *SIC 5083*

REIS, H.J. INTERNATIONAL LTD *p849*
479 O'BRIEN RD, RENFREW, ON, K7V 3Z3
(613) 432-4133 *SIC 5083*

RICHARDSON INTERNATIONAL (QUEBEC) LIMITEE *p1376*
10 RUE DE LA REINE, SOREL-TRACY, QC, J3P 4R2
(450) 743-3893 *SIC 5083*

ROBERT'S FARM EQUIPMENT SALES INC *p544*
14945 COUNTY RD 10, CHESLEY, ON, N0G 1L0
(519) 363-3192 *SIC 5083*

ROCKY MOUNTAIN DEALERSHIPS INC *p135*
4802 57TH AVE, GRIMSHAW, AB, T0H 1W0
(780) 332-4691 *SIC 5083*

S. H. DAYTON LTD *p356*
144 INDUSTRIAL RD, SHOAL LAKE, MB, R0J 1Z0
(204) 759-2065 *SIC 5083*

SERVICE AGROMECANIQUE INC *p1297*
24 RUE PRINCIPALE O, SAINT-CLEMENT, QC, G0L 2N0
(418) 963-2177 *SIC 5083*

STEWART'S NEW HOLLAND LTD *p569*
9410 WELLINGTON RD 124, ERIN, ON, N0B 1T0
(519) 833-9384 *SIC 5083*

STOLTZ SALES & SERVICE (ELMIRA) LTD *p568*
GD LCD MAIN, ELMIRA, ON, N3B 2Z4
(519) 669-1561 *SIC 5083*

SYDOR FARM EQUIPMENT LTD *p349*
GD, DAUPHIN, MB, R7N 2T3
(204) 638-6443 *SIC 5083*

TRISTAR DAIRY CENTRE LTD *p350*
26147 WIENS RD, GRUNTHAL, MB, R0A 0R0
(204) 434-6801 *SIC 5083*

VANDEN BUSSCHE IRRIGATION & EQUIPMENT LIMITED *p564*
2515 PINEGROVE RD, DELHI, ON, N4B 2E5
(519) 582-2380 *SIC 5083*

VANDENBRINK FARM EQUIPMENT INC *p882*
7565 QUAKER RD, SPARTA, ON, N0L 2H0
(519) 775-2601 *SIC 5083*

VANDER ZAAG, H. J. FARM EQUIPMENT LTD *p476*
5900 COUNTY RD 10 SUITE 2, ALLISTON, ON, L9R 1V2
(705) 435-3226 *SIC 5083*

VANEE FARM CENTRE INC *p141*
510 36 ST N, LETHBRIDGE, AB, T1H 5H6
(403) 327-1100 *SIC 5083*

VINCENT FARM EQUIPMENT (SEAFORTH) INC *p879*
42787 HYDROLINE RD, SEAFORTH, ON, N0K 1W0
(519) 527-0120 *SIC 5083*

WALCO EQUIPMENT LTD *p568*
20 ARTHUR ST N, ELMIRA, ON, N3B 1Z9
(519) 669-4025 *SIC 5083*

WARDALE EQUIPMENT (1998) LTD *p1439*
230 BROADWAY ST E, YORKTON, SK, S3N 4C6
(306) 783-8508 *SIC 5083*

WESTERN SALES (1986) LTD *p1423*
405 HWY 7 W, ROSETOWN, SK, S0L 2V0
(306) 882-4291 *SIC 5083*

WESTERN TRACTOR COMPANY INC *p141*
3214 5 AVE N, LETHBRIDGE, AB, T1H 0P4
(403) 327-5512 *SIC 5083*

WESTWARD PARTS SERVICES LTD *p156*
6517 67 ST, RED DEER, AB, T4P 1A3

▲ Public Company   ■ Public Company Family Member   **HQ** Headquarters   **BR** Branch   **SL** Single Location

(403) 347-2200   *SIC* 5083
WHEAT BELT EQUIPMENT LTD   *p*347
10 CAMPBELL'S TRAILER CRT, BRANDON, MB, R7A 5Y5
(204) 725-2273   *SIC* 5083

WILMAR IMPLEMENT CO LTD   *p*153
5803 47 AVE, PROVOST, AB, T0B 3S0
(780) 753-2278   *SIC* 5083

YETMAN'S LTD   *p*373
949 JARVIS AVE, WINNIPEG, MB, R2X 0A1
(204) 586-8046   *SIC* 5083

SIC 5084 Industrial machinery and equipment

10079952 CANADA INC   *p*1327
2431 RUE GUENETTE, SAINT-LAURENT, QC, H4R 2E9
(514) 337-0566   *SIC* 5084

1124965 ONTARIO LTD   *p*489
800 ESSA RD, BARRIE, ON, L9J 0A8
(705) 728-9211   *SIC* 5084

120601 CANADA INC   *p*1040
26 FOURTH ST, CHARLOTTETOWN, PE, C1E 2B3
(902) 566-1220   *SIC* 5084

121352 CANADA INC   *p*1288
1156 AV LARIVIERE, ROUYN-NORANDA, QC, J9X 4K8
(819) 797-3300   *SIC* 5084

1253207 ALBERTA LTD   *p*27
4040 BLACKFOOT TRAIL SE SUITE 120, CALGARY, AB, T2G 4E6
(403) 252-5366   *SIC* 5084

1509611 ONTARIO INC   *p*547
577 EDGELEY BLVD SUITE 1, CONCORD, ON, L4K 4B2
(905) 660-4200   *SIC* 5084

2747-6035 QUEBEC INC   *p*1126
2302 52E AV, LACHINE, QC, H8T 2Y3
(514) 631-1988   *SIC* 5084

2778751 CANADA INC   *p*1354
220 RUE PRINCIPALE, SAINT-ZOTIQUE, QC, J0P 1Z0
(450) 267-5955   *SIC* 5084

2971038 CANADA INC   *p*1231
5535 RUE ERNEST-CORMIER, MONTREAL, QC, H7C 2S9
(450) 665-8780   *SIC* 5084

599681 SASKATCHEWAN LTD   *p*1417
HWY 1 E, REGINA, SK, S4P 3R8
(306) 791-7777   *SIC* 5084

6654100 CANADA INC   *p*1116
2400 RUE ALEXIS-LE-TROTTEUR, JONQUIERE, QC, G7X 0J7
(418) 542-6164   *SIC* 5084

9071-2670 QUEBEC INC   *p*1145
2400 CH DU LAC, LONGUEUIL, QC, J4N 1G8
(450) 670-5445   *SIC* 5084

9093451 CANADA INC   *p*1093
10475 CH COTE-DE-LIESSE, DORVAL, QC, H9P 1A7
(514) 685-9444   *SIC* 5084

9111735 CANADA INC   *p*816
1730 ST. LAURENT BLVD SUITE 800, OTTAWA, ON, K1G 5L1
(343) 996-8101   *SIC* 5084

9192-2773 QUEBEC INC   *p*1147
2620 RUE MACPHERSON, MAGOG, QC, J1X 0E6
(819) 868-4215   *SIC* 5084

990731 ONTARIO INC   *p*1034
1401 DUNDAS ST, WOODSTOCK, ON, N4S 7V9
(519) 537-8095   *SIC* 5084

995843 ONTARIO LTD   *p*736
6691 EDWARDS BLVD SUITE 1, MISSISSAUGA, ON, L5T 2H8
(905) 795-2610   *SIC* 5084

A.T.L.A.S. AERONAUTIQUE INC   *p*1108
420 RUE EDOUARD, GRANBY, QC, J2G 3Z3

(450) 378-8107   *SIC* 5084
ACCU-FLO METER SERVICE LTD   *p*27
4024 7 ST SE, CALGARY, AB, T2G 2Y8
(403) 243-1425   *SIC* 5084

ACE INSTRUMENTS LTD   *p*213
11207 TAHLTAN RD, FORT ST. JOHN, BC, V1J 6G8
(250) 785-1207   *SIC* 5084

ACIERS J.P. INC, LES   *p*1123
15 3E AV E, LA REINE, QC, J0Z 2L0
(819) 947-8291   *SIC* 5084

ACKLANDS - GRAINGER INC   *p*903
50 MINTHORN BLVD, THORNHILL, ON, L3T 7X8
(905) 763-3474   *SIC* 5084

ACTIVE EXHAUST CORP   *p*870
1865 BIRCHMOUNT RD, SCARBOROUGH, ON, M1P 2J5
(416) 445-9610   *SIC* 5084

ADF DIESEL MONTREAL INC   *p*1353
5 CH DE LA COTE-SAINT-PAUL, SAINT-STANISLAS-DE-CHAMPLAIN, QC, G0X 3E0
(418) 328-8713   *SIC* 5084

ADF DIESEL SAINT-STANISLAS INC   *p*1353
5 CH DE LA COTE-SAINT-PAUL, SAINT-STANISLAS-DE-CHAMPLAIN, QC, G0X 3E0
(418) 328-8713   *SIC* 5084

ADP DISTRIBUTORS INC   *p*281
18940 94 AVE SUITE 100, SURREY, BC, V4N 4X5
(604) 888-3726   *SIC* 5084

ADVANCED ENERGY MANAGEMENT LTD   *p*445
60 DOREY AVE SUITE 103, DARTMOUTH, NS, B3B 0B1
(902) 453-4498   *SIC* 5084

AGILENT TECHNOLOGIES CANADA INC   *p*719
6705 MILLCREEK DR UNIT 5, MISSISSAUGA, ON, L5N 5M4
(289) 290-3859   *SIC* 5084

AIR-SERV CANADA INC.   *p*501
80 DEVON RD UNIT 4, BRAMPTON, ON, L6T 5B3
   SIC 5084

AIRDEX CORP   *p*485
230 SAUNDERS RD, BARRIE, ON, L4N 9A2
   SIC 5084

AIRIA RESIDENTIAL SYSTEMS INC   *p*650
511 MCCORMICK BLVD, LONDON, ON, N5W 4C8
(519) 457-1904   *SIC* 5084

AKHURST HOLDINGS LIMITED   *p*205
1669 FOSTER'S WAY, DELTA, BC, V3M 6S7
(604) 540-1430   *SIC* 5084

AKHURST MACHINERY LIMITED   *p*112
9615 63 AVE NW, EDMONTON, AB, T6E 0G2
(780) 435-3936   *SIC* 5084

AKHURST MACHINERY LIMITED   *p*205
1669 FOSTER'S WAY, DELTA, BC, V3M 6S7
(604) 540-1430   *SIC* 5084

ALCOS MACHINERY INC   *p*754
190 HARRY WALKER PKY N, NEWMARKET, ON, L3Y 7B4
(905) 836-6030   *SIC* 5084

ALL-LIFT LTD   *p*508
320 CLARENCE ST SUITE 7-10, BRAMPTON, ON, L6W 1T5
(905) 459-5348   *SIC* 5084

ALLEGION CANADA INC   *p*582
51 WORCESTER RD, ETOBICOKE, ON, M9W 4K2
(800) 900-1434   *SIC* 5084

ALTEC INDUSTRIES LTD   *p*682
831 NIPISSING RD, MILTON, ON, L9T 4Z4
(905) 875-2000   *SIC* 5084

AMADA CANADA LTD   *p*1110
885 RUE GEORGES-CROS, GRANBY, QC, J2J 1E8
(450) 378-0111   *SIC* 5084

AMBYINT INC   *p*20
1440 AVIATION PK NE SUITE 119, CALGARY, AB, T2E 7E2

(800) 205-1311   *SIC* 5084
AMIMAC (2002) LTEE   *p*1116
3499 RUE DE L'ENERGIE, JONQUIERE, QC, G7X 0C1
(418) 542-3531   *SIC* 5084

ANDRITZ LTEE   *p*1127
2260 32E AV, LACHINE, QC, H8T 3H4
(514) 631-7700   *SIC* 5084

APEX DISTRIBUTION INC   *p*43
407 2 ST SW SUITE 550, CALGARY, AB, T2P 2Y3
(403) 268-7333   *SIC* 5084

AQUATECK WATER SYSTEMS DISTRIBUTORS LTD   *p*815
2700 LANCASTER RD SUITE 116, OTTAWA, ON, K1B 4T7
(613) 526-4613   *SIC* 5084

AQUIFER PUMP DISTRIBUTING LTD   *p*1426
227A VENTURE CRES, SASKATOON, SK, S7K 6N8
(306) 242-1567   *SIC* 5084

ARROW WELDING & INDUSTRIAL SUPPLIES INC   *p*99
17811 107 AVE NW, EDMONTON, AB, T5S 1R8
(780) 483-2050   *SIC* 5084

ASCENSEURS DESIGN INC   *p*1263
1865 RUE A.-R.-DECARY, QUEBEC, QC, G1N 3Z8
(418) 681-2023   *SIC* 5084

ASTRA DESIGN SYSTEMS INC   *p*692
5155 CREEKBANK RD, MISSISSAUGA, ON, L4W 1X2
(905) 282-9000   *SIC* 5084

ATLANTIC COMPRESSED AIR LTD   *p*408
484 EDINBURGH DR, MONCTON, NB, E1E 2L1
(506) 858-9500   *SIC* 5084

ATLANTIS POMPE STE-FOY INC   *p*1263
1844 BOUL WILFRID-HAMEL, QUEBEC, QC, G1N 3Z2
(418) 681-7301   *SIC* 5084

ATLAS POLAR COMPANY LIMITED   *p*916
60 NORTHLINE RD, TORONTO, ON, M4B 3E5
(416) 751-7740   *SIC* 5084

AUSTIN METAL LIMITED PARTNERSHIP   *p*183
5414 GORING ST, BURNABY, BC, V5B 3A3
(604) 291-7381   *SIC* 5084

AVENSYS SOLUTIONS INC   *p*1338
178 RUE MERIZZI, SAINT-LAURENT, QC, H4T 1S4
(514) 738-6766   *SIC* 5084

AVENUE INDUSTRIAL SUPPLY COMPANY LIMITED   *p*850
35 STAPLES AVE SUITE 110, RICHMOND HILL, ON, L4B 4W6
(877) 304-1270   *SIC* 5084

B. MCDOWELL EQUIPMENT LIMITED   *p*899
2018 KINGSWAY, SUDBURY, ON, P3B 4J8
(705) 566-8190   *SIC* 5084

BAKER HUGHES CANADA COMPANY   *p*44
401 9 AVE SW SUITE 1000, CALGARY, AB, T2P 3C5
(403) 537-3400   *SIC* 5084

BAKER HUGHES CANADA COMPANY   *p*139
7016 45 ST, LEDUC, AB, T9E 7E7
(780) 986-5559   *SIC* 5084

BAR HYDRAULICS INC   *p*615
1632 UPPER OTTAWA ST, HAMILTON, ON, L8W 3P2
(905) 385-2257   *SIC* 5084

BARON OILFIELD SUPPLY   *p*131
9515 108 ST, GRANDE PRAIRIE, AB, T8V 5R7
(780) 532-5661   *SIC* 5084

BEAUDRY MORIN INC   *p*1347
565 RUE PRINCIPALE, SAINT-LEONARD-D'ASTON, QC, J0C 1M0
(819) 399-2403   *SIC* 5084

BELTERRA CORPORATION   *p*205
1609 DERWENT WAY, DELTA, BC, V3M 6K8

(604) 540-0044   *SIC* 5084
BERENDSEN FLUID POWER LTD   *p*878
35 IRONSIDE CRES UNIT A, SCARBOROUGH, ON, M1X 1G5
(416) 335-5557   *SIC* 5084

BEVCO SALES INTERNATIONAL INC   *p*281
9354 194 ST, SURREY, BC, V4N 4E9
(604) 888-1455   *SIC* 5084

BIESSE CANADA INC   *p*1152
18005 RUE LAPOINTE, MIRABEL, QC, J7J 0G2
(450) 437-5534   *SIC* 5084

BIK HYDRAULICS LTD   *p*582
41 CLAIREVILLE DR UNIT A, ETOBICOKE, ON, M9W 5Z7
(416) 679-3838   *SIC* 5084

BIZERBA CANADA INC   *p*720
2810 ARGENTIA RD UNIT 9, MISSISSAUGA, ON, L5N 8L2
(905) 816-0498   *SIC* 5084

BLACK & DECKER CANADA INC   *p*519
100 CENTRAL AVE W, BROCKVILLE, ON, K6V 4N8
(613) 342-6641   *SIC* 5084

BOBCAT OF REGINA LTD   *p*1417
GD LCD MAIN, REGINA, SK, S4P 2Z4
(306) 347-7600   *SIC* 5084

BOIS OUVRES WATERVILLE INC   *p*1400
525 RUE PRINCIPALE N, WATERVILLE, QC, J0B 3H0
(819) 837-2476   *SIC* 5084

BONUS METAL CANADA INC   *p*1240
10171 AV PELLETIER, MONTREAL-NORD, QC, H1H 3R2
(514) 321-4820   *SIC* 5084

BORETS CANADA LTD   *p*148
2305 8 ST, NISKU, AB, T9E 7Z3
(780) 955-4795   *SIC* 5084

BOSCH REXROTH CANADA CORP   *p*1011
490 PRINCE CHARLES DR S, WELLAND, ON, L3B 5X7
(905) 735-0510   *SIC* 5084

BRADVIN TRAILER SALES LTD   *p*131
10920 87 AVE, GRANDE PRAIRIE, AB, T8V 8K4
(780) 539-6260   *SIC* 5084

BRANDT TRACTOR LTD   *p*99
10630 176 ST NW, EDMONTON, AB, T5S 1M2
(780) 484-6613   *SIC* 5084

BRANDT TRACTOR LTD   *p*1417
HWY 1 E, REGINA, SK, S4P 3R8
(306) 791-7777   *SIC* 5084

BUNZL CANADA INC   *p*537
400 JAMIESON PKY, CAMBRIDGE, ON, N3C 4N3
(519) 651-2233   *SIC* 5084

C B ENGINEERING LTD   *p*27
5040 12A ST SE, CALGARY, AB, T2G 5K9
(403) 259-6220   *SIC* 5084

CANADA FOOD EQUIPMENT LTD   *p*573
45 VANSCO RD, ETOBICOKE, ON, M8Z 5Z8
(416) 253-5100   *SIC* 5084

CANADA PUMP AND POWER (CPP) CORPORATION   *p*4
53113 RANGE ROAD 211, ARDROSSAN, AB, T8G 2C5
(780) 922-1178   *SIC* 5084

CANADIAN DEWATERING (2006) LTD   *p*122
8350 1 ST NW, EDMONTON, AB, T6P 1X2
(780) 400-2260   *SIC* 5084

CANADIAN DEWATERING L.P.   *p*122
8350 1 ST NW, EDMONTON, AB, T6P 1X2
(780) 400-2260   *SIC* 5084

CANADIAN IPG CORPORATION   *p*889
130 WOODWORTH AVE, ST THOMAS, ON, N5P 3K1
(519) 637-1945   *SIC* 5084

CANADIAN N D E TECHNOLOGY LTD   *p*583
124 SKYWAY AVE, ETOBICOKE, ON, M9W 4Y9
(416) 213-8000   *SIC* 5084

CANADO/NACAN EQUIPEMENT INC   *p*1328

5782 BOUL THIMENS, SAINT-LAURENT, QC, H4R 2K9

(514) 333-0077 SIC 5084

CANALTA CONTROLS LTD p155
6759 65 AVE, RED DEER, AB, T4P 1X5

(403) 342-4494 SIC 5084

CANCARD INC p667
177 IDEMA RD SUITE 8, MARKHAM, ON, L3R 1A9

(416) 449-8111 SIC 5084

CANWEST PROPANE PARTNERSHIP p46
440 2 AVE SW SUITE 1700, CALGARY, AB, T2P 5E9

(403) 206-4000 SIC 5084

CAPITAL INDUSTRIAL SALES & SERVICE LTD p122
851 77 AVE NW, EDMONTON, AB, T6P 1S9

(780) 440-4467 SIC 5084

CARGESCO (2002) INC p1297
2325 BOUL INDUSTRIEL, SAINT-CESAIRE, QC, J0L 1T0

(450) 469-3168 SIC 5084

CB INDUSTRIAL PART NETWORK p526
2100 CLIPPER CRES, BURLINGTON, ON, L7M 2P5

(905) 639-1907 SIC 5084

CCTF CORPORATION p648
2124 OXFORD ST E, LONDON, ON, N5V 0B7

(519) 453-3488 SIC 5084

CENTRAL AIR EQUIPMENT LTD p28
1322 HASTINGS CRES SE, CALGARY, AB, T2G 4C9

(403) 243-8003 SIC 5084

CENTRE DE MECANIQUE DU GOLFE INC p1367
336 AV NOEL, SEPT-ILES, QC, G4R 1L7

(418) 962-4057 SIC 5084

CERVUS EQUIPMENT CORPORATION p76
333 96 AVE NE SUITE 5201, CALGARY, AB, T3K 0S3

(403) 567-0339 SIC 5084

CHAMCO INDUSTRIES LTD p2
553 KINGSVIEW WAY SE SUITE 110, AIRDRIE, AB, T4A 0C9

(403) 945-8134 SIC 5084

CHAMCO INDUSTRIES LTD p77
8900 VENTURE AVE SE, CALGARY, AB, T3S 0A2

(403) 777-1200 SIC 5084

CHARLES LAPIERRE INC p1333
5600 RUE KIERAN, SAINT-LAURENT, QC, H4S 2B5

(514) 337-6990 SIC 5084

CISOLIFT DISTRIBUTION INC p1306
192 RUE SYLVESTRE, SAINT-GERMAIN-DE-GRANTHAM, QC, J0C 1K0

(819) 395-3838 SIC 5084

CLARK'S SUPPLY AND SERVICE LTD p1410
1650 STADACONA ST W, MOOSE JAW, SK, S6H 4P8

(306) 693-4334 SIC 5084

CLARK, KENNEDY COMPANY, LIMITED p580
15 LEADING RD, ETOBICOKE, ON, M9V 4B7

(416) 743-5911 SIC 5084

COG-VEYOR SYSTEMS INC p1030
371 HANLAN RD, WOODBRIDGE, ON, L4L 3T1

(416) 798-7333 SIC 5084

COLUMBIA CONTAINERS LTD p285
2319 COMMISSIONER ST, VANCOUVER, BC, V5L 1A4

(604) 254-9461 SIC 5084

COMMANDER WAREHOUSE EQUIPMENT LTD p241
930 1ST ST W SUITE 119, NORTH VANCOUVER, BC, V7P 3N4

(604) 980-8511 SIC 5084

COMPAIR CANADA INC p803
2390 SOUTH SERVICE RD W, OAKVILLE, ON, L6L 5M9

(905) 847-0688 SIC 5084

COMPRESSCO CANADA INC p15
5050 76 AVE SE, CALGARY, AB, T2C 2X2

(403) 279-5866 SIC 5084

COMPRESSEURS QUEBEC A K ENR p1328
2431 RUE GUENETTE, SAINT-LAURENT, QC, H4R 2E9

(514) 337-0566 SIC 5084

CONCEPTION GENIK INC p1321
715 RUE NOBEL BUREAU 108, SAINT-JEROME, QC, J7Z 7A3

(450) 436-7706 SIC 5084

CONTINENTAL ALLOYS & SERVICES INC p47
1440-530 8 AVE SW, CALGARY, AB, T2P 3S8

(403) 216-5150 SIC 5084

CONTINENTAL CONVEYOR (ONTARIO) LIMITED p747
100 RICHMOND BLVD, NAPANEE, ON, K7R 4A4

(613) 354-3318 SIC 5084

CONTROLES PROVAN ASSOCIES INC, LES p1333
2315 RUE HALPERN, SAINT-LAURENT, QC, H4S 1S3

(514) 332-3230 SIC 5084

CORBETT CREEK WATER POLLUTION CONTROL PLANT p1013
2400 FORBES ST, WHITBY, ON, L1N 8M3

(905) 576-9844 SIC 5084

CORES WORLDWIDE INCORPORATED p440
674 HIGHWAY 214, BELNAN, NS, B2S 2N2

(902) 883-1611 SIC 5084

CORPORATION INTERNATIONAL BROTHER (CANADA) LTEE, LA p1091
1 RUE HOTEL-DE-VILLE, DOLLARD-DES-ORMEAUX, QC, H9B 3H6

(514) 685-0600 SIC 5084

COWPER INC p1126
677 7E AV, LACHINE, QC, H8S 3A1

(514) 637-6746 SIC 5084

CPT CANADA POWER TECHNOLOGY LIMITED p705
161 WATLINE AVE, MISSISSAUGA, ON, L4Z 1P2

(905) 890-6900 SIC 5084

CRANESMART SYSTEMS INC p113
4908 97 ST NW, EDMONTON, AB, T6E 5S1

(780) 437-2986 SIC 5084

CRAWFORD PACKAGING INC p502
115 WALKER DR UNIT A, BRAMPTON, ON, L6T 5P5

(800) 265-4993 SIC 5084

CULLEN DIESEL POWER LTD p281
9300 192 ST, SURREY, BC, V4N 3R8

(604) 888-1211 SIC 5084

CUMMINS EST DU CANADA SEC p738
7175 PACIFIC CIR, MISSISSAUGA, ON, L5T 2A8

(905) 795-0050 SIC 5084

CUMMINS EST DU CANADA SEC p1250
7200 RTE TRANSCANADIENNE, POINTE-CLAIRE, QC, H9R 1C2

(514) 695-8410 SIC 5084

CUMMINS WESTERN CANADA LIMITED PARTNERSHIP p12
4887 35 ST SE, CALGARY, AB, T2B 3H6

(403) 569-1122 SIC 5084

CUMMINS WESTERN CANADA LIMITED PARTNERSHIP p100
11751 181 ST NW, EDMONTON, AB, T5S 2K5

(780) 455-2151 SIC 5084

CUMMINS WESTERN CANADA LIMITED PARTNERSHIP p281
18452 96 AVE, SURREY, BC, V4N 3P8

(604) 882-5000 SIC 5084

CUT TECHNOLOGIES p1138
460 3E AV BUREAU 100, LEVIS, QC, G6W 5M6

(418) 834-7772 SIC 5084

D.J. INDUSTRIAL SALES AND MANUFAC-

TURING INC p551
25 NORTH RIVERMEDE RD UNIT 1, CONCORD, ON, L4K 5V4

(416) 798-7575 SIC 5084

DATEK INDUSTRIAL TECHNOLOGIES LTD p199
3268 CHARTWELL GREEN, COQUITLAM, BC, V3E 3M9

(604) 468-8615 SIC 5084

DAVIS CONTROLS LIMITED p797
2200 BRISTOL CIR, OAKVILLE, ON, L6H 5R3

(905) 829-2000 SIC 5084

DECOUPAGE M.P.S. INC p1339
123 MONTEE DE LIESSE, SAINT-LAURENT, QC, H4T 1S6

(514) 744-8291 SIC 5084

DEMATIC LIMITED p721
6750 CENTURY AVE SUITE 302, MISSISSAUGA, ON, L5N 2V8

(877) 567-7300 SIC 5084

DESCH CANADA LTD p535
240 SHEARSON CRES, CAMBRIDGE, ON, N1T 1J6

(519) 621-4560 SIC 5084

DICKNER INC p1284
559 RUE DE LAUSANNE, RIMOUSKI, QC, G5L 4A7

(418) 723-7936 SIC 5084

DIGICON BUILDING CONTROL SOLUTIONS LIMITED p446
201 BROWNLOW AVE UNIT 11, DARTMOUTH, NS, B3B 1W2

(902) 468-2633 SIC 5084

DIMATEC INC p385
180 CREE CRES, WINNIPEG, MB, R3J 3W1

(204) 832-2828 SIC 5084

DISCOVERY CANADA MERCHANDISERS LTD p385
311 SAULTEAUX CRES, WINNIPEG, MB, R3J 3C7

(204) 885-7792 SIC 5084

DIXON GROUP CANADA LIMITED p369
2200 LOGAN AVE, WINNIPEG, MB, R2R 0J2

(204) 633-5650 SIC 5084

DNOW CANADA ULC p48
401 9 AVE SW SUITE 845, CALGARY, AB, T2P 3C5

(403) 531-5600 SIC 5084

DNOW CANADA ULC p122
2603 76 AVE NW, EDMONTON, AB, T6P 1P6

(780) 944-1000 SIC 5084

DNOW CANADA ULC p122
2603 76 AVE NW, EDMONTON, AB, T6P 1P6

(780) 944-1000 SIC 5084

DNOW CANADA ULC p139
6621 45 ST, LEDUC, AB, T9E 7E3

(780) 980-1490 SIC 5084

DNOW CANADA ULC p144
6452 66 ST, LLOYDMINSTER, AB, T9V 3T6

(780) 875-5504 SIC 5084

DNOW CANADA ULC p144
GD RPO 10, LLOYDMINSTER, AB, T9V 2H2

SIC 5084

DRIVE PRODUCTS INC p1
26230 TWP RD 531A UNIT 111, ACHESON, AB, T7X 5A4

(780) 960-6826 SIC 5084

DRIVE PRODUCTS INC p694
1665 SHAWSON DR, MISSISSAUGA, ON, L4W 1T7

(905) 564-5800 SIC 5084

E. M. PRECISE TOOL LTD p891
216 ARVIN AVE UNIT A, STONEY CREEK, ON, L8E 2L8

(905) 664-2644 SIC 5084

EAB TOOL COMPANY INC p205
584 EBURY PL, DELTA, BC, V3M 6M8

(604) 526-4595 SIC 5084

EARLSCOURT METAL INDUSTRIES LTD p738
6660 ORDAN DR, MISSISSAUGA, ON, L5T 1J7

(905) 564-9000 SIC 5084

ECO TABS CANADA INC p797
2429 LAMOKA CRT, OAKVILLE, ON, L6H 5Z7

(888) 732-6822 SIC 5084

EDDYFI NDT INC p1266
3425 RUE PIERRE-ARDOUIN, QUEBEC, QC, G1P 0B3

(418) 780-1565 SIC 5084

EJ ENTERPRISE p228
20179 56 AVE, LANGLEY, BC, V3A 3Y6

(604) 514-2224 SIC 5084

ELECTROMEGA LIMITEE p1072
105 AV LIBERTE, CANDIAC, QC, J5R 3X8

(450) 635-1020 SIC 5084

ELLIOTT-MATSUURA CANADA INC p797
2120 BUCKINGHAM RD, OAKVILLE, ON, L6H 5X2

(905) 829-2211 SIC 5084

EMBALLAGES JEAN CARTIER INC p1297
2325 BOUL INDUSTRIEL, SAINT-CESAIRE, QC, J0L 1T0

(450) 469-3168 SIC 5084

EMEC MACHINE TOOLS INC p739
205 ADMIRAL BLVD, MISSISSAUGA, ON, L5T 2T3

(905) 565-3570 SIC 5084

EN-PLAS INC p864
1395 MORNINGSIDE AVE, SCARBOROUGH, ON, M1B 3J1

(416) 286-3030 SIC 5084

ENDRESS + HAUSER CANADA LTD p522
1075 SUTTON DR, BURLINGTON, ON, L7L 5Z8

(905) 681-9292 SIC 5084

ENTREPRISES LARRY INC p1224
4200 RUE SAINT-PATRICK, MONTREAL, QC, H4E 1A5

(514) 767-5363 SIC 5084

EPSCAN INDUSTRIES LTD p213
10012 94 AVE, FORT ST. JOHN, BC, V1J 5J6

(250) 787-9659 SIC 5084

EQUIPEMENT COMAIRCO LTEE p1231
5535 RUE ERNEST-CORMIER, MONTREAL, QC, H7C 2S9

(450) 665-8780 SIC 5084

EQUIPEMENT MOORE LTEE p1333
4955 CH SAINT-FRANCOIS, SAINT-LAURENT, QC, H4S 1P3

(514) 333-1212 SIC 5084

EQUIPEMENTS CONTRO VALVE INC, LES p1070
9610 RUE IGNACE UNIT B, BROSSARD, QC, J4Y 2R3

(450) 444-5858 SIC 5084

EQUIPEMENTS E.M.U. LTEE p1276
3975 RUE JEAN-MARCHAND, QUEBEC, QC, G2C 2J2

(418) 767-2277 SIC 5084

EQUIPEMENTS PLANNORD LTEE p1293
70 RUE D'ANVERS, SAINT-AUGUSTIN-DE-DESMAURES, QC, G3A 1S4

(418) 878-4007 SIC 5084

EQUIPMENT D'EMBALLAGE M.M.C. LTEE p1134
2040 BOUL DAGENAIS O, LAVAL-OUEST, QC, H7L 5W2

(450) 625-4662 SIC 5084

EQUIPMENT WORLD INC p908
988 ALLOY DR, THUNDER BAY, ON, P7B 6A5

(807) 623-9561 SIC 5084

ESAB GROUP CANADA INC p731
6200 CANTAY RD UNIT 20, MISSISSAUGA, ON, L5R 3Y9

(905) 670-0220 SIC 5084

ESC AUTOMATION INC p271
5265 185A ST SUITE 100, SURREY, BC, V3S 7A4

(604) 574-7790   *SIC 5084*
EVEREST AUTOMATION INC   *p1250*
227D BOUL BRUNSWICK, POINTE-CLAIRE, QC, H9R 4X5
(514) 630-9290   *SIC 5084*

EXACTA TOOL 2010 ULC   *p513*
120 VAN KIRK DR, BRAMPTON, ON, L7A 1B1
(905) 840-2240   *SIC 5084*

FANUC CANADA, LTD   *p722*
6774 FINANCIAL DR, MISSISSAUGA, ON, L5N 7J6
(905) 812-2300   *SIC 5084*

FELDCAMP EQUIPMENT LIMITED   *p763*
701 GRAHAM DR, NORTH BAY, ON, P1B 9E6
(705) 472-5885   *SIC 5084*

FERRO TECHNIQUE LTEE   *p1339*
819 RUE MCCAFFREY, SAINT-LAURENT, QC, H4T 1N3
(514) 341-3450   *SIC 5084*

FICODIS INC   *p1188*
465 RUE SAINT-JEAN BUREAU 708, MONTREAL, QC, H2Y 2R6
(514) 360-4007   *SIC 5084*

FINNING INTERNATIONAL INC   *p289*
565 GREAT NORTHERN WAY SUITE 300, VANCOUVER, BC, V5T 0H8
(604) 331-4816   *SIC 5084*

FIREBALL EQUIPMENT LTD   *p100*
17509 109A AVE NW, EDMONTON, AB, T5S 2W4
(780) 944-4818   *SIC 5084*

FISHER AND LUDLOW   *p1247*
12450 BOUL INDUSTRIEL, POINTE-AUX-TREMBLES, QC, H1B 5M5
SIC 5084

FIVES MACHINING SYSTEMS CANADA INC   *p537*
70 COOPER ST, CAMBRIDGE, ON, N3C 2N4
(905) 673-7007   *SIC 5084*

FIVES SOLIOS INC   *p1196*
625 AV DU PRESIDENT-KENNEDY, MONTREAL, QC, H3A 1K2
(514) 284-0341   *SIC 5084*

FLEX-O-MARK INC   *p685*
2633 DREW RD, MISSISSAUGA, ON, L4T 1G1
(905) 678-7997   *SIC 5084*

FLO-DRAULIC CONTROLS LTD   *p593*
45 SINCLAIR AVE, GEORGETOWN, ON, L7G 4X4
(905) 702-9456   *SIC 5084*

FLO-SKID MANUFACTURING INC   *p16*
6725 86 AVE SE, CALGARY, AB, T2C 2S4
(403) 279-6602   *SIC 5084*

FLUID HOSE & COUPLING INC   *p739*
6150 DIXIE RD UNIT 1, MISSISSAUGA, ON, L5T 2E2
(905) 670-0955   *SIC 5084*

FLUKE ELECTRONICS CANADA LP   *p705*
400 BRITANNIA RD E UNIT 1, MISSISSAUGA, ON, L4Z 1X9
(905) 890-7601   *SIC 5084*

FMC TECHNOLOGIES COMPANY   *p109*
6703 68 AVE NW, EDMONTON, AB, T6B 3E3
(780) 468-9231   *SIC 5084*

FPH GROUP INC   *p649*
570 INDUSTRIAL RD, LONDON, ON, N5V 1V1
(519) 686-9965   *SIC 5084*

FRANK HENRY EQUIPMENT (1987) LTD   *p114*
9810 60 AVE NW, EDMONTON, AB, T6E 0C5
(780) 434-8778   *SIC 5084*

FREUD CANADA, INC   *p739*
7450 PACIFIC CIR, MISSISSAUGA, ON, L5T 2A3
(905) 670-1025   *SIC 5084*

FRONTLINE SYSTEMS INC   *p592*
210 JAMES A. BRENNAN RD,

GANANOQUE, ON, K7G 1N7
(613) 463-9575   *SIC 5084*

FUJITEC CANADA, INC   *p852*
15 EAST WILMOT ST, RICHMOND HILL, ON, L4B 1A3
(905) 731-8681   *SIC 5084*

FUNDY GRINDING & MACHINING LIMITED   *p468*
9 FARNHAM RD, TRURO, NS, B2N 2X6
(902) 893-4274   *SIC 5084*

FURNACE BELT COMPANY LIMITED, THE   *p735*
1874 DREW RD UNIT 7, MISSISSAUGA, ON, L5S 1J6
(905) 677-5068   *SIC 5084*

FUTURE HYDRAULIK INC   *p1085*
1597 RUE CUNARD, COTE SAINT-LUC, QC, H7S 2B4
(514) 687-0187   *SIC 5084*

G K D INDUSTRIES LTD   *p16*
7939 54 ST SE, CALGARY, AB, T2C 4R7
(403) 279-8087   *SIC 5084*

G.A.L. CANADA ELEVATOR PRODUCTS CORP   *p739*
6500 GOTTARDO CRT, MISSISSAUGA, ON, L5T 2A2
(905) 564-0838   *SIC 5084*

G.E.'S ALL TRUCKING LIMITED   *p441*
385 YORK ST, BRIDGEWATER, NS, B4V 3K1
SIC 5084

G.N. JOHNSTON EQUIPMENT CO. LTD.   *p731*
5990 AVEBURY RD, MISSISSAUGA, ON, L5R 3R2
(905) 712-6000   *SIC 5084*

G.N. JOHNSTON EQUIPMENT CO. LTD.   *p731*
5990 AVEBURY RD, MISSISSAUGA, ON, L5R 3R2
(905) 712-6000   *SIC 5084*

G.N. JOHNSTON EQUIPMENT CO. LTD.   *p1329*
5000 RUE LEVY, SAINT-LAURENT, QC, H4R 2P1
(514) 956-0020   *SIC 5084*

GARNET INSTRUMENTS LTD   *p161*
286 KASKA RD, SHERWOOD PARK, AB, T8A 4G7
(780) 467-1010   *SIC 5084*

GASTALDO PUMP SALES LTD   *p206*
482 FRASERVIEW PL, DELTA, BC, V3M 6H4
(604) 526-6262   *SIC 5084*

GE ENERGY OILFIELD TECHNOLGY CANADA INC   *p12*
2880 45 AVE SE SUITE 432, CALGARY, AB, T2B 3M1
SIC 5084

GONDERFLEX INTERNATIONAL INC *p1141*
530 BOUL GUIMOND, LONGUEUIL, QC, J4G 1P8
(450) 651-2224   *SIC 5084*

GRANT AGGREGATE & INDUSTRIAL SUPPLY INC   *p898*
2578 LASALLE BLVD, SUDBURY, ON, P3A 4R7
(705) 524-2711   *SIC 5084*

GREAT WEST EQUIPMENT LTD   *p331*
123 L & A CROSS RD, VERNON, BC, V1B 3S1
(250) 549-4232   *SIC 5084*

GROUPE FORDIA INC   *p1091*
3 RUE HOTEL-DE-VILLE, DOLLARD-DES-ORMEAUX, QC, H9B 3G4
(514) 336-9211   *SIC 5084*

GROUPE JLD LAGUE   *p1082*
544 RUE MAIN O, COATICOOK, QC, J1A 2S5
(819) 849-0300   *SIC 5084*

GROUPE LD INC   *p1115*
2370 RUE BAUMAN, JONQUIERE, QC, G7S 4S4
(418) 699-4350   *SIC 5084*

GROUPE MASKA INC   *p1312*
550 AV VAUDREUIL, SAINT-HYACINTHE, QC, J2S 4H2
(450) 372-1676   *SIC 5084*

GRUNDFOS CANADA INC   *p797*
2941 BRIGHTON RD, OAKVILLE, ON, L6H 6C9
(905) 829-9533   *SIC 5084*

H. B. MORNINGSTAR INDUSTRIES LIMITED   *p794*
335 CLAYSON RD, NORTH YORK, ON, M9M 2H4
(416) 745-3547   *SIC 5084*

HANDLING TECHNOLOGIES INC   *p553*
21 CORRINE CRT, CONCORD, ON, L4K 4W2
(905) 739-1350   *SIC 5084*

HANDTMANN CANADA LIMITED   *p1010*
654 COLBY DR, WATERLOO, ON, N2V 1A2
(519) 725-3666   *SIC 5084*

HARDING FORKLIFT SERVICES LTD   *p282*
18623 96 AVE, SURREY, BC, V4N 3P6
(604) 888-1412   *SIC 5084*

HARDROCK BITS & OILFIELD SUPPLIES LTD   *p158*
2200 SOUTH HIGHWAY DR SE, REDCLIFF, AB, T0J 2P0
(403) 529-2100   *SIC 5084*

HARVEY & COMPANY LIMITED   *p430*
88 KENMOUNT RD, ST. JOHN'S, NL, A1B 3R1
(709) 738-8911   *SIC 5084*

HAYWARD GORDON ULC   *p593*
5 BRIGDEN GATE, GEORGETOWN, ON, L7G 0A3
(905) 693-8595   *SIC 5084*

HAZMASTERS ENVIRONMENTAL CONTROLS INC   *p182*
3131 UNDERHILL AVE, BURNABY, BC, V5A 3C8
(604) 420-0025   *SIC 5084*

HEADWATER EQUIPMENT SALES LTD *p80*
592041 RIVER RIDGE RD UNIT 2, COALHURST, AB, T0L 0V0
(403) 327-3681   *SIC 5084*

HEIDELBERG CANADA GRAPHIC EQUIPMENT LIMITED   *p740*
6285 KENWAY DR, MISSISSAUGA, ON, L5T 2L3
(905) 362-4400   *SIC 5084*

HEWITT MATERIAL HANDLING INC   *p554*
425 MILLWAY AVE, CONCORD, ON, L4K 3V8
(905) 669-6590   *SIC 5084*

HIBON INC   *p1250*
100 RUE VOYAGEUR, POINTE-CLAIRE, QC, H9R 6A8
(514) 631-3501   *SIC 5084*

HOLWIN TOOLING SYSTEMS INC   *p1023*
5270 BURKE ST, WINDSOR, ON, N9A 6J3
(519) 737-7550   *SIC 5084*

HOMAG CANADA INC   *p740*
5090 EDWARDS BLVD, MISSISSAUGA, ON, L5T 2W3
(905) 670-1700   *SIC 5084*

HOWARD MARTEN FLUID TECHNOLOGIES INC   *p844*
902 DILLINGHAM RD, PICKERING, ON, L1W 1Z6
(905) 831-2901   *SIC 5084*

HYDAC CORPORATION   *p1011*
14 FEDERAL RD, WELLAND, ON, L3B 3P2
(905) 714-9322   *SIC 5084*

HYDRACO INDUSTRIES LTD   *p145*
2111 9 AVE SW, MEDICINE HAT, AB, T1A 8M9
(403) 528-4400   *SIC 5084*

HYDREXCEL INC   *p1056*
665 AV DUTORD BUREAU 294, BECANCOUR, QC, G9H 2Z6
(819) 294-2728   *SIC 5084*

HYDRIL CANADIAN COMPANY LIMITED PARTNERSHIP   *p148*
2307 8 ST, NISKU, AB, T9E 7Z3

(780) 955-2045   *SIC 5084*
I-D BEVERAGES INC   *p1237*
1800 SUD LAVAL (A-440) O, MONTREAL, QC, H7S 2E7
(450) 687-2680   *SIC 5084*

ICE WESTERN SALES LTD   *p16*
9765 54 ST SE, CALGARY, AB, T2C 5J6
(403) 252-5577   *SIC 5084*

IDENTIFICATION MULTI SOLUTIONS INC *p1334*
9000 BOUL HENRI-BOURASSA O, SAINT-LAURENT, QC, H4S 1L5
(514) 336-3213   *SIC 5084*

IMPORT TOOL CORPORATION LTD   *p115*
10340 71 AVE NW, EDMONTON, AB, T6E 0W8
(780) 434-3464   *SIC 5084*

INDUSTRIAL TRUCK SERVICE LTD   *p365*
89 DURAND RD, WINNIPEG, MB, R2J 3T1
(204) 663-9325   *SIC 5084*

INDUSTRIES ELIRA INC   *p1356*
1600 RUE JEAN-LACHAINE, SAINTE-CATHERINE, QC, J5C 1C2
(450) 638-4694   *SIC 5084*

INDUSTRIES RAINVILLE INC   *p1316*
175 RTE 104, SAINT-JEAN-SUR-RICHELIEU, QC, J2X 5T7
(450) 347-5521   *SIC 5084*

INNOVAIR INDUSTRIAL LIMITED   *p381*
150 MCPHILLIPS ST, WINNIPEG, MB, R3E 2J9
(204) 772-9476   *SIC 5084*

INSTRUMENTS I.T.M. INC, LES   *p1355*
20800 BOUL INDUSTRIEL, SAINTE-ANNE-DE-BELLEVUE, QC, H9X 0A1
(514) 457-7280   *SIC 5084*

INTEGRATED DISTRIBUTION SYSTEMS LIMITED PARTNERSHIP   *p1*
26313 TWP RD 531A, ACHESON, AB, T7X 5A3
(780) 487-6700   *SIC 5084*

INTEGRATED DISTRIBUTION SYSTEMS LIMITED PARTNERSHIP   *p101*
17604 105 AVE NW, EDMONTON, AB, T5S 1G4
(780) 483-6641   *SIC 5084*

INTEGRATED DISTRIBUTION SYSTEMS LIMITED PARTNERSHIP   *p703*
3280 WHARTON WAY, MISSISSAUGA, ON, L4X 2C5
(905) 212-3300   *SIC 5084*

INTEGRATED DISTRIBUTION SYSTEMS LIMITED PARTNERSHIP   *p1086*
2000 RUE JOHN-MOLSON, COTE SAINT-LUC, QC, H7T 0H4
(450) 682-3737   *SIC 5084*

INTEGRATED DISTRIBUTION SYSTEMS LIMITED PARTNERSHIP   *p1086*
2000 RUE JOHN-MOLSON, COTE SAINT-LUC, QC, H7T 0H4
(450) 682-3737   *SIC 5084*

INTEGRATED DISTRIBUTION SYSTEMS LIMITED PARTNERSHIP   *p1275*
2997 AV WATT, QUEBEC, QC, G1X 3W1
(418) 651-4236   *SIC 5084*

INTEGRATED DISTRIBUTION SYSTEMS LIMITED PARTNERSHIP   *p1306*
243 RUE DES ARTISANS, SAINT-GERMAIN-DE-GRANTHAM, QC, J0C 1K0
(819) 472-4076   *SIC 5084*

ITRON CANADA INC   *p1386*
3260 RUE DU CHANOINE-CHAMBERLAND, TROIS-RIVIERES, QC, G8Z 2T2
(819) 373-5303   *SIC 5084*

ITW CANADA INC   *p678*
120 TRAVAIL RD, MARKHAM, ON, L3S 3J1
(905) 201-8399   *SIC 5084*

JAMES ELECTRIC MOTOR SERVICES LTD *p30*
4020 8 ST SE, CALGARY, AB, T2G 3A7
(403) 252-5477   *SIC 5084*

JET EQUIPMENT & TOOLS LTD   *p201*
49 SCHOONER ST, COQUITLAM, BC, V3K

0B3

(604) 523-8665 *SIC 5084*

JOHN BROOKS COMPANY LIMITED *p723*
2625 MEADOWPINE BLVD, MISSISSAUGA, ON, L5N 7K5
(905) 624-4200 *SIC 5084*

K.W. PETROLEUM SERVICES LTD *p1428*
849 56TH ST E, SASKATOON, SK, S7K 5Y9
(306) 244-4468 *SIC 5084*

KAESER COMPRESSEURS CANADA INC *p1062*
3760 RUE LA VERENDRYE, BOISBRIAND, QC, J7H 1R5
(450) 971-1414 *SIC 5084*

KAR INDUSTRIEL INC *p1251*
100 AV COLUMBUS, POINTE-CLAIRE, QC, H9R 4K4
(514) 694-4711 *SIC 5084*

KITO CANADA INC *p186*
3815 1ST AVE SUITE 309, BURNABY, BC, V5C 3V6
(888) 322-5486 *SIC 5084*

KO-REC-TYPE (CANADA) LTD *p740*
1100 COURTNEYPARK DR E UNIT 4, MISSISSAUGA, ON, L5T 1L7
SIC 5084

KREATOR EQUIPMENT & SERVICES INCORPORATED *p863*
473036 COUNTY RD 11, SCARBOROUGH, ON, L9W 0R2
(519) 941-7876 *SIC 5084*

KRONES MACHINERY CO. LIMITED *p688*
6285 NORTHAM DR SUITE 108, MISSISSAUGA, ON, L4V 1X5
(905) 364-4900 *SIC 5084*

KSM INC *p149*
1904 4 ST, NISKU, AB, T9E 7T8
(780) 955-3456 *SIC 5084*

KUBOTA CANADA LTD *p678*
5900 14TH AVE, MARKHAM, ON, L3S 4K4
(905) 294-7477 *SIC 5084*

KUDU INDUSTRIES INC *p17*
9112 40 ST SE, CALGARY, AB, T2C 2P3
(403) 279-5838 *SIC 5084*

KURT'S IRON WORKS LTD *p146*
933 19 ST SW, MEDICINE HAT, AB, T1B 0A2
(403) 527-2844 *SIC 5084*

LAKESIDE PROCESS CONTROLS LTD *p723*
2475 HOGAN DR, MISSISSAUGA, ON, L5N 0E9
(905) 412-0500 *SIC 5084*

LANGEN PACKAGING INC *p723*
6500 KITIMAT RD UNIT 1, MISSISSAUGA, ON, L5N 2B8
(905) 670-7200 *SIC 5084*

LEMMER SPRAY SYSTEMS LTD *p24*
4624 12 ST NE, CALGARY, AB, T2E 4R4
(403) 250-7735 *SIC 5084*

LIFCO HYDRAULICS LTD *p887*
250 MARTINDALE RD, ST CATHARINES, ON, L2S 0B2
(905) 641-0033 *SIC 5084*

LIFT BOSS INC *p84*
7912 YELLOWHEAD TRAIL NW, EDMONTON, AB, T5B 1G3
(780) 474-9900 *SIC 5084*

LIFT LINE MACHINERY LTD *p1012*
495 PRINCE CHARLES DR S, WELLAND, ON, L3B 5X1
(905) 788-0971 *SIC 5084*

LIFTOW LIMITED *p740*
1400 COURTNEYPARK DR E, MISSISSAUGA, ON, L5T 1H1
(905) 677-3270 *SIC 5084*

LIFTOW LIMITED *p1128*
1936 32E AV, LACHINE, QC, H8T 3J7
(514) 633-9360 *SIC 5084*

LIFTWAY LIMITED *p517*
GD LCD MAIN, BRANTFORD, ON, N3T 5M2
(519) 759-5590 *SIC 5084*

LIGNAREX INC *p1121*
7700 CH DE LA BATTURE, LA BAIE, QC,

G7B 3P6

(418) 306-5049 *SIC 5084*

LUKE'S MACHINERY CO. LTD *p375*
318 NOTRE DAME AVE, WINNIPEG, MB, R3B 1P5
(204) 943-3421 *SIC 5084*

M.T.E. CONTROLS CORPORATION *p807*
5135 HENNIN DR, OLDCASTLE, ON, N0R 1L0
(519) 737-7555 *SIC 5084*

MACHINERIES B.V. LTEE *p1097*
5555 RUE SAINT-ROCH S, DRUMMONDVILLE, QC, J2B 6V4
(819) 474-4444 *SIC 5084*

MACHINERIES ST-JOVITE INC., LES *p1159*
1313 RUE DE SAINT-JOVITE, MONT-TREMBLANT, QC, J8E 3J9
(819) 425-3737 *SIC 5084*

MACKENZIE PULP MILL CORPORATION *p230*
1000 COQUAWALDY RD, MACKENZIE, BC, V0J 2C0
(250) 997-2431 *SIC 5084*

MADSEN DIESEL & TURBINE INC *p426*
141 GLENCOE DR, MOUNT PEARL, NL, A1N 4S7
(709) 726-6774 *SIC 5084*

MAGIC NORTH AMERICA INC *p678*
110 TRAVAIL RD, MARKHAM, ON, L3S 3J1
(905) 471-7780 *SIC 5084*

MAINLINE EQUIPMENT LTD *p96*
14535 114 AVE NW, EDMONTON, AB, T5M 2Y8
(780) 453-3695 *SIC 5084*

MAINWAY HANDLING SYSTEMS INC *p528*
3345 NORTH SERVICE RD UNIT 101, BURLINGTON, ON, L7N 3G2
(905) 335-0133 *SIC 5084*

MAN ENERGY SOLUTIONS CANADA LTD *p314*
1177 HASTINGS ST W SUITE 1930, VANCOUVER, BC, V6E 2K3
(604) 235-2254 *SIC 5084*

MANULIFT E.M.I. LTEE *p1293*
100 RUE D'ANVERS, SAINT-AUGUSTIN-DE-DESMAURES, QC, G3A 1S4
(418) 878-5424 *SIC 5084*

MANUTENTION QUEBEC INC *p1251*
100A BOUL HYMUS, POINTE-CLAIRE, QC, H9R 1E4
(514) 694-4223 *SIC 5084*

MAR-CON WIRE BELT INC *p255*
2431 VAUXHALL PL, RICHMOND, BC, V6V 1Z5
(604) 278-8922 *SIC 5084*

MARCOTTE SYSTEMES LTEE *p1393*
1471 BOUL LIONEL-BOULET UNITE 28, VARENNES, QC, J3X 1P7
(450) 652-6000 *SIC 5084*

MARIE, F. LIMITED *p672*
123 DENISON ST, MARKHAM, ON, L3R 1B5
(905) 475-0093 *SIC 5084*

MARINDUSTRIAL ONTARIO INC *p717*
4090 RIDGEWAY DR UNIT 8, MISSISSAUGA, ON, L5L 5X5
(905) 607-5052 *SIC 5084*

MARKEM-IMAJE INC *p735*
7075 EDWARDS BLVD UNIT 2, MISSISSAUGA, ON, L5S 1Z2
(800) 267-5108 *SIC 5084*

MAZAK CORPORATION CANADA *p537*
50 COMMERCE CRT, CAMBRIDGE, ON, N3C 4P7
(519) 658-2021 *SIC 5084*

MBI DRILLING PRODUCTS INC *p1290*
110 RUE JACQUES-BIBEAU, ROUYN-NORANDA, QC, J9Y 0A3
(819) 762-9645 *SIC 5084*

MBI PACIFIC DRILLING PRODUCTS LTD *p1428*
3150 FAITHFULL AVE, SASKATOON, SK, S7K 8H3
(306) 955-9560 *SIC 5084*

MCCANN EQUIPMENT LTD *p1094*
10255 CH COTE-DE-LIESSE, DORVAL, QC, H9P 1A3
(514) 636-6344 *SIC 5084*

MEGATEL INFORMATION SYSTEMS INC *p1340*
3930 RUE GRIFFITH, SAINT-LAURENT, QC, H4T 1A7
(514) 333-0717 *SIC 5084*

MEGTEC TURBOSONIC INC *p1008*
550 PARKSIDE DR UNIT A14, WATERLOO, ON, N2L 5V4
(519) 885-5513 *SIC 5084*

MEGTEC TURBOSONIC TECHNOLOGIES INC *p1008*
550 PARKSIDE DR UNIT A14, WATERLOO, ON, N2L 5V4
(519) 885-5513 *SIC 5084*

METCON SALES AND ENGINEERING LIMITED *p555*
15 CONNIE CRES UNIT 3, CONCORD, ON, L4K 1L3
(905) 738-2355 *SIC 5084*

METSO FLOW CONTROL CANADA LTD *p1330*
4716 BOUL THIMENS, SAINT-LAURENT, QC, H4R 2B2
(514) 908-7045 *SIC 5084*

METSO MINERALS CANADA INC *p1330*
4000 BOUL THIMENS, SAINT-LAURENT, QC, H4R 2B2
(514) 335-5426 *SIC 5084*

MICRO-WATT CONTROL DEVICES LTD *p76*
11141 15 ST NE, CALGARY, AB, T3K 0Z5
(403) 250-1594 *SIC 5084*

MILRON METAL FABRICATORS INC *p106*
12145 156 ST NW, EDMONTON, AB, T5V 1N4
(780) 451-3258 *SIC 5084*

MILTEX CONSTRUCTION LIMITED *p586*
31 RACINE RD SUITE 416, ETOBICOKE, ON, M9W 2Z4
SIC 5084

MITUTOYO CANADA INC *p725*
2121 MEADOWVALE BLVD, MISSISSAUGA, ON, L5N 5N1
(905) 821-1261 *SIC 5084*

MODERN TOOL LTD *p17*
11488 70 ST SE, CALGARY, AB, T2C 4Y3
(403) 236-1150 *SIC 5084*

MONTREAL TRACTEUR INC *p1053*
21601 AV CLARK-GRAHAM, BAIE-D'URFE, QC, H9X 3T5
(514) 457-8100 *SIC 5084*

MOORE INDUSTRIAL LTD *p369*
169 OMANDS CREEK BLVD, WINNIPEG, MB, R2R 1V9
(204) 632-4092 *SIC 5084*

MORMAK INVESTMENTS LTD *p331*
8140 BECKETTS RD, VERNON, BC, V1B 3V3
(250) 542-7350 *SIC 5084*

MULDOWNEY HOLDINGS LTD *p81*
GD, DE WINTON, AB, T0L 0X0
(403) 253-0399 *SIC 5084*

MULTI-TECH SYSTEMS INTERNATIONAL INC *p1010*
592 COLBY DRIVE, WATERLOO, ON, N2V 1A2
(905) 825-3825 *SIC 5084*

NATIONAL ENERGY EQUIPMENT INC *p735*
1850 DERRY RD E, MISSISSAUGA, ON, L5S 1Y6
(905) 564-2422 *SIC 5084*

NCS FLUID HANDLING SYSTEMS INC *p163*
280 PORTAGE CLOSE UNIT 530, SHERWOOD PARK, AB, T8H 2R6
(780) 910-7951 *SIC 5084*

ND GRAPHICS INC *p556*
55 INTERCHANGE WAY UNIT 1, CONCORD, ON, L4K 5W3
(416) 663-6416 *SIC 5084*

NEW AGE ROBOTICS AND CONTROLS INC *p483*

515 WAYDOM DR, AYR, ON, N0B 1E0
(519) 621-3333 *SIC 5084*

NEXUS ENERGY TECHNOLOGIES INC *p157*
175 CLEARVIEW DR UNIT 100, RED DEER COUNTY, AB, T4E 0A1
(403) 314-0607 *SIC 5084*

NJM PACKAGING INC *p1335*
5600 RUE KIERAN, SAINT-LAURENT, QC, H4S 2B5
(514) 337-6990 *SIC 5084*

NKC OF CANADA INC *p706*
55 VILLAGE CENTRE PL SUITE 213, MISSISSAUGA, ON, L4Z 1V9
(905) 273-4011 *SIC 5084*

NORDSON CANADA, LIMITED *p673*
1211 DENISON ST, MARKHAM, ON, L3R 4B3
(905) 475-6730 *SIC 5084*

NORMAND, J.R. INC *p1140*
752 CH OLIVIER, LEVIS, QC, G7A 2N2
(418) 831-3226 *SIC 5084*

NORPINE AUTO SUPPLY (96) LTD *p138*
10533 100 ST, LA CRETE, AB, T0H 2H0
(780) 928-3912 *SIC 5084*

NORTHERN BLOWER INC *p363*
901 REGENT AVE W, WINNIPEG, MB, R2C 2Z8
(204) 222-4216 *SIC 5084*

NORTRAX QUEBEC INC *p1342*
4500 DESSTE CHOMEDEY (A-13) O, SAINT-LAURENT, QC, H7R 6E9
(450) 625-3221 *SIC 5084*

NOVA INDUSTRIAL SUPPLIES LIMITED *p464*
1006 NOVA DR, NEW MINAS, NS, B4N 3X7
(902) 681-1665 *SIC 5084*

NUCLEUS DISTRIBUTION INC *p698*
5220 GENERAL RD, MISSISSAUGA, ON, L4W 1G8
(800) 263-4283 *SIC 5084*

OCTAGON DISTRIBUTION COMPANY LIMITED *p698*
5220 GENERAL RD, MISSISSAUGA, ON, L4W 1G8
SIC 5084

OLYMPIC MATERIAL HANDLING LTD *p556*
300 BRADWICK DR, CONCORD, ON, L4K 1K8
(416) 661-4609 *SIC 5084*

OMCAN MANUFACTURING & DISTRIBUTING COMPANY INC *p717*
3115 PEPPER MILL CRT, MISSISSAUGA, ON, L5L 4X5
(905) 828-0234 *SIC 5084*

OMNIFLEX HOSE & EQUIPMENT LTD *p534*
78 COWANSVIEW RD SUITE 3, CAMBRIDGE, ON, N1R 7N3
(519) 622-0261 *SIC 5084*

OTTAWA EQUIPMENT & HYDRAULIC INC *p816*
2628 EDINBURGH PL, OTTAWA, ON, K1B 5M1
(613) 748-9000 *SIC 5084*

OUTIL MAG INC *p1398*
10 BOUL LABBE S, VICTORIAVILLE, QC, G6S 1B5
(819) 751-2424 *SIC 5084*

OUTIL-PAC INC *p1158*
5895 AV ANDOVER, MONT-ROYAL, QC, H4T 1H8
(514) 733-3555 *SIC 5084*

OUTILLAGE INDUSTRIEL QUEBEC LTEE *p1265*
395 AV MARCONI, QUEBEC, QC, G1N 4A5
(418) 683-2527 *SIC 5084*

OUTILLAGE PLACIDE MATHIEU INC *p1057*
670 RUE PICARD, BELOEIL, QC, J3G 5X9
(450) 467-3565 *SIC 5084*

OUTILLAGES KING CANADA INC *p1094*
700 AV MELOCHE, DORVAL, QC, H9P 2Y4
(514) 636-5464 *SIC 5084*

OUTILS DE COUPE DRILLMEX INC *p1359*
2105 RUE BOMBARDIER, SAINTE-JULIE,

QC, J3E 2N1
(450) 922-1929   *SIC* 5084

P.R. DISTRIBUTIONS INC   *p1276*
6500 RUE ZEPHIRIN-PAQUET, QUEBEC, QC, G2C 0M3
(418) 872-6018   *SIC* 5084

P.T.I. PUNCH TOOLS INC   *p201*
211 SCHOOLHOUSE ST SUITE 11, CO-QUITLAM, BC, V3K 4X9
(604) 521-3143   *SIC* 5084

PACA INDUSTRIAL DISTRIBUTION LTD
p642
84 MCBRINE PL, KITCHENER, ON, N2R 1H3
(519) 748-5650   *SIC* 5084

PACIFIC TRUCK & EQUIPMENT   *p215*
2226 NORTH NADINA AVE, HOUSTON, BC, V0J 1Z0
(250) 845-0061   *SIC* 5084

PALFINGER INC   *p759*
7942 DORCHESTER RD, NIAGARA FALLS, ON, L2G 7W7
(905) 374-3363   *SIC* 5084

PEERLESS ENGINEERING SALES LTD
p186
4015 1ST AVE, BURNABY, BC, V5C 3W5
(604) 659-4100   *SIC* 5084

PENTAIR CANADA, INC   *p637*
269 TRILLIUM DR, KITCHENER, ON, N2E 1W9
(519) 748-5470   *SIC* 5084

PERFEXIA INC   *p637*
111 BLEAMS RD, KITCHENER, ON, N2C 2G2
(519) 884-8650   *SIC* 5084

PICKFORD GROUP LTD, THE   *p151*
1237-200 SOUTHRIDGE DR, OKOTOKS, AB, T1S 0N8
(403) 571-0571   *SIC* 5084

PLEXPACK CORP   *p871*
1160 BIRCHMOUNT RD UNIT 2, SCARBOROUGH, ON, M1P 2B8
(416) 291-8085   *SIC* 5084

PNEUTECH-ROUSSEAU GROUP INC *p1128*
1475 32E AV, LACHINE, QC, H8T 3J1
(514) 635-7000   *SIC* 5084

POINT FOUR SYSTEMS INC   *p201*
16 FAWCETT RD UNIT 103, COQUITLAM, BC, V3K 6X9
SIC 5084

POLAR BEAR WATER GROUP (1978) LTD
p152
1 MAIN ST, PICKARDVILLE, AB, T0G 1W0
(780) 349-4872   *SIC* 5084

POLYWEST LTD   *p389*
3700 MCGILLIVRAY BLVD UNIT B, WINNIPEG, MB, R3P 5S3
(204) 924-8265   *SIC* 5084

POMPACTION INC   *p1252*
119 BOUL HYMUS, POINTE-CLAIRE, QC, H9R 1E5
(514) 697-8600   *SIC* 5084

POMPES ET FILTRATIONS DE THETFORD INC   *p1383*
221 RUE JALBERT O, THETFORD MINES, QC, G6G 7W1
(418) 335-9348   *SIC* 5084

PRAIRIE HYDRAULIC EQUIPMENT LTD *p17*
7824 56 ST SE, CALGARY, AB, T2C 4S9
(403) 279-2070   *SIC* 5084

PRESSTEK CANADA CORP   *p742*
400 AMBASSADOR DR, MISSISSAUGA, ON, L5T 2J3
(905) 362-0610   *SIC* 5084

PRIME FASTENERS (MANITOBA) LIMITED
p384
1501 KING EDWARD ST, WINNIPEG, MB, R3H 0R8
(204) 633-6624   *SIC* 5084

PRIME MATERIAL HANDLING EQUIPMENT LIMITED   *p444*
1 CANAL ST, DARTMOUTH, NS, B2Y 2W1
(902) 468-1210   *SIC* 5084

PRIMO INSTRUMENT INC   *p1240*

4407 RUE DE CHARLEROI, MONTREAL-NORD, QC, H1H 1T6
(514) 329-3242   *SIC* 5084

PRITCHARD ENGINEERING COMPANY LIMITED   *p391*
100 OTTER ST, WINNIPEG, MB, R3T 0M8
(204) 452-2344   *SIC* 5084

PRO-AB EQUIPEMENTS 2003 INC   *p753*
883304 HWY 65, NEW LISKEARD, ON, P0J 1P0
(705) 647-6065   *SIC* 5084

PRO-BEL ENTERPRISES LIMITED   *p474*
765 WESTNEY RD S, AJAX, ON, L1S 6W1
(905) 427-0616   *SIC* 5084

PRO-LINE AUTOMATION SYSTEMS LTD
p1028
303 VAUGHAN VALLEY BLVD, WOODBRIDGE, ON, L4H 3B5
(905) 264-6230   *SIC* 5084

PRO-LINE MANUFACTURING INC   *p6*
27323 TOWNSHIP RD 394 LOT 48, BLACKFALDS, AB, T0M 0J0
(403) 885-2527   *SIC* 5084

PROAX TECHNOLOGIES LTD   *p799*
2552 BRISTOL CIR, OAKVILLE, ON, L6H 5S1
(905) 829-2006   *SIC* 5084

PROCON SYSTEMS (2013) INC   *p68*
9504 HORTON RD SW, CALGARY, AB, T2V 2X4
(403) 255-2921   *SIC* 5084

PROCON SYSTEMS INC   *p42*
1403 29 ST NW, CALGARY, AB, T2N 2T9
(780) 499-7088   *SIC* 5084

PROFILE DRILLING INC   *p689*
6525 NORTHAM DR, MISSISSAUGA, ON, L4V 1J2
(416) 650-6444   *SIC* 5084

PROMAC INDUSTRIES LIMITED PARTNERSHIP   *p17*
7150 112 AVE SE, CALGARY, AB, T2C 4Z1
(403) 279-8333   *SIC* 5084

PRONGHORN CONTROLS LTD   *p17*
4919 72 AVE SE UNIT 101, CALGARY, AB, T2C 3H3
(403) 720-2526   *SIC* 5084

PROSON UTILITY SOLUTIONS INC   *p606*
355 ELMIRA RD N UNIT 138, GUELPH, ON, N1K 1S5
(519) 767-2843   *SIC* 5084

PROTECTION INCENDIE ROBERTS LTEE
p152
26A BOUL HYMUS BUREAU 49, POINTE-CLAIRE, QC, H9R 1C9
(514) 695-7070   *SIC* 5084

PROTOTECH SERVICES LTD   *p110*
6916 68 AVE NW, EDMONTON, AB, T6B 3C5
(780) 433-2133   *SIC* 5084

PROTOTIER-1 INC   *p490*
3690 ADJALA-TECUMSETH TOWNLINE SUITE 2, BEETON, ON, L0G 1A0
(705) 434-0457   *SIC* 5084

PSC-POWER SOURCE CANADA LTD   *p806*
8400 PARKHILL DR, OAKVILLE, ON, L9T 5V7
(289) 851-6690   *SIC* 5084

PSI PROLEW INC   *p1252*
975 AV SELKIRK, POINTE-CLAIRE, QC, H9R 4S4
(514) 697-7867   *SIC* 5084

PT PAPERTECH INC   *p239*
219 1ST ST E, NORTH VANCOUVER, BC, V7L 1B4
(604) 990-1600   *SIC* 5084

PUMPS & PRESSURE INC   *p156*
7018 JOHNSTONE DR, RED DEER, AB, T4P 3Y6
(403) 340-3666   *SIC* 5084

QM BEARINGS & POWER TRANSMISSION LTD   *p207*
1511 DERWENT WAY SUITE 205, DELTA, BC, V3M 6N4
(604) 521-7226   *SIC* 5084

RAM INDUSTRIES INC   *p1438*
33 YORK RD E, YORKTON, SK, S3N 3Z4
(306) 786-2677   *SIC* 5084

RAM MANUFACTURING LTD   *p102*
10203 184 ST NW, EDMONTON, AB, T5S 2J4
(780) 484-4776   *SIC* 5084

RECTOR MACHINE WORKS LTD   *p863*
190 SACKVILLE RD, SAULT STE. MARIE, ON, P6B 4T6
(705) 256-6221   *SIC* 5084

RECUP ESTRIE   *p1371*
2180 RUE CLAUDE-GREFFARD, SHERBROOKE, QC, J1H 5H1
(819) 346-2111   *SIC* 5084

RECUPERACTION MARRONNIERS INC
p1131
2555 AV DOLLARD, LASALLE, QC, H8N 3A9
(514) 595-1212   *SIC* 5084

REDHEAD EQUIPMENT LTD   *p1416*
BOX 32098 HWY 1 E, REGINA, SK, S4N 7L2
(306) 721-2666   *SIC* 5084

REGIONAL HOSE & EQUIPMENT LTD *p536*
175 TURNBULL CRT, CAMBRIDGE, ON, N1T 1C6
(519) 740-1662   *SIC* 5084

REGIONAL HOSE TORONTO LTD   *p558*
15 CONNIE CRES UNIT 2223, CONCORD, ON, L4K 1L3
(905) 660-5560   *SIC* 5084

REGULVAR INC   *p1235*
3985 BOUL INDUSTRIEL, MONTREAL, QC, H7L 4S3
(450) 629-0435   *SIC* 5084

REISER (CANADA) CO.   *p529*
1549 YORKTON CRT UNIT 4, BURLINGTON, ON, L7P 5B7
(905) 631-6611   *SIC* 5084

RELCO INC   *p558*
7700 KEELE ST UNIT 10, CONCORD, ON, L4K 2A1
(416) 740-8632   *SIC* 5084

RELIABLE CORPORATION   *p791*
100 WINGOLD AVE UNIT 5, NORTH YORK, ON, M6B 4K7
(905) 785-0200   *SIC* 5084

RI-GO LIFT TRUCK LIMITED   *p558*
175 COURTLAND AVE, CONCORD, ON, L4K 4T2
(416) 213-7277   *SIC* 5084

RICHWAY ENVIRONMENTAL TECHNOLOGIES LTD   *p264*
11300 NO. 5 RD SUITE 100, RICHMOND, BC, V7A 5J7
(604) 275-2201   *SIC* 5084

RIDEOUT LABRADOR LIMITED   *p424*
GD, HAPPY VALLEY-GOOSE BAY, NL, A0P 1C0
(709) 754-2240   *SIC* 5084

RIDEOUT TOOL AND MACHINE INC   *p431*
222 KENMOUNT RD, ST. JOHN'S, NL, A1B 3R2
(709) 754-2240   *SIC* 5084

ROBOTSHOP INC   *p1153*
18005 RUE LAPOINTE BUREAU 305, MIRABEL, QC, J7J 0G2
(450) 420-1446   *SIC* 5084

RODAN ENERGY SOLUTIONS INC   *p707*
165 MATHESON BLVD E SUITE 6, MISSISSAUGA, ON, L4Z 3K2
(905) 625-9900   *SIC* 5084

ROGER'S ELECTRIC MOTOR SERVICE (1998) LTD   *p394*
1990 CONNOLLY AVE, BATHURST, NB, E2A 4W7
(506) 548-8711   *SIC* 5084

ROLLINS MACHINERY LIMITED   *p227*
21869 56 AVE, LANGLEY, BC, V2Y 2M9
(604) 533-0048   *SIC* 5084

ROTALEC CANADA INC   *p1341*
900 RUE MCCAFFREY, SAINT-LAURENT, QC, H4T 2C7

(514) 341-3685   *SIC* 5084

RUSHTON GAS & OIL EQUIPMENT (1991) LTD   *p124*
2331 121 AVE NE, EDMONTON, AB, T6S 1B2
(780) 475-8801   *SIC* 5084

RYDER MATERIAL HANDLING ULC   *p742*
210 ANNAGEM BLVD, MISSISSAUGA, ON, L5T 2V5
(905) 565-2100   *SIC* 5084

S.N.S. INDUSTRIAL PRODUCTS LIMITED
p888
142 SUGAR MAPLE RD, ST GEORGE BRANT, ON, N0E 1N0
(519) 448-3055   *SIC* 5084

SAMSON CONTROLS INC   *p674*
105 RIVIERA DR UNIT 1, MARKHAM, ON, L3R 5J7
(905) 474-0354   *SIC* 5084

SANCTON GROUP INC   *p413*
85 MCILVEEN DR, SAINT JOHN, NB, E2J 4Y6
(506) 635-8500   *SIC* 5084

SANDVIK CANADA, INC   *p727*
2550 MEADOWVALE BLVD UNIT 3, MISSISSAUGA, ON, L5N 8C2
(905) 826-8900   *SIC* 5084

SANSOM EQUIPMENT LIMITED   *p469*
100 UPHAM DR, TRURO, NS, B2N 6W8
(902) 895-2885   *SIC* 5084

SCM GROUP CANADA INC   *p736*
1180 LORIMAR DR, MISSISSAUGA, ON, L5S 1M9
(905) 670-5110   *SIC* 5084

SCN INDUSTRIEL INC   *p1367*
22555 AUT TRANSCANADIENNE, SENNEVILLE, QC, H9X 3L7
(514) 457-1709   *SIC* 5084

SERVICES FORESTIERS DE MONT-LAURIER LTEE   *p1124*
327 CH DU GOLF RR 1, LAC-DES-ECORCES, QC, J0W 1H0
(819) 623-3143   *SIC* 5084

SHELLEY INDUSTRIAL AUTOMATION INC
p777
41 COLDWATER RD, NORTH YORK, ON, M3B 1Y8
(416) 447-6471   *SIC* 5084

SHELLEY, R G ENTERPRISES (1990) INC
p777
41 COLDWATER RD, NORTH YORK, ON, M3B 1Y8
(416) 447-6471   *SIC* 5084

SICK LTD   *p854*
2 EAST BEAVER CREEK RD UNIT 3, RICHMOND HILL, ON, L4B 2N3
(905) 771-1444   *SIC* 5084

SIMARK CONTROLS LTD   *p18*
10509 46 ST SE, CALGARY, AB, T2C 5C2
(403) 236-0580   *SIC* 5084

SIMSON MAXWELL   *p116*
8750 58 AVE NW, EDMONTON, AB, T6E 6G6
(780) 434-6431   *SIC* 5084

SIRCO MACHINERY COMPANY LIMITED
p576
40 JUTLAND RD, ETOBICOKE, ON, M8Z 2G9
(416) 255-1321   *SIC* 5084

SMC PNEUMATICS (CANADA) LTD   *p799*
2715 BRISTOL CIR SUITE 2, OAKVILLE, ON, L6H 6X5
(905) 812-0400   *SIC* 5084

SMITH CAMERON PUMP SOLUTIONS INC
p277
13478 78 AVE UNIT 1, SURREY, BC, V3W 8J6
(604) 596-5522   *SIC* 5084

SOCIETE XYLEM CANADA   *p604*
55 ROYAL RD, GUELPH, ON, N1H 1T1
(519) 821-1900   *SIC* 5084

SODASTREAM CANADA LTD   *p700*
5450 EXPLORER DR SUITE 202, MISSISSAUGA, ON, L4W 5N1

(905) 629-4450   *SIC* 5084
SOLAR TURBINES CANADA LTD   *p*123
2510 84 AVE NW, EDMONTON, AB, T6P
1K3
(780) 464-8900   *SIC* 5084
SOURCE ATLANTIC LIMITED   *p*414
331 CHESLEY DR, SAINT JOHN, NB, E2K
5P2
(506) 632-1000   *SIC* 5084
SOURCE ATLANTIC LIMITED   *p*414
331 CHESLEY DR, SAINT JOHN, NB, E2K
5P2
(506) 635-7711   *SIC* 5084
SOUTHWEST BINDING SYSTEMS LTD*p*875
20 DOVEDALE CRT, SCARBOROUGH, ON,
M1S 5A7
(416) 285-7044   *SIC* 5084
SPARTAN CONTROLS LTD   *p*11
305 27 ST SE, CALGARY, AB, T2A 7V2
(403) 207-0797   *SIC* 5084
**STANDARD MANUFACTURERS SERVICES
LTD**   *p*367
691 GOLSPIE ST, WINNIPEG, MB, R2K
2V3
(204) 956-6300   *SIC* 5084
STAR PACKAGING EQUIPMENT LIMITED
*p*743
6935 DAVAND DR, MISSISSAUGA, ON,
L5T 1L5
(905) 564-0092   *SIC* 5084
STAR SUPPLY INC   *p*884
530   EASTCHESTER   AVE   E,   ST
CATHARINES, ON, L2M 7P3
(905) 641-1240   *SIC* 5084
STIHL LIMITED   *p*662
1515 SISE RD SUITE 5666, LONDON, ON,
N6N 1E1
(519) 681-3000   *SIC* 5084
STRICTLY SALES & SERVICE INC   *p*448
125 TRIDER CRES, DARTMOUTH, NS,
B3B 1V6
(902) 468-5308   *SIC* 5084
SUREPOINT SERVICES INC   *p*150
1211 8A ST, NISKU, AB, T9E 7R3
(780) 955-3939   *SIC* 5084
SURPLEC INDUSTRIEL INC   *p*1376
155 CH GODIN, SHERBROOKE, QC, J1R
0S6
(819) 821-3634   *SIC* 5084
SYNTEC PROCESS EQUIPMENT LTD *p*495
77 PILLSWORTH RD UNIT 12, BOLTON,
ON, L7E 4G4
(905) 951-8000   *SIC* 5084
SYSTECH INSTRUMENTATION INC   *p*18
3-4351 104 AVE SE, CALGARY, AB, T2C
5C6
(403) 291-3535   *SIC* 5084
SYSTEMES ACCESSAIR INC, LES   *p*1356
1905   RUE   PASTEUR,   SAINTE-
CATHERINE, QC, J5C 1B7
(450) 638-5441   *SIC* 5084
**TARPON ENERGY SERVICES(PROCESS
SYSTEMS)LTD**   *p*19
7020 81 ST SE, CALGARY, AB, T2C 5B8
(403) 234-8647   *SIC* 5084
TATRO EQUIPMENT SALES LTD   *p*543
7744 SEVENTH LINE E, CHATHAM, ON,
N7M 5J6
(519) 354-4352   *SIC* 5084
TAURUS CRACO MACHINERY INC   *p*507
282 ORENDA RD, BRAMPTON, ON, L6T
4X6
(905) 451-8430   *SIC* 5084
TEAM EAGLE LTD   *p*540
10 TRENT DR, CAMPBELLFORD, ON, K0L
1L0
(705) 653-2956   *SIC* 5084
**TECHMATION ELECTRIC & CONTROLS
LTD**   *p*3
117 KINGSVIEW RD SE, AIRDRIE, AB, T4A
0A8
(403) 243-0990   *SIC* 5084
**TECUMSEH PRODUCTS OF CANADA, LIM-
ITED**   *p*482

200 ELM ST, AYLMER, ON, N5H 2M8
(519) 765-1556   *SIC* 5084
TETRA PAK CANADA INC   *p*784
20 DE BOERS DR SUITE 420, NORTH
YORK, ON, M3J 0H1
(647) 775-1837   *SIC* 5084
THOMAS SKINNER & SON LIMITED   *p*256
13880 VULCAN WAY, RICHMOND, BC, V6V
1K6
(604) 276-2131   *SIC* 5084
THUNDER BAY HYDRAULICS LTD   *p*910
701 MONTREAL ST, THUNDER BAY, ON,
P7E 3P2
(807) 623-3151   *SIC* 5084
TKS CONTROLS LTD   *p*167
4605 41 ST, STETTLER, AB, T0C 2L0
(403) 740-4071   *SIC* 5084
TMG NORTH AMERICA INC   *p*589
155 REXDALE BLVD SUITE 207, ETOBI-
COKE, ON, M9W 5Z8
(416) 303-3504   *SIC* 5084
TOMRA CANADA INC   *p*1054
20500   AV   CLARK-GRAHAM,   BAIE-
D'URFE, QC, H9X 4B6
(514) 457-4177   *SIC* 5084
TOOLWAY INDUSTRIES LTD   *p*1028
31 CONAIR PKY, WOODBRIDGE, ON, L4H
0S4
(905) 326-5450   *SIC* 5084
TOP LIFT ENTERPRISES INC   *p*893
42 PINELANDS AVE, STONEY CREEK,
ON, L8E 5X9
(905) 662-4137   *SIC* 5084
TORCAN LIFT EQUIPMENT LTD   *p*559
166 BOWES RD, CONCORD, ON, L4K 1J6
(905) 760-1582   *SIC* 5084
TRANSCAT CANADA INC   *p*1091
90A BOUL BRUNSWICK BUREAU A,
DOLLARD-DES-ORMEAUX, QC, H9B 2C5
(514) 685-9626   *SIC* 5084
TRC HYDRAULICS INC   *p*398
855 RUE CHAMPLAIN, DIEPPE, NB, E1A
1P6
(506) 853-1986   *SIC* 5084
**TRICENTRIS - TRI, TRANSFORMATION,
SENSIBILISATION**   *p*1103
45   RUE   PIERRE-MENARD,   GATINEAU,
QC, J8R 3X3
(819) 643-4448   *SIC* 5084
TRIONEX INC   *p*1046
121 RUE DES METIERS, AMOS, QC, J9T
4M4
(819) 732-5327   *SIC* 5084
TRIUMPH TOOL LTD   *p*606
91 ARROW RD, GUELPH, ON, N1K 1S8
(519) 836-4811   *SIC* 5084
TS LP   *p*111
5135 67 AVE NW, EDMONTON, AB, T6B
2R8
(780) 481-1122   *SIC* 5084
TYSON TOOL COMPANY LIMITED   *p*794
75 ORMONT DR, NORTH YORK, ON, M9L
2S3
(416) 746-3688   *SIC* 5084
UNI-RAM CORPORATION   *p*676
381 BENTLEY ST SUITE 117, MARKHAM,
ON, L3R 9T2
(905) 477-5911   *SIC* 5084
UNITEC WELDING ALLOYS   *p*560
61 VILLARBOIT CRES, CONCORD, ON,
L4K 4R2
(905) 669-4249   *SIC* 5084
VAN DE WATER-RAYMOND 1960 LTEE
*p*1084
1600A BOUL SAINT-MARTIN E UNITE 680,
COTE SAINT-LUC, QC, H7G 4R8
(888) 597-5538   *SIC* 5084
VERMEER CANADA INC   *p*893
1100 SOUTH SERVICE RD SUITE 423,
STONEY CREEK, ON, L8E 0C5
(289) 765-5260   *SIC* 5084
VIKING PUMP OF CANADA INC   *p*1024
661 GROVE AVE, WINDSOR, ON, N9A 6G7
(519) 256-5438   *SIC* 5084

**VIKING SURPLUS OIL FIELD EQUIPMENT
LTD**   *p*1406
36 HWY 39 E, ESTEVAN, SK, S4A 2L7
SIC 5084
VISUASCAN INC   *p*1345
9066   RUE   PASCAL-GAGNON,   SAINT-
LEONARD, QC, H1P 2X4
(514) 322-2725   *SIC* 5084
WAINBEE LIMITED   *p*707
5789 COOPERS AVE, MISSISSAUGA, ON,
L4Z 3S6
(905) 568-1700   *SIC* 5084
WAINBEE S H C N INC   *p*1367
453 AV NOEL, SEPT-ILES, QC, G4R 1M1
(418) 962-4949   *SIC* 5084
WAJAX CORPORATION   *p*703
3280 WHARTON WAY, MISSISSAUGA, ON,
L4X 2C5
(905) 212-3300   *SIC* 5084
**WAJAX INDUSTRIAL COMPONENTS LIM-
ITED PARTNERSHIP**   *p*1129
2202 52E AV, LACHINE, QC, H8T 2Y3
(514) 636-3333   *SIC* 5084
**WAJAX INDUSTRIAL COMPONENTS LIM-
ITED PARTNERSHIP**   *p*1129
2200 52E AV, LACHINE, QC, H8T 2Y3
(514) 636-3333   *SIC* 5084
WAJAX LIMITED   *p*728
2250 ARGENTIA RD, MISSISSAUGA, ON,
L5N 6A5
(905) 212-3300   *SIC* 5084
WALL GRAIN HANDLING SYSTEMS LTD
*p*392
1460 CHEVRIER BLVD UNIT 202, WIN-
NIPEG, MB, R3T 1Y6
(204) 269-7616   *SIC* 5084
WALLACE EQUIPMENT LTD   *p*402
25 GILLIS RD, FREDERICTON, NB, E3C
2G3
(506) 458-8380   *SIC* 5084
WALLMARC WOOD INDUSTRIES LIMITED
*p*905
59 GLEN CAMERON RD, THORNHILL, ON,
L3T 5W2
(905) 889-1342   *SIC* 5084
WARRIOR RIG TECHNOLOGIES LIMITED
*p*12
1515 28 ST NE, CALGARY, AB, T2A 3T1
(403) 291-6444   *SIC* 5084
WEIR CANADA, INC   *p*728
2360 MILLRACE CRT, MISSISSAUGA, ON,
L5N 1W2
(905) 812-7100   *SIC* 5084
WEIR CANADA, INC   *p*1133
9401 RUE WANKLYN, LASALLE, QC, H8R
1Z2
(514) 366-4310   *SIC* 5084
WESTECH INDUSTRIAL LTD   *p*38
5636 BURBANK CRES SE, CALGARY, AB,
T2H 1Z6
(403) 252-8803   *SIC* 5084
WESTERN BELTING & HOSE (1986) LTD
*p*187
6468 BERESFORD ST, BURNABY, BC, V5E
1B6
(604) 451-4133   *SIC* 5084
**WESTERN   MATERIALS   HANDLING   &
EQUIPMENT LTD**   *p*19
7805 46 ST SE, CALGARY, AB, T2C 2Y5
(403) 236-0305   *SIC* 5084
WESTERN OIL SERVICES LTD   *p*228
19840 57A AVE, LANGLEY, BC, V3A 6G6
(604) 514-4787   *SIC* 5084
WESTPOWER EQUIPMENT LTD   *p*19
4451 54 AVE SE, CALGARY, AB, T2C 2A2
(403) 720-3300   *SIC* 5084
WESTQUIP DIESEL SALES (ALTA) LTD *p*2
11162 261 ST, ACHESON, AB, T7X 6C7
(780) 960-5560   *SIC* 5084
WESTVAC INDUSTRIAL LTD   *p*2
26609 111 AVE, ACHESON, AB, T7X 6E1
(780) 962-1218   *SIC* 5084
WESTWAY MACHINERY LTD   *p*709
2370 CAWTHRA RD, MISSISSAUGA, ON,

L5A 2X1
(905) 803-9999   *SIC* 5084
WF STEEL & CRANE LTD   *p*150
705 23 AVE, NISKU, AB, T9E 7Y5
(587) 410-0625   *SIC* 5084
**WILLIAMS MACHINERY LIMITED PART-
NERSHIP**   *p*275
10240 GRACE RD, SURREY, BC, V3V 3V6
(604) 930-3300   *SIC* 5084
WOLFTEK INDUSTRIES INC   *p*251
4944   CONTINENTAL   WAY,   PRINCE
GEORGE, BC, V2N 5S5
(250) 561-1556   *SIC* 5084
WOODLAND EQUIPMENT INC   *p*216
2015 TRANS CANADA HWY W, KAM-
LOOPS, BC, V1S 1A7
(250) 372-2855   *SIC* 5084
WULFTEC INTERNATIONAL INC   *p*1052
209 RUE WULFTEC, AYER'S CLIFF, QC,
J0B 1C0
(819) 838-4232   *SIC* 5084
YALE INDUSTRIAL TRUCKS INC   *p*1034
340 HANLAN RD, WOODBRIDGE, ON, L4L
3P6
(905) 851-6620   *SIC* 5084
YASKAWA CANADA INC   *p*718
3530 LAIRD RD UNIT 3, MISSISSAUGA,
ON, L5L 5Z7
(905) 569-6686   *SIC* 5084
ZAZULA PROCESS EQUIPMENT LTD *p*33
4609 MANITOBA RD SE, CALGARY, AB,
T2G 4B9
(403) 244-0751   *SIC* 5084
ZEDI CANADA INC   *p*66
902 11 AVE SW, CALGARY, AB, T2R 0E7
(403) 444-1100   *SIC* 5084

SIC 5085 *Industrial supplies*

1669051 NOVA SCOTIA LIMITED   *p*781
680 STEEPROCK DR, NORTH YORK, ON,
M3J 2X1
(416) 635-6500   *SIC* 5085
190394 CANADA INC   *p*1248
5977 RTE TRANSCANADIENNE, POINTE-
CLAIRE, QC, H9R 1C1
(514) 630-2800   *SIC* 5085
2962-9060 QUEBEC INC   *p*1151
12770 RUE BRAULT, MIRABEL, QC, J7J
0W3
(450) 420-1839   *SIC* 5085
3033441 NOVA SCOTIA COMPANY   *p*162
172 TURBO DR, SHERWOOD PARK, AB,
T8H 2J6
(780) 464-7774   *SIC* 5085
519728 ONTARIO LTD   *p*839
38 LANARK RD, PERTH, ON, K7H 3C9
(613) 267-5880   *SIC* 5085
5BLUE PROCESS EQUIPMENT INC   *p*148
2303 8 ST, NISKU, AB, T9E 7Z3
(780) 955-2040   *SIC* 5085
680061 ONTARIO LIMITED   *p*648
44 BELLEISLE CRT, LONDON, ON, N5V
4L2
(519) 659-2696   *SIC* 5085
A. C. T. EQUIPMENT SALES LTD   *p*184
4455 ALASKA ST, BURNABY, BC, V5C 5T3
(604) 294-6271   *SIC* 5085
ABRASIFS J.J.S. INC   *p*1140
900 CH OLIVIER, LEVIS, QC, G7A 2N1
(418) 836-0557   *SIC* 5085
ABRASIVE BLAST & PAINT INC   *p*148
1207 16 AVE, NISKU, AB, T9E 0A8
(780) 955-3616   *SIC* 5085
ABRASIVE TECHNOLOGY NA, INC *p*1093
2250 BOUL HYMUS, DORVAL, QC, H9P
1J9
(514) 421-7396   *SIC* 5085
ACCURATE FASTENERS LTD   *p*548
550 APPLEWOOD CRES SUITE 1, CON-
CORD, ON, L4K 4B4
(416) 798-7887   *SIC* 5085
ACIERS INOXYDABLES C.F.F. (QUEBEC)

INC   p1332
4900 CH DU BOIS-FRANC, SAINT-LAURENT, QC, H4S 1A7
(514) 337-7700   SIC 5085

ACKLANDS - GRAINGER INC   p92
14360 123 AVE NW, EDMONTON, AB, T5L 2Y3
SIC 5085

ACKLANDS - GRAINGER INC   p95
11708 167 ST NW, EDMONTON, AB, T5M 3Z2
(780) 453-0300   SIC 5085

ACKLANDS - GRAINGER INC   p903
123 COMMERCE VALLEY DR E SUITE 700, THORNHILL, ON, L3T 7W8
(905) 731-5516   SIC 5085

ACKLANDS - GRAINGER INC   p1434
3602 MILLAR AVE, SASKATOON, SK, S7P 0B1
(306) 664-5500   SIC 5085

ALFA LAVAL INC   p873
101 MILNER AVE, SCARBOROUGH, ON, M1S 4S6
(416) 299-6101   SIC 5085

ALFAGOMMA CANADA INC   p1332
6550 RUE ABRAMS BUREAU 6540, SAINT-LAURENT, QC, H4S 1Y2
(514) 333-5577   SIC 5085

ALICE-ALIYA (CANADA) INC   p850
92 SPRINGBROOK DR, RICHMOND HILL, ON, L4B 3P9
(905) 886-1172   SIC 5085

ALIMENTS SERVAL CANADA LTEE, LES p1146
303 RUE SAINT-MARC, LOUISEVILLE, QC, J5V 2G2
(819) 228-5551   SIC 5085

ALTA WEST INDUSTRIES   p136
141 HAMPSHIRE RD, HINTON, AB, T7V 1G8
(780) 865-2930   SIC 5085

AMCAN-JUMAX INC   p1307
3300 2E RUE, SAINT-HUBERT, QC, J3Y 8Y7
(450) 445-8888   SIC 5085

AMPAK INC   p1134
4225 DES LAURENTIDES (A-15) E, LAVAL-OUEST, QC, H7L 5W5
(450) 682-4141   SIC 5085

ANIXTER POWER SOLUTIONS CANADA INC p546
188 PURDY RD, COLBORNE, ON, K0K 1S0
(905) 355-2474   SIC 5085

APPLIED INDUSTRIAL TECHNOLOGIES, LP p1434
143 WHEELER ST, SASKATOON, SK, S7P 0A4
(306) 931-0888   SIC 5085

ARCTEC ALLOYS LIMITED   p20
4304 10 ST NE, CALGARY, AB, T2E 6K3
(403) 250-9355   SIC 5085

ARMOUR VALVE LTD   p873
126 MILNER AVE, SCARBOROUGH, ON, M1S 3R2
(416) 299-0780   SIC 5085

ATLAS BEARINGS CORPORATION   p501
8043 DIXIE RD, BRAMPTON, ON, L6T 3V1
(905) 790-0283   SIC 5085

ATTACHES INDUSTRIELLES USCAN LTEE, LES p1091
87A BOUL BRUNSWICK, DOLLARD-DES-ORMEAUX, QC, H9B 2J5
(514) 684-2940   SIC 5085

B.C. FASTENERS & TOOLS (2000) LTD p275
12824 78 AVE UNIT 101, SURREY, BC, V3W 8E7
(604) 599-5455   SIC 5085

B.C. FASTENERS & TOOLS LTD   p221
1960 WINDSOR RD SUITE 3, KELOWNA, BC, V1Y 4R5
(250) 868-9222   SIC 5085

B.G.E. SERVICE & SUPPLY LTD   p118
5711 103A ST NW, EDMONTON, AB, T6H 2J6

(780) 436-6960   SIC 5085
BDI CANADA INC   p737
6235 TOMKEN RD, MISSISSAUGA, ON, L5T 1K2
(905) 238-3392   SIC 5085

BERICAP INC   p521
835 SYSCON CRT, BURLINGTON, ON, L7L 6C5
(905) 634-2248   SIC 5085

BISSETT FASTENERS LIMITED   p200
63 FAWCETT RD, COQUITLAM, BC, V3K 6V2
(604) 540-0200   SIC 5085

BOHNE SPRING INDUSTRIES LIMITED p573
60 CORONET RD, ETOBICOKE, ON, M8Z 2M1
(416) 231-9000   SIC 5085

BOLT AND NUT SUPPLY LIMITED   p532
384 FRANKLIN BLVD, CAMBRIDGE, ON, N1R 8G5
(519) 623-0370   SIC 5085

BOLT SUPPLY HOUSE LTD, THE   p27
3909 MANCHESTER RD SE UNIT C, CALGARY, AB, T2G 4A1
(403) 245-2818   SIC 5085

BOSHART INDUSTRIES INC   p685
25 WHALEY AVE, MILVERTON, ON, N0K 1M0
(519) 595-4444   SIC 5085

BRIGHTON-BEST INTERNATIONAL, (CANADA) INC p501
7900 GOREWAY DR SUITE 1, BRAMPTON, ON, L6T 5W6
(905) 791-2000   SIC 5085

BRITISH FASTENING SYSTEMS LIMITED p782
155 CHAMPAGNE DR UNIT 10, NORTH YORK, ON, M3J 2C6
(416) 631-9400   SIC 5085

BUCKET SHOP INC, THE   p913
24 GOVERNMENT RD S, TIMMINS, ON, P4R 1N4
(705) 531-2658   SIC 5085

BURKERT CONTROMATIC INC   p521
5002 SOUTH SERVICE RD, BURLINGTON, ON, L7L 5Y7
(905) 632-3033   SIC 5085

C.G. INDUSTRIAL SPECIALTIES LTD p290
558 E KENT AVE SOUTH, VANCOUVER, BC, V5X 4V6
(604) 263-1671   SIC 5085

CALGARY FASTENERS & TOOLS LTD p28
1288 42 AVE SE UNIT 1, CALGARY, AB, T2G 5P1
(403) 287-5340   SIC 5085

CALGARY VALVE & FITTING INC   p10
3202 12 AVE NE, CALGARY, AB, T2A 6N8
(403) 243-5646   SIC 5085

CAM DISTRIBUTORS LTD   p14
7095 64 ST SE UNIT 20, CALGARY, AB, T2C 5C3
(403) 720-0076   SIC 5085

CAMFIL CANADA INC   p1233
2785 AV FRANCIS-HUGHES, MONTREAL, QC, H7L 3J6
(450) 629-3030   SIC 5085

CANADIAN BABBITT BEARINGS LTD p513
64 DALKEITH DR, BRANTFORD, ON, N3P 1N6
(519) 752-5471   SIC 5085

CANADIAN BEARINGS LTD   p734
1600 DREW RD, MISSISSAUGA, ON, L5S 1S5
(905) 670-7422   SIC 5085

CANADIAN INTERMODAL SERVICES LTD p14
5402 44 ST SE, CALGARY, AB, T2C 4M8
(403) 920-0577   SIC 5085

CANADIAN MEASUREMENT-METROLOGY INC p720
2433 MEADOWVALE BLVD, MISSISSAUGA, ON, L5N 5S2
(905) 819-7878   SIC 5085

CANADIAN THREADALL LIMITED   p535
130 TURNBULL CRT, CAMBRIDGE, ON, N1T 1J2
(519) 576-3360   SIC 5085

CANMEC LA BAIE INC   p1121
3453 CH DES CHUTES, LA BAIE, QC, G7B 3N8
(418) 544-3391   SIC 5085

CAOUTCHOUC ET PLASTIQUES FALPACO INC p1110
825 RUE J.-A.-BOMBARDIER, GRANBY, QC, J2J 1E9
(450) 378-3348   SIC 5085

CARLSTAR GROUP ULC, THE   p1010
645 MCMURRAY RD, WATERLOO, ON, N2V 2B7
(519) 885-0630   SIC 5085

CARTOUCHES CERTIFIEES INC   p1183
160 RUE SAINT-VIATEUR E BUREAU 411, MONTREAL, QC, H2T 1A8
(888) 573-6787   SIC 5085

CHECKER INDUSTRIAL LTD   p1022
3345 WYANDOTTE ST E, WINDSOR, ON, N8Y 1E9
(519) 258-2022   SIC 5085

CHEMLINE PLASTICS LIMITED   p904
55 GUARDSMAN RD, THORNHILL, ON, L3T 6L2
(905) 889-7890   SIC 5085

CHENG SHIN RUBBER CANADA, INC p499
400 CHRYSLER DR UNIT C, BRAMPTON, ON, L6S 5Z5
(905) 789-0882   SIC 5085

CITERNES EXPERTS INC   p1231
4545 AV DES INDUSTRIES, MONTREAL, QC, H7C 1A1
(514) 323-5510   SIC 5085

CLOW CANADA INC   p609
1757 BURLINGTON ST E, HAMILTON, ON, L8H 3L5
(905) 548-9604   SIC 5085

COMMERCIAL BEARING SERVICE (1966) LTD. p113
4203 95 ST NW SUITE 1966, EDMONTON, AB, T6E 5R6
(780) 432-1611   SIC 5085

COMMERCIAL SOLUTIONS INC   p113
4203 95 ST NW, EDMONTON, AB, T6E 5R6
(780) 432-1611   SIC 5085

COMPAGNIE MOTOPARTS INC   p1246
1124 RUE SAINT-CALIXTE, PLESSISVILLE, QC, G6L 1N8
(819) 362-7373   SIC 5085

CONCEPTS ON WHEELS INC   p668
2600 JOHN ST UNIT 224, MARKHAM, ON, L3R 3W3
(905) 513-1595   SIC 5085

CONCORD SCREEN INC   p755
1311 KERRISDALE BLVD, NEWMARKET, ON, L3Y 8Z8
(905) 953-8100   SIC 5085

CONNECT CONVEYOR BELTING INC p683
405 INDUSTRIAL DR UNIT 128, MILTON, ON, L9T 5B1
(905) 878-5552   SIC 5085

CONSTRUCTION FASTENERS & TOOLS LTD p1426
504 45TH A ST E, SASKATOON, SK, S7K 0W7
(306) 668-8880   SIC 5085

CONTAINERWEST MANUFACTURING LTD p254
11660 MITCHELL RD, RICHMOND, BC, V6V 1T7
(604) 322-0533   SIC 5085

CONTROLES LAURENTIDE LTEE   p1118
18000 RTE TRANSCANADIENNE, KIRKLAND, QC, H9J 4A1
(514) 697-9230   SIC 5085

CORPORATION DE VALVES TRUELINE, LA p1355
20675 BOUL INDUSTRIEL, SAINTE-ANNE-DE-BELLEVUE, QC, H9X 4B2
(514) 457-5777   SIC 5085

CRANE CANADA CO.   p1027
141 ROYAL GROUP CRES, WOODBRIDGE, ON, L4H 1X9
(416) 244-5351   SIC 5085

CYNTECH CONSTRUCTION LTD   p159
235061 WRANGLER LINK, ROCKY VIEW COUNTY, AB, T1X 0K3
(403) 228-1767   SIC 5085

DAVID & CLAUDE HOLDINGS CANADA INC p533
30 COWANSVIEW RD, CAMBRIDGE, ON, N1R 7N3
(519) 622-2320   SIC 5085

DEETAG LTD   p648
649 THIRD ST, LONDON, ON, N5V 2C1
(519) 659-4673   SIC 5085

DISTRIBUTIONS J.R.V. INC   p1367
818 BOUL LAURE BUREAU 101, SEPT-ILES, QC, G4R 1Y8
(418) 962-9457   SIC 5085

DIVERSCO SUPPLY INC   p533
495 CONESTOGA BLVD, CAMBRIDGE, ON, N1R 7P4
(519) 740-1210   SIC 5085

DOALL CANADA INC   p797
2715 BRISTOL CIR, OAKVILLE, ON, L6H 6X5
(800) 923-6255   SIC 5085

DRESSER-RAND CANADA, ULC   p114
9330 45 AVE NW, EDMONTON, AB, T6E 6S1
(780) 436-0604   SIC 5085

DRILLING FLUIDS TREATMENT SYSTEMS INC p15
7530 114 AVE SE, CALGARY, AB, T2C 4T3
(403) 279-0123   SIC 5085

DYNA-FLO CONTROL VALVE SERVICES LTD p122
1911 66 AVE NW, EDMONTON, AB, T6P 1M5
(780) 469-4000   SIC 5085

DYNALINE INDUSTRIES INC   p100
18070 109 AVE NW, EDMONTON, AB, T5S 2K2
(780) 453-3964   SIC 5085

DYNAMEX INDUSTRIAL SUPPLY LTD p120
6558 28 AVE NW UNIT 295, EDMONTON, AB, T6L 6N3
(780) 904-3451   SIC 5085

EAGLEBURGMANN CANADA INC   p683
8699 ESCARPMENT WAY SUITE 9, MILTON, ON, L9T 0J5
(905) 693-8782   SIC 5085

EARLS INDUSTRIES LTD   p246
1616 KEBET WAY, PORT COQUITLAM, BC, V3C 5W9
(604) 941-8388   SIC 5085

EDMONTON FASTENERS & TOOLS LTD p95
16409 111 AVE NW, EDMONTON, AB, T5M 2S2
(780) 484-3113   SIC 5085

EDMONTON VALVE & FITTING INC p114
4503 93 ST NW, EDMONTON, AB, T6E 5S9
(780) 437-0640   SIC 5085

ENDRIES INTERNATIONAL CANADA INC p536
255 PINEBUSH RD UNIT A, CAMBRIDGE, ON, N1T 1B9
(519) 740-3523   SIC 5085

ENGRENAGE PROVINCIAL INC   p1080
1001 RUE DE LA RUPERT, CHICOUTIMI, QC, G7K 0A2
(418) 693-8132   SIC 5085

ENGRENAGE PROVINCIAL INC   p1260
165 BOUL DES CEDRES, QUEBEC, QC, G1L 1M8
(418) 683-2745   SIC 5085

ENGRENAGES POWER-LINK2 INC, LES p1309
5405 RUE J.-A.-BOMBARDIER, SAINT-HUBERT, QC, J3Z 1K3
(450) 678-0588   SIC 5085

ENGRENAGES SPECIALISES INC   p1283

620 RUE DESMARAIS, RICHMOND, QC, J0B 2H0
(819) 826-3379   SIC 5085

ENTREPRISES ELECTRIQUES NADCO INC p1157
8550 CH DELMEADE, MONT-ROYAL, QC, H4T 1L7
(514) 342-2748   SIC 5085

EQUIPMENT LEASING COMPANY LTD, THE p480
106 BROOKEVIEW DR, AURORA, ON, L4G 6R5
(905) 629-3210   SIC 5085

EQUIPMENTS INDUSTRIELS I.B.S. VAL D'OR INC, LES p1390
85 RUE DES DISTRIBUTEURS, VAL-D'OR, QC, J9P 6Y1
(819) 825-3179   SIC 5085

ERIKS INDUSTRIAL SERVICES LP p125
9748 12 AVE SW, EDMONTON, AB, T6X 0J5
(780) 437-1260   SIC 5085

EUTECTIC CANADA INC p1394
428 RUE AIME-VINCENT, VAUDREUIL-DORION, QC, J7V 5V5
(514) 695-7500   SIC 5085

EXOCOR LTD p886
271 RIDLEY RD W SUITE 2, ST CATHARINES, ON, L2S 0B3
(905) 704-0603   SIC 5085

F. K. MACHINERY LIMITED p486
475 WELHAM RD, BARRIE, ON, L4N 8Z6
(705) 721-4200   SIC 5085

FAIRVIEW LTD p797
1170 INVICTA DR UNIT C, OAKVILLE, ON, L6H 6G1
(905) 338-0800   SIC 5085

FASTENAL CANADA LTD p636
900 WABANAKI DR, KITCHENER, ON, N2C 0B7
(519) 748-6566   SIC 5085

FASTENAL CANADA, LTEE p636
900 WABANAKI DR, KITCHENER, ON, N2C 0B7
(519) 748-6566   SIC 5085

FASTENER WAREHOUSE LTD p1427
820 46TH ST E, SASKATOON, SK, S7K 3V7
(306) 374-1199   SIC 5085

FASTENERS & FITTINGS INC p683
901 STEELES AVE E, MILTON, ON, L9T 5H3
(905) 670-2503   SIC 5085

FASTENING HOUSE INC p552
160 BASS PRO MILLS DR, CONCORD, ON, L4K 0A7
(905) 669-7448   SIC 5085

FENNER DUNLOP (BRACEBRIDGE), INC p496
700 ECCLESTONE DR, BRACEBRIDGE, ON, P1L 1W1
(705) 645-4431   SIC 5085

FESTO INC p695
5300 EXPLORER DR, MISSISSAUGA, ON, L4W 5G4
(905) 624-9000   SIC 5085

FIBRES DE VERRE RIOUX INC, LES p1358
10 RANG COTE BIC, SAINTE-FRANCOISE, QC, G0L 3B0
(418) 851-1240   SIC 5085

FLUIDSEAL INC p254
13680 BRIDGEPORT RD SUITE 5, RICHMOND, BC, V6V 1V3
(604) 278-6808   SIC 5085

GATES CANADA INC p515
225 HENRY ST BLDG 8, BRANTFORD, ON, N3S 7R4
(519) 759-4141   SIC 5085

GENERAL BEARING SERVICE INC p834
490 KENT ST, OTTAWA, ON, K2P 2B7
(613) 238-8100   SIC 5085

GLASROCK PRODUCTS INC p892
274 SOUTH SERVICE RD SUITE 268, STONEY CREEK, ON, L8E 2N9
(905) 664-5300   SIC 5085

GOULD FASTENERS p688
6209 NORTHWEST DR, MISSISSAUGA, ON, L4V 1P6
(905) 677-8253   SIC 5085

GREEN LINE HOSE & FITTINGS LTD p206
1477 DERWENT WAY, DELTA, BC, V3M 6N3
(604) 670-1647   SIC 5085

GREEN LINE SALES LTD p206
1477 DERWENT WAY, DELTA, BC, V3M 6N3
(604) 525-6800   SIC 5085

GREGG DISTRIBUTORS (FORT MCMURRAY) LTD p128
325 MACALPINE CRES, FORT MCMURRAY, AB, T9H 4Y4
(780) 715-4000   SIC 5085

GREGG DISTRIBUTORS LIMITED PARTNERSHIP p35
5755 11 ST SE, CALGARY, AB, T2H 1M7
(403) 253-6463   SIC 5085

GRIMCO CANADA, INC p783
680 STEEPROCK DR, NORTH YORK, ON, M3J 2X1
(416) 635-6500   SIC 5085

GRK CANADA LIMITED p910
1499 ROSSLYN RD, THUNDER BAY, ON, P7E 6W1
(807) 474-4300   SIC 5085

GROUPE J.S.V. INC, LE p1162
8015 AV MARCO-POLO, MONTREAL, QC, H1E 5Y8
(514) 842-8351   SIC 5085

GROUPE VIF INC p1312
4000 BOUL CASAVANT O, SAINT-HYACINTHE, QC, J2S 9E3
(450) 774-6953   SIC 5085

HALL FILTER SERVICE (2013) LTD, LES p239
338 ESPLANADE E, NORTH VANCOUVER, BC, V7L 1A4
(604) 986-5366   SIC 5085

HANSLER SMITH LIMITED p519
1385 CALIFORNIA AVE, BROCKVILLE, ON, K6V 5V5
(613) 342-4408   SIC 5085

HARVAN MANUFACTURING LTD p1036
612 JACK ROSS AVE, WOODSTOCK, ON, N4V 1B6
(519) 537-8311   SIC 5085

HASKINS INDUSTRIAL INC p762
1371 FRANKLIN ST, NORTH BAY, ON, P1A 2W1
(705) 474-4420   SIC 5085

HB SEALING PRODUCTS LTD p487
30 SAUNDERS RD SUITE 1, BARRIE, ON, L4N 9A8
(705) 739-6735   SIC 5085

HI-TECH SEALS INC p115
9211 41 AVE NW, EDMONTON, AB, T6E 6R5
(780) 438-6055   SIC 5085

HIGGINSON EQUIPMENT INC p522
1175 CORPORATE DR UNIT 1, BURLINGTON, ON, L7L 5V5
(905) 335-2211   SIC 5085

HOWELL PLUMBING SUPPLIES DASCO LIMITED p593
11 ARMSTRONG AVE, GEORGETOWN, ON, L7G 4S1
(905) 877-2293   SIC 5085

HUOT, REAL INC p1267
2550 AV DALTON, QUEBEC, QC, G1P 3S4
(418) 634-5967   SIC 5085

HYDAC INTERNATIONAL p1369
83 RUE DU TOURNESOL, SHEFFORD, QC, J2M 1K9
(450) 539-3388   SIC 5085

I.R.P. INDUSTRIAL RUBBER LTD p740
6300 EDWARDS BLVD UNIT 1, MISSISSAUGA, ON, L5T 2V7
(905) 670-5700   SIC 5085

ICS UNIVERSAL DRUM RECONDITIONING LIMITED PARTNERSHIP p713

2460 ROYAL WINDSOR DR, MISSISSAUGA, ON, L5J 1K7
(905) 822-3280   SIC 5085

IDEAL GEAR AND MACHINE WORKS INC p210
6415 RIVER RD, DELTA, BC, V4K 5B9
(604) 952-4327   SIC 5085

INCOM MANUFACTURING GROUP LTD p477
1259 SANDHILL DR SUITE 76, ANCASTER, ON, L9G 4V5
(905) 648-0774   SIC 5085

INDUSTRIAL, PETROLEUM AND MINING SUPPLIES LIMITED p474
395 WESTNEY RD S, AJAX, ON, L1S 6M6
(905) 686-4071   SIC 5085

INDUSTRIES GENO INC, LES p1334
5750 CH SAINT-FRANCOIS, SAINT-LAURENT, QC, H4S 1B7
(514) 331-4915   SIC 5085

INLAND INDUSTRIAL SUPPLY LTD p120
9949 29A AVE NW, EDMONTON, AB, T6N 1A9
(780) 413-0029   SIC 5085

INNOVATION PCM INC p1356
21 RUE INDUSTRIELLE, SAINTE-CLAIRE, QC, G0R 2V0
(418) 883-4009   SIC 5085

INNOVATIVE CONTROL SOLUTIONS INC p671
3115 14TH AVE SUITE 8, MARKHAM, ON, L3R 0H1
(905) 709-4220   SIC 5085

INTERCITY INDUSTRIAL SUPPLY LIMITED p908
669 SQUIER ST, THUNDER BAY, ON, P7B 4A7
(807) 345-2324   SIC 5085

INVESTISSEMENTS MICHAEL WILSON INC, LES p1401
642 AV MURRAY HILL, WESTMOUNT, QC, H3Y 2W6
(450) 465-3330   SIC 5085

ISCO CANADA, INC p373
2901 STURGEON RD, WINNIPEG, MB, R2Y 2L9
(204) 831-8625   SIC 5085

J/E BEARING & MACHINE LTD p911
68 SPRUCE ST, TILLSONBURG, ON, N4G 5V3
(519) 842-8476   SIC 5085

JET EQUIPMENT & TOOLS LTD p182
3260 PRODUCTION WAY, BURNABY, BC, V5A 4W4
(800) 472-7686   SIC 5085

JOINTS ETANCHES R.B. INC, LES p1334
8585 BOUL HENRI-BOURASSA O, SAINT-LAURENT, QC, H4S 1P7
(514) 334-2220   SIC 5085

JONES, CHARLES INDUSTRIAL LIMITED p892
237 ARVIN AVE, STONEY CREEK, ON, L8E 5S6
(905) 664-8448   SIC 5085

K&D PRATT GROUP INC p426
126 GLENCOE DR, MOUNT PEARL, NL, A1N 4S9
(709) 722-5690   SIC 5085

KAMAN INDUSTRIAL TECHNOLOGIES, LTD p206
746 CHESTER RD, DELTA, BC, V3M 6J1
(604) 523-2356   SIC 5085

KEYENCE CANADA INC p723
6775 FINANCIAL DR SUITE 202, MISSISSAUGA, ON, L5N 0A4
(905) 366-7655   SIC 5085

KEYMAY INTERNATIONAL INC p161
53169 RANGE ROAD 225, SHERWOOD PARK, AB, T8A 4T7
(780) 417-1955   SIC 5085

KILIAN CANADA ULC p575
75 TORLAKE CRES, ETOBICOKE, ON, M8Z 1B7
(416) 252-5936   SIC 5085

KING MANUFACTURING p435
9 ASPEN RD, HAY RIVER, NT, X0E 0R6
(867) 874-2373   SIC 5085

KING'S ENERGY SERVICES LTD p158
277 BURNT PARK DR, RED DEER COUNTY, AB, T4S 0K7
(403) 343-2822   SIC 5085

KLINGSPOR INC p892
1175 BARTON ST UNIT 1, STONEY CREEK, ON, L8E 5H1
(905) 643-0770   SIC 5085

KOYO BEARINGS CANADA INC p1056
4 RUE VICTORIA S, BEDFORD, QC, J0J 1A0
(450) 248-3316   SIC 5085

KSB PUMPS INC p696
5205 TOMKEN RD, MISSISSAUGA, ON, L4W 3N8
(905) 568-9200   SIC 5085

KTI LIMITED p481
33 ISAACSON CRES, AURORA, ON, L4G 0A4
(905) 727-8807   SIC 5085

LAFCO OUTILLAGE INC p1049
7700 RUE BOMBARDIER, ANJOU, QC, H1J 0A2
(514) 327-7556   SIC 5085

LAKESHORE MILL SUPPLIES LTD p813
150 WENTWORTH ST E, OSHAWA, ON, L1H 3V5
(905) 579-5222   SIC 5085

LAWSON PRODUCTS INC. (ONTARIO) p724
7315 RAPISTAN CRT, MISSISSAUGA, ON, L5N 5Z4
(905) 567-0089   SIC 5085

LEGERE INDUSTRIAL SUPPLIES LTD p832
1140 MORRISON DR UNIT 110, OTTAWA, ON, K2H 8S9
(613) 829-8010   SIC 5085

LENNOX DRUM LIMITED p474
233 FULLER RD, AJAX, ON, L1S 2E1
(905) 427-1441   SIC 5085

LEVAC SUPPLY LIMITED p630
25 RAILWAY ST, KINGSTON, ON, K7K 2L7
(613) 546-6663   SIC 5085

M & Z INDUSTRIAL SUPPLY LTD p122
7823 25 ST NW, EDMONTON, AB, T6P 1N4
(780) 440-2737   SIC 5085

M. LEMIEUX INC p1276
5005 RUE HUGUES-RANDIN, QUEBEC, QC, G2C 0G5
(418) 688-5050   SIC 5085

M.A. STEWART & SONS LTD p277
12900 87 AVE, SURREY, BC, V3W 3H9
(604) 594-8431   SIC 5085

MADDOCKS ENGINEERED MACHINERY INC p609
663 WOODWARD AVE, HAMILTON, ON, L8H 6P3
(905) 549-9626   SIC 5085

MAGNA POWERTRAIN FPC LIMITED PARTNERSHIP p555
800 TESMA WAY, CONCORD, ON, L4K 5C2
(905) 303-1689   SIC 5085

MANUS ABRASIVE SYSTEMS INC p122
1040 78 AVE NW, EDMONTON, AB, T6P 1L7
(780) 468-2588   SIC 5085

MAPLE LEAF METALS (A PARTNERSHIP) p110
4510 68 AVE NW, EDMONTON, AB, T6B 2P3
(780) 468-3951   SIC 5085

MARTIN SPROCKET & GEAR CANADA INC p740
896 MEYERSIDE DR, MISSISSAUGA, ON, L5T 1R9
(905) 670-1991   SIC 5085

MATHESON VALVES & FITTINGS LTD p1330
4060 BOUL POIRIER, SAINT-LAURENT, QC, H4R 2A5
(514) 337-1106   SIC 5085

MCALLISTER INDUSTRIES LTD p282
9678 186 ST, SURREY, BC, V4N 3N7

(604) 888-1871 *SIC* 5085
MEI MILLER ENTERPRISES INC *p36*
7523 FLINT RD SE, CALGARY, AB, T2H 1G3
SIC 5085
MOTION INDUSTRIES (CANADA), INC *p193*
8985 FRASERWOOD CT, BURNABY, BC, V5J 5E8
(604) 521-3207 *SIC* 5085
MOULES MIRPLEX INC, LES *p1318*
765 RUE PIERRE-CAISSE, SAINT-JEAN-SUR-RICHELIEU, QC, J3B 8C6
(450) 348-6611 *SIC* 5085
MOULES PLASTICOR INC, LES *p1128*
1170 50E AV, LACHINE, QC, H8T 2V3
(514) 636-9630 *SIC* 5085
MRC CANADA ULC *p110*
4103 53 AVE NW SUITE 726, EDMONTON, AB, T6B 3R5
(780) 466-0328 *SIC* 5085
MSC INDUSTRIAL SUPPLY ULC *p697*
2595 SKYMARK AVE SUITE 202, MISSISSAUGA, ON, L4W 4L5
(905) 219-6300 *SIC* 5085
MUELLER CANADA LTD *p487*
82 HOOPER RD, BARRIE, ON, L4N 8Z9
(705) 719-9965 *SIC* 5085
MUIR TAPES & ADHESIVES LTD *p798*
2815 BRISTOL CIR, OAKVILLE, ON, L6H 6X5
(905) 820-6847 *SIC* 5085
MULLER MARTINI CANADA INC *p556*
20 CALDARI RD SUITE 2, CONCORD, ON, L4K 4N8
(905) 660-9595 *SIC* 5085
MULTI-LINE FASTENER SUPPLY CO. LTD *p741*
1100 COURTNEYPARK DR E UNIT 5, MISSISSAUGA, ON, L5T 1L7
(905) 677-5088 *SIC* 5085
NATIONAL ENGINEERED FASTENERS INC *p518*
1747 GREENHOUSE RD, BRESLAU, ON, N0B 1M0
(519) 886-0919 *SIC* 5085
NCI CANADA INC *p804*
2305 WYECROFT ROAD, OAKVILLE, ON, L6L 6R2
(905) 727-5545 *SIC* 5085
NEW-LINE PRODUCTS LTD *p282*
9415 189 ST UNIT 1, SURREY, BC, V4N 5L8
(604) 455-5400 *SIC* 5085
NEWMAN'S VALVE LIMITED *p484*
92 DAVIDSON ST, BARRIE, ON, L4M 3R8
(705) 737-4216 *SIC* 5085
NIFAST CANADA CORPORATION *p622*
12 UNDERWOOD RD, INGERSOLL, ON, N5C 3J9
(519) 485-1050 *SIC* 5085
NIS NORTHERN INDUSTRIAL SALES LTD *p96*
11440 163 ST NW, EDMONTON, AB, T5M 3T3
(780) 454-2682 *SIC* 5085
NORTHERN INDUSTRIAL SALES B.C. LTD *p251*
3526 OPIE CRES, PRINCE GEORGE, BC, V2N 2P9
(250) 562-4435 *SIC* 5085
NORTHERN METALIC SALES (F.S.J.) LTD *p214*
10407 ALASKA RD, FORT ST. JOHN, BC, V1J 1B1
(250) 787-0717 *SIC* 5085
NORTHERN OASIS MARKETING & DIRECT SALES *p910*
701 MONTREAL ST, THUNDER BAY, ON, P7E 3P2
(807) 623-5249 *SIC* 5085
NSK CANADA INC *p706*
5585 MCADAM RD, MISSISSAUGA, ON, L4Z 1N4
(905) 890-0740 *SIC* 5085

NTN BEARING CORPORATION OF CANADA LIMITED *p745*
305 COURTNEYPARK DR W, MISSISSAUGA, ON, L5W 1Y4
(905) 564-2700 *SIC* 5085
NUERA INC *p1134*
1980 BOUL DAGENAIS O, LAVAL-OUEST, QC, H7L 5W2
(514) 955-1024 *SIC* 5085
OCEANSIDE EQUIPMENT LIMITED *p447*
181 JOSEPH ZATZMAN DR UNIT 12, DARTMOUTH, NS, B3B 1R5
(902) 468-4844 *SIC* 5085
OIL-DRI CANADA ULC *p1237*
730 RUE SALABERRY, MONTREAL, QC, H7S 1H3
(450) 663-5750 *SIC* 5085
ONTARIO BELTING & POWER TRANSMISSION CO. LTD *p1032*
371 HANLAN RD, WOODBRIDGE, ON, L4L 3T1
(416) 798-7333 *SIC* 5085
ONTARIO HOSE SPECIALTIES LIMITED *p741*
7245 PACIFIC CIR, MISSISSAUGA, ON, L5T 1V1
(905) 670-0113 *SIC* 5085
OPTIMOULE INC *p1383*
275 RUE MONFETTE E, THETFORD MINES, QC, G6G 7H4
(418) 338-6106 *SIC* 5085
PACE INVESTCO LTD *p1252*
193 BOUL BRUNSWICK, POINTE-CLAIRE, QC, H9R 5N2
(514) 630-6820 *SIC* 5085
PALL (CANADA) ULC *p717*
3450 RIDGEWAY DR UNIT 6, MISSISSAUGA, ON, L5L 0A2
(905) 542-0330 *SIC* 5085
PARIS SPRING LTD *p837*
41 WOODSLEE AVE, PARIS, ON, N3L 3T5
(519) 442-1502 *SIC* 5085
PARR METAL FABRICATORS LTD *p371*
717 JARVIS AVE, WINNIPEG, MB, R2W 3B4
(204) 586-8121 *SIC* 5085
PENN ENGINEERED FASTENERS CORPORATION *p557*
590 BASALTIC RD, CONCORD, ON, L4K 5A2
(905) 879-0433 *SIC* 5085
PERFORMANCE POLYMERS INC *p534*
36 RAGLIN PL, CAMBRIDGE, ON, N1R 7J2
(519) 622-1792 *SIC* 5085
PETRO SERVICE LIMITED *p413*
11 MCILVEEN DR, SAINT JOHN, NB, E2J 4Y6
(506) 632-1000 *SIC* 5085
POLYGON INTERNATIONAL TECHNOLOGY INC *p57*
400 5 AVE SW SUITE 300, CALGARY, AB, T2P 0L6
(403) 984-2759 *SIC* 5085
PRECIMOLD INC *p1073*
9 BOUL MARIE-VICTORIN, CANDIAC, QC, J5R 4S8
(450) 659-2921 *SIC* 5085
PREFERRED POLYMER COATINGS LTD *p572*
31 PORTLAND ST, ETOBICOKE, ON, M8Y 1A6
(416) 201-9003 *SIC* 5085
PRIMESOURCE BUILDING PRODUCTS CANADA CORPORATION *p258*
7431 NELSON RD SUITE 110, RICHMOND, BC, V6W 1G3
(604) 231-0473 *SIC* 5085
PRO-TECH VALVE SALES INC *p110*
5880 56 AVE NW, EDMONTON, AB, T6B 3E4
(780) 466-4405 *SIC* 5085
PROCESS PRODUCTS LIMITED *p557*
50 LOCKE ST UNIT 1, CONCORD, ON, L4K 5R4

(416) 781-3399 *SIC* 5085
PROGRESSIVE RUBBER INDUSTRIES INC *p218*
597A CHILCOTIN RD, KAMLOOPS, BC, V2H 1G6
(250) 851-0611 *SIC* 5085
PULTRALL INC *p1383*
700 9E RUE N, THETFORD MINES, QC, G6G 6Z5
(418) 335-3202 *SIC* 5085
R.M. & S. COMPANY LIMITED *p434*
1 COMMERCIAL ST, WABUSH, NL, A0R 1B0
(709) 282-3644 *SIC* 5085
RASTALL MINE SUPPLY LIMITED *p900*
268 HEMLOCK ST, SUDBURY, ON, P3C 1H9
(705) 675-2431 *SIC* 5085
RDP MARATHON INC *p1087*
2583 BOUL CHOMEDEY, COTE SAINT-LUC, QC, H7T 2R2
(450) 687-7262 *SIC* 5085
RED-L DISTRIBUTORS LTD *p149*
3675 13 ST, NISKU, AB, T9E 1C5
(780) 437-2630 *SIC* 5085
REGIONAL HOSE TORONTO LTD *p576*
236 NORSEMAN ST, ETOBICOKE, ON, M8Z 2R4
(416) 239-9555 *SIC* 5085
RINGBALL CORPORATION *p726*
2160 MEADOWPINE BLVD, MISSISSAUGA, ON, L5N 6H6
(905) 826-1100 *SIC* 5085
RITE CORPORATION *p1050*
10250 BOUL PARKWAY, ANJOU, QC, H1J 2K4
(514) 324-8900 *SIC* 5085
ROBERT BOSCH INC *p726*
6955 CREDITVIEW RD, MISSISSAUGA, ON, L5N 1R1
(905) 826-6060 *SIC* 5085
ROBERTSON INC *p524*
1185 CORPORATE DR SUITE 1, BURLINGTON, ON, L7L 5V5
(905) 332-7776 *SIC* 5085
ROTEX SUPPLY INC *p94*
14360 123 AVE NW, EDMONTON, AB, T5L 2Y3
(780) 465-0637 *SIC* 5085
ROTOPRECISION INC *p707*
304 WATLINE AVE, MISSISSAUGA, ON, L4Z 1P4
(905) 712-3800 *SIC* 5085
ROTORK CONTROLS (CANADA) LTD *p726*
6705 MILLCREEK DR UNIT 3, MISSISSAUGA, ON, L5N 5M4
(905) 363-0313 *SIC* 5085
ROUSSEAU CONTROLS INC. *p1128*
1475 32E AV, LACHINE, QC, H8T 3J1
(506) 859-8992 *SIC* 5085
RUBBERLINE PRODUCTS LIMITED *p637*
81 BLEAMS RD, KITCHENER, ON, N2C 2G2
(519) 894-0400 *SIC* 5085
SCS SUPPLY GROUP INC *p652*
145 ADELAIDE ST S, LONDON, ON, N5Z 3K7
(519) 686-2650 *SIC* 5085
SDF ABRASIF INC *p1388*
8750 BOUL INDUSTRIEL BUREAU 202, TROIS-RIVIERES, QC, G9A 5E1
(819) 697-2408 *SIC* 5085
SHAW'S ENTERPRISES LTD *p149*
2801 5 ST, NISKU, AB, T9E 0C2
(780) 955-7222 *SIC* 5085
SKF CANADA LIMITED *p875*
40 EXECUTIVE CRT, SCARBOROUGH, ON, M1S 4N4
(416) 299-1220 *SIC* 5085
SKYLINE HOLDINGS INCORPORATED *p414*
331 CHESLEY DR, SAINT JOHN, NB, E2K 5P2
SIC 5085

SOCIETE INDUSTRIELLE JASON (CANADA) LTEE *p1095*
9135 CH COTE-DE-LIESSE, DORVAL, QC, H9P 2N9
(514) 631-6781 *SIC* 5085
SPACESAVER SOLUTIONS INC *p481*
115 ENGELHARD DR, AURORA, ON, L4G 3V1
(905) 726-3933 *SIC* 5085
SPAENAUR INC *p635*
815 VICTORIA ST N, KITCHENER, ON, N2B 3C3
(519) 578-0381 *SIC* 5085
SPARTAN CONTROLS LTD *p116*
8403 51 AVE NW, EDMONTON, AB, T6E 5L9
(780) 468-5463 *SIC* 5085
STELFAST INC *p506*
5 PARKSHORE DR, BRAMPTON, ON, L6T 5M1
(905) 670-9400 *SIC* 5085
STELLAR INDUSTRIAL SALES LIMITED *p448*
520 WINDMILL RD, DARTMOUTH, NS, B3B 1B3
(902) 468-5499 *SIC* 5085
SUNOX INDUSTRIAL GASES INC *p536*
440 SHELDON DR, CAMBRIDGE, ON, N1T 2C1
(519) 624-4413 *SIC* 5085
SUPER SLINGS INC *p150*
505 11 AVE, NISKU, AB, T9E 7N5
(780) 955-7111 *SIC* 5085
SWAGELOK CENTRAL CANADA *p389*
118 COMMERCE DR, WINNIPEG, MB, R3P 0Z6
(204) 633-4446 *SIC* 5085
SYLVAN AUTOMATION LTD *p863*
1018 MCNABB ST, SAULT STE. MARIE, ON, P6B 6J1
(705) 254-4669 *SIC* 5085
T.J. TRADING CO. INC *p787*
260 BARTLEY DR, NORTH YORK, ON, M4A 1G5
(416) 661-9506 *SIC* 5085
TALBOT SALES LIMITED *p865*
120 VENTURE DR, SCARBOROUGH, ON, M1B 3L6
(416) 286-3666 *SIC* 5085
TASCO SUPPLIES LTD *p344*
336 MACKENZIE AVE N, WILLIAMS LAKE, BC, V2G 1N7
(250) 392-6232 *SIC* 5085
TAYLOR FLUID SYSTEMS INC *p897*
81 GRIFFITH RD, STRATFORD, ON, N5A 6S4
(519) 273-2811 *SIC* 5085
TENAQUIP LIMITEE *p1367*
22555 AUT TRANSCANADIENNE, SENNEVILLE, QC, H9X 3L7
(514) 457-7801 *SIC* 5085
THORDON BEARINGS INC *p526*
3225 MAINWAY, BURLINGTON, ON, L7M 1A6
(905) 335-1440 *SIC* 5085
TIMBERWOLF FOREST PRODUCTS INC *p477*
7781 HOWARD AVE, AMHERSTBURG, ON, N0R 1J0
(519) 726-9653 *SIC* 5085
TIMBERWOLF FOREST PRODUCTS INC *p1024*
2015 NORTH TALBOT RD, WINDSOR, ON, N9A 6J3
SIC 5085
TOPRINGS LTEE *p1111*
1020 BOUL INDUSTRIEL, GRANBY, QC, J2J 1A4
(450) 375-1828 *SIC* 5085
TORY TAPE LTD *p1034*
230 TROWERS RD UNIT 9-11, WOODBRIDGE, ON, L4L 7J1
(416) 410-1404 *SIC* 5085
TRANS AM PIPING PRODUCTS LTD *p78*

9335 ENDEAVOR DR SE, CALGARY, AB, T3S 0A1

(403) 236-0601   SIC 5085

TRICAN PACKAGING INC   p541
1078 KOHLER RD, CAYUGA, ON, N0A 1E0
(905) 772-0711   SIC 5085

TRY HARD INDUSTRIAL SUPPLY CO LTD
p743
1411 COURTNEYPARK DR E, MISSISSAUGA, ON, L5T 2E3
(905) 565-8700   SIC 5085

TSUBAKI OF CANADA LIMITED   p736
1630 DREW RD, MISSISSAUGA, ON, L5S 1J6
(905) 676-0400   SIC 5085

TUNDRA PROCESS SOLUTIONS LTD   p71
3200 118 AVE SE, CALGARY, AB, T2Z 3X1
(403) 255-5222   SIC 5085

TURK, ROY INDUSTRIAL SALES LIMITED
p589
106 VULCAN ST, ETOBICOKE, ON, M9W 1L2
(416) 742-2777   SIC 5085

VALLEN CANADA INC   p111
4810 92 AVE NW, EDMONTON, AB, T6B 2X4
(780) 468-3366   SIC 5085

VALTROL EQUIPMENT LIMITED   p805
2305 WYECROFT RD, OAKVILLE, ON, L6L 6R2
(905) 828-9900   SIC 5085

VANNES ET RACCORDS LAURENTIEN LTEE   p1337
2425 RUE HALPERN, SAINT-LAURENT, QC, H4S 1S3
(418) 872-3622   SIC 5085

WATTS   WATER   TECHNOLOGIES (CANADA) INC   p525
5435 NORTH SERVICE RD, BURLINGTON, ON, L7L 5H7
(905) 332-4090   SIC 5085

WEBER SUPPLY COMPANY INC   p642
1830 STRASBURG RD, KITCHENER, ON, N2R 1E9
(519) 888-4200   SIC 5085

WESCO AIRCRAFT EUROPE, LTD   p589
22 WORCESTER RD, ETOBICOKE, ON, M9W 5X2
(416) 674-0770   SIC 5085

WESCO INDUSTRIES LTD   p226
9663 199A ST UNIT 1, LANGLEY, BC, V1M 2X7
(604) 881-3000   SIC 5085

WESTERN EQUIPMENT LTD   p273
5219 192 ST UNIT 114, SURREY, BC, V3S 4P6
(604) 574-3311   SIC 5085

WESTERN POLYMERS CORP   p26
1003 55 AVE NE SUITE A, CALGARY, AB, T2E 6W1
(403) 295-7194   SIC 5085

WFS ENTERPRISES INC   p1022
730 NORTH SERVICE RD E, WINDSOR, ON, N8X 3J3
(519) 966-2202   SIC 5085

WFS LTD   p1022
730 NORTH SERVICE RD E, WINDSOR, ON, N8X 3J3
(519) 966-2202   SIC 5085

WILLIAMS, R. B. INDUSTRIAL SUPPLY LTD
p150
3280 10 ST, NISKU, AB, T9E 1E7
(780) 955-9332   SIC 5085

WINDSOR PALLET LIMITED   p1017
2890 N TALBOT, WINDSOR, ON, N0R 1K0
(519) 737-1406   SIC 5085

WORLD SOURCE FILTRATION INC   p861
321 QUEEN ST SUITE 1, SARNIA, ON, N7T 2S3
(519) 383-7771   SIC 5085

WURTH CANADA LIMITED   p600
345 HANLON CREEK BLVD, GUELPH, ON, N1C 0A1
(905) 564-6225   SIC 5085

SIC 5087 Service establishment equipment

1459243 ONTARIO INC   p690
2180 MATHESON BLVD E UNIT 1, MISSISSAUGA, ON, L4W 5E1
(905) 206-5500   SIC 5087

1558775 ONTARIO LIMITED   p901
80 NATIONAL ST, SUDBURY, ON, P3L 1M5
(705) 673-8218   SIC 5087

1638-2723 QUEBEC INC.   p1307
2805 BOUL LOSCH, SAINT-HUBERT, QC, J3Y 3V6
(514) 866-8683   SIC 5087

1688150 ALBERTA LTD   p121
2004 80 AVE NW, EDMONTON, AB, T6P 1N2
(780) 462-4430   SIC 5087

3635112 CANADA INC   p622
14935 COUNTY RD 2, INGLESIDE, ON, K0C 1M0
(613) 537-9559   SIC 5087

821373 ONTARIO LTD   p500
3 BREWSTER RD SUITE 5, BRAMPTON, ON, L6T 5G9
(905) 794-2074   SIC 5087

A-1 BAGS & SUPPLIES INC   p736
6400 KENNEDY RD, MISSISSAUGA, ON, L5T 2Z5
(905) 676-9950   SIC 5087

ACME SUPPLIES LTD   p334
2311 GOVERNMENT ST, VICTORIA, BC, V8T 4P4
(250) 383-8822   SIC 5087

ADVANCE BEAUTY SUPPLY LIMITEDp1019
2979 TECUMSEH RD E, WINDSOR, ON, N8W 1G6
(519) 944-0904   SIC 5087

ADVANTAGE MAINTENANCE PRODUCTS LTD   p836
105 SCOTT AVE, PARIS, ON, N3L 3K4
(519) 442-7881   SIC 5087

AGENCES W PELLETIER (1980) INC p1325
1400 BOUL JULES-POITRAS, SAINT-LAURENT, QC, H4N 1X7
(514) 276-6700   SIC 5087

AJAX MAINTENANCE & SHIPPING SUPPLIES CO LTD   p873
100 COMMANDER BLVD, SCARBOROUGH, ON, M1S 3H7
(416) 291-7601   SIC 5087

ALTERNATIVE BEAUTY SERVICES LTD
p737
1680 COURTNEYPARK DR E UNIT 9, MISSISSAUGA, ON, L5T 1R4
(905) 670-0611   SIC 5087

AOF SERVICE ALIMENTAIRE INC   p1098
2150 RUE SIGOUIN, DRUMMONDVILLE, QC, J2C 5Z4
(819) 477-5353   SIC 5087

AREO-FEU LTEE   p1309
5205 RUE J.-A.-BOMBARDIER, SAINT-HUBERT, QC, J3Z 1G4
(450) 651-2240   SIC 5087

B & B SALES LIMITED   p422
27 UNION ST, CORNER BROOK, NL, A2H 5P9
(709) 639-8991   SIC 5087

BATESVILLE CANADA LTD   p734
2390 ANSON DR, MISSISSAUGA, ON, L5S 1G2
(905) 673-7717   SIC 5087

BEAUTY SYSTEMS GROUP (CANADA) INC
p720
2345 ARGENTIA RD SUITE 102, MISSISSAUGA, ON, L5N 8K4
(905) 696-2600   SIC 5087

BOUTRY CANADA LTEE   p1169
2170 AV CHARLAND, MONTREAL, QC, H1Z 1B1
SIC 5087

BUSY-BEE SANITARY SUPPLIES INC p113
4004 97 ST NW UNIT 24, EDMONTON, AB, T6E 6N1

(780) 462-0075   SIC 5087

C.G. MAINTENANCE & SANITARY PRODUCTS INC   p782
40 SAINT REGIS CRES, NORTH YORK, ON, M3J 1Y5
SIC 5087

CAN-RAD BEAUTY LIMITED   p786
125 NORFINCH DR SUITE 100, NORTH YORK, ON, M3N 1W8
(416) 663-7373   SIC 5087

CANADIAN MARKETING TEST CASE 201 LIMITED   p730
5770 HURONTARIO ST, MISSISSAUGA, ON, L5R 3G5
SIC 5087

CANTIN BEAUTE LTEE   p1266
2495 AV DALTON, QUEBEC, QC, G1P 3S5
(418) 654-0444   SIC 5087

CAPILEX-BEAUTE LTEE   p1266
2670 AV DALTON, QUEBEC, QC, G1P 3S4
(418) 653-2500   SIC 5087

CAPT-AIR INC   p1183
5860 BOUL SAINT-LAURENT, MONTREAL, QC, H2T 1T3
(514) 273-4331   SIC 5087

CARPET CARE SYSTEMS   p580
34 ASHMOUNT CRES, ETOBICOKE, ON, M9R 1C7
(416) 247-7311   SIC 5087

CENTRAL BEAUTY SUPPLY LIMITED p650
300 ASHLAND AVE, LONDON, ON, N5W 4E4
(519) 453-4590   SIC 5087

CHEMNORTH SYSTEMS AND SERVICES COMPANY LTD   p568
30 TIMBER RD SUITE 2, ELLIOT LAKE, ON, P5A 2T1
(705) 461-9821   SIC 5087

CONCEPT JP INC   p1101
2089 RUE MICHELIN, FABREVILLE, QC, H7L 5B7
(800) 795-2595   SIC 5087

CORTEX DISTRIBUTION LTD   p1058
40 RUE EMILIEN-MARCOUX BUREAU 10, BLAINVILLE, QC, J7C 0B5
(450) 686-9999   SIC 5087

COSBEC INC   p1338
699 RUE GOUGEON, SAINT-LAURENT, QC, H4T 2B4
(514) 336-2411   SIC 5087

COSIMO MINNELLA INVESTMENTS INC
p384
1680 NOTRE DAME AVE UNIT 7, WINNIPEG, MB, R3H 1H6
(204) 786-0001   SIC 5087

DALEX CANADA INC   p551
157 ADESSO DR, CONCORD, ON, L4K 3C3
(905) 738-2070   SIC 5087

DOMINION VOTING SYSTEMS CORPORATION   p977
215 SPADINA AVE SUITE 200, TORONTO, ON, M5T 2C7
(416) 762-8683   SIC 5087

DUROX FLOOR ACCESSORIES LIMITED
p783
255 STEEPROCK DR, NORTH YORK, ON, M3J 2Z5
(416) 630-4883   SIC 5087

DYSON CANADA LIMITED   p980
312 ADELAIDE ST W, TORONTO, ON, M5V 1R2
(416) 849-5821   SIC 5087

E.E. ENGRAVER'S EXPRESS INC   p227
20381 62 AVE SUITE 705, LANGLEY, BC, V3A 5E6
(604) 533-3467   SIC 5087

EQUIPEMENT D'INCENDIE GLOBE INC
p1126
590 19E AV, LACHINE, QC, H8S 3M5
(514) 637-2534   SIC 5087

FIBRECLEAN SUPPLIES LTD   p23
3750 19 ST NE SUITE 101, CALGARY, AB, T2E 6V2

(403) 291-3991   SIC 5087

FILTEX VACUUMS OF CANADA   p23
3103 CENTRE ST NW, CALGARY, AB, T2E 2X3
(403) 277-5511   SIC 5087

FLEXO PRODUCTS LIMITED   p760
4777 KENT AVE, NIAGARA FALLS, ON, L2H 1J5
(905) 354-2723   SIC 5087

GUARD-X INC   p1049
10600 BOUL PARKWAY, ANJOU, QC, H1J 1R6
(514) 277-2127   SIC 5087

GUAY BEAUTE INC   p1061
585 BOUL DU CURE-BOIVIN, BOISBRIAND, QC, J7G 2A8
(514) 273-9991   SIC 5087

H. CHALUT LTEE   p1320
2172 BOUL DU CURE-LABELLE, SAINT-JEROME, QC, J7Y 1T3
(450) 438-4153   SIC 5087

HARCO CO. LTD   p705
1600 MCADAM RD, MISSISSAUGA, ON, L4Z 1P1
(905) 890-1220   SIC 5087

HI-TECH BEAUTY SUPPLIES LTD   p35
5718 BURBANK CRES SE, CALGARY, AB, T2H 1Z6
(403) 253-3113   SIC 5087

HOLLYWOOD BEAUTY SUPPLY   p862
44 GREAT NORTHERN RD SUITE 51, SAULT STE. MARIE, ON, P6B 4Y5
(705) 949-9132   SIC 5087

INSTITUTION QUEBEC   p1296
1395 RUE MARIE-VICTORIN, SAINT-BRUNO, QC, J3V 6B7
(450) 482-0724   SIC 5087

JACKSON, GEORGE N. LIMITED   p381
1139 MCDERMOT AVE, WINNIPEG, MB, R3E 0V2
(204) 786-3821   SIC 5087

JAN-MAR SALES LIMITED   p740
6976 COLUMBUS RD, MISSISSAUGA, ON, L5T 2G1
(416) 255-8535   SIC 5087

JOHNSON-ROSE INC   p723
7300 EAST DANBRO CRES, MISSISSAUGA, ON, L5N 6C2
(905) 817-1470   SIC 5087

JOYLYPSO INC   p1340
4850 RUE BOURG, SAINT-LAURENT, QC, H4T 1J2
(514) 735-4255   SIC 5087

MAISON AMI-CO (1981) INC, LA   p1344
8455   BOUL   LANGELIER,   SAINT-LEONARD, QC, H1P 2C5
(514) 351-7520   SIC 5087

MARITIME BEAUTY SUPPLY CO LTD p455
3695 BARRINGTON ST, HALIFAX, NS, B3K 2Y3
(902) 429-8510   SIC 5087

METRO BEAUTY SUPPLY LIMITED p1028
315 NEW HUNTINGTON RD, WOODBRIDGE, ON, L4H 0R5
(800) 263-2365   SIC 5087

MICHAEL'S EQUIPMENT LTD   p837
105 SCOTT AVE, PARIS, ON, N3L 3K4
(519) 442-0317   SIC 5087

MISTER CHEMICAL LTD   p556
101 JACOB KEFFER PKY, CONCORD, ON, L4K 5N8
(905) 761-9995   SIC 5087

MODERN BEAUTY SUPPLIES INC   p31
415 MANITOU RD SE, CALGARY, AB, T2G 4C2
(403) 259-4442   SIC 5087

MODERN JANITORIAL SERVICES (1978) LTD   p1412
2521 COMMERCE DR, NORTH BATTLEFORD, SK, S9A 2X5
(306) 445-4774   SIC 5087

NATIONAL FIRE EQUIPMENT LIMITEDp556
40 EDILCAN DR, CONCORD, ON, L4K 3S6
(905) 761-6355   SIC 5087

NELLA CUTLERY (TORONTO) INC p787
148 NORFINCH DR, NORTH YORK, ON, M3N 1X8
(416) 740-2424 SIC 5087

NILFISK CANADA COMPANY p741
240 SUPERIOR BLVD, MISSISSAUGA, ON, L5T 2L2
(905) 696-4840 SIC 5087

OUGH FIRE SYSTEMS LTD p488
16 LENNOX DR, BARRIE, ON, L4N 9V8
(705) 720-0570 SIC 5087

PLAYER ONE AMUSEMENT GROUP INC p689
6420 VISCOUNT RD, MISSISSAUGA, ON, L4V 1H3
(416) 251-2122 SIC 5087

PROTECTION INCENDIE POLYGON INC p1062
1935 BOUL LIONEL-BERTRAND, BOIS-BRIAND, QC, J7H 1N8
(450) 430-7516 SIC 5087

RELIABLE WINDOW CLEANERS (SUDBURY) LIMITED p900
345 REGENT ST, SUDBURY, ON, P3C 4E1
(705) 675-5281 SIC 5087

REX BEAUTY INC. p786
3304 KEELE ST, NORTH YORK, ON, M3M 2H7
(416) 398-9494 SIC 5087

ROBERTSON PYROTECHEM LIMITED p576
50 CHAUNCEY AVE, ETOBICOKE, ON, M8Z 2Z4
(416) 233-3934 SIC 5087

ROBINSON FORGIONE GROUP INC p700
1200 AEROWOOD DR SUITE 50, MISSISSAUGA, ON, L4W 2S7
(905) 602-1965 SIC 5087

ROMADOR ENTERPRISES LTD p96
11348 142 ST NW, EDMONTON, AB, T5M 1T9
(780) 454-3388 SIC 5087

SECURITE POLYGON INC p1062
1935 BOUL LIONEL-BERTRAND, BOIS-BRIAND, QC, J7H 1N8
(450) 430-7516 SIC 5087

SERVICE & MAINTENANCE DE CASTEL (1997) INC p1162
11650 AV J.-J.-JOUBERT, MONTREAL, QC, H1E 7E7
(514) 648-5166 SIC 5087

SHAIR SALES LTD p280
3557 190 ST UNIT 101, SURREY, BC, V3Z 0P6
(604) 514-7005 SIC 5087

SPROUSE FIRE & SAFETY (1996) CORP p18
5329 72 AVE SE, CALGARY, AB, T2C 4X6
(403) 265-3891 SIC 5087

STAXI CORPORATION LIMITED p1034
120 JEVLAN DR UNIT 4B, WOODBRIDGE, ON, L4L 8G3
(877) 677-8294 SIC 5087

STEEL FIRE EQUIPMENT LIMITED p743
150 SUPERIOR BLVD, MISSISSAUGA, ON, L5T 2L2
(905) 564-1500 SIC 5087

STOGRYN SALES LTD p111
6808 82 AVE NW, EDMONTON, AB, T6B 0E7
(780) 465-6408 SIC 5087

SUEDE MASTER (1975) INC p791
25 CONNIE ST, NORTH YORK, ON, M6L 2H8
(416) 614-8000 SIC 5087

SUMMIT SALON SERVICES INC p18
10905 48 ST SE SUITE 105, CALGARY, AB, T2C 1G8
(403) 252-6201 SIC 5087

SUPERIOR SOLUTIONS LTD p805
851 PROGRESS CRT, OAKVILLE, ON, L6L 6K1
(800) 921-5527 SIC 5087

SYLON INC p707
5610 MCADAM RD, MISSISSAUGA, ON,

L4Z 1P1
(905) 890-1220 SIC 5087

TAKARA COMPANY, CANADA, LTD p714
2076 SOUTH SHERIDAN WAY, MISSISSAUGA, ON, L5J 2M4
(905) 822-2755 SIC 5087

THREE AMIGO'S BEAUTY SUPPLY CO LTD p339
555 ARDERSIER RD UNIT A8, VICTORIA, BC, V8Z 1C8
(250) 475-3099 SIC 5087

TIGER-VAC INTERNATIONAL INC p1134
2020 BOUL DAGENAIS O, LAVAL-OUEST, QC, H7L 5W2
(450) 622-0100 SIC 5087

TRANSTAR SANITATION SUPPLY LTD. p194
3975 NORTH FRASER WAY, BURNABY, BC, V5J 5H9
(604) 439-9585 SIC 5087

UNIVERSAL FOOD & PAPER PRODUCTS LTD p291
8595 FRASER ST, VANCOUVER, BC, V5X 3Y1
(604) 324-0331 SIC 5087

WESCLEAN EQUIPMENT & CLEANING SUPPLIES LTD p97
11450 149 ST NW, EDMONTON, AB, T5M 1W7
(780) 451-1533 SIC 5087

WESCLEAN NORTHERN SALES LTD p435
15 INDUSTRIAL DR, HAY RIVER, NT, X0E 0R6
(867) 875-5100 SIC 5087

SIC 5088 Transportation equipment and supplies

260304 BC LTD p334
2120 QUADRA ST, VICTORIA, BC, V8T 4C5
(250) 382-7722 SIC 5088

3 POINTS AVIATION CORP p1040
91 WATTS AVE, CHARLOTTETOWN, PE, C1E 2B7
(902) 628-8846 SIC 5088

AIRSTART INC p691
2680 SKYMARK AVE SUITE 901, MISSISSAUGA, ON, L4W 5L6
(905) 366-8730 SIC 5088

APPROVISIONNEMENT DE NAVIRES CLIPPER INC p1209
770 RUE MILL, MONTREAL, QC, H3C 1Y3
(514) 937-9561 SIC 5088

ARTON BEADS CRAFT INC p978
523 QUEEN ST W, TORONTO, ON, M5V 2B4
(416) 504-1168 SIC 5088

ASPEN CUSTOM TRAILERS p139
3914 81 AVE, LEDUC, AB, T9E 0C3
(780) 980-1925 SIC 5088

AVIALL (CANADA) LTD p685
7150 TORBRAM RD SUITE 15, MISSISSAUGA, ON, L4T 3Z8
(905) 676-1695 SIC 5088

AVMAX AIRCRAFT LEASING INC p21
380 MCTAVISH RD NE SUITE 3, CALGARY, AB, T2E 7G5
(403) 735-3299 SIC 5088

BLUE WATER AGENCIES LIMITED p445
40 TOPPLE DR, DARTMOUTH, NS, B3B 1L6
(902) 468-4900 SIC 5088

BOMBARDIER TRANSPORTATION CANADA INC p1122
230 RTE O BUREAU 130, LA POCATIERE, QC, G0R 1Z0
(418) 856-1232 SIC 5088

C.C. MARINE DISTRIBUTORS INC p755
460 HARRY WALKER PKY S, NEWMARKET, ON, L3Y 8E3
(905) 830-0000 SIC 5088

COMTEK ADVANCED STRUCTURES LTD p521
1360 ARTISANS CRT, BURLINGTON, ON,

L7L 5Y2
(905) 331-8121 SIC 5088

DART AEROSPACE LTD p619
1270 ABERDEEN ST, HAWKESBURY, ON, K6A 1K7
(613) 632-5200 SIC 5088

DISTRIBUTION LAURENT LEBLANC INC p1317
370 RUE SAINT-LOUIS, SAINT-JEAN-SUR-RICHELIEU, QC, J3B 1Y4
(450) 346-7044 SIC 5088

EQUIPEMENT D'ESSAI AEROSPATIAL C.E.L. LTEE p1141
715 RUE DELAGE BUREAU 400, LONGUEUIL, QC, J4G 2P8
(450) 442-9994 SIC 5088

HOPE AERO PROPELLER & COMPONENTS INC p685
7605 BATH RD, MISSISSAUGA, ON, L4T 3T1
(905) 677-8747 SIC 5088

INDUSTRIES MARINE SEAGULF INC p1211
815 RUE MILL, MONTREAL, QC, H3C 1Y5
(514) 935-6933 SIC 5088

KADEX AERO SUPPLY LTD p841
925 AIRPORT RD UNIT 211A, PETERBOROUGH, ON, K9J 0E7
(705) 742-9725 SIC 5088

KARLO CORPORATION SUPPLY & SERVICES p1049
10801 BOUL RAY-LAWSON BUREAU 100, ANJOU, QC, H1J 1M5
(514) 255-5017 SIC 5088

L.B. FOSTER TECHNOLOGIES FERROVIAIRES CANADA LTEE p1251
172 BOUL BRUNSWICK, POINTE-CLAIRE, QC, H9R 5P9
(514) 695-8500 SIC 5088

LAGUE ET GOYETTE LTEE p1291
124 RUE AUTHIER, SAINT-ALPHONSE-DE-GRANBY, QC, J0E 2A0
(450) 777-1101 SIC 5088

MECHANICAL SYSTEMS REMANUFACTURING INC p735
1740 DREW RD, MISSISSAUGA, ON, L5S 1J6
(905) 673-5733 SIC 5088

MERCER'S MARINE EQUIPMENT LIMITED p422
210 MARINE DR, CLARENVILLE, NL, A5A 1L8
(709) 466-7430 SIC 5088

MHD - ROCKLAND INC p1355
21250 BOUL INDUSTRIEL, SAINTE-ANNE-DE-BELLEVUE, QC, H9X 0B4
(514) 453-1632 SIC 5088

NORTH AMERICAN TRANSIT SUPPLY CORPORATION p684
375 BRONTE ST N, MILTON, ON, L9T 3N7
(905) 876-0255 SIC 5088

OCEAN PACIFIC MARINE SUPPLY LTD p195
1370 ISLAND HWY SUITE 102, CAMPBELL RIVER, BC, V9W 8C9
(250) 286-1011 SIC 5088

OSI GEOSPATIAL INC p189
4585 CANADA WAY SUITE 400, BURNABY, BC, V5G 4L6
(778) 373-4600 SIC 5088

PATLON AIRCRAFT & INDUSTRIES LIMITED p594
8130 FIFTH LINE, GEORGETOWN, ON, L7G 0B8
(905) 864-8706 SIC 5088

PAYNE MACHINE COMPANY LTD p646
46 MOUNT HOPE ST, LINDSAY, ON, K9V 5G4
(705) 324-8990 SIC 5088

PEERLESS, E.B. LTD p265
6651 ELMBRIDGE WAY SUITE 130, RICHMOND, BC, V7C 5C2
(604) 279-9907 SIC 5088

PRODUITS MOBILICAB CANADA INC p1044
280 RUE BONIN, ACTON VALE, QC, J0H 1A0

(450) 546-0999 SIC 5088

QUALITE PERFORMANCE MAGOG INC p1148
2400 RUE SHERBROOKE, MAGOG, QC, J1X 4E6
(819) 843-0099 SIC 5088

RONSCO INC p1088
75 RUE INDUSTRIELLE, COTEAU-DU-LAC, QC, J0P 1B0
(514) 866-1033 SIC 5088

SIMEX DEFENCE INC p1252
216 BOUL BRUNSWICK, POINTE-CLAIRE, QC, H9R 1A6
(514) 697-7655 SIC 5088

STRIGHT-MACKAY LIMITED p463
209 TERRA COTTA DR, NEW GLASGOW, NS, B2H 6A8
(902) 928-1900 SIC 5088

UNITED MARITIME SUPPLIERS INC p285
1854 FRANKLIN ST, VANCOUVER, BC, V5L 1P8
(255) 255-6525 SIC 5088

WESTCAN RAIL LTD p178
31220 SOUTH FRASER WAY, ABBOTSFORD, BC, V2T 6L5
(604) 534-0124 SIC 5088

WESTERN MARINE COMPANY p286
1494 POWELL ST, VANCOUVER, BC, V5L 5B5
(604) 253-7721 SIC 5088

SIC 5091 Sporting and recreation goods

6861083 CANADA INC p1107
53 RUE DU BLIZZARD, GATINEAU, QC, J9A 0C8
(819) 777-2222 SIC 5091

ACAPULCO POOLS LIMITED p635
1550 VICTORIA ST N, KITCHENER, ON, N2B 3E2
(519) 743-6357 SIC 5091

ACUSHNET CANADA INC p754
500 HARRY WALKER PKY NE, NEWMARKET, ON, L3Y 8T6
(905) 898-7575 SIC 5091

ADIDAS CANADA LIMITED p1026
8100 27 HWY SUITE 1, WOODBRIDGE, ON, L4H 3N2
(905) 266-4200 SIC 5091

AMER SPORTS CANADA INC p238
2220 DOLLARTON HWY UNIT 110, NORTH VANCOUVER, BC, V7H 1A8
(604) 960-3001 SIC 5091

AQUIFORM DISTRIBUTORS LTD p278
19296 25 AVE, SURREY, BC, V3Z 3X1
(604) 541-0500 SIC 5091

BARRETT CORPORATION p419
300 LOCKHART MILL RD, WOODSTOCK, NB, E7M 6B9
(506) 328-8853 SIC 5091

BEACHCOMBER HOT TUBS INC p275
13245 COMBER WAY, SURREY, BC, V3W 5V8
(604) 591-8611 SIC 5091

BMG HOLDINGS LTD p404
32 SAWYER RD, JACKSONVILLE, NB, E7M 3B7
(506) 328-8853 SIC 5091

BRS CANADA ACQUISITION INC p486
92 CAPLAN AVE SUITE 108, BARRIE, ON, L4N 9J2
(705) 719-7922 SIC 5091

CANADIAN MARKETING TEST CASE 204 LIMITED p730
5770 HURONTARIO ST, MISSISSAUGA, ON, L5R 3G5
SIC 5091

CARBERRY INTERNATIONAL SPORTS INC p383
820 BRADFORD ST, WINNIPEG, MB, R3H 0N5
(204) 632-4222 SIC 5091

CENTRE SKATEBOARD DISTRIBUTION

LTD   *p285*
1486 E PENDER ST, VANCOUVER, BC, V5L 1V8
(604) 629-0000   *SIC 5091*

CENTURY INTERNATIONAL ARMS LTD *p1338*
353 RUE ISABEY, SAINT-LAURENT, QC, H4T 1Y2
(514) 731-8883   *SIC 5091*

CHARIOT CARRIERS INC   *p34*
5760 9 ST SE UNIT 105, CALGARY, AB, T2H 1Z9
(403) 640-0822   *SIC 5091*

CINTEX INTERNATIONAL (CANADA) LIMITED   *p693*
5195 MAINGATE DR, MISSISSAUGA, ON, L4W 1G4
(905) 795-8052   *SIC 5091*

COGHLAN'S LTD   *p390*
121 IRENE ST, WINNIPEG, MB, R3T 4C7
(204) 284-9550   *SIC 5091*

COMPAGNIE OTTO JANGL LTEE   *p1376*
294 RANG SAINT-PAUL, SHERRINGTON, QC, J0L 2N0
(450) 247-2758   *SIC 5091*

COSMOPOLITAN INDUSTRIES GOLF CANADA LTD   *p1426*
1302B ALBERTA AVE, SASKATOON, SK, S7K 1R5
(306) 477-4653   *SIC 5091*

DB PERKS & ASSOCIATES LTD   *p238*
2411 DOLLARTON HWY SUITE 102, NORTH VANCOUVER, BC, V7H 0A3
(604) 980-2805   *SIC 5091*

DYACO CANADA INC   *p758*
5955 DON MURIE ST, NIAGARA FALLS, ON, L2G 0A9
(905) 353-8955   *SIC 5091*

EASTON HOCKEY CANADA, INC   *p1118*
17550 RTE TRANSCANADIENNE, KIRKLAND, QC, H9J 3A3
(514) 630-9669   *SIC 5091*

FITNESS DEPOT INC   *p563*
700 WALLRICH AVE, CORNWALL, ON, K6J 5X4
(613) 938-8196   *SIC 5091*

GOBA SPORTS GROUP INC   *p670*
151 WHITEHALL DR, MARKHAM, ON, L3R 9T1
(888) 989-4015   *SIC 5091*

GROUPE SPORTS-INTER PLUS INC, LE *p1264*
420 RUE FARADAY, QUEBEC, QC, G1N 4E5
(418) 527-0244   *SIC 5091*

GSM (CANADA) PTY LTD   *p1334*
5900 RUE KIERAN, SAINT-LAURENT, QC, H4S 2B5
(514) 336-6382   *SIC 5091*

GULFSTREAM INC   *p533*
145 SHELDON DR, CAMBRIDGE, ON, N1R 5X5
(519) 622-0950   *SIC 5091*

HIGH OUTPUT SPORTS CANADA INC *p239*
1465 CHARLOTTE RD, NORTH VANCOUVER, BC, V7J 1H1
(604) 985-3933   *SIC 5091*

ICON DU CANADA INC   *p1320*
900 RUE DE L'INDUSTRIE, SAINT-JEROME, QC, J7Y 4B8
(450) 565-2955   *SIC 5091*

INA INTERNATIONAL LTD   *p16*
110250 QUARRY PARK BLVD SE, CALGARY, AB, T2C 3E7
(403) 717-1400   *SIC 5091*

INFINITY SPORTS GROUP LTD, THE *p229*
27452 52 AVE, LANGLEY, BC, V4W 4B2
SIC 5091

JIGGERNAUT TACKLE INC   *p563*
1235 CUMBERLAND ST, CORNWALL, ON, K6J 4K6
(613) 932-3474   *SIC 5091*

KAHUNAVERSE SPORTS GROUP INC *p279*
19036 22 AVE SUITE 101, SURREY, BC,

V3Z 3S6
(604) 536-2441   *SIC 5091*

KORTH GROUP LTD   *p150*
64186 393 LOOP E, OKOTOKS, AB, T1S 0L1
(403) 938-3255   *SIC 5091*

KREVCO LIFESTYLES INC   *p384*
700 BERRY ST, WINNIPEG, MB, R3H 0S6
(204) 786-6957   *SIC 5091*

LITZEN, T. SPORTS LIMITED   *p566*
433 OFIELD RD S, DUNDAS, ON, L9H 5E2
(905) 628-3344   *SIC 5091*

LIVE TO PLAY SPORTS   *p247*
1465 KEBET WAY, PORT COQUITLAM, BC, V3C 6L3
(604) 552-2930   *SIC 5091*

MARCHANT'S SCHOOL SPORT LIMITED *p867*
849 PROGRESS AVE, SCARBOROUGH, ON, M1H 2X4
(416) 439-9400   *SIC 5091*

MERCURY MARINE LIMITED   *p684*
8698 ESCARPMENT WAY, MILTON, ON, L9T 0M1
(905) 567-6372   *SIC 5091*

MERRITHEW CORPORATION   *p924*
2200 YONGE ST SUITE 500, TORONTO, ON, M4S 2C6
(416) 482-4050   *SIC 5091*

MIZUNO CANADA LTD   *p697*
5206 TIMBERLEA BLVD, MISSISSAUGA, ON, L4W 2S5
(905) 629-0500   *SIC 5091*

MOMENTUM DISTRIBUTION INC   *p1310*
2045 RUE FRANCIS BUREAU 200, SAINT-HUBERT, QC, J4T 0A6
(450) 466-5115   *SIC 5091*

NIKE CANADA CORP   *p869*
260 BRIMLEY RD, SCARBOROUGH, ON, M1M 3H8
(416) 264-8505   *SIC 5091*

NIKE CANADA CORP   *p982*
200 WELLINGTON ST W, TORONTO, ON, M5V 3C7
(416) 581-1585   *SIC 5091*

NORMARK INC   *p814*
1350 PHILLIP MURRAY AVE, OSHAWA, ON, L1J 6Z9
(905) 571-3001   *SIC 5091*

NORTHEASTERN SWIMMING POOL DISTRIBUTORS INC   *p556*
282 NORTH RIVERMEDE RD, CONCORD, ON, L4K 3N6
(905) 761-7946   *SIC 5091*

OAKCREEK GOLF & TURF LP   *p17*
3816 64 AVE SE, CALGARY, AB, T2C 2B4
(403) 279-2907   *SIC 5091*

PACIFIC NET & TWINE LTD   *p266*
3731 MONCTON ST, RICHMOND, BC, V7E 3A5
(604) 274-7238   *SIC 5091*

PING CANADA CORPORATION   *p799*
2790 BRIGHTON RD, OAKVILLE, ON, L6H 5T4
(905) 829-8004   *SIC 5091*

PPL AQUATIC, FITNESS & SPA GROUP INC *p699*
5170 TIMBERLEA BLVD UNIT A, MISSISSAUGA, ON, L4W 2S5
(905) 501-7210   *SIC 5091*

PROSLIDE TECHNOLOGY INC   *p830*
2650 QUEENSVIEW DR SUITE 150, OTTAWA, ON, K2B 8H6
(613) 526-5522   *SIC 5091*

PUMA CANADA INC   *p998*
175 BOUL GALAXY SUITE 201, TORONTO, ON, M9W 0C9
(416) 481-7862   *SIC 5091*

R.B. INC   *p791*
79 WINGOLD AVE UNIT 10, NORTH YORK, ON, M6B 1P8
(416) 787-4998   *SIC 5091*

RAMPION ENTERPRISES LTD   *p207*
1555 CLIVEDEN AVE, DELTA, BC, V3M 6P7

(604) 395-8225   *SIC 5091*

RAYMOND LANCTOT LTEE   *p1330*
5290 BOUL THIMENS, SAINT-LAURENT, QC, H4R 2B2
(514) 731-6841   *SIC 5091*

SCP DISTRIBUTORS CANADA INC   *p516*
373 ELGIN ST, BRANTFORD, ON, N3S 7P5
(519) 720-9219   *SIC 5091*

SERVICE PLUS AQUATICS INC   *p717*
3600B LAIRD RD UNIT 7, MISSISSAUGA, ON, L5L 6A7
(905) 569-7899   *SIC 5091*

SHIMANO CANADA LTD   *p842*
427 PIDO RD, PETERBOROUGH, ON, K9J 6X7
(705) 745-3232   *SIC 5091*

SPARTAN ATHLETIC PRODUCTS LIMITED *p448*
10 MORRIS DR UNIT 13, DARTMOUTH, NS, B3B 1K8
(902) 482-0330   *SIC 5091*

TAYLOR MADE GOLF CANADA LTD *p1028*
6240 HIGHWAY 7 SUITE 100, WOODBRIDGE, ON, L4H 4G3
(800) 668-9883   *SIC 5091*

TOURNAMENT SPORTS MARKETING INC *p1007*
185 WEBER ST S, WATERLOO, ON, N2J 2B1
(519) 888-6500   *SIC 5091*

TRICOT MONDIAL INC   *p1327*
490 BOUL MONTPELLIER, SAINT-LAURENT, QC, H4N 2G7
(514) 279-9333   *SIC 5091*

WHITEWATER WEST INDUSTRIES LTD *p259*
6700 MCMILLAN WAY, RICHMOND, BC, V6W 1J7
(604) 273-1068   *SIC 5091*

WORLD FAMOUS SALES OF CANADA INC *p561*
333 CONFEDERATION PKY SUITE 1, CONCORD, ON, L4K 4S1
(905) 738-4777   *SIC 5091*

YAMAHA MOTOR CANADA LTD   *p766*
480 GORDON BAKER RD, NORTH YORK, ON, M2H 3B4
(416) 498-1911   *SIC 5091*

YARMOUTH SEA PRODUCTS LTD   *p462*
GD, METEGHAN, NS, B0W 2J0
(902) 645-2417   *SIC 5091*

SIC 5092 Toys and hobby goods and supplies

1271591 ONTARIO INC   *p887*
261 MARTINDALE RD UNIT 14, ST CATHARINES, ON, L2W 1A2
(905) 688-7755   *SIC 5092*

2961-4765 QUEBEC INC   *p1261*
595 BOUL PIERRE-BERTRAND BUREAU 125, QUEBEC, QC, G1M 3T8
(418) 622-5126   *SIC 5092*

9135-3904 QUEBEC INC   *p1061*
2515 AV DE LA RENAISSANCE, BOISBRIAND, QC, J7H 1T9
(514) 667-0623   *SIC 5092*

9341-6246 QUEBEC INC   *p1101*
523 BOUL CURE-LABELLE, FABREVILLE, QC, H7P 2P5
(450) 628-9901   *SIC 5092*

ARROW GAMES CORPORATION   *p758*
6199 DON MURIE ST, NIAGARA FALLS, ON, L2G 0B1
(905) 354-7300   *SIC 5092*

ARROW GAMES CORPORATION   *p848*
9515 MONTROSE RD UNIT 2, PORT ROBINSON, ON, L0S 1K0
(905) 354-7300   *SIC 5092*

ASMODEE CANADA INC   *p1283*
31 RUE DE LA COOPERATIVE, RIGAUD, QC, J0P 1P0
(450) 424-0655   *SIC 5092*

ASSOCIATION ECHEC ET MATHEMATIQUES *p1185*
3423 RUE SAINT-DENIS BUREAU 400, MONTREAL, QC, H2X 3L2
(514) 845-8352   *SIC 5092*

BEST MADE TOYS INTERNATIONAL INC *p782*
120 SAINT REGIS CRES N, NORTH YORK, ON, M3J 1Z3
(416) 630-6665   *SIC 5092*

BINGO VEZINA INC   *p1343*
6125 BOUL METROPOLITAIN E, SAINT-LEONARD, QC, H1P 1X7
(514) 321-5555   *SIC 5092*

CANADIAN GROUP, THE   *p792*
430 SIGNET DR SUITE A, NORTH YORK, ON, M9L 2T6
(416) 746-3388   *SIC 5092*

CANADIAN HOBBYCRAFT LIMITED   *p550*
445 EDGELEY BLVD UNIT 1, CONCORD, ON, L4K 4G1
(905) 738-6556   *SIC 5092*

CANUCK AMUSEMENTS AND MERCHANDISING LTD   *p73*
3911 37 ST SW, CALGARY, AB, T3E 6L6
(403) 249-6641   *SIC 5092*

CIE DANAWARES   *p1127*
1860 32E AV, LACHINE, QC, H8T 3J7
(514) 342-5555   *SIC 5092*

CITIWELL INTERNATIONAL INC   *p782*
401 MAGNETIC DR UNIT 9, NORTH YORK, ON, M3J 3H9
SIC 5092

COATS CANADA INC   *p1027*
10 ROYBRIDGE GATE SUITE 200, WOODBRIDGE, ON, L4H 3M8
(905) 850-9200   *SIC 5092*

COMET STRIP ENTERPRISES (CANADA) LTD *p254*
5375 PARKWOOD PL SUITE 1, RICHMOND, BC, V6V 2N1
(604) 278-4005   *SIC 5092*

CTG BRANDS INC   *p551*
123 GREAT GULF DR, CONCORD, ON, L4K 5V1
(905) 761-3330   *SIC 5092*

DISTIL INTERACTIVE LTD   *p751*
16 FITZGERALD RD SUITE 200, NEPEAN, ON, K2H 8R6
SIC 5092

EDITION JEUX INFINIS INC   *p1213*
2110 RUE DRUMMOND BUREAU 200, MONTREAL, QC, H3G 1W9
SIC 5092

GROSNOR DISTRIBUTION INC   *p513*
4 LOWRY DR, BRAMPTON, ON, L7A 1C4
(416) 744-3344   *SIC 5092*

HASBRO CANADA CORPORATION   *p695*
2645 SKYMARK AVE SUITE 200, MISSISSAUGA, ON, L4W 4H2
(905) 238-3374   *SIC 5092*

INTERNATIONAL PLAYING CARD COMPANY LIMITED   *p504*
845 INTERMODAL DR UNIT 1, BRAMPTON, ON, L6T 0C6
(905) 488-7102   *SIC 5092*

JOHN BEAD CORPORATION LIMITED *p868*
20 BERTRAND AVE, SCARBOROUGH, ON, M1L 2P4
(416) 757-3287   *SIC 5092*

JOUET K.I.D. INC   *p1276*
4000 RUE JEAN-MARCHAND BUREAU 120, QUEBEC, QC, G2C 1Y6
(418) 627-0101   *SIC 5092*

KROEGER INC   *p878*
455 FINCHDENE SQ, SCARBOROUGH, ON, M1X 1B7
(416) 752-4382   *SIC 5092*

LA GALERIE DU JOUET JFA INC   *p1045*
1435 AV DU PONT S, ALMA, QC, G8B 2V9
(418) 662-6221   *SIC 5092*

LION RAMPANT IMPORTS LTD   *p513*
36 EASTON RD, BRANTFORD, ON, N3P 1J5

▲ Public Company   ■ Public Company Family Member   **HQ** Headquarters   **BR** Branch   **SL** Single Location

(905) 572-6446   *SIC* 5092
LOUISE KOOL & GALT LIMITED   *p874*
2123 MCCOWAN RD, SCARBOROUGH, ON, M1S 3Y6
(416) 293-0312   *SIC* 5092
LUDIA INC   *p1189*
410 RUE SAINT-NICOLAS BUREAU 400, MONTREAL, QC, H2Y 2P5
(514) 313-3370   *SIC* 5092
MAISON JOSEPH BATTAT LTEE   *p1158*
8440 CH DARNLEY, MONT-ROYAL, QC, H4T 1M4
(866) 665-5524   *SIC* 5092
MATTEL CANADA INC   *p732*
6155 FREEMONT BLVD, MISSISSAUGA, ON, L5R 3W2
(905) 501-0404   *SIC* 5092
MYSTICAL DISTRIBUTING COMPANY LTD   *p999*
6 FOSTER STEARNS RD, TRENTON, ON, K8V 5R5
(613) 394-7056   *SIC* 5092
NINTENDO OF CANADA LTD   *p287*
2925 VIRTUAL WAY SUITE 150, VANCOUVER, BC, V5M 4X5
(604) 279-1600   *SIC* 5092
ORB FACTORY LIMITED, THE   *p458*
225 HERRING COVE RD, HALIFAX, NS, B3P 1L3
(902) 477-9570   *SIC* 5092
OUTSET MEDIA CORPORATION   *p338*
4226 COMMERCE CIR UNIT 106, VICTORIA, BC, V8Z 6N6
(250) 592-7374   *SIC* 5092
PIERRE BELVEDERE INC   *p1131*
2555 AV DOLLARD, LASALLE, QC, H8N 3A9
(514) 286-2880   *SIC* 5092
REVE ALCHIMIQUE INC   *p1216*
1751 RUE RICHARDSON, MONTREAL, QC, H3K 1G6
(514) 904-3700   *SIC* 5092
SKYBOX LABS INC   *p186*
4190 LOUGHEED HWY SUITE 200, BURNABY, BC, V5C 6A8
(604) 558-4330   *SIC* 5092
SOLUTIONS 2 GO LATAM INC   *p506*
15 PRODUCTION RD, BRAMPTON, ON, L6T 4N8
(905) 564-1140   *SIC* 5092
SONY INTERACTIVE ENTERTAINMENT CANADA INC   *p745*
1 PROLOGIS BLVD SUITE 103, MISSISSAUGA, ON, L5W 0G2
(905) 795-5152   *SIC* 5092
TRIBAL NOVA INC   *p1185*
4200 BOUL SAINT-LAURENT BUREAU 1203, MONTREAL, QC, H2W 2R2
(514) 598-0444   *SIC* 5092
UDISCO LTEE   *p1220*
4660 BOUL DECARIE, MONTREAL, QC, H3X 2H5
(514) 481-8107   *SIC* 5092
V & L ASSOCIATES INC   *p743*
6315 DANVILLE RD, MISSISSAUGA, ON, L5T 2H7
(905) 565-7535   *SIC* 5092
WHYTE, J. G. & SON LIMITED   *p750*
15 CAPELLA CRT SUITE 124, NEPEAN, ON, K2E 7X1
SIC 5092
WILLOW FUN WORLD LTD   *p227*
19609 WILLOWBROOK DR UNIT 2, LANGLEY, BC, V2Y 1A5
(604) 530-5324   *SIC* 5092
WOOLFITT'S ART ENTERPRISES INC *p991*
1153 QUEEN ST W, TORONTO, ON, M6J 1J4
(416) 536-7878   *SIC* 5092

SIC 5093 Scrap and waste materials

1222433 ONTARIO INC   *p993*

144 UNION ST, TORONTO, ON, M6N 3M9
(416) 654-3464   *SIC* 5093
1650473 ONTARIO INC   *p610*
10 HILLYARD ST, HAMILTON, ON, L8L 8J9
SIC 5093
4271815 CANADA INC   *p1248*
61 BOUL HYMUS, POINTE-CLAIRE, QC, H9R 1E2
(514) 428-0848   *SIC* 5093
A.B.C. HOLDINGS LTD   *p180*
8081 MEADOW AVE, BURNABY, BC, V3N 2V9
SIC 5093
A.B.C. RECYCLING LTD   *p180*
8081 MEADOW AVE, BURNABY, BC, V3N 2V9
(604) 522-9727   *SIC* 5093
ACIER CENTURY INC   *p1125*
600 RUE DE LA BERGE-DU-CANAL, LACHINE, QC, H8R 1H4
(514) 364-1505   *SIC* 5093
ACIERS REMI LATULIPPE INC, LES *p1392*
481 112 RTE E, VALLEE-JONCTION, QC, G0S 3J0
(418) 253-5521   *SIC* 5093
ALLIED TEXTILES & REFUSE INC   *p1223*
3700 RUE SAINT-PATRICK BUREAU 200, MONTREAL, QC, H4E 1A2
(514) 932-5962   *SIC* 5093
ATTAR METALS INC   *p737*
1856 ROMANI CRT, MISSISSAUGA, ON, L5T 1J1
(905) 670-1491   *SIC* 5093
BARRY GROUP INC   *p421*
GD, CATALINA, NL, A0C 1J0
(709) 469-2849   *SIC* 5093
BASTILLE, J. M. INC   *p1285*
396 RUE TEMISCOUATA BUREAU 744, RIVIERE-DU-LOUP, QC, G5R 2Z2
(418) 862-3346   *SIC* 5093
BENNY STARK LIMITED   *p993*
200 UNION ST, TORONTO, ON, M6N 3M9
(416) 654-3464   *SIC* 5093
BOURQUE, A ACIER ET METAUX INC *p1375*
737 CH GODIN, SHERBROOKE, QC, J1R 0S6
(819) 569-6960   *SIC* 5093
CALGARY METAL RECYCLING INC   *p28*
3415 OGDEN RD SE, CALGARY, AB, T2G 4N4
(403) 262-4542   *SIC* 5093
CANADA FIBERS LTD   *p997*
130 ARROW RD, TORONTO, ON, M9M 2M1
(416) 253-0400   *SIC* 5093
CANADIAN TEXTILE RECYCLING LIMITED   *p521*
5385 MUNRO CRT, BURLINGTON, ON, L7L 5M7
(905) 632-1464   *SIC* 5093
CANN-AMM EXPORTS INC   *p230*
23638 RIVER RD UNIT 1, MAPLE RIDGE, BC, V2W 1B7
(604) 466-9121   *SIC* 5093
COMBINED METAL INDUSTRIES INC *p792*
505 GARYRAY DR, NORTH YORK, ON, M9L 1P9
(416) 743-7730   *SIC* 5093
COOKSTOWN AUTO CENTRE LTD   *p561*
5046 5TH, COOKSTOWN, ON, L0L 1L0
(416) 364-0743   *SIC* 5093
COOPER'S IRON & METAL INC   *p933*
130 COMMISSIONERS ST, TORONTO, ON, M5A 1A8
(416) 461-0733   *SIC* 5093
CORPORATION COPNICK, LA   *p1222*
6198 RUE NOTRE-DAME O, MONTREAL, QC, H4C 1V4
(514) 937-9306   *SIC* 5093
DOMINION NICKEL INVESTMENTS LTD *p522*
834 APPLEBY LINE SUITE 1, BURLINGTON, ON, L7L 2Y7
(905) 639-9939   *SIC* 5093
DONALD E. CHARLTON LTD   *p176*

2035 QUEEN ST, ABBOTSFORD, BC, V2T 6J3
(604) 854-6499   *SIC* 5093
EYES N. OPTICS   *p998*
73 DUNDAS ST W SUITE A, TRENTON, ON, K8V 3P4
(613) 392-3040   *SIC* 5093
FAGEN & FILS   *p1204*
625 RUE BELMONT, MONTREAL, QC, H3B 2M1
SIC 5093
FIBRES J. C. INC, LES   *p1074*
3718 CH DE LA GRANDE-LIGNE, CHAMBLY, QC, J3L 4A7
(450) 359-4545   *SIC* 5093
GALLANT ENTERPRISES LTD   *p399*
194 RUE ST-FRANCOIS SUITE 210, EDMUNDSTON, NB, E3V 1E9
(506) 739-9390   *SIC* 5093
GENERAL RECYCLING INDUSTRIES LTD *p109*
4120 84 AVE NW, EDMONTON, AB, T6B 3H3
(780) 461-5555   *SIC* 5093
GENERAL SCRAP IRON & METALS LTD *p109*
4120 84 AVE NW, EDMONTON, AB, T6B 3H3
(780) 452-5865   *SIC* 5093
GENERAL SCRAP PARTNERSHIP   *p362*
135 BISMARCK ST, WINNIPEG, MB, R2C 2W3
(877) 495-6314   *SIC* 5093
GENOR RECYCLING SERVICES LIMITED *p515*
434 HENRY ST, BRANTFORD, ON, N3S 7W1
(519) 756-5264   *SIC* 5093
GERDAU AMERISTEEL CORPORATION *p356*
1 RAILWAY ST, SELKIRK, MB, R1A 2B3
(204) 482-6701   *SIC* 5093
GOLD, A. & SONS LTD   *p543*
7659 QUEENS LINE, CHATHAM, ON, N7M 5J5
(519) 352-0360   *SIC* 5093
GOLDY METALS INC   *p878*
1216 SEWELLS RD, SCARBOROUGH, ON, M1X 1S1
(416) 286-8686   *SIC* 5093
GRATTON COULEE AGRI PARTS LTD *p137*
HWY 881 S, IRMA, AB, T0B 2H0
(780) 754-2303   *SIC* 5093
HARVEST FRASER RICHMOND ORGANICS LTD   *p258*
7028 YORK RD, RICHMOND, BC, V6W 0B1
(604) 270-7500   *SIC* 5093
HOTZ AND SONS COMPANY INC   *p610*
39 LOTTRIDGE ST, HAMILTON, ON, L8L 6W1
(905) 545-2665   *SIC* 5093
INDUSTRIAL METALS (2011)   *p365*
550 MESSIER ST, WINNIPEG, MB, R2J 0G5
(204) 233-1908   *SIC* 5093
INDUSTRIES ASSOCIEES DE L'ACIER LTEE, LES   *p1356*
7140 132 RTE, SAINTE-CATHERINE, QC, J5C 1B6
(450) 632-1881   *SIC* 5093
J. FAGEN & FILS INC   *p1322*
201 RUE MONTCALM BUREAU 100, SAINT-JOSEPH-DE-SOREL, QC, J3R 1B9
(450) 742-8880   *SIC* 5093
J.M. BASTILLE ACIER INC   *p1286*
396 RUE TEMISCOUATA, RIVIERE-DU-LOUP, QC, G5R 2Z2
(418) 862-3346   *SIC* 5093
JAMEL METALS INC   *p374*
316 NOTRE DAME AVE, WINNIPEG, MB, R3B 1P4
(204) 947-3066   *SIC* 5093
JOSEPH & COMPANY INC   *p640*
257 VICTORIA ST N, KITCHENER, ON,

N2H 5C9
(519) 743-0205   *SIC* 5093
K-SCRAP RESOURCES LTD   *p1025*
110 HILL AVE, WINDSOR, ON, N9C 3B8
(519) 254-5188   *SIC* 5093
KAR-BASHER MANITOBA LTD   *p346*
855 49TH ST E, BRANDON, MB, R7A 7R2
(204) 726-8080   *SIC* 5093
L. BELANGER METAL INC   *p1386*
2950 RUE DE LA SIDBEC N, TROIS-RIVIERES, QC, G8Z 4E1
(819) 375-6600   *SIC* 5093
LONDON SALVAGE AND TRADING COMPANY LIMITED   *p652*
333 EGERTON ST, LONDON, ON, N5Z 2H3
(519) 451-0680   *SIC* 5093
MAINSTREAM METALS INC   *p523*
4350 HARVESTER RD, BURLINGTON, ON, L7L 5S4
(905) 631-5945   *SIC* 5093
MARX METALS LIMITED   *p686*
2520 RENA RD, MISSISSAUGA, ON, L4T 3C9
SIC 5093
MAXUC TRADING LTD   *p784*
79 MARTIN ROSS AVE, NORTH YORK, ON, M3J 2L5
(416) 667-0888   *SIC* 5093
MCDONALD METALS (1983) LTD   *p1414*
GD, PRINCE ALBERT, SK, S6V 8A4
(306) 764-9333   *SIC* 5093
MET-RECY LTEE   *p1362*
2975 BOUL INDUSTRIEL, SAINTE-ROSE, QC, H7L 3W9
(450) 668-6008   *SIC* 5093
METALLISATION DU NORD INC   *p1077*
876 RUE PERREAULT, CHIBOUGAMAU, QC, G8P 2K3
(418) 748-6442   *SIC* 5093
MISSISSAUGA PAPER FIBRES LTD   *p741*
1111 TRISTAR DR UNIT 1, MISSISSAUGA, ON, L5T 1W5
(905) 564-7260   *SIC* 5093
MOFFATT SCRAP IRON & METAL INC *p540*
9620 GUELPH LINE, CAMPBELLVILLE, ON, L0P 1B0
(905) 854-2792   *SIC* 5093
NASHA METAL EXPORT INC   *p878*
88 MISTY HILLS TRAIL, SCARBOROUGH, ON, M1X 1T3
(647) 765-8952   *SIC* 5093
NI-MET METALS INC   *p798*
2939 PORTLAND DR SUITE 300, OAKVILLE, ON, L6H 5S4
(289) 291-1111   *SIC* 5093
NIM DISPOSAL LTD   *p898*
2755 LASALLE BLVD, SUDBURY, ON, P3A 4R7
(705) 566-9363   *SIC* 5093
OGO FIBERS INC   *p853*
9140 LESLIE ST SUITE 312, RICHMOND HILL, ON, L4B 0A9
(905) 762-9300   *SIC* 5093
PACIFIC METALS LIMITED   *p291*
8360 ONTARIO ST, VANCOUVER, BC, V5X 3E5
(604) 327-1148   *SIC* 5093
PAPER FIBRES INC   *p689*
6405 NORTHWEST DR, MISSISSAUGA, ON, L4V 1K2
(905) 672-7222   *SIC* 5093
PAPIER REBUT CENTRAL INC   *p1173*
4270 RUE HOGAN, MONTREAL, QC, H2H 2N4
(514) 526-4965   *SIC* 5093
POPOW & SONS BODY SHOP LTD   *p138*
5017 49 ST, LACOMBE, AB, T4L 1Y2
(403) 782-6941   *SIC* 5093
POSCOR METAL RECOVERY CORP   *p498*
10095 BRAMALEA RD SUITE 201, BRAMPTON, ON, L6R 0K1
(647) 641-3928   *SIC* 5093
POSNER METALS LIMITED   *p609*
610 BEACH RD, HAMILTON, ON, L8H 3L1

(905) 544-1881   *SIC 5093*

RECYCLAGE DE PAPIER HANNA LTEE *p1322*
760 AV GUY-POULIN, SAINT-JOSEPH-DE-BEAUCE, QC, G0S 2V0
(418) 397-5859   *SIC 5093*

ROSS, JOHN AND SONS LIMITED *p459*
171 CHAIN LAKE DR, HALIFAX, NS, B3S 1B3
(902) 450-5633   *SIC 5093*

RUTMET INC *p799*
2939 PORTLAND DR SUITE 300, OAKVILLE, ON, L6H 5S4
(289) 291-1111   *SIC 5093*

S.R.V. INDUSTRIAL SUPPLY INC *p872*
2500 LAWRENCE AVE E SUITE 12, SCARBOROUGH, ON, M1P 2R7
(416) 757-1020   *SIC 5093*

SAM ADELSTEIN & CO. LIMITED *p883*
492 WELLAND AVE, ST CATHARINES, ON, L2M 5V5
(905) 988-9336   *SIC 5093*

SCHAEFER SYSTEM INTERNATIONAL LIMITED *p506*
140 NUGGETT CRT, BRAMPTON, ON, L6T 5H4
(905) 458-5399   *SIC 5093*

SCHNITZER STEEL CANADA LTD *p275*
12195 MUSQUEAM DR, SURREY, BC, V3V 3T2
(604) 580-0251   *SIC 5093*

SCOTIA RECYCLING LIMITED *p448*
5 BROWN AVE, DARTMOUTH, NS, B3B 1Z7
(902) 468-5650   *SIC 5093*

SL MARKETING INC *p1012*
555 BROWN RD, WELLAND, ON, L3B 5N4
(905) 714-4000   *SIC 5093*

THYSSENKRUPP MATERIALS CA, LTD *p1336*
4700 CH DU BOIS-FRANC, SAINT-LAURENT, QC, H4S 1A7
(514) 337-0161   *SIC 5093*

TMS INTERNATIONAL CANADA LIMITED *p971*
199 BAY ST SUITE 5300, TORONTO, ON, M5L 1B9
SIC 5093

TRANSATLANTIC ANGELS TRADING CO LTD *p262*
11482 RIVER RD, RICHMOND, BC, V6X 1Z7
(604) 231-1960   *SIC 5093*

TRIPLE M METAL LP *p610*
1640 BRAMPTON ST, HAMILTON, ON, L8H 3S1
(905) 545-7083   *SIC 5093*

TRISTAR INDUSTRIES LTD *p589*
160 BETHRIDGE RD, ETOBICOKE, ON, M9W 1N3
(416) 747-5767   *SIC 5093*

URBANMINE INC *p389*
72 ROTHWELL RD, WINNIPEG, MB, R3P 2H7
(204) 774-0192   *SIC 5093*

WAXMAN INDUSTRIAL SERVICES CORP *p525*
4350 HARVESTER RD, BURLINGTON, ON, L7L 5S4
(905) 639-1111   *SIC 5093*

WIPECO INDUSTRIES INC, LES *p1228*
3333 RUE DOUGLAS-B.-FLOREANI, MONTREAL, QC, H4S 1Y6
(514) 935-2551   *SIC 5093*

ZALEV BROTHERS CO *p1022*
200 GRAND MARAIS RD E, WINDSOR, ON, N8X 3H2
(519) 966-0620   *SIC 5093*

ZUBICK, JOHN LIMITED *p651*
105 CLARKE RD, LONDON, ON, N5W 5C9
(519) 451-5470   *SIC 5093*

SIC 5094 Jewelry and precious stones

9106-5235 QUEBEC INC *p1058*
1044 BOUL DU CURE-LABELLE, BLAINVILLE, QC, J7C 2M5
(450) 939-4799   *SIC 5094*

9217-5041 QUEBEC INC *p1263*
1095 RUE EUGENE-CHINIC, QUEBEC, QC, G1N 4N2
(581) 741-3233   *SIC 5094*

A.T. STORRS LTD *p285*
1353 PENDER ST E, VANCOUVER, BC, V5L 1V7
(800) 561-5800   *SIC 5094*

BIJOUTERIE CARMEN INC *p1325*
700 RUE HODGE AVE SUITE 200, SAINT-LAURENT, QC, H4N 2V2
(514) 273-1718   *SIC 5094*

BONICA PRECISION (CANADA) INC *p253*
3830 JACOMBS RD UNIT 105, RICHMOND, BC, V6V 1Y6
(604) 270-0812   *SIC 5094*

BULOVA WATCH COMPANY LIMITED *p864*
39 CASEBRIDGE CRT, SCARBOROUGH, ON, M1B 5N4
(416) 751-7151   *SIC 5094*

CANADIAN COIN & CURRENCY CORP *p855*
10355 YONGE ST, RICHMOND HILL, ON, L4C 3C1
(905) 883-5300   *SIC 5094*

DAVID SHAW SILVERWARE NORTH AMERICA LTD *p783*
85 MARTIN ROSS AVE, NORTH YORK, ON, M3J 2L5
(416) 736-0492   *SIC 5094*

DAVIS & WILLMOT INC *p917*
2060 QUEEN ST E SUITE 51504, TORONTO, ON, M4E 1C9
SIC 5094

DIAMANTS BASAL INC *p1203*
1255 BOUL ROBERT-BOURASSA BUREAU 460, MONTREAL, QC, H3B 3B6
(514) 861-6675   *SIC 5094*

DOMINION DIAMOND CORPORATION *p436*
4920 52 ST UNIT 900, YELLOWKNIFE, NT, X1A 3T1
(867) 669-6100   *SIC 5094*

EMBIX COMPAGNIE D'IMPORTATIONS DE MONTRES LTEE *p1218*
2550 CH BATES BUREAU 301, MONTREAL, QC, H3S 1A7
(514) 731-3978   *SIC 5094*

FIFTH AVENUE COLLECTION LTD *p1411*
30 STADACONA ST W, MOOSE JAW, SK, S6H 1Z1
(306) 694-8188   *SIC 5094*

FRABELS INC *p1156*
5580 RUE PARE, MONT-ROYAL, QC, H4P 2M1
(514) 842-8561   *SIC 5094*

GARBO GROUP INC *p791*
34 WINGOLD AVE, NORTH YORK, ON, M6B 1P5
(416) 782-9500   *SIC 5094*

GEMME CANADIENNE P.A. INC *p1196*
1002 RUE SHERBROOKE O BUREAU 2525, MONTREAL, QC, H3A 3L6
(514) 287-1951   *SIC 5094*

GEMPERLE INC *p1196*
1002 RUE SHERBROOKE O BUREAU 2525, MONTREAL, QC, H3A 3L6
(514) 287-9017   *SIC 5094*

GLOBAL ROYALTIES LIMITED *p705*
145 TRADERS BLVD E UNIT 1, MISSISSAUGA, ON, L4Z 3L3
(905) 890-3000   *SIC 5094*

H.R.A. INVESTMENTS LTD *p313*
1021 HASTINGS ST W UNIT 2300, VANCOUVER, BC, V6E 0C3
(604) 669-9562   *SIC 5094*

INTERNATIONAL SILVER DEVELOPMENT INC *p712*
1260 LAKESHORE RD E, MISSISSAUGA, ON, L5E 3B8
SIC 5094

KLASSEN JEWELLERS LTD *p1431*
2318 AVENUE C N, SASKATOON, SK, S7L 5X5
(306) 652-2112   *SIC 5094*

KUNG'S MANUFACTORY LTD *p289*
18 2ND AVE E, VANCOUVER, BC, V5T 1B1
(604) 873-6341   *SIC 5094*

MAINLINE FASHIONS INC *p789*
42 DUFFLAW RD UNIT 100, NORTH YORK, ON, M6A 2W1
(416) 368-1522   *SIC 5094*

MASTER DESIGN JEWELLERY LIMITED *p784*
1001 PETROLIA RD, NORTH YORK, ON, M3J 2X7
SIC 5094

NATIONAL TIME EQUIPMENT CO LTD *p996*
31 CORONET RD, TORONTO, ON, M8Z 2L8
(416) 252-2293   *SIC 5094*

ODYSSEY TIME INC *p780*
60 PRINCE ANDREW PL, NORTH YORK, ON, M3C 2H4
(647) 288-2222   *SIC 5094*

OLYMPIA JEWELLERY CORP *p784*
312 DOLOMITE DR SUITE 208, NORTH YORK, ON, M3J 2N2
SIC 5094

PAJ CANADA COMPANY *p673*
168 KONRAD CRES UNIT 1, MARKHAM, ON, L3R 9T9
(905) 752-2080   *SIC 5094*

PANDORA JEWELRY LTD *p579*
5535 EGLINTON AVE W SUITE 234, ETOBICOKE, ON, M9C 5K5
(416) 626-1211   *SIC 5094*

RAND ACCESSORIES INC *p1179*
9350 AV DE L'ESPLANADE BUREAU 222, MONTREAL, QC, H2N 1V6
(514) 385-3482   *SIC 5094*

RICHEMONT CANADA, INC *p700*
4610 EASTGATE PKY UNIT 1, MISSISSAUGA, ON, L4W 3W6
(905) 602-8532   *SIC 5094*

ROLEX CANADA LTD *p927*
50 ST CLAIR AVE W, TORONTO, ON, M4V 3B7
(416) 968-1100   *SIC 5094*

ROYAL CANADIAN MINT *p366*
520 LAGIMODIERE BLVD, WINNIPEG, MB, R2J 3E7
(204) 983-6400   *SIC 5094*

ROYAL CANADIAN MINT *p815*
320 SUSSEX DR, OTTAWA, ON, K1A 0G8
(613) 993-8990   *SIC 5094*

ROYAL INTERNATIONAL COLLECTABLES INC *p924*
2161 YONGE ST SUITE 608, TORONTO, ON, M4S 3A6
SIC 5094

ST. JOHN'S TROPHIES LTD *p743*
1750 BONHILL RD, MISSISSAUGA, ON, L5T 1C8
(905) 564-2001   *SIC 5094*

SWATCH GROUP (CANADA) LTD, THE *p984*
555 RICHMOND ST W SUITE 1105, TORONTO, ON, M5V 3B1
(416) 703-1667   *SIC 5094*

TIMEX GROUP CANADA, INC *p676*
7300 WARDEN AVE 115, MARKHAM, ON, L3R 9Z6
(905) 477-8463   *SIC 5094*

VANITY FASHIONS LIMITED *p448*
34 PAYZANT AVE, DARTMOUTH, NS, B3B 1Z6
(902) 468-6763   *SIC 5094*

WENGER LTEE *p1331*
3521 BOUL THIMENS, SAINT-LAURENT, QC, H4R 1V5
(514) 337-4455   *SIC 5094*

WESTMINSTER SELECT TRADING CORPORATION *p935*
397 DUNDAS ST E, TORONTO, ON, M5A 2A7

---

(416) 363-2727   *SIC 5094*

SIC 5099 Durable goods, nec

163453 CANADA INC *p1248*
6800 RTE TRANSCANADIENNE, POINTE-CLAIRE, QC, H9R 1C2
(514) 956-7482   *SIC 5099*

167986 CANADA INC *p1093*
1901 RTE TRANSCANADIENNE, DORVAL, QC, H9P 1J1
(514) 685-2202   *SIC 5099*

2956-1198 QUEBEC INC *p1222*
3974 RUE NOTRE-DAME O BUREAU 101, MONTREAL, QC, H4C 1R1
(514) 573-2850   *SIC 5099*

9097-4775 QUEBEC INC *p1161*
9100 BOUL MAURICE-DUPLESSIS, MONTREAL, QC, H1E 7C2
(514) 494-4798   *SIC 5099*

9191-7906 QUEBEC INC *p1072*
200 RUE STRASBOURG, CANDIAC, QC, J5R 0B4
(450) 659-3434   *SIC 5099*

9210-7556 QUEBEC INC *p1100*
3954D BOUL LEMAN, FABREVILLE, QC, H7E 1A1
SIC 5099

ABOND CORPORATION INC *p1126*
10050 CH DE LA COTE-DE-LIESSE, LACHINE, QC, H8T 1A3
(514) 636-7979   *SIC 5099*

ACTIVE FIRE & SAFETY SERVICES LTD *p275*
12110 86 AVE, SURREY, BC, V3W 3H7
(604) 590-0149   *SIC 5099*

AGT CLIC FOODS INC *p1084*
2185 AV FRANCIS-HUGHES, COTE SAINT-LUC, QC, H7S 1N5
(450) 669-2663   *SIC 5099*

ALCO ELECTRONICS INC *p666*
725 DENISON ST, MARKHAM, ON, L3R 1B8
(905) 477-7878   *SIC 5099*

ANDERSON MERCHANDISERS-CANADA, INC. *p850*
60 LEEK CRES SUITE B, RICHMOND HILL, ON, L4B 1H1
SIC 5099

ANNETTE'S KEEPSAKES *p343*
GD, WHITE ROCK, BC, V4B 5L5
(604) 538-5890   *SIC 5099*

APPLIED ELECTRONICS LIMITED *p691*
1260 KAMATO RD, MISSISSAUGA, ON, L4W 1Y1
(905) 625-4321   *SIC 5099*

ARCTIC CO-OPERATIVES LIMITED *p371*
1645 INKSTER BLVD, WINNIPEG, MB, R2X 2W7
(204) 697-1625   *SIC 5099*

B SQUARED AIRSOFT LTD *p95*
14574 116 AVE NW, EDMONTON, AB, T5M 3E9
(780) 884-8292   *SIC 5099*

BALTA IMPORTS LTD *p754*
17600 YONGE ST SUITE 43, NEWMARKET, ON, L3Y 4Z1
(905) 853-5281   *SIC 5099*

BATH MILL INC *p176*
2637 DEACON ST, ABBOTSFORD, BC, V2T 6L4
(604) 302-2284   *SIC 5099*

BOIS D'OEUVRE CEDRICO INC *p1074*
562 RTE 132 E, CAUSAPSCAL, QC, G0J 1J0
(418) 756-5727   *SIC 5099*

BOIS PRECIEUX QUEBEC CANADA 1993 INC *p1082*
3100 RTE 108 BUREAU 4, COOKSHIRE-EATON, QC, J0B 1M0
(866) 624-0243   *SIC 5099*

BROGAN SAFETY SUPPLY LTD *p131*
12002 101 AVE SUITE 101, GRANDE

PRAIRIE, AB, T8V 8B1
(780) 539-9004   *SIC* 5099
BUCHANAN SALES INC *p908*
1120 PREMIER WAY, THUNDER BAY, ON,
P7B 0A3
SIC 5099
BUGABOOS EYEWEAR (U.S.A) INC *p241*
758 HARBOURSIDE DR, NORTH VAN-
COUVER, BC, V7P 3R7
(604) 924-2393   *SIC* 5099
CALEGO INTERNATIONAL INC *p1338*
6265 CH DE LA COTE-DE-LIESSE BU-
REAU 200, SAINT-LAURENT, QC, H4T 1C3
(514) 334-2117   *SIC* 5099
CASIO CANADA LTD *p667*
141 MCPHERSON ST, MARKHAM, ON,
L3R 3L3
(905) 248-4400   *SIC* 5099
CATALYST PULP AND PAPER SALES INC
p264
3600 LYSANDER LANE 2ND FL, RICH-
MOND, BC, V7B 1C3
(604) 247-4400   *SIC* 5099
CATHAY IMPORTERS 2000 LIMITED *p254*
12631 VULCAN WAY, RICHMOND, BC, V6V
1J7
(604) 233-0050   *SIC* 5099
CCT GLOBAL SOURCING INC *p550*
40 BRADWICK DR UNIT 5, CONCORD, ON,
L4K 1K9
(905) 326-8452   *SIC* 5099
COAST TO COAST VIDEO SALES LTD *p237*
1109 ROYAL AVE, NEW WESTMINSTER,
BC, V3M 1K4
(604) 525-9355   *SIC* 5099
CORPORATE SECURITY SUPPLY LTD *p384*
891 CENTURY ST SUITE A, WINNIPEG,
MB, R3H 0M3
(204) 989-1000   *SIC* 5099
COSTCO WHOLESALE CANADA LTD *p8*
2853 32 ST NE, CALGARY, AB, T1Y 6T7
(403) 299-1610   *SIC* 5099
COSTCO WHOLESALE CANADA LTD *p34*
99 HERITAGE GATE SE, CALGARY, AB,
T2H 3A7
(403) 313-7650   *SIC* 5099
COSTCO WHOLESALE CANADA LTD *p77*
11588 SARCEE TRAIL NW SUITE 543,
CALGARY, AB, T3R 0A1
(403) 516-3700   *SIC* 5099
COSTCO WHOLESALE CANADA LTD *p105*
12450 149 ST NW SUITE 154, EDMON-
TON, AB, T5V 1G9
(780) 453-8470   *SIC* 5099
COSTCO WHOLESALE CANADA LTD *p131*
9901 116 ST UNIT 102, GRANDE PRAIRIE,
AB, T8V 6H6
(780) 538-2911   *SIC* 5099
COSTCO WHOLESALE CANADA LTD *p143*
3200 MAYOR MAGRATH DR S, LETH-
BRIDGE, AB, T1K 6Y6
(403) 320-8917   *SIC* 5099
COSTCO WHOLESALE CANADA LTD *p147*
2350 BOX SPRINGS BLVD NW BOX SUITE
593, MEDICINE HAT, AB, T1C 0C8
(403) 581-5700   *SIC* 5099
COSTCO WHOLESALE CANADA LTD *p157*
37400 HIGHWAY 2 UNIT 162, RED DEER
COUNTY, AB, T4E 1B9
(403) 340-3736   *SIC* 5099
COSTCO WHOLESALE CANADA LTD *p160*
293020 CROSSIRON COMMON SUITE
300, ROCKY VIEW COUNTY, AB, T4A 0J6
(403) 516-5050   *SIC* 5099
COSTCO WHOLESALE CANADA LTD *p162*
2201 BROADMOOR BLVD, SHERWOOD
PARK, AB, T8H 0A1
(780) 410-2520   *SIC* 5099
COSTCO WHOLESALE CANADA LTD *p174*
1127 SUMAS WAY, ABBOTSFORD, BC,
V2S 8H2
(604) 850-3458   *SIC* 5099
COSTCO WHOLESALE CANADA LTD *p182*
3550 BRIGHTON AVE SUITE 51, BURN-

ABY, BC, V5A 4W3
(604) 420-2668   *SIC* 5099
COSTCO WHOLESALE CANADA LTD *p216*
1675 VERSATILE DR, KAMLOOPS, BC,
V1S 1W7
(250) 374-5336   *SIC* 5099
COSTCO WHOLESALE CANADA LTD *p219*
2479 HIGHWAY 97 N, KELOWNA, BC, V1X
4J2
(250) 868-9515   *SIC* 5099
COSTCO WHOLESALE CANADA LTD *p226*
20499 64 AVE, LANGLEY, BC, V2Y 1N5
(604) 539-8901   *SIC* 5099
COSTCO WHOLESALE CANADA LTD *p245*
2370 OTTAWA ST, PORT COQUITLAM, BC,
V3B 7Z1
(604) 552-2228   *SIC* 5099
COSTCO WHOLESALE CANADA LTD *p250*
2555 RANGE RD SUITE 158, PRINCE
GEORGE, BC, V2N 4G8
(250) 561-0784   *SIC* 5099
COSTCO WHOLESALE CANADA LTD *p259*
9151 BRIDGEPORT RD SUITE 54, RICH-
MOND, BC, V6X 3L9
(604) 270-3647   *SIC* 5099
COSTCO WHOLESALE CANADA LTD *p276*
7423 KING GEORGE BLVD SUITE 55,
SURREY, BC, V3W 5A8
(604) 596-7435   *SIC* 5099
COSTCO WHOLESALE CANADA LTD *p298*
605 EXPO BLVD, VANCOUVER, BC, V6B
1V4
(604) 622-5050   *SIC* 5099
COSTCO WHOLESALE CANADA LTD *p340*
799 MCCALLUM RD, VICTORIA, BC, V9B
6A2
(250) 391-1151   *SIC* 5099
COSTCO WHOLESALE CANADA LTD *p362*
1499 REGENT AVE W, WINNIPEG, MB,
R2C 4M4
(204) 654-4214   *SIC* 5099
COSTCO WHOLESALE CANADA LTD *p384*
1315 ST JAMES ST SUITE 57, WINNIPEG,
MB, R3H 0K9
(204) 788-4415   *SIC* 5099
COSTCO WHOLESALE CANADA LTD *p458*
230 CHAIN LAKE DR, HALIFAX, NS, B3S
1C5
(902) 450-1078   *SIC* 5099
COSTCO WHOLESALE CANADA LTD *p475*
150 KINGSTON RD E, AJAX, ON, L1Z 1E5
(905) 619-6677   *SIC* 5099
COSTCO WHOLESALE CANADA LTD *p478*
100 LEGEND CRT SUITE 1105, AN-
CASTER, ON, L9K 1J3
(905) 304-0344   *SIC* 5099
COSTCO WHOLESALE CANADA LTD *p486*
41 MAPLEVIEW DR E, BARRIE, ON, L4N
9A9
(705) 728-2350   *SIC* 5099
COSTCO WHOLESALE CANADA LTD *p509*
100 BISCAYNE CRES, BRAMPTON, ON,
L6W 4S1
(905) 450-2092   *SIC* 5099
COSTCO WHOLESALE CANADA LTD *p529*
1225 BRANT ST, BURLINGTON, ON, L7P
1X7
(905) 336-6714   *SIC* 5099
COSTCO WHOLESALE CANADA LTD *p658*
693 WONDERLAND RD N SUITE 530,
LONDON, ON, N6H 4L1
(519) 474-5301   *SIC* 5099
COSTCO WHOLESALE CANADA LTD *p678*
65 KIRKHAM DR SUITE 545, MARKHAM,
ON, L3S 0A9
(905) 201-3502   *SIC* 5099
COSTCO WHOLESALE CANADA LTD *p680*
1 YORKTECH DR SUITE 151, MARKHAM,
ON, L6G 1A6
(905) 477-5718   *SIC* 5099
COSTCO WHOLESALE CANADA LTD *p716*
3180 LAIRD RD, MISSISSAUGA, ON, L5L
6A5
(905) 828-3340   *SIC* 5099

COSTCO WHOLESALE CANADA LTD *p730*
5900 RODEO DR SUITE 526, MISSIS-
SAUGA, ON, L5R 3S9
(905) 568-4828   *SIC* 5099
COSTCO WHOLESALE CANADA LTD *p749*
415 WEST HUNT CLUB RD, NEPEAN, ON,
K2E 1C5
(613) 221-2010   *SIC* 5099
COSTCO WHOLESALE CANADA LTD *p856*
35 JOHN BIRCHALL RD SUITE 592, RICH-
MOND HILL, ON, L4S 0B2
(905) 780-2100   *SIC* 5099
COSTCO WHOLESALE CANADA LTD *p872*
1411 WARDEN AVE SUITE 537, SCAR-
BOROUGH, ON, M1R 2S3
(416) 288-0033   *SIC* 5099
COSTCO WHOLESALE CANADA LTD *p1048*
7373 RUE BOMBARDIER, ANJOU, QC, H1J
2V2
(514) 493-4814   *SIC* 5099
COSTCO WHOLESALE CANADA LTD *p1061*
3600 AV DES GRANDES TOURELLES,
BOISBRIAND, QC, J7H 0A1
(450) 420-4500   *SIC* 5099
COSTCO WHOLESALE CANADA LTD *p1064*
635 CH DE TOURAINE, BOUCHERVILLE,
QC, J4B 5E4
(450) 645-2631   *SIC* 5099
COSTCO WHOLESALE CANADA LTD *p1072*
60 RUE STRASBOURG, CANDIAC, QC,
J5R 0B4
(450) 444-3453   *SIC* 5099
COSTCO WHOLESALE CANADA LTD *p1104*
1100 BOUL MALONEY O BUREAU 542,
GATINEAU, QC, J8T 6G3
(819) 246-4005   *SIC* 5099
COSTCO WHOLESALE CANADA LTD *p1236*
2999 NORD LAVAL A-440 O, MONTREAL,
QC, H7P 5P4
(450) 686-7420   *SIC* 5099
COSTCO WHOLESALE CANADA LTD *p1249*
5701 RTE TRANSCANADIENNE, POINTE-
CLAIRE, QC, H9R 1B7
(514) 426-5052   *SIC* 5099
COSTCO WHOLESALE CANADA LTD *p1275*
3233 AV WATT, QUEBEC, QC, G1X 4W2
(418) 656-0666   *SIC* 5099
COSTCO WHOLESALE CANADA LTD *p1278*
440 RUE BOUVIER, QUEBEC, QC, G2J
1E3
(418) 627-5100   *SIC* 5099
COSTCO WHOLESALE CANADA LTD *p1308*
5025 BOUL COUSINEAU, SAINT-HUBERT,
QC, J3Y 3K7
(450) 443-3618   *SIC* 5099
COSTCO WHOLESALE CANADA LTD *p1422*
665 UNIVERSITY PARK DR SUITE 520,
REGINA, SK, S4V 2V8
(306) 789-8838   *SIC* 5099
COSTCO WHOLESALE CANADA LTD *p1435*
115 MARQUIS DR W, SASKATOON, SK,
S7R 1C7
(306) 933-4262   *SIC* 5099
D. R. BRENTON LIMITED *p460*
2 LAKESIDE PARK DR UNIT 5, LAKESIDE,
NS, B3T 1L7
(902) 876-7879   *SIC* 5099
DATAVISUAL MARKETING INC *p819*
1101 POLYTEK ST SUITE 500, OTTAWA,
ON, K1J 0B3
(613) 741-9898   *SIC* 5099
DIVERTISSEMENT SONOMA S.E.C. *p1402*
1 CAR WESTMOUNT BUREAU 1100,
WESTMOUNT, QC, H3Z 2P9
(514) 341-5600   *SIC* 5099
DOMINION & GRIMM INC *p1048*
8250 RUE MARCONI, ANJOU, QC, H1J 1B2
(514) 351-3000   *SIC* 5099
DSS AVIATION INC *p446*
71 WRIGHT AVE, DARTMOUTH, NS, B3B
1H4
(902) 444-3788   *SIC* 5099
DUBORD & RAINVILLE INC *p1329*
4045 BOUL POIRIER, SAINT-LAURENT,

QC, H4R 2G9
(514) 735-6111   *SIC* 5099
DUO COMMUNICATIONS OF CANADA LTD
p1224
10000 BOUL CAVENDISH, MONTREAL,
QC, H4M 2V1
SIC 5099
E M I MUSIC CANADA *p688*
3109 AMERICAN DR, MISSISSAUGA, ON,
L4V 0A2
SIC 5099
EAGLE CINEMATRONICS INC *p276*
8299 129 ST UNIT 104, SURREY, BC, V3W
0A6
(604) 592-5511   *SIC* 5099
ECHO BRAND MANAGEMENT LTD *p276*
8065 130 ST, SURREY, BC, V3W 7X4
(604) 590-4020   *SIC* 5099
ELECTROGAS MONITORS LTD *p155*
7961 49 AVE SUITE 1, RED DEER, AB, T4P
2V5
(403) 341-6167   *SIC* 5099
EMBALLAGE D'ALIMENTS LATINA INC
p1162
9200 RUE ROBERT-ARMOUR BUREAU 1,
MONTREAL, QC, H1E 2H1
(514) 643-0784   *SIC* 5099
ENSEIGNES CMD INC *p1070*
3615B RUE ISABELLE, BROSSARD, QC,
J4Y 2R2
(450) 465-1100   *SIC* 5099
ENTERTAINMENT ONE GP LIMITED *p502*
70 DRIVER RD UNIT 1, BRAMPTON, ON,
L6T 5V2
(905) 624-7337   *SIC* 5099
ENTREPRISE T.R.A. (2011) INC *p1301*
145 RUE DAOUST BUREAU 101, SAINT-
EUSTACHE, QC, J7R 6P4
(450) 491-2940   *SIC* 5099
EQUIPEMENT D'INCENDIE PRIORITE INC
p1339
7528 CH DE LA COTE-DE-LIESSE, SAINT-
LAURENT, QC, H4T 1E7
(514) 636-2431   *SIC* 5099
**EQUIPEMENTS D'ERABLIERE C.D.L. INC,
LES** *p1343*
257 RTE 279, SAINT-LAZARE-DE-
BELLECHASSE, QC, G0R 3J0
(418) 883-5158   *SIC* 5099
ESSENDANT CANADA, INC *p739*
6400 ORDAN DR, MISSISSAUGA, ON, L5T
2H6
(905) 670-1223   *SIC* 5099
**EVERLITE LUGGAGE MANUFACTURING
LIMITED** *p993*
451 ALLIANCE AVE, TORONTO, ON, M6N
2J1
(416) 763-4040   *SIC* 5099
FABRICATION SCANDINAVE INC *p1074*
452 BOUL PERRON, CARLETON, QC, G0C
1J0
(418) 364-6701   *SIC* 5099
FANTAISIE D'ETAIN INC *p1402*
21 AV GLADSTONE BUREAU 2, WEST-
MOUNT, QC, H3Z 1Z3
(514) 735-4141   *SIC* 5099.
FIBRECO EXPORT INC *p241*
1209 MCKEEN AVE, NORTH VANCOU-
VER, BC, V7P 3H9
(604) 980-6543   *SIC* 5099
FISKARS CANADA, INC *p670*
675 COCHRANE DR, MARKHAM, ON, L3R
0B8
(905) 940-8460   *SIC* 5099
FLAME-TAMER FIRE & SAFETY LTD *p503*
8058 TORBRAM RD, BRAMPTON, ON, L6T
3T2
(905) 791-3102   *SIC* 5099
G.A. PAPER INTERNATIONAL INC *p670*
327 RENFREW DR SUITE 102, MARKHAM,
ON, L3R 9S8
(905) 479-7600   *SIC* 5099
GAGNON IMAGE INC *p1285*
70 MONTEE INDUSTRIELLE-ET-

COMMERCIALE BUREAU F, RIMOUSKI, QC, G5M 1B1
(418) 723-2394   *SIC* 5099

GENCO MARINE LIMITED   *p712*
1008 RANGEVIEW RD, MISSISSAUGA, ON, L5E 1H3
(416) 504-2891   *SIC* 5099

GENTEC INTERNATIONAL   *p670*
90 ROYAL CREST CRT, MARKHAM, ON, L3R 9X6
(905) 513-7733   *SIC* 5099

GEORGIAN BAY FIRE & SAFETY LTD *p835*
1700 20TH ST E, OWEN SOUND, ON, N4K 5W9
(519) 376-6120   *SIC* 5099

GESTION QUEMAR INC   *p1264*
194 AV SAINT-SACREMENT, QUEBEC, QC, G1N 3X6
(418) 681-5088   *SIC* 5099

GLAZERS INC   *p1334*
7800 BOUL HENRI-BOURASSA O, SAINT-LAURENT, QC, H4S 1P4
(514) 335-1500   *SIC* 5099

GLOBAL PACIFIC RESOURCES INC *p298*
134 ABBOTT ST SUITE 500, VANCOUVER, BC, V6B 2K4
(604) 685-4411   *SIC* 5099

GROUPE BUGATTI INC, LE   *p1061*
1963 BOUL LIONEL-BERTRAND, BOIS-BRIAND, QC, J7H 1N8
(514) 832-1010   *SIC* 5099

HAZMASTERS ENVIRONMENTAL INC *p334*
575 HILLSIDE AVE, VICTORIA, BC, V8T 1Y8
(250) 384-0025   *SIC* 5099

HAZMASTERS INC   *p475*
651 HARWOOD AVE N UNIT 4, AJAX, ON, L1Z 0K4
(905) 231-0011   *SIC* 5099

HEYS INTERNATIONAL LTD   *p731*
333 FOSTER CRES SUITE 1, MISSISSAUGA, ON, L5R 4E5
(905) 565-8100   *SIC* 5099

HONTA TRADING INTERNATIONAL INC *p671*
110A COCHRANE DR, MARKHAM, ON, L3R 5S7
(905) 305-0688   *SIC* 5099

HUDSON'S BAY COMPANY   *p585*
145 CARRIER DR, ETOBICOKE, ON, M9W 5N5
(416) 798-5755   *SIC* 5099

ICON MEDIA COMMUNICATIONS INC *p671*
7495 BIRCHMOUNT RD, MARKHAM, ON, L3R 5G2
(905) 889-1944   *SIC* 5099

IMPORTATIONS CARA INC, LES   *p1383*
805 BOUL FRONTENAC E, THETFORD MINES, QC, G6G 6L5
(418) 335-3593   *SIC* 5099

INDUSTRIES JAM LTEE, LES   *p1053*
21000 AUT TRANSCANADIENNE, BAIE-D'URFE, QC, H9X 4B7
(514) 457-2555   *SIC* 5099

INTELLIGENT IMAGING SYSTEMS, INC *p119*
6325 GATEWAY BLVD NW SUITE 170, EDMONTON, AB, T6H 5H6
(780) 461-3355   *SIC* 5099

J.B. HAND & SONS LIMITED   *p433*
690 TOPSAIL RD, ST. JOHN'S, NL, A1E 2E2
(709) 364-2300   *SIC* 5099

JELINEK CORK LIMITED   *p804*
2260 SPEERS RD, OAKVILLE, ON, L6L 2X8
(905) 827-4666   *SIC* 5099

KIDDE CANADA INC   *p554*
340 FOUR VALLEY DR, CONCORD, ON, L4K 5Z1
(905) 695-6060   *SIC* 5099

KIEF MUSIC LTD   *p276*
13139 80 AVE SUITE 1, SURREY, BC, V3W 3B1
SIC 5099

LATOPLAST LTD   *p713*

1661 FINFAR CRT, MISSISSAUGA, ON, L5J 4K1
(905) 823-6150   *SIC* 5099

LEVITT-SAFETY LIMITED   *p798*
2872 BRISTOL CIR, OAKVILLE, ON, L6H 5T5
(905) 829-3668   *SIC* 5099

LONG ISLAND DISTRIBUTING CO. LIMITED   *p916*
425 ALNESS ST, TORONTO, ON, M3J 2H4
SIC 5099

MAGASIN DE MUSIQUE STEVE INC *p1192*
51 RUE SAINT-ANTOINE O, MONTREAL, QC, H2Z 1G9
(514) 878-2216   *SIC* 5099

MARTEL FILS INC   *p1109*
688 RUE PRINCIPALE, GRANBY, QC, J2G 2Y4
(450) 361-6445   *SIC* 5099

MAUI JIM CANADA ULC   *p724*
2830 ARGENTIA RD UNIT 3, MISSISSAUGA, ON, L5N 8G4
(905) 286-9714   *SIC* 5099

MCFEETERS G., ENTERPRISES INC *p882*
2825 SOUTH GRIMSBY RD 21, SMITHVILLE, ON, L0R 2A0
(905) 643-6167   *SIC* 5099

MORTON CLARKE & CO. LTD   *p255*
2551 NO. 6 RD UNIT 1105, RICHMOND, BC, V6V 1P3
(604) 273-1055   *SIC* 5099

MUSKOKA TIMBER MILLS LTD   *p497*
2152 MANITOBA ST, BRACEBRIDGE, ON, P1L 1X4
(705) 645-7757   *SIC* 5099

NADEL ENTERPRISES INC   *p689*
3320 CAROGA DR, MISSISSAUGA, ON, L4V 1L4
(416) 745-2622   *SIC* 5099

NEWELL BRANDS CANADA ULC   *p801*
586 ARGUS RD SUITE 400, OAKVILLE, ON, L6J 3J3
(866) 595-0525   *SIC* 5099

OPTIMAX EYEWEAR INCORPORATED *p513*
55 REGAN RD UNIT 2, BRAMPTON, ON, L7A 1B2
(905) 846-6103   *SIC* 5099

OSMOCO LABORATORIES INC   *p1253*
260 CH DU BORD-DU-LAC LAKESHORE, POINTE-CLAIRE, QC, H9S 4K9
(514) 694-4567   *SIC* 5099

OUTLOOK EYEWEAR CANADA LIMITED *p706*
290 BRUNEL RD, MISSISSAUGA, ON, L4Z 2C2
(905) 890-1391   *SIC* 5099

P.K. DOUGLASS INC   *p698*
1033 JAYSON CRT, MISSISSAUGA, ON, L4W 2P4
(905) 624-3300   *SIC* 5099

PACIFIC BIOENERGY CORPORATION *p315*
1111 HASTINGS ST W SUITE 780, VANCOUVER, BC, V6E 2J3
(604) 602-1099   *SIC* 5099

PACIFIC VEND DISTRIBUTORS LTD *p291*
8250 FRASER ST, VANCOUVER, BC, V5X 3X6
(604) 324-2164   *SIC* 5099

PF RESOLU CANADA INC   *p1053*
1 CH DE LA SCIERIE, BAIE-COMEAU, QC, G5C 2S9
(418) 589-9229   *SIC* 5099

PLANET GASTRONOMIE   *p1190*
465 RUE SAINT-JEAN, MONTREAL, QC, H2Y 2R6
SIC 5099

POWER TRADING INC   *p1252*
2555 BOUL DES SOURCES, POINTE-CLAIRE, QC, H9R 5Z3
(514) 421-2225   *SIC* 5099

PRECISION TRANSFER TECHNOLOGIES INC   *p831*
1750 COURTWOOD CRES SUITE 104, OT-

TAWA, ON, K2C 2B5
(613) 729-8987   *SIC* 5099

PRESENCE INFORMATIQUE INC   *p1257*
4600 BOUL HENRI-BOURASSA LOCAL 130, QUEBEC, QC, G1H 3A5
(418) 681-2470   *SIC* 5099

PROMOBOIS G.D.S. INC   *p1089*
207 295 RTE, DEGELIS, QC, G5T 1R1
(418) 853-5050   *SIC* 5099

QUANTUM PLUS LTD   *p1028*
500 NEW ENTERPRISE WAY, WOODBRIDGE, ON, L4H 0R3
(905) 264-3700   *SIC* 5099

QUATREX ENVIRONNEMENT INC   *p1381*
2085 BOUL DES ENTREPRISES, TERREBONNE, QC, J6Y 1W9
(450) 963-4747   *SIC* 5099

RICHARDS PACKAGING INCOME FUND *p742*
6095 ORDAN DR, MISSISSAUGA, ON, L5T 2M7
(905) 670-7760   *SIC* 5099

ROLAND CANADA LTD   *p256*
5480 PARKWOOD WAY, RICHMOND, BC, V6V 2M4
(604) 270-6626   *SIC* 5099

RONCO DISPOSABLE PRODUCTS LTD *p558*
70 PLANCHET RD, CONCORD, ON, L4K 2C7
(905) 660-6700   *SIC* 5099

ROYAL CITY FIRE SUPPLIES LTD   *p237*
633 TWELFTH ST, NEW WESTMINSTER, BC, V3M 4J5
(604) 522-4240   *SIC* 5099

RUBIE'S COSTUME COMPANY (CANADA) *p674*
2710 14TH AVE, MARKHAM, ON, L3R 0J1
(905) 470-0300   *SIC* 5099

SAFETY EXPRESS LTD   *p717*
4190 SLADEVIEW CRES UNIT 1-2, MISSISSAUGA, ON, L5L 0A1
(905) 608-0111   *SIC* 5099

SAMSONITE CANADA INC   *p896*
305 C H MEIER BLVD, STRATFORD, ON, N5A 0H4
(519) 271-5040   *SIC* 5099

SBC FIREMASTER LTD   *p252*
275 COPPER MOUNTAIN RD, PRINCETON, BC, V0X 1W0
(250) 295-7685   *SIC* 5099

SECURITE PLUS MODE PLEIN AIR INC *p1388*
5426 BOUL GENE-H.-KRUGER, TROIS-RIVIERES, QC, G9A 4N8
(819) 379-2434   *SIC* 5099

SECURO VISION INC   *p1142*
2285 RUE DE LA METROPOLE, LONGUEUIL, QC, J4G 1E5
(450) 679-2330   *SIC* 5099

SIGNALISATION JP INC   *p1356*
1980 RUE LAURIER, SAINTE-CATHERINE, QC, J5C 1B8
(450) 845-3461   *SIC* 5099

SMARTREND SUPPLY LTD   *p392*
1249 CLARENCE AVE UNIT 9, WINNIPEG, MB, R3T 1T4
(204) 489-7237   *SIC* 5099

SOLUS SECURITE INC   *p1386*
2545 RUE DE LA SIDBEC S, TROIS-RIVIERES, QC, G8Z 4M6
(819) 373-2053   *SIC* 5099

SONY MUSIC ENTERTAINMENT CANADA INC   *p780*
150 FERRAND DR SUITE 300, NORTH YORK, ON, M3C 3E5
(416) 589-3000   *SIC* 5099

SPECSAUDIO 1990 INC   *p1107*
79 RUE CREMAZIE, GATINEAU, QC, J8Y 3P1
(819) 777-3681   *SIC* 5099

ST. REGIS CRYSTAL INC   *p680*
271 YORKTECH DR, MARKHAM, ON, L6G 1A6

(905) 754-3355   *SIC* 5099

SUNDOG DISTRIBUTING INC   *p40*
83 SKYLINE CRES NE, CALGARY, AB, T2K 5X2
(403) 516-6600   *SIC* 5099

SUNTECH OPTICS INC   *p242*
758 HARBOURSIDE DR, NORTH VANCOUVER, BC, V7P 3R7
(604) 929-8141   *SIC* 5099

SUPERIOR SAFETY INC   *p909*
782 MACDONELL ST, THUNDER BAY, ON, P7B 4A6
(807) 344-3473   *SIC* 5099

SUPERTEK CANADA INC   *p1158*
8605 CH DARNLEY, MONT-ROYAL, QC, H4T 1X2
(514) 737-8354   *SIC* 5099

SURVIVAL SYSTEMS HOLDING LIMITED *p444*
20 ORION CRT SUITE 1, DARTMOUTH, NS, B2Y 4W6
(902) 466-7878   *SIC* 5099

TARGUS (CANADA) LTD   *p743*
6725 EDWARDS BLVD, MISSISSAUGA, ON, L5T 2V9
(905) 564-9300   *SIC* 5099

TIMBERWEST FOREST CORP   *p316*
2000-1055 HASTINGS ST W, VANCOUVER, BC, V6E 2E9
(604) 654-4600   *SIC* 5099

TP-HOLIDAY GROUP LIMITED   *p1165*
4875 BOUL DES GRANDES-PRAIRIES, MONTREAL, QC, H1R 1X4
(514) 325-0660   *SIC* 5099

TRADEX SUPPLY LTD   *p26*
3505 EDMONTON TRAIL NE, CALGARY, AB, T2E 3N9
(403) 250-7842   *SIC* 5099

TRANSFORMATEUR FEDERAL LTEE *p1248*
5059 BOUL SAINT-JEAN-BAPTISTE, POINTE-AUX-TREMBLES, QC, H1B 5V3
(514) 640-5059   *SIC* 5099

TRANSWORLD IMPORTS INC   *p258*
22071 FRASERWOOD WAY SUITE 100, RICHMOND, BC, V6W 1J5
(604) 272-3432   *SIC* 5099

TRICORBRAUN CANADA, INC   *p202*
1650 BRIGANTINE DR SUITE 500, COQUITLAM, BC, V3K 7B5
(604) 540-8166   *SIC* 5099

UNIVERSAL MUSIC CANADA INC   *p768*
2450 VICTORIA PARK AVE SUITE 1, NORTH YORK, ON, M2J 5H3
(416) 718-4000   *SIC* 5099

VARIETES PIERRE PRUD'HOMME INC, LES   *p1320*
801 RUE PRICE, SAINT-JEROME, QC, J7Y 4E2
(450) 438-2977   *SIC* 5099

VISIONCORP INTERNATIONAL INC   *p97*
16715 113 AVE NW, EDMONTON, AB, T5M 2X2
(780) 489-2012   *SIC* 5099

VISUAL PLANNING CORPORATION   *p703*
3071 UNIVERSAL DR, MISSISSAUGA, ON, L4X 2E2
(905) 629-7397   *SIC* 5099

W.H.B. IDENTIFICATION SOLUTIONS INC *p677*
710 COCHRANE DR, MARKHAM, ON, L3R 5N7
(905) 764-1122   *SIC* 5099

WASIP LTD   *p878*
3771 VICTORIA PARK AVE, SCARBOROUGH, ON, M1W 3Z5
(416) 297-5020   *SIC* 5099

WAYNE SAFETY INC   *p786*
1250 SHEPPARD AVE W, NORTH YORK, ON, M3K 2A6
(416) 661-1100   *SIC* 5099

WEISDORF GROUP OF COMPANIES INC, THE   *p677*
2801 JOHN ST, MARKHAM, ON, L3R 2Y8
(905) 477-9901   *SIC* 5099

▲ Public Company   ■ Public Company Family Member   **HQ** Headquarters   **BR** Branch   **SL** Single Location

WEISDORF, IRVING HOLDINGS INC *p677*
2801 JOHN ST, MARKHAM, ON, L3R 2Y8
(905) 477-9901   *SIC 5099*

WESTWOOD FIBRE PRODUCTS INC *p341*
2677 KYLE RD SUITE E, WEST KELOWNA,
BC, V1Z 2M9
(250) 769-1427   *SIC 5099*

**WHOLESALE LETTERING AND CARVING
LIMITED** *p744*
6215 NETHERHART RD, MISSISSAUGA,
ON, L5T 1G5
SIC 5099

YAMAHA CANADA MUSIC LTD *p875*
135 MILNER AVE, SCARBOROUGH, ON,
M1S 3R1
(416) 298-1311   *SIC 5099*

SIC 5111 Printing and writing paper

3427277 CANADA INC *p1393*
887 RTE HARWOOD BUREAU 53,
VAUDREUIL-DORION, QC, J7V 8P2
(450) 424-2323   *SIC 5111*

COPAP COMMERCE INC *p1249*
755 BOUL SAINT-JEAN BUREAU 305,
POINTE-CLAIRE, QC, H9R 5M9
(514) 693-9150   *SIC 5111*

DOMTAR INC *p738*
1330 COURTNEYPARK DR E, MISSIS-
SAUGA, ON, L5T 1K5
(905) 670-1330   *SIC 5111*

DOMTAR INC *p1127*
2125 23E AV, LACHINE, QC, H8T 1X5
(514) 636-5006   *SIC 5111*

ENTREPRISES ROLLAND INC, LES *p1319*
980 RUE DE L'INDUSTRIE, SAINT-
JEROME, QC, J7Y 4B8
(450) 569-0040   *SIC 5111*

**FIDUCIE TECHNOLOGIES DE FIBRES
AIKAWA** *p1374*
72 RUE QUEEN, SHERBROOKE, QC, J1M
2C3
(819) 562-4754   *SIC 5111*

LINKMAX PAPER LTD *p801*
2904 SOUTH SHERIDAN WAY SUITE 303,
OAKVILLE, ON, L6J 7L7
(905) 829-0053   *SIC 5111*

LOUKIL, SAID *p1300*
247 RUE ISABELLE, SAINT-EUSTACHE,
QC, J7P 4E9
(450) 491-3366   *SIC 5111*

S.O.F. WHITE PAPER COMPANY LTD *p210*
9990 RIVER WAY, DELTA, BC, V4G 1M9
(604) 951-3900   *SIC 5111*

SPICERS CANADA ULC *p1033*
200 GALCAT DR, WOODBRIDGE, ON, L4L
0B9
(905) 265-5000   *SIC 5111*

SPICERS CANADA ULC *p1033*
200 GALCAT DR, WOODBRIDGE, ON, L4L
0B9
(905) 265-5000   *SIC 5111*

VERITIV CANADA, INC *p26*
6040 11 ST NE, CALGARY, AB, T2E 9B1
(403) 250-5416   *SIC 5111*

VERITIV CANADA, INC *p1342*
4300 RUE HICKMORE, SAINT-LAURENT,
QC, H4T 1K2
(514) 367-3111   *SIC 5111*

XPEDX CANADA, INC *p507*
156 PARKSHORE DR, BRAMPTON, ON,
L6T 5M1
(905) 595-4351   *SIC 5111*

SIC 5112 Stationery and office supplies

2172004 ONTARIO INC *p547*
200 CONNIE CRES UNIT 4, CONCORD,
ON, L4K 1M1
(905) 738-1688   *SIC 5112*

605494 ALBERTA LTD *p104*
15462 131 AVE NW, EDMONTON, AB, T5V
0A1
(780) 454-4321   *SIC 5112*

864884 ONTARIO INC *p1026*
180 NEW HUNTINGTON RD UNIT 1,
WOODBRIDGE, ON, L4H 0P5
(905) 264-6670   *SIC 5112*

9019-4002 QUEBEC INC *p1047*
9601 BOUL PARKWAY, ANJOU, QC, H1J
1P3
(514) 352-0858   *SIC 5112*

989116 ONTARIO LIMITED *p865*
503 CENTENNIAL RD N, SCARBOROUGH,
ON, M1C 2A5
(416) 208-5441   *SIC 5112*

A-LINE ATLANTIC INC *p422*
43 MAPLE VALLEY RD SUITE 6, CORNER
BROOK, NL, A2H 6T3
(709) 634-1280   *SIC 5112*

ACME UNITED LIMITED *p808*
210 BROADWAY SUITE 204, OR-
ANGEVILLE, ON, L9W 5G4
(519) 940-8755   *SIC 5112*

BELLA FLOR CANADA *p657*
444 NEWBOLD ST, LONDON, ON, N6E 1K3
(800) 667-1902   *SIC 5112*

BRASSARD BURO INC *p1266*
2747 AV WATT, QUEBEC, QC, G1P 3X3
(418) 657-5500   *SIC 5112*

BUREAUTIQUE COTE-SUD INC *p1159*
49 RUE SAINT-JEAN-BAPTISTE E, MONT-
MAGNY, QC, G5V 1J6
(418) 248-4949   *SIC 5112*

BUROPRO CITATION INC *p1397*
505 BOUL JUTRAS E, VICTORIAVILLE,
QC, G6P 7H4
(819) 752-7777   *SIC 5112*

BUSINESS FURNISHINGS (1996) LTD *p383*
1741 WELLINGTON AVE, WINNIPEG, MB,
R3H 0G1
(204) 489-4191   *SIC 5112*

CAPITAL PRINTING & FORMS INC *p93*
14133 128A AVE NW, EDMONTON, AB,
T5L 4P5
(780) 453-5039   *SIC 5112*

CARLTON CARDS LIMITED *p692*
1820 MATHESON BLVD UNIT B1, MISSIS-
SAUGA, ON, L4W 0B3
(905) 219-6410   *SIC 5112*

CHESTOVAN STATIONERY LIMITED *p668*
100 STEELCASE RD E SUITE 105,
MARKHAM, ON, L3R 1E8
(905) 475-5542   *SIC 5112*

COVEY OFFICE GROUP INC *p402*
250 ALISON BLVD, FREDERICTON, NB,
E3C 0A9
(506) 458-8333   *SIC 5112*

CRITES & RIDDELL INC *p1130*
2695 AV DOLLARD, LASALLE, QC, H8N
2J8
(514) 368-8641   *SIC 5112*

**DATA COMMUNICATIONS MANAGEMENT
CORP** *p125*
9503 12 AVE SW, EDMONTON, AB, T6X
0C3
(780) 462-9700   *SIC 5112*

DENIS OFFICE SUPPLIES *p406*
123 LUTZ ST, MONCTON, NB, E1C 5E8
(506) 853-8920   *SIC 5112*

DISTRIBUTEURS JARDEL INC, LES *p1339*
7575 RTE TRANSCANADIENNE BUREAU
405, SAINT-LAURENT, QC, H4T 1V6
(514) 321-3983   *SIC 5112*

DIXON TICONDEROGA INC *p755*
210 PONY DR UNIT 1, NEWMARKET, ON,
L3Y 7B6
(905) 895-5122   *SIC 5112*

EDITIONS VAUDREUIL INC *p1394*
480 BOUL HARWOOD, VAUDREUIL-
DORION, QC, J7V 7H4
(450) 455-7974   *SIC 5112*

**ENTREPRISES DOMINION BLUELINE INC,
LES** *p1317*
230 RUE FOCH BUREAU 450, SAINT-
JEAN-SUR-RICHELIEU, QC, J3B 2B2

(450) 346-6827   *SIC 5112*

ETELLIGENT SOLUTIONS INC *p93*
11820 121 ST NW, EDMONTON, AB, T5L
5H5
(780) 452-3033   *SIC 5112*

FACTOR FORMS WEST LTD *p114*
8411 MCINTYRE RD NW, EDMONTON, AB,
T6E 6G3
(780) 468-1111   *SIC 5112*

FOURNITURES DE BUREAU DENIS INC
p1234
2990 BOUL LE CORBUSIER, MONTREAL,
QC, H7L 3M2
(450) 687-8682   *SIC 5112*

GRAND & TOY LIMITED *p96*
11522 168 ST NW, EDMONTON, AB, T5M
3T9
(866) 391-8111   *SIC 5112*

GRAND & TOY LIMITED *p818*
900 BELFAST RD, OTTAWA, ON, K1G 0Z6
(866) 391-8111   *SIC 5112*

GRAND & TOY LIMITED *p1031*
200 AVIVA PARK DR, WOODBRIDGE, ON,
L4L 9C7
(866) 391-8111   *SIC 5112*

GREEN IMAGING SUPPLIES INC *p717*
3330 RIDGEWAY DR UNIT 17, MISSIS-
SAUGA, ON, L5L 5Z9
(905) 607-2525   *SIC 5112*

HBI OFFICE PLUS INC *p1420*
1162 OSLER ST, REGINA, SK, S4R 5G9
(306) 757-5678   *SIC 5112*

JANNEX ENTERPRISES (1980) LIMITED
p679
280 HILLMOUNT RD UNIT 7, MARKHAM,
ON, L6C 3A1
(905) 284-8484   *SIC 5112*

MEDIA CASH REGISTER INC *p1245*
9580 BOUL GOUIN O, PIERREFONDS,
QC, H8Y 1R3
(514) 685-3630   *SIC 5112*

MERANGUE INTERNATIONAL LIMITED
p678
55 TRAVAIL RD UNIT 2, MARKHAM, ON,
L3S 3J1
(905) 209-0955   *SIC 5112*

MILLS PRINTING & STATIONERY CO. LTD
p285
1111 CLARK DR, VANCOUVER, BC, V5L
3K5
(604) 254-7211   *SIC 5112*

**NATIONAL FOCUS DISTRIBU-
TION/LOGISTICS INC** *p476*
151 CHURCH ST S, ALLISTON, ON, L9R
1E5
(705) 434-9995   *SIC 5112*

OBJECTIF LUNE INC *p1166*
2030 BOUL PIE-IX BUREAU 500, MON-
TREAL, QC, H1V 2C8
(514) 875-5863   *SIC 5112*

ONIX LAZER CORPORATION *p818*
645 BELFAST RD UNIT 1, OTTAWA, ON,
K1G 4V3
SIC 5112

PAPETERIE ST-REMI INC *p1351*
725 RUE NOTRE-DAME, SAINT-REMI, QC,
J0L 2L0
(450) 454-6065   *SIC 5112*

PC PARTS NOW INC *p678*
5990 14TH AVE, MARKHAM, ON, L3S 4M4
(905) 752-0222   *SIC 5112*

**PENTEL STATIONERY OF CANADA LIM-
ITED** *p265*
5900 NO. 2 RD SUITE 140, RICHMOND,
BC, V7C 4R9
(604) 270-1566   *SIC 5112*

PROMEX DATA PUBLISHING INC *p557*
37 STAFFERN DR, CONCORD, ON, L4K
2X2
(905) 738-0288   *SIC 5112*

QRX TECHNOLOGY GROUP INC *p557*
200 CONNIE CRES UNIT 4, CONCORD,
ON, L4K 1M1
(905) 738-1688   *SIC 5112*

QUALITY CLASSROOMS INC *p385*
840 BRADFORD ST, WINNIPEG, MB, R3H
0N5
(204) 775-6566   *SIC 5112*

S.P. RICHARDS CO. CANADA INC *p207*
820 CLIVEDEN PL UNIT 4, DELTA, BC, V3M
6C7
(604) 540-0444   *SIC 5112*

SCRAPBOOK, EH WHOLESALE LTD *p25*
5421 11 ST NE UNIT 109, CALGARY, AB,
T2E 6M4
(403) 229-1058   *SIC 5112*

SOLUTIONS *p361*
777 NORQUAY DR, WINKLER, MB, R6W
2S2
(204) 325-1006   *SIC 5112*

SPECTOR & CO. INC *p1336*
5700 RUE KIERAN, SAINT-LAURENT, QC,
H4S 2B5
(514) 337-7721   *SIC 5112*

SS LASER TECH LTD *p256*
13560 MAYCREST WAY UNIT 2115, RICH-
MOND, BC, V6V 2W9
(604) 821-0058   *SIC 5112*

SUPREME OFFICE PRODUCTS LIMITED
p1416
310 HENDERSON DR, REGINA, SK, S4N
5W7
(306) 566-8800   *SIC 5112*

SUTHERLAND UNION INC *p957*
335 BAY ST SUITE 1000, TORONTO, ON,
M5H 2R3
SIC 5112

TEC BUSINESS SOLUTIONS LTD *p700*
1048 RONSA CRT, MISSISSAUGA, ON,
L4W 3Y4
(905) 828-8132   *SIC 5112*

---
*SIC 5113 Industrial and personal service
paper*

A. & R. BELLEY INC *p1372*
1035 RUE PANNETON, SHERBROOKE,
QC, J1K 2B3
(819) 823-1843   *SIC 5113*

AMERICAN PAPER EXPORT INC *p326*
1080 HOWE ST UNIT 506, VANCOUVER,
BC, V6Z 2T1
(604) 298-7092   *SIC 5113*

ASIA PULP & PAPER (CANADA) LTD *p511*
20 HEREFORD ST SUITE 15, BRAMPTON,
ON, L6Y 0M1
(905) 450-2100   *SIC 5113*

BUNZL CANADA INC *p527*
3150 HARVESTER RD SUITE 100,
BURLINGTON, ON, L7N 3W8
(289) 289-1200   *SIC 5113*

CALIBRE SALES INC *p549*
8162 KEELE ST, CONCORD, ON, L4K 2A5
(905) 660-3603   *SIC 5113*

CANADIAN PAPER CONNECTION INC *p550*
200 VICEROY RD UNIT 1, CONCORD, ON,
L4K 3N8
(905) 669-2222   *SIC 5113*

CAPITAL PAPER PRODUCTS LIMITED *p459*
27 CALKIN DR, KENTVILLE, NS, B4N 3V7
(902) 678-6767   *SIC 5113*

CHAMPION PRODUCTS CORP *p1022*
2601 WYANDOTTE ST E, WINDSOR, ON,
N8Y 0A5
(519) 252-5414   *SIC 5113*

**CIE CANADIENNE DE PAPIER &
D'EMBALLAGE LTEE** *p1333*
3001 RUE BRABANT-MARINEAU, SAINT-
LAURENT, QC, H4S 1V5
(514) 333-4040   *SIC 5113*

COLET SHIPPING SUPPLIES INC *p738*
165 ANNAGEM BLVD, MISSISSAUGA, ON,
L5T 2V1
(905) 670-4919   *SIC 5113*

**COMPAGNIE DIVERSIFIEE EDELSTEIN
LTEE, LA** *p1241*
9001 CH AVON BUREAU 100, MONTREAL-

OUEST, QC, H4X 2G8
(514) 489-8689   *SIC 5113*

CONVERTER CORE INC   p509
155 ORENDA RD UNIT 1, BRAMPTON, ON, L6W 1W3
(905) 459-6566   *SIC 5113*

CREATIVE BAG CO. LTD, THE   p783
1100 LODESTAR RD UNIT 1, NORTH YORK, ON, M3J 2Z4
(416) 631-6444   *SIC 5113*

DORFIN INC   p1329
5757 BOUL THIMENS, SAINT-LAURENT, QC, H4R 2H6
(514) 335-0333   *SIC 5113*

DOVERCO INC   p1127
2111 32E AV, LACHINE, QC, H8T 3J1
(514) 420-6000   *SIC 5113*

EL-EN PACKAGING COMPANY LIMITED   p552
200 GREAT GULF DR, CONCORD, ON, L4K 5W1
(905) 761-5975   *SIC 5113*

EMBALLAGES BOUDREAULT CANADA LTEE, LES   p1106
45 RUE ADRIEN-ROBERT, GATINEAU, QC, J8Y 3S3
(819) 777-1603   *SIC 5113*

EMBALLAGES CARROUSEL INC, LES   p1064
1401 RUE AMPERE, BOUCHERVILLE, QC, J4B 6C5
(450) 655-2025   *SIC 5113*

EMBALLAGES DELTAPAC INC   p1048
7575 BOUL METROPOLITAIN E, ANJOU, QC, H1J 1J8
(514) 352-5546   *SIC 5113*

EMBALLAGES L. BOUCHER INC, LES   p1266
1360 AV GALILEE, QUEBEC, QC, G1P 4E3
(418) 681-2320   *SIC 5113*

EMBALLAGES MASKA INC   p1310
7450 AV PION, SAINT-HYACINTHE, QC, J2R 1R9
(450) 796-2040   *SIC 5113*

EMPAQUETAGES MESSIER INC   p1245
1050 RTE 133, PHILIPSBURG, QC, J0J 1N0
(450) 248-3921   *SIC 5113*

ENTERPRISE PAPER CO. LTD   p200
95 BRIGANTINE DR, COQUITLAM, BC, V3K 6Y9
(604) 522-6295   *SIC 5113*

EUGENE   ALLARD   PRODUITS D'EMBALLAGE ET D'ENTRETIEN INC   p1116
2244 RUE CHAPAIS, JONQUIERE, QC, G7X 4B4
(418) 547-6654   *SIC 5113*

FELLOWES CANADA LTD   p914
1261 TAPSCOTT RD, TORONTO, ON, M1X 1S9
(905) 475-6320   *SIC 5113*

G. T. FRENCH PAPER LIMITED   p615
90 GLOVER RD, HAMILTON, ON, L8W 3T7
(905) 574-0275   *SIC 5113*

HEARTLAND SHIPPING SUPPLIES INC   p740
6690 INNOVATOR DR, MISSISSAUGA, ON, L5T 2J3
(905) 564-9777   *SIC 5113*

JUNISE VENTES INC   p1234
4001 BOUL INDUSTRIEL, MONTREAL, QC, H7L 4S3
(514) 858-7777   *SIC 5113*

LILY CUPS INC   p865
2121 MARKHAM RD, SCARBOROUGH, ON, M1B 2W3
(416) 293-2877   *SIC 5113*

MARTIN-BROWER OF CANADA CO   p724
6985 FINANCIAL DR 3RD FL, MISSISSAUGA, ON, L5N 0G3
(905) 363-7000   *SIC 5113*

MAYERS PACKAGING LTD   p372
50 MANDALAY DR, WINNIPEG, MB, R2X

2Z2
(204) 774-1651   *SIC 5113*

MERCHANTS PAPER COMPANY WINDSOR LIMITED   p1023
975 CRAWFORD AVE, WINDSOR, ON, N9A 5C8
(519) 977-9977   *SIC 5113*

PACTIV CANADA INC   p853
33 STAPLES AVE, RICHMOND HILL, ON, L4B 4W6
(905) 770-8810   *SIC 5113*

PAPIERS ET EMBALLAGES ARTEAU INC   p1162
11420 BOUL ARMAND-BOMBARDIER, MONTREAL, QC, H1E 2W9
(514) 494-2222   *SIC 5113*

PLACEMENTS JULES CHAMBERLAND LTEE   p1096
2540 139 RTE, DRUMMONDVILLE, QC, J2A 2P9
(819) 478-4967   *SIC 5113*

PRODUITS M.G.D. INC, LES   p1059
680 BOUL INDUSTRIEL, BLAINVILLE, QC, J7C 3V4
(450) 437-1414   *SIC 5113*

REBOX CORP   p1341
7500 CH DE LA COTE-DE-LIESSE, SAINT-LAURENT, QC, H4T 1E7
(514) 335-1717   *SIC 5113*

ROSENBLOOM GROUPE INC   p1327
1225 RUE HODGE, SAINT-LAURENT, QC, H4N 2B5
(514) 748-7711   *SIC 5113*

SHIPPERS SUPPLY INC   p110
5219 47 ST NW, EDMONTON, AB, T6B 3N4
(780) 444-7777   *SIC 5113*

SNELLING PAPER & SANITATION LTD p816
1410 TRIOLE ST, OTTAWA, ON, K1B 3M5
(613) 745-7184   *SIC 5113*

STIR STICKS & PICKS INTERNATIONAL INC   p588
50 FASKEN DR UNIT 9, ETOBICOKE, ON, M9W 1K5
(416) 675-2064   *SIC 5113*

TORONTO SUN WAH TRADING INC   p576
18 CANMOTOR AVE, ETOBICOKE, ON, M8Z 4E5
(416) 252-7757   *SIC 5113*

ULINE CANADA CORPORATION   p685
3333 JAMES SNOW PKY N, MILTON, ON, L9T 8L1
(866) 295-5510   *SIC 5113*

VERITIV CANADA, INC   p743
1475 COURTNEYPARK DR E, MISSISSAUGA, ON, L5T 2R1
(905) 795-7400   *SIC 5113*

ZEBRA PAPER CONVERTERS INC   p702
5130 CREEKBANK RD, MISSISSAUGA, ON, L4W 2G2
(905) 602-1100   *SIC 5113*

SIC 5122 Drugs, proprietaries, and sundries

1506369 ALBERTA ULC   p1328
6635 BOUL HENRI-BOURASSA O, SAINT-LAURENT, QC, H4R 1E1
SIC 5122

1561109 ONTARIO INC   p972
40 BERNARD AVE, TORONTO, ON, M5R 1R2
(416) 460-0980   *SIC 5122*

1737868 ONTARIO INC.   p625
200 TERENCE MATTHEWS CRES, KANATA, ON, K2M 2C6
(613) 591-0044   *SIC 5122*

3762530 CANADA INC   p1157
5775 AV ANDOVER, MONT-ROYAL, QC, H4T 1H6
(514) 739-3633   *SIC 5122*

711620 ONTARIO LIMITED   p769
20 MANGO DR, NORTH YORK, ON, M2K 2G1
(416) 733-8285   *SIC 5122*

9051-1916 QUEBEC INC   p1384
65 BOUL SAINTE-MADELEINE, TROIS-RIVIERES, QC, G8T 3K8
(819) 694-9050   *SIC 5122*

9180-9582 QUEBEC INC   p1090
2500 BOUL DES PROMENADES, DEUX-MONTAGNES, QC, J7R 6L2
(450) 472-6444   *SIC 5122*

ABCANN MEDICINALS INC   p747
126 VANLUVEN RD, NAPANEE, ON, K7R 3L2
(613) 354-6384   *SIC 5122*

ACIC PHARMACEUTICALS INC   p515
81 SINCLAIR BLVD, BRANTFORD, ON, N3S 7X6
(519) 751-3668   *SIC 5122*

ACTELION PHARMACEUTIQUES CANADA INC   p1133
3111 BOUL SAINT-MARTIN O BUREAU 300, LAVAL, QC, H7T 0K2
(450) 681-1664   *SIC 5122*

ADENAT INC   p500
3 BREWSTER RD UNIT 1, BRAMPTON, ON, L6T 5G9
(905) 794-2808   *SIC 5122*

ADVANCED   ORTHOMOLECULAR   RESEARCH INC   p20
3900 12 ST NE, CALGARY, AB, T2E 8H9
(403) 250-9997   *SIC 5122*

ADVANZ PHARMA CORP   p729
5770 HURONTARIO ST SUITE 310, MISSISSAUGA, ON, L5R 3G5
(905) 842-5150   *SIC 5122*

AITON DRUG COMPANY, LIMITED   p403
20 AITON CRES, HARTLAND, NB, E7P 2H2
(506) 375-4469   *SIC 5122*

AKUNA INTERNATIONAL CORP   p691
5115 SATELLITE DR, MISSISSAUGA, ON, L4W 5B6
(905) 848-0428   *SIC 5122*

ALCON CANADA INC   p719
2665 MEADOWPINE BLVD, MISSISSAUGA, ON, L5N 8C7
(905) 826-6700   *SIC 5122*

ALEAFIA HEALTH INC   p548
8810 JANE ST 2ND FL, CONCORD, ON, L4K 2M9
(416) 860-5665   *SIC 5122*

ALEXION PHARMA CANADA CORP   p548
3100 RUTHERFORD RD, CONCORD, ON, L4K 0G6
(866) 393-1188   *SIC 5122*

AMGEN BRITISH COLUMBIA INC   p182
7990 ENTERPRISE ST, BURNABY, BC, V5A 1V7
(604) 415-1800   *SIC 5122*

AMGEN CANADA INC   p719
6775 FINANCIAL DR SUITE 100, MISSISSAUGA, ON, L5N 0A4
(905) 285-3000   *SIC 5122*

AMWAY CANADA CORPORATION   p657
375 EXETER RD, LONDON, ON, N6E 2Z3
(519) 685-7700   *SIC 5122*

ANB CANADA INC   p754
25 MILLARD AVE W UNIT 1, NEWMARKET, ON, L3X 7R5
(905) 953-9777   *SIC 5122*

ANSELL CANADA INC   p1088
105 RUE LAUDER, COWANSVILLE, QC, J2K 2K8
(450) 266-1850   *SIC 5122*

AP MARTIN PHARMACEUTICAL SUPPLIES LTD   p253
13711 MAYFIELD PL UNIT 150, RICHMOND, BC, V6V 2G9
(604) 273-8899   *SIC 5122*

APEX BRANDED SOLUTIONS INC   p548
21 GRANITERIDGE RD SUITE 1, CONCORD, ON, L4K 5M9
(905) 760-9946   *SIC 5122*

APTALIS PHARMA CANADA ULC   p1158
597 BOUL SIR-WILFRID-LAURIER, MONT-SAINT-HILAIRE, QC, J3H 6C4
(450) 467-5138   *SIC 5122*

ASTELLAS PHARMA CANADA, INC   p666
675 COCHRANE DR SUITE 500, MARKHAM, ON, L3R 0B8
(905) 470-7990   *SIC 5122*

AUSTRALIS CAPITAL INC.   p297
510 SEYMOUR ST SUITE 900, VANCOUVER, BC, V6B 3J5
SIC 5122

AVON CANADA INC   p1249
5500 RTE TRANSCANADIENNE, POINTE-CLAIRE, QC, H9R 1B6
(514) 695-3371   *SIC 5122*

AXEL KRAFT INTERNATIONAL LIMITED   p480
99 ENGELHARD DR, AURORA, ON, L4G 3V1
(905) 841-6840   *SIC 5122*

BABESKIN BODYCARE INC   p341
815 MARGAREE PL, WEST VANCOUVER, BC, V7T 2J5
(604) 922-1883   *SIC 5122*

BAXTER CORPORATION   p476
89 CENTRE ST S, ALLISTON, ON, L9R 1J4
(705) 435-6261   *SIC 5122*

BAYER INC   p692
2920 MATHESON BLVD E SUITE 1, MISSISSAUGA, ON, L4W 5R6
(416) 248-0771   *SIC 5122*

BEAUTE STAR BEDARD INC   p1133
1700 RUE FLEETWOOD, LAVAL, QC, H7N 0C6
(450) 967-7827   *SIC 5122*

BEAUTE STAR BEDARD INC   p1133
1700 RUE FLEETWOOD, LAVAL, QC, H7N 0C6
(450) 967-7827   *SIC 5122*

BEAUTYNEXT GROUP INC   p782
436 LIMESTONE CRES, NORTH YORK, ON, M3J 2S4
(416) 665-6616   *SIC 5122*

BEIERSDORF CANADA INC   p1332
2344 BOUL ALFRED-NOBEL BUREAU 100A, SAINT-LAURENT, QC, H4S 0A4
(514) 956-4330   *SIC 5122*

BELCAM INC   p1072
9 BOUL MONTCALM N BUREAU 400, CANDIAC, QC, J5R 3L5
(450) 619-1112   *SIC 5122*

BELL LIFESTYLE PRODUCTS INC   p716
3164 PEPPER MILL CRT UNIT 1-8, MISSISSAUGA, ON, L5L 4X4
(905) 820-7000   *SIC 5122*

BESCO BEAUTE (1980) LTEE   p1221
5770 CH UPPER-LACHINE, MONTREAL, QC, H4A 2B3
(514) 481-1115   *SIC 5122*

BIC INC   p786
155 OAKDALE RD, NORTH YORK, ON, M3N 1W2
(416) 742-9173   *SIC 5122*

BIG BRANDS INC   p14
5329 72 AVE SE, CALGARY, AB, T2C 4X6
(587) 470-5810   *SIC 5122*

BIOMATIK CORPORATION   p538
140 MCGOVERN DR UNIT 9, CAMBRIDGE, ON, N3H 4R7
(519) 489-7195   *SIC 5122*

BIOSTEEL SPORTS NUTRITION INC   p790
1-87 WINGOLD AVE, NORTH YORK, ON, M6B 1P8
(416) 322-7833   *SIC 5122*

BODY PLUS   p183
6200 DARNLEY ST SUITE 204, BURNABY, BC, V5B 3B1
SIC 5122

BOEHRINGER INGELHEIM (CANADA) LTD
p521
5180 SOUTH SERVICE RD, BURLINGTON, ON, L7L 5H4
(905) 639-0333   *SIC 5122*

BOIRON CANADA INC   p1295
1300 RUE RENE-DESCARTES, SAINT-BRUNO, QC, J3V 0B7
(450) 723-2066   *SIC 5122*

C. DECICCO AGENCIES INC   *p692*
1035 STACEY CRT, MISSISSAUGA, ON,
L4W 2X7
(905) 238-1485   *SIC* 5122
CALEA LTD   *p692*
2785 SKYMARK AVE UNIT 2, MISSIS-
SAUGA, ON, L4W 4Y3
(905) 238-1234   *SIC* 5122
**CANADIAN ADDICTION TREATMENT
PHARMACY LP**   *p678*
175 COMMERCE VALLEY DR W,
MARKHAM, ON, L3T 7P6
(905) 773-3884   *SIC* 5122
CANARX SERVICES INC   *p1021*
235 EUGENIE ST W SUITE 105D, WIND-
SOR, ON, N8X 2X7
(519) 973-1735   *SIC* 5122
CELGENE CANADA INC   *p721*
6755 MISSISSAUGA RD SUITE 600, MIS-
SISSAUGA, ON, L5N 7Y2
(289) 291-0200   *SIC* 5122
CENTURA BRANDS INC   *p693*
1200 AEROWOOD DR UNIT 50, MISSIS-
SAUGA, ON, L4W 2S7
(905) 602-1965   *SIC* 5122
CHANEL CANADA ULC   *p1072*
55 BOUL MARIE-VICTORIN, CANDIAC,
QC, J5R 1B6
(450) 659-1981   *SIC* 5122
CLARINS CANADA INC   *p1363*
815 CHOMEDEY (A-13) E, SAINTE-ROSE,
QC, H7W 5N4
(450) 688-0144   *SIC* 5122
CLT LOGISTICS, INC   *p864*
5900 FINCH AVE E, SCARBOROUGH, ON,
M1B 5P8
(416) 646-4199   *SIC* 5122
CMI COSMETIC MANUFACTURERS INC
p550
90 MOYAL CRT, CONCORD, ON, L4K 4R8
(905) 879-1999   *SIC* 5122
COLLEGA INTERNATIONAL INC   *p776*
210 LESMILL RD, NORTH YORK, ON, M3B
2T5
(416) 754-1444   *SIC* 5122
CONGLOM INC   *p1328*
4600 BOUL POIRIER, SAINT-LAURENT,
QC, H4R 2C5
(514) 333-6666   *SIC* 5122
CONTINENTAL COSMETICS LTD   *p551*
390 MILLWAY AVE, CONCORD, ON, L4K
3V8
(905) 660-0622   *SIC* 5122
**CORPORATION BIONETIX INTERNA-
TIONAL**   *p1355*
21040 RUE DAOUST, SAINTE-ANNE-DE-
BELLEVUE, QC, H9X 4C7
(514) 457-2914   *SIC* 5122
CORPORATION GROUPE PHARMESSOR
p1346
5000 BOUL METROPOLITAIN E, SAINT-
LEONARD, QC, H1S 3G7
(514) 725-1212   *SIC* 5122
CORPORATION MCKESSON CANADA, LA
p100
10931 177 ST NW, EDMONTON, AB, T5S
1P6
(780) 486-8700   *SIC* 5122
CORPORATION MCKESSON CANADA, LA
p200
71 GLACIER ST, COQUITLAM, BC, V3K
5Z1
(604) 942-7111   *SIC* 5122
CORPORATION MCKESSON CANADA, LA
p687
6355 VISCOUNT RD, MISSISSAUGA, ON,
L4V 1W2
(905) 671-4586   *SIC* 5122
CORPORATION MCKESSON CANADA, LA
p1098
650 RUE BERGERON, DRUMMONDVILLE,
QC, J2C 0E2
(819) 850-5400   *SIC* 5122
CORPORATION MCKESSON CANADA, LA

p1169
8290 BOUL PIE-IX BUREAU 1, MON-
TREAL, QC, H1Z 4E8
(514) 593-4531   *SIC* 5122
CORPORATION MCKESSON CANADA, LA
p1276
2655 RUE DE CELLES, QUEBEC, QC, G2C
1K7
(418) 845-3061   *SIC* 5122
CORPORATION MCKESSON CANADA, LA
p1328
4705 RUE DOBRIN, SAINT-LAURENT, QC,
H4R 2P7
(514) 745-2100   *SIC* 5122
COTY CANADA INC   *p1093*
1255 RTE TRANSCANADIENNE BUREAU
200, DORVAL, QC, H9P 2V4
(514) 421-5050   *SIC* 5122
COVER FX SKIN CARE INC   *p782*
1681 FLINT RD, NORTH YORK, ON, M3J
2W8
(866) 424-3332   *SIC* 5122
DERMALOGICA (CANADA) LTD   *p980*
720 KING ST W SUITE 300, TORONTO,
ON, M5V 2T3
(416) 368-2286   *SIC* 5122
**DISPENSARIES WHOLESALE (1991) LIM-
ITED**   *p92*
10326 112 ST NW, EDMONTON, AB, T5K
1N2
(780) 426-1664   *SIC* 5122
DISTRIBUTEURS TOWN LTEE   *p1156*
5473 RUE PARE, MONT-ROYAL, QC, H4P
1P7
(514) 735-4555   *SIC* 5122
DISTRIBUTION PHARMAPLUS INC   *p1276*
2905 RUE DE CELLES BUREAU 102, QUE-
BEC, QC, G2C 1W7
(418) 667-5499   *SIC* 5122
DIVA INTERNATIONAL INC   *p642*
222 MCINTYRE DR, KITCHENER, ON, N2R
1E8
(519) 896-9103   *SIC* 5122
**DR. REDDY'S LABORATORIES CANADA
INC**   *p694*
2425 MATHESON BLVD E 7TH FL, MISSIS-
SAUGA, ON, L4W 5K4
(289) 201-2299   *SIC* 5122
**DSM NUTRITIONAL PRODUCTS CANADA
INC**   *p483*
395 WAYDOM DR SUITE 2, AYR, ON, N0B
1E0
(519) 622-2200   *SIC* 5122
**DUPUIS MAGNA COSMETIQUES INTER-
NATIONAL INC**   *p1303*
191 RUE LEVEILLE, SAINT-FRANCOIS-
DU-LAC, QC, J0G 1M0
(450) 568-3517   *SIC* 5122
ECOLOPHARM INC   *p1074*
8100 RUE SAMUEL-HATT, CHAMBLY, QC,
J3L 6W4
(450) 447-6307   *SIC* 5122
ELIZABETH ARDEN (CANADA) LIMITED
p694
1590 SOUTH GATEWAY RD, MISSIS-
SAUGA, ON, L4W 0A8
(905) 276-4500   *SIC* 5122
ELIZABETH GRANT INTERNATIONAL INC
p868
381 KENNEDY RD, SCARBOROUGH, ON,
M1K 2A1
(877) 751-1999   *SIC* 5122
EMD INC   *p715*
2695 NORTH SHERIDAN WAY SUITE 200,
MISSISSAUGA, ON, L5K 2N6
(905) 919-0200   *SIC* 5122
EMERAUD CANADA LIMITED   *p578*
145 THE WEST MALL, ETOBICOKE, ON,
M9C 5P5
(416) 767-4200   *SIC* 5122
EMERGENT BIOSOLUTIONS CANADA INC
p390
155 INNOVATION DR, WINNIPEG, MB, R3T
5Y3

(204) 275-4200   *SIC* 5122
ENTREPRISES MARC DONTIGNY INC
p1384
701 BOUL THIBEAU, TROIS-RIVIERES,
QC, G8T 7A2
(819) 378-4549   *SIC* 5122
ERFA CANADA 2012 INC   *p1227*
8250 BOUL DECARIE BUREAU 110, MON-
TREAL, QC, H4P 2P5
(514) 931-3133   *SIC* 5122
ESTEE LAUDER COSMETICS LTD   *p874*
161 COMMANDER BLVD, SCARBOR-
OUGH, ON, M1S 3K9
(416) 292-1111   *SIC* 5122
**EURO-PHARM INTERNATIONAL CANADA
INC**   *p1344*
9400 BOUL LANGELIER, SAINT-
LEONARD, QC, H1P 3H8
(514) 324-1073   *SIC* 5122
FAMILIPRIX INC   *p1276*
6000 RUE ARMAND-VIAU BUREAU 418,
QUEBEC, QC, G2C 2C5
(418) 847-3311   *SIC* 5122
FARLEYCO MARKETING INC   *p852*
30 EAST WILMOT ST, RICHMOND HILL,
ON, L4B 1A4
(905) 709-2650   *SIC* 5122
FERRING INC   *p767*
200 YORKLAND BLVD SUITE 500, NORTH
YORK, ON, M2J 5C1
(416) 490-0121   *SIC* 5122
FOREST LABORATORIES CANADA INC
p552
610 APPLEWOOD CRES UNIT 302, CON-
CORD, ON, L4K 0E3
(289) 695-4700   *SIC* 5122
FRECHETTE, JOSEE PHARMACIE   *p1052*
525 1RE AV, ASBESTOS, QC, J1T 4R1
(819) 879-6969   *SIC* 5122
FRESENIUS KABI CANADA LTD   *p997*
165 GALAXY BLVD SUITE 100, TORONTO,
ON, M9W 0C8
(905) 770-3711   *SIC* 5122
FRUITS & PASSION BOUTIQUES INC *p1070*
9180 BOUL LEDUC BUREAU 280,
BROSSARD, QC, J4Y 0N7
(450) 678-9620   *SIC* 5122
FUSION BRANDS INC   *p926*
40 ST CLAIR AVE W SUITE 200,
TORONTO, ON, M4V 1M2
(800) 261-9110   *SIC* 5122
GALDERMA CANADA INC   *p904*
55 COMMERCE VALLEY DR W SUITE 400,
THORNHILL, ON, L3T 7V9
(905) 762-2500   *SIC* 5122
GALENOVA INC   *p1312*
4555 AV BEAUDRY, SAINT-HYACINTHE,
QC, J2S 8W2
(450) 778-2837   *SIC* 5122
GENUINE HEALTH INC   *p989*
200-491 COLLEGE ST, TORONTO, ON,
M6G 1A5
(877) 500-7888   *SIC* 5122
GENZYME CANADA INC   *p695*
2700 MATHESON BLVD E SUITE 800, MIS-
SISSAUGA, ON, L4W 4V9
(905) 625-0011   *SIC* 5122
**GLASSHOUSE PHARMACEUTICALS LIM-
ITED CANADA**   *p722*
2145 MEADOWPINE BLVD, MISSIS-
SAUGA, ON, L5N 6R8
(905) 821-7600   *SIC* 5122
**GLAXOSMITHKLINE CONSUMER HEALTH-
CARE INC**   *p722*
7333 MISSISSAUGA RD, MISSISSAUGA,
ON, L5N 6L4
(905) 819-3000   *SIC* 5122
**GLAXOSMITHKLINE CONSUMER HEALTH-
CARE INC**   *p797*
2030 BRISTOL CIR, OAKVILLE, ON, L6H
0H2
(800) 387-7374   *SIC* 5122
GLG LIFE TECH CORPORATION   *p260*
10271 SHELLBRIDGE WAY SUITE 100,

RICHMOND, BC, V6X 2W8
(604) 285-2602   *SIC* 5122
GMS CAPITAL CORP   *p1164*
3055 BOUL DE L'ASSOMPTION, MON-
TREAL, QC, H1N 2H1
SIC 5122
GROUPE JEAN COUTU (PJC) INC, LE
p1392
245 RUE JEAN-COUTU, VARENNES, QC,
J3X 0E1
(450) 646-9760   *SIC* 5122
GROUPE SANI-TECH INC   *p1140*
1450 RUE THOMAS-POWERS, LEVIS, QC,
G7A 0P9
(418) 836-0616   *SIC* 5122
GUERLAIN (CANADA) LTD   *p1131*
2515 RUE LEGER, LASALLE, QC, H8N 2V9
(514) 363-0432   *SIC* 5122
HERBALIFE OF CANADA LTD   *p12*
4550 25 ST SE SUITE 120, CALGARY, AB,
T2B 3P1
(403) 204-2264   *SIC* 5122
**HFC PRESTIGE INTERNATIONAL CANADA
INC**   *p1094*
1255 RTE TRANSCANADIENNE BUREAU
200, DORVAL, QC, H9P 2V4
(514) 421-5050   *SIC* 5122
HOFFMANN-LA ROCHE LIMITED   *p1092*
201 BOUL ARMAND-FRAPPIER, DORVAL,
QC, H7V 4A2
(450) 686-7050   *SIC* 5122
HYLAND'S HOMEOPATHIC CANADA INC
p1378
381 139 RTE N, SUTTON, QC, J0E 2K0
(450) 538-6636   *SIC* 5122
IMPERIAL DISTRIBUTORS CANADA INC
p105
16504 121A AVE NW, EDMONTON, AB,
T5V 1J9
(780) 484-2287   *SIC* 5122
IMPRES PHARMA INC   *p533*
1165 FRANKLIN BLVD SUITE J, CAM-
BRIDGE, ON, N1R 8E1
(866) 781-0491   *SIC* 5122
INOYAN LABORATORIES INC   *p554*
97 SARAMIA CRES UNIT 1, CONCORD,
ON, L4K 4P7
(905) 267-0721   *SIC* 5122
INSTITUT NEOMED   *p1334*
7171 RUE FREDERICK-BANTING, SAINT-
LAURENT, QC, H4S 1Z9
(514) 367-1212   *SIC* 5122
INTERPHARM LTD   *p914*
30 NOVOPHARM CRT, TORONTO, ON,
M1B 2K9
(800) 663-5903   *SIC* 5122
IOGEN ENERGY CORPORATION   *p827*
310 HUNT CLUB RD, OTTAWA, ON, K1V
1C1
(613) 733-9830   *SIC* 5122
JOHNSTON DRUG WHOLESALE LTD *p234*
2286 DORMAN RD, NANAIMO, BC, V9S
5G2
(250) 758-3341   *SIC* 5122
KAMINS DERMATOLOGIQUE, INC   *p1251*
325 AV STILLVIEW, POINTE-CLAIRE, QC,
H9R 2Y6
(514) 428-1628   *SIC* 5122
KAO CANADA INC   *p745*
75 COURTNEYPARK DR W UNIT 2, MIS-
SISSAUGA, ON, L5W 0E3
(905) 670-7890   *SIC* 5122
KOHL & FRISCH LIMITED   *p554*
7622 KEELE ST, CONCORD, ON, L4K 2R5
(905) 660-7622   *SIC* 5122
KOPPERT CANADA LIMITED   *p878*
40 IRONSIDE CRES UNIT 3, SCARBOR-
OUGH, ON, M1X 1G4
(416) 291-0040   *SIC* 5122
KRIKORIAN, S.H. & CO LTD   *p671*
1 VALLEYWOOD DR UNIT 4, MARKHAM,
ON, L3R 5L9
(905) 479-4080   *SIC* 5122
LA COMPAGNIE D'IMPORTATION DE COS-

METIQUES LIMITEE p1066
1380 RUE NEWTON BUREAU 203, BOUCHERVILLE, QC, J4B 5H2
(450) 449-1236 SIC 5122

LABORATOIRES CHEZ-NOUS INC., LES p1303
606 BOUL DU SACRE-COEUR, SAINT-FELICIEN, QC, G8K 1T5
(418) 679-2694 SIC 5122

LABORATOIRES G.M.F. (1983) INC p1310
7485 AV DUPLESSIS, SAINT-HYACINTHE, QC, J2R 1S5
(450) 796-4772 SIC 5122

LABORATOIRES LALCO INC p1379
1542 RUE NATIONALE, TERREBONNE, QC, J6W 6M1
(450) 492-6435 SIC 5122

LABORATOIRES NICAR INC, LES p1059
10 RUE GASTON-DUMOULIN BUREAU 500, BLAINVILLE, QC, J7C 0A3
(450) 979-0400 SIC 5122

LABORATOIRES SUISSE INC, LES p1066
1310 RUE NOBEL, BOUCHERVILLE, QC, J4B 5H3
(450) 444-9808 SIC 5122

LANCASTER MEDICAL SUPPLIES AND PRESCRIPTIONS LTD p181
6741 CARIBOO RD UNIT 203, BURNABY, BC, V3N 4A3
(604) 708-8181 SIC 5122

LAWTON'S DRUG STORES LIMITED p447
81 THORNHILL DR, DARTMOUTH, NS, B3B 1R9
(902) 468-4637 SIC 5122

LEO PHARMA INC p904
123 COMMERCE VALLEY DR E SUITE 400, THORNHILL, ON, L3T 7W8
(905) 886-9822 SIC 5122

LIFESTYLES NETWORK SERVICES INC p555
8100 KEELE ST, CONCORD, ON, L4K 2A3
(905) 761-9342 SIC 5122

LUNDBECK CANADA INC p1228
2600 BOUL ALFRED-NOBEL BUREAU 400, MONTREAL, QC, H4S 0A9
(514) 844-8515 SIC 5122

M.C.P. MCCAUGHEY CONSUMER PRODUCTS MANAGEMENT INC p528
3365 HARVESTER RD SUITE 204, BURLINGTON, ON, L7N 3N2
(905) 319-2246 SIC 5122

MANSFIELD MEDICAL DISTRIBUTORS LTD p1158
5775 AV ANDOVER, MONT-ROYAL, QC, H4T 1H6
(514) 739-3633 SIC 5122

MANTRA PHARMA INC p1071
4605B BOUL LAPINIERE BUREAU 250, BROSSARD, QC, J4Z 3T5
(450) 678-7088 SIC 5122

MARC ANTHONY COSMETICS LTD p555
190 PIPPIN RD, CONCORD, ON, L4K 4X9
(905) 530-2500 SIC 5122

MARCAN PHARMACEUTICALS INC p749
2 GURDWARA RD SUITE 112, NEPEAN, ON, K2E 1A2
(613) 228-2600 SIC 5122

MARKWINS CANADA CORPORATION p706
267 MATHESON BLVD E SUITE 1, MISSISSAUGA, ON, L4Z 1X8
(905) 507-4545 SIC 5122

MARY KAY COSMETICS LTD p724
2020 MEADOWVALE BLVD, MISSISSAUGA, ON, L5N 6Y2
(905) 858-0020 SIC 5122

MCKESSON CORPORATION p672
131 MCNABB ST, MARKHAM, ON, L3R 5V7
(905) 943-9499 SIC 5122

MCKESSON SPECIALIZED DISTRIBUTION INC p684
8449 LAWSON RD UNIT 102, MILTON, ON, L9T 9L1
(905) 827-1300 SIC 5122

MCMAHON DISTRIBUTEUR PHARMACEU-

TIQUE INC p1247
12225 BOUL INDUSTRIEL BUREAU 100, POINTE-AUX-TREMBLES, QC, H1B 5M7
(514) 355-8350 SIC 5122

MEDISCA PHARMACEUTIQUE INC p1330
6090 BOUL HENRI-BOURASSA O, SAINT-LAURENT, QC, H4R 3A6
(800) 932-1039 SIC 5122

MEDISYSTEM PHARMACY LIMITED p776
75 LESMILL RD SUITE 3, NORTH YORK, ON, M3B 2T8
(416) 441-2293 SIC 5122

MENTHOLATUM COMPANY OF CANADA LIMITED, THE p887
45 HANNOVER DR UNIT 2, ST CATHARINES, ON, L2W 1A3
(905) 688-1665 SIC 5122

MERCK CANADA INC p1117
16750 RTE TRANSCANADIENNE, KIRKLAND, QC, H9H 4M7
(514) 428-7920 SIC 5122

MERZ PHARMA CANADA LTD p523
5515 NORTH SERVICE RD SUITE 202, BURLINGTON, ON, L7L 6G4
(905) 315-1193 SIC 5122

METAGENICS CANADA, INC p712
851 RANGEVIEW RD SUITE 1, MISSISSAUGA, ON, L5E 1H1
(905) 891-1300 SIC 5122

METHAPHARM INC p516
81 SINCLAIR BLVD, BRANTFORD, ON, N3S 7X6
(519) 751-3602 SIC 5122

METRO RICHELIEU INC p1247
12225 BOUL INDUSTRIEL BUREAU 100, POINTE-AUX-TREMBLES, QC, H1B 5M7
(514) 355-8350 SIC 5122

MOROCCANOIL CANADA INC p1157
5742 RUE FERRIER, MONT-ROYAL, QC, H4P 1M7
(514) 448-8967 SIC 5122

MPX INTERNATIONAL CORPORATION p772
5255 YONGE ST STE 701, NORTH YORK, ON, M2N 6P4
(416) 840-6632 SIC 5122

NATCO PHARMA (CANADA) INC p725
2000 ARGETIA RD PLAZA 1 SUITE 200, MISSISSAUGA, ON, L5N 1P7
(905) 997-3353 SIC 5122

NATURAL FACTORS NUTRITIONAL PRODUCTS LTD p201
1550 UNITED BLVD, COQUITLAM, BC, V3K 6Y2
(604) 777-1757 SIC 5122

NATURE'S WAY OF CANADA LIMITED p447
15 GARLAND AVE UNIT 4, DARTMOUTH, NS, B3B 0A6
(902) 334-1468 SIC 5122

NEW DIRECTIONS AROMATICS INC p741
6781 COLUMBUS RD, MISSISSAUGA, ON, L5T 2G9
(905) 362-1915 SIC 5122

NOVARTIS ANIMAL HEALTH CANADA INC p725
2000 ARGENTIA RD SUITE 400, MISSISSAUGA, ON, L5N 1P7
(905) 814-0840 SIC 5122

NOVO NORDISK CANADA INC p725
2476 ARGENTIA RD UNIT 101, MISSISSAUGA, ON, L5N 6M1
(905) 629-4222 SIC 5122

NU SKIN CANADA, INC p717
4085 SLADEVIEW CRES, MISSISSAUGA, ON, L5L 5X3
(905) 569-5100 SIC 5122

NUTRI-DYN PRODUCTS LTD p137
4307 49 ST, INNISFAIL, AB, T4G 1P3
(403) 227-3926 SIC 5122

OASIS ESTHETIQUE DISTRIBUTION INC p1214
1231 RUE SAINTE-CATHERINE O BUREAU 303, MONTREAL, QC, H3G 1P5
(514) 286-9148 SIC 5122

ORCHARD INTERNATIONAL INC p741
275 SUPERIOR BLVD UNIT 1, MISSISSAUGA, ON, L5T 2L6
(905) 564-9848 SIC 5122

ORGANIKA HEALTH PRODUCTS INC p255
13480 VERDUN PL, RICHMOND, BC, V6V 1V2
(604) 277-3302 SIC 5122

PARAZA PHARMA INC p1228
2525 AV MARIE-CURIE, MONTREAL, QC, H4S 2E1
(514) 337-7200 SIC 5122

PCCA CORP p649
744 THIRD ST, LONDON, ON, N5V 5J2
(519) 455-0690 SIC 5122

PERFUMES ETC. LTD p742
6880 COLUMBUS RD UNIT 2, MISSISSAUGA, ON, L5T 2G1
(905) 850-8060 SIC 5122

PHARMACIE GAETAN, JACQUES ET MARCOT, JULIE p1253
196 1RE AV, PORTNEUF, QC, G0A 2Y0
(418) 286-3301 SIC 5122

PHARMAPAR INC p1393
1565 BOUL LIONEL-BOULET, VARENNES, QC, J3X 1P7
(514) 731-2003 SIC 5122

PHARMASYSTEMS INC p674
151 TELSON RD, MARKHAM, ON, L3R 1E7
(905) 475-2500 SIC 5122

PIERRE FABRE DERMO-COSMETIQUE CANADA INC p1071
9955 RUE DE CHATEAUNEUF UNITE 115, BROSSARD, QC, J4Z 3V5
(450) 676-9035 SIC 5122

PINNACLE PHARMACEUTICS LTD p1033
7611 PINE VALLEY DR SUITE 31, WOODBRIDGE, ON, L4L 0A2
(905) 430-7541 SIC 5122

PLATINUM NATURALS LTD p853
11 SIMS CRES SUITE 2, RICHMOND HILL, ON, L4B 1C9
(905) 731-8097 SIC 5122

PRAIRIE NATURALS HEALTH PRODUCTS INC p201
56 FAWCETT RD, COQUITLAM, BC, V3K 6V5
(800) 931-4247 SIC 5122

PRESTILUX INC p1234
3537 BOUL LE CORBUSIER, MONTREAL, QC, H7L 4Z4
(514) 963-5096 SIC 5122

PRODUITS SANITAIRES LEPINE INC, LES p1105
134 AV GATINEAU, GATINEAU, QC, J8T 4J8
(819) 205-1626 SIC 5122

PROVIMI CANADA ULC p1377
557 CH DE SAINT-DOMINIQUE BUREAU 1, ST-VALERIEN, QC, J0H 2B0
(450) 549-2629 SIC 5122

PURITY LIFE HEALTH PRODUCTS LP p473
6 COMMERCE CRES, ACTON, ON, L7J 2X3
(519) 853-3511 SIC 5122

REDKEN CONCEPT J P INC p1101
2089 RUE MICHELIN, FABREVILLE, QC, H7L 5B7
(450) 687-2595 SIC 5122

REJUDICARE SYNERGY LTD p1026
6220 WESTAR DR, WINDSOR, ON, N9J 0B5
(519) 734-6600 SIC 5122

RXSOURCE CORP p855
556 EDWARD AVE UNIT 74, RICHMOND HILL, ON, L4C 9Y5
(905) 883-4333 SIC 5122

SANI-PLUS INC p1119
1600 RUE DU PINCELIER, L'ANCIENNE-LORETTE, QC, G2E 6B7
(418) 871-4683 SIC 5122

SANOFI SANTE GRAND PUBLIC INC p1087
2905 PLACE LOUIS-R.-RENAUD, COTE SAINT-LUC, QC, H7V 0A3

(514) 956-6200 SIC 5122

SANOFI-AVENTIS CANADA INC p1087
2905 PLACE LOUIS-R.-RENAUD, COTE SAINT-LUC, QC, H7V 0A3
(514) 331-9220 SIC 5122

SEROYAL INTERNATIONAL INC p855
490 ELGIN MILLS RD E, RICHMOND HILL, ON, L4C 0L8
(905) 508-2050 SIC 5122

SERVICES HEALTHMARK LTEE, LES p1336
8827 BOUL HENRI-BOURASSA O, SAINT-LAURENT, QC, H4S 1P7
(514) 336-0012 SIC 5122

SERVIER CANADA INC p1343
235 BOUL ARMAND-FRAPPIER, SAINT-LAURENT, QC, H7V 4A7
(450) 978-9700 SIC 5122

SHAKLEE CANADA INC p528
3100 HARVESTER RD UNIT 7, BURLINGTON, ON, L7N 3W8
(905) 681-1422 SIC 5122

SHISEIDO (CANADA) INC p675
303 ALLSTATE PKY, MARKHAM, ON, L3R 5P9
(905) 763-1250 SIC 5122

SISU INC p193
7635 NORTH FRASER WAY SUITE 102, BURNABY, BC, V5J 0B8
(604) 420-6610 SIC 5122

SIVEM PHARMACEUTICALS ULC p1330
4800 RUE LEVY, SAINT-LAURENT, QC, H4R 2P1
(514) 832-1290 SIC 5122

SMARTPRACTICE CANADA ULC p11
720 28TH STREET NE, STE 210, CALGARY, AB, T2A 6R3
(403) 450-9997 SIC 5122

SOINS ESTHETIQUES PHYTODERM INC p1327
68 RUE STINSON, SAINT-LAURENT, QC, H4N 2E7
(514) 735-1531 SIC 5122

SOMAK INTERNATIONAL INC p1235
1985 RUE MONTEREY, MONTREAL, QC, H7L 3T6
(450) 688-0123 SIC 5122

SOSEN INC p1212
995 RUE WELLINGTON BUREAU 210, MONTREAL, QC, H3C 1V3
(514) 789-1255 SIC 5122

SSI SUSTAINABLE SOLUTIONS INTERNATIONAL PARTNERS p181
8395 RIVERBEND CRT, BURNABY, BC, V3N 5E7
(604) 430-2020 SIC 5122

SUMMUM BEAUTE INTERNATIONAL INC p1309
4400 BOUL KIMBER, SAINT-HUBERT, QC, J3Y 8L4
(450) 678-3231 SIC 5122

TAKEDA CANADA INC p806
435 NORTH SERVICE RD W SUITE 101, OAKVILLE, ON, L6M 4X8
(905) 469-9333 SIC 5122

TALLGRASS NATURAL HEALTH LTD p292
375 5TH AVE W SUITE 201, VANCOUVER, BC, V5Y 1J6
(604) 709-0101 SIC 5122

TEVA CANADA INNOVATION G.P. -S.E.N.C. p1192
1080 COTE DU BEAVER HALL, MONTREAL, QC, H2Z 1S8
(514) 878-0095 SIC 5122

TFB & ASSOCIATES LIMITED p676
7300 WARDEN AVE SUITE 210, MARKHAM, ON, L3R 9Z6
(905) 940-0889 SIC 5122

TORONTO BARBER & BEAUTY SUPPLY LIMITED p790
112 ORFUS RD, NORTH YORK, ON, M6A 1L9
(416) 787-1211 SIC 5122

TRANSPORT TFI 1, S.E.C. p1337
8801 RTE TRANSCANADIENNE BUREAU

500, SAINT-LAURENT, QC, H4S 1Z6
(514) 331-4000   *SIC 5122*
UNICITY NETWORK CANADA, LTD   *p278*
7495 132 ST SUITE 1007, SURREY, BC, V3W 1J8
SIC 5122
UNIPHARM WHOLESALE DRUGS LTD*p257*
2051 VAN DYKE PL SUITE 100, RICHMOND, BC, V6V 1X6
(604) 270-9745   *SIC 5122*
UNIPRIX DANIEL GUAY & JULIE BEAUPRE (AFFILIATED PHARMACY)   *p1075*
1682 RUE PRINCIPALE, CHAMBORD, QC, G0W 1G0
(418) 342-6263   *SIC 5122*
VALEANT CANADA S.E.C.   *p1363*
2150 BOUL SAINT-ELZEAR O, SAINTE-ROSE, QC, H7L 4A8
(514) 744-6792   *SIC 5122*
VANGUARD NETWORKING INC   *p890*
1217 TALBOT ST, ST THOMAS, ON, N5P 1G8
SIC 5122
VETOQUINOL N.-A. INC   *p1134*
2000 CH GEORGES, LAVALTRIE, QC, J5T 3S5
(450) 586-2252   *SIC 5122*
WELCOME PHARMACY (QUEEN) LTD*p992*
1488 QUEEN ST W, TORONTO, ON, M6K 1M4
(416) 533-2391   *SIC 5122*

SIC 5131 Piece goods and notions

1079746 ONTARIO LIMITED   *p781*
1021 FINCH AVE W, NORTH YORK, ON, M3J 2C7
(416) 650-9996   *SIC 5131*
2960-2778 QUEBEC INC   *p1337*
7300 RTE TRANSCANADIENNE, SAINT-LAURENT, QC, H4T 1A3
(514) 448-9455   *SIC 5131*
3727513 CANADA INC   *p1169*
8920 BOUL PIE-IX BUREAU 300, MONTREAL, QC, H1Z 4H9
(514) 328-7212   *SIC 5131*
ALENDEL FABRICS LIMITED   *p548*
274 EDGELEY BLVD, CONCORD, ON, L4K 3Y4
(905) 669-1998   *SIC 5131*
ALES GROUPE CANADA INC   *p1187*
420 RUE NOTRE-DAME O BUREAU 500, MONTREAL, QC, H2Y 1V3
(514) 932-3636   *SIC 5131*
ANDOLA FIBRES LTD   *p631*
740 PROGRESS AVE, KINGSTON, ON, K7M 4W9
(613) 389-1261   *SIC 5131*
ARTCRAFT COMPANY INC   *p548*
309 PENNSYLVANIA AVE, CONCORD, ON, L4K 5R9
(905) 660-1919   *SIC 5131*
AZIZ, J. & A. LIMITED   *p782*
1635 FLINT RD, NORTH YORK, ON, M3J 2J6
(416) 787-0365   *SIC 5131*
CANTEX CANADA LIMITED   *p872*
2 ROLARK DR, SCARBOROUGH, ON, M1R 4G2
(416) 751-4567   *SIC 5131*
COLOMER CANADA, LTD   *p738*
1055 COURTNEYPARK DR E SUITE A, MISSISSAUGA, ON, L5T 1M7
(905) 565-7047   *SIC 5131*
DECORS DE MAISON COMMONWEALTH INC   *p1169*
8800 BOUL PIE-IX, MONTREAL, QC, H1Z 3V1
(514) 384-8290   *SIC 5131*
DEE, ROSE E. (INTERNATIONAL) LIMITED   *p992*
1450 CASTLEFIELD AVE, TORONTO, ON, M6M 1Y6

(416) 658-2222   *SIC 5131*
DELTA TEXTILES INC   *p200*
61 GLACIER ST, COQUITLAM, BC, V3K 5Z1
(604) 942-2214   *SIC 5131*
DESIGNER FABRIC OUTLET LTD   *p991*
1360 QUEEN ST W, TORONTO, ON, M6K 1L7
(416) 531-2810   *SIC 5131*
ENNIS, J. FABRICS LTD   *p114*
6111 91 ST NW, EDMONTON, AB, T6E 6V6
(780) 474-5414   *SIC 5131*
EUGENE TEXTILES (2003) INC   *p1333*
1391 RUE SAINT-AMOUR, SAINT-LAURENT, QC, H4S 1T4
(514) 382-2400   *SIC 5131*
FABRICMASTER INC   *p989*
76 MIRANDA AVE SUITE 2, TORONTO, ON, M6E 5A1
(416) 658-2205   *SIC 5131*
FABTRENDS INTERNATIONAL INC   *p1178*
9350 AV DE L'ESPLANADE, MONTREAL, QC, H2N 1V6
(514) 382-2210   *SIC 5131*
FLAG WORKS INC   *p35*
5622 BURLEIGH CRES SE UNIT 1-4, CALGARY, AB, T2H 1Z8
(403) 265-5595   *SIC 5131*
FLAMCAN TEXTILES INC   *p1178*
9600 RUE MEILLEUR BUREAU 101, MONTREAL, QC, H2N 2E3
SIC 5131
GA INTERNATIONAL INC   *p1236*
3208 AV JACQUES-BUREAU, MONTREAL, QC, H7P 0A9
(450) 973-9420   *SIC 5131*
HAMDANI TEXTILES INC   *p885*
55 CATHERINE ST, ST CATHARINES, ON, L2R 5E9
(905) 682-6666   *SIC 5131*
HAMILTON ARTS & CRAFTS   *p608*
303 HIGHRIDGE AVE, HAMILTON, ON, L8E 3W1
(905) 578-0750   *SIC 5131*
ICON SALON SYSTEMS LTD   *p276*
13361 78 AVE SUITE 610, SURREY, BC, V3W 5B9
(604) 591-2339   *SIC 5131*
JOANNE FABRICS INC   *p800*
2610 SHERIDAN GARDEN DR, OAKVILLE, ON, L6J 7Z4
(905) 491-3900   *SIC 5131*
KRAVET FABRICS CANADA COMPANY   *p717*
3600B LAIRD RD UNIT 5, MISSISSAUGA, ON, L5L 6A7
(905) 607-0706   *SIC 5131*
MARSHALL FABRICS LTD   *p384*
575 BERRY ST, WINNIPEG, MB, R3H 0S2
(204) 783-1939   *SIC 5131*
MORI LEE ASSOCIATES (CANADA)   *p789*
1293 CALEDONIA RD, NORTH YORK, ON, M6A 2X7
(416) 789-9911   *SIC 5131*
NEMCOR INC   *p534*
501 FRANKLIN BLVD, CAMBRIDGE, ON, N1R 8G9
(519) 740-0595   *SIC 5131*
NILEX INC   *p122*
6810 8 ST NW, EDMONTON, AB, T6P 0C5
(780) 463-9535   *SIC 5131*
RAYMOND PARENT TEXTILES INC   *p1376*
33 RUE DU PRINCE, SOREL-TRACY, QC, J3P 4J5
(450) 743-9666   *SIC 5131*
ROBERT ALLEN FABRICS (CANADA) LTD   *p726*
2880 ARGENTIA RD UNIT 11, MISSISSAUGA, ON, L5N 7X8
(905) 826-7750   *SIC 5131*
SAFDIE & CO. INC   *p1157*
8191 CH MONTVIEW, MONT-ROYAL, QC, H4P 2P2
(514) 344-7599   *SIC 5131*

SPRINGS CANADA, INC   *p733*
110 MATHESON BLVD W SUITE 200, MISSISSAUGA, ON, L5R 3T4
(905) 890-4994   *SIC 5131*
STAFFORD TEXTILES LIMITED   *p580*
1 EVA RD SUITE 101, ETOBICOKE, ON, M9C 4Z5
(416) 252-3133   *SIC 5131*
SUM IT CORPORATION   *p86*
10934 120 ST NW, EDMONTON, AB, T5H 3P7
(780) 452-7200   *SIC 5131*
TELIO & CIE INC   *p1327*
625 RUE DESLAURIERS, SAINT-LAURENT, QC, H4N 1W8
(514) 271-4607   *SIC 5131*
TEXTILE PRODUCTS LTD   *p701*
1581 MATHESON BLVD, MISSISSAUGA, ON, L4W 1H9
(905) 361-1831   *SIC 5131*
TEXTILES BAKER INC, LES   *p1129*
1812 RUE ONESIME-GAGNON, LACHINE, QC, H8T 3M6
(514) 931-0831   *SIC 5131*
TEXTILES D. ZINMAN LTEE   *p1226*
459 RUE DESLAURIERS, MONTREAL, QC, H4N 1W2
(514) 276-2597   *SIC 5131*
TEXTILES ELITE INC   *p1051*
9200 RUE CLAVEAU, ANJOU, QC, H1J 1Z4
(514) 352-2291   *SIC 5131*
TEXTILES J.P. DOUMAK INC   *p1341*
855 RUE MCCAFFREY, SAINT-LAURENT, QC, H4T 1N3
(514) 342-9397   *SIC 5131*
TEXTILES ROBLIN INC   *p1051*
9151 BOUL LOUIS-H.-LAFONTAINE, ANJOU, QC, H1J 1Z1
(514) 353-8100   *SIC 5131*
TISSUS MASTER LTEE, LES   *p1051*
7963 RUE ALFRED, ANJOU, QC, H1J 1J3
(514) 351-9715   *SIC 5131*
TREND-TEX FABRICS INC   *p247*
1317 KEBET WAY, PORT COQUITLAM, BC, V3C 6G1
(604) 941-4620   *SIC 5131*
TRIDEN DISTRIBUTORS LIMITED   *p845*
22 DILLINGHAM RD, PICKERING, ON, L1W 1Z6
(416) 291-2955   *SIC 5131*
VANCOUVER QUILTING MANUFACTURING LTD   *p285*
188 VICTORIA DR, VANCOUVER, BC, V5L 4C3
(604) 253-7744   *SIC 5131*
WELLA CANADA, INC   *p733*
5800 AVEBURY RD UNIT 1, MISSISSAUGA, ON, L5R 3M3
(905) 568-2494   *SIC 5131*
WORLD WIDE IOZZA LTD   *p589*
240 HUMBERLINE DR SUITE D, ETOBICOKE, ON, M9W 5X1
(416) 675-1930   *SIC 5131*

SIC 5136 Men's and boy's clothing

109652 CANADA LTD/LTEE   *p1337*
8750 CH DE LA COTE-DE-LIESSE BUREAU 100, SAINT-LAURENT, QC, H4T 1H2
(514) 344-9660   *SIC 5136*
11292580 ONTARIO LIMITED   *p652*
649 RICHMOND ST, LONDON, ON, N6A 3G7
(519) 238-2720   *SIC 5136*
119155 CANADA LIMITED   *p831*
159 CLEOPATRA DR SUITE 100, OTTAWA, ON, K2G 5X4
(613) 226-8680   *SIC 5136*
2810221 CANADA INC   *p1177*
9500 RUE MEILLEUR BUREAU 800, MONTREAL, QC, H2N 2B7
(514) 388-0284   *SIC 5136*
3727513 CANADA INC   *p1169*

8920 BOUL PIE-IX BUREAU 300, MONTREAL, QC, H1Z 4H9
(514) 328-9220   *SIC 5136*
4207602 CANADA INC   *p1192*
2024 RUE PEEL BUREAU 400, MONTREAL, QC, H3A 1W5
(514) 881-2525   *SIC 5136*
4453166 CANADA INC   *p1328*
1420 RUE BEAULAC, SAINT-LAURENT, QC, H4R 1R7
(514) 744-5559   *SIC 5136*
7886395 CANADA INC   *p832*
1120 MORRISON DR UNIT 1, OTTAWA, ON, K2H 8M7
(613) 736-8288   *SIC 5136*
9168-8820 QUEBEC INC   *p1156*
5771 RUE FERRIER, MONT-ROYAL, QC, H4P 1N3
(514) 735-6622   *SIC 5136*
9227-6898 QUEBEC INC   *p1233*
1527 NORD LAVAL (A-440) O BUREAU 230, MONTREAL, QC, H7L 3W3
(514) 381-4392   *SIC 5136*
9292-1394 QUEBEC INC   *p1179*
225 RUE DE LIEGE O BUREAU A, MONTREAL, QC, H2P 1H4
(514) 381-4392   *SIC 5136*
A.J.M. PROMOTIONS SPORTIVES INTERNATIONALES LTEE   *p1338*
350 RUE MCCAFFREY, SAINT-LAURENT, QC, H4T 1N1
(514) 344-6767   *SIC 5136*
A.Y.K. INTERNATIONAL INC   *p1047*
8250 RUE EDISON, ANJOU, QC, H1J 1S8
(514) 279-4648   *SIC 5136*
ANTONACCI CLOTHES LIMITED   *p786*
99 NORFINCH DR, NORTH YORK, ON, M3N 1W8
(416) 663-4093   *SIC 5136*
ARDENT SPORTSWEAR INCORPORATED   *p291*
125 3RD AVE W, VANCOUVER, BC, V5Y 1E6
(604) 879-3268   *SIC 5136*
ATELIERS MANUTEX INC, LES   *p1289*
230 AV MARCEL-BARIL, ROUYN-NORANDA, QC, J9X 7C1
(819) 764-4415   *SIC 5136*
ATTRACTION INC   *p1124*
672 RUE DU PARC, LAC-DROLET, QC, G0Y 1C0
(819) 549-2477   *SIC 5136*
AUTHENTIC T-SHIRT COMPANY ULC, THE   *p323*
850 KENT AVE SOUTH W, VANCOUVER, BC, V6P 3G1
(778) 732-0258   *SIC 5136*
AVIV INTERNATIONAL TRADE CORPORATION   *p666*
31 TELSON RD SUITE 2, MARKHAM, ON, L3R 1E4
(905) 479-5047   *SIC 5136*
BENISTI USA LLC   *p1225*
1650 RUE CHABANEL O, MONTREAL, QC, H4N 3M8
(514) 384-0140   *SIC 5136*
BESTILE APPAREL INC   *p866*
841 PROGRESS AVE, SCARBOROUGH, ON, M1H 2X4
SIC 5136
BESTSELLER VENTES EN GROS CANADA INC   *p1180*
225 RUE DE LIEGE O, MONTREAL, QC, H2P 1H4
(514) 381-4392   *SIC 5136*
BOB DALE GLOVES & IMPORTS LTD *p108*
4504 82 AVE NW, EDMONTON, AB, T6B 2S4
(780) 469-2100   *SIC 5136*
BULA CANADA INC   *p1332*
4005 RUE SARTELON, SAINT-LAURENT, QC, H4S 2A6
(514) 270-4222   *SIC 5136*
CANADA SPORTSWEAR CORP   *p792*

230 BARMAC DR, NORTH YORK, ON, M9L
2Z3

(416) 740-8020   *SIC* 5136

CANADIAN GRAPHICS WEST INC   p290
8285 MAIN ST, VANCOUVER, BC, V5X 3L7

(604) 324-1246   *SIC* 5136

CAPITAL STIKLY INC   p1178
225 RUE CHABANEL O BUREAU 200,
MONTREAL, QC, H2N 2C9

(514) 381-5393   *SIC* 5136

CAULFEILD APPAREL GROUP LTD   p782
1400 WHITEHORSE RD, NORTH YORK,
ON, M3J 3A7

(416) 636-5900   *SIC* 5136

CHOKO MOTORSPORTS INC   p1001
19 ANDERSON BLVD, UXBRIDGE, ON,
L9P 0C7

(905) 642-1010   *SIC* 5136

**COLUMBIA SPORTSWEAR CANADA LIM-
ITED**   p661
1425 MAX BROSE DR SUITE 1, LONDON,
ON, N6N 0A2

(519) 644-5000   *SIC* 5136

COLUMBIA SPORTSWEAR CANADA LP
p661
1425 MAX BROSE DR SUITE 1, LONDON,
ON, N6N 0A2

(519) 644-5000   *SIC* 5136

**COMMERCE INTERNATIONAL MANHAT-
TAN INC**   p1338
6150 RTE TRANSCANADIENNE, SAINT-
LAURENT, QC, H4T 1X5

(514) 388-5588   *SIC* 5136

**COMPAGNIE DE COMMERCE A.S. & F.
LTEE**   p1216
9850 RUE MEILLEUR, MONTREAL, QC,
H3L 3J4

(514) 385-5568   *SIC* 5136

COMPAGNIE DE VETEMENTS C-IN2 INC
p1338
8750 CH DE LA COTE-DE-LIESSE BU-
REAU 100, SAINT-LAURENT, QC, H4T 1H2

(514) 344-9660   *SIC* 5136

CONCORD COORDINATES INC   p871
2220 MIDLAND AVE UNIT 21 23, SCAR-
BOROUGH, ON, M1P 3E6

SIC 5136

CONSENSO CREATIONS INC   p1225
1565 RUE CHABANEL O, MONTREAL, QC,
H4N 2W3

SIC 5136

COPPLEY LTD   p613
56 YORK BLVD, HAMILTON, ON, L8R 0A2

(905) 529-1112   *SIC* 5136

DE CHAMPLAIN DESIGN INC   p1350
812 BOUL DE L'INDUSTRIE, SAINT-PAUL,
QC, J0K 3E0

(450) 760-2098   *SIC* 5136

DREW BRADY COMPANY INC   p805
1155 NORTH SERVICE RD W UNIT 6,
OAKVILLE, ON, L6M 3E3

(905) 815-1534   *SIC* 5136

DUBWEAR INC   p735
7880 TRANMERE DR, MISSISSAUGA, ON,
L5S 1L9

(905) 362-1334   *SIC* 5136

FANA SPORTS INC   p1344
6140 RUE MARIVAUX, SAINT-LEONARD,
QC, H1P 3K3

(514) 648-8888   *SIC* 5136

FANTASTIC-T KNITTERS INC   p285
1374 VENABLES ST, VANCOUVER, BC,
V5L 2G4

(604) 255-8883   *SIC* 5136

FXR FACTORY RACING INC   p353
155 OAKLAND RD, OAK BLUFF, MB, R4G
0A4

(204) 736-4406   *SIC* 5136

GANT PARIS DU CANADA LTEE, LE p1329
2315 RUE COHEN, SAINT-LAURENT, QC,
H4R 2N7

(514) 345-0135   *SIC* 5136

GETRACAN INC   p1229
130 MONTEE DE LIESSE, MONTREAL,

QC, H4T 1N4

(514) 382-4860   *SIC* 5136

GRAND NATIONAL APPAREL INC   p794
100 MARMORA ST SUITE 3, NORTH
YORK, ON, M9M 2X5

(416) 746-3511   *SIC* 5136

GRIFFEN MANIMPEX LTD   p785
945 WILSON AVE SUITE 2, NORTH YORK,
ON, M3K 1E8

(416) 630-7007   *SIC* 5136

GROUPE BBH INC   p1339
4400 RUE HICKMORE, SAINT-LAURENT,
QC, H4T 1K2

(514) 633-6765   *SIC* 5136

GROUPE MINT GREEN INC, LE   p1250
6900 RTE TRANSCANADIENNE, POINTE-
CLAIRE, QC, H9R 1C2

(514) 333-4461   *SIC* 5136

GUESS? CANADA CORPORATION   p1170
8275 19E AV, MONTREAL, QC, H1Z 4K2

(514) 593-4107   *SIC* 5136

HAGGAR CANADA CO.   p783
777 SUPERTEST RD, NORTH YORK, ON,
M3J 2M9

(416) 652-3777   *SIC* 5136

HOME GAME INC, THE   p554
114B FERNSTAFF CRT, CONCORD, ON,
L4K 3L9

SIC 5136

HOUSE INC, THE   p783
620 SUPERTEST RD UNIT 9, NORTH
YORK, ON, M3J 2M5

SIC 5136

HUGO BOSS CANADA INC   p554
2600 STEELES AVE W SUITE 2, CON-
CORD, ON, L4K 3C8

(905) 739-2677   *SIC* 5136

IMPORTATIONS RALLYE INC   p1179
433 RUE CHABANEL O BUREAU 1000,
MONTREAL, QC, H2N 2J8

(514) 381-5941   *SIC* 5136

**IMPORTATIONS-EXPORTATIONS BENISTI
INC**   p1226
1650 RUE CHABANEL O, MONTREAL, QC,
H4N 3M8

(514) 384-0140   *SIC* 5136

**INDUSTRIES MAJESTIC (CANADA) LTEE,
LES**   p1334
5905 RUE KIERAN, SAINT-LAURENT, QC,
H4S 0A3

(514) 727-2000   *SIC* 5136

INDUSTRIES MIDWAY LTEE   p1170
8270 BOUL PIE-IX, MONTREAL, QC, H1Z
3T6

(514) 722-1122   *SIC* 5136

INNOVATIVE GLOBAL SOLUTIONS INC p23
320 19 ST SE, CALGARY, AB, T2E 6J6

(403) 204-1198   *SIC* 5136

JAMBO KITMEEN LTD   p504
1810 STEELES AVE E, BRAMPTON, ON,
L6T 1A7

(905) 792-3009   *SIC* 5136

JAYTEX OF CANADA LIMITED   p791
29 GURNEY CRES, NORTH YORK, ON,
M6B 1S9

(416) 785-1099   *SIC* 5136

JCORP INC   p1326
95 RUE GINCE, SAINT-LAURENT, QC, H4N
1J7

(514) 384-3872   *SIC* 5136

KNP HEADWEAR INC   p865
50 MELHAM CRT, SCARBOROUGH, ON,
M1B 2E5

(416) 298-8516   *SIC* 5136

LACOSTE CANADA INC   p1184
4200 BOUL SAINT-LAURENT BUREAU
901, MONTREAL, QC, H2W 2R2

(514) 286-1212   *SIC* 5136

LEVY CANADA FASHION COMPANY p1179
225 RUE CHABANEL O BUREAU 200,
MONTREAL, QC, H2N 2C9

(514) 908-0104   *SIC* 5136

LOUIS-HEBERT UNIFORME INC   p1083
1963 RUE NOTRE-DAME-DE-FATIMA,

COTE SAINT-LUC, QC, H7G 4R9

(450) 668-3766   *SIC* 5136

**MANHATTAN INTERNATIONAL CONCEPTS
INC**   p1340
6150 RTE TRANSCANADIENNE, SAINT-
LAURENT, QC, H4T 1X5

(514) 388-5588   *SIC* 5136

**MANUFACTURE DE LINGERIE CHATEAU
INC**   p1184
215 RUE SAINT-ZOTIQUE O, MONTREAL,
QC, H2V 1A2

(514) 274-7505   *SIC* 5136

MANUFACTURE TRIPLE G. INC   p1134
2705 RUE MICHELIN, LAVAL-OUEST, QC,
H7L 5X6

(450) 681-2700   *SIC* 5136

MARK'S WORK WEARHOUSE LTD   p36
1035 64 AVE SE SUITE 30, CALGARY, AB,
T2H 2J7

(403) 255-9220   *SIC* 5136

**MARQUES DE VETEMENTS FREEMARK
INC**   p1157
5640 RUE PARE, MONT-ROYAL, QC, H4P
2M1

(514) 341-7333   *SIC* 5136

MAVI JEANS INC   p295
580 INDUSTRIAL AVE, VANCOUVER, BC,
V6A 2P3

(604) 708-2373   *SIC* 5136

MCGREGOR INDUSTRIES INC   p934
63 POLSON ST, TORONTO, ON, M5A 1A4

(416) 591-9191   *SIC* 5136

MEN'S DEN, THE   p171
4902 50 AVE, VERMILION, AB, T9X 1A4

(780) 581-0100   *SIC* 5136

MODASUITE INC   p1183
160 RUE SAINT-VIATEUR E BUREAU 610,
MONTREAL, QC, H2T 1A8

(438) 384-0824   *SIC* 5136

MODES DO-GREE LTEE, LES   p1218
3205 CH DE BEDFORD, MONTREAL, QC,
H3S 1G3

(514) 904-2109   *SIC* 5136

MONDETTA CANADA, INC   p381
1109 WINNIPEG AVE, WINNIPEG, MB,
R3E 0S2

(204) 786-1700   *SIC* 5136

NEXT CYCLE INC   p641
275 GAGE AVE, KITCHENER, ON, N2M
2C9

(519) 747-7776   *SIC* 5136

NOXS INC   p1179
9500 RUE MEILLEUR BUREAU 200, MON-
TREAL, QC, H2N 2B7

(514) 385-0636   *SIC* 5136

OMNITEX INC   p575
120 THE EAST MALL, ETOBICOKE, ON,
M8Z 5V5

SIC 5136

ORIENTEX IND. INC   p673
155 TORBAY RD, MARKHAM, ON, L3R 1G7

(905) 475-8540   *SIC* 5136

OUTDOOR OUTFITS LIMITED   p982
372 RICHMOND ST W SUITE 400,
TORONTO, ON, M5V 1X6

(416) 598-4111   *SIC* 5136

P.Y.A. IMPORTER LTD   p789
15 APEX RD, NORTH YORK, ON, M6A 2V6

(416) 929-3300   *SIC* 5136

PEDS LEGWEAR INC   p1198
1501 AV MCGILL COLLEGE BUREAU 914,
MONTREAL, QC, H3A 3M8

(514) 875-5575   *SIC* 5136

PERRIN INC   p1157
5711 RUE FERRIER, MONT-ROYAL, QC,
H4P 1N3

(514) 341-4321   *SIC* 5136

PHILCOS ENTERPRISER LTD   p706
120 BRUNEL RD, MISSISSAUGA, ON, L4Z
1T5

(905) 568-1823   *SIC* 5136

PRODUCTION ACYPOL INC   p1226
1350 RUE MAZURETTE BUREAU 409,
MONTREAL, QC, H4N 1H2

(514) 388-8888   *SIC* 5136

PVH CANADA, INC   p744
775 BRITANNIA RD W UNIT 1, MISSIS-
SAUGA, ON, L5V 2Y1

(905) 826-9645   *SIC* 5136

PVH CANADA, INC   p983
555 RICHMOND ST W SUITE 1106,
TORONTO, ON, M5V 3B1

(416) 309-7200   *SIC* 5136

PVH CANADA, INC   p1341
7445 CH DE LA COTE-DE-LIESSE, SAINT-
LAURENT, QC, H4T 1G2

(514) 278-6000   *SIC* 5136

RUDSACK   p1173
829 AV DU MONT-ROYAL E, MONTREAL,
QC, H2J 1W9

(514) 508-4100   *SIC* 5136

SALB, H. INTERNATIONAL   p795
49 RIVALDA RD, NORTH YORK, ON, M9M
2M4

(416) 746-1944   *SIC* 5136

SCHURE SPORTS INC   p558
345 CONNIE CRES, CONCORD, ON, L4K
5R2

(905) 669-6021   *SIC* 5136

SIGA INTERNATIONAL   p784
81 SAINT REGIS CRES S, NORTH YORK,
ON, M3J 1Y6

(416) 504-7442   *SIC* 5136

SML CANADA ACQUISITION CORP p1331
2328 RUE COHEN, SAINT-LAURENT, QC,
H4R 2N8

(514) 858-7272   *SIC* 5136

SOUCIE-SALO SAFETY INC   p900
1300 LORNE ST, SUDBURY, ON, P3C 5N1

(705) 674-8092   *SIC* 5136

**STORMTECH PERFORMANCE APPAREL
LTD**   p187
3773 STILL CREEK AVE, BURNABY, BC,
V5C 4E2

(866) 407-2222   *SIC* 5136

SUMAGGO COLLECTION INC   p707
5715 COOPERS AVE SUITE 7, MISSIS-
SAUGA, ON, L4Z 2C7

(905) 712-9777   *SIC* 5136

SUNICE INC   p1341
850 RUE MCCAFFREY, SAINT-LAURENT,
QC, H4T 1N1

(514) 341-6767   *SIC* 5136

**SUPREME INTERNATIONAL CO. CANADA
LTD**   p795
100 MARMORA ST SUITE 3, NORTH
YORK, ON, M9M 2X5

(416) 746-3511   *SIC* 5136

TAMODA APPAREL INC   p289
319 2ND AVE E SUITE 315, VANCOUVER,
BC, V5T 1B9

(604) 877-2282   *SIC* 5136

TECHNO SPORT INTERNATIONAL LTEE
p1051
7850 RUE BOMBARDIER BUREAU 263,
ANJOU, QC, H1J 2G3

(514) 356-2151   *SIC* 5136

THREAD COLLECTIVE INC   p1341
850 RUE MCCAFFREY, SAINT-LAURENT,
QC, H4T 1N1

(514) 345-1777   *SIC* 5136

TRISTAR CAP & GARMENT LTD   p257
12671 BATHGATE WAY UNIT 1, RICH-
MOND, BC, V6V 1Y5

(604) 279-4287   *SIC* 5136

TXT CARBON FASHIONS INC   p1179
433 RUE CHABANEL O BUREAU 400,
MONTREAL, QC, H2N 2J4

(514) 382-8271   *SIC* 5136

V.I.C. SAFETY INCORPORATED   p1028
377 VAUGHAN VALLEY BLVD, WOOD-
BRIDGE, ON, L4H 3B5

(905) 850-0838   *SIC* 5136

**VENTE AU DETAIL BESTSELLER CANADA
INC**   p1181
225A RUE DE LIEGE O, MONTREAL, QC,
H2P 1H4

(514) 381-4392   *SIC* 5136

▲ Public Company   ■ Public Company Family Member   **HQ** Headquarters   **BR** Branch   **SL** Single Location

VETEMENTS DE SPORT R.G.R. INC *p1305*
4100 10E AV, SAINT-GEORGES, QC, G5Y
7S3
(418) 228-9458 *SIC* 5136
VETEMENTS GOLDEN BRAND (CANADA)
LTEE *p1051*
9393 BOUL METROPOLITAIN E, ANJOU,
QC, H1J 3C7
(514) 272-8841 *SIC* 5136
VETEMENTS NTD INC, LES *p1342*
700 RUE MCCAFFREY, SAINT-LAURENT,
QC, H4T 1N1
(514) 341-8330 *SIC* 5136
WATSON, JOHN LIMITED *p194*
7955 NORTH FRASER WAY, BURNABY,
BC, V5J 0A4
(604) 874-1105 *SIC* 5136
WEARWELL GARMENTS LIMITED *p466*
126 ACADIA AVE, STELLARTON, NS, B0K
1S0
(902) 752-4190 *SIC* 5136
WILLYS URBANE CULTURE *p921*
276 CARLAW AVE SUITE 218B,
TORONTO, ON, M4M 3L1
(416) 462-2038 *SIC* 5136

SIC 5137 Women's and children's clothing

0998236 B.C. LTD *p259*
4151 HAZELBRIDGE WAY SUITE 1700,
RICHMOND, BC, V6X 4J7
(604) 288-1002 *SIC* 5137
125338 CANADA INC *p1181*
5800 RUE SAINT-DENIS BUREAU 402,
MONTREAL, QC, H2S 3L5
(514) 274-2407 *SIC* 5137
1422545 ONTARIO INC *p547*
74 EDILCAN DR UNIT 1, CONCORD, ON,
L4K 3S5
(905) 660-3357 *SIC* 5137
152258 CANADA INC *p1177*
555 RUE CHABANEL O BUREAU M53B,
MONTREAL, QC, H2N 2H7
SIC 5137
163288 CANADA INC *p1244*
47 AV COURCELETTE, OUTREMONT, QC,
H2V 3A5
(514) 277-0880 *SIC* 5137
2900319 CANADA INC *p1240*
146 PROM RONALD, MONTREAL-OUEST,
QC, H4X 1M8
(514) 489-9159 *SIC* 5137
4113993 CANADA INC *p1177*
555 RUE CHABANEL O BUREAU 707,
MONTREAL, QC, H2N 2H8
(514) 382-7066 *SIC* 5137
576195 ONTARIO LIMITED *p792*
500 BARMAC DR SUITE 2, NORTH YORK,
ON, M9L 2X8
(416) 789-1477 *SIC* 5137
6356036 CANADA INC *p1325*
590 RUE HODGE, SAINT-LAURENT, QC,
H4N 2A4
(514) 389-8885 *SIC* 5137
8463859 CANADA INC *p829*
416 RICHMOND RD, OTTAWA, ON, K2A
0G2
(613) 695-3416 *SIC* 5137
9071-7851 QUEBEC INC *p1325*
200 BOUL LEBEAU, SAINT-LAURENT, QC,
H4N 1R4
(514) 332-5437 *SIC* 5137
9149-5077 QUEBEC INC *p1177*
333 RUE CHABANEL O BUREAU 504,
MONTREAL, QC, H2N 2E7
(514) 381-2886 *SIC* 5137
9189-8718 QUEBEC INC *p1177*
350 RUE DE LOUVAIN O BUREAU 310,
MONTREAL, QC, H2N 2E8
(514) 389-7297 *SIC* 5137
9213-0699 QUEBEC INC *p1084*
2555 BOUL LE CORBUSIER BUREAU 090,
COTE SAINT-LUC, QC, H7S 1Z4

(450) 686-6767 *SIC* 5137
9381-0455 QUEBEC INC *p1275*
1450 RUE ESTHER-BLONDIN BUREAU
100, QUEBEC, QC, G1Y 3N7
(418) 254-6464 *SIC* 5137
ACI BRANDS INC *p800*
2616 SHERIDAN GARDEN DR, OAKVILLE,
ON, L6J 7Z2
(905) 829-1566 *SIC* 5137
AGENCES LISETTE LIMOGES INC, LES
p1177
9250 AV DU PARC BUREAU 300, MON-
TREAL, QC, H2N 1Z2
(514) 385-1222 *SIC* 5137
AGENCES WANT INC, LES *p1180*
8480 RUE JEANNE-MANCE, MONTREAL,
QC, H2P 2S3
(514) 868-9268 *SIC* 5137
AJPRO DISTRIBUTION INC *p1233*
2047 NORD LAVAL (A-440) O, MONTREAL,
QC, H7L 3W3
(450) 681-0666 *SIC* 5137
ALCA DISTRIBUTION INC *p278*
2153 192 ST UNIT 4, SURREY, BC, V3Z
3X2
(604) 635-3901 *SIC* 5137
ALPHA SPORTSWEAR LIMITED *p288*
112 6TH AVE E, VANCOUVER, BC, V5T
1J5
(604) 873-2621 *SIC* 5137
APPAREL RESOURCE GROUP INC *p872*
80 ROLARK DR, SCARBOROUGH, ON,
M1R 4G2
SIC 5137
B.L. INTIMATE APPAREL CANADA INC
p1178
9500 RUE MEILLEUR BUREAU 111, MON-
TREAL, QC, H2N 2B7
(514) 858-9254 *SIC* 5137
BEAUMARCHE INC *p1178*
9124 BOUL SAINT-LAURENT, MONTREAL,
QC, H2N 1M9
(514) 382-4062 *SIC* 5137
BENCHMARK ATHLETIC INC *p729*
6085 BELGRAVE RD, MISSISSAUGA, ON,
L5R 4E6
(905) 361-2390 *SIC* 5137
BERNARD ATHLETIC KNIT & ENTER-
PRISES LIMITED *p993*
2 SCARLETT RD, TORONTO, ON, M6N 4J6
(416) 766-6151 *SIC* 5137
BRAVADO DESIGNS LTD *p775*
60 SCARSDALE RD UNIT 100, NORTH
YORK, ON, M3B 2R7
(416) 466-8652 *SIC* 5137
CABRELLI INC *p1178*
9200 RUE MEILLEUR BUREAU 300, MON-
TREAL, QC, H2N 2A9
(514) 384-4750 *SIC* 5137
CALGARY CO-OP HOME HEALTH CARE
LIMITED *p39*
9309 MACLEOD TRAIL SW SUITE 3, CAL-
GARY, AB, T2J 0P6
(403) 252-2266 *SIC* 5137
CANADIAN CLOTHING INTERNATIONAL
INC *p864*
541 CONLINS RD, SCARBOROUGH, ON,
M1B 5S1
(416) 335-1300 *SIC* 5137
CANADIAN TEST CASE 117 *p730*
5770 HURONTARIO ST, MISSISSAUGA,
ON, L5R 3G5
SIC 5137
CHANDELLES ET CREATIONS ROBIN INC
p1249
151 AV ALSTON, POINTE-CLAIRE, QC,
H9R 5V9
(514) 426-5999 *SIC* 5137
CHAPELLERIE JEAN MYRIAM INC, LA
p1178
555 RUE CHABANEL O UNITE 303, MON-
TREAL, QC, H2N 2H8
(514) 383-0549 *SIC* 5137
CIE D'HABILLEMENT SE CE LTEE, LA

p1338
6445 CH DE LA COTE-DE-LIESSE, SAINT-
LAURENT, QC, H4T 1S9
(514) 341-4440 *SIC* 5137
CIE D'IMPORTATION DE NOUVEAUTES
STEIN INC, LA *p1325*
865 RUE DESLAURIERS, SAINT-
LAURENT, QC, H4N 1X3
(514) 334-3366 *SIC* 5137
COLLECTIONS DE STYLE R.D. INTERNA-
TIONALES LTEE, LES *p1227*
5275 RUE FERRIER BUREAU 200, MON-
TREAL, QC, H4P 1L7
(514) 342-1222 *SIC* 5137
COMO DIFFUSION INC *p1325*
103 BOUL MARCEL-LAURIN, SAINT-
LAURENT, QC, H4N 2M3
(514) 286-2666 *SIC* 5137
COMPAGNIE MEXX CANADA *p1325*
905 RUE HODGE, SAINT-LAURENT, QC,
H4N 2B3
(514) 383-5555 *SIC* 5137
CONCEPT SAINT-BRUNO INC *p1112*
3844 BOUL TASCHEREAU, GREENFIELD
PARK, QC, J4V 2H9
(450) 466-0422 *SIC* 5137
CREATIONS CLAIRE BELL INC *p1178*
8955 BOUL SAINT-LAURENT BUREAU
301, MONTREAL, QC, H2N 1M5
(514) 270-1477 *SIC* 5137
CREATIONS G.S.L. INC *p1178*
9494 BOUL SAINT-LAURENT BUREAU
800, MONTREAL, QC, H2N 1P4
(514) 273-0422 *SIC* 5137
CREATIONS NOC NOC INC *p1178*
9600 RUE MEILLEUR BUREAU 750, MON-
TREAL, QC, H2N 2E3
(514) 381-2554 *SIC* 5137
CREATIONS ROBO INC *p1225*
1205 RUE DE LOUVAIN O, MONTREAL,
QC, H4N 1G6
(514) 382-6501 *SIC* 5137
DACURY AGENCIES CORPORATION *p789*
59 SAMOR RD, NORTH YORK, ON, M6A
1J2
(416) 781-2171 *SIC* 5137
DEBRADEE ENTERPRISES LTD *p1432*
2 AUDITORIUM AVE, SASKATOON, SK,
S7M 5S8
(306) 525-8600 *SIC* 5137
DEX BROS. CIE DE VETEMENTS LTEE
p1325
390 RUE DESLAURIERS, SAINT-
LAURENT, QC, H4N 1V8
(514) 383-2474 *SIC* 5137
DIANA DOLLS FASHIONS INC *p891*
555 BARTON ST, STONEY CREEK, ON,
L8E 5S1
(905) 643-9118 *SIC* 5137
DOT-LINE DESIGN LTD *p851*
19 EAST WILMOT ST, RICHMOND HILL,
ON, L4B 1A3
(905) 760-1133 *SIC* 5137
EI BRAND MANAGEMENT INC *p1333*
2520 AV MARIE-CURIE, SAINT-LAURENT,
QC, H4S 1N1
(514) 344-3533 *SIC* 5137
ELEVENTH FLOOR APPAREL LTD *p584*
100 RONSON DR, ETOBICOKE, ON, M9W
1B6
(416) 696-2818 *SIC* 5137
EQUIPE H.B. HELLER INC, L' *p1377*
175 RUE PASSENGER RR 4, STANSTEAD,
QC, J0B 3E2
(819) 876-2709 *SIC* 5137
EURO VERVE CO. LTD *p670*
951 DENISON ST UNIT 16, MARKHAM,
ON, L3R 3W9
(905) 513-8283 *SIC* 5137
EUROPEAN CREATIONS LTD *p263*
12240 HORSESHOE WAY UNIT 14, RICH-
MOND, BC, V7A 4X9
(604) 275-0440 *SIC* 5137
FDJ FRENCH DRESSING INC *p1178*

225 RUE CHABANEL O BUREAU 200,
MONTREAL, QC, H2N 2C9
(514) 333-7171 *SIC* 5137
GASPARD REGALIA INC *p372*
1266 FIFE ST, WINNIPEG, MB, R2X 2N6
(204) 949-5700 *SIC* 5137
GAYA CANADA ENTERPRISE LTD *p295*
1868 GLEN DR SUITE 232, VANCOUVER,
BC, V6A 4K4
(604) 738-0971 *SIC* 5137
GENUINE CANADIAN CORP, THE *p744*
1 PROLOGIS BLVD, MISSISSAUGA, ON,
L5W 0G2
(519) 624-6574 *SIC* 5137
GERTEX HOSIERY INC *p791*
9 DENSLEY AVE, NORTH YORK, ON, M6M
2P5
(416) 241-2345 *SIC* 5137
GLOBAL FURS INC *p1196*
400 BOUL DE MAISONNEUVE O BUREAU
100, MONTREAL, QC, H3A 1L4
(514) 288-6644 *SIC* 5137
GROUPE CABRELLI INC *p1178*
9200 RUE MEILLEUR BUREAU 300, MON-
TREAL, QC, H2N 2A9
(514) 384-4750 *SIC* 5137
GROUPE DE TISSUS NINO MARCELLO
INC, LE *p1178*
555 RUE CHABANEL O UNITE 902, MON-
TREAL, QC, H2N 2H7
(514) 441-3555 *SIC* 5137
GROUPE HEXAVOGUE INC, LE *p1184*
4200 BOUL SAINT-LAURENT BUREAU
200, MONTREAL, QC, H2W 2R2
(514) 286-4392 *SIC* 5137
GROUPE LEMUR INC, LE *p1326*
275 RUE STINSON BUREAU 201, SAINT-
LAURENT, QC, H4N 2E1
(514) 748-6234 *SIC* 5137
GROUPE MINIMOME INC *p1178*
225 RUE CHABANEL O BUREAU 800,
MONTREAL, QC, H2N 2C9
(514) 383-3408 *SIC* 5137
GROUPE STERLING INTIMITE INC, LE
p1178
9600 RUE MEILLEUR BUREAU 930, MON-
TREAL, QC, H2N 2E3
(514) 385-0500 *SIC* 5137
HAPPY KIDS CANADA INC *p1179*
8955 BOUL SAINT-LAURENT BUREAU
301, MONTREAL, QC, H2N 1M5
(514) 270-1477 *SIC* 5137
HATLEY - P'TITE MAISON BLEUE INC
p1132
860 90E AV, LASALLE, QC, H8R 3A2
(514) 272-8444 *SIC* 5137
HYP GOLF LTD *p258*
21320 GORDON WAY UNIT 110, RICH-
MOND, BC, V6W 1J8
(604) 270-6060 *SIC* 5137
I.E.I. INC *p1250*
39 BOUL HYMUS, POINTE-CLAIRE, QC,
H9R 4T2
(514) 630-8149 *SIC* 5137
IMPORTATIONS INTERNATIONALES BO-
CHITEX INC, LES *p1340*
225 MONTEE DE LIESSE, SAINT-
LAURENT, QC, H4T 1P5
(514) 381-3310 *SIC* 5137
IMPORTATIONS N & N INC, LES *p1293*
109 RUE D'AMSTERDAM, SAINT-
AUGUSTIN-DE-DESMAURES, QC, G3A
2V5
(418) 878-9555 *SIC* 5137
IMPORTATIONS S.M.D. LTEE, LES *p1179*
555 RUE CHABANEL O, MONTREAL, QC,
H2N 2H7
(514) 389-3474 *SIC* 5137
IMPORTATIONS VENETO LIMITEE *p1334*
2569 RUE DE MINIAC, SAINT-LAURENT,
QC, H4S 1E5
(514) 735-1898 *SIC* 5137
IRVING PERSONAL CARE LIMITED *p397*
100 PROM MIDLAND, DIEPPE, NB, E1A

6X4

(506) 857-7713   *SIC* 5137
IRWIN TOGS INC   p1180
8484 AV DE L'ESPLANADE, MONTREAL,
QC, H2P 2R7

(514) 384-7760   *SIC* 5137
JANA AND COMPANY IMPORTS   p323
8680 CAMBIE ST, VANCOUVER, BC, V6P
6M9

(604) 688-3657   *SIC* 5137
JENO NEUMAN ET FILS INC   p1061
95 BOUL DES ENTREPRISES, BOIS-
BRIAND, QC, J7G 2T1

(450) 430-5901   *SIC* 5137
JJM MANUFACTURING LTD   p696
5430 TIMBERLEA BLVD SUITE 2, MISSIS-
SAUGA, ON, L4W 2T7

(905) 206-2150   *SIC* 5137
JMAX GLOBAL DISTRIBUTORS INC   p323
8680 CAMBIE ST, VANCOUVER, BC, V6P
6M9

(604) 688-3657   *SIC* 5137
**JOHN FORSYTH SHIRT COMPANY INC,
THE**   p696
2645 SKYMARK AVE UNIT 105, MISSIS-
SAUGA, ON, L4W 4H2

(905) 362-4040   *SIC* 5137
JONES APPAREL CANADA GROUP, LP
p554
388 APPLEWOOD CRES, CONCORD, ON,
L4K 4B4

(888) 880-8730   *SIC* 5137
KIANGTEX COMPANY LIMITED   p917
46 HOLLINGER RD, TORONTO, ON, M4B
3G5

(416) 750-3771   *SIC* 5137
KIM-LAUREN & CIE INC   p1179
9400 BOUL SAINT-LAURENT BUREAU
402, MONTREAL, QC, H2N 1P3

(514) 385-3582   *SIC* 5137
KOMBI SPORTS INC   p1156
5711 RUE FERRIER, MONT-ROYAL, QC,
H4P 1N3

(514) 341-4321   *SIC* 5137
L. DAVIS TEXTILES (1991) INC   p1111
780 RUE GEORGES-CROS, GRANBY, QC,
J2J 1N2

(450) 375-1665   *SIC* 5137
LINGERIE HAGO INC   p1182
7070 RUE SAINT-URBAIN, MONTREAL,
QC, H2S 3H6

(514) 276-2518   *SIC* 5137
M J FASHIONS LTD   p261
8571 BRIDGEPORT RD, RICHMOND, BC,
V6X 1R7

(604) 273-9233   *SIC* 5137
MAISON PIACENTE   p1369
805 111E RUE, SHAWINIGAN-SUD, QC,
G9P 2T5

SIC 5137
**MANUFACTURIER DE BAS DE NYLON
SPLENDID INC**   p1179
55 RUE DE LOUVAIN O BUREAU 200,
MONTREAL, QC, H2N 1A4

(514) 381-7687   *SIC* 5137
METALSMITH ACCESSORIES   p94
PO BOX 3391 STN D, EDMONTON, AB, T5L
4J2

(780) 454-0736   *SIC* 5137
MODE CAPITAL INC, LA   p1326
1200 BOUL JULES-POITRAS BUREAU
200, SAINT-LAURENT, QC, H4N 1X7

(514) 337-4444   *SIC* 5137
MODE PETIT BOUFFON INC, LA   p1183
5425 AV CASGRAIN BUREAU 401, MON-
TREAL, QC, H2T 1X6

(514) 276-9828   *SIC* 5137
MODES CORWIK INC   p1179
225 RUE CHABANEL O BUREAU 200,
MONTREAL, QC, H2N 2C9

(514) 381-5393   *SIC* 5137
MODES HOW INTERNATIONAL INC, LES
p1182
6595 RUE SAINT-URBAIN, MONTREAL,

QC, H2S 3G6

(514) 904-0055   *SIC* 5137
MODES KNIT SET (2010) LTEE, LES   p1179
9500 RUE MEILLEUR BUREAU 510, MON-
TREAL, QC, H2N 2B7

SIC 5137
MODES MORSAM INC   p1179
350 RUE DE LOUVAIN O BUREAU 101,
MONTREAL, QC, H2N 2E8

(514) 383-0033   *SIC* 5137
MODES ZERO II 60 INC   p1179
9400 BOUL SAINT-LAURENT BUREAU
200, MONTREAL, QC, H2N 1P3

(514) 383-3580   *SIC* 5137
NASRI INTERNATIONAL INC   p1326
500 BOUL LEBEAU, SAINT-LAURENT, QC,
H4N 1R5

(514) 334-8282   *SIC* 5137
**NATIONAL LOGISTICS SERVICES (2006)
INC**   p745
150 COURTNEYPARK DR W, MISSIS-
SAUGA, ON, L5W 1Y6

(905) 364-0033   *SIC* 5137
NO LIMITS SPORTSWEAR INC   p292
68 5TH AVE W, VANCOUVER, BC, V5Y 1H6

(604) 431-7330   *SIC* 5137
NORTH AMERICAN CLOTHING INC   p795
22 LIDO RD, NORTH YORK, ON, M9M 1M6

(416) 741-2626   *SIC* 5137
PANAXIS INC   p791
70 WINGOLD AVE, NORTH YORK, ON,
M6B 1P5

(416) 256-5800   *SIC* 5137
PEEPERS INTERNATIONAL LTD   p611
360 WENTWORTH ST N, HAMILTON, ON,
L8L 5W3

SIC 5137
POINT ZERO GIRLS CLUB INC   p1226
1650 RUE CHABANEL O, MONTREAL, QC,
H4N 3M8

(514) 384-0140   *SIC* 5137
**PRODUCTIONS MIGHTY MAC CANADA
INC, LES**   p1335
5555 RUE CYPIHOT, SAINT-LAURENT, QC,
H4S 1R3

(514) 388-8888   *SIC* 5137
R.M.P. ATHLETIC LOCKER LIMITED   p706
135 MATHESON BLVD UNIT 201, MISSIS-
SAUGA, ON, L4Z 1R2

(905) 361-2390   *SIC* 5137
ROADRUNNER APPAREL INC   p1128
2005 23E AV, LACHINE, QC, H8T 1X1

(514) 631-4669   *SIC* 5137
S.D.R. DISTRIBUTION SERVICES   p700
1880 MATHESON BLVD E, MISSISSAUGA,
ON, L4W 5N4

(905) 625-7377   *SIC* 5137
SGS SPORTS INC   p1341
6400 CH DE LA COTE-DE-LIESSE, SAINT-
LAURENT, QC, H4T 1E3

(514) 737-5665   *SIC* 5137
SHANDEX SALES GROUP LIMITED   p845
1100 SQUIRES BEACH RD, PICKERING,
ON, L1W 3N8

(905) 420-7407   *SIC* 5137
SINGGA ENTERPRISES INC   p288
3373 KINGSWAY, VANCOUVER, BC, V5R
5K6

SIC 5137
SOCIETE DE COMMERCE ACADEX INC
p1179
350 RUE DE LOUVAIN O BUREAU 310,
MONTREAL, QC, H2N 2E8

(514) 389-7297   *SIC* 5137
SOCIETE EN COMMANDITE CANADELLE
p1345
4405 BOUL METROPOLITAIN E, SAINT-
LEONARD, QC, H1R 1Z4

(514) 376-6240   *SIC* 5137
SUPER-FIT KNITTING MILLS INC   p974
1191 BATHURST ST, TORONTO, ON, M5R
3H4

(416) 537-2137   *SIC* 5137
TORA WESTERN CANADA LTD   p11

4710 17 AVE SE SUITE G2, CALGARY, AB,
T2A 0V1

(403) 207-5200   *SIC* 5137
**TRANS-CONTINENTAL TEXTILE EX-
PORTERS INC**   p869
16 UPTON RD, SCARBOROUGH, ON, M1L
2B8

(416) 285-8951   *SIC* 5137
TRICOTS LELA INC, LES   p1183
5425 AV CASGRAIN BUREAU 601, MON-
TREAL, QC, H2T 1X6

(514) 271-3102   *SIC* 5137
TRIO-SELECTION INC   p1341
8305 CH DE LA C?TE-DE-LIESSE, SAINT-
LAURENT, QC, H4T 1G5

(514) 387-2591   *SIC* 5137
TRIUMPH FASHIONS LTD   p296
1275 VENABLES ST SUITE 300, VANCOU-
VER, BC, V6A 2E4

(604) 254-6969   *SIC* 5137
UGO-SAC IMPORTS LTD   p1179
9500 RUE MEILLEUR BUREAU 600, MON-
TREAL, QC, H2N 2B7

(514) 382-4271   *SIC* 5137
V I P GARMENTS OF CANADA LTD   p26
1339 40 AVE NE SUITE 11, CALGARY, AB,
T2E 8N6

SIC 5137
VETEMENTS MAJCO INC   p1327
1200 BOUL JULES-POITRAS BUREAU
100, SAINT-LAURENT, QC, H4N 1X7

(514) 956-0322   *SIC* 5137
VETEMENTS MARK-EDWARDS INC   p1181
8480 RUE JEANNE-MANCE BUREAU 201,
MONTREAL, QC, H2P 2S3

(514) 388-2353   *SIC* 5137
VETEMENTS URBAN RAGS INC   p1179
9130 AV DU PARC, MONTREAL, QC, H2N
1Z2

(514) 384-6922   *SIC* 5137
VETEMENTS VA-YOLA LTEE, LES   p1327
550 RUE DESLAURIERS, SAINT-
LAURENT, QC, H4N 1V8

(514) 337-4175   *SIC* 5137
WERTEX HOSIERY INCORPORATED   p974
1191 BATHURST ST, TORONTO, ON, M5R
3H4

(416) 537-2137   *SIC* 5137
WESTERN GLOVE WORKS   p373
555 LOGAN AVE, WINNIPEG, MB, R3A 0S4

(204) 788-4249   *SIC* 5137

SIC 5139 Footwear

602667 ONTARIO LTD   p526
4551 PALLADIUM WAY, BURLINGTON, ON,
L7M 0W9

(905) 335-9951   *SIC* 5139
ADIDAS CANADA LIMITED   p1026
8100 27 HWY SUITE 1, WOODBRIDGE,
ON, L4H 3N2

(905) 266-4200   *SIC* 5139
C. & J. CLARK CANADA LIMITED   p796
2881 BRIGHTON RD, OAKVILLE, ON, L6H
6C9

(905) 829-1825   *SIC* 5139
CALERES CANADA, INC   p839
1857 ROGERS RD, PERTH, ON, K7H 1P7

(613) 267-0348   *SIC* 5139
CHAUSSURES L'INTERVALLE INC   p1228
4345 BOUL POIRIER, MONTREAL, QC,
H4R 2A4

(438) 386-4555   *SIC* 5139
CHAUSSURES M & M INC   p1328
4350 BOUL THIMENS, SAINT-LAURENT,
QC, H4R 2P2

(514) 738-8210   *SIC* 5139
CHAUSSURES S T C INC, LES   p1048
10100 RUE COLBERT, ANJOU, QC, H1J
2J8

(514) 351-0675   *SIC* 5139
**COMPAGNIE COMMERCIALE EMEGO
LTEE, LA**   p1130

7373 RUE CORDNER, LASALLE, QC, H8N
2R5

(514) 365-0202   *SIC* 5139
CORPORATION ASICS CANADA   p1370
101 RUE DES ABENAQUIS BUREAU 201,
SHERBROOKE, QC, J1H 1H1

(819) 566-8866   *SIC* 5139
COTE-RECO INC   p1089
100 12E AV, DESCHAILLONS-SUR-SAINT-
LAURENT, QC, G0S 1G0

(819) 292-2323   *SIC* 5139
COUGAR SHOES INC   p531
2 MASONRY CRT, BURLINGTON, ON, L7T
4A8

(905) 639-0100   *SIC* 5139
ECCO SHOES CANADA INC   p669
10 WHITEHALL DR, MARKHAM, ON, L3R
5Z7

(905) 947-8148   *SIC* 5139
GREDICO FOOTWEAR LIMITED   p739
415 ANNAGEM BLVD, MISSISSAUGA, ON,
L5T 3A7

(866) 855-0755   *SIC* 5139
GROUPE ALDO INC, LE   p1329
3665 BOUL POIRIER, SAINT-LAURENT,
QC, H4R 3J2

(514) 747-5892   *SIC* 5139
INDEKA IMPORTS LTD   p798
2120 BRISTOL CIR, OAKVILLE, ON, L6H
5R3

(905) 829-3000   *SIC* 5139
PAJAR DISTRIBUTION LTD   p1183
4509 AV COLONIALE, MONTREAL, QC,
H2T 1V8

(514) 844-3067   *SIC* 5139
PRODUCTION PAJAR LTEE   p1183
4509 AV COLONIALE, MONTREAL, QC,
H2T 1V8

(514) 844-3067   *SIC* 5139
ROBLIN ATHLETIC INC   p391
1457 CHEVRIER BLVD SUITE A, WIN-
NIPEG, MB, R3T 1Y7

(204) 477-5100   *SIC* 5139
SERUM INTERNATIONAL INC   p1342
4400 DESSTE CHOMEDEY (A-13) O,
SAINT-LAURENT, QC, H7R 6E9

(450) 625-8511   *SIC* 5139
SHOES FOR CREWS   p745
199 LONGSIDE DR, MISSISSAUGA, ON,
L5W 1Z9

SIC 5139
SKECHERS USA CANADA, INC   p700
5055 SATELLITE DR UNIT 6, MISSIS-
SAUGA, ON, L4W 5K7

(905) 238-7121   *SIC* 5139
SUGI CANADA LTEE   p1236
3255 RUE JULES-BRILLANT, MONTREAL,
QC, H7P 6C9

SIC 5139
TIME BOMB TRADING INC   p194
8067 NORTH FRASER WAY, BURNABY,
BC, V5J 5M8

(604) 251-1097   *SIC* 5139
TOTES ISOTONER CANADA LIMITED p743
6335 SHAWSON DR, MISSISSAUGA, ON,
L5T 1S7

(905) 564-4798   *SIC* 5139
TREND MARKETING WHOLESALE INC
p785
1500 LODESTAR RD, NORTH YORK, ON,
M3J 3C1

(416) 663-3939   *SIC* 5139
TT GROUP LIMITED   p661
1806 WHARNCLIFFE RD S, LONDON, ON,
N6L 1K1

(519) 652-0080   *SIC* 5139
WOLVERINE WORLD WIDE CANADA ULC
p728
6225 MILLCREEK DR, MISSISSAUGA, ON,
L5N 0G2

(905) 285-9560   *SIC* 5139

SIC 5141 Groceries, general line

0561768 B.C. LTD *p322*
3080 BROADWAY W, VANCOUVER, BC, V6K 2H1
(604) 733-4191   *SIC* 5141

10373532 CANADA LTD *p171*
10851 100 ST, WESTLOCK, AB, T7P 2R5
(780) 349-7040   *SIC* 5141

1496519 ONTARIO INC *p815*
2675 BLACKWELL ST UNIT 8, OTTAWA, ON, K1B 4E4
(613) 747-6660   *SIC* 5141

2012865 ONTARIO INC *p1029*
71 SILTON RD UNIT 8, WOODBRIDGE, ON, L4L 7Z8
(905) 856-8252   *SIC* 5141

2022839 ONTARIO INC *p1002*
8500 KEELE ST, VAUGHAN, ON, L4K 2A6
(905) 532-1455   *SIC* 5141

21 CENTURY TRADING INC *p208*
6951 72 ST UNIT 110, DELTA, BC, V4G 0A2
(604) 952-4565   *SIC* 5141

3374840 CANADA INC *p1093*
565 AV EDWARD VII, DORVAL, QC, H9P 1E7

   SIC 5141

3523462 CANADA INC *p1307*
3400 BOUL LOSCH BUREAU 35, SAINT-HUBERT, QC, J3Y 5T6
(450) 443-0060   *SIC* 5141

3764605 CANADA INC *p1069*
9600 RUE IGNACE BUREAU G, BROSSARD, QC, J4Y 2R4
(450) 444-2956   *SIC* 5141

394045 ALBERTA LTD *p84*
8007 127 AVE NW, EDMONTON, AB, T5C 1R9
(780) 473-6567   *SIC* 5141

4019636 CANADA INC *p1169*
3733 RUE JARRY E BUREAU A, MONTREAL, QC, H1Z 2G1
(514) 727-8919   *SIC* 5141

4069838 CANADA INC *p1235*
2750 AV JACQUES-BUREAU, MONTREAL, QC, H7P 6B3
(450) 681-0400   *SIC* 5141

633569 ONTARIO LIMITED *p906*
206 RICHMOND ST, THOROLD, ON, L2V 4L8
(905) 227-1575   *SIC* 5141

9155- 5714 QUEBEC INC *p1304*
17850 BOUL LACROIX, SAINT-GEORGES, QC, G5Y 5B8
(418) 228-8661   *SIC* 5141

994421 N.W.T. LTD *p435*
353A OLD AIRPORT RD, YELLOWKNIFE, NT, X1A 3T4
(867) 873-5338   *SIC* 5141

996660 ONTARIO LIMITED *p792*
63 SIGNET DR, NORTH YORK, ON, M9L 2W5
(416) 747-8707   *SIC* 5141

A. BOSA & CO. LTD *p284*
1465 KOOTENAY ST, VANCOUVER, BC, V5K 4Y3
(604) 253-5578   *SIC* 5141

A.K.D. TRADING INC *p878*
10 NEWGALE GATE SUITE 5, SCARBOROUGH, ON, M1X 1C5
(416) 299-7384   *SIC* 5141

A.S. MAY POWELL CORPORATION *p691*
2475 SKYMARK AVE UNIT 1, MISSISSAUGA, ON, L4W 4Y6
(905) 625-9306   *SIC* 5141

ACEMA IMPORTATIONS INC *p1145*
2616 BOUL JACQUES-CARTIER E, LONGUEUIL, QC, J4N 1P8
(450) 646-2591   *SIC* 5141

ACOSTA CANADA CORPORATION *p1029*
250 ROWNTREE DAIRY RD, WOODBRIDGE, ON, L4L 9J7
(905) 264-0466   *SIC* 5141

ALIMENTS CONAN INC, LES *p1332*
7007 BOUL HENRI-BOURASSA O, SAINT-LAURENT, QC, H4S 2E2
(514) 334-7977   *SIC* 5141

ALIMENTS IMEX INC *p1225*
1605 RUE DE BEAUHARNOIS O BUREAU 100, MONTREAL, QC, H4N 1J6
   SIC 5141

ALIMENTS PROLIMER INC *p1261*
650 BOUL PERE-LELIEVRE BUREAU 200, QUEBEC, QC, G1M 3T2
   SIC 5141

ALIMENTS SAPUTO LIMITEE *p1343*
6869 BOUL METROPOLITAIN E, SAINT-LEONARD, QC, H1P 1X8
(514) 328-6662   *SIC* 5141

ALIMENTS TOUSAIN INC *p1325*
95 RUE STINSON, SAINT-LAURENT, QC, H4N 2E1
(514) 748-7353   *SIC* 5141

ALIMENTS VALLI INC., LES *p1307*
3400 BOUL LOSCH BUREAU 35, SAINT-HUBERT, QC, J3Y 5T6
(450) 443-0060   *SIC* 5141

ALIMENTS WHYTE'S INC, LES *p1233*
1540 RUE DES PATRIOTES, MONTREAL, QC, H7L 2N6
(450) 625-1976   *SIC* 5141

ALIMPLUS INC *p1047*
9777 RUE COLBERT, ANJOU, QC, H1J 1Z9
(514) 274-5662   *SIC* 5141

ALIMPLUS INC *p1047*
340 235 RTE, ANGE-GARDIEN, QC, J0E 1E0
(450) 293-3626   *SIC* 5141

ALL CITY IMPORTERS LTD *p285*
1290 ODLUM DR, VANCOUVER, BC, V5L 3L9
(604) 251-1045   *SIC* 5141

AMCA SALES LIMITED *p445*
1000 WINDMILL RD SUITE 22, DARTMOUTH, NS, B3B 1L7
(902) 468-1501   *SIC* 5141

ANDERSON WATTS LTD *p183*
6336 DARNLEY ST, BURNABY, BC, V5B 3B1
(604) 291-7751   *SIC* 5141

APO PRODUCTS LTD *p913*
5590 FINCH AVE E UNIT 1, TORONTO, ON, M1B 1T1
(416) 321-5412   *SIC* 5141

ARTHUR ROGER & ASSOCIES INC *p1134*
2010 BOUL DAGENAIS O, LAVAL-OUEST, QC, H7L 5W2
(450) 963-5080   *SIC* 5141

ASM CANADA, INC *p666*
160 MCNABB ST SUITE 330, MARKHAM, ON, L3R 4E4
(905) 475-9623   *SIC* 5141

ATLANTIC GROCERY DISTRIBUTORS LIMITED *p421*
1 HOPE AVE, BAY ROBERTS, NL, A0A 1G0
(709) 786-9720   *SIC* 5141

ATLANTIC RETAIL CO-OPERATIVES FEDERATION *p406*
123 HALIFAX ST, MONCTON, NB, E1C 9R6
(506) 858-6000   *SIC* 5141

ATLANTIC WHOLESALERS LTD *p408*
100 BAIG BLVD, MONCTON, NB, E1E 1C8
(506) 852-2000   *SIC* 5141

AVRON FOODS LIMITED *p549*
277 BASALTIC RD, CONCORD, ON, L4K 4W8
(800) 997-9752   *SIC* 5141

B. TERFLOTH + CIE (CANADA) INC *p1401*
3500 BOUL DE MAISONNEUVE O UNITE 2360, WESTMOUNT, QC, H3Z 3C1
(514) 939-2341   *SIC* 5141

BEAUDRY, JEAN-PAUL LTEE *p1247*
12225 BOUL METROPOLITAIN E, POINTE-AUX-TREMBLES, QC, H1B 5R3
(514) 352-5620   *SIC* 5141

BELLEMONT POWELL LTEE *p1064*
1570 RUE AMPERE UNITE 508, BOUCHERVILLE, QC, J4B 7L4
(450) 641-2661   *SIC* 5141

BEN DESHAIES INC *p1045*
431 6E RUE O, AMOS, QC, J9T 2V5
(819) 732-6466   *SIC* 5141

BERTOZZI, ADRIANO IMPORTING INC *p582*
2070 CODLIN CRES UNIT 2, ETOBICOKE, ON, M9W 7J2
(416) 213-0075   *SIC* 5141

BIDCOR SALES AND MARKETING INC *p692*
2785 SKYMARK AVE SUITE 14, MISSISSAUGA, ON, L4W 4Y3
   SIC 5141

BOESE FOODS INTERNATIONAL INC *p521*
4145 NORTH SERVICE RD 2ND FL, BURLINGTON, ON, L7L 6A3
(289) 288-5304   *SIC* 5141

BOUCHERIE VEILLEUX INC *p1360*
1000 BOUL VACHON N, SAINTE-MARIE, QC, G6E 1M2
(418) 386-5744   *SIC* 5141

BRANDVENTURE INC *p667*
335 RENFREW DR SUITE 202, MARKHAM, ON, L3R 9S9
(888) 277-9737   *SIC* 5141

BRAZILIAN CANADIAN COFFEE ALBERTA INC *p33*
6812 6 ST SE BAY SUITE J, CALGARY, AB, T2H 2K4
   SIC 5141

BREWMASTER COFFEE ENTERPRISES (M.H.) INC *p145*
764 7 ST SE, MEDICINE HAT, AB, T1A 1K6
(403) 526-0791   *SIC* 5141

BRIGHT HARVEST ENTERPRISE INC *p259*
2620 SIMPSON RD SUITE 140, RICHMOND, BC, V6X 2P9
(604) 278-6680   *SIC* 5141

BRUNO & NICK INC *p1182*
6766 RUE MARCONI, MONTREAL, QC, H2S 3J7
(514) 272-8998   *SIC* 5141

BUGDEN, E L LIMITED *p422*
199 RIVERSIDE DR, CORNER BROOK, NL, A2H 4A1
(709) 634-6177   *SIC* 5141

BULK BARN FOODS LIMITED *p480*
320 DON HILLOCK DR, AURORA, ON, L4G 0G9
(905) 726-5000   *SIC* 5141

BURLODGE CANADA LTD *p716*
3400 RIDGEWAY DR UNIT 14, MISSISSAUGA, ON, L5L 0A2
(905) 790-1881   *SIC* 5141

C.B. POWELL LIMITED *p692*
2475 SKYMARK AVE SUITE 1, MISSISSAUGA, ON, L4W 4Y6
(905) 206-7797   *SIC* 5141

CANADA FENG TAI INTERNATIONAL INC *p764*
1100 GORDON BAKER RD, NORTH YORK, ON, M2H 3B3
(416) 497-6666   *SIC* 5141

CANADIAN ROCKIE MATSUTAKE LTD *p259*
8740 BECKWITH RD SUITE 110, RICHMOND, BC, V6X 1V5
   SIC 5141

CANEAST FOODS LIMITED *p851*
70 EAST BEAVER CREEK RD UNIT 204, RICHMOND HILL, ON, L4B 3B2
(905) 771-6051   *SIC* 5141

CAPOL INC *p1309*
5132 RUE J.-A.-BOMBARDIER, SAINT-HUBERT, QC, J3Z 1H1
(450) 766-8707   *SIC* 5141

CARIBBEAN ICE CREAM COMPANY LTD *p787*
130 BERMONDSEY RD, NORTH YORK, ON, M4A 1X5
(416) 759-3277   *SIC* 5141

CDC FOODS INC *p851*
21 EAST WILMOT ST UNIT 2, RICHMOND HILL, ON, L4B 1A3
(905) 763-2929   *SIC* 5141

CENTRAL ONTARIO DAIRY DISTRIBUTION *p705*
260 BRUNEL RD SUITE B, MISSISSAUGA, ON, L4Z 1T5
(905) 507-0084   *SIC* 5141

CHISHOLM, RONALD A. LIMITED *p928*
2 BLOOR ST W SUITE 3300, TORONTO, ON, M4W 3K3
(416) 967-6000   *SIC* 5141

CHUNG HING CO. LTD *p290*
8595 FRASER ST, VANCOUVER, BC, V5X 3Y1
(604) 324-7411   *SIC* 5141

CLARK, DROUIN, LEFEBVRE INC *p1064*
1301 RUE GAY-LUSSAC, BOUCHERVILLE, QC, J4B 7K1
(450) 449-4171   *SIC* 5141

COLABOR LIMITED PARTNERSHIP *p648*
580 INDUSTRIAL RD, LONDON, ON, N5V 1V1
(800) 265-9267   *SIC* 5141

COLABOR LIMITED PARTNERSHIP *p648*
580 INDUSTRIAL RD, LONDON, ON, N5V 1V1
(519) 453-3410   *SIC* 5141

COLABOR LIMITED PARTNERSHIP *p817*
100 LEGACY RD, OTTAWA, ON, K1G 5T8
(613) 737-7000   *SIC* 5141

COMEAU, C. L. CO, LTD *p396*
117 BOUL ST-PIERRE O, CARAQUET, NB, E1W 1B6
(506) 727-3411   *SIC* 5141

COMPASS FOOD SALES COMPANY LIMITED *p480*
260 INDUSTRIAL PKY N, AURORA, ON, L4G 4C3
(905) 713-0167   *SIC* 5141

CONCORD SALES INC *p240*
1124 LONSDALE AVE SUITE 400, NORTH VANCOUVER, BC, V7M 2H1
(604) 986-7341   *SIC* 5141

CONGLOM INC *p254*
11488 EBURNE WAY UNIT 130, RICHMOND, BC, V6V 3E1
(604) 629-1338   *SIC* 5141

CORINTHIAN DISTRIBUTORS LTD *p192*
8118 NORTH FRASER WAY UNIT 1, BURNABY, BC, V5J 0E5
(604) 431-5058   *SIC* 5141

CORNWALL FRUIT SUPPLY LIMITED *p562*
1424 LASCELLE AVE, CORNWALL, ON, K6H 3L2
   SIC 5141

CORPORATION DES ALIMENTS I-D *p1237*
1800 SUD LAVAL (A-440) O, MONTREAL, QC, H7S 2E7
(450) 687-2680   *SIC* 5141

COSTCO WHOLESALE CANADA LTD *p428*
28 STAVANGER DR, ST. JOHN'S, NL, A1A 5E8
(709) 738-8610   *SIC* 5141

COSTCO WHOLESALE CANADA LTD *p633*
1015 CENTENNIAL DR, KINGSTON, ON, K7P 3B7
(613) 549-2527   *SIC* 5141

COSTCO WHOLESALE CANADA LTD *p657*
4313 WELLINGTON RD S, LONDON, ON, N6E 2Z8
(519) 680-1027   *SIC* 5141

COSTCO WHOLESALE CANADA LTD *p750*
1849 MERIVALE RD SUITE 540, NEPEAN, ON, K2G 1E3
(613) 727-4786   *SIC* 5141

COSTCO WHOLESALE CANADA LTD *p884*
3 NORTH SERVICE RD, ST CATHARINES, ON, L2N 7R1
(905) 646-2008   *SIC* 5141

COSTCO WHOLESALE CANADA LTD *p899*
1465 KINGSWAY, SUDBURY, ON, P3B 0A5
(705) 524-8255   *SIC* 5141

COURTNEY'S DISTRIBUTING INC *p847*
1941 CONCESSION RD 5, PORT HOPE, ON, L1A 3V5
(905) 786-1106   *SIC* 5141

CROSS PACIFIC INVESTMENT GROUP INC

p200
62 FAWCETT RD SUITE 13, COQUITLAM, BC, V3K 6V5
(604) 522-8144   *SIC* 5141
CYBA STEVENS MANAGEMENT GROUP INC   *p22*
5735 7 ST NE SUITE 100, CALGARY, AB, T2E 8V3
(403) 291-3288   *SIC* 5141
DAN-D FOODS (TORONTO) LTD   *p551*
45 BASALTIC RD UNIT 5, CONCORD, ON, L4K 1G5
(905) 889-7807   *SIC* 5141
DAN-D FOODS LTD   *p263*
11760 MACHRINA WAY, RICHMOND, BC, V7A 4V1
(604) 274-3263   *SIC* 5141
DISTRIBUTEURS D'ALIMENTS DEFEDIS INC   *p1363*
755 CHOMEDEY (A-13) E, SAINTE-ROSE, QC, H7W 5N4
(450) 681-9500   *SIC* 5141
DISTRIBUTION EPICERIE C.T.S. INC *p1127*
5025 RUE FRANCOIS-CUSSON, LA-CHINE, QC, H8T 3K1
(514) 335-3586   *SIC* 5141
DISTRIBUTIONS ALIMENTAIRES LE MAR-QUIS INC   *p1064*
1250 RUE NOBEL BUREAU 190, BOUCHERVILLE, QC, J4B 5H1
(450) 655-4764   *SIC* 5141
DISTRIBUTIONS MISSUM INC   *p1101*
3838 BOUL LEMAN, FABREVILLE, QC, H7E 1A1
(450) 661-0281   *SIC* 5141
DOT FOODS CANADA, INC   *p502*
12 BARTON CRT, BRAMPTON, ON, L6T 5H6
SIC 5141
DUNNE, WILLIAM M & ASSOCIATES LIM-ITED   *p1031*
10 DIRECTOR CRT SUITE 300, WOOD-BRIDGE, ON, L4L 7E8
(905) 856-5240   *SIC* 5141
DUTCH MARKET LIMITED, THE   *p542*
80 WILLIAM ST S, CHATHAM, ON, N7M 4S3
(519) 352-2831   *SIC* 5141
EBERHARDT FOODS LTD   *p105*
12165 154 ST NW, EDMONTON, AB, T5V 1J3
(780) 454-8331   *SIC* 5141
EDOKO FOOD IMPORTERS LTD   *p246*
1335 KEBET WAY, PORT COQUITLAM, BC, V3C 6G1
(604) 944-7332   *SIC* 5141
ELCO FINE FOODS INC   *p669*
233 ALDEN RD, MARKHAM, ON, L3R 3W6
(604) 651-1551   *SIC* 5141
ELCO FINE FOODS LTD   *p254*
13100 MITCHELL RD SUITE 120, RICH-MOND, BC, V6V 1M8
(604) 324-1551   *SIC* 5141
EMPIRE FOODS LIMITED   *p669*
205 TORBAY RD UNIT 7, MARKHAM, ON, L3R 3W4
(905) 475-9988   *SIC* 5141
ESPACE HOUBLON INC   *p1300*
180 25E AV, SAINT-EUSTACHE, QC, J7P 2V2
(450) 983-7122   *SIC* 5141
ESSLINGER FOODS LTD   *p522*
5035 NORTH SERVICE RD, BURLINGTON, ON, L7L 5V2
(905) 332-3777   *SIC* 5141
EUCLID'S HOLDINGS LTD   *p878*
275 FINCHDENE SQ UNIT 1, SCARBOR-OUGH, ON, M1X 1B9
(416) 321-8002   *SIC* 5141
EUROPEAN FINE FOODS CO. INC   *p694*
1191 CRESTLAWN DR, MISSISSAUGA, ON, L4W 1A7
(905) 206-0964   *SIC* 5141
EXEL LOGISTICS CANADA INC   *p688*

6700 NORTHWEST DR, MISSISSAUGA, ON, L4V 1L5
SIC 5141
EXPORT-IMPORT TRADE CENTRE OF CANADA AND U.S.A. LIMITED   *p944*
481 UNIVERSITY AVE UNIT 301, TORONTO, ON, M5G 2E9
(416) 979-7967   *SIC* 5141
EXTRA FOODS & DRUGS LTD   *p286*
3189 GRANDVIEW HWY, VANCOUVER, BC, V5M 2E9
(604) 439-5402   *SIC* 5141
FEDERATED CO-OPERATIVES LIMITED *p11*
2626 10 AVE NE, CALGARY, AB, T2A 2M3
(403) 531-6665   *SIC* 5141
FEDERATED CO-OPERATIVES LIMITED *p12*
3333 52 ST SE, CALGARY, AB, T2B 1N3
(403) 531-6600   *SIC* 5141
FEDERATED CO-OPERATIVES LIMITED *p105*
13232 170 ST NW, EDMONTON, AB, T5V 1M7
(780) 447-5700   *SIC* 5141
FEDERATED CO-OPERATIVES LIMITED *p384*
1615 KING EDWARD ST, WINNIPEG, MB, R3H 0R7
(204) 633-8950   *SIC* 5141
FEDERATED CO-OPERATIVES LIMITED *p1427*
607 46TH ST E, SASKATOON, SK, S7K 0X1
SIC 5141
FINDLAY FOODS (KINGSTON) LTD   *p632*
675 PROGRESS AVE, KINGSTON, ON, K7M 0C7
(613) 384-5331   *SIC* 5141
FIRST NATIONAL FOOD BROKERAGE*p584*
26 CLAIREVILLE DR, ETOBICOKE, ON, M9W 5T9
(416) 679-0833   *SIC* 5141
FISHER BRANCH CO-OP GAS B   *p350*
22 CACHE, FISHER BRANCH, MB, R0C 0Z0
(204) 372-6202   *SIC* 5141
FLANAGAN FOODSERVICE INC   *p636*
145 OTONABEE DR, KITCHENER, ON, N2C 1L7
(519) 748-6878   *SIC* 5141
FONG TAI INTERNATIONAL FOOD LIMITED *p765*
1100 GORDON BAKER RD, NORTH YORK, ON, M2H 3B3
(416) 497-6666   *SIC* 5141
FORTINOS SUPERMARKET LTD   *p615*
1275 RYMAL RD E SUITE 2, HAMILTON, ON, L8W 3N1
(905) 318-4532   *SIC* 5141
FORTINOS SUPERMARKET LTD   *p894*
102 HIGHWAY 8, STONEY CREEK, ON, L8G 4H3
(905) 664-2886   *SIC* 5141
FRUIT OF THE LAND INC   *p906*
1 PROMENADE CIR, THORNHILL, ON, L4J 4P8
(905) 761-9611   *SIC* 5141
G-P DISTRIBUTING INC   *p1440*
29 MACDONALD RD, WHITEHORSE, YT, Y1A 4L1
(867) 667-4500   *SIC* 5141
G. D. BROKERAGE INC   *p446*
21 WILLIAMS AVE UNIT 4, DARTMOUTH, NS, B3B 1X3
(902) 468-1777   *SIC* 5141
GARDEN CITY WAREHOUSING & DISTRI-BUTION LTD   *p233*
839 OLD VICTORIA RD, NANAIMO, BC, V9R 5Z9
(250) 754-5447   *SIC* 5141
GARROD FOOD BROKERS LTD   *p23*
7777 10 ST NE SUITE 120, CALGARY, AB, T2E 8X2
(403) 291-2818   *SIC* 5141

GEORGE WESTON LIMITED   *p925*
22 ST CLAIR AVE E SUITE 1901, TORONTO, ON, M4T 2S7
(416) 922-2500   *SIC* 5141
GORDON FOOD SERVICE CANADA LTD *p160*
290212 TOWNSHIP ROAD 261, ROCKY VIEW COUNTY, AB, T4A 0V6
(403) 235-8555   *SIC* 5141
GORDON FOOD SERVICE CANADA LTD *p389*
310 STERLING LYON PKY, WINNIPEG, MB, R3P 0Y2
(204) 224-0134   *SIC* 5141
GORDON FOOD SERVICE CANADA LTD *p683*
2999 JAMES SNOW PKY N, MILTON, ON, L9T 5G4
(905) 864-3700   *SIC* 5141
GOUDAS FOOD PRODUCTS AND INVEST-MENTS LIMITED   *p553*
241 SNIDERCROFT RD, CONCORD, ON, L4K 2J8
SIC 5141
GOUDAS FOOD PRODUCTS CO. LTD *p553*
241 SNIDERCROFT RD, CONCORD, ON, L4K 2J8
(905) 660-3233   *SIC* 5141
GRACE FOODS CANADA INC   *p852*
70 WEST WILMOT ST, RICHMOND HILL, ON, L4B 1H8
(905) 886-1002   *SIC* 5141
GREAT WEST ITALIAN IMPORTERS LTD *p23*
5130 SKYLINE WAY NE, CALGARY, AB, T2E 6V1
(403) 275-8222   *SIC* 5141
GREENWORLD FOOD EXPRESS INC *p695*
5380 MAINGATE DR, MISSISSAUGA, ON, L4W 1R8
(905) 212-7720   *SIC* 5141
GROUPE COLABOR INC   *p1065*
1620 BOUL DE MONTARVILLE, BOUCHERVILLE, QC, J4B 8P4
(450) 449-4911   *SIC* 5141
GROUPE DE COURTAGE OMNI LTEE*p1101*
3838 BOUL LEMAN, FABREVILLE, QC, H7E 1A1
(450) 661-0281   *SIC* 5141
GROUPE F.G.B. 2000 INC, LE   *p1234*
1225 RUE BERGAR, MONTREAL, QC, H7L 4Z7
(450) 967-0076   *SIC* 5141
HOLLSHOP IMPORTS LTD   *p228*
20215 62 AVE UNIT 102, LANGLEY, BC, V3A 5E6
(604) 533-8822   *SIC* 5141
HOUSE OF SHER 2018 LTD   *p176*
3120 QUEEN ST SUITE 104, ABBOTS-FORD, BC, V2T 6J3
(604) 859-3030   *SIC* 5141
IMPORTATIONS & DISTRIBUTIONS B.H. INC   *p1160*
12880 RUE JEAN-GROU, MONTREAL, QC, H1A 3N5
(514) 356-1276   *SIC* 5141
IMPORTATIONS CACHERES INC.   *p1334*
6600 BOUL THIMENS, SAINT-LAURENT, QC, H4S 1S5
SIC 5141
INFORM BROKERAGE INC   *p184*
2286 HOLDOM AVE, BURNABY, BC, V5B 4Y5
(604) 324-0565   *SIC* 5141
INTERNATIONAL PACIFIC SALES LTD*p258*
22111 FRASERWOOD WAY, RICHMOND, BC, V6W 1J5
(604) 273-7035   *SIC* 5141
IQBAL FOODS CORPORATION   *p919*
2 THORNCLIFFE PARK DR UNIT 10, TORONTO, ON, M4H 1H2
(416) 467-0177   *SIC* 5141
ISLAND INDEPENDENT BUYING GROUP LTD   *p196*

3110 HOPE PL, CHEMAINUS, BC, V0R 1K4
(250) 246-1828   *SIC* 5141
ITAL-PLUS IMPORTS INC   *p825*
925 GLADSTONE AVE, OTTAWA, ON, K1R 6Y3
(613) 230-7166   *SIC* 5141
J & S BROKERAGE LTD   *p119*
6040 GATEWAY BLVD NW, EDMONTON, AB, T6H 2H6
(780) 435-5446   *SIC* 5141
J B FOOD SERVICES INC   *p1018*
7605 TECUMSEH RD E, WINDSOR, ON, N8T 3H1
(519) 251-1125   *SIC* 5141
J.L. FREEMAN, S.E.C.   *p1066*
1250 RUE NOBEL BUREAU 200, BOUCHERVILLE, QC, J4B 5H1
(450) 641-4520   *SIC* 5141
J.L. INTERNATIONAL   *p852*
21 EAST WILMOT ST UNIT 2, RICHMOND HILL, ON, L4B 1A3
(905) 763-2929   *SIC* 5141
JACE HOLDINGS LTD   *p238*
1893 MILLS RD, NORTH SAANICH, BC, V8L 5S9
(250) 483-1709   *SIC* 5141
JACE HOLDINGS LTD   *p267*
6649 BUTLER CRES, SAANICHTON, BC, V8M 1Z7
(250) 483-1600   *SIC* 5141
JACE HOLDINGS LTD   *p337*
3475 QUADRA ST SUITE 13, VICTORIA, BC, V8X 1G8
(250) 382-2751   *SIC* 5141
JAM-BEC INC   *p1114*
380 BOUL DE L'INDUSTRIE, JOLIETTE, QC, J6E 8V2
(450) 759-5130   *SIC* 5141
JAN K. OVERWEEL LIMITED   *p1031*
3700 STEELES AVE W SUITE 702, WOOD-BRIDGE, ON, L4L 8K8
(905) 850-9010   *SIC* 5141
JEFO NUTRITION INC   *p1310*
4900 RUE MARTINEAU, SAINT-HYACINTHE, QC, J2R 1K3
(450) 799-4454   *SIC* 5141
JFC INTERNATIONAL (CANADA) INC *p696*
1025 KAMATO RD, MISSISSAUGA, ON, L4W 0C1
(905) 629-0993   *SIC* 5141
JOHN'S YOUR INDEPENDENT GROCER *p198*
215 PORT AUGUSTA ST UNIT C, COMOX, BC, V9M 3M9
(250) 339-7651   *SIC* 5141
KARRYS BROS., LIMITED   *p740*
180 COURTNEYPARK DR E, MISSIS-SAUGA, ON, L5T 2S5
(905) 565-1000   *SIC* 5141
KASSELER FOOD PRODUCTS INC   *p696*
1031 BREVIK PL, MISSISSAUGA, ON, L4W 3R7
(905) 629-2142   *SIC* 5141
KIMMEL SALES LIMITED   *p554*
126 EDILCAN DR UNIT 1, CONCORD, ON, L4K 3S5
(905) 669-2083   *SIC* 5141
KIN'S FARM LTD   *p263*
12151 HORSESHOE WAY, RICHMOND, BC, V7A 4V4
(604) 272-2551   *SIC* 5141
KRAFT HEINZ CANADA ULC   *p1395*
401 RUE MARIE-CURIE, VAUDREUIL-DORION, QC, J7V 0B9
(450) 455-5576   *SIC* 5141
KRONOS FOODS LTD   *p868*
371 DANFORTH RD, SCARBOROUGH, ON, M1L 3X8
(416) 690-1990   *SIC* 5141
L. N. REYNOLDS CO. LIMITED   *p513*
10160 HURONTARIO ST SUITE 1, BRAMP-TON, ON, L7A 0E4
(905) 840-3700   *SIC* 5141
LABORATOIRES C.O.P. INC   *p1107*

▲ Public Company   ■ Public Company Family Member   **HQ** Headquarters   **BR** Branch   **SL** Single Location

60 RUE JEAN-PROULX, GATINEAU, QC, J8Z 1W1

(819) 772-4447 *SIC* 5141

LAROSA FINE FOODS INC *p295*
855 TERMINAL AVE, VANCOUVER, BC, V6A 2M9

(604) 688-8306 *SIC* 5141

LEMIEUX, JACQUES (GROSSISTE) INC *p1160*
179 RUE DES INDUSTRIES, MONT-MAGNY, QC, G5V 4G2

(418) 248-8117 *SIC* 5141

LEO'S DISTRIBUTING COMPANY CANADA LIMITED *p654*
149 PICCADILLY ST, LONDON, ON, N6A 1R9

(519) 439-2730 *SIC* 5141

LID BROKERAGE & REALTY CO. (1977) LTD.
1171 8TH ST E, SASKATOON, SK, S7H 0S3

(306) 668-3000 *SIC* 5141

LOBLAWS INC *p24*
2928 23 ST NE, CALGARY, AB, T2E 8R7

(403) 291-2810 *SIC* 5141

LOBLAWS INC *p75*
5858 SIGNAL HILL CTR SW SUITE 1577, CALGARY, AB, T3H 3P8

(403) 686-8035 *SIC* 5141

LOBLAWS INC *p96*
14740 111 AVE NW, EDMONTON, AB, T5M 2P5

(780) 452-5411 *SIC* 5141

LOBLAWS INC *p101*
17303 STONY PLAIN RD NW SUITE 1573, EDMONTON, AB, T5S 1B5

(780) 486-8452 *SIC* 5141

LOBLAWS INC *p121*
9711 23 AVE NW, EDMONTON, AB, T6N 1K7

(780) 490-3935 *SIC* 5141

LOBLAWS INC *p212*
291 COWICHAN WAY SUITE 1563, DUNCAN, BC, V9L 6P5

(250) 746-0529 *SIC* 5141

LOBLAWS INC *p260*
4651 NO. 3 RD SUITE 1557, RICHMOND, BC, V6X 2C4

(604) 233-2418 *SIC* 5141

LOBLAWS INC *p277*
7550 KING GEORGE BLVD SUITE 1, SURREY, BC, V3W 2T2

SIC 5141

LOBLAWS INC *p287*
3185 GRANDVIEW HWY, VANCOUVER, BC, V5M 2E9

(604) 439-5479 *SIC* 5141

LOBLAWS INC *p344*
1000 SOUTH LAKESIDE DR, WILLIAMS LAKE, BC, V2G 3A6

(250) 305-2150 *SIC* 5141

LOBLAWS INC *p367*
1035 GATEWAY RD SUITE 1512, WINNIPEG, MB, R2K 4C1

(204) 987-7534 *SIC* 5141

LOBLAWS INC *p381*
1385 SARGENT AVE, WINNIPEG, MB, R3E 3P8

(204) 784-7901 *SIC* 5141

LOBLAWS INC *p384*
1725 ELLICE AVE, WINNIPEG, MB, R3H 1A6

(204) 775-8280 *SIC* 5141

LOBLAWS INC *p511*
1 PRESIDENTS CHOICE CIR, BRAMPTON, ON, L6Y 5S5

(905) 459-2500 *SIC* 5141

LOBLAWS INC *p751*
2065A ROBERTSON RD, NEPEAN, ON, K2H 5Y9

(613) 829-4680 *SIC* 5141

LOBLAWS INC *p816*
2625 SHEFFIELD RD, OTTAWA, ON, K1B 1A8

(613) 741-4756 *SIC* 5141

LOBLAWS INC *p1390*
502 RUE GIGUERE, VAL-D'OR, QC, J9P 7G6

(819) 825-5000 *SIC* 5141

LOBLAWS INC *p1431*
411 CONFEDERATION DR, SASKATOON, SK, S7L 5C3

(306) 683-5634 *SIC* 5141

LOBLAWS SUPERMARKETS LIMITED *p989*
650 DUPONT ST SUITE 1029, TORONTO, ON, M6G 4B1

(416) 588-3756 *SIC* 5141

LOEB CLUB PLUS GILLES DIONNE INC *p1104*
900 BOUL MALONEY O, GATINEAU, QC, J8T 3R6

(514) 243-5231 *SIC* 5141

MAPLE LEAF FOODS INC *p801*
178 SOUTH SERVICE RD E, OAKVILLE, ON, L6J 0A5

(905) 815-6500 *SIC* 5141

MARKETWEST FOOD GROUP LIMITED PARTNERSHIP *p201*
1580 BRIGANTINE DR SUITE 200, COQUITLAM, BC, V3K 7C1

(604) 526-1788 *SIC* 5141

MARTIN-BROWER OF CANADA CO *p24*
4242 21 ST NE, CALGARY, AB, T2E 9A6

(403) 255-3278 *SIC* 5141

MARTIN-BROWER OF CANADA CO *p1053*
475 AV LEE, BAIE-D'URFE, QC, H9X 3S3

(514) 457-4411 *SIC* 5141

MAYRAND LIMITEE *p1049*
9701 BOUL LOUIS-H.-LAFONTAINE, ANJOU, QC, H1J 2A3

(514) 255-9330 *SIC* 5141

MCRAE, W. R. COMPANY LIMITED *p630*
549 MONTREAL ST, KINGSTON, ON, K7K 3J1

(613) 544-6611 *SIC* 5141

MEDICINE HAT WHOLESALE FOODS LTD *p146*
702 INDUSTRIAL AVE SE, MEDICINE HAT, AB, T1A 3L8

(403) 527-4481 *SIC* 5141

METRO INC *p1052*
7151 RUE JEAN-TALON E, ANJOU, QC, H1M 3N8

(514) 356-5800 *SIC* 5141

METRO INC *p1083*
1600 BOUL SAINT-MARTIN E BUREAU A, COTE SAINT-LUC, QC, H7G 4S7

(514) 643-1000 *SIC* 5141

METRO INC *p1161*
11011 BOUL MAURICE-DUPLESSIS, MONTREAL, QC, H1C 1V6

(514) 643-1000 *SIC* 5141

METRO ONTARIO INC *p534*
95 WATER ST N, CAMBRIDGE, ON, N1R 3B5

(519) 623-3652 *SIC* 5141

METRO ONTARIO INC *p577*
25 VICKERS RD, ETOBICOKE, ON, M9B 1C1

(416) 234-6590 *SIC* 5141

METRO ONTARIO INC *p751*
1811 ROBERTSON RD, NEPEAN, ON, K2H 8X3

(613) 721-7028 *SIC* 5141

METRO ONTARIO INC *p811*
4510 INNES RD, ORLEANS, ON, K4A 4C5

(613) 824-8850 *SIC* 5141

METRO ONTARIO INC *p818*
490 INDUSTRIAL AVE, OTTAWA, ON, K1G 0Y9

(613) 737-1300 *SIC* 5141

METRO ONTARIO INC *p830*
1360 RICHMOND RD, OTTAWA, ON, K2B 8L4

(613) 828-4207 *SIC* 5141

METRO RICHELIEU INC *p1161*
11011 BOUL MAURICE-DUPLESSIS, MONTREAL, QC, H1C 1V6

(514) 643-1000 *SIC* 5141

METRO RICHELIEU INC *p1267*
635 AV NEWTON, QUEBEC, QC, G1P 4C4

(418) 871-7101 *SIC* 5141

METRO RICHELIEU INC *p1283*
85 BOUL BRIEN BUREAU 101, REPENTIGNY, QC, J6A 8B6

(450) 581-3072 *SIC* 5141

METRO RICHELIEU INC *p1313*
3800 AV CUSSON, SAINT-HYACINTHE, QC, J2S 8V6

(450) 771-1651 *SIC* 5141

MILLER & SMITH FOODS INC *p575*
33 CONNELL CRT, ETOBICOKE, ON, M8Z 1E8

(416) 253-2000 *SIC* 5141

MITCHELL AGENCIES LIMITED *p447*
55 WESTON CRT, DARTMOUTH, NS, B3B 2C8

(902) 468-8990 *SIC* 5141

MORRIS WHOLESALE LTD *p405*
125 PETRIE ST, MIRAMICHI, NB, E1V 1S4

(506) 836-9012 *SIC* 5141

NATIONAL IMPORTERS CANADA LTD *p255*
13100 MITCHELL RD SUITE 120, RICHMOND, BC, V6V 1M8

(604) 324-1551 *SIC* 5141

NEWFOUNDLAND SALES & MARKETING INC *p428*
18 ARGYLE ST UNIT 201, ST. JOHN'S, NL, A1A 1V3

(709) 722-6706 *SIC* 5141

NORTH AMERICAN TEA & COFFEE INC *p209*
7861 82 ST, DELTA, BC, V4G 1L9

(604) 940-7861 *SIC* 5141

OFC DISTRIBUTION INC *p708*
580 ORWELL ST, MISSISSAUGA, ON, L5A 3V7

(905) 270-2009 *SIC* 5141

OFIELD, CRAIG GROUP LTD *p853*
55 LEEK CRES, RICHMOND HILL, ON, L4B 3Y2

(905) 726-5000 *SIC* 5141

OLSON INTERNATIONAL TRADING LTD *p182*
4098 MCCONNELL DR, BURNABY, BC, V5A 3Y9

(604) 420-8022 *SIC* 5141

P.J. IMPEX INC *p1224*
5532 RUE SAINT-PATRICK BUREAU 300, MONTREAL, QC, H4E 1A8

(514) 369-2035 *SIC* 5141

PANTRY SHELF FOOD CORPORATION *p689*
3983 NASHUA DR UNIT B, MISSISSAUGA, ON, L4V 1P3

(905) 677-7200 *SIC* 5141

PASTENE ENTERPRISES ULC *p1050*
9101 RUE DE L'INNOVATION, ANJOU, QC, H1J 2X9

(514) 353-7997 *SIC* 5141

PETER IGEL GROUP INC *p768*
2235 SHEPPARD AVE E SUITE 909, NORTH YORK, ON, M2J 5B5

(416) 493-8800 *SIC* 5141

PILAROS INTERNATIONAL TRADING INC *p1363*
755 CHOMEDEY (A-13) E, SAINTE-ROSE, QC, H7W 5N4

(450) 681-6900 *SIC* 5141

POULIN, NIKOL INC *p1305*
3100 BOUL DIONNE, SAINT-GEORGES, QC, G5Y 3Y4

(418) 228-3267 *SIC* 5141

PRATTS FOOD SERVICE (ALBERTA) LTD *p160*
291196 WAGON WHEEL RD SUITE 403, ROCKY VIEW COUNTY, AB, T4A 0E2

(403) 476-7728 *SIC* 5141

PRATTS WHOLESALE (SASK.) LTD *p1420*
1616 4TH AVE, REGINA, SK, S4R 8C3

(306) 522-0101 *SIC* 5141

PRIMELINE FOOD PARTNERS LTD *p201*
1580 BRIGANTINE DR SUITE 200, CO-

QUITLAM, BC, V3K 7C1

(604) 526-1788 *SIC* 5141

PROVIGO DISTRIBUTION INC *p633*
775 BAYRIDGE DR, KINGSTON, ON, K7P 2P1

(613) 384-8800 *SIC* 5141

PROVIGO DISTRIBUTION INC *p1125*
3560 RUE LAVAL, LAC-MEGANTIC, QC, G6B 2X4

(819) 583-4001 *SIC* 5141

PROVIGO DISTRIBUTION INC *p1327*
400 AV SAINTE-CROIX, SAINT-LAURENT, QC, H4N 3L4

(514) 383-3000 *SIC* 5141

PROVIGO DISTRIBUTION INC *p1356*
480 BOUL SAINTE-ANNE, SAINTE-ANNE-DES-PLAINES, QC, J0N 1H0

(450) 478-1864 *SIC* 5141

PROVIGO DISTRIBUTION INC *p1398*
60 RUE CARIGNAN, VICTORIAVILLE, QC, G6P 4Z6

SIC 5141

PSC NATURAL FOODS LTD *p340*
2924 JACKLIN RD SUITE 117, VICTORIA, BC, V9B 3Y5

(250) 386-3880 *SIC* 5141

PUBNICO TRAWLERS LIMITED *p461*
155 HWY 3, LOWER EAST PUBNICO, NS, B0W 2A0

(902) 762-3202 *SIC* 5141

QUALIFIRST FOODS LTD *p587*
89 CARLINGVIEW DR, ETOBICOKE, ON, M9W 5E4

(416) 244-1177 *SIC* 5141

ROLAND & FRERES LIMITEE *p1349*
22 RUE FORTIER, SAINT-PACOME, QC, G0L 3X0

(418) 852-2191 *SIC* 5141

ROMAN CHEESE PRODUCTS LIMITED *p760*
7770 CANADIAN DR, NIAGARA FALLS, ON, L2H 0X3

(905) 356-2639 *SIC* 5141

S & F FOOD IMPORTERS INC *p558*
565 EDGELEY BLVD, CONCORD, ON, L4K 4G4

(416) 410-9091 *SIC* 5141

S. BOURASSA (STE-AGATHE) LTEE *p1354*
680 RUE PRINCIPALE, SAINTE-AGATHE-DES-MONTS, QC, J8C 1L3

(819) 326-1707 *SIC* 5141

SABRINA WHOLESALE FOODS INC *p558*
1950 HIGHWAY 7 UNIT 18, CONCORD, ON, L4K 3P2

(416) 665-1533 *SIC* 5141

SAPUTO PRODUITS LAITIERS CANADA S.E.N.C. *p97*
16110 116 AVE NW, EDMONTON, AB, T5M 3V4

(514) 328-3366 *SIC* 5141

SARDO, MARIO SALES INC *p495*
99 PILLSWORTH RD, BOLTON, ON, L7E 4E4

(905) 951-9096 *SIC* 5141

SASKATOON CO-OPERATIVE ASSOCIATION LIMITED, THE *p1432*
1624 33RD ST W, SASKATOON, SK, S7L 0X3

(306) 933-3865 *SIC* 5141

SCOTIA FOODSERVICE LTD *p460*
4 DOMINION CRES, LAKESIDE, NS, B3T 1M1

(902) 876-2356 *SIC* 5141

SESHA ONTARIO INC *p569*
476 ROBINSON RD, ENNISMORE, ON, K0L 1T0

(705) 292-6719 *SIC* 5141

SHAPE FOODS, INC *p347*
2001 VICTORIA AVE E, BRANDON, MB, R7A 7L2

(204) 727-3529 *SIC* 5141

SHEUNG KEE TRADING COMPANY INC *p877*
3411 MCNICOLL AVE UNIT 11, SCARBOR-

OUGH, ON, M1V 2V6
(905) 471-4481   *SIC 5141*

SHOPPERS WHOLESALE FOOD COMPANY *p251*
1959 NICHOLSON ST S, PRINCE GEORGE, BC, V2N 2Z9
(250) 562-6655   *SIC 5141*

SOBEYS CAPITAL INCORPORATED *p18*
7704 30 ST SE, CALGARY, AB, T2C 1M8
   SIC 5141

SOBEYS CAPITAL INCORPORATED *p106*
12910 156 ST NW, EDMONTON, AB, T5V 1E9
(780) 447-1440   *SIC 5141*

SOBEYS CAPITAL INCORPORATED *p373*
1800 INKSTER BLVD, WINNIPEG, MB, R2X 2Z5
(204) 632-7100   *SIC 5141*

SOBEYS CAPITAL INCORPORATED *p466*
115 KING ST, STELLARTON, NS, B0K 0A2
(902) 752-8371   *SIC 5141*

SOBEYS CAPITAL INCORPORATED *p764*
2555 TROUT LAKE RD, NORTH BAY, ON, P1B 7S8
(705) 495-4221   *SIC 5141*

SOBEYS CAPITAL INCORPORATED *p920*
1015 BROADVIEW AVE SUITE 718, TORONTO, ON, M4K 2S1
(416) 421-5906   *SIC 5141*

SOBEYS CAPITAL INCORPORATED *p1240*
11281 BOUL ALBERT-HUDON, MONTREAL-NORD, QC, H1G 3J5
(514) 324-1010   *SIC 5141*

SOBEYS CAPITAL INCORPORATED *p1240*
11281 BOUL ALBERT-HUDON, MONTREAL-NORD, QC, H1G 3J5
(514) 324-1010   *SIC 5141*

SOBEYS CAPITAL INCORPORATED *p1268*
950 AV GALILEE BUREAU 2008, QUEBEC, QC, G1P 4B7
(418) 681-1922   *SIC 5141*

SOBEYS CAPITAL INCORPORATED *p1290*
333 AV MONTEMURRO, ROUYN-NORANDA, QC, J9X 7C6
(819) 797-1900   *SIC 5141*

SOBEYS CAPITAL INCORPORATED *p1346*
7150 BOUL LANGELIER, SAINT-LEONARD, QC, H1S 2X6
(514) 254-5454   *SIC 5141*

SOBEYS QUEBEC INC *p1067*
1500 BOUL DE MONTARVILLE, BOUCHERVILLE, QC, J4B 5Y3
(514) 324-1010   *SIC 5141*

SOBEYS QUEBEC INC *p1220*
4885 AV VAN HORNE, MONTREAL, QC, H3W 1J2
(514) 731-8336   *SIC 5141*

SOCIETE EN COMMANDITE PASQUIER *p1315*
87 BOUL SAINT-LUC BUREAU A, SAINT-JEAN-SUR-RICHELIEU, QC, J2W 1E2
(450) 299-9999   *SIC 5141*

ST. PHILLIPS FOODS LIMITED *p664*
2563 MAJOR MACKENZIE DR SUITE 8, MAPLE, ON, L6A 2E8
(905) 832-5688   *SIC 5141*

STANTON DISTRIBUTING CO LTD *p435*
49 NAVY RD, INUVIK, NT, X0E 0T0
(867) 777-4381   *SIC 5141*

STAR MARKETING LTD *p280*
3289 190 ST, SURREY, BC, V3Z 1A7
(778) 574-0778   *SIC 5141*

STEWART FOODSERVICE INC *p488*
201 SAUNDERS RD, BARRIE, ON, L4N 9A3
(705) 728-3051   *SIC 5141*

SUNFRESH LIMITED *p512*
1 PRESIDENTS CHOICE CIR, BRAMPTON, ON, L6Y 5S5
(905) 459-2500   *SIC 5141*

SUNWEST FOOD PROCESSORS LTD *p177*
31100 WHEEL AVE, ABBOTSFORD, BC, V2T 6H1
(604) 852-3760   *SIC 5141*

SYSCO CANADA, INC *p18*

4639 72 AVE SE, CALGARY, AB, T2C 4H7
(403) 720-1300   *SIC 5141*

SYSCO CANADA, INC *p247*
1346 KINGSWAY AVE, PORT COQUITLAM, BC, V3C 6G4
(604) 944-4410   *SIC 5141*

SYSCO CANADA, INC *p340*
2881 AMY RD, VICTORIA, BC, V9B 0B2
(250) 475-3333   *SIC 5141*

SYSCO CANADA, INC *p398*
611 BOUL FERDINAND, DIEPPE, NB, E1A 7G1
(506) 857-6000   *SIC 5141*

SYSCO CANADA, INC *p410*
460 MACNAUGHTON AVE, MONCTON, NB, E1H 2K1
(866) 447-9726   *SIC 5141*

SYSCO CANADA, INC *p578*
21 FOUR SEASONS PL SUITE 400, ETOBICOKE, ON, M9B 6J8
(416) 234-2666   *SIC 5141*

SYSCO CANADA, INC *p633*
650 CATARAQUI WOODS DR, KINGSTON, ON, K7P 2Y4
(613) 384-6666   *SIC 5141*

SYSCO CANADA, INC *p842*
65 ELMDALE RD, PETERBOROUGH, ON, K9J 6X4
(705) 748-6701   *SIC 5141*

SYSCO CANADA, INC *p898*
106 BAY ST, STURGEON FALLS, ON, P2B 3G6
(705) 753-4444   *SIC 5141*

SYSCO CANADA, INC *p1162*
11625 AV 55E BUREAU 864, MONTREAL, QC, H1E 2K2
(514) 494-5200   *SIC 5141*

SYSCO CANADA, INC *p1416*
266 E DEWDNEY AVE, REGINA, SK, S4N 4G2
(306) 347-5200   *SIC 5141*

SYSCO CENTRAL ONTARIO, INC *p842*
65 ELMDALE RD, PETERBOROUGH, ON, K9J 0G5
(705) 748-6701   *SIC 5141*

SYSCO FOUR SEASONS PRODUCE LTD *p291*
127 E KENT AVE NORTH, VANCOUVER, BC, V5X 2X5
   SIC 5141

SYSCO VICTORIA, INC *p340*
2881 AMY RD, VICTORIA, BC, V9B 0B2
(250) 475-3333   *SIC 5141*

T-BROTHERS FOOD AND TRADING LTD *p202*
88 BRIGANTINE DR SUITE 100, COQUITLAM, BC, V3K 6Z6
(604) 540-0306   *SIC 5141*

THAI INDOCHINE TRADING INC *p678*
50 TRAVAIL RD, MARKHAM, ON, L3S 3J1
(416) 292-2228   *SIC 5141*

THOMAS, LARGE & SINGER INC *p676*
15 ALLSTATE PKY SUITE 500, MARKHAM, ON, L3R 5B4
(800) 268-5542   *SIC 5141*

TOPMADE ENTERPRISES LTD *p19*
7177 40 ST SE, CALGARY, AB, T2C 2H7
(403) 236-7557   *SIC 5141*

TRA STELLARTON *p466*
GD, STELLARTON, NS, B0K 1S0
(902) 752-1525   *SIC 5141*

TREE OF LIFE CANADA ULC *p733*
6185 MCLAUGHLIN RD, MISSISSAUGA, ON, L5R 3W7
(905) 507-6161   *SIC 5141*

U-BUY DISCOUNT FOODS LIMITED *p560*
8811 KEELE ST, CONCORD, ON, L4K 2N1
(905) 669-8002   *SIC 5141*

UNIBEL COMPANY LTD *p576*
44 ATOMIC AVE, ETOBICOKE, ON, M8Z 5L1
(416) 533-3591   *SIC 5141*

UNICER FOODS LTD *p994*
370 ALLIANCE AVE, TORONTO, ON, M6N

2H8
(416) 766-9535   *SIC 5141*

UNICO INC *p560*
8000 KEELE ST, CONCORD, ON, L4K 2A4
(905) 669-9633   *SIC 5141*

VALOROSO FOODS (1996) LTD *p223*
1467 SUTHERLAND AVE, KELOWNA, BC, V1Y 5Y4
(250) 860-3631   *SIC 5141*

WALLACE & CAREY (B.C.) LTD *p207*
551 CHESTER RD, DELTA, BC, V3M 6G7
(604) 522-9930   *SIC 5141*

WEBB, J.N. & SONS LIMITED *p592*
930 FIFTH ST W, FORT FRANCES, ON, P9A 3C7
(807) 274-5613   *SIC 5141*

WESTERN IMPACT SALES & MARKETING INC *p12*
3223 5 AVE NE UNIT 309, CALGARY, AB, T2A 6E9
(403) 272-3065   *SIC 5141*

WESTROW FOOD BROKERS INC *p19*
2880 GLENMORE TRAIL SE SUITE 115, CALGARY, AB, T2C 2E7
(403) 720-0703   *SIC 5141*

WILBY COMMERCIAL LTD *p677*
110 TORBAY RD UNIT 3-4, MARKHAM, ON, L3R 1G6
(905) 513-7505   *SIC 5141*

WISMETTAC ASIAN FOODS, INC *p264*
11388 NO. 5 RD SUITE 130, RICHMOND, BC, V7A 4E7
(604) 303-8620   *SIC 5141*

YOUNG & YOUNG TRADING CO. LIMITED *p872*
328 NANTUCKET BLVD UNIT 8, SCARBOROUGH, ON, M1P 2P4
(416) 288-9298   *SIC 5141*

YUILL'S VALU-MART *p489*
19625 OPEONGO ST, BARRYS BAY, ON, K0J 1B0
(613) 756-2023   *SIC 5141*

ZARA *p936*
220 YONGE ST SUITE C-4A, TORONTO, ON, M5B 2H1
(647) 288-0333   *SIC 5141*

ZENAR GROUP INC, THE *p66*
1508 8 ST SW SUITE 203, CALGARY, AB, T2R 1R6
(403) 261-1566   *SIC 5141*

ZUCKER, SIMON & ASSOCIATES *p921*
3080 YONGE ST SUITE 5010, TORONTO, ON, M4N 3N1
(416) 489-8277   *SIC 5141*

SIC 5142 Packaged frozen goods

0429746 B.C. LTD *p205*
1345 CLIVEDEN AVE, DELTA, BC, V3M 6C7
(604) 515-4555   *SIC 5142*

0429746 B.C. LTD *p661*
2825 INNOVATION DR, LONDON, ON, N6M 0B6
(519) 937-7777   *SIC 5142*

2 SISTERS POULTRY & MEAT LTD *p191*
5791 SIDLEY ST, BURNABY, BC, V5J 5E6
(604) 327-5526   *SIC 5142*

9309-6774 QUEBEC INC *p1387*
9300 BOUL INDUSTRIEL, TROIS-RIVIERES, QC, G9A 5E1
(819) 539-8058   *SIC 5142*

ALIMENTS ALASKO INC *p1165*
6810 BOUL DES GRANDES-PRAIRIES, MONTREAL, QC, H1P 3P3
(514) 328-6661   *SIC 5142*

ALIMENTS CONGELES MOOV INC *p1343*
6810 BOUL DES GRANDES-PRAIRIES, SAINT-LEONARD, QC, H1P 3P3
(514) 328-6661   *SIC 5142*

ALIMENTS MULTIBAR INC, LES *p1047*
9000 BOUL DES SCIENCES, ANJOU, QC, H1J 3A9
(514) 355-1151   *SIC 5142*

ALIMENTS VLM INC, LES *p1091*
1651 RUE SAINT-REGIS, DOLLARD-DES-ORMEAUX, QC, H9B 3H7
(514) 426-4100   *SIC 5142*

ALSAFA FOODS CANADA LIMITED *p704*
57 VILLAGE CENTRE PL SUITE 302, MISSISSAUGA, ON, L4Z 1V9
(800) 268-8174   *SIC 5142*

BASSETT & WALKER INTERNATIONAL INC *p932*
2 BERKELEY ST SUITE 502, TORONTO, ON, M5A 4J5
(416) 363-7070   *SIC 5142*

BEDESSEE IMPORTS LTD *p870*
2 GOLDEN GATE CRT, SCARBOROUGH, ON, M1P 3A5
(416) 292-2400   *SIC 5142*

BIRCH STREET SEAFOODS LTD *p449*
31 BIRCH ST, DIGBY, NS, B0V 1A0
(902) 245-6551   *SIC 5142*

BLEUETIERES SENCO INC, LES *p1302*
1459 BOUL DU SACRE-COEUR, SAINT-FELICIEN, QC, G8K 1B3
(418) 679-1472   *SIC 5142*

BLEUETS FORTIN & FILS INC *p1090*
555 RUE DE QUEN, DOLBEAU-MISTASSINI, QC, G8L 5M3
(418) 276-8611   *SIC 5142*

BLEUETS MISTASSINI LTEE *p1090*
555 RUE DE QUEN, DOLBEAU-MISTASSINI, QC, G8L 5M3
(418) 276-8611   *SIC 5142*

BLEUETS SAUVAGES DU QUEBEC INC, LES *p1296*
698 RUE MELANCON BUREAU 160, SAINT-BRUNO-LAC-SAINT-JEAN, QC, G0W 2L0
(418) 343-2410   *SIC 5142*

BONDUELLE CANADA INC *p621*
583278 HAMILTON RD, INGERSOLL, ON, N5C 3J7
(519) 485-0282   *SIC 5142*

BOULANGERIES COMAS INC, LES *p1343*
6325 BOUL DES GRANDES-PRAIRIES BUREAU 5, SAINT-LEONARD, QC, H1P 1A5
(514) 323-1880   *SIC 5142*

BOUVILLIONS-BELLERIVE INC *p1135*
80 RUE JACQUES-NAU BUREAU 102, LEVIS, QC, G6V 9J4
(418) 838-9611   *SIC 5142*

BRAVO PRODUCTS & EXPORTS INC *p771*
170 SHEPPARD AVE E SUITE 303A, NORTH YORK, ON, M2N 3A4
(416) 590-9605   *SIC 5142*

BRECON FOODS INC *p1249*
189 BOUL HYMUS BUREAU 406, POINTE-CLAIRE, QC, H9R 1E9
(514) 426-8140   *SIC 5142*

CAMPBELL COMPANY OF CANADA *p646*
1400 MITCHELL RD S, LISTOWEL, ON, N4W 3G7
   SIC 5142

CAMPBELL RIVER FISHING CO LTD *p194*
1330 HOMEWOOD RD, CAMPBELL RIVER, BC, V9W 6Y5
(250) 286-0887   *SIC 5142*

CANAFRIC INC *p883*
15 SEAPARK DR, ST CATHARINES, ON, L2M 6S5
(905) 688-9588   *SIC 5142*

CAVENDISH FARMS CORPORATION *p397*
100 MIDLAND DR, DIEPPE, NB, E1A 6X4
(506) 858-7777   *SIC 5142*

CDA-TEQ QUEBEC INC *p1215*
1201 RUE DE CONDE, MONTREAL, QC, H3K 2E4
(514) 789-0529   *SIC 5142*

CENTENNIAL FOODSERVICE *p28*
4412 MANILLA RD SE SUITE 1, CALGARY, AB, T2G 4B7
(403) 214-0044   *SIC 5142*

CHARLEBOIS, MAURICE ALIMENTATION LTEE *p1245*
267 RUE MARIE-CLAUDE, PLAISANCE,

QC, J0V 1S0
SIC 5142

COLABOR LIMITED PARTNERSHIP *p738*
6270 KENWAY DR, MISSISSAUGA, ON,
L5T 2N3
(905) 795-2400 *SIC 5142*

DINAMIX ALLIANCE INC *p891*
35 SUNNYHURST AVE SUITE 2, STONEY
CREEK, ON, L8E 5M9
(905) 643-9979 *SIC 5142*

DISTRIBUTION COTE-NORD INC *p1052*
12 AV ROMEO-VEZINA, BAIE-COMEAU,
QC, G4Z 2W2
(418) 296-3300 *SIC 5142*

**DISTRIBUTIONS ALIMENTAIRES MAN-
SION INC, LES** *p1072*
255 AV LIBERTE, CANDIAC, QC, J5R 3X8
(450) 632-5088 *SIC 5142*

ENTREPRISES P.P. HALLE LTEE *p1266*
2610 BOUL WILFRID-HAMEL, QUEBEC,
QC, G1P 2J1
(418) 687-4740 *SIC 5142*

**EXPORT PACKERS COMPANY INCORPO-
RATED** *p502*
107 WALKER DR, BRAMPTON, ON, L6T
5K5
(905) 792-9700 *SIC 5142*

EXPORT PACKERS COMPANY LIMITED
p503
107 WALKER DR, BRAMPTON, ON, L6T
5K5
(905) 792-9700 *SIC 5142*

FRUITION MANUFACTURING LIMITEDp803
2379 SPEERS RD, OAKVILLE, ON, L6L 2X9
(905) 337-6400 *SIC 5142*

FRUITS DE MER LIBERIO INC *p1162*
7337 AV JEAN-VALETS, MONTREAL, QC,
H1E 3H4
(514) 750-4022 *SIC 5142*

GASTRONOMIA ALIMENTS FINS INCp1215
1619B RUE WILLIAM, MONTREAL, QC,
H3J 1R1
(514) 281-6400 *SIC 5142*

**GOLDEN FLEECE FOOD DISTRIBUTORS
AND WHOLESALERS LTD** *p503*
16 BAKER RD, BRAMPTON, ON, L6T 4E3
(905) 458-1101 *SIC 5142*

INTERPROVINCIAL MEAT SALES LIMITED
p446
65 THORNHILL DR, DARTMOUTH, NS,
B3B 1R9
(902) 468-5884 *SIC 5142*

JIM PATTISON ENTERPRISES LTD *p306*
1067 CORDOVA ST W UNIT 1800, VAN-
COUVER, BC, V6C 1C7
(604) 688-6764 *SIC 5142*

JOHN O'S FOODS INC *p1013*
827 DROVERS RD, WHEATLEY, ON, N0P
2P0
(519) 825-4673 *SIC 5142*

LEGUPRO INC *p1291*
1424 RANG DES CHUTES, SAINT-
AMBROISE, QC, G7P 2V4
(418) 672-4717 *SIC 5142*

MANNARICH FOOD INC *p878*
131 FINCHDENE SQ UNIT 10, SCARBOR-
OUGH, ON, M1X 1A6
(905) 471-9656 *SIC 5142*

MEILLEURES MARQUES LTEE *p1062*
1755 BOUL LIONEL-BERTRAND, BOIS-
BRIAND, QC, J7H 1N8
(450) 435-0674 *SIC 5142*

METRO RICHELIEU INC *p1376*
250 BOUL FISET, SOREL-TRACY, QC, J3P
3P7
(450) 742-4563 *SIC 5142*

MILLER & SMITH FOODS INCORPORATED
p575
33 CONNELL CRT, ETOBICOKE, ON, M8Z
1E8
(416) 253-2000 *SIC 5142*

MIMI FOOD PRODUCTS INC *p556*
1260 CREDITSTONE RD UNIT 2-3, CON-
CORD, ON, L4K 5T7

(905) 660-0010 *SIC 5142*
MOM'S PANTRY PRODUCTS LTD *p368*
3241 ST MARY'S RD, WINNIPEG, MB, R2N
4B4
(204) 954-2060 *SIC 5142*

NATURE'S TOUCH FROZEN FOODS INC
p1340
5105-M RUE FISHER, SAINT-LAURENT,
QC, H4T 1J8
(514) 737-7790 *SIC 5142*

NEWFOUNDLAND MULTI-FOODS LIMITED
p424
43 ASPEN RD, HAPPY VALLEY-GOOSE
BAY, NL, A0P 1C0
(709) 896-3543 *SIC 5142*

NOUVEAU TASTE INC *p920*
38 MCGEE ST, TORONTO, ON, M4M 2K9
(416) 778-6300 *SIC 5142*

OLIGEL DISTRIBUTION INC *p1313*
2775 AV BOURDAGES N, SAINT-
HYACINTHE, QC, J2S 5S3
(450) 774-2900 *SIC 5142*

PERREAULT, YVAN & FILS INC *p1154*
235 AV PERREAULT, MONT-JOLI, QC, G5H
3K6
(418) 775-7743 *SIC 5142*

PLACEMENTS BOIVAIN INC *p1293*
149 RUE D'AMSTERDAM, SAINT-
AUGUSTIN-DE-DESMAURES, QC, G3A
2V5
(418) 878-3373 *SIC 5142*

**POISSONERIE ARSENEAU FISH MARKET
LTEE/LTD** *p410*
221 RUE PRINCIPALE, NIGADOO, NB, E8K
3S8
(506) 783-2195 *SIC 5142*

POISSONNERIE COWIE (1985) INC, LA
p1111
660 RUE BERNARD, GRANBY, QC, J2J
0H6
(450) 375-7500 *SIC 5142*

R.J.T. BLUEBERRY PARK INC *p179*
25990 48 AVE, ALDERGROVE, BC, V4W
1J2
(604) 381-4562 *SIC 5142*

RELIANCE FOODS INTERNATIONAL INC
p1120
549 GRAND BOULEVARD, L'ILE-PERROT,
QC, J7V 4X4
(514) 425-1880 *SIC 5142*

REUVEN INTERNATIONAL LIMITED *p924*
1881 YONGE ST SUITE 201, TORONTO,
ON, M4S 3C4
(416) 929-1496 *SIC 5142*

ROUSSE, RAYMOND INC *p1365*
569 RUE ELLEN, SALABERRY-DE-
VALLEYFIELD, QC, J6S 0B1
(450) 373-5085 *SIC 5142*

SKOR FOOD SERVICE LTD *p558*
10 RONROSE DR, CONCORD, ON, L4K
4R3
(905) 660-1212 *SIC 5142*

SYSCO CANADA, INC *p427*
10 OLD PLACENTIA RD, MOUNT PEARL,
NL, A1N 4P5
(709) 748-1200 *SIC 5142*

TERRA NOVA FOODS INC *p434*
49 JAMES LANE, ST. JOHN'S, NL, A1E 3H3
(709) 579-2121 *SIC 5142*

TROCHU MEAT PROCESSORS LTD *p170*
233 NORTH RD, TROCHU, AB, T0M 2C0
(403) 442-4202 *SIC 5142*

TRUMPS FOOD INTEREST LTD *p296*
646 POWELL ST, VANCOUVER, BC, V6A
1H4
(604) 732-8473 *SIC 5142*

TYSON FOODS CANADA INC *p707*
226 BRITANNIA RD E, MISSISSAUGA, ON,
L4Z 1S6
(905) 206-0443 *SIC 5142*

VICTOR CUSTOM QUALITY MEATS LTD
p560
101 CITATION DR UNIT 14, CONCORD,
ON, L4K 2S4

SIC 5142
WYMAN, JASPER & SON CANADA INC
p1042
41 MCQUIN RD, MORELL, PE, C0A 1S0
(902) 961-3330 *SIC 5142*

---

*SIC 5143 Dairy products, except dried or
canned*

2737-2895 QUEBEC INC *p1121*
2152 CH SAINT-JOSEPH, LA BAIE, QC,
G7B 3N9
(418) 544-2622 *SIC 5143*

2747-8353 QUEBEC INC *p1235*
530 PLACE FORAND, MONTREAL, QC,
H7P 5L9
(450) 622-0070 *SIC 5143*

9140-5621 QUEBEC INC *p1357*
222 RUE PRINCIPALE, SAINTE-
ELIZABETH-DE-WARWICK, QC, J0A 1M0
(819) 358-6555 *SIC 5143*

9314-8591 QUEBEC INC *p1063*
1250 RUE NOBEL BUREAU 200,
BOUCHERVILLE, QC, J4B 5H1
(450) 645-2211 *SIC 5143*

AGROPUR COOPERATIVE *p334*
2220 DOWLER PL, VICTORIA, BC, V8T
4H3
(250) 360-5200 *SIC 5143*

AGROPUR COOPERATIVE *p405*
256 LAWLOR LANE, MIRAMICHI, NB, E1V
3Z9
(506) 627-7720 *SIC 5143*

AGROPUR COOPERATIVE *p811*
1001 DAIRY DR, ORLEANS, ON, K4A 3N3
(613) 834-5700 *SIC 5143*

AGROPUR COOPERATIVE *p1063*
81 RUE SAINT-FELIX, BON-CONSEIL, QC,
J0C 1A0
(819) 336-2727 *SIC 5143*

AGROPUR COOPERATIVE *p1309*
4600 RUE ARMAND-FRAPPIER, SAINT-
HUBERT, QC, J3Z 1G5
(450) 878-2333 *SIC 5143*

AGROPUR COOPERATIVE *p1311*
995 RUE DANIEL-JOHNSON E, SAINT-
HYACINTHE, QC, J2S 7V6
(450) 773-6493 *SIC 5143*

ALBERT PERRON INC *p1350*
156 AV ALBERT-PERRON, SAINT-PRIME,
QC, G8J 1L4
(418) 251-3164 *SIC 5143*

ALIMENTS MATRIX INC, LES *p618*
896 CECILE BLVD, HAWKESBURY, ON,
K6A 3R5
(613) 632-8623 *SIC 5143*

BARRY'S BAY DAIRY LTD *p489*
15 DUNN ST, BARRYS BAY, ON, K0J 1B0
(613) 756-2018 *SIC 5143*

BERARDINI, FERNANDO INC *p1325*
80 RUE STINSON, SAINT-LAURENT, QC,
H4N 2E7
(514) 744-9412 *SIC 5143*

BRR LOGISTICS LIMITED *p542*
24 MCGREGOR PL, CHATHAM, ON, N7M
5J4
(519) 352-4120 *SIC 5143*

**CENTRAL ONTARIO DAIRY DISTRIBUTING
INC** *p705*
5820 KENNEDY RD, MISSISSAUGA, ON,
L4Z 2C3
(905) 501-9168 *SIC 5143*

CHRISTIE'S DAIRY LIMITED *p489*
4819 UNION RD, BEAMSVILLE, ON, L0R
1B4
(905) 563-8841 *SIC 5143*

CLOVER LEAF CHEESE LTD *p22*
1201 45 AVE NE, CALGARY, AB, T2E 2P2
(403) 250-3780 *SIC 5143*

DAIRY FARMERS OF NEW BRUNSWICK
p412
29 MILK BOARD RD, ROACHVILLE, NB,
E4G 2G7
(506) 432-4330 *SIC 5143*

DAIRY PRODUCTS IN MOTION INC *p738*
6045 EDWARDS BLVD, MISSISSAUGA,
ON, L5T 2W7
(905) 565-5210 *SIC 5143*

DEVELOPPEMENT BONNET INC *p1298*
54 RUE PRINCIPALE, SAINT-DAMASE, QC,
J0H 1J0
(450) 797-3301 *SIC 5143*

DISTRIBUTION MFG INC *p1225*
387 RUE DESLAURIERS, MONTREAL, QC,
H4N 1W2
(514) 344-5558 *SIC 5143*

**EMPIRE CHEESE & BUTTER CO-
OPERATIVE** *p539*
1120 COUNTY RD 8, CAMPBELLFORD,
ON, K0L 1L0
(705) 653-3187 *SIC 5143*

FARMERS CO-OPERATIVE DAIRY LIMITED
p455
GD, HALIFAX, NS, B3K 5Y6
SIC 5143

FINICA FOOD SPECIALTIES LIMITED *p739*
65 SUPERIOR BLVD UNIT 1, MISSIS-
SAUGA, ON, L5T 2X9
(905) 696-2770 *SIC 5143*

FROMAGE LA CHAUDIERE INC *p1125*
3226 RUE LAVAL, LAC-MEGANTIC, QC,
G6B 1A4
(819) 583-4664 *SIC 5143*

FROMAGERIE DES BASQUES ENR *p1384*
69 132 RTE O, TROIS-PISTOLES, QC, G0L
4K0
(418) 851-2189 *SIC 5143*

FROMAGERIE DES NATIONS INC *p1236*
3535 NORD LAVAL (A-440) O UNITE 440,
MONTREAL, QC, H7P 5G9
(450) 682-3862 *SIC 5143*

FROMAGES CDA INC *p1049*
8895 3E CROISSANT, ANJOU, QC, H1J
1B6
(514) 648-7997 *SIC 5143*

FRULACT CANADA INC *p633*
1295 CENTENNIAL DR, KINGSTON, ON,
K7P 0R6
(613) 507-7500 *SIC 5143*

GLACIER BILBOQUET INC, LE *p1217*
6833 AV DU PARC, MONTREAL, QC, H3N
1W8
SIC 5143

HEWITT'S DAIRY LIMITED *p607*
128 KING ST E, HAGERSVILLE, ON, N0A
1H0
(905) 768-3524 *SIC 5143*

IMPORTATION BERCHICCI LTEE *p1344*
6205 BOUL COUTURE, SAINT-LEONARD,
QC, H1P 3G7
(514) 325-2020 *SIC 5143*

KAWARTHA DAIRY LIMITED *p494*
3332 COUNTY RD 36 S, BOBCAYGEON,
ON, K0M 1A0
(705) 738-5123 *SIC 5143*

KRINOS FOODS CANADA LTD *p554*
251 DONEY CRES, CONCORD, ON, L4K
1P6
(905) 669-4414 *SIC 5143*

MAPLE DALE CHEESE INC *p846*
2864 HWY 37, PLAINFIELD, ON, K0K 2V0
(613) 477-2454 *SIC 5143*

MARC VILLENEUVE INC *p1395*
2050 RUE CHICOINE, VAUDREUIL-
DORION, QC, J7V 8P2
(450) 424-4616 *SIC 5143*

MONDO FOODS CO. LTD *p391*
40 OTTER ST, WINNIPEG, MB, R3T 4J7
(204) 453-7722 *SIC 5143*

**ORGANIC MEADOW LIMITED PARTNER-
SHIP** *p601*
335 LAIRD RD UNIT 1, GUELPH, ON, N1G
4P7
(519) 767-9694 *SIC 5143*

PARENT, ALAIN INC *p1057*
640 RUE NOTRE-DAME, BERTHIERVILLE,
QC, J0K 1A0
(450) 836-4480 *SIC 5143*

PARMALAT CANADA INC *p1222*
1900 AV WESTMORE, MONTREAL, QC, H4B 1Z3
(514) 369-3534 *SIC 5143*

PARMX CHEESE CO. LTD *p31*
4117 16A ST SE, CALGARY, AB, T2G 3T7
(403) 237-0707 *SIC 5143*

PHIPPS DESSERTS LTD *p777*
1875 LESLIE ST UNIT 21, NORTH YORK, ON, M3B 2M5
(416) 391-5800 *SIC 5143*

PRODUITS ALIMENTAIRES ANCO LTEE, LES *p1309*
4700 RUE ARMAND-FRAPPIER, SAINT-HUBERT, QC, J3Z 1G5
(450) 443-4838 *SIC 5143*

PRODUITS SAINT-HENRI INC, LES *p1067*
91 RUE DE LA BARRE BUREAU 2, BOUCHERVILLE, QC, J4B 2X6
(450) 449-9799 *SIC 5143*

SAPUTO INC *p175*
1799 RIVERSIDE RD SUITE 48, ABBOTS-FORD, BC, V2S 4J8
(604) 853-2225 *SIC 5143*

SAPUTO PRODUITS LAITIERS CANADA S.E.N.C. *p1327*
100 RUE STINSON, SAINT-LAURENT, QC, H4N 2E7
(514) 328-3312 *SIC 5143*

SAPUTO PRODUITS LAITIERS CANADA S.E.N.C. *p1327*
2365 CH DE LA COTE-DE-LIESSE, SAINT-LAURENT, QC, H4N 2M7
(514) 328-6663 *SIC 5143*

TOTALE ALIMENTATION INC *p1089*
130 CH SAINT-MICHEL RR 3, CRABTREE, QC, J0K 1B0
(450) 754-3785 *SIC 5143*

TRANSCOLD DISTRIBUTION LTD *p207*
1460 CLIVEDEN AVE, DELTA, BC, V3M 6L9
(604) 519-0600 *SIC 5143*

TRANSPORT DP INC *p1154*
1213 RUE INDUSTRIELLE, MONT-JOLI, QC, G5H 3T9
(418) 775-1311 *SIC 5143*

VIANDEX INC *p1261*
199 RUE JOLY, QUEBEC, QC, G1L 1N7
(418) 780-3211 *SIC 5143*

SIC 5144 Poultry and poultry products

116278 CANADA INC *p1183*
365 RUE BEAUBIEN O, MONTREAL, QC, H2V 1C8
(514) 495-2435 *SIC 5144*

1426420 ONTARIO INC *p566*
161 HWY 8, DUNDAS, ON, L9H 5E1
(905) 627-2228 *SIC 5144*

149942 CANADA INC *p1233*
1955 RUE MONTEREY, MONTREAL, QC, H7L 3T6
(450) 688-7660 *SIC 5144*

1729787 ONTARIO LIMITED *p906*
133 FRONT ST N SUITE 1, THOROLD, ON, L2V 0A3
(905) 227-2015 *SIC 5144*

9181-2958 QUEBEC INC *p1154*
2443 CH DU 5E-RANG S, MONT-LAURIER, QC, J9L 3G7
(819) 623-5672 *SIC 5144*

ADP DIRECT POULTRY LTD *p573*
34 VANSCO RD, ETOBICOKE, ON, M8Z 5J4
(416) 658-0911 *SIC 5144*

ALIMENTS LA BROCHETTE INC, LES *p1158*
404 RTE 104, MONT-SAINT-GREGOIRE, QC, J0J 1K0
(450) 346-4144 *SIC 5144*

BELWOOD POULTRY LIMITED *p477*
4272 4TH CONC N, AMHERSTBURG, ON, N9V 2Y9
(519) 736-2236 *SIC 5144*

BURNBRAE FARMS LIMITED *p663*

3356 COUNTY ROAD 27, LYN, ON, K0E 1M0
(613) 345-5651 *SIC 5144*

CANADIAN EGG MARKETING AGENCY *p833*
21 FLORENCE ST, OTTAWA, ON, K2P 0W6
(613) 238-2514 *SIC 5144*

CANTON POULTRY MEATS INC *p1010*
670 SUPERIOR DR, WATERLOO, ON, N2V 2C6
(519) 746-1390 *SIC 5144*

CHAI POULTRY INC *p920*
115 SAULTER ST S, TORONTO, ON, M4M 3K8
SIC 5144

COOP FEDEREE, LA *p1310*
3250 BOUL LAURIER E, SAINT-HYACINTHE, QC, J2R 2B6
(450) 773-6661 *SIC 5144*

DUNN-RITE FOOD PRODUCTS LTD *p390*
199 HAMELIN ST, WINNIPEG, MB, R3T 0P2
(204) 452-8379 *SIC 5144*

EGGSOLUTIONS - VANDERPOLS INC *p176*
3911 MT LEHMAN RD, ABBOTSFORD, BC, V2T 5W5
(604) 856-4127 *SIC 5144*

ENTREPRISES ROBERT CHARETTE INC, LES *p1303*
1003 3E RANG, SAINT-GABRIEL-DE-BRANDON, QC, J0K 2N0
(450) 835-7988 *SIC 5144*

EPIC FOODS INC *p702*
3258 WHARTON WAY, MISSISSAUGA, ON, L4X 2C1
SIC 5144

FERME ST-OURS INC *p1349*
8 RUE BOURGEOIS, SAINT-OURS, QC, J0G 1P0
(450) 785-2148 *SIC 5144*

FERME ST-ZOTIQUE LTEE *p1354*
200 69E AV, SAINT-ZOTIQUE, QC, J0P 1Z0
(450) 267-3521 *SIC 5144*

FLINTSHIRE FARMS INC *p591*
79 PHEASANT FARM RD, FLINTON, ON, K0H 1P0
(613) 336-8552 *SIC 5144*

GRANNY'S POULTRY COOPERATIVE (MANITOBA) LTD *p362*
750 PANDORA AVE E, WINNIPEG, MB, R2C 4G5
(204) 925-6260 *SIC 5144*

GRAY, L. H. & SON LIMITED *p897*
644 WRIGHT ST, STRATHROY, ON, N7G 3H8
(519) 245-0480 *SIC 5144*

GROUPE NUTRI INC *p1312*
6655 RUE PICARD, SAINT-HYACINTHE, QC, J2S 1H3
(514) 745-1045 *SIC 5144*

HUTTERITE BRETHREN CHURCH OF BELLE PLAINE *p1404*
GD, BELLE PLAINE, SK, S0G 0G0
(306) 345-2544 *SIC 5144*

J & K POULTRY LTD *p295*
771 CORDOVA ST E, VANCOUVER, BC, V6A 1M2
(604) 253-8292 *SIC 5144*

KING CAPON LIMITED *p880*
18347 WARDEN AVE, SHARON, ON, L0G 1V0
(905) 478-2382 *SIC 5144*

LEKIU POULTRY (2006) LTD *p295*
458 PRIOR ST, VANCOUVER, BC, V6A 2E5
(604) 681-1999 *SIC 5144*

MAN-KWONG ENTERPRISES LTD *p295*
1233 GLEN DR, VANCOUVER, BC, V6A 3M8
(604) 254-3688 *SIC 5144*

MAPLE LEAF FOODS INC *p617*
90 10TH AVE, HANOVER, ON, N4N 3B8
(519) 364-3200 *SIC 5144*

MARITIME PRIDE EGGS INC *p438*
50 TANTRAMAR CRES, AMHERST, NS,

B4H 0A1
(800) 563-2246 *SIC 5144*

NATIONAL EGG INC *p897*
644 WRIGHT ST, STRATHROY, ON, N7G 3H8
(519) 245-0480 *SIC 5144*

NEPCO INC *p1172*
6569 AV PAPINEAU, MONTREAL, QC, H2G 2X3
(514) 729-0404 *SIC 5144*

NEWFOUNDLAND EGGS, INC *p422*
1 ROACHES LINE, CLARKES BEACH, NL, A0A 1W0
(709) 528-4595 *SIC 5144*

NIKOLAOS FINE FOODS INC. *p615*
225 NEBO RD UNIT 5, HAMILTON, ON, L8W 2E1
(905) 388-8074 *SIC 5144*

OEUFS OVALE S.E.C., LES *p1323*
205 RUE DAMASE-BRETON, SAINT-LAMBERT-DE-LAUZON, QC, G0S 2W0
(418) 889-8088 *SIC 5144*

OVALE SEC *p1323*
205 RUE DAMASE-BRETON, SAINT-LAMBERT-DE-LAUZON, QC, G0S 2W0
(418) 889-8088 *SIC 5144*

PHLYN HOLDINGS LTD *p391*
199 HAMELIN ST, WINNIPEG, MB, R3T 0P2
(204) 452-8379 *SIC 5144*

PLANWAY POULTRY INC *p575*
26 CANMOTOR AVE, ETOBICOKE, ON, M8Z 4E5
(416) 252-7676 *SIC 5144*

POULETS RIVERVIEW INC *p1364*
287 RUE MASSON, SAINTE-SOPHIE-DE-LEVRARD, QC, G0X 3C0
(450) 431-1140 *SIC 5144*

PRODUCTIONS AGRICOLES OUELLET, LES *p404*
1119 ROUTE 280, MCLEODS, NB, E3N 5W6
(506) 753-3736 *SIC 5144*

SARGENT FARMS LIMITED *p684*
189 MILL ST, MILTON, ON, L9T 1S3
(905) 878-4401 *SIC 5144*

STAR EGG CO. LTD *p1430*
1302 QUEBEC AVE, SASKATOON, SK, S7K 1V5
(306) 244-4041 *SIC 5144*

STARBRITE HUTTERIAN BRETHREN *p127*
GD, FOREMOST, AB, T0K 0X0
(403) 867-2299 *SIC 5144*

SUPERIOR POULTRY PROCESSORS LTD *p199*
2784 ABERDEEN AVE, COQUITLAM, BC, V3B 1A3
(604) 464-0533 *SIC 5144*

SURE FRESH FOODS INC *p497*
3855 LINE 4, BRADFORD, ON, L3Z 0Z1
(905) 939-2962 *SIC 5144*

T & R SARGENT FARMS LIMITED *p685*
189 MILL ST, MILTON, ON, L9T 1S3
(905) 878-4401 *SIC 5144*

TNT FOODS INTERNATIONAL INC *p507*
20 WESTWYN CRT, BRAMPTON, ON, L6T 4T5
(905) 672-1787 *SIC 5144*

UNION POULTRY CANADA INC *p676*
70 DENISON ST SUITE 2, MARKHAM, ON, L3R 1B6
(905) 305-1913 *SIC 5144*

UNITED POULTRY CO LTD *p296*
534 CORDOVA ST E, VANCOUVER, BC, V6A 1L7
(604) 255-9308 *SIC 5144*

VIANDES BERNARD CENTRALE INC, LES *p1129*
2001 AV 32E, LACHINE, QC, H8T 3J1
(514) 780-8585 *SIC 5144*

VOLAILLES ET VIANDE AMGA LTEE *p1337*
9555 RTE TRANSCANADIENNE, SAINT-LAURENT, QC, H4S 1V3
(514) 273-8848 *SIC 5144*

VOLAILLES REGAL INC *p1363*
955 RUE MICHELIN, SAINTE-ROSE, QC, H7L 5B6
(450) 667-7070 *SIC 5144*

VYEFIELD ENTERPRISES LTD *p32*
3815 16 ST SE, CALGARY, AB, T2G 4W5
(403) 290-1838 *SIC 5144*

SIC 5145 Confectionery

1161396 ONTARIO INC *p796*
2965 BRISTOL CIR BLDG C, OAKVILLE, ON, L6H 6P9
(905) 829-2229 *SIC 5145*

620126 ALBERTA LTD *p108*
6803 72 AVE NW, EDMONTON, AB, T6B 3A5
(780) 465-3499 *SIC 5145*

9252-9064 QUEBEC INC *p1358*
2090 RUE BOMBARDIER, SAINTE-JULIE, QC, J3E 2J9
(450) 649-1331 *SIC 5145*

ARYZTA CANADA CO *p515*
115 SINCLAIR BLVD SUITE 1, BRANT-FORD, ON, N3S 7X6
(519) 720-2000 *SIC 5145*

BASSE FRERES ALIMENTATION ORIEN-TALE (2013) INC *p1235*
4555 NORD LAVAL (A-440) O, MONTREAL, QC, H7P 4W6
(450) 781-1255 *SIC 5145*

CENTRAL ROAST INC *p738*
6880 COLUMBUS RD, MISSISSAUGA, ON, L5T 2G1
(416) 661-7366 *SIC 5145*

CONFISERIE MONDOUX INC *p1083*
1610 PLACE DE LIERRE, COTE SAINT-LUC, QC, H7G 4X7
(450) 669-1311 *SIC 5145*

CONFISERIES REGAL INC *p1233*
1625 BOUL DAGENAIS O, MONTREAL, QC, H7L 5A3
(450) 628-6700 *SIC 5145*

CONFISERIES REGAL INC *p1328*
4620 BOUL THIMENS, SAINT-LAURENT, QC, H4R 2B2
(514) 333-8540 *SIC 5145*

COURTNEY WHOLESALE CONFEC-TIONERY LIMITED *p648*
600 THIRD ST, LONDON, ON, N5V 2C2
(519) 451-7440 *SIC 5145*

DISTRIBUTIONS YVAN NADEAU INC, LES *p1377*
11 RANG SAINT-LEON N, STANDON, QC, G0R 4L0
(418) 642-5035 *SIC 5145*

EXCLUSIVE CANDY AND NOVELTY DIS-TRIBUTING LIMITED *p739*
1832 BONHILL RD, MISSISSAUGA, ON, L5T 1C4
(905) 795-8781 *SIC 5145*

FKK WHOLESALE CASH & CARRY INC *p790*
920 CALEDONIA RD SUITE 2, NORTH YORK, ON, M6B 3Y1
(416) 783-1197 *SIC 5145*

HUER FOODS INC *p229*
5543 275 ST, LANGLEY, BC, V4W 3X9
(604) 626-4888 *SIC 5145*

HUSKY FOOD IMPORTERS & DISTRIBU-TORS LIMITED *p1027*
155 RAINBOW CREEK DR, WOOD-BRIDGE, ON, L4H 0A4
(905) 850-8288 *SIC 5145*

INDULBEC INC *p1236*
3625 BOUL CURE-LABELLE BUREAU 100, MONTREAL, QC, H7P 0A5
(450) 689-5726 *SIC 5145*

ITWAL LIMITED *p513*
440 RAILSIDE DR, BRAMPTON, ON, L7A 1L1
(905) 840-9400 *SIC 5145*

JOHNVINCE FOODS *p783*

555 STEEPROCK DR, NORTH YORK, ON, M3J 2Z6

(416) 636-6146   *SIC* 5145

KL FOODS INC   *p671*

235 HOOD RD UNIT 3, MARKHAM, ON, L3R 4N3

(905) 479-9048   *SIC* 5145

LEESE ENTERPRISES INTERNATIONAL INC   *p988*

1210 EGLINTON AVE W, TORONTO, ON, M6C 2E3

(416) 781-8404   *SIC* 5145

LINDT & SPRUNGLI (CANADA), INC   *p954*

181 UNIVERSITY AVE SUITE 900, TORONTO, ON, M5H 3M7

(416) 351-8566   *SIC* 5145

LUDIK DESIGNER CONFISEUR INC   *p1297*

660 RTE 112, SAINT-CESAIRE, QC, J0L 1T0

(450) 469-0514   *SIC* 5145

MARVIN ENTERPRISES INC   *p1016*

3627 COCHRANE ST, WHITBY, ON, L1R 2T2

(905) 665-5686   *SIC* 5145

MAY, J. K. INVESTMENTS LTD   *p379*

149 PIONEER AVE, WINNIPEG, MB, R3C 0H2

(204) 943-8525   *SIC* 5145

MENTHES RITO LTEE, LES   *p1388*

1055 RUE LA VERENDRYE, TROIS-RIVIERES, QC, G9A 2T1

(819) 379-1449   *SIC* 5145

MORRIS NATIONAL INC   *p556*

100 JACOB KEFFER PKY, CONCORD, ON, L4K 4W3

(905) 879-7777   *SIC* 5145

MORRIS NATIONAL INC   *p1131*

2235 RUE LAPIERRE, LASALLE, QC, H8N 1B7

(514) 368-1000   *SIC* 5145

NOR-LAB LIMITED   *p424*

8 LONDON ST, HAPPY VALLEY-GOOSE BAY, NL, A0P 1E0

(709) 896-3795   *SIC* 5145

P. A. FINE FOODS AND DISTRIBUTORS LTD   *p1414*

3850 5TH AVE E, PRINCE ALBERT, SK, S6W 0A1

(306) 763-7061   *SIC* 5145

PEPSICO CANADA ULC   *p275*

11811 103A AVE, SURREY, BC, V3V 0B5

(604) 587-8300   *SIC* 5145

PEPSICO CANADA ULC   *p510*

12 CLIPPER CRT, BRAMPTON, ON, L6W 4T9

(905) 460-2400   *SIC* 5145

PEPSICO CANADA ULC   *p662*

40 ENTERPRISE DR SUITE 2, LONDON, ON, N6N 1A1

(519) 668-4004   *SIC* 5145

PEPSICO CANADA ULC   *p865*

1 WATER TOWER GATE, SCARBOROUGH, ON, M1B 6C5

(416) 284-3200   *SIC* 5145

POPPA CORN CORP   *p699*

5135 CREEKBANK RD UNIT C, MISSISSAUGA, ON, L4W 1R3

(905) 212-9855   *SIC* 5145

PREMIER BRANDS CANADA LTD   *p845*

680 GRANITE CRT, PICKERING, ON, L1W 4A3

(416) 750-8807   *SIC* 5145

PUR COMPANY INC, THE   *p784*

23 KODIAK CRES, NORTH YORK, ON, M3J 3E5

(416) 941-7557   *SIC* 5145

ROBERTS, DAVID FOOD CORPORATION   *p799*

2351 UPPER MIDDLE RD E, OAKVILLE, ON, L6H 6P7

(905) 502-7700   *SIC* 5145

ROTISSERIES ST-HUBERT LTEE, LES   *p1050*

9050 IMP DE L'INVENTION, ANJOU, QC,

H1J 3A7

(514) 324-5400   *SIC* 5145

SCOTT-BATHGATE LTD   *p379*

149 PIONEER AVE, WINNIPEG, MB, R3C 0H2

(204) 943-8525   *SIC* 5145

SINCERE TRADING OF K.B.A. CO-OPERATIVE LTD   *p579*

169 THE WEST MALL, ETOBICOKE, ON, M9C 1C2

(416) 789-7544   *SIC* 5145

TAYLOR & GRANT SPECIALTIES LIMITED   *p1007*

151 WEBER ST S SUITE 2, WATERLOO, ON, N2J 2A9

SIC 5145

TOOTSI IMPEX INC   *p1336*

8800 BOUL HENRI-BOURASSA O, SAINT-LAURENT, QC, H4S 1P4

(514) 381-9790   *SIC* 5145

TOOTSIE ROLL OF CANADA ULC   *p559*

345 COURTLAND AVE, CONCORD, ON, L4K 5A6

(905) 660-8989   *SIC* 5145

TROPHY FOODS INC   *p743*

71 ADMIRAL BLVD, MISSISSAUGA, ON, L5T 2T1

(905) 670-8050   *SIC* 5145

TURKEY HILL SUGARBUSH LIMITED   *p1400*

10 RUE DE WATERLOO, WATERLOO, QC, J0E 2N0

(450) 539-4822   *SIC* 5145

VENDING PRODUCTS OF CANADA LIMITED   *p589*

108 WOODBINE DOWNS BLVD UNIT 1, ETOBICOKE, ON, M9W 5S6

(416) 213-8363   *SIC* 5145

WADDEN, F.J. & SONS LIMITED   *p427*

51 GLENCOE DR, MOUNT PEARL, NL, A1N 4S6

(709) 364-1444   *SIC* 5145

SIC 5146 Fish and seafoods

11108204 CANADA INC   *p547*

235 RAYETTE RD UNIT 1A, CONCORD, ON, L4K 2G1

(437) 218-3702   *SIC* 5146

1294711 ALBERTA LTD   *p8*

3515 27 ST NE SUITE 8, CALGARY, AB, T1Y 5E4

(403) 250-8222   *SIC* 5146

1750769 ONTARIO INC   *p833*

504A KENT ST, OTTAWA, ON, K2P 2B9

(613) 231-3474   *SIC* 5146

2210961 ONTARIO LIMITED   *p542*

135 BOTHWELL ST, CHATHAM, ON, N7M 5K5

(519) 354-4600   *SIC* 5146

3092983 NOVA SCOTIA LIMITED   *p459*

877 HIGHWAY 203, KEMPTVILLE, NS, B5A 5R3

(902) 761-2334   *SIC* 5146

310104 ALBERTA LTD   *p161*

278 CREE RD, SHERWOOD PARK, AB, T8A 4G2

(780) 449-3710   *SIC* 5146

3274876 NOVA SCOTIA LIMITED   *p442*

55 ORION WHARF RD, CLARKS HARBOUR, NS, B0W 1P0

(902) 745-2943   *SIC* 5146

602390 ONTARIO LIMITED   *p873*

81 SCOTTFIELD DR, SCARBOROUGH, ON, M1S 5R4

(416) 740-9000   *SIC* 5146

658612 ONTARIO LTD   *p633*

215 INDUSTRY RD, KINGSVILLE, ON, N9Y 1K9

(519) 733-9100   *SIC* 5146

9036-4514 QUEBEC INC   *p1287*

45 RUE WHITELEY, RIVIERE-SAINT-PAUL, QC, G0G 2P0

(418) 379-2087   *SIC* 5146

A & L SEAFOODS LIMITED   *p461*

20 MINTO ST, LOUISBOURG, NS, B1C 1L1

(902) 733-2900   *SIC* 5146

ACADIAN SUPREME INC   *p1043*

8323 11 RTE, WELLINGTON STATION, PE, C0B 2E0

(902) 854-2675   *SIC* 5146

AERO TRADING CO LTD   *p290*

8592 FRASER ST SUITE 200, VANCOUVER, BC, V5X 3Y3

(604) 327-6331   *SIC* 5146

ALIMENTATION TRACY INC   *p1168*

4900 RUE MOLSON, MONTREAL, QC, H1Y 3J8

(450) 743-0644   *SIC* 5146

ALIMENTS FIDAS LTEE, LES   *p1343*

6575 BOUL DES GRANDES-PRAIRIES, SAINT-LEONARD, QC, H1P 3G8

(514) 322-7575   *SIC* 5146

ALL TEMP FOODS LTD   *p644*

15 INDUSTRIAL RD, LEAMINGTON, ON, N8H 4W4

(519) 326-8611   *SIC* 5146

ALLSEAS FISHERIES INC   *p573*

55 VANSCO RD, ETOBICOKE, ON, M8Z 5Z8

(416) 255-3474   *SIC* 5146

ANGEL SEAFOODS LTD   *p290*

8475 FRASER ST, VANCOUVER, BC, V5X 3Y1

(604) 254-2824   *SIC* 5146

ARBUTUS COVE ENTERPRISES INC   *p336*

650 HERALD ST, VICTORIA, BC, V8W 1S7

(250) 598-1387   *SIC* 5146

ATKINSON, LEO G FISHERIES LIMITED   *p442*

89 DANIELS HEAD RD RR 1, CLARKS HARBOUR, NS, B0W 1P0

(902) 745-3047   *SIC* 5146

AZUMA FOODS (CANADA) CO., LTD   *p253*

11451 TWIGG PL, RICHMOND, BC, V6V 3C9

(604) 325-1129   *SIC* 5146

BARRY GROUP INC   *p422*

415 GRIFFIN DR, CORNER BROOK, NL, A2H 3E9

(709) 785-7387   *SIC* 5146

BAYNES SOUND OYSTER LTD   *p284*

5848 ISLAND HWY, UNION BAY, BC, V0R 3B0

(250) 335-2111   *SIC* 5146

BLUNDELL SEAFOODS LTD   *p259*

11351 RIVER RD, RICHMOND, BC, V6X 1Z6

(604) 270-3300   *SIC* 5146

BOTSFORD FISHERIES LTD   *p411*

2112 ROUTE 950, PETIT-CAP, NB, E4N 2J8

(506) 577-4327   *SIC* 5146

BREAKWATER FISHERIES LIMITED   *p462*

13311 HWY 104 AULD'S COVE, MULGRAVE, NS, B0E 2G0

SIC 5146

BROAD COVE FISHERIES   *p449*

1631 CULLODEN RD, DIGBY, NS, B0V 1A0

(902) 532-7301   *SIC* 5146

BRUN FISHERIES LTD   *p411*

73 CH DE L'ILE, PETIT-CAP, NB, E4N 2G6

(506) 577-1157   *SIC* 5146

CALKINS & BURKE LIMITED   *p318*

1500 GEORGIA ST W SUITE 800, VANCOUVER, BC, V6G 2Z6

(604) 669-3741   *SIC* 5146

CANADIAN FISHING COMPANY LIMITED, THE   *p294*

301 WATERFRONT RD E, VANCOUVER, BC, V6A 0B3

(604) 681-0211   *SIC* 5146

CAPE BALD PACKERS, LIMITED   *p396*

2618 CH ACADIE, CAP-PELE, NB, E4N 1E3

(506) 577-4316   *SIC* 5146

CHOICE CANNING COMPANY INC   *p1002*

3100 STEELES AVE W SUITE 603, VAUGHAN, ON, L4K 3R1

(905) 918-3866   *SIC* 5146

CLEAR PACIFIC TRADING LTD   *p263*

12160 HORSESHOE WAY SUITE 120, RICHMOND, BC, V7A 4V5

SIC 5146

CLEARWATER SEAFOODS LIMITED PARTNERSHIP   *p423*

1 PLANT RD, GRAND BANK, NL, A0E 1W0

(709) 832-1550   *SIC* 5146

COASTAL ENTERPRISES LTD   *p398*

48 DIPPER HARBOUR RD, DIPPER HARBOUR, NB, E5J 1X2

SIC 5146

COLD NORTH SEAFOODS LIMITED   *p426*

157 GLENCOE DR SUITE 200, MOUNT PEARL, NL, A1N 4S7

(709) 368-9953   *SIC* 5146

COMEAUVILLE SEAFOOD PRODUCTS LIMITED   *p465*

GD, SAULNIERVILLE, NS, B0W 2Z0

(902) 769-2266   *SIC* 5146

COMPAGNIE DE POISSONS DE MONTREAL LTEE, LA   *p1216*

1647 RUE SAINT-PATRICK, MONTREAL, QC, H3K 3G9

(514) 486-9537   *SIC* 5146

CONCHE SEAFOODS LTD   *p422*

2 HAMBOUR DR, CONCHE, NL, A0K 1Y0

(709) 622-4111   *SIC* 5146

CONNORS BROS. CLOVER LEAF SEAFOODS LIMITED   *p395*

180 BRUNSWICK ST, BLACKS HARBOUR, NB, E5H 1G6

(506) 456-3391   *SIC* 5146

CONNORS BROS. CLOVER LEAF SEAFOODS COMPANY   *p668*

80 TIVERTON CRT SUITE 600, MARKHAM, ON, L3R 0G4

(905) 474-0608   *SIC* 5146

COWIE INC   *p1110*

660 RUE BERNARD, GRANBY, QC, J2J 0H6

(450) 375-7500   *SIC* 5146

D.B. KENNEY FISHERIES LIMITED   *p470*

301 WATER ST, WESTPORT, NS, B0V 1H0

(902) 839-2023   *SIC* 5146

DAILY SEAFOOD INC   *p919*

135 BLAKE ST, TORONTO, ON, M4J 3E2

(416) 461-9449   *SIC* 5146

DAVIS STRAIT FISHERIES LIMITED   *p458*

71 MCQUADE LAKE CRES, HALIFAX, NS, B3S 1C4

(902) 450-5115   *SIC* 5146

DOM INTERNATIONAL LIMITED   *p871*

10 GOLDEN GATE CRT, SCARBOROUGH, ON, M1P 3A5

(416) 265-3993   *SIC* 5146

EMPAQUETEURS UNIS DE FRUITS DE MER LTEE, LES   *p1344*

6575 BOUL DES GRANDES-PRAIRIES, SAINT-LEONARD, QC, H1P 3G8

(514) 322-5888   *SIC* 5146

EVERGREEN INTERNATIONAL FOODSTUFFS LTD   *p285*

1944 FRANKLIN ST, VANCOUVER, BC, V5L 1R2

(604) 253-8835   *SIC* 5146

FATHOM FISH & SEAFOOD INC   *p458*

339 HERRING COVE SUITE 215, HALIFAX, NS, B3R 1V5

(902) 407-0700   *SIC* 5146

FISHERMAN'S MARKET INTERNATIONAL INCORPORATED   *p457*

607 BEDFORD HWY, HALIFAX, NS, B3M 2L6

(902) 443-3474   *SIC* 5146

FROBISHER INTERNATIONAL ENTERPRISE LTD   *p205*

787 CLIVEDEN PL UNIT 600, DELTA, BC, V3M 6C7

(604) 523-8108   *SIC* 5146

FRUITS DE MER LAGOON INC   *p1127*

1301 32E AV, LACHINE, QC, H8T 3H2

(514) 383-1383   *SIC* 5146

FRUITS DE MER MADELEINE INC, LES

p1120
546 CH FOUGERE, L'ETANG-DU-NORD,
QC, G4T 3B3
(418) 986-6016   *SIC* 5146

FRUITS DE MER MADELEINE INC, LES
p1120
546 CH FOUGERE, L'ETANG-DU-NORD,
QC, G4T 3B3
(418) 986-6016   *SIC* 5146

FRUITS DE MER STARBOARD INC   p1094
560 AV LEPINE, DORVAL, QC, H9P 1G2
(514) 780-1818   *SIC* 5146

FUNDY BAY ENTERPRISES LTD   p398
65 DIPPER HARBOUR RD, DIPPER HAR-
BOUR, NB, E5J 1X3
(506) 659-2890   *SIC* 5146

FUTURE SEAFOODS INC   p1038
358 NEW RD, BEDEQUE, PE, C0B 1C0
(902) 887-3012   *SIC* 5146

GERRET ENTERPRISES INCORPORATED
p439
58 BOUNDARY ST, BARRINGTON PAS-
SAGE, NS, B0W 1G0
(902) 745-3899   *SIC* 5146

GI-OCEAN INTERNATIONAL LTEE   p1334
9899 RTE TRANSCANADIENNE, SAINT-
LAURENT, QC, H4S 1V1
(514) 339-9994   *SIC* 5146

GIDNEY FISHERIES LIMITED   p449
136 DAKIN PARK RD, DIGBY, NS, B0V 1A0
(902) 834-2775   *SIC* 5146

GOLDEN CROWN FOODS INC   p797
1154 BALLANTRY RD, OAKVILLE, ON, L6H
5M9
(905) 334-9178   *SIC* 5146

**GRAND HALE MARINE PRODUCTS COM-
PANY LIMITED**   p254
11551 TWIGG PL, RICHMOND, BC, V6V
2Y2
(604) 325-9393   *SIC* 5146

GROUPE BELLE-ILE INC   p419
3113 RUE PRINCIPALE, TRACADIE-
SHEILA, NB, E1X 1A2
(506) 395-3374   *SIC* 5146

GROUPE MDMP INC   p1272
2960 BOUL LAURIER BUREAU 380, QUE-
BEC, QC, G1V 4S1
(418) 657-4444   *SIC* 5146

H & H FISHERIES LIMITED   p449
100 GOVERNMENT WHARF RD, EAST-
ERN PASSAGE, NS, B3G 1M5
SIC 5146

HERVIC ENTERPRISES LTD   p439
2896 MELBOURNE RD RR 1, ARCADIA,
NS, B0W 1B0
(902) 742-3981   *SIC* 5146

HOPKINS, H LIMITED   p465
11 BREAKWATER ST, PORT MORIEN, NS,
B1B 1Y5
(902) 737-2244   *SIC* 5146

I. DEVEAU FISHERIES LIMITED   p439
508 HWY 330 NE, BARRINGTON PAS-
SAGE, NS, B0W 1G0
(902) 745-2877   *SIC* 5146

IFC SEAFOOD INC   p1362
5584 BOUL DES ROSSIGNOLS, SAINTE-
ROSE, QC, H7L 5Z1
(450) 682-9144   *SIC* 5146

IVY FISHERIES LTD   p465
3762 OLD SAMBRO RD, SAMBRO, NS,
B3V 1G1
SIC 5146

J & K FISHERY (2001) LIMITED   p462
GD, MERIGOMISH, NS, B0K 1G0
SIC 5146

J K MARINE SERVICES LIMITED   p461
5 COMMERCIAL ST, LOUISBOURG, NS,
B1C 1B5
(902) 733-2739   *SIC* 5146

KENDALL'S FISHERY LIMITED   p427
GD, PORT AU PORT, NL, A0N 1T0
(709) 642-5711   *SIC* 5146

L. & S. MARKETING LTD   p1043
142 DALTON AVE, TIGNISH, PE, C0B 2B0

(902) 882-3105   *SIC* 5146

L. R. JACKSON FISHERIES LIMITED   p848
172 MAIN ST, PORT STANLEY, ON, N5L
1H6
(519) 782-3562   *SIC* 5146

LA NASSA FOODS INC   p634
215 INDUSTRY RD, KINGSVILLE, ON, N9Y
1K9
(519) 733-9100   *SIC* 5146

LAKESHORE FISH MARKET INC   p847
1 PASSMORE AVE, PORT DOVER, ON,
N0A 1N0
(519) 428-8949   *SIC* 5146

LAPOINTE FISH LIMITED   p825
445 CATHERINE ST, OTTAWA, ON, K1R
5T7
(613) 241-1115   *SIC* 5146

LIONS GATE FISHERIES LTD   p210
4179 RIVER RD W, DELTA, BC, V4K 1R9
(604) 946-1361   *SIC* 5146

M. G. FISHERIES LTD   p402
7 NORMAN RD, GRAND MANAN, NB, E5G
2G5
(506) 662-3696   *SIC* 5146

**M.B. PRODUCT RESEARCH DISTRIBUT-
ING INC**   p555
270 PENNSYLVANIA AVE UNIT 11-13,
CONCORD, ON, L4K 3Z7
(905) 660-1421   *SIC* 5146

MACDONALD, J A COMPANY   p1038
4557 WHARF RD, CARDIGAN, PE, C0A
1G0
(902) 583-2020   *SIC* 5146

MARCHE BLAIS INC   p1244
204 BOUL PABOS, PABOS, QC, G0C 2H0
(418) 689-3564   *SIC* 5146

**MARINER NEPTUNE FISH & SEAFOOD
COMPANY LTD**   p371
472 DUFFERIN AVE, WINNIPEG, MB, R2W
2Y6
(204) 589-5341   *SIC* 5146

**MEDEX. FISH IMPORTING & EXPORTING
CO. LTD**   p1032
189 WESTCREEK DR, WOODBRIDGE,
ON, L4L 9N6
(905) 856-8188   *SIC* 5146

MENU-MER LTEE   p1102
153 BOUL RENARD E, GASPE, QC, G4X
5K9
(418) 269-7714   *SIC* 5146

MERSEY SEAFOODS LIMITED   p460
26 BRISTOL AVE, LIVERPOOL, NS, B0T
1K0
(902) 354-3467   *SIC* 5146

MIDLAND FOOD PRODUCTS INC   p586
195 REXDALE BLVD, ETOBICOKE, ON,
M9W 1P7
(416) 741-0123   *SIC* 5146

MIDLAND FOODS (WINNIPEG), INC   p368
900 NAIRN AVE, WINNIPEG, MB, R2L 0X8
(204) 663-3883   *SIC* 5146

MILLS AQUACULTURE INC   p395
5 RUE MILLS, BOUCTOUCHE, NB, E4S
3S3
SIC 5146

MINIGOO FISHERIES INC   p1041
195 EAGLE FEATHER TRAIL, LENNOX IS-
LAND, PE, C0B 1P0
SIC 5146

MURPHY, R & K ENTERPRISES LIMITED
p461
2871 HIGHWAY 334, LOWER WEDGE-
PORT, NS, B0W 2B0
(902) 663-2503   *SIC* 5146

NAGEOIRE LTEE, LA   p404
144 CH DU HAVRE, LE GOULET, NB, E8S
2H1
(506) 336-8808   *SIC* 5146

**NATIONAL HERRING IMPORTING COM-
PANY LTD**   p1050
9820 BOUL RAY-LAWSON, ANJOU, QC,
H1J 1L1
(514) 274-4774   *SIC* 5146

NORTH DELTA SEAFOODS LTD   p209

7857 HUSTON RD, DELTA, BC, V4G 1M1
(604) 582-8268   *SIC* 5146

NORTHERN LIGHTS SEAFOOD INC   p425
44 WATERS ST SUITE 40, MAIN BROOK,
NL, A0K 3N0
(709) 865-3333   *SIC* 5146

OCEANFOOD INDUSTRIES LIMITED   p255
11520 EBURNE WAY, RICHMOND, BC, V6V
2G7
(604) 324-1666   *SIC* 5146

OCEANFOOD SALES LIMITED   p285
1909 HASTINGS ST E, VANCOUVER, BC,
V5L 1T5
(604) 255-1414   *SIC* 5146

OCI HOLDINGS INC   p1042
20 HOPE ST, SOURIS, PE, C0A 2B0
(902) 687-1245   *SIC* 5146

PACIFIC SALMON INDUSTRIES INC   p277
8305 128 ST, SURREY, BC, V3W 4G1
(604) 501-7600   *SIC* 5146

PACIFIC SEAFOODS INTERNATIONAL LTD
p247
9300 TRUSTEE RD, PORT HARDY, BC,
V0N 2P0
(250) 949-8781   *SIC* 5146

PECHERIES NORREF QUEBEC INC, LES
p1169
4900 RUE MOLSON, MONTREAL, QC, H1Y
3J8
(514) 593-9999   *SIC* 5146

PEERLESS FISH COMPANY LIMITED   p427
GD, PETTY HARBOUR, NL, A0A 3H0
(709) 747-1521   *SIC* 5146

PNL INTERNATIONAL TRADING INC   p440
1496 BEDFORD HWY SUITE 212, BED-
FORD, NS, B4A 1E5
(902) 307-2117   *SIC* 5146

POISSONNERIE BLANCHETTE INC   p1355
150 BOUL PERRON E, SAINTE-ANNE-
DES-MONTS, QC, G4V 3A4
(418) 763-9494   *SIC* 5146

POISSONNERIE UNIMER INC   p1273
2500 CH DES QUATRE-BOURGEOIS,
QUEBEC, QC, G1V 4P9
(418) 654-1880   *SIC* 5146

POISSONNERIE VERSEAU II   p1384
152 132 RTE O, TROIS-PISTOLES, QC,
G0L 4K0
(418) 851-1516   *SIC* 5146

PREMIUM SEAFOODS LIMITED   p439
449 VETERANS MEMORIAL DR, ARICHAT,
NS, B0E 1A0
(902) 226-3474   *SIC* 5146

PRESTEVE FOODS LIMITED   p1013
20954 ERIE ST S, WHEATLEY, ON, N0P
2P0
(519) 825-4677   *SIC* 5146

PRESTEVE FOODS LIMITED   p1013
20954 ERIE ST S, WHEATLEY, ON, N0P
2P0
(519) 825-4677   *SIC* 5146

PRODUITS MARINS ST-GODEFROI INC
p1306
157 RUE PRINCIPALE, SAINT-GODEFROI,
QC, G0C 3C0
(418) 752-5578   *SIC* 5146

QUALITY SEAFOODS LIMITED   p471
306 HILTON RD, YARMOUTH, NS, B5A 4A6
(902) 742-9238   *SIC* 5146

RBN FISHERIES LIMITED   p462
65 NEWELL RD, MILL VILLAGE, NS, B0J
2H0
(902) 677-2491   *SIC* 5146

RED ROCK SEAFOODS LTD   p1041
546 MAIN ST, MONTAGUE, PE, C0A 1R0
(902) 549-5087   *SIC* 5146

RUBY SEAS INTERNATIONAL INC   p989
1061 EGLINTON AVE W SUITE 202,
TORONTO, ON, M6C 2C9
(416) 787-3474   *SIC* 5146

RYCOTT WHOLESALE FOODS INC   p608
504 KENORA AVE, HAMILTON, ON, L8E
3X8
(905) 560-2424   *SIC* 5146

S.M. PRODUCTS (B.C.) LTD   p210
3827 RIVER RD W, DELTA, BC, V4K 3N2
(604) 946-7665   *SIC* 5146

SAMBRO FISHERIES LIMITED   p465
40 LENNYS LANE, SAMBRO, NS, B3V 1L5
(902) 868-2140   *SIC* 5146

**SCOTIA GARDEN SEAFOOD INCORPO-
RATED**   p471
112 WATER ST, YARMOUTH, NS, B5A 1L5
(902) 742-2411   *SIC* 5146

SCOTIA HARVEST INC   p449
144 WATER ST, DIGBY, NS, B0V 1A0
(902) 245-6528   *SIC* 5146

SEA AGRA SEAFOOD BROKERAGE LTD
p240
1078 ADDERLEY ST, NORTH VANCOU-
VER, BC, V7L 1T3
(604) 984-3303   *SIC* 5146

SEA MERCHANTS INC   p576
55 VANSCO RD, ETOBICOKE, ON, M8Z
5Z8
(416) 255-2700   *SIC* 5146

SEACORE SEAFOOD INC   p1033
81 AVIVA PARK DR, WOODBRIDGE, ON,
L4L 9C1
(905) 856-6222   *SIC* 5146

SEVEN SEAS FISH CO. LTD   p256
12411 VULCAN WAY, RICHMOND, BC, V6V
1J7
(604) 247-1266   *SIC* 5146

SHEDIAC LOBSTER SHOP LTD   p417
261 MAIN ST, SHEDIAC, NB, E4P 2A6
(506) 532-4302   *SIC* 5146

SMITH, EMERY FISHERIES LIMITED   p465
5309 HWY 3, SHAG HARBOUR, NS, B0W
3B0
(902) 723-2115   *SIC* 5146

SOGELCO INTERNATIONAL INC   p1190
715 RUE DU SQUARE-VICTORIA BUREAU
400, MONTREAL, QC, H2Y 2H7
(514) 849-2414   *SIC* 5146

SOLINE TRADING LTD   p1336
9899 RTE TRANSCANADIENNE, SAINT-
LAURENT, QC, H4S 1V1
(514) 339-1818   *SIC* 5146

SOUTH SHORE SEAFOODS LTD   p1038
6 FOY RD, BLOOMFIELD STATION, PE,
C0B 1E0
(902) 853-4052   *SIC* 5146

SOUTH SHORE TRADING CO. LTD   p419
36 JOHN A TRENHOLM RD, UPPER CAPE,
NB, E4M 2R6
(506) 538-7619   *SIC* 5146

ST ANNS LOBSTER GALLEY LIMITEDp439
51943 CABOT TRAIL, BADDECK, NS, B0E
1B0
(902) 295-3100   *SIC* 5146

ST. HELEN SEAFOODS INC   p990
138 SAINT HELENS AVE, TORONTO, ON,
M6H 0B8
(416) 536-5111   *SIC* 5146

STARBOARD SEAFOOD (ONTARIO) INC
p869
33 UPTON RD, SCARBOROUGH, ON, M1L
2C1
(416) 752-2828   *SIC* 5146

STRICTLY LOBSTER LIMITED   p471
72 WATER ST, YARMOUTH, NS, B5A 1K9
(902) 742-6272   *SIC* 5146

TAI FOONG INVESTMENTS LTD   p879
2900 MARKHAM RD, SCARBOROUGH,
ON, M1X 1E6
(416) 299-7575   *SIC* 5146

TFI FOODS LTD   p875
44 MILNER AVE, SCARBOROUGH, ON,
M1S 3P8
(416) 299-7575   *SIC* 5146

TOPPITS FOODS LTD   p1034
301 CHRISLEA RD, WOODBRIDGE, ON,
L4L 8N4
(905) 850-8900   *SIC* 5146

TRADEX FOODS INC   p338
3960 QUADRA ST UNIT 410, VICTORIA,
BC, V8X 4A3

(250) 479-1355   *SIC* 5146
TRI-STAR SEAFOOD SUPPLY LTD   *p262*
11751 VOYAGEUR WAY, RICHMOND, BC,
V6X 3J4
(604) 273-3324   *SIC* 5146
TWIN SEAFOOD LIMITED   *p461*
6689 WOOD HARBOUR RD, LOWER
WOODS HARBOUR, NS, B0W 2E0
(902) 723-9003   *SIC* 5146
VALIA TRADING CORP   *p707*
4 ROBERT SPECK PKWY 15 FL SUITE
1530, MISSISSAUGA, ON, L4Z 1S1
(647) 701-9656   *SIC* 5146
WAH LOONG LTD   *p257*
5388 PARKWOOD PL, RICHMOND, BC,
V6V 2N1
(604) 273-1688   *SIC* 5146
WORLD LINK FOOD DISTRIBUTORS INC
p450
209 AEROTECH DR UNIT 10-12B, GOFFS,
NS, B2T 1K3
(902) 423-0787   *SIC* 5146

SIC 5147 Meats and meat products

1197283 ONTARIO LIMITED   *p858*
1030 CONFEDERATION ST UNIT 2, SAR-
NIA, ON, N7S 6H1
(519) 383-8837   *SIC* 5147
1376371 ONTARIO INC   *p702*
3066 JARROW AVE, MISSISSAUGA, ON,
L4X 2C7
(905) 238-9818   *SIC* 5147
566735 ONTARIO INC   *p567*
GD LCD MAIN, DUNNVILLE, ON, N1A 2W9
(905) 774-5900   *SIC* 5147
573349 ONTARIO LIMITED   *p573*
121 SHORNCLIFFE RD, ETOBICOKE, ON,
M8Z 5K7
(416) 234-2290   *SIC* 5147
9168-9406 QUEBEC INC   *p1237*
1033 CHOMEDEY (A-13) E, MONTREAL,
QC, H7W 4V3
(450) 668-5888   *SIC* 5147
9256-5589 QUEBEC INC   *p1157*
8593 CH DELMEADE, MONT-ROYAL, QC,
H4T 1M1
(514) 522-1196   *SIC* 5147
9273-9127 QUEBEC INC   *p1231*
575 MONTEE SAINT-FRANCOIS, MON-
TREAL, QC, H7C 2S8
(514) 935-5446   *SIC* 5147
9278-3455 QUEBEC INC   *p1215*
2715 RUE DE READING, MONTREAL, QC,
H3K 1P7
(514) 937-8571   *SIC* 5147
9387-0616 QUEBEC INC   *p1240*
10035 AV PLAZA, MONTREAL-NORD, QC,
H1H 4L5
(514) 321-8260   *SIC* 5147
9387-0616 QUEBEC INC   *p1361*
6625 RUE ERNEST-CORMIER, SAINTE-
ROSE, QC, H7C 2V2
(450) 665-6100   *SIC* 5147
9395-8098 QUEBEC INC   *p1047*
9595 BOUL METROPOLITAIN E, ANJOU,
QC, H1J 3C1
(514) 744-6641   *SIC* 5147
A.C.D. WHOLESALE MEATS LTD   *p993*
140 RYDING AVE, TORONTO, ON, M6N
1H2
(416) 766-2200   *SIC* 5147
ALIMENTATION ASIE-MONTREAL INC
p1381
3010A RUE ANDERSON, TERREBONNE,
QC, J6Y 1W1
(450) 621-3288   *SIC* 5147
ALIMENTS CHATEL INC, LES   *p1231*
575 MONTEE ST FRANCOIS, MONTREAL,
QC, H7C 2S8
(514) 935-5446   *SIC* 5147
ALIMENTS PREMONT INC   *p1354*
1505 RTE LUPIEN, SAINTE-ANGELE-DE-

PREMONT, QC, J0K 1R0
(819) 268-2820   *SIC* 5147
ALIMENTS UNI INC, LES   *p1338*
6100 CH DE LA COTE-DE-LIESSE BU-
REAU 200, SAINT-LAURENT, QC, H4T 1E3
(514) 731-3401   *SIC* 5147
ARMSTRONG, O.H. LIMITED   *p460*
1478 PARK ST, KINGSTON, NS, B0P 1R0
(902) 765-3311   *SIC* 5147
B & C FOOD DISTRIBUTORS LTD   *p266*
6711 BUTLER CRES, SAANICHTON, BC,
V8M 1Z7
(250) 544-2333   *SIC* 5147
BEARTOOTH HOLDINGS LIMITED   *p432*
689 WATER ST, ST. JOHN'S, NL, A1E 1B5
(709) 726-6932   *SIC* 5147
BEEFEATERS INC   *p866*
885 PROGRESS AVE SUITE 318, SCAR-
BOROUGH, ON, M1H 3G3
(416) 289-1554   *SIC* 5147
BOUCHER, O. & FILS LIMITEE   *p1357*
2045 BOUL SAINT-ELZEAR O, SAINTE-
DOROTHEE, QC, H7L 3N7
(450) 682-2400   *SIC* 5147
BOUCHERIE CHARCUTERIE PERRON INC
p1350
145 AV ALBERT-PERRON, SAINT-PRIME,
QC, G8J 1L3
(418) 251-3131   *SIC* 5147
BROTHERS MEAT LIMITED   *p455*
2665 AGRICOLA ST, HALIFAX, NS, B3K
4C7
(902) 455-8774   *SIC* 5147
C.T.S. FOOD BROKERS INC   *p1127*
5025 RUE FRANCOIS-CUSSON, LA-
CHINE, QC, H8T 3K1
(514) 956-0356   *SIC* 5147
CALAHOO MEATS LTD   *p168*
3 54416 RGE RD 280, STURGEON
COUNTY, AB, T8R 1Z5
(780) 458-2136   *SIC* 5147
**CANADIAN AMERICAN BOXED MEAT
CORP**   *p737*
6905 KENDERRY GATE SUITE 2, MISSIS-
SAUGA, ON, L5T 2Y8
(905) 949-8882   *SIC* 5147
CANWORLD FOODS LTD   *p996*
320 NORTH QUEEN ST SUITE 100,
TORONTO, ON, M9C 5K4
(416) 233-1900   *SIC* 5147
CHARCUTERIE LA TOUR EIFFEL INC   *p1261*
485 RUE DES ENTREPRENEURS, QUE-
BEC, QC, G1M 2V2
(418) 687-2840   *SIC* 5147
**CHARLIE'S MEAT & SEAFOOD SUPPLY
LTD**   *p869*
61 SKAGWAY AVE, SCARBOROUGH, ON,
M1M 3T9
(416) 261-1312   *SIC* 5147
CHEF-REDI MEATS INC   *p1431*
501 45TH ST W SUITE 11, SASKATOON,
SK, S7L 5Z9
(306) 665-3266   *SIC* 5147
CHICAGO 58 FOOD PRODUCTS LIMITED
p1030
135 HAIST AVE, WOODBRIDGE, ON, L4L
5V6
(905) 265-1044   *SIC* 5147
CHOYS HOLDINGS INCORPORATED   *p259*
4751 SHELL RD SUITE 2, RICHMOND, BC,
V6X 3H4
(604) 270-6882   *SIC* 5147
CONCORD PREMIUM MEATS LTD   *p551*
125 EDILCAN DR, CONCORD, ON, L4K
3S6
(905) 738-7979   *SIC* 5147
CONCORD PREMIUM MEATS LTD   *p1301*
160 RUE WILLIAMS, SAINT-EUSTACHE,
QC, J7R 0A4
(450) 623-7676   *SIC* 5147
CONESTOGA MEAT PACKERS LTD   *p518*
313 MENNO ST, BRESLAU, ON, N0B 1M0
(519) 648-2506   *SIC* 5147
CONTINENTAL SAUSAGE CO. LTD   *p290*

3585 MAIN ST, VANCOUVER, BC, V5V 3N4
(604) 874-0332   *SIC* 5147
D & S MEAT PRODUCTS LTD   *p473*
220 CLEMENTS RD W UNIT 1, AJAX, ON,
L1S 3K5
(905) 427-9229   *SIC* 5147
DELICANA NORD-OUEST INC   *p1289*
680 AV CHAUSSE, ROUYN-NORANDA,
QC, J9X 4B9
(819) 762-3555   *SIC* 5147
DISTRIBUTIONS PAUL-EMILE DUBE LTEE
p1384
489 RUE NOTRE-DAME E RR 1, TROIS-
PISTOLES, QC, G0L 4K0
(418) 851-1862   *SIC* 5147
EASTERN MEAT SOLUTIONS INC   *p996*
302 THE EAST MALL SUITE 500,
TORONTO, ON, M9B 6C7
(416) 252-2791   *SIC* 5147
FRESHOUSE FOODS LTD   *p593*
71 TODD RD, GEORGETOWN, ON, L7G
4R8
(905) 671-0220   *SIC* 5147
GIBIERS CANABEC INC, LES   *p1293*
115 RUE DES GRANDS-LACS, SAINT-
AUGUSTIN-DE-DESMAURES, QC, G3A 2T9
(418) 843-0782   *SIC* 5147
GLOBE WHOLESALE MEATS INC   *p793*
61 SIGNET DR, NORTH YORK, ON, M9L
2W5
(416) 745-7000   *SIC* 5147
GROBER INC   *p536*
425 DOBBIE DR, CAMBRIDGE, ON, N1T
1S9
(519) 622-2500   *SIC* 5147
H. A. VAILLANCOURT INC   *p1089*
30 BOUL MARIE-VICTORIN, DELSON, QC,
J5B 1A9
(450) 632-2109   *SIC* 5147
HARDY SALES (ALBERTA) LTD   *p229*
27417 GLOUCESTER WAY, LANGLEY, BC,
V4W 3Z8
(604) 856-3911   *SIC* 5147
HARDY SALES LTD   *p229*
27417 GLOUCESTER WAY, LANGLEY, BC,
V4W 3Z8
(604) 856-3911   *SIC* 5147
INNISFAIL MEAT PACKERS LTD   *p137*
5107 47 AVE, INNISFAIL, AB, T4G 1P8
(403) 277-5166   *SIC* 5147
INTERCITY PACKERS LTD   *p255*
1900 NO. 6 RD, RICHMOND, BC, V6V 1W3
(604) 295-2010   *SIC* 5147
LAVERGNE WESTERN BEEF INC   *p748*
3971 NAVAN RD, NAVAN, ON, K4B 1H9
(613) 824-8175   *SIC* 5147
LAWRENCE MEAT PACKING CO. LTD   *p204*
11088 4TH ST, DAWSON CREEK, BC, V1G
4H8
(250) 782-5111   *SIC* 5147
LEAVOY ROWE BEEF CO. LTD   *p703*
3066 JARROW AVE, MISSISSAUGA, ON,
L4X 2C7
(905) 272-2330   *SIC* 5147
LEKKER FOOD DISTRIBUTORS LTD   *p340*
2670 WILFERT RD, VICTORIA, BC, V9B
5Z3
(250) 388-0377   *SIC* 5147
MAISON DU GIBIER INC, LA   *p1280*
585 RUE DE L'ARGON, QUEBEC, QC, G2N
2G7
(418) 849-8427   *SIC* 5147
MAPLE LEAF FOODS INC   *p523*
5100 HARVESTER RD, BURLINGTON, ON,
L7L 4X4
(905) 681-5050   *SIC* 5147
MULDER'S MEAT MARKET (1983) LTD   *p410*
1400 ONONDAGA ST, OROMOCTO, NB,
E2V 2H6
(506) 357-8862   *SIC* 5147
NEW MARKET MEAT PACKERS LTD   *p756*
15452 WARDEN AVE, NEWMARKET, ON,
L3Y 4W1
(905) 836-7001   *SIC* 5147

**NEW ZEALAND AND AUSTRALIAN LAMB
COMPANY LIMITED, THE**   *p577*
10 SHORNCLIFFE RD UNIT 1, ETOBI-
COKE, ON, M9B 3S3
(416) 231-5262   *SIC* 5147
NEWTON'S HI QUALITY MEATS LTD   *p277*
12481 80 AVE, SURREY, BC, V3W 3A4
(604) 596-1528   *SIC* 5147
NORTHBUD DISTRIBUTORS LTD   *p732*
6030 FREEMONT BLVD, MISSISSAUGA,
ON, L5R 3X4
    SIC 5147
NOSSACK FINE MEATS LTD   *p156*
7240 JOHNSTONE DR SUITE 100, RED
DEER, AB, T4P 3Y6
(403) 346-5006   *SIC* 5147
OAK RIDGE MEATS LIMITED   *p352*
1055 BOUNDARY RD, MCCREARY, MB,
R0J 1B0
(204) 835-2365   *SIC* 5147
OLSENS MEAT & PRODUCE LTD   *p416*
391 LANCASTER AVE, SAINT JOHN, NB,
E2M 2L3
(506) 657-0000   *SIC* 5147
OLYMEL S.E.C.   *p1066*
1580 RUE EIFFEL, BOUCHERVILLE, QC,
J4B 5Y1
(514) 858-9000   *SIC* 5147
OLYMEL S.E.C.   *p1385*
531 RUE DES ERABLES, TROIS-
RIVIERES, QC, G8T 7Z7
(819) 376-3770   *SIC* 5147
PENGUIN MEAT SUPPLY LTD   *p279*
19195 33 AVE UNIT 1, SURREY, BC, V3Z
1A1
(604) 531-1447   *SIC* 5147
PIONEER MEATS LTD   *p79*
104 ELK RUN BLVD, CANMORE, AB, T1W
1L1
(403) 678-4109   *SIC* 5147
PRAIRIE MEATS   *p1429*
2326 MILLAR AVE, SASKATOON, SK, S7K
2Y2
(306) 244-4024   *SIC* 5147
PRODUITS ALIMENTAIRES VIAU INC, LES
p1361
6625 RUE ERNEST-CORMIER, SAINTE-
ROSE, QC, H7C 2V2
(450) 665-6100   *SIC* 5147
PRODUITS DE VIANDE PAC-RITE INC, LES
p1162
9090 RUE PIERRE-BONNE, MONTREAL,
QC, H1E 6W5
(514) 524-3557   *SIC* 5147
RETAIL READY FOODS INC   *p956*
130 ADELAIDE ST W SUITE 810,
TORONTO, ON, M5H 3P5
(905) 812-8555   *SIC* 5147
RICHMOND HILL WHOLESALE MEAT LTD
p674
70 DENISON ST SUITE 8, MARKHAM, ON,
L3R 1B6
(905) 513-1817   *SIC* 5147
ROMAN DELI LTD   *p887*
87 HANNOVER DR SUITE 3, ST
CATHARINES, ON, L2W 1A3
(905) 641-5211   *SIC* 5147
ROWE FARM MEATS LIMITED   *p995*
105 RONCESVALLES AVE, TORONTO,
ON, M6R 2K9
(416) 532-3738   *SIC* 5147
RUSS PATERSON LTD   *p369*
49 OMANDS CREEK BLVD, WINNIPEG,
MB, R2R 2V2
(204) 985-5400   *SIC* 5147
RYDING-REGENCY MEAT PACKERS LTD
p994
70 GLEN SCARLETT RD, TORONTO, ON,
M6N 1P4
(416) 763-1611   *SIC* 5147
SALAISON ALPHA LTEE   *p1050*
10800 BOUL DU GOLF, ANJOU, QC, H1J
2Y7
(514) 593-8430   *SIC* 5147

SALAISON LA MAISON DU ROTI INC *p1173*
1969 AV DU MONT-ROYAL E, MONTREAL, QC, H2H 1J5
(514) 521-2448   *SIC 5147*

SALAISON LEVESQUE INC *p1218*
500 AV BEAUMONT, MONTREAL, QC, H3N 1T7
(514) 273-1702   *SIC 5147*

SASKATOON SPECIALTY MEATS LTD *p1425*
106 MELVILLE ST, SASKATOON, SK, S7J 0R1
(306) 653-9292   *SIC 5147*

SMITH QUALITY MEAT & POULTRY INC *p1341*
125 RUE BARR, SAINT-LAURENT, QC, H4T 1W6
(514) 735-2100   *SIC 5147*

SPRINGER'S MEATS INC *p610*
544 PARKDALE AVE N, HAMILTON, ON, L8H 5Y7
(905) 544-0782   *SIC 5147*

ST. HELEN'S MEAT PACKERS LIMITED *p994*
55 GLEN SCARLETT RD, TORONTO, ON, M6N 1P5
(416) 769-1788   *SIC 5147*

SUNRISE POULTRY PROCESSORS LTD *p273*
17565 65A AVE, SURREY, BC, V3S 7B6
(604) 596-9505   *SIC 5147*

SUPREME MEAT SUPPLIES LTD *p187*
1725 MACDONALD AVE, BURNABY, BC, V5C 4P3
(604) 299-0541   *SIC 5147*

SURE GOOD FOODS LTD *p715*
2333 NORTH SHERIDAN WAY SUITE 100, MISSISSAUGA, ON, L5K 1A7
(905) 286-1619   *SIC 5147*

TO-LE-DO FOODSERVICE REALTY HOLDINGS LTD *p393*
2430 MCGILLIVRAY BLVD, WINNIPEG, MB, R3Y 1G6
(204) 487-3340   *SIC 5147*

TOWNSEND BUTCHERS INC *p881*
419 CONCESSION 14 TOWNSEND, SIMCOE, ON, N3Y 4K3
(519) 426-6750   *SIC 5147*

TRANSPORT LOGI-PRO INC. *p1051*
9001 RUE DU PARCOURS, ANJOU, QC, H1J 2Y1
(514) 493-1717   *SIC 5147*

TREEN PACKERS LTD *p1437*
GD, SWIFT CURRENT, SK, S9H 3V4
(306) 773-4473   *SIC 5147*

VIANDES AGRO INC *p1331*
3100 BOUL DE LA COTE-VERTU BUREAU 210, SAINT-LAURENT, QC, H4R 2J8
(514) 335-6606   *SIC 5147*

VIANDES BOVITENDRES INC *p1235*
95 RUE DE LA POINTE-LANGLOIS, MONTREAL, QC, H7L 3J4
(450) 653-4375   *SIC 5147*

VIANDES C.D.S. INC, LES *p1080*
598 BOUL DU SAGUENAY O, CHICOUTIMI, QC, G7J 1H4
(418) 549-9614   *SIC 5147*

VIANDES FRANCOEUR INC, LES *p1359*
1841 RUE LAVOISIER, SAINTE-JULIE, QC, J3E 1Y6
(450) 922-4538   *SIC 5147*

VIANDES MONTCALM INC, LES *p1051*
7755 RUE GRENACHE, ANJOU, QC, H1J 1C4
(514) 327-1310   *SIC 5147*

VIANDES OR-FIL INTERNATIONAL INC, LES *p1235*
2080 RUE MONTEREY, MONTREAL, QC, H7L 3S3
(450) 687-5664   *SIC 5147*

VIANDES P.P. HALLE LTEE, LES *p1268*
2610 BOUL WILFRID-HAMEL, QUEBEC, QC, G1P 2J1
(418) 687-4740   *SIC 5147*

VIANDES PERREAULT PELLERIN INC *p1350*
11 RUE DU CURE-VALOIS, SAINT-PAUL, QC, J6E 7L8
(450) 759-8023   *SIC 5147*

VIANDES RIENDEAU LTEE *p1282*
399 RUE DES INDUSTRIES, REPENTIGNY, QC, J5Z 4Y8
(450) 654-6262   *SIC 5147*

VICTORY MEAT MARKET LTD *p402*
334 KING ST, FREDERICTON, NB, E3B 1E3
(506) 458-8480   *SIC 5147*

WHITE VEAL MEAT PACKERS LTD *p561*
5136 9TH LINE, COOKSTOWN, ON, L0L 1L0
(416) 745-7448   *SIC 5147*

WINKLER MEATS LTD *p361*
270 GEORGE AVE, WINKLER, MB, R6W 3M4
(204) 325-9593   *SIC 5147*

WOODWARD MEAT PURVEYORS INC *p805*
1346 SPEERS RD, OAKVILLE, ON, L6L 5V3
(905) 847-7200   *SIC 5147*

WORLD MEATS INC *p718*
2255 DUNWIN DR UNIT 1, MISSISSAUGA, ON, L5L 1A3
(905) 569-0559   *SIC 5147*

SIC 5148 Fresh fruits and vegetables

056729 N.B. LTD *p403*
18 DIVOT DR, HANWELL, NB, E3C 0L2
(506) 457-0305   *SIC 5148*

1068409 ONTARIO LIMITED *p633*
2237 COUNTY RD 31, KINGSVILLE, ON, N9Y 2E5
(519) 326-5919   *SIC 5148*

1248671 ONTARIO INC *p594*
1481 MICHAEL ST UNIT C, GLOUCESTER, ON, K1B 3R5
(613) 742-9999   *SIC 5148*

1362385 ONTARIO LIMITED *p633*
1932 SETTERINGTON DR, KINGSVILLE, ON, N9Y 2E5
SIC 5148

1758691 ONTARIO INC *p620*
21360 BATHURST ST, HOLLAND LANDING, ON, L9N 1P6
(905) 830-0333   *SIC 5148*

2619-0645 QUEBEC INC *p1365*
1658 BOUL SAINTE-MARIE, SALABERRY-DE-VALLEYFIELD, QC, J6T 6M2
(450) 373-0690   *SIC 5148*

2944715 CANADA INC *p1224*
9150 RUE CHARLES-DE LA TOUR, MONTREAL, QC, H4N 1M2
(514) 389-3815   *SIC 5148*

3095-6395 QUEBEC INC *p1097*
1175 BOUL LEMIRE, DRUMMONDVILLE, QC, J2C 7X8
(819) 474-7281   *SIC 5148*

480412 B.C. LTD *p294*
645 MALKIN AVE, VANCOUVER, BC, V6A 3V7
(604) 255-6684   *SIC 5148*

9058-7239 QUEBEC INC *p1169*
9250 BOUL PIE-IX, MONTREAL, QC, H1Z 4H7
(514) 850-0020   *SIC 5148*

927912 ONTARIO LIMITED *p816*
3150 HAWTHORNE RD SUITE B-1, OTTAWA, ON, K1G 5H5
(613) 247-0099   *SIC 5148*

971016 ONTARIO LIMITED *p858*
1621 ROAD 3, RUTHVEN, ON, N0P 2G0
SIC 5148

A.J. LANZAROTTA WHOLESALE FRUIT & VEGETABLES LTD *p712*
1000 LAKESHORE RD E, MISSISSAUGA, ON, L5E 1E4
(905) 891-0510   *SIC 5148*

AENOS FOOD SERVICES INC *p826*

2455 KALADAR AVE, OTTAWA, ON, K1V 8B9
(613) 736-0310   *SIC 5148*

AGRISTAR INC *p10*
720 28 ST NE SUITE 208, CALGARY, AB, T2A 6R3
(403) 873-5177   *SIC 5148*

AMCO PRODUCE INC *p644*
523 WILKINSON DR, LEAMINGTON, ON, N8H 3V5
(519) 326-9095   *SIC 5148*

AQUAFUCHSIA *p1401*
4881 RUE SHERBROOKE O, WESTMOUNT, QC, H3Z 1G9
(514) 489-8466   *SIC 5148*

ATLANTIC POTATO DISTRIBUTORS LTD *p411*
42 INDUSTRIAL PARK ST, PERTH-ANDOVER, NB, E7H 2J2
(506) 273-6501   *SIC 5148*

B.C. TREE FRUITS LIMITED *p221*
1473 WATER ST, KELOWNA, BC, V1Y 1J6
(250) 470-4200   *SIC 5148*

BAMFORD PRODUCE COMPANY LIMITED *p703*
2501 STANFIELD RD SUITE A, MISSISSAUGA, ON, L4Y 1R6
(905) 615-9400   *SIC 5148*

BASSANO FARMS LTD *p10*
923 28 ST NE, CALGARY, AB, T2A 7X1
(403) 273-4557   *SIC 5148*

BC FRESH VEGETABLES INC *p210*
4363 KING ST, DELTA, BC, V4K 0A5
(604) 946-3139   *SIC 5148*

BC TREE FRUITS COOPERATIVE *p221*
1473 WATER ST, KELOWNA, BC, V1Y 1J6
(250) 470-4200   *SIC 5148*

BEAUVAIS LTEE *p1072*
264 AV LIBERTE, CANDIAC, QC, J5R 6X1
(514) 871-0226   *SIC 5148*

BLUSH LANE ORGANIC PRODUCE LTD *p75*
10 ASPEN STONE BLVD SW SUITE 3000, CALGARY, AB, T3H 0K3
(403) 210-1247   *SIC 5148*

BONCHEFF GREENHOUSES INC *p573*
382 OLIVEWOOD RD, ETOBICOKE, ON, M8Z 2Z9
(416) 233-1800   *SIC 5148*

BONDI PRODUCE CO. LTD *p995*
188 NEW TORONTO ST, TORONTO, ON, M8V 2E8
(416) 252-7799   *SIC 5148*

BRADFORD & DISTRICT PRODUCE LTD *p497*
355 DISSETTE ST, BRADFORD, ON, L3Z 3H1
(905) 775-9633   *SIC 5148*

BURNAC PRODUCE LIMITED *p1027*
80 ZENWAY BLVD, WOODBRIDGE, ON, L4H 3H1
(905) 856-9064   *SIC 5148*

CAN-AM PRODUCE & TRADING LTD *p294*
886 MALKIN AVE, VANCOUVER, BC, V6A 2K7
(604) 253-8834   *SIC 5148*

CANADA GARLIC IMPORTING INC *p705*
315 TRADERS BLVD E UNIT 2, MISSISSAUGA, ON, L4Z 3E4
(905) 501-8868   *SIC 5148*

CANADAWIDE FRUIT WHOLESALERS INC *p1225*
1370 RUE DE BEAUHARNOIS O BUREAU 200, MONTREAL, QC, H4N 1J5
(514) 382-3232   *SIC 5148*

CANADIAN FRUIT & PRODUCE COMPANY INC *p572*
165 THE QUEENSWAY SUITE 306, ETOBICOKE, ON, M8Y 1H8
(416) 259-5007   *SIC 5148*

CANNEBERGES BECANCOUR MANAGEMENT INC *p1347*
94 RANG SAINT-FRANCOIS, SAINT-LOUIS-DE-BLANDFORD, QC, G0Z 1B0
(819) 364-3853   *SIC 5148*

CAPESPAN NORTH AMERICA INC *p1338*
6700 CH DE LA COTE-DE-LIESSE BUREAU 301, SAINT-LAURENT, QC, H4T 2B5
(514) 739-9181   *SIC 5148*

CAPESPAN NORTH AMERICA INC *p1338*
6700 CH DE LA COTE-DE-LIESSE BUREAU 301, SAINT-LAURENT, QC, H4T 2B5
(514) 739-9181   *SIC 5148*

CAROPAC INC *p1357*
736 3E RANG, SAINTE-CLOTILDE-DE-CHATEAUGUAY, QC, J0L 1W0
(450) 826-3145   *SIC 5148*

CATANIA, M. L. COMPANY LIMITED *p708*
575 ORWELL ST SUITE 3, MISSISSAUGA, ON, L5A 2W4
(416) 236-9394   *SIC 5148*

CHENAIL FRUITS ET LEGUMES INC *p1180*
340 RUE BELLARMIN, MONTREAL, QC, H2P 1G5
(514) 858-7540   *SIC 5148*

CHILL FRESH PRODUCE INC *p533*
1170 FRANKLIN BLVD UNIT B, CAMBRIDGE, ON, N1R 7J2
(519) 896-0124   *SIC 5148*

CHIOVITTI BANANA COMPANY LIMITED *p574*
26 MAGNIFICENT RD, ETOBICOKE, ON, M8Z 4T3
(416) 251-3774   *SIC 5148*

COMMERCE JARDINO FRESH INC *p1161*
8145 AV MARCO-POLO, MONTREAL, QC, H1E 5Y8
(514) 664-5566   *SIC 5148*

COURCHESNE, LAROSE, LIMITEE *p1048*
9761 BOUL DES SCIENCES, ANJOU, QC, H1J 0A6
(514) 525-6381   *SIC 5148*

DAN'S PRODUCE LIMITED *p760*
7201 BEECHWOOD RD, NIAGARA FALLS, ON, L2H 0W8
(905) 356-1560   *SIC 5148*

DEL SOL GREENHOUSES INC *p633*
1665 GRAHAM, KINGSVILLE, ON, N9Y 2E4
(519) 733-8373   *SIC 5148*

DEODATO, TONY & SONS LIMITED *p632*
100 BINNINGTON CRT, KINGSTON, ON, K7M 8N1
(613) 548-3073   *SIC 5148*

DISTAMAX INC *p1384*
522 RUE DES ERABLES, TROIS-RIVIERES, QC, G8T 7Z6
(819) 375-2147   *SIC 5148*

DISTRIBUTEURS ESSEX CONTINENTALE INC, LES *p1225*
985 RUE DU MARCHE-CENTRAL, MONTREAL, QC, H4N 1K2
(514) 745-1222   *SIC 5148*

DISTRIBUTION FISHER CAPESPAN CANADA *p1339*
6700 CH DE LA COTE-DE-LIESSE BUREAU 301, SAINT-LAURENT, QC, H4T 2B5
(514) 739-9181   *SIC 5148*

DISTRIBUTIONS AGRI-SOL INC *p1225*
1509 RUE ANTONIO-BARBEAU, MONTREAL, QC, H4N 2R5
(514) 381-4804   *SIC 5148*

DISTROBEL INC *p1394*
436 RUE VALOIS, VAUDREUIL-DORION, QC, J7V 1T4
SIC 5148

DOMINION CITRUS LIMITED *p996*
165 THE QUEENSWAY SUITE 302, TORONTO, ON, M8Y 1H8
(416) 242-8341   *SIC 5148*

DON'S PRODUCE INC *p842*
1535 SNYDER'S RD E, PETERSBURG, ON, N0B 2H0
(519) 634-1077   *SIC 5148*

DONATO FRUITS ET LEGUMES INC *p1225*
1605 RUE DE BEAUHARNOIS O, MONTREAL, QC, H4N 1J6
(514) 388-1622   *SIC 5148*

EARTHFRESH FARMS INC *p522*

1095 CLAY AVE, BURLINGTON, ON, L7L
0A1

(416) 251-2271   *SIC* 5148

EARTHFRESH FOODS CORP   *p*522

1095 CLAY AVE, BURLINGTON, ON, L7L
0A1

(416) 251-2271   *SIC* 5148

**EDMONTON POTATO GROWERS COOPER-
ATIVE INC**   *p*105

12220 170 ST NW, EDMONTON, AB, T5V
1L7

(780) 447-1860   *SIC* 5148

EL DORADO VEGETABLE FARMS LTD*p*158

860 BROADWAY AVE W, REDCLIFF, AB,
T0J 2P0

(403) 548-6671   *SIC* 5148

ELISSA GROUP CO   *p*626

4 MARICONA WAY, KANATA, ON, K2T 1H1

(613) 799-6473   *SIC* 5148

ERIE-JAMES LIMITED   *p*644

102 QUEENS AVE, LEAMINGTON, ON,
N8H 3H4

(519) 326-4417   *SIC* 5148

EVERGREEN HERBS LTD   *p*279

3727 184 ST, SURREY, BC, V3Z 1B8

(604) 576-2567   *SIC* 5148

**EXETER PRODUCE AND STORAGE COM-
PANY, LIMITED**   *p*590

215 THAMES RD W SS 3, EXETER, ON,
N0M 1S3

(519) 235-0141   *SIC* 5148

F.G. LISTER & CO., LIMITED   *p*571

475 HORNER AVE, ETOBICOKE, ON, M8W
4X7

(416) 259-7621   *SIC* 5148

F.P.D. EAST INC   *p*1127

2300 23E AV, LACHINE, QC, H8T 0A3

(514) 428-0331   *SIC* 5148

F.W. WARD & SONS INC   *p*1326

515 DESLAURIERS ST, SAINT-LAURENT,
QC, H4N 1W2

(514) 858-9331   *SIC* 5148

FERME H. DAIGNEAULT & FILS INC   *p*1357

1582 1ER RANG, SAINTE-CLOTILDE-DE-
CHATEAUGUAY, QC, J0L 1W0

(450) 826-0555   *SIC* 5148

FERMES LUFA INC, LES   *p*1225

1400 RUE ANTONIO-BARBEAU BUREAU
201, MONTREAL, QC, H4N 1H5

(514) 669-3559   *SIC* 5148

FERMES V. FORINO & FILS INC, LES*p*1376

298 RANG SAINTE-MELANIE, SHERRING-
TON, QC, J0L 2N0

(450) 454-6307   *SIC* 5148

FINNIGAN GREENHOUSE PRODUCE LTD
*p*412

11021 RUE PRINCIPALE, ROGERSVILLE,
NB, E4Y 2L7

(506) 775-6042   *SIC* 5148

FRESH ADVANCEMENTS INC   *p*572

165 THE QUEENSWAY SUITE 333, ETOBI-
COKE, ON, M8Y 1H8

(416) 259-5400   *SIC* 5148

FRESH DIRECT PRODUCE LTD   *p*294

890 MALKIN AVE, VANCOUVER, BC, V6A
2K6

(604) 255-1330   *SIC* 5148

FRESH START FOODS CANADA LTD   *p*683

2705 DURANTE WAY, MILTON, ON, L9T
5J1

(905) 878-9000   *SIC* 5148

FRESH TASTE PRODUCE LIMITED   *p*572

165 THE QUEENSWAY SUITE 343, ETOBI-
COKE, ON, M8Y 1H8

(416) 255-0157   *SIC* 5148

FRESHLINE FOODS LTD   *p*703

2501 STANFIELD RD SUITE A, MISSIS-
SAUGA, ON, L4Y 1R6

(416) 253-6040   *SIC* 5148

FRESHPOINT VANCOUVER LTD   *p*294

1020 MALKIN AVE, VANCOUVER, BC, V6A
3S9

(604) 253-1551   *SIC* 5148

FRESHPOINT VANCOUVER LTD   *p*1002

1400 CREDITSTONE RD UNIT A,
VAUGHAN, ON, L4K 0E2

SIC 5148

FRUITICANA PRODUCE LTD   *p*276

7676 129A ST, SURREY, BC, V3W 4H7

(604) 502-0005   *SIC* 5148

**FRUITS & LEGUMES ERIC FRECHETTE
INC, LES**   *p*1139

750 RUE JEAN-MARCHAND, LEVIS, QC,
G6Y 9G6

(418) 835-6997   *SIC* 5148

FRUITS & LEGUMES GAETAN BONO INC
*p*1225

995 RUE DU MARCHE-CENTRAL, MON-
TREAL, QC, H4N 1K2

(514) 381-1387   *SIC* 5148

FRUITS DORES INC   *p*1068

1650 RUE PANAMA BUREAU 510,
BROSSARD, QC, J4W 2W4

(450) 923-5856   *SIC* 5148

FRUITS ET LEGUMES BEAUPORT INC
*p*1255

275 AV DU SEMOIR, QUEBEC, QC, G1C
7V5

(418) 661-6938   *SIC* 5148

FRUITS ET LEGUMES BOTSIS INC, LES
*p*1326

140 RUE STINSON, SAINT-LAURENT, QC,
H4N 2E7

(514) 389-7676   *SIC* 5148

GAMBLES ONTARIO PRODUCE INC   *p*572

165 THE QUEENSWAY SUITE 240, ETOBI-
COKE, ON, M8Y 1H8

(416) 259-6391   *SIC* 5148

**GARDEN GROVE DISTRIBUTION (2013)
LTD**   *p*371

440 JARVIS AVE, WINNIPEG, MB, R2W
3A6

SIC 5148

GLOBAL M.J.L. LTEE   *p*1180

8355 RUE JEANNE-MANCE, MONTREAL,
QC, H2P 2Y1

(514) 858-5566   *SIC* 5148

GMASJ ONTARIO INC   *p*793

1290 ORMONT DR, NORTH YORK, ON,
M9L 2V4

(416) 241-9151   *SIC* 5148

GREENFIELD PRODUCE LTD   *p*263

12151 HORSESHOE WAY, RICHMOND,
BC, V7A 4V4

(604) 272-2551   *SIC* 5148

GREENGROCER INC, THE   *p*739

6110 SHAWSON DR, MISSISSAUGA, ON,
L5T 1E6

(416) 253-9070   *SIC* 5148

GROUPE ETHIER INC   *p*1152

16800 CH CHARLES UNITE 123,
MIRABEL, QC, J7J 0V9

(450) 435-9581   *SIC* 5148

GROUPE TOMAPURE INC   *p*1234

1790 PLACE MARTENOT, MONTREAL,
QC, H7L 5B5

(450) 663-6444   *SIC* 5148

HECTOR LARIVEE INC   *p*1174

1755 RUE BERCY, MONTREAL, QC, H2K
2T9

(514) 521-8331   *SIC* 5148

HILITE FINE FOODS INC   *p*571

415 HORNER AVE UNIT 4, ETOBICOKE,
ON, M8W 4W3

(416) 503-0499   *SIC* 5148

HILLSIDE GARDENS LIMITED   *p*497

1383 RIVER RD, BRADFORD, ON, L3Z 4A6

(905) 775-3356   *SIC* 5148

HURON PRODUCE LIMITED   *p*590

40534 THAMES RD, EXETER, ON, N0M
1S5

(519) 235-2650   *SIC* 5148

IMEX AGRO INC   *p*1106

128 BOUL SAINT-RAYMOND, GATINEAU,
QC, J8Y 1T2

(819) 483-1515   *SIC* 5148

IMPORTATIONS KROPS INC   *p*1163

9761 BOUL DES SCIENCES, MONTREAL,

QC, H1J 0A6

(514) 525-6464   *SIC* 5148

**INVESTISSEMENTS CAPESPAN CANADA
INC, LES**   *p*1340

6700 CH DE LA COTE-DE-LIESSE BU-
REAU 301, SAINT-LAURENT, QC, H4T 2B5

(514) 739-9181   *SIC* 5148

IPPOLITO FRUIT AND PRODUCE LIMITED
*p*529

201 NORTH SERVICE RD, BURLINGTON,
ON, L7P 5C4

(905) 631-7700   *SIC* 5148

ISLAND HOLDINGS LTD   *p*398

100 MIDLAND DR, DIEPPE, NB, E1A 6X4

(506) 858-7777   *SIC* 5148

ISLANDS WEST MANUFACTURERS LTD
*p*337

4247 DOUGLAS ST, VICTORIA, BC, V8X
3Y7

(250) 727-0744   *SIC* 5148

ITALIAN PRODUCE CO. LIMITED   *p*572

165 THE QUEENSWAY RM 314, ETOBI-
COKE, ON, M8Y 1H8

(416) 259-7641   *SIC* 5148

J-D MARKETING (LEAMINGTON) INC *p*634

2400 GRAHAM, KINGSVILLE, ON, N9Y
2E5

(519) 733-3663   *SIC* 5148

J.B. LAVERDURE INC   *p*1180

400 BOUL CREMAZIE O, MONTREAL, QC,
H2P 1C7

(514) 382-7520   *SIC* 5148

J.B.M. ENTERPRISES   *p*179

5000 256 ST, ALDERGROVE, BC, V4W 1J4

(604) 856-1466   *SIC* 5148

J.G. RIVE-SUD FRUITS & LEGUMES INC
*p*1074

1963 RUE PATRICK-FARRAR, CHAMBLY,
QC, J3L 4N7

(450) 447-3092   *SIC* 5148

JARDINS G & R LTEE, LES   *p*1347

1043 RUE GARIEPY, SAINT-LIN-
LAURENTIDES, QC, J5M 2N1

(450) 439-3425   *SIC* 5148

JARDINS M.G. S.E.N.C., LES   *p*1359

985 RANG SAINT-SIMON, SAINTE-
MADELEINE, QC, J0H 1S0

(450) 795-3459   *SIC* 5148

JEM D INTERNATIONAL PARTNERS LP
*p*634

2400 GRAHAM, KINGSVILLE, ON, N9Y
2E5

(519) 733-3663   *SIC* 5148

JOHN SANFILIPPO AND CO. LTD   *p*546

333 PEEL ST, COLLINGWOOD, ON, L9Y
3W3

(705) 445-4200   *SIC* 5148

JOSEPH S. CHOW LTD   *p*263

11780 HAMMERSMITH WAY SUITE 120,
RICHMOND, BC, V7A 5E9

(604) 271-0255   *SIC* 5148

JOYCE FRUIT MARKETS LIMITED   *p*795

28 RIVALDA RD SUITE A, NORTH YORK,
ON, M9M 2M3

(416) 745-4411   *SIC* 5148

KARAM FRUITS ET LEGUMES INC *p*1297

700 RUE DE LA VISITATION, SAINT-
CHARLES-BORROMEE, QC, J6E 7S3

(450) 753-5881   *SIC* 5148

KNIGHT'S APPLEDEN FRUIT LIMITED*p*546

11687 COUNTY ROAD 2 RR 3, COL-
BORNE, ON, K0K 1S0

(905) 349-2521   *SIC* 5148

KOO, JIM M. PRODUCE INC   *p*285

777 CLARK DR, VANCOUVER, BC, V5L
3J3

(604) 253-6622   *SIC* 5148

KOORNNEEF PRODUCE LTD   *p*572

165 THE QUEENSWAY SUITE 151, ETOBI-
COKE, ON, M8Y 1H8

(416) 255-5188   *SIC* 5148

KROWN PRODUCE INC   *p*12

4923 47 ST SE, CALGARY, AB, T2B 3S5

SIC 5148

**LAKEVIEW VEGETABLE PROCESSING
INC**   *p*849

21413 LESLIE ST RR 1, QUEENSVILLE,
ON, L0G 1R0

(905) 478-2521   *SIC* 5148

LANGLEY FARM MARKET (1997) INC *p*190

4820 KINGSWAY SUITE 316, BURNABY,
BC, V5H 4P1

(604) 521-2883   *SIC* 5148

LEGUBEC INC   *p*1262

905 RUE FERNAND-DUFOUR, QUEBEC,
QC, G1M 3B2

(418) 681-3531   *SIC* 5148

LEGUMES R. & M. INC, LES   *p*1376

26 RANG CONTANT, SHERRINGTON, QC,
J0L 2N0

(514) 977-3840   *SIC* 5148

LITTLE POTATO COMPANY LTD, THE *p*101

11749 180 ST NW, EDMONTON, AB, T5S
2H6

(780) 414-6075   *SIC* 5148

LONGO BROTHERS FRUIT MARKETS INC
*p*526

2900 WALKER'S LINE, BURLINGTON, ON,
L7M 4M8

(905) 331-1645   *SIC* 5148

**LUC CHARBONNEAU FRUITS & LEGUMES
INC**   *p*1162

8135 AV MARCO-POLO, MONTREAL, QC,
H1E 5Y8

(514) 337-3955   *SIC* 5148

MAPLE LEAF FOODS INC   *p*141

2720 2A AVE N, LETHBRIDGE, AB, T1H
5B4

(403) 380-9900   *SIC* 5148

MASTRONARDI PRODUCE LIMITED   *p*634

2100 ROAD 4 E, KINGSVILLE, ON, N9Y
2E5

(519) 326-3218   *SIC* 5148

MCCAIN PRODUCE INC   *p*399

8734 MAIN ST UNIT 1, FLORENCEVILLE-
BRISTOL, NB, E7L 3G6

(506) 392-3036   *SIC* 5148

MCKENNA BROS (1989) LIMITED   *p*1038

4109 48 RD, CARDIGAN, PE, C0A 1G0

(902) 583-2951   *SIC* 5148

**MELVIN HARTMAN ENTERPRISES LIM-
ITED**   *p*818

3150 HAWTHORNE RD SUITE B-1, OT-
TAWA, ON, K1G 5H5

(613) 247-0099   *SIC* 5148

METRO RICHELIEU INC   *p*1164

5400 AV PIERRE-DE COUBERTIN, MON-
TREAL, QC, H1N 1P7

SIC 5148

MISTER PRODUCE LTD   *p*575

50 JUTLAND RD, ETOBICOKE, ON, M8Z
2H1

(416) 252-9191   *SIC* 5148

MISTY MOUNTAIN INDUSTRIES LTD *p*255

13900 MAYCREST WAY SUITE 130, RICH-
MOND, BC, V6V 3E2

(604) 273-8299   *SIC* 5148

MOUNTAIN VIEW PACKERS LTD   *p*399

9112 ROUTE 130, FLORENCEVILLE-
BRISTOL, NB, E7K 2R2

(506) 392-6017   *SIC* 5148

NATIONAL PRODUCE MARKETING INC
*p*575

55 PLYWOOD PL UNIT 102, ETOBICOKE,
ON, M8Z 5J3

(416) 259-0833   *SIC* 5148

NATURE FRESH FARMS SALES INC *p*644

4 SENECA RD, LEAMINGTON, ON, N8H
5H7

(519) 326-1111   *SIC* 5148

NATURE'S VINE PRODUCE INC.   *p*793

5601 STEELES AVE W UNIT 11, NORTH
YORK, ON, M9L 1S7

SIC 5148

NIAGARA ORCHARD & VINEYARD CORP
*p*1004

1550 HWY 55, VIRGIL, ON, L0S 1T0

(905) 468-3297   *SIC* 5148

NORFOLK FRUIT GROWERS' ASSOCIATION, THE *p881*
99 QUEENSWAY E, SIMCOE, ON, N3Y 4M5
(519) 426-6931   *SIC* 5148

NORTH AMERICAN PRODUCE BUYERS LIMITED *p572*
165 THE QUEENSWAY SUITE 336, ETOBICOKE, ON, M8Y 1H8
(416) 255-5544   *SIC* 5148

NORTH HOUSE FOODS LTD *p595*
1169 PARISIEN ST, GLOUCESTER, ON, K1B 4W4
(613) 746-6662   *SIC* 5148

O'LEARY POTATO PACKERS LTD *p1042*
85 ELLIS AVE, O'LEARY, PE, C0B 1V0
SIC 5148

ONTARIO POTATO DIST. (ALLISTON) INC. 1991 *p476*
GD STN MAIN, ALLISTON, ON, L9R 1T8
(705) 435-6902   *SIC* 5148

OPPENHEIMER, DAVID AND COMPANY I, LLC *p201*
11 BURBIDGE ST SUITE 101, COQUITLAM, BC, V3K 7B2
(604) 461-6779   *SIC* 5148

P.E.I. VEGETABLE GROWERS COOPERATIVE ASSOCIATION, LIMITED *p1040*
280 SHERWOOD RD, CHARLOTTETOWN, PE, C1E 0E4
(902) 892-5361   *SIC* 5148

PATATES DINO INC *p1109*
71 RUE FOCH, GRANBY, QC, J2G 6B4
(450) 372-3373   *SIC* 5148

PATATES DOLBEC INC *p1353*
295 363 RTE S, SAINT-UBALDE, QC, G0A 4L0
(418) 277-2442   *SIC* 5148

PFENNING'S ORGANIC VEGETABLES INC *p753*
1209 WATERLOO ST, NEW HAMBURG, ON, N3A 1T1
(519) 662-3468   *SIC* 5148

PRIDE PAK NFLD LTD *p427*
107 MCNAMARA DR, PARADISE, NL, A1L 0A7
(709) 782-8000   *SIC* 5148

PRODUITS FRAIS FMS INC *p1376*
298 RANG SAINTE-MELANIE, SHERRINGTON, QC, J0L 2N0
(450) 454-6499   *SIC* 5148

PRODUITS VEGKISS INC *p1115*
1400 CH LASALLE, JOLIETTE, QC, J6E 0L8
(450) 752-2250   *SIC* 5148

PROPUR INC *p1277*
5185 RUE RIDEAU, QUEBEC, QC, G2E 5S2
(418) 862-7739   *SIC* 5148

PROVIGO DISTRIBUTION INC *p1067*
180 CH DU TREMBLAY, BOUCHERVILLE, QC, J4B 7W3
(450) 449-8000   *SIC* 5148

PROVINCIAL FRUIT CO. LIMITED *p572*
165 THE QUEENSWAY, ETOBICOKE, ON, M8Y 1H8
(416) 259-5001   *SIC* 5148

PURE HOTHOUSE FOODS INC *p644*
459 HIGHWAY 77, LEAMINGTON, ON, N8H 3V6
(519) 326-8444   *SIC* 5148

QUATTROCCHI, JOSEPH & COMPANY LIMITED *p882*
63 CHURCH ST W, SMITHS FALLS, ON, K7A 1R2
(613) 283-4980   *SIC* 5148

RED HAT CO-OPERATIVE LTD *p158*
809 BROADWAY AVE E, REDCLIFF, AB, T0J 2P0
(403) 548-6453   *SIC* 5148

RITE-PAK PRODUCE CO. LIMITED *p573*
165 THE QUEENSWAY, ETOBICOKE, ON, M8Y 1H8
(416) 252-3121   *SIC* 5148

ROBINSON, ERIC C. INC *p1038*

1804 RTE 115, ALBANY, PE, C0B 1A0
(902) 437-6666   *SIC* 5148

ROOTS ORGANIC INC *p280*
3585 184 ST, SURREY, BC, V3Z 1B8
(604) 576-2567   *SIC* 5148

RUSSELL, J.E. PRODUCE LTD *p573*
165 THE QUEENSWAY SUITE 332, ETOBICOKE, ON, M8Y 1H8
(416) 252-7838   *SIC* 5148

SAHOTA FARMS LTD *p178*
40990 NO. 3 RD, ABBOTSFORD, BC, V3G 2S1
(604) 823-2341   *SIC* 5148

SCOTIAN GOLD CO-OPERATIVE LIMITED *p442*
2900 LOVETT RD, COLDBROOK, NS, B4R 1A6
(902) 679-2191   *SIC* 5148

SERRES ROYALES INC, LES *p1321*
1954 BOUL SAINT-ANTOINE, SAINT-JEROME, QC, J7Z 7M2
(450) 438-1334   *SIC* 5148

SMITH, L & H FRUIT COMPANY LIMITED *p656*
22 MAITLAND ST, LONDON, ON, N6B 3L2
(519) 433-4004   *SIC* 5148

SOBEYS CAPITAL INCORPORATED *p426*
10 OLD PLACENTIA RD, MOUNT PEARL, NL, A1N 4P5
(709) 748-1200   *SIC* 5148

STAR PRODUCE LTD *p1425*
2941 PORTAGE AVE, SASKATOON, SK, S7J 3S6
(306) 934-0999   *SIC* 5148

STREEF PRODUCE LIMITED *p848*
447 HWY 2, PRINCETON, ON, N0J 1V0
(519) 458-4311   *SIC* 5148

STRONACH & SONS INC *p573*
165 THE QUEENSWAY SUITE 318, ETOBICOKE, ON, M8Y 1H8
(416) 259-5009   *SIC* 5148

SUN PARLOUR GREENHOUSE GROWERS CO-OPERATIVE LIMITED *p645*
230 COUNTY RD 31, LEAMINGTON, ON, N8H 3V5
(519) 326-8681   *SIC* 5148

SUN PROCESSING LTD *p194*
7580 LOWLAND DR, BURNABY, BC, V5J 5A4
(604) 688-8372   *SIC* 5148

SUNDINE PRODUCE INC *p743*
6075 KESTREL RD, MISSISSAUGA, ON, L5T 1Y8
(905) 364-1600   *SIC* 5148

TERMINAL FRUIT & PRODUCE LTD *p296*
788 MALKIN AVE, VANCOUVER, BC, V6A 2K2
(604) 251-3383   *SIC* 5148

THOMAS FRESH INC *p19*
5470 76 AVE SE, CALGARY, AB, T2C 4S3
(403) 236-8234   *SIC* 5148

TOBIQUE FARMS OPERATING (2012) LIMITED *p398*
2424 ROUTE 108, DSL DE DRUMMOND, NB, E3Y 2K7
(506) 553-9913   *SIC* 5148

TOMATO KING 2010 INC *p996*
165 THE QUEENSWAY SUITE 232, TORONTO, ON, M8Y 1H8
(416) 259-5410   *SIC* 5148

TRI-B ACRES INC *p645*
132 MERSEA ROAD 5, LEAMINGTON, ON, N8H 3V5
(519) 326-0042   *SIC* 5148

VAN MEEKEREN FARMS LTD *p460*
237 THORPE RD, KENTVILLE, NS, B4N 3V7
(902) 678-2366   *SIC* 5148

VANCO FARMS LTD *p1042*
9311 TRANS CANADA HWY - RTE 1, MOUNT ALBION, PE, C1B 0R4
(902) 651-2005   *SIC* 5148

VEG-PAK PRODUCE LIMITED *p573*
165 THE QUEENSWAY RM 249, ETOBI-

COKE, ON, M8Y 1H8
(416) 259-4686   *SIC* 5148

VEGPRO INTERNATIONAL INC *p1376*
147 RANG SAINT-PAUL, SHERRINGTON, QC, J0L 2N0
(450) 454-7712   *SIC* 5148

VERGER BELLIVEAU ORCHARD LTD *p405*
1209 RUE PRINCIPALE, MEMRAMCOOK, NB, E4K 2S6
(506) 758-0295   *SIC* 5148

VERGER DU PERE DE LA FRAISE, LE *p1350*
1740 RUE PRINCIPALE E, SAINT-PAUL-D'ABBOTSFORD, QC, J0E 1A0
(450) 379-5271   *SIC* 5148

VERGER LACROIX INC *p1322*
649 CH PRINCIPAL, SAINT-JOSEPH-DU-LAC, QC, J0N 1M0
(450) 623-4888   *SIC* 5148

VINELAND GROWERS CO-OPERATIVE LIMITED *p623*
4150 JORDAN RD SUITE 700, JORDAN STATION, ON, L0R 1S0
(905) 562-4133   *SIC* 5148

VISSER, GERRIT & SONS (1991) INC *p1043*
6346 TRANS CANADA HWY - RTE 1, VERNON BRIDGE, PE, C0A 2E0
(902) 651-2371   *SIC* 5148

WALLACE & CAREY INC *p207*
551 CHESTER RD, DELTA, BC, V3M 6G7
(604) 522-9930   *SIC* 5148

YEN BROS. FOOD SERVICE LTD *p296*
1988 VERNON DR, VANCOUVER, BC, V6A 3Y6
(604) 255-6522   *SIC* 5148

SIC 5149 Groceries and related products, nec

10167819 CANADA INC *p1381*
460 RUE FERNAND-POITRAS, TERREBONNE, QC, J6Y 1Y4
(514) 493-9423   *SIC* 5149

106203 CANADA LTD *p545*
158 SECOND AVE, COCHRANE, ON, P0L 1C0
(705) 272-4305   *SIC* 5149

113712 CANADA INC *p1061*
3780 RUE LA VERENDRYE, BOISBRIAND, QC, J7H 1R5
(450) 437-7077   *SIC* 5149

1277487 ONTARIO LIMITED *p513*
20 SAGE CRT, BRANTFORD, ON, N3R 7T4
(519) 752-4937   *SIC* 5149

1350950 ONTARIO LTD *p750*
1558 MERIVALE RD, NEPEAN, ON, K2G 3J9
(613) 225-3470   *SIC* 5149

160841 CANADA INC *p1239*
10671 AV BRUNET, MONTREAL-NORD, QC, H1G 5E1
(514) 325-3680   *SIC* 5149

1649338 ONTARIO INC *p540*
266 WESTBROOK RD, CARP, ON, K0A 1L0
(613) 831-4446   *SIC* 5149

1928321 ONTARIO INC *p1006*
23 KING ST N, WATERLOO, ON, N2J 2W6
(519) 954-6622   *SIC* 5149

2075894 ONTARIO INC *p665*
170 ESNA PARK DR UNIT 14, MARKHAM, ON, L3R 1E3
(905) 752-0460   *SIC* 5149

2443499 ONTARIO INC *p1029*
48 CASTER AVE, WOODBRIDGE, ON, L4L 5Z1
(905) 771-0637   *SIC* 5149

2920409 CANADA INC *p1169*
8575 8E AV, MONTREAL, QC, H1Z 2X2
(514) 374-2700   *SIC* 5149

3059714 NOVA SCOTIA COMPANY *p539*
103 SECOND ST, CAMPBELLFORD, ON, K0L 1L0
(705) 653-3590   *SIC* 5149

3213463 CANADA INC *p1047*

7545 AV M.-B.-JODOIN, ANJOU, QC, H1J 2H9
(514) 528-1150   *SIC* 5149

327494 B.C. LTD *p208*
7763 PROGRESS WAY, DELTA, BC, V4G 1A3
(604) 420-3511   *SIC* 5149

3367771 CANADA INC *p1393*
189 BOUL HARWOOD, VAUDREUIL-DORION, QC, J7V 1Y3
(450) 455-2827   *SIC* 5149

340532 ONTARIO LIMITED *p548*
565 EDGELEY BLVD, CONCORD, ON, L4K 4G4
(905) 669-9930   *SIC* 5149

386140 ONTARIO LIMITED *p611*
191 VICTORIA AVE S, HAMILTON, ON, L8N 0A4
(905) 522-2730   *SIC* 5149

3D DISTRIBUTION CANADA INC *p184*
5045 STILL CREEK AVE, BURNABY, BC, V5C 5V1
(604) 299-5045   *SIC* 5149

5 SAISONS INC *p1401*
1250 AV GREENE, WESTMOUNT, QC, H3Z 2A3
(514) 931-0249   *SIC* 5149

596042 ONTARIO LIMITED *p711*
720 BURNHAMTHORPE RD W UNIT 28, MISSISSAUGA, ON, L5C 3G1
(905) 270-9840   *SIC* 5149

6 MILE BAKERY & DELI LTD *p338*
3950 CAREY RD, VICTORIA, BC, V8Z 4E2
(250) 727-7737   *SIC* 5149

6702601 CANADA INC *p1292*
4919 RUE SAINT-FELIX, SAINT-AUGUSTIN-DE-DESMAURES, QC, G3A 1B4
(418) 571-0705   *SIC* 5149

9098-8585 QUEBEC INC *p1397*
59 RUE GIROUARD, VICTORIAVILLE, QC, G6P 5T2
(819) 357-8395   *SIC* 5149

9104-7332 QUEBEC INC *p1185*
351 RUE EMERY, MONTREAL, QC, H2X 1J2
(514) 286-4002   *SIC* 5149

9138-1616 QUEBEC INC *p1168*
4600 RUE MOLSON, MONTREAL, QC, H1Y 0A3
(514) 223-2600   *SIC* 5149

9141-1967 QUEBEC INC *p1345*
4815 BOUL COUTURE, SAINT-LEONARD, QC, H1R 3H7
(514) 326-0185   *SIC* 5149

9192-4548 QUEBEC INC *p1390*
539 CH DE LA BAIE-DOREE, VAL-D'OR, QC, J9P 7B3
(819) 637-2444   *SIC* 5149

91933614 QUEBEC INC *p1141*
844 RUE JEAN-NEVEU, LONGUEUIL, QC, J4G 2M1
(514) 721-3016   *SIC* 5149

9195-4750 QUEBEC INC *p1227*
8255 AV MOUNTAIN SIGHTS BUREAU 408, MONTREAL, QC, H4P 2B5
(514) 340-7737   *SIC* 5149

9256-8971 QUEBEC INC *p1093*
22 AV LINDSAY, DORVAL, QC, H9P 2T8
SIC 5149

AIDUS INTERNATIONAL *p259*
2560 SHELL RD UNIT 1048, RICHMOND, BC, V6X 0B8
(604) 304-7889   *SIC* 5149

ALBI BEVERAGES LIMITED *p284*
3440 BRIDGEWAY, VANCOUVER, BC, V5K 1B6
SIC 5149

ALIMENTATION POIVRE ET SEL LA CHARCUTIERE INC *p1168*
3245 RUE MASSON, MONTREAL, QC, H1Y 1Y4
(514) 374-3611   *SIC* 5149

ALIMENTS BRETON INC *p1294*

1312 RUE SAINT-GEORGES, SAINT-BERNARD, QC, G0S 2G0
(418) 475-6601   *SIC* 5149

ALIMENTS DAINTY FOODS INC, LES p1401
2 PLACE ALEXIS NIHON NO1777 3500 DE MAISONNEUVE O, WESTMOUNT, QC, H3Z 3C1
(514) 908-7777   *SIC* 5149

ALIMENTS KOYO INC p1338
4605 RUE HICKMORE, SAINT-LAURENT, QC, H4T 1S5
(514) 744-1299   *SIC* 5149

ALIMENTS MARTEL INC p1381
460 RUE FERNAND-POITRAS, TERRE-BONNE, QC, J6Y 1Y4
(514) 493-9423   *SIC* 5149

ALIMENTS ROSEHILL INC, LES p1332
7171 BOUL THIMENS, SAINT-LAURENT, QC, H4S 2A2
(514) 745-1153   *SIC* 5149

ALIMENTS RUSTICA INC, LES p1047
10301 RUE COLBERT, ANJOU, QC, H1J 2G5
(514) 325-9009   *SIC* 5149

ALL GOLD IMPORTS INC p666
4255 14TH AVE, MARKHAM, ON, L3R 0J2
(416) 740-4653   *SIC* 5149

AMARO INC p1298
4061 GRAND RANG SAINTE-CATHERINE, SAINT-CUTHBERT, QC, J0K 2C0
(514) 593-5144   *SIC* 5149

ANDREWS & GEORGE COMPANY LIMITED p291
125 3RD AVE W, VANCOUVER, BC, V5Y 1E6
(604) 876-0466   *SIC* 5149

APEX FOODSOURCE LTD p176
30530 PROGRESSIVE WAY, ABBOTSFORD, BC, V2T 6W3
(604) 854-1492   *SIC* 5149

AQUATERRA CORPORATION p691
1200 BRITANNIA RD E, MISSISSAUGA, ON, L4W 4T5
(905) 795-6500   *SIC* 5149

ARCTIC BEVERAGES LP p356
107 MOUNTAIN VIEW RD UNIT 2, ROSSER, MB, R0H 1E0
(204) 633-8686   *SIC* 5149

ARCTIC CHILLER LTD p161
100 CREE RD, SHERWOOD PARK, AB, T8A 3X8
(780) 449-0459   *SIC* 5149

AURORA IMPORTING & DISTRIBUTING LIMITED p734
815· GANA CRT, MISSISSAUGA, ON, L5S 1P2
(905) 670-1855   *SIC* 5149

BAKEMARK INGREDIENTS CANADA LIMITED p253
2480 VIKING WAY, RICHMOND, BC, V6V 1N2
(604) 303-1700   *SIC* 5149

BAKER STREET BAKERY INC p578
130 THE WEST MALL, ETOBICOKE, ON, M9C 1B9
(416) 785-9666   *SIC* 5149

BD APD INC p1167
3075 RUE DE ROUEN, MONTREAL, QC, H1W 3Z2
(514) 528-8877   *SIC* 5149

BEAUCE EAU INC p1353
175 CH DES FONDS, SAINT-VICTOR, QC, G0M 2B0
(418) 588-3289   *SIC* 5149

BEAUDRY & CADRIN INC p1247
12225 BOUL METROPOLITAIN E, POINTE-AUX-TREMBLES, QC, H1B 5R3
(514) 352-5620   *SIC* 5149

BEE MAID HONEY LIMITED p383
625 ROSEBERRY ST, WINNIPEG, MB, R3H 0T4
(204) 786-8977   *SIC* 5149

BENNETT'S BAKERY LIMITED p907
899 TUNGSTEN ST, THUNDER BAY, ON,

P7B 6H2
(807) 344-2931   *SIC* 5149

BEST BAKING INC p573
166 NORSEMAN ST, ETOBICOKE, ON, M8Z 2R4
(416) 536-1330   *SIC* 5149

BIOFORCE CANADA INC p1091
66 BOUL BRUNSWICK, DOLLARD-DES-ORMEAUX, QC, H9B 2L3
(514) 421-3441   *SIC* 5149

BIONEUTRA GLOBAL CORPORATION p120
9608 25 AVE NW, EDMONTON, AB, T6N 1J4
(780) 466-1481   *SIC* 5149

BLUE STAR NUTRACEUTICALS INC p492
180 NORTH FRONT ST UNIT 6, BELLEVILLE, ON, K8P 3B9
(613) 968-2278   *SIC* 5149

BLUERIVER TRADING LTD p782
369 RIMROCK ROAD, NORTH YORK, ON, M3J 3G2
(416) 638-8543   *SIC* 5149

BODY PLUS NUTRITIONAL PRODUCTS INC p864
130 MCLEVIN AVE UNIT 5, SCARBOROUGH, ON, M1B 3R6
(416) 332-1881   *SIC* 5149

BONDUELLE CANADA INC p1297
1055 RTE 112, SAINT-CESAIRE, QC, J0L 1T0
(450) 469-3159   *SIC* 5149

BONNES GATERIES 2007 INC p1349
710 RTE LAGUEUX, SAINT-NICOLAS, QC, G7A 1A7
(418) 831-4948   *SIC* 5149

BOULANGERIE CASCHER DE MONTREAL LTEE p1227
7005 AV VICTORIA, MONTREAL, QC, H4P 2N9
(514) 739-3651   *SIC* 5149

BOULANGERIE GONDOLE INC p1325
225 RUE BENJAMIN-HUDON, SAINT-LAURENT, QC, H4N 1J1
(514) 956-5555   *SIC* 5149

BOULANGERIE VACHON INC p1343
8770 BOUL LANGELIER BUREAU 230, SAINT-LEONARD, QC, H1P 3C6
(514) 326-5084   *SIC* 5149

BOULANGERIE VACHON INC p1360
380 RUE NOTRE-DAME N, SAINTE-MARIE, QC, G6E 2K7
(418) 387-5421   *SIC* 5149

BRAZILIAN CANADIAN COFFEE CO. LTD p582
1260 MARTIN GROVE RD, ETOBICOKE, ON, M9W 4X3
(416) 749-2000   *SIC* 5149

BREUVAGES APPALACHES INC, LES p1397
925 RUE NOTRE-DAME O, VICTORIAVILLE, QC, G6P 7L1
SIC 5149

BROSSARD FRERES INC p1239
10848 AV MOISAN, MONTREAL-NORD, QC, H1G 4N7
(514) 321-4121   *SIC* 5149

BRULERIE GRANDE RESERVE INC p1372
930 RUE BLAIS, SHERBROOKE, QC, J1K 2B7
(819) 564-8844   *SIC* 5149

BURRITO BOYZ DISTRIBUTION INC p573
21 JUTLAND RD, ETOBICOKE, ON, M8Z 2G6
(416) 251-8536   *SIC* 5149

C.P. VEGETABLE OIL INC p501
10 CARSON CRT UNIT 2, BRAMPTON, ON, L6T 4P8
(905) 792-2309   *SIC* 5149

CAFE FARO INC p1372
930 RUE BLAIS, SHERBROOKE, QC, J1K 2B7
(819) 564-8844   *SIC* 5149

CAFE MARC ROBITAILLE INC p1044
850 AV TANGUAY, ALMA, QC, G8B 5Y3

(418) 668-8022   *SIC* 5149

CAFE VITTORIA INC p1370
1625 RUE BELVEDERE S, SHERBROOKE, QC, J1H 4E4
(819) 564-8226   *SIC* 5149

CANADA BREAD COMPANY, LIMITED p615
155 NEBO RD SUITE 1, HAMILTON, ON, L8W 2E1
(905) 387-3935   *SIC* 5149

CANADA COMPOUND CORPORATION p1030
391 ROWNTREE DAIRY RD, WOODBRIDGE, ON, L4L 8H1
(905) 856-5005   *SIC* 5149

CANDA SIX FORTUNE ENTERPRISE CO. LTD p192
8138 NORTH FRASER WAY, BURNABY, BC, V5J 0E7
(604) 432-9000   *SIC* 5149

CANTERBURY COFFEE CORPORATION p192
8080 NORTH FRASER WAY UNIT 1, BURNABY, BC, V5J 0E6
(604) 431-4400   *SIC* 5149

CANTERBURY FOOD SERVICE (ALTA) LTD p108
4803 93 AVE NW, EDMONTON, AB, T6B 3A2
(780) 468-6363   *SIC* 5149

CAPWORK LABORATORY INC p254
13982 CAMBIE RD SUITE 113, RICHMOND, BC, V6V 2K2
(604) 233-7060   *SIC* 5149

CEDAROME CANADA INC p1072
21 RUE PAUL-GAUGUIN, CANDIAC, QC, J5R 3X8
(450) 659-8000   *SIC* 5149

CHOCOLAT PERFECTION INC p1142
570 BOUL ROLAND-THERRIEN BUREAU 217, LONGUEUIL, QC, J4H 3V9
(450) 674-4546   *SIC* 5149

CHOCOLATS COLOMBE p1047
128 235 RTE, ANGE-GARDIEN, QC, J0E 1E0
(450) 293-0129   *SIC* 5149

CHUANG'S COMPANY LTD p668
110 DENISON ST UNIT 8, MARKHAM, ON, L3R 1B6
(905) 415-2812   *SIC* 5149

CLUB COFFEE L.P. p583
55 CARRIER DR SUITE 1, ETOBICOKE, ON, M9W 5V9
(416) 675-1300   *SIC* 5149

COCA-COLA CANADA BOTTLING LIMITED p1415
355 HENDERSON DR, REGINA, SK, S4N 6B9
(800) 218-2653   *SIC* 5149

COCA-COLA LTD p460
20 LAKESIDE PARK DR, LAKESIDE, NS, B3T 1L8
(902) 876-8661   *SIC* 5149

COCA-COLA LTD p765
3389 STEELES AVE E SUITE 500, NORTH YORK, ON, M2H 3S8
SIC 5149

COCA-COLA REFRESHMENTS CANADA COMPANY p1261
990 AV GODIN, QUEBEC, QC, G1M 2X9
(418) 686-4884   *SIC* 5149

COLD PRESS CORP, THE p972
176 ST GEORGE ST, TORONTO, ON, M5R 2M7
(416) 934-5034   *SIC* 5149

COMMUNITY FARM STORE LTD, THE p211
330 DUNCAN ST SUITE 101, DUNCAN, BC, V9L 3W4
(250) 748-6223   *SIC* 5149

COMPAGNIE 2 AMERIKS INC, LA p1233
2300 RUE MICHELIN, MONTREAL, QC, H7L 5C3
(438) 380-3330   *SIC* 5149

COMPAGNIE INTERNATIONALE DE PRODUITS ALIMENTAIRES ET COMMERCE DE

DETAIL INC p1185
1615 RUE SAINT-DENIS, MONTREAL, QC, H2X 3K3
(514) 287-3555   *SIC* 5149

CONCEPT GOURMET DU VILLAGE ULC p1242
539 CH DU VILLAGE, MORIN-HEIGHTS, QC, J0R 1H0
(800) 668-2314   *SIC* 5149

CONSORTIUM DES MARQUES PRIVEES PBC INC, LES p1396
3000 BOUL RENE-LEVESQUE BUREAU 330, VERDUN, QC, H3E 1T9
(514) 768-4122   *SIC* 5149

COOPERATIVE D'ALENTOUR, GROSSISTE EN ALIMENTATION NATURELLE DES CANTONS DE L'EST p1373
4740 BOUL INDUSTRIEL, SHERBROOKE, QC, J1L 3A3
(819) 562-3443   *SIC* 5149

CROSBY MOLASSES COMPANY LIMITED p413
327 ROTHESAY AVE, SAINT JOHN, NB, E2J 2C3
(506) 634-7515   *SIC* 5149

DAWN FOOD PRODUCTS (CANADA), LTD p502
275 STEELWELL RD, BRAMPTON, ON, L6T 0C8
(289) 505-4640   *SIC* 5149

DELICOUKI INC p1345
5695 BOUL DES GRANDES-PRAIRIES BUREAU 118, SAINT-LEONARD, QC, H1R 1B3
(514) 731-2705   *SIC* 5149

DELTA COUNTRY FARMS (BC) LTD p210
3752 ARTHUR DR, DELTA, BC, V4K 3N2
(604) 940-1881   *SIC* 5149

DIMA IMPORT-EXPORT INC p1239
12020 BOUL ALBERT-HUDON, MONTREAL-NORD, QC, H1G 3K7
(514) 955-7295   *SIC* 5149

DISCOVERY ISLANDS ORGANICS LTD p294
880 MALKIN AVE, VANCOUVER, BC, V6A 2K6
(604) 299-1684   *SIC* 5149

DISTRIBUTIONS CHRISTIAN PELLERIN INC p1058
719 BOUL INDUSTRIEL BUREAU 101, BLAINVILLE, QC, J7C 3V3
(450) 434-4641   *SIC* 5149

DOMINO'S PIZZA NS CO p535
490 PINEBUSH RD UNIT 2, CAMBRIDGE, ON, N1T 0A5
(519) 748-1330   *SIC* 5149

DUBE & LOISELLE INC p1110
583 RUE DUFFERIN, GRANBY, QC, J2H 0Y5
(450) 378-9996   *SIC* 5149

EARLY'S FARM & GARDEN CENTRE p1424
2615 LORNE AVE, SASKATOON, SK, S7J 0S5
(306) 931-1982   *SIC* 5149

EAUX NAYA INC, LES p1166
2030 BOUL PIE-IX BUREAU 214.4, MONTREAL, QC, H1V 2C8
(514) 525-6292   *SIC* 5149

EBAM ENTERPRISES LTD p815
1616 MICHAEL ST, OTTAWA, ON, K1B 3T7
(613) 745-8998   *SIC* 5149

ELITE INTERNATIONAL FOODS INC p77
10725 25 ST NE BAY 124 BLDG B, CALGARY, AB, T3N 0A4
(403) 291-0660   *SIC* 5149

EMPIRE COMPANY LIMITED p466
115 KING ST, STELLARTON, NS, B0K 1S0
(902) 752-8371   *SIC* 5149

ENTREPRISES AMIRA INC, LES p1329
5375 BOUL HENRI-BOURASSA O, SAINT-LAURENT, QC, H4R 1C1
(514) 382-9823   *SIC* 5149

ESSENCES ET FRAGRANCES BELL CANADA INC p1070
3800 RUE ISABELLE, BROSSARD, QC,

J4Y 2R3

(450) 444-3819   *SIC* 5149

EUROTRADE IMPORT-EXPORT INC   *p694*
5484 TIMBERLEA BLVD, MISSISSAUGA, ON, L4W 2T7

(905) 624-2064   *SIC* 5149

FABRIQUE ARHOMA INC, LA   *p1175*
1700 RUE ONTARIO E, MONTREAL, QC, H2L 1S7

(514) 598-1700   *SIC* 5149

FALCON BAKERY   *p349*
21 PARK BLVD, FALCON BEACH, MB, R0E 0N0

(204) 349-8993   *SIC* 5149

FERN BROOK SPRINGS BOTTLED WATER COMPANY LIMITED   *p593*
10 BRIGDEN GATE, GEORGETOWN, ON, L7G 0A3

SIC 5149

FESTA JUICE COMPANY LTD   *p1031*
271 CHRISLEA RD, WOODBRIDGE, ON, L4L 8N6

(905) 850-5557   *SIC* 5149

FGF BRANDS INC   *p793*
1295 ORMONT DR, NORTH YORK, ON, M9L 2W6

(416) 742-7434   *SIC* 5149

FIELD GATE ORGANICS INC   *p621*
194338 19TH LINE, INGERSOLL, ON, N5C 3J6

(519) 425-8799   *SIC* 5149

FIRST CHOICE FOODS INC   *p192*
8125 NORTH FRASER WAY, BURNABY, BC, V5J 5M8

(604) 515-8885   *SIC* 5149

FOOD SUPPLIES DISTRIBUTING COMPANY INC   *p552*
355 RAYETTE RD UNIT 10, CONCORD, ON, L4K 2G2

SIC 5149

FOODFEST INTERNATIONAL 2000 INC   *p552*
361 CONNIE CRES, CONCORD, ON, L4K 5R2

(905) 709-4775   *SIC* 5149

FORTIER BEVERAGES LIMITED   *p545*
158 SECOND AVE, COCHRANE, ON, P0L 1C0

(705) 272-4305   *SIC* 5149

FREEDOM PET SUPPLIES INC   *p536*
480 THOMPSON DR, CAMBRIDGE, ON, N1T 2K8

(519) 624-8069   *SIC* 5149

FRENCH'S FOOD COMPANY INC, THE   *p695*
1680 TECH AVE UNIT 2, MISSISSAUGA, ON, L4W 5S9

(905) 283-7000   *SIC* 5149

FRESHOUSE FOODS LTD   *p497*
65 REAGEN'S INDUSTRIAL PKY, BRADFORD, ON, L3Z 0Z9

(905) 775-8880   *SIC* 5149

FRUIT D'OR INC   *p1399*
306 RTE 265, VILLEROY, QC, G0S 3K0

(819) 385-1126   *SIC* 5149

FRUIT DOME INC   *p1157*
5975 AV ANDOVER, MONT-ROYAL, QC, H4T 1H8

(514) 664-4470   *SIC* 5149

G.D. NIRVANA INC   *p1339*
955 RUE MCCAFFREY, SAINT-LAURENT, QC, H4T 1N3

(514) 739-9111   *SIC* 5149

GABRIELLA'S KITCHEN INC   *p203*
910 FITZGERALD AVE UNIT 301, COURTENAY, BC, V9N 2R5

(250) 334-3209   *SIC* 5149

GESTION P. A. T. INC   *p1351*
371 BOUL ST-PIERRE, SAINT-RAPHAEL, QC, G0R 4C0

(418) 243-2022   *SIC* 5149

GIVAUDAN CANADA CO   *p695*
2400 MATHESON BLVD E, MISSISSAUGA, ON, L4W 5G9

(905) 282-9808   *SIC* 5149

GOURMET NUTRITION F.B INC   *p1358*
2121 RUE LEONARD-DE VINCI BUREAU 4, SAINTE-JULIE, QC, J3E 1Z2

(450) 922-2885   *SIC* 5149

GOURMET TRADING CO. LTD   *p716*
3750A LAIRD RD SUITE 7, MISSISSAUGA, ON, L5L 0A6

(905) 826-6800   *SIC* 5149

GREENSPACE BRANDS INC   *p973*
176 ST GEORGE ST, TORONTO, ON, M5R 2M7

(416) 934-5034   *SIC* 5149

GRENIER ELPHEGE INC   *p1057*
40 BOUL SIR-WILFRID-LAURIER, BELOEIL, QC, J3G 4E8

(450) 467-4279   *SIC* 5149

GRIFFIN, HAROLD T. INC   *p739*
7491 PACIFIC CIR, MISSISSAUGA, ON, L5T 2A4

(905) 564-1710   *SIC* 5149

GROUPE FOODAROM INC   *p1309*
5400 RUE ARMAND-FRAPPIER, SAINT-HUBERT, QC, J3Z 1G5

(450) 443-3113   *SIC* 5149

GROUPE PHOENICIA INC   *p1334*
2605 BOUL PITFIELD, SAINT-LAURENT, QC, H4S 1T2

(514) 389-6363   *SIC* 5149

GUNN'S HOMEMADE CAKES & PASTRY LTD   *p371*
247 SELKIRK AVE, WINNIPEG, MB, R2W 2L5

(204) 582-2364   *SIC* 5149

HANNIGAN'S HONEY INC   *p1435*
GD, SHELLBROOK, SK, S0J 2E0

(306) 747-7782   *SIC* 5149

HARMONY WHOLE FOODS MARKET (ORANGEVILLE) LTD   *p808*
163 FIRST ST UNIT A, ORANGEVILLE, ON, L9W 3J8

(519) 941-8961   *SIC* 5149

HAYHOE EQUIPMENT AND SUPPLY LTD   *p554*
45 VILLARBOIT CRES SUITE 2, CONCORD, ON, L4K 4R2

(905) 669-5118   *SIC* 5149

HEALTH4ALL PRODUCTS LIMITED   *p487*
545 WELHAM RD, BARRIE, ON, L4N 8Z6

(705) 733-2117   *SIC* 5149

HELA SPICE CANADA INC   *p1001*
119 FRANKLIN ST, UXBRIDGE, ON, L9P 1J5

(905) 852-5100   *SIC* 5149

HERBORISTERIE LA CLEF DES CHAMPS INC   *p1391*
2205 CH DE LA RIVIERE, VAL-DAVID, QC, J0T 2N0

(819) 322-1561   *SIC* 5149

HERITAGE COFFEE CO. LTD   *p657*
97 BESSEMER RD UNIT 8, LONDON, ON, N6E 1P9

(519) 686-3620   *SIC* 5149

HILLS FOODS LTD   *p201*
130 GLACIER ST UNIT 1, COQUITLAM, BC, V3K 5Z6

(604) 472-1500   *SIC* 5149

HONAJI FOOD LTD   *p201*
42 FAWCETT RD UNIT 109, COQUITLAM, BC, V3K 6X9

(604) 759-2886   *SIC* 5149

HORIZON DISTRIBUTORS LTD   *p181*
5589 TRAPP AVE, BURNABY, BC, V3N 0B2

(604) 524-6610   *SIC* 5149

HORTON SPICE MILLS LIMITED   *p671*
256 STEELCASE RD W, MARKHAM, ON, L3R 1B3

(905) 475-6130   *SIC* 5149

ICE RIVER SPRINGS WATER CO. INC   *p880*
485387 COUNTY RD 11, SHELBURNE, ON, L9V 3N5

(519) 925-2929   *SIC* 5149

IGA ST-AUGUSTIN   *p1153*
14995 RUE DES SAULES, MIRABEL, QC, J7N 2A3

(450) 475-1118   *SIC* 5149

IMMUNOTEC INC   *p1394*
300 RUE JOSEPH-CARRIER, VAUDREUIL-DORION, QC, J7V 5V5

(450) 424-9992   *SIC* 5149

INDULBEC INC   *p1086*
3035 BOUL LE CARREFOUR, COTE SAINT-LUC, QC, H7T 1C8

(450) 687-5083   *SIC* 5149

INSTITUT DE RECHERCHE BIOLOGIQUE YVES PONROY (CANADA) INC   *p1128*
2035 RUE ONESIME-GAGNON, LACHINE, QC, H8T 3M5

(514) 448-4325   *SIC* 5149

INTERNATIONAL HERBS (B.C.) LTD   *p279*
4151 184 ST, SURREY, BC, V3Z 1B7

(604) 576-2345   *SIC* 5149

INVESTISSEMENTS PROSPA INC   *p1215*
1262 RUE SAINT-MATHIEU, MONTREAL, QC, H3H 2H8

SIC 5149

IQBAL HALAL FOODS INC   *p567*
2 THORNCLIFFE PARK DR UNIT 7-15, EAST YORK, ON, M4H 1H2

(416) 467-0177   *SIC* 5149

ISLAND ABBEY FOODS LTD   *p1040*
20 INNOVATION WAY, CHARLOTTETOWN, PE, C1E 0K4

(902) 367-9722   *SIC* 5149

ITN FOOD CORPORATION   *p874*
40 COMMANDER BLVD, SCARBOROUGH, ON, M1S 3S2

(416) 321-2052   *SIC* 5149

J.L. BRISSETTE LTEE   *p1354*
24 RUE BRISSETTE, SAINTE-AGATHE-DES-MONTS, QC, J8C 1T4

(819) 326-3263   *SIC* 5149

JEG ENTERPRISES   *p512*
57 CHEVIOT CRES, BRAMPTON, ON, L6Z 4G8

SIC 5149

JOHNNY'S BAKERY (1981) LTD   *p235*
660 BAKER ST, NELSON, BC, V1L 4J4

SIC 5149

KHALSA UNION TRADING COMPANY   *p1032*
418 HANLAN RD SUITE 17, WOODBRIDGE, ON, L4L 4Z1

(905) 851-7999   *SIC* 5149

KILO GATEAUX LTEE   *p1217*
6744 RUE HUTCHISON, MONTREAL, QC, H3N 1Y4

(514) 270-3024   *SIC* 5149

KOREA FOOD TRADING LTD   *p1002*
8500 KEELE ST, VAUGHAN, ON, L4K 2A6

(905) 532-0325   *SIC* 5149

KOYO FOODS QUEBEC INC   *p1340*
4605 RUE HICKMORE, SAINT-LAURENT, QC, H4T 1S5

(514) 744-1299   *SIC* 5149

KRAFT HEINZ CANADA ULC   *p182*
2700 PRODUCTION WAY SUITE 450, BURNABY, BC, V5A 4X1

(604) 420-2511   *SIC* 5149

KREMBLO INTERNATIONAL TRADE COMPANY INC   *p779*
49 THE DONWAY W SUITE 1401, NORTH YORK, ON, M3C 3M9

(416) 445-3474   *SIC* 5149

LA ROCCA CREATIVE CAKES INC   *p857*
45 VIA RENZO DR, RICHMOND HILL, ON, L4S 0B4

(905) 884-7275   *SIC* 5149

LABRADOR LAURENTIENNE INC   *p1242*
2540 BOUL LOUIS-FRECHETTE, NICOLET, QC, J3T 1N1

(819) 293-4555   *SIC* 5149

LANTIC INC   *p169*
5405 64 ST, TABER, AB, T1G 2C4

(403) 223-3535   *SIC* 5149

LATHAM DISTRIBUTORS   *p885*
475 GLENDALE AVE, ST CATHARINES, ON, L2P 3Y2

(905) 682-3344   *SIC* 5149

LEE LI HOLDINGS INC   *p740*
299 COURTNEYPARK DR E, MISSISSAUGA, ON, L5T 2T6

(905) 565-5968   *SIC* 5149

LEIS PET DISTRIBUTING INC   *p1013*
1315 HUTCHISON RD, WELLESLEY, ON, N0B 2T0

(519) 656-3559   *SIC* 5149

LEVEL GROUND TRADING LTD   *p267*
1757 SEAN HTS, SAANICHTON, BC, V8M 0B3

(250) 544-0932   *SIC* 5149

MADDIES NATURAL PET PRODUCTS LTD   *p209*
6655 DENNETT PL, DELTA, BC, V4G 1N4

(604) 946-7977   *SIC* 5149

MADISON COUNTY FOOD & BEVERAGE CO. LTD., THE   *p809*
43 ONTARIO ST, ORILLIA, ON, L3V 0T7

(705) 326-3586   *SIC* 5149

MAISON BERGEVIN INC, LA   *p1260*
199 RUE JOLY, QUEBEC, QC, G1L 1N7

SIC 5149

MANITOBA COOPERATIVE HONEY PRODUCERS LIMITED   *p384*
625 ROSEBERRY ST, WINNIPEG, MB, R3H 0T4

(204) 783-2240   *SIC* 5149

MARCATUS QED INC   *p991*
43 HANNA AVE UNIT C-424, TORONTO, ON, M6K 1X1

(416) 255-0099   *SIC* 5149

MAZZA INNOVATION LTD   *p209*
7901 PROGRESS WAY, DELTA, BC, V4G 1A3

(604) 337-1578   *SIC* 5149

MEAD JOHNSON NUTRITION (CANADA) CO   *p624*
535 LEGGET DR SUITE 900, KANATA, ON, K2K 3B8

(613) 595-4700   *SIC* 5149

METROPOLITAN TEA COMPANY LTD, THE   *p571*
41 BUTTERICK RD, ETOBICOKE, ON, M8W 4W4

(416) 588-0089   *SIC* 5149

MIG HOLDINGS INC   *p801*
156 REYNOLDS ST, OAKVILLE, ON, L6J 3K9

(905) 339-0229   *SIC* 5149

MIKE AND MIKE'S INC   *p1032*
1 ROYAL GATE BLVD UNIT F, WOODBRIDGE, ON, L4L 8Z7

(416) 987-2772   *SIC* 5149

MILFORA DAIRY SUPPLIES INC   *p620*
743 SKYHILLS RD, HUNTSVILLE, ON, P1H 2N5

(705) 789-4557   *SIC* 5149

MIXOLOGY CANADA INC   *p504*
45 ARMTHORPE RD, BRAMPTON, ON, L6T 5M4

(905) 793-9100   *SIC* 5149

MOSTI MONDIALE INC   *p1356*
6865 RTE 132, SAINTE-CATHERINE, QC, J5C 1B6

(450) 638-6380   *SIC* 5149

MOULIN HUBERT LACOSTE INC   *p1356*
114 RTE SAINT-JEAN N, SAINTE-CLAIRE, QC, G0R 2V0

(418) 883-3688   *SIC* 5149

MR. SNACK (1997) INC   *p119*
6551 GATEWAY BLVD NW, EDMONTON, AB, T6H 2J1

(780) 414-0505   *SIC* 5149

MULDOON'S OWN AUTHENTIC COFFEE CORP   *p697*
5680 TIMBERLEA BLVD, MISSISSAUGA, ON, L4W 4M6

(905) 712-2233   *SIC* 5149

MULTI-MARQUES INC   *p1357*
3443 AV FRANCIS-HUGHES BUREAU 1, SAINTE-DOROTHEE, QC, H7L 5A6

(450) 629-9444   *SIC* 5149

MUSKOKA SPRINGS NATURAL SPRING

WATER INC p598
220 BAY ST, GRAVENHURST, ON, P1P
1H1
(705) 687-8852 *SIC* 5149

NAKA SALES LIMITED p586
252 BROCKPORT DR, ETOBICOKE, ON,
M9W 5S1
(416) 748-3073 *SIC* 5149

**NATIONAL SAFETY ASSOCIATES OF
CANADA INC / NSA CANADA INC** p698
2785 SKYMARK AVE SUITE 15, MISSIS-
SAUGA, ON, L4W 4Y3
(905) 624-6368 *SIC* 5149

NATRA CHOCOLATE AMERICA INC p662
2800 ROXBURGH RD, LONDON, ON, N6N
1K9
(519) 681-9494 *SIC* 5149

NATURAL LIFE NUTRITION INC p193
7337 NORTH FRASER WAY UNIT 108,
BURNABY, BC, V5J 0G7
(604) 207-0493 *SIC* 5149

NATURALLY FIT SUPPLEMENTS INC p404
125 ROUTE 105, LOWER ST MARYS, NB,
E3A 8P8
(506) 451-8707 *SIC* 5149

NATURE'S PATH BAKING INC p261
9100 VAN HORNE WAY, RICHMOND, BC,
V6X 1W3
(604) 248-8806 *SIC* 5149

NATURE'S PATH FOODS INC p261
9100 VAN HORNE WAY, RICHMOND, BC,
V6X 1W3
(604) 248-8777 *SIC* 5149

**NATURE'S SUNSHINE PRODUCTS OF
CANADA LTD** p505
44 PEEL CENTRE DR UNIT 402, BRAMP-
TON, ON, L6T 4B5
(905) 458-6100 *SIC* 5149

NATURISTE INC p1330
5900 BOUL HENRI-BOURASSA O, SAINT-
LAURENT, QC, H4R 1V9
(514) 336-2244 *SIC* 5149

NEAL BROTHERS INC p853
50 VOGELL RD UNIT 6, RICHMOND HILL,
ON, L4B 3K6
(905) 738-7955 *SIC* 5149

NESTLE CANADA INC p215
66700 OTHELLO RD, HOPE, BC, V0X 1L1
(604) 860-4888 *SIC* 5149

NESTLE CANADA INC p586
65 CARRIER DR, ETOBICOKE, ON, M9W
5V9
(416) 675-1300 *SIC* 5149

NESTLE CANADA INC p849
101 BROCK RD S, PUSLINCH, ON, N0B
2J0
(519) 763-9462 *SIC* 5149

**NEW AGE MARKETING & BRAND MAN-
AGEMENT INC** p36
7210H 5 ST SE, CALGARY, AB, T2H 2L9
(403) 212-1055 *SIC* 5149

NITTA CASINGS (CANADA) INC p673
57 STEELCASE RD W, MARKHAM, ON,
L3R 2M4
(905) 475-6441 *SIC* 5149

**NOR-COM INVESTMENT ENTERPRISES
LTD** p132
10525 100 AVE SUITE 200, GRANDE
PRAIRIE, AB, T8V 0V8
(780) 539-6080 *SIC* 5149

**NORTH AMERICAN IMPEX INCORPO-
RATED** p673
600 HOOD RD, MARKHAM, ON, L3R 3K9
SIC 5149

NOTHING BUT NATURE INC p973
176 ST. GEORGE ST, TORONTO, ON, M5R
2M7
(416) 934-5034 *SIC* 5149

NUMAGE TRADING INC p556
894 EDGELEY BLVD, CONCORD, ON, L4K
4V4
(905) 660-4172 *SIC* 5149

NUTRACELLE p1042
9 CARRIAGE LANE, STRATFORD, PE, C1B

2G9
(877) 229-1207 *SIC* 5149

NUTRAFARMS INC p487
261 KING ST, BARRIE, ON, L4N 6B5
(705) 739-0669 *SIC* 5149

NUTTER'S BULK & NATURAL FOODS INC
p146
1601 DUNMORE RD SE SUITE 107,
MEDICINE HAT, AB, T1A 1Z8
(403) 529-1664 *SIC* 5149

ODEM INTERNATIONAL INC p1288
483 CH DE LA GRANDE-COTE, ROSE-
MERE, QC, J7A 1M1
(450) 965-1412 *SIC* 5149

OLAM CANADA COMPANY p741
1100 MID-WAY BLVD UNIT 7, MISSIS-
SAUGA, ON, L5T 1V8
(905) 795-8871 *SIC* 5149

OLIVE THE SENSES p336
1701 DOUGLAS ST UNIT 9, VICTORIA, BC,
V8W 0C1
(250) 590-8418 *SIC* 5149

OLIVIER'S CANDIES LTD p17
2828 54 AVE SE BAY CTR, CALGARY, AB,
T2C 0A7
(403) 266-6028 *SIC* 5149

**OLYMPIC WHOLESALE COMPANY LIM-
ITED** p474
75 GREEN CRT, AJAX, ON, L1S 6W9
(905) 426-5188 *SIC* 5149

OMEGA FOOD IMPORTERS CO. LTD p741
395 PENDANT DR UNIT 2, MISSISSAUGA,
ON, L5T 2W9
(905) 212-9252 *SIC* 5149

ONTARIO BAKERY SUPPLIES LIMITED
p787
84 OAKDALE RD, NORTH YORK, ON, M3N
1V9
(416) 742-6741 *SIC* 5149

ONTARIO NATURAL FOOD COMPANY INC
p732
5800 KEATON CRES, MISSISSAUGA, ON,
L5R 3K2
(905) 507-2021 *SIC* 5149

ORANGE MAISON INC p1110
904 RUE DUFFERIN, GRANBY, QC, J2H
0T8
SIC 5149

ORGANIC MEADOW INC p601
335 LAIRD RD UNIT 1, GUELPH, ON, N1G
4P7
(519) 767-9694 *SIC* 5149

ORIGINAL JOE'S p139
5411 DISCOVERY WAY UNIT 101, LEDUC,
AB, T9E 8N4
(780) 986-6965 *SIC* 5149

OZERY'S PITA BREAK PARTNERSHIP
p1032
11 DIRECTOR CRT, WOODBRIDGE, ON,
L4L 4S5
(905) 265-1143 *SIC* 5149

**PACE PROCESSING AND PRODUCT DE-
VELOPMENT LTD** p272
19495 55 AVE SUITE 107, SURREY, BC,
V3S 8P7
(604) 539-9201 *SIC* 5149

PACIFIC BLENDS LTD p247
1625 KEBET WAY UNIT 100, PORT CO-
QUITLAM, BC, V3C 5W9
(604) 945-4600 *SIC* 5149

PACIFIC VETERINARY SALES LIMITED
p175
34079 GLADYS AVE, ABBOTSFORD, BC,
V2S 2E8
(604) 850-1510 *SIC* 5149

**PACIFIC WELLFARE RESOURCE INVEST-
MENT INC** p181
8218 NORTH FRASER WAY, BURNABY,
BC, V3N 0E9
(778) 989-6678 *SIC* 5149

PAN PACIFIC PET LIMITED p175
34079 GLADYS AVE, ABBOTSFORD, BC,
V2S 2E8
(604) 850-1510 *SIC* 5149

PEPSI BOTTLING GROUP p141
2400 31 ST N, LETHBRIDGE, AB, T1H 5K8
(403) 327-1310 *SIC* 5149

**PEPSI BOTTLING GROUP (CANADA), ULC,
THE** p662
40 ENTERPRISE DR SUITE 1, LONDON,
ON, N6N 1A7
(519) 681-0030 *SIC* 5149

**PEPSI BOTTLING GROUP (CANADA), ULC,
THE** p818
869 BELFAST RD, OTTAWA, ON, K1G 0Z4
(613) 244-9961 *SIC* 5149

**PEPSI BOTTLING GROUP (CANADA), ULC,
THE** p1079
1800 BOUL TALBOT, CHICOUTIMI, QC,
G7H 7Y1
(418) 549-3135 *SIC* 5149

PEPSI COLA CANADA LTEE p1285
401 BOUL DE LA RIVIERE, RIMOUSKI, QC,
G5L 7R1
(418) 722-8080 *SIC* 5149

PET SCIENCE LTD p513
14 REGAN RD UNIT 1, BRAMPTON, ON,
L7A 1B9
(905) 840-1300 *SIC* 5149

**PETITE BRETONNE (DISTRIBUTION) INC,
LA** p1059
1210 BOUL MICHELE-BOHEC,
BLAINVILLE, QC, J7C 5S4
(450) 420-9159 *SIC* 5149

PILOT COFFEE CORP p920
50 WAGSTAFF DR, TORONTO, ON, M4L
3W9
(416) 546-4006 *SIC* 5149

PLACEMENTS ROGERCAN INC, LES p1134
2010 BOUL DAGENAIS O, LAVAL-OUEST,
QC, H7L 5W2
(450) 963-5080 *SIC* 5149

PLANET BEAN INC p600
259 GRANGE RD UNIT 2, GUELPH, ON,
N1E 6R5
(519) 837-1040 *SIC* 5149

PLANET FOODS INC p17
4040E 80 AVE SE, CALGARY, AB, T2C 2J7
(403) 281-7911 *SIC* 5149

POLAR FOODS INC p350
GD, FISHER BRANCH, MB, R0C 0Z0
(204) 372-6132 *SIC* 5149

POWERBEV INC p512
60 HEREFORD ST, BRAMPTON, ON, L6Y
0N3
(905) 453-2855 *SIC* 5149

PRANA BIOVEGETALIENS INC p1327
1440 BOUL JULES-POITRAS, SAINT-
LAURENT, QC, H4N 1X7
(514) 276-4864 *SIC* 5149

PREMIUM BRANDS BAKERY GROUP INC
p261
10991 SHELLBRIDGE WAY, RICHMOND,
BC, V6X 3C6
(604) 656-3100 *SIC* 5149

**PRODUITS & BASES DE SOUPE MAJOR
DU CANADA INC, LES** p1335
7171 BOUL THIMENS, SAINT-LAURENT,
QC, H4S 2A2
(514) 745-1163 *SIC* 5149

PRODUITS ANDALOS INC p1327
230 BOUL LEBEAU, SAINT-LAURENT, QC,
H4N 1R4
(514) 832-1000 *SIC* 5149

**PRODUITS DE L'ERABLE BOLDUC & FILS
INC, LES** p1353
292 3E RANG N, SAINT-VICTOR, QC, G0M
2B0
(418) 588-3315 *SIC* 5149

PRODUITS DE PATISSERIE MICHAUD INC
p1281
1520 AV DES AFFAIRES, QUEBEC, QC,
G3J 1Y8
(418) 843-3712 *SIC* 5149

PUR BRANDS INC p287
2642 NOOTKA ST, VANCOUVER, BC, V5M
3M5
(604) 299-5045 *SIC* 5149

PURESOURCE INC p604
5068 WHITELAW RD UNIT 5, GUELPH,
ON, N1H 6J3
(519) 837-2140 *SIC* 5149

PURETAP WATER DISTILLERS LTD p742
950 VERBENA RD, MISSISSAUGA, ON,
L5T 1T6
(905) 670-7400 *SIC* 5149

QUALITY NATURAL FOODS CANADA INC
p874
420 NUGGET AVE SUITE 1, SCARBOR-
OUGH, ON, M1S 4A4
(416) 261-8700 *SIC* 5149

QZINA SPECIALTY FOODS INC p94
12547 129 ST NW, EDMONTON, AB, T5L
1H7
(780) 447-4499 *SIC* 5149

RED DEER BOTTLING COMPANY LTD p156
6855 EDGAR INDUSTRIAL DR, RED
DEER, AB, T4P 3R2
(403) 346-2585 *SIC* 5149

RFI CANADA PARTNERSHIP p1000
178 MAIN ST, UNIONVILLE, ON, L3R 2G9
(905) 534-1044 *SIC* 5149

ROLAND'S SEA VEGETABLES p402
174 HILL RD, GRAND MANAN, NB, E5G
4C4
(506) 662-3468 *SIC* 5149

ROYAL CANIN CANADA INC p849
100 BEIBER RD, PUSLINCH, ON, N0B 2J0
(519) 780-6700 *SIC* 5149

SATAU INC p1091
71 BOUL BRUNSWICK, DOLLARD-DES-
ORMEAUX, QC, H9B 2N4
(514) 631-5775 *SIC* 5149

SCHAAF FOODS INC p1011
130 FROBISHER DR SUITE 6, WATER-
LOO, ON, N2V 1Z9
(519) 747-1655 *SIC* 5149

SEASIA FOODS LTD p291
8310 PRINCE EDWARD ST, VANCOUVER,
BC, V5X 3R9
(604) 618-8680 *SIC* 5149

SEED-EX INC p351
GD, LETELLIER, MB, R0G 1C0
(204) 737-2000 *SIC* 5149

SEQUEL NATURALS ULC p189
3001 WAYBURNE DR UNIT 101, BURN-
ABY, BC, V5G 4W3
(866) 839-8863 *SIC* 5149

SERVICES ALIMENTAIRES WOLFE INC
p1342
2624 BOUL DES OISEAUX, SAINT-
LAURENT, QC, H7L 4N9
(450) 628-5760 *SIC* 5149

SHAFER - HAGGART LTD p316
1100 MELVILLE ST SUITE 938, VANCOU-
VER, BC, V6E 4A6
(604) 669-5512 *SIC* 5149

SHERIDAN VENTURES LTD p714
2222 SOUTH SHERIDAN WAY UNIT 210,
MISSISSAUGA, ON, L5J 2M4
(905) 823-7780 *SIC* 5149

SIGNALISATION DES CANTONS INC p1376
1001 CH DION, SHERBROOKE, QC, J1R
0R8
(819) 987-1483 *SIC* 5149

SIMPLY THE BEST GOURMET PRODUCTS
p273
17665 66A AVE SUITE 110, SURREY, BC,
V3S 2A7
(604) 576-9395 *SIC* 5149

SMALL POTATOES URBAN DELIVERY INC
p285
1660 HASTINGS ST E, VANCOUVER, BC,
V5L 1S6
(604) 215-7783 *SIC* 5149

**SNOWCAP INTERIOR FOOD SERVICES
LTD** p180
4130 SPALLUMCHEEN DR, ARMSTRONG,
BC, V0E 1B6
(250) 546-8781 *SIC* 5149

SOURCES VEO INC, LES p1112
1335 CH DE LA RIVIERE-ROUGE,

GRENVILLE-SUR-LA-ROUGE, QC, J0V 1B0

(819) 242-2882   *SIC* 5149

SOUTHERN GLAZER'S WINE AND SPIRITS OF CANADA, LLC   *p572*
3250 BLOOR ST W SUITE 901, ETOBI-COKE, ON, M8X 2X9

(647) 347-7711   *SIC* 5149

SPECIAL D. BAKING LTD   *p116*
6003 92 ST NW, EDMONTON, AB, T6E 3A5

(780) 436-9650   *SIC* 5149

ST JOSEPHS BAKERY (NIAGARA) INC*p884*
53 FACER ST, ST CATHARINES, ON, L2M 5H7

(905) 937-4411   *SIC* 5149

ST-PIERRE, JULES LTEE   *p1155*
1054 BOUL ALBINY-PAQUETTE, MONT-LAURIER, QC, J9L 1M1

SIC 5149

STAR SALT INC   *p1224*
3351 RUE SAINT-PATRICK, MONTREAL, QC, H4E 1A1

(514) 933-1117   *SIC* 5149

STARR CULINARY DELIGHTS INC   *p689*
3880 NASHUA DR, MISSISSAUGA, ON, L4V 1M5

(905) 612-1958   *SIC* 5149

STORCK CANADA INC   *p707*
2 ROBERT SPECK PKY SUITE 695, MIS-SISSAUGA, ON, L4Z 1H8

(905) 272-4480   *SIC* 5149

STOWE, LESLEY FINE FOODS LTD   *p321*
1685 5TH AVE W, VANCOUVER, BC, V6J 1N5

SIC 5149

STRATOS PIZZERIA   *p1385*
5030 BOUL DES FORGES, TROIS-RIVIERES, QC, G8Y 1X2

(819) 694-7777   *SIC* 5149

SUNCO FOODS INC   *p194*
9208 NORTH FRASER CRES, BURNABY, BC, V5J 0E3

(604) 451-9208   *SIC* 5149

SUNNY CRUNCH FOODS LIMITED   *p675*
200 SHIELDS CRT, MARKHAM, ON, L3R 9T5

(905) 475-0422   *SIC* 5149

SUNOPTA INC   *p559*
8755 KEELE ST, CONCORD, ON, L4K 2N1

(905) 738-4304   *SIC* 5149

SUNOPTA INC   *p727*
2233 ARGENTIA RD SUITE 401, MISSIS-SAUGA, ON, L5N 2X7

(905) 821-9669   *SIC* 5149

SWEET POTATO INCORPORATED, THE   *p994*
108 VINE AVE, TORONTO, ON, M6P 1V7

(416) 762-4848   *SIC* 5149

SWISS WATER DECAFFEINATED COFFEE INC   *p183*
3131 LAKE CITY WAY, BURNABY, BC, V5A 3A3

(604) 420-4050   *SIC* 5149

TANNIS TRADING INC   *p819*
2390 STEVENAGE DR, OTTAWA, ON, K1G 3W3

(613) 736-6000   *SIC* 5149

TASTE OF NATURE FOODS INC   *p675*
230 FERRIER ST, MARKHAM, ON, L3R 2Z5

(905) 415-8218   *SIC* 5149

TATA GLOBAL BEVERAGES CANADA INC   *p588*
10 CARLSON CRT SUITE 700, ETOBI-COKE, ON, M9W 6L2

(416) 798-1224   *SIC* 5149

TEMPLE LIFESTYLE INCORPORATED   *p1179*
9600 RUE MEILLEUR BUREAU 932, MON-TREAL, QC, H2N 2E3

(514) 382-3805   *SIC* 5149

TERRA BEATA FARMS LTD   *p462*
161 MONK POINT RD, LUNENBURG, NS, B0J 2C0

(902) 634-4435   *SIC* 5149

THAI UNITED FOOD TRADING LTD   *p194*
7978 NORTH FRASER WAY SUITE 2, BURNABY, BC, V5J 0C7

(604) 437-4933   *SIC* 5149

TIFFANY GATE FOODS INC   *p588*
195 STEINWAY BLVD, ETOBICOKE, ON, M9W 6H6

(416) 213-9720   *SIC* 5149

TOUT-PRET INC   *p1275*
2950 AV WATT BUREAU 12, QUEBEC, QC, G1X 4A8

(418) 527-5557   *SIC* 5149

TROPHY FOODS INC   *p19*
6210 44 ST SE, CALGARY, AB, T2C 4L3

(403) 571-6887   *SIC* 5149

TRUEMAN DISTRIBUTION LTD   *p19*
6280 76 AVE SE UNIT 10, CALGARY, AB, T2C 5N5

(403) 236-3008   *SIC* 5149

UNFI CANADA, INC   *p187*
4535 STILL CREEK AVE, BURNABY, BC, V5C 5W1

(604) 253-6549   *SIC* 5149

UNFI CANADA, INC   *p560*
8755 KEELE ST, CONCORD, ON, L4K 2N1

(905) 738-4204   *SIC* 5149

UNFI CANADA, INC   *p560*
8755 KEELE ST, CONCORD, ON, L4K 2N1

(905) 738-4204   *SIC* 5149

VAN HOUTTE COFFEE SERVICE   *p650*
775 INDUSTRIAL RD UNIT 1, LONDON, ON, N5V 3N5

SIC 5149

VANCOUVER WATER ENTERPRISES CANADA CO., LTD   *p198*
44488 SOUTH SUMAS RD SUITE 125, CHILLIWACK, BC, V2R 5M3

(604) 824-7455   *SIC* 5149

VENTES RUDOLPH 2000 INC, LES   *p1173*
4625 RUE D'IBERVILLE, MONTREAL, QC, H2H 2L9

(514) 596-1998   *SIC* 5149

VICTORIAN EPICURE INC   *p268*
10555 WEST SAANICH RD, SIDNEY, BC, V8L 6A8

(250) 656-5751   *SIC* 5149

VINCENT S. VARIETE LIMITEE   *p1282*
433 RUE SAINT-PAUL, REPENTIGNY, QC, J5Z 0C9

(450) 585-1687   *SIC* 5149

VISCOFAN CANADA INC   *p1327*
290 RUE BENJAMIN-HUDON BUREAU 2, SAINT-LAURENT, QC, H4N 1J4

(514) 333-1700   *SIC* 5149

WESTERN RICE MILLS LTD   *p266*
6231 WESTMINSTER HWY UNIT 120, RICHMOND, BC, V7C 4V4

(604) 321-0338   *SIC* 5149

WESTERN WATER INDUSTRIES   *p1434*
301 CENTRAL AVE, SASKATOON, SK, S7N 2E9

(306) 374-8555   *SIC* 5149

WORLEE INTERNATIONAL INC   *p1342*
750 RUE GOUGEON, SAINT-LAURENT, QC, H4T 4L5

(514) 332-6455   *SIC* 5149

YOUR PETSCHOICE ULC   *p677*
7300 WARDEN AVE SUITE 106, MARKHAM, ON, L3R 9Z6

(905) 946-1200   *SIC* 5149

ZARCONE BROTHERS LTD   *p615*
20 HEMPSTEAD DR, HAMILTON, ON, L8W 2E7

(905) 574-1500   *SIC* 5149

ZAVIDA COFFEE COMPANY INC   *p561*
70 CONNIE CRES UNIT 12, CONCORD, ON, L4K 1L6

(905) 738-0103   *SIC* 5149

ZORBA'S BAKERY & FOODS LTD   *p194*
7173 BULLER AVE, BURNABY, BC, V5J 4S1

(604) 439-7731   *SIC* 5149

SIC 5153 Grain and field beans

0695602 BC LTD   *p241*
998 HARBOURSIDE DR SUITE 211, NORTH VANCOUVER, BC, V7P 3T2

(604) 988-3833   *SIC* 5153

1309497 ALBERTA LTD   *p136*
4923 50 ST, INNISFAIL, AB, T4G 1T1

(403) 227-2774   *SIC* 5153

1815264 ONTARIO INC   *p718*
251 QUEEN ST S UNIT 252, MISSIS-SAUGA, ON, L5M 1L7

(905) 593-4204   *SIC* 5153

5465461 MANITOBA INC   *p362*
28 CHRISTOPHER ST, WINNIPEG, MB, R2C 2Z2

(204) 989-7696   *SIC* 5153

8956995 CANADA INC   *p1116*
3450 RUE SAINT-DOMINIQUE BUREAU 100, JONQUIERE, QC, G8A 2M3

(514) 374-1315   *SIC* 5153

AGRICOM INTERNATIONAL INC   *p241*
828 HARBOURSIDE DR SUITE 213, NORTH VANCOUVER, BC, V7P 3R9

(604) 983-6922   *SIC* 5153

ALPHA COMMODITIES CORP   *p691*
5750 TIMBERLEA BLVD UNIT 17, MISSIS-SAUGA, ON, L4W 5N8

(416) 907-5505   *SIC* 5153

BAR-B-DEE FARMS LTD   *p496*
GD, BORNHOLM, ON, N0K 1A0

(519) 347-2966   *SIC* 5153

BEECHWOOD AGRI SERVICES INC   *p837*
123 KING ST, PARKHILL, ON, N0M 2K0

(519) 294-0474   *SIC* 5153

BROADGRAIN COMMODITIES INC   *p937*
18 KING ST E SUITE 900, TORONTO, ON, M5C 1C4

(416) 504-0070   *SIC* 5153

BUNGE GRAIN DU CANADA INC   *p1310*
6120 RUE DES SEIGNEURS E, SAINT-HYACINTHE, QC, J2R 1Z9

SIC 5153

BUNGE GRAIN DU CANADA INC   *p1359*
60 RUE SAINT-SIMON, SAINTE-MADELEINE, QC, J0H 1S0

SIC 5153

CANADIAN OATS MILLING LTD   *p168*
55021 RGE RD 234A, STURGEON COUNTY, AB, T8T 2A9

(780) 973-9102   *SIC* 5153

CANFARM PULSE INC   *p390*
1427 SOMERVILLE AVE, WINNIPEG, MB, R3T 1C3

(204) 298-3595   *SIC* 5153

CARGILL LIMITED   *p377*
240 GRAHAM AVE SUITE 300, WINNIPEG, MB, R3C 0J7

(204) 947-0141   *SIC* 5153

CARGILL LIMITED   *p1074*
7901 RUE SAMUEL-HATT, CHAMBLY, QC, J3L 6V7

(450) 447-4600   *SIC* 5153

CENTURY AGRO LTD   *p1420*
845 BROAD ST UNIT 207, REGINA, SK, S4R 8G9

(306) 949-7182   *SIC* 5153

CEREALEX INC   *p1352*
666 RANG DU RUISSEAU-DES-ANGES S, SAINT-ROCH-DE-L'ACHIGAN, QC, J0K 3H0

(450) 588-3132   *SIC* 5153

COOP DES CANTONS COOPERATIVE AGRICOLE   *p1081*
96 RUE MAIN E, COATICOOK, QC, J1A 1N2

(819) 849-9833   *SIC* 5153

COOP UNIFRONTIERES, LA   *p1298*
4 RANG SAINT-ANDRE, SAINT-CYPRIEN-DE-NAPIERVILLE, QC, J0J 1L0

(450) 245-3308   *SIC* 5153

CYRILLE FRIGON (1996) INC   *p1146*
1351 BOUL SAINT-LAURENT O, LOUI-SEVILLE, QC, J5V 2L4

(819) 228-9491   *SIC* 5153

DENNIS JACKSON SEED SERVICE LTD   *p565*
1315 JACKSON ST, DRESDEN, ON, N0P 1M0

(519) 683-4413   *SIC* 5153

DUNNINGTON HOLDINGS LTD   *p1436*
1 COMMODITY DR, SUCCESS, SK, S0N 2R0

(306) 773-9748   *SIC* 5153

ELEVATEUR RIVE-SUD INC   *p1082*
4065 RUE INDUSTRIELLE, CONTRE-COEUR, QC, J0L 1C0

(450) 587-2500   *SIC* 5153

FAIRCREST FARMS LIMITED   *p1035*
455017 45TH LINE, WOODSTOCK, ON, N4S 7V7

(519) 537-8713   *SIC* 5153

FERGUSON BROS. OF ST. THOMAS LIMITED   *p889*
43850 FERGUSON LINE SUITE 6, ST THOMAS, ON, N5P 3T1

(519) 631-3463   *SIC* 5153

FERMES PROLIX INC   *p1315*
705 BOUL SAINT-LUC, SAINT-JEAN-SUR-RICHELIEU, QC, J2W 2G6

(450) 348-9436   *SIC* 5153

FILL-MORE SEEDS INC   *p1407*
1 RAILWAY AVE, FILLMORE, SK, S0G 1N0

(306) 722-3353   *SIC* 5153

GARDINER DAM TERMINAL JOINT VENTURE   *p1436*
GD, STRONGFIELD, SK, S0H 3Z0

(306) 857-2134   *SIC* 5153

GARDINER DAM TERMINAL LTD   *p1409*
HWY 19 OLD HWY SUITE 44, LOREBURN, SK, S0H 2S0

(306) 857-2134   *SIC* 5153

GEDCO   *p974*
1033 BAY ST SUITE 212, TORONTO, ON, M5S 3A5

(416) 961-1777   *SIC* 5153

GLOBEWAYS CANADA INC   *p695*
2570 MATHESON BLVD E SUITE 110, MIS-SISSAUGA, ON, L4W 4Z3

(905) 712-1010   *SIC* 5153

GRAIN ST-LAURENT INC   *p1188*
407 RUE MCGILL BUREAU 315, MON-TREAL, QC, H2Y 2G3

(514) 871-2037   *SIC* 5153

GRAINS ELITE S.E.C.   *p1226*
9001 BOUL DE L'ACADIE BUREAU 200, MONTREAL, QC, H4N 3H7

SIC 5153

GRAINSCONNECT CANADA OPERATIONS INC   *p16*
48 QUARRY PARK BLVD SE SUITE 260, CALGARY, AB, T2C 5P2

(403) 879-2727   *SIC* 5153

GREAT CANADIAN BEAN COMPANY INC, THE   *p473*
26831 NEW ONTARIO RD, AILSA CRAIG, ON, N0M 1A0

(519) 232-4449   *SIC* 5153

HALIFAX GRAIN ELEVATOR LIMITED *p451*
951 SOUTH BLAND ST, HALIFAX, NS, B3H 4S6

(902) 421-1714   *SIC* 5153

HEGGIE, R. K. GRAIN LTD   *p153*
GD, RAYMOND, AB, T0K 2S0

SIC 5153

HENSALL DISTRICT CO-OPERATIVE, IN-CORPORATED   *p620*
1 DAVIDSON DR, HENSALL, ON, N0M 1X0

(519) 262-3002   *SIC* 5153

HORIZON AGRO INC   *p352*
1086 HORIZON RD, MORRIS, MB, R0G 1K0

(204) 746-2026   *SIC* 5153

ILTA GRAIN INC   *p282*
8427 160 ST, SURREY, BC, V4N 0V6

(604) 597-5060   *SIC* 5153

INGREDIENTS PLUS DISTRIBUTION INC   *p245*
585 SEABORNE AVE UNIT 2120, PORT

COQUITLAM, BC, V3B 0M3
(604) 468-7146   *SIC* 5153
KALSHEA COMMODITIES INC
42 PARKROYAL BAY, WINNIPEG, MB, R3P
1P2
(204) 272-3773   *SIC* 5153
LD ENERGY CANADA LP   *p53*
350 7 AVE SW, CALGARY, AB, T2P 3N9
(403) 410-1199   *SIC* 5153
LINEAR GRAIN INC   *p348*
67 CENTER AVE W, CARMAN, MB, R0G
0J0
(204) 745-6747   *SIC* 5153
LOUIS DREYFUS COMPANY CANADA ULC
p65
525 11 AVE SW SUITE 500, CALGARY, AB,
T2R 0C9
(403) 205-3322   *SIC* 5153
**LOUIS DREYFUS COMPANY YORKTON
TRADING LP**   *p65*
525 11 AVE SW SUITE 500, CALGARY, AB,
T2R 0C9
(403) 205-3322   *SIC* 5153
MARINA COMMODITIES INC   *p710*
90 BURNHAMTHORPE RD W SUITE 1102,
MISSISSAUGA, ON, L5B 3C3
(905) 828-0777   *SIC* 5153
MAXWELL FARM ELEVATOR   *p544*
604 CONCESSION 2, CHESLEY, ON, N0G
1L0
(519) 363-3423   *SIC* 5153
MILLTOWN COLONY FARMS LTD   *p349*
GD, ELIE, MB, R0H 0H0
(204) 353-2838   *SIC* 5153
MILLTOWN METAL SHOP LTD   *p349*
GD, ELIE, MB, R0H 0H0
(204) 353-2741   *SIC* 5153
MUNRO AGROMART LTD   *p643*
6011 34 HWY, LANCASTER, ON, K0C 1N0
(613) 347-3063   *SIC* 5153
**NEGOCIANTS DE GRAINS OCCIDENTAUX
INC**   *p1117*
16766 RTE TRANSCANADIENNE BUREAU
400, KIRKLAND, QC, H9H 4M7
(514) 509-2119   *SIC* 5153
NEWCO GRAIN LTD   *p80*
GD, COALDALE, AB, T1M 1K8
(403) 345-3335   *SIC* 5153
NORAG RESOURCES INC   *p847*
4476 COUNTY 10 RD, PORT HOPE, ON,
L1A 3V5
(905) 753-1180   *SIC* 5153
NOVA GRAIN INC   *p1318*
800 RUE BOUCHER, SAINT-JEAN-SUR-
RICHELIEU, QC, J3B 7Z8
(450) 348-0976   *SIC* 5153
NUVISION COMMODITIES INC   *p357*
49 ELEVATOR RD, ST JEAN BAPTISTE,
MB, R0G 2B0
(204) 758-3401   *SIC* 5153
PARKLAND PULSE GRAIN CO. LTD   *p1412*
GD LCD MAIN, NORTH BATTLEFORD, SK,
S9A 2X5
(306) 445-4199   *SIC* 5153
PARRISH & HEIMBECKER, LIMITED   *p375*
201 PORTAGE AVE SUITE 1400, WIN-
NIPEG, MB, R3B 3K6
(204) 956-2030   *SIC* 5153
PATERSON GLOBALFOODS INC   *p379*
333 MAIN ST 22ND FL, WINNIPEG, MB,
R3C 4E2
(204) 956-2090   *SIC* 5153
PATTERSON GRAIN LIMITED   *p888*
23364 WELLBURN RD SUITE 3, ST
MARYS, ON, N4X 1C6
(519) 461-1829   *SIC* 5153
PRAIRIE HERITAGE SEEDS INC   *p1415*
HIGHWAY 28 N MILE 4, RADVILLE, SK,
S0C 2G0
(306) 869-2926   *SIC* 5153
PRAIRIE PULSE INC   *p1437*
700 CAMPBELL DR, VANSCOY, SK, S0L
3J0
(306) 249-9236   *SIC* 5153

**PRINCE EDWARD ISLAND GRAIN ELEVA-
TORS CORPORATION**   *p1041*
62 VICTORIA ST, KENSINGTON, PE, C0B
1M0
(902) 836-8935   *SIC* 5153
RICHARDSON INTERNATIONAL LIMITED
p239
375 LOW LEVEL RD, NORTH VANCOU-
VER, BC, V7L 1A7
(604) 987-8855   *SIC* 5153
RICHARDSON INTERNATIONAL LIMITED
p375
1 LOMBARD PL SUITE 2800, WINNIPEG,
MB, R3B 0X3
(204) 934-5961   *SIC* 5153
RICHARDSON MILLING LIMITED   *p355*
1 CAN-OAT DR, PORTAGE LA PRAIRIE,
MB, R1N 3W1
(204) 857-9700   *SIC* 5153
RICHARDSON PIONEER LIMITED   *p375*
1 LOMBARD PL SUITE 2700, WINNIPEG,
MB, R3B 0X8
(204) 934-5961   *SIC* 5153
RICHARDSON, JAMES & SONS, LIMITED
p375
3000 ONE LOMBARD PL, WINNIPEG, MB,
R3B 0Y1
(204) 953-7970   *SIC* 5153
RIESE INVESTMENTS LTD   *p1408*
1 RIESE BAY, LA RONGE, SK, S0J 1L0
(306) 425-2314   *SIC* 5153
ROSENDALE FARMS LIMITED   *p1007*
544 SAWMILL RD, WATERLOO, ON, N2J
4G8
(519) 744-4941   *SIC* 5153
SEMICAN INTERNATIONAL INC   *p1246*
366 10E RANG, PLESSISVILLE, QC, G6L
2Y2
(819) 362-6759   *SIC* 5153
SEVITA INTERNATIONAL CORPORATION
p622
11451 CAMERON RD, INKERMAN, ON,
K0E 1J0
(613) 989-3000   *SIC* 5153
SG CERESCO INC   *p1353*
164 CH DE LA GRANDE-LIGNE, SAINT-
URBAIN-PREMIER, QC, J0S 1Y0
(450) 427-3831   *SIC* 5153
SHADY LANE GRAIN FACILITY   *p171*
GD, WANHAM, AB, T0H 3P0
(780) 694-3005   *SIC* 5153
SIMPSON SEEDS INC   *p1411*
1170 NORTH SERVICE RD, MOOSE JAW,
SK, S6H 4P8
(306) 693-2132   *SIC* 5153
SNOBELEN FARMS LTD   *p663*
323 HAVELOCK ST, LUCKNOW, ON, N0G
2H0
(519) 528-2092   *SIC* 5153
SOUTH WEST AG PARTNERS INC   *p543*
40 CENTRE ST SUITE 200, CHATHAM,
ON, N7M 5W3
(519) 380-0002   *SIC* 5153
STEEGRAIN INC   *p1314*
103 RUE SAINTE-GENEVIEVE, SAINT-
ISIDORE, QC, G0S 2S0
(418) 882-3731   *SIC* 5153
SUNRISE FOODS INTERNATIONAL INC
p1430
306 QUEEN ST SUITE 200, SASKATOON,
SK, S7K 0M2
(306) 931-4576   *SIC* 5153
TASLAR TRADING CORP   *p1415*
100 SHERWOOD FOREST RD, REGINA,
SK, S0G 3W0
(306) 500-5522   *SIC* 5153
THOMPSONS LIMITED   *p493*
2 HYLAND DR, BLENHEIM, ON, N0P 1A0
(519) 676-5411   *SIC* 5153
WESTLOCK TERMINALS (NGC) LTD   *p172*
9921 108 ST, WESTLOCK, AB, T7P 2J1
(780) 349-7034   *SIC* 5153
WOODRILL LTD   *p605*
7861 7 HWY, GUELPH, ON, N1H 6H8

(519) 821-1018   *SIC* 5153

SIC 5154 Livestock

2623-4419 QUEBEC INC   *p1131*
9615 RUE CLEMENT, LASALLE, QC, H8R
4B4
(514) 363-0276   *SIC* 5154
324007 ALBERTA LTD   *p1437*
GD LCD MAIN, WEYBURN, SK, S4H 2J7
SIC 5154
65548 MANITOBA LTD   *p355*
GD, ROBLIN, MB, R0L 1P0
(204) 937-2106   *SIC* 5154
BALOG AUCTION SERVICES INC   *p142*
GD, LETHBRIDGE, AB, T1J 3Y2
(403) 320-1980   *SIC* 5154
BARTSIDE FARMS   *p1037*
3302 HALDIMAND ROAD 9, YORK., ON,
N0A 1R0
(905) 692-2766   *SIC* 5154
BEAVER HILL AUCTION SERVICES LTD
p169
GD, TOFIELD, AB, T0B 4J0
(780) 662-9384   *SIC* 5154
CALGARY STOCKYARDS LTD   *p34*
5925 12 ST SE RM 200, CALGARY, AB, T2H
2M3
(403) 234-7429   *SIC* 5154
CATTLEX LTD   *p351*
GD, HAMIOTA, MB, R0M 0T0
(204) 764-2471   *SIC* 5154
**COOPERATIVE DES ENCANS D'ANIMAUX
DU BAS-SAINT-LAURENT**   *p1284*
3229 132 RTE O, RIMOUSKI, QC, G0L 1B0
(418) 736-5788   *SIC* 5154
**DAVID CARSON FARMS & AUCTION SER-
VICES LTD**   *p646*
5531 PERTH LINE 86, LISTOWEL, ON,
N4W 3G8
(519) 291-2049   *SIC* 5154
DENFIELD LIVESTOCK SALES LTD   *p564*
12952 SIXTEEN MILE RD, DENFIELD, ON,
N0M 1P0
(519) 666-1140   *SIC* 5154
ENCAN OUTAOUAIS LAURENTIDES   *p1103*
655 CH INDUSTRIEL, GATINEAU, QC, J8R
3M1
(819) 669-5775   *SIC* 5154
ENCAN SAWYERVILLE INC   *p1082*
512 RUE MAIN O, COATICOOK, QC, J1A
1P9
(819) 875-3577   *SIC* 5154
**ENCANS D'ANIMAUX DU LAC ST-JEAN
INC, LES**   *p1243*
1360 RANG NORD, NORMANDIN, QC,
G8M 4P5
(418) 274-2233   *SIC* 5154
ENTREPRISES MAX FRIED INC, LES   *p1071*
9125 GRANDE-ALLEE BUREAU 1,
BROSSARD, QC, J4Z 3H8
SIC 5154
FOOTHILLS LIVESTOCK AUCTION LTD
p167
GD, STAVELY, AB, T0L 1Z0
(403) 549-2120   *SIC* 5154
FRASER VALLEY AUCTIONS (1983) LTD
p226
21801 56 AVE, LANGLEY, BC, V2Y 2M9
(604) 534-3241   *SIC* 5154
GIBSON LIVESTOCK (1981) LTD   *p1411*
GD LCD MAIN, MOOSE JAW, SK, S6H 4N6
(306) 692-9668   *SIC* 5154
GLADSTONE AUCTION MART LTD   *p350*
GD, GLADSTONE, MB, R0J 0T0
(204) 385-2537   *SIC* 5154
GRAND PRAIRIE LIVESTOCK MARKET
p132
14809 100 ST, GRANDE PRAIRIE, AB, T8V
7C2
SIC 5154
**GRUNTHAL LIVESTOCK AUCTION MART
LIMITED**   *p350*

GD, GRUNTHAL, MB, R0A 0R0
(204) 434-6519   *SIC* 5154
HAMS MARKETING SERVICES CO-OP INC
p365
750 MARION ST, WINNIPEG, MB, R2J 0K4
(204) 233-4991   *SIC* 5154
INTERNATIONAL GENETICS LIMITED   *p546*
GD STN MAIN, COLLINGWOOD, ON, L9Y
3Z3
(705) 445-2734   *SIC* 5154
**KAWARTHA LAKES COOPERATIVE AUC-
TION MARKET INC**   *p1036*
580 WOODVILLE RD, WOODVILLE, ON,
K0M 2T0
(705) 439-4444   *SIC* 5154
KILLARNEY AUCTION MART LTD   *p351*
2 17 W SUITE 27, KILLARNEY, MB, R0K
1G0
(204) 523-8477   *SIC* 5154
LEMAY LAND & LIVESTOCK CO   *p170*
GD, TROCHU, AB, T0M 2C0
(403) 442-3022   *SIC* 5154
LEO'S LIVESTOCK EXCHANGE LIMITED
p599
1643 SALE BARN RD, GREELY, ON, K4P
1N6
(613) 821-2634   *SIC* 5154
MACIOCIA MARIO & FILS LTEE   *p1123*
131 RANG DES PETITS-ETANGS, LA PRE-
SENTATION, QC, J0H 1B0
(450) 796-3354   *SIC* 5154
**MANKOTA STOCKMEN'S WEIGH COM-
PANY LIMITED**   *p1409*
178 RAILWAY AVE E, MANKOTA, SK, S0H
2W0
(306) 478-2229   *SIC* 5154
MARCHE D'ANIMAUX DE L'EST   *p1314*
2020 RANG DE LA RIVIERE, SAINT-
ISIDORE, QC, G0S 2S0
(418) 882-6301   *SIC* 5154
**MARCHE D'ANIMAUX VIVANTS VEILLEUX
& FRERES INC**   *p1122*
1287 14E AV, LA GUADELOUPE, QC, G0M
1G0
(418) 459-6832   *SIC* 5154
MCCLARY STOCKYARDS LIMITED   *p175*
34559 MCCLARY AVE, ABBOTSFORD, BC,
V2S 7N3
(604) 864-2381   *SIC* 5154
MCF HOLDINGS LTD   *p166*
101 RIEL DR SUITE 100, ST. ALBERT, AB,
T8N 3X4
(780) 477-2233   *SIC* 5154
NORQUAY HOLDING CO LTD   *p354*
23042 ROAD 68N, OAKVILLE, MB, R0H
0Y0
(204) 267-2139   *SIC* 5154
NORTH COUNTRY LIVESTOCK LTD   *p107*
24040 17 ST NE, EDMONTON, AB, T5Y 6J6
(780) 478-2333   *SIC* 5154
PARKLAND LIVESTOCK MARKET LTD
p1408
GD, KELLIHER, SK, S0A 1V0
SIC 5154
PERKINS FARMS INC   *p171*
GD STN MAIN, WAINWRIGHT, AB, T9W
1M3
(780) 842-3642   *SIC* 5154
**PICTURE BUTTE AUCTION MARKET 2001
LTD**   *p152*
GD, PICTURE BUTTE, AB, T0K 1V0
(403) 732-4400   *SIC* 5154
PRAIRIE LIVESTOCK LTD   *p1411*
GD, MOOSOMIN, SK, S0G 3N0
(306) 435-3327   *SIC* 5154
QUINTAINE, P & SON LTD   *p347*
GD, BRANDON, MB, R7A 5Y5
(204) 729-8565   *SIC* 5154
RAFFAN INVESTMENTS LTD   *p179*
903 HWY 97A RR 7, ARMSTRONG, BC,
V0E 1B7
(250) 546-9420   *SIC* 5154
RIMBEY AUCTION MART (1996) LTD   *p158*
4831 47 ST, RIMBEY, AB, T0C 2J0

(403) 843-2439   *SIC 5154*
SELECT FARM & EXPORT SERVICES INC
p618
GD LCD MAIN, HANOVER, ON, N4N 3C2
(519) 369-6000   *SIC 5154*
SHAUNAVON LIVESTOCK SALES (1988) LTD   *p1435*
GD, SHAUNAVON, SK, S0N 2M0
(306) 297-2457   *SIC 5154*
STE ROSE AUCTION MART LTD   *p358*
GD, STE ROSE DU LAC, MB, R0L 1S0
(204) 447-2266   *SIC 5154*
STETTLER AUCTION MART (1990) LTD
p167
4305 52 AVE, STETTLER, AB, T0C 2L0
(403) 742-2369   *SIC 5154*
SUNDERLAND HOG FARMS LTD   *p151*
GD, PARADISE VALLEY, AB, T0B 3R0
(780) 745-2214   *SIC 5154*
SYNERGY SERVICES INC   *p647*
515 MAITLAND AVE S, LISTOWEL, ON, N4W 2M7
(519) 291-4638   *SIC 5154*
TRIPLE J LIVESTOCK LTD   *p172*
9004 110A ST, WESTLOCK, AB, T7P 2N4
(780) 349-3153   *SIC 5154*
VALLEY AUCTION LTD   *p180*
903 HWY 97A, ARMSTRONG, BC, V0E 1B7
(250) 546-9420   *SIC 5154*
VANKLEEK HILL LIVESTOCK EXCHANGE LIMITED   *p1001*
1239 RIDGE RD, VANKLEEK HILL, ON, K0B 1R0
(613) 678-3008   *SIC 5154*
VENTES INTERNATIONALES D'ANIMAUX - TRUDEAU INC   *p1359*
726 MONT?E SAINTE-JULIE, SAINTE-JULIE, QC, J3E 1W9
(450) 649-1122   *SIC 5154*
VOLD, JONES & VOLD AUCTION CO LTD
p152
4410 HIGHWAY 2A, PONOKA, AB, T4J 1J8
(403) 783-5561   *SIC 5154*
WALKER DAIRY INC   *p482*
50828 TALBOT ST E, AYLMER, ON, N5H 2R1
(519) 765-2406   *SIC 5154*
WEAVERCROFT INTERNATIONAL   *p565*
3038 HAMILTON RD SUITE 119, DORCHESTER, ON, N0L 1G5
(519) 868-0330   *SIC 5154*
WESTERN HOG EXCHANGE   *p85*
10319 PRINCESS ELIZABETH AVE NW, EDMONTON, AB, T5G 0Y5
(780) 474-8292   *SIC 5154*
WHITEWOOD AUCTION SERVICE LTD
p1438
HWY 1, WHITEWOOD, SK, S0G 5C0
(306) 735-2822   *SIC 5154*
WINNIPEG LIVESTOCK SALES LTD   *p380*
GD, WINNIPEG, MB, R3C 2E6
(204) 694-8328   *SIC 5154*

SIC 5159 Farm-product raw materials, nec

ACCORD INTERNATIONAL LEAF INC *p1249*
193 AV LABROSSE, POINTE-CLAIRE, QC, H9R 1A3
SIC 5159
ALTA GENETICS INC   *p160*
263090 RGE RD 11, ROCKY VIEW COUNTY, AB, T4B 2T3
(403) 226-0666   *SIC 5159*
B. & K. INTERNATIONAL CORPORATION
p392
34 WATERFRONT RD, WINNIPEG, MB, R3X 1L2
(204) 654-4785   *SIC 5159*
BARNSTON ISLAND HERB CORPORATION
p281
148 BARNSTON ISLAND, SURREY, BC, V4N 4R1
(604) 581-8017   *SIC 5159*

BARRETT HIDES INC   *p486*
75 WELHAM RD, BARRIE, ON, L4N 8Y3
(705) 734-9905   *SIC 5159*
ERIEVIEW ACRES INC   *p633*
1930 SEACLIFF DR, KINGSVILLE, ON, N9Y 2N1
(519) 326-3013   *SIC 5159*
GLADWIN FARMS LTD   *p178*
5327 GLADWIN RD, ABBOTSFORD, BC, V4X 1X8
(604) 859-6820   *SIC 5159*
GLOBAL COMMODITIES TRADERS INC
p723
2430 MEADOWPINE BLVD SUITE 103, MISSISSAUGA, ON, L5N 6S2
(905) 908-0092   *SIC 5159*
HALFORD HIDE TRADING CO. LTD   *p83*
8629 126 AVE NW, EDMONTON, AB, T5B 1G8
(780) 474-4989   *SIC 5159*
HI-POINT INDUSTRIES (1991) LTD   *p421*
141 SUNSET DR, BISHOPS FALLS, NL, A0H 1C0
(709) 258-6274   *SIC 5159*
NORTH AMERICAN FUR AUCTIONS INC
p586
65 SKYWAY AVE, ETOBICOKE, ON, M9W 6C7
(416) 675-9320   *SIC 5159*
PREMIER HORTICULTURE LTD   *p355*
302 NORTH, RICHER, MB, R0E 1S0
(204) 422-8805   *SIC 5159*
PRO INGREDIENTS INC   *p1309*
7750 BOUL COUSINEAU BUREAU 402, SAINT-HUBERT, QC, J3Z 0C8
(450) 632-1199   *SIC 5159*
SCHENCK FARMS & GREENHOUSES CO. LIMITED   *p886*
1396 SOUTH SERVICE RD, ST CATHARINES, ON, L2R 6P9
(905) 684-5478   *SIC 5159*
SELECT SIRES CANADA INC   *p627*
2 INDUSTRIAL RD, KEMPTVILLE, ON, K0G 1J0
(613) 258-3800   *SIC 5159*
SOLS CALCO SOILS INC, LES   *p746*
17354 ALLAIRE RD, MOOSE CREEK, ON, K0C 1W0
(613) 538-2885   *SIC 5159*
SPUD PLAINS FARMS LTD   *p360*
12 14W NE SUITE 32, WELLWOOD, MB, R0K 2H0
(204) 834-3866   *SIC 5159*
SUN GRO HORTICULTURE CANADA LTD
p160
52130 RANGE RD, SEBA BEACH, AB, T0E 2B0
(780) 797-3019   *SIC 5159*
SUN GRO HORTICULTURE CANADA LTD
p403
4492 ROUTE 113, HAUT-LAMEQUE, NB, E8T 3L3
(506) 336-2229   *SIC 5159*
TOTAL SWINE GENETICS INC   *p912*
223277 OSTRANDER RD SUITE 7, TILLSONBURG, ON, N4G 4H1
(519) 877-4350   *SIC 5159*
TOURBES NIROM PEAT MOSS INC, LES
p1287
315 CH DES RAYMOND, RIVIERE-DU-LOUP, QC, G5R 5Y5
(418) 862-0075   *SIC 5159*
TOURBIERES BERGER LTEE, LES   *p1349*
121 1ER RANG, SAINT-MODESTE, QC, G0L 3W0
(418) 862-4462   *SIC 5159*
VICTOR'S SPECIALTY FOODS LTD   *p856*
280 STOUFFVILLE RD, RICHMOND HILL, ON, L4E 3P4
SIC 5159
WESTGEN, WESTERN CANADA'S GENETICS CENTRE   *p232*
6681 GLOVER RD, MILNER, BC, V0X 1T0
(604) 530-1141   *SIC 5159*

WIGMORE CROP PRODUCTION PRODUCTS LTD   *p1404*
140 NELSON INDUSTRIAL DR, AVONLEA, SK, S0H 0C0
(306) 868-2252   *SIC 5159*

SIC 5162 Plastics materials and basic shapes

629728 ONTARIO LIMITED   *p858*
1271 LOUGAR AVE, SARNIA, ON, N7S 5N5
(519) 332-0430   *SIC 5162*
ACRYLCO MFG. LTD   *p205*
711 DERWENT WAY, DELTA, BC, V3M 5P9
(604) 524-9441   *SIC 5162*
ALLIED PLASTIC GROUP OF COMPANIES LTD   *p794*
707 ARROW RD, NORTH YORK, ON, M9M 2L4
(416) 749-7070   *SIC 5162*
ALPATECH VINYL INC   *p498*
100 EXCHANGE DR, BRAMPTON, ON, L6S 0C8
(905) 678-4695   *SIC 5162*
ANTEK MADISON PLASTICS CORP   *p878*
100 FINCHDENE SQ, SCARBOROUGH, ON, M1X 1C1
(416) 321-1170   *SIC 5162*
BAMBERGER POLYMERS (CANADA) CORP   *p720*
2000 ARGENTIA RD SUITE 306, MISSISSAUGA, ON, L5N 1P7
(905) 821-9400   *SIC 5162*
BAYCOMP COMPANY   *p521*
5035 NORTH SERVICE RD, BURLINGTON, ON, L7L 5V2
(905) 332-0991   *SIC 5162*
CANADA COLORS AND CHEMICALS LIMITED   *p928*
175 BLOOR ST E SUITE 1300, TORONTO, ON, M4W 3R8
(416) 443-5500   *SIC 5162*
DUBOIS AGRINOVATION INC   *p1351*
478 RANG NOTRE-DAME, SAINT-REMI, QC, J0L 2L0
(450) 454-4641   *SIC 5162*
EXCALIBUR PLASTICS LTD   *p633*
1397 ROAD 3 E, KINGSVILLE, ON, N9Y 2E5
(519) 326-6000   *SIC 5162*
FABCO PLASTICS WHOLESALE (ONTARIO) LIMITED   *p1003*
2175 TESTON RD, VAUGHAN, ON, L6A 1T3
(905) 832-0600   *SIC 5162*
FABCO PLASTIQUES INC   *p664*
2175 TESTON RD PO BOX 2175 STN MAIN, MAPLE, ON, L6A 1T3
(905) 832-0600   *SIC 5162*
G.R.T. GENESIS INC   *p509*
173 GLIDDEN RD SUITE 1, BRAMPTON, ON, L6W 3L9
(905) 452-0552   *SIC 5162*
GROUPE POLYALTO INC   *p1339*
4105 RUE HICKMORE, SAINT-LAURENT, QC, H4T 1S5
(514) 738-6817   *SIC 5162*
JAY CEE ENTERPRISES LIMITED   *p499*
165 SUN PAC BLVD UNIT 4, BRAMPTON, ON, L6S 5Z6
(905) 791-1303   *SIC 5162*
KAL-TRADING INC   *p711*
3440 WOLFEDALE RD, MISSISSAUGA, ON, L5C 1W4
(905) 273-7400   *SIC 5162*
LAIRD PLASTICS (CANADA) INC   *p509*
155 ORENDA RD UNIT 4, BRAMPTON, ON, L6W 1W3
(905) 595-4800   *SIC 5162*
MULTI-PLASTICS CANADA CO   *p1014*
55 MOORE CRT, WHITBY, ON, L1N 9Z8
(905) 430-7511   *SIC 5162*
OCTOPUS PRODUCTS LIMITED   *p791*

23 GURNEY CRES, NORTH YORK, ON, M6B 1S9
(416) 531-5051   *SIC 5162*
PLASTIQUES DURA (1977) LIMITEE, LES
p1125
110 RUE RICHER, LACHINE, QC, H8R 1R2
(514) 369-8980   *SIC 5162*
PLASTIVAL INC   *p1103*
312 RUE SAINT-LOUIS, GATINEAU, QC, J8P 8B3
(819) 770-2018   *SIC 5162*
PLASTRUCT CANADA INC   *p1003*
4305 SPRING CREEK RD, VINELAND, ON, L0R 2C0
(905) 563-4000   *SIC 5162*
POLYMERSHAPES DISTRIBUTION CANADA INC   *p500*
9150 AIRPORT RD, BRAMPTON, ON, L6S 6G1
(905) 789-3111   *SIC 5162*
RAVAGO CANADA CO   *p587*
180 ATTWELL DR SUITE 260, ETOBICOKE, ON, M9W 6A9
(416) 977-5456   *SIC 5162*
SABIC INNOVATIVE PLASTICS CANADA INC   *p545*
44 NORMAR RD, COBOURG, ON, K9A 4L7
(905) 372-6801   *SIC 5162*
SABIC INNOVATIVE PLASTICS CANADA INC   *p662*
1 STRUCTURED PRODUCT DR, LONG SAULT, ON, K0C 1P0
(905) 372-6801   *SIC 5162*
SENTINEL POLYMERS CANADA INC *p651*
1105 FRANCES ST, LONDON, ON, N5W 2L9
(519) 451-7677   *SIC 5162*
TRICLO INC   *p571*
241 BIRMINGHAM ST, ETOBICOKE, ON, M8V 2C7
(416) 252-4777   *SIC 5162*
VI-LUX BUILDING PRODUCTS INC   *p748*
105 RICHMOND BLVD, NAPANEE, ON, K7R 3Z8
(613) 354-4830   *SIC 5162*

SIC 5169 Chemicals and allied products, nec

425579 ALBERTA LTD   *p72*
130 BOWNESS CTR NW, CALGARY, AB, T3B 5M5
(403) 242-1020   *SIC 5169*
ACTIVATION PRODUCTS (CAN) INC *p544*
975A ELGIN ST W SUITE 357, COBOURG, ON, K9A 5J3
(416) 702-2962   *SIC 5169*
ADHESIFS PROMA INC   *p1047*
9801 BOUL PARKWAY, ANJOU, QC, H1J 1P3
(514) 852-8585   *SIC 5169*
ADJUVANTS EUCLID CANADA INC *p1310*
2835 GRANDE ALLEE BUREAU 300, SAINT-HUBERT, QC, J4T 3K3
(450) 465-2233   *SIC 5169*
AIR LIQUIDE CANADA INC   *p13*
3004 54 AVE SE, CALGARY, AB, T2C 0A7
(403) 310-9353   *SIC 5169*
AIR LIQUIDE GLOBAL E&C SOLUTIONS CANADA INC   *p42*
140 4 AVE SW SUITE 550, CALGARY, AB, T2P 3N3
(403) 774-4300   *SIC 5169*
AIR LIQUIDE GLOBAL E&C SOLUTIONS CANADA LP   *p42*
1404 AVE SW SUITE 550, CALGARY, AB, T2P 3N3
(403) 774-4300   *SIC 5169*
AIR PRODUCTS CANADA LTD   *p719*
2233 ARGENTIA RD, MISSISSAUGA, ON, L5N 2X7
(905) 816-6670   *SIC 5169*
AIRGAS CANADA INC   *p205*
634 DERWENT WAY, DELTA, BC, V3M 5P8

SIC 5169

ANCO CHEMICALS INC *p664*
85 MALMO CRT, MAPLE, ON, L6A 1R4
(905) 832-2276 *SIC 5169*

ARCH CHEMICALS CANADA, INC *p803*
160 WARNER DR, OAKVILLE, ON, L6L 6E7
(905) 847-9878 *SIC 5169*

ASHLAND CANADA CORP *p713*
2620 ROYAL WINDSOR DR, MISSISSAUGA, ON, L5J 4E7
(800) 274-5263 *SIC 5169*

AUSTIN POWDER LTD *p202*
4919 ISLAND HWY N, COURTENAY, BC, V9N 5Z2
(250) 334-2624 *SIC 5169*

AVALON COAL SALT & OIL LTD *p422*
69 COLEY'S PT N, COLEYS POINT SOUTH, NL, A0A 1X0
(709) 753-4000 *SIC 5169*

AZELIS CANADA INC *p1063*
1570 RUE AMPERE BUREAU 106, BOUCHERVILLE, QC, J4B 7L4
(450) 449-6363 *SIC 5169*

BAKER HUGHES CANADA COMPANY *p44*
401 9 AVE SW SUITE 1300, CALGARY, AB, T2P 3C5
SIC 5169

BEHCHO KO DEVELOPMENT CORPORATION *p436*
25 STANTON PLAZA, YELLOWKNIFE, NT, X1A 2P3
(867) 920-7288 *SIC 5169*

BIO BASIC CANADA INC *p667*
20 KONRAD CRES SUITE 1, MARKHAM, ON, L3R 8T4
(905) 474-4493 *SIC 5169*

BLAKE, A. E. VENTES LTEE *p1328*
3588 BOUL POIRIER, SAINT-LAURENT, QC, H4R 2J5
(514) 332-4214 *SIC 5169*

BLENDTEK FINE INGREDIENTS INC *p538*
32 CHERRY BLOSSOM RD, CAMBRIDGE, ON, N3H 4R7
(519) 279-4401 *SIC 5169*

BRENNTAG CANADA INC *p573*
43 JUTLAND RD, ETOBICOKE, ON, M8Z 2G6
(416) 259-8231 *SIC 5169*

BRENNTAG CANADA INC *p1332*
9999 RTE TRANSCANADIENNE, SAINT-LAURENT, QC, H4S 1V1
(514) 333-7820 *SIC 5169*

BRUDERHEIM ENERGY TERMINAL LTD *p27*
500 CENTRE ST SE SUITE 2600, CALGARY, AB, T2G 1A6
(403) 766-2000 *SIC 5169*

C.T.M. ADHESIVES INC *p1047*
8320 RUE GRENACHE, ANJOU, QC, H1J 1C5
(514) 321-5540 *SIC 5169*

CALSCO SOLVENTS LIMITED *p876*
4120 MIDLAND AVE, SCARBOROUGH, ON, M1V 4S8
(416) 293-0123 *SIC 5169*

CAMBRIAN SOLUTIONS INC *p800*
627 LYONS LANE SUITE 300, OAKVILLE, ON, L6J 5Z7
(905) 338-3172 *SIC 5169*

CAMCARB CO2 LTD *p792*
155 SIGNET DR, NORTH YORK, ON, M9L 1V1
(416) 745-1304 *SIC 5169*

CANADA COLORS AND CHEMICALS (EASTERN) LIMITED *p928*
175 BLOOR ST E SUITE 1300, TORONTO, ON, M4W 3R8
(416) 443-5500 *SIC 5169*

CANADIAN KROWN DEALERS INC *p879*
35 MAGNUM DR, SCHOMBERG, ON, L0G 1T0
(905) 939-8750 *SIC 5169*

CANEXUS CHEMICALS CANADA LTD *p45*
144 4 AVE SW UNIT 2100, CALGARY, AB, T2P 3N4
(403) 571-7300 *SIC 5169*

CASCADE AQUA-TECH LTD *p184*
3215 NORLAND AVE SUITE 100, BURNABY, BC, V5B 3A9
(604) 291-6101 *SIC 5169*

CERVO-POLYGAZ INC *p1080*
1371 RUE DE LA MANIC, CHICOUTIMI, QC, G7K 1G7
(418) 696-1212 *SIC 5169*

CFR CHEMICALS INC *p46*
525 8 AVE SW SUITE 1920, CALGARY, AB, T2P 1G1
(587) 320-1097 *SIC 5169*

CHARTON-HOBBS INC *p1396*
3000 BOUL RENE-LEVESQUE BUREAU 400, VERDUN, QC, H3E 1T9
(514) 353-8955 *SIC 5169*

CHEMARKETING INDUSTRIES INC *p716*
2155 DUNWIN DR UNIT 15, MISSISSAUGA, ON, L5L 4M1
(905) 607-6800 *SIC 5169*

CHEMETALL CANADA, LIMITED *p501*
1 KENVIEW BLVD SUITE 110, BRAMPTON, ON, L6T 5E6
(905) 791-1628 *SIC 5169*

CHEMROY CANADA INC *p501*
106 SUMMERLEA RD, BRAMPTON, ON, L6T 4X3
(905) 789-0701 *SIC 5169*

CHEMROY CHEMICALS LIMITED *p501*
106 SUMMERLEA RD, BRAMPTON, ON, L6T 4X3
(905) 789-0701 *SIC 5169*

CHEMSYNERGY INC *p521*
1100 BURLOAK DR SUITE 101, BURLINGTON, ON, L7L 6B2
(905) 827-4900 *SIC 5169*

CHEMTRADE LOGISTICS (US) INC *p764*
155 GORDON BAKER RD SUITE 300, NORTH YORK, ON, M2H 3N5
(416) 496-5856 *SIC 5169*

CHEMTRADE PERFORMANCE CHEMICALS CANADA INC *p765*
155 GORDON BAKER RD SUITE 300, NORTH YORK, ON, M2H 3N5
(416) 496-5856 *SIC 5169*

CHEMTRADE PERFORMANCE CHEMICALS US, LLC *p765*
155 GORDON BAKER RD SUITE 300, NORTH YORK, ON, M2H 3N5
(416) 496-5856 *SIC 5169*

CHEMTRADE WEST LIMITED PARTNERSHIP *p765*
155 GORDON BAKER RD SUITE 300, NORTH YORK, ON, M2H 3N5
(416) 496-5856 *SIC 5169*

CLARIANT (CANADA) INC *p1333*
4600 RUE COUSENS, SAINT-LAURENT, QC, H4S 1X3
(514) 334-1117 *SIC 5169*

CLARIANT PLASTICS & COATINGS CANADA INC *p578*
2 LONE OAK CRT, ETOBICOKE, ON, M9C 5R9
(416) 847-7000 *SIC 5169*

CLARKE ROLLER & RUBBER LIMITED *p601*
485 SOUTHGATE DR, GUELPH, ON, N1G 3W6
(519) 763-7655 *SIC 5169*

CLEARTECH INDUSTRIES LIMITED PARTNERSHIP *p1426*
1500 QUEBEC AVE, SASKATOON, SK, S7K 1V7
(306) 664-2522 *SIC 5169*

CLOROX COMPANY OF CANADA, LTD, THE *p509*
150 BISCAYNE CRES, BRAMPTON, ON, L6W 4V3
(905) 595-8200 *SIC 5169*

COMET CHEMICAL COMPANY LTD *p622*
3463 THOMAS ST, INNISFIL, ON, L9S 3W4
(705) 436-5580 *SIC 5169*

COMMERCE KOLTECH LTEE *p1338*
943 RUE REVERCHON, SAINT-LAURENT, QC, H4T 4L2
(514) 739-4111 *SIC 5169*

CONFORTCHEM INC *p1249*
76 BOUL HYMUS, POINTE-CLAIRE, QC, H9R 1E3
(514) 332-1140 *SIC 5169*

CRODA CANADA LIMITED *p906*
221 RACCO PKY UNIT A, THORNHILL, ON, L4J 8X9
(905) 886-1383 *SIC 5169*

CSI CHEMICAL COMPANY LTD *p259*
2560 SHELL RD SUITE 3013, RICHMOND, BC, V6X 0B8
(604) 278-1071 *SIC 5169*

DEBRO INC. *p499*
11 AUTOMATIC RD, BRAMPTON, ON, L6S 4K6
(905) 799-8200 *SIC 5169*

DEMPSEY CORPORATION *p920*
47 DAVIES AVE, TORONTO, ON, M4M 2A9
(416) 461-0844 *SIC 5169*

DISTRIBUTION SOGITEX INC *p1390*
1201 RUE DES MANUFACTURIERS, VAL-D'OR, QC, J9P 6Y7
(819) 825-2331 *SIC 5169*

DISTRIBUTIONS MULTI-PRO INC *p1344*
8480 RUE CHAMP D'EAU, SAINT-LEONARD, QC, H1P 1Y3
(514) 955-1128 *SIC 5169*

DIVERSITY TECHNOLOGIES CORPORATION *p114*
8750 53 AVE NW, EDMONTON, AB, T6E 5G2
(780) 440-4923 *SIC 5169*

DOWBICO SUPPLIES LIMITED *p574*
50 TITAN RD, ETOBICOKE, ON, M8Z 2J8
(416) 252-7137 *SIC 5169*

DRYTAC CANADA INC *p502*
105 NUGGETT CRT, BRAMPTON, ON, L6T 5A9
(905) 660-1748 *SIC 5169*

ENERCON WATER TREATMENT LTD *p140*
3606 6 AVE N, LETHBRIDGE, AB, T1H 5C4
(403) 328-9730 *SIC 5169*

ENX INC *p1*
53016 HWY 60 UNIT 703, ACHESON, AB, T7X 5A7
(780) 962-7993 *SIC 5169*

EPI ENVIRONMENTAL PRODUCTS INC *p320*
1788 BROADWAY W SUITE 801, VANCOUVER, BC, V6J 1Y1
(604) 738-6281 *SIC 5169*

EQUIPEMENT SANITAIRE CHERBOURG (1977) INC *p1370*
1051 RUE GALT E, SHERBROOKE, QC, J1G 1Y7
(819) 566-2266 *SIC 5169*

EVONIK CANADA INC *p527*
3380 SOUTH SERVICE RD SUITE 5, BURLINGTON, ON, L7N 3J5
(905) 336-3423 *SIC 5169*

EVONIK OIL ADDITIVES CANADA INC *p746*
12695 COUNTY ROAD 28, MORRISBURG, ON, K0C 1X0
(613) 543-2983 *SIC 5169*

FANCHEM LTD *p592*
1012 GORE RD, FREELTON, ON, L8B 0Z5
(905) 659-3351 *SIC 5169*

FC GEOSYNTHETIQUES INC *p1360*
1300 2E RUE DU PARC-INDUSTRIEL, SAINTE-MARIE, QC, G6E 1G8
(418) 658-0200 *SIC 5169*

FLOCHEM LTD *p603*
6986 WELLINGTON ROAD 124, GUELPH, ON, N1H 6J4
(519) 763-5441 *SIC 5169*

FORT DISTRIBUTORS LTD *p357*
938 MCPHILLIPS RD, ST ANDREWS, MB, R1A 4E7
(204) 785-2180 *SIC 5169*

GALATA CHEMICALS (CANADA) INC *p497*

10 REAGEN'S INDUSTRIAL PKY, BRADFORD, ON, L3Z 0Z8
(905) 775-5000 *SIC 5169*

GESTION INFILISE INC *p1394*
3901 RUE F.-X.-TESSIER, VAUDREUIL-DORION, QC, J7V 5V5
(450) 424-0161 *SIC 5169*

GOLDEN FLOORING ACCESSORIES PS LTD *p96*
11662 154 ST NW, EDMONTON, AB, T5M 3N8
(780) 451-4222 *SIC 5169*

GREER, W.E. LIMITED *p93*
14704 119 AVE NW, EDMONTON, AB, T5L 2P1
(780) 451-1516 *SIC 5169*

GRENHALL INDUSTRIES INC *p503*
1 IMPERIAL CRT, BRAMPTON, ON, L6T 4X4
(905) 458-8549 *SIC 5169*

HC-TECH INC *p609*
665 PARKDALE AVE N, HAMILTON, ON, L8H 5Z1
(905) 547-5693 *SIC 5169*

HENKEL CANADA CORPORATION *p723*
2515 MEADOWPINE BLVD UNIT 1, MISSISSAUGA, ON, L5N 6C3
(905) 814-6511 *SIC 5169*

HOLLAND CLEANING SOLUTIONS LTD *p1020*
4590 RHODES DR, WINDSOR, ON, N8W 5C2
(519) 948-4373 *SIC 5169*

HURONIA/MED-E-OX LTD *p597*
282 SUNCOAST DR E, GODERICH, ON, N7A 4K4
(519) 524-5363 *SIC 5169*

IFC NORTH AMERICA INC *p886*
63 CHURCH ST SUITE 301, ST CATHARINES, ON, L2R 3C4
(905) 685-8560 *SIC 5169*

IMCD CANADA LIMITED *p504*
99 SUMMERLEA RD, BRAMPTON, ON, L6T 4V2
(800) 575-3382 *SIC 5169*

INDUSTRIES CHEMI-3 INC *p1340*
346 RUE ISABEY, SAINT-LAURENT, QC, H4T 1W1
(514) 365-0050 *SIC 5169*

INTER PROPANE INC *p1149*
460 RUE SICARD, MASCOUCHE, QC, J7K 3G5
(450) 474-4000 *SIC 5169*

INTERNATIONAL CORROSION CONTROL INC *p523*
930 SHELDON CRT, BURLINGTON, ON, L7L 5K6
(905) 634-7751 *SIC 5169*

INTERNATIONAL SUPPLIERS AND CONTRACTORS INC *p1053*
19400 AV CRUICKSHANK, BAIE-D'URFE, QC, H9X 3P1
(514) 457-5362 *SIC 5169*

INTRACHEM INDUSTRIES INC *p995*
476 ARMADALE AVE, TORONTO, ON, M6S 3X9
(416) 760-0929 *SIC 5169*

INVISTA (CANADA) COMPANY *p663*
1400 COUNTY RD 2, MAITLAND, ON, K0E 1P0
(613) 348-4204 *SIC 5169*

KISSNER MILLING COMPANY LIMITED *p636*
148 MANITOU DR SUITE 301, KITCHENER, ON, N2C 1L3
(519) 279-4860 *SIC 5169*

LA PANTHERE VERTE *p1213*
2153 RUE MACKAY, MONTREAL, QC, H3G 2J2
(514) 903-4744 *SIC 5169*

LEWIS-GOETZ ULC *p182*
3181 THUNDERBIRD CRES, BURNABY, BC, V5A 3G1
(604) 444-4885 *SIC 5169*

MAGCHEM INC *p1066*
1271 RUE AMPERE BUREAU 101, BOUCHERVILLE, QC, J4B 5Z5
(450) 641-8500   *SIC* 5169

MAGIC WHITE INC *p872*
80 CROCKFORD BLVD, SCARBOROUGH, ON, M1R 3C3
(416) 751-2802   *SIC* 5169

MATCO PACKAGING INC *p1330*
2519 RUE COHEN, SAINT-LAURENT, QC, H4R 2N5
(514) 337-6050   *SIC* 5169

MEGLOBAL CANADA INC *p130*
BAG 16 HWY 15, FORT SASKATCHEWAN, AB, T8L 2P4
(780) 992-4250   *SIC* 5169

MEGLOBAL CANADA INC *p154*
HWY 597 PRENTISS RD, RED DEER, AB, T4N 6N1
(403) 885-7000   *SIC* 5169

MESSER CANADA INC *p732*
5860 CHEDWORTH WAY, MISSISSAUGA, ON, L5R 0A2
(905) 501-1700   *SIC* 5169

MILACRON CANADA CORP *p523*
1175 APPLEBY LINE UNIT B1, BURLINGTON, ON, L7L 5H9
(905) 319-1919   *SIC* 5169

MIN-CHEM CANADA LTD *p802*
460 WYECROFT RD, OAKVILLE, ON, L6K 2G7
(905) 842-8300   *SIC* 5169

NALCO CANADA ULC *p54*
815 8 AVE SW SUITE 1400, CALGARY, AB, T2P 3P2
(403) 234-7881   *SIC* 5169

NCH CANADA INC *p505*
247 ORENDA RD, BRAMPTON, ON, L6T 1E6
(905) 457-5220   *SIC* 5169

NCH CANADA INC *p1226*
9001 BOUL DE L'ACADIE BUREAU 800, MONTREAL, QC, H4N 3H5
(514) 733-4572   *SIC* 5169

NETCHEM INC *p514*
35 ROY BLVD, BRANTFORD, ON, N3R 7K1
(519) 751-4700   *SIC* 5169

NEXEO SOLUTIONS CANADA CORP *p798*
2450 BRISTOL CIR, OAKVILLE, ON, L6H 6P6
(800) 387-2376   *SIC* 5169

NSC MINERALS LTD *p1431*
2241 SPEERS AVE, SASKATOON, SK, S7L 5X6
(306) 934-6477   *SIC* 5169

PACE CHEMICALS LTD *p206*
1597 DERWENT WAY FL 2, DELTA, BC, V3M 6K8
(604) 520-6211   *SIC* 5169

PARKLAND RESPIRATORY CARE LTD *p121*
3152 PARSONS RD NW, EDMONTON, AB, T6N 1L6
(780) 430-8999   *SIC* 5169

PELECANUS HOLDINGS LTD *p289*
887 GREAT NORTHERN WAY SUITE 101, VANCOUVER, BC, V5T 4T5
(604) 263-9994   *SIC* 5169

PNE CORPORATION *p1002*
279 ENTREPRISE RD, VARS, ON, K0A 3H0
(613) 443-2181   *SIC* 5169

POLAR EXPLOSIVES LTD *p436*
349 OLD AIRPORT RD SUITE 104, YELLOWKNIFE, NT, X1A 3X6
(867) 880-4613   *SIC* 5169

POLYTECH CANADA INC *p1017*
5505 RHODES DR, WINDSOR, ON, N8N 2M1
SIC 5169

PRAIRIE PETRO-CHEM HOLDINGS LTD *p1406*
738 6TH ST, ESTEVAN, SK, S4A 1A4
(306) 634-5808   *SIC* 5169

PRAXAIR *p659*
1435 HYDE PARK RD, LONDON, ON, N6H 0B5
(519) 473-7834   *SIC* 5169

PRAXAIR CANADA INC *p207*
1470 DERWENT WAY, DELTA, BC, V3M 6H9
(604) 527-0700   *SIC* 5169

PRAXAIR CANADA INC *p510*
165 BISCAYNE CRES, BRAMPTON, ON, L6W 4R3
(905) 450-9353   *SIC* 5169

PRAXAIR CANADA INC *p1050*
8151 BOUL METROPOLITAIN E, ANJOU, QC, H1J 1X6
(514) 353-3340   *SIC* 5169

PRO-SHIELD CORPORATION *p575*
33 CORONET RD, ETOBICOKE, ON, M8Z 2L8
(800) 561-4272   *SIC* 5169

PROCTER & GAMBLE INC *p773*
4711 YONGE ST, NORTH YORK, ON, M2N 6K8
(416) 730-4711   *SIC* 5169

PRODUITS CHIMIQUES AMPLEX LTEE, LES *p1252*
600 AV DELMAR, POINTE-CLAIRE, QC, H9R 4A8
(514) 630-3309   *SIC* 5169

PRODUITS SANITAIRES CLOUTIER INC *p1102*
11 BOUL DE GASPE, GASPE, QC, G4X 1A1
(418) 368-7376   *SIC* 5169

PRODUITS SANITAIRES NORFIL INC *p1289*
320 AV TURPIN, ROUYN-NORANDA, QC, J9X 7E1
(819) 762-8129   *SIC* 5169

PROMOTION LEPINE INC *p1267*
2800 BOUL WILFRID-HAMEL, QUEBEC, QC, G1P 2J1
(418) 687-0084   *SIC* 5169

PROSOL INC *p1327*
165 RUE DESLAURIERS BUREAU 254, SAINT-LAURENT, QC, H4N 2S4
(514) 745-1212   *SIC* 5169

QUADRA CHIMIE LTEE *p1395*
3901 RUE F.-X.-TESSIER, VAUDREUIL-DORION, QC, J7V 5V5
(450) 424-0161   *SIC* 5169

R.M. FERGUSON & COMPANY INC *p505*
235 ADVANCE BLVD SUITE 1, BRAMPTON, ON, L6T 4J2
(905) 458-5553   *SIC* 5169

RBF INTERNATIONAL LTEE *p1321*
780 RUE NOBEL, SAINT-JEROME, QC, J7Z 7A3
(450) 438-4416   *SIC* 5169

RDI CHEMICAL CORPORATION *p736*
1875 DREW RD, MISSISSAUGA, ON, L5S 1J5
(905) 673-2556   *SIC* 5169

REHO INTERNATIONAL INC *p765*
7 EQUESTRIAN CRT, NORTH YORK, ON, M2H 3M9
(416) 269-2950   *SIC* 5169

SAJE NATURAL BUSINESS INC *p289*
22 5TH AVE E SUITE 500, VANCOUVER, BC, V5T 1G8
(877) 275-7253   *SIC* 5169

SANI-SOL INC *p891*
149 IBER RD, STITTSVILLE, ON, K2S 1E7
(613) 831-3698   *SIC* 5169

SARDIS EXPLOSIVES (2000) LTD *p197*
6890 LICKMAN RD, CHILLIWACK, BC, V2R 4A9
(604) 858-6919   *SIC* 5169

SHARE CORPORATION CANADA LTD *p373*
1691 CHURCH AVE, WINNIPEG, MB, R2X 2Y7
(204) 633-8553   *SIC* 5169

SHELL GLOBAL SOLUTIONS CANADA INC *p59*
400 4 AVE SW, CALGARY, AB, T2P 0J4
(403) 691-3540   *SIC* 5169

SIGMA-ALDRICH CANADA CO. *p799*

2149 WINSTON PARK DR, OAKVILLE, ON, L6H 6J8
(905) 829-9500   *SIC* 5169

SIRCO CLEANERS (1980) LTD *p385*
1393 BORDER ST UNIT 5, WINNIPEG, MB, R3H 0N1
(204) 831-8551   *SIC* 5169

SKY TECK LABS INC *p703*
3289 LENWORTH DR SUITE B, MISSISSAUGA, ON, L4X 2H1
(905) 602-8007   *SIC* 5169

SNOWLINE ENTERPRISES LTD *p224*
3121 HILL RD SUITE 214, LAKE COUNTRY, BC, V4V 1G1
(250) 766-0068   *SIC* 5169

SOCIETE EN COMMANDITE USINE DE SOUFRE SUNCOR MONTREAL *p1238*
11450 RUE CHERRIER, MONTREAL-EST, QC, H1B 1A6
(514) 645-1636   *SIC* 5169

SODROX CHEMICALS LTD *p604*
7040 WELLINGTON ROAD 124, GUELPH, ON, N1H 6J3
(519) 837-2330   *SIC* 5169

STATE CHEMICAL LTD *p743*
1745 MEYERSIDE DR SUITE 1, MISSISSAUGA, ON, L5T 1C6
(905) 670-4669   *SIC* 5169

STORCHEM INC *p528*
855 HARRINGTON CRT, BURLINGTON, ON, L7N 3P3
(905) 639-9700   *SIC* 5169

SUEZ WATER TECHNOLOGIES & SOLUTIONS CANADA *p806*
3239 DUNDAS ST W, OAKVILLE, ON, L6M 4B2
(905) 465-3030   *SIC* 5169

SUPERIOR GENERAL PARTNER INC *p1102*
101 CH DONALDSON, GATINEAU, QC, J8L 3X3
(819) 986-1135   *SIC* 5169

T.F. WARREN GROUP INC *p518*
57 OLD ONONDAGA RD W, BRANTFORD, ON, N3T 5M1
(519) 756-8222   *SIC* 5169

TAIL RISK SYSTEMS SOLUTIONS LTD *p60*
202 6 AVE SW SUITE 1110, CALGARY, AB, T2P 2R9
(587) 352-5071   *SIC* 5169

TEMPO CANADA ULC *p806*
1175 NORTH SERVICE RD W SUITE 200, OAKVILLE, ON, L6M 2W1
(905) 339-3309   *SIC* 5169

THAMES RIVER CHEMICAL CORP *p525*
5230 HARVESTER RD, BURLINGTON, ON, L7L 4X4
(905) 681-5353   *SIC* 5169

UBA INC *p1389*
3450 BOUL GENE-H.-KRUGER BUREAU 100, TROIS-RIVIERES, QC, G9A 4M3
(819) 379-3311   *SIC* 5169

UNIVAR CANADA LTD *p262*
9800 VAN HORNE WAY, RICHMOND, BC, V6X 1W5
(604) 273-1441   *SIC* 5169

UNIVAR CANADA LTD *p795*
64 ARROW RD, NORTH YORK, ON, M9M 2L9
(416) 740-5300   *SIC* 5169

UNIVAR CANADA LTD *p1095*
2200 CH SAINT-FRANCOIS, DORVAL, QC, H9P 1K2
(514) 421-0303   *SIC* 5169

VAC OXYGENE ULC *p1145*
1733 BOUL TASCHEREAU, LONGUEUIL, QC, J4K 2X9
(450) 679-3406   *SIC* 5169

VITALAIRE CANADA INC *p728*
6990 CREDITVIEW RD UNIT 6, MISSISSAUGA, ON, L5N 8R9
(905) 855-0414   *SIC* 5169

VOPAK TERMINALS OF CANADA INC *p1239*
2775 AV GEORGES-V, MONTREAL-EST, QC, H1L 6J7
(514) 687-3193   *SIC* 5169

VOPAK TERMINAUX DE L'EST DU CANADA INC *p1239*
2775 AV GEORGES-V, MONTREAL-EST, QC, H1L 6J7
(514) 687-3193   *SIC* 5169

WILSON, J C CHEMICALS LTD *p650*
1900 HURON ST UNIT 2, LONDON, ON, N5V 4A3
SIC 5169

WORX ENVIRONMENTAL PRODUCTS OF CANADA INC *p19*
2305 52 AVE SE UNIT 10, CALGARY, AB, T2C 4X7
(403) 538-0203   *SIC* 5169

XTECH EXPLOSIVE DECONTAMINATION INC *p151*
900 VILLAGE LANE SUITE 14, OKOTOKS, AB, T1S 1Z6
(403) 938-3883   *SIC* 5169

SIC 5171 Petroleum bulk stations and terminals

13089980 ONTARIO LTD *p881*
1 BLACK BEAR RD, SIOUX LOOKOUT, ON, P8T 1B3
(807) 737-2250   *SIC* 5171

73502 MANITOBA LIMITED *p348*
1873 1ST ST N, BRANDON, MB, R7C 1A9
(204) 728-4554   *SIC* 5171

74829 MANITOBA LTD *p359*
945 GARDEN AVE, THE PAS, MB, R9A 1L6
(204) 623-2581   *SIC* 5171

ADVANTAGE CO-OPERATIVE ASSOCIATION LTD *p1415*
3 BROADWAY ST S, REDVERS, SK, S0C 2H0
(306) 452-3513   *SIC* 5171

AGCOM PETROLEUM SALES LTD *p7*
600 INDUSTRIAL RD, BROOKS, AB, T1R 1B6
(403) 362-5700   *SIC* 5171

ANDRE TARDIFF AGENCY LIMITED *p565*
140 COLONISATION AVE N, DRYDEN, ON, P8N 2Z5
(807) 223-4324   *SIC* 5171

ARCOLA CO-OPERATIVE ASSOCIATION LIMITED *p1404*
HWY 13, ARCOLA, SK, S0C 0G0
(306) 455-2393   *SIC* 5171

ARCTIC DOVE LIMITED *p435*
8 TANK FARM RD, INUVIK, NT, X0E 0T0
(867) 777-3226   *SIC* 5171

ARMAND H. COUTURE LTD *p619*
1226 FRONT ST, HEARST, ON, P0L 1N0
(705) 362-4941   *SIC* 5171

ARMSTRONG REGIONAL COOPERATIVE *p179*
973 OTTER LAKE CROSS RD, ARMSTRONG, BC, V0E 1B6
(250) 546-9438   *SIC* 5171

BASSETT PETROLEUM DISTRIBUTORS LTD *p435*
43013 MACKENZIE HWY, HAY RIVER, NT, X0E 0R9
(867) 874-8500   *SIC* 5171

BATTLEFORDS AND DISTRICT CO-OPERATIVE LTD *p1412*
9800 TERRITORIAL DR SUITE 1, NORTH BATTLEFORD, SK, S9A 3W6
(306) 445-9800   *SIC* 5171

BEAUSEJOUR CONSUMERS CO-OPERATIVE LIMITED *p345*
605 PARK AVE, BEAUSEJOUR, MB, R0E 0C0
(204) 268-2605   *SIC* 5171

BEAVER CREEK CO-OP ASSN LIMITED *p139*
HWY 15 & 831, LAMONT, AB, T0B 2R0
(780) 895-2241   *SIC* 5171

BEELAND CO-OPERATIVE ASSOCIATION LIMITED *p1437*

1101 99 ST, TISDALE, SK, S0E 1T0
(306) 873-2688 *SIC* 5171
BENGOUGH CO-OPERATIVE LIMITED
p1404
140 3 ST E, BENGOUGH, SK, S0C 0K0
(306) 268-2040 *SIC* 5171
BENSON B A & SON LTD *p284*
266 1ST AVE, TRAIL, BC, V1R 4V2
(250) 368-6428 *SIC* 5171
BOUCHER & JONES INC *p1006*
155 ROGER ST SUITE 1, WATERLOO, ON, N2J 1B1
(519) 653-3501 *SIC* 5171
BRANDON PETROLEUM SALES LTD *p108*
3515 76 AVE NW, EDMONTON, AB, T6B 2S8
(780) 413-1826 *SIC* 5171
BRENDONN HOLDINGS LTD *p356*
JUNCTION OF HWY SUITE 16, RUSSELL, MB, R0J 1W0
(204) 773-2268 *SIC* 5171
BULYEA COMMUNITY CO-OPERATIVE ASSOCIATION LIMITED *p1404*
GD, BULYEA, SK, S0G 0L0
(306) 725-4911 *SIC* 5171
CENTENNIAL SUPPLY LTD *p361*
526 CENTENNIAL ST, WINKLER, MB, R6W 1J4
(204) 325-8261 *SIC* 5171
CENTRAL PLAINS CO-OPERATIVE LTD *p1423*
117 1ST AVE E, ROSETOWN, SK, S0L 2V0
(306) 882-2601 *SIC* 5171
CHINOOK FUELS LTD *p127*
160 MACKAY CRES, FORT MCMURRAY, AB, T9H 4W8
(780) 743-2381 *SIC* 5171
CORONACH CO-OPERATIVE ASSOCIATION LIMITED, THE *p1405*
112 CENTRE ST, CORONACH, SK, S0H 0Z0
(306) 267-2010 *SIC* 5171
CRAIK CO-OPERATIVE ASSOCIATION LIMITED, THE *p1405*
309 3RD ST, CRAIK, SK, S0G 0V0
(306) 734-2612 *SIC* 5171
DALL CONTRACTING LTD *p212*
GD, FORT NELSON, BC, V0C 1R0
(250) 774-7251 *SIC* 5171
DAWSON CO-OPERATIVE UNION *p204*
10200 8 ST SUITE 3, DAWSON CREEK, BC, V1G 3P8
(250) 782-2217 *SIC* 5171
DERKO'S SERVICE LTD *p134*
5008 50 AVE, GRASSLAND, AB, T0A 1V0
(780) 525-3931 *SIC* 5171
DIAMOND CO-OPERATIVE ASSOCIATION LTD *p1408*
223 1ST AVE NE, ITUNA, SK, S0A 1N0
(306) 795-2441 *SIC* 5171
DOAK'S PETROLEUM LTD *p359*
945 GORDON AVE, THE PAS, MB, R9A 1L6
(204) 623-2581 *SIC* 5171
DONALD L. DAVIDSON FUELS LTD *p1011*
54 PINEWOOD DR, WAWA, ON, P0S 1K0
(705) 856-2166 *SIC* 5171
EDWARD CONSUMERS COOPERATIVE LTD *p354*
13 BROADWAY ST, PIERSON, MB, R0M 1S0
(204) 634-2418 *SIC* 5171
ELM CREEK CO-OPERATIVE OIL & SUPPLIES LTD *p349*
43 CHURCH AVE, ELM CREEK, MB, R0G 0N0
(204) 436-2493 *SIC* 5171
FORT ST JOHN CO-OPERATIVE ASSOCIATION
10808 91 AVE, FORT ST. JOHN, BC, V1J 5R1
(250) 785-4471 *SIC* 5171
FOUR RIVERS CO-OPERATIVE *p331*
188 EAST STEWART ST, VANDERHOOF, BC, V0J 3A0

(250) 567-4414 *SIC* 5171
FOXTON FUELS LIMITED *p1026*
50 NORTH ST W, WINGHAM, ON, N0G 2W0
(519) 357-2664 *SIC* 5171
FRANK LOGAN *p1392*
485 249 RTE, VAL-JOLI, QC, J1S 0E8
(819) 845-4901 *SIC* 5171
GIRARD BULK SERVICE LTD *p1406*
134 4TH ST, ESTEVAN, SK, S4A 0T4
(306) 637-4370 *SIC* 5171
GRANT FUELS INC. *p753*
251 GRAY RD, NEW LISKEARD, ON, P0J 1P0
(705) 647-6566 *SIC* 5171
GRASSROOTS CO-OPERATIVE LTD *p1407*
216 MAIN ST, HAZENMORE, SK, S0N 1C0
(306) 264-5111 *SIC* 5171
HANCOCK PETROLEUM INC *p144*
5904 44 ST, LLOYDMINSTER, AB, T9V 1V7
(780) 875-2495 *SIC* 5171
INTERLAKE CONSUMERS CO-OPERATIVE LIMITED *p345*
253 MAIN ST, ARBORG, MB, R0C 0A0
(204) 376-5245 *SIC* 5171
JANICO INVESTMENTS LTD *p366*
928 MARION ST, WINNIPEG, MB, R2J 0K8
(204) 949-7281 *SIC* 5171
KAYFORE HOLDINGS LTD *p144*
5310 52ND ST, LLOYDMINSTER, AB, T9V 3B5
(780) 875-2266 *SIC* 5171
KINDERSLEY AND DISTRICT CO-OPERATIVE LIMITED *p1408*
214 MAIN ST, KINDERSLEY, SK, S0L 1S0
(306) 463-2624 *SIC* 5171
KOCH FUEL PRODUCTS INC *p169*
1221 2ND ST N, THREE HILLS, AB, T0M 2A0
(403) 443-5770 *SIC* 5171
L & R DISTRIBUTORS LTD *p155*
8120 EDGAR INDUSTRIAL DR, RED DEER, AB, T4P 3R2
SIC 5171
LA RONGE PETROLEUM LTD *p1408*
1420 FINNLAYSON ST, LA RONGE, SK, S0J 1L0
(306) 425-6841 *SIC* 5171
LAKE LENORE CO-OPERATIVE ASSOCIATION LIMITED *p1408*
300 LAKE DR HWY SUITE 368, LAKE LENORE, SK, S0K 2J0
(306) 368-2255 *SIC* 5171
LAMON, J.J. INC *p1412*
1007 BATTLEFORD RD, NORTH BATTLEFORD, SK, S9A 2P2
(306) 445-3592 *SIC* 5171
LANGBANK CO-OPERATIVE ASSOCIATION LIMITED, THE *p1408*
1ST AVE W, LANGBANK, SK, S0G 2X0
(306) 538-2125 *SIC* 5171
LOAD'EM UP PETROLEUMS LTD *p250*
1064 GREAT ST, PRINCE GEORGE, BC, V2N 2K8
(250) 562-8166 *SIC* 5171
LOWE FARM CO-OP SERVICES (1959) LTD *p351*
78 MAIN ST, LOWE FARM, MB, R0G 1E0
(204) 746-8476 *SIC* 5171
MARQUETTE CONSUMERS COOPERATIVE LIMITED *p352*
GD, MARQUETTE, MB, R0H 0V0
(204) 375-6570 *SIC* 5171
MATONABEE PETROEUM LTD *p436*
117 KAM LAKE RD, YELLOWKNIFE, NT, X1A 0G3
(867) 873-4001 *SIC* 5171
MATONABEE PETROLEUM LTD *p436*
PO BOX 2697 STN MAIN, YELLOWKNIFE, NT, X1A 2R1
(867) 873-4001 *SIC* 5171
MAX FUEL DISTRIBUTORS LTD *p163*
701 12 AVE NE, SLAVE LAKE, AB, T0G 2A2
(780) 849-3820 *SIC* 5171

MCROBERT FUELS LIMITED *p897*
4755 EGREMONT DR SUITE 1, STRATHROY, ON, N7G 3H3
(519) 246-1019 *SIC* 5171
MILLER SUPPLY LTD. *p150*
48223 338 AVE E, OKOTOKS, AB, T1S 1B2
(403) 995-4797 *SIC* 5171
MONTMARTRE CO-OPERATIVE ASSOCIATION LIMITED *p1410*
104 CENTRAL AVE, MONTMARTRE, SK, S0G 3M0
(306) 424-2144 *SIC* 5171
MOOSE JAW CO-OPERATIVE ASSOCIATION LIMITED, THE *p1411*
500 1ST AVE NW SUITE B10, MOOSE JAW, SK, S6H 3M5
(306) 692-2351 *SIC* 5171
MOOSEHORN CONSUMERS COOPERATIVE LTD *p352*
1 MAIN ST, MOOSEHORN, MB, R0C 2E0
(204) 768-2770 *SIC* 5171
NAL RESOURCES LIMITED *p54*
550 6 AVE SW SUITE 600, CALGARY, AB, T2P 0S2
(403) 294-3600 *SIC* 5171
PARKLAND CO-OPERATIVE ASSOCIATION LIMITED, THE *p1413*
108 ASH ST, PORCUPINE PLAIN, SK, S0E 1H0
(306) 278-2022 *SIC* 5171
PRAIRIE FUELS *p170*
4744 51 AVE, VEGREVILLE, AB, T9C 1S1
(780) 632-4987 *SIC* 5171
R. KIDD FUELS CORP *p784*
3993 KEELE ST, NORTH YORK, ON, M3J 2X6
(416) 741-2343 *SIC* 5171
RIDGEDALE CO-OPERATIVE ASSOCIATION LTD *p1423*
119 MAIN ST, RIDGEDALE, SK, S0E 1L0
(306) 277-2042 *SIC* 5171
ROCK GLEN CO-OPERATIVE ASSOCIATION LIMITED, THE *p1423*
150 HWY 2 S, ROCKGLEN, SK, S0H 3R0
(306) 476-2210 *SIC* 5171
ROSS AGRI-SUPPLIES (CAMROSE) INC *p78*
3838 47 AVE, CAMROSE, AB, T4V 3W8
(780) 672-2529 *SIC* 5171
SHELLBROOK CO-OPERATIVE ASSOCIATION LIMITED, THE *p1435*
GD, SHELLBROOK, SK, S0J 2E0
(306) 747-2122 *SIC* 5171
SHERWOOD CO-OPERATIVE ASSOCIATION LIMITED *p1415*
615 WINNIPEG ST N, REGINA, SK, P0T 2S0
(306) 791-9300 *SIC* 5171
SMOOK FUELS LTD *p360*
HWY 201, VITA, MB, R0A 2K0
(204) 425-3997 *SIC* 5171
SOUTH COUNTRY CO-OP LIMITED *p146*
969 16 ST SW, MEDICINE HAT, AB, T1A 4X5
(403) 528-6600 *SIC* 5171
TDC CONTRACTING LTD *p435*
1 BREYNAT ST, FORT SMITH, NT, X0E 0P0
(867) 872-2458 *SIC* 5171
UKRAINIAN FARMERS CO-OPERATIVE LIMITED *p350*
22 TACHE ST, FISHER BRANCH, MB, R0C 0Z0
(204) 372-6202 *SIC* 5171
UNIFIED HOLDINGS LTD *p1414*
99 RIVER ST E, PRINCE ALBERT, SK, S6V 0A1
(306) 922-2770 *SIC* 5171
YELLOWHEAD PETROLEUM PRODUCTS LTD *p123*
8901 20 ST NW, EDMONTON, AB, T6P 1K8
(780) 449-1111 *SIC* 5171
YORKTON CO-OPERATIVE ASSOCIATION LIMITED, THE *p1439*
30 ARGYLE ST, YORKTON, SK, S3N 0P6

(306) 783-3601 *SIC* 5171
YOUNG, GARY AGENCIES LTD *p251*
1085 GREAT ST, PRINCE GEORGE, BC, V2N 2K8
(250) 563-1725 *SIC* 5171

SIC 5172 Petroleum products, nec

1443635 ONTARIO INC *p618*
3235 FRONT RD, HAWKESBURY, ON, K6A 2R2
(613) 632-6256 *SIC* 5172
1670747 ONTARIO INC *p907*
720 HEWITSON ST, THUNDER BAY, ON, P7B 5Z1
(807) 623-3996 *SIC* 5172
1673594 ALBERTA LTD *p79*
10702 79 AVE, CLAIRMONT, AB, T8X 5G9
(780) 538-2445 *SIC* 5172
1796640 ONTARIO LIMITED *p910*
920 COMMERCE ST, THUNDER BAY, ON, P7E 6E9
(807) 475-9555 *SIC* 5172
2124688 ONTARIO LIMITED *p781*
3975 KEELE ST, NORTH YORK, ON, M3J 1P1
(416) 665-7594 *SIC* 5172
2618-7922 QUEBEC INC *p1343*
8055 BOUL LANGELIER, SAINT-LEONARD, QC, H1P 2B7
(514) 852-9181 *SIC* 5172
4REFUEL CANADA LP *p224*
9440 202 ST SUITE 215, LANGLEY, BC, V1M 4A6
(604) 513-0386 *SIC* 5172
673927 ONTARIO INC *p665*
3175 14TH AVE UNIT 2, MARKHAM, ON, L3R 0H1
(905) 479-8444 *SIC* 5172
682880 B.C. LTD *p243*
7338 INDUSTRIAL WAY, PEMBERTON, BC, V0N 2L0
(604) 894-6220 *SIC* 5172
9016-0003 QUEBEC INC *p1360*
1315 BOUL SAINT-JEAN-BAPTISTE O, SAINTE-MARTINE, QC, J0S 1V0
(450) 427-1999 *SIC* 5172
976576 ALBERTA LTD *p146*
1433 30 ST SW, MEDICINE HAT, AB, T1B 3N4
(403) 529-9099 *SIC* 5172
993106 ALBERTA LTD *p121*
1444 78 AVE NW, EDMONTON, AB, T6P 1L7
(780) 438-5930 *SIC* 5172
AFD PETROLEUM LTD *p121*
1444 78 AVE NW, EDMONTON, AB, T6P 1L7
(780) 438-5930 *SIC* 5172
AGCOM LTD *p140*
3240 2 AVE N, LETHBRIDGE, AB, T1H 0C6
(403) 328-9228 *SIC* 5172
AIRCONSOL AVIATION SERVICES ULC *p423*
GD LCD MAIN, GANDER, NL, A1V 1W4
(709) 256-3042 *SIC* 5172
ALDUS CAPITAL CORP *p748*
28 CONCOURSE GATE SUITE 105, NEPEAN, ON, K2E 7T7
(613) 723-4567 *SIC* 5172
ALLARD DISTRIBUTING LIMITED *p425*
208 HUMPHRY RD, LABRADOR CITY, NL, A2V 2K7
(709) 944-5144 *SIC* 5172
AOT ENERGY CANADA INC *p43*
520 3 AVE SW SUITE 3120, CALGARY, AB, T2P 0R3
(403) 770-2700 *SIC* 5172
AOT ENERGY CANADA NATURAL GAS INC *p43*
520 3 AVE SW UNIT 3120, CALGARY, AB, T2P 0R3
(403) 770-2700 *SIC* 5172

APRIL SUPER FLO INC p1121
9 RUE BELAND, L'ISLE-VERTE, QC, G0L 1K0
(418) 898-5151   SIC 5172

ARLYN ENTERPRISES LTD p13
6303 30 ST SE UNIT 112, CALGARY, AB, T2C 1R4
(403) 279-2223   SIC 5172

ASIG CANADA LTD p511
8501 MISSISSAUGA RD SUITE 302, BRAMPTON, ON, L6Y 5G8
(905) 497-4114   SIC 5172

ASIG CANADA LTD p728
5600 SILVER DART DR, MISSISSAUGA, ON, L5P 1C4
(905) 694-2846   SIC 5172

ASIG CANADA LTD p1431
2515 AIRPORT RD SUITE 7, SASKATOON, SK, S7L 1M4
(306) 651-6018   SIC 5172

ATHABASCA OIL CORPORATION p43
215 9 AVE SW SUITE 1200, CALGARY, AB, T2P 1K3
(403) 237-8227   SIC 5172

AVJET HOLDING INC p1098
1525 BOUL SAINT-JOSEPH, DRUM-MONDVILLE, QC, J2C 2E9
(819) 479-1000   SIC 5172

BIG RED OIL PRODUCTS INC p844
1915 CLEMENTS RD SUITE 7, PICKER-ING, ON, L1W 3V1
(905) 420-0001   SIC 5172

BLACK TIGER FUELS LTD p163
GD, SLAVE LAKE, AB, T0G 2A0
(780) 849-3616   SIC 5172

BOWMAN FUELS LTD p486
265 BURTON AVE, BARRIE, ON, L4N 2R9
(705) 726-6071   SIC 5172

BP CANADA ENERGY MARKETING CORP p45
240 4 AVE SW, CALGARY, AB, T2P 4H4
(403) 233-1313   SIC 5172

BRAY'S FUELS LIMITED p755
19870 HWY 11, NEWMARKET, ON, L3Y 4V9
(905) 775-3120   SIC 5172

CAFAS FUELING, ULC p1092
780 BOUL STUART-GRAHAM S, DORVAL, QC, H4Y 1G2
(514) 636-3770   SIC 5172

CANADA IMPERIAL OIL LIMITED p45
237 4 AVE SW SUITE 2480, CALGARY, AB, T2P 0H6
(800) 567-3776   SIC 5172

CANADA IMPERIAL OIL LIMITED p859
602 CHRISTINA ST S, SARNIA, ON, N7T 7M5
(519) 339-2000   SIC 5172

CANADIAN BIOENERGY CORPORATION p240
221 ESPLANADE W SUITE 310, NORTH VANCOUVER, BC, V7M 3J3
(604) 947-0040   SIC 5172

CASE 'N DRUM OIL INC p657
3462 WHITE OAK RD, LONDON, ON, N6E 2Z9
(519) 681-3772   SIC 5172

CASTLE FUELS (2008) INC p216
1639 TRANS CANADA HWY E, KAM-LOOPS, BC, V2C 3Z5
(250) 372-5035   SIC 5172

CENTRAL CANADA FUELS & LUBRI-CANTS INC p910
910 COMMERCE ST, THUNDER BAY, ON, P7E 6E9
(807) 475-4259   SIC 5172

CHAUFFAGE RDL PG INC p1286
160 RUE LOUIS-PHILIPPE-LEBRUN, RIVIERE-DU-LOUP, QC, G5R 5W8
(418) 862-5351   SIC 5172

CLARK OIL CO. LTD p419
GD STN MAIN, WOODSTOCK, NB, E7M 6B9
(506) 328-3243   SIC 5172

COMPLETE AVIATION SERVICES LTD p840
SS 5 STN DELIVERY CENTRE, PETER-BOROUGH, ON, K9J 6X6
(705) 745-8626   SIC 5172

CONSOLIDATED AVIATION FUELING OF TORONTO, ULC p728
5600 SILVER DART DR, MISSISSAUGA, ON, L5P 1A2
(905) 694-2846   SIC 5172

CR 92 HOLDINGS LTD p195
1720 MAPLE ST, CAMPBELL RIVER, BC, V9W 3G2
(250) 287-4214   SIC 5172

D.D. DISTRIBUTION LUBRIFIANTS INC p1351
69 BOUL SAINT-REMI, SAINT-REMI, QC, J0L 2L0
(450) 454-3978   SIC 5172

D.W.P. DISTRIBUTORS LTD p271
5504 176 ST, SURREY, BC, V3S 4C3
(604) 576-2961   SIC 5172

DANDY OIL PRODUCTS LTD p105
15630 118 AVE NW, EDMONTON, AB, T5V 1C4
(780) 452-1104   SIC 5172

DAVE MOORE FUELS LTD p589
315 MAIN ST N SUITE 3, EXETER, ON, N0M 1S3
(519) 235-0853   SIC 5172

DAVIS & MCCAULEY FUELS LTD p648
660 CLARKE RD, LONDON, ON, N5V 3A9
(519) 453-6960   SIC 5172

DAVIS FUEL COMPANY LIMITED p520
22 KING ST, BURFORD, ON, N0E 1A0
(519) 449-2417   SIC 5172

DEPMAR FLIGHT HOLDINGS INC p1431
HANGAR 10 JOHN G. DIEFENBAKER AIR-PORT, SASKATOON, SK, S7L 6S1
(306) 931-8552   SIC 5172

DESERT CARDLOCK FUEL SERVICES LIM-ITED p216
1885 VERSATILE DR, KAMLOOPS, BC, V1S 1C5
(250) 374-8144   SIC 5172

DESHAIES, JEAN-PAUL INC p1056
14875 BOUL BECANCOUR, BECANCOUR, QC, G9H 2L7
(819) 222-5623   SIC 5172

DEVON CANADA CORPORATION p168
GD, SWAN HILLS, AB, T0G 2C0
(780) 333-7800   SIC 5172

DOUBLE C. DISTRIBUTORS LTD p126
6330 4 AVE, EDSON, AB, T7E 1M1
(780) 723-3141   SIC 5172

DOWLER-KARN LIMITED p889
43841 TALBOT LINE, ST THOMAS, ON, N5P 3S7
(519) 631-3810   SIC 5172

DUPUIS, PIERRE ET CAMILLE INC p1163
2150 BOUL PIERRE-BERNARD, MON-TREAL, QC, H1L 4P4
(514) 351-9950   SIC 5172

EDWARD FUELS LIMITED p597
263 HURON RD, GODERICH, ON, N7A 2Z8
(519) 524-8386   SIC 5172

ELBOW RIVER MARKETING LTD p48
335 8 AVE SW SUITE 810, CALGARY, AB, T2P 1C9
(403) 232-6868   SIC 5172

ENERGIE VALERO INC p1195
1801 AV MCGILL COLLEGE BUREAU 1300, MONTREAL, QC, H3A 2N4
(514) 982-8200   SIC 5172

ENTREPRISES EMILE CREVIER INC p1329
2025 RUE LUCIEN-THIMENS, SAINT-LAURENT, QC, H4R 1K8
(514) 331-2951   SIC 5172

ENTREPRISES PAUL F. DELANEY INC p1073
165 CH PRINCIPAL, CAP-AUX-MEULES, QC, G4T 1C4
(418) 986-2135   SIC 5172

ESSO AVITAT INTERDEL AVIATION SER-VICES INC p264

5360 AIRPORT RD S, RICHMOND, BC, V7B 1B4
(604) 270-2222   SIC 5172

EXECUTIVE FLIGHT CENTRE FUEL SER-VICES LTD p23
680 PALMER RD NE SUITE 200, CAL-GARY, AB, T2E 7R3
(403) 291-2825   SIC 5172

FEDERATION DES COOPERATIVES DU NOUVEAU-QUEBEC p1053
19950 AV CLARK-GRAHAM, BAIE-D'URFE, QC, H9X 3R8
(514) 457-9371   SIC 5172

FLITE LINE SERVICES (KITCHENER) INC p518
4881 FOUNTAIN ST N SUITE 4, BRESLAU, ON, N0B 1M0
(519) 648-3404   SIC 5172

FREW ENERGY LIMITED p883
180 CUSHMAN RD, ST CATHARINES, ON, L2M 6T6
(905) 685-7334   SIC 5172

FREW PETROLEUM CORPORATION p812
190 WENTWORTH ST E, OSHAWA, ON, L1H 3V5
(905) 723-3742   SIC 5172

FT NELSON BULK SALES LTD p213
MILE 293 ALASKA HWY, FORT NELSON, BC, V0C 1R0
(250) 774-7340   SIC 5172

FUCHS LUBRICANTS CANADA LTD p536
405 DOBBIE DR, CAMBRIDGE, ON, N1T 1S8
(519) 622-2040   SIC 5172

FUEL TRADE INTERNATIONAL INC p951
180 UNIVERSITY AVE UNIT 5204, TORONTO, ON, M5H 0A2
(416) 313-2912   SIC 5172

FUELS INC p613
136 CANNON ST W, HAMILTON, ON, L8R 2B9
(905) 528-0241   SIC 5172

GAETAN VERREAULT FUELS LIMITED p913
HIGHWAY 101 W, TIMMINS, ON, P4N 7H9
(705) 268-4199   SIC 5172

GARDNER DENVER CANADA CORP p803
2390 SOUTH SERVICE RD W, OAKVILLE, ON, L6L 5M9
(905) 847-0688   SIC 5172

GIBSON ENERGY ULC p50
440 2 AVE SW SUITE 1700, CALGARY, AB, T2P 5E9
(403) 206-4000   SIC 5172

GIBSON ENERGY ULC p132
9502 42 AVE, GRANDE PRAIRIE, AB, T8V 5N3
(780) 539-4427   SIC 5172

GLANFORD AVIATION SERVICES LTD p747
9300 AIRPORT RD SUITE 200, MOUNT HOPE, ON, L0R 1W0
(905) 679-4127   SIC 5172

GLOBAL FUELS INC p531
1463 ONTARIO ST SUITE C, BURLING-TON, ON, L7S 1G6
(289) 288-0433   SIC 5172

GOYER PETROLE HUILE A CHAUFFGE INC p1301
794 BOUL ARTHUR-SAUV?, SAINT-EUSTACHE, QC, J7R 4K3
(450) 473-4794   SIC 5172

GROUPE ENERGIE BDL INC p1049
10390 BOUL LOUIS-H.-LAFONTAINE, AN-JOU, QC, H1J 2T3
(514) 493-3576   SIC 5172

GROUPE HARNOIS INC, LE p1353
80 RTE 158, SAINT-THOMAS, QC, J0K 3L0
(450) 756-1660   SIC 5172

GROUPE PETROLIER OLCO ULC p1239
2775 AV GEORGES-V, MONTREAL-EST, QC, H1L 6J7
(514) 645-6526   SIC 5172

HARNOIS ENERGIES INC p1150
1640 BOUL INDUSTRIEL, MATAGAMI, QC, J0Y 2A0

(819) 739-2563   SIC 5172

HIWAY FUEL SERVICES LTD p246
1485 COAST MERIDIAN RD SUITE 200, PORT COQUITLAM, BC, V3C 5P1
(604) 552-8586   SIC 5172

HUILES BERTRAND INC, LES p1237
4949 BOUL LEVESQUE O, MONTREAL, QC, H7W 2R8
(450) 682-2845   SIC 5172

INTER PIPELINE US MARKETING LTD p52
215 2ND ST SW SUITE 3200, CALGARY, AB, T2P 1M4
(403) 538-9015   SIC 5172

JBI (CANADA) INC p848
1783 ALLANPORT RD RR 1, PORT ROBIN-SON, ON, L0S 1K0
SIC 5172

JEPSON PETROLEUM (ALBERTA) LTD p16
5215 61 AVE SE, CALGARY, AB, T2C 3Y6
(403) 215-1449   SIC 5172

JOE MARTIN & SONS LTD p101
18335 105 AVE NW UNIT 201, EDMON-TON, AB, T5S 2K9
(780) 455-0550   SIC 5172

KELLER EQUIPMENT SUPPLY LTD p30
1228 26 AVE SE, CALGARY, AB, T2G 5S2
(403) 243-8666   SIC 5172

KELLY WESTERN SERVICES LTD p386
30 HANGAR LINE RD, WINNIPEG, MB, R3J 3Y7
(204) 948-9500   SIC 5172

KENT PETROLEUM LIMITED p543
280 RICHMOND ST, CHATHAM, ON, N7M 1P6
(519) 623-7411   SIC 5172

KILDAIR SERVICE ULC p1379
1000 MONTEE DES PIONNIERS BUREAU 110, TERREBONNE, QC, J6V 1S8
(450) 756-8091   SIC 5172

KLONDIKE LUBRICANTS CORPORATION p179
3078 275 ST, ALDERGROVE, BC, V4W 3L4
(604) 856-5335   SIC 5172

LEADER AUTO RESSOURCES LAR INC p1251
2525 AUT TRANSCANADIENNE BUREAU 937, POINTE-CLAIRE, QC, H9R 4V6
(514) 694-6880   SIC 5172

LOCATION LOUIS ANDRE PELLETIER LTEE p1154
233 BOUL ALBINY-PAQUETTE, MONT-LAURIER, QC, J9L 1K2
(819) 623-4015   SIC 5172

LUBRICOR INC p1008
475 CONESTOGO RD, WATERLOO, ON, N2L 4C9
(519) 884-8455   SIC 5172

M & M MOTOR PRODUCTS LTD p1420
1400 TORONTO ST, REGINA, SK, S4R 8S8
(306) 757-2001   SIC 5172

M K IMPEX CANADA p724
6382 LISGAR DR, MISSISSAUGA, ON, L5N 6X1
(416) 509-4462   SIC 5172

M&A ENTERPRISES p1435
315 MARQUIS DR W, SASKATOON, SK, S7R 1B6
(306) 653-2744   SIC 5172

MACDONNELL FUELS LIMITED p835
317504 HWY 6 & 10, OWEN SOUND, ON, N4K 5N6
(519) 376-1916   SIC 5172

MACEWEN PETROLEUM INC p680
18 ADELAIDE ST, MAXVILLE, ON, K0C 1T0
(613) 527-2100   SIC 5172

MACKENZIE OIL LIMITED p860
1486 PLANK RD, SARNIA, ON, N7T 7H3
(519) 336-0521   SIC 5172

MACNAMARA, SAMUEL P. ENTERPRISES LIMITED p755
2220 DAVIS DR, NEWMARKET, ON, L3Y 4W1
(905) 898-5678   SIC 5172

MAGNUM OIL (MB) LTD p372

450 SHEPPARD ST, WINNIPEG, MB, R2X 2P8

(204) 594-0440   *SIC* 5172

MAINTAIR AVIATION SERVICES LTD *p910*
316 HECTOR DOUGALL WAY, THUNDER BAY, ON, P7E 6M6

(807) 475-5915   *SIC* 5172

MARINE PETROBULK LTD *p241*
10 PEMBERTON AVE, NORTH VANCOUVER, BC, V7P 2R1

(604) 987-4415   *SIC* 5172

MARYN INTERNATIONAL SALES LTD *p17*
4216 54 AVE SE SUITE 8, CALGARY, AB, T2C 2E3

(403) 252-2239   *SIC* 5172

MAX FUEL DISTRIBUTORS (1998) LTD *p173*
5503 KEPLER ST, WHITECOURT, AB, T7S 1X7

(780) 778-2346   *SIC* 5172

MAYES-MARTIN LIMITED *p487*
150 VESPRA ST, BARRIE, ON, L4N 2G9

(705) 728-5027   *SIC* 5172

MENZIES AVIATION FUELING CANADA LIMITED *p586*
10 CARLSON CT UNIT 301, ETOBICOKE, ON, M9W 6A2

(647) 798-3890   *SIC* 5172

MFP RESOURCES CORP *p110*
5920 76 AVE NW, EDMONTON, AB, T6B 0A6

(780) 465-9668   *SIC* 5172

MIDNIGHT MECHANICAL LIMITED *p435*
42099 MACKENZIE HWY, HAY RIVER, NT, X0E 0R9

(867) 874-2201   *SIC* 5172

MIDSTREAM ENERGY PARTNERS (USA), LLC *p54*
205 5 AVE SW SUITE 3900, CALGARY, AB, T2P 2V7

(403) 296-1660   *SIC* 5172

MIDSTREAM LPG PARTNERSHIP *p54*
205 5 AVE SW SUITE 3900, CALGARY, AB, T2P 2V7

(403) 266-1985   *SIC* 5172

MILLSAP FUEL DISTRIBUTORS LTD *p1432*
905 AVENUE P S, SASKATOON, SK, S7M 2X3

(306) 244-7916   *SIC* 5172

MONARCH OIL (KITCHENER) LIMITED *p635*
808 VICTORIA ST N, KITCHENER, ON, N2B 3C1

(519) 743-8241   *SIC* 5172

MOTOSEL INDUSTRIAL GROUP INC *p201*
204 CAYER ST UNIT 407, COQUITLAM, BC, V3K 5B1

(604) 629-8733   *SIC* 5172

NGL SUPPLY CO. LTD *p55*
435 4 AVE SW SUITE 550, CALGARY, AB, T2P 3A8

(403) 265-1977   *SIC* 5172

NOCO CANADA COMPANY *p577*
5468 DUNDAS ST W SUITE 401, ETOBICOKE, ON, M9B 6E3

(416) 232-6626   *SIC* 5172

NORSTAN SALES LTD *p247*
1530 KINGSWAY AVE SUITE 201, PORT COQUITLAM, BC, V3C 6N6

(604) 257-5555   *SIC* 5172

NORTH ARM TRANSPORTATION LTD *p288*
2582 E KENT AVE SOUTH, VANCOUVER, BC, V5S 2H8

(604) 321-9171   *SIC* 5172

NORTH ATLANTIC *p430*
86 THORBURN RD, ST. JOHN'S, NL, A1B 3M3

(709) 738-5542   *SIC* 5172

NORTHWEST FUELS LIMITED *p283*
5138 KEITH AVE, TERRACE, BC, V8G 1K9

(250) 635-2066   *SIC* 5172

OTTAWA VALLEY GRAIN PRODUCTS INC *p849*
558 RAGLAN ST S, RENFREW, ON, K7V 1R8

SIC 5172

OULTON FUELS LTD *p470*
1699 KING ST, WINDSOR, NS, B0N 2T0

(902) 798-1118   *SIC* 5172

PACESETTER PETROLEUM LIMITED *p1440*
126 INDUSTRIAL RD, WHITEHORSE, YT, Y1A 2T9

(867) 633-5908   *SIC* 5172

PAGE, CHRIS AND ASSOCIATES LTD *p94*
14435 124 AVE NW, EDMONTON, AB, T5L 3B2

(780) 451-4373   *SIC* 5172

PAL AERO SERVICES LTD *p428*
HANGAR NO 4 ST JOHN'S INTERNATIONAL AIRPORT, ST. JOHN'S, NL, A1A 5B5

(709) 576-4615   *SIC* 5172

PAQUET & FILS LTEE *p1137*
4 RUE DU TERROIR, LEVIS, QC, G6V 9J3

(418) 833-9602   *SIC* 5172

PEACE FUEL DISTRIBUTORS LTD *p152*
7510 99 AVE, PEACE RIVER, AB, T8S 1M5

(780) 624-3003   *SIC* 5172

PEARSON INTERNATIONAL FUEL FACILITIES CORPORATION *p689*
5915 AIRPORT RD UNIT 110, MISSISSAUGA, ON, L4V 1T1

(905) 677-1020   *SIC* 5172

PENNER, LARRY ENTERPRISES INC *p379*
29 MOUNTAIN VIEW, WINNIPEG, MB, R3C 2E6

(204) 989-4300   *SIC* 5172

PEPCO CORP *p619*
25 GASPESIE RD, HEARST, ON, P0L 1N0

(844) 362-4523   *SIC* 5172

PEPCO ENERGY CORP *p619*
25 CH. GASPESIE RD, HEARST, ON, P0L 1N0

(844) 362-4523   *SIC* 5172

PEPCO ENERGY CORP *p1050*
10220 BOUL LOUIS-H.-LAFONTAINE, ANJOU, QC, H1J 2T3

(514) 493-7000   *SIC* 5172

PERFORMA LUBRICANTS INTERNATIONAL INC *p1016*
42 MONTROSE CRES, WHITBY, ON, L1R 1C5

(905) 668-1440   *SIC* 5172

PETRO MONTESTRIE INC *p1109*
619 RUE LAURENT, GRANBY, QC, J2G 8Y3

(450) 378-9771   *SIC* 5172

PETRO-CANADA LUBRICANTS INC *p714*
2310 LAKESHORE RD W, MISSISSAUGA, ON, L5J 1K2

(866) 335-3369   *SIC* 5172

PETROGAS ENERGY CORP *p56*
205 5 AVE SW SUITE 3900, CALGARY, AB, T2P 2V7

(403) 266-1985   *SIC* 5172

PETROLE J.M.B INC *p1072*
85 RUE COMMERCIALE, CABANO, QC, G0L 1E0

(418) 854-2267   *SIC* 5172

PETROLES ALCASYNA (1993) INC, LES *p1046*
511 RUE PRINCIPALE S, AMOS, QC, J9T 2J8

(819) 732-5334   *SIC* 5172

PETROLES CADEKO INC *p1262*
455 RUE DES ENTREPRENEURS BUREAU 652, QUEBEC, QC, G1M 2V2

(418) 688-9188   *SIC* 5172

PETROLES CARUFEL INC, LES *p1123*
78 8E AV O, LA SARRE, QC, J9Z 1N3

(819) 762-0765   *SIC* 5172

PETROLES COULOMBE & FILS INC, LES *p1109*
226 RUE ROBINSON S BUREAU 1, GRANBY, QC, J2G 7M6

(450) 375-2080   *SIC* 5172

PETROLES CREVIER INC *p1330*
2025 RUE LUCIEN-THIMENS, SAINT-LAURENT, QC, H4R 1K8

(514) 331-2951   *SIC* 5172

PETROLES J.C. TRUDEL INC *p1366*
1220 10E AV, SENNETERRE, QC, J0Y 2M0

(819) 737-2477   *SIC* 5172

PETROLES J.D. INC *p1151*
60 RUE DU PORT, MATANE, QC, G4W 3M6

(418) 562-0969   *SIC* 5172

PETROLES R.L. INC, LES *p1079*
460 RUE RACINE E, CHICOUTIMI, QC, G7H 1T7

(418) 543-0775   *SIC* 5172

PETROLES R.TURMEL INC, LES *p1125*
4575 RUE LATULIPPE, LAC-MEGANTIC, QC, G6B 3H1

(819) 583-3838   *SIC* 5172

PETRONOR INC *p1391*
1401 CH SULLIVAN, VAL-D'OR, QC, J9P 6V6

(819) 824-5505   *SIC* 5172

PETROVALUE PRODUCTS CANADA INC *p273*
19402 54 AVE UNIT 104, SURREY, BC, V3S 7H9

(604) 576-0004   *SIC* 5172

PHILIPPE GOSSELIN & ASSOCIES LIMITEE *p1360*
1133 BOUL VACHON N, SAINTE-MARIE, QC, G6E 1M9

(418) 387-5449   *SIC* 5172

PIONEER LAND SERVICES LTD *p133*
10537 98 AVE SUITE 201, GRANDE PRAIRIE, AB, T8V 4L1

(780) 532-7707   *SIC* 5172

POINTS NORTH FREIGHT FORWARDING INC *p1431*
2405B WHEATON AVE, SASKATOON, SK, S7L 5Y3

(306) 633-2137   *SIC* 5172

PRODUITS ORAPI-DRY SHINE INC., LES *p1162*
7521 BOUL HENRI-BOURASSA E, MONTREAL, QC, H1E 1N9

(514) 735-3272   *SIC* 5172

PRODUITS PETROLIERS NORCAN S.E.N.C., LES *p1165*
6370 RUE NOTRE-DAME E, MONTREAL, QC, H1N 2E1

(514) 253-2222   *SIC* 5172

PROLAB TECHNOLOGIES INC *p1383*
4531 RUE INDUSTRIELLE, THETFORD MINES, QC, G6H 2J1

(418) 423-2777   *SIC* 5172

R & P PETROLEUM INC *p568*
2236 COUNTY ROAD 92, ELMVALE, ON, L0L 1P0

(705) 429-5179   *SIC* 5172

R. BRUCE GRAHAM LIMITED *p622*
203 BELL ST, INGERSOLL, ON, N5C 2P2

SIC 5172

R. P. OIL LIMITED *p1015*
1111 BURNS ST E UNIT 3, WHITBY, ON, L1N 6A6

(905) 666-2313   *SIC* 5172

ROBERTSON BULK SALES CALGARY LTD *p18*
6811 52 ST SE, CALGARY, AB, T2C 4J5

(403) 531-5700   *SIC* 5172

ROMA LUBE LTD *p784*
3975 KEELE ST, NORTH YORK, ON, M3J 1P1

(416) 656-4189   *SIC* 5172

SAM HOLDINGS LTD *p68*
1623 96 AVE SW, CALGARY, AB, T2V 5E5

(403) 266-1985   *SIC* 5172

SCRUTON-EDWARD CORP *p544*
268 ALBERT ST, CLINTON, ON, N0M 1L0

(519) 482-7381   *SIC* 5172

SEMINOLE CANADA GAS CO *p59*
350 7 AVE SW SUITE 2200, CALGARY, AB, T2P 3N9

SIC 5172

SERVICE D'ECHANGE RAPIDGAZ INC *p1110*
241 RUE SAINT-CHARLES S, GRANBY, QC, J2G 7A7

(450) 375-6644   *SIC* 5172

SERVICES DE LUBRIFIANTS INDUS-

TRIELS & COMMERCIAUX (SLIC) INC *p1371*
402 RUE ALEXANDRE, SHERBROOKE, QC, J1H 4T3

(819) 562-1411   *SIC* 5172

SHELL CANADA PRODUCTS *p59*
400 4 AVE SW, CALGARY, AB, T2P 0J4

(403) 691-3111   *SIC* 5172

SHORELINE LUBE DISTRIBUTION INC *p402*
55 CH RAYMEL, GRAND-BARACHOIS, NB, E4P 7M7

(506) 577-4440   *SIC* 5172

SINOCANADA PETROLEUM CORPORATION *p59*
444 7 AVE SW UNIT 800, CALGARY, AB, T2P 0X8

SIC 5172

SMITH, JACK FUELS LTD *p911*
351 QUEEN ST N, TILBURY, ON, N0P 2L0

(519) 682-0111   *SIC* 5172

SMITH, M.R. LIMITED *p183*
3100 UNDERHILL AVE, BURNABY, BC, V5A 3C6

(604) 420-4331   *SIC* 5172

SOCAR TRADING (CANADA) LTD *p59*
118 8 AVE SW UNIT 200, CALGARY, AB, T2P 1B3

(587) 956-1100   *SIC* 5172

SOCIETE DE GESTION REJEAN & SERGE AUCOIN INTERNATIONAL INC *p1174*
2359 RUE FRONTENAC, MONTREAL, QC, H2K 2Z8

(514) 356-3545   *SIC* 5172

SOUTH PEACE DISTRIBUTORS LTD *p136*
AB-43, HYTHE, AB, T0H 2C0

(780) 356-3970   *SIC* 5172

SPRING FUEL DISTRIBUTORS INC *p220*
275 CAMPION ST, KELOWNA, BC, V1X 7S9

(250) 491-0427   *SIC* 5172

SUNCOR ENERGY MARKETING INC *p60*
150 6 AVE SW, CALGARY, AB, T2P 3Y7

(403) 296-8000   *SIC* 5172

SUNCOR ENERGY PRODUCTS INC *p861*
1900 RIVER RD, SARNIA, ON, N7T 7J3

(519) 337-2301   *SIC* 5172

SUPERLINE FUELS (2009) LIMITED *p456*
3479 BARRINGTON ST SUITE 3451, HALIFAX, NS, B3K 2X8

(902) 429-0740   *SIC* 5172

TARGRAY AMERIQUES INC *p1118*
18105 RTE TRANSCANADIENNE, KIRKLAND, QC, H9J 3Z4

(514) 695-8095   *SIC* 5172

THUNDER BAY FLIGHT REFUELING LIMITED *p910*
304 HECTOR DOUGALL WAY, THUNDER BAY, ON, P7E 6M6

(807) 577-1178   *SIC* 5172

TIDAL ENERGY MARKETING INC *p61*
237 4 AVE SW SUITE 2000, CALGARY, AB, T2P 4K3

(403) 205-7770   *SIC* 5172

TRANSIT PETROLEUM *p604*
516 IMPERIAL RD N, GUELPH, ON, N1H 1G4

(519) 571-1220   *SIC* 5172

TRAVEL CENTRE CANADA INC, THE *p1036*
535 MILL ST, WOODSTOCK, ON, N4S 7V6

(519) 421-3144   *SIC* 5172

TRINITY CAPITAL GP LTD *p62*
205 5 AVE SW SUITE 3030, CALGARY, AB, T2P 2V7

(403) 266-1985   *SIC* 5172

UNITECH LUBRICANTS AMERICA *p1011*
155 FROBISHER DR UNIT 218, WATERLOO, ON, N2V 2E1

(519) 208-2900   *SIC* 5172

UNITED FARMERS OF ALBERTA CO-OPERATIVE LIMITED *p74*
4838 RICHARD RD SW SUITE 700, CALGARY, AB, T3E 6L1

(403) 570-4500   *SIC* 5172

UNIVERSAL AVIATION SERVICES CORPO-

RATION
GD LCD MAIN, FORT MCMURRAY, AB, T9H 3E2
(780) 791-9881 *SIC 5172*

UPI OIL LP *p658*
3462 WHITE OAK RD, LONDON, ON, N6E 2Z9
(519) 681-3772 *SIC 5172*

UPPER CANADA FUELS (2001) LIMITED *p842*
660 THE QUEENSWAY, PETERBOROUGH, ON, K9J 7H2
(705) 742-8815 *SIC 5172*

W O STINSON & SON LTD *p628*
2955 HWY 43, KEMPTVILLE, ON, K0G 1J0
(613) 258-1826 *SIC 5172*

W.H. LUBRICANTS LTD *p1011*
185 FROBISHER DR, WATERLOO, ON, N2V 2E6
(519) 513-9805 *SIC 5172*

WAKEFIELD CANADA INC *p571*
3620 LAKE SHORE BLVD W, ETOBICOKE, ON, M8W 1N6
(416) 252-5511 *SIC 5172*

WD-40 COMPANY (CANADA) LTD *p996*
5399 EGLINTON AVE W SUITE 214, TORONTO, ON, M9C 5K6
(416) 622-9881 *SIC 5172*

WEST NOVA FUELS LIMITED *p462*
73 FALKLAND ST, LUNENBURG, NS, B0J 2C0
(902) 634-3835 *SIC 5172*

WILBUR, DAVID PRODUCTS LTD *p1040*
155 BELVEDERE AVE, CHARLOTTETOWN, PE, C1A 2Y9
SIC 5172

WILSON FUEL CO. LIMITED *p456*
3617 BARRINGTON ST SUITE 289, HALIFAX, NS, B3K 2Y3
(902) 429-3835 *SIC 5172*

WN BIRD FINANCIAL GROUP INC *p547*
387 RAGLAN ST, COLLINGWOOD, ON, L9Y 3Z1
(705) 445-4501 *SIC 5172*

WOODS, DON FUELS LIMITED *p999*
20 RIVER ST, TWEED, ON, K0K 3J0
(613) 478-3039 *SIC 5172*

YYJ FBO SERVICES LTD *p238*
1962 CANSO RD SUITE 101, NORTH SAANICH, BC, V8L 5V5
(250) 655-8833 *SIC 5172*

SIC 5181 Beer and ale

BRASSEURS DU MONDE INC *p1311*
3755 RUE PICARD PORTE 2, SAINT-HYACINTHE, QC, J2S 1H3
(450) 250-2611 *SIC 5181*

BREWERS RETAIL INC *p508*
69 FIRST GULF BLVD, BRAMPTON, ON, L6W 4T8
(905) 450-2799 *SIC 5181*

BREWERS' DISTRIBUTOR LTD *p246*
1711 KINGSWAY AVE, PORT COQUITLAM, BC, V3C 0B6
(604) 927-4055 *SIC 5181*

COOL BEER BREWING CO. INCORPORATED *p574*
164 EVANS AVE, ETOBICOKE, ON, M8Z 1J4
(416) 255-7100 *SIC 5181*

INDIA BREWERIES INC *p942*
1 YONGE ST SUITE 1801, TORONTO, ON, M5E 1W7
(416) 214-1855 *SIC 5181*

MOLSON BREWERIES OF CANADA LIMITED *p586*
33 CARLINGVIEW DR, ETOBICOKE, ON, M9W 5E4
(416) 679-1786 *SIC 5181*

MOLSON INC *p1176*
1555 RUE NOTRE-DAME E, MONTREAL, QC, H2L 2R5

(514) 521-1786 *SIC 5181*

PREMIUM BEER COMPANY INC, THE *p587*
275 BELFIELD RD, ETOBICOKE, ON, M9W 7H9
(905) 855-7743 *SIC 5181*

PRODUITS STAR APPETIZING INC, LES *p1224*
1685 RUE CABOT, MONTREAL, QC, H4E 1C9
(514) 765-0614 *SIC 5181*

SIC 5182 Wine and distilled beverages

9127-2021 QUEBEC INC *p1225*
1350 RUE MAZURETTE BUREAU 314, MONTREAL, QC, H4N 1H2
(514) 739-9112 *SIC 5182*

ARTERRA WINES CANADA, INC *p1288*
175 CH DE MARIEVILLE, ROUGEMONT, QC, J0L 1M0
(450) 469-3104 *SIC 5182*

AUTHENTIC WINE AND SPIRITS MERCHANTS *p191*
7432 FRASER PARK DR, BURNABY, BC, V5J 5B9
(604) 708-5022 *SIC 5182*

BEAM CANADA INC *p572*
3280 BLOOR ST W UNIT 510, ETOBICOKE, ON, M8X 2X3
(416) 849-7300 *SIC 5182*

CAVE SPRING CELLARS LTD *p623*
3836 MAIN ST RR 1, JORDAN STATION, ON, L0R 1S0
(905) 562-3581 *SIC 5182*

DIAGEO CANADA INC *p1366*
1 RUE SALABERRY, SALABERRY-DE-VALLEYFIELD, QC, J6T 2G9
(450) 373-3230 *SIC 5182*

DIAMOND ESTATES WINES & SPIRITS INC *p805*
435 NORTH SERVICE RD W UNIT 100, OAKVILLE, ON, L6M 4X8
(905) 641-1042 *SIC 5182*

DIAMOND ESTATES WINES & SPIRITS LTD *p761*
1067 NIAGARA STONE RD, NÍAGARA ON THE LAKE, ON, L0S 1J0
(905) 685-5673 *SIC 5182*

DISTILLERIES SAZERAC DU CANADA INC, LES *p1210*
950 CH DES MOULINS, MONTREAL, QC, H3C 3W5
(514) 395-3200 *SIC 5182*

FREE SPIRIT MARKET LTD *p1407*
615 MAIN STREET, HUMBOLDT, SK, S0K 2A0
(306) 682-2223 *SIC 5182*

HIGHWOOD DISTILLERS LTD *p70*
4948 126 AVE SE UNIT 23, CALGARY, AB, T2Z 0A9
(403) 216-2440 *SIC 5182*

INTERNATIONAL CELLARS INC *p298*
1122 MAINLAND ST SUITE 200, VANCOUVER, BC, V6B 5L1
(604) 689-5333 *SIC 5182*

KIRKWOOD GROUP LTD, THE *p806*
1155 NORTH SERVICE RD W SUITE 8, OAKVILLE, ON, L6M 3E3
(905) 849-4346 *SIC 5182*

MAISON DES FUTAILLES, S.E.C. *p1066*
500 RUE D'AVAUGOUR BUREAU 2050, BOUCHERVILLE, QC, J4B 0G6
(450) 645-9777 *SIC 5182*

MIELZYNSKI, PETER AGENCIES LIMITED *p798*
231 OAK PARK BLVD SUITE 400, OAKVILLE, ON, L6H 7S8
(905) 257-2116 *SIC 5182*

PACIFIC WINE & SPIRITS INC *p74*
2505 17 AVE SW UNIT 208, CALGARY, AB, T3E 7V3
(403) 226-0214 *SIC 5182*

PENINSULA RIDGE ESTATES WINERY LIM-

ITED *p490*
5600 KING ST RR 3, BEAMSVILLE, ON, L0R 1B3
(905) 563-0900 *SIC 5182*

PHILIPPE DANDURAND WINES LIMITED *p699*
1660 TECH AVE SUITE 3, MISSISSAUGA, ON, L4W 5S7
(416) 368-3344 *SIC 5182*

RENAISSANCE WINE MERCHANTS LTD *p31*
3303 8 ST SE, CALGARY, AB, T2G 3A4
(403) 296-0170 *SIC 5182*

SELECT WINE MERCHANTS LTD *p300*
1122 MAINLAND ST SUITE 470, VANCOUVER, BC, V6B 5L1
(604) 687-8199 *SIC 5182*

SOBEYS WESTERN CELLARS *p107*
15353 CASTLE DOWNS RD NW, EDMONTON, AB, T5X 6C3
(780) 473-7800 *SIC 5182*

SOCIETE DE VIN INTERNATIONALE LTEE *p1101*
3838 BOUL LEMAN, FABREVILLE, QC, H7E 1A1
(450) 661-0281 *SIC 5182*

SPIRITUEUX UNGAVA CIE LTEE, LES *p1088*
291 RUE MINER, COWANSVILLE, QC, J2K 3Y6
(450) 263-5835 *SIC 5182*

TRIALTO WINE GROUP LTD *p300*
1260 HAMILTON ST SUITE 300, VANCOUVER, BC, V6B 2S8
(778) 331-8999 *SIC 5182*

UNIVINS ET SPIRITUEUX (CANADA) INC *p1226*
1350 RUE MAZURETTE BUREAU 326, MONTREAL, QC, H4N 1H2
(514) 522-9339 *SIC 5182*

VENTURI-SCHULZE LTD *p198*
4235 VINEYARD RD, COBBLE HILL, BC, V0R 1L5
(250) 743-5630 *SIC 5182*

VINTNERS CELLAR SASKATOON *p1435*
1824 MCORMOND DR SUITE 146, SASKATOON, SK, S7S 0A6
(306) 371-9463 *SIC 5182*

SIC 5191 Farm supplies

489425 ALBERTA LTD *p20*
1204 EDMONTON TRAIL NE UNIT 1, CALGARY, AB, T2E 3K5
(403) 276-5156 *SIC 5191*

68235 MANITOBA LTD *p351*
5461 PORTAGE AVE UNIT B, HEADINGLEY, MB, R4H 1H8
(204) 885-8120 *SIC 5191*

963488 ONTARIO LIMITED *p537*
255 HOLIDAY INN DR SUITE 312, CAMBRIDGE, ON, N3C 3T2
(519) 220-1151 *SIC 5191*

AGRACITY CROP & NUTRITION LTD *p1426*
320 22ND ST E, SASKATOON, SK, S7K 0H1
(306) 665-2294 *SIC 5191*

AGRICO CANADA LIMITED *p685*
7420 AIRPORT RD UNIT 202, MISSISSAUGA, ON, L4T 4E5
(905) 672-5700 *SIC 5191*

AGROCENTRE TECHNOVA INC *p1242*
515 RUE DE MONSEIGNEUR-COURCHESNE, NICOLET, QC, J3T 1C8
(819) 293-5851 *SIC 5191*

AGRONOMY COMPANY OF CANADA LTD *p903*
17554 PLOVER MILLS RD, THORNDALE, ON, N0M 2P0
(519) 461-9057 *SIC 5191*

ALBERTA NURSERIES & SEEDS LTD *p6*
GD, BOWDEN, AB, T0M 0K0
SIC 5191

ALIMENTS PRO-LACTO INC, LES *p1399*

303 RTE 265, VILLEROY, QC, G0S 3K0
(819) 385-1232 *SIC 5191*

ALLTECH CANADA INC *p601*
20 CUTTEN PL, GUELPH, ON, N1G 4Z7
(519) 763-3331 *SIC 5191*

ANSWER GARDEN PRODUCTS LTD, THE *p178*
27715 HUNTINGDON RD, ABBOTSFORD, BC, V4X 1B6
(604) 856-6221 *SIC 5191*

APPLIED WIRING ASSEMBLIES INC *p593*
2 ROSETTA ST, GEORGETOWN, ON, L7G 3P2
(905) 873-1717 *SIC 5191*

ARCHER'S POULTRY FARM LIMITED *p518*
15738 COUNTY ROAD 2, BRIGHTON, ON, K0K 1H0
(613) 475-0820 *SIC 5191*

BARR-AG LTD *p151*
5837 IMPERIAL DR, OLDS, AB, T4H 1G6
(403) 507-8660 *SIC 5191*

BAYER CROPSCIENCE INC *p1415*
295 HENDERSON DR, REGINA, SK, S4N 6C2
(306) 721-4500 *SIC 5191*

BAYER CROPSCIENCE INC *p1426*
5 CLUMBERS HWY 41, SASKATOON, SK, S7K 7E9
(306) 477-9400 *SIC 5191*

BELCHIM CROP PROTECTION CANADA INC *p600*
104 COOPER DR UNIT 3, GUELPH, ON, N1C 0A4
(519) 826-7878 *SIC 5191*

BLAIR'S FERTILIZER LTD *p1409*
GD, LANIGAN, SK, S0K 2M0
(306) 365-3150 *SIC 5191*

BRADFORD GREENHOUSES LIMITED *p497*
2433 12TH CONC, BRADFORD, ON, L3Z 2B2
(905) 775-4769 *SIC 5191*

BRETT-YOUNG SEEDS LIMITED *p392*
HWY 330 AND HWY 100 SW CORNER, WINNIPEG, MB, R3V 1L5
(204) 261-7932 *SIC 5191*

BRETT-YOUNG SEEDS LIMITED PARTNERSHIP *p392*
GD, WINNIPEG, MB, R3V 1L5
(204) 261-7932 *SIC 5191*

C & M SEEDS MANUFACTURING INC *p836*
6180 5TH LINE RR 3, PALMERSTON, ON, N0G 2P0
(519) 343-2126 *SIC 5191*

CANADA AGRIGROW *p1021*
1243 ELM AVE, WINDSOR, ON, N8X 2B6
(519) 915-8882 *SIC 5191*

CANPOTEX LIMITED *p1426*
111 2ND AVE S SUITE 400, SASKATOON, SK, S7K 3R7
(306) 931-2200 *SIC 5191*

CANTERRA SEEDS (2002) LTD *p390*
1475 CHEVRIER BLVD UNIT 201, WINNIPEG, MB, R3T 1Y7
(204) 988-9750 *SIC 5191*

CANTERRA SEEDS HOLDINGS LTD *p390*
1475 CHEVRIER BLVD UNIT 201, WINNIPEG, MB, R3T 1Y7
(204) 988-9750 *SIC 5191*

CARGILL LIMITED *p1307*
5928 BOUL COUSINEAU BUREAU 300, SAINT-HUBERT, QC, J3Y 7R9
(450) 676-8607 *SIC 5191*

CO-OPERATIVE REGIONALE DE NIPISSING-SUDBURY LIMITED *p1003*
4 RUE PRINCIPALE, VERNER, ON, P0H 2M0
(705) 594-2354 *SIC 5191*

COOP AVANTIS *p1360*
500 RTE CAMERON BUREAU 100, SAINTE-MARIE, QC, G6E 0L9
(418) 386-2667 *SIC 5191*

COOP DES MONTEREGIENNES, LA *p1109*
61 RUE SAINTE-THERESE, GRANBY, QC, J2G 7K2

---

(450) 378-2667 *SIC* 5191

COOP FEDEREE, LA p1064
1580 RUE EIFFEL, BOUCHERVILLE, QC,
J4B 5Y1
(450) 449-6344 *SIC* 5191

COOP FEDEREE, LA p1225
9001 BOUL DE L'ACADIE BUREAU 200,
MONTREAL, QC, H4N 3H7
(514) 858-2222 *SIC* 5191

COOP FEDEREE, LA p1298
249 RUE PRINCIPALE, SAINT-DAMASE,
QC, J0H 1J0
(450) 797-2691 *SIC* 5191

**COOPERATIVE AGRICOLE D'EMBRUN
LIMITED, LA** p569
926 NOTRE DAME ST, EMBRUN, ON, K0A
1W0
(613) 443-2892 *SIC* 5191

COOPERATIVE AGRICOLE PROFID'OR
p1114
839 RUE PAPINEAU, JOLIETTE, QC, J6E
2L6
(450) 759-4041 *SIC* 5191

**COOPERATIVE AGRO-ALIMENTAIRE DES
VALLEES, OUTAOUAIS-LAURENTIDES**
p1384
340 RUE LYON, THURSO, QC, J0X 3B0
(819) 985-4839 *SIC* 5191

CROP MANAGEMENT NETWORK INC p78
4232 41 ST SUITE 110, CAMROSE, AB,
T4V 4E5
(587) 322-2767 *SIC* 5191

DALZIEL ENTERPRISES LTD p81
3439 HWY 580, CREMONA, AB, T0M 0R0
(403) 337-3264 *SIC* 5191

DECOR STRUCTURES CORP p866
735 PROGRESS AVE, SCARBOROUGH,
ON, M1H 2W7
(416) 498-9379 *SIC* 5191

DEGOEYS NURSERY AND FLOWERS
p1013
1501 RD 6, WHEATLEY, ON, N0P 2P0
(519) 326-8813 *SIC* 5191

DISTRIBUTION WESTCO INC p416
9 RUE WESTCO, SAINT-FRANCOIS-DE-
MADAWASKA, NB, E7A 1A5
(506) 992-3112 *SIC* 5191

DLF PICKSEED CANADA INC p645
1 GREENFIELD RD, LINDSAY, ON, K9V
4S3
(705) 878-9240 *SIC* 5191

DSD INTERNATIONAL INC p1382
2515 CH DE L'AEROPORT, THETFORD
MINES, QC, G6G 5R7
(418) 338-3507 *SIC* 5191

DUPONT PIONEER p721
1919 MINNESOTA CRT, MISSISSAUGA,
ON, L5N 0C9
(519) 352-6350 *SIC* 5191

EARTHCO SOIL MIXTURES INC p552
401 BOWES RD SUITE 1, CONCORD, ON,
L4K 1J4
(905) 761-6599 *SIC* 5191

**ENTREPRISES D'ALIMENTATION POUR
ANIMAUX FAMILIER (A.P.A.F) INC, LES**
p1333
4850 CH DU BOIS-FRANC BUREAU 200,
SAINT-LAURENT, QC, H4S 1A7
(514) 745-1262 *SIC* 5191

FINNIE DISTRIBUTING (1997) INC p888
4188 PERTH LINE SUITE 9, ST MARYS,
ON, N4X 1C5
(519) 284-2080 *SIC* 5191

FLAMAN SALES LTD p1436
GD, SOUTHEY, SK, S0G 4P0
(306) 726-4403 *SIC* 5191

FLEMING FEED MILL LIMITED p544
60 IRWIN ST, CLINTON, ON, N0M 1L0
(519) 482-3438 *SIC* 5191

FORTIFIED NUTRITION LIMITED p140
3613 9 AVE N, LETHBRIDGE, AB, T1H 6G8
(403) 320-0401 *SIC* 5191

FOSTER'S SEED AND FEED LTD p5
1120 8TH AVE W, BEAVERLODGE, AB,

T0H 0C0
(780) 354-2107 *SIC* 5191

**FURST-MCNESS COMPANY OF CANADA
LIMITED** p621
30 WILSON ST, INGERSOLL, ON, N5C 4E8
(519) 485-5600 *SIC* 5191

GASTRONOME ANIMAL INC, LE p1356
300 RANG DES ECOSSAIS, SAINTE-
BRIGIDE-D'IBERVILLE, QC, J0J 1X0
(450) 469-0921 *SIC* 5191

GLANBIA NUTRITIONALS (CANADA) INC
p345
190 MAIN ST S, ANGUSVILLE, MB, R0J
0A0
(204) 773-2575 *SIC* 5191

GREEN PRAIRIE INTERNATIONAL INC
p142
210072 TOWNSHIP RD 90B, LETH-
BRIDGE, AB, T1J 5P1
(403) 327-9941 *SIC* 5191

GREENSTAR PLANT PRODUCTS INC p224
9430 198 ST, LANGLEY, BC, V1M 3C8
(604) 882-7699 *SIC* 5191

GRISE, OLIER & CIE LTEE p1350
1 RUE MARTIN, SAINT-PIE, QC, J0H 1W0
(450) 772-2445 *SIC* 5191

GROBER NUTRITION INC p536
415 DOBBIE DR, CAMBRIDGE, ON, N1T
1S8
(519) 622-2500 *SIC* 5191

GROWERS GREENHOUSE SUPPLIES INC
p1003
3559 NORTH SERVICE RD, VINELAND
STATION, ON, L0R 2E0
(905) 562-7341 *SIC* 5191

GROWERS SUPPLY COMPANY LIMITED
p220
2605 ACLAND RD, KELOWNA, BC, V1X
7J4
(250) 765-4500 *SIC* 5191

GUILLEMETTE, MAURICE INC p1056
3635 BOUL DE PORT-ROYAL, BECAN-
COUR, QC, G9H 1Y2
(819) 233-2354 *SIC* 5191

**HALIFAX SEED COMPANY INCORPO-
RATED** p455
5860 KANE ST, HALIFAX, NS, B3K 2B7
(902) 454-7456 *SIC* 5191

HANFENG EVERGREEN INC p926
2 ST CLAIR AVE W SUITE 610, TORONTO,
ON, M4V 1L5

HARVEX AGROMART INC p836
2109B COUNTY ROAD 20 RR 2, OXFORD
STATION, ON, K0G 1T0
(613) 258-3445 *SIC* 5191

HARWIL FARMS MOBILE FEEDS LTD p607
4410 HIGHWAY 6 RR 6, HAGERSVILLE,
ON, N0A 1H0
(905) 768-1118 *SIC* 5191

HI-HOG FARM & RANCH EQUIPMENT LTD
p8
8447 23 AVE NE, CALGARY, AB, T1Y 7G9
(403) 280-8300 *SIC* 5191

**INTERNATIONAL COMMODITIES EXPORT
COMPANY OF CANADA LIMITED** p52
606 4 ST SW SUITE 1020, CALGARY, AB,
T2P 1T1
(403) 264-8954 *SIC* 5191

J. MCEWEN'S PETROLEUMS LTD p130
11141 89 AVE, FORT SASKATCHEWAN,
AB, T8L 2S6
(780) 997-4120 *SIC* 5191

JACK VAN KLAVEREN LIMITED p886
1894 SEVENTH ST, ST CATHARINES, ON,
L2R 6P9
(905) 641-5599 *SIC* 5191

JEFO NUTRITION INC p1310
5020 AV JEFO, SAINT-HYACINTHE, QC,
J2R 2E7
(450) 799-2000 *SIC* 5191

JOHNSON, S. S. SEEDS LTD p345
GD, ARBORG, MB, R0C 0A0
(204) 376-5228 *SIC* 5191

JONES FEED MILLS LIMITED p646
1024 ALFRED ST, LINWOOD, ON, N0B 2A0
(519) 698-2082 *SIC* 5191

KEEPSAKE PLANTS LTD p644
268 SEACLIFF DR W, LEAMINGTON, ON,
N8H 4C8
(519) 326-6121 *SIC* 5191

LAKESIDE GRAIN & FEED LIMITED p591
7858 RAWLINGS RD SUITE 1, FOREST,
ON, N0N 1J0
(519) 786-2106 *SIC* 5191

LEIS FEED AND SUPPLY LIMITED p1013
1214 QUEENS BUSH RD, WELLESLEY,
ON, N0B 2T0
(519) 656-2810 *SIC* 5191

LEWIS CATTLE OILER CO. LTD p354
GD, OAK LAKE, MB, R0M 1P0
(204) 855-2775 *SIC* 5191

MACEWEN AGRICENTRE INC p680
40 CATHERINE ST W, MAXVILLE, ON, K0C
1T0
(613) 527-2175 *SIC* 5191

MAHEU, GERARD INC p1347
289 5E RANG, SAINT-LOUIS-DE-
GONZAGUE, QC, J0S 1T0
(450) 377-1420 *SIC* 5191

MAR-JOHN'S NURSERY LTD p1006
1060 LOBSINGER LINE, WATERLOO, ON,
N2J 4G8
(519) 664-2482 *SIC* 5191

MATERIAUX PAYSAGERS SAVARIA LTEE
p1066
950 CH DE LORRAINE, BOUCHERVILLE,
QC, J4B 5E4
(450) 655-6147 *SIC* 5191

**MAX UNDERHILL'S FARM SUPPLY LIM-
ITED** p1003
56532 CALTON LINE SUITE 1, VIENNA,
ON, N0J 1Z0
(519) 866-3632 *SIC* 5191

MCCAIN FERTILIZERS LIMITED p399
9109 ROUTE 130, FLORENCEVILLE-
BRISTOL, NB, E7L 1Y8
(506) 392-2810 *SIC* 5191

MCEWEN'S FUELS & FERTILIZERS INC
p130
11141 89 AVE, FORT SASKATCHEWAN,
AB, T8L 2S6
(780) 998-2058 *SIC* 5191

MEUNERIE CHARLEVOIX INC p1353
31 RANG SAINT-GEORGES, SAINT-
URBAIN-DE-CHARLEVOIX, QC, G0A 4K0
(418) 639-2472 *SIC* 5191

MEUNERIE SAWYERVILLE INC p1082
100 RUE DE LA MEUNERIE, COOKSHIRE-
EATON, QC, J0B 1M0
(819) 875-5471 *SIC* 5191

MOLESWORTH FARM SUPPLY LTD p647
44743 PERTH LINE 86, LISTOWEL, ON,
N4W 3G6
(519) 291-3740 *SIC* 5191

MORAND INDUSTRIES LTD p151
5502 LAC SUITE ANNE, ONOWAY, AB, T0E
1V0
(780) 967-2500 *SIC* 5191

N. M. BARTLETT INC p490
4509 BARTLETT RD, BEAMSVILLE, ON,
L0R 1B1
(905) 563-8261 *SIC* 5191

NEWS-GLOBAL SOURCING COMPANY
p698
1109 BRITANNIA RD E, MISSISSAUGA,
ON, L4W 3X1
(905) 564-2100 *SIC* 5191

NIEUWLAND FEED & SUPPLY LIMITED
p565
96 WELLINGTON ST, DRAYTON, ON, N0G
1P0
(519) 638-3008 *SIC* 5191

NORSECO INC p1236
2914 BOUL CURE-LABELLE, MONTREAL,
QC, H7P 5R9
(514) 332-2275 *SIC* 5191

NORTH WELLINGTON CO-OPERATIVE

SERVICES p618
56 MARGARET ST, HARRISTON, ON, N0G
1Z0
(519) 338-2331 *SIC* 5191

ONTARIO SEED CO LIMITED p639
77 WELLINGTON ST S, KITCHENER, ON,
N2G 2E6
(519) 886-0557 *SIC* 5191

OTTER FARM & HOME CO-OPERATIVE
p229
3650 248 ST, LANGLEY, BC, V4W 1X7
(604) 607-6924 *SIC* 5191

PESTELL MINERALS & INGREDIENTS INC
p752
141 HAMILTON RD, NEW HAMBURG, ON,
N3A 2H1
(519) 662-2877 *SIC* 5191

PESTELL SHAVINGS LIMITED p752
141 HAMILTON RD SUITE 794, NEW HAM-
BURG, ON, N3A 2H1
(519) 662-6565 *SIC* 5191

PLACEMENTS RRJ INC, LES p1335
5800 RUE KIERAN, SAINT-LAURENT, QC,
H4S 2B5
SIC 5191

PLANT PRODUCTS INC p644
50 HAZELTON ST, LEAMINGTON, ON, N8H
1B8
(519) 326-9037 *SIC* 5191

PRAIRIE MICRO-TECH (1996) INC p1420
2641 ALBERT ST N, REGINA, SK, S4R 8R7
(306) 721-6066 *SIC* 5191

PRAIRIE STEEL PRODUCTS LTD p1405
GD, CLAVET, SK, S0K 0Y0
(306) 933-1141 *SIC* 5191

RACK PETROLEUM LTD p1404
901 HWY 4 S, BIGGAR, SK, S0K 0M0
(306) 948-1800 *SIC* 5191

RAY AGRO & PETROLEUM LTD p167
18 BOULDER BLVD, STONY PLAIN, AB,
T7Z 1V7
(780) 963-2078 *SIC* 5191

RONA INC p392
1530 GAMBLE PL SUITE 453, WINNIPEG,
MB, R3T 1N6
SIC 5191

SEMICAN ATLANTIC INC p1246
366 10E RANG, PLESSISVILLE, QC, G6L
2Y2
(819) 362-6759 *SIC* 5191

SHAFER COMMODITIES INC p316
1100 MELVILLE ST SUITE 938, VANCOU-
VER, BC, V6E 4A6
(604) 669-5512 *SIC* 5191

SHARPE'S SOIL SERVICES LTD p1411
205 PARK AVE, MOOSOMIN, SK, S0G 3N0
(306) 435-3319 *SIC* 5191

SOLOMON, M.J. LTD p356
124 INDUSTRIAL PARK RD, SHOAL LAKE,
MB, R0J 1Z0
(204) 759-2626 *SIC* 5191

SOUTH ESSEX FABRICATING INC p645
4 SENECA RD, LEAMINGTON, ON, N8H
5H7
(519) 322-5995 *SIC* 5191

SPEARE SEEDS p618
99 JOHN ST N, HARRISTON, ON, N0G 1Z0
(519) 338-3840 *SIC* 5191

SPRUCEDALE AGROMART LIMITED p902
291 YOUNG ST, TARA, ON, N0H 2N0
(519) 934-2340 *SIC* 5191

SUN PARLOUR GROWER SUPPLY LIMITED
p645
230 COUNTY RD 31, LEAMINGTON, ON,
N8H 3W2
(519) 326-8681 *SIC* 5191

SUNRIDGE FORAGE LTD p356
15 2128 NW, RUSSELL, MB, R0J 1W0
SIC 5191

SUPREME INTERNATIONAL LIMITED p172
6010 47 ST, WETASKIWIN, AB, T9A 2R3
(780) 352-6061 *SIC* 5191

SYLVITE AGRI-SERVICES LTD p528
3221 NORTH SERVICE RD SUITE 200,

▲ Public Company ■ Public Company Family Member **HQ** Headquarters **BR** Branch **SL** Single Location

BURLINGTON, ON, L7N 3G2
(519) 485-5770   *SIC* 5191
SYLVITE HOLDINGS INC   p528
3221 NORTH SERVICE RD SUITE 200, BURLINGTON, ON, L7N 3G2
(905) 331-8365   *SIC* 5191
SYNGENTA CANADA INC   p602
140 RESEARCH LANE, GUELPH, ON, N1G 4Z3
(519) 836-5665   *SIC* 5191
TERIS SERVICES D'APPROVISIONNEMENT INC   p1362
3180 MONTEE SAINT-AUBIN, SAINTE-ROSE, QC, H7L 3H8
(450) 622-2710   *SIC* 5191
THORLAKSON FEEDYARDS INC   p3
GD STN MAIN, AIRDRIE, AB, T4A 0H4
(403) 948-5434   *SIC* 5191
TIDAL ORGANICS INCORPORATED   p465
2433 HIGHWAY UNIT 3, PUBNICO, NS, B0W 2W0
(902) 762-3525   *SIC* 5191
UNICOOP, COOPERATIVE AGRICOLE   p1360
500 RTE CAMERON BUREAU 100, SAINTE-MARIE, QC, G6E 0L9
(418) 386-2667   *SIC* 5191
UNITED AGRI PRODUCTS CANADA INC   p565
789 DONNYBROOK DR SUITE 2, DORCHESTER, ON, N0L 1G5
(519) 268-5900   *SIC* 5191
VANDAELE SEEDS LTD   p352
GD, MEDORA, MB, R0M 1K0
(204) 665-2384   *SIC* 5191
VANTREIGHT FARMS   p267
8277 CENTRAL SAANICH RD, SAANICHTON, BC, V8M 1T7
(250) 652-7777   *SIC* 5191
VIVACO, GROUPE COOPERATIF   p1398
5 AV PIE-X, VICTORIAVILLE, QC, G6P 4R8
(819) 758-4770   *SIC* 5191
WALLENSTEIN FEED & SUPPLY LTDp1005
7307 WELLINGTON ROAD 86, WALLENSTEIN, ON, N0B 2S0
(519) 669-5143   *SIC* 5191
WANSTEAD FARMERS CO-OPERATIVE CO., LIMITED   p1037
5495 ELEVATOR ST, WYOMING, ON, N0N 1T0
(519) 845-3301   *SIC* 5191
WEST COAST SEEDS LTD   p211
5344 34B AVE, DELTA, BC, V4L 2P1
(604) 952-8820   *SIC* 5191
WESTWAY HOLDINGS CANADA INC p1069
6 RUE DE LA PLACE-DU-COMMERCE BUREAU 202, BROSSARD, QC, J4W 3J9
(450) 465-1715   *SIC* 5191
WILBUR-ELLIS COMPANY OF CANADA LIMITED   p143
212084 TOWNSHIP ROAD 81A, LETHBRIDGE, AB, T1K 8G6
(403) 328-3311   *SIC* 5191
WINTERMAR FARMS (1989) LTD   p1013
265 KATHERINE ST S SUITE 1, WEST MONTROSE, ON, N0B 2V0
(519) 664-3701   *SIC* 5191
WOODSTREAM CANADA CORPORATION
p513
4 LOWRY DR, BRAMPTON, ON, L7A 1C4
(905) 840-2640   *SIC* 5191
YARA CANADA INC   p1419
1874 SCARTH ST SUITE 1800, REGINA, SK, S4P 4B3
(306) 525-7600   *SIC* 5191

SIC 5192 Books, periodicals, and newspapers

ABEBOOKS INC   p339
655 TYEE RD SUITE 500, VICTORIA, BC, V9A 6X5
(250) 412-3200   *SIC* 5192

AMAZON CANADA FULFILLMENT SERVICES INC   p719
6363 MILLCREEK DR, MISSISSAUGA, ON, L5N 1L8
(289) 998-0300   *SIC* 5192
BELL MEDIA INC   p978
444 FRONT ST W, TORONTO, ON, M5V 2S9
(416) 585-5000   *SIC* 5192
BIBLAIRIE G.G.C. LTEE   p1371
1567 RUE KING O, SHERBROOKE, QC, J1J 2C6
(819) 566-0344   *SIC* 5192
BOOK DEPOT INC   p907
67 FRONT ST N, THOROLD, ON, L2V 1X3
(905) 680-7230   *SIC* 5192
BROUGHTON, B. COMPANY LIMITED p766
322 CONSUMERS RD, NORTH YORK, ON, M2J 1P8
(416) 690-4777   *SIC* 5192
CANADIAN LAWYER MAGAZINE INC p480
240 EDWARD ST, AURORA, ON, L4G 3S9
(905) 841-6480   *SIC* 5192
COAST TO COAST NEWSSTAND SERVICES LTD   p873
5230 FINCH AVE E SUITE 1, SCARBOROUGH, ON, M1S 4Z9
(416) 754-3900   *SIC* 5192
DACKIR DISTRIBUTIONS   p211
5305 12 AVE, DELTA, BC, V4M 2B1
(604) 318-1235   *SIC* 5192
DIFFUSION DIMEDIA INC   p1325
539 BOUL LEBEAU, SAINT-LAURENT, QC, H4N 1S2
(514) 336-3941   *SIC* 5192
DISTICOR DIRECT RETAILER SERVICES INC   p473
695 WESTNEY RD S UNIT 14, AJAX, ON, L1S 6M9
(905) 619-6565   *SIC* 5192
DISTRIBUTION HMH INC   p1174
1815 AV DE LORIMIER, MONTREAL, QC, H2K 3W6
(514) 523-1523   *SIC* 5192
EDILIVRE INC   p1156
5740 RUE FERRIER, MONT-ROYAL, QC, H4P 1M7
(514) 738-0202   *SIC* 5192
EDITIONS HURTUBISE INC   p1174
1815 AV DE LORIMIER, MONTREAL, QC, H2K 3W6
(514) 523-1523   *SIC* 5192
FITZHENRY & WHITESIDE LIMITED   p670
195 ALLSTATE PKY, MARKHAM, ON, L3R 4T8
(905) 477-9700   *SIC* 5192
GALLIMARD LTEE   p1185
3700A BOUL SAINT-LAURENT, MONTREAL, QC, H2X 2V4
(514) 499-0072   *SIC* 5192
GLOBE AND MAIL INC, THE   p933
351 KING ST E SUITE 1600, TORONTO, ON, M5A 0N1
(416) 585-5000   *SIC* 5192
GTC (MEDIA)-HEBDO COURRIER LAVAL
p1237
2700 AV FRANCIS-HUGHES BUREAU 200, MONTREAL, QC, H7S 2B9
(450) 667-4360   *SIC* 5192
HACHETTE CANADA INC   p1226
9001 BOUL DE L'ACADIE BUREAU 1002, MONTREAL, QC, H4N 3H5
(514) 382-3034   *SIC* 5192
HARPERCOLLINS CANADA LIMITED p952
22 ADELAIDE ST W, TORONTO, ON, M5H 4E3
(416) 975-9334   *SIC* 5192
INDIGO BOOKS & MUSIC INC   p504
100 ALFRED KUEHNE BLVD, BRAMPTON, ON, L6T 4K4
(905) 789-1234   *SIC* 5192
INTERFORUM CANADA INC   p1175
1001 BOUL DE MAISONNEUVE E BUREAU 1001, MONTREAL, QC, H2L 4P9

(514) 281-1050   *SIC* 5192
JOURNAL LA RELEVE INC   p1066
528 RUE SAINT-CHARLES, BOUCHERVILLE, QC, J4B 3M5
(450) 641-4844   *SIC* 5192
JOURNAL LE PEUPLE LEVIS   p1136
5790 BOUL ETIENNE-DALLAIRE, LEVIS, QC, G6V 8V6
(418) 833-9398   *SIC* 5192
LEBLANC & DAVID MARKETING INCp1175
425 RUE SHERBROOKE E BUREAU 12, MONTREAL, QC, H2L 1J9
(514) 982-0180   *SIC* 5192
LIBRARY BOUND INC   p1010
100 BATHURST DR UNIT 2, WATERLOO, ON, N2V 1V6
(519) 885-3233   *SIC* 5192
LIBRARY SERVICES CENTRE   p637
131 SHOEMAKER ST, KITCHENER, ON, N2E 3B5
(519) 746-4420   *SIC* 5192
MANITOBAN NEWSPAPER PUBLICATIONS CORPORATION, THE   p391
105 UNIVERSITY CRES, WINNIPEG, MB, R3T 2N5
(204) 474-6535   *SIC* 5192
MESSAGERIES A.D.P. INC   p1176
955 RUE AMHERST, MONTREAL, QC, H2L 3K4
(514) 523-1182   *SIC* 5192
MICROVITE INVESTMENTS LIMITED p814
1000 THORNTON RD S UNIT B, OSHAWA, ON, L1J 7E2
(905) 619-6565   *SIC* 5192
MONAHAN AGENCY LTD   p332
2506 41 ST, VERNON, BC, V1T 6J9
(250) 545-3235   *SIC* 5192
MOUNTAIN VIEW PUBLISHING INC   p151
5021 51 ST, OLDS, AB, T4H 1P6
(403) 556-7510   *SIC* 5192
NEWS THE CLASSIFIED   p272
5450 152 ST, SURREY, BC, V3S 5J9
(604) 575-5555   *SIC* 5192
NEWSWEST INC   p36
5716 BURBANK RD SE, CALGARY, AB, T2H 1Z4
(403) 253-8856   *SIC* 5192
OTTAWA X PRESS PUBLISHING INC p834
309 COOPER ST SUITE 401, OTTAWA, ON, K2P 0G5
(613) 237-8226   *SIC* 5192
PALMER, JACKIE DISTRIBUTORS LTD p17
6957 48 ST SE, CALGARY, AB, T2C 5A4
   SIC 5192
PARASOURCE MARKETING AND DISTRIBUTION LIMITED   p837
55 WOODSLEE AVE, PARIS, ON, N3L 3E5
(519) 442-7853   *SIC* 5192
PEACE LIBRARY SYSTEM   p134
8301 110 ST, GRANDE PRAIRIE, AB, T8W 6T2
(780) 538-4656   *SIC* 5192
PROLOGIX DISTRIBUTION SERVICESp869
120 SINNOTT RD, SCARBOROUGH, ON, M1L 4N1
(416) 615-3064   *SIC* 5192
PROLOGUE INC   p1062
1650 BOUL LIONEL-BERTRAND, BOISBRIAND, QC, J7H 1N7
(450) 434-0306   *SIC* 5192
QUEBEC LOISIRS ULC   p1327
253 BOUL DECARIE, SAINT-LAURENT, QC, H4N 2L7
(514) 340-2932   *SIC* 5192
RAINCOAST BOOK DISTRIBUTION LTD
p256
2440 VIKING WAY, RICHMOND, BC, V6V 1N2
(604) 448-7100   *SIC* 5192
ROYAL CITY RECORDS NOW   p183
3430 BRIGHTON AVE SUITE 201A, BURNABY, BC, V5A 3H4
   SIC 5192
SCHOLASTIC CANADA LTD   p679

175 HILLMOUNT RD, MARKHAM, ON, L6C 1Z7
(905) 887-7323   *SIC* 5192
SING TAO NEWSPAPERS (CANADA 1988) LIMITED   p324
8508 ASH ST, VANCOUVER, BC, V6P 3M2
(604) 909-1122   *SIC* 5192
SOCADIS INC   p1327
420 RUE STINSON, SAINT-LAURENT, QC, H4N 3L7
(514) 331-3300   *SIC* 5192
STEELE DISTRIBUTORS INC   p266
3351 FRANCIS RD, RICHMOND, BC, V7C 1J1
(604) 278-4569   *SIC* 5192
STERLING NEWSPAPERS GROUP   p324
1200 73RD AVE W SUITE 920, VANCOUVER, BC, V6P 6G5
(604) 732-4443   *SIC* 5192
TECK NEWS AGENCY (1977) LIMITEDp634
5 KIRKLAND ST E, KIRKLAND LAKE, ON, P2N 1N9
   SIC 5192
THOMAS ALLEN & SON LIMITED   p676
195 ALLSTATE PKWY, MARKHAM, ON, L3R 4T8
(905) 475-9126   *SIC* 5192
TILWOOD DIRECT MARKETING INC p507
300 ORENDA RD, BRAMPTON, ON, L6T 1G2
(905) 793-8225   *SIC* 5192
TILWOOD PUBLISHING SERVICES INC
p507
300 ORENDA RD, BRAMPTON, ON, L6T 1G2
(905) 793-8225   *SIC* 5192
UNITED LIBRARY SERVICES INC   p38
7140 FAIRMOUNT DR SE, CALGARY, AB, T2H 0X4
(403) 252-4426   *SIC* 5192
WHITEHOTS INC   p482
205 INDUSTRIAL PKY N UNIT 3, AURORA, ON, L4G 4C4
(905) 727-9188   *SIC* 5192

SIC 5193 Flowers and florists supplies

1254711 ONTARIO LIMITED   p539
437 MARK RD SUITE 1, CAMERON, ON, K0M 1G0
(705) 374-4700   *SIC* 5193
1882540 ONTARIO INC   p994
1444 DUPONT ST UNIT 11, TORONTO, ON, M6P 4H3
(416) 516-1569   *SIC* 5193
2436-3392 QUEBEC INC   p1301
807 BOUL ARTHUR-SAUVE, SAINT-EUSTACHE, QC, J7R 4K3
(450) 472-8400   *SIC* 5193
3856011 CANADA INC   p691
4800 EASTGATE PKY UNIT 4, MISSISSAUGA, ON, L4W 3W6
(905) 366-0800   *SIC* 5193
542144 ONTARIO LTD   p760
1695 NIAGARA STONE RD, NIAGARA ON THE LAKE, ON, L0S 1J0
(905) 468-3217   *SIC* 5193
615317 NB INC   p395
891 ROUTE 880, BERWICK, NB, E5P 3H5
(506) 433-6168   *SIC* 5193
7169311 MANITOBA LTD   p383
975 SHERWIN RD UNIT 1, WINNIPEG, MB, R3H 0T8
(855) 838-7852   *SIC* 5193
968502 ONTARIO INC   p590
1050 CANBORO RD, FENWICK, ON, L0S 1C0
(905) 892-4766   *SIC* 5193
A.M.A. HOLICULTURE INC   p633
2011 SPINKS DR, KINGSVILLE, ON, N9Y 2E5
(519) 322-1397   *SIC* 5193
A.V.K. NURSERY HOLDINGS INC   p857

1724 CONCESSION 4, ROCKTON, ON, L0R 1X0
(905) 659-1518　*SIC* 5193

ACCESS FLOWER TRADING INC　*p802*
700 DORVAL DR SUITE 405, OAKVILLE, ON, L6K 3V3
(905) 849-1343　*SIC* 5193

ALBERTA BUILDING CONTRACTORS LTD *p67*
9232 HORTON RD SW, CALGARY, AB, T2V 2X4
(403) 888-1960　*SIC* 5193

ARANA GARDENING SUPPLIES LIMITED *p737*
6300 KENNEDY RD UNIT 1, MISSISSAUGA, ON, L5T 2X5
(905) 670-8500　*SIC* 5193

BAJAR, ANTONIO GREENHOUSES LIMITED　*p754*
18545 KEELE ST, NEWMARKET, ON, L3Y 4V9
(905) 775-2773　*SIC* 5193

BAKKER, J. C. & SONS LIMITED　*p885*
1360 THIRD ST SUITE 3, ST CATHARINES, ON, L2R 6P9
(905) 935-4533　*SIC* 5193

BAYVIEW FLOWERS (JORDAN STATION) LTD　*p623*
3764 JORDAN RD, JORDAN STATION, ON, L0R 1S0
(905) 562-7321　*SIC* 5193

BOURBEAU, GERARD & FILS INC　*p1256*
8285 1RE AV, QUEBEC, QC, G1G 4C1
(418) 623-5401　*SIC* 5193

BRON & SONS NURSERY CO. LTD　*p215*
3315 CARSON RD, GRAND FORKS, BC, V0H 1H4
(250) 442-2014　*SIC* 5193

CAMBRIAN TRADING HOUSE LTD　*p833*
153 GILMOUR ST, OTTAWA, ON, K2P 0N8
(613) 233-3111　*SIC* 5193

CEDARWAY FLORAL INC　*p489*
4665 BARTLETT RD, BEAMSVILLE, ON, L0R 1B1
(905) 563-4338　*SIC* 5193

CELLAY CANADA INC　*p668*
30 ROYAL CREST CRT SUITE 8, MARKHAM, ON, L3R 9W8
SIC 5193

CENTRAL ALBERTA GREENHOUSES LTD *p5*
GD, BLACKFALDS, AB, T0M 0J0
(403) 885-4606　*SIC* 5193

CENTRE DU PIN LIMITEE, LE　*p1184*
225 RUE JOSEPH-TISON, MONTREAL, QC, H2V 4S5
(514) 278-5551　*SIC* 5193

DOWNHAM NURSERIES (1993) INC　*p897*
390 YORK ST, STRATHROY, ON, N7G 2E5
SIC 5193

DUTCHMASTER NURSERIES LIMITED*p520*
3735 SIDELINE 16, BROUGHAM, ON, L0H 1A0
(905) 683-8211　*SIC* 5193

ENTREPRISES MARSOLAIS INC, LES *p1166*
5045 RUE ONTARIO, MONTREAL, QC, H1V 1M7
(514) 254-7171　*SIC* 5193

EVERGRO CANADA INC　*p208*
7430 HOPCOTT RD SUITE 1, DELTA, BC, V4G 1B6
(604) 940-0290　*SIC* 5193

FERME DES RASADES INC　*p1384*
118 132 RTE E BUREAU 3095, TROIS-PISTOLES, QC, G0L 4K0
(418) 851-2366　*SIC* 5193

FLEURIGROS 1995 INC　*p1266*
2365 AV WATT BUREAU 1, QUEBEC, QC, G1P 3X2
(418) 654-2888　*SIC* 5193

FLORA-DEI　*p682*
632 SAFARI RD, MILLGROVE, ON, L8B 1S8
(905) 659-3354　*SIC* 5193

FLORISTS SUPPLY LTD　*p384*
35 AIRPORT RD, WINNIPEG, MB, R3H 0V5
(800) 665-7378　*SIC* 5193

FOLIERA INC　*p489*
4655 BARTLETT RD, BEAMSVILLE, ON, L0R 1B1
(905) 563-1066　*SIC* 5193

GALE'S WHOLESALE LTD　*p1416*
1602 ELLIOTT ST, REGINA, SK, S4N 6L1
(306) 757-8545　*SIC* 5193

GROBE NURSERY LIMITED　*p518*
1787 GREENHOUSE RD, BRESLAU, ON, N0B 1M0
(519) 648-2247　*SIC* 5193

INLINE NURSERIES (2010) INC　*p198*
49944 YALE RD, CHILLIWACK, BC, V4Z 0B3
(604) 794-7096　*SIC* 5193

M. VAN NOORT & SONS BULB COMPANY LIMITED　*p226*
22264 NO 10 HWY, LANGLEY, BC, V2Y 2K6
(604) 888-6555　*SIC* 5193

MAKE SCENTS FLOWER DISTRIBUTORS INC　*p193*
3777 MARINE WAY, BURNABY, BC, V5J 5A7
(604) 433-3552　*SIC* 5193

MEX Y CAN TRADING (EAST) INC.　*p741*
6799 PACIFIC CIR UNIT 4, MISSISSAUGA, ON, L5T 1S6
(905) 670-3355　*SIC* 5193

MEYERS FRUIT FARMS LTD　*p761*
1444 IRVINE RD RR 4, NIAGARA ON THE LAKE, ON, L0S 1J0
(905) 934-3925　*SIC* 5193

MORGAN CREEK TROPICALS LTD　*p279*
4148 184 ST, SURREY, BC, V3Z 1B7
(604) 576-1156　*SIC* 5193

MORI NURSERIES LIMITED　*p761*
1695 NIAGARA STONE RD, NIAGARA ON THE LAKE, ON, L0S 1J0
(905) 468-3217　*SIC* 5193

NEIL VANDER KRUK HOLDINGS INC *p566*
1155 HWY 5, DUNDAS, ON, L9H 5E2
(905) 628-0112　*SIC* 5193

NORQUAY NURSERIES LTD　*p355*
GD LCD MAIN 28168 1 HWY E, PORTAGE LA PRAIRIE, MB, R1N 3B2
(204) 239-6507　*SIC* 5193

NORTH WEST WHOLESALE FLORISTS LTD　*p193*
8580 GREENALL AVE, BURNABY, BC, V5J 3M6
(604) 430-0593　*SIC* 5193

NORTHLAND FLORAL INC　*p886*
1703 SOUTH SERVICE RD, ST CATHARINES, ON, L2R 6P9
(905) 646-2828　*SIC* 5193

PAN AMERICAN NURSERY PRODUCTS INC　*p279*
5151 152 ST, SURREY, BC, V3Z 1G9
(604) 576-8641　*SIC* 5193

PETALS WEST INC　*p384*
975 SHERWIN RD UNIT 1, WINNIPEG, MB, R3H 0T8
(204) 786-1801　*SIC* 5193

PIROCHE PLANTS INC　*p244*
20542 MCNEIL RD, PITT MEADOWS, BC, V3Y 2T9
(604) 465-7101　*SIC* 5193

PLANTES D'INTERIEUR VERONNEAU INC, LES　*p1234*
2965 BOUL LE CORBUSIER, MONTREAL, QC, H7L 3M3
(450) 680-1989　*SIC* 5193

QUALITREE PROPAGATORS INC　*p266*
51546 FERRY RD, ROSEDALE, BC, V0X 1X2
(604) 794-3375　*SIC* 5193

QUEBEC MULTIPLANTS　*p1262*
755 RUE DU MARAIS, QUEBEC, QC, G1M 3R7
(418) 687-1616　*SIC* 5193

ROYAL GARDENS LIMITED　*p411*

30 ROYAL GARDENS RD, PENOBSQUIS, NB, E4G 2C5
(506) 433-2030　*SIC* 5193

SCOTT'S NURSERY LTD　*p404*
2192 ROUTE 102, LINCOLN, NB, E3B 8N1
(506) 458-9208　*SIC* 5193

SERRES RIEL INC, LES　*p1351*
1851 RANG NOTRE-DAME, SAINT-REMI, QC, J0L 2L0
(450) 454-9425　*SIC* 5193

SIPKENS NURSERIES LTD　*p1037*
3261 LONDON LINE, WYOMING, ON, N0N 1T0
(519) 542-8353　*SIC* 5193

SPRING VALLEY GARDENS (NIAGARA) INC　*p886*
1330 FIFTH ST LOUTH, ST CATHARINES, ON, L2R 6P9
(905) 935-9002　*SIC* 5193

TRANSAMERICAS TRADING INC　*p389*
1248 WILKES AVE, WINNIPEG, MB, R3P 1C2
(204) 831-3663　*SIC* 5193

TSC NURSERY SALES LIMITED　*p257*
18071 WESTMINSTER HWY, RICHMOND, BC, V6V 1B1
(604) 214-4575　*SIC* 5193

UNITED FLORAL INC　*p194*
4085 MARINE WAY, BURNABY, BC, V5J 5E2
(604) 438-3535　*SIC* 5193

VAN BELLE NURSERY INC　*p178*
34825 HALLERT RD, ABBOTSFORD, BC, V3G 1R3
(604) 853-3415　*SIC* 5193

VANDERGRIFT WHOLESALE FLORIST LTD　*p600*
353 ELIZABETH ST, GUELPH, ON, N1E 2X9
(519) 822-8097　*SIC* 5193

VANDERMEER GREENHOUSES LTD *p351*
21065 DUMAINE RD, ILE DES CHENES, MB, R0A 0T0
(204) 878-3420　*SIC* 5193

WATERDALE INC　*p702*
1303 AEROWOOD DR, MISSISSAUGA, ON, L4W 2P6
(905) 624-2600　*SIC* 5193

WATERLOO FLOWERS LIMITED　*p518*
1001 KRAMP RD, BRESLAU, ON, N0B 1M0
SIC 5193

WESTBROOK FLORAL LTD　*p490*
4994 NORTH SERVICE RD, BEAMSVILLE, ON, L0R 1B3
(905) 945-9611　*SIC* 5193

SIC 5194 Tobacco and tobacco products

8268533 CANADA INC　*p1225*
155 BOUL MONTPELLIER, MONTREAL, QC, H4N 2G3
(514) 385-2509　*SIC* 5194

99767 CANADA LTEE　*p1401*
4795 RUE SAINTE-CATHERINE O, WESTMOUNT, QC, H3Z 1S8
(514) 731-5654　*SIC* 5194

CAMPBELLFORD WHOLESALE COMPANY LTD　*p539*
11 INDUSTRIAL DR SUITE 1, CAMPBELLFORD, ON, K0L 1L0
(705) 653-3640　*SIC* 5194

CHAREST, F. LTEE　*p1305*
1085 42E RUE N, SAINT-GEORGES, QC, G5Z 0T9
(418) 228-9747　*SIC* 5194

COMPAGNIE REGITAN LTEE, LA　*p1093*
1420 RTE TRANSCANADIENNE, DORVAL, QC, H9P 1H7
(514) 685-8282　*SIC* 5194

G.T. WHOLESALE LIMITED　*p817*
2480 WALKLEY RD, OTTAWA, ON, K1G 6A9
(613) 521-8222　*SIC* 5194

GROUPE TABAC SCANDINAVE CANADA INC　*p1144*
1000 RUE DE SERIGNY BUREAU 600, LONGUEUIL, QC, J4K 5B1
(450) 677-1807　*SIC* 5194

HOUSE OF HORVATH INC　*p991*
77 OSSINGTON AVE, TORONTO, ON, M6J 2Z2
(416) 534-4254　*SIC* 5194

IMPERIAL TOBACCO COMPAGNIE LIMITEE　*p1223*
3711 RUE SAINT-ANTOINE O, MONTREAL, QC, H4C 3P6
(514) 932-6161　*SIC* 5194

JOHN PLAYER & FILS LTEE　*p1223*
3711 RUE SAINT-ANTOINE O, MONTREAL, QC, H4C 3P6
(514) 932-6161　*SIC* 5194

LOUDON BROS. LIMITED　*p909*
830A ATHABASCA ST, THUNDER BAY, ON, P7C 3E6
(807) 623-5458　*SIC* 5194

MASSEY WHOLESALE LTD　*p680*
400 CARLALBERT ST, MASSEY, ON, P0P 1P0
(705) 865-2051　*SIC* 5194

PRATTS LIMITED　*p372*
101 HUTCHINGS ST, WINNIPEG, MB, R2X 2V4
(204) 949-2800　*SIC* 5194

ROLLY'S WHOLESALE LTD　*p410*
10 MACNAUGHTON AVE, MONCTON, NB, E1H 3L9
(506) 859-7110　*SIC* 5194

SPIKE MARKS INC　*p1327*
275 RUE STINSON, SAINT-LAURENT, QC, H4N 2E1
(514) 737-0066　*SIC* 5194

TEL-STAR MARKETING GROUP (1993) LTD *p1034*
64 TROWERS RD UNIT 2, WOODBRIDGE, ON, L4L 7K5
SIC 5194

WALLACE & CAREY INC　*p40*
5445 8 ST NE, CALGARY, AB, T2K 5R9
(403) 275-7360　*SIC* 5194

SIC 5198 Paints, varnishes, and supplies

2164-1204 QUEBEC INC　*p1216*
9795 RUE WAVERLY, MONTREAL, QC, H3L 2V7
(514) 381-8524　*SIC* 5198

AKZO NOBEL WOOD COATINGS LTD*p1400*
274 RUE SAINT-LOUIS BUREAU 6, WARWICK, QC, J0A 1M0
(819) 358-7500　*SIC* 5198

BEHR PROCESS CANADA LTD　*p10*
2750 CENTRE AVE NE, CALGARY, AB, T2A 2L3
(403) 273-0226　*SIC* 5198

BELLARE INDUSTRIAL COATINGS INC*p21*
636 36 AVE NE, CALGARY, AB, T2E 2L7
(403) 295-9676　*SIC* 5198

CORONET WALLPAPERS (ONTARIO) LIMITED　*p583*
88 RONSON DR, ETOBICOKE, ON, M9W 1B9
(416) 245-2900　*SIC* 5198

DATRAN BAS ST-LAURENT INC　*p1285*
290 AV DE L'INDUSTRIE, RIMOUSKI, QC, G5M 1W4
SIC 5198

DYNAMIC PAINT PRODUCTS INC　*p721*
7040 FINANCIAL DR, MISSISSAUGA, ON, L5N 7H5
(905) 812-9319　*SIC* 5198

ENDUITS STEF INC　*p1373*
4365 RUE ROBITAILLE, SHERBROOKE, QC, J1L 2K2
(819) 820-1188　*SIC* 5198

FARGEYS PAINT & WALL COVERINGS LTD *p153*

3433 50 AVE, RED DEER, AB, T4N 3Y3

(403) 343-3133   *SIC 5198*

FIBREWALL CANADA LTD   *p122*
1309 77 AVE NW, EDMONTON, AB, T6P 1M8

(780) 945-0561   *SIC 5198*

HEER'S DECORATING AND DESIGN CENTRES INC   *p641*
428 GAGE AVE UNIT 4, KITCHENER, ON, N2M 5C9

(519) 578-5330   *SIC 5198*

INNOVATIVE MANUFACTURING INC   *p206*
861 DERWENT WAY SUITE 877, DELTA, BC, V3M 5R4

(604) 522-2811   *SIC 5198*

JET ICE LIMITED   *p755*
1091 KERRISDALE BLVD, NEWMARKET, ON, L3Y 8W1

(905) 853-4204   *SIC 5198*

METRO ACQUISITION 2004, INC   *p555*
2600 STEELES AVE W, CONCORD, ON, L4K 3C8

(905) 738-5177   *SIC 5198*

NORWALL GROUP INC   *p505*
150 DELTA PARK BLVD, BRAMPTON, ON, L6T 5T6

(905) 791-2700   *SIC 5198*

P.S. ATLANTIC LIMITED   *p426*
102 CLYDE AVE, MOUNT PEARL, NL, A1N 4S2

(709) 747-5432   *SIC 5198*

PEINTURE SYLTECK INC   *p1399*
1521 BOUL JUTRAS O, VICTORIAVILLE, QC, G6T 2A9

(819) 758-3662   *SIC 5198*

PEINTURES PROLUX INC   *p1162*
11430 56E AV, MONTREAL, QC, H1E 2L5

(514) 648-4911   *SIC 5198*

PRODUITS B.C.M. LTEE   *p1079*
340 RUE EMILE-COUTURE, CHICOUTIMI, QC, G7H 8B6

(418) 545-1698   *SIC 5198*

REVETEMENTS AGRO INC, LES   *p1111*
1195 RUE PRINCIPALE, GRANBY, QC, J2J 0M3

(450) 776-1010   *SIC 5198*

SAWILL LTD   *p558*
54 AUDIA CRT UNIT 2, CONCORD, ON, L4K 3N4

(905) 669-0341   *SIC 5198*

SHERWIN-WILLIAMS CANADA INC   *p905*
8500 LESLIE ST SUITE 220, THORNHILL, ON, L3T 7M8

SIC 5198

SHERWIN-WILLIAMS STORE GROUP INC   *p707*
170 BRUNEL RD UNIT B, MISSISSAUGA, ON, L4Z 1T5

(905) 507-0166   *SIC 5198*

WALLS ALIVE LTD   *p67*
1328 17 AVE SW, CALGARY, AB, T2T 0C3

(403) 244-8931   *SIC 5198*

YORKE TOWNE SUPPLIES LIMITED   *p854*
1235 REID ST, RICHMOND HILL, ON, L4B 1G4

(905) 762-1200   *SIC 5198*

SIC 5199 Nondurable goods, nec

120348 CANADA INC   *p1331*
4600 CH DU BOIS-FRANC, SAINT-LAURENT, QC, H4S 1A7

(514) 331-3130   *SIC 5199*

121409 CANADA INC   *p848*
3425 HANDS RD, PRESCOTT, ON, K0E 1T0

(613) 925-4502   *SIC 5199*

135456 CANADA INC   *p1052*
5547 RTE 112, ASCOT CORNER, QC, J0B 1A0

(819) 822-1833   *SIC 5199*

1531011 ONTARIO INC   *p581*
185 CARLINGVIEW DR SUITE 1, ETOBI-

COKE, ON, M9W 5E8

(416) 285-0041   *SIC 5199*

2010162 ONTARIO LTD   *p759*
6868 KINSMEN CRT, NIAGARA FALLS, ON, L2H 0Y5

(905) 358-3674   *SIC 5199*

2920654 CANADA INC   *p1156*
5785 RUE PARE, MONT-ROYAL, QC, H4P 1S1

(514) 736-0810   *SIC 5199*

6669409 CANADA INC   *p1233*
3504 AV FRANCIS-HUGHES, MONTREAL, QC, H7L 5A9

(450) 696-1090   *SIC 5199*

788265 ONTARIO LIMITED   *p665*
250 SHIELDS CRT UNIT 1, MARKHAM, ON, L3R 9W7

(905) 415-8020   *SIC 5199*

9199-4467 QUEBEC INC   *p1225*
1350 RUE MAZURETTE BUREAU 228, MONTREAL, QC, H4N 1H2

(514) 316-2404   *SIC 5199*

987217 ONTARIO LIMITED   *p666*
168 KONRAD CRES UNIT 2, MARKHAM, ON, L3R 9T9

(905) 474-9304   *SIC 5199*

A & A ENTERPRISES INC   *p1034*
354 DUNDAS ST, WOODSTOCK, ON, N4S 1B4

SIC 5199

A & R DECORATIONS   *p1242*
166 RTE 299, NEW RICHMOND, QC, G0C 2B0

(418) 392-4686   *SIC 5199*

ABBOTT OF ENGLAND 1981 LIMITED   *p791*
545 TRETHEWEY DR, NORTH YORK, ON, M6M 2J4

(416) 789-7663   *SIC 5199*

ADLER INTERNATIONAL, LTD   *p864*
5610 FINCH AVE E, SCARBOROUGH, ON, M1B 6A6

(416) 291-9000   *SIC 5199*

AFFIRMATIVE DYNAMIC INDUSTRY INC   *p762*
1765 JANE ST, NORTH BAY, ON, P1B 3K3

(705) 476-8809   *SIC 5199*

ALTIUM PACKAGING CANADA INC   *p971*
199 BAY ST SUITE 4000, TORONTO, ON, M5L 1A9

SIC 5199

AMSCAN DISTRIBUTORS (CANADA) LTD   *p782*
1225 FINCH AVE W, NORTH YORK, ON, M3J 2E8

(800) 363-6662   *SIC 5199*

ANIPET ANIMAL SUPPLIES INC   *p278*
19038 24 AVE, SURREY, BC, V3Z 3S9

(604) 536-3367   *SIC 5199*

ARBRE JOYEUX INC   *p1356*
1077 271 RTE, SAINTE-CLOTILDE-DE-BEAUCE, QC, G0N 1C0

(418) 427-3363   *SIC 5199*

ARCTIC PACKAGING INDUSTRIES INC   *p1010*
295 FROBISHER DR, WATERLOO, ON, N2V 2G4

(519) 885-2161   *SIC 5199*

ARTICLES EN CUIR C.B.M. INC   *p1227*
8370 RUE LABARRE, MONTREAL, QC, H4P 2E7

(514) 738-5858   *SIC 5199*

ATLAS GRAPHIC SUPPLY INC   *p666*
121 WHITEHALL DR, MARKHAM, ON, L3R 9T1

(905) 948-9800   *SIC 5199*

ATTITUDES IMPORT INC   *p1101*
3025 BOUL LE CORBUSIER, FABREVILLE, QC, H7L 4C3

(450) 681-4147   *SIC 5199*

AUTRUCHE VARIETES INC   *p1141*
715 RUE DELAGE BUREAU 700, LONGUEUIL, QC, J4G 2P8

(450) 670-2323   *SIC 5199*

B.R.T. DISTRIBUTING LTD   *p627*

1368 HIGHWAY 7, KEENE, ON, K9J 0G6

(705) 295-6832   *SIC 5199*

BAG TEX PACKAGING INC   *p836*
10 SPRUCE ST, PARIS, ON, N3L 1R6

(519) 442-0499   *SIC 5199*

BALCO INC   *p383*
1610 ST JAMES ST, WINNIPEG, MB, R3H 0L2

(204) 772-2421   *SIC 5199*

BASIC SPIRIT INCORPORATED   *p465*
73 WATER ST, PUGWASH, NS, B0K 1L0

(902) 243-3390   *SIC 5199*

BELER HOLDINGS INC   *p716*
4050A SLADEVIEW CRES SUITE 1A, MISSISSAUGA, ON, L5L 5Y5

(905) 569-1277   *SIC 5199*

BRANDALLIANCE ONTARIO INC   *p1007*
640 BRIDGE ST W, WATERLOO, ON, N2K 4M9

(519) 746-2055   *SIC 5199*

BRANDALLIANCE, INC   *p1002*
10 ROYBRIDGE GATE SUITE 202, VAUGHAN, ON, L4H 3M8

(905) 819-0155   *SIC 5199*

C.J. MARKETING LTD   *p851*
50 EAST WILMOT ST, RICHMOND HILL, ON, L4B 3Z3

(905) 886-8885   *SIC 5199*

CALCULATED INCENTIVES INC   *p906*
109 ROSEDALE HEIGHTS DR, THORNHILL, ON, L4J 4V9

SIC 5199

CAN-PET DISTRIBUTORS INC   *p550*
84 DONEY CRES SUITE C, CONCORD, ON, L4K 3A8

(905) 738-3663   *SIC 5199*

CANA IMPORT EXPORT LTD   *p573*
1589 THE QUEENSWAY UNIT 1, ETOBICOKE, ON, M8Z 5W9

(416) 252-8652   *SIC 5199*

CANADIAN ART PRINTS INC   *p265*
6311 WESTMINSTER HWY UNIT 110, RICHMOND, BC, V7C 4V4

(604) 207-0165   *SIC 5199*

CANADIAN TEST CASE 31 LTD   *p720*
6750 CENTURY AVE SUITE 305, MISSISSAUGA, ON, L5N 2V8

(905) 812-5920   *SIC 5199*

CANDYM ENTERPRISES LTD   *p680*
95 CLEGG RD, MARKHAM, ON, L6G 1B9

(905) 474-1555   *SIC 5199*

CENTRE DE CONFORMITE ICC INC   *p1093*
88 AV LINDSAY, DORVAL, QC, H9P 2T8

(514) 636-8146   *SIC 5199*

CHANNEL CONTROL MERCHANTS CORPORATION   *p515*
225 HENRY ST UNIT 5B, BRANTFORD, ON, N3S 7R4

(519) 770-3403   *SIC 5199*

CHERISON ENTERPRISES INC   *p550*
53 COURTLAND AVE SUITE 1, CONCORD, ON, L4K 3T2

(905) 882-6168   *SIC 5199*

CICHLID WHOLESALE LTD   *p14*
7503 35 ST SE UNIT 25, CALGARY, AB, T2C 1V3

(403) 720-8355   *SIC 5199*

CIE MATERIAUX DE CONSTRUCTION BP CANADA, LA   *p1130*
2850 AV DOLLARD, LASALLE, QC, H8N 2V2

(514) 364-0161   *SIC 5199*

CONSOLIDATED BOTTLE CORPORATION   *p993*
77 UNION ST, TORONTO, ON, M6N 3N2

(800) 561-1354   *SIC 5199*

COSTCO WHOLESALE CANADA LTD   *p594*
1900 CYRVILLE RD, GLOUCESTER, ON, K1B 1A5

(613) 748-9966   *SIC 5199*

COSTCO WHOLESALE CANADA LTD   *p840*
485 THE PARKWAY, PETERBOROUGH, ON, K9J 0B3

(705) 750-2600   *SIC 5199*

COSTCO WHOLESALE CANADA LTD   *p1030*
71 COLOSSUS DR SUITE 547, WOODBRIDGE, ON, L4L 9J8

(905) 264-8337   *SIC 5199*

COSTCO WHOLESALE CANADA LTD   *p1078*
2500 BOUL TALBOT, CHICOUTIMI, QC, G7H 5B1

(418) 696-1112   *SIC 5199*

COSTCO WHOLESALE CANADA LTD   *p1373*
3400 RUE KING O, SHERBROOKE, QC, J1L 1C9

(819) 822-2121   *SIC 5199*

COTTON CANDY INC   *p721*
2600 ARGENTIA RD, MISSISSAUGA, ON, L5N 5V4

(905) 858-2600   *SIC 5199*

CRAWFORD PACKAGING INC   *p648*
3036 PAGE ST, LONDON, ON, N5V 4P2

(519) 659-0507   *SIC 5199*

CREATIVE CONCEPTS D.V.R. INC   *p113*
4404 94 ST NW, EDMONTON, AB, T6E 6T7

(780) 438-3044   *SIC 5199*

CROWNHILL PACKAGING LTD   *p502*
8905 GOREWAY DR, BRAMPTON, ON, L6T 0B7

(905) 494-1191   *SIC 5199*

CTM INTERNATIONAL GIFTWARE INC   *p1239*
11420 BOUL ALBERT-HUDON, MONTREAL-NORD, QC, H1G 3J6

(514) 324-4200   *SIC 5199*

D & L SALES LIMITED   *p873*
150 MIDDLEFIELD RD, SCARBOROUGH, ON, M1S 4L6

(416) 423-1133   *SIC 5199*

DANSON DECOR INC   *p1333*
3425 RUE DOUGLAS-B.-FLOREANI, SAINT-LAURENT, QC, H4S 1Y6

(514) 335-2435   *SIC 5199*

DAVID YOUNGSON & ASSOCIATES LIMITED   *p916*
12 CRANFIELD RD UNIT 200, TORONTO, ON, M4B 3G8

(416) 441-9696   *SIC 5199*

DETAIL K2 INC   *p522*
1080 CLAY AVE UNIT 2, BURLINGTON, ON, L7L 0A1

(905) 335-2152   *SIC 5199*

DEZINECORP INC   *p705*
369 BRITANNIA RD E, MISSISSAUGA, ON, L4Z 2H5

SIC 5199

DIAMOND YARNS OF CANADA LTD   *p783*
155 MARTIN ROSS AVE SUITE 3, NORTH YORK, ON, M3J 2L9

(416) 736-6111   *SIC 5199*

DIFFUSION ARTEQ INC   *p1159*
10 ST-JEAN-BAPTISTE E, MONTMAGNY, QC, G5V 1J7

(418) 248-3332   *SIC 5199*

DISTRIBUTION COUCHE-TARD INC   *p1234*
4204 BOUL INDUSTRIEL, MONTREAL, QC, H7L 0E3

(450) 662-6632   *SIC 5199*

EAGLE, JAMES R. HOLDINGS LIMITED   *p646*
172 MAIN ST W, LISTOWEL, ON, N4W 1A1

(519) 291-1011   *SIC 5199*

EDDIE'S HANG-UP DISPLAY LTD   *p291*
60 3RD AVE W, VANCOUVER, BC, V5Y 1E4

(604) 708-3100   *SIC 5199*

ELASTO PROXY INC   *p1061*
4035 RUE LAVOISIER, BOISBRIAND, QC, J7H 1N1

(450) 434-2744   *SIC 5199*

EMBALLAGE CADEAU NOBLE INC   *p1183*
5623 AV CASGRAIN, MONTREAL, QC, H2T 1Y1

(514) 278-8500   *SIC 5199*

EMBALLAGES FESTIVAL INC   *p1339*
8286 CH DE LA COTE-DE-LIESSE, SAINT-LAURENT, QC, H4T 1G7

(514) 731-3713   *SIC 5199*

EMBALLAGES L.P. AUBUT INC   *p1264*

1135 RUE TAILLON, QUEBEC, QC, G1N 4G7

(418) 523-2956   *SIC* 5199

ENCHANTED MEADOW ESSENTIALS INC p205
1480 CLIVEDEN AVE, DELTA, BC, V3M 6L9

(604) 540-2999   *SIC* 5199

ENTREPRISES PNH INC, LES p1093
1985 BOUL HYMUS, DORVAL, QC, H9P 1J8

(514) 683-3279   *SIC* 5199

EXAGON MARKETING INC p552
300 CONFEDERATION PKY UNIT 4, CONCORD, ON, L4K 4T8

(905) 669-9627   *SIC* 5199

FAIRDEAL IMPORT & EXPORT LTD p185
3855 HENNING DR UNIT 116, BURNABY, BC, V5C 6N3

(604) 257-2939   *SIC* 5199

FILS PROMPTEX YARNS INC p1094
30 AV JENKINS, DORVAL, QC, H9P 2R1

(514) 636-9928   *SIC* 5199

FLAIR FLEXIBLE PACKAGING (CANADA) CORPORATION p16
4100 72 AVE SE, CALGARY, AB, T2C 2C1

(403) 207-3226   *SIC* 5199

G & B SMITH FISHERIES LIMITED p471
50 ROUTE 304, YARMOUTH, NS, B5A 4J8

(902) 742-5478   *SIC* 5199

G.A.R. TREE FARMS LTD p439
595 FARMINGTON RD, BARSS CORNER, NS, B0R 1A0

(902) 644-3415   *SIC* 5199

GANZ p1031
1 PEARCE RD, WOODBRIDGE, ON, L4L 3T2

(905) 851-6661   *SIC* 5199

GEM-SEN HOLDINGS CORP p553
266 APPLEWOOD CRES, CONCORD, ON, L4K 4B4

(905) 660-3110   *SIC* 5199

GENUMARK PROMOTIONAL MERCHANDISE INC p765
707 GORDON BAKER RD, NORTH YORK, ON, M2H 2S6

(416) 391-9191   *SIC* 5199

GERMAN ADVERTISING ADVANTAGE INC, THE p224
19770 94A AVE, LANGLEY, BC, V1M 3B7

(604) 888-8008   *SIC* 5199

GOLDEN GATE HIDE & LEATHER LTD p871
21A COSENTINO DR, SCARBOROUGH, ON, M1P 3A3

(416) 299-7195   *SIC* 5199

GREENSPAR WHOLESALE LIMITED p424
125 HARVEY ST, HARBOUR GRACE, NL, A0A 2M0

(709) 596-3538   *SIC* 5199

GROUPE INTERNATIONAL TRAVELWAY INC p1334
4600 CH DU BOIS-FRANC, SAINT-LAURENT, QC, H4S 1A7

(514) 331-3130   *SIC* 5199

GROUPE TRIUM INC p1179
9031 AV DU PARC, MONTREAL, QC, H2N 1Z1

(514) 355-1625   *SIC* 5199

HARTZ CANADA INC p889
1125 TALBOT ST, ST THOMAS, ON, N5P 3W7

(519) 631-7660   *SIC* 5199

HERSCHEL SUPPLY COMPANY LTD p295
611 ALEXANDER ST SUITE 327, VANCOUVER, BC, V6A 1E1

(800) 307-5597   *SIC* 5199

HT PRODUCTIONS INC p609
690 RENNIE ST, HAMILTON, ON, L8H 3R2

(905) 544-7575   *SIC* 5199

IG IMAGE GROUP INC p292
34 2ND AVE W, VANCOUVER, BC, V5Y 1B3

(604) 873-3333   *SIC* 5199

IMPORTATIONS EXPORTATIONS LAM INC p1185
2115 BOUL SAINT-LAURENT, MONTREAL,

QC, H2X 2T5

(514) 843-3030   *SIC* 5199

IMPORTATIONS JACQUES FOURNIER LTEE, LES p1305
2525 127E RUE, SAINT-GEORGES, QC, G5Y 5G4

(418) 228-8594   *SIC* 5199

IMPORTATIONS MIRDO CANADA INC., LES p1223
6312 RUE NOTRE-DAME O, MONTREAL, QC, H4C 1V4

(514) 932-1523   *SIC* 5199

IMPORTATIONS NOSTALGIA MARKETING & DESIGN LTEE p1160
20 AV DE LA COUR, MONTMAGNY, QC, G5V 2V9

(418) 248-2600   *SIC* 5199

INDUSTRIES F.M. INC p1109
176 RUE FRONTENAC, GRANBY, QC, J2G 7R4

(450) 378-0148   *SIC* 5199

KIRKWOOD & MURPHY LTD p696
5150 TIMBERLEA BLVD, MISSISSAUGA, ON, L4W 2S5

(905) 602-6900   *SIC* 5199

KOREAN BUSINESSMEN'S COOPERATIVE ASSOCIATION p187
6373 ARBROATH ST, BURNABY, BC, V5E 1C3

(604) 431-7373   *SIC* 5199

LAODAS-WAY HEALING LTD p3
GD, ALDER FLATS, AB, T0C 0A0

(780) 621-0765   *SIC* 5199

LEXAR INTERNATIONAL LTD p366
16 MAZENOD RD SUITE 3, WINNIPEG, MB, R2J 4H2

(204) 661-9000   *SIC* 5199

MCCABE PROMOTIONAL ADVERTISING INC p661
384 SOVEREIGN RD, LONDON, ON, N6M 1A5

(519) 455-7009   *SIC* 5199

MCM GROUP LTD p1010
730 BRIDGE ST W SUITE 1, WATERLOO, ON, N2V 2J4

(519) 725-3800   *SIC* 5199

MEADE RAY INTERNATIONAL INC p1227
8370 RUE LABARRE, MONTREAL, QC, H4P 2E7

(514) 738-5858   *SIC* 5199

METROMEDIA MARKETING LTD p24
5774 10 ST NE, CALGARY, AB, T2E 8W7

(403) 291-3912   *SIC* 5199

MTI POLYFAB INC p741
7381 PACIFIC CIR, MISSISSAUGA, ON, L5T 2A4

(800) 265-1840   *SIC* 5199

MULTIPLUS D.M. INC p1094
10389 CH COTE-DE-LIESSE, DORVAL, QC, H9P 2Z3

(514) 422-8881   *SIC* 5199

MYRON MANUFACTURING CORP (USA) p865
5610 FINCH AVE E, SCARBOROUGH, ON, M1B 6A6

(647) 288-5300   *SIC* 5199

NATIONAL BAIT INC p712
946 LAKESHORE RD E, MISSISSAUGA, ON, L5E 1E4

(905) 278-0180   *SIC* 5199

NATURE 3M INC p1243
943 RUE SAINT-CYRILLE, NORMANDIN, QC, G8M 4H9

(418) 274-2511   *SIC* 5199

NORTH EASTERN CHRISTMAS TREE ASSOCIATION p450
799 SOUTH RIVER LAKE RD, GOSHEN, NS, B0H 1M0

(902) 783-2430   *SIC* 5199

NORTHCOTT SILK INC p556
101 COURTLAND AVE, CONCORD, ON, L4K 3T5

(905) 760-0072   *SIC* 5199

NORTHERN ICE SUPPLY LTD p249

1835 1ST AVE, PRINCE GEORGE, BC, V2L 2Y8

(778) 763-0945   *SIC* 5199

O'DONNELL SPECIALTY ADVERTISING LTD p474
487 WESTNEY RD S UNIT 16, AJAX, ON, L1S 6W8

(905) 427-8818   *SIC* 5199

PARIS SOUTHERN LIGHTS INC p837
6 ADAMS ST SUITE A, PARIS, ON, N3L 3X4

(519) 442-2988   *SIC* 5199

PARTYLITE GIFTS, LTD p853
55 EAST BEAVER CREEK RD UNIT A, RICHMOND HILL, ON, L4B 1E8

(905) 881-6161   *SIC* 5199

PEMBINA PROMOTIONS INC p387
421 MULVEY AVE, WINNIPEG, MB, R3L 0R6

(204) 453-4132   *SIC* 5199

PINE VALLEY PACKAGING GROUP INC p1001
1 PARRATT RD, UXBRIDGE, ON, L9P 1R1

(905) 862-0830   *SIC* 5199

PINECORE ENTERPRISES INC p241
828 HARBOURSIDE DR SUITE 117, NORTH VANCOUVER, BC, V7P 3R9

(604) 990-9679   *SIC* 5199

POLARIS TRADING CORP p261
2030-10013 RIVER DR, RICHMOND, BC, V6X 0N2

(778) 834-2701   *SIC* 5199

PREMIER TECH HOME & GARDEN INC p726
1900 MINNESOTA CRT SUITE 125, MISSISSAUGA, ON, L5N 3C9

(905) 812-8556   *SIC* 5199

PRODUITS DE PREMIERS SOINS EMERGENCY (2011) INC p1327
700 BOUL LEBEAU, SAINT-LAURENT, QC, H4N 1R5

SIC 5199

PRODUITS MENAGERS FREUDENBERG INC p674
15 ALLSTATE PKY, MARKHAM, ON, L3R 5B4

(905) 669-9949   *SIC* 5199

PRODUITS MENAGERS FREUDENBERG INC p1084
666 BOUL SAINT-MARTIN O BUREAU 220, COTE SAINT-LUC, QC, H7M 5G4

(450) 975-4535   *SIC* 5199

PROMOTIONS C.D. INC p1067
165 RUE JULES-LEGER, BOUCHERVILLE, QC, J4B 7K8

(450) 641-1161   *SIC* 5199

PUBL TRANS CANADA ADVERTISING (QUEBEC) LTD p1142
625 BOUL GUIMOND, LONGUEUIL, QC, J4G 1L9

SIC 5199

PUBLICITE MALGA INC p1111
625 RUE GEORGES-CROS, GRANBY, QC, J2J 1B4

(450) 378-4448   *SIC* 5199

RODNEY ENTERPRISES LIMITED p448
20 RADDALL AVE, DARTMOUTH, NS, B3B 1T2

(902) 468-2601   *SIC* 5199

ROLF C. HAGEN INC p1054
20500 AUT TRANSCANADIENNE, BAIE-D'URFE, QC, H9X 0A2

(514) 457-0914   *SIC* 5199

ROLF C. HAGEN INC p1336
2450 AV MARIE-CURIE, SAINT-LAURENT, QC, H4S 1N1

SIC 5199

RUBBER TECH. INTERNATIONAL LTD p140
GD, LEGAL, AB, T0G 1L0

(780) 961-3229   *SIC* 5199

S.K.S. NOVELTY COMPANY LTD p547
30 SANDFORD FLEMING RD, COLLINGWOOD, ON, L9Y 4V7

(705) 444-5653   *SIC* 5199

S.L.K. MARKETING LIMITED p1033

126 TROWERS RD, WOODBRIDGE, ON, L4L 5Z4

(905) 856-4343   *SIC* 5199

SAFECROSS FIRST AID LTD p784
21 KODIAK CRES SUITE 200, NORTH YORK, ON, M3J 3E5

(416) 665-0050   *SIC* 5199

SCOTTS CANADA LTD p727
2000 ARGENTIA RD SUITE 300, MISSISSAUGA, ON, L5N 1P7

(905) 814-7425   *SIC* 5199

SEAGULL COMPANY INCORPORATED, THE p588
20 VOYAGER CRT S SUITE A, ETOBICOKE, ON, M9W 5M7

(416) 847-4612   *SIC* 5199

SELECT BAIT & FISHING SUPPLIES INC p918
45 RESEARCH RD, TORONTO, ON, M4G 2G8

(416) 429-5656   *SIC* 5199

SHIPPAM & ASSOCIATES INC p385
865 KING EDWARD ST, WINNIPEG, MB, R3H 0P8

(204) 925-3696   *SIC* 5199

SPAFAX CANADA INC p930
2 BLOOR ST E SUITE 1020, TORONTO, ON, M4W 1A8

(416) 350-2425   *SIC* 5199

SPARTA 2002 DESIGNS & PROMOTIONS INC p1132
9246 RUE BOIVIN, LASALLE, QC, H8R 2E7

(514) 363-5674   *SIC* 5199

SPECIALTY DISTRIBUTING LTD p1430
829 48TH ST E, SASKATOON, SK, S7K 0X5

(306) 975-9867   *SIC* 5199

SPLASH INTERNATIONAL MARKETING INC p675
395 COCHRANE DR SUITE 3, MARKHAM, ON, L3R 9R5

(905) 947-4440   *SIC* 5199

SPORTOP MARKETING INC p909
875 TUNGSTEN ST UNIT C, THUNDER BAY, ON, P7B 6H2

(807) 346-5400   *SIC* 5199

SS RIG & VAC LTD p150
1801 8 ST, NISKU, AB, T9E 7S8

(780) 979-9987   *SIC* 5199

STAEDTLER-MARS LIMITED p744
850 MATHESON BLVD W UNIT 4, MISSISSAUGA, ON, L5V 0B4

(905) 501-9008   *SIC* 5199

STINCOR SPECIALTIES LTD p791
15 DENSLEY AVE, NORTH YORK, ON, M6M 2P5

(416) 243-0293   *SIC* 5199

SUN-GLO PRODUCTS INC p743
6681 EXCELSIOR CRT, MISSISSAUGA, ON, L5T 2J2

(905) 678-6456   *SIC* 5199

TALBOT MARKETING INC p661
383 SOVEREIGN RD, LONDON, ON, N6M 1A3

(519) 659-5862   *SIC* 5199

TRILLIUM MARKETING GROUP LTD. p785
77 MARTIN ROSS AVE, NORTH YORK, ON, M3J 2L5

(416) 667-3030   *SIC* 5199

TWINKLE ENTERPRISES LTD p300
308 WATER ST, VANCOUVER, BC, V6B 1B6

SIC 5199

UPPER CANADA SOAP & CANDLE MAKERS CORPORATION p733
5875 CHEDWORTH WAY, MISSISSAUGA, ON, L5R 3L9

(905) 897-1710   *SIC* 5199

USACAN MEDIA DISTRIBUTION SERVICE INC p1331
1459 RUE BEGIN, SAINT-LAURENT, QC, H4R 1V8

SIC 5199

VERITIV CANADA, INC p207
1425 DERWENT WAY, DELTA, BC, V3M

6N3
(604) 520-7500 *SIC* 5199
WAL-MART CANADA CORP *p7*
917 3 ST W SUITE 3658, BROOKS, AB,
T1R 1L5
(403) 793-2111 *SIC* 5199
WEDDINGSTAR INC *p83*
2032 BULLSHEAD RD, DUNMORE, AB,
T1B 0K9
(403) 529-1110 *SIC* 5199
WESTFAIR DRUGS LTD *p19*
3916 72 AVE SE, CALGARY, AB, T2C 2E2
(403) 279-1600 *SIC* 5199
WHITE STORE EQUIPMENT LTD *p837*
21 WOODSLEE AVE, PARIS, ON, N3L 3T6
(519) 442-4461 *SIC* 5199
WINDSOR WHOLESALE BAIT LTD *p1025*
500 NORTHWOOD ST, WINDSOR, ON,
N9E 4Z2
(519) 966-8540 *SIC* 5199
WING ON CHEONG (CANADA) LIMITED
p677
235 HOOD RD UNIT 2, MARKHAM, ON,
L3R 4N3
SIC 5199
XENTEX TRADING INC *p702*
5960 SHAWSON DR, MISSISSAUGA, ON,
L4W 3W5
(905) 696-9329 *SIC* 5199

---

*SIC 5211 Lumber and other building
materials*

1020012 ONTARIO INC *p617*
580 24TH AVE SUITE 1, HANOVER, ON,
N4N 3B8
(519) 364-3410 *SIC* 5211
139464 CANADA LIMITED *p476*
4920 COUNTY ROAD 17, ALFRED, ON,
K0B 1A0
(613) 679-2252 *SIC* 5211
1853865 ONTARIO INC *p840*
1699 CHEMONG RD, PETERBOROUGH,
ON, K9J 6X2
(705) 748-9111 *SIC* 5211
1959612 ONTARIO INC *p480*
194 EARL STEWART DR, AURORA, ON,
L4G 6V7
(905) 726-4933 *SIC* 5211
2171-0751 QUEBEC INC *p1377*
74A 132 RTE O, ST-ADELME-DE-MATANE,
QC, G0L 2R0
(418) 498-2405 *SIC* 5211
2321-1998 QUEBEC INC *p1231*
1070 MONTEE MASSON, MONTREAL,
QC, H7C 2R2
(450) 661-1515 *SIC* 5211
2699001 CANADA LIMITED *p565*
509 GOVERNMENT ST, DRYDEN, ON, P8N
2P6
(807) 223-3381 *SIC* 5211
2757-5158 QUEBEC INC *p1134*
4589 AUT 440 O BUREAU 103, LAVAL, QC,
H7W 0J7
(450) 688-9050 *SIC* 5211
3084761 MANITOBA LTD *p353*
262 MAIN ST, NIVERVILLE, MB, R0A 1E0
(204) 883-2327 *SIC* 5211
3490051 MANITOBA LTD *p361*
880 MEMORIAL DR, WINKLER, MB, R6W
0M6
(204) 325-9133 *SIC* 5211
581976 SASKATCHEWAN LTD *p1409*
802 1ST ST W, MEADOW LAKE, SK, S9X
1E2
(306) 236-4467 *SIC* 5211
616536 B.C. LTD *p331*
4601 27 ST, VERNON, BC, V1T 4Y8
(250) 545-5384 *SIC* 5211
669021 ALBERTA LTD *p108*
5104 55 AVE NW, EDMONTON, AB, T6B
3C6
(780) 865-4183 *SIC* 5211
727849 ONTARIO LIMITED *p599*

1357 BARFIELD RD, GREELY, ON, K4P
1A1
(613) 821-0166 *SIC* 5211
7577010 CANADA INC *p1063*
1501 RUE AMPERE BUREAU 200,
BOUCHERVILLE, QC, J4B 5Z5
(450) 655-2441 *SIC* 5211
891934 ONTARIO LIMITED *p808*
60 FOURTH AVE SUITE 1, ORANGEVILLE,
ON, L9W 3Z7
(519) 941-5407 *SIC* 5211
9060-5015 QUEBEC INC *p1300*
440 RUE DUBOIS, SAINT-EUSTACHE, QC,
J7P 4W9
(450) 623-1438 *SIC* 5211
9067-6628 QUEBEC INC *p1083*
164 BOUL DES LAURENTIDES, COTE
SAINT-LUC, QC, H7G 4P6
(450) 667-0255 *SIC* 5211
9095-6988 QUEBEC INC *p1348*
3120 RUE BERNARD-PILON, SAINT-
MATHIEU-DE-BELOEIL, QC, J3G 4S5
(450) 467-8181 *SIC* 5211
9214-6489 QUEBEC INC *p1116*
3590 RUE DE L'ENERGIE, JONQUIERE,
QC, G7X 9H3
(418) 695-1793 *SIC* 5211
921983 ONTARIO INC *p1013*
119 CONSUMERS DR, WHITBY, ON, L1N
1C4
(905) 665-9565 *SIC* 5211
ABB INC *p1126*
2117 32E AV, LACHINE, QC, H8T 3J1
SIC 5211
ACTIVE MARBLE & TILE LTD *p39*
5355 8 ST NE, CALGARY, AB, T2K 5R9
(403) 274-2111 *SIC* 5211
AERLOC INDUSTRIES LTD *p566*
64 HEAD ST, DUNDAS, ON, L9H 3H7
(905) 628-6061 *SIC* 5211
ALF CURTIS HOME IMPROVEMENTS INC
p842
370 PARKHILL RD E, PETERBOROUGH,
ON, K9L 1C3
(705) 742-4690 *SIC* 5211
ALLIANCE READY MIX LTD *p165*
47 ELLIOT ST, ST. ALBERT, AB, T8N 5S5
(780) 459-1090 *SIC* 5211
ALLIED LUMBERLAND LTD *p1410*
240 5TH AVE NW, MOOSE JAW, SK, S6H
4R3
(306) 694-4000 *SIC* 5211
**ALWEATHER WINDOWS & DOORS LIM-
ITED** *p445*
27 TROOP AVE, DARTMOUTH, NS, B3B
2A7
(902) 468-2605 *SIC* 5211
AMBASSADOR SALES (SOUTHERN) LTD
p13
4110 76 AVE SE, CALGARY, AB, T2C 2J2
(403) 720-2012 *SIC* 5211
AMC FORM TECHNOLOGIES *p351*
35 HEADINGLEY ST, HEADINGLEY, MB,
R4H 0A8
(204) 633-8800 *SIC* 5211
ANCTIL, J. INC *p1299*
3110 RTE 222, SAINT-DENIS-DE-
BROMPTON, QC, J0B 2P0
(819) 846-2747 *SIC* 5211
ARCADIAN PROJECTS INC *p483*
1439 GINGERICH RD UNIT 2, BADEN, ON,
N3A 3J7
(519) 804-9697 *SIC* 5211
ARENS, MIKE BUILDING MATERIALS LTD
p542
124 KEIL DR S SUITE 1719, CHATHAM,
ON, N7M 3H1
(519) 354-0700 *SIC* 5211
ARISE TECHNOLOGIES CORP *p535*
150 WERLICH DR SUITE 5, CAMBRIDGE,
ON, N1T 1N6
SIC 5211
ARMOIRES DISTINCTION INC *p1284*
180 AV LEONIDAS S, RIMOUSKI, QC, G5L

2T2
(418) 723-6857 *SIC* 5211
BANNEX PARTNERSHIP *p167*
6610 50 AVE, STETTLER, AB, T0C 2L2
(403) 742-4737 *SIC* 5211
BARCOL DOOR LTD *p92*
14820 YELLOWHEAD TRAIL NW, EDMON-
TON, AB, T5L 3C5
(780) 452-7140 *SIC* 5211
**BARRY'S BAY CUSTOM WOODWORKING
AND BUILDERS' SUPPLY LTD** *p489*
306 JOHN ST, BARRYS BAY, ON, K0J 1B0
(613) 756-2794 *SIC* 5211
BARZOTTI WOODWORKING LIMITED *p606*
2 WATSON RD S, GUELPH, ON, N1L 1E2
(519) 821-3670 *SIC* 5211
BENNETT'S HOME FURNISHINGS LIMITED
p539
13 FRONT ST S, CAMPBELLFORD, ON,
K0L 1L0
(705) 653-1188 *SIC* 5211
BERNIER, A D INC *p1129*
229 2E AV, LAMBTON, QC, G0M 1H0
(418) 486-7461 *SIC* 5211
BEST BUY HOUSING INC *p351*
4250 PORTAGE AVE, HEADINGLEY, MB,
R4H 1C6
(204) 895-2393 *SIC* 5211
BETHEL WINDOWS & DOORS LTD *p80*
1504 12 ST, COALDALE, AB, T1M 1M3
(403) 345-4401 *SIC* 5211
BETON CHEVALIER INC *p1055*
152 39E AV, BEAUCEVILLE, QC, G5X 3S4
(418) 774-4747 *SIC* 5211
BLACKWOOD BUILDING CENTRE LTD
p174
33050 SOUTH FRASER WAY, ABBOTS-
FORD, BC, V2S 2A9
(604) 853-6471 *SIC* 5211
BLAIR BUILDING MATERIALS INC *p664*
10445 KEELE ST, MAPLE, ON, L6A 3Y9
(416) 798-4996 *SIC* 5211
BMP (1985) LIMITED *p618*
5276 HINCHINBROOKE RD, HARTING-
TON, ON, K0H 1W0
(613) 372-2838 *SIC* 5211
**BOIS DE CONSTRUCTION CHENEVILLE
INC, LES** *p1077*
99 RUE ALBERT-FERLAND, CHENEVILLE,
QC, J0V 1E0
(819) 428-3903 *SIC* 5211
BROUILLETTE & FRERE INC *p1096*
4500 BOUL SAINT-JOSEPH, DRUM-
MONDVILLE, QC, J2A 1A7
(819) 475-7114 *SIC* 5211
BROWN WINDOW CORPORATION *p549*
185 SNOW BLVD SUITE 2, CONCORD, ON,
L4K 4N9
(905) 738-6045 *SIC* 5211
**BUTLER RIDGE ENERGY SERVICES (2011)
LTD** *p216*
8908 CLARKE AVE, HUDSON'S HOPE, BC,
V0C 1V0
(250) 783-2363 *SIC* 5211
BYTOWN LUMBER INC *p597*
1740 QUEENSDALE AVE, GLOUCESTER,
ON, K1T 1J6
(613) 733-9303 *SIC* 5211
C.A. FISCHER LUMBER CO. LTD *p95*
16210 114 AVE NW SUITE 200, EDMON-
TON, AB, T5M 2Z5
(780) 453-1994 *SIC* 5211
CADROPORTE MANUFACTURIER INC
p1058
700 BOUL INDUSTRIEL, BLAINVILLE, QC,
J7C 3V4
(450) 434-9000 *SIC* 5211
CALLBECKS LTD *p1042*
613 WATER ST E, SUMMERSIDE, PE, C1N
4H8
(902) 436-1100 *SIC* 5211
CANAC IMMOBILIER INC *p1119*
6235 BOUL WILFRID-HAMEL,
L'ANCIENNE-LORETTE, QC, G2E 5W2

(418) 872-2874 *SIC* 5211
CANAC IMMOBILIER INC *p1285*
228 RUE DES NEGOCIANTS, RIMOUSKI,
QC, G5M 1B6
(418) 723-0007 *SIC* 5211
CANADIAN LUMBER LTD *p361*
139 NORTH RAILWAY AVE, WINKLER, MB,
R6W 1J4
(204) 325-5319 *SIC* 5211
CANADIAN MDF PRODUCTS COMPANY
p93
14810 131 AVE NW SUITE 2, EDMONTON,
AB, T5L 4Y3
(780) 452-5406 *SIC* 5211
**CANADIAN VINYLTEK WINDOWS CORPO-
RATION** *p205*
587 EBURY PL, DELTA, BC, V3M 6M8
(604) 540-0029 *SIC* 5211
CANROOF CORPORATION INC *p920*
560 COMMISSIONERS ST, TORONTO, ON,
M4M 1A7
(416) 461-8122 *SIC* 5211
CARON & GUAY INC *p1261*
615 BOUL PIERRE-BERTRAND, QUEBEC,
QC, G1M 3J3
(418) 683-7534 *SIC* 5211
CARON, CAMILLE INC *p1150*
9 RUE NOTTAWAY, MATAGAMI, QC, J0Y
2A0
SIC 5211
CARRINGTONS BUILDING CENTRE LTD
p899
82 LORNE ST, SUDBURY, ON, P3C 4N8
(705) 673-9511 *SIC* 5211
CASH & CARRY LUMBER MART LTD *p1412*
11301 6TH AVE, NORTH BATTLEFORD,
SK, S9A 2N5
(306) 445-4350 *SIC* 5211
CEDAR GROVE BUILDING PRODUCTS LTD
p276
8073 132 ST, SURREY, BC, V3W 4N5
(604) 590-3106 *SIC* 5211
CENTRAL HARDWARE LTD *p212*
701 BASS AVE, ENDERBY, BC, V0E 1V2
(250) 838-6474 *SIC* 5211
**CENTRE DE RENOVATION ANDRE LES-
PERANCE INC** *p1364*
227 BOUL RENE-A.-ROBERT, SAINTE-
THERESE, QC, J7E 4L1
(450) 430-6220 *SIC* 5211
CENTRE DE RENOVATION F D S INC *p1116*
3460 BOUL SAINT-FRANCOIS UNITE
B001, JONQUIERE, QC, G7X 8L3
(418) 548-4676 *SIC* 5211
**CENTRE DE RENOVATION RAYMOND
BOIES INC** *p1055*
215 RUE LACHANCE, BEAUPRE, QC, G0A
1E0
(418) 827-4531 *SIC* 5211
**CENTRE DE RENOVATION RAYMOND
BOIES INC** *p1075*
8540 BOUL SAINTE-ANNE, CHATEAU-
RICHER, QC, G0A 1N0
(418) 824-4533 *SIC* 5211
CENTURY GLASS (85) LTD *p216*
1110 VICTORIA ST, KAMLOOPS, BC, V2C
2C5
(250) 374-1274 *SIC* 5211
CLEARVIEW COLONY LTD *p349*
GD, ELM CREEK, MB, R0G 0N0
(204) 436-2187 *SIC* 5211
CO-OP DES DEUX RIVES *p1243*
1455 AV DU ROCHER BUREAU 102, NOR-
MANDIN, QC, G8M 3X5
(418) 274-2910 *SIC* 5211
**COMMERCIAL DRYWALL SUPPLY (ON-
TARIO) INC** *p668*
235 DON PARK RD, MARKHAM, ON, L3R
1C2
(905) 415-7777 *SIC* 5211
COMPAGNIE EAGLE LUMBER LIMITEE, LA
p1321
435 BOUL JEAN-BAPTISTE-ROLLAND E.,
SAINT-JEROME, QC, J7Z 4J4

---

(450) 432-4004   *SIC 5211*
**CONSTRUCTION DISTRIBUTION & SUP-
PLY COMPANY INC**   *p1002*
300 CONFEDERATION PKWY UNIT 3,
VAUGHAN, ON, L4K 4T8
(416) 665-8006   *SIC 5211*
COOPER INDUSTRIES (ELECTRICAL) INC
p730
5925 MCLAUGHLIN RD, MISSISSAUGA,
ON, L5R 1B8
(905) 501-3000   *SIC 5211*
COUNTRY LUMBER LTD   *p227*
22538 FRASER HWY, LANGLEY, BC, V2Z
2T8
(604) 533-4447   *SIC 5211*
COUPAL & FILS INC   *p1159*
349 117 RTE, MONT-TREMBLANT, QC, J8E
2X4
(819) 425-8771   *SIC 5211*
CUISINES BEAUREGARD INC   *p1110*
655 RUE SIMONDS S, GRANBY, QC, J2J
1C2
(450) 375-0707   *SIC 5211*
CUISITEC LTEE   *p1321*
175 RUE MICHENER, SAINT-JOSEPH-DE-
BEAUCE, QC, G0S 2V0
(418) 397-5432   *SIC 5211*
DASHWOOD INDUSTRIES INC   *p541*
69323 RICHMOND ST, CENTRALIA, ON,
N0M 1K0
(519) 228-6624   *SIC 5211*
DAVIDSON ENMAN LUMBER LIMITED   *p29*
452 42 AVE SE, CALGARY, AB, T2G 1Y5
(403) 243-2566   *SIC 5211*
DAWE, STAN LTD   *p422*
191 RIVERSIDE DR, CORNER BROOK,
NL, A2H 2N2
(709) 639-9131   *SIC 5211*
DECK STORE INC, THE   *p997*
789 ARROW RD SUITE 10, TORONTO, ON,
M9M 2L4
(416) 749-3963   *SIC 5211*
DELTON CABINET MFG LTD   *p93*
14135 128 AVE NW, EDMONTON, AB, T5L
3H3
(780) 413-2260   *SIC 5211*
DISTRIBUTION BATH FITTER INC   *p1301*
225 RUE ROY, SAINT-EUSTACHE, QC, J7R
5R5
(450) 472-0024   *SIC 5211*
DOIDGE BUILDING CENTRES LTD   *p629*
1768 HIGHWAY 21, KINCARDINE, ON, N2Z
2Y6
(705) 645-8284   *SIC 5211*
DOWNEY BUILDING SUPPLIES LTD   *p411*
1106 CLEVELAND AVE, RIVERVIEW, NB,
E1B 5V8
(506) 388-2400   *SIC 5211*
**DURWEST CONSTRUCTION SYSTEMS
(ALBERTA) LTD**   *p15*
10665 46 ST SE, CALGARY, AB, T2C 5C2
(403) 253-7385   *SIC 5211*
E.G. PENNER BUILDING CENTRES LTD
p358
200 PARK RD W, STEINBACH, MB, R5G
1A1
(204) 326-1325   *SIC 5211*
EFP DESIGNS INC   *p552*
50 VICEROY RD SUITE 23, CONCORD,
ON, L4K 3A7
(905) 669-0368   *SIC 5211*
ELITE FORMWORK INC   *p77*
9935 ENTERPRISE WAY SE, CALGARY,
AB, T3S 0A1
(403) 236-7751   *SIC 5211*
ELMWOOD HARDWARE LTD   *p405*
257 ELMWOOD DR, MONCTON, NB, E1A
1X4
(506) 858-8100   *SIC 5211*
EMARD BROS. LUMBER CO. LTD   *p562*
840 TENTH ST E, CORNWALL, ON, K6H
7S2
(613) 932-5660   *SIC 5211*
EMMERSON LUMBER LIMITED   *p607*

63 MAPLE AVE, HALIBURTON, ON, K0M
1S0
(705) 457-1550   *SIC 5211*
EMPIRE KITCHEN & BATH LTD   *p35*
5539 1 ST SE, CALGARY, AB, T2H 1H9
(403) 252-2458   *SIC 5211*
ENTABLATURE FRIEZE & PILLARS INC
p552
50 VICEROY RD UNIT 23, CONCORD, ON,
L4K 3A7
(905) 669-0368   *SIC 5211*
**ENTREPRISES A & R SAVOIE ET FILS
LTEE, LES**   *p419*
2650 RUE PRINCIPALE, TRACADIE-
SHEILA, NB, E1X 1A1
(506) 395-6997   *SIC 5211*
ENTREPRISES P. BONHOMME LTEE, LES
p1107
921 BOUL SAINT-JOSEPH, GATINEAU,
QC, J8Z 1S8
(819) 561-5577   *SIC 5211*
ENVIROTEC SERVICES INCORPORATED
p1427
100 CORY RD, SASKATOON, SK, S7K 8B7
(306) 244-9500   *SIC 5211*
**EVANS LUMBER AND BUILDERS SUPPLY
LIMITED**   *p900*
172 PINE ST, SUDBURY, ON, P3C 1X3
(705) 674-1921   *SIC 5211*
FABRICANA IMPORTS LTD   *p260*
4591 GARDEN CITY RD, RICHMOND, BC,
V6X 2K4
(604) 273-5316   *SIC 5211*
FEATURE MILLWORK INC   *p200*
204 CAYER ST UNIT 301, COQUITLAM,
BC, V3K 5B1
(604) 522-7951   *SIC 5211*
FENERGIC INC   *p1400*
17 RUE SAINTE-JEANNE-D'ARC, WAR-
WICK, QC, J0A 1M0
(819) 358-3400   *SIC 5211*
FENETRES ELITE INC, LES   *p1306*
264 RUE DEMERS, SAINT-GILLES, QC,
G0S 2P0
(418) 888-4342   *SIC 5211*
FERRELL BUILDERS SUPPLY LIMITED
p615
1549 RYMAL RD E, HAMILTON, ON, L8W
3N2
(905) 387-1948   *SIC 5211*
FILSINGER, W. & SONS LIMITED   *p602*
55 DAWSON RD SUITE 1, GUELPH, ON,
N1H 1B1
(519) 821-5744   *SIC 5211*
FISCHER, C.A. LIMBER, CO. LTD   *p132*
11105 100 AVE, GRANDE PRAIRIE, AB,
T8V 3J9
(780) 538-1340   *SIC 5211*
FLEMING DOOR PRODUCTS LTD.   *p1031*
101 ASHBRIDGE CIR, WOODBRIDGE, ON,
L4L 3R5
(800) 263-7515   *SIC 5211*
FLOORRIGHT INTERIORS LTD   *p143*
3021 32 ST S, LETHBRIDGE, AB, T1K 7B1
(587) 800-0848   *SIC 5211*
FORESCO HOLDING INC   *p1130*
498 BOUL DU ROYAUME, LAROUCHE,
QC, G0W 1Z0
(418) 542-8243   *SIC 5211*
FRASER SUPPLIES (1980) LIMITED   *p441*
4147 MAIN HWY, BERWICK, NS, B0P 1E0
(902) 538-3183   *SIC 5211*
FRIES TALLMAN LUMBER (1976) LTD
p1420
1737 DEWDNEY AVE, REGINA, SK, S4R
1G5
(306) 525-2791   *SIC 5211*
**G & B MCNABB LUMBER COMPANY LIM-
ITED**   *p837*
22 SEGUIN ST, PARRY SOUND, ON, P2A
1B1
(705) 746-5825   *SIC 5211*
GABRIEL COUTURE & FILS LTEE   *p1081*
2 CH ST-ONGE, CLEVELAND, QC, J0B 2H0

(819) 826-3777   *SIC 5211*
GABRIELE FLOOR & HOME   *p644*
55 TALBOT ST W, LEAMINGTON, ON, N8H
1M5
(519) 326-5786   *SIC 5211*
**GAMMA MURS ET FENETRES INTERNA-
TIONAL INC**   *p1119*
6130 BOUL SAINTE-ANNE, L'ANGE GAR-
DIEN, QC, G0A 2K0
(418) 822-1448   *SIC 5211*
GARLAND CANADA INC   *p584*
209 CARRIER DR, ETOBICOKE, ON, M9W
5Y8
(416) 747-7995   *SIC 5211*
GATHER INVESTMENTS LIMITED   *p990*
172 OSSINGTON AVE, TORONTO, ON,
M6J 2Z7
(416) 532-2813   *SIC 5211*
GEM CABINETS LTD   *p93*
14019 128 AVE NW, EDMONTON, AB, T5L
3H3
(780) 454-8652   *SIC 5211*
GIBSONS BUILDING SUPPLIES LTD   *p214*
924 GIBSONS WAY, GIBSONS, BC, V0N
1V7
(604) 886-8141   *SIC 5211*
GILBERT SMITH FOREST PRODUCTS LTD
p180
4411 BORTHWICK AVE, BARRIERE, BC,
V0E 1E0
(250) 672-9435   *SIC 5211*
GOLDWOOD INDUSTRIES LTD   *p254*
12691 MITCHELL RD, RICHMOND, BC,
V6V 1M7
(604) 327-2935   *SIC 5211*
GRANDEUR HOUSING LTD   *p361*
401 PEMBINA AVE E, WINKLER, MB, R6W
4B9
(204) 325-9558   *SIC 5211*
GRANDOR LUMBER INC   *p597*
5224 BANK ST, GLOUCESTER, ON, K1X
1H2
(613) 822-3390   *SIC 5211*
GRANIT DESIGN INC   *p1378*
77 RUE INDUSTRIELLE, STANSTEAD, QC,
J0B 3E0
(819) 876-7111   *SIC 5211*
GRANT LUMBER BUILDING CENTRES LTD
p753
GD, NEW LISKEARD, ON, P0J 1P0
(705) 647-9311   *SIC 5211*
GRAY, TOM BUILDING CENTRES INC   *p1021*
700 TECUMSEH RD W, WINDSOR, ON,
N8X 1H2
(519) 254-1143   *SIC 5211*
GREELY SAND & GRAVEL INC   *p599*
1971 OLD PRESCOTT RD, GREELY, ON,
K4P 1L3
(613) 821-3003   *SIC 5211*
GROUPE PATRICK MORIN INC   *p1247*
11850 RUE SHERBROOKE E, POINTE-
AUX-TREMBLES, QC, H1B 1C4
(514) 645-1115   *SIC 5211*
GROUPE PATRICK MORIN INC   *p1282*
567 BOUL PIERRE-LE GARDEUR, RE-
PENTIGNY, QC, J5Z 5H1
(450) 585-8564   *SIC 5211*
GROUPE PATRICK MORIN INC   *p1361*
4300 BOUL ROBERT-BOURASSA,
SAINTE-ROSE, QC, H7E 0C2
(450) 781-4466   *SIC 5211*
GROUPE PATRICK MORIN INC   *p1376*
369 BOUL POLIQUIN, SOREL-TRACY, QC,
J3P 7W1
(450) 742-4567   *SIC 5211*
GSL FAMILY TRUST   *p334*
780 TOPAZ AVE, VICTORIA, BC, V8T 2M1
(250) 384-3003   *SIC 5211*
H. MATTEAU ET FILS (1987) INC   *p1369*
891 7E AV, SHAWINIGAN, QC, G9T 2B9
(819) 538-3381   *SIC 5211*
H. MATTEAU ET FILS (1987) INC   *p1385*
15 RUE PHILIPPE-FRANCOEUR, TROIS-
RIVIERES, QC, G8T 9L7

(819) 374-4735   *SIC 5211*
HABITAFLEX CONCEPT INC   *p1160*
240 AV DES ATELIERS, MONTMAGNY, QC,
G5V 4G4
(418) 248-8886   *SIC 5211*
HAMILTON BUILDERS' SUPPLY INC   *p615*
164 LIMERIDGE RD E, HAMILTON, ON,
L9A 2S3
(905) 388-2352   *SIC 5211*
HANEY BUILDERS SUPPLIES (1964) LTD
p231
22740 DEWDNEY TRUNK RD, MAPLE
RIDGE, BC, V2X 3K2
(604) 820-0444   *SIC 5211*
HANEY BUILDERS' SUPPLIES (1971) LTD
p231
22740 DEWDNEY TRUNK RD, MAPLE
RIDGE, BC, V2X 3K2
(604) 463-6206   *SIC 5211*
HARRISON, C. ERNEST & SONS LIMITED
p438
404 MACDONALD RD, AMHERST, NS, B4H
3Y4
(902) 667-3306   *SIC 5211*
HAUSER, R BUILDING MATERIALS LTD
p78
6809 48 AVE, CAMROSE, AB, T4V 4W1
(780) 672-8818   *SIC 5211*
**HAWKESBURY LUMBER SUPPLY COM-
PANY LIMITED**   *p619*
900 ALEXANDER SIVERSKY ST,
HAWKESBURY, ON, K6A 3N4
(613) 632-4663   *SIC 5211*
HENGAB INVESTMENTS LIMITED   *p989*
804 DUPONT ST, TORONTO, ON, M6G 1Z6
(416) 531-2401   *SIC 5211*
HI-TEC PROFILES INC   *p1418*
2301 INDUSTRIAL DR, REGINA, SK, S4P
3C6
(306) 721-3800   *SIC 5211*
HOME DEPOT OF CANADA INC   *p77*
11320 SARCEE TRAIL NW, CALGARY, AB,
T3R 0A1
(403) 374-3866   *SIC 5211*
HOME DEPOT OF CANADA INC   *p132*
11222 103 AVE, GRANDE PRAIRIE, AB,
T8V 7H1
(780) 831-3160   *SIC 5211*
HOME DEPOT OF CANADA INC   *p150*
101 SOUTHBANK BLVD UNIT 10, OKO-
TOKS, AB, T1S 0G1
(403) 995-4710   *SIC 5211*
HOME DEPOT OF CANADA INC   *p175*
1956 VEDDER WAY, ABBOTSFORD, BC,
V2S 8K1
(604) 851-4400   *SIC 5211*
HOME DEPOT OF CANADA INC   *p203*
388 LERWICK RD, COURTENAY, BC, V9N
9E5
(250) 334-5400   *SIC 5211*
HOME DEPOT OF CANADA INC   *p458*
368 LACEWOOD DR, HALIFAX, NS, B3S
1L8
(902) 457-3480   *SIC 5211*
HOME DEPOT OF CANADA INC   *p475*
260 KINGSTON RD E, AJAX, ON, L1Z 1G1
(905) 428-7939   *SIC 5211*
HOME DEPOT OF CANADA INC   *p478*
122 MARTINDALE CRES, ANCASTER, ON,
L9K 1J9
(905) 304-6826   *SIC 5211*
HOME DEPOT OF CANADA INC   *p478*
122 MARTINDALE CRES, ANCASTER, ON,
L9K 1J9
(905) 304-5900   *SIC 5211*
HOME DEPOT OF CANADA INC   *p509*
49 FIRST GULF BLVD, BRAMPTON, ON,
L6W 4R8
(905) 457-1800   *SIC 5211*
HOME DEPOT OF CANADA INC   *p526*
3050 DAVIDSON CRT, BURLINGTON, ON,
L7M 4M9
(905) 331-1700   *SIC 5211*
HOME DEPOT OF CANADA INC   *p533*
35 PINEBUSH RD, CAMBRIDGE, ON, N1R

8E2
(519) 624-2700 *SIC* 5211

HOME DEPOT OF CANADA INC *p543*
8582 PIONEER LINE, CHATHAM, ON, N7M 5J1
(519) 380-2040 *SIC* 5211

HOME DEPOT OF CANADA INC *p563*
1825 BROOKDALE AVE, CORNWALL, ON, K6J 5X7
(613) 930-4470 *SIC* 5211

HOME DEPOT OF CANADA INC *p637*
1400 OTTAWA ST S, KITCHENER, ON, N2E 4E2
(519) 569-4300 *SIC* 5211

HOME DEPOT OF CANADA INC *p678*
50 KIRKHAM DR, MARKHAM, ON, L3S 4K7
(905) 201-2590 *SIC* 5211

HOME DEPOT OF CANADA INC *p758*
7190 MORRISON ST, NIAGARA FALLS, ON, L2E 7K5
(905) 371-7470 *SIC* 5211

HOME DEPOT OF CANADA INC *p831*
1900 BASELINE RD, OTTAWA, ON, K2C 3Z6
(613) 723-5900 *SIC* 5211

HOME DEPOT OF CANADA INC *p841*
500 LANSDOWNE ST W, PETERBOROUGH, ON, K9J 8J7
(705) 876-4560 *SIC* 5211

HOME DEPOT OF CANADA INC *p1010*
600 KING ST N, WATERLOO, ON, N2V 2J5
(519) 883-0580 *SIC* 5211

HOME DEPOT OF CANADA INC *p1182*
100 RUE BEAUBIEN O, MONTREAL, QC, H2S 3S1
(514) 490-8030 *SIC* 5211

HOME DEPOT OF CANADA INC *p1278*
1516 AV JULES-VERNE, QUEBEC, QC, G2G 2R5
(418) 872-8007 *SIC* 5211

HOME DEPOT OF CANADA INC *p1279*
300 RUE BOUVIER, QUEBEC, QC, G2J 1R8
(418) 634-8880 *SIC* 5211

HOME DEPOT OF CANADA INC *p1378*
660 MONTEE DES PIONNIERS, TERREBONNE, QC, J6V 1N9
(450) 657-4400 *SIC* 5211

HOME DEPOT OF CANADA INC *p1387*
4500 RUE REAL-PROULX, TROIS-RIVIERES, QC, G9A 6P9
(819) 379-3900 *SIC* 5211

HOME HARDWARE STORES LIMITED *p172*
6410 36 ST, WETASKIWIN, AB, T9A 3B6
(780) 352-1984 *SIC* 5211

HOME HARDWARE STORES LIMITED *p449*
336 LANCASTER CRES, DEBERT, NS, B0M 1G0
(902) 662-2800 *SIC* 5211

HOME HARDWARE STORES LIMITED *p888*
34 HENRY ST, ST JACOBS, ON, N0B 2N0
(519) 664-2252 *SIC* 5211

HOME HARDWARE STORES LIMITED *p1042*
14 KINLOCK RD, STRATFORD, PE, C1B 1R1
SIC 5211

HOMEWAY COMPANY LIMITED *p651*
1801 TRAFALGAR ST, LONDON, ON, N5W 1X7
(519) 453-6400 *SIC* 5211

IMPERIAL ROOFING (SARNIA) LTD *p860*
313 GLADWISH DR, SARNIA, ON, N7T 7H3
(519) 336-6146 *SIC* 5211

INLAND STEEL PRODUCTS INC *p1432*
1520 17TH ST W, SASKATOON, SK, S7M 4A4
(306) 652-5353 *SIC* 5211

INOVACO LTEE *p1104*
777 BOUL DE LA CITE, GATINEAU, QC, J8T 8J9
(819) 568-3400 *SIC* 5211

INVERMERE HARDWARE & BUILDING SUPPLIES CO LTD *p216*

9980 ARROW RD, INVERMERE, BC, V0A 1K2
(250) 342-6908 *SIC* 5211

IRVING, J. D. LIMITED *p396*
290 MAIN ST, CHIPMAN, NB, E4A 2M7
(506) 339-7900 *SIC* 5211

IRVING, J. D. LIMITED *p426*
60 OLD PLACENTIA RD, MOUNT PEARL, NL, A1N 4Y1
(709) 748-3500 *SIC* 5211

J. DROLET & FILS LTEE *p1399*
11 RUE DES OBLATS S, VILLE-MARIE, QC, J9V 1J9
(819) 629-2885 *SIC* 5211

J.H. ENTERPRISES (1969) LIMITED *p1431*
2505 AVENUE C N, SASKATOON, SK, S7L 6A6
(306) 652-5322 *SIC* 5211

J.L. BELISLE BUILDING MATERIALS LTD *p603*
389 SPEEDVALE AVE W, GUELPH, ON, N1H 1C7
(519) 822-8230 *SIC* 5211

JACK FRENCH LIMITED *p632*
200 BINNINGTON CRT, KINGSTON, ON, K7M 8R6
(613) 547-6666 *SIC* 5211

JACQUES LAFERTE LTEE *p1099*
1650 BOUL LEMIRE, DRUMMONDVILLE, QC, J2C 5A4
(819) 477-8950 *SIC* 5211

JONELJIM INVESTMENTS LIMITED *p467*
199 TOWNSEND ST, SYDNEY, NS, B1P 5E4
(902) 564-5554 *SIC* 5211

JULIAN TILE INC *p225*
9688 203 ST, LANGLEY, BC, V1M 4B9
(604) 299-4085 *SIC* 5211

KEMPTVILLE BUILDING CENTRE LTD *p627*
2540 HWY 43, KEMPTVILLE, ON, K0G 1J0
(613) 258-6000 *SIC* 5211

KERRISDALE LUMBER CO LTD *p322*
6191 WEST BOULEVARD, VANCOUVER, BC, V6M 3X3
(604) 261-4274 *SIC* 5211

KINGDON LUMBER LIMITED *p643*
34 DEYNCOURT ST, LAKEFIELD, ON, K0L 2H0
(705) 652-3361 *SIC* 5211

KOTOWICH HARDWARE LTD *p165*
4001 50 AVE, ST PAUL, AB, T0A 3A2
(780) 645-3173 *SIC* 5211

KRUGER INDUSTRIES INC *p75*
28 CROWFOOT TERRACE NW, CALGARY, AB, T3G 5W2
(403) 276-6900 *SIC* 5211

LAMPREA BUILDING MATERIALS LTD *p1035*
1147 DUNDAS ST SUITE 1, WOODSTOCK, ON, N4S 8W3
(519) 421-0484 *SIC* 5211

LANGEVIN & FOREST LTEE *p1170*
9995 BOUL PIE-IX, MONTREAL, QC, H1Z 3X1
(514) 322-9330 *SIC* 5211

LESPERANCE, FRANCOIS INC *p1083*
164 BOUL DES LAURENTIDES, COTE SAINT-LUC, QC, H7G 4P6
(450) 667-0255 *SIC* 5211

LEXSUCO CORP *p688*
3275 ORLANDO DR, MISSISSAUGA, ON, L4V 1C5
(905) 792-8800 *SIC* 5211

LOGIC LUMBER (LETH.) LTD *p141*
1217 39 ST N, LETHBRIDGE, AB, T1H 6Y8
(403) 328-7755 *SIC* 5211

LOMBARD PRE-CAST INC *p340*
661 LOMBARD DR, VICTORIA, BC, V9C 3Y9
(250) 478-9581 *SIC* 5211

LORTIE & MARTIN LTEE *p1354*
20 RUE SAINT-PAUL E, SAINTE-AGATHE-DES-MONTS, QC, J8C 3M3
(819) 326-3844 *SIC* 5211

LOUIS MAGLIO ENTERPRISES LTD *p235*
29 GOVERNMENT RD, NELSON, BC, V1L 4L9
(250) 352-6661 *SIC* 5211

LOWE'S COMPANIES CANADA, ULC *p9*
2909 SUNRIDGE WAY NE, CALGARY, AB, T1Y 7K7
(403) 277-0044 *SIC* 5211

LOWE'S COMPANIES CANADA, ULC *p101*
10225 186 ST NW, EDMONTON, AB, T5S 0G5
(780) 486-2508 *SIC* 5211

LOWE'S COMPANIES CANADA, ULC *p121*
10141 13 AVE NW, EDMONTON, AB, T6N 0B6
(780) 430-1344 *SIC* 5211

LOWE'S COMPANIES CANADA, ULC *p160*
261199 CROSSIRON BLVD UNIT 300, ROCKY VIEW COUNTY, AB, T4A 0J6
(403) 567-7440 *SIC* 5211

LOWE'S COMPANIES CANADA, ULC *p237*
1085 TANAKA CRT, NEW WESTMINSTER, BC, V3M 0G2
(604) 527-7239 *SIC* 5211

LOWE'S COMPANIES CANADA, ULC *p487*
71 BRYNE DR, BARRIE, ON, L4N 8V8
(905) 952-2950 *SIC* 5211

LOWE'S COMPANIES CANADA, ULC *p512*
10111 HEART LAKE RD, BRAMPTON, ON, L6Z 0E4
(905) 840-2351 *SIC* 5211

LOWE'S COMPANIES CANADA, ULC *p664*
200 MCNAUGHTON RD E, MAPLE, ON, L6A 4E2
(905) 879-2450 *SIC* 5211

LOWE'S COMPANIES CANADA, ULC *p697*
5150 SPECTRUM WAY, MISSISSAUGA, ON, L4W 5G2
(905) 219-1000 *SIC* 5211

LOWE'S COMPANIES CANADA, ULC *p755*
18401 YONGE ST, NEWMARKET, ON, L3Y 4V8
(905) 952-2950 *SIC* 5211

LOWE'S COMPANIES CANADA, ULC *p760*
7959 MCLEOD RD, NIAGARA FALLS, ON, L2H 0G5
(905) 374-5520 *SIC* 5211

LOWE'S COMPANIES CANADA, ULC *p772*
5160 YONGE ST SUITE 2, NORTH YORK, ON, M2N 6L9
(416) 730-7300 *SIC* 5211

LOWE'S COMPANIES CANADA, ULC *p843*
1899 BROCK RD, PICKERING, ON, L1V 4H7
(905) 619-7530 *SIC* 5211

LOWE'S COMPANIES CANADA, ULC *p876*
6005 STEELES AVE E, SCARBOROUGH, ON, M1V 5P7
(416) 940-4827 *SIC* 5211

LOWE'S COMPANIES CANADA, ULC *p899*
1199 MARCUS DR, SUDBURY, ON, P3B 4K6
(705) 521-7200 *SIC* 5211

LOWE'S COMPANIES CANADA, ULC *p1016*
4005 GARRARD RD, WHITBY, ON, L1R 0J1
(905) 433-2870 *SIC* 5211

LOWE'S COMPANIES CANADA, ULC *p1420*
489 N ALBERT ST, REGINA, SK, S4R 3C3
(306) 545-1386 *SIC* 5211

LYONS LTD *p863*
500 WELLINGTON ST W, SAULT STE. MARIE, ON, P6C 3T5
(705) 759-1555 *SIC* 5211

MAGLIO BUILDING CENTRE LTD *p235*
29 GOVERNMENT RD, NELSON, BC, V1L 4L9
(250) 352-6661 *SIC* 5211

MAINLAND CONSTRUCTION MATERIALS ULC *p225*
9525 201 ST UNIT 317, LANGLEY, BC, V1M 4A5
(604) 882-5650 *SIC* 5211

MAR-SPAN TRUSS INC *p565*
7873 WELLINGTON RD 8, DRAYTON, ON,

N0G 1P0
(519) 638-3086 *SIC* 5211

MARITIME HOME IMPROVEMENT LIMITED *p415*
300 UNION ST, SAINT JOHN, NB, E2L 4Z2
(506) 632-4100 *SIC* 5211

MARLBORO WINDOW AND DOOR MANUFACTURER LTD *p818*
2370 STEVENAGE DR, OTTAWA, ON, K1G 3W3
(613) 736-1441 *SIC* 5211

MARVIN WINDOWS INC *p740*
1455 COURTNEYPARK DR E, MISSISSAUGA, ON, L5T 2E3
(905) 670-5052 *SIC* 5211

MATERIAUX BONHOMME INC *p1103*
225 MONTEE PAIEMENT, GATINEAU, QC, J8P 6M7
(819) 561-5577 *SIC* 5211

MATERIAUX CAMPAGNA (2003) INC *p1290*
1200 RUE MANTHA, ROUYN-NORANDA, QC, J9Y 0G2
(819) 797-1200 *SIC* 5211

MATERIAUX DE CONSTRUCTION LETOURNEAU INC *p1400*
4855 143 RTE, WATERVILLE, QC, J0B 3H0
(819) 566-5633 *SIC* 5211

MATERIAUX LAURENTIENS INC *p1320*
2159 BOUL DU CURE-LABELLE, SAINT-JEROME, QC, J7Y 1T1
(450) 438-9780 *SIC* 5211

MATERIAUX LAURENTIENS INC *p1382*
7700 BOUL LAURIER, TERREBONNE, QC, J7M 2K8
(450) 478-7557 *SIC* 5211

MATERIAUX MIRON INC *p1365*
230 BOUL MONSEIGNEUR-LANGLOIS, SALABERRY-DE-VALLEYFIELD, QC, J6S 0A7
(450) 373-7272 *SIC* 5211

MATERIAUX PONT MASSON INC *p1365*
2715 BOUL MONSEIGNEUR-LANGLOIS, SALABERRY-DE-VALLEYFIELD, QC, J6S 5P7
(450) 371-2041 *SIC* 5211

MATTAMY HOMES LIMITED *p684*
1550 DERRY RD, MILTON, ON, L9T 1A1
(905) 875-2692 *SIC* 5211

MCKECHNIE, ANDY BUILDING MATERIALS LTD *p569*
830 CENTRE ST, ESPANOLA, ON, P5E 1J1
(705) 869-2100 *SIC* 5211

MCLEOD MERCANTILE LTD *p164*
135 SOUTH AVE, SPRUCE GROVE, AB, T7X 3A5
(780) 962-2575 *SIC* 5211

MCMUNN & YATES BUILDING SUPPLIES LTD *p387*
600 PEMBINA HWY, WINNIPEG, MB, R3M 2M5
(204) 940-4040 *SIC* 5211

MCNAUGHTON AUTOMOTIVE LIMITED *p753*
22789 HAGERTY RD, NEWBURY, ON, N0L 1Z0
(519) 693-4449 *SIC* 5211

MCRAE MILLS LIMITED *p1016*
160 HAY CREEK RD, WHITNEY, ON, K0J 2M0
(613) 637-2977 *SIC* 5211

MIDLAND LUMBER & BUILDING SUPPLIES LTD *p681*
200 THIRD ST, MIDLAND, ON, L4R 3R9
(705) 526-2264 *SIC* 5211

MIDWAY LUMBER MILLS LIMITED *p903*
41 SHERWOOD RD, THESSALON, ON, P0R 1L0
(705) 842-3246 *SIC* 5211

MILL & TIMBER PRODUCTS LTD *p275*
12770 116 AVE, SURREY, BC, V3V 7H9
(604) 580-2781 *SIC* 5211

MILLTECH MILLWORK LTD *p94*
12410 142 ST NW, EDMONTON, AB, T5L 4K2

(780) 455-6655   *SIC* 5211

MINTECH CANADA INC   *p*1251
1870 BOUL DES SOURCES BUREAU 100, POINTE-CLAIRE, QC, H9R 5N4
(514) 697-8260   *SIC* 5211

MODERN MOSAIC LIMITED   *p*759
8620 OAKWOOD DR, NIAGARA FALLS, ON, L2G 0J2
(905) 356-3045   *SIC* 5211

MOFFATT & POWELL LIMITED   *p*658
1282 HYDE PARK RD, LONDON, ON, N6H 5K5
(519) 472-2000   *SIC* 5211

MOISAN, ELOI INC   *p*1306
20 354 RTE, SAINT-GILBERT, QC, G0A 3T0
(418) 268-3232   *SIC* 5211

MONETTE, EUGENE INC   *p*1391
2650 1ER RANG DE DONCASTER, VAL-DAVID, QC, J0T 2N0
(819) 322-3833   *SIC* 5211

MONTALCO CABINETS (1991) LTD   *p*261
2700 SIMPSON RD UNIT 125, RICHMOND, BC, V6X 2P9
(604) 273-5105   *SIC* 5211

MOSCONE TILE LTD   *p*556
8830 JANE ST SUITE 1, CONCORD, ON, L4K 2M9
(905) 761-5722   *SIC* 5211

MOULURES M. WARNET INC   *p*1059
100 RUE MARIUS-WARNET, BLAINVILLE, QC, J7C 5P9
(450) 437-1209   *SIC* 5211

MUSKOKA LUMBER AND BUILDING SUPPLIES CENTRE LIMITED   *p*846
3687 HWY 118, PORT CARLING, ON, P0B 1J0
(705) 765-3105   *SIC* 5211

MYROWICH, A BUILDING MATERIAL LTD   *p*1438
145 BROADWAY ST E, YORKTON, SK, S3N 3K5
(306) 783-3608   *SIC* 5211

NAUD, PIERRE INC   *p*1369
405 AV DU CAPITAINE-VEILLEUX, SHAW-INIGAN, QC, G9P 1Z7
(819) 537-1877   *SIC* 5211

NELSON LUMBER COMPANY LTD   *p*94
12727 ST ALBERT TRAIL NW, EDMONTON, AB, T5L 4H5
(780) 452-9151   *SIC* 5211

NEWTON ENTERPRISES (1983)   *p*353
1 MAIN ST, NEWTON SIDING, MB, R0H 0X0
(204) 267-2211   *SIC* 5211

NORQUAY CO-OPERATIVE ASSOCIATION LIMITED, THE   *p*1412
13 HWY 49, NORQUAY, SK, S0A 2V0
(306) 594-2215   *SIC* 5211

NORTH AMERICAN LUMBER LIMITED *p*379
205 FORT ST SUITE 200, WINNIPEG, MB, R3C 1E3
(204) 942-8121   *SIC* 5211

NORTHERN ENERGY CONSTRUCTORS LTD   *p*251
9368 MILWAUKEE WAY SUITE 101, PRINCE GEORGE, BC, V2N 5T3
(250) 562-8100   *SIC* 5211

NORTHUMBERLAND BUILDING MATERIALS LTD   *p*847
205 PETER ST SUITE 368, PORT HOPE, ON, L1A 3V6
(416) 759-8542   *SIC* 5211

NOVA CAPITAL INCORPORATED   *p*467
530 GRAND LAKE RD, SYDNEY, NS, B1P 5T4
(902) 562-7000   *SIC* 5211

NUCASA MILLING COMPANY LIMITED *p*184
6150 LOUGHEED HWY, BURNABY, BC, V5B 2Z9
(604) 294-3232   *SIC* 5211

PARK PACIFIC LUMBERWORLD LTD *p*337
3955 QUADRA ST, VICTORIA, BC, V8X 1J7
(250) 479-7151   *SIC* 5211

PAYZANT BUILDING PRODUCTS LIMITED *p*461
250 SACKVILLE DR, LOWER SACKVILLE, NS, B4C 2R4
(902) 864-0000   *SIC* 5211

PENNER LUMBER & BUILDERS' SUPPLIES LIMITED   *p*1004
700 PENNER ST, VIRGIL, ON, L0S 1T0
(905) 468-3242   *SIC* 5211

PHANTOM MFG. (INT'L) LTD   *p*177
30451 SIMPSON RD, ABBOTSFORD, BC, V2T 6C7
SIC 5211

PIONEER BUILDING SUPPLIES LTD   *p*196
45754 YALE RD, CHILLIWACK, BC, V2P 2N4
(604) 795-7238   *SIC* 5211

PLACEMENTS JACQUES LAFERTE INC, LES   *p*1099
1650 BOUL LEMIRE, DRUMMONDVILLE, QC, J2C 5A4
(819) 477-8950   *SIC* 5211

PLANCHERS SEQUOIA INC, LES   *p*1357
2800 RUE ETIENNE-LENOIR, SAINTE-DOROTHEE, QC, H7R 0A3
(450) 622-8899   *SIC* 5211

PORTES DE GARAGE CEDO INC   *p*1283
605 BOUL IBERVILLE BUREAU 2061, REPENTIGNY, QC, J6A 5H9
(450) 585-4224   *SIC* 5211

PORTES ET FENETRES ROYALTY   *p*1393
17 BOULEVARD CITE DES JEUNES, VAUDREUIL-DORION, QC, G7V 9E8
(450) 218-4411   *SIC* 5211

POWELL RIVER BUILDING SUPPLY LTD *p*248
4750 JOYCE AVE, POWELL RIVER, BC, V8A 3B6
(604) 485-2791   *SIC* 5211

PREMIER BATHROOMS CANADA LTD *p*270
14716 104 AVE, SURREY, BC, V3R 1M3
(604) 588-9688   *SIC* 5211

PRENDIVILLE CORPORATION   *p*369
165 RYAN ST, WINNIPEG, MB, R2R 0N9
(204) 989-9600   *SIC* 5211

PRO BUILDING SUPPLY LTD   *p*244
150 FAIRVIEW PL, PENTICTON, BC, V2A 6A5
(250) 492-6635   *SIC* 5211

PRODUITS FLEURCO INC, LES   *p*1330
4575 BOUL POIRIER, SAINT-LAURENT, QC, H4R 2A4
(514) 326-2222   *SIC* 5211

QUEST BRANDS INC   *p*505
1 VAN DER GRAAF CRT, BRAMPTON, ON, L6T 5E5
(905) 789-6868   *SIC* 5211

RAFUSE BUILDING SUPPLIES (1977) LTD *p*471
200 DYKELAND ST, WOLFVILLE, NS, B4P 1A2
(902) 542-2211   *SIC* 5211

RAY-DONN TOEWS BUILDING MATERIALS LTD   *p*1411
506 HIGH ST W, MOOSE JAW, SK, S6H 1T4
(306) 693-0211   *SIC* 5211

REGAL ALUMINUM (1993) INC   *p*558
177 DRUMLIN CIR SUITE 1, CONCORD, ON, L4K 3E7
(905) 738-4375   *SIC* 5211

REGAL BUILDING MATERIALS LTD   *p*37
7131 6 ST SE SUITE D, CALGARY, AB, T2H 2M8
(403) 253-2010   *SIC* 5211

RENOVAPRIX INC   *p*1301
226 25E AV, SAINT-EUSTACHE, QC, J7P 4Z8
(450) 472-3000   *SIC* 5211

RENOVATEUR REGIONAL   *p*1320
1025 BOUL JEAN-BAPTISTE-ROLLAND O, SAINT-JEROME, QC, J7Y 4Y7
(450) 560-3979   *SIC* 5211

RENOVATIONS MARTIN MARTIN INC *p*1173
5187 AV PAPINEAU, MONTREAL, QC, H2H

1W1
(514) 270-6599   *SIC* 5211

REVETEMENT R.H.R. INC   *p*1318
755 RUE BOUCHER, SAINT-JEAN-SUR-RICHELIEU, QC, J3B 8P4
(450) 359-7868   *SIC* 5211

RICK KURZAC BUILDING MATERIALS LTD *p*218
1325 JOSEP WAY, KAMLOOPS, BC, V2H 1N6
(250) 377-7234   *SIC* 5211

RIDEAU LUMBER (SMITH'S FALLS) LIMITED   *p*882
58 ABBOTT ST N, SMITHS FALLS, ON, K7A 1W5
(613) 283-2211   *SIC* 5211

RK SCHEPERS HOLDINGS LTD   *p*204
1608 NORTHWEST BLVD, CRESTON, BC, V0B 1G6
(250) 428-9388   *SIC* 5211

ROB ROLSTON BUILDING MATERIALS LTD   *p*621
35 CRESCENT RD, HUNTSVILLE, ON, P1H 1Y3
(705) 789-4111   *SIC* 5211

RONA INC   *p*9
2665 32 ST NE, CALGARY, AB, T1Y 6Z7
(403) 219-5800   *SIC* 5211

RONA INC   *p*282
16659 FRASER HWY, SURREY, BC, V4N 0E7
(604) 576-2955   *SIC* 5211

RONA INC   *p*367
775 PANET RD, WINNIPEG, MB, R2K 4C6
(204) 663-7389   *SIC* 5211

RONA INC   *p*1309
5035 BOUL COUSINEAU, SAINT-HUBERT, QC, J3Y 3K7
(450) 656-4422   *SIC* 5211

ROUSSEAU, MARC LTEE   *p*1241
520 BOUL CURE-LABELLE, MONTREAL-OUEST, QC, H7V 2T2
(450) 688-1170   *SIC* 5211

ROYAL DOORS LTD   *p*409
105 HENRI DUNANT ST, MONCTON, NB, E1E 1E4
(506) 857-4075   *SIC* 5211

SANGROUP INC   *p*225
25583 88 AVE, LANGLEY, BC, V1M 3N8
(604) 881-4848   *SIC* 5211

SCHELL LUMBER LIMITED   *p*895
33 EDWARD ST, STOUFFVILLE, ON, L4A 1A4
(905) 640-3440   *SIC* 5211

SHEPHERD'S HARDWARE LIMITED   *p*180
3525 MILL ST, ARMSTRONG, BC, V0E 1B0
(250) 546-3002   *SIC* 5211

SHERWOOD TIMBER MART INC   *p*1041
423 MOUNT EDWARD RD, CHARLOTTETOWN, PE, C1E 2A1
(902) 368-3648   *SIC* 5211

SOLARIS INTERNATIONAL INC   *p*1119
6150 BOUL SAINTE-ANNE, L'ANGE GARDIEN, QC, G0A 2K0
(418) 822-0643   *SIC* 5211

SOO MILL & LUMBER COMPANY LIMITED *p*863
539 GREAT NORTHERN RD, SAULT STE. MARIE, ON, P6B 5A1
(705) 759-0533   *SIC* 5211

SPAR ROOFING & METAL SUPPLIES LIMITED   *p*990
1360 BLOOR ST W, TORONTO, ON, M6H 1P2
(416) 534-8421   *SIC* 5211

SPRATT AGGREGATES LTD   *p*541
2300 CARP RD, CARP, ON, K0A 1L0
(613) 831-0717   *SIC* 5211

STAR BUILDING MATERIALS (ALBERTA) LTD   *p*32
2345 ALYTH RD SE, CALGARY, AB, T2G 5T8
(403) 720-0010   *SIC* 5211

STAR BUILDING MATERIALS (ALBERTA)

LTD   *p*366
16 SPEERS RD, WINNIPEG, MB, R2J 1L8
(204) 233-8687   *SIC* 5211

STAR BUILDING MATERIALS LTD   *p*367
16 SPEERS RD SUITE 118, WINNIPEG, MB, R2J 1L8
(204) 233-8687   *SIC* 5211

STORDOR INVESTMENTS LTD   *p*97
11703 160 ST NW, EDMONTON, AB, T5M 3Z3
(780) 451-0060   *SIC* 5211

SUNPLY CORPORATION   *p*385
551 CENTURY ST, WINNIPEG, MB, R3H 0L8
(204) 786-5555   *SIC* 5211

SURMONT SAND & GRAVEL LTD   *p*129
431 MACKENZIE BLVD UNIT 8, FORT MC-MURRAY, AB, T9H 4C5
(780) 743-2533   *SIC* 5211

SURPLUS MALOUIN INC   *p*1400
6400 RUE FOSTER, WATERLOO, QC, J0E 2N0
(450) 539-3722   *SIC* 5211

SWANSON, JIM LUMBER LTD   *p*639
166 PARK ST, KITCHENER, ON, N2G 1M8
(519) 743-1404   *SIC* 5211

TAMARACK LUMBER INC   *p*528
3255 SERVICE RD NORTH, BURLINGTON, ON, L7N 3G2
(905) 335-1115   *SIC* 5211

TARPIN LUMBER INCORPORATED   *p*622
2267 BOWMAN ST, INNISFIL, ON, L9S 3V5
(705) 436-5373   *SIC* 5211

TAYLOR LUMBER COMPANY LIMITED *p*462
12111 HWY 224 RR 4, MIDDLE MUSQUODOBOIT, NS, B0N 1X0
(902) 384-2444   *SIC* 5211

TBM HOLDCO LTD   *p*25
1601 AIRPORT RD NE SUITE 705, CALGARY, AB, T2E 6Z8
(800) 663-3342   *SIC* 5211

TEAHEN & TEAHEN BUILDING SUPPLIES LTD   *p*651
1780 DUNDAS ST, LONDON, ON, N5W 3E5
(519) 455-0660   *SIC* 5211

THOMAS, RENE & FILS INC   *p*1393
10 RUE BEAUREGARD, VARENNES, QC, J3X 1R1
(450) 652-2927   *SIC* 5211

TIMBERTOWN BUILDING CENTRE LTD *p*26
3440 12 ST NE SUITE G, CALGARY, AB, T2E 6N1
(403) 291-1317   *SIC* 5211

TITAN LUMBER CORP   *p*78
4615 39 ST, CAMROSE, AB, T4V 0Z4
(780) 608-1236   *SIC* 5211

TOMLINSON, R. W. LIMITED   *p*1002
8125 RUSSELL RD, VARS, ON, K0A 3H0
(613) 835-3395   *SIC* 5211

TOP SHOP INC, THE   *p*650
502 FIRST ST, LONDON, ON, N5V 1Z3
(519) 455-9400   *SIC* 5211

TRAIL BUILDING SUPPLIES LTD   *p*117
9450 45 AVE NW, EDMONTON, AB, T6E 5V3
(780) 463-1737   *SIC* 5211

TREMBLAY ET FRERES LTEE   *p*1391
97 BOUL LAMAQUE, VAL-D'OR, QC, J9P 2H7
(819) 825-7470   *SIC* 5211

TRUEFOAM LIMITED   *p*448
11 MOSHER DR, DARTMOUTH, NS, B3B 1L8
(902) 468-5440   *SIC* 5211

TSI INSULATION LTD   *p*2
27392 ELLIS RD, ACHESON, AB, T7X 6N3
(780) 484-1344   *SIC* 5211

TURKSTRA LUMBER COMPANY LIMITED *p*616
1050 UPPER WELLINGTON ST, HAMILTON, ON, L9A 3S6
(905) 388-8220   *SIC* 5211

UNICON CONCRETE SPECIALTIES LTD *p*97
11740 156 ST NW, EDMONTON, AB, T5M

3T5

(780) 455-3737　*SIC 5211*

UNITED LUMBER AND BUILDING SUP-PLIES COMPANY LIMITED p485
520 BAYFIELD ST, BARRIE, ON, L4M 5A2

(705) 726-8132　*SIC 5211*

UPPAL BUILDING SUPPLIES LTD p278
7846 128 ST, SURREY, BC, V3W 4E8

(604) 594-4142　*SIC 5211*

VALMONT WC ENGINEERING GROUP LTD p210
7984 RIVER RD, DELTA, BC, V4G 1E3

(604) 946-1256　*SIC 5211*

VAN'ISLE WINDOWS LTD p335
404 HILLSIDE AVE, VICTORIA, BC, V8T 1Y7

(250) 383-7128　*SIC 5211*

VISIONWALL CORPORATION p103
17915 118 AVE NW, EDMONTON, AB, T5S 1L6

(780) 451-4000　*SIC 5211*

WARMAN HOME CENTRE LP p1437
601 SOUTH RAILWAY ST W, WARMAN, SK, S0K 4S0

(306) 933-4950　*SIC 5211*

WEATHERHAVEN GLOBAL RESOURCES LTD p202
2120 HARTLEY AVE, COQUITLAM, BC, V3K 6W5

(604) 451-8900　*SIC 5211*

WEST FRASER MILLS LTD p136
99 WEST RIVER RD, HINTON, AB, T7V 1Y7

(780) 865-8900　*SIC 5211*

WESTCOAST MOULDING & MILLWORK LIMITED p282
18810 96 AVE, SURREY, BC, V4N 3R1

(604) 513-1138　*SIC 5211*

WESTECK WINDOWS MFG. INC p198
8104 EVANS RD, CHILLIWACK, BC, V2R 5R8

(604) 792-6700　*SIC 5211*

WESTERN BUILDING LTD p423
25 POPLAR RD, CORNER BROOK, NL, A2H 4T6

(709) 634-3163　*SIC 5211*

WESTRUM LUMBER LTD p1423
611 WECKMAN DR, ROULEAU, SK, S0G 4K0

(306) 776-2505　*SIC 5211*

WHITE-WOOD DISTRIBUTORS LTD p373
119 PLYMOUTH ST, WINNIPEG, MB, R2X 2T3

(204) 982-9450　*SIC 5211*

WHITING DOOR MANUFACTURING LIMITED p528
3435 SOUTH SERVICE RD, BURLINGTON, ON, L7N 3W6

(905) 333-6745　*SIC 5211*

WIEBE, J. BUILDING MATERIALS LTD p645
241 OAK ST E, LEAMINGTON, ON, N8H 4W8

(519) 326-4474　*SIC 5211*

SIC 5231 Paint, glass, and wallpaper stores

HOME DEPOT OF CANADA INC p814
1481 HARMONY RD N, OSHAWA, ON, L1K 0Z6

(905) 743-5600　*SIC 5231*

HOME DEPOT OF CANADA INC p867
2911 EGLINTON AVE E, SCARBOROUGH, ON, M1J 2E5

(416) 289-2500　*SIC 5231*

HOME DEPOT OF CANADA INC p1103
243 MONTEE PAIEMENT, GATINEAU, QC, J8P 6M7

(819) 246-4060　*SIC 5231*

LAURENTIDE RE-SOURCES INC p1399
345 RUE DE LA BULSTRODE, VICTORIAV-ILLE, QC, G6T 1P7

(819) 752-9744　*SIC 5231*

LOOP RECYCLED PRODUCTS INC p758
940 CHIPPAWA CREEK RD, NIAGARA

FALLS, ON, L2E 6S5

(905) 353-0068　*SIC 5231*

RANDALL'S PAINTS LIMITED p826
555 BANK ST, OTTAWA, ON, K1S 5L7

(613) 233-8441　*SIC 5231*

VITRERIE LABERGE (1988) INC p1255
415 RUE DES ALLEGHANYS, QUEBEC, QC, G1C 4N4

(418) 663-6363　*SIC 5231*

SIC 5251 Hardware stores

1439037 ONTARIO LTD p645
220 LINDSAY ST S, LINDSAY, ON, K9V 2N3

(705) 324-3516　*SIC 5251*

1441246 ONTARIO INC p895
3010 LINE 34, STRATFORD, ON, N5A 6S5

(519) 271-4370　*SIC 5251*

2030413 ONTARIO LIMITED p514
10 KING GEORGE RD, BRANTFORD, ON, N3R 5J7

(519) 751-3333　*SIC 5251*

2950-4602 QUEBEC INC p1347
435 RUE SAINT-ISIDORE, SAINT-LIN-LAURENTIDES, QC, J5M 2V1

(450) 439-2000　*SIC 5251*

3100-6588 QUEBEC INC p1114
920 BOUL FIRESTONE, JOLIETTE, QC, J6E 2W5

(450) 756-4545　*SIC 5251*

321124 B.C. LTD p213
9820 108 ST, FORT ST. JOHN, BC, V1J 0A7

(250) 787-0371　*SIC 5251*

645373 ALBERTA LTD p151
6307 46 ST, OLDS, AB, T4H 1L7

(403) 556-2550　*SIC 5251*

697739 ONTARIO INC p849
555 O'BRIEN RD, RENFREW, ON, K7V 3Z3

(613) 432-5138　*SIC 5251*

734046 ONTARIO LIMITED p1017
1613 LESPERANCE RD, WINDSOR, ON, N8N 1Y2

(519) 735-3400　*SIC 5251*

9027-0653 QUEBEC INC p1149
175 MONTEE MASSON, MASCOUCHE, QC, J7K 3B4

(450) 474-6181　*SIC 5251*

AL'S POWER PLUS p214
921 GIBSONS WAY, GIBSONS, BC, V0N 1V8

(604) 886-3700　*SIC 5251*

APEX-NIAGARA TOOL LTD p885
54 CATHERINE ST, ST CATHARINES, ON, L2R 7R5

(905) 704-1797　*SIC 5251*

ARROW PLUMBING INC p862
594 SECOND LINE E, SAULT STE. MARIE, ON, P6B 4K1

(705) 759-8316　*SIC 5251*

AYLWARDS (1986) LIMITED p425
200 ATLANTIC ST SUITE 192, MARYS-TOWN, NL, A0E 2M0

(709) 279-2202　*SIC 5251*

BARFITT BROS. HARDWARE (AURORA) LTD p480
289 WELLINGTON ST E, AURORA, ON, L4G 6H6

(905) 727-4751　*SIC 5251*

BEEBE, D LUMBER CO LTD p747
199 JIM KIMMETT BLVD, NAPANEE, ON, K7R 3L1

(613) 354-3315　*SIC 5251*

BORDER CITY BUILDING CENTRE LTD p143
2802 50 AVE, LLOYDMINSTER, AB, T9V 2S3

(780) 875-7762　*SIC 5251*

BRETON & THIBAULT LTEE p1289
333 BOUL RIDEAU, ROUYN-NORANDA, QC, J9X 5Y6

(819) 797-4444　*SIC 5251*

BRIAN DOMELLE ENTERPRISES LIMITED p918

459-825 EGLINTON AVE E, TORONTO, ON, M4G 4G9

(416) 422-0303　*SIC 5251*

BROCKVILLE HARDWARE ENTERPRISES INC p519
584 STEWART BLVD, BROCKVILLE, ON, K6V 7H2

(613) 342-4421　*SIC 5251*

BRYAN, J GASCON INVESTMENTS INC p283
5100 16 HWY W SUITE 486, TERRACE, BC, V8G 5S5

(250) 635-7178　*SIC 5251*

BUSY BEE MACHINE TOOLS LTD p549
130 GREAT GULF DR, CONCORD, ON, L4K 5W1

(905) 738-5115　*SIC 5251*

C. HEAD LIMITED p10
8 AVE NE SUITE 326, CALGARY, AB, T2A 6K5

(403) 248-6400　*SIC 5251*

CALDWELL, C. MARK ENTERPRISE LTD p76
388 COUNTRY HILLS BLVD NE UNIT 200, CALGARY, AB, T3K 5J6

(403) 226-9550　*SIC 5251*

CANADIAN TIRE p259
3511 NO. 3 RD, RICHMOND, BC, V6X 2B8

(604) 273-2939　*SIC 5251*

CANADIAN TIRE p458
16 DENTITH RD, HALIFAX, NS, B3R 2H9

(902) 477-5608　*SIC 5251*

CANADIAN TIRE p494
99 MCEWAN DR E SUITE 2, BOLTON, ON, L7E 2Z7

(905) 857-5425　*SIC 5251*

CANADIAN TIRE ASSOCIATE STORE p456
6203 QUINPOOL RD SUITE 44, HALIFAX, NS, B3L 4P6

(902) 422-4598　*SIC 5251*

CANADIAN TIRE ASSOCIATES STORE p450
130 RESERVE ST, GLACE BAY, NS, B1A 4W5

(902) 842-0700　*SIC 5251*

CAPITAL IRON (1997) LTD p334
1900 STORE ST, VICTORIA, BC, V8T 4R4

(250) 385-9703　*SIC 5251*

CASSIE CO ENTERPRISES LTD p646
500 MITCHELL RD S, LISTOWEL, ON, N4W 3G7

(519) 291-1960　*SIC 5251*

CENTRE DE RENOVATION TERREBONNE INC p1380
1505 CH GASCON, TERREBONNE, QC, J6X 2Z6

(450) 471-6631　*SIC 5251*

COOPERATIVE AGRICOLE DU PRE-VERT p1384
1316 RUE SAINTE-MARIE, TINGWICK, QC, J0A 1L0

(819) 359-2255　*SIC 5251*

CORPORATION ALLIANCE DYNAMIQUE p1086
3065 BOUL LE CARREFOUR, COTE SAINT-LUC, QC, H7T 1C7

(450) 688-0688　*SIC 5251*

D & F CLOUTIER GROUP ENTERPRISES INC p837
30 PINE DR, PARRY SOUND, ON, P2A 3B8

(705) 746-4033　*SIC 5251*

D & K CROSS SALES LTD. p267
1151 10 AVE SW SUITE 300, SALMON ARM, BC, V1E 1T3

(250) 832-9600　*SIC 5251*

D & L GUITARD SALES INC p470
5130 ST MARGARETS BAY RD, UPPER TANTALLON, NS, B3Z 1E2

(902) 826-2800　*SIC 5251*

DAVE DEPLAEDT RETAIL SALES LTD p1433
1731 PRESTON AVE N SUITE 133, SASKA-TOON, SK, S7N 4V2

(306) 373-3666　*SIC 5251*

DEREK HUTCHISON SALES LIMITED p463
9212 COMMERCIAL ST, NEW MINAS, NS, B4N 5J5

(902) 681-4576　*SIC 5251*

DRAVES, BRIAN H MERCHANDISING LTD p886
431 LOUTH ST SUITE 90, ST CATHARINES, ON, L2S 4A2

(905) 682-9275　*SIC 5251*

ELIK, MIKE LIMITED p711
3050 MAVIS RD SUITE 346, MISSIS-SAUGA, ON, L5C 1T8

(905) 270-9200　*SIC 5251*

ELLARD ENTERPRISES LIMITED p839
115 DRUMMOND ST W, PERTH, ON, K7H 2K8

(613) 267-4501　*SIC 5251*

ENTREPRISES PAUL WOODSTOCK LTEE p1089
65 132 RTE, DELSON, QC, J5B 1H1

(450) 632-1700　*SIC 5251*

ENTREPRISES ROLAND DOYON p1162
7555 BOUL MAURICE-DUPLESSIS BU-REAU 454, MONTREAL, QC, H1E 7N2

(514) 643-2232　*SIC 5251*

FERLAC INC p1303
1039 RUE DE CARILLON, SAINT-FELICIEN, QC, G8K 2A2

(418) 679-1676　*SIC 5251*

FINES HOME HARDWARE & BUILDING CENTRE p622
9 THOROLD LN, INGLESIDE, ON, K0C 1M0

(613) 537-2233　*SIC 5251*

FYNBO, IB HARDWARE LTD p570
47 WILSON AVE, ESSEX, ON, N8M 2L9

(519) 776-4646　*SIC 5251*

G & M PLUMBING & HEATING LTD p132
10944 96 AVE, GRANDE PRAIRIE, AB, T8V 3J5

(780) 538-3222　*SIC 5251*

GEERLINKS BUILDING CENTRE AND FUR-NITURE LIMITED p890
295 WELLINGTON ST, ST THOMAS, ON, N5R 2S6

(519) 631-2910　*SIC 5251*

GESTION J. M. LEROUX LTEE p1262
30 BOUL WILFRID-HAMEL, QUEBEC, QC, G1M 2P7

(418) 687-2111　*SIC 5251*

GESTION REJEAN LEGER INC p1138
600 RUE DE LA CONCORDE, LEVIS, QC, G6W 8A8

(418) 839-9797　*SIC 5251*

GILLAM FAMILY HOLDINGS LIMITED p880
725 STEELES ST, SHELBURNE, ON, L9V 3M7

(519) 925-3991　*SIC 5251*

GILMER'S BUILDING CENTRE LIMITED p847
177 TORONTO RD SUITE 1, PORT HOPE, ON, L1A 3V5

(905) 885-4568　*SIC 5251*

GLENBRIAR HOME HARDWARE p1006
262 WEBER ST N, WATERLOO, ON, N2J 3H6

(519) 886-2950　*SIC 5251*

GOODLAD, JOHN P. SALES INC p906
8081 DUFFERIN ST, THORNHILL, ON, L4J 8R9

(905) 889-7455　*SIC 5251*

GOW'S HARDWARE LIMITED p441
76 HIGH ST, BRIDGEWATER, NS, B4V 1V8

(902) 543-7121　*SIC 5251*

GREEN LINE HOSE & FITTINGS (AL-BERTA) LTD p109
7003 ROPER RD NW, EDMONTON, AB, T6B 3K3

(780) 465-5216　*SIC 5251*

GREEN LINE MANUFACTURING LTD p1434
3711 MITCHELMORE AVE, SASKATOON, SK, S7P 0C5

(306) 934-8886　*SIC 5251*

GREG SAARI MERCHANDISING LTD p70

4155 126 AVE SE, CALGARY, AB, T2Z 0A1
(403) 257-4729   *SIC* 5251

GUILLEMETTE, JEAN-PAUL INC   p1276
4500 RUE ARMAND-VIAU BUREAU 342, QUEBEC, QC, G2C 2B9
(418) 872-6221   *SIC* 5251

H. MATTEAU ET FILS (1987) INC   p1368
1650 RUE TRUDEL, SHAWINIGAN, QC, G9N 0A2
(819) 539-8328   *SIC* 5251

HANSON HARDWARE LTD   p1407
191 BROADWAY AVE, FORT QU'APPELLE, SK, S0G 1S0
SIC 5251

HENLEY DEVELOPMENT CORP   p266
3560 MONCTON ST, RICHMOND, BC, V7E 3A2
(604) 275-2317   *SIC* 5251

HOME DEPOT OF CANADA INC   p3
2925 MAIN ST SE, AIRDRIE, AB, T4B 3G5
(403) 945-3865   *SIC* 5251

HOME DEPOT OF CANADA INC   p11
343 36 ST NE, CALGARY, AB, T2A 7S9
(403) 248-3040   *SIC* 5251

HOME DEPOT OF CANADA INC   p41
1818 16 AVE NW, CALGARY, AB, T2M 0L8
(403) 284-7931   *SIC* 5251

HOME DEPOT OF CANADA INC   p69
390 SHAWVILLE BLVD SE, CALGARY, AB, T2Y 3S4
(403) 201-5611   *SIC* 5251

HOME DEPOT OF CANADA INC   p70
5125 126 AVE SE, CALGARY, AB, T2Z 0B2
(403) 257-8756   *SIC* 5251

HOME DEPOT OF CANADA INC   p76
388 COUNTRY HILLS BLVD NE UNIT 100, CALGARY, AB, T3K 5J6
(403) 226-7500   *SIC* 5251

HOME DEPOT OF CANADA INC   p77
5019 NOSE HILL DR NW, CALGARY, AB, T3L 0A2
(403) 241-4060   *SIC* 5251

HOME DEPOT OF CANADA INC   p83
13304 50 ST NW, EDMONTON, AB, T5A 4Z8
(780) 478-7133   *SIC* 5251

HOME DEPOT OF CANADA INC   p96
1 WESTMOUNT SHOPPING CTR NW SUITE 604, EDMONTON, AB, T5M 3L7
(780) 732-9225   *SIC* 5251

HOME DEPOT OF CANADA INC   p104
17404 99 AVE NW, EDMONTON, AB, T5T 5L5
(780) 484-5100   *SIC* 5251

HOME DEPOT OF CANADA INC   p118
6725 104 ST NW, EDMONTON, AB, T6H 2L3
(780) 431-4743   *SIC* 5251

HOME DEPOT OF CANADA INC   p124
4430 17 ST NW, EDMONTON, AB, T6T 0B4
(780) 577-3575   *SIC* 5251

HOME DEPOT OF CANADA INC   p125
6218 CURRENTS DR NW, EDMONTON, AB, T6W 0L8
(780) 989-7460   *SIC* 5251

HOME DEPOT OF CANADA INC   p143
3708 MAYOR MAGRATH DR S, LETHBRIDGE, AB, T1K 7V1
(403) 331-3581   *SIC* 5251

HOME DEPOT OF CANADA INC   p144
7705 44 ST, LLOYDMINSTER, AB, T9V 0X9
(780) 870-9420   *SIC* 5251

HOME DEPOT OF CANADA INC   p146
1851 STRACHAN RD SE, MEDICINE HAT, AB, T1B 4V7
(403) 581-4300   *SIC* 5251

HOME DEPOT OF CANADA INC   p157
2030 50 AVE, RED DEER, AB, T4R 3A2
(403) 358-7550   *SIC* 5251

HOME DEPOT OF CANADA INC   p162
390 BASELINE RD SUITE 200, SHERWOOD PARK, AB, T8H 1X1
(780) 417-7875   *SIC* 5251

HOME DEPOT OF CANADA INC   p164

168 16A HWY, SPRUCE GROVE, AB, T7X 3X3
(780) 960-5600   *SIC* 5251

HOME DEPOT OF CANADA INC   p165
750 ST ALBERT TRAIL, ST. ALBERT, AB, T8N 7H5
(780) 458-4026   *SIC* 5251

HOME DEPOT OF CANADA INC   p185
3950 HENNING DR, BURNABY, BC, V5C 6M2
(604) 294-3077   *SIC* 5251

HOME DEPOT OF CANADA INC   p201
1900 UNITED BLVD SUITE D, COQUITLAM, BC, V3K 6Z1
(604) 540-6277   *SIC* 5251

HOME DEPOT OF CANADA INC   p204
2000 MCPHEE RD, CRANBROOK, BC, V1C 0A3
(250) 420-4250   *SIC* 5251

HOME DEPOT OF CANADA INC   p211
2980 DRINKWATER RD UNIT 1, DUNCAN, BC, V9L 6C6
(250) 737-2360   *SIC* 5251

HOME DEPOT OF CANADA INC   p218
1020 HILLSIDE DR, KAMLOOPS, BC, V2E 2N1
(250) 371-4300   *SIC* 5251

HOME DEPOT OF CANADA INC   p220
2515 ENTERPRISE WAY, KELOWNA, BC, V1X 7K2
(250) 979-4501   *SIC* 5251

HOME DEPOT OF CANADA INC   p226
6550 200 ST, LANGLEY, BC, V2Y 1P2
(604) 514-1788   *SIC* 5251

HOME DEPOT OF CANADA INC   p234
6555 METRAL DR, NANAIMO, BC, V9T 2L9
(250) 390-9093   *SIC* 5251

HOME DEPOT OF CANADA INC   p245
1069 NICOLA AVE, PORT COQUITLAM, BC, V3B 8B2
(604) 468-3360   *SIC* 5251

HOME DEPOT OF CANADA INC   p250
5959 O'GRADY RD, PRINCE GEORGE, BC, V2N 6Z5
(250) 906-3610   *SIC* 5251

HOME DEPOT OF CANADA INC   p255
2700 SWEDEN WAY, RICHMOND, BC, V6V 2W8
(604) 303-7360   *SIC* 5251

HOME DEPOT OF CANADA INC   p274
12701 110 AVE, SURREY, BC, V3V 3J7
(604) 580-2159   *SIC* 5251

HOME DEPOT OF CANADA INC   p279
2525 160 ST, SURREY, BC, V3Z 0C8
(604) 542-3520   *SIC* 5251

HOME DEPOT OF CANADA INC   p293
2388 CAMBIE ST, VANCOUVER, BC, V5Z 2T8
(604) 675-1260   *SIC* 5251

HOME DEPOT OF CANADA INC   p295
900 TERMINAL AVE, VANCOUVER, BC, V6A 4G4
(604) 608-1423   *SIC* 5251

HOME DEPOT OF CANADA INC   p332
5501 ANDERSON WAY, VERNON, BC, V1T 9V1
(250) 550-1600   *SIC* 5251

HOME DEPOT OF CANADA INC   p333
3986 SHELBOURNE ST, VICTORIA, BC, V8N 3E3
(250) 853-5350   *SIC* 5251

HOME DEPOT OF CANADA INC   p340
2400 MILLSTREAM RD, VICTORIA, BC, V9B 3R3
(250) 391-6001   *SIC* 5251

HOME DEPOT OF CANADA INC   p341
840 MAIN ST SUITE E1, WEST VANCOUVER, BC, V7T 2Z3
(604) 913-2630   *SIC* 5251

HOME DEPOT OF CANADA INC   p346
801 18TH ST N, BRANDON, MB, R7A 7S1
(204) 571-3300   *SIC* 5251

HOME DEPOT OF CANADA INC   p362
1590 REGENT AVE W, WINNIPEG, MB,

R2C 3B4
(204) 654-5400   *SIC* 5251

HOME DEPOT OF CANADA INC   p368
1999 BISHOP GRANDIN BLVD, WINNIPEG, MB, R2M 5S1
(204) 253-7649   *SIC* 5251

HOME DEPOT OF CANADA INC   p370
845 LEILA AVE, WINNIPEG, MB, R2V 3J7
(204) 336-5530   *SIC* 5251

HOME DEPOT OF CANADA INC   p382
727 EMPRESS ST, WINNIPEG, MB, R3G 3P5
(204) 779-0703   *SIC* 5251

HOME DEPOT OF CANADA INC   p402
1450 REGENT ST, FREDERICTON, NB, E3C 0A4
(506) 462-9460   *SIC* 5251

HOME DEPOT OF CANADA INC   p407
235 MAPLETON RD, MONCTON, NB, E1C 0G9
(506) 853-8150   *SIC* 5251

HOME DEPOT OF CANADA INC   p413
55 LCD CRT, SAINT JOHN, NB, E2J 5E5
(506) 632-9440   *SIC* 5251

HOME DEPOT OF CANADA INC   p430
70 KELSEY DR, ST. JOHN'S, NL, A1B 5C7
(709) 570-2400   *SIC* 5251

HOME DEPOT OF CANADA INC   p446
40 FINNIAN ROW, DARTMOUTH, NS, B3B 0B6
(902) 460-4700   *SIC* 5251

HOME DEPOT OF CANADA INC   p467
50 SYDNEY PORT ACCESS RD, SYDNEY, NS, B1P 7H2
(902) 564-3250   *SIC* 5251

HOME DEPOT OF CANADA INC   p481
15360 BAYVIEW AVE, AURORA, ON, L4G 7J1
(905) 726-4500   *SIC* 5251

HOME DEPOT OF CANADA INC   p487
10 BARRIE VIEW DR, BARRIE, ON, L4N 8V4
(705) 733-2800   *SIC* 5251

HOME DEPOT OF CANADA INC   p492
210 BELL BLVD, BELLEVILLE, ON, K8P 5L8
(613) 961-5340   *SIC* 5251

HOME DEPOT OF CANADA INC   p497
470 HOLLAND ST W, BRADFORD, ON, L3Z 0A2
(905) 778-2100   *SIC* 5251

HOME DEPOT OF CANADA INC   p497
20 DEPOT DR, BRACEBRIDGE, ON, P1L 0A1
(705) 646-5600   *SIC* 5251

HOME DEPOT OF CANADA INC   p498
60 GREAT LAKES DR, BRAMPTON, ON, L6R 2K7
(905) 792-5430   *SIC* 5251

HOME DEPOT OF CANADA INC   p510
9515 MISSISSAUGA RD, BRAMPTON, ON, L6X 0Z8
(905) 453-3900   *SIC* 5251

HOME DEPOT OF CANADA INC   p514
25 HOLIDAY DR, BRANTFORD, ON, N3R 7J4
(519) 757-3534   *SIC* 5251

HOME DEPOT OF CANADA INC   p540
570 MCNEELY AVE, CARLETON PLACE, ON, K7C 0A7
(613) 253-3870   *SIC* 5251

HOME DEPOT OF CANADA INC   p545
1050 DEPALMA DR, COBOURG, ON, K9A 0A8
(905) 377-7600   *SIC* 5251

HOME DEPOT OF CANADA INC   p579
193 NORTH QUEEN ST, ETOBICOKE, ON, M9C 1A7
(416) 626-9800   *SIC* 5251

HOME DEPOT OF CANADA INC   p585
1983 KIPLING AVE, ETOBICOKE, ON, M9W 4J4
(416) 746-1357   *SIC* 5251

HOME DEPOT OF CANADA INC   p595

1616 CYRVILLE RD, GLOUCESTER, ON, K1B 3L8
(613) 744-1700   *SIC* 5251

HOME DEPOT OF CANADA INC   p603
63 WOODLAWN RD W, GUELPH, ON, N1H 1G8
(519) 780-3400   *SIC* 5251

HOME DEPOT OF CANADA INC   p608
350 CENTENNIAL PKY N, HAMILTON, ON, L8E 2X4
(905) 561-9755   *SIC* 5251

HOME DEPOT OF CANADA INC   p626
10 FRANK NIGHBOR PL SUITE FRNT, KANATA, ON, K2V 1B9
(613) 271-7577   *SIC* 5251

HOME DEPOT OF CANADA INC   p632
606 GARDINERS RD, KINGSTON, ON, K7M 3X9
(613) 384-3511   *SIC* 5251

HOME DEPOT OF CANADA INC   p641
100 GATEWAY PARK DR, KITCHENER, ON, N2P 2J4
(519) 650-3900   *SIC* 5251

HOME DEPOT OF CANADA INC   p651
448 CLARKE RD, LONDON, ON, N5W 6H1
(519) 457-5800   *SIC* 5251

HOME DEPOT OF CANADA INC   p660
3035 WONDERLAND RD S, LONDON, ON, N6L 1R4
(519) 691-1400   *SIC* 5251

HOME DEPOT OF CANADA INC   p671
3155 HIGHWAY 7 E, MARKHAM, ON, L3R 0T9
(905) 940-5900   *SIC* 5251

HOME DEPOT OF CANADA INC   p679
1201 CASTLEMORE AVE, MARKHAM, ON, L6E 0G5
(905) 201-5500   *SIC* 5251

HOME DEPOT OF CANADA INC   p683
1013 MAPLE AVE, MILTON, ON, L9T 0A5
(905) 864-1200   *SIC* 5251

HOME DEPOT OF CANADA INC   p711
3065 MAVIS RD, MISSISSAUGA, ON, L5C 1T7
(905) 281-6230   *SIC* 5251

HOME DEPOT OF CANADA INC   p723
2920 ARGENTIA RD, MISSISSAUGA, ON, L5N 8C5
(905) 814-3860   *SIC* 5251

HOME DEPOT OF CANADA INC   p731
650 MATHESON BLVD W, MISSISSAUGA, ON, L5R 3T2
SIC 5251

HOME DEPOT OF CANADA INC   p755
17850 YONGE ST, NEWMARKET, ON, L3Y 8S1
(905) 898-0090   *SIC* 5251

HOME DEPOT OF CANADA INC   p763
1275 SEYMOUR ST, NORTH BAY, ON, P1B 9V6
(705) 845-2300   *SIC* 5251

HOME DEPOT OF CANADA INC   p779
1 CONCORDE GATE SUITE 900, NORTH YORK, ON, M3C 4H9
(416) 609-0852   *SIC* 5251

HOME DEPOT OF CANADA INC   p783
2375 STEELES AVE W, NORTH YORK, ON, M3J 3A8
(416) 664-9800   *SIC* 5251

HOME DEPOT OF CANADA INC   p786
90 BILLY BISHOP WAY, NORTH YORK, ON, M3K 2C8
(416) 373-6000   *SIC* 5251

HOME DEPOT OF CANADA INC   p791
825 CALEDONIA RD, NORTH YORK, ON, M6B 3X8
(416) 780-4730   *SIC* 5251

HOME DEPOT OF CANADA INC   p795
2233 SHEPPARD AVE W, NORTH YORK, ON, M9M 2Z7
SIC 5251

HOME DEPOT OF CANADA INC   p797
2555 BRISTOL CIR, OAKVILLE, ON, L6H 5W9

(905) 829-5900   *SIC* 5251
HOME DEPOT OF CANADA INC   *p800*
99 CROSS AVE, OAKVILLE, ON, L6J 2W7
(905) 815-5000   *SIC* 5251
HOME DEPOT OF CANADA INC   *p804*
3300 SOUTH SERVICE RD W, OAKVILLE, ON, L6L 0B1
(905) 469-7110   *SIC* 5251
HOME DEPOT OF CANADA INC   *p808*
49 FOURTH AVE, ORANGEVILLE, ON, L9W 1G7
(519) 940-9061   *SIC* 5251
HOME DEPOT OF CANADA INC   *p811*
2121 TENTH LINE RD SUITE 1, ORLEANS, ON, K4A 4C5
(613) 590-2030   *SIC* 5251
HOME DEPOT OF CANADA INC   *p826*
2056 BANK ST, OTTAWA, ON, K1V 7Z8
(613) 739-5300   *SIC* 5251
HOME DEPOT OF CANADA INC   *p835*
1590 20TH AVE E, OWEN SOUND, ON, N4K 5N3
(519) 372-3970   *SIC* 5251
HOME DEPOT OF CANADA INC   *p838*
27 ROBINSON LANE, PEMBROKE, ON, K8A 0A5
(613) 732-6550   *SIC* 5251
HOME DEPOT OF CANADA INC   *p843*
1105A KINGSTON RD, PICKERING, ON, L1V 1B5
(905) 421-2000   *SIC* 5251
HOME DEPOT OF CANADA INC   *p852*
50 RED MAPLE RD, RICHMOND HILL, ON, L4B 4K1
(905) 763-2311   *SIC* 5251
HOME DEPOT OF CANADA INC   *p857*
1706 ELGIN MILLS RD E, RICHMOND HILL, ON, L4S 1M6
(905) 787-7200   *SIC* 5251
HOME DEPOT OF CANADA INC   *p858*
1350 QUINN DR, SARNIA, ON, N7S 6L5
(519) 333-2300   *SIC* 5251
HOME DEPOT OF CANADA INC   *p862*
530 GREAT NORTHERN RD, SAULT STE. MARIE, ON, P6B 4Z9
(705) 254-1150   *SIC* 5251
HOME DEPOT OF CANADA INC   *p864*
60 GRAND MARSHALL DR, SCARBOROUGH, ON, M1B 5N6
(416) 283-3166   *SIC* 5251
HOME DEPOT OF CANADA INC   *p884*
20 YMCA DR, ST CATHARINES, ON, L2N 7R6
(905) 937-5900   *SIC* 5251
HOME DEPOT OF CANADA INC   *p899*
1500 MARCUS DR, SUDBURY, ON, P3B 4K5
(705) 525-2960   *SIC* 5251
HOME DEPOT OF CANADA INC   *p908*
359 MAIN ST, THUNDER BAY, ON, P7B 5L6
(807) 624-1100   *SIC* 5251
HOME DEPOT OF CANADA INC   *p913*
2143 RIVERSIDE DR, TIMMINS, ON, P4R 0A1
(705) 360-8750   *SIC* 5251
HOME DEPOT OF CANADA INC   *p918*
101 WICKSTEED AVE, TORONTO, ON, M4G 4H9
(416) 467-2300   *SIC* 5251
HOME DEPOT OF CANADA INC   *p993*
2121 ST CLAIR AVE W, TORONTO, ON, M6N 5A8
(416) 766-2800   *SIC* 5251
HOME DEPOT OF CANADA INC   *p1014*
1700 VICTORIA ST E, WHITBY, ON, L1N 9K6
(905) 571-5900   *SIC* 5251
HOME DEPOT OF CANADA INC   *p1018*
6570 TECUMSEH RD E, WINDSOR, ON, N8T 1E6
(519) 974-5420   *SIC* 5251
HOME DEPOT OF CANADA INC   *p1020*
1925 DIVISION RD, WINDSOR, ON, N8W 1Z7

(519) 967-3700   *SIC* 5251
HOME DEPOT OF CANADA INC   *p1031*
140 NORTHVIEW BLVD, WOODBRIDGE, ON, L4L 8T2
(905) 851-1800   *SIC* 5251
HOME DEPOT OF CANADA INC   *p1036*
901 JULIANA DR, WOODSTOCK, ON, N4V 1B9
(519) 421-5500   *SIC* 5251
HOME DEPOT OF CANADA INC   *p1049*
11300 RUE RENAUDE-LAPOINTE, ANJOU, QC, H1J 2V7
(514) 356-3650   *SIC* 5251
HOME DEPOT OF CANADA INC   *p1062*
2400 BOUL DU FAUBOURG, BOISBRIAND, QC, J7H 1S3
(450) 971-6061   *SIC* 5251
HOME DEPOT OF CANADA INC   *p1111*
165 RUE SIMONDS N, GRANBY, QC, J2J 0R7
(450) 375-5544   *SIC* 5251
HOME DEPOT OF CANADA INC   *p1112*
500 AV AUGUSTE, GREENFIELD PARK, QC, J4V 3R4
(450) 462-5020   *SIC* 5251
HOME DEPOT OF CANADA INC   *p1138*
500 RUE DE LA CONCORDE, LEVIS, QC, G6W 8A8
(418) 834-7050   *SIC* 5251
HOME DEPOT OF CANADA INC   *p1226*
1000 RUE SAUVE O BUREAU 1000, MONTREAL, QC, H4N 3L5
(514) 333-6868   *SIC* 5251
HOME DEPOT OF CANADA INC   *p1235*
1400 BOUL LE CORBUSIER, MONTREAL, QC, H7N 6J5
(450) 680-2225   *SIC* 5251
HOME DEPOT OF CANADA INC   *p1250*
185 BOUL HYMUS, POINTE-CLAIRE, QC, H9R 1E9
(514) 630-8631   *SIC* 5251
HOME DEPOT OF CANADA INC   *p1295*
901 RUE DE L'ETANG, SAINT-BRUNO, QC, J3V 6N8
(450) 461-2000   *SIC* 5251
HOME DEPOT OF CANADA INC   *p1298*
490 VOIE DE LA DESSERTE, SAINT-CONSTANT, QC, J5A 2S6
(450) 633-2030   *SIC* 5251
HOME DEPOT OF CANADA INC   *p1320*
1045 BOUL DU GRAND-HERON, SAINT-JEROME, QC, J7Y 3P2
(450) 565-6020   *SIC* 5251
HOME DEPOT OF CANADA INC   *p1373*
1355 BOUL DU PLATEAU-SAINT-JOSEPH, SHERBROOKE, QC, J1L 3E2
(819) 348-4481   *SIC* 5251
HOME DEPOT OF CANADA INC   *p1394*
55 BOUL DE LA CITE-DES-JEUNES, VAUDREUIL-DORION, QC, J7V 8C1
(450) 510-2600   *SIC* 5251
HOME DEPOT OF CANADA INC   *p1398*
160 BOUL ARTHABASKA O, VICTORIAVILLE, QC, G6S 0P2
(819) 752-0700   *SIC* 5251
HOME DEPOT OF CANADA INC   *p1416*
1867 E VICTORIA AVE, REGINA, SK, S4N 6E6
(306) 761-1919   *SIC* 5251
HOME DEPOT OF CANADA INC   *p1423*
1030 N PASQUA ST, REGINA, SK, S4X 4V3
(306) 564-5700   *SIC* 5251
HOME DEPOT OF CANADA INC   *p1427*
707 CIRCLE DR E, SASKATOON, SK, S7K 0V1
(306) 651-6250   *SIC* 5251
HOME DEPOT OF CANADA INC   *p1435*
3043 CLARENCE AVE S SUITE 1, SASKATOON, SK, S7T 0B5
(306) 657-4100   *SIC* 5251
HOME HARDWARE BUILDING CENTRE   *p213*
9820 108 ST, FORT ST. JOHN, BC, V1J 0A7
(250) 787-0371   *SIC* 5251

HOME LUMBER INC   *p868*
714 BIRCHMOUNT RD, SCARBOROUGH, ON, M1K 1R4
(416) 759-4441   *SIC* 5251
INDEXABLE CUTTING TOOLS OF CANADA LIMITED   *p1011*
66 CLARK ST, WELLAND, ON, L3B 5W6
(905) 735-8665   *SIC* 5251
INTERNATIONAL MINICUT INC   *p1049*
8400 BOUL DU GOLF, ANJOU, QC, H1J 3A1
(514) 352-6464   *SIC* 5251
INVESTISSEMENT CRB INC   *p1066*
585 CH DE TOURAINE, BOUCHERVILLE, QC, J4B 5E4
(450) 655-1340   *SIC* 5251
JEMARICA INC   *p857*
9040 COUNTY ROAD 17 SUITE 623, ROCKLAND, ON, K4K 1V5
(613) 446-4410   *SIC* 5251
JOBAL INDUSTRIES LIMITED   *p499*
2 EDVAC DR, BRAMPTON, ON, L6S 5P2
(905) 799-8555   *SIC* 5251
JUUSOLA, JACK SALES LTD   *p218*
1441 HILLSIDE DR, KAMLOOPS, BC, V2E 1A9
(250) 374-3115   *SIC* 5251
K & J PECK SALES LTD   *p420*
388 CONNELL ST, WOODSTOCK, NB, E7M 5G9
(506) 328-3353   *SIC* 5251
K. M. S. TOOLS & EQUIPMENT LTD   *p201*
110 WOOLRIDGE ST, COQUITLAM, BC, V3K 5V4
(604) 522-5599   *SIC* 5251
KELLY, JIM BUILDING MATERIALS LTD *p82*
4221 50 ST, DRAYTON VALLEY, AB, T7A 1S1
(780) 542-4044   *SIC* 5251
LANCASHIRE SAW SALES & SERVICE (CANADA) LTD   *p1420*
2413 6TH AVE SUITE 306, REGINA, SK, S4R 1B5
(306) 565-0033   *SIC* 5251
LEE VALLEY TOOLS LTD   *p832*
1090 MORRISON DR, OTTAWA, ON, K2H 1C2
(613) 596-0350   *SIC* 5251
LEGER, D L SALES INC   *p619*
1525 CAMERON ST, HAWKESBURY, ON, K6A 3R3
(613) 632-3399   *SIC* 5251
LEGRESLEY, FRANCOIS LTEE/LTD   *p410*
790 RUE PRINCIPALE, NEGUAC, NB, E9G 1N5
(506) 776-8334   *SIC* 5251
LEROUX, SYLVAIN M. ENTREPRISES LTD *p1220*
1500 AV ATWATER BUREAU G, MONTREAL, QC, H3Z 1X5
(514) 939-1820   *SIC* 5251
MARTINEAU, REAL INC   *p1287*
10 BOUL BOUTHILLIER, ROSEMERE, QC, J7A 4B4
(450) 437-2007   *SIC* 5251
MCDONALD, PHIL ENTERPRISES LTD *p1006*
400 WEBER ST N, WATERLOO, ON, N2J 3J3
(519) 885-1050   *SIC* 5251
MEADOW LAKE HOME HARDWARE BUILDING CENTRE LTD   *p1410*
802 1ST ST W, MEADOW LAKE, SK, S9X 1E2
(306) 236-4467   *SIC* 5251
METRO HARDWARE & MAINTENANCE INC *p784*
72 MARTIN ROSS AVE, NORTH YORK, ON, M3J 2L4
(416) 633-4293   *SIC* 5251
MICHEL THIBAUDEAU INC   *p1111*
70 RUE SIMONDS N, GRANBY, QC, J2J 2L1
(450) 378-9884   *SIC* 5251

MILLS-ROY ENTERPRISES LIMITED   *p591*
240 GARRISON RD, FORT ERIE, ON, L2A 1M7
(905) 871-8081   *SIC* 5251
MILTON HARDWARE & BUILDING SUPPLIES LTD   *p684*
385 STEELES AVE E, MILTON, ON, L9T 3G6
(905) 878-9222   *SIC* 5251
MINDEN HARDWARE LTD   *p685*
16 BOBCAYGION RD, MINDEN, ON, K0M 2K0
(705) 286-1351   *SIC* 5251
MISTEREL INC   *p562*
201 NINTH ST E, CORNWALL, ON, K6H 2V1
(613) 933-0592   *SIC* 5251
NELSON BUILDING CENTRE LTD   *p236*
101 MCDONALD DR, NELSON, BC, V1L 6B9
(250) 352-1919   *SIC* 5251
NEW WORLD TECHNOLOGIES INCORPORATED   *p177*
30580 PROGRESSIVE WAY, ABBOTSFORD, BC, V2T 6Z2
(604) 852-0405   *SIC* 5251
NORTHERN HARDWARE & FURNITURE CO., LTD   *p249*
1386 3RD AVE, PRINCE GEORGE, BC, V2L 3E9
(250) 563-7161   *SIC* 5251
NORTHERN METALIC SALES (G.P.) LTD *p133*
9708 108 ST, GRANDE PRAIRIE, AB, T8V 4E2
(780) 539-9555   *SIC* 5251
ONWARD CLUTHE HARDWARE PRODUCTS INC   *p635*
10 CENTENNIAL RD, KITCHENER, ON, N2B 3G1
(519) 742-8446   *SIC* 5251
ORILLIA BUILDING SUPPLIES (2001) LIMITED   *p809*
5 KING ST, ORILLIA, ON, L3V 1R2
(705) 326-7371   *SIC* 5251
OUTILLEUR S.E.C., L'   *p1314*
236 RUE SAINTE-GENEVIEVE, SAINT-ISIDORE, QC, G0S 2S0
(418) 882-5656   *SIC* 5251
OUTILS A. RICHARD CO   *p1057*
120 RUE JACQUES-CARTIER, BERTHIERVILLE, QC, J0K 1A0
(450) 836-3766   *SIC* 5251
PEAVEY INDUSTRIES LIMITED   *p156*
7740 40 AVE, RED DEER, AB, T4P 2H9
(403) 346-8991   *SIC* 5251
PEMBINA CONSUMERS CO-OP (2000) LTD *p357*
61 MAIN ST, ST LEON, MB, R0G 2E0
(204) 744-2228   *SIC* 5251
PENNER BUILDING CENTRE AND BUILDERS SUPPLIES LIMITED   *p1004*
700 PENNER ST, VIRGIL, ON, L0S 1T0
(905) 468-3242   *SIC* 5251
PENNY POWER HARDWARE LTD   *p356*
917 MANITOBA AVE, SELKIRK, MB, R1A 3T7
(204) 785-2773   *SIC* 5251
PRESTON HARDWARE (1980) LIMITED *p825*
248 PRESTON ST UNIT 234, OTTAWA, ON, K1R 7R4
(613) 230-7166   *SIC* 5251
PRINCESS AUTO LTD   *p363*
475 PANET RD, WINNIPEG, MB, R2C 2Z1
(204) 667-4630   *SIC* 5251
PRINCESS GROUP INC   *p363*
475 PANET RD, WINNIPEG, MB, R2C 2Z1
(204) 667-4630   *SIC* 5251
PRO BUILDERS LTD   *p244*
150 FAIRVIEW PL, PENTICTON, BC, V2A 6A5
(250) 493-7844   *SIC* 5251
PROUDFOOTS INCORPORATED   *p466*

130 VISTA DR, STELLARTON, NS, B0K 0A2
(902) 752-1500 *SIC 5251*

PROUDFOOTS INCORPORATED *p466*
130 VISTA DR, STELLARTON, NS, B0K 1S0
(902) 752-4600 *SIC 5251*

QUAD CITY BUILDING MATERIALS LTD
p204
1901 MCPHEE RD, CRANBROOK, BC, V1C
7J2
(250) 426-6288 *SIC 5251*

QUINCAILLERIE NOTRE-DAME DE ST-HENRI INC *p1215*
2371 RUE NOTRE-DAME O BUREAU 1,
MONTREAL, QC, H3J 1N3
(514) 932-5616 *SIC 5251*

R. B. BELL (SUPPLIES) LIMITED *p500*
2850 QUEEN ST E, BRAMPTON, ON, L6S
6E8
(905) 792-9301 *SIC 5251*

RATTRAY, WILLIAM HOLDINGS LTD *p760*
3770 MONTROSE RD, NIAGARA FALLS,
ON, L2H 3C8
(905) 354-3848 *SIC 5251*

REDDEN, C. I. LTD *p442*
50 EMPIRE LANE, CURRYS CORNER, NS,
B0N 2T0
(902) 798-3222 *SIC 5251*

RENO-VALLEE INC *p1046*
358 BOUL SAINT-BENOIT O, AMQUI, QC,
G5J 2G3
(418) 629-3800 *SIC 5251*

ROCH GAUTHIER ET FILS INC *p1350*
68 RUE SAINTE-CATHERINE, SAINT-POLYCARPE, QC, J0P 1X0
(450) 265-3256 *SIC 5251*

RON DITTBERNER LTD *p195*
1444 ISLAND HWY, CAMPBELL RIVER,
BC, V9W 8C9
(250) 286-0122 *SIC 5251*

RONA INC *p129*
8408 MANNING AVE, FORT MCMURRAY,
AB, T9H 5G2
(780) 743-4666 *SIC 5251*

RONA INC *p1226*
1011 RUE DU MARCHE-CENTRAL, MON-TREAL, QC, H4N 3J6
(514) 385-6888 *SIC 5251*

RONA INC *p1237*
1505 BOUL LE CORBUSIER, MONTREAL,
QC, H7S 1Z3
(450) 682-2220 *SIC 5251*

RONA INC *p1262*
999 RUE DU MARAIS, QUEBEC, QC, G1M
3T9
(418) 688-2220 *SIC 5251*

ROSBACK, R A ENTERPRISES LTD *p248*
1700 BROUGHTON BLVD, PORT MC-NEILL, BC, V0N 2R0
(250) 956-3323 *SIC 5251*

SHERWOOD HARDWARE LTD *p1040*
115 ST. PETERS RD, CHARLOTTETOWN,
PE, C1A 5P3
(902) 892-8509 *SIC 5251*

SIMPSON, S. B. GROUP INC *p526*
3210 MAINWAY, BURLINGTON, ON, L7M
1A5
(905) 335-6575 *SIC 5251*

**SOCIETE COOPERATIVE AGRICOLE DE
LA RIVIERE-DU-SUD** *p1377*
34 CH SAINT-FRANCOIS O, ST-FRANCOIS-DE-LA-RIVIERE-DU-S, QC,
G0R 3A0
(418) 259-7715 *SIC 5251*

**SOCIETE COOPERATIVE AGRICOLE DES
APPALACHES** *p1133*
156 RUE GRENIER, LAURIERVILLE, QC,
G0S 1P0
(819) 365-4372 *SIC 5251*

STEGG LIMITED *p492*
294 UNIVERSITY AVE, BELLEVILLE, ON,
K8N 5S6
(613) 966-4000 *SIC 5251*

TCB TRI-CITIES BUILDERS SUPPLY LTD
p223

1650 SPRINGFIELD RD, KELOWNA, BC,
V1Y 5V4
(250) 763-5040 *SIC 5251*

TEAHEN, R & R BUILDING SUPPLIES LTD
p859
1272 LONDON RD SUITE 1707, SARNIA,
ON, N7S 1P5
(519) 337-3783 *SIC 5251*

THORBURN FLEX INC *p1252*
173 AV ONEIDA, POINTE-CLAIRE, QC,
H9R 1A9
(514) 695-8710 *SIC 5251*

TREVOR J LOWE INC *p596*
2010 OGILVIE RD, GLOUCESTER, ON, K1J
8X3
(613) 748-0637 *SIC 5251*

TROUNCY INC *p535*
200 FRANKLIN BLVD SUITE 16A, CAM-BRIDGE, ON, N1R 8N8
(519) 623-2361 *SIC 5251*

TSC STORES L.P. *p650*
1000 CLARKE RD, LONDON, ON, N5V 3A9
(519) 453-5270 *SIC 5251*

TURNER, GRANT C. T. ENTERPRISES INC
p332
SUITE 345 4900 27 ST, VERNON, BC, V1T
7G7
(250) 549-2131 *SIC 5251*

UNIROPE LIMITED *p703*
3070 UNIVERSAL DR, MISSISSAUGA, ON,
L4X 2C8
(905) 624-5131 *SIC 5251*

VELANOFF, JACK HOLDINGS LIMITED
p560
3200 RUTHERFORD RD SUITE 653, CON-CORD, ON, L4K 5R3
(905) 303-9148 *SIC 5251*

VOLUMAT INC *p1391*
1716 CH SULLIVAN, VAL-D'OR, QC, J9P
1M5
(819) 825-3070 *SIC 5251*

WILD'S TIMBER CONTRACTORS LTD *p168*
HIGHWAY 584 W, SUNDRE, AB, T0M 1X0
(403) 638-3508 *SIC 5251*

---

*SIC 5261 Retail nurseries and garden
stores*

1044912 ONTARIO LIMITED *p843*
2215 BROCK RD N, PICKERING, ON, L1V
2R4
(905) 683-5952 *SIC 5261*

5517509 MANITOBA LTD *p346*
1329 ROSSER AVE E, BRANDON, MB,
R7A 7J2
(204) 728-7540 *SIC 5261*

9260-8553 QUEBEC INC *p1119*
6029 BOUL WILFRID-HAMEL,
L'ANCIENNE-LORETTE, QC, G2E 2H3
(418) 872-9705 *SIC 5261*

ANGELO'S GARDEN CENTRE LIMITED
p548
1801 HIGHWAY 7, CONCORD, ON, L4K
1V4
(905) 669-9220 *SIC 5261*

ARRK CANADA HOLDINGS, INC *p1004*
17 ELM DR S, WALLACEBURG, ON, N8A
5E8
(519) 627-6078 *SIC 5261*

BERGER PEAT MOSS ENR *p395*
149 BAY DU VIN RIVER RD, BAY DU VIN,
NB, E1N 5P4
(800) 463-5582 *SIC 5261*

BLYLEVEN ENTERPRISES INC *p836*
363 GOVERNORS RD E, PARIS, ON, N3L
3E1
(519) 752-4436 *SIC 5261*

BRADFORD GREENHOUSES LIMITED *p883*
4346 HWY 90, SPRINGWATER, ON, L9X
1T7
(705) 725-9913 *SIC 5261*

CANADA GARDENWORKS LTD *p184*
6250 LOUGHEED HWY, BURNABY, BC,
V5B 2Z9

(604) 299-0621 *SIC 5261*

CANNOR NURSERIES (1989) LTD *p174*
34261 MARSHALL RD, ABBOTSFORD, BC,
V2S 1L8
SIC 5261

CAVENDISH AGRI SERVICES LIMITED *p397*
100 MIDLAND DR, DIEPPE, NB, E1A 6X4
(506) 858-7777 *SIC 5261*

**DAVEY TREE EXPERT CO. OF CANADA,
LIMITED** *p233*
13 VICTORIA CRES SUITE 20, NANAIMO,
BC, V9R 5B9
(250) 755-1288 *SIC 5261*

DEVRY GREENHOUSES (1989) LTD *p196*
49259 CASTLEMAN RD, CHILLIWACK, BC,
V2P 6H4
(604) 794-3874 *SIC 5261*

**EDDI'S WHOLESALE GARDEN SUPPLIES
LTD** *p229*
5744 268 ST, LANGLEY, BC, V4W 0B2
(604) 607-4447 *SIC 5261*

G-MAC'S AGTEAM INC *p1408*
908 MAIN ST, KINDERSLEY, SK, S0L 1S0
(306) 463-4769 *SIC 5261*

**GREENLAND NURSERY & LANDSCAPING
LTD** *p161*
23108 16 HWY, SHERWOOD PARK, AB,
T8A 4V2
(780) 467-7557 *SIC 5261*

HOME DEPOT OF CANADA INC *p809*
3225 MONARCH DR, ORILLIA, ON, L3V
7Z4
(705) 327-6500 *SIC 5261*

JARDINERIE FERNAND FORTIER INC, LA
p1254
99 116 RTE E, PRINCEVILLE, QC, G6L 4K6
(819) 364-5009 *SIC 5261*

LYONS LANDSCAPING LTD *p218*
1271 SALISH RD, KAMLOOPS, BC, V2H
1P6
(250) 374-6965 *SIC 5261*

MANDERLEY TURF PRODUCTS INC *p130*
55403 RANGE RD 222, FORT
SASKATCHEWAN, AB, T8L 2N9
(780) 998-1995 *SIC 5261*

MOUNTAINVIEW TURF FARM LTD *p1281*
4790 5E CONC, QUYON, QC, J0X 2V0
(819) 458-2632 *SIC 5261*

MUD BAY NURSERIES LTD *p279*
4391 KING GEORGE BLVD, SURREY, BC,
V3Z 1G6
(604) 596-9201 *SIC 5261*

MUNRO FARM SUPPLIES LTD *p355*
GD LCD MAIN, PORTAGE LA PRAIRIE, MB,
R1N 3A7
(204) 857-8741 *SIC 5261*

NUTRIEN AG SOLUTIONS (CANADA) INC
p1422
2625 VICTORIA AVE 6TH FL, REGINA, SK,
S4T 1Z8
(306) 569-4379 *SIC 5261*

PEPINIERE CHARLEVOIX INC *p1122*
2375 BOUL DE COMPORTE, LA MALBAIE,
QC, G5A 3C6
(418) 439-4646 *SIC 5261*

PEPINIERE PIERREFONDS INC *p1290*
11409 BOUL GOUIN O, ROXBORO, QC,
H8Y 1X7
(514) 684-5051 *SIC 5261*

POTTERS FARM & NURSERY INC *p279*
19158 48 AVE, SURREY, BC, V3Z 1B2
(604) 576-5011 *SIC 5261*

PRAIRIE SOIL SERVICES LTD *p1412*
1 MILE W HWY 49, NORQUAY, SK, S0A
2V0
(306) 594-2330 *SIC 5261*

REDFERN FARM SERVICES LTD *p347*
922 DOUGLAS ST, BRANDON, MB, R7A
7B2
(204) 725-8580 *SIC 5261*

RITCHIE FEED & SEED INC *p595*
1390 WINDMILL LANE, GLOUCESTER,
ON, K1B 4V5
(613) 741-4430 *SIC 5261*

SHERIDAN NURSERIES LIMITED *p594*
12302 TENTH LINE, GEORGETOWN, ON,
L7G 4S7
(905) 873-0522 *SIC 5261*

VAN DONGEN LANDSCAPING & NURS-ERIES LTD *p620*
6750 TRAFALGAR RD SUITE 1, HORNBY,
ON, L0P 1E0
(905) 878-1105 *SIC 5261*

VANDERMEER NURSERY LTD *p475*
588 LAKE RIDGE RD S SUITE 1, AJAX,
ON, L1Z 1X3
(905) 427-2525 *SIC 5261*

VESEY'S SEEDS LTD *p1043*
411 YORK RD, YORK, PE, C0A 1P0
(902) 368-7333 *SIC 5261*

WIMCO NURSERIES LTD *p246*
1300 DOMINION AVE, PORT COQUITLAM,
BC, V3B 8G7
(604) 942-7518 *SIC 5261*

SIC 5271 Mobile home dealers

JANDEL HOMES *p132*
9407 153 AVE, GRANDE PRAIRIE, AB, T8V
0B6
(780) 402-3170 *SIC 5271*

N R MOTORS LTD *p249*
805 1ST AVE, PRINCE GEORGE, BC, V2L
2Y4
(250) 563-8891 *SIC 5271*

WILLIAMS SCOTSMAN OF CANADA INC *p2*
9529 266 ST, ACHESON, AB, T7X 6H9
(780) 638-9210 *SIC 5271*

SIC 5311 Department stores

A B C COMPANY LIMITED *p570*
123 FOURTH ST, ETOBICOKE, ON, M8V
2Y6
(905) 812-5941 *SIC 5311*

A. SETLAKWE LIMITEE *p1382*
188 RUE NOTRE-DAME O, THETFORD
MINES, QC, G6G 1J6
(418) 335-9121 *SIC 5311*

ARMY & NAVY DEPT. STORE LIMITED *p236*
502 COLUMBIA ST, NEW WESTMINSTER,
BC, V3L 1B1
(604) 526-4661 *SIC 5311*

ARMY & NAVY DEPT. STORE LIMITED *p296*
27 HASTINGS ST W SUITE 25, VANCOU-VER, BC, V6B 1G5
(604) 682-6644 *SIC 5311*

ARMY & NAVY DEPT. STORE LIMITED *p296*
74 CORDOVA ST W, VANCOUVER, BC,
V6B 1C9
(604) 683-9660 *SIC 5311*

BPSR CORPORATION *p570*
123 FOURTH ST, ETOBICOKE, ON, M8V
2Y6
(905) 999-9999 *SIC 5311*

BYLES, A. S. SUPPLIES LIMITED *p393*
1711 KENASTON BLVD, WINNIPEG, MB,
R3Y 1V5
(204) 269-9630 *SIC 5311*

CANADIAN TEST CASE 172 *p720*
6750 CENTURY AVE SUITE 305, MISSIS-SAUGA, ON, L5N 0B7
SIC 5311

CANTIN, DENIS R LTEE *p1235*
1450 BOUL LE CORBUSIER, MONTREAL,
QC, H7N 6J5
(450) 682-9922 *SIC 5311*

COMPUTER TRENDS CANADA *p34*
5738 BURBANK CRES SE, CALGARY, AB,
T2H 1Z6
SIC 5311

COSTCO WHOLESALE CANADA LTD *p567*
18182 YONGE ST, EAST GWILLIMBURY,
ON, L9N 0J3
(905) 954-4733 *SIC 5311*

DAND AUTO PARTS LIMITED *p39*

9940 MACLEOD TRAIL SE SUITE 3, CALGARY, AB, T2J 3K9

(403) 278-4040   *SIC* 5311

DOTY, RONALD T. LIMITED   p496
HWY 118 W, BRACEBRIDGE, ON, P1L 1V4

(705) 645-5261   *SIC* 5311

E.D.M. LASALLE INC   p1130
7427 BOUL NEWMAN BUREAU 36, LASALLE, QC, H8N 1X3

(514) 365-6633   *SIC* 5311

ENTREPRISES FRANCOIS BRIEN LTEE, LES   p1070
9900 BOUL LEDUC BUREAU 643, BROSSARD, QC, J4Y 0B4

(450) 443-0005   *SIC* 5311

ENTREPRISES JACQUES CARIGNAN LTEE, LES   p1104
700 BOUL MALONEY O, GATINEAU, QC, J8T 8K7

(819) 246-1234   *SIC* 5311

FRENETTE, GEFFREY LTEE   p1282
115 BOUL BRIEN, REPENTIGNY, QC, J6A 8J3

(450) 585-9840   *SIC* 5311

GESTION ALAIN LAFOREST INC   p1045
50 BOUL SAINT-LUC, ALMA, QC, G8B 6K1

(418) 662-6618   *SIC* 5311

GESTION JEAN PAQUETTE INC   p1255
705 RUE CLEMENCEAU BUREAU 184, QUEBEC, QC, G1C 7T9

(418) 663-4334   *SIC* 5311

GESTION M.L.B. CARDINAL LTEE   p1059
500 BOUL DE LA SEIGNEURIE O BUREAU 649, BLAINVILLE, QC, J7C 5T7

(450) 419-4700   *SIC* 5311

GESTION MICHAEL ROSSY LTEE   p1326
450 BOUL LEBEAU, SAINT-LAURENT, QC, H4N 1R7

(514) 335-6255   *SIC* 5311

GESTION RENE J. BEAUDOIN INC   p1170
2225 BOUL CREMAZIE E, MONTREAL, QC, H1Z 4N4

(514) 729-1861   *SIC* 5311

GESTIONS REJEAN POITRAS INC, LES
p1394
50 BOUL DE LA CITE-DES-JEUNES BUREAU 646, VAUDREUIL-DORION, QC, J7V 9L5

(450) 424-2744   *SIC* 5311

GIANT TIGER STORES LIMITED   p818
2480 WALKLEY RD, OTTAWA, ON, K1G 6A9

(613) 521-8222   *SIC* 5311

GRANITE DEPARTMENT STORE INC p433
681 TOPSAIL RD, ST. JOHN'S, NL, A1E 2E3

(709) 368-2416   *SIC* 5311

HOLT, RENFREW & CIE, LIMITEE   p305
737 DUNSMUIR ST, VANCOUVER, BC, V6C 1N5

(604) 681-3121   *SIC* 5311

HONEST ED'S LIMITED   p989
581 BLOOR ST W SUITE 1, TORONTO, ON, M6G 1K3

(416) 537-1574   *SIC* 5311

HOPE DISTRIBUTION & SALES INC p245
2125 HAWKINS ST SUITE 609, PORT COQUITLAM, BC, V3B 0G6

(604) 468-6951   *SIC* 5311

HUDSON'S BAY COMPANY   p8
2525 36 ST NE, CALGARY, AB, T1Y 5T4

(403) 261-0759   *SIC* 5311

HUDSON'S BAY COMPANY   p8
3333 SUNRIDGE WAY NE, CALGARY, AB, T1Y 7H5

SIC 5311

HUDSON'S BAY COMPANY   p35
6455 MACLEOD TRAIL SW, CALGARY, AB, T2H 0K8

(403) 255-6121   *SIC* 5311

HUDSON'S BAY COMPANY   p39
100 ANDERSON RD SE, CALGARY, AB, T2J 3V1

(403) 278-9520   *SIC* 5311

HUDSON'S BAY COMPANY   p51

200 8 AVE SW, CALGARY, AB, T2P 1B5

(403) 262-0345   *SIC* 5311

HUDSON'S BAY COMPANY   p71
3625 SHAGANAPPI TRAIL NW, CALGARY, AB, T3A 0E2

(403) 286-1220   *SIC* 5311

HUDSON'S BAY COMPANY   p84
1 LONDONDERRY MALL NW UNIT 86, EDMONTON, AB, T5C 3C8

(780) 478-2931   *SIC* 5311

HUDSON'S BAY COMPANY   p85
650 KINGSWAY GARDEN MALL NW, EDMONTON, AB, T5G 3E6

(780) 479-7100   *SIC* 5311

HUDSON'S BAY COMPANY   p104
8882 170 ST NW SUITE 1001, EDMONTON, AB, T5T 3J7

(780) 444-1550   *SIC* 5311

HUDSON'S BAY COMPANY   p119
150 SOUTHGATE SHOPPING CTR NW, EDMONTON, AB, T6H 4M7

(780) 435-9211   *SIC* 5311

HUDSON'S BAY COMPANY   p120
9738 19 AVE NW, EDMONTON, AB, T6N 1K6

(780) 414-5850   *SIC* 5311

HUDSON'S BAY COMPANY   p142
200 4 AVE S SUITE 200, LETHBRIDGE, AB, T1J 4C9

(403) 329-3131   *SIC* 5311

HUDSON'S BAY COMPANY   p146
3292 DUNMORE RD SE SUITE F7, MEDICINE HAT, AB, T1B 2R4

(403) 526-7888   *SIC* 5311

HUDSON'S BAY COMPANY   p157
4900 MOLLY BANNISTER DR, RED DEER, AB, T4R 1N9

(403) 347-2211   *SIC* 5311

HUDSON'S BAY COMPANY   p165
375 ST ALBERT TRAIL SUITE 300, ST. ALBERT, AB, T8N 3K8

(780) 458-5800   *SIC* 5311

HUDSON'S BAY COMPANY   p175
32900 SOUTH FRASER WAY SUITE 2, ABBOTSFORD, BC, V2S 5A1

(604) 853-7711   *SIC* 5311

HUDSON'S BAY COMPANY   p190
4850 KINGSWAY, BURNABY, BC, V5H 4P2

(604) 436-1196   *SIC* 5311

HUDSON'S BAY COMPANY   p198
2929 BARNET HWY SUITE 100, COQUITLAM, BC, V3B 5R9

(604) 468-4453   *SIC* 5311

HUDSON'S BAY COMPANY   p216
1320 TRANS CANADA HWY W SUITE 300, KAMLOOPS, BC, V1S 1J1

(250) 372-8271   *SIC* 5311

HUDSON'S BAY COMPANY   p222
2271 HARVEY AVE SUITE 1415, KELOWNA, BC, V1Y 6H3

(250) 860-2483   *SIC* 5311

HUDSON'S BAY COMPANY   p228
19705 FRASER HWY SUITE 320, LANGLEY, BC, V3A 7E9

(604) 530-8434   *SIC* 5311

HUDSON'S BAY COMPANY   p234
6631 ISLAND HWY N SUITE 1A, NANAIMO, BC, V9T 4T7

(250) 390-3141   *SIC* 5311

HUDSON'S BAY COMPANY   p237
805 BOYD ST, NEW WESTMINSTER, BC, V3M 5X2

(604) 525-7362   *SIC* 5311

HUDSON'S BAY COMPANY   p243
2111 MAIN ST SUITE 160, PENTICTON, BC, V2A 6V1

(250) 493-1900   *SIC* 5311

HUDSON'S BAY COMPANY   p249
1600 15TH AVE SUITE 140, PRINCE GEORGE, BC, V2L 3X3

(250) 563-0211   *SIC* 5311

HUDSON'S BAY COMPANY   p262
6060 MINORU BLVD SUITE 100, RICHMOND, BC, V6Y 1Y2

(604) 273-3844   *SIC* 5311

HUDSON'S BAY COMPANY   p270
1400 GUILDFORD TOWN CTR, SURREY, BC, V3R 7B7

(604) 588-2111   *SIC* 5311

HUDSON'S BAY COMPANY   p293
650 41ST AVE W, VANCOUVER, BC, V5Z 2M9

(604) 261-3311   *SIC* 5311

HUDSON'S BAY COMPANY   p305
674 GRANVILLE ST SUITE 9999, VANCOUVER, BC, V6C 1Z6

(604) 681-6211   *SIC* 5311

HUDSON'S BAY COMPANY   p332
4900 27 ST SUITE 10, VERNON, BC, V1T 2C7

(250) 545-5331   *SIC* 5311

HUDSON'S BAY COMPANY   p336
1150 DOUGLAS ST SUITE 1, VICTORIA, BC, V8W 2C8

(250) 385-1311   *SIC* 5311

HUDSON'S BAY COMPANY   p338
3125 DOUGLAS ST, VICTORIA, BC, V8Z 3K3

(250) 386-3322   *SIC* 5311

HUDSON'S BAY COMPANY   p341
725 PARK ROYAL N, WEST VANCOUVER, BC, V7T 1H9

(604) 925-1411   *SIC* 5311

HUDSON'S BAY COMPANY   p378
450 PORTAGE AVE, WINNIPEG, MB, R3C 0E7

(204) 783-2112   *SIC* 5311

HUDSON'S BAY COMPANY   p382
1485 PORTAGE AVE, WINNIPEG, MB, R3G 0W4

(204) 975-3228   *SIC* 5311

HUDSON'S BAY COMPANY   p407
1100 MAIN ST, MONCTON, NB, E1C 1H4
SIC 5311

HUDSON'S BAY COMPANY   p457
7067 CHEBUCTO RD SUITE 111, HALIFAX, NS, B3L 4R5
SIC 5311

HUDSON'S BAY COMPANY   p503
8925 TORBRAM RD, BRAMPTON, ON, L6T 4G1

(905) 792-4400   *SIC* 5311

HUDSON'S BAY COMPANY   p503
8925 TORBRAM RD, BRAMPTON, ON, L6T 4G1

(905) 792-4400   *SIC* 5311

HUDSON'S BAY COMPANY   p503
25 PEEL CENTRE DR SUITE 3, BRAMPTON, ON, L6T 3R5

(905) 793-5100   *SIC* 5311

HUDSON'S BAY COMPANY   p530
777 GUELPH LINE UNIT 8, BURLINGTON, ON, L7R 3N2

(905) 634-8866   *SIC* 5311

HUDSON'S BAY COMPANY   p531
900 MAPLE AVE, BURLINGTON, ON, L7S 2J8

(905) 681-0030   *SIC* 5311

HUDSON'S BAY COMPANY   p533
355 HESPELER RD UNIT 1, CAMBRIDGE, ON, N1R 6B3

(519) 622-4919   *SIC* 5311

HUDSON'S BAY COMPANY   p579
25 THE WEST MALL, ETOBICOKE, ON, M9C 1B8

(416) 626-4711   *SIC* 5311

HUDSON'S BAY COMPANY   p585
500 REXDALE BLVD, ETOBICOKE, ON, M9W 6K5

(416) 674-6000   *SIC* 5311

HUDSON'S BAY COMPANY   p616
999 UPPER WENTWORTH ST, HAMILTON, ON, L9A 4X5

(905) 318-8008   *SIC* 5311

HUDSON'S BAY COMPANY   p632
945 GARDINERS RD, KINGSTON, ON, K7M 7H4

(613) 384-3888   *SIC* 5311

HUDSON'S BAY COMPANY   p657
1105 WELLINGTON RD SUITE 5, LONDON, ON, N6E 1V4

(519) 685-4100   *SIC* 5311

HUDSON'S BAY COMPANY   p658
1680 RICHMOND ST, LONDON, ON, N6G 3Y9

(519) 675-0080   *SIC* 5311

HUDSON'S BAY COMPANY   p671
5000 HIGHWAY 7 E, MARKHAM, ON, L3R 4M9

(905) 513-1770   *SIC* 5311

HUDSON'S BAY COMPANY   p710
100 CITY CENTRE DR SUITE 200, MISSISSAUGA, ON, L5B 2C9

(905) 270-7600   *SIC* 5311

HUDSON'S BAY COMPANY   p718
5100 ERIN MILLS PKY UNIT Y001, MISSISSAUGA, ON, L5M 4Z5

(905) 820-8300   *SIC* 5311

HUDSON'S BAY COMPANY   p767
1800 SHEPPARD AVE E SUITE 1, NORTH YORK, ON, M2J 5A7

(416) 491-2010   *SIC* 5311

HUDSON'S BAY COMPANY   p770
6500 YONGE ST, NORTH YORK, ON, M2M 3X4

(416) 226-4202   *SIC* 5311

HUDSON'S BAY COMPANY   p789
3401 DUFFERIN ST, NORTH YORK, ON, M6A 2T9

(416) 789-8011   *SIC* 5311

HUDSON'S BAY COMPANY   p797
240 LEIGHLAND AVE, OAKVILLE, ON, L6H 3H6

(905) 842-4811   *SIC* 5311

HUDSON'S BAY COMPANY   p810
110 PLACE D'ORLEANS DR, ORLEANS, ON, K1C 2L9

(613) 837-8274   *SIC* 5311

HUDSON'S BAY COMPANY   p814
419 KING ST W, OSHAWA, ON, L1J 2K5

(905) 571-1211   *SIC* 5311

HUDSON'S BAY COMPANY   p820
1200 ST. LAURENT BLVD, OTTAWA, ON, K1K 3B8

(613) 748-6105   *SIC* 5311

HUDSON'S BAY COMPANY   p821
73 RIDEAU ST, OTTAWA, ON, K1N 5W8

(613) 241-7511   *SIC* 5311

HUDSON'S BAY COMPANY   p855
9350 YONGE ST SUITE 1999, RICHMOND HILL, ON, L4C 5G2

(905) 883-1222   *SIC* 5311

HUDSON'S BAY COMPANY   p868
1 EGLINTON SQ, SCARBOROUGH, ON, M1L 2K1

(416) 759-4771   *SIC* 5311

HUDSON'S BAY COMPANY   p871
300 BOROUGH DR SUITE 2, SCARBOROUGH, ON, M1P 4P5

(416) 296-0555   *SIC* 5311

HUDSON'S BAY COMPANY   p887
221 GLENDALE AVE, ST CATHARINES, ON, L2T 2K9

(905) 688-4441   *SIC* 5311

HUDSON'S BAY COMPANY   p929
2 BLOOR ST E SUITE 52, TORONTO, ON, M4W 3H7

(416) 972-3313   *SIC* 5311

HUDSON'S BAY COMPANY   p929
2 BLOOR ST E SUITE 52, TORONTO, ON, M4W 3H7

(416) 972-3333   *SIC* 5311

HUDSON'S BAY COMPANY   p939
176 YONGE ST, TORONTO, ON, M5C 2L7

(416) 861-6251   *SIC* 5311

HUDSON'S BAY COMPANY   p952
401 BAY ST SUITE 601, TORONTO, ON, M5H 2Y4

(866) 225-8251   *SIC* 5311

HUDSON'S BAY COMPANY   p1021
3030 HOWARD AVE, WINDSOR, ON, N8X 4T3

▲ Public Company   ■ Public Company Family Member   **HQ** Headquarters   **BR** Branch   **SL** Single Location

(519) 966-4666   *SIC* 5311
HUDSON'S BAY COMPANY   p1086
3045 BOUL LE CARREFOUR, COTE SAINT-LUC, QC, H7T 1C7
(450) 687-1540   *SIC* 5311
HUDSON'S BAY COMPANY   p1104
1100 BOUL MALONEY O, GATINEAU, QC, J8T 6G3
(819) 243-7036   *SIC* 5311
HUDSON'S BAY COMPANY   p1250
6790 AUT TRANSCANADIENNE, POINTE-CLAIRE, QC, H9R 1C5
(514) 697-4870   *SIC* 5311
HUDSON'S BAY COMPANY   p1280
5401 BOUL DES GALERIES, QUEBEC, QC, G2K 1N4
(418) 627-5922   *SIC* 5311
HUDSON'S BAY COMPANY   p1287
401 BOUL LABELLE, ROSEMERE, QC, J7A 3T2
(450) 433-6991   *SIC* 5311
HUDSON'S BAY COMPANY   p1296
800 BOUL DES PROMENADES, SAINT-BRUNO, QC, J3V 5J9
(450) 653-4455   *SIC* 5311
HUDSON'S BAY COMPANY   p1418
2150 11TH AVE, REGINA, SK, S4P 0J5
(306) 525-8511   *SIC* 5311
HUDSON'S BAY COMPANY   p1427
201 1ST AVE S, SASKATOON, SK, S7K 1J5
(306) 242-7611   *SIC* 5311
INVESTISSEMENT PIERRE MARCOTTE LIMITEE, LES   p1296
900 RUE DE L'ETANG, SAINT-BRUNO, QC, J3V 6K8
(450) 653-0222   *SIC* 5311
JOCELYN CROTEAU INC   p1062
2300 BOUL DU FAUBOURG, BOISBRIAND, QC, J7H 1S3
(450) 435-0216   *SIC* 5311
K.F.S. LIMITED   p562
27 FIRST ST E, CORNWALL, ON, K6H 1K5
(613) 933-7110   *SIC* 5311
MACEACHERN, K & A HOLDINGS LTD   p1040
202 BUCHANAN DR, CHARLOTTETOWN, PE, C1E 2H8
(902) 892-8586   *SIC* 5311
MAGASIN LATULIPPE INC   p1264
637 RUE SAINT-VALLIER O, QUEBEC, QC, G1N 1C6
(418) 529-0024   *SIC* 5311
MAGASINS C.P.C. INC, LES   p1375
4500 BOUL BOURQUE, SHERBROOKE, QC, J1N 1S2
(819) 348-0620   *SIC* 5311
MAGASINS HART INC   p1231
900 PLACE PAUL-KANE, MONTREAL, QC, H7C 2T2
(450) 661-4155   *SIC* 5311
MAGASINS KORVETTE LTEE, LES   p1386
2325 BOUL DES RECOLLETS, TROIS-RIVIERES, QC, G8Z 3X6
(819) 374-4625   *SIC* 5311
MAISON SIMONS INC, LA   p1296
600 BOUL DES PROMENADES, SAINT-BRUNO, QC, J3V 6L9
(514) 282-1840   *SIC* 5311
MARGOLIANS MARITIMES LIMITED   p469
65 INGLIS PL SUITE 49, TRURO, NS, B2N 4B5
SIC 5311
MICHAEL ROSSY LTEE   p1326
450 BOUL LEBEAU, SAINT-LAURENT, QC, H4N 1R7
(514) 335-6255   *SIC* 5311
MURRAY, DON A. HOLDINGS LTD   p154
6380 50 AVE SUITE 300, RED DEER, AB, T4N 4C6
(403) 346-1497   *SIC* 5311
NORDSTROM CANADA RETAIL, INC   p36
6455 MACLEOD TRAIL SW, CALGARY, AB, T2H 0K8
(780) 291-2000   *SIC* 5311

NORDSTROM CANADA RETAIL, INC   p315
745 THURLOW ST SUITE 2400, VANCOUVER, BC, V6E 0C5
SIC 5311
NORDSTROM CANADA RETAIL, INC   p330
799 ROBSON ST, VANCOUVER, BC, V7Y 0A2
(604) 699-2100   *SIC* 5311
NORDSTROM CANADA RETAIL, INC   p579
25 THE WEST MALL UNIT 1150A, ETOBICOKE, ON, M9C 1B8
(647) 798-4200   *SIC* 5311
NORDSTROM CANADA RETAIL, INC   p789
3401 DUFFERIN ST UNIT 500, NORTH YORK, ON, M6A 2T9
(416) 780-6630   *SIC* 5311
NORDSTROM CANADA RETAIL, INC   p821
50 RIDEAU ST SUITE 500, OTTAWA, ON, K1N 9J7
(613) 567-7005   *SIC* 5311
NORTH WEST COMPANY INC, THE   p379
77 MAIN ST, WINNIPEG, MB, R3C 1A3
(204) 943-0881   *SIC* 5311
PILON, RAYMOND J. ENTERPRISES LTD   p542
575 GRAND AVE W, CHATHAM, ON, N7L 1C5
(519) 351-9510   *SIC* 5311
PIONEER CO-OPERATIVE ASSOCIATION LIMITED, THE   p1436
1150 CENTRAL AVE N SUITE 2000, SWIFT CURRENT, SK, S9H 0G1
(306) 778-8800   *SIC* 5311
PLACEMENTS MICHEL MAYRAND INC, LES   p1106
355 BOUL DE LA CARRIERE BUREAU 176, GATINEAU, QC, J8Y 6W4
(819) 777-4381   *SIC* 5311
PYXIS REAL ESTATE EQUITIES INC   p940
95 KING ST E SUITE 201, TORONTO, ON, M5C 1G4
(416) 815-0201   *SIC* 5311
QUALITY STORES LTD   p732
5770 HURONTARIO ST, MISSISSAUGA, ON, L5R 3G5
SIC 5311
RICHARD, MARIAN ENTERPRISES LTD   p645
262 ERIE ST S, LEAMINGTON, ON, N8H 3C5
(519) 326-8191   *SIC* 5311
RIFF'S LIMITED   p424
2 HARDY AVE, GRAND FALLS-WINDSOR, NL, A2A 2P9
(709) 489-5631   *SIC* 5311
SEARS CANADA INC   p936
290 YONGE ST SUITE 700, TORONTO, ON, M5B 2C3
SIC 5311
SPORTS DIX 30 INC   p1070
9550 BOUL LEDUC BUREAU 15, BROSSARD, QC, J4Y 0B3
(450) 926-2000   *SIC* 5311
STONE, BRUCE ENTERPRISES LTD   p911
1221 ARTHUR ST W, THUNDER BAY, ON, P7K 1A7
(807) 475-4235   *SIC* 5311
SUPER DISCOUNT STORE INC   p678
46 NORMAN ROSS DR, MARKHAM, ON, L3S 2Z1
(416) 939-5451   *SIC* 5311
TIGRE VAL D'OR LIMITEE   p1391
825 3E AV, VAL-D'OR, QC, J9P 1T2
(819) 825-8106   *SIC* 5311
TIM CURRY SALES LIMITED   p340
855 LANGFORD PKY, VICTORIA, BC, V9B 4V5
(250) 474-2291   *SIC* 5311
TORA CAP-DE-LA-MADELEINE LIMITEE   p1385
800 BOUL THIBEAU, TROIS-RIVIERES, QC, G8T 7A6
(819) 697-3833   *SIC* 5311
TORA SAINT-CHARLES-BORROMEE LIMI-

TEE   p1297
197 RUE DE LA VISITATION BUREAU 109, SAINT-CHARLES-BORROMEE, QC, J6E 4N6
(450) 760-3568   *SIC* 5311
WAL-MART CANADA CORP   p3
2881 MAIN ST SE SUITE 1050, AIRDRIE, AB, T4B 3G5
(403) 945-1295   *SIC* 5311
WAL-MART CANADA CORP   p12
3800 MEMORIAL DR NE SUITE 1100, CALGARY, AB, T2A 2K2
(403) 235-2352   *SIC* 5311
WAL-MART CANADA CORP   p26
1110 57 AVE NE SUITE 3013, CALGARY, AB, T2E 9B7
(403) 730-0990   *SIC* 5311
WAL-MART CANADA CORP   p39
9650 MACLEOD TRAIL SE, CALGARY, AB, T2J 0P7
(403) 258-3988   *SIC* 5311
WAL-MART CANADA CORP   p41
5005 NORTHLAND DRIVE NW, CALGARY, AB, T2L 2K1
(403) 247-8585   *SIC* 5311
WAL-MART CANADA CORP   p70
310 SHAWVILLE BLVD SE SUITE 100, CALGARY, AB, T2Y 3S4
(403) 201-5415   *SIC* 5311
WAL-MART CANADA CORP   p73
1212 37 ST SW SUITE 3009, CALGARY, AB, T3C 1S3
(403) 242-2205   *SIC* 5311
WAL-MART CANADA CORP   p75
8888 COUNTRY HILLS BLVD NW SUITE 200, CALGARY, AB, T3G 5T4
(403) 567-1502   *SIC* 5311
WAL-MART CANADA CORP   p78
6800 48 AVE UNIT 400, CAMROSE, AB, T4V 4T1
(780) 608-1211   *SIC* 5311
WAL-MART CANADA CORP   p81
4702 43 AVE SUITE 3640, COLD LAKE, AB, T9M 1M9
(780) 840-2340   *SIC* 5311
WAL-MART CANADA CORP   p82
1801 SOUTH RAILWAY AVE, DRUMHELLER, AB, T0J 0Y2
(403) 820-7744   *SIC* 5311
WAL-MART CANADA CORP   p82
5217 POWER CENTRE BLVD, DRAYTON VALLEY, AB, T7A 0A5
(780) 514-3207   *SIC* 5311
WAL-MART CANADA CORP   p103
18521 STONY PLAIN RD NW SUITE 3027, EDMONTON, AB, T5S 2V9
(780) 487-8626   *SIC* 5311
WAL-MART CANADA CORP   p107
5004 98 AVE NW SUITE 1, EDMONTON, AB, T6A 0A1
(780) 466-2002   *SIC* 5311
WAL-MART CANADA CORP   p107
13703 40 ST NW SUITE 3028, EDMONTON, AB, T5Y 3B5
(780) 476-4460   *SIC* 5311
WAL-MART CANADA CORP   p121
1203 PARSONS RD NW SUITE 3029, EDMONTON, AB, T6N 0A9
(780) 468-1755   *SIC* 5311
WAL-MART CANADA CORP   p126
5750 2 AVE, EDSON, AB, T7E 0A1
(780) 723-6357   *SIC* 5311
WAL-MART CANADA CORP   p129
2 HOSPITAL ST, FORT MCMURRAY, AB, T9H 5E4
(780) 790-6012   *SIC* 5311
WAL-MART CANADA CORP   p130
9551 87 AVE, FORT SASKATCHEWAN, AB, T8L 4N3
(780) 998-3633   *SIC* 5311
WAL-MART CANADA CORP   p133
11050 103 AVE, GRANDE PRAIRIE, AB, T8V 7H1
(780) 513-3740   *SIC* 5311
WAL-MART CANADA CORP   p136

900 CARMICHAEL LANE SUITE 100, HINTON, AB, T7V 1Y6
(780) 865-1421   *SIC* 5311
WAL-MART CANADA CORP   p140
5302 DISCOVERY WAY, LEDUC, AB, T9E 8J7
(780) 986-7574   *SIC* 5311
WAL-MART CANADA CORP   p141
3195 26 AVE N SUITE 1078, LETHBRIDGE, AB, T1H 5P3
(403) 380-6722   *SIC* 5311
WAL-MART CANADA CORP   p143
3700 MAYOR MAGRATH DR S SUITE 3048, LETHBRIDGE, AB, T1K 7T6
(403) 328-6277   *SIC* 5311
WAL-MART CANADA CORP   p144
4210 70 AVE SUITE 3168, LLOYDMINSTER, AB, T9V 2X3
(780) 875-4777   *SIC* 5311
WAL-MART CANADA CORP   p147
2051 STRACHAN RD SE, MEDICINE HAT, AB, T1B 0G4
(403) 504-4410   *SIC* 5311
WAL-MART CANADA CORP   p152
1100 TABLE MOUNTAIN RD, PINCHER CREEK, AB, T0K 1W0
(403) 627-1790   *SIC* 5311
WAL-MART CANADA CORP   p155
6375 50 AVE, RED DEER, AB, T4N 4C7
(403) 346-6650   *SIC* 5311
WAL-MART CANADA CORP   p157
2010 50 AVE SUITE 3194, RED DEER, AB, T4R 3A2
(403) 358-5842   *SIC* 5311
WAL-MART CANADA CORP   p162
239 WYE RD, SHERWOOD PARK, AB, T8B 1N1
(780) 464-2105   *SIC* 5311
WAL-MART CANADA CORP   p164
1500 MAIN ST SW, SLAVE LAKE, AB, T0G 2A4
(780) 849-9579   *SIC* 5311
WAL-MART CANADA CORP   p166
700 ST ALBERT TRAIL SUITE 3087, ST. ALBERT, AB, T8N 7A5
(780) 458-1629   *SIC* 5311
WAL-MART CANADA CORP   p167
4724 70TH ST, STETTLER, AB, T0C 2L1
(403) 742-4404   *SIC* 5311
WAL-MART CANADA CORP   p168
200 RANCH MARKET, STRATHMORE, AB, T1P 0A8
(403) 934-9776   *SIC* 5311
WAL-MART CANADA CORP   p169
4500 64 ST SUITE 1, TABER, AB, T1G 0A4
(403) 223-3458   *SIC* 5311
WAL-MART CANADA CORP   p169
3420 47 AVE, SYLVAN LAKE, AB, T4S 0B6
(403) 887-7590   *SIC* 5311
WAL-MART CANADA CORP   p170
6809 16A HWY W, VEGREVILLE, AB, T9C 0A2
(780) 632-6016   *SIC* 5311
WAL-MART CANADA CORP   p171
2901 13 AVE SUITE 1062, WAINWRIGHT, AB, T9W 0A2
(780) 842-3144   *SIC* 5311
WAL-MART CANADA CORP   p173
5005 DAHL DR, WHITECOURT, AB, T7S 1X6
(780) 706-3323   *SIC* 5311
WAL-MART CANADA CORP   p176
1812 VEDDER WAY SUITE 3019, ABBOTSFORD, BC, V2S 8K1
(604) 854-3575   *SIC* 5311
WAL-MART CANADA CORP   p180
9855 AUSTIN RD SUITE 300, BURNABY, BC, V3J 1N5
(604) 421-0661   *SIC* 5311
WAL-MART CANADA CORP   p198
45610 LUCKAKUCK WAY UNIT 200, CHILLIWACK, BC, V2R 1A2
(604) 858-5100   *SIC* 5311
WAL-MART CANADA CORP   p204

▲ Public Company   ■ Public Company Family Member   **HQ** Headquarters   **BR** Branch   **SL** Single Location

2100 WILLOWBROOK DR SUITE 3183, CRANBROOK, BC, V1C 7H2
(250) 489-3202 SIC 5311

WAL-MART CANADA CORP p205
600 HIGHWAY 2, DAWSON CREEK, BC, V1G 0A4
(250) 719-0128 SIC 5311

WAL-MART CANADA CORP p212
3020 DRINKWATER RD, DUNCAN, BC, V9L 6C6
(250) 748-2566 SIC 5311

WAL-MART CANADA CORP p214
9007 96A ST, FORT ST. JOHN, BC, V1J 7B6
(250) 261-5544 SIC 5311

WAL-MART CANADA CORP p218
1055 HILLSIDE DR UNIT 100, KAMLOOPS, BC, V2E 2S5
(250) 374-1591 SIC 5311

WAL-MART CANADA CORP p220
1555 BANKS RD, KELOWNA, BC, V1X 7Y8
(250) 860-8811 SIC 5311

WAL-MART CANADA CORP p232
3900 CRAWFORD AVE SUITE 100, MERRITT, BC, V1K 0A4
(250) 315-1366 SIC 5311

WAL-MART CANADA CORP p233
31956 LOUGHEED HWY SUITE 1119, MISSION, BC, V2V 0C6
(604) 820-0048 SIC 5311

WAL-MART CANADA CORP p235
6801 ISLAND HWY N SUITE 3059, NANAIMO, BC, V9T 6N8
(250) 758-0343 SIC 5311

WAL-MART CANADA CORP p236
1000 LAKESIDE DR, NELSON, BC, V1L 5Z4
(250) 352-3782 SIC 5311

WAL-MART CANADA CORP p242
925 MARINE DR SUITE 3057, NORTH VANCOUVER, BC, V7P 1S2
(604) 984-6830 SIC 5311

WAL-MART CANADA CORP p244
275 GREEN AVE W SUITE 135, PENTICTON, BC, V2A 7J2
(250) 493-6681 SIC 5311

WAL-MART CANADA CORP p245
3355 JOHNSTON RD, PORT ALBERNI, BC, V9Y 8K1
(250) 720-0912 SIC 5311

WAL-MART CANADA CORP p248
7100 ALBERNI ST SUITE 23, POWELL RIVER, BC, V8A 5K9
(604) 485-9811 SIC 5311

WAL-MART CANADA CORP p251
6565 SOUTHRIDGE AVE SUITE 3651, PRINCE GEORGE, BC, V2N 6Z4
(250) 906-3203 SIC 5311

WAL-MART CANADA CORP p252
890 RITA RD, QUESNEL, BC, V2J 7J3
(250) 747-4464 SIC 5311

WAL-MART CANADA CORP p269
39210 DISCOVERY WAY SUITE 1015, SQUAMISH, BC, V8B 0N1
(604) 815-4625 SIC 5311

WAL-MART CANADA CORP p271
1000 GUILDFORD TOWN CTR, SURREY, BC, V3R 7C3
(604) 581-1932 SIC 5311

WAL-MART CANADA CORP p278
12451 88 AVE, SURREY, BC, V3W 1P8
(604) 597-7117 SIC 5311

WAL-MART CANADA CORP p280
2355 160 ST, SURREY, BC, V3Z 9N6
(604) 541-9015 SIC 5311

WAL-MART CANADA CORP p283
4427 16 HWY W, TERRACE, BC, V8G 5L5
(250) 615-4728 SIC 5311

WAL-MART CANADA CORP p284
1601 MARCOLIN DR SUITE 1011, TRAIL, BC, V1R 4Y1
(250) 364-1802 SIC 5311

WAL-MART CANADA CORP p284
1601 MARCOLIN DR SUITE 1011, TRAIL, BC, V1R 4Y1

(250) 364-2688 SIC 5311

WAL-MART CANADA CORP p332
2200 58 AVE SUITE 3169, VERNON, BC, V1T 9T2
(250) 558-0425 SIC 5311

WAL-MART CANADA CORP p339
3460 SAANICH RD SUITE 3109, VICTORIA, BC, V8Z 0B9
(250) 475-3356 SIC 5311

WAL-MART CANADA CORP p347
903 18TH ST N, BRANDON, MB, R7A 7S1
(204) 726-5821 SIC 5311

WAL-MART CANADA CORP p349
1450 MAIN ST S UNIT A, DAUPHIN, MB, R7N 3H4
(204) 638-4808 SIC 5311

WAL-MART CANADA CORP p355
2348 SISSONS DR, PORTAGE LA PRAIRIE, MB, R1N 0G5
(204) 857-5011 SIC 5311

WAL-MART CANADA CORP p360
300 MYSTERY LAKE RD SUITE 3102, THOMPSON, MB, R8N 0M2
(204) 778-4669 SIC 5311

WAL-MART CANADA CORP p361
1000 NAVIGATOR RD, WINKLER, MB, R6W 0L8
(204) 325-4160 SIC 5311

WAL-MART CANADA CORP p368
1225 ST MARY'S RD SUITE 54, WINNIPEG, MB, R2M 5E6
(204) 256-7027 SIC 5311

WAL-MART CANADA CORP p370
2370 MCPHILLIPS ST SUITE 3118, WINNIPEG, MB, R2V 4J6
(204) 334-2273 SIC 5311

WAL-MART CANADA CORP p382
1001 EMPRESS ST, WINNIPEG, MB, R3G 3P8
(204) 284-6900 SIC 5311

WAL-MART CANADA CORP p387
3655 PORTAGE AVE, WINNIPEG, MB, R3K 2G6
(204) 897-3410 SIC 5311

WAL-MART CANADA CORP p389
1665 KENASTON BLVD, WINNIPEG, MB, R3P 2M4
(204) 488-2052 SIC 5311

WAL-MART CANADA CORP p394
4 RUE JAGOE, ATHOLVILLE, NB, E3N 5C3
(506) 753-7105 SIC 5311

WAL-MART CANADA CORP p395
900 ST. ANNE ST, BATHURST, NB, E2A 6X2
(506) 546-0500 SIC 5311

WAL-MART CANADA CORP p399
805 RUE VICTORIA SUITE 1033, EDMUNDSTON, NB, E3V 3T3
(506) 735-8412 SIC 5311

WAL-MART CANADA CORP p400
125 TWO NATIONS XG SUITE 1067, FREDERICTON, NB, E3A 0T3
SIC 5311

WAL-MART CANADA CORP p402
1399 REGENT ST, FREDERICTON, NB, E3C 1A3
(506) 452-1511 SIC 5311

WAL-MART CANADA CORP p405
200 DOUGLASTOWN BLVD, MIRAMICHI, NB, E1V 7K4
(506) 778-8224 SIC 5311

WAL-MART CANADA CORP p407
25 PLAZA BLVD SUITE 3659, MONCTON, NB, E1C 0G3
(506) 858-7394 SIC 5311

WAL-MART CANADA CORP p413
450 WESTMORLAND RD SUITE 3091, SAINT JOHN, NB, E2J 4Z2
(506) 634-6600 SIC 5311

WAL-MART CANADA CORP p418
80 MAIN ST, SUSSEX, NB, E4E 1Y6
(506) 432-9333 SIC 5311

WAL-MART CANADA CORP p420
430 CONNELL ST, WOODSTOCK, NB, E7M

5R5
(506) 324-8099 SIC 5311

WAL-MART CANADA CORP p421
120 COLUMBUS DR, CARBONEAR, NL, A1Y 1B3
(709) 596-5009 SIC 5311

WAL-MART CANADA CORP p422
16 MURPHY SQ, CORNER BROOK, NL, A2H 1R4
(709) 634-2310 SIC 5311

WAL-MART CANADA CORP p423
55 AV ROE, GANDER, NL, A1V 0H6
(709) 256-7581 SIC 5311

WAL-MART CANADA CORP p424
19 CROMER AVE, GRAND FALLS-WINDSOR, NL, A2A 2K5
(709) 489-5739 SIC 5311

WAL-MART CANADA CORP p425
500 VANIER AVE SUITE 1035, LABRADOR CITY, NL, A2V 2W7
(709) 944-3378 SIC 5311

WAL-MART CANADA CORP p427
60 MERCHANT DR, MOUNT PEARL, NL, A1N 5J5
(709) 364-4214 SIC 5311

WAL-MART CANADA CORP p431
75 KELSEY DR, ST. JOHN'S, NL, A1B 0C7
(709) 722-6707 SIC 5311

WAL-MART CANADA CORP p434
42 QUEEN ST, STEPHENVILLE, NL, A2N 3A7
(709) 643-5018 SIC 5311

WAL-MART CANADA CORP p436
313 OLD AIRPORT RD, YELLOWKNIFE, NT, X1A 3T3
(867) 873-4545 SIC 5311

WAL-MART CANADA CORP p438
50 MARKET ST, ANTIGONISH, NS, B2G 3B4
(902) 867-1279 SIC 5311

WAL-MART CANADA CORP p438
46 ROBERT ANGUS DR, AMHERST, NS, B4H 4R7
(902) 661-3476 SIC 5311

WAL-MART CANADA CORP p440
141 DAMASCUS RD, BEDFORD, NS, B4A 0C2
(902) 865-4000 SIC 5311

WAL-MART CANADA CORP p441
60 PINE GROVE RD, BRIDGEWATER, NS, B4V 4H2
(902) 543-8680 SIC 5311

WAL-MART CANADA CORP p448
90 LAMONT TERR, DARTMOUTH, NS, B3B 0B5
(902) 461-4474 SIC 5311

WAL-MART CANADA CORP p457
6990 MUMFORD RD SUITE 3636, HALIFAX, NS, B3L 4W4
(902) 454-7990 SIC 5311

WAL-MART CANADA CORP p459
220 CHAIN LAKE DR, HALIFAX, NS, B3S 1C5
(902) 450-5570 SIC 5311

WAL-MART CANADA CORP p463
713 WESTVILLE RD SUITE 3061, NEW GLASGOW, NS, B2H 2J6
(902) 928-0008 SIC 5311

WAL-MART CANADA CORP p464
9097 COMMERCIAL ST SUITE 3738, NEW MINAS, NS, B4N 3E6
(902) 681-4271 SIC 5311

WAL-MART CANADA CORP p465
47 PAINT ST UNIT 17, PORT HAWKESBURY, NS, B9A 3J9
(902) 625-0954 SIC 5311

WAL-MART CANADA CORP p467
800 GRAND LAKE RD, SYDNEY, NS, B1P 6S9
(902) 562-1110 SIC 5311

WAL-MART CANADA CORP p468
65 KELTIC DR, SYDNEY, NS, B1S 1P4
(902) 562-3353 SIC 5311

WAL-MART CANADA CORP p469

140 WADE RD, TRURO, NS, B2N 7H3
(902) 893-5582 SIC 5311

WAL-MART CANADA CORP p471
108 STARRS RD, YARMOUTH, NS, B5A 2T5
(902) 749-2306 SIC 5311

WAL-MART CANADA CORP p475
270 KINGSTON RD E, AJAX, ON, L1Z 1G1
(905) 426-6160 SIC 5311

WAL-MART CANADA CORP p478
1051 GARNER RD W SUITE 3127, ANCASTER, ON, L9G 3K9
(905) 648-9980 SIC 5311

WAL-MART CANADA CORP p482
135 FIRST COMMERCE DR, AURORA, ON, L4G 0G2
(905) 841-0300 SIC 5311

WAL-MART CANADA CORP p485
450 BAYFIELD ST, BARRIE, ON, L4M 5A2
(705) 728-2833 SIC 5311

WAL-MART CANADA CORP p488
35 MAPLEVIEW DR W, BARRIE, ON, L4N 9H5
(705) 728-9122 SIC 5311

WAL-MART CANADA CORP p492
274 MILLENNIUM PKY, BELLEVILLE, ON, K8N 4Z5
(613) 966-9466 SIC 5311

WAL-MART CANADA CORP p507
30 COVENTRY RD, BRAMPTON, ON, L6T 5P9
(905) 793-1983 SIC 5311

WAL-MART CANADA CORP p508
50 QUARRY EDGE DR, BRAMPTON, ON, L6V 4K2
(905) 874-0112 SIC 5311

WAL-MART CANADA CORP p515
300 KING GEORGE RD SUITE 1, BRANTFORD, ON, N3R 5L7
(519) 759-3450 SIC 5311

WAL-MART CANADA CORP p520
1942 PARKEDALE AVE SUITE 3006, BROCKVILLE, ON, K6V 7N4
(613) 342-9293 SIC 5311

WAL-MART CANADA CORP p527
4515 DUNDAS ST SUITE 1, BURLINGTON, ON, L7M 5B4
(905) 331-0027 SIC 5311

WAL-MART CANADA CORP p535
22 PINEBUSH RD, CAMBRIDGE, ON, N1R 8K5
(519) 624-7467 SIC 5311

WAL-MART CANADA CORP p542
881 ST CLAIR ST, CHATHAM, ON, N7L 0E9
(519) 352-1142 SIC 5311

WAL-MART CANADA CORP p545
73 STRATHY RD, COBOURG, ON, K9A 5W8
(905) 373-1239 SIC 5311

WAL-MART CANADA CORP p547
10 CAMBRIDGE, COLLINGWOOD, ON, L9Y 0A1
(705) 445-9262 SIC 5311

WAL-MART CANADA CORP p561
101 EDGELEY BLVD SUITE 3145, CONCORD, ON, L4K 4Z4
(905) 761-7945 SIC 5311

WAL-MART CANADA CORP p563
950 BROOKDALE AVE, CORNWALL, ON, K6J 4P5
(613) 933-8366 SIC 5311

WAL-MART CANADA CORP p565
HWY 17 E, DRYDEN, ON, P8N 2Y6
(807) 223-7190 SIC 5311

WAL-MART CANADA CORP p580
165 NORTH QUEEN ST SUITE 3031, ETOBICOKE, ON, M9C 1A7
(416) 239-7090 SIC 5311

WAL-MART CANADA CORP p589
2245 ISLINGTON AVE SUITE 3740, ETOBICOKE, ON, M9W 3W6
(416) 747-6499 SIC 5311

WAL-MART CANADA CORP p592
1250 KING'S HWY, FORT FRANCES, ON,

P9A 2X6
(807) 274-1373   *SIC* 5311
WAL-MART CANADA CORP   p592
750 GARRISON RD, FORT ERIE, ON, L2A 1N7
(905) 991-9971   *SIC* 5311
WAL-MART CANADA CORP   p597
35400 HURON RD, GODERICH, ON, N7A 3X8
(519) 524-5060   *SIC* 5311
WAL-MART CANADA CORP   p604
11 WOODLAWN RD W, GUELPH, ON, N1H 1G8
(519) 767-1600   *SIC* 5311
WAL-MART CANADA CORP   p617
2190 RYMAL RD E SUITE 1042, HANNON, ON, L0R 1P0
(905) 692-7000   *SIC* 5311
WAL-MART CANADA CORP   p617
675 UPPER JAMES ST, HAMILTON, ON, L9C 2Z5
(905) 389-6333   *SIC* 5311
WAL-MART CANADA CORP   p618
1100 10TH ST, HANOVER, ON, N4N 3B8
(519) 364-0867   *SIC* 5311
WAL-MART CANADA CORP   p621
111 HOWLAND DR UNIT 10, HUNTSVILLE, ON, P1H 2P4
(705) 787-1137   *SIC* 5311
WAL-MART CANADA CORP   p626
500 EARL GREY DR, KANATA, ON, K2T 1B6
(613) 599-6765   *SIC* 5311
WAL-MART CANADA CORP   p627
350 GOVERNMENT RD E, KAPUSKASING, ON, P5N 2X7
(705) 335-6111   *SIC* 5311
WAL-MART CANADA CORP   p628
24 MIIKANA WAY UNIT 1, KENORA, ON, P9N 4J1
(807) 468-6379   *SIC* 5311
WAL-MART CANADA CORP   p633
1130 MIDLAND AVE, KINGSTON, ON, K7P 2X9
(613) 384-9071   *SIC* 5311
WAL-MART CANADA CORP   p637
2960 KINGSWAY DR SUITE 3045, KITCHENER, ON, N2C 1X1
(519) 894-6600   *SIC* 5311
WAL-MART CANADA CORP   p638
1400 OTTAWA ST S UNIT E, KITCHENER, ON, N2E 4E2
(519) 576-0921   *SIC* 5311
WAL-MART CANADA CORP   p645
304 ERIE ST S, LEAMINGTON, ON, N8H 3C5
(519) 326-3900   *SIC* 5311
WAL-MART CANADA CORP   p651
330 CLARKE RD, LONDON, ON, N5W 6G4
(519) 455-8910   *SIC* 5311
WAL-MART CANADA CORP   p658
1105 WELLINGTON RD SUITE 3051, LONDON, ON, N6E 1V4
(519) 681-7500   *SIC* 5311
WAL-MART CANADA CORP   p677
5000 HIGHWAY 7 E UNIT Y006A, MARKHAM, ON, L3R 4M9
(905) 477-6060   *SIC* 5311
WAL-MART CANADA CORP   p682
16845 12 HWY, MIDLAND, ON, L4R 0A9
(705) 526-4754   *SIC* 5311
WAL-MART CANADA CORP   p685
1280 STEELES AVE E SUITE 1000, MILTON, ON, L9T 6R1
(905) 864-6027   *SIC* 5311
WAL-MART CANADA CORP   p711
100 CITY CENTRE DR SUITE 100, MISSISSAUGA, ON, L5B 2G7
(905) 270-9300   *SIC* 5311
WAL-MART CANADA CORP   p718
2160 BURNHAMTHORPE RD W, MISSISSAUGA, ON, L5L 5Z5
(905) 608-0922   *SIC* 5311
WAL-MART CANADA CORP   p728

1940 ARGENTIA RD, MISSISSAUGA, ON, L5N 1P9
(905) 821-2111   *SIC* 5311
WAL-MART CANADA CORP   p728
1940 ARGENTIA RD, MISSISSAUGA, ON, L5N 1P9
(800) 328-0402   *SIC* 5311
WAL-MART CANADA CORP   p728
6600 KITIMAT RD, MISSISSAUGA, ON, L5N 1L9
(905) 817-1824   *SIC* 5311
WAL-MART CANADA CORP   p728
3155 ARGENTIA RD, MISSISSAUGA, ON, L5N 8E1
(905) 821-8150   *SIC* 5311
WAL-MART CANADA CORP   p752
3651 STRANDHERD DR, NEPEAN, ON, K2J 4G8
(613) 823-8714   *SIC* 5311
WAL-MART CANADA CORP   p757
17940 YONGE ST, NEWMARKET, ON, L3Y 8S4
(905) 853-8811   *SIC* 5311
WAL-MART CANADA CORP   p759
7481 OAKWOOD DR, NIAGARA FALLS, ON, L2G 0J5
(905) 371-3999   *SIC* 5311
WAL-MART CANADA CORP   p764
1500 FISHER ST SUITE 102, NORTH BAY, ON, P1B 3H3
(705) 472-1704   *SIC* 5311
WAL-MART CANADA CORP   p799
234 HAYS BLVD, OAKVILLE, ON, L6H 6M4
(905) 257-5740   *SIC* 5311
WAL-MART CANADA CORP   p810
175 MURPHY RD, ORILLIA, ON, L3V 0B5
(705) 325-7403   *SIC* 5311
WAL-MART CANADA CORP   p811
3900 INNES RD, ORLEANS, ON, K1W 1K9
(613) 837-9399   *SIC* 5311
WAL-MART CANADA CORP   p814
1471 HARMONY RD N SUITE 3161, OSHAWA, ON, L1K 0Z6
(905) 404-6581   *SIC* 5311
WAL-MART CANADA CORP   p819
450 TERMINAL AVE SUITE 1031, OTTAWA, ON, K1G 0Z3
(613) 562-0500   *SIC* 5311
WAL-MART CANADA CORP   p827
2210 BANK ST, OTTAWA, ON, K1V 1J5
(613) 247-1184   *SIC* 5311
WAL-MART CANADA CORP   p836
1555 18TH AVE E, OWEN SOUND, ON, N4K 0E2
(519) 371-6900   *SIC* 5311
WAL-MART CANADA CORP   p837
1 PINE DR, PARRY SOUND, ON, P2A 3C3
(705) 746-1573   *SIC* 5311
WAL-MART CANADA CORP   p838
1108 PEMBROKE ST E, PEMBROKE, ON, K8A 8P7
(613) 735-4997   *SIC* 5311
WAL-MART CANADA CORP   p840
1002 CHEMONG RD SUITE 3071, PETERBOROUGH, ON, K9H 7E2
(705) 742-1685   *SIC* 5311
WAL-MART CANADA CORP   p844
1899 BROCK RD UNIT B, PICKERING, ON, L1V 4H7
(905) 619-9588   *SIC* 5311
WAL-MART CANADA CORP   p850
980 O'BRIEN RD SUITE 1, RENFREW, ON, K7V 0B4
(613) 432-4676   *SIC* 5311
WAL-MART CANADA CORP   p859
1444 QUINN DR, SARNIA, ON, N7S 6M8
(519) 542-4272   *SIC* 5311
WAL-MART CANADA CORP   p861
GD LCD MAIN, SARNIA, ON, N7T 7H7
(519) 542-1854   *SIC* 5311
WAL-MART CANADA CORP   p865
785 MILNER AVE, SCARBOROUGH, ON, M1B 3C3
(416) 281-2929   *SIC* 5311

WAL-MART CANADA CORP   p869
800 WARDEN AVE, SCARBOROUGH, ON, M1L 4T7
(416) 615-2697   *SIC* 5311
WAL-MART CANADA CORP   p872
300 BOROUGH DR SUITE 2, SCARBOROUGH, ON, M1P 4P5
(416) 290-1916   *SIC* 5311
WAL-MART CANADA CORP   p875
3850 SHEPPARD AVE E SUITE 3000, SCARBOROUGH, ON, M1T 3L4
(416) 291-4100   *SIC* 5311
WAL-MART CANADA CORP   p877
5995 STEELES AVE E SUITE SIDE, SCARBOROUGH, ON, M1V 5P7
(416) 298-1210   *SIC* 5311
WAL-MART CANADA CORP   p882
114 LOMBARD ST, SMITHS FALLS, ON, K7A 5B8
(613) 284-0838   *SIC* 5311
WAL-MART CANADA CORP   p884
525 WELLAND AVE, ST CATHARINES, ON, L2M 6P3
(905) 685-4100   *SIC* 5311
WAL-MART CANADA CORP   p887
420 VANSICKLE RD SUITE 2, ST CATHARINES, ON, L2S 0C7
(905) 687-9212   *SIC* 5311
WAL-MART CANADA CORP   p890
1063 TALBOT ST UNIT 60, ST THOMAS, ON, N5P 1G4
(519) 631-1253   *SIC* 5311
WAL-MART CANADA CORP   p895
1050 HOOVER PARK DR, STOUFFVILLE, ON, L4A 0K2
(905) 640-8848   *SIC* 5311
WAL-MART CANADA CORP   p897
150 CARROLL ST E, STRATHROY, ON, N7G 4G2
(519) 245-7200   *SIC* 5311
WAL-MART CANADA CORP   p899
1349 LASALLE BLVD SUITE 3097, SUDBURY, ON, P3A 1Z2
(705) 566-3700   *SIC* 5311
WAL-MART CANADA CORP   p909
777 MEMORIAL AVE, THUNDER BAY, ON, P7B 6S2
(807) 346-9441   *SIC* 5311
WAL-MART CANADA CORP   p912
400 SIMCOE ST, TILLSONBURG, ON, N4G 4X1
(519) 842-7770   *SIC* 5311
WAL-MART CANADA CORP   p990
900 DUFFERIN ST SUITE 3106, TORONTO, ON, M6H 4B1
(416) 537-2561   *SIC* 5311
WAL-MART CANADA CORP   p992
1305 LAWRENCE AVE W, TORONTO, ON, M6L 1A5
(416) 244-1171   *SIC* 5311
WAL-MART CANADA CORP   p994
2525 ST CLAIR AVE W, TORONTO, ON, M6N 4Z5
(416) 763-7325   *SIC* 5311
WAL-MART CANADA CORP   p999
HWY 2 AT 2ND DUGHILL RD, TRENTON, ON, K8V 5P7
(613) 394-2191   *SIC* 5311
WAL-MART CANADA CORP   p1001
6 WELWOOD DR, UXBRIDGE, ON, L9P 1Z7
(905) 862-0721   *SIC* 5311
WAL-MART CANADA CORP   p1005
60 MCNAUGHTON AVE UNIT 16, WALLACEBURG, ON, N8A 1R9
(519) 627-8840   *SIC* 5311
WAL-MART CANADA CORP   p1012
102 PRIMEWAY DR, WELLAND, ON, L3B 0A1
(905) 735-3500   *SIC* 5311
WAL-MART CANADA CORP   p1016
4100 BALDWIN ST S, WHITBY, ON, L1R 3H8
(905) 655-0206   *SIC* 5311

WAL-MART CANADA CORP   p1019
7100 TECUMSEH RD E SUITE 3115, WINDSOR, ON, N8T 1E6
(519) 945-3065   *SIC* 5311
WAL-MART CANADA CORP   p1025
3120 DOUGALL AVE, WINDSOR, ON, N9E 1S7
(519) 969-8121   *SIC* 5311
WAL-MART CANADA CORP   p1036
499 NORWICH AVE, WOODSTOCK, ON, N4S 9A2
(519) 539-5120   *SIC* 5311
WAL-MART CANADA CORP   p1041
80 BUCHANAN DR, CHARLOTTETOWN, PE, C1E 2E5
(902) 628-4600   *SIC* 5311
WAL-MART CANADA CORP   p1043
511 GRANVILLE ST, SUMMERSIDE, PE, C1N 5J4
(902) 432-3570   *SIC* 5311
WAL-MART CANADA CORP   p1045
1755 AV DU PONT S BUREAU 5795, ALMA, QC, G8B 7W7
(418) 480-3887   *SIC* 5311
WAL-MART CANADA CORP   p1053
630 BOUL LAFLECHE BUREAU 3002, BAIE-COMEAU, QC, G5C 2Y3
(418) 589-9971   *SIC* 5311
WAL-MART CANADA CORP   p1071
9000 BOUL LEDUC UNITE 102, BROSSARD, QC, J4Y 0E6
(450) 672-5000   *SIC* 5311
WAL-MART CANADA CORP   p1080
3017-1451 BOUL TALBOT, CHICOUTIMI, QC, G7H 5N8
(418) 693-1500   *SIC* 5311
WAL-MART CANADA CORP   p1085
1660 BOUL LE CORBUSIER, COTE SAINT-LUC, QC, H7S 1Z2
(450) 681-1126   *SIC* 5311
WAL-MART CANADA CORP   p1089
1770 RUE DU SUD, COWANSVILLE, QC, J2K 3G8
(450) 263-6006   *SIC* 5311
WAL-MART CANADA CORP   p1100
1205 BOUL RENE-LEVESQUE, DRUMMONDVILLE, QC, J2C 7V4
(819) 472-7446   *SIC* 5311
WAL-MART CANADA CORP   p1105
640 BOUL MALONEY O, GATINEAU, QC, J8T 8K7
(819) 246-8808   *SIC* 5311
WAL-MART CANADA CORP   p1108
35 BOUL DU PLATEAU, GATINEAU, QC, J9A 3G1
(819) 772-1911   *SIC* 5311
WAL-MART CANADA CORP   p1111
75 RUE SIMONDS N, GRANBY, QC, J2J 2S3
(450) 777-8863   *SIC* 5311
WAL-MART CANADA CORP   p1115
1505 BOUL FIRESTONE BUREAU 521, JOLIETTE, QC, J6E 9E5
(450) 752-8210   *SIC* 5311
WAL-MART CANADA CORP   p1118
17000 RTE TRANSCANADIENNE, KIRKLAND, QC, H9J 2M5
(514) 695-3040   *SIC* 5311
WAL-MART CANADA CORP   p1125
3130 RUE LAVAL, LAC-MEGANTIC, QC, G6B 1A4
(819) 583-2882   *SIC* 5311
WAL-MART CANADA CORP   p1129
480 AV BETHANY, LACHUTE, QC, J8H 4H5
(450) 562-0258   *SIC* 5311
WAL-MART CANADA CORP   p1131
6797 BOUL NEWMAN, LASALLE, QC, H8N 3E4
(514) 368-2248   *SIC* 5311
WAL-MART CANADA CORP   p1137
5303 RUE LOUIS-H.-LA FONTAINE, LEVIS, QC, G6V 8X4
(418) 833-8555   *SIC* 5311
WAL-MART CANADA CORP   p1139

700 RUE DE LA CONCORDE, LEVIS, QC, G6W 8A8
(418) 834-5115   *SIC* 5311

WAL-MART CANADA CORP   *p*1146
1999 BOUL ROLAND-THERRIEN, LONGUEUIL, QC, J4N 1A3
(450) 448-2688   *SIC* 5311

WAL-MART CANADA CORP   *p*1148
1935 RUE SHERBROOKE, MAGOG, QC, J1X 2T5
(819) 868-9775   *SIC* 5311

WAL-MART CANADA CORP   *p*1150
155 MONTEE MASSON BUREAU 3149, MASCOUCHE, QC, J7K 3B4
(450) 474-2679   *SIC* 5311

WAL-MART CANADA CORP   *p*1151
150 RUE PIUZE, MATANE, QC, G4W 4T2
(418) 566-4779   *SIC* 5311

WAL-MART CANADA CORP   *p*1228
5400 RUE JEAN-TALON O, MONTREAL, QC, H4P 2T5
(514) 735-0913   *SIC* 5311

WAL-MART CANADA CORP   *p*1240
6140 BOUL HENRI-BOURASSA E, MONTREAL-NORD, QC, H1G 5X3
(514) 324-7853   *SIC* 5311

WAL-MART CANADA CORP   *p*1278
1470 AV JULES-VERNE BUREAU 3146, QUEBEC, QC, G2G 2R5
(418) 874-6068   *SIC* 5311

WAL-MART CANADA CORP   *p*1283
100 BOUL BRIEN BUREAU 66, REPENTIGNY, QC, J6A 5N4
(450) 654-8886   *SIC* 5311

WAL-MART CANADA CORP   *p*1285
415 MONTEE INDUSTRIELLE-ET-COMMERCIALE BUREAU 3198, RIMOUSKI, QC, G5M 1Y1
(418) 722-1990   *SIC* 5311

WAL-MART CANADA CORP   *p*1287
100 RUE DES CERISIERS, RIVIERE-DU-LOUP, QC, G5R 6E8
(418) 862-3003   *SIC* 5311

WAL-MART CANADA CORP   *p*1288
401 BOUL LABELLE BUREAU 3080, ROSEMERE, QC, J7A 3T2
(450) 435-2982   *SIC* 5311

WAL-MART CANADA CORP   *p*1290
275 BOUL RIDEAU BUREAU 3136, ROUYN-NORANDA, QC, J9X 5Y6
(819) 762-0619   *SIC* 5311

WAL-MART CANADA CORP   *p*1296
1475 BOUL SAINT-BRUNO, SAINT-BRUNO, QC, J3V 6J1
(450) 653-9996   *SIC* 5311

WAL-MART CANADA CORP   *p*1298
500 VOIE DE LA DESSERTE UNITE 132, SAINT-CONSTANT, QC, J5A 2S5
(450) 632-2192   *SIC* 5311

WAL-MART CANADA CORP   *p*1302
764 BOUL ARTHUR-SAUVE BUREAU 3089, SAINT-EUSTACHE, QC, J7R 4K3
(450) 491-6922   *SIC* 5311

WAL-MART CANADA CORP   *p*1305
750 107E RUE, SAINT-GEORGES, QC, G5Y 0A1
(418) 220-0010   *SIC* 5311

WAL-MART CANADA CORP   *p*1311
5950 RUE MARTINEAU, SAINT-HYACINTHE, QC, J2R 2H6
(450) 796-4001   *SIC* 5311

WAL-MART CANADA CORP   *p*1315
100 BOUL OMER-MARCIL, SAINT-JEAN-SUR-RICHELIEU, QC, J2W 2X2
(450) 349-0666   *SIC* 5311

WAL-MART CANADA CORP   *p*1320
1030 BOUL DU GRAND-HERON, SAINT-JEROME, QC, J7Y 5K8
(450) 438-6776   *SIC* 5311

WAL-MART CANADA CORP   *p*1346
7445 BOUL LANGELIER, SAINT-LEONARD, QC, H1S 1V6
(514) 899-1889   *SIC* 5311

WAL-MART CANADA CORP   *p*1354

400 RUE LAVERDURE, SAINTE-AGATHE-DES-MONTS, QC, J8C 0A2
(819) 326-9559   *SIC* 5311

WAL-MART CANADA CORP   *p*1361
5205 BOUL ROBERT-BOURASSA, SAINTE-ROSE, QC, H7E 0A3
(450) 661-7447   *SIC* 5311

WAL-MART CANADA CORP   *p*1363
700 CHOMEDEY (A-13) O, SAINTE-ROSE, QC, H7X 3S9
(450) 969-3226   *SIC* 5311

WAL-MART CANADA CORP   *p*1365
2050 BOUL MONSEIGNEUR-LANGLOIS, SALABERRY-DE-VALLEYFIELD, QC, J6S 5R1
(450) 371-9026   *SIC* 5311

WAL-MART CANADA CORP   *p*1367
1005 BOUL LAURE BUREAU 500, SEPT-ILES, QC, G4R 4S6
(418) 968-5151   *SIC* 5311

WAL-MART CANADA CORP   *p*1369
1600 BOUL ROYAL, SHAWINIGAN, QC, G9N 8S8
(819) 537-0113   *SIC* 5311

WAL-MART CANADA CORP   *p*1374
4050 BOUL JOSAPHAT-RANCOURT BUREAU 3086, SHERBROOKE, QC, J1L 3C6
(819) 823-1661   *SIC* 5311

WAL-MART CANADA CORP   *p*1383
1025 BOUL FRONTENAC E, THETFORD MINES, QC, G6G 6S7
(418) 338-4884   *SIC* 5311

WAL-MART CANADA CORP   *p*1385
300 RUE BARKOFF, TROIS-RIVIERES, QC, G8T 2A3
(819) 379-2992   *SIC* 5311

WAL-MART CANADA CORP   *p*1391
1855 3E AV BUREAU 3139, VAL-D'OR, QC, J9P 7A9
(819) 874-8411   *SIC* 5311

WAL-MART CANADA CORP   *p*1395
3050 BOUL DE LA GARE, VAUDREUIL-DORION, QC, J7V 0H1
(450) 510-3314   *SIC* 5311

WAL-MART CANADA CORP   *p*1398
110 BOUL ARTHABASKA O, VICTORIAVILLE, QC, G6S 0P2
(819) 758-5136   *SIC* 5311

WAL-MART CANADA CORP   *p*1407
413 KENSINGTON AVE, ESTEVAN, SK, S4A 2A5
(306) 634-2110   *SIC* 5311

WAL-MART CANADA CORP   *p*1408
710 11TH AVENUE E, KINDERSLEY, SK, S0L 1S2
(306) 463-1330   *SIC* 5311

WAL-MART CANADA CORP   *p*1411
551 THATCHER DR E SUITE 3173, MOOSE JAW, SK, S6J 1L8
(306) 693-3218   *SIC* 5311

WAL-MART CANADA CORP   *p*1413
601 CARLTON TRAIL SUITE 1, NORTH BATTLEFORD, SK, S9A 4A9
(306) 445-8105   *SIC* 5311

WAL-MART CANADA CORP   *p*1414
800 15TH ST E SUITE 100, PRINCE ALBERT, SK, S6V 8E3
(306) 764-9770   *SIC* 5311

WAL-MART CANADA CORP   *p*1422
2715 GORDON RD, REGINA, SK, S4S 6H7
(306) 584-0061   *SIC* 5311

WAL-MART CANADA CORP   *p*1422
2150 PRINCE OF WALES DR, REGINA, SK, S4V 3A6
(306) 780-3700   *SIC* 5311

WAL-MART CANADA CORP   *p*1423
3939 ROCHDALE BLVD, REGINA, SK, S4X 4P7
(306) 543-3237   *SIC* 5311

WAL-MART CANADA CORP   *p*1433
225 BETTS AVE, SASKATOON, SK, S7M 1L2
(306) 382-5454   *SIC* 5311

WAL-MART CANADA CORP   *p*1434

1706 PRESTON AVE N SUITE 3084, SASKATOON, SK, S7N 4Y1
(306) 373-2300   *SIC* 5311

WAL-MART CANADA CORP   *p*1435
3035 CLARENCE AVE S, SASKATOON, SK, S7T 0B6
(306) 653-8200   *SIC* 5311

WAL-MART CANADA CORP   *p*1437
1800 22ND AVE NE, SWIFT CURRENT, SK, S9H 0E5
(306) 778-3489   *SIC* 5311

WAL-MART CANADA CORP   *p*1438
1000 SIMS AVE, WEYBURN, SK, S4H 3N9
(306) 842-6030   *SIC* 5311

WAL-MART CANADA CORP   *p*1439
240 HAMILTON RD, YORKTON, SK, S3N 4C6
(306) 782-9820   *SIC* 5311

WAL-MART CANADA CORP   *p*1440
9021 QUARTZ RD, WHITEHORSE, YT, Y1A 4P9
(867) 667-2652   *SIC* 5311

SIC 5331 Variety stores

CANADIAN TEST CASE 36 LIMITED   *p*720
6750 CENTURY AVE SUITE 305, MISSISSAUGA, ON, L5N 2V8
SIC 5331

DOLLARAMA L.P.   *p*1156
5805 AV ROYALMOUNT, MONT-ROYAL, QC, H4P 0A1
(514) 737-1006   *SIC* 5331

HUDSON'S BAY COMPANY   *p*1155
2435 CH ROCKLAND, MONT-ROYAL, QC, H3P 2Z3
(514) 739-5521   *SIC* 5331

MAGI-PRIX INC   *p*1083
3194 AV DES ARISTOCRATES, COTE SAINT-LUC, QC, H7E 5H8
(450) 963-0410   *SIC* 5331

ROMAX VARIETY LIMITED   *p*860
900 WELLINGTON ST, SARNIA, ON, N7T 1J5
(519) 336-6660   *SIC* 5331

SUPER FRESHMART LTD   *p*932
524 CHURCH ST, TORONTO, ON, M4Y 2E1
SIC 5331

SIC 5399 Miscellaneous general merchandise

AERRIANTA INTERNATIONAL (AMERIQUE DU NORD) INC   *p*1332
6400 RUE ABRAMS, SAINT-LAURENT, QC, H4S 1Y2
(514) 335-0254   *SIC* 5399

AMBURG LIMITED   *p*747
13 INDUSTRIAL BLVD, NAPANEE, ON, K7R 1M7
(613) 354-4371   *SIC* 5399

ARMY & NAVY DEPT. STORE LIMITED   *p*84
100 LONDONDERRY MALL UNIT A, EDMONTON, AB, T5C 3C8
SIC 5399

ARZ GROUP OF COMPANIES LIMITED   *p*766
279 YORKLAND BLVD, NORTH YORK, ON, M2J 1S5
(416) 847-0350   *SIC* 5399

AUTO LAC INC   *p*405
2491 KING GEORGE HWY, MIRAMICHI, NB, E1V 6W3
(506) 773-9448   *SIC* 5399

BRODY COMPANY LTD, THE   *p*411
199 HAMPTON RD SUITE 606, QUISPAMSIS, NB, E2E 4L9
(506) 849-4123   *SIC* 5399

CENTRAL PLAINS CO-OPERATIVE LTD   *p*1407
203 MAIN ST, ESTON, SK, S0L 1A0
(306) 882-2601   *SIC* 5399

COSTCO WHOLESALE CANADA LTD   *p*393

2365 MCGILLIVRAY BLVD SUITE 1, WINNIPEG, MB, R3Y 0A1
(204) 487-5100   *SIC* 5399

COSTCO WHOLESALE CANADA LTD   *p*409
25 TRINITY DR SUITE 217, MONCTON, NB, E1G 2J7
(506) 858-7959   *SIC* 5399

COSTCO WHOLESALE CANADA LTD   *p*574
50 QUEEN ELIZABETH BLVD SUITE 524, ETOBICOKE, ON, M8Z 1M1
(416) 251-2832   *SIC* 5399

COSTCO WHOLESALE CANADA LTD   *p*641
4438 KING ST E SUITE 512, KITCHENER, ON, N2P 2G4
(519) 650-3662   *SIC* 5399

COSTCO WHOLESALE CANADA LTD   *p*1019
4411 WALKER RD SUITE 534, WINDSOR, ON, N8W 3T6
(519) 972-1899   *SIC* 5399

COSTCO WHOLESALE CANADA LTD   *p*1216
300 RUE BRIDGE, MONTREAL, QC, H3K 2C3
(514) 938-5170   *SIC* 5399

COSTCO WHOLESALE CANADA LTD   *p*1225
1015 RUE DU MARCHE-CENTRAL, MONTREAL, QC, H4N 3J8
(514) 381-1251   *SIC* 5399

COSTCO WHOLESALE CANADA LTD   *p*1387
3000 BOUL DES RECOLLETS, TROIS-RIVIERES, QC, G9A 6J2
(819) 693-5758   *SIC* 5399

DILLABOUGH, D M HOLDINGS LIMITED   *p*346
1655 18TH ST, BRANDON, MB, R7A 5C6
SIC 5399

ENGLAND, PAUL SALES LTD   *p*382
750 ST JAMES ST, WINNIPEG, MB, R3G 3J7
(204) 943-0311   *SIC* 5399

ENTREPRISES HENRI RAVARY LTEE, LES   *p*1167
3025 RUE SHERBROOKE E BUREAU 400, MONTREAL, QC, H1W 1B2
(514) 521-8888   *SIC* 5399

FHC ENTERPRISES LTD   *p*205
766 CLIVEDEN PL SUITE 150, DELTA, BC, V3M 6C7
(604) 549-9280   *SIC* 5399

GATEWAY CO-OPERATIVE LTD   *p*1405
707 NORWAY RD, CANORA, SK, S0A 0L0
(306) 563-5637   *SIC* 5399

GESTION ANDRE R. VAILLANCOURT LTEE   *p*1160
3500 BOUL DU TRICENTENAIRE BUREAU 303, MONTREAL, QC, H1B 0A3
(514) 645-2761   *SIC* 5399

GESTION GILLES ST-MICHEL INC   *p*1289
245 BOUL RIDEAU, ROUYN-NORANDA, QC, J9X 5Y6
(819) 762-4375   *SIC* 5399

GIRTON MANAGEMENT LTD   *p*365
157 VERMILLION RD SUITE 266, WINNIPEG, MB, R2J 3Z7
(204) 254-5169   *SIC* 5399

HAMILTON STORES LIMITED   *p*424
445 HAMILTON RIVER RD, HAPPY VALLEY-GOOSE BAY, NL, A0P 1S0
(709) 896-5451   *SIC* 5399

HUTCHISON, W A LTD   *p*362
1519 REGENT AVE W, WINNIPEG, MB, R2C 4M4
(204) 667-2454   *SIC* 5399

INDUSTRIES GOODWILL RENAISSANCE MONTREAL INC   *p*1181
7250 BOUL SAINT-LAURENT, MONTREAL, QC, H2R 2X9
(514) 276-3626   *SIC* 5399

J. GRANT WALLACE HOLDINGS LTD   *p*346
1655 18TH ST, BRANDON, MB, R7A 5C6
(204) 728-7120   *SIC* 5399

LAMONT, PAUL AUTOMOTIVE LTD   *p*763
890 MCKEOWN AVE, NORTH BAY, ON, P1B 8M1
(705) 472-3000   *SIC* 5399

LAURION, S. & J. LIMITED   *p139*
5402 DISCOVERY WAY, LEDUC, AB, T9E 8L9
(780) 986-5229   *SIC 5399*

LOBLAWS INC   *p166*
101 ST ALBERT RD SUITE 1, ST. ALBERT, AB, T8N 6L5
(780) 418-6818   *SIC 5399*

LOBLAWS INC   *p386*
3193 PORTAGE AVE, WINNIPEG, MB, R3K 0W4
(204) 831-3528   *SIC 5399*

LOBLAWS INC   *p1423*
4450 ROCHDALE BLVD SUITE 1585, REGINA, SK, S4X 4N9
(306) 546-6618   *SIC 5399*

MAGASINS LECOMPTE INC   *p1398*
119 RUE NOTRE-DAME E, VICTORIAVILLE, QC, G6P 3Z8
(819) 758-2626   *SIC 5399*

MEADOW LAKE CO-OPERATIVE ASSOCIATION LIMITED   *p1410*
107 2ND ST W, MEADOW LAKE, SK, S9X 1C6
(306) 236-5678   *SIC 5399*

MOUAT'S TRADING CO. LTD   *p268*
106 FULFORD-GANGES RD, SALT SPRING ISLAND, BC, V8K 2S3
(250) 537-5551   *SIC 5399*

MTF MAINLAND DISTRIBUTORS INC   *p229*
26868 56 AVE UNIT 101, LANGLEY, BC, V4W 1N9
(604) 626-4465   *SIC 5399*

NATIONAL RECYCLING INC   *p505*
5 COPPER RD, BRAMPTON, ON, L6T 4W5
(905) 790-2828   *SIC 5399*

NIMA VANI ENTERPRISES LIMITED   *p443*
1 MATTHEW FRANCIS CRT, DARTMOUTH, NS, B2W 6A1
SIC 5399

NUANCE GROUP (CANADA) INC, THE *p689*
5925 AIRPORT RD SUITE 300, MISSISSAUGA, ON, L4V 1W1
(905) 673-7299   *SIC 5399*

OSIRIS INC   *p505*
1 WILKINSON RD, BRAMPTON, ON, L6T 4M6
(905) 452-0392   *SIC 5399*

PEACE BRIDGE DUTY FREE INC   *p592*
1 PEACE BRIDGE PLAZA, FORT ERIE, ON, L2A 5N1
(905) 871-5400   *SIC 5399*

PRAIRIE CO-OPERATIVE LIMITED   *p1410*
304 1ST AVE E, MELVILLE, SK, S0A 2P0
(306) 728-5497   *SIC 5399*

PRINCE ALBERT CO-OPERATIVE ASSOCIATION LIMITED, THE   *p1414*
801 15TH ST E SUITE 791, PRINCE ALBERT, SK, S6V 0C7
(306) 764-9393   *SIC 5399*

PUGLIA, P. M. SALES LTD   *p1411*
1350 MAIN ST N, MOOSE JAW, SK, S6H 8B9
(306) 693-0888   *SIC 5399*

R.J. BONNEVILLE ENTERPRISES INC *p751*
1820 MERIVALE RD DOOR # 258, NEPEAN, ON, K2G 1E6
(613) 224-9330   *SIC 5399*

RED APPLE STORES INC   *p689*
6877 GOREWAY DR SUITE 3, MISSISSAUGA, ON, L4V 1L9
(905) 293-9700   *SIC 5399*

SOCIETE CO-OPERATIVE DE LAMEQUE LTEE, LA   *p404*
68 RUE PRINCIPALE, LAMEQUE, NB, E8T 1M6
(506) 344-2206   *SIC 5399*

SOUTHERN PLAINS CO-OPERATIVE LIMITED   *p1406*
826 4TH ST, ESTEVAN, SK, S4A 0W1
(306) 637-4300   *SIC 5399*

SURPLUS R.D. INC   *p1399*
500 RUE DE L'ACADIE, VICTORIAVILLE, QC, G6T 1A6

---

(819) 758-2466   *SIC 5399*

SWAN VALLEY CONSUMERS COOPERATIVE LIMITED   *p359*
811 MAIN ST E, SWAN RIVER, MB, R0L 1Z0
(204) 734-3431   *SIC 5399*

TORA LONDON LIMITED   *p652*
1251 HURON ST, LONDON, ON, N5Y 4V1
(613) 521-8222   *SIC 5399*

TORA MAGOG LIMITEE   *p1148*
1730 RUE SHERBROOKE, MAGOG, QC, J1X 2T3
(819) 843-3043   *SIC 5399*

TORA STRATFORD LIMITED   *p897*
477 HURON ST, STRATFORD, ON, N5A 5T8
(519) 272-2029   *SIC 5399*

VALUE VILLAGE STORES, INC   *p10*
3405 34 ST NE, CALGARY, AB, T1Y 6T6
(403) 291-3323   *SIC 5399*

VALUE VILLAGE STORES, INC   *p143*
1708 MAYOR MAGRATH DR S, LETHBRIDGE, AB, T1K 2R5
(403) 320-5358   *SIC 5399*

VALUE VILLAGE STORES, INC   *p181*
7350 EDMONDS ST, BURNABY, BC, V3N 0G7
(604) 540-4916   *SIC 5399*

VALUE VILLAGE STORES, INC   *p1020*
4322 WALKER RD, WINDSOR, ON, N8W 3T5
(519) 250-0199   *SIC 5399*

WAL-MART CANADA CORP   *p857*
3001 RICHELIEU ST, ROCKLAND, ON, K4K 0B5
(613) 446-5730   *SIC 5399*

WAL-MART CANADA CORP   *p1389*
4520 BOUL GENE-H.-KRUGER, TROIS-RIVIERES, QC, G9A 4N1
(819) 372-1181   *SIC 5399*

WDFG CANADA INC   *p265*
3211 GRANT MCCONACHIE WAY, RICHMOND, BC, V7B 0A4
(604) 273-1708   *SIC 5399*

WEST COAST DUTY FREE STORE LTD *p280*
111 176 ST SUITE 1, SURREY, BC, V3Z 9S4
(604) 538-3222   *SIC 5399*

YOUR DOLLAR STORE WITH MORE INC *p220*
160 DOUGALL RD S UNIT 200, KELOWNA, BC, V1X 3J4
(250) 860-4225   *SIC 5399*

SIC 5411 Grocery stores

1011191 ONTARIO INC   *p1001*
3140 OLD HWY 69 N SUITE 28, VAL CARON, ON, P3N 1G3
(705) 897-4958   *SIC 5411*

1023714 ONTARIO INC   *p855*
10488 YONGE ST, RICHMOND HILL, ON, L4C 3G7
(905) 884-2600   *SIC 5411*

1031647 ONTARIO LTD   *p682*
575 ONTARIO ST S UNIT 9, MILTON, ON, L9T 2N2
SIC 5411

1032002 ONTARIO INC   *p520*
4025 NEW ST, BURLINGTON, ON, L7L 1S8
(905) 639-0319   *SIC 5411*

1048271 ONTARIO LTD   *p837*
1200 PEMBROKE ST W, PEMBROKE, ON, K8A 7T1
(613) 735-5335   *SIC 5411*

1057362 ONTARIO LTD   *p578*
460 RENFORTH DR SUITE 1, ETOBICOKE, ON, M9C 2N2
(416) 622-1840   *SIC 5411*

1124029 ONTARIO INC   *p664*
217 TORONTO ST S, MARKDALE, ON, N0C 1H0

---

(519) 986-3683   *SIC 5411*

1127919 ONTARIO LIMITED   *p598*
290 FIRST ST N, GRAVENHURST, ON, P1P 1H3
(705) 687-0554   *SIC 5411*

1132145 ONTARIO LIMITED   *p631*
1030 COVERDALE DR, KINGSTON, ON, K7M 9E1
(613) 389-0090   *SIC 5411*

113559 ONTARIO LIMITED   *p837*
425 PEMBROKE ST E, PEMBROKE, ON, K8A 3L1
(613) 735-4136   *SIC 5411*

11375644 CANADA INC   *p1323*
1935 BOUL KELLER, SAINT-LAURENT, QC, H4K 2V6
(514) 727-9999   *SIC 5411*

1144257 ONTARIO LIMITED   *p477*
181 SANDWICH ST S, AMHERSTBURG, ON, N9V 1Z9
(519) 736-7378   *SIC 5411*

1144259 ONTARIO LIMITED   *p647*
65 REGIONAL RD 24, LIVELY, ON, P3Y 1H3
(705) 692-3514   *SIC 5411*

1148956 ONTARIO LTD   *p569*
745 CENTRE ST, ESPANOLA, ON, P5E 1S8
(705) 869-0284   *SIC 5411*

1151377 ONTARIO INC   *p518*
14 MAIN ST, BRIGHTON, ON, K0K 1H0
(613) 475-0200   *SIC 5411*

116260 CANADA INC   *p1354*
350 RUE PRINCIPALE, SAINT-ZOTIQUE, QC, J0P 1Z0
(450) 267-3343   *SIC 5411*

1179131 ONTARIO LIMITED   *p493*
101 EAST ST S SUITE 7, BOBCAYGEON, ON, K0M 1A0
(705) 738-9811   *SIC 5411*

1179132 ONTARIO LIMITED   *p826*
2681 ALTA VISTA DR, OTTAWA, ON, K1V 7T5
(613) 733-2311   *SIC 5411*

1184038 ONTARIO LIMITED   *p778*
747 DON MILLS RD SUITE 60, NORTH YORK, ON, M3C 1T2
(416) 239-7171   *SIC 5411*

1195149 ONTARIO LIMITED   *p632*
1586 CENTENNIAL DR, KINGSTON, ON, K7P 0C7
(613) 389-8010   *SIC 5411*

1214288 ONTARIO LIMITED   *p482*
125 JOHN ST N, AYLMER, ON, N5H 2A7
(519) 773-9219   *SIC 5411*

123 ENTERPRISES LTD   *p268*
374 LOWER GANGES RD, SALT SPRING ISLAND, BC, V8K 2V7
(250) 537-4144   *SIC 5411*

1262510 ONTARIO LIMITED   *p563*
1414 HIGHWAY 2 UNIT 8, COURTICE, ON, L1E 3B4
(905) 433-7735   *SIC 5411*

1265767 ONTARIO LIMITED   *p857*
311 GORHAM RD, RIDGEWAY, ON, L0S 1N0
(905) 894-5266   *SIC 5411*

1265768 ONTARIO LTD   *p769*
3259 BAYVIEW AVE, NORTH YORK, ON, M2K 1G4
(416) 221-6702   *SIC 5411*

127113 CANADA INC   *p1096*
960 CH HERRON, DORVAL, QC, H9S 1B3
SIC 5411

1290357 ONTARIO LIMITED   *p905*
1054 CENTRE ST, THORNHILL, ON, L4J 3M8
(905) 882-2240   *SIC 5411*

1290685 ONTARIO INC   *p610*
135 BARTON ST E, HAMILTON, ON, L8L 8A8
(905) 523-0641   *SIC 5411*

1291292 ONTARIO INC   *p809*
43 ONTARIO ST, ORILLIA, ON, L3V 0T7
(705) 326-3586   *SIC 5411*

1307299 ONTARIO INC.   *p840*

1200 LANSDOWNE ST W, PETERBOROUGH, ON, K9J 2A1
(705) 748-5655   *SIC 5411*

132087 CANADA INC   *p1223*
6675 BOUL MONK, MONTREAL, QC, H4E 3J2
(514) 767-5323   *SIC 5411*

1323339 ONTARIO LIMITED   *p902*
20954 DALTON RD, SUTTON WEST, ON, L0E 1R0
(905) 722-5671   *SIC 5411*

1327187 ONTARIO INC   *p484*
2 7 ST, BALMERTOWN, ON, P0V 1C0
(807) 735-2132   *SIC 5411*

1340123 ONTARIO LTD   *p754*
869 MULOCK DR SUITE 6, NEWMARKET, ON, L3Y 8S3
(905) 853-3356   *SIC 5411*

13601 YUKON INC.   *p1440*
4220 4TH AVE, WHITEHORSE, YT, Y1A 1K1
(867) 667-2527   *SIC 5411*

1365992 ONTARIO LTD   *p923*
710 MOUNT PLEASANT RD, TORONTO, ON, M4S 2N6
(416) 483-1290   *SIC 5411*

1389773 ONTARIO INC   *p610*
399 GREENHILL AVE, HAMILTON, ON, L8K 6N5
(905) 561-2221   *SIC 5411*

1401911 ONTARIO LIMITED   *p842*
4136 PETROLIA LINE, PETROLIA, ON, N0N 1R0
(519) 882-2211   *SIC 5411*

1408939 ONTARIO LIMITED   *p510*
345 MAIN ST N, BRAMPTON, ON, L6X 1N6
(905) 452-9122   *SIC 5411*

1416018 ONTARIO LIMITED   *p993*
853 JANE ST, TORONTO, ON, M6N 4C4
(416) 762-7975   *SIC 5411*

1426159 ONTARIO LIMITED   *p842*
400 LANSDOWNE ST E SUITE 1, PETERBOROUGH, ON, K9L 0B2
(705) 740-9365   *SIC 5411*

1437384 ONTARIO LIMITED   *p917*
1500 BAYVIEW AVE, TORONTO, ON, M4G 3B4
(416) 486-8294   *SIC 5411*

1437716 ONTARIO LIMITED   *p820*
596 MONTREAL RD, OTTAWA, ON, K1K 0T9
(613) 745-0778   *SIC 5411*

1441571 ONTARIO INC   *p839*
501 TOWERHILL RD, PETERBOROUGH, ON, K9H 7S3
(705) 740-9026   *SIC 5411*

1460932 ONTARIO LIMITED   *p832*
2577 BASELINE RD, OTTAWA, ON, K2H 7B3
(613) 726-9513   *SIC 5411*

1470341 ONTARIO INC   *p751*
1581 GREENBANK RD SUITE 16, NEPEAN, ON, K2J 4Y6
(613) 825-5495   *SIC 5411*

1476182 ONTARIO LIMITED   *p990*
22 NORTHCOTE AVE, TORONTO, ON, M6J 3K3
(416) 537-4124   *SIC 5411*

1500451 ONTARIO LIMITED   *p484*
165 WELLINGTON ST E, BARRIE, ON, L4M 2C7
(705) 737-0389   *SIC 5411*

1520202 ONTARIO LTD   *p493*
286 CHATHAM ST N RR 5, BLENHEIM, ON, N0P 1A0
(519) 676-0353   *SIC 5411*

1530431 ONTARIO LIMITED   *p677*
7075 MARKHAM RD, MARKHAM, ON, L3S 3J9
(905) 471-0089   *SIC 5411*

1540886 ONTARIO INC   *p526*
2180 ITABASHI WAY SUITE 1A, BURLINGTON, ON, L7M 5A5
(905) 319-7272   *SIC 5411*

1543892 ONTARIO LTD *p645*
42 RUSSELL ST W, LINDSAY, ON, K9V
2W9
(705) 328-0622 *SIC* 5411

1571921 ONTARIO LIMITED *p864*
51 TAPSCOTT RD, SCARBOROUGH, ON,
M1B 4Y7
SIC 5411

1576610 ONTARIO LTD *p870*
2471 KINGSTON RD, SCARBOROUGH,
ON, M1N 1V4
(416) 261-4569 *SIC* 5411

1594058 ONTARIO LTD *p658*
1190 OXFORD ST W, LONDON, ON, N6H
4N2
(519) 474-2561 *SIC* 5411

1594414 ONTARIO LIMITED *p866*
4473 KINGSTON RD, SCARBOROUGH,
ON, M1E 2N7
(416) 281-9140 *SIC* 5411

1633936 ONTARIO INC *p599*
1349 MEADOW DR, GREELY, ON, K4P 1N3
(613) 821-3016 *SIC* 5411

167395 CANADA INC *p1183*
5242 AV DU PARC, MONTREAL, QC, H2V
4G7
(514) 273-8782 *SIC* 5411

1690651 ONTARIO INC *p577*
5559 DUNDAS ST W, ETOBICOKE, ON,
M9B 1B9
(416) 239-7171 *SIC* 5411

1692038 ONTARIO LTD *p788*
1811 AVENUE RD, NORTH YORK, ON,
M5M 3Z3
(416) 781-3917 *SIC* 5411

169727 CANADA INC *p1103*
720 MONTEE PAIEMENT BUREAU 100,
GATINEAU, QC, J8R 4A3
(819) 643-4233 *SIC* 5411

1784007 ONTARIO LTD *p932*
200 FRONT ST E SUITE 3458, TORONTO,
ON, M5A 4T9
(416) 368-8484 *SIC* 5411

1791884 ONTARIO LIMITED *p781*
3685 KEELE ST SUITE 5, NORTH YORK,
ON, M3J 3H6
(866) 987-6453 *SIC* 5411

1794318 ONTARIO INC *p580*
1701 MARTIN GROVE RD SUITE 1, ETOBI-
COKE, ON, M9V 4N4
(416) 742-8688 *SIC* 5411

1827212 ONTARIO LIMITED *p648*
1925 DUNDAS ST SUITE 3453, LONDON,
ON, N5V 1P7
(519) 453-8226 *SIC* 5411

1847674 ONTARIO INC *p1012*
609 SOUTH PELHAM RD, WELLAND, ON,
L3C 3C7
(905) 735-7467 *SIC* 5411

1992013 ONTARIO LTD *p868*
1880 EGLINTON AVE E, SCARBOROUGH,
ON, M1L 2L1
(416) 750-4400 *SIC* 5411

2004104 ONTARIO LIMITED *p618*
857 CECILE BLVD, HAWKESBURY, ON,
K6A 1P4
(613) 632-5994 *SIC* 5411

2018775 ONTARIO LIMITED *p652*
234 OXFORD ST E, LONDON, ON, N6A
1T7
(519) 432-1127 *SIC* 5411

2023649 ONTARIO LIMITED *p906*
9 PINE ST N, THOROLD, ON, L2V 3Z9
(905) 227-0533 *SIC* 5411

2024232 ONTARIO INC *p906*
7040 YONGE ST UNIT B1, THORNHILL,
ON, L4J 1V7
(905) 882-0040 *SIC* 5411

2026798 ONTARIO LIMITED *p745*
120 ONTARIO RD, MITCHELL, ON, N0K
1N0
(519) 348-8446 *SIC* 5411

2032244 ONTARIO LIMITED *p746*
121 MAIN ST S, MOUNT FOREST, ON,

N0G 2L0
(519) 323-1390 *SIC* 5411

2037247 ONTARIO LIMITED *p618*
52 BRIDGE ST, HASTINGS, ON, K0L 1Y0
(705) 696-3504 *SIC* 5411

2037247 ONTARIO LIMITED *p1077*
1155 BOUL TALBOT, CHICOUTIMI, QC,
G7H 4B5
(418) 690-0063 *SIC* 5411

2043665 ONTARIO LIMITED *p620*
131 HOWLAND DR, HUNTSVILLE, ON,
P1H 2P7
(705) 789-6972 *SIC* 5411

2051183 ONTARIO LIMITED *p875*
2555 VICTORIA PARK AVE SUITE 19,
SCARBOROUGH, ON, M1T 1A3
(416) 773-1166 *SIC* 5411

2079421 ONTARIO LIMITED *p1003*
1551 NIAGARA STONE RD, VIRGIL, ON,
L0S 1T0
(905) 468-3286 *SIC* 5411

2100050 ONTARIO INC *p766*
3030 DON MILLS RD SUITE 26, NORTH
YORK, ON, M2J 3C1
(416) 756-1668 *SIC* 5411

2125341 ALBERTA LTD *p172*
4802 51 ST SUITE 1, WHITECOURT, AB,
T7S 1R9
(780) 778-5900 *SIC* 5411

2144011 ONTARIO INC *p628*
443 THE QUEENSWAY S SUITE 26,
KESWICK, ON, L4P 3J4
(905) 476-7773 *SIC* 5411

2156110 ONTARIO LIMITED *p1005*
115 HAMILTON ST N SUITE 81, WATER-
DOWN, ON, L8B 1A8
(905) 690-6446 *SIC* 5411

2169319 ONTARIO INC *p778*
747 DON MILLS RD UNIT 60, NORTH
YORK, ON, M3C 1T2
(416) 900-1699 *SIC* 5411

2360083 ONTARIO LIMITED *p780*
4750 DUFFERIN ST, NORTH YORK, ON,
M3H 5S7
(416) 736-6606 *SIC* 5411

2408234 ONTARIO INC *p882*
239 ST CATHARINES ST, SMITHVILLE,
ON, L0R 2A0
(905) 957-3374 *SIC* 5411

2625-8368 QUEBEC INC *p1304*
16850 BOUL LACROIX, SAINT-GEORGES,
QC, G5Y 8G9
(418) 228-8661 *SIC* 5411

2627 W 16TH AVENUE HOLDINGS LTD *p322*
2627 16TH AVE W, VANCOUVER, BC, V6K
3C2
(604) 736-0009 *SIC* 5411

2704242 CANADA INC *p1161*
9025 BOUL MAURICE-DUPLESSIS, MON-
TREAL, QC, H1E 6M3
(514) 648-1883 *SIC* 5411

2747-6761 QUEBEC INC *p1317*
400 BOUL DU SEMINAIRE N BUREAU
2747, SAINT-JEAN-SUR-RICHELIEU, QC,
J3B 5L2
(450) 349-2878 *SIC* 5411

2788331 CANADA INC *p1306*
701 AV SAINT-GEORGES, SAINT-
GEORGES-DE-CHAMPLAIN, QC, G7T 5K4
(819) 533-5445 *SIC* 5411

2857-4077 QUEBEC INC *p1369*
850 7E AV, SHAWINIGAN, QC, G9T 2B8
(819) 533-4553 *SIC* 5411

2858-6691 QUEBEC INC *p1282*
305 BOUL IBERVILLE, REPENTIGNY, QC,
J6A 2A6
(450) 581-2630 *SIC* 5411

2875446 CANADA INC *p1384*
266 RUE VICTORIA, THURSO, QC, J0X
3B0
(819) 985-3259 *SIC* 5411

2875448 CANADA INC *p1105*
2505 RUE SAINT-LOUIS, GATINEAU, QC,
J8V 1A4

(819) 561-3772 *SIC* 5411

2941902 CANADA INC *p1346*
6852A RUE JEAN-TALON E, SAINT-
LEONARD, QC, H1S 1N1
(514) 252-8277 *SIC* 5411

2956-2584 QUEBEC INC *p1046*
98 235 RTE, ANGE-GARDIEN, QC, J0E
1E0
(450) 293-6115 *SIC* 5411

3093-9920 QUEBEC INC *p1116*
2350 RUE SAINT-HUBERT, JONQUIERE,
QC, G7X 5N4
(418) 547-6611 *SIC* 5411

3095-0497 QUEBEC INC *p1311*
1340 BOUL CHOQUETTE, SAINT-
HYACINTHE, QC, J2S 6G1
(450) 778-5558 *SIC* 5411

3105-4521 QUEBEC INC *p1302*
1200 BOUL SAINT-FELICIEN, SAINT-
FELICIEN, QC, G8K 2N6
(418) 679-1431 *SIC* 5411

3183441 CANADA INC *p1245*
4957 BOUL SAINT-JEAN, PIERREFONDS,
QC, H9H 2A9
SIC 5411

320364 ALBERTA LTD *p80*
5411 55 ST, COLD LAKE, AB, T9M 1R6
(780) 594-3311 *SIC* 5411

3424626 CANADA INC *p1323*
1855 AV O'BRIEN, SAINT-LAURENT, QC,
H4L 3W6
(450) 681-4100 *SIC* 5411

3855515 CANADA INC *p1184*
5029 AV DU PARC, MONTREAL, QC, H2V
4E9
(514) 271-8788 *SIC* 5411

3855155 CANADA INC *p1214*
1420 RUE DU FORT, MONTREAL, QC, H3H
2C4
SIC 5411

3881793 MANITOBA LTD *p370*
2575 MAIN ST, WINNIPEG, MB, R2V 4W3
(204) 334-1211 *SIC* 5411

399837 BC LTD *p212*
4823 50TH AVE S, FORT NELSON, BC,
V0C 1R0
(250) 774-2791 *SIC* 5411

4128001 CANADA INC *p1237*
4919 BOUL NOTRE-DAME, MONTREAL,
QC, H7W 1V3
(450) 681-4300 *SIC* 5411

4259238 CANADA INC *p1346*
5915 RUE BELANGER, SAINT-LEONARD,
QC, H1T 1G8
(514) 259-4216 *SIC* 5411

4501403 CANADA INC *p1246*
3478 32E AV, POINTE-AUX-TREMBLES,
QC, H1A 3M1
(514) 498-7227 *SIC* 5411

4501403 CANADA INC *p1248*
230 BOUL HYMUS, POINTE-CLAIRE, QC,
H9R 5P5
(514) 694-3747 *SIC* 5411

450252 ONTARIO LTD *p879*
95 MAIN ST S, SEAFORTH, ON, N0K 1W0
(519) 527-1631 *SIC* 5411

49TH PARALLEL GROCERY LIMITED *p224*
1020 1ST AVE, LADYSMITH, BC, V9G 1A5
(250) 245-3221 *SIC* 5411

510127 ONTARIO LIMITED *p861*
219 TRUNK RD, SAULT STE. MARIE, ON,
P6A 3S7
(705) 254-7466 *SIC* 5411

526293 BC LTD *p195*
1502 COLUMBIA AVE UNIT 1, CASTLE-
GAR, BC, V1N 4G5
(250) 304-2470 *SIC* 5411

563769 B.C. LTD *p214*
1900 GARIBALDI WAY, GARIBALDI HIGH-
LANDS, BC, V0N 1T0
(604) 898-6810 *SIC* 5411

574852 ALBERTA LIMITED *p20*
2202 CENTRE ST NE, CALGARY, AB, T2E
2T5

(403) 277-9166 *SIC* 5411

576794 ONTARIO LTD *p978*
69 SPADINA AVE, TORONTO, ON, M5V
3P8
(416) 979-8155 *SIC* 5411

600038 SASKATCHEWAN LTD *p350*
557 SOUTH HUDSON ST, FLIN FLON, MB,
R8A 1E1
(306) 688-3426 *SIC* 5411

602726 ONTARIO LTD *p919*
623 DANFORTH AVE, TORONTO, ON, M4K
1R2
(416) 466-5371 *SIC* 5411

61401 MANITOBA LTD *p370*
1650 MAIN ST, WINNIPEG, MB, R2V 1Y9
(204) 339-0213 *SIC* 5411

616813 N.B. LTD *p412*
1350 HICKEY RD, SAINT JOHN, NB, E2J
5C9
(506) 657-8463 *SIC* 5411

625056 SASKATCHEWAN LTD *p369*
1050 KEEWATIN ST, WINNIPEG, MB, R2R
2E2
(204) 694-0085 *SIC* 5411

677957 ONTARIO INC *p880*
19101 LESLIE ST, SHARON, ON, L0G 1V0
(905) 478-8241 *SIC* 5411

7-ELEVEN CANADA, INC *p253*
3531 VIKING WAY UNIT 7, RICHMOND,
BC, V6V 1W1
(604) 273-2008 *SIC* 5411

7-ELEVEN CANADA, INC *p273*
13450 102 AVE SUITE 2400, SURREY, BC,
V3T 0C3
(604) 586-0711 *SIC* 5411

717940 ONTARIO LIMITED *p611*
435 MAIN ST E, HAMILTON, ON, L8N 1K1
(905) 528-5493 *SIC* 5411

727432 ONTARIO LIMITED *p758*
6460 LUNDY'S LANE, NIAGARA FALLS,
ON, L2G 1T6
(905) 357-4623 *SIC* 5411

749416 ONTARIO INC *p568*
40 HILLSIDE DR S, ELLIOT LAKE, ON, P5A
1M7
(705) 848-9790 *SIC* 5411

779173 ONTARIO LIMITED *p564*
75 DEEP RIVER ROAD, DEEP RIVER, ON,
K0J 1P0
(613) 584-3893 *SIC* 5411

783312 ONTARIO LIMITED *p708*
2281 CAMILLA RD, MISSISSAUGA, ON,
L5A 2K2
(905) 848-4840 *SIC* 5411

783814 ALBERTA LTD *p146*
1960 STRACHAN RD SE, MEDICINE HAT,
AB, T1B 4K4
(403) 504-5400 *SIC* 5411

784704 ONTARIO LTD *p617*
832 10TH ST, HANOVER, ON, N4N 1S3
(519) 364-4661 *SIC* 5411

808269 ONTARIO INC *p890*
20 WILLIAM ST, ST THOMAS, ON, N5R
3G9
(519) 633-9370 *SIC* 5411

81918 ONTARIO LTD *p800*
125 CROSS AVE SUITE 1, OAKVILLE, ON,
L6J 2W8
(905) 844-7493 *SIC* 5411

8273537 CANADA LIMITED *p155*
3 CLEARVIEW MARKET WAY, RED DEER,
AB, T4P 0M9
(403) 342-1265 *SIC* 5411

868971 ONTARIO INC *p837*
1751 PAUL MARTIN DR, PEMBROKE, ON,
K8A 6W5
(613) 735-7066 *SIC* 5411

892316 ONTARIO LIMITED *p665*
4476 16TH AVE, MARKHAM, ON, L3R 0M1
(905) 940-0655 *SIC* 5411

900261 ONTARIO INC *p913*
670 AIRPORT RD SUITE 200, TIMMINS,
ON, P4P 1J2
(705) 268-5020 *SIC* 5411

▲ Public Company   ■ Public Company Family Member   **HQ** Headquarters   **BR** Branch   **SL** Single Location

9008-4013 QUEBEC INC   p1394
585 AV SAINT-CHARLES BUREAU 500, VAUDREUIL-DORION, QC, J7V 8P9
(450) 424-3550   SIC 5411

9020-7424 QUEBEC INC   p1280
3373 RUE DE L'HETRIERE, QUEBEC, QC, G3A 0M2
(418) 872-4113   SIC 5411

9023-4683 QUEBEC INC   p1319
2012 RUE SAINT-GEORGES, SAINT-JEROME, QC, J7Y 1M8
(450) 565-8890   SIC 5411

9026-4979 QUEBEC INC   p1313
2260 RUE SAINT-CHARLES, SAINT-HYACINTHE, QC, J2T 1V5
(450) 774-4189   SIC 5411

9045-9827 QUEBEC INC   p1385
6060 BOUL JEAN-XXIII, TROIS-RIVIERES, QC, G8Z 4B5
(819) 374-6060   SIC 5411

9067-3476 QUEBEC INC   p1287
348 CH DE LA GRANDE-COTE, ROSE-MERE, QC, J7A 1K3
(450) 621-3510   SIC 5411

9069-7897 QUEBEC INC   p1291
790   343   RTE,   SAINT-ALPHONSE-RODRIGUEZ, QC, J0K 1W0
(450) 883-2963   SIC 5411

9070-5245 QUEBEC INC   p1257
272 RUE SAINT-JOSEPH E, QUEBEC, QC, G1K 3A9
(418) 648-2805   SIC 5411

9084-4622 QUEBEC INC   p1103
1205 RUE DE NEUVILLE, GATINEAU, QC, J8M 2E7
(819) 986-7579   SIC 5411

9085-1379 QUEBEC INC   p1261
1035 BOUL WILFRID-HAMEL, QUEBEC, QC, G1M 2R7
(418) 683-4775   SIC 5411

9093-3789 QUEBEC INC   p1389
1801 3E AV BUREAU 180, VAL-D'OR, QC, J9P 5K1
(819) 874-7741   SIC 5411

9093-6907 QUEBEC INC   p1246
13155 RUE SHERBROOKE E, POINTE-AUX-TREMBLES, QC, H1A 1B9
(514) 498-2220   SIC 5411

9094-0594 QUEBEC INC   p1130
1255 BOUL SHEVCHENKO, LASALLE, QC, H8N 1N8
(514) 595-9111   SIC 5411

911803 ONTARIO INC   p594
370 WILLIAM ST, GEORGIAN BLUFFS, ON, N0H 2T0
(519) 534-0760   SIC 5411

9120-9734 QUEBEC INC   p1256
4250 1RE AV BUREAU 95, QUEBEC, QC, G1H 2S5
(418) 627-0660   SIC 5411

9125-9051 QUEBEC INC.   p1242
120 BOUL PERRON O, NEW RICHMOND, QC, G0C 2B0
(418) 392-4237   SIC 5411

9128-0453 QUEBEC INC   p1360
2950 BOUL DES PROMENADES, SAINTE-MARTHE-SUR-LE-LAC, QC, J0N 1P0
(450) 623-3010   SIC 5411

9128-3820 QUEBEC INC   p1147
1526 RUE SHERBROOKE, MAGOG, QC, J1X 2T3
(819) 868-1122   SIC 5411

9139-6317 QUEBEC INC   p1322
3765 CH D'OKA, SAINT-JOSEPH-DU-LAC, QC, J0N 1M0
(450) 413-2789   SIC 5411

9142-5454 QUEBEC INC   p1078
2000 BOUL TALBOT, CHICOUTIMI, QC, G7H 7Y2
(418) 698-9556   SIC 5411

9157-5548 QUEBEC INC   p1075
40   RUE   EMILE-DESPINS,   CHARLE-MAGNE, QC, J5Z 3L6
(450) 581-6611   SIC 5411

9158-7022 QUEBEC INC   p1361
3595 BOUL DE LA CONCORDE E, SAINTE-ROSE, QC, H7E 2E1
(450) 661-2525   SIC 5411

9158-9093 QUEBEC INC   p1319
1005 BOUL DU GRAND-HERON, SAINT-JEROME, QC, J7Y 3P2
(450) 438-5214   SIC 5411

9158-9325 QUEBEC INC   p1139
1015 RUE DU BASILIC, LEVIS, QC, G6Z 3K4
(418) 834-8077   SIC 5411

9165-1588 QUEBEC INC   p1311
5445   BOUL   LAURIER   O,   SAINT-HYACINTHE, QC, J2S 3V6
(450) 773-0333   SIC 5411

9171-2802 QUEBEC INC   p1243
450 BOUL DON-QUICHOTTE, NOTRE-DAME-DE-L'ILE-PERROT, QC, J7V 0J9
(514) 425-6111   SIC 5411

9175-6429 QUEBEC INC   p1364
214 BOUL RENE-A.-ROBERT, SAINTE-THERESE, QC, J7E 4L2
(450) 971-0458   SIC 5411

9181-8153 QUEBEC INC   p1242
680 CH DU VILLAGE, MORIN-HEIGHTS, QC, J0R 1H0
(450) 226-5769   SIC 5411

9190-4144 QUEBEC INC.   p1349
400 AV CHAPLEAU, SAINT-PASCAL, QC, G0L 3Y0
(418) 492-2902   SIC 5411

9191-0174 QUEBEC INC   p1184
5600 AV DU PARC, MONTREAL, QC, H2V 4H1
(514) 272-5258   SIC 5411

9215-9516 QUEBEC INC   p1071
3260 BOUL LAPINIERE, BROSSARD, QC, J4Z 3L8
(450) 445-1224   SIC 5411

9222-0524 QUEBEC INC   p1287
1395 RUE L'ANNONCIATION S, RIVIERE-ROUGE, QC, J0T 1T0
SIC 5411

9230-9970 QUEBEC INC   p1276
2295 AV CHAUVEAU BUREAU 200, QUE-BEC, QC, G2C 0G7
(418) 842-3381   SIC 5411

974475 ONTARIO LIMITED   p748
200 GRANT CARMAN DR, NEPEAN, ON, K2E 7Z8
(613) 727-1672   SIC 5411

974479 ONTARIO LIMITED   p762
1 LAURENTIAN AVE, NORTH BAY, ON, P1B 9T2
(705) 472-8866   SIC 5411

976736 ONTARIO LIMITED   p477
7 MANITOU CRES W, AMHERSTVIEW, ON, K7N 1B7
(613) 389-4184   SIC 5411

987112 ONTARIO INC   p607
32 KING ST E, HAGERSVILLE, ON, N0A 1H0
(905) 768-3571   SIC 5411

98946 CANADA INC   p1375
6185 CH DE SAINT-ELIE, SHERBROOKE, QC, J1R 0L1
(819) 566-8555   SIC 5411

994731 ONTARIO LTD   p894
5710 MAIN ST, STOUFFVILLE, ON, L4A 8B1
(866) 987-6453   SIC 5411

A & F GALATI LIMITED   p764
5845 LESLIE ST, NORTH YORK, ON, M2H 1J8
(416) 756-2000   SIC 5411

ABERNETHY FOODS (ORILLIA) INC   p809
80 FITTONS RD W, ORILLIA, ON, L3V 7A1
(705) 325-9072   SIC 5411

ABOUGOUCHE BROS ENTERPRISES LTD
p138
10114 101 ST, LAC LA BICHE, AB, T0A 2C0
(780) 623-4234   SIC 5411

ACME FOOD CO, THE   p233

14 COMMERCIAL ST, NANAIMO, BC, V9R 5G2
(250) 753-0042   SIC 5411

ADVANCE FOODS LTD   p98
9106 142 ST NW, EDMONTON, AB, T5R 0M7
(780) 483-1525   SIC 5411

AGOSTINO & NANCY'S NO FRILLS   p812
151 BLOOR ST E, OSHAWA, ON, L1H 3M3
(905) 571-6488   SIC 5411

ALIMENTATION A.D.R. INC   p1280
795 BOUL DU LAC BUREAU 264, QUE-BEC, QC, G2M 0E4
(418) 849-3674   SIC 5411

ALIMENTATION ANDREA JOLICOEUR INC
p1246
3000 BOUL DE LA ROUSSELIERE, POINTE-AUX-TREMBLES, QC, H1A 4G3
(514) 498-7117   SIC 5411

ALIMENTATION BENOIT ROBERT INC
p1385
1375 RUE AUBUCHON, TROIS-RIVIERES, QC, G8Y 5K4
(819) 373-5166   SIC 5411

ALIMENTATION   BLANCHETTE   & CYRENNE INC   p1163
9280 RUE SHERBROOKE E, MONTREAL, QC, H1L 1E5
(514) 351-1252   SIC 5411

ALIMENTATION CHRISTIAN VERREAULT INC   p1121
150 6E RUE, LA BAIE, QC, G7B 4V9
(418) 544-8251   SIC 5411

ALIMENTATION COATICOOK (1986) INC
p1081
265 RUE CHILD, COATICOOK, QC, J1A 2B5
(819) 849-6226   SIC 5411

ALIMENTATION COUCHE-TARD INC   p1233
4204 BOUL INDUSTRIEL, MONTREAL, QC, H7L 0E3
(450) 662-3272   SIC 5411

ALIMENTATION D.M. ST-GEORGES INC
p1349
110 RUE BRASSARD, SAINT-MICHEL-DES-SAINTS, QC, J0K 3B0
(450) 833-1313   SIC 5411

ALIMENTATION DANIEL BRUYERE INC
p1173
1955 RUE SAINTE-CATHERINE E, MON-TREAL, QC, H2K 2H6
(514) 525-5090   SIC 5411

ALIMENTATION DANIEL INC   p1245
13057 BOUL GOUIN O, PIERREFONDS, QC, H8Z 1X1
(514) 620-7370   SIC 5411

ALIMENTATION DANIEL LAROUCHE INC
p1369
1100 13E AV N, SHERBROOKE, QC, J1E 3J7
(819) 562-6788   SIC 5411

ALIMENTATION DE LA MITIS INC   p1154
1330 BOUL BENOIT-GABOURY, MONT-JOLI, QC, G5H 4B2
(418) 775-8915   SIC 5411

ALIMENTATION DENIS GODIN INC   p1166
4405 RUE SAINTE-CATHERINE E, MON-TREAL, QC, H1V 1Y4
(514) 254-0126   SIC 5411

ALIMENTATION DOMINIC POTVIN INC
p1163
6550 RUE SHERBROOKE E, MONTREAL, QC, H1N 1C6
(514) 259-8403   SIC 5411

ALIMENTATION DUPLESSIS, MARTIN INC
p1219
5150 CH DE LA COTE-DES-NEIGES, MON-TREAL, QC, H3T 1X8
(514) 738-7377   SIC 5411

ALIMENTATION ERIC DA PONTE INC   p1167
3800 RUE ONTARIO E, MONTREAL, QC, H1W 1S4
(514) 524-8850   SIC 5411

ALIMENTATION FRANCIS LAMONTAGNE

INC   p1104
1100 BOUL MALONEY O, GATINEAU, QC, J8T 6G3
SIC 5411

ALIMENTATION GAETAN PLANTE INC
p1134
53 PLACE QUEVILLON, LEBEL-SUR-QUEVILLON, QC, J0Y 1X0
(819) 755-4803   SIC 5411

ALIMENTATION HOCHELAGA G.S. INC
p1163
7975 RUE HOCHELAGA, MONTREAL, QC, H1L 2K9
(514) 351-7340   SIC 5411

ALIMENTATION J. G. D. INC   p1122
975 BOUL TASCHEREAU BUREAU 302, LA PRAIRIE, QC, J5R 1W7
(450) 659-1611   SIC 5411

ALIMENTATION L'EPICIER INC   p1161
11460 BOUL ARMAND-BOMBARDIER, MONTREAL, QC, H1E 2W9
(514) 351-1991   SIC 5411

ALIMENTATION LAPOINTE & FRERES INC
p1122
25 BOUL KANE, LA MALBAIE, QC, G5A 1J2
(418) 665-3954   SIC 5411

ALIMENTATION LAROCHE & FILS INC
p1135
3045 RTE LAGUEUX BUREAU 100, LEVIS, QC, G6J 1K6
(418) 831-7987   SIC 5411

ALIMENTATION LE SIEUR ENR   p1379
1415 GRANDE ALLEE, TERREBONNE, QC, J6W 5M9
(450) 492-7272   SIC 5411

ALIMENTATION LEBEL INC   p1122
615 RUE 1 RE, LA POCATIERE, QC, G0R 1Z0
(418) 856-3827   SIC 5411

ALIMENTATION MARC BOUGIE INC   p1168
3185 RUE BEAUBIEN E, MONTREAL, QC, H1Y 1H5
(514) 721-2433   SIC 5411

ALIMENTATION MARIE GIGNAC INC   p1271
2450 BOUL LAURIER BUREAU 418, QUE-BEC, QC, G1V 2L1
(418) 651-8150   SIC 5411

ALIMENTATION MARQUIS, YVES INC   p1359
1116 BOUL VACHON N, SAINTE-MARIE, QC, G6E 1N7
(418) 387-3120   SIC 5411

ALIMENTATION OLIVIER,GUY INC   p1292
3525 RUE DE L'HETRIERE, SAINT-AUGUSTIN-DE-DESMAURES,   QC,   G3A 0C1
(418) 872-4444   SIC 5411

ALIMENTATION R DENIS INC   p1235
255 BOUL DE LA CONCORDE O, MON-TREAL, QC, H7N 5T1
(450) 668-0793   SIC 5411

ALIMENTATION RAYMOND DROUIN INC
p1142
369 RUE SAINT-JEAN O, LONGUEUIL, QC, J4H 2X7
(450) 679-4570   SIC 5411

ALIMENTATION RAYMOND ROUSSEAU INC   p1270
1580 CH SAINT-LOUIS, QUEBEC, QC, G1S 1G6
(418) 527-7758   SIC 5411

ALIMENTATION RICHARD GAGNON S C INC   p1322
1461 AV VICTORIA, SAINT-LAMBERT, QC, J4R 1R5
(450) 671-6205   SIC 5411

ALIMENTATION ROBERT DESROCHER INC   p1135
44 RTE DU PRESIDENT-KENNEDY, LEVIS, QC, G6V 6C5
(418) 835-6313   SIC 5411

ALIMENTATION ROBERT DUFOUR INC
p1122
375 BOUL DE COMPORTE BUREAU 129, LA MALBAIE, QC, G5A 1H9

(418) 665-4473   *SIC 5411*
ALIMENTATION SERRO INC   p1263
707 BOUL CHAREST O, QUEBEC, QC,
G1N 4P6
(418) 681-7385   *SIC 5411*
ALIMENTATION SOGESCO INC   p1311
3000 BOUL LAFRAMBOISE, SAINT-
HYACINTHE, QC, J2S 4Z4
(450) 773-7582   *SIC 5411*
ALIMENTATION ST-DENIS INC   p1084
307 BOUL CARTIER O, COTE SAINT-LUC,
QC, H7N 2J1
(450) 669-7501   *SIC 5411*
ALIMENTATION ST-ONGE INC   p1307
972 CH DES HAUTEURS, SAINT-
HIPPOLYTE, QC, J8A 1L2
(450) 224-5179   *SIC 5411*
ALIMENTATION ST-RAYMOND INC   p1351
333 COTE JOYEUSE BUREAU 100, SAINT-
RAYMOND, QC, G3L 4A8
(418) 337-6781   *SIC 5411*
ALIMENTATION SYLVAIN BRIERE INC
p1377
7000 AV DE LA PLAZA BUREAU 2036,
SOREL-TRACY, QC, J3R 4L8
(450) 742-8227   *SIC 5411*
**ALIMENTATION THOMASSIN, STEPHANE
INC**   p1271
815 AV MYRAND, QUEBEC, QC, G1V 2V7
(418) 683-1981   *SIC 5411*
ALIMENTATIONS BECHAR INC   p1104
455 BOUL GREBER, GATINEAU, QC, J8T
5T7
(819) 243-0011   *SIC 5411*
ALIMENTATIONS GAREAU INC   p1281
3450 RUE QUEEN, RAWDON, QC, J0K 1S0
(450) 834-2633   *SIC 5411*
**ALIMENTATIONS GOVANNI ROUSSO 2004
INC**   p1229
6645 AV SOMERLED, MONTREAL, QC,
H4V 1T3
(514) 486-3042   *SIC 5411*
**ALIMENTATIONS SHNAIDMAN PAGANO
INC, LES**   p1083
5800 BOUL CAVENDISH BUREAU 111,
COTE SAINT-LUC, QC, H4W 2T5
(514) 482-4710   *SIC 5411*
ALIMENTS CHEVREFILS INC, LES   p1354
555 BOUL DE SAINTE-ADELE BUREAU
205, SAINTE-ADELE, QC, J8B 1A7
(450) 227-2712   *SIC 5411*
**ALIMENTS ESPOSITO (ST-MICHEL) LTEE,
LES**   p1171
7030 BOUL SAINT-MICHEL, MONTREAL,
QC, H2A 2Z4
(514) 722-1069   *SIC 5411*
ALIMENTS S.R.C. INC, LES   p1345
4617 BOUL DES GRANDES-PRAIRIES,
SAINT-LEONARD, QC, H1R 1A5
(514) 721-2421   *SIC 5411*
ALWAYS A DOLLAR PLUS   p788
496 LAWRENCE AVE W, NORTH YORK,
ON, M6A 1A1
(416) 785-8500   *SIC 5411*
ANNABLE FOODS LTD   p284
850 FARWELL ST, TRAIL, BC, V1R 3T8
(250) 368-3363   *SIC 5411*
ARMSTRONG PLAZA LTD   p839
142 HUNTER ST E, PETERBOROUGH,
ON, K9H 1G6
(705) 743-8253   *SIC 5411*
ARMSTRONG STORE LIMITED   p840
760 SHERBROOKE ST, PETERBOR-
OUGH, ON, K9J 2R1
(705) 742-3321   *SIC 5411*
ASKEW'S FOOD SERVICE LTD   p267
111 LAKESHORE DR NE, SALMON ARM,
BC, V1E 4N3
(250) 832-2064   *SIC 5411*
ATLANTIC WHOLESALERS LTD   p394
700 ST. PETER AVE, BATHURST, NB, E2A
2Y7
(506) 547-3180   *SIC 5411*
ATLANTIC WHOLESALERS LTD   p409

89 TRINITY DR, MONCTON, NB, E1G 2J7
(506) 383-4919   *SIC 5411*
ATLANTIC WHOLESALERS LTD   p410
1198 ONONDAGA ST, OROMOCTO, NB,
E2V 1B8
(506) 357-5982   *SIC 5411*
ATLANTIC WHOLESALERS LTD   p411
425 COVERDALE RD, RIVERVIEW, NB,
E1B 3K3
(506) 387-5992   *SIC 5411*
ATLANTIC WHOLESALERS LTD   p412
168 ROTHESAY AVE, SAINT JOHN, NB,
E2J 2B5
(506) 648-1320   *SIC 5411*
ATLANTIC WHOLESALERS LTD   p413
650 SOMERSET ST, SAINT JOHN, NB, E2K
2Y7
(506) 658-6054   *SIC 5411*
ATLANTIC WHOLESALERS LTD   p418
10 LOWER COVE RD, SUSSEX, NB, E4E
0B7
(506) 433-9820   *SIC 5411*
ATLANTIC WHOLESALERS LTD   p419
350 CONNELL ST, WOODSTOCK, NB, E7M
5G8
(506) 328-1100   *SIC 5411*
ATLANTIC WHOLESALERS LTD   p419
3409 RUE PRINCIPALE SUITE 31,
TRACADIE-SHEILA, NB, E1X 1C7
(506) 393-1155   *SIC 5411*
ATLANTIC WHOLESALERS LTD   p438
126 ALBION ST S, AMHERST, NS, B4H 2X3
(902) 661-0703   *SIC 5411*
ATLANTIC WHOLESALERS LTD   p439
1650 BEDFORD HWY, BEDFORD, NS, B4A
4J7
(902) 832-3117   *SIC 5411*
ATLANTIC WHOLESALERS LTD   p441
21 DAVISON DR, BRIDGEWATER, NS, B4V
3K8
(902) 543-1809   *SIC 5411*
ATLANTIC WHOLESALERS LTD   p442
920 COLE HARBOUR RD, DARTMOUTH,
NS, B2V 2J5
(902) 462-4500   *SIC 5411*
ATLANTIC WHOLESALERS LTD   p449
470 WARWICK ST, DIGBY, NS, B0V 1A0
(902) 245-4108   *SIC 5411*
ATLANTIC WHOLESALERS LTD   p449
295 HIGHWAY 214, ELMSDALE, NS, B2S
2L1
(902) 883-1180   *SIC 5411*
ATLANTIC WHOLESALERS LTD   p450
155 RESERVE ST, GLACE BAY, NS, B1A
4W3
(902) 842-9609   *SIC 5411*
ATLANTIC WHOLESALERS LTD   p451
1075 BARRINGTON ST, HALIFAX, NS, B3H
4P1
(902) 492-3240   *SIC 5411*
ATLANTIC WHOLESALERS LTD   p456
3711 JOSEPH HOWE DR, HALIFAX, NS,
B3L 4H8
(902) 468-8866   *SIC 5411*
ATLANTIC WHOLESALERS LTD   p458
210 CHAIN LAKE DR, HALIFAX, NS, B3S
1C5
(902) 450-5317   *SIC 5411*
ATLANTIC WHOLESALERS LTD   p461
745 SACKVILLE DR, LOWER SACKVILLE,
NS, B4E 2R2
(902) 864-2299   *SIC 5411*
ATLANTIC WHOLESALERS LTD   p463
9064 COMMERCIAL ST, NEW MINAS, NS,
B4N 3E4
(902) 681-0665   *SIC 5411*
ATLANTIC WHOLESALERS LTD   p464
125 KING ST SUITE 321, NORTH SYDNEY,
NS, B2A 3S1
(902) 794-7111   *SIC 5411*
ATLANTIC WHOLESALERS LTD   p467
1225 KINGS RD, SYDNEY, NS, B1S 1E1
(902) 539-7657   *SIC 5411*
ATLANTIC WHOLESALERS LTD   p470

11 COLE DR, WINDSOR, NS, B0N 2T0
(902) 798-9537   *SIC 5411*
ATLANTIC WHOLESALERS LTD   p1038
465 UNIVERSITY AVE, CHARLOTTE-
TOWN, PE, C1A 4N9
(902) 569-2850   *SIC 5411*
ATLANTIC WHOLESALERS LTD   p1041
509 MAIN ST, MONTAGUE, PE, C0A 1R0
(902) 838-5421   *SIC 5411*
ATLANTIC WHOLESALERS LTD   p1042
535 GRANVILLE ST, SUMMERSIDE, PE,
C1N 6N4
(902) 888-1581   *SIC 5411*
ATM FOODS LTD   p207
8037 120 ST, DELTA, BC, V4C 6P7
SIC 5411
AVONDALE STORES LIMITED   p623
4520 JORDAN RD, JORDAN STATION, ON,
L0R 1S0
(905) 562-4173   *SIC 5411*
BAIE STE-ANNE CO-OPERATIVE LTD p394
5575 ROUTE 117, BAIE-SAINTE-ANNE,
NB, E9A 1E6
(506) 228-4211   *SIC 5411*
BALMORAL SAVE EASY   p394
647 DES PIONNIERS AVE, BALMORAL,
NB, E8E 1B3
(506) 826-2545   *SIC 5411*
BAR DEN FOODS LTD   p219
590 HIGHWAY 33 W UNIT 12, KELOWNA,
BC, V1X 6A8
(250) 762-9234   *SIC 5411*
BARBOUR'S FOOD MARKET LIMITEDp544
6708 35 HWY RR 1, COBOCONK, ON, K0M
1K0
(705) 454-1414   *SIC 5411*
BARRY'S BAY METRO   p489
28 BAY ST, BARRYS BAY, ON, K0J 1B0
(613) 756-7097   *SIC 5411*
BATEMAN FOODS (1995) LTD   p83
13504 VICTORIA TRAIL NW, EDMONTON,
AB, T5A 5C9
(780) 432-1535   *SIC 5411*
BAXTROM INDEPENDENT GROCERY p561
31 NINTH ST E, CORNWALL, ON, K6H 6R3
(613) 938-8040   *SIC 5411*
BEACH SUPERMARKETS LIMITED   p920
2040 QUEEN ST E, TORONTO, ON, M4L
1J4
(416) 694-3011   *SIC 5411*
BELFIRE'S VALUMART   p639
385 FREDERICK ST, KITCHENER, ON,
N2H 2P2
(519) 571-7248   *SIC 5411*
BEST COST FOOD LTD   p338
3555 DOUGLAS ST, VICTORIA, BC, V8Z
3L6
SIC 5411
BEVENDALE ENTERPRISES LTD   p343
1380 ALPHA LAKE RD SUITE 4,
WHISTLER, BC, V8E 0H9
(604) 932-5506   *SIC 5411*
BIDGOOD'S WHOLESALE LIMITED   p423
355 MAIN RD, GOULDS, NL, A1S 1J9
(709) 368-3125   *SIC 5411*
BIGNUCOLO INCORPORATED   p541
13 BEECH ST, CHAPLEAU, ON, P0M 1K0
(705) 864-0774   *SIC 5411*
BILLY GRUFF MARKETING LTD   p198
2310 ALBERNI HWY, COOMBS, BC, V0R
1M0
(250) 248-6272   *SIC 5411*
BLENHEIM SOBEY'S   p493
20210 COMMUNICATION RD, BLENHEIM,
ON, N0P 1A0
(519) 676-9044   *SIC 5411*
BLETSOE ENTERPRISES INC   p643
1 QUEEN ST, LAKEFIELD, ON, K0L 2H0
(705) 652-3202   *SIC 5411*
BLUE WATER IGA   p563
420 LYNDOCH ST, CORUNNA, ON, N0N
1G0
(519) 862-5213   *SIC 5411*
BLUMENSCHEIN HOLDINGS LTD   p124

11750 30 AVE SW, EDMONTON, AB, T6W
1A8
SIC 5411
BOB'S NO FRILLS   p529
571 BRANT ST, BURLINGTON, ON, L7R
2G6
(866) 987-6453   *SIC 5411*
BOLTON SUPERMARKETS LTD   p737
6790 PACIFIC CIR, MISSISSAUGA, ON,
L5T 1N8
(905) 670-1204   *SIC 5411*
BORDERLAND CO-OPERATIVE LIMITED
p1411
704 MAIN ST, MOOSOMIN, SK, S0G 3N0
(306) 435-4655   *SIC 5411*
BOTTEGA NICASTRO INC, LA   p821
64 GEORGE ST, OTTAWA, ON, K1N 5V9
(613) 789-7575   *SIC 5411*
BOUCHER RONALD & FILS INC   p1360
851 RTE PRINCIPALE, SAINTE-MELANIE,
QC, J0K 3A0
(450) 889-8363   *SIC 5411*
BOUCHERIE DENIS COUTURE INC   p1257
825 4E AV, QUEBEC, QC, G1J 3A6
(418) 648-2633   *SIC 5411*
BOURASSA, S. (ST-SAUVEUR) LTEE p1352
105B AV GUINDON RR 6, SAINT-
SAUVEUR, QC, J0R 1R6
(450) 227-4737   *SIC 5411*
BOURDON, EDOUARD & FILS INC   p1181
760 RUE JEAN-TALON E, MONTREAL, QC,
H2R 1V1
(514) 270-5226   *SIC 5411*
BOWMANVILLE FOOD LAND   p496
225 KING ST E, BOWMANVILLE, ON, L1C
1P8
(905) 697-7256   *SIC 5411*
BRAXCO LIMITED   p414
130 STATION ST, SAINT JOHN, NB, E2L
3H6
(506) 633-9040   *SIC 5411*
BROMLEY FOODS LTD   p139
5421 50 ST, LEDUC, AB, T9E 6Z7
(780) 986-2289   *SIC 5411*
BROWNLEE, RONALD (1994) LTD   p839
50 WILSON ST W, PERTH, ON, K7H 2N4
(613) 267-4921   *SIC 5411*
BRUNO'S FINE FOODS (ETOBICOKE) LTD
p572
4242 DUNDAS ST W SUITE 15, ETOBI-
COKE, ON, M8X 1Y6
(416) 234-1106   *SIC 5411*
BRUNO'S FINE FOODS (NORTH) LTD p855
9665 BAYVIEW AVE SUITE 29, RICHMOND
HILL, ON, L4C 9V4
(905) 737-4280   *SIC 5411*
BUTCHER BOYS ENTERPRISES LTD p331
4803 PLEASANT VALLEY RD, VERNON,
BC, V1B 3L7
(250) 542-2968   *SIC 5411*
BUY-LOW FOODS LTD   p14
7100 44 ST SE, CALGARY, AB, T2C 2V7
(403) 236-6300   *SIC 5411*
BUY-LOW FOODS LTD   p281
19580 TELEGRAPH TRAIL, SURREY, BC,
V4N 4H1
(604) 888-1121   *SIC 5411*
BUYNFLY FOOD LIMITED   p425
208 HUMBER AVE, LABRADOR CITY, NL,
A2V 1K9
(709) 944-4003   *SIC 5411*
C-MAC MICROCIRCUITS ULC   p1373
3000 BOUL INDUSTRIEL, SHERBROOKE,
QC, J1L 1V8
(819) 821-4524   *SIC 5411*
CALABRIA MARKET & DELI INC   p393
139 SCURFIELD BLVD, WINNIPEG, MB,
R3Y 1L6
(204) 487-1700   *SIC 5411*
CALEDON EAST FOODLAND   p531
15771 AIRPORT RD SUITE 4A, CALEDON
EAST, ON, L7C 1K2
(905) 584-9677   *SIC 5411*
CALGARY CO-OPERATIVE ASSOCIATION

▲ Public Company   ■ Public Company Family Member   **HQ** Headquarters   **BR** Branch   **SL** Single Location

LIMITED *p10*
3330 17 AVE SE SUITE 5, CALGARY, AB, T2A 0P9
(403) 299-4461   *SIC* 5411

CALGARY CO-OPERATIVE ASSOCIATION LIMITED *p21*
540 16 AVE NE, CALGARY, AB, T2E 1K4
(403) 299-4276   *SIC* 5411

CALGARY CO-OPERATIVE ASSOCIATION LIMITED *p34*
151 86 AVE SE UNIT 110, CALGARY, AB, T2H 3A5
(403) 219-6025   *SIC* 5411

CALGARY CO-OPERATIVE ASSOCIATION LIMITED *p39*
1221 CANYON MEADOWS DR SE SUITE 95, CALGARY, AB, T2J 6G2
(403) 299-4350   *SIC* 5411

CALGARY CO-OPERATIVE ASSOCIATION LIMITED *p40*
4122 BRENTWOOD RD NW SUITE 4, CALGARY, AB, T2L 1K8
(403) 299-4301   *SIC* 5411

CALGARY CO-OPERATIVE ASSOCIATION LIMITED *p74*
35 CROWFOOT WAY NW, CALGARY, AB, T3G 2L4
(403) 216-4500   *SIC* 5411

CALGARY CO-OPERATIVE ASSOCIATION LIMITED *p168*
320 2ND ST, STRATHMORE, AB, T1P 1K1
(403) 934-3121   *SIC* 5411

CALHOUN FOODS LAND *p682*
6 CENTURY BLVD, MILLBROOK, ON, L0A 1G0
(705) 932-2139   *SIC* 5411

CAMCOURT HOLDINGS LTD *p203*
660 ENGLAND AVE, COURTENAY, BC, V9N 2N4
(250) 338-1383   *SIC* 5411

CAMROSE SOBEYS CORP *p78*
4820 66 ST, CAMROSE, AB, T4V 4P6
(780) 672-5969   *SIC* 5411

CANAWAY HOLDINGS LTD *p333*
3651 SHELBOURNE ST SUITE 4, VICTORIA, BC, V8P 4H1
(250) 477-2218   *SIC* 5411

CANTOR'S GROCERY LTD *p380*
1445 LOGAN AVE, WINNIPEG, MB, R3E 1S1
(204) 774-1679   *SIC* 5411

CARLETON CO-OPERATIVE LIMITED *p399*
8818 MAIN ST, FLORENCEVILLE-BRISTOL, NB, E7L 3G2
(506) 392-5587   *SIC* 5411

CAROL WABUSH CO-OP SOCIETY LIMITED *p425*
500 VANIER AVE, LABRADOR CITY, NL, A2V 2W7
SIC 5411

CARRINGTON-O'BRIEN FOODS LTD *p158*
GD, ROCKY MOUNTAIN HOUSE, AB, T4T 1T1
(403) 845-2110   *SIC* 5411

CAVANAGH'S FOOD MARKET LIMITED *p468*
86 MAIN ST, TRURO, NS, B2N 4G6
SIC 5411

CELIA HARBOUR HOLDINGS LTD *p1440*
29 LEWES BLVD, WHITEHORSE, YT, Y1A 4S5
(867) 667-7860   *SIC* 5411

CENTRAL ALBERTA CO-OP LTD *p153*
6201 46 AVE, RED DEER, AB, T4N 6Z1
(403) 309-8913   *SIC* 5411

CENTRAL MEAT MARKET (KITCHENER) LIMITED *p638*
760 KING ST W, KITCHENER, ON, N2G 1E6
(519) 576-9400   *SIC* 5411

CENTRE OASIS SURF INC *p1069*
9520 BOUL LEDUC BUREAU 1, BROSSARD, QC, J4Y 0B3
(450) 486-7873   *SIC* 5411

CHAMARD, JACQUES & FILS INC *p1282*
619 BOUL IBERVILLE, REPENTIGNY, QC, J6A 2C5
(450) 581-0101   *SIC* 5411

CHAMPAGNE, GERARD LTEE *p1396*
5144 RUE BANNANTYNE, VERDUN, QC, H4G 1G5
(514) 766-3536   *SIC* 5411

CHARTRAND'S INDEPENDENT INC *p544*
4764 REGIONAL ROAD 15 RR 4, CHELMSFORD, ON, P0M 1L0
(705) 855-4588   *SIC* 5411

CHARTRAND, R. J. HOLDINGS LIMITED *p753*
55 SCOTT ST, NEW LISKEARD, ON, P0J 1P0
(705) 647-8844   *SIC* 5411

CHRIS & STACEY'S NO FRILLS *p712*
1250 SOUTH SERVICE RD, MISSISSAUGA, ON, L5E 1V4
(905) 891-1021   *SIC* 5411

CHRIS AND BETH NO FRILLS LTD *p811*
1050 SIMCOE ST N SUITE 754, OSHAWA, ON, L1G 4W5
(905) 728-3100   *SIC* 5411

CLACE HOLDINGS LTD *p335*
903 YATES ST, VICTORIA, BC, V8V 3M4
(250) 381-6000   *SIC* 5411

CLARENCE ENTERPRISES LIMITED *p465*
10029 HIGHWAY 1, SAULNIERVILLE, NS, B0W 2Z0
(902) 769-3458   *SIC* 5411

CLARENVILLE AREA CONSUMERS CO-OPERATIVE SOCIETY LTD *p421*
238 MEMORIAL DR, CLARENVILLE, NL, A5A 1N9
(709) 466-2622   *SIC* 5411

CLEARVIEW CONSUMER CO-OP LTD *p358*
365 PTH 12 N, STEINBACH, MB, R5G 1V1
(204) 346-2667   *SIC* 5411

CLEMENT FOODS LTD *p385*
1881 PORTAGE AVE, WINNIPEG, MB, R3J 0H3
(204) 988-4810   *SIC* 5411

CLOVERLEAF GROCERY (EMO) LIMITED *p569*
5970 HWY 11, EMO, ON, P0W 1E0
(807) 482-2793   *SIC* 5411

CLUB COOPERATIF DE CONSOMMATION D'AMOS *p1046*
421 12E AV E, AMOS, QC, J9T 3H1
(819) 732-5281   *SIC* 5411

CO-OP SASKATOON STONEBRID *p1435*
106 STONEBRIDGE BLVD, SASKATOON, SK, S7T 0J1
(306) 933-0306   *SIC* 5411

CO-OPERATIVE DE BOUCTOUCHE LTD , (LA) *p395*
191 IRVING BLVD, BOUCTOUCHE, NB, E4S 3K3
(506) 743-1960   *SIC* 5411

CO-OPERATIVE DE SAINT-QUENTIN LTEE *p417*
145 RUE CANADA, SAINT-QUENTIN, NB, E8A 1J4
(506) 235-2083   *SIC* 5411

COBB'S AG FOODS LTD *p169*
5015 50 ST SUITE 2, SYLVAN LAKE, AB, T4S 1P9
SIC 5411

COLCHESTER CO-OPERATIVE SERVICES LIMITED *p468*
339 WILLOW ST SUITE A, TRURO, NS, B2N 5A6
(902) 893-9470   *SIC* 5411

COLDWATER FOODLAND *p546*
77 COLDWATER RD, COLDWATER, ON, L0K 1E0
(705) 686-7700   *SIC* 5411

COLUMBUS LINE CANADA INC *p303*
900 HASTINGS ST W SUITE 600, VANCOUVER, BC, V6C 1E5
SIC 5411

COMMUNITY NATURAL FOODS LTD *p34*
202 61 AVE SW, CALGARY, AB, T2H 0B4
(403) 930-6363   *SIC* 5411

CONCORD FOOD CENTRE INC *p906*
1438 CENTRE ST, THORNHILL, ON, L4J 3N1
(905) 886-2180   *SIC* 5411

CONSUMERS COMMUNITY CO-OP *p416*
3300 WESTFIELD RD, SAINT JOHN, NB, E2M 7A4
SIC 5411

COOP ALIMENTAIRE DE LA REGION D'ASBESTOS *p1052*
511 1RE AV, ASBESTOS, QC, J1T 3P6
(819) 879-5427   *SIC* 5411

COOPER MARKET LTD *p216*
804 LAVAL CRES, KAMLOOPS, BC, V2C 5P3
SIC 5411

COOPERATIVE AGRICOLE D'EMBRUN LIMITEE, LA *p569*
GD, EMBRUN, ON, K0A 1W0
(613) 443-2892   *SIC* 5411

COOPERATIVE CARTIER LTEE, LA *p411*
25 BOUL CARTIER UNIT 105, RICHIBUCTO, NB, E4W 3W7
(506) 523-4461   *SIC* 5411

COOPERATIVE D'ALBANEL *p1044*
287 RUE DE L'EGLISE, ALBANEL, QC, G8M 3J9
(418) 279-3183   *SIC* 5411

COOPERATIVE D'APPROVISIONNEMENT DE CHAMBORD *p1075*
1945 RTE 169, CHAMBORD, QC, G0W 1G0
(418) 342-6495   *SIC* 5411

COOPERATIVE DE CARAQUET LIMITEE, LA *p396*
121 BOUL ST-PIERRE O, CARAQUET, NB, E1W 1B6
(506) 727-1930   *SIC* 5411

COOPERATIVE DE L'UNIVERSITE DE SHERBROOKE *p1372*
2500 BOUL DE L'UNIVERSITE BUREAU B5 014, SHERBROOKE, QC, J1K 2R1
(819) 821-3599   *SIC* 5411

COOPERATIVE DE ROGERSVILLE LIMITEE, LA *p412*
28 BOUCHER ST, ROGERSVILLE, NB, E4Y 1X5
(506) 775-6131   *SIC* 5411

COOPERATIVE DE SHEDIAC LIMITEE, LA *p417*
335 MAIN ST, SAINT-LEOLIN, NB, E4P 2B1
(506) 532-4441   *SIC* 5411

COOPERATIVE DES CONSOMATEURS DE CHARLESBOURG *p1280*
1233 BOUL LOUIS-XIV, QUEBEC, QC, G2L 1L9
(418) 628-2525   *SIC* 5411

COOPERATIVE DES CONSOMMATEURS D'ALMA *p1045*
705 AV DU PONT N, ALMA, QC, G8B 6T5
(418) 662-7405   *SIC* 5411

COOPERATIVE DES CONSOMMATEURS DE FERMONT *p1102*
299 LE CARREFOUR, FERMONT, QC, G0G 1J0
SIC 5411

COOPERATIVE DES CONSOMMATEURS DE LORETTEVILLE *p1275*
250 RUE LOUIS-IX, QUEBEC, QC, G2B 1L4
(418) 842-2341   *SIC* 5411

COOPERATIVE DES CONSOMMATEURS DE STE-FOY *p1274*
999 AV DE BOURGOGNE, QUEBEC, QC, G1W 4S6
(418) 658-6472   *SIC* 5411

COOPERATIVE NOTRE-DAME LIMITEE , LA *p419*
2616 CH VAL-DOUCET, VAL-DOUCET, NB, E8R 1Z2
(506) 764-3394   *SIC* 5411

COOPERATIVE REGIONALE DE LA BAIE LTEE, LA *p419*
3430 RUE PRINCIPALE, TRACADIE-

SHEILA, NB, E1X 1C8
(506) 395-1700   *SIC* 5411

COQUITLAM SUPERMARKETS LTD *p198*
1163 PINETREE WAY SUITE 1056, COQUITLAM, BC, V3B 8A9
(604) 552-6108   *SIC* 5411

CORNERSTONE CO-OPERATIVE *p165*
5017 42 ST SUITE 3, ST PAUL, AB, T0A 3A2
(780) 645-3351   *SIC* 5411

CREEKSIDE MARKET INC *p343*
2071 LAKE PLACID RD SUITE 305, WHISTLER, BC, V8E 0B6
(604) 938-9301   *SIC* 5411

DAUPHIN CONSUMERS COOPERATIVE LTD *p348*
18 3RD AVE NE, DAUPHIN, MB, R7N 0Y6
(204) 638-6003   *SIC* 5411

DAVID SULLIVAN GROUP OF COMPANIES LTD, THE *p298*
489 ROBSON ST, VANCOUVER, BC, V6B 6L9
(604) 684-5714   *SIC* 5411

DAVIS YOUR INDEPENDENT GROCER *p847*
20 JOCELYN ST, PORT HOPE, ON, L1A 3V5
(905) 885-1867   *SIC* 5411

DAVIS, GARY FOOD STORES LIMITED *p847*
177 TORONTO RD, PORT HOPE, ON, L1A 3V5
SIC 5411

DEAN MILLS NO FRILLS *p542*
100 WILLIAM ST S, CHATHAM, ON, N7M 4S4
(519) 351-0355   *SIC* 5411

DEAN'S FOOD BASICS *p862*
701 PINE ST, SAULT STE. MARIE, ON, P6B 3G2
(705) 949-8929   *SIC* 5411

DEE ENTERPRISES LTD *p200*
455 NORTH RD, COQUITLAM, BC, V3K 3V9
(604) 937-1205   *SIC* 5411

DELHI IGA *p564*
227 MAIN STREET OF DELHI, DELHI, ON, N4B 2M4
(519) 582-0990   *SIC* 5411

DELLA SIEGA ENTERPRISES LTD *p151*
6700 46 ST SUITE 300, OLDS, AB, T4H 0A2
(403) 556-7384   *SIC* 5411

DELMAS CO-OPERATIVE ASSOCIATION *p231*
1562 MAIN ST, MASSET, BC, V0T 1M0
(250) 626-3933   *SIC* 5411

DELTA CO-OPERATIVE ASSOCIATION LTD, THE *p1437*
130 SECOND AVE W, UNITY, SK, S0K 4L0
(306) 228-2662   *SIC* 5411

DEPANNEUR CADEKO *p1366*
43 BOUL JOUBERT E, SAYABEC, QC, G0J 3K0
(418) 536-5495   *SIC* 5411

DEPANNEUR NEWVIQ'VI INC *p1118*
1285 RUE GORDON, KUUJJUAQ, QC, J0M 1C0
(819) 964-2228   *SIC* 5411

DEPANNEUR VAL MAHER INC *p1109*
1000 CH DENISON E, GRANBY, QC, J2G 8C7
(450) 375-2041   *SIC* 5411

DESPRES H LTEE *p1378*
44 RUE PRINCIPALE N, SUTTON, QC, J0E 2K0
(450) 538-2211   *SIC* 5411

DIPIETRO FRESH MEAT & DELICATESSEN LTD *p533*
30 GLAMIS RD, CAMBRIDGE, ON, N1R 7H5
(519) 622-3222   *SIC* 5411

DISCOVERY FOODS LTD *p194*
2207 GLENMORE RD UNIT 1, CAMPBELL RIVER, BC, V9H 1E1
(250) 923-7733   *SIC* 5411

DJD DEVELOPMENT CORPORATION *p630*
235 GORE RD SUITE 1, KINGSTON, ON,

K7L 0C3
(613) 542-3406   *SIC* 5411
DOLLAR FOOD MFG INC   p285
1410 ODLUM DR, VANCOUVER, BC, V5L 4X7
(604) 253-1422   *SIC* 5411
DOLLO BROS. FOOD MARKET LIMITED p685
123 25 HWY SUITE 35, MINDEN, ON, K0M 2K0
(705) 286-1121   *SIC* 5411
DONALD'S MARKET LTD   p285
2342 HASTINGS ST E, VANCOUVER, BC, V5L 1V5
(604) 254-3014   *SIC* 5411
DONG-PHUONG ORIENTAL MARKET LTD p93
14810 131 AVE NW, EDMONTON, AB, T5L 4Y3
(780) 447-2883   *SIC* 5411
DORING ENTERPRISES INC   p350
94 7TH AVE, GIMLI, MB, R0C 1B1
(204) 642-5995   *SIC* 5411
DOUBLE O MARKETS LTD   p242
GD, OLIVER, BC, V0H 1T0
SIC 5411
DRUMHELLER CO-OP LTD   p82
555 HWY 10 E, DRUMHELLER, AB, T0J 0Y0
(403) 823-5555   *SIC* 5411
DUBE, R. LTEE   p1045
370 AV BEGIN, ALMA, QC, G8B 2W8
(418) 662-3611   *SIC* 5411
DUFRESNE, L. & FILS LTEE   p1391
2500 RUE DE L'EGLISE, VAL-DAVID, QC, J0T 2N0
(819) 322-2030   *SIC* 5411
DUMAS YOUR INDEPENDENT GROCERS p900
82 LORNE ST, SUDBURY, ON, P3C 4N8
(705) 671-3051   *SIC* 5411
E & T FOODS LTD   p170
5203 50 AVE, VALLEYVIEW, AB, T0H 3N0
(780) 524-4424   *SIC* 5411
E88TLC90 HOLDINGS LTD   p340
772 GOLDSTREAM AVE, VICTORIA, BC, V9B 2X3
(250) 478-8306   *SIC* 5411
EAST CENTRAL CO-OPERATIVE LIMITED p1408
211 1ST AVE, KELVINGTON, SK, S0A 1W0
(306) 327-4745   *SIC* 5411
EMPIRE SUPERMARKET (2010) LTD p260
4600 NO. 3 RD UNIT 111, RICHMOND, BC, V6X 2C2
SIC 5411
ENTREPRISES B J T BOULIANNE INC, LES p1378
335 CH DU HIBOU, STONEHAM-ET-TEWKESBURY, QC, G3C 1R9
(418) 848-2637   *SIC* 5411
ENTREPRISES CD VARIN INC, LES p1281
285 RUE VALMONT, REPENTIGNY, QC, J5Y 3H6
(450) 654-9253   *SIC* 5411
ENTREPRISES CLEMENT RUEL (2000) INC p1096
4565 BOUL SAINT-JOSEPH, DRUM-MONDVILLE, QC, J2A 1B4
(819) 472-1107   *SIC* 5411
ENTREPRISES EMILE CHARLES & FILS LTEE   p1400
1716 RTE 105, WAKEFIELD, QC, J0X 3G0
(819) 459-2326   *SIC* 5411
ENTREPRISES G.A. LEBLANC INC, LES p1077
45 RUE ALBERT-FERLAND, CHENEVILLE, QC, J0V 1E0
(819) 428-3966   *SIC* 5411
ENTREPRISES LA CHARCUTIERE LAVAL INC   p1232
3315 BOUL DE LA CONCORDE E, MON-TREAL, QC, H7E 2C3
SIC 5411

EPICERIE CENTRE-MATIC INC   p1323
1233 RUE DES ERABLES, SAINT-LAMBERT-DE-LAUZON, QC, G0S 2W0
(418) 889-9723   *SIC* 5411
EPICERIE QUINTAL & FRERES 1978 INC p1342
4805 BOUL ARTHUR-SAUVE, SAINT-LAURENT, QC, H7R 3X2
(450) 627-3123   *SIC* 5411
EPICERIE R. BUTEAU INC   p1350
2650 25E AV, SAINT-PROSPER-DE-DORCHESTER, QC, G0M 1Y0
(418) 594-8244   *SIC* 5411
EPICERIE R. CADIEUX & FILS INC   p1284
461 CH DE LA GRANDE-LIGNE, RIGAUD, QC, J0P 1P0
(450) 451-5318   *SIC* 5411
EPICERIE SALTARELLI ET FILS INC p1224
11847 BOUL LAURENTIEN, MONTREAL, QC, H4J 2M1
(514) 331-5879   *SIC* 5411
EPICIERS HOGUE ET FRERES INC, LES p1355
7 BOUL SAINTE-ANNE, SAINTE-ANNE-DES-PLAINES, QC, J0N 1H0
(450) 478-1765   *SIC* 5411
ESKIMO POINT LUMBER SUP-PLY/AIRPORT SERVICES LTD   p472
GD, ARVIAT, NU, X0C 0E0
(867) 857-2752   *SIC* 5411
EXCEL PRIX GROSSISTE EN ALIMENTA-TION INC   p1234
1225 RUE BERGAR, MONTREAL, QC, H7L 4Z7
(450) 967-0076   *SIC* 5411
F. P. RIDEAUVIEW INC   p831
1430 PRINCE OF WALES DR, OTTAWA, ON, K2C 1N6
(613) 225-1240   *SIC* 5411
FAIRWAY HOLDINGS (1994) LTD   p339
272 GORGE RD W, VICTORIA, BC, V9A 1M7
(250) 385-4814   *SIC* 5411
FALHER AND DISTRICT COOPERATIVE ASSOCIATION LTD, THE   p126
108 MAIN ST, FALHER, AB, T0H 1M0
(780) 837-2261   *SIC* 5411
FAMILY FOODS PORTAGE AVENUE   p385
1881 PORTAGE AVE, WINNIPEG, MB, R3J 0H3
(204) 988-4810   *SIC* 5411
FAMOUS FOODS MARKETS LTD   p287
1595 KINGSWAY UNIT 101, VANCOUVER, BC, V5N 2R8
(604) 872-3019   *SIC* 5411
FARM BOY SUPERMARKET   p830
1495 RICHMOND RD, OTTAWA, ON, K2B 6R9
(613) 688-2882   *SIC* 5411
FARMBOY MARKETS LIMITED   p840
754 LANSDOWNE ST W, PETERBOR-OUGH, ON, K9J 1Z3
(705) 745-2811   *SIC* 5411
FIESTA FARMS INC   p989
200 CHRISTIE ST, TORONTO, ON, M6G 3B6
(416) 537-1235   *SIC* 5411
FIRST GROCERY LTD   p288
7190 KERR ST, VANCOUVER, BC, V5S 4W2
(604) 433-0434   *SIC* 5411
FIRST STREET FOODS LTD   p171
221 2 S, VULCAN, AB, T0L 2B0
(403) 485-6955   *SIC* 5411
FISHER'S NO FRILLS   p539
15 CANROBERT ST, CAMPBELLFORD, ON, K0L 1L0
(866) 987-6453   *SIC* 5411
FOCENCO LIMITED   p434
383 CONNECTICUT DR, STEPHENVILLE, NL, A2N 2Y6
(709) 637-6600   *SIC* 5411
FOCENCO LIMITED   p434
127 MAIN ST SUITE 125, STEPHENVILLE,

NL, A2N 1J5
(709) 643-2885   *SIC* 5411
FOODLAND   p563
420 LYNDOCH ST, CORUNNA, ON, N0N 1G0
(519) 862-5213   *SIC* 5411
FOREST LAWN SOBEYS   p11
5115 17 AVE SE, CALGARY, AB, T2A 0V8
(403) 273-9339   *SIC* 5411
FORTINO'S (HIGHWAY 7 & ANSLEY) LTD p1031
3940 HIGHWAY 7, WOODBRIDGE, ON, L4L 9C3
(905) 851-5642   *SIC* 5411
FORTINO'S (LAWRENCE & ALLEN) LTD p789
700 LAWRENCE AVE W, NORTH YORK, ON, M6A 3B4
(416) 785-9843   *SIC* 5411
FORTINO'S (NEW STREET) LTD   p522
5111 NEW ST SUITE 50, BURLINGTON, ON, L7L 1V2
(905) 631-7227   *SIC* 5411
FORTINOS (DUNDURN) LTD   p612
50 DUNDURN ST S, HAMILTON, ON, L8P 4W3
(905) 529-4290   *SIC* 5411
FORTINOS (MALL 1994) LTD   p614
65 MALL RD, HAMILTON, ON, L8V 5B8
(905) 387-7673   *SIC* 5411
FORTINOS (OAKVILLE) LTD   p802
173 LAKESHORE RD W, OAKVILLE, ON, L6K 1E7
(905) 845-3654   *SIC* 5411
FORTINOS FIESTA MALL LTD   p894
102 HIGHWAY 8, STONEY CREEK, ON, L8G 4H3
(905) 662-3772   *SIC* 5411
FORTINOS SUPERMARKET LTD   p508
60 QUARRY EDGE DR, BRAMPTON, ON, L6V 4K2
(905) 453-3600   *SIC* 5411
FRANCIS FOODSTORE LTD   p461
143 VICTORIA RD, LUNENBURG, NS, B0J 2C0
(902) 634-3751   *SIC* 5411
FREDERICTON DIRECT CHARGE CO-OPERATIVE LIMITED   p402
170 DOAK RD, FREDERICTON, NB, E3C 2G2
(506) 453-1300   *SIC* 5411
FRESHSTONE BRANDS INC   p635
1326 VICTORIA ST N, KITCHENER, ON, N2B 3E2
(519) 578-2940   *SIC* 5411
FRESON MARKET LTD   p7
330 FAIRVIEW AVE W, BROOKS, AB, T1R 1K7
SIC 5411
FRESON MARKET LTD   p132
11417 99 ST, GRANDE PRAIRIE, AB, T8V 2H6
(780) 532-2920   *SIC* 5411
FRESON MARKET LTD   p135
5032 53RD AVE, HIGH PRAIRIE, AB, T0G 1E0
(780) 523-3253   *SIC* 5411
FRESON MARKET LTD   p167
4401 48 ST UNIT 130, STONY PLAIN, AB, T7Z 1N3
(780) 968-6924   *SIC* 5411
FUNKS FOODS LTD   p176
2580 CLEARBROOK RD, ABBOTSFORD, BC, V2T 2Y5
SIC 5411
GALATI BROS. SUPERMARKETS (JANE) LIMITED   p787
4734 JANE ST, NORTH YORK, ON, M3N 2L2
SIC 5411
GALATI MARKET FRESH INC   p765
5845 LESLIE ST, NORTH YORK, ON, M2H 1J8
(416) 747-1899   *SIC* 5411

GALATI SUPERMARKETS (FINCH) LIM-ITED   p794
2592 FINCH AVE W, NORTH YORK, ON, M9M 2G3
SIC 5411
GANDER CONSUMERS CO-OPERATIVE SOCIETY LIMITED   p423
72 ELIZABETH DR, GANDER, NL, A1V 1J8
(709) 256-4843   *SIC* 5411
GARDEN BASKET FOOD MARKETS IN-CORPORATED, THE   p670
7676 WOODBINE AVE UNIT 1, MARKHAM, ON, L3R 2N2
(905) 305-8220   *SIC* 5411
GARDEN BASKET FOOD MARKETS IN-CORPORATED, THE   p679
9271 MARKHAM RD, MARKHAM, ON, L6E 1A1
(905) 471-0777   *SIC* 5411
GARDEN FOODS - BOLTON LTD   p494
501 QUEEN ST S, BOLTON, ON, L7E 1A1
(905) 857-1227   *SIC* 5411
GESTION FAMILLE DEZIEL INC   p1343
1869 CH SAINTE-ANGELIQUE, SAINT-LAZARE, QC, J7T 2X9
(450) 455-6165   *SIC* 5411
GESTION GAETAN BOUCHER   p1292
405 273 RTE, SAINT-APOLLINAIRE, QC, G0S 2E0
(418) 881-3112   *SIC* 5411
GESTION GILLES-GENEST INC   p1082
35 RUE PRINCIPALE E, COOKSHIRE-EATON, QC, J0B 1M0
(819) 875-5455   *SIC* 5411
GESTION MASSON, ST-PIERRE INC p1385
165 BOUL SAINTE-MADELEINE, TROIS-RIVIERES, QC, G8T 3L7
(819) 375-4824   *SIC* 5411
GESTION QUADRIVIUM LTEE   p1169
2506 RUE BEAUBIEN E, MONTREAL, QC, H1Y 1G2
SIC 5411
GESTION RENE J. BEAUDOIN INC   p1283
115 BOUL BRIEN, REPENTIGNY, QC, J6A 8J3
(450) 585-9840   *SIC* 5411
GESTION TREMBLAY LEBOEUF INC p1243
1130 RUE SAINT-CYRILLE, NORMANDIN, QC, G8M 4J7
(418) 274-2009   *SIC* 5411
GILBERT HOLDINGS LTD   p150
201 SOUTHRIDGE DR UNIT 700, OKO-TOKS, AB, T1S 2E1
(403) 938-3439   *SIC* 5411
GIRARD, B & FILS INC   p1303
1199 BOUL SAINT-FELICIEN, SAINT-FELICIEN, QC, G8K 3J1
(418) 679-1304   *SIC* 5411
GLENCOE FOODLAND   p594
195 MAIN ST, GLENCOE, ON, N0L 1M0
(519) 287-2776   *SIC* 5411
GLOGOWSKI EURO FOOD LTD   p641
403 HIGHLAND RD W, KITCHENER, ON, N2M 3C6
(519) 584-7190   *SIC* 5411
GRAND MARCHE COL-FAX INC   p1236
3699 NORD LAVAL (A-440) O, MONTREAL, QC, H7P 5P6
(450) 688-7773   *SIC* 5411
GREAT PACIFIC INDUSTRIES INC   p185
4399 LOUGHEED HWY SUITE 996, BURN-ABY, BC, V5C 3Y7
(604) 298-8412   *SIC* 5411
GREAT PACIFIC INDUSTRIES INC   p213
10345 100 ST, FORT ST. JOHN, BC, V1J 3Z2
(250) 785-2985   *SIC* 5411
GREAT PACIFIC INDUSTRIES INC   p222
1876 COOPER RD SUITE 101, KELOWNA, BC, V1Y 9N6
(250) 860-1444   *SIC* 5411
GREAT PACIFIC INDUSTRIES INC   p224
19855 92A AVE, LANGLEY, BC, V1M 3B6
(604) 888-1213   *SIC* 5411

GREAT PACIFIC INDUSTRIES INC *p231*
20395 LOUGHEED HWY SUITE 300, MAPLE RIDGE, BC, V2X 2P9
(604) 465-8665   *SIC* 5411

GREAT PACIFIC INDUSTRIES INC *p232*
32555 LONDON AVE SUITE 400, MISSION, BC, V2V 6M7
(604) 826-9564   *SIC* 5411

GREAT PACIFIC INDUSTRIES INC *p234*
3200 ISLAND HWY N, NANAIMO, BC, V9T 1W1
(250) 751-1414   *SIC* 5411

GREAT PACIFIC INDUSTRIES INC *p243*
2111 MAIN ST SUITE 161, PENTICTON, BC, V2A 6W6
(250) 492-2011   *SIC* 5411

GREEN'S POP SHOP LTD *p140*
613 13 ST N, LETHBRIDGE, AB, T1H 2S7
(403) 329-4848   *SIC* 5411

GROUPE ADONIS INC *p1086*
2425 BOUL CURE-LABELLE, COTE SAINT-LUC, QC, H7T 1R3
(450) 978-2333   *SIC* 5411

GROUPE ADONIS INC *p1226*
2001 RUE SAUVE O, MONTREAL, QC, H4N 3L6
(514) 382-8606   *SIC* 5411

GROUPE ADONIS INC *p1290*
4601 BOUL DES SOURCES, ROXBORO, QC, H8Y 3C5
(514) 685-5050   *SIC* 5411

GROUPE EPICIERS ANGUS INC *p1100*
150 RUE ANGUS S BUREAU 10, EAST ANGUS, QC, J0B 1R0
(819) 832-2449   *SIC* 5411

H & B INVESTMENTS LTD *p222*
3033 PANDOSY ST, KELOWNA, BC, V1Y 1W3
(250) 763-0819   *SIC* 5411

H & W FOOD COUNTRY *p233*
82 TWELFTH ST, NANAIMO, BC, V9R 6R6
(250) 753-7545   *SIC* 5411

H. W. M. STORES LTD *p214*
900 GIBSONS WAY, GIBSONS, BC, V0N 1V7
(604) 886-2424   *SIC* 5411

H.Y. LOUIE CO. LIMITED *p182*
2821 PRODUCTION WAY, BURNABY, BC, V5A 3G7
(604) 421-4242   *SIC* 5411

HAMAN, B. & A. LIMITED *p1011*
36 MISSION RD, WAWA, ON, P0S 1K0
(705) 856-2555   *SIC* 5411

HANAHREUM MART INC *p201*
329 NORTH RD SUITE 100, COQUITLAM, BC, V3K 3V8
(604) 939-0135   *SIC* 5411

HANAHREUM MART INC *p553*
193 JARDIN DR, CONCORD, ON, L4K 1X5
(416) 792-1131   *SIC* 5411

HARE FOODS LTD *p170*
4902 51 AVE, TOFIELD, AB, T0B 4J0
(780) 662-3718   *SIC* 5411

HARTEK HOLDINGS LTD *p143*
2920 26 AVE S, LETHBRIDGE, AB, T1K 7K8
(403) 320-2272   *SIC* 5411

HENDRIKS INDEPENDENT GROCER *p839*
80 DUFFERIN ST, PERTH, ON, K7H 3A7
SIC 5411

HERITAGE CO-OP 1997 LTD *p352*
120 MAIN ST, MINNEDOSA, MB, R0J 1E0
(204) 867-2295   *SIC* 5411

HIGHLAND FARMS INC *p706*
50 MATHESON BLVD E, MISSISSAUGA, ON, L4Z 1N5
(905) 501-9545   *SIC* 5411

HIGHLAND FARMS INC *p871*
850 ELLESMERE RD, SCARBOROUGH, ON, M1P 2W5
(416) 298-1999   *SIC* 5411

HURLEY FOODS LTD *p621*
273 KING ST W, INGERSOLL, ON, N5C 2K9

(519) 425-4406   *SIC* 5411

I.G.A. PLUS SUMMERLAND NO 155 *p270*
7519 PRAIRIE VALLEY RD, SUMMERLAND, BC, V0H 1Z4
(250) 494-4376   *SIC* 5411

IGA DAIGLE *p1364*
220 RUE SAINT-CHARLES, SAINTE-THERESE, QC, J7E 2B4
(450) 435-1370   *SIC* 5411

IGA #8113 *p1316*
435 9E AV, SAINT-JEAN-SUR-RICHELIEU, QC, J2X 1K5
(450) 358-2804   *SIC* 5411

IGA ALIMENTATION COOP POR *p1253*
26 BOUL DES ILES, PORT-CARTIER, QC, G5B 0A4
(418) 766-0008   *SIC* 5411

IGA EXTRA MARCHE LACAS INC *p1365*
1366 BOUL MONSEIGNEUR-LANGLOIS, SALABERRY-DE-VALLEYFIELD, QC, J6S 1E3
(450) 373-0251   *SIC* 5411

IGA EXTRA MARCHE PAQUETTE INC *p1385*
3925 BOUL DES FORGES, TROIS-RIVIERES, QC, G8Y 1V9
(819) 379-2397   *SIC* 5411

IGA MARCHE LACOSTE HEBERT *p1143*
1401 CH DE CHAMBLY, LONGUEUIL, QC, J4J 3X6
(450) 677-2869   *SIC* 5411

IGLOOLIK CO-OPERATIVE LIMITED *p472*
GD, IGLOOLIK, NU, X0A 0L0
(867) 934-8958   *SIC* 5411

INDIAN HEAD CONSUMERS CO-OPERATIVE SOCIETY LTD *p434*
50 CAROLINA AVE, STEPHENVILLE, NL, A2N 2S3
(709) 643-5675   *SIC* 5411

INKAS CORPORATION *p793*
3605 WESTON RD, NORTH YORK, ON, M9L 1V7
(416) 645-8725   *SIC* 5411

IROQUOIS FALLS FOODLAND *p623*
171 AMBRIDGE DR, IROQUOIS FALLS, ON, P0K 1G0
(705) 232-4071   *SIC* 5411

ITALIAN CENTRE SHOP SOUTH LTD *p86*
10878 95 ST NW, EDMONTON, AB, T5H 2E4
(780) 424-4869   *SIC* 5411

ITALIAN CENTRE SHOP SOUTH LTD *p119*
5028 104A ST NW, EDMONTON, AB, T6H 6A2
(780) 989-4869   *SIC* 5411

JACE HOLDINGS LTD *p211*
1270 56 ST, DELTA, BC, V4L 2A4
(604) 948-9210   *SIC* 5411

JACE HOLDINGS LTD *p233*
650 TERMINAL AVE UNIT 3, NANAIMO, BC, V9R 5E2
(250) 754-6273   *SIC* 5411

JACE HOLDINGS LTD *p267*
6772 KIRKPATRICK CRES, SAANICHTON, BC, V8M 1Z9
(250) 483-1616   *SIC* 5411

JEFF'S NO FRILLS *p570*
53 ARTHUR AVE, ESSEX, ON, N8M 2N1
(519) 776-4944   *SIC* 5411

JELSCHEN FOODS LTD *p6*
4501 50 AVE, BONNYVILLE, AB, T9N 2N5
(780) 826-2048   *SIC* 5411

JESSE & KELLY'S NO FRILLS *p591*
1135 THOMPSON RD, FORT ERIE, ON, L2A 6T7
(866) 987-6453   *SIC* 5411

JOE'S NO FRILLS 796 LIMITED *p863*
369 KORAH RD, SAULT STE. MARIE, ON, P6C 4J4
(866) 987-6453   *SIC* 5411

JOLY, ERNEST & FILS INC *p1044*
1530 RUE D'ACTON, ACTON VALE, QC, J0H 1A0
(450) 546-7733   *SIC* 5411

JUNVIR INVESTMENTS LIMITED *p929*

446 SUMMERHILL AVE, TORONTO, ON, M4W 2E4
(416) 921-2714   *SIC* 5411

JUSTIN & STACEY'S NO FRILLS *p478*
285 MILL ST, ANGUS, ON, L0M 1B4
(705) 424-7090   *SIC* 5411

K-TILBURY FOOD MARKET LTD *p911*
15 QUEEN ST S, TILBURY, ON, N0P 2L0
(519) 682-3245   *SIC* 5411

KAROB FOODS LTD *p272*
17710 56 AVE SUITE 10, SURREY, BC, V3S 1C7
SIC 5411

KELLAND PROPERTIES INC *p234*
2350 DELINEA PL, NANAIMO, BC, V9T 5L9
(250) 585-1482   *SIC* 5411

KELLAND PROPERTIES INC *p245*
2943 10TH AVE, PORT ALBERNI, BC, V9Y 2N5
(250) 723-3397   *SIC* 5411

KENNY ENTERPRISES LIMITED *p433*
462 TOPSAIL RD, ST. JOHN'S, NL, A1E 2C2
(709) 364-3207   *SIC* 5411

KITCHEN TABLE INCORPORATED, THE *p964*
12 QUEENS QUAY W SUITE 416, TORONTO, ON, M5J 2V7
(416) 778-4800   *SIC* 5411

KLEIN, ROBERT ENTERPRISES INC *p1422*
1005 PASQUA ST, REGINA, SK, S4T 4K9
(306) 791-6362   *SIC* 5411

KNECHTEL'S FOOD MARKET *p911*
15 QUEEN S, TILBURY, ON, N0P 2L0
(519) 682-3245   *SIC* 5411

KOOTENAY COUNTRY STORE CO-OP *p235*
295 BAKER ST, NELSON, BC, V1L 4H4
(250) 354-4077   *SIC* 5411

KOOTENAY MARKET LTD *p204*
2 CRANBROOK ST N SUITE 320, CRANBROOK, BC, V1C 3P6
(250) 426-1846   *SIC* 5411

KYSY INC *p681*
795 BALM BEACH RD E, MIDLAND, ON, L4R 4K4
(705) 527-4067   *SIC* 5411

L & M FOOD MARKET (ONTARIO) LIMITED *p569*
181 GEDDES ST, ELORA, ON, N0B 1S0
(519) 846-1188   *SIC* 5411

L. A. DAIGNEAULT & FILS LTEE *p1088*
1531 RUE DU SUD, COWANSVILLE, QC, J2K 2Z4
(450) 263-3686   *SIC* 5411

LA CRETE CO-OP LIMITED *p137*
10502 100 ST, LA CRETE, AB, T0H 2H0
(780) 928-2900   *SIC* 5411

LADY YORK HOLDINGS LTD *p791*
2939 DUFFERIN ST, NORTH YORK, ON, M6B 3S7
(416) 781-8585   *SIC* 5411

LAFLAMME, HENRI INC *p1106*
425 BOUL SAINT-JOSEPH, GATINEAU, QC, J8Y 3Z8
(819) 770-9131   *SIC* 5411

LAMANTIA, J & B LTD *p646*
50 WILLIAM ST S, LINDSAY, ON, K9V 3A5
(705) 324-6625   *SIC* 5411

LANGCO FOODS LTD *p1412*
9801 TERRITORIAL DR, NORTH BATTLEFORD, SK, S9A 3Z8
(306) 445-1934   *SIC* 5411

LANSDOWNE I G A *p119*
5120 122 ST NW, EDMONTON, AB, T6H 3S2
(780) 436-8387   *SIC* 5411

LARNY HOLDINGS LIMITED *p819*
2520 ST. LAURENT BLVD SUITE 201, OTTAWA, ON, K1H 1B1
(613) 736-7962   *SIC* 5411

LAURA'S YOUR INDEPENDENT GROCERY *p626*
300 EAGLESON RD, KANATA, ON, K2M 1C9

(613) 592-3850   *SIC* 5411

LEWISPORTE AREA CONSUMERS CO-OP SOCIETY LTD *p425*
423 MAIN ST SUITE 415, LEWISPORTE, NL, A0G 3A0
(709) 535-6728   *SIC* 5411

LEWISPORTE CO-OP LTD *p425*
465 MAIN ST, LEWISPORTE, NL, A0G 3A0
(709) 535-6728   *SIC* 5411

LING & LING ENTERPRISES LTD *p884*
533 LAKE ST, ST CATHARINES, ON, L2N 4H6
(905) 937-7719   *SIC* 5411

LITTLE SHORT STOP STORES LIMITED *p539*
201B PRESTON PKY, CAMBRIDGE, ON, N3H 5E8
(519) 653-3171   *SIC* 5411

LIZZI, C. ENTERPRISES INC *p684*
327 BRONTE ST S UNIT 1, MILTON, ON, L9T 4A4
(905) 875-0303   *SIC* 5411

LLAP HOLDINGS LTD *p39*
14939 DEER RIDGE DR SE, CALGARY, AB, T2J 7C4
(403) 278-2626   *SIC* 5411

LLOYDMINSTER AND DISTRICT CO-OPERATIVE LIMITED *p1409*
4090 41 ST SUITE 101, LLOYDMINSTER, SK, S9V 2J1
(306) 825-2271   *SIC* 5411

LOBLAW COMPANIES LIMITED *p24*
3225 12 ST NE, CALGARY, AB, T2E 7S9
(403) 291-7700   *SIC* 5411

LOBLAW COMPANIES LIMITED *p421*
GD, BAY ROBERTS, NL, A0A 1G0
(709) 786-6001   *SIC* 5411

LOBLAW COMPANIES LIMITED *p511*
1 PRESIDENTS CHOICE CIR, BRAMPTON, ON, L6Y 5S5
(905) 459-2500   *SIC* 5411

LOBLAW COMPANIES LIMITED *p697*
925 RATHBURN RD E UNIT A, MISSISSAUGA, ON, L4W 4C3
(905) 276-6560   *SIC* 5411

LOBLAW COMPANIES LIMITED *p826*
64 ISABELLA ST, OTTAWA, ON, K1S 1V4
(613) 232-4831   *SIC* 5411

LOBLAW COMPANIES LIMITED *p1313*
2000 BOUL CASAVANT O, SAINT-HYACINTHE, QC, J2S 7K2
(450) 771-6601   *SIC* 5411

LOBLAW FINANCIAL HOLDINGS INC *p434*
62 PRINCE RUPERT DR, STEPHENVILLE, NL, A2N 3W7
(709) 643-0862   *SIC* 5411

LOBLAW PROPERTIES LIMITED *p457*
3711 JOSEPH HOWE DR, HALIFAX, NS, B3L 4H8
SIC 5411

LOBLAW PROPERTIES LIMITED *p469*
46 ELM ST, TRURO, NS, B2N 3H6
(902) 895-4306   *SIC* 5411

LOBLAW PROPERTIES LIMITED *p993*
605 ROGERS RD SUITE 208, TORONTO, ON, M6M 1B9
(416) 653-1951   *SIC* 5411

LOBLAW QUEBEC LIMITEE *p1326*
330 AV SAINTE-CROIX, SAINT-LAURENT, QC, H4N 3K4
(514) 747-0606   *SIC* 5411

LOBLAWS INC *p3*
1050 YANKEE VALLEY BLVD SE, AIRDRIE, AB, T4A 2E4
(403) 912-3800   *SIC* 5411

LOBLAWS INC *p9*
3575 20 AVE NE, CALGARY, AB, T1Y 6R3
(403) 280-8222   *SIC* 5411

LOBLAWS INC *p17*
6810 40 ST SE, CALGARY, AB, T2C 2A5
(905) 459-2500   *SIC* 5411

LOBLAWS INC *p40*
7020 4 ST NW, CALGARY, AB, T2K 1C4
(403) 516-8519   *SIC* 5411

LOBLAWS INC   *p69*
10505 SOUTHPORT RD SW SUITE 1, CALGARY, AB, T2W 3N2
(403) 225-6207   *SIC 5411*

LOBLAWS INC   *p70*
15915 MACLEOD TRAIL SE UNIT 100, CALGARY, AB, T2Y 3R9
(403) 254-3637   *SIC 5411*

LOBLAWS INC   *p71*
5251 COUNTRY HILLS BLVD NW SUITE 1575, CALGARY, AB, T3A 5H8
(403) 241-4027   *SIC 5411*

LOBLAWS INC   *p76*
3633 WESTWINDS DR NE UNIT 100, CALGARY, AB, T3J 5K3
(403) 590-3347   *SIC 5411*

LOBLAWS INC   *p94*
12350 137 AVE NW, EDMONTON, AB, T5L 4X6
(780) 406-3768   *SIC 5411*

LOBLAWS INC   *p119*
4821 CALGARY TRAIL NW SUITE 1570, EDMONTON, AB, T6H 5W8
(780) 430-2797   *SIC 5411*

LOBLAWS INC   *p124*
4410 17 ST NW, EDMONTON, AB, T6T 0C1
(780) 450-2041   *SIC 5411*

LOBLAWS INC   *p128*
9 HAINEAULT ST, FORT MCMURRAY, AB, T9H 1R8
(780) 790-3827   *SIC 5411*

LOBLAWS INC   *p132*
12225 99 ST SUITE 1544, GRANDE PRAIRIE, AB, T8V 6X9
(780) 831-3827   *SIC 5411*

LOBLAWS INC   *p144*
5031 44 ST, LLOYDMINSTER, AB, T9V 0A6
(780) 871-8060   *SIC 5411*

LOBLAWS INC   *p146*
1792 TRANS CANADA WAY SE SUITE 1550, MEDICINE HAT, AB, T1B 4C6
(403) 528-5727   *SIC 5411*

LOBLAWS INC   *p154*
5016A 51 AVE, RED DEER, AB, T4N 4H5
(403) 350-3531   *SIC 5411*

LOBLAWS INC   *p163*
410 BASELINE RD SUITE 100, SHERWOOD PARK, AB, T8H 2A7
(780) 417-5212   *SIC 5411*

LOBLAWS INC   *p164*
100 JENNIFER HEIL WAY SUITE 10, SPRUCE GROVE, AB, T7X 4B8
(780) 960-7400   *SIC 5411*

LOBLAWS INC   *p179*
3100 272 ST, ALDERGROVE, BC, V4W 3N7
(604) 859-6501   *SIC 5411*

LOBLAWS INC   *p195*
1424 ISLAND HWY SUITE 1524, CAMPBELL RIVER, BC, V9W 8C9
(250) 830-2736   *SIC 5411*

LOBLAWS INC   *p201*
1301 LOUGHEED HWY, COQUITLAM, BC, V3K 6P9
(604) 520-8339   *SIC 5411*

LOBLAWS INC   *p207*
8195 120 ST, DELTA, BC, V4C 6P7
(604) 592-5218   *SIC 5411*

LOBLAWS INC   *p217*
910 COLUMBIA ST W SUITE 1522, KAMLOOPS, BC, V2C 1L2
(250) 371-6418   *SIC 5411*

LOBLAWS INC   *p239*
333 SEYMOUR BLVD SUITE 1560, NORTH VANCOUVER, BC, V7J 2J4
(604) 904-5537   *SIC 5411*

LOBLAWS INC   *p244*
19800 LOUGHEED HWY SUITE 201, PITT MEADOWS, BC, V3Y 2W1
(604) 460-4319   *SIC 5411*

LOBLAWS INC   *p250*
2155 FERRY AVE, PRINCE GEORGE, BC, V2N 5E8
(250) 960-1300   *SIC 5411*

LOBLAWS INC   *p252*

2335 MAPLE DR E, QUESNEL, BC, V2J 7J6
(250) 747-2803   *SIC 5411*

LOBLAWS INC   *p347*
920 VICTORIA AVE, BRANDON, MB, R7A 1A7
(204) 729-4600   *SIC 5411*

LOBLAWS INC   *p358*
276 MAIN ST, STEINBACH, MB, R5G 1Y8
(204) 346-6304   *SIC 5411*

LOBLAWS INC   *p358*
130 PTH 12 N, STEINBACH, MB, R5G 1T4
(204) 320-4101   *SIC 5411*

LOBLAWS INC   *p370*
2132 MCPHILLIPS ST, WINNIPEG, MB, R2V 3C8
(204) 631-6250   *SIC 5411*

LOBLAWS INC   *p391*
80 BISON DR SUITE 1509, WINNIPEG, MB, R3T 4Z7
(204) 275-4118   *SIC 5411*

LOBLAWS INC   *p418*
195 KING ST, ST STEPHEN, NB, E3L 2E4
(506) 465-1457   *SIC 5411*

LOBLAWS INC   *p422*
5 MURPHY SQ SUITE 926, CORNER BROOK, NL, A2H 1R4
(709) 634-9450   *SIC 5411*

LOBLAWS INC   *p475*
30 KINGSTON RD W SUITE 1012, AJAX, ON, L1T 4K8
(905) 683-2272   *SIC 5411*

LOBLAWS INC   *p511*
85 STEELES AVE W, BRAMPTON, ON, L6Y 0K3
(905) 451-0917   *SIC 5411*

LOBLAWS INC   *p519*
1972 PARKEDALE AVE SUITE 1017, BROCKVILLE, ON, K6V 7N4
(613) 498-0994   *SIC 5411*

LOBLAWS INC   *p542*
791 ST CLAIR ST, CHATHAM, ON, N7L 0E9
(519) 352-4982   *SIC 5411*

LOBLAWS INC   *p593*
171 GUELPH ST SUITE 2811, GEORGETOWN, ON, L7G 4A1
(905) 877-7005   *SIC 5411*

LOBLAWS INC   *p599*
361 SOUTH SERVICE RD SUITE 2806, GRIMSBY, ON, L3M 4E8
(905) 309-3911   *SIC 5411*

LOBLAWS INC   *p626*
760 EAGLESON RD, KANATA, ON, K2M 0A7
(613) 254-6050   *SIC 5411*

LOBLAWS INC   *p628*
538 PARK ST, KENORA, ON, P9N 1A1
(807) 468-1868   *SIC 5411*

LOBLAWS INC   *p641*
875 HIGHLAND RD W SUITE 178, KITCHENER, ON, N2N 2Y2
(519) 745-4781   *SIC 5411*

LOBLAWS INC   *p644*
201 TALBOT ST E, LEAMINGTON, ON, N8H 3X5
(519) 322-1371   *SIC 5411*

LOBLAWS INC   *p658*
1205 OXFORD ST W, LONDON, ON, N6H 1V9
(519) 641-3653   *SIC 5411*

LOBLAWS INC   *p664*
2911 MAJOR MACKENZIE DR SUITE 80, MAPLE, ON, L6A 3N9
(905) 417-0490   *SIC 5411*

LOBLAWS INC   *p681*
9292 93 HWY, MIDLAND, ON, L4R 4K4
(705) 527-0388   *SIC 5411*

LOBLAWS INC   *p684*
820 MAIN ST E SUITE 2810, MILTON, ON, L9T 0J4
(905) 875-3600   *SIC 5411*

LOBLAWS INC   *p711*
3045 MAVIS RD SUITE 2841, MISSISSAUGA, ON, L5C 1T7
(905) 275-6171   *SIC 5411*

LOBLAWS INC   *p783*
51 GERRY FITZGERALD DR SUITE 1033, NORTH YORK, ON, M3J 3N4
(416) 665-7636   *SIC 5411*

LOBLAWS INC   *p787*
3501 YONGE ST, NORTH YORK, ON, M4N 2N5
(416) 481-8105   *SIC 5411*

LOBLAWS INC   *p798*
201 OAK PARK BLVD SUITE 1024, OAKVILLE, ON, L6H 7T4
(905) 257-9330   *SIC 5411*

LOBLAWS INC   *p814*
1385 HARMONY RD N SUITE 1043, OSHAWA, ON, L1K 0Z6
(905) 433-9569   *SIC 5411*

LOBLAWS INC   *p827*
2210C BANK ST SUITE 1188, OTTAWA, ON, K1V 1J5
(613) 733-1377   *SIC 5411*

LOBLAWS INC   *p829*
190 RICHMOND RD SUITE 1009, OTTAWA, ON, K1Z 6W6
(613) 722-5890   *SIC 5411*

LOBLAWS INC   *p858*
600 MURPHY RD, SARNIA, ON, N7S 5T7
(519) 383-8133   *SIC 5411*

LOBLAWS INC   *p867*
755 BRIMLEY RD, SCARBOROUGH, ON, M1J 1C5
(416) 279-0802   *SIC 5411*

LOBLAWS INC   *p889*
1063 TALBOT ST UNIT 50, ST THOMAS, ON, N5P 1G4
(519) 637-6358   *SIC 5411*

LOBLAWS INC   *p898*
1485 LASALLE BLVD, SUDBURY, ON, P3A 5H7
(705) 521-1031   *SIC 5411*

LOBLAWS INC   *p908*
600 HARBOUR EXPY, THUNDER BAY, ON, P7B 6P4
(807) 343-4500   *SIC 5411*

LOBLAWS INC   *p920*
17 LESLIE ST, TORONTO, ON, M4M 3H9
(416) 469-2897   *SIC 5411*

LOBLAWS INC   *p920*
720 BROADVIEW AVE, TORONTO, ON, M4K 2P1
(416) 778-8762   *SIC 5411*

LOBLAWS INC   *p997*
2549 WESTON RD, TORONTO, ON, M9N 2A7
(416) 246-1906   *SIC 5411*

LOBLAWS INC   *p1001*
100 MCARTHUR AVE, VANIER, ON, K1L 8H5
(613) 744-0705   *SIC 5411*

LOBLAWS INC   *p1005*
25 45TH ST S, WASAGA BEACH, ON, L9Z 1A7
(705) 429-4315   *SIC 5411*

LOBLAWS INC   *p1016*
200 TAUNTON RD W SUITE 1058, WHITBY, ON, L1R 3H8
(905) 665-1164   *SIC 5411*

LOBLAWS INC   *p1020*
4371 WALKER RD SUITE 567, WINDSOR, ON, N8W 3T6
(519) 972-8335   *SIC 5411*

LOBLAWS INC   *p1066*
1001 BOUL DE MONTARVILLE BUREAU 1, BOUCHERVILLE, QC, J4B 6P5
(450) 449-0081   *SIC 5411*

LOBLAWS INC   *p1097*
1850 BOUL SAINT-JOSEPH, DRUMMONDVILLE, QC, J2B 1R3
(819) 472-1197   *SIC 5411*

LOBLAWS INC   *p1108*
375 CH D'AYLMER BUREAU 5, GATINEAU, QC, J9H 1A5
(819) 682-4433   *SIC 5411*

LOBLAWS INC   *p1240*
10200 BOUL PIE-IX, MONTREAL-NORD,

QC, H1H 3Z1
(514) 321-3111   *SIC 5411*

LOBLAWS INC   *p1255*
699 RUE CLEMENCEAU, QUEBEC, QC, G1C 4N6
(418) 666-0155   *SIC 5411*

LOBLAWS INC   *p1279*
350 RUE BOUVIER, QUEBEC, QC, G2J 1R8
(418) 623-5475   *SIC 5411*

LOBLAWS INC   *p1283*
86 BOUL BRIEN, REPENTIGNY, QC, J6A 5K7
(450) 581-8866   *SIC 5411*

LOBLAWS INC   *p1385*
3725 BOUL DES FORGES, TROIS-RIVIERES, QC, G8Y 4P2
(819) 374-8980   *SIC 5411*

LOBLAWS INC   *p1410*
620A SASKETCHEWAN AVE, MELFORT, SK, S0E 1A0
(306) 752-9725   *SIC 5411*

LOBLAWS INC   *p1410*
290 PRINCE WILLIAM DR, MELVILLE, SK, S0A 2P0
(306) 728-6615   *SIC 5411*

LOBLAWS INC   *p1420*
921 BROAD ST, REGINA, SK, S4R 8G9
(306) 525-2125   *SIC 5411*

LOBLAWS INC   *p1421*
3960 ALBERT ST SUITE 9037, REGINA, SK, S4S 3R1
(306) 584-9444   *SIC 5411*

LOBLAWS INC   *p1422*
2055 PRINCE OF WALES DR SUITE 1584, REGINA, SK, S4V 3A3
(306) 546-6518   *SIC 5411*

LOBLAWS INC   *p1424*
2901 8TH ST E SUITE 1535, SASKATOON, SK, S7H 0V4
(306) 978-7040   *SIC 5411*

LOBLAWS INC   *p1428*
2815 WANUSKEWIN RD, SASKATOON, SK, S7K 8E6
(306) 249-9200   *SIC 5411*

LOBLAWS INC   *p1435*
315 HEROLD RD, SASKATOON, SK, S7V 1J7
(306) 664-5033   *SIC 5411*

LOBLAWS SUPERMARKETS LIMITED *p475*
30 KINGSTON RD W SUITE 1012, AJAX, ON, L1T 4K8
(905) 683-5573   *SIC 5411*

LOBLAWS SUPERMARKETS LIMITED *p482*
657 JOHN ST N, AYLMER, ON, N5H 2R2
(519) 765-2811   *SIC 5411*

LOBLAWS SUPERMARKETS LIMITED *p511*
1 PRESIDENTS CHOICE CIR, BRAMPTON, ON, L6Y 5S5
(905) 459-2500   *SIC 5411*

LOBLAWS SUPERMARKETS LIMITED *p546*
12 HURONTARIO ST, COLLINGWOOD, ON, L9Y 2L6
(705) 445-0461   *SIC 5411*

LOBLAWS SUPERMARKETS LIMITED *p576*
270 THE KINGSWAY, ETOBICOKE, ON, M9A 3T7
(416) 231-0931   *SIC 5411*

LOBLAWS SUPERMARKETS LIMITED *p577*
380 THE EAST MALL, ETOBICOKE, ON, M9B 6L5
(416) 695-8990   *SIC 5411*

LOBLAWS SUPERMARKETS LIMITED *p593*
300 GUELPH ST, GEORGETOWN, ON, L7G 4B1
(905) 877-4711   *SIC 5411*

LOBLAWS SUPERMARKETS LIMITED *p596*
1980 OGILVIE RD, GLOUCESTER, ON, K1J 9L3
(613) 746-5724   *SIC 5411*

LOBLAWS SUPERMARKETS LIMITED *p619*
1560 CAMERON ST SUITE 820, HAWKESBURY, ON, K6A 3S5
(613) 632-9215   *SIC 5411*

LOBLAWS SUPERMARKETS LIMITED p633
1048 MIDLAND AVE, KINGSTON, ON, K7P 2X9
(613) 389-4119   *SIC 5411*

LOBLAWS SUPERMARKETS LIMITED p646
400 KENT ST W, LINDSAY, ON, K9V 6K2
(705) 878-4605   *SIC 5411*

LOBLAWS SUPERMARKETS LIMITED p657
635 SOUTHDALE RD E, LONDON, ON, N6E 3W6
(519) 686-8007   *SIC 5411*

LOBLAWS SUPERMARKETS LIMITED p713
250 LAKESHORE RD W, MISSISSAUGA, ON, L5H 1G6
(905) 271-9925   *SIC 5411*

LOBLAWS SUPERMARKETS LIMITED p749
1460 MERIVALE RD, NEPEAN, ON, K2E 5P2
(613) 226-6001   *SIC 5411*

LOBLAWS SUPERMARKETS LIMITED p752
3201 GREENBANK RD SUITE 1035, NEPEAN, ON, K2J 4H9
(613) 825-0812   *SIC 5411*

LOBLAWS SUPERMARKETS LIMITED p755
18120 YONGE ST, NEWMARKET, ON, L3Y 4V8
(905) 830-4072   *SIC 5411*

LOBLAWS SUPERMARKETS LIMITED p802
173 LAKESHORE RD W, OAKVILLE, ON, L6K 1E7
(905) 845-4946   *SIC 5411*

LOBLAWS SUPERMARKETS LIMITED p810
1226 PLACE D'ORLEANS DR SUITE 3935, ORLEANS, ON, K1C 7K3
(613) 834-4074   *SIC 5411*

LOBLAWS SUPERMARKETS LIMITED p814
481 GIBB ST, OSHAWA, ON, L1J 1Z4
(905) 743-0043   *SIC 5411*

LOBLAWS SUPERMARKETS LIMITED p831
1980 BASELINE RD, OTTAWA, ON, K2C 0C6
(613) 723-3200   *SIC 5411*

LOBLAWS SUPERMARKETS LIMITED p843
1792 LIVERPOOL RD, PICKERING, ON, L1V 4G6
(905) 831-6301   *SIC 5411*

LOBLAWS SUPERMARKETS LIMITED p867
3401 LAWRENCE AVE E, SCARBOROUGH, ON, M1H 1B2
(416) 438-4392   *SIC 5411*

LOBLAWS SUPERMARKETS LIMITED p918
301 MOORE AVE, TORONTO, ON, M4G 1E1
(416) 425-0604   *SIC 5411*

LOBLAWS SUPERMARKETS LIMITED p925
12 ST CLAIR AVE E, TORONTO, ON, M4T 1L7
(416) 960-8108   *SIC 5411*

LOBLAWS SUPERMARKETS LIMITED p1012
821 NIAGARA ST, WELLAND, ON, L3C 1M4
(905) 732-9010   *SIC 5411*

LOBLAWS SUPERMARKETS LIMITED p1016
3100 GARDEN ST UNIT 2, WHITBY, ON, L1R 2G8
(866) 987-6453   *SIC 5411*

LOBLAWS SUPERMARKETS LIMITED p1167
2925 RUE RACHEL E, MONTREAL, QC, H1W 3Z8
(514) 522-4442   *SIC 5411*

LOGAN GROUP PARTNERSHIP p269
6661 SOOKE RD SUITE 103, SOOKE, BC, V9Z 0A1
SIC 5411

LONGO BROTHERS FRUIT MARKETS INC p672
3085 HIGHWAY 7 E, MARKHAM, ON, L3R 0J5
(905) 479-8877   *SIC 5411*

LONGO BROTHERS FRUIT MARKETS INC p686
7085 GOREWAY DR, MISSISSAUGA, ON,

L4T 3X6
(905) 677-3481   *SIC 5411*

LONGO BROTHERS FRUIT MARKETS INC p717
3163 WINSTON CHURCHILL BLVD, MISSISSAUGA, ON, L5L 2W1
(905) 828-0008   *SIC 5411*

LONGO BROTHERS FRUIT MARKETS INC p718
5636 GLEN ERIN DR UNIT 1, MISSISSAUGA, ON, L5M 6B1
(905) 567-4450   *SIC 5411*

LONGO BROTHERS FRUIT MARKETS INC p1027
8800 HUNTINGTON RD, WOODBRIDGE, ON, L4H 3M6
(905) 264-4100   *SIC 5411*

LONGO BROTHERS FRUIT MARKETS INC p1032
8401 WESTON RD, WOODBRIDGE, ON, L4L 1A6
(905) 850-6161   *SIC 5411*

LORETTE MARKET PLACE LIMITED p351
11 LARAMEE DR, LORETTE, MB, R0A 0Y0
(204) 878-2510   *SIC 5411*

LU & SONS ENTERPRISE LTD p266
12051 NO. 1 RD SUITE 604, RICHMOND, BC, V7E 1T5
(604) 274-7878   *SIC 5411*

LUCKETT RETAIL MANAGEMENT INC p439
1595 BEDFORD HWY SUITE 122, BEDFORD, NS, B4A 3Y4
(902) 835-4997   *SIC 5411*

LUM & SON FINE FOODS LTD p335
1058 PANDORA AVE, VICTORIA, BC, V8V 3P5
(250) 384-3543   *SIC 5411*

M & M MARKETS LTD p999
58A VICTORIA ST N, TWEED, ON, K0K 3J0
(613) 478-2014   *SIC 5411*

M & M MEAT SHOPS LTD p724
2240 ARGENTIA RD SUITE 100, MISSISSAUGA, ON, L5N 2K7
(905) 465-6325   *SIC 5411*

MAC CHAIN COMPANY LIMITED p282
9445 193A ST, SURREY, BC, V4N 4N5
(604) 888-1229   *SIC 5411*

MAC'S OYSTERS LTD p212
7162 ISLAND HWY S, FANNY BAY, BC, V0R 1W0
(250) 335-2129   *SIC 5411*

MACDEN HOLDINGS LTD p849
HWY 105, RED LAKE, ON, P0V 2M0
(807) 727-2855   *SIC 5411*

MACKENZIE CONSUMERS CO-OPERATIVE ASSOCIATION p230
403 MACKENZIE BLVD SUITE 103, MACKENZIE, BC, V0J 2C0
(250) 997-3335   *SIC 5411*

MACSWEEN ENTERPRISES LTD p1040
161 MAYPOINT RD SUITE 14, CHARLOTTETOWN, PE, C1E 1X6
(902) 892-8002   *SIC 5411*

MAGASIN CO-OP DE BONAVENTURE p1063
168 AV DE GRAND-PRE, BONAVENTURE, QC, G0C 1E0
(418) 534-2020   *SIC 5411*

MAGASIN CO-OP DE MONTMAGNY p1160
70 BOUL TACHE O, MONTMAGNY, QC, G5V 3A4
(418) 248-1230   *SIC 5411*

MAGASIN CO-OP DE PLESSISVILLE p1246
1971 RUE BILODEAU, PLESSISVILLE, QC, G6L 3J1
(819) 362-6357   *SIC 5411*

MAGASIN CO-OP DE STE-PERPETUE, CTE L'ISLET p1361
358 RUE PRINCIPALE S, SAINTE-PERPETUE-DE-L'ISLET, QC, G0R 3Z0
(418) 359-2221   *SIC 5411*

MAGASIN COOP DE MARIA IGA p1149
524 BOUL PERRON, MARIA, QC, G0C 1Y0
(418) 759-3440   *SIC 5411*

MAGASIN COOP DE RIVIERE-DU-LOUP p1286
298 BOUL ARMAND-THERIAULT BUREAU 60, RIVIERE-DU-LOUP, QC, G5R 4C2
(418) 862-3590   *SIC 5411*

MAGASIN COOP DE ST-ANSELME p1292
70 RUE PRINCIPALE, SAINT-ANSELME, QC, G0R 2N0
(418) 885-4461   *SIC 5411*

MAGASIN COOP LA PAIX p1315
321 RTE DE L'EGLISE, SAINT-JEAN-PORT-JOLI, QC, G0R 3G0
(418) 598-3385   *SIC 5411*

MAGASIN COOP ST-GEDEON p1304
800 BOUL CANAM S, SAINT-GEDEON-DE-BEAUCE, QC, G0M 1T0
(418) 582-3977   *SIC 5411*

MAGASINS MAXI p1075
1601 BOUL DE PERIGNY, CHAMBLY, QC, J3L 1W9
(450) 447-7500   *SIC 5411*

MAPLE LEAF FOODS INC p1292
254 RUE PRINCIPALE, SAINT-ANSELME, QC, G0R 2N0
SIC 5411

MARCHE A. LAROUCHE LTEE p1079
992 BOUL DU SAGUENAY E, CHICOUTIMI, QC, G7H 1L5
(418) 543-4521   *SIC 5411*

MARCHE ALIMENTATION THIBAULT INC p1380
2120 CH GASCON, TERREBONNE, QC, J6X 3A1
(450) 964-2050   *SIC 5411*

MARCHE ANDRE MARTEL INC p1301
219 RUE SAINT-LAURENT, SAINT-EUSTACHE, QC, J7P 4W4
(450) 472-7720   *SIC 5411*

MARCHE ANDRE TELLIER INC p1376
411 BOUL POLIQUIN, SOREL-TRACY, QC, J3P 7V9
(450) 743-3693   *SIC 5411*

MARCHE AYLMER INC p1108
799 BOUL WILFRID-LAVIGNE BUREAU 1098, GATINEAU, QC, J9J 1V2
(819) 685-3490   *SIC 5411*

MARCHE BEAUBIEN INC p1163
RUE BEAUBIEN E, MONTREAL, QC, H1M 3E6
(514) 254-6081   *SIC 5411*

MARCHE BELANGER INC p1289
680 AV CHAUSSE, ROUYN-NORANDA, QC, J9X 4B9
(819) 762-2992   *SIC 5411*

MARCHE BELLEMARE INC p1069
2121 BOUL LAPINIERE, BROSSARD, QC, J4W 1L7
(450) 445-3044   *SIC 5411*

MARCHE BELLEMARE INC p1308
5350 GRANDE ALLEE BUREAU 1353, SAINT-HUBERT, QC, J3Y 1A3
(450) 676-0220   *SIC 5411*

MARCHE BOURGEAULT INC p1303
160 RUE SAINT-GABRIEL, SAINT-GABRIEL-DE-BRANDON, QC, J0K 2N0
(450) 835-4794   *SIC 5411*

MARCHE C.D.L. TELLIER INC p1239
6190 BOUL HENRI-BOURASSA E, MONTREAL-NORD, QC, H1G 5X3
(514) 321-0120   *SIC 5411*

MARCHE CENTRAL C.J.C. LTEE p1145
2642 CH DE CHAMBLY, LONGUEUIL, QC, J4L 1M5
(450) 651-4123   *SIC 5411*

MARCHE CHEVREFILS SAINT-SAUVEUR INC p1352
222A CH DU LAC-MILLETTE, SAINT-SAUVEUR, QC, J0R 1R3
(450) 227-8734   *SIC 5411*

MARCHE CHEVREFILS STE-AGATHE INC p1354
1050 RUE PRINCIPALE, SAINTE-AGATHE-DES-MONTS, QC, J8C 1L6
(819) 326-2822   *SIC 5411*

MARCHE CLEMENT DEFORGES INC p1097
1910 BOUL SAINT-JOSEPH, DRUMMONDVILLE, QC, J2B 1R2
(819) 477-7700   *SIC 5411*

MARCHE CREVIER IGA (S.C.B.) INC p1297
655 RUE DE LA VISITATION, SAINT-CHARLES-BORROMEE, QC, J6E 4P9
(450) 752-1441   *SIC 5411*

MARCHE CREVIER IGA INC p1243
17 RUE GAUTHIER N, NOTRE-DAME-DES-PRAIRIES, QC, J6E 1T7
(450) 759-2554   *SIC 5411*

MARCHE CROISETIERE BERTHIER INC p1057
1071 AV GILLES-VILLENEUVE, BERTHIERVILLE, QC, J0K 1A0
(450) 836-3775   *SIC 5411*

MARCHE D'ALIMENTATION BECK INC p1131
8130 BOUL CHAMPLAIN, LASALLE, QC, H8P 1B4
(514) 364-4777   *SIC 5411*

MARCHE D'ALIMENTATION DIANE RODRIGUE INC p1146
714 BOUL SAINT-LAURENT O, LOUISEVILLE, QC, J5V 1K7
(819) 228-5818   *SIC 5411*

MARCHE D'ALIMENTATION MARCANIO & FILS INC p1172
1550 RUE BELANGER, MONTREAL, QC, H2G 1A8
(514) 729-1866   *SIC 5411*

MARCHE D'ALIMENTATION MARCANIO (ANJOU) INC p1049
7172 RUE BOMBARDIER, ANJOU, QC, H1J 2Z9
(514) 352-5447   *SIC 5411*

MARCHE D. BOUTIN ST-FELICIEN INC p1090
99 8E AV, DOLBEAU-MISTASSINI, QC, G8L 1Z1
(418) 276-0361   *SIC 5411*

MARCHE DE LA ROUSSELIERE INC p1247
3000 RUE DE LA ROUSSELIERE, POINTE-AUX-TREMBLES, QC, H1A 4G3
(514) 498-7117   *SIC 5411*

MARCHE DENIGIL (1984) INC p1363
500 BOUL SAMSON, SAINTE-ROSE, QC, H7X 1J5
(450) 689-2282   *SIC 5411*

MARCHE DES OISEAUX INC p1362
580 BOUL CURE-LABELLE, SAINTE-ROSE, QC, H7L 4V6
(450) 963-1072   *SIC 5411*

MARCHE DOMINIC PICHE INC p1253
3023 BOUL LABELLE, PREVOST, QC, J0R 1T0
SIC 5411

MARCHE DU FAUBOURG STE-JULIE INC p1359
2055 RUE PRINCIPALE BUREAU 187, SAINTE-JULIE, QC, J3E 1W1
(450) 649-4078   *SIC 5411*

MARCHE DU VIEUX BEAUPORT INC p1256
771 AV ROYALE, QUEBEC, QC, G1E 1Z1
(418) 661-9181   *SIC 5411*

MARCHE DUBREUIL VEILLETTE INC p1308
6250 BOUL COUSINEAU BUREAU 100, SAINT-HUBERT, QC, J3Y 8X9
(450) 462-4420   *SIC 5411*

MARCHE DUCHEMIN ET FRERES INC p1323
1947 BOUL KELLER, SAINT-LAURENT, QC, H4K 2V6
(514) 336-8085   *SIC 5411*

MARCHE DUCHEMIN ET LACAS INC p1151
927 BOUL SAINT-JEAN-BAPTISTE, MERCIER, QC, J6R 2K8
(450) 691-7647   *SIC 5411*

MARCHE ELITE ST-ANTOINE INC p1321
633 BOUL DES LAURENTIDES, SAINT-JEROME, QC, J7Z 4M4
(450) 432-3433   *SIC 5411*

MARCHE ELITE ST-JEROME INC p1320

430 BOUL MONSEIGNEUR-DUBOIS, SAINT-JEROME, QC, J7Y 3L8
(450) 432-3433   SIC 5411

MARCHE EMERY & FILS INC   p1146
80 RUE SAINT-MARC, LOUISEVILLE, QC, J5V 2E6
(819) 228-2764   SIC 5411

MARCHE FRECHETTE INC   p1089
276 RUE PRINCIPALE, DAVELUYVILLE, QC, G0Z 1C0
(819) 367-2352   SIC 5411

MARCHE G. CARDINAL INC   p1356
5480 BOUL SAINT-LAURENT, SAINTE-CATHERINE, QC, J5C 1B1
(450) 638-0360   SIC 5411

MARCHE GAOUETTE INC   p1109
40 RUE EVANGELINE, GRANBY, QC, J2G 8K1
(450) 378-4447   SIC 5411

MARCHE HEBERT SENECAL INC   p1232
5805 BOUL ROBERT-BOURASSA, MONTREAL, QC, H7E 0A4
(450) 665-4441   SIC 5411

MARCHE IGA LOUISE MENARD ST-LAMBERT INC   p1322
371 AV VICTORIA, SAINT-LAMBERT, QC, J4P 2H7
(450) 466-3880   SIC 5411

MARCHE IGA ST-HENRI DE LEVIS INC
p1306
59 RTE CAMPAGNA, SAINT-HENRI-DE-LEVIS, QC, G0R 3E0
(418) 882-5375   SIC 5411

MARCHE J P FONTAINE INC   p1100
382 RUE PRINCIPALE, EASTMAN, QC, J0E 1P0
(450) 297-2815   SIC 5411

MARCHE J.C. MESSIER INC   p1066
535 RUE SAMUEL-DE CHAMPLAIN BUREAU 200, BOUCHERVILLE, QC, J4B 6B6
(450) 641-3032   SIC 5411

MARCHE J.C. MESSIER INC   p1083
155 BOUL DE LA CONCORDE E, COTE SAINT-LUC, QC, H7G 2C6
(450) 667-3277   SIC 5411

MARCHE J.C. MESSIER INC   p1149
875 MONT?E MASSON, MASCOUCHE, QC, J7K 3T3
(450) 966-9996   SIC 5411

MARCHE J.C. MESSIER INC   p1168
3600 BOUL SAINT-JOSEPH E, MONTREAL, QC, H1X 1W6
(514) 254-2950   SIC 5411

MARCHE J.R. GRAVEL INC   p1081
110 RUE NOTRE-DAME, CLERMONT, QC, G4A 1G3
(418) 439-3922   SIC 5411

MARCHE KELLY MALONEY INC   p1103
910 BOUL MALONEY E, GATINEAU, QC, J8P 1H5
(819) 643-2353   SIC 5411

MARCHE L. ETHIER & FILS INC   p1153
9300 RUE SAINT-ETIENNE, MIRABEL, QC, J7N 2N2
(450) 258-2084   SIC 5411

MARCHE L.V. LTEE   p1074
686 BOUL PERRON GD, CARLETON, QC, G0C 1J0
(418) 364-7380   SIC 5411

MARCHE LA PERADE INC   p1355
185 RUE PRINCIPALE, SAINTE-ANNE-DE-LA-PERADE, QC, G0X 2J0
(418) 325-2233   SIC 5411

MARCHE LABRIE & LANDRY INC   p1389
1010 BOUL LAURE, UASHAT, QC, G4R 5P1
(418) 962-7797   SIC 5411

MARCHE LAMBERT ET FRERES INCp1294
2400 BOUL DU MILLENAIRE, SAINT-BASILE-LE-GRAND, QC, J3N 1T8
(450) 441-3800   SIC 5411

MARCHE LAMBERT ET FRERES INCp1296
23 BOUL SEIGNEURIAL O, SAINT-BRUNO, QC, J3V 2G9
(450) 653-4466   SIC 5411

MARCHE LAMBERT ET FRERES INCp1298
400 132 RTE, SAINT-CONSTANT, QC, J5A 2J8
SIC 5411

MARCHE LAPLANTE FARNHAM INCp1101
999 RUE PRINCIPALE E, FARNHAM, QC, J2N 1M9
(450) 293-4210   SIC 5411

MARCHE LEBLANC INC   p1154
101 RUE HEBERT, MONT-LAURIER, QC, J9L 3H9
(819) 623-3200   SIC 5411

MARCHE LEBLANC MONTEE PAIEMENT INC   p1103
435 MONTEE PAIEMENT, GATINEAU, QC, J8P 0B1
(819) 561-5478   SIC 5411

MARCHE LOUISE MENARD (ILE-DES-SOEURS) INC, LES   p1396
30 PLACE DU COMMERCE, VERDUN, QC, H3E 1V7
(514) 362-6330   SIC 5411

MARCHE MARCANIO ET FILS INC   p1172
1550 RUE BELANGER, MONTREAL, QC, H2G 1A8
(514) 729-1866   SIC 5411

MARCHE MARIO DOIRON INC   p1075
500 AV DAIGNEAULT UNITE 101, CHANDLER, QC, G0C 1K0
(418) 689-6999   SIC 5411

MARCHE MICHEL LEMIEUX INC   p1283
450 CH RICHELIEU, RICHELIEU, QC, J3L 3R8
(450) 658-1831   SIC 5411

MARCHE MONTEE GAGNON INC   p1060
50 MONTEE GAGNON, BOIS-DES-FILION, QC, J6Z 2L1
(450) 621-2266   SIC 5411

MARCHE PERREAULT & GELINAS INC
p1315
318 BOUL SAINT-LUC, SAINT-JEAN-SUR-RICHELIEU, QC, J2W 2A3
(450) 359-4110   SIC 5411

MARCHE PIERRE JOBIDON INC   p1322
1021 AV DU PALAIS, SAINT-JOSEPH-DE-BEAUCE, QC, G0S 2V0
(418) 397-5213   SIC 5411

MARCHE PLOUFFE GRANBY INC   p1109
65 RUE PRINCIPALE, GRANBY, QC, J2G 2T7
(450) 378-9926   SIC 5411

MARCHE PLOUFFE SHERBROOKE INC
p1370
1175 RUE KING E, SHERBROOKE, QC, J1G 1E6
(819) 346-2229   SIC 5411

MARCHE PLOUFFE WATERLOO INCp1400
4615 RUE FOSTER, WATERLOO, QC, J0E 2N0
(450) 534-2648   SIC 5411

MARCHE PLUS SHAWINIGAN INC   p1369
4175 12E AV, SHAWINIGAN-SUD, QC, G9P 4G3
(819) 537-3724   SIC 5411

MARCHE RHEAUME INC   p1281
1501 RUE JACQUES-BEDARD, QUEBEC, QC, G3G 1P9
(418) 849-4416   SIC 5411

MARCHE RIENDEAU BELOEIL INC   p1057
1030 RUE SAINT-JEAN-BAPTISTE, BELOEIL, QC, J3G 0J1
(450) 536-1113   SIC 5411

MARCHE ROBERT DESROCHERS INC
p1077
7000 125 RTE, CHERTSEY, QC, J0K 3K0
(450) 882-2332   SIC 5411

MARCHE ROBERT TELLIER (1990) INC
p1319
872 MONTEE SAINTE-THERESE, SAINT-JEROME, QC, J5L 2L1
(450) 565-5977   SIC 5411

MARCHE ROMEO ROY & FILS INC   p1299
108 RTE 108 E, SAINT-EPHREM-DE-BEAUCE, QC, G0M 1R0

(418) 484-2085   SIC 5411

MARCHE SABREVOIS INC   p1066
535 RUE SAMUEL-DE CHAMPLAIN BUREAU 2, BOUCHERVILLE, QC, J4B 6B6
(450) 655-2634   SIC 5411

MARCHE SENNETERRE INC   p1366
760 10E AV, SENNETERRE, QC, J0Y 2M0
(819) 737-2232   SIC 5411

MARCHE SHAWINIGAN-SUD INC   p1369
2105 105E AV, SHAWINIGAN, QC, G9P 1N9
(819) 537-6997   SIC 5411

MARCHE ST-CANUT INC   p1153
9600 RUE HENRI-PICHE, MIRABEL, QC, J7N 0T4
(450) 431-3244   SIC 5411

MARCHE ST-JANVIER INC   p1152
13380 BOUL DU CURE-LABELLE, MIRABEL, QC, J7J 1G9
(450) 971-7881   SIC 5411

MARCHE ST-PIERRE & FILS INC   p1383
780 BOUL FRONTENAC E, THETFORD MINES, QC, G6G 6H1
(418) 335-6222   SIC 5411

MARCHE ST-PIERRE ET FILS INC   p1110
585 RUE SAINT-HUBERT, GRANBY, QC, J2H 1Y5
(450) 777-0898   SIC 5411

MARCHE STE-MADELEINE INC   p1359
30 RUE SAINT-JEAN-BAPTISTE, SAINTE-MADELEINE, QC, J0H 1S0
(450) 795-3355   SIC 5411

MARCHE STEPHANE BEAULIEU INCp1359
1535 125 RTE, SAINTE-JULIENNE, QC, J0K 2T0
(450) 831-2166   SIC 5411

MARCHE TELLIER JEAN-TALON INCp1346
5000 RUE JEAN-TALON E, SAINT-LEONARD, QC, H1S 1K6
(514) 728-3535   SIC 5411

MARCHES D'ALIMENTS NATURELS TAU INC, LES   p1173
4238 RUE SAINT-DENIS, MONTREAL, QC, H2J 2K8
(514) 843-4420   SIC 5411

MARCHES LOUISE MENARD (PREVILLE) INC, LES   p1323
299 BOUL SIR-WILFRID-LAURIER BUREAU 201, SAINT-LAMBERT, QC, J4R 2L1
(450) 923-9399   SIC 5411

MARCHES LOUISE MENARD INC, LES
p1322
34 AV ARGYLE, SAINT-LAMBERT, QC, J4P 2H4
(514) 843-6116   SIC 5411

MARCHES PEPIN INC, LES   p1057
865 BOUL YVON-L'HEUREUX N, BELOEIL, QC, J3G 6P5
(450) 467-3512   SIC 5411

MARINO'S MARKET LTD   p242
3230 CONNAUGHT CRES, NORTH VANCOUVER, BC, V7R 0A5
SIC 5411

MARK-CREST FOODS LTD   p225
19670 92A AVE SUITE 100, LANGLEY, BC, V1M 3B2
(604) 882-2066   SIC 5411

MARKET PLACE IGA   p323
3535 41ST AVE W, VANCOUVER, BC, V6N 3E7
(604) 261-2423   SIC 5411

MARKETPLACE IGA 48   p244
19150 LOUGHEED HWY, PITT MEADOWS, BC, V3Y 2H6
SIC 5411

MARLER MINI MART (CAMROSE) LTD   p53
350 7 AVE SW SUITE 2900, CALGARY, AB, T2P 3N9
SIC 5411

MARMORA FOOD MARKET LIMITED   p680
42 MATHEW ST, MARMORA, ON, K0K 2M0
(613) 472-2706   SIC 5411

MASSINE ENTERPRISES INC   p834
296 BANK ST, OTTAWA, ON, K2P 1X8
(613) 234-8692   SIC 5411

MAXI 8619   p1121
2100 RUE BAGOT, LA BAIE, QC, G7B 3Z3
(418) 544-2848   SIC 5411

MAXI MANIWAKI INC   p1148
170 RUE PRINCIPALE S, MANIWAKI, QC, J9E 1Z7
(819) 449-6822   SIC 5411

MAXI PREFONTAINE   p1167
2925 RUE SHERBROOKE E, MONTREAL, QC, H1W 1B2
(514) 521-0660   SIC 5411

MAXI ROBERVAL   p1287
150 AV SAINT-ALPHONSE, ROBERVAL, QC, G8H 3P8
(418) 275-4471   SIC 5411

MAYFAIR VILLAGE FOODS   p333
2187 OAK BAY AVE UNIT 101, VICTORIA, BC, V8R 1G1
(250) 592-8911   SIC 5411

MCAULEY'S NOFRILLS   p284
8100 3B HWY SUITE 142, TRAIL, BC, V1R 4N7
(250) 368-8577   SIC 5411

MCKEEN, D & J HOLDINGS (OTTAWA) INC
p826
754 BANK ST, OTTAWA, ON, K1S 3V6
(613) 232-9466   SIC 5411

MCLELLAN'S SUPERMARKET LTD   p315
1255 DAVIE ST, VANCOUVER, BC, V6E 1N4
(604) 688-0911   SIC 5411

MEDICINE HAT CO-OP LIMITED   p146
3030 13 AVE SE SUITE 100, MEDICINE HAT, AB, T1B 1E3
(403) 528-6604   SIC 5411

MEINHARDT FINE FOODS INC   p319
3002 GRANVILLE ST, VANCOUVER, BC, V6H 3J8
(604) 732-4405   SIC 5411

METRO CHARNY INC   p1139
8032 AV DES EGLISES, LEVIS, QC, G6X 1X7
(418) 832-5346   SIC 5411

METRO INC   p519
237 KING ST W, BROCKVILLE, QC, K6V 3S2
(613) 345-4260   SIC 5411

METRO INC   p1051
6500 BOUL JOSEPH-RENAUD, ANJOU, QC, H1K 3V4
(514) 354-0282   SIC 5411

METRO MARCHE CHEVREFILS MT-TREMBLANT   p1159
1011 RUE DE SAINT-JOVITE, MONT-TREMBLANT, QC, J8E 3J9
(819) 425-3381   SIC 5411

METRO ONTARIO INC   p428
55 STAVANGER DR, ST. JOHN'S, NL, A1A 5E8
(709) 576-3576   SIC 5411

METRO ONTARIO INC   p474
280 HARWOOD AVE S, AJAX, ON, L1S 2J1
(905) 683-6951   SIC 5411

METRO ONTARIO INC   p479
375 DANIEL ST S, ARNPRIOR, ON, K7S 3K6
(613) 623-6273   SIC 5411

METRO ONTARIO INC   p481
1 HENDERSON DR UNIT 1, AURORA, ON, L4G 4J7
(905) 727-0185   SIC 5411

METRO ONTARIO INC   p484
400 BAYFIELD ST SUITE 1, BARRIE, ON, L4M 5A1
(705) 722-8284   SIC 5411

METRO ONTARIO INC   p492
110 NORTH FRONT ST, BELLEVILLE, ON, K8P 5J8
(613) 962-0056   SIC 5411

METRO ONTARIO INC   p497
505 MUSKOKA RD HWY SUITE 118, BRACEBRIDGE, ON, P1L 1T3
(705) 645-8751   SIC 5411

METRO ONTARIO INC   p498

20 GREAT LAKES DR, BRAMPTON, ON, L6R 2K7
(905) 789-6161   *SIC* 5411

METRO ONTARIO INC   p508
227 VODDEN ST E, BRAMPTON, ON, L6V 1N2
(905) 451-7842   *SIC* 5411

METRO ONTARIO INC   p509
156 MAIN ST S, BRAMPTON, ON, L6W 2C9
(905) 459-6212   *SIC* 5411

METRO ONTARIO INC   p512
180 SANDALWOOD PKY E, BRAMPTON, ON, L6Z 1Y4
(905) 846-2222   *SIC* 5411

METRO ONTARIO INC   p513
10088 MCLAUGHLIN RD SUITE 1, BRAMPTON, ON, L7A 2X6
SIC 5411

METRO ONTARIO INC   p514
371 ST PAUL AVE, BRANTFORD, ON, N3R 4N5
(519) 758-0300   *SIC* 5411

METRO ONTARIO INC   p523
5353 LAKESHORE RD, BURLINGTON, ON, L7L 1C8
(905) 634-1804   *SIC* 5411

METRO ONTARIO INC   p523
2010 APPLEBY LINE, BURLINGTON, ON, L7L 6M6
(905) 331-7900   *SIC* 5411

METRO ONTARIO INC   p528
3365 FAIRVIEW ST, BURLINGTON, ON, L7N 3N9
(905) 634-1896   *SIC* 5411

METRO ONTARIO INC   p537
100 JAMIESON PKY, CAMBRIDGE, ON, N3C 4B3
(519) 658-1150   *SIC* 5411

METRO ONTARIO INC   p546
640 FIRST ST, COLLINGWOOD, ON, L9Y 4Y7
(705) 444-5252   *SIC* 5411

METRO ONTARIO INC   p562
1315 SECOND ST E, CORNWALL, ON, K6H 7C4
(613) 932-0514   *SIC* 5411

METRO ONTARIO INC   p566
119 OSLER DR, DUNDAS, ON, L9H 6X4
(905) 628-0177   *SIC* 5411

METRO ONTARIO INC   p566
15 GOVERNORS RD, DUNDAS, ON, L9H 6L9
(905) 627-4791   *SIC* 5411

METRO ONTARIO INC   p577
201 LLOYD MANOR RD, ETOBICOKE, ON, M9B 6H6
(416) 236-3217   *SIC* 5411

METRO ONTARIO INC   p577
250 THE EAST MALL, ETOBICOKE, ON, M9B 3Y8
(416) 233-4149   *SIC* 5411

METRO ONTARIO INC   p577
5559 DUNDAS ST W, ETOBICOKE, ON, M9B 1B9
(416) 239-7171   *SIC* 5411

METRO ONTARIO INC   p593
333 KING ST E, GANANOQUE, ON, K7G 1G6
(613) 382-7090   *SIC* 5411

METRO ONTARIO INC   p596
1930 MONTREAL RD, GLOUCESTER, ON, K1J 6N2
(613) 744-2961   *SIC* 5411

METRO ONTARIO INC   p600
380 ERAMOSA RD, GUELPH, ON, N1E 6R2
(519) 824-8700   *SIC* 5411

METRO ONTARIO INC   p601
500 EDINBURGH RD S, GUELPH, ON, N1G 4Z1
(519) 763-3552   *SIC* 5411

METRO ONTARIO INC   p608
2500 BARTON ST E, HAMILTON, ON, L8E 4A2

(905) 578-5454   *SIC* 5411

METRO ONTARIO INC   p610
1900 KING ST E, HAMILTON, ON, L8K 1W1
(905) 545-5929   *SIC* 5411

METRO ONTARIO INC   p614
845 KING ST W, HAMILTON, ON, L8S 1K4
(905) 523-5044   *SIC* 5411

METRO ONTARIO INC   p615
505 RYMAL RD E SUITE 3, HAMILTON, ON, L8W 3X1
(905) 574-5298   *SIC* 5411

METRO ONTARIO INC   p615
1070 STONE CHURCH RD E, HAMILTON, ON, L8W 3K8
SIC 5411

METRO ONTARIO INC   p617
751 UPPER JAMES ST, HAMILTON, ON, L9C 3A1
(905) 575-5545   *SIC* 5411

METRO ONTARIO INC   p620
70 KING WILLIAM ST SUITE 5A, HUNTSVILLE, ON, P1H 2A5
(705) 789-9619   *SIC* 5411

METRO ONTARIO INC   p631
310 BARRIE ST, KINGSTON, ON, K7L 5L4
(613) 542-5795   *SIC* 5411

METRO ONTARIO INC   p632
466 GARDINERS RD, KINGSTON, ON, K7M 7W8
(613) 384-6334   *SIC* 5411

METRO ONTARIO INC   p632
1300 BATH RD, KINGSTON, ON, K7M 4X4
(613) 544-9317   *SIC* 5411

METRO ONTARIO INC   p633
775 BAYRIDGE DR, KINGSTON, ON, K7P 2P1
(613) 384-8800   *SIC* 5411

METRO ONTARIO INC   p636
655 FAIRWAY RD S, KITCHENER, ON, N2C 1X4
(519) 896-5100   *SIC* 5411

METRO ONTARIO INC   p641
370 HIGHLAND RD W SUITE 1, KITCHENER, ON, N2M 5J9
(519) 744-4100   *SIC* 5411

METRO ONTARIO INC   p641
851 FISCHER HALLMAN RD, KITCHENER, ON, N2M 5N8
(519) 570-2500   *SIC* 5411

METRO ONTARIO INC   p644
288 ERIE ST S, LEAMINGTON, ON, N8H 3C5
(519) 322-1414   *SIC* 5411

METRO ONTARIO INC   p646
363 KENT ST W, LINDSAY, ON, K9V 2Z7
(705) 878-3300   *SIC* 5411

METRO ONTARIO INC   p651
155 CLARKE RD, LONDON, ON, N5W 5C9
(519) 455-5604   *SIC* 5411

METRO ONTARIO INC   p652
1299 OXFORD ST E, LONDON, ON, N5Y 4W5
(519) 453-8510   *SIC* 5411

METRO ONTARIO INC   p652
1030 ADELAIDE ST N, LONDON, ON, N5Y 2M9
(519) 672-8994   *SIC* 5411

METRO ONTARIO INC   p656
395 WELLINGTON RD, LONDON, ON, N6C 5Z6
(519) 680-2317   *SIC* 5411

METRO ONTARIO INC   p658
1225 WONDERLAND RD N, LONDON, ON, N6G 2V9
(519) 472-5601   *SIC* 5411

METRO ONTARIO INC   p658
301 OXFORD ST W, LONDON, ON, N6H 1S6
(519) 433-1708   *SIC* 5411

METRO ONTARIO INC   p659
509 COMMISSIONERS RD W, LONDON, ON, N6J 1Y5
(519) 473-2857   *SIC* 5411

METRO ONTARIO INC   p679

1220 CASTLEMORE AVE, MARKHAM, ON, L6E 0H7
(905) 209-9200   *SIC* 5411

METRO ONTARIO INC   p697
4141 DIXIE RD UNIT 2, MISSISSAUGA, ON, L4W 1V5
(905) 238-1366   *SIC* 5411

METRO ONTARIO INC   p704
1077 NORTH SERVICE RD SUITE 41, MISSISSAUGA, ON, L4Y 1A6
SIC 5411

METRO ONTARIO INC   p708
377 BURNHAMTHORPE RD E, MISSISSAUGA, ON, L5A 3Y1
(905) 270-2143   *SIC* 5411

METRO ONTARIO INC   p708
1585 MISSISSAUGA VALLEY BLVD, MISSISSAUGA, ON, L5A 3W9
(905) 566-9100   *SIC* 5411

METRO ONTARIO INC   p714
910 SOUTHDOWN RD UNIT 46, MISSISSAUGA, ON, L5J 2Y4
(905) 823-4800   *SIC* 5411

METRO ONTARIO INC   p715
2225 ERIN MILLS PKY, MISSISSAUGA, ON, L5K 1T9
(905) 829-3737   *SIC* 5411

METRO ONTARIO INC   p717
3476 GLEN ERIN DR, MISSISSAUGA, ON, L5L 3R4
(905) 569-2162   *SIC* 5411

METRO ONTARIO INC   p724
3221 DERRY RD W SUITE 16, MISSISSAUGA, ON, L5N 7L7
(905) 785-1844   *SIC* 5411

METRO ONTARIO INC   p724
6677 MEADOWVALE TOWN CENTRE CIR, MISSISSAUGA, ON, L5N 2R5
(905) 826-2717   *SIC* 5411

METRO ONTARIO INC   p748
35 ALKENBRACK ST, NAPANEE, ON, K7R 4C4
(613) 354-2882   *SIC* 5411

METRO ONTARIO INC   p752
3201 STRANDHERD DR, NEPEAN, ON, K2J 5N1
(613) 823-8825   *SIC* 5411

METRO ONTARIO INC   p752
900 GREENBANK RD, NEPEAN, ON, K2J 4P6
(613) 823-4458   *SIC* 5411

METRO ONTARIO INC   p754
16640 YONGE ST UNIT 1, NEWMARKET, ON, L3X 2N8
(905) 853-5100   *SIC* 5411

METRO ONTARIO INC   p755
1111 DAVIS DR, NEWMARKET, ON, L3Y 9E5
(905) 853-5355   *SIC* 5411

METRO ONTARIO INC   p755
17725 YONGE ST SUITE 1, NEWMARKET, ON, L3Y 7C1
(905) 895-9700   *SIC* 5411

METRO ONTARIO INC   p760
3770 MONTROSE RD, NIAGARA FALLS, ON, L2H 3C8
(905) 371-3200   *SIC* 5411

METRO ONTARIO INC   p762
390 LAKESHORE DR, NORTH BAY, ON, P1A 2C7
(705) 840-2424   *SIC* 5411

METRO ONTARIO INC   p768
2452 SHEPPARD AVE E, NORTH YORK, ON, M2J 1X1
(416) 756-2513   *SIC* 5411

METRO ONTARIO INC   p769
291 YORK MILLS RD, NORTH YORK, ON, M2L 1L3
(416) 444-5809   *SIC* 5411

METRO ONTARIO INC   p772
20 CHURCH AVE, NORTH YORK, ON, M2N 0B7
(416) 229-6200   *SIC* 5411

METRO ONTARIO INC   p775

1277 YORK MILLS RD, NORTH YORK, ON, M3A 1Z5
(416) 444-7921   *SIC* 5411

METRO ONTARIO INC   p781
600 SHEPPARD AVE W, NORTH YORK, ON, M3H 2S1
(416) 636-5136   *SIC* 5411

METRO ONTARIO INC   p786
2200 JANE ST, NORTH, YORK, ON, M3M 1A4
(416) 241-5732   *SIC* 5411

METRO ONTARIO INC   p789
3090 BATHURST ST, NORTH YORK, ON, M6A 2A1
(416) 783-1227   *SIC* 5411

METRO ONTARIO INC   p791
1411 LAWRENCE AVE W, NORTH YORK, ON, M6L 1A4
(416) 248-5846   *SIC* 5411

METRO ONTARIO INC   p798
1011 UPPER MIDDLE RD E SUITE 412, OAKVILLE, ON, L6H 5Z9
(905) 849-4911   *SIC* 5411

METRO ONTARIO INC   p804
1521 REBECCA ST, OAKVILLE, ON, L6L 1Z8
(905) 827-5421   *SIC* 5411

METRO ONTARIO INC   p808
150 FIRST ST SUITE 7, ORANGEVILLE, ON, L9W 3T7
(519) 941-6391   *SIC* 5411

METRO ONTARIO INC   p809
70 FRONT ST N, ORILLIA, ON, L3V 4R8
(705) 323-9334   *SIC* 5411

METRO ONTARIO INC   p810
1675E TENTH LINE RD, ORLEANS, ON, K1E 3P6
(613) 837-2614   *SIC* 5411

METRO ONTARIO INC   p812
285 TAUNTON RD E SUITE 4, OSHAWA, ON, L1G 3V2
(905) 432-2197   *SIC* 5411

METRO ONTARIO INC   p814
555 ROSSLAND RD E, OSHAWA, ON, L1K 1K8
(905) 579-5862   *SIC* 5411

METRO ONTARIO INC   p814
149 MIDTOWN DR, OSHAWA, ON, L1J 3Z7
SIC 5411

METRO ONTARIO INC   p827
2515 BANK ST, OTTAWA, ON, K1V 0Y4
(613) 731-7410   *SIC* 5411

METRO ONTARIO INC   p827
1670 HERON RD, OTTAWA, ON, K1V 0C2
(613) 731-0066   *SIC* 5411

METRO ONTARIO INC   p827
3310 MCCARTHY RD, OTTAWA, ON, K1V 9S1
(613) 523-2774   *SIC* 5411

METRO ONTARIO INC   p835
1070 2ND AVE E, OWEN SOUND, ON, N4K 2H7
(519) 371-0222   *SIC* 5411

METRO ONTARIO INC   p838
1100 PEMBROKE ST E SUITE 891, PEMBROKE, ON, K8A 6Y7
(613) 735-1846   *SIC* 5411

METRO ONTARIO INC   p840
1154 CHEMONG RD SUITE 9, PETERBOROUGH, ON, K9H 7J6
(705) 745-3381   *SIC* 5411

METRO ONTARIO INC   p843
1822 WHITES RD SUITE 11, PICKERING, ON, L1V 4M1
(905) 420-8838   *SIC* 5411

METRO ONTARIO INC   p846
124 CLARENCE ST, PORT COLBORNE, ON, L3K 3G3
(905) 834-8800   *SIC* 5411

METRO ONTARIO INC   p857
1070 MAJOR MACKENZIE DR E, RICHMOND HILL, ON, L4S 1P3
(905) 770-1400   *SIC* 5411

METRO ONTARIO INC   p860

▲ Public Company   ■ Public Company Family Member   **HQ** Headquarters   **BR** Branch   **SL** Single Location

560 EXMOUTH ST, SARNIA, ON, N7T 5P5
(519) 337-8308   SIC 5411
METRO ONTARIO INC   p860
191 INDIAN RD S, SARNIA, ON, N7T 3W3
(519) 344-1500   SIC 5411
METRO ONTARIO INC   p862
625 TRUNK RD, SAULT STE. MARIE, ON,
P6A 3T1
(705) 949-7260   SIC 5411
METRO ONTARIO INC   p862
150 CHURCHILL BLVD, SAULT STE.
MARIE, ON, P6A 3Z9
(705) 254-3923   SIC 5411
METRO ONTARIO INC   p863
275 SECOND LINE W, SAULT STE. MARIE,
ON, P6C 2J4
(705) 949-0350   SIC 5411
METRO ONTARIO INC   p865
261 PORT UNION RD, SCARBOROUGH,
ON, M1C 2L3
(416) 284-7792   SIC 5411
METRO ONTARIO INC   p866
2900 ELLESMERE RD SUITE 587, SCAR-
BOROUGH, ON, M1E 4B8
(416) 284-5320   SIC 5411
METRO ONTARIO INC   p867
3221 EGLINTON AVE E, SCARBOROUGH,
ON, M1J 2H7
(416) 261-4204   SIC 5411
METRO ONTARIO INC   p871
16 WILLIAM KITCHEN RD SUITE 535,
SCARBOROUGH, ON, M1P 5B7
(416) 321-0500   SIC 5411
METRO ONTARIO INC   p872
15 ELLESMERE RD, SCARBOROUGH,
ON, M1R 4B7
(416) 391-0626   SIC 5411
METRO ONTARIO INC   p877
2900 WARDEN AVE, SCARBOROUGH,
ON, M1W 2S8
(416) 497-6734   SIC 5411
METRO ONTARIO INC   p881
150 WEST ST, SIMCOE, ON, N3Y 5C1
(519) 426-2010   SIC 5411
METRO ONTARIO INC   p884
101 LAKESHORE RD, ST CATHARINES,
ON, L2N 2T6
(905) 934-0131   SIC 5411
METRO ONTARIO INC   p890
417 WELLINGTON ST SUITE 1, ST
THOMAS, ON, N5R 5J5
(519) 633-8780   SIC 5411
METRO ONTARIO INC   p894
5612 MAIN ST, STOUFFVILLE, ON, L4A
8B7
(905) 642-8600   SIC 5411
METRO ONTARIO INC   p900
400 NOTRE DAME AVE, SUDBURY, ON,
P3C 5K5
(705) 675-5845   SIC 5411
METRO ONTARIO INC   p901
1933 REGENT ST, SUDBURY, ON, P3E
5R2
    SIC 5411
METRO ONTARIO INC   p904
8190 BAYVIEW AVE, THORNHILL, ON, L3T
2S2
(905) 731-2300   SIC 5411
METRO ONTARIO INC   p907
640 RIVER ST, THUNDER BAY, ON, P7A
3S4
(807) 345-8342   SIC 5411
METRO ONTARIO INC   p910
505 ARTHUR ST W, THUNDER BAY, ON,
P7E 5R5
(807) 475-0276   SIC 5411
METRO ONTARIO INC   p910
1101 ARTHUR ST W, THUNDER BAY, ON,
P7E 5S2
(807) 577-3910   SIC 5411
METRO ONTARIO INC   p912
225 BROADWAY ST, TILLSONBURG, ON,
N4G 3R2
(519) 842-3625   SIC 5411

METRO ONTARIO INC   p917
1500 WOODBINE AVE, TORONTO, ON,
M4C 4G9
(416) 422-0076   SIC 5411
METRO ONTARIO INC   p919
45 OVERLEA BLVD SUITE 2, TORONTO,
ON, M4H 1C3
(416) 421-1732   SIC 5411
METRO ONTARIO INC   p922
656 EGLINTON AVE E, TORONTO, ON,
M4P 1P1
(416) 482-7422   SIC 5411
METRO ONTARIO INC   p922
40 EGLINTON AVE E, TORONTO, ON, M4P
3A2
(416) 759-1952   SIC 5411
METRO ONTARIO INC   p922
2300 YONGE ST SUITE 752, TORONTO,
ON, M4P 1E4
(416) 483-7340   SIC 5411
METRO ONTARIO INC   p935
89 GOULD ST, TORONTO, ON, M5B 2R1
(416) 862-7171   SIC 5411
METRO ONTARIO INC   p942
80 FRONT ST E SUITE 804, TORONTO,
ON, M5E 1T4
(416) 703-9393   SIC 5411
METRO ONTARIO INC   p976
425 BLOOR ST W, TORONTO, ON, M5S
1X6
(416) 923-9099   SIC 5411
METRO ONTARIO INC   p989
735 COLLEGE ST, TORONTO, ON, M6G
1C5
(416) 533-2515   SIC 5411
METRO ONTARIO INC   p991
100 LYNN WILLIAMS ST SUITE 572,
TORONTO, ON, M6K 3N6
(416) 588-1300   SIC 5411
METRO ONTARIO INC   p999
53 QUINTE ST, TRENTON, ON, K8V 3S8
(613) 394-2525   SIC 5411
METRO ONTARIO INC   p1001
50 BEECHWOOD AVE, VANIER, ON, K1L
8B3
(613) 744-6676   SIC 5411
METRO ONTARIO INC   p1014
70 THICKSON RD S, WHITBY, ON, L1N 7T2
(905) 668-5334   SIC 5411
METRO ONTARIO INC   p1016
4111 THICKSON RD N, WHITBY, ON, L1R
2X3
(905) 655-1553   SIC 5411
METRO ONTARIO INC   p1017
11729 TECUMSEH RD E, WINDSOR, ON,
N8N 1L8
(519) 979-9366   SIC 5411
METRO ONTARIO INC   p1018
2090 LAUZON RD, WINDSOR, ON, N8T
2Z3
(519) 944-7335   SIC 5411
METRO ONTARIO INC   p1018
6740 WYANDOTTE ST E, WINDSOR, ON,
N8S 1P6
(519) 948-5676   SIC 5411
METRO ONTARIO INC   p1023
880 GOYEAU ST, WINDSOR, ON, N9A 1H8
(519) 258-3064   SIC 5411
METRO ONTARIO INC   p1024
2750 TECUMSEH RD W, WINDSOR, ON,
N9B 3P9
(519) 256-1891   SIC 5411
METRO ONTARIO INC   p1028
9600 ISLINGTON AVE, WOODBRIDGE,
ON, L4H 2T1
(905) 893-1618   SIC 5411
METRO ONTARIO INC   p1035
868 DUNDAS ST, WOODSTOCK, ON, N4S
1G7
(519) 537-7021   SIC 5411
METRO ONTARIO PHARMACIES LIMITED
p806
280 NORTH SERVICE RD W, OAKVILLE,
ON, L6M 2S2

(905) 337-7694   SIC 5411
METRO PLUS MARIO LAVOIE   p1079
1550 BOUL TALBOT, CHICOUTIMI, QC,
G7H 4C2
(418) 543-7394   SIC 5411
METRO RICHELIEU CANDIAC INC   p1073
50 BOUL MONTCALM N, CANDIAC, QC,
J5R 3L8
(450) 444-2300   SIC 5411
METRO RICHELIEU INC   p614
967 FENNELL AVE E, HAMILTON, ON, L8T
1R1
(905) 318-7777   SIC 5411
METRO RICHELIEU INC   p1054
50 BOUL SAINT-CHARLES BUREAU 17,
BEACONSFIELD, QC, H9W 2X3
(514) 695-5811   SIC 5411
METRO RICHELIEU INC   p1076
200 BOUL D'ANJOU BUREAU 626,
CHATEAUGUAY, QC, J6K 1C5
(450) 691-2880   SIC 5411
METRO RICHELIEU INC   p1079
299 RUE DES SAGUENEENS,
CHICOUTIMI, QC, G7H 3A5
(418) 696-4114   SIC 5411
METRO RICHELIEU INC   p1099
565 BOUL SAINT-JOSEPH BUREAU 4,
DRUMMONDVILLE, QC, J2C 2B6
(819) 474-2702   SIC 5411
METRO RICHELIEU INC   p1104
720 BOUL MALONEY O, GATINEAU, QC,
J8T 8K7
(819) 243-5117   SIC 5411
METRO RICHELIEU INC   p1106
725A BOUL DE LA CARRIERE, GATINEAU,
QC, J8Y 6T9
(819) 595-1344   SIC 5411
METRO RICHELIEU INC   p1112
5012 BOUL TASCHEREAU, GREENFIELD
PARK, QC, J4V 2J2
(450) 672-8966   SIC 5411
METRO RICHELIEU INC   p1145
2901 CH DE CHAMBLY, LONGUEUIL, QC,
J4L 1M7
(450) 651-6886   SIC 5411
METRO RICHELIEU INC   p1240
6000 BOUL HENRI-BOURASSA E,
MONTREAL-NORD, QC, H1G 2T6
(514) 323-4370   SIC 5411
METRO RICHELIEU INC   p1251
325 BOUL SAINT-JEAN, POINTE-CLAIRE,
QC, H9R 3J1
(514) 697-6520   SIC 5411
METRO RICHELIEU INC   p1315
61 2E RANG E, SAINT-JEAN-PORT-JOLI,
QC, G0R 3G0
(418) 598-3371   SIC 5411
METRO RICHELIEU INC   p1317
600 RUE PIERRE-CAISSE BUREAU 2000,
SAINT-JEAN-SUR-RICHELIEU, QC, J3A 1M1
(450) 348-0927   SIC 5411
METRO RICHELIEU INC   p1346
6775 RUE JEAN-TALON E, SAINT-
LEONARD, QC, H1S 1N2
(514) 252-0230   SIC 5411
METRO RICHELIEU INC   p1366
398 CH LAROCQUE, SALABERRY-DE-
VALLEYFIELD, QC, J6T 4C5
(450) 370-1444   SIC 5411
METRO RICHELIEU INC   p1371
350 RUE BELVEDERE N, SHERBROOKE,
QC, J1H 4B1
(819) 564-6014   SIC 5411
METRO RICHELIEU INC   p1388
750 BOUL DU SAINT-MAURICE, TROIS-
RIVIERES, QC, G9A 3P6
(819) 371-1120   SIC 5411
METRO RICHELIEU INC   p1398
601 BOUL JUTRAS E, VICTORIAVILLE,
QC, G6P 7H4
(819) 752-6659   SIC 5411
METRO RICHELIEU INC   p1402
4840 RUE SHERBROOKE O, WEST-
MOUNT, QC, H3Z 1G8

(514) 488-4083   SIC 5411
MIC-MAC BEVERAGE ROOM LIMITED p443
219 WAVERLEY RD, DARTMOUTH, NS,
B2X 2C3
(902) 434-7600   SIC 5411
MICHEL'S SUPER A FOODS LTD   p131
3100 PINE PLAZA, GRANDE CACHE, AB,
T0E 0Y0
(780) 827-2434   SIC 5411
MICHIELI'S SUPERMARKET LIMITED p881
79 QUEEN ST, SIOUX LOOKOUT, ON, P8T
1A3
(807) 737-1630   SIC 5411
MIDISLAND HOLDINGS LTD   p234
4750 RUTHERFORD RD SUITE 103,
NANAIMO, BC, V9T 4K6
(250) 729-2611   SIC 5411
MIKE AND LORI'S NO FRILLS   p763
975 MCKEOWN AVE, NORTH BAY, ON,
P1B 9P2
(866) 987-6453   SIC 5411
MIKE DEAN BUTCHER LIMITED   p544
19 KING ST, CHESTERVILLE, ON, K0C
1H0
(613) 448-2822   SIC 5411
MIKE'S NO FRILLS   p860
889 EXMOUTH ST, SARNIA, ON, N7T 5R3
(866) 987-6453   SIC 5411
MOHAWK IMPERIAL SALES   p565
406 HWY 2 & HWY SUITE 49, DE-
SERONTO, ON, K0K 1X0
(613) 396-3700   SIC 5411
MORRISH HOLDINGS LTD   p359
GD STN MAIN, THE PAS, MB, R9A 1K2
(204) 623-6469   SIC 5411
MORTON WHOLESALE LTD   p1023
5188 WALKER RD, WINDSOR, ON, N9A
6J3
(519) 737-6961   SIC 5411
MRT ENTERPRISES INC   p24
817 19 ST NE SUITE 109, CALGARY, AB,
T2E 4X5
(403) 216-8800   SIC 5411
MURPHY'S VALU-MART   p1004
1200 YOUNGE ST S, WALKERTON, ON,
N0G 2V0
(519) 881-2280   SIC 5411
NESTERS MARKET LTD   p343
7019 NESTERS RD, WHISTLER, BC, V8E
0X1
(604) 932-3545   SIC 5411
NEW HORIZON CO-OPERATIVE LTD p132
9831 100 AVE, GRANDE PRAIRIE, AB, T8V
0T7
(780) 539-6111   SIC 5411
NEWCASTLE FOODLAND INC   p753
131 KING AVE E, NEWCASTLE, ON, L1B
1H3
(905) 987-4627   SIC 5411
NO FRILLS   p1412
11403 RAILWAY AVENUE E, NORTH BAT-
TLEFORD, SK, S9A 0A1
(306) 445-3375   SIC 5411
**NORTH CENTRAL CO-OPERATIVE ASSO-
CIATION LTD**   p167
4917 50 AVE, STONY PLAIN, AB, T7Z 1W6
(780) 963-2272   SIC 5411
NORTH FRONT PRICE CHOPPER   p492
305 NORTH FRONT ST SUITE 5,
BELLEVILLE, ON, K8P 3C3
(613) 966-0270   SIC 5411
NORTH WEST COMPANY LP, THE   p107
14097 VICTORIA TRAIL NW, EDMONTON,
AB, T5Y 2B6
(780) 472-7780   SIC 5411
NORTH WEST COMPANY LP, THE   p353
GD, NORWAY HOUSE, MB, R0B 1B0
(204) 359-6258   SIC 5411
NORTH WEST COMPANY LP, THE   p1420
2735 AVONHURST DR, REGINA, SK, S4R
3J3
(306) 789-3155   SIC 5411
NORTOWN FOODS LIMITED   p988
892 EGLINTON AVE W, TORONTO, ON,

▲ Public Company   ■ Public Company Family Member   **HQ** Headquarters   **BR** Branch   **SL** Single Location

M6C 2B6

(416) 789-2921 *SIC 5411*

O & P SUPERMARKETS LTD *p333*
3829 CADBORO BAY RD, VICTORIA, BC, V8N 4G1
(250) 477-6513 *SIC 5411*

O'REILLY'S INDEPENDENT GROCER *p848*
150 PRESCOTT CENTRE DR, PRESCOTT, ON, K0E 1T0
(613) 925-4625 *SIC 5411*

OAK LANE ENTERPRISES LTD *p338*
4420 WEST SAANICH RD, VICTORIA, BC, V8Z 3E9
(250) 708-3900 *SIC 5411*

OFRIGIDAIRE ALIMENTATION INC *p1124*
1575 RTE 277, LAC-ETCHEMIN, QC, G0R 1S0
(418) 625-6301 *SIC 5411*

ORGANIC GARAGE LTD *p802*
579 KERR ST, OAKVILLE, ON, L6K 3E1
(905) 849-1648 *SIC 5411*

ORR'S LITTLE CURRENT VALUE MART *p647*
40 MEREDITH, LITTLE CURRENT, ON, P0P 1K0
(705) 368-0617 *SIC 5411*

P.R. ST-GERMAIN INC *p1376*
50 RUE VICTORIA, SOREL-TRACY, QC, J3P 1Y6
(450) 743-5738 *SIC 5411*

PARLIAMENT, ART FOODS LIMITED *p592*
54 FRANKFORD RD, FOXBORO, ON, K0K 2B0
(613) 968-5721 *SIC 5411*

PAS IGA 1979 FOOD PRODUCTS LTD, THE *p354*
HWY 10 N, OPASKWAYAK, MB, R0B 2J0
SIC 5411

PATRICE INDEPENDENT GROCER INC *p477*
401 OTTAWA ST, ALMONTE, ON, K0A 1A0
(613) 256-2080 *SIC 5411*

PEACE COUNTRY CO-OP LIMITED *p152*
9714 96 AVE, PEACE RIVER, AB, T8S 1H8
(780) 624-1096 *SIC 5411*

PELLY BANKS TRADING CO. LTD *p1440*
1406 CENTENNIAL ST, WHITEHORSE, YT, Y1A 3Z3
(867) 633-2265 *SIC 5411*

PETER'S FOOD & DRUG BASICS *p872*
2131 LAWRENCE AVE E, SCARBOROUGH, ON, M1R 5G4
(416) 759-7625 *SIC 5411*

PINCHER CREEK CO-OPERATIVE ASSOCIATION LIMITED *p152*
GD, PINCHER CREEK, AB, T0K 1W0
(403) 627-2607 *SIC 5411*

PINELAND CO-OPERATIVE ASSOCIATION LIMITED *p1412*
1511 8 ST W, NIPAWIN, SK, S0E 1E0
(306) 862-4668 *SIC 5411*

PLATEAU FOODS LTD *p199*
1410 PARKWAY BLVD UNIT A, COQUITLAM, BC, V3E 3J7
(604) 464-8506 *SIC 5411*

POIRIER & FILS LTEE *p1113*
484 RUE PRINCIPALE, HUDSON, QC, J0P 1H0
(450) 458-5573 *SIC 5411*

POIRIER & FILS LTEE *p1343*
1869 CH SAINTE-ANGELIQUE, SAINT-LAZARE, QC, J7T 2X9
(450) 455-6165 *SIC 5411*

PONOKA FOODS LTD *p152*
4502 50 ST UNIT 1, PONOKA, AB, T4J 1J5
(403) 783-4528 *SIC 5411*

PORT MCNEIL FOODS LTD *p247*
1705 CAMPBELL WAY UNIT 44, PORT MCNEIL, BC, V0N 2R0
(250) 956-4404 *SIC 5411*

POTTIER'S GENERAL STORES LIMITED *p469*
8175 HWY 3, TUSKET, NS, B0W 3M0
(902) 648-2212 *SIC 5411*

POWELL'S SUPERMARKET LIMITED *p421*
160 CONCEPTION BAY HWY SUITE 152, BAY ROBERTS, NL, A0A 1G0
(709) 786-2101 *SIC 5411*

PRAIRIE NORTH CO-OPERATIVE LIMITED *p1410*
1141 MAIN ST, MELFORT, SK, S0E 1A0
(306) 752-9381 *SIC 5411*

PRINGLE CREEK I G A *p1015*
728 ANDERSON ST UNIT 4, WHITBY, ON, L1N 3V6
(905) 668-5538 *SIC 5411*

PROVIGO DISTRIBUTION INC *p632*
1225 PRINCESS ST, KINGSTON, ON, K7M 3E1
(613) 544-8202 *SIC 5411*

PROVIGO DISTRIBUTION INC *p1053*
570 BOUL LAFLECHE, BAIE-COMEAU, QC, G5C 1C3
(418) 589-9020 *SIC 5411*

PROVIGO DISTRIBUTION INC *p1089*
31 BOUL GEORGES-GAGNE S, DELSON, QC, J5B 2E4
(450) 638-5041 *SIC 5411*

PROVIGO DISTRIBUTION INC *p1102*
130 AV LEPINE, GATINEAU, QC, J8L 4M4
(819) 281-5232 *SIC 5411*

PROVIGO DISTRIBUTION INC *p1105*
800 BOUL MALONEY O, GATINEAU, QC, J8T 3R6
(819) 561-9244 *SIC 5411*

PROVIGO DISTRIBUTION INC *p1107*
775 BOUL SAINT-JOSEPH, GATINEAU, QC, J8Y 4C1
(819) 771-7701 *SIC 5411*

PROVIGO DISTRIBUTION INC *p1107*
1 BOUL DU PLATEAU, GATINEAU, QC, J9A 3G1
(819) 777-2747 *SIC 5411*

PROVIGO DISTRIBUTION INC *p1115*
909 BOUL FIRESTONE, JOLIETTE, QC, J6E 2W4
(450) 755-2781 *SIC 5411*

PROVIGO DISTRIBUTION INC *p1119*
1201 AUT DUPLESSIS, L'ANCIENNE-LORETTE, QC, G2G 2B4
(418) 872-2400 *SIC 5411*

PROVIGO DISTRIBUTION INC *p1146*
1150 RUE KING-GEORGE, LONGUEUIL, QC, J4N 1P3
(450) 647-1717 *SIC 5411*

PROVIGO DISTRIBUTION INC *p1148*
1350 RUE SHERBROOKE, MAGOG, QC, J1X 2T3
(819) 868-8630 *SIC 5411*

PROVIGO DISTRIBUTION INC *p1165*
7600 RUE SHERBROOKE E, MONTREAL, QC, H1N 3W1
(514) 257-4511 *SIC 5411*

PROVIGO DISTRIBUTION INC *p1177*
8305 AV PAPINEAU, MONTREAL, QC, H2M 2G2
(514) 376-6457 *SIC 5411*

PROVIGO DISTRIBUTION INC *p1186*
3421 AV DU PARC, MONTREAL, QC, H2X 2H6
(514) 281-0488 *SIC 5411*

PROVIGO DISTRIBUTION INC *p1218*
375 RUE JEAN-TALON O, MONTREAL, QC, H3N 2Y8
(514) 948-2600 *SIC 5411*

PROVIGO DISTRIBUTION INC *p1247*
12780 RUE SHERBROOKE E, POINTE-AUX-TREMBLES, QC, H1A 4Y3
(514) 498-2675 *SIC 5411*

PROVIGO DISTRIBUTION INC *p1262*
552 BOUL WILFRID-HAMEL, QUEBEC, QC, G1M 3E5
(418) 640-1700 *SIC 5411*

PROVIGO DISTRIBUTION INC *p1267*
5150 BOUL DE L'ORMIERE, QUEBEC, QC, G1P 4B2
(418) 872-3866 *SIC 5411*

PROVIGO DISTRIBUTION INC *p1274*

3440 CH DES QUATRE-BOURGEOIS BUREAU 8143, QUEBEC, QC, G1W 4T3
(418) 653-6241 *SIC 5411*

PROVIGO DISTRIBUTION INC *p1288*
339 BOUL LABELLE, ROSEMERE, QC, J7A 2H7
(450) 437-0471 *SIC 5411*

PROVIGO DISTRIBUTION INC *p1315*
200 BOUL OMER-MARCIL, SAINT-JEAN-SUR-RICHELIEU, QC, J2W 2V1
(450) 348-0998 *SIC 5411*

PROVIGO DISTRIBUTION INC *p1320*
900 BOUL GRIGNON, SAINT-JEROME, QC, J7Y 3S7
(450) 436-3824 *SIC 5411*

PROVIGO DISTRIBUTION INC *p1330*
1757 BOUL MARCEL-LAURIN, SAINT-LAURENT, QC, H4R 1J5
(514) 747-2203 *SIC 5411*

PROVIGO DISTRIBUTION INC *p1352*
50 AV SAINT-DENIS, SAINT-SAUVEUR, QC, J0R 1R4
(450) 227-2827 *SIC 5411*

PROVIGO DISTRIBUTION INC *p1363*
444 BOUL CURE-LABELLE, SAINTE-ROSE, QC, H7P 4W7
(450) 625-4221 *SIC 5411*

PROVIGO DISTRIBUTION INC *p1379*
1345 BOUL MOODY, TERREBONNE, QC, J6W 3L1
(450) 471-1009 *SIC 5411*

PROVIGO DISTRIBUTION INC *p1385*
320 RUE BARKOFF, TROIS-RIVIERES, QC, G8T 2A3
(819) 378-4932 *SIC 5411*

PROVIGO DISTRIBUTION INC *p1386*
5875 BOUL JEAN-XXIII, TROIS-RIVIERES, QC, G8Z 4N8
(819) 378-8759 *SIC 5411*

PROVISIONS ROCK ISLAND INC *p1378*
14 CH DE FAIRFAX RR 1, STANSTEAD, QC, J0B 3E0
(819) 876-7262 *SIC 5411*

PUPO'S SUPERMARKET LIMITED *p1012*
195 MAPLE AVE, WELLAND, ON, L3C 5G6
(905) 735-5615 *SIC 5411*

PUSATERI'S LIMITED *p788*
1539 AVENUE RD, NORTH YORK, ON, M5M 3X4
(416) 785-9124 *SIC 5411*

PUSATERI'S LIMITED *p976*
77 BLOOR ST W SUITE 1803, TORONTO, ON, M5S 1M2
(416) 785-9100 *SIC 5411*

QUALITY FOODS LTD *p212*
1581 ALBERNI HWY, ERRINGTON, BC, V0R 1V0
(250) 248-4004 *SIC 5411*

QUALITY MARKET (THUNDER BAY) INC *p910*
146 CENTENNIAL SQ, THUNDER BAY, ON, P7E 1H3
SIC 5411

QUEENSDALE SUPERMARKET LTD *p240*
3030 LONSDALE AVE, NORTH VANCOUVER, BC, V7N 3J5
(604) 987-6644 *SIC 5411*

R & L CONVENIENCE ENTERPRISES INC *p412*
1 ELLIS DR, ROTHESAY, NB, E2E 1A1
(506) 847-1603 *SIC 5411*

R K R FOODS LTD *p135*
5023 54 AVE, GRIMSHAW, AB, T0H 1W0
(780) 332-4495 *SIC 5411*

R. GREEN SUPERMARKETS INC *p651*
1595 ADELAIDE ST N, LONDON, ON, N5X 4E8
(519) 645-8868 *SIC 5411*

RABBA, J. COMPANY LIMITED, THE *p706*
5820 KENNEDY RD, MISSISSAUGA, ON, L4Z 2C3
(905) 890-2436 *SIC 5411*

RADCO FOOD STORES LTD *p147*
10003 100 ST, MORINVILLE, AB, T8R 1R5

(780) 939-4418 *SIC 5411*

RAINBOW NATURAL FOODS INC *p830*
1487 RICHMOND RD, OTTAWA, ON, K2B 6R9
(613) 726-9200 *SIC 5411*

RAINVILLE, ROGER & FILS INC *p1303*
3100 RUE HENRI-L.-CHEVRETTE, SAINT-FELIX-DE-VALOIS, QC, J0K 2M0
(450) 889-4747 *SIC 5411*

RAVEN ENTERPRISES INC. *p1414*
200 28TH ST E, PRINCE ALBERT, SK, S6V 1X2
(306) 922-3663 *SIC 5411*

RED BARN COUNTRY MARKET LTD *p338*
751 VANALMAN AVE, VICTORIA, BC, V8Z 3B8
(250) 479-6817 *SIC 5411*

RED DEER CO-OP LIMITED *p154*
5118 47 AVE, RED DEER, AB, T4N 3P7
(403) 340-1766 *SIC 5411*

REID'S FOODLAND *p1003*
6145 HIGHWAY 38, VERONA, ON, K0H 2W0
(613) 374-2112 *SIC 5411*

RENCO FOODS LTD *p909*
161 COURT ST S, THUNDER BAY, ON, P7B 2X7
(807) 345-3947 *SIC 5411*

RIENDEAU, GAETAN INC *p1314*
2030 BOUL LAURIER E, SAINT-HYACINTHE, QC, J2T 1K7
(450) 774-2311 *SIC 5411*

RIMBEY CO-OP ASSOCIATION LTD *p158*
4625 51 ST, RIMBEY, AB, T0C 2J0
(403) 843-2258 *SIC 5411*

RIVERBEND CO-OPERATIVE LTD *p1413*
101 SASKATCHEWAN AVE E, OUTLOOK, SK, S0L 2N0
(306) 867-8614 *SIC 5411*

RJ'S FRUGAL MARKETS INC *p600*
63 MAIN ST W, GRIMSBY, ON, L3M 4H1
(905) 945-3323 *SIC 5411*

ROB'S NO FRILLS *p510*
295 QUEEN ST E, BRAMPTON, ON, L6W 3R1
(905) 452-9200 *SIC 5411*

ROBERT'S NO FRILLS *p484*
319 BLAKE ST, BARRIE, ON, L4M 1K7
(705) 725-8607 *SIC 5411*

ROBINSON'S YOUR INDEPENDENT GROCER *p663*
1160 BEAVERWOOD DR, MANOTICK, ON, K4M 1A5
(613) 692-2828 *SIC 5411*

RON'S NO FRILLS *p883*
525 WELLAND AVE SUITE 1316, ST CATHARINES, ON, L2M 6P3
(905) 685-4096 *SIC 5411*

RONALD D. BAILEY GROCERY LIMITED *p888*
GD, ST MARYS, ON, N4X 1A6
(519) 284-2631 *SIC 5411*

ROUILLARD & FRERES INC *p1245*
21 RUE GEORGES, PIERREVILLE, QC, J0G 1J0
(450) 568-3510 *SIC 5411*

RUNDLES NO FRILLS *p657*
635 SOUTHDALE RD E, LONDON, ON, N6E 3W6
(866) 987-6453 *SIC 5411*

S.A.D.E HOLDINGS LTD *p235*
2345 ISLAND HWY E, NANOOSE BAY, BC, V9P 9E2
(250) 468-7441 *SIC 5411*

SAFETY MART #5 (1994) LTD *p198*
74 YOUNG RD, CLEARWATER, BC, V0E 1N2
(250) 674-2213 *SIC 5411*

SAFETY MART NO. 7 (2001) LTD *p196*
305 BROOK DR UNIT 6, CHASE, BC, V0E 1M0
(250) 679-8515 *SIC 5411*

SASKATOON CO-OPERATIVE ASSOCIATION LIMITED, THE *p1435*

503 WELLMAN CRES SUITE 201, SASKA-
TOON, SK, S7T 0J1

(306) 933-3801   SIC 5411

SAVE-ON-FOODS LIMITED PARTNERSHIP
p225
19855 92A AVE, LANGLEY, BC, V1M 3B6

(604) 888-1213   SIC 5411

SAVE-ON-FOODS LIMITED PARTNERSHIP
p239
1199 LYNN VALLEY RD UNIT 1221,
NORTH VANCOUVER, BC, V7J 3H2

(604) 980-4857   SIC 5411

SAVE-ON-FOODS LIMITED PARTNERSHIP
p316
1133 ALBERNI ST, VANCOUVER, BC, V6E
4T9

(604) 648-2053   SIC 5411

SAVE-ON-FOODS LIMITED PARTNERSHIP
p340
759 MCCALLUM RD, VICTORIA, BC, V9B
6A2

(250) 475-3157   SIC 5411

SEA FRESH FISH LTD   p230
23963 LOUGHEED HWY, MAPLE RIDGE,
BC, V2W 1J1

(604) 463-9817   SIC 5411

SEIGNEURIE BLAINVILLE INC, LA p1060
9 BOUL DE LA SEIGNEURIE E,
BLAINVILLE, QC, J7C 4G6

(450) 434-3313   SIC 5411

SELFLAND CO-OP LTD   p1404
409 CENTRE ST, ASSINIBOIA, SK, S0H
0B0

(306) 642-3347   SIC 5411

SHANNON'S, GREG FOOD BASICS   p885
149 HARTZEL RD, ST CATHARINES, ON,
L2P 1N6

(905) 684-7439   SIC 5411

SHARPE FOODS LTD   p540
85 FRONT ST N, CAMPBELLFORD, ON,
K0L 1L0

(705) 653-2326   SIC 5411

**SHERWOOD CO-OPERATIVE ASSOCIA-
TION LIMITED**   p1422
2925 E QUANCE ST, REGINA, SK, S4V 3B7

(306) 791-9300   SIC 5411

SHERWOOD PARK IGA   p161
688 WYE RD, SHERWOOD PARK, AB, T8A
6G3

(780) 416-7920   SIC 5411

SMYLIE'S YOUR INDEPENDENT GROCER
p999
293 DUNDAS ST E, TRENTON, ON, K8V
1M1

(613) 392-0297   SIC 5411

SOBEYS CAPITAL INCORPORATED   p5
5700 50 ST, BEAUMONT, AB, T4X 1M8

(780) 929-2749   SIC 5411

SOBEYS CAPITAL INCORPORATED   p70
150 MILLRISE BLVD SW UNIT 3109, CAL-
GARY, AB, T2Y 5G7

(403) 873-5085   SIC 5411

SOBEYS CAPITAL INCORPORATED   p70
2335 162 AVE SW SUITE 100, CALGARY,
AB, T2Y 4S6

(403) 873-0101   SIC 5411

SOBEYS CAPITAL INCORPORATED   p71
20 MCKENZIE TOWNE AVE SE, CALGARY,
AB, T2Z 3S7

(403) 257-4343   SIC 5411

SOBEYS CAPITAL INCORPORATED   p77
11300 TUSCANY BLVD NW SUITE 2020,
CALGARY, AB, T3L 2V7

(403) 375-0595   SIC 5411

SOBEYS CAPITAL INCORPORATED   p81
6403 51 ST, COLD LAKE, AB, T9M 1C8

(780) 594-3335   SIC 5411

SOBEYS CAPITAL INCORPORATED   p94
13140 ST ALBERT TRAIL NW, EDMON-
TON, AB, T5L 4P6

(780) 486-4800   SIC 5411

SOBEYS CAPITAL INCORPORATED   p107
5119 167 AVE NW, EDMONTON, AB, T5Y
0L2

(780) 478-4740   SIC 5411

SOBEYS CAPITAL INCORPORATED   p107
15367 CASTLE DOWNS RD NW, EDMON-
TON, AB, T5X 6C3

(780) 472-0100   SIC 5411

SOBEYS CAPITAL INCORPORATED   p119
2011 111 ST NW, EDMONTON, AB, T6J
4V9

(780) 435-1224   SIC 5411

SOBEYS CAPITAL INCORPORATED   p120
5011 23 AVE NW, EDMONTON, AB, T6L
7G5

(780) 485-6622   SIC 5411

SOBEYS CAPITAL INCORPORATED   p123
2430 RABBIT HILL RD NW, EDMONTON,
AB, T6R 3B5

(780) 989-1610   SIC 5411

SOBEYS CAPITAL INCORPORATED   p129
210 THICKWOOD BLVD, FORT MCMUR-
RAY, AB, T9K 1X9

(780) 743-9339   SIC 5411

SOBEYS CAPITAL INCORPORATED   p130
10004 99 AVE, FORT SASKATCHEWAN,
AB, T8L 3Y1

(780) 998-5429   SIC 5411

SOBEYS CAPITAL INCORPORATED   p141
327 BLUEFOX BLVD N, LETHBRIDGE, AB,
T1H 6T3

(403) 320-5154   SIC 5411

SOBEYS CAPITAL INCORPORATED   p144
4227 75 AVE, LLOYDMINSTER, AB, T9V
2X4

(780) 871-0955   SIC 5411

SOBEYS CAPITAL INCORPORATED   p144
4227 75 AVE, LLOYDMINSTER, AB, T9V
2X4

(780) 875-3215   SIC 5411

SOBEYS CAPITAL INCORPORATED   p151
6700 46 ST SUITE 300, OLDS, AB, T4H 0A2

(403) 556-3113   SIC 5411

SOBEYS CAPITAL INCORPORATED   p151
201 SOUTHRIDGE DR SUITE 700, OKO-
TOKS, AB, T1S 2E1

(403) 995-4088   SIC 5411

SOBEYS CAPITAL INCORPORATED   p157
2110 50 AVE, RED DEER, AB, T4R 2K1

(403) 348-0848   SIC 5411

SOBEYS CAPITAL INCORPORATED   p159
4419 52 AVE, ROCKY MOUNTAIN HOUSE,
AB, T4T 1A3

(403) 846-0038   SIC 5411

SOBEYS CAPITAL INCORPORATED   p159
5427 52 AVE, ROCKY MOUNTAIN HOUSE,
AB, T4T 1S9

(403) 845-3371   SIC 5411

SOBEYS CAPITAL INCORPORATED   p163
590 BASELINE RD UNIT 100, SHERWOOD
PARK, AB, T8H 1Y4

(780) 417-0419   SIC 5411

SOBEYS CAPITAL INCORPORATED   p166
392 ST ALBERT RD, ST. ALBERT, AB, T8N
5J9

(780) 459-5909   SIC 5411

SOBEYS CAPITAL INCORPORATED   p167
4607 50 ST, STETTLER, AB, T0C 2L0

(403) 742-5025   SIC 5411

SOBEYS CAPITAL INCORPORATED   p172
4703 50 ST, WETASKIWIN, AB, T9A 1J6

(780) 352-2227   SIC 5411

SOBEYS CAPITAL INCORPORATED   p348
3409 VICTORIA AVE, BRANDON, MB, R7B
2L8

(204) 727-3443   SIC 5411

SOBEYS CAPITAL INCORPORATED   p348
3409 VICTORIA AVE, BRANDON, MB, R7B
2L8

(204) 727-3443   SIC 5411

SOBEYS CAPITAL INCORPORATED   p358
178 PTH 12 N UNIT 1, STEINBACH, MB,
R5G 1T7

(204) 326-1316   SIC 5411

SOBEYS CAPITAL INCORPORATED   p367
965 HENDERSON HWY, WINNIPEG, MB,
R2K 2M2

(204) 338-0349   SIC 5411

SOBEYS CAPITAL INCORPORATED   p368
1500 DAKOTA ST SUITE 1, WINNIPEG, MB,
R2N 3Y7

(204) 253-3663   SIC 5411

SOBEYS CAPITAL INCORPORATED   p368
1939 BISHOP GRANDIN BLVD, WINNIPEG,
MB, R2M 5S1

(204) 255-5064   SIC 5411

SOBEYS CAPITAL INCORPORATED   p373
1870 BURROWS AVE, WINNIPEG, MB,
R2X 3C3

(204) 697-1997   SIC 5411

SOBEYS CAPITAL INCORPORATED   p387
3635 PORTAGE AVE, WINNIPEG, MB, R3K
2G6

(204) 832-8605   SIC 5411

SOBEYS CAPITAL INCORPORATED   p389
1660 KENASTON BLVD, WINNIPEG, MB,
R3P 2M6

(204) 489-7007   SIC 5411

SOBEYS CAPITAL INCORPORATED   p396
140 ROSEBERRY ST, CAMPBELLTON, NB,
E3N 2G9

(506) 753-5339   SIC 5411

SOBEYS CAPITAL INCORPORATED   p400
463 BROOKSIDE DR SUITE 349, FREDER-
ICTON, NB, E3A 8V4

(506) 450-7109   SIC 5411

SOBEYS CAPITAL INCORPORATED   p401
1150 PROSPECT ST, FREDERICTON, NB,
E3B 3C1

(506) 458-8891   SIC 5411

SOBEYS CAPITAL INCORPORATED   p407
1380 MOUNTAIN RD, MONCTON, NB, E1C
2T8

(506) 858-8283   SIC 5411

SOBEYS CAPITAL INCORPORATED   p411
1160 FINDLAY BLVD, RIVERVIEW, NB, E1B
0J6

(506) 386-4616   SIC 5411

SOBEYS CAPITAL INCORPORATED   p411
1 LEWIS ST, OROMOCTO, NB, E2V 4K5

(506) 357-9831   SIC 5411

SOBEYS CAPITAL INCORPORATED   p412
140A HAMPTON RD, ROTHESAY, NB, E2E
2R1

(506) 847-5697   SIC 5411

SOBEYS CAPITAL INCORPORATED   p413
519 WESTMORLAND RD, SAINT JOHN,
NB, E2J 3W9

(506) 633-1187   SIC 5411

SOBEYS CAPITAL INCORPORATED   p414
149 LANSDOWNE AVE SUITE 233, SAINT
JOHN, NB, E2K 2Z9

(506) 652-4470   SIC 5411

SOBEYS CAPITAL INCORPORATED   p416
1 PLAZA AVE, SAINT JOHN, NB, E2M 0C2

(506) 674-1460   SIC 5411

SOBEYS CAPITAL INCORPORATED   p417
183 MAIN ST SUITE 738, SHEDIAC, NB,
E4P 2A5

(506) 532-0842   SIC 5411

SOBEYS CAPITAL INCORPORATED   p420
370 CONNELL ST UNIT 11, WOODSTOCK,
NB, E7M 5G9

(506) 328-6819   SIC 5411

SOBEYS CAPITAL INCORPORATED   p422
350 CONCEPTION BAY HWY, CONCEP-
TION BAY SOUTH, NL, A1X 7A3

(709) 834-9052   SIC 5411

SOBEYS CAPITAL INCORPORATED   p422
1 MOUNT BERNARD AVE SUITE 861,
CORNER BROOK, NL, A2H 6Y5

(709) 639-7193   SIC 5411

SOBEYS CAPITAL INCORPORATED   p429
10 ELIZABETH AVE SUITE 744, ST.
JOHN'S, NL, A1A 5L4

(709) 753-3402   SIC 5411

SOBEYS CAPITAL INCORPORATED   p433
45 ROPEWALK LANE, ST. JOHN'S, NL,
A1E 4P1

(709) 739-8663   SIC 5411

SOBEYS CAPITAL INCORPORATED   p433

470 TOPSAIL RD SUITE 340, ST. JOHN'S,
NL, A1E 2C3

(709) 748-1250   SIC 5411

SOBEYS CAPITAL INCORPORATED   p438
151 CHURCH ST, ANTIGONISH, NS, B2G
2E2

(902) 863-6022   SIC 5411

SOBEYS CAPITAL INCORPORATED   p439
3552 HWY 3, BARRINGTON PASSAGE,
NS, B0W 1G0

(902) 637-3063   SIC 5411

SOBEYS CAPITAL INCORPORATED   p441
349 LAHAVE ST SUITE 322, BRIDGEWA-
TER, NS, B4V 2T6

(902) 543-9244   SIC 5411

SOBEYS CAPITAL INCORPORATED   p443
4 FOREST HILLS PKY, DARTMOUTH, NS,
B2W 5G7

(902) 435-3909   SIC 5411

SOBEYS CAPITAL INCORPORATED   p443
100 MAIN ST SUITE 250, DARTMOUTH,
NS, B2X 1R5

(902) 434-6696   SIC 5411

SOBEYS CAPITAL INCORPORATED   p443
612 MAIN ST SUITE 622, DARTMOUTH,
NS, B2W 5M5

(902) 433-0140   SIC 5411

SOBEYS CAPITAL INCORPORATED   p444
6 PRIMROSE ST, DARTMOUTH, NS, B3A
4C5

(902) 463-2910   SIC 5411

SOBEYS CAPITAL INCORPORATED   p444
551 PORTLAND ST, DARTMOUTH, NS,
B2Y 4B1

(902) 469-8396   SIC 5411

SOBEYS CAPITAL INCORPORATED   p449
246 LANCASTER CRES, DEBERT, NS,
B0M 1G0

(902) 752-8371   SIC 5411

SOBEYS CAPITAL INCORPORATED   p450
269 HIGHWAY 214 UNIT 1, ELMSDALE,
NS, B2S 1K1

(902) 883-8111   SIC 5411

SOBEYS CAPITAL INCORPORATED   p451
1120 QUEEN ST, HALIFAX, NS, B3H 2R9

(902) 422-7605   SIC 5411

SOBEYS CAPITAL INCORPORATED   p456
2651 WINDSOR ST SUITE 554, HALIFAX,
NS, B3K 5C7

(902) 455-8508   SIC 5411

SOBEYS CAPITAL INCORPORATED   p457
287 LACEWOOD DR SUITE 644, HALIFAX,
NS, B3M 3Y7

(902) 457-2102   SIC 5411

SOBEYS CAPITAL INCORPORATED   p458
279 HERRING COVE RD, HALIFAX, NS,
B3P 1M2

(902) 477-2817   SIC 5411

SOBEYS CAPITAL INCORPORATED   p460
180 BRISTOL AVE, LIVERPOOL, NS, B0T
1K0

(902) 354-4225   SIC 5411

SOBEYS CAPITAL INCORPORATED   p461
752 SACKVILLE DR SUITE 670, LOWER
SACKVILLE, NS, B4E 1R7

(902) 865-5057   SIC 5411

SOBEYS CAPITAL INCORPORATED   p463
38 GEORGE ST SUITE 652, NEW GLAS-
GOW, NS, B2H 2K1

(902) 752-6258   SIC 5411

SOBEYS CAPITAL INCORPORATED   p464
622 REEVES ST UNIT 1, PORT HAWKES-
BURY, NS, B9A 2R7

(902) 625-1242   SIC 5411

SOBEYS CAPITAL INCORPORATED   p464
239 WEST RIVER RD, PICTOU, NS, B0K
1H0

(902) 485-5841   SIC 5411

SOBEYS CAPITAL INCORPORATED   p464
9256 COMMERCIAL ST, NEW MINAS, NS,
B4N 4A9

(902) 681-3723   SIC 5411

SOBEYS CAPITAL INCORPORATED   p467
272B PRINCE ST, SYDNEY, NS, B1P 5K6

▲ Public Company   ■ Public Company Family Member   **HQ** Headquarters   **BR** Branch   **SL** Single Location

(902) 562-1762   *SIC* 5411
SOBEYS CAPITAL INCORPORATED   *p*469
68 ROBIE ST SUITE 594, TRURO, NS, B2N
1L2
(902) 893-9388   *SIC* 5411
SOBEYS CAPITAL INCORPORATED   *p*469
985 PRINCE ST, TRURO, NS, B2N 1H7
(902) 895-9579   *SIC* 5411
SOBEYS CAPITAL INCORPORATED   *p*470
50 EMPIRE LANE WENTWORTH RD,
WINDSOR, NS, B0N 2T0
(902) 798-0992   *SIC* 5411
SOBEYS CAPITAL INCORPORATED   *p*475
260 KINGSTON RD W, AJAX, ON, L1T 4E4
(905) 426-7144   *SIC* 5411
SOBEYS CAPITAL INCORPORATED   *p*476
161 YOUNG ST, ALLISTON, ON, L9R 2A9
(705) 434-9512   *SIC* 5411
SOBEYS CAPITAL INCORPORATED   *p*477
83 SANDWICH ST S, AMHERSTBURG,
ON, N9V 1Z5
(519) 736-4520   *SIC* 5411
SOBEYS CAPITAL INCORPORATED   *p*478
247 MILL ST, ANGUS, ON, L0M 1B2
(705) 424-1588   *SIC* 5411
SOBEYS CAPITAL INCORPORATED   *p*478
977 GOLF LINKS RD, ANCASTER, ON, L9K
1K1
(905) 648-3534   *SIC* 5411
SOBEYS CAPITAL INCORPORATED   *p*481
15500 BAYVIEW AVE, AURORA, ON, L4G
7J1
(905) 726-2530   *SIC* 5411
SOBEYS CAPITAL INCORPORATED   *p*485
409 BAYFIELD ST SUITE C1, BARRIE, ON,
L4M 6E5
(705) 739-1100   *SIC* 5411
SOBEYS CAPITAL INCORPORATED   *p*488
37 MAPLEVIEW DR W, BARRIE, ON, L4N
9H5
(705) 728-9858   *SIC* 5411
SOBEYS CAPITAL INCORPORATED   *p*490
4610 ONTARIO ST, BEAMSVILLE, ON, L0R
1B3
(905) 563-1088   *SIC* 5411
SOBEYS CAPITAL INCORPORATED   *p*500
930 NORTH PARK DR, BRAMPTON, ON,
L6S 3Y5
(905) 458-7673   *SIC* 5411
SOBEYS CAPITAL INCORPORATED   *p*512
380 BOVAIRD DR E SUITE 29, BRAMP-
TON, ON, L6Z 2S8
(905) 840-0770   *SIC* 5411
SOBEYS CAPITAL INCORPORATED   *p*512
11965 HURONTARIO ST, BRAMPTON, ON,
L6Z 4P7
(905) 846-5658   *SIC* 5411
SOBEYS CAPITAL INCORPORATED   *p*512
8975 CHINGUACOUSY RD, BRAMPTON,
ON, L6Y 0J2
(905) 796-1517   *SIC* 5411
SOBEYS CAPITAL INCORPORATED   *p*534
75 DUNDAS ST, CAMBRIDGE, ON, N1R
6G5
(519) 620-9022   *SIC* 5411
SOBEYS CAPITAL INCORPORATED   *p*535
130 CEDAR ST, CAMBRIDGE, ON, N1S
1W4
(519) 622-8906   *SIC* 5411
SOBEYS CAPITAL INCORPORATED   *p*573
125 THE QUEENSWAY, ETOBICOKE, ON,
M8Y 1H6
(416) 259-1758   *SIC* 5411
SOBEYS CAPITAL INCORPORATED   *p*590
15 LINDSAY ST, FENELON FALLS, ON,
K0M 1N0
(705) 887-3611   *SIC* 5411
SOBEYS CAPITAL INCORPORATED   *p*591
110 20 HWY E, FONTHILL, ON, L0S 1E0
(905) 892-2570   *SIC* 5411
SOBEYS CAPITAL INCORPORATED   *p*598
55 MAIN ST E, GRAND BEND, ON, N0M
1T0
(519) 238-8944   *SIC* 5411

SOBEYS CAPITAL INCORPORATED   *p*600
44 LIVINGSTON AVE, GRIMSBY, ON, L3M
1L1
(905) 945-9973   *SIC* 5411
SOBEYS CAPITAL INCORPORATED   *p*609
700 QUEENSTON RD UNIT A, HAMILTON,
ON, L8G 1A3
(905) 560-8111   *SIC* 5411
SOBEYS CAPITAL INCORPORATED   *p*615
905 RYMAL RD E, HAMILTON, ON, L8W
3M2
(905) 383-9930   *SIC* 5411
SOBEYS CAPITAL INCORPORATED   *p*618
236 10TH ST, HANOVER, ON, N4N 1N9
(519) 364-2891   *SIC* 5411
SOBEYS CAPITAL INCORPORATED   *p*627
840 MARCH RD, KANATA, ON, K2W 0C9
(613) 599-8965   *SIC* 5411
SOBEYS CAPITAL INCORPORATED   *p*629
814 DURHAM ST, KINCARDINE, ON, N2Z
3B9
(519) 395-0022   *SIC* 5411
SOBEYS CAPITAL INCORPORATED   *p*638
1187 FISCHER HALLMAN RD SUITE 852,
KITCHENER, ON, N2E 4H9
(519) 576-1280   *SIC* 5411
SOBEYS CAPITAL INCORPORATED   *p*641
274 HIGHLAND RD W, KITCHENER, ON,
N2M 3C5
(519) 744-6561   *SIC* 5411
SOBEYS CAPITAL INCORPORATED   *p*686
7205 GOREWAY DR UNIT1, MISSIS-
SAUGA, ON, L4T 2T9
(905) 677-0239   *SIC* 5411
SOBEYS CAPITAL INCORPORATED   *p*719
5602 TENTH LINE W, MISSISSAUGA, ON,
L5M 7L9
(905) 858-2899   *SIC* 5411
SOBEYS CAPITAL INCORPORATED   *p*760
3714 PORTAGE RD, NIAGARA FALLS, ON,
L2J 2K9
(905) 371-2270   *SIC* 5411
SOBEYS CAPITAL INCORPORATED   *p*764
1899 ALGONQUIN AVE, NORTH BAY, ON,
P1B 4Y8
(705) 472-4001   *SIC* 5411
SOBEYS CAPITAL INCORPORATED   *p*775
6201 BATHURST ST, NORTH YORK, ON,
M2R 2A5
SIC 5411
SOBEYS CAPITAL INCORPORATED   *p*801
511 MAPLE GROVE DR SUITE 4,
OAKVILLE, ON, L6J 6X8
(905) 849-0691   *SIC* 5411
SOBEYS CAPITAL INCORPORATED   *p*805
2441 LAKESHORE RD W, OAKVILLE, ON,
L6L 5V5
(905) 825-2278   *SIC* 5411
SOBEYS CAPITAL INCORPORATED   *p*806
1500 UPPER MIDDLE RD W, OAKVILLE,
ON, L6M 0C2
(905) 847-1909   *SIC* 5411
SOBEYS CAPITAL INCORPORATED   *p*809
500 RIDDELL RD, ORANGEVILLE, ON,
L9W 5L1
(519) 941-1339   *SIC* 5411
SOBEYS CAPITAL INCORPORATED   *p*813
564 KING ST E, OSHAWA, ON, L1H 1G5
(905) 571-4835   *SIC* 5411
SOBEYS CAPITAL INCORPORATED   *p*814
1377 WILSON RD N, OSHAWA, ON, L1K
2Z5
(905) 440-4687   *SIC* 5411
SOBEYS CAPITAL INCORPORATED   *p*837
307 GRAND RIVER ST N, PARIS, ON, N3L
2N9
(519) 442-4485   *SIC* 5411
SOBEYS CAPITAL INCORPORATED   *p*881
438 NORFOLK ST S, SIMCOE, ON, N3Y
2X3
(519) 426-4799   *SIC* 5411
SOBEYS CAPITAL INCORPORATED   *p*883
400 SCOTT ST, ST CATHARINES, ON, L2M
3W4

(905) 935-9974   *SIC* 5411
SOBEYS CAPITAL INCORPORATED   *p*895
30 QUEENSLAND RD, STRATFORD, ON,
N4Z 1H4
(519) 273-2631   *SIC* 5411
SOBEYS CAPITAL INCORPORATED   *p*906
9200 BATHURST ST, THORNHILL, ON, L4J
8W1
(905) 731-7600   *SIC* 5411
SOBEYS CAPITAL INCORPORATED   *p*912
678 BROADWAY ST, TILLSONBURG, ON,
N4G 3S9
(519) 688-1734   *SIC* 5411
SOBEYS CAPITAL INCORPORATED   *p*917
2451 DANFORTH AVE SUITE 938,
TORONTO, ON, M4C 1L1
(416) 698-6868   *SIC* 5411
SOBEYS CAPITAL INCORPORATED   *p*990
840 DUPONT ST, TORONTO, ON, M6G 1Z8
(416) 534-3588   *SIC* 5411
SOBEYS CAPITAL INCORPORATED   *p*998
260 QUEEN ST N, TOTTENHAM, ON, L0G
1W0
(905) 936-1077   *SIC* 5411
SOBEYS CAPITAL INCORPORATED   *p*999
30 ONTARIO ST, TRENTON, ON, K8V 5S9
(613) 394-2791   *SIC* 5411
SOBEYS CAPITAL INCORPORATED   *p*1007
94 BRIDGEPORT RD E, WATERLOO, ON,
N2J 2J9
(519) 885-4170   *SIC* 5411
SOBEYS CAPITAL INCORPORATED   *p*1009
450 COLUMBIA ST W, WATERLOO, ON,
N2T 2W1
(519) 880-9143   *SIC* 5411
SOBEYS CAPITAL INCORPORATED   *p*1026
19 AMY CROFT DR, WINDSOR, ON, N9K
1C7
(519) 735-4110   *SIC* 5411
SOBEYS CAPITAL INCORPORATED   *p*1036
379 SPRINGBANK AVE N, WOODSTOCK,
ON, N4T 1R3
(519) 421-3340   *SIC* 5411
SOBEYS CAPITAL INCORPORATED   *p*1041
GD, MONTAGUE, PE, C0A 1R0
(902) 838-3388   *SIC* 5411
SOBEYS CAPITAL INCORPORATED   *p*1041
679 UNIVERSITY AVE, CHARLOTTE-
TOWN, PE, C1E 1E5
(902) 566-3218   *SIC* 5411
SOBEYS CAPITAL INCORPORATED   *p*1042
9 KINLOCK RD SUITE 621, STRATFORD,
PE, C1B 1P8
(902) 894-3800   *SIC* 5411
SOBEYS CAPITAL INCORPORATED   *p*1043
868-475 GRANVILLE ST, SUMMERSIDE,
PE, C1N 3N9
(902) 436-5795   *SIC* 5411
SOBEYS CAPITAL INCORPORATED   *p*1076
90 BOUL D'ANJOU, CHATEAUGUAY, QC,
J6K 1C3
(450) 692-3446   *SIC* 5411
SOBEYS CAPITAL INCORPORATED   *p*1240
11281 BOUL ALBERT-HUDON,
MONTREAL-NORD, QC, H1G 3J5
(514) 324-1010   *SIC* 5411
SOBEYS CAPITAL INCORPORATED   *p*1255
969 AV NORDIQUE BUREAU 458, QUE-
BEC, QC, G1C 7S8
(418) 667-5700   *SIC* 5411
SOBEYS CAPITAL INCORPORATED   *p*1268
5005 BOUL DE L'ORMIERE BUREAU 445,
QUEBEC, QC, G1P 1K6
(418) 877-3922   *SIC* 5411
SOBEYS CAPITAL INCORPORATED   *p*1270
255 CH SAINTE-FOY, QUEBEC, QC, G1R
1T5
(418) 524-9890   *SIC* 5411
SOBEYS CAPITAL INCORPORATED   *p*1279
5555 BOUL DES GRADINS, QUEBEC, QC,
G2J 1C8
(418) 622-5262   *SIC* 5411
SOBEYS CAPITAL INCORPORATED   *p*1285
395 AV SIROIS, RIMOUSKI, QC, G5L 8R2

(418) 724-2244   *SIC* 5411
SOBEYS CAPITAL INCORPORATED   *p*1287
254 BOUL DE L'HOTEL-DE-VILLE BUREAU
451, RIVIERE-DU-LOUP, QC, G5R 1M4
(418) 862-7861   *SIC* 5411
SOBEYS CAPITAL INCORPORATED   *p*1371
775 RUE GALT O BUREAU 514, SHER-
BROOKE, QC, J1H 1Z1
(819) 564-8686   *SIC* 5411
SOBEYS CAPITAL INCORPORATED   *p*1374
3950 RUE KING O BUREAU B, SHER-
BROOKE, QC, J1L 1P6
(819) 563-5172   *SIC* 5411
SOBEYS CAPITAL INCORPORATED   *p*1385
645 BOUL THIBEAU, TROIS-RIVIERES,
QC, G8T 6Z6
(819) 376-1551   *SIC* 5411
SOBEYS CAPITAL INCORPORATED   *p*1395
585 AV SAINT-CHARLES, VAUDREUIL-
DORION, QC, J7V 8P9
(450) 424-3549   *SIC* 5411
SOBEYS CAPITAL INCORPORATED   *p*1406
440 KING ST, ESTEVAN, SK, S4A 2B4
(306) 637-2550   *SIC* 5411
SOBEYS CAPITAL INCORPORATED   *p*1407
2304 QUILL CTR, HUMBOLDT, SK, S0K
2A1
(306) 682-2130   *SIC* 5411
SOBEYS CAPITAL INCORPORATED   *p*1423
4101 ROCHDALE BLVD, REGINA, SK, S4X
4P7
(306) 546-5881   *SIC* 5411
SOBEYS CAPITAL INCORPORATED   *p*1424
1550 8TH ST E, SASKATOON, SK, S7H 0T3
(306) 477-5800   *SIC* 5411
SOBEYS INC   *p*466
115 KING ST, SHELBURNE, NS, B0T 1W0
(902) 752-8371   *SIC* 5411
SOBEYS QUEBEC INC   *p*1079
1324 BOUL TALBOT, CHICOUTIMI, QC,
G7H 4B8
(418) 549-9751   *SIC* 5411
SOBEYS QUEBEC INC   *p*1090
850 CH D'OKA, DEUX-MONTAGNES, QC,
J7R 1L7
(450) 473-6280   *SIC* 5411
SOBEYS QUEBEC INC   *p*1131
8130 BOUL CHAMPLAIN, LASALLE, QC,
H8P 1B4
(514) 364-4777   *SIC* 5411
SOBEYS QUEBEC INC   *p*1138
1060 BOUL GUILLAUME-COUTURE,
LEVIS, QC, G6W 5M6
(418) 834-3811   *SIC* 5411
SOBEYS QUEBEC INC   *p*1149
65 MONTEE MASSON, MASCOUCHE, QC,
J7K 3B4
(450) 474-2444   *SIC* 5411
SOBEYS QUEBEC INC   *p*1301
299 BOUL ARTHUR-SAUVE, SAINT-
EUSTACHE, QC, J7P 2B1
(450) 472-1558   *SIC* 5411
SOBEYS QUEBEC INC   *p*1370
2240 RUE KING E, SHERBROOKE, QC,
J1G 5G8
(819) 566-8282   *SIC* 5411
SOBEYS QUEBEC INC   *p*1380
675 BOUL DES SEIGNEURS, TERRE-
BONNE, QC, J6W 1T5
(450) 492-5580   *SIC* 5411
SOBEYS QUEBEC INC   *p*1393
1777 RTE 132, VARENNES, QC, J3X 1P7
(450) 929-0405   *SIC* 5411
SOBEYS WEST INC   *p*7
550 CASSILS RD W SUITE 100, BROOKS,
AB, T1R 0W3
(403) 362-6851   *SIC* 5411
SOBEYS WEST INC   *p*9
3550 32 AVE NE SUITE 286, CALGARY, AB,
T1Y 6J2
(403) 291-2035   *SIC* 5411
SOBEYS WEST INC   *p*11
399 36 ST NE, CALGARY, AB, T2A 7R4
(403) 248-0848   *SIC* 5411

▲ Public Company   ■ Public Company Family Member   **HQ** Headquarters   **BR** Branch   **SL** Single Location

SOBEYS WEST INC *p18*
7740 18 ST SE, CALGARY, AB, T2C 2N5
(403) 236-0559 *SIC* 5411

SOBEYS WEST INC *p25*
1818 CENTRE ST NE SUITE 20, CALGARY, AB, T2E 2S6
(403) 276-3328 *SIC* 5411

SOBEYS WEST INC *p25*
1020 64 AVE NE, CALGARY, AB, T2E 7V8
(403) 730-3500 *SIC* 5411

SOBEYS WEST INC *p39*
9737 MACLEOD TRAIL SW, CALGARY, AB, T2J 0P6
(403) 252-8199 *SIC* 5411

SOBEYS WEST INC *p39*
1755 LAKE BONAVISTA DR SE SUITE 1, CALGARY, AB, T2J 0N3
(403) 271-1616 *SIC* 5411

SOBEYS WEST INC *p40*
3636 BRENTWOOD RD NW, CALGARY, AB, T2L 1K8
(403) 289-1424 *SIC* 5411

SOBEYS WEST INC *p40*
5607 4 ST NW, CALGARY, AB, T2K 1B3
(403) 730-5080 *SIC* 5411

SOBEYS WEST INC *p41*
3636 MORLEY TR NW, CALGARY, AB, T2L 1K8
(403) 289-9890 *SIC* 5411

SOBEYS WEST INC *p42*
410 10 ST NW, CALGARY, AB, T2N 1V9
(403) 270-3054 *SIC* 5411

SOBEYS WEST INC *p42*
1632 14 AVE NW UNIT 1846, CALGARY, AB, T2N 1M7
(403) 210-0002 *SIC* 5411

SOBEYS WEST INC *p65*
813 11 AVE SW, CALGARY, AB, T2R 0E6
(403) 264-1375 *SIC* 5411

SOBEYS WEST INC *p67*
524 ELBOW DR SW, CALGARY, AB, T2S 2H6
(403) 228-6141 *SIC* 5411

SOBEYS WEST INC *p68*
1600 90 AVE SW, CALGARY, AB, T2V 5A8
(403) 255-2755 *SIC* 5411

SOBEYS WEST INC *p69*
2525 WOODVIEW DR SW, CALGARY, AB, T2W 4N4
(403) 238-1400 *SIC* 5411

SOBEYS WEST INC *p78*
6800 48 AVE SUITE 200, CAMROSE, AB, T4V 4T1
(780) 672-1211 *SIC* 5411

SOBEYS WEST INC *p79*
135 CHESTERMERE STATION WAY UNIT 100, CHESTERMERE, AB, T1X 1V2
(403) 410-9700 *SIC* 5411

SOBEYS WEST INC *p83*
500 MANNING CROSS NW, EDMONTON, AB, T5A 5A1
(780) 475-2896 *SIC* 5411

SOBEYS WEST INC *p91*
1858230 82ND AVE, EDMONTON, AB, T5J 2K2
(780) 469-9452 *SIC* 5411

SOBEYS WEST INC *p92*
11410 104 AVE NW, EDMONTON, AB, T5K 2S5
(780) 424-0666 *SIC* 5411

SOBEYS WEST INC *p94*
12950 137 AVE NW, EDMONTON, AB, T5L 4Y8
(780) 377-2402 *SIC* 5411

SOBEYS WEST INC *p97*
601 WESTMOUNT SHOPPING CENTER, EDMONTON, AB, T5M 3L7
(780) 451-1860 *SIC* 5411

SOBEYS WEST INC *p104*
6655 178 ST NW SUITE 600, EDMONTON, AB, T5T 4J5
(780) 481-7646 *SIC* 5411

SOBEYS WEST INC *p107*
3004 118 AVE NW, EDMONTON, AB, T5W 4W3
(780) 477-6923 *SIC* 5411

SOBEYS WEST INC *p107*
8720 156 AVE NW, EDMONTON, AB, T5Z 3B4
(780) 486-0584 *SIC* 5411

SOBEYS WEST INC *p112*
8330 82 AVE NW, EDMONTON, AB, T6C 0Y6
(780) 469-9464 *SIC* 5411

SOBEYS WEST INC *p119*
2304 109 ST NW, EDMONTON, AB, T6J 3S8
(780) 430-4278 *SIC* 5411

SOBEYS WEST INC *p120*
2331 66 ST NW SUITE 341, EDMONTON, AB, T6K 4B4
(780) 450-8180 *SIC* 5411

SOBEYS WEST INC *p120*
38 AVENUE & MILLWOODS RD SUITE 100, EDMONTON, AB, T6K 3L6
(780) 462-4424 *SIC* 5411

SOBEYS WEST INC *p123*
576 RIVERBEND SQ NW SUITE 802, EDMONTON, AB, T6R 2E3
(780) 434-6124 *SIC* 5411

SOBEYS WEST INC *p129*
131 SIGNAL RD, FORT MCMURRAY, AB, T9H 4N6
(780) 791-3909 *SIC* 5411

SOBEYS WEST INC *p129*
9601 FRANKLIN AVE, FORT MCMURRAY, AB, T9H 2J8
(780) 790-1988 *SIC* 5411

SOBEYS WEST INC *p133*
9925 114 AVE, GRANDE PRAIRIE, AB, T8V 4A9
(780) 532-1627 *SIC* 5411

SOBEYS WEST INC *p140*
6112 50 ST SUITE 6112, LEDUC, AB, T9E 6N7
(780) 986-0390 *SIC* 5411

SOBEYS WEST INC *p141*
1702 23 ST N, LETHBRIDGE, AB, T1H 5B3
(403) 320-2231 *SIC* 5411

SOBEYS WEST INC *p143*
2750 FAIRWAY PLAZA RD S, LETHBRIDGE, AB, T1K 6Z3
(403) 328-0330 *SIC* 5411

SOBEYS WEST INC *p144*
5211 44 ST, LLOYDMINSTER, AB, T9V 0A7
(780) 875-3448 *SIC* 5411

SOBEYS WEST INC *p151*
610 BIG ROCK LN, OKOTOKS, AB, T1S 1L2
(403) 938-9341 *SIC* 5411

SOBEYS WEST INC *p154*
4408 50 AVE, RED DEER, AB, T4N 3Z6
(403) 346-1886 *SIC* 5411

SOBEYS WEST INC *p161*
985 FIR ST, SHERWOOD PARK, AB, T8A 4N5
(780) 467-0177 *SIC* 5411

SOBEYS WEST INC *p161*
2020 SHERWOOD DR, SHERWOOD PARK, AB, T8A 3H9
(780) 467-3037 *SIC* 5411

SOBEYS WEST INC *p166*
395 ST ALBERT TRAIL, ST. ALBERT, AB, T8N 5Z9
(780) 458-3620 *SIC* 5411

SOBEYS WEST INC *p166*
2 HEBERT RD SUITE 300, ST. ALBERT, AB, T8N 5T8
(780) 460-9356 *SIC* 5411

SOBEYS WEST INC *p169*
4926 46 AVE, TABER, AB, T1G 2A4
(403) 223-5749 *SIC* 5411

SOBEYS WEST INC *p179*
27566 FRASER HWY, ALDERGROVE, BC, V4W 3N5
(604) 857-1351 *SIC* 5411

SOBEYS WEST INC *p180*
9855 AUSTIN RD, BURNABY, BC, V3J 1N4
(604) 420-8091 *SIC* 5411

SOBEYS WEST INC *p186*
4440 HASTINGS ST SUITE E, BURNABY, BC, V5C 2K2
(604) 205-7497 *SIC* 5411

SOBEYS WEST INC *p199*
3051 LOUGHEED HWY SUITE 100, COQUITLAM, BC, V3B 1C6
SIC 5411

SOBEYS WEST INC *p202*
1033 AUSTIN AVE, COQUITLAM, BC, V3K 3P2
(604) 939-2850 *SIC* 5411

SOBEYS WEST INC *p204*
1200 BAKER ST, CRANBROOK, BC, V1C 1A8
(250) 417-0221 *SIC* 5411

SOBEYS WEST INC *p218*
945 COLUMBIA ST W, KAMLOOPS, BC, V2C 1L5
(250) 374-2811 *SIC* 5411

SOBEYS WEST INC *p227*
6153 200 ST, LANGLEY, BC, V2Y 1A2
(604) 530-6131 *SIC* 5411

SOBEYS WEST INC *p231*
20201 LOUGHEED HWY SUITE 300, MAPLE RIDGE, BC, V2X 2P6
(604) 460-7200 *SIC* 5411

SOBEYS WEST INC *p238*
1175 MT SEYMOUR RD, NORTH VANCOUVER, BC, V7H 2Y4
(604) 924-1302 *SIC* 5411

SOBEYS WEST INC *p238*
800 CARNARVON ST SUITE 220, NEW WESTMINSTER, BC, V3M 0G3
(604) 522-2019 *SIC* 5411

SOBEYS WEST INC *p239*
1170 27TH ST E, NORTH VANCOUVER, BC, V7J 1S1
(604) 988-7095 *SIC* 5411

SOBEYS WEST INC *p268*
2345 BEACON AVE, SIDNEY, BC, V8L 1W9
(250) 656-2735 *SIC* 5411

SOBEYS WEST INC *p268*
360 TRANS CANADA HWY SW UNIT 1, SALMON ARM, BC, V1E 1B4
(250) 832-8086 *SIC* 5411

SOBEYS WEST INC *p269*
3664 16 HWY E, SMITHERS, BC, V0J 2N6
(250) 847-4744 *SIC* 5411

SOBEYS WEST INC *p277*
7165 138 ST, SURREY, BC, V3W 7T9
(604) 594-4515 *SIC* 5411

SOBEYS WEST INC *p278*
7450 120 ST, SURREY, BC, V3W 3M9
(604) 594-7341 *SIC* 5411

SOBEYS WEST INC *p281*
12825 16 AVE, SURREY, BC, V4A 1N5
(604) 531-3422 *SIC* 5411

SOBEYS WEST INC *p287*
1780 BROADWAY E, VANCOUVER, BC, V5N 1W3
(604) 873-0225 *SIC* 5411

SOBEYS WEST INC *p293*
990 KING EDWARD AVE W, VANCOUVER, BC, V5Z 2E2
(604) 733-0073 *SIC* 5411

SOBEYS WEST INC *p293*
650 41ST AVE W, VANCOUVER, BC, V5Z 2M9
(604) 263-5502 *SIC* 5411

SOBEYS WEST INC *p318*
1641 DAVIE ST, VANCOUVER, BC, V6G 1W1
(604) 669-8131 *SIC* 5411

SOBEYS WEST INC *p318*
1766 ROBSON ST, VANCOUVER, BC, V6G 1E2
(604) 683-0202 *SIC* 5411

SOBEYS WEST INC *p322*
2733 BROADWAY W, VANCOUVER, BC, V6K 2G5
(604) 732-5030 *SIC* 5411

SOBEYS WEST INC *p332*
4300 32 ST, VERNON, BC, V1T 9H1
(250) 542-2627 *SIC* 5411

SOBEYS WEST INC *p342*
5385 HEADLAND DR, WEST VANCOUVER, BC, V7W 3C7
(604) 926-2034 *SIC* 5411

SOBEYS WEST INC *p356*
318 MANITOBA AVE, SELKIRK, MB, R1A 0Y7
(204) 482-5775 *SIC* 5411

SOBEYS WEST INC *p358*
143 PTH 12 N, STEINBACH, MB, R5G 1T5
(204) 346-1555 *SIC* 5411

SOBEYS WEST INC *p363*
1615 REGENT AVE W UNIT 500, WINNIPEG, MB, R2C 5C6
(204) 663-6862 *SIC* 5411

SOBEYS WEST INC *p363*
105 PANDORA AVE E, WINNIPEG, MB, R2C 0A1
(204) 222-6878 *SIC* 5411

SOBEYS WEST INC *p370*
850 KEEWATIN ST SUITE 12, WINNIPEG, MB, R2R 0Z5
(204) 632-6763 *SIC* 5411

SOBEYS WEST INC *p382*
1485 PORTAGE AVE SUITE 160E, WINNIPEG, MB, R3G 0W4
(204) 775-6348 *SIC* 5411

SOBEYS WEST INC *p387*
655 OSBORNE ST, WINNIPEG, MB, R3L 2B7
(204) 475-0793 *SIC* 5411

SOBEYS WEST INC *p388*
1120 GRANT AVE, WINNIPEG, MB, R3M 2A6
(204) 452-7197 *SIC* 5411

SOBEYS WEST INC *p389*
2025 CORYDON AVE SUITE 150, WINNIPEG, MB, R3P 0N5
(204) 489-6498 *SIC* 5411

SOBEYS WEST INC *p389*
3900 GRANT AVE SUITE 20, WINNIPEG, MB, R3R 3C2
(204) 837-5339 *SIC* 5411

SOBEYS WEST INC *p392*
1319 PEMBINA HWY, WINNIPEG, MB, R3T 2B6
(204) 284-0973 *SIC* 5411

SOBEYS WEST INC *p565*
75 WHYTE AVE, DRYDEN, ON, P8N 3E6
(807) 223-3276 *SIC* 5411

SOBEYS WEST INC *p628*
400 FIRST AVE S, KENORA, ON, P9N 1W4
(807) 468-5868 *SIC* 5411

SOBEYS WEST INC *p1411*
200 1ST AVE NW, MOOSE JAW, SK, S6H 1K9
(306) 693-8033 *SIC* 5411

SOBEYS WEST INC *p1421*
3859 SHERWOOD DR, REGINA, SK, S4R 4A8
(306) 949-7488 *SIC* 5411

SOBEYS WEST INC *p1424*
3310 8TH ST E, SASKATOON, SK, S7H 5M3
(306) 955-4644 *SIC* 5411

SOBEYS WEST INC *p1430*
134 PRIMROSE DR, SASKATOON, SK, S7K 5S6
(306) 242-6090 *SIC* 5411

SOBEYS WEST INC *p1432*
300 CONFEDERATION DR SUITE 100, SASKATOON, SK, S7L 4R6
(306) 384-9599 *SIC* 5411

SOBEYS WEST INC *p1434*
1739 PRESTON AVE N, SASKATOON, SK, S7N 4V2
(306) 668-9901 *SIC* 5411

SOCIETE COOPERATIVE AGRICOLE DE SAINT-UBALD *p1353*
464 RUE SAINT-PAUL, SAINT-UBALDE, QC, G0A 4L0
(418) 277-2225 *SIC* 5411

SOUTHLAND CANADA STORE *p37*

▲ Public Company ■ Public Company Family Member   **HQ** Headquarters   **BR** Branch   **SL** Single Location

6015 4 ST SE, CALGARY, AB, T2H 2A5
(403) 253-6218   *SIC* 5411
SOUTHLAND CO-OPERATIVE LTD   *p1404*
409 CENTRE ST, ASSINIBOIA, SK, S0H 0B0
(306) 642-4128   *SIC* 5411
SPOLETINI/PALUMBO INC   *p32*
1308 9 AVE SE, CALGARY, AB, T2G 0T3
(403) 537-1161   *SIC* 5411
ST MARY'S ECONOMIC DEVELOPMENT CORP   *p400*
150 CLIFFE ST, FREDERICTON, NB, E3A 0A1
(506) 452-9367   *SIC* 5411
ST. MARY'S RETAIL SALES   *p400*
150 CLIFFE ST, FREDERICTON, NB, E3A 0A1
(506) 452-9367   *SIC* 5411
STARSKY FINE FOODS MISSISSAUGA INC   *p703*
2040 DUNDAS ST E UNIT 2, MISSISSAUGA, ON, L4X 2X8
(905) 279-8889   *SIC* 5411
STARSKY FINE FOODS MISSISSAUGA INC   *p717*
3115 DUNDAS ST W, MISSISSAUGA, ON, L5L 3R8
(905) 363-2000   *SIC* 5411
STEVE'S NO FRILLS LTD   *p836*
1020 10TH ST W, OWEN SOUND, ON, N4K 5S1
(866) 987-6453   *SIC* 5411
STEWART DRUGS HANNA (1984) LTD *p135*
610 2ND AVE W, HANNA, AB, T0J 1P0
(403) 854-4154   *SIC* 5411
STONEWALL GROCERS LIMITED, THE *p359*
330 3RD AVE S UNIT 3, STONEWALL, MB, R0C 2Z0
(204) 467-5553   *SIC* 5411
STONG'S MARKETS LTD   *p324*
4560 DUNBAR ST, VANCOUVER, BC, V6S 2G6
(604) 266-1401   *SIC* 5411
STUDENT ASSOCIATION OF THE BRITISH COLUMBIA INSTITUTE OF TECHNOLOGY *p189*
3700 WILLINGDON AVE SUITE 260, BURNABY, BC, V5G 3H2
(604) 432-8847   *SIC* 5411
SUN VALLEY SUPERMARKET INCORPORATED   *p868*
468 DANFORTH RD, SCARBOROUGH, ON, M1K 1C6
(416) 264-2323   *SIC* 5411
SUNTERRA ENTERPRISES INC   *p119*
5728 111 ST NW, EDMONTON, AB, T6H 3G1
(780) 434-2610   *SIC* 5411
SUPER MARCHE CLEMENT NICOLET INC *p1242*
2000 BOUL LOUIS-FRECHETTE UNITE 100, NICOLET, QC, J3T 1M9
(819) 293-6937   *SIC* 5411
SUPER MARCHE COLLIN INC   *p1069*
2004 BOUL DE ROME, BROSSARD, QC, J4W 3M7
(450) 671-8885   *SIC* 5411
SUPER MARCHE DONAT THERIAULT LIMITEE   *p399*
570 RUE VICTORIA, EDMUNDSTON, NB, E3V 3N1
(506) 735-1860   *SIC* 5411
SUPER MARCHE FRONTENAC INC *p1110*
320 BOUL LECLERC O, GRANBY, QC, J2G 1V3
(450) 372-8014   *SIC* 5411
SUPER MARCHE IBERVILLE INC   *p1283*
305 BOUL IBERVILLE, REPENTIGNY, QC, J6A 2A6
(450) 581-2630   *SIC* 5411
SUPER MARCHE J.C. BEDARD LTEE *p1253*
169 RUE DUPONT, PONT-ROUGE, QC, G3H 1N3

(418) 873-2415   *SIC* 5411
SUPER MARCHE LAPLANTE INC   *p1316*
420 2E AV BUREAU 171, SAINT-JEAN-SUR-RICHELIEU, QC, J2X 2B8
(450) 357-1258   *SIC* 5411
SUPER MARCHE MONT-ROYAL (1988) INC *p1173*
2185 AV DU MONT-ROYAL E, MONTREAL, QC, H2H 1K2
(514) 522-5146   *SIC* 5411
SUPER MARCHE PLOUFFE INC   *p1056*
5 AV DES PINS, BEDFORD, QC, J0J 1A0
(450) 248-2968   *SIC* 5411
SUPER MARCHE RACICOT (1980) INC *p1155*
1280 AV BEAUMONT, MONT-ROYAL, QC, H3P 3E5
(514) 737-3511   *SIC* 5411
SUPER MARCHE ROBERVAL INC   *p1287*
1221 BOUL MARCOTTE BUREAU 1, ROBERVAL, QC, G8H 3B8
(418) 275-4692   *SIC* 5411
SUPER MARCHE ROY INC   *p1290*
240 AV LARIVIERE, ROUYN-NORANDA, QC, J9X 4G8
(819) 762-5783   *SIC* 5411
SUPER MARCHE SIROIS INC   *p1285*
465 BOUL SAINT-GERMAIN, RIMOUSKI, QC, G5L 3P2
(418) 722-0722   *SIC* 5411
SUPER MARCHE ST-RAPHAEL INC *p1120*
640 BOUL JACQUES-BIZARD, L'ILE-BIZARD, QC, H9C 2H2
(514) 620-4443   *SIC* 5411
SUPERMARCH DJS COUSINEAU INC *p1142*
455 BOUL JEAN-PAUL-VINCENT, LONGUEUIL, QC, J4G 1R3
(450) 646-4302   *SIC* 5411
SUPERMARCHE A R G INC   *p1088*
175 RUE PRINCIPALE, COWANSVILLE, QC, J2K 3L9
SIC 5411
SUPERMARCHE ANDRE GRASSET INC *p1177*
8935 AV ANDRE-GRASSET, MONTREAL, QC, H2M 2E9
(514) 382-1465   *SIC* 5411
SUPERMARCHE BELSERA INC   *p1268*
2300 BOUL PERE-LELIEVRE, QUEBEC, QC, G1P 2X5
(418) 682-4197   *SIC* 5411
SUPERMARCHE BERGERON INC   *p1108*
2195 CH RIDGE, GODMANCHESTER, QC, J0S 1H0
(450) 264-2909   *SIC* 5411
SUPERMARCHE BOUCHER INC   *p1281*
3528 RUE METCALFE, RAWDON, QC, J0K 1S0
(450) 834-2561   *SIC* 5411
SUPERMARCHE BOUCHER INC   *p1315*
841 RTE LOUIS-CYR, SAINT-JEAN-DE-MATHA, QC, J0K 2S0
(450) 886-1010   *SIC* 5411
SUPERMARCHE CLAKA INC   *p1263*
1625 RUE DU MARAIS, QUEBEC, QC, G1M 0A2
(418) 688-1441   *SIC* 5411
SUPERMARCHE CREVIER (LACHENAIE) INC   *p1379*
325 MONTEE DES PIONNIERS, TERREBONNE, QC, J6V 1H4
(450) 582-2271   *SIC* 5411
SUPERMARCHE CREVIER (REPENTIGNY) INC   *p1283*
180 BOUL BRIEN, REPENTIGNY, QC, J6A 7E9
(450) 582-0201   *SIC* 5411
SUPERMARCHE CREVIER (VALMONT) INC *p1282*
315 RUE VALMONT, REPENTIGNY, QC, J5Y 0Y5
(450) 657-5082   *SIC* 5411
SUPERMARCHE CREVIER L'ASSOMPTION INC   *p1120*

860 BOUL DE L'ANGE-GARDIEN N, L'ASSOMPTION, QC, J5W 1P1
(450) 589-5738   *SIC* 5411
SUPERMARCHE D.D.O. INC   *p1091*
11800 BOUL DE SALABERRY, DOLLARD-DES-ORMEAUX, QC, H9B 2R8
(514) 685-5252   *SIC* 5411
SUPERMARCHE DEZIEL INC   *p1180*
1155 RUE JARRY E, MONTREAL, QC, H2P 1W9
(514) 725-9323   *SIC* 5411
SUPERMARCHE DON QUICHOTTE INC *p1121*
110 BOUL DON-QUICHOTTE, L'ILE-PERROT, QC, J7V 6L7
(514) 453-3027   *SIC* 5411
SUPERMARCHE FAMILLE ROUSSEAU INC *p1140*
1855 RTE DES RIVIERES, LEVIS, QC, G7A 4X8
(418) 831-5400   *SIC* 5411
SUPERMARCHE G.C. INC   *p1054*
1020 BOUL MONSEIGNEUR-DE-LAVAL BUREAU 1, BAIE-SAINT-PAUL, QC, G3Z 2W6
(418) 435-5210   *SIC* 5411
SUPERMARCHE GEORGES BADRA INC *p1112*
300 AV AUGUSTE, GREENFIELD PARK, QC, J4V 3R4
(450) 656-7055   *SIC* 5411
SUPERMARCHE GUY CORRIVEAU INC *p1046*
511 7E RUE O, AMOS, QC, J9T 2Y3
SIC 5411
SUPERMARCHE J C J PLOUFFE INC *p1375*
4801 BOUL BOURQUE, SHERBROOKE, QC, J1N 2G6
(819) 564-7733   *SIC* 5411
SUPERMARCHE J.P.V. PLOUFFE INC *p1148*
460 RUE SAINT-PATRICE O, MAGOG, QC, J1X 1W9
(819) 843-9202   *SIC* 5411
SUPERMARCHE LACHUTE INC   *p1129*
501 AV BETHANY, LACHUTE, QC, J8H 4A6
(450) 562-7919   *SIC* 5411
SUPERMARCHE LAFRANCE INC   *p1051*
7172 RUE BOMBARDIER, ANJOU, QC, H1J 2Z9
(514) 352-1386   *SIC* 5411
SUPERMARCHE LAROCHE (1991) INC *p1133*
122 BOUL LAURIER, LAURIER-STATION, QC, G0S 1N0
(418) 728-2882   *SIC* 5411
SUPERMARCHE LEFEBVRE ET FILLES INC   *p1221*
1500 AV ATWATER, MONTREAL, QC, H3Z 1X5
(514) 933-0995   *SIC* 5411
SUPERMARCHE MARQUIS L'ASSOMPTION INC   *p1120*
790 MONTEE DE SAINT-SULPICE, L'ASSOMPTION, QC, J5W 0M6
(450) 589-0442   *SIC* 5411
SUPERMARCHE MARQUIS REPENTIGNY INC   *p1283*
150 RUE LOUVAIN, REPENTIGNY, QC, J6A 8J7
(450) 585-1445   *SIC* 5411
SUPERMARCHE MELLON INC   *p1115*
2085 BOUL MELLON, JONQUIERE, QC, G7S 3G4
(418) 548-7557   *SIC* 5411
SUPERMARCHE MONT ST-HILAIRE   *p1158*
345 BOUL HONORIUS-CHARBONNEAU, MONT-SAINT-HILAIRE, QC, J3H 5H6
(450) 467-8977   *SIC* 5411
SUPERMARCHE N.G. INC   *p1084*
1855 BOUL RENE-LAENNEC, COTE SAINT-LUC, QC, H7M 5E2
(450) 629-1850   *SIC* 5411
SUPERMARCHE ORNAWKA INC   *p1220*
4885 AV VAN HORNE, MONTREAL, QC, H3W 1J2

(514) 731-8336   *SIC* 5411
SUPERMARCHE PAGANO ET SHNAIDMAN INC   *p1083*
7151 CH DE LA COTE-SAINT-LUC BUREAU 108, COTE SAINT-LUC, QC, H4V 1J2
(514) 486-3254   *SIC* 5411
SUPERMARCHE PELLETIER INC   *p1391*
1177 8E RUE, VAL-D'OR, QC, J9P 1R1
(819) 825-6608   *SIC* 5411
SUPERMARCHE PERRIER ET MARTEL INC *p1342*
6155 BOUL ARTHUR-SAUVE, SAINT-LAURENT, QC, H7R 3X8
(450) 627-4496   *SIC* 5411
SUPERMARCHE PIERRE M LEDUC INC *p1217*
2820 RUE DE SALABERRY, MONTREAL, QC, H3M 1L3
(514) 745-1640   *SIC* 5411
SUPERMARCHE RAYMOND MARTIN INC *p1398*
11 RUE DE L'AQUEDUC, VICTORIAVILLE, QC, G6P 1L4
(819) 752-9797   *SIC* 5411
SUPERMARCHE ROBERT PILON LTEE *p1365*
1380 BOUL MONSEIGNEUR-LANGLOIS, SALABERRY-DE-VALLEYFIELD, QC, J6S 1E3
(450) 373-0251   *SIC* 5411
SUPERMARCHE ROY INC   *p1290*
240 AV LARIVIERE BUREAU 550, ROUYN-NORANDA, QC, J9X 4G8
(819) 762-7739   *SIC* 5411
SUPERMARCHE SARAZIN, GILLES INC *p1145*
825 RUE SAINT-LAURENT O, LONGUEUIL, QC, J4K 2V1
(450) 677-5237   *SIC* 5411
SUPERMARCHE ST-BRUNO INC   *p1296*
750 MONTEE MONTARVILLE, SAINT-BRUNO, QC, J3V 6B1
(450) 461-0792   *SIC* 5411
SUPERMARCHES DAIGLE, JACQUES INC *p1061*
25 BOUL DES ENTREPRISES, BOIS-BRIAND, QC, J7G 3K6
(450) 430-1396   *SIC* 5411
SUPERMARCHES GP INC, LES   *p1151*
750 AV DU PHARE O BUREAU 4415, MATANE, QC, G4W 3W8
(418) 562-4434   *SIC* 5411
SUPERMARCHES GP INC, LES   *p1154*
40 AV DOUCET, MONT-JOLI, QC, G5H 0B8
(418) 775-8848   *SIC* 5411
SUPERMARCHES GP INC, LES   *p1378*
633 RUE COMMERCIALE N UNITE 100, TEMISCOUATA-SUR-LE-LAC, QC, G0L 1E0
(418) 854-2177   *SIC* 5411
SYSCO CANADA, INC   *p392*
1570 CLARENCE AVE, WINNIPEG, MB, R3T 1T6
(204) 478-4000   *SIC* 5411
T & T SUPERMARKET INC   *p11*
999 36 ST NE SUITE 800, CALGARY, AB, T2A 7X6
(403) 569-6888   *SIC* 5411
T & T SUPERMARKET INC   *p104*
8882 170 ST NW SUITE 2580, EDMONTON, AB, T5T 4M2
(780) 483-6638   *SIC* 5411
T & T SUPERMARKET INC   *p191*
4800 KINGSWAY SUITE 147, BURNABY, BC, V5H 4J2
(604) 436-4881   *SIC* 5411
T & T SUPERMARKET INC   *p258*
21500 GORDON WAY, RICHMOND, BC, V6W 1J8
(604) 276-9889   *SIC* 5411
T & T SUPERMARKET INC   *p262*
8181 CAMBIE RD SUITE 1000, RICHMOND, BC, V6X 3X9
(604) 284-5550   *SIC* 5411
T & T SUPERMARKET INC   *p262*

3700 NO. 3 RD SUITE 1000, RICHMOND, BC, V6X 3X2

(604) 276-8808   SIC 5411

T & T SUPERMARKET INC   p300
179 KEEFER PL, VANCOUVER, BC, V6B 6L4

(604) 899-8836   SIC 5411

T & T SUPERMARKET INC   p906
1 PROMENADE CIR, THORNHILL, ON, L4J 4P8

(905) 763-8113   SIC 5411

TERRINGTON CONSUMERS CO-OPERATIVE SOCIETY LIMITED   p424
1 ABBOTT DR, HAPPY VALLEY-GOOSE BAY, NL, A0P 1E0

(709) 896-5737   SIC 5411

THIARA SUPERMARKET LTD.   p728
3899 TRELAWNY CIR SUITE 1, MISSISSAUGA, ON, L5N 6S3

(905) 824-8960   SIC 5411

THREE HILLS FOOD STORES LTD   p169
119 4TH AVE N, THREE HILLS, AB, T0M 2A0

(403) 443-5022   SIC 5411

TODD'S YIG 803 LTD   p607
5121 COUNTY RD 21 RR 3, HALIBURTON, ON, K0M 1S0

(705) 455-9775   SIC 5411

TOM'S INDEPENDENT GROCER   p1421
336 N MCCARTHY BLVD SUITE A, REGINA, SK, S4R 7M2

(306) 949-1255   SIC 5411

TONY'S NO FRILLS LTD   p617
770 UPPER JAMES ST SUITE 723, HAMILTON, ON, L9C 3A2

(905) 574-2069   SIC 5411

TRA MARITIMES   p395
3917 MAIN ST, BELLEDUNE, NB, E8G 2K3
SIC 5411

TRAIL BAY DEVELOPMENTS LTD   p268
5755 COWRIE ST SUITE 1, SECHELT, BC, V0N 3A0

(604) 885-9812   SIC 5411

TREATY ENTERPRISE INC   p461
10 TREATY TRAIL, LOWER TRURO, NS, B6L 1V9

(902) 897-2650   SIC 5411

TRIPLE CROWN FOODS LTD   p340
2945 JACKLIN RD SUITE 200, VICTORIA, BC, V9B 5E3

(250) 478-8998   SIC 5411

TROUSDALE'S I G A   p902
5 GEORGE ST, SYDENHAM, ON, K0H 2T0

(613) 376-6609   SIC 5411

TRUE VALUE FOOD CENTRE LTD   p180
7108 WEST SAANICH RD, BRENTWOOD BAY, BC, V8M 1P8

(250) 544-8183   SIC 5411

TWIN VALLEY CO-OP LTD   p345
861 VINE ST, BIRTLE, MB, R0M 0C0

(204) 842-3387   SIC 5411

UNATA INC   p984
504 WELLINGTON ST W SUITE 200, TORONTO, ON, M5V 1E3

(416) 305-9977   SIC 5411

UNIPAC PACKAGING PRODUCTS LTD p103
11133 184 ST NW, EDMONTON, AB, T5S 2L6

(780) 466-3121   SIC 5411

UPPER JAMES 2004 LTD   p616
1550 UPPER JAMES ST, HAMILTON, ON, L9B 2L6

(905) 383-9700   SIC 5411

VALLEYVIEW CONSUMERS CO-OP LTD p360
250 PRINCESS ST W, VIRDEN, MB, R0M 2C0

(204) 748-2520   SIC 5411

VALU-MART INC   p646
42 RUSSELL ST W, LINDSAY, ON, K9V 2W9

(705) 328-0622   SIC 5411

VALUMART LTD   p931
55 BLOOR ST W, TORONTO, ON, M4W

1A5

(416) 923-8831   SIC 5411

VANAN FOODS LIMITED   p98
9106 142 ST NW, EDMONTON, AB, T5R 0M7

(780) 483-1525   SIC 5411

VEGREVILLE & DISTRICT CO-OP LTD p170
4914 51 AVE GD, VEGREVILLE, AB, T9C 1V5

(780) 632-2884   SIC 5411

VIATEUR PAQUETTE & FILS INC   p1113
1026 133 RTE, HENRYVILLE, QC, J0J 1E0
SIC 5411

VICTORIA FUJIYA FOODS LTD   p333
3624 SHELBOURNE ST, VICTORIA, BC, V8P 4H2

(250) 598-3711   SIC 5411

VO'S YIG #00835   p848
1893 SCUGOG ST, PORT PERRY, ON, L9L 1H9

(905) 985-9772   SIC 5411

VODDEN FOODLAND   p500
456 VODDEN ST E, BRAMPTON, ON, L6S 5Y7

(905) 453-3100   SIC 5411

VOYER & JOBIN LTEE   p1351
268 RUE SAINT-JOSEPH, SAINT-RAYMOND, QC, G3L 1J3

(418) 337-2278   SIC 5411

W.R.A. ENTERPRISES PORTAGE LA PRAIRIE LTD   p355
2100 SASKATCHEWAN AVE W, PORTAGE LA PRAIRIE, MB, R1N 0P3

(204) 857-4700   SIC 5411

WALKER'S GROCERY LTD   p5
1040 FIRST AVE, BEAVERLODGE, AB, T0H 0C0

(780) 354-2092   SIC 5411

WALTERS VALU-MART   p850
6179 PERTH ST, RICHMOND, ON, K0A 2Z0

(613) 838-8800   SIC 5411

WATSON HOLDINGS LTD   p1411
468 LILLOOET ST W, MOOSE JAW, SK, S6H 7T1

(306) 692-1516   SIC 5411

WESDAN HOLDINGS INC   p215
1100 SUNSHINE COAST HWY, GIBSONS, BC, V0N 1V7

(604) 886-3487   SIC 5411

WESTFAIR FOODS LTD   p368
215 ST ANNE'S RD, WINNIPEG, MB, R2M 2Z9

(204) 258-2419   SIC 5411

WESTFORT FOODS INC   p910
111 FREDERICA ST E, THUNDER BAY, ON, P7E 3V4

(807) 623-4220   SIC 5411

WESTVIEW CO-OPERATIVE ASSOCIATION LIMITED   p151
5330 46 ST, OLDS, AB, T4H 1P6

(403) 556-3335   SIC 5411

WESTWARD ENTERPRISES LTD   p196
5001 50TH AVE, CHETWYND, BC, V0C 1J0

(250) 788-2422   SIC 5411

WHOLE FOODS MARKET CANADA INC p342
925 MAIN ST, WEST VANCOUVER, BC, V7T 2Z3

(604) 678-0500   SIC 5411

WING ON NEW GROUP CANADA INC p677
351 FERRIER ST SUITE 6, MARKHAM, ON, L3R 5Z2

(905) 604-4677   SIC 5411

WOODSTOCK INDEPENDENT GROCER ASSOCIATE, INC.   p1036
645 DUNDAS ST SUITE 1, WOODSTOCK, ON, N4S 1E4

(519) 421-3420   SIC 5411

YELLOWKNIFE DIRECT CHARGE CO-OPERATIVE LIMITED   p436
321 OLD AIRPORT RD, YELLOWKNIFE, NT, X1A 3T3

(867) 873-5770   SIC 5411

YUMMY MARKET INC   p664

1390 MAJOR MACKENZIE DR, MAPLE, ON, L6A 4H6

(905) 417-4117   SIC 5411

YUMMY MARKET INC   p781
4400 DUFFERIN ST UNIT B-4, NORTH YORK, ON, M3H 6A8

(416) 665-0040   SIC 5411

ZECHNER'S LIMITED   p761
155 RAILWAY ST, NIPIGON, ON, P0T 2J0

(807) 887-2910   SIC 5411

ZEHRMART INC   p489
620 YONGE ST, BARRIE, ON, L4N 4E6

(705) 735-2390   SIC 5411

ZEHRMART INC   p496
487 QUEEN ST S, BOLTON, ON, L7E 2B4

(905) 951-7505   SIC 5411

ZEHRMART INC   p512
1 PRESIDENTS CHOICE CIR, BRAMPTON, ON, L6Y 5S5

(905) 459-2500   SIC 5411

ZEHRMART INC   p515
410 FAIRVIEW DR SUITE 1, BRANTFORD, ON, N3R 7V7

(519) 754-4932   SIC 5411

ZEHRMART INC   p535
400 CONESTOGA BLVD, CAMBRIDGE, ON, N1R 7L7

(519) 620-1376   SIC 5411

ZEHRMART INC   p590
800 TOWER ST S, FERGUS, ON, N1M 2R3

(519) 843-5500   SIC 5411

ZEHRMART INC   p598
HWY 8 S, GODERICH, ON, N7A 4C6

(519) 524-2229   SIC 5411

ZEHRMART INC   p601
297 ERAMOSA RD, GUELPH, ON, N1E 2M7

(519) 763-4550   SIC 5411

ZEHRMART INC   p635
1375 WEBER ST E, KITCHENER, ON, N2A 3Y7

(519) 748-4570   SIC 5411

ZEHRMART INC   p643
5890 MALDEN RD, LASALLE, ON, N9H 1S4

(519) 966-6030   SIC 5411

ZEHRMART INC   p881
125 QUEENSWAY E, SIMCOE, ON, N3Y 5M7

(519) 426-7743   SIC 5411

ZEHRMART INC   p1007
315 LINCOLN RD SUITE 1, WATERLOO, ON, N2J 4H7

(519) 885-1360   SIC 5411

ZEHRMART INC   p1009
450 ERB ST W, WATERLOO, ON, N2T 1H4

(519) 886-4900   SIC 5411

ZEHRMART INC   p1012
821 NIAGARA ST, WELLAND, ON, L3C 1M4

(905) 732-9380   SIC 5411

ZEIDCO INC   p383
905 PORTAGE AVE, WINNIPEG, MB, R3G 0P3

(204) 987-8840   SIC 5411

SIC 5421 Meat and fish markets

347942 B. C. LTD   p285
57 LAKEWOOD DR, VANCOUVER, BC, V5L 4W4

(604) 251-9168   SIC 5421

887252 ONTARIO LIMITED   p990
1042 BLOOR ST W, TORONTO, ON, M6H 1M3

(416) 531-7462   SIC 5421

BARRY GROUP INC   p394
12 ALLEE FRIGAULT, ANSE-BLEUE, NB, E8N 2J2
SIC 5421

CHOUINARD, A. & FILS INC   p1354
10505 BOUL SAINTE-ANNE, SAINTE-ANNE-DE-BEAUPRE, QC, G0A 3C0

(418) 827-5569   SIC 5421

COOPERATIVE DES PECHEURS DE CAP

DAUPHIN   p1112
51 CH SHORE, GROSSE-ILE, QC, G4T 6A4

(418) 985-2321   SIC 5421

FABKO FOOD LTD   p83
8715 126 AVE NW, EDMONTON, AB, T5B 1G8

SIC 5421

FRASER VALLEY MEAT SUPPLIES LTD p196
45735 ALEXANDER AVE, CHILLIWACK, BC, V2P 1L6

(604) 792-4723   SIC 5421

FRIGOVIANDE INC   p1164
6065 RUE HOCHELAGA, MONTREAL, QC, H1N 1X7

(514) 256-0400   SIC 5421

HALENDA'S FINE FOODS LTD   p812
915 NELSON ST, OSHAWA, ON, L1H 5N7

(905) 576-6328   SIC 5421

KANATA HOLDINGS LTD   p260
11251 RIVER RD UNIT 200, RICHMOND, BC, V6X 1Z6

(604) 273-6005   SIC 5421

LOBLAWS INC   p1087
3500 BOUL SAINT-MARTIN O, COTE SAINT-LUC, QC, H7T 2W4

(450) 688-2969   SIC 5421

MISSFRESH INC   p1340
4220 RUE GRIFFITH, SAINT-LAURENT, QC, H4T 1A7

(844) 647-7373   SIC 5421

MOUNTAIN TOP FOODS LTD   p148
2301 18 AVE, NANTON, AB, T0L 1R0

(403) 646-0038   SIC 5421

OCEAN CHOICE INTERNATIONAL   p421
28 CAMPBELL ST SUITE 10, BONAVISTA, NL, A0C 1B0

(709) 468-7840   SIC 5421

OCEAN CHOICE INTERNATIONAL   p430
1315 TOPSAIL RD, ST. JOHN'S, NL, A1B 3N4

(709) 782-6244   SIC 5421

PERL'S MEAT PRODUCTS LIMITED   p791
3015 BATHURST ST, NORTH YORK, ON, M6B 3B5

SIC 5421

POISSONNERIE ODESSA INC., LES   p1172
6569 AV PAPINEAU BUREAU 100, MONTREAL, QC, H2G 2X3

(450) 743-9999   SIC 5421

POISSONNERIE DU HAVRE LTEE   p1113
968 RUE DE LA BERGE, HAVRE-SAINT-PIERRE, QC, G0G 1P0

(418) 538-2515   SIC 5421

POSEIDON 'LES POISSONS ET CRUSTACES' INC   p1140
259 RUE DU BORD-DE-LA-MER, LONGUE-POINTE-DE-MINGAN, QC, G0G 1V0

(418) 949-2331   SIC 5421

SHIGS ENTERPRISES LTD   p296
450 ALEXANDER ST, VANCOUVER, BC, V6A 1C5

(604) 251-9093   SIC 5421

STAWNICHY'S HOLDINGS LTD   p148
5212 50 ST, MUNDARE, AB, T0B 3H0

(780) 764-3912   SIC 5421

STEMMLER MEATS & CHEESE (HEIDELBERG) INCORPORATED   p619
3031 LOBSINGER LINE, HEIDELBERG, ON, N0B 2M1

(519) 699-4590   SIC 5421

SUNTERRA MEATS LTD   p137
4312 51 ST, INNISFAIL, AB, T4G 1A3

(403) 442-4202   SIC 5421

TAYLOR SHELLFISH CANADA ULC   p212
8260 ISLAND HWY S, FANNY BAY, BC, V0R 1W0

(250) 335-0125   SIC 5421

SIC 5431 Fruit and vegetable markets

2739-9708 QUEBEC INC   p1218

▲ Public Company   ■ Public Company Family Member   **HQ** Headquarters   **BR** Branch   **SL** Single Location

5192 CH DE LA COTE-DES-NEIGES, MONTREAL, QC, H3T 1X8
(514) 738-1384   *SIC 5431*

509334 ONTARIO INC   p861
1141 LAKESHORE RD, SARNIA, ON, N7V 2V5
(519) 542-1241   *SIC 5431*

657720 ONTARIO LTD   p658
1260 GAINSBOROUGH RD, LONDON, ON, N6H 5K8
(519) 473-2273   *SIC 5431*

658771 ONTARIO LTD   p1020
2727 HOWARD AVE, WINDSOR, ON, N8X 3X4
(519) 972-1440   *SIC 5431*

964211 ONTARIO LTD   p1104
215 RUE BELLEHUMEUR, GATINEAU, QC, J8T 8H3
SIC 5431

ATRIUM GROUP INC, THE   p452
1515 DRESDEN ROW, HALIFAX, NS, B3J 4B1
(902) 425-5700   *SIC 5431*

AVERY'S FARM MARKETS LIMITED   p451
619 CENTRAL AVE, GREENWOOD, NS, B0P 1R0
(902) 765-0224   *SIC 5431*

BOLTHOUSE FARMS CANADA INC   p1013
303 MILO RD, WHEATLEY, ON, N0P 2P0
(519) 825-3412   *SIC 5431*

BRANT FOOD CENTER LTD   p516
94 GREY ST, BRANTFORD, ON, N3T 2T5
(519) 756-8002   *SIC 5431*

BRENNEIS MARKET GARDENS INC   p87
GD STN MAIN, EDMONTON, AB, T5J 2G8
(780) 473-7733   *SIC 5431*

CARLING FRUIT INC   p829
1855 CARLING AVE, OTTAWA, ON, K2A 1E4
(613) 722-6106   *SIC 5431*

CENTRAL FOODS CO. LTD   p263
12160 HORSESHOE WAY, RICHMOND, BC, V7A 4V5
(604) 271-9797   *SIC 5431*

COUNTRY PRODUCE (ORILLIA) LTD   p809
301 WESTMOUNT DR N, ORILLIA, ON, L3V 6Y4
(705) 325-9902   *SIC 5431*

FARM BOY COMPANY INC   p562
814 SYDNEY ST, CORNWALL, ON, K6H 3J8
(613) 938-8566   *SIC 5431*

FINES HERBES DE CHEZ NOUS INC, LES   p1348
116 CH TRUDEAU, SAINT-MATHIEU-DE-BELOEIL, QC, J3G 0E3
(450) 464-2969   *SIC 5431*

FRUITERIE VAL-MONT INC, LA   p1172
2147 AV DU MONT-ROYAL E, MONTREAL, QC, H2H 1J9
(514) 523-8212   *SIC 5431*

FRUITS ET LEGUMES GRANDE-ALLEE INC   p1071
4635 GRANDE-ALLEE, BROSSARD, QC, J4Z 3E9
(450) 678-3167   *SIC 5431*

FRUITS ET LEGUMES TARDIF INC   p1123
559 CH DE SAINT-JEAN, LA PRAIRIE, QC, J5R 2L2
(450) 659-6449   *SIC 5431*

H & W PRODUCE CORPORATION   p93
12510 132 AVE NW, EDMONTON, AB, T5L 3P9
(780) 451-3700   *SIC 5431*

HARVEST BARN OF NIAGARA LTD   p761
1822 NIAGARA STONE RD, NIAGARA ON THE LAKE, ON, L0S 1J0
(905) 468-3224   *SIC 5431*

LOCOCO, A. WHOLESALE LTD   p758
4167 VICTORIA AVE, NIAGARA FALLS, ON, L2E 4B2
(905) 358-3281   *SIC 5431*

LONGO BROTHERS FRUIT MARKETS INC   p511

7700 HURONTARIO ST SUITE 202, BRAMPTON, ON, L6Y 4M3
(905) 455-3135   *SIC 5431*

LONGO BROTHERS FRUIT MARKETS INC   p531
1225 FAIRVIEW ST, BURLINGTON, ON, L7S 1Y3
(905) 637-3804   *SIC 5431*

LONGO BROTHERS FRUIT MARKETS INC   p798
338 DUNDAS ST E, OAKVILLE, ON, L6H 6Z9
(905) 257-5633   *SIC 5431*

MAISON DE LA POMME DE FRELIGHSBURG INC   p1102
32 RTE 237 N, FRELIGHSBURG, QC, J0J 1C0
(450) 298-5275   *SIC 5431*

MAISON SAMI T.A. FRUITS INC, LA   p1226
1505 RUE LEGENDRE O, MONTREAL, QC, H4N 1H6
(514) 858-6363   *SIC 5431*

MARCHE DORE & FILS INC   p1154
939 BOUL ALBINY-PAQUETTE BUREAU 1, MONT-LAURIER, QC, J9L 3J1
(819) 623-6984   *SIC 5431*

MASSTOWN MARKET LIMITED   p449
10622 HIGHWAY 2, DEBERT, NS, B0M 1G0
(902) 662-2816   *SIC 5431*

METRO RICHELIEU INC   p1256
2968 BOUL SAINTE-ANNE, QUEBEC, QC, G1E 3J3
SIC 5431

METRO RICHELIEU INC   p1293
60 RUE D'ANVERS, SAINT-AUGUSTIN-DE-DESMAURES, QC, G3A 1S4
SIC 5431

NATURE'S FINEST PRODUCE LTD   p836
6874 PAIN COURT LINE RR 1, PAIN COURT, ON, N0P 1Z0
(519) 380-9520   *SIC 5431*

OLIFRUITS LTEE   p1084
290 BOUL DE LA CONCORDE E, COTE SAINT-LUC, QC, H7G 2E6
(450) 667-4031   *SIC 5431*

ORGANIC BOX LTD   p110
5712 59 ST NW, EDMONTON, AB, T6B 3L4
(780) 469-1900   *SIC 5431*

PERES NATURE INC, LES   p1305
10735 1RE AV, SAINT-GEORGES, QC, G5Y 2B8
(418) 227-4444   *SIC 5431*

POLYCULTURE PLANTE (1987) INC   p1361
8683 CH ROYAL, SAINTE-PETRONILLE, QC, G0A 4C0
(418) 828-9603   *SIC 5431*

QUALITY GREENS CANADA LTD   p222
1889 SPALL RD UNIT 101, KELOWNA, BC, V1Y 4R2
(250) 763-8200   *SIC 5431*

SANDHER FRUIT PACKERS LTD   p220
4525 SCOTTY CREEK RD, KELOWNA, BC, V1X 6N3
(250) 491-9176   *SIC 5431*

SMITH'S MARKETS INC   p899
971 LASALLE BLVD, SUDBURY, ON, P3A 1X7
(705) 560-3663   *SIC 5431*

SOUTHBANK FRUIT INC   p827
2446 BANK ST UNIT 131, OTTAWA, ON, K1V 1A4
(613) 521-9653   *SIC 5431*

STRAWBERRY TYME INC   p881
1250 ST JOHN'S RD W, SIMCOE, ON, N3Y 4K1
(519) 426-3099   *SIC 5431*

SUE'S PRODUCE WORLD LTD   p856
205 DON HEAD VILLAGE BLVD SUITE 7, RICHMOND HILL, ON, L4C 7R4
(905) 737-0520   *SIC 5431*

SUN VALLEY FRUIT MARKET & GROCERIES (DANFORTH) LTD   p920
583 DANFORTH AVE, TORONTO, ON, M4K 1P9

(416) 264-2323   *SIC 5431*

VEGETARIEN TROIS RIVIERES INC   p1385
3960 BOUL DES FORGES, TROIS-RIVIERES, QC, G8Y 1V7
(819) 372-9730   *SIC 5431*

WALKERS OWN PRODUCE INTERNATIONAL INC   p38
7711 MACLEOD TRAIL SW, CALGARY, AB, T2H 0M1
(587) 583-8050   *SIC 5431*

WESTCOAST VEGETABLES LTD   p211
5369 49B AVE, DELTA, BC, V4K 4R7
(604) 940-4748   *SIC 5431*

SIC 5441 Candy, nut, and confectionery stores

1199893 ONTARIO LIMITED   p581
1850 ALBION RD UNIT 6, ETOBICOKE, ON, M9W 6J9
(416) 213-1165   *SIC 5441*

4542410 CANADA INC   p1261
550 AV GODIN, QUEBEC, QC, G1M 2K2
(418) 687-5320   *SIC 5441*

HUDSON DUFRY - EDMONTON   p126
PO BOX 9898, EDMONTON, AB, T9E 0V3
(780) 890-7263   *SIC 5441*

IMMACULATE CONFECTION LTD   p186
5284 STILL CREEK AVE, BURNABY, BC, V5C 4E4
(604) 293-1600   *SIC 5441*

KERNELS POPCORN LIMITED   p922
40 EGLINTON AVE E SUITE 250, TORONTO, ON, M4P 3A2
(416) 487-4194   *SIC 5441*

NUT MAN COMPANY INC, THE   p31
4112 8 ST SE, CALGARY, AB, T2G 3A7
(403) 287-1983   *SIC 5441*

NUTTY CHOCOLATIER CO LTD, THE   p848
182 QUEEN ST, PORT PERRY, ON, L9L 1B8
(905) 985-2210   *SIC 5441*

SIC 5451 Dairy products stores

ARLA FOODS INC   p548
675 RIVERMEDE RD, CONCORD, ON, L4K 2G9
(905) 669-9393   *SIC 5451*

BIG MOO ICE CREAM PARLOURS, THE   p169
4603 LAKESHORE DR, SYLVAN LAKE, AB, T4S 1C3
(403) 887-5533   *SIC 5451*

DICKIE-DEE ICE CREAM VENDING BIKES & TRUCKS   p371
530 DUFFERIN AVE, WINNIPEG, MB, R2W 2Y6
(204) 586-5218   *SIC 5451*

FROMAGERIE POLYETHNIQUE INC, LA   p1352
235 CH DE SAINT-ROBERT, SAINT-ROBERT, QC, J0G 1S0
(450) 782-2111   *SIC 5451*

FROMAGERIES PIMAR INC, LES   p1181
220 RUE JEAN-TALON E, MONTREAL, QC, H2R 1S7
(514) 272-1161   *SIC 5451*

LA TRAPPE A FROMAGE DE L'OUTAOUAIS   p1106
114 BOUL SAINT-RAYMOND, GATINEAU, QC, J8Y 1S9
(819) 243-6411   *SIC 5451*

MADE BY MARCUS LTD   p67
1013 17 AVE SW SUITE 121, CALGARY, AB, T2T 0A7
(403) 452-1692   *SIC 5451*

MAISON D'AFFINAGE BERGERON INC, LA   p1140
865 RTE DES RIVIERES, LEVIS, QC, G7A 2V2
(418) 831-0991   *SIC 5451*

MORISSETTE, MARCEL INC   p1356
171 BOUL BEGIN, SAINTE-CLAIRE, QC, G0R 2V0
(418) 883-3388   *SIC 5451*

PETITS DELICES G.T. INC, AUX   p1265
2022 RUE LAVOISIER BUREAU 198, QUEBEC, QC, G1N 4L5
(418) 683-8099   *SIC 5451*

SIC 5461 Retail bakeries

053944 NB INC   p400
546 KING ST SUITE A, FREDERICTON, NB, E3B 1E6
(506) 459-0067   *SIC 5461*

1087299 ONTARIO LTD   p1004
10 MCNAB ST, WALKERTON, ON, N0G 2V0
(519) 881-2794   *SIC 5461*

1129822 ONTARIO INC   p618
1000 MCGILL ST, HAWKESBURY, ON, K6A 1R6
(613) 632-8278   *SIC 5461*

1279028 ONTARIO LIMITED   p658
755 WONDERLAND RD N, LONDON, ON, N6H 4L1
(519) 473-7772   *SIC 5461*

1360548 ONTARIO LIMITED   p547
370 NORTH RIVERMEDE RD UNIT 1, CONCORD, ON, L4K 3N2
(905) 669-5883   *SIC 5461*

1456882 ONTARIO LTD   p788
3401 DUFFERIN ST, NORTH YORK, ON, M6A 2T9
(416) 789-3533   *SIC 5461*

1459564 ONTARIO LTD   p568
68 YONGE ST S, ELMVALE, ON, L0L 1P0
(705) 322-5504   *SIC 5461*

1555965 ONTARIO INC   p615
473 CONCESSION ST, HAMILTON, ON, L9A 1C1
(905) 383-7160   *SIC 5461*

1788741 ONTARIO INC   p760
6161 THOROLD STONE RD SUITE 3, NIAGARA FALLS, ON, L2J 1A4
(905) 357-6600   *SIC 5461*

2104225 ONTARIO LTD   p1103
255 CH INDUSTRIEL, GATINEAU, QC, J8R 3V8
(819) 669-7246   *SIC 5461*

2318-4211 QUEBEC INC   p1299
413 RUE PRINCIPALE, SAINT-DONAT-DE-MONTCALM, QC, J0T 2C0
(819) 424-2220   *SIC 5461*

2549204 ONTARIO INC   p870
1 WILLIAM KITCHEN RD SUITE 1, SCARBOROUGH, ON, M1P 5B7
(416) 293-1010   *SIC 5461*

2551194 ONTARIO INC   p625
74 OSPREY CRES, KANATA, ON, K2M 2Z8
(613) 567-7100   *SIC 5461*

3116506 CANADA INC   p1145
2479 CH DE CHAMBLY, LONGUEUIL, QC, J4L 1M2
(450) 468-4406   *SIC 5461*

3122298 CANADA INC   p1166
4445 RUE ONTARIO E BUREAU 4, MONTREAL, QC, H1V 3V3
(514) 259-5929   *SIC 5461*

3169693 CANADA INC   p1200
895 RUE DE LA GAUCHETIERE O BUREAU 401, MONTREAL, QC, H3B 4G1
(514) 393-1247   *SIC 5461*

3761045 CANADA INC   p1085
2888 AV DU COSMODOME BUREAU 2, COTE SAINT-LUC, QC, H7T 2X1
(450) 682-1800   *SIC 5461*

4048873 CANADA INC   p1173
860 AV DU MONT-ROYAL E, MONTREAL, QC, H2J 1X1
(514) 523-2751   *SIC 5461*

593631 ONTARIO LIMITED   p788
3522 BATHURST ST, NORTH YORK, ON,

M6A 2C6
SIC 5461

651233 ONTARIO INC   *p616*
630 STONE CHURCH RD W, HAMILTON, ON, L9B 1A7
(905) 389-3487   *SIC 5461*

683060 ALBERTA LTD   *p86*
8 EDMONTON CITY CENTRE NW, EDMONTON, AB, T5J 2Y7
(780) 477-6853   *SIC 5461*

770976 ONTARIO LIMITED   *p1029*
100 WHITMORE RD, WOODBRIDGE, ON, L4L 7K4
(905) 850-1477   *SIC 5461*

828590 ONTARIO INC   *p1006*
94 BRIDGEPORT RD E, WATERLOO, ON, N2J 2J9
(519) 746-6804   *SIC 5461*

849432 ONTARIO LIMITED   *p531*
29 PLAINS RD W UNIT 1, BURLINGTON, ON, L7T 1E8
(905) 634-2669   *SIC 5461*

9015-9492 QUEBEC INC   *p1222*
3025 RUE SAINT-AMBROISE, MONTREAL, QC, H4C 2C2
(514) 932-0328   *SIC 5461*

9038-7200 QUEBEC INC   *p1300*
255 25E AV BUREAU 926, SAINT-EUSTACHE, QC, J7P 4Y1
(450) 974-3493   *SIC 5461*

9154-4742 QUEBEC INC   *p1084*
2000 BOUL RENE-LAENNEC, COTE SAINT-LUC, QC, H7M 4J8
(450) 629-5115   *SIC 5461*

ACE BAKERY LIMITED   *p733*
580 SECRETARIAT CRT, MISSISSAUGA, ON, L5S 2A5
(905) 565-8138   *SIC 5461*

ADAMS 22 HOLDINGS LTD   *p211*
2628 BEVERLY ST, DUNCAN, BC, V9L 5C7
(250) 709-2205   *SIC 5461*

ALYRIN OPERATIONS LTD   *p458*
10 RAGGED LAKE BLVD SUITE 8, HALIFAX, NS, B3S 1C2
(902) 450-0056   *SIC 5461*

ART-IS-IN BAKERY INC   *p824*
250 CITY CENTRE AVE UNIT 112, OTTAWA, ON, K1R 6K7
(613) 695-1226   *SIC 5461*

BAGOS BUN BAKERY LTD   *p371*
232 JARVIS AVE, WINNIPEG, MB, R2W 3A1
(204) 586-8409   *SIC 5461*

BD CANADA LTD   *p311*
1100 MELVILLE ST UNIT 210, VANCOUVER, BC, V6E 4A6
(604) 296-3500   *SIC 5461*

BEAULIEU BAKERY LTD   *p810*
2122 ST. JOSEPH BLVD, ORLEANS, ON, K1C 1E6
(613) 837-2525   *SIC 5461*

BEE BELL HEALTH BAKERY INC   *p112*
10416 80 AVE NW, EDMONTON, AB, T6E 5T7

SIC 5461

BEIGNES M.W.M. INC., LES   *p1144*
895 RUE SAINT-LAURENT O, LONGUEUIL, QC, J4K 2V1
(450) 677-6363   *SIC 5461*

BISCUITERIE DOMINIC INC   *p1114*
285 RUE SAINT-CHARLES-BORROMEE N, JOLIETTE, QC, J6E 4R8
(450) 756-2637   *SIC 5461*

BOSS BAKERY & RESTAURANT LTD, THE   *p294*
532 MAIN ST, VANCOUVER, BC, V6A 2T9
(604) 683-3860   *SIC 5461*

BOULANGERIE ARTISANALE LA BOITE A PAIN INC   *p1258*
289 RUE SAINT-JOSEPH E, QUEBEC, QC, G1K 3B1
(418) 647-3666   *SIC 5461*

BOULANGERIE GADOUA LTEE   *p1353*
561 RUE PRINCIPALE, SAINT-THOMAS,

QC, J0K 3L0
SIC 5461

BOULANGERIE GEORGES INC   *p1370*
2000 RUE KING E, SHERBROOKE, QC, J1G 5G6
(819) 564-3002   *SIC 5461*

BOULANGERIE ST-METHODE   *p1071*
6000 AV AUTEUIL, BROSSARD, QC, J4Z 1N3
(450) 766-0678   *SIC 5461*

BOULANGERIE ST-METHODE INC   *p1044*
14 RUE PRINCIPALE E, ADSTOCK, QC, G0N 1S0
(418) 422-2246   *SIC 5461*

BREADKO NATIONAL BAKING LTD   *p737*
6310 KESTREL RD, MISSISSAUGA, ON, L5T 1Z3
(905) 670-4949   *SIC 5461*

BREEN'S ENTERPRISES LIMITED   *p428*
104 CHARTER AVE, ST. JOHN'S, NL, A1A 1P2
(709) 726-9040   *SIC 5461*

BRULE FOODS LTD   *p526*
4000 MAINWAY SUITE 3, BURLINGTON, ON, L7M 4B9
(905) 319-2663   *SIC 5461*

C & R VENTURES INC   *p388*
1857 GRANT AVE SUITE A, WINNIPEG, MB, R3N 1Z2
(204) 489-1086   *SIC 5461*

CANADA BREAD COMPANY, LIMITED   *p1361*
3455 AV FRANCIS-HUGHES, SAINTE-ROSE, QC, H7L 5A5
(450) 669-2222   *SIC 5461*

CHEZ PIGGY RESTAURANT LIMITED   *p630*
44 PRINCESS ST, KINGSTON, ON, K7L 1A4
(613) 544-7790   *SIC 5461*

CHUDLEIGH'S LTD   *p683*
8501 CHUDLEIGH WAY, MILTON, ON, L9T 0L9
(905) 878-8781   *SIC 5461*

CINNAROLL BAKERIES LIMITED   *p22*
2140 PEGASUS RD NE, CALGARY, AB, T2E 8G8
(403) 255-4556   *SIC 5461*

COFFEE COOP, THE   *p895*
693 ERIE ST, STRATFORD, ON, N4Z 1A1
(519) 271-6127   *SIC 5461*

COOKIES GRILL   *p197*
44335 YALE RD SUITE 3A, CHILLIWACK, BC, V2R 4H2
(604) 792-0444   *SIC 5461*

CRUST CRAFT INC   *p93*
13211 146 ST NW, EDMONTON, AB, T5L 4S8
(780) 466-1333   *SIC 5461*

D'AVERSA, NINO BAKERY LIMITED   *p783*
1 TORO RD, NORTH YORK, ON, M3J 2A4
(416) 638-3271   *SIC 5461*

DIVA DELIGHTS INC   *p384*
548 KING EDWARD ST, WINNIPEG, MB, R3H 1H8
(204) 885-4376   *SIC 5461*

DR. DONUT INC   *p617*
2200 RYMAL RD E, HANNON, ON, L0R 1P0
(905) 692-3556   *SIC 5461*

DUCHESS BAKE SHOP LTD   *p95*
10718 124 ST, EDMONTON, AB, T5M 0H1
(780) 488-4999   *SIC 5461*

ELYOD INVESTMENTS LIMITED   *p860*
775 EXMOUTH ST, SARNIA, ON, N7T 5P7
(519) 332-6741   *SIC 5461*

EPIC FOOD SERVICES INC   *p231*
22987 DEWDNEY TRUNK RD, MAPLE RIDGE, BC, V2X 3K8
(604) 466-0671   *SIC 5461*

FANCY POKKET CORPORATION   *p408*
1220 ST GEORGE BLVD, MONCTON, NB, E1E 4K7
(506) 853-7299   *SIC 5461*

GOLDEN WEST BAKING COMPANY ULC   *p206*

1111 DERWENT WAY, DELTA, BC, V3M 5R4
(604) 525-2491   *SIC 5461*

GOLDILOCKS BAKE SHOP (CANADA) INC   *p321*
1606 BROADWAY W, VANCOUVER, BC, V6J 1X6
(604) 736-2464   *SIC 5461*

GRAHAM, L.G. HOLDINGS INC   *p634*
1020 OTTAWA ST N SUITE 510, KITCHENER, ON, N2A 3Z3
(519) 894-1499   *SIC 5461*

GRANDMOTHER'S PIE SHOPPE INC   *p988*
65 SAMOR RD, TORONTO, ON, M6A 1J2
(416) 782-9000   *SIC 5461*

HANLEY CORPORATION   *p491*
289 FRONT ST, BELLEVILLE, ON, K8N 2Z6
(613) 967-1771   *SIC 5461*

HKH OPPORTUNITIES INC   *p497*
118 HOLLAND ST W, BRADFORD, ON, L3Z 2B4
(905) 775-0282   *SIC 5461*

HOT OVEN BAKERY LTD, THE   *p577*
250 THE EAST MALL SUITE 285, ETOBICOKE, ON, M9B 3Y8
(416) 233-6771   *SIC 5461*

I & G BISMARKATING LTD   *p178*
2054 WHATCOM RD SUITE 1, ABBOTSFORD, BC, V3G 2K8
(604) 855-9655   *SIC 5461*

J & S HOLDINGS INC   *p365*
1040 BEAVERHILL BLVD SUITE 1, WINNIPEG, MB, R2J 4B1
(204) 255-8431   *SIC 5461*

K.M. BAKERY   *p977*
438 DUNDAS ST W, TORONTO, ON, M5T 1G7

SIC 5461

KINNIKINNICK FOODS INC   *p86*
10940 120 ST NW, EDMONTON, AB, T5H 3P7
(780) 732-7527   *SIC 5461*

LAARK ENTERPRISES LIMITED   *p1014*
516 BROCK ST N, WHITBY, ON, L1N 4J2
(905) 430-3703   *SIC 5461*

MACDONALD, R & G ENTERPRISES LIMITED   *p464*
603 REEVES ST, PORT HAWKESBURY, NS, B9A 2R8
(902) 625-1199   *SIC 5461*

MAISON DU BAGEL INC   *p1184*
263 RUE SAINT-VIATEUR O, MONTREAL, QC, H2V 1Y1
(514) 276-8044   *SIC 5461*

MAJA HOLDINGS LTD   *p443*
4 FOREST HILLS PKY SUITE 317, DARTMOUTH, NS, B2W 5G7
(902) 462-2032   *SIC 5461*

MATTCO SERVICES LIMITED   *p496*
350 WAVERLEY RD, BOWMANVILLE, ON, L1C 4Y4
(905) 623-0175   *SIC 5461*

MAXIMS BAKERY LTD   *p287*
3596 COMMERCIAL ST, VANCOUVER, BC, V5N 4E9
(604) 876-8266   *SIC 5461*

MCGLINCHEY ENTERPRISES LIMITED   *p534*
275 WATER ST N, CAMBRIDGE, ON, N1R 3B9
(519) 621-2360   *SIC 5461*

MONTREAL PITA INC   *p1218*
654 AV BEAUMONT, MONTREAL, QC, H3N 1V5
(514) 495-4513   *SIC 5461*

MORZOC INVESTMENT INC   *p884*
275 GENEVA ST, ST CATHARINES, ON, L2N 2E9
(905) 935-0071   *SIC 5461*

MULTI-MARQUES INC   *p1139*
845 RUE JEAN-MARCHAND, LEVIS, QC, G6Y 9G4
(418) 837-3611   *SIC 5461*

MURPHY, D.P. INC   *p1039*

250 BRACKLEY POINT RD, CHARLOTTETOWN, PE, C1A 6Y9
(902) 368-3727   *SIC 5461*

NATURAL BAKERY LTD   *p381*
769 HENRY AVE, WINNIPEG, MB, R3E 1V2
(204) 783-7344   *SIC 5461*

NELSON, NELSON FOODS INC   *p881*
15 QUEENSWAY E, SIMCOE, ON, N3Y 4Y2
(519) 428-0101   *SIC 5461*

OJEKA GALLERY INC   *p886*
212 WELLAND AVE, ST CATHARINES, ON, L2R 2P3
(905) 682-4129   *SIC 5461*

OTTAWA BAGEL SHOP INC   *p828*
1321 WELLINGTON ST W, OTTAWA, ON, K1Y 3B6
(613) 722-8753   *SIC 5461*

PANERA BREAD ULC   *p780*
1066 DON MILLS RD, NORTH YORK, ON, M3C 0H8
(416) 384-1116   *SIC 5461*

PEFOND INC   *p1376*
170 BOUL FISET, SOREL-TRACY, QC, J3P 3P4
(450) 742-8295   *SIC 5461*

PIONEER FOOD SERVICES LIMITED   *p524*
5100 SOUTH SERVICE RD SUITE 1, BURLINGTON, ON, L7L 6A5
(905) 333-9887   *SIC 5461*

REDPATH FOODS INC   *p261*
2560 SIMPSON RD, RICHMOND, BC, V6X 2P9
(604) 873-1393   *SIC 5461*

RIDEAU BAKERY LIMITED   *p827*
1666 BANK ST, OTTAWA, ON, K1V 7Y6
(613) 737-3355   *SIC 5461*

RYASH COFFEE CORPORATION   *p679*
9251 WOODBINE AVE, MARKHAM, ON, L6C 1Y9
(905) 887-8444   *SIC 5461*

S & K NG ENTERPRISES LTD   *p296*
158 PENDER ST E, VANCOUVER, BC, V6A 1T3
(604) 689-7835   *SIC 5461*

S. GUMPERT CO. OF CANADA LTD   *p708*
2500 TEDLO ST, MISSISSAUGA, ON, L5A 4A9
(905) 279-2600   *SIC 5461*

SNOW CAP ENTERPRISES LTD   *p181*
5698 TRAPP AVE SUITE 564, BURNABY, BC, V3N 5G4
(604) 515-3202   *SIC 5461*

SPRINGER INVESTMENTS LTD   *p413*
97 LOCH LOMOND RD, SAINT JOHN, NB, E2J 1X6
(506) 847-9168   *SIC 5461*

SWEET GALLERY EXCLUSIVE PASTRY LIMITED   *p576*
350 BERING AVE, ETOBICOKE, ON, M8Z 3A9
(416) 232-1539   *SIC 5461*

SWISS PASTRIES & DELICATESSEN OF OTTAWA LIMITED   *p595*
1423 STAR TOP RD, GLOUCESTER, ON, K1B 3W5

SIC 5461

TETI BAKERY INC   *p588*
27 SIGNAL HILL AVE SUITE 3, ETOBICOKE, ON, M9W 6V8
(416) 798-8777   *SIC 5461*

TIM HORTONS   *p26*
1185 49 AVE NE, CALGARY, AB, T2E 8V2
(403) 730-0556   *SIC 5461*

TIM HORTONS   *p38*
5A HERITAGE GATE SE, CALGARY, AB, T2H 3A7
(403) 692-6629   *SIC 5461*

TIM HORTONS   *p71*
11488 24 ST SE SUITE 400, CALGARY, AB, T2Z 4C9
(403) 236-3749   *SIC 5461*

TIM HORTONS   *p107*
9902 153 AVE NW, EDMONTON, AB, T5X 6A4

TIM HORTONS *p144*
4301 75 AVE, LLOYDMINSTER, AB, T9V 2X4
(780) 448-9722   *SIC 5461*

TIM HORTONS *p370*
2500 MAIN ST, WINNIPEG, MB, R2V 4Y1
(780) 808-2600   *SIC 5461*

TIM HORTONS *p388*
570 PEMBINA HWY, WINNIPEG, MB, R3M 2M5
(204) 334-3126   *SIC 5461*

TIM HORTONS *p411*
280 RESTIGOUCHE RD, OROMOCTO, NB, E2V 2G9
(204) 452-2531   *SIC 5461*

TIM HORTONS *p421*
8 TRANS CANADA HWY, BISHOPS FALLS, NL, A0H 1C0
(506) 446-9343   *SIC 5461*

TIM HORTONS *p492*
165 COLLEGE ST W, BELLEVILLE, ON, K8P 2G7
(709) 258-2156   *SIC 5461*

TIM HORTONS *p610*
136 KENILWORTH AVE N SUITE 130, HAMILTON, ON, L8H 4R8
(613) 967-2197   *SIC 5461*

TIM HORTONS *p623*
20945 DALTON RD, JACKSONS POINT, ON, L0E 1R0
(905) 543-1811   *SIC 5461*

TIM HORTONS *p848*
925 EDWARD ST, PRESCOTT, ON, K0E 1T0
(905) 722-7762   *SIC 5461*

TIM HORTONS *p897*
166 ONTARIO ST, STRATFORD, ON, N5A 3H4
(613) 925-1465   *SIC 5461*

TIM HORTONS *p909*
1127 OLIVER RD, THUNDER BAY, ON, P7B 7A4
(519) 273-2421   *SIC 5461*

TIM HORTONS LTD *p604*
1 NICHOLAS BEAVER RD, GUELPH, ON, N1H 6H9
(807) 344-0880   *SIC 5461*

TIM HORTONS RESTAURANTS *p1119*
1225 AUT DUPLESSIS, L'ANCIENNE-LORETTE, QC, G2G 2B4
(519) 822-4748   *SIC 5461*

UNGER FARM MARKET INC *p659*
1010 GAINSBOROUGH RD, LONDON, ON, N6H 5L4
(418) 877-0989   *SIC 5461*

UNIFILLER SYSTEMS INC *p210*
7621 MACDONALD RD, DELTA, BC, V4G 1N3
(519) 472-8126   *SIC 5461*

VEGFRESH INC *p794*
1290 ORMONT DR, NORTH YORK, ON, M9L 2V4
(604) 940-2233   *SIC 5461*

WILSON'S INVESTMENTS LIMITED *p467*
197 CHARLOTTE ST SUITE 203, SYDNEY, NS, B1P 1C4
(416) 667-0518   *SIC 5461*

YIKES ENTERPRISES LTD *p10*
3508 32 AVE NE UNIT 500, CALGARY, AB, T1Y 6J2
(902) 564-4399   *SIC 5461*

YORKDALE CAFE LTD *p923*
2377 YONGE ST SUITE 823, TORONTO, ON, M4P 2C8
(403) 291-2925   *SIC 5461*

(416) 484-4231   *SIC 5461*

SIC 5499 Miscellaneous food stores

1122630 ONTARIO LIMITED *p718*
5399 DURIE RD, MISSISSAUGA, ON, L5M 2C8
(905) 567-6457   *SIC 5499*

1148290 ONTARIO INC *p535*
95 SAGINAW PKY SUITE A, CAMBRIDGE, ON, N1T 1W2
(519) 623-1856   *SIC 5499*

1529813 ALBERTA LTD *p165*
5 GIROUX RD SUITE 420, ST. ALBERT, AB, T8N 6J8
(780) 460-7499   *SIC 5499*

1574942 ONTARIO LIMITED *p811*
1802 SIMCOE ST N, OSHAWA, ON, L1G 4X9
(905) 576-2092   *SIC 5499*

3248 KING GEORGE HWY HOLDINGS LTD *p283*
3248 KING GEORGE BLVD, SURREY, BC, V4P 1A5
(604) 541-3902   *SIC 5499*

4174071 CANADA INC *p1126*
4905 RUE FAIRWAY, LACHINE, QC, H8T 1B7
(514) 633-7455   *SIC 5499*

546073 ONTARIO LIMITED *p919*
348 DANFORTH AVE SUITE 8, TORONTO, ON, M4K 1N8
(416) 466-2129   *SIC 5499*

9020-5758 QUEBEC INC *p1108*
11 RUE EVANGELINE, GRANBY, QC, J2G 6N3
(450) 994-4794   *SIC 5499*

A. LASSONDE INC *p1343*
9420 BOUL LANGELIER, SAINT-LEONARD, QC, H1P 3H8
(514) 351-4010   *SIC 5499*

AKUNA CANADA INC *p691*
5115 SATELLITE DR, MISSISSAUGA, ON, L4W 5B6
(905) 290-0326   *SIC 5499*

ALIVE HEALTH CENTRE LTD *p259*
2680 SHELL RD SUITE 228, RICHMOND, BC, V6X 4C9
(604) 273-6266   *SIC 5499*

AMARANTH WHOLE FOODS MARKET INC *p74*
7 ARBOUR LAKE DR NW, CALGARY, AB, T3G 5G8
(403) 547-6333   *SIC 5499*

ARROWHEAD SPRING WATER LTD *p33*
5730 BURBANK RD SE, CALGARY, AB, T2H 1Z4
SIC 5499

BARIATRIX NUTRITION INC *p1127*
4905 RUE FAIRWAY, LACHINE, QC, H8T 1B7
(514) 633-7455   *SIC 5499*

BOITE A GRAINS INC, LA *p1106*
581 BOUL SAINT-JOSEPH, GATINEAU, QC, J8Y 4A6
(819) 771-3000   *SIC 5499*

BRULERIE DES MONTS INC. *p1352*
197 RUE PRINCIPALE, SAINT-SAUVEUR, QC, J0R 1R0
(450) 227-6157   *SIC 5499*

CAFE MORGANE ROYALE INC *p1387*
4945 BOUL GENE-H.-KRUGER, TROIS-RIVIERES, QC, G9A 4N5
(819) 694-1118   *SIC 5499*

CANADIAN TEST CASE 158 *p1194*
505 BOUL DE MAISONNEUVE O BUREAU 906, MONTREAL, QC, H3A 3C2
(514) 904-1496   *SIC 5499*

CANTERBURY FOOD SERVICE LTD *p192*
8080 NORTH FRASER WAY UNIT 1, BURNABY, BC, V5J 0E6
(604) 431-4400   *SIC 5499*

COMMUNITY NATURAL FOODS LTD *p34*
6120 1A ST SW, CALGARY, AB, T2H 0G3
(403) 252-0011   *SIC 5499*

COMMUNITY NATURAL FOODS LTD *p72*
1304 10 AVE SW, CALGARY, AB, T3C 0J2
(403) 930-6363   *SIC 5499*

DAMSAR INC *p1171*
8115 AV PAPINEAU, MONTREAL, QC, H2E 2H7
(514) 374-0177   *SIC 5499*

DAVIDSTEA INC *p1156*
5430 RUE FERRIER, MONT-ROYAL, QC, H4P 1M2
(514) 739-0006   *SIC 5499*

ECS COFFEE INC *p527*
3100 HARVESTER RD UNIT 6, BURLINGTON, ON, L7N 3W8
(905) 631-1524   *SIC 5499*

GENERAL NUTRITION CENTRES COMPANY *p688*
6299 AIRPORT RD SUITE 300, MISSISSAUGA, ON, L4V 1N3
(905) 612-1016   *SIC 5499*

GREENHOUSE JUICE COMPANY ULC *p990*
9 OSSINGTON AVE, TORONTO, ON, M6J 2Y8
(647) 351-0188   *SIC 5499*

GROUPE JOHANNE VERDON INC *p1181*
1274 RUE JEAN-TALON E BUREAU 200, MONTREAL, QC, H2R 1W3
(514) 272-0018   *SIC 5499*

GROUPE WESTCO INC *p416*
9 RUE WESTCO, SAINT-FRANCOIS-DE-MADAWASKA, NB, E7A 1A5
(506) 992-3112   *SIC 5499*

HEALTH VENTURES LTD *p334*
2950 DOUGLAS ST SUITE 180, VICTORIA, BC, V8T 4N4
(250) 384-3388   *SIC 5499*

HOLTMANN, J. HOLDINGS INC *p387*
106 OSBORNE ST SUITE 200, WINNIPEG, MB, R3L 1Y5
(204) 984-9561   *SIC 5499*

JARDINS VAL-MONT INC., LES *p1359*
488 AV JULES-CHOQUET, SAINTE-JULIE, QC, J3E 1W6
(450) 649-1863   *SIC 5499*

JAYCEE HERB TRADERS LTD *p606*
21 AIRPARK PL, GUELPH, ON, N1L 1B2
(519) 829-3535   *SIC 5499*

LIBERTE NATURAL FOODS INC *p1309*
5000 RUE J.-A.-BOMBARDIER, SAINT-HUBERT, QC, J3Z 1H1
(450) 926-5222   *SIC 5499*

LIQUID NUTRITION INC *p1213*
2007 RUE BISHOP, MONTREAL, QC, H3G 2E8
SIC 5499

METRO PLUS *p1076*
105 RUE PRINCIPALE, CHATEAUGUAY, QC, J6K 1G2
(450) 699-8796   *SIC 5499*

MIDEAST FOOD DISTRIBUTORS (1987) LTD *p818*
1010 BELFAST RD, OTTAWA, ON, K1G 4A2
(613) 244-2525   *SIC 5499*

MURCHIE'S TEA & COFFEE (2007) LTD *p209*
8028 RIVER WAY, DELTA, BC, V4G 1K9
(604) 231-7501   *SIC 5499*

NATURE'S EMPORIUM BULK & HEALTH FOODS LTD *p754*
16655 YONGE ST SUITE 27, NEWMARKET, ON, L3X 1V6
(905) 898-1844   *SIC 5499*

NATURE'S FARE NATURAL FOODS INC *p217*
1350 SUMMIT DR SUITE 5, KAMLOOPS, BC, V2C 1T8
(250) 314-9560   *SIC 5499*

OPTIMUM HEALTH CHOICES INC *p118*
7115 109 ST NW SUITE 2, EDMONTON, AB, T6G 1B9
(780) 432-5464   *SIC 5499*

PROVIGO DISTRIBUTION INC *p1105*
800 BOUL MALONEY O, GATINEAU, QC, J8T 3R6
(819) 561-9244   *SIC 5499*

ROMARAH INCORPORATED *p614*
1000 UPPER GAGE AVE SUITE 14, HAMILTON, ON, L8V 4R5
(905) 388-8400   *SIC 5499*

SAND HILLS COLONY *p5*
GD, BEISEKER, AB, T0M 0G0

(403) 947-2042   *SIC 5499*

TRANSPORT DIANE PICHE INC *p1118*
3862 BOUL SAINT-CHARLES, KIRKLAND, QC, H9H 3C3
(514) 693-9059   *SIC 5499*

VOLUNTEER ENTERPRISES OF THE HEALTH SCIENCES CENTRE INC *p373*
820 SHERBROOK ST SUITE MS210, WINNIPEG, MB, R3A 1R9
(204) 787-7313   *SIC 5499*

SIC 5511 New and used car dealers

0092584 B.C. LTD *p219*
1200 LEATHEAD RD, KELOWNA, BC, V1X 2K4
(250) 491-2475   *SIC 5511*

0127494 B.C. LTD *p331*
4608 27 ST, VERNON, BC, V1T 4Y6
(250) 275-4004   *SIC 5511*

045502 N. B. LTD *p412*
312 ROTHESAY AVE, SAINT JOHN, NB, E2J 2B9
(506) 634-6060   *SIC 5511*

050537 N.B. LTEE *p398*
475 RUE VICTORIA, EDMUNDSTON, NB, E3V 2K7
(506) 739-7716   *SIC 5511*

055841 NB LTD *p397*
1170 AV AVIATION, DIEPPE, NB, E1A 9A3
(506) 853-1116   *SIC 5511*

0705507 BC LTD *p219*
3260 HIGHWAY 97 N, KELOWNA, BC, V1X 5C1
(250) 491-9467   *SIC 5511*

0769510 B.C. LTD *p243*
510 DUNCAN AVE W, PENTICTON, BC, V2A 7N1
(250) 492-0100   *SIC 5511*

0794856 B.C. LTD *p243*
448 DUNCAN AVE W, PENTICTON, BC, V2A 7N1
(250) 492-0205   *SIC 5511*

0809021 B.C. LTD *p331*
6417 HWY 97, VERNON, BC, V1B 3R4
(250) 542-0371   *SIC 5511*

0859710 B.C. LTD *p219*
2767 HIGHWAY 97 N, KELOWNA, BC, V1X 4J8
(250) 448-0990   *SIC 5511*

0889541 BC LTD *p203*
1027 VICTORIA AVE N, CRANBROOK, BC, V1C 3Y6
(250) 489-4311   *SIC 5511*

1002495 B.C. LTD *p246*
2060 OXFORD CONNECTOR, PORT COQUITLAM, BC, V3C 0A4
(604) 464-3330   *SIC 5511*

1004907 ALBERTA LTD *p33*
22 HERITAGE MEADOWS RD SE, CALGARY, AB, T2H 3C1
(403) 250-4930   *SIC 5511*

1009931 ALBERTA LTD *p75*
20 FREEPORT LANDNG NE, CALGARY, AB, T3J 5H6
(403) 290-1111   *SIC 5511*

101013121 SASKATCHEWAN LTD *p1424*
730 BRAND RD, SASKATOON, SK, S7J 5J3
(306) 955-5080   *SIC 5511*

101105464 SASKATCHEWAN LTD *p1425*
635 CIRCLE DR E, SASKATOON, SK, S7K 7Y2
(306) 955-8877   *SIC 5511*

1015605 SALES LIMITED *p467*
1124 KINGS RD, SYDNEY, NS, B1S 1C8
(902) 562-1298   *SIC 5511*

1028918 ONTARIO INC *p528*
1249 GUELPH LINE, BURLINGTON, ON, L7P 2T1
(905) 335-0223   *SIC 5511*

1034250 ONTARIO LTD *p631*
401 BATH RD, KINGSTON, ON, K7M 7C9
(613) 634-4000   *SIC 5511*

1035312 ONTARIO LIMITED *p512*
190 CANAM CRES, BRAMPTON, ON, L7A 1A9
(905) 459-1810   *SIC 5511*

1042735 ONTARIO INC *p512*
15 VAN KIRK DR, BRAMPTON, ON, L7A 1W4
(905) 459-0290   *SIC 5511*

1049054 B.C. LTD. *p234*
3612 ISLAND HWY N, NANAIMO, BC, V9T 1W2
(250) 756-1515   *SIC 5511*

105262 CANADA INC *p1218*
3500 RUE JEAN-TALON O, MONTREAL, QC, H3R 2E8
(514) 739-3175   *SIC 5511*

1053038 ONTARIO LIMITED *p616*
1495 UPPER JAMES ST, HAMILTON, ON, L9B 1K2
(905) 574-8200   *SIC 5511*

1055551 ONTARIO INC *p618*
341 TUPPER ST, HAWKESBURY, ON, K6A 3T6
(613) 632-6598   *SIC 5511*

1079259 B.C. LTD *p246*
2060 OXFORD CONNECTOR, PORT CO-QUITLAM, BC, V3C 0A4
(604) 464-3330   *SIC 5511*

1083153 ONTARIO LTD *p715*
2400 MOTORWAY BLVD, MISSISSAUGA, ON, L5L 1X3
(905) 828-0070   *SIC 5511*

11084836 CANADA INC. *p1103*
1205 RUE ODILE-DAOUST, GATINEAU, QC, J8M 1Y7
(819) 986-2224   *SIC 5511*

1121121 ONTARIO INC *p762*
240 LAKESHORE DR, NORTH BAY, ON, P1A 2B6
(705) 476-5100   *SIC 5511*

1123932 ONTARIO INC *p872*
2124 LAWRENCE AVE E, SCARBOR-OUGH, ON, M1R 3A3
(416) 752-0970   *SIC 5511*

1125278 ONTARIO LTD *p788*
3180 DUFFERIN ST, NORTH YORK, ON, M6A 2T1
(416) 256-1405   *SIC 5511*

1131898 ALBERTA LTD *p146*
1450 STRACHAN RD SE, MEDICINE HAT, AB, T1B 4V2
(403) 526-3633   *SIC 5511*

1133571 ALBERTA LTD *p172*
4120 56 ST, WETASKIWIN, AB, T9A 1V3
(780) 352-2225   *SIC 5511*

11336 NEWFOUNDLAND INC *p429*
73 KENMOUNT RD, ST. JOHN'S, NL, A1B 3P8
(709) 753-4051   *SIC 5511*

1137283 ONTARIO LTD *p867*
2594 EGLINTON AVE E SUITE 2592, SCARBOROUGH, ON, M1K 2R5
(416) 266-4594   *SIC 5511*

1145678 ONTARIO LIMITED *p616*
1221 UPPER JAMES ST, HAMILTON, ON, L9C 3B2
(905) 574-8989   *SIC 5511*

1155760 ONTARIO LIMITED *p873*
5500 FINCH AVE E, SCARBOROUGH, ON, M1S 0C7
(416) 283-7100   *SIC 5511*

1166709 ONTARIO LIMITED *p498*
2250 QUEEN ST E SUITE 2000, BRAMP-TON, ON, L6S 5X9
(905) 458-7100   *SIC 5511*

1168170 ONTARIO LTD *p647*
10 DUHAMEL RD, LIVELY, ON, P3Y 1L4
(705) 692-4746   *SIC 5511*

1176356 ONTARIO INC *p809*
385 WEST ST S, ORILLIA, ON, L3V 5H2
(705) 329-4277   *SIC 5511*

1185140 ALBERTA LTD *p162*
31 AUTOMALL RD, SHERWOOD PARK, AB, T8H 0C7

(780) 410-2455   *SIC 5511*

1191460 ONTARIO INC *p907*
545 THIRTEENTH AVE, THUNDER BAY, ON, P7B 7B4
(807) 345-2552   *SIC 5511*

1197243 ONTARIO LTD *p1037*
425 BROADWAY ST, WYOMING, ON, N0N 1T0
(519) 845-3352   *SIC 5511*

1216809 ONTARIO LIMITED *p868*
1897 EGLINTON AVE E, SCARBOROUGH, ON, M1L 2L6
(416) 751-4892   *SIC 5511*

1249592 ONTARIO LTD *p872*
2110 LAWRENCE AVE E, SCARBOR-OUGH, ON, M1R 3A3
(416) 750-8885   *SIC 5511*

1263815 ONTARIO INC *p903*
7079 YONGE ST, THORNHILL, ON, L3T 2A7
(905) 763-3688   *SIC 5511*

1270477 ONTARIO INC *p815*
1556 MICHAEL ST, OTTAWA, ON, K1B 3T7
(613) 741-0337   *SIC 5511*

1341805 ONTARIO INC *p682*
1245 STEELES AVE E, MILTON, ON, L9T 0K2
(905) 875-1700   *SIC 5511*

1364279 ONTARIO INC *p597*
2559 BANK ST, GLOUCESTER, ON, K1T 1M8
(613) 736-7022   *SIC 5511*

1389984 ONTARIO INC *p690*
5525 AMBLER DR, MISSISSAUGA, ON, L4W 3Z1
(905) 602-0884   *SIC 5511*

1390835 ONTARIO INC *p978*
528 FRONT ST W SUITE 325, TORONTO, ON, M5V 1B8
(416) 703-7700   *SIC 5511*

1412873 ALBERTA LTD *p125*
1205 101 ST SW, EDMONTON, AB, T6X 1A1
(780) 486-5100   *SIC 5511*

1422718 ONTARIO INC *p485*
125 MAPLEVIEW DR W, BARRIE, ON, L4N 9H7
(705) 727-0000   *SIC 5511*

1426195 ONTARIO LIMITED *p690*
1257 EGLINTON AVE E, MISSISSAUGA, ON, L4W 1K7
(905) 629-4044   *SIC 5511*

1428309 ONTARIO LTD *p1029*
5585 HIGHWAY 7, WOODBRIDGE, ON, L4L 1T5
(877) 694-8654   *SIC 5511*

1443237 ONTARIO INC *p807*
713003 1ST LINE, ORANGEVILLE, ON, L9W 2Z2
(519) 941-9291   *SIC 5511*

1443803 ALBERTA LTD *p162*
30 AUTOMALL RD, SHERWOOD PARK, AB, T8H 2N1
(780) 417-0005   *SIC 5511*

1454615 ALBERTA LTD *p125*
830 100 ST SW, EDMONTON, AB, T6X 0S8
(780) 989-2222   *SIC 5511*

1461616 ONTARIO INC *p1017*
10280 TECUMSEH RD E, WINDSOR, ON, N8R 1A2
(519) 735-7706   *SIC 5511*

1470754 ONTARIO INC *p498*
2280 QUEEN ST E, BRAMPTON, ON, L6S 5X9
(905) 494-1000   *SIC 5511*

147766 CANADA INC *p1018*
7180 TECUMSEH RD E, WINDSOR, ON, N8T 1E6
(519) 945-8100   *SIC 5511*

1478575 ONTARIO LIMITED *p690*
5505 AMBLER DR, MISSISSAUGA, ON, L4W 3Z1
(905) 206-8886   *SIC 5511*

1497665 ONTARIO INC *p562*

1107 BROOKDALE AVE, CORNWALL, ON, K6J 4P6
(613) 933-7555   *SIC 5511*

1502026 ONTARIO LTD *p864*
80 AUTO MALL DR, SCARBOROUGH, ON, M1B 5N5
(416) 291-2929   *SIC 5511*

1511905 ONTARIO INC *p602*
359 WOODLAWN RD W, GUELPH, ON, N1H 7K9
(519) 824-9150   *SIC 5511*

1512804 ONTARIO INC *p510*
47 BOVAIRD DR W, BRAMPTON, ON, L6X 0G9
(905) 459-2600   *SIC 5511*

1527619 ONTARIO LIMITED *p1013*
5 SUNRAY ST, WHITBY, ON, L1N 8Y3
(905) 668-6881   *SIC 5511*

1543738 ONTARIO LIMITED *p905*
222 STEELES AVE W, THORNHILL, ON, L4J 1A1
(416) 221-8876   *SIC 5511*

156023 CANADA INC *p1151*
20900 CH DE LA COTE N, MIRABEL, QC, J7J 0E5
(450) 437-8000   *SIC 5511*

1583647 ALBERTA LTD *p98*
10220 184 ST NW, EDMONTON, AB, T5S 0B9
(780) 483-4024   *SIC 5511*

1607408 ONTARIO INC *p490*
720 DUNDAS ST W, BELLEVILLE, ON, K8N 4Z2
(613) 969-1166   *SIC 5511*

1633578 ONTARIO LIMITED *p906*
434 STEELES AVE W, THORNHILL, ON, L4J 6X6
(905) 889-0080   *SIC 5511*

166606 CANADA INC *p1324*
3333 CH DE LA COTE-DE-LIESSE, SAINT-LAURENT, QC, H4N 3C2
(514) 748-7777   *SIC 5511*

1673612 ONTARIO INC *p788*
3400 DUFFERIN ST, NORTH YORK, ON, M6A 2V1
(416) 789-4101   *SIC 5511*

1675001 ONTARIO LIMITED *p856*
11188 YONGE ST, RICHMOND HILL, ON, L4S 1K9
(905) 884-5100   *SIC 5511*

1681230 ONTARIO INC *p1018*
10380 TECUMSEH RD E, WINDSOR, ON, N8R 1A7
(519) 979-9900   *SIC 5511*

168360 CANADA INC *p1281*
845 RUE NOTRE-DAME BUREAU 1989, REPENTIGNY, QC, J5Y 1C4
(450) 582-3182   *SIC 5511*

1712318 ONTARIO LIMITED *p334*
2546 GOVERNMENT ST, VICTORIA, BC, V8T 4P7
(250) 385-1408   *SIC 5511*

174741 CANADA INC *p1107*
961 BOUL SAINT-JOSEPH, GATINEAU, QC, J8Z 1W8
(819) 776-6700   *SIC 5511*

174762 CANADA INC *p1107*
961 BOUL SAINT-JOSEPH, GATINEAU, QC, J8Z 1W8
(819) 776-6700   *SIC 5511*

177786 CANADA INC *p1104*
850 BOUL MALONEY O, GATINEAU, QC, J8T 3R6
(819) 568-0066   *SIC 5511*

178011 CANADA INC *p386*
3636 PORTAGE AVE, WINNIPEG, MB, R3K 0Z8
(204) 837-3636   *SIC 5511*

178023 CANADA LTD *p386*
3965 PORTAGE AVE SUITE 100, WIN-NIPEG, MB, R3K 2H4
(204) 837-4000   *SIC 5511*

1850178 ONTARIO LIMITED *p906*
7064 YONGE ST, THORNHILL, ON, L4J

1V7
(905) 882-9660   *SIC 5511*

1857-2123 QUEBEC INC *p1354*
2330 117 RTE, SAINTE-AGATHE-NORD, QC, J8C 2Z8
(819) 326-1044   *SIC 5511*

188461 CANADA INC *p1221*
7100 RUE SAINT-JACQUES, MONTREAL, QC, H4B 1V2
(514) 487-7777   *SIC 5511*

190937 CANADA LTEE *p1139*
6000 RUE DES MOISSONS, LEVIS, QC, G6Y 0Z6
(418) 830-2834   *SIC 5511*

1911661 ONTARIO INC *p498*
5 COACHWORKS CRES, BRAMPTON, ON, L6R 3Y2
(416) 981-9400   *SIC 5511*

191191 CANADA LTD *p383*
670 CENTURY ST, WINNIPEG, MB, R3H 0A1
(204) 788-1100   *SIC 5511*

1937225 NOVA SCOTIA LIMITED *p444*
224 WYSE RD, DARTMOUTH, NS, B3A 1M9
(902) 466-0086   *SIC 5511*

1971041 ONTARIO INC *p778*
1155 LESLIE ST, NORTH YORK, ON, M3C 2J6
(416) 444-4269   *SIC 5511*

1991943 ONTARIO INC *p884*
155 SCOTT ST, ST CATHARINES, ON, L2N 1H3
(888) 511-2862   *SIC 5511*

2020455 ONTARIO INC *p805*
1525 NORTH SERVICE RD W, OAKVILLE, ON, L6M 2W2
(905) 825-8777   *SIC 5511*

2031113 ONTARIO LIMITED *p785*
600 WILSON AVE, NORTH YORK, ON, M3K 1C9
(416) 741-7480   *SIC 5511*

2071848 ALBERTA LTD *p125*
1235 101 ST SW, EDMONTON, AB, T6X 1A1
(780) 462-2834   *SIC 5511*

2079608 ONTARIO INC *p1034*
1455 DUNDAS ST, WOODSTOCK, ON, N4S 7V9
(519) 537-5614   *SIC 5511*

2088941 CANADA INC *p1107*
1235 BOUL SAINT-JOSEPH, GATINEAU, QC, J8Z 3J6
(819) 776-0077   *SIC 5511*

2095008 ONTARIO INC *p682*
170 STEELES AVE E, MILTON, ON, L9T 2Y5
(905) 864-8588   *SIC 5511*

2142242 ONTARIO INC *p635*
1800 VICTORIA ST N, KITCHENER, ON, N2B 3E5
(519) 747-0269   *SIC 5511*

2145150 ONTARIO INC *p617*
150 7TH AVE, HANOVER, ON, N4N 2G9
(519) 364-1010   *SIC 5511*

2154781 CANADA LTD *p581*
25 VICE REGENT BLVD, ETOBICOKE, ON, M9W 6N2
(416) 748-2900   *SIC 5511*

2176069 ONTARIO INC *p475*
100 ACHILLES RD, AJAX, ON, L1Z 0C5
(905) 619-5522   *SIC 5511*

2177761 ONTARIO INC *p716*
2477 MOTORWAY BLVD SUITE 3, MISSIS-SAUGA, ON, L5L 3R2
(905) 828-8488   *SIC 5511*

2178320 CANADA LTD *p458*
12 LAKELANDS BLVD, HALIFAX, NS, B3S 1S8
(902) 454-2369   *SIC 5511*

2187878 NOVA SCOTIA LIMITED *p454*
2672 ROBIE ST, HALIFAX, NS, B3K 4N8
(902) 453-4115   *SIC 5511*

219 AUTOMOTIVE INC *p442*

580 PORTLAND ST, DARTMOUTH, NS, B2W 2M3
(902) 434-7700   *SIC* 5511

2194737 ONTARIO INC   *p*894
1288 MILLARD ST, STOUFFVILLE, ON, L4A 0W7
(416) 921-1288   *SIC* 5511

2207412 NOVA SCOTIA LTD   *p*442
580 PORTLAND ST, DARTMOUTH, NS, B2W 2M3
(902) 434-4000   *SIC* 5511

2231737 NOVA SCOTIA LIMITED   *p*471
45 STARRS RD, YARMOUTH, NS, B5A 2T2
(902) 742-7191   *SIC* 5511

2232556 ONTARIO INC   *p*920
11 SUNLIGHT PARK RD, TORONTO, ON, M4M 1B5
(416) 623-6464   *SIC* 5511

2248085 ONTARIO INC   *p*691
5500 DIXIE RD, MISSISSAUGA, ON, L4W 4N3
(905) 238-7188   *SIC* 5511

2275510 ONTARIO LTD   *p*656
35 SOUTHDALE RD E, LONDON, ON, N6C 4X5
(519) 668-0600   *SIC* 5511

2310884 ONTARIO INC   *p*831
350 WEST HUNT CLUB RD, OTTAWA, ON, K2E 1A5
(613) 688-6000   *SIC* 5511

2311390 ONTARIO INC   *p*622
2484 DORAL DR, INNISFIL, ON, L9S 0A3
(705) 431-9393   *SIC* 5511

2333-2224 QUEBEC INC   *p*1265
2400 AV DALTON, QUEBEC, QC, G1P 3X1
(418) 654-9292   *SIC* 5511

2394748 ONTARIO INC   *p*855
9144 YONGE ST, RICHMOND HILL, ON, L4C 7A1
(905) 763-3688   *SIC* 5511

2410147 ONTARIO INC   *p*691
4505 DIXIE RD, MISSISSAUGA, ON, L4W 5K3
(905) 625-7533   *SIC* 5511

242747 ONTARIO LIMITED   *p*658
680 OXFORD ST W, LONDON, ON, N6H 1T9
(519) 472-4890   *SIC* 5511

2445120 ONTARIO INC   *p*631
1412 BATH RD, KINGSTON, ON, K7M 4X6
(613) 817-1808   *SIC* 5511

2449616 ONTARIO INC   *p*894
35 AUTOMALL BLVD, STOUFFVILLE, ON, L4A 0W7
(289) 451-0087   *SIC* 5511

2463103 NOVA SCOTIA LTD   *p*442
7181 HIGHWAY 1, COLDBROOK, NS, B4R 1A2
(902) 678-2155   *SIC* 5511

2486535 ONTARIO LTD   *p*578
2000 THE QUEENSWAY, ETOBICOKE, ON, M9C 5H5
(416) 913-5780   *SIC* 5511

2489736 ONTARIO LIMITED   *p*855
10414 YONGE ST, RICHMOND HILL, ON, L4C 3C3
(905) 780-9999   *SIC* 5511

2494719 ONTARIO INC   *p*1018
10980 TECUMSEH RD E, WINDSOR, ON, N8R 1A8
(519) 956-7700   *SIC* 5511

2507246 ONTARIO INC   *p*802
2270 SOUTH SERVICE RD W, OAKVILLE, ON, L6L 5M9
(905) 827-7191   *SIC* 5511

2508046 ONTARIO LTD   *p*847
50 BENSON CRT, PORT HOPE, ON, L1A 3V6
(905) 885-6421   *SIC* 5511

2527-9829 QUEBEC INC   *p*1375
4367 BOUL BOURQUE, SHERBROOKE, QC, J1N 1S4
(819) 564-1600   *SIC* 5511

2531-7504 QUEBEC INC   *p*1104

850 BOUL MALONEY O, GATINEAU, QC, J8T 3R6
(819) 568-0066   *SIC* 5511

2552-4018 QUEBEC INC   *p*1085
2480 BOUL CURE-LABELLE, COTE SAINT-LUC, QC, H7T 1R1
(450) 682-6000   *SIC* 5511

2585693 ONTARIO INC   *p*787
1681 EGLINTON AVE E SUITE 1671, NORTH YORK, ON, M4A 1J6
(416) 752-6666   *SIC* 5511

2625-2106 QUEBEC INC   *p*1354
155 BOUL NORBERT-MORIN, SAINTE-AGATHE-DES-MONTS, QC, J8C 3M2
(819) 326-1600   *SIC* 5511

2634912 ONTARIO INC   *p*856
11262 YONGE ST, RICHMOND HILL, ON, L4S 1K9
(905) 770-0005   *SIC* 5511

2709970 CANADA INC   *p*1147
2500 RUE SHERBROOKE, MAGOG, QC, J1X 4E8
(819) 843-9883   *SIC* 5511

2732-2304 QUEBEC INC   *p*1288
1225 AV LARIVIERE, ROUYN-NORANDA, QC, J9X 6M6
(819) 762-6565   *SIC* 5511

2734-7681 QUEBEC INC   *p*1104
850 BOUL MALONEY O, GATINEAU, QC, J8T 3R6
(819) 568-0066   *SIC* 5511

2782677 CANADA INC   *p*1058
1053 BOUL DU CURE-LABELLE, BLAINVILLE, QC, J7C 2M2
(450) 434-5484   *SIC* 5511

2846-3826 QUEBEC INC   *p*1284
210 AV LEONIDAS S, RIMOUSKI, QC, G5L 2T2
(418) 722-6633   *SIC* 5511

2848-7403 QUEBEC INC   *p*1058
700 BOUL DU CURE-LABELLE, BLAINVILLE, QC, J7C 2J6
(450) 435-1122   *SIC* 5511

2853167 CANADA INC   *p*529
2016 PLAINS RD E, BURLINGTON, ON, L7R 5B3
(905) 633-8811   *SIC* 5511

2864-4920 QUEBEC INC   *p*1364
120 BOUL DESJARDINS E, SAINTE-THERESE, QC, J7E 1C8
(450) 435-3685   *SIC* 5511

2938286 CANADA INC   *p*1142
60 BOUL ROLAND-THERRIEN, LONGUEUIL, QC, J4H 3V8
(450) 928-2000   *SIC* 5511

2945-9344 QUEBEC INC   *p*1063
1540 RUE AMPERE, BOUCHERVILLE, QC, J4B 7L4
(450) 449-7929   *SIC* 5511

294557 ALBERTA LTD   *p*6
GD STN MAIN, BONNYVILLE, AB, T9N 2J6
(780) 826-3278   *SIC* 5511

2948-7659 QUEBEC INC   *p*1075
411 BOUL SAINT-FRANCIS, CHATEAU-GUAY, QC, J6J 1Z6
(450) 699-8555   *SIC* 5511

2955-4201 QUEBEC INC   *p*1375
4620 BOUL BOURQUE, SHERBROOKE, QC, J1N 2A8
(819) 821-9272   *SIC* 5511

2960-7082 QUEBEC INC   *p*1393
115 RUE JOSEPH-CARRIER, VAUDREUIL-DORION, QC, J7V 5V5
(450) 455-5555   *SIC* 5511

2970-7528 QUEBEC INC   *p*1300
625 RUE DUBOIS, SAINT-EUSTACHE, QC, J7P 3W1
(450) 472-7272   *SIC* 5511

2972344 CANADA INC   *p*1144
900 RUE SAINT-LAURENT O, LONGUEUIL, QC, J4K 1C5
(450) 674-7474   *SIC* 5511

3039214 NOVA SCOTIA LIMITED   *p*454
3625 KEMPT RD, HALIFAX, NS, B3K 4X6

(902) 454-1000   *SIC* 5511

3041000 CANADA INC   *p*1107
951 BOUL SAINT-JOSEPH, GATINEAU, QC, J8Z 1S8
(819) 777-2611   *SIC* 5511

3041518 NOVA SCOTIA LIMITED   *p*454
3773 WINDSOR ST, HALIFAX, NS, B3K 0A2
(902) 453-1130   *SIC* 5511

3067419 NOVA SCOTIA LIMITED   *p*442
15 LANSING CRT, DARTMOUTH, NS, B2W 0K3
(902) 462-6600   *SIC* 5511

307711 ALBERTA LTD   *p*156
1824 49 AVE, RED DEER, AB, T4R 2N7
(403) 347-7700   *SIC* 5511

3100-8410 QUEBEC INC   *p*1110
1165 RUE PRINCIPALE, GRANBY, QC, J2J 0M3
(450) 994-4220   *SIC* 5511

3188192 NOVA SCOTIA INCORPORATED   *p*459
971 PARK ST, KENTVILLE, NS, B4N 3X1
(902) 678-3323   *SIC* 5511

3213695 NOVA SCOTIA LIMITED   *p*463
300 WESTVILLE RD, NEW GLASGOW, NS, B2H 2J5
(902) 752-8321   *SIC* 5511

3248224 CANADA INC   *p*1104
1255 BOUL LA VERENDRYE O, GATINEAU, QC, J8T 8K2
(819) 568-4646   *SIC* 5511

3278724 NOVA SCOTIA LIMITED   *p*468
126 MAIN ST, TRURO, NS, B2N 4G9
(902) 897-1700   *SIC* 5511

328633 BC LTD   *p*271
19265 LANGLEY BYPASS, SURREY, BC, V3S 6K1
(604) 534-0181   *SIC* 5511

3286509 CANADA INC   *p*1311
450 RUE DANIEL-JOHNSON E, SAINT-HYACINTHE, QC, J2S 8W5
(450) 774-1679   *SIC* 5511

3302775 NOVA SCOTIA LTD   *p*441
15133 HEBBVILLE RD, BRIDGEWATER, NS, B4V 2W4
(902) 543-2493   *SIC* 5511

330542 BC LTD   *p*252
259 MCLEAN ST, QUESNEL, BC, V2J 2N8
(250) 992-9293   *SIC* 5511

3347818 CANADA INC   *p*1120
12 BOUL DON-QUICHOTTE, L'ILE-PERROT, QC, J7V 6N5
(514) 425-2255   *SIC* 5511

3370160 CANADA INC   *p*1281
839 RUE NOTRE-DAME, REPENTIGNY, QC, J5Y 1C4
(450) 654-7111   *SIC* 5511

351684 BC LTD   *p*331
6425 HWY 97, VERNON, BC, V1B 3R4
(250) 545-0531   *SIC* 5511

3566072 CANADA INC   *p*1214
1920 RUE SAINTE-CATHERINE O, MONTREAL, QC, H3H 1M4
(514) 937-7777   *SIC* 5511

3588025 CANADA INC   *p*1093
2291 PLACE TRANSCANADIENNE, DOR-VAL, QC, H9P 2X7
(514) 683-3880   *SIC* 5511

3595650 CANADA INC   *p*1107
1135 BOUL SAINT-JOSEPH, GATINEAU, QC, J8Z 1W8
(819) 770-7768   *SIC* 5511

3617581 CANADA INC   *p*1104
346 BOUL GREBER, GATINEAU, QC, J8T 5R6
(819) 561-6669   *SIC* 5511

3652548 CANADA INC   *p*1311
3400 AV CUSSON, SAINT-HYACINTHE, QC, J2S 8N9
(450) 774-1332   *SIC* 5511

3725766 CANADA INC   *p*1047
7050 BOUL HENRI-BOURASSA E, ANJOU, QC, H1E 7K7
(514) 354-7901   *SIC* 5511

3725839 CANADA INC   *p*1092
4600B BOUL SAINT-JEAN, DOLLARD-DES-ORMEAUX, QC, H9H 2A6
(514) 624-7777   *SIC* 5511

3729451 CANADA INC   *p*1125
230 BOUL MONTREAL-TORONTO, LA-CHINE, QC, H8S 1B8
(514) 637-1155   *SIC* 5511

388010 ALBERTA LTD   *p*157
142 LEVA AVE, RED DEER COUNTY, AB, T4E 1B9
(403) 342-2923   *SIC* 5511

401 DIXIE NISSAN LTD   *p*691
5500 DIXIE RD UNIT B, MISSISSAUGA, ON, L4W 4N3
(905) 238-5500   *SIC* 5511

401 TRUCKSOURCE INC   *p*663
4293 COUNTY RD 46, MAIDSTONE, ON, N0R 1K0
(519) 737-6956   *SIC* 5511

405 AUTO SALES INC   *p*532
227 HESPELER RD, CAMBRIDGE, ON, N1R 3H8
(519) 623-5991   *SIC* 5511

405-4547 CANADA INC   *p*1220
6100 BOUL DECARIE, MONTREAL, QC, H3X 2J8
(514) 342-2222   *SIC* 5511

4093640 CANADA INC   *p*1085
2350 BOUL CHOMEDEY, COTE SAINT-LUC, QC, H7T 2W3
(450) 682-3336   *SIC* 5511

41068 TORONTO HYUNDAI   *p*989
2460 DUFFERIN ST, TORONTO, ON, M6E 3T3
(416) 787-9789   *SIC* 5511

4134320 CANADA INC   *p*1285
379 BOUL ARTHUR-BUIES E, RIMOUSKI, QC, G5M 0C7
(418) 724-5180   *SIC* 5511

414067 B.C. LTD   *p*227
20622 LANGLEY BYPASS, LANGLEY, BC, V3A 6K8
(604) 530-3156   *SIC* 5511

415841 ONTARIO LIMITED   *p*989
2000 EGLINTON AVE W, TORONTO, ON, M6E 2J9
(416) 751-1530   *SIC* 5511

417 COLLISION CENTER   *p*594
1599 STAR TOP RD, GLOUCESTER, ON, K1B 5P5
(613) 749-8382   *SIC* 5511

417 INFINITI NISSAN LTD   *p*594
1599 STAR TOP RD, GLOUCESTER, ON, K1B 5P5
(613) 749-9417   *SIC* 5511

421342 ONTARIO LIMITED   *p*631
775 GARDINERS RD, KINGSTON, ON, K7M 7H8
(613) 384-2531   *SIC* 5511

4236009 MANITOBA LTD   *p*348
1445 18TH ST N SUITE 1445, BRANDON, MB, R7C 1A6
(204) 728-8554   *SIC* 5511

4247728 CANADA INC   *p*691
1600 TOYO CIRCLE, MISSISSAUGA, ON, L4W 0E7
(905) 238-6000   *SIC* 5511

4247744 CANADA INC   *p*691
1700 TOYO CIR, MISSISSAUGA, ON, L4W 0E7
(905) 816-4200   *SIC* 5511

425507 ALBERTA LTD   *p*150
100 NORTHGATE BLVD, OKOTOKS, AB, T1S 0H9
(403) 842-1100   *SIC* 5511

4259891 CANADA LTD   *p*617
2260 RYMAL RD E, HANNON, ON, L0R 1P0
(905) 528-7001   *SIC* 5511

4335325 CANADA INC   *p*1241
1530 BOUL CHOMEDEY, MONTREAL-OUEST, QC, H7V 3N8
(450) 680-1000   *SIC* 5511

435809 B.C. LTD   *p*219

2580 ENTERPRISE WAY, KELOWNA, BC, V1X 7X5

(250) 712-0505 *SIC* 5511

440 CHEVROLET BUICK GMC LTEE *p1085*
3670 SUD LAVAL (A-440) O, COTE SAINT-LUC, QC, H7T 2H6

(450) 682-3670 *SIC* 5511

4427378 CANADA INC *p1074*
830 BOUL DE PERIGNY, CHAMBLY, QC, J3L 1W3

(450) 658-6623 *SIC* 5511

4475518 CANADA INC *p618*
455 COUNTY RD 17, HAWKESBURY, ON, K6A 3R4

(613) 632-5222 *SIC* 5511

4486404 CANADA INC *p1300*
312 RUE DUBOIS, SAINT-EUSTACHE, QC, J7P 4W9

(450) 623-8977 *SIC* 5511

4486404 CANADA INC. *p1074*
840 BOUL DE PERIGNY, CHAMBLY, QC, J3L 1W3

(450) 447-6699 *SIC* 5511

4544391 CANADA INC *p1104*
1299 BOUL LA VERENDRYE O, GATINEAU, QC, J8T 8K2

(819) 243-5454 *SIC* 5511

465912 ONTARIO INC *p760*
343 AIRPORT RD, NIAGARA ON THE LAKE, ON, L0S 1J0

(905) 682-1711 *SIC* 5511

498326 ONTARIO LIMITED *p920*
677 QUEEN ST E, TORONTO, ON, M4M 1G6

(416) 465-5471 *SIC* 5511

501548 ONTARIO LTD *p830*
955 RICHMOND RD, OTTAWA, ON, K2B 6R1

(613) 726-0333 *SIC* 5511

502386 ALBERTA LTD *p10*
888 MERIDIAN RD NE, CALGARY, AB, T2A 2N8

(403) 291-1444 *SIC* 5511

504147 ALBERTA LTD *p33*
34 HERITAGE MEADOWS RD SE, CALGARY, AB, T2H 3C1

(403) 253-0338 *SIC* 5511

504148 ALBERTA INC *p38*
11700 LAKE FRASER DR SE, CALGARY, AB, T2J 7J5

(403) 253-6531 *SIC* 5511

530664 ALBERTA LTD *p131*
13116 100 ST SUITE 780, GRANDE PRAIRIE, AB, T8V 4H9

(780) 532-8010 *SIC* 5511

547121 ONTARIO LTD *p496*
380 ECCLESTONE DR, BRACEBRIDGE, ON, P1L 1R1

(705) 645-8763 *SIC* 5511

548050 ONTARIO INC *p631*
1388 BATH RD, KINGSTON, ON, K7M 4X6

(613) 546-2211 *SIC* 5511

551546 ALBERTA LTD *p151*
6207 46 ST, OLDS, AB, T4H 1L7

(403) 556-7332 *SIC* 5511

564205 ONTARIO INC *p839*
1370 CHEMONG RD, PETERBOROUGH, ON, K9H 0E7

(705) 876-6591 *SIC* 5511

583455 SASKATCHEWAN LTD *p1419*
700 BROAD ST, REGINA, SK, S4R 8H7

(306) 522-2222 *SIC* 5511

587577 ALBERTA LIMITED *p72*
909 15 ST SW, CALGARY, AB, T3C 1E5

(403) 232-6400 *SIC* 5511

588388 ALBERTA LTD *p40*
4849 NORTHLAND DR NW, CALGARY, AB, T2L 2K3

(403) 286-4849 *SIC* 5511

591226 SASKATCHEWAN LTD *p1425*
110A CIRCLE DR E, SASKATOON, SK, S7K 4K1

(306) 373-7477 *SIC* 5511

598755 B.C. LTD *p227*

20257 LANGLEY BYPASS, LANGLEY, BC, V3A 6K9

(604) 539-2111 *SIC* 5511

598840 SASKATCHEWAN LTD *p1411*
1788 MAIN ST N, MOOSE JAW, SK, S6J 1L4

(306) 692-1808 *SIC* 5511

604329 SASKATCHEWAN LTD *p1420*
444 BROAD ST, REGINA, SK, S4R 1X3

(306) 525-8848 *SIC* 5511

609173 N.B. LTD *p402*
1165 HANWELL RD, FREDERICTON, NB, E3C 1A5

(506) 450-0800 *SIC* 5511

612111 NB LTD *p402*
505 BISHOP DR, FREDERICTON, NB, E3C 2M6

(506) 454-3634 *SIC* 5511

614568 ALBERTA LTD *p10*
1100 MERIDIAN RD NE, CALGARY, AB, T2A 2N9

(403) 571-3077 *SIC* 5511

617274 SASKATCHEWAN LTD *p1411*
1743 MAIN ST N, MOOSE JAW, SK, S6J 1L6

(306) 694-1355 *SIC* 5511

621509 ONTARIO INC *p490*
658 DUNDAS ST W, BELLEVILLE, ON, K8N 4Z2

(613) 966-9936 *SIC* 5511

625974 SASKATCHEWAN LTD *p1431*
2035 IDYLWYLD DR N, SASKATOON, SK, S7L 4R3

(306) 664-6767 *SIC* 5511

6304966 CANADA INC *p1085*
3475 BOUL LE CARREFOUR, COTE SAINT-LUC, QC, H7T 3A3

(450) 688-1880 *SIC* 5511

6358101 CANADA INC *p1106*
7 BOUL DU CASINO, GATINEAU, QC, J8Y 6V7

(819) 777-1771 *SIC* 5511

636066 ALBERTA LTD *p146*
16 STRACHAN CRT SE, MEDICINE HAT, AB, T1B 4R7

(403) 526-0626 *SIC* 5511

638691 ONTARIO LIMITED *p846*
658 MAIN ST W, PORT COLBORNE, ON, L3K 5V4

(905) 835-8120 *SIC* 5511

641100 ALBERTA LTD *p80*
544 RAILWAY ST W, COCHRANE, AB, T4C 2E2

(403) 932-4072 *SIC* 5511

646371 B.C. LTD *p216*
1355 CARIBOO PL, KAMLOOPS, BC, V2C 5Z3

(250) 828-7966 *SIC* 5511

650124 ONTARIO LIMITED *p485*
261 MAPLEVIEW DR W, BARRIE, ON, L4N 9E8

(705) 737-3440 *SIC* 5511

699215 ONTARIO LIMITED *p605*
949 WOODLAWN RD W, GUELPH, ON, N1K 1C9

(519) 837-3020 *SIC* 5511

709226 ONTARIO LIMITED *p748*
370 WEST HUNT CLUB RD, NEPEAN, ON, K2E 1A5

(613) 523-9951 *SIC* 5511

715837 ONTARIO INC *p1013*
1520 DUNDAS ST E, WHITBY, ON, L1N 2K7

(905) 430-2351 *SIC* 5511

724053 ALBERTA LTD *p74*
125 CROWFOOT WAY NW, CALGARY, AB, T3G 2R2

(403) 239-6677 *SIC* 5511

724412 ONTARIO LIMITED *p597*
2555 BANK ST, GLOUCESTER, ON, K1T 1M8

(613) 526-5202 *SIC* 5511

7255721 CANADA INC *p1395*
1003 BOUL RENE-LEVESQUE, VERDUN,

QC, H3E 0B2

(514) 769-3555 *SIC* 5511

734393 ONTARIO LIMITED *p518*
555 STEWART BLVD, BROCKVILLE, ON, K6V 7H2

(613) 342-9111 *SIC* 5511

75040 MANITOBA LTD *p390*
1717 WAVERLEY ST UNIT 900, WINNIPEG, MB, R3T 6A9

(204) 261-9580 *SIC* 5511

7531877 CANADA LTEE *p1103*
1265 RUE ODILE-DAOUST, GATINEAU, QC, J8M 1Y7

(819) 281-7788 *SIC* 5511

7618280 CANADA INC *p1103*
1255 RUE ODILE-DAOUST, GATINEAU, QC, J8M 1Y7

(819) 281-1110 *SIC* 5511

765620 ONTARIO INC *p691*
5500 DIXIE RD UNIT F, MISSISSAUGA, ON, L4W 4N3

(905) 238-9888 *SIC* 5511

765620 ONTARIO INC *p830*
955 RICHMOND RD, OTTAWA, ON, K2B 6R1

(613) 726-0333 *SIC* 5511

767405 ALBERTA LTD *p98*
10220 170 ST NW, EDMONTON, AB, T5S 1N9

(780) 420-1111 *SIC* 5511

771922 ALBERTA INC *p20*
1211 CENTRE ST NW, CALGARY, AB, T2E 2R3

(403) 930-0610 *SIC* 5511

798983 ONTARIO INC *p639*
663 VICTORIA ST N, KITCHENER, ON, N2H 5G3

SIC 5511

805658 ONTARIO INC *p520*
4100 HARVESTER RD SUITE 1, BURLINGTON, ON, L7L 0C1

(905) 632-5371 *SIC* 5511

8421722 CANADA INC *p1112*
4844 BOUL TASCHEREAU, GREENFIELD PARK, QC, J4V 2J2

(450) 672-2720 *SIC* 5511

845453 ONTARIO LTD *p618*
959 MCGILL ST, HAWKESBURY, ON, K6A 3K8

(613) 632-4125 *SIC* 5511

859689 ONTARIO INC *p884*
158 SCOTT ST, ST CATHARINES, ON, L2N 1H1

SIC 5511

862390 ONTARIO INC *p898*
1035 FALCONBRIDGE RD, SUDBURY, ON, P3A 4M9

(705) 560-6625 *SIC* 5511

864475 ALBERTA LTD *p98*
10151 179 ST NW, EDMONTON, AB, T5S 1P9

(780) 444-8645 *SIC* 5511

8863377 CANADA INC *p1247*
12277 BOUL METROPOLITAIN E, POINTE-AUX-TREMBLES, QC, H1B 5R3

(514) 645-1694 *SIC* 5511

894812 ONTARIO INC *p681*
806 KING ST, MIDLAND, ON, L4R 0B8

(705) 526-6640 *SIC* 5511

898984 ONTARIO INC *p855*
10427 YONGE ST SUITE 2, RICHMOND HILL, ON, L4C 3C2

SIC 5511

9003-4406 QUEBEC INC *p1285*
169 BOUL SAINTE-ANNE, RIMOUSKI, QC, G5M 1C3

(418) 725-0911 *SIC* 5511

9014-5467 QUEBEC INC *p1080*
2315 BOUL SAINT-PAUL, CHICOUTIMI, QC, G7K 1E5

(418) 543-6477 *SIC* 5511

9020-7697 QUEBEC INC *p1361*
250 BOUL CURE-LABELLE, SAINTE-ROSE, QC, H7L 3A2

SIC 5511

9027-9118 QUEBEC INC *p1389*
3115 BOUL SAINT-JEAN, TROIS-RIVIERES, QC, G9B 2M3

(819) 377-7500 *SIC* 5511

9039-4735 QUEBEC INC *p1069*
9100 BOUL TASCHEREAU, BROSSARD, QC, J4X 1C3

(450) 659-1616 *SIC* 5511

9039-7571 QUEBEC INC *p1069*
9425 BOUL TASCHEREAU, BROSSARD, QC, J4Y 2J3

(450) 659-6688 *SIC* 5511

9039-8082 QUEBEC INC *p1247*
12150 RUE SHERBROOKE E, POINTE-AUX-TREMBLES, QC, H1B 1C7

(514) 645-6700 *SIC* 5511

9042-0209 QUEBEC INC *p1343*
5625 BOUL METROPOLITAIN E, SAINT-LEONARD, QC, H1P 1X3

(514) 362-2872 *SIC* 5511

9045-4604 QUEBEC INC *p1097*
1200 BOUL RENE-LEVESQUE, DRUMMONDVILLE, QC, J2C 5W4

(819) 474-3930 *SIC* 5511

9056-4725 QUEBEC INC *p1045*
1151 111 RTE E, AMOS, QC, J9T 1N2

(819) 732-7000 *SIC* 5511

9075-5125 QUEBEC INC *p1044*
2625 AV DU PONT S BUREAU 1, ALMA, QC, G8B 5V2

(418) 480-4776 *SIC* 5511

9080-3404 QUEBEC INC *p1239*
6464 BOUL HENRI-BOURASSA E, MONTREAL-NORD, QC, H1G 5W9

(514) 256-1010 *SIC* 5511

9085327 CANADA INC *p1282*
225 BOUL BRIEN, REPENTIGNY, QC, J6A 6M4

(450) 585-5824 *SIC* 5511

9096-9080 QUEBEC INC *p1069*
8450 BOUL TASCHEREAU, BROSSARD, QC, J4X 1C2

(450) 466-0999 *SIC* 5511

9097-8875 QUEBEC INC *p1355*
671 RUE PRINCIPALE, SAINTE-ANNE-DE-LA-PERADE, QC, G0X 2J0

(418) 325-2444 *SIC* 5511

9101-2468 QUEBEC INC *p1375*
5119 BOUL BOURQUE, SHERBROOKE, QC, J1N 2K6

(819) 564-8664 *SIC* 5511

9106-3644 QUEBEC INC *p1110*
1289 RUE PRINCIPALE, GRANBY, QC, J2J 0M3

(450) 372-2007 *SIC* 5511

9118-8706 QUEBEC INC *p1254*
585 RUE CLEMENCEAU, QUEBEC, QC, G1C 7Z9

(418) 667-3131 *SIC* 5511

9119-8523 QUEBEC INC *p1069*
9200 BOUL TASCHEREAU, BROSSARD, QC, J4X 1C3

(450) 465-3200 *SIC* 5511

9122-4568 QUEBEC INC *p1097*
10 RUE CORMIER, DRUMMONDVILLE, QC, J2C 0L4

(819) 477-1777 *SIC* 5511

9122-8171 QUEBEC INC *p1088*
165 RUE DE SALABERRY, COWANSVILLE, QC, J2K 5G9

(450) 263-8888 *SIC* 5511

9123-2165 QUEBEC INC *p1072*
185 BOUL DE L'INDUSTRIE, CANDIAC, QC, J5R 1J4

(450) 659-6511 *SIC* 5511

9127-7509 QUEBEC INC *p1081*
151 116 RTE, CLEVELAND, QC, J0B 2H0

(819) 826-5923 *SIC* 5511

9146-3000 QUEBEC INC *p1364*
120 BOUL DESJARDINS E, SAINTE-THERESE, QC, J7E 1C8

(450) 435-3685 *SIC* 5511

9151-8100 QUEBEC INC *p1294*

▲ Public Company ■ Public Company Family Member **HQ** Headquarters **BR** Branch **SL** Single Location

141 BOUL SIR-WILFRID-LAURIER, SAINT-BASILE-LE-GRAND, QC, J3N 1M2

(450) 653-1003   SIC 5511

9153-7639 QUEBEC INC   p1263
1600 RUE CYRILLE-DUQUET, QUEBEC, QC, G1N 2E5

(418) 654-2929   SIC 5511

9171-1440 QUEBEC INC.   p1090
42 BOUL SAINT-MICHEL, DOLBEAU-MISTASSINI, QC, G8L 5J3

(418) 276-6511   SIC 5511

9180-6166 QUEBEC INC   p1281
1507 BOUL PIE-XI S, QUEBEC, QC, G3K 1Y1

(418) 845-6060   SIC 5511

9182-2452 QUEBEC INC   p1261
215 RUE ETIENNE-DUBREUIL, QUEBEC, QC, G1M 4A6

(418) 681-5000   SIC 5511

9204-6424 QUEBEC INC   p1367
5570 BOUL ROYAL, SHAWINIGAN, QC, G9N 4R8

(819) 539-8333   SIC 5511

9207-8922 QUEBEC INC   p1394
29 BOUL DE LA CITE-DES-JEUNES, VAUDREUIL-DORION, QC, J7V 0N3

(450) 455-7941   SIC 5511

9211-6409 QUEBEC INC   p1075
33 BOUL SAINT-JEAN-BAPTISTE, CHATEAUGUAY, QC, J6J 3H5

(450) 699-9000   SIC 5511

9218-8069 QUEBEC INC   p1139
5990 BOUL WILFRID-CARRIER, LEVIS, QC, G6Y 9X9

(418) 837-9199   SIC 5511

9220-3785 QUEBEC INC   p1279
4901 BOUL DES GALERIES, QUEBEC, QC, G2K 1X1

(418) 622-8180   SIC 5511

9229-3786 QUEBEC INC   p1355
671 RUE PRINCIPALE, SAINTE-ANNE-DE-LA-PERADE, QC, G0X 2J0

(418) 325-2444   SIC 5511

9264-1711 QUEBEC INC   p1151
179 BOUL SAINT-JEAN-BAPTISTE, MERCIER, QC, J6R 2C1

(450) 844-7888   SIC 5511

9268-8241 QUEBEC INC   p1158
230 RUE DE SAINT-JOVITE BUREAU 229, MONT-TREMBLANT, QC, J8E 2Z9

(819) 425-3711   SIC 5511

9274-8706 QUEBEC INC   p1063
5740 BOUL SAINTE-ANNE, BOISCHATEL, QC, G0A 1H0

(418) 822-2424   SIC 5511

9308-3152 QUEBEC INC   p1367
10303 BOUL DES HETRES, SHAWINIGAN, QC, G9N 4Y2

(819) 539-5457   SIC 5511

9308-5934 QUEBEC INC   p1384
300 RUE VACHON, TROIS-RIVIERES, QC, G8T 8Y2

(819) 691-3025   SIC 5511

9311-9089 QUEBEC INC   p1281
1459 BOUL PIE-XI S, QUEBEC, QC, G3K 0P8

(418) 767-2500   SIC 5511

9351-8371 QUEBEC INC   p1295
1905 BOUL SIR-WILFRID-LAURIER, SAINT-BRUNO, QC, J3V 0G8

(450) 653-1553   SIC 5511

942599 ONTARIO LIMITED   p593
316 GUELPH ST, GEORGETOWN, ON, L7G 4B5

(905) 873-1818   SIC 5511

949043 ONTARIO INC   p473
500 BAYLY ST W, AJAX, ON, L1S 4G6

(905) 686-0555   SIC 5511

953866 ONTARIO LIMITED   p754
17735 LESLIE ST, NEWMARKET, ON, L3Y 3E3

(905) 898-2721   SIC 5511

965515 ALBERTA LTD   p98
17920 100 AVE NW SUITE SIDE, EDMON-

TON, AB, T5S 2T6

(780) 481-0924   SIC 5511

967210 ALBERTA LTD   p20
2256 23 ST NE, CALGARY, AB, T2E 8N3

(403) 250-2502   SIC 5511

967530 ALBERTA LTD   p112
9820 34 AVE NW, EDMONTON, AB, T6E 6L1

(780) 989-8888   SIC 5511

967961 ONTARIO LIMITED   p754
349 MULOCK DR, NEWMARKET, ON, L3Y 5W2

(416) 798-7877   SIC 5511

969642 ALBERTA LIMITED   p69
14750 5 ST SW, CALGARY, AB, T2Y 2E7

(403) 256-4788   SIC 5511

979094 ALBERTA LTD   p112
9605 34 AVE NW, EDMONTON, AB, T6E 5W8

(780) 465-5252   SIC 5511

982874 ONTARIO LIMITED   p716
3045 GLEN ERIN DR, MISSISSAUGA, ON, L5L 1J3

(905) 828-5923   SIC 5511

982875 ONTARIO LIMITED   p637
44 ALPINE RD, KITCHENER, ON, N2E 1A1

(519) 749-1314   SIC 5511

985178 ONTARIO INC   p512
30 VAN KIRK DR, BRAMPTON, ON, L7A 2Y4

(905) 454-1434   SIC 5511

990550 ONTARIO INC   p659
766 WHARNCLIFFE RD S, LONDON, ON, N6J 2N4

(519) 685-2277   SIC 5511

998699 ALBERTA LTD   p33
168 GLENDEER CIR SE, CALGARY, AB, T2H 2V4

(403) 253-6800   SIC 5511

AAA PRECISION TIRE AND AUTOMOTIVE   p425
86 CLYDE AVE, MOUNT PEARL, NL, A1N 4S2

(709) 747-9595   SIC 5511

AB COX AUTOMOTIVE LTD   p480
305 WELLINGTON ST E, AURORA, ON, L4G 6C3

(905) 841-2121   SIC 5511

ABBOTSFORD CHRYSLER DODGE JEEP RAM LTD   p176
30285 AUTOMALL DR, ABBOTSFORD, BC, V2T 5M1

(604) 857-1000   SIC 5511

ABBOTSFORD NISSAN LTD   p176
30180 AUTOMALL DR, ABBOTSFORD, BC, V2T 5M1

(604) 857-7755   SIC 5511

ACADIA MOTORS LTD   p407
22 BAIG BLVD, MONCTON, NB, E1E 1C8

(506) 857-8611   SIC 5511

ACTION CHEVROLET INC   p1307
7955 CH DE CHAMBLY, SAINT-HUBERT, QC, J3Y 5K2

(450) 445-7333   SIC 5511

ADDISON CHEVROLET BUICK GMC (WEST)   p719
6600 TURNER VALLEY RD, MISSISSAUGA, ON, L5N 5Z1

(866) 980-6928   SIC 5511

ADESA MONTREAL CORPORATION   p1301
300 BOUL ALBERT-MONDOU, SAINT-EUSTACHE, QC, J7R 7A7

(450) 472-4400   SIC 5511

ADVANCE AUTOMOTIVE INDUSTRIES INC   p687
6520 VISCOUNT RD, MISSISSAUGA, ON, L4V 1H3

(905) 677-0912   SIC 5511

ADVANTAGE FORD SALES LTD   p39
12800 MACLEOD TRAIL SE, CALGARY, AB, T2J 7E5

(403) 225-3636   SIC 5511

AGENCES KYOTO LTEE, LES   p1152
16500 MONTEE GUENETTE, MIRABEL,

QC, J7J 2E2

(450) 438-1255   SIC 5511

AGINCOURT NISSAN LIMITED   p873
1871 MCCOWAN RD, SCARBOROUGH, ON, M1S 4L4

(416) 291-1188   SIC 5511

AIRPORT FORD LINCOLN SALES LIMITED   p616
49 RYMAL RD E, HAMILTON, ON, L9B 1B9

(905) 388-6665   SIC 5511

AITKEN MOTORS LTD   p880
51 QUEENSWAY E, SIMCOE, ON, N3Y 4M5

(519) 426-1793   SIC 5511

AJAX JEEP EAGLE LTD   p1013
1602 CHAMPLAIN AVE, WHITBY, ON, L1N 6A7

(905) 683-4100   SIC 5511

AJAX SALES & SERVICE INC   p473
301 BAYLY ST W, AJAX, ON, L1S 6M2

(905) 428-0088   SIC 5511

ALBERNI ECHO TOYOTA   p245
2555 PORT ALBERNI HWY, PORT ALBERNI, BC, V9Y 8P2

(250) 723-9448   SIC 5511

ALBERT, PAUL CHEVROLET BUICK CADILLAC GMC LTEE   p1078
870 BOUL TALBOT, CHICOUTIMI, QC, G7H 4B4

(418) 696-4444   SIC 5511

ALBI FORD LINCOLN JOLIETTE INC   p1243
525 131 RTE, NOTRE-DAME-DES-PRAIRIES, QC, J6E 0M1

(450) 759-7750   SIC 5511

ALBI LE GEANT INC   p1149
3550 AV DE LA GARE, MASCOUCHE, QC, J7K 3C1

(450) 474-7000   SIC 5511

ALBI LE GEANT INC   p1149
3550 AV DE LA GARE, MASCOUCHE, QC, J7K 3C1

(450) 474-5555   SIC 5511

ALEX WILLIAMSON MOTOR SALES LIMITED   p1001
259 TORONTO ST S, UXBRIDGE, ON, L9P 1R1

(905) 852-3332   SIC 5511

ALLIANCE FORD INC   p1354
90 BOUL NORBERT-MORIN, SAINTE-AGATHE-DES-MONTS, QC, J8C 3K8

(819) 326-8944   SIC 5511

ALMA FORD INC   p1044
1570 AV DU PONT S, ALMA, QC, G8B 6N1

(418) 662-6695   SIC 5511

AMI AUTO INC   p1076
191 BOUL SAINT-JEAN-BAPTISTE, CHATEAUGUAY, QC, J6K 3B9

(450) 692-9600   SIC 5511

ANCASTER TOYOTA INC   p477
30 MASON DR, ANCASTER, ON, L9G 3K9

(905) 648-9910   SIC 5511

ANDERSON MOTORS LTD   p1413
3333 6TH AVE E, PRINCE ALBERT, SK, S6V 8C8

(306) 765-3000   SIC 5511

ANDERSON, GORD AUTOMOTIVE GROUP INC   p1034
1267 DUNDAS ST, WOODSTOCK, ON, N4S 7V9

(519) 537-2326   SIC 5511

ANDREWS, DENNY FORD SALES INC   p99
18208 STONY PLAIN RD NW, EDMONTON, AB, T5S 1A7

(780) 489-9999   SIC 5511

ANIKA HOLDINGS INC   p390
1700 WAVERLEY ST SUITE B, WINNIPEG, MB, R3T 5V7

(204) 269-9551   SIC 5511

ANNANDALE LEASING LIMITED   p843
GD, PICKERING, ON, L1V 2R1

(905) 683-5722   SIC 5511

ANTHONY'S AUTO SALES INC   p219
2759 HIGHWAY 97 N, KELOWNA, BC, V1X 4J8

(250) 861-6163   SIC 5511

APPLEWOOD HOLDINGS INC   p716
3000 WOODCHESTER DR, MISSISSAUGA, ON, L5L 2R4

(905) 828-2221   SIC 5511

APPLEWOOD MOTORS INC   p227
19764 LANGLEY BYPASS, LANGLEY, BC, V3A 7B1

(604) 533-7881   SIC 5511

APPLEWOOD NISSAN INC   p270
15257 FRASER HWY, SURREY, BC, V3R 3P3

(604) 589-1775   SIC 5511

ARCHER TRUCK SERVICES LIMITED   p885
260 DUNKIRK RD, ST CATHARINES, ON, L2R 7K6

(905) 685-6532   SIC 5511

ARMAND AUTOMOBILES LTEE   p1074
542 BOUL PERRON, CARLETON, QC, G0C 1J0

(418) 364-3382   SIC 5511

ARMANEAU AUTOS INC   p1159
140 BOUL TACHE O, MONTMAGNY, QC, G5V 3A5

(418) 248-2323   SIC 5511

ARNPRIOR CHRYSLER LTD   p478
205 MADAWASKA BLVD, ARNPRIOR, ON, K7S 1S6

(613) 623-4256   SIC 5511

ARSLAN AUTOMOTIVE CANADA LTEE   p1249
84 AV LEACOCK, POINTE-CLAIRE, QC, H9R 1H1

(514) 694-1113   SIC 5511

ARTHUR CHRYSLER DODGE JEEP LIMITED   p479
165 CATHERINE ST W, ARTHUR, ON, N0G 1A0

(519) 848-2016   SIC 5511

ASPOL MOTORS (1982) LTD   p204
1125 102 AVE, DAWSON CREEK, BC, V1G 2C2

(250) 782-5804   SIC 5511

ATKIN, MICHAEL HOLDINGS INC   p99
17415 103 AVE NW, EDMONTON, AB, T5S 1J4

(780) 486-5100   SIC 5511

ATLANTIC MOTORS LTD   p397
665 BOUL FERDINAND, DIEPPE, NB, E1A 7G1

(506) 852-8225   SIC 5511

ATTRELL AUTO HOLDINGS LIMITED   p513
110 CANAM CRES, BRAMPTON, ON, L7A 1A9

(905) 451-7235   SIC 5511

ATTRELL MOTOR CORPORATION   p513
100 CANAM CRES, BRAMPTON, ON, L7A 1A9

(905) 451-1699   SIC 5511

AU CARROSSIER INC   p1289
1355 AV LARIVIERE, ROUYN-NORANDA, QC, J9X 6M6

(819) 762-5000   SIC 5511

AU ROYAUME CHRYSLER DODGE JEEP   p1354
700 RUE PRINCIPALE, SAINTE-AGATHE-DES-MONTS, QC, J8C 1L3

(819) 326-4524   SIC 5511

AUDI AUTOHAUS   p335
1101 YATES ST, VICTORIA, BC, V8V 3N1

(250) 590-5849   SIC 5511

AUDI CANADA INC   p473
777 BAYLY ST W, AJAX, ON, L1S 7G7

(905) 428-4826   SIC 5511

AUTO AMBASSADEUR INC   p1085
2000 BOUL CHOMEDEY, COTE SAINT-LUC, QC, H7T 2W3

(450) 686-2710   SIC 5511

AUTO BOULEVARD SAINT-MARTIN INC   p1085
2450 BOUL CHOMEDEY, COTE SAINT-LUC, QC, H7T 2X3

(450) 682-1212   SIC 5511

AUTO BUGATTI INC   p1093

825 AV AVOCA, DORVAL, QC, H9P 1G4

(514) 636-8750 *SIC* 5511

AUTO CLASSIQUE DE LAVAL INC *p1363*
3131 DESSTE NORD LAVAL (A-440) O, SAINTE-ROSE, QC, H7P 5P2

(450) 681-2500 *SIC* 5511

AUTO FRANK & MICHEL INC *p1063*
5790 BOUL SAINTE-ANNE RR 1, BOIS-CHATEL, QC, G0A 1H0

(418) 822-2252 *SIC* 5511

AUTO FRANK ET MICHEL INC *p1063*
5790 BOUL SAINTE-ANNE, BOISCHATEL, QC, G0A 1H0

(418) 822-6686 *SIC* 5511

AUTO FRANK MICHEL CHARLEVOIX INC *p1122*
2060 BOUL DE COMPORTE, LA MALBAIE, QC, G5A 3C5

(418) 665-6431 *SIC* 5511

AUTO GALLERY 1994 LTD *p1420*
609 WINNIPEG ST, REGINA, SK, S4R 8P2

(306) 525-6700 *SIC* 5511

AUTO GROUP AURORA INC *p480*
669 WELLINGTON ST E, AURORA, ON, L4G 0C9

(905) 727-1948 *SIC* 5511

AUTO GROUP NEWMARKET INC *p754*
1171 DAVIS DR, NEWMARKET, ON, L3Y 8R1

(905) 953-2890 *SIC* 5511

AUTO HAUS FORT GARRY (1981) LTD *p387*
660 PEMBINA HWY, WINNIPEG, MB, R3M 2M5

(204) 284-7520 *SIC* 5511

AUTO IMPORTATION TERREBONNE INC *p1379*
1295 CAR MASSON, TERREBONNE, QC, J6W 6J7

SIC 5511

AUTO L.P. TREMBLAY, LTEE *p1078*
1330 BOUL DU ROYAUME O, CHICOUTIMI, QC, G7H 5B1

(418) 549-3320 *SIC* 5511

AUTO METIVIER INC *p1135*
160 RTE DU PRESIDENT-KENNEDY, LEVIS, QC, G6V 6E1

(418) 837-4701 *SIC* 5511

AUTO MONT CHEVROLET BUICK GMC LTEE *p1154*
1300 BOUL ALBINY-PAQUETTE, MONT-LAURIER, QC, J9L 1M7

(819) 623-1122 *SIC* 5511

AUTO MSHOP *p1307*
4535 AV THIBAULT BUREAU 1, SAINT-HUBERT, QC, J3Y 7N1

(579) 720-7747 *SIC* 5511

AUTO PLUS J.F. HAMEL INC *p1058*
255 BOUL DE LA SEIGNEURIE O, BLAINVILLE, QC, J7C 4N3

(450) 435-4455 *SIC* 5511

AUTO SENATEUR INC *p1235*
255 BOUL SAINT-MARTIN E, MONTREAL, QC, H7M 1Z1

(450) 663-2020 *SIC* 5511

AUTO WEST INFINITI LTD *p253*
13720 SMALLWOOD PL, RICHMOND, BC, V6V 1W8

SIC 5511

AUTO-NET AUTOMOBILE SALES LTD *p162*
10 BROADWAY BLVD, SHERWOOD PARK, AB, T8H 2A2

(780) 449-5775 *SIC* 5511

AUTOCANADA INC *p104*
15511 123 AVE NW UNIT 200, EDMONTON, AB, T5V 0C3

(866) 938-0561 *SIC* 5511

AUTOMOBILE EN DIRECT.COM INC *p1297*
360 RTE 132, SAINT-CONSTANT, QC, J5A 1M3

(450) 638-6664 *SIC* 5511

AUTOMOBILE G.R. COREE LONGUEUIL LTEE *p1141*
1680 BOUL MARIE-VICTORIN, LONGUEUIL, QC, J4G 1A5

(450) 670-2080 *SIC* 5511

AUTOMOBILE KAMOURASKA (1992) INC *p1349*
255 AV PATRY, SAINT-PASCAL, QC, G0L 3Y0

(418) 492-3432 *SIC* 5511

AUTOMOBILE NATIONAL (1999) INC *p1304*
585 90E RUE, SAINT-GEORGES, QC, G5Y 3L1

(418) 228-8838 *SIC* 5511

AUTOMOBILE PAILLE INC *p1057*
700 AV GILLES-VILLENEUVE, BERTHIERVILLE, QC, J0K 1A0

(450) 836-6291 *SIC* 5511

AUTOMOBILE PAQUIN LTEE *p1296*
17 RUE PRINCIPALE N, SAINT-BRUNO-DE-GUIGUES, QC, J0Z 2G0

(819) 728-2289 *SIC* 5511

AUTOMOBILE PIERRE METHOT INC *p1397*
885 RUE NOTRE-DAME E, VICTORIAV-ILLE, QC, G6P 4B8

(819) 758-5858 *SIC* 5511

AUTOMOBILES AUMONT (1977) INC, LES *p1243*
357 BOUL ANTONIO-BARRETTE, NOTRE-DAME-DES-PRAIRIES, QC, J6E 1G1

(450) 759-3449 *SIC* 5511

AUTOMOBILES B. G. P. INC *p1304*
8800 BOUL LACROIX, SAINT-GEORGES, QC, G5Y 2B5

(418) 228-5825 *SIC* 5511

AUTOMOBILES BAURORE 2000 LTEE, LES *p1103*
975 CH DE MASSON, GATINEAU, QC, J8M 1R4

(819) 986-6714 *SIC* 5511

AUTOMOBILES BELLEM INC, LES *p1154*
2050 BOUL ALBINY-PAQUETTE BUREAU 3, MONT-LAURIER, QC, J9L 3G5

(819) 623-7341 *SIC* 5511

AUTOMOBILES BERNIER & CREPEAU LTEE *p1389*
3100 BOUL SAINT-JEAN, TROIS-RIVIERES, QC, G9B 2M9

(819) 377-3077 *SIC* 5511

AUTOMOBILES BOUCHARD & FILS INC *p1154*
1800 BOUL JACQUES-CARTIER, MONT-JOLI, QC, G5H 2W8

(418) 775-4378 *SIC* 5511

AUTOMOBILES BOUCHARD & FILS INC *p1285*
401 AV LEONIDAS S, RIMOUSKI, QC, G5M 1A1

(418) 722-4388 *SIC* 5511

AUTOMOBILES CANDIAC INC, LES *p1089*
30 132 RTE, DELSON, QC, J5B 1H3

(450) 632-2220 *SIC* 5511

AUTOMOBILES CARMER 1990 INC *p1075*
417 BOUL RENE-LEVESQUE O, CHAN-DLER, QC, G0C 1K0

(418) 689-4467 *SIC* 5511

AUTOMOBILES CHICOUTIMI (1986) INC *p1078*
545 BOUL DU ROYAUME O, CHICOUTIMI, QC, G7H 5B1

(418) 545-6555 *SIC* 5511

AUTOMOBILES DES SEIGNEURS INC *p1379*
893 RUE L?ON-MARTEL, TERREBONNE, QC, J6W 2K4

(450) 471-6602 *SIC* 5511

AUTOMOBILES DONALD BRASSARD INC *p1380*
2850 CH GASCON, TERREBONNE, QC, J6X 4H6

(450) 477-0555 *SIC* 5511

AUTOMOBILES FAIRVIEW INC *p1249*
15 AV AUTO PLAZA, POINTE-CLAIRE, QC, H9R 5Z7

(514) 630-3666 *SIC* 5511

AUTOMOBILES ILE-PERROT INC *p1120*
40 BOUL DON-QUICHOTTE, L'ILE-PERROT, QC, J7V 6N5

(514) 453-8416 *SIC* 5511

AUTOMOBILES J. D. A. INC *p1311*
3395 BOUL LAFRAMBOISE, SAINT-HYACINTHE, QC, J2S 4Z7

(450) 774-9191 *SIC* 5511

AUTOMOBILES L F B INC, LES *p1149*
118 MONTEE MASSON, MASCOUCHE, QC, J7K 3B5

(450) 474-2428 *SIC* 5511

AUTOMOBILES LA SEIGNEURIE (1990) INC, LES *p1074*
850 BOUL DE PERIGNY BUREAU 112, CHAMBLY, QC, J3L 1W3

(450) 658-6699 *SIC* 5511

AUTOMOBILES LAPORTE, REJEAN & FILS LTEE *p1349*
1881 RUE PRINCIPALE, SAINT-NORBERT, QC, J0K 3C0

(450) 836-3783 *SIC* 5511

AUTOMOBILES LEVEILLE INC *p1379*
1369 MONTEE MASSON, TERREBONNE, QC, J6W 6A6

(450) 471-4117 *SIC* 5511

AUTOMOBILES LEVIKO (1991) LTEE *p1135*
144 RTE DU PRESIDENT-KENNEDY, LEVIS, QC, G6V 6C9

(418) 833-7140 *SIC* 5511

AUTOMOBILES MAUGER FORD INC *p1112*
119 GRANDE ALLEE E, GRANDE-RIVIERE, QC, G0C 1V0

(418) 385-2118 *SIC* 5511

AUTOMOBILES MAURICE PARENT INC *p1261*
205 RUE ETIENNE-DUBREUIL, QUEBEC, QC, G1M 4A6

(418) 627-4601 *SIC* 5511

AUTOMOBILES MET-HAM INC *p1249*
575 BOUL SAINT-JEAN, POINTE-CLAIRE, QC, H9R 3K1

(514) 685-5555 *SIC* 5511

AUTOMOBILES PERRON (CHICOUTIMI) INC *p1078*
930 BOUL TALBOT, CHICOUTIMI, QC, G7H 4B4

(418) 549-7633 *SIC* 5511

AUTOMOBILES POPULAR INC, LES *p1173*
5441 RUE SAINT-HUBERT, MONTREAL, QC, H2J 2Y4

(514) 274-5471 *SIC* 5511

AUTOMOBILES REGATE INC *p1365*
1325 BOUL MONSEIGNEUR-LANGLOIS, SALABERRY-DE-VALLEYFIELD, QC, J6S 1C1

(450) 373-4372 *SIC* 5511

AUTOMOBILES RELAIS 2000 INC *p1371*
2059 RUE KING O, SHERBROOKE, QC, J1J 2E9

(819) 563-6622 *SIC* 5511

AUTOMOBILES RIMAR INC *p1346*
5500 BOUL METROPOLITAIN E, SAINT-LEONARD, QC, H1S 1A6

(514) 253-4888 *SIC* 5511

AUTOMOBILES ROBERGE LTEE *p1254*
545 RUE CLEMENCEAU, QUEBEC, QC, G1C 7B6

(418) 666-2000 *SIC* 5511

AUTOMOBILES ROCHMAT INC *p1191*
1124 RUE DE BLEURY, MONTREAL, QC, H2Z 1N4

(514) 879-1550 *SIC* 5511

AUTOMOBILES ROYAUME LTEE *p1078*
533 BOUL DU ROYAUME O, CHICOUTIMI, QC, G7H 5B1

(418) 543-9393 *SIC* 5511

AUTOMOBILES SENEX LTEE *p1366*
851 7E AV, SENNETERRE, QC, J0Y 2M0

(819) 737-2291 *SIC* 5511

AUTOMOBILES SILVER STAR (MON-TREAL) INC *p1227*
7800 BOUL DECARIE, MONTREAL, QC, H4P 2H4

(514) 735-5501 *SIC* 5511

AUTOMOBILES ST-EUSTACHE INC *p1058*
16 RUE DE BRAINE, BLAINVILLE, QC, J7B

1Z1

(514) 927-8977 *SIC* 5511

AUTOMOBILES ULSAN LTEE *p1093*
1625 BOUL HYMUS, DORVAL, QC, H9P 1J5

(514) 683-5702 *SIC* 5511

AUTOMOBILES VAL ESTRIE INC *p1373*
4141 RUE KING O, SHERBROOKE, QC, J1L 1P5

(819) 563-4466 *SIC* 5511

AUTOMOBILES VIEILLES FORGES LTEE *p1389*
1500 BOUL ARTHUR-ROUSSEAU, TROIS-RIVIERES, QC, G9B 0X4

(819) 373-2355 *SIC* 5511

AUTOMOBILES VILLENEUVE JOLIETTE (1996) INC *p1243*
570 131 RTE, NOTRE-DAME-DES-PRAIRIES, QC, J6E 0M2

(450) 759-8155 *SIC* 5511

AUTOMOTIVE WHOLESALE INC *p870*
2380 LAWRENCE AVE E, SCARBOR-OUGH, ON, M1P 2R5

(416) 285-6363 *SIC* 5511

AUTOPLUS RESOURCES LTD *p27*
4620 BLACKFOOT TRAIL SE, CALGARY, AB, T2G 4G2

(403) 243-6200 *SIC* 5511

AUTOS ECONOMIQUES CASAVANT INC, LES *p1311*
350 RUE DANIEL-JOHNSON E, SAINT-HYACINTHE, QC, J2S 8W5

(450) 774-1724 *SIC* 5511

AUTOS J. G. PINARD & FILS LTEE *p1359*
1219 125 RTE, SAINTE-JULIENNE, QC, J0K 2T0

(450) 831-2211 *SIC* 5511

AUTOS JEAN-FRANCOIS HAMEL LTEE *p1300*
332 RUE DUBOIS, SAINT-EUSTACHE, QC, J7P 4W9

(450) 491-0440 *SIC* 5511

AUTOS R. CHAGNON DE GRANBY INC *p1110*
1711 RUE PRINCIPALE, GRANBY, QC, J2J 0M9

(450) 378-9963 *SIC* 5511

AUTOS YOMO INC, LES *p1386*
5225 BOUL JEAN-XXIII, TROIS-RIVIERES, QC, G8Z 4A5

(819) 374-3330 *SIC* 5511

AUTOTEK CAR SALES & SERVICE (1996) LTD *p692*
1630 MATHESON BLVD SUITE 1, MISSIS-SAUGA, ON, L4W 1Y4

(905) 625-4100 *SIC* 5511

AVALON FORD SALES 1996 LIMITED *p429*
80 WYATT BLVD, ST. JOHN'S, NL, A1B 3N9

(709) 754-7500 *SIC* 5511

AVANTAGE FORD INC *p1120*
30 BOUL DON-QUICHOTTE, L'ILE-PERROT, QC, J7V 6N5

(514) 453-5850 *SIC* 5511

AVANTGARD INVESTMENTS INC *p571*
3526 LAKE SHORE BLVD W, ETOBICOKE, ON, M8W 1N6

(416) 252-0066 *SIC* 5511

AVENUE PONTIAC BUICK GMC INC *p1285*
140 MONTEE INDUSTRIELLE-ET-COMMERCIALE, RIMOUSKI, QC, G5M 1B1

(418) 725-2001 *SIC* 5511

B M W ELITE AUTOMOBILES INC *p595*
1040 OGILVIE RD, GLOUCESTER, ON, K1J 8G9

(613) 749-7700 *SIC* 5511

BADANAI MOTORS LTD *p907*
399 MEMORIAL AVE, THUNDER BAY, ON, P7B 3Y4

(807) 683-4900 *SIC* 5511

BAIG BLVD MOTORS INC *p408*
1820 MAIN ST, MONCTON, NB, E1E 4S7

(506) 857-2950 *SIC* 5511

BAILLOT, JULES & FILS LIMITEE *p1107*

960 BOUL SAINT-JOSEPH, GATINEAU, QC, J8Z 1T3
(819) 777-5261   *SIC* 5511
BANCROFT MOTORS LTD   *p484*
29668 HWY 62 NORTH RR 2, BANCROFT, ON, K0L 1C0
(613) 332-3437   *SIC* 5511
BANLIEUE FORD INC   *p1292*
344 RUE LAURIER, SAINT-APOLLINAIRE, QC, G0S 2E0
(418) 881-2323   *SIC* 5511
BANNERMAN, BOB MOTORS LIMITED*p778*
888 DON MILLS RD, NORTH YORK, ON, M3C 1V6
(416) 444-0888   *SIC* 5511
BANNISTER CHEVROLET BUICK GMC VERNON INC   *p331*
4703 27 ST, VERNON, BC, V1T 4Y8
(250) 542-2647   *SIC* 5511
BARBER MOTORS (1963) LTD   *p1437*
1 GOVERNMENT RD, WEYBURN, SK, S4H 0N8
(306) 842-6531   *SIC* 5511
BARIL FORD LINCOLN INC   *p1311*
6875 BOUL LAURIER O, SAINT-HYACINTHE, QC, J2S 9A5
(514) 454-7070   *SIC* 5511
BARNABE NISSAN DE CHATEAUGUAY INC
p1076
187 BOUL SAINT-JEAN-BAPTISTE, CHATEAUGUAY, QC, J6K 3B4
(450) 691-9541   *SIC* 5511
BARNES WHEATON CHEVROLET CADIL-LAC LTD   *p196*
46125 OLDS DR, CHILLIWACK, BC, V2P 0B5
(604) 792-1391   *SIC* 5511
BARRIE FORD   *p486*
55 MAPLEVIEW DR W, BARRIE, ON, L4N 9H7
(705) 737-2310   *SIC* 5511
BARRY, ART FORD SALES LTD   *p139*
8012 SPARROW CRES, LEDUC, AB, T9E 7G1
(780) 986-1100   *SIC* 5511
BATHURST FINE CARS INC   *p394*
2300 ST. PETER AVE, BATHURST, NB, E2A 7K2
(506) 548-4569   *SIC* 5511
BAVARIA AUTOHAUS (1997) LTD   *p99*
18925 STONY PLAIN RD NW, EDMONTON, AB, T5S 2Y4
(780) 484-0000   *SIC* 5511
BAYSIDE CHRYSLER DODGE LTD   *p394*
1374 ST. PETER AVE, BATHURST, NB, E2A 3A5
(506) 546-6606   *SIC* 5511
BAYVIEW CHRYSLER DODGE LTD   *p859*
255 INDIAN RD S, SARNIA, ON, N7T 3W5
(519) 336-2189   *SIC* 5511
BAYVIEW TRUCKS & EQUIPMENT LTD
p412
315 MCALLISTER DR, SAINT JOHN, NB, E2J 2S8
(800) 561-9911   *SIC* 5511
BEAR, JOHN PONTIAC BUICK CADILLAC LTD   *p616*
1200 UPPER JAMES ST, HAMILTON, ON, L9C 3B1
(905) 575-9400   *SIC* 5511
BEAUCE AUTO (2000) INC   *p1055*
405 BOUL RENAULT, BEAUCEVILLE, QC, G5X 1N7
(418) 774-9801   *SIC* 5511
BEAUDRY & LAPOINTE LTEE   *p1123*
1 111 RTE O BUREAU 1110, LA SARRE, QC, J9Z 1R5
(819) 333-2266   *SIC* 5511
BEAUPRE CAPITALE CHRYSLER INC
p1261
225 RUE DU MARAIS, QUEBEC, QC, G1M 3C8
(418) 687-2604   *SIC* 5511
BEL-AIR AUTOMOBILES INC   *p820*

450 MCARTHUR AVE, OTTAWA, ON, K1K 1G4
(613) 741-3270   *SIC* 5511
BELANGER FORD LINCOLN CENTRE LTD, THE   *p543*
204 MICHAEL ST, CHELMSFORD, ON, P0M 1L0
(705) 855-4504   *SIC* 5511
BELL CITY AUTO CENTRE INC   *p516*
100 OLD ONONDAGA RD E, BRANTFORD, ON, N3T 5L4
(800) 265-8498   *SIC* 5511
BELLAMY AUTOTECHNIC LTD   *p1420*
2640 AVONHURST DR, REGINA, SK, S4R 3J4
(306) 525-4555   *SIC* 5511
BELLIVEAU MOTORS LIMITED   *p442*
1484 HIGHWAY 1, CHURCH POINT, NS, B0W 1M0
(902) 769-0706   *SIC* 5511
BEMA IMPORTS INC   *p1424*
607 BRAND CRT, SASKATOON, SK, S7J 5L3
(306) 955-0900   *SIC* 5511
BENNETT CHEVROLET CADILLAC LTD
p532
445 HESPELER RD, CAMBRIDGE, ON, N1R 6J2
(519) 621-1250   *SIC* 5511
BENNETT DUNLOP FORD SALES (1993) LIMITED   *p1420*
770 BROAD ST, REGINA, SK, S4R 8H7
(306) 522-6612   *SIC* 5511
BERCO AUTOMOTIVE SUPPLY LIMITED
p792
163 MILVAN DR SUITE 1, NORTH YORK, ON, M9L 1Z8
(416) 749-0231   *SIC* 5511
BERK'S INTERTRUCK LTD   *p234*
2230 MCCULLOUGH RD, NANAIMO, BC, V9S 4M8
(250) 758-5217   *SIC* 5511
BERNIER & CREPEAU (1988) LTEE   *p1098*
160 BOUL SAINT-JOSEPH, DRUM-MONDVILLE, QC, J2C 2A8
(819) 477-8503   *SIC* 5511
BERO INVESTMENTS LTD   *p283*
14948 32 AVE, SURREY, BC, V4P 3R5
(604) 536-3644   *SIC* 5511
BERUBE CHEVROLET CADILLAC BUICK GMC LTEE   *p1286*
101 BOUL CARTIER, RIVIERE-DU-LOUP, QC, G5R 2N3
(418) 862-6324   *SIC* 5511
BESSETTE AUTOMOBILE INC   *p1088*
395 RUE DE LA RIVIERE, COWANSVILLE, QC, J2K 1N4
(450) 263-4000   *SIC* 5511
BICKNELL, PETER AUTOMOTIVE INC *p883*
117 CUSHMAN RD, ST CATHARINES, ON, L2M 6S9
(905) 685-3184   *SIC* 5511
BIG 4 MOTORS LTD   *p33*
7330 MACLEOD TRAIL SE, CALGARY, AB, T2H 0L9
(403) 252-6671   *SIC* 5511
BIG LAKES DODGE LTD   *p135*
5109 41 ST, HIGH PRAIRIE, AB, T0G 1E0
(780) 523-5007   *SIC* 5511
BIG M FORD LINCOLN LTD   *p146*
1312 TRANS CANADA WAY SE, MEDICINE HAT, AB, T1B 3Z9
(403) 527-4406   *SIC* 5511
BILL HOWICH CHRYSLER LTD   *p194*
2777 ISLAND HWY, CAMPBELL RIVER, BC, V9W 2H4
(250) 287-9133   *SIC* 5511
BILL MATTHEWS' AUTOHAUS LIMITED
p429
575 KENMOUNT RD, ST. JOHN'S, NL, A1B 3P9
(709) 726-4424   *SIC* 5511
BILODEAU, CECIL AUTOS LTEE   *p1354*
9641 BOUL SAINTE-ANNE, SAINTE-

ANNE-DE-BEAUPRE, QC, G0A 3C0
(418) 827-3773   *SIC* 5511
BIRCHWOOD HONDA WEST   *p386*
3965 PORTAGE AVE SUITE 75, WIN-NIPEG, MB, R3K 2H5
(204) 888-4542   *SIC* 5511
BIRCHWOOD PONTIAC BUICK LIMITED
p386
3965 PORTAGE AVE UNIT 40, WINNIPEG, MB, R3K 2H1
(204) 837-5811   *SIC* 5511
BISSON CHEVROLET INC   *p1382*
2257 RUE NOTRE-DAME E, THETFORD MINES, QC, G6G 2W4
(418) 335-7571   *SIC* 5511
BLACK PALM AVIARIES OF CANADA INC
p866
4251 KINGSTON RD, SCARBOROUGH, ON, M1E 2M5
(416) 283-4262   *SIC* 5511
BLACKSTOCK FORD LINCOLN SALES LTD
p808
207155 9 HWY, ORANGEVILLE, ON, L9W 2Z7
(519) 941-5431   *SIC* 5511
BLAIKIES DODGE CHRYSLER LIMITED
p468
28 WADDELL ST, TRURO, NS, B2N 4A2
(902) 893-4381   *SIC* 5511
BLAINVILLE CHRYSLER DODGE INC*p1058*
249 BOUL DE LA SEIGNEURIE O, BLAINVILLE, QC, J7C 4N3
(450) 419-5337   *SIC* 5511
BLAINVILLE FORD INC   *p1058*
600 BOUL DU CURE-LABELLE, BLAINVILLE, QC, J7C 2H9
(450) 430-9181   *SIC* 5511
BLANCHARD, A. INC   *p1056*
4350 AV ARSENEAULT, BECANCOUR, QC, G9H 1V8
(819) 233-2349   *SIC* 5511
BLUE MOUNTAIN CHRYSLER LTD   *p546*
9950 26 HWY, COLLINGWOOD, ON, L9Y 3Z1
(705) 445-2740   *SIC* 5511
BLUE STAR FORD LINCOLN SALES LTD
p880
121 QUEENSWAY E, SIMCOE, ON, N3Y 4M5
(519) 426-3673   *SIC* 5511
BMW STORE LTD, THE   *p320*
2040 BURRARD ST, VANCOUVER, BC, V6J 3H5
(604) 659-3200   *SIC* 5511
BODYLINE INC   *p607*
185 BANCROFT ST, HAMILTON, ON, L8E 4L4
(905) 573-7000   *SIC* 5511
BOISVERT PONTIAC BUICK LTD   *p1058*
470 BOUL DU CURE-LABELLE, BLAINVILLE, QC, J7C 2H2
(450) 430-9400   *SIC* 5511
BOISVERT, P.E. AUTO LTEE   *p1064*
2 BOUL MARIE-VICTORIN, BOUCHERVILLE, QC, J4B 1V5
(514) 527-8215   *SIC* 5511
BONNYMAN MITSUBISHI   *p463*
29 CRESCENT DR, NEW MINAS, NS, B4N 3G7
SIC 5511
BONNYVILLE DODGE LTD   *p6*
5605 50 AVE, BONNYVILLE, AB, T9N 2L1
(780) 826-2999   *SIC* 5511
BOSTON'S CHEV-OLDS-CADILLAC-GEO LTD   *p862*
415 PIM ST, SAULT STE. MARIE, ON, P6B 2T9
SIC 5511
BOULEVARD CHEVROLET INC   *p1285*
374 MONTEE INDUSTRIELLE-ET-COMMERCIALE, RIMOUSKI, QC, G5M 1X1
(888) 844-5490   *SIC* 5511
BOULEVARD DODGE CHRYSLER JEEP

(2000) INC   *p1325*
2955 CH DE LA COTE-DE-LIESSE, SAINT-LAURENT, QC, H4N 2N3
(514) 748-2955   *SIC* 5511
BOULEVARD METROPOLITAIN AUTOMO-BILE INC   *p1325*
100 BOUL MONTPELLIER, SAINT-LAURENT, QC, H4N 0H8
(514) 748-0100   *SIC* 5511
BOUNDARY FORD SALES LTD   *p143*
2502 50 AVE, LLOYDMINSTER, AB, T9V 2S3
(780) 872-7755   *SIC* 5511
BOUNDARY FORD SALES LTD   *p1409*
2405 50 AVE, LLOYDMINSTER, SK, S9V 1Z7
(306) 825-4481   *SIC* 5511
BOURASSA AUTOMOBILES INTERNA-TIONAL INC   *p1363*
2800 BOUL CHOMEDEY, SAINTE-ROSE, QC, H7P 5Z9
(450) 681-0028   *SIC* 5511
BOURASSA WEST ISLAND INC   *p1093*
2000 PLACE TRANSCANADIENNE, DOR-VAL, QC, H9P 2X5
(514) 683-2000   *SIC* 5511
BOURGEOIS MOTORS LIMITED   *p681*
281 CRANSTON CRES, MIDLAND, ON, L4R 4L1
(705) 526-2278   *SIC* 5511
BOW CYCLE & MOTOR CO LTD   *p72*
8525 BOWFORT RD NW, CALGARY, AB, T3B 2V2
(403) 288-5421   *SIC* 5511
BOW MEL CHRYSLER LTD   *p211*
461 TRANS CANADA HWY, DUNCAN, BC, V9L 3R7
(250) 748-8144   *SIC* 5511
BOYER, MICHAEL PONTIAC BUICK GMC (1988) LTD   *p843*
715 KINGSTON RD, PICKERING, ON, L1V 1A9
(905) 831-2693   *SIC* 5511
BRABY MOTORS LTD   *p267*
1250 TRANS CANADA HWY SW, SALMON ARM, BC, V1E 1T1
(250) 832-8053   *SIC* 5511
BRAMGATE AUTOMOTIVE INC   *p508*
268 QUEEN ST E, BRAMPTON, ON, L6V 1B9
(905) 459-6040   *SIC* 5511
BRAMGATE LEASING INC   *p508*
268 QUEEN ST E, BRAMPTON, ON, L6V 1B9
(905) 459-6040   *SIC* 5511
BRAMPTON NORTH NISSAN   *p513*
195 CANAM CRES, BRAMPTON, ON, L7A 1G1
(905) 459-1600   *SIC* 5511
BRANTFORD CHRYSLER DODGE JEEP LTD   *p514*
180 LYNDEN RD, BRANTFORD, ON, N3R 8A3
(519) 753-7331   *SIC* 5511
BRANTFORD FINE CARS LIMITED   *p517*
378 KING GEORGE RD SUITE 6, BRANT-FORD, ON, N3T 5L8
(519) 753-3168   *SIC* 5511
BRANTFORD NISSAN INC   *p514*
338 KING GEORGE RD, BRANTFORD, ON, N3R 5M1
(519) 756-9240   *SIC* 5511
BRASSO NISSAN LTD   *p33*
195 GLENDEER CIR SE, CALGARY, AB, T2H 2S8
(403) 253-5555   *SIC* 5511
BRENNAN PONTIAC BUICK GMC LTD*p918*
1860 BAYVIEW AVE, TORONTO, ON, M4G 0C3
(416) 485-0350   *SIC* 5511
BRENTRIDGE FORD SALES LTD   *p172*
5604 41 AVE, WETASKIWIN, AB, T9A 3M7
(780) 352-6048   *SIC* 5511
BRETON, DENIS CHEVROLET LTEE *p1300*

364 RUE DUBOIS, SAINT-EUSTACHE, QC, J7P 4W9

(450) 472-3200 *SIC 5511*

BRETT CHEVROLET CADILLAC *p412*
183 ROTHESAY AVE, SAINT JOHN, NB, E2J 2B4

(506) 634-5555 *SIC 5511*

BREWIS, CHARLES LIMITED *p605*
995 WOODLAWN RD W, GUELPH, ON, N1K 1C9

(519) 836-0645 *SIC 5511*

BRIDGE CITY CHRYSLER DODGE JEEP LTD *p142*
3216 1 AVE S, LETHBRIDGE, AB, T1J 4H2

(403) 328-3325 *SIC 5511*

BRIDGEWATER MAZDA *p459*
15230 HIGHWAY 3, HEBBVILLE, NS, B4V 6X5

(902) 530-9666 *SIC 5511*

BRIMELL MOTORS LIMITED *p873*
5060 SHEPPARD AVE E, SCARBOROUGH, ON, M1S 4N3

(416) 292-2241 *SIC 5511*

BRITISH FINE CARS LTD *p99*
17007-111 AVE, EDMONTON, AB, T5S 0J5

(780) 484-1818 *SIC 5511*

BROCKVILLE MOTOR SALES LIMITED *p519*
1240 STEWART BLVD, BROCKVILLE, ON, K6V 7H2

(613) 342-5244 *SIC 5511*

BROSSARD CHEVROLET BUICK GMC INC *p1069*
2555 BOUL MATTE, BROSSARD, QC, J4Y 2P4

(450) 619-6666 *SIC 5511*

BROUILLETTE AUTOMOBILE INC *p1311*
2750 RUE LAFONTAINE, SAINT-HYACINTHE, QC, J2S 2N6

(450) 773-8551 *SIC 5511*

BROWN BROS MANAGEMENT LTD *p290*
270 MARINE DR SE, VANCOUVER, BC, V5X 2S6

(604) 321-5100 *SIC 5511*

BROWN, BARRIE PONTIAC BUICK GMC LTD *p194*
2700 ISLAND HWY, CAMPBELL RIVER, BC, V9W 2H5

SIC 5511

BROWN, BOB BUICK GMC LTD *p243*
1010 WESTMINSTER AVE W, PENTICTON, BC, V2A 1L6

(250) 493-7121 *SIC 5511*

BROWNE'S AUTO SUPPLIES LIMITED *p426*
1075 TOPSAIL RD, MOUNT PEARL, NL, A1N 5G1

(709) 364-9397 *SIC 5511*

BROWNS' CHEVROLET LIMITED *p204*
12109 8 ST, DAWSON CREEK, BC, V1G 5A5

(250) 782-9155 *SIC 5511*

BRUCE CHEVROLET PONTIAC BUICK GMC LIMITED *p462*
394 MAIN ST, MIDDLETON, NS, B0S 1P0

(902) 825-3494 *SIC 5511*

BRUHAM AUTOMOTIVE INC *p1000*
5201 HIGHWAY 7 E, UNIONVILLE, ON, L3R 1N3

(905) 948-8222 *SIC 5511*

BRUNSWICK HINO INC *p411*
20 SMITH ST, PETITCODIAC, NB, E4Z 4W1

(506) 756-2250 *SIC 5511*

BUDD'S MAZDA *p805*
1501 NORTH SERVICE RD W, OAKVILLE, ON, L6M 2W2

(905) 827-4242 *SIC 5511*

BUDD, STUART & SONS LIMITED *p803*
2454 SOUTH SERVICE RD W, OAKVILLE, ON, L6L 5M9

(905) 845-3577 *SIC 5511*

BUDDS CHEVROLET CADILLAC BUICK *p802*
410 SOUTH SERVICE RD W, OAKVILLE, ON, L6K 2H4

(888) 992-2620 *SIC 5511*

BUDDS HAMILTON LIMITED *p803*
2454 SOUTH SERVICE RD W, OAKVILLE, ON, L6L 5M9

(905) 845-3577 *SIC 5511*

BUIST MOTOR PRODUCTS LTD *p158*
4230 50 AVE, RIMBEY, AB, T0C 2J0

(403) 843-2244 *SIC 5511*

BUPONT MOTORS INC *p913*
1180 RIVERSIDE DR, TIMMINS, ON, P4R 1A2

(705) 268-2226 *SIC 5511*

BURKE'S AUTO SALES *p463*
2757 WESTVILLE RD, NEW GLASGOW, NS, B2H 5C6

(902) 755-2522 *SIC 5511*

BURLINGTON MAZDA *p527*
805 WALKER'S LINE, BURLINGTON, ON, L7N 2G1

(905) 333-1790 *SIC 5511*

BURRARD IMPORTS LTD *p320*
2430 BURRARD ST, VANCOUVER, BC, V6J 5L3

(604) 736-8890 *SIC 5511*

BUSTARD BROTHERS LIMITED *p1008*
575 DAVENPORT RD, WATERLOO, ON, N2L 5Z3

(519) 884-5888 *SIC 5511*

BUTLER AUTO SALES LTD *p216*
142 TRANQUILLE RD, KAMLOOPS, BC, V2B 3G1

(250) 554-2518 *SIC 5511*

BUTLER CHEVROLET PONTIAC BUICK CADILLAC LTD *p837*
1370 PEMBROKE ST W, PEMBROKE, ON, K8A 7M3

(613) 735-3147 *SIC 5511*

BYTEK AUTOMOBILES INC *p817*
1325 ST. LAURENT BLVD, OTTAWA, ON, K1G 0Z7

(613) 745-6885 *SIC 5511*

C & C MOTOR SALES LTD *p1015*
1705 DUNDAS ST W, WHITBY, ON, L1P 1Y9

(905) 430-6666 *SIC 5511*

CABOT FORD LINCOLN SALES LIMITED *p429*
177 KENMOUNT RD, ST. JOHN'S, NL, A1B 3P9

(709) 722-6600 *SIC 5511*

CADILLAC CHEVROLET BUICK GMC DU WEST ISLAND LTEE *p1091*
3650 BOUL DES SOURCES, DOLLARD-DES-ORMEAUX, QC, H9B 1Z9

(514) 683-6555 *SIC 5511*

CADILLAC HUMMER OF LONDON *p658*
600 OXFORD ST W, LONDON, ON, N6H 1T9

(519) 472-1199 *SIC 5511*

CALGARY C MOTORS LP *p34*
125 GLENDEER CIR SE, CALGARY, AB, T2H 2S8

(403) 255-8111 *SIC 5511*

CALGARY H MOTORS LP *p21*
1920 23 ST NE, CALGARY, AB, T2E 8N3

(403) 250-9990 *SIC 5511*

CALGARY M VEHICLES GP INC *p34*
168 GLENDEER CIRCLE SE, CALGARY, AB, T2H 2V4

(403) 253-6800 *SIC 5511*

CALGARY V MOTORS LP *p40*
4849 NORTHLAND DR NW, CALGARY, AB, T2L 2K3

(403) 286-4849 *SIC 5511*

CALMONT TRUCK CENTRE LTD *p99*
11403 174 ST NW, EDMONTON, AB, T5S 2P4

(780) 451-2680 *SIC 5511*

CAM CLARK FORD SALES LTD *p2*
925 VETERANS BLVD NW BAY 1, AIRDRIE, AB, T4A 2G6

(403) 948-6660 *SIC 5511*

CAMBRIAN FORD SALES INC *p898*
1615 KINGSWAY ST, SUDBURY, ON, P3A

4S9

(705) 560-3673 *SIC 5511*

CAMBRIDGE VOLKSWAGEN INC *p532*
275 HESPELER RD, CAMBRIDGE, ON, N1R 3H8

(519) 621-8989 *SIC 5511*

CAMCO AUTOMOBILES INC *p828*
1475 CARLING AVE, OTTAWA, ON, K1Z 7L9

(613) 728-8888 *SIC 5511*

CAMION FREIGHTLINER MONT-LAURIER INC *p1124*
325 CH DU GOLF, LAC-DES-ECORCES, QC, J0W 1H0

(819) 623-7177 *SIC 5511*

CAMIONS FREIGHTLINER M.B. TROIS-RIVIERES LTEE *p1389*
300 RUE QUENNEVILLE, TROIS-RIVIERES, QC, G9B 1X6

(819) 377-9997 *SIC 5511*

CAMIONS FREIGHTLINER QUEBEC DIVISION LEVIS INC *p1135*
865 RUE ARCHIMEDE, LEVIS, QC, G6V 7M5

(418) 837-3661 *SIC 5511*

CAMIONS FREIGHTLINER QUEBEC INC *p1266*
2380 AV DALTON, QUEBEC, QC, G1P 3X1

(418) 657-2425 *SIC 5511*

CAMIONS INTER-ESTRIE (1991) INC, LES *p1373*
250 RUE LEGER, SHERBROOKE, QC, J1L 1M1

(819) 564-6677 *SIC 5511*

CAMIONS INTERNATIONAL ELITE LTEE *p1261*
265 RUE ETIENNE-DUBREUIL, QUEBEC, QC, G1M 4A6

(418) 687-9510 *SIC 5511*

CAMPBELL & CAMERON INC *p1130*
1855 AV DOLLARD, LASALLE, QC, H8N 1T9

(514) 762-9777 *SIC 5511*

CAMPBELL FORD SALES LTD *p828*
1500 CARLING AVE, OTTAWA, ON, K1Z 0A3

(613) 725-3611 *SIC 5511*

CAMPBELL, BOB MOTORS LTD *p542*
296 RICHMOND ST, CHATHAM, ON, N7M 1P6

(519) 352-4740 *SIC 5511*

CAMPBELL, SCOTT DODGE LTD *p1412*
3042 99TH ST HWY SUITE 4, NORTH BATTLEFORD, SK, S9A 3W8

(306) 445-6640 *SIC 5511*

CAMROSE CHRYSLER LTD *p78*
3511 48 AVE, CAMROSE, AB, T4V 0K9

(780) 672-2476 *SIC 5511*

CAN-AM MOTORS LTD *p405*
40 MORTON AVE, MONCTON, NB, E1A 3H9

(506) 852-8210 *SIC 5511*

CAN-BOW MOTORS LTD *p78*
707 RAILWAY AVE, CANMORE, AB, T1W 1P2

(403) 678-4222 *SIC 5511*

CANBEC AUTOMOBILE INC *p1227*
4070 RUE JEAN-TALON O, MONTREAL, QC, H4P 1V5

(514) 289-6464 *SIC 5511*

CANUSA AUTOMOTIVE WAREHOUSING INC *p650*
2290 SCANLAN ST, LONDON, ON, N5W 6G7

(519) 268-7070 *SIC 5511*

CANYON CREEK TOYOTA INC *p39*
370 CANYON MEADOWS DR SE, CALGARY, AB, T2J 7C6

(403) 278-6066 *SIC 5511*

CAPILANO VOLKSWAGEN INC *p241*
1151 MARINE DR, NORTH VANCOUVER, BC, V7P 1T1

(604) 985-0694 *SIC 5511*

CAPITAL DODGE CHRYSLER JEEP LIM-

ITED *p626*
2500 PALLADIUM DR SUITE 1200, KANATA, ON, K2V 1E2

(613) 271-7114 *SIC 5511*

CAPITAL FORD LINCOLN INC *p1423*
1201 N PASQUA ST, REGINA, SK, S4X 4P7

(306) 543-5410 *SIC 5511*

CAPITAL MOTORS (1985) LTD *p204*
1609 ALASKA AVE, DAWSON CREEK, BC, V1G 1Z9

(250) 782-8589 *SIC 5511*

CAPITAL MOTORS LIMITED *p429*
479 KENMOUNT RD, ST. JOHN'S, NL, A1B 3P9

(709) 726-0288 *SIC 5511*

CAPITAL MOTORS LP *p125*
1311 101 ST SW, EDMONTON, AB, T6X 1A1

(780) 435-4711 *SIC 5511*

CAPITAL PONTIAC BUICK CADILLAC GMC LTD *p1423*
4020 ROCHDALE BLVD, REGINA, SK, S4X 4P7

(306) 525-5211 *SIC 5511*

CARCANADA CORPORATION *p663*
5791 REGIONAL ROAD 73, MANOTICK, ON, K4M 1A5

(613) 489-1212 *SIC 5511*

CARDEAGER FORD SALES SERVICE & AUTO BODY LTD *p355*
GD, ROBLIN, MB, R0L 1P0

(204) 937-8386 *SIC 5511*

CARIBOO CHEVROLET BUICK GMC LTD *p344*
370 MACKENZIE AVE S, WILLIAMS LAKE, BC, V2G 1C7

(250) 392-7185 *SIC 5511*

CARIBOO CHEVROLET OLDSMOBILE PONTIAC BUICK GMC LTD *p344*
370 MACKENZIE AVE S, WILLIAMS LAKE, BC, V2G 1C7

(250) 392-7185 *SIC 5511*

CARLE FORD INC *p1102*
901 RUE DOLLARD, GATINEAU, QC, J8L 3T4

(819) 986-3000 *SIC 5511*

CARLING MOTORS CO LTD *p829*
1638 CARLING AVE, OTTAWA, ON, K2A 1C5

(613) 706-8082 *SIC 5511*

CARLYLE MOTOR PRODUCTS LTD *p1405*
GD, CARLYLE, SK, S0C 0R0

(306) 453-6741 *SIC 5511*

CARMEN & FRANKS GARAGE LTD *p867*
2584 EGLINTON AVE E, SCARBOROUGH, ON, M1K 2R5

(416) 261-7219 *SIC 5511*

CAROL AUTOMOBILE LIMITED *p425*
55 AVALON DR, LABRADOR CITY, NL, A2V 1K3

(709) 944-2000 *SIC 5511*

CARON AUTOMOBILES INC *p1159*
75 BOUL TACHE E, MONTMAGNY, QC, G5V 1B6

(418) 248-7877 *SIC 5511*

CARREFOUR DE LA VOITURE IMPORTEE INC *p1311*
200 RUE DANIEL-JOHNSON E, SAINT-HYACINTHE, QC, J2S 8W5

(514) 856-7878 *SIC 5511*

CARRIER CENTERS INC *p1035*
645 ATHLONE AVE, WOODSTOCK, ON, N4S 7V8

(519) 539-0971 *SIC 5511*

CARRIER TRUCK CENTER INC *p514*
6 EDMONDSON ST, BRANTFORD, ON, N3R 7J3

(519) 752-5431 *SIC 5511*

CARROLL SOUTH SHORE MOTORS INC *p441*
GD LCD MAIN, BRIDGEWATER, NS, B4V 2V8

(902) 543-2493 *SIC 5511*

CARRUS INVESTMENTS LTD *p808*

GD STN A, ORANGEVILLE, ON, L9W 2Z4
(519) 941-6221   SIC 5511
CARTER CHEVROLET CADILLAC BUICK GMC BURNABY LTD   p185
4550 LOUGHEED HWY, BURNABY, BC, V5C 3Z5
(604) 291-6474   SIC 5511
CARTER CHEVROLET CADILLAC BUICK GMC NORTHSHORE LTD   p241
800 AUTOMALL DR, NORTH VANCOUVER, BC, V7P 3R8
(604) 987-5231   SIC 5511
CARTER DODGE CHRYSLER LTD   p185
4650 LOUGHEED HWY, BURNABY, BC, V5C 4A6
(604) 299-2681   SIC 5511
CARTER MOTOR CARS LTD   p320
2390 BURRARD ST, VANCOUVER, BC, V6J 3J1
(604) 736-2821   SIC 5511
CARTIER CHEVROLET BUICK GMC LTEE   p1281
1475 BOUL PIE-XI S, QUEBEC, QC, G3K 1H1
(418) 847-6000   SIC 5511
CAVALCADE FORD LTD   p496
420 ECCLESTONE DR, BRACEBRIDGE, ON, P1L 1R1
(705) 645-8731   SIC 5511
CENTAUR IMPORT MOTORS (1977) LTD p28
3819 MACLEOD TRAIL SW, CALGARY, AB, T2G 2R3
(403) 287-2544   SIC 5511
CENTENNIAL PONTIAC BUICK GMC LTD p413
160 ROTHESAY AVE, SAINT JOHN, NB, E2J 2B5
(506) 634-2020   SIC 5511
CENTRAL AUTOMOTIVE SERVICES LIMITED   p533
1220 FRANKLIN BLVD, CAMBRIDGE, ON, N1R 8B7
(519) 653-7161   SIC 5511
CENTRAL GARAGE LTD   p394
76 RUE NOTRE DAME, ATHOLVILLE, NB, E3N 3Z2
(506) 753-7731   SIC 5511
CENTRAL MOTORS (PELHAM) LTD   p591
227 HWY 20, FONTHILL, ON, L0S 1E6
(905) 892-2653   SIC 5511
CENTRAL TRUCK EQUIPMENT INC   p142
3521 1 AVE S, LETHBRIDGE, AB, T1J 4H1
(403) 328-4189   SIC 5511
CENTRE DE L'AUTO BLAIN, MARIO INC, LE p1151
545 BOUL LAURIER, MCMASTERVILLE, QC, J3G 6P2
(450) 464-4551   SIC 5511
CENTRE DU CAMION (AMIANTE) INC p1383
4680 BOUL FRONTENAC E, THETFORD MINES, QC, G6H 4G5
(418) 338-8588   SIC 5511
CENTRE DU CAMION BEAUDOIN INC p1096
5360 RUE SAINT-ROCH S, DRUMMONDVILLE, QC, J2B 6V4
(819) 478-8186   SIC 5511
CENTRE DU CAMION STE-MARIE INC, LE p1310
5400 RUE MARTINEAU, SAINT-HYACINTHE, QC, J2R 1T8
(450) 796-4004   SIC 5511
CGW AUTOMOTIVE GROUP LIMITED p438
34 LORD AMHERST DR, AMHERST, NS, B4H 4W6
(902) 667-8348   SIC 5511
CHALET CHEVROLET OLDSMOBILE LTD p223
1142 304TH ST, KIMBERLEY, BC, V1A 3H6
(250) 427-4895   SIC 5511
CHALUT, A . AUTO LTEE   p1243
250 BOUL ANTONIO-BARRETTE, NOTRE-DAME-DES-PRAIRIES, QC, J6E 6J5
(450) 756-1638   SIC 5511
CHAMPION CHEVROLET BUICK GMC LTD

p284
2880 HIGHWAY DR, TRAIL, BC, V1R 2T3
(250) 368-9134   SIC 5511
CHAMPLAIN DODGE CHRYSLER LTEE p1396
3350 RUE WELLINGTON, VERDUN, QC, H4G 1T5
(514) 761-4801   SIC 5511
CHAMPLAIN MOTORS LIMITED   p408
1810 MAIN ST, MONCTON, NB, E1E 4S7
(506) 857-1800   SIC 5511
CHAREST AUTOMOBILE LTEE   p1399
275 BOUL PIERRE-ROUX E BUREAU 443, VICTORIAVILLE, QC, G6T 1S9
(819) 758-8271   SIC 5511
CHARLAND CHEVROLET CADILLAC BUICK GMC LTEE   p1109
595 RUE BOIVIN, GRANBY, QC, J2G 2M1
(450) 372-4242   SIC 5511
CHARLESBOURG AUTOMOBILES LTEE p1256
16070 BOUL HENRI-BOURASSA, QUEBEC, QC, G1G 3Z8
(418) 623-9843   SIC 5511
CHARLESGLEN LTD   p77
7687 110 AVE NW SUITE 7687, CALGARY, AB, T3R 1R8
(403) 241-0888   SIC 5511
CHARLOTTE COUNTY CHEVROLET BUICK GMC LTD   p398
137 ROUTE 170, DUFFERIN CHARLOTTE CO, NB, E3L 3X5
(506) 466-0640   SIC 5511
CHARTRAND FORD (VENTES) INC   p1083
1610 BOUL SAINT-MARTIN E, COTE SAINT-LUC, QC, H7G 4W6
(450) 669-6110   SIC 5511
CHECKPOINT CHRYSLER LTD   p885
357 ONTARIO ST, ST CATHARINES, ON, L2R 5L3
(905) 688-2802   SIC 5511
CHECKPOINT GMC PONTIAC BUICK LTD p405
349 KING GEORGE HWY, MIRAMICHI, NB, E1V 1L2
(506) 622-7091   SIC 5511
CHEVALIER AUTOMOBILES INC   p866
4334 KINGSTON RD, SCARBOROUGH, ON, M1E 2M8
(416) 281-1234   SIC 5511
CHEVALIER CHRYSLER INC   p480
14535 YONGE ST, AURORA, ON, L4G 6L1
(905) 841-1233   SIC 5511
CHEVROLET TRUCKS LTD   p113
10727 82 AVE NW, EDMONTON, AB, T6E 2B1
(780) 439-0071   SIC 5511
CHIBOUGAMAU AUTOMOBILE INC p1077
859 3E RUE, CHIBOUGAMAU, QC, G8P 1R1
(418) 748-2634   SIC 5511
CHICOUTIMI CHRYSLER DODGE JEEP INC p1078
829 BOUL TALBOT, CHICOUTIMI, QC, G7H 4B5
(418) 549-2873   SIC 5511
CHIVA AUTO GOUP INC   p721
2290 BATTLEFORD RD, MISSISSAUGA, ON, L5N 3K6
(905) 812-8882   SIC 5511
CHOMEDEY NISSAN INC   p1086
2465 BOUL CURE-LABELLE, COTE SAINT-LUC, QC, H7T 1R3
(450) 682-4400   SIC 5511
CHOMEDEY/DESLAURIERS FORD LINCOLN INC   p1235
2705 BOUL CHOMEDEY, MONTREAL, QC, H7P 0C2
(450) 666-3673   SIC 5511
CHUDD'S CHRYSLER LTD   p350
231 GD, GIMLI, MB, R0C 1B0
(204) 642-8555   SIC 5511
CITADELLE CHEVROLET CADILLAC BUICK GMC LTEE   p1136

89 RTE DU PRESIDENT-KENNEDY, LEVIS, QC, G6V 6C8
(418) 835-1171   SIC 5511
CITY AUTO SERVICE LTD   p235
803 BAKER ST, NELSON, BC, V1L 4J8
(250) 352-5346   SIC 5511
CITY BUICK CHEVROLET CADILLAC GMC LTD   p764
1900 VICTORIA PARK AVE, NORTH YORK, ON, M1R 1T6
(416) 751-5920   SIC 5511
CITY CHEVROLET GEO OLDSMOBILE LTD p610
155 CANNON ST E, HAMILTON, ON, L8L 2A6
SIC 5511
CITY FORD SALES LTD   p124
14750 MARK MESSIER TRAIL NW, EDMONTON, AB, T6V 1H5
(780) 454-2000   SIC 5511
CITY MOTORS A LIMITED PARTNERSHIP p422
119 O'CONNELL DR, CORNER BROOK, NL, A2H 5M6
(709) 637-1000   SIC 5511
CITY PLYMOUTH CHRYSLER (MEDICINE HAT) LTD   p145
982 REDCLIFF DR SW, MEDICINE HAT, AB, T1A 5E4
(403) 526-6944   SIC 5511
CIVIC MOTORS LTD   p820
1171 ST. LAURENT BLVD, OTTAWA, ON, K1K 3B7
(613) 741-6676   SIC 5511
CLARK'S AUTO CENTRE LTD   p1042
110 WALKER AVE, SUMMERSIDE, PE, C1N 6V9
(902) 436-5800   SIC 5511
CLARK, J & SON LIMITED   p400
820 PROSPECT ST, FREDERICTON, NB, E3B 4Z2
(506) 452-1010   SIC 5511
CLARK, JIM MOTORS LTD   p400
35 ALISON BLVD, FREDERICTON, NB, E3B 4Z9
(506) 452-2200   SIC 5511
CLARKDALE MOTORS LTD   p290
4575 MAIN ST, VANCOUVER, BC, V5V 3R4
(604) 872-5431   SIC 5511
CLASSIC DODGE CHRYSLER INC   p486
145 BRADFORD ST, BARRIE, ON, L4N 3B2
(705) 795-1431   SIC 5511
CLAUDE AUTO (1984) INC   p1154
330 BOUL ALBINY-PAQUETTE, MONT-LAURIER, QC, J9L 1J9
(819) 623-3511   SIC 5511
CLAYTON AUTOMOTIVE GROUP INC p496
29 SPICER SQ, BOWMANVILLE, ON, L1C 5M2
(905) 697-2333   SIC 5511
CLEMENT, CHRYSLER DODGE LTEE p1146
77 RUE DE L'EGLISE N, LORRAINVILLE, QC, J0Z 2R0
(819) 625-2187   SIC 5511
CLOUTHIER, BILL & SONS LTD   p838
17 BRANDON AVE, PEMBROKE, ON, K8A 6W5
(613) 735-4194   SIC 5511
CLOUTIER, N. V. INC   p1371
2550 RUE KING O, SHERBROOKE, QC, J1J 2H1
(819) 346-3911   SIC 5511
CLUTE, BOB PONTIAC BUICK GMC LTD p491
6692 HWY 62, BELLEVILLE, ON, K8N 4Z5
(613) 962-4584   SIC 5511
COAL VALLEY MOTOR PRODUCTS LTD p212
16 MANITOU RD, FERNIE, BC, V0B 1M5
(250) 423-9288   SIC 5511
COAST MOUNTAIN CHEVROLET PONTIAC BUICK GMC LTD   p269
4038 16 HWY E RR 6, SMITHERS, BC, V0J 2N6

(250) 847-2214   SIC 5511
COBOURG NISSAN LTD   p545
831 DIVISION ST, COBOURG, ON, K9A 5R9
(905) 372-3963   SIC 5511
COCHRANE MOTOR PRODUCTS LTD   p80
6 RIVER HEIGHTS DR, COCHRANE, AB, T4C 0N8
(403) 932-4072   SIC 5511
COLLEGE FORD LINCOLN LTD   p142
3975 1 AVE S, LETHBRIDGE, AB, T1J 4P8
(403) 329-0333   SIC 5511
COLLEGE PARK MOTOR PRODUCTS LTD p170
4512 RAILWAY AVE, VERMILION, AB, T9X 1E9
(780) 853-4646   SIC 5511
COLLINGWOOD CARS INC   p546
10230 26 HWY, COLLINGWOOD, ON, L9Y 0A5
(705) 444-1414   SIC 5511
COLLINS FAMILY CARS INC   p660
1035 WHARNCLIFFE RD S, LONDON, ON, N6L 1J9
(519) 690-1600   SIC 5511
COLONIAL CHEVROLET LTD   p755
18100 YONGE ST, NEWMARKET, ON, L3Y 8V1
(905) 895-1171   SIC 5511
COLONY FORD LINCOLN SALES INC p508
300 QUEEN ST E, BRAMPTON, ON, L6V 1C2
(905) 451-4094   SIC 5511
COLONY PONTIAC BUICK LTD   p1407
331 MAIN ST, HUMBOLDT, SK, S0K 2A1
(306) 682-2661   SIC 5511
COMMERCE AUTOMOBILE S.G.C. CORPORATION   p1047
7010 BOUL HENRI-BOURASSA E, ANJOU, QC, H1E 7K7
(514) 324-7777   SIC 5511
COMOX VALLEY DODGE CHRYSLER JEEP LTD   p203
4847 ISLAND HWY N, COURTENAY, BC, V9N 5Y8
(250) 338-5451   SIC 5511
COMPETITION CHEVROLET LTD   p167
40 BOULDER BLVD, STONY PLAIN, AB, T7Z 1V7
(780) 963-6121   SIC 5511
COMPETITION TOYOTA LTD   p651
1515 ROB PANZER RD, LONDON, ON, N5X 0M7
(519) 451-3880   SIC 5511
COMPLEXE AUTO 440 DE LAVAL INC p1086
3670 SUD LAVAL (A-440) O, COTE SAINT-LUC, QC, H7T 2H6
(450) 682-3670   SIC 5511
COMPLEXE DE L'AUTO PARK AVENUE INC p1345
4505 BOUL METROPOLITAIN E BUREAU 201, SAINT-LEONARD, QC, H1R 1Z4
(514) 899-9000   SIC 5511
COMPTON, CLARKE FINANCIAL INC p172
5402 56 ST, WETASKIWIN, AB, T9A 2B3
(780) 352-3311   SIC 5511
CONCESSIONNAIRE HONDA DE   p1316
400 RUE LABERGE, SAINT-JEAN-SUR-RICHELIEU, QC, J3A 1G5
(450) 347-7567   SIC 5511
CONCORDE AUTOMOBILE (1990) LTEE p1312
3003 RUE PICARD, SAINT-HYACINTHE, QC, J2S 1H2
(450) 774-5336   SIC 5511
CONNEXION TRUCK CENTRE LTD   p369
440 OAK POINT HWY, WINNIPEG, MB, R2R 1V3
(204) 633-3333   SIC 5511
CONVENTRY MOTORS LIMITED   p390
1717 WAVERLEY ST UNIT 520, WINNIPEG, MB, R3T 6A9
(204) 475-3982   SIC 5511
COOKSON MOTORS LTD   p221

1150 GORDON DR, KELOWNA, BC, V1Y 3E4

(250) 763-2327 *SIC* 5511

COOKSVILLE DODGE CHRYSLER INCp708
290 DUNDAS ST E, MISSISSAUGA, ON, L5A 1W9

(905) 279-3031 *SIC* 5511

COQUITLAM CHRYSLER DODGE JEEP LTD p199
2960 CHRISTMAS WAY, COQUITLAM, BC, V3C 4E6

(604) 464-6611 *SIC* 5511

COREY FORD LTD p420
336 CONNELL ST, WOODSTOCK, NB, E7M 5E2

(506) 328-8828 *SIC* 5511

CORNWALLIS CHEVROLET BUICK GMC LIMITED p463
9184 COMMERCIAL ST, NEW MINAS, NS, B4N 3E5

(902) 681-8300 *SIC* 5511

CORVETTE SPECIALTIES AUTO GROUP LTD p274
11180 SCOTT RD, SURREY, BC, V3V 8B8

(604) 580-8388 *SIC* 5511

COSMO MOTORS LTD p259
3511 NO. 3 RD, RICHMOND, BC, V6X 2B8

(604) 273-0333 *SIC* 5511

COTRAC FORD LINCOLN SALES INC p567
204 CURRIE RD, DUTTON, ON, N0L 1J0

(519) 762-3536 *SIC* 5511

COUNTRY ENTERPRISES LTD p136
1103 14 ST SE, HIGH RIVER, AB, T1V 1L5

SIC 5511

COUNTRYSIDE CHRYSLER DODGE LIMITED p569
458 TALBOT ST N, ESSEX, ON, N8M 2W6

(519) 776-5287 *SIC* 5511

COURTESY CHEVROLET LTD. p574
1635 THE QUEENSWAY, ETOBICOKE, ON, M8Z 1T8

SIC 5511

COURTESY CHRYSLER DODGE (1987) LTD
p34
125 GLENDEER CIR SE, CALGARY, AB, T2H 2S8

(403) 255-8111 *SIC* 5511

COURTESY CHRYSLER DODGE JEEP p35
125 GLENDEER CIR SE, CALGARY, AB, T2H 2S8

(403) 255-9100 *SIC* 5511

COURTESY FORD LINCOLN SALES LIMITED p659
684 WHARNCLIFFE RD S, LONDON, ON, N6J 2N4

(519) 680-1200 *SIC* 5511

COURVILLE, DAN CHEVROLET LTD p900
2601 REGENT ST, SUDBURY, ON, P3E 6K6

(705) 523-2438 *SIC* 5511

COVENTRY NORTH JAGUAR LAND ROVER
p1030
123 AUTO PARK CIR, WOODBRIDGE, ON, L4L 9S5

(647) 990-3433 *SIC* 5511

COWAN BUICK GMC LTD p496
166 KING ST E, BOWMANVILLE, ON, L1C 1N8

(905) 623-3396 *SIC* 5511

COWELL IMPORTS INC p254
5680 PARKWOOD CRES, RICHMOND, BC, V6V 0B5

(604) 273-6068 *SIC* 5511

COWELL MOTORS LTD p254
5600 PARKWOOD CRES, RICHMOND, BC, V6V 0B5

(604) 279-9663 *SIC* 5511

CRESTVIEW CHRYSLER DODGE JEEP
p1420
601 ALBERT ST, REGINA, SK, S4R 2P4

(306) 992-2443 *SIC* 5511

CROPPER, A.G. ENTERPRISES LTD p1412
501 5TH AVE N, NAICAM, SK, S0K 2Z0

(306) 874-2011 *SIC* 5511

CROSBY AUDI INC p635

2350 SHIRLEY DR, KITCHENER, ON, N2B 3X5

(519) 514-0100 *SIC* 5511

CROSS & NORMAN (1986) LTD p227
20027 FRASER HWY, LANGLEY, BC, V3A 4E4

(604) 534-7927 *SIC* 5511

CROSSROADS PONTIAC BUICK LIMITED
p423
295 AIRPORT BLVD, GANDER, NL, A1V 1Y9

(709) 651-3500 *SIC* 5511

CROSSTOWN OLDSMOBILE CHEVROLET LTD p898
280 FALCONBRIDGE RD, SUDBURY, ON, P3A 5K3

(705) 566-4804 *SIC* 5511

CROWFOOT DODGE CHRYSLER INC p74
20 CROWFOOT RISE NW, CALGARY, AB, T3G 3S7

(403) 241-0300 *SIC* 5511

CROWFOOT H MOTORS LP p75
710 CROWFOOT CRESCENT NW, CALGARY, AB, T3G 4S3

(403) 252-8833 *SIC* 5511

CROWFOOT IMAGE AUTO BODY LTD p75
141 CROWFOOT WAY NW UNIT 25, CALGARY, AB, T3G 4B7

(403) 547-4932 *SIC* 5511

CROWN NISSAN p390
1717 WAVERLEY ST SUITE 700, WINNIPEG, MB, R3T 6A9

(204) 269-4685 *SIC* 5511

CRUICKSHANK FORD p795
2062 WESTON RD, NORTH YORK, ON, M9N 1X5

(416) 244-6461 *SIC* 5511

CULLEN WESTERN STAR TRUCK INCp174
380 RIVERSIDE RD SUITE 3, ABBOTSFORD, BC, V2S 7M4

(604) 504-5904 *SIC* 5511

CULLEN, BARRY CHEVROLET CADILLAC LTD p605
905 WOODLAWN RD W, GUELPH, ON, N1K 1B7

(519) 824-0210 *SIC* 5511

CULLEN, BRIAN MOTORS LIMITED p885
386 ONTARIO ST, ST CATHARINES, ON, L2R 5L8

(905) 684-8745 *SIC* 5511

CULLEN, RAY CHEVROLET LTD p659
730 WHARNCLIFFE RD S, LONDON, ON, N6J 2N4

(519) 686-2875 *SIC* 5511

CURRY MOTORS LIMITED p607
5065 COUNTY RD 21 RR 3, HALIBURTON, ON, K0M 1S0

(705) 457-2765 *SIC* 5511

CUSTOM TRUCK SALES INC p1415
520 PARK ST, REGINA, SK, S4N 0T6

(306) 569-9021 *SIC* 5511

CVH AUTO INC p203
250 OLD ISLAND HWY, COURTENAY, BC, V9N 3P1

(250) 334-2441 *SIC* 5511

CYPRESS MOTORS (SC) p1436
2234 SOUTH SERVICE RD W, SWIFT CURRENT, SK, S9H 5J7

(306) 778-3673 *SIC* 5511

CYRVILLE CHRYSLER DODGE JEEP LTD
p820
900 ST. LAURENT BLVD, OTTAWA, ON, K1K 3B3

(613) 745-7051 *SIC* 5511

CYV CHEVROLET PONTIAC BUICK GMC LTD p420
324 CONNELL ST, WOODSTOCK, NB, E7M 5E2

(506) 799-0110 *SIC* 5511

D B D AUTO INC p1235
1215 BOUL DES LAURENTIDES, MONTREAL, QC, H7M 2Y1

(450) 668-6393 *SIC* 5511

D K FORD SALES LTD p139

6559 SPARROW DR, LEDUC, AB, T9E 7L1

(780) 986-2929 *SIC* 5511

D'ALESSANDRO INVESTMENTS LIMITED
p571
3526 LAKE SHORE BLVD W, ETOBICOKE, ON, M8W 1N6

(416) 252-2277 *SIC* 5511

DAIGNEAULT & FRERE (1966) INC p1316
400 RUE LABERGE, SAINT-JEAN-SUR-RICHELIEU, QC, J3A 1G5

(450) 347-7567 *SIC* 5511

DAJO HOLDINGS LTD p408
1810 MAIN ST, MONCTON, NB, E1E 4S7

(506) 852-8210 *SIC* 5511

DALMAR MOTORS LIMITED p659
475 WHARNCLIFFE RD S, LONDON, ON, N6J 2N1

(519) 433-3181 *SIC* 5511

DAMS FORD LINCOLN SALES LTD p271
19330 LANGLEY BYPASS, SURREY, BC, V3S 7R2

(604) 532-9921 *SIC* 5511

DAVIES AUTO ELECTRIC LIMITED p702
2571 WHARTON GLEN AVE, MISSISSAUGA, ON, L4X 2A8

(905) 279-6300 *SIC* 5511

DAVIS GMC BUICK LTD p142
115 WT HILL BLVD S, LETHBRIDGE, AB, T1J 4T6

(403) 329-4444 *SIC* 5511

DCH MOTORS LTD p260
4211 NO. 3 RD, RICHMOND, BC, V6X 2C3

(604) 278-8999 *SIC* 5511

DDJLR ONTARIO LTD p716
2477 MOTORWAY BLVD, MISSISSAUGA, ON, L5L 3R2

(905) 828-8488 *SIC* 5511

DEALERSHIP INVESTMENTS LIMITED p84
13145 97 ST NW, EDMONTON, AB, T5E 4C4

(780) 476-6221 *SIC* 5511

DEARBORN MOTORS LTD p217
2555 TRANS CANADA HWY E, KAMLOOPS, BC, V2C 4B1

(250) 372-7101 *SIC* 5511

DECKER MOTORS LIMITED p422
245 MEMORIAL DR, CLARENVILLE, NL, A5A 1R4

(709) 466-2394 *SIC* 5511

DEER LAKE SALES & SERVICE LTD p192
5965 KINGSWAY, BURNABY, BC, V5J 1H1

(604) 434-2488 *SIC* 5511

DEGROOT-HILL CHEVROLET BUICK GMC LTD p911
HWY 3, TILLSONBURG, ON, N4G 4H3

(519) 842-9026 *SIC* 5511

DELISLE AUTO LTEE p1174
2815 RUE SHERBROOKE E, MONTREAL, QC, H2K 1H2

(514) 523-1122 *SIC* 5511

DEMEYERE CHRYSLER LIMITED p880
144 QUEENSWAY E, SIMCOE, ON, N3Y 4K8

(519) 426-3010 *SIC* 5511

DENHAM FORD SALES LTD p172
5601 45 AVE, WETASKIWIN, AB, T9A 2G2

(780) 352-6043 *SIC* 5511

DENNIS CHEVROLET PONTIAC BUICK GMC LTD p422
24 CONFEDERATION DR, CORNER BROOK, NL, A2H 6G7

(709) 634-8248 *SIC* 5511

DENNISON AUTO LTD p241
828 AUTOMALL DR, NORTH VANCOUVER, BC, V7P 3R8

(604) 929-6736 *SIC* 5511

DERAGON AUTO-CITE INC p1088
797 BOUL JEAN-JACQUES-BERTRAND, COWANSVILLE, QC, J2K 0H9

(450) 266-0101 *SIC* 5511

DEROUARD MOTOR PRODUCTS LTD p628
1405 RAILWAY ST, KENORA, ON, P9N 0B3

(807) 467-4450 *SIC* 5511

DERRICK DODGE (1980) LTD p118

6211 104 ST NW, EDMONTON, AB, T6H 2K8

(780) 435-9500 *SIC* 5511

DERY AUTOMOBILE LTEE p1316
1055 BOUL DU SEMINAIRE N, SAINT-JEAN-SUR-RICHELIEU, QC, J3A 1R7

(450) 359-9000 *SIC* 5511

DERY TOYOTA LTEE p1315
250 RUE MOREAU, SAINT-JEAN-SUR-RICHELIEU, QC, J2W 0E9

(450) 359-9000 *SIC* 5511

DES SOURCES DODGE CHRYSLER LTEE
p1091
3400 BOUL DES SOURCES, DOLLARD-DES-ORMEAUX, QC, H9B 1Z9

(514) 685-3310 *SIC* 5511

DESCHAMPS CHEVROLET BUICK CADILLAC GMC LTEE p1358
333 BOUL ARMAND-FRAPPIER, SAINTE-JULIE, QC, J3E 0C7

(450) 649-9333 *SIC* 5511

DESJARDINS FORD LTEE p1329
1150 BOUL MARCEL-LAURIN, SAINT-LAURENT, QC, H4R 1J7

(514) 332-3850 *SIC* 5511

DESMEULES AUTOMOBILES INC p1135
182 138 RTE, LES ESCOUMINS, QC, G0T 1K0

(418) 233-2490 *SIC* 5511

DESTINATION AUTO ENTERPRISES INC
p185
4278 LOUGHEED HWY, BURNABY, BC, V5C 3Y5

(604) 294-2111 *SIC* 5511

DESTINATION AUTO SALES INC p289
368 KINGSWAY, VANCOUVER, BC, V5T 3J6

(604) 873-3676 *SIC* 5511

DESTINATION AUTO VENTURES INC p185
4278 LOUGHEED HWY, BURNABY, BC, V5C 3Y5

(604) 294-2111 *SIC* 5511

DESTINATION CHRYSLER LTD p241
1600 MARINE DR, NORTH VANCOUVER, BC, V7P 1T9

(888) 461-4138 *SIC* 5511

DEVON CHRYSLER DODGE JEEP RAM LTD p81
7 SASKATCHEWAN AVE W, DEVON, AB, T9G 1B2

(888) 342-9117 *SIC* 5511

DEVONIAN MOTOR CORPORATION p118
5220 GATEWAY BLVD, EDMONTON, AB, T6H 4J7

(780) 462-8846 *SIC* 5511

DEWILDT CAR SALES LIMITED p610
1600 MAIN ST E, HAMILTON, ON, L8K 1E7

(905) 312-0404 *SIC* 5511

DFC AUTO LTD p220
2350 HIGHWAY 97 N, KELOWNA, BC, V1X 4H8

(250) 860-6000 *SIC* 5511

DIAMOND INTERNATIONAL TRUCKS LTD
p100
17020 118 AVE NW, EDMONTON, AB, T5S 1S4

(780) 454-1541 *SIC* 5511

DICK'S GARAGE LIMITED p861
967 TRUNK RD, SAULT STE. MARIE, ON, P6A 5K9

(705) 759-1133 *SIC* 5511

DIEPPE AUTO LTEE/LTD p397
600 RUE CHAMPLAIN, DIEPPE, NB, E1A 1P4

(506) 857-0444 *SIC* 5511

DILAWRI CHEVROLET BUICK GMC INC
p1104
868 BOUL MALONEY O, GATINEAU, QC, J8T 3R6

(819) 568-5811 *SIC* 5511

DILAWRI HOLDINGS INC p390
1700 WAVERLEY ST SUITE C, WINNIPEG, MB, R3T 5V7

(204) 269-1572 *SIC* 5511

DINGWALL FORD SALES LTD   p628
927 HIGHWAY 17 E, KENORA, ON, P9N 1L9
(807) 468-6443   SIC 5511

DIRECT MOTOR COMPANY LTD   p597
2575 BANK ST, GLOUCESTER, ON, K1T 1M8
(613) 739-3088   SIC 5511

DISBROWE PONTIAC BUICK CADILLAC LTD   p889
116 EDWARD ST, ST THOMAS, ON, N5P 4E6
(519) 631-2224   SIC 5511

DISCOVERY FORD SALES BURLINGTON LIMITED   p530
850 BRANT ST, BURLINGTON, ON, L7R 2J5
(905) 632-8696   SIC 5511

DISCOVERY MOTORS LTD   p211
6466 BELL MCKINNON RD, DUNCAN, BC, V9L 6C1
(250) 748-5814   SIC 5511

DISTINCTIVE AUTOBODY & COLLISON CENTER LTD   p413
1265 LOCH LOMOND RD, SAINT JOHN, NB, E2J 3V4
(506) 634-1765   SIC 5511

DIXIE FORD SALES LIMITED   p694
5495 DIXIE RD, MISSISSAUGA, ON, L4W 1E6
(905) 629-1300   SIC 5511

DIXIE MOTORS LP   p694
5515 AMBLER DR, MISSISSAUGA, ON, L4W 3Z1
(905) 238-8080   SIC 5511

DIXIE PLYMOUTH CHRYSLER LTD   p502
8050 DIXIE RD, BRAMPTON, ON, L6T 4W6
(905) 452-1000   SIC 5511

DOLBEAU AUTOMOBILES LTEE   p1090
1770 BOUL WALLBERG, DOLBEAU-MISTASSINI, QC, G8L 1H8
(418) 276-0580   SIC 5511

DOMINION MOTORS (THUNDER BAY-1984) LTD   p908
882 COPPER CRES, THUNDER BAY, ON, P7B 6C9
(807) 343-2277   SIC 5511

DON DOCKSTEADER MOTORS LTD   p323
8530 CAMBIE ST, VANCOUVER, BC, V6P 6N6
(604) 323-2200   SIC 5511

DON VALLEY VOLKSWAGEN LIMITED p787
1695 EGLINTON AVE E, NORTH YORK, ON, M4A 1J6
(647) 956-0498   SIC 5511

DONMAR CAR SALES LTD   p100
17990 102 AVE NW, EDMONTON, AB, T5S 1M9
(780) 454-0422   SIC 5511

DONNELLY PONTIAC BUICK GMC LTD p826
2496 BANK ST, OTTAWA, ON, K1V 8S2
(613) 737-5000   SIC 5511

DONPAT INVESTMENTS LIMITED   p455
2657 ROBIE ST, HALIFAX, NS, B3K 4N9
(902) 453-1940   SIC 5511

DONWAY FORD SALES LIMITED   p868
1975 EGLINTON AVE E, SCARBOROUGH, ON, M1L 2N1
(416) 751-2200   SIC 5511

DOUG MARSHALL MOTOR CITY LTD p131
11044 100 ST, GRANDE PRAIRIE, AB, T8V 2N1
(780) 532-9333   SIC 5511

DOUGLAS FORD LINCOLN SALES LTD p484
379 BAYFIELD ST, BARRIE, ON, L4M 3C5
(705) 728-5558   SIC 5511

DOW MOTORS (OTTAWA) LIMITED   p825
845 CARLING AVE, OTTAWA, ON, K1S 2E7
(613) 237-2777   SIC 5511

DOWNEY FORD SALES LTD   p413
35 CONSUMERS DR, SAINT JOHN, NB, E2J 4Z7

(506) 632-6519   SIC 5511

DOWNIE, DALE NISSAN INC   p651
1111 OXFORD ST E, LONDON, ON, N5Y 3L7
(519) 451-4560   SIC 5511

DOWNSVIEW CHRYSLER PLYMOUTH (1964) LTD   p783
199 RIMROCK RD, NORTH YORK, ON, M3J 3C6
(416) 635-1660   SIC 5511

DOWNTOWN AUTOMOTIVE INC   p933
259 LAKE SHORE BLVD E, TORONTO, ON, M5A 3T7
SIC 5511

DOWNTOWN FINE CARS INC   p933
68 PARLIAMENT ST, TORONTO, ON, M5A 0B2
(416) 603-9988   SIC 5511

DRAYTON VALLEY FORD SALES LTD   p82
5214 POWER CENTRE BLVD, DRAYTON VALLEY, AB, T7A 0A5
(780) 542-4438   SIC 5511

DRIVING FORCE INC, THE   p100
17631 103 AVE NW, EDMONTON, AB, T5S 1N8
(780) 483-9559   SIC 5511

DRUMMOND, SCOTT MOTORS LTD   p539
501 GRAND RD RR 1, CAMPBELLFORD, ON, K0L 1L0
(705) 653-2020   SIC 5511

DRYDEN CHEVROLET BUICK GMC LTD p565
489 GOVERNMENT ST, DRYDEN, ON, P8N 2P6
(807) 223-7123   SIC 5511

DUBE AUTO SALES LIMITED   p398
454 RUE VICTORIA, EDMUNDSTON, NB, E3V 2K5
SIC 5511

DUBOIS & FRERES LIMITEE   p1246
637 AV SAINT-LOUIS, PLESSISVILLE, QC, G6L 2L9
(819) 362-7377   SIC 5511

DUCHARME MOTORS LTD   p6
5714 50 AVE, BONNYVILLE, AB, T9N 2K8
(780) 826-3278   SIC 5511

DUCHESNE AUTO LTEE   p1045
450 RUE DE QUEN, ALMA, QC, G8B 5P5
(418) 662-3431   SIC 5511

DUCLOS LONGUEUIL CHRYSLER DODGE JEEP RAM INC   p1308
5055 BOUL COUSINEAU, SAINT-HUBERT, QC, J3Y 3K7
(450) 656-4110   SIC 5511

DUECK CHEVROLET BUICK CADILLAC GMC LIMITED   p290
400 MARINE DR SE, VANCOUVER, BC, V5X 4X2
(604) 324-7222   SIC 5511

DUECK PONTIAC BUICK GMC LIMITED p294
888 TERMINAL AVE, VANCOUVER, BC, V6A 0A9
(604) 675-7900   SIC 5511

DUFOUR PONTIAC CHEVROLET INC p1122
2040 BOUL DE COMPORTE, LA MALBAIE, QC, G5A 3C4
(418) 665-7511   SIC 5511

DUNN, CRAIG PONTIAC BUICK GMC LTD p354
2345 SISSONS DR, PORTAGE LA PRAIRIE, MB, R1N 3P1
(204) 239-5770   SIC 5511

DUPONT FORD LTEE   p1315
190 RUE MOREAU, SAINT-JEAN-SUR-RICHELIEU, QC, J2W 2M4
(450) 359-3673   SIC 5511

DUPORTAGE FORD LTEE   p1107
949 BOUL SAINT-JOSEPH, GATINEAU, QC, J8Z 1S8
(819) 778-2751   SIC 5511

DUPUIS, FORD LINCOLN INC   p541
603 RUE ST ISIDORE, CASSELMAN, ON, K0A 1M0

(613) 764-2994   SIC 5511

DUVAL VOLKSWAGEN INC   p1064
1301 RUE AMPERE, BOUCHERVILLE, QC, J4B 5Z5
(450) 679-0890   SIC 5511

DYSON & ARMSTRONG INC   p1283
555 RUE CRAIG, RICHMOND, QC, J0B 2H0
(819) 826-3306   SIC 5511

EAGLE CREEK MOTOR PRODUCTS LTD p1409
809 9TH ST W SUITE 2, MEADOW LAKE, SK, S9X 1Y2
(306) 236-4482   SIC 5511

EAGLE NORTH HOLDINGS INC   p539
2400 EAGLE ST N, CAMBRIDGE, ON, N3H 4R7
(519) 653-7030   SIC 5511

EAGLE RIDGE CHEVROLET BUICK GMC LTD   p199
2595 BARNET HWY, COQUITLAM, BC, V3E 1K9
(604) 464-3941   SIC 5511

EAGLE RIVER CHRYSLER LTD   p173
3315 CAXTON ST, WHITECOURT, AB, T7S 1P4
(780) 778-2844   SIC 5511

EAST-COURT FORD LINCOLN SALES LIMITED   p874
4700 SHEPPARD AVE E, SCARBOROUGH, ON, M1S 3V6
(416) 292-1171   SIC 5511

EASTGATE FORD SALES & SERVICE (82) COMPANY INC   p609
350 PARKDALE AVE N, HAMILTON, ON, L8H 5Y3
(905) 547-2521   SIC 5511

EASTSIDE CHEVROLET BUICK GMC LTD p669
8435 WOODBINE AVE SUITE 7, MARKHAM, ON, L3R 2P4
(905) 475-7373   SIC 5511

EASTSIDE DODGE CHRYSLER LTD   p11
815 36 ST NE, CALGARY, AB, T2A 4W3
(403) 273-4313   SIC 5511

EASTVIEW CHEVROLET BUICK GMC LTD p627
222 GOVERNMENT RD, KAPUSKASING, ON, P5N 2X2
(705) 335-6187   SIC 5511

EASTWAY CHRYSLER DODGE JEEP LTD p867
2851 EGLINTON AVE E, SCARBOROUGH, ON, M1J 2E2
(416) 264-2501   SIC 5511

EASTWAY SALES & LEASING INC   p1018
9375 TECUMSEH RD E, WINDSOR, ON, N8R 1A1
(519) 979-1900   SIC 5511

ECONOMY WHEELS LTD   p645
129 ANGELINE ST N, LINDSAY, ON, K9V 4M9
(705) 324-5566   SIC 5511

EDMONDS CHEVROLET PONTIAC BUICK GMC LTD   p620
138 HANES RD, HUNTSVILLE, ON, P1H 1M4
(705) 789-5507   SIC 5511

EDMONTON KENWORTH LTD   p100
17335 118 AVE NW, EDMONTON, AB, T5S 2P5
(780) 453-3431   SIC 5511

EDMONTON MOTORS LIMITED   p92
11445 JASPER AVE NW, EDMONTON, AB, T5K 0M6
(780) 482-7809   SIC 5511

EDMUNDSTON AUTO LTD. - EDMUNDSTON AUTO LTEE   p398
121 CH CANADA, EDMUNDSTON, NB, E3V 1V7
(506) 735-4741   SIC 5511

EDSON CHRYSLER DODGE JEEP LTD p126
7440 4TH AVE, EDSON, AB, T7E 1V8
(780) 723-9500   SIC 5511

EDWARDS GARAGE LIMITED   p159

4403 42ND AVE, ROCKY MOUNTAIN HOUSE, AB, T4T 1A6
(403) 845-3328   SIC 5511

EICHENBERG MOTORS (1971) LIMITED p911
39 BROADWAY ST, TILLSONBURG, ON, N4G 3P2
(519) 842-5953   SIC 5511

ELGIN CHRYSLER LTD   p890
275 WELLINGTON ST, ST THOMAS, ON, N5R 2S6
(519) 633-2200   SIC 5511

ELITE CHRYSLER JEEP INC   p1376
6138 CH DE SAINT-ELIE, SHERBROOKE, QC, J1R 0L1
(819) 571-5540   SIC 5511

EMBRUN FORD SALES LTD   p569
608 NOTRE DAME ST, EMBRUN, ON, K0A 1W0
(613) 443-2985   SIC 5511

ENCORE AUTOMOBILE LTEE   p1076
266 BOUL SAINT-JEAN-BAPTISTE, CHATEAUGUAY, QC, J6K 3C2
(450) 698-1060   SIC 5511

ENERGY DODGE LTD   p1408
801 11TH AVE E, KINDERSLEY, SK, S0L 1S0
(306) 463-4131   SIC 5511

ENS MOTORS LTD   p1427
285 VENTURE CRES, SASKATOON, SK, S7K 6N8
(306) 653-5611   SIC 5511

ENSIGN CHRYSLER DODGE JEEP LTD p335
1061 YATES ST, VICTORIA, BC, V8V 3M5
(250) 386-2981   SIC 5511

ENTERPRISE LOCATION D'AUTOS CANADA LIMITEE   p1092
600 RUE ARTHUR-FECTEAU, DORVAL, QC, H4Y 1K5
SIC 5511

ENTOUR AUTOMOBILES INC   p1297
270 RTE 132, SAINT-CONSTANT, QC, J5A 2C9
(450) 632-7155   SIC 5511

ERICKSEN M-B LTD   p124
2120 103A ST SW, EDMONTON, AB, T6W 2P6
(780) 431-5100   SIC 5511

ERIN DODGE CHRYSLER LTD   p716
2365 MOTORWAY BLVD, MISSISSAUGA, ON, L5L 2M4
(905) 828-2004   SIC 5511

ERIN MILLS IMPORT INC   p716
3025 WOODCHESTER DR, MISSISSAUGA, ON, L5L 3V3
(905) 828-5800   SIC 5511

ERIN PARK AUTOMOTIVE PARTNERSHIP p716
2411 MOTORWAY BLVD, MISSISSAUGA, ON, L5L 3R2
(905) 828-7711   SIC 5511

ERINMOTORWAY INVESTMENTS LIMITED p716
2380 MOTORWAY BLVD, MISSISSAUGA, ON, L5L 1X3
(905) 828-1650   SIC 5511

ERINWOOD FORD SALES LIMITED   p716
2395 MOTORWAY BLVD, MISSISSAUGA, ON, L5L 1V4
(905) 828-1600   SIC 5511

ERNIE DEAN CHEVROLET BUICK GMC LTD   p476
4906 CONCESSION RD 7, ALLISTON, ON, L9R 1V3
(705) 435-4318   SIC 5511

ETOILE DODGE CHRYSLER INC, L' p1116
3311 BOUL DU ROYAUME, JONQUIERE, QC, G7X 0C4
(418) 542-9518   SIC 5511

EVANS, KEN FORD SALES LTD   p211
439 TRANS CANADA HWY, DUNCAN, BC, V9L 3R7
(250) 748-5555   SIC 5511

EXCEL AUTOMOBILES MONTREAL LTEE *p1156*
5400 RUE PARE, MONT-ROYAL, QC, H4P 1R3
(514) 342-6360   *SIC 5511*

EXCELLENCE DODGE CHRYSLER INC *p1300*
250 RUE DUBOIS, SAINT-EUSTACHE, QC, J7P 4W9
(450) 491-5555   *SIC 5511*

EXPERT CHEVROLET BUICK GMC LTD *p619*
500 HWY 11 E, HEARST, ON, P0L 1N0
(705) 362-8001   *SIC 5511*

EXPERT GARAGE LIMITED *p619*
420 HWY 11 E, HEARST, ON, P0L 1N0
(705) 362-4301   *SIC 5511*

EXPRESSWAY MOTORS LTD *p752*
1554 HAYSVILLE RD, NEW HAMBURG, ON, N3A 1A3
(519) 662-3900   *SIC 5511*

FADY AUTO INC *p1092*
4648 BOUL SAINT-JEAN, DOLLARD-DES-ORMEAUX, QC, H9H 2A6
(514) 696-7777   *SIC 5511*

FAIR ISLE FORD SALES LTD *p1039*
GD STN CENTRAL, CHARLOTTETOWN, PE, C1A 7K1
(902) 368-3673   *SIC 5511*

FAIR, MIKE CHEVROLET BUICK GMC CADILLAC LTD *p881*
199 LOMBARD ST, SMITHS FALLS, ON, K7A 5B8
(613) 283-3882   *SIC 5511*

FAIRLEY & STEVENS LIMITED *p446*
580 WINDMILL RD, DARTMOUTH, NS, B3B 1B5
(902) 468-6271   *SIC 5511*

FAIRVIEW COVE AUTO LIMITED *p457*
30 BEDFORD HWY, HALIFAX, NS, B3M 2J2
(902) 457-1555   *SIC 5511*

FAIRVIEW IMPORT MOTORS INC *p635*
2385 SHIRLEY DR, KITCHENER, ON, N2B 3X4
(519) 893-9000   *SIC 5511*

FAIRVIEW NISSAN LIMITEE *p1250*
345 BOUL BRUNSWICK, POINTE-CLAIRE, QC, H9R 4S1
(514) 697-5222   *SIC 5511*

FAIRVIEW PLYMOUTH CHRYSLER LTD *p402*
1065 HANWELL RD, FREDERICTON, NB, E3C 1A5
(506) 458-8955   *SIC 5511*

FAIRWAY FORD SALES LTD *p358*
236 MAIN ST, STEINBACH, MB, R5G 1Y6
(204) 326-3412   *SIC 5511*

FALLS CHEVROLET CADILLAC LTD *p760*
5888 THOROLD STONE RD, NIAGARA FALLS, ON, L2J 1A2
(905) 353-9123   *SIC 5511*

FENWICK, GLEN MOTORS LIMITED *p860*
836 ONTARIO ST, SARNIA, ON, N7T 1N2
(519) 344-7473   *SIC 5511*

FERRI, R AUTOMOBILES INC *p695*
4505 DIXIE RD, MISSISSAUGA, ON, L4W 5K3
(905) 625-7533   *SIC 5511*

FERRO AUTOMOBILES INC *p1367*
690 AV BROCHU, SEPT-ILES, QC, G4R 2X5
(418) 962-3301   *SIC 5511*

FESTIVAL FORD SALES (1983) LTD *p157*
37400 HIGHWAY 2 SUITE 421, RED DEER COUNTY, AB, T4E 1B9
(403) 343-3673   *SIC 5511*

FIDDLEHEAD AUTO SALES LIMITED *p467*
70 DODD ST, SYDNEY, NS, B1P 1T6
(902) 539-0771   *SIC 5511*

FIFTH AVENUE AUTO HAUS LTD *p11*
1120 MERIDIAN RD NE, CALGARY, AB, T2A 2N9
(403) 273-2500   *SIC 5511*

FINCH CHEVROLET CADILLAC BUICK

GMC LTD *p658*
640 WONDERLAND RD N, LONDON, ON, N6H 3E5
(519) 657-9411   *SIC 5511*

FINCHAM AUTOMOTIVE SUPPLIES LIMITED *p574*
70 ADVANCE RD SUITE 2484, ETOBICOKE, ON, M8Z 2T7
(416) 233-5896   *SIC 5511*

FINES FORD LINCOLN SALES & SERVICE LTD *p494*
12435 50 HWY, BOLTON, ON, L7E 1M3
(905) 857-1252   *SIC 5511*

FINES FORD LINCOLN SALES&SERVICE LTD *p494*
10 SIMONA DR, BOLTON, ON, L7E 4C7
(905) 857-1252   *SIC 5511*

FIRST TRUCK CENTRE INC *p95*
11313 170 ST NW, EDMONTON, AB, T5M 3P5
(780) 413-8800   *SIC 5511*

FLAG CHEVROLET-CHEVROLET TRUCK LTD *p270*
15250 104 AVE, SURREY, BC, V3R 6N8
(604) 584-7411   *SIC 5511*

FLECHE AUTO (1987) LTEE, LA *p1053*
707 BOUL LAFLECHE, BAIE-COMEAU, QC, G5C 1C6
(418) 589-3714   *SIC 5511*

FOCUS AUTO DESIGN INC *p16*
6159 40 ST SE, CALGARY, AB, T2C 2B1
(403) 255-4711   *SIC 5511*

FOCUS MOTORS LIMITED *p368*
1066 NAIRN AVE, WINNIPEG, MB, R2L 0Y4
(204) 663-3814   *SIC 5511*

FOLK, DON CHEVROLET INC *p220*
2350 HIGHWAY 97 N, KELOWNA, BC, V1X 4H8
(250) 860-6000   *SIC 5511*

FORBES BROS. INC *p514*
21 LYNDEN RD SUITE 19, BRANTFORD, ON, N3R 8B8
(519) 759-8220   *SIC 5511*

FORBES MOTORS INC *p640*
165 WEBER ST S, KITCHENER, ON, N2J 4A6
(519) 742-4463   *SIC 5511*

FORD LINCOLN *p1006*
455 KING ST N, WATERLOO, ON, N2J 2Z5
(877) 339-6067   *SIC 5511*

FORD LINCOLN GABRIEL, S.E.C. *p1222*
7100 RUE SAINT-JACQUES, MONTREAL, QC, H4B 1V2
(514) 487-7777   *SIC 5511*

FOREST PARK MOTORS INC *p813*
799 BLOOR ST W, OSHAWA, ON, L1J 5Y6
(905) 404-0525   *SIC 5511*

FORMAN FORD SALES LIMITED *p348*
36 2ND AVE NW, DAUPHIN, MB, R7N 1H2
(204) 622-3673   *SIC 5511*

FORMO MOTORS LTD *p359*
1550 MAIN ST, SWAN RIVER, MB, R0L 1Z0
(204) 734-4577   *SIC 5511*

FORMULA FORD SALES LIMITED *p843*
940 KINGSTON RD, PICKERING, ON, L1V 1B3
(905) 420-1449   *SIC 5511*

FORMULE FORD LINCOLN INC *p1111*
1144 RUE PRINCIPALE, GRANBY, QC, J2J 0M2
(450) 777-1777   *SIC 5511*

FORT CITY CHRYSLER SALES LTD *p213*
8424 ALASKA RD, FORT ST. JOHN, BC, V1J 5L6
(250) 787-5220   *SIC 5511*

FORT MOTORS LTD *p213*
11104 ALASKA RD, FORT ST. JOHN, BC, V1J 5T5
(250) 785-6661   *SIC 5511*

FORT YORK C MOTORS LP *p933*
321 FRONT ST E, TORONTO, ON, M5A 1G3
(416) 368-7000   *SIC 5511*

FORTIER AUTO (MONTREAL) LTEE *p1052*

7000 BOUL LOUIS-H.-LAFONTAINE, ANJOU, QC, H1M 2X3
(514) 353-9821   *SIC 5511*

FOSTER PONTIAC BUICK INC *p875*
3445 SHEPPARD AVE E, SCARBOROUGH, ON, M1T 3K5
(416) 291-9745   *SIC 5511*

FOURLANE FORD SALES LTD *p137*
4412 50 ST, INNISFAIL, AB, T4G 1P7
(403) 227-3311   *SIC 5511*

FOURNIER CHEVROLET OLDSMOBILE INC *p1262*
305 RUE DU MARAIS, QUEBEC, QC, G1M 3C8
(418) 687-5200   *SIC 5511*

FRASER CITY MOTORS LTD *p271*
19418 LANGLEY BYPASS, SURREY, BC, V3S 7R2
(604) 534-5355   *SIC 5511*

FRASER FORD SALES LIMITED *p813*
815 KING ST W, OSHAWA, ON, L1J 2L4
(905) 576-1800   *SIC 5511*

FRASER RIVER CHEVROLET BUICK GMC LTD *p252*
340 CARSON AVE, QUESNEL, BC, V2J 2B3
(250) 992-5515   *SIC 5511*

FREEBORN MOTORS LTD *p197*
44954 YALE RD W, CHILLIWACK, BC, V2R 4H1
(604) 792-2724   *SIC 5511*

FREEDOM FORD SALES LIMITED *p112*
7505 75 ST NW, EDMONTON, AB, T6C 4H8
(780) 465-9411   *SIC 5511*

FREEWAY FORD SALES LIMITED *p864*
958 MILNER AVE, SCARBOROUGH, ON, M1B 5V7
(416) 293-3077   *SIC 5511*

FREEWAY IMPORTS LTD *p270*
15420 104 AVE, SURREY, BC, V3R 1N8
(604) 583-7121   *SIC 5511*

FREIGHTLINER MANITOBA LTD *p369*
2058 LOGAN AVE, WINNIPEG, MB, R2R 0H9
(204) 694-3000   *SIC 5511*

FREIGHTLINER OF RED DEER INC *p155*
8046 EDGAR INDUSTRIAL CRES, RED DEER, AB, T4P 3R3
(403) 309-8225   *SIC 5511*

FRONTIER AUTOMOTIVE INC *p362*
1486 REGENT AVE W, WINNIPEG, MB, R2C 3A8
(204) 944-6600   *SIC 5511*

FRONTIER PETERBILT SALES LTD *p1427*
303 50TH ST E, SASKATOON, SK, S7K 6C1
(306) 242-3411   *SIC 5511*

FROST CHEVROLET BUICK GMC CADILLAC LTD *p513*
150 BOVAIRD DR W, BRAMPTON, ON, L7A 0H3
(905) 459-0126   *SIC 5511*

FRY, BENTON FORD SALES LTD *p492*
321 NORTH FRONT ST, BELLEVILLE, ON, K8P 3C6
(613) 962-9141   *SIC 5511*

FUNDY MOTORS (1995) LTD *p413*
160 ROTHESAY AVE, SAINT JOHN, NB, E2J 2B5
(506) 633-1333   *SIC 5511*

FUNK'S TOYOTA LTD *p358*
57 PTH 12 N, STEINBACH, MB, R5G 1T3
(204) 326-9808   *SIC 5511*

FUTUROTO INC *p1351*
279 AV SAINT-JACQUES, SAINT-RAYMOND, QC, G3L 4A2
(418) 337-6745   *SIC 5511*

G & M CHEVROLET-CADILLAC LTD *p399*
605 RUE VICTORIA, EDMUNDSTON, NB, E3V 3M8
(506) 735-3331   *SIC 5511*

G.B. BUSINESS ENTERPRISES LTD *p147*
8704 100 ST, MORINVILLE, AB, T8R 1K6
(780) 939-3666   *SIC 5511*

G.E. COWELL HOLDINGS LTD *p254*

13611 SMALLWOOD PL, RICHMOND, BC, V6V 1W8
(604) 273-3922   *SIC 5511*

GABRIEL MONTREAL-NORD, S.E.C. *p1239*
6464 BOUL HENRI-BOURASSA E, MONTREAL-NORD, QC, H1G 5W9
(514) 323-7777   *SIC 5511*

GALERIES FORD INC, LES *p1116*
3443 BOUL DU ROYAUME, JONQUIERE, QC, G7X 0C5
(418) 542-9551   *SIC 5511*

GALLINGER MOTORS LIMITED *p683*
655 MAIN ST E, MILTON, ON, L9T 3J2
(905) 875-3673   *SIC 5511*

GALT CHRYSLER DODGE LTD *p539*
2440 EAGLE ST N, CAMBRIDGE, ON, N3H 4R7
(519) 650-2440   *SIC 5511*

GANANOQUE MOTORS LTD *p592*
439 KING ST E, GANANOQUE, ON, K7G 1G9
(613) 382-2168   *SIC 5511*

GARAGE CIVIC LIMITEE *p1091*
3650 BOUL DES SOURCES, DOLLARD-DES-ORMEAUX, QC, H9B 1Z9
(514) 683-5533   *SIC 5511*

GARAGE DODGE CHRYSLER DE SAINT-BASILE INC *p1294*
225 BOUL SIR-WILFRID-LAURIER, SAINT-BASILE-LE-GRAND, QC, J3N 1M2
(450) 653-0114   *SIC 5511*

GARAGE F COSSETTE INC *p1368*
10303 BOUL DES HETRES, SHAWINIGAN, QC, G9N 4Y2
(819) 539-5457   *SIC 5511*

GARAGE FLORENT BEGIN INC *p1124*
1483 277 RTE, LAC-ETCHEMIN, QC, G0R 1S0
(418) 625-6101   *SIC 5511*

GARAGE FRANKE INC *p1354*
180 RUE PRINCIPALE E, SAINTE-AGATHE-DES-MONTS, QC, J8C 1K3
(819) 326-4775   *SIC 5511*

GARAGE JEAN-ROCH THIBEAULT INC *p1054*
909 BOUL MONSEIGNEUR-DE LAVAL, BAIE-SAINT-PAUL, QC, G3Z 2V9
(418) 435-2379   *SIC 5511*

GARAGE P VENNE INC *p1283*
94 RUE NOTRE-DAME, REPENTIGNY, QC, J6A 2P3
(514) 343-3428   *SIC 5511*

GARAGE REJEAN ROY INC *p1397*
465 BOUL DES BOIS-FRANCS N, VICTORIAVILLE, QC, G6P 1H1
(819) 758-8000   *SIC 5511*

GARAGE RENAUD FORTIER INC *p1375*
4320 BOUL BOURQUE, SHERBROOKE, QC, J1N 1S3
(819) 562-1700   *SIC 5511*

GARAGE SAVIGNAC, P E LTEE *p1114*
671 RUE SAINT-THOMAS, JOLIETTE, QC, J6E 3R6
(450) 756-4563   *SIC 5511*

GARAGE WINDSOR LTEE *p1286*
287 RUE TEMISCOUATA, RIVIERE-DU-LOUP, QC, G5R 2Y7
(418) 862-3586   *SIC 5511*

GARDEN CITY CHRYSLER PLYMOUTH LTD *p352*
220 STEPHEN ST, MORDEN, MB, R6M 1T4
(204) 822-6296   *SIC 5511*

GARDNER CHEVROLET OLDSMOBILE LTD *p215*
945 WATER AVE, HOPE, BC, V0X 1L0
(604) 869-2002   *SIC 5511*

GARDNER CHEVROLET PONTIAC BUICK GMC LTD *p215*
945 WATER ST, HOPE, BC, V0X 1L0
(604) 869-9511   *SIC 5511*

GARDNER MOTORS (1981) LTD *p146*
1500 STRACHAN RD SE, MEDICINE HAT, AB, T1B 4V2
(403) 527-2248   *SIC 5511*

GAREAU AUTO INC *p1390*
1100 3E AV E, VAL-D'OR, QC, J9P 0J6
(819) 825-6880   *SIC* 5511

GATEWAY CHEVROLET INC *p503*
2 GATEWAY BLVD, BRAMPTON, ON, L6T 4A7
(905) 791-7111   *SIC* 5511

GATEWAY CHEVROLET OLDSMOBILE INC *p503*
2 GATEWAY BLVD, BRAMPTON, ON, L6T 4A7
(905) 791-7111   *SIC* 5511

GATEWAY MOTORS (EDMONTON) LTD *p124*
2020 103A ST SW, EDMONTON, AB, T6W 2P6
(780) 439-3939   *SIC* 5511

GAUTHIER CHRYSLER DODGE JEEP *p362*
1375 REGENT AVE W, WINNIPEG, MB, R2C 3B2
(204) 661-8999   *SIC* 5511

GAUTHIER, JIM CHEVROLET LTD *p370*
1400 MCPHILLIPS ST, WINNIPEG, MB, R2V 4G6
(204) 697-1400   *SIC* 5511

GEAR-O-RAMA SUPPLY LTD *p204*
9300 GOLF COURSE RD, DAWSON CREEK, BC, V1G 4E9
(250) 782-8126   *SIC* 5511

GEMINI MOTORS LIMITED *p636*
26 MANITOU DR, KITCHENER, ON, N2C 1L1
(519) 894-2050   *SIC* 5511

GENDRON CHRYSLER JEEP DODGE *p1148*
259 BOUL DESJARDINS, MANIWAKI, QC, J9E 2E4
(819) 449-1611   *SIC* 5511

GENEEN AUTOMOBILES LIMITED *p989*
740 DUPONT ST, TORONTO, ON, M6G 1Z6
(416) 530-1880   *SIC* 5511

GEORGETOWN CHEVROLET BUICK GMC LTD *p593*
33 MOUNTAINVIEW RD N, GEORGE-TOWN, ON, L7G 4J7
(905) 877-6944   *SIC* 5511

GEORGIAN INTERNATIONAL LIMITED *p484*
85 BAYFIELD ST SUITE 500, BARRIE, ON, L4M 3A7
(705) 730-5900   *SIC* 5511

GERARD HUBERT AUTOMOBILES LTEE *p1148*
241 BOUL DESJARDINS, MANIWAKI, QC, J9E 2E3
(819) 449-2266   *SIC* 5511

GERRY'S TRUCK CENTRE LTD *p660*
4049 EASTGATE CRES, LONDON, ON, N6L 1B7
(519) 652-2100   *SIC* 5511

GESTION 47 LTEE *p1083*
1601 BOUL SAINT-MARTIN E, COTE SAINT-LUC, QC, H7G 4R4
(450) 669-7070   *SIC* 5511

GESTION ANKABETH INC *p1375*
4880 BOUL BOURQUE, SHERBROOKE, QC, J1N 2A7
(819) 823-1400   *SIC* 5511

GESTION CARBO LTEE *p1076*
117 BOUL SAINT-JEAN-BAPTISTE, CHATEAUGUAY, QC, J6K 3B1
(450) 691-4130   *SIC* 5511

GESTION GAEVAN INC *p1280*
625 RUE DE L'ARGON, QUEBEC, QC, G2N 2G7
(418) 841-2001   *SIC* 5511

GESTION GREGOIRE INC *p1315*
210 RUE MOREAU, SAINT-JEAN-SUR-RICHELIEU, QC, J2W 0E9
(450) 347-2835   *SIC* 5511

GESTION PONTIAC INC *p1391*
91 CH DU FORT, VAL-DES-MONTS, QC, J8N 4H4
   SIC 5511

GESTION RENE FORTIN INC *p1098*
150 BOUL SAINT-JOSEPH, DRUM-

MONDVILLE, QC, J2C 2A8
(819) 478-8148   *SIC* 5511

GESTION S. BISAILLON INC *p1308*
4645 CH DE CHAMBLY, SAINT-HUBERT, QC, J3Y 3M9
(450) 462-2828   *SIC* 5511

GESTIONS J.B. GREGOIRE INC *p1315*
96 RUE MOREAU, SAINT-JEAN-SUR-RICHELIEU, QC, J2W 2M4
(450) 348-6835   *SIC* 5511

GIBBONS, JOHN AUTOMOTIVE GROUP 2010 LTD *p543*
725 RICHMOND ST, CHATHAM, ON, N7M 5J5
(519) 352-6200   *SIC* 5511

GIESBRECHT & SONS LTD *p350*
GD, GIMLI, MB, R0C 1B0
(204) 642-5133   *SIC* 5511

GILLESPIE PONTIAC BUICK CADILLAC LIMITED *p1012*
16 LINCOLN ST, WELLAND, ON, L3C 5J1
(905) 735-7151   *SIC* 5511

GIRALDEAU INTER-AUTO INC *p1320*
2180 BOUL DU CURE-LABELLE, SAINT-JEROME, QC, J7Y 1T3
(450) 476-0720   *SIC* 5511

GIRARD AUTOMOBILE INC *p1282*
283 RUE VALMONT, REPENTIGNY, QC, J5Y 3H5
(450) 581-1490   *SIC* 5511

GLASSFORD MOTORS LIMITED *p621*
30 SAMNAH CRES SUITE 4, INGERSOLL, ON, N5C 3J7
(519) 485-0940   *SIC* 5511

GLENLEVEN MOTORS LIMITED *p800*
2388 ROYAL WINDSOR DR, OAKVILLE, ON, L6J 7Y2
(905) 845-7575   *SIC* 5511

GLENMAC CORPORATION LTD *p70*
11555 29 ST SE, CALGARY, AB, T2Z 0N4
(403) 258-6300   *SIC* 5511

GLOBOCAM (MONTREAL) INC *p1248*
155 AV REVERCHON, POINTE-CLAIRE, QC, H9P 1K1
(514) 344-4000   *SIC* 5511

GO AUTO CORPORATION *p101*
10220 184 ST NW, EDMONTON, AB, T5S 0B9
(780) 701-9999   *SIC* 5511

GO AUTO RED DEER CHRYSLER DODGE JEEP RAM LTD *p153*
3115 50 AVE, RED DEER, AB, T4N 3X8
(403) 352-7999   *SIC* 5511

GOLD KEY AUTOMOTIVE LTD *p271*
19545 LANGEY BYPASS, SURREY, BC, V3S 6K1
(604) 534-7431   *SIC* 5511

GOLD KEY PONTIAC BUICK (1984) LTD *p271*
19545 LANGLEY BYPASS, SURREY, BC, V3S 6K1
(604) 534-7431   *SIC* 5511

GOLD KEY SALES & SERVICES LTD *p280*
2092 152 ST, SURREY, BC, V4A 4N8
(604) 536-7212   *SIC* 5511

GOLD KEY SALES AND LEASE LTD *p271*
19545 LANGEY BYPASS, SURREY, BC, V3S 6K1
(604) 534-7431   *SIC* 5511

GOYETTE, MAURICE PONTIAC BUICK 1983 INC *p1392*
1623 132 RTE, VARENNES, QC, J3X 1P7
   SIC 5511

GRAEMOND HOLDINGS LTD *p234*
2535 BOWEN RD, NANAIMO, BC, V9T 3L2
(250) 758-3361   *SIC* 5511

GRAHAM AUTOMOTIVE SALES INC *p751*
2185 ROBERTSON RD, NEPEAN, ON, K2H 5Z2
(613) 596-1515   *SIC* 5511

GRAHAM AUTOMOTIVE SALES LTD *p751*
2195 ROBERTSON RD, NEPEAN, ON, K2H 5Z2
(613) 596-1515   *SIC* 5511

GRAHAM, TONY MOTORS (1980) LIMITED *p750*
1855 MERIVALE RD, NEPEAN, ON, K2G 1E3
(613) 225-1212   *SIC* 5511

GRAND-PORTAGE VOLKSWAGEN INC *p1286*
157 RUE FRASER, RIVIERE-DU-LOUP, QC, G5R 1C9
(418) 862-3490   *SIC* 5511

GRAND-PRIX AUTOMOTIVE DISTRIBU-TORS INC *p30*
4313 MANHATTAN RD SE, CALGARY, AB, T2G 4B1
(403) 243-5622   *SIC* 5511

GRANDWEST ENTERPRISES INC *p1427*
815 CIRCLE DR E, SASKATOON, SK, S7K 3S4
(306) 665-7755   *SIC* 5511

GREAT PLAINS FORD SALES (1978) LTD *p1437*
206 SIMS AVE, WEYBURN, SK, S4H 2H6
(306) 842-2645   *SIC* 5511

GREAT WEST CHRYSLER INC *p101*
17817 STONY PLAIN RD NW, EDMONTON, AB, T5S 1B4
(780) 483-5337   *SIC* 5511

GREAT WEST KENWORTH LTD *p35*
5909 6 ST SE, CALGARY, AB, T2H 1L8
(403) 253-7555   *SIC* 5511

GREAVETTE CHEVROLET PONTIAC BUICK CADILLAC GMC LTD *p497*
375 ECCLESTONE DR, BRACEBRIDGE, ON, P1L 1T6
(705) 645-2241   *SIC* 5511

GREEN ISLAND G AUTO LTD *p211*
6300 TRANS CANADA HWY, DUNCAN, BC, V9L 0C1
(250) 746-7131   *SIC* 5511

GRENIER CHEVROLET BUICK GMC INC *p1379*
1325 CAR MASSON, TERREBONNE, QC, J6W 6J7
(450) 471-3746   *SIC* 5511

GRENIER DODGE CHRYSLER INC *p1379*
1245 MONTEE MASSON, TERREBONNE, QC, J6W 6A6
(450) 471-4111   *SIC* 5511

GREY MOTORS AUTOMOTIVE GROUP LTD *p835*
717936 HIGHWAY 6 N, OWEN SOUND, ON, N4K 5W9
(519) 376-2240   *SIC* 5511

GRIMSBY CHRYSLER DODGE JEEP LTD. *p599*
421 SOUTH SERVICE RD, GRIMSBY, ON, L3M 4E8
(905) 945-9606   *SIC* 5511

GROGAN FORD LINCOLN INC *p1011*
5271 NAUVOO RD, WATFORD, ON, N0M 2S0
(519) 876-2730   *SIC* 5511

GROUPE AUBE LTEE *p1390*
1908 3E AV, VAL-D'OR, QC, J9P 7B1
(819) 825-6440   *SIC* 5511

GROUPE AUTO STE-FOY INC *p1272*
2777 BOUL DU VERSANT-NORD, QUE-BEC, QC, G1V 1A4
(418) 658-1340   *SIC* 5511

GROUPE CHASSE INC *p1173*
819 RUE RACHEL E, MONTREAL, QC, H2J 2H7
(514) 527-3411   *SIC* 5511

GROVE PONTIAC BUICK GMC LTD *p164*
HIGHWAY 16A W, SPRUCE GROVE, AB, T7X 3B2
   SIC 5511

GRV C MOTORS LP *p164*
200 ST. MATTHEWS AVE, SPRUCE GROVE, AB, T7X 3A6
(780) 809-9971   *SIC* 5511

GSL CHEVROLET OLDSMOBILE CADIL-LAC (1986) LIMITED *p72*
1720 BOW TRAIL SW, CALGARY, AB, T3C

2E4
(403) 781-1519   *SIC* 5511

GUELPH NISSAN INFINITI INC *p605*
805 WOODLAWN RD W, GUELPH, ON, N1K 1E9
(519) 822-9200   *SIC* 5511

GUILDFORD MOTORS INC *p274*
13820 104 AVE, SURREY, BC, V3T 1W9
(604) 584-1304   *SIC* 5511

GUSTAFSON'S AUTO SERVICE LTD *p344*
122 BROADWAY AVE N, WILLIAMS LAKE, BC, V2G 2X8
(250) 392-2305   *SIC* 5511

GUSTAFSON'S AUTOMOBILE CO LTD *p344*
122 BROADWAY AVE N, WILLIAMS LAKE, BC, V2G 2X8
(250) 392-3035   *SIC* 5511

HALFORD & VALENTINE (1991) LTD *p73*
11 RICHARD WAY SW, CALGARY, AB, T3E 7M8
(403) 217-1722   *SIC* 5511

HALLMARK FORD SALES LIMITED *p270*
10025 152 ST, SURREY, BC, V3R 4G6
(604) 584-1222   *SIC* 5511

HAMEL AUTOS DE MIRABEL INC *p1152*
10000 RUE DU PLEIN-AIR, MIRABEL, QC, J7J 1S5
(450) 435-1313   *SIC* 5511

HAMEL CHEVROLET BUICK GMC LTEE *p1345*
9455 BOUL LACORDAIRE, SAINT-LEONARD, QC, H1R 3E8
(514) 327-3540   *SIC* 5511

HAMEL HYUNDAI INC *p1300*
130 RUE DUBOIS, SAINT-EUSTACHE, QC, J7P 4W9
(450) 974-0440   *SIC* 5511

HANI AUTO INC *p1239*
7000 BOUL HENRI-BOURASSA E, MONTREAL-NORD, QC, H1G 6C4
(514) 327-7777   *SIC* 5511

HARBOURVIEW AUTOHAUS LTD *p234*
4921 WELLINGTON RD, NANAIMO, BC, V9T 2H5
(250) 751-1411   *SIC* 5511

HARDY RINGUETTE AUTOMOBILE INC *p1390*
1842 3E AV BUREAU 610, VAL-D'OR, QC, J9P 7A9
(819) 874-5151   *SIC* 5511

HARMONY AUTO SALES LTD *p220*
2550 ENTERPRISE WAY, KELOWNA, BC, V1X 7X5
(250) 860-6500   *SIC* 5511

HARMONY PREMIUM MOTORS LTD *p220*
2552 ENTERPRISE WAY, KELOWNA, BC, V1X 7X5
(250) 861-3003   *SIC* 5511

HARVEST INVESTMENTS LTD *p358*
144 PTH 12 N, STEINBACH, MB, R5G 1T4
(204) 326-1311   *SIC* 5511

HARWOOD FORD SALES LTD *p7*
1303 SUTHERLAND DR E, BROOKS, AB, T1R 1C8
(403) 362-6900   *SIC* 5511

HATHEWAY (TRACADIE) LIMITED *p419*
3318 RUE LACHAPELLE, TRACADIE-SHEILA, NB, E1X 1G5
(506) 395-2208   *SIC* 5511

HATHEWAY LIMITED *p394*
1030 ST. ANNE ST, BATHURST, NB, E2A 6X2
(506) 546-4464   *SIC* 5511

HATHEWAY, JIM FORD SALES LIMITED *p438*
76 ROBERT ANGUS DR, AMHERST, NS, B4H 4R7
(902) 667-6000   *SIC* 5511

HAWKINS TRUCK MART LTD *p403*
125 GREENVIEW DR, HANWELL, NB, E3C 0E4
(506) 452-7946   *SIC* 5511

HAYWORTH EQUIPMENT SALES INC *p1*
26180 114 AVE, ACHESON, AB, T7X 6R1

(780) 962-9100   *SIC* 5511
HCN MOTORS LTD   *p749*
275 WEST HUNT CLUB RD, NEPEAN, ON, K2E 1A6
(613) 521-6262   *SIC* 5511
HEALY FORD SALES LIMITED   *p89*
10616 103 AVE NW, EDMONTON, AB, T5J 0J2
    SIC 5511
HEASLIP FORD SALES LTD   *p607*
18 MAIN ST S, HAGERSVILLE, ON, N0A 1H0
(905) 768-3393   *SIC* 5511
HEFFNER MOTORS LIMITED   *p634*
3121 KING ST E, KITCHENER, ON, N2A 1B1
(519) 748-9666   *SIC* 5511
HEMPHILL PONTIAC BUICK CHEVROLET GMC LIMITED   *p1042*
34 WATER ST, SUMMERSIDE, PE, C1N 4T8
(877) 759-1458   *SIC* 5511
HENINGER TOYOTA   *p30*
3640 MACLEOD TRAIL SE, CALGARY, AB, T2G 2P9
(403) 243-8000   *SIC* 5511
HENLEY MOTORS LIMITED   *p884*
308 LAKE ST, ST CATHARINES, ON, L2N 4H3
(905) 934-3379   *SIC* 5511
HENTSCHEL, HART INC   *p860*
755 CONFEDERATION ST, SARNIA, ON, N7T 1M8
(519) 344-1123   *SIC* 5511
HERBLENS MOTORS INC   *p101*
11204 170 ST NW, EDMONTON, AB, T5S 2X1
(780) 466-8300   *SIC* 5511
HERITAGE FORD SALES LIMITED   *p869*
2660 KINGSTON RD, SCARBOROUGH, ON, M1M 1L6
(416) 261-3311   *SIC* 5511
HERRON CHEVROLET PONTIAC BUICK GMC LIMITED   *p463*
465 WESTVILLE RD, NEW GLASGOW, NS, B2H 2J6
(902) 752-1534   *SIC* 5511
HEUVELMANS CHEVROLET BUICK GMC CADILLAC LIMITED   *p542*
755 GRAND AVE E, CHATHAM, ON, N7L 1X5
(519) 352-9200   *SIC* 5511
HICKMAN MOTORS LIMITED   *p430*
85 KENMOUNT RD, ST. JOHN'S, NL, A1B 3P8
(709) 726-6990   *SIC* 5511
HIGH COUNTRY CHEVROLET BUICK GMC LTD   *p136*
702 11 AVE SE, HIGH RIVER, AB, T1V 1M3
(403) 652-2000   *SIC* 5511
HIGH PRAIRIE FORD SALES & SERVICE LTD   *p135*
5404 40 ST, HIGH PRAIRIE, AB, T0G 1E0
(780) 523-4193   *SIC* 5511
HIGH RIVER FORD SALES   *p136*
1103 11 AVE SE, HIGH RIVER, AB, T1V 1P2
    SIC 5511
HIGHBURY FORD SALES LIMITED   *p651*
1365 DUNDAS ST LONDON, ON, N5W 3B5
(519) 455-1800   *SIC* 5511
HIGHLAND CHEVROLET CADILLAC LTD   *p480*
15783 YONGE ST, AURORA, ON, L4G 1P4
(905) 727-1900   *SIC* 5511
HIGHLAND FORD SALES LIMITED   *p470*
35 BALODIS DR, WESTVILLE, NS, B0K 2A0
(902) 396-2020   *SIC* 5511
HIGHLAND FORD SALES LIMITED   *p862*
68 GREAT NORTHERN RD, SAULT STE. MARIE, ON, P6B 4Y5
(705) 759-5050   *SIC* 5511
HIGHWAY STERLING WESTERN STAR INC

p483
1021 INDUSTRIAL RD, AYR, ON, N0B 1E0
(519) 740-2405   *SIC* 5511
HILDEBRAND MOTORS LTD   *p151*
6401 46 ST, OLDS, AB, T4H 1L7
(403) 556-3371   *SIC* 5511
HILLCREST VOLKSWAGON (1979) LTD   *p455*
3154 ROBIE ST, HALIFAX, NS, B3K 4P9
(902) 453-2790   *SIC* 5511
HILLSIDE MOTORS (1973) LTD   *p1039*
113 ST. PETERS RD, CHARLOTTETOWN, PE, C1A 5P3
(902) 368-2438   *SIC* 5511
HILLSIDE NISSAN LTD   *p401*
580 PROSPECT ST, FREDERICTON, NB, E3B 6G9
(506) 458-9423   *SIC* 5511
HILLTOP SALES & SERVICE LTD   *p332*
4407 27 ST, VERNON, BC, V1T 4Y5
(250) 542-2324   *SIC* 5511
HIND, CRAIG DODGE CHRYSLER LIMITED   *p871*
2180 LAWRENCE AVE E, SCARBOROUGH, ON, M1P 2P8
    SIC 5511
HING LEE MOTORS LIMITED   *p920*
601 EASTERN AVE, TORONTO, ON, M4M 1E3
(416) 461-2323   *SIC* 5511
HODGSCO EQUITIES LTD   *p165*
5 GALARNEAU PL, ST. ALBERT, AB, T8N 2Y3
(780) 458-7100   *SIC* 5511
HOGAN CHEVROLET BUICK GMC LIMITED   *p874*
5000 SHEPPARD AVE E, SCARBOROUGH, ON, M1S 4L9
(416) 291-5054   *SIC* 5511
HOGEWONING MOTORS LTD   *p514*
5 WOODYATT DR, BRANTFORD, ON, N3R 7K3
(519) 752-5010   *SIC* 5511
HOLLIS FORD INC   *p469*
266 ROBIE ST, TRURO, NS, B2N 1L1
(902) 895-5000   *SIC* 5511
HOMETOWN SERVICE LTD   *p361*
690 MEMORIAL DR, WINKLER, MB, R6W 0M6
(204) 325-4777   *SIC* 5511
HONDA CANADA INC   *p241*
816 AUTOMALL DR, NORTH VANCOUVER, BC, V7P 3R8
(604) 984-0331   *SIC* 5511
HOPPER AUTOMOBILES LTD   *p763*
550 MCKEOWN AVE, NORTH BAY, ON, P1B 7M2
(888) 392-9178   *SIC* 5511
HORIZON EXPORTS INC   *p214*
1028 GIBSONS WAY, GIBSONS, BC, V0N 1V7
(604) 886-3433   *SIC* 5511
HOTTE AUTOMOBILE INC   *p619*
640 MAIN ST W, HAWKESBURY, ON, K6A 2J3
(613) 632-1159   *SIC* 5511
HOULE & FRERES GARAGE (TERREBONNE) LTEE   *p1149*
290 MONTEE MASSON, MASCOUCHE, QC, J7K 3B5
(450) 474-1110   *SIC* 5511
HOULE AUTOMOBILE LTEE   *p1163*
9080 RUE HOCHELAGA, MONTREAL, QC, H1L 2N9
(514) 351-5010   *SIC* 5511
HOULE TOYOTA LTEE   *p1247*
12305 RUE SHERBROOKE E, POINTE-AUX-TREMBLES, QC, H1B 1C8
(514) 640-5010   *SIC* 5511
HOWARD MOTORS INC   *p430*
46 KENMOUNT RD, ST. JOHN'S, NL, A1B 1W2
(709) 726-9900   *SIC* 5511
HUDSON, LARRY PONTIAC BUICK GMC

(1995) INC   *p647*
1000 WALLACE AVE N, LISTOWEL, ON, N4W 1M5
(519) 291-3791   *SIC* 5511
HULL NISSAN   *p1107*
959 BOUL SAINT-JOSEPH, GATINEAU, QC, J8Z 1W8
(819) 776-0100   *SIC* 5511
HULLY GULLY AUTOMOBILES INC   *p660*
940 WHARNCLIFFE RD S, LONDON, ON, N6L 1K3
(519) 686-3754   *SIC* 5511
HUMBER MOTORS LIMITED   *p422*
8 MOUNT BERNARD AVE, CORNER BROOK, NL, A2H 0C6
(709) 634-4371   *SIC* 5511
HUMBERVIEW GROUP LTD   *p995*
2500 BLOOR ST W, TORONTO, ON, M6S 1R7
    SIC 5511
HUNT CHRYSLER LTD   *p684*
500 BRONTE ST S, MILTON, ON, L9T 9H5
(905) 876-2580   *SIC* 5511
HUNT CLUB AUTOMOTIVE LTD   *p826*
92 TERRY FOX DR, OTTAWA, ON, K1V 0W8
(613) 733-7500   *SIC* 5511
HUNT CLUB MOTORS LIMITED   *p597*
2655 BANK ST, GLOUCESTER, ON, K1T 1N1
(613) 521-2300   *SIC* 5511
HURON MOTOR PRODUCTS LIMITED   *p590*
70704 LONDON RD, EXETER, ON, N0M 1S1
(514) 700-0180   *SIC* 5511
HYATT AUTO SALES & LEASING INC   *p35*
161 GLENDEER CIR SE, CALGARY, AB, T2H 2S8
(403) 252-8833   *SIC* 5511
HYUNDAI AUTOMOBILES ULSAN LTEE   *p1094*
1625 BOUL HYMUS, DORVAL, QC, H9P 1J5
(514) 336-4613   *SIC* 5511
IMAGE AUTOMOBILES INC   *p608*
155 CENTENNIAL PKY N, HAMILTON, ON, L8E 1H8
(905) 561-4100   *SIC* 5511
INDIAN HEAD CHRYSLER DODGE JEEP RAM LTD   *p1408*
501 JOHNSTON AVE, INDIAN HEAD, SK, S0G 2K0
(306) 695-2254   *SIC* 5511
INFINITI LAVAL INC   *p1086*
1950 BOUL CHOMEDEY, COTE SAINT-LUC, QC, H7T 2W3
(514) 382-8550   *SIC* 5511
INFINITI QUEBEC INC   *p1275*
2766 RUE EINSTEIN, QUEBEC, QC, G1X 4N8
(418) 658-3535   *SIC* 5511
INLAND AUTO CENTRE LTD   *p204*
11600 8 ST, DAWSON CREEK, BC, V1G 4R7
(250) 782-5507   *SIC* 5511
INTER-BOUCHERVILLE INC   *p1066*
50 CH DU TREMBLAY, BOUCHERVILLE, QC, J4B 6Z5
(450) 655-5050   *SIC* 5511
INVESTISSEMENTS J.B. GREGOIRE INC   *p1069*
8450 BOUL TASCHEREAU, BROSSARD, QC, J4X 1C2
(450) 466-0999   *SIC* 5511
IRL INTERNATIONAL TRUCK CENTRES LTD   *p331*
7156 MEADOWLARK RD, VERNON, BC, V1B 3R6
(877) 463-0292   *SIC* 5511
ISFELD, LOU LINCOLN MERCURY SALES LTD   *p177*
32562 SOUTH FRASER WAY, ABBOTSFORD, BC, V2T 1X6
(604) 857-1327   *SIC* 5511

ISLINGTON CHRYSLER PLYMOUTH (1963) LTD   *p577*
5476 DUNDAS ST W, ETOBICOKE, ON, M9B 1B6
(416) 239-3541   *SIC* 5511
ISLINGTON MOTOR SALES LIMITED *p1031*
7625 MARTIN GROVE RD SUITE B, WOODBRIDGE, ON, L4L 2C5
(905) 851-1279   *SIC* 5511
ISON T.H. AUTO SALES INC   *p917*
2300 DANFORTH AVE, TORONTO, ON, M4C 1K6
(416) 423-2300   *SIC* 5511
J.B.'S AUTOMOTIVE CENTRE LTD   *p101*
11670 170 ST NW SUITE 80, EDMONTON, AB, T5S 1J7
(780) 435-3681   *SIC* 5511
J.L. DESJARDINS AUTO COLLECTION INC *p1275*
3330 AV WATT, QUEBEC, QC, G1X 4S6
(418) 650-0063   *SIC* 5511
JACOBSON FORD SALES LTD   *p268*
450 TRANS CANADA HWY SW, SALMON ARM, BC, V1E 1S9
(250) 832-2101   *SIC* 5511
JAGO AUTO LTD   *p422*
31 CONFEDERATION DR, CORNER BROOK, NL, A2H 0A6
(709) 639-7575   *SIC* 5511
JAMES CAMPBELL SERVICES LTD   *p815*
550 TAUNTON RD W, OSHAWA, ON, L1L 0N8
(905) 571-5420   *SIC* 5511
JAMES WESTERN STAR TRUCK & TRAILER LTD   *p250*
5239 CONTINENTAL WAY, PRINCE GEORGE, BC, V2N 5S5
(250) 561-0646   *SIC* 5511
JANZEN CHEVROLET BUICK GMC LTD *p361*
145 BOUNDARY TRAIL, WINKLER, MB, R6W 0L7
(204) 325-9511   *SIC* 5511
JAPAN AUTO LEASING INC   *p1008*
545 KING ST N, WATERLOO, ON, N2L 5Z6
(519) 746-4120   *SIC* 5511
JEFFREY BEST MOTORS INCORPORATED *p459*
843 PARK ST, KENTVILLE, NS, B4N 3V7
(902) 678-6000   *SIC* 5511
JERRY FORD SALES LTD   *p126*
5908 4 AVE, EDSON, AB, T7E 1L9
(780) 723-4441   *SIC* 5511
JESSEL, BRIAN AUTOSPORT INC   *p286*
2311 BOUNDARY RD, VANCOUVER, BC, V5M 4W5
(604) 222-7788   *SIC* 5511
JIM PENNEY LIMITED   *p423*
105 LAURELL RD, GANDER, NL, A1V 0A9
(709) 256-4821   *SIC* 5511
JIM TUBMAN HOLDINGS LTD   *p827*
1770 BANK ST, OTTAWA, ON, K1V 7Y6
(613) 733-4050   *SIC* 5511
JIM WILSON CHEVROLET BUICK GMC INC *p809*
20 MULCAHY CT, ORILLIA, ON, L3V 6H9
(705) 329-2000   *SIC* 5511
JL DESJARDINS AUTO COLLECTION INC *p1262*
175 RUE DU MARAIS, QUEBEC, QC, G1M 3C8
(418) 683-4450   *SIC* 5511
JLV ENTERPRISES   *p386*
3965 PORTAGE AVE UNIT 10, WINNIPEG, MB, R3K 2G8
(204) 452-0756   *SIC* 5511
JOHN BEAR BUICK GMC LTD   *p884*
333 LAKE ST, ST CATHARINES, ON, L2N 7T3
(905) 934-2571   *SIC* 5511
JOHNSTON MOTOR SALES CO. LIMITED *p617*
1350 UPPER JAMES ST, HAMILTON, ON, L9C 3B4

▲ Public Company   ■ Public Company Family Member   **HQ** Headquarters   **BR** Branch   **SL** Single Location

(905) 388-5502 *SIC* 5511
JOHNSTON, KERV MOTORS (1996) LTD
p487
80 MAPLEVIEW DR W, BARRIE, ON, L4N
9H6
(705) 733-2100 *SIC* 5511
JOLIETTE DODGE CHRYSLER LTEE *p1114*
305 RUE DU CURE-MAJEAU, JOLIETTE,
QC, J6E 8S9
(450) 586-6002 *SIC* 5511
JOLIETTE MITSUBISHI *p1355*
661 RUE PRINCIPALE, SAINTE-ANNE-DE-
LA-PERADE, QC, G0X 2J0
(418) 325-2444 *SIC* 5511
JOLOWAY LTD *p1040*
40 LOWER MALPEQUE RD, CHARLOTTE-
TOWN, PE, C1E 1R3
(902) 566-1101 *SIC* 5511
JONES, MARV LTD *p231*
20611 LOUGHEED HWY, MAPLE RIDGE,
BC, V2X 2P9
(604) 465-5464 *SIC* 5511
JONKER AUTO LTD *p272*
19515 LANGLEY BYPASS, SURREY, BC,
V3S 6K1
(604) 530-6281 *SIC* 5511
**JONSSON, DENNIS MOTOR PRODUCTS
LTD** *p245*
3800 JOHNSTON RD, PORT ALBERNI, BC,
V9Y 5N7
(250) 723-3541 *SIC* 5511
JUBILEE FORD SALES (1983) LTD *p1425*
419 BRAND PL, SASKATOON, SK, S7J 5L6
(306) 373-4444 *SIC* 5511
JUNCTION MOTORS LTD *p135*
5309 50 ST, GRIMSHAW, AB, T0H 1W0
(780) 332-2886 *SIC* 5511
K.L. FINE CARS LTD *p804*
2500 SOUTH SERVICE RD W, OAKVILLE,
ON, L6L 5M9
(905) 845-7791 *SIC* 5511
**KALAWSKY PONTIAC BUICK G M C (1989)
LTD** *p195*
1700 COLUMBIA AVE, CASTLEGAR, BC,
V1N 2W4
(250) 365-2155 *SIC* 5511
**KAMLOOPS DODGE CHRYSLER JEEP
LIMITED** *p217*
2525 TRANS CANADA HWY E, KAM-
LOOPS, BC, V2C 4A9
(250) 374-4477 *SIC* 5511
KAMLOOPS HYUNDAI *p217*
948 NOTRE DAME DR, KAMLOOPS, BC,
V2C 6J2
(250) 851-9380 *SIC* 5511
KANTOLA MOTORS LIMITED *p628*
200 LAKEVIEW DR, KENORA, ON, P9N
0H2
(807) 468-8984 *SIC* 5511
KEAY, JIM FORD LINCOLN SALES LTD
p810
1438 YOUVILLE DR, ORLEANS, ON, K1C
2X8
(613) 841-1010 *SIC* 5511
KECHNIE CHEVROLET OLDSMOBILE LTD
p597
74 KINGSTON ST, GODERICH, ON, N7A
3K4
SIC 5511
KEIJ ENTERPRISES LTD *p243*
2405 SKAHA LAKE RD, PENTICTON, BC,
V2A 6E8
(250) 493-1107 *SIC* 5511
KELLY & BELL HOLDINGS LTD *p1425*
819 MELVILLE ST, SASKATOON, SK, S7J
5L2
(306) 242-8688 *SIC* 5511
KELOWNA CHRYSLER DODGE JEEP *p220*
2440 ENTERPRISE WAY, KELOWNA, BC,
V1X 6X6
(250) 763-6121 *SIC* 5511
KELOWNA FORD LINCOLN SALES LTD
p220
2540 ENTERPRISE WAY, KELOWNA, BC,

V1X 7X5
(250) 868-2330 *SIC* 5511
KELOWNA MOTORS LTD *p220*
2560 ENTERPRISE WAY, KELOWNA, BC,
V1X 7X5
(250) 762-2068 *SIC* 5511
KELOWNA NISSAN LTD *p220*
2741 HIGHWAY 97 N, KELOWNA, BC, V1X
4J8
(250) 712-0404 *SIC* 5511
KEN SARGENT GMC BUICK LTD *p132*
12308 100 ST, GRANDE PRAIRIE, AB, T8V
4H7
(780) 532-8865 *SIC* 5511
KEN SHAW MOTORS LIMITED *p993*
2336 ST CLAIR AVE W, TORONTO, ON,
M6N 1K8
(416) 766-0055 *SIC* 5511
KENMOUNT MOTORS INC *p430*
547 KENMOUNT RD, ST. JOHN'S, NL, A1B
3P9
(709) 579-1999 *SIC* 5511
KENNEBEC DODGE CHRYSLER INC *p1305*
10240 BOUL LACROIX, SAINT-GEORGES,
QC, G5Y 1K1
(418) 228-5575 *SIC* 5511
KENNEDY FORD SALES LIMITED *p802*
280 SOUTH SERVICE RD W, OAKVILLE,
ON, L6K 3X5
(905) 845-1646 *SIC* 5511
**KENTVILLE CHRYSLER DODGE JEEP
(2005) INC** *p459*
800 PARK ST, KENTVILLE, NS, B4N 3V7
(902) 678-2134 *SIC* 5511
KENTWOOD FORD SALES INC *p84*
13344 97 ST NW, EDMONTON, AB, T5E
4C9
(780) 476-8600 *SIC* 5511
KEY LEASE CANADA LTD *p249*
2005 REDWOOD ST, PRINCE GEORGE,
BC, V2L 2N5
(250) 564-7205 *SIC* 5511
KEY WEST FORD SALES LTD *p237*
301 STEWARDSON WAY, NEW WESTMIN-
STER, BC, V3M 2A5
(604) 239-7832 *SIC* 5511
KIA MOTORS LP *p94*
13634 ST ALBERT TRAIL NW, EDMON-
TON, AB, T5L 4P3
(780) 509-1550 *SIC* 5511
KIA OF TIMMINS *p913*
1285 RIVERSIDE DR, TIMMINS, ON, P4R
1A6
(705) 267-8291 *SIC* 5511
KIA SOUTH VANCOUVER *p290*
396 MARINE DR SW, VANCOUVER, BC,
V5X 2R6
(604) 326-6868 *SIC* 5511
KING GEORGE CARRIAGE LTD *p283*
2466 KING GEORGE BLVD, SURREY, BC,
V4P 1H5
(604) 536-2884 *SIC* 5511
KING MAZDA INC *p413*
440 ROTHESAY AVE, SAINT JOHN, NB,
E2J 2C4
(506) 634-8370 *SIC* 5511
KINGLAND FORD SALES LTD *p435*
922 MACKENZIE HWY SS 22, HAY RIVER,
NT, X0E 0R8
SIC 5511
**KINGSCROSS HYUNDAI MOTOR SPORTS
INC** *p868*
23 CIVIC RD, SCARBOROUGH, ON, M1L
2K6
(416) 757-7700 *SIC* 5511
KINGSCROSS MOTOR SPORTS INC *p868*
1957 EGLINTON AVE E, SCARBOROUGH,
ON, M1L 2M3
(416) 755-6283 *SIC* 5511
KINGSTON DODGE CHRYSLER (1980) LTD
p632
1429 PRINCESS ST, KINGSTON, ON, K7M
3E9
(613) 549-8900 *SIC* 5511

KINGSTON DODGE JEEP EAGLE LTD *p632*
1429 PRINCESS ST, KINGSTON, ON, K7M
3E9
(613) 549-8900 *SIC* 5511
KINGSWAY MOTORS (1982) LTD *p84*
12820 97 ST NW, EDMONTON, AB, T5E
4C3
(780) 478-8300 *SIC* 5511
KIRBY INTERNATIONAL TRUCKS LTD*p636*
48 ARDELT AVE, KITCHENER, ON, N2C
2C0
(519) 578-6680 *SIC* 5511
KIRK CHITICK PETERBOROUGH AUTO
p841
898 FORD ST, PETERBOROUGH, ON, K9J
5V3
(705) 536-0050 *SIC* 5511
KITCHENER NISSAN (2009) INC *p635*
1450 VICTORIA ST N, KITCHENER, ON,
N2B 3E2
(519) 744-1188 *SIC* 5511
KLONDIKE MOTORS LTD *p1440*
191 RANGE RD, WHITEHORSE, YT, Y1A
3E5
(867) 668-3362 *SIC* 5511
KNAPP, KEN FORD SALES LTD *p570*
390 TALBOT ST N, ESSEX, ON, N8M 2W4
(519) 776-6447 *SIC* 5511
KOCH FORD LINCOLN SALES LTD *p119*
5121 GATEWAY BLVD NW, EDMONTON,
AB, T6H 5W5
(780) 434-8411 *SIC* 5511
**KOLLBEC GATINEAU CHRYSLER JEEP
INC** *p1104*
812 BOUL MALONEY O, GATINEAU, QC,
J8T 3R6
(819) 568-1414 *SIC* 5511
KROTZ, HARVEY LIMITED *p647*
1199 WALLACE AVE N, LISTOWEL, ON,
N4W 1M6
(519) 291-3520 *SIC* 5511
L.D. AUTO (1986) INC *p1303*
854 BOUL DU SACRE-COEUR, SAINT-
FELICIEN, QC, G8K 1S2
(418) 679-1546 *SIC* 5511
LABRADOR MOTORS LIMITED *p424*
12 LORING DR, HAPPY VALLEY-GOOSE
BAY, NL, A0P 1C0
(709) 896-2452 *SIC* 5511
LACOMBE FORD SALES LTD *p138*
5610 HIGHWAY 2A, LACOMBE, AB, T4L
1A3
(403) 782-6811 *SIC* 5511
LAKE CITY FORD SALES INC *p344*
800 BROADWAY AVE N, WILLIAMS LAKE,
BC, V2G 3P4
(250) 392-4455 *SIC* 5511
LAKELAND FORD SALES LTD *p1413*
3434 2ND AVE W, PRINCE ALBERT, SK,
S6V 5G2
(306) 764-3325 *SIC* 5511
LAKERIDGE CHRYSLER DODGE JEEP LTD
p847
152 PETER ST, PORT HOPE, ON, L1A 1C6
(905) 885-6550 *SIC* 5511
LAKEVIEW MOTORS LP *p220*
2690 HIGHWAY 97 N, KELOWNA, BC, V1X
4J4
(250) 763-5337 *SIC* 5511
LAKEWOOD CHEVROLET LTD *p115*
9150 34 AVE NW, EDMONTON, AB, T6E
5P2
(780) 462-5959 *SIC* 5511
LAKING MOTORS INC *p899*
695 KINGSWAY, SUDBURY, ON, P3B 2E4
(705) 674-7534 *SIC* 5511
**LALLIER AUTOMOBILE (CHARLES-
BOURG) INC** *p1256*
4650 3E AV O, QUEBEC, QC, G1H 6E7
(418) 627-1010 *SIC* 5511
LALLIER AUTOMOBILE (HULL) INC *p1107*
981 BOUL SAINT-JOSEPH, GATINEAU,
QC, J8Z 1W8
(819) 778-1444 *SIC* 5511

LALLIER AUTOMOBILE (MONTREAL) INC
p1224
12435 BOUL LAURENTIEN, MONTREAL,
QC, H4K 2J2
(514) 337-2330 *SIC* 5511
LALLIER AUTOMOBILE (QUEBEC) INC
p1264
2000 RUE CYRILLE-DUQUET, QUEBEC,
QC, G1N 2E8
(418) 687-2525 *SIC* 5511
**LALLIER AUTOMOBILE (REPENTIGNY)
INC** *p1379*
215 RUE DES MIGRATEURS, TERRE-
BONNE, QC, J6V 0A8
(450) 581-7575 *SIC* 5511
LALLY KIA *p543*
725 RICHMOND ST, CHATHAM, ON, N7M
5J5
(519) 352-6200 *SIC* 5511
LAMB FORD SALES LTD *p78*
3771 48 AVE, CAMROSE, AB, T4V 3T4
(780) 672-2411 *SIC* 5511
LAMBTON MOTORS LIMITED, THE *p860*
101 INDIAN RD S, SARNIA, ON, N7T 3W1
(519) 464-4020 *SIC* 5511
LANDAU FORD LINCOLN SALES LIMITED
p382
555 EMPRESS ST, WINNIPEG, MB, R3G
3H1
(204) 772-2411 *SIC* 5511
LANGE & FETTER MOTORS LIMITED *p999*
52 DUNDAS ST E, TRENTON, ON, K8V 1K7
(613) 392-6561 *SIC* 5511
LANGLEY HYUNDAI LTD *p272*
19459 LANGLEY BYPASS, SURREY, BC,
V3S 6K1
(604) 539-8549 *SIC* 5511
LANOUE, ANDRE ORGANIZATION INC
p911
85 MILL ST W, TILBURY, ON, N0P 2L0
(519) 682-2424 *SIC* 5511
**LAPLANTE CHEVROLET PONTIAC BUICK
GMC LTD** *p541*
632 PRINCIPALE ST, CASSELMAN, ON,
K0A 1M0
(613) 764-2846 *SIC* 5511
LAPOINTE AUTOMOBILES INC *p1160*
160 BOUL TACHE O, MONTMAGNY, QC,
G5V 3A5
(418) 248-8899 *SIC* 5511
LAPOINTE BROS PEMBROKE LIMITED
p838
1398 PEMBROKE ST W, PEMBROKE, ON,
K8A 7M3
(613) 735-0634 *SIC* 5511
LAPOINTE CHRYSLER BROS JEEP *p838*
1398 PEMBROKE ST W, PEMBROKE, ON,
K8A 7M3
(613) 735-3128 *SIC* 5511
LAQUERRE CHRYSLER INC *p1399*
34 BOUL ARTHABASKA E, VICTORIAV-
ILLE, QC, G6T 0S7
(819) 752-5252 *SIC* 5511
LAURIA HYUNDAI *p847*
50 BENSON CRT, PORT HOPE, ON, L1A
3V6
(905) 885-2880 *SIC* 5511
LAVAL AUTOS HAMEL INC *p1086*
2500 BOUL CHOMEDEY, COTE SAINT-
LUC, QC, H7T 2W1
(450) 682-4050 *SIC* 5511
LAVAL VOLKSWAGEN LTEE *p1264*
777 BOUL CHAREST O, QUEBEC, QC,
G1N 2C6
(418) 687-4451 *SIC* 5511
LE CENTRE ROUTIER (1994) INC *p1286*
375 RUE TEMISCOUATA BUREAU 998,
RIVIERE-DU-LOUP, QC, G5R 2Y9
SIC 5511
LEAMINGTON CHRYSLER (1992) LTD *p644*
170 OAK ST W, LEAMINGTON, ON, N8H
2B6
(519) 326-9052 *SIC* 5511
LEATHEAD INVESTMENTS LTD *p220*

2727 HIGHWAY 97 N, KELOWNA, BC, V1X 4J8

(250) 860-7700   SIC 5511

LEAVENS VOLKSWAGEN INC   p649
2360 AUTO MALL AVE, LONDON, ON, N5V 0B4

(519) 455-2580   SIC 5511

LECOURS, JEAN PAUL LIMITED   p619
733 FRONT ST, HEARST, ON, P0L 1N0

(705) 362-4011   SIC 5511

LEDINGHAM PONTIAC BUICK GMC   p358
200 PTH 12 N, STEINBACH, MB, R5G 1T6

(204) 326-3451   SIC 5511

LEDUC CHRYSLER LTD   p139
6102 46A ST, LEDUC, AB, T9E 7A7

(780) 986-2051   SIC 5511

LEGACY FORD PONOKA   p152
6305 42 AVE, PONOKA, AB, T4J 1J8

(403) 783-5501   SIC 5511

LEO AUTOMOBILE LTEE   p1079
1849 BOUL TALBOT, CHICOUTIMI, QC, G7H 7Y4

(418) 545-1190   SIC 5511

LESLIE MOTORS LTD   p618
73 ELORA ST, HARRISTON, ON, N0G 1Z0

(519) 338-2310   SIC 5511

LESSARD, M LTEE   p1280
300 BOUL LOUIS-XIV, QUEBEC, QC, G2K 1W7

(418) 623-5471   SIC 5511

LESTAGE & FILS LTEE   p1351
699 RUE NOTRE-DAME, SAINT-REMI, QC, J0L 2L0

(450) 454-7591   SIC 5511

LEWIS MOTOR SALES (NORTH BAY) INC   p763
19 HEWITT DR, NORTH BAY, ON, P1B 8K5

(705) 472-7220   SIC 5511

LEWIS MOTOR SALES INC   p487
76 MAPLEVIEW DR W, BARRIE, ON, L4N 9H6

(705) 728-3026   SIC 5511

LEWIS, MAITLAND ENTERPRISES LTD   p863
1124 GREAT NORTHERN RD, SAULT STE. MARIE, ON, P6B 0B6

(705) 759-4545   SIC 5511

LINCOLN HEIGHTS FORD SALES LIMITED   p830
1377 RICHMOND RD, OTTAWA, ON, K2B 6R7

(613) 829-2120   SIC 5511

LINDSAY BUICK   p646
150 ANGELINE ST N SUITE 484, LINDSAY, ON, K9V 4N1

(705) 324-2148   SIC 5511

LMB AUTOMOBILE INC   p53
520 3 AVE SW SUITE 1900, CALGARY, AB, T2P 0R3

SIC 5511

LOCATION 18E RUE INC   p1255
455 RUE CLEMENCEAU, QUEBEC, QC, G1C 7B6

(418) 647-1822   SIC 5511

LOCATION HEBERT 2000 LTEE   p1246
750 AV SAINT-LOUIS, PLESSISVILLE, QC, G6L 2M1

(819) 362-8816   SIC 5511

LOCATION JEAN LEGARE LTEE   p1167
3035 RUE HOCHELAGA, MONTREAL, QC, H1W 1G1

(514) 522-6466   SIC 5511

LOGI-TEC MANAGEMENT LIMITED PARTNERSHIP   p101
18110 118 AVE NW, EDMONTON, AB, T5S 2G2

(780) 452-6225   SIC 5511

LOMBARDI AUTO LTEE   p1346
4356 BOUL METROPOLITAIN E, SAINT-LEONARD, QC, H1S 1A2

(514) 728-2222   SIC 5511

LONDON AUTOMOTIVE & MANUFACTURING LTD   p661
1477 SISE RD, LONDON, ON, N6N 1E1

(519) 686-0489   SIC 5511

LONDON FINE CARS LTD   p659
560 WHARNCLIFFE RD S, LONDON, ON, N6J 2N4

(519) 649-0889   SIC 5511

LONDONDERRY DODGE CHRYSLER JEEP LTD   p83
13333 FORT RD NW, EDMONTON, AB, T5A 1C3

(780) 665-4851   SIC 5511

LONE STAR INC   p36
10 HERITAGE MEADOWS RD SE, CALGARY, AB, T2H 3C1

(403) 253-1333   SIC 5511

LONGUE POINTE CHRYSLER DODGE (1987) LTEE   p1346
6200 BOUL METROPOLITAIN E, SAINT-LEONARD, QC, H1S 1A9

(514) 256-5092   SIC 5511

LONGUEUIL NISSAN INC   p1143
760 RUE SAINT-CHARLES E, LONGUEUIL, QC, J4H 1C3

(450) 442-2000   SIC 5511

LOTLINX INC   p612
8 MAIN ST E SUITE 200, HAMILTON, ON, L8N 1E8

SIC 5511

LOUISEVILLE AUTOMOBILE LTEE   p1146
871 BOUL SAINT-LAURENT O, LOUISEVILLE, QC, J5V 1L3

SIC 5511

LOUNSBURY AUTOMOTIVE LIMITED   p407
2155 WEST MAIN ST, MONCTON, NB, E1C 9P2

(506) 857-4300   SIC 5511

LOUNSBURY COMPANY LIMITED   p407
2155 MAIN ST W, MONCTON, NB, E1C 9P2

(506) 857-4300   SIC 5511

LOUNSBURY COMPANY LIMITED   p409
1655 MOUNTAIN RD, MONCTON, NB, E1G 1A5

(506) 857-4385   SIC 5511

LUCIANI AUTOMOBILES INC   p1227
4040 RUE JEAN-TALON O, MONTREAL, QC, H4P 1V5

(514) 340-1344   SIC 5511

LUKANDA HOLDINGS LTD   p201
1288 LOUGHEED HWY, COQUITLAM, BC, V3K 6S4

(604) 523-3009   SIC 5511

LUSSIER PONTIAC BUICK G M C LTEE   p1313
3000 RUE DESSAULLES, SAINT-HYACINTHE, QC, J2S 2V8

(450) 778-1112   SIC 5511

M T K AUTO WEST LTD   p261
10780 CAMBIE RD, RICHMOND, BC, V6X 1K8

(604) 233-0700   SIC 5511

M.G.M. FORD LINCOLN SALES LTD   p157
3010 50 AVE, RED DEER, AB, T4R 1M5

(403) 346-6621   SIC 5511

MACCARTHY MOTORS (TERRACE) LTD   p283
5004 16 HWY W, TERRACE, BC, V8G 5S5

(250) 635-4941   SIC 5511

MACDONALD BUICK GMC CADILLAC LTD   p408
111 BAIG BLVD, MONCTON, NB, E1E 1C9

(506) 853-6202   SIC 5511

MACDONALD, D. ALEX LIMITED   p1042
25 WATER ST, SUMMERSIDE, PE, C1N 1A3

(902) 436-6653   SIC 5511

MACDONALD, JIM MOTORS LTD   p592
1324 KING'S HWY, FORT FRANCES, ON, P9A 2X6

(807) 274-5321   SIC 5511

MACFARLANE CHEVROLET LIMITED   p843
4219 OIL HERITAGE RD RR 1, PETROLIA, ON, N0N 1R0

(519) 882-3804   SIC 5511

MACINTYRE CHEVROLET CADILLAC LIMITED   p467

101 DISCO ST, SYDNEY, NS, B1P 5V7

(902) 564-4491   SIC 5511

MACIVER DODGE LIMITED   p755
17615 YONGE ST, NEWMARKET, ON, L3Y 5H6

(905) 898-1900   SIC 5511

MACIVER DODGE-JEEP LTD   p755
17615 YONGE ST, NEWMARKET, ON, L3Y 5H6

(905) 898-1900   SIC 5511

MACK MACKENZIE MOTORS LIMITED p849
547 NEW ST, RENFREW, ON, K7V 1H1

(613) 432-3684   SIC 5511

MACK SALES & SERVICE OF DURHAM INC   p474
610 FINLEY AVE UNIT 9, AJAX, ON, L1S 2E3

(905) 426-6225   SIC 5511

MACK SALES & SERVICE OF MANITOBA LTD   p384
385 EAGLE DR, WINNIPEG, MB, R3H 0G7

(204) 772-0316   SIC 5511

MACK SALES & SERVICE OF NANAIMO LTD   p234
2213 MCCULLOUGH RD, NANAIMO, BC, V9S 4M7

(250) 758-0185   SIC 5511

MACK SALES & SERVICE OF STONEY CREEK LTD   p892
330 SOUTH SERVICE RD, STONEY CREEK, ON, L8E 2R4

(905) 662-4240   SIC 5511

MACLIN MOTORS LIMITED   p36
135 GLENDEER CIR SE, CALGARY, AB, T2H 2S8

(403) 252-0101   SIC 5511

MACMASTER CHEVROLET LTD   p649
1350 DRIVER LANE, LONDON, ON, N5V 0B4

(519) 455-6200   SIC 5511

MAGNUSON FORD SALES LTD   p177
32562 SOUTH FRASER WAY, ABBOTSFORD, BC, V2T 1X6

(604) 853-7401   SIC 5511

MAGOG TOYOTA INC   p1148
2500 RUE SHERBROOKE, MAGOG, QC, J1X 4E8

(819) 843-9883   SIC 5511

MAISON CHRYSLER DE CHARLESBOURG LTEE, LA   p1256
15070 BOUL HENRI-BOURASSA, QUEBEC, QC, G1G 3Z4

(418) 622-4700   SIC 5511

MANN-NORTHWAY AUTO SOURCE LTD p1414
500 MARQUIS RD E, PRINCE ALBERT, SK, S6V 8B3

(306) 765-2200   SIC 5511

MAPLE ACURA   p664
111 AUTO VAUGHAN DR, MAPLE, ON, L6A 4A1

(289) 342-5100   SIC 5511

MAPLE VOLKSWAGEN   p664
260 SWEETRIVER BLVD, MAPLE, ON, L6A 4V3

(905) 832-5711   SIC 5511

MAR-HAM AUTOMOTIVE INC   p616
57 RYMAL RD W, HAMILTON, ON, L9B 1B5

(905) 389-7111   SIC 5511

MARANELLO MOTORS LIMITED   p1032
55 AUTO PARK CIR, WOODBRIDGE, ON, L4L 8R1

(416) 213-5699   SIC 5511

MARANELLO SPORTS INC   p1032
200 AUTO PARK CIR, WOODBRIDGE, ON, L4L 8R1

(416) 749-5325   SIC 5511

MARIGOLD FORD LINCOLN SALES LIMITED   p1014
1120 DUNDAS ST E, WHITBY, ON, L1N 2K2

(905) 668-5893   SIC 5511

MARINE CHRYSLER DODGE JEEP LTD p290

450 MARINE DR SE, VANCOUVER, BC, V5X 4V2

(604) 321-1236   SIC 5511

MARINE DRIVE IMPORTED CARS LTD p323
850 MARINE DR SW, VANCOUVER, BC, V6P 5Z1

(604) 324-6632   SIC 5511

MARITIME EXHAUST LTD   p408
191 HENRI DUNANT ST UNIT 4, MONCTON, NB, E1E 1E4

(506) 857-8733   SIC 5511

MARK MOTORS OF OTTAWA (1987) LIMITED   p820
611 MONTREAL RD SUITE 1, OTTAWA, ON, K1K 0T8

(613) 749-4275   SIC 5511

MARKHAM INFINITI LIMITED   p1000
4340 HIGHWAY 7 E, UNIONVILLE, ON, L3R 1L9

(905) 752-0881   SIC 5511

MARKVILLE FORD LINCOLN LIMITED p1000
8210 KENNEDY RD, UNIONVILLE, ON, L3R 5X3

(905) 474-1350   SIC 5511

MAROSTICA MOTORS LIMITED   p908
1142 ALLOY DR, THUNDER BAY, ON, P7B 6M9

(807) 346-5809   SIC 5511

MARQUIS AUTOMOBILES INC   p1150
1065 AV DU PHARE O, MATANE, QC, G4W 3M6

(418) 562-3333   SIC 5511

MARSH MOTORS CHRYSLER LIMITED p424
GD, GRAND FALLS-WINDSOR, NL, A2A 2J9

(709) 489-2151   SIC 5511

MARSHALL AUTOMOTIVE (PEACE RIVER) LTD   p152
7501 100 AVE, PEACE RIVER, AB, T8S 1M5

(780) 428-0563   SIC 5511

MARSHALL, STEVE FORD LINCOLN LTD p234
3851 SHENTON RD SUITE 3, NANAIMO, BC, V9T 2H1

(250) 758-7311   SIC 5511

MARSHALL, STEVE MOTORS (1996) LTD p195
2300 ISLAND HWY, CAMPBELL RIVER, BC, V9W 2G8

(250) 287-9171   SIC 5511

MARTIN CHRYSLER LTD   p7
879 3 ST W, BROOKS, AB, T1R 1L5

(403) 362-3354   SIC 5511

MASON, GREG SERVICES INC   p1014
1505 DUNDAS ST E, WHITBY, ON, L1N 2K6

(905) 668-5100   SIC 5511

MASSULLO MOTORS LIMITED   p248
4493 JOYCE AVE, POWELL RIVER, BC, V8A 3A8

(604) 485-7981   SIC 5511

MAURICIE TOYOTA INC   p1368
8823 BOUL DES HETRES, SHAWINIGAN, QC, G9N 4X3

(819) 539-8393   SIC 5511

MAXIM TRANSPORTATION SERVICES INC p379
1860 BROOKSIDE BLVD, WINNIPEG, MB, R3C 2E6

(204) 790-6599   SIC 5511

MAY, JACK CHEVROLET BUICK GMC LIMITED   p748
3788 PRINCE OF WALES DR, NEPEAN, ON, K2C 3H1

(613) 692-3553   SIC 5511

MAY, RON PONTIAC BUICK GMC LTD p467
303 WELTON ST, SYDNEY, NS, B1P 5S3

(902) 539-6494   SIC 5511

MCALPINE FORD LINCOLN SALES LTD p481
15815 YONGE ST, AURORA, ON, L4G 1P4

▲ Public Company   ■ Public Company Family Member   **HQ** Headquarters   **BR** Branch   **SL** Single Location

(905) 841-2424   *SIC* 5511

MCCLELLAN WHEATON CHEVROLET LTD *p78*
3850 48 AVE, CAMROSE, AB, T4V 3Z8
(780) 672-2355   *SIC* 5511

MCCURDY CHEVROLET OLSMOBILE PONTIAC BUICK GMC LTD *p999*
174 TRENTON-FRANKFORD RD, TRENTON, ON, K8V 5R6
(613) 392-1245   *SIC* 5511

MCDONNELL MOTORS LTD *p897*
359 CARADOC ST S, STRATHROY, ON, N7G 2P5
(519) 245-0840   *SIC* 5511

MCGEE MOTORS LTD *p597*
180 SUNCOAST DR E, GODERICH, ON, N7A 4N4
(519) 524-8391   *SIC* 5511

MCGEE, JACK CHEVROLET CADILLAC LIMITED *p841*
1053 CLONSILLA AVE, PETERBOROUGH, ON, K9J 5Y2
(705) 741-9000   *SIC* 5511

MCGRAW ET FRERE LIMITEE *p419*
2892 RUE PRINCIPALE, TRACADIE-SHEILA, NB, E1X 1A2
(506) 395-2263   *SIC* 5511

MCKAY PONTIAC BUICK (1979) LTD *p36*
7711 MACLEOD TRAIL SW, CALGARY, AB, T2H 0M1
(403) 243-0109   *SIC* 5511

MCKEOWN MOTORS LIMITED *p632*
805 GARDINERS RD, KINGSTON, ON, K7M 7E6
(613) 389-4426   *SIC* 5511

MCKINSTRY, WILLIAM LIMITED *p565*
176 GOVERNMENT ST, DRYDEN, ON, P8N 2N9
(807) 223-4214   *SIC* 5511

MCL MOTOR CARS 1992 INC *p321*
1718 3RD AVE W, VANCOUVER, BC, V6J 1K4
(604) 736-7911   *SIC* 5511

MCLEAN, BRIAN CHEVROLET LTD *p203*
2145 CLIFFE AVE, COURTENAY, BC, V9N 2L5
(250) 334-3400   *SIC* 5511

MCMILLAN & SAUNDERS INC *p744*
797 BANCROFT DR, MISSISSAUGA, ON, L5V 2Y6
(905) 858-0712   *SIC* 5511

MCNAUGHT PONTIAC BUICK CADILLAC GMC LTD *p391*
1717 WAVERLEY ST UNIT 1000, WINNIPEG, MB, R3T 6A9
(204) 786-3811   *SIC* 5511

MCPHILLIPS HOLDINGS (WINNIPEG) LTD *p370*
2425 MCPHILLIPS ST, WINNIPEG, MB, R2V 4J7
(204) 338-7985   *SIC* 5511

MCQUARRIE MOTOR PRODUCTS INC *p569*
228 CENTRE ST, ESPANOLA, ON, P5E 1G1
(705) 869-1351   *SIC* 5511

MEADOWVALE FORD SALES AND SERVICE LIMITED *p724*
2230 BATTLEFORD RD, MISSISSAUGA, ON, L5N 3K6
(905) 542-3673   *SIC* 5511

MECANICAM AUTO *p1172*
5612 RUE CARTIER, MONTREAL, QC, H2G 2T9
(514) 495-1007   *SIC* 5511

MELNICK MOTORS LTD *p345*
1012 PARK AVE, BEAUSEJOUR, MB, R0E 0C0
(204) 268-1514   *SIC* 5511

MERCEDES BENZ PETERBOROUGH INC *p841*
995 CRAWFORD DR, PETERBOROUGH, ON, K9J 3X1
(705) 742-9000   *SIC* 5511

MERCEDES-BENZ SURREY *p270*

15508 104 AVE, SURREY, BC, V3R 1N8
(604) 581-7662   *SIC* 5511

MERLIN FORD LINCOLN INC *p1431*
3750 IDYLWYLD DR N, SASKATOON, SK, S7L 6G3
(306) 931-6611   *SIC* 5511

MERLIN MOTORS INC *p1431*
3750 IDYLWYLD DR N SUITE 107, SASKATOON, SK, S7L 6G3
(306) 931-6611   *SIC* 5511

MERTIN CHEVROLET CADILLAC PONTIAC BUICK GMC LTD *p196*
45930 AIRPORT RD, CHILLIWACK, BC, V2P 1A2
(604) 795-9104   *SIC* 5511

MERTIN HYUNDAI *p196*
45753 YALE RD, CHILLIWACK, BC, V2P 2N5
(604) 702-1000   *SIC* 5511

MERTIN NISSAN *p196*
8287 YOUNG RD, CHILLIWACK, BC, V2P 4N8
(604) 792-8218   *SIC* 5511

MERVYN MOTORS LIMITED *p222*
1717 HARVEY AVE, KELOWNA, BC, V1Y 6G3
(250) 860-6278   *SIC* 5511

METCALFE'S GARAGE LTD *p360*
HWY 2 E, TREHERNE, MB, R0G 2V0
(204) 723-2175   *SIC* 5511

METRO CHRYSLER LTD *p1440*
5 2 MILE HILL RD, WHITEHORSE, YT, Y1A 0A4
(867) 667-2525   *SIC* 5511

METRO FORD SALES LTD *p54*
1111 9 AVE SW, CALGARY, AB, T2P 1L3
(403) 263-4530   *SIC* 5511

METRO FREIGHTLINER HAMILTON INC *p892*
475 SEAMAN ST, STONEY CREEK, ON, L8E 2R2
(905) 561-6110   *SIC* 5511

METRO MOTORS LTD *p246*
2505 LOUGHEED HWY, PORT COQUITLAM, BC, V3B 1B2
(604) 464-6631   *SIC* 5511

METRO NISSAN INC *p1131*
8686 BOUL NEWMAN, LASALLE, QC, H8N 1Y5
(514) 366-8931   *SIC* 5511

METRO PLYMOUTH CHRYSLER LTD *p830*
1047 RICHMOND RD, OTTAWA, ON, K2B 6R1
(613) 596-1006   *SIC* 5511

MICHAEL JACKSON MOTOR SALES LIMITED *p547*
480 HUME ST, COLLINGWOOD, ON, L9Y 1W6
(705) 445-2222   *SIC* 5511

MID-ONTARIO DIESEL LIMITED *p487*
400 DUNLOP ST W, BARRIE, ON, L4N 1C2
(705) 722-1122   *SIC* 5511

MID-TOWN FORD SALES LIMITED *p391*
1717 WAVERLEY ST SUITE 100, WINNIPEG, MB, R3T 6A9
(204) 284-7650   *SIC* 5511

MID-WAY MOTORS (QUINTE) LIMITED *p491*
48 MILLENNIUM PKY, BELLEVILLE, ON, K8N 4Z5
(613) 968-4538   *SIC* 5511

MIDLAND AUTOMOTIVE CORPORATION *p681*
868 KING ST, MIDLAND, ON, L4R 0B8
(705) 526-1344   *SIC* 5511

MIDWAY MOTORS LTD *p439*
2499 CABOT TRAIL, BADDECK, NS, B0E 1B0
(902) 295-2290   *SIC* 5511

MIEDEMA'S MOTOR SALES LTD *p476*
1 ADDISON RD, ALLISTON, ON, L9R 1V2
(705) 435-7609   *SIC* 5511

MIKE DOYLE DODGE CHRYSLER INC *p901*
2555 REGENT ST, SUDBURY, ON, P3E 6K6
(705) 523-1101   *SIC* 5511

MIKE KNAPP FORD SALES LIMITED *p1012*
607 NIAGARA ST, WELLAND, ON, L3C 1L9
(905) 732-3673   *SIC* 5511

MIKE PRIESTNER AUTOMOTIVE GROUP LTD *p115*
3603 99 ST NW SUITE 780, EDMONTON, AB, T6E 6K6
(780) 450-1021   *SIC* 5511

MILLER-HUGHES FORD SALES LIMITED *p563*
711 PITT ST, CORNWALL, ON, K6J 3S1
(613) 932-2584   *SIC* 5511

MILLS NISSAN LTD *p125*
1275 101 ST SW, EDMONTON, AB, T6X 1A1
(780) 463-5700   *SIC* 5511

MILLS PONTIAC BUICK GMC LTD *p812*
240 BOND ST E, OSHAWA, ON, L1G 1B5
(905) 432-7333   *SIC* 5511

MILLTOWN MOTORS LIMITED *p493*
237 CAUSLEY ST, BLIND RIVER, ON, P0R 1B0
(705) 356-2207   *SIC* 5511

MILTON CHRYSLER DODGE LIMITED *p684*
81 ONTARIO ST N, MILTON, ON, L9T 2T2
(905) 878-8877   *SIC* 5511

MINI OTTAWA EAST (6125) *p596*
1020 OGILVIE RD, GLOUCESTER, ON, K1J 8G9
(613) 728-8888   *SIC* 5511

MIRAMICHI CHRYSLER DODGE JEEP INC *p405*
1155 KING GEORGE HWY, MIRAMICHI, NB, E1V 5J7
(506) 622-3900   *SIC* 5511

MISSISSAUGA AUTOMOTIVE INC *p714*
1800 LAKESHORE RD W, MISSISSAUGA, ON, L5J 1J7
(905) 567-8881   *SIC* 5511

MISSISSAUGA TOYOTA INC *p703*
2215 DUNDAS ST E, MISSISSAUGA, ON, L4X 2X2
(905) 625-3420   *SIC* 5511

MJY AUTO SALES & LEASING LTD *p132*
12709 100 ST, GRANDE PRAIRIE, AB, T8V 4H2
(780) 532-5005   *SIC* 5511

MOFFITT DODGE CHRYSLER LTD *p410*
205 ROUTE 170, OAK BAY, NB, E3L 3X7
(506) 466-3061   *SIC* 5511

MOHAWK FORD SALES LIMITED *p617*
930 UPPER JAMES ST, HAMILTON, ON, L9C 3A5
(905) 388-1711   *SIC* 5511

MONTEITH VENTURES INC *p402*
433 BISHOP DR, FREDERICTON, NB, E3C 2M6
(506) 455-2277   *SIC* 5511

MONTESTRIE AUTORAMA INC *p1111*
6 RUE IRWIN, GRANBY, QC, J2J 2P1
(450) 378-8404   *SIC* 5511

MONTGOMERY FORD SALES LIMITED *p663*
701 CAMPBELL ST, LUCKNOW, ON, N0G 2H0
(519) 528-2813   *SIC* 5511

MONTMORENCY FORD (1997) INC *p1070*
7225 BOUL TASCHEREAU, BROSSARD, QC, J4Y 1A1
(450) 678-9940   *SIC* 5511

MORREY AUTO GROUP LTD *p241*
818 AUTOMALL DR, NORTH VANCOUVER, BC, V7P 3R8
(604) 984-9211   *SIC* 5511

MORREY NISSAN OF COQUITLAM LTD *p246*
2710 LOUGHEED HWY, PORT COQUITLAM, BC, V3B 6P2
(604) 464-1216   *SIC* 5511

MORRIS, DAVID FINE CARS LTD *p102*
17407 111 AVE NW, EDMONTON, AB, T5S 0A1
(780) 484-9000   *SIC* 5511

MORSTAR HOLDINGS LTD *p356*

230 MAIN ST, SELKIRK, MB, R1A 1R9
SIC 5511

MOTEURS DECARIE INC, LES *p1227*
8255 RUE BOUGAINVILLE, MONTREAL, QC, H4P 2T3
(514) 334-9910   *SIC* 5511

MOTION MAZDA *p808*
753007 2ND LINE E, ORANGEVILLE, ON, L9W 2Z2
(519) 943-1100   *SIC* 5511

MOTOR WORKS ONE HOLDINGS INC *p835*
510 MOTOR WORKS PVT, OTTAWA, ON, K2R 0A5
(613) 656-6526   *SIC* 5511

MOTOR WORKS TWO HOLDINGS INC *p835*
520 MOTOR WORKS PVT, OTTAWA, ON, K2R 0A5
(613) 656-6536   *SIC* 5511

MR MOTORS LP *p231*
11911 WEST ST, MAPLE RIDGE, BC, V2X 3M6
(604) 465-8931   *SIC* 5511

MSA FORD SALES LTD *p177*
30295 AUTOMALL DR, ABBOTSFORD, BC, V2T 5M1
(604) 856-9000   *SIC* 5511

MT. BRYDGES FORD SALES LTD *p746*
8791 GLENDON DR, MOUNT BRYDGES, ON, N0L 1W0
(519) 264-1912   *SIC* 5511

MURPHY FORD SALES LTD *p838*
1341 PEMBROKE ST W, PEMBROKE, ON, K8A 5R3
(613) 735-6861   *SIC* 5511

MURPHY, DAN FORD SALES LTD *p663*
1346 BANKFIELD RD, MANOTICK, ON, K4M 1A7
(613) 692-3594   *SIC* 5511

MURRAY AUTO GROUP BRANDON LTD *p347*
1500 RICHMOND AVE, BRANDON, MB, R7A 7E3
(204) 728-0130   *SIC* 5511

MURRAY AUTO GROUP FORT ST. JOHN LTD *p214*
11204 ALASKA RD, FORT ST. JOHN, BC, V1J 5T5
(250) 785-8005   *SIC* 5511

MURRAY AUTO GROUP LETHBRIDGE LTD *p143*
2815 26 AVE S, LETHBRIDGE, AB, T1K 7K7
(403) 328-1101   *SIC* 5511

MURRAY AUTO GROUP POCK LP *p283*
3150 KING GEORGE BLVD, SURREY, BC, V4P 1A2
(604) 538-7022   *SIC* 5511

MURRAY AUTO GROUP WINNIPEG LTD *p391*
1700 WAVERLEY ST SUITE C, WINNIPEG, MB, R3T 5V7
(204) 261-6200   *SIC* 5511

MURRAY BUICK GMC PENTICTON *p243*
1010 WESTMINSTER AVE W, PENTICTON, BC, V2A 1L6
(250) 493-7121   *SIC* 5511

MURRAY CHEVROLET CADILLAC BUICK GMC MOOSE JAW *p1411*
15 CHESTER RD, MOOSE JAW, SK, S6J 1N3
(306) 693-4605   *SIC* 5511

MURRAY CHEVROLET OLDSMOBILE CADILLAC LTD *p146*
1270 TRANS CANADA WAY SE, MEDICINE HAT, AB, T1B 1J5
(403) 527-5544   *SIC* 5511

MURRAY CHEVROLET PONTIAC BUICK GMC ESTEVAN *p1406*
801 13TH AVE, ESTEVAN, SK, S4A 2L9
(306) 634-3661   *SIC* 5511

MURRAY CHEVROLET PONTIAC BUICK GMC MERRITT LIMITED PARTNERSHIP *p232*
2049 NICOLA AVE, MERRITT, BC, V1K 1B8

(250) 378-9255   SIC 5511
**MURRAY MOTOR SALES WINNIPEG LIM-
ITED PARTNERSHIP**   p387
300 PEMBINA HWY, WINNIPEG, MB, R3L
2E2
(204) 284-6650   SIC 5511
**MURRAY MOTORS CHILLIWACK LIMITED
PARTNERSHIP**   p197
44954 YALE RD W, CHILLIWACK, BC, V2R
4H1
(604) 792-2724   SIC 5511
MURRAY MOTORS FORT ST. JOHN LTD
p214
11204 ALASKA RD, FORT ST. JOHN, BC,
V1J 5T5
(250) 785-6661   SIC 5511
**MURRAY MOTORS THE PAS LIMITED
PARTNERSHIP**   p359
212 LAROSE AVE, THE PAS, MB, R9A 1L1
(204) 623-3481   SIC 5511
**MURRAY MOTORS YARMOUTH LIMITED
PARTNERSHIP**   p471
45 STARRS RD, YARMOUTH, NS, B5A 2T2
(902) 742-7191   SIC 5511
**MURRAY PONTIAC BUICK GMC LIMITED
PARTNERSHIP**   p177
30355 AUTOMALL DR, ABBOTSFORD, BC,
V2T 5M1
(604) 857-0742   SIC 5511
MYERS BARRHAVEN NIS INC   p752
530 MOTOR WORKS PVT, NEPEAN, ON,
K2R 0A5
(613) 778-8893   SIC 5511
**MYERS CADILLAC CHEVROLET BUICK
GMC INC**   p831
1200 BASELINE RD, OTTAWA, ON, K2C
0A6
(613) 225-2277   SIC 5511
MYERS HY WEST INC   p752
4115 STRANDHERD DR, NEPEAN, ON,
K2J 6H8
(613) 714-8888   SIC 5511
MYERS KANATA CHEV BUICK GMC INC
p626
2500 PALLADIUM DR SUITE 200, KANATA,
ON, K2V 1E2
(613) 592-9221   SIC 5511
MYERS KANATA NISSAN INC   p751
2185 ROBERTSON RD, NEPEAN, ON, K2H
5Z2
(613) 596-1515   SIC 5511
**MYERS KEMPTVILLE CHEVROLET BUICK
GMC INC**   p627
104 ELVIRA ST E, KEMPTVILLE, ON, K0G
1J0
(613) 258-3403   SIC 5511
**MYERS ORLEANS CHEVROLET BUICK
GMC INC**   p810
1875 ST. JOSEPH BLVD, ORLEANS, ON,
K1C 7J2
(613) 834-6397   SIC 5511
MYERS VOLKSWAGEN   p626
2500 PALLADIUM DR SUITE 501, KANATA,
ON, K2V 1E2
(613) 592-8484   SIC 5511
**MYERS, BOB CHEVROLET OLDSMOBILE
LTD**   p474
425 BAYLY ST W, AJAX, ON, L1S 6M3
(905) 427-2500   SIC 5511
N.S.M. AUTO LTD   p85
9670 125A AVE NW SUITE SIDE, EDMON-
TON, AB, T5G 3E5
(780) 479-5700   SIC 5511
NANAIMO CHRYSLER LTD   p234
4170 WELLINGTON RD, NANAIMO, BC,
V9T 2H3
(250) 758-1191   SIC 5511
NATIONAL TRUCK CENTRE INC   p225
9758 203 ST, LANGLEY, BC, V1M 4B9
(604) 888-5577   SIC 5511
NBFG AUTO LTD   p1412
2501 99TH ST, NORTH BATTLEFORD, SK,
S9A 2X6
(306) 445-3300   SIC 5511

**NELSON CHEVROLET OLDSMOBILE PON-
TIAC BUICK GMC LTD**   p1404
201 1ST AVE W, ASSINIBOIA, SK, S0H 0B0
(306) 642-5995   SIC 5511
NELSON FORD SALES (2003) INC   p236
623 RAILWAY ST, NELSON, BC, V1L 1H5
(250) 352-7202   SIC 5511
NEW MARKET INVESTMENT LIMITEDp756
75 MULOCK DR, NEWMARKET, ON, L3Y
8V2
(416) 798-7854   SIC 5511
NEW WEST FREIGHTLINER INC   p12
3444 44 AVE SE, CALGARY, AB, T2B 3J9
(403) 569-4800   SIC 5511
NEWTYPE MOTORS LTD   p261
9200 BRIDGEPORT RD, RICHMOND, BC,
V6X 1S1
(604) 231-9200   SIC 5511
NIAGARA MOTORS LIMITED   p1004
1537 NIAGARA STONE RD, VIRGIL, ON,
L0S 1T0
(905) 468-2145   SIC 5511
NICHOLS, ROY MOTORS LIMITED   p564
2728 COURTICE RD, COURTICE, ON, L1E
2M7
(905) 436-2228   SIC 5511
NICOL AUTO INC   p1123
400 2E RUE E, LA SARRE, QC, J9Z 2J1
(819) 333-5467   SIC 5511
NIPAWIN CHRYSLER DODGE LTD   p1412
301 1 AVE W, NIPAWIN, SK, S0E 1E0
(306) 862-4755   SIC 5511
NOR-LAN CHRYSLER INC   p133
12517 100 ST, GRANDE PRAIRIE, AB, T8V
4H2
(780) 978-9335   SIC 5511
NORAL MOTORS (1983) LTD   p128
10129 MACDONALD AVE, FORT MCMUR-
RAY, AB, T9H 1T2
(780) 743-5444   SIC 5511
NORDEN VOLKSWAGEN LIMITED   p102
17820 STONY PLAIN RD NW, EDMONTON,
AB, T5S 1A4
(780) 426-3000   SIC 5511
NORDEST VOLKSWAGEN INC   p1240
10395 BOUL PIE-IX, MONTREAL-NORD,
QC, H1H 3Z7
(514) 325-3422   SIC 5511
NORRIS FORD SALES LTD   p171
2929 15 AVE, WAINWRIGHT, AB, T9W 0A4
(780) 842-4400   SIC 5511
NORTH BAY CHRYSLER LTD   p762
352 LAKESHORE DR, NORTH BAY, ON,
P1A 2C2
(705) 472-0820   SIC 5511
NORTH FRONT MOTORS INC   p492
239 NORTH FRONT ST, BELLEVILLE, ON,
K8P 3C3
(613) 966-3333   SIC 5511
NORTH HILL MOTORS (1975) LTD   p3
139 EAST LAKE CRES NE, AIRDRIE, AB,
T4A 2H7
(403) 948-2600   SIC 5511
NORTH MARKHAM MOTORS LTD   p1000
8220 KENNEDY RD, UNIONVILLE, ON, L3R
5X3
(905) 477-2451   SIC 5511
**NORTH YORK CHEVROLET OLDSMOBILE
LTD**   p906
7200 YONGE ST, THORNHILL, ON, L4J
1V8
(905) 881-5000   SIC 5511
**NORTHGATE CHEVROLET BUICK GMC
LIMITED PARTNERSHIP**   p84
13215 97 ST NW, EDMONTON, AB, T5E
4C7
(780) 476-3371   SIC 5511
NORTHLAND FORD SALES LTD   p359
HIGHWAY 10 S, THE PAS, MB, R9A 1K9
(204) 623-4350   SIC 5511
NORTHLAND MOTORS LP   p249
2021 HIGHWAY 16 W, PRINCE GEORGE,
BC, V2L 0A4
(250) 564-6663   SIC 5511

NORTHSTAR MOTORS LTD   p94
13634 ST ALBERT TRAIL NW, EDMON-
TON, AB, T5L 4P3
(780) 478-7669   SIC 5511
NORTHTOWN AUTO LP   p251
2844 RECPLACE DR, PRINCE GEORGE,
BC, V2N 0G2
(250) 562-5254   SIC 5511
**NORTHWAY CHEVROLET OLDSMOBILE
LTD**   p1414
500 MARQUIS RD E, PRINCE ALBERT, SK,
S6V 8B3
(306) 765-2200   SIC 5511
NORTHWAY FORD LINCOLN LTD   p517
388 KING GEORGE RD, BRANTFORD, ON,
N3T 5L8
(519) 753-8691   SIC 5511
**NORTHWEST MOTORS (RED DEER) LIM-
ITED**   p154
3115 50 AVE, RED DEER, AB, T4N 3X8
(403) 346-2035   SIC 5511
NOTMAN MOTOR SALES LTD   p562
2205 VINCENT MASSEY DR, CORNWALL,
ON, K6H 5R6
(613) 938-0934   SIC 5511
NOVA ENTERPRISES LIMITED   p447
670 AV WILKINSON, DARTMOUTH, NS,
B3B 0J4
(902) 468-5900   SIC 5511
NURSE CHEVROLET CADILLAC LTDp1014
1530 DUNDAS ST E, WHITBY, ON, L1N
2K7
(905) 668-4044   SIC 5511
O'CONNOR MOTORS LTD   p196
45730 HOCKING AVE, CHILLIWACK, BC,
V2P 1B3
(604) 792-2754   SIC 5511
O'LEARY BUICK GMC LTD   p402
1135 HANWELL RD, FREDERICTON, NB,
E3C 1A5
(506) 453-7000   SIC 5511
O'REGAN HALIFAX LIMITED   p456
3575 KEMPT RD, HALIFAX, NS, B3K 4X6
(902) 453-2331   SIC 5511
O'REGAN'S NISSAN DARTMOUTH LTD
p443
60 BAKER DR UNIT C, DARTMOUTH, NS,
B2W 6L4
(902) 469-8484   SIC 5511
**OAK-LAND FORD LINCOLN SALES LIM-
ITED**   p801
570 TRAFALGAR RD, OAKVILLE, ON, L6J
3J2
(905) 844-3273   SIC 5511
OAKGROUP AUTOMOTIVE CORPORATION
p698
1035 RONSA CRT, MISSISSAUGA, ON,
L4W 2N6
(905) 614-0777   SIC 5511
OAKRIDGE FORD SALES (1981) LIMITED
p659
601 OXFORD ST W, LONDON, ON, N6H
1T8
(519) 472-0944   SIC 5511
OAKVILLE AUTOMOTIVE GROUP INC p804
2375 WYECROFT RD, OAKVILLE, ON, L6L
6L4
(905) 842-8400   SIC 5511
OAKVILLE VOLKSWAGEN INC   p806
1345 NORTH SERVICE RD W, OAKVILLE,
ON, L6M 2W2
(905) 844-3285   SIC 5511
OAKWOOD MOTORS INC   p1425
635 BRAND CRT, SASKATOON, SK, S7J
5L3
(306) 664-3333   SIC 5511
OCEAN PARK FORD SALES LTD   p283
3050 KING GEORGE BLVD, SURREY, BC,
V4P 1A2
(604) 531-8883   SIC 5511
OGILVIE MOTORS LTD   p596
1020 OGILVIE RD, GLOUCESTER, ON, K1J
8G9
(613) 745-9191   SIC 5511

OGILVIE SUBARU   p816
1040 PARISIEN ST, OTTAWA, ON, K1B 3M8
(613) 745-9191   SIC 5511
OKOTOKS LINCOLN MERCURY   p151
4 WESTLAND RD, OKOTOKS, AB, T1S 1N1
(403) 938-2255   SIC 5511
**OLD MILL PONTIAC BUICK CADILLAC LIM-
ITED**   p994
2595 ST CLAIR AVE W, TORONTO, ON,
M6N 4Z5
(416) 766-2443   SIC 5511
**OLIVIER SEPT-ILES CHRYSLER DODGE
JEEP RAM INC**   p1367
119 RUE MONSEIGNEUR-BLANCHE,
SEPT-ILES, QC, G4R 3G7
(418) 962-2555   SIC 5511
OLIVIER, JACQUES FORD INC   p1308
4405 CH DE CHAMBLY, SAINT-HUBERT,
QC, J3Y 3M7
(450) 445-3673   SIC 5511
ONTARIO CHRYSLER JEEP DODGE INC
p698
5280 DIXIE RD, MISSISSAUGA, ON, L4W
2A7
(905) 625-8801   SIC 5511
ONTARIO MOTOR SALES LIMITED   p814
140 BOND ST W, OSHAWA, ON, L1J 8M2
(905) 725-6501   SIC 5511
OPEN ROAD AUTO GROUP LTD   p299
1039 HAMILTON ST, VANCOUVER, BC,
V6B 5T4
SIC 5511
OPEN ROAD MOTORS INC   p756
87 MULOCK DR, NEWMARKET, ON, L3Y
8V2
(905) 895-8700   SIC 5511
OPENROAD AUTO GROUP LIMITED   p255
5631 PARKWOOD WAY, RICHMOND, BC,
V6V 2M6
(604) 273-5533   SIC 5511
OPENROAD AUTO GROUP LIMITED   p255
13251 SMALLWOOD PL, RICHMOND, BC,
V6V 1W8
(604) 273-3766   SIC 5511
ORANGEVILLE CHRYSLER LIMITED   p808
207 163 HWY SUITE 9, ORANGEVILLE,
ON, L9W 2Z7
(519) 942-8400   SIC 5511
ORCHARD FORD SALES LTD   p220
911 STREMEL RD, KELOWNA, BC, V1X
5E6
(250) 860-1000   SIC 5511
ORILLIA DODGE CHRYSLER JEEP INC
p809
450 MEMORIAL AVE, ORILLIA, ON, L3V
0T7
(705) 325-1331   SIC 5511
ORLEANS DODGE CHRYSLER INC   p810
1465 YOUVILLE DR, ORLEANS, ON, K1C
4R1
(613) 830-1777   SIC 5511
ORTYNSKY AUTOMOTIVE COMPANY LTD
p368
980 NAIRN AVE, WINNIPEG, MB, R2L 0Y2
(204) 654-0440   SIC 5511
ORTYNSKY NISSAN LTD   p368
980 NAIRN AVE, WINNIPEG, MB, R2L 0Y2
(204) 669-0791   SIC 5511
OTTAWA MOTOR SALES (1987) LIMITED
p827
2496 BANK ST SUITE 40010, OTTAWA,
ON, K1V 8S2
(613) 733-6931   SIC 5511
OTTO'S COLLISION CENTER   p829
1551 LAPERRIERE AVE, OTTAWA, ON,
K1Z 7T1
(613) 728-7032   SIC 5511
OTTO'S SERVICE CENTRE LIMITED   p827
660 HUNT CLUB RD, OTTAWA, ON, K1V
1C1
(613) 725-3048   SIC 5511
OTWA N MOTORS LTD   p595
1599 STAR TOP RD SUITE 417,
GLOUCESTER, ON, K1B 5P5

▲ Public Company   ■ Public Company Family Member   **HQ** Headquarters   **BR** Branch   **SL** Single Location

(613) 749-9417   *SIC* 5511
OVERSEAS MOTORS (WINDSOR) INC
p1018
9225 TECUMSEH RD E, WINDSOR, ON,
N8R 1A1
(519) 254-0358   *SIC* 5511
OWEN SOUND MOTORS LIMITED   p836
202423 SUNSET STRIP HWY 6&21, OWEN
SOUND, ON, N4K 5N7
(519) 376-5580   *SIC* 5511
OXFORD DODGE CHRYSLER (1992) LTD
p659
1249 HYDE PARK RD, LONDON, ON, N6H
5K6
(519) 473-1010   *SIC* 5511
PACCAR OF CANADA LTD   p1340
7500 RTE TRANSCANADIENNE, SAINT-
LAURENT, QC, H4T 1A5
(514) 735-2581   *SIC* 5511
PACIFIC MAINLAND HOLDINGS LTD p201
1288 LOUGHEED HWY, COQUITLAM, BC,
V3K 6S4
(604) 522-6140   *SIC* 5511
PACIFIC MOTOR SALES AND SERVICE LTD
p335
1060 YATES ST, VICTORIA, BC, V8V 3M6
(250) 385-5747   *SIC* 5511
PALLISER CHEVROLET LTD   p137
4604 42 AVE, INNISFAIL, AB, T4G 1P6
(403) 227-1434   *SIC* 5511
PAQUET NISSAN INC   p1138
3580 BOUL GUILLAUME-COUTURE,
LEVIS, QC, G6W 6N7
(418) 838-3838   *SIC* 5511
PAQUIN FORD LTEE   p1289
1155 AV LARIVIERE, ROUYN-NORANDA,
QC, J9X 4K9
(819) 797-3673   *SIC* 5511
**PARE CENTRE DU CAMION WHITE GMC
INC**   p1137
250 RTE DU PRESIDENT-KENNEDY,
LEVIS, QC, G6V 9J6
(418) 833-5333   *SIC* 5511
PARE CHEVROLET OLDSMOBILE INC
p1292
1239 RTE BEGIN, SAINT-ANSELME, QC,
G0R 2N0
SIC 5511
PARK AVENUE ENTERPRISES LTD   p177
30360 AUTOMALL DR, ABBOTSFORD, BC,
V2T 5M1
(604) 857-1430   *SIC* 5511
PARK LANE CHEVROLET CADILLAC LTD
p858
1290 LONDON RD, SARNIA, ON, N7S 1P5
(519) 541-8883   *SIC* 5511
PARK SHORE MOTORS LTD   p241
835 AUTOMALL DR, NORTH VANCOU-
VER, BC, V7P 3R8
(604) 985-9344   *SIC* 5511
PARKER'S CHRYSLER DODGE JEEP LTD
p244
1765 MAIN ST, PENTICTON, BC, V2A 5H1
(250) 492-2839   *SIC* 5511
PARKSIDE FORD LINCOLN LTD   p370
2000 MAIN ST, WINNIPEG, MB, R2V 2B8
(204) 339-2000   *SIC* 5511
PARKSVILLE CHRYSLER   p243
230 SHELLY RD, PARKSVILLE, BC, V9P
1V6
(250) 248-3281   *SIC* 5511
PARKWAY FORD SALES (1996) LTD p1007
455 KING ST N, WATERLOO, ON, N2J 2Z5
(519) 884-5110   *SIC* 5511
PARKWAY PLYMOUTH CHRYSLER LTD
p725
2260 BATTLEFORD RD, MISSISSAUGA,
ON, L5N 3K6
(905) 567-1700   *SIC* 5511
PASCAL CHEVROLET LTEE   p1253
80 BOUL DU PORTAGE-DES-MOUSSES,
PORT-CARTIER, QC, G5B 1E1
(418) 766-4343   *SIC* 5511
PATTISON, JIM GROUP INC   p308

1067 CORDOVA ST W SUITE 1800, VAN-
COUVER, BC, V6C 1C7
(604) 688-6764   *SIC* 5511
PATTISON, JIM INDUSTRIES LTD   p308
1067 CORDOVA ST W SUITE 1800, VAN-
COUVER, BC, V6C 1C7
(604) 688-6764   *SIC* 5511
PAULDONLAM INVESTMENTS INC   p865
2240 MARKHAM RD, SCARBOROUGH,
ON, M1B 2W4
(416) 754-4555   *SIC* 5511
PAULTOM MOTORS LIMITED   p641
3800 KING ST E, KITCHENER, ON, N2P
2G5
(519) 744-4119   *SIC* 5511
PEACE ARCH MOTORS LTD   p283
3174 KING GEORGE BLVD, SURREY, BC,
V4P 1A2
(604) 531-2916   *SIC* 5511
PEEL CHRYSLER PLYMOUTH (1991) INC
p713
212 LAKESHORE RD W, MISSISSAUGA,
ON, L5H 1G6
(905) 278-6181   *SIC* 5511
PENINSULA MOTOR SALES LTD   p836
202392 SUNSET STRIP, OWEN SOUND,
ON, N4K 5N7
(519) 376-3252   *SIC* 5511
PENTICTON KIA   p244
550 DUNCAN AVE W, PENTICTON, BC,
V2A 7N1
(250) 276-1200   *SIC* 5511
PERADE FORD INC, LA   p1355
727 RUE PRINCIPALE BUREAU 512,
SAINTE-ANNE-DE-LA-PERADE, QC, G0X
2J0
(418) 325-2244   *SIC* 5511
**PERFORMANCE CARS (ST CATHARINES)
LIMITED**   p886
371 ONTARIO ST, ST CATHARINES, ON,
L2R 5L3
(905) 685-3838   *SIC* 5511
PERFORMANCE EQUIPMENT LTD   p741
6950 TOMKEN RD, MISSISSAUGA, ON,
L5T 2S3
(905) 564-8333   *SIC* 5511
PERFORMANCE FORD SALES INC p1020
1150 PROVINCIAL RD, WINDSOR, ON,
N8W 5W2
(519) 972-6500   *SIC* 5511
PERFORMANCE GROUP 262 LAKE INC
p884
262 LAKE ST, ST CATHARINES, ON, L2N
4H1
(905) 934-7246   *SIC* 5511
PERFORMANCE HYUNDAI   p884
268 LAKE ST, ST CATHARINES, ON, L2N
4H1
(905) 937-7000   *SIC* 5511
PERFORMANCE LAURENTIDES INC p1155
1435 BOUL ALBINY-PAQUETTE, MONT-
LAURIER, QC, J9L 1M8
(819) 623-6331   *SIC* 5511
PERFORMANCE MOTORS (OTTAWA) INC
p810
1469 YOUVILLE DR, ORLEANS, ON, K1C
4R1
(613) 830-6320   *SIC* 5511
PETERBILT MANITOBA LTD   p369
1895 BROOKSIDE BLVD, WINNIPEG, MB,
R2R 2Y3
(204) 633-0071   *SIC* 5511
PETERBILT OF ONTARIO INC   p652
31 BUCHANAN CRT, LONDON, ON, N5Z
4P9
(519) 686-1000   *SIC* 5511
PETERBILT PACIFIC INC   p282
19470 96 AVE, SURREY, BC, V4N 4C2
(604) 888-1411   *SIC* 5511
PETERBILT QUEBEC EAST LTD   p1349
195 AV DU PARC, SAINT-PASCAL, QC, G0L
3Y0
(418) 492-7383   *SIC* 5511
PETERSEN PONTIAC BUICK GMC (ALTA)

INC   p163
10 AUTOMALL RD, SHERWOOD PARK,
AB, T8H 2N1
(587) 805-0959   *SIC* 5511
PETRIE FORD SALES (KINGSTON) LTD
p632
1388 BATH RD, KINGSTON, ON, K7M 4X6
(613) 544-6203   *SIC* 5511
PFAFF AUTOMOTIVE PARTNERS INC p557
9088 JANE ST, CONCORD, ON, L4K 2M9
(905) 907-2834   *SIC* 5511
PFAFF MOTORS INC   p557
220 CALDARI RD, CONCORD, ON, L4K 4L1
(905) 761-7890   *SIC* 5511
PHAETON AUTOMOTIVE GROUP INC p660
1065 WHARNCLIFFE RD S, LONDON, ON,
N6L 1J9
(519) 680-1800   *SIC* 5511
PICKERING CAR CORP   p843
557 KINGSTON RD, PICKERING, ON, L1V
3N7
(416) 798-4800   *SIC* 5511
PIE IX DODGE CHRYSLER 2000 INC p1170
9350 BOUL PIE-IX, MONTREAL, QC, H1Z
4E9
(514) 342-8500   *SIC* 5511
PIE IX TOYOTA INC   p1240
6767 BOUL HENRI-BOURASSA E,
MONTREAL-NORD, QC, H1G 2V6
(514) 329-0909   *SIC* 5511
**PIKE WHEATON CHEVROLET OLDSMO-
BILE LTD**   p157
3110 50 AVE, RED DEER, AB, T4R 1M6
(403) 343-8918   *SIC* 5511
PINEWOOD FORD LIMITED   p909
640 MEMORIAL AVE, THUNDER BAY, ON,
P7B 3Z5
(807) 344-9611   *SIC* 5511
PINNACLE AUTO SALES   p389
23 ROTHWELL RD, WINNIPEG, MB, R3P
2M5
(204) 667-2467   *SIC* 5511
PINNACLE CHRYSLER JEEP DODGE INC
p1020
2300 TECUMSEH RD E, WINDSOR, ON,
N8W 1E5
(519) 254-1196   *SIC* 5511
PIONEER GARAGE LIMITED   p232
33320 1ST AVE, MISSION, BC, V2V 1G8
(604) 462-7333   *SIC* 5511
PITMAN, WAYNE FORD LINCOLN INC p606
895 WOODLAWN RD W, GUELPH, ON,
N1K 1B7
(519) 824-6400   *SIC* 5511
PLACEMENTS BERIVES INC, LES   p1286
101 BOUL CARTIER, RIVIERE-DU-LOUP,
QC, G5R 2N3
(418) 862-6324   *SIC* 5511
PLACEMENTS GILLES ARNOLD INC p1115
2595 RUE GODBOUT, JONQUIERE, QC,
G7S 5S9
(418) 548-0821   *SIC* 5511
PLANTE, PAT AUTOS LTEE   p1107
850 BOUL SAINT-JOSEPH, GATINEAU,
QC, J8Z 1S9
(819) 770-0220   *SIC* 5511
PLAZA AUTO GROUP LTD   p855
9144 YONGE ST SUITE 200, RICHMOND
HILL, ON, L4C 7A1
(613) 890-4078   *SIC* 5511
**PLAZA CHEVROLET HUMMER CADILLAC
INC**   p1335
10480 BOUL HENRI-BOURASSA O, SAINT-
LAURENT, QC, H4S 1N6
(514) 332-1673   *SIC* 5511
PLAZA FORD SALES LIMITED   p467
33 TERMINAL RD, SYDNEY, NS, B1P 7B3
(902) 567-1616   *SIC* 5511
PLAZA NISSAN LIMITED   p616
1545 UPPER JAMES ST, HAMILTON, ON,
L9B 1K2
(905) 389-3588   *SIC* 5511
PLAZA PONTIAC BUICK LIMITED   p789
3400 DUFFERIN ST, NORTH YORK, ON,

M6A 2V1
(416) 781-5271   *SIC* 5511
PLUTO INVESTMENTS LTD   p102
10152 179 ST NW, EDMONTON, AB, T5S
1S1
(780) 486-1780   *SIC* 5511
POIRIER CHRYSLER JEEP DODGE LTEE
p1289
1265 AV LARIVIERE, ROUYN-NORANDA,
QC, J9X 6M6
(819) 764-7437   *SIC* 5511
POIRIER, ROGER AUTOMOBILE INC p1377
2325 RUE LAPRADE, SOREL-TRACY, QC,
J3R 2C1
(450) 742-2743   *SIC* 5511
POLICARO INVESTMENTS LIMITED   p500
2 MARITIME ONTARIO BLVD, BRAMPTON,
ON, L6S 0C2
(905) 791-3500   *SIC* 5511
POLITO FORD LINCOLN SALES LTD   p646
2 HARVEST ST, LINDSAY, ON, K9V 4S5
(705) 328-3673   *SIC* 5511
PONOKA CHEVROLET OLDSMOBILE LTD
p152
6305 44 AVE, PONOKA, AB, T4J 1J8
(403) 783-4494   *SIC* 5511
PORSCHE CANADIAN INVESTMENT ULC
p456
3367 KEMPT RD, HALIFAX, NS, B3K 4X5
(902) 453-8800   *SIC* 5511
PORSCHE CENTRE CALGARY   p37
5512 MACLEOD TRAIL SW, CALGARY, AB,
T2H 0J5
(403) 243-8101   *SIC* 5511
POTHIER MOTORS LTD   p450
18 FALMOUTH BACK RD, FALMOUTH, NS,
B0P 1L0
(877) 286-0154   *SIC* 5511
POWELL MOTORS LTD   p359
804 MAIN ST E, SWAN RIVER, MB, R0L
1Z0
(204) 734-3464   *SIC* 5511
PRAIRIE TRUCK LTD   p133
9916 108 ST, GRANDE PRAIRIE, AB, T8V
4E2
(780) 532-3541   *SIC* 5511
PRECISION HOLDINGS LTD   p347
404 18TH ST N, BRANDON, MB, R7A 7P3
(204) 725-0508   *SIC* 5511
PRECISION MOTORS LTD   p37
130 GLENDEER CIR SE, CALGARY, AB,
T2H 2V4
(403) 243-8344   *SIC* 5511
PREMIER AUTOMOTIVE GROUP INC p806
1453 NORTH SERVICE RD W, OAKVILLE,
ON, L6M 2W2
(905) 847-8400   *SIC* 5511
**PREMIER CHEVROLET CADILLAC BUICK
GMC INC**   p1023
500 DIVISION RD, WINDSOR, ON, N9A
6M9
(519) 969-6000   *SIC* 5511
**PREMIER TRUCK GROUP OF MISSIS-
SAUGA**   p742
7035 PACIFIC CIR, MISSISSAUGA, ON,
L5T 2A8
(905) 564-8270   *SIC* 5511
PREMIUM TRUCK & TRAILER INC   p251
1015 GREAT ST, PRINCE GEORGE, BC,
V2N 2K8
(250) 563-0696   *SIC* 5511
PRESTIGE FORD INC   p1365
1275 BOUL MONSEIGNEUR-LANGLOIS,
SALABERRY-DE-VALLEYFIELD, QC, J6S
1C1
(450) 371-0711   *SIC* 5511
**PRESTON CHEVROLET BUICK GMC
CADILLAC LTD**   p228
19990 LANGLEY BYPASS, LANGLEY, BC,
V3A 4Y1
(604) 534-4154   *SIC* 5511
PRIMA AUTO SALES LIMITED   p1033
7635 MARTIN GROVE RD, WOODBRIDGE,
ON, L4L 2C5

(905) 850-8111   *SIC* 5511
PRIMA AUTOMOBILES INC   *p*1287
136 CH DES RAYMOND, RIVIERE-DU-LOUP, QC, G5R 5X6
(418) 867-1420   *SIC* 5511
PRINCE GEORGE MOTORS LTD   *p*250
1331 CENTRAL ST W, PRINCE GEORGE, BC, V2M 3E2
(250) 563-8111   *SIC* 5511
PRINCIPALE AUTOS LTEE   *p*1111
1196 RUE PRINCIPALE, GRANBY, QC, J2J 0M2
(450) 378-4666   *SIC* 5511
PROBART MOTORS LIMITED   *p*659
652 WHARNCLIFFE RD S, LONDON, ON, N6J 2N4
(519) 649-1800   *SIC* 5511
PROVINCIAL CHRYSLER LTD   *p*1020
1001 PROVINCIAL RD, WINDSOR, ON, N8W 5V9
(519) 250-5500   *SIC* 5511
PTC AUTOMOTIVE LTD   *p*921
777 DUNDAS ST E, TORONTO, ON, M4M 0E2
(416) 530-1366   *SIC* 5511
QUANTRILL, CHEVROLET BUICK GMC CADILLAC LTD   *p*847
265 PETER ST, PORT HOPE, ON, L1A 3V6
(905) 885-4573   *SIC* 5511
QUANTUM AUTOMOTIVE GROUP INCORPORATED   *p*529
441 NORTH SERVICE RD, BURLINGTON, ON, L7P 0A3
(905) 632-4222   *SIC* 5511
QUEENSTON CHEVROLET INC   *p*608
282 CENTENNIAL PKY N, HAMILTON, ON, L8E 2X4
(905) 560-2020   *SIC* 5511
QUERIN, ARMAND AUTOMOBILES LTEE   *p*1087
2385 BOUL CHOMEDEY, COTE SAINT-LUC, QC, H7T 2W5
(450) 688-4787   *SIC* 5511
QUEST AUTOMOTIVE LEASING SERVICES LTD   *p*874
4960 SHEPPARD AVE E, SCARBOROUGH, ON, M1S 4A7
(416) 298-7600   *SIC* 5511
R.J.R. INVESTMENTS LTD   *p*385
670 CENTURY ST, WINNIPEG, MB, R3H 0A1
(204) 788-1100   *SIC* 5511
RACEWAY PLYMOUTH CHRYSLER LTD   *p*587
150 REXDALE BLVD, ETOBICOKE, ON, M9W 1P6
(416) 743-9900   *SIC* 5511
RACINE CHEVROLET BUICK GMC LTEE   *p*1317
1080 RUE DOUGLAS, SAINT-JEAN-SUR-RICHELIEU, QC, J3A 0A2
(450) 359-5900   *SIC* 5511
RAF ENTERPRISES INC   *p*1007
300 WEBER ST N, WATERLOO, ON, N2J 3H6
(519) 885-2000   *SIC* 5511
RAINBOW FORD SALES INC   *p*159
HWY 11E 42 AVE, ROCKY MOUNTAIN HOUSE, AB, T4T 1A9
(403) 845-3673   *SIC* 5511
RAINVILLE AUTOMOBILE 1975 INC   *p*1109
15 RUE DUTILLY, GRANBY, QC, J2G 6N6
(450) 378-3943   *SIC* 5511
RALLY MOTORS LTD   *p*1414
60 38TH ST E, PRINCE ALBERT, SK, S6W 1A6
(306) 922-6363   *SIC* 5511
RALLYE MOTORS LTD   *p*407
199 CARSON DR, MONCTON, NB, E1C 0K4
(506) 852-8200   *SIC* 5511
RALLYE MOTORS MITSUBISHI   *p*409
1837 MAIN ST, MONCTON, NB, E1E 1H6
(506) 857-8677   *SIC* 5511

RALY AUTOMOTIVE GROUP LTD   *p*911
76 MILL ST W, TILBURY, ON, N0P 2L0
(519) 682-3131   *SIC* 5511
RAMSAY'S AUTO SALES LIMITED   *p*468
229 KINGS RD, SYDNEY, NS, B1S 1A5
(902) 539-0112   *SIC* 5511
READY IMPORT LIMITED   *p*708
230 DUNDAS ST E, MISSISSAUGA, ON, L5A 1W9
(905) 896-3500   *SIC* 5511
REAUME CHEVROLET LTD   *p*1026
500 FRONT RD, WINDSOR, ON, N9J 1Z9
(519) 734-7844   *SIC* 5511
RED HILL TOYOTA   *p*608
2333 BARTON ST E, HAMILTON, ON, L8E 2W8
(905) 561-1202   *SIC* 5511
REGENCY AUTO ENTERPRISE INC   *p*186
4278 LOUGHEED HWY, BURNABY, BC, V5C 3Y5
(604) 291-8122   *SIC* 5511
REGENCY AUTO INVESTMENTS INC   *p*289
401 KINGSWAY, VANCOUVER, BC, V5T 3K1
(604) 879-8411   *SIC* 5511
REGENCY LEXUS TOYOTA INC   *p*289
401 KINGSWAY, VANCOUVER, BC, V5T 3K1
(604) 879-6241   *SIC* 5511
REGINA SPORT & IMPORT AUTOMOTIVE GROUP LTD   *p*1421
755 BROAD ST, REGINA, SK, S4R 8G3
(306) 757-2369   *SIC* 5511
RELIABLE MOTORS LTD   *p*1041
14 JOHN YEO DR, CHARLOTTETOWN, PE, C1E 3H6
(902) 566-4409   *SIC* 5511
RENAUD, LARRY FORD & RV SALES   *p*618
175 KING ST W, HARROW, ON, N0R 1G0
(519) 738-6767   *SIC* 5511
RENDEZ-VOUS CHRYSLER LTD   *p*403
795 BOUL EVERARD H DAIGLE, GRAND-SAULT/GRAND FALLS, NB, E3Z 3C7
(506) 473-5000   *SIC* 5511
RENFREW CHRYSLER INC.   *p*73
1920 PUMPHOUSE RD SW, CALGARY, AB, T3C 3N4
(403) 266-1920   *SIC* 5511
RENFREW NATIONAL LEASING LTD   *p*73
1920 PUMPHOUSE RD SW, CALGARY, AB, T3C 3N4
(403) 266-1920   *SIC* 5511
REPENTIGNY CHEVROLET BUICK GMC INC   *p*1283
612 RUE NOTRE-DAME, REPENTIGNY, QC, J6A 2T9
(450) 581-9500   *SIC* 5511
RESTIGOUCHE MOTORS LTD   *p*396
388 DOVER ST, CAMPBELLTON, NB, E3N 3M7
(506) 753-5019   *SIC* 5511
REVELL MOTORS SALES LIMITED   *p*1003
6628 38 HWY, VERONA, ON, K0H 2W0
(613) 374-2133   *SIC* 5511
REVENBERG, GUS PONTIAC BUICK HUMMER GMC LTD   *p*1018
10150 TECUMSEH RD E, WINDSOR, ON, N8R 1A2
(519) 979-2800   *SIC* 5511
RICE AUTOMOTIVE INVESTMENTS LTD   *p*203
445 CROWN ISLE BLVD, COURTENAY, BC, V9N 9W1
(250) 338-6761   *SIC* 5511
RICHMOND CHRYSLER DODGE JEEP LTD   *p*256
5491 PARKWOOD WAY, RICHMOND, BC, V6V 2M9
(604) 273-7521   *SIC* 5511
RICHMOND HILL AUTO PARK LIMITED   *p*857
11240 YONGE ST, RICHMOND HILL, ON, L4S 1K9
(905) 889-1189   *SIC* 5511

RICHMOND IMPORTS LTD   *p*256
13600 SMALLWOOD PL, RICHMOND, BC, V6V 1W8
(604) 207-1846   *SIC* 5511
RICHMOND NISSAN LTD   *p*256
13220 SMALLWOOD PL, RICHMOND, BC, V6V 1W8
(604) 273-1661   *SIC* 5511
RICHWIL TRUCK CENTRE LTD   *p*404
314 LOCKHART MILL RD, JACKSONVILLE, NB, E7M 3S4
(506) 328-9379   *SIC* 5511
RIDGEHILL FORD SALES (1980) LIMITED   *p*534
217 HESPELER RD SUITE 637, CAMBRIDGE, ON, N1R 3H8
(519) 621-0720   *SIC* 5511
RINFRET AUTO INC   *p*1137
5355 BOUL GUILLAUME-COUTURE, LEVIS, QC, G6V 4Z3
(418) 833-2133   *SIC* 5511
RIVE SUD CHRYSLER DODGE INC   *p*1069
9400 BOUL TASCHEREAU, BROSSARD, QC, J4X 1C3
(450) 444-9400   *SIC* 5511
RIVE SUD PONTIAC BUICK GMC INC   *p*1143
395 RUE SAINT-CHARLES O, LONGUEUIL, QC, J4H 1G1
    SIC 5511
RIVER CITY NISSAN   *p*217
2405 TRANS CANADA HWY E, KAMLOOPS, BC, V2C 4A9
(250) 377-8850   *SIC* 5511
RIVER SIDE FORD SALES LIMITED   *p*520
25 ELEANOR ST, BROCKVILLE, ON, K6V 4H9
(613) 342-0234   *SIC* 5511
RIVERSIDE DODGE CHRYSLER JEEP LTD   *p*1414
160 38TH ST E, PRINCE ALBERT, SK, S6W 1A6
(306) 764-4217   *SIC* 5511
RIVERSIDE PONTIAC BUICK LTD   *p*848
101 DEVELOPMENT DR, PRESCOTT, ON, K0E 1T0
(613) 925-5941   *SIC* 5511
RIVERVIEW AUTOMOBILE LIMITED   *p*1005
854 MURRAY ST, WALLACEBURG, ON, N8A 1W4
(519) 627-6014   *SIC* 5511
RIVERVIEW MOTORS LIMITED   *p*424
75 LINCOLN RD, GRAND FALLS-WINDSOR, NL, A2A 1N3
(709) 489-2138   *SIC* 5511
RIVERVIEW SERVICE CENTRE LIMITED   *p*543
351 RICHMOND ST, CHATHAM, ON, N7M 1P5
(519) 352-4937   *SIC* 5511
RJAMES MANAGEMENT GROUP LTD   *p*217
2072 FALCON RD, KAMLOOPS, BC, V2C 4J3
(250) 374-1431   *SIC* 5511
ROADSPORT LIMITED   *p*872
940 ELLESMERE RD, SCARBOROUGH, ON, M1P 2W8
(416) 291-9501   *SIC* 5511
ROBERT MOTORS (1980) LIMITED   *p*578
5450 DUNDAS ST W, ETOBICOKE, ON, M9B 1B4
(416) 231-1984   *SIC* 5511
ROBINSON BUICK GMC LTD   *p*606
875 WOODLAWN RD W, GUELPH, ON, N1K 1B7
(519) 821-0520   *SIC* 5511
ROBINSON LEASING AND SALES LIMITED   *p*606
875 WOODLAWN RD W, GUELPH, ON, N1K 1B7
(519) 821-0520   *SIC* 5511
ROCK COUNTRY CHEVROLET BUICK GMC LTD   *p*360
121 NELSON RD, THOMPSON, MB, R8N 0B7

(204) 778-7081   *SIC* 5511
ROCKY MOUNTAIN DODGE CHRYSLER JEEP LTD   *p*159
4415 42ND AVE, ROCKY MOUNTAIN HOUSE, AB, T4T 1B6
(403) 845-2851   *SIC* 5511
ROCOTO LTEE   *p*1079
1540 BOUL DU ROYAUME O BUREAU 4, CHICOUTIMI, QC, G7H 5B1
(418) 549-5574   *SIC* 5511
RODEO FORD SALES LIMITED   *p*147
1788 SAAMIS DR NW, MEDICINE HAT, AB, T1C 1W7
(403) 529-2777   *SIC* 5511
RON HODGSON CHEVROLET BUICK GMC LTD   *p*166
5 GALARNEAU PL, ST. ALBERT, AB, T8N 2Y3
(780) 458-7100   *SIC* 5511
RONDEAU CHRYSLER JEEP DODGE INC   *p*1315
180 RUE MOREAU, SAINT-JEAN-SUR-RICHELIEU, QC, J2W 2M4
(450) 359-7333   *SIC* 5511
ROSE CITY FORD SALES LIMITED   *p*1019
6333 TECUMSEH RD E, WINDSOR, ON, N8T 1E7
(519) 948-7800   *SIC* 5511
ROSETOWN MAINLINE MOTOR PRODUCTS LIMITED   *p*1423
505 7 HWY W, ROSETOWN, SK, S0L 2V0
(306) 882-2691   *SIC* 5511
ROUSSEL TOYOTA   *p*405
323 KING GEORGE HWY, MIRAMICHI, NB, E1V 1L2
(506) 622-1867   *SIC* 5511
ROY FOSS MOTORS LTD   *p*906
7200 YONGE ST UNIT 1, THORNHILL, ON, L4J 1V8
(905) 886-2000   *SIC* 5511
ROY FOSS SATURN SAAB OF LEASIDE LTD   *p*918
957 EGLINTON AVE E, TORONTO, ON, M4G 4B5
    SIC 5511
ROY'S CHEVROLET BUICK GMC INC   *p*599
4000 COUNTY RD 34, GREEN VALLEY, ON, K0C 1L0
(613) 525-2300   *SIC* 5511
ROYAL CHEVROLET-CADILLAC INC   *p*808
1 MONORA PARK DR, ORANGEVILLE, ON, L9W 0E1
(519) 941-0420   *SIC* 5511
ROYAL CITY MOTORS LTD   *p*606
635 WOODLAWN RD W, GUELPH, ON, N1K 1E9
(519) 837-3431   *SIC* 5511
ROYAL FORD LINCOLN SALES LTD   *p*1438
117 BROADWAY ST E, YORKTON, SK, S3N 3B2
(306) 782-2261   *SIC* 5511
ROYAL GARAGE LIMITED, THE   *p*426
709 TOPSAIL RD, MOUNT PEARL, NL, A1N 3N4
(709) 748-2110   *SIC* 5511
ROYAL OAK LEXUS   *p*77
7677 112 AVE NW, CALGARY, AB, T3R 1R8
(403) 261-9977   *SIC* 5511
RUSH TRUCK CENTRES OF CANADA LIMITED   *p*686
7450 TORBRAM RD, MISSISSAUGA, ON, L4T 1G9
(905) 671-7600   *SIC* 5511
RUSSELLE ENTERPRISES INC   *p*842
1400 LANSDOWNE ST W, PETERBOROUGH, ON, K9J 2A2
(705) 742-4288   *SIC* 5511
RUSSELLE TOYOTA INC   *p*842
1400 LANSDOWNE ST W, PETERBOROUGH, ON, K9J 2A2
(705) 742-4288   *SIC* 5511
S & B KESWICK MOTORS LIMITED   *p*628
475 THE QUEENSWAY S, KESWICK, ON, L4P 2E2

▲ Public Company   ■ Public Company Family Member   **HQ** Headquarters   **BR** Branch   **SL** Single Location

(905) 476-3111   *SIC 5511*

S-304 HOLDINGS LTD   *p273*
19505 LANGLEY BYPASS, SURREY, BC, V3S 6K1
(604) 534-7957   *SIC 5511*

S.L. FORD SALES LTD   *p163*
309 1A AVE SE SS 3, SLAVE LAKE, AB, T0G 2A3
(780) 849-4419   *SIC 5511*

SADLON, PAUL MOTORS INCORPORATED   *p484*
550 BAYFIELD ST, BARRIE, ON, L4M 5A2
(705) 721-7733   *SIC 5511*

SAINT JOHN VOLKSWAGEN   *p413*
297 ROTHESAY AVE, SAINT JOHN, NB, E2J 2C1
(506) 658-1313   *SIC 5511*

SAINT-CONSTANT AUTO 2010 INC   *p1298*
48 RUE SAINT-PIERRE, SAINT-CONSTANT, QC, J5A 1B9
(450) 632-0700   *SIC 5511*

SALMON ARM CHEV BUICK GMC LTD *p268*
3901 11 AVE NE, SALMON ARM, BC, V1E 2S2
(250) 832-6066   *SIC 5511*

SARCEE MOTORS LTD   *p74*
55 GLENBROOK PL SW, CALGARY, AB, T3E 6W4
(403) 249-9166   *SIC 5511*

SASKATOON C AUTO LP   *p1424*
2200 8TH ST E, SASKATOON, SK, S7H 0V3
(306) 374-2120   *SIC 5511*

SATISFACTION PLYMOUTH CHRLSER INC   *p1399*
1475 BOUL JUTRAS O, VICTORIAVILLE, QC, G6T 2A9
(819) 752-5252   *SIC 5511*

SATURN SAAB ISUZU OF EDMONTON *p94*
14803 137 AVE NW, EDMONTON, AB, T5L 2L5
(780) 484-4455   *SIC 5511*

SAULNIER AUTOMOBILES INC   *p1302*
445 BOUL INDUSTRIEL, SAINT-EUSTACHE, QC, J7R 5R3
(450) 623-7446   *SIC 5511*

SAUNDERS AUTOMOTIVE LIMITED   *p896*
640 LORNE AVE E, STRATFORD, ON, N5A 6S4
(519) 271-9227   *SIC 5511*

SCARBOROUGH NISSAN (1989) LIMITED *p869*
1941 EGLINTON AVE E, SCARBOROUGH, ON, M1L 2M4
(416) 751-3511   *SIC 5511*

SCARBOROUGH TRUCK CENTRE INC *p865*
1810 MARKHAM RD, SCARBOROUGH, ON, M1B 2W2
SIC 5511

SCARSVIEW MOTORS LTD   *p865*
951 MILNER AVE, SCARBOROUGH, ON, M1B 5X4
(416) 281-6200   *SIC 5511*

SCHLUETER CHEVROLET OLDSMOBILE LIMITED   *p637*
2685 KINGSWAY DR, KITCHENER, ON, N2C 1A7
(519) 884-9000   *SIC 5511*

SCHON, GEORGE MOTORS LIMITED *p1033*
7685 MARTIN GROVE RD, WOODBRIDGE, ON, L4L 1B5
(905) 851-3993   *SIC 5511*

SCOCHI HOLDINGS INC   *p228*
19820 FRASER HWY, LANGLEY, BC, V3A 4C9
(604) 533-7881   *SIC 5511*

SCOTIA CHRYSLER INC   *p467*
325 WELTON ST, SYDNEY, NS, B1P 5S3
(902) 539-2280   *SIC 5511*

SCOTT, GORD NISSAN INC   *p154*
6863 50 AVE, RED DEER, AB, T4N 4E2
(403) 347-2258   *SIC 5511*

SCOTT, KIPP PONTIAC BUICK LTD   *p154*
6841 50 AVE, RED DEER, AB, T4N 4E2
(403) 343-6633   *SIC 5511*

SCOTT-FISHER ENTERPRISES INC *p578*
5507 DUNDAS ST W, ETOBICOKE, ON, M9B 1B8
(416) 207-0565   *SIC 5511*

SEA TO SKY FORD SALES LTD   *p269*
1100 COMMERCIAL PL, SQUAMISH, BC, V8B 0S7
(604) 892-3673   *SIC 5511*

SEARLES, DENNIS CHEVROLET LIMITED *p532*
160 ARGYLE ST S, CALEDONIA, ON, N3W 1K7
(905) 765-4424   *SIC 5511*

SEASIDE CHEVROLET LIMITED   *p417*
13 HARBOUR VIEW DR, SCOUDOUC, NB, E4P 3L5
(506) 532-6666   *SIC 5511*

SEAWAY CHEVROLET CADILLAC BUICK GMC LTD   *p563*
2695 BROOKDALE AVE, CORNWALL, ON, K6J 5X9
(613) 933-3000   *SIC 5511*

SELKIRK CHRYSLER (MB) LTD   *p356*
1011 MANITOBA AVE, SELKIRK, MB, R1A 3T7
(204) 482-4151   *SIC 5511*

SENCHUK FORD SALES LTD   *p1406*
118 SOURIS AVE, ESTEVAN, SK, S4A 1J6
(306) 634-3696   *SIC 5511*

SENTES CHEVROLET LTD   *p244*
933 WESTMINSTER AVE W, PENTICTON, BC, V2A 1L1
(250) 493-2333   *SIC 5511*

SERAY AUTO INC   *p1075*
730 BOUL DE PERIGNY, CHAMBLY, QC, J3L 1W3
(450) 658-4482   *SIC 5511*

SERVICES DE MECANIQUE MOBILE B L INC   *p1111*
50 RUE SAINT-JUDE S, GRANBY, QC, J2J 2N4
(450) 378-0413   *SIC 5511*

SETAY MOTORS INC   *p608*
282 CENTENNIAL PKY N, HAMILTON, ON, L8E 2X4
(905) 549-4656   *SIC 5511*

SEVEN VIEW PLYMOUTH CHRYSLER LTD *p558*
2685 HIGHWAY 7, CONCORD, ON, L4K 1V8
(905) 669-5051   *SIC 5511*

SHAGANAPPI MOTORS (1976) LTD   *p72*
4720 CROWCHILD TRAIL NW, CALGARY, AB, T3A 2N2
(403) 288-0444   *SIC 5511*

SHANAHAN CARRIAGE CO. LTD, THE *p756*
567 DAVIS DR, NEWMARKET, ON, L3Y 2P5
(416) 798-4858   *SIC 5511*

SHEEHAN'S TRUCK CENTRE INC   *p524*
4320 HARVESTER RD, BURLINGTON, ON, L7L 5S4
(905) 632-0300   *SIC 5511*

SHELLBROOK CHEVROLET OLDSMOBILE LTD   *p1435*
43 MAIN ST, SHELLBROOK, SK, S0J 2E0
(306) 747-2411   *SIC 5511*

SHERBROOKE AUTOMOBILE INC   *p1375*
4465 BOUL BOURQUE, SHERBROOKE, QC, J1N 1S4
(819) 569-9111   *SIC 5511*

SHERBROOKE NISSAN INC   *p1375*
4280 BOUL BOURQUE, SHERBROOKE, QC, J1N 1W7
(819) 823-8008   *SIC 5511*

SHERIDAN FORD LINCOLN SALES LTD *p712*
1345 LAKESHORE RD E, MISSISSAUGA, ON, L5E 1G5
SIC 5511

SHERMAN, L.E. MOTORS LTD   *p252*
1001 CHAMBERLIN AVE, PRINCE RUPERT, BC, V8J 4J5
(250) 624-9171   *SIC 5511*

SHERWAY NISSAN (2000) LIMITED   *p578*
5448 DUNDAS ST W, ETOBICOKE, ON, M9B 1B4
(416) 239-1217   *SIC 5511*

SHERWOOD CHEVROLET INC   *p1425*
550 BRAND RD, SASKATOON, SK, S7J 5J3
(306) 374-6330   *SIC 5511*

SHERWOOD PARK DODGE CHRYSLER JEEP LTD   *p163*
230 PROVINCIAL AVE, SHERWOOD PARK, AB, T8H 0E1
(780) 410-4100   *SIC 5511*

SHERWOOD PARK VEHICLES LP   *p163*
41 AUTOMALL RD, SHERWOOD PARK, AB, T8H 0C7
(780) 410-2450   *SIC 5511*

SILVER CROSS AUTOMOTIVE INC   *p588*
14 GOODMARK PL, ETOBICOKE, ON, M9W 6R1
(905) 799-5533   *SIC 5511*

SILVER RIDGE MOTOR PRODUCTS LTD *p143*
3524 2 AVE S, LETHBRIDGE, AB, T1J 4T9
(403) 329-6888   *SIC 5511*

SILVER STAR AUTO MB INC   *p271*
15508 104 AVE, SURREY, BC, V3R 1N8
(604) 581-7806   *SIC 5511*

SILVERHILL MOTORS LTD   *p37*
5728 MACLEOD TRAIL SW, CALGARY, AB, T2H 0J6
(403) 253-6060   *SIC 5511*

SILVERWOOD MOTOR PRODUCTS LTD *p144*
5103 25 ST, LLOYDMINSTER, AB, T9V 3G2
(780) 870-5166   *SIC 5511*

SIMMONS AUTO SALES & SERVICE LIMITED   *p423*
461 JAMES BLVD, GANDER, NL, A1V 2V4
(709) 256-3415   *SIC 5511*

SIMPSON AUTOMOBILES INC   *p1102*
112 BOUL DE GASPE, GASPE, QC, G4X 1A9
(800) 368-2279   *SIC 5511*

SISLEY MOTORS LIMITED   *p906*
88 STEELES AVE W, THORNHILL, ON, L4J 1A1
(416) 223-3111   *SIC 5511*

SKAHA FORD INC   *p244*
198 PARKWAY PL, PENTICTON, BC, V2A 8G8
(250) 492-3800   *SIC 5511*

SLAVE LAKE CHRYSLER DODGE JEEP RAM LTD   *p163*
701 15 AVE SW, SLAVE LAKE, AB, T0G 2A4
(780) 849-5225   *SIC 5511*

SLESSOR AUTO WORLD   *p600*
569 MAIN ST W, GRIMSBY, ON, L3M 1V1
(905) 643-1221   *SIC 5511*

SMALL CAR CENTRE LTD   *p856*
77 16TH AVE, RICHMOND HILL, ON, L4C 7A5
(905) 731-8899   *SIC 5511*

SMITH CHEVROLET OLDSMOBILE LTD *p218*
950 NOTRE DAME DR SUITE 3310, KAMLOOPS, BC, V2C 6J2
(250) 377-3302   *SIC 5511*

SMITH, BYRON FORD SALES INC   *p168*
1040 WESTRIDGE RD, STRATHMORE, AB, T1P 1H8
(403) 934-2100   *SIC 5511*

SMITH, PETER CHEVROLET CADILLAC LTD   *p492*
42 TOWNCENTRE RD, BELLEVILLE, ON, K8N 4Z5
(613) 968-6767   *SIC 5511*

SMITH, TOM CHEVROLET LIMITED   *p682*
824 KING ST, MIDLAND, ON, L4R 0B8
(705) 526-0193   *SIC 5511*

SMYL CHEVROLET PONTIAC BUICK GMC LTD   *p173*
3520 KEPLER ST, WHITECOURT, AB, T7S 1N9
(780) 778-2202   *SIC 5511*

SMYL MOTORS LTD   *p165*
5015 44 ST SS 2, ST PAUL, AB, T0A 3A2
(780) 645-4414   *SIC 5511*

SOLUTION FORD INC   *p1077*
117 BOUL SAINT-JEAN-BAPTISTE, CHATEAUGUAY, QC, J6K 3B1
(450) 691-4130   *SIC 5511*

SOMA AUTO INC   *p1046*
42 10E AV O, AMOS, QC, J9T 1W8
(819) 732-3205   *SIC 5511*

SOMERSET CHEVROLET CORVETTE LTD *p934*
291 LAKE SHORE BLVD E, TORONTO, ON, M5A 1B9
(416) 368-8878   *SIC 5511*

SOMI INC   *p744*
6160 MAVIS RD, MISSISSAUGA, ON, L5V 2X4
(905) 569-7777   *SIC 5511*

SOR HOLDINGS LTD   *p363*
1364 REGENT AVE W, WINNIPEG, MB, R2C 3A8
(204) 667-9993   *SIC 5511*

SOUTH COAST FORD SALES LTD   *p268*
5606 WHARF RD, SECHELT, BC, V0N 3A0
(604) 885-3281   *SIC 5511*

SOUTH FORT CHEVROLET LTD   *p130*
10109 89 AVE, FORT SASKATCHEWAN, AB, T8L 3V5
(780) 998-7881   *SIC 5511*

SOUTH LONDON INFINITI-NISSAN INC *p660*
1055 WHARNCLIFFE RD S, LONDON, ON, N6L 1J9
(519) 685-5497   *SIC 5511*

SOUTH OAKVILLE CHRYSLER DODGE JEEP RAM LTD   *p802*
175 WYECROFT RD, OAKVILLE, ON, L6K 3S3
(905) 845-6653   *SIC 5511*

SOUTH POINT CHEVROLET PONTIAC BUICK GMC LTD   *p645*
108 ERIE ST N, LEAMINGTON, ON, N8H 0A9
(519) 326-3206   *SIC 5511*

SOUTH WEST CHRYSLER DODGE INC *p659*
658 WHARNCLIFFE RD S, LONDON, ON, N6J 2N4
(519) 649-2121   *SIC 5511*

SOUTHBANK DODGE CHRYSLER (1982) LTD   *p827*
1255 JOHNSTON RD, OTTAWA, ON, K1V 8Z1
(613) 731-1970   *SIC 5511*

SOUTHCENTER AUTO INC   *p1432*
321 CIRCLE DR W, SASKATOON, SK, S7L 5S8
(306) 373-3711   *SIC 5511*

SOUTHGATE CHEVROLET BUICK GMC LTD   *p39*
13103 LAKE FRASER DR SE, CALGARY, AB, T2J 3H5
(403) 256-4960   *SIC 5511*

SOUTHGATE PONTIAC BUICK GMC LTD *p116*
9751 34 AVE NW, EDMONTON, AB, T6E 5X9
(855) 971-6989   *SIC 5511*

SOUTHLAND INTERNATIONAL TRUCKS LTD   *p141*
4310 9 AVE N, LETHBRIDGE, AB, T1H 6N1
(403) 328-0808   *SIC 5511*

SOUTHRIDGE CHRYSLER LTD   *p151*
12 SOUTHRIDGE DR, OKOTOKS, AB, T1S 1N1
(403) 938-3636   *SIC 5511*

SOUTHSIDE MOTORS LTD   *p39*
11888 MACLEOD TRAIL SE, CALGARY, AB, T2J 7J2
(403) 252-4327   *SIC 5511*

SOUTHSIDE NISSAN LTD   *p291*
290 MARINE DR SW, VANCOUVER, BC, V5X 2R5

▲ Public Company   ■ Public Company Family Member   **HQ** Headquarters   **BR** Branch   **SL** Single Location

(604) 324-4644 *SIC 5511*
SOUTHSIDE PLYMOUTH CHRYSLER LTD
p157
2804 50 AVE, RED DEER, AB, T4R 1M4
(403) 346-5577 *SIC 5511*
SOUTHTOWN CHRYSLER INC *p120*
4404 66 ST NW, EDMONTON, AB, T6K 4E7
(780) 490-3200 *SIC 5511*
SOUTHWEST AUTO CENTRE LTD *p348*
2080 CURRIE BLVD, BRANDON, MB, R7B 4E7
(204) 728-8740 *SIC 5511*
SOVEA AUTOS LTEE *p1262*
125 RUE DU MARAIS, QUEBEC, QC, G1M 3C8
(418) 681-0011 *SIC 5511*
SPEEDWAY MOTORS LTD *p338*
3329 DOUGLAS ST, VICTORIA, BC, V8Z 3L2
(250) 386-6650 *SIC 5511*
SPELMER CHRYSLER JEEP DODGE SALES LTD *p999*
51 HIGHWAY 33, TRENTON, ON, K8V 5R1
(613) 394-3945 *SIC 5511*
SPENCER, BILL CHEVROLET OLDSMOBILE LTD *p545*
1090 ELGIN ST W SUITE 12, COBOURG, ON, K9A 5V5
(905) 372-8773 *SIC 5511*
SPINELLI TOYOTA (1981) INC *p1252*
10 AV AUTO PLAZA, POINTE-CLAIRE, QC, H9R 3H9
(514) 694-1510 *SIC 5511*
SPINELLI TOYOTA (1981) INC *p1252*
10 AV AUTO PLAZA, POINTE-CLAIRE, QC, H9R 3H9
(514) 694-1510 *SIC 5511*
SPINELLI TOYOTA (1981) INC *p1252*
12 AV AUTO PLAZA, POINTE-CLAIRE, QC, H9R 4W6
(514) 694-1510 *SIC 5511*
SPRUCELAND FORD SALES LTD *p173*
4144 KEPLER ST, WHITECOURT, AB, T7S 0A3
(780) 778-4777 *SIC 5511*
SPV MOTORS LP *p163*
2365 BROADMOOR BLVD, SHERWOOD PARK, AB, T8H 1B4
(780) 400-4800 *SIC 5511*
ST PAUL DODGE LTD *p165*
4014 50 AVE, ST PAUL, AB, T0A 3A2
SIC 5511
ST-GEORGES CHEVROLET PONTIAC BUICK CADILLAC GMC INC *p1305*
520 87E RUE, SAINT-GEORGES, QC, G5Y 7L9
(418) 228-8801 *SIC 5511*
ST-JEROME CHEVROLET BUICK GMC INC *p1320*
265 RUE JOHN-F.-KENNEDY, SAINT-JEROME, QC, J7Y 4B5
(450) 438-1203 *SIC 5511*
ST-LEONARD NISSAN INC *p1346*
4400 BOUL METROPOLITAIN E, SAINT-LEONARD, QC, H1S 1A2
(514) 365-7777 *SIC 5511*
ST. ALBERT DODGE CHRYSLER LTD *p166*
184 ST ALBERT TRAIL, ST. ALBERT, AB, T8N 0P7
(780) 238-8787 *SIC 5511*
ST. THOMAS FORD LINCOLN SALES LIMITED *p889*
1012 TALBOT ST, ST THOMAS, ON, N5P 1G3
(519) 631-5080 *SIC 5511*
STACY'S AUTO RANCH LIMITED *p441*
366 DUFFERIN ST, BRIDGEWATER, NS, B4V 2H2
(902) 212-0024 *SIC 5511*
STADIUM NISSAN INC *p41*
2420 CROWCHILD TRAIL NW, CALGARY, AB, T2M 4N5
(403) 284-4611 *SIC 5511*
STAHL PETERBILT INC *p103*

18020 118 AVE NW, EDMONTON, AB, T5S 2G2
(780) 483-6666 *SIC 5511*
STAMPEDE PONTIAC BUICK (1988) LTD *p60*
1110 9 AVE SW, CALGARY, AB, T2P 1M1
SIC 5511
STAMPEDE TOYOTA & LEASING LTD *p9*
2508 24 AVE NE, CALGARY, AB, T1Y 6R8
(403) 291-2111 *SIC 5511*
STANDARD MOTORS (77) LTD *p1436*
44 2ND AVE NW, SWIFT CURRENT, SK, S9H 0N9
(306) 773-3131 *SIC 5511*
STANG'S AUTOMOTIVE ENTERPRISES INC *p9*
3003 32 AVE NE, CALGARY, AB, T1Y 6J1
(403) 291-7060 *SIC 5511*
STAR ONE MOTOR CO *p1015*
250 THICKSON RD S, WHITBY, ON, L1N 9Z1
(905) 666-8805 *SIC 5511*
STARR, MARVIN PONTIAC BUICK CADILLAC INC *p867*
3132 EGLINTON AVE E, SCARBOROUGH, ON, M1J 2H1
SIC 5511
STAUFFER MOTORS LIMITED *p912*
685 BROADWAY ST, TILLSONBURG, ON, N4G 4H1
(519) 842-3646 *SIC 5511*
STE-MARIE AUTOMOBILES LTEE *p1351*
540 RANG NOTRE-DAME, SAINT-REMI, QC, J0L 2L0
(514) 861-5529 *SIC 5511*
STEDELBAUER CHEVROLET INC *p84*
13145 97 ST NW, EDMONTON, AB, T5E 4C4
(780) 476-6221 *SIC 5511*
STEELE AUTO GROUP LIMITED *p448*
8 BASINVIEW DR, DARTMOUTH, NS, B3B 1G4
(902) 454-3185 *SIC 5511*
STEELE CHEVROLET BUICK GMC CADILLAC *p443*
636 PORTLAND ST, DARTMOUTH, NS, B2W 2M3
(902) 434-4100 *SIC 5511*
STEELE CHRYSLER PLYMOUTH LIMITED *p457*
44 BEDFORD HWY, HALIFAX, NS, B3M 2J2
(902) 454-7341 *SIC 5511*
STEELE VOLKSWAGEN LIMITED *p448*
696 WINDMILL RD, DARTMOUTH, NS, B3B 2A5
(902) 468-6411 *SIC 5511*
STEELTOWN FORD SALES 1980 LTD *p356*
933 MANITOBA AVE, SELKIRK, MB, R1A 3T7
(888) 485-3230 *SIC 5511*
STEINBACH DODGE CHRYSLER LTD *p359*
208 MAIN ST, STEINBACH, MB, R5G 1Y6
(204) 326-4461 *SIC 5511*
STEPHANI MOTORS LTD *p5*
4811 53 ST, BARRHEAD, AB, T7N 1G2
(780) 674-2211 *SIC 5511*
STERLING FORD SALES (OTTAWA) INC *p596*
1425 OGILVIE RD, GLOUCESTER, ON, K1J 7P3
(613) 741-3720 *SIC 5511*
STERLING TRUCKS OF CALGARY LTD *p9*
2800 BARLOW TRAIL NE SUITE 291, CALGARY, AB, T1Y 1A2
(866) 792-1443 *SIC 5511*
STERLING WESTERN STAR TRUCKS ALBERTA LTD *p18*
9115 52 ST SE, CALGARY, AB, T2C 2R4
(403) 720-3400 *SIC 5511*
STERNE MOTORS LTD *p482*
625 ST. JOHN'S SIDEROAD E, AURORA, ON, L4G 0Z7
(905) 841-1400 *SIC 5511*
STETSON MOTORS (2000) LTD *p82*

2451 50TH ST, DRAYTON VALLEY, AB, T7A 1S4
(780) 542-5391 *SIC 5511*
STETTLER DODGE LTD *p167*
4406 44 AVE, STETTLER, AB, T0C 2L0
(403) 742-3000 *SIC 5511*
STETTLER MOTORS (1998) LTD *p167*
6115 50 AVE SS 2, STETTLER, AB, T0C 2L2
(403) 742-3407 *SIC 5511*
STM BG AUTO INC *p889*
449 QUEEN ST W, ST MARYS, ON, N4X 1B7
(519) 284-3310 *SIC 5511*
STOCKFISH, GEORGE FORD SALES (1987) LTD *p764*
HWY 17 E, NORTH BAY, ON, P1B 8J5
(705) 476-1506 *SIC 5511*
STOCKIE, GARY CHEVROLET LIMITED *p640*
20 OTTAWA ST N, KITCHENER, ON, N2H 0A4
SIC 5511
STONELEIGH MOTORS LIMITED *p682*
9186 COUNTY ROAD HWY SUITE 93, MIDLAND, ON, L4R 4K6
(705) 526-3724 *SIC 5511*
STONY PLAIN CHRYSLER LTD *p168*
4004 51 ST, STONY PLAIN, AB, T7Z 0A2
(780) 963-2236 *SIC 5511*
STOP 23 AUTO SALES LTD *p647*
910 WALLACE AVE N, LISTOWEL, ON, N4W 1M5
(519) 291-5757 *SIC 5511*
STOTHART AUTOMOTIVE INC *p395*
335 MURRAY AVE, BATHURST, NB, E2A 1T4
(506) 548-8988 *SIC 5511*
STRATFORD MOTOR PRODUCTS (1984) LTD *p896*
824 ONTARIO ST, STRATFORD, ON, N5A 3K1
(519) 271-5900 *SIC 5511*
STRATHMORE MOTOR PRODUCTS LTD *p168*
900 WESTRIDGE RD, STRATHMORE, AB, T1P 1H8
(403) 934-3334 *SIC 5511*
STREETSVILLE HYUNDAI *p727*
6225 MISSISSAUGA RD, MISSISSAUGA, ON, L5N 1A4
(905) 812-5401 *SIC 5511*
SUBARU OF KINGSTON *p632*
399 BATH RD, KINGSTON, ON, K7M 7C9
(613) 546-7000 *SIC 5511*
SULLIVAN MOTOR PRODUCTS LTD *p216*
2760 YELLOWHEAD HWY SUITE 16, HOUSTON, BC, V0J 1Z0
(250) 845-2244 *SIC 5511*
SUMMERSIDE CHRYSLER DODGE (1984) LTD *p1043*
3 WATER ST, SUMMERSIDE, PE, C1N 1A2
(902) 436-9141 *SIC 5511*
SUMMIT DODGE CHRYSLER JEEP LIMITED *p495*
10 SIMONA DR, BOLTON, ON, L7E 4C7
SIC 5511
SUMMIT FORD SALES (1982) LIMITED *p580*
12 CARRIER DR, ETOBICOKE, ON, M9V 2C1
(416) 741-6221 *SIC 5511*
SUN TOYOTA LTD *p117*
10130 82 AVE NW, EDMONTON, AB, T6E 1Z4
(780) 433-2411 *SIC 5511*
SUNDRE MOTORS LTD *p168*
104 MAIN AVE NE, SUNDRE, AB, T0M 1X0
SIC 5511
SUNRIDGE NISSAN LTD *p9*
3131 32 AVE NE, CALGARY, AB, T1Y 6J1
(403) 291-2626 *SIC 5511*
SUNRISE FORD SALES LTD *p174*
872 ALPINE RD, 100 MILE HOUSE, BC, V0K 2E0

(250) 395-2414 *SIC 5511*
SUNRISE SERVICE ABBOTSFORD LTD *p177*
30210 AUTOMALL DR, ABBOTSFORD, BC, V2T 5M1
(604) 857-2658 *SIC 5511*
SUNRISE VEHICLE SALES LTD *p218*
2477 TRANS CANADA HWY E, KAMLOOPS, BC, V2C 4A9
(250) 372-5588 *SIC 5511*
SUNWEST AUTO CENTRE LTD *p203*
401 RYAN RD, COURTENAY, BC, V9N 3R5
(250) 338-7565 *SIC 5511*
SUPER DAVE'S GOLDEN EARS MOTORS LTD *p230*
23213 LOUGHEED HWY, MAPLE RIDGE, BC, V2W 1C1
(604) 467-3401 *SIC 5511*
SUPERCARS INC *p431*
220 KENMOUNT RD, ST. JOHN'S, NL, A1B 3T2
(709) 726-8555 *SIC 5511*
SUPERIOR DODGE CHRYSLER (1978) LIMITED *p862*
311 TRUNK RD, SAULT STE. MARIE, ON, P6A 3S8
(705) 256-7481 *SIC 5511*
SURGENOR GATINEAU CHEVROLET CADILLAC LTEE *p1107*
950 BOUL SAINT-JOSEPH, GATINEAU, QC, J8Z 1S9
(819) 777-2731 *SIC 5511*
SURGENOR PONTIAC BUICK LIMITED *p816*
1571 LIVERPOOL CRT, OTTAWA, ON, K1B 4L1
(613) 745-0024 *SIC 5511*
SURGENOR PONTIAC BUICK LIMITED *p820*
939 ST. LAURENT BLVD, OTTAWA, ON, K1K 3B1
(613) 741-0741 *SIC 5511*
SURREY IMPORTS LTD *p271*
15291 FRASER HWY, SURREY, BC, V3R 3P3
(604) 583-7421 *SIC 5511*
SUTHERLAND EQUIPMENT LTD *p401*
911 HANWELL RD, FREDERICTON, NB, E3B 9Z1
(506) 452-1155 *SIC 5511*
SUZANNE ROY FORD INC *p1137*
61 RTE DU PRESIDENT-KENNEDY, LEVIS, QC, G6V 6C7
(418) 835-1915 *SIC 5511*
SUZUKI CANADA INC *p854*
100 EAST BEAVER CREEK RD, RICHMOND HILL, ON, L4B 1J6
(905) 764-1574 *SIC 5511*
SUZUKI SUBARU REPENTIGNY INC *p1283*
575 RUE NOTRE-DAME, REPENTIGNY, QC, J6A 2T6
(514) 891-9950 *SIC 5511*
T.R.Y. JACKSON BROTHERS LIMITED *p488*
181 MAPLEVIEW DR W, BARRIE, ON, L4N 9E8
(705) 726-0288 *SIC 5511*
TALLMAN TRUCK CENTRE LIMITED *p686*
7450 TORBRAM RD, MISSISSAUGA, ON, L4T 1G9
(905) 671-7600 *SIC 5511*
TANDET EASTERN LIMITED *p630*
191 DALTON AVE, KINGSTON, ON, K7K 6C2
(613) 544-1212 *SIC 5511*
TANTRAMAR CHEVROLET BUICK GMC (2009) LIMITED *p438*
88 ROBERT ANGUS DR, AMHERST, NS, B4H 4R7
(902) 667-9975 *SIC 5511*
TARTAN SALES (1973) LTD *p5*
202 10 ST, BEAVERLODGE, AB, T0H 0C0
SIC 5511
TAYLOR CHRYSLER DODGE INC *p608*
260 CENTENNIAL PKY N, HAMILTON, ON,

L8E 2X4
(905) 561-0333 *SIC 5511*
TAYLOR FORD SALES LTD *p406*
10 LEWISVILLE RD, MONCTON, NB, E1A 2K2
(506) 857-2300 *SIC 5511*
TAYLOR MOTOR SALES LTD *p1421*
655 BROAD ST, REGINA, SK, S4R 1X5
(306) 569-8777 *SIC 5511*
TAYLOR VOLKSWAGEN INC *p1421*
775 BROAD ST, REGINA, SK, S4R 8G3
(306) 757-9657 *SIC 5511*
TAYLOR, JEROME D CHEVROLET CADILLAC LIMITED *p632*
2440 PRINCESS ST, KINGSTON, ON, K7M 3G4
(613) 549-1311 *SIC 5511*
TEAM CHRYSLER JEEP DODGE INC *p744*
777 BANCROFT DR, MISSISSAUGA, ON, L5V 2Y6
(905) 819-0001 *SIC 5511*
TEAM FORD SALES LIMITED *p121*
3304 91 ST NW, EDMONTON, AB, T6N 1C1
(780) 462-8300 *SIC 5511*
TEAM TRUCK CENTRES LIMITED *p662*
1040 WILTON GROVE RD, LONDON, ON, N6N 1C7
(519) 453-2970 *SIC 5511*
TEAM TRUCK CENTRES LIMITED *p662*
795 WILTON GROVE RD, LONDON, ON, N6N 1N7
(519) 681-6868 *SIC 5511*
TERCIER MOTORS LTD *p6*
6413 50 AVE, BONNYVILLE, AB, T9N 2L9
(780) 826-3301 *SIC 5511*
TERRA NOVA MOTORS LIMITED *p431*
595 KENMOUNT RD, ST. JOHN'S, NL, A1B 3P9
(709) 364-4130 *SIC 5511*
TERRACE FORD LINCOLN SALES INC *p528*
900 WALKER'S LINE, BURLINGTON, ON, L7N 2G2
(905) 632-6252 *SIC 5511*
TERRACE TOTEM FORD SALES LTD *p283*
4631 KEITH AVE, TERRACE, BC, V8G 1K3
(250) 635-4978 *SIC 5511*
TERREBONNE FORD INC *p1381*
2730 CH GASCON, TERREBONNE, QC, J6X 4H6
(450) 968-9000 *SIC 5511*
THIBAULT CHEVROLET CADILLAC BUICK GMC DE ROUYN-NORANDA LTEE *p1290*
375 BOUL RIDEAU, ROUYN-NORANDA, QC, J9X 5Y7
(819) 762-1751 *SIC 5511*
THIBAULT, RONALD CHEVROLET CADILLAC BUICK GMC LTEE *p1374*
3839 RUE KING O, SHERBROOKE, QC, J1L 1W7
(819) 563-7878 *SIC 5511*
THOMAS MOTORS LTD *p1410*
1955 HWY 6TH S, MELFORT, SK, S0E 1A0
(306) 752-5663 *SIC 5511*
THOMAS PONTIAC BUICK GMC LTD *p545*
100 UNIVERSITY AVE E, COBOURG, ON, K9A 1C8
(905) 372-5447 *SIC 5511*
THOMPSON FORD SALES LTD *p360*
15 STATION RD, THOMPSON, MB, R8N 0N6
(204) 778-6386 *SIC 5511*
THORNCREST SHERWAY INC *p576*
1575 THE QUEENSWAY, ETOBICOKE, ON, M8Z 1T9
(416) 521-7000 *SIC 5511*
THRASHER SALES & LEASING LTD *p477*
251 SIMCOE ST, AMHERSTBURG, ON, N9V 1M5
(519) 736-6481 *SIC 5511*
TILBURY AUTO SALES AND RV INC. *p911*
20600 COUNTY ROAD 42, TILBURY, ON, N0P 2L0
(866) 980-2512 *SIC 5511*
TIMBERLAND FORD INC *p913*

445 ALGONQUIN BLVD W, TIMMINS, ON, P4N 2S4
(705) 268-3673 *SIC 5511*
TIMMINS GARAGE INCORPORATED *p913*
1395 RIVERSIDE DR, TIMMINS, ON, P4R 1A6
(705) 268-4122 *SIC 5511*
TIMMINS KENWORTH LTD *p913*
4041 HWY 101 W, TIMMINS, ON, P4R 0E8
(705) 268-7800 *SIC 5511*
TISDALE SALES & SERVICES LTD *p1408*
105 11 AVE E, KINDERSLEY, SK, S0L 1S0
(306) 463-2686 *SIC 5511*
TITAN AUTOMOTIVE GROUP LTD *p1421*
755 BROAD ST, REGINA, SK, S4R 8G3
(306) 775-3388 *SIC 5511*
TONER CHEVROLET BUICK GMC LTD *p403*
877 BOUL EVERARD H DAIGLE, GRAND-SAULT/GRAND FALLS, NB, E3Z 3C7
(506) 473-2727 *SIC 5511*
TONY GRAHAM KANATA LIMITED *p627*
2500 PALLADIUM DR SUITE 600, KANATA, ON, K2V 1E2
(613) 271-8200 *SIC 5511*
TORONTO KIA *p917*
2222 DANFORTH AVE, TORONTO, ON, M4C 1K3
(416) 421-9000 *SIC 5511*
TORONTO SMART CARS LTD *p906*
7200 YONGE ST SUITE 1, THORNHILL, ON, L4J 1V8
(905) 762-1020 *SIC 5511*
TOTAL LEASE & TRUCK SALES LTD *p220*
2655 ENTERPRISE WAY, KELOWNA, BC, V1X 7Y6
(250) 712-0668 *SIC 5511*
TOWER CHRYSLER PLYMOUTH LTD *p39*
10901 MACLEOD TRAIL SW, CALGARY, AB, T2J 4L3
(403) 278-2020 *SIC 5511*
TOWN & COUNTRY CHRYSLER LIMITED *p882*
245 LOMBARD ST, SMITHS FALLS, ON, K7A 5B8
(613) 283-7555 *SIC 5511*
TOWN & COUNTRY MOTORS (1989) LIMITED *p1000*
8111 KENNEDY RD, UNIONVILLE, ON, L3R 5M2
(905) 948-2948 *SIC 5511*
TOWNE SALES AND SERVICE LIMITED *p405*
2227 KING GEORGE HWY, MIRAMICHI, NB, E1V 6N1
(506) 622-9020 *SIC 5511*
TOYOTA CANADA *p157*
413 LANTERN ST, RED DEER COUNTY, AB, T4E 0A5
(403) 343-3444 *SIC 5511*
TRADITION FORD (VENTES) LTEE *p1099*
1163 BOUL SAINT-JOSEPH, DRUMMONDVILLE, QC, J2C 2C8
(819) 477-3050 *SIC 5511*
TRANS CANADA MOTORS (PETERBOROUGH) LIMITED *p842*
1189 LANSDOWNE ST W, PETERBOROUGH, ON, K9J 7M2
(705) 743-4141 *SIC 5511*
TRANSASIAN FINE CARS LTD *p934*
183 FRONT ST E, TORONTO, ON, M5A 1E7
(416) 867-1577 *SIC 5511*
TRANSASIAN FINE CARS LTD *p1000*
5201 HIGHWAY 7 E, UNIONVILLE, ON, L3R 1N3
(905) 948-8866 *SIC 5511*
TRANSCONTINENTAL FINE CARS LTD *p934*
328 BAYVIEW AVE, TORONTO, ON, M5A 3R7
(416) 961-2834 *SIC 5511*
TRANSDIFF INC *p1275*
2901 AV WATT, QUEBEC, QC, G1X 3W1
(418) 653-3422 *SIC 5511*

TRANSGLOBAL FINE CARS LTD *p906*
480 STEELES AVE W, THORNHILL, ON, L4J 1A2
(905) 886-3380 *SIC 5511*
TRANSOCEANIC FINE CARS LTD *p906*
220 STEELES AVE W, THORNHILL, ON, L4J 1A1
(905) 886-8800 *SIC 5511*
TRANSWORLD FINE CARS LTD *p906*
222 STEELES AVE W, THORNHILL, ON, L4J 1A1
(905) 886-6880 *SIC 5511*
TREND AUTO GROUP INC *p262*
11631 BRIDGEPORT RD, RICHMOND, BC, V6X 1T5
(604) 638-9899 *SIC 5511*
TRILLIUM FORD LINCOLN LTD *p476*
1 ADDISON RD HWY 89 E, ALLISTON, ON, L9R 1W1
(705) 435-7609 *SIC 5511*
TRIUS AUTOMOBILE INC *p530*
629 BRANT ST, BURLINGTON, ON, L7R 2H1
(905) 333-4144 *SIC 5511*
TROIS DIAMANTS AUTOS (1987) LTEE *p1150*
3035 CH GASCON, MASCOUCHE, QC, J7L 3X7
(450) 477-6348 *SIC 5511*
TROIS-RIVIERES CHEVROLET BUICK GMC CADILLAC INC *p1389*
4201 BOUL GENE-H.-KRUGER, TROIS-RIVIERES, QC, G9A 4M9
(819) 376-3791 *SIC 5511*
TROIS-RIVIERES NISSAN INC *p1389*
4700 RUE REAL-PROULX, TROIS-RIVIERES, QC, G9A 6P9
(819) 379-2611 *SIC 5511*
TRUE NORTH CHEVROLET CADILLAC LTD *p764*
1370 SEYMOUR ST, NORTH BAY, ON, P1B 9V6
(705) 472-1210 *SIC 5511*
TURPIN GROUP LTD *p627*
2500 PALLADIUM DR UNIT 200, KANATA, ON, K2V 1E2
SIC 5511
TURPIN SATURN SAAB ISUZU LIMITED *p627*
2500 PALLADIUM DR UNIT 400, KANATA, ON, K2V 1E2
SIC 5511
TWIN HILLS FORD LINCOLN LIMITED *p856*
10801 YONGE ST, RICHMOND HILL, ON, L4C 3E3
(905) 884-4441 *SIC 5511*
TWIN MOTORS LTD *p360*
1637 GORDON AVE, THE PAS, MB, R9A 1L1
(204) 623-6402 *SIC 5511*
TWR C MOTORS LP *p39*
10901 MACLEOD TRAIL SW, CALGARY, AB, T2J 4L3
(403) 225-6193 *SIC 5511*
TYEE CHEVROLET BUICK GMC LTD *p195*
570 13TH AVE, CAMPBELL RIVER, BC, V9W 4G8
(250) 287-9511 *SIC 5511*
ULMER, ROSS CHEVROLET CADILLAC LTD *p1409*
2101 50 AVE, LLOYDMINSTER, SK, S9V 1Z7
(306) 825-8866 *SIC 5511*
UNIONVILLE MOTORS (1973) LIMITED *p1000*
4630 HIGHWAY 7 E, UNIONVILLE, ON, L3R 1M5
SIC 5511
UNIQUE CHRYSLER DODGE JEEP LTD *p528*
915 WALKER'S LINE, BURLINGTON, ON, L7N 3V8
(905) 631-8100 *SIC 5511*
UNIQUE MOTORS LTD *p528*

915 WALKER'S LINE, BURLINGTON, ON, L7N 3V8
(905) 631-8100 *SIC 5511*
UNITED AUTO SALES & SERVICE LTD *p402*
14 AVONLEA CRT, FREDERICTON, NB, E3C 1N8
(506) 454-2886 *SIC 5511*
UNIVERSAL FORD LINCOLN SALES LTD *p10*
2800 BARLOW TRAIL NE, CALGARY, AB, T1Y 1A2
(403) 291-2850 *SIC 5511*
UNIVERSAL TRUCK & TRUCK TRAILER *p398*
925 RUE CHAMPLAIN, DIEPPE, NB, E1A 5T6
(506) 857-2222 *SIC 5511*
UPPER CANADA MOTOR SALES LIMITED *p746*
12375 COUNTY ROAD 28, MORRISBURG, ON, K0C 1X0
(613) 543-2925 *SIC 5511*
UPTOWN AUTOMOBILES INC *p1157*
8665 BOUL DECARIE, MONT-ROYAL, QC, H4P 2T9
(514) 737-6666 *SIC 5511*
V J L R H LONDON INC *p661*
1035 WHARNCLIFFE RD S, LONDON, ON, N6L 1J9
(519) 681-9400 *SIC 5511*
V.I.P. SALES LTD *p177*
30270 AUTOMALL DR, ABBOTSFORD, BC, V2T 5M1
(604) 857-1600 *SIC 5511*
VAL ALBERT MOTORS LIMITED *p627*
392 GOVERNMENT RD E RR 1, KAPUSKASING, ON, P5N 2X7
(705) 335-5000 *SIC 5511*
VALLEY EQUIPMENT LIMITED *p403*
289 MCLEAN AVE, HARTLAND, NB, E7P 2K7
(506) 375-4412 *SIC 5511*
VALLEY FORD LIMITED *p460*
898 PARK ST, KENTVILLE, NS, B4N 3V7
(902) 678-1330 *SIC 5511*
VALLEY FORD SALES *p1407*
224 EAST SERVICE RD, HAGUE, SK, S0K 1X0
(306) 225-3673 *SIC 5511*
VANCOUVER ISLAND AUTO SALES LTD *p235*
2575 BOWEN RD, NANAIMO, BC, V9T 3L4
(250) 751-1168 *SIC 5511*
VANN, GREG NISSAN INC *p539*
2386 EAGLE ST N, CAMBRIDGE, ON, N3H 4R7
(519) 650-9200 *SIC 5511*
VARSITY CHRYSLER JEEP DODGE RAM LTD *p40*
665 GODDARD AVE NE, CALGARY, AB, T2K 6K1
(403) 730-4000 *SIC 5511*
VAUDREUIL HONDA INC *p1395*
9 BOUL DE LA CITE-DES-JEUNES, VAUDREUIL-DORION, QC, J7V 0N3
(450) 424-2500 *SIC 5511*
VEGREVILLE FORD SALES & SERVICE INC *p170*
6106 50 AVE, VEGREVILLE, AB, T9C 1N6
(780) 632-2060 *SIC 5511*
VENTES FORD BRUNELLE LTEE, LES *p1301*
500 RUE DUBOIS, SAINT-EUSTACHE, QC, J7P 4W9
(450) 491-1110 *SIC 5511*
VENTES FORD ELITE (1978) INC *p1320*
2171 BOUL DU CURE-LABELLE, SAINT-JEROME, QC, J7Y 1T1
(450) 436-3142 *SIC 5511*
VERCHERES AUTO INC *p1145*
3551 CH DE CHAMBLY, LONGUEUIL, QC, J4L 4E2
(450) 679-4710 *SIC 5511*
VERNON CHRYSLER DODGE LTD *p332*

4607 27 ST, VERNON, BC, V1T 4Y8

(250) 545-2261   *SIC* 5511

VERSATILE LEASING   p235
3851 SHENTON RD SUITE 3, NANAIMO, BC, V9T 2H1

(250) 758-7311   *SIC* 5511

VIC AUTORAMA INC   p1399
21 BOUL ARTHABASKA E, VICTORIAV-ILLE, QC, G6T 0S4

(819) 758-1588   *SIC* 5511

VICKAR COMMUNITY CHEVROLET LTD
p363
964 REGENT AVE W, WINNIPEG, MB, R2C 3A8

(204) 661-8391   *SIC* 5511

VICTORIA FORD ALLIANCE LTD   p339
3377 DOUGLAS ST, VICTORIA, BC, V8Z 3L4

(250) 475-2255   *SIC* 5511

VICTORIA STAR MOTORS INC   p636
125 CENTENNIAL RD, KITCHENER, ON, N2B 3E9

(519) 579-4460   *SIC* 5511

VIKING TRUCK SALES INC   p483
2943 CEDAR CREEK RD SUITE 1187, AYR, ON, N0B 1E0

(519) 740-1656   *SIC* 5511

VILLAGE CHRYSLER DODGE JEEP LTD
p475
201 BAYLY ST W, AJAX, ON, L1S 3K3

(905) 683-5429   *SIC* 5511

VILLAGE FORD LINCOLN SALES LTD
p1411
1708 MAIN ST N, MOOSE JAW, SK, S6J 1L4

(306) 693-3673 - *SIC* 5511

VILLAGE NISSAN LIMITED   p1000
25   SOUTH   UNIONVILLE   AVE, UNIONVILLE, ON, L3R 6B8

(905) 604-0147   *SIC* 5511

VILLE MARIE SUZUKI AUTOMOBILE INC
p1168
2995 RUE HOCHELAGA, MONTREAL, QC, H1W 1G1

(514) 598-8666   *SIC* 5511

VIOLETTE LTEE   p403
157   MADAWASKA   RD,   GRAND-SAULT/GRAND FALLS, NB, E3Z 3E8

(506) 473-1770   *SIC* 5511

VIRDEN MAINLINE MOTOR PRODUCTS LIMITED   p360
HWY 1 W, VIRDEN, MB, R0M 2C0

(204) 748-3811   *SIC* 5511

VISION CHEVROLET BUICK GMC INC
p1089
30 RTE 132, DELSON, QC, J5B 1H3

(450) 632-2220   *SIC* 5511

VISION FORD INC   p394
105 SISTER GREEN RD, ATHOLVILLE, NB, E3N 5C5

(506) 753-5001   *SIC* 5511

VOIE RAPIDE DES LAURENTIDES   p1321
155 BOUL LACHAPELLE BUREAU 158, SAINT-JEROME, QC, J7Z 7L2

(450) 436-2264   *SIC* 5511

VOL-HAM AUTOMOTIVE INC   p934
43 EASTERN AVE, TORONTO, ON, M5A 1H1

(416) 868-1880   *SIC* 5511

VOLKSWAGEN MIDTOWN   p914
3450 SHEPPARD AVE E, TORONTO, ON, M1T 3K4

(416) 291-6456   *SIC* 5511

VOLVO OF DURHAM   p844
920 KINGSTON RD, PICKERING, ON, L1V 1B3

(905) 421-9515   *SIC* 5511

VOLVO OF NORTH VANCOUVER   p242
809 AUTOMALL DR, NORTH VANCOU-VER, BC, V7P 3R8

(604) 986-9889   *SIC* 5511

VOLVO OF OAKVILLE   p805
770 PACIFIC RD, OAKVILLE, ON, L6L 6M5

(905) 825-8088   *SIC* 5511

VT VENTURES INC   p197
8750 YOUNG RD, CHILLIWACK, BC, V2P 4P4

(604) 792-1167   *SIC* 5511

VULCAN AUTOMOTIVE EQUIPMENT LTD
p207
788 CALDEW ST UNIT 121, DELTA, BC, V3M 5S2

(604) 526-1167   *SIC* 5511

W.J.B. MOTORS LIMITED   p805
1291 SPEERS RD, OAKVILLE, ON, L6L 2X5

(905) 827-4242   *SIC* 5511

WAINALTA MOTORS (1988) LTD   p171
2110 15 AVE, WAINWRIGHT, AB, T9W 1L2

(780) 842-4255   *SIC* 5511

WALLACEBURG AUTOMOTIVE INC p1005
330 SELKIRK ST, WALLACEBURG, ON, N8A 3X7

(519) 627-2288   *SIC* 5511

WAM MOTORS GP INC   p389
485 STERLING LYON PKY, WINNIPEG, MB, R3P 2S8

(204) 284-2834   *SIC* 5511

WARNER TRUCK INDUSTRIES LTD p1416
330 E 4TH AVE, REGINA, SK, S4N 4Z6

(306) 359-1930   *SIC* 5511

WATERLOO DODGE CHRYSLER LTD p1007
150 WEBER ST S, WATERLOO, ON, N2J 2A8

(519) 743-0300   *SIC* 5511

WATERLOO NISSAN INC   p1009
141 NORTHFIELD DR W, WATERLOO, ON, N2L 5A6

(866) 978-9411   *SIC* 5511

WATKIN MOTORS PARTNERSHIP   p332
4602 27 ST, VERNON, BC, V1T 4Y6

(250) 260-3411   *SIC* 5511

WATROUS MAINLINE MOTOR PRODUCTS LIMITED   p1437
208 1ST AVE E HWY SUITE 2, WATROUS, SK, S0K 4T0

(306) 946-3336   *SIC* 5511

WEEDON AUTOMOBILE (1977) INC p1401
326 2E AV, WEEDON, QC, J0B 3J0

(819) 877-2833   *SIC* 5511

WEIDNER MOTORS LIMITED   p138
5640 HIGHWAY 2A, LACOMBE, AB, T4L 1A3

(403) 782-3626   *SIC* 5511

WEINS CANADA INC   p677
3120 STEELES AVE E, MARKHAM, ON, L3R 1G9

(905) 475-0308   *SIC* 5511

WELLINGTON MOTORS LIMITED   p606
935 WOODLAWN RD W, GUELPH, ON, N1K 1B7

(519) 651-2422   *SIC* 5511

WELLS FORD SALES LTD   p890
48 BELLEVILLE RD, STIRLING, ON, K0K 3E0

(613) 395-3375   *SIC* 5511

WENDELL MOTOR SALES LTD   p637
549 FAIRWAY RD S, KITCHENER, ON, N2C 1X4

(519) 893-1501   *SIC* 5511

WEST AUTO SALES LTD   p202
1881 UNITED BLVD SUITE D, COQUIT-LAM, BC, V3K 0B6

(604) 777-1292   *SIC* 5511

WEST COAST IMPORT VEHICLES LTD p245
19950 LOUGHEED HWY, PITT MEADOWS, BC, V3Y 2S9

(604) 465-3209   *SIC* 5511

WEST COAST MOTORS LTD   p231
20370 LOUGHEED HWY, MAPLE RIDGE, BC, V2X 2P8

(604) 465-5481   *SIC* 5511

WEST END MOTORS (FORT FRANCES) IN-CORPORATED   p592
600 KING'S HWY, FORT FRANCES, ON, P9A 2W9

(807) 274-7751   *SIC* 5511

WEST PARK MOTORS LTD   p345
248 CENTRE AVE SE SS 3, ALTONA, MB, R0G 0B3

(204) 324-6494   *SIC* 5511

WEST YORK CHEVROLET INC   p994
1785 ST CLAIR AVE W, TORONTO, ON, M6N 1J6

(416) 656-1200   *SIC* 5511

WESTBORO AUTO IMPORTS LTD   p829
225 RICHMOND RD, OTTAWA, ON, K1Z 6W7

(613) 728-5813   *SIC* 5511

WESTCASTLE MOTORS LTD   p152
1100 WATERTON AVE, PINCHER CREEK, AB, T0K 1W0

(403) 627-3223   *SIC* 5511

WESTERN CHEVROLET PONTIAC BUICK GMC LTD   p83
906 HWY 9 S, DRUMHELLER, AB, T0J 0Y0

(403) 823-3371   *SIC* 5511

WESTERN HYUNDAI   p1411
1774 MAIN ST N, MOOSE JAW, SK, S6J 1L4

(306) 691-5444   *SIC* 5511

WESTERN PONTIAC BUICK GMC (1999) LTD   p103
18325 STONY PLAIN RD NW, EDMONTON, AB, T5S 1C6

(780) 486-3333   *SIC* 5511

WESTERN PONTIAC GMC 1999 LTD p103
18325 STONY PLAIN RD, EDMONTON, AB, T5S 1C6

(780) 486-3333   *SIC* 5511

WESTERN STAR SALES THUNDER BAY LTD   p909
3150 ARTHUR ST W, THUNDER BAY, ON, P7C 4V1

(807) 939-2537   *SIC* 5511

WESTERN STAR TRUCKS (NORTH) LTD p2
26229 TOWNSHIP ROAD 531A, ACHE-SON, AB, T7X 5A4

(780) 453-3452   *SIC* 5511

WESTERN STERLING TRUCKS LTD p104
18353 118 AVE NW, EDMONTON, AB, T5S 1M8

(780) 481-7400   *SIC* 5511

WESTGATE CHEVROLET LTD   p104
10145 178 ST NW, EDMONTON, AB, T5S 1E4

(780) 483-3320   *SIC* 5511

WESTMINSTER VOLKSWAGEN LTD p199
2555 BARNET HWY, COQUITLAM, BC, V3H 1W4

(604) 461-5000   *SIC* 5511

WESTOWNE MOTORS (1983) LIMITED p578
5511 DUNDAS ST W, ETOBICOKE, ON, M9B 1B8

(416) 232-2011   *SIC* 5511

WESTRIDGE PONTIAC BUICK GMC LTD
p144
2406 50 AVE, LLOYDMINSTER, AB, T9V 2W7

(780) 875-3366   *SIC* 5511

WESTVIEW FORD SALES LTD   p203
4901 ISLAND HWY N, COURTENAY, BC, V9N 5Y9

(250) 334-3161   *SIC* 5511

WETASKIWIN CHEVROLET OLDSMOBILE (2001) LTD   p172
4710 56 ST, WETASKIWIN, AB, T9A 1V7

SIC 5511

WHEATON CHEVROLET LTD   p1421
260 N ALBERT ST, REGINA, SK, S4R 3C1

(306) 543-1555   *SIC* 5511

WHEATON GMC BUICK CADILLAC LTD
p1430
2102 MILLAR AVE, SASKATOON, SK, S7K 6P4

(306) 244-8131   *SIC* 5511

WHEATON   PONTIAC   BUICK   GMC (NANAIMO) LTD   p235
2590 BOWEN RD, NANAIMO, BC, V9T 3L3

(250) 758-2438   *SIC* 5511

WHEEL'S AUTOMOTIVE DEALER SUP-PLIES INC   p893
600 ARVIN AVE, STONEY CREEK, ON, L8E 5P1

(800) 465-8831   *SIC* 5511

WHITBY TOYOTA COMPANY   p1016
1025 DUNDAS ST W, WHITBY, ON, L1P 1Z1

(905) 668-4792   *SIC* 5511

WHITE ROCK CHRYSLER LTD   p283
3050 KING GEORGE BLVD UNIT 7, SUR-REY, BC, V4P 1A2

(604) 531-9156   *SIC* 5511

WHITECAP MOTORS   p164
804 MAIN ST SW, SLAVE LAKE, AB, T0G 2A0

(780) 849-2600   *SIC* 5511

WHITECOURT FORD INC   p173
4144 KEPLER ST, WHITECOURT, AB, T7S 0A3

(780) 778-4777   *SIC* 5511

WHITEHORSE MOTORS LIMITED   p1440
4178 4TH AVE, WHITEHORSE, YT, Y1A 1J6

(867) 667-7866   *SIC* 5511

WHITEOAK FORD LINCOLN SALES LIM-ITED   p712
3285 MAVIS RD, MISSISSAUGA, ON, L5C 1T7

(905) 270-8210   *SIC* 5511

WHITEROCK CHRYSLER JEEP LIMITED
p283
3050 KING GEORGE BLVD, SURREY, BC, V4P 1A2

(604) 531-9156   *SIC* 5511

WIETZES MOTORS LIMITED   p561
7080 DUFFERIN ST, CONCORD, ON, L4K 0A1

(905) 761-5133   *SIC* 5511

WILF'S ELIE FORD SALES LTD   p349
HWY 1, ELIE, MB, R0H 0H0

(204) 353-2481   *SIC* 5511

WILKINS LIMITED   p443
36 BAKER DR, DARTMOUTH, NS, B2W 6K1

(902) 435-3330   *SIC* 5511

WILLE DODGE CHRYSLER LTD   p339
3240 DOUGLAS ST, VICTORIA, BC, V8Z 3K7

(250) 475-3511   *SIC* 5511

WILLIAMS CHRYSLER LTD   p129
324 GREGOIRE DR, FORT MCMURRAY, AB, T9H 3R2

(780) 790-9000   *SIC* 5511

WILLIAMS, JIM LEASING LIMITED p489
191 MAPLEVIEW DR W, BARRIE, ON, L4N 9E8

(705) 734-1200   *SIC* 5511

WILLOWBROOK MOTORS LTD   p228
19611 LANGLEY BYPASS, LANGLEY, BC, V3A 4K8

(604) 530-7361   *SIC* 5511

WILLOWDALE NISSAN LTD   p906
7200 YONGE ST SUITE 881, THORNHILL, ON, L4J 1V8

(905) 881-3900   *SIC* 5511

WILLS CHEVROLET   p600
337 MAIN ST E, GRIMSBY, ON, L3M 5N9

(905) 309-3356   *SIC* 5511

WILSON CHEVROLET LIMITED   p753
100 WILSON ST, NEW LISKEARD, ON, P0J 1P0

(705) 647-2031   *SIC* 5511

WILSON, JIM PONTIAC CHEVROLET BUICK GMC INC   p810
MULCAHY PO BOX 20 STN MAIN, ORIL-LIA, ON, L3V 6H9

(705) 325-1322   *SIC* 5511

WILSON-NIBLETT MOTORS LIMITED p856
10675 YONGE ST, RICHMOND HILL, ON, L4C 3E1

(905) 884-0991   *SIC* 5511

WILTON GROVE TRUCK SALES & SER-VICES LIMITED   p662
1445 SISE RD SUITE 1, LONDON, ON, N6N 1E1

(519) 649-1771   *SIC* 5511

▲ Public Company   ■ Public Company Family Member   **HQ** Headquarters   **BR** Branch   **SL** Single Location

WINDJAMMER INVESTMENTS INC p423
30 CONFEDERATION DR, CORNER BROOK, NL, A2H 6T2
(709) 634-8881 SIC 5511

WINDSOR MOTORS (1975) LTD p133
13105 100 ST, GRANDE PRAIRIE, AB, T8V 4H3
(780) 532-9153 SIC 5511

WINEGARD MOTORS LIMITED p532
140 ARGYLE ST S, CALEDONIA, ON, N3W 1E5
(905) 765-4444 SIC 5511

WINNIPEG C MOTORS LP p370
1900 MAIN ST, WINNIPEG, MB, R2V 3S9
(204) 339-2011 SIC 5511

WINNIPEG DODGE CHRYSLER LTD p387
3965 PORTAGE AVE UNIT 90, WINNIPEG, MB, R3K 2H3
(204) 774-4444 SIC 5511

WINSLOW-GEROLAMY MOTORS LIMITED
p842
1018 LANSDOWNE ST W, PETERBOROUGH, ON, K9J 1Z9
(705) 742-3411 SIC 5511

WLT HOLDINGS LTD p387
3965 PORTAGE AVE SUITE 70, WINNIPEG, MB, R3K 2H8
(204) 889-3700 SIC 5511

WOLFE MOTORS LTD p285
1595 BOUNDARY RD, VANCOUVER, BC, V5K 5C4
(604) 293-1311 SIC 5511

WOLVERINE FORD SALES (2006) LTD p135
10102 97 ST SS 1, HIGH LEVEL, AB, T0H 1Z0
(780) 926-2291 SIC 5511

WOOD MOTORS (1972) LIMITED p402
880 PROSPECT ST, FREDERICTON, NB, E3B 2T8
(506) 452-6611 SIC 5511

WOODBINE CHRYSLER LTD p677
8280 WOODBINE AVE, MARKHAM, ON, L3R 2N8
(905) 415-2260 SIC 5511

WOODCHESTER IMPORTS INC p718
3089 WOODCHESTER DR, MISSISSAUGA, ON, L5L 1J2
(905) 828-2289 SIC 5511

WOODCHESTER NISSAN INC p718
2560 MOTORWAY BLVD, MISSISSAUGA, ON, L5L 1X3
(905) 828-7001 SIC 5511

WOODLAND VERDUN LTEE p1397
1009 RUE WOODLAND, VERDUN, QC, H4H 1V7
(514) 761-3444 SIC 5511

WOODRIDGE FORD LINCOLN LTD p71
11580 24 ST SE, CALGARY, AB, T2Z 3K1
(403) 253-2211 SIC 5511

WORLD AUTO PARTS (CANADA) LTD p589
355 CARLINGVIEW DR UNIT 1, ETOBICOKE, ON, M9W 5G8
(416) 675-6750 SIC 5511

XTOWN MOTORS LP p106
15520 123 AVE NW, EDMONTON, AB, T5V 1K8
(780) 488-4881 SIC 5511

YELLOWKNIFE CHRYSLER LTD p436
340 OLD AIRPORT RD, YELLOWKNIFE, NT, X1A 3T3
(867) 873-4222 SIC 5511

YORKDALE FORD LINCOLN SALES LIMITED
p790
3130 DUFFERIN ST, NORTH YORK, ON, M6A 2S6
(416) 787-4534 SIC 5511

YORKTON DODGE p1439
270 HAMILTON RD, YORKTON, SK, S3N 4C6
(306) 783-9022 SIC 5511

ZACH & KAYLYN ENTERPRISES INC p104
17707 111 AVE NW, EDMONTON, AB, T5S 0A1
(780) 484-5444 SIC 5511

ZAROWNY MOTORS (ST PAUL) LTD p165
5508 50 AVE, ST PAUL, AB, T0A 3A1
(780) 645-4468 SIC 5511

ZENCOR EQUITIES LIMITED p164
HWY 16A GOLDEN SPIKE RD, SPRUCE GROVE, AB, T7X 2Y3
(780) 962-3000 SIC 5511

ZENDER FORD SALES LTD p164
HWY 16A GOLDEN SPIKE RD, SPRUCE GROVE, AB, T7X 2Y3
SIC 5511

ZIMMER WHEATON BUICK GMC LTD p218
685 NOTRE DAME DR, KAMLOOPS, BC, V2C 5N7
(250) 374-1148 SIC 5511

ZOMEL HOLDINGS LTD p335
506 FINLAYSON ST, VICTORIA, BC, V8T 5C8
(250) 388-6921 SIC 5511

ZP HOLDINGS INC p111
7450 ROPER RD NW, EDMONTON, AB, T6B 3L9
(780) 490-5269 SIC 5511

SIC 5521 Used car dealers

1068827 ONTARIO INC p564
11211 LONGWOODS RD RR 1, DELAWARE, ON, N0L 1E0
(519) 652-9766 SIC 5521

1076528 ALBERTA LTD p155
6720 JOHNSTONE DR, RED DEER, AB, T4P 3Y2
(403) 347-7777 SIC 5521

1076634 ONTARIO INC p788
3080 DUFFERIN ST, NORTH YORK, ON, M6A 2S6
(416) 243-1550 SIC 5521

2176542 ONTARIO LTD p920
11 SUNLIGHT PARK RD, TORONTO, ON, M4M 1B5
(416) 623-4269 SIC 5521

435682 ONTARIO LIMITED p497
19990 11 HWY S, BRADFORD, ON, L3Z 2B6
(905) 775-6497 SIC 5521

4695900 MANITOBA LTD p386
3777 PORTAGE AVE, WINNIPEG, MB, R3K 0X6
(204) 895-3777 SIC 5521

5 STAR DEALERS INC p650
1500 DUNDAS ST, LONDON, ON, N5W 3B9
(519) 455-4227 SIC 5521

715137 ONTARIO LTD p830
1071 RICHMOND RD, OTTAWA, ON, K2B 6R2
SIC 5521

9067-7246 QUEBEC INC p1097
1355 BOUL SAINT-JOSEPH, DRUMMONDVILLE, QC, J2C 2E4
(819) 477-1414 SIC 5521

970207 ONTARIO LIMITED p815
851 HIGHWAY 7, OTONABEE, ON, K9J 6X7
(705) 748-2777 SIC 5521

970910 ONTARIO INC p988
147 BENTWORTH AVE, TORONTO, ON, M6A 1P6
SIC 5521

975002 ALBERTA INC p33
161 GLENDEER CIR SE, CALGARY, AB, T2H 2S8
(403) 275-6464 SIC 5521

ALBERNI CHRYSLER LTD p245
2611 ALBERTA HWY, PORT ALBERNI, BC, V9Y 8P2
(250) 723-5331 SIC 5521

ALC - AUTO LIST OF CANADA INC p362
823 REGENT AVE W, WINNIPEG, MB, R2C 3A7
(204) 224-0636 SIC 5521

ARBOUR AUTOMOBILES LTEE p1085
2475 BOUL CHOMEDEY, COTE SAINT-LUC, QC, H7T 2R2

(450) 681-8110 SIC 5521

AUTOMOBILES DU BOULEVARD 2000 INC
p1243
3260 RTE DU PRESIDENT-KENNEDY, NOTRE-DAME-DES-PINS, QC, G0M 1K0
(418) 774-4100 SIC 5521

AUTOMOBILES FRANCOIS ST-JEAN INC, LES p1243
560 131 RTE, NOTRE-DAME-DES-PRAIRIES, QC, J6E 0M2
(450) 752-1212 SIC 5521

AUTOMOBILES HYUNDAI RUBY AUTO p1382
2272 RUE NOTRE-DAME E, THETFORD MINES, QC, G6G 2W2
(418) 338-4665 SIC 5521

AUTOTOWN SALES CORPORATION p390
1717 WAVERLEY ST SUITE 400, WINNIPEG, MB, R3T 6A9
(204) 269-1600 SIC 5521

AUTOWEST INC p370
2150 MCPHILLIPS ST, WINNIPEG, MB, R2V 3C8
(204) 632-7135 SIC 5521

BMW STE-JULIE p1358
1633 BOUL ARMAND-FRAPPIER, SAINTE-JULIE, QC, J3E 3R6
(450) 922-1633 SIC 5521

BURLINGTON-FAIRVIEW NISSAN LTD p521
4111 NORTH SERVICE RD, BURLINGTON, ON, L7L 4X6
(905) 681-2162 SIC 5521

CAMIONS INTERNATIONAL WEST ISLAND INC p1333
6100 CH SAINT-FRANCOIS, SAINT-LAURENT, QC, H4S 1B7
(514) 333-4412 SIC 5521

CANADIAN FINE MOTORS INC p872
1882 LAWRENCE AVE E, SCARBOROUGH, ON, M1R 2Y5
(416) 588-8899 SIC 5521

CAPITAL S ENTERPRISES LTD p346
GD, BRANDON, MB, R7A 5Y1
(204) 730-0097 SIC 5521

CAR LOT ETC INC, THE p898
2231 LASALLE BLVD, SUDBURY, ON, P3A 2A9
(705) 560-3999 SIC 5521

CAREFREE RV LTD p108
4510 51 AVE NW, EDMONTON, AB, T6B 2W2
(780) 438-2008 SIC 5521

CARS R US LTD p461
183 SACKVILLE DR, LOWER SACKVILLE, NS, B4C 2R5
(902) 864-1109 SIC 5521

CENTRE DU CAMION GAMACHE INC p1113
609 RUE PRINCIPALE, ILE-AUX-NOIX, QC, J0J 1G0
(450) 246-3881 SIC 5521

CORPORATIF RENAUD INC p1314
3445 BOUL LAFRAMBOISE, SAINT-HYACINTHE, QC, J4T 2G1
(450) 462-9991 SIC 5521

CRANBROOK DODGE p203
1725 CRANBROOK ST N, CRANBROOK, BC, V1C 3S9
(888) 697-0855 SIC 5521

DON VALLEY NORTH TOYOTA LIMITED
p665
5362 HIGHWAY 7 E, MARKHAM, ON, L3P 1B9
(905) 294-8100 SIC 5521

ECONAUTO (1985) LTEE p1371
2615 RUE KING O, SHERBROOKE, QC, J1J 2H3
(819) 566-5322 SIC 5521

FIND-A-CAR AUTO SALES & BROKERING INC p850
6104 PERTH ST, RICHMOND, ON, K0A 2Z0
SIC 5521

FORD MOTOR COMPANY OF CANADA, LIMITED p1023
3223 LAUZON PKY, WINDSOR, ON, N9A 6X3
(519) 944-8784 SIC 5521

FORT ROUGE AUTO SALES p387
680 PEMBINA HWY, WINNIPEG, MB, R3M 2M5
(877) 792-9521 SIC 5521

GARAGE POIRIER & FILS LTEE p1390
1780 3E AV, VAL-D'OR, QC, J9P 1W4
(819) 825-5214 SIC 5521

GARAGE TARDIF LTEE p1046
1222 111 RTE E, AMOS, QC, J9T 1N1
(819) 732-5314 SIC 5521

GEORDY RENTALS INC p283
2576 KING GEORGE BLVD, SURREY, BC, V4P 1H5
(604) 668-7230 SIC 5521

GORRUR LIMITED p683
410 STEELES AVE E, MILTON, ON, L9T 1Y4
(905) 875-2277 SIC 5521

GORRUD'S AUTO GROUP p683
410 STEELES AVE E, MILTON, ON, L9T 1Y4
(905) 875-2277 SIC 5521

GROUPE AUTOMOTIVE HOLAND LEVIS INC p1136
5303 RUE LOUIS-H.-LA FONTAINE, LEVIS, QC, G6V 8X4
(418) 830-5000 SIC 5521

HALDIMAND MOTORS LTD p541
42 TALBOT ST E, CAYUGA, ON, N0A 1E0
(905) 772-3511 SIC 5521

HAMEL AUTOS DE BLAINVILLE INC p1059
620 BOUL DE LA SEIGNEURIE O BUREAU 517, BLAINVILLE, QC, J7C 5T7
(450) 437-5050 SIC 5521

HEARTLAND MOTORS LIMITED p344
106 BROADWAY AVE N, WILLIAMS LAKE, BC, V2G 2X7
(250) 392-3225 SIC 5521

HOLIDAY FORD LINCOLN LTD p841
1555 LANSDOWNE ST W, PETERBOROUGH, ON, K9J 7M3
(705) 742-5432 SIC 5521

IMPORT AUTO PLAZA INC p430
475 KENMOUNT RD, ST. JOHN'S, NL, A1B 3P9
(709) 579-6487 SIC 5521

JOHN SCOTTI AUTOMOTIVE LTEE p1345
4315 BOUL METROPOLITAIN E, SAINT-LEONARD, QC, H1R 1Z4
(514) 725-9394 SIC 5521

JOHNSON, O M HOLDINGS INC p861
311 TRUNK RD, SAULT STE. MARIE, ON, P6A 3S8
(705) 256-7481 SIC 5521

KIESWETTER MOTORS INC p641
4202 KING ST E, KITCHENER, ON, N2P 2G5
(519) 653-2540 SIC 5521

LAKEHEAD MOTORS LIMITED, THE p908
951 MEMORIAL AVE, THUNDER BAY, ON, P7B 4A1
(807) 344-0584 SIC 5521

LE RELAIS CHEVROLET CADILLAC BUICK GMC LTEE p1177
9411 AV PAPINEAU, MONTREAL, QC, H2M 2G5
(514) 384-6380 SIC 5521

LOCURETT ENTERPRISES LTD p260
5660 MINORU BLVD, RICHMOND, BC, V6X 2A9
(604) 273-1001 SIC 5521

MACDONALD, LARRY CHEVROLET LTD p897
28380 CENTRE RD, STRATHROY, ON, N7G 3C4
(519) 245-0410 SIC 5521

MANDEX CORPORATION p386
3081 PORTAGE AVE, WINNIPEG, MB, R3K 0W4
SIC 5521

MCCLURE, F. & SONS LTD p403
55 RUE OUELLETTE, GRAND-

SAULT/GRAND FALLS, NB, E3Z 0A6
(506) 473-2024   *SIC 5521*

MEGA FORMULE D'OCCASION   *p1285*
169 BOUL SAINTE-ANNE, RIMOUSKI, QC, G5M 1C3
(418) 723-5955   *SIC 5521*

MILLER'S COLLISION & CAR SALES *p591*
1557 BOWEN RD, FORT ERIE, ON, L2A 5M4
(905) 871-5105   *SIC 5521*

MONTCALM VENTURES LTD   *p324*
1404 MARINE DR SW, VANCOUVER, BC, V6P 5Z9
(604) 261-3343   *SIC 5521*

MONTREAL AUTO PRIX INC   *p1346*
4900 BOUL METROPOLITAIN E, SAINT-LEONARD, QC, H1S 3A4
(514) 593-9020   *SIC 5521*

NORCAN LEASING LTD   *p1440*
213 RANGE RD, WHITEHORSE, YT, Y1A 3E5
(867) 668-2137   *SIC 5521*

O'REGAN I-N LIMITED   *p456*
3461 KEMPT RD, HALIFAX, NS, B3K 5T7
(902) 453-2020   *SIC 5521*

OBRIANS   *p1429*
2112 MILLAR AVE, SASKATOON, SK, S7K 6P4
(306) 955-5626   *SIC 5521*

ONE-EIGHTY CORP   *p1008*
20 ERB ST W SUITE 803, WATERLOO, ON, N2L 1T2
(519) 884-2003   *SIC 5521*

OPENLANE CANADA INC   *p982*
370 KING ST W SUITE 500, TORONTO, ON, M5V 1J9
(416) 861-5777   *SIC 5521*

PATHWAY HYUNDAI   *p810*
1375 YOUVILLE DR, ORLEANS, ON, K1C 4R1
(613) 837-4222   *SIC 5521*

PLATINUM MOTOR CARS INC   *p9*
2720 BARLOW TRAIL NE, CALGARY, AB, T1Y 1A1
(403) 276-4878   *SIC 5521*

R & D AUTO SALES   *p1421*
979 WINNIPEG ST SUITE C, REGINA, SK, S4R 1J1
(306) 565-2929   *SIC 5521*

REVELL FORD LINCOLN   *p1003*
6715 MAIN ST, VERONA, ON, K0H 2W0
(613) 374-2612   *SIC 5521*

SASKATOON MOTOR PRODUCTS (1973) LTD   *p1429*
715 CIRCLE DR E, SASKATOON, SK, S7K 0V1
(306) 242-0276   *SIC 5521*

SHERWAY FINE CARS LTD   *p579*
2000 THE QUEENSWAY, ETOBICOKE, ON, M9C 5H5
(416) 620-1987   *SIC 5521*

SHERWOOD INVESTMENTS LIMITED *p1425*
550 BRAND RD, SASKATOON, SK, S7J 5J3
(306) 374-6330   *SIC 5521*

SHERWOOD PARK AUTO SALES LTD *p163*
20 BROADWAY BLVD, SHERWOOD PARK, AB, T8H 2A2
(780) 449-4499   *SIC 5521*

SLIPP, SCOTT NISSAN LIMITED   *p460*
975 PARK ST, KENTVILLE, NS, B4N 4H8
(902) 679-4000   *SIC 5521*

SOUTH TRAIL CHRYSLER LTD   *p71*
6103 130 AVE SE, CALGARY, AB, T2Z 5E1
(587) 349-7272   *SIC 5521*

SPADONI MOTORS LIMITED   *p902*
HWY 17, TERRACE BAY, ON, P0T 2W0
(807) 825-4561   *SIC 5521*

STEWART, J. J. MOTORS LIMITED   *p796*
2239 8 LINE, NORWOOD, ON, K0L 2V0
(705) 639-5383   *SIC 5521*

STOP 23 SERVICE LIMITED   *p647*
910 WALLACE AVE N, LISTOWEL, ON, N4W 1M5

(519) 291-3628   *SIC 5521*
STREET MOTOR SALES LTD   *p882*
171 LOMBARD ST, SMITHS FALLS, ON, K7A 5B8
(613) 284-0023   *SIC 5521*

SUBARU OF MAPLE   *p664*
250 SWEETRIVER BLVD, MAPLE, ON, L6A 4V3
(289) 342-7800   *SIC 5521*

T R SAND & GRAVEL INC   *p883*
1417 NOTRE DAME DR RR 1, ST AGATHA, ON, N0B 2L0
(519) 747-4173   *SIC 5521*

TOYOTA DEALERS ADVERTISING ASSOCI-ATION   *p32*
411 11 AVE SE, CALGARY, AB, T2G 0Y5
(403) 237-2388   *SIC 5521*

VARSITY PLYMOUTH CHRYSLER (1994) LTD   *p40*
4914 6 ST NE, CALGARY, AB, T2K 4W5
(403) 250-5541   *SIC 5521*

VIOLETTE MOTORS LTD   *p399*
70 CHIEF JOANNA BLVD MMFN, ED-MUNDSTON, NB, E7C 0C1
(506) 737-9520   *SIC 5521*

WHEELS & DEALS LTD   *p400*
402 SAINT MARYS ST, FREDERICTON, NB, E3A 8H5
(506) 459-6832   *SIC 5521*

WILSON'S, MARK BETTER USED CAR LIMITED   *p601*
700 YORK RD, GUELPH, ON, N1E 6A5
(519) 836-2900   *SIC 5521*

WRIGHT AUTO SALES INC   *p1007*
35 WEBER ST N, WATERLOO, ON, N2J 3G5
(519) 742-5622   *SIC 5521*

SIC 5531 Auto and home supply stores

0756271 B.C. LTD   *p275*
13412 72 AVE, SURREY, BC, V3W 2N8
(604) 591-6064   *SIC 5531*

1146490 ONTARIO INC   *p628*
1229 HIGHWAY 17 E SUITE 1, KENORA, ON, P9N 1L9
(807) 468-3014   *SIC 5531*

1371500 ONTARIO INC   *p690*
1770 BRITANNIA RD E, MISSISSAUGA, ON, L4W 1J3
(905) 565-8406   *SIC 5531*

1519950 ONTARIO INC   *p508*
25 CLARK BLVD, BRAMPTON, ON, L6W 1X4
(905) 452-0111   *SIC 5531*

1557483 ONTARIO INC   *p988*
2471 DUFFERIN ST, TORONTO, ON, M6B 3P6
SIC 5531

1562067 ONTARIO INC   *p826*
1720 BANK ST, OTTAWA, ON, K1V 7Y6
SIC 5531

2742-7608 QUEBEC INC   *p1044*
225 AV DU PONT S, ALMA, QC, G8B 2T7
(418) 668-3061   *SIC 5531*

2891379 CANADA INC   *p468*
90 ROBIE ST, TRURO, NS, B2N 1L1
(902) 897-4466   *SIC 5531*

2931621 CANADA INC   *p795*
2625B WESTON RD, NORTH YORK, ON, M9N 3W1
(416) 247-2196   *SIC 5531*

3-D AUTO PARTS LTD   *p466*
17 BRIDGE AVE, STELLARTON, NS, B0K 0A2
(902) 752-9370   *SIC 5531*

381616 ALBERTA LTD   *p158*
4315 44 ST, ROCKY MOUNTAIN HOUSE, AB, T4T 1A4
(403) 845-3633   *SIC 5531*

389987 ALBERTA LTD   *p136*
120 NORTH ST, HINTON, AB, T7V 1S8
(780) 865-8800   *SIC 5531*

4137566 CANADA LTD   *p807*
99 FIRST ST, ORANGEVILLE, ON, L9W 2E8
(519) 941-1090   *SIC 5531*

4178963 CANADA INC   *p1328*
11200 BOUL CAVENDISH, SAINT-LAURENT, QC, H4R 2J7
(514) 337-4862   *SIC 5531*

581917 ONTARIO INC   *p906*
1108 BEAVER DAM RD, THOROLD, ON, L2V 3Y7
(905) 227-4118   *SIC 5531*

822099 ONTARIO LIMITED   *p573*
12 LOCKPORT AVE, ETOBICOKE, ON, M8Z 2R7
(416) 236-1277   *SIC 5531*

9032-8402 QUEBEC INC   *p1078*
1257 BOUL TALBOT BUREAU 268, CHICOUTIMI, QC, G7H 4C1
(418) 549-5014   *SIC 5531*

9050-4283 QUEBEC INC   *p1159*
488 AV SAINT-DAVID, MONTMAGNY, QC, G5V 4P9
(418) 248-2602   *SIC 5531*

905364 ONTARIO LIMITED   *p663*
3817 COUNTY RD 46 RR 3, MAIDSTONE, ON, N0R 1K0
(519) 737-2630   *SIC 5531*

9183-9530 QUEBEC INC   *p1284*
401 RUE SAINT-JEAN-BAPTISTE E, RI-MOUSKI, QC, G5L 1Z2
(418) 723-1156   *SIC 5531*

9215-0770 QUEBEC INC   *p1357*
2650 RUE ETIENNE-LENOIR, SAINTE-DOROTHEE, QC, H7R 0A3
(450) 504-9866   *SIC 5531*

944746 ONTARIO INC   *p1021*
2594 HOWARD AVE, WINDSOR, ON, N8X 3W5
(519) 966-2006   *SIC 5531*

970426 ALBERTA INC   *p98*
11754 170 ST NW, EDMONTON, AB, T5S 1J7
(780) 452-0220   *SIC 5531*

99 TRUCK PARTS & INDUSTRIAL EQUIP-MENT LTD   *p273*
12905 KING GEORGE BLVD, SURREY, BC, V3T 2T1
(604) 580-1677   *SIC 5531*

A & E WARDELL LTD   *p450*
130 RESERVE ST, GLACE BAY, NS, B1A 4W5
(902) 842-0077   *SIC 5531*

A-A-A BATTERIES LTD   *p757*
5559 GEORGE ST, NIAGARA FALLS, ON, L2E 7K9
(905) 371-0666   *SIC 5531*

A.P.T. AUTO PARTS TRADING CO. LTD*p181*
7342 WINSTON ST UNIT 10, BURNABY, BC, V5A 2H1
(604) 421-2781   *SIC 5531*

ABBSRY USED TIRES LTD   *p176*
31088 PEARDONVILLE RD UNIT 1, AB-BOTSFORD, BC, V2T 6K5
(604) 870-0490   *SIC 5531*

ACHESON, A.J. SALES LIMITED   *p444*
30 LAMONT TERR, DARTMOUTH, NS, B3B 0B5
(902) 434-2823   *SIC 5531*

ACTIVE TIRE & AUTO CENTRE INC   *p571*
580 EVANS AVE, ETOBICOKE, ON, M8W 2W1
(416) 255-5581   *SIC 5531*

AIRDRIE MOTORS (1986) LTD   *p2*
149 EAST LAKE CRES NE, AIRDRIE, AB, T4A 2H7
(403) 948-6912   *SIC 5531*

ALDER AUTO PARTS LTD   *p281*
19414 96 AVE SUITE 3, SURREY, BC, V4N 4C2
(604) 888-3722   *SIC 5531*

ANDRE SIMON INC   *p1384*
425 RUE DESSUREAULT, TROIS-RIVIERES, QC, G8T 2L8

(819) 373-1013   *SIC 5531*
ANDRE, JEAN-GUY LTEE   *p1105*
692 BOUL GREBER, GATINEAU, QC, J8V 3P8
(819) 243-6181   *SIC 5531*

ANDY'S TIRE SHOP LIMITED   *p468*
146 ROBIE ST, TRURO, NS, B2N 1L1
(902) 897-1669   *SIC 5531*

ANE STEWART LTD   *p451*
730 CENTRAL AVE, GREENWOOD, NS, B0P 1N0
(902) 765-6338   *SIC 5531*

ARNPRIOR OTTAWA AUTO PARTS LTD *p478*
5445 MADAWASKA BLVD, ARNPRIOR, ON, K7S 3H4
(613) 623-7361   *SIC 5531*

ATLANTIC CAR STEREO LIMITED   *p443*
26 LAKECREST DR, DARTMOUTH, NS, B2X 1T8
(902) 435-0600   *SIC 5531*

ATTACHES ET SUSPENSION MONTREAL-NORD   *p1161*
8065 BOUL HENRI-BOURASSA E, MON-TREAL, QC, H1E 2Z3
(514) 643-4106   *SIC 5531*

AVG (OEAM) INC   *p876*
605 MIDDLEFIELD RD UNIT 1, SCARBOR-OUGH, ON, M1V 5B9

B & G KERR SALES LTD   *p629*
1040 DIVISION ST SUITE 694, KINGSTON, ON, K7K 0C3
(613) 546-1922   *SIC 5531*

B & I TRUCK PARTS INC   *p486*
480 DUNLOP ST W, BARRIE, ON, L4N 9W5
(705) 737-3201   *SIC 5531*

B J'S TRUCK PARTS INC   *p1038*
502 BRACKLEY PT RD, CHARLOTTE-TOWN, PE, C1A 8C2
(902) 566-4205   *SIC 5531*

BAKER, WALTER & CHANTAL SALES LTD *p477*
1060 WILSON ST W, ANCASTER, ON, L9G 3K9
(905) 304-0000   *SIC 5531*

BANNERMAN ENTERPRISES INC   *p213*
9820 93 AVE, FORT ST. JOHN, BC, V1J 6J8
(250) 787-1142   *SIC 5531*

BAST TIRECRAFT   *p1006*
1 BAST PL, WATERLOO, ON, N2J 4G8
(519) 664-2282   *SIC 5531*

BENNETT, KEN ENTERPRISES INC   *p417*
173 MAIN ST, SHEDIAC, NB, E4P 2A5
(506) 533-9788   *SIC 5531*

BENSON, GARRY W ENTERPRISES LTD *p39*
40 HUNTERHORN DR NE, CALGARY, AB, T2K 6H2
SIC 5531

BEVERLY GROUP INC, THE   *p566*
525 6 HWY, DUNDAS, ON, L9H 7K1
(905) 525-9240   *SIC 5531*

BOCCIOLETTI, J & M SALES LTD   *p131*
11311 99 ST, GRANDE PRAIRIE, AB, T8V 2H6
(780) 539-9292   *SIC 5531*

BODNAR, KEN ENTERPRISES INC   *p532*
75 DUNDAS ST, CAMBRIDGE, ON, N1R 6G5
(519) 621-8180   *SIC 5531*

BRACKENRIG ENTERPRISES INC   *p678*
2900 MAJOR MACKENZIE DR E, MARKHAM, ON, L6C 0G6
(416) 907-8237   *SIC 5531*

BRANCY ONE HOLDINGS LTD   *p848*
140 PRESCOTT CENTRE DR, PRESCOTT, ON, K0E 1T0
(613) 925-4217   *SIC 5531*

BRIDGER, BOB ENTERPRISES INC   *p211*
2929 GREEN RD, DUNCAN, BC, V9L 0C1
(250) 748-5557   *SIC 5531*

BUTORAC, DON LIMITED   *p532*
90 PINEBUSH RD, CAMBRIDGE, ON, N1R

8J8

(519) 623-3360   SIC 5531

CAM CLARK FORD RICHMOND LTD   p253
13580 SMALLWOOD PL, RICHMOND, BC, V6V 2C1
(604) 273-7331   SIC 5531

CAMIONS A & R DUBOIS INC   p1314
2745 RUE PRINCIPALE, SAINT-JEAN-BAPTISTE, QC, J0L 2B0
(450) 464-4631   SIC 5531

CAMPBELL, RON G SALES LTD   p140
1240 2A AVE N SUITE 2, LETHBRIDGE, AB, T1H 0E4
(403) 320-6191   SIC 5531

CANADIAN AUTO RECYCLING LIMITED   p426
6 COREY KING DR, MOUNT PEARL, NL, A1N 0A2
(709) 747-2000   SIC 5531

CANADIAN TIRE   p135
1 GATEWAY BLVD SS 1 SUITE 908, HIGH LEVEL, AB, T0H 1Z0
(780) 926-1908   SIC 5531

CANADIAN TIRE   p168
900 PINE RD SUITE 109, STRATHMORE, AB, T1P 0A2
(403) 934-9733   SIC 5531

CANADIAN TIRE   p169
62 THEVENAZ IND. TRAIL UNIT 200, SYL-VAN LAKE, AB, T4S 0B6
(403) 887-0581   SIC 5531

CANADIAN TIRE   p176
32513 SOUTH FRASER WAY SUITE 434, ABBOTSFORD, BC, V2T 4N5
(604) 870-4134   SIC 5531

CANADIAN TIRE   p439
150 DAMASCUS RD, BEDFORD, NS, B4A 0E5
(902) 835-1060   SIC 5531

CANADIAN TIRE   p514
30 LYNDEN RD, BRANTFORD, ON, N3R 8A4
(519) 751-2878   SIC 5531

CANADIAN TIRE   p519
2360 PARKEDALE AVE, BROCKVILLE, ON, K6V 7J5
(613) 342-5841   SIC 5531

CANADIAN TIRE   p617
896 10TH ST, HANOVER, ON, N4N 3P2
(519) 364-2870   SIC 5531

CANADIAN TIRE   p633
640 CATARAQUI WOODS DR, KINGSTON, ON, K7P 2Y5
(613) 384-1766   SIC 5531

CANADIAN TIRE   p851
250 SILVER LINDEN DR SUITE 87, RICH-MOND HILL, ON, L4B 4W7
(905) 731-3100   SIC 5531

CANADIAN TIRE   p856
11720 YONGE ST, RICHMOND HILL, ON, L4E 0K4
(905) 884-9009   SIC 5531

CANADIAN TIRE   p917
2681 DANFORTH AVE SUITE 273, TORONTO, ON, M4C 1L4
(416) 690-6069   SIC 5531

CANADIAN TIRE   p1004
74 MCNAUGHTON AVE SUITE 135, WAL-LACEBURG, ON, N8A 1R9
(519) 627-4251   SIC 5531

CANADIAN TIRE   p1091
3079 BOUL DES SOURCES, DOLLARD-DES-ORMEAUX, QC, H9B 1Z6
(514) 684-9750   SIC 5531

CANADIAN TIRE   p1135
100 RTE DU PRESIDENT-KENNEDY, LEVIS, QC, G6V 6C9
(418) 833-5525   SIC 5531

CANADIAN TIRE   p1346
6565 RUE JEAN-TALON E, SAINT-LEONARD, QC, H1S 1N2
(514) 257-9350   SIC 5531

CANADIAN TIRE   p1382
4785 BOUL LAURIER, TERREBONNE, QC,

J7M 1C3
(450) 477-4013   SIC 5531

CANADIAN TIRE   p1440
18 CHILKOOT WAY, WHITEHORSE, YT, Y1A 6T5
(867) 668-3652   SIC 5531

CANADIAN TIRE ASSOCIATE STORE p127
1 HOSPITAL ST, FORT MCMURRAY, AB, T9H 5C1
(780) 791-6400   SIC 5531

CANADIAN TIRE ASSOCIATE STORE p136
868 CARMICHAEL LANE, HINTON, AB, T7V 1Y6
(780) 865-6198   SIC 5531

CANADIAN TIRE ASSOCIATE STORE p192
7200 MARKET CROSS, BURNABY, BC, V5J 0A2
(604) 451-5888   SIC 5531

CANADIAN TIRE ASSOCIATE STORE p203
1100 VICTORIA AVE N, CRANBROOK, BC, V1C 6G7
(250) 489-5563   SIC 5531

CANADIAN TIRE ASSOCIATE STORE p276
7599 KING GEORGE BLVD, SURREY, BC, V3W 5A8
(604) 572-3739   SIC 5531

CANADIAN TIRE ASSOCIATE STORE p418
250 KING ST, ST STEPHEN, NB, E3L 2E5
(506) 466-4110   SIC 5531

CANADIAN TIRE ASSOCIATE STORE p565
409 GOVERNMENT ST, DRYDEN, ON, P8N 2P4
(807) 223-6644   SIC 5531

CANADIAN TIRE ASSOCIATE STORE LTD p267
2090 10 AVE SW, SALMON ARM, BC, V1E 0E1
(250) 832-5474   SIC 5531

CANADIAN TIRE ASSOCIATE STORES & AUTO CENTRES   p1117
16821 RTE TRANSCANADIENNE UNITE 149, KIRKLAND, QC, H9H 5J1
(514) 697-4761   SIC 5531

CANADIAN TIRE ASSOCIATES STORES ALL DEPARTMENTS   p1420
655 ALBERT ST, REGINA, SK, S4R 2P4
(306) 525-9027   SIC 5531

CANADIAN TIRE CORPORATION, LIMITED p924
2180 YONGE ST, TORONTO, ON, M4S 2B9
(416) 480-3000   SIC 5531

CANADIAN TIRE KINCARDINE   p629
811 DURHAM ST, KINCARDINE, ON, N2Z 3B8
(519) 395-2886   SIC 5531

CANADIANTIRE   p629
811 DURHAM ST, KINCARDINE, ON, N2Z 3B8
(519) 395-2886   SIC 5531

CARKAE ENGLISH SALES LTD   p635
1080 VICTORIA ST N SUITE 139, KITCH-ENER, ON, N2B 3C4
(519) 744-1153   SIC 5531

CARRIER TRUCK CENTER INC   p1035
645 ATHLONE AVE, WOODSTOCK, ON, N4S 7V8
(519) 539-9837   SIC 5531

CAYEN, J.C. HOLDINGS LTD   p1437
1240 SIMS AVE, WEYBURN, SK, S4H 3N9
(306) 842-4600   SIC 5531

CEDM TOWER LTD   p405
2491 KING GEORGE HWY, MIRAMICHI, NB, E1V 6W3
(506) 773-9446   SIC 5531

CENTRE DU CAMION D'AMOS INC   p1046
145 RTE 111 E, AMOS, QC, J9T 3A2
(819) 732-6471   SIC 5531

CENTRE DU CAMION MONT-LAURIER INC, LE   p1154
3763 CH DE LA LIEVRE N, MONT-LAURIER, QC, J9L 3G4
(819) 623-3433   SIC 5531

CENTRE TECHNO-PNEU INC   p1285
445 RUE DE L'EXPANSION, RIMOUSKI,

QC, G5M 1B4
(418) 724-4104   SIC 5531

CIERE, PIETER ENTERPRISES INC   p836
31 MECHANIC ST, PARIS, ON, N3L 1K1
(519) 442-2312   SIC 5531

CIVIC TIRE & BATTERY (WESTLOCK) LTD p172
10111 107 ST, WESTLOCK, AB, T7P 1W9
(780) 349-3351   SIC 5531

CLAUDE L'HEUREUX HOLDINGS INC p811
3910 INNES RD SUITE 422, ORLEANS, ON, K1W 1K9
(613) 830-7000   SIC 5531

CML BOSWELL HOLDINGS LTD   p159
5440 46 ST, ROCKY MOUNTAIN HOUSE, AB, T4T 1B3
(403) 846-0077   SIC 5531

COAST POWERTRAIN LTD   p236
420 CANFOR AVE, NEW WESTMINSTER, BC, V3L 5G2
(604) 520-6125   SIC 5531

COAST TIRE & AUTO SERVICE LTD   p414
130 SOMERSET ST SUITE 150, SAINT JOHN, NB, E2K 2X4
(506) 674-9620   SIC 5531

COLLIN & DIANA PARKER SALES LTD p805
1100 KERR ST, OAKVILLE, ON, L6M 0L4
(905) 844-0202   SIC 5531

CRONIER, J.P. ENTERPRISES INC   p619
1330 FRONT ST, HEARST, ON, P0L 1N0
(705) 362-5822   SIC 5531

CROPLEY, PAUL J & D SALES LTD   p897
24614 ADELAIDE RD, STRATHROY, ON, N7G 2P8
(519) 245-2704   SIC 5531

CROZIER, DONNA & JOHN LIMITED   p83
13211 FORT RD NW, EDMONTON, AB, T5A 1C3
(780) 473-2394   SIC 5531

DANDCO ENTERPRISES LTD   p157
2510 50 AVE, RED DEER, AB, T4R 1M3
(403) 342-2223   SIC 5531

DANIEL S. WEBSTER HOLDINGS LIMITED p546
89 BALSAM ST, COLLINGWOOD, ON, L9Y 3Y6
(705) 445-4169   SIC 5531

DAVENPORT SALES & AUTO SERVICE LTD p71
5404 DALTON DR NW SUITE 299, CAL-GARY, AB, T3A 2C3
(403) 288-1100   SIC 5531

DAVENPORT SALES & AUTO SERVICE LTD p84
11839 KINGSWAY NW, EDMONTON, AB, T5G 3J7
(780) 413-8473   SIC 5531

DEGUIRE, MICHEL HOLDINGS INC   p1436
1811 22ND AVE NE, SWIFT CURRENT, SK, S9H 5B7
(306) 773-0654   SIC 5531

DEMERS, MICHEL STORE INC   p900
2259 REGENT ST, SUDBURY, ON, P3E 5M9
(705) 523-5800   SIC 5531

DENANCO SALES LTD   p838
1104 PEMBROKE ST E, PEMBROKE, ON, K8A 8S2
(613) 735-0000   SIC 5531

DERBYSHIRE E.D. & SONS LIMITED   p633
2560 PRINCESS ST SUITE 417, KINGSTON, ON, K7P 2S8
(613) 384-4414   SIC 5531

DERBYSHIRE, D MERCHANDISING LTD p486
75 MAPLEVIEW DR W, BARRIE, ON, L4N 9H7
(705) 792-0920   SIC 5531

DESUTTER INVESTMENTS INC   p252
570 NEWMAN RD, QUESNEL, BC, V2J 6Z8
(250) 747-5275   SIC 5531

DEWLING, S & C SALES LTD   p172
3851 56 ST, WETASKIWIN, AB, T9A 2B1
(780) 352-7175   SIC 5531

DODSON, JIM SALES LTD   p660
3100 WONDERLAND RD S, LONDON, ON, N6L 1A6
(519) 680-2277   SIC 5531

DOM'S AUTO PARTS CO LIMITED   p563
1604 BASELINE RD, COURTICE, ON, L1E 2S5
(905) 434-4566   SIC 5531

DONALD F. JOHNSTON HOLDINGS LTD p660
1020 WONDERLAND RD S, LONDON, ON, N6K 3S4
(519) 680-1770   SIC 5531

DUNCAN AUTO PARTS (1983) LTD   p211
5829 DUNCAN ST, DUNCAN, BC, V9L 3W7
(250) 746-5431   SIC 5531

DUNGEY, D.B. HOLDINGS INC   p423
8 CROMER AVE, GRAND FALLS-WINDSOR, NL, A2A 1X2
(709) 489-9270   SIC 5531

ED'S TIRE SERVICE (1993) LTD   p352
80 THORNHILL ST, MORDEN, MB, R6M 1C7
SIC 5531

ENDRESS SALES AND DISTRIBUTION LTD p268
4380 SUNSHINE COAST HWY RR 1, SECHELT, BC, V0N 3A1
(604) 885-6611   SIC 5531

ENTREPRISES BOULOS,PIERRE L INC, LES   p1254
705 RUE CLEMENCEAU, QUEBEC, QC, G1C 7T9
(418) 663-4334   SIC 5531

ENTREPRISES GHISLAIN G FORTIN LTEE p1284
419 BOUL JESSOP BUREAU 320, RI-MOUSKI, QC, G5L 7Y5
(418) 722-8426   SIC 5531

ENTREPRISES J.P. LAROCHELLE INC, LES   p1115
2290 BOUL RENE-LEVESQUE, JON-QUIERE, QC, G7S 5Y5
(418) 542-3909   SIC 5531

ENTREPRISES JOEL GIRARD INC, LES p1397
3180 RUE WELLINGTON, VERDUN, QC, H4G 1T3
(514) 766-8561   SIC 5531

ENTREPRISES MARIO LAROCHELLE INC, LES   p1367
402 BOUL LAURE, SEPT-ILES, QC, G4R 1X5
(418) 968-1415   SIC 5531

ENTREPRISES MICHEL CHOINIERE INC, LES   p1365
1770 BOUL MONSEIGNEUR-LANGLOIS, SALABERRY-DE-VALLEYFIELD, QC, J6S 5R1
(450) 373-0123   SIC 5531

ENTREPRISES MICHEL HAMELIN INC, LES p1092
223 138 RTE, DONNACONA, QC, G3M 1C1
(418) 285-1331   SIC 5531

ENTREPRISES PIERRE LAUZON LTEE p1090
1751 BOUL VEZINA BUREAU 284, DOLBEAU-MISTASSINI, QC, G8L 3S4
(418) 276-2385   SIC 5531

ENTREPRISES RAYMOND LEWIS INC, LES p1317
855 BOUL DU SEMINAIRE N BUREAU 153, SAINT-JEAN-SUR-RICHELIEU, QC, J3A 1J2
(450) 348-3851   SIC 5531

ERSSER, A. J. HOLDINGS LTD   p835
1605 16TH ST E, OWEN SOUND, ON, N4K 5N3
(519) 376-5220   SIC 5531

EXCEL RETAIL LIMITED   p758
6840 MCLEOD RD, NIAGARA FALLS, ON, L2G 3G6
(905) 358-0161   SIC 5531

EXCEL TIRE CENTRES INC   p289
615 KINGSWAY, VANCOUVER, BC, V5T

3K5

(604) 876-1225   *SIC 5531*

FILES, JIM & DEANNA SALES & SERVICES LIMITED   *p1005*

11 CLAPPISON AVE SUITE 220, WATER-DOWN, ON, L8B 0Y2

(905) 690-3486   *SIC 5531*

FINCH, BARRY ENTERPRISES LTD   *p896*

1093 ONTARIO ST, STRATFORD, ON, N5A 6W6

(519) 273-2080   *SIC 5531*

FITCHCO ENTERPRISES INC   *p410*

345 MIRAMICHI RD, OROMOCTO, NB, E2V 4T4

(506) 357-3304   *SIC 5531*

FORD, WAYNE SALES LIMITED   *p755*

17750 YONGE ST, NEWMARKET, ON, L3Y 8P4

(905) 895-4565   *SIC 5531*

FOUNTAIN TIRE (EDSON) LTD   *p126*

4619 2 AVE, EDSON, AB, T7E 1C1

(780) 723-7666   *SIC 5531*

FOUNTAIN TIRE (G.P.) LTD   *p132*

13003 100 ST, GRANDE PRAIRIE, AB, T8V 4H3

(780) 539-1710   *SIC 5531*

FOUNTAIN TIRE (SAULT STE. MARIE) LTD   *p862*

55 BLACK RD, SAULT STE. MARIE, ON, P6B 0A3

(705) 254-6664   *SIC 5531*

FOUNTAIN TIRE LTD   *p124*

1006 103A ST SW SUITE 103, EDMON-TON, AB, T6W 2P6

(780) 464-3700   *SIC 5531*

FOX, DOMINIC LIMITED   *p646*

377 KENT ST W, LINDSAY, ON, K9V 2Z7

(705) 324-8301   *SIC 5531*

FOX, JOHN A LTD   *p867*

3553 LAWRENCE AVE E, SCARBOR-OUGH, ON, M1H 1B2

(416) 431-3888   *SIC 5531*

FRISBY TIRE CO. (1974) LIMITED   *p750*

1377 CLYDE AVE, NEPEAN, ON, K2G 3H7

(613) 224-2200   *SIC 5531*

G. C. LOH MERCHANDISING LTD   *p580*

1530 ALBION RD, ETOBICOKE, ON, M9V 1B4

(416) 745-9070   *SIC 5531*

G.G.C.S. HOLDINGS LTD   *p203*

820 CRANBROOK ST N, CRANBROOK, BC, V1C 3R9

(250) 426-5208   *SIC 5531*

GALLANT, RAYMOND & SONS LTD   *p412*

11055 RUE PRINCIPALE, ROGERSVILLE, NB, E4Y 2L8

(506) 775-2797   *SIC 5531*

GAMEX INC   *p1113*

609 RUE PRINCIPALE, ILE-AUX-NOIX, QC, J0J 1G0

(450) 246-3881   *SIC 5531*

GARON, LAWRENCE M ENTERPRISES LTD   *p846*

287 WEST SIDE RD, PORT COLBORNE, ON, L3K 5L2

(905) 835-1155   *SIC 5531*

GAUDREAU, MARC INC   *p394*

384 OLD VAL D'AMOUR RD, ATHOLVILLE, NB, E3N 4E3

(506) 789-0220   *SIC 5531*

GENERAL MOTORS OF CANADA COM-PANY   *p101*

17707 118 AVE NW, EDMONTON, AB, T5S 1P7

(780) 451-7000   *SIC 5531*

GEORGE, JS ENTERPRISES LTD   *p418*

138 MAIN ST SUITE 17, SUSSEX, NB, E4E 3E1

(506) 433-3201   *SIC 5531*

GESTION BENOIT GUILLEMETTE INC   *p1053*

650 RUE DE PARFONDEVAL BUREAU 265, BAIE-COMEAU, QC, G5C 3R3

(418) 589-9924   *SIC 5531*

GESTION C. & L. LAROCHELLE INC   *p1382*

70 BOUL FRONTENAC E BUREAU 156, THETFORD MINES, QC, G6G 1N4

(418) 338-3535   *SIC 5531*

GESTION D. PRESSAULT INC   *p1150*

145 RUE PIUZE, MATANE, QC, G4W 0H7

(418) 562-5144   *SIC 5531*

GESTION DOMINIC PAQUETTE INC   *p627*

25 BRUNETVILLE RD SUITE 30, KA-PUSKASING, ON, P5N 2E9

(705) 335-6066   *SIC 5531*

GESTION FAMILLE BUCCI INC   *p1379*

1250 BOUL MOODY BUREAU 312, TERRE-BONNE, QC, J6W 3K9

(450) 961-9011   *SIC 5531*

GESTION GIACOMO D'AMICO INC   *p403*

383   CH   MADAWASKA,   GRAND-SAULT/GRAND FALLS, NB, E3Y 1A4

(506) 473-3550   *SIC 5531*

GESTION GILLES CHARTRAND INC   *p394*

520 ST. PETER AVE, BATHURST, NB, E2A 2Y7

(506) 547-8120   *SIC 5531*

GESTION GUY L'HEUREUX INC   *p1101*

544 BOUL CURE-LABELLE BUREAU 690, FABREVILLE, QC, H7P 2P4

(450) 963-8686   *SIC 5531*

GESTION MARIO ROY INC   *p1122*

375 BOUL DE COMPORTE BUREAU 118, LA MALBAIE, QC, G5A 1H9

(418) 665-6483   *SIC 5531*

GESTION MICHEL SEGUIN INC   *p1070*

9900 BOUL LEDUC, BROSSARD, QC, J4Y 0B4

(450) 443-0005   *SIC 5531*

GESTION REJEAN TROTTIER INC   *p1182*

6275 BOUL SAINT-LAURENT BUREAU 343, MONTREAL, QC, H2S 3C3

(514) 273-2428   *SIC 5531*

GESTION REMI GAUTHIER INC   *p407*

1106 MOUNTAIN RD, MONCTON, NB, E1C 2T3

(506) 852-2970   *SIC 5531*

GESTION ROGER THERIAULT   *p394*

384 OLD VAL D'AMOUR RD, ATHOLVILLE, NB, E3N 4E3

(506) 789-0230   *SIC 5531*

GESTION STEFANO ROVER INC   *p1125*

3642 RUE LAVAL, LAC-MEGANTIC, QC, G6B 1A4

(819) 583-3332   *SIC 5531*

GESTIONS GILBERT ROY INC   *p1224*

3180 RUE WELLINGTON, MONTREAL, QC, H4G 1T3

(514) 766-8561   *SIC 5531*

GESTIONS REJEAN SAVARD LTEE   *p1232*

4975 BOUL ROBERT-BOURASSA BU-REAU 231, MONTREAL, QC, H7E 0A4

(450) 665-4747   *SIC 5531*

GESTIONS SYLVAIN BERUBE INC   *p1363*

500 DESSTE CHOMEDEY (A-13) O, SAINTE-ROSE, QC, H7X 3S9

(450) 969-4141   *SIC 5531*

GOSTLIN, K E ENTERPRISES LTD   *p220*

1655 LECKIE RD, KELOWNA, BC, V1X 6E4

(250) 860-4331   *SIC 5531*

GRANDVIEW SALES & DISTRIBUTION LTD   *p874*

4630 SHEPPARD AVE E SUITE 264, SCAR-BOROUGH, ON, M1S 3V5

(416) 291-7791   *SIC 5531*

GRANT, JAMIE & BARB SALES LTD   *p683*

1210 STEELES AVE E, MILTON, ON, L9T 6R1

(905) 878-2349   *SIC 5531*

GREATER   VANCOUVER   ASSOCIATE STORES LTD   *p287*

2220 KINGSWAY, VANCOUVER, BC, V5N 2T7

SIC 5531

GRIFA, BLAISE LTD   *p73*

5200 RICHMOND RD SW SUITE 302, CAL-GARY, AB, T3E 6M9

(403) 246-1961   *SIC 5531*

GWENAL HOLDINGS LTD   *p235*

6900 ISLAND HWY N, NANAIMO, BC, V9V 1P6

SIC 5531

H.G. CAMPBELL ENTERPRISES LTD   *p681*

HWY 93 S, MIDLAND, ON, L4R 5K9

(705) 526-9321   *SIC 5531*

H.S. PIKE HOLDINGS INC   *p564*

366 BURKES RD RR 1, DEEP RIVER, ON, K0J 1P0

(613) 584-3337   *SIC 5531*

HALDEX LIMITED   *p536*

500 PINEBUSH RD UNIT 1, CAMBRIDGE, ON, N1T 0A5

(519) 621-6722   *SIC 5531*

HARVEY, R & J ADVENTURES LTD   *p1438*

205 HAMILTON RD, YORKTON, SK, S3N 4B9

(306) 783-9733   *SIC 5531*

HATCH, ROBERT RETAIL INC   *p80*

320 5 AVE W, COCHRANE, AB, T4C 2E3

(403) 851-0894   *SIC 5531*

HAYHURST, GEORGE LIMITED   *p814*

441 GIBB ST, OSHAWA, ON, L1J 1Z4

(905) 728-6272   *SIC 5531*

HIGGINS, PATRICK J ENTERPRISES LTD   *p1001*

327 TORONTO ST S, UXBRIDGE, ON, L9P 1Z7

(905) 852-3315   *SIC 5531*

HLADY, RONALD H. AUTO SALES LTD   *p69*

250 SHAWVILLE WAY SE, CALGARY, AB, T2Y 3J1

SIC 5531

HODGKINSON A & G SALES LTD   *p484*

320 BAYFIELD ST SUITE M103, BARRIE, ON, L4M 3C1

(705) 726-2861   *SIC 5531*

HUTTON, B. MARKETING LTD   *p231*

11969 200 ST, MAPLE RIDGE, BC, V2X 3M7

(604) 460-4664   *SIC 5531*

I & D MCEWEN LTD   *p498*

10 GREAT LAKES DR, BRAMPTON, ON, L6R 2K7

(905) 793-4800   *SIC 5531*

INGLIS, D.W. LIMITED   *p723*

6670 MEADOWVALE TOWN CENTRE CIR, MISSISSAUGA, ON, L5N 4B7

(905) 821-1087   *SIC 5531*

INVESTISSEMENTS MICHEL DESLAURI-ERS INC, LES   *p1159*

370 117 RTE, MONT-TREMBLANT, QC, J8E 2X3

(819) 425-1110   *SIC 5531*

J.B. PRECISION ENGINES & PARTS LTD   *p337*

3340 OAK ST, VICTORIA, BC, V8X 1R1

(250) 475-2520   *SIC 5531*

J.D. MCARTHUR TIRE SERVICES INC *p835*

1066 3RD AVE E, OWEN SOUND, ON, N4K 2L2

(519) 376-3520   *SIC 5531*

J.M. DUBRIS LTEE   *p1302*

500   BOUL   ARTHUR-SAUVE,   SAINT-EUSTACHE, QC, J7R 4Z3

(450) 472-2270   *SIC 5531*

JBE HOME & AUTO LIMITED   *p177*

32513 SOUTH FRASER WAY SUITE 434, ABBOTSFORD, BC, V2T 4N5

(604) 870-4125   *SIC 5531*

JEAN C. DUPONT LTEE   *p399*

260 CH CANADA, EDMUNDSTON, NB, E3V 1W1

(506) 739-8343   *SIC 5531*

JENKINS, MALCOLM J. MERCHANDISING LTD   *p1414*

3725 2ND AVE W, PRINCE ALBERT, SK, S6W 1A1

(306) 764-9000   *SIC 5531*

JHAJ HOLDINGS LTD   *p252*

156 MALCOLM DR, QUESNEL, BC, V2J 1E4

(604) 594-8800   *SIC 5531*

K & J FAMILY HOLDINGS LTD   *p590*

100 THAMES RD W SS 3 SUITE 3, EX-ETER, ON, N0M 1S3

(519) 235-0160   *SIC 5531*

K A R INDUSTRIES LIMITED   *p339*

1519 ADMIRALS RD, VICTORIA, BC, V9A 2P8

(250) 381-3111   *SIC 5531*

K C AUTOMOTIVE PARTS INC   *p835*

222 14TH ST W SUITE 130, OWEN SOUND, ON, N4K 3X8

(519) 376-2501   *SIC 5531*

K.K. PENNER TIRE CENTERS INC   *p346*

39 PENNER DR, BLUMENORT, MB, R0A 0C0

(204) 326-6419   *SIC 5531*

KAL TIRE ALBERTA LTD   *p16*

5375 68 AVE SE, CALGARY, AB, T2C 5A7

(403) 236-7171   *SIC 5531*

KAVANAGH INVESTMENTS LTD   *p144*

4215 70 AVE, LLOYDMINSTER, AB, T9V 2X2

(780) 875-4410   *SIC 5531*

KING-O-MATIC INDUSTRIES LIMITED *p696*

955 PANTERA DR, MISSISSAUGA, ON, L4W 2T4

(905) 624-1956   *SIC 5531*

L & L MCCAW HOLDINGS LTD   *p430*

50 KELSEY DR, ST. JOHN'S, NL, A1B 5C7

(709) 722-5530   *SIC 5531*

L & M MERCIER ENTERPRISES INC *p1406*

200 KING ST SUITE 146, ESTEVAN, SK, S4A 2W4

(306) 634-6407   *SIC 5531*

LACHANCE, B.D. SALES LTD   *p143*

2720 FAIRWAY RD S, LETHBRIDGE, AB, T1K 7A5

(403) 394-9633   *SIC 5531*

LANDRY, CLAUDE INVESTMENTS INC *p420*

388 CONNELL ST, WOODSTOCK, NB, E7M 5G9

(506) 328-3353   *SIC 5531*

LATTANVILLE HOLDINGS CORPORATION *p656*

378 HORTON ST E SUITE 494, LONDON, ON, N6B 1L7

(519) 642-7142   *SIC 5531*

LEGARE, DUPERRE INC   *p1346*

4250   RUE   JEAN-TALON   E,   SAINT-LEONARD, QC, H1S 1J7

(514) 723-2233   *SIC 5531*

LEMAY, G & S HOLDINGS INC   *p419*

450 RUE DU MOULIN SUITE 491, TRACADIE-SHEILA, NB, E1X 1A4

(506) 395-4313   *SIC 5531*

LEROUX, K. D. SALES LTD   *p869*

1901 EGLINTON AVE E, SCARBOROUGH, ON, M1L 2L8

(416) 615-2666   *SIC 5531*

LESAGE, L.T. HOLDINGS LTD   *p4*

2913 48 AVE, ATHABASCA, AB, T9S 0A4

(780) 675-3019   *SIC 5531*

LEVY, JEFF INVESTMENTS LTD   *p781*

4400 DUFFERIN ST SUITE 1, NORTH YORK, ON, M3H 6A8

(416) 667-9777   *SIC 5531*

LINCIA CORPORATION   *p77*

11940 SARCEE TRAIL NW, CALGARY, AB, T3R 0A1

(403) 295-0200   *SIC 5531*

LKQ SHAW AUTO RECYCLERS INC   *p651*

1765 PENSION LANE, LONDON, ON, N5V 6C7

(519) 455-1200   *SIC 5531*

LKQ UPPER BROOKSIDE INC   *p470*

466 BROOKSIDE RD, UPPER BROOK-SIDE, NS, B6L 2B3

(902) 897-0252   *SIC 5531*

LOMBARDI, ALDO SALES INC   *p566*

50 COOTES DR, DUNDAS, ON, L9H 1B6

(905) 627-3534   *SIC 5531*

LORDCO PARTS LTD   *p231*

22866 DEWDNEY TRUNK RD, MAPLE RIDGE, BC, V2X 3K6

▲ Public Company   ■ Public Company Family Member   **HQ** Headquarters   **BR** Branch   **SL** Single Location

(604) 467-1581   *SIC* 5531
M. A. S. CHIBOUGAMAU INC   *p*1077
874 3E RUE, CHIBOUGAMAU, QC, G8P
1P9
(418) 748-7674   *SIC* 5531
M.C.T. PNEUS INC   *p*1243
1293 RUE DU PARC-INDUSTRIEL, NOR-
MANDIN, QC, G8M 4C6
(418) 274-3765   *SIC* 5531
M.R. BAULDIC ENTERPRISES INC   *p*204
11628 8 ST, DAWSON CREEK, BC, V1G
4R7
(250) 782-9552   *SIC* 5531
MA FEENER SALES LTD   *p*416
885 FAIRVILLE BLVD, SAINT JOHN, NB,
E2M 5T9
(506) 635-1711   *SIC* 5531
MACKINTOSH, K.J. SALES LTD   *p*107
9603 162 AVE NW SUITE 397, EDMON-
TON, AB, T5Z 3T6
(780) 495-9696   *SIC* 5531
MACLEAN, K. T. (KEN) LIMITED   *p*157
2510 50 AVE, RED DEER, AB, T4R 1M3
(403) 342-2222   *SIC* 5531
MACMILLAN, DOUG ENTERPRISES LTD
*p*243
960 RAILWAY ST, PENTICTON, BC, V2A
8N2
(250) 492-3586   *SIC* 5531
MAGASIN JEAN DUMAS INC   *p*1354
50 BOUL NORBERT-MORIN, SAINTE-
AGATHE-DES-MONTS, QC, J8C 2V6
(819) 326-8900   *SIC* 5531
MAGASIN MARC-ANDRE ST-JACQUES INC
*p*1385
6 RUE FUSEY, TROIS-RIVIERES, QC, G8T
2T1
(819) 376-6866   *SIC* 5531
MAGASIN MYRLANIE INC   *p*1226
9050 BOUL DE L'ACADIE, MONTREAL,
QC, H4N 2S5
(514) 388-6464   *SIC* 5531
MAGASIN ST-JEAN, ALAIN INC   *p*1099
715 BOUL SAINT-JOSEPH BUREAU 158,
DRUMMONDVILLE, QC, J2C 7V2
(819) 478-1471   *SIC* 5531
MAGOG FORD (2000) INC   *p*1147
2000 RUE SHERBROOKE, MAGOG, QC,
J1X 2T3
(819) 843-3673   *SIC* 5531
MAL WHITLOCK ENTERPRISES LTD   *p*570
300 MAIDSTONE AVE W, ESSEX, ON, N8M
2X6
(519) 776-5224   *SIC* 5531
MALGO, JA SALES LTD   *p*170
6623 16A HWY W, VEGREVILLE, AB, T9C
0A3
SIC 5531
MARCHAND, PIERRE STORE INC   *p*898
12011 HIGHWAY 17 E, STURGEON FALLS,
ON, P2B 2S7
(705) 753-2630   *SIC* 5531
MARKET TIRE (1976) LTD   *p*1432
115 IDYLWYLD DR S, SASKATOON, SK,
S7M 1L4
(306) 244-5442   *SIC* 5531
MARSHALL, JAMES B ENTERPRISES LTD
*p*428
60 ELIZABETH AVE SUITE 144, ST.
JOHN'S, NL, A1A 1W4
(709) 722-1860   *SIC* 5531
MARTIN HOME & AUTO LTD   *p*887
300 GLENDALE AVE, ST CATHARINES,
ON, L2T 2L5
(905) 227-7481   *SIC* 5531
MARTIN, LOUIS MERCHANDISING LTD
*p*482
605 JOHN ST N, AYLMER, ON, N5H 2B6
(519) 773-8424   *SIC* 5531
MCCARTHY ELLIS MERCANTILE LTD *p*988
700 LAWRENCE AVE W, TORONTO, ON,
M6A 3B4
(289) 442-2851   *SIC* 5531
MCCULLOUGH, D.E. ENTERPRISES LTD

*p*492
101 BELL BLVD, BELLEVILLE, ON, K8P
4V2
(613) 968-6701   *SIC* 5531
**MCMASTER, PAT & MARLEEN ENTER-
PRISES LTD**   *p*569
801 CENTRE ST, ESPANOLA, ON, P5E
1N2
(705) 869-3807   *SIC* 5531
MCNAMARA, MERVIN J. INC   *p*898
1066 BARRYDOWNE RD SUITE 278, SUD-
BURY, ON, P3A 3V3
(705) 566-9735   *SIC* 5531
MEDEIROS, PAUL ENTERPRISES LIMITED
*p*634
146 GOVERNMENT RD W, KIRKLAND
LAKE, ON, P2N 2E9
(705) 567-9281   *SIC* 5531
MORRISON, DAVID W. ENTERPRISES LTD
*p*1024
2650 TECUMSEH RD W, WINDSOR, ON,
N9B 3R1
(519) 252-7743   *SIC* 5531
MOSER, K.G. LIMITED   *p*620
77 KING WILLIAM ST, HUNTSVILLE, ON,
P1H 1E5
(705) 789-5569   *SIC* 5531
MUSKOKA AUTO PARTS LIMITED   *p*620
11 KING WILLIAM ST, HUNTSVILLE, ON,
P1H 1G6
(705) 789-2321   *SIC* 5531
NADEAU, MARCEL MANAGEMENT INC
*p*197
7560 VEDDER RD, CHILLIWACK, BC, V2R
4E7
(604) 858-7230   *SIC* 5531
NAPA AUTO PARTS   *p*1131
7214 BOUL NEWMAN, LASALLE, QC, H8N
1X2
(514) 365-5116   *SIC* 5531
NAPA AUTO PARTS   *p*1234
2999 BOUL LE CORBUSIER, MONTREAL,
QC, H7L 3M3
(450) 681-6495   *SIC* 5531
NAPA PIECES D'AUTO   *p*1347
557 RUE SAINT-LOUIS, SAINT-LIN-
LAURENTIDES, QC, J5M 2X2
(450) 439-2006   *SIC* 5531
NATIONAL 4WD CENTRE INC   *p*523
5379 HARVESTER RD, BURLINGTON, ON,
L7L 5K4
(905) 634-0001   *SIC* 5531
NATIONAL TIRE DISTRIBUTORS   *p*622
311 INGERSOLL ST S, INGERSOLL, ON,
N5C 3J7
(519) 425-1228   *SIC* 5531
NIAGARA BATTERY & TIRE LTD   *p*885
79 HARTZEL RD, ST CATHARINES, ON,
L2P 1M9
(905) 682-1844   *SIC* 5531
NURKKALA, HJ INVESTMENTS   *p*358
131 PTH 12 N, STEINBACH, MB, R5G 1T5
(204) 326-3436   *SIC* 5531
O M B PARTS & INDUSTRIAL LTD   *p*422
7 BLACKMORE AVE SUITE 1,
CLARENVILLE, NL, A5A 1B8
(709) 466-6491   *SIC* 5531
O.K. TIRE STORES INC   *p*279
19082 21 AVE, SURREY, BC, V3Z 3M3
(604) 542-7999   *SIC* 5531
OLIVER, PETER M SALES LTD   *p*920
1015 LAKE SHORE BLVD E SUITE 654,
TORONTO, ON, M4M 1B4
(416) 778-0102   *SIC* 5531
ONTARIO TIRE RECOVERY INC   *p*607
2985 CONCESSION 12 WALPOLE,
HAGERSVILLE, ON, N0A 1H0
SIC 5531
ORFORD SALES LTD   *p*587
2025 KIPLING AVE, ETOBICOKE, ON,
M9W 4J8
(416) 743-6950   *SIC* 5531
P & R HOFSTATTER SALES LTD   *p*839
45 DUFFERIN ST, PERTH, ON, K7H 3A5

(613) 267-3412   *SIC* 5531
PAC BRAKE MANUFACTURING   *p*282
19594 96 AVE, SURREY, BC, V4N 4C3
(604) 882-0183   *SIC* 5531
PACO LTEE   *p*1079
870 BOUL TALBOT, CHICOUTIMI, QC, G7H
4B4
(418) 696-4444   *SIC* 5531
PARAMOUNT PARTS INC   *p*128
36 RIEDEL ST SUITE 1, FORT MCMUR-
RAY, AB, T9H 3E1
(780) 791-3000   *SIC* 5531
PARISIEN, J.W. ENTERPRISES LTD   *p*882
10 FERRARA DR SUITE 98, SMITHS
FALLS, ON, K7A 5K4
(613) 283-3906   *SIC* 5531
PARTSMAN INC, THE   *p*814
278 PARK RD S, OSHAWA, ON, L1J 4H5
(905) 436-3227   *SIC* 5531
PEINTURE & PIECES D.R. INC   *p*1148
2509 RUE SHERBROOKE, MAGOG, QC,
J1X 4E7
(819) 843-0550   *SIC* 5531
PENNER, P & A SALES INC   *p*1410
300 STONEGATE 500 HWY SUITE 6,
MELFORT, SK, S0E 1A0
(306) 752-7277   *SIC* 5531
**PERFORMANCE IMPROVEMENTS SPEED
SHOPS LIMITED**   *p*575
87 ADVANCE RD, ETOBICOKE, ON, M8Z
2S6
(416) 259-9656   *SIC* 5531
**PETER CHARLES ANSLEY HOLDINGS
LIMITED**   *p*858
1380 LONDON RD UNIT 300, SARNIA, ON,
N7S 1P8
(519) 542-3403   *SIC* 5531
PIECES D'AUTO ALAIN COTE INC *p*1119
6315 BOUL WILFRID-HAMEL,
L'ANCIENNE-LORETTE, QC, G2E 5W2
(418) 780-4770   *SIC* 5531
PIECES D'AUTO SUPER INC   *p*1308
7803 CH DE CHAMBLY, SAINT-HUBERT,
QC, J3Y 5K2
(450) 676-1850   *SIC* 5531
**PIECES D'AUTOS CHAMBLY RICHELIEU
INC**   *p*1283
2000 CH DES PATRIOTES BUREAU 299,
RICHELIEU, QC, J3L 6M1
(450) 658-7474   *SIC* 5531
PIECES D'AUTOS FERNAND BEGIN INC
*p*1350
416 RANG F.-BEGIN, SAINT-PHILIBERT,
QC, G0M 1X0
(418) 228-2413   *SIC* 5531
PIECES D'AUTOS JEAN LEBLANC LTEE
*p*1388
3780 BOUL GENE-H.-KRUGER, TROIS-
RIVIERES, QC, G9A 4M3
(819) 370-1212   *SIC* 5531
PIECES D'AUTOS M.R. INC., LES   *p*1057
125 RUE D'IBERVILLE, BERTHIERVILLE,
QC, J0K 1A0
(450) 836-7001   *SIC* 5531
PIECES D'AUTOS TRANSBEC INC, LES
*p*1231
5505 RUE ERNEST-CORMIER, MON-
TREAL, QC, H7C 0A1
(450) 665-4440   *SIC* 5531
PMD RETAIL SALES INC   *p*604
10 WOODLAWN RD E SUITE 260,
GUELPH, ON, N1H 1G7
(519) 821-2244   *SIC* 5531
PNEU-HYD INDUSTRIES LIMITED   *p*893
375 GREEN RD UNIT 1, STONEY CREEK,
ON, L8E 4A5
(905) 664-5540   *SIC* 5531
PNEUS BEAUCERONS INC, LES   *p*1055
538 BOUL RENAULT, BEAUCEVILLE, QC,
G5X 1N2
(418) 774-3404   *SIC* 5531
PNEUS BERNARD, ROBERT, LES   *p*1398
900 RUE NOTRE-DAME E, VICTORIAV-
ILLE, QC, G6P 4B7

(819) 752-4567   *SIC* 5531
PNEUS DU BOULEVARD LTEE   *p*396
461 BOUL ST-PIERRE O, CARAQUET, NB,
E1W 1A3
(506) 727-7488   *SIC* 5531
PNEUS RATTE INC   *p*1261
103 3E AV, QUEBEC, QC, G1L 2V3
(418) 529-5378   *SIC* 5531
PNEUS SP INC   *p*1050
9135 RUE EDISON, ANJOU, QC, H1J 1T4
(514) 354-7444   *SIC* 5531
POLLOCK, PAUL S. ENTERPRISES LTD
*p*637
1400 OTTAWA ST S, KITCHENER, ON, N2E
4E2
(519) 743-1113   *SIC* 5531
PORTENGEN, R. HOME AND AUTO INC
*p*568
50 HILLSIDE DR S, ELLIOT LAKE, ON, P5A
1M7
(705) 848-3663   *SIC* 5531
PRECISION TRUCK ACCESSORIES   *p*172
9024 100 ST, WESTLOCK, AB, T7P 2L4
(780) 349-3010   *SIC* 5531
PROULX, MICHEL STORE INC   *p*746
12329 COUNTY RD 2, MORRISBURG, ON,
K0C 1X0
(613) 543-2845   *SIC* 5531
QUALITY TIRE SERVICE LTD   *p*1416
2150 E VICTORIA AVE SUITE 201,
REGINA, SK, S4N 7B9
(306) 721-2155   *SIC* 5531
R J J HOLDINGS LTD   *p*599
44 LIVINGSTON AVE SUITE 40, GRIMSBY,
ON, L3M 1L1
(905) 945-5441   *SIC* 5531
RACETTE, J. P. INC   *p*1347
557 RUE SAINT-LOUIS, SAINT-LIN-
LAURENTIDES, QC, J5M 2X2
(450) 439-2006   *SIC* 5531
RADAR AUTO PARTS INC   *p*544
20 KING ST, CLINTON, ON, N0M 1L0
(519) 482-3445   *SIC* 5531
RALPH'S AUTO SUPPLY (B.C.) LTD *p*256
12011 MITCHELL RD, RICHMOND, BC,
V6V 1M7
(604) 572-5747   *SIC* 5531
RAPID ELECTRIC VEHICLES INC   *p*285
1570 CLARK DR, VANCOUVER, BC, V5L
3L3
SIC 5531
RELAIS   *p*1374
260 RUE LEGER, SHERBROOKE, QC, J1L
1Y5
(819) 566-7317   *SIC* 5531
**RELAIS PNEUS FREINS ET SUSPENSIONS
INC, LE**   *p*1375
4255 BOUL BOURQUE, SHERBROOKE,
QC, J1N 1S4
(819) 566-7722   *SIC* 5531
RICHARD REINDERS SALES LTD   *p*204
1100 VICTORIA AVE N SUITE 395, CRAN-
BROOK, BC, V1C 6G7
(250) 489-3300   *SIC* 5531
RIDETONES INC   *p*1007
161 ROGER ST, WATERLOO, ON, N2J 1B1
(519) 745-8887   *SIC* 5531
ROBERT G. AYLWARD SALES LTD   *p*422
4 MURPHY SQ UNIT 185, CORNER
BROOK, NL, A2H 1R4
(709) 634-8531   *SIC* 5531
ROSS DREY LIMITED   *p*1015
155 CONSUMERS DR, WHITBY, ON, L1N
1C4
(905) 668-5828   *SIC* 5531
ROSSDREY LTD   *p*1422
2965 GORDON RD SUITE 65, REGINA, SK,
S4S 6H7
(306) 585-1355   *SIC* 5531
RUBIN, MARILYN D. SALES & SERVICE INC
*p*597
35430 HURON RD RR 2 SUITE 2,
GODERICH, ON, N7A 3X8
(519) 524-2121   *SIC* 5531

RYAN, D.C. SALES INC p567
1002 BROAD ST E, DUNNVILLE, ON, N1A 2Z2
(905) 774-2545 SIC 5531

SALKELD, C. & S. ENTERPRISES LTD p842
1200 LANSDOWNE ST W SUITE 81, PETERBOROUGH, ON, K9J 2A1
(705) 742-0406 SIC 5531

SAMETCO AUTO INC p375
233 PORTAGE AVE SUITE 200, WINNIPEG, MB, R3B 2A7
(204) 925-7278 SIC 5531

SANDY MCTYRE RETAIL LTD p657
1125 WELLINGTON RD, LONDON, ON, N6E 1M1
(519) 681-2655 SIC 5531

SASKATOON WHOLESALE TIRE LTD p1430
2705 WENTZ AVE, SASKATOON, SK, S7K 4B6
(306) 244-9512 SIC 5531

SCHMIDT, JACK SUPPLIES LIMITED p889
1063 TALBOT ST UNIT 25, ST THOMAS, ON, N5P 1G4
(519) 631-4910 SIC 5531

SCOTIA TIRE SERVICES LIMITED p457
267 BEDFORD HWY, HALIFAX, NS, B3M 2K5
(902) 443-3150 SIC 5531

SEARS, WC HOLDINGS INC p422
27 MANITOBA DR, CLARENVILLE, NL, A5A 1K3
(709) 466-8080 SIC 5531

SELLORS, ERIC R. HOLDINGS LIMITED p769
1019 SHEPPARD AVE E SUITE 4, NORTH YORK, ON, M2K 1C2
(416) 226-4415 SIC 5531

SEMEGEN, MICHEL HOLDINGS LTD p400
75 TWO NATIONS XG SUITE 337, FREDERICTON, NB, E3A 0T3
(506) 450-8933 SIC 5531

SERVICE DE PNEU K & S KELLY INC p1108
627 RUE AUGUSTE-MONDOUX, GATINEAU, QC, J9J 3K2
(819) 600-1061 SIC 5531

SERVICE DE PNEUS AUCLAIR INC p1268
3755 BOUL WILFRID-HAMEL, QUEBEC, QC, G1P 2J4
(418) 871-6740 SIC 5531

SERVICES DE PNEUS DESHARNAIS INC p1265
710 BOUL CHAREST O, QUEBEC, QC, G1N 2C1
(418) 681-6041 SIC 5531

SHIRLEY, STEWART A ENTERPRISES LIMITED p438
133 CHURCH ST SUITE 1, ANTIGONISH, NS, B2G 2E3
(902) 863-4753 SIC 5531

SIDNEY TIRE LTD p268
9817 RESTHAVEN DR, SIDNEY, BC, V8L 3E7
(250) 656-5544 SIC 5531

SKELLY, ROBERT E. LIMITED p1019
5415 TECUMSEH RD E, WINDSOR, ON, N8T 1C5
(519) 948-8111 SIC 5531

SOEHNER SALES LIMITED p438
152 ALBION ST S, AMHERST, NS, B4H 4H4
(902) 667-7218 SIC 5531

SPACE AGE TIRE LTD p358
8 PTH 52 W, STEINBACH, MB, R5G 1X7
(204) 326-6039 SIC 5531

SPINELLI HONDA p1126
220 BOUL MONTREAL-TORONTO, LACHINE, QC, H8S 1B8
(514) 637-6565 SIC 5531

ST-HYACINTHE CHRYSLER JEEP DODGE INC p1313
1155 BOUL CHOQUETTE, SAINT-HYACINTHE, QC, J2S 0C4
(450) 924-0568 SIC 5531

SUN COUNTRY HIGHWAY LTD p520
76000 LONDON RD RR 1, BRUCEFIELD,

ON, N0M 1J0
(866) 467-6920 SIC 5531

SUNSTRUM, GARRY W. SALES LIMITED p484
341 HASTINGS ST N RR 2 SUITE 130, BANCROFT, ON, K0L 1C0
(613) 332-0145 SIC 5531

T & L GREGORINI ENTERPRISES INC p284
8238 3B HWY, TRAIL, BC, V1R 4W4
(250) 364-3333 SIC 5531

TALKA ENTERPRISES LTD p576
1608 THE QUEENSWAY, ETOBICOKE, ON, M8Z 1V1
(416) 255-5531 SIC 5531

TALLON, DENNIS M. & ASSOCIATES INC p476
400 MAIN ST S, ALEXANDRIA, ON, K0C 1A0
(613) 525-2383 SIC 5531

TALLON, TIMOTHY J SALES INC p994
2129 ST CLAIR AVE W SUITE 182, TORONTO, ON, M6N 5B4
(416) 766-8141 SIC 5531

TCBC HOLDINGS INC p229
26712 BLOUCESTER WAY SUITE 203, LANGLEY, BC, V3W 3V6
(604) 626-4412 SIC 5531

TEX-DON LTD p751
2135 ROBERTSON RD, NEPEAN, ON, K2H 5Z2
(613) 829-9580 SIC 5531

TIGER AUTO PARTS INC p869
117 SINNOTT RD, SCARBOROUGH, ON, M1L 4S6
(888) 664-6618 SIC 5531

TIRE RECYCLING ATLANTIC CANADA CORPORATION p405
149 INDUSTRIAL PARK RD, MINTO, NB, E4B 3A6
(506) 327-4355 SIC 5531

TIRECRAFT EDMONTON TRUCK CENTRE INC p103
17803 118 AVE NW, EDMONTON, AB, T5S 1L6
(780) 452-4481 SIC 5531

TIRECRAFT WESTERN CANADA LTD p94
14404 128 AVE NW, EDMONTON, AB, T5L 3H6
(780) 509-1664 SIC 5531

TOM MARA ENTERPRISE LIMITED p463
699 WESTVILLE RD, NEW GLASGOW, NS, B2H 2J6
(902) 755-5581 SIC 5531

TOUCHETTE PNEUS & MECANIQUE p1397
4101 BOUL CHAMPLAIN, VERDUN, QC, H4G 1A6
(514) 766-4291 SIC 5531

TOYO TIRE CANADA INC p258
7791 NELSON RD UNIT 120, RICHMOND, BC, V6W 1G3
(604) 304-1941 SIC 5531

TRAVALE TIRE & SERVICE INC p611
340 WENTWORTH ST N, HAMILTON, ON, L8L 5W3
(905) 777-8473 SIC 5531

TREMBLAY, C.J. INVESTMENTS INC p714
900 SOUTHDOWN RD, MISSISSAUGA, ON, L5J 2Y4
(905) 822-6234 SIC 5531

TRUCK OUTFITTERS INC, THE p119
6525 GATEWAY BLVD NW, EDMONTON, AB, T6H 2J1
(780) 439-2360 SIC 5531

UAP/NAPA AUTO PARTS INC p409
325 EDINBURGH DR, MONCTON, NB, E1E 4A6
(506) 857-1111 SIC 5531

ULTIMATE DRIVING COMPANY INC, THE p431
120 KENMOUNT RD, ST. JOHN'S, NL, A1B 3R2
(709) 754-3269 SIC 5531

UNI-SELECT QUEBEC INC p1068
170 BOUL INDUSTRIEL, BOUCHERVILLE,

QC, J4B 2X3
(450) 641-2440 SIC 5531

UNITED MALWOOD MERCHANTS INC p626
8181 CAMPEAU DR SUITE 457, KANATA, ON, K2T 1B7
(613) 599-5105 SIC 5531

VALIFF SALES INC p830
1660 CARLING AVE SUITE 290, OTTAWA, ON, K2A 1C5
(613) 725-3111 SIC 5531

VANDERVAART SALES & SERVICE LTD p565
409 GOVERNMENT ST, DRYDEN, ON, P8N 2P4
(807) 223-4026 SIC 5531

VANZUYLEN'S ALIGNMENT SERVICE LIMITED p630
213 CONCESSION ST, KINGSTON, ON, K7K 2B6
(613) 548-7444 SIC 5531

VOLCO ENTERPRISES LTD p257
12291 BRIDGEPORT RD, RICHMOND, BC, V6V 1J4
(604) 270-4727 SIC 5531

W. GORDON INC p1222
2125 BOUL CAVENDISH, MONTREAL, QC, H4B 2Y2
(514) 481-7771 SIC 5531

W.J. PARISEAU SALES LTD p436
328 OLD AIRPORT RD, YELLOWKNIFE, NT, X1A 3T3
(867) 873-2403 SIC 5531

WAI CANADA INC p1003
535 MILLWAY AVE SUITE 1, VAUGHAN, ON, L4K 3V4
(905) 660-7274 SIC 5531

WAKEHAM TAYLOR HOLDINGS INC p578
5363 DUNDAS ST W, ETOBICOKE, ON, M9B 1B1
SIC 5531

WAL-MART CANADA CORP p227
20202 66 AVE, LANGLEY, BC, V2Y 1P3
(604) 539-5210 SIC 5531

WALDIE, D.S. HOLDINGS INCORPORATED p278
8140 120 ST, SURREY, BC, V3W 3N3
SIC 5531

WARD TIRES, INC p13
3307 48 AVE SE, CALGARY, AB, T2B 2Y8
(403) 273-0202 SIC 5531

WARDELL, A & M SALES LTD p167
6607 50 AVE, STETTLER, AB, T0C 2L2
(403) 742-8319 SIC 5531

WAYNE'S TIRE WAREHOUSE LTD p117
4717 99 ST NW, EDMONTON, AB, T6E 4Y1
(780) 437-4555 SIC 5531

WEAVER, J & D HOLDINGS LTD p333
3993 CEDAR HILL RD, VICTORIA, BC, V8N 4M9
(250) 721-1125 SIC 5531

WEICKERT, C & R ENTERPRISES LTD p457
10 RADCLIFFE DR SUITE 465, HALIFAX, NS, B3M 4K7
(902) 823-2499 SIC 5531

WEST END TIRE (1990) LTD p367
1991 DUGALD RD, WINNIPEG, MB, R2J 0H3
(204) 663-9037 SIC 5531

WILLIAMS, DAVE & PAT SALES LTD p274
13665 102 AVE SUITE 489, SURREY, BC, V3T 1N7
(604) 583-8473 SIC 5531

WOOD AUTOMOTIVE GROUP p71
11580 24 ST SE, CALGARY, AB, T2Z 3K1
(403) 640-8494 SIC 5531

WRANK ENTERPRISES LTD p1026
3920 DOUGALL AVE, WINDSOR, ON, N9G 1X2
(519) 966-3650 SIC 5531

YOKOHAMA TIRE (CANADA) INC p226
9325 200 ST SUITE 500, LANGLEY, BC, V1M 3A7
(604) 546-9656 SIC 5531

YOUNG, J. & S. MERCHANTS LTD p1009

656 ERB ST W, WATERLOO, ON, N2T 2Z7
(519) 884-1255 SIC 5531

ZYWOT, T. HOLDINGS LIMITED p748
476 CENTRE ST N, NAPANEE, ON, K7R 1P8
(613) 354-2222 SIC 5531

SIC 5541 Gasoline service stations

1008803 ONTARIO LTD p1000
4780 HIGHWAY 7 E, UNIONVILLE, ON, L3R 1M8
(905) 477-2003 SIC 5541

1085453 ONTARIO LTD p623
2054 JOYCEVILLE RD, JOYCEVILLE, ON, K0H 1Y0
(613) 546-5025 SIC 5541

1107078 ONTARIO INC p773
4021 YONGE ST, NORTH YORK, ON, M2P 1N6
(416) 223-0837 SIC 5541

1126194 ONTARIO LIMITED p528
1150 GUELPH LINE, BURLINGTON, ON, L7P 2S8
(905) 335-5595 SIC 5541

1162095 ALBERTA LTD p5
5204 50 ST, BEAUMONT, AB, T4X 1E5
(780) 929-6466 SIC 5541

1197767 ONTARIO LTD p597
2536 BANK ST, GLOUCESTER, ON, K1T 1M9
(613) 260-7331 SIC 5541

1211084 ONTARIO LTD p490
6521 HWY 62, BELLEVILLE, ON, K8N 4Z5
(613) 968-6811 SIC 5541

1213475 ONTARIO INC p811
4358 INNES RD, ORLEANS, ON, K4A 3W3
(613) 834-6533 SIC 5541

1249932 ONTARIO INC p547
1514 STEELES AVE W, CONCORD, ON, L4K 2P7
(905) 738-0338 SIC 5541

1319691 ONTARIO INCORPORATED p651
1845 ADELAIDE ST N, LONDON, ON, N5X 0E3
(519) 660-1205 SIC 5541

1435207 ONTARIO INC p496
2305 HIGHWAY 2, BOWMANVILLE, ON, L1C 3K7
(905) 623-8521 SIC 5541

1461148 ONTARIO CORP p918
8 THORNCLIFFE PARK DR, TORONTO, ON, M4H 1H4
(416) 421-3723 SIC 5541

1475541 ONTARIO LTD p547
2651 RUTHERFORD RD, CONCORD, ON, L4K 2N6
(905) 856-0662 SIC 5541

1491222 ONTARIO LTD p796
450 DUNDAS ST E, OAKVILLE, ON, L6H 7L4
(905) 257-5185 SIC 5541

1498403 ONTARIO LTD p1018
7400 TECUMSEH RD E, WINDSOR, ON, N8T 1E9
(519) 974-7116 SIC 5541

1514660 ONTARIO INC p826
2498 BANK ST, OTTAWA, ON, K1V 8S2
(613) 523-2027 SIC 5541

1530460 ONTARIO INC p762
390 LAKESHORE DR SUITE 7, NORTH BAY, ON, P1A 2C7
(705) 476-1230 SIC 5541

1535477 ONTARIO LIMITED p619
GD, HEARST, ON, P0L 1N0
(705) 362-4085 SIC 5541

1553690 ONTARIO INC p652
277 HIGHBURY AVE N, LONDON, ON, N5Z 2W8
(519) 455-0329 SIC 5541

1579149 ONTARIO LTD p1006
106 BRIDGEPORT RD E, WATERLOO, ON, N2J 2J9

(519) 746-0139   *SIC* 5541
2041188 ONTARIO INC   *p718*
2632 CREDIT VALLEY RD, MISSISSAUGA, ON, L5M 4J6
(647) 986-0000   *SIC* 5541
2097738 ONTARIO INC   *p591*
1637 PETTIT RD, FORT ERIE, ON, L2A 5M4
  SIC 5541
2116160 ONTARIO INC   *p685*
7355 GOREWAY DR, MISSISSAUGA, ON, L4T 2T8
(905) 405-0881   *SIC* 5541
2124964 ONTARIO INC   *p511*
471 MAIN ST S, BRAMPTON, ON, L6Y 1N6
(905) 451-6489   *SIC* 5541
22 ENTERPRISES LTD   *p262*
11131 NO. 5 RD, RICHMOND, BC, V7A 4E8
(604) 204-0047   *SIC* 5541
2714159 CANADA INC   *p850*
44 EAST BEAVER CREEK RD UNIT 16, RICHMOND HILL, ON, L4B 1G8
(905) 886-5432   *SIC* 5541
2792924 MANITOBA LTD   *p373*
228 ISABEL ST, WINNIPEG, MB, R3A 1G9
  SIC 5541
3025906 NOVA SCOTIA LIMITED   *p456*
6389 QUINPOOL RD, HALIFAX, NS, B3L 1A6
(902) 424-1397   *SIC* 5541
327989 BC LTD   *p218*
1271 SALISH RD, KAMLOOPS, BC, V2H 1P6
(250) 828-1515   *SIC* 5541
4-HOWELL BROTHERS INC   *p718*
3030 ARTESIAN DR, MISSISSAUGA, ON, L5M 7P5
(905) 828-5926   *SIC* 5541
413877 ALBERTA LTD   *p134*
4703 50 AVE UNIT A, GRASSLAND, AB, T0A 1V0
(780) 525-2295   *SIC* 5541
470695 BC LTD   *p252*
2712 ISLAND HWY W, QUALICUM BEACH, BC, V9K 2C4
(250) 752-3111   *SIC* 5541
4TH & BURRARD ESSO SERVICE   *p320*
1790 4TH AVE W, VANCOUVER, BC, V6J 1M1
  SIC 5541
5195684 MANITOBA INC   *p392*
3357 PEMBINA HWY, WINNIPEG, MB, R3V 1A2
(204) 261-3014   *SIC* 5541
6132511 CANADA LTD   *p1405*
GD, DAVIDSON, SK, S0G 1A0
(306) 567-3222   *SIC* 5541
6842071 CANADA INC   *p168*
436 RIDGE RD SUITE 1, STRATHMORE, AB, T1P 1B5
  SIC 5541
846840 ALBERTA LTD   *p165*
174 ST ALBERT TRAIL, ST. ALBERT, AB, T8N 0P7
(780) 418-1165   *SIC* 5541
9035-2022 QUEBEC INC   *p1358*
546 3E RANG BUREAU 3, SAINTE-HELENE-DE-BAGOT, QC, J0H 1M0
(450) 791-2304   *SIC* 5541
9050-6015 QUEBEC INC   *p1083*
500 BOUL DES LAURENTIDES, COTE SAINT-LUC, QC, H7G 2V1
  SIC 5541
9081-9012 QUEBEC INC   *p1403*
4 RUE SAINTE-ANNE, YAMACHICHE, QC, G0X 3L0
(819) 228-5620   *SIC* 5541
908593 ONTARIO LIMITED   *p911*
3613 QUEEN'S LINE, TILBURY, ON, N0P 2L0
(519) 682-3235   *SIC* 5541
9109-9861 QUEBEC INC   *p1061*
2525 BOUL DE LA GRANDE-ALLEE, BOIS-BRIAND, QC, J7H 1E3

(450) 430-4475   *SIC* 5541
963618 ALBERTA LTD   *p84*
13205 97 ST NW, EDMONTON, AB, T5E 4C7
(780) 478-7833   *SIC* 5541
ABHAY ENTERPRISES LTD   *p199*
1401 JOHNSON ST, COQUITLAM, BC, V3E 3J3
(604) 464-1347   *SIC* 5541
ACTTON SUPER-SAVE GAS STATIONS LTD   *p271*
19395 LANGLEY BYPASS, SURREY, BC, V3S 6K1
(604) 533-4423   *SIC* 5541
ARCHEAN ENERGY LTD   *p43*
324 8 AVE SW SUITE 1000, CALGARY, AB, T2P 2Z2
(403) 237-9600   *SIC* 5541
ARMSTRONG REGIONAL CO-OPERATIVE *p179*
973 OTTER LAKE CROSS RD, ARMSTRONG, BC, V0E 1B6
(250) 546-9438   *SIC* 5541
ARROWHEAD DEVELOPMENT CORPORATION   *p349*
101 YELLOWQUILL TRAIL W, EDWIN, MB, R0H 0G0
(204) 252-2731   *SIC* 5541
ASHERN GARAGE LTD   *p345*
2 MAIN ST, ASHERN, MB, R0C 0E0
(204) 768-2835   *SIC* 5541
ASPEN-DUNHILL HOLDINGS LTD   *p880*
HIGHWAY 2 W SUITE 6, SHANNONVILLE, ON, K0K 3A0
(613) 966-6895   *SIC* 5541
ATRC ENTERPRISES   *p165*
5005 42 ST SS 2, ST PAUL, AB, T0A 3A2
(780) 645-3227   *SIC* 5541
BENEDICT HOLDINGS LTD   *p165*
390 ST ALBERT TRAIL, ST. ALBERT, AB, T8N 5J9
(780) 459-5447   *SIC* 5541
BENICK SERVICES INC   *p394*
170 AULAC RD, AULAC, NB, E4L 2X2
(506) 536-1339   *SIC* 5541
BENNETT'S LIMITED   *p424*
165 HAMILTON RIVER RD, HAPPY VALLEY-GOOSE BAY, NL, A0P 1E0
(709) 896-5024   *SIC* 5541
BLACK TOP CABS LTD   *p326*
777 PACIFIC ST, VANCOUVER, BC, V6Z 2R7
(604) 683-4567   *SIC* 5541
BLUEWAVE ENERGY LTD   *p445*
30 OLAND CRT, DARTMOUTH, NS, B3B 1V2
(902) 481-0515   *SIC* 5541
BRI-AL FISHER SERVICES INC   *p883*
1678 ERB'S RD, ST AGATHA, ON, N0B 2L0
(519) 747-1606   *SIC* 5541
BTK INVESTMENTS LIMITED   *p409*
2600 MOUNTAIN RD, MONCTON, NB, E1G 3T6
(506) 859-6000   *SIC* 5541
BUFFALO RIVER MINI MART & GAS BAR INC   *p1405*
GD, DILLON, SK, S0M 0S0
(306) 282-2177   *SIC* 5541
C & G VILLAGE INN   *p353*
2193 HWY 59, NIVERVILLE, MB, R0A 1E0
(204) 388-4283   *SIC* 5541
CAMIONS FREIGHTLINER STERLING DRUMMONDVILLE INC   *p1096*
5770 PLACE KUBOTA BUREAU 4, DRUMMONDVILLE, QC, J2B 6V4
(819) 474-2264   *SIC* 5541
CAN-AM TRAVEL STOPS INC   *p1438*
1203 HWY 1, WHITEWOOD, SK, S0G 5C0
(306) 735-2565   *SIC* 5541
CANADIAN METAL AND FIBRE LTD   *p343*
1392 JOHNSTON RD, WHITE ROCK, BC, V4B 3Z2
(604) 535-2793   *SIC* 5541
CANADIAN TIRE   *p678*

7650 MARKHAM RD, MARKHAM, ON, L3S 4S1
(905) 472-1638   *SIC* 5541
CANADIAN TIRE   *p806*
1550 SIMMONS, ODESSA, ON, K0H 2H0
(613) 386-3457   *SIC* 5541
CANADIAN TIRE   *p1438*
277 BROADWAY ST E SUITE 287, YORKTON, SK, S3N 3G7
(306) 783-9744   *SIC* 5541
CANADIAN TIRE ASSOCIATE STORE *p814*
1333 WILSON RD N SUITE 336, OSHAWA, ON, L1K 2B8
(905) 433-5575   *SIC* 5541
CANADIAN TIRE GAS BAR   *p908*
943 FORT WILLIAM RD, THUNDER BAY, ON, P7B 3A6
(807) 346-8070   *SIC* 5541
CANADIAN TRUCKSTOPS LTD   *p12*
2515 50 AVE SE, CALGARY, AB, T2B 3R8
(403) 236-2515   *SIC* 5541
CANSO FORD SALES (2005) LIMITED *p464*
9 MACINTOSH RD, PORT HAWKESBURY, NS, B9A 3K4
(902) 625-1338   *SIC* 5541
CARLING PROPANE INC   *p620*
19752 HOLLAND LANDING RD UNIT 201, HOLLAND LANDING, ON, L9N 0A1
(905) 952-0146   *SIC* 5541
CHAVES GAS BARS LIMITED   *p533*
31 DUNDAS ST S, CAMBRIDGE, ON, N1R 8N9
(519) 622-1301   *SIC* 5541
CHENIER MOTORS LTD   *p913*
1276 RIVERSIDE DR, TIMMINS, ON, P4R 1A4
(705) 264-9528   *SIC* 5541
CO DARA VENTURES LTD   *p243*
5500 CLEMENTS CRES SUITE 80, PEACHLAND, BC, V0H 1X5
(250) 767-9054   *SIC* 5541
CO-OP, REGINA GAS BAR   *p1422*
4705 GORDON RD, REGINA, SK, S4W 0B7
(306) 791-9388   *SIC* 5541
COPPER BAY HOLDINGS INC   *p520*
9 BENNETT ST, BRUCE MINES, ON, P0R 1C0
(705) 785-3506   *SIC* 5541
COUCHE-TARD INC   *p1233*
4204 BOUL INDUSTRIEL, MONTREAL, QC, H7L 0E3
(450) 662-6632   *SIC* 5541
COUNTRY CROSS ROADS SERVICE *p1437*
GD, WAKAW, SK, S0K 4P0
(306) 233-5553   *SIC* 5541
CRAWFORD MARINE SERVICES   *p286*
2985 VIRTUAL WAY SUITE 280, VANCOUVER, BC, V5M 4X7
(604) 436-2277   *SIC* 5541
CREE WAY GAS WEST LTD   *p1432*
2511 22ND ST W, SASKATOON, SK, S7M 0V9
(306) 975-0125   *SIC* 5541
CREE-WAY GAS LTD   *p1433*
343 PACKHAM AVE, SASKATOON, SK, S7N 4S1
(306) 955-8823   *SIC* 5541
CROSSROADS ESSO   *p639*
593 VICTORIA ST N, KITCHENER, ON, N2H 5E9
(519) 741-0424   *SIC* 5541
D'ENTREMONT, PAUL MARINE LTD   *p470*
2616 HWY 3, WEST PUBNICO, NS, B0W 3S0
(902) 762-3301   *SIC* 5541
DAMAR HOLDINGS LTD   *p1410*
1920 HWY 6 S, MELFORT, SK, S0E 1A0
(306) 752-9066   *SIC* 5541
DARVIC ENTERPRISES LTD   *p340*
2435 MILLSTREAM RD, VICTORIA, BC, V9B 3R5
(250) 391-6082   *SIC* 5541
DASKO HOLDINGS LTD   *p220*
1830 UNDERHILL ST, KELOWNA, BC, V1X

5P8
(250) 862-5242   *SIC* 5541
DIAMO ENTERPRISES INC   *p502*
1795 STEELES AVE E, BRAMPTON, ON, L6T 4L5
(905) 792-7108   *SIC* 5541
DOMO GASOLINE CORPORATION LTD *p377*
270 FORT ST, WINNIPEG, MB, R3C 1E5
(204) 943-5920   *SIC* 5541
DRUMMOND FUELS (OTTAWA) LTD   *p749*
30 RIDEAU HEIGHTS DR, NEPEAN, ON, K2E 7A6
(613) 226-4444   *SIC* 5541
DRYDEN TRUCK STOP INC   *p565*
GD LCD MAIN, DRYDEN, ON, P8N 2Y6
(807) 223-2085   *SIC* 5541
DSM INVESTMENTS INC   *p194*
959 TRANS CANADA HWY S, CACHE CREEK, BC, V0K 1H0
(250) 457-9312   *SIC* 5541
EAGLE BUTTE CROSSING (TEMPO)   *p83*
7 3RD AVE E, DUNMORE, AB, T0J 1A1
(403) 526-6552   *SIC* 5541
EAST LAKE HUSKY MARKET TRUCK STOP   *p15*
5225 106 AVE SE, CALGARY, AB, T2C 5N2
(403) 236-5225   *SIC* 5541
EASTON'S 28 SERVICE CENTRE LTD *p669*
3100 STEELES AVE E SUITE 401, MARKHAM, ON, L3R 8T3
(905) 940-9409   *SIC* 5541
EDDY'S RESTAURANT SERVICES LTD *p427*
GD, SOUTH BROOK GB, NL, A0J 1S0
(709) 657-2590   *SIC* 5541
ENCANA CORPORATION   *p134*
11040 70 AVE, GRANDE PRAIRIE, AB, T8W 2M2
(780) 539-4422   *SIC* 5541
ENGLISH RIVER ENTERPRISES INC *p1405*
2553 GRASSWOOD RD E, CORMAN PARK, SK, S7T 1C8
(306) 374-9181   *SIC* 5541
ENTREPRISES CLEMENT LAVOIE INC *p1082*
92 RUE SAINT-JACQUES S, COATICOOK, QC, J1A 2N8
(819) 849-6374   *SIC* 5541
ENTREPRISES ELAINE ROY INC, LES *p1260*
2600 RUE DE LA CONCORDE, QUEBEC, QC, G1L 6A5
(418) 621-9802   *SIC* 5541
ESSO SERVICE STATION   *p5*
THE TRANSCANADA HWY 1 SERVICE RD, BASSANO, AB, T0J 0B0
(403) 641-3916   *SIC* 5541
F C C REPAIRS   *p155*
7493 49 AVE CRES SUITE 5, RED DEER, AB, T4P 1X6
(403) 343-0092   *SIC* 5541
FIRST CHOICE TRUCK & CAR WASH INC *p173*
3530 KEPLER ST, WHITECOURT, AB, T7S 0B5
(780) 778-3377   *SIC* 5541
FLYING J CANADA INC   *p747*
628 COUNTY RD 41, NAPANEE, ON, K7R 3L1
(613) 354-7044   *SIC* 5541
G.A. VALLANCE HOLDINGS LIMITED *p226*
6312 200 ST SUITE 426, LANGLEY, BC, V2Y 1A1
(604) 532-4411   *SIC* 5541
G.M. PACE ENTERPRISES INC   *p211*
4801 TRANS CANADA HWY SUITE 3, DUNCAN, BC, V9L 6L3
(250) 246-4448   *SIC* 5541
GALE'S GAS BARS LIMITED   *p757*
4388 PORTAGE RD, NIAGARA FALLS, ON, L2E 6A4
(905) 356-4820   *SIC* 5541
GARAGE CLEMENT FOURNIER INC *p1138*
4560 BOUL GUILLAUME-COUTURE,

LEVIS, QC, G6W 6M7
(418) 837-0859 *SIC* 5541
GAS KING OIL CO. LTD   *p142*
1604 2 AVE S, LETHBRIDGE, AB, T1J 0G2
(403) 320-2142 *SIC* 5541
GRA HAM ENERGY LIMITED   *p888*
88 QUEEN ST W, ST MARYS, ON, N4X 1A9
(519) 284-3420 *SIC* 5541
GRAEME'S AUTO SERVICE   *p81*
PO BOX 115, DELBURNE, AB, T0M 0V0
(403) 318-6088 *SIC* 5541
GWAALAGAA NAAY CORPORATION *p252*
226 HWY 16, QUEEN CHARLOTTE, BC,
V0T 1S1
SIC 5541
H & I ENTERPRISES (VANKLEEK) LTD
p1001
21160 SERVICE RD, VANKLEEK HILL, ON,
K0B 1R0
(613) 525-2120 *SIC* 5541
HALTE DU BOIS INC   *p1134*
250 AUT FELIX-LECLERC, LAVALTRIE,
QC, J5T 3K4
SIC 5541
HANNAFIN, E.J. ENTERPRISES LIMITED
p491
57 CANNIFTON RD, BELLEVILLE, ON, K8N
4V1
(613) 966-7017 *SIC* 5541
HERLE'S HOLDINGS LTD   *p144*
6214 50 AVE, LLOYDMINSTER, AB, T9V
2C9
(780) 875-3422 *SIC* 5541
HUNTER'S ONE STOP LTD   *p398*
2046 ROUTE 690, DOUGLAS HARBOUR,
NB, E4B 1Y7
(506) 385-2292 *SIC* 5541
HUNTING ENERGY SERVICES (CANADA)
LTD   *p23*
5550 SKYLINE WAY NE, CALGARY, AB,
T2E 7Z7
(403) 543-4477 *SIC* 5541
J.D. FOX ENTERPRISES INC   *p1038*
141 ABEGWEIT BLVD, BORDEN-
CARLETON, PE, C0B 1X0
(902) 437-2600 *SIC* 5541
J.D.I. VENTURES LIMITED   *p460*
957 CENTRAL AVE, KINGSTON, NS, B0P
1R0
SIC 5541
JCF AUTO SPORT   *p1394*
904 RTE HARWOOD, VAUDREUIL-
DORION, QC, J7V 8P2
SIC 5541
JOHN SK LTD   *p487*
151 MAPLEVIEW DR W, BARRIE, ON, L4N
9E8
(705) 734-0819 *SIC* 5541
JUTZI, D.H. LIMITED   *p896*
279 LORNE AVE E, STRATFORD, ON, N5A
6S4
(519) 271-9831 *SIC* 5541
KARISS ENTERPRISES LIMITED   *p426*
65 CLYDE AVE, MOUNT PEARL, NL, A1N
4R8
(709) 745-3403 *SIC* 5541
KAST HOLDINGS INC   *p1422*
2020 COLEMAN CRES, REGINA, SK, S4V
3B9
(306) 721-3335 *SIC* 5541
KB HOLDINGS LTD   *p217*
411 10TH AVE, KAMLOOPS, BC, V2C 6J8
(250) 372-1734 *SIC* 5541
KIANI MOTORS LTD   *p241*
1980 MARINE DR, NORTH VANCOUVER,
BC, V7P 1V6
(604) 987-4490 *SIC* 5541
KISA ENTERPRISES LTD   *p240*
2305 LONSDALE AVE, NORTH VANCOU-
VER, BC, V7M 2K9
(604) 986-0288 *SIC* 5541
KITSUMKALUM TEMPLE GAS BAR   *p283*
14309 HWY 16E, TERRACE, BC, V8G 0A6
(250) 635-0017 *SIC* 5541

KOCA AB SERVICES LTD   *p5*
610 HWY 9, BEISEKER, AB, T0M 0G0
(403) 947-0006 *SIC* 5541
KTW HOLDINGS LTD   *p252*
580 HIGHWAY W, PRINCETON, BC, V0X
1W0
(250) 372-0451 *SIC* 5541
LAWDAN INVESTMENTS LTD   *p331*
683 COMMONAGE RD, VERNON, BC, V1H
1G3
(250) 542-1707 *SIC* 5541
LEDUC CO-OP LTD   *p139*
5403 50 ST, LEDUC, AB, T9E 6Z7
(780) 986-3036 *SIC* 5541
LOVELY IMPORTS & RETAILS LTD   *p783*
3720 KEELE ST, NORTH YORK, ON, M3J
2V9
(416) 636-0568 *SIC* 5541
LOVELY IMPORTS & RETAILS LTD   *p786*
2205 JANE ST, NORTH YORK, ON, M3M
1A5
(416) 248-9814 *SIC* 5541
MAILLETTE HOLDINGS INC   *p606*
80 IMPERIAL RD S, GUELPH, ON, N1K 2A1
(519) 822-2175 *SIC* 5541
MANITOWABI, ANDREW GROUP   *p1016*
2174 WIKWEMIKONG WAY, WIK-
WEMIKONG, ON, P0P 2J0
(705) 859-3788 *SIC* 5541
MAZENC FUELS LTD   *p1416*
529 E 1ST AVE, REGINA, SK, S4N 4Z3
(306) 721-6667 *SIC* 5541
MCKEOWN, WILLIAM MOTOR SALES LIM-
ITED   *p883*
2589 SPRINGBROOK RD, SPRING-
BROOK, ON, K0K 3C0
(613) 395-3883 *SIC* 5541
MIKE'S ONE STOP INC   *p607*
229 RORKE AVE S, HAILEYBURY, ON, P0J
1K0
(705) 672-3667 *SIC* 5541
MOULTON, RALPH HOLDINGS LTD   *p545*
1125 ELGIN ST W, COBOURG, ON, K9A
5T9
(905) 372-8781 *SIC* 5541
MR. GAS LIMITED   *p810*
1420 YOUVILLE DR SUITE 1, ORLEANS,
ON, K1C 7B3
(613) 824-6777 *SIC* 5541
MUNN ENTERPRISES LTD   *p186*
1969 WILLINGDON AVE, BURNABY, BC,
V5C 5J3
(604) 299-1124 *SIC* 5541
NEEPAWA-GLADSTONE COOPERATIVE
LIMITED   *p353*
32 MAIN ST E, NEEPAWA, MB, R0J 1H0
(204) 476-2328 *SIC* 5541
NICOLANI SERVICES LTD   *p216*
995 ARLINGTON CRT, KAMLOOPS, BC,
V2B 8T5
(250) 372-0451 *SIC* 5541
NISKU TRUCK STOP LTD   *p139*
8020 SPARROW DR SUITE 201, LEDUC,
AB, T9E 7G3
(780) 986-5312 *SIC* 5541
NOCO CANADA INC   *p579*
133 THE WEST MALL UNIT 11, ETOBI-
COKE, ON, M9C 1C2
(416) 232-6626 *SIC* 5541
NRZ INVESTMENTS INC   *p659*
491 OXFORD ST W, LONDON, ON, N6H
1T2
(519) 472-5410 *SIC* 5541
OBOR HOLDINGS LTD   *p216*
228 TRANQUILLE RD, KAMLOOPS, BC,
V2B 3G1
(250) 376-1710 *SIC* 5541
OCEANS RETAIL INVESTMENTS INC *p177*
2096 CLEARBROOK RD, ABBOTSFORD,
BC, V2T 2X2
(604) 852-1950 *SIC* 5541
OGILVIE, BRIAN HOLDING LTD   *p154*
88 HOWARTH ST SUITE 5, RED DEER, AB,
T4N 6V9

(403) 342-6307 *SIC* 5541
OSPREY TRUCK STOP   *p399*
2 MARTIN DR, EEL RIVER BAR FIRST NA-
TION, NB, E8C 3C7
(506) 685-8210 *SIC* 5541
OUELLET & JOBIN INC   *p1303*
50 RTE DE TADOUSSAC BUREAU 2,
SAINT-FULGENCE, QC, G0V 1S0
(418) 674-2811 *SIC* 5541
PBCN P.A. FUEL AND CONVENIENCE LIM-
ITED PARTNERSHIP   *p1414*
3451 2ND AVE W, PRINCE ALBERT, SK,
S6V 5G1
(306) 953-1490 *SIC* 5541
PC 96 HOLDINGS LTD   *p235*
2345 ISLAND HWY E, NANOOSE BAY, BC,
V9P 9E2
(250) 468-7441 *SIC* 5541
PELP LIMITED PARTNERSHIP   *p524*
1122 INTERNATIONAL BLVD SUITE 700,
BURLINGTON, ON, L7L 6Z8
(905) 639-2060 *SIC* 5541
PENINSULA CONSUMER SERVICES CO-
OPERATIVE   *p267*
2132 KEATING CROSS RD UNIT 1,
SAANICHTON, BC, V8M 2A6
(250) 652-5752 *SIC* 5541
PEPPERS HIGHWAY SERVICE INC   *p171*
HIGHWAY 28, WASKATENAU, AB, T0A 3P0
(780) 358-2644 *SIC* 5541
PETROLE LEGER INC   *p1120*
460 GRAND BOULEVARD, L'ILE-PERROT,
QC, J7V 4X5
(514) 453-5766 *SIC* 5541
PETROLES C.L. INC, LES   *p1316*
25 104 RTE, SAINT-JEAN-SUR-
RICHELIEU, QC, J2X 1H2
(450) 346-7555 *SIC* 5541
PETROSOL INC   *p1139*
1023 RUE RENAULT BUREAU 100, LEVIS,
QC, G6Z 1B6
(418) 647-3800 *SIC* 5541
PLACEMENTS M DROUIN INC, LES *p1305*
14920 BOUL LACROIX, SAINT-GEORGES,
QC, G5Y 1R6
(418) 228-0051 *SIC* 5541
POWER PLUS TECHNOLOGY INC   *p409*
2731 MOUNTAIN RD, MONCTON, NB, E1G
2W5
(506) 857-9212 *SIC* 5541
R M KOMAR ENTERPRISES LIMITED *p368*
1621 ST MARY'S RD, WINNIPEG, MB, R2M
3W8
(204) 254-4955 *SIC* 5541
RAYMOND BEAUSEJOUR (1989) INC *p1391*
202 3E AV, VAL-D'OR, QC, J9P 1R5
(819) 824-4185 *SIC* 5541
RED RIVER COOPERATIVE LTD   *p366*
10 PRAIRIE WAY, WINNIPEG, MB, R2J 3J8
(204) 631-4600 *SIC* 5541
RESEAU GLP & CIE INC   *p1283*
95 BOUL BRIEN, REPENTIGNY, QC, J6A
8B6
(450) 654-8787 *SIC* 5541
RESTAURANT-BAR LA ROCHELIERE INC
p1323
1370 RUE DU PONT, SAINT-LAMBERT-DE-
LAUZON, QC, G0S 2W0
(418) 889-0183 *SIC* 5541
ROADKING TRAVEL CENTRE STRATH-
CONA INC   *p163*
26 STRATHMOOR DR SUITE 164, SHER-
WOOD PARK, AB, T8H 2B6
(780) 417-9400 *SIC* 5541
ROYAL CANADIAN SECURITIES LIMITED
p379
320 GRAHAM AVE SUITE 800, WINNIPEG,
MB, R3C 0J7
(204) 947-2835 *SIC* 5541
RPM ENTERPRISES LTD   *p356*
395 MAIN ST, SELKIRK, MB, R1A 1T9
(204) 482-4131 *SIC* 5541
S & L PROPERTIES LTD   *p363*
605 REGENT AVE W, WINNIPEG, MB, R2C

1R9
(204) 222-9431 *SIC* 5541
S MALIK INVESTMENTS LTD   *p18*
8338 18 ST SE SUITE 432, CALGARY, AB,
T2C 4E4
(403) 236-2776 *SIC* 5541
SAC DRUMMOND INC   *p1306*
192 CH DE LA STATION, SAINT-GERMAIN-
DE-GRANTHAM, QC, J0C 1K0
(819) 395-4286 *SIC* 5541
SELKIRK CHEVROLET PONTIAC BUICK
GMC LTD   *p356*
1010 MANITOBA AVE, SELKIRK, MB, R1A
3T7
(204) 482-1010 *SIC* 5541
SHAW, JACK ENTERPRISES LIMITED
p1416
225 E 6TH AVE, REGINA, SK, S4N 6A6
(306) 545-5454 *SIC* 5541
SHELL CANADA LIMITED   *p520*
250 LAURIER BLVD, BROCKVILLE, ON,
K6V 5V7
(613) 498-5700 *SIC* 5541
SHELL O'TRENTE ENR   *p1290*
630 BOUL RIDEAU, ROUYN-NORANDA,
QC, J9X 7G1
(819) 764-3530 *SIC* 5541
SIMSAK CORPORATION   *p497*
133 HOLLAND ST E, BRADFORD, ON, L3Z
2A8
(905) 778-9600 *SIC* 5541
SIX PILLARS LTD   *p594*
375 MOUNTAINVIEW RD S, GEORGE-
TOWN, ON, L7G 5X3
(905) 873-9982 *SIC* 5541
STATION INNU ENR   *p1389*
100 BOUL DES MONTAGNAIS, UASHAT,
QC, G4R 5P9
(418) 968-4866 *SIC* 5541
STURGEON LAKE FINE FOODS & GAS
BAR   *p1436*
1 ECONOMIC LANE, STURGEON LAKE,
SK, S0J 2E1
(306) 764-1222 *SIC* 5541
SUPER SPLASH AUTO CLEANING LTD
p359
53 PTH 12 N, STEINBACH, MB, R5G 1T3
(204) 326-3474 *SIC* 5541
T C ENTERPRISES LTD   *p1437*
HWY 6 & 5 SW CORNER, WATSON, SK,
S0K 4V0
(306) 287-3636 *SIC* 5541
TAKBRO ENTERPRISES LIMITED   *p498*
10115 BRAMALEA RD, BRAMPTON, ON,
L6R 1W6
(905) 789-0753 *SIC* 5541
TALL TIMBER LTD   *p79*
GD, CARDSTON, AB, T0K 0K0
SIC 5541
TALLBOYS GRILL & PUB   *p357*
10 PTH 2, ST CLAUDE, MB, R0G 1Z0
(204) 379-2491 *SIC* 5541
TAXI COOP QUEBEC 525-5191   *p1261*
496 2E AV, QUEBEC, QC, G1L 3B1
(418) 525-4953 *SIC* 5541
TERRACE BAY ENTERPRISES LIMITED
p903
HWY 17 3 SIMCOE PLAZA, TERRACE BAY,
ON, P0T 2W0
(807) 825-3226 *SIC* 5541
TRANSCANADA PIPELINE USA LTD   *p62*
450 1 ST SW, CALGARY, AB, T2P 5H1
(403) 920-2000 *SIC* 5541
TRANSCANADA TRUCK STOP LTD   *p158*
1900 HWY DR S UNIT 2, REDCLIFF, AB,
T0J 2P0
(403) 548-7333 *SIC* 5541
TREATY ENTERPRISES   *p442*
600 CALDWELL RD, DARTMOUTH, NS,
B2V 2S8
(902) 434-7777 *SIC* 5541
TRI STAR GAS MART (1992) LTD   *p332*
3308 48 AVE, VERNON, BC, V1T 3R6
(250) 558-7800 *SIC* 5541

▲ Public Company   ■ Public Company Family Member   **HQ** Headquarters   **BR** Branch   **SL** Single Location

TUNCER TRADE INC *p685*
235 STEELES AVE E, MILTON, ON, L9T
1Y2
(905) 878-5829 *SIC 5541*

TURBOTRONICS *p1432*
230 29TH ST E, SASKATOON, SK, S7L 6Y6
(306) 242-7644 *SIC 5541*

UNIPETRO DIXIE INC *p733*
6035 MCLAUGHLIN RD, MISSISSAUGA,
ON, L5R 1B9
(905) 712-8800 *SIC 5541*

UPI INC *p604*
105 SILVERCREEK PKY N SUITE 200,
GUELPH, ON, N1H 8M1
(519) 821-2667 *SIC 5541*

UPLANDS MOTORING COMPANY LTD *p333*
3095 SHELBOURNE ST, VICTORIA, BC,
V8R 4M9
(250) 592-2444 *SIC 5541*

V.H. FUELS INC *p869*
1896 EGLINTON AVE E, SCARBOROUGH,
ON, M1L 2L9
(416) 751-8896 *SIC 5541*

VAL RITA TIRE SALES LTD *p1001*
96 GOVERNMENT RD, VAL RITA, ON, P0L
2G0
(705) 335-8496 *SIC 5541*

VAN DEN ELZEN DEVELOPMENTS LTD
p223
2949 PANDOSY ST SUITE 103, KELOWNA,
BC, V1Y 1W1
(250) 769-5315 *SIC 5541*

VICTORIA ST GAS BAR LTD *p640*
593 VICTORIA ST N, KITCHENER, ON,
N2H 5E9
(519) 741-0424 *SIC 5541*

VIRGIN & ALL SAINTS CO. LTD, THE *p1015*
1755 DUNDAS ST W, WHITBY, ON, L1P
1Y9
(905) 665-9270 *SIC 5541*

W.O. STINSON & SON LIMITED *p597*
4726 BANK ST, GLOUCESTER, ON, K1T
3W7
(613) 822-7400 *SIC 5541*

WEST EDMONTON TRUCKLAND LTD *p106*
16806 118 AVE NW, EDMONTON, AB, T5V
1M8
(780) 452-3532 *SIC 5541*

**WESTERN PETROLEUM NEWFOUND-
LAND LIMITED** *p427*
4 RIVERHEAD CENTER UNIT 2, RIVER-
HEAD HARBOUR GRACE, NL, A0A 3P0
(709) 596-4181 *SIC 5541*

**XPRESS FOOD AND GAS (MOOSE JAW)
LTD** *p1437*
1510 SOUTH SERVICE RD W, SWIFT
CURRENT, SK, S9H 3T1
(306) 773-6444 *SIC 5541*

YUKON TIRE CENTRE LTD *p1440*
107 INDUSTRIAL RD, WHITEHORSE, YT,
Y1A 2T7
(867) 667-6102 *SIC 5541*

SIC 5551 Boat dealers

9003-2723 QUEBEC INC *p1243*
576 131 RTE, NOTRE-DAME-DES-
PRAIRIES, QC, J6E 0M2
(450) 752-1224 *SIC 5551*

9147-8453 QUEBEC INC *p1371*
2325 RUE KING O, SHERBROOKE, QC,
J1J 2G2
(819) 566-8882 *SIC 5551*

BARRIE RECREATION LTD *p486*
65 HART DR, BARRIE, ON, L4N 5M3
(705) 733-2280 *SIC 5551*

BOULET LEMELIN YACHT INC *p1258*
1125 BOUL CHAMPLAIN, QUEBEC, QC,
G1K 0A2
(418) 681-5655 *SIC 5551*

COASTAL MARINE LIMITED *p426*
1256 TOPSAIL RD, MOUNT PEARL, NL,
A1N 5E8

(709) 747-0159 *SIC 5551*

**CUSTOM MARINE DESIGN & SUPPLY LIM-
ITED** *p468*
29 GREENS POINT RD, TRENTON, NS,
B0K 1X0
(902) 752-2827 *SIC 5551*

DUFORT INDUSTRIES LTD *p384*
999 KING EDWARD ST UNIT 6, WIN-
NIPEG, MB, R3H 0R1
(204) 633-3381 *SIC 5551*

DUNN HOLDINGS INC *p598*
1035 MARINA RD, GRAVENHURST, ON,
P1P 1R2
(705) 687-7793 *SIC 5551*

G & L WILCOX LIMITED *p567*
698 SNO-DRIFTERS RD, EGANVILLE, ON,
K0J 1T0
(613) 628-2424 *SIC 5551*

GORDON BAY MARINE LTD *p663*
55A HATHERLEY RD SUITE 1, MACTIER,
ON, P0C 1H0
(705) 375-2623 *SIC 5551*

GROUPE THOMAS MARINE INC *p1392*
550 BOUL LIONEL-BOULET, VARENNES,
QC, J3X 1P7
(877) 652-2999 *SIC 5551*

HURST MARINA LTD *p663*
2726 RIVER RD, MANOTICK, ON, K4M 1B4
(613) 692-1234 *SIC 5551*

MARINE DEPOT INC *p1393*
550 BOUL LIONEL-BOULET, VARENNES,
QC, J3X 1P7
(450) 652-2999 *SIC 5551*

MARINE PLAZA TVT *p809*
1753 DIVISION RD W, ORILLIA, ON, L3V
6H2
(705) 329-1646 *SIC 5551*

P & E MANUFACTURING LTD *p394*
1524 ROUTE 950, BAS-CAP-PELE, NB,
E4N 1A9
(506) 577-4356 *SIC 5551*

PARIS MARINE LIMITED *p841*
2980 LAKEFIELD RD, PETERBOROUGH,
ON, K9J 6X5
(705) 652-6444 *SIC 5551*

PRIDE OF MUSKOKA MARINE LIMITED
p497
1785 BEAUMONT DR RR 4, BRACE-
BRIDGE, ON, P1L 1X2
(705) 645-9151 *SIC 5551*

QUINN'S MARINA LTD *p837*
25 QUINN RD, PEFFERLAW, ON, L0E 1N0
(705) 437-1122 *SIC 5551*

RAYBURN'S MARINE WORLD LTD *p220*
2330 ENTERPRISE WAY, KELOWNA, BC,
V1X 4H7
(250) 860-4232 *SIC 5551*

REMBOURRAGE PRINCEVILLE TECH
p1254
105 RUE BEAUDET, PRINCEVILLE, QC,
G6L 4L3
(819) 364-2645 *SIC 5551*

S G POWER PRODUCTS LTD *p335*
730 HILLSIDE AVE, VICTORIA, BC, V8T
1Z4
(250) 382-8291 *SIC 5551*

SEAMASTERS SERVICES LIMITED *p448*
647 WINDMILL RD, DARTMOUTH, NS, B3B
1B7
(902) 468-5967 *SIC 5551*

SHERWOOD MARINE CENTRE LTD *p267*
6771 OLDFIELD RD, SAANICHTON, BC,
V8M 2A2
(250) 652-6520 *SIC 5551*

STERLING MARINE FUELS *p1025*
3565 RUSSELL ST, WINDSOR, ON, N9C
1E8
(519) 253-4694 *SIC 5551*

**TRU-NORTH RV, AUTO & MARINE SALES
INC** *p1414*
4189 2ND AVE W, PRINCE ALBERT, SK,
S6W 1A1
(306) 763-8100 *SIC 5551*

SIC 5561 Recreational vehicle dealers

1000 ISLANDS R.V. CENTRE INC *p592*
409 COUNTY ROAD 2 E, GANANOQUE,
ON, K7G 2V4
(613) 382-4400 *SIC 5561*

125173 CANADA INC *p1232*
2380 MONTEE MASSON, MONTREAL,
QC, H7E 4P2
(450) 666-2444 *SIC 5561*

1541094 ONTARIO INC *p996*
1581 THE QUEENSWAY SUITE 2,
TORONTO, ON, M8Z 1T8
(416) 253-5001 *SIC 5561*

2474761 MANITOBA LTD *p364*
1272 DUGALD RD, WINNIPEG, MB, R2J
0H2
(204) 987-5640 *SIC 5561*

3320235 CANADA INC *p1120*
175 MONTEE DE SAINT-SULPICE,
L'ASSOMPTION, QC, J5W 2T3
(450) 589-5718 *SIC 5561*

392268 ALBERTA LTD *p118*
5305 ALLARD WAY NW SUITE 310, ED-
MONTON, AB, T6H 5X8
(780) 777-7776 *SIC 5561*

539290 ONTARIO LTD *p907*
940 COBALT CRES, THUNDER BAY, ON,
P7B 5W3
(807) 346-9399 *SIC 5561*

618382 ALBERTA LTD *p135*
102 24 ST SE, HIGH RIVER, AB, T1V 0B3
(403) 652-3171 *SIC 5561*

**ARRKANN TRAILER & SPORT CENTRE
LTD** *p121*
1904 80 AVE NW, EDMONTON, AB, T6P
1N2
(780) 440-4811 *SIC 5561*

BRUCE'S FOUR SEASONS (1984) LTD *p360*
TRANSCANADA HWY N, VIRDEN, MB,
R0M 2C0
(204) 748-1539 *SIC 5561*

CAN-AM TRAILERS LIMITED *p662*
6068 COLONEL TALBOT RD, LONDON,
ON, N6P 1J1
(519) 652-3284 *SIC 5561*

CAREFREE COACH & RV LTD *p108*
4510 51 AVE NW, EDMONTON, AB, T6B
2W2
(780) 438-2008 *SIC 5561*

CENTRE DU SPORT LAC-ST-JEAN INC
p1075
1454 RUE PRINCIPALE, CHAMBORD, QC,
G0W 1G0
(418) 342-6202 *SIC 5561*

DON MCPHAIL MOTORS LTD *p618*
6332 WELLINGTON RD, HARRISTON, ON,
N0G 1Z0
(519) 338-3422 *SIC 5561*

ELDORADO R V SALES LTD *p140*
711 2A AVE N, LETHBRIDGE, AB, T1H 0E1
(403) 329-3933 *SIC 5561*

FIELD OF DREAMS RV LTD *p3*
45 KINGSVIEW RD SE, AIRDRIE, AB, T4A
0A8
(403) 249-2123 *SIC 5561*

FRASERWAY RV GP LTD *p220*
3732 HIGHWAY 97 N, KELOWNA, BC, V1X
5C2
(250) 807-2898 *SIC 5561*

FRASERWAY RV LIMITED PARTNERSHIP
p176
30440 SOUTH FRASER WAY, ABBOTS-
FORD, BC, V2T 6L4
(604) 850-1976 *SIC 5561*

G N R TRAVEL CENTRE LTD *p365*
1370 DUGALD RD, WINNIPEG, MB, R2J
0H2
(204) 233-4478 *SIC 5561*

GEANT MOTORISE INC, LE *p1291*
173 RTE 172, SAINT-AMBROISE, QC, G7P
2N5
(418) 672-4744 *SIC 5561*

HAPPY TRAILS R.V. INC *p132*
15211 100 ST, GRANDE PRAIRIE, AB, T8V
7C2
(780) 538-2120 *SIC 5561*

KIA CAP SANTE INC *p1074*
5 CH DU BOIS-DE-L'AIL, CAP-SANTE, QC,
G0A 1L0
(418) 285-5555 *SIC 5561*

KIMPEX INC *p1100*
5355 RUE SAINT-ROCH S BUREAU 4,
DRUMMONDVILLE, QC, J2E 0B4
(819) 472-3326 *SIC 5561*

LACOMBE RV 2000 LTD *p138*
27211 HIGHWAY 12 SUITE 96, LACOMBE
COUNTY, AB, T4L 0E3
(403) 782-4544 *SIC 5561*

LAZY DAYS RV CENTRE INC *p162*
137 TURBO DR, SHERWOOD PARK, AB,
T8H 2J6
(780) 449-6177 *SIC 5561*

**LEISURE MART & RV CANADA CORPORA-
TION** *p749*
2098 PRINCE OF WALES DR, NEPEAN,
ON, K2E 7A5
(613) 226-8228 *SIC 5561*

MINARD'S LEISURE WORLD LTD *p1437*
921 GOVERNMENT RD S, WEYBURN, SK,
S4H 3R3
(306) 842-3288 *SIC 5561*

O'CONNOR RV CENTRES *p197*
44430 YALE RD, CHILLIWACK, BC, V2R
4H1
(604) 792-2747 *SIC 5561*

OTTO MOBILE VANCOUVER *p272*
17535 55B AVE, SURREY, BC, V3S 5V2
SIC 5561

**OWASCO CANADIAN CAR & CAMPER
RENTAL LTD** *p1015*
2030 CHAMPLAIN AVE, WHITBY, ON, L1N
6A7
(905) 579-7573 *SIC 5561*

PINE ACRES (HAMPTON) LIMITED *p1041*
24965 ROUTE 2, KENSINGTON, PE, C0B
1M0
(902) 836-5040 *SIC 5561*

POSITOR INC. *p1067*
1356 RUE NEWTON, BOUCHERVILLE, QC,
J4B 5H2
(450) 449-0327 *SIC 5561*

R V OUTFITTERS *p662*
6068 COLONEL TALBOT RD, LONDON,
ON, N6P 1J1
(519) 652-3284 *SIC 5561*

RED DEER RV COUNTRY LTD *p157*
1 GASOLINE ALLEY E, RED DEER
COUNTY, AB, T4E 1B3
(403) 340-1132 *SIC 5561*

ROSKI COMPOSITES INC *p1290*
130 RUE DE L'EGLISE BUREAU 3, ROX-
TON FALLS, QC, J0H 1E0
(450) 548-5821 *SIC 5561*

ROULOTTES E. TURMEL INC *p1075*
7010 BOUL SAINTE-ANNE, CHATEAU-
RICHER, QC, G0A 1N0
(418) 824-3401 *SIC 5561*

ROULOTTES R. G. GAGNON INC *p1120*
175 MONTEE DE SAINT-SULPICE,
L'ASSOMPTION, QC, J5W 2T3
(450) 589-5718 *SIC 5561*

ROULOTTES STE-ANNE INC *p1381*
3306 BOUL DES ENTREPRISES, TERRE-
BONNE, QC, J6X 4J8
(450) 477-1803 *SIC 5561*

SICARD HOLIDAY CAMPERS LIMITED *p882*
7526 REGIONAL ROAD 20, SMITHVILLE,
ON, L0R 2A0
(905) 957-3344 *SIC 5561*

SUN-VIEW INDUSTRIES LTD *p270*
15915 BENTLEY PL, SUMMERLAND, BC,
V0H 1Z3
(250) 494-1327 *SIC 5561*

TRANSCONA TRAILER SALES LTD *p367*
1330 DUGALD RD, WINNIPEG, MB, R2J
0H2

---

(204) 237-7272   *SIC* 5561
TRAVELAND LEISURE CENTRE (REGINA) LTD   p1419
GD LCD MAIN, REGINA, SK, S4P 2Z4
(306) 789-3311   *SIC* 5561
TRAVELAND LEISURE VEHICLES LTD p228
20529 LANGLEY BYPASS, LANGLEY, BC, V3A 5E8
(604) 530-8141   *SIC* 5561
VELLNER LEISURE PRODUCTS (1980) LTD   p157
1890 49 AVE, RED DEER, AB, T4R 2N7
(403) 343-1464   *SIC* 5561
VILLAGE MOBILE HOMES LTD   p1416
2901 POWERHOUSE DR, REGINA, SK, S4N 0A1
(306) 525-5666   *SIC* 5561
VOYAGER R.V. CENTRE LTD   p224
9250 HIGHWAY 97, LAKE COUNTRY, BC, V4V 1P9
(250) 766-4607   *SIC* 5561
WESTERN RV COUNTRY LTD   p3
61 EAST LAKE RAMP NE, AIRDRIE, AB, T4A 2K4
(403) 912-2634   *SIC* 5561
WOODY'S RV WORLD LTD   p157
1702 49 AVE, RED DEER, AB, T4R 2N7
(403) 346-1130   *SIC* 5561

SIC 5571 Motorcycle dealers

1235054 ONTARIO LIMITED   p485
311 BRYNE DR, BARRIE, ON, L4N 8V4
(705) 728-5322   *SIC* 5571
1268558 ONTARIO LIMITED   p813
880 CHAMPLAIN AVE, OSHAWA, ON, L1J 7A6
(905) 434-6550   *SIC* 5571
127897 CANADA LTD   p629
295 DALTON AVE, KINGSTON, ON, K7K 6Z1
(613) 544-4600   *SIC* 5571
129157 CANADA INC   p1263
1831 BOUL WILFRID-HAMEL, QUEBEC, QC, G1N 3Z1
(418) 527-4489   *SIC* 5571
136562 CANADA INC   p1221
6695 RUE SAINT-JACQUES BUREAU 514, MONTREAL, QC, H4B 1V3
(514) 483-6686   *SIC* 5571
1496201 ONTARIO INC   p750
1963 MERIVALE RD, NEPEAN, ON, K2G 1G1
(613) 736-8899   *SIC* 5571
2630-6241 QUEBEC INC   p1052
305 BOUL LA SALLE, BAIE-COMEAU, QC, G4Z 2L5
(418) 296-9191   *SIC* 5571
293564 ALBERTA LTD   p165
15 INGLEWOOD DR SUITE 2, ST. ALBERT, AB, T8N 5E2
(780) 458-7227   *SIC* 5571
393346 ALBERTA LTD   p165
15 INGLEWOOD DR UNIT 2, ST. ALBERT, AB, T8N 5E2
(780) 458-7227   *SIC* 5571
4223373 CANADA INC   p1311
3003 RUE PICARD, SAINT-HYACINTHE, QC, J2S 1H2
(450) 252-4488   *SIC* 5571
6535577 CANADA INC   p1282
47 RUE DE LYON, REPENTIGNY, QC, J5Z 4Z3
(450) 582-2442   *SIC* 5571
775757 ONTARIO INC   p602
55473 HIGHWAY 6 N, GUELPH, ON, N1H 6J2
(519) 836-1957   *SIC* 5571
883481 ONTARIO INC   p839
17100 HIGHWAY 7 RR 6, PERTH, ON, K7H 3C8
SIC 5571
9185-9322 QUEBEC INC   p1316

1000 RUE DOUGLAS, SAINT-JEAN-SUR-RICHELIEU, QC, J3A 1V1
(450) 348-6816   *SIC* 5571
ADRENALINE SPORTS INC   p1119
6280 BOUL WILFRID-HAMEL, L'ANCIENNE-LORETTE, QC, G2E 2H8
(418) 687-0383   *SIC* 5571
ARBUTUS RV & MARINE SALES LTD p232
2603 SACKVILLE RD, MERVILLE, BC, V0R 2M0
(250) 337-2174   *SIC* 5571
BLACKFOOT MOTORCYCLE LTD   p27
6 HIGHFIELD CIR SE, CALGARY, AB, T2G 5N5
(403) 243-2636   *SIC* 5571
BORDER CITY R.V. CENTRE LTD   p1409
GD LCD MAIN, LLOYDMINSTER, SK, S9V 0X5
(403) 875-0345   *SIC* 5571
CANADIAN WILDERNESS ADVENTURES LTD   p342
4545 BLACKCOMB WAY, WHISTLER, BC, V0N 1B4
(604) 938-1554   *SIC* 5571
CANDAN ENTERPRISES LTD   p227
20257 LANGLEY BYPASS, LANGLEY, BC, V3A 6K9
(604) 530-3645   *SIC* 5571
CENTRE DE MOTOS INC   p1069
8705 BOUL TASCHEREAU, BROSSARD, QC, J4Y 1A4
(450) 443-4488   *SIC* 5571
CENTRE DU SPORT ALARY INC   p1321
1324 BOUL SAINT-ANTOINE, SAINT-JEROME, QC, J7Z 7M2
(450) 436-2242   *SIC* 5571
CLARE'S CYCLE & SPORTS LTD   p590
799 HWY 20, FENWICK, ON, L0S 1C0
(905) 892-2664   *SIC* 5571
DEELEY, TREV MOTORCYCLES (1991) LTD   p286
1875 BOUNDARY RD, VANCOUVER, BC, V5M 3Y7
(604) 291-1875   *SIC* 5571
DION MOTO INC   p1351
840 COTE JOYEUSE, SAINT-RAYMOND, QC, G3L 4B3
(418) 337-2776   *SIC* 5571
DRANE, STEVE MOTERCYCLES LTD p340
2940 ED NIXON TERR, VICTORIA, BC, V9B 0B2
(250) 475-1345   *SIC* 5571
ECHO CYCLE LTD   p104
21220 100 AVE NW, EDMONTON, AB, T5T 5X8
(780) 447-3246   *SIC* 5571
EXCALIBUR MOTORCYCLE WORKS LIMITED   p910
1425 WALSH ST W, THUNDER BAY, ON, P7E 4X6
(807) 622-0007   *SIC* 5571
GO RV & MARINE RED DEER LTD   p157
29 PETROLIA DR, RED DEER COUNTY, AB, T4E 1B3
(403) 347-5546   *SIC* 5571
GORDON AULENBACK LTD   p248
3034 ST JOHNS ST, PORT MOODY, BC, V3H 2C5
(604) 461-3434   *SIC* 5571
HARLEY DAVIDSON MOTORCYCLES OF EDMONTON (1980) LTD   p83
7420 YELLOWHEAD TRAIL NW, EDMONTON, AB, T5B 1G3
(780) 451-7857   *SIC* 5571
HARLEY DAVIDSON OF KINGSTON   p630
295 DALTON AVE, KINGSTON, ON, K7K 6Z1
(613) 544-4600   *SIC* 5571
HARLEY-DAVIDSON OF SOUTHERN ALBERTA INC   p23
2245 PEGASUS RD NE, CALGARY, AB, T2E 8C3
(403) 250-3141   *SIC* 5571
HERITAGE HARLEY-DAVIDSON LTD   p124

1616 CALGARY TRAIL SW, EDMONTON, AB, T6W 1A1
(780) 430-7200   *SIC* 5571
HIGH ROLLERS CUSTOM MOTOR PARTS   p130
11091 86 AVE, FORT SASKATCHEWAN, AB, T8L 3T7
(780) 992-3225   *SIC* 5571
HITCH HOUSE INC, THE   p880
1490 11 HWY S, SHANTY BAY, ON, L0L 2L0
(705) 722-0008   *SIC* 5571
HOLESHOT MOTORSPORTS LTD   p226
8867 201 ST, LANGLEY, BC, V2Y 0C8
(604) 882-3800   *SIC* 5571
JACOX HARLEY-DAVIDSON INC   p723
2815 ARGENTIA RD, MISSISSAUGA, ON, L5N 8G6
(905) 858-0966   *SIC* 5571
KANE'S MOTOR CYCLE SHOP LTD   p30
914 11 ST SE, CALGARY, AB, T2G 3E8
(403) 262-5462   *SIC* 5571
KELOWNA TRUCK & R.V. LTD   p341
1780 BYLAND RD, WEST KELOWNA, BC, V1Z 1A9
(250) 769-1000   *SIC* 5571
LAC LA BICHE SPORTING GOODS LTD   p138
13337 101 AVE, LAC LA BICHE, AB, T0A 2C0
(780) 623-4145   *SIC* 5571
MACLEAN'S SPORTS LTD   p399
489 UNION ST, FREDERICTON, NB, E3A 3M9
(506) 450-6090   *SIC* 5571
MEDICINE HAT HARLEY-DAVIDSON   p83
1923 2 AVE, DUNMORE, AB, T1B 0K3
(403) 527-9235   *SIC* 5571
MIKEY'S GENERAL SALES & REPAIR LTD   p913
1301 AIRPORT RD, TIMMINS, ON, P4P 0A8
(705) 268-6050   *SIC* 5571
MOTO M.T.L. INTERNATIONAL INC   p1222
6695 RUE SAINT-JACQUES, MONTREAL, QC, H4B 1V3
(514) 483-6686   *SIC* 5571
MOTOCYCLETTES & ARTICLES DE SPORTS PONT-VIAU INC   p1236
4501 NORD LAVAL (A-440) O, MONTREAL, QC, H7P 4W6
(450) 973-4501   *SIC* 5571
MOTOS DAYTONA INC   p1222
6695 RUE SAINT-JACQUES, MONTREAL, QC, H4B 1V3
(514) 483-6686   *SIC* 5571
NADON SPORT INC   p1302
62 RUE SAINT-LOUIS, SAINT-EUSTACHE, QC, J7R 1X7
(450) 473-2381   *SIC* 5571
NADON SPORT SAINT-EUSTACHE INC   p1301
645 RUE DUBOIS, SAINT-EUSTACHE, QC, J7P 3W1
(450) 473-2381   *SIC* 5571
OTTAWA GOODTIME CENTRE LIMITED   p749
450 WEST HUNT CLUB RD, NEPEAN, ON, K2E 1B2
(613) 731-9071   *SIC* 5571
POWER SPORTS CANADA INC   p750
1 LASER ST, NEPEAN, ON, K2E 7V1
(613) 224-7899   *SIC* 5571
PRAIRIE MOTORCYCLE LTD   p1420
1355 MCINTYRE ST, REGINA, SK, S4R 2M9
(306) 522-1747   *SIC* 5571
PRO CYCLE LIMITED   p448
360 HIGNEY AVE, DARTMOUTH, NS, B3B 0L4
(902) 468-2518   *SIC* 5571
RALLY MOTOR SPORTS LTD   p1414
10 38TH ST E, PRINCE ALBERT, SK, S6W 1A6
(306) 922-6363   *SIC* 5571
REDHEAD EQUIPMENT LTD   p1429

9010 NORTH SERVICE ROAD, SASKATOON, SK, S7K 7E8
(306) 931-4600   *SIC* 5571
RIVERSIDE SALES LTD   p166
15 INGLEWOOD DR SUITE 2, ST. ALBERT, AB, T8N 5E2
(780) 458-7272   *SIC* 5571
ROBERTSON IMPLEMENTS (1988) LTD   p1436
2464 SOUTH SERVICE RD W, SWIFT CURRENT, SK, S9H 5J8
(306) 773-4948   *SIC* 5571
ROCHELEAU CHEVROLET & OLDS   p1088
434 RUE DE LA RIVIERE, COWANSVILLE, QC, J2K 1N5
(450) 263-1541   *SIC* 5571
ROCKY'S HARLEY DAVIDSON LTD   p662
900 WILTON GROVE RD, LONDON, ON, N6N 1C7
(519) 438-1450   *SIC* 5571
ROULOTTES LUPIEN (2000) INC   p1298
2700 RTE 122, SAINT-CYRILLE-DE-WENDOVER, QC, J1Z 1C1
(819) 397-4949   *SIC* 5571
SIMPLY MOBILE LTD   p650
1920 DUNDAS ST, LONDON, ON, N5V 3P1
(519) 451-5120   *SIC* 5571
SPORT S.M. INC   p1275
11337 BOUL VALCARTIER, QUEBEC, QC, G2A 2M4
(418) 842-2703   *SIC* 5571
STE-MARIE, CLAUDE SPORT INC   p1309
5925 CH DE CHAMBLY, SAINT-HUBERT, QC, J3Y 3R4
(450) 678-4700   *SIC* 5571
STONE'S SUPERIOR HOMES LIMITED p463
2689 WESTVILLE RD, NEW GLASGOW, NS, B2H 5C6
(902) 752-3164   *SIC* 5571
TOYS FOR BIG BOYS LTD   p409
633 SALISBURY RD, MONCTON, NB, E1E 1B9
(506) 858-8088   *SIC* 5571
TRAILBLAZER R.V. CENTRE LTD   p150
2302 SPARROW DR, NISKU, AB, T9E 8A2
(780) 955-0300   *SIC* 5571
TRAVELAND R.V. RENTALS LTD   p228
20257 LANGLEY BYPASS, LANGLEY, BC, V3A 6K9
(604) 532-8128   *SIC* 5571
TURPLE BROS LTD   p157
175 LEVA AVE, RED DEER COUNTY, AB, T4E 0A5
(403) 346-5238   *SIC* 5571
ULTIMATE POWER SPORTS INC   p492
1037 WALLBRIDGE RD, BELLEVILLE, ON, K8N 4Z5
SIC 5571
V.R. SOULIERE INC   p1130
179 RUE DU PARC-INDUSTRIEL, LANORAIE, QC, J0K 1E0
(450) 589-1110   *SIC* 5571
VISION R.V. CORPORATION   p2
26301A TWP RD 531A, ACHESON, AB, T7X 5A3
(780) 962-0012   *SIC* 5571
VR ST-CYR INC   p1348
3465 CH DE L'INDUSTRIE, SAINT-MATHIEU-DE-BELOEIL, QC, J3G 0R9
(450) 446-3660   *SIC* 5571
WESTERN RV CENTRE LEDUC INC   p140
7503 SPARROW DR, LEDUC, AB, T9E 0H3
(780) 986-2880   *SIC* 5571

SIC 5599 Automotive dealers, nec

375414 ONTARIO LIMITED   p900
2240 LONG LAKE RD, SUDBURY, ON, P3E 5H4
(705) 682-4463   *SIC* 5599
9258-0547 QUEBEC INC   p1261
215 RUE ETIENNE-DUBREUIL, QUEBEC, QC, G1M 4A6

▲ Public Company   ■ Public Company Family Member   **HQ** Headquarters   **BR** Branch   **SL** Single Location

(418) 681-5000   *SIC 5599*
CYCLE WORKS MOTORSPORTS LTD *p113*
5688 75 ST NW, EDMONTON, AB, T6E 5X6
(780) 440-3200   *SIC 5599*
ECKO MARINE LTD *p3*
4200 47 ST, ALBERTA BEACH, AB, T0E 0A1
(780) 924-3250   *SIC 5599*
EQUIPEMENTS PIERRE CHAMPIGNY LTEE *p1044*
280 RUE BONIN RR 4, ACTON VALE, QC, J0H 1A0
(450) 546-0999   *SIC 5599*
EQUIPEMENTS VILLENEUVE INC *p1077*
1178   BOUL   SAINTE-GENEVIEVE, CHICOUTIMI, QC, G7G 2G6
(418) 543-3600   *SIC 5599*
FACTORY OUTLET TRAILERS INC *p136*
80010 475 AVE, HIGH RIVER, AB, T1V 1M3
(403) 603-3311   *SIC 5599*
G E MOTEURS D'AVIONS INC *p1068*
2 BOUL DE L'AEROPORT, BROMONT, QC, J2L 1S6
(450) 534-0917   *SIC 5599*
GREGOIRE SPORT INC *p1147*
2061 BOUL BARRETTE, LOURDES-DE-JOLIETTE, QC, J0K 1K0
(450) 752-2201   *SIC 5599*
GROUPE CONTANT INC *p1230*
6310 BOUL DES MILLE-ILES, MONTREAL, QC, H7B 1B3
(450) 666-6676   *SIC 5599*
J & B CYCLE & MARINE CO. LTD *p913*
950 RIVERSIDE DR, TIMMINS, ON, P4N 3W2
(705) 267-1417   *SIC 5599*
K.M.K. SALES LTD *p1407*
HWY 20 S, HUMBOLDT, SK, S0K 2A1
(306) 682-0738   *SIC 5599*
LEVAERO AVIATION INC *p911*
2039 DEREK BURNEY DR, THUNDER BAY, ON, P7K 0A1
(807) 475-5353   *SIC 5599*
MOTOS ILLIMITEES INC *p1380*
3250 BOUL DES ENTREPRISES, TERREBONNE, QC, J6X 4J8
(450) 477-4000   *SIC 5599*
OAK CREEK DEVELOPMENTS *p17*
3816 64 AVE SE, CALGARY, AB, T2C 2B4
(403) 279-2904   *SIC 5599*
PRO-PERFORMANCE G. P. L INC *p1063*
5750 BOUL SAINTE-ANNE, BOISCHATEL, QC, G0A 1H0
(418) 822-3838   *SIC 5599*
WASAGA 500 GO-KARTS LTD *p1005*
152 RIVER RD W, WASAGA BEACH, ON, L9Z 2X2
(705) 322-2594   *SIC 5599*

SIC 5611 Men's and boys' clothing stores

BELOW THE BELT LTD *p112*
5611 86 ST NW, EDMONTON, AB, T6E 6H7
(780) 469-5301   *SIC 5611*
BELOW THE BELT STORE (VANCOUVER) LTD *p112*
5611 86 ST NW, EDMONTON, AB, T6E 6H7
(780) 469-5301   *SIC 5611*
BOUTIQUE UNISEXE JOVEN INC *p1328*
3616 BOUL POIRIER, SAINT-LAURENT, QC, H4R 2J5
(514) 382-5940   *SIC 5611*
CANADA GOOSE INC *p989*
250 BOWIE AVE, TORONTO, ON, M6E 4Y2
(416) 780-9850   *SIC 5611*
ENTREPRISES ERNEST (MTL) LTEE, LES *p1178*
9200 RUE MEILLEUR BUREAU 101, MONTREAL, QC, H2N 2A9
(514) 858-5258   *SIC 5611*
FREED STORAGE LIMITED *p1021*
1526 OTTAWA ST, WINDSOR, ON, N8X 2G5

---

(519) 258-6532   *SIC 5611*
GCO CANADA INC *p739*
6300 DIXIE RD, MISSISSAUGA, ON, L5T 1A7
(905) 670-2514   *SIC 5611*
HARRY ROSEN INC *p975*
77 BLOOR ST W SUITE 5, TORONTO, ON, M5S 1M2
(416) 935-9200   *SIC 5611*
HARRY ROSEN INC *p975*
82 BLOOR ST W, TORONTO, ON, M5S 1L9
(416) 972-0556   *SIC 5611*
HENRY SINGER FASHION GROUP LTD *p89*
10180 101 ST NW SUITE 165, EDMONTON, AB, T5J 3S4
(780) 420-0909   *SIC 5611*
HOLT, RENFREW & CIE, LIMITEE *p89*
10180 101 ST NW, EDMONTON, AB, T5J 3S4
(780) 425-5300   *SIC 5611*
HOLT, RENFREW & CIE, LIMITEE *p1272*
2452 BOUL LAURIER, QUEBEC, QC, G1V 2L1
(514) 842-5111   *SIC 5611*
INC GROUP INC *p789*
1185 CALEDONIA RD, NORTH YORK, ON, M6A 2X1
(416) 785-1771   *SIC 5611*
JEAN BLEU INC, LE *p1128*
1895 46E AV, LACHINE, QC, H8T 2N9
(514) 631-3300   *SIC 5611*
MARQUES DE VETEMENTS FREEMARK TEC INC *p1157*
5640 RUE PARE, MONT-ROYAL, QC, H4P 2M1
(514) 341-7333   *SIC 5611*
MOORES THE SUIT PEOPLE INC *p586*
129 CARLINGVIEW DR, ETOBICOKE, ON, M9W 5E7
(416) 675-1900   *SIC 5611*
NATHAR LIMITED *p562*
27 FIRST ST E, CORNWALL, ON, K6H 1K5
(613) 932-8854   *SIC 5611*
PANTORAMA INDUSTRIES INC, LES *p1091*
2 RUE LAKE, DOLLARD-DES-ORMEAUX, QC, H9B 3H9
(514) 421-1850   *SIC 5611*
RANDY RIVER INC *p790*
111 ORFUS RD, NORTH YORK, ON, M6A 1M4
(416) 785-1771   *SIC 5611*
STOLLERY, FRANK LIMITED *p930*
1 BLOOR ST W, TORONTO, ON, M4W 1A3
SIC 5611
STRAUSSCO HOLDINGS LTD *p784*
601 MAGNETIC DR UNIT 41, NORTH YORK, ON, M3J 3J2
(416) 650-1404   *SIC 5611*

SIC 5621 Women's clothing stores

157503 CANADA INC *p1155*
4360 CH DE LA COTE-DE-LIESSE, MONT-ROYAL, QC, H4N 2P7
(514) 344-5140   *SIC 5621*
163972 CANADA INC *p1177*
9600 RUE MEILLEUR BUREAU 730, MONTREAL, QC, H2N 2E3
(514) 385-3629   *SIC 5621*
2518879 ONTARIO INC *p650*
1712 DUNDAS ST, LONDON, ON, N5W 3C9
(519) 659-8725   *SIC 5621*
4233964 CANADA INC *p1331*
2575 BOUL PITFIELD, SAINT-LAURENT, QC, H4S 1T2
(514) 383-4442   *SIC 5621*
595028 ALBERTA LTD *p85*
11825 105 AVE NW, EDMONTON, AB, T5H 0L9
(780) 421-7361   *SIC 5621*
6938001 CANADA INC *p1177*
433 RUE CHABANEL O UNITE 801, MONTREAL, QC, H2N 2J7

---

(514) 383-0026   *SIC 5621*
7098961 CANADA INC *p1337*
4600 RUE HICKMORE, SAINT-LAURENT, QC, H4T 1K2
(514) 733-4666   *SIC 5621*
9264-6231 QUEBEC INC *p1378*
281   RUE   EDWARD-ASSH,   STE-CATHERINE-DE-LA-J-CARTIE, QC, G3N 1A3
(418) 875-1839   *SIC 5621*
ARITZIA LP *p294*
611 ALEXANDER ST SUITE 118, VANCOUVER, BC, V6A 1E1
(604) 251-3132   *SIC 5621*
ARITZIA LP *p329*
701 GEORGIA ST W SUITE 53D, VANCOUVER, BC, V7Y 1K8
(604) 681-9301   *SIC 5621*
ARLIE'S SPORT SHOP (DOWNTOWN) LTD *p883*
17 KEEFER RD, ST CATHARINES, ON, L2M 6K4
(905) 684-8134   *SIC 5621*
AULD PHILLIPS LTD *p197*
8040 EVANS RD, CHILLIWACK, BC, V2R 5R8
(604) 792-8518   *SIC 5621*
BLU'S CLOTHING LTD *p113*
4719 101 ST NW, EDMONTON, AB, T6E 5C6
(780) 437-3991   *SIC 5621*
BOOTLEGGER CLOTHING INC *p257*
6651 FRASERWOOD PL UNIT 250, RICHMOND, BC, V6W 1J3
(604) 276-8400   *SIC 5621*
BOUTIQUE COLORI INC *p1325*
2255 CH DE LA COTE-DE-LIESSE, SAINT-LAURENT, QC, H4N 2M6
(514) 858-7494   *SIC 5621*
BOUTIQUE LE PENTAGONE INC *p1378*
301   RUE   EDWARD-ASSH,   STE-CATHERINE-DE-LA-J-CARTIE, QC, G3N 1A3
(418) 875-1839   *SIC 5621*
BOUTIQUE MARIE CLAIRE INC *p1047*
8501 BOUL RAY-LAWSON, ANJOU, QC, H1J 1K6
(514) 354-0650   *SIC 5621*
BOUTIQUE OPTION INC *p1060*
120 CH DE LA GRANDE-COTE, BOIS-BRIAND, QC, J7G 1B9
(450) 433-2999   *SIC 5621*
BOUTIQUE TRISTAN & ISEUT INC *p1215*
20 RUE DES SEIGNEURS, MONTREAL, QC, H3K 3K3
(514) 937-4601   *SIC 5621*
BRYAN'S FASHIONS LTD *p285*
1950 FRANKLIN ST, VANCOUVER, BC, V5L 1R2
(604) 255-1890   *SIC 5621*
CHATEAU INC, LE *p1325*
105   BOUL   MARCEL-LAURIN,   SAINT-LAURENT, QC, H4N 2M3
(514) 738-7000   *SIC 5621*
CLUB MONACO CORP *p974*
157 BLOOR ST W, TORONTO, ON, M5S 1P7
(416) 591-8837   *SIC 5621*
CONCEPT MODE STE-FOY INC *p1274*
999 AV DE BOURGOGNE BUREAU A1, QUEBEC, QC, G1W 4S6
(418) 653-3214   *SIC 5621*
CROTEAU, PIERRE INC *p1173*
1490 AV DU MONT-ROYAL E BUREAU 3, MONTREAL, QC, H2J 1Y9
(514) 521-0059   *SIC 5621*
CYRS LTEE *p1235*
1789 BOUL DES LAURENTIDES, MONTREAL, QC, H7M 2P7
SIC 5621
ECLIPSE STORES INC *p431*
354 WATER ST SUITE 401, ST. JOHN'S, NL, A1C 1C4
(709) 722-0311   *SIC 5621*

ENTREPRISES VAGABOND INC, LES *p1285*
451 RUE DE L'EXPANSION, RIMOUSKI, QC, G5M 1B4
(418) 724-2243   *SIC 5621*
FAIRWEATHER LTD *p789*
1185 CALEDONIA RD, NORTH YORK, ON, M6A 2X1
(416) 785-1771   *SIC 5621*
GESTION JOCELYNE CROTEAU INC *p1283*
91 RUE OUIMET, REPENTIGNY, QC, J6A 1E1
(450) 581-2092   *SIC 5621*
GREAT GARB BOUTIQUE (TABER) LTD *p169*
5221 48 AVE, TABER, AB, T1G 1S8
SIC 5621
GROUPE DYNAMITE INC *p1156*
5592 RUE FERRIER, MONT-ROYAL, QC, H4P 1M2
(514) 733-3962   *SIC 5621*
GROUPE JACOB INC *p1339*
6125 CH DE LA COTE-DE-LIESSE, SAINT-LAURENT, QC, H4T 1C8
(514) 731-8877   *SIC 5621*
HOLT, RENFREW & CIE, LIMITEE *p305*
737 DUNSMUIR ST, VANCOUVER, BC, V6C 1N5
(604) 681-3121   *SIC 5621*
HOLT, RENFREW & CIE, LIMITEE *p929*
60 BLOOR ST W SUITE 1100, TORONTO, ON, M4W 3B8
(416) 922-2333   *SIC 5621*
HOLT, RENFREW & CIE, LIMITEE *p929*
50 BLOOR ST W SUITE 200, TORONTO, ON, M4W 1A1
(416) 922-2333   *SIC 5621*
JM (RETAIL) INC *p585*
110 RONSON DR, ETOBICOKE, ON, M9W 1B6
(416) 674-7433   *SIC 5621*
LTS TG LTD *p697*
5045 ORBITOR DR BLDG 12 SUITE 202, MISSISSAUGA, ON, L4W 4Y4
(905) 890-2430   *SIC 5621*
MAGASIN LAURA (P.V.) INC *p1234*
3000 BOUL LE CORBUSIER, MONTREAL, QC, H7L 3W2
(450) 973-6090   *SIC 5621*
MANTIQUE FASHIONS LTD *p289*
5 5TH AVE E, VANCOUVER, BC, V5T 1G7
(604) 736-7161   *SIC 5621*
MENDOCINO CLOTHING COMPANY LTD *p989*
496 GILBERT AVE, TORONTO, ON, M6E 4X5
(416) 847-0590   *SIC 5621*
MILLS COMPANY LIMITED *p453*
5486 SPRING GARDEN RD, HALIFAX, NS, B3J 1G4
SIC 5621
MODE LE GRENIER INC *p1049*
8501 BOUL RAY-LAWSON, ANJOU, QC, H1J 1K6
(514) 354-0650   *SIC 5621*
MODES CAZZA INC *p1179*
433 RUE CHABANEL O UNITE 801, MONTREAL, QC, H2N 2J7
(514) 383-0026   *SIC 5621*
NORTHERN REFLECTIONS LTD *p577*
21 FOUR SEASONS PL 2ND FLR, ETOBICOKE, ON, M9B 6J8
(416) 626-2500   *SIC 5621*
NORTHERN REFLECTIONS LTD *p995*
2198 BLOOR ST W, TORONTO, ON, M6S 1N4
(416) 769-8378   *SIC 5621*
NYGARD INTERNATIONAL PARTNERSHIP *p372*
1771 INKSTER BLVD, WINNIPEG, MB, R2X 1R3
(204) 982-5000   *SIC 5621*
OLSEN FASHION CANADA INC *p698*
5112 TIMBERLEA BLVD, MISSISSAUGA, ON, L4W 2S5

---

(905) 290-1919   *SIC 5621*
PLACEMENTS ARDEN INC, LES   *p1335*
2575 BOUL PITFIELD, SAINT-LAURENT, QC, H4S 1T2
(514) 383-4442   *SIC 5621*
RAYNA PEARL INVESTMENT LTD   *p587*
19 SHAFT RD, ETOBICOKE, ON, M9W 4M3
(416) 241-1521   *SIC 5621*
REITMANS (CANADA) LIMITEE   *p1217*
250 RUE SAUVE O, MONTREAL, QC, H3L 1Z2
(514) 384-1140   *SIC 5621*
SAMUEL & CO. APPAREL LIMITED   *p459*
127 CHAIN LAKE DR UNIT 9, HALIFAX, NS, B3S 1B3
(902) 454-7093   *SIC 5621*
SERENA FASHIONS (ALBERTA) LTD   *p37*
6737 FAIRMOUNT DR SE SUITE 60, CALGARY, AB, T2H 0X6
(403) 255-1551   *SIC 5621*
SERENA FASHIONS LTD   *p322*
2700 BROADWAY W, VANCOUVER, BC, V6K 2G4
(604) 733-8508   *SIC 5621*
TRIPLE FLIP INC   *p38*
6120 11 ST SE UNIT 7, CALGARY, AB, T2H 2L7
(403) 769-3547   *SIC 5621*
VETEMENTS EFG INC   *p1337*
3335 BOUL PITFIELD, SAINT-LAURENT, QC, H4S 1H3
(514) 333-9119   *SIC 5621*
YM INC. (SALES)   *p790*
50 DUFFLAW RD SUITE 364, NORTH YORK, ON, M6A 2W1
(416) 789-1071   *SIC 5621*

SIC 5632 Women's accessory and specialty stores

168662 CANADA INC   *p1177*
333 RUE CHABANEL O BUREAU 800, MONTREAL, QC, H2N 2E7
(514) 384-7691   *SIC 5632*
168662 CANADA INC   *p1181*
260 RUE GARY-CARTER, MONTREAL, QC, H2R 2V7
(514) 384-7691   *SIC 5632*
BOUTIQUE LA VIE EN ROSE INC   *p1166*
4320 AV PIERRE-DE COUBERTIN, MONTREAL, QC, H1V 1A6
(514) 256-9446   *SIC 5632*
CLAIRE'S STORES CANADA CORP   *p986*
100 KING ST W SUITE 6600, TORONTO, ON, M5X 2A1
(800) 252-4737   *SIC 5632*
COACH STORES CANADA CORPORATION   *p452*
1959 UPPER WATER ST SUITE 900, HALIFAX, NS, B3J 3N2
(866) 995-9956   *SIC 5632*
CORPORATION SENZA, LA   *p551*
8960 JANE ST, CONCORD, ON, L4K 2M9
SIC 5632
CORPORATION SENZA, LA   *p1093*
1608 BOUL SAINT-REGIS, DORVAL, QC, H9P 1H6
(514) 684-7700   *SIC 5632*
DIRECTIONS EAST TRADING LIMITED   *p783*
995 FINCH AVE W, NORTH YORK, ON, M3J 2C7
(416) 661-7188   *SIC 5632*
GROUPE ATALLAH INC   *p1178*
333 RUE CHABANEL O BUREAU 900, MONTREAL, QC, H2N 2E7
(514) 600-5818   *SIC 5632*
HOLT, RENFREW & CIE, LIMITEE   *p997*
396 HUMBERLINE DR, TORONTO, ON, M9W 6J7
(416) 675-9200   *SIC 5632*
KNIX WEAR INC   *p991*
70 CLAREMONT ST 2ND FL, TORONTO, ON, M6J 2M5
(647) 715-9446   *SIC 5632*

LEVI STRAUSS & CO. (CANADA) INC   *p852*
1725 16TH AVE SUITE 200, RICHMOND HILL, ON, L4B 4C6
(905) 763-4400   *SIC 5632*
LXRANDCO, INC   *p1181*
7399 BOUL SAINT-LAURENT, MONTREAL, QC, H2R 1W7
(514) 654-9993   *SIC 5632*
MEJURI INC   *p991*
18 MOWAT AVE, TORONTO, ON, M6K 3E8
(416) 731-2600   *SIC 5632*
MICHAEL KORS (CANADA) CO   *p1213*
3424 RUE SIMPSON, MONTREAL, QC, H3G 2J3
(514) 737-5677   *SIC 5632*
MICHAEL KORS (CANADA) HOLDINGS LTD   *p1213*
3424 RUE SIMPSON, MONTREAL, QC, H3G 2J3
(514) 737-5677   *SIC 5632*
UNDERCOVER WEAR FASHIONS & LINGERIE   *p227*
4888 236 ST, LANGLEY, BC, V2Z 2S5
SIC 5632
VICTORIA'S SECRET (CANADA) CORP.   *p1095*
1608 BOUL SAINT-REGIS, DORVAL, QC, H9P 1H6
(514) 684-7700   *SIC 5632*

SIC 5641 Children's and infants' wear stores

CHILDREN'S PLACE (CANADA), LP, THE   *p730*
6040 CANTAY RD, MISSISSAUGA, ON, L5R 4J2
(905) 502-0353   *SIC 5641*
J.M. CLEMENT LTEE   *p1279*
5830 BOUL PIERRE-BERTRAND BUREAU 400, QUEBEC, QC, G2J 1B7
(418) 626-0006   *SIC 5641*

SIC 5651 Family clothing stores

1404136 ONTARIO LIMITED   *p925*
1510 YONGE ST, TORONTO, ON, M4T 1Z6
(416) 962-8662   *SIC 5651*
1905405 ONTARIO LIMITED   *p870*
300 BOROUGH DR UNIT 267, SCARBOROUGH, ON, M1P 4P5
(416) 290-6863   *SIC 5651*
9008-6398 QUEBEC INC   *p1357*
80 RUE DE L'HOTEL-DE-VILLE, SAINTE-ELIZABETH-DE-WARWICK, QC, J0A 1M0
(819) 358-9008   *SIC 5651*
9028-3409 QUEBEC INC   *p1400*
210 RUE SAINT-LOUIS, WARWICK, QC, J0A 1M0
(819) 559-8484   *SIC 5651*
9368-1476 QUEBEC INC   *p1397*
575 BOUL DES BOIS-FRANCS S, VICTORIAVILLE, QC, G6P 5X5
(819) 357-2055   *SIC 5651*
9381-0596 QUEBEC INC   *p1265*
2530 BOUL WILFRID-HAMEL BUREAU 101, QUEBEC, QC, G1P 2J1
(418) 524-6464   *SIC 5651*
AMERICAN EAGLE OUTFITTERS CANADA CORPORATION   *p744*
450 COURTNEYPARK DR W, MISSISSAUGA, ON, L5W 1Y6
(289) 562-8000   *SIC 5651*
ARITZIA INC   *p294*
611 ALEXANDER ST SUITE 118, VANCOUVER, BC, V6A 1E1
(604) 251-3132   *SIC 5651*
AUBAINERIE CONCEPT MODE INC, L'   *p1390*
965 RUE GERMAIN, VAL-D'OR, QC, J9P 7H7
(819) 824-4377   *SIC 5651*
AUBAINERIE CONCEPT MODE, L   *p1076*

80 BOUL D'ANJOU, CHATEAUGUAY, QC, J6K 1C3
(450) 699-0444   *SIC 5651*
C. CROTEAU INC   *p1282*
220 BOUL BRIEN, REPENTIGNY, QC, J6A 7E9
(450) 581-7373   *SIC 5651*
CLAUDE CROTEAU ET FILLES INC   *p1384*
500 RUE BARKOFF, TROIS-RIVIERES, QC, G8T 9P5
(819) 379-4566   *SIC 5651*
CONCEPT MASCOUCHE INC   *p1149*
161 MONTEE MASSON BUREAU 44, MASCOUCHE, QC, J7K 3B4
(450) 474-3315   *SIC 5651*
CORPORATION A.U.B. INC   *p1236*
1605 BOUL LE CORBUSIER, MONTREAL, QC, H7S 1Z3
(450) 681-3317   *SIC 5651*
CROTEAU, J. A. (1989) INC   *p1225*
1001 RUE DU MARCHE-CENTRAL LOCAL A11, MONTREAL, QC, H4N 1J8
(514) 382-3403   *SIC 5651*
CROTEAU, MARCEL INC   *p1114*
990 RUE PAPINEAU BUREAU 5, JOLIETTE, QC, J6E 2L7
(450) 756-1221   *SIC 5651*
DENIS CROTEAU INC   *p1106*
9 BOUL MONTCLAIR BUREAU 19, GATINEAU, QC, J8Y 2E2
(819) 770-6886   *SIC 5651*
DON MICHAEL HOLDINGS INC   *p790*
75 TYCOS DR, NORTH YORK, ON, M6B 1W3
(416) 781-7540   *SIC 5651*
FOREVER XXI ULC   *p767*
1800 SHEPPARD AVE E, NORTH YORK, ON, M2J 5A7
(416) 494-6363   *SIC 5651*
FREEMARK APPAREL BRANDS RETAIL BE INC   *p1156*
5640 RUE PARE, MONT-ROYAL, QC, H4P 2M1
(514) 341-7333   *SIC 5651*
FRENCH CONNECTION (CANADA) LIMITED   *p980*
111 PETER ST SUITE 406, TORONTO, ON, M5V 2H1
(416) 640-6160   *SIC 5651*
GAP (CANADA) INC   *p35*
6455 MACLEOD TRAIL SW SUITE 210, CALGARY, AB, T2H 0K8
(403) 640-1303   *SIC 5651*
GAP (CANADA) INC   *p35*
6455 MACLEOD TRAIL SW SUITE 151, CALGARY, AB, T2H 0K3
(403) 640-1305   *SIC 5651*
GAP (CANADA) INC   *p71*
3625 SHAGANAPPI TRAIL NW, CALGARY, AB, T3A 0E2
(403) 288-5188   *SIC 5651*
GAP (CANADA) INC   *p190*
4700 KINGSWAY SUITE 2138, BURNABY, BC, V5H 4M1
(604) 431-6559   *SIC 5651*
GAP (CANADA) INC   *p503*
89 WALKER DR, BRAMPTON, ON, L6T 5K5
(905) 793-8888   *SIC 5651*
GAP (CANADA) INC   *p510*
9500 MCLAUGHLIN RD, BRAMPTON, ON, L6X 0B8
(905) 460-2060   *SIC 5651*
GAP (CANADA) INC   *p553*
1 BASS PRO MILLS DR, CONCORD, ON, L4K 5W4
(905) 761-7577   *SIC 5651*
GAP (CANADA) INC   *p928*
60 BLOOR ST W SUITE 1501, TORONTO, ON, M4W 3B8
(416) 921-2225   *SIC 5651*
GAP (CANADA) INC   *p935*
220 YONGE ST, TORONTO, ON, M5B 2H1
(416) 595-6336   *SIC 5651*
GAP (CANADA) INC   *p935*

260 YONGE ST, TORONTO, ON, M5B 2L9
(416) 599-8802   *SIC 5651*
GESTION CAVEAU DES JEANS INC   *p1106*
84 RUE LOIS, GATINEAU, QC, J8Y 3R4
SIC 5651
H & M HENNES & MAURITZ INC   *p553*
1 BASS PRO MILLS DR, CONCORD, ON, L4K 5W4
(905) 760-1769   *SIC 5651*
H&M HENNES & MAURITZ INC   *p945*
1 DUNDAS ST W SUITE 1808, TORONTO, ON, M5G 1Z3
(416) 623-4300   *SIC 5651*
H&M HENNES & MAURITZ INC   *p1205*
1100 RUE SAINTE-CATHERINE O, MONTREAL, QC, H3B 1H4
(514) 788-4590   *SIC 5651*
HOLT, RENFREW & CIE, LIMITEE   *p51*
8 AVE SW UNIT 510, CALGARY, AB, T2P 4H9
(403) 269-7341   *SIC 5651*
HOLT, RENFREW & CIE, LIMITEE   *p1213*
1300 RUE SHERBROOKE O, MONTREAL, QC, H3G 1H9
(514) 842-5111   *SIC 5651*
ICEBREAKER MERINO CLOTHING INC   *p298*
21 WATER ST SUITE 502, VANCOUVER, BC, V6B 1A1
(778) 338-9666   *SIC 5651*
ISLAND BEACH COMPANY CLOTHING & GRAPHICS INCORPORATED   *p469*
82 PURDY DR, TRURO, NS, B2N 5W8
(902) 897-0560   *SIC 5651*
MAGASIN LAURA (P.V.) INC   *p1104*
1076 BOUL MALONEY O, GATINEAU, QC, J8T 3R6
(819) 561-8071   *SIC 5651*
MAGASINS J.L. TAYLOR INC, LES   *p1322*
525 AV NOTRE-DAME BUREAU 672, SAINT-LAMBERT, QC, J4P 2K6
(450) 672-9722   *SIC 5651*
MAGASINS J.L. TAYLOR INC, LES   *p1322*
556 AV VICTORIA, SAINT-LAMBERT, QC, J4P 2J5
(450) 672-9722   *SIC 5651*
MAISON SIMONS INC, LA   *p1269*
20 COTE DE LA FABRIQUE, QUEBEC, QC, G1R 3V9
(418) 692-3630   *SIC 5651*
MAISON SIMONS INC, LA   *p1374*
3050 BOUL DE PORTLAND, SHERBROOKE, QC, J1L 1K1
(819) 829-1840   *SIC 5651*
MARK'S WORK WEARHOUSE LTD   *p804*
3449 SUPERIOR CRT, OAKVILLE, ON, L6L 0C4
(800) 461-4378   *SIC 5651*
ME TO WE STYLE INC   *p934*
145 BERKELEY ST, TORONTO, ON, M5A 2X1
(416) 964-8942   *SIC 5651*
MODE CHOC (ALMA) LTEE   *p1045*
1055 AV DU PONT S BUREAU 50, ALMA, QC, G8B 2V7
(418) 668-2346   *SIC 5651*
MODE CHOC (ALMA) LTEE   *p1305*
610 RUE 90E, SAINT-GEORGES, QC, G5Y 3L2
(418) 221-6850   *SIC 5651*
MODE CHOC (DOLBEAU) LTEE   *p1090*
361 BOUL VEZINA, DOLBEAU-MISTASSINI, QC, G8L 3K6
(418) 276-7189   *SIC 5651*
OAK AND FORT CORP   *p289*
7 6TH AVE E UNIT 200, VANCOUVER, BC, V5T 1J3
(604) 559-6911   *SIC 5651*
OLD NAVY (CANADA) INC   *p710*
100 CITY CENTRE DR UNIT E6, MISSISSAUGA, ON, L5B 2C9
(905) 275-5155   *SIC 5651*
OLD NAVY (CANADA) INC   *p789*
1 YORKDALE RD, NORTH YORK, ON, M6A

3A1

(416) 787-9384 *SIC 5651*

OLD NAVY (CANADA) INC *p930*
60 BLOOR ST W SUITE 1501, TORONTO, ON, M4W 3B8

(416) 921-2711 *SIC 5651*

PLENTY STORES INC *p295*
1352 VERNON DR, VANCOUVER, BC, V6A 3P7

(604) 733-4484 *SIC 5651*

PLUM CLOTHING LTD *p285*
1543 VENABLES ST, VANCOUVER, BC, V5L 2G8

(604) 254-5034 *SIC 5651*

PNB NATION LLC *p1326*
95 RUE GINCE, SAINT-LAURENT, QC, H4N 1J7

(514) 384-3872 *SIC 5651*

R. CROTEAU RIMOUSKI INC *p1285*
400 BOUL JESSOP, RIMOUSKI, QC, G5L 1N1

(418) 723-1614 *SIC 5651*

REID'S DRY GOODS LTD *p322*
2125 41ST AVE W, VANCOUVER, BC, V6M 1Z3

(604) 266-9177 *SIC 5651*

RETAIL DIMENSIONS INCORPORATED *p524*
4335 MAINWAY, BURLINGTON, ON, L7L 5N9

SIC 5651

SHERLOCK CLOTHING LIMITED *p459*
127 CHAIN LAKE DR UNIT 9, HALIFAX, NS, B3S 1B3

(902) 454-7098 *SIC 5651*

STILES' CLOTHIERS INC *p25*
1435 40 AVE NE UNIT 4, CALGARY, AB, T2E 8N6

(403) 230-8515 *SIC 5651*

WAREHOUSE ONE CLOTHING LTD *p392*
1530 GAMBLE PL, WINNIPEG, MB, R3T 1N6

(204) 885-4200 *SIC 5651*

WINNER SPORTSWEAR LTD *p296*
1223 FRANCES ST, VANCOUVER, BC, V6A 1Z4

(604) 253-0411 *SIC 5651*

WINNERS MERCHANTS INTERNATIONAL L.P. *p41*
5111 NORTHLAND DR NW SUITE 200, CALGARY, AB, T2L 2J8

(403) 247-8100 *SIC 5651*

WINNERS MERCHANTS INTERNATIONAL L.P. *p75*
5498 SIGNAL HILL CTR SW, CALGARY, AB, T3H 3P8

(403) 246-4999 *SIC 5651*

WINNERS MERCHANTS INTERNATIONAL L.P. *p245*
19800 LOUGHEED HWY SUITE 160, PITT MEADOWS, BC, V3Y 2W1

(604) 465-4330 *SIC 5651*

WINNERS MERCHANTS INTERNATIONAL L.P. *p327*
798 GRANVILLE ST SUITE 300, VANCOUVER, BC, V6Z 3C3

(604) 683-1058 *SIC 5651*

WINNERS MERCHANTS INTERNATIONAL L.P. *p507*
55 WEST DR, BRAMPTON, ON, L6T 4A1

(905) 451-7200 *SIC 5651*

WINNERS MERCHANTS INTERNATIONAL L.P. *p677*
5000 HIGHWAY 7 E, MARKHAM, ON, L3R 4M9

(905) 415-1441 *SIC 5651*

WINNERS MERCHANTS INTERNATIONAL L.P. *p690*
3185 AMERICAN DR, MISSISSAUGA, ON, L4V 1B8

(905) 672-2228 *SIC 5651*

WINNERS MERCHANTS INTERNATIONAL L.P. *p733*
60 STANDISH CRT, MISSISSAUGA, ON,

L5R 0G1

(905) 405-8000 *SIC 5651*

WINNERS MERCHANTS INTERNATIONAL L.P. *p748*
100 BAYSHORE DR, NEPEAN, ON, K2B 8C1

(613) 721-6451 *SIC 5651*

WINNERS MERCHANTS INTERNATIONAL L.P. *p790*
3090 BATHURST ST SUITE 1, NORTH YORK, ON, M6A 2A1

(416) 782-4469 *SIC 5651*

WINNERS MERCHANTS INTERNATIONAL L.P. *p799*
2460 WINSTON CHURCHILL BLVD SUITE 1, OAKVILLE, ON, L6H 6J5

(905) 829-9086 *SIC 5651*

WINNERS MERCHANTS INTERNATIONAL L.P. *p936*
444 YONGE ST UNIT G3, TORONTO, ON, M5B 2H4

(416) 598-8800 *SIC 5651*

WINNERS MERCHANTS INTERNATIONAL L.P. *p1082*
6900 BOUL DECARIE BUREAU 3550, COTE SAINT-LUC, QC, H3X 2T8

(514) 733-4200 *SIC 5651*

WINNERS MERCHANTS INTERNATIONAL L.P. *p1165*
7275 RUE SHERBROOKE E BUREAU 2000, MONTREAL, QC, H1N 1E9

(514) 798-1908 *SIC 5651*

WINNERS MERCHANTS INTERNATIONAL L.P. *p1200*
1500 AV MCGILL COLLEGE, MONTREAL, QC, H3A 3J5

(514) 788-4949 *SIC 5651*

WINNERS MERCHANTS INTERNATIONAL L.P. *p1248*
1050 CHOMEDEY (A-13) O, POINTE-CLAIRE, QC, H7X 4C9

(450) 969-2007 *SIC 5651*

WINNERS MERCHANTS INTERNATIONAL L.P. *p1389*
4125 BOUL DES RECOLLETS, TROIS-RIVIERES, QC, G9A 6M1

(819) 370-2001 *SIC 5651*

ZARA CANADA INC *p1209*
1200 AV MCGILL COLLEGE BUREAU 1550, MONTREAL, QC, H3B 4G7

(514) 868-1516 *SIC 5651*

SIC 5661 Shoe stores

1125151 ONTARIO LIMITED *p581*
6931 STEELES AVE W, ETOBICOKE, ON, M9W 6K7

(416) 675-9235 *SIC 5661*

2076631 ONTARIO LIMITED *p581*
151 CARLINGVIEW DR UNIT 6, ETOBICOKE, ON, M9W 5S4

(416) 679-8884 *SIC 5661*

2169-5762 QUEBEC INC *p1378*
281 RUE EDWARD-ASSH, STE-CATHERINE-DE-LA-J-CARTIE, QC, G3N 1A3

(418) 875-1839 *SIC 5661*

2302659 MANITOBA LTD *p393*
59 SCURFIELD BLVD SUITE 9, WINNIPEG, MB, R3Y 1V2

(204) 925-6880 *SIC 5661*

991909 ONTARIO INC *p514*
595 WEST ST UNIT 5, BRANTFORD, ON, N3R 7C5

(519) 754-4775 *SIC 5661*

CANADA WEST SHOE MANUFACTURING INC
1250 FIFE ST, WINNIPEG, MB, R2X 2N6

(204) 632-4110 *SIC 5661*

CANADIAN FOOTWEAR (1982) LTD *p373*
128 ADELAIDE ST, WINNIPEG, MB, R3A 0W5

(204) 944-7463 *SIC 5661*

CHAUSSURES BO-PIEDS INC *p1144*
2626 RUE PAPINEAU, LONGUEUIL, QC, J4K 3M4

(450) 651-9222 *SIC 5661*

CHAUSSURES BROWNS INC *p1328*
2255 RUE COHEN, SAINT-LAURENT, QC, H4R 2N7

(514) 334-5000 *SIC 5661*

CHAUSSURES RUBINO INC, LES *p1343*
9300 RUE DU PRADO, SAINT-LEONARD, QC, H1P 3B4

(514) 326-0566 *SIC 5661*

CHURGIN, ARNOLD SHOES LIMITED *p46*
227 8 AVE SW, CALGARY, AB, T2P 1B7

(403) 262-3366 *SIC 5661*

EDMONTON RUNNING ROOM LTD *p114*
9750 47 AVE NW, EDMONTON, AB, T6E 5P3

(780) 439-3099 *SIC 5661*

FACTORY SHOE (KITCHENER) LTD *p639*
686 VICTORIA ST N, KITCHENER, ON, N2H 5G1

(519) 743-2021 *SIC 5661*

FLUEVOG, JOHN BOOTS & SHOES LTD *p326*
837 GRANVILLE ST, VANCOUVER, BC, V6Z 1K7

(604) 688-5245 *SIC 5661*

FOOT LOCKER CANADA CO *p793*
230 BARMAC DR, NORTH YORK, ON, M9L 2Z3

(416) 748-4210 *SIC 5661*

GENFOOT INC *p1127*
1940 55E AV, LACHINE, QC, H8T 3H3

(514) 341-3950 *SIC 5661*

GEOX CANADA INC *p695*
2110 MATHESON BLVD E SUITE 100, MISSISSAUGA, ON, L4W 5E1

(905) 629-8500 *SIC 5661*

GESTION TREE ROOTS INC *p1329*
2300 RUE EMILE-BELANGER, SAINT-LAURENT, QC, H4R 3J4

(514) 747-2536 *SIC 5661*

GROUPE ALDO INC, LE *p1329*
2300 RUE EMILE-BELANGER, SAINT-LAURENT, QC, H4R 3J4

(514) 747-2536 *SIC 5661*

GROUPE PANDA DETAIL INC *p1059*
1060 BOUL MICHELE-BOHEC BUREAU 108, BLAINVILLE, QC, J7C 5E2

(579) 637-9741 *SIC 5661*

GROUPE YELLOW INC *p1183*
5665 BOUL SAINT-LAURENT, MONTREAL, QC, H2T 1S9

(514) 273-0424 *SIC 5661*

GROUPE YELLOW INC *p1183*
5665 BOUL SAINT-LAURENT, MONTREAL, QC, H2T 1S9

(514) 273-0424 *SIC 5661*

JEAN-PAUL FORTIN (1997) INC *p1276*
2050 RUE DE CELLES, QUEBEC, QC, G2C 1X8

(418) 845-5369 *SIC 5661*

MARKIO DESIGNS INC *p973*
1200 BAY ST SUITE 600, TORONTO, ON, M5R 2A5

(416) 929-9629 *SIC 5661*

PAYLESS SHOESOURCE CANADA INC *p579*
191 THE WEST MALL SUITE 1100, ETOBICOKE, ON, M9C 5K8

(416) 626-3666 *SIC 5661*

PAYLESS SHOESOURCE GP INC *p971*
4000-199 ST BAY, COMMERCE COURT W, TORONTO, ON, M5L 1A9

SIC 5661

PAYLESS SHOESOURCE LP *p971*
4000-199 ST BAY, TORONTO, ON, M5L 1A9

SIC 5661

RONSONS SHOE STORES LTD *p264*
12495 HORSESHOE WAY, RICHMOND, BC, V7A 4X6

(604) 270-9974 *SIC 5661*

RUNNING ROOM CANADA INC *p116*

9750 47 AVE NW SUITE 60, EDMONTON, AB, T6E 5P3

(780) 439-3099 *SIC 5661*

SANPAUL INVESTMENTS LIMITED *p784*
365 FLINT RD UNIT 1, NORTH YORK, ON, M3J 2J2

(416) 667-8929 *SIC 5661*

SOFT-MOC INC *p1015*
1400 HOPKINS ST UNIT 3-4, WHITBY, ON, L1N 2C3

(905) 665-8119 *SIC 5661*

STERLING SHOES LIMITED PARTNERSHIP *p256*
2580 VISCOUNT WAY, RICHMOND, BC, V6V 1N1

(604) 270-6640 *SIC 5661*

VELLA, PAUL SHOES (MISSISSAUGA) LIMITED *p785*
365 FLINT RD UNIT 1, NORTH YORK, ON, M3J 2J2

(416) 667-8929 *SIC 5661*

SIC 5699 Miscellaneous apparel and accessory stores

9099-9012 QUEBEC INC *p1081*
709 RUE MERRILL, COATICOOK, QC, J1A 2S2

SIC 5699

9119-6188 QUEBEC INC *p1145*
2786 CH DU LAC BUREAU 1, LONGUEUIL, QC, J4N 1B8

(450) 646-2888 *SIC 5699*

BEKAR & ASSOCIATES ENTERPRISES LIMITED *p197*
45737 LUCKAKUCK WAY, CHILLIWACK, BC, V2R 4E8

(604) 858-4199 *SIC 5699*

COLLECTIONS UNIMAGE INC *p1231*
5620 RUE ERNEST-CORMIER, MONTREAL, QC, H7C 2T5

(450) 661-6444 *SIC 5699*

EDDIE BAUER OF CANADA INC *p1031*
201 AVIVA PARK DR, WOODBRIDGE, ON, L4L 9C1

(800) 426-8020 *SIC 5699*

GESTION SETR INC *p1385*
4125 BOUL DES FORGES BUREAU 1, TROIS-RIVIERES, QC, G8Y 1W1

(819) 376-4343 *SIC 5699*

GESTION TREMBLAY ET LAPOINTE INC *p1385*
300 RUE BARKOFF BUREAU 302, TROIS-RIVIERES, QC, G8T 2A3

(819) 375-3858 *SIC 5699*

GROUPE APP (CANADA) INC *p1178*
600 RUE CHABANEL O, MONTREAL, QC, H2N 2K6

(514) 388-5287 *SIC 5699*

LAMMLE'S WESTERN WEAR LTD *p71*
12012 44 ST SE, CALGARY, AB, T2Z 4A2

(403) 255-0272 *SIC 5699*

MIMRAN, JOSEPH & ASSOCIATES INC *p994*
1485 DUPONT ST, TORONTO, ON, M6P 3S2

(416) 516-0641 *SIC 5699*

MOMO SPORTS INC *p1374*
530 RUE JEAN-PAUL-PERRAULT, SHERBROOKE, QC, J1L 3A6

(819) 822-3077 *SIC 5699*

RJM56 INVESTMENTS INC *p576*
360 EVANS AVE, ETOBICOKE, ON, M8Z 1K5

(416) 593-6900 *SIC 5699*

ROYAL J & M DISTRIBUTING INC *p606*
925 WOODLAWN RD W, GUELPH, ON, N1K 1B7

(519) 822-7081 *SIC 5699*

ST-BRUNO MODES ET SPORTS INC *p1296*
750 BOUL DES PROMENADES, SAINT-BRUNO, QC, J3V 6A8

(450) 372-0368 *SIC 5699*

SWIMCO AQUATIC SUPPLIES LTD *p38*
6403 BURBANK RD SE SUITE 1, CALGARY, AB, T2H 2E1
(403) 259-6113   *SIC 5699*

TILLEY ENDURABLES, INC *p780*
60 GERVAIS DR, NORTH YORK, ON, M3C 1Z3
(416) 441-6141   *SIC 5699*

SIC 5712 Furniture stores

1342205 ONTARIO LIMITED *p485*
90 ANNE STREET S, BARRIE, ON, L4N 2E3
(613) 247-3300   *SIC 5712*

1562246 ONTARIO INC *p912*
108 THIRD AVE, TIMMINS, ON, P4N 1C3
(705) 264-2274   *SIC 5712*

1569243 ONTARIO INC *p485*
316 BAYVIEW DR, BARRIE, ON, L4N 8X9
(705) 719-4870   *SIC 5712*

1692246 ONTARIO INC *p665*
91 ESNA PARK DR UNIT 8, MARKHAM, ON, L3R 2S2
(905) 845-6556   *SIC 5712*

3717291 CANADA INC *p1084*
2205 BOUL INDUSTRIEL, COTE SAINT-LUC, QC, H7S 1P8
(450) 669-2323   *SIC 5712*

446987 ONTARIO INC *p500*
3389 STEELES AVE E, BRAMPTON, ON, L6T 5W4
(905) 494-1118   *SIC 5712*

4507525 CANADA INC *p1343*
8755 BOUL LANGELIER, SAINT-LEONARD, QC, H1P 2C6
(514) 356-0677   *SIC 5712*

648781 ALBERTA LTD *p98*
17109 109 AVE NW, EDMONTON, AB, T5S 2H8
(780) 481-7800   *SIC 5712*

7902476 CANADA INC *p594*
1750 CYRVILLE RD, GLOUCESTER, ON, K1B 3L8
(613) 749-0001   *SIC 5712*

99702 CANADA LTEE *p594*
1750 CYRVILLE RD, GLOUCESTER, ON, K1B 3L8
(613) 749-0001   *SIC 5712*

ABI/ADVANCED BUSINESS INTERIORS INC *p816*
2355 ST. LAURENT BLVD, OTTAWA, ON, K1G 4L2
(613) 738-1003   *SIC 5712*

AMEUBLEMENTS ARTELITE INC *p1047*
10251 BOUL RAY-LAWSON, ANJOU, QC, H1J 1L6
(514) 493-6113   *SIC 5712*

AMEUBLEMENTS TANGUAY INC *p1078*
1990 BOUL TALBOT, CHICOUTIMI, QC, G7H 7Y3
(418) 698-4411   *SIC 5712*

AMEUBLEMENTS TANGUAY INC *p1276*
7200 RUE ARMAND-VIAU, QUEBEC, QC, G2C 2A7
(800) 826-4829   *SIC 5712*

AMEUBLEMENTS TANGUAY INC *p1385*
2200 BOUL DES RECOLLETS, TROIS-RIVIERES, QC, G8Z 3X5
(819) 373-1111   *SIC 5712*

ARROW FURNITURE LTD *p794*
35 ARROW RD, NORTH YORK, ON, M9M 2L4
(416) 743-1530   *SIC 5712*

ART SHOPPE LIMITED *p923*
2131 YONGE ST, TORONTO, ON, M4S 2A7
(416) 487-3211   *SIC 5712*

ASHKYLE LTD *p405*
101 LEWISVILLE RD, MONCTON, NB, E1A 2K5
(506) 859-6969   *SIC 5712*

B.B. BARGOON'S (1996) CORP *p549*
8201 KEELE ST UNIT 1, CONCORD, ON,

L4K 1Z4
(905) 761-5065   *SIC 5712*

BAD BOY FURNITURE WAREHOUSE LIMITED *p792*
500 FENMAR DR, NORTH YORK, ON, M9L 2V5
(416) 667-7546   *SIC 5712*

BONDAR'S FINE FURNITURE LTD *p33*
6999 11 ST SE BAY SUITE 110, CALGARY, AB, T2H 2S1
(403) 253-8200   *SIC 5712*

BOOMCO DECOR INC *p549*
255 BASS PRO MILLS DR SUITE, CONCORD, ON, L4K 0A2
(905) 660-0677   *SIC 5712*

BOOMCO DECOR INC *p659*
760 WHARNCLIFFE RD S, LONDON, ON, N6J 2N4
(519) 686-1441   *SIC 5712*

BRICK LTD, THE *p95*
16930 114 AVE NW, EDMONTON, AB, T5M 3S2
(780) 930-6000   *SIC 5712*

BRICK WAREHOUSE LP, THE *p182*
3100 PRODUCTION WAY SUITE 103, BURNABY, BC, V5A 4R4
(604) 415-4900   *SIC 5712*

BRICK WAREHOUSE LP, THE *p219*
948 MCCURDY RD SUITE 100, KELOWNA, BC, V1X 2P7
(250) 765-2220   *SIC 5712*

BRICK WAREHOUSE LP, THE *p702*
1607 DUNDAS ST E, MISSISSAUGA, ON, L4X 1L5
(905) 629-2900   *SIC 5712*

BRICK WAREHOUSE LP, THE *p737*
6765 KENNEDY RD, MISSISSAUGA, ON, L5T 0A2
(905) 696-3400   *SIC 5712*

BRICK WAREHOUSE LP, THE *p870*
19 WILLIAM KITCHEN RD, SCARBOROUGH, ON, M1P 5B7
(416) 751-3383   *SIC 5712*

BRICK WAREHOUSE LP, THE *p1030*
137 CHRISLEA RD, WOODBRIDGE, ON, L4L 8N6
(905) 850-5300   *SIC 5712*

C.J.C. COULTER INVESTMENTS 2006 INC *p1021*
1324 WINDSOR AVE, WINDSOR, ON, N8X 3L9
(519) 253-7422   *SIC 5712*

CARDINAL FINE CABINETRY CORPORATION *p660*
165 EXETER RD, LONDON, ON, N6L 1A4
(519) 652-3295   *SIC 5712*

CENTRE MASSICOTTE INC *p1261*
687 BOUL PIERRE-BERTRAND, QUEBEC, QC, G1M 3E4
(418) 687-4340   *SIC 5712*

CLEAR VIEW HOME FURNISHINGS LTD *p413*
428 ROTHESAY AVE, SAINT JOHN, NB, E2J 2C4
(506) 634-1966   *SIC 5712*

CLERMONT, MARIETTE INC *p1236*
2300 BOUL LE CORBUSIER, MONTREAL, QC, H7S 2C9
(450) 934-7502   *SIC 5712*

COHEN'S HOME FURNISHINGS LIMITED *p426*
24 GLENCOE DR, MOUNT PEARL, NL, A1N 4P6
(709) 739-6631   *SIC 5712*

COMFORT FURNITURE GALLERIES *p100*
17109 109 AVE NW, EDMONTON, AB, T5S 2H8
(780) 481-7800   *SIC 5712*

CONCORDIA FURNITURE LTD *p1048*
11001 RUE SECANT, ANJOU, QC, H1J 1S6
(514) 355-5100   *SIC 5712*

CRATE AND BARREL CANADA INC *p39*
100 ANDERSON RD SE SUITE 273, CALGARY, AB, T2J 3V1

(403) 278-7020   *SIC 5712*

D & S FURNITURE GALLERIES LTD *p382*
1425 ELLICE AVE, WINNIPEG, MB, R3G 0G3
(204) 783-8500   *SIC 5712*

D.O.T FURNITURE LIMITED *p703*
3105 DIXIE RD, MISSISSAUGA, ON, L4Y 4E3
(416) 252-2228   *SIC 5712*

DICKS AND COMPANY LIMITED *p433*
385 EMPIRE AVE, ST. JOHN'S, NL, A1E 1W6
(709) 579-5111   *SIC 5712*

DODD'S FURNITURE LTD *p334*
715 FINLAYSON ST, VICTORIA, BC, V8T 2T4
(250) 388-6663   *SIC 5712*

DOMON LTEE *p1126*
1950 RUE REMEMBRANCE, LACHINE, QC, H8S 1W9
(514) 637-5835   *SIC 5712*

EBENISTERIE NORCLAIR INC *p1064*
155 RUE JULES-LEGER, BOUCHERVILLE, QC, J4B 7K8
(450) 641-1737   *SIC 5712*

EBENISTERIES SAMSON SAMUEL INC, LES *p1074*
7900 BOUL INDUSTRIEL, CHAMBLY, QC, J3L 4X3
(450) 447-7503   *SIC 5712*

EQ3 LTD *p363*
170 FURNITURE PARK, WINNIPEG, MB, R2G 1B9
(204) 957-8018   *SIC 5712*

ETHAN ALLEN (CANADA) INC *p1027*
205 TRADE VALLEY DR SUITE B, WOODBRIDGE, ON, L4H 3N6
(905) 264-7686   *SIC 5712*

FINESSE HOME LIVING INC *p119*
4210 GATEWAY BLVD NW, EDMONTON, AB, T6J 7K1
(780) 444-7100   *SIC 5712*

FOURNITURES DE BUREAU DENIS INC *p1134*
2725 RUE MICHELIN, LAVAL-OUEST, QC, H7L 5X6
(450) 681-5300   *SIC 5712*

FURNCO FURNITURE INTERNATIONAL DISTRIBUTORS LTD *p783*
363 SUPERTEST RD, NORTH YORK, ON, M3J 2M4
(416) 736-6120   *SIC 5712*

FURNITURE INVESTMENT GROUP INC *p892*
563 BARTON ST, STONEY CREEK, ON, L8E 5S1
SIC 5712

G2MC INC *p1225*
1215 BOUL CREMAZIE O, MONTREAL, QC, H4N 2W1
(514) 382-1443   *SIC 5712*

G2MC INC *p1237*
2323 DES LAURENTIDES (A-15) E, MONTREAL, QC, H7S 1Z7
(450) 682-3022   *SIC 5712*

GAGNON FRERES INC *p1079*
1460 BOUL TALBOT, CHICOUTIMI, QC, G7H 4C2
(418) 690-3366   *SIC 5712*

GERMAIN LARIVIERE (1970) LTEE *p1310*
4370 BOUL LAURIER E, SAINT-HYACINTHE, QC, J2R 2C1
(450) 799-5522   *SIC 5712*

GESTION MAISON ETHIER INC *p1294*
267 BOUL SIR-WILFRID-LAURIER, SAINT-BASILE-LE-GRAND, QC, J3N 1M8
(450) 653-1556   *SIC 5712*

GRENIER POPULAIRE DES BASSES LAURENTIDES *p1300*
217 RUE SAINT-LAURENT, SAINT-EUSTACHE, QC, J7P 4W4
(450) 623-5891   *SIC 5712*

GROUPE BMTC INC *p1104*
500 BOUL DE LA GAPPE, GATINEAU, QC,

J8T 8A8
(819) 561-5007   *SIC 5712*

GROUPE DAGENAIS M.D.C. INC *p1068*
117 BOUL DE BROMONT, BROMONT, QC, J2L 2K7
SIC 5712

GUNNAR MANUFACTURING INC *p70*
3200 118 AVE SE, CALGARY, AB, T2Z 3X1
(403) 236-1828   *SIC 5712*

HAUSER INDUSTRIES INC *p1006*
330 WEBER ST N, WATERLOO, ON, N2J 3H6
(800) 268-7328   *SIC 5712*

HBI - HERITAGE BUSINESS INTERIORS INC *p30*
2600 PORTLAND ST SE SUITE 2050, CALGARY, AB, T2G 4M6
(403) 252-2888   *SIC 5712*

HERITAGE OFFICE FURNISHINGS LTD *p323*
1588 RAND AVE, VANCOUVER, BC, V6P 3G2
(604) 688-2381   *SIC 5712*

HOGEBOOM, PAUL W. HOLDINGS LTD *p659*
760 WHARNCLIFFE RD S, LONDON, ON, N6J 2N4
(519) 686-1441   *SIC 5712*

IKEA CANADA LIMITED PARTNERSHIP *p531*
1065 PLAINS RD E, BURLINGTON, ON, L7T 4K1
(905) 637-9440   *SIC 5712*

IKEA CANADA LIMITED PARTNERSHIP *p574*
1475 THE QUEENSWAY, ETOBICOKE, ON, M8Z 1T3
(866) 866-4532   *SIC 5712*

IKEA CANADA LIMITED PARTNERSHIP *p1065*
586 CH DE TOURAINE, BOUCHERVILLE, QC, J4B 5E4
SIC 5712

IKEA CANADA LIMITED PARTNERSHIP *p1339*
9090 BOUL CAVENDISH, SAINT-LAURENT, QC, H4T 1Z8
(514) 904-8619   *SIC 5712*

IKEA LIMITED *p120*
1311 102 ST NW, EDMONTON, AB, T6N 1M3
(866) 866-4532   *SIC 5712*

IMMEUBLES STRUC-TUBE LTEE *p1340*
6000 RTE TRANSCANADIENNE, SAINT-LAURENT, QC, H4T 1X9
(514) 333-9747   *SIC 5712*

INSIDEOUT BURLINGTON LTD *p529*
1515 NORTH SERVICE RD, BURLINGTON, ON, L7P 0A2
(905) 681-7173   *SIC 5712*

INSPIRATION FURNITURE INC *p319*
1275 6TH AVE W, VANCOUVER, BC, V6H 1A6
(604) 730-1275   *SIC 5712*

INTERIEURS MOBILIA INC, LES *p1251*
2525 BOUL DES SOURCES, POINTE-CLAIRE, QC, H9R 5Z9
(514) 685-7557   *SIC 5712*

JORDANS INTERIORS LTD *p319*
1470 BROADWAY W, VANCOUVER, BC, V6H 1H4
(604) 733-1174   *SIC 5712*

JYSK LINEN'N FURNITURE INC *p201*
25 KING EDWARD ST UNIT 101, COQUITLAM, BC, V3K 4S8
(604) 472-0769   *SIC 5712*

KETER CANADA INC *p684*
205 MARKET DR, MILTON, ON, L9T 4Z7
(905) 864-6695   *SIC 5712*

LEON'S FURNITURE LIMITED *p487*
81 BRYNE DR, BARRIE, ON, L4N 8V8
(705) 730-1777   *SIC 5712*

LEON'S FURNITURE LIMITED *p706*
201 BRITANNIA RD E, MISSISSAUGA, ON,

L4Z 3X8
(905) 501-9505 *SIC 5712*
LEON'S FURNITURE LIMITED p761
440 TAYLOR RD, NIAGARA ON THE LAKE, ON, L0S 1J0
(905) 682-8519 *SIC 5712*
LEON'S FURNITURE LIMITED p795
10 SUNTRACT RD, NORTH YORK, ON, M9N 3N9
SIC 5712
LEON'S FURNITURE LIMITED p795
45 GORDON MACKAY RD, NORTH YORK, ON, M9N 3X3
(416) 243-7880 *SIC 5712*
LEON'S FURNITURE LIMITED p830
2600 QUEENSVIEW DR, OTTAWA, ON, K2B 8H6
(613) 820-6446 *SIC 5712*
LEON'S FURNITURE LIMITED p1087
2000 BOUL DANIEL-JOHNSON, COTE SAINT-LUC, QC, H7T 1A3
(450) 688-3851 *SIC 5712*
LEON'S FURNITURE LIMITED p1275
2840 RUE EINSTEIN, QUEBEC, QC, G1X 5H3
(418) 683-9600 *SIC 5712*
M.J.M. FURNITURE CENTRE LTD p277
13570 77 AVE, SURREY, BC, V3W 6Y3
(604) 596-9901 *SIC 5712*
MCCRUM'S DIRECT SALES LTD p36
5310 1 ST SW, CALGARY, AB, T2H 0C8
(403) 259-4939 *SIC 5712*
MCKERCHER KINGSTON LIMITED p633
2730 PRINCESS ST, KINGSTON, ON, K7P 2W6
(613) 384-2418 *SIC 5712*
MEGABURO INC p1045
440 RUE COLLARD, ALMA, QC, G8B 1N2
(418) 668-4591 *SIC 5712*
MEGABURO INC p1383
236 RUE NOTRE-DAME O, THETFORD MINES, QC, G6G 1J6
(418) 338-8808 *SIC 5712*
MERCEDES CORP p888
1386 KING ST N, ST JACOBS, ON, N0B 2N0
(519) 664-2293 *SIC 5712*
MEUBLES DENIS RIEL INC p1101
1555 BOUL INDUSTRIEL, FARNHAM, QC, J2N 2X3
(450) 293-3605 *SIC 5712*
MEUBLES JCPERREAULT INC p1352
5 RUE INDUSTRIELLE, SAINT-ROCH-DE-L'ACHIGAN, QC, J0K 3H0
(450) 588-7211 *SIC 5712*
MEUBLES MARCHAND INC, LES p1391
1767 3E AV, VAL-D'OR, QC, J9P 1W3
(819) 874-8777 *SIC 5712*
MEUBLES REAL LEVASSEUR & FILS INC p1246
1907 RUE PRINCIPALE, POHENEGAMOOK, QC, G0L 1J0
(418) 859-3159 *SIC 5712*
MILLWOOD FURNITURE ENT. LTD p201
1365 UNITED BLVD, COQUITLAM, BC, V3K 6Y3
(604) 777-1365 *SIC 5712*
MMP OFFICE INTERIORS INCORPORATED p447
656 WINDMILL RD SUITE 1, DARTMOUTH, NS, B3B 1B8
(902) 422-4011 *SIC 5712*
MONK OFFICE SUPPLY LTD p339
800 VIEWFIELD RD, VICTORIA, BC, V9A 4V1
(800) 735-3433 *SIC 5712*
MULTIWOOD INC p71
11580 40 ST SE, CALGARY, AB, T2Z 4V6
(403) 279-7789 *SIC 5712*
NORDIC HOLDINGS LTD p125
2303 91 ST SW, EDMONTON, AB, T6X 1V8
(780) 437-1527 *SIC 5712*
NOTRE DAME AGENCIES LIMITED p425
391 MAIN ST, LEWISPORTE, NL, A0G 3A0

(709) 535-8691 *SIC 5712*
PACIFIC RIM CABINETS LTD p206
640 BELGRAVE WAY, DELTA, BC, V3M 5R7
(604) 515-7377 *SIC 5712*
PARAMOUNT INDUSTRIES LTD p261
5520 MINORU BLVD, RICHMOND, BC, V6X 2A9
(604) 273-0155 *SIC 5712*
PORTE EVOLUTION INC p1045
1500 BOUL SAINT-JUDE, ALMA, QC, G8B 3L4
(418) 668-6688 *SIC 5712*
RENOVATION EXPO INC p1254
40 RUE SAINT-PIERRE, PRINCEVILLE, QC, G6L 5A9
(819) 364-2616 *SIC 5712*
S. SETLAKWE LTEE p1383
493 BOUL FRONTENAC O, THETFORD MINES, QC, G6G 6K2
(418) 338-8511 *SIC 5712*
SANDY'S FURNITURE LTD p202
1335 UNITED BLVD SUITE D, COQUITLAM, BC, V3K 6V3
(604) 520-0800 *SIC 5712*
SCAN DESIGNS LTD p202
140 UNITED BLVD, COQUITLAM, BC, V3K 6Y2
(604) 524-3444 *SIC 5712*
SCHWARTZ & CO LTD p467
325 VULCAN AVE, SYDNEY, NS, B1P 5X1
(902) 539-4404 *SIC 5712*
SCHWARTZ & COMPANY (2006) LIMITED p467
30 REEVES ST, SYDNEY, NS, B1P 3C5
(902) 539-4404 *SIC 5712*
SIM'S FURNITURE LIMITED p157
2811 BREMNER AVE UNIT A, RED DEER, AB, T4R 1P7
(403) 342-7467 *SIC 5712*
SLEEP COUNTRY CANADA HOLDINGS INC p506
7920 AIRPORT RD, BRAMPTON, ON, L6T 4N8
(289) 748-0206 *SIC 5712*
SLEEP COUNTRY CANADA INC p238
805 BOYD ST SUITE 100, NEW WESTMINSTER, BC, V3M 5X2
(604) 515-9711 *SIC 5712*
SLEEP COUNTRY CANADA INC p506
7920 AIRPORT RD, BRAMPTON, ON, L6T 4N8
(289) 748-0206 *SIC 5712*
SMITTY'S SHOPPING CENTRE LIMITED p618
170 3RD ST, HANOVER, ON, N4N 1B2
(519) 364-3800 *SIC 5712*
SOFA TO GO p1047
12900 BOUL INDUSTRILLE, ANJOU, QC, H1A 4X9
(514) 387-7632 *SIC 5712*
STAR QUALITY OFFICE FURNITURE MFG LTD p1033
10 WESTCREEK DR SUITE 16, WOODBRIDGE, ON, L4L 9R5
(416) 741-8000 *SIC 5712*
STONEY CREEK FURNITURE LIMITED p893
395 LEWIS RD, STONEY CREEK, ON, L8E 5N5
(905) 643-4121 *SIC 5712*
STRUC-TUBE LTEE p1341
6000 RTE TRANSCANADIENNE, SAINT-LAURENT, QC, H4T 1X9
(514) 333-9747 *SIC 5712*
TDG FURNITURE INC p389
116 NATURE PARK WAY, WINNIPEG, MB, R3P 0X8
(204) 989-9898 *SIC 5712*
TEPPERMAN, N. LIMITED p661
1150 WHARNCLIFFE RD S, LONDON, ON, N6L 1K3
(519) 433-5353 *SIC 5712*
TEPPERMAN, N. LIMITED p1021
2595 OUELLETTE AVE, WINDSOR, ON, N8X 4V8

(519) 969-9700 *SIC 5712*
THREE-H MANUFACTURING LTD p753
156462 CLOVER VALLEY RD, NEW LISKEARD, ON, P0J 1P0
(705) 647-4323 *SIC 5712*
TODAY'S COLONIAL FURNITURE 2000 INC p811
1680 VIMONT CRT SUITE 100, ORLEANS, ON, K4A 3M3
(613) 837-5900 *SIC 5712*
TRIAL DESIGN INC p1366
570 BOUL DES ERABLES, SALABERRY-DE-VALLEYFIELD, QC, J6T 6G4
(450) 370-1377 *SIC 5712*
UPPER ROOM HOME FURNISHINGS INC, THE p751
545 WEST HUNT CLUB RD, NEPEAN, ON, K2G 5W5
(613) 721-5873 *SIC 5712*
URBAN BARN LTD p194
4085 MARINE WAY UNIT 1, BURNABY, BC, V5J 5E2
(604) 456-2200 *SIC 5712*
WHEATON, GARNET FARM LIMITED p441
518 SHAW RD RR 3, BERWICK, NS, B0P 1E0
(902) 538-9793 *SIC 5712*
WHITE OAK CUSTOM WOODWORKING LTD p496
10 BROWNING CRT, BOLTON, ON, L7E 1G8
(905) 669-0919 *SIC 5712*
WIELER HUNT INVESTMENTS INC p822
60 BY WARD MARKET SQ, OTTAWA, ON, K1N 7A2
(613) 562-9111 *SIC 5712*
WILLIAMS-SONOMA CANADA, INC p790
3401 DUFFERIN ST SUITE 215, NORTH YORK, ON, M6A 2T9
(416) 785-1233 *SIC 5712*
WILSON'S SHOPPING CENTRE LIMITED p439
3536 HWY 3, BARRINGTON PASSAGE, NS, B0W 1G0
(902) 637-2300 *SIC 5712*
WORLDWIDE SLEEP CENTRE LIMITED p1019
2525 JEFFERSON BLVD, WINDSOR, ON, N8T 2W5
(519) 944-3552 *SIC 5712*

SIC 5713 Floor covering stores

9240-9770 QUEBEC INC p1149
500 RUE SICARD, MASCOUCHE, QC, J7K 3G5
(450) 474-5002 *SIC 5713*
98599 CANADA LTD p444
30 AKERLEY BLVD, DARTMOUTH, NS, B3B 1N1
(902) 481-1010 *SIC 5713*
ALEXANIAN FLOORING LIMITED p612
601 MAIN ST W, HAMILTON, ON, L8P 1K9
(905) 527-2857 *SIC 5713*
ASHLEY CARPETS LTD p95
14340 111 AVE NW, EDMONTON, AB, T5M 2P4
(780) 454-9503 *SIC 5713*
BEAULIEU DECOR D'ASTOUS & FRERES INC p1284
385 2E RUE E, RIMOUSKI, QC, G5L 2G4
(418) 723-9487 *SIC 5713*
CERAMIQUE DECORS M.S.F. INC p1266
2750 AV DALTON, QUEBEC, QC, G1P 3S4
(418) 781-0955 *SIC 5713*
COUVRE-PLANCHERS PELLETIER INC p1138
4600 BOUL GUILLAUME-COUTURE, LEVIS, QC, G6W 5N6
(418) 837-3681 *SIC 5713*
CURTIS CARPETS LTD p390
1280 PEMBINA HWY, WINNIPEG, MB, R3T 2B2

(204) 452-8100 *SIC 5713*
ELTE CARPETS LIMITED p989
80 RONALD AVE, TORONTO, ON, M6E 5A2
(416) 785-7885 *SIC 5713*
INSTALL-A-FLOR LIMITED p446
31 STERNS CRT, DARTMOUTH, NS, B3B 1W7
(902) 468-3111 *SIC 5713*
JORDANS RUGS LTD p319
1470 BROADWAY W, VANCOUVER, BC, V6H 1H4
(604) 733-1174 *SIC 5713*
JOUJAN BROTHERS FLOORING INC p145
941 SOUTH RAILWAY ST SE UNIT 3, MEDICINE HAT, AB, T1A 2W3
(403) 528-8008 *SIC 5713*
LANCTOT, J.C. INC p1314
148 RUE BOYER, SAINT-ISIDORE-DE-LAPRAIRIE, QC, J0L 2A0
(450) 692-4655 *SIC 5713*
RITCHIE, KEVIN A LTD p402
1250 HANWELL RD, FREDERICTON, NB, E3C 1A7
(506) 458-8588 *SIC 5713*
TAYLOR FLOORING LIMITED p443
114 WOODLAWN RD SUITE 257, DARTMOUTH, NS, B2W 2S7
(902) 435-3567 *SIC 5713*

SIC 5714 Drapery and upholstery stores

BOUTIQUE LINEN CHEST (PHASE II) INC p1155
2305 CH ROCKLAND BUREAU 500, MONTROYAL, QC, H3P 3E9
(514) 341-7810 *SIC 5714*
INTEGRITY WALL SYSTEMS INC p341
1371 COURTLAND AVE, VICTORIA, BC, V9E 2C5
(250) 480-5500 *SIC 5714*

SIC 5719 Miscellaneous homefurnishings

1348441 ONTARIO INC p690
1775 SISMET RD, MISSISSAUGA, ON, L4W 1P9
(905) 282-9371 *SIC 5719*
1619214 ONTARIO LIMITED p921
2552 YONGE ST, TORONTO, ON, M4P 2J2
(416) 485-0303 *SIC 5719*
3237681 CANADA INC p1038
489 BRACKLEY POINT RD -RTE 15, BRACKLEY, PE, C1E 1Z3
(902) 629-1500 *SIC 5719*
333308 ONTARIO LTD p927
55 BLOOR ST W SUITE 506, TORONTO, ON, M4W 1A5
(416) 964-2900 *SIC 5719*
429149 B.C. LTD p180
8168 GLENWOOD DR, BURNABY, BC, V3N 5E9
(604) 549-2000 *SIC 5719*
AAA ENTERPRISES INC p184
3918 KITCHENER ST, BURNABY, BC, V5C 3M2
(604) 558-2250 *SIC 5719*
ADVANCED PREFABS LIMITED p829
1722 CARLING AVE, OTTAWA, ON, K2A 1C7
(613) 728-1775 *SIC 5719*
AU LIT FINE LINENS INC p923
2049 YONGE ST, TORONTO, ON, M4S 2A2
(416) 489-7992 *SIC 5719*
BAIN DEPOT INC p1058
1200 BOUL MICHELE-BOHEC, BLAINVILLE, QC, J7C 5S4
(450) 433-6930 *SIC 5719*
BATH & BODY WORKS (CANADA) CORP p1093
1608 BOUL SAINT-REGIS, DORVAL, QC, H9P 1H6
(514) 684-7700 *SIC 5719*

BATH & BODY WORKS INC   p718
5100 ERIN MILLS PKY, MISSISSAUGA,
ON, L5M 4Z5
(905) 820-1112   *SIC 5719*

BENIX & CO. INC   p788
98 ORFUS RD, NORTH YORK, ON, M6A
1L9
(416) 784-0732   *SIC 5719*

BLINDS BY VERTICAN INC   p145
549 17 ST SW, MEDICINE HAT, AB, T1A
7W5
(403) 527-9084   *SIC 5719*

BLINDS TO GO INC   p1168
3510 BOUL SAINT-JOSEPH E, MON-
TREAL, QC, H1X 1W6
(514) 255-4000   *SIC 5719*

BOUCLAIR INC   p1249
152 AV ALSTON, POINTE-CLAIRE, QC,
H9R 6B4
(514) 426-0115   *SIC 5719*

BOUTIQUE LINEN CHEST (PHASE II) INC
p1134
4455 DES LAURENTIDES (A-15) E, LAVAL-
OUEST, QC, H7L 5X8
(514) 331-5260   *SIC 5719*

BRITE BLINDS LTD   p182
4275 PHILLIPS AVE SUITE C, BURNABY,
BC, V5A 2X4
(604) 420-8820   *SIC 5719*

**CHINTZ & COMPANY DECORATIVE FUR-
NISHINGS INC**   p336
1720 STORE ST, VICTORIA, BC, V8W 1V5
(250) 381-2404   *SIC 5719*

CONCEPTS ZONE INC, LES   p1173
4246 RUE SAINT-DENIS, MONTREAL, QC,
H2J 2K8
(514) 845-3530   *SIC 5719*

DANIADOWN QUILTS LTD   p290
1270 MARINE DR SE, VANCOUVER, BC,
V5X 2V9
(604) 324-8766   *SIC 5719*

EQUIPEMENTS ARES DORVAL LTEE, LES
p1093
2000 BOUL HYMUS BUREAU 201, DOR-
VAL, QC, H9P 1J7
(514) 683-4337   *SIC 5719*

FIREPLACE CENTRE, THE   p829
811 BOYD AVE, OTTAWA, ON, K2A 2C8
(613) 728-1775   *SIC 5719*

FIREPLACE PRODUCTS U.S., INC   p209
6988 VENTURE ST, DELTA, BC, V4G 1H4
(604) 946-5155   *SIC 5719*

GESTION MADELEINE DE VILLERS INC
p1173
4246 RUE SAINT-DENIS, MONTREAL, QC,
H2J 2K8
(514) 845-4090   *SIC 5719*

GROUPE LUMINAIRES INC, LE   p1250
260 AV LABROSSE, POINTE-CLAIRE, QC,
H9R 5L5
(514) 683-3883   *SIC 5719*

GROUPE MULTI LUMINAIRE INC, LE p1086
2591 BOUL DANIEL-JOHNSON, COTE
SAINT-LUC, QC, H7T 1S8
(450) 681-3939   *SIC 5719*

HODDOR LIGHTING INC   p992
1461 CASTLEFIELD AVE, TORONTO, ON,
M6M 1Y4
(416) 651-6570   *SIC 5719*

HUDSON'S BAY COMPANY   p190
4800 KINGSWAY SUITE 118, BURNABY,
BC, V5H 4J2
    SIC 5719

KITCHEN STUFF PLUS INC   p988
125 TYCOS DR, TORONTO, ON, M6B 1W6
(416) 944-2847   *SIC 5719*

**OXFORD MILLS HOME FASHION FACTORY
OUTLET INC, THE**   p534
425 HESPELER RD UNIT 1C, CAM-
BRIDGE, ON, N1R 6J2
(519) 342-3026   *SIC 5719*

PARK LIGHTING AND FURNITURE LTD p98
10353 170 ST NW, EDMONTON, AB, T5P
4V4

(780) 434-9600   *SIC 5719*

PASSION CUISINE ET GOURMET   p1393
2020 BOUL RENE-GAULTIER BUREAU 36,
VARENNES, QC, J3X 1N9
(450) 929-2942   *SIC 5719*

PRODUITS CLAIR DE LUNE INC   p1340
361 RUE LOCKE, SAINT-LAURENT, QC,
H4T 1X7
(514) 389-5757   *SIC 5719*

ROB MCINTOSH CHINA INC   p882
20369 SOUTH SERVICE RD, SOUTH LAN-
CASTER, ON, K0C 2C0
(613) 347-2461   *SIC 5719*

ROBINSON LIGHTING LTD   p382
995 MILT STEGALL DR, WINNIPEG, MB,
R3G 3H7
(204) 784-0099   *SIC 5719*

SINOBEC TRADING INC   p1336
4455 RUE COUSENS, SAINT-LAURENT,
QC, H4S 1X5
(514) 339-9333   *SIC 5719*

STOKES CANADA INC   p1157
5660 RUE FERRIER, MONT-ROYAL, QC,
H4P 1M7
(514) 341-4334   *SIC 5719*

STOKES INC   p1157
5660 RUE FERRIER, MONT-ROYAL, QC,
H4P 1M7
(514) 341-4334   *SIC 5719*

UNION ELECTRIC LIGHTING CO. LTD p993
1491 CASTLEFIELD AVE, TORONTO, ON,
M6M 1Y3
(416) 652-2200   *SIC 5719*

SIC 5722 Household appliance stores

1100833 ONTARIO LIMITED   p989
672 DUPONT ST SUITE 201, TORONTO,
ON, M6G 1Z6
(416) 535-1555   *SIC 5722*

COAST WHOLESALE APPLIANCES INC
p290
8488 MAIN ST, VANCOUVER, BC, V5X
4W8
(604) 321-6644   *SIC 5722*

CUSTOM VACUUM SERVICES LTD   p148
904 29 AVE, NISKU, AB, T9E 1B7
(780) 955-9344   *SIC 5722*

GERMAIN LARIVIERE INC   p1310
4370 BOUL LAURIER E, SAINT-
HYACINTHE, QC, J2R 2C1
(450) 799-5522   *SIC 5722*

ICS GROUP INC   p78
250081 MOUNTAIN VIEW TRAIL, CAL-
GARY, AB, T3Z 3S3
(403) 247-4440   *SIC 5722*

MIDWESTERN ONTARIO SERVICE EXPERT
p1006
826 KING ST N UNIT 14, WATERLOO, ON,
N2J 4G8
(519) 664-2974   *SIC 5722*

NAIRN VACUUM & APPLIANCE   p368
929 NAIRN AVE, WINNIPEG, MB, R2L 0X9
(204) 668-4901   *SIC 5722*

RELIABLE PARTS LTD   p201
85 NORTH BEND ST, COQUITLAM, BC,
V3K 6N1
(604) 941-1355   *SIC 5722*

**SERVICE DE L'ESTRIE (VENTE & REPARA-
TION) INC**   p1371
225 RUE WELLINGTON S, SHERBROOKE,
QC, J1H 5E1
(819) 563-0563   *SIC 5722*

**SOUTHAMPTON-TRANE AIR CONDITION-
ING (CALGARY) INC**   p18
10905 48 ST SE SUITE 157, CALGARY, AB,
T2C 1G8
(403) 301-0090   *SIC 5722*

**SPECIALISTES DE L'ELECTROMENAGER,
LES**   p1388
3215 BOUL DES RECOLLETS, TROIS-
RIVIERES, QC, G9A 6M1
(819) 693-3393   *SIC 5722*

**TACKABERRY HEATING SUPPLIES LIM-
ITED**   p630
60 DALTON AVE, KINGSTON, ON, K7K 6C3
(613) 549-3320   *SIC 5722*

TASCO DISTRIBUTORS INC   p794
84 KENHAR DR, NORTH YORK, ON, M9L
1N2
(416) 642-5600   *SIC 5722*

TRAIL APPLIANCES HOLDINGS LTD   p38
6880 11 ST SE, CALGARY, AB, T2H 2T9
(403) 253-5442   *SIC 5722*

TRAIL APPLIANCES LTD   p38
6880 11 ST SE, CALGARY, AB, T2H 2T9
(403) 253-5442   *SIC 5722*

TRAIL APPLIANCES LTD   p38
6880 11 ST SE, CALGARY, AB, T2H 2T9
(403) 253-5442   *SIC 5722*

TRAIL APPLIANCES LTD   p257
3388 SWEDEN WAY, RICHMOND, BC, V6V
0B2
(604) 233-2030   *SIC 5722*

---

*SIC 5731 Radio, television, and electronic
stores*

1039658 ONTARIO INC   p825
1123 BANK ST, OTTAWA, ON, K1S 3X4

149667 CANADA INC   p1346
6925 RUE JEAN-TALON E, SAINT-
LEONARD, QC, H1S 1N2
(514) 254-2153   *SIC 5731*

668824 ALBERTA LTD   p33
6009 1A ST SW SUITE 1, CALGARY, AB,
T2H 0G5
(403) 255-2270   *SIC 5731*

9114-9534 QUEBEC INC   p1371
2424 RUE KING O BUREAU 200, SHER-
BROOKE, QC, J1J 2E8
(819) 780-9505   *SIC 5731*

ANDRE'S T.V. SALES & SERVICE LTD p220
2153 SPRINGFIELD RD, KELOWNA, BC,
V1Y 7X1
(250) 861-4101   *SIC 5731*

AUDIO WAREHOUSE LTD   p1420
1329 LORNE ST, REGINA, SK, S4R 2K2
(306) 525-8128   *SIC 5731*

B & B ELECTRONICS LTD   p125
4316 SAVARYN DR SW, EDMONTON, AB,
T6X 1Z9
(780) 439-3901   *SIC 5731*

BAY-BLOOR RADIO INC   p928
55 BLOOR ST W, TORONTO, ON, M4W
1A5
(416) 967-1122   *SIC 5731*

BELL MOBILITE INC   p692
5055 SATELLITE DR UNIT 1, MISSIS-
SAUGA, ON, L4W 5K7
    SIC 5731

BEST BUY CANADA LTD   p87
10304 109 ST NW, EDMONTON, AB, T5J
1M3
(780) 498-5505   *SIC 5731*

BEST BUY CANADA LTD   p156
5001 19 ST UNIT 800, RED DEER, AB, T4R
3R1
(403) 314-5645   *SIC 5731*

BEST BUY CANADA LTD   p192
8800 GLENLYON PKY, BURNABY, BC, V5J
5K3
(604) 435-8223   *SIC 5731*

BEST BUY CANADA LTD   p341
2100 PARK ROYAL S, WEST VANCOUVER,
BC, V7T 2W4
(604) 913-3336   *SIC 5731*

BEST BUY CANADA LTD   p445
119 GALE TERR, DARTMOUTH, NS, B3B
0C4
(902) 468-0075   *SIC 5731*

BEST BUY CANADA LTD   p529
1200 BRANT ST UNIT 1, BURLINGTON,
ON, L7P 5C6
(905) 332-4758   *SIC 5731*

BEST BUY CANADA LTD   p567

175 GREEN LANE E, EAST GWILLIM-
BURY, ON, L9N 0C9
(905) 954-1262   *SIC 5731*

BEST BUY CANADA LTD   p596
1525 CITY PARK DR, GLOUCESTER, ON,
K1J 1H3
(613) 747-7636   *SIC 5731*

BEST BUY CANADA LTD   p626
745 KANATA AVE SUITE GG1, KANATA,
ON, K2T 1H9
(613) 287-3912   *SIC 5731*

BEST BUY CANADA LTD   p636
215 FAIRWAY RD S, KITCHENER, ON, N2C
1X2
(519) 783-0333   *SIC 5731*

BEST BUY CANADA LTD   p641
50 GATEWAY PARK DR, KITCHENER, ON,
N2P 2J4
    SIC 5731

BEST BUY CANADA LTD   p651
1735 RICHMOND ST SUITE 111, LONDON,
ON, N5X 3Y2
(519) 640-2900   *SIC 5731*

BEST BUY CANADA LTD   p795
2625A WESTON RD, NORTH YORK, ON,
M9N 3V8
(416) 242-6162   *SIC 5731*

BEST BUY CANADA LTD   p814
1471 HARMONY RD N, OSHAWA, ON, L1K
0Z6
(905) 433-4455   *SIC 5731*

BEST BUY CANADA LTD   p820
380 COVENTRY RD, OTTAWA, ON, K1K
2C6
(613) 212-0333   *SIC 5731*

BEST BUY CANADA LTD   p826
2210 BANK ST UNIT B1, OTTAWA, ON, K1V
1J5
(613) 526-7450   *SIC 5731*

BEST BUY CANADA LTD   p858
1380 EXMOUTH ST, SARNIA, ON, N7S 3X9
(519) 542-4388   *SIC 5731*

BEST BUY CANADA LTD   p870
480 PROGRESS AVE, SCARBOROUGH,
ON, M1P 5J1
(416) 296-7020   *SIC 5731*

BEST BUY CANADA LTD   p1000
8601 WARDEN AVE SUITE 1,
UNIONVILLE, ON, L3R 0B5
    SIC 5731

BEST BUY CANADA LTD   p1030
7850 WESTON RD SUITE 1, WOOD-
BRIDGE, ON, L4L 9N8
(905) 264-3191   *SIC 5731*

BEST BUY CANADA LTD   p1069
8480 BOUL LEDUC UNIT 100, BROSSARD,
QC, J4Y 0K7
(450) 766-2300   *SIC 5731*

BEST BUY CANADA LTD   p1078
1401 BOUL TALBOT, CHICOUTIMI, QC,
G7H 5N6
(418) 698-6701   *SIC 5731*

BEST BUY CANADA LTD   p1130
7077 BOUL NEWMAN, LASALLE, QC, H8N
1X1
(514) 368-6570   *SIC 5731*

BEST BUY CANADA LTD   p1214
2313 RUE SAINTE-CATHERINE O BU-
REAU 108, MONTREAL, QC, H3H 1N2
    SIC 5731

DOYON, G. T. V. (SHERBROOKE) INC p1373
525 RUE NORTHROP-FRYE, SHER-
BROOKE, QC, J1L 2Y3
(819) 565-3177   *SIC 5731*

FILLION, LOUIS ELECTRONIQUE INC
p1164
5690 RUE SHERBROOKE E, MONTREAL,
QC, H1N 1A1
(514) 254-6041   *SIC 5731*

GLOBALSTAR CANADA SATELLITE CO.
p731
115 MATHESON BLVD W UNIT 100, MIS-
SISSAUGA, ON, L5R 3L1
(905) 890-1377   *SIC 5731*

SOURCE (BELL) ELECTRONICS INC, THE *p485*
279 BAYVIEW DR, BARRIE, ON, L4M 4W5
(705) 728-2262 *SIC 5731*

SIC 5734 Computer and software stores

170260 CANADA INC *p862*
773 GREAT NORTHERN RD, SAULT STE. MARIE, ON, P6B 0B7
(705) 946-0876 *SIC 5734*

AFFINIO INC *p456*
2717 JOSEPH HOWE DR SUITE 300, HALIFAX, NS, B3L 4T9
(866) 991-3263 *SIC 5734*

AUDCOMP GROUP INC *p477*
611 TRADEWIND DR SUITE 100, ANCASTER, ON, L9G 4V5
(905) 304-1775 *SIC 5734*

BCOM COMPUTER CENTRE INC *p105*
15051 118 AVE NW, EDMONTON, AB, T5V 1H9
(780) 481-8855 *SIC 5734*

BEST BUY CANADA LTD *p33*
6909 MACLEOD TRAIL SW, CALGARY, AB, T2H 0L6
SIC 5734

BEST BUY CANADA LTD *p69*
350 SHAWVILLE BLVD SE UNIT 110, CALGARY, AB, T2Y 3S4
(403) 509-9120 *SIC 5734*

BIG BLUE BUBBLE INC *p653*
220 DUNDAS ST SUITE 900, LONDON, ON, N6A 1H3
(519) 649-0071 *SIC 5734*

BUILT TO SELL INC *p917*
2175 QUEEN ST E UNIT 302, TORONTO, ON, M4E 1E5
(416) 628-9754 *SIC 5734*

CARETEK INTEGRATED BUSINESS SOLUTIONS INC *p501*
1900 CLARK BLVD UNIT 8, BRAMPTON, ON, L6T 0E9
(416) 630-9555 *SIC 5734*

CEB CANADA INC *p1258*
400 BOULEVARD JEAN-LESAGE UNITE 500, QUEBEC, QC, G1K 8W1
(418) 523-6663 *SIC 5734*

COMPUTER DATA SOURCE CANADA CORP *p668*
3780 14TH AVE UNIT 106, MARKHAM, ON, L3R 9Y5
(905) 474-2100 *SIC 5734*

COOPSCO SAINT-HYACINTHE *p1312*
3000 AV BOULLE, SAINT-HYACINTHE, QC, J2S 1H9
(450) 774-2727 *SIC 5734*

D-WAVE SYSTEMS INC *p188*
3033 BETA AVE, BURNABY, BC, V5G 4M9
(604) 630-1428 *SIC 5734*

DISTRIBUTION HARTCO SOCIETE EN COMMANDITE *p1048*
9393 BOUL METROPOLITAIN E, ANJOU, QC, H1J 3C7
(514) 354-0580 *SIC 5734*

DRUMMOND INFORMATIQUE LTEE *p1096*
412 RUE HERIOT BUREAU 101, DRUMMONDVILLE, QC, J2B 1B5
(819) 477-8886 *SIC 5734*

DYMAXION RESEARCH LIMITED *p452*
5515 COGSWELL ST, HALIFAX, NS, B3J 1R2
(902) 422-1973 *SIC 5734*

EASTSIDE GAMES INC *p293*
555 12TH AVE W SUITE 550, VANCOUVER, BC, V5Z 3X7
(604) 568-5051 *SIC 5734*

ELECTRONICS BOUTIQUE CANADA INC *p502*
8995 AIRPORT RD SUITE 512, BRAMPTON, ON, L6T 5T2
(905) 790-9262 *SIC 5734*

ESIT CANADA ENTERPRISE SERVICES CO *p453*
1969 UPPER WATER ST, HALIFAX, NS, B3J 3R7
(902) 000-0000 *SIC 5734*

GEEP CANADA INC *p1234*
2995 BOUL LE CORBUSIER, MONTREAL, QC, H7L 3M3
(450) 506-0220 *SIC 5734*

INSIGHT CANADA INC *p1220*
5410 BOUL DECARIE, MONTREAL, QC, H3X 4B2
(514) 344-3500 *SIC 5734*

INTERTAIN GROUP LIMITED, THE *p981*
24 DUNCAN ST 2 FL, TORONTO, ON, M5V 2B8
(647) 641-8404 *SIC 5734*

JOLERA INC *p929*
365 BLOOR ST E 2 FL, TORONTO, ON, M4W 3L4
(416) 410-1011 *SIC 5734*

JUMP PLUS STORES ULC *p977*
275 COLLEGE ST, TORONTO, ON, M5T 1S2
(416) 927-8000 *SIC 5734*

LIFT CO. LTD *p981*
77 PETER ST SUITE 200, TORONTO, ON, M5V 2G4
(647) 239-6804 *SIC 5734*

MEMORY EXPRESS INC *p9*
3333 34 AVE NE, CALGARY, AB, T1Y 6H2
(403) 398-4533 *SIC 5734*

MID-RANGE COMPUTER GROUP INC *p672*
85 IDEMA RD, MARKHAM, ON, L3R 1A9
(905) 940-1814 *SIC 5734*

NETSUITE INC *p698*
5800 EXPLORER DR SUITE 100, MISSISSAUGA, ON, L4W 5K9
(905) 219-8534 *SIC 5734*

NORTHERN MICRO INC *p1274*
3107 AV DES HOTELS BUREAU 2, QUEBEC, QC, G1W 4W5
(418) 654-1733 *SIC 5734*

NOVIPRO INC *p1206*
1010 RUE DE LA GAUCHETIERE O BUREAU 1900, MONTREAL, QC, H3B 2N2
(514) 744-5353 *SIC 5734*

PCM VENTES CANADA INC *p1207*
1100 BOUL ROBERT-BOURASSA, MONTREAL, QC, H3B 3A5
(514) 373-8700 *SIC 5734*

POWERLAND COMPUTERS LTD *p364*
170 MARION ST, WINNIPEG, MB, R2H 0T4
(204) 237-3800 *SIC 5734*

RLOGISTICS LIMITED PARTNERSHIP *p558*
501 APPLEWOOD CRES, CONCORD, ON, L4K 4J3
(905) 660-5030 *SIC 5734*

SHOPPER+ INC *p1128*
2210 52E AV, LACHINE, QC, H8T 2Y3
(514) 631-5216 *SIC 5734*

SIMPLY COMPUTING INC *p321*
1690 BROADWAY W SUITE 203, VANCOUVER, BC, V6J 1X6
(604) 714-1450 *SIC 5734*

SOLUTIONS INFORMATIQUES INSO INC *p1184*
6615 AV DU PARC, MONTREAL, QC, H2V 4J1
(514) 270-4477 *SIC 5734*

T L D COMPUTERS INC *p264*
12251 HORSESHOE WAY UNIT 100, RICHMOND, BC, V7A 4V4
(604) 272-6000 *SIC 5734*

TOON BOOM ANIMATION INC *p1184*
4200 BOUL SAINT-LAURENT BUREAU 1020, MONTREAL, QC, H2W 2R2
(514) 278-8666 *SIC 5734*

WESTKEY GRAPHICS LTD *p183*
3212 LAKE CITY WAY, BURNABY, BC, V5A 3A4
(604) 421-7778 *SIC 5734*

SIC 5735 Record and prerecorded tape stores

GROUPE ARCHAMBAULT INC *p1175*
500 RUE SAINTE-CATHERINE E, MONTREAL, QC, H2L 2C6
(514) 849-6201 *SIC 5735*

SIC 5736 Musical instrument stores

1449132 ONTARIO LIMITED *p1006*
343 WEBER ST N, WATERLOO, ON, N2J 3H8
(519) 579-8243 *SIC 5736*

2428391 ONTARIO INC *p477*
1430 CORMORANT RD, ANCASTER, ON, L9G 4V5
(905) 304-1010 *SIC 5736*

501479 NB LTD *p406*
48 BONACCORD ST, MONCTON, NB, E1C 5K7
(506) 857-0000 *SIC 5736*

AXE MUSIC INC *p83*
11931 WAYNE GRETZKY DRIVE NORTHBOUND NW, EDMONTON, AB, T5B 1Y4
(780) 471-2001 *SIC 5736*

COSMO MUSIC COMPANY LTD *p856*
10 VIA RENZO DR, RICHMOND HILL, ON, L4S 0B6
(905) 770-5222 *SIC 5736*

GROUPE ARCHAMBAULT INC *p1164*
5655 AV PIERRE-DE COUBERTIN, MONTREAL, QC, H1N 1R2
(514) 272-4049 *SIC 5736*

LONG & MCQUADE LIMITED *p295*
368 TERMINAL AVE, VANCOUVER, BC, V6A 3W9
(604) 734-4886 *SIC 5736*

LONG & MCQUADE LIMITED *p845*
722 ROSEBANK RD, PICKERING, ON, L1W 4B2
(905) 837-9785 *SIC 5736*

LONG HOLDINGS INC *p845*
722 ROSEBANK RD, PICKERING, ON, L1W 4B2
(905) 837-9785 *SIC 5736*

ORGUES LETOURNEAU LTEE *p1314*
16355 AV SAVOIE, SAINT-HYACINTHE, QC, J2T 3N1
(450) 774-2698 *SIC 5736*

PRICE, GORDON MUSIC LTD *p116*
10828 82 AVE NW, EDMONTON, AB, T6E 2B3
(780) 439-0007 *SIC 5736*

ST JOHN'S MUSIC LTD *p373*
1570 CHURCH AVE, WINNIPEG, MB, R2X 1G8
(204) 694-1818 *SIC 5736*

TOM LEE MUSIC CO. LTD *p300*
650 GEORGIA ST W SUITE 310, VANCOUVER, BC, V6B 4N7
(604) 685-2521 *SIC 5736*

SIC 5812 Eating places

0319637 B.C. LTD *p317*
8901 STANLEY PARK DR, VANCOUVER, BC, V6G 3E2
SIC 5812

1004839 ONTARIO LIMITED *p715*
3105 DUNDAS ST W SUITE 101, MISSISSAUGA, ON, L5L 3R8
(905) 569-7000 *SIC 5812*

10087408 CANADA INC *p1200*
1280 AVE DES CANADIENS-DE-MONTREAL, MONTREAL, QC, H3B 3B3
(514) 261-7661 *SIC 5812*

101055401 SASKATCHEWAN LTD *p1423*
2404 8TH ST E, SASKATOON, SK, S7H 0V6
SIC 5812

1025091 ONTARIO LIMITED *p659*
585 SPRINGBANK DR SUITE 204, LONDON, ON, N6J 1H3
(519) 641-1178 *SIC 5812*

1051107 ONTARIO LTD *p843*
1725 KINGSTON RD SUITE 25, PICKERING, ON, L1V 4L9
(905) 619-1000 *SIC 5812*

1094285 ONTARIO LIMITED *p931*
112 ISABELLA ST, TORONTO, ON, M4Y 1P1
(416) 920-9410 *SIC 5812*

1095141 ONTARIO LIMITED *p665*
7225 WOODBINE AVE SUITE 119, MARKHAM, ON, L3R 1A3
(905) 940-2199 *SIC 5812*

1172413 ONTARIO INC *p625*
651 TERRY FOX DR SUITE SIDE, KANATA, ON, K2L 4E7
(613) 836-3680 *SIC 5812*

1174976 ONTARIO INC *p936*
19 TORONTO ST, TORONTO, ON, M5C 2R1
(416) 214-5888 *SIC 5812*

1184892 ALBERTA LTD *p26*
115 9 AVE SE SUITE 294, CALGARY, AB, T2G 0P5
(403) 246-3636 *SIC 5812*

1212551 ONTARIO INC *p652*
95 POND MILLS RD, LONDON, ON, N5Z 3X3
(519) 645-1917 *SIC 5812*

126677 CANADA LIMITED *p815*
1620 MICHAEL ST, OTTAWA, ON, K1B 3T7
(613) 741-2800 *SIC 5812*

1327601 ONTARIO INC *p736*
50 COURTNEYPARK DR E, MISSISSAUGA, ON, L5T 2Y3
(905) 565-6225 *SIC 5812*

1335270 ONTARIO LTD *p704*
87 MATHESON BLVD E, MISSISSAUGA, ON, L4Z 2Y5
(905) 502-8000 *SIC 5812*

139670 CANADA LTEE *p1103*
1885 RUE SAINT-LOUIS BUREAU 100, GATINEAU, QC, J8T 6G4
(819) 568-1723 *SIC 5812*

1413249 ONTARIO INC *p1013*
75 CONSUMERS DR SUITE 17, WHITBY, ON, L1N 9S2
(905) 665-6575 *SIC 5812*

1498882 ONTARIO INC *p648*
1915 DUNDAS ST SUITE SIDE, LONDON, ON, N5V 5J9
(519) 451-5737 *SIC 5812*

1561716 ONTARIO LTD *p581*
930 DIXON RD, ETOBICOKE, ON, M9W 1J9
(416) 674-7777 *SIC 5812*

1561716 ONTARIO LTD *p843*
705 KINGSTON RD, PICKERING, ON, L1V 6K3
(905) 420-3334 *SIC 5812*

175246 CANADA INC *p1245*
4928 BOUL DES SOURCES BUREAU 2545, PIERREFONDS, QC, H8Y 3E1
(514) 684-0779 *SIC 5812*

2389807 ONTARIO INC *p787*
3885 YONGE ST, NORTH YORK, ON, M4N 2P2
(416) 322-5544 *SIC 5812*

28 AUGUSTA FUND LTD *p33*
6920 MACLEOD TRAIL SE, CALGARY, AB, T2H 0L3
(403) 259-3119 *SIC 5812*

293967 ALBERTA LTD *p92*
13080 ST ALBERT TRAIL NW, EDMONTON, AB, T5L 4Y6
(780) 482-5696 *SIC 5812*

2954-8682 QUEBEC INC *p1256*
475 BOUL DE L'ATRIUM BUREAU 104, QUEBEC, QC, G1H 7H9
SIC 5812

301726 ALBERTA LTD *p129*
8751 94 ST, FORT SASKATCHEWAN, AB, T8L 4P7
(780) 998-9999 *SIC 5812*

3111326 CANADA INC *p1077*

1611 BOUL TALBOT, CHICOUTIMI, QC, G7H 4C3
(418) 698-8611 *SIC* 5812

3177743 MANITOBA LTD *p356*
1018 MANITOBA AVE, SELKIRK, MB, R1A 4M2
(204) 785-7777 *SIC* 5812

340107 ALBERTA LTD *p85*
10665 109 ST NW, EDMONTON, AB, T5H 3B5
(780) 474-6466 *SIC* 5812

35790 MANITOBA LTD *p347*
1836 BRANDON AVE, BRANDON, MB, R7B 3G8
(204) 725-4223 *SIC* 5812

360641 BC LTD *p292*
555 12TH AVE W UNIT 201, VANCOUVER, BC, V5Z 3X7
(604) 879-8038 *SIC* 5812

4359241 MANITOBA INC *p72*
1002 37 ST SW, CALGARY, AB, T3C 1S1
(403) 249-7799 *SIC* 5812

458890 B.C. LTD *p211*
101 TRANS CANADA HWY, DUNCAN, BC, V9L 3P8
(250) 748-5151 *SIC* 5812

476982 BRITISH COLUMBIA LTD *p1013*
75 CONSUMERS DR, WHITBY, ON, L1N 9S2
SIC 5812

483696 ALBERTA LTD *p112*
7921 CORONET RD NW, EDMONTON, AB, T6E 4N7
SIC 5812

570230 ONTARIO INC *p656*
387 WELLINGTON RD, LONDON, ON, N6C 4P9
(519) 680-1830 *SIC* 5812

6131646 CANADA INC *p548*
120 INTERCHANGE WAY, CONCORD, ON, L4K 5C3
(905) 760-7600 *SIC* 5812

6143580 CANADA INC. *p1257*
10 RUE SAINT-ANTOINE, QUEBEC, QC, G1K 4C9
(418) 692-1022 *SIC* 5812

668977 ALBERTA INC *p69*
235 SHAWVILLE BLVD SE, CALGARY, AB, T2Y 3H9
(403) 256-6999 *SIC* 5812

7073674 CANADA LTD *p822*
77 BANK ST, OTTAWA, ON, K1P 5N2
(613) 831-2235 *SIC* 5812

718695 ONTARIO INC *p616*
1170 UPPER JAMES ST, HAMILTON, ON, L9C 3B1
(905) 574-7880 *SIC* 5812

817936 ALBERTA LTD *p42*
513 8 AVE SW SUITE 126, CALGARY, AB, T2P 1G1
(403) 508-9999 *SIC* 5812

882547 ONTARIO INC *p530*
1235 FAIRVIEW ST SUITE 1, BURLINGTON, ON, L7S 2H9
(905) 632-6000 *SIC* 5812

9010-5826 QUEBEC INC *p1212*
1459 RUE CRESCENT, MONTREAL, QC, H3G 2B2
(514) 288-3814 *SIC* 5812

9030-5582 QUEBEC INC *p1380*
1460 CH GASCON BUREAU 101, TERREBONNE, QC, J6X 2Z5
(450) 492-5225 *SIC* 5812

9064-4048 QUEBEC INC *p1114*
1505 BOUL BASE-DE-ROC, JOLIETTE, QC, J6E 0L1
(450) 759-6900 *SIC* 5812

9070-9734 QUEBEC INC *p1356*
1580 BOUL DES ECLUSES, SAINTE-CATHERINE, QC, J5C 2B4
(450) 638-9018 *SIC* 5812

9098-2067 QUEBEC INC *p1319*
1 RUE JOHN-F.-KENNEDY, SAINT-JEROME, QC, J7Y 4B4

(450) 660-6200 *SIC* 5812

9098-2067 QUEBEC INC *p1319*
2001 BOUL DU CURE-LABELLE, SAINT-JEROME, QC, J7Y 1S2
(450) 431-6411 *SIC* 5812

9122-6910 QUEBEC INC *p1387*
4520 BOUL DES RECOLLETS, TROIS-RIVIERES, QC, G9A 4N2
(819) 370-1099 *SIC* 5812

9124-4269 QUEBEC INC *p1044*
1049 AV DU PONT S, ALMA, QC, G8B 0E8
(418) 662-1178 *SIC* 5812

9317-3649 QUEBEC INC *p1370*
31 RUE KING O BUREAU 203, SHERBROOKE, QC, J1H 1N5
(819) 791-3123 *SIC* 5812

9342-6484 QUEBEC INC *p1187*
425 RUE SAINT-NICOLAS, MONTREAL, QC, H2Y 2P4
(514) 619-9649 *SIC* 5812

939927 ONTARIO LIMITED *p581*
200 QUEEN'S PLATE DR, ETOBICOKE, ON, M9W 6Y9
(416) 746-6000 *SIC* 5812

940734 ONTARIO LIMITED *p636*
670 FAIRWAY RD S, KITCHENER, ON, N2C 1X3
(519) 894-0811 *SIC* 5812

945575 ALBERTA LTD *p150*
10 SOUTHRIDGE DR, OKOTOKS, AB, T1S 1N1
(403) 995-0224 *SIC* 5812

9458778 CANADA LIMITED *p1295*
1917 BOUL SIR-WILFRID-LAURIER, SAINT-BRUNO, QC, J3V 0G8
(514) 443-5648 *SIC* 5812

959009 ONTARIO INC *p492*
390 NORTH FRONT ST, BELLEVILLE, ON, K8P 3E1
(613) 962-8440 *SIC* 5812

975445 ONTARIO INC *p529*
2084 OLD LAKESHORE RD, BURLINGTON, ON, L7R 1A3
(905) 634-2084 *SIC* 5812

979786 ONTARIO LIMITED *p958*
146 FRONT ST W, TORONTO, ON, M5J 1G2
(416) 977-8840 *SIC* 5812

985907 ONTARIO LIMITED *p862*
389 GREAT NORTHERN RD, SAULT STE. MARIE, ON, P6B 4Z8
(705) 941-9993 *SIC* 5812

994486 N.W.T LTD *p435*
GD LCD MAIN, YELLOWKNIFE, NT, X1A 2L8
(867) 873-5600 *SIC* 5812

A & W FOOD SERVICES OF CANADA INC *p240*
171 ESPLANADE W SUITE 300, NORTH VANCOUVER, BC, V7M 3K9
(604) 988-2141 *SIC* 5812

A AND W RESTAURANT *p463*
689 WESTVILLE RD, NEW GLASGOW, NS, B2H 2J6
SIC 5812

A POWER INTERNATIONAL TRADING COMPANY *p318*
1575 ROBSON ST, VANCOUVER, BC, V6G 1C3
(604) 872-0712 *SIC* 5812

ABBOTSFORD RESTAURANTS LTD *p174*
2142 WEST RAILWAY ST, ABBOTSFORD, BC, V2S 2E2
(604) 855-9893 *SIC* 5812

ABREY ENTERPRISES INC *p236*
815 MCBRIDE BLVD, NEW WESTMINSTER, BC, V3L 2B9
(604) 718-1189 *SIC* 5812

ADLYS HOTELS INC *p1006*
59 KING ST N, WATERLOO, ON, N2J 2X2
(519) 886-3350 *SIC* 5812

AFFINITY FOOD GROUP INC *p661*
480 SOVEREIGN RD UNIT 3, LONDON, ON, N6M 1A4

(519) 453-6873 *SIC* 5812

AGNEW, J. E. FOOD SERVICES LTD *p631*
83 TERRY FOX DR SUITE A, KINGSTON, ON, K7M 8N4
(613) 544-9400 *SIC* 5812

ALBERTS RESTAURANTS LTD *p85*
10550 115 ST NW, EDMONTON, AB, T5H 3K6
(780) 429-1259 *SIC* 5812

ALBERTS RESTAURANTS LTD *p104*
1640 BURLINGTON AVE, EDMONTON, AB, T5T 3J7
(780) 444-3105 *SIC* 5812

ALBERTS RESTAURANTS LTD *p118*
10362 51 AVE NW, EDMONTON, AB, T6H 5X6
(780) 437-7081 *SIC* 5812

ALEX MARION RESTAURANTS LTD *p1415*
940 E VICTORIA AVE, REGINA, SK, S4N 7A9
SIC 5812

ALIK ENTERPRISES LTD *p342*
4222 VILLAGE SQ, WHISTLER, BC, V0N 1B4
(604) 932-4540 *SIC* 5812

ANGIE'S KITCHEN LIMITED *p883*
1761 ERB'S RD, ST AGATHA, ON, N0B 2L0
(519) 747-1700 *SIC* 5812

ANGUS G FOODS INC *p442*
588 PORTLAND ST, DARTMOUTH, NS, B2W 2M3
(902) 435-3181 *SIC* 5812

ARAMARK CANADA LTD. *p117*
125 UNIVERSITY CAMPUS NW, EDMONTON, AB, T6G 2H6
(780) 492-5800 *SIC* 5812

ARAMARK CANADA LTD. *p451*
923 ROBIE ST, HALIFAX, NS, B3H 3C3
(902) 420-5599 *SIC* 5812

ARAMARK CANADA LTD. *p573*
811 ISLINGTON AVE, ETOBICOKE, ON, M8Z 5W8
(416) 255-1331 *SIC* 5812

ARAMARK CANADA LTD. *p842*
2151 EAST BANK DR, PETERBOROUGH, ON, K9L 1Z8
SIC 5812

ARAMARK CANADA LTD. *p907*
955 OLIVER RD, THUNDER BAY, ON, P7B 5E1
(807) 343-8142 *SIC* 5812

ARAMARK CANADA LTD. *p974*
21 CLASSIC AVE SUITE 1008, TORONTO, ON, M5S 2Z3
(416) 598-2424 *SIC* 5812

ARAMARK QUEBEC INC *p1338*
4900 RUE FISHER, SAINT-LAURENT, QC, H4T 1J6
(514) 341-7770 *SIC* 5812

ARAMARK REMOTE WORKPLACE SERVICES LTD *p112*
9647 45 AVE NW, EDMONTON, AB, T6E 5Z8
(780) 437-5665 *SIC* 5812

ARCTIC OIL & GAS SERVICES INC *p435*
170 MACKENZIE RD, INUVIK, NT, X0E 0T0
(867) 777-8700 *SIC* 5812

ARGYLE COBBLERS LTD *p451*
1663 ARGYLE ST, HALIFAX, NS, B3J 2B5
(902) 492-3018 *SIC* 5812

ASHTON CASSE-CROUTE INC *p1261*
1100 AV GALIBOIS BUREAU 250, QUEBEC, QC, G1M 3M7
(418) 682-2288 *SIC* 5812

ATHABASCA CATERING LIMITED PARTNERSHIP *p1433*
335 PACKHAM AVE SUITE 120, SASKATOON, SK, S7N 4S1
(306) 242-8008 *SIC* 5812

AUBE, J.-P. RESTAURANT SERVICES LTD *p912*
522 ALGONQUIN BLVD E UNIT 520, TIMMINS, ON, P4N 1B7
(705) 264-7323 *SIC* 5812

B.B. INVESTMENTS INC *p76*
388 COUNTRY HILLS BLVD NE SUITE 600, CALGARY, AB, T3K 5J6
(403) 226-7171 *SIC* 5812

BADALI'S, JOE PIAZZA ON FRONT INC *p959*
156 FRONT ST W, TORONTO, ON, M5J 2L6
(416) 977-3064 *SIC* 5812

BEATTY FOODS LTD *p473*
374 QUEEN ST E, ACTON, ON, L7J 2Y5
(519) 853-9128 *SIC* 5812

BEATTY FOODS LTD *p508*
372 MAIN ST N, BRAMPTON, ON, L6V 1P8
(905) 455-2841 *SIC* 5812

BEATTY FOODS LTD *p512*
160 SANDALWOOD PKY E, BRAMPTON, ON, L6Z 1Y5
(905) 840-0700 *SIC* 5812

BEAUGARTE (QUEBEC INC) *p1271*
2590 BOUL LAURIER UNITE 150, QUEBEC, QC, G1V 4M6
SIC 5812

BEAUGARTE (QUEBEC) INC *p1271*
2600 BOUL LAURIER, QUEBEC, QC, G1V 4W1
SIC 5812

BENNETT RESTAURANT LTD *p429*
54 KENMOUNT RD, ST. JOHN'S, NL, A1B 1W2
(709) 754-1254 *SIC* 5812

BENTO INC *p667*
25 CENTURIAN DR SUITE 208, MARKHAM, ON, L3R 5N8
(905) 513-0028 *SIC* 5812

BIAMONTE INVESTMENTS LTD *p760*
7600 LUNDY'S LANE, NIAGARA FALLS, ON, L2H 1H1
(905) 354-2211 *SIC* 5812

BIG SHO FOODS LTD *p998*
130 QUEEN ST N, TOTTENHAM, ON, L0G 1W0
(905) 936-6157 *SIC* 5812

BINGEMANS INC *p635*
425 BINGEMANS CENTRE DR, KITCHENER, ON, N2B 3X7
(519) 744-1555 *SIC* 5812

BLT FOODS LTD *p412*
499 ROTHESAY AVE, SAINT JOHN, NB, E2J 2C6
(506) 633-1098 *SIC* 5812

BOATHOUSE RESTAURANTS OF CANADA *p343*
14935 MARINE DR, WHITE ROCK, BC, V4B 1C3
(604) 536-7320 *SIC* 5812

BOONE FOOD SERVICES LIMITED *p456*
6960 MUMFORD RD SUITE 300, HALIFAX, NS, B3L 4P1
(902) 453-5330 *SIC* 5812

BOSTON PIZZA INTERNATIONAL INC *p840*
821 RYE ST, PETERBOROUGH, ON, K9J 6X1
(705) 740-2775 *SIC* 5812

BOSTON PIZZA INTERNATIONAL INC *p1051*
7300 BOUL DES ROSERAIES, ANJOU, QC, H1M 2T5
(514) 788-4848 *SIC* 5812

BOSTON PIZZA INTERNATIONAL INC *p1086*
450 PROM DU CENTROPOLIS, COTE SAINT-LUC, QC, H7T 3C2
(450) 688-2229 *SIC* 5812

BOSTON PIZZA ORLEANS *p811*
3884 INNES RD, ORLEANS, ON, K1W 1K9
(613) 590-0881 *SIC* 5812

BOSTON PIZZA ROYALTIES INCOME FUND *p259*
10760 SHELLBRIDGE WAY UNIT 100, RICHMOND, BC, V6X 3H1
(604) 270-1108 *SIC* 5812

BOUVIER INC, LE *p1275*
2335 BOUL BASTIEN, QUEBEC, QC, G2B 1B3

(418) 842-9160   *SIC 5812*
BRANTMAC MANAGEMENT LIMITED *p514*
73 KING GEORGE RD, BRANTFORD, ON,
N3R 5K2
(519) 756-7350   *SIC 5812*
BRIDGEHEAD (2000) INC *p824*
130 ANDERSON ST, OTTAWA, ON, K1R
6T7
(613) 231-5488   *SIC 5812*
BROWN'S FINE FOOD SERVICES INC *p630*
844 DIVISION ST, KINGSTON, ON, K7K
4C3
(613) 546-3246   *SIC 5812*
**BURGESS, JOHN WILLIAM ENTERPRISES
INC** *p703*
799 DUNDAS ST E, MISSISSAUGA, ON,
L4Y 2B7
(905) 566-4982   *SIC 5812*
CACTUS CAFE BARLOW LTD *p292*
550 BROADWAY W, VANCOUVER, BC, V5Z
0E9
(604) 714-2025   *SIC 5812*
CACTUS RESTAURANTS LTD *p184*
4219B LOUGHEED HWY, BURNABY, BC,
V5C 3Y6
(604) 291-6606   *SIC 5812*
CACTUS RESTAURANTS LTD *p219*
1575 BANKS RD SUITE 200, KELOWNA,
BC, V1X 7Y8
(250) 763-6752   *SIC 5812*
CACTUS RESTAURANTS LTD *p259*
5500 NO. 3 RD, RICHMOND, BC, V6X 2C8
(604) 244-9969   *SIC 5812*
CACTUS RESTAURANTS LTD *p292*
550 BROADWAY W SUITE 201, VANCOU-
VER, BC, V5Z 0E9
(604) 714-2025   *SIC 5812*
CACTUS RESTAURANTS LTD *p320*
1530 BROADWAY W, VANCOUVER, BC,
V6J 5K9
(604) 733-0434   *SIC 5812*
CALGARY TOWER FACILITIES LTD *p45*
101 9 AVE SW, CALGARY, AB, T2P 1J9
(403) 266-7171   *SIC 5812*
CAMPBELL, JAMES INC *p645*
333 KENT ST W, LINDSAY, ON, K9V 2Z7
(705) 324-6668   *SIC 5812*
CAMPBELL, JAMES INC *p840*
978 LANSDOWNE ST W, PETERBOR-
OUGH, ON, K9J 1Z9
(705) 743-6731   *SIC 5812*
CANADIAN DINERS (1995) L.P. LTD *p820*
1130 ST. LAURENT BLVD, OTTAWA, ON,
K1K 3B6
(613) 747-9190   *SIC 5812*
CANADIAN TEST CASE 176 *p720*
6750 CENTURY AVE SUITE 305, MISSIS-
SAUGA, ON, L5N 2V8
(905) 812-5920   *SIC 5812*
CANADIAN TEST CASE 177 CORP *p720*
6750 CENTURY AVE SUITE 305, MISSIS-
SAUGA, ON, L5N 2V8
(905) 812-5920   *SIC 5812*
CANADIAN TEST CASE 187 *p720*
6750 CENTURY AVE SUITE 305, MISSIS-
SAUGA, ON, L5N 2V8
(905) 812-5920   *SIC 5812*
CAPITAL TRAITEUR MONTREAL INC *p1191*
159 RUE SAINT-ANTOINE O BUREAU 400,
MONTREAL, QC, H2Z 2A7
(514) 875-1897   *SIC 5812*
CAPITAL TRAITEUR MONTREAL INC *p1191*
201 AV VIGER O, MONTREAL, QC, H2Z
1X7
(514) 871-3111   *SIC 5812*
CARA FOODS *p368*
1221 ST MARY'S RD, WINNIPEG, MB, R2M
5L5
(204) 254-2128   *SIC 5812*
CARA FOODS INTERNATIONAL LTD *p856*
1620 ELGIN MILLS RD E, RICHMOND
HILL, ON, L4S 0B2
(905) 508-4139   *SIC 5812*
CARA HOLDINGS LIMITED *p972*

21 BEDFORD RD SUITE 200, TORONTO,
ON, M5R 2J9
(905) 760-2244   *SIC 5812*
CARA OPERATIONS QUEBEC LTD *p550*
199 FOUR VALLEY DR, CONCORD, ON,
L4K 0B8
(905) 760-2244   *SIC 5812*
CARA OPERATIONS QUEBEC LTD *p573*
1001 THE QUEENSWAY, ETOBICOKE, ON,
M8Z 6C7
(416) 255-0464   *SIC 5812*
CARTER, DWAYNE ENTERPRISES LTD
p386
3401 PORTAGE AVE, WINNIPEG, MB, R3K
0W9
(204) 949-6022   *SIC 5812*
CATERERS (YORK) LIMITED *p781*
37 SOUTHBOURNE AVE, NORTH YORK,
ON, M3H 1A4
SIC 5812
CAUSEWAY RESTAURANTS LTD *p336*
812 WHARF ST, VICTORIA, BC, V8W 1T3
(250) 381-2244   *SIC 5812*
CAVCO FOOD SERVICES LTD *p637*
715 OTTAWA ST S, KITCHENER, ON, N2E
3H5
(519) 569-7224   *SIC 5812*
CAVCO FOOD SERVICES LTD *p641*
431 HIGHLAND RD W, KITCHENER, ON,
N2M 3C6
(519) 578-8630   *SIC 5812*
CCFGLM ONTARIO LIMITED *p574*
1255 THE QUEENSWAY, ETOBICOKE, ON,
M8Z 1S1
(416) 252-5000   *SIC 5812*
CENTRE ISLAND FOOD SERVICES LTD
p574
84 ADVANCE RD, ETOBICOKE, ON, M8Z
2T7
(416) 234-2345   *SIC 5812*
**CHADWICK FOOD SERVICE MANAGE-
MENT INCORPORATED** *p439*
200 WATERFRONT DR SUITE 225, BED-
FORD, NS, B4A 4J4
SIC 5812
CHALMERS INVESTMENT CORP LTD *p28*
727 42 AVE SE, CALGARY, AB, T2G 1Y8
(403) 243-6642   *SIC 5812*
CHARCOAL STEAK HOUSE INC *p634*
2980 KING ST E, KITCHENER, ON, N2A
1A9
(519) 893-6570   *SIC 5812*
CHARLTOM RESTAURANTS LIMITED *p455*
3630 KEMPT RD, HALIFAX, NS, B3K 4X8
(902) 832-2103   *SIC 5812*
CHEBUCTO VENTURES CORP *p213*
8911 117 AVE, FORT ST. JOHN, BC, V1J
6B8
(250) 787-7501   *SIC 5812*
**CHENOY'S DELICATESSEN & STEAK
HOUSE INC** *p1091*
3616 BOUL SAINT-JEAN, DOLLARD-DES-
ORMEAUX, QC, H9G 1X1
(514) 620-2584   *SIC 5812*
CHEZ HENRI MAJEAU ET FILS INC *p1297*
30 RUE DE LA VISITATION, SAINT-
CHARLES-BORROMEE, QC, J6E 4M8
(450) 759-1113   *SIC 5812*
CHG BLOOR HOLDINGS INC *p972*
1221 BAY ST, TORONTO, ON, M5R 3P5
(647) 348-7000   *SIC 5812*
CHIC RESTO-POP INC, LE *p1167*
1500 AV D'ORLEANS, MONTREAL, QC,
H1W 3R1
(514) 521-4089   *SIC 5812*
CHIRO FOODS LIMITED *p104*
17118 90 AVE NW, EDMONTON, AB, T5T
4C8
(780) 438-8848   *SIC 5812*
CHIRO FOODS LIMITED *p118*
5041 GATEWAY BLVD NW UNIT 100, ED-
MONTON, AB, T6H 4R7
(780) 438-8848   *SIC 5812*
CHISHOLM, R. FOOD SERVICES INC *p762*

140 LAKESHORE DR, NORTH BAY, ON,
P1A 2A8
(705) 474-9770   *SIC 5812*
CLS CATERING SERVICES LTD *p264*
3560 JERICHO RD, RICHMOND, BC, V7B
1C2
(604) 273-4438   *SIC 5812*
CLS CATERING SERVICES LTD *p728*
2950 CONVAIR DR, MISSISSAUGA, ON,
L5P 1A2
(416) 676-3218   *SIC 5812*
COJALY INC *p1394*
601 AV SAINT-CHARLES, VAUDREUIL-
DORION, QC, J7V 8G4
(450) 455-0409   *SIC 5812*
COLASANTI FARMS LIMITED *p858*
1550 ROAD 3 E, RUTHVEN, ON, N0P 2G0
(519) 326-3287   *SIC 5812*
COMEX FOOD PRODUCTION INC *p303*
586 HORNBY ST, VANCOUVER, BC, V6C
2E7
(604) 971-4745   *SIC 5812*
COMPASS GROUP CANADA LTD *p238*
1640 ELECTRA BLVD SUITE 123, NORTH
SAANICH, BC, V8L 5V4
(250) 655-3718   *SIC 5812*
COMPASS GROUP CANADA LTD *p452*
1800 ARGYLE ST SUITE 401, HALIFAX,
NS, B3J 3N8
SIC 5812
COMPASS GROUP CANADA LTD *p542*
285 MCNAUGHTON AVE E, CHATHAM,
ON, N7L 2G7
(519) 358-7111   *SIC 5812*
COMPASS GROUP CANADA LTD *p744*
1 PROLOGIS BLVD SUITE 400, MISSIS-
SAUGA, ON, L5W 0G2
(905) 795-5100   *SIC 5812*
COMPASS GROUP CANADA LTD *p1426*
35 22ND ST E, SASKATOON, SK, S7K 0C8
(306) 975-7790   *SIC 5812*
**CONCEPT ECO-PLEIN AIR LE BALUCHON
INC** *p1350*
3550 CH DES TREMBLES RR 3, SAINT-
PAULIN, QC, J0K 3G0
(819) 268-2695   *SIC 5812*
CONCORDE FOOD SERVICES (1996) LTD
p1424
1171 8TH ST E, SASKATOON, SK, S7H 0S3
(306) 668-3000   *SIC 5812*
CONSOLIDATED RESTAURANTS LIMITED
p443
620 PORTLAND ST, DARTMOUTH, NS,
B2W 2M3
(902) 434-8814   *SIC 5812*
**COOPERATIVE DES TRAVAILLEURS ET
TRAVAILLEUSES PREMIER DEFI LAVAL**
p1342
1111 BOUL DES LAURENTIDES, SAINT-
LAURENT, QC, H7N 5B5
(450) 668-7085   *SIC 5812*
**COOPERATIVE DES TRAVAILLEUSES ET
TRAVAILLEURS EN RESTAURATION LA
DEMOCRATE** *p1167*
2901 RUE SHERBROOKE E, MONTREAL,
QC, H1W 1B2
SIC 5812
COREY CRAIG LTD *p406*
713 MAIN ST, MONCTON, NB, E1C 1E3
(506) 856-8050   *SIC 5812*
CUISINES NUTRI-DELI INC, LES *p1321*
535 RUE FILION, SAINT-JEROME, QC, J7Z
1J6
(450) 438-5278   *SIC 5812*
CULINARY CAPERS CATERING INC *p320*
1545 3RD AVE W, VANCOUVER, BC, V6J
1J8
(604) 875-0123   *SIC 5812*
**DANA HOSPITALITY LIMITED PARTNER-
SHIP** *p800*
2898 SOUTH SHERIDAN WAY SUITE 200,
OAKVILLE, ON, L6J 7L5
(905) 829-0292   *SIC 5812*
DANIEL ET DANIEL CATERING INC *p933*

248 CARLTON ST, TORONTO, ON, M5A
2L1
(416) 968-9275   *SIC 5812*
DAWNAL QUICK SERVE LTD *p216*
1465 TRANS CANADA HWY W, KAM-
LOOPS, BC, V1S 1A1
(250) 374-1922   *SIC 5812*
DAWNAL QUICK SERVE LTD *p216*
661 FORTUNE DR, KAMLOOPS, BC, V2B
2K7
(250) 376-0222   *SIC 5812*
DAWNAL QUICK SERVE LTD *p217*
500 NOTRE DAME DR UNIT 800, KAM-
LOOPS, BC, V2C 6T6
(250) 314-3686   *SIC 5812*
DENCAN RESTAURANTS INC *p320*
1755 BROADWAY W SUITE 310, VANCOU-
VER, BC, V6J 4S5
(604) 730-6620   *SIC 5812*
DENCAN RESTAURANTS INC *p331*
4201 32 ST SUITE 6501, VERNON, BC,
V1T 5P3
(250) 542-0079   *SIC 5812*
DHILLON FOOD SERVICES LTD *p249*
820 VICTORIA ST, PRINCE GEORGE, BC,
V2L 5P1
(250) 563-2331   *SIC 5812*
DONATO GROUP INC, THE *p802*
700 KERR ST SUITE 100, OAKVILLE, ON,
L6K 3W5
(905) 337-7777   *SIC 5812*
DOPKO FOOD SERVICES LTD *p172*
5517 37A AVE, WETASKIWIN, AB, T9A 3A5
(780) 986-5322   *SIC 5812*
DOUBLE ARROW VENTURES LTD *p40*
3630 BRENTWOOD RD NW SUITE 500,
CALGARY, AB, T2L 1K8
(403) 284-4404   *SIC 5812*
**DOWN EAST HOSPITALITY INCORPO-
RATED** *p443*
335 PRINCE ALBERT RD SUITE 1, DART-
MOUTH, NS, B2Y 1N7
(902) 434-7500   *SIC 5812*
DRUXY'S INC *p894*
52 ABBOTSFORD RD, STOUFFVILLE, ON,
L4A 2C1
(416) 385-9500   *SIC 5812*
**EAGLE'S NEST COFFEE AND BAKED
GOODS INC** *p484*
234 HASTINGS ST N, BANCROFT, ON, K0L
1C0
(613) 332-0299   *SIC 5812*
EARL'S ON TOP RESTAURANT LTD *p221*
211 BERNARD AVE, KELOWNA, BC, V1Y
6N2
(250) 763-2777   *SIC 5812*
EARL'S RESTAURANT (CLAREVIEW) LTD
p83
13330 50 ST NW, EDMONTON, AB, T5A
4Z8
(780) 473-9008   *SIC 5812*
**EARL'S RESTAURANT (SHERWOOD PARK)
LTD** *p162*
194 ORDZE AVE, SHERWOOD PARK, AB,
T8B 1M6
(780) 449-2575   *SIC 5812*
EARL'S RESTAURANT (WHITE ROCK) LTD
p280
1767 152 ST SUITE 7, SURREY, BC, V4A
4N3
SIC 5812
EARL'S RESTAURANTS CARRELL LTD *p22*
3030 23 ST NE, CALGARY, AB, T2E 8R7
(403) 291-6700   *SIC 5812*
EARL'S RESTAURANTS CARRELL LTD
p326
905 HORNBY ST, VANCOUVER, BC, V6Z
1V3
(604) 682-6700   *SIC 5812*
EARL'S RESTAURANTS LTD *p39*
10640 MACLEOD TRAIL SE, CALGARY,
AB, T2J 0P8
(403) 278-7860   *SIC 5812*
EARL'S RESTAURANTS LTD *p41*

1110 16 AVE NW, CALGARY, AB, T2M 0K8
(403) 289-2566   SIC 5812

EARL'S RESTAURANTS LTD   p66
2401 4 ST SW, CALGARY, AB, T2S 1X5
(403) 228-4141   SIC 5812

EARL'S RESTAURANTS LTD   p71
5005 DALHOUSIE DR NW SUITE 605,
CALGARY, AB, T3A 5R8
(403) 247-1143   SIC 5812

EARL'S RESTAURANTS LTD   p92
11830 JASPER AVE NW, EDMONTON, AB,
T5K 0N7
(780) 488-6582   SIC 5812

EARL'S RESTAURANTS LTD   p117
8629 112 ST NW, EDMONTON, AB, T6G
1K8
(780) 439-4848   SIC 5812

EARL'S RESTAURANTS LTD   p174
32900 SOUTH FRASER WAY SUITE 1, AB-
BOTSFORD, BC, V2S 5A1
SIC 5812

EARL'S RESTAURANTS LTD   p185
3850 LOUGHEED HWY, BURNABY, BC,
V5C 6N4
(604) 291-1019   SIC 5812

EARL'S RESTAURANTS LTD   p217
1210 SUMMIT DR SUITE 800, KAMLOOPS,
BC, V2C 6M1
(250) 372-3275   SIC 5812

EARL'S RESTAURANTS LTD   p246
2850 SHAUGHNESSY ST SUITE 5100,
PORT COQUITLAM, BC, V3C 6K5
(604) 941-1733   SIC 5812

EARL'S RESTAURANTS LTD   p276
7236 120 ST, SURREY, BC, V3W 3M9
SIC 5812

EARL'S RESTAURANTS LTD   p320
1601 BROADWAY W, VANCOUVER, BC,
V6J 1W9
(604) 736-5663   SIC 5812

EARL'S RESTAURANTS LTD   p336
1703 BLANSHARD ST, VICTORIA, BC,
V8W 2J8
SIC 5812

EARL'S RESTAURANTS LTD   p341
303 MARINE DR, WEST VANCOUVER, BC,
V7P 3J8
SIC 5812

EARL'S RESTAURANTS LTD   p377
191 MAIN ST, WINNIPEG, MB, R3C 1A7
(204) 989-0103   SIC 5812

EARL'S RESTAURANTS LTD   p390
2005 PEMBINA HWY, WINNIPEG, MB, R3T
5W7
SIC 5812

EARL'S RESTAURANTS LTD   p1421
2606 28TH AVE, REGINA, SK, S4S 6P3
(306) 584-7733   SIC 5812

EARL'S RESTAURANTS LTD   p1427
610 2ND AVE N, SASKATOON, SK, S7K
2C8
(306) 664-4060   SIC 5812

EARLS MARKET SQUARE LTD   p131
9825 100 ST, GRANDE PRAIRIE, AB, T8V
6X3
(780) 538-3275   SIC 5812

EARLS RESTAURANT (RED DEER) LTD
p157
2111 50 AVE, RED DEER, AB, T4R 1Z4
(403) 342-4055   SIC 5812

EAST SIDE MARIO'S   p1006
450 KING ST N SUITE SIDE, WATERLOO,
ON, N2J 2Z6
(226) 647-2587   SIC 5812

EASTON'S 28 RESTAURANTS LTD   p847
HWY 28 & 401, PORT HOPE, ON, L1A 3V6
(905) 885-1400   SIC 5812

**EDMONTON CITY CENTRE CHURCH COR-
PORATION**   p85
9321 JASPER AVE NW, EDMONTON, AB,
T5H 3T7
(780) 424-1201   SIC 5812

EK'ATI SERVICES LTD   p436
4910 50 AVE, YELLOWKNIFE, NT, X1A 3S5

(867) 873-8873   SIC 5812

EL-RANCHO FOOD SERVICES LIMITED
p1433
218 103RD ST E, SASKATOON, SK, S7N
1Y7
(306) 668-2600   SIC 5812

ELECTRIC FOODS INC   p11
3663 12 AVE NE, CALGARY, AB, T2A 7T1
(403) 248-7640   SIC 5812

ELITE CAMP SERVICES INC   p164
340 ACHESON RD, SPRUCE GROVE, AB,
T7X 5A7
SIC 5812

ELIZABETHAN CATERING SERVICES LTD
p164
55 ALBERTA AVE, SPRUCE GROVE, AB,
T7X 4B9
(780) 962-3663   SIC 5812

ELIZABETHS BAKERY LTD   p75
79 CROWFOOT WAY NW, CALGARY, AB,
T3G 2R2
(403) 239-2583   SIC 5812

ENTERPRISE PARIS INC   p857
2875 RUE LAPORTE, ROCKLAND, ON,
K4K 1R3
(613) 446-9948   SIC 5812

**ENTERPRISES MICHEL MARCHAND INC,
LES**   p1379
1400 BOUL MOODY, TERREBONNE, QC,
J6W 3K9
(450) 471-9022   SIC 5812

ENTREPRISES DORO J.C.S. INC, LES
p1344
6050 BOUL DES GRANDES-PRAIRIES BU-
REAU 204, SAINT-LEONARD, QC, H1P 1A2
(514) 722-3676   SIC 5812

ENTREPRISES JMC (1973) LTEE, LES
p1072
101 CH SAINT-FRANCOIS-XAVIER, CAN-
DIAC, QC, J5R 4V4
(450) 632-4723   SIC 5812

ENTREPRISES MACBAIE INC, LES   p1079
999 BOUL TALBOT, CHICOUTIMI, QC, G7H
4B5
(418) 545-3593   SIC 5812

ENTREPRISES MACBAIE INC, LES   p1079
1401 BOUL TALBOT BUREAU 1,
CHICOUTIMI, QC, G7H 5N6
(418) 545-3593   SIC 5812

ENTREPRISES MACBAIE INC, LES   p1121
1082 RUE AIME-GRAVEL, LA BAIE, QC,
G7B 2M5
(418) 545-3593   SIC 5812

**ENTREPRISES MICHEL MARCHAND INC,
LES**   p1130
8300 BOUL NEWMAN, LASALLE, QC, H8N
1X9
(514) 365-1223   SIC 5812

ENTREPRISES PANTHERE VERTE INC
p1183
160 RUE SAINT-VIATEUR E BUREAU 101,
MONTREAL, QC, H2T 1A8
(514) 507-2620   SIC 5812

EQUIPE PCJ INC   p1144
822 RUE SAINT-LAURENT O, LONGUEUIL,
QC, J4K 1C3
(450) 651-1154   SIC 5812

**ESPLANADE (TORONTO) SPAGHETTI
CORP**   p942
54 THE ESPLANADE, TORONTO, ON, M5E
1A6
(416) 864-9761   SIC 5812

**FACULTY CLUB OF THE UNIVERSITY OF
ALBERTA EDMONTON, THE**   p117
11435 SASKATCHEWAN DR NW, EDMON-
TON, AB, T6G 2G9
(780) 492-4231   SIC 5812

FAMOUS COFFEE SHOP, THE   p759
6380 FALLSVIEW BLVD UNIT R 1, NIA-
GARA FALLS, ON, L2G 7Y6
(905) 354-7775   SIC 5812

FOREVER IN DOUGH INC   p120
9804 22 AVE NW, EDMONTON, AB, T6N
1L1

(780) 463-9086   SIC 5812

FORT MCMURRAY PIZZA LTD   p128
10202 MACDONALD AVE, FORT MCMUR-
RAY, AB, T9H 1T4
(780) 743-5056   SIC 5812

**FORTES, JOE SEAFOOD & CHOP HOUSE
LTD**   p313
777 THURLOW ST, VANCOUVER, BC, V6E
3V5
(604) 669-1940   SIC 5812

FRANCHISE MANAGEMENT INC   p420
417 CONNELL ST SUITE 7, WOODSTOCK,
NB, E7M 5G5
(506) 328-4631   SIC 5812

FRATELLI GOUP INC   p829
309 RICHMOND RD, OTTAWA, ON, K1Z
6X3
(613) 722-6772   SIC 5812

FRESHII INC   p928
1055 YONGE ST, TORONTO, ON, M4W 2L2
(647) 350-2001   SIC 5812

**FULMER DEVELOPMENT CORPORATION,
THE**   p318
1500 GEORGIA ST W SUITE 1290, VAN-
COUVER, BC, V6G 2Z6
(604) 558-5492   SIC 5812

G.R.R. HOLDINGS LTD   p385
2553 PORTAGE AVE, WINNIPEG, MB, R3J
0P3
(204) 885-5275   SIC 5812

GATE GOURMET CANADA INC   p695
2498 BRITANNIA RD E, MISSISSAUGA,
ON, L4W 2P7
(905) 405-4100   SIC 5812

GENERAL MILLS RESTAURANTS INC p688
5915 AIRPORT RD SUITE 910, MISSIS-
SAUGA, ON, L4V 1T1
(905) 673-7898   SIC 5812

GESTION ASSELIN INC   p1379
934 RUE SAINT-SACREMENT, TERRE-
BONNE, QC, J6W 3G2
(450) 964-8448   SIC 5812

GESTION CEJEMAR INC   p1057
1040   AV   GILLES-VILLENEUVE,
BERTHIERVILLE, QC, J0K 1A0
(450) 836-1238   SIC 5812

GESTION DENISON TH INC   p1369
211 CH SAXBY S, SHEFFORD, QC, J2M
1S3
(450) 775-6845   SIC 5812

GESTION GEORGES ABRAHAM INC p1079
433 RUE RACINE E, CHICOUTIMI, QC,
G7H 1T5
(418) 543-2875   SIC 5812

GESTION LOUMA INC   p1370
1325 12E AV N, SHERBROOKE, QC, J1E
3P6
(819) 566-4844   SIC 5812

GESTION MAHEL INC   p1300
130 RUE DUBOIS, SAINT-EUSTACHE, QC,
J7P 4W9
(450) 974-0440   SIC 5812

GESTION N. AUGER INC   p1136
5480 RUE SAINT-GEORGES, LEVIS, QC,
G6V 4M6
(418) 833-3241   SIC 5812

GESTION RESTO GRANBY INC   p1109
940 RUE PRINCIPALE, GRANBY, QC, J2G
2Z4
(450) 378-4656   SIC 5812

GESTION RESTO ST-HYACINTHE INC p1312
1315 RUE DANIEL-JOHNSON O, SAINT-
HYACINTHE, QC, J2S 8S4
(450) 774-7770   SIC 5812

GESTION VALMIRA INC   p1107
25 RUE DE L'EMBELLIE, GATINEAU, QC,
J9A 3K3
(819) 595-4989   SIC 5812

GESTION VINNY INC   p1272
2950 BOUL LAURIER, QUEBEC, QC, G1V
2M4
(418) 659-4484   SIC 5812

GESTIONS G.D. BERUBE INC, LES p1398
1111 BOUL JUTRAS E BUREAU 11, VIC-

TORIAVILLE, QC, G6S 1C1
(819) 357-3657   SIC 5812

GESTIONS PARKER-SCOTT INC   p1131
8080 BOUL CHAMPLAIN BUREAU 1439,
LASALLE, QC, H8P 1B3
(514) 368-2114   SIC 5812

GIBBYS RESTAURANT INC   p1188
298 PLACE D'YOUVILLE, MONTREAL, QC,
H2Y 2B6
(514) 282-1837   SIC 5812

**GIBSON'S, TIM HOLDINGS PARRY SOUND
LTD**   p837
1 MALL DR, PARRY SOUND, ON, P2A 3A9
(705) 746-8467   SIC 5812

GLOBAL SEA SERVICES LTD   p705
2 ROBERT SPECK PKY SUITE 750, MIS-
SISSAUGA, ON, L4Z 1H8
(905) 908-2141   SIC 5812

GMRI CANADA, INC   p711
790 BURNHAMTHORPE RD W, MISSIS-
SAUGA, ON, L5C 4G3
(905) 848-8477   SIC 5812

GOLDEN ARCH FOOD SERVICES LTD p487
80 BARRIE VIEW DR, BARRIE, ON, L4N
8V4
(705) 735-1700   SIC 5812

GOLFBC HOLDINGS INC   p343
8080   NICKLAUS   NORTH   BLVD,
WHISTLER, BC, V8E 1J7
(604) 938-9898   SIC 5812

GRANDI COMPANY LIMITED   p590
870 TOWER ST S, FERGUS, ON, N1M 3N7
(519) 787-5125   SIC 5812

GRANDI COMPANY LIMITED   p601
372 STONE RD W, GUELPH, ON, N1G 4T8
(519) 763-8842   SIC 5812

GRANDI COMPANY LIMITED   p603
243 WOODLAWN RD W, GUELPH, ON,
N1H 8J1
(519) 826-0507   SIC 5812

GREAT EVENTS CATERING INC   p35
7207 FAIRMOUNT DR SE, CALGARY, AB,
T2H 0X6
(403) 256-7150   SIC 5812

GREAT STEAK HOUSE INC, THE   p249
582 GEORGE ST, PRINCE GEORGE, BC,
V2L 1R7
(250) 563-1768   SIC 5812

GRIZZLY GRILL INC, THE   p630
395 PRINCESS ST, KINGSTON, ON, K7L
1B9
(613) 544-7566   SIC 5812

GROUPE NORMANDIN INC   p1256
15021 BOUL HENRI-BOURASSA, QUE-
BEC, QC, G1G 3Z2
(418) 626-7216   SIC 5812

GROUPE NORMANDIN INC   p1286
83 BOUL CARTIER, RIVIERE-DU-LOUP,
QC, G5R 2N1
(418) 867-1366   SIC 5812

GROUPE RESTOS PLAISIRS INC, LE p1259
46 BOUL CHAMPLAIN, QUEBEC, QC, G1K
4H7
(418) 694-0303   SIC 5812

GROUPE RESTOS PLAISIRS INC, LE p1259
84 RUE DALHOUSIE BUREAU 140, QUE-
BEC, QC, G1K 8M5
(418) 692-4455   SIC 5812

GROUPE RESTOS PLAISIRS INC, LE p1269
1225 COURS DU GENERAL-DE MONT-
CALM BUREAU 419, QUEBEC, QC, G1R
4W6
(418) 694-9222   SIC 5812

GROUPE SPORTSCENE INC   p1065
1180 PLACE NOBEL BUREAU 102,
BOUCHERVILLE, QC, J4B 5L2
(450) 641-3011   SIC 5812

GROUPE SPORTSCENE INC   p1205
1212 RUE DE LA GAUCHETIERE O, MON-
TREAL, QC, H3B 2S2
(514) 925-2255   SIC 5812

GROUPE SPORTSCENE INC   p1227
5485 RUE DES JOCKEYS, MONTREAL,
QC, H4P 2T7

(514) 731-2020   *SIC* 5812
HANSON RESTAURANTS (TB) INC   p101
10114 175 ST NW, EDMONTON, AB, T5S 1L1
(780) 484-2896   *SIC* 5812
HANSON RESTAURANTS INC   p104
9768 170 ST NW SUITE 284, EDMONTON, AB, T5T 5L4
(780) 484-2896   *SIC* 5812
HARADROS FOOD SERVICES INC   p1424
1820 8TH ST E SUITE 200, SASKATOON, SK, S7H 0T6
(306) 955-5555   *SIC* 5812
HARD ROCK CAFE   p759
5685 FALLS AVE, NIAGARA FALLS, ON, L2G 3K6
(905) 356-7625   *SIC* 5812
HARPO ENTERPRISES   p272
17960 56 AVE, SURREY, BC, V3S 1C7
(604) 575-1690   *SIC* 5812
HAWTHORNE PARK INC   p270
14476 104 AVE, SURREY, BC, V3R 1L9
(604) 587-1040   *SIC* 5812
HDQ INVESTMENTS LTD   p153
4202 50 AVE, RED DEER, AB, T4N 3Z3
(403) 346-3518   *SIC* 5812
HIP RESTAURANTS LTD   p797
1011 UPPER MIDDLE RD E SUITE C3, OAKVILLE, ON, L6H 5Z9
(647) 403-2494   *SIC* 5812
HOAM LTD   p1035
525 NORWICH AVE, WOODSTOCK, ON, N4S 9A2
(519) 421-7300   *SIC* 5812
HOCO LIMITED   p759
4960 CLIFTON HILL, NIAGARA FALLS, ON, L2G 3N4
(905) 357-5911   *SIC* 5812
HORIZON NORTH CAMP & CATERING PARTNERSHIP   p51
240 4 AVE SW SUITE 900, CALGARY, AB, T2P 4H4
(403) 517-4654   *SIC* 5812
HOST INTERNATIONAL OF CANADA, LTD   p23
2000 AIRPORT RD NE SUITE 160, CALGARY, AB, T2E 6W5
(403) 503-2214   *SIC* 5812
HOT HOUSE RESTAURANT AND BAR   p942
35 CHURCH ST, TORONTO, ON, M5E 1T3
(416) 366-7800   *SIC* 5812
HOUGHTAM ENTERPRISES   p368
1225 ST MARY'S RD SUITE 49, WINNIPEG, MB, R2M 5E5
(204) 257-1132   *SIC* 5812
HRC CANADA INC   p1213
1458 RUE CRESCENT, MONTREAL, QC, H3G 2B6
SIC 5812
HU-A-KAM ENTERPRISES INC   p918
1787 BAYVIEW AVE, TORONTO, ON, M4G 3C5
(416) 292-0459   *SIC* 5812
HY'S OF CANADA LTD   p298
128 PENDER ST W UNIT 303, VANCOUVER, BC, V6B 1R8
(604) 684-3311   *SIC* 5812
HY'S OF CANADA LTD   p952
120 ADELAIDE ST W SUITE 101, TORONTO, ON, M5H 1T1
(416) 364-6600   *SIC* 5812
IDH INVESTMENTS LTD   p175
2455 WEST RAILWAY ST, ABBOTSFORD, BC, V2S 2E3
(604) 744-2444   *SIC* 5812
INCH FOODS INC   p616
20 RYMAL RD E, HAMILTON, ON, L9B 1T7
(905) 387-9282   *SIC* 5812
INN ON THE TWENTY LTD   p623
3836 MAIN ST, JORDAN STATION, ON, L0R 1S0
(905) 562-7313   *SIC* 5812
ISLANDSAND HOLDINGS INC   p1039
150 QUEEN ST, CHARLOTTETOWN, PE,

C1A 4B5
(902) 368-1728   *SIC* 5812
J.F. & L. RESTAURANTS LIMITED   p579
25 THE WEST MALL SUITE 1019, ETOBICOKE, ON, M9C 1B8
(416) 621-4465   *SIC* 5812
J.F. & L. RESTAURANTS LIMITED   p671
110 DENISON ST UNIT 3, MARKHAM, ON, L3R 1B6
(905) 479-2402   *SIC* 5812
J.F. & L. RESTAURANTS LIMITED   p765
5941 LESLIE ST, NORTH YORK, ON, M2H 1J8
(416) 493-4444   *SIC* 5812
J.F. & L. RESTAURANTS LIMITED   p906
1 PROMENADE CIR, THORNHILL, ON, L4J 4P8
SIC 5812
J.W. VENTURES INC   p348
1790 HIGHLAND AVE, BRANDON, MB, R7C 1A7
(204) 571-3152   *SIC* 5812
JACK FRIDAY'S LIMITED   p453
1740 ARGYLE ST, HALIFAX, NS, B3J 2B6
(902) 454-9344   *SIC* 5812
JACOBS CATERING LTD   p988
2828 BATHURST ST SUITE 502, TORONTO, ON, M6B 3A7
(905) 886-3832   *SIC* 5812
JARDINS NELSON INC   p1188
407 PLACE JACQUES-CARTIER, MONTREAL, QC, H2Y 3B1
(514) 861-5731   *SIC* 5812
JERITRISH COMPANY LTD   p628
900 HIGHWAY 17 E, KENORA, ON, P9N 1L9
(807) 468-3018   *SIC* 5812
JOE KOOL'S RESTAURANTS LIMITED p654
595 RICHMOND ST, LONDON, ON, N6A 3G2
(519) 663-5665   *SIC* 5812
JOEY CROWFOOT   p75
50 CROWFOOT WAY NW, CALGARY, AB, T3G 4C8
(403) 547-5639   *SIC* 5812
JOEY TOMATO'S   p328
505 BURRARD ST UNIT 950, VANCOUVER, BC, V7X 1M5
(604) 699-5639   *SIC* 5812
JOEY TOMATO'S (EAU CLAIRE) INC   p52
208 BARCLAY PARADE SW, CALGARY, AB, T2P 4R4
(403) 263-6336   *SIC* 5812
JOEY TOMATO'S KITCHENS INC   p92
11228 JASPER AVE NW, EDMONTON, AB, T5K 0V2
(780) 420-1996   *SIC* 5812
JOEY TOMATO'S KITCHENS INC   p162
222 BASELINE RD UNIT 250, SHERWOOD PARK, AB, T8H 1S8
(780) 449-1161   *SIC* 5812
JOEY TOMATO'S KITCHENS INC   p201
550 LOUGHEED HWY, COQUITLAM, BC, V3K 3S3
(604) 939-3077   *SIC* 5812
JOPAMAR HOLDINGS INC   p808
93 FIRST ST, ORANGEVILLE, ON, L9W 2E8
(519) 941-4009   *SIC* 5812
K.A.S.A. HOLDINGS LTD   p348
1907 RICHMOND AVE, BRANDON, MB, R7B 0T4
(204) 725-2244   *SIC* 5812
KEG RESTAURANT   p241
800 MARINE DR, NORTH VANCOUVER, BC, V7P 1R8
SIC 5812
KEG RESTAURANTS LTD   p36
7104 MACLEOD TRAIL SE, CALGARY, AB, T2H 0L3
(403) 253-2534   *SIC* 5812
KEG RESTAURANTS LTD   p41
1923 UXBRIDGE DR NW, CALGARY, AB, T2N 2V2

(403) 282-0020   *SIC* 5812
KEG RESTAURANTS LTD   p104
9960 170 ST NW, EDMONTON, AB, T5T 6G7
(780) 414-1114   *SIC* 5812
KEG RESTAURANTS LTD   p115
8020 105 ST NW, EDMONTON, AB, T6E 4Z4
SIC 5812
KEG RESTAURANTS LTD   p120
1631 102 ST NW, EDMONTON, AB, T6N 1M3
(780) 485-6530   *SIC* 5812
KEG RESTAURANTS LTD   p198
2991 LOUGHEED HWY UNIT 130, COQUITLAM, BC, V3B 6J6
(604) 464-5340   *SIC* 5812
KEG RESTAURANTS LTD   p260
10100 SHELLBRIDGE WAY, RICHMOND, BC, V6X 2W7
(604) 276-0242   *SIC* 5812
KEG RESTAURANTS LTD   p276
7948 120 ST, SURREY, BC, V3W 3N2
(604) 591-6161   *SIC* 5812
KEG RESTAURANTS LTD   p279
15180 32 AVE DIVERS, SURREY, BC, V3Z 3M1
(604) 542-9733   *SIC* 5812
KEG RESTAURANTS LTD   p319
1499 ANDERSON ST, VANCOUVER, BC, V6H 3R5
(604) 685-4735   *SIC* 5812
KEG RESTAURANTS LTD   p378
115 GARRY ST, WINNIPEG, MB, R3C 1G5
(204) 942-7619   *SIC* 5812
KEG RESTAURANTS LTD   p393
2034 MCGILLIVRAY BLVD, WINNIPEG, MB, R3Y 1V5
(204) 477-5300   *SIC* 5812
KEG RESTAURANTS LTD   p432
135 HARBOUR DR, ST. JOHN'S, NL, A1C 6N6
(709) 726-4534   *SIC* 5812
KEG RESTAURANTS LTD   p511
70 GILLINGHAM DR, BRAMPTON, ON, L6X 4X7
(905) 456-3733   *SIC* 5812
KEG RESTAURANTS LTD   p585
927 DIXON RD, ETOBICOKE, ON, M9W 1J8
(416) 675-2311   *SIC* 5812
KEG RESTAURANTS LTD   p776
1977 LESLIE ST, NORTH YORK, ON, M3B 2M3
(416) 446-1045   *SIC* 5812
KEG RESTAURANTS LTD   p798
300 HAYS BLVD, OAKVILLE, ON, L6H 7P3
(905) 257-2700   *SIC* 5812
KEG RESTAURANTS LTD   p804
3130 SOUTH SERVICE RD W, OAKVILLE, ON, L6L 6T1
(905) 681-1810   *SIC* 5812
KEG RESTAURANTS LTD   p821
75 YORK ST, OTTAWA, ON, K1N 5T2
(613) 241-8514   *SIC* 5812
KEG RESTAURANTS LTD   p867
60 ESTATE DR, SCARBOROUGH, ON, M1H 2Z1
(416) 438-1452   *SIC* 5812
KEG RESTAURANTS LTD   p887
344 GLENDALE AVE, ST CATHARINES, ON, L2T 4E3
(905) 680-4585   *SIC* 5812
KEG RESTAURANTS LTD   p908
735 HEWITSON ST, THUNDER BAY, ON, P7B 6B5
(807) 623-1960   *SIC* 5812
KEG RESTAURANTS LTD   p932
515 JARVIS ST, TORONTO, ON, M4Y 2H7
(416) 964-6609   *SIC* 5812
KEG RESTAURANTS LTD   p942
56 THE ESPLANADE, TORONTO, ON, M5E 1A7
(416) 367-0685   *SIC* 5812

KEG RESTAURANTS LTD   p981
560 KING ST W, TORONTO, ON, M5V 0L5
(416) 364-7227   *SIC* 5812
KEG STEAKHOUSE & BAR, THE   p1008
42 NORTHFIELD DR E, WATERLOO, ON, N2L 6A1
(519) 725-4444   *SIC* 5812
KEG STEAKHOUSE AND BAR   p94
13960 137 AVE NW, EDMONTON, AB, T5L 5H1
(780) 472-0707   *SIC* 5812
KELSEY'S RESTAURANTS INC   p554
199 FOUR VALLEY DR, CONCORD, ON, L4K 0B8
(905) 760-2244   *SIC* 5812
KENMAR FOOD SERVICES LTD   p378
444 ST MARY AVE SUITE 135, WINNIPEG, MB, R3C 3T1
(204) 942-4414   *SIC* 5812
KERRIO CORPORATION   p759
6546 FALLSVIEW BLVD, NIAGARA FALLS, ON, L2G 3W2
(905) 356-6965   *SIC* 5812
KIL INVESTMENTS LTD   p401
251 WOODSTOCK RD, FREDERICTON, NB, E3B 2H8
(506) 457-4386   *SIC* 5812
KIOV INCORPORATED   p860
411 CHRISTINA ST N, SARNIA, ON, N7T 5V8
(519) 336-1320   *SIC* 5812
KJMAL ENTERPRISES LTD   p1413
800 15TH ST E UNIT 800, PRINCE ALBERT, SK, S6V 8E3
(306) 922-6366   *SIC* 5812
KJMAL ENTERPRISES LTD   p1421
4651 ALBERT ST, REGINA, SK, S4S 6B6
(306) 584-5656   *SIC* 5812
KOKANEE FOOD SERVICES INC   p204
1405 CRANBROOK ST N, CRANBROOK, BC, V1C 3S7
(250) 426-7767   *SIC* 5812
KOOLINI ITALIAN CUISINI LIMITED   p1020
1520 TECUMSEH RD E, WINDSOR, ON, N8W 1C4
(519) 254-5665   *SIC* 5812
KOTSOVOS RESTAURANTS LIMITED   p999
35 FRONT ST, TRENTON, ON, K8V 4N3
(613) 392-4333   *SIC* 5812
KRAN MANAGEMENT SERVICES LIMITED   p545
805 WILLIAM ST, COBOURG, ON, K9A 3A8
(905) 372-6335   *SIC* 5812
L'AVIATIC CLUB INC   p1259
450 RUE DE LA GARE-DU-PALAIS BUREAU 104, QUEBEC, QC, G1K 3X2
(418) 522-3555   *SIC* 5812
LAKEHEAD UNIVERSITY STUDENT UNION   p908
955 OLIVER RD, THUNDER BAY, ON, P7B 5E1
(807) 343-8500   *SIC* 5812
LAST BEST PLACE CORP, THE   p981
145 JOHN ST, TORONTO, ON, M5V 2E4
SIC 5812
LAST CLASS, THE   p484
1 GEORGIAN DR, BARRIE, ON, L4M 3X9
(705) 722-1526   *SIC* 5812
LAVOIE, J. P. & SONS LTD   p417
2986 FREDERICTON RD, SALISBURY, NB, E4J 2G1
(506) 372-3333   *SIC* 5812
LAVTOR HOLDINGS (ALBERTA) LTD   p85
1 KINGSWAY GARDEN MALL NW SUITE 555, EDMONTON, AB, T5G 3A6
(780) 479-1313   *SIC* 5812
LAVTOR HOLDINGS (ALBERTA) LTD   p101
17865 106A AVE NW UNIT 101, EDMONTON, AB, T5S 1V8
(780) 483-7545   *SIC* 5812
LE BIFTHEQUE INC   p1340
6705 CH DE LA COTE-DE-LIESSE, SAINT-LAURENT, QC, H4T 1E5
SIC 5812

LE PUB UNIVERSITAIRE INC p1273
2325 RUE DE L'UNIVERSITE BUREAU 1312, QUEBEC, QC, G1V 0B3
(418) 656-7075   *SIC* 5812

LOCAL PUBLIC EATERY LTD p163
222 BASELINE RD SUITE 330, SHERWOOD PARK, AB, T8H 1S8
(780) 417-3182   *SIC* 5812

LONE STAR GROUP OF COMPANIES LIMITED p596
1211 LEMIEUX ST, GLOUCESTER, ON, K1J 1A2
(613) 742-9378   *SIC* 5812

LONE STAR GROUP OF COMPANIES LIMITED p802
472 MORDEN RD SUITE 101, OAKVILLE, ON, L6K 3W4
(905) 845-5852   *SIC* 5812

LOUIS LUNCHEONETTE INC p1370
386 RUE KING E, SHERBROOKE, QC, J1G 1A8
(819) 563-5581   *SIC* 5812

LUCAS & MARCO INC p575
1000 ISLINGTON AVE, ETOBICOKE, ON, M8Z 4P8
(416) 255-4152   *SIC* 5812

LUCIANO'S RESTAURANT GROUP p30
316 3 ST SE, CALGARY, AB, T2G 2S4
SIC 5812

LUDWICK CATERING LTD p349
3184 BIRDS HILL RD, EAST ST PAUL, MB, R2E 1H1
(204) 668-8091   *SIC* 5812

LYNSOS INC p898
1463 LASALLE BLVD, SUDBURY, ON, P3A 1Z8
(705) 560-2500   *SIC* 5812

M & V ENTERPRISES LTD p107
5515 101 AVE NW, EDMONTON, AB, T6A 3Z7
(780) 465-0771   *SIC* 5812

MAC'S FOODS LTD p414
5 WELLESLEY AVE, SAINT JOHN, NB, E2K 2V1
(506) 642-2424   *SIC* 5812

MACKINNON RESTAURANTS INC p476
137 YONGE ST W, ALLISTON, ON, L9R 1V1
(705) 434-0003   *SIC* 5812

MACRI CATERING LIMITED p1032
71 WINGES RD, WOODBRIDGE, ON, L4L 6B5
(905) 851-8030   *SIC* 5812

MANCHU WOK (CANADA) INC p680
85 CITIZEN CRT UNIT 9, MARKHAM, ON, L6G 1A8
(905) 946-7200   *SIC* 5812

MANU FORTI CORPORATION LTD p474
222 BAYLY ST W, AJAX, ON, L1S 3V4
(905) 686-2133   *SIC* 5812

MARBLE RESTAURANTS LTD p115
9054 51 AVE NW SUITE 200, EDMONTON, AB, T6E 5X4
(780) 462-5755   *SIC* 5812

MAREK HOSPITALITY INC p801
2898 SOUTH SHERIDAN WAY UNIT 200, OAKVILLE, ON, L6J 7L5
(905) 829-0292   *SIC* 5812

MARLU INC p1385
300 RUE BARKOFF, TROIS-RIVIERES, QC, G8T 2A3
(819) 373-7921   *SIC* 5812

MARLU INC p1388
4520 BOUL DES RECOLLETS, TROIS-RIVIERES, QC, G9A 4N2
(819) 373-5408   *SIC* 5812

MARTIN DESSERT INC p1140
500 RUE DE BERNIERES, LEVIS, QC, G7A 1E1
(418) 836-1234   *SIC* 5812

MARTIN, CLAUDE & MARCEL INC p1137
49C RTE DU PRESIDENT-KENNEDY, LEVIS, QC, G6V 6C3
(418) 835-1234   *SIC* 5812

MARTIN, CLAUDE & MARCEL INC p1256
3410 BOUL SAINTE-ANNE, QUEBEC, QC, G1E 3L7
(418) 663-1234   *SIC* 5812

MARTIN, CLAUDE & MARCEL INC p1256
7352 BOUL HENRI-BOURASSA, QUEBEC, QC, G1H 3E4
(418) 622-0220   *SIC* 5812

MARTIN, CLAUDE & MARCEL INC p1279
701 RUE DES ROCAILLES, QUEBEC, QC, G2J 1A9
(418) 622-0220   *SIC* 5812

MCAMM ENTERPRIZES LTD p681
9195 HWY 93, MIDLAND, ON, L4R 4K4
(705) 526-4631   *SIC* 5812

MCBURL CORP p530
689 GUELPH LINE, BURLINGTON, ON, L7R 3M7
(905) 639-1661   *SIC* 5812

MCBURL CORP p531
623 PLAINS RD E, BURLINGTON, ON, L7T 2E8
(905) 632-0072   *SIC* 5812

MCCRAM INC p419
3458 RUE PRINCIPALE, TRACADIE-SHEILA, NB, E1X 1C8
(506) 394-1111   *SIC* 5812

MCDONALD'S RESTAURANT p1420
525 N ALBERT ST, REGINA, SK, S4R 8E2
(306) 543-0236   *SIC* 5812

MCDONALD'S RESTAURANTS p401
1177 PROSPECT ST, FREDERICTON, NB, E3B 3B9
(506) 444-6231   *SIC* 5812

MCDONALD'S RESTAURANTS p847
175 ROSE GLEN RD, PORT HOPE, ON, L1A 3V6
(905) 885-2480   *SIC* 5812

MCDONALD'S RESTAURANTS p886
385 ONTARIO ST, ST CATHARINES, ON, L2R 5L3
(905) 688-0244   *SIC* 5812

MCDONALD'S RESTAURANTS LTD p217
1751 TRANS CANADA HWY E, KAMLOOPS, BC, V2C 3Z6
(250) 374-1718   *SIC* 5812

MCDONALD'S RESTAURANTS LTD p334
1644 HILLSIDE AVE, VICTORIA, BC, V8T 2C5
SIC 5812

MCDONALD'S RESTAURANTS OF CANADA LIMITED p120
5360 23 AVE NW, EDMONTON, AB, T6L 6X2
(780) 414-8449   *SIC* 5812

MCDONALD'S RESTAURANTS OF CANADA LIMITED p128
450 GREGOIRE DR, FORT MCMURRAY, AB, T9H 3R2
(780) 791-0551   *SIC* 5812

MCDONALD'S RESTAURANTS OF CANADA LIMITED p161
950 ORDZE RD, SHERWOOD PARK, AB, T8A 4L8
(780) 467-6490   *SIC* 5812

MCDONALD'S RESTAURANTS OF CANADA LIMITED p186
4400 STILL CREEK DR, BURNABY, BC, V5C 6C6
(604) 718-1090   *SIC* 5812

MCDONALD'S RESTAURANTS OF CANADA LIMITED p186
4805 HASTINGS ST, BURNABY, BC, V5C 2L1
(604) 718-1015   *SIC* 5812

MCDONALD'S RESTAURANTS OF CANADA LIMITED p186
4400 STILL CREEK DR, BURNABY, BC, V5C 6C6
(604) 294-2181   *SIC* 5812

MCDONALD'S RESTAURANTS OF CANADA LIMITED p190
4700 KINGSWAY SUITE 1160, BURNABY, BC, V5H 4M1

(604) 718-1005   *SIC* 5812

MCDONALD'S RESTAURANTS OF CANADA LIMITED p196
45816 YALE RD, CHILLIWACK, BC, V2P 2N7
(604) 795-5911   *SIC* 5812

MCDONALD'S RESTAURANTS OF CANADA LIMITED p208
7005 120 ST, DELTA, BC, V4E 2A9
(604) 592-1330   *SIC* 5812

MCDONALD'S RESTAURANTS OF CANADA LIMITED p212
5883 TRANS CANADA HWY, DUNCAN, BC, V9L 3R9
(250) 715-2370   *SIC* 5812

MCDONALD'S RESTAURANTS OF CANADA LIMITED p228
19780 FRASER HWY, LANGLEY, BC, V3A 4C9
(604) 514-1820   *SIC* 5812

MCDONALD'S RESTAURANTS OF CANADA LIMITED p231
22780 LOUGHEED HWY, MAPLE RIDGE, BC, V2X 2V6
(604) 463-7858   *SIC* 5812

MCDONALD'S RESTAURANTS OF CANADA LIMITED p241
1219 MARINE DR, NORTH VANCOUVER, BC, V7P 1T3
(604) 904-4390   *SIC* 5812

MCDONALD'S RESTAURANTS OF CANADA LIMITED p241
925 MARINE DR, NORTH VANCOUVER, BC, V7P 1S2
(604) 985-6757   *SIC* 5812

MCDONALD'S RESTAURANTS OF CANADA LIMITED p261
8191 ALDERBRIDGE WAY, RICHMOND, BC, V6X 3A9
SIC 5812

MCDONALD'S RESTAURANTS OF CANADA LIMITED p270
1000 GUILDFORD TOWN CTR, SURREY, BC, V3R 7C3
SIC 5812

MCDONALD'S RESTAURANTS OF CANADA LIMITED p270
10250 152 ST, SURREY, BC, V3R 6N7
(604) 587-3380   *SIC* 5812

MCDONALD'S RESTAURANTS OF CANADA LIMITED p272
15749 FRASER HWY, SURREY, BC, V3S 2V9
(604) 507-7900   *SIC* 5812

MCDONALD'S RESTAURANTS OF CANADA LIMITED p275
12930 96 AVE, SURREY, BC, V3V 6A8
(604) 587-3390   *SIC* 5812

MCDONALD'S RESTAURANTS OF CANADA LIMITED p287
2021 KINGSWAY, VANCOUVER, BC, V5N 2T2
(604) 718-1060   *SIC* 5812

MCDONALD'S RESTAURANTS OF CANADA LIMITED p295
1527 MAIN ST, VANCOUVER, BC, V6A 2W5
(604) 718-1075   *SIC* 5812

MCDONALD'S RESTAURANTS OF CANADA LIMITED p299
86 PENDER ST W UNIT 1001, VANCOUVER, BC, V6B 6N8
(604) 718-1165   *SIC* 5812

MCDONALD'S RESTAURANTS OF CANADA LIMITED p318
1701 ROBSON ST, VANCOUVER, BC, V6G 1C9
(604) 718-1020   *SIC* 5812

MCDONALD'S RESTAURANTS OF CANADA LIMITED p362
15 REENDERS DR, WINNIPEG, MB, R2C 5K5
(204) 949-3221   *SIC* 5812

MCDONALD'S RESTAURANTS OF

CANADA LIMITED p363
1460 HENDERSON HWY, WINNIPEG, MB, R2G 1N4
(204) 949-6074   *SIC* 5812

MCDONALD'S RESTAURANTS OF CANADA LIMITED p364
77 GOULET ST, WINNIPEG, MB, R2H 0R5
(204) 949-6018   *SIC* 5812

MCDONALD'S RESTAURANTS OF CANADA LIMITED p366
65 VERMILLION RD, WINNIPEG, MB, R2J 3W7
(204) 949-6015   *SIC* 5812

MCDONALD'S RESTAURANTS OF CANADA LIMITED p369
994 KEEWATIN ST, WINNIPEG, MB, R2R 2V1
(204) 949-6079   *SIC* 5812

MCDONALD'S RESTAURANTS OF CANADA LIMITED p370
847 LEILA AVE, WINNIPEG, MB, R2V 3J7
(204) 949-6066   *SIC* 5812

MCDONALD'S RESTAURANTS OF CANADA LIMITED p382
1440 ELLICE AVE, WINNIPEG, MB, R3G 0G4
(204) 949-5123   *SIC* 5812

MCDONALD'S RESTAURANTS OF CANADA LIMITED p387
425 NATHANIEL ST SUITE 1187, WINNIPEG, MB, R3M 3X1
(204) 949-6031   *SIC* 5812

MCDONALD'S RESTAURANTS OF CANADA LIMITED p393
1725 KENASTON BLVD, WINNIPEG, MB, R3Y 1V5
(204) 949-5128   *SIC* 5812

MCDONALD'S RESTAURANTS OF CANADA LIMITED p487
201 FAIRVIEW RD, BARRIE, ON, L4N 9B1
(905) 823-8500   *SIC* 5812

MCDONALD'S RESTAURANTS OF CANADA LIMITED p487
85 DUNLOP ST W, BARRIE, ON, L4N 1A5
(705) 726-6500   *SIC* 5812

MCDONALD'S RESTAURANTS OF CANADA LIMITED p498
45 MOUNTAINASH RD, BRAMPTON, ON, L6R 1W4
(905) 458-7488   *SIC* 5812

MCDONALD'S RESTAURANTS OF CANADA LIMITED p499
2450 QUEEN ST E, BRAMPTON, ON, L6S 5X9
(905) 793-5295   *SIC* 5812

MCDONALD'S RESTAURANTS OF CANADA LIMITED p508
344 QUEEN ST E, BRAMPTON, ON, L6V 1C3
(905) 459-8800   *SIC* 5812

MCDONALD'S RESTAURANTS OF CANADA LIMITED p513
30 BRISDALE DR, BRAMPTON, ON, L7A 3G1
(905) 495-1122   *SIC* 5812

MCDONALD'S RESTAURANTS OF CANADA LIMITED p519
2454 PARKEDALE AVE, BROCKVILLE, ON, K6V 3G8
(613) 342-5551   *SIC* 5812

MCDONALD'S RESTAURANTS OF CANADA LIMITED p534
GD STN GALT, CAMBRIDGE, ON, N1R 5S8
SIC 5812

MCDONALD'S RESTAURANTS OF CANADA LIMITED p537
401 WESTBOUND HWY, CAMBRIDGE, ON, N3C 4B1
SIC 5812

MCDONALD'S RESTAURANTS OF CANADA LIMITED p561
3464 COUNTY RD 89, COOKSTOWN, ON, L0L 1L0
SIC 5812

MCDONALD'S RESTAURANTS OF CANADA LIMITED *p652*
1159 HIGHBURY AVE N, LONDON, ON, N5Y 1A6
(519) 451-6830   *SIC* 5812

MCDONALD'S RESTAURANTS OF CANADA LIMITED *p657*
1074 WELLINGTON RD, LONDON, ON, N6E 1M2
(519) 691-1042   *SIC* 5812

MCDONALD'S RESTAURANTS OF CANADA LIMITED *p659*
462 WHARNCLIFFE RD S, LONDON, ON, N6J 2M9
(519) 673-0680   *SIC* 5812

MCDONALD'S RESTAURANTS OF CANADA LIMITED *p686*
3510 DERRY RD E, MISSISSAUGA, ON, L4T 3V7
(905) 677-8711   *SIC* 5812

MCDONALD'S RESTAURANTS OF CANADA LIMITED *p752*
3773 STRANDHERD DR, NEPEAN, ON, K2J 4B1
(613) 823-7838   *SIC* 5812

MCDONALD'S RESTAURANTS OF CANADA LIMITED *p769*
1125 SHEPPARD AVE E, NORTH YORK, ON, M2K 1C5
SIC 5812

MCDONALD'S RESTAURANTS OF CANADA LIMITED *p779*
1 MCDONALDS PL, NORTH YORK, ON, M3C 3L4
(416) 443-1000   *SIC* 5812

MCDONALD'S RESTAURANTS OF CANADA LIMITED *p779*
747 DON MILLS RD SUITE 13, NORTH YORK, ON, M3C 1T2
(416) 429-1266   *SIC* 5812

MCDONALD'S RESTAURANTS OF CANADA LIMITED *p784*
150 RIMROCK RD, NORTH YORK, ON, M3J 3A6
(416) 630-8381   *SIC* 5812

MCDONALD'S RESTAURANTS OF CANADA LIMITED *p787*
1831 FINCH AVE W SUITE 56, NORTH YORK, ON, M3N 2V2
(416) 636-7601   *SIC* 5812

MCDONALD'S RESTAURANTS OF CANADA LIMITED *p795*
2625F WESTON RD, NORTH YORK, ON, M9N 3X2
(416) 241-5505   *SIC* 5812

MCDONALD'S RESTAURANTS OF CANADA LIMITED *p795*
2020 JANE ST, NORTH YORK, ON, M9N 2V3
(416) 248-6648   *SIC* 5812

MCDONALD'S RESTAURANTS OF CANADA LIMITED *p808*
95 FIRST ST, ORANGEVILLE, ON, L9W 2E8
(519) 940-0197   *SIC* 5812

MCDONALD'S RESTAURANTS OF CANADA LIMITED *p811*
4416 INNES RD, ORLEANS, ON, K4A 3W3
(613) 841-6633   *SIC* 5812

MCDONALD'S RESTAURANTS OF CANADA LIMITED *p820*
594 MONTREAL RD, OTTAWA, ON, K1K 0T9
(613) 741-0093   *SIC* 5812

MCDONALD'S RESTAURANTS OF CANADA LIMITED *p827*
2380 BANK ST, OTTAWA, ON, K1V 8S1
(613) 526-1258   *SIC* 5812

MCDONALD'S RESTAURANTS OF CANADA LIMITED *p827*
1771 WALKLEY RD, OTTAWA, ON, K1V 1L2
(613) 733-8354   *SIC* 5812

MCDONALD'S RESTAURANTS OF CANADA LIMITED *p843*

MCDONALD'S RESTAURANTS OF CANADA LIMITED
1300 KINGSTON RD, PICKERING, ON, L1V 3M9
(905) 839-5665   *SIC* 5812

MCDONALD'S RESTAURANTS OF CANADA LIMITED *p869*
3150 ST CLAIR AVE E, SCARBOROUGH, ON, M1L 1V6
(416) 751-9014   *SIC* 5812

MCDONALD'S RESTAURANTS OF CANADA LIMITED *p902*
1631 MANNING RD, TECUMSEH, ON, N8N 2L9
(519) 735-8122   *SIC* 5812

MCDONALD'S RESTAURANTS OF CANADA LIMITED *p990*
1185 DUPONT ST, TORONTO, ON, M6H 2A5
(416) 536-4188   *SIC* 5812

MCDONALD'S RESTAURANTS OF CANADA LIMITED *p993*
630 KEELE ST, TORONTO, ON, M6N 3E2
(416) 604-1496   *SIC* 5812

MCDONALD'S RESTAURANTS OF CANADA LIMITED *p1000*
5225 HIGHWAY 7 E, UNIONVILLE, ON, L3R 1N3
(905) 477-2891   *SIC* 5812

MCDONALD'S RESTAURANTS OF CANADA LIMITED *p1018*
7777 TECUMSEH RD E, WINDSOR, ON, N8T 1G3
(519) 945-4751   *SIC* 5812

MCDONALD'S RESTAURANTS OF CANADA LIMITED *p1020*
2780 TECUMSEH RD E, WINDSOR, ON, N8W 1G3
(519) 945-3634   *SIC* 5812

MCDONALD'S RESTAURANTS OF CANADA LIMITED *p1025*
883 HURON CHURCH RD, WINDSOR, ON, N9C 2K3
(519) 258-3531   *SIC* 5812

MCDONALD'S RESTAURANTS OF CANADA LIMITED *p1025*
3354 DOUGALL AVE, WINDSOR, ON, N9E 1S6
(519) 966-0454   *SIC* 5812

MCDONALD'S RESTAURANTS OF CANADA LIMITED *p1025*
5631 OJIBWAY PKY, WINDSOR, ON, N9C 4J5
(519) 250-5311   *SIC* 5812

MCDONALD'S RESTAURANTS OF CANADA LIMITED *p1059*
797 BOUL DU CURE-LABELLE, BLAINVILLE, QC, J7C 3P5
(450) 979-7131   *SIC* 5812

MCDONALD'S RESTAURANTS OF CANADA LIMITED *p1104*
80 BOUL GR?BER, GATINEAU, QC, J8T 3P8
(819) 561-1436   *SIC* 5812

MCDONALD'S RESTAURANTS OF CANADA LIMITED *p1189*
1 RUE NOTRE-DAME E, MONTREAL, QC, H2Y 1B6
(514) 285-8720   *SIC* 5812

MCDONALD'S RESTAURANTS OF CANADA LIMITED *p1283*
185 RUE NOTRE-DAME, REPENTIGNY, QC, J6A 2R3
(450) 581-8520   *SIC* 5812

MCDONALD'S RESTAURANTS OF CANADA LIMITED *p1286*
100 RUE DES CERISIERS, RIVIERE-DU-LOUP, QC, G5R 6E8
(418) 863-4242   *SIC* 5812

MCDONALD'S RESTAURANTS OF CANADA LIMITED *p1346*
7445 BOUL LANGELIER, SAINT-LEONARD, QC, H1S 1V6
(514) 252-1105   *SIC* 5812

MCDONALD'S RESTAURANTS OF CANADA LIMITED *p1422*

2620 DEWDNEY AVE, REGINA, SK, S4T 0X3
(306) 525-6611   *SIC* 5812

MCDONALD'S RESTAURANTS OF CANADA LIMITED *p1423*
6210 ROCHDALE BLVD, REGINA, SK, S4X 4K8
(306) 543-6300   *SIC* 5812

MCDONALD'S RESTAURANTS OF CANADA LIMITED *p1423*
1955 PRINCE OF WALES DR, REGINA, SK, S4Z 1A5
(306) 781-1340   *SIC* 5812

MCDONALD'S RESTAURANTS OF CANADA LIMITED *p1424*
1706 PRESTON AVE, SASKATOON, SK, S7H 2V8
(306) 955-8677   *SIC* 5812

MCDONALD'S RESTAURANTS OF CANADA LIMITED *p1432*
2225 22ND ST W, SASKATOON, SK, S7M 0V5
(306) 955-8660   *SIC* 5812

MCDONALDS RESTAURANT *p1424*
3510 8TH ST E UNIT 1, SASKATOON, SK, S7H 0W6
(306) 955-8674   *SIC* 5812

MCDONALDS RESTAURANT OF CANADA INC *p1028*
9200 WESTON RD UNIT E, WOODBRIDGE, ON, L4H 2P8
(905) 832-0424   *SIC* 5812

MCG RESTAURANTS LTD *p85*
10628 KINGSWAY NW, EDMONTON, AB, T5G 0W8
(780) 944-0232   *SIC* 5812

MCKENNCO INC *p1042*
481 GRANVILLE ST, SUMMERSIDE, PE, C1N 4P7
(902) 436-5462   *SIC* 5812

MCPHILLIPS LIMITED PARTNERSHIP *p366*
123 VERMILLION RD, WINNIPEG, MB, R2J 4A9
(204) 253-1928   *SIC* 5812

MEDIEVAL TIMES DINNER & TOURNAMENT (TORONTO) INC *p991*
10 DUFFERIN ST, TORONTO, ON, M6K 3C3
(416) 260-1170   *SIC* 5812

MERCATO INTERNATIONAL LTD *p67*
2224 4 ST SW, CALGARY, AB, T2S 1W9
(403) 263-5535   *SIC* 5812

MIDWEST RESTAURANT INC *p1416*
2037 PARK ST, REGINA, SK, S4N 6S2
(306) 781-5655   *SIC* 5812

MIDWEST RESTAURANT INC *p1424*
3134 8TH ST E, SASKATOON, SK, S7H 0W2
(306) 374-9800   *SIC* 5812

MILLER, P.G. ENTERPRISES LIMITED *p481*
2 ALLAURA BLVD, AURORA, ON, L4G 3S5
(905) 713-1850   *SIC* 5812

MILLER, P.G. ENTERPRISES LIMITED *p756*
17760 YONGE ST, NEWMARKET, ON, L3Y 8P4
(905) 895-1222   *SIC* 5812

MILLER, P.G. ENTERPRISES LIMITED *p756*
1100 DAVIS DR, NEWMARKET, ON, L3Y 8W8
(905) 853-0118   *SIC* 5812

MILLS GROUP INC, THE *p509*
285 QUEEN ST E, BRAMPTON, ON, L6W 2C2
(905) 453-5818   *SIC* 5812

MITTON, V CO LTD *p1039*
365 UNIVERSITY AVE, CHARLOTTETOWN, PE, C1A 4N2
(902) 892-1892   *SIC* 5812

MON 3047 INC *p626*
140 EARL GREY DR, KANATA, ON, K2T 1B6
(613) 270-0518   *SIC* 5812

MONTANA'S COOKHOUSE *p338*
315 BURNSIDE RD W, VICTORIA, BC, V8Z 7L6
(250) 978-9333   *SIC* 5812

MONTANA'S COOKHOUSE SALOON *p121*
1720 99 ST NW, EDMONTON, AB, T6N 1M5
(780) 466-8520   *SIC* 5812

MONTANA'S COOKHOUSE SALOON *p487*
66 BARRIE VIEW DR, BARRIE, ON, L4N 8V4
(705) 726-3375   *SIC* 5812

MOORE ENTERPRISES INC *p401*
1050 WOODSTOCK RD, FREDERICTON, NB, E3B 7R8
(506) 450-3778   *SIC* 5812

MOR-WEN RESTAURANTS LTD *p891*
1010 STITTSVILLE MAIN ST, STITTSVILLE, ON, K2S 1B9
(613) 831-2738   *SIC* 5812

MOTEL BOULEVARD CARTIER INC *p1286*
80 BOUL CARTIER, RIVIERE-DU-LOUP, QC, G5R 2M9
(418) 867-1830   *SIC* 5812

MOXIE'S CLASSIC GRILL *p382*
1485 PORTAGE AVE SUITE 234, WINNIPEG, MB, R3G 0W4
(204) 783-1840   *SIC* 5812

MOXIE'S CLASSIC GRILL *p484*
509 BAYFIELD ST, BARRIE, ON, L4M 4Z8
(705) 733-5252   *SIC* 5812

MOXIE'S CLASSIC GRILL *p1021*
3100 HOWARD AVE UNIT 20, WINDSOR, ON, N8X 3Y8
(519) 250-3390   *SIC* 5812

MOXIE'S RESTAURANTS INC *p146*
3090 DUNMORE RD SE, MEDICINE HAT, AB, T1B 2X2
(403) 528-8628   *SIC* 5812

MOXIE'S RESTAURANTS, LIMITED PARTNERSHIP *p71*
3625 SHAGANAPPI TRAIL NW, CALGARY, AB, T3A 0E2
(403) 288-2663   *SIC* 5812

MOXIE'S RESTAURANTS, LIMITED PARTNERSHIP *p76*
25 HOPEWELL WAY NE, CALGARY, AB, T3J 4V7
(403) 291-4636   *SIC* 5812

MOXIE'S RESTAURANTS, LIMITED PARTNERSHIP *p142*
1621 3 AVE S, LETHBRIDGE, AB, T1J 0L1
(403) 320-1102   *SIC* 5812

MOXIE'S RESTAURANTS, LIMITED PARTNERSHIP *p250*
1804 CENTRAL ST E, PRINCE GEORGE, BC, V2M 3C3
(250) 564-4700   *SIC* 5812

MOXIE'S RESTAURANTS, LIMITED PARTNERSHIP *p362*
1615 REGENT AVE W SUITE 200, WINNIPEG, MB, R2C 5C6
(204) 654-3345   *SIC* 5812

MOXIE'S RESTAURANTS, LIMITED PARTNERSHIP *p710*
100 CITY CENTRE DR UNIT 2-730, MISSISSAUGA, ON, L5B 2C9
(905) 276-6555   *SIC* 5812

MOXIE'S RESTAURANTS, LIMITED PARTNERSHIP *p772*
4950 YONGE ST SUITE 105, NORTH YORK, ON, M2N 6K1
SIC 5812

MUGGS, J J INC *p976*
500 BLOOR ST W, TORONTO, ON, M5S 1Y3
(416) 531-7638   *SIC* 5812

NEW GLASGOW RECREATION CENTRE (1980) INC *p1041*
604 RTE 258 RR 3, HUNTER RIVER, PE, C0A 1N0
(902) 964-2870   *SIC* 5812

NEWGEN RESTAURANT SERVICES INC *p586*
15 CARLSON CRT, ETOBICOKE, ON, M9W 6A2
(416) 675-8818   *SIC* 5812

NEWGEN RESTAURANT SERVICES INC p732
5975 MAVIS RD, MISSISSAUGA, ON, L5R 3T7
(905) 502-8555   SIC 5812

NEWGEN RESTAURANT SERVICES INC p780
895 DON MILLS RD SUITE 208, NORTH YORK, ON, M3C 1W3
(416) 751-8731   SIC 5812

NEWGEN RESTAURANT SERVICES INC p821
61 YORK ST, OTTAWA, ON, K1N 5T2
(613) 241-6525   SIC 5812

NIAGARA PARKS COMMISSION, THE p758
6650 NIAGARA PKY, NIAGARA FALLS, ON, L2E 6T2
(877) 642-7275   SIC 5812

NIAGARA PARKS COMMISSION, THE p758
6345 NIAGARA PKWY, NIAGARA FALLS, ON, L2E 6T2
(905) 356-2217   SIC 5812

NORMA DONUTS LIMITED p591
141 GARRISON RD, FORT ERIE, ON, L2A 1M3
(905) 871-1743   SIC 5812

NORTH-ED (1994) LTD p83
12996 50 ST NW, EDMONTON, AB, T5A 4L2
(780) 457-0221   SIC 5812

NORVAN ENTERPRISES (1982) LTD p368
246 DUNKIRK DR, WINNIPEG, MB, R2M 3W9
(204) 257-0373   SIC 5812

OKANAGAN GENERAL PARTNER LIMITED p219
3333 UNIVERSITY WAY, KELOWNA, BC, V1V 1V7
(250) 807-9851   SIC 5812

OLD SPAGHETTI FACTORY (EDMONTON) LTD p104
8882 170 ST NW SUITE 1632, EDMONTON, AB, T5T 4M2
(780) 444-2181   SIC 5812

OLD SPAGHETTI FACTORY (WHISTLER) LTD p343
4154 VILLAGE GREEN, WHISTLER, BC, V8E 1H1
(604) 938-1015   SIC 5812

OLIVE GARDEN ITALIAN RESTAURANT p228
20080 LANGLEY BYPASS, LANGLEY, BC, V3A 9J7
(604) 514-3499   SIC 5812

OLIVER & BONACINI HOSPITALITY INC p922
2323 YONGE ST SUITE 303, TORONTO, ON, M4P 2C9
(416) 485-8047   SIC 5812

ONTARIO RIBS INC p943
56 THE ESPLANADE SUITE 201, TORONTO, ON, M5E 1A7
(416) 864-9775   SIC 5812

PANACHE ROTISSEURS (1990) INC p575
1633 THE QUEENSWAY, ETOBICOKE, ON, M8Z 1T8
(416) 251-3129   SIC 5812

PANZEX VANCOUVER INC p343
4270 MOUNTAIN SQ, WHISTLER, BC, V0N 1B4
(604) 932-6945   SIC 5812

PASLEY, MAX ENTERPRISES LIMITED p9
1920 68 ST, CALGARY, AB, T1Y 6Y7
(403) 280-6388   SIC 5812

PASLEY, MAX ENTERPRISES LIMITED p40
6820 4 ST NW, CALGARY, AB, T2K 1C2
(403) 295-1004   SIC 5812

PASLEY, MAX ENTERPRISES LIMITED p75
100 STEWART GREEN SW UNIT 100, CALGARY, AB, T3H 3C8
(403) 246-1577   SIC 5812

PASLEY, MAX ENTERPRISES LIMITED p76
5219 FALSBRIDGE DR NE, CALGARY, AB, T3J 3C1

(403) 293-4052   SIC 5812

PASLEY, MAX ENTERPRISES LIMITED p142
217 3 AVE S, LETHBRIDGE, AB, T1J 4L6
(403) 328-8844   SIC 5812

PASLEY, MAX ENTERPRISES LIMITED p154
7149 50 AVE, RED DEER, AB, T4N 4E4
(403) 342-2226   SIC 5812

PEARN, ROY E. ENTERPRISES LIMITED p810
320 MEMORIAL AVE, ORILLIA, ON, L3V 5X6
(705) 325-9851   SIC 5812

PEPPERS, SAMMY J GOURMET GRILL AND BAR p226
19925 WILLOWBROOK DR SUITE 101, LANGLEY, BC, V2Y 1A7
(604) 514-0224   SIC 5812

PETERS DAIRY BAR LTD p143
1152 MAYOR MAGRATH DR S, LETHBRIDGE, AB, T1K 2P8
(403) 327-6440   SIC 5812

PETERS' DRIVE INN p24
219 16 AVE NE, CALGARY, AB, T2E 1J9
(403) 277-2747   SIC 5812

PHOENIX GRILL LTD, THE p70
16061 MACLEOD TRAIL SE SUITE 335, CALGARY, AB, T2Y 3S5
(403) 509-9111   SIC 5812

PINEHILL MANAGEMENT CORP p9
2121 36 ST NE, CALGARY, AB, T1Y 5S3
SIC 5812

PINNACLE CATERERS LTD p965
40 BAY ST SUITE 300, TORONTO, ON, M5J 2X2
(416) 815-6036   SIC 5812

PIONEER FOOD SERVICES LIMITED p477
1180 2 HWY SUITE 2, ANCASTER, ON, L9G 3K9
(905) 648-5222   SIC 5812

PIZZA NOVA RESTAURANTS LIMITED p871
2247 MIDLAND AVE SUITE 12, SCARBOROUGH, ON, M1P 4R1
(416) 439-0051   SIC 5812

PIZZA PIZZA LIMITED p575
500 KIPLING AVE, ETOBICOKE, ON, M8Z 5E5
(416) 967-1010   SIC 5812

PIZZERIA DEMERS INC p1370
936 RUE DU CONSEIL, SHERBROOKE, QC, J1G 1L7
(819) 564-2811   SIC 5812

PLACE TEVERE INC p1345
8610 RUE DU CREUSOT, SAINT-LEONARD, QC, H1P 2A7
(514) 322-9762   SIC 5812

PLACEMENTS SERGAKIS INC p1131
7373 RUE CORDNER, LASALLE, QC, H8N 2R5
(514) 937-0531   SIC 5812

POINT PLUS RESTAURANT-BAR INC, AU p1398
192 BOUL DES BOIS-FRANCS S, VICTORIAVILLE, QC, G6P 4S7
(819) 758-9927   SIC 5812

PORTE DE LA MAURICIE INC, LA p1403
4 RUE SAINTE-ANNE, YAMACHICHE, QC, G0X 3L0
(819) 228-9434   SIC 5812

PRIME RESTAURANTS p601
370 STONE RD W SUITE SIDE, GUELPH, ON, N1G 4V9
(519) 763-7861   SIC 5812

PRIME RESTAURANTS INC p616
1389 UPPER JAMES ST SUITE SIDE, HAMILTON, ON, L9B 1K2
(905) 574-3890   SIC 5812

PRIME RESTAURANTS INC p732
10 KINGSBRIDGE GARDEN CIR SUITE 600, MISSISSAUGA, ON, L5R 3K6
(905) 568-0000   SIC 5812

PRIME RESTAURANTS INC p869
12 LEBOVIC AVE SUITE 9, SCARBOROUGH, ON, M1L 4V9
(416) 285-6631   SIC 5812

PRINCE ALBERT DEVELOPMENT CORPORATION p1414
3680 2ND AVE W, PRINCE ALBERT, SK, S6V 5G2
(306) 763-1362   SIC 5812

QUALIDEC CORPORATION p1007
55 NORTHFIELD DR E, WATERLOO, ON, N2K 3T6
SIC 5812

QUARTERDECK BREWING CO LTD p299
601 CORDOVA ST W, VANCOUVER, BC, V6B 1G1
(604) 689-9151   SIC 5812

R-MAG 118 INC p1148
1615 CH DE LA RIVIERE-AUX-CERISES BUREAU 2, MAGOG, QC, J1X 3W3
(819) 847-3366   SIC 5812

R. G. MC. GROUP LIMITED p394
620 ST. PETER AVE, BATHURST, NB, E2A 2Y7
(506) 548-9555   SIC 5812

R.A.F. HOLDINGS INC p474
1 HARWOOD AVE S, AJAX, ON, L1S 2C1
(905) 683-6497   SIC 5812

RCR HOSPITALITY GROUP LIMITED p456
6009 QUINPOOL RD SUITE 300, HALIFAX, NS, B3K 5J7
(902) 454-8533   SIC 5812

RECIPE UNLIMITED CORPORATION p265
6260 MILLER RD, RICHMOND, BC, V7B 1B3
(604) 278-9144   SIC 5812

RECIPE UNLIMITED CORPORATION p484
397 BAYFIELD ST, BARRIE, ON, L4M 3C5
(705) 737-5272   SIC 5812

RECIPE UNLIMITED CORPORATION p488
85 BARRIE VIEW DR, BARRIE, ON, L4N 8V4
(705) 733-0791   SIC 5812

RECIPE UNLIMITED CORPORATION p515
84 LYNDEN RD SUITE 1771, BRANTFORD, ON, N3R 6B8
(519) 759-6990   SIC 5812

RECIPE UNLIMITED CORPORATION p557
199 FOUR VALLEY DR, CONCORD, ON, L4K 0B8
(905) 760-2244   SIC 5812

RECIPE UNLIMITED CORPORATION p563
960 BROOKDALE AVE SUITE 18, CORNWALL, ON, K6J 4P5
(416) 852-4714   SIC 5812

RECIPE UNLIMITED CORPORATION p608
200 CENTENNIAL PKY N, HAMILTON, ON, L8E 4A1
(905) 599-4133   SIC 5812

RECIPE UNLIMITED CORPORATION p652
1141 HIGHBURY AVE N, LONDON, ON, N5Y 1A5
(519) 453-8100   SIC 5812

RECIPE UNLIMITED CORPORATION p751
1711 MERIVALE RD, NEPEAN, ON, K2G 3K2
(613) 288-0517   SIC 5812

RECIPE UNLIMITED CORPORATION p759
4960 CLIFTON HILL, NIAGARA FALLS, ON, L2G 3N4
(905) 353-0051   SIC 5812

RECIPE UNLIMITED CORPORATION p808
115 FIFTH AVE, ORANGEVILLE, ON, L9W 5B7
(519) 940-4004   SIC 5812

RECIPE UNLIMITED CORPORATION p831
1100 BAXTER RD, OTTAWA, ON, K2C 4B1
SIC 5812

RECIPE UNLIMITED CORPORATION p875
2555 VICTORIA PARK AVE SUITE 19, SCARBOROUGH, ON, M1T 1A3
(416) 494-9693   SIC 5812

RECIPE UNLIMITED CORPORATION p905
2910 STEELES AVE E, THORNHILL, ON, L3T 7X1
(905) 709-0550   SIC 5812

RECIPE UNLIMITED CORPORATION p983
132 JOHN ST, TORONTO, ON, M5V 2E3

SIC 5812

RECIPE UNLIMITED CORPORATION p994
590 KEELE ST, TORONTO, ON, M6N 3E2
(416) 760-7893   SIC 5812

RECIPE UNLIMITED CORPORATION p1000
3760 HIGHWAY 7 E, UNIONVILLE, ON, L3R 0N2
(905) 760-2244   SIC 5812

RECIPE UNLIMITED CORPORATION p1015
175 CONSUMERS DR, WHITBY, ON, L1N 1C4
(905) 666-1411   SIC 5812

RECIPE UNLIMITED CORPORATION p1092
1185 RUE RODOLPHE-PAGE BUREAU 1, DORVAL, QC, H4Y 1H3
(514) 636-5824   SIC 5812

RED LOBSTER HOSPITALITY LLC p11
312 35 ST NE, CALGARY, AB, T2A 6S7
(403) 248-8111   SIC 5812

RED LOBSTER HOSPITALITY LLC p37
6100 MACLEOD TRAIL SW SUITE 100, CALGARY, AB, T2H 0K5
(403) 252-8818   SIC 5812

RED LOBSTER HOSPITALITY LLC p102
10121 171 ST NW, EDMONTON, AB, T5S 1S6
(780) 484-0700   SIC 5812

RED LOBSTER HOSPITALITY LLC p102
10111 171 ST NW, EDMONTON, AB, T5S 1S6
(780) 484-0660   SIC 5812

RED LOBSTER HOSPITALITY LLC p119
4110 CALGARY TRL NW, EDMONTON, AB, T6J 6Y6
(780) 437-3434   SIC 5812

RED LOBSTER HOSPITALITY LLC p119
4111 CALGARY TRAIL NW, EDMONTON, AB, T6J 6S6
(780) 436-8510   SIC 5812

RED LOBSTER HOSPITALITY LLC p363
51 REENDERS DR, WINNIPEG, MB, R2C 5E8
(204) 661-8129   SIC 5812

RED LOBSTER HOSPITALITY LLC p382
1544 PORTAGE AVE, WINNIPEG, MB, R3G 0W9
(204) 783-9434   SIC 5812

RED LOBSTER HOSPITALITY LLC p382
1540 PORTAGE AVE, WINNIPEG, MB, R3G 0W9
(204) 783-9434   SIC 5812

RED LOBSTER HOSPITALITY LLC p484
319 BAYFIELD ST, BARRIE, ON, L4M 3C2
(705) 728-2401   SIC 5812

RED LOBSTER HOSPITALITY LLC p515
67 KING GEORGE RD, BRANTFORD, ON, N3R 5K2
(519) 759-7121   SIC 5812

RED LOBSTER HOSPITALITY LLC p579
1790 THE QUEENSWAY, ETOBICOKE, ON, M9C 5H5
(416) 620-9990   SIC 5812

RED LOBSTER HOSPITALITY LLC p656
667 WELLINGTON RD, LONDON, ON, N6C 4R4
(519) 668-0220   SIC 5812

RED LOBSTER HOSPITALITY LLC p751
1595 MERIVALE RD, NEPEAN, ON, K2G 3J4
(613) 727-0035   SIC 5812

RED LOBSTER HOSPITALITY LLC p759
6220 LUNDY'S LANE, NIAGARA FALLS, ON, L2G 1T6
(905) 357-1303   SIC 5812

RED LOBSTER HOSPITALITY LLC p790
3200 DUFFERIN ST, NORTH YORK, ON, M6A 3B2
(416) 785-7930   SIC 5812

RED LOBSTER HOSPITALITY LLC p818
1499 ST. LAURENT BLVD, OTTAWA, ON, K1G 0Z9
(613) 744-7560   SIC 5812

RED LOBSTER HOSPITALITY LLC p875
3252 SHEPPARD AVE E, SCARBOR-

OUGH, ON, M1T 3K3
(416) 491-2507   *SIC* 5812

RED LOBSTER HOSPITALITY LLC   *p*905
7291 YONGE ST, THORNHILL, ON, L3T 2A9
(905) 731-3550   *SIC* 5812

RED LOBSTER HOSPITALITY LLC   *p*1019
6575 TECUMSEH RD E, WINDSOR, ON, N8T 1E7
(519) 948-7677   *SIC* 5812

RED LOBSTER HOSPITALITY LLC   *p*1424
2501 8TH ST E, SASKATOON, SK, S7H 0V4
(306) 373-8333   *SIC* 5812

RED OAK CATERING INC   *p*433
50 HAMLYN RD SUITE 466, ST. JOHN'S, NL, A1E 5X7
(709) 368-6808   *SIC* 5812

RED ROBIN RESTAURANT (CAPILANO) LTD   *p*241
801 MARINE DR SUITE 100, NORTH VANCOUVER, BC, V7P 3K6
SIC 5812

RESTAURANT A LA RIVE INC   *p*1160
153 RUE SAINT-LOUIS, MONTMAGNY, QC, G5V 1N4
(418) 248-3494   *SIC* 5812

RESTAURANT AIX INC   *p*1190
711 COTE DE LA PLACE-D'ARMES, MONTREAL, QC, H2Y 2X6
(514) 904-1201   *SIC* 5812

RESTAURANT B.C.L. INC   *p*1398
609 BOUL DES BOIS-FRANCS S, VICTORIAVILLE, QC, G6P 5X1
(819) 357-9226   *SIC* 5812

RESTAURANT BRANDS INTERNATIONAL INC   *p*987
130 KING ST W SUITE 300, TORONTO, ON, M5X 1E1
(905) 339-5724   *SIC* 5812

RESTAURANT CONTINENTAL INC   *p*1269
26 RUE SAINT-LOUIS, QUEBEC, QC, G1R 3Y9
(418) 694-9995   *SIC* 5812

RESTAURANT DU VIEUX PORT INC   *p*1190
39 RUE SAINT-PAUL E, MONTREAL, QC, H2Y 1G2
(514) 866-3175   *SIC* 5812

RESTAURANT INNOVATIONS INC   *p*641
20 HELDMANN RD, KITCHENER, ON, N2P 0A6
(519) 653-9660   *SIC* 5812

RESTAURANT MACGEORGES INC   *p*1228
7475 BOUL DECARIE, MONTREAL, QC, H4P 2G9
(514) 738-3588   *SIC* 5812

RESTAURANT NEWTOWN INC   *p*1214
1476 RUE CRESCENT, MONTREAL, QC, H3G 2B6
(514) 284-6555   *SIC* 5812

RESTAURANT NORMANDIN (2014) INC   *p*1275
2335 BOUL BASTIEN, QUEBEC, QC, G2B 1B3
(418) 842-9160   *SIC* 5812

RESTAURANT NORMANDIN (2014) INC   *p*1349
530 RTE DU PONT, SAINT-NICOLAS, QC, G7A 2N9
(418) 831-1991   *SIC* 5812

RESTAURANT SAINT-PAUL (MONTREAL) LTEE   *p*1190
25 RUE SAINT-PAUL E, MONTREAL, QC, H2Y 1G2
(514) 871-9093   *SIC* 5812

RESTAURANTS DUMAS LTEE, LES   *p*1101
410 BOUL CURE-LABELLE, FABREVILLE, QC, H7P 2P1
(450) 628-0171   *SIC* 5812

RESTAURANTS IANA INC   *p*1370
975 RUE KING E, SHERBROOKE, QC, J1G 1E3
(819) 571-9623   *SIC* 5812

RESTAURANTS MAC-VIC INC, LES   *p*1313
3005 BOUL LAFRAMBOISE, SAINT-

HYACINTHE, QC, J2S 4Z6
(450) 774-5955   *SIC* 5812

RESTAURANTS MAC-VIC INC, LES   *p*1313
3200 BOUL LAFRAMBOISE, SAINT-HYACINTHE, QC, J2S 4Z5
(450) 261-8880   *SIC* 5812

RESTAURANTS MIKA INC, LES   *p*1281
1154 RUE DE LA FAUNE, QUEBEC, QC, G3E 1T2
(418) 845-6323   *SIC* 5812

RESTAURANTS SERQUA INC, LES   *p*1381
1415 BOUL MOODY, TERREBONNE, QC, J6X 4C8
(450) 471-1161   *SIC* 5812

RESTAURANTS T.S.N.A. INC   *p*1143
365 RUE SAINT-JEAN, LONGUEUIL, QC, J4H 2X7
(450) 670-5609   *SIC* 5812

RESTAURATION MIMAR INC   *p*1352
725 CH JEAN-ADAM, SAINT-SAUVEUR, QC, J0R 1R3
(450) 227-4664   *SIC* 5812

RICARDA'S INC   *p*536
240 SHEARSON CRES, CAMBRIDGE, ON, N1T 1J6
(416) 304-9134   *SIC* 5812

RICHTREE MARKET RESTAURANTS INC   *p*821
50 RIDEAU ST SUITE 115, OTTAWA, ON, K1N 9J7
SIC 5812

RICHTREE MARKET RESTAURANTS INC   *p*956
14 QUEEN ST W, TORONTO, ON, M5H 3X4
(416) 366-8986   *SIC* 5812

RICHTREE MARKET RESTAURANTS INC   *p*971
40 YONGE BLVD, TORONTO, ON, M5M 3G5
(416) 366-8986   *SIC* 5812

RICMAR ENTERPRISES LTD   *p*587
925 DIXON RD, ETOBICOKE, ON, M9W 1J8
(416) 674-3031   *SIC* 5812

RJMB RESTAURANTS LTD   *p*225
20394 88 AVE, LANGLEY, BC, V1M 2Y6
(604) 881-6220   *SIC* 5812

ROBIE & KEMPT SERVICES LIMITED   *p*456
3630 KEMPT RD, HALIFAX, NS, B3K 4X8
(902) 832-2103   *SIC* 5812

ROCK THE BYWARD MARKET CORPORATION   *p*821
73 YORK ST, OTTAWA, ON, K1N 5T2
(613) 241-2442   *SIC* 5812

ROTISSERIE ROUYN-NORANDA INC *p*1290
60 AV QUEBEC, ROUYN-NORANDA, QC, J9X 6P9
(819) 797-2151   *SIC* 5812

ROTISSERIES DE SHERBROOKE INC, LES   *p*1374
3070 RUE KING O, SHERBROOKE, QC, J1L 1C9
(819) 563-5111   *SIC* 5812

ROTISSERIES DU HAUT RICHELIEU LTEE, LES   *p*1317
960 BOUL DU SEMINAIRE N, SAINT-JEAN-SUR-RICHELIEU, QC, J3A 1L2
(450) 348-6876   *SIC* 5812

ROTISSERIES ST-HUBERT LTEE, LES   *p*1067
500 RUE ALBANEL, BOUCHERVILLE, QC, J4B 2Z6
(450) 449-9366   *SIC* 5812

ROTISSERIES ST-HUBERT LTEE, LES   *p*1071
6325 BOUL TASCHEREAU, BROSSARD, QC, J4Z 1A6
SIC 5812

ROTISSERIES ST-HUBERT LTEE, LES   *p*1165
6225 RUE SHERBROOKE E, MONTREAL, QC, H1N 1C3
(514) 259-6939   *SIC* 5812

ROTISSERIES ST-HUBERT LTEE, LES

*p*1208
1180 AV DES CANADIENS-DE-MONTREAL, MONTREAL, QC, H3B 2S2
(514) 866-0500   *SIC* 5812

ROWENDA INVESTMENTS LTD   *p*591
124 HWY 20 E, FONTHILL, ON, L0S 1E6
(905) 892-7906   *SIC* 5812

ROXSON ENTERPRISES LIMITED   *p*479
80 MCGONIGAL ST W, ARNPRIOR, ON, K7S 1M3
SIC 5812

RRGB RESTAURANTS CANADA INC   *p*103
10010 171 ST NW, EDMONTON, AB, T5S 1S3
(780) 484-6735   *SIC* 5812

RRGB RESTAURANTS CANADA INC   *p*107
4950 137 AVE NW, EDMONTON, AB, T5Y 2V4
(780) 456-8700   *SIC* 5812

RRGB RESTAURANTS CANADA INC   *p*163
8005 EMERALD DR SUITE 250, SHERWOOD PARK, AB, T8H 0P1
(587) 269-4401   *SIC* 5812

RRGB RESTAURANTS CANADA INC   *p*175
33011 SOUTH FRASER WAY, ABBOTSFORD, BC, V2S 2A6
(604) 853-8185   *SIC* 5812

RRGB RESTAURANTS CANADA INC   *p*191
4640 KINGSWAY SUITE 112, BURNABY, BC, V5H 4L9
SIC 5812

RRGB RESTAURANTS CANADA INC   *p*270
10237 152 ST, SURREY, BC, V3R 4G6
(604) 930-2415   *SIC* 5812

RRGB RESTAURANTS CANADA INC   *p*337
800 TOLMIE AVE, VICTORIA, BC, V8X 3W4
(250) 386-4440   *SIC* 5812

RUTH'S CHRIS STEAK HOUSE EDMONTON   *p*90
10103 100 ST NW, EDMONTON, AB, T5J 0N8
(780) 990-0123   *SIC* 5812

S & T ALLARD FOOD LTD   *p*133
10206 100 ST SUITE 640, GRANDE PRAIRIE, AB, T8V 3K1
(780) 532-6660   *SIC* 5812

SABRITIN HOSPITALITY INC   *p*512
370 BOVAIRD DR E, BRAMPTON, ON, L6Z 2S8
(905) 846-3321   *SIC* 5812

SALISBURY HOUSE OF CANADA LTD *p*370
787 LEILA AVE, WINNIPEG, MB, R2V 3J7
(204) 594-7257   *SIC* 5812

SALISBURY HOUSE OF CANADA LTD *p*392
1941 PEMBINA HWY, WINNIPEG, MB, R3T 2G7
SIC 5812

SAN MIGUEL FOODS LTD   *p*481
1 HENDERSON DR UNIT 4, AURORA, ON, L4G 4J7
(905) 727-7918   *SIC* 5812

SAWMILL RESTAURANT GROUP LTD *p*119
4810 CALGARY TRAIL NW, EDMONTON, AB, T6H 5H5
(780) 463-4499   *SIC* 5812

SCARLETT HOUSE FOOD GROUP INC*p*736
7615 KIMBEL ST UNIT 8, MISSISSAUGA, ON, L5S 1A8
(905) 672-6302   *SIC* 5812

SECOND CUP LTD, THE   *p*689
6303 AIRPORT RD FLR 2, MISSISSAUGA, ON, L4V 1R8
(905) 362-1827   *SIC* 5812

SECOND CUP LTD, THE   *p*773
5095 YONGE ST, NORTH YORK, ON, M2N 6Z4
(416) 227-9332   *SIC* 5812

SEQUOIA COMPANY OF RESTAURANTS INC   *p*318
1583 COAL HARBOUR QUAY, VANCOUVER, BC, V6G 3E7
(604) 687-5684   *SIC* 5812

SEQUOIA COMPANY OF RESTAURANTS INC   *p*318

1583 COAL HARBOUR QUAY, VANCOUVER, BC, V6G 3E7
(604) 687-5684   *SIC* 5812

SERVICE CUISINE G.P. INC   *p*1060
82 RUE REAL-BENOIT, BLAINVILLE, QC, J7C 5J1
(450) 979-9921   *SIC* 5812

SHARK CLUBS OF CANADA INC   *p*76
31 HOPEWELL WAY NE, CALGARY, AB, T3J 4V7
(403) 543-2600   *SIC* 5812

SHOPSY'S HOSPITALITY INC   *p*943
33 YONGE ST, TORONTO, ON, M5E 1G4
(905) 474-3333   *SIC* 5812

SILVERBIRCH NO. 41 OPERATIONS LIMITED PARTNERSHIP   *p*285
2205 COMMISSIONER ST, VANCOUVER, BC, V5L 1A4
SIC 5812

SIR CORP   *p*459
184 CHAIN LAKE DR, HALIFAX, NS, B3S 1C5
(902) 450-1370   *SIC* 5812

SIR CORP   *p*478
839 GOLF LINKS RD, ANCASTER, ON, L9K 1L5
(905) 304-1721   *SIC* 5812

SIR CORP   *p*506
154 WEST DR, BRAMPTON, ON, L6T 5P1
(905) 457-5200   *SIC* 5812

SIR CORP   *p*525
5360 SOUTH SERVICE RD SUITE 200, BURLINGTON, ON, L7L 5L1
(905) 681-2997   *SIC* 5812

SIR CORP   *p*588
25 CARLSON CRT, ETOBICOKE, ON, M9W 6A2
(416) 213-1688   *SIC* 5812

SIR CORP   *p*657
1070 WELLINGTON RD SUITE 1, LONDON, ON, N6E 3V8
(519) 680-3800   *SIC* 5812

SIR CORP   *p*711
299 RATHBURN RD W, MISSISSAUGA, ON, L5B 4C1
(905) 279-3342   *SIC* 5812

SIR CORP   *p*711
219 RATHBURN RD W, MISSISSAUGA, ON, L5B 4C1
(905) 566-4662   *SIC* 5812

SIR CORP   *p*711
209 RATHBURN RD W, MISSISSAUGA, ON, L5B 4C1
(905) 281-1721   *SIC* 5812

SIR CORP   *p*967
144 FRONT ST W, TORONTO, ON, M5J 2L7
(416) 585-2121   *SIC* 5812

SJR FOOD SERVICES LTD   *p*211
1835 56 ST UNIT 44, DELTA, BC, V4L 2M1
(604) 948-3630   *SIC* 5812

SKY BAR LTD   *p*327
938 HOWE ST SUITE 615, VANCOUVER, BC, V6Z 1N9
(604) 697-0990   *SIC* 5812

SMITH & SCOTT STEAKHOUSE LIMITED *p*456
6061 YOUNG ST, HALIFAX, NS, B3K 2A3
(902) 454-8814   *SIC* 5812

SMITTY'S CANADA INC   *p*67
501 18 AVE SW SUITE 600, CALGARY, AB, T2S 0C7
(403) 229-3838   *SIC* 5812

SMSI TRAVEL CENTRES INC   *p*773
45 SHEPPARD AVE E SUITE 302, NORTH YORK, ON, M2N 5W9
(416) 221-4900   *SIC* 5812

SNOWLINE RESTAURANTS INC   *p*343
4429 SUNDIAL PL, WHISTLER, BC, V0N 1B4
(604) 932-5151   *SIC* 5812

SNUG HARBOUR SEAFOOD BAR & GRILL *p*713
14 STAVEBANK RD S, MISSISSAUGA, ON, L5G 2T1

(905) 274-5000   *SIC* 5812
SODEXO CANADA LTD   p227
7600 GLOVER RD, LANGLEY, BC, V2Y 1Y1
(604) 513-2009   *SIC* 5812
SODEXO CANADA LTD   p438
GD, ANTIGONISH, NS, B2G 2W5
(902) 867-2491   *SIC* 5812
SODEXO CANADA LTD   p525
5420 NORTH SERVICE RD SUITE 501, BURLINGTON, ON, L7L 6C7
(905) 632-8592   *SIC* 5812
SODEXO CANADA LTD   p562
1950 MONTREAL RD, CORNWALL, ON, K6H 6L2
(613) 936-5800   *SIC* 5812
SODEXO CANADA LTD   p631
75 BADER LANE, KINGSTON, ON, K7L 3N8
(613) 533-2953   *SIC* 5812
SODEXO CANADA LTD   p976
21 SUSSEX AVE UNIT 3, TORONTO, ON, M5S 1J6
SIC 5812
SODEXO CANADA LTD   p976
41 CLASSIC AVE, TORONTO, ON, M5S 2Z3
SIC 5812
SODEXO QUEBEC LIMITEE   p1108
100 RUE LAURIER, GATINEAU, QC, K1A 0M8
(819) 776-8391   *SIC* 5812
SODEXO QUEBEC LIMITEE   p1108
100 RUE LAURIER, GATINEAU, QC, K1A 0M8
(819) 776-8391   *SIC* 5812
SOTTO SOTTO RISTORANTE LIMITED p973
116 AVENUE RD UNIT A, TORONTO, ON, M5R 2H4
(416) 962-0011   *SIC* 5812
SOURCES 40 WESTT INC   p1252
2305 RTE TRANSCANADIENNE, POINTE-CLAIRE, QC, H9R 5Z5
(514) 428-9378   *SIC* 5812
SOUTH ALBERTA RIBS (2002) LTD   p37
6712 MACLEOD TRAIL SE, CALGARY, AB, T2H 0L3
(403) 301-7427   *SIC* 5812
SPATSIZI REMOTE SERVICES CORPORATION p205
GD, DEASE LAKE, BC, V0C 1L0
(250) 771-5484   *SIC* 5812
SPECTRA GROUP OF GREAT RESTAURANTS INC, THE   p238
900 QUAYSIDE DR, NEW WESTMINSTER, BC, V3M 6G1
(604) 525-3474   *SIC* 5812
SPECTRA GROUP OF GREAT RESTAURANTS INC, THE   p338
3195 DOUGLAS ST, VICTORIA, BC, V8Z 3K3
SIC 5812
SPEEDI GOURMET CO LTD   p321
1650 4TH AVE W, VANCOUVER, BC, V6J 1L9
(604) 731-8877   *SIC* 5812
SPEEDY CREEK (2011) LTD   p103
17724 102 AVE NW, EDMONTON, AB, T5S 1H5
SIC 5812
SPEEDY CREEK (2011) LTD   p119
10333 34 AVE NW, EDMONTON, AB, T6J 6V1
SIC 5812
SPRUCE GROVE PIZZA LTD   p164
201 CALAHOO RD, SPRUCE GROVE, AB, T7X 1R1
(780) 962-0224   *SIC* 5812
STARBUCKS COFFEE CANADA, INC p773
5140 YONGE ST SUITE 1205, NORTH YORK, ON, M2N 6L7
(416) 228-7300   *SIC* 5812
STEVESTON RESTAURANTS LTD   p264
11151 NO. 5 RD, RICHMOND, BC, V7A 4E8
(604) 272-1399   *SIC* 5812

STONEWATER GROUP OF FRANCHISES
p214
9324 ALASKA RD, FORT ST. JOHN, BC, V1J 6L5
(250) 262-4151   *SIC* 5812
STUDY BREAK LIMITED   p596
5480 CANOTEK RD SUITE 20, GLOUCESTER, ON, K1J 9H7
(613) 745-6389   *SIC* 5812
SUN SUI WAH SEAFOOD RESTAURANT
p262
4940 NO. 3 RD SUITE 102, RICHMOND, BC, V6X 3A5
(604) 273-8208   *SIC* 5812
SUNNY HOLDINGS LIMITED   p41
1140 16 AVE NW, CALGARY, AB, T2M 0K8
SIC 5812
SWENSON, LARRY ENTERPRISES LTD
p463
689 WESTVILLE RD, NEW GLASGOW, NS, B2H 2J6
(902) 752-6442   *SIC* 5812
SYDAX DEVELOPMENTS LIMITED   p444
300 PRINCE ALBERT RD, DARTMOUTH, NS, B2Y 4J2
(902) 468-8817   *SIC* 5812
SYMONS THE BAKER LTD   p1406
1305 9TH ST, ESTEVAN, SK, S4A 1J1
(306) 634-6456   *SIC* 5812
SYSCO CANADA, INC   p460
1 DUCK POND RD SUITE 1, LAKESIDE, NS, B3T 1M5
(902) 876-2311   *SIC* 5812
T.T.O.C.S. LIMITED   p814
419 KING ST W SUITE SIDE, OSHAWA, ON, L1J 2K5
SIC 5812
TACORPORATION RESTAURANT LTD p285
1622 COMMERCIAL DR UNIT A, VANCOUVER, BC, V5L 3Y4
(604) 559-8226   *SIC* 5812
TAYLYX LTD   p748
475 CENTRE ST N, NAPANEE, ON, K7R 3S4
(613) 354-9707   *SIC* 5812
TDL GROUP CORP, THE   p19
7460 51 ST SE, CALGARY, AB, T2C 4B4
(403) 203-7400   *SIC* 5812
TDL GROUP CORP, THE   p79
120 JOHN MORRIS WAY SUITE 300, CHESTERMERE, AB, T1X 1V3
(403) 248-0000   *SIC* 5812
TDL GROUP CORP, THE   p607
950 SOUTHGATE DR, GUELPH, ON, N1L 1S7
(519) 824-1304   *SIC* 5812
TEE-BEE-QUE LIMITED   p1025
1855 HURON CHURCH RD, WINDSOR, ON, N9C 2L6
SIC 5812
TEJAZZ MANAGEMENT SERVICES INC
p241
4238 ST. PAULS AVE, NORTH VANCOUVER, BC, V7N 1T5
(604) 986-9475   *SIC* 5812
TEMPERENCECO INC   p957
10 TEMPERANCE ST SUITE 202, TORONTO, ON, M5H 1Y4
(647) 348-7000   *SIC* 5812
TISDELLE ENTERPRISES (EXPRESS) LIMITED   p890
6 PRINCESS AVE SUITE 5, ST THOMAS, ON, N5R 3V2
(519) 631-0116   *SIC* 5812
TOMANICK GROUP, THE   p151
10 SOUTHRIDGE DR, OKOTOKS, AB, T1S 1N1
(403) 995-0224   *SIC* 5812
TOOR & ASSOCIATES INC   p806
270 NORTH SERVICE RD W, OAKVILLE, ON, L6M 2R8
(905) 849-8100   *SIC* 5812
TORBA RESTAURANTS INC   p879
6 FATHER COSTELLO DR, SCHU-

MACHER, ON, P0N 1G0
(705) 267-4150   *SIC* 5812
TURTLE JACK'S RESTAURANT INC p528
3370 SOUTH SERVICE RD SUITE 102, BURLINGTON, ON, L7N 3M6
(905) 332-6833   *SIC* 5812
TWINCORP INC   p1007
316 MARSLAND DR, WATERLOO, ON, N2J 3Z1
(519) 885-4600   *SIC* 5812
UNCLE RAY'S RESTAURANT CO. LTD p195
1361 16TH AVE, CAMPBELL RIVER, BC, V9W 2C9
(250) 287-2631   *SIC* 5812
UNDERHILL FOOD SERVICES LTD   p140
6504 SPARROW DR, LEDUC, AB, T9E 6T9
(780) 986-5323   *SIC* 5812
UPPER CRUST CATERERS LTD   p118
10909 86 AVE NW, EDMONTON, AB, T6G 0W8
(780) 758-5599   *SIC* 5812
URBAN DINING GROUP INC   p976
192 BLOOR ST W SUITE 201, TORONTO, ON, M5S 1T8
(416) 967-9671   *SIC* 5812
VINNIE ZUCCHINI'S CORPORATION   p560
9100 JANE ST BLDG G UNIT 48, CONCORD, ON, L4K 0A4
(905) 761-1361   *SIC* 5812
WAHA ENTERPRISES INC   p748
100 BAYSHORE DR, NEPEAN, ON, K2B 8C1
(613) 721-2918   *SIC* 5812
WATER STREET (VANCOUVER) SPAGHETTI CORP   p337
703 DOUGLAS ST, VICTORIA, BC, V8W 2B4
(250) 381-8444   *SIC* 5812
WATSON, T.J. ENTERPRISES INC p1020
4255 TECUMSEH RD E, WINDSOR, ON, N8W 1K2
(519) 250-0955   *SIC* 5812
WATTS' GROUP LIMITED   p968
156 FRONT ST W SUITE 610, TORONTO, ON, M5J 2L6
(416) 755-1374   *SIC* 5812
WAY, G RESTAURANTS SERVICES LTD
p515
299 WAYNE GRETZKY PKY, BRANTFORD, ON, N3R 8A5
(519) 751-2304   *SIC* 5812
WENDCORP HOLDINGS INC   p518
202 GRAND RIVER AVE SUITE 1, BRANTFORD, ON, N3T 4X9
(519) 756-8431   *SIC* 5812
WENDY'S RESTAURANTS OF CANADA INC
p802
240 WYECROFT RD, OAKVILLE, ON, L6K 2G7
(905) 337-8041   *SIC* 5812
WHITE SPOT LIMITED   p180
4075 NORTH RD, BURNABY, BC, V3J 1S3
(604) 421-4620   *SIC* 5812
WHITE SPOT LIMITED   p199
3025 LOUGHEED HWY SUITE 500, COQUITLAM, BC, V3B 6S2
(604) 942-9224   *SIC* 5812
WHITE SPOT LIMITED   p239
333 BROOKSBANK AVE SUITE 1100, NORTH VANCOUVER, BC, V7J 3S8
(604) 988-6717   *SIC* 5812
WHITE SPOT LIMITED   p262
5880 NO. 3 RD, RICHMOND, BC, V6X 2E1
(604) 273-3699   *SIC* 5812
WHITE SPOT LIMITED   p291
1126 MARINE DR SE, VANCOUVER, BC, V5X 2V7
(604) 321-6631   *SIC* 5812
WHITE SPOT LIMITED   p294
650 41ST AVE W SUITE 613A, VANCOUVER, BC, V5Z 2M9
(604) 261-2820   *SIC* 5812
WHITE SPOT LIMITED   p342
752 MARINE DR UNIT 1108, WEST VAN-

COUVER, BC, V7T 1A6
(604) 922-4520   *SIC* 5812
WILD BILL'S SALOON INC   p79
737 MAIN ST, CANMORE, AB, T1W 2B2
(403) 762-0333   *SIC* 5812
WILSON FOODS CENTRE LTD   p753
1000 REGIONAL RD 17, NEWCASTLE, ON, L1B 0T7
(905) 987-0505   *SIC* 5812
WILSON FOODS KINGSWAY LTD   p813
1300 KING ST E, OSHAWA, ON, L1H 8J4
(905) 442-3545   *SIC* 5812
YANJACO INC   p1395
435 BOUL HARWOOD, VAUDREUIL-DORION, QC, J7V 7W1
(450) 455-3336   *SIC* 5812
YATSEN GROUP INC   p677
7650 BIRCHMOUNT RD, MARKHAM, ON, L3R 6B9
(905) 474-0710   *SIC* 5812
YELLOWKNIFE INN LTD   p436
5010 49TH ST, YELLOWKNIFE, NT, X1A 2N4
(867) 873-2601   *SIC* 5812
YESNABY INVESTMENTS LTD   p253
105 NORTH STAR RD, QUESNEL, BC, V2J 5K2
(250) 992-6868   *SIC* 5812
ZUCHTER BERK CREATIVE CATERERS INC   p778
1895 LESLIE ST, NORTH YORK, ON, M3B 2M3
(416) 386-1086   *SIC* 5812

SIC 5813 Drinking places

1263528 ONTARIO LIMITED   p932
132 QUEENS QUAY E, TORONTO, ON, M5A 0S1
SIC 5813
2166-2440 QUEBEC INC   p1397
19 BOUL DES BOIS-FRANCS S, VICTORIAVILLE, QC, G6P 4S2
(819) 758-7176   *SIC* 5813
376599 ALBERTA INC   p27
4630 MACLEOD TRAIL SW, CALGARY, AB, T2G 5E8
(403) 287-2500   *SIC* 5813
599515 ALBERTA LTD   p66
730 17 AVE SW, CALGARY, AB, T2S 0B7
(403) 228-3566   *SIC* 5813
793337 ONTARIO INC   p1006
341 MARSLAND DR, WATERLOO, ON, N2J 3Z2
(519) 886-7730   *SIC* 5813
9065-1837 QUEBEC INC   p1387
300 RUE DES FORGES, TROIS-RIVIERES, QC, G9A 2G8
(819) 370-2005   *SIC* 5813
AIRLINER MOTOR HOTEL (1972) LTD p320
2233 BURRARD ST SUITE 309, VANCOUVER, BC, V6J 3H9
SIC 5813
BOURGABEC INC   p1268
600 GRANDE ALLEE E, QUEBEC, QC, G1R 2K5
(418) 522-0393   *SIC* 5813
CAMPUS   p1175
1111 RUE SAINTE-CATHERINE E, MONTREAL, QC, H2L 2G6
(514) 526-9867   *SIC* 5813
CLUB PRO ADULT ENTERTAINMENT INC
p550
170 DOUGHTON RD, CONCORD, ON, L4K 1R4
(905) 669-6422   *SIC* 5813
COWBOYS COUNTRY SALOON LTD p100
10102 180 ST NW, EDMONTON, AB, T5S 1N4
SIC 5813
GOTHAM STEAKHOUSE & COCKTAIL BAR LIMITED PARTNERSHIP   p298
615 SEYMOUR ST, VANCOUVER, BC, V6B

3K3

(604) 605-8282   *SIC 5813*

GRAFTONS CONNOR PROPERTY INC *p453*
1741 GRAFTON ST, HALIFAX, NS, B3J 2C6

(902) 454-9344   *SIC 5813*

HRC CANADA INC *p935*
279 YONGE ST, TORONTO, ON, M5B 1N8

(416) 362-3636   *SIC 5813*

IMMOBILIER JACK ASTOR'S (DORVAL) INC *p1091*
3051 BOUL DES SOURCES, DOLLARD-DES-ORMEAUX, QC, H9B 1Z6

(514) 685-5225   *SIC 5813*

IMMOBILIER SKI BROMONT INC *p1068*
150 RUE CHAMPLAIN, BROMONT, QC, J2L 1A2

(450) 534-2200   *SIC 5813*

IRISH TIMES PUB CO LTD *p336*
1200 GOVERNMENT ST, VICTORIA, BC, V8W 1Y3

(250) 383-5531   *SIC 5813*

JACKS *p654*
539 RICHMOND ST, LONDON, ON, N6A 3E9

(519) 438-1876   *SIC 5813*

LABATT BREWING COMPANY LIMITED *p1131*
2505 RUE SENKUS, LASALLE, QC, H8N 2X8

(514) 595-2505   *SIC 5813*

MILLERS LANDING PUB LTD *p247*
1979 BROWN ST, PORT COQUITLAM, BC, V3C 2N4

(604) 941-8822   *SIC 5813*

NEW PALACE CABARET LIMITED, THE *p453*
1721 BRUNSWICK ST, HALIFAX, NS, B3J 2G4

(902) 420-0015   *SIC 5813*

OUTLAWS GROUP INC *p36*
7400 MACLEOD TRAIL SE SUITE 24, CALGARY, AB, T2H 0L9

(403) 255-4646   *SIC 5813*

SHARK CLUBS OF CANADA INC *p133*
9898 99 ST, GRANDE PRAIRIE, AB, T8V 2H2

(780) 513-5450   *SIC 5813*

SIR CORP *p579*
1900 THE QUEENSWAY, ETOBICOKE, ON, M9C 5H5

(416) 626-2700   *SIC 5813*

SIR CORP *p626*
125 ROLAND MICHENER DR SUITE B1, KANATA, ON, K2T 1G7

(613) 271-1041   *SIC 5813*

SKI BROMONT.COM, SOCIETE EN COMMANDITE *p1068*
150 RUE CHAMPLAIN, BROMONT, QC, J2L 1A2

(450) 534-2200   *SIC 5813*

STRATHCONA HOTEL OF VICTORIA LTD *p337*
919 DOUGLAS ST, VICTORIA, BC, V8W 2C2

(250) 383-7137   *SIC 5813*

SWANS ENTERPRISES LTD *p337*
506 PANDORA AVE SUITE 203, VICTORIA, BC, V8W 1N6

(250) 361-3310   *SIC 5813*

VILLAGE MANOR (TO) LTD *p974*
14 MADISON AVE, TORONTO, ON, M5R 2S1

(416) 927-1722   *SIC 5813*

SIC 5912 Drug stores and proprietary stores

056186 N.B. INC *p396*
101 WATER ST, CAMPBELLTON, NB, E3N 1B2

(506) 759-8547   *SIC 5912*

1124980 ONTARIO INC *p898*
1276 LASALLE BLVD SUITE 683, SUDBURY, ON, P3A 1Y8

(705) 566-5551   *SIC 5912*

123273 CANADA INC *p1319*
298 RUE DE MARTIGNY O UNITE 101, SAINT-JEROME, QC, J7Y 4C9

(450) 436-1022   *SIC 5912*

139273 CANADA INC *p1083*
5800 BOUL CAVENDISH, COTE SAINT-LUC, QC, H4W 2T5

(514) 482-6340   *SIC 5912*

153924 CANADA INC *p1396*
4061 RUE WELLINGTON, VERDUN, QC, H4G 1V6

(514) 761-4591   *SIC 5912*

153927 CANADA INC *p1106*
15 BOUL MONTCLAIR BUREAU 203, GATINEAU, QC, J8Y 2E2

(819) 770-4232   *SIC 5912*

1548732 ONTARIO LIMITED *p907*
640 RIVER ST, THUNDER BAY, ON, P7A 3S4

(807) 345-8012   *SIC 5912*

2058658 ONTARIO INC *p618*
1275 TUPPER ST, HAWKESBURY, ON, K6A 3T5

(613) 675-1515   *SIC 5912*

2310-3393 QUEBEC INC *p1097*
520 BOUL SAINT-JOSEPH BUREAU 10, DRUMMONDVILLE, QC, J2C 2B8

(819) 472-3003   *SIC 5912*

2737-1822 QUEBEC INC *p1260*
3417 1RE AV, QUEBEC, QC, G1L 3R4

(418) 622-1237   *SIC 5912*

2739-0988 QUEBEC INC *p1346*
4675 RUE JEAN-TALON E, SAINT-LEONARD, QC, H1S 1K3

(514) 722-4664   *SIC 5912*

2741-3327 QUEBEC INC *p1184*
5692 AV DU PARC, MONTREAL, QC, H2V 4H1

(514) 270-6500   *SIC 5912*

2759-1106 QUEBEC INC *p1119*
1415 RUE NOTRE-DAME, L'ANCIENNE-LORETTE, QC, G2E 3A8

(418) 872-2864   *SIC 5912*

2846-6589 QUEBEC INC *p1300*
509 BOUL ARTHUR-SAUVE, SAINT-EUSTACHE, QC, J7P 4X4

(450) 473-4169   *SIC 5912*

2965-6311 QUEBEC INC *p1084*
2065 BOUL DES LAURENTIDES BUREAU 84, COTE SAINT-LUC, QC, H7M 4M2

(514) 663-0672   *SIC 5912*

2968-4305 QUEBEC INC *p1246*
12800 RUE SHERBROOKE E BUREAU 61, POINTE-AUX-TREMBLES, QC, H1A 4Y3

(514) 498-4840   *SIC 5912*

2970-9177 QUEBEC INC *p1323*
1051 RUE DECARIE, SAINT-LAURENT, QC, H4L 3M8

(514) 748-7725   *SIC 5912*

3097-8217 QUEBEC INC *p1235*
3475 BOUL DAGENAIS O BUREAU 119, MONTREAL, QC, H7P 4V9

(450) 963-0846   *SIC 5912*

4 CORNERS PHARMACYSTEMS INC *p900*
1935 PARIS ST SUITE 69, SUDBURY, ON, P3E 3C6

(705) 523-3730   *SIC 5912*

5043680 MANITOBA INC *p360*
17 SELKIRK AVE SUITE 549, THOMPSON, MB, R8N 0M5

(204) 778-8391   *SIC 5912*

640039 BC LTD *p292*
885 BROADWAY W SUITE 263, VANCOUVER, BC, V5Z 1J9

(604) 708-1135   *SIC 5912*

653457 B.C. LTD *p211*
1215C 56 ST UNIT C, DELTA, BC, V4L 2A6

(604) 943-1144   *SIC 5912*

662942 BC LTD *p232*
32530 LOUGHEED HWY SUITE 206, MISSION, BC, V2V 1A5

(604) 826-1244   *SIC 5912*

663353 B.C. LTD *p259*

11800 CAMBIE RD, RICHMOND, BC, V6X 1L5

(604) 278-9105   *SIC 5912*

7818696 CANADA INC *p1222*
642 RUE DE COURCELLE BUREAU 101, MONTREAL, QC, H4C 3C5

(514) 659-1681   *SIC 5912*

837705 ONTARIO LTD *p561*
5 NINTH ST E, CORNWALL, ON, K6H 6R3

(613) 938-7339   *SIC 5912*

9007-8361 QUEBEC INC *p1054*
50 BOUL SAINT-CHARLES, BEACONS-FIELD, QC, H9W 2X3

(514) 697-4550   *SIC 5912*

9013-5617 QUEBEC INC *p1221*
6411 RUE SHERBROOKE O, MONTREAL, QC, H4B 1N3

(819) 823-2295   *SIC 5912*

9026-2437 QUEBEC INC *p1167*
3845 RUE ONTARIO E, MONTREAL, QC, H1W 1S5

(514) 524-7727   *SIC 5912*

9029-0917 QUEBEC INC *p1092*
4301 BOUL SAINT-JEAN BUREAU 77, DOLLARD-DES-ORMEAUX, QC, H9H 2A4

(514) 626-4477   *SIC 5912*

9051-8051 QUEBEC INC *p1130*
8371 BOUL NEWMAN BUREAU 79, LASALLE, QC, H8N 1Y4

(514) 595-8550   *SIC 5912*

9070-4701 QUEBEC INC *p1218*
2635 AV VAN HORNE, MONTREAL, QC, H3S 1P6

(514) 731-3366   *SIC 5912*

9072-3917 QUEBEC INC *p1117*
3790 BOUL SAINT-CHARLES BUREAU 69, KIRKLAND, QC, H9H 3C3

(514) 426-1011   *SIC 5912*

9080-0822 QUEBEC INC *p1161*
8222 BOUL MAURICE-DUPLESSIS, MONTREAL, QC, H1E 2Y5

(514) 494-8888   *SIC 5912*

9100-9720 QUEBEC INC *p1395*
38 PLACE DU COMMERCE BUREAU 7, VERDUN, QC, H3E 1T8

(514) 762-6666   *SIC 5912*

9115-7776 QUEBEC INC *p1361*
580 BOUL CURE-LABELLE, SAINTE-ROSE, QC, H7L 4V6

(450) 963-9507   *SIC 5912*

9132-9326 QUEBEC INC *p1398*
1111 BOUL JUTRAS E BUREAU 20, VICTORIAVILLE, QC, G6S 1C1

(819) 357-4748   *SIC 5912*

9141-9721 QUEBEC INC *p1287*
401 BOUL LABELLE, ROSEMERE, QC, J7A 3T2

(450) 971-4664   *SIC 5912*

9159-9159 QUEBEC INC *p1248*
6815 RTE TRANSCANADIENNE, POINTE-CLAIRE, QC, H9R 5J1

(514) 695-4211   *SIC 5912*

9206-5580 QUEBEC INC *p1287*
1221 BOUL MARCOTTE, ROBERVAL, QC, G8H 3B8

(418) 275-5288   *SIC 5912*

9214-1142 QUEBEC INC *p1354*
10459 BOUL SAINTE-ANNE, SAINTE-ANNE-DE-BEAUPRE, QC, G0A 3C0

(418) 827-3714   *SIC 5912*

9223-0846 QUEBEC INC *p1155*
1365 AV BEAUMONT, MONT-ROYAL, QC, H3P 2H7

(514) 738-2401   *SIC 5912*

9255-8097 QUEBEC INC. *p1112*
185 GRANDE ALLEE E, GRANDE-RIVIERE, QC, G0C 1V0

(418) 385-2121   *SIC 5912*

9306-8906 QUEBEC INC *p1058*
1083 BOUL DU CURE-LABELLE BUREAU 110, BLAINVILLE, QC, J7C 3M9

(450) 435-1981   *SIC 5912*

A L NEILSON FAMILY PHARMACY LTD *p998*
90 DUNDAS ST W, TRENTON, ON, K8V

3P3

(613) 392-1212   *SIC 5912*

A. JAFFER PHARMACY LTD *p778*
946 LAWRENCE AVE E SUITE 1330, NORTH YORK, ON, M3C 1R1

(416) 444-4445   *SIC 5912*

A.D.H. DRUGS LIMITED *p971*
550 EGLINTON AVE W SUITE 506, TORONTO, ON, M5N 1B6

(416) 485-3093   *SIC 5912*

ABRAHAM, R.J. DRUGS LTD *p658*
1186 OXFORD ST W, LONDON, ON, N6H 4N2

(519) 471-7151   *SIC 5912*

ADAMS PHARMACY LTD *p630*
797 PRINCESS ST, KINGSTON, ON, K7L 1G1

(613) 544-2500   *SIC 5912*

AHMAD, J DRUGS LTD *p770*
6428 YONGE ST, NORTH YORK, ON, M2M 3X4

(416) 223-6250   *SIC 5912*

AJRAM'S, ANNY PHARMACY LTD *p592*
615 KING ST E, GANANOQUE, ON, K7G 1H4

(613) 382-2303   *SIC 5912*

ALAM DRUGS LIMITED *p601*
615 SCOTTSDALE DR SUITE 1089, GUELPH, ON, N1G 3P4

(519) 823-8000   *SIC 5912*

AMOPHARM INC *p1045*
82 1RE AV E, AMOS, QC, J9T 4B2

(819) 727-1234   *SIC 5912*

ANDRE ROY ET SYLVAIN BOISSELLE PHARMACIENS INC *p1376*
369 BOUL FISET, SOREL-TRACY, QC, J3P 3R3

(450) 746-7840   *SIC 5912*

ANGELS PHARMACEUTICAL SERVICES LTD *p714*
2458 DUNDAS ST W UNIT 13, MISSISSAUGA, ON, L5K 1R8

(905) 823-7895   *SIC 5912*

AQUINOX PHARMACEUTICALS INC *p288*
887 GREAT NORTHERN WAY SUITE 450, VANCOUVER, BC, V5T 4T5

(604) 629-9223   *SIC 5912*

ARCHAMBAULT, J. L. PHARMACIEN *p1295*
12 BOUL CLAIREVUE O BUREAU 39, SAINT-BRUNO, QC, J3V 1P8

(450) 653-1528   *SIC 5912*

AROMATHAULT *p1154*
26 AV DU DOCTEUR-RENE-A.-LEPAGE, MONT-JOLI, QC, G5H 1R2

(418) 775-8841   *SIC 5912*

ASSOCIATED MARITIME PHARMACIES LIMITED *p449*
269 HIGHWAY 214 UNIT 2, ELMSDALE, NS, B2S 1K1

(902) 883-8018   *SIC 5912*

AURIUM PHARMA INC *p549*
7941 JANE ST SUITE 105, CONCORD, ON, L4K 4L6

(905) 669-9057   *SIC 5912*

BABINEAU, D. DRUGS INC *p1017*
11500 TECUMSEH RD E SUITE 1118, WINDSOR, ON, N8N 1L7

(519) 735-2121   *SIC 5912*

BAJAJ DRUGS LIMITED *p580*
1530 ALBION RD SUITE 925, ETOBICOKE, ON, M9V 1B4

(416) 741-7711   *SIC 5912*

BARRY PHARMACY LTD *p400*
1040 PROSPECT ST SUITE 172, FREDERICTON, NB, E3B 3C1

(506) 451-1567   *SIC 5912*

BARRY PHILLIPS DRUGS LIMITED *p572*
3010 BLOOR ST W, ETOBICOKE, ON, M8X 1C2

(416) 234-0136   *SIC 5912*

BELZILE, BEAUMIER ET BELZILE SENC *p1111*
765 6E AV, GRAND-MERE, QC, G9T 2H8

(819) 538-8606   *SIC 5912*

BERTOLIN, S. PHARMACY LTD p33
6455 MACLEOD TRAIL S UNIT Y003, CALGARY, AB, T2H 0K4
(403) 253-2424 SIC 5912

BETTER WELLNESS JMC LTD p634
1221 WEBER ST E SUITE 1086, KITCHENER, ON, N2A 1C2
(519) 748-2430 SIC 5912

BISHARA PHARMA INC p1185
3575 AV DU PARC BUREAU 5602, MONTREAL, QC, H2X 3P9
(514) 849-6176 SIC 5912

BOUCHER, MARC PHARMACIEN p1261
5 RUE MARIE-DE-L'INCARNATION, QUEBEC, QC, G1M 3J4
SIC 5912

BOUCTOUCHE PHARMACY LTD p395
30 IRVING BLVD SUITE 200, BOUCTOUCHE, NB, E4S 3L2
(506) 743-2434 SIC 5912

BOVE DRUGS LIMITED p516
320 COLBORNE ST W SUITE 1152, BRANTFORD, ON, N3T 1M2
(519) 759-8133 SIC 5912

BOYLAN GROUP LTD, THE p145
540 18 ST SW, MEDICINE HAT, AB, T1A 8A7
(403) 526-7799 SIC 5912

BREAU, RAYMOND LTD p398
131 RUE DE L'EGLISE, EDMUNDSTON, NB, E3V 1J9
(506) 735-5559 SIC 5912

BRIDGEWATER PHARMACY LIMITED p441
215 DOMINION ST, BRIDGEWATER, NS, B4V 2K7
(902) 543-3418 SIC 5912

BRISTOW, TERRY DRUGS LTD p900
2015 LONG LAKE RD, SUDBURY, ON, P3E 4M8
(705) 522-3030 SIC 5912

BROWN'S GENERAL STORE LTD p150
31 SOUTHRIDGE DR SUITE 171, OKOTOKS, AB, T1S 2N3
(403) 995-3798 SIC 5912

C H S PHARMACY LIMITED p812
117 KING ST E, OSHAWA, ON, L1H 1B9
(905) 576-9096 SIC 5912

C H S PHARMACY LIMITED p844
590 GRANITE CRT SUITE 4, PICKERING, ON, L1W 3X6
(905) 420-7335 SIC 5912

C.J.W. PHARMACY INCORPORATED p602
104 SILVERCREEK PKY N, GUELPH, ON, N1H 7B4
(519) 821-5080 SIC 5912

CANADA DRUGS LTD p365
16 TERRACON PL, WINNIPEG, MB, R2J 4G7
SIC 5912

CARLETON PLACE DRUG MART INC p540
47 LANSDOWNE AVE, CARLETON PLACE, ON, K7C 3S9
(613) 257-1414 SIC 5912

CAROPHIL INC p1219
5122 CH DE LA COTE-DES-NEIGES BUREAU 2, MONTREAL, QC, H3T 1X8
(514) 738-8464 SIC 5912

CASPEN DRUGS LTD p124
3945 34 ST NW SUITE 371, EDMONTON, AB, T6T 1L5
(780) 461-6768 SIC 5912

CENTRAL DRUG STORES LTD, THE p233
495 DUNSMUIR ST, NANAIMO, BC, V9R 6B9
(250) 753-6401 SIC 5912

CHAUHAN PHARMACY SERVICES LTD p509
160 MAIN ST S SUITE 2, BRAMPTON, ON, L6W 2E1
(905) 451-0111 SIC 5912

CHESTER PHARMACY LTD p441
3785 HWY 3, CHESTER, NS, B0J 1J0
(902) 275-3518 SIC 5912

CHEUNG, ARTHUR PHARMACY LIMITED
p796
240 LEIGHLAND AVE, OAKVILLE, ON, L6H 3H6
(905) 842-3730 SIC 5912

CHEUNG, HARRY PHARMACIES LTD p920
970 QUEEN ST E SUITE 823, TORONTO, ON, M4M 1J8
(416) 462-0062 SIC 5912

CHIU, WALLY DRUGS LTD p769
2528 BAYVIEW AVE, NORTH YORK, ON, M2L 1A9
(416) 816-1823 SIC 5912

CHOO KIN ENTERPRISES LTD p195
984 SHOPPERS ROW, CAMPBELL RIVER, BC, V9W 2C5
SIC 5912

CHRISTINE'S HOLDINGS INC p1424
3310 8TH ST E UNIT 440, SASKATOON, SK, S7H 5M3
(306) 373-5556 SIC 5912

CHRISTOPHER YEE DRUGS LTD p668
5000 HIGHWAY 7 E, MARKHAM, ON, L3R 4M9
(905) 477-6320 SIC 5912

CHUNG, A. T. PHARMACY LIMITED p995
2290 BLOOR ST W SUITE 989, TORONTO, ON, M6S 1N9
(416) 769-1105 SIC 5912

CLARK, H. PHARMACY INC p880
454 NORFOLK ST S, SIMCOE, ON, N3Y 2X3
(519) 426-6580 SIC 5912

CLEMENT GAGNON ET JACINTHE DESJARDINS, PHARMACIENS (S.E.N.C.) p1242
145 CH CYR, NEW RICHMOND, QC, G0C 2B0
(418) 392-4451 SIC 5912

COCHRANE, D. ROSS PHARMACY LIMITED p471
442 MAIN ST, WOLFVILLE, NS, B4P 1E2
(902) 542-3624 SIC 5912

CONPHARM LTD p1420
303 N ALBERT ST, REGINA, SK, S4R 3C3
(306) 777-8010 SIC 5912

CORPORATION DE GESTION E.A. MICHOT, LA p1221
5038 RUE SHERBROOKE O, MONTREAL, QC, H4A 1S7
(514) 484-3531 SIC 5912

COSTINIUK, D PHARMACY LTD p884
600 ONTARIO ST, ST CATHARINES, ON, L2N 7H8
(905) 937-3532 SIC 5912

COTNAM, DAN DRUGS LTD p911
200 BROADWAY ST, TILLSONBURG, ON, N4G 5A7
(519) 842-3521 SIC 5912

COULTER'S PHARMACY (LONDON) LTD p660
1051 WONDERLAND RD S, LONDON, ON, N6K 3X4
(519) 472-2222 SIC 5912

COUNTRY DRUG STORES LTD p540
6 CAMERON ST E, CANNINGTON, ON, L0E 1E0
(705) 432-2644 SIC 5912

COVE VIEW PHARMACY INC p413
407 WESTMORLAND RD SUITE 194, SAINT JOHN, NB, E2J 3S9
(506) 636-7777 SIC 5912

CRAIG, JAN DRUG STORE LTD p1026
6020 MALDEN RD, WINDSOR, ON, N9H 1S8
(519) 969-9971 SIC 5912

CROWELLS PHARMACY LTD p458
205 HERRING COVE RD SUITE 505, HALIFAX, NS, B3P 1L1
(902) 477-4650 SIC 5912

CUMMINGS PHARMACY LTD p420
370 CONNELL ST, WOODSTOCK, NB, E7M 5G9
(506) 328-8801 SIC 5912

D'SA, MEL M. INC p184
6508 HASTINGS ST SUITE 214, BURNABY, BC, V5B 1S2
(604) 291-0638 SIC 5912

D. R. PERRY PHARMACY LTD p143
2045 MAYOR MAGRATH DR S UNIT 102, LETHBRIDGE, AB, T1K 2S2
(403) 328-5509 SIC 5912

D.C. DRUGS LIMITED p933
467 PARLIAMENT ST, TORONTO, ON, M5A 3A3
(416) 925-4121 SIC 5912

D.M. SERVANT PHARMACY LIMITED p444
21 MICMAC BLVD SUITE 129, DARTMOUTH, NS, B3A 4K6
(902) 463-3321 SIC 5912

DALIMONTE, M. PHARMACY LTD p664
2943 MAJOR MACKENZIE DR SUITE 1, MAPLE, ON, L6A 3N9
(905) 832-9954 SIC 5912

DANIEL LAVOIE PHARMACIEN INC p1304
11400 1RE AVE, SAINT-GEORGES, QC, G5Y 5S4
(418) 227-1515 SIC 5912

DEFFOSSES ET VALLEE S.E.N.C p1281
1065 BOUL PIE-XI N BUREAU 263, QUEBEC, QC, G3K 2S5
(418) 840-0337 SIC 5912

DELBIGIO, KEN PHARMACY LTD p387
43 OSBORNE ST, WINNIPEG, MB, R3L 1Y2
(204) 958-7000 SIC 5912

DELTA PHARMA INC p1093
1655 RTE TRANSCANADIENNE, DORVAL, QC, H9P 1J1
(514) 685-7311 SIC 5912

DEREK K. HO PHARMACY LTD p1000
8601 WARDEN AVE, UNIONVILLE, ON, L3R 0B5
(905) 479-0772 SIC 5912

DESSUREAULT, JEAN-CLAUDE PHARMACIEN p1297
113 RUE SAINT-PIERRE UNITE 101, SAINT-CONSTANT, QC, J5A 0M3
(450) 632-2730 SIC 5912

DHAMI, TEJI DRUGS LTD p658
1680 RICHMOND ST SUITE 764, LONDON, ON, N6G 3Y9
(519) 663-9370 SIC 5912

DINOFF, S. DRUGS LIMITED p988
523 ST CLAIR AVE W, TORONTO, ON, M6C 1A1
(416) 538-1155 SIC 5912

DISTRIBUTIONS JOSEE PERRAULT INC p1281
3285 1E AV BUREAU 100, RAWDON, QC, J0K 1S0
(450) 834-2582 SIC 5912

DISTRIBUTIONS NORYVE INC p1046
76 1RE AV O BUREAU 108, AMOS, QC, J9T 1T8
(819) 732-3306 SIC 5912

DN PHARMACY INC p1009
658 ERB ST W, WATERLOO, ON, N2T 2Z7
(519) 886-3530 SIC 5912

DOLARIAN, STEPHAN p1219
5510 CH DE LA COTE-DES-NEIGES BUREAU 215, MONTREAL, QC, H3T 1Y9
(514) 344-8338 SIC 5912

DREVER, S. PHARMACY LIMITED p590
710 TOWER ST S, FERGUS, ON, N1M 2R3
(519) 843-3160 SIC 5912

DTS PHARMA INC p1143
1049 BOUL ROLAND-THERRIEN BUREAU 236, LONGUEUIL, QC, J4J 4L3
(450) 928-0030 SIC 5912

DUOPHARM INC p1090
4894 BOUL DES SOURCES BUREAU 66, DOLLARD-DES-ORMEAUX, QC, H8Y 3C7
(514) 684-6131 SIC 5912

DZOMBETA DRUG LTD p190
4827 KINGSWAY SUITE 2283, BURNABY, BC, V5H 4T6
(604) 433-2721 SIC 5912

E & L DRUGS LTD p399
269 MAIN ST, FREDERICTON, NB, E3A 1E1
(506) 451-1550 SIC 5912

ECONOFAR (1988) INC p1068
7400 BOUL TASCHEREAU BUREAU 71, BROSSARD, QC, J4W 1M9
SIC 5912

ECONOMY DRUGS LTD p390
2211 PEMBINA HWY, WINNIPEG, MB, R3T 2H1
(204) 269-8113 SIC 5912

ELAINE MAH PHARMACY LTD p165
140 ST ALBERT TRAIL SUITE 570, ST. ALBERT, AB, T8N 7C8
(780) 460-9222 SIC 5912

ENTREPRISES CHRISTIAN CHADI INC, LES p1364
95 BOUL DU CURE-LABELLE BUREAU 15, SAINTE-THERESE, QC, J7E 2X6
(450) 437-5555 SIC 5912

ENTREPRISES DONTIGNY ET TREMBLAY INC, LES p1384
15 RUE FUSEY, TROIS-RIVIERES, QC, G8T 2T3
(819) 378-2828 SIC 5912

ENTREPRISES ISABELLE DESJARDINS INC, LES p1319
900 BOUL GRIGNON BUREAU 116, SAINT-JEROME, QC, J7Y 3S7
(450) 438-1293 SIC 5912

ENTREPRISES JULIE LESSARD INC, LES p1382
5333 BOUL LAURIER BUREAU 180, TERREBONNE, QC, J7M 1W1
(450) 477-4401 SIC 5912

ENTREPRISES KIM LUU INC, LES p1240
10551 BOUL PIE-IX, MONTREAL-NORD, QC, H1H 4A3
(514) 321-1230 SIC 5912

ENTREPRISES MICHEL CAPLETTE INC p1130
1819 AV DOLLARD, LASALLE, QC, H8N 1T9
(514) 364-1644 SIC 5912

EPP'S PHARMACY LTD p358
382 MAIN ST, STEINBACH, MB, R5G 1Z3
(204) 326-3747 SIC 5912

ESCOMPTE CHEZ LAFORTUNE INC p1071
5635 GRANDE-ALLEE BUREAU 100, BROSSARD, QC, J4Z 3G3
(450) 462-2120 SIC 5912

ESCOMPTES C.F.M. INC p1358
800 MONTEE SAINTE-JULIE BUREAU 100, SAINTE-JULIE, QC, J3E 2C4
(450) 922-6000 SIC 5912

ESCOMPTES FERNAND LACHANCE INC. p1317
947 BOUL DU SEMINAIRE N, SAINT-JEAN-SUR-RICHELIEU, QC, J3A 1K1
(450) 348-9251 SIC 5912

ESCOPHAR INC p1308
5245 BOUL COUSINEAU BUREAU 149, SAINT-HUBERT, QC, J3Y 6J8
(450) 462-2200 SIC 5912

EXUS PHARMACEUTICALS LTD p637
700 STRASBURG RD, KITCHENER, ON, N2E 2M2
(519) 576-8340 SIC 5912

F D PHARMACY INC p788
1500 AVENUE RD, NORTH YORK, ON, M5M 3X2
(416) 781-6146 SIC 5912

FAMILIPRIX-ROY ET LEBLOND INC p1304
899 17E RUE, SAINT-GEORGES, QC, G5Y 4W1
(418) 228-1017 SIC 5912

FATIMA AIT ADDI p1180
370 RUE JARRY E, MONTREAL, QC, H2P 1T9
(514) 382-4730 SIC 5912

FELBER INC p1346
7275 BOUL LANGELIER, SAINT-LEONARD, QC, H1S 1V6
(514) 259-4614 SIC 5912

FERGUSON, N. DRUGS LTD p759
6565 LUNDY'S LANE SUITE 799, NIAGARA

FALLS, ON, L2G 1V1
(905) 354-3845 *SIC* 5912
FESUK, ROBERT S. PHARMACY LTD *p652*
759 ADELAIDE ST N, LONDON, ON, N5Y 2L7
(519) 679-4567 *SIC* 5912
FILEK, STEVE DRUGS LIMITED *p862*
44 GREAT NORTHERN RD SUITE 669, SAULT STE. MARIE, ON, P6B 4Y5
(705) 949-2143 *SIC* 5912
FINDLAY'S DRUG STORE (NEW LISKEARD) LIMITED *p753*
237 WHITEWOOD AVE UNIT 25, NEW LISKEARD, ON, P0J 1P0
(705) 647-8186 *SIC* 5912
FLAGEC INC *p1279*
1220 BOUL LEBOURGNEUF BUREAU 200, QUEBEC, QC, G2K 2G4
(418) 523-7015 *SIC* 5912
FORD'S, SCOTT PHARMACY LTD *p633*
775 STRAND BLVD SUITE 11, KINGSTON, ON, K7P 2Z4
(613) 384-7477 *SIC* 5912
FOREWEST HOLDINGS INC *p228*
5769 201A ST UNIT 169, LANGLEY, BC, V3A 8H9
(604) 514-8303 *SIC* 5912
FOUZIA AKHTAR DRUGS LTD *p580*
415 THE WESTWAY SUITE 1, ETOBICOKE, ON, M9R 1H5
(416) 249-8344 *SIC* 5912
FRATUM PHARMA INC *p1344*
9380 BOUL LANGELIER, SAINT-LEONARD, QC, H1P 3H8
(514) 322-6111 *SIC* 5912
FRESON MARKET LTD *p4*
5020 49 AVE, BARRHEAD, AB, T7N 1G4
(780) 674-3784 *SIC* 5912
FWS PHARMACY SERVICES LTD *p222*
2271 HARVEY AVE SUITE 1360, KELOWNA, BC, V1Y 6H2
(250) 860-3764 *SIC* 5912
G AND G WHITE HOWLEY PHARMACY LTD *p464*
131 KING ST SUITE 148, NORTH SYDNEY, NS, B2A 3S1
(902) 794-7211 *SIC* 5912
G. PELLERIN C. DESBIENS, PHARMACIENS *p1369*
1920 105E AV, SHAWINIGAN, QC, G9P 1N4
(819) 537-1869 *SIC* 5912
GARY DANIELS PHARMACIES LTD *p606*
7 CLAIR RD W SUITE 1213, GUELPH, ON, N1L 0A6
(519) 763-3431 *SIC* 5912
GAUTHIER, VINCE R. DRUGS LTD *p1021*
500 TECUMSEH RD E, WINDSOR, ON, N8X 2S2
(519) 253-1115 *SIC* 5912
GEDILEX INC *p1282*
515 BOUL LACOMBE BUREAU 255, REPENTIGNY, QC, J5Z 1P5
(450) 581-6545 *SIC* 5912
GEEN'S PRESCRIPTION PHARMACY LIMITED *p491*
276 FRONT ST, BELLEVILLE, ON, K8N 2Z8
(613) 962-4579 *SIC* 5912
GENTES ET BOLDUC PHARMACIENS S.E.N.C *p1312*
4555 AV BEAUDRY, SAINT-HYACINTHE, QC, J2S 8W2
(450) 778-2837 *SIC* 5912
GEO JACK ENTERPRISES INC *p1421*
4130 ALBERT ST SUITE 425, REGINA, SK, S4S 3R8
(306) 777-8040 *SIC* 5912
GESTION BBFD INC *p1275*
3730 RUE DU CAMPANILE, QUEBEC, QC, G1X 4G6
(418) 658-1337 *SIC* 5912
GESTION CHRISTIAN BASTIEN INC *p1367*
770 BOUL LAURE UNITE 270, SEPT-ILES, QC, G4R 1Y5
(418) 962-3333 *SIC* 5912

GESTION CHRISTIAN DUGUAY INC *p1232*
3100 BOUL DE LA CONCORDE E BUREAU 50D, MONTREAL, QC, H7E 2B8
(450) 661-7748 *SIC* 5912
GESTION CHRISTIAN J. OUELLET INC *p1255*
3333 RUE DU CARREFOUR, QUEBEC, QC, G1C 5R9
(418) 667-7534 *SIC* 5912
GESTION CLAUDE MEILLEUR INC *p1373*
3050 BOUL DE PORTLAND, SHERBROOKE, QC, J1L 1K1
(819) 569-9621 *SIC* 5912
GESTION CLAUDIUS INC *p1317*
1000 BOUL DU SEMINAIRE N BUREAU 4, SAINT-JEAN-SUR-RICHELIEU, QC, J3A 1E5
(450) 348-6813 *SIC* 5912
GESTION CLAUMOND INC *p1372*
2235 RUE GALT O, SHERBROOKE, QC, J1K 1K6
(819) 569-9349 *SIC* 5912
GESTION DOMINIQUE BOND INC *p1275*
2160 BOUL BASTIEN, QUEBEC, QC, G2B 1B7
(418) 842-3648 *SIC* 5912
GESTION FRANCOIS MALTAIS INC *p1370*
1363 RUE BELVEDERE S, SHERBROOKE, QC, J1H 4E4
(819) 565-9595 *SIC* 5912
GESTION G.G.V.M. INC *p1097*
511 RUE HERIOT, DRUMMONDVILLE, QC, J2B 7R3
(819) 477-3777 *SIC* 5912
GESTION HEROUX ET SAUCIER INC *p1247*
12675 RUE SHERBROOKE E, POINTE-AUX-TREMBLES, QC, H1A 3W7
(514) 642-2251 *SIC* 5912
GESTION JACQUES BOURGET INC *p1232*
2955 BOUL DE LA CONCORDE E BUREAU 76, MONTREAL, QC, H7E 2B5
(450) 661-6921 *SIC* 5912
GESTION KM INC *p1224*
5855 BOUL GOUIN O, MONTREAL, QC, H4J 1E5
(514) 334-8641 *SIC* 5912
GESTION LISE HAMEL-CHARTRAND INC *p1219*
4815 AV VAN HORNE, MONTREAL, QC, H3W 1J2
(514) 739-1758 *SIC* 5912
GESTION MAGDI TEBECHRANI INC., LES *p1239*
6000 BOUL HENRI-BOURASSA E, MONTREAL-NORD, QC, H1G 2T6
(514) 323-5010 *SIC* 5912
GESTION MICHEL LANG INC *p1131*
8096 BOUL CHAMPLAIN, LASALLE, QC, H8P 1B3
(514) 367-3300 *SIC* 5912
GESTION PERREAULT ET BEAULIEU INC *p1072*
15 BOUL MONTCALM N, CANDIAC, QC, J5R 3L4
(450) 659-5426 *SIC* 5912
GESTION PHARMASSO INC *p1345*
9235 BOUL LACORDAIRE, SAINT-LEONARD, QC, H1R 2B6
(514) 324-2600 *SIC* 5912
GESTION PICARD-DUBUC INC *p1126*
2880 RUE REMEMBRANCE BUREAU 74, LACHINE, QC, H8S 1X8
(514) 637-3578 *SIC* 5912
GESTION RITEAL INC *p1220*
1500 AV ATWATER, MONTREAL, QC, H3Z 1X5
(514) 931-4283 *SIC* 5912
GESTION ROSLYN-ALVIN LTEE *p1106*
320 BOUL SAINT-JOSEPH BUREAU 221, GATINEAU, QC, J8Y 3Y8
(819) 770-6668 *SIC* 5912
GESTION SARMASO INC *p1155*
2305 CH ROCKLAND BUREAU 191, MONT-ROYAL, QC, H3P 3E9
(514) 739-5551 *SIC* 5912

GESTION SYLVAIN GOUDREAULT INC *p1399*
1768 BOUL DES LAURENTIDES BUREAU 1, VIMONT, QC, H7M 2P6
(450) 663-3197 *SIC* 5912
GESTIONS DOROTHEE MINVILLE INC *p1204*
390 RUE SAINTE-CATHERINE O, MONTREAL, QC, H3B 1A1
(514) 875-7070 *SIC* 5912
GESTIONS FERNANDA CIVITELLA INC, LES *p1096*
330 AV DORVAL BUREAU 11, DORVAL, QC, H9S 3H7
(514) 631-1827 *SIC* 5912
GESTIONS FORTIER-ALLAN 29 INC *p1175*
901 RUE SAINTE-CATHERINE E BUREAU 29, MONTREAL, QC, H2L 2E5
(514) 842-4915 *SIC* 5912
GESTIONS LUCAP INC *p1213*
1500 RUE SAINTE-CATHERINE O, MONTREAL, QC, H3G 1S8
(514) 933-4744 *SIC* 5912
GGP DRUGS LTD *p794*
2550 FINCH AVE W SUITE 854, NORTH YORK, ON, M9M 2G3
(416) 749-5271 *SIC* 5912
GRAVELUNI INC *p1250*
277 BOUL SAINT-JEAN, POINTE-CLAIRE, QC, H9R 3J1
(514) 695-1122 *SIC* 5912
GREAT WEST DRUGS (SOUTHGATE) LTD *p114*
4484 97 ST NW, EDMONTON, AB, T6E 5R9
(780) 496-9366 *SIC* 5912
GRECO, ROBERTO DRUGS LTD *p644*
269 ERIE ST S SUITE 1117, LEAMINGTON, ON, N8H 3C4
(519) 326-2663 *SIC* 5912
GREEN, ESTHER DRUGS LTD *p775*
6205 BATHURST ST, NORTH YORK, ON, M2R 2A5
(416) 222-5464 *SIC* 5912
GREGOIRE RAKELIAN PHARMACIEN *p1363*
3000 AV JACQUES-BUREAU BUREAU BUREAU, SAINTE-ROSE, QC, H7P 5P7
(450) 682-0099 *SIC* 5912
GROUPE J.C.F. LTEE *p1059*
1083 BOUL DU CURE-LABELLE BUREAU 110, BLAINVILLE, QC, J7C 3M9
(450) 435-1981 *SIC* 5912
HACKMAN, RICHARD B. DRUGS LTD *p161*
2020 SHERWOOD DR UNIT 600, SHERWOOD PARK, AB, T8A 3H9
(780) 464-9788 *SIC* 5912
HANBALI, JEFF DRUGS LTD *p613*
620 KING ST W SUITE 1458, HAMILTON, ON, L8P 1C2
(905) 522-0599 *SIC* 5912
HANBALI, JEFF DRUGS LTD *p616*
999 UPPER WENTWORTH ST SUITE 200, HAMILTON, ON, L9A 4X5
(905) 388-8450 *SIC* 5912
HANNA, NABIL DRUGS LTD *p826*
2515 BANK ST, OTTAWA, ON, K1V 0Y4
(613) 523-9999 *SIC* 5912
HAUNSLA PHARMACY LTD *p705*
5035 HURONTARIO ST SUITE 1100, MISSISSAUGA, ON, L4Z 3X7
(905) 890-1313 *SIC* 5912
HENDERSON'S PHARMACY LIMITED *p907*
15 FRONT ST S, THOROLD, ON, L2V 1W8
(905) 227-2511 *SIC* 5912
HENRY, KATHERINE PHARMACY LTD *p812*
300 TAUNTON RD E SUITE 2, OSHAWA, ON, L1G 7T4
(905) 579-1900 *SIC* 5912
HIGGINS FAMILY PHARMACY LTD *p467*
1174 KINGS RD SUITE 149, SYDNEY, NS, B1S 1C9
(902) 539-8111 *SIC* 5912
HOANA DRUGS LTD *p196*
45905 YALE RD UNIT 30, CHILLIWACK,

BC, V2P 2M6
(604) 792-7377 *SIC* 5912
HOLOWAYCHUK, L.B. PHARMACY LTD *p107*
16504 95 ST NW SUITE 375, EDMONTON, AB, T5Z 3L7
(780) 456-5557 *SIC* 5912
HOLTZMAN, JACK DRUGS LIMITED *p481*
14729 YONGE ST SUITE 970, AURORA, ON, L4G 1N1
(905) 727-4275 *SIC* 5912
HUYNH, KIM DRUGS LTD *p671*
7060 WARDEN AVE, MARKHAM, ON, L3R 5Y2
(905) 474-1414 *SIC* 5912
I.R.A.S. PHARMACY LTD *p577*
5230 DUNDAS ST W, ETOBICOKE, ON, M9B 1A8
(416) 233-3269 *SIC* 5912
IBRAHIM, YASSER PHARMACY LIMITED *p531*
900 MAPLE AVE SUITE 747, BURLINGTON, ON, L7S 2J8
(905) 681-1277 *SIC* 5912
IP, JERRY PHARMACY INC *p867*
1235 MCCOWAN RD, SCARBOROUGH, ON, M1H 3K3
(416) 412-1353 *SIC* 5912
J AHMAD DRUGS LTD *p703*
700 BURNHAMTHORPE RD E, MISSISSAUGA, ON, L4Y 2X3
(905) 279-1812 *SIC* 5912
J D M PHARMACY INC *p203*
310 8TH ST, COURTENAY, BC, V9N 1N3
(250) 334-3134 *SIC* 5912
J M S PHARMACY SERVICE INC *p457*
3430 JOSEPH HOWE DR SUITE 138, HALIFAX, NS, B3L 4H7
(902) 443-6084 *SIC* 5912
J.R. GIUDICE PHARMACY INC *p614*
902 MOHAWK RD E, HAMILTON, ON, L8T 2R8
(905) 387-2300 *SIC* 5912
JALALDIN, NARMIN DRUGS LTD *p829*
1309 CARLING AVE, OTTAWA, ON, K1Z 7L3
(613) 722-4277 *SIC* 5912
JAMAL, OME PHARMACY LTD *p865*
265 PORT UNION RD, SCARBOROUGH, ON, M1C 2L3
(416) 284-9229 *SIC* 5912
JAMIE D. TEMPLE PHARMACY LTD *p627*
2727 HWY 43, KEMPTVILLE, ON, K0G 1J0
(613) 258-2557 *SIC* 5912
JAMIESON PHARMACY LTD *p453*
5524 SPRING GARDEN RD, HALIFAX, NS, B3J 1G5
(902) 429-2400 *SIC* 5912
JEAN COUTU ANNIE LAROCHE & MICHEL ST-GEORGES (AFFILIATED PHARMACIES) *p1171*
1221 RUE FLEURY E, MONTREAL, QC, H2C 1R2
SIC 5912
JEAN COUTU GERMAIN CHARTIER & LIVIO PAROLIN (AFFILIATED PHARMACIES) *p1057*
790 AV GILLES-VILLENEUVE, BERTHIERVILLE, QC, J0K 1A0
(450) 836-3733 *SIC* 5912
JEAN COUTU JACQUES BOUILLON (AFFILIATED PHARMACIES) *p1287*
253B BOUL LABELLE, ROSEMERE, QC, J7A 2H3
(450) 437-9151 *SIC* 5912
JEAN COUTU JEAN-PHILIPPE ROY (AFFILIATED PHARMACIES) *p1075*
3300 BOUL FRECHETTE, CHAMBLY, QC, J3L 6Z6
(450) 447-5511 *SIC* 5912
JEAN COUTU MARIE-CLAUDE OUELLET & ANNIE SANFACON *p1275*
1221 RUE CHARLES-ALBANEL, QUEBEC, QC, G1X 4Y5

(418) 874-0275   *SIC* 5912
JEAN-COUTU   *p1110*
505 RUE DU RUBIS, GRANBY, QC, J2H
2S3

(450) 266-3966   *SIC* 5912
**JEAN-FRANCOIS GAUTHIER ET ALEXAN-
DRE RIVARD, PHARMACIENS S.E.N.C**
p1385
200 RUE FUSEY, TROIS-RIVIERES, QC,
G8T 2V8

(819) 375-8941   *SIC* 5912
**JEAN-SEBASTIEN CROTEAU ISABELLE
ANNE ROBITAILLE INC**   *p1398*
141 RUE NOTRE-DAME E, VICTORIAV-
ILLE, QC, G6P 3Z8

(819) 752-4554   *SIC* 5912
JIM BROWN PHARMACY LTD   *p161*
2020 SHERWOOD DR UNIT 600, SHER-
WOOD PARK, AB, T8A 3H9

(780) 464-9788   *SIC* 5912
JODHA PHARMACY INC   *p718*
128 QUEEN ST S SUITE 3, MISSISSAUGA,
ON, L5M 1K8

(905) 567-0744   *SIC* 5912
K CRAWFORD PHARMACY INC   *p1039*
403 UNIVERSITY AVE, CHARLOTTE-
TOWN, PE, C1A 4N7

(902) 892-3433   *SIC* 5912
K.B. BORISENKO PHARMACY LTD   *p382*
1485 PORTAGE AVE SUITE 178, WIN-
NIPEG, MB, R3G 0W4

(204) 775-2478   *SIC* 5912
KA DJORDJEVIC PHARMACY INC   *p704*
1077 NORTH SERVICE RD SUITE 27, MIS-
SISSAUGA, ON, L4Y 1A6

(905) 277-3661   *SIC* 5912
KANJEE ENTERPRISES LTD   *p71*
3625 SHAGANAPPI TRAIL NW SUITE 356,
CALGARY, AB, T3A 0E2

(403) 288-0111   *SIC* 5912
KANJI RX DRUG LTD   *p76*
600 SADDLETOWNE CIR NE SUITE 101,
CALGARY, AB, T3J 5M1

(403) 568-7143   *SIC* 5912
KAPOOR, VINAY DRUGS LTD   *p910*
900 ARTHUR ST E, THUNDER BAY, ON,
P7E 5M8

(807) 623-2390   *SIC* 5912
KATES' PHARMACY LTD   *p132*
11801 100 ST SUITE 137, GRANDE
PRAIRIE, AB, T8V 3Y2

(780) 357-9301   *SIC* 5912
KATZ GROUP INC   *p89*
10104 103 AVE NW SUITE 1702, EDMON-
TON, AB, T5J 0H8

(780) 990-0505   *SIC* 5912
KELLY, MARIA ENTERPRISES INC   *p92*
11408 JASPER AVE NW, EDMONTON, AB,
T5K 0M1

(780) 482-1011   *SIC* 5912
KELLY, PAUL (1993) LIMITED   *p491*
411 BRIDGE ST E, BELLEVILLE, ON, K8N
1P7

(613) 962-5387   *SIC* 5912
KENNEBECASIS DRUGS LTD   *p412*
1A MARR RD, ROTHESAY, NB, E2E 3L4

(506) 847-7581   *SIC* 5912
KHETIA PHARMACY INC   *p786*
1084 WILSON AVE, NORTH YORK, ON,
M3K 1G6

(416) 633-9884   *SIC* 5912
KIN LEM DRUGS LIMITED   *p632*
1875 BATH RD, KINGSTON, ON, K7M 4Y3

(613) 384-6990   *SIC* 5912
KNAUER, CLAIRE PHARMACY LTD   *p657*
395 SOUTHDALE RD E SUITE 1, LONDON,
ON, N6E 1A2

(519) 685-1160   *SIC* 5912
KOLANDJIAN, A. PHARMACY LTD   *p767*
4865 LESLIE ST, NORTH YORK, ON, M2J
2K8

(416) 493-2111   *SIC* 5912
KONA DRUGS LTD   *p250*
737 CENTRAL ST W, PRINCE GEORGE,

BC, V2M 3C6

(250) 562-2311   *SIC* 5912
KRISINGER DRUG LTD   *p283*
4647 LAKELSE AVE SUITE 102, TER-
RACE, BC, V8G 1R3

(250) 635-7261   *SIC* 5912
KURT RYAN PHARMACY SERVICES LTD
p458
315 HERRING COVE RD, HALIFAX, NS,
B3R 1V5

(902) 477-1210   *SIC* 5912
L.J.M. MARKETING INC   *p1164*
6420 RUE SHERBROOKE E BUREAU 55,
MONTREAL, QC, H1N 3P6

(514) 259-6991   *SIC* 5912
LAM, MICHELLE PHARMACY LTD   *p107*
3812 118 AVE NW SUITE 318, EDMON-
TON, AB, T5W 5C7

(780) 474-2424   *SIC* 5912
LAPORTE, MARCEL PHARMACY INC *p860*
260 INDIAN RD S, SARNIA, ON, N7T 3W4

(519) 337-3727   *SIC* 5912
LAU, REGINALD DRUGS LTD   *p867*
685 MCCOWAN RD, SCARBOROUGH, ON,
M1J 1K2

(416) 431-4822   *SIC* 5912
LAWTON'S DRUG STORES LIMITED   *p447*
236 BROWNLOW AVE SUITE 270, DART-
MOUTH, NS, B3B 1V5

(902) 468-1000   *SIC* 5912
LAWTON'S INCORPORATED   *p447*
236 BROWNLOW AVE SUITE 270, DART-
MOUTH, NS, B3B 1V5

(902) 468-1000   *SIC* 5912
LEITNER, IRVING DRUGS LTD   *p855*
9350 YONGE ST SUITE 966, RICHMOND
HILL, ON, L4C 5G2

(905) 884-0555   *SIC* 5912
LIVRAISON WILLIAM LTEE   *p1094*
610 AV ORLY, DORVAL, QC, H9P 1E9

(514) 526-5901   *SIC* 5912
LOBLAWS INC   *p1420*
336 N MCCARTHY BLVD, REGINA, SK,
S4R 7M2

(306) 924-2620   *SIC* 5912
LONDON DRUGS EXECUTIVE   *p263*
12151 HORSESHOE WAY, RICHMOND,
BC, V7A 4V4

(604) 272-7400   *SIC* 5912
LONDON DRUGS LIMITED   *p9*
3545 32 AVE NE, CALGARY, AB, T1Y 6M6

(403) 571-4931   *SIC* 5912
LONDON DRUGS LIMITED   *p74*
5255 RICHMOND RD SW SUITE 300, CAL-
GARY, AB, T3E 7C4

(403) 571-4932   *SIC* 5912
LONDON DRUGS LIMITED   *p98*
14951 STONY PLAIN RD NW, EDMONTON,
AB, T5P 4W1

(780) 944-4522   *SIC* 5912
LONDON DRUGS LIMITED   *p142*
905 1 AVE S SUITE 110, LETHBRIDGE, AB,
T1J 4M7

(403) 320-8899   *SIC* 5912
LONDON DRUGS LIMITED   *p166*
19 BELLEROSE DR SUITE 10, ST. AL-
BERT, AB, T8N 5E1

(780) 944-4548   *SIC* 5912
LONDON DRUGS LIMITED   *p177*
32700 SOUTH FRASER WAY SUITE 26,
ABBOTSFORD, BC, V2T 4M5

(604) 852-0936   *SIC* 5912
LONDON DRUGS LIMITED   *p190*
4970 KINGSWAY, BURNABY, BC, V5H 2E2

(604) 448-4806   *SIC* 5912
LONDON DRUGS LIMITED   *p217*
450 LANSDOWNE ST SUITE 68, KAM-
LOOPS, BC, V2C 1Y3

(250) 372-0028   *SIC* 5912
LONDON DRUGS LIMITED   *p237*
60 TENTH ST, NEW WESTMINSTER, BC,
V3M 3X3

(604) 524-1326   *SIC* 5912
LONDON DRUGS LIMITED   *p263*

12251 HORSESHOE WAY, RICHMOND,
BC, V7A 4X5

(604) 272-7400   *SIC* 5912
LONDON DRUGS LIMITED   *p270*
2340 GUILDFORD TOWN CTR, SURREY,
BC, V3R 7B9

(604) 588-7881   *SIC* 5912
LONDON DRUGS LIMITED   *p293*
525 BROADWAY W, VANCOUVER, BC, V5Z
1E6

(604) 448-4804   *SIC* 5912
LONDON DRUGS LIMITED   *p318*
1650 DAVIE ST, VANCOUVER, BC, V6G
1V9

(604) 448-4850   *SIC* 5912
LONDON DRUGS LIMITED   *p322*
2091 42ND AVE W SUITE 10, VANCOU-
VER, BC, V6M 2B4

(604) 448-1036   *SIC* 5912
LONDON DRUGS LIMITED   *p326*
710 GRANVILLE ST, VANCOUVER, BC,
V6Z 1E4

(604) 448-4002   *SIC* 5912
LONDON DRUGS LIMITED   *p332*
4400 32 ST SUITE 700, VERNON, BC, V1T
9H2

(250) 549-1551   *SIC* 5912
LONDON DRUGS LIMITED   *p340*
1907 SOOKE RD, VICTORIA, BC, V9B 1V8

(604) 474-0900   *SIC* 5912
LOVELL DRUGS LIMITED   *p812*
52 1/2 SIMCOE ST N, OSHAWA, ON, L1G
4S1

(905) 723-2276   *SIC* 5912
LOWES PHARMACY LIMITED   *p104*
6655 178 ST NW UNIT 610, EDMONTON,
AB, T5T 4J5

(780) 487-1013   *SIC* 5912
LUSSIER, BERNARD INC   *p1302*
378 BOUL ARTHUR-SAUVE, SAINT-
EUSTACHE, QC, J7R 2J4

(450) 473-3911   *SIC* 5912
M & L PHARMACY LTD   *p410*
1198 ONONDAGA ST SUITE 16, ORO-
MOCTO, NB, E2V 1B8

(506) 357-8435   *SIC* 5912
**M & N CROWELL PHARMACY SERVICES
LTD**   *p438*
303 MAIN ST SUITE 143, ANTIGONISH,
NS, B2G 2C3

(902) 863-6522   *SIC* 5912
M. VERNESCU DRUGS LTD   *p566*
101 OSLER DR SUITE 102, DUNDAS, ON,
L9H 4H4

(905) 628-2251   *SIC* 5912
MACLAI DRUGS LIMITED   *p718*
5100 ERIN MILLS PKY SUITE 904, MISSIS-
SAUGA, ON, L5M 4Z5

(905) 569-3939   *SIC* 5912
MACQUARRIES DRUGS LIMITED   *p469*
920 PRINCE ST SUITE 513, TRURO, NS,
B2N 1H5

(902) 896-1600   *SIC* 5912
MAGASIN FARMAJEM INC   *p1120*
405 GRAND BOULEVARD, L'ILE-PERROT,
QC, J7V 4X3

(514) 453-2896   *SIC* 5912
**MAGASINS D'ESCOMPTE ALMICO INC,
LES**   *p1229*
6624 AV SOMERLED, MONTREAL, QC,
H4V 1T2

(514) 487-6530   *SIC* 5912
MARK S. LESLIE APATHECARY LTD *p519*
2399 PARKEDALE AVE SUITE 27,
BROCKVILLE, ON, K6V 3G9

(613) 342-6701   *SIC* 5912
MARSH, GLENDA PHARMACY LTD   *p347*
809 18TH ST, BRANDON, MB, R7A 5B8

(204) 729-8100   *SIC* 5912
MARTEL, DAN PHARMACY LIMITED *p484*
524 BAYFIELD ST SUITE 650, BARRIE,
ON, L4M 5A2

(705) 722-6300   *SIC* 5912
MARTIN & BELZILE INC   *p1053*

691 BOUL LAFLECHE BUREAU 89, BAIE-
COMEAU, QC, G5C 1C4

(418) 589-4969   *SIC* 5912
MARTIN, DENNIS M DRUGS INC   *p760*
3701 PORTAGE RD UNIT 1, NIAGARA
FALLS, ON, L2J 2K8

(905) 354-6511   *SIC* 5912
MATTHEWS, MARK PHARMACY LTD *p546*
119 HURONTARIO ST, COLLINGWOOD,
ON, L9Y 2L9

(705) 444-6055   *SIC* 5912
MAY BALIAN & EMAD GABRA S.E.N.C.R.L.
p1330
2085 BOUL MARCEL-LAURIN, SAINT-
LAURENT, QC, H4R 1K4

(514) 334-1823   *SIC* 5912
MCKENZIE, C. PHARMACY INC   *p1432*
2410 22ND ST W UNIT 20, SASKATOON,
SK, S7M 5S6

(306) 382-5005   *SIC* 5912
MCQUAID, S. PHARMACY LTD   *p860*
510 EXMOUTH ST, SARNIA, ON, N7T 0A5

(519) 344-2409   *SIC* 5912
MEDI-PARE LTEE   *p1115*
2075 BOUL MELLON BUREAU 100, JON-
QUIERE, QC, G7S 5Z8

(418) 548-3188   *SIC* 5912
MEDICAL HALL (1978) LIMITED   *p450*
135 COMMERCIAL ST, GLACE BAY, NS,
B1A 3B9

(902) 849-6552   *SIC* 5912
MEDICAL PHARMACIES GROUP LIMITED
p672
300 TOWN CENTRE BLVD 4TH FL,
MARKHAM, ON, L3R 5Z6

(866) 689-3169   *SIC* 5912
MELROSE DRUGS LTD   *p3*
209 CENTRE AVE SW UNIT 100, AIRDRIE,
AB, T4B 3L8

(403) 948-0010   *SIC* 5912
MENDRINOS, B. DRUGS LTD   *p659*
467 WHARNCLIFFE RD S, LONDON, ON,
N6J 2M8

(519) 672-4970   *SIC* 5912
METRO ONTARIO PHARMACIES LIMITED
p577
5559 DUNDAS ST W, ETOBICOKE, ON,
M9B 1B9

(416) 239-7171   *SIC* 5912
MICHAEL S WONG PHARMACY LTD *p781*
1881 STEELES AVE W SUITE 819, NORTH
YORK, ON, M3H 5Y4

(416) 665-2631   *SIC* 5912
MILESTEP PHARMACY SERVICES INC
p251
5240 DOMANO BLVD UNIT 470, PRINCE
GEORGE, BC, V2N 4A1

(250) 964-1888   *SIC* 5912
MONTY PHARMACY LTD   *p917*
812 O'CONNOR DR, TORONTO, ON, M4B
2S9

(416) 285-5822   *SIC* 5912
MORIN, JEAN-GUY INC   *p1164*
5955 RUE SHERBROOKE E, MONTREAL,
QC, H1N 1B7

(514) 254-7513   *SIC* 5912
MOSLIM, M. PHARMACY LTD   *p531*
484 PLAINS RD E, BURLINGTON, ON, L7T
2E1

(905) 632-3365   *SIC* 5912
MULVIHILL DRUG MART LIMITED   *p838*
1231 PEMBROKE ST W, PEMBROKE, ON,
K8A 5R3

(613) 735-1079   *SIC* 5912
MUZYK, D.J. DRUGS LTD   *p770*
1515 STEELES AVE E, NORTH YORK, ON,
M2M 3Y7

(416) 226-1313   *SIC* 5912
N WELCH PHARMACY SERVICES INC *p889*
107 EDWARD ST SUITE 101, ST THOMAS,
ON, N5P 1Y8

(519) 633-4402   *SIC* 5912
NART DRUGS INC   *p973*
292 DUPONT ST, TORONTO, ON, M5R 1V9

(416) 972-0232   *SIC 5912*
NATIONAL PHARMACY   *p865*
70 MELFORD DR SUITE 7, SCARBOR-
OUGH, ON, M1B 1Y9
(416) 265-9000   *SIC 5912*
NEUFELD, C. M. PHARMACY LTD   *p41*
1632 14 AVE NW UNIT 1790, CALGARY,
AB, T2N 1M7
(403) 289-6761   *SIC 5912*
NO FRILLS   *p168*
900 PINE RD SUITE 101, STRATHMORE,
AB, T1P 0A2
(403) 934-6500   *SIC 5912*
NORTHEND PHARMACY LTD   *p409*
1633 MOUNTAIN RD, MONCTON, NB, E1G
1A5
(506) 858-0055   *SIC 5912*
NPS ALLELIX CORP   *p689*
6850 GOREWAY DR, MISSISSAUGA, ON,
L4V 1V7
(905) 677-0831   *SIC 5912*
O'BRIAIN DRUGS LTD   *p406*
320 ELMWOOD DR, MONCTON, NB, E1A
6V2
(506) 383-8303   *SIC 5912*
OCIMAC INC   *p1114*
504 BOUL MANSEAU BUREAU 25, JOLI-
ETTE, QC, J6E 3E2
(450) 759-2560   *SIC 5912*
OLOINGSIGH DRUGS LIMITED   *p428*
141 TORBAY RD, ST. JOHN'S, NL, A1A 2H1
(709) 722-6270   *SIC 5912*
ORANO LIMITED   *p862*
625 TRUNK RD, SAULT STE. MARIE, ON,
P6A 3T1
(705) 945-8088   *SIC 5912*
ORCHARD, VALI PHARMACY INC   *p909*
1186 MEMORIAL AVE UNIT 1, THUNDER
BAY, ON, P7B 5K5
(807) 623-3601   *SIC 5912*
OTSUKA CANADA PHARMACEUTICAL INC
p1335
2250 BOUL ALFRED-NOBEL BUREAU 301,
SAINT-LAURENT, QC, H4S 2C9
(514) 332-3001   *SIC 5912*
OUELLET, PATRICK 1843 INC   *p1254*
1 RUE GUYON BUREAU 1843, QUEBEC,
QC, G1B 1T1
(418) 666-1410   *SIC 5912*
OUELLETTE, RONALD INC   *p399*
160 BOUL HEBERT, EDMUNDSTON, NB,
E3V 2S7
(506) 735-8459   *SIC 5912*
PAGGOS, MARIO DRUGS LTD   *p1032*
4000 HIGHWAY 7, WOODBRIDGE, ON, L4L
8Z2
(905) 851-2199   *SIC 5912*
**PAQUET, CHRISTINE ET CHARLES
BOISVERT, PHARMACIENS S.E.N.C.** *p1259*
138 RUE SAINT-VALLIER O BUREAU 175,
QUEBEC, QC, G1K 1K1
(418) 525-4981   *SIC 5912*
PAR-S DRUGS LTD   *p932*
465 YONGE ST, TORONTO, ON, M4Y 1X4
(416) 408-4000   *SIC 5912*
PARAMOUNT PHARMACIES LIMITED *p464*
3435 PLUMMER AVE SUITE 529, NEW
WATERFORD, NS, B1H 1Z4
(902) 862-7186   *SIC 5912*
PARM'S PRESCRIPTIONS LTD   *p277*
12080 NORDEL WAY SUITE 101, SURREY,
BC, V3W 1P6
(604) 543-8155   *SIC 5912*
PARTROSE DRUGS LIMITED   *p579*
666 BURNHAMTHORPE RD, ETOBICOKE,
ON, M9C 2Z4
(416) 621-2330   *SIC 5912*
PASLOSKI, DARRELL PHARMACY LTD
p1440
303 OGILVIE ST SUITE 2, WHITEHORSE,
YT, Y1A 2S3
(867) 667-6633   *SIC 5912*
PATEL, SAMIR PHARMACY LTD   *p905*
298 JOHN ST, THORNHILL, ON, L3T 6M8

(905) 886-3711   *SIC 5912*
PAUL GOLDMAN DRUGS LTD   *p936*
220 YONGE ST SUITE 824, TORONTO,
ON, M5B 2H1
(416) 979-9373   *SIC 5912*
PEDERSON FAMILY PHARMACY LTD *p129*
8600 FRANKLIN AVE SUITE 501, FORT
MCMURRAY, AB, T9H 4G8
(780) 743-1251   *SIC 5912*
PHARLEM INC   *p1316*
795 BOUL D'IBERVILLE, SAINT-JEAN-
SUR-RICHELIEU, QC, J2X 4S7
(450) 347-2000   *SIC 5912*
PHARMA NTK INC   *p1323*
740 BOUL DE LA COTE-VERTU, SAINT-
LAURENT, QC, H4L 5C8
(514) 744-2555   *SIC 5912*
PHARMA PLUS DRUGMARTS LTD   *p706*
5965 COOPERS AVE, MISSISSAUGA, ON,
L4Z 1R9
(905) 501-7800   *SIC 5912*
PHARMA-SANTE JONQUIERE INC   *p1116*
2340 RUE SAINT-HUBERT BUREAU 23,
JONQUIERE, QC, G7X 5N4
(418) 547-5795   *SIC 5912*
PHARMACIE ANIK BERTRAND INC *p1372*
1470 RUE KING O, SHERBROOKE, QC,
J1J 2C2
(819) 564-3111   *SIC 5912*
**PHARMACIE BEDARD LYNE PHARMACI-
ENNE INC**   *p1322*
490 AV VICTORIA, SAINT-LAMBERT, QC,
J4P 2J4
(450) 671-5563   *SIC 5912*
PHARMACIE BRUNET-CANTIN INC *p619*
4 NINTH ST, HEARST, ON, P0L 1N0
(705) 372-1212   *SIC 5912*
PHARMACIE CAROLINE MILETTE   *p1166*
5700 RUE SAINT-ZOTIQUE E BUREAU
100, MONTREAL, QC, H1T 3Y7
(514) 255-5797   *SIC 5912*
**PHARMACIE CHRISTIAN BOURQUE,
PHAMACIEN INC**   *p1375*
4870 BOUL BOURQUE, SHERBROOKE,
QC, J1N 3S5
(819) 820-0222   *SIC 5912*
**PHARMACIE CHRISTINE LEGER & MAR-
TIN COTE INC**   *p1242*
1693 BOUL LOUIS-FRECHETTE, NICO-
LET, QC, J3T 1Z6
(819) 293-6111   *SIC 5912*
**PHARMACIE DENNIS ABUD PHARMACY
INC**   *p398*
123 RUE CHAMPLAIN, DIEPPE, NB, E1A
1N5
(506) 859-1990   *SIC 5912*
PHARMACIE JEAN COUTU   *p1282*
155 BOUL LACOMBE UNITE 160, RE-
PENTIGNY, QC, J5Z 3C4
(450) 654-6747   *SIC 5912*
PHARMACIE JEAN COUTU   *p1330*
2085 BOUL MARCEL-LAURIN, SAINT-
LAURENT, QC, H4R 1K4
(514) 745-3003   *SIC 5912*
**PHARMACIE JEAN-MICHEL COUTU ET
TRISTAN GIGUERE INC**   *p1145*
3245 CH DE CHAMBLY BUREAU 305,
LONGUEUIL, QC, J4L 4K5
(450) 670-2496   *SIC 5912*
PHARMACIE KANOU & YOUSSEF S.E.N.C.
p1240
6405 BOUL LEGER BUREAU 38,
MONTREAL-NORD, QC, H1G 1L4
(514) 323-6270   *SIC 5912*
PHARMACIE LEBLANC, PIERRE INC *p417*
338 MAIN ST, SHEDIAC, NB, E4P 2E5
(506) 532-4410   *SIC 5912*
**PHARMACIE LOUIS LEGAULT, LYETTE
BOULE, PHARMACIENS INC**   *p1091*
3353 BOUL DES SOURCES, DOLLARD-
DES-ORMEAUX, QC, H9B 1Z8
(514) 683-5460   *SIC 5912*
**PHARMACIE MARTINE CLAVEAU ET
KEVIN MARK KIRKCALDY INC**   *p1076*

103 RUE PRINCIPALE, CHATEAUGUAY,
QC, J6K 1G2
(450) 691-3636   *SIC 5912*
PHARMACIE MORIN INC   *p1165*
5955 RUE SHERBROOKE E, MONTREAL,
QC, H1N 1B7
(514) 254-7513   *SIC 5912*
PHARMACIE NICOLAS CARBONNEAU INC
p1236
4515 BOUL ARTHUR-SAUVE, MONTREAL,
QC, H7R 5P8
(450) 962-7455   *SIC 5912*
PHARMACIE QUOC HUY HOANG INC *p1229*
6624 AV SOMERLED BUREAU 258, MON-
TREAL, QC, H4V 1T2
(514) 487-6530   *SIC 5912*
**PHARMACIE RAYMOND BEAUCAIRE
PHARMACIEN INC**   *p1168*
3452 RUE ONTARIO E, MONTREAL, QC,
H1W 1R2
(514) 522-1126   *SIC 5912*
PHARMACIE RENE RIVARD   *p1171*
2330 RUE FLEURY E, MONTREAL, QC,
H2B 1K9
(514) 387-7102   *SIC 5912*
**PHARMACIE S GAGNON & L MARMEN
S.E.N.C**   *p1273*
2766 CH SAINTE-FOY, QUEBEC, QC, G1V
1V5
(418) 657-2956   *SIC 5912*
**PHARMACIE SONIA GUIMONT PHARMACI-
ENNE INC**   *p1294*
275 BOUL SIR-WILFRID-LAURIER BU-
REAU 100, SAINT-BASILE-LE-GRAND, QC,
J3N 1V6
(450) 441-1944   *SIC 5912*
**PHARMACIE SYLVIE GELINAS ET CHAN-
TAL BELLEMARE PHARMACIENNES INC**
p1386
940 BOUL DES RECOLLETS, TROIS-
RIVIERES, QC, G8Z 3W9
(819) 379-1444   *SIC 5912*
PHARMACIE SYRHAK PHARMACY INC
p619
80 MAIN ST E SUITE 159, HAWKESBURY,
ON, K6A 1A3
(613) 632-2743   *SIC 5912*
**PHARMACIEN A. LAJEUNESSE & ASSO-
CIES**   *p1182*
6461 AV CHRISTOPHE-COLOMB, MON-
TREAL, QC, H2S 2G5
(514) 273-7373   *SIC 5912*
PHARMACIEN MARTIN GAGNON INC *p1102*
39 MONTEE DE SANDY BEACH BUREAU
31, GASPE, QC, G4X 2A9
(418) 368-3341   *SIC 5912*
PHARMACIES AFFILIEES A PROXIM *p1370*
624 RUE BOWEN S, SHERBROOKE, QC,
J1G 2E9
(819) 569-5561   *SIC 5912*
PHARMAPRIX   *p1346*
4420 RUE JEAN-TALON E, SAINT-
LEONARD, QC, H1S 1J7
(514) 723-1000   *SIC 5912*
PHARMAPRIX CLAUDINE LOUBERT INC
p1323
1031 AV VICTORIA, SAINT-LAMBERT, QC,
J4R 1P6
(450) 671-8367   *SIC 5912*
PHARWAHA DRUGS LIMITED   *p686*
7205 GOREWAY DR SUITE B1, MISSIS-
SAUGA, ON, L4T 2T9
(905) 677-7181   *SIC 5912*
PINEO, P. PHARMACEUTICALS INC *p752*
3151 STRANDHERD DR SUITE 1302, NE-
PEAN, ON, K2J 5N1
(613) 825-8717   *SIC 5912*
**PLACEMENTS JACQUES FELIX THIBAULT
INC., LES**   *p1076*
237 BOUL SAINT-JEAN-BAPTISTE BU-
REAU 124, CHATEAUGUAY, QC, J6K 3C3
(450) 692-7981   *SIC 5912*
**PLACEMENTS JACQUES FELIX
THIBEAULT INC, LES**   *p1151*

777 BOUL SAINT-JEAN-BAPTISTE,
MERCIER, QC, J6R 1G1
(450) 692-5990   *SIC 5912*
PLACEMENTS RABPHAR INC   *p1241*
610 BOUL CURE-LABELLE, MONTREAL-
OUEST, QC, H7V 2T7
(450) 687-5910   *SIC 5912*
PLACEMENTS ROBERT SIMARD INC *p1166*
4466 RUE BEAUBIEN E, MONTREAL, QC,
H1T 3Y8
(514) 728-3674   *SIC 5912*
POTVIN, PIERRE INC   *p1084*
1859 BOUL RENE-LAENNEC BUREAU
101, COTE SAINT-LUC, QC, H7M 5E2
(450) 662-6064   *SIC 5912*
PROSPECT HUMAN SERVICES SOCIETY
p11
915 33 ST NE, CALGARY, AB, T2A 6T2
(403) 273-2822   *SIC 5912*
PVK DRUGS LIMITED   *p894*
5710 MAIN ST UNIT 3, STOUFFVILLE, ON,
L4A 8A9
(905) 640-2700   *SIC 5912*
QUINN'S PHARMACY LIMITED (1987) *p646*
74 KENT ST W SUITE 948, LINDSAY, ON,
K9V 2Y4
(705) 324-7400   *SIC 5912*
R & T PHARMACY LTD   *p1413*
11412 RAILWAY AVE E UNIT 12, NORTH
BATTLEFORD, SK, S9A 3P7
(306) 445-6253   *SIC 5912*
R.C. PHARMACY LTD   *p600*
380 ERAMOSA RD, GUELPH, ON, N1E
6R2
(519) 822-2480   *SIC 5912*
R.D.-PHAR INC   *p1162*
8315 BOUL MAURICE-DUPLESSIS, MON-
TREAL, QC, H1E 3B5
(514) 643-2808   *SIC 5912*
RAMVAL INC   *p1182*
6500 RUE SAINT-HUBERT, MONTREAL,
QC, H2S 2M3
(514) 272-8233   *SIC 5912*
RATHI, KANU PRIYA PHARMACY INC *p534*
499 HESPELER RD, CAMBRIDGE, ON,
N1R 6J2
(519) 623-6770   *SIC 5912*
REINGOLD, M. DRUGS LIMITED   *p926*
1507 YONGE ST, TORONTO, ON, M4T 1Z2
(416) 923-7700   *SIC 5912*
REMEDY HOLDINGS INC   *p674*
675 COCHRANE DR SUITE 110,
MARKHAM, ON, L3R 0B8
(647) 794-3388   *SIC 5912*
RENNSTADD PHARMA INC   *p477*
47 WILSON ST W, ANCASTER, ON, L9G
1N1
(905) 648-4493   *SIC 5912*
REXALL PHARMACY GROUP LTD   *p706*
5965 COOPERS AVE, MISSISSAUGA, ON,
L4Z 1R9
(905) 501-7800   *SIC 5912*
RIBAK PHARMA LTD   *p894*
377 HIGHWAY 8 SUITE 369, STONEY
CREEK, ON, L8G 1E7
(905) 662-9996   *SIC 5912*
**RIVET, PATRICE & MANON ST-JEAN PHAR-
MACIENS SENC**   *p1171*
1465 RUE JEAN-TALON E BUREAU 282,
MONTREAL, QC, H2E 1S8
(514) 270-2151   *SIC 5912*
ROMANO, DOMENIC PHARMACY INC *p510*
1 KENNEDY RD S UNIT 1, BRAMPTON,
ON, L6W 3C9
(905) 454-4464   *SIC 5912*
RONPIEN INC   *p1149*
3131 BOUL DE MASCOUCHE, MAS-
COUCHE, QC, J7K 3B7
(450) 474-6171   *SIC 5912*
ROULSTON PHARMACY LTD   *p896*
211 ONTARIO ST UNIT 1, STRATFORD,
ON, N5A 3H3
(519) 271-8600   *SIC 5912*
ROULSTON'S DISCOUNT DRUGS LIMITED

▲ Public Company   ■ Public Company Family Member   **HQ** Headquarters   **BR** Branch   **SL** Single Location

p881
17 NORFOLK ST S, SIMCOE, ON, N3Y 2V8
(519) 426-1731   *SIC 5912*

ROYMICK INC p1391
823 3E AV BUREAU 31, VAL-D'OR, QC, J9P 1S8
(819) 824-3645   *SIC 5912*

RUBICON PHARMACIES CANADA INC p1438
117 3RD ST UNIT 206, WEYBURN, SK, S4H 0W3
(306) 848-3855   *SIC 5912*

RX FRASER LTD p9
2525 36 ST NE SUITE 135, CALGARY, AB, T1Y 5T4
(403) 280-6667   *SIC 5912*

S.L. DEVISON PHARMACIES INC p831
888 MEADOWLANDS DR, OTTAWA, ON, K2C 3R2
(613) 225-6204   *SIC 5912*

SALAMEH DRUGS LTD p713
321 LAKESHORE RD W, MISSISSAUGA, ON, L5H 1G9
(905) 271-4581   *SIC 5912*

SANTE-BEAUTE DANMOR INC p1368
1 RUE LA PLAZA-DE-MAURICIE BUREAU 27, SHAWINIGAN, QC, G9N 7C1
(819) 539-5416   *SIC 5912*

SB PHARMACY SERVICES LTD p1015
1801 DUNDAS ST E, WHITBY, ON, L1N 7C5
(905) 436-1050   *SIC 5912*

SCEPTER DRUGS LTD p195
1297 SHOPPERS ROW SUITE 209, CAMPBELL RIVER, BC, V9W 2C7
(250) 286-1166   *SIC 5912*

SCRIPTECH MEDS INC p512
8965 CHINGUACOUSY RD SUITE 1092, BRAMPTON, ON, L6Y 0J2
(905) 454-1620   *SIC 5912*

SEHDEV PHARMACY INC p498
51 MOUNTAINASH RD SUITE 1, BRAMPTON, ON, L6R 1W4
(905) 458-5526   *SIC 5912*

SENTINEL DRUGS LIMITED p457
3711 JOSEPH HOWE DR, HALIFAX, NS, B3L 4H8
(902) 468-8866   *SIC 5912*

SERVICE DRUG LTD p342
5331 HEADLAND DR, WEST VANCOUVER, BC, V7W 3C6
(604) 926-5331   *SIC 5912*

SERVICE SANTE CLAUDE GERVAIS INC, LES p1067
520 BOUL DU FORT-SAINT-LOUIS BUREAU 1, BOUCHERVILLE, QC, J4B 1S5
(450) 655-6651   *SIC 5912*

SERVICES PHARMACEUTIQUES SOCJETI LTEE p822
50 RIDEAU ST SUITE 125, OTTAWA, ON, K1N 9J7
(613) 236-2533   *SIC 5912*

SGS PHARMACY INC p1424
2105 8TH ST E UNIT 42, SASKATOON, SK, S7H 0T8
(306) 374-4888   *SIC 5912*

SHAREAN DRUGS LTD p631
445 PRINCESS ST, KINGSTON, ON, K7L 1C3
(613) 546-3696   *SIC 5912*

SHOPPERS DRUG MART p243
140 ISLAND HWY E, PARKSVILLE, BC, V9P 2G5
(250) 248-3521   *SIC 5912*

SHOPPERS DRUG MART p398
477 RUE PAUL SUITE 181, DIEPPE, NB, E1A 4X5
(506) 857-0820   *SIC 5912*

SHOPPERS DRUG MART p457
278 LACEWOOD DR SUITE 136, HALIFAX, NS, B3M 3N8
(902) 443-5214   *SIC 5912*

SHOPPERS DRUG MART p540
315 MCNEELY AVE, CARLETON PLACE, ON, K7C 4S6
(613) 253-5595   *SIC 5912*

SHOPPERS DRUG MART p843
1355 KINGSTON RD SUITE 618, PICKERING, ON, L1V 1B8
(905) 839-4488   *SIC 5912*

SHOPPERS DRUG MART p847
60 ONTARIO ST, PORT HOPE, ON, L1A 2T8
(905) 885-1294   *SIC 5912*

SHOPPERS DRUG MART p855
10660 YONGE ST, RICHMOND HILL, ON, L4C 3C9
(905) 884-5233   *SIC 5912*

SHOPPERS DRUG MART CORPORATION p768
243 CONSUMERS RD, NORTH YORK, ON, M2J 4W8
(416) 493-1220   *SIC 5912*

SILVA, MANUEL J DRUGS LTD p512
180 SANDALWOOD PKY E, BRAMPTON, ON, L6Z 1Y4
(905) 846-4700   *SIC 5912*

SILVERTHORNE PHARMACY LTD p1035
959 DUNDAS ST SUITE 1, WOODSTOCK, ON, N4S 1H2
(519) 537-2042   *SIC 5912*

SINCLAIR PHARMACY (1980) LTD p896
12 WELLINGTON ST, STRATFORD, ON, N5A 2L2
(519) 271-8940   *SIC 5912*

SOBEYS WEST INC p39
11011 BONAVENTURE DR SE, CALGARY, AB, T2J 6S1
(403) 278-5225   *SIC 5912*

SOCIETE DE GESTION RENE RAINVILLE LTEE p1115
1075 BOUL FIRESTONE BUREAU 1240, JOLIETTE, QC, J6E 6X6
(450) 759-8800   *SIC 5912*

SOCIETE IMMOBILIERE LAFLECHE INC, LA p1112
765 6E AV, GRAND-MERE, QC, G9T 2H8
(819) 538-8606   *SIC 5912*

SOCIETE PRIBEX LTEE, LA p1057
350 BOUL SIR-WILFRID-LAURIER, BELOEIL, QC, J3G 4G7
(450) 467-0296   *SIC 5912*

SOLARIS PHARMACEUTICALS INC p278
8322 130 ST SUITE 201, SURREY, BC, V3W 8J9
(778) 218-2655   *SIC 5912*

SONAL BACHU PHARMACY LTD p363
1555 REGENT AVE W UNIT 32T, WINNIPEG, MB, R2C 4J2
(204) 661-8068   *SIC 5912*

SPEARS & MACLEOD PHARMACY LIMITED p471
333 MAIN ST SUITE 519, YARMOUTH, NS, B5A 1E5
(902) 742-7825   *SIC 5912*

SPINA, JOHN DRUGS LTD p475
15 WESTNEY RD N SUITE 2, AJAX, ON, L1T 1P5
(905) 426-3355   *SIC 5912*

ST. PIERRE, BARRY PHARMACY LTD p917
1500 WOODBINE AVE, TORONTO, ON, M4C 4G9
(416) 429-2529   *SIC 5912*

STEPHEN MACDONALD PHARMACY INC p822
334 CUMBERLAND ST, OTTAWA, ON, K1N 7J2
(705) 325-2377   *SIC 5912*

STEVE DOUCET PHARMACUETICAL INC p395
939 ST. PETER AVE, BATHURST, NB, E2A 2Z3
(506) 547-8023   *SIC 5912*

SULLIVAN, EVAN PHARMACY LIMITED p492
150 SIDNEY ST SUITE 1, BELLEVILLE, ON, K8P 5E2
(613) 962-3406   *SIC 5912*

SUPER THRIFTY DRUGS CANADA LTD p347
381 PARK AVE E UNIT F, BRANDON, MB, R7A 7A5
(204) 728-1522   *SIC 5912*

SURANI, B. DRUGS LTD p824
161 BANK ST, OTTAWA, ON, K1P 5N7
(613) 232-5723   *SIC 5912*

TAILOR DRUGS LIMITED p727
6975 MEADOWVALE TOWN CENTRE CIR, MISSISSAUGA, ON, L5N 2V7
(905) 826-7112   *SIC 5912*

TALBOT, JOHANNE PHARMACIENNE p1270
110 BOUL RENE-LEVESQUE O BUREAU 118, QUEBEC, QC, G1R 2A5
(418) 522-1235   *SIC 5912*

TAN, KENNY PHARMACY INC p976
360 BLOOR ST W SUITE 806, TORONTO, ON, M5S 1X1
(416) 961-2121   *SIC 5912*

TEE, FRANK PHARMACIES LTD p826
702 BANK ST SUITE 700, OTTAWA, ON, K1S 3V2
(613) 233-3202   *SIC 5912*

THIBAULT, JACQUES ENTREPRISES INC p1076
97 BOUL D'ANJOU, CHATEAUGUAY, QC, J6J 2R1
(450) 691-2622   *SIC 5912*

TIRCONNELL PHARMACY LIMITED p718
3163 WINSTON CHURCHILL BLVD SUITE 1098, MISSISSAUGA, ON, L5L 2W1
(905) 607-7871   *SIC 5912*

TOLMIE, M. B. DRUGS LTD p682
9226 93 HWY, MIDLAND, ON, L4R 4K4
(705) 526-7855   *SIC 5912*

TONA, ALAN PHARMACY LIMITED p545
270 SPRING ST, COBOURG, ON, K9A 3K2
(905) 372-3333   *SIC 5912*

TRANSPHARM INC p1395
585 AV SAINT-CHARLES BUREAU 180, VAUDREUIL-DORION, QC, J7V 8P9
(450) 455-5568   *SIC 5912*

TREMBLAY, ANDREE P. PHARMACIEN ENR p1057
350 BOUL SIR-WILFRID-LAURIER, BELOEIL, QC, J3G 4G7
(450) 467-0296   *SIC 5912*

TREMBLAY, FRANCOIS PHARMACIE p1105
640 BOUL MALONEY O, GATINEAU, QC, J8T 8K7
(819) 246-9662   *SIC 5912*

TRIPLE A PHARMACY INC p811
1675E TENTH LINE RD, ORLEANS, ON, K1E 3P6
(613) 837-6078   *SIC 5912*

TRIPLE J PHARMACY LTD p500
980 CENTRAL PARK DR, BRAMPTON, ON, L6S 3L7
(905) 791-1797   *SIC 5912*

TSANG, A.J. PHARMACY LTD p244
19150 LOUGHEED HWY SUITE 110, PITT MEADOWS, BC, V3Y 2H6
(604) 465-8122   *SIC 5912*

UNIPRIX INC p1346
5000 BOUL METROPOLITAIN E BUREAU 100, SAINT-LEONARD, QC, H1S 3G7
(514) 725-1212   *SIC 5912*

UNIPRIX PHARMACY p1116
2095 RUE SAINTE-FAMILLE, JONQUIERE, QC, G7X 4W8
(418) 547-3689   *SIC 5912*

UNIPRIX PIERRE BERGERON ET MARISA SGRO (PHARMACIE AFFILIEE) p1118
2963 BOUL SAINT-CHARLES, KIRKLAND, QC, H9H 3B5
(514) 694-3074   *SIC 5912*

V.A. HEALTH CARE INC p1007
50 WEBER ST N, WATERLOO, ON, N2J 3G7
(519) 880-8083   *SIC 5912*

VALERIO, TOMASELLI p1245
4930 BOUL SAINT-JEAN, PIERREFONDS, QC, H9H 4B2
(514) 620-7920   *SIC 5912*

VANDENBURG, ROMEO DRUG COMPANY LTD p917
3003 DANFORTH AVE, TORONTO, ON, M4C 1M9
(416) 694-2131   *SIC 5912*

VARIETES CHARRON & LECLERC, SENC p1125
6240 RUE SALABERRY, LAC-MEGANTIC, QC, G6B 1H8
(819) 583-2123   *SIC 5912*

VARTEGEZ SIMONIAN PHARMACY LTD p728
6040 GLEN ERIN DR SUITE 1, MISSISSAUGA, ON, L5N 3M4
(905) 821-8020   *SIC 5912*

VITAL PHARMACY INC p434
250 LEMARCHANT RD, ST. JOHN'S, NL, A1E 1P7
(709) 739-9751   *SIC 5912*

VIVA PHARMACEUTICAL INC p257
13880 VIKING PL, RICHMOND, BC, V6V 1K8
(604) 718-0816   *SIC 5912*

WADE, R.S. HEALTH CARE LTD p398
18 RUE CHAMPLAIN UNIT 1, DIEPPE, NB, E1A 1N3
(506) 389-1680   *SIC 5912*

WADLAND PHARMACY LIMITED p512
1 PRESIDENTS CHOICE CIR, BRAMPTON, ON, L6Y 5S5
(905) 459-2500   *SIC 5912*

WANG, MAURICE DRUGS LTD p931
20 BLOOR ST E, TORONTO, ON, M4W 3G7
(416) 967-7787   *SIC 5912*

WARDILL, J.A. ENTERPRISES INC p340
2945 JACKLIN RD SUITE 300, VICTORIA, BC, V9B 5E3
(250) 474-1114   *SIC 5912*

WARRIAN, KAREN PHARMACY p573
125 THE QUEENSWAY, ETOBICOKE, ON, M8Y 1H6
(416) 766-6196   *SIC 5912*

WAY'S PHARMACY LIMITED p434
390 TOPSAIL RD, ST. JOHN'S, NL, A1E 2B8
(709) 368-6084   *SIC 5912*

WEINGARTEN, ALAN DRUGS LTD p571
2850 LAKE SHORE BLVD W, ETOBICOKE, ON, M8V 1H9
(416) 255-2397   *SIC 5912*

WEST SIDE PHARMACY INC p416
667 FAIRVILLE BLVD, SAINT JOHN, NB, E2M 3W2
(506) 636-7740   *SIC 5912*

WEYLAND, LAURA PHARMACY LTD p984
388 KING ST W SUITE 1320, TORONTO, ON, M5V 1K2
(416) 597-6550   *SIC 5912*

WIERSEMA, TRACY PHARMACY LTD p488
649 YONGE ST, BARRIE, ON, L4N 4E7
(705) 792-4388   *SIC 5912*

WILF'S DRUG STORE LTD p490
330 NOTRE DAME ST, BELLE RIVER, ON, N0R 1A0
(519) 728-1610   *SIC 5912*

WOLFF, MARY ANN DRUGS LTD p477
199 SANDWICH ST S, AMHERSTBURG, ON, N9V 1Z9
(519) 736-5435   *SIC 5912*

WONG, VICKY C.K. DRUGS LTD p679
9255 WOODBINE AVE SUITE 27, MARKHAM, ON, L6C 1Y9
(905) 887-3000   *SIC 5912*

YOUNGS PHARMACY LIMITED p594
47 MAIN ST S, GEORGETOWN, ON, L7G 3G2
(905) 877-2711   *SIC 5912*

ZABS PHARMACY LTD p1419
2202 BROAD ST SUITE 422, REGINA, SK, S4P 4V6
(306) 777-8166   *SIC 5912*

ZAHID, M. DRUGS LTD p757
1111 DAVIS DR SUITE 46, NEWMARKET,

▲ Public Company   ■ Public Company Family Member   **HQ** Headquarters   **BR** Branch   **SL** Single Location

ON, L3Y 8X2
(905) 898-7771   *SIC* 5912

SIC 5921 Liquor stores

1046809 ALBERTA INC   *p41*
2112 CROWCHILD TRAIL NW, CALGARY,
AB, T2M 3Y7
(403) 338-1268   *SIC* 5921

30TH STREET LIQUOR STORE LTD   *p331*
2901 30 ST, VERNON, BC, V1T 5C9
(250) 545-5800   *SIC* 5921

527758 B.C. LTD   *p343*
14995 MARINE DR SUITE 6, WHITE
ROCK, BC, V4B 1C3
   SIC 5921

586307 ALBERTA LTD   *p74*
7422 CROWFOOT RD NW UNIT 201, CAL-
GARY, AB, T3G 3N7
(403) 296-2200   *SIC* 5921

675122 ALBERTA LTD   *p112*
4207 98 ST NW SUITE 102, EDMONTON,
AB, T6E 5R7
   SIC 5921

9191-1404 QUEBEC INC   *p1193*
420 RUE SHERBROOKE O, MONTREAL,
QC, H3A 1B2
(514) 499-7777   *SIC* 5921

ALCANNA INC   *p99*
17220 STONY PLAIN RD SUITE 101, ED-
MONTON, AB, T5S 1K6
(780) 944-9994   *SIC* 5921

BARLEY MILL PUB LTD, THE   *p243*
2460 SKAHA LAKE RD, PENTICTON, BC,
V2A 6E9
(250) 493-8000   *SIC* 5921

BREWERS RETAIL INC   *p661*
280 SOVEREIGN RD, LONDON, ON, N6M
1B3
(519) 451-3699   *SIC* 5921

BREWERS RETAIL INC   *p692*
5900 EXPLORER DR, MISSISSAUGA, ON,
L4W 5L2
(905) 361-1005   *SIC* 5921

BREWERS RETAIL INC   *p817*
2750 SWANSEA CRES, OTTAWA, ON, K1G
6R8
(613) 738-8615   *SIC* 5921

BREWERS RETAIL INC   *p891*
414 DEWITT RD, STONEY CREEK, ON,
L8E 4B7
(905) 664-7921   *SIC* 5921

**CENTRAL CITY BREWERS & DISTILLERS
LTD**   *p270*
11411 BRIDGEVIEW DR, SURREY, BC,
V3R 0C2
(604) 588-2337   *SIC* 5921

CHATEAU DES CHARMES WINES LTD *p888*
1025 YORK RD, ST DAVIDS, ON, L0S 1P0
(905) 262-4219   *SIC* 5921

COLIO ESTATE WINES INC   *p693*
5900 AMBLER DR SUITE 7, MISSIS-
SAUGA, ON, L4W 2N3
(905) 949-4246   *SIC* 5921

FOUR SEASONS PALACE CATERERS LTD
p1416
909 E ARCOLA AVE, REGINA, SK, S4N
0S2
(306) 525-8338   *SIC* 5921

**FOUR WINDS HOTELS MANAGEMENT
CORP**   *p135*
10302 97 ST, HIGH LEVEL, AB, T0H 1Z0
(780) 220-1840   *SIC* 5921

HILLSIDE CELLARS WINERY LTD   *p243*
1350 NARAMATA RD, PENTICTON, BC,
V2A 8T6
(250) 493-6274   *SIC* 5921

JOHN B PUB LTD   *p201*
1000 AUSTIN AVE, COQUITLAM, BC, V3K
3P1
(604) 931-5115   *SIC* 5921

KIRKFIELD HOTEL LIMITED   *p386*
3317 PORTAGE AVE, WINNIPEG, MB, R3K

0W8
(204) 837-1314   *SIC* 5921

LIBERTY WINE MERCHANTS LTD   *p289*
291 2ND AVE E SUITE 100, VANCOUVER,
BC, V5T 1B8
(604) 739-7801   *SIC* 5921

**LIQUOR CONTROL BOARD OF ONTARIO,
THE**   *p942*
55 LAKE SHORE BLVD E SUITE 876,
TORONTO, ON, M5E 1A4
(416) 365-5900   *SIC* 5921

**LIQUOR CONTROL BOARD OF ONTARIO,
THE**   *p942*
1 YONGE ST 13TH FLOOR, TORONTO,
ON, M5E 1E5
(416) 365-5778   *SIC* 5921

**LIQUOR DEPOT AT WINDERMERE CROSS-
ING**   *p115*
10508 82 AVE NW UNIT 300, EDMONTON,
AB, T6E 2A4
(780) 702-7400   *SIC* 5921

LIQUOR STORE CABARET   *p1273*
2600 BOUL LAURIER BUREAU 180, QUE-
BEC, QC, G1V 4T3
   SIC 5921

LIQUOR STORES GP INC   *p115*
10508 82 AVE NW SUITE 300, EDMON-
TON, AB, T6E 2A4
(780) 944-9994   *SIC* 5921

LIQUOR STORES LIMITED PARTNERSHIP
p115
10508 82 AVE NW SUITE 300, EDMON-
TON, AB, T6E 2A4
(780) 944-9994   *SIC* 5921

**NEW BRUNSWICK LIQUOR CORPORA-
TION**   *p401*
170 WILSEY RD, FREDERICTON, NB, E3B
5J1
(506) 452-6826   *SIC* 5921

**NEWFOUNDLAND LABRADOR LIQUOR
CORPORATION**   *p430*
90 KENMOUNT RD, ST. JOHN'S, NL, A1B
3R1
(709) 724-1100   *SIC* 5921

**NORTHWEST   TERRITORIES   LIQUOR
COMMISSION**   *p435*
31 CAPITAL DR SUITE 201, HAY RIVER,
NT, X0E 1G2
(867) 874-8700   *SIC* 5921

NOVA SCOTIA LIQUOR CORPORATION
p459
93 CHAIN LAKE DR, HALIFAX, NS, B3S
1A3
(902) 450-6752   *SIC* 5921

PIONEER'S PUB LTD, THE   *p263*
10111 NO. 3 RD SUITE 200, RICHMOND,
BC, V7A 1W6
(604) 271-6611   *SIC* 5921

**PRINCE EDWARD ISLAND LIQUOR CON-
TROL COMMISSION**   *p1039*
3 GARFIELD ST, CHARLOTTETOWN, PE,
C1A 6A4
(902) 368-5710   *SIC* 5921

RIVER'S REACH PUB INC   *p236*
320 SIXTH ST, NEW WESTMINSTER, BC,
V3L 3A8
(604) 777-0101   *SIC* 5921

ROCKY MOUNTAIN LIQUOR INC   *p96*
11478 149 ST, EDMONTON, AB, T5M 1W7
(780) 483-8183   *SIC* 5921

ROYAL COACHMAN INN LTD, THE   *p195*
84 DOGWOOD ST, CAMPBELL RIVER, BC,
V9W 2X7
(250) 286-0231   *SIC* 5921

SOCIETE DES ALCOOLS DU QUEBEC
p1165
560 RUE HECTOR-BARSALOU, MON-
TREAL, QC, H1N 3T2
(514) 254-6000   *SIC* 5921

SOCIETE DES ALCOOLS DU QUEBEC
p1165
7500 RUE TELLIER, MONTREAL, QC, H1N
3W5
(514) 254-6000   *SIC* 5921

SUMMERHILL ESTATE WINERY CO   *p219*
4870 CHUTE LAKE RD SUITE 1,
KELOWNA, BC, V1W 4M3
(250) 764-8000   *SIC* 5921

TIMBERLAND HOTEL CORPORATION *p136*
114 PARK ST, HINTON, AB, T7V 2B1
(780) 865-2231   *SIC* 5921

WATERLOO BREWING LTD   *p636*
400 BINGEMANS CENTRE DR, KITCH-
ENER, ON, N2B 3X9
(519) 742-2732   *SIC* 5921

WOODY'S ON BRUNETTE   *p202*
935 BRUNETTE AVE, COQUITLAM, BC,
V3K 1C8
(604) 526-1718   *SIC* 5921

YUKON LIQUOR CORPORATION   *p1440*
9031 QUARTZ RD, WHITEHORSE, YT, Y1A
4P9
(867) 667-5245   *SIC* 5921

SIC 5932 Used merchandise stores

CANADIAN TEST CASE 87   *p720*
6750 CENTURY AVE SUITE 305, MISSIS-
SAUGA, ON, L5N 2V8
(905) 812-5920   *SIC* 5932

**CORPORATION REGIONALE DE DEVEL-
OPPEMENT DE LA RECUPERATION ET DU
RECYCLAGE REGION 02**   *p1045*
1000 BOUL SAINT-JUDE, ALMA, QC, G8B
3L1
(418) 668-8502   *SIC* 5932

DYN EXPORTERS CANADA INC   *p783*
387 LIMESTONE CRES, NORTH YORK,
ON, M3J 2R1
(905) 761-9559   *SIC* 5932

FIVE STAR RAGS INC   *p735*
7500 KIMBEL ST, MISSISSAUGA, ON, L5S
1A2
(905) 405-8365   *SIC* 5932

FRIPES EXPORT LTD   *p871*
310 MIDWEST RD, SCARBOROUGH, ON,
M1P 3A9
(416) 752-5046   *SIC* 5932

GOODWILL INDUSTRIES NIAGARA   *p885*
111 CHURCH ST, ST CATHARINES, ON,
L2R 3C9
(905) 641-5285   *SIC* 5932

**GOODWILL   INDUSTRIES,   ONTARIO
GREAT LAKES**   *p655*
255 HORTON ST E, LONDON, ON, N6B
1L1
(519) 645-1455   *SIC* 5932

**GOODWILL   INDUSTRIES-ESSEX   KENT
LAMBTON INC**   *p860*
439 PALMERSTON ST S, SARNIA, ON,
N7T 3P4
(519) 332-0440   *SIC* 5932

GROUPE COMPTANT QUEBEC INC *p1172*
2024 AV DU MONT-ROYAL E, MONTREAL,
QC, H2H 1J6
(514) 527-6023   *SIC* 5932

**LEBLANC, GUY ENTERPRISES (1984) LIM-
ITED**   *p449*
343 CONWAY RD, DIGBY, NS, B0V 1A0
(902) 245-2171   *SIC* 5932

MAPLE COMPUTERS INC   *p708*
20 DUNDAS ST E UNIT 4, MISSISSAUGA,
ON, L5A 1W2
(905) 272-1446   *SIC* 5932

**MENNONITE   CENTRAL   COMMITTEE
CANADA**   *p347*
414 PACIFIC AVE, BRANDON, MB, R7A
0H5
(204) 727-1162   *SIC* 5932

MILLER'S AUTO RECYCLING (1992) LTD
p591
1557 BOWEN RD, FORT ERIE, ON, L2A
5M4
(800) 263-8104   *SIC* 5932

RECYCLO-CENTRE INC   *p1376*
165 AV DE L'HOTEL-DIEU, SOREL-TRACY,
QC, J3P 1M2

---

(450) 746-4559   *SIC* 5932

RIO TEXTILES EXPORTERS LTD   *p867*
1840 ELLESMERE RD, SCARBOROUGH,
ON, M1H 2V5
   SIC 5932

SIB ENTERPRISES INC   *p875*
393 NUGGET AVE, SCARBOROUGH, ON,
M1S 4G3
(416) 292-7792   *SIC* 5932

SIC 5941 Sporting goods and bicycle shops

1249413 ALBERTA LTD   *p41*
1632 14 AVE NW SUITE 1774, CALGARY,
AB, T2N 1M7
(403) 289-4441   *SIC* 5941

2173-4108 QUEBEC INC   *p1363*
640 CHOMEDEY (A-13) O, SAINTE-ROSE,
QC, H7X 3S9
   SIC 5941

2427-9028 QUEBEC INC   *p1279*
5401 BOUL DES GALERIES BUREAU 240,
QUEBEC, QC, G2K 1N4
(418) 627-0062   *SIC* 5941

3100-2504 QUEBEC INC   *p1077*
1401 BOUL TALBOT   BUREAU   3,
CHICOUTIMI, QC, G7H 5N6
(418) 545-4945   *SIC* 5941

4094590 CANADA INC   *p1069*
9550 BOUL LEDUC BUREAU 15,
BROSSARD, QC, J4Y 0B3
   SIC 5941

4094590 CANADA INC   *p1278*
200 RUE BOUVIER UNITE 100, QUEBEC,
QC, G2J 1R8
(418) 627-6665   *SIC* 5941

9023-4436 QUEBEC INC   *p1271*
2700 BOUL LAURIER, QUEBEC, QC, G1V
2L8
(418) 658-1820   *SIC* 5941

910259 ONTARIO INC   *p748*
100 BAYSHORE DR UNIT 301, NEPEAN,
ON, K2B 8C1
(613) 829-7680   *SIC* 5941

ATMOSPHERE   *p1104*
1100 BOUL MALONEY O, GATINEAU, QC,
J8T 6G3
(819) 243-3711   *SIC* 5941

BASS PRO SHOPS CANADA INC   *p549*
1 BASS PRO MILLS DR, CONCORD, ON,
L4K 5W4
(905) 761-4000   *SIC* 5941

BEAULIEU, CLAUDE SPORT INC   *p1352*
75 AV DE LA GARE BUREAU E1, SAINT-
SAUVEUR, QC, J0R 1R6
(450) 227-8632   *SIC* 5941

BICYCLES QUILICOT INC, LES   *p1364*
232 RUE SAINT-CHARLES LOCAL 90,
SAINTE-THERESE, QC, J7E 2B4
(450) 420-2222   *SIC* 5941

BOLIVAR HOLDINGS LTD   *p273*
10280 CITY PKY, SURREY, BC, V3T 4C2
(604) 589-8299   *SIC* 5941

BOW CYCLE & SPORTS LTD   *p72*
6501 BOWNESS RD NW, CALGARY, AB,
T3B 0E8
(403) 288-5422   *SIC* 5941

BUSHTUKAH INC   *p828*
203 RICHMOND RD, OTTAWA, ON, K1Z
6W4
   SIC 5941

CABELA'S RETAIL CANADA INC   *p21*
851 64 AVE NE, CALGARY, AB, T2E 3B8
(403) 910-0200   *SIC* 5941

CABELA'S RETAIL CANADA INC   *p365*
25 DE BAETS ST, WINNIPEG, MB, R2J 4G5
(204) 788-4867   *SIC* 5941

CABELA'S RETAIL CANADA INC   *p388*
580 STERLING LYON PKY, WINNIPEG, MB,
R3P 1E9
(204) 786-8966   *SIC* 5941

CLEVE'S SPORTING GOODS LIMITED *p445*
30 THORNHILL DR, DARTMOUTH, NS,

B3B 1S1
(902) 468-1885   *SIC* 5941
CLEVE'S SPORTING GOODS LIMITEDp471
76 STARRS RD, YARMOUTH, NS, B5A 2T5
(902) 742-8135   *SIC* 5941
COMOR SPORTS CENTRE LTD   p320
1793 4TH AVE W, VANCOUVER, BC, V6J
1M2
(604) 734-0212   *SIC* 5941
CORBETT'S SKIS & SNOWBOARDS INC
p803
2278 SPEERS RD, OAKVILLE, ON, L6L 2X8
(905) 338-7713   *SIC* 5941
CORDEE PLEIN AIR INC, LA   p1086
2777 BOUL SAINT-MARTIN O, COTE
SAINT-LUC, QC, H7T 2Y7
(514) 524-1326   *SIC* 5941
CORDEE PLEIN AIR INC, LA   p1174
2159 RUE SAINTE-CATHERINE E, MON-
TREAL, QC, H2K 2H9
(514) 524-1326   *SIC* 5941
DECATHLON CANADA INC   p1068
2151 BOUL LAPINIERE, BROSSARD, QC,
J4W 2T5
(514) 962-7545   *SIC* 5941
DISTRIBUTIONS LMC LTEE, LES   p1378
600 CH DU HIBOU, STONEHAM-ET-
TEWKESBURY, QC, G3C 1T3
(418) 848-2415   *SIC* 5941
DIVERSION P.L. SPORTS INC   p1155
2305 CH ROCKLAND BUREAU 320, MONT-
ROYAL, QC, H3P 3E9
(514) 735-4751   *SIC* 5941
EAST LONDON SPORTS LIMITED   p659
406 WHARNCLIFFE RD S, LONDON, ON,
N6J 2M4
(519) 673-3810   *SIC* 5941
EMPIRE SPORTS INC   p1064
1155C PLACE NOBEL, BOUCHERVILLE,
QC, J4B 7L3
(450) 645-9998   *SIC* 5941
EMPIRE SPORTS INC   p1146
2786 CH DU LAC BUREAU 1, LONGUEUIL,
QC, J4N 1B8
(450) 646-2888   *SIC* 5941
ERNIE'S FITNESS EXPERTS   p131
11500 100 ST SUITE 1, GRANDE PRAIRIE,
AB, T8V 4C2
(780) 539-9505   *SIC* 5941
ERNIE'S SPORT CENTRE (1983) LTD p131
11500 100 ST UNIT 1, GRANDE PRAIRIE,
AB, T8V 4C2
(780) 539-6262   *SIC* 5941
ERNIE'S SPORTS (S3) INC   p131
11500 100 ST UNIT 1, GRANDE PRAIRIE,
AB, T8V 4C2
(780) 539-6262   *SIC* 5941
FGL SPORTS LTD   p23
824 41 AVE NE, CALGARY, AB, T2E 3R3
(403) 717-1400   *SIC* 5941
FGL SPORTS LTD   p1021
3100 HOWARD AVE, WINDSOR, ON, N8X
3Y8
(519) 972-8379   *SIC* 5941
FGL SPORTS LTD   p1236
4855 RUE LOUIS-B.-MAYER, MONTREAL,
QC, H7P 6C8
(450) 687-5200   *SIC* 5941
FISHIN' HOLE (1982) LTD, THE   p105
11829 154 ST NW, EDMONTON, AB, T5V
1G6
(780) 469-6630   *SIC* 5941
GESTION GERALD SAVARD INC   p1278
5500 BOUL DES GRADINS BUREAU 405,
QUEBEC, QC, G2J 1A1
(418) 622-7333   *SIC* 5941
GOLF TOWN LIMITED   p553
610 APPLEWOOD CRES UNIT 302, CON-
CORD, ON, L4K 0E3
(905) 479-0343   *SIC* 5941
**GOLF TOWN OPERATING LIMITED PART-
NERSHIP**   p553
610 APPLEWOOD CRES UNIT 302, CON-
CORD, ON, L4K 0E3

(905) 479-0343   *SIC* 5941
GRAND BAZAR DE GRANBY INC, AUp1111
1141 RUE PRINCIPALE BUREAU 378,
GRANBY, QC, J2J 0M3
(450) 378-2022   *SIC* 5941
GREENHAWK INC   p731
5665 MCLAUGHLIN RD, MISSISSAUGA,
ON, L5R 3K5
(905) 238-0311   *SIC* 5941
GROUPE LALIBERTE SPORTS INC p1379
1185 BOUL MOODY BUREAU 90, TERRE-
BONNE, QC, J6W 3Z5
(450) 824-1091   *SIC* 5941
K RICE RETAILING INC   p162
169 ORDZE AVE SUITE 428, SHERWOOD
PARK, AB, T8B 1M6
(780) 449-1577   *SIC* 5941
LEVESQUE, A. ET S. (1993) INC   p1358
430 RUE COUTURE, SAINTE-HELENE-
DE-BAGOT, QC, J0H 1M0
(450) 791-2727   *SIC* 5941
MICON SPORTS LTD   p811
2085 TENTH LINE RD, ORLEANS, ON, K4A
4C5
(613) 731-6006   *SIC* 5941
MODES ET SPORTS 3050 INC   p1374
3050 BOUL DE PORTLAND BUREAU 528,
SHERBROOKE, QC, J1L 1K1
(819) 346-5286   *SIC* 5941
MONTREAL CENTRE SPORTS INC p1206
930 RUE SAINTE-CATHERINE O, MON-
TREAL, QC, H3B 1E2
(514) 866-1914   *SIC* 5941
MOUNTAIN EQUIPMENT CO-OPERATIVE
p65
830 10 AVE SW, CALGARY, AB, T2R 0A9
(403) 269-2420   *SIC* 5941
MOUNTAIN EQUIPMENT CO-OPERATIVE
p289
1077 GREAT NORTHERN WAY, VANCOU-
VER, BC, V5T 1E1
(604) 707-3300   *SIC* 5941
MOUNTAIN EQUIPMENT CO-OPERATIVE
p829
366 RICHMOND RD, OTTAWA, ON, K2A
0E8
(613) 729-2700   *SIC* 5941
NAUTILUS PLUS INC   p1308
3550 1RE RUE, SAINT-HUBERT, QC, J3Y
8Y5
(514) 666-5814   *SIC* 5941
NEW AGE SPORTS INC   p290
8206 ONTARIO ST SUITE 200, VANCOU-
VER, BC, V5X 3E3
(604) 324-9943   *SIC* 5941
QUICK SPORTS   p242
4740 CAPILANO RD, NORTH VANCOU-
VER, BC, V7R 4K3
SIC 5941
ROYAL SPORTS SHOP LTD   p367
650 RALEIGH ST, WINNIPEG, MB, R2K 3Z9
(204) 668-4584   *SIC* 5941
SAIL PLEIN AIR INC   p1133
2850 AV JACQUES-BUREAU, LAVAL, QC,
H7P 0B7
(450) 688-6264   *SIC* 5941
SHOOTING EDGE INC, THE   p37
510 77 AVE SE SUITE 4, CALGARY, AB,
T2H 1C3
(403) 720-4867   *SIC* 5941
SKI MOJO INC   p1070
8025 BOUL TASCHEREAU, BROSSARD,
QC, J4Y 1A4
(450) 462-4040   *SIC* 5941
SKI MOJO INC   p1241
1355   BOUL   DES   LAURENTIDES,
MONTREAL-OUEST, QC, H7N 4Y5
(450) 669-5123   *SIC* 5941
SKIIS LTD   p703
1945 DUNDAS ST E SUITE 210, MISSIS-
SAUGA, ON, L4X 2T8
(905) 896-1206   *SIC* 5941
SNOW COVERS SPORTS INC   p321
1701 3RD AVE W, VANCOUVER, BC, V6J

1K7
(604) 738-3715   *SIC* 5941
SPORTING LIFE INC   p580
25 THE WEST MALL SUITE 7, ETOBI-
COKE, ON, M9C 1B8
(416) 620-7002   *SIC* 5941
SPORTING LIFE INC   p924
130 MERTON ST 6TH FL, TORONTO, ON,
M4S 1A4
(416) 485-1685   *SIC* 5941
SPORTS 12345 INC   p1087
3035 BOUL LE CARREFOUR BUREAU
T02, COTE SAINT-LUC, QC, H7T 1C8
(450) 682-0032   *SIC* 5941
SPORTSMAN LIMITED, THE   p67
1442 17 AVE SW, CALGARY, AB, T2T 0C8
(403) 245-4311   *SIC* 5941
STM SPORTS TRADE MALL LTD   p335
508 DISCOVERY ST, VICTORIA, BC, V8T
1G8
(250) 383-6443   *SIC* 5941
SUMMIT SKI LIMITED   p343
4293   MOUNTAIN   SQ   UNIT   118,
WHISTLER, BC, V8E 1B8
(604) 932-6225   *SIC* 5941
**UNITED CYCLE & MOTOR COMPANY
(1975) LIMITED**   p117
7620 GATEWAY BLVD NW, EDMONTON,
AB, T6E 4Z8
(780) 433-1181   *SIC* 5941
VALHALLA PURE OUTFITTERS INC p332
2700 30 AVE, VERNON, BC, V1T 2B6
(250) 542-9800   *SIC* 5941
VERNON D'EON FISHING SUPPLIES LTD
p462
373 ROUTE 335, MIDDLE WEST PUB-
NICO, NS, B0W 2M0
(902) 762-2217   *SIC* 5941

SIC 5942 Book stores

9210-7580 QUEBEC INC   p1282
29 RUE DE LYON, REPENTIGNY, QC, J5Z
4Z3
(450) 585-9909   *SIC* 5942
BLACK BOND BOOKS LTD   p232
32555 LONDON AVE SUITE 344, MISSION,
BC, V2V 6M7
(604) 814-2650   *SIC* 5942
BLACK BOND BOOKS LTD   p280
15562 24 AVE UNIT 1, SURREY, BC, V4A
2J5
(604) 536-4444   *SIC* 5942
BOOKMASTERS LTD   p974
501 BLOOR ST W SUITE 30, TORONTO,
ON, M5S 1Y2
(416) 961-4496   *SIC* 5942
BOOKSHELF OF GUELPH LIMITED p602
41 QUEBEC ST, GUELPH, ON, N1H 2T1
(519) 821-3311   *SIC* 5942
CMIC SUCCESS LTD   p916
4850 KEELE ST, TORONTO, ON, M3J 3K1
(416) 736-0123   *SIC* 5942
**COOPERATIVE DE L'ECOLE DES HAUTES
ETUDES COMMERCIALES**   p1219
5255 AV DECELLES BUREAU 2340, MON-
TREAL, QC, H3T 2B1
(514) 340-6396   *SIC* 5942
COOPSCO SAINTE-FOY   p1272
2410 CH SAINTE-FOY, QUEBEC, QC, G1V
1T3
(418) 659-6600   *SIC* 5942
FOLLETT OF CANADA, INC   p834
381 KENT ST SUITE 327, OTTAWA, ON,
K2P 2A8
(613) 230-6148   *SIC* 5942
INDIGO BOOKS & MUSIC INC   p9
2555 32 ST NE SUITE 500, CALGARY, AB,
T1Y 7J6
(403) 250-9171   *SIC* 5942
INDIGO BOOKS & MUSIC INC   p929
55 BLOOR ST W, TORONTO, ON, M4W
1A5

INDIGO BOOKS & MUSIC INC   p935
220 YONGE ST SUITE 103, TORONTO,
ON, M5B 2H1
(416) 591-3622   *SIC* 5942
INDIGO BOOKS & MUSIC INC   p981
82 PETER ST SUITE 300, TORONTO, ON,
M5V 2G5
(416) 598-8000   *SIC* 5942
INDIGO BOOKS & MUSIC INC   p981
620 KING ST W, TORONTO, ON, M5V 1M6
(416) 364-4499   *SIC* 5942
INDIGO BOOKS & MUSIC INC   p1205
1171 RUE SAINTE-CATHERINE O BU-
REAU 777, MONTREAL, QC, H3B 1K4
SIC 5942
LIBRAIRIE RENAUD-BRAY INC   p1164
5655 AV PIERRE-DE COUBERTIN, MON-
TREAL, QC, H1N 1R2
(514) 272-4049   *SIC* 5942
RAKUTEN KOBO INC   p992
135 LIBERTY ST SUITE 101, TORONTO,
ON, M6K 1A7
(416) 977-8737   *SIC* 5942
**SAUNDERS OFFICE AND SCHOOL SUP-
PLIES LIMITED**   p547
29 STEWART RD, COLLINGWOOD, ON,
L9Y 4M7
(705) 444-1696   *SIC* 5942
SIMON FRASER UNIVERSITY   p300
555 HASTINGS ST W SUITE 17U, VAN-
COUVER, BC, V6B 4N5
(778) 782-5235   *SIC* 5942
SOCIETE BIBLIQUE CANADIEN   p1173
2700 RUE RACHEL E BUREAU 100, MON-
TREAL, QC, H2H 1S7
(514) 524-7873   *SIC* 5942

SIC 5943 Stationery stores

A.J. BUS LINES LIMITED   p568
2 CHARLES WALK, ELLIOT LAKE, ON, P5A
2A3
(705) 848-3013   *SIC* 5943
BEATTIE STATIONERY LIMITED   p886
399 VANSICKLE RD SUITE 3056, ST
CATHARINES, ON, L2S 3T4
(905) 688-4040   *SIC* 5943
CAN ALTA BINDERY CORP   p113
8445 DAVIES RD NW, EDMONTON, AB,
T6E 4N3
(780) 466-9973   *SIC* 5943
CHRISTIE SCHOOL SUPPLY MANITOBA
p346
705 PACIFIC AVE, BRANDON, MB, R7A
0H8
(204) 727-1423   *SIC* 5943
CHRISTIE, B. L. INVESTMENTS INC p908
581 RED RIVER RD, THUNDER BAY, ON,
P7B 1H4
(807) 344-6666   *SIC* 5943
**COOP DE LA POLYVALENTE DE
THETFORD-MINES**   p1382
561 RUE SAINT-PATRICK, THETFORD
MINES, QC, G6G 5W1
(418) 338-7832   *SIC* 5943
GRAND & TOY LIMITED   p192
4560 TILLICUM ST, BURNABY, BC, V5J 5L4
(866) 391-8111   *SIC* 5943
GRAND & TOY LIMITED   p393
15 SCURFIELD BLVD, WINNIPEG, MB,
R3Y 1V4
(204) 284-5100   *SIC* 5943
GRAND & TOY LIMITED   p1031
200 AVIVA PARK DR, WOODBRIDGE, ON,
L4L 9C7
(416) 401-6300   *SIC* 5943
GRAND & TOY LIMITED   p1128
2275 52E AV, LACHINE, QC, H8T 2Y8
(866) 391-8111   *SIC* 5943
LIBRAIRIES BOYER LTEE   p1366
10 RUE NICHOLSON, SALABERRY-DE-
VALLEYFIELD, QC, J6T 4M2

(450) 373-6211   *SIC 5943*
LOWERYS, LIMITED   p908
540 CENTRAL AVE, THUNDER BAY, ON,
P7B 6B4
(807) 344-6666   *SIC 5943*
RGO OFFICE PRODUCTS EDMONTON LTD
p85
11624 120 ST NW, EDMONTON, AB, T5G
2Y2
(780) 413-6600   *SIC 5943*
STAPLES CANADA ULC   p456
2003 GOTTINGEN ST, HALIFAX, NS, B3K
3B1
(902) 474-5100   *SIC 5943*
STAPLES CANADA ULC   p854
6 STAPLES AVE, RICHMOND HILL, ON,
L4B 4W3
(905) 737-1147   *SIC 5943*
WESTKEY GRAPHICS LTD   p181
8315 RIVERBEND CRT, BURNABY, BC,
V3N 5E7
(604) 549-2350   *SIC 5943*
WILSON, ROY V (1984) LTD   p565
32 KING ST, DRYDEN, ON, P8N 1B3
(807) 223-3316   *SIC 5943*

SIC 5944 Jewelry stores

1170760 ONTARIO LTD   p788
1 YORKDALE RD UNIT 402, NORTH YORK,
ON, M6A 3A1
(416) 785-8801   *SIC 5944*
137448 CANADA INC   p1241
734 BOUL CURE-LABELLE, MONTREAL-
OUEST, QC, H7V 2T9
(450) 978-5638   *SIC 5944*
ANN-LOUISE JEWELLERS LTD   p288
18 2ND AVE E, VANCOUVER, BC, V5T 1B1
(604) 873-6341   *SIC 5944*
APPELT'S JEWELLERY LTD   p385
305 MADISON ST UNIT C, WINNIPEG, MB,
R3J 1H9
(204) 774-2829   *SIC 5944*
BEAUMONT STANLEY INC   p322
2125 41ST AVE W, VANCOUVER, BC, V6M
1Z3
(604) 266-9177   *SIC 5944*
**BEN MOSS JEWELLERS WESTERN
CANADA LTD**   p374
201 PORTAGE AVE SUITE 300, WIN-
NIPEG, MB, R3B 3K6
(204) 947-6682   *SIC 5944*
BIJOUTERIE LAVIGUEUR LTEE   p1310
3981 RUE DE MONT-ROYAL BUREAU 100,
SAINT-HUBERT, QC, J4T 2H4
(450) 672-3233   *SIC 5944*
BIJOUTIERS DOUCET 1993 INC, LES p1178
9250 RUE MEILLEUR BUREAU 201, MON-
TREAL, QC, H2N 2A5
(514) 385-4500   *SIC 5944*
BIZOU INTERNATIONAL INC   p1304
8585 BOUL LACROIX, SAINT-GEORGES,
QC, G5Y 5L6
(418) 227-0424   *SIC 5944*
BIZOU INTERNATIONAL INC   p1359
1490 3E AV DU PARC-INDUSTRIEL,
SAINTE-MARIE, QC, G6E 3T9
(418) 387-8481   *SIC 5944*
CHARM JEWELRY LIMITED   p443
140 PORTLAND ST, DARTMOUTH, NS,
B2Y 1J1
(902) 463-7177   *SIC 5944*
DIAMANT ELINOR INC.   p1250
987 BOUL SAINT-JEAN, POINTE-CLAIRE,
QC, H9R 5M3
(450) 688-6288   *SIC 5944*
GRIFFIN JEWELLERY DESIGNS INC p852
50 WEST WILMOT ST SUITE 201, RICH-
MOND HILL, ON, L4B 1M5
(905) 882-0004   *SIC 5944*
GROUPE BIRKS INC   p1196
2020 BOUL ROBERT-BOURASSA BU-
REAU 200, MONTREAL, QC, H3A 2A5

(514) 397-2501   *SIC 5944*
GROUPE JACOBUS INC   p1274
3175 CH DES QUATRE-BOURGEOIS BU-
REAU 35, QUEBEC, QC, G1W 2K7
(418) 658-7373   *SIC 5944*
LUGARO JEWELLERS LTD   p194
3114 BOUNDARY RD, BURNABY, BC, V5M
4A2
(604) 454-1200   *SIC 5944*
MEJURI INC   p991
18 MOWAT AVE UNIT C, TORONTO, ON,
M6K 3E8
(416) 731-2600   *SIC 5944*
**METALSMITHS MASTER ARCHITECTS OF
JEWELRY INC**   p101
17410 107 AVE NW, EDMONTON, AB, T5S
1E9
(780) 454-0736   *SIC 5944*
MICHAEL HILL JEWELLER (CANADA) LTD
p315
1090 PENDER ST W SUITE 530, VANCOU-
VER, BC, V6E 2N7
(604) 913-3114   *SIC 5944*
MONTRES BIG TIME INC   p1226
9250 BOUL DE L'ACADIE BUREAU 340,
MONTREAL, QC, H4N 3C5
(514) 384-6464   *SIC 5944*
NATURE'S COIN GROUP LTD   p4
225A BEAR ST, BANFF, AB, T1L 1B4
(403) 762-3018   *SIC 5944*
PARIS JEWELLERS LTD   p102
18913 111 AVE NW, EDMONTON, AB, T5S
2X4
(780) 930-1418   *SIC 5944*
PUGWASH HOLDINGS LTD   p102
11248 170 ST NW, EDMONTON, AB, T5S
2X1
(780) 484-6342   *SIC 5944*
SPENCE DIAMONDS LTD   p293
550 6TH AVE W SUITE 410, VANCOUVER,
BC, V5Z 1A1
(604) 739-9928   *SIC 5944*
SWAROVSKI CANADA LIMITED   p675
80 GOUGH RD UNIT 2, MARKHAM, ON,
L3R 6E8
(905) 752-0498   *SIC 5944*
TIFFANY & CO. CANADA   p976
150 BLOOR ST W SUITE M108,
TORONTO, ON, M5S 2X9
(416) 921-3900   *SIC 5944*

SIC 5945 Hobby, toy, and game shops

BENJO INC   p1258
520 BOUL CHAREST E BUREAU 233,
QUEBEC, QC, G1K 3J3
(418) 640-0001   *SIC 5945*
BRAIN BUSTER INC   p667
206 TELSON RD, MARKHAM, ON, L3R 1E6
(905) 604-5055   *SIC 5945*
**CALENDAR CLUB OF CANADA LIMITED
PARTNERSHIP**   p836
6 ADAMS ST SUITE A, PARIS, ON, N3L 3X4
(519) 442-8355   *SIC 5945*
GREAT HOBBIES INC   p1042
17 GLEN STEWART DR SUITE 1, STRAT-
FORD, PE, C1B 2A8
(902) 569-3289   *SIC 5945*
MASTERMIND LP   p865
415 MILNER AVE SUITE 4, SCARBOR-
OUGH, ON, M1B 2L1
(416) 321-8984   *SIC 5945*
MICHAELS OF CANADA, ULC   p509
547 STEELES AVE E UNIT 3, BRAMPTON,
ON, L6W 4S2
(905) 874-9640   *SIC 5945*
MRS. TIGGY WINKLE'S LTD   p828
75 BREEZEHILL AVE N, OTTAWA, ON, K1Y
2H6
(613) 523-3663   *SIC 5945*
PLAYIT INCORPORATED   p845
831 BROCK RD UNIT 1, PICKERING, ON,
L1W 3L8

(905) 837-7650   *SIC 5945*
SAM KOTZER LIMITED   p571
77 FIMA CRES, ETOBICOKE, ON, M8W
3R1
(416) 532-1114   *SIC 5945*
TOYS 'R' US (CANADA) LTD   p560
2777 LANGSTAFF RD, CONCORD, ON,
L4K 4M5
(905) 660-2000   *SIC 5945*
TOYS 'R' US (CANADA) LTD   p923
2300 YONGE ST, TORONTO, ON, M4P 1E4
(416) 322-1599   *SIC 5945*
TOYS, TOYS, TOYS INC   p915
1800 SHEPPARD AVE E, TORONTO, ON,
M2J 5A7
(416) 773-1950   *SIC 5945*

---

*SIC 5946 Camera and photographic supply
stores*

**CRANBROOK GLEN ENTERPRISES LIM-
ITED**   p937
119 CHURCH ST, TORONTO, ON, M5C
2G5
(416) 868-0572   *SIC 5946*
**CRANBROOK GLEN ENTERPRISES LIM-
ITED**   p1182
6229 RUE SAINT-HUBERT, MONTREAL,
QC, H2S 2L9
(514) 274-6577   *SIC 5946*
DON'S PHOTO SHOP LTD   p370
1839 MAIN ST, WINNIPEG, MB, R2V 2A4
(204) 942-7887   *SIC 5946*
KERRISDALE CAMERAS LTD   p322
2170 41ST AVE W, VANCOUVER, BC, V6M
1Z5
(604) 263-3221   *SIC 5946*
LENS & SHUTTER CAMERAS LTD   p322
2902 BROADWAY W SUITE 201, VANCOU-
VER, BC, V6K 2G8
SIC 5946
MCBAIN CAMERA LTD   p86
10805 107 AVE NW, EDMONTON, AB, T5H
0W9
(780) 420-0404   *SIC 5946*
SANEAL CAMERA SUPPLIES LTD   p73
1402 11 AVE SW, CALGARY, AB, T3C 0M8
(403) 228-1865   *SIC 5946*
VISTEK LTD   p934
496 QUEEN ST E, TORONTO, ON, M5A
4G8
(416) 365-1777   *SIC 5946*
VISTEK WEST CALGARY INC   p86
10569 109 ST NW, EDMONTON, AB, T5H
3B1
(780) 484-0333   *SIC 5946*

SIC 5947 Gift, novelty, and souvenir shop

2982651 MANITOBA LIMITED   p359
333 MAIN ST SUITE 17, STONEWALL, MB,
R0C 2Z0
(204) 467-8113   *SIC 5947*
647802 ONTARIO LIMITED   p757
4199 RIVER RD, NIAGARA FALLS, ON, L2E
3E7
(905) 357-1133   *SIC 5947*
8603600 CANADA INC   p751
27 NORTHSIDE RD UNIT 2710, NEPEAN,
ON, K2H 8S1
(613) 265-4095   *SIC 5947*
9297-6232 QUEBEC INC   p1338
361 RUE LOCKE, SAINT-LAURENT, QC,
H4T 1X7
(514) 389-5757   *SIC 5947*
ABBEY CARDS & GIFTS LIMITED, THE
p762
126 MAIN ST W, NORTH BAY, ON, P1B 2T5
(705) 472-2760   *SIC 5947*
AZ TRADING CO. LTD   p259
7080 RIVER RD SUITE 223, RICHMOND,
BC, V6X 1X5

(604) 214-3600   *SIC 5947*
BEAUDEV GESTIONS INC   p1063
102 CH DU TREMBLAY, BOUCHERVILLE,
QC, J4B 6Z6
SIC 5947
COASTAL CULTURE INC   p1038
156 QUEEN ST, CHARLOTTETOWN, PE,
C1A 4B5
(902) 894-3146   *SIC 5947*
COUTTS, WILLIAM E. COMPANY, LIMITED
p480
100 VANDORF SIDEROAD, AURORA, ON,
L4G 3G9
SIC 5947
DAVIS AGENCY OF OTTAWA LIMITED p751
3161 GREENBANK RD UNIT A7, NEPEAN,
ON, K2J 4H9
(613) 825-0755   *SIC 5947*
**ETOBICOKE HOSPITAL VOLUNTEER AS-
SOCIATION GIFT SHOP**   p580
101 HUMBER COLLEGE BLVD, ETOBI-
COKE, ON, M9V 1R8
(416) 747-3400   *SIC 5947*
**FORTRESS OF LOUISBOURG ASSOCIA-
TION**   p450
259 PARK SERVICE RD, FORTRESS OF
LOUISBOURG, NS, B1C 2L2
(902) 733-2280   *SIC 5947*
**HACHETTE DISTRIBUTION SERVICES
(CANADA) INC**   p981
370 KING ST W SUITE 600, TORONTO,
ON, M5V 1J9
(416) 863-6400   *SIC 5947*
HUDSON GROUP CANADA, INC   p450
1 BELL BLVD SUITE 1621, ENFIELD, NS,
B2T 1K2
(902) 873-3282   *SIC 5947*
INTERNATIONAL CIGAR STORES LIMITED
p1000
170 MAIN ST, UNIONVILLE, ON, L3R 2G9
(905) 940-1515   *SIC 5947*
LS TRAVEL RETAIL NORTH AMERICA INC
p981
370 KING ST W SUITE 703, TORONTO,
ON, M5V 1J9
(416) 863-6400   *SIC 5947*
MARIPOSA MARKET LTD   p809
109 MISSISSAGA ST E, ORILLIA, ON, L3V
1V6
(705) 325-8885   *SIC 5947*
NIAGARA PARKS COMMISSION, THE p759
7400 PORTAGE RD, NIAGARA FALLS, ON,
L2G 0E5
(905) 356-2241   *SIC 5947*
NICKEL CENTRE PHARMACY INC   p1001
3140 OLD HWY 69 N SUITE 17, VAL
CARON, ON, P3N 1G3
(705) 897-1867   *SIC 5947*
PANIER & CADEAU INC, LE   p1253
274 CH DU BORD-DU-LAC LAKESHORE,
POINTE-CLAIRE, QC, H9S 4K9
(514) 695-7038   *SIC 5947*
PARTY CITY CANADA INC   p784
1225 FINCH AVE W, NORTH YORK, ON,
M3J 2E8
(416) 631-8455   *SIC 5947*
QUESNEL CRAFTERS SOCIETY   p252
102 CARSON AVE, QUESNEL, BC, V2J
2A8
(250) 991-0419   *SIC 5947*
SFP CANADA LTD   p1131
7077 BOUL NEWMAN BUREAU 15,
LASALLE, QC, H8N 1X1
(514) 366-7660   *SIC 5947*
ST JOSEPH'S HEALTH CENTRE AUXILARY
p655
268 GROSVENOR ST, LONDON, ON, N6A
4L6
(519) 646-6000   *SIC 5947*
TC BIZZ.COM CORP   p932
449 CHURCH ST, TORONTO, ON, M4Y 2C5
(416) 323-0772   *SIC 5947*
TELFORD INVESTMENTS LTD   p103
17551 108 AVE NW, EDMONTON, AB, T5S

1G2

(780) 489-9562   *SIC 5947*

THINGS ENGRAVED INC   p642
61 MCBRINE PL, KITCHENER, ON, N2R 1H5

(519) 748-2211   *SIC 5947*

TORONTO EAST GENERAL GIFT SHOP p917
825 COXWELL AVE, TORONTO, ON, M4C 3E7

(416) 469-6050   *SIC 5947*

TRILLIUM HEALTH PARTNERS VOLUNTEERS   p711
100 QUEENSWAY W, MISSISSAUGA, ON, L5B 1B8

(905) 848-7276   *SIC 5947*

WRAP-IT-UP INC   p918
660 EGLINTON AVE E, TORONTO, ON, M4G 2K2

SIC 5947

SIC 5948 Luggage and leather goods stores

BOUTIQUE OF LEATHERS LTD, THE   p70
12012 44 ST SE, CALGARY, AB, T2Z 4A2

(403) 259-2726   *SIC 5948*

CANADIAN FUR SHOP OF SAITOH LIMITED   p960
65 HARBOUR SQ SUITE 1204, TORONTO, ON, M5J 2L4

(416) 364-5885   *SIC 5948*

CUIRS BENTLEY INC   p1338
6125 CH DE LA COTE-DE-LIESSE, SAINT-LAURENT, QC, H4T 1C8

(514) 341-9333   *SIC 5948*

KUNY'S LEATHER MANUFACTURING COMPANY LTD   p139
5901 44A ST, LEDUC, AB, T9E 7B8

(780) 986-1151   *SIC 5948*

LEVY'S LEATHERS LIMITED   p375
190 DISRAELI FWY, WINNIPEG, MB, R3B 2Z4

(204) 957-5139   *SIC 5948*

SAXON LEATHER LTD   p373
310 ROSS AVE, WINNIPEG, MB, R3A 0L4

(204) 956-4011   *SIC 5948*

SIC 5949 Sewing, needlework, and piece goods

ATLANTIC FABRICS LIMITED   p443
114 WOODLAWN RD, DARTMOUTH, NS, B2W 2S7

(902) 434-1440   *SIC 5949*

C & M TEXTILES INC   p1181
7500 RUE SAINT-HUBERT, MONTREAL, QC, H2R 2N6

(514) 272-0247   *SIC 5949*

DISTRIBUTION CLUB TISSUS (1994) INC p1308
1651 BOUL DES PROMENADES BUREAU 676, SAINT-HUBERT, QC, J3Y 5K2

(450) 462-1717   *SIC 5949*

FABRICLAND DISTRIBUTORS (WESTERN) CORP   p992
1450 CASTLEFIELD AVE, TORONTO, ON, M6M 1Y6

(416) 658-2200   *SIC 5949*

FABRICLAND DISTRIBUTORS INC   p992
1450 CASTLEFIELD AVE, TORONTO, ON, M6M 1Y6

(416) 658-2200   *SIC 5949*

FABRICLAND PACIFIC LIMITED   p11
495 36 ST NE SUITE 104, CALGARY, AB, T2A 6K3

(855) 554-4840   *SIC 5949*

FABRICLAND PACIFIC LIMITED   p217
2121 TRANS CANADA HWY E, KAMLOOPS, BC, V2C 4A6

(250) 374-3360   *SIC 5949*

FABRICVILLE CO. INC   p1225
9195 RUE CHARLES-DE LA TOUR, MON-

TREAL, QC, H4N 1M3

(514) 383-3942   *SIC 5949*

GEO. SHEARD FABRICS LTD   p1082
84 RUE MERRILL, COATICOOK, QC, J1A 1X4

(819) 849-6311   *SIC 5949*

NORFOLK KNITTERS LIMITED   p537
50 GROH AVE, CAMBRIDGE, ON, N3C 1Y9

(519) 743-4672   *SIC 5949*

SIC 5961 Catalog and mail-order houses

2144205 ONTARIO INC   p703
3415 DIXIE RD SUITE 113, MISSISSAUGA, ON, L4Y 2B1

(905) 670-7677   *SIC 5961*

3619842 CANADA INC   p1192
666 RUE SHERBROOKE O STE 801, MONTREAL, QC, H3A 1E7

SIC 5961

5177007 MANITOBA LTD   p364
24 TERRACON PL SUITE 467, WINNIPEG, MB, R2J 4G7

(204) 654-5194   *SIC 5961*

9208-3179 QUEBEC INC   p1240
10240 AV ARMAND-LAVERGNE, MONTREAL-NORD, QC, H1H 3N4

(514) 664-4646   *SIC 5961*

9267-8010 QUEBEC INC   p1108
338 RUE SAINT-JACQUES, GRANBY, QC, J2G 3N2

(450) 372-4447   *SIC 5961*

ATELIER KOLLONTAI INC   p1174
2065 RUE PARTHENAIS BUREAU 389, MONTREAL, QC, H2K 3T1

(514) 223-4899   *SIC 5961*

B.O.B. HEADQUARTERS INC   p346
658 18TH ST UNIT 2, BRANDON, MB, R7A 5B4

(204) 728-7470   *SIC 5961*

BARNETT, WINNIFRED MARY KAY CONSULTANT   p658
185 HUNT CLUB DR, LONDON, ON, N6H 3Y8

(519) 471-7227   *SIC 5961*

BAYSHORE SPECIALTY RX LTD   p667
233 ALDEN RD, MARKHAM, ON, L3R 3W6

(905) 474-0822   *SIC 5961*

BOUTIQUES SAN FRANCISCO   p1385
4125 BOUL DES FORGES, TROIS-RIVIERES, QC, G8Y 1W1

(819) 375-8727   *SIC 5961*

BUYATAB ONLINE INC   ,p297
B1 788 BEATTY ST, VANCOUVER, BC, V6B 2M1

(604) 678-3275   *SIC 5961*

CHANNEL GATE TECHNOLOGIES INC p185
4170 STILL CREEK DR SUITE 310, BURNABY, BC, V5C 6C6

(604) 683-0313   *SIC 5961*

DISTRIBUTIONS MONTREX INC, LES p1157
5934 CH DE LA COTE-DE-LIESSE, MONTROYAL, QC, H4T 2A5

(514) 737-8929   *SIC 5961*

FLICKA GYM CLUB   p239
123 23RD ST E, NORTH VANCOUVER, BC, V7L 3E2

(604) 985-7918   *SIC 5961*

FOREST CITY SURPLUS (1986) LIMITED p650
1712 DUNDAS ST, LONDON, ON, N5W 3C9

(519) 451-0246   *SIC 5961*

GAMBO DRUGS LIMITED   p424
GD, HILLVIEW, NL, A0E 2A0

(709) 546-2460   *SIC 5961*

INTERNATIONAL DIRECT RESPONSE SERVICES LTD   p209
10159 NORDEL CRT, DELTA, BC, V4G 1J8

(604) 951-6855   *SIC 5961*

ISODIOL INTERNATIONAL INC   p306
200 GRANVILLE ST SUITE 2710, VANCOUVER, BC, V6C 1S4

(604) 409-4409   *SIC 5961*

KABUNI TECHNOLOGIES INC   p299
375 WATER ST SUITE 200, VANCOUVER, BC, V6B 0M9

(778) 686-2243   *SIC 5961*

MILOMA INVESTMENTS LTD   p556
3280 STEELES AVE W UNIT 18, CONCORD, ON, L4K 2Y2

(905) 738-4545   *SIC 5961*

MISS MARY MAXIM LTD   p837
75 SCOTT AVE, PARIS, ON, N3L 3G5

(519) 442-2266   *SIC 5961*

NATIONAL PHILATELIC CENTRE   p438
75 ST NINIAN ST, ANTIGONISH, NS, B2G 2R8

(902) 863-6550   *SIC 5961*

PEACOCK PARADE INC, THE   p991
828 RICHMOND ST W, TORONTO, ON, M6J 1C9

SIC 5961

PHARMAPLUS #4950   p356
366 MAIN ST, SELKIRK, MB, R1A 2J7

(204) 482-6003   *SIC 5961*

PHARMAPRIX   p1066
100 BOUL DE MONTARVILLE UNITE 120, BOUCHERVILLE, QC, J4B 5M4

(450) 655-3010   *SIC 5961*

PLANET DRUGS DIRECT INC   p277
7455 132 ST SUITE 100, SURREY, BC, V3W 1J8

(604) 501-6902   *SIC 5961*

RADIOWORLD CENTRAL INC   p31
711 48 AVE SE UNIT 8, CALGARY, AB, T2G 4X2

(587) 317-2000   *SIC 5961*

REGAL GIFTS CORPORATION   p488
360 SAUNDERS RD, BARRIE, ON, L4N 9Y2

(800) 565-3130   *SIC 5961*

RIZWAN CHAMPSI PHARMACY INC   p923
2345 YONGE ST, TORONTO, ON, M4P 2E5

(416) 487-5411   *SIC 5961*

SATRANG DESIGNER WEAR INC   p126
2956 ELLWOOD DR SW, EDMONTON, AB, T6X 0A9

(780) 245-0043   *SIC 5961*

SCOTT'S PARABLE CHRISTIAN STORES INC   p1430
810 CIRCLE DR E SUITE 106B, SASKATOON, SK, S7K 3T8

(306) 244-3700   *SIC 5961*

SPECTRUM EDUCATIONAL SUPPLIES LIMITED   p756
150 PONY DR, NEWMARKET, ON, L3Y 7B6

(905) 898-0031   *SIC 5961*

STOCKADE INVESTMENTS LTD   p606
785 IMPERIAL RD N, GUELPH, ON, N1K 1X4

(519) 763-1050   *SIC 5961*

SUBIR BAINS PHARMACY LTD   p684
265 MAIN ST E UNIT 104, MILTON, ON, L9T 1P1

(905) 878-4492   *SIC 5961*

TEXTBOOKRENTAL CA, INC   p916
34 ASHWARRREN RD, TORONTO, ON, M3J 1Z7

SIC 5961

UNIVERSAL DRUG STORE LTD   p367
1329 NIAKWA RD E UNIT 9, WINNIPEG, MB, R2J 3T4

(204) 255-9911   *SIC 5961*

WILLIAM DAM SEEDS LIMITED   p566
279 HWY 8, DUNDAS, ON, L9H 5E1

(905) 628-6641   *SIC 5961*

WORLD WIDE ENTERPRISES LIMITED p325
10991 SHELLBRIDGE WAY STE 490, VANCOUVER, BC, V6X 3C6

SIC 5961

SIC 5962 Merchandising machine operators

128388 CANADA INC   p1140
1100 RUE HERELLE BUREAU 4, LONGUEUIL, QC, J4G 2M8

(450) 646-3949   *SIC 5962*

A.R.P. AUTO-AUXILIARIES INC   p1125
2300 RUE VICTORIA, LACHINE, QC, H8S 1Z3

(514) 634-7000   *SIC 5962*

ATS AUTOMATION   p968
100 WELLINGTON ST W, TORONTO, ON, M5K 1J3

(416) 601-1555   *SIC 5962*

AUTOMATED SOLUTIONS INTERNATIONAL INC   p537
25 MILLING RD SUITE 204, CAMBRIDGE, ON, N3C 1C3

(519) 220-0071   *SIC 5962*

AUTOMATES VEN INC   p1098
2375 RUE POWER, DRUMMONDVILLE, QC, J2C 6Z5

(819) 477-1133   *SIC 5962*

BROKERHOUSE DISTRIBUTORS INC p582
108 WOODBINE DOWNS BLVD UNIT 4, ETOBICOKE, ON, M9W 5S6

(416) 798-3537   *SIC 5962*

BUNNY'S FOOD SERVICE LIMITED   p563
1540 HIGHWAY 2, COURTICE, ON, L1E 2R6

(905) 434-2444   *SIC 5962*

CANADIAN AUTOMATED MANAGEMENT SYSTEMS LTD   p188
3707 WAYBURNE DR, BURNABY, BC, V5G 3L1

(604) 430-5677   *SIC 5962*

CANADIAN AUTOMATION & TOOL INTERNATIONAL INC   p738
6811 EDWARDS BLVD, MISSISSAUGA, ON, L5T 2S2

(905) 795-1232   *SIC 5962*

CITY COIN VENDING SERVICES LTD   p68
9212 HORTON RD SW UNIT J, CALGARY, AB, T2V 2X4

(403) 253-0324   *SIC 5962*

DISTRIBUTION LE PERCO INC   p1314
16535 AV PETIT, SAINT-HYACINTHE, QC, J2T 3J5

(450) 773-7146   *SIC 5962*

EDMONTON COIN VENDING (1970) LTD p95
11690 147 ST NW, EDMONTON, AB, T5M 1W2

(780) 452-2727   *SIC 5962*

J. C. VENDING (ONTARIO) LIMITED   p636
625 WABANAKI DR UNIT 6, KITCHENER, ON, N2C 2G3

SIC 5962

OMEX MANUFACTURING ULC   p896
251 LORNE AVE W, STRATFORD, ON, N5A 6S4

(519) 273-5760   *SIC 5962*

PANOPTIC AUTOMATION SOLUTIONS INC p71
3320 114 AVE SE, CALGARY, AB, T2Z 3V6

(587) 315-1450   *SIC 5962*

PRO AUTOMATION INC   p1293
243 RUE DE BORDEAUX, SAINT AUGUSTIN-DE-DESMAURES, QC, G3A 2M8

(418) 878-4500   *SIC 5962*

QUALITY VENDING & COFFEE SERVICES LTD   p372
91 PLYMOUTH ST, WINNIPEG, MB, R2X 2V5

(204) 633-2405   *SIC 5962*

RYAN COMPANY LIMITED   p338
723A VANALMAN AVE, VICTORIA, BC, V8Z 3B6

(250) 388-4254   *SIC 5962*

SELKIRK BEVERAGES LTD   p204
604 INDUSTRIAL ROAD C, CRANBROOK, BC, V1C 4Y8

(250) 426-2731   *SIC 5962*

T.A.C. CONTROLS & AUTOMATION INC p559
259 EDGELEY BLVD UNIT 5, CONCORD, ON, L4K 3Y5

(905) 660-0878   *SIC 5962*

TRAITEURS J. D. INC, LES   p1110

▲ Public Company   ■ Public Company Family Member   **HQ** Headquarters   **BR** Branch   **SL** Single Location

635 RUE COWIE, GRANBY, QC, J2G 8J2
SIC 5962

SIC 5963 Direct selling establishments

1748271 ONTARIO INC *p880*
36 MAPLEHYRN AVE, SHARON, ON, L0G 1V0
(519) 457-2863   *SIC* 5963

753146 ALBERTA LTD *p118*
10755 69 AVE NW, EDMONTON, AB, T6H 2C9
(780) 432-6535   *SIC* 5963

7643454 CANADA INC *p1108*
35 RUE DUFFERIN BUREAU 204, GRANBY, QC, J2G 4W5
(450) 776-3930   *SIC* 5963

888930 ONTARIO INC *p691*
1290 FEWSTER DR, MISSISSAUGA, ON, L4W 1A4
(905) 625-4447   *SIC* 5963

9248-9202 QUEBEC INC *p1337*
235 RUE NESS, SAINT-LAURENT, QC, H4T 1S1
(514) 508-2529   *SIC* 5963

ADVANTAGE DATASYSTEMS CORPORATION *p181*
8061 LOUGHEED HWY SUITE 110, BURNABY, BC, V5A 1W9
(604) 415-3950   *SIC* 5963

ALIMENTS MARTEL INC *p1103*
212 BOUL DE L'AEROPORT, GATINEAU, QC, J8R 3X3
(819) 663-0835   *SIC* 5963

AQUATERRA CORPORATION *p257*
6560 MCMILLAN WAY, RICHMOND, BC, V6W 1L2
(604) 232-7610   *SIC* 5963

AWNBCO FOODS LTD *p1412*
2142 100TH ST, NORTH BATTLEFORD, SK, S9A 0X6
(306) 445-9453   *SIC* 5963

BERMAN FALK INC *p224*
9499 198 ST, LANGLEY, BC, V1M 3B8
(604) 882-8903   *SIC* 5963

CAISSEN WATER TECHNOLOGIES INC *p538*
265 INDUSTRIAL RD, CAMBRIDGE, ON, N3H 4R7
(800) 265-7841   *SIC* 5963

CANKOSH INC *p667*
7030 WOODBINE AVE SUITE 500, MARKHAM, ON, L3R 6G2
(905) 943-7990   *SIC* 5963

CANTINE LUCIE INC *p1311*
5825 AV DESJARDINS, SAINT-HYACINTHE, QC, J2S 1A4
(450) 774-8585   *SIC* 5963

COM-TEL MARKETING INC *p550*
163 BUTTERMILL AVE SUITE 1, CONCORD, ON, L4K 3X8
(905) 738-1494   *SIC* 5963

COMMUNITY SUPPORT CONNECTIONS-MEALS ON WHEELS AND MORE *p1008*
420 WEBER ST N UNIT L, WATERLOO, ON, N2L 4E7
(519) 772-8787   *SIC* 5963

COMPAGNIE DE TELEPHONE BELL DU CANADA OU BELL CANADA, LA *p286*
2980 VIRTUAL WAY, VANCOUVER, BC, V5M 4X3
SIC 5963

COMPASS GROUP CANADA LTD *p445*
10 MORRIS DR SUITE 35, DARTMOUTH, NS, B3B 1K8
(902) 466-0150   *SIC* 5963

CULLIGAN WEST TORONTO *p502*
8985 AIRPORT RD, BRAMPTON, ON, L6T 5T2
(416) 798-7670   *SIC* 5963

DEWPOINT BOTTLING COMPANY LTD *p372*
326 KEEWATIN ST, WINNIPEG, MB, R2X 2R9

(204) 774-7770   *SIC* 5963
EVERYDAY STYLE LTD *p1018*
7675 TRANBY AVE, WINDSOR, ON, N8S 2B7
(519) 258-7905   *SIC* 5963

GRANDE EPOQUE INC, LA *p1191*
1099 RUE CLARK BUREAU 3, MONTREAL, QC, H2Z 1K3
(514) 954-0756   *SIC* 5963

ICT GROUP *p839*
360 GEORGE ST N SUITE 100, PETERBOROUGH, ON, K9H 7E7
SIC 5963

INSTORE FOCUS INC *p841*
485 THE PARKWAY, PETERBOROUGH, ON, K9J 0B3
SIC 5963

J A T INVESTMENTS INC *p413*
535 WESTMORLAND RD SUITE 3, SAINT JOHN, NB, E2J 3T3
(506) 649-2002   *SIC* 5963

K F C *p463*
674 EAST RIVER RD, NEW GLASGOW, NS, B2H 3S1
(902) 752-8184   *SIC* 5963

KOOTENAY MADE NATURAL PRODUCTS *p235*
377 BAKER ST, NELSON, BC, V1L 4H6
(250) 352-2333   *SIC* 5963

LHS ENTERPRISES *p858*
2916 COUNTY RD 31, RUSCOM STATION, ON, N0R 1R0
SIC 5963

LXRANDCO INC *p1181*
40 JEAN-TALON ST W 17TH FL SUITE 34, MONTREAL, QC, H2R 2W5
(514) 623-2052   *SIC* 5963

MAPLE RIDGE PITT MEADOWS NEWS *p231*
22328 119 AVE, MAPLE RIDGE, BC, V2X 2Z3
(604) 467-1122   *SIC* 5963

METROLAND MEDIA GROUP LTD *p481*
250 INDUSTRIAL PKY N, AURORA, ON, L4G 4C3
SIC 5963

MOE'S CLASSIC RUGS & HOME ACCESSORIES LTD *p295*
1728 GLEN DR, VANCOUVER, BC, V6A 4L5
(604) 688-0633   *SIC* 5963

NORTHERN RESPONSE (INTERNATIONAL) LTD *p853*
50 STAPLES AVE, RICHMOND HILL, ON, L4B 0A7
(866) 584-1694   *SIC* 5963

OXFORD MILKWAY TRANSPORT CO-OPERATIVE *p1036*
103 LONGWORTH LANE, WOODSTOCK, ON, N4V 1G6
(519) 539-2302   *SIC* 5963

PARNALL MAILING CORP *p649*
555 ADMIRAL DR SUITE 6, LONDON, ON, N5V 4L6
(519) 452-3000   *SIC* 5963

REID'S FURNITURE OF BARRIE LIMITED *p488*
491 BRYNE DR, BARRIE, ON, L4N 9P7
(705) 735-3337   *SIC* 5963

ROSENEATH DIRECT OPERATING CORPORATION *p854*
91 GRANTON DR, RICHMOND HILL, ON, L4B 2N5
SIC 5963

SECOND NATURE BATH AND BODY PRODUCTS INC *p530*
385 SMITH AVE, BURLINGTON, ON, L7R 2T9
SIC 5963

SERENDIPITY CLOTHING CO *p223*
2903 PANDOSY ST SUITE 102, KELOWNA, BC, V1Y 1W1
(250) 861-4166   *SIC* 5963

TIM HORTONS *p508*
15 BOVAIRD DR E, BRAMPTON, ON, L6V

0A2
(905) 456-0263   *SIC* 5963
TRENTWAY-WAGAR INC *p492*
75 BRIDGE ST E, BELLEVILLE, ON, K8N 1L9
(613) 962-2163   *SIC* 5963

TWIN CITY REFRESHMENTS LIMITED *p909*
637 SQUIER ST, THUNDER BAY, ON, P7B 4A7
(807) 344-8651   *SIC* 5963

WINSUN DISTRIBUTING *p389*
2025 CORYDON AVE SUITE 267, WINNIPEG, MB, R3P 0N5
(204) 888-1873   *SIC* 5963

SIC 5983 Fuel oil dealers

120033 CANADA INC *p1103*
581 BOUL SAINT-REN? E, GATINEAU, QC, J8P 8A6
(819) 663-5868   *SIC* 5983

941-2401 HEATING LTD *p808*
400 RICHARDSON RD, ORANGEVILLE, ON, L9W 4W8
(519) 941-2401   *SIC* 5983

ALPHA OIL INC *p792*
490 GARYRAY DR, NORTH YORK, ON, M9L 1P8
(416) 745-6131   *SIC* 5983

B & A PETROLEUM LTD *p1436*
2004 SOUTH SERVICE RD W, SWIFT CURRENT, SK, S9H 5J5
(306) 773-8890   *SIC* 5983

BRADSHAW BROS. PETROLEUM LTD. *p1006*
308 MAIN ST S, WATERFORD, ON, N0E 1Y0
(519) 443-8611   *SIC* 5983

BRITISH EMPIRE FUELS INC *p494*
41 COUNTRY RD SUITE 36, BOBCAYGEON, ON, K0M 1A0
(705) 738-2121   *SIC* 5983

CANADIAN ULTRAMAR COMPANY *p429*
39 PIPPY PL, ST. JOHN'S, NL, A1B 3X2
(709) 754-1880   *SIC* 5983

CHALMERS FUELS INC *p836*
6630 HWY 23, PALMERSTON, ON, N0G 2P0
(519) 343-3023   *SIC* 5983

COMMANDER HOLDINGS INC *p1038*
3 MOUNT EDWARD RD, CHARLOTTETOWN, PE, C1A 5R7
(902) 566-2295   *SIC* 5983

COOL CREEK ENERGY LTD *p218*
455 DENE DR, KAMLOOPS, BC, V2H 1J1
(250) 374-0614   *SIC* 5983

CORNWALL IRVING 24 & MAINWAY CENTRE *p563*
3250 BROOKDALE AVE, CORNWALL, ON, K6K 1W3
(613) 933-5668   *SIC* 5983

COUGAR FUELS LTD *p6*
5602 54 AVE, BONNYVILLE, AB, T9N 2N3
(780) 826-3043   *SIC* 5983

DUFRESNE, FERNAND INC *p1261*
455 RUE DES ENTREPRENEURS BUREAU 513, QUEBEC, QC, G1M 2V2
(418) 688-1820   *SIC* 5983

DUFRESNE, MARC (1978) INC *p1386*
5345 RUE SAINT-JOSEPH, TROIS-RIVIERES, QC, G8Z 4M5
(819) 374-1433   *SIC* 5983

ELIE, JOSEPH LTEE *p1052*
7400 BOUL DES GALERIES D'ANJOU UNITE 300, ANJOU, QC, H1M 3M2
(514) 493-2930   *SIC* 5983

ENERGIE VALERO INC *p1195*
2200 AV MCGILL COLLEGE UNITE 400, MONTREAL, QC, H3A 3P8
(514) 493-5201   *SIC* 5983

FRANCIS FUELS LTD *p749*
28 CONCOURSE GATE SUITE 105, NEPEAN, ON, K2E 7T7

(613) 723-4567   *SIC* 5983
GUINDON GLENOCO LIMITED *p563*
1310 PITT ST, CORNWALL, ON, K6J 3T6
(613) 933-5120   *SIC* 5983

HARVEY'S OIL LIMITED *p431*
87 WATER ST, ST. JOHN'S, NL, A1C 1A5
(709) 726-1680   *SIC* 5983

HOGG FUEL & SUPPLY LIMITED *p639*
5 HILL ST, KITCHENER, ON, N2H 5T4
(519) 579-5330   *SIC* 5983

HUILES NORCO LTEE, LES *p1125*
230 RUE NORMAN, LACHINE, QC, H8R 1A1
(514) 486-9000   *SIC* 5983

HUILES THUOT ET BEAUCHEMIN INC, LES *p1318*
775 RUE GAUDETTE, SAINT-JEAN-SUR-RICHELIEU, QC, J3B 7S7
(450) 359-4440   *SIC* 5983

KENMAC ENERGY INC *p1039*
3 MOUNT EDWARD RD, CHARLOTTETOWN, PE, C1A 5R7
(902) 566-2295   *SIC* 5983

KINGSTON FUELS LTD *p405*
249 DUKE ST, MIRAMICHI, NB, E1N 1J5
(506) 773-6426   *SIC* 5983

MAURICE'S SERVICE CENTRE LIMITED *p428*
4 BARN RD, ST. ANTHONY, NL, A0K 4S0
(709) 454-3434   *SIC* 5983

MCDOUGALL ENERGY INC *p863*
900 MCNABB ST, SAULT STE. MARIE, ON, P6B 6J1
(705) 949-6202   *SIC* 5983

MICHAUD PETROLEUM INC *p403*
866 BOUL EVERARD H DAIGLE, GRAND-SAULT/GRAND FALLS, NB, E3Z 3C8
(506) 473-1197   *SIC* 5983

PAUL GRAND'MAISON INC *p1321*
200 BOUL LACHAPELLE, SAINT-JEROME, QC, J7Z 7L2
(450) 438-1266   *SIC* 5983

PETROLE PAGE INC *p1253*
2899 BOUL DU CURE-LABELLE BUREAU 100, PREVOST, QC, J0R 1T0
(450) 224-1795   *SIC* 5983

PETROLES SHERBROOKE INC, LES *p1372*
125 RUE DES QUATRE-PINS, SHERBROOKE, QC, J1J 2L5
(819) 565-1770   *SIC* 5983

SANDS BULK SALES LTD *p251*
1059 EASTERN ST, PRINCE GEORGE, BC, V2N 5R8
(250) 563-2855   *SIC* 5983

SCOTIA FUELS LIMITED *p456*
6380 LADY HAMMOND RD, HALIFAX, NS, B3K 2S3
(902) 453-2121   *SIC* 5983

SYDCO FUELS LIMITED *p467*
452 GEORGE ST, SYDNEY, NS, B1P 1K3
(902) 539-6444   *SIC* 5983

WOODWARD'S OIL LIMITED *p424*
16 LORING DR, HAPPY VALLEY-GOOSE BAY, NL, A0P 1C0
(709) 896-2421   *SIC* 5983

SIC 5984 Liquefied petroleum gas dealers

1649313 ONTARIO INC *p888*
5552 RUE ST CATHARINE, ST ISIDORE, ON, K0C 2B0
(613) 524-2079   *SIC* 5984

9049-1135 QUEBEC INC *p1360*
1325 BOUL SAINT-JEAN-BAPTISTE O, SAINTE-MARTINE, QC, J0S 1V0
(450) 427-1706   *SIC* 5984

AUTOGAS PROPANE LTD *p191*
5605 BYRNE RD, BURNABY, BC, V5J 3J1
(604) 433-4900   *SIC* 5984

BELL-GAZ LTEE *p1303*
5300 CH DE SAINT-GABRIEL, SAINT-FELIX-DE-VALOIS, QC, J0K 2M0
(450) 889-5944   *SIC* 5984

CALEDON PROPANE INC *p494*
1 BETOMAT CRT, BOLTON, ON, L7E 2V9
(905) 857-1448 *SIC 5984*

EDPRO ENERGY GROUP INC *p649*
5 CUDDY BLVD, LONDON, ON, N5V 3Y3
(519) 690-0000 *SIC 5984*

ENERGIE P38 INC *p1366*
683 CH LAROCQUE, SALABERRY-DE-VALLEYFIELD, QC, J6T 4E1
(450) 373-4333 *SIC 5984*

GAZ PROPANE RAINVILLE INC *p1109*
280 RUE SAINT-CHARLES S, GRANBY, QC, J2G 7A9
(450) 378-4108 *SIC 5984*

LO-COST PROPANE LTD *p141*
3191 5 AVE N, LETHBRIDGE, AB, T1H 0P2
(403) 380-3536 *SIC 5984*

MUTUAL PROPANE LIMITED *p96*
16203 114 AVE NW, EDMONTON, AB, T5M 2Z3
(780) 451-4454 *SIC 5984*

MUTUAL TANKS LTD *p96*
16203 114 AVE NW, EDMONTON, AB, T5M 2Z3
(780) 451-4454 *SIC 5984*

PRIMEMAX ENERGY INC *p483*
2558 CEDAR CREEK RD SUITE 1, AYR, ON, N0B 1E0
(519) 740-8209 *SIC 5984*

PROPANE NORD-OUEST INC *p1391*
2701 BOUL JEAN-JACQUES-COSSETTE, VAL-D'OR, QC, J9P 6Y3
(819) 824-6778 *SIC 5984*

SAVE-X-LP GAS LTD *p141*
3195 5 AVE N, LETHBRIDGE, AB, T1H 0P2
(403) 380-3536 *SIC 5984*

SIMCOE ENERGY & TECHNICAL SERVICES INC *p497*
285 DISSETTE ST, BRADFORD, ON, L3Z 3G9
(905) 778-8105 *SIC 5984*

SPARLING'S PROPANE CO. LIMITED *p493*
82948 LONDON RD, BLYTH, ON, N0M 1H0
(519) 523-4256 *SIC 5984*

STERLING O&G INTERNATIONAL CORPORATION *p389*
99 ROYAL CREST DR, WINNIPEG, MB, R3P 2R1
(204) 952-1505 *SIC 5984*

STITTCO ENERGY LIMITED *p67*
255 17 AVE SW UNIT 303, CALGARY, AB, T2S 2T8
(403) 228-5815 *SIC 5984*

SUPER-SAVE ENTERPRISES LTD *p273*
19395 LANGLEY BYPASS, SURREY, BC, V3S 6K1
(604) 533-4423 *SIC 5984*

SUPERIEUR PROPANE *p1155*
252 AV DU MOULIN, MONT-LAURIER, QC, J9L 3W1
SIC 5984

SUPERIOR PLUS LP *p604*
7022 WELLINGTON RD, GUELPH, ON, N1H 6H8
(807) 223-2980 *SIC 5984*

SUPERIOR PLUS LP *p984*
200 WELLINGTON ST W SUITE 401, TORONTO, ON, M5V 3C7
(416) 345-8050 *SIC 5984*

SUPERIOR PROPANE INC *p94*
14820 123 AVE NW, EDMONTON, AB, T5L 2Y3
(780) 732-3636 *SIC 5984*

SUPERIOR PROPANE INC *p144*
6210 44 ST, LLOYDMINSTER, AB, T9V 1V9
SIC 5984

SUPREME TANK INCORPORATED *p449*
26 HARBOUR DR, EDWARDSVILLE, NS, B2A 4T4
(902) 564-9504 *SIC 5984*

VOMAR INDUSTRIES INC *p351*
GD, LA SALLE, MB, R0G 1B0
(204) 736-4288 *SIC 5984*

SIC 5989 Fuel dealers, nec

H. E. FORESTRY LTD *p394*
1990 ROUTE 380, ANDERSON ROAD, NB, E7G 4C1
(506) 356-2310 *SIC 5989*

SIC 5992 Florists

1801794 ONTARIO INC *p1337*
935 RUE REVERCHON, SAINT-LAURENT, QC, H4T 4L2
(514) 733-3515 *SIC 5992*

421229 ONTARIO LIMITED *p736*
7255 PACIFIC CIR, MISSISSAUGA, ON, L5T 1V1
(905) 564-5581 *SIC 5992*

BAY GROWERS INC *p544*
828114 GREY ROAD 40, CLARKSBURG, ON, N0H 1J0
(519) 599-7568 *SIC 5992*

BUNCHES FLOWER COMPANY *p117*
7108 109 ST NW, EDMONTON, AB, T6G 1B8
(780) 447-5359 *SIC 5992*

CLEARVIEW HORTICULTURAL PRODUCTS INC *p229*
5343A 264 ST SUITE 1, LANGLEY, BC, V4W 1J7
(604) 856-6131 *SIC 5992*

GARDEN CITY GROWERS INC *p761*
405 CONCESSION 5 RD, NIAGARA ON THE LAKE, ON, L0S 1J0
(905) 685-1120 *SIC 5992*

GROWER'S CHOICE LANDSCAPE PRODUCTS INC *p642*
1720 HURON RD, KITCHENER, ON, N2R 1R6
(519) 748-6551 *SIC 5992*

HAMER TREE SERVICES LTD *p81*
GD, DE WINTON, AB, T0L 0X0
(403) 938-6245 *SIC 5992*

HOFLAND, JOHN G LTD. *p740*
6695 PACIFIC CIR, MISSISSAUGA, ON, L5T 1V6
(905) 670-8220 *SIC 5992*

HOLE'S GREENHOUSES & GARDENS LTD *p165*
101 RIEL DR, ST. ALBERT, AB, T8N 3X4
(780) 651-7355 *SIC 5992*

ISLINGTON NURSERIES LIMITED *p575*
1000 ISLINGTON AVE SUITE 5, ETOBICOKE, ON, M8Z 4P8
(416) 231-8416 *SIC 5992*

JACKMAN FLOWER SHOP LIMITED *p763*
157 WORTHINGTON ST E, NORTH BAY, ON, P1B 1G4
(705) 494-8000 *SIC 5992*

LOBLAWS *p626*
200 EARL GREY DR, KANATA, ON, K2T 1B6
(613) 599-9934 *SIC 5992*

MARCHE D'ALIMENTATION CREVIER INC *p1363*
550 CHOMEDEY (A-13) O, SAINTE-ROSE, QC, H7X 3S9
(450) 689-3131 *SIC 5992*

MEXICAN FLOWER TRADING INC *p741*
1240 MID-WAY BLVD UNIT A, MISSISSAUGA, ON, L5T 2B8
(905) 670-0870 *SIC 5992*

PENGLAD FARMS INC *p886*
3930 NINTH ST, ST CATHARINES, ON, L2R 6P9
(905) 684-7861 *SIC 5992*

PLANTERRA LTEE *p1095*
2275 CH SAINT-FRANCOIS, DORVAL, QC, H9P 1K3
(514) 684-0310 *SIC 5992*

ROSA FLORA GROWERS LIMITED *p567*
GD LCD MAIN, DUNNVILLE, ON, N1A 2W9
(905) 774-8044 *SIC 5992*

ROSE DRUMMOND INC *p1097*
210 BOUL LEMIRE O, DRUMMONDVILLE, QC, J2B 8A9
(819) 474-3488 *SIC 5992*

RUTLEDGE FLOWERS AT YORKDALE INC *p924*
635 MOUNT PLEASANT RD SUITE A, TORONTO, ON, M4S 2M9
(416) 783-6355 *SIC 5992*

SIGNE GARNEAU PAYSAGISTE INC *p1399*
29 BOUL ARTHABASKA E, VICTORIAVILLE, QC, G6T 0S5
(819) 758-3887 *SIC 5992*

STAALDUINEN FLORAL LIMITED *p893*
1255 ARVIN AVE, STONEY CREEK, ON, L8E 0H7
(905) 643-2703 *SIC 5992*

VERMEER GREENHOUSES (WELLAND) INC *p1012*
684 SOUTH PELHAM RD, WELLAND, ON, L3C 3C8
(905) 735-5744 *SIC 5992*

WEST VAN FLORIST LTD *p342*
1821 MARINE DR, WEST VANCOUVER, BC, V7V 1J7
(604) 922-4171 *SIC 5992*

SIC 5993 Tobacco stores and stands

CANNTRUST HOLDINGS INC *p1027*
9200 WESTON RD, WOODBRIDGE, ON, L4H 2P8
(647) 872-2300 *SIC 5993*

HAVANA HOUSE CIGAR AND TOBACCO MERCHANTS LTD *p920*
9 DAVIES AVE SUITE 112, TORONTO, ON, M4M 2A6
(416) 406-6644 *SIC 5993*

SIC 5994 News dealers and newsstands

CORPORATION PRESSE COMMERCE *p1338*
3339 RUE GRIFFITH BUREAU 4, SAINT-LAURENT, QC, H4T 1W5
(514) 333-5041 *SIC 5994*

GEDDES ENTERPRISES OF LONDON LIMITED *p653*
140 FULLARTON ST SUITE 604, LONDON, ON, N6A 5P2
SIC 5994

HACHETTE DISTRIBUTION SERVICES (CANADA) INC *p729*
GD, MISSISSAUGA, ON, L5P 1B2
(905) 694-9696 *SIC 5994*

QUEBECOR MEDIA INC *p1153*
12800 RUE BRAULT, MIRABEL, QC, J7J 0W4
(450) 663-9000 *SIC 5994*

SIC 5995 Optical goods stores

9085-7160 QUEBEC INC *p1289*
75 RUE MONSEIGNEUR-TESSIER O, ROUYN-NORANDA, QC, J9X 2S5
(819) 764-4747 *SIC 5995*

A.B. IMAGE OPTICS INC *p198*
2764 BARNET HWY SUITE 101, COQUITLAM, BC, V3B 1B9
(604) 942-1642 *SIC 5995*

ABBOTT MEDICAL OPTICAL INC *p666*
80 WHITEHALL DR, MARKHAM, ON, L3R 0P3
(905) 305-3305 *SIC 5995*

ARCHIBALD, GRAY & MCKAY LTD *p657*
3514 WHITE OAK RD, LONDON, ON, N6E 2Z9
(519) 685-5300 *SIC 5995*

BONLOOK INC *p1222*
4020 RUE SAINT-AMBROISE BUREAU 489, MONTREAL, QC, H4C 2C7

---

(855) 943-5566 *SIC 5995*

CARL ZEISS CANADA LIMITED *p776*
45 VALLEYBROOK DR, NORTH YORK, ON, M3B 2S6
(416) 449-4660 *SIC 5995*

DOWNTOWN EATERY (1993) LTD *p980*
563 KING ST W, TORONTO, ON, M5V 1M1
(416) 585-9200 *SIC 5995*

EYESTAR OPTICAL LTD *p254*
2639 VIKING WAY UNIT 150, RICHMOND, BC, V6V 3B7
(604) 303-9760 *SIC 5995*

EYEWEAR PLACE LTD, THE *p119*
2065 111 ST NW, EDMONTON, AB, T6J 4V9
(780) 433-4888 *SIC 5995*

FAMILY VISION CARE LTD *p89*
10088 102 AVE NW SUITE 1805, EDMONTON, AB, T5J 2Z1
(780) 423-2128 *SIC 5995*

FORWARD VISION GROUP INC. *p658*
1828 BLUE HERON DR SUITE 37, LONDON, ON, N6H 0B7
(519) 471-6665 *SIC 5995*

FUJI OPTICAL CO LTD *p852*
550 HIGHWAY 7 E, RICHMOND HILL, ON, L4B 3Z4
(905) 882-5665 *SIC 5995*

FYI SERVICES ET PRODUITS QUEBEC INC *p1262*
1100 AV GALIBOIS BUREAU A200, QUEBEC, QC, G1M 3M7
(418) 527-6682 *SIC 5995*

GRAY, L. H. & SON LIMITED *p647*
955 TREMAINE AVE S, LISTOWEL, ON, N4W 3G9
(519) 291-5150 *SIC 5995*

GRIMARD OPTIQUE INC *p1169*
3108 RUE BEAUBIEN E, MONTREAL, QC, H1Y 1H3
(514) 439-0602 *SIC 5995*

GROUPE MARCHAND RENE INC *p1262*
1100 AV GALIBOIS BUREAU A200, QUEBEC, QC, G1M 3M7
(418) 527-6682 *SIC 5995*

GROUPE VISION NEW LOOK INC *p1205*
1 PLACE VILLE-MARIE SUITE 3670, MONTREAL, QC, H3B 3P2
(514) 877-4119 *SIC 5995*

HAKIM OPTICAL LABORATORY LIMITED *p867*
3430 LAWRENCE AVE E, SCARBOROUGH, ON, M1H 1A9
(416) 439-3416 *SIC 5995*

IRIS THE VISUAL GROUP WESTERN CANADA INC *p225*
9440 202 ST SUITE 315, LANGLEY, BC, V1M 4A6
(604) 881-0353 *SIC 5995*

LNLC INC *p1280*
1100 RUE BOUVIER BUREAU 100, QUEBEC, QC, G2K 1L9
(418) 624-6100 *SIC 5995*

LUNETTERIE BRANCHES INC., LES *p1321*
509 RUE SAINT-GEORGES, SAINT-JEROME, QC, J7Z 5B6
(450) 432-3914 *SIC 5995*

LUXOTTICA CANADA INC *p724*
2000 ARGENTIA RD SUITE 2, MISSISSAUGA, ON, L5N 1P7
(905) 858-0008 *SIC 5995*

LUXOTTICA RETAIL CANADA INC *p724*
2000 ARGENTIA RD UNIT 2, MISSISSAUGA, ON, L5N 1P7
(905) 858-0008 *SIC 5995*

METROTOWN OPTICAL LTD *p190*
6411 NELSON AVE SUITE 105, BURNABY, BC, V5H 4H3
SIC 5995

MMG CANADA LIMITED *p575*
10 VANSCO RD, ETOBICOKE, ON, M8Z 5J4
(416) 251-2831 *SIC 5995*

OPTAGEX INC *p1371*

---

243 RUE KING O, SHERBROOKE, QC, J1H 1P8

(819) 563-1191   *SIC 5995*

VEZINA OPTICIANS   *p810*
5929 JEANNE D'ARC BLVD S SUITE AA, ORLEANS, ON, K1C 6V8

(613) 837-1119   *SIC 5995*

VOGUE OPTICAL GROUP INC   *p1040*
5 BRACKLEY POINT RD, CHARLOTTE-TOWN, PE, C1A 6X8

(902) 566-3326   *SIC 5995*

SIC 5999 Miscellaneous retail stores, nec

1001943 ONTARIO LIMITED   *p473*
725 WESTNEY RD S UNIT 1, AJAX, ON, L1S 7J7

(905) 686-1212   *SIC 5999*

1009833 ALBERTA LTD   *p160*
261116 WAGON WHEEL WAY, ROCKY VIEW COUNTY, AB, T4A 0E3

(403) 250-8484   *SIC 5999*

1152174 ONTARIO LIMITED   *p769*
6464 YONGE ST, NORTH YORK, ON, M2M 3X4

SIC 5999

144503 CANADA INC   *p1248*
6361 RTE TRANSCANADIENNE BUREAU 119, POINTE-CLAIRE, QC, H9R 5A5

(514) 694-6843   *SIC 5999*

191837 CANADA INC   *p1218*
3901 RUE JEAN-TALON O BUREAU 301, MONTREAL, QC, H3R 2G4

(514) 373-3131   *SIC 5999*

2330-2029 QUEBEC INC   *p1168*
5135 10E AV, MONTREAL, QC, H1Y 2G5

(514) 525-3757   *SIC 5999*

2758792 CANADA INC   *p1091*
3352 BOUL DES SOURCES, DOLLARD-DES-ORMEAUX, QC, H9B 1Z9

(514) 684-6846   *SIC 5999*

3294269 CANADA INC   *p1337*
7020 CH DE LA C?TE-DE-LIESSE, SAINT-LAURENT, QC, H4T 1E7

(514) 344-8883   *SIC 5999*

3474534 CANADA INC   *p1241*
800 BOUL CHOMEDEY BUREAU 160, MONTREAL-OUEST, QC, H7V 3Y4

(450) 682-7711   *SIC 5999*

3499481 CANADA INC   *p578*
25 THE WEST MALL, ETOBICOKE, ON, M9C 1B8

(905) 593-3179   *SIC 5999*

3499481 CANADA INC   *p716*
4161 SLADEVIEW CRES UNIT 12, MISSISSAUGA, ON, L5L 5R3

(905) 593-3177   *SIC 5999*

4L COMMUNICATIONS INC   *p361*
1555 REGENT AVE W SUITE T58, WINNIPEG, MB, R2C 4J2

(204) 927-6363   *SIC 5999*

619020 SASKATCHEWAN LTD   *p1415*
HWY 6 N, RAYMORE, SK, S0A 3J0

(306) 746-2911   *SIC 5999*

9044-4928 QUEBEC INC   *p1372*
2980 RUE KING O, SHERBROOKE, QC, J1L 1Y7

(819) 566-5555   *SIC 5999*

9047-6334 QUEBEC INC   *p1370*
1597 RUE GALT E, SHERBROOKE, QC, J1G 3H4

(819) 566-8558   *SIC 5999*

9060-1899 QUEBEC INC   *p1097*
126 RUE HERIOT, DRUMMONDVILLE, QC, J2C 1J8

(819) 472-1121   *SIC 5999*

9378-7471 QUEBEC INC   *p1261*
909 BOUL PIERRE-BERTRAND BUREAU 150, QUEBEC, QC, G1M 3R8

(418) 687-1988   *SIC 5999*

994794 ONTARIO INC   *p1001*
4 BANFF RD SUITE 3, UXBRIDGE, ON, L9P 1S9

(905) 852-6977   *SIC 5999*

ABLE COPIERS LTD   *p238*
12 ORWELL ST, NORTH VANCOUVER, BC, V7J 2G1

(604) 904-9858   *SIC 5999*

ADVANCE ELECTRONICS LTD   *p381*
1300 PORTAGE AVE, WINNIPEG, MB, R3G 0V1

(204) 786-6541   *SIC 5999*

ADVANCED 2000 SYSTEMS INC   *p1425*
718 CIRCLE DR E, SASKATOON, SK, S7K 3T7

(306) 955-2355   *SIC 5999*

ADVANCED MOBILITY PRODUCTS LTD   *p191*
8620 GLENLYON PKY SUITE 101, BURNABY, BC, V5J 0B6

(604) 293-0002   *SIC 5999*

ADVANCED PRESENTATION PRODUCTS INC   *p716*
4180 SLADEVIEW CRES UNIT 4, MISSISSAUGA, ON, L5L 0A1

(905) 502-1110   *SIC 5999*

ADVANTAGE FARM EQUIPMENT LTD   *p1037*
392 BROADWAY ST, WYOMING, ON, N0N 1T0

(519) 845-3346   *SIC 5999*

AGRATURF EQUIPMENT SERVICES INC   *p564*
170 COUNTY ROAD 13, COURTLAND, ON, N0J 1E0

(519) 688-1011   *SIC 5999*

AGRIS CO-OPERATIVE LTD   *p542*
835 PARK AVE W, CHATHAM, ON, N7M 0N1

(519) 354-7178   *SIC 5999*

ALTEL INC   *p1233*
3150 BOUL LE CORBUSIER, MONTREAL, QC, H7L 4S8

(450) 682-9788   *SIC 5999*

AMPRO ELECTRIC LTD   *p650*
406 FIRST ST, LONDON, ON, N5W 4N1

(519) 439-9748   *SIC 5999*

ANIMALERIE DYNO INC   *p1254*
2377 BOUL LOUIS-XIV, QUEBEC, QC, G1C 1B2

(418) 661-7128   *SIC 5999*

APEX COMMUNICATIONS INC   *p273*
13734 104 AVE SUITE 201, SURREY, BC, V3T 1W5

(604) 583-6685   *SIC 5999*

ARCHANGEL FIREWORKS INC   *p387*
104 PEMBINA HWY, WINNIPEG, MB, R3L 2C8

(204) 943-3332   *SIC 5999*

AUDIO VISUAL SYSTEMS INTEGRATION INC   *p27*
3636 7 ST SE, CALGARY, AB, T2G 2Y8

(403) 255-4123   *SIC 5999*

BAINS ULTRA INC   *p1140*
1200 CH INDUSTRIEL BUREAU 4, LEVIS, QC, G7A 1B1

(418) 831-7132   *SIC 5999*

BAKA COMMUNICATIONS, INC   *p577*
630 THE EAST MALL, ETOBICOKE, ON, M9B 4B1

(416) 641-2800   *SIC 5999*

BATTLE RIVER IMPLEMENTS LTD   *p78*
4717 38 ST, CAMROSE, AB, T4V 3W9

(780) 672-4463   *SIC 5999*

BEAVER VALLEY STONE LIMITED   *p667*
8081 WOODBINE AVE, MARKHAM, ON, L3R 2P1

(416) 222-2424   *SIC 5999*

BELL MOBILITE INC   *p1096*
200 BOUL BOUCHARD BUREAU 500, DORVAL, QC, H9S 5X5

(514) 333-3336   *SIC 5999*

BEST BUY CANADA LTD   *p224*
19890 92A AVE, LANGLEY, BC, V1M 3A9

(604) 419-5500   *SIC 5999*

BEST BUY CANADA LTD   *p626*
255 KANATA AVE UNIT D1, KANATA, ON, K2T 1K5

SIC 5999

BEST BUY CANADA LTD   *p729*
6075 MAVIS RD UNIT 1, MISSISSAUGA, ON, L5R 4G6

(905) 361-8251   *SIC 5999*

BEST BUY CANADA LTD   *p754*
17890 YONGE ST, NEWMARKET, ON, L3Y 8S1

SIC 5999

BEST BUY CANADA LTD   *p1064*
584 CH DE TOURAINE BUREAU 101, BOUCHERVILLE, QC, J4B 8S5

SIC 5999

BEST BUY CANADA LTD   *p1249*
6321 RTE TRANSCANADIENNE UNITE 121, POINTE-CLAIRE, QC, H9R 5A5

(514) 428-1999   *SIC 5999*

BEST WEST PET FOODS INC   *p383*
1150 ST JAMES ST, WINNIPEG, MB, R3H 0K7

(204) 783-0952   *SIC 5999*

BOLDT POOL CONSTRUCTION LTD   *p884*
20 NIHAN DR, ST CATHARINES, ON, L2N 1L1

(905) 934-0937   *SIC 5999*

BRANT TELEPHONE INC   *p527*
3190 HARVESTER RD SUITE 101, BURLINGTON, ON, L7N 3T1

(905) 632-2000   *SIC 5999*

BROOKS INDUSTRIAL METALS LTD   *p7*
221 7TH ST E, BROOKS, AB, T1R 1B3

(403) 362-3544   *SIC 5999*

BWIRELESS COMMUNICATIONS INC   *p297*
555 ROBSON ST UNIT 1, VANCOUVER, BC, V6B 1A6

(604) 689-8488   *SIC 5999*

CAISSIECO ENTERPRISES LTD   *p443*
24 FOREST HILLS PKY, DARTMOUTH, NS, B2W 6E4

(902) 462-6100   *SIC 5999*

CAM-TRAC BERNIERES INC   *p1140*
830 CH OLIVIER, LEVIS, QC, G7A 2N1

(418) 831-2324   *SIC 5999*

CAMPBELL MONUMENT COMPANY LIMITED   *p490*
712 DUNDAS ST W, BELLEVILLE, ON, K8N 4Z2

(613) 966-5154   *SIC 5999*

CANADIAN HEARING SOCIETY   *p972*
271 SPADINA RD, TORONTO, ON, M5R 2V3

(416) 928-2502   *SIC 5999*

CANADIAN WIRELESS COMMUNICATIONS INC   *p480*
10-91 FIRST COMMERCE DR, AURORA, ON, L4G 0G2

(905) 726-2652   *SIC 5999*

CANON CANADA INC   *p928*
175 BLOOR ST E SUITE 1200, TORONTO, ON, M4W 3R8

(416) 491-9330   *SIC 5999*

CASCADES CANADA ULC   *p486*
35 FRASER CRT, BARRIE, ON, L4N 5J5

(705) 737-0470   *SIC 5999*

CELLULAR BABY CELL PHONE ACCESSORIES SPECIALIST LTD   *p190*
4710 KINGSWAY UNIT 1028, BURNABY, BC, V5H 4M2

(604) 437-9977   *SIC 5999*

CELLULAR CONCEPTS OF NOVA SCOTIA LIMITED   *p455*
3232 BARRINGTON ST, HALIFAX, NS, B3K 2X7

(902) 423-0167   *SIC 5999*

CENTRE DE TELEPHONE MOBILE LTEE   *p1048*
9680 BOUL DU GOLF BUREAU 1, ANJOU, QC, H1J 2Y7

(514) 645-9271   *SIC 5999*

CERVUS LP   *p76*
333 96 AVE NE SUITE 5201, CALGARY, AB, T3K 0S3

(403) 275-2215   *SIC 5999*

CHAPITEAUX CLASSIC INC, LES   *p1247*

12301 BOUL METROPOLITAIN E, POINTE-AUX-TREMBLES, QC, H1B 5R3

(514) 645-4555   *SIC 5999*

CHINA EDUCATION RESOURCES INC   *p297*
515 PENDER ST W SUITE 300, VANCOUVER, BC, V6B 6H5

(604) 331-2388   *SIC 5999*

CISCO SYSTEMS CANADA CO   *p1194*
1800 AV MCGILL COLLEGE BUREAU 700, MONTREAL, QC, H3A 3J6

(514) 847-6800   *SIC 5999*

CLASSIC CARE PHARMACY CORPORATION   *p521*
1320 HEINE CRT, BURLINGTON, ON, L7L 6L9

(905) 631-9027   *SIC 5999*

CLEARWEST SOLUTIONS INC   *p226*
8700 200 ST SUITE 310, LANGLEY, BC, V2Y 0G4

(604) 888-5050   *SIC 5999*

CLEF DE SOL INC, LA   *p1277*
445 AV SAINT-JEAN-BAPTISTE BUREAU 220, QUEBEC, QC, G2E 5N7

(418) 627-0840   *SIC 5999*

CLUB PISCINE PLUS C.P.P.Q. (LONGUEUIL) INC, LE   *p1141*
620 RUE JEAN-NEVEU, LONGUEUIL, QC, J4G 1P1

(450) 463-3112   *SIC 5999*

CLUB PISCINE PLUS C.P.P.Q. (WEST ISLAND) INC, LE   *p1245*
14920 BOUL DE PIERREFONDS, PIERREFONDS, QC, H9H 4G2

(514) 696-2582   *SIC 5999*

COMPLETE COMMUNICATION SYSTEMS INC   *p893*
905 QUEENSTON RD, STONEY CREEK, ON, L8G 1B6

(905) 664-1158   *SIC 5999*

COUTURE PARFUMS & COSMETICS LTD   *p574*
997 THE QUEENSWAY, ETOBICOKE, ON, M8Z 1P3

(416) 597-3232   *SIC 5999*

CROOKS, J R HEALTH CARE SERVICES INC   *p908*
285 MEMORIAL AVE, THUNDER BAY, ON, P7B 6H4

(807) 345-6564   *SIC 5999*

CUI-CANADA, INC   *p783*
39 KODIAK CRES, NORTH YORK, ON, M3J 3E5

(416) 630-8108   *SIC 5999*

CULLIGAN OF CANADA ULC   *p1438*
76 SEVENTH AVE S SUITE 1, YORKTON, SK, S3N 3V2

(306) 782-2648   *SIC 5999*

D & W GROUP INC   *p623*
2173 HIGHWAY 3, JARVIS, ON, N0A 1J0

(519) 587-2273   *SIC 5999*

D. & A.'S PET FOOD 'N MORE LTD   *p279*
19347 24 AVE UNIT 105, SURREY, BC, V3Z 3S9

(604) 591-5990   *SIC 5999*

D2 TECHNOLOGIE INC   *p1328*
2119 BOUL MARCEL-LAURIN, SAINT-LAURENT, QC, H4R 1K4

(514) 904-5888   *SIC 5999*

DANS UN JARDIN CANADA INC   *p1064*
240 BOUL INDUSTRIEL, BOUCHERVILLE, QC, J4B 2X4

(450) 449-2121   *SIC 5999*

DBRAND INC   *p980*
500 KING ST W 3RD FL, TORONTO, ON, M5V 1L9

(647) 282-3711   *SIC 5999*

DCB BUSINESS SYSTEMS GROUP INC   *p491*
175 LAHR DR, BELLEVILLE, ON, K8N 5S2

(613) 966-6315   *SIC 5999*

DECIEM DISTRIBUTION INC   *p933*
511 RICHMOND ST E, TORONTO, ON, M5A 1R4

(416) 203-3992   *SIC 5999*

DECIEM INC p933
517 RICHMOND ST E, TORONTO, ON, M5A 1R4
(416) 203-3992 *SIC* 5999

DEERMART EQUIPMENT SALES LTD p155
6705 GOLDEN WEST AVE, RED DEER, AB, T4P 1A7
(403) 343-2238 *SIC* 5999

DELTA POWER EQUIPMENT LTD p589
71301 LONDON RD, EXETER, ON, N0M 1S3
(519) 235-2121 *SIC* 5999

DIGITCOM TELECOMMUNICATIONS CANADA INC p783
250 RIMROCK RD, NORTH YORK, ON, M3J 3A6
(416) 783-7890 *SIC* 5999

DIGITEL SYSTEMS INC p260
10851 SHELLBRIDGE WAY SUITE 110, RICHMOND, BC, V6X 2W8
(604) 231-0101 *SIC* 5999

DOLLAR TREE STORES CANADA, INC p188
3185 WILLINGDON GREEN SUITE 206, BURNABY, BC, V5G 4P3
(604) 321-2550 *SIC* 5999

DOLLARAMA INC p1156
5805 AV ROYALMOUNT, MONT-ROYAL, QC, H4P 0A1
(514) 737-1006 *SIC* 5999

DYAND MECHANICAL SYSTEMS INC p95
14840 115 AVE NW, EDMONTON, AB, T5M 3C1
(780) 452-5800 *SIC* 5999

EAST HAMILTON RADIO LIMITED p609
1325 BARTON ST E, HAMILTON, ON, L8H 2W2
(905) 549-3581 *SIC* 5999

EASTERN ONTARIO WATER TECHNOLOGY LTD p519
240 WALTHAM RD, BROCKVILLE, ON, K6V 7K3
(613) 498-2830 *SIC* 5999

ELECTROTEMP TECHNOLOGIES INC p705
406 WATLINE AVE, MISSISSAUGA, ON, L4Z 1X2
(905) 488-9263 *SIC* 5999

ELITE SPORTSWEAR & AWARDS LTD p93
14703 118 AVE NW, EDMONTON, AB, T5L 2M7
(780) 454-9775 *SIC* 5999

FACES COSMETICS INC p997
520 GARYRAY DR, TORONTO, ON, M9L 1R1
(416) 746-7575 *SIC* 5999

FITCH SECURITY INTEGRATION INC p584
14 METEOR DR, ETOBICOKE, ON, M9W 1A4
(416) 235-1818 *SIC* 5999

FORGET & SAUVE, AUDIOPROTHESISTES S.E.N.C. p1329
5255 BOUL HENRI-BOURASSA O BUREAU 410, SAINT-LAURENT, QC, H4R 2M6
(514) 353-0001 *SIC* 5999

FRANK FLAMAN SALES LTD p148
2310 SPARROW DR, NISKU, AB, T9E 8A2
(780) 955-3400 *SIC* 5999

FULL LINE AG SALES LTD p1427
2 YELLOWHEAD INDUSTRIAL PARK LOT 2 RR 4 LCD MAIN, SASKATOON, SK, S7K 3J7
(306) 934-1546 *SIC* 5999

G F LTD p30
2270 PORTLAND ST SE, CALGARY, AB, T2G 4M6
(403) 287-7111 *SIC* 5999

GESTION GCL INC p1159
1595 RTE 117, MONT-TREMBLANT, QC, J8E 2X9
(819) 425-2711 *SIC* 5999

GESTION LITTLE MOUSE INC p1264
1350 RUE CYRILLE-DUQUET, QUEBEC, QC, G1N 2E5
(418) 681-6381 *SIC* 5999

GESTION MARC DESERRES INC p1175
1265 RUE BERRI BUREAU 1000, MONTREAL, QC, H2L 4X4
(514) 842-6695 *SIC* 5999

GESTION SYNER-PHARM INC p1397
141 RUE NOTRE-DAME E, VICTORIAVILLE, QC, G6P 3Z8
(819) 752-4554 *SIC* 5999

GLOBAL WIRELESS SOLUTIONS INC p580
22 DIXON RD SUITE 2, ETOBICOKE, ON, M9P 2L1
(416) 246-1656 *SIC* 5999

GOLDWELL COSMETICS (CANADA) LTD p739
1045 TRISTAR DR, MISSISSAUGA, ON, L5T 1W5
(905) 670-2844 *SIC* 5999

GREEN ESSENTIAL SERVICES INC p952
250 UNIVERSITY AVE SUITE 200, TORONTO, ON, M5H 3E5
(866) 820-2284 *SIC* 5999

GREEN TRACTORS INC p762
6770 KING RD, NOBLETON, ON, L0G 1N0
(905) 859-0581 *SIC* 5999

GREENVALLEY EQUIPMENT INC p352
25016 ROAD 25W HIGHWAY 3 E, MORDEN, MB, R6M 2B9
(204) 325-7742 *SIC* 5999

GROUP CONNECT LTD, THE p262
8010 SABA RD SUITE 110, RICHMOND, BC, V6Y 4B2
(604) 821-1852 *SIC* 5999

GROUPE AGRITEX INC, LE p1296
230 RUE MARQUIS, SAINT-CELESTIN, QC, J0C 1G0
(819) 229-3686 *SIC* 5999

GROUPE CDREM INC p1128
10200 CH DE LA COTE-DE-LIESSE, LACHINE, QC, H8T 1A3
(514) 636-4512 *SIC* 5999

HEARING LOSS CLINIC INC, THE p41
1632 14 AVE NW SUITE 251, CALGARY, AB, T2N 1M7
(403) 289-3290 *SIC* 5999

HEARX HEARING INC p619
290 MCGILL ST SUITE A, HAWKESBURY, ON, K6A 1P8
(877) 268-1045 *SIC* 5999

HELIX ADVANCED COMMUNICATIONS & INFRASTRUCTURE, INC p93
12540 129 ST NW, EDMONTON, AB, T5L 4R4
(780) 451-2357 *SIC* 5999

HI-PRO FEEDS LP p150
HWY 2A 306 AVE, OKOTOKS, AB, T1S 1A2
(403) 938-8350 *SIC* 5999

HOME DEPOT OF CANADA INC p276
7350 120 ST, SURREY, BC, V3W 3M9
(604) 590-2796 *SIC* 5999

HOME DOCTOR LIMITED, THE p438
3067 HIGHWAY 104 UNIT C, ANTIGONISH, NS, B2G 2K5
(902) 735-9100 *SIC* 5999

HOWELL DATA SYSTEMS INC p1021
250 TECUMSEH RD E, WINDSOR, ON, N8X 2R3
SIC 5999

HURON BAY CO-OPERATIVE INC p902
15 HILCREST ST, TEESWATER, ON, N0G 2S0
(519) 392-6862 *SIC* 5999

HYDROPOOL INC p740
335 SUPERIOR BLVD, MISSISSAUGA, ON, L5T 2L6
(800) 465-2933 *SIC* 5999

IMAGINE WIRELESS INC p74
4550 17 AVE SW UNIT 28, CALGARY, AB, T3E 7B9
(403) 974-3150 *SIC* 5999

INTERNATIONAL AQUATIC SERVICES LTD p783
4496 CHESSWOOD DR, NORTH YORK, ON, M3J 2B9
(416) 665-6400 *SIC* 5999

ISLAND ACOUSTICS (OAK BAY) INC p336
645 FORT ST UNIT 309, VICTORIA, BC, V8W 1G2
(250) 385-3103 *SIC* 5999

J. E. MONDOU LTEE p1049
10400 RUE RENAUDE-LAPOINTE, ANJOU, QC, H1J 2V7
(514) 322-5300 *SIC* 5999

K.M. TURNBULL SALES INC p1410
290 PRINCE WILLIAM DR, MELVILLE, SK, S0A 2P0
(306) 728-8810 *SIC* 5999

KOST FIRE EQUIPMENT LTD p145
677 14 ST SW, MEDICINE HAT, AB, T1A 4V5
(403) 527-1500 *SIC* 5999

KOYMAN GALLERIES LIMITED p818
1771 ST. LAURENT BLVD, OTTAWA, ON, K1G 3V4
(613) 526-1562 *SIC* 5999

KRAMER AUCTIONS LTD p1412
GD LCD MAIN, NORTH BATTLEFORD, SK, S9A 2X5
(306) 445-2377 *SIC* 5999

L'OCCITANE CANADA CORP p988
2700 DUFFERIN ST UNIT 89, TORONTO, ON, M6B 4J3
(416) 782-0005 *SIC* 5999

LABORATOIRE POULIOT INC p1272
2815 CH DES QUATRE-BOURGEOIS, QUEBEC, QC, G1V 1X8
(418) 652-0100 *SIC* 5999

LEISURE MANUFACTURING INC p599
317 SOUTH SERVICE RD SUITE 2, GRIMSBY, ON, L3M 4E8
(905) 309-1800 *SIC* 5999

LEVITT-SAFETY LIMITED p918
33 LAIRD DR, TORONTO, ON, M4G 3S8
(416) 425-6659 *SIC* 5999

MAGASINS TREVI INC p1152
12775 RUE BRAULT, MIRABEL, QC, J7J 0C4
(450) 973-1249 *SIC* 5999

MAGNACHARGE BATTERY CORPORATION p206
1279 DERWENT WAY UNIT 1, DELTA, BC, V3M 5V9
(604) 525-0391 *SIC* 5999

MAPLE CITY OFFICE EQUIPMENT LTD p543
170 QUEEN ST, CHATHAM, ON, N7M 2G8
(519) 352-2940 *SIC* 5999

MARKUSSON NEW HOLLAND OF REGINA LTD p1406
26 GREAT PLAINS RD, EMERALD PARK, SK, S4L 1B6
(306) 781-2828 *SIC* 5999

MATAPEDIENNE COOPERATIVE AGRICOLE, LA p1046
90 RUE PROULX BUREAU 550, AMQUI, QC, G5J 3G3
(418) 629-4401 *SIC* 5999

MAZER IMPLEMENTS p348
1908 CURRIE BLVD, BRANDON, MB, R7B 4E7
(204) 728-2244 *SIC* 5999

MAZERGROUP LTD p348
1908 CURRIE BLVD, BRANDON, MB, R7B 4E7
(204) 728-2244 *SIC* 5999

MAZERGROUP LTD p351
GD, HARTNEY, MB, R0M 0X0
(204) 858-2000 *SIC* 5999

MCCOWAN DESIGN & MANUFACTURING LTD p871
1760 BIRCHMOUNT RD, SCARBOROUGH, ON, M1P 2H7
(416) 291-7111 *SIC* 5999

MCGRAIL FARM EQUIPMENT LIMITED PARTNERSHIP p547
8705 COUNTY RD 46 RR 1, COMBER, ON, N0P 1J0
(519) 687-6662 *SIC* 5999

ME TO WE SHOP INC p934

145 BERKELEY ST, TORONTO, ON, M5A 2X1
(416) 964-8942 *SIC* 5999

MILANI PLUMBING DRAINAGE & HEATING LTD p190
5526 KINGSWAY, BURNABY, BC, V5H 2G2
(604) 453-1234 *SIC* 5999

MINOR BROS. FARM SUPPLY LTD p567
9 MILL AVE, DUNNVILLE, ON, N1A 2W1
(905) 774-7591 *SIC* 5999

MODERN BUSINESS EQUIPMENT LIMITED p433
172 HAMILTON AVE, ST. JOHN'S, NL, A1E 1J5
(709) 579-2147 *SIC* 5999

MOTEYO INC p789
3111 DUFFERIN ST, NORTH YORK, ON, M6A 2S7
(416) 785-3031 *SIC* 5999

MR P'S & MR PET'S LTD p232
33560 1ST AVE, MISSION, BC, V2V 1H4
(604) 814-2994 *SIC* 5999

MUELLER CANADA LTD p1320
230 RUE CASTONGUAY, SAINT-JEROME, QC, J7Y 2J7
SIC 5999

NATIONAL CELLULAR INC p798
2679 BRISTOL CIR SUITE 8, OAKVILLE, ON, L6H 6Z8
(905) 828-9200 *SIC* 5999

NATIONAL HEARING SERVICES p640
50 QUEEN ST N, KITCHENER, ON, N2H 6M2
SIC 5999

NATIONAL HEARING SERVICES INC p336
1007 LANGLEY ST SUITE 301, VICTORIA, BC, V8W 1V7
(250) 413-2100 *SIC* 5999

NELSON MONUMENTS LTD p418
23 WESTERN ST, SUSSEX, NB, E4E 1E7
(506) 432-9000 *SIC* 5999

NELSON MOTORS & EQUIPMENT (1976) LTD p1404
HWY 334, AVONLEA, SK, S0H 0C0
(306) 868-5000 *SIC* 5999

OMER DESERRES INC p1176
1265 RUE BERRI BUREAU 1000, MONTREAL, QC, H2L 4X4
(514) 842-6695 *SIC* 5999

OPTIMA COMMUNICATIONS INC p1015
1615 DUNDAS ST E SUITE 300, WHITBY, ON, L1N 2L1
(905) 448-2300 *SIC* 5999

OPUS FRAMING LTD p321
1677 2ND AVE W, VANCOUVER, BC, V6J 1H3
(604) 736-7535 *SIC* 5999

ORION BUILDING MAINTENANCE (OBM) LTD p110
5503 76 AVE NW, EDMONTON, AB, T6B 0A7
(780) 440-0136 *SIC* 5999

PADDOCK WOOD BREWING SUPPLIES LTD p1433
116 103RD ST E SUITE B1, SASKATOON, SK, S7N 1Y7
(306) 477-5632 *SIC* 5999

PARADISE PET CENTER LTD p166
580 ST ALBERT TRAIL SUITE 50, ST. ALBERT, AB, T8N 6M9
(780) 459-6896 *SIC* 5999

PARKLAND FARM EQUIPMENT (1990) LTD p167
34 BOULDER BLVD, STONY PLAIN, AB, T7Z 1V7
(780) 963-7411 *SIC* 5999

PATTISON AGRICULTURE LIMITED p1436
2777 NORTH SERVICE RD W, SWIFT CURRENT, SK, S9H 5M1
(306) 773-9351 *SIC* 5999

PDL MOBILITY LIMITED p24
2420 42 AVE NE, CALGARY, AB, T2E 7T6
(403) 291-5400 *SIC* 5999

PENTAGON FARM CENTRE LTD p138

4950 HARRINGTON RIDGE UNIT 1, LA-COMBE, AB, T4L 1A8
(403) 782-6873　*SIC 5999*

PET PLANET LTD　*p31*
600 MANITOU RD SE, CALGARY, AB, T2G 4C5
(403) 777-4664　*SIC 5999*

PINE ENVIRONMENTAL CANADA, INC *p750*
159 COLONNADE RD S UNITS 3 AND 4, NEPEAN, ON, K2E 7J4
(343) 882-1470　*SIC 5999*

PISCES EXOTICA PET EMPORIUM LTD *p24*
4921 SKYLINE WAY NE, CALGARY, AB, T2E 4G5
(403) 274-3314　*SIC 5999*

PISCINES LAUNIER INC　*p1388*
5825 BOUL GENE-H.-KRUGER, TROIS-RIVIERES, QC, G9A 4P1
(819) 375-7771　*SIC 5999*

PLANTERS EQUIPMENT LIMITED　*p460*
GD, KENTVILLE, NS, B4N 3V6
(902) 678-5555　*SIC 5999*

PODOLINSKY EQUIPMENT LTD　*p843*
6057 PETROLIA LINE, PETROLIA, ON, N0N 1R0
(519) 844-2360　*SIC 5999*

PRAIRIE COMMUNICATIONS LTD　*p384*
1305 KING EDWARD ST, WINNIPEG, MB, R3H 0R6
(204) 632-7800　*SIC 5999*

PREMIER EQUIPMENT LTD.　*p568*
275 CHURCH ST W, ELMIRA, ON, N3B 1N3
(519) 669-5453　*SIC 5999*

PREMIER SCHOOL AGENDAS LTD　*p226*
20230 64 AVE UNIT 103, LANGLEY, BC, V2Y 1N3
(604) 857-1707　*SIC 5999*

PRICE'S ALARM SYSTEMS (2009) LTD *p338*
4243 GLANFORD AVE UNIT 100, VICTORIA, BC, V8Z 4B9
(250) 384-4104　*SIC 5999*

QUADRANT COSMETICS CORP　*p853*
20 WEST BEAVER CREEK RD, RICHMOND HILL, ON, L4B 3L6
(416) 921-2913　*SIC 5999*

RAZOR SHARP MAGNETICS INC　*p25*
314 11 AVE NE, CALGARY, AB, T2E 0Z1
SIC 5999

REN'S FEED AND SUPPLIES LIMITED *p849*
20 BROCK RD N UNIT 3, PUSLINCH, ON, N0B 2J0
(519) 767-5858　*SIC 5999*

RIMER ALCO NORTH AMERICA INC *p352*
205 STEPHEN ST, MORDEN, MB, R6M 1V2
(204) 822-6595　*SIC 5999*

RITCHIE BROS. AUCTIONEERS (INTERNATIONAL) LTD　*p193*
9500 GLENLYON PKY SUITE 300, BURNABY, BC, V5J 0C6
(778) 331-5500　*SIC 5999*

SAVARD ORTHO CONFORT INC　*p1265*
1350 RUE CYRILLE-DUQUET, QUEBEC, QC, G1N 2E5
(418) 681-6381　*SIC 5999*

SCHIPPERS CANADA LTD　*p138*
27211 HIGHWAY 12 SUITE 120, LACOMBE COUNTY, AB, T4L 0E3
(403) 786-9911　*SIC 5999*

SCOTT SAFETY SUPPLY SERVICES LTD *p173*
3365 33 ST, WHITECOURT, AB, T7S 0A2
(780) 778-3389　*SIC 5999*

SECURASSURE CANADA INC　*p1218*
3901 RUE JEAN-TALON O BUREAU 301, MONTREAL, QC, H3R 2G4
(514) 373-3131　*SIC 5999*

SECURITAS CANADA LIMITED　*p443*
175 MAIN ST SUITE 201, DARTMOUTH, NS, B2X 1S1
(902) 434-2442　*SIC 5999*

SEPHORA BEAUTY CANADA, INC　*p710*
100 CITY CENTRE DR UNIT 2-930, MISSISSAUGA, ON, L5B 2C9
(905) 279-4400　*SIC 5999*

SERVICES INDUSTRIELS SYSTEMEX (S.I.S.) INC　*p1157*
8260 CH DEVONSHIRE UNITE 240, MONT-ROYAL, QC, H4P 2P7
(514) 738-6323　*SIC 5999*

SHOPPERS DRUG MART CORPORATION *p787*
104 BARTLEY DR, NORTH YORK, ON, M4A 1C5
(416) 752-8885　*SIC 5999*

SHOPPERS HOME HEALTH CARE (CANADA) INC　*p768*
243 CONSUMERS RD, NORTH YORK, ON, M2J 4W8
(416) 493-1220　*SIC 5999*

SHOPPERS HOME HEALTH CARE (ONTARIO) INC　*p787*
104 BARTLEY DR, NORTH YORK, ON, M4A 1C5
(416) 752-8885　*SIC 5999*

SIEMENS CANADA LIMITED　*p1171*
8455 19E AV, MONTREAL, QC, H1Z 4J2
SIC 5999

SOURCE ATLANTIC LIMITED　*p448*
14 AKERLEY BLVD, DARTMOUTH, NS, B3B 1J3
(902) 494-5377　*SIC 5999*

SOUTH COUNTRY EQUIPMENT LTD *p1411*
1731 MAIN ST N, MOOSE JAW, SK, S6J 1L6
(306) 642-3366　*SIC 5999*

SOUTHEASTERN FARM EQUIPMENT LTD *p358*
300 PTH 12 N, STEINBACH, MB, R5G 1T6
(204) 326-9834　*SIC 5999*

SPACES INC　*p111*
9319 47 ST NW, EDMONTON, AB, T6B 2R7
(587) 855-6684　*SIC 5999*

SPECTRUM COMMUNICATIONS INTERNATIONAL INC　*p656*
79 WELLINGTON ST, LONDON, ON, N6B 2K4
(519) 663-2109　*SIC 5999*

SPI SANTE SECURITE INC　*p1060*
60 RUE GASTON-DUMOULIN, BLAINVILLE, QC, J7C 0A3
(450) 420-2012　*SIC 5999*

STEWART'S, ED GARAGE & EQUIPMENT LTD　*p569*
9410 WELLINGTON RD 124 RR 2, ERIN, ON, N0B 1T0
(519) 833-9616　*SIC 5999*

STRAIGHT SHOOTER SAFETY INC　*p136*
GD, HIGH RIVER, AB, T1V 1M3
(403) 336-1124　*SIC 5999*

STRATECOM INC　*p1134*
1940 BOUL TASCHEREAU BUREAU 100A, LEMOYNE, QC, J4P 3N2
(450) 466-6640　*SIC 5999*

SUNDERLAND CO-OPERATIVE INC　*p901*
1 RIVER ST, SUNDERLAND, ON, L0C 1H0
(705) 357-3491　*SIC 5999*

SUNRAY MANUFACTURING INC　*p111*
7509 72A ST NW, EDMONTON, AB, T6B 1Z3
(780) 440-1595　*SIC 5999*

SUPERMARCHE CREVIER (IBERVILLE) INC　*p1282*
1124 BOUL IBERVILLE BUREAU 110, REPENTIGNY, QC, J5Y 3M6
(450) 704-4750　*SIC 5999*

SWISH MAINTENANCE LIMITED　*p842*
2060 FISHER DR, PETERBOROUGH, ON, K9J 6X6
(705) 745-5763　*SIC 5999*

TEN BUSS LIMITED　*p497*
430 HOLLAND ST W SUITE 446, BRADFORD, ON, L3Z 0G1
(905) 778-4330　*SIC 5999*

TIME BUSINESS MACHINES LTD　*p103*
17620 107 AVE NW, EDMONTON, AB, T5S 1G8
(780) 483-3040　*SIC 5999*

TOM HARRIS CELLULAR LTD　*p339*

3680 UPTOWN BLVD UNIT 209, VICTORIA, BC, V8Z 0B9
(250) 360-0606　*SIC 5999*

TOTALLY ONE COMMUNICATIONS INC *p560*
60 SARAMIA CRES SUITE 3, CONCORD, ON, L4K 4J7
(905) 761-1331　*SIC 5999*

TRENDWEST　*p228*
20258 FRASER HWY SUITE 104, LANGLEY, BC, V3A 4E6
(604) 534-5044　*SIC 5999*

TREVI FABRICATION INC　*p1068*
1235 RUE AMPERE, BOUCHERVILLE, QC, J4B 7M6
(514) 228-7384　*SIC 5999*

TRICOM SECURITY SERVICES INC　*p958*
20 QUEEN ST W, TORONTO, ON, M5H 3R3
(416) 651-7890　*SIC 5999*

TROCHU MOTORS LTD　*p170*
102 ECKENFELDER ST, TROCHU, AB, T0M 2C0
(403) 442-3866　*SIC 5999*

UPTOWN COMMUNICATION HOUSE INC *p854*
10 WEST PEARCE ST, RICHMOND HILL, ON, L4B 1B6
(905) 731-7318　*SIC 5999*

VALLEY INDUSTRIES (2007) LTD　*p460*
110 LAWRENCETOWN LANE, LAWRENCETOWN., NS, B0S 1M0
(902) 584-2211　*SIC 5999*

VECTOR COMMUNICATIONS LTD　*p133*
11213 97 AVE, GRANDE PRAIRIE, AB, T8V 5N5
(780) 532-2555　*SIC 5999*

WAL-MART CANADA CORP　*p530*
2065 FAIRVIEW ST, BURLINGTON, ON, L7R 0B4
(905) 637-3100　*SIC 5999*

WATER BLAST MANUFACTURING LP *p106*
16712 118 AVE NW, EDMONTON, AB, T5V 1P7
(780) 451-4521　*SIC 5999*

WEAGANT FARM SUPPLIES LIMITED *p1016*
11250 COUNTY RD 43, WINCHESTER, ON, K0C 2K0
(613) 774-2887　*SIC 5999*

WESTERN GASCO CYLINDERS LTD *p282*
18925 94 AVE UNIT 4, SURREY, BC, V4N 4X5
(604) 513-4429　*SIC 5999*

WINDMULLER, MONICA & KLAUS　*p496*
1 WARBRICK LANE, BOLTON, ON, L7E 1G3
(905) 857-0882　*SIC 5999*

WIRELESS PERSONAL COMMUNICATIONS INC　*p790*
166 BENTWORTH AVE, NORTH YORK, ON, M6A 1P7
(416) 667-4189　*SIC 5999*

XEROX CANADA LTD　*p775*
20 YORK MILLS RD SUITE 500, NORTH YORK, ON, M2P 2C2
(416) 733-6501　*SIC 5999*

YVES ROCHER AMERIQUE DU NORD INC *p1142*
2199 BOUL FERNAND-LAFONTAINE, LONGUEUIL, QC, J4G 2V7
(450) 442-9555　*SIC 5999*

SIC 6011 Federal reserve banks

BANK OF CANADA　*p815*
234 WELLINGTON ST, OTTAWA, ON, K1A 0G9
(613) 782-8111　*SIC 6011*

SIC 6021 National commercial banks

B2B BANK　*p944*

199 BAY ST SUITE 600, TORONTO, ON, M5G 1M5
(647) 826-7979　*SIC 6021*

BANK OF CHINA (CANADA) LTD　*p903*
50 MINTHORN BLVD SUITE 600, THORNHILL, ON, L3T 7X8
(905) 771-6886　*SIC 6021*

BANK OF MONTREAL　*p236*
610 SIXTH ST SUITE 125, NEW WESTMINSTER, BC, V3L 3C2
(604) 665-3770　*SIC 6021*

BANK OF MONTREAL　*p527*
865 HARRINGTON CRT, BURLINGTON, ON, L7N 3P3
SIC 6021

BANK OF MONTREAL　*p877*
3550 PHARMACY AVE, SCARBOROUGH, ON, M1W 3Z3
(416) 490-4300　*SIC 6021*

BANK OF MONTREAL　*p1187*
119 RUE SAINT-JACQUES, MONTREAL, QC, H2Y 1L6
(514) 877-7373　*SIC 6021*

BANK OF NOVA SCOTIA TRUST COMPANY, THE　*p937*
1 QUEEN ST E SUITE 1200, TORONTO, ON, M5C 2W5
(416) 866-7829　*SIC 6021*

BANK OF NOVA SCOTIA, THE　*p302*
815 HASTINGS ST W SUITE 300, VANCOUVER, BC, V6C 1B4
SIC 6021

BANK OF NOVA SCOTIA, THE　*p302*
409 GRANVILLE ST UNIT 700, VANCOUVER, BC, V6C 1T2
(604) 630-4000　*SIC 6021*

BANK OF NOVA SCOTIA, THE　*p377*
200 PORTAGE AVE, WINNIPEG, MB, R3C 2R7
(204) 985-3011　*SIC 6021*

BANK OF NOVA SCOTIA, THE　*p1193*
1002 RUE SHERBROOKE O BUREAU 200, MONTREAL, QC, H3A 3L6
(514) 499-5432　*SIC 6021*

BANK OF NOVA SCOTIA, THE　*p1193*
1002 RUE SHERBROOKE O BUREAU 600, MONTREAL, QC, H3A 3L6
(514) 287-3600　*SIC 6021*

BANK OF NOVA SCOTIA, THE　*p1214*
1922 RUE SAINTE-CATHERINE O BUREAU 300, MONTREAL, QC, H3H 1M4
SIC 6021

BANQUE NATIONALE DU CANADA　*p44*
407 8 AVE SW SUITE 1000, CALGARY, AB, T2P 1E5
(403) 294-4917　*SIC 6021*

BANQUE NATIONALE DU CANADA　*p985*
130 KING ST W SUITE 3200, TORONTO, ON, M5X 2A2
(647) 252-5380　*SIC 6021*

BANQUE NATIONALE DU CANADA　*p1187*
500 PLACE D'ARMES BUREAU 500, MONTREAL, QC, H2Y 2W3
(514) 394-6642　*SIC 6021*

BANQUE NATIONALE DU CANADA　*p1201*
600 RUE DE LA GAUCHETIERE O BUREAU 4E, MONTREAL, QC, H3B 4L3
(514) 394-4385　*SIC 6021*

BANQUE NATIONALE DU CANADA　*p1268*
333 GRANDE ALLEE E BUREAU 400, QUEBEC, QC, G1R 5W3
(418) 521-6400　*SIC 6021*

BANQUE NATIONALE DU CANADA　*p1328*
1130 BOUL MARCEL-LAURIN, SAINT-LAURENT, QC, H4R 1J7
(514) 332-4220　*SIC 6021*

BRIDGEWATER BANK　*p45*
926 5 AVE SW SUITE 150, CALGARY, AB, T2P 0N7
(866) 243-4301　*SIC 6021*

CANADIAN IMPERIAL BANK OF COMMERCE　*p971*
199 BAY ST COMMERCE CRT W, TORONTO, ON, M5L 1A2

▲ Public Company　■ Public Company Family Member　**HQ** Headquarters　**BR** Branch　**SL** Single Location

(416) 980-3096   *SIC 6021*
CANADIAN TEST CASE 174   *p730*
5770 HURONTARIO ST, MISSISSAUGA, ON, L5R 3G5
  SIC 6021
CANADIAN WESTERN BANK   *p87*
10303 JASPER AVE NW SUITE 3000, EDMONTON, AB, T5J 3N6
(780) 423-8888   *SIC 6021*
CANADIAN WESTERN BANK   *p303*
666 BURRARD ST 22ND FL, VANCOUVER, BC, V6C 2X8
(604) 669-0081   *SIC 6021*
CITIBANK CANADA   *p961*
123 FRONT ST W SUITE 1900, TORONTO, ON, M5J 2M3
(416) 947-5500   *SIC 6021*
CONCENTRA BANK   *p1426*
333 3RD AVE N, SASKATOON, SK, S7K 2M2
(306) 956-5100   *SIC 6021*
CORPORATION BNP PARIBAS CANADA
p1194
1981 AV MCGILL COLLEGE BUREAU 515, MONTREAL, QC, H3A 2W8
(514) 285-6000   *SIC 6021*
DEUTSCHE BANK AG- CANADA BRANCH
p971
199 BAY ST SUITE 4700, TORONTO, ON, M5L 1E9
(416) 682-8000   *SIC 6021*
EFFORT TRUST COMPANY, THE   *p611*
240 MAIN ST E, HAMILTON, ON, L8N 1H5
(905) 528-8956   *SIC 6021*
EQUITABLE BANK   *p926*
30 ST CLAIR AVE W SUITE 700, TORONTO, ON, M4V 3A1
(416) 515-7000   *SIC 6021*
FINANCIERE BANQUE NATIONALE INC
p374
200 WATERFRONT DR SUITE 400, WINNIPEG, MB, R3B 3P1
(204) 925-2250   *SIC 6021*
FINANC!ERE BANQUE NATIONALE INC
p1204
5E ETAGE 1155, RUE METCALFE, MONTREAL, QC, H3B 2V6
(514) 879-2222   *SIC 6021*
FIRM CAPITAL PROPERTY TRUST   *p988*
163 CARTWRIGHT AVE, TORONTO, ON, M6A 1V5
(416) 635-0221   *SIC 6021*
FIRST NATIONS BANK OF CANADA *p1427*
224 4TH AVE S SUITE 406, SASKATOON, SK, S7K 5M5
(306) 955-6739   *SIC 6021*
HOME TRUST COMPANY   *p952*
145 KING ST W SUITE 2300, TORONTO, ON, M5H 1J8
(416) 775-5000   *SIC 6021*
HSBC BANK CANADA   *p305*
885 GEORGIA ST W, VANCOUVER, BC, V6C 3G1
(604) 685-1000   *SIC 6021*
HSBC BANK CANADA   *p963*
70 YORK ST SUITE 800, TORONTO, ON, M5J 1S9
(416) 868-8000   *SIC 6021*
ICICI BANK CANADA   *p779*
150 FERRAND DR SUITE 1200, NORTH YORK, ON, M3C 3E5
(416) 847-7881   *SIC 6021*
INDUSTRIAL AND COMMERCIAL BANK OF CHINA (CANADA)   *p953*
333 BAY ST SUITE 3710, TORONTO, ON, M5H 2R2
(416) 366-5588   *SIC 6021*
KEB HANA BANK CANADA   *p772*
4950 YONGE ST SUITE 103, NORTH YORK, ON, M2N 6K1
(416) 222-5200   *SIC 6021*
KEB HANA BANK CANADA   *p772*
4950 YONGE ST UNIT 1101, NORTH YORK, ON, M2N 6K1

(416) 536-8046   *SIC 6021*
MANULIFE BANK OF CANADA   *p640*
500 KING ST N SUITE 500-MA, KITCHENER, ON, N2J 4Z6
(519) 747-7000   *SIC 6021*
MBNA CANADA BANK   *p595*
1600 JAMES NAISMITH DR SUITE 800, GLOUCESTER, ON, K1B 5N8
(613) 907-4800   *SIC 6021*
MOTUS BANK   *p996*
3280 BLOOR ST W CENTRE TOWER SUITE 700, TORONTO, ON, M8X 2X3
(905) 988-1000   *SIC 6021*
NATIONAL BANK TRUST INC   *p1206*
600 RUE DE LA GAUCHETIERE O BUREAU 2800, MONTREAL, QC, H3B 4L2
(514) 871-7100   *SIC 6021*
PEACE HILLS TRUST COMPANY   *p90*
10011 109 ST NW 10TH FL, EDMONTON, AB, T5J 3S8
(780) 421-1606   *SIC 6021*
PEOPLES TRUST COMPANY/COMPAGNIE DE FIDUCIE PEOPLES   *p308*
888 DUNSMUIR ST SUITE 1400, VANCOUVER, BC, V6C 3K4
(604) 683-2881   *SIC 6021*
ROYAL BANK OF CANADA   *p966*
200 BAY ST, TORONTO, ON, M5J 2J5
(416) 974-3940   *SIC 6021*
ROYAL BANK OF CANADA   *p966*
88 QUEENS QUAY W SUITE 300, TORONTO, ON, M5J 0B8
(416) 955-2777   *SIC 6021*
ROYAL TRUST CORPORATION OF CANADA   *p970*
77 KING ST W SUITE 3800, TORONTO, ON, M5K 2A1
(416) 974-1400   *SIC 6021*
SBI CANADA BANK   *p710*
77 CITY CENTRE DR SUITE 106, MISSISSAUGA, ON, L5B 1M5
(905) 896-6540   *SIC 6021*
TORONTO-DOMINION BANK, THE   *p91*
10004 JASPER AVE NW SUITE 500, EDMONTON, AB, T5J 1R3
(780) 448-8251   *SIC 6021*
TORONTO-DOMINION BANK, THE   *p701*
4880 TAHOE BLVD 5TH FL, MISSISSAUGA, ON, L4W 5P3
(905) 293-5613   *SIC 6021*
TORONTO-DOMINION BANK, THE   *p733*
20 MILVERTON DR SUITE 10, MISSISSAUGA, ON, L5R 3G2
(905) 568-3600   *SIC 6021*
TORONTO-DOMINION BANK, THE   *p970*
55 KING ST W, TORONTO, ON, M5K 1A2
(416) 982-5722   *SIC 6021*
TORONTO-DOMINION BANK, THE   *p970*
66 WELLINGTON ST W, TORONTO, ON, M5K 1A2
(416) 982-7650   *SIC 6021*
UBS BANK (CANADA)   *p958*
154 UNIVERSITY AVE SUITE 700, TORONTO, ON, M5H 3Y9
(416) 343-1800   *SIC 6021*
VANCITY COMMUNITY INVESTMENT BANK   *p300*
401 HASTINGS ST W SUITE 401, VANCOUVER, BC, V6B 1L5
(604) 708-7800   *SIC 6021*
VANCITY COMMUNITY INVESTMENT BANK   *p310*
815 HASTINGS ST W SUITE 401, VANCOUVER, BC, V6C 1B4
(604) 708-7800   *SIC 6021*
VERSABANK   *p655*
140 FULLARTON ST SUITE 2002, LONDON, ON, N6A 5P2
(519) 645-1919   *SIC 6021*
WPT INDUSTRIAL REAL ESTATE INVESTMENT TRUST   *p971*
199 BAY ST SUITE 4000, TORONTO, ON, M5L 1A9
(800) 230-9505   *SIC 6021*

SIC 6036 Savings institutions, except federal

ATB FINANCIAL   *p87*
10020 100 ST NW SUITE 2100, EDMONTON, AB, T5J 0N3
(780) 408-7000   *SIC 6036*
CAISSE DESJARDINS DU LAC-MEMPHREMAGOG   *p1148*
342 RUE PRINCIPALE, MANSONVILLE, QC, J0E 1X0
(819) 843-3328   *SIC 6036*
TANGERINE BANK   *p765*
3389 STEELES AVE E, NORTH YORK, ON, M2H 3S8
(416) 497-5157   *SIC 6036*

SIC 6062 State credit unions

1ST CHOICE SAVINGS AND CREDIT UNION LTD   *p143*
45 FAIRMONT BLVD S, LETHBRIDGE, AB, T1K 1T1
(403) 320-4600   *SIC 6062*
ACCESS CREDIT UNION LIMITED   *p361*
23111 PTH 14 UNIT 2, WINKLER, MB, R6W 4B4
(204) 331-1612   *SIC 6062*
ADVANTAGE CREDIT UNION   *p1410*
114 MAIN ST, MELFORT, SK, S0E 1A0
(306) 752-2744   *SIC 6062*
ALTERNA SAVINGS   *p582*
165 ATTWELL DR, ETOBICOKE, ON, M9W 5Y5
(416) 213-7900   *SIC 6062*
ALTERNA SAVINGS AND CREDIT UNION LIMITED   *p828*
319 MCRAE AVE, OTTAWA, ON, K1Z 0B9
(613) 560-0150   *SIC 6062*
ASSINIBOINE CREDIT UNION LIMITED, THE   *p376*
200 MAIN ST 6TH FL, WINNIPEG, MB, R3C 1A8
(204) 958-8588   *SIC 6062*
BLUESHORE FINANCIAL CREDIT UNION
p240
1250 LONSDALE AVE, NORTH VANCOUVER, BC, V7M 2H6
(604) 983-4500   *SIC 6062*
CAISSE D'ECONOMIE SOLIDAIRE DESJARDINS   *p1258*
155 BOUL CHAREST E BUREAU 500, QUEBEC, QC, G1K 3G6
(418) 647-1527   *SIC 6062*
CAISSE DESJARDINS CHARLES-LEMOYNE   *p1322*
477 AV VICTORIA, SAINT-LAMBERT, QC, J4P 2J1
(450) 671-3733   *SIC 6062*
CAISSE DESJARDINS D'AMOS   *p1046*
2 RUE PRINCIPALE N, AMOS, QC, J9T 2K6
  SIC 6062
CAISSE DESJARDINS DE BEAUPORT
p1254
799 RUE CLEMENCEAU, QUEBEC, QC, G1C 8J7
(418) 660-3119   *SIC 6062*
CAISSE DESJARDINS DE BOUCHERVILLE
p1064
1071 BOUL DE MONTARVILLE, BOUCHERVILLE, QC, J4B 6R2
(450) 655-9041   *SIC 6062*
CAISSE DESJARDINS DE CHICOUTIMI
p1078
245 RUE RACINE E, CHICOUTIMI, QC, G7H 1S4
(418) 549-3224   *SIC 6062*
CAISSE DESJARDINS DE CHOMEDEY
p1087
3075 BOUL CARTIER O, COTE SAINT-LUC, QC, H7V 1J4
(450) 688-0900   *SIC 6062*
CAISSE DESJARDINS DE DRUM-

MONDVILLE   *p1098*
460 BOUL SAINT-JOSEPH, DRUMMONDVILLE, QC, J2C 2A8
(819) 474-2524   *SIC 6062*
CAISSE DESJARDINS DE DRUMMONDVILLE   *p1098*
460 BOUL SAINT-JOSEPH, DRUMMONDVILLE, QC, J2C 2A8
(819) 474-2524   *SIC 6062*
CAISSE DESJARDINS DE GRANBY-HAUTE-YAMASKA   *p1108*
450 RUE PRINCIPALE, GRANBY, QC, J2G 2X1
(450) 777-5353   *SIC 6062*
CAISSE DESJARDINS DE HULL-AYLMER
p1106
250 BOUL SAINT-JOSEPH, GATINEAU, QC, J8Y 3X6
(819) 776-3000   *SIC 6062*
CAISSE DESJARDINS DE HULL-AYLMER
p1107
219 BOUL DU PLATEAU, GATINEAU, QC, J9A 0N4
(819) 776-3000   *SIC 6062*
CAISSE DESJARDINS DE JONQUIERE
p1116
2358 RUE SAINT-DOMINIQUE, JONQUIERE, QC, G7X 0M7
(418) 695-1850   *SIC 6062*
CAISSE DESJARDINS DE L'ERABLE *p1246*
1658 RUE SAINT-CALIXTE, PLESSISVILLE, QC, G6L 1P9
(819) 362-3236   *SIC 6062*
CAISSE DESJARDINS DE L'OUEST DE LA MAURICIE   *p1146*
75 AV SAINT-LAURENT BUREAU 300, LOUISEVILLE, QC, J5V 1J6
(819) 228-9422   *SIC 6062*
CAISSE DESJARDINS DE L'OUEST DE LA MONTEREGIE   *p1151*
724 BOUL SAINT-JEAN-BAPTISTE, MERCIER, QC, J6R 0B2
(450) 698-2204   *SIC 6062*
CAISSE DESJARDINS DE L'OUEST DE LAVAL   *p1363*
440 CHOMEDEY (A-13) O, SAINTE-ROSE, QC, H7X 3S9
(450) 962-1800   *SIC 6062*
CAISSE DESJARDINS DE LA CHAUDIERE
p1137
1190B RUE DE COURCHEVEL BUREAU 103, LEVIS, QC, G6W 0M6
(418) 839-8819   *SIC 6062*
CAISSE DESJARDINS DE LA REGION DE SAINT-HYACINTHE   *p1311*
1697 RUE GIROUARD O, SAINT-HYACINTHE, QC, J2S 2Z9
(450) 768-3030   *SIC 6062*
CAISSE DESJARDINS DE LA REGION DE THETFORD   *p1382*
300 BOUL FRONTENAC E, THETFORD MINES, QC, G6G 7M8
(418) 338-3591   *SIC 6062*
CAISSE DESJARDINS DE LA VALLEE DES PAYS-D'EN-HAUT   *p1352*
218 RUE PRINCIPALE, SAINT-SAUVEUR, QC, J0R 1R0
(450) 227-3712   *SIC 6062*
CAISSE DESJARDINS DE LORIMIER-VILLERAY   *p1171*
2050 BOUL ROSEMONT, MONTREAL, QC, H2G 1T1
(514) 376-7676   *SIC 6062*
CAISSE DESJARDINS DE MERCIER-ROSEMONT   *p1346*
6955 RUE JEAN-TALON E, SAINT-LEONARD, QC, H1S 1N2
(514) 254-7878   *SIC 6062*
CAISSE DESJARDINS DE QUEBEC *p1258*
135 RUE SAINT-VALLIER O, QUEBEC, QC, G1K 1J9
(418) 687-2810   *SIC 6062*
CAISSE DESJARDINS DE QUEBEC *p1263*
150 RUE MARIE-DE-L'INCARNATION,

QUEBEC, QC, G1N 4G8
(418) 687-2810   *SIC* 6062

CAISSE DESJARDINS DE RIMOUSKI *p*1284
100 RUE JULIEN-REHEL, RIMOUSKI, QC, G5L 0G6
(418) 723-3368   *SIC* 6062

CAISSE DESJARDINS DE SAINT-ANTOINE-DES-LAURENTIDES *p*1320
663 BOUL SAINT-ANTOINE, SAINT-JEROME, QC, J7Z 3B8
(450) 436-5331   *SIC* 6062

CAISSE DESJARDINS DE SAINT-HUBERT *p*1307
2400 BOUL GAETAN-BOUCHER, SAINT-HUBERT, QC, J3Y 5B7
(450) 443-0047   *SIC* 6062

CAISSE DESJARDINS DE SAINTE-FOY *p*1274
990 AV DE BOURGOGNE BUREAU 200, QUEBEC, QC, G1W 0E8
(418) 653-0515   *SIC* 6062

CAISSE DESJARDINS DE SAINTE-FOY *p*1275
3211 CH SAINTE-FOY, QUEBEC, QC, G1X 1R3
(418) 653-0515   *SIC* 6062

CAISSE DESJARDINS DE SALABERRY-DE-VALLEYFIELD *p*1365
120 RUE ALEXANDRE, SALABERRY-DE-VALLEYFIELD, QC, J6S 3K4
(450) 377-4177   *SIC* 6062

CAISSE DESJARDINS DE SALABERRY-DE-VALLEYFIELD *p*1366
15 RUE SAINT-THOMAS, SALABERRY-DE-VALLEYFIELD, QC, J6T 4J1
(450) 377-4177   *SIC* 6062

CAISSE DESJARDINS DE SAULT-AU-RECOLLET-MONTREAL-NORD *p*1240
10205 BOUL PIE-IX, MONTREAL-NORD, QC, H1H 3Z4
(514) 322-9310   *SIC* 6062

CAISSE DESJARDINS DE SILLERY–SAINT-LOUIS-DE-FRANCE *p*1271
1444 AV MAGUIRE, QUEBEC, QC, G1T 1Z3
(418) 681-3566   *SIC* 6062

CAISSE DESJARDINS DE VIMONT-AUTEUIL *p*1232
5350 BOUL DES LAURENTIDES, MON-TREAL, QC, H7K 2J8
(450) 669-2694   *SIC* 6062

CAISSE DESJARDINS DES BOIS-FRANCS *p*1397
300 BOUL DES BOIS-FRANCS S, VICTO-RIAVILLE, QC, G6P 7W7
(819) 758-9421   *SIC* 6062

CAISSE DESJARDINS DES GRANDS BOULEVARDS DE LAVAL *p*1133
3111 BOUL SAINT-MARTIN O, LAVAL, QC, H7T 0K2
(450) 667-9950   *SIC* 6062

CAISSE DESJARDINS DES POLICIERS ET POLICIERES *p*1173
460 RUE GILFORD, MONTREAL, QC, H2J 1N3
(514) 847-1004   *SIC* 6062

CAISSE DESJARDINS DES RIVIERES DE QUEBEC *p*1276
2287 AV CHAUVEAU, QUEBEC, QC, G2C 0G7
(418) 842-1214   *SIC* 6062

CAISSE DESJARDINS DES SEIGNEURIES DE BELLECHASE *p*1297
2807 AV ROYALE, SAINT-CHARLES-DE-BELLECHASSE, QC, G0R 2T0
(418) 887-3337   *SIC* 6062

CAISSE DESJARDINS DES SEIGNEURIES DE LA FRONTIERE *p*1242
373 RUE SAINT-JACQUES, NAPIERVILLE, QC, J0J 1L0
(450) 245-3391   *SIC* 6062

CAISSE DESJARDINS DES TROIS-RIVIERES *p*1387
1200 RUE ROYALE, TROIS-RIVIERES, QC,

G9A 4J2
(819) 376-1200   *SIC* 6062

CAISSE DESJARDINS DES VERTS-SOMMETS DE L'ESTRIE *p*1081
155 RUE CHILD, COATICOOK, QC, J1A 2B4
(819) 849-0434   *SIC* 6062

CAISSE DESJARDINS DU CARREFOUR DES LACS *p*1090
572 AV JACQUES-CARTIER, DISRAELI, QC, G0N 1E0
(418) 449-2652   *SIC* 6062

CAISSE DESJARDINS DU CENTRE-DE-LA-MAURICIE *p*1368
444 5E RUE DE LA POINTE, SHAWINIGAN, QC, G9N 1E6
(819) 536-4404   *SIC* 6062

CAISSE DESJARDINS DU COEUR DE BEL-LECHASSE *p*1291
730 RTE BEGIN, SAINT-ANSELME, QC, G0R 2N0
(418) 885-4421   *SIC* 6062

CAISSE DESJARDINS DU COEUR-DE-L'ILE *p*1171
2050 BOUL ROSEMONT, MONTREAL, QC, H2G 1T1
(514) 376-7676   *SIC* 6062

CAISSE DESJARDINS DU HAUT-RICHELIEU *p*1315
175 BOUL OMER-MARCIL, SAINT-JEAN-SUR-RICHELIEU, QC, J2W 0A3
(450) 359-5933   *SIC* 6062

CAISSE DESJARDINS DU HAUT-RICHELIEU *p*1316
730 BOUL D'IBERVILLE, SAINT-JEAN-SUR-RICHELIEU, QC, J2X 3Z9
(450) 357-5000   *SIC* 6062

CAISSE DESJARDINS DU LAC-MEMPHREMAGOG *p*1147
230 RUE PRINCIPALE O, MAGOG, QC, J1X 2A5
SIC 6062

CAISSE DESJARDINS DU MONT-SAINT-BRUNO *p*1295
1649 RUE MONTARVILLE, SAINT-BRUNO, QC, J3V 3T8
(450) 653-3646   *SIC* 6062

CAISSE DESJARDINS DU NORD DE LAVAL *p*1361
396 BOUL CURE-LABELLE, SAINTE-ROSE, QC, H7L 4T7
(450) 622-8130   *SIC* 6062

CAISSE DESJARDINS DU NORD DE SHER-BROOKE *p*1371
1845 RUE KING O, SHERBROOKE, QC, J1J 2E4
(819) 566-0050   *SIC* 6062

CAISSE DESJARDINS DU SUD DE LA CHAUDIERE *p*1304
10555 BOUL LACROIX, SAINT-GEORGES, QC, G5Y 1K2
(418) 228-8824   *SIC* 6062

CAISSE DESJARDINS GODEFROY *p*1056
4265 BOUL DE PORT-ROYAL, BECAN-COUR, QC, G9H 1Z3
(819) 233-2333   *SIC* 6062

CAISSE DESJARDINS PIERRE-BOUCHER *p*1145
2401 BOUL ROLAND-THERRIEN, LONGUEUIL, QC, J4N 1C5
(450) 468-7411   *SIC* 6062

CAISSE DESJARDINS PIERRE-LE GARDEUR *p*1282
477 RUE NOTRE-DAME, REPENTIGNY, QC, J6A 2T6
(450) 585-5555   *SIC* 6062

CAISSE DESJARDINS THERESE-DE BLAINVILLE *p*1364
201 BOUL DU CURE-LABELLE, SAINTE-THERESE, QC, J7E 2X6
(450) 430-6550   *SIC* 6062

CAISSE POPULAIRE DE LA PRAIRIE *p*1123
450 BOUL TASCHEREAU, LA PRAIRIE, QC, J5R 1V1

(450) 659-5431   *SIC* 6062

CAISSE POPULAIRE DES VOYAGEURS INC *p*899
531 NOTRE DAME AVE, SUDBURY, ON, P3C 5L1
(705) 674-4234   *SIC* 6062

CAISSE POPULAIRE DESJARDINS CANA-DIENNE ITALIENNE *p*1182
6999 BOUL SAINT-LAURENT, MONTREAL, QC, H2S 3E1
(514) 270-4124   *SIC* 6062

CAISSE POPULAIRE DESJARDINS D'ALMA *p*1044
600 RUE COLLARD, ALMA, QC, G8B 1N4
(418) 669-1414   *SIC* 6062

CAISSE POPULAIRE DESJARDINS DE CHARLESBOURG *p*1256
155 76E RUE E, QUEBEC, QC, G1H 1G4
(418) 626-1146   *SIC* 6062

CAISSE POPULAIRE DESJARDINS DE L'ENVOLEE *p*1058
1070 BOUL DU CURE-LABELLE, BLAINVILLE, QC, J7C 2M7
(450) 430-4603   *SIC* 6062

CAISSE POPULAIRE DESJARDINS DE L'ENVOLEE *p*1152
13845 BOUL DU CURE-LABELLE, MIRABEL, QC, J7J 1A1
(450) 430-4603   *SIC* 6062

CAISSE POPULAIRE DESJARDINS DE RICHELIEU-SAINT-MATHIAS *p*1283
1111 3E RUE, RICHELIEU, QC, J3L 3Z2
(450) 658-0649   *SIC* 6062

CAISSE POPULAIRE DESJARDINS DE SAINT-LAURENT, LA *p*1323
1460 RUE DE L'EGLISE, SAINT-LAURENT, QC, H4L 2H6
(514) 748-8821   *SIC* 6062

CAISSE POPULAIRE DESJARDINS DES MILLE-ILES *p*1231
4433 BOUL DE LA CONCORDE E, MON-TREAL, QC, H7C 1M4
(450) 661-7274   *SIC* 6062

CAISSE POPULAIRE DESJARDINS DES RAMEES *p*1120
1278 CH DE LA VERNIERE, L'ETANG-DU-NORD, QC, G4T 3E6
(418) 986-2319   *SIC* 6062

CAISSE POPULAIRE DESJARDINS DU BASSIN-DE-CHAMBLY *p*1074
455 BOUL BRASSARD, CHAMBLY, QC, J3L 4V6
(450) 658-0691   *SIC* 6062

CAISSE POPULAIRE DESJARDINS DU PIEMONT LAURENTIEN *p*1119
1638 RUE NOTRE-DAME, L'ANCIENNE-LORETTE, QC, G2E 3B6
(418) 872-1445   *SIC* 6062

CAISSE POPULAIRE DESJARDINS LE MANOIR *p*1149
820 MONTEE MASSON, MASCOUCHE, QC, J7K 3B6
(450) 474-2474   *SIC* 6062

CAISSE POPULAIRE KENT-SUD LTEE *p*395
196 IRVING BLVD, BOUCTOUCHE, NB, E4S 3L7
(506) 576-6666   *SIC* 6062

CAISSE POPULAIRE LA PRAIRIE LTEE *p*357
130 CENTRALE AVE, STE ANNE, MB, R5H 1J3
(204) 422-8896   *SIC* 6062

CAISSE POPULAIRE LA VALLEE LTEE *p*403
181 BOUL BROADWAY, GRAND-SAULT/GRAND FALLS, NB, E3Z 2J8
(506) 473-3660   *SIC* 6062

CAISSE POPULAIRE TRILLIUM INC *p*596
1173 CYRVILLE RD, GLOUCESTER, ON, K1J 7S6
(613) 745-2123   *SIC* 6062

CAISSES DESJARDINS DES BERGES DE ROUSSILLON *p*1297
296 VOIE DE LA DESSERTE, SAINT-

CONSTANT, QC, J5A 2C9
(450) 632-2820   *SIC* 6062

CAMBRIAN CREDIT UNION LIMITED *p*377
225 BROADWAY, WINNIPEG, MB, R3C 5R4
(204) 925-2600   *SIC* 6062

CASERA CREDIT UNION LIMITED *p*362
1300 PLESSIS RD, WINNIPEG, MB, R2C 2Y6
(204) 958-6300   *SIC* 6062

CHINOOK CREDIT UNION LTD *p*7
99 2 ST W, BROOKS, AB, T1R 1B9
(403) 362-4233   *SIC* 6062

COAST CAPITAL SAVINGS FEDERAL CREDIT UNION *p*273
9900 KING GEORGE BLVD SUITE 800, SURREY, BC, V3T 0K7
(604) 517-7400   *SIC* 6062

COASTAL COMMUNITY CREDIT UNION *p*233
59 WHARF ST UNIT 220, NANAIMO, BC, V9R 2X3
(250) 716-2331   *SIC* 6062

COASTAL COMMUNITY CREDIT UNION *p*233
59 WHARF ST SUITE 220, NANAIMO, BC, V9R 2X3
(250) 741-3200   *SIC* 6062

COMMUNITY SAVINGS CREDIT UNION *p*274
13450 102 AVE SUITE 1600, SURREY, BC, V3T 5X3
(604) 654-2000   *SIC* 6062

CONEXUS CREDIT UNION 2006 *p*1413
2800 2ND AVE W, PRINCE ALBERT, SK, S6V 5Z4
(306) 953-6100   *SIC* 6062

CONEXUS CREDIT UNION 2006 *p*1417
1960 ALBERT ST SUITE 205, REGINA, SK, S4P 2T1
(800) 667-7477   *SIC* 6062

CREDIT UNION CENTRAL ALBERTA LIM-ITED *p*35
8500 MACLEOD TRAIL SE SUITE 350N, CALGARY, AB, T2H 2N1
(403) 258-5900   *SIC* 6062

CREDIT UNION CENTRAL OF CANADA *p*179
2941 272 ST, ALDERGROVE, BC, V4W 3R3
(604) 856-7724   *SIC* 6062

CREDIT UNION CENTRAL OF CANADA *p*455
6074 LADY HAMMOND RD, HALIFAX, NS, B3K 2R7
(902) 453-0680   *SIC* 6062

DUCA FINANCIAL SERVICES CREDIT UNION LTD *p*771
5290 YONGE ST, NORTH YORK, ON, M2N 5P9
(416) 223-8502   *SIC* 6062

EAST COAST CREDIT UNION LIMITED *p*438
257 MAIN ST, ANTIGONISH, NS, B2G 2C1
SIC 6062

FEDERATION DES CAISSES DESJARDINS DU QUEBEC *p*1076
235 CH DE LA HAUTE-RIVIERE, CHATEAUGUAY, QC, J6K 5B1
(450) 692-1000   *SIC* 6062

FEDERATION DES CAISSES DESJARDINS DU QUEBEC *p*1136
100 RUE DES COMMANDEURS, LEVIS, QC, G6V 7N5
(418) 835-8444   *SIC* 6062

FEDERATION DES CAISSES DESJARDINS DU QUEBEC *p*1191
425 AV VIGER O BUREAU 900, MON-TREAL, QC, H2Z 1W5
(514) 397-4789   *SIC* 6062

FEDERATION DES CAISSES DESJARDINS DU QUEBEC *p*1230
1 COMPLEX DESJARDINS, MONTREAL, QC, H5B 1B2
(514) 281-7000   *SIC* 6062

FEDERATION DES CAISSES POPULAIRE ACADIENNES INC, LA *p*396

295 BOUL ST-PIERRE O, CARAQUET, NB, E1W 1A4
(506) 726-4000 *SIC 6062*
FIRST WEST CREDIT UNION p196
9240 YOUNG RD, CHILLIWACK, BC, V2P 4R2
(604) 539-7300 *SIC 6062*
FIRSTONTARIO CREDIT UNION LIMITED p609
1299 BARTON ST E, HAMILTON, ON, L8H 2V4
(800) 616-8878 *SIC 6062*
FIRSTONTARIO CREDIT UNION LIMITED p885
3969 MONTROSE, ST CATHARINES, ON, L2R 6Z4
(905) 685-5555 *SIC 6062*
FIRSTONTARIO CREDIT UNION LIMITED p892
970 SOUTH SERVICE RD SUITE 301, STONEY CREEK, ON, L8E 6A2
(905) 387-0770 *SIC 6062*
GULF AND FRASER FISHERMEN'S CREDIT UNION p181
7375 KINGSWAY, BURNABY, BC, V3N 3B5
(604) 517-5100 *SIC 6062*
GULF AND FRASER FISHERMEN'S CREDIT UNION p181
7375 KINGSWAY, BURNABY, BC, V3N 3B5
(604) 419-8888 *SIC 6062*
INNOVATION CREDIT UNION LIMITED p1412
1202 102ND ST, NORTH BATTLEFORD, SK, S9A 1G3
(306) 446-7000 *SIC 6062*
INTERIOR SAVINGS CREDIT UNION p222
678 BERNARD AVE SUITE 300, KELOWNA, BC, V1Y 6P3
(250) 869-8300 *SIC 6062*
ISLAND SAVINGS CREDIT UNION p211
499 CANADA AVE SUITE 300, DUNCAN, BC, V9L 1T7
(250) 748-4728 *SIC 6062*
KOOTENAY SAVINGS CREDIT UNION p284
1101 DEWDNEY AVE SUITE 106, TRAIL, BC, V1R 4T1
(250) 368-2686 *SIC 6062*
LIBRO CREDIT UNION LIMITED p654
217 YORK ST SUITE 100, LONDON, ON, N6A 5P9
(519) 672-0124 *SIC 6062*
MERIDIAN CREDIT UNION LIMITED p572
3280 BLOOR ST W, ETOBICOKE, ON, M8X 2X3
(416) 597-4400 *SIC 6062*
MERIDIAN CREDIT UNION LIMITED p887
75 CORPORATE PARK DR SUITE 1, ST CATHARINES, ON, L2S 3W3
(905) 937-4222 *SIC 6062*
MOUNTAIN VIEW CREDIT UNION LTD p151
4920 50 AVE, OLDS, AB, T4H 1P5
(403) 556-3306 *SIC 6062*
NEWFOUNDLAND & LABRADOR CREDIT UNION LIMITED p432
240 WATER ST, ST. JOHN'S, NL, A1C 1B7
(709) 722-5824 *SIC 6062*
NORTH PEACE SAVINGS AND CREDIT UNION p214
10344 100 ST, FORT ST. JOHN, BC, V1J 3Z1
(250) 787-0361 *SIC 6062*
NORTHERN CREDIT UNION LIMITED p863
280 MCNABB ST, SAULT STE. MARIE, ON, P6B 1Y6
(705) 949-2644 *SIC 6062*
NORTHERN CREDIT UNION LTD p863
681 PINE ST, SAULT STE. MARIE, ON, P6B 3G2
(705) 253-9868 *SIC 6062*
NORTHERN SAVINGS CREDIT UNION p251
138 3RD AVE W, PRINCE RUPERT, BC, V8J 1K8
(250) 627-3612 *SIC 6062*
PACE SAVINGS & CREDIT UNION LIMITED

p557
8111 JANE ST UNIT 1, CONCORD, ON, L4K 4L7
(905) 738-8900 *SIC 6062*
PENFINANCIAL CREDIT UNION LIMITED p1012
247 EAST MAIN ST, WELLAND, ON, L3B 3X1
(905) 735-4801 *SIC 6062*
RAPPORT CREDIT UNION LIMITED p932
18 GRENVILLE ST SUITE 1, TORONTO, ON, M4Y 3B3
(416) 314-6772 *SIC 6062*
SALMON ARM SAVINGS AND CREDIT UNION p268
370 LAKESHORE DR NE, SALMON ARM, BC, V1E 1E4
(250) 832-8011 *SIC 6062*
SERVUS CREDIT UNION LTD p121
151 KARL CLARK RD NW, EDMONTON, AB, T6N 1H5
(780) 496-2000 *SIC 6062*
SERVUS CREDIT UNION LTD p154
4901 48 ST SUITE 201, RED DEER, AB, T4N 6M4
(403) 342-5533 *SIC 6062*
ST STANISLAUS-ST CASIMIR'S POLISH PARISHES CREDIT UNION LIMITED p995
220 RONCESVALLES AVE, TORONTO, ON, M6R 2L7
(416) 537-2181 *SIC 6062*
STEINBACH CREDIT UNION LIMITED p358
305 MAIN ST, STEINBACH, MB, R5G 1B1
(204) 326-3495 *SIC 6062*
SUNOVA CREDIT UNION LIMITED p356
233 MAIN ST, SELKIRK, MB, R1A 1S1
(204) 785-7625 *SIC 6062*
SUNOVA CREDIT UNION LIMITED p359
410 CENTRE AVE, STONEWALL, MB, R0C 2Z0
(204) 467-5574 *SIC 6062*
SUNRISE CREDIT UNION LIMITED p360
220 7TH AVE S, VIRDEN, MB, R0M 2C0
(204) 748-2907 *SIC 6062*
SUNSHINE COAST CREDIT UNION p214
985 GIBSONS WAY RR 8, GIBSONS, BC, V0N 1V8
(604) 740-2662 *SIC 6062*
SYNERGY CREDIT UNION LTD p1409
4907 50 ST, LLOYDMINSTER, SK, S9V 0N1
(306) 825-3301 *SIC 6062*
TANDIA FINANCIAL CREDIT UNION LIMITED p613
75 JAMES ST S, HAMILTON, ON, L8P 2Y9
(800) 598-2891 *SIC 6062*
TCU FINANCIAL GROUP p1435
307 LUDLOW ST, SASKATOON, SK, S7S 1N6
(306) 651-6700 *SIC 6062*
TEACHERS CREDIT UNION LIMITED p613
75 JAMES ST S, HAMILTON, ON, L8P 2Y9
(905) 525-8131 *SIC 6062*
VALLEY FIRST CREDIT UNION p244
184 MAIN ST, PENTICTON, BC, V2A 8G7
(250) 490-2720 *SIC 6062*
VANCOUVER CITY SAVINGS CREDIT UNION p296
183 TERMINAL AVE, VANCOUVER, BC, V6A 4G2
(604) 877-7013 *SIC 6062*
WESTMINSTER SAVINGS CREDIT UNION p274
13450 102 AVE SUITE 1900, SURREY, BC, V3T 5Y1
(604) 517-0100 *SIC 6062*
WEYBURN CREDIT UNION LIMITED p1438
205 COTEAU AVE, WEYBURN, SK, S4H 0G5
(306) 842-6641 *SIC 6062*
WINDSOR FAMILY CREDIT UNION LIMITED p1022
3000 MARENTETTE AVE, WINDSOR, ON, N8X 4G2
(519) 974-1181 *SIC 6062*

YOUR CREDIT UNION LTD p826
14 CHAMBERLAIN AVE SUITE 200, OTTAWA, ON, K1S 1V9
(613) 238-8001 *SIC 6062*
YOUR NEIGHBOURHOOD CREDIT UNION LIMITED p641
38 EXECUTIVE PL, KITCHENER, ON, N2P 2N4
(519) 804-9190 *SIC 6062*

SIC 6081 Foreign bank and branches and agencies

SOCIETE GENERALE (CANADA) p1199
1501 AV MCGILL COLLEGE BUREAU 1800, MONTREAL, QC, H3A 3M8
(514) 841-6000 *SIC 6081*

SIC 6091 Nondeposit trust facilities

CANADIAN WESTERN TRUST COMPANY p297
750 CAMBIE ST SUITE 300, VANCOUVER, BC, V6B 0A2
(604) 685-2081 *SIC 6091*
CIBC MELLON GLOBAL SECURITIES SERVICES COMPANY p653
150 DUFFERIN AVE 5TH FL, LONDON, ON, N6A 5N6
(519) 873-2218 *SIC 6091*
CIBC MELLON GLOBAL SECURITIES SERVICES COMPANY p961
1 YORK ST SUITE 500, TORONTO, ON, M5J 0B6
(416) 643-5000 *SIC 6091*
OLYMPIA FINANCIAL GROUP INC p31
125 9 AVE SE SUITE 2300, CALGARY, AB, T2G 0P6
(403) 261-0900 *SIC 6091*
OLYMPIA TRUST COMPANY p31
125 9 AVE SE SUITE 2300, CALGARY, AB, T2G 0P6
(403) 261-0900 *SIC 6091*

SIC 6099 Functions related to deposit banking

1022481 ONTARIO INC p813
419 KING ST W SUITE 2482, OSHAWA, ON, L1J 2K5
(905) 576-1600 *SIC 6099*
ACCESS CASH GENERAL PARTNERSHIP p581
191 ATTWELL DR UNIT 4, ETOBICOKE, ON, M9W 5Z2
(416) 247-0200 *SIC 6099*
AMEX CANADA INC p766
2225 SHEPPARD AVE E, NORTH YORK, ON, M2J 5C2
(905) 474-8000 *SIC 6099*
CALGARY FOREIGN EXCHANGE LTD p45
255 5 AVE SUITE 480, CALGARY, AB, T2P 3G6
(403) 290-0400 *SIC 6099*
CAMBRIDGE MERCANTILE CORP p949
212 KING ST W SUITE 400, TORONTO, ON, M5H 1K5
(416) 646-6401 *SIC 6099*
CARDTRONICS CANADA HOLDINGS INC p10
1420 28 ST NE SUITE 6, CALGARY, AB, T2A 7W6
(403) 207-1500 *SIC 6099*
CARDTRONICS CANADA HOLDINGS INC p687
3269 AMERICAN DR SUITE 1, MISSISSAUGA, ON, L4V 1V4
(905) 678-7373 *SIC 6099*
CASH 4 YOU CORP p533
250 DUNDAS ST S UNIT 10, CAMBRIDGE, ON, N1R 8A8

(519) 620-1900 *SIC 6099*
CASH NOWPLUS INC p667
3100 STEELES AVE E SUITE 906, MARKHAM, ON, L3R 8T3
(905) 470-0084 *SIC 6099*
CUSTOM HOUSE ULC p279
409-2626 CROYDON DR, SURREY, BC, V3Z 0S8
(604) 560-8060 *SIC 6099*
DIRECT CASH (LNET) p10
1420 28 ST NE SUITE 6, CALGARY, AB, T2A 7W6
(403) 207-1500 *SIC 6099*
ENCOREFX INC p336
517 FORT ST FL 2, VICTORIA, BC, V8W 1E7
(250) 412-5253 *SIC 6099*
EVERLINK PAYMENT SERVICES INC p904
125 COMMERCE VALLEY DR W UNIT 100, THORNHILL, ON, L3T 7W4
(905) 946-5898 *SIC 6099*
EXCHANGE CORPORATION CANADA INC p264
4831 MILLER RD SUITE 206, RICHMOND, BC, V7B 1K7
(604) 656-1700 *SIC 6099*
FIRMA FOREIGN EXCHANGE CORPORATION p89
10205 101 ST NW SUITE 400, EDMONTON, AB, T5J 2P4
(780) 426-4946 *SIC 6099*
FIRST DATA CANADA LIMITED p695
2630 SKYMARK AVE SUITE 400, MISSISSAUGA, ON, L4W 5A4
(905) 602-3509 *SIC 6099*
HOCK SHOP INC p484
400 BAYFIELD ST, BARRIE, ON, L4M 5A1
(705) 728-2274 *SIC 6099*
MERCANTILE EXCHANGE CORPORATION p939
8 KING ST E 14TH FL, TORONTO, ON, M5C 1B5
(416) 368-3680 *SIC 6099*
NATIONAL MONEY MART COMPANY p334
401 GARBALLY RD, VICTORIA, BC, V8T 5M3
(250) 595-5211 *SIC 6099*
NT SERVICES LIMITED p24
215 16 ST SE 3RD FL, CALGARY, AB, T2E 7P5
(403) 769-3600 *SIC 6099*
PACNET SERVICES LTD p308
595 HOWE ST 4 FL, VANCOUVER, BC, V6C 2T5
(604) 689-0399 *SIC 6099*
PNB REMITTANCE COMPANY (CANADA) p710
3050 CONFEDERATION PKY UNIT 104, MISSISSAUGA, ON, L5B 3Z6
(905) 897-9600 *SIC 6099*
REVENUEWIRE INC p333
3962 BORDEN ST SUITE 102, VICTORIA, BC, V8P 3H8
(250) 590-2273 *SIC 6099*
TRAVELEX CANADA LIMITED p941
100 YONGE ST, TORONTO, ON, M5C 2W1
(416) 359-3700 *SIC 6099*
TULLETT PREBON CANADA LIMITED p941
1 TORONTO ST SUITE 803, TORONTO, ON, M5C 2V6
(416) 941-0606 *SIC 6099*
VANCOUVER BULLION AND CURRENCY EXCHANGE LTD p310
800 PENDER ST W SUITE 120, VANCOUVER, BC, V6C 2V6
(604) 685-1008 *SIC 6099*
VELOCITY TRADE HOLDINGS LTD p941
100 YONGE ST SUITE 1800, TORONTO, ON, M5C 2W1
(416) 855-2800 *SIC 6099*
VOGOGO INC p974
5 HAZELTON AVE SUITE 300, TORONTO, ON, M5R 2E1
(647) 715-3707 *SIC 6099*

SIC 6111 Federal and federally sponsored credit agencies

CREDIT UNION CENTRAL OF CANADA p937
151 YONGE ST SUITE 1000, TORONTO, ON, M5C 2W7
(416) 232-1262   *SIC 6111*

EXPORT DEVELOPMENT CANADA p815
150 SLATER ST, OTTAWA, ON, K1A 1K3
(613) 598-2500   *SIC 6111*

FEDERATION DES PRODUCTEURS DE CULTURES COMMERCIALES DU QUEBEC p1143
555 BOUL ROLAND-THERRIEN BUREAU 505, LONGUEUIL, QC, J4H 4G4
(450) 679-0530   *SIC 6111*

IMPORTATIONS DE-RO-MA (1983) LTEE p1362
2055 BOUL DAGENAIS O, SAINTE-ROSE, QC, H7L 5V1
(450) 629-7689   *SIC 6111*

LANGLEY, CORPORATION OF THE TOWNSHIP OF p227
4700 224 ST, LANGLEY, BC, V2Z 1N4
(604) 532-7300   *SIC 6111*

LANYAP TRADE p570
88 PALACE PIER CRT SUITE 603, ETOBICOKE, ON, M8V 4C2
(647) 808-2186   *SIC 6111*

NEW BRUNSWICK MUNICIPAL FINANCE CORPORATION p401
670 KING ST RM 376, FREDERICTON, NB, E3B 1G1
(506) 453-2515   *SIC 6111*

NOVA SCOTIA BUSINESS INC p453
1800 ARGYLE ST SUITE 701, HALIFAX, NS, B3J 3N8
(902) 424-6650   *SIC 6111*

ONTARIO TRILLIUM FOUNDATION p976
800 BAY ST SUITE 2, TORONTO, ON, M5S 3A9
(416) 963-4927   *SIC 6111*

PROVINCE OF PEI p1039
94 EUSTON ST, CHARLOTTETOWN, PE, C1A 1W4
(902) 368-6300   *SIC 6111*

SUNKATCHERS RV PARK COOPERATIVE p223
4155 HWY 3, KEREMEOS, BC, V0X 1N1
(250) 499-2065   *SIC 6111*

UNITED BUNKERS INVESTORS CORPORATION p958
180 UNIVERSITY AVE SUITE 04, TORONTO, ON, M5H 0A2
(416) 567-0089   *SIC 6111*

SIC 6141 Personal credit institutions

1005199 B.C. LTD p327
555 BURRARD ST SUITE 600, VANCOUVER, BC, V7X 1M8
(604) 559-4322   *SIC 6141*

AUTOLOAN SOLUTIONS LTD p996
80 JUTLAND RD, TORONTO, ON, M8Z 2G6
(888) 300-9769   *SIC 6141*

BANQUE DE DEVELOPPEMENT DU CANADA p1201
5 PLACE VILLE-MARIE BUREAU 400, MONTREAL, QC, H3B 5E7
(514) 283-5904   *SIC 6141*

BELMONT PROPERTIES p319
1401 BROADWAY W SUITE 302, VANCOUVER, BC, V6H 1H6
(604) 736-2841   *SIC 6141*

CANADA DRIVES LTD p328
555 BURRARD ST SUITE 600, VANCOUVER, BC, V7X 1M8
(888) 865-6402   *SIC 6141*

CASH STORE FINANCIAL SERVICES INC, THE p105
15511 123 AVE NW, EDMONTON, AB, T5V 0C3
(780) 408-5110   *SIC 6141*

CASH STORE INC, THE p99
17631 103 AVE NW, EDMONTON, AB, T5S 1N8
(780) 408-5110   *SIC 6141*

EASYFINANCIAL SERVICES INC p709
33 CITY CENTRE DR SUITE 510, MISSISSAUGA, ON, L5B 2N5
(905) 272-2788   *SIC 6141*

FAIRSTONE FINANCIERE INC p1204
630 BOUL RENE-LEVESQUE O BUREAU 1400, MONTREAL, QC, H3B 1S6
(800) 995-2274   *SIC 6141*

FORD CREDIT CANADA LIMITED p800
THE CANADIAN RD, OAKVILLE, ON, L6J 5C7
(905) 845-2511   *SIC 6141*

HONDA CANADA FINANCE INC p679
180 HONDA BLVD SUITE 200, MARKHAM, ON, L6C 0H9
(905) 888-4188   *SIC 6141*

INGLE INTERNATIONAL INC. p981
460 RICHMOND ST W SUITE 100, TORONTO, ON, M5V 1Y1
(416) 730-8488   *SIC 6141*

LENDCARE CAPITAL INC p843
1315 PICKERING PKWY FL 4, PICKERING, ON, L1V 7G5
(905) 839-1009   *SIC 6141*

RIFCO INC p154
4909 49 ST SUITE 702, RED DEER, AB, T4N 1V1
(403) 314-1288   *SIC 6141*

RIFCO NATIONAL AUTO FINANCE CORPORATION p154
4909 49 ST SUITE 702, RED DEER, AB, T4N 1V1
(403) 314-1288   *SIC 6141*

TD FINANCING SERVICES HOME INC p921
25 BOOTH AVE SUITE 101, TORONTO, ON, M4M 2M3
(416) 463-4422   *SIC 6141*

TOYOTA CREDIT CANADA INC p676
80 MICRO CRT SUITE 200, MARKHAM, ON, L3R 9Z5
(905) 513-8200   *SIC 6141*

VICTORIA FIREMAN'S MUTUAL BENEFIT SOCIETY p335
1234 YATES ST, VICTORIA, BC, V8V 3M8
SIC 6141

SIC 6153 Short-term business credit institutions, except agricultural

AMEX CANADA INC p666
80 MICRO CRT SUITE 300, MARKHAM, ON, L3R 9Z5
(905) 475-2177   *SIC 6153*

CANADIAN TIRE SERVICES LIMITED p1011
1000 EAST MAIN ST, WELLAND, ON, L3B 3Z3
(905) 735-3131   *SIC 6153*

CAPITAL ONE BANK (CANADA BRANCH) p1217
950 AV BEAUMONT, MONTREAL, QC, H3N 1V5
(800) 481-3239   *SIC 6153*

CAPITAL ONE SERVICES (CANADA) INC p771
5140 YONGE ST SUITE 1900, NORTH YORK, ON, M2N 6L7
(416) 549-2500   *SIC 6153*

CHRYSLER FINANCIAL SERVICES CANADA INC p1023
1 RIVERSIDE DR W, WINDSOR, ON, N9A 5K3
(519) 973-2000   *SIC 6153*

CITI CARDS CANADA INC p730
5900 HURONTARIO ST, MISSISSAUGA, ON, L5R 0B8
(905) 285-7500   *SIC 6153*

CITIBANK CANADA p937
1 TORONTO ST SUITE 1200, TORONTO, ON, M5C 2V6
(416) 369-6399   *SIC 6153*

COMMANDITE FPI PRO INC p1194
2000 RUE MANSFIELD BUREAU 920, MONTREAL, QC, H3A 2Z6
(514) 933-9552   *SIC 6153*

GE VFS CANADA LIMITED PARTNERSHIP p722
2300 MEADOWVALE BLVD SUITE 200, MISSISSAUGA, ON, L5N 5P9
(905) 858-5100   *SIC 6153*

GENERAL ELECTRIC CAPITAL CANADA p722
2300 MEADOWVALE BLVD, MISSISSAUGA, ON, L5N 5P9
(905) 858-5100   *SIC 6153*

GENERAL MOTORS ACCEPTANCE CORPORATION OF CANADA, LIMITED p1096
455 BOUL FENELON BUREAU 310, DORVAL, QC, H9S 5K1
(514) 633-6933   *SIC 6153*

IPS OF CANADA, U.L.C. p585
170 ATTWELL DR UNIT 550, ETOBICOKE, ON, M9W 5Z5
(800) 293-1136   *SIC 6153*

JOHN DEERE FINANCIAL INC p804
3430 SUPERIOR CRT, OAKVILLE, ON, L6L 0C4
(905) 319-9100   *SIC 6153*

MASTERCARD CANADA, INC p930
121 BLOOR ST E SUITE 600, TORONTO, ON, M4W 3M5
(416) 365-6655   *SIC 6153*

MOGO FINANCE TECHNOLOGY INC p299
401 GEORGIA ST W SUITE 2100, VANCOUVER, BC, V6B 5A1
(604) 659-4380   *SIC 6153*

SIEMENS FINANCIAL LTD p525
1550 APPLEBY LINE, BURLINGTON, ON, L7L 6X7
(905) 315-6868   *SIC 6153*

SIC 6159 Miscellaneous business credit institutions

ACCORD FINANCIAL CORP p974
77 BLOOR ST W 18 FL, TORONTO, ON, M5S 1M2
(416) 961-0007   *SIC 6159*

AGRICULTURE FINANCIAL SERVICES CORPORATION p138
5718 56 AVE, LACOMBE, AB, T4L 1B1
(403) 782-8200   *SIC 6159*

ALARIS ROYALTY CORP p66
333 24TH AVE SW SUITE 250, CALGARY, AB, T2S 3E6
(888) 228-0873   *SIC 6159*

BODKIN FINANCIAL CORPORATION p716
2150 DUNWIN DR SUITE 1, MISSISSAUGA, ON, L5L 5M8
(905) 820-4550   *SIC 6159*

CAISSE DESJARDINS - CENTRE DE SERVICE p1173
1685 RUE RACHEL E, MONTREAL, QC, H2J 2K6
(514) 524-3551   *SIC 6159*

CAPITAL TRANSIT INC p1263
2035 RUE DU HAUT-BORD BUREAU 300, QUEBEC, QC, G1N 4R7
(418) 914-0777   *SIC 6159*

CITICORP VENDOR FINANCE, LTD p961
123 FRONT ST W SUITE 1500, TORONTO, ON, M5J 2M3
(800) 991-4046   *SIC 6159*

CLE CAPITAL INC p1386
2200 RUE DE LA SIDBEC S, TROIS-RIVIERES, QC, G8Z 4H1
(819) 373-8000   *SIC 6159*

COAST CAPITAL SAVINGS FEDERAL CREDIT UNION p274
9900 KING GEORGE BLVD 4TH FL, SURREY, BC, V3T 0K7
(778) 945-3225   *SIC 6159*

CREDIT VW CANADA, INC p1328
4865 RUE MARC-BLAIN BUREAU 300, SAINT-LAURENT, QC, H4R 3B2
(514) 332-4333   *SIC 6159*

CTL CORP p797
1660 NORTH SERVICE RD E SUITE 102, OAKVILLE, ON, L6H 7G3
(905) 815-9510   *SIC 6159*

CWB MAXIUM FINANCIAL INC p851
30 VOGELL RD SUITE 1, RICHMOND HILL, ON, L4B 3K6
(905) 780-6150   *SIC 6159*

CWB NATIONAL LEASING INC p390
1525 BUFFALO PL, WINNIPEG, MB, R3T 1L9
(204) 954-9000   *SIC 6159*

DE LAGE LANDEN FINANCIAL SERVICES CANADA INC p803
3450 SUPERIOR CRT UNIT 1, OAKVILLE, ON, L6L 0C4
(905) 465-3160   *SIC 6159*

DEALNET CAPITAL CORP p950
4 KING ST W SUITE 1700, TORONTO, ON, M5H 1B6
(905) 695-8557   *SIC 6159*

DELL FINANCIAL SERVICES CANADA LIMITED p765
155 GORDON BAKER RD SUITE 501, NORTH YORK, ON, M2H 3N5
(800) 864-8156   *SIC 6159*

DOMAINE LAFOREST p1245
485 170 RTE, PETIT-SAGUENAY, QC, G0V 1N0
(418) 638-5408   *SIC 6159*

EAGLE COPTERS LTD p22
823 MCTAVISH RD NE, CALGARY, AB, T2E 7G9
(403) 250-7370   *SIC 6159*

ECN CAPITAL CORP p962
200 BAY ST NORTH TOWER SUITE 1625, TORONTO, ON, M5J 2J1
(416) 646-4710   *SIC 6159*

EQUIREX LEASING CORP p802
700 DORVAL DR UNIT 302, OAKVILLE, ON, L6K 3V3
(905) 844-4424   *SIC 6159*

FARM CREDIT CANADA p1417
1800 HAMILTON ST, REGINA, SK, S4P 4L3
(306) 780-8100   *SIC 6159*

FEDERATION DES CAISSES DESJARDINS DU QUEBEC p1255
3333 RUE DU CARREFOUR BUREAU 280, QUEBEC, QC, G1C 5R9
(418) 660-2229   *SIC 6159*

FIRST INSURANCE FUNDING OF CANADA INC p938
20 TORONTO ST SUITE 700, TORONTO, ON, M5C 2B8
(888) 232-2238   *SIC 6159*

FULCRUM CAPITAL PARTNERS INC p304
885 GEORGIA ST W SUITE 1020, VANCOUVER, BC, V6C 3E8
(604) 631-8088   *SIC 6159*

GCIC LTD p939
1 ADELAIDE ST E SUITE 2800, TORONTO, ON, M5C 2V9
(416) 350-3250   *SIC 6159*

GENERAL MOTORS FINANCIAL OF CANADA, LTD. p767
2001 SHEPPARD AVE E UNIT 600, NORTH YORK, ON, M2J 4Z8
(416) 753-4000   *SIC 6159*

GHR SYSTEMS INC p951
11 KING ST W SUITE 600, TORONTO, ON, M5H 4C7
(416) 360-5775   *SIC 6159*

GOVERNMENT OF THE PROVINCE OF ALBERTA p138
5718 56 AVE, LACOMBE, AB, T4L 1B1
(403) 782-8309   *SIC 6159*

GROUPE AGF ACCES INC p1120
125 RUE DE L'INDUSTRIE, L'ASSOMPTION, QC, J5W 2T9
(450) 589-8100   *SIC 6159*

LBC CAPITAL INC p523
5035 SOUTH SERVICE RD, BURLINGTON, ON, L7L 6M9
(905) 633-2400 *SIC 6159*

LEASE LINK CANADA CORP p101
17220 STONY PLAIN RD NW SUITE 201A, EDMONTON, AB, T5S 1K6
(780) 414-0616 *SIC 6159*

LUSSIER DALE PARIZEAU INC p1376
80 RUE AUGUSTA, SOREL-TRACY, QC, J3P 1A5
(450) 746-1000 *SIC 6159*

MANITOBA AGRICULTURAL SERVICES CORPORATION p355
50 24TH ST NW SUITE 400, PORTAGE LA PRAIRIE, MB, R1N 3V9
(204) 239-3499 *SIC 6159*

MERIDIAN ONECAP CREDIT CORP p190
4710 KINGSWAY SUITE 1500, BURNABY, BC, V5H 4M2
(604) 646-2247 *SIC 6159*

METALLA ROYALTY & STREAMING LTD p307
543 GRANVILLE ST SUITE 501, VANCOUVER, BC, V6C 1X8
(604) 696-0741 *SIC 6159*

MFL MANAGEMENT LIMITED p987
100 KING ST W, TORONTO, ON, M5X 2A1
(416) 362-0714 *SIC 6159*

PACIFIC & WESTERN PUBLIC SECTOR FINANCING CORP p654
140 FULLARTON ST, LONDON, ON, N6A 5P2
(519) 645-1919 *SIC 6159*

PCL CONSTRUCTION HOLDINGS LTD p115
9915 56 AVE NW, EDMONTON, AB, T6E 5L7
(780) 733-5000 *SIC 6159*

PCL CONSTRUCTION RESOURCES INC p115
5410 99 ST NW, EDMONTON, AB, T6E 3P4
(780) 733-5400 *SIC 6159*

PENNECON LIMITED p431
1309 TOPSAIL RD, ST. JOHN'S, NL, A1B 3N4
(709) 782-3404 *SIC 6159*

RCAP LEASING INC p524
5575 NORTH SERVICE RD SUITE 300, BURLINGTON, ON, L7L 6M1
(905) 639-3995 *SIC 6159*

ROYAL BANK OF CANADA p572
3250 BLOOR ST W SUITE 800, ETOBICOKE, ON, M8X 2X9
SIC 6159

ROYNAT CAPITAL INC p956
40 KING ST W, TORONTO, ON, M5H 3Y2
(416) 933-2730 *SIC 6159*

ROYNAT INC p1199
1002 RUE SHERBROOKE O BUREAU 1100, MONTREAL, QC, H3A 3L6
(514) 987-4947 *SIC 6159*

SKIDMORE DEVELOPMENT GROUP LTD p309
837 HASTINGS ST W SUITE 715, VANCOUVER, BC, V6C 3N6
(604) 757-7461 *SIC 6159*

TD ASSET FINANCE CORP p970
55 KING ST W, TORONTO, ON, M5K 1A2
(416) 982-2322 *SIC 6159*

TERRA FIRMA CAPITAL CORPORATION p926
22 ST CLAIR AVE E SUITE 200, TORONTO, ON, M4T 2S3
(416) 792-4700 *SIC 6159*

TRAVELLERS FINANCE LTD p274
800-9900 KING GEORGE BLVD, SURREY, BC, V3T 0K7
(604) 293-0202 *SIC 6159*

WELLS FARGO FINANCIAL CORPORATION CANADA p958
40 KING ST W SUITE 3200, TORONTO, ON, M5H 3Y2
(800) 626-2805 *SIC 6159*

SIC 6162 Mortgage bankers and loan correspondents

4549440 MANITOBA LTD p393
99 SCURFIELD BLVD UNIT 100, WINNIPEG, MB, R3Y 1Y1
(204) 954-7620 *SIC 6162*

9121196 CANADA INC p1395
14 PLACE DU COMMERCE, VERDUN, QC, H3E 1T5
(514) 287-1211 *SIC 6162*

ARDENTON CAPITAL CORPORATION p311
1021 WEST HASTINGS ST UNIT 2400, VANCOUVER, BC, V6E 0C3
(604) 833-4899 *SIC 6162*

BOREALIS INFRASTRUCTURE MANAGEMENT INC p960
200 BAY ST SUITE 2100, TORONTO, ON, M5J 2J2
(416) 361-1011 *SIC 6162*

CAPITAL MORTGAGES p748
18 DEAKIN ST SUITE 106, NEPEAN, ON, K2E 8B7
(613) 228-3888 *SIC 6162*

DOMINION LENDING CENTRES INC p245
2215 COQUITLAM AVE SUITE 16, PORT COQUITLAM, BC, V3B 1J6
(604) 696-1221 *SIC 6162*

FEDERATION DES CAISSES DESJARDINS DU QUEBEC p1051
7755 BOUL LOUIS-H.-LAFONTAINE BUREAU 30711, ANJOU, QC, H1K 4M6
(514) 376-4420 *SIC 6162*

FIRST NATIONAL FINANCIAL LP p962
100 UNIVERSITY AVE SUITE 1200, TORONTO, ON, M5J 1V6
(416) 593-1100 *SIC 6162*

GET A BETTER MORTGAGE p572
642 THE QUEENSWAY, ETOBICOKE, ON, M8Y 1K5
(416) 252-9000 *SIC 6162*

INVESTORS GROUP INC p865
305 MILNER AVE SUITE 701, SCARBOROUGH, ON, M1B 3V4
(416) 292-7229 *SIC 6162*

LEAGUE SAVINGS & MORTGAGE COMPANY p455
6074 LADY HAMMOND RD, HALIFAX, NS, B3K 2R7
(902) 453-4220 *SIC 6162*

MCAP COMMERCIAL LP p954
200 KING ST W SUITE 400, TORONTO, ON, M5H 3T4
(416) 598-2665 *SIC 6162*

MCAP SERVICE CORPORATION p640
101 FREDERICK ST SUITE 600, KITCHENER, ON, N2H 6R2
(519) 743-7800 *SIC 6162*

MCAP SERVICE CORPORATION p954
200 KING ST W SUITE 400, TORONTO, ON, M5H 3T4
(416) 598-2665 *SIC 6162*

MONTROSE MORTGAGE CORPORATION LTD p379
200 GRAHAM AVE SUITE 1110, WINNIPEG, MB, R3C 4L5
(204) 982-1110 *SIC 6162*

NEIGHBOURHOOD DOMINION LENDING CENTRES p484
39 COLLIER ST SUITE 300, BARRIE, ON, L4M 1G5
(705) 720-1001 *SIC 6162*

NOVACAP TMT V, S.E.C p1071
3400 RUE DE L'ECLIPSE BUREAU 700, BROSSARD, QC, J4Z 0P3
(450) 651-5000 *SIC 6162*

ONTARIO MORTGAGE ACTION CENTRE LTD p848
288 BRIDGE ST, PORT STANLEY, ON, N5L 1C3
SIC 6162

PARADIGM QUEST INC p956
390 BAY ST SUITE 1800, TORONTO, ON, M5H 2Y2

(416) 366-8606 *SIC 6162*

PEOPLES FINANCIAL CORPORATION p965
95 WELLINGTON ST W SUITE 915, TORONTO, ON, M5J 2N7
(416) 861-1315 *SIC 6162*

SCOTIA MORTGAGE AUTHORITY p970
79 WELLINGSTON ST W SUITE 3400, TORONTO, ON, M5K 1K7
(416) 350-7400 *SIC 6162*

SELECT MORTGAGE CORP p339
1497 ADMIRALS RD SUITE 205, VICTORIA, BC, V9A 2P8
(250) 483-1373 *SIC 6162*

SOCIETE D'HYPOTHEQUE DE LA BANQUE ROYALE p1212
1 PLACE VILLE-MARIE, MONTREAL, QC, H3C 3A9
(514) 874-7222 *SIC 6162*

TIMBERCREEK FINANCIAL CORP p930
25 PRICE ST, TORONTO, ON, M4W 1Z1
(416) 923-9967 *SIC 6162*

WESTMOUNT MORTGAGE CORPORATION p63
605 5 AVE SW SUITE 2300, CALGARY, AB, T2P 3H5
(403) 269-1027 *SIC 6162*

SIC 6163 Loan brokers

2786591 CANADA INC p1395
14 PLACE DU COMMERCE BUREAU 600, VERDUN, QC, H3E 1T5
(514) 287-1211 *SIC 6163*

ATRIUM MORTGAGE INVESTMENT CORPORATION p936
20 ADELAIDE ST E SUITE 900, TORONTO, ON, M5C 2T6
(416) 867-1053 *SIC 6163*

CANADA ICI CAPITAL CORPORATION p87
10180 101 ST NW SUITE 3540, EDMONTON, AB, T5J 3S4
(780) 990-1144 *SIC 6163*

CANADA LIFE MORTGAGE SERVICES LTD p944
330 UNIVERSITY AVE, TORONTO, ON, M5G 1R8
(416) 597-6981 *SIC 6163*

CASH CANADA FINANCIAL CENTERS LTD p108
8170 50 ST NW SUITE 325, EDMONTON, AB, T6B 1E6
(780) 424-1080 *SIC 6163*

CIBC MORTGAGES INC p942
33 YONGE ST SUITE 700, TORONTO, ON, M5E 1G4
(416) 865-1999 *SIC 6163*

EQUITABLE GROUP INC p926
30 ST CLAIR AVE W SUITE 700, TORONTO, ON, M4V 3A1
(416) 515-7000 *SIC 6163*

FLEXITI FINANCIAL INC p986
130 KING ST W SUITE 1740, TORONTO, ON, M5X 1E1
(416) 583-1860 *SIC 6163*

HOMEGUARD FUNDING LTD p754
83 DAWSON MANOR BLVD, NEWMARKET, ON, L3X 2H5
(905) 895-1777 *SIC 6163*

MA PMGI BROKERAGE INC p724
6505 MISSISSAUGA RD UNIT A, MISSISSAUGA, ON, L5N 1A6
(905) 542-9100 *SIC 6163*

MORTGAGE 1 CORPORATION p54
700 4 AVE SW SUITE 1700, CALGARY, AB, T2P 3J4
SIC 6163

MORTGAGE BROKERS CITY INC p828
788 ISLAND PARK DR, OTTAWA, ON, K1Y 0C2
(613) 274-3490 *SIC 6163*

MORTGAGE INTELLIGENCE INC p732
5770 HURONTARIO ST SUITE 600, MISSISSAUGA, ON, L5R 3G5

(905) 283-3600 *SIC 6163*

NORTHWOOD MORTGAGE LTD p673
7676 WOODBINE AVE SUITE 300, MARKHAM, ON, L3R 2N2
(416) 969-8130 *SIC 6163*

ORIANA FINANCIAL GROUP OF CANADA LTD p1032
4300 STEELES AVE W UNIT 34, WOODBRIDGE, ON, L4L 4C2
(905) 265-8315 *SIC 6163*

XEVA MORTGAGE p342
1455 BELLEVUE AVE SUITE 213, WEST VANCOUVER, BC, V7T 1C3
SIC 6163

SIC 6211 Security brokers and dealers

1067863 ALBERTA LTD p86
10250 101 ST NW SUITE 1550, EDMONTON, AB, T5J 3P4
(780) 428-1522 *SIC 6211*

20/20 PROPERTIES INC p292
638 MILLBANK, VANCOUVER, BC, V5Z 4B7
(604) 620-3130 *SIC 6211*

3653340 CANADA INC p1324
9800 BOUL CAVENDISH BUREAU 200, SAINT-LAURENT, QC, H4M 2V9
SIC 6211

ACADEMY FABRICATORS GROUP LIMITED PARTNERSHIP p108
4066-78 AVE, EDMONTON, AB, T6B 3M8
(780) 395-4914 *SIC 6211*

ACUMEN CAPITAL FINANCE PARTNERS LIMITED p42
404 6 AVE SW UNIT 700, CALGARY, AB, T2P 0R9
(403) 571-0300 *SIC 6211*

AGF MANAGEMENT LIMITED p968
66 WELLINGTON ST W SUITE 3300, TORONTO, ON, M5K 1E9
(416) 367-1900 *SIC 6211*

APVE INVESTMENTS INC p1401
9 AV FORDEN, WESTMOUNT, QC, H3Y 2Y6
SIC 6211

AR-LINE SECURITY AND INVESTIGATION LTD p568
34 BIRCH RD, ELLIOT LAKE, ON, P5A 2E2
SIC 6211

ARMSTRONG & QUAILE ASSOCIATES INC p663
5858 RIDEAU VALLEY DR N, MANOTICK, ON, K4M 1B3
(613) 692-0751 *SIC 6211*

ARROW CAPITAL MANAGEMENT INC p936
36 TORONTO ST SUITE 750, TORONTO, ON, M5C 2C5
(416) 323-0477 *SIC 6211*

ASSANTE CAPITAL MANAGEMENT LTD p936
2 QUEEN ST E SUITE 1900, TORONTO, ON, M5C 3G7
(416) 348-9994 *SIC 6211*

ATLANTIC ALARM & SOUND LTD p397
489 AV ACADIE SUITE 200, DIEPPE, NB, E1A 1H7
(506) 853-9315 *SIC 6211*

BANK OF MONTREAL HOLDING INC p985
100 KING ST W 21ST FLOOR, TORONTO, ON, M5X 1A1
(416) 359-5003 *SIC 6211*

BAROMETER CAPITAL MANAGEMENT INC p959
1 UNIVERSITY AVE SUITE 1800, TORONTO, ON, M5J 2P1
(416) 775-3080 *SIC 6211*

BAYCOR INDUSTRIES LTD p44
404 6 AVE SW SUITE 300, CALGARY, AB, T2P 0R9
(403) 294-0600 *SIC 6211*

BBS SECURITIES INC p773
4100 YONGE ST SUITE 506, NORTH

YORK, ON, M2P 2B5
(416) 235-0200   *SIC* 6211

BIRCH HILL EQUITY PARTNERS II LTD*p969*
100 WELLINGTON ST W SUITE 2300, TORONTO, ON, M5K 1B7
(416) 775-3800   *SIC* 6211

BLACK DIAMOND MANAGEMENT GROUP CORPORATION   *p709*
77 CITY CENTRE DR, MISSISSAUGA, ON, L5B 1M5
(289) 201-7898   *SIC* 6211

BMO INVESTORLINE INC   *p985*
100 KING ST W 21ST FLOOR, TORONTO, ON, M5X 2A1
(416) 867-6300   *SIC* 6211

BMO NESBITT BURNS INC   *p44*
525 8 AVE SW SUITE 3200, CALGARY, AB, T2P 1G1
(403) 261-9550   *SIC* 6211

BMO NESBITT BURNS INC   *p377*
360 MAIN ST SUITE 1400, WINNIPEG, MB, R3C 3Z3
(204) 949-2183   *SIC* 6211

BMO NESBITT BURNS INC   *p825*
979 BANK ST 6TH FL, OTTAWA, ON, K1S 5K5
(613) 562-6400   *SIC* 6211

BMO NESBITT BURNS INC   *p985*
100 KING ST W UNIT 1, TORONTO, ON, M5X 2A1
(416) 643-1778   *SIC* 6211

BMO NESBITT BURNS INC   *p985*
100 KING ST W FL 38, TORONTO, ON, M5X 1H3
(416) 365-6029   *SIC* 6211

BMO NESBITT BURNS INC   *p986*
1 FIRST CANADIAN PL 21ST FL, TORONTO, ON, M5X 1H3
(416) 359-4000   *SIC* 6211

BMO PRIVATE INVESTMENT COUNSEL INC   *p986*
100 KING ST W, TORONTO, ON, M5X 1H3
(416) 359-5001   *SIC* 6211

BORDER INVESTIGATION AND SECURITY INC   *p410*
303 ROUTE 170, OAK BAY, NB, E3L 3Y2
(506) 466-6303   *SIC* 6211

BRADSHAW CANADA HOLDINGS, INC   *p1027*
200 ZENWAY BLVD SUITE 3, WOODBRIDGE, ON, L4H 0L6
(905) 264-2246   *SIC* 6211

BRAHAM & ASSOCIATES INC   *p833*
251 BANK ST, OTTAWA, ON, K2P 1X3
(613) 294-4589   *SIC* 6211

BRANT SECURITIES LIMITED   *p960*
220 BAY ST SUITE 300, TORONTO, ON, M5J 2W4
(416) 596-4599   *SIC* 6211

BULLETPROOF SOLUTIONS INC   *p402*
25 ALISON BLVD, FREDERICTON, NB, E3C 2N5
(506) 452-8558   *SIC* 6211

BURGEONVEST BICK SECURITIES LIMITED   *p612*
21 KING ST W SUITE 1100, HAMILTON, ON, L8P 4W7
(905) 528-6505   *SIC* 6211

BURGUNDY ASSET MANAGEMENT LTD   *p960*
181 BAY ST SUITE 4510, TORONTO, ON, M5J 2T3
(416) 869-3222   *SIC* 6211

CALDWELL SECURITIES LTD   *p949*
150 KING ST W SUITE 1710, TORONTO, ON, M5H 1J9
(416) 862-7755   *SIC* 6211

CANACCORD GENUITY CORP   *p45*
450 1 ST SW SUITE 2200, CALGARY, AB, T2P 5H1
(403) 508-3800   *SIC* 6211

CANACCORD GENUITY CORP   *p330*
609 GRANVILLE ST SUITE 2200, VANCOUVER, BC, V7Y 1H2

(604) 643-7300   *SIC* 6211

CANACCORD GENUITY CORP   *p1202*
1250 BOUL RENE-LEVESQUE O BUREAU 2000, MONTREAL, QC, H3B 4W8
SIC 6211

CANACCORD GENUITY GROUP INC   *p330*
609 GRANVILLE ST VAN UNIT 2200, VANCOUVER, BC, V7Y 1H2
(604) 643-7300   *SIC* 6211

CANADA-ISRAEL SECURITIES LIMITED   *p782*
801-1120 FINCH AVE W, NORTH YORK, ON, M3J 3H7
(416) 789-3351   *SIC* 6211

CANADIAN PROTECTION PROVIDERS INC   *p766*
251 CONSUMERS RD SUITE 1200, NORTH YORK, ON, M2J 4R3
(647) 330-0313   *SIC* 6211

CATLIN CANADA INC   *p937*
100 YONGE ST SUITE 1200, TORONTO, ON, M5C 2W1
(416) 928-5586   *SIC* 6211

CDS CLEARING AND DEPOSITORY SERVICES INC   *p950*
85 RICHMOND ST W, TORONTO, ON, M5H 2C9
(416) 365-8400   *SIC* 6211

CERES GLOBAL AG CORP   *p846*
2 SHERWOOD FOREST LN, PORT COLBORNE, ON, L3K 5V8
(905) 834-5924   *SIC* 6211

CIBC MELLON TRUST COMPANY   *p961*
1 YORK ST SUITE 900, TORONTO, ON, M5J 0B6
(416) 643-5000   *SIC* 6211

CIBC WORLD MARKETS INC   *p88*
10180 101 ST NW SUITE 1800, EDMONTON, AB, T5J 3S4
(780) 429-8900   *SIC* 6211

CIBC WORLD MARKETS INC   *p374*
1 LOMBARD PL SUITE 1000, WINNIPEG, MB, R3B 3N9
(204) 942-0311   *SIC* 6211

CIBC WORLD MARKETS INC   *p833*
150 ELGIN ST, OTTAWA, ON, K2P 1L4
(613) 237-5775   *SIC* 6211

CIBC WORLD MARKETS INC   *p904*
123 COMMERCE VALLEY DR E SUITE 100, THORNHILL, ON, L3T 7W8
(905) 762-2300   *SIC* 6211

CIBC WORLD MARKETS INC   *p961*
161 BAY ST, TORONTO, ON, M5J 2S1
(416) 594-7000   *SIC* 6211

CIBC WORLD MARKETS INC   *p961*
181 BAY ST SUITE 600, TORONTO, ON, M5J 2T3
SIC 6211

CIBC WORLD MARKETS INC   *p1194*
600 BOUL DE MAISONNEUVE O BUREAU 3050, MONTREAL, QC, H3A 3J2
(514) 847-6300   *SIC* 6211

CIBC WORLD MARKETS INC   *p1202*
1 PLACE VILLE-MARIE BUREAU 4125, MONTREAL, QC, H3B 3P9
(514) 392-7600   *SIC* 6211

CITIGROUP GLOBAL MARKETS CANADA INC   *p961*
161 BAY ST SUITE 4600, TORONTO, ON, M5J 2S1
(416) 866-2300   *SIC* 6211

CONCERT INFRASTRUCTURE LTD   *p326*
1190 HORNBY ST, VANCOUVER, BC, V6Z 2K5
(604) 688-9460   *SIC* 6211

CONNOR, CLARK & LUNN WHOLESALE FINANCE INC   *p986*
130 KING STREET W SUITE 1400, TORONTO, ON, M5X 1C8
(416) 862-2020   *SIC* 6211

CORMARK SECURITIES (USA) LIMITED   *p961*
220 BAY ST SUITE 2800, TORONTO, ON, M5J 2W4

(416) 362-7485   *SIC* 6211

CORMARK SECURITIES INC   *p961*
200 BAY ST S SUITE 2800, TORONTO, ON, M5J 2J2
(416) 362-7485   *SIC* 6211

CORPORATION FINANCIERE THINKING CAPITAL   *p1220*
4200 BOUL DORCHESTER O BUREAU 300, MONTREAL, QC, H3Z 1V2
(866) 889-9412   *SIC* 6211

CORPORATION GARDAWORLD SERVICES TRANSPORT DE VALEURS CANADA*p1248*
1390 RUE BARRE, POINTE-AUX-TREMBLES, QC, H3C 5X9
(514) 281-2811   *SIC* 6211

COUGAR GLOBAL INVESTMENTS LIMITED PARTNERSHIP   *p950*
357 BAY ST SUITE 1001, TORONTO, ON, M5H 2T7
(416) 368-5255   *SIC* 6211

COUNSEL GROUP FUNDS   *p693*
2680 SKYMARK AVE SUITE 700, MISSISSAUGA, ON, L4W 5L6
(905) 625-9885   *SIC* 6211

COVENTREE INC   *p961*
161 BAY ST 27TH FL, TORONTO, ON, M5J 2S1
(416) 815-0700   *SIC* 6211

CPPIB EQUITY INVESTMENTS INC   *p937*
1 QUEEN ST E SUITE 2500, TORONTO, ON, M5C 2W5
(416) 868-4075   *SIC* 6211

CREDENTIAL SECURITIES INC   *p312*
1111 GEORGIA ST W SUITE 800, VANCOUVER, BC, V6E 4T6
(604) 714-3900   *SIC* 6211

CREDIT SUISSE SECURITIES (CANADA) INC   *p986*
1 FIRST CANADIAN PL SUITE 2900, TORONTO, ON, M5X 1C9
(416) 352-4500   *SIC* 6211

D C SECURITY INC   *p583*
22 GOODMARK PL UNIT 20, ETOBICOKE, ON, M9W 6R2
(416) 213-1995   *SIC* 6211

D&D SECURITIES INC   *p950*
150 YORK ST SUITE 1714, TORONTO, ON, M5H 3S5
(416) 363-0201   *SIC* 6211

D+H LIMITED PARTNERSHIP   *p962*
120 BREMNER BLVD 30TH FL, TORONTO, ON, M5J 0A8
(416) 696-7700   *SIC* 6211

DESJARDINS SOCIETE DE PLACEMENT INC   *p1230*
2 COMPLEXE DESJARDINS, MONTREAL, QC, H5B 1H5
(866) 666-1280   *SIC* 6211

DESSERT CITY INVESTIGATIONS AND SECURITY INC   *p217*
6968 FURRER RD, KAMLOOPS, BC, V2C 4V9
(250) 828-8778   *SIC* 6211

DH CORPORATION   *p669*
81 WHITEHALL DR, MARKHAM, ON, L3R 9T1
(905) 944-1231   *SIC* 6211

DH CORPORATION   *p1141*
830 RUE DELAGE, LONGUEUIL, QC, J4G 2V4
(450) 463-6372   *SIC* 6211

DIVERSIFIED GLOBAL ASSET MANAGEMENT CORP   *p938*
77 KING ST E SUITE 4310, TORONTO, ON, M5C 1G3
(416) 644-7587   *SIC* 6211

DOUBLE RAINBOW CANADA CHINA HOLDINGS GROUP INC   *p856*
127 FRANK ENDEAN RD, RICHMOND HILL, ON, L4S 1V2
SIC 6211

DUNDEE CORPORATION   *p938*
1 ADELAIDE ST E SUITE 2000, TORONTO, ON, M5C 2V9

(416) 350-3388   *SIC* 6211

EDWARD D. JONES & CO. CANADA HOLDING CO., INC   *p709*
90 BURNHAMTHORPE RD W SUITE 902, MISSISSAUGA, ON, L5B 3C3
(905) 306-8600   *SIC* 6211

ENDEAVOUR FINANCIAL LTD   *p328*
595 BURRARD ST SUITE 3123, VANCOUVER, BC, V7X 1J1
(604) 685-4554   *SIC* 6211

EQUICAPITA INCOME TRUST   *p75*
8561 8A AVE SW SUITE 2210, CALGARY, AB, T3H 0V5
(587) 887-1538   *SIC* 6211

ESTATE MORTGAGE INC   *p406*
19 KATHERINE AVE, MONCTON, NB, E1C 7M7
(506) 855-5626   *SIC* 6211

EVANGELINE SECURITIES LIMITED   *p470*
1051 KING ST, WINDSOR, NS, B0N 2T0
(902) 792-1035   *SIC* 6211

FENGATE CAPITAL MANAGEMENT LTD   *p969*
77 KING ST W UNIT 4230, TORONTO, ON, M5K 2A1
(416) 488-4184   *SIC* 6211

FIDELITY CLEARING CANADA ULC   *p945*
483 BAY ST, TORONTO, ON, M5G 2N7
(416) 216-6357   *SIC* 6211

FINANCIERE BANQUE NATIONALE INC   *p304*
666 BURRARD ST SUITE 100, VANCOUVER, BC, V6C 2X8
(604) 623-6777   *SIC* 6211

FIRST ASSET OPPORTUNITY FUND   *p962*
95 WELLINGTON ST W SUITE 1400, TORONTO, ON, M5J 2N7
(416) 642-1289   *SIC* 6211

FIRST FINANCIAL UNDERWRITING SERVICES INC   *p867*
111 GRANGEWAY AVE SUITE 300, SCARBOROUGH, ON, M1H 3E9
(416) 750-7388   *SIC* 6211

FIRSTENERGY CAPITAL CORP   *p49*
311 6 AVE SW SUITE 1100, CALGARY, AB, T2P 3H2
(403) 262-0600   *SIC* 6211

FOUNDERS ADVANTAGE CAPITAL CORP   *p66*
2207 4TH ST SW SUITE 400, CALGARY, AB, T2S 1X1
(403) 455-9660   *SIC* 6211

FREEDOM INTERNATIONAL BROKERAGE COMPANY   *p951*
181 UNIVERSITY AVE SUITE 1500, TORONTO, ON, M5H 3M7
(416) 367-2588   *SIC* 6211

FRONTIER DISCOUNT HOBBIES LTD *p491*
277 FRONT ST, BELLEVILLE, ON, K8N 2Z6
(613) 967-2845   *SIC* 6211

FUNDEX INVESTMENTS INC   *p553*
400 APPLEWOOD CRES, CONCORD, ON, L4K 0C3
(905) 305-1651   *SIC* 6211

GATEWAY SECURITIES INC   *p313*
1177 HASTINGS ST W SUITE 168, VANCOUVER, BC, V6E 2K3
SIC 6211

GLC ASSET MANAGEMENT GROUP LTD   *p653*
255 DUFFERIN AVE, LONDON, ON, N6A 4K1
(519) 432-7229   *SIC* 6211

GLOBAL MAXFIN CAPITAL INC   *p939*
15 TORONTO ST SUITE 202, TORONTO, ON, M5C 2E3
(416) 741-1445   *SIC* 6211

GLOBAL SECURITIES CORPORATION   *p328*
3 BENTALL CTR SUITE 1100, VANCOUVER, BC, V7X 1C4
(604) 689-5400   *SIC* 6211

GLOBAL SECURITIES CORPORATION   *p328*

595 BURRARD ST, VANCOUVER, BC, V7X
1C4

(604) 689-5400   *SIC* 6211

GMP CAPITAL INC   *p952*
145 KING ST W SUITE 300, TORONTO,
ON, M5H 1J8

(416) 367-8600   *SIC* 6211

GMP SECURITIES L.P.   *p952*
145 KING ST W SUITE 300, TORONTO,
ON, M5H 1J8

(416) 367-8600   *SIC* 6211

GOLDMAN SACHS CANADA INC   *p969*
77 KING ST W SUITE 3400, TORONTO,
ON, M5K 2A1

(416) 343-8900   *SIC* 6211

GRIFFITHS MCBURNEY CANADA CORP
p952
145 KING ST W SUITE 1100, TORONTO,
ON, M5H 1J8

(416) 367-8600   *SIC* 6211

GROWTH WORKS LTD   *p313*
2600-1055 GEORGIA ST W, VANCOUVER,
BC, V6E 3G6

(604) 688-9631   *SIC* 6211

GROWTHWORKS ENTERPRISES LTD *p453*
1801 HOLLIS ST SUITE 310, HALIFAX, NS,
B3J 3N4

(902) 423-9367   *SIC* 6211

HAMPTON SECURITIES LIMITED   *p952*
141 ADELAIDE ST W SUITE 1800,
TORONTO, ON, M5H 3L5

(416) 862-7800   *SIC* 6211

HAYWOOD SECURITIES INC   *p305*
200 BURRARD ST SUITE 700, VANCOUVER, BC, V6C 3L6

(604) 697-7100   *SIC* 6211

HELCIM INC   *p64*
1300 8 ST SW SUITE 403, CALGARY, AB,
T2R 1B2

(403) 291-1172   *SIC* 6211

HERITAGE SURFACE SOLUTIONS   *p23*
6815 8 ST NE SUITE 165, CALGARY, AB,
T2E 7H7

(403) 291-2804   *SIC* 6211

HSBC CAPITAL (CANADA) INC   *p305*
885 GEORGIA ST W SUITE 1100, VANCOUVER, BC, V6C 3E8

(604) 631-8088   *SIC* 6211

HSBC SECURITIES (CANADA) INC   *p963*
70 YORK ST SUITE 800, TORONTO, ON,
M5J 1S9

(416) 868-8000   *SIC* 6211

ICON INFRASTRUCTURE LLP   *p981*
155 WELLINGTON ST W SUITE 2930,
TORONTO, ON, M5V 3H1

(416) 649-1331   *SIC* 6211

IGM FINANCIAL INC   *p378*
447 PORTAGE AVE, WINNIPEG, MB, R3C
3B6

(204) 943-0361   *SIC* 6211

IMPERIAL CAPITAL CORPORATION *p953*
200 KING ST W SUITE 1701, TORONTO,
ON, M5H 3T4

(416) 362-3658   *SIC* 6211

INDEPENDENT FINANCIAL SERVICES LTD
p1428
1001 3RD AVE N, SASKATOON, SK, S7K
2K5

(306) 244-7385   *SIC* 6211

INDEPENDENT TRADING GROUP (ITG) INC
p953
4 KING ST W SUITE 402, TORONTO, ON,
M5H 1B6

(416) 941-0046   *SIC* 6211

INDUSTRIELLE ALLIANCE VALEURS MOBILIERES INC   *p1197*
2200 AV MCGILL COLLEGE BUREAU 350,
MONTREAL, QC, H3A 3P8

(514) 499-1066   *SIC* 6211

INFINIUM CAPITAL CORPORATION   *p934*
106 FRONT ST E SUITE 200, TORONTO,
ON, M5A 1E1

SIC 6211

INTEGRAL WEALTH SECURITIES LIMITED

p953
56 TEMPERANCE ST SUITE 900,
TORONTO, ON, M5H 3V5

(416) 203-2000   *SIC* 6211

**INVESTISSEMENTS LACORDAIRE INC,
LES**   *p1361*
6625 RUE ERNEST-CORMIER, SAINTE-
ROSE, QC, H7C 2V2

(514) 321-8260   *SIC* 6211

JAYMOR SECURITIES LTD   *p852*
105 WEST BEAVER CREEK RD UNIT 9-10,
RICHMOND HILL, ON, L4B 1C6

(905) 882-1212   *SIC* 6211

JENNINGS CAPITAL INC   *p52*
308 4 AVE SW SUITE 2700, CALGARY, AB,
T2P 0H7

(403) 292-0970   *SIC* 6211

JORDAN CAPITAL MARKETS INC   *p314*
1075 GEORGIA ST W SUITE 1920, VANCOUVER, BC, V6E 3C9

(778) 373-4091   *SIC* 6211

LABRADOR IRON ORE ROYALTY CORPORATION   *p985*
40 KING ST W, TORONTO, ON, M5W 2X6

(416) 863-7133   *SIC* 6211

LANDSOLUTIONS LP   *p65*
601 10 AVE SW SUITE 200, CALGARY, AB,
T2R 0B2

(403) 290-0008   *SIC* 6211

LEEDE JONES GABLE INC   *p939*
110 YONGE ST SUITE 600, TORONTO,
ON, M5C 1T4

(416) 365-8000   *SIC* 6211

LEEDE JONES GABLE INC.   *p53*
421 7 AVE SW SUITE 3415, CALGARY, AB,
T2P 4K9

(403) 531-6800   *SIC* 6211

LIBERTY SECURITY SYSTEMS INC   *p119*
5640 104 ST NW, EDMONTON, AB, T6H
2K2

(780) 988-7233   *SIC* 6211

LOEWEN, ONDAATJE, MCCUTCHEON LIMITED   *p973*
148 YORKVILLE AVE SUITE 3, TORONTO,
ON, M5R 1C2

(416) 964-4400   *SIC* 6211

MACDOUGALL, MACDOUGALL & MACTIER INC   *p1206*
1010 RUE DE LA GAUCHETIERE O BUREAU 2000, MONTREAL, QC, H3B 4J1

(514) 394-3000   *SIC* 6211

MACKIE RESEACH CAPITAL CORPORATION   *p971*
199 BAY ST SUITE 4500, TORONTO, ON,
M5L 1G2

(416) 860-7600   *SIC* 6211

**MACQUARIE CAPITAL MARKETS CANADA
LTD**   *p307*
550 BURRARD ST SUITE 500, VANCOUVER, BC, V6C 2B5

(604) 605-3944   *SIC* 6211

**MACQUARIE CAPITAL MARKETS CANADA
LTD**   *p964*
181 BAY ST SUITE 3100, TORONTO, ON,
M5J 2T3

(416) 848-3500   *SIC* 6211

**MACQUARIE CAPITAL MARKETS CANADA
LTD**   *p964*
181 BAY ST SUITE 900, TORONTO, ON,
M5J 2T3

(416) 848-3500   *SIC* 6211

MARWA HOLDINGS INC   *p973*
61 YORKVILLE AVE PH 914, TORONTO,
ON, M5R 1B7

SIC 6211

MCA VALEURS MOBILIERES INC   *p1192*
555 BOUL RENE-LEVESQUE O BUREAU
140, MONTREAL, QC, H2Z 1B1

SIC 6211

MCLEAN WATSON INVESTMENTS INC
p954
141 ADELAIDE ST W SUITE 1200,
TORONTO, ON, M5H 3L5

(416) 363-2000   *SIC* 6211

MERITIGROUP LTD   *p672*
7100 WOODBINE AVE SUITE 218,
MARKHAM, ON, L3R 5J2

(905) 489-8299   *SIC* 6211

MERRILL LYNCH & CO., CANADA LTD *p964*
181 BAY ST SUITE 400, TORONTO, ON,
M5J 2V8

(416) 369-7400   *SIC* 6211

MERRILL LYNCH CANADA INC   *p964*
181 BAY ST SUITE 400, TORONTO, ON,
M5J 2V8

(416) 369-7400   *SIC* 6211

MERRILL LYNCH CANADA INC   *p1206*
1250 BOUL RENE-LEVESQUE O BUREAU
3100, MONTREAL, QC, H3B 4W8

(514) 846-1050   *SIC* 6211

MGI SECURITIES INC   *p942*
26 WELLINGTON ST E SUITE 900,
TORONTO, ON, M5E 1S2

(416) 864-6477   *SIC* 6211

MILLENNIUM III PROPERTIES CORPORATION   *p1431*
2612 KOYL AVE, SASKATOON, SK, S7L
5X9

(306) 955-4174   *SIC* 6211

MILLENNUIM MANAGEMENT CORP   *p330*
609 GRANVILLE ST SUITE 1600, VANCOUVER, BC, V7Y 1C3

(604) 669-1322   *SIC* 6211

MORGAN STANLEY CANADA LIMITED
p965
181 BAY ST SUITE 3700, TORONTO, ON,
M5J 2T3

(416) 943-8400   *SIC* 6211

MORTGAGEATLANTIC   *p458*
14 MCQUADE LAKE CRES UNIT 202, HALIFAX, NS, B3S 1B6

(902) 493-3326   *SIC* 6211

MOTION MICRO SOLUTIONS INC   *p624*
300 MARCH RD SUITE 400, KANATA, ON,
K2K 2E2

(613) 667-9157   *SIC* 6211

MUFG BANK, LTD., CANADA BRANCH *p965*
200 BAY ST SUITE 1700, TORONTO, ON,
M5J 2J1

(416) 865-0220   *SIC* 6211

NORSTONE FINANCIAL CORPORATION
p997
130 KING ST, TORONTO, ON, M9N 1L5

(416) 860-6245   *SIC* 6211

ODLUM BROWN LIMITED   *p308*
250 HOWE ST SUITE 1100, VANCOUVER,
BC, V6C 3S9

(604) 669-1600   *SIC* 6211

ONTARIO ECONOMIC DEVELOPMENT
p640
30 DUKE ST W SUITE 906, KITCHENER,
ON, N2H 3W5

(519) 571-6074   *SIC* 6211

OTTAWA-CARLETON MORTGAGE INC *p830*
381 RICHMOND RD, OTTAWA, ON, K2A
0E7

(613) 563-3447   *SIC* 6211

PARADIGM CAPITAL INC   *p965*
95 WELLINGTON ST W SUITE 2101,
TORONTO, ON, M5J 2N7

(416) 361-9892   *SIC* 6211

PAYMENTECH CANADA DEBIT, INC *p868*
888 BIRCHMOUNT RD SUITE 7, SCARBOROUGH, ON, M1K 5L1

(416) 288-3027   *SIC* 6211

**PENDER NDI LIFE SCIENCES FUND (VCC)
INC**   *p308*
885 GEORGIA ST W SUITE 200, VANCOUVER, BC, V6C 3E8

(604) 688-1511   *SIC* 6211

PETERS & CO. LIMITED   *p56*
308 4 AVE SW SUITE 2300, CALGARY, AB,
T2P 0H7

(403) 261-4850   *SIC* 6211

PI FINANCIAL CORP   *p308*
666 BURRARD ST SUITE 1900, VANCOUVER, BC, V6C 3N1

(604) 664-2900   *SIC* 6211

PICTET CANADA S.E.C.   *p1207*
1000 RUE DE LA GAUCHETIERE O BUREAU 3100, MONTREAL, QC, H3B 4W5

(514) 288-8161   *SIC* 6211

PINNACLE WEALTH BROKERS INC   *p77*
15 ROYAL VISTA PL NW SUITE 250, CALGARY, AB, T3R 0P3

(855) 628-4286   *SIC* 6211

PLATINUM PROPERTIES GROUP CORP
p293
777 BROADWAY W SUITE 707, VANCOUVER, BC, V5Z 4J7

(604) 638-3300   *SIC* 6211

POLAR CAPITAL CORPORATION   *p956*
372 BAY ST, TORONTO, ON, M5H 2W9

(416) 367-4364   *SIC* 6211

POLLITT & CO. INC   *p956*
330 BAY ST SUITE 405, TORONTO, ON,
M5H 2S8

(416) 365-3313   *SIC* 6211

POWER CORPORATION DU CANADA
p1190
751 RUE DU SQUARE-VICTORIA, MONTREAL, QC, H2Y 2J3

(514) 286-7400   *SIC* 6211

PRIMCORP SECURITY LTD   *p295*
211 GEORGIA ST E SUITE 303, VANCOUVER, BC, V6A 1Z6

(604) 801-6899   *SIC* 6211

**PROFESSIONAL   INVESTMENTS
(KINGSTON) INC**   *p633*
1180 CLYDE CRT, KINGSTON, ON, K7P
2E4

(613) 384-7511   *SIC* 6211

QTRADE CANADA INC   *p329*
505 BURRARD ST SUITE 1920, VANCOUVER, BC, V7X 1M6

(604) 605-4111   *SIC* 6211

QUESTRADE, INC   *p770*
5650 YONGE ST SUITE 1700, NORTH
YORK, ON, M2M 4G3

(416) 227-9876   *SIC* 6211

R.J. O'BRIEN & ASSOCIATES CANADA INC
p389
195 COMMERCE DR, WINNIPEG, MB, R3P
1A2

(204) 594-1440   *SIC* 6211

RAYMOND JAMES LTD   *p58*
525 8 AVE SW SUITE 161, CALGARY, AB,
T2P 1G1

(403) 221-0333   *SIC* 6211

RAYMOND JAMES LTD   *p309*
925 GEORGIA ST W SUITE 2100, VANCOUVER, BC, V6C 3L2

(604) 659-8000   *SIC* 6211

RBC DEXIA INVESTORS SERVICES   *p58*
335 8 AVE SW, CALGARY, AB, T2P 1C9

(403) 292-3978   *SIC* 6211

RBC DOMINION SECURITIES INC   *p375*
201 PORTAGE AVE SUITE 3100, WINNIPEG, MB, R3B 3K6

(204) 982-3450   *SIC* 6211

RBC DOMINION SECURITIES LIMITED *p966*
200 BAY ST 9TH FLOOR, TORONTO, ON,
M5J 2J5

(416) 842-4088   *SIC* 6211

RBC PHILLIPS, HAGER & NORTH INVESTMENT COUNSEL INC   *p983*
155 WELLINGTON ST W FL 17, TORONTO,
ON, M5V 3H1

(416) 956-9618   *SIC* 6211

ROTHSCHILD (CANADA) INC   *p966*
161 BAY ST SUITE 4230, TORONTO, ON,
M5J 2S1

(416) 369-9600   *SIC* 6211

ROYAL BANK HOLDING INC   *p966*
200 BAY ST 9TH FLOOR, TORONTO, ON,
M5J 2J5

(416) 974-7493   *SIC* 6211

S.R.E.P.E. INC   *p1173*
4837 RUE BOYER BUREAU 240, MONTREAL, QC, H2J 3E6

(514) 525-3447   *SIC* 6211

SALMAN PARTNERS INC   *p316*

1095 PENDER ST W SUITE 1702, VAN-
COUVER, BC, V6E 2M6
SIC 6211
SCOTIA CAPITAL INC *p59*
119 6 AVE SW SUITE 300, CALGARY, AB,
T2P 0P8
(403) 298-4000 *SIC 6211*
SCOTIA CAPITAL INC *p90*
10104 103 AVE NW SUITE 2000, EDMON-
TON, AB, T5J 0H8
(780) 497-3200 *SIC 6211*
SCOTIA CAPITAL INC *p825*
350 ALBERT ST SUITE 2100, OTTAWA,
ON, K1R 1A4
(613) 563-0991 *SIC 6211*
SCOTIA CAPITAL INC *p956*
40 KING ST W, TORONTO, ON, M5H 3Y2
(416) 863-7411 *SIC 6211*
SCOTIA CAPITAL INC *p1199*
1002 RUE SHERBROOKE O BUREAU 600,
MONTREAL, QC, H3A 3L6
(514) 287-3600 *SIC 6211*
SCOTIA PRIVATE CLIENT GROUP *p379*
200 PORTAGE AVE SUITE 845, WIN-
NIPEG, MB, R3C 3X2
(204) 985-3104 *SIC 6211*
SCOTIA WATEROUS INC *p59*
225 6 AVE SW STE 1700, CALGARY, AB,
T2P 1M2
(403) 410-9947 *SIC 6211*
SCOTT LAND & LEASE LTD *p59*
202 6 AVE SW SUITE 900, CALGARY, AB,
T2P 2R9
(403) 261-1000 *SIC 6211*
SECURITAS CANADA LIMITED *p813*
1908 COLONEL SAM DR, OSHAWA, ON,
L1H 8P7
(905) 644-6370 *SIC 6211*
SENVEST CAPITAL INC *p1199*
1000 RUE SHERBROOKE O BUREAU
2400, MONTREAL, QC, H3A 3G4
(514) 281-8082 *SIC 6211*
SERVICES AIRBASE INC, LES *p1095*
81 AV LINDSAY, DORVAL, QC, H9P 2S6
(514) 735-5260 *SIC 6211*
SI ALARMS LIMITED *p381*
1380 NOTRE DAME AVE UNIT 200, WIN-
NIPEG, MB, R3E 0P7
(204) 231-1606 *SIC 6211*
SILVERTIP SECURITY LTD *p248*
7100 ALBERNI ST SUITE 24, POWELL
RIVER, BC, V8A 5K9
SIC 6211
SKYLINK SECURITY INC *p930*
1027 YONGE ST, TORONTO, ON, M4W 2K9
(416) 922-5017 *SIC 6211*
SOCIETE DE FIDUCIE BMO *p1208*
1250 BOUL RENE-LEVESQUE O UNITE
4600, MONTREAL, QC, H3B 5J5
(514) 877-7373 *SIC 6211*
SOLIUM CAPITAL INC *p59*
600 3 AVE SW SUITE 1500, CALGARY, AB,
T2P 0G5
(403) 515-3910 *SIC 6211*
**STANDARD SECURITIES CAPITAL COR-
PORATION** *p973*
24 HAZELTON AVE, TORONTO, ON, M5R
2E2
SIC 6211
STERLING MUTUALS INC *p1024*
880 OUELLETTE AVE, WINDSOR, ON,
N9A 1C7
(519) 256-8999 *SIC 6211*
STERN PARTNERS INC *p300*
650 GEORGIA ST W UNIT 2900, VANCOU-
VER, BC, V6B 4N8
(604) 681-8817 *SIC 6211*
SUCCESSION CAPITAL CORPORATION
p997
88 ARROW RD, TORONTO, ON, M9M 2L8
(416) 223-1700 *SIC 6211*
SWIFT TRADE SECURITIES LTD *p927*
55 ST CLAIR AVE W SUITE 900,
TORONTO, ON, M4V 2Y7

(416) 351-0000 *SIC 6211*
TAG INTERNATIONAL INC *p809*
75 FIRST ST SUITE 321, ORANGEVILLE,
ON, L9W 2E7
(519) 943-0074 *SIC 6211*
TD CAPITAL GROUP LIMITED *p970*
100 WELLINGTON ST W, TORONTO, ON,
M5K 1A2
(800) 430-6095 *SIC 6211*
TD SECURITIES INC *p970*
66 WELLINGTON ST W, TORONTO, ON,
M5K 1A2
(416) 307-8500 *SIC 6211*
TD WATERHOUSE CANADA INC *p970*
79 WELLINGTON ST W 10TH FL,
TORONTO, ON, M5K 1A1
(416) 307-6672 *SIC 6211*
TD WATERHOUSE CANADA INC *p976*
77 BLOOR ST W SUITE 3, TORONTO, ON,
M5S 1M2
(416) 982-7686 *SIC 6211*
THOMSON, WILLIAM E ASSOCIATES INC
p958
390 BAY ST SUITE 1102, TORONTO, ON,
M5H 2Y2
(416) 947-1300 *SIC 6211*
TIO NETWORKS CORP *p310*
250 HOWE ST UNIT 1550, VANCOUVER,
BC, V6C 3R8
(604) 298-4636 *SIC 6211*
**TRAFIGURA CANADA GENERAL PART-
NERSHIP** *p61*
400 3 AVE SW SUITE 3450, CALGARY, AB,
T2P 4H2
(403) 294-0400 *SIC 6211*
TRI-CORP CANADA INVESTMENTS INC
p91
203 TRI-CORP CENTRE, EDMONTON, AB,
T5J 1V8
(780) 496-9607 *SIC 6211*
**VALEURS MOBILIERES BANQUE LAU-
RENTIENNE INC** *p1214*
1360 BOUL RENE-LEVESQUE O BUREAU
620, MONTREAL, QC, H3G 0E8
(514) 350-2800 *SIC 6211*
VALEURS MOBILIERES DESJARDINS INC
p1209
1170 RUE PEEL BUREAU 300, MON-
TREAL, QC, H3B 0A9
(514) 987-1749 *SIC 6211*
VALEURS MOBILIERES DESJARDINS INC
p1230
2 COMPLEXE DESJARDINS TOUR E 15
+TAGE, MONTREAL, QC, H5B 1J2
(514) 286-3180 *SIC 6211*
VELOCITY TRADE CANADA LTD. *p941*
100 YONGE ST UNIT 1800, TORONTO, ON,
M5C 2W1
(416) 855-2800 *SIC 6211*
**VERICO CML CANADIAN MORTGAGE
LENDER INC** *p26*
2316 6 ST NE, CALGARY, AB, T2E 3Z1
(866) 265-7988 *SIC 6211*
VIRTU ITG CANADA CORP *p988*
130 KING ST W SUITE 1040, TORONTO,
ON, M5X 2A2
(416) 874-0900 *SIC 6211*
VISUALGATE SYSTEMS INC *p785*
64 BAKERSFIELD ST, NORTH YORK, ON,
M3J 2W7
SIC 6211
WATT CARMICHAEL INC *p941*
1 QUEEN ST E SUITE 1900, TORONTO,
ON, M5C 2W6
(416) 864-1500 *SIC 6211*
**WEALTHTERRA CAPITAL MANAGEMENT
INC** *p80*
105 1ST ST W SUITE 104, COCHRANE,
AB, T4C 1A4
(403) 981-1156 *SIC 6211*
WESTAIM CORPORATION, THE *p968*
70 YORK ST SUITE 1700, TORONTO, ON,
M5J 1S9
(416) 969-3333 *SIC 6211*

**YI JIA INTERNATIONAL GROUP (CANADA)
LTD** *p191*
4720 KINGSWAY UNIT 2335, BURNABY,
BC, V5H 4N2
(778) 379-0118 *SIC 6211*

---

*SIC 6221 Commodity contracts brokers,
dealers*

FRIEDBERG MERCANTILE GROUP LTD
p962
181 BAY ST SUITE 250, TORONTO, ON,
M5J 2T3
(416) 364-1171 *SIC 6221*
GREAT LAKES COMMODITIES INC *p952*
320 BAY ST, TORONTO, ON, M5H 4A6
(416) 864-0856 *SIC 6221*
**GROUPE D'APPROVISIONNEMENT EN
COMMUN DE L'EST DU QUEBEC** *p1278*
710 RUE BOUVIER BUREAU 296, QUE-
BEC, QC, G2J 1C2
(418) 780-8111 *SIC 6221*
IMPACT DETAIL INC *p1380*
2625 BOUL DES ENTREPRISES, TERRE-
BONNE, QC, J6X 4J9
(514) 767-1555 *SIC 6221*
LIMSON CANADA, LTD *p263*
12411 HORSESHOE WAY, RICHMOND,
BC, V7A 4X6
(604) 529-5275 *SIC 6221*
MARTECH MARKETING LIMITED *p89*
10060 JASPER AVE NW SUITE 1701, ED-
MONTON, AB, T5J 3R8
(780) 454-2006 *SIC 6221*
THYSSENKRUPP MATERIALS CA, LTD
p559
2821 LANGSTAFF RD, CONCORD, ON,
L4K 5C6
(905) 669-0247 *SIC 6221*

---

*SIC 6231 Security and commodity
exchanges*

BOURSE DE MONTREAL INC *p1229*
800 RUE DU SQUARE-VICTORIA 4E
ETAGE, MONTREAL, QC, H4Z 1A1
(514) 871-2424 *SIC 6231*
CANDEAL.CA INC *p932*
152 KING ST E SUITE 400, TORONTO, ON,
M5A 1J3
(416) 814-7800 *SIC 6231*
CNSX MARKETS INC *p986*
100 KING ST W SUITE 7210, TORONTO,
ON, M5X 1E1
(416) 572-2000 *SIC 6231*
COOPERATION ECHANGE CANADA INC
p1229
975 BOUL ROMEO-VACHON-AEROPORT
N, MONTREAL, QC, H4V 1H1
(514) 828-0068 *SIC 6231*
CST INVESTOR SERVICES INC *p950*
320 BAY ST SUITE 1000, TORONTO, ON,
M5H 4A6
(888) 402-1644 *SIC 6231*
JITNEYTRADE INC *p1189*
360 RUE SAINT-JACQUES, MONTREAL,
QC, H2Y 1P5
(514) 985-8080 *SIC 6231*
TMX GROUP LIMITED *p958*
100 ADELAIDE ST W SUITE 300,
TORONTO, ON, M5H 1S3
(416) 947-4670 *SIC 6231*
TSX INC *p958*
100 ADELAIDE ST W SUITE 300,
TORONTO, ON, M5H 4H1
(888) 873-8392 *SIC 6231*

SIC 6282 Investment advice

1556890 ONTARIO LTD *p788*
1 YORKDALE RD SUITE 404, NORTH

YORK, ON, M6A 3A1
(416) 787-1612 *SIC 6282*
6142974 CANADA INC *p927*
175 BLOOR ST E SUITE 606, TORONTO,
ON, M4W 3R8
(416) 934-1436 *SIC 6282*
9218-4118 QUEBEC INC *p1395*
507 RTE MARIE-VICTORIN, VERCHERES,
QC, J0L 2R0
(450) 583-3513 *SIC 6282*
ADDENDA CAPITAL INC *p1201*
800 BOUL RENE-LEVESQUE O BUREAU
2750, MONTREAL, QC, H3B 1X9
(514) 287-0223 *SIC 6282*
AGF MANAGEMENT LIMITED *p968*
66 WELLINGTON ST W FL 31, TORONTO,
ON, M5K 1E9
(800) 268-8583 *SIC 6282*
ALTACORP CAPITAL INC *p43*
585 8 AVE SW UNIT 410, CALGARY, AB,
T2P 1G1
(403) 539-8600 *SIC 6282*
AP FOUNDERS LP *p968*
79 WELLINGTON ST W SUITE 3500,
TORONTO, ON, M5K 1K7
(416) 306-9800 *SIC 6282*
ARCA FINANCIAL GROUP INC *p1007*
237 LABRADOR DR, WATERLOO, ON, N2K
4M8
(519) 745-8500 *SIC 6282*
ASSANTE FINANCIAL MANAGEMENT *p630*
264 KING ST E, KINGSTON, ON, K7L 3A9
(613) 549-8602 *SIC 6282*
**ASSOCIATION OF MUNICIPALITIES OF ON-
TARIO** *p948*
200 UNIVERSITY AVE SUITE 801,
TORONTO, ON, M5H 3C6
(416) 971-9856 *SIC 6282*
ASSURANCES ETERNA INC *p1270*
1134 GRANDE ALLEE O BUREAU 400,
QUEBEC, QC, G1S 1E5
(418) 266-1000 *SIC 6282*
B2B BANK FINANCIAL SERVICES INC *p944*
199 BAY ST SUITE 610, TORONTO, ON,
M5G 1M5
(416) 926-0221 *SIC 6282*
BALANCED FINANCIAL SERVICES LTD
p322
2309 41ST AVE W SUITE 202, VANCOU-
VER, BC, V6M 2A3
(604) 261-8509 *SIC 6282*
BANRO INVESTMENT SOLUTIONS CORP
p985
100 KING ST W UNIT 5602, TORONTO,
ON, M5X 2A2
(416) 948-5271 *SIC 6282*
BARNES COMMUNICATIONS INC *p941*
1 YONGE ST SUITE 1504, TORONTO, ON,
M5E 1E5
(416) 367-5000 *SIC 6282*
BASKIN FINANCIAL SERVICES INC *p926*
95 ST CLAIR AVE W SUITE 900,
TORONTO, ON, M4V 1N6
(416) 969-9540 *SIC 6282*
BCA RESEARCH INC *p1193*
1002 RUE SHERBROOKE O BUREAU
1600, MONTREAL, QC, H3A 3L6
(514) 499-9550 *SIC 6282*
BENTALL KENNEDY LP *p959*
1 YORK ST SUITE 1100, TORONTO, ON,
M5J 0B6
(416) 681-3400 *SIC 6282*
BIMCOR INC *p1202*
1000 RUE DE LA GAUCHETIERE O BU-
REAU 1300, MONTREAL, QC, H3B 5A7
(514) 394-4750 *SIC 6282*
BLACKWOOD PARTNERS CORPORATION
p937
110 YONGE ST SUITE 1500, TORONTO,
ON, M5C 1T4
(416) 603-3900 *SIC 6282*
BMO ASSET MANAGEMENT INC *p985*
100 KING ST W 43RD FLOOR, TORONTO,
ON, M5X 1A1

(416) 359-5000   *SIC 6282*
BOREALIS CAPITAL CORPORATION *p960*
200 BAY ST SUITE 200, TORONTO, ON, M5J 2J2
(416) 361-1011   *SIC 6282*
BRANDES INVESTMENT PARTNERS & CO. *p960*
20 BAY ST SUITE 400, TORONTO, ON, M5J 2N8
(416) 306-5700   *SIC 6282*
BROWNSTONE INVESTMENT PLANNING INC *p377*
444 ST MARY AVE SUITE 1122, WINNIPEG, MB, R3C 3T1
(204) 944-9911   *SIC 6282*
CANADIAN SHAREOWNERS ASSOCIATION *p949*
170 UNIVERSITY AVE SUITE 704, TORONTO, ON, M5H 3B3
(416) 595-9600   *SIC 6282*
CARDINAL CAPITAL MANAGEMENT INC *p383*
1780 WELLINGTON AVE SUITE 506, WINNIPEG, MB, R3H 1B3
(204) 783-0716   *SIC 6282*
CI FINANCIAL CORP *p937*
2 QUEEN ST E, TORONTO, ON, M5C 3G7
(416) 364-1145   *SIC 6282*
CI INVESTMENTS INC *p937*
1 QUEEN ST E SUITE 2000, TORONTO, ON, M5C 3W5
(416) 364-1145   *SIC 6282*
CIBC ASSET MANAGEMENT HOLDINGS INC *p971*
COMMERCE CRT W, TORONTO, ON, M5L 1A2
(416) 980-2211   *SIC 6282*
CIBC ASSET MANAGEMENT INC *p961*
18 YORK ST SUITE 140, TORONTO, ON, M5J 2T8
(416) 364-5620   *SIC 6282*
CIBC ASSET MANAGEMENT INC *p1194*
1500 BOUL ROBERT-BOURASSA BUREAU 800, MONTREAL, QC, H3A 3S6
(514) 875-7040   *SIC 6282*
CIBC INVESTOR SERVICES INC *p971*
199 BAY ST, TORONTO, ON, M5L 1A2
(416) 980-3343   *SIC 6282*
CIBC INVESTOR SERVICES INC *p1202*
1155 BOUL RENE-LEVESQUE O BUREAU 1501, MONTREAL, QC, H3B 2J6
(514) 876-3343   *SIC 6282*
CIBT EDUCATION GROUP INC *p293*
777 BROADWAY W UNIT 1200, VANCOUVER, BC, V5Z 4J7
(604) 871-9909   *SIC 6282*
CONNOR, CLARK & LUNN INVESTMENT MANAGEMENT LTD *p312*
1111 GEORGIA ST W UNIT 2300, VANCOUVER, BC, V6E 4M3
(604) 685-2020   *SIC 6282*
DE THOMAS WEALTH MANAGEMENT CORP *p851*
9033 LESLIE ST UNIT 1, RICHMOND HILL, ON, L4B 4K3
(905) 731-9800   *SIC 6282*
DESJARDINS SECURITE FINANCIERE INVESTISSEMENTS INC *p1269*
1150 RUE DE CLAIRE-FONTAINE, QUEBEC, QC, G1R 5G4
(877) 647-5435   *SIC 6282*
DIBRINA SURE FINANCIAL GROUP INC *p900*
62 FROOD RD SUITE 302, SUDBURY, ON, P3C 4Z3
(705) 688-9011   *SIC 6282*
DOHENY SECURITIES LIMITED *p385*
1661 PORTAGE AVE SUITE 702, WINNIPEG, MB, R3J 3T7
(204) 925-1250   *SIC 6282*
DOHERTY & ASSOCIATES LTD *p823*
56 SPARKS ST SUITE 700, OTTAWA, ON, K1P 5A9
(613) 238-6727   *SIC 6282*

DRISCOLL, J. F. INVESTMENT CORP *p997*
130 KING ST, TORONTO, ON, M9N 1L5
(416) 365-7532   *SIC 6282*
E-L FINANCIAL CORPORATION LIMITED *p950*
165 UNIVERSITY AVE 10TH FL, TORONTO, ON, M5H 3B8
(416) 947-2578   *SIC 6282*
FAIRFAX FINANCIAL HOLDINGS LIMITED *p962*
95 WELLINGTON ST SUITE 800, TORONTO, ON, M5J 2N7
(416) 367-4941   *SIC 6282*
FIERA CAPITAL CORPORATION *p1195*
1981 MCGILL COLLEGE AVE SUITE 1500, MONTREAL, QC, H3A 0H5
(514) 954-3300   *SIC 6282*
FORMULA GROWTH LIMITED *p1196*
1010 RUE SHERBROOKE O BUREAU 2300, MONTREAL, QC, H3A 2R7
(514) 288-5136   *SIC 6282*
FRANKLIN TEMPLETON INVESTMENTS CORP *p771*
5000 YONGE ST SUITE 900, NORTH YORK, ON, M2N 0A7
(416) 957-6000   *SIC 6282*
GENERATION ADVISORS INC *p925*
22 ST CLAIR AVE E, TORONTO, ON, M4T 2S3
(416) 361-1498   *SIC 6282*
GENERATION PORTFOLIO MANAGEMENT CORP *p925*
22 ST CLAIR AVE E, TORONTO, ON, M4T 2S3
(416) 361-1498   *SIC 6282*
GESTION D'ACTIFS SECTORIELS INC *p1196*
1000 RUE SHERBROOKE O BUREAU 2120, MONTREAL, QC, H3A 3G4
(514) 849-8777   *SIC 6282*
GLUSKIN SHEFF + ASSOCIATES INC *p952*
333 BAY ST SUITE 5100, TORONTO, ON, M5H 2R2
(416) 681-6000   *SIC 6282*
GOLDEN OPPORTUNITIES FUND INC *p1427*
410 22ND ST E SUITE 830, SASKATOON, SK, S7K 5T6
(306) 652-5557   *SIC 6282*
GOLDENLIFE FINANCIAL CORP *p578*
555 BURNHAMTHORPE RD SUITE 305, ETOBICOKE, ON, M9C 2Y3
(416) 620-0615   *SIC 6282*
GOODMAN & COMPANY, INVESTMENT COUNSEL LTD *p939*
1 ADELAIDE ST E SUITE 2100, TORONTO, ON, M5C 2V9
(416) 363-9097   *SIC 6282*
GRANVILLE WEST GROUP LTD *p313*
1075 GEORGIA ST W SUITE 1425, VANCOUVER, BC, V6E 3C9
(604) 687-5570   *SIC 6282*
GRAVITAS FINANCIAL INC *p952*
333 BAY ST SUITE 1700, TORONTO, ON, M5H 2R2
(647) 252-1674   *SIC 6282*
GREYSTONE CAPITAL MANAGEMENT INC *p1421*
1230 BLACKFOOT DR UNIT 300, REGINA, SK, S4S 7G4
(306) 779-6400   *SIC 6282*
GREYSTONE MANAGED INVESTMENTS INC *p1421*
1230 BLACKFOOT DR UNIT 300, REGINA, SK, S4S 7G4
(306) 779-6400   *SIC 6282*
GUARDIAN CAPITAL GROUP LIMITED *p971*
199 BAY ST SUITE 3100, TORONTO, ON, M5L 1E8
(416) 364-8341   *SIC 6282*
GUARDIAN CAPITAL LP *p971*
199 BAY ST SUITE 3100, TORONTO, ON, M5L 1E8
(416) 364-8341   *SIC 6282*

GWL REALTY ADVISORS INC *p945*
330 UNIVERSITY AVE SUITE 300, TORONTO, ON, M5G 1R7
(416) 552-5959   *SIC 6282*
HAMBLIN, WATSA INVESTMENT COUNSEL LTD *p963*
95 WELLINGTON ST W SUITE 802, TORONTO, ON, M5J 2N7
(416) 366-9544   *SIC 6282*
HILLSDALE INVESTMENT MANAGEMENT INC *p969*
100 WELLINGTON ST W SUITE 2100, TORONTO, ON, M5K 1J3
(416) 913-3900   *SIC 6282*
IA CLARINGTON INVESTMENTS INC *p946*
522 UNIVERSITY AVE SUITE 700, TORONTO, ON, M5G 1W7
(416) 860-9880   *SIC 6282*
INDEPENDANT PLANNING GROUP INC/GROUPE INDEPENDANT DE PLANIFICATION INC *p749*
35 ANTARES DR, NEPEAN, ON, K2E 8B1
(613) 738-3388   *SIC 6282*
INFRA-PSP CANADA INC *p1205*
1250 BOUL RENE-LEVESQUE O BUREAU 1400, MONTREAL, QC, H3B 4W8
(514) 937-2772   *SIC 6282*
INTACT INVESTMENT MANAGEMENT, INC *p946*
700 UNIVERSITY AVE SUITE 1500, TORONTO, ON, M5G 0A1
(416) 341-1464   *SIC 6282*
INVESTIA SERVICES FINANCIERS INC *p1279*
6700 BOUL PIERRE-BERTRAND BUREAU 300, QUEBEC, QC, G2J 0B4
(418) 684-5548   *SIC 6282*
INVESTORS GROUP TRUST CO. LTD *p767*
200 YORKLAND BLVD UNIT 300, NORTH YORK, ON, M2J 5C1
(647) 456-5160   *SIC 6282*
JARISLOWSKY, FRASER LIMITEE *p1197*
1010 RUE SHERBROOKE O BUREAU 2005, MONTREAL, QC, H3A 2R7
(514) 842-2727   *SIC 6282*
LEGG MASON CANADA INC *p964*
220 BAY ST SUITE 1400, TORONTO, ON, M5J 2W4
(416) 860-0616   *SIC 6282*
LEITH WHEELER INVESTMENT COUNSEL LTD *p306*
400 BURRARD ST SUITE 1500, VANCOUVER, BC, V6C 3A6
(604) 683-3391   *SIC 6282*
MACCOUL INVESTMENTS LIMITED *p442*
211 DUKE ST, CHESTER, NS, B0J 1J0
(902) 275-3262   *SIC 6282*
MAVRIX FUND MANAGEMENT INC *p954*
212 KING ST W SUITE 501, TORONTO, ON, M5H 1K5
(416) 362-3077   *SIC 6282*
MCKELLAR STRUCTURED SETTLEMENTS INC *p601*
649 SCOTTSDALE DR SUITE 100, GUELPH, ON, N1G 4T7
(519) 836-1672   *SIC 6282*
MCLEAN & PARTNERS WEALTH MANAGEMENT LTD *p65*
801 10 AVE SW, CALGARY, AB, T2R 0B4
(403) 234-0005   *SIC 6282*
MFS INVESTMENT MANAGEMENT CANADA LIMITED *p970*
77 KING ST W SUITE 3500, TORONTO, ON, M5K 2A1
(416) 862-9800   *SIC 6282*
NEWPORT PRIVATE WEALTH INC *p982*
469 KING ST W SUITE C, TORONTO, ON, M5V 1K4
(416) 867-7555   *SIC 6282*
NEXGEN FINANCIAL LIMITED PARTNERSHIP *p940*
36 TORONTO ST SUITE 1070, TORONTO, ON, M5C 2C5
(416) 775-3700   *SIC 6282*

NINEPOINT PARTNERS LP *p965*
200 BAY ST SUITE 2700, TORONTO, ON, M5J 2J1
(416) 362-7172   *SIC 6282*
NORTHPOINT CAPITAL PARTNERS (CANADA) LTD *p970*
79 WELLINGTON ST W, TORONTO, ON, M5K 1N9
(866) 964-4141   *SIC 6282*
NORTHLEAF INFRASTRUCTURE CAPITAL PARTNERS II LP *p970*
79 WELLINGTON ST W FL 6, TORONTO, ON, M5K 1N9
(866) 964-4141   *SIC 6282*
NT GLOBAL ADVISORS INC *p955*
145 KING ST W SUITE 1910, TORONTO, ON, M5H 1J8
(416) 366-2020   *SIC 6282*
OMBUDSMAN FOR BANKING SERVICES AND INVESTMENTS *p955*
401 BAY ST SUITE 1505, TORONTO, ON, M5H 2Y4
(416) 287-2877   *SIC 6282*
OMERS PRIVATE EQUITY INC *p955*
100 ADELAIDE ST W SUITE 900, TORONTO, ON, M5H 0E2
(416) 864-3200   *SIC 6282*
ONEX CORPORATION *p965*
161 BAY ST, TORONTO, ON, M5J 2S1
(416) 362-7711   *SIC 6282*
ONEX PARTNERS ADVISOR GP INC *p965*
161 BAY ST SUITE 4900, TORONTO, ON, M5J 2S1
(416) 362-7711   *SIC 6282*
OPTIMUM GESTION DE PLACEMENTS INC *p1198*
425 BOUL DE MAISONNEUVE O BUREAU 1620, MONTREAL, QC, H3A 3G5
(514) 288-7545   *SIC 6282*
ORBIS INVESTMENTS (CANADA) LIMITED *p190*
4710 KINGSWAY SUITE 2600, BURNABY, BC, V5H 4M2
(778) 331-3000   *SIC 6282*
OSISKO GOLD ROYALTIES LTD *p1207*
1100 AV DES CANADIENS-DE-MONTREAL BUREAU 300, MONTREAL, QC, H3B 2S2
(514) 940-0670   *SIC 6282*
PACIFIC REALM INVESTMENT GROUP INC. *p831*
20E CASTLEBROOK LANE, OTTAWA, ON, K2G 5G3
SIC 6282
PADDON + YORKE INC *p708*
95 DUNDAS ST E, MISSISSAUGA, ON, L5A 1W7
(905) 272-3204   *SIC 6282*
PAROUSIA INVESTMETS LTD *p628*
3152 DONALD B MUNRO DR, KINBURN, ON, K0A 2H0
(613) 254-6599   *SIC 6282*
PLACEMENTS MONTRUSCO BOLTON INC *p1198*
1501 AV MCGILL COLLEGE BUREAU 1200, MONTREAL, QC, H3A 3M8
(514) 842-6464   *SIC 6282*
PORTLAND INVESTMENT COUNSEL INC *p529*
1375 KERNS RD SUITE 100, BURLINGTON, ON, L7P 4V7
(905) 331-4242   *SIC 6282*
PRIME QUADRANT CORP *p926*
2 ST CLAIR AVE E SUITE 800, TORONTO, ON, M4T 2T5
(647) 749-4118   *SIC 6282*
PRIMERICA FINANCIAL SERVICES LTD *p596*
839 SHEFFORD RD SUITE 200, GLOUCESTER, ON, K1J 9K8
(613) 742-0768   *SIC 6282*
PRIMERICA FINANCIAL SERVICES LTD *p703*
1425 DUNDAS ST E SUITE 207, MISSIS-

SAUGA, ON, L4X 2W4
(905) 602-1167   *SIC 6282*

PROFESSIONALS' FINANCIAL INC. *p1230*
2 COMPLEXE DESJARDINS E, MONTREAL, QC, H5B 1C2
(514) 350-5075   *SIC 6282*

PROLIFIO INVESTMENT & ASSET MANAGEMENT CORP *p966*
161 BAY ST, TORONTO, ON, M5J 2S1
(416) 948-5505   *SIC 6282*

QUADRAS INVESTMENT SERVICES LTD *p655*
255 DUFFERIN AVE, LONDON, ON, N6A 4K1
(519) 435-4826   *SIC 6282*

RBC ASSET MANAGEMENT INC *p966*
200 BAY ST, TORONTO, ON, M5J 2J5
(416) 974-9419   *SIC 6282*

RBC DOMINION SECURITIES INC *p966*
200 BAY ST, TORONTO, ON, M5J 2W7
(416) 842-2000   *SIC 6282*

RBC INVESTOR SERVICES TRUST *p966*
200 BAY ST, TORONTO, ON, M5J 2J5
SIC 6282

RBC INVESTOR SERVICES TRUST *p983*
155 WELLINGTON ST W 7 FL, TORONTO, ON, M5V 3H1
(416) 955-6251   *SIC 6282*

RECOGNIA INC *p751*
301 MOODIE DR SUITE 200, NEPEAN, ON, K2H 9C4
(613) 789-2267   *SIC 6282*

RED ISLE PRIVATE INVESTMENTS INC *p1207*
1250 BOUL RENE-LEVESQUE O, MONTREAL, QC, H3B 4W8
SIC 6282

REGION 9 REGIONAL TOURISM ORGANIZATION *p631*
945 PRINCESS ST SUITE 202, KINGSTON, ON, K7L 5L9
(613) 344-2095   *SIC 6282*

ROTHENBERG & ROTHENBERG ANNUITIES LTD *p1402*
4420 RUE SAINTE-CATHERINE O, WESTMOUNT, QC, H3Z 1R2
(514) 934-0586   *SIC 6282*

SANDFORD - BLACKSTOCK INVESTMENTS LIMITED *p895*
37 SANDIFORD DR UNIT 300, STOUFFVILLE, ON, L4A 3Z2
SIC 6282

SCIERADE INVESTMENT CORPORATION *p973*
1235 BAY ST, TORONTO, ON, M5R 3K4
(647) 244-6707   *SIC 6282*

SELECT FINANCIAL SERVICES INC *p534*
193 PINEBUSH RD SUITE 200, CAMBRIDGE, ON, N1R 7H8
(519) 622-9613   *SIC 6282*

SENTRY INVESTMENTS *p940*
2 QUEEN ST E FL 12, TORONTO, ON, M5C 3G7
(416) 861-8729   *SIC 6282*

SHELTER CANADIAN PROPERTIES LIMITED *p387*
2600 SEVEN EVERGREEN PLACE, WINNIPEG, MB, R3L 2T3
(204) 475-9090   *SIC 6282*

SPROTT ASSET MANAGEMENT INC *p967*
200 BAY ST SUITE 2700, TORONTO, ON, M5J 2J1
(416) 955-5885   *SIC 6282*

SPROTT INC *p967*
200 BAY ST SUITE 2600, TORONTO, ON, M5J 2J1
(416) 943-8099   *SIC 6282*

SPRUCEGROVE INVESTMENT MANAGEMENT LTD *p957*
181 UNIVERSITY AVE SUITE 1300, TORONTO, ON, M5H 3M7
(416) 363-5854   *SIC 6282*

STUART, W H HOLDINGS LIMITED *p675*
11 ALLSTATE PKY SUITE 410, MARKHAM,

ON, L3R 9T8
(905) 305-0880   *SIC 6282*

T.E. FINANCIAL CONSULTANTS LTD *p943*
26 WELLINGTON ST E SUITE 800, TORONTO, ON, M5E 1S2
(416) 366-1451   *SIC 6282*

TALISKER RESOURCES LTD *p987*
100 KING STREET W 70 FLOOR, TORONTO, ON, M5X 1A9
(416) 361-2808   *SIC 6282*

TD INVESTMENT SERVICES INC *p970*
55 KING ST W, TORONTO, ON, M5K 1A2
(416) 944-5728   *SIC 6282*

TIMBERCREEK ASSET MANAGEMENT INC *p930*
25 PRICE ST, TORONTO, ON, M4W 1Z1
(416) 306-9967   *SIC 6282*

TIMBERCREEK INVESTMENT MANAGEMENT INC *p931*
25 PRICE ST, TORONTO, ON, M4W 1Z1
(416) 306-9967   *SIC 6282*

TRADE ALLIANCE & INVESTMENT CORP *p968*
161 BAY ST, TORONTO, ON, M5J 2S1
SIC 6282

UBS GLOBAL ASSET MANAGEMENT (CANADA) INC *p968*
161 BAY ST SUITE 4000, TORONTO, ON, M5J 2S1
(416) 681-5200   *SIC 6282*

VANGUARD INVESTMENTS CANADA INC. *p984*
155 WELLINGTON ST W SUITE 3720, TORONTO, ON, M5V 3H1
(416) 263-7100   *SIC 6282*

VARSHNEY CAPITAL CORPORATION *p310*
925 GEORGIA ST W SUITE 1304, VANCOUVER, BC, V6C 3L2
(604) 684-2181   *SIC 6282*

VERTEX ONE ASSET MANAGEMENT INC *p317*
1021 HASTINGS ST W SUITE 3200, VANCOUVER, BC, V6E 0C3
(604) 681-5787   *SIC 6282*

W.C.S. FINANCIAL SERVICES INC *p854*
20 WERTHEIM CRT SUITE 40, RICHMOND HILL, ON, L4B 3A8
(905) 731-1984   *SIC 6282*

WECAN- WINDSOR ETHICS CAPITAL ANGEL NETWORK *p1024*
720 OUELLETTE AVE, WINDSOR, ON, N9A 1C2
(519) 259-9836   *SIC 6282*

WESTCAP MGT. LTD *p1430*
410 22ND ST E SUITE 830, SASKATOON, SK, S7K 5T6
(306) 652-5557   *SIC 6282*

WORLDSOURCE FINANCIAL MANAGEMENT INC *p677*
625 COCHRANE DR SUITE 700, MARKHAM, ON, L3R 9R9
(905) 940-0044   *SIC 6282*

SIC 6289 Security and commodity service

ARC PROTECTION CORP *p208*
7351 VANTAGE WAY UNIT 3, DELTA, BC, V4G 1C9
(604) 345-0215   *SIC 6289*

BOURQUE SECURITY SERVICES NS *p457*
176 BEDFORD HWY, HALIFAX, NS, B3M 2J8
(902) 832-2456   *SIC 6289*

CANADIAN CORPS OF COMMISSIONAIRES NATIONAL OFFICE, THE *p490*
314 PINNACLE ST UNIT 2, BELLEVILLE, ON, K8N 3B4
(613) 962-6500   *SIC 6289*

CANADIAN DEPOSITORY FOR SECURITIES LIMITED, THE *p949*
85 RICHMOND ST W, TORONTO, ON, M5H 2C9
(416) 365-8400   *SIC 6289*

CONNECT INSURE *p831*
1111 PRINCE OF WALES DR, OTTAWA, ON, K2C 3T2
(613) 723-0670   *SIC 6289*

CORPORATION DE SECURITE GARDA CANADA *p128*
8600 FRANKLIN AVE SUITE 606, FORT MCMURRAY, AB, T9H 4G8
(780) 791-7087   *SIC 6289*

CREDIT UNION CENTRAL OF NOVA SCOTIA *p455*
6074 LADY HAMMOND RD, HALIFAX, NS, B3K 2R7
(902) 453-0680   *SIC 6289*

DBRS LIMITED *p950*
181 UNIVERSITY AVE SUITE 700, TORONTO, ON, M5H 3M7
(416) 593-5577   *SIC 6289*

EIGEN DEVELOPMENT LTD *p320*
1807 10TH AVE W SUITE 300, VANCOUVER, BC, V6J 2A9
(604) 484-0211   *SIC 6289*

EQUITY FINANCIAL TRUST COMPANY *p951*
200 UNIVERSITY AVE SUITE 400, TORONTO, ON, M5H 3C6
(416) 504-5050   *SIC 6289*

FUNDATA CANADA INC *p776*
26 LESMILL RD SUITE 1B, NORTH YORK, ON, M3B 2T5
(416) 445-5443   *SIC 6289*

GOVERNMENT OF THE PROVINCE OF ALBERTA *p92*
9820 106 ST NW SUITE 534, EDMONTON, AB, T5K 2J6
(780) 427-3076   *SIC 6289*

HAMILTON TECH DRIVE INC *p616*
1030 UPPER JAMES ST SUITE 308, HAMILTON, ON, L9C 6X6
(888) 723-3183   *SIC 6289*

INTERNATIONAL CROWD MANAGEMENT INC *p192*
6881 RUSSELL AVE, BURNABY, BC, V5J 4R8
(604) 688-0070   *SIC 6289*

INTERNATIONAL FINANCIAL DATA SERVICES (CANADA) LIMITED *p939*
30 ADELAIDE ST E SUITE 1, TORONTO, ON, M5C 3G9
(416) 506-8000   *SIC 6289*

SERVICES FINANCIERS PENSON CANADA INC *p1190*
360 RUE SAINT-JACQUES BUREAU 1201, MONTREAL, QC, H2Y 1P5
SIC 6289

STANDARD & POORS'S RATING SERVICES *p987*
130 KING ST W SUITE 1100, TORONTO, ON, M5X 2A2
(416) 507-2500   *SIC 6289*

STORECHECK -CONCORD *p559*
2180 STEELES AVE W, CONCORD, ON, L4K 2Z5
(905) 660-1334   *SIC 6289*

TRIAD INTERNATIONAL CORP *p1034*
690 ROWNTREE DAIRY RD SUITE 201, WOODBRIDGE, ON, L4L 5T7
(905) 264-9031   *SIC 6289*

UNICORN SECURITY *p237*
624 SIXTH ST UNIT 201, NEW WESTMINSTER, BC, V3L 3C4
(604) 593-5454   *SIC 6289*

SIC 6311 Life insurance

4256344 CANADA INC *p1212*
1245 RUE SHERBROOKE O BUREAU 2100, MONTREAL, QC, H3G 1G3
(877) 499-9555   *SIC 6311*

AA MUNRO INSURANCE *p461*
209 COBEQUID RD, LOWER SACKVILLE, NS, B4C 3P3
(902) 864-2510   *SIC 6311*

AACE FINANCIAL SERVICES LTD *p500*
5 MELANIE DR UNIT 10, BRAMPTON, ON, L6T 4K8
(905) 799-9004   *SIC 6311*

AGENCE D'ASSURANCE VIE MANUEL SMITH LTEE *p1328*
3333 BOUL DE LA COTE-VERTU STE 450, SAINT-LAURENT, QC, H4R 2N1
(514) 343-0200   *SIC 6311*

AIL CANADA *p368*
1549 ST MARY'S RD SUITE 101, WINNIPEG, MB, R2M 5G9
(204) 942-9477   *SIC 6311*

ASSUMPTION MUTUAL LIFE INSURANCE COMPANY *p406*
770 MAIN ST, MONCTON, NB, E1C 1E7
(506) 853-6040   *SIC 6311*

ASSURANCES ROBILLARD & ASSOCIES INC, LES *p1303*
461 CH DE JOLIETTE BUREAU 100, SAINT-FELIX-DE-VALOIS, QC, J0K 2M0
(450) 889-5557   *SIC 6311*

ASSURANT LIFE OF CANADA *p754*
1111 DAVIS DRIVE, NEWMARKET, ON, L3Y 9E5
(888) 977-3752   *SIC 6311*

ASSURANT LIFE OF CANADA MARKHAM *p666*
95 ROYAL CREST CRT UNIT 19, MARKHAM, ON, L3R 9X5
(905) 943-4447   *SIC 6311*

AUBERGE SUR LA ROUTE, L' *p1187*
426 RUE SAINT-GABRIEL, MONTREAL, QC, H2Y 2Z9
(514) 954-1041   *SIC 6311*

AXA ASSURANCES INC *p311*
1090 GEORGIA ST W SUITE 1350, VANCOUVER, BC, V6E 3V7
SIC 6311

AXA ASSURANCES INC *p432*
35 BLACKMARSH RD, ST. JOHN'S, NL, A1E 1S4
(709) 726-8974   *SIC 6311*

AXA ASSURANCES INC *p1193*
2020 BOUL ROBERT-BOURASSA BUREAU 100, MONTREAL, QC, H3A 2A5
(514) 282-1914   *SIC 6311*

AXA ASSURANCES INC *p1271*
2640 BOUL LAURIER BUREAU 900, QUEBEC, QC, G1V 5C2
SIC 6311

BERKSHIRE HATHAWAY SPECIALTY INSURANCE *p959*
200 BAY ST, TORONTO, ON, M5J 2J2
(647) 846-7803   *SIC 6311*

BFL CANADA INSURANCE SERVICES INC *p41*
1167 KENSINGTON CRES NW SUITE 200, CALGARY, AB, T2N 1X7
(403) 451-4132   *SIC 6311*

BLUE CROSS LIFE INSURANCE COMPANY OF CANADA *p406*
644 MAIN ST SUITE 500, MONCTON, NB, E1C 1E2
(506) 853-1811   *SIC 6311*

BMO LIFE INSURANCE COMPANY *p941*
60 YONGE ST 11TH FLOOR, TORONTO, ON, M5E 1H5
(416) 596-3900   *SIC 6311*

BRANT MUTUAL INSURANCE COMPANY *p514*
20 HOLIDAY DR, BRANTFORD, ON, N3R 7J4
(519) 752-0088   *SIC 6311*

BRITISH COLUMBIA LIFE AND CASUALTY COMPANY *p188*
4250 CANADA WAY, BURNABY, BC, V5G 4W6
(604) 419-8000   *SIC 6311*

CANADA LIFE ASSURANCE COMPANY, THE *p944*
330 UNIVERSITY AVE SUITE 2, TORONTO, ON, M5G 1R8
(416) 597-1440   *SIC 6311*

CANADA LIFE ASSURANCE COMPANY, THE *p1417*
1901 SCARTH ST SUITE 414, REGINA, SK, S4P 4L4
(306) 751-6000 *SIC* 6311

CANADA LOYAL FINANCIAL LIMITED *p796*
2866 PORTLAND DR, OAKVILLE, ON, L6H 5W8
(905) 829-5514 *SIC* 6311

CANADIAN LIFE AND HEALTH INSURANCE OMBUDSERVICE *p937*
20 TORONTO ST SUITE 710, TORONTO, ON, M5C 2B8
(416) 777-9002 *SIC* 6311

CANADIAN PREMIER LIFE INSURANCE COMPANY *p771*
25 SHEPPARD AVE W, NORTH YORK, ON, M2N 6S6
(416) 883-6300 *SIC* 6311

CANADIAN TEST CASE 49 LTD *p720*
6750 CENTURY AVE SUITE 305, MISSISSAUGA, ON, L5N 2V8
(905) 812-5920 *SIC* 6311

CAPITALE ASSUREUR DE L'ADMINISTRATION PUBLIQUE INC, LA *p1268*
625 RUE JACQUES-PARIZEAU, QUEBEC, QC, G1R 2G5
(418) 644-4106 *SIC* 6311

CAPITALE MUTUELLE DE L'ADMINISTRATION PUBLIQUE, LA *p1268*
625 RUE JACQUES-PARIZEAU, QUEBEC, QC, G1R 2G5
(418) 644-4229 *SIC* 6311

CARNAGHAN THORNE INSURANCE GROUP INC. *p415*
10 CROWN ST, SAINT JOHN, NB, E2L 2X5
(506) 634-1177 *SIC* 6311

CENTRE FINANCIER S.F.L. DU LITTORAL INC *p1286*
290 BOUL DE L'HOTEL-DE-VILLE BUREAU 200, RIVIERE-DU-LOUP, QC, G5R 5C6
(418) 862-4980 *SIC* 6311

CHEVRIER LAPORTE & ASSOCIES INC *p1290*
319 RUE NOTRE-DAME, ROXTON FALLS, QC, J0H 1E0
SIC 6311

CLARICA LIFE INSURANCE COMPANY *p1019*
3200 DEZIEL DR SUITE 508, WINDSOR, ON, N8W 5K8
(519) 974-3200 *SIC* 6311

CLARKE, DOUGLAS K INSURANCE BROKERS LIMITED *p668*
151 ESNA PARK DR SUITE 26, MARKHAM, ON, L3R 3B1
SIC 6311

CO-OPERATORS GENERAL INSURANCE COMPANY *p406*
10 RECORD ST, MONCTON, NB, E1C 0B2
(506) 853-1215 *SIC* 6311

COASTAL COMMUNITY INSURANCE SERVICES 2007 LTD *p233*
59 WHARF ST SUITE 220, NANAIMO, BC, V9R 2X3
(888) 741-1010 *SIC* 6311

COMPAGNIE D'ASSURANCES GENERALES TD *p1180*
50 BOUL CREMAZIE O BUREAU 1200, MONTREAL, QC, H2P 1B6
(514) 382-6060 *SIC* 6311

CONWAY JACQUES COURTIERS *p1203*
1250 BOUL RENE-LEVESQUE O, MONTREAL, QC, H3B 4W8
(514) 935-4242 *SIC* 6311

CRAIG MCDONALD REDDON INSURANCE BROKERS LTD *p617*
467 10TH ST SUITE 200, HANOVER, ON, N4N 1R3
(519) 364-3540 *SIC* 6311

CUMIS GROUP LIMITED, THE *p530*
151 NORTH SERVICE RD, BURLINGTON, ON, L7R 4C2

(800) 263-9120 *SIC* 6311
CUMIS LIFE INSURANCE COMPANY *p530*
151 NORTH SERVICE RD, BURLINGTON, ON, L7R 4C2
(905) 632-1221 *SIC* 6311

DAIGNEAULT FERLAND ASSURANCES INC *p1060*
181 RUE HENRY-BESSEMER BUREAU 103, BOIS-DES-FILION, QC, J6Z 4S9
(450) 621-3666 *SIC* 6311

DESJARDINS SECURITE FINANCIERE, COMPAGNIE D'ASSURANCE VIE *p926*
95 ST CLAIR AVE W SUITE 100, TORONTO, ON, M4V 1N7
(416) 926-2700 *SIC* 6311

DESJARDINS SECURITE FINANCIERE, COMPAGNIE D'ASSURANCE VIE *p1136*
200 RUE DES COMMANDEURS, LEVIS, QC, G6V 6R2
(418) 838-7800 *SIC* 6311

DESJARDINS SECURITE FINANCIERE, COMPAGNIE D'ASSURANCE VIE *p1230*
1 COMPLEXE DESJARDINS, MONTREAL, QC, H5B 1E2
(514) 285-3000 *SIC* 6311

DESJARDINS SECURITE FINANCIERE, COMPAGNIE D'ASSURANCE VIE *p1230*
2 COMPLEXE DESJARDINS TOUR E, MONTREAL, QC, H5B 1E2
(514) 350-8700 *SIC* 6311

DOT BENEFITS CORP *p781*
555 WILSON AVE, NORTH YORK, ON, M3H 0C5
(416) 636-4411 *SIC* 6311

EMPIRE LIFE INSURANCE COMPANY, THE *p630*
259 KING ST E, KINGSTON, ON, K7L 3A8
(613) 548-1881 *SIC* 6311

EQUITABLE LIFE INSURANCE COMPANY OF CANADA, THE *p1006*
1 WESTMOUNT RD N, WATERLOO, ON, N2J 4C7
(519) 886-5210 *SIC* 6311

EVALUATIONS BIGRAS INC, LES *p1061*
1919 BOUL LIONEL-BERTRAND BUREAU 103, BOISBRIAND, QC, J7H 1N8
(450) 420-6555 *SIC* 6311

EXCELLENCE LIFE INSURANCE COMPANY, THE *p1176*
1611 BOUL CREMAZIE E BUREAU 900, MONTREAL, QC, H2M 2P2
(514) 327-0020 *SIC* 6311

FAITHLIFE FINANCIAL *p1008*
470 WEBER ST N, WATERLOO, ON, N2L 6J2
(519) 886-4610 *SIC* 6311

FAMILY WEALTH ADVISORS LTD *p839*
22 FOSTER ST, PERTH, ON, K7H 1R6
(613) 264-8267 *SIC* 6311

FAVREAU, GENDRON ASSURANCE ET SERVICES FINANCIERS INC *p1055*
505 RUE DES E?RABLES, BEAUHARNOIS, QC, J6N 1T3
(450) 429-3755 *SIC* 6311

FERNANDES GROUP, THE *p705*
260 BRUNEL RD, MISSISSAUGA, ON, L4Z 1T5
SIC 6311

FINANCIAL HORIZONS INCORPORATED *p639*
22 FREDERICK ST SUITE 112, KITCHENER, ON, N2H 6M6
(519) 742-4474 *SIC* 6311

FORESTERS LIFE INSURANCE COMPANY *p731*
100 MILVERTON DR SUITE 400, MISSISSAUGA, ON, L5R 4H1
(905) 219-8000 *SIC* 6311

FRIENDS OF CHARLESTON LAKE PARK, THE *p643*
148 WOODVALE RD, LANSDOWNE, ON, K0E 1L0
(613) 659-2065 *SIC* 6311

GESTION LEGALIS INC *p1272*

1195 AV LAVIGERIE BUREAU 200, QUEBEC, QC, G1V 4N3
(418) 658-9966 *SIC* 6311

GREAT WEST LIFE ASSURANCE *p530*
360 TORRANCE ST, BURLINGTON, ON, L7R 2R9
(905) 637-6561 *SIC* 6311

GREAT-WEST LIFE ASSURANCE COMPANY, THE *p378*
60 OSBORNE ST N, WINNIPEG, MB, R3C 1V3
(204) 946-8100 *SIC* 6311

GREAT-WEST LIFE ASSURANCE COMPANY, THE *p945*
330 UNIVERSITY AVE SUITE 400, TORONTO, ON, M5G 1R7
(416) 552-5050 *SIC* 6311

GREAT-WEST LIFE ASSURANCE COMPANY, THE *p977*
190 SIMCOE ST, TORONTO, ON, M5T 3M3
(416) 597-1440 *SIC* 6311

GREAT-WEST LIFECO INC *p378*
100 OSBORNE ST N, WINNIPEG, MB, R3C 1V3
(204) 946-1190 *SIC* 6311

GROUPE PROMUTUEL FEDERATION DE SOCIETE MUTUELLES D'ASSURANCES GENERALES *p1279*
2000 BOUL LEBOURGNEUF BUREAU 400, QUEBEC, QC, G2K 0B6
(418) 840-1313 *SIC* 6311

H & A FINANCIAL ADVISORS *p1418*
2445 13TH AVE SUITE 200, REGINA, SK, S4P 0W1
(306) 584-2523 *SIC* 6311

HALLE COUTURE & ASSOCIES LTEE *p1122*
475 RUE SAINT-ETIENNE, LA MALBAIE, QC, G5A 1H5
(418) 665-3978 *SIC* 6311

HAMILTON AND PARTNERS *p51*
734 7 AVE SW SUITE 1100, CALGARY, AB, T2P 3P8
(403) 262-2080 *SIC* 6311

HIROC INSURANCE SERVICES LIMITED *p772*
4711 YONGE ST SUITE 1600, NORTH YORK, ON, M2N 6K8
(416) 733-2773 *SIC* 6311

HOLLIS INSURANCE INC *p1278*
6700 BOUL PIERRE-BERTRAND BUREAU 300, QUEBEC, QC, G2J 0B4
(418) 623-4330 *SIC* 6311

HUMANIA ASSURANCE INC *p1312*
1555 RUE GIROUARD O BUREAU 201, SAINT-HYACINTHE, QC, J2S 2Z6
(514) 866-6051 *SIC* 6311

IMMIGRANT WOMEN'S ASSOCIATION OF MANITOBA INC *p374*
515 PORTAGE AVE, WINNIPEG, MB, R3B 2E9
SIC 6311

INDEPENDENT ORDER OF FORESTERS, THE *p779*
789 DON MILLS RD SUITE 1200, NORTH YORK, ON, M3C 1T9
(416) 429-3000 *SIC* 6311

INDUSTRIELLE ALLIANCE, ASSURANCE ET SERVICES FINANCIERS INC *p1270*
1080 GRANDE ALLEE O, QUEBEC, QC, G1S 1C7
(418) 684-5000 *SIC* 6311

IVARI CANADA ULC *p772*
5000 YONGE ST UNIT 500, NORTH YORK, ON, M2N 7J8
(416) 883-5000 *SIC* 6311

KNIGHTS OF COLUMBUS INSURANCE *p617*
26 DAVIS CRT, HAMPTON, ON, L0B 1J0
(905) 263-4212 *SIC* 6311

L'HEBDO DU ST-MAURICE *p1368*
1672 AV SAINT-MARC BUREAU A, SHAWINIGAN, QC, G9N 2H4
(819) 537-4161 *SIC* 6311

LA CAPITALE SERVICES CONSEILS INC *p1269*
625 RUE JACQUES-PARIZEAU, QUEBEC, QC, G1R 2G5
(418) 747-7600 *SIC* 6311

LIFEBRIDGE HEALTH MANAGEMENT INC *p710*
90 BURNHAMTHORPE RD W SUITE 206, MISSISSAUGA, ON, L5B 3C3
SIC 6311

LINDSAY LLP *p299*
564 BEATTY ST SUITE 1000, VANCOUVER, BC, V6B 2L3
(778) 945-5188 *SIC* 6311

LONDON INSURANCE GROUP INC *p654*
255 DUFFERIN AVE SUITE 540, LONDON, ON, N6A 4K1
(519) 432-5281 *SIC* 6311

LONDON LIFE, COMPAGNIE D'ASSURANCE-VIE *p314*
1111 GEORGIA ST W SUITE 1200, VANCOUVER, BC, V6E 4M3
(604) 685-6521 *SIC* 6311

LONDON LIFE, COMPAGNIE D'ASSURANCE-VIE *p596*
1223 MICHAEL ST N SUITE 300, GLOUCESTER, ON, K1J 7T2
(613) 748-3455 *SIC* 6311

LONDON LIFE, COMPAGNIE D'ASSURANCE-VIE *p654*
255 DUFFERIN AVE SUITE 273, LONDON, ON, N6A 4K1
(519) 432-5281 *SIC* 6311

LONDON LIFE, COMPAGNIE D'ASSURANCE-VIE *p710*
1 CITY CENTRE DR SUITE 1600, MISSISSAUGA, ON, L5B 1M2
(905) 276-1177 *SIC* 6311

LONDON LIFE, COMPAGNIE D'ASSURANCE-VIE *p789*
970 LAWRENCE AVE W SUITE 600, NORTH YORK, ON, M6A 3B6
SIC 6311

LONDON LIFE, COMPAGNIE D'ASSURANCE-VIE *p1197*
1800 AV MCGILL COLLEGE UNITE 1100, MONTREAL, QC, H3A 3J6
(514) 931-4242 *SIC* 6311

LONDON LIFE, COMPAGNIE D'ASSURANCE-VIE *p1330*
3773 BOUL DE LA COTE-VERTU BUREAU 200, SAINT-LAURENT, QC, H4R 2M3
SIC 6311

MANUFACTURERS LIFE INSURANCE COMPANY, THE *p929*
200 BLOOR ST E SUITE 1, TORONTO, ON, M4W 1E5
(416) 926-3000 *SIC* 6311

MANUFACTURERS LIFE INSURANCE COMPANY, THE *p1008*
500 KING ST N, WATERLOO, ON, N2L 5W6
(519) 747-7000 *SIC* 6311

MANUFACTURERS LIFE INSURANCE COMPANY, THE *p1198*
2000 RUE MANSFIELD UNITE 300, MONTREAL, QC, H3A 2Z4
(514) 288-6268 *SIC* 6311

MANULIFE CANADA LTD *p640*
500 KING ST N, KITCHENER, ON, N2J 4Z6
(519) 747-7000 *SIC* 6311

MAY-MCCONVILLE-OMNI INSURANCE BROKERS LIMITED *p654*
685 RICHMOND ST SUITE 300, LONDON, ON, N6A 5M1
(519) 673-0880 *SIC* 6311

METROPOLITAN LIFE INSURANCE COMPANY *p825*
360 ALBERT ST SUITE 1750, OTTAWA, ON, K1R 7X7
SIC 6311

MUNICH LIFE MANAGEMENT CORPORATION LTD *p954*
390 BAY ST SUITE 2600, TORONTO, ON, M5H 2Y2

(416) 359-2200   *SIC* 6311

OPTIMUM REASSURANCE   *p1073*
8 PLACE AVILA, CANDIAC, QC, J5R 5R5
(450) 984-1462   *SIC* 6311

OSI-WORLDWIDE INC   *p932*
10 ST MARY ST SUITE 602, TORONTO, ON, M4Y 1P9
(416) 960-9752   *SIC* 6311

PPI QUEBEC ADVISORY INC   *p1396*
3000 BOUL RENE-LEVESQUE BUREAU 340, VERDUN, QC, H3E 1T9
(514) 765-7400   *SIC* 6311

PPI SOLUTIONS INC   *p31*
340 50 AVE SE SUITE 1340, CALGARY, AB, T2G 2B1
(403) 243-6163   *SIC* 6311

PRAIRIE FINANCIAL GROUP LTD   *p735*
2355 DERRY RD E UNIT 29, MISSISSAUGA, ON, L5S 1V6
(905) 612-0800   *SIC* 6311

PRIMERICA LIFE INSURANCE COMPANY OF CANADA   *p726*
2000 ARGENTIA RD SUITE 5, MISSISSAUGA, ON, L5N 1P7
(905) 812-3520   *SIC* 6311

RBC INSURANCE SERVICES INC   *p726*
6880 FINANCIAL DR WEST TOWER, MISSISSAUGA, ON, L5N 7Y5
(905) 949-3663   *SIC* 6311

RBC LIFE INSURANCE COMPANY   *p726*
6880 FINANCIAL DR SUITE 1000, MISSISSAUGA, ON, L5N 8E8
(905) 816-2746   *SIC* 6311

REINSURANCE MANAGEMENT ASSOCIATES INC   *p956*
170 UNIVERSITY AVE SUITE 500, TORONTO, ON, M5H 3B3
(416) 408-2602   *SIC* 6311

RELIABLE LIFE INSURANCE COMPANY   *p613*
100 KING ST W, HAMILTON, ON, L8P 1A2
(905) 525-5031   *SIC* 6311

RGA LIFE REINSURANCE COMPANY OF CANADA   *p970*
77 KING ST W SUITE 2300, TORONTO, ON, M5K 2A1
(416) 682-0000   *SIC* 6311

RGA LIFE REINSURANCE COMPANY OF CANADA   *p1199*
1981 AV MCGILL COLLEGE UNITE 1300, MONTREAL, QC, H3A 3A8
(514) 985-5260   *SIC* 6311

RGA LIFE REINSURANCE COMPANY OF CANADA   *p1208*
1255 RUE PEEL BUREAU 1000, MONTREAL, QC, H3B 2T9
(514) 985-5502   *SIC* 6311

S & V PLANNING CORPORATION   *p335*
968 MEARES ST, VICTORIA, BC, V8V 3J4
(250) 388-6774   *SIC* 6311

SCDA (2015) INC   *p1214*
1245 RUE SHERBROOKE O BUREAU 2100, MONTREAL, QC, H3G 1G3
(514) 499-8855   *SIC* 6311

SCHMUNK GATT SMITH & ASSOCIATES   *p228*
20334 56 AVE SUITE 204, LANGLEY, BC, V3A 3Y7
(604) 533-9813   *SIC* 6311

SHENGLIN FINANCIAL INC   *p773*
170 SHEPPARD AVE E SUITE 500, NORTH YORK, ON, M2N 3A4
(416) 789-3691   *SIC* 6311

SOCIETE SAINT-JEAN-BAPTISTE DE LA MAURICIE OBNL   *p1386*
3239 RUE PAPINEAU, TROIS-RIVIERES, QC, G8Z 1P4
(819) 375-4881   *SIC* 6311

SSQ SOCIETE D'ASSURANCE-VIE INC   *p1273*
2525 BOUL LAURIER, QUEBEC, QC, G1V 4Z6
(418) 651-7000   *SIC* 6311

SSQ, SOCIETE D'ASSURANCE INC   *p1273*

2525 BOUL LAURIER, QUEBEC, QC, G1V 2L2
(418) 651-7000   *SIC* 6311

STROUD AGENCIES LTD   *p107*
9945 50 ST NW UNIT 304, EDMONTON, AB, T6A 0L4
(780) 426-2400   *SIC* 6311

SUN LIFE ASSURANCE COMPANY OF CANADA   *p967*
1 YORK ST, TORONTO, ON, M5J 0B6
(416) 979-9966   *SIC* 6311

SUN LIFE ASSURANCE COMPANY OF CANADA   *p1208*
1155 RUE METCALFE BUREAU 20, MONTREAL, QC, H3B 2V9
(514) 866-6411   *SIC* 6311

SUN LIFE ASSURANCE COMPANY OF CANADA   *p1208*
1001 RUE DU SQUARE-DORCHESTER BUREAU 600, MONTREAL, QC, H3B 1N1
(514) 731-7961   *SIC* 6311

SUN LIFE DU CANADA, COMPAGNIE D'ASSURANCE-VIE   *p1208*
1155 RUE METCALFE BUREAU 1410, MONTREAL, QC, H3B 2V9
(514) 393-8820   *SIC* 6311

TANSEY INSURANCE SERVICE LTD   *p227*
4769 222 ST UNIT 103, LANGLEY, BC, V2Z 3C1
(604) 539-7783   *SIC* 6311

TD LIFE INSURANCE COMPANY   *p970*
55 KING ST W, TORONTO, ON, M5K 1A2
SIC 6311

TEACHERS LIFE INSURANCE SOCIETY (FRATERNAL)   *p578*
916 THE EAST MALL SUITE C, ETOBICOKE, ON, M9B 6K1
(416) 620-1140   *SIC* 6311

TRANS GLOBAL LIFE INSURANCE COMPANY   *p97*
16930 114 AVE NW SUITE 275, EDMONTON, AB, T5M 3S2
(780) 930-6000   *SIC* 6311

UKRAINIAN FRATERNAL SOCIETY OF CANADA   *p371*
235 MCGREGOR ST, WINNIPEG, MB, R2W 4W5
(204) 586-4482   *SIC* 6311

UNION-VIE, COMPAGNIE MUTUELLE D'ASSURANCE, L'   *p1100*
142 RUE HERIOT, DRUMMONDVILLE, QC, J2C 1J8
(819) 478-1315   *SIC* 6311

UNISON INSURANCE & FINANCIAL SERVICES INC.   *p703*
2077 DUNDAS ST E SUITE 103, MISSISSAUGA, ON, L4X 1M2
(905) 624-5300   *SIC* 6311

VITAL BENEFITS INCORPORATED   *p66*
224 11 AVE SW SUITE 301, CALGARY, AB, T2R 0C3
(403) 209-3817   *SIC* 6311

WAWANESA LIFE INSURANCE COMPANY, THE   *p66*
708 11 AVE SW SUITE 600, CALGARY, AB, T2R 0E4
(403) 536-9258   *SIC* 6311

WAWANESA LIFE INSURANCE COMPANY, THE   *p380*
200 MAIN ST SUITE 400, WINNIPEG, MB, R3C 1A8
(204) 985-3940   *SIC* 6311

WAWANESA LIFE INSURANCE COMPANY, THE   *p774*
4110 YONGE ST SUITE 100, NORTH YORK, ON, M2P 2B7
(519) 886-4320   *SIC* 6311

WESTERN FINANCIAL GROUP INC   *p136*
1010 24 ST SE, HIGH RIVER, AB, T1V 2A7
(403) 652-2663   *SIC* 6311

WESTERN LIFE ASSURANCE COMPANY   *p382*
717 PORTAGE AVE 4TH FLOOR, WINNIPEG, MB, R3G 0M8

(204) 786-6431   *SIC* 6311

WORLD FINANCIAL GROUP INSURANCE AGENCY OF CANADA INC   *p773*
5000 YONGE ST SUITE 800, NORTH YORK, ON, M2N 7E9
SIC 6311

SIC 6321 Accident and health insurance

ABC BENEFITS CORPORATION   *p86*
10009 108 ST NW, EDMONTON, AB, T5J 3C5
(780) 498-8000   *SIC* 6321

ACADIA STUDENTS' UNION INC   *p471*
30 HIGHLAND AVE, WOLFVILLE, NS, B4P 1Y7
(902) 585-2110   *SIC* 6321

ACCIDENT BENEFIT SOLUTION   *p719*
6300 PRAIRIE CIR, MISSISSAUGA, ON, L5N 5Y9
(905) 824-4476   *SIC* 6321

ACCIDENT INJURY MEDICAL ASSESSMENT   *p782*
1280 FINCH AVE W SUITE 507, NORTH YORK, ON, M3J 3K6
(416) 665-4010   *SIC* 6321

ASSOCIATION D'HOSPITALISATION CANASSURANCE   *p1193*
550 RUE SHERBROOKE O, MONTREAL, QC, H3A 1B9
(514) 286-7658   *SIC* 6321

BALL HARRISON HANSELL EMPLOYEE BENEFITS INSURANCE AGENCY LTD *p891*
1040 SOUTH SERVICE RD, STONEY CREEK, ON, L8E 6G3
(905) 643-1017   *SIC* 6321

CANADIAN BENEFITS CONSULTING GROUP INC   *p922*
2300 YONGE ST SUITE 3000, TORONTO, ON, M4P 1E4
(416) 483-5896   *SIC* 6321

CANADIAN UNIVERSITIES RECIPROCAL INSURANCE EXCHANGE   *p521*
5500 NORTH SERVICE RD SUITE 901, BURLINGTON, ON, L7L 6W6
(905) 336-3366   *SIC* 6321

CANASSURANCE COMPAGNIE D'ASSURANCE INC   *p1194*
550 RUE SHERBROOKE O BUREAU B9, MONTREAL, QC, H3A 3S3
(514) 286-8400   *SIC* 6321

CAPITALE ASSURANCES GENERALES INC, LA   *p1268*
625 RUE JACQUES-PARIZEAU, QUEBEC, QC, G1R 2G5
(418) 781-1618   *SIC* 6321

CIGNA LIFE INSURANCE COMPANY OF CANADA   *p866*
100 CONSILIUM PL SUITE 301, SCARBOROUGH, ON, M1H 3E3
(416) 290-6666   *SIC* 6321

COLIN PLOTKIN & SONS CONSULTING INC   *p258*
12011 RIVERSIDE WAY SUITE 210, RICHMOND, BC, V6W 1K6
(604) 241-9639   *SIC* 6321

D. KRAHN INSURANCE & FINANCIAL SERVICES INC   *p1427*
75 LENORE DR SUITE 1, SASKATOON, SK, S7K 7Y1
(306) 384-7216   *SIC* 6321

DESTINATION TRAVEL HEALTH PLAN*p767*
211 CONSUMERS RD SUITE 200, NORTH YORK, ON, M2J 4G8
(416) 499-6616   *SIC* 6321

F D D C H DE JONQUIERE   *p1287*
989 RUE COLLARD, ROBERVAL, QC, G8H 1X9
(418) 765-3444   *SIC* 6321

FIRST GENERAL SERVICES (EDMONTON) INC   *p109*
7311 77 AVE NW, EDMONTON, AB, T6B 0B7

(780) 463-4040   *SIC* 6321

FOCUS ASSESSMENTS INC   *p634*
1601 RIVER RD E UNIT 10, KITCHENER, ON, N2A 3Y4
(519) 893-5972   *SIC* 6321

GEAR PELLING INSURANCE LTD   *p260*
7340 WESTMINSTER HWY SUITE 110, RICHMOND, BC, V6X 1A1
(604) 276-2474   *SIC* 6321

GREAT-WEST LIFE ASSURANCE COMPANY, THE   *p89*
10110 104 ST NW SUITE 202, EDMONTON, AB, T5J 4R5
(780) 917-7800   *SIC* 6321

GREAT-WEST LIFE ASSURANCE COMPANY, THE   *p313*
1075 GEORGIA ST W SUITE 900, VANCOUVER, BC, V6E 4N4
(604) 646-1200   *SIC* 6321

HEALTHSOURCE PLUS INC   *p767*
2225 SHEPPARD AVE E SUITE 1400, NORTH YORK, ON, M2J 5C2
SIC 6321

LA CAPITALE FINANCIAL SECURITY INSURANCE COMPANY   *p745*
7150 DERRYCREST DR SUITE 1150, MISSISSAUGA, ON, L5W 0E5
(905) 795-2300   *SIC* 6321

MEDAVIE INC   *p407*
644 MAIN ST, MONCTON, NB, E1C 1E2
(506) 853-1811   *SIC* 6321

MEDAVIE INC   *p407*
644 MAIN ST, MONCTON, NB, E1C 1E2
(506) 853-1811   *SIC* 6321

MEDAVIE INC   *p1198*
550 RUE SHERBROOKE O BUREAU 1200, MONTREAL, QC, H3A 1B9
(514) 286-7778   *SIC* 6321

MEDICAL SERVICES INCORPORATED *p1428*
516 2ND AVE N, SASKATOON, SK, S7K 2C5
(306) 244-1192   *SIC* 6321

MEDIPAC INTERNATIONAL INC   *p776*
180 LESMILL RD, NORTH YORK, ON, M3B 2T5
(416) 441-7070   *SIC* 6321

NORFOLK MOBILITY BENEFITS INC   *p65*
999 8 ST SW SUITE 300, CALGARY, AB, T2R 1N7
(403) 232-8545   *SIC* 6321

NORTH AMERICAN AIR TRAVEL INSURANCE AGENTS LTD   *p262*
6081 NO. 3 RD 11 FL SUITE 1101, RICHMOND, BC, V6Y 2B2
(604) 276-9900   *SIC* 6321

NORTH YORK REHABILITATION CENTRE CORP   *p915*
2255 SHEPPARD AVE E SUITE 300, TORONTO, ON, M2J 4Y1
(416) 497-4477   *SIC* 6321

ODYSSEY HEALTH SERVICES   *p523*
1100 BURLOAK DR SUITE 603, BURLINGTON, ON, L7L 6B2
(905) 319-0202   *SIC* 6321

ORION TRAVEL INSURANCE COMPANY COMPAGNIE D'ASSURANCE VOYAGE ORION   *p905*
60 COMMERCE VALLEY DR E, THORNHILL, ON, L3T 7P9
(905) 771-3000   *SIC* 6321

PACIFIC FIRST   *p186*
3993 HENNING DR UNIT 215, BURNABY, BC, V5C 6P7
(604) 293-1974   *SIC* 6321

PBC HEALTH BENEFITS SOCIETY   *p189*
4250 CANADA WAY, BURNABY, BC, V5G 4W6
(604) 419-2200   *SIC* 6321

PROFORMANCE ADJUSTING SOLUTIONS *p843*
1101 KINGSTON RD SUITE 280, PICKERING, ON, L1V 1B5
SIC 6321

QOC HEALTH INC p983
436 WELLINGTON ST W UNIT 601, TORONTO, ON, M5V 1E3
(647) 725-9660　SIC 6321

RCU INSURANCE SERVICES LTD p253
110 2ND ST W, REVELSTOKE, BC, V0E 2S0
(250) 837-6291　SIC 6321

SCOTIALIFE FINANCIAL SERVICES INC p940
100 YONGE ST SUITE 400, TORONTO, ON, M5C 2W1
(416) 866-7075　SIC 6321

SECURIGLOBE INC p1199
1450 RUE CITY COUNCILLORS BUREAU 1000, MONTREAL, QC, H3A 2E6
(450) 462-2444　SIC 6321

SELECTCARE WORLDWIDE CORP p947
438 UNIVERSITY AVE SUITE 1201, TORONTO, ON, M5G 2K8
(416) 340-7265　SIC 6321

SOCIETE SAINT-JEAN BAPTISTE DU CENTRE-DU-QUEBEC INC, LA p1097
449 RUE NOTRE-DAME, DRUMMONDVILLE, QC, J2B 2K9
(819) 478-2519　SIC 6321

SWISS RE LIFE & HEALTH CANADA p957
150 KING ST W SUITE 1000, TORONTO, ON, M5H 1J9
(416) 947-3800　SIC 6321

TOTAL HEALTH AND FAMILY CENTRE p704
1090 DUNDAS ST E SUITE 1105, MISSISSAUGA, ON, L4Y 2B8
(905) 275-4993　SIC 6321

TRAVEL HEALTHCARE INSURANCE SOLUTIONS INC p905
300 JOHN ST SUITE 405, THORNHILL, ON, L3T 5W4
(905) 731-8140　SIC 6321

TRAVEL INSURANCE OFFICE INC p665
190 BULLOCK DR SUITE 2, MARKHAM, ON, L3P 7N3
(905) 201-1571　SIC 6321

VISIONS OF INDEPENDENCE INC p380
190 SHERBROOK ST, WINNIPEG, MB, R3C 2B6
(204) 453-5982　SIC 6321

WORK ABLE CENTRES INC p769
4 LANSING SQ SUITE 102, NORTH YORK, ON, M2J 5A2
(416) 496-6166　SIC 6321

SIC 6324 Hospital and medical service plans

A 1 MEDICAL CENTRE INC p751
3161 STRANDHERD DR UNIT 305, NEPEAN, ON, K2J 5N1
(613) 823-7766　SIC 6324

ALBERTA HEALTH SERVICES p78
1100 HOSPITAL PL, CANMORE, AB, T1W 1N2
(403) 678-3769　SIC 6324

ALLIANCE POUR LA SANTE ETUDIANTE AU QUEBEC INC p1201
1200 AV MCGILL COLLEGE BUREAU 2200, MONTREAL, QC, H3B 4G7
(514) 844-4423　SIC 6324

ALTERNATIVE BENEFIT SOLUTIONS INC p486
556 BRYNE DR UNIT 19 & 20, BARRIE, ON, L4N 9P6
(705) 726-6100　SIC 6324

AMG LONDON INC p653
230 VICTORIA ST, LONDON, ON, N6A 2C2
(519) 667-0660　SIC 6324

CANADIAN TEST CASE 29-B p720
6750 CENTURY AVE SUITE 305, MISSISSAUGA, ON, L5N 2V8
(905) 812-5922　SIC 6324

CHAMPLAIN LHIN p596
1900 CITY PARK DR SUITE 204, GLOUCESTER, ON, K1J 1A3

(613) 747-6784　SIC 6324

CLAIMSECURE INC p709
1 CITY CENTRE DR SUITE 620, MISSISSAUGA, ON, L5B 1M2
(705) 673-2541　SIC 6324

CLAIMSECURE INC p899
40 ELM ST SUITE 225, SUDBURY, ON, P3C 0A2
(705) 673-2541　SIC 6324

CUT KNIFE HEALTH COMPLEX PRAIRIE NORTH HEALTH DISTRICT p1405
102 DION AVE, CUT KNIFE, SK, S0M 0N0
(306) 398-4977　SIC 6324

ESTON HEALTH CENTRE p1407
822 MAIN ST, ESTON, SK, S0L 1A0
(306) 962-3667　SIC 6324

GREAT-WEST LIFE ASSURANCE COMPANY, THE p378
100 OSBORNE ST N, WINNIPEG, MB, R3C 1V3
(204) 946-1190　SIC 6324

GREEN SHIELD CANADA p1017
8677 ANCHOR DR, WINDSOR, ON, N8N 5G1
(519) 739-1133　SIC 6324

GROUP MEDICAL SERVICES p1417
2055 ALBERT ST, REGINA, SK, S4P 2T8
(306) 352-7638　SIC 6324

INTER TRIBAL HEALTH AUTHORITY p233
534 CENTRE ST, NANAIMO, BC, V9R 4Z3
(250) 753-0590　SIC 6324

LAKERIDGE HEALTH p496
47 LIBERTY ST S, BOWMANVILLE, ON, L1C 2N4
(905) 623-3331　SIC 6324

LAKERIDGE HEALTH p812
1 HOSPITAL CRT, OSHAWA, ON, L1G 2B9
(905) 576-8711　SIC 6324

NORTHERN HEALTH AUTHORITY p194
741 CTR ST, BURNS LAKE, BC, V0J 1E0
(250) 692-2400　SIC 6324

ORDRE DES DENTISTES DU QUEBEC p1198
2020 BOUL ROBERT-BOURASSA BUREAU 2160, MONTREAL, QC, H3A 2A5
(514) 281-0300　SIC 6324

PACIFIC COMPANION ENTERPRISES INC p180
7083 SILVERDALE PL, BRENTWOOD BAY, BC, V8M 1G9
SIC 6324

PLATINUM HEALTH BENEFITS SOLUTIONS INC p699
5090 EXPLORER DR SUITE 501, MISSISSAUGA, ON, L4W 4T9
(905) 602-0404　SIC 6324

RED SUCKER LAKE HEALTH AUTHORITY INC p355
GD, RED SUCKER LAKE, MB, R0B 1H0
(204) 469-5229　SIC 6324

SASKATCHEWAN HEALTH-CARE ASSOCIATION p1419
2002 VICTORIA AVE SUITE 500, REGINA, SK, S4P 0R7
(306) 347-1740　SIC 6324

SCARBOROUGH AND ROUGE HOSPITAL p474
580 HARWOOD AVE S SUITE 199, AJAX, ON, L1S 2J4
(905) 683-2320　SIC 6324

SERVICES DE SOINS DE SANTE OPTISOINS p1115
2655 BOUL DU ROYAUME BUREAU 550, JONQUIERE, QC, G7S 4S9
(418) 548-0010　SIC 6324

SHAUNAVON HOSPITAL & CARE CENTRE p1435
GD, SHAUNAVON, SK, S0N 2M0
(306) 297-2644　SIC 6324

SOCIETE DE SERVICES DENTAIRES (A.C.D.Q.) INC p1199
425 BOUL DE MAISONNEUVE O BUREAU 1450, MONTREAL, QC, H3A 3G5
(514) 282-1425　SIC 6324

UNITED HEALTH SERVICES CORPORATION p382
599 EMPRESS ST, WINNIPEG, MB, R3G 3P3
(204) 775-0151　SIC 6324

SIC 6331 Fire, marine, and casualty insurance

563737 SASKATCHEWAN LTD p1423
3502 TAYLOR ST E SUITE 103, SASKATOON, SK, S7H 5H9
(306) 955-1330　SIC 6331

911 RESTORATION OF DURHAM REGION p812
500 RALEIGH AVE UNIT 11, OSHAWA, ON, L1H 3T2
(905) 436-9911　SIC 6331

ACE INA INSURANCE p959
25 YORK ST SUITE 1400, TORONTO, ON, M5J 2V5
(416) 368-2911　SIC 6331

AGRICORP p601
1 STONE RD W, GUELPH, ON, N1G 4Y2
(888) 247-4999　SIC 6331

AIG INSURANCE COMPANY OF CANADA p959
145 WELLINGTON ST W SUITE 1400, TORONTO, ON, M5J 1H8
(416) 596-3000　SIC 6331

ALGOMA MUTUAL INSURANCE COMPANY p903
131 MAIN ST, THESSALON, ON, P0R 1L0
(705) 842-3345　SIC 6331

ALLIED WORLD SPECIALTY INSURANCE COMPANY p948
200 KING ST W SUITE 1600, TORONTO, ON, M5H 3T4
(647) 558-1120　SIC 6331

ALLSTATE INSURANCE COMPANY OF CANADA p666
27 ALLSTATE PKY SUITE 100, MARKHAM, ON, L3R 5P8
(905) 477-6900　SIC 6331

APRIL MARINE CANADA INC p1071
4405 BOUL LAPINIERE, BROSSARD, QC, J4Z 3T5
(450) 671-6147　SIC 6331

ASSOCIATION DES CROISIERES DU SAINT-LAURENT p1284
84 RUE SAINT-GERMAIN E BUREAU 206, RIMOUSKI, QC, G5L 1A6
(418) 725-0135　SIC 6331

ASSURANCES FORTIN, GAGNON ET LEBRUN INC p1124
4138 RUE LAVAL, LAC-MEGANTIC, QC, G6B 1B3
(819) 583-1208　SIC 6331

ASSURANCES GENERALES BANQUE NATIONAL INC p1201
1100 BOUL ROBERT-BOURASSA UNITE 11, MONTREAL, QC, H3B 3A5
(514) 871-7507　SIC 6331

ASSURANCES GROUPE CONCORDE INC p1087
3820 BOUL LEVESQUE O BUREAU 101, COTE SAINT-LUC, QC, H7V 1E8
(450) 973-2822　SIC 6331

AVIVA CANADA INC p1201
630 BOUL RENE-LEVESQUE O BUREAU 900, MONTREAL, QC, H3B 1S6
(514) 876-5029　SIC 6331

AVIVA INSURANCE COMPANY OF CANADA p43
140 4 AVE SW SUITE 2400, CALGARY, AB, T2P 3W4
(403) 750-0600　SIC 6331

AVIVA INSURANCE COMPANY OF CANADA p87
10250 101 ST NW SUITE 1700, EDMONTON, AB, T5J 3P4
(780) 428-1822　SIC 6331

AVIVA INSURANCE COMPANY OF CANADA p326

1125 HOWE ST SUITE 1100, VANCOUVER, BC, V6Z 2Y6
(604) 669-2626　SIC 6331

AVIVA INSURANCE COMPANY OF CANADA p612
1 KING ST W SUITE 600, HAMILTON, ON, L8P 1A4
(289) 391-2600　SIC 6331

AVIVA INSURANCE COMPANY OF CANADA p653
255 QUEENS AVE SUITE 1500, LONDON, ON, N6A 5R8
(519) 672-2880　SIC 6331

AVIVA INSURANCE COMPANY OF CANADA p868
2206 EGLINTON AVE E SUITE 160, SCARBOROUGH, ON, M1L 4S8
(416) 288-1800　SIC 6331

AVIVA INSURANCE COMPANY OF CANADA p1201
630 BOUL RENE-LEVESQUE O BUREAU 700, MONTREAL, QC, H3B 1S6
(514) 399-1200　SIC 6331

AXA INSURANCE (CANADA) p770
5700 YONGE ST SUITE 1400, NORTH YORK, ON, M2M 4K2
(416) 218-4175　SIC 6331

AYR FARMERS' MUTUAL INSURANCE COMPANY p482
1400 NORTHUMBERLAND ST RR 1, AYR, ON, N0B 1E0
(519) 632-7413　SIC 6331

B & W INSURANCE AGENCIES p275
8434 120 ST SUITE 108, SURREY, BC, V3W 7S2
(604) 591-7891　SIC 6331

BASF AGRICULTURAL SPECIALTIES LTD p1435
3835 THATCHER AVE, SASKATOON, SK, S7R 1A3
(306) 373-3060　SIC 6331

BAY OF QUINTE MUTUAL INSURANCE CO p845
13379 LOYALIST PKY, PICTON, ON, K0K 2T0
(613) 476-2145　SIC 6331

BEACON UNDERWRITING LTD p329
700 GEORGIA ST W SUITE 1488, VANCOUVER, BC, V7Y 1K8
(604) 685-6533　SIC 6331

BERTIE AND CLINTON MUTUAL INSURANCE COMPANY p1012
1003 NIAGARA ST, WELLAND, ON, L3C 1M5
(905) 735-1234　SIC 6331

BILODEAU COUTURE ASSURANCES INC p1080
31 RUE RACINE O, CHICOUTIMI, QC, G7J 1E4
(418) 698-0999　SIC 6331

BOILER INSPECTION AND INSURANCE COMPANY OF CANADA, THE p949
390 BAY ST SUITE 2000, TORONTO, ON, M5H 2Y2
(416) 363-5491　SIC 6331

CAA INSURANCE COMPANY p903
60 COMMERCE VALLEY DR E, THORNHILL, ON, L3T 7P9
(905) 771-3000　SIC 6331

CERTAS DIRECT COMPAGNIE D'ASSURANCE p705
3 ROBERT SPECK PKY, MISSISSAUGA, ON, L4Z 2G5
(905) 306-3900　SIC 6331

CHUBB INSURANCE COMPANY OF CANADA p971
199 BAY ST SUITE 2500, TORONTO, ON, M5L 1E2
(416) 863-0550　SIC 6331

CHUBB INSURANCE COMPANY OF CANADA p1202
1250 BOUL RENE-LEVESQUE O BUREAU 2700, MONTREAL, QC, H3B 4W8
(514) 938-4000　SIC 6331

CO-OPERATORS GROUP LIMITED, THE
p602
130 MACDONELL ST, GUELPH, ON, N1H
2Z6
(519) 824-4400   SIC 6331
COACHMAN INSURANCE COMPANY p577
10 FOUR SEASONS PL SUITE 200, ETO-
BICOKE, ON, M9B 6H7
(416) 255-3417   SIC 6331
COAST UNDERWRITERS LTD   p297
650 GEORGIA ST W UNIT 2690, VANCOU-
VER, BC, V6B 4N7
(604) 683-5631   SIC 6331
**COMMISSION DES NORMES, DE L'EQUITE,
DE LA SANTE ET DE LA SECURITE DU
TRAVAIL, LA**   p1258
524 RUE BOURDAGES BUREAU 370,
QUEBEC, QC, G1K 7E2
(877) 639-0744   SIC 6331
**COMMONWELL MUTUAL INSURANCE
GROUP, THE**   p645
336 ANGELINE ST S, LINDSAY, ON, K9V
0J8
(705) 324-2146   SIC 6331
**COMPAGNIE D'ASSURANCE BELAIR INC,
LA**   p944
700 UNIVERSITY AVE SUITE 1100,
TORONTO, ON, M5G 0A2
(416) 250-6363   SIC 6331
**COMPAGNIE D'ASSURANCE BELAIR INC,
LA**   p1051
7101 RUE JEAN-TALON E BUREAU 300,
ANJOU, QC, H1M 3T6
(514) 270-1700   SIC 6331
**COMPAGNIE D'ASSURANCE BELAIR INC,
LA**   p1279
5400 BOUL DES GALERIES BUREAU 500,
QUEBEC, QC, G2K 2B4
(418) 877-1199   SIC 6331
COMPAGNIE D'ASSURANCE DU QUEBEC
p1194
1001 BOUL DE MAISONNEUVE O BU-
REAU 1400, MONTREAL, QC, H3A 3C8
(514) 844-1116   SIC 6331
**COMPAGNIE D'ASSURANCE MISSISQUOI,
LA**   p1203
5 PLACE VILLE-MARIE UNITE 1400, MON-
TREAL, QC, H3B 2G2
(514) 875-5790   SIC 6331
COMPAGNIE D'ASSURANCE SONNET
p1203
5 PLACE VILLE-MARIE BUREAU 1400,
MONTREAL, QC, H3B 0A8
(514) 875-5790   SIC 6331
CONTINENTAL CASUALTY COMPANY p969
66 WELLINGTON ST W SUITE 3700,
TORONTO, ON, M5K 1E9
(416) 542-7300   SIC 6331
COSECO INSURANCE INC.   p730
5600 CANCROSS CRT, MISSISSAUGA,
ON, L5R 3E9
(905) 507-6156   SIC 6331
CUMIS GENERAL INSURANCE COMPANY
p530
151 NORTH SERVICE RD, BURLINGTON,
ON, L7R 4C2
(905) 632-1221   SIC 6331
DALTON TIMMIS INSURANCE GROUP INC
p478
35 STONE CHURCH RD, ANCASTER, ON,
L9K 1S5
(905) 648-3922   SIC 6331
**DAS LEGAL PROTECTION INSURANCE
COMPANY LIMITED**   p950
390 BAY ST SUITE 1610, TORONTO, ON,
M5H 2Y2
(416) 342-5400   SIC 6331
DATA GATHERING SERVICE INC   p161
320 SIOUX RD SUITE 110, SHERWOOD
PARK, AB, T8A 3X6
(780) 467-9575   SIC 6331
**DESJARDINS ASSURANCES GENERALES
INC**   p1136
6300 BOUL DE LA RIVE-SUD, LEVIS, QC,

G6V 6P9
(418) 835-4850   SIC 6331
DOME INSURANCE CORP LTD   p377
240 GRAHAM AVE SUITE 800, WINNIPEG,
MB, R3C 0J7
(204) 947-2835   SIC 6331
**DOMINION OF CANADA GENERAL INSUR-
ANCE COMPANY, THE**   p950
165 UNIVERSITY AVE SUITE 101,
TORONTO, ON, M5H 3B9
(416) 362-7231   SIC 6331
**ECONOMICAL MUTUAL INSURANCE COM-
PANY**   p48
801 6 AVE SW SUITE 2700, CALGARY, AB,
T2P 3W2
(403) 265-8590   SIC 6331
**ECONOMICAL MUTUAL INSURANCE COM-
PANY**   p312
1055 GEORGIA ST W SUITE 1900, VAN-
COUVER, BC, V6E 0B6
(800) 951-6665   SIC 6331
**ECONOMICAL MUTUAL INSURANCE COM-
PANY**   p446
238A BROWNLOW AVE SUITE 310, DART-
MOUTH, NS, B3B 2B4
(902) 835-6214   SIC 6331
**ECONOMICAL MUTUAL INSURANCE COM-
PANY**   p612
120 KING ST W SUITE 750, HAMILTON,
ON, L8P 4V2
(519) 570-8200   SIC 6331
**ECONOMICAL MUTUAL INSURANCE COM-
PANY**   p640
590 RIVERBEND DR, KITCHENER, ON,
N2K 3S2
(519) 570-8335   SIC 6331
**ECONOMICAL MUTUAL INSURANCE COM-
PANY**   p653
148 FULLARTON ST SUITE 1200, LON-
DON, ON, N6A 5P3
(800) 265-4441   SIC 6331
**ECONOMICAL MUTUAL INSURANCE COM-
PANY**   p770
5700 YONGE ST SUITE 1600, NORTH
YORK, ON, M2M 4K2
(800) 268-8801   SIC 6331
**ECONOMICAL MUTUAL INSURANCE COM-
PANY**   p825
343 PRESTON ST SUITE 500, OTTAWA,
ON, K1S 1N4
(613) 567-7060   SIC 6331
**ECONOMICAL MUTUAL INSURANCE COM-
PANY**   p1008
111 WESTMOUNT RD S, WATERLOO, ON,
N2L 2L6
(519) 570-8200   SIC 6331
**ECONOMICAL MUTUAL INSURANCE COM-
PANY**   p1203
5 PLACE VILLE-MARIE UNITE 1400, MON-
TREAL, QC, H3B 2G2
(514) 875-5790   SIC 6331
ERB AND ERB INSURANCE BROKERS LTD
p635
818 VICTORIA ST N, KITCHENER, ON,
N2B 3C1
(519) 579-4270   SIC 6331
FACILITY ASSOCIATION   p944
777 BAY ST SUITE 2400, TORONTO, ON,
M5G 2C8
(416) 863-1750   SIC 6331
FARM MUTUAL REINSURANCE PLAN INC
p536
350 PINEBUSH RD, CAMBRIDGE, ON, N1T
1Z6
(519) 740-6415   SIC 6331
**FEDERATED INSURANCE COMPANY OF
CANADA**   p377
255 COMMERCE DRIVE, WINNIPEG, MB,
R3C 3C9
(204) 786-6431   SIC 6331
FUNDY MUTUAL INSURANCE LTD   p418
1022 MAIN ST, SUSSEX, NB, E4E 2M3
(506) 432-1535   SIC 6331
GLENSTONE CAPITAL CORPORATION

p951
181 UNIVERSITY AVE SUITE 1000,
TORONTO, ON, M5H 3M7
(416) 682-5300   SIC 6331
GOLDEN TRIANGLE RESTORATION INC
p533
2302 DUMFRIES RD, CAMBRIDGE, ON,
N1R 5S3
(519) 624-4487   SIC 6331
GORE MUTUAL INSURANCE COMPANY
p328
505 BURRARD ST UNIT 1780, VANCOU-
VER, BC, V7X 1M6
(604) 682-0998   SIC 6331
GORE MUTUAL INSURANCE COMPANY
p533
252 DUNDAS ST S, CAMBRIDGE, ON, N1R
8A8
(519) 623-1910   SIC 6331
**GOUVERNEMENT DE LA PROVINCE DE
QUEBEC**   p1106
15 RUE GAMELIN, GATINEAU, QC, J8Y
6N5
(819) 778-8600   SIC 6331
**GRENVILLE MUTUAL INSURANCE COM-
PANY**   p882
3005 COUNTY RD 21, SPENCERVILLE,
ON, K0E 1X0
(613) 258-9988   SIC 6331
**GROUPE ESTRIE-RICHELIEU, COMPAG-
NIE D'ASSURANCE, LE**   p1109
770 RUE PRINCIPALE, GRANBY, QC, J2G
2Y7
(450) 378-0101   SIC 6331
**H.B. GROUP INSURANCE MANAGEMENT
LTD**   p731
5600 CANCROSS CRT, MISSISSAUGA,
ON, L5R 3E9
(905) 507-6156   SIC 6331
HARLOCK MURRAY UNDERWRITING LTD
p237
960 QUAYSIDE DR UNIT 103, NEW WEST-
MINSTER, BC, V3M 6G2
(604) 669-7745   SIC 6331
HEARTLAND FARM MUTUAL INC   p1006
100 ERB ST E, WATERLOO, ON, N2J 1L9
(519) 886-4530   SIC 6331
HICKMAN MOUNT RECONSTRUCTION INC
p649
562 SOVEREIGN RD UNIT 5, LONDON,
ON, N5V 4K6
(519) 457-1970   SIC 6331
HOMETURF LTD   p735
7123 FIR TREE DR, MISSISSAUGA, ON,
L5S 1G4
(905) 791-8873   SIC 6331
**INDUSTRIELLE ALLIANCE, ASSURANCE
AUTO ET HABITATION INC**   p1270
925 GRANDE ALLEE O BUREAU 230,
QUEBEC, QC, G1S 1C1
(418) 650-4600   SIC 6331
**INSURANCE COMPANY OF PRINCE ED-
WARD ISLAND, THE**   p1039
14 GREAT GEORGE ST SUITE 3, CHAR-
LOTTETOWN, PE, C1A 4J6
(902) 368-3675   SIC 6331
**INSURANCE CORPORATION OF BRITISH
COLUMBIA**   p201
1575 HARTLEY AVE, COQUITLAM, BC,
V3K 6Z7
(604) 777-4627   SIC 6331
**INSURANCE CORPORATION OF BRITISH
COLUMBIA**   p228
6000 PRODUCTION WAY, LANGLEY, BC,
V3A 6L5
(604) 530-7111   SIC 6331
**INSURANCE CORPORATION OF BRITISH
COLUMBIA**   p240
151 ESPLANADE W, NORTH VANCOU-
VER, BC, V7M 3H9
(604) 661-2800   SIC 6331
**INSURANCE CORPORATION OF BRITISH
COLUMBIA**   p270
10262 152A ST, SURREY, BC, V3R 6T8

(604) 584-3211   SIC 6331
**INSURANCE CORPORATION OF BRITISH
COLUMBIA**   p276
13665 68 AVE, SURREY, BC, V3W 0Y6
(604) 597-7600   SIC 6331
**INSURANCE CORPORATION OF BRITISH
COLUMBIA**   p334
425 DUNEDIN ST, VICTORIA, BC, V8T 5H7
(250) 480-5600   SIC 6331
INTACT FINANCIAL CORPORATION p946
700 UNIVERSITY AVE SUITE 1500,
TORONTO, ON, M5G 0A1
(416) 341-1464   SIC 6331
INTACT INSURANCE COMPANY   p52
321 6 AVE SW SUITE 1200, CALGARY, AB,
T2P 3H3
(403) 269-7961   SIC 6331
INTACT INSURANCE COMPANY   p305
999 HASTINGS ST W SUITE 1100, VAN-
COUVER, BC, V6C 2W2
(604) 891-5400   SIC 6331
INTACT INSURANCE COMPANY   p446
20 HECTOR GATE SUITE 200, DART-
MOUTH, NS, B3B 0K3
(902) 420-1732   SIC 6331
INTACT INSURANCE COMPANY   p654
255 QUEENS AVE SUITE 900, LONDON,
ON, N6A 5R8
(519) 432-6721   SIC 6331
INTACT INSURANCE COMPANY   p723
6925 CENTURY AVE SUITE 900, MISSIS-
SAUGA, ON, L5N 0E3
(905) 858-1070   SIC 6331
INTACT INSURANCE COMPANY   p820
1400 ST. LAURENT BLVD SUITE 300, OT-
TAWA, ON, K1K 4H4
(800) 267-1836   SIC 6331
INTACT INSURANCE COMPANY   p946
700 UNIVERSITY AVE SUITE 1500,
TORONTO, ON, M5G 0A1
(416) 341-1464   SIC 6331
INTACT INSURANCE COMPANY   p1052
7101 RUE JEAN-TALON E BUREAU 1000,
ANJOU, QC, H1M 0A5
(514) 388-5466   SIC 6331
JIMSAR BUSINESS SERVICES INC p105
13141 156 ST NW, EDMONTON, AB, T5V
1V2
(780) 476-1600   SIC 6331
JOHNSON INC   p97
12220 STONY PLAIN RD NW SUITE 301,
EDMONTON, AB, T5N 3Y4
SIC 6331
**KENT & ESSEX MUTUAL INSURANCE
COMPANY**   p543
10 CREEK RD, CHATHAM, ON, N7M 5J3
SIC 6331
KINGSWAY FINANCIAL SERVICES INC
p927
45 ST CLAIR AVE W STE 400, TORONTO,
ON, M4V 1K9
(416) 848-1171   SIC 6331
MAX CANADA INSURANCE COMPANY
p640
50 QUEEN ST N UNIT 710, KITCHENER,
ON, N2H 6P4
(519) 634-5267   SIC 6331
MELOCHE MONNEX INC   p457
6940 MUMFORD RD SUITE 301, HALIFAX,
NS, B3L 0B7
(902) 420-1112   SIC 6331
**MENNONITE MUTUAL INSURANCE CO.
(ALBERTA) LTD**   p9
2946 32 ST NE SUITE 300, CALGARY, AB,
T1Y 6J7
(403) 275-6996   SIC 6331
**METRO GENERAL INSURANCE CORPO-
RATION LIMITED**   p430
20 CROSBIE PL, ST. JOHN'S, NL, A1B 3Y8
SIC 6331
**MUNICH REINSURANCE COMPANY OF
CANADA**   p954
390 BAY ST SUITE 2300, TORONTO, ON,
M5H 2Y2

(416) 366-9206   *SIC 6331*
MUTUAL FIRE INSURANCE COMPANY OF BRITISH COLUMBIA, THE   *p225*
9366 200A ST SUITE 201, LANGLEY, BC, V1M 4B3
(604) 881-1250   *SIC 6331*
NORDIC INSURANCE COMPANY OF CANADA, THE   *p946*
700 UNIVERSITY AVE SUITE 1500, TORONTO, ON, M5G 0A1
(416) 932-0044   *SIC 6331*
NORTH BLENHEIM MUTUAL INSURANCE COMPANY   *p518*
11 BAIRD ST N, BRIGHT, ON, N0J 1B0
(519) 454-8661   *SIC 6331*
NORTHBRIDGE GENERAL INSURANCE CORPORATION   *p955*
105 ADELAIDE ST W 4TH FL, TORONTO, ON, M5H 1P9
(416) 350-4400   *SIC 6331*
NORTHBRIDGE GENERAL INSURANCE CORPORATION   *p955*
105 ADELAIDE ST W UNIT 700, TORONTO, ON, M5H 1P9
(416) 350-4300   *SIC 6331*
NORTHBRIDGE PERSONAL INSURANCE CORPORATION   *p955*
105 ADELAIDE ST W, TORONTO, ON, M5H 1P9
(416) 350-4400   *SIC 6331*
NOVEX INSURANCE COMPANY   *p770*
5775 YONGE ST SUITE 600, NORTH YORK, ON, M2M 4J1
(416) 228-2618   *SIC 6331*
OLD REPUBLIC INSURANCE COMPANY OF CANADA   *p613*
100 KING ST W UNIT 1100, HAMILTON, ON, L8P 1A2
(905) 523-5936   *SIC 6331*
OPTIMUM ASSURANCE AGRICOLE INC   *p1388*
25 RUE DES FORGES BUREAU 422, TROIS-RIVIERES, QC, G9A 6A7
(819) 373-2040   *SIC 6331*
OPTIMUM GENERAL INC   *p1198*
425 BOUL DE MAISONNEUVE O BUREAU 1500, MONTREAL, QC, H3A 3G5
(514) 288-8725   *SIC 6331*
OPTIMUM WEST INSURANCE COMPANY INC   *p190*
4211 KINGSWAY SUITE 600, BURNABY, BC, V5H 1Z6
(604) 688-1541   *SIC 6331*
PEEL MUTUAL INSURANCE COMPANY   *p512*
103 QUEEN ST W, BRAMPTON, ON, L6Y 1M3
(905) 451-2386   *SIC 6331*
PEMBRIDGE INSURANCE COMPANY   *p673*
27 ALLSTATE PKWY SUITE 100, MARKHAM, ON, L3R 5P8
(905) 513-4013   *SIC 6331*
PERSONNELLE ASSURANCES GENERALES INC, LA   *p1137*
6300 BOUL DE LA RIVE-SUD, LEVIS, QC, G6V 6P9
(418) 835-4850   *SIC 6331*
PERSONNELLE, COMPAGNIE D'ASSURANCES, LA   *p706*
3 ROBERT SPECK PKY SUITE 550, MISSISSAUGA, ON, L4Z 3Z9
(905) 306-5252   *SIC 6331*
PREMIER MARINE INSURANCE MANAGERS GROUP (WEST) INC   *p308*
625 HOWE ST SUITE 300, VANCOUVER, BC, V6C 2T6
(604) 669-5211   *SIC 6331*
PRIMMUM INSURANCE COMPANY   *p1180*
50 BOUL CREMAZIE O BUREAU 1200, MONTREAL, QC, H2P 1B6
(514) 382-6060   *SIC 6331*
PRINCE EDWARD ISLAND MUTUAL INSURANCE COMPANY   *p1043*
116 WALKER AVE, SUMMERSIDE, PE,

C1N 6V9
(902) 436-2185   *SIC 6331*
PROMUTUEL CHARLEVOIX-MONTMORENCY   *p1054*
951 BOUL MONSEIGNEUR-DE LAVAL, BAIE-SAINT-PAUL, QC, G3Z 2W3
(418) 435-2793   *SIC 6331*
PROMUTUEL DU LAC AU FLEUVE   *p1113*
11 RUE COMMERCIALE, HEBERTVILLE, QC, G8N 1N3
(418) 344-1565   *SIC 6331*
PROMUTUEL LANAUDIERE, SOCIETE MUTUELLE D'ASSURANCE GENERALE   *p1115*
1075 BOUL FIRESTONE BUREAU 4100, JOLIETTE, QC, J6E 6X6
(450) 755-5555   *SIC 6331*
PYROTECH BEI INC   *p1362*
1455 RUE MICHELIN, SAINTE-ROSE, QC, H7L 4S2
(450) 967-1515   *SIC 6331*
RAIN AND HAIL INSURANCE SERVICE INC   *p1421*
4303 ALBERT ST SUITE 200, REGINA, SK, S4S 3R6
(306) 584-8844   *SIC 6331*
RBC GENERAL INSURANCE COMPANY   *p726*
6880 FINANCIAL DR SUITE 200, MISSISSAUGA, ON, L5N 7Y5
(905) 816-5400   *SIC 6331*
ROINS FINANCIAL SERVICES LIMITED   *p966*
18 YORK ST SUITE 410, TORONTO, ON, M5J 2T8
(416) 366-7511   *SIC 6331*
ROY, SPEED & ROSS LTD   *p524*
5500 NORTH SERVICE RD SUITE 300, BURLINGTON, ON, L7L 6W6
(905) 331-3113   *SIC 6331*
ROYAL & SUN ALLIANCE INSURANCE COMPANY OF CANADA   *p65*
326 11 AVE SW SUITE 300, CALGARY, AB, T2R 0C5
(403) 233-6000   *SIC 6331*
ROYAL & SUN ALLIANCE INSURANCE COMPANY OF CANADA   *p448*
50 GARLAND AVE SUITE 101, DARTMOUTH, NS, B3B 0A3
(902) 493-1500   *SIC 6331*
ROYAL & SUN ALLIANCE INSURANCE COMPANY OF CANADA   *p715*
2225 ERIN MILLS PKY SUITE 1000, MISSISSAUGA, ON, L5K 2S9
(905) 403-2333   *SIC 6331*
ROYAL & SUN ALLIANCE INSURANCE COMPANY OF CANADA   *p966*
18 YORK ST SUITE 800, TORONTO, ON, M5J 2T8
(416) 366-7511   *SIC 6331*
SAGE OTTAWA   *p821*
700 SUSSEX DR SUITE 200, OTTAWA, ON, K1N 1K4
SIC 6331
SASKATCHEWAN CROP INSURANCE CORPORATION   *p1410*
484 PRINCE WILLIAM DR, MELVILLE, SK, S0A 2P0
(306) 728-7200   *SIC 6331*
SASKATCHEWAN GOVERNMENT INSURANCE   *p1418*
2260 11TH AVE SUITE 18, REGINA, SK, S4P 0J9
(306) 751-1200   *SIC 6331*
SASKATCHEWAN MOTOR CLUB SERVICES LIMITED   *p1421*
200 ALBERT ST, REGINA, SK, S4R 2N4
(306) 791-4321   *SIC 6331*
SASKATCHEWAN MUNICIPAL HAIL INSURANCE ASSOCIATION   *p1419*
2100 CORNWALL ST, REGINA, SK, S4P 2K7
(306) 569-1852   *SIC 6331*
SASKATCHEWAN MUTUAL INSURANCE

COMPANY   *p1429*
279 3RD AVE N, SASKATOON, SK, S7K 2H8
(306) 653-4232   *SIC 6331*
SASKATCHEWAN WORKERS' COMPENSATION BOARD   *p1419*
1881 SCARTH ST SUITE 200, REGINA, SK, S4P 4L1
(800) 667-7590   *SIC 6331*
SCOR CANADA REINSURANCE COMPANY   *p971*
199 BAY ST SUITE 2800, TORONTO, ON, M5L 1G1
(416) 869-3670   *SIC 6331*
SF INSURANCE PLACEMENT CORPORATION OF CANADA   *p481*
333 FIRST COMMERCE DR, AURORA, ON, L4G 8A4
(905) 750-4100   *SIC 6331*
SGI CANADA INSURANCE SERVICES LTD   *p1419*
2260 11TH AVE SUITE 18, REGINA, SK, S4P 0J9
(306) 751-1200   *SIC 6331*
SHEPEHERD GROUP, THE   *p795*
140 WENDELL AVE SUITE 9, NORTH YORK, ON, M9N 3R2
(416) 249-1700   *SIC 6331*
SMARTCOVERAGE INSURANCE AGENCY INC   *p1020*
3600 RHODES DR, WINDSOR, ON, N8W 5A4
(519) 974-7067   *SIC 6331*
SOVEREIGN GENERAL INSURANCE COMPANY, THE   *p37*
6700 MACLEOD TRAIL SE SUITE 140, CALGARY, AB, T2H 0L3
SIC 6331
STANLEY MUTUAL INSURANCE COMPANY   *p418*
32 IRISHTOWN RD, STANLEY, NB, E6B 1B6
(506) 367-2273   *SIC 6331*
SWISS REINSURANCE COMPANY CANADA   *p957*
150 KING ST W SUITE 2200, TORONTO, ON, M5H 1J9
(416) 408-0272   *SIC 6331*
TERRA RESTORATION STEAMATIC HAMILTON   *p615*
115 HEMPSTEAD DR SUITE 5, HAMILTON, ON, L8W 2Y6
(905) 387-0662   *SIC 6331*
THINKUNSURE LTD   *p676*
11 ALLSTATE PKY UNIT 206, MARKHAM, ON, L3R 9T8
(905) 415-8800   *SIC 6331*
TOWN & COUNTRY MUTUAL INSURANCE COMPANY   *p897*
79 CARADOC ST N, STRATHROY, ON, N7G 2M5
(519) 246-1132   *SIC 6331*
TREMBLAY ASSURANCE LTEE   *p1045*
575 BOUL DE QUEN, ALMA, QC, G8B 5Z1
(418) 662-6413   *SIC 6331*
TWEEDIE BRUNSWICK & LAVESQUE   *p399*
36 RUE DE L'EGLISE, EDMUNDSTON, NB, E3V 1J2
(506) 735-5515   *SIC 6331*
UNICA INSURANCE INC   *p745*
7150 DERRYCREST DR SUITE 1, MISSISSAUGA, ON, L5W 0E5
(905) 677-9777   *SIC 6331*
UNIFUND ASSURANCE COMPANY   *p432*
10 FACTORY LANE, ST. JOHN'S, NL, A1C 6H5
(709) 737-1500   *SIC 6331*
UNIQUE ASSURANCES GENERALES INC, L'   *p1260*
625 RUE SAINT AMABLE, QUEBEC, QC, G1K 0E1
(418) 683-2711   *SIC 6331*
WABISA MUTUAL INSURANCE COMPANY   *p623*

35 TALBOT ST W, JARVIS, ON, N0A 1J0
(519) 587-4454   *SIC 6331*
WATERBORNE UNDERWRITING SERVICES LTD   *p310*
409 GRANVILLE ST SUITE 1157, VANCOUVER, BC, V6C 1T2
SIC 6331
WAWANESA MUTUAL INSURANCE COMPANY   *p66*
708 11 AVE SW SUITE 600, CALGARY, AB, T2R 0E4
(403) 266-8600   *SIC 6331*
WAWANESA MUTUAL INSURANCE COMPANY, THE   *p117*
8657 51 AVE NW SUITE 100, EDMONTON, AB, T6E 6A8
(780) 469-5700   *SIC 6331*
WAWANESA MUTUAL INSURANCE COMPANY, THE   *p321*
1985 BROADWAY W SUITE 400, VANCOUVER, BC, V6J 4Y3
(800) 665-2778   *SIC 6331*
WAWANESA MUTUAL INSURANCE COMPANY, THE   *p380*
191 BROADWAY SUITE 900, WINNIPEG, MB, R3C 3P1
(204) 985-3923   *SIC 6331*
WAWANESA MUTUAL INSURANCE COMPANY, THE   *p409*
1010 ST GEORGE BLVD, MONCTON, NB, E1E 4R5
(506) 853-1010   *SIC 6331*
WAWANESA MUTUAL INSURANCE COMPANY, THE   *p774*
4110 YONGE ST SUITE 100, NORTH YORK, ON, M2P 2B7
(416) 250-9292   *SIC 6331*
WAWANESA MUTUAL INSURANCE COMPANY, THE   *p1157*
8585 BOUL DECARIE, MONT-ROYAL, QC, H4P 2J4
(514) 342-2211   *SIC 6331*
WEST WAWANOSH MUTUAL INSURANCE COMPANY, THE   *p567*
81 SOUTHAMPTON ST SUITE 1, DUNGANNON, ON, N0M 1R0
(519) 529-7921   *SIC 6331*
WESTERN ASSURANCE COMPANY   *p715*
2225 ERIN MILLS PKY SUITE 1000, MISSISSAUGA, ON, L5K 2S9
(905) 403-2333   *SIC 6331*
WESTMINSTER MUTUAL INSURANCE COMPANY   *p493*
14122 BELMONT RD, BELMONT, ON, N0L 1B0
(519) 644-1663   *SIC 6331*
WORK COMP TECH LTD   *p33*
1401 1 ST SE SUITE 200, CALGARY, AB, T2G 2J3
(403) 294-0501   *SIC 6331*
WORKERS COMPENSATION BOARD OF NOVA SCOTIA   *p454*
5668 SOUTH ST, HALIFAX, NS, B3J 1A6
(902) 491-8999   *SIC 6331*
WORKERS COMPENSATION BOARD OF PRINCE EDWARD ISLAND   *p1040*
14 WEYMOUTH ST, CHARLOTTETOWN, PE, C1A 4Y1
(902) 368-5680   *SIC 6331*
WORKERS' COMPENSATION BOARD ALBERTA   *p26*
4311 12 ST NE SUITE 150, CALGARY, AB, T2E 4P9
(403) 517-6000   *SIC 6331*
WORKERS' COMPENSATION BOARD ALBERTA   *p92*
9912 107 ST NW, EDMONTON, AB, T5K 1G5
(780) 498-3999   *SIC 6331*
WORKERS' COMPENSATION BOARD OF BRITISH COLUMBIA   *p235*
4980 WILLS RD, NANAIMO, BC, V9T 6C6
(604) 273-2266   *SIC 6331*
WORKERS' COMPENSATION BOARD OF

BRITISH COLUMBIA p250
1066 VANCOUVER ST, PRINCE GEORGE, BC, V2L 5M4
(250) 561-3715 *SIC* 6331

WORKERS' COMPENSATION BOARD OF BRITISH COLUMBIA p266
6951 WESTMINSTER HWY, RICHMOND, BC, V7C 1C6
(604) 231-8888 *SIC* 6331

WORKERS' SAFETY AND COMPENSATION COMMISSION OF THE NORTHWEST TERRITORIES AND NUNAVUT p436
5022 49 ST, YELLOWKNIFE, NT, X1A 3R8
(867) 920-3888 *SIC* 6331

WORKPLACE HEALTH SAFETY & COMPENSATION COMMISSION OF NEWFOUNDLAND AND LABRADOR p429
148 FOREST RD UNIT 146, ST. JOHN'S, NL, A1A 1E6
(709) 778-1000 *SIC* 6331

WORKPLACE HEALTH, SAFETY & COMPENSATION COMMISSION OF NEW BRUNSWICK p416
1 PORTLAND ST, SAINT JOHN, NB, E2L 3X9
(506) 632-2200 *SIC* 6331

WORKPLACE SAFETY & INSURANCE BOARD, THE p613
120 KING ST W, HAMILTON, ON, L8P 4V2
(800) 387-0750 *SIC* 6331

WORKPLACE SAFETY & INSURANCE BOARD, THE p639
55 KING ST W SUITE 502, KITCHENER, ON, N2G 4W1
(800) 387-0750 *SIC* 6331

WORKPLACE SAFETY & INSURANCE BOARD, THE p655
148 FULLARTON ST SUITE 402, LONDON, ON, N6A 5P3
(800) 387-0750 *SIC* 6331

WORKPLACE SAFETY & INSURANCE BOARD, THE p824
180 KENT ST SUITE 400, OTTAWA, ON, K1P 0B6
(416) 344-1000 *SIC* 6331

WORKPLACE SAFETY & INSURANCE BOARD, THE p901
30 CEDAR ST, SUDBURY, ON, P3E 1A4
(705) 677-4260 *SIC* 6331

WORKPLACE SAFETY & INSURANCE BOARD, THE p985
200 FRONT ST W SUITE 101, TORONTO, ON, M5V 3J1
(416) 344-1000 *SIC* 6331

WORKPLACE SAFETY & INSURANCE BOARD, THE p1022
2485 OUELLETTE AVE, WINDSOR, ON, N8X 1L5
(800) 387-0750 *SIC* 6331

WORKPLACE SAFETY NORTH p764
690 MCKEOWN AVE, NORTH BAY, ON, P1B 7M2
(705) 474-7233 *SIC* 6331

WORKSAFEBC p266
6951 WESTMINSTER HWY SUITE 600, RICHMOND, BC, V7C 1C6
(604) 231-8888 *SIC* 6331

WYNWARD INSURANCE GROUP p376
1 LOMBARD PL SUITE 1240, WINNIPEG, MB, R3B 0V9
(204) 943-0721 *SIC* 6331

SIC 6351 Surety insurance

AGENCES D'ASSURANCE COPOLOFF INC, LES p1227
5500 AV ROYALMOUNT BUREAU 325, MONTREAL, QC, H4P 1H7
(514) 731-9605 *SIC* 6351

ALBERTA NEW HOME WARRANTY PROGRAM, THE p75
30 SPRINGBOROUGH BLVD SW SUITE 301, CALGARY, AB, T3H 0N9

(403) 253-3636 *SIC* 6351

ASSURANT SERVICES CANADA INC p771
5000 YONGE ST SUITE 2000, NORTH YORK, ON, M2N 7E9
(416) 733-3360 *SIC* 6351

ATLANTIC CENTRAL p455
6074 LADY HAMMOND RD SUITE B, HALIFAX, NS, B3K 2R7
(902) 453-0680 *SIC* 6351

BERKLEY CANADA INC p949
145 KING ST W SUITE 1000, TORONTO, ON, M5H 1J8
(416) 304-1178 *SIC* 6351

CAN-SURE UNDERWRITING LTD p329
700 GEORGIA ST W SUITE 1488, VANCOUVER, BC, V7Y 1A1
(604) 685-6533 *SIC* 6351

CANADA GUARANTY MORTGAGE INSURANCE COMPANY p937
1 TORONTO ST SUITE 400, TORONTO, ON, M5C 2V6
(416) 640-8924 *SIC* 6351

CANADA LIFE FINANCIAL CORPORATION p944
330 UNIVERSITY AVE, TORONTO, ON, M5G 1R7
(416) 597-1440 *SIC* 6351

CHAMBRE DE LA SECURITE FINANCIERE p1185
300 RUE LEO-PARISEAU BUREAU 2600, MONTREAL, QC, H2X 4B8
(514) 282-5777 *SIC* 6351

CORPORATION FINANCIERE BROME INC p1194
550 RUE SHERBROOKE O BUREAU 700, MONTREAL, QC, H3A 1B9
(514) 842-2975 *SIC* 6351

DION SERVICES FINANCIERS p1289
1380 AV LARIVIERE, ROUYN-NORANDA, QC, J9X 4L1
(819) 797-4400 *SIC* 6351

FOND D'ASSURANCE RESPONSABILITE PROFESSIONNELLE DE LA CHAMBRE DES NOTAIRES DU QUEBEC p1204
1200 AV MCGILL COLLEGE BUREAU 1500, MONTREAL, QC, H3B 4G7
(514) 871-4999 *SIC* 6351

FONDS D'ASSURANCE RESPONSABILITE PROFESSIONNELLE DU BARREAU DU QUEBEC p1188
445 BOUL SAINT-LAURENT BUREAU 300, MONTREAL, QC, H2Y 3T8
(514) 954-3452 *SIC* 6351

FONDS DE SECURITE DESJARDINS p1136
100 AV DES COMMANDEURS, LEVIS, QC, G6V 7N5
SIC 6351

GARANTIE DE CONSTRUCTION RESIDENTIELLE (GCR), LA p1052
7171 RUE JEAN-TALON E BUREAU 200, ANJOU, QC, H1M 3N2
(514) 657-2333 *SIC* 6351

GE CANADA EQUIPMENT FINANCING AND CAPITALIST FUNDS p304
400 BURRARD ST SUITE 1050, VANCOUVER, BC, V6C 3A6
SIC 6351

GENWORTH FINANCIAL MORTGAGE INSURANCE COMPANY CANADA p797
2060 WINSTON PARK DR SUITE 300, OAKVILLE, ON, L6H 5R7
(905) 287-5300 *SIC* 6351

GENWORTH MI CANADA INC p797
2060 WINSTON PARK DR SUITE 300, OAKVILLE, ON, L6H 5R7
(905) 287-5300 *SIC* 6351

GROUPE PPP LTEE, LE p1279
1165 BOUL LEBOURGNEUF BUREAU 250, QUEBEC, QC, G2K 2C9
(418) 623-8155 *SIC* 6351

HEALTHCARE INSURANCE RECIPROCAL OF CANADA p771
4711 YONGE ST SUITE 1600, NORTH YORK, ON, M2N 6K8

(416) 733-2773 *SIC* 6351

IDC WORLDSOURCE INSURANCE NETWORK INC p313
1075 GEORGIA ST W, VANCOUVER, BC, V6E 3C9
(604) 689-8289 *SIC* 6351

LSBC CAPTIVE INSURANCE COMPANY LTD p299
845 CAMBIE ST SUITE 800, VANCOUVER, BC, V6B 4Z9
(604) 669-2533 *SIC* 6351

MUNICIPAL INSURANCE ASSOCIATION OF BRITISH COLUMBIA p292
429 2ND AVE W UNIT 200, VANCOUVER, BC, V5Y 1E3
(604) 683-6266 *SIC* 6351

NATIONAL HOME WARRANTY PROGRAMS LTD p125
9808 12 AVE SW, EDMONTON, AB, T6X 0J5
(780) 425-2981 *SIC* 6351

O.C. TANNER RECOGNITION COMPANY LIMITED p523
4200 FAIRVIEW ST, BURLINGTON, ON, L7L 4Y8
(905) 632-7255 *SIC* 6351

OMNI WARRANTY CORP p308
355 BURRARD ST SUITE 350, VANCOUVER, BC, V6C 2G8
(604) 806-5300 *SIC* 6351

PLAN DE PROTECTION MECANIQUE P.P.M. INC p1252
2525 AUT TRANSCANADIENNE, POINTE-CLAIRE, QC, H9R 4V6
SIC 6351

SAL MARKETING INC p300
2165 BROADWAY W, VANCOUVER, BC, V6B 5H6
(604) 737-3816 *SIC* 6351

SERVICES COMERCO INC p1087
3300 BOUL SAINT-MARTIN O BUREAU 300, COTE SAINT-LUC, QC, H7T 1A1
(450) 682-9900 *SIC* 6351

SOUTH COUNTRY AGENCIES p169
5300 47 AVE, TABER, AB, T1G 1R1
(403) 223-8123 *SIC* 6351

SPORTS-CAN INSURANCE CONSULTANTS LTD p227
8411 200 ST SUITE 103, LANGLEY, BC, V2Y 0E7
(604) 888-0050 *SIC* 6351

SSQ SOCIETE D'ASSURANCE-VIE INC p773
110 SHEPPARD AVE E UNIT 500, NORTH YORK, ON, M2N 6Y8
(416) 221-3477 *SIC* 6351

TABOR MANOR LONG TERM CARE FACILITY p884
1 TABOR DR, ST CATHARINES, ON, L2N 1V9
(905) 934-2548 *SIC* 6351

TACAMOR INC p427
1 AUGUSTA PL, PLACENTIA, NL, A0B 2Y0
SIC 6351

TARION WARRANTY CORPORATION p773
5160 YONGE ST 12TH FL, NORTH YORK, ON, M2N 6L9
(416) 229-3828 *SIC* 6351

TRAVELERS INSURANCE COMPANY OF CANADA p958
20 QUEEN ST W SUITE 300, TORONTO, ON, M5H 3R3
(416) 360-8183 *SIC* 6351

TRAVELERS INSURANCE COMPANY OF CANADA p958
165 UNIVERSITY AVE SUITE 101, TORONTO, ON, M5H 3B9
(416) 362-7231 *SIC* 6351

VAC SERVICE OF CANADA INC p819
1001 THOMAS SPRATT PL, OTTAWA, ON, K1G 5L5
SIC 6351

VERI-CHEQUE LTD p905
8500 LESLIE ST SUITE 500, THORNHILL,

ON, L3T 7M8
(905) 709-0928 *SIC* 6351

WESTERN SURETY COMPANY p1419
1881 SCARTH ST UNIT 2100, REGINA, SK, S4P 4K9
(306) 791-3735 *SIC* 6351

WGI SERVICE PLAN DIVISION INC p342
1455 BELLEVUE AVE SUITE 300, WEST VANCOUVER, BC, V7T 1C3
(604) 922-6563 *SIC* 6351

WORLD WIDE WARRANTY INC p342
1455 BELLEVUE AVE SUITE 300, WEST VANCOUVER, BC, V7T 1C3
(604) 922-0305 *SIC* 6351

XPV WATER PARTNERS INC p968
40 UNIVERSITY AVE SUITE 801, TORONTO, ON, M5J 1T1
(416) 581-8850 *SIC* 6351

YOUNGS INSURANCE BROKERS INC p887
110B HANNOVER DR SUITE 106, ST CATHARINES, ON, L2W 1A4
(905) 688-1100 *SIC* 6351

SIC 6361 Title insurance

FIRST CANADIAN TITLE COMPANY LIMITED p800
2235 SHERIDAN GARDEN DR SUITE 745, OAKVILLE, ON, L6J 7Y5
(905) 287-1000 *SIC* 6361

FIRST CANADIAN TITLE COMPANY LIMITED p800
2235 SHERIDAN GARDEN DR SUITE 745, OAKVILLE, ON, L6J 7Y5
(800) 307-0370 *SIC* 6361

FIRST CANADIAN TITLE COMPANY LIMITED p1326
333 BOUL DECARIE BUREAU 200, SAINT-LAURENT, QC, H4N 3M9
(514) 744-1210 *SIC* 6361

FNF CANADA COMPANY p722
2700 ARGENTIA RD, MISSISSAUGA, ON, L5N 5V4
(905) 813-7174 *SIC* 6361

SUTTON GROUP - WEST COAST REALTY p227
19653 WILLOWBROOK DR UNIT 156, LANGLEY, BC, V2Y 1A5
(604) 533-3939 *SIC* 6361

SIC 6371 Pension, health, and welfare funds

ALBERTA SCHOOL EMPLOYEE BENEFIT PLAN, THE p118
6104 104 ST NW SUITE 301, EDMONTON, AB, T6H 2K7
(780) 438-5300 *SIC* 6371

ALBERTA TEACHERS' RETIREMENT FUND BOARD p97
11010 142 ST NW SUITE 600, EDMONTON, AB, T5N 2R1
(780) 451-4166 *SIC* 6371

ASSOCIATION DE BIENFAISANCE ET DE RETRAITE DES POLICIERS DE LA VILLE DE MONTREAL p1173
480 RUE GILFORD BUREAU 200, MONTREAL, QC, H2J 1N3
(514) 527-8061 *SIC* 6371

B C FEDERATION OF LABOUR (CLC) p288
5118 JOYCE ST SUITE 200, VANCOUVER, BC, V5R 4H1
(604) 430-1421 *SIC* 6371

BC PENSION CORPORATION p334
2995 JUTLAND RD, VICTORIA, BC, V8T 5J9
(250) 356-8548 *SIC* 6371

BOILERMAKER'S NATIONAL BENEFIT PLANS p667
45 MCINTOSH DR, MARKHAM, ON, L3R 8C7
(905) 946-2530 *SIC* 6371

BRITISH COLUMBIA FEDERATION OF RE-TIRED UNION MEMBERS   *p288*
5118 JOYCE ST SUITE 200, VANCOUVER, BC, V5R 4H1
(604) 688-4565   *SIC 6371*

CALGARY DISTRICT PIPE TRADES HEALTH & WELFARE AND PENSION PLANS   *p8*
2635 37 AVE NE SUITE 110, CALGARY, AB, T1Y 5Z6
(403) 250-3534   *SIC 6371*

CAPITAL D'AMERIQUE CDPQ INC   *p1191*
1000 PLACE JEAN-PAUL-RIOPELLE BU-REAU 12E, MONTREAL, QC, H2Z 2B3
(514) 842-3261   *SIC 6371*

CBC PENSION BOARD OF TRUSTEES   *p822*
99 BANK ST SUITE 191, OTTAWA, ON, K1P 6B9
(613) 688-3900   *SIC 6371*

CIVIL SERVICE SUPERANNUATION BOARD   *p377*
444 ST MARY AVE SUITE 1200, WIN-NIPEG, MB, R3C 3T1
(204) 946-3200   *SIC 6371*

CO-OPERATIVE SUPERANNUATION SOCI-ETY   *p1426*
333 3RD AVE N SUITE 501, SASKATOON, SK, S7K 2M2
(306) 244-1539   *SIC 6371*

COLLEGES OF APPLIED ARTS & TECH-NOLOGY PENSION PLAN   *p935*
250 YONGE ST UNIT 2900, TORONTO, ON, M5B 2L7
(416) 673-9000   *SIC 6371*

CWSDS PASSPORT   *p683*
917 NIPISSING RD UNIT 1A, MILTON, ON, L9T 5E3
(905) 693-8885   *SIC 6371*

ELLEMENT CONSULTING GROUP   *p384*
503-1780 WELLINGTON AVE, WINNIPEG, MB, R3H 1B3
(204) 954-7300   *SIC 6371*

EMPLOYEE BENEFIT FUNDS ADMINIS-TRATION LTD   *p114*
4224 93 ST NW SUITE 200, EDMONTON, AB, T6E 5P5
(780) 465-2882   *SIC 6371*

FORESTERS ASSET MANAGEMENT INC   *p938*
20 ADELAIDE ST E SUITE 1500, TORONTO, ON, M5C 2T6
(800) 828-1540   *SIC 6371*

GRAPHIC COMMUNICATIONS BENEFITS ADMINISTRATION COR   *p695*
5025 ORBITOR DR SUITE 210, MISSIS-SAUGA, ON, L4W 4Y5
SIC 6371

GREINER-PACAUD MANAGEMENT ASSO-CIATES   *p963*
70 UNIVERSITY AVE SUITE 1200, TORONTO, ON, M5J 2M4
(416) 864-0040   *SIC 6371*

HEALTHCARE EMPLOYEES PENSION PLAN - MANITOBA   *p378*
200 GRAHAM AVE SUITE 900, WINNIPEG, MB, R3C 4L5
(204) 942-6591   *SIC 6371*

HOOPP INVESTMENT MANAGEMENT LIM-ITED   *p963*
1 YORK ST SUITE 1900, TORONTO, ON, M5J 0B6
(416) 369-9212   *SIC 6371*

INTERNATIONAL ASSOCIATION OF MA-CHINISTS LABOUR MANAGEMENT PEN-SION FUND (CANADA)   *p825*
200 ISABELLA ST UNIT 400, OTTAWA, ON, K1S 1V7
(613) 567-8259   *SIC 6371*

IWA-FOREST INDUSTRY PENSION PLAN   *p286*
2955 VIRTUAL WAY SUITE 150, VANCOU-VER, BC, V5M 4X6
(604) 433-6310   *SIC 6371*

KINGSTON INDEPENDENT NYLON WORK-

ERS UNION OFFICE & RECREATION CEN-TRE   *p632*
725 ARLINGTON PARK PL, KINGSTON, ON, K7M 7E4
(613) 389-5255   *SIC 6371*

LABOURERS' PENSION FUND OF CEN-TRAL AND EASTERN CANADA   *p798*
1315 NORTH SERVICE RD E, OAKVILLE, ON, L6H 1A7
(289) 291-3663   *SIC 6371*

METALLURGISTES UNIS D'AMERIQUE   *p1177*
565 BOUL CREMAZIE E BUREAU 5100, MONTREAL, QC, H2M 2V8
(514) 599-2000   *SIC 6371*

NORTHERN INTERIOR WOODWORKERS HOLDING SOCIETY   *p249*
1777 3RD AVE SUITE 100, PRINCE GEORGE, BC, V2L 3G7
(250) 563-7771   *SIC 6371*

NOVA SCOTIA PENSION SERVICES COR-PORATION   *p453*
1949 UPPER WATER ST SUITE 400, HALI-FAX, NS, B3J 3N3
(902) 424-5070   *SIC 6371*

OMERS ADMINISTRATION CORPORATION   *p955*
100 ADELAIDE ST W SUITE 900, TORONTO, ON, M5H 0E2
(416) 369-2400   *SIC 6371*

ONTARIO PENSION BOARD   *p955*
200 KING ST W SUITE 2200, TORONTO, ON, M5H 3X6
(416) 364-8558   *SIC 6371*

ONTARIO PUBLIC SERVICE EMPLOYEES UNION PENSION PLAN TRUST FUND   *p940*
1 ADELAIDE ST E SUITE 1200, TORONTO, ON, M5C 3A7
(416) 681-6161   *SIC 6371*

ONTARIO TEACHERS' INSURANCE PLAN INC   *p1008*
125 NORTHFIELD DR W SUITE 100, WA-TERLOO, ON, N2L 6K4
(519) 888-9683   *SIC 6371*

ONTARIO TEACHERS' PENSION PLAN BOARD   *p770*
5650 YONGE ST SUITE 300, NORTH YORK, ON, M2M 4H5
(416) 228-5900   *SIC 6371*

PUBLIC SERVICE PENSION PLAN   *p125*
5103 WINDERMERE BLVD SW, EDMON-TON, AB, T6W 0S9
(800) 358-0840   *SIC 6371*

SASKATCHEWAN HEALTHCARE EMPLOY-EES' PENSION PLAN   *p1423*
4581 PARLIAMENT AVE SUITE 201, REGINA, SK, S4W 0G3
(306) 751-8300   *SIC 6371*

STRATHBRIDGE ASSET MANAGEMENT INC   *p957*
121 KING ST W SUITE 2600, TORONTO, ON, M5H 3T9
(416) 681-3900   *SIC 6371*

TEACHERS RETIREMENT ALLOWANCES FUND BOARD   *p379*
25 FORKS MARKET RD SUITE 330, WIN-NIPEG, MB, R3C 4S8
(204) 949-0048   *SIC 6371*

TELECOMMUNICATION WORKERS PEN-SION PLAN   *p191*
4603 KINGSWAY SUITE 303, BURNABY, BC, V5H 4M4
(604) 430-1317   *SIC 6371*

U.B.P. SERVICES LIMITED   *p1011*
151 FROBISHER DR SUITE E220, WATER-LOO, ON, N2V 2C9
(519) 725-8818   *SIC 6371*

WINNIPEG CIVIC EMPLOYEES BENEFITS PROGRAM, THE   *p376*
317 DONALD ST SUITE 5, WINNIPEG, MB, R3B 2H6
(204) 986-2522   *SIC 6371*

SIC 6399 Insurance carriers, nec

CANADA DEPOSIT INSURANCE CORPO-RATION   *p822*
50 O'CONNOR ST 17TH FL, OTTAWA, ON, K1P 6L2
(613) 996-2081   *SIC 6399*

COAST TO COAST DEALER SERVICES INC   *p610*
1945 KING ST E SUITE 100, HAMILTON, ON, L8K 1W2
(905) 578-7477   *SIC 6399*

CREDIT UNION DEPOSIT GUARANTEE CORPORATION   *p88*
10104 103 AVE NW SUITE 2000, EDMON-TON, AB, T5J 0H8
(780) 428-6680   *SIC 6399*

CREDIT UNION DEPOSIT GUARANTEE CORPORATION   *p377*
200 GRAHAM AVE SUITE 390, WINNIPEG, MB, R3C 4L5
(204) 942-8480   *SIC 6399*

DEPOSIT INSURANCE CORPORATION OF ONTARIO   *p771*
4711 YONGE ST SUITE 700, NORTH YORK, ON, M2N 6K8
(416) 325-9444   *SIC 6399*

FONDS SOCIAL DES EMPLOYES DE LA CAISSE DE DEPOT ET PLACEMENT DU QUEBEC   *p1191*
1000 PLACE JEAN-PAUL-RIOPELLE BU-REAU A12, MONTREAL, QC, H2Z 2B3
(514) 842-3261   *SIC 6399*

GARANTIES NATIONALES MRWV LIMI-TEE, LES   *p1236*
4605 RUE LOUIS-B.-MAYER, MONTREAL, QC, H7P 6G5
(450) 688-9496   *SIC 6399*

GLOBAL WARRANTY CORPORATION   *p655*
471 WATERLOO ST, LONDON, ON, N6B 2P4
(519) 672-9356   *SIC 6399*

LUBRICO WARRANTY INC   *p649*
2124 JETSTREAM RD, LONDON, ON, N5V 3P5
(519) 451-1900   *SIC 6399*

MASSCOMP ELECTRONICS LTD   *p853*
40 EAST PEARCE ST, RICHMOND HILL, ON, L4B 1B7
(905) 764-9533   *SIC 6399*

SYM-TECH INC   *p854*
150 WEST BEAVER CREEK RD SUITE 1, RICHMOND HILL, ON, L4B 1B4
(905) 889-5390   *SIC 6399*

WAGONMASTER ENTERPRISES B.C. INC   *p856*
561 EDWARD AVE UNIT 11, RICHMOND HILL, ON, L4C 9W6
(905) 737-4627   *SIC 6399*

SIC 6411 Insurance agents, brokers, and service

1 UP INSURANCE INC   *p76*
36 PANATELLA LINK NW, CALGARY, AB, T3K 0T6
(403) 910-2442   *SIC 6411*

1192901 ONTARIO LTD   *p498*
14 AUTOMATIC RD SUITE 38, BRAMP-TON, ON, L6S 5N5
(905) 458-1400   *SIC 6411*

2158124 ONTARIO INC   *p477*
1336 SANDHILL DR UNIT 3, ANCASTER, ON, L9G 4V5
(905) 648-6767   *SIC 6411*

2421593 CANADA INC   *p602*
130 MACDONELL ST, GUELPH, ON, N1H 2Z6
(519) 824-4400   *SIC 6411*

370271 ONTARIO LIMITED   *p548*
1600 STEELES AVE W SUITE 426, CON-CORD, ON, L4K 4M2
(905) 660-4006   *SIC 6411*

3823202 CANADA INC   *p653*

130 DUFFERIN AVE SUITE 204, LONDON, ON, N6A 5R2
(519) 675-1415   *SIC 6411*

4211596 CANADA INC   *p63*
326 11 AVE SW SUITE 500, CALGARY, AB, T2R 0C5
(403) 262-8868   *SIC 6411*

89536 BC LTD   *p240*
132 ESPLANADE W SUITE 200, NORTH VANCOUVER, BC, V7M 1A2
(604) 982-3100   *SIC 6411*

A C & D INSURANCE SERVICES LTD   *p241*
1196 MARINE DR, NORTH VANCOUVER, BC, V7P 1S8
(604) 985-0581   *SIC 6411*

A HIGH RISK   *p800*
349 DAVIS RD, OAKVILLE, ON, L6J 2X2
(905) 845-5252   *SIC 6411*

A-WIN INSURANCE LTD   *p38*
10325 BONAVENTURE DR SE SUITE 100, CALGARY, AB, T2J 7E4
(403) 278-1050   *SIC 6411*

A.A. MUNRO INSURANCE BROKERS INC   *p470*
9492 TRANS CANADA HWY, WHYCOCO-MAGH, NS, B0E 3M0
(902) 756-2700   *SIC 6411*

A.M.A. INSURANCE AGENCY LTD   *p118*
10310 39A AVE, EDMONTON, AB, T6H 5X9
(780) 430-5555   *SIC 6411*

ABLE INSURANCE BROKERS LTD   *p691*
2560 MATHESON BLVD E SUITE 400, MIS-SISSAUGA, ON, L4W 4Y9
(905) 629-2253   *SIC 6411*

ACCESS INSURANCE GROUP LTD   *p112*
4435 99 ST NW, EDMONTON, AB, T6E 5B6
(780) 435-2400   *SIC 6411*

ACUMEN INSURANCE GROUP INC   *p894*
835 PARAMOUNT DR SUITE 301, STONEY CREEK, ON, L8J 0B4
(905) 574-7000   *SIC 6411*

ADRIATIC INSURANCE BROKERS LTD   *p1029*
10 DIRECTOR CRT SUITE 100, WOOD-BRIDGE, ON, L4L 7E8
(905) 851-8555   *SIC 6411*

AGENCE ANDRE BEAULNE LTEE   *p1345*
5055 BOUL METROPOLITAIN E BUREAU 200, SAINT-LEONARD, QC, H1R 1Z7
(514) 329-3333   *SIC 6411*

AGENCE D'ASSURANCES ANDRE DUFRESNE   *p1167*
4061 RUE HOCHELAGA, MONTREAL, QC, H1W 1K4
(514) 256-3626   *SIC 6411*

AGENCES D'ASSURANCE RANDLE INC   *p1117*
17001 RTE TRANSCANADIENNE, KIRK-LAND, QC, H9H 0A7
(514) 694-4161   *SIC 6411*

AIG INSURANCE COMPANY OF CANADA   *p1193*
2000 AV MCGILL COLLEGE BUREAU 1200, MONTREAL, QC, H3A 3H3
(514) 842-0603   *SIC 6411*

ALBERTA INSURANCE COUNCIL   *p87*
10104 103 AVE NW SUITE 600, EDMON-TON, AB, T5J 0H8
(780) 421-4148   *SIC 6411*

ALIA CONSEIL INC   *p1193*
550 RUE SHERBROOKE O, MONTREAL, QC, H3A 1B9
(418) 652-1737   *SIC 6411*

ALL-RISKS INSURANCE BROKERS LIM-ITED   *p1021*
1591 OUELLETTE AVE, WINDSOR, ON, N8X 1K5
(519) 253-6376   *SIC 6411*

ALLEN, G & B INSURANCE BROKERS LIM-ITED   *p1005*
45 DOMINION ST, WARKWORTH, ON, K0K 3K0
(705) 924-2632   *SIC 6411*

ALLIANCE ASSURANCE INC   *p403*

---

166 BOUL BROADWAY SUITE 200, GRAND-SAULT/GRAND FALLS, NB, E3Z 2J9

(506) 473-9400   *SIC* 6411

ALLSTATE INSURANCE COMPANY OF CANADA   *p1278*

1150 AUT DUPLESSIS UNIT 600, QUEBEC, QC, G2G 2B5

(819) 569-5911   *SIC* 6411

ALLWEST INSURANCE SERVICES LTD *p320*

2-1855 BURRARD ST, VANCOUVER, BC, V6J 3G9

(604) 736-1969   *SIC* 6411

ALPER, SEYMOUR INC   *p1156*

5520 RUE PARE BUREAU 1, MONT-ROYAL, QC, H4P 2M1

(514) 737-3434   *SIC* 6411

ALPHA COMPAGNIE D'ASSURANCE INC, L'   *p1097*

430 RUE SAINT-GEORGES UNITE 119, DRUMMONDVILLE, QC, J2C 4H4

(819) 474-7958   *SIC* 6411

ALPINE INSURANCE & FINANCIAL INC *p39*

8820 BLACKFOOT TRAIL SE SUITE 123, CALGARY, AB, T2J 3J1

(403) 270-8822   *SIC* 6411

ANDERSON-MCTAGUE & ASSOCIATES LTD   *p414*

154 PRINCE WILLIAM ST, SAINT JOHN, NB, E2L 2B6

(506) 632-5020   *SIC* 6411

ANDERSON-MCTAGUE INSURANCE AGENCY   *p414*

158 PRINCE WILLIAM ST, SAINT JOHN, NB, E2L 2B6

(506) 632-5000   *SIC* 6411

ANDREW AGENCIES LTD   *p360*

322 7TH AVE S, VIRDEN, MB, R0M 2C0

(204) 748-2734   *SIC* 6411

ANGUS-MILLER LTD   *p414*

40 WELLINGTON ROW, SAINT JOHN, NB, E2L 3H3

(506) 633-7000   *SIC* 6411

ANTHONY INSURANCE INCORPORATED *p432*

35 BLACKMARSH RD, ST. JOHN'S, NL, A1E 1S4

(709) 758-5500   *SIC* 6411

AON CANADA INC   *p326*

900 HOWE ST, VANCOUVER, BC, V6Z 2M4

(604) 688-4442   *SIC* 6411

AON CANADA INC   *p959*

20 BAY ST SUITE 2400, TORONTO, ON, M5J 2N8

(416) 868-5500   *SIC* 6411

AON CANADA INC   *p1201*

700 RUE DE LA GAUCHETIERE O UNITE 1800, MONTREAL, QC, H3B 0A5

(514) 842-5000   *SIC* 6411

AON PARIZEAU INC   *p1201*

700 RUE DE LA GAUCHETIERE O BUREAU 1700, MONTREAL, QC, H3B 0A4

(514) 842-5000   *SIC* 6411

AON REED STENHOUSE INC   *p43*

600 3 AVE SW SUITE 1800, CALGARY, AB, T2P 0G5

(403) 267-7010   *SIC* 6411

AON REED STENHOUSE INC   *p87*

10025 102A AVE NW SUITE 900, EDMONTON, AB, T5J 0Y2

(780) 423-9801   *SIC* 6411

AON REED STENHOUSE INC   *p296*

401 GEORGIA ST W SUITE 1200, VANCOUVER, BC, V6B 5A1

(604) 688-4442   *SIC* 6411

AON REED STENHOUSE INC   *p959*

20 BAY ST SUITE 2400, TORONTO, ON, M5J 2N8

(416) 868-5500   *SIC* 6411

AON REED STENHOUSE INC   *p1201*

700 DE LA GAUCHETIERE O BUREAU 1800, MONTREAL, QC, H3B 0A4

(514) 842-5000   *SIC* 6411

APRI INSURANCE SOLUTIONS INC   *p850*

165 EAST BEAVER CREEK RD SUITE 18, RICHMOND HILL, ON, L4B 2N2

(866) 877-3600   *SIC* 6411

APRIL CANADA INC   *p1071*

3250 BOUL LAPINIERE BUREAU 100, BROSSARD, QC, J4Z 3T8

(855) 745-2020   *SIC* 6411

AQUA INSURAQUA INSURANCE   *p92*

13220 ST ALBERT TRAIL NW SUITE 302, EDMONTON, AB, T5L 4W1

(780) 448-0100   *SIC* 6411

ARCHWAY INSURANCE INC   *p438*

81 VICTORIA ST E, AMHERST, NS, B4H 1X7

(902) 667-0800   *SIC* 6411

ASSURANCE 5000 INC   *p1151*

89 RUE SAINT-ANDRE, METABETCHOUAN-LAC-A-LA-CROIX, QC, G8G 1V5

(418) 349-5000   *SIC* 6411

ASSURANCE BURROWES INC   *p1168*

2600 BOUL SAINT-JOSEPH E BUREAU 206, MONTREAL, QC, H1Y 2A4

(514) 522-2661   *SIC* 6411

ASSURANCE ET GESTION DE RISQUES *p1106*

815 BOUL DE LA CARRIERE BUREAU 102, GATINEAU, QC, J8Y 6T4

SIC 6411

ASSURANCE JONES INC   *p1129*

103 AV BETHANY, LACHUTE, QC, J8H 2L2

(450) 562-8555   *SIC* 6411

ASSURANCE ROY YELLE INC   *p1088*

106 RUE CHURCH, COWANSVILLE, QC, J2K 1T8

(450) 263-0110   *SIC* 6411

ASSURANCE VOYAGE RSA INC   *p1371*

1910 RUE KING O BUREAU 200, SHERBROOKE, QC, J1J 2E2

(819) 780-0064   *SIC* 6411

ASSURANCES COTE, GUIMOND, LAFOND & ASSOCIES INC   *p1045*

221 1RE AV E, AMOS, QC, J9T 1H5

(819) 732-5371   *SIC* 6411

ASSURANCES FONTAINE LEMAY & ASS INC, LES   *p1135*

5331 RUE SAINT-GEORGES, LEVIS, QC, G6V 4N4

(418) 835-1150   *SIC* 6411

ASSURANCES GROUPE VEZINA   *p1084*

999 BOUL SAINT-MARTIN O, COTE SAINT-LUC, QC, H7S 1M5

(450) 663-6880   *SIC* 6411

ASSURANCES J.Y. MARCOUX & ASSOCIES INC   *p1359*

1017 BOUL VACHON N BUREAU 100, SAINTE-MARIE, QC, G6E 1M3

(418) 387-6604   *SIC* 6411

ASSURANCES JEAN-CLAUDE LECLERC INC   *p1100*

230 BOUL SAINT-JOSEPH O, DRUMMONDVILLE, QC, J2E 0G3

(819) 477-3156   *SIC* 6411

ASSURANCES JOE ANGELONE INC *p1051*

7811 BOUL LOUIS-H.-LAFONTAINE BUREAU 201, ANJOU, QC, H1K 4E4

(514) 353-1331   *SIC* 6411

ASSURANCES MICHEL BROSSEAU LTEE *p1156*

5665 AV ROYALMOUNT BUREAU 200, MONT-ROYAL, QC, H4P 2P9

(514) 288-9141   *SIC* 6411

ASSURANCES PROVENCHER VERREAULT & ASSOCIES INC   *p1071*

7055 BOUL TASCHEREAU BUREAU 620, BROSSARD, QC, J4Z 1A7

(450) 676-7707   *SIC* 6411

ASSURANCES ROBICHAUD INSURANCE BROKERS INC   *p627*

37 RIVERSIDE DR, KAPUSKASING, ON, P5N 1A7

(705) 335-2371   *SIC* 6411

ASSURANCES ROLAND GROULX INC, LES   *p1105*

540 BOUL DE L'HOPITAL BUREAU 200, GATINEAU, QC, J8V 3T2

(819) 243-0242   *SIC* 6411

ASSURANCES SAGUENAY INC   *p1115*

2655 BOUL DU ROYAUME BUREAU 102, JONQUIERE, QC, G7S 4S9

(418) 699-1100   *SIC* 6411

ASSURANCIA GROUPE BROSSEAU INC *p1072*

1 AV LIBERTE, CANDIAC, QC, J5R 3X8

(450) 635-1155   *SIC* 6411

ASSURANCIA SHINK DECELLES INC *p1365*

45 RUE VICTORIA E, SALABERRY-DE-VALLEYFIELD, QC, J6T 2L4

(450) 377-8585   *SIC* 6411

ASSUREXPERTS INC   *p1277*

540 RUE MICHEL-FRAGASSO, QUEBEC, QC, G2E 5N4

(418) 871-2289   *SIC* 6411

ASSURIS   *p935*

250 YONGE ST SUITE 3110, TORONTO, ON, M5B 2L7

(416) 359-2001   *SIC* 6411

ASTRO INSURANCE 1000 INC   *p142*

542 7 ST S UNIT 100, LETHBRIDGE, AB, T1J 2H1

(403) 320-6700   *SIC* 6411

ATKINSON & TERRY INSURANCE BROKERS   *p207*

8067 120 ST SUITE 120, DELTA, BC, V4C 6P7

(604) 596-3350   *SIC* 6411

ATRENS-COUNSEL INSURANCE BROKERS INC   *p719*

7111 SYNTEX DR SUITE 200, MISSISSAUGA, ON, L5N 8C3

(905) 567-6222   *SIC* 6411

ATTO & ASSOCIATES INSURANCE BROKERS INC   *p704*

5660 MCADAM RD SUITE A1, MISSISSAUGA, ON, L4Z 1T2

(905) 890-1412   *SIC* 6411

AURREA SIGNATURE INC   *p1063*

1205 RUE AMPERE BUREAU 201, BOUCHERVILLE, QC, J4B 7M6

(450) 650-2151   *SIC* 6411

AVIVA CANADA INC   *p444*

99 WYSE RD SUITE 1600, DARTMOUTH, NS, B3A 4S5

(902) 460-3100   *SIC* 6411

AVIVA CANADA INC   *p679*

10 AVIVA WAY SUITE 100, MARKHAM, ON, L6G 0G1

(416) 288-1800   *SIC* 6411

AVIVA CANADA INC   *p1177*

555 RUE CHABANEL O BUREAU 900, MONTREAL, QC, H2N 2H8

(514) 850-4100   *SIC* 6411

AVIVA INSURANCE COMPANY OF CANADA   *p948*

121 KING ST W SUITE 1400, TORONTO, ON, M5H 3T9

SIC 6411

AXA ASSISTANCE CANADA INC   *p1193*

2001 BOUL ROBERT-BOURASSA BUREAU 1850, MONTREAL, QC, H3A 2L8

(514) 285-9053   *SIC* 6411

AXION INSURANCE SERVICES INC   *p851*

95 MURAL ST SUITE 205, RICHMOND HILL, ON, L4B 3G2

(905) 731-3118   *SIC* 6411

AXIS INSURANCE MANAGERS INC   *p327*

555 BURRARD ST BOX 275 UNIT 400, VANCOUVER, BC, V7X 1M8

(604) 731-5328   *SIC* 6411

AZGA INSURANCE AGENCY CANADA LTD *p641*

4273 KING ST E, KITCHENER, ON, N2P 2E9

(519) 742-2800   *SIC* 6411

B S I INSURANCE BROKERS LTD   *p351*

16 3RD AVENUE EAST, LETELLIER, MB, R0G 1C0

(204) 737-2471   *SIC* 6411

B.C.A.A. HOLDINGS LTD   *p187*

4567 CANADA WAY, BURNABY, BC, V5G 4T1

(604) 268-5000   *SIC* 6411

BAIRD MACGREGOR INSURANCE BROKERS INC   *p920*

825 QUEEN ST E, TORONTO, ON, M4M 1H8

(416) 778-8000   *SIC* 6411

BAKER, BERTRAND, CHASSE & GOGUEN CLAIM SERVICES LIMITED   *p709*

3660 HURONTARIO ST SUITE 601, MISSISSAUGA, ON, L5B 3C4

(905) 279-8880   *SIC* 6411

BARBER STEWART MCVITTIE & WALLACE INSURANCE BROKERS LTD   *p766*

6 LANSING SQ SUITE 230, NORTH YORK, ON, M2J 1T5

(416) 493-0050   *SIC* 6411

BARON INSURANCE AGENCIES GROUP INC   *p331*

5301 25 AVE SUITE 119, VERNON, BC, V1T 9R1

(250) 545-6565   *SIC* 6411

BARTON, BLACK & ROBERTSON INSURANCE SERVICES LTD   *p216*

206 SEYMOUR ST UNIT 100, KAMLOOPS, BC, V2C 6P5

(250) 314-6217   *SIC* 6411

BAY CITY INSURANCE SERVICES LTD *p238*

1199 LYNN VALLEY RD SUITE 121, NORTH VANCOUVER, BC, V7J 3H2

(604) 986-1155   *SIC* 6411

BEACH & ASSOCIATES LIMITED   *p959*

95 WELLINGTON ST W SUITE 1120, TORONTO, ON, M5J 2N7

(416) 368-9680   *SIC* 6411

BEAZLEY CANADA LIMITED   *p959*

55 UNIVERSITY AVE SUITE 550, TORONTO, ON, M5J 2H7

(416) 601-2155   *SIC* 6411

BECK, WILSON M INSURANCE SERVICES INC   *p192*

8678 GREENALL AVE SUITE 303, BURNABY, BC, V5J 3M6

(604) 437-6200   *SIC* 6411

BELMONT FINANCIAL GROUP INC, THE *p443*

33 ALDERNEY DR UNIT 7TH, DARTMOUTH, NS, B2Y 2N4

(902) 465-5687   *SIC* 6411

BELYER INSURANCE LTD   *p1019*

3390 WALKER RD SUITE 300, WINDSOR, ON, N8W 3S1

(519) 915-4667   *SIC* 6411

BENEFITS BY DESIGN INC   *p245*

2755 LOUGHEED HWY SUITE 500, PORT COQUITLAM, BC, V3B 5Y9

(604) 464-0313   *SIC* 6411

BENSON KEARLEY & ASSOCIATES INSURANCE BROKERS LTD   *p754*

17705 LESLIE ST SUITE 101, NEWMARKET, ON, L3Y 3E3

(905) 898-3815   *SIC* 6411

BFL CANADA INSURANCE SERVICES INC *p311*

1177 HASTINGS ST W SUITE 200, VANCOUVER, BC, V6E 2K3

(604) 669-9600   *SIC* 6411

BFL CANADA RISK AND INSURANCE SERVICES INC   *p949*

181 UNIVERSITY AVE SUITE 1700, TORONTO, ON, M5H 3M7

(416) 599-5530   *SIC* 6411

BFL CANADA RISQUES ET ASSURANCES INC   *p1193*

2001 AV MCGILL COLLEGE BUREAU 2200, MONTREAL, QC, H3A 1G1

(514) 843-3632   *SIC* 6411

BILGEN, BERK INSURANCE LTD   *p112*

8925 51 AVE NW SUITE 311, EDMONTON, AB, T6E 5J3

(780) 822-6042   *SIC* 6411

BINKS INSURANCE BROKERS LIMITED p830
2625 QUEENSVIEW DR SUITE 100B, OTTAWA, ON, K2B 8K2
(613) 226-1350 *SIC* 6411

BLUE CIRCLE INSURANCE LTD p27
3402 8 ST SE UNIT 200, CALGARY, AB, T2G 5S7
(403) 770-4949 *SIC* 6411

BLUE CROSS LIFE INSURANCE COMPANY OF CANADA p1417
1870 ALBERT ST SUITE 100, REGINA, SK, S4P 4B7
(306) 525-5025 *SIC* 6411

BLUE SKY FINANCIAL GROUP INC p762
128 MCINTYRE ST W SUITE 100, NORTH BAY, ON, P1B 2Y6
(705) 497-3723 *SIC* 6411

BMO LIFE ASSURANCE COMPANY p941
60 YONGE ST, TORONTO, ON, M5E 1H5
(416) 596-3900 *SIC* 6411

BMT INSURANCE BROKERS LTD p912
65 MAPLE ST S, TIMMINS, ON, P4N 1Y6
(705) 268-9988 *SIC* 6411

BOURGEOIS-COTE-FORGET & ASSOCIATES INSURANCE BROKERS p810
2712 ST. JOSEPH BLVD, ORLEANS, ON, K1C 1G5
(613) 824-0441 *SIC* 6411

BOW VALLEY INSURANCE SERVICES (1992) LTD p67
9805 HORTON RD SW, CALGARY, AB, T2V 2X5
(403) 297-9400 *SIC* 6411

BOXBERG HOLDING LTD p520
6124 ANNA ST, BRUNNER, ON, N0K 1C0
(519) 595-8903 *SIC* 6411

BRADLEY'S COMMERCIAL INSURANCE LIMITED p890
1469 STITTSVILLE MAIN ST, STITTSVILLE, ON, K2S 0C8
(613) 836-2473 *SIC* 6411

BRECKLES INSURANCE BROKERS LIMITED p1000
85 ENTERPRISE BLVD SUITE 401, UNIONVILLE, ON, L6G 0B5
(905) 752-4747 *SIC* 6411

BRIGHTER FUTURES p846
GD, PIKANGIKUM, ON, P0V 2L0
(807) 773-5300 *SIC* 6411

BRIO INSURANCE p358
13 BRANDT ST SUITE 1, STEINBACH, MB, R5G 0C2
(204) 326-3870 *SIC* 6411

BRISTER INSURANCE BROKERS LTD p746
83 MAIN ST, MORRISBURG, ON, K0C 1X0
(613) 543-3731 *SIC* 6411

BROKERFORCE INSURANCE INC p766
200 CONSUMERS RD SUITE 608, NORTH YORK, ON, M2J 4R4
(416) 494-2696 *SIC* 6411

BROKERS TRUST INSURANCE GROUP INC p549
2780 HIGHWAY 7 SUITE 201, CONCORD, ON, L4K 3R9
(416) 427-5251 *SIC* 6411

BROWN BROS. AGENCIES LIMITED p336
1125 BLANSHARD ST, VICTORIA, BC, V8W 2H7
(250) 385-8771 *SIC* 6411

BROWN, AL G. & ASSOCIATES p788
970 LAWRENCE AVE W SUITE 501, NORTH YORK, ON, M6A 3B6
(416) 787-6176 *SIC* 6411

BRYSON & ASSOCIATES INSURANCE BROKERS LTD p475
541 BAYLY ST E, AJAX, ON, L1Z 1W7
(905) 426-8787 *SIC* 6411

BUCKLEY INSURANCE BROKERS LTD p755
247 MAIN ST S, NEWMARKET, ON, L3Y 3Z4
(905) 836-7283 *SIC* 6411

BUNTAIN INSURANCE AGENCIES LTD p324

3707 10TH AVE W, VANCOUVER, BC, V6R 2G5
(604) 224-2373 *SIC* 6411

BURROWES COURTIERS D'ASSURANCES p1168
2647 PLACE CHASSE, MONTREAL, QC, H1Y 2C3
(514) 522-2661 *SIC* 6411

BUTLER BYERS INSURANCE LTD p1426
301 4TH AVE N, SASKATOON, SK, S7K 2L8
(306) 653-2233 *SIC* 6411

C & C INSURANCE CONSULTANTS LTD p643
22425 JEFFERIES RD UNIT 6, KOMOKA, ON, N0L 1R0
(519) 657-1446 *SIC* 6411

CAISSE POPULAIRE LES GRANDS BOULEVARD p1085
1535 BOUL SAINT-MARTIN O, COTE SAINT-LUC, QC, H7S 1N1
(450) 668-4000 *SIC* 6411

CALDWELL-ROACH AGENCIES LIMITED p468
643 PRINCE ST, TRURO, NS, B2N 1G5
(902) 893-4204 *SIC* 6411

CAM-RON INSURANCE BROKERS LIMITED p806
4579 OIL SPRINGS LINE, OIL SPRINGS, ON, N0N 1P0
(519) 834-2833 *SIC* 6411

CAMBRIAN INSURANCE BROKERS LIMITED p900
130 PARIS ST SUITE 1, SUDBURY, ON, P3E 3E1
(705) 673-5000 *SIC* 6411

CAMERON & ASSOCIATES INSURANCE CONSULTANTS LTD p960
55 YORK ST SUITE 400, TORONTO, ON, M5J 1R7
(416) 350-5822 *SIC* 6411

CANADA BROKERLINK (ONTARIO) INC p68
1201 GLENMORE TRAIL SW SUITE 100, CALGARY, AB, T2V 4Y8
(403) 209-6300 *SIC* 6411

CANADA BROKERLINK INC p64
1400 1 ST SW SUITE 200, CALGARY, AB, T2R 0V8
(403) 290-1541 *SIC* 6411

CANADA LOYAL INSURANCE AGENCY LIMITED p796
2866 PORTLAND DR, OAKVILLE, ON, L6H 5W8
(905) 829-5514 *SIC* 6411

CANADA PROTECTION PLAN INC p779
250 FERRAND DR SUITE 1100, NORTH YORK, ON, M3C 3G8
(416) 447-6060 *SIC* 6411

CANADIAN AVIATION INSURANCE MANAGERS LTD p960
200 BAY ST SUITE 2310, TORONTO, ON, M5J 2J1
(416) 865-0252 *SIC* 6411

CANADIAN CLAIMS SERVICES INC p99
17958 106 AVE, EDMONTON, AB, T5S 1V4
(780) 443-1185 *SIC* 6411

CANADIAN INSURANCE BROKERS INC p922
1 EGLINTON AVE E SUITE 415, TORONTO, ON, M4P 3A1
(416) 486-0951 *SIC* 6411

CANADIAN NORTHERN SHIELD INSURANCE COMPANY p297
555 HASTINGS ST W UNIT 1900, VANCOUVER, BC, V6B 4N6
(604) 662-2900 *SIC* 6411

CANTIN GAGNON ASSURANCES INC p1116
2463 RUE SAINT-DOMINIQUE, JONQUIERE, QC, G7X 6K4
(418) 542-7575 *SIC* 6411

CANWELL INSURANCE AND FINANCIAL SERVICES INC p665
121 ROBINSON ST, MARKHAM, ON, L3P 1P2

SIC 6411

CAPITAL WEST INSURANCE SERVICES p231
22785 DEWDNEY TRUNK RD, MAPLE RIDGE, BC, V2X 3K4
(604) 476-1227 *SIC* 6411

CAPITALE GESTION FINANCIERE INC, LA p1271
650-2875 BOUL LAURIER, QUEBEC, QC, G1V 5B1
(418) 644-0038 *SIC* 6411

CAPRICMW INSURANCE SERVICES LTD p221
1500 HARDY ST SUITE 100, KELOWNA, BC, V1Y 8H2
(250) 860-2426 *SIC* 6411

CARPROOF CORPORATION p653
130 DUFFERIN AVE SUITE 1101, LONDON, ON, N6A 5R2
(866) 835-8612 *SIC* 6411

CARR & COMPANY INSURANCE BROKERS LTD p819
1980 OGILVIE RD, OTTAWA, ON, K1J 9L3
(613) 706-1806 *SIC* 6411

CARRUTHERS NICOL INSURANCE INC p835
1230 2ND AVE E, OWEN SOUND, ON, N4K 2J3
(519) 376-5350 *SIC* 6411

CARSON & WEEKS INSURANCE BROKERS LIMITED p665
59 MAIN ST N, MARKHAM, ON, L3P 1X7
(905) 294-0722 *SIC* 6411

CASCADE INSURANCE AGENCIES (BURNABY) INC p190
4683 KINGSWAY, BURNABY, BC, V5H 2B3
SIC 6411

CAYUGA MUTUAL INSURANCE COMPANY p541
23 KING ST, CAYUGA, ON, N0A 1E0
(905) 772-5498 *SIC* 6411

CCS ADJUSTERS INC p99
10120 175 ST NW, EDMONTON, AB, T5S 1L1
(780) 443-1185 *SIC* 6411

CCV INSURANCE & FINANCIAL SERVICES INC p510
32 QUEEN ST W, BRAMPTON, ON, L6X 1A1
(905) 459-6066 *SIC* 6411

CDSPI p776
155 LESMILL RD, NORTH YORK, ON, M3B 2T8
(416) 296-9401 *SIC* 6411

CENTRAL AGENCIES INC p78
4870 51 ST, CAMROSE, AB, T4V 1S1
(780) 679-2170 *SIC* 6411

CERTAS HOME AND AUTO INSURANCE COMPANY p1136
6300 BOUL GUILLAUME-COUTURE, LEVIS, QC, G6V 6P9
(418) 835-4900 *SIC* 6411

CHAPDELAINE ASSURANCE ET SERVICES FINANCIERS INC p1056
220 RUE BREBEUF, BELOEIL, QC, J3G 5P3
(450) 464-2112 *SIC* 6411

CHARLEBOIS-TREPANIER ET ASSOCIES 2009 INC p1106
815 BOUL DE LA CARRIERE BUREAU 102, GATINEAU, QC, J8Y 6T4
(819) 777-5246 *SIC* 6411

CHARLES TAYLOR CONSULTING SERVICES (CANADA) INC p46
321 6 AVE SW SUITE 910, CALGARY, AB, T2P 3H3
(403) 266-3336 *SIC* 6411

CHATEAU DE CHAMPLAIN p414
300 BOARS HEAD RD SUITE 119, SAINT JOHN, NB, E2K 5C2
(506) 633-1195 *SIC* 6411

CHEEP INSURANCE p443
GD, DARTMOUTH, NS, B2Y 3Y3
(902) 463-1675 *SIC* 6411

CHERRY INSURANCE LTD p1426
350 3RD AVE S, SASKATOON, SK, S7K 1M5
(306) 653-2313 *SIC* 6411

CHES SPECIAL RISK INC p986
130 KING ST W 19TH FL, TORONTO, ON, M5X 1C9
(647) 480-1515 *SIC* 6411

CIS INSURANCE BROKERS (CANADA) LTD p904
505 HIGHWAY 7 E SUITE 328, THORNHILL, ON, L3T 7T1
(905) 889-2268 *SIC* 6411

CLAIMSPRO LP p693
1550 ENTERPRISE RD SUITE 310, MISSISSAUGA, ON, L4W 4P4
(905) 671-0185 *SIC* 6411

CLOVER INSURANCE GROUP p1030
3800 STEELES AVE W SUITE 201, WOODBRIDGE, ON, L4L 4G9
(905) 851-7774 *SIC* 6411

CMW INSURANCE SERVICES LTD p185
1901 ROSSER AVE UNIT 700, BURNABY, BC, V5C 6R6
(604) 294-3301 *SIC* 6411

CNA CANADA, INC p969
66 WELLINGTON ST W SUITE 3700, TORONTO, ON, M5K 1J5
(416) 542-7300 *SIC* 6411

CO-OPERATORS GENERAL INSURANCE COMPANY p602
130 MACDONELL ST, GUELPH, ON, N1H 2Z6
(519) 824-4400 *SIC* 6411

CO-OPERATORS GENERAL INSURANCE COMPANY p711
1270 CENTRAL PKY W SUITE 600, MISSISSAUGA, ON, L5C 4P4
SIC 6411

CO-OPERATORS GROUP LIMITED, THE p668
7300 WARDEN AVE SUITE 110, MARKHAM, ON, L3R 9Z6
(905) 470-7300 *SIC* 6411

CO-OPERATORS GROUP LIMITED, THE p1417
1920 COLLEGE AVE, REGINA, SK, S4P 1C4
(306) 347-6200 *SIC* 6411

COAST CAPITAL INSURANCE SERVICES LTD p339
1499 ADMIRALS RD, VICTORIA, BC, V9A 2P8
(250) 483-7000 *SIC* 6411

COAST CLAIM SERVICE LTD p334
2727 QUADRA ST SUITE 6, VICTORIA, BC, V8T 4E5
(250) 386-3111 *SIC* 6411

COAST COUNTRY INSURANCE SERVICES LTD p203
426 8TH ST, COURTENAY, BC, V9N 1N5
(250) 334-3443 *SIC* 6411

COASTAL COMMUNITY INSURANCE AGENCIES LTD p233
50 TENTH ST SUITE 111, NANAIMO, BC, V9R 6L1
SIC 6411

COASTAL INSURANCE SERVICES LTD p185
4350 STILL CREEK DR SUITE 400, BURNABY, BC, V5C 0G5
(604) 269-1000 *SIC* 6411

COLES RETIREMENT PLANNING CONSULTANTS p452
2000 BARRINGTON ST, HALIFAX, NS, B3J 3K1
(902) 423-0350 *SIC* 6411

COLLEY, BORLAND & VALE INSURANCE BROKERS LIMITED p1000
4591 HIGHWAY 7 E SUITE 200, UNIONVILLE, ON, L3R 1M6
(905) 477-2720 *SIC* 6411

COLLINS RANKIN INSURANCE BROKERS p637

645 WESTMOUNT RD E, KITCHENER, ON, N2E 3S3

SIC 6411

COMPAGNIE D'ASSURANCE BELAIR INC, LA *p831*

1111 PRINCE OF WALES DR SUITE 200, OTTAWA, ON, K2C 3T2

(613) 744-3279   *SIC 6411*

COMPAGNIE D'ASSURANCE HABITATION ET AUTO TD *p668*

675 COCHRANE DR SUITE 100, MARKHAM, ON, L3R 0B8

(905) 415-8400   *SIC 6411*

COOKE, CHARLIE INSURANCE AGENCY LTD *p1039*

125 POWNAL ST SUITE 1, CHARLOTTE-TOWN, PE, C1A 3W4

(902) 566-5666   *SIC 6411*

CORE INSURANCE CLAIMS CONTRACTING INC *p792*

94 KENHAR DR UNIT 10, NORTH YORK, ON, M9L 1N2

(416) 740-9400   *SIC 6411*

CORNELL INSURANCE BROKERS LTD *p668*

275 RENFREW DR SUITE 208, MARKHAM, ON, L3R 0C8

(905) 471-3868   *SIC 6411*

CORNERSTONE INSURANCE BROKERS LTD *p1030*

8001 WESTON RD SUITE 300, WOOD-BRIDGE, ON, L4L 9C8

(905) 856-1981   *SIC 6411*

COTE, CLAUDE ASSURANCES ENR *p1088*

106 RUE CHURCH, COWANSVILLE, QC, J2K 1T8

(450) 263-0597   *SIC 6411*

COUGHLIN & ASSOCIATES LTD *p817*

466 TREMBLAY RD, OTTAWA, ON, K1G 3R1

(613) 231-2266   *SIC 6411*

COUGHLIN, GUY INSURANCE AGENCY LTD *p387*

1170 TAYLOR AVE UNIT 4, WINNIPEG, MB, R3M 3Z4

(204) 953-4600   *SIC 6411*

COURTIER MULTI PLUS INC *p1172*

5650 RUE D'IBERVILLE BUREAU 630, MONTREAL, QC, H2G 2B3

(514) 376-0313   *SIC 6411*

COURTIKA ASSURANCES INC *p1109*

800 RUE PRINCIPALE SUITE 206, GRANBY, QC, J2G 2Y8

(450) 372-5801   *SIC 6411*

COWAN INSURANCE GROUP LTD *p538*

705 FOUNTAIN ST N, CAMBRIDGE, ON, N3H 4R7

(519) 650-6360   *SIC 6411*

COWAN, FRANK COMPANY LIMITED *p848*

75 MAIN ST N, PRINCETON, ON, N0J 1V0

(519) 458-4331   *SIC 6411*

CRAIG, MCDONALD, REDDON INSURANCE BROKERS LTD *p1004*

12 COLBORNE ST S, WALKERTON, ON, N0G 2V0

(519) 881-2701   *SIC 6411*

CRAWFORD & COMPANY (CANADA) INC *p640*

539 RIVERBEND DR, KITCHENER, ON, N2K 3S3

(519) 578-5540   *SIC 6411*

CRAWFORD & COMPANY (CANADA) INC *p1006*

180 KING ST S UNIT 610, WATERLOO, ON, N2J 1P8

(519) 578-9800   *SIC 6411*

CREIGHTON & COMPANY INSURANCE BROKERS LTD *p705*

315 MATHESON BLVD E, MISSISSAUGA, ON, L4Z 1X8

(905) 890-0090   *SIC 6411*

CRI CREDIT GROUP SERVICES INC *p185*

4185 STILL CREEK DR UNIT 350A, BURNABY, BC, V5C 6G9

(604) 438-7785   *SIC 6411*

CROSBIE JOB INSURANCE LIMITED *p430*

1 CROSBIE PL SUITE 201, ST. JOHN'S, NL, A1B 3Y8

(709) 726-5414   *SIC 6411*

CUNNINGHAM LINDSEY CANADA LIMITED *p611*

46 JACKSON ST E, HAMILTON, ON, L8N 1L1

(905) 528-1481   *SIC 6411*

CUNNINGHAM LINDSEY CANADA LIMITED *p612*

25 MAIN ST W SUITE 1810, HAMILTON, ON, L8P 1H1

(905) 528-1481   *SIC 6411*

CUNNINGHAM LINDSEY CANADA LIMITED *p1317*

523 BOUL DU SEMINAIRE N BUREAU 103, SAINT-JEAN-SUR-RICHELIEU, QC, J3B 5L8

SIC 6411

CURTIS INSURANCE LIMITED *p776*

1500 DON MILLS RD SUITE 501, NORTH YORK, ON, M3B 3K4

(416) 447-4499   *SIC 6411*

D G DUNBAR INSURANCE BROKER LIMITED *p653*

255 QUEENS AVE SUITE 1050, LONDON, ON, N6A 5R8

(519) 642-0858   *SIC 6411*

D. A. TOWNLEY & ASSOCIATES LTD *p188*

4400 DOMINION ST SUITE 160, BURN-ABY, BC, V5G 4G3

(604) 299-7482   *SIC 6411*

D. G. BEVAN INSURANCE BROKERS LTD *p486*

166 SAUNDERS RD UNIT 6, BARRIE, ON, L4N 9A4

(705) 726-3381   *SIC 6411*

DAIGNEAULT PROVOST JOLY LEBRUN INC *p1076*

185 BOUL SAINT-JEAN-BAPTISTE BU-REAU 100, CHATEAUGUAY, QC, J6K 3B4

(450) 691-9913   *SIC 6411*

DAV-BAR-DAL INSURANCE SERVICES LTD *p142*

300 10 ST S, LETHBRIDGE, AB, T1J 2M6

(403) 320-1010   *SIC 6411*

DAVIDSON DELAPLANTE INSURANCE BROKERS LTD *p912*

100 THIRD AVE, TIMMINS, ON, P4N 1C3

(705) 268-1011   *SIC 6411*

DAWSON & KEENAN INSURANCE LTD *p861*

121 BROCK ST, SAULT STE. MARIE, ON, P6A 3B6

(705) 949-3740   *SIC 6411*

DAY, GUY R. & SON LIMITED *p418*

78 MILLTOWN BLVD, ST STEPHEN, NB, E3L 1G6

(506) 466-3330   *SIC 6411*

DESJARDINS GROUPE D'ASSURANCES GENERALES INC *p694*

5070 DIXIE RD, MISSISSAUGA, ON, L4W 1C9

(905) 366-4430   *SIC 6411*

DESJARDINS GROUPE D'ASSURANCES GENERALES INC *p1136*

6300 BOUL GUILLAUME-COUTURE, LEVIS, QC, G6V 6P9

(418) 835-4850   *SIC 6411*

DESJARDINS GROUPE D'ASSURANCES GENERALES INC *p1230*

1 COMPLEXE DESJARDINS BUREAU 1, MONTREAL, QC, H5B 1B1

(514) 350-8300   *SIC 6411*

DESJARDINS GROUPE D'ASSURANCES GENERALES INC *p1304*

15590 8E AV, SAINT-GEORGES, QC, G5Y 7X6

SIC 6411

DESJARDINS HOLDING FINANCIER INC *p1230*

1 RUE COMPLEXE DESJARDINS S 40E ETAGE, MONTREAL, QC, H5B 1J1

(418) 838-7870   *SIC 6411*

DESLAURIERS & ASSOCIES INC *p1064*

210 BOUL DE MONTARVILLE BUREAU 3015, BOUCHERVILLE, QC, J4B 6T3

(450) 641-1911   *SIC 6411*

DESPRES-PACEY INSURANCE BROKERS LIMITED *p753*

26 ARMSTRONG ST, NEW LISKEARD, ON, P0J 1P0

(705) 647-6713   *SIC 6411*

DIBRINA & ASSOCIATES *p900*

7 CEDAR ST SUITE 202, SUDBURY, ON, P3E 1A2

(705) 688-9011   *SIC 6411*

DIBRINA SURE BENEFITS CONSULTING INC *p900*

62 FROOD RD SUITE 302, SUDBURY, ON, P3C 4Z3

(705) 688-9393   *SIC 6411*

DISABILITY CONCEPTS INC *p48*

736 6 AVE SW SUITE 1500, CALGARY, AB, T2P 3T7

(403) 262-2080   *SIC 6411*

DLK INSURANCE BROKERS LTD *p519*

35 KING ST W, BROCKVILLE, ON, K6V 3P7

(613) 342-8663   *SIC 6411*

DOIRON, RENEE *p411*

8 RUE CENTENNIAL, RICHIBUCTO, NB, E4W 3X2

(506) 523-9403   *SIC 6411*

DOMINION OF CANADA GENERAL INSURANCE COMPANY, THE *p48*

777 8 AVE SW SUITE 1700, CALGARY, AB, T2P 3R5

(403) 231-6600   *SIC 6411*

DOMINION OF CANADA GENERAL INSURANCE COMPANY, THE *p805*

1275 NORTH SERVICE RD W SUITE 103, OAKVILLE, ON, L6M 3G4

(905) 825-6400   *SIC 6411*

DOMINION OF CANADA GENERAL INSURANCE COMPANY, THE *p950*

165 UNIVERSITY AVE., TORONTO, ON, M5H 3B9

(416) 362-7231   *SIC 6411*

DONOVAN INSURANCE BROKERS INC *p1006*

72 REGINA ST N, WATERLOO, ON, N2J 3A5

(519) 886-3150   *SIC 6411*

DORSEY GROUP INSURANCE PLANNERS INC, THE *p514*

330 WEST ST UNIT 7, BRANTFORD, ON, N3R 7V5

(519) 759-0033   *SIC 6411*

DOWLING INSURANCE BROKERS INC *p384*

1045 ST JAMES ST UNIT A, WINNIPEG, MB, R3H 1B1

(204) 949-2600   *SIC 6411*

DPM INSURANCE GROUP *p911*

31 QUEEN ST N, TILBURY, ON, N0P 2L0

(519) 682-0202   *SIC 6411*

DRAYDEN INSURANCE LTD *p97*

10310 124 ST NW SUITE 100, EDMONTON, AB, T5N 1R2

(780) 482-6300   *SIC 6411*

DUBE COOKE PEDICELLI INC *p1159*

370 RUE DE SAINT-JOVITE BUREAU 202, MONT-TREMBLANT, QC, J8E 2Z9

(450) 537-3646   *SIC 6411*

DUFRESNE, ANDRE INSURANCE *p1167*

4061 RUE HOCHELAGA, MONTREAL, QC, H1W 1K4

(514) 256-3626   *SIC 6411*

DULIBAN INSURANCE BROKERS LIMITED *p591*

165 HWY 20 SUITE 7, FONTHILL, ON, L0S 1E5

(905) 892-5723   *SIC 6411*

DUSYK & BARLOW INSURANCE BROKERS LTD *p1422*

302 UNIVERSITY PARK DR, REGINA, SK, S4V 0Y8

(306) 791-3474   *SIC 6411*

DYCK INSURANCE AGENCY (WETASKIWIN) LTD. *p172*

5105 47 AVE, WETASKIWIN, AB, T9A 0K4

(780) 352-9222   *SIC 6411*

DYCK INSURANCE SERVICE LTD *p67*

24 ST SW, CALGARY, AB, T2T 5H9

(403) 246-4600   *SIC 6411*

E-DJUSTER INC *p749*

28 CONCOURSE GATE UNIT 203, NE-PEAN, ON, K2E 7T7

(866) 779-5950   *SIC 6411*

ECHELON FINANCIAL HOLDINGS INC *p694*

2680 MATHESON BLVD E SUITE 300, MISSISSAUGA, ON, L4W 0A5

(905) 214-7880   *SIC 6411*

ECHELON GENERAL INSURANCE COMPANY *p694*

2680 MATHESON BLVD E SUITE 300, MISSISSAUGA, ON, L4W 0A5

(905) 214-7880   *SIC 6411*

EDMONDS GALLAGHER MCLAUGHLIN INSURANCE BROKERS LIMITED *p838*

270 LAKE ST, PEMBROKE, ON, K8A 7Y9

(613) 735-0621   *SIC 6411*

EGI FINANCIAL HOLDINGS INC *p694*

2680 MATHESON BLVD E SUITE 300, MISSISSAUGA, ON, L4W 0A5

(905) 214-7880   *SIC 6411*

EGR INC *p1203*

1100 BOUL ROBERT-BOURASSA 6E ETAGE, MONTREAL, QC, H3B 3A5

(514) 370-4800   *SIC 6411*

EISENHAUER INSURANCE INCORPORATED *p458*

362 LACEWOOD DR SUITE 205, HALIFAX, NS, B3S 1M7

(902) 454-5888   *SIC 6411*

ELFA INSURANCE SERVICES INC *p669*

3950 14TH AVE UNIT 105, MARKHAM, ON, L3R 0A9

(905) 470-1038   *SIC 6411*

ELITE INSURANCE COMPANY *p326*

1125 HOWE ST SUITE 1100, VANCOUVER, BC, V6Z 2Y6

(604) 669-2626   *SIC 6411*

ELITE WEALTH MANAGEMENT INC *p260*

7080 RIVER RD SUITE 241, RICHMOND, BC, V6X 1X5

(604) 276-8081   *SIC 6411*

ENCON GROUP INC *p596*

1400 BLAIR PL SUITE 50, GLOUCESTER, ON, K1J 9B8

(613) 786-2000   *SIC 6411*

ESSOR ASSURANCES PLACEMENTS CONSEILS INC *p1204*

1100 BOUL ROBERT-BOURASSA, MONTREAL, QC, H3B 3A5

(514) 878-9373   *SIC 6411*

ESSOR ASSURANCES PLACEMENTS CONSEILS INC *p1279*

5600 BOUL DES GALERIES BUREAU 600, QUEBEC, QC, G2K 2H6

(418) 692-0660   *SIC 6411*

ESTIMATIONS GUY JALBERT 1997 INC, LES *p1373*

4520 BOUL INDUSTRIEL, SHERBROOKE, QC, J1L 2S8

(819) 566-7222   *SIC 6411*

EVEREST INSURANCE COMPANY OF CANADA *p986*

130 KING ST W SUITE 2520, TORONTO, ON, M5X 2A2

(416) 487-3900   *SIC 6411*

EXCEL INSURANCE AGENCY INC *p670*

80 ACADIA AVE SUITE 205, MARKHAM, ON, L3R 9V1

(905) 470-8222   *SIC 6411*

EXCEL INSURANCE BROKERS (METRO VANCOUVER) INC *p190*

4720 KINGSWAY UNIT 2600, BURNABY, BC, V5H 4N2

(604) 282-7719   *SIC 6411*

EXPERTISES SCM LES *p1103*

510 BOUL MALONEY E BUREAU 104, GATINEAU, QC, J8P 1E7

(819) 663-6068 *SIC* 6411

FAIRWAY INSURANCE SERVICES INCORPORATED *p449*

104 MONTAGUE ROW, DIGBY, NS, B0V 1A0

(902) 245-4741 *SIC* 6411

FAMILY INSURANCE SOLUTIONS INC *p313*

1177 HASTINGS ST W SUITE 1400, VANCOUVER, BC, V6E 2K3

(604) 687-2655 *SIC* 6411

FENA INSURANCE SOLUTIONS INC *p757*

4056 DORCHESTER RD UNIT 2, NIAGARA FALLS, ON, L2E 6M9

(905) 356-3362 *SIC* 6411

FIRST CANADIAN INSURANCE CORPORATION *p161*

320 SIOUX RD SUITE 110, SHERWOOD PARK, AB, T8A 3X6

(780) 410-9182 *SIC* 6411

FIRST CANADIAN TITLE COMPANY LIMITED *p406*

1234 MAIN ST SUITE 2001, MONCTON, NB, E1C 1H7

(506) 383-6326 *SIC* 6411

FIRST GENERAL SERVICES (PA) LTD *p1413*

32 NORTH INDUSTRIAL, PRINCE ALBERT, SK, S6V 5P7

(306) 764-7000 *SIC* 6411

FIRST GENERAL SERVICES (WINNIPEG) LTD *p390*

125 FENNOLL ST UNIT 1, WINNIPEG, MB, R3T 0M2

(204) 477-0560 *SIC* 6411

FIRST LION HOLDINGS INC *p1196*

2001 AV MCGILL COLLEGE BUREAU 2200, MONTREAL, QC, H3A 1G1

(514) 843-3632 *SIC* 6411

FIRSTBROOK CASSIE & ANDERSON LIMITED *p924*

1867 YONGE ST SUITE 300, TORONTO, ON, M4S 1Y5

(416) 486-1421 *SIC* 6411

FONDS D'ASSURANCE RESPONSABILITE PROFESSIONNELLE DE L'ORDRE DES PHARMACIENS DU QUEBEC *p1196*

2020 BOUL ROBERT-BOURASSA BUREAU 2160, MONTREAL, QC, H3A 2A5

(514) 281-0300 *SIC* 6411

FOSTER PARK BROKERS INC *p101*

17704 103 AVE NW SUITE 200, EDMONTON, AB, T5S 1J9

(780) 489-4961 *SIC* 6411

FOUNDERS INSURANCE GROUP INC *p471*

260 MAIN ST, WOLFVILLE, NS, B4P 1C4

SIC 6411

FOUNDERS INSURANCE GROUP INC. *p446*

250 BROWNLOW AVE SUITE 18, DARTMOUTH, NS, B3B 1W9

(902) 468-3529 *SIC* 6411

FRED C RYALL INSURANCE INC *p705*

53 VILLAGE CENTRE PL, MISSISSAUGA, ON, L4Z 1V9

(416) 419-0240 *SIC* 6411

FS REALTY CENTRE CORPORATION *p709*

2150 HURONTARIO ST UNIT 202E, MISSISSAUGA, ON, L5B 1M8

(416) 253-0066 *SIC* 6411

G T I BROKER GROUP INC *p417*

177 RUE ST-JEAN, SAINT-LEONARD, NB, E7E 2B3

(506) 423-7777 *SIC* 6411

GALLAGHER BASSETT CANADA INC *p774*

4311 YONGE ST SUITE 404, NORTH YORK, ON, M2P 1N6

(416) 861-8212 *SIC* 6411

GALLAGHER, ARTHUR J (CANADA) GROUP *p578*

185 THE WEST MALL SUITE 1710, ETOBICOKE, ON, M9C 5L5

(416) 620-8030 *SIC* 6411

GALLAGHER, ARTHUR J. CANADA LIMITED *p951*

181 UNIVERSITY AVE UNIT 1200, TORONTO, ON, M5H 3M7

(416) 260-5333 *SIC* 6411

GALON MANAGEMENT LTD *p1427*

909 3RD AVE N, SASKATOON, SK, S7K 2K4

(306) 244-7000 *SIC* 6411

GATEWAY INSURANCE BROKERS LTD *p457*

371 ST MARGARETS BAY RD SUITE 101, HALIFAX, NS, B3N 1J8

(902) 431-9300 *SIC* 6411

GAUTHIER, J C INSURANCE BROKER & ASSOCIATES INC *p821*

428 RIDEAU ST SUITE 101, OTTAWA, ON, K1N 5Z2

(613) 789-4140 *SIC* 6411

GENEX SERVICES OF CANADA INC *p695*

2800 SKYMARK AVE SUITE 401, MISSISSAUGA, ON, L4W 5A6

SIC 6411

GILLONS' INSURANCE BROKERS LTD *p592*

326 CHURCH ST, FORT FRANCES, ON, P9A 1E1

(807) 274-7716 *SIC* 6411

GLOBAL AEROSPACE UNDERWRITING MANAGERS (CANADA) LIMITED *p670*

100 RENFREW DR SUITE 200, MARKHAM, ON, L3R 9R6

(905) 479-2244 *SIC* 6411

GLOBAL EXCEL MANAGEMENT INC *p1374*

73 RUE QUEEN, SHERBROOKE, QC, J1M 0C9

(819) 566-8833 *SIC* 6411

GLOBALEX GESTION DE RISQUES INC *p1196*

1130 RUE SHERBROOKE O, MONTREAL, QC, H3A 2M8

(514) 382-9625 *SIC* 6411

GLOBALEX GESTION DE RISQUES INC *p1196*

999 BOUL DE MAISONNEUVE O, MONTREAL, QC, H3A 3L4

(514) 382-6674 *SIC* 6411

GODFREY-MORROW INSURANCE & FINANCIAL SERVICES LTD *p64*

1003 11 AVE SW, CALGARY, AB, T2R 0G2

(403) 244-4945 *SIC* 6411

GOLD KEY INSURANCE SERVICES LTD *p287*

4038 KNIGHT ST, VANCOUVER, BC, V5N 5Y7

(604) 325-1241 *SIC* 6411

GOODISON INSURANCE & FINANCIAL SERVICES LTD *p508*

36 QUEEN ST E SUITE 200, BRAMPTON, ON, L6V 1A2

(905) 451-1236 *SIC* 6411

GPL ASSURANCE INC *p1086*

3131 BOUL SAINT-MARTIN O BUREAU 600, COTE SAINT-LUC, QC, H7T 2Z5

SIC 6411

GREAT-WEST LIFE ASSURANCE COMPANY, THE *p1196*

2001 BOUL ROBERT-BOURASSA UNITE 1000, MONTREAL, QC, H3A 2A6

(514) 350-7975 *SIC* 6411

GROUPE ASSURANCE ELCO INC *p1071*

4405 BOUL LAPINIERE, BROSSARD, QC, J4Z 3T5

(450) 672-7070 *SIC* 6411

GROUPE CENSEO INC *p1241*

1200 BOUL CHOMEDEY BUREAU 1050, MONTREAL-OUEST, QC, H7V 3Z3

(450) 973-8000 *SIC* 6411

GROUPE D'ASSURANCES VERRIER INC *p1098*

430 RUE SAINT-GEORGES BUREAU 121, DRUMMONDVILLE, QC, J2C 4H4

(819) 477-6131 *SIC* 6411

GROUPE DESMARAIS PINSONNEAULT & AVARD INC *p1312*

3395 RUE PICARD, SAINT-HYACINTHE,

QC, J2S 1H3

(450) 250-3321 *SIC* 6411

GROUPE DPJL INC *p1076*

185 BOUL SAINT-JEAN-BAPTISTE BUREAU 100, CHATEAUGUAY, QC, J6K 3B4

(450) 691-9913 *SIC* 6411

GROUPE FINANCIER AGA INC *p1402*

3500 BOUL DE MAISONNEUVE O BUREAU 2200, WESTMOUNT, QC, H3Z 3C1

(514) 935-5444 *SIC* 6411

GROUPE FINANCIER FORT INC *p1220*

3400 BOUL DE MAISONNEUVE O BUREAU 1115, MONTREAL, QC, H3Z 3B8

(514) 288-6161 *SIC* 6411

GROUPE JETTE ASSURANCES INC *p1314*

153 RUE SAINT-JACQUES, SAINT-JACQUES, QC, J0K 2R0

(450) 839-3911 *SIC* 6411

GROUPE LEDOR INC, MUTUELLE D'ASSURANCE *p1356*

78 BOUL BEGIN, SAINTE-CLAIRE, QC, G0R 2V0

(418) 883-2251 *SIC* 6411

GROUPE PREMIER MEDICAL INC *p1235*

2 PLACE LAVAL BUREAU 250, MONTREAL, QC, H7N 5N6

(450) 667-7737 *SIC* 6411

GROUPE PROMUTUEL FEDERATION DE SOCIETE MUTUELLES D'ASSURANCES GENERALES *p1123*

48 BOUL TASCHEREAU, LA PRAIRIE, QC, J5R 6C1

(450) 444-0988 *SIC* 6411

GROUPE SANTE PHYSIMED *p1280*

1300 BOUL LEBOURGNEUF BUREAU 300, QUEBEC, QC, G2K 2N1

(418) 624-2001 *SIC* 6411

GROUPE ULTIMA INC *p1052*

7100 RUE JEAN-TALON E BUREAU 210, ANJOU, QC, H1M 3S3

(514) 722-0024 *SIC* 6411

GROUPE VEZINA & ASSOCIES LTEE, LE *p1085*

999 BOUL SAINT-MARTIN O, COTE SAINT-LUC, QC, H7S 1M5

(450) 663-6880 *SIC* 6411

GROUPE VIAU INC *p1143*

550 CH DE CHAMBLY BUREAU 300, LONGUEUIL, QC, J4H 3L8

SIC 6411

GROUPEMENT DES ASSUREURS AUTOMOBILES *p1229*

800 PLACE-VICTORIA BUREAU 2410, MONTREAL, QC, H4Z 0A2

(514) 288-1537 *SIC* 6411

GROUPHEALTH BENEFIT SOLUTIONS *p279*

2626 CROYDON DR SUITE 200, SURREY, BC, V3Z 0S8

(604) 542-4100 *SIC* 6411

GUARANTEE CO OF NORTH AMERICA, (THE) *p595*

36 PARKRIDGE CRES, GLOUCESTER, ON, K1B 3E7

SIC 6411

GUARANTEE COMPANY OF NORTH AMERICA, THE *p771*

4950 YONGE ST SUITE 1400, NORTH YORK, ON, M2N 6K1

(416) 223-9580 *SIC* 6411

GUARANTEE COMPANY OF NORTH AMERICA, THE *p1035*

954 DUNDAS ST, WOODSTOCK, ON, N4S 7Z9

(519) 539-9868 *SIC* 6411

GUAY BUSSIERES & ASSOCIES INC *p1267*

3405 BOUL WILFRID-HAMEL BUREAU 200, QUEBEC, QC, G1P 2J3

SIC 6411

GUILD INSURANCE BROKERS INC *p347*

2830 VICTORIA AVE, BRANDON, MB, R7B 3X1

(204) 729-4949 *SIC* 6411

GUTHRIE INSURANCE BROKERS LTD *p767*

505 CONSUMERS RD SUITE 308, NORTH YORK, ON, M2J 4V8

(416) 487-5200 *SIC* 6411

H D F INSURANCE & FINANCIAL GROUP *p173*

5111 50 AVE, WHITECOURT, AB, T7S 1S8

(780) 778-8828 *SIC* 6411

H. L. STAEBLER COMPANY LIMITED *p635*

871 VICTORIA ST N SUITE 7B, KITCHENER, ON, N2B 3S4

(519) 743-5221 *SIC* 6411

H.B. GROUP INSURANCE MANAGEMENT LTD *p731*

5600 CANCROSS CRT SUITE A, MISSISSAUGA, ON, L5R 3E9

(905) 507-6156 *SIC* 6411

H.W. HOLLINGER (CANADA) INC *p1197*

550 RUE SHERBROOKE O BUREAU 2070, MONTREAL, QC, H3A 1B9

(514) 842-8421 *SIC* 6411

HALPENNY INSURANCE BROKERS LTD *p829*

1550 LAPERRIERE AVE SUITE 100, OTTAWA, ON, K1Z 7T2

(613) 722-7626 *SIC* 6411

HAMILTON TOWNSHIP MUTUAL INSURANCE COMPANY *p545*

1185 ELGIN ST W, COBOURG, ON, K9A 4K5

(905) 372-0186 *SIC* 6411

HAMILTON WARD AND CATHERS INSURANCE SERVICE LIMITED *p482*

75 TALBOT ST E, AYLMER, ON, N5H 1H3

(519) 773-8471 *SIC* 6411

HARBORD INSURANCE SERVICES LTD *p337*

805 CLOVERDALE AVE SUITE 150, VICTORIA, BC, V8X 2S9

(250) 388-5533 *SIC* 6411

HARDIMAN, MOUNT &ASSOCIATES INSURANCE BROKERS LIMITED *p1014*

1032 BROCK ST S SUITE 5, WHITBY, ON, L1N 4L8

(905) 668-1477 *SIC* 6411

HARMONIA ASSURANCE INC *p1390*

1100 3E AV, VAL-D'OR, QC, J9P 1T6

(819) 825-8673 *SIC* 6411

HARVARD WESTERN VENTURES INC *p1418*

2151 ALBERT ST, REGINA, SK, S4P 2V1

(306) 757-1633 *SIC* 6411

HARVEST INSURANCE AGENCY LTD *p358*

304 MAIN ST, STEINBACH, MB, R5G 1Z1

(204) 326-2323 *SIC* 6411

HARVEST RETIREMENT *p518*

15 HARVEST AVE, BRANTFORD, ON, N4G 0E2

(519) 688-0448 *SIC* 6411

HEALTHCARE INSURANCE RECIPROCAL OF CANADA *p363*

1200 ROTHESAY ST, WINNIPEG, MB, R2G 1T7

(204) 943-4125 *SIC* 6411

HENDRY SWINTON MCKENZIE INSURANCE SERVICES INC *p336*

830 PANDORA AVE, VICTORIA, BC, V8W 1P4

(250) 388-5555 *SIC* 6411

HERITAGE HILL INSURANCE LTD *p68*

10333 SOUTHPORT RD SW SUITE 355, CALGARY, AB, T2W 3X6

SIC 6411

HOMELIFE PROSPERITY LAND REALTY INC *p904*

2900 STEELES AVE E SUITE 211, THORNHILL, ON, L3T 4X1

(905) 707-8020 *SIC* 6411

HOOPER-HOLMES CANADA LIMITED *p877*

1059 MCNICOLL AVE, SCARBOROUGH, ON, M1W 3W6

(416) 493-2800 *SIC* 6411

HOOPER-HOLMES CANADA LIMITED *p877*

1059 MCNICOLL AVE, SCARBOROUGH, ON, M1W 3W6

(416) 493-2800   *SIC 6411*
HOPE & HARDER INSURANCE BROKERS INC   *p883*
512 WELLAND AVE, ST CATHARINES, ON, L2M 5V5
(905) 935-4667   *SIC 6411*
HUB FINANCIAL (BC) INC, THE   *p313*
1185 GEORGIA ST W SUITE 800, VANCOUVER, BC, V6E 4E6
(604) 684-0086   *SIC 6411*
HUB FINANCIAL INC   *p1031*
3700 STEELES AVE W UNIT 1001, WOODBRIDGE, ON, L4L 8K8
(905) 264-1634   *SIC 6411*
HUB INTERNATIONAL   *p1197*
1010 SHERBROOKE ST W STE 2510, MONTREAL, QC, H3A 2R7
(514) 787-7200   *SIC 6411*
HUB INTERNATIONAL CANADA WEST ULC   *p196*
8346 NOBLE RD, CHILLIWACK, BC, V2P 6R5
(604) 703-7070   *SIC 6411*
HUB INTERNATIONAL HKMB LIMITED   *p945*
595 BAY ST SUITE 900, TORONTO, ON, M5G 2E3
(416) 597-0008   *SIC 6411*
HUB INTERNATIONAL INSURANCE BROKERS   *p185*
4350 STILL CREEK DR SUITE 400, BURNABY, BC, V5C 0G5
(604) 293-1481   *SIC 6411*
HUB INTERNATIONAL MANITOBA   *p386*
1661 PORTAGE AVE SUITE 500, WINNIPEG, MB, R3J 3T7
(204) 988-4800   *SIC 6411*
HUB INTERNATIONAL ONTARIO LIMITED   *p797*
2265 UPPER MIDDLE RD E SUITE 700, OAKVILLE, ON, L6H 0G5
(905) 847-5500   *SIC 6411*
HUB INTERNATIONAL QUEBEC LIMITEE   *p1227*
8500 BOUL DECARIE, MONTREAL, QC, H4P 2N2
(514) 374-9600   *SIC 6411*
HUESTIS INSURANCE & ASSOCIATES LTD   *p416*
11 LLOYD ST, SAINT JOHN, NB, E2M 4N4
(506) 635-1515   *SIC 6411*
HUESTIS INSURANCE GROUP   *p416*
11 LLOYD ST, SAINT JOHN, NB, E2M 4N4
(506) 635-1515   *SIC 6411*
HUGH WOOD CANADA LTD   *p774*
4120 YONGE ST SUITE 201, NORTH YORK, ON, M2P 2B8
(416) 229-6600   *SIC 6411*
HYNDMAN & COMPANY LTD   *p1039*
57 QUEEN ST, CHARLOTTETOWN, PE, C1A 4A5
(902) 566-4244   *SIC 6411*
ICD INSURANCE BROKERS LTD   *p755*
569 STEVEN CRT SUITE 5, NEWMARKET, ON, L3Y 6Z3
(905) 830-9000   *SIC 6411*
IMAGINE FINANCIAL LTD   *p981*
460 RICHMOND ST W SUITE 100, TORONTO, ON, M5V 1Y1
(416) 730-8488   *SIC 6411*
INDEPENDENT REHABILITATION SERVICES INC   *p715*
2155 LEANNE BLVD SUITE 240, MISSISSAUGA, ON, L5K 2K8
(905) 823-8895   *SIC 6411*
INDUSTRIELLE ALLIANCE, ASSURANCE ET SERVICES FINANCIERS INC   *p898*
1210 LASALLE BLVD, SUDBURY, ON, P3A 1Y5
(705) 524-5755   *SIC 6411*
INDUSTRIELLE ALLIANCE, ASSURANCE ET SERVICES FINANCIERS INC   *p1071*
9935 RUE DE CHATEAUNEUF STE 230, BROSSARD, QC, J4Z 3V4
(450) 672-6410   *SIC 6411*

INDUSTRIELLE ALLIANCE, ASSURANCE ET SERVICES FINANCIERS INC   *p1270*
925 GRANDE ALLEE O BUREAU 200, QUEBEC, QC, G1S 4Z4
(418) 686-7738   *SIC 6411*
INDUSTRIELLE ALLIANCE, ASSURANCE ET SERVICES FINANCIERS INC   *p1344*
6555 BOUL METROPOLITAIN E BUREAU 403, SAINT-LEONARD, QC, H1P 3H3
(514) 324-3811   *SIC 6411*
ING & MCKEE INSURANCE LTD   *p157*
2830 BREMNER AVE, RED DEER, AB, T4R 1M9
(403) 346-5547   *SIC 6411*
INSURANCE BANK   *p96*
16403 111 AVE NW, EDMONTON, AB, T5M 2S2
(780) 439-2265   *SIC 6411*
INSURANCE BUREAU OF CANADA   *p767*
2235 SHEPPARD AVE E SUITE 1100, NORTH YORK, ON, M2J 5B5
(416) 445-5912   *SIC 6411*
INSURANCE BUREAU OF CANADA   *p946*
777 BAY ST SUITE 2400, TORONTO, ON, M5G 2C8
(416) 362-2031   *SIC 6411*
INSURANCE BUREAU OF CANADA   *p1229*
800 RUE DU SQUARE-VICTORIA BUREAU 2410, MONTREAL, QC, H4Z 0A2
(514) 288-4321   *SIC 6411*
INSURANCE CENTRE INC, THE   *p630*
321 CONCESSION ST, KINGSTON, ON, K7K 2B9
(613) 544-5313   *SIC 6411*
INSURANCE COUNCIL OF BRITISH COLUMBIA   *p314*
1040 GEORGIA ST W SUITE 300, VANCOUVER, BC, V6E 4H1
(604) 688-0321   *SIC 6411*
INSURANCE GUYS INC, THE   *p98*
16612 109 AVE NW, EDMONTON, AB, T5P 1C2
(780) 448-2298   *SIC 6411*
INSURANCE PORTFOLIO INC   *p865*
10 MILNER BUSINESS CRT SUITE 800, SCARBOROUGH, ON, M1B 3C6
(416) 754-3910   *SIC 6411*
INSURANCE SEARCH BUREAU OF CANADA INC   *p684*
8160 PARKHILL DR, MILTON, ON, L9T 5V7
(905) 875-0556   *SIC 6411*
INSURANCE SUPERMARKET INC   *p554*
A101-8000 JANE ST, CONCORD, ON, L4K 5B8
(888) 818-1963   *SIC 6411*
INSURANCELAND INC   *p696*
2585 SKYMARK AVE UNIT 300, MISSISSAUGA, ON, L4W 4L5
(905) 238-0668   *SIC 6411*
INTACT INSURANCE COMPANY   *p286*
2955 VIRTUAL WAY SUITE 400, VANCOUVER, BC, V5M 4X6
(604) 891-5400   *SIC 6411*
INTEGRATED FINANCIAL GROUP INC   *p98*
10220 156 ST NW SUITE 200, EDMONTON, AB, T5P 2R1
(780) 454-6505   *SIC 6411*
INTER-GROUPE ASSURANCES INC   *p1272*
1175 AV LAVIGERIE BUREAU 475, QUEBEC, QC, G1V 4P1
(418) 682-5666   *SIC 6411*
INTERCITY EQUITY CORPORATION   *p321*
1847 BROADWAY W SUITE 104, VANCOUVER, BC, V6J 1Y6
(604) 731-6541   *SIC 6411*
INVESSA ASSURANCES ET SERVICES FINANCIERS INC   *p1086*
225 PROM DU CENTROPOLIS BUREAU 220, COTE SAINT-LUC, QC, H7T 0B3
(450) 781-6560   *SIC 6411*
INVESTISSEMENTS ALT2 INC   *p1374*
73 RUE QUEEN, SHERBROOKE, QC, J1M 0C9
(819) 566-8833   *SIC 6411*

IVES INSURANCE BROKERS LTD   *p570*
347 MAIDSTONE AVE E, ESSEX, ON, N8M 2K1
(519) 776-7371   *SIC 6411*
JARDINE LLOYD THOMPSON CANADA INC   *p314*
1111 GEORGIA ST W SUITE 1600, VANCOUVER, BC, V6E 4G2
(604) 682-4211   *SIC 6411*
JMHI INSURANCE GROUP INC   *p543*
550 RICHMOND ST, CHATHAM, ON, N7M 1R3
(226) 312-2020   *SIC 6411*
JOHNSON CORPORATION, THE   *p432*
10 FACTORY LANE, ST. JOHN'S, NL, A1C 6H5
(709) 737-1500   *SIC 6411*
JOHNSON INC   *p430*
95 ELIZABETH AVE, ST. JOHN'S, NL, A1B 1R6
(709) 737-1500   *SIC 6411*
JOHNSON INC   *p432*
10 FACTORY LANE, ST. JOHN'S, NL, A1C 6H5
(888) 737-1680   *SIC 6411*
JOHNSON INC   *p852*
1595 16TH AVE SUITE 700, RICHMOND HILL, ON, L4B 3S5
(905) 764-4900   *SIC 6411*
JOHNSTON, MEIER INSURANCE AGENCIES LTD   *p231*
22367 DEWDNEY TRUNK RD, MAPLE RIDGE, BC, V2X 3J4
(604) 467-4184   *SIC 6411*
JOHNSTON, RON INSURANCE LTD   *p809*
448 WEST ST N, ORILLIA, ON, L3V 5E8
(705) 325-6200   *SIC 6411*
JONES BROWN INC   *p963*
145 WELLINGTON ST W SUITE 1200, TORONTO, ON, M5J 1H8
(416) 408-1920   *SIC 6411*
JONES DESLAURIERS INSURANCE MANAGEMENT INC   *p696*
2375 SKYMARK AVE, MISSISSAUGA, ON, L4W 4Y6
(416) 259-4625   *SIC 6411*
JOSEPH D'ONOFRIO ET ASSOCIES INC   *p1346*
5045 RUE JEAN-TALON E BUREAU 201, SAINT-LEONARD, QC, H1S 0B6
(514) 328-2555   *SIC 6411*
JOSSLIN INSURANCE BROKERS LIMITED   *p752*
118 PEEL ST, NEW HAMBURG, ON, N3A 1E3
(519) 662-1644   *SIC 6411*
JRP GROUP INSURANCE SOLUTIONS INC   *p915*
2 LANSING SQ UNIT 207, TORONTO, ON, M2J 4P8
(647) 776-0906   *SIC 6411*
KANE, BRIAN INSURANCE AGENCIES LTD   *p23*
6815 8 ST NE SUITE 120, CALGARY, AB, T2E 7H7
(403) 276-8766   *SIC 6411*
KANETIX LTD   *p981*
360 ADELAIDE ST W SUITE 100, TORONTO, ON, M5V 1R7
(416) 599-9779   *SIC 6411*
KANNEGIETER-ZIMMERMAN INSURANCE BROKERS LIMITED   *p886*
131 ONTARIO ST, ST CATHARINES, ON, L2R 5J9
(905) 688-9170   *SIC 6411*
KENNEDY INSURANCE BROKERS INC   *p763*
414 FRASER ST, NORTH BAY, ON, P1B 3W9
(705) 472-5950   *SIC 6411*
KERNAGHAN, S J ADJUSTERS LIMITED   *p318*
1445 GEORGIA ST W SUITE 300, VANCOUVER, BC, V6G 2T3

(604) 688-5651   *SIC 6411*
KINGS MUTUAL INSURANCE COMPANY, THE   *p441*
220 COMMERCIAL ST, BERWICK, NS, B0P 1E0
(902) 538-3187   *SIC 6411*
KNIGHT ARCHER INSURANCE LTD   *p1416*
512 E VICTORIA AVE, REGINA, SK, S4N 0N7
(306) 569-2288   *SIC 6411*
KNOX INSURANCE BROKERS LTD   *p763*
705 CASSELLS ST, NORTH BAY, ON, P1B 4A3
(705) 474-4000   *SIC 6411*
LA CAPITALE - COMPAGNIE D'ASSURANCE   *p1269*
525 BOUL RENE-LEVESQUE E, QUEBEC, QC, G1R 5S9
(418) 266-1700   *SIC 6411*
LACKNER MCLENNAN INSURANCE LTD   *p635*
818 VICTORIA ST N, KITCHENER, ON, N2B 3C1
(519) 579-3330   *SIC 6411*
LANDMARK CANADA   *p801*
2902 SOUTH SHERIDAN WAY SUITE 10, OAKVILLE, ON, L6J 7L6
(905) 829-5511   *SIC 6411*
LANGELIER ASSURANCES INC   *p1313*
2500 BOUL CASAVANT O, SAINT-HYACINTHE, QC, J2S 7R8
(514) 745-8435   *SIC 6411*
LANKI INVESTIGATIONS INC   *p270*
9547 152 ST SUITE 113, SURREY, BC, V3R 5Y5
(604) 930-0399   *SIC 6411*
LAREAU - COURTIERS D'ASSURANCES INC   *p1242*
4 RTE 219 BUREAU 707, NAPIERVILLE, QC, J0J 1L0
(450) 245-3322   *SIC 6411*
LAWYERS PROFESSIONAL INDEMNITY COMPANY   *p935*
250 YONGE ST SUITE 3101, TORONTO, ON, M5B 2L7
(416) 598-5800   *SIC 6411*
LEBLANC, GERARD COURTIER D'ASSURANCES LTEE   *p1082*
6920 RTE LOUIS-S.-SAINT-LAURENT, COMPTON, QC, J0B 1L0
(819) 823-3311   *SIC 6411*
LEDOUX, LEW & PATTERSON INSURANCE BROKERS LIMITED   *p732*
115 MATHESON BLVD W SUITE 202, MISSISSAUGA, ON, L5R 3L1
(905) 890-1877   *SIC 6411*
LEDOUX, LEW & PATTERSON INSURANCE BROKERS LTD   *p672*
7030 WOODBINE AVE SUITE 100, MARKHAM, ON, L3R 6G2
(905) 944-1188   *SIC 6411*
LEFEBVRE, PAYETTE ET ASSOCIES INC   *p1318*
170 RUE SAINT-JACQUES, SAINT-JEAN-SUR-RICHELIEU, QC, J3B 2K5
(514) 856-7751   *SIC 6411*
LEGROW, CAL INSURANCE LIMITED   *p430*
189 HIGGINS LINE, ST. JOHN'S, NL, A1B 4N4
(709) 722-3282   *SIC 6411*
LEIBEL INSURANCE GROUP CORP   *p101*
17415 102 AVE NW SUITE 102, EDMONTON, AB, T5S 1J8
(780) 484-8880   *SIC 6411*
LEMIEUX ASSURANCES INC   *p1137*
1610 BOUL ALPHONSE-DESJARDINS, LEVIS, QC, G6V 0H1
(418) 835-0939   *SIC 6411*
LEMIEUX ASSURANCES INC   *p1306*
186 RUE COMMERCIALE, SAINT-HENRI-DE-LEVIS, QC, G0R 3E0
(418) 882-0801   *SIC 6411*
LGM FINANCIAL SERVICES INC   *p314*
1021 HASTINGS ST W UNIT 400, VAN-

COUVER, BC, V6E 0C3

(604) 806-5300   *SIC* 6411

LLOYD SADD INSURANCE BROKERS LTD *p97*

10240 124 ST NW UNIT 700, EDMONTON, AB, T5N 3W6

(780) 483-4544   *SIC* 6411

LMG INSURANCE BROKERS LTD *p212*

2640 BEVERLY ST SUITE 200, DUNCAN, BC, V9L 5C7

(250) 748-3200   *SIC* 6411

LMS PROLINK LTD *p946*

480 UNIVERSITY AVE SUITE 800, TORONTO, ON, M5G 1V2

(416) 595-7484   *SIC* 6411

LOGIQ3 CORP *p939*

60 ADELAIDE ST E UNIT 1300, TORONTO, ON, M5C 3E4

(416) 340-7435   *SIC* 6411

LONDON DRUGS INSURANCE SERVICES LTD *p260*

5971 NO. 3 RD, RICHMOND, BC, V6X 3Y6

(604) 821-0808   *SIC* 6411

LONDON LIFE, COMPAGNIE D'ASSURANCE-VIE *p875*

2075 KENNEDY RD SUITE 300, SCARBOROUGH, ON, M1T 3V3

SIC 6411

LONDON LIFE, COMPAGNIE D'ASSURANCE-VIE *p1197*

2001 BOUL ROBERT-BOURASSA UNITE 800, MONTREAL, QC, H3A 2A6

(514) 350-5500   *SIC* 6411

LOYALIST INSURANCE BROKERS LIMITED *p478*

911 GOLF LINKS RD SUITE 111, ANCASTER, ON, L9K 1H9

(905) 648-6767   *SIC* 6411

LUNDGREN & YOUNG INSURANCE LTD *p68*

9705 HORTON RD SW SUITE 200C, CALGARY, AB, T2V 2X5

(403) 253-1980   *SIC* 6411

LUSSIER DALE PARIZEAU INC *p1269*

900 BOUL RENE-LEVESQUE E BUREAU 700, QUEBEC, QC, G1R 2B5

(418) 647-1111   *SIC* 6411

M.E POWELL INSURANCE BROKERS LTD *p801*

349 DAVIS RD, OAKVILLE, ON, L6J 2X2

(905) 844-3629   *SIC* 6411

MACDONALD CHISHOLM INC *p471*

396 MAIN ST SUITE 100, YARMOUTH, NS, B5A 1E9

(902) 742-3531   *SIC* 6411

MACDONALD CHISHOLM INCORPORATED *p459*

6 MASTERS AVE, KENTVILLE, NS, B4N 2N6

(902) 678-6277   *SIC* 6411

MACLEOD-LORWAY FINANCIAL GROUP LIMITED *p467*

215 CHARLOTTE ST, SYDNEY, NS, B1P 1C4

(902) 539-6666   *SIC* 6411

MAGNA INSURANCE CORP *p74*

5 RICHARD WAY SW UNIT 104, CALGARY, AB, T3E 7M8

(403) 930-0466   *SIC* 6411

MAGNES GROUP INC, THE *p801*

1540 CORNWALL RD SUITE 100, OAKVILLE, ON, L6J 7W5

(905) 845-9793   *SIC* 6411

MAHONE INSURANCE GROUP INC *p462*

201 MAIN ST, MAHONE BAY, NS, B0J 2E0

(902) 624-9600   *SIC* 6411

MAINWAY HUNTER CREIGHTON INSURANCE INC *p718*

101 QUEEN ST S SUITE 100, MISSISSAUGA, ON, L5M 1K7

(905) 826-3215   *SIC* 6411

MAISONNEUVE LALONDE SOULIGNY COURTIERS D'ASSURANCE LTEE *p888*

GD, ST ISIDORE, ON, K0C 2B0

(613) 524-2174   *SIC* 6411

MANN, R. E. BROKERS LTD *p881*

28 COLBORNE ST N, SIMCOE, ON, N3Y 3T9

(519) 426-2551   *SIC* 6411

MANTHA INSURANCE BROKERS LTD *p1001*

295 MONTREAL RD, VANIER, ON, K1L 6B8

(613) 746-1450   *SIC* 6411

MANTHA REAL ESTATE & INSURANCE INC *p1001*

295 MONTREAL RD, VANIER, ON, K1L 6B8

(613) 830-3000   *SIC* 6411

MANULIFE FINANCIAL CORPORATION *p929*

200 BLOOR ST E, TORONTO, ON, M4W 1E5

(416) 926-3000   *SIC* 6411

MANULIFE SECURITIES INSURANCE *p774*

4101 YONGE ST SUITE 700, NORTH YORK, ON, M2P 1N6

(416) 218-8707   *SIC* 6411

MARSH ADJUSTMENT BUREAU LIMITED *p439*

1550 BEDFORD HWY SUITE 711, BEDFORD, NS, B4A 1E6

(902) 469-3537   *SIC* 6411

MARSH CANADA LIMITED *p53*

222 3 AVE SW SUITE 1100, CALGARY, AB, T2P 0B4

(403) 290-7900   *SIC* 6411

MARSH CANADA LIMITED *p307*

550 BURRARD ST SUITE 800, VANCOUVER, BC, V6C 2K1

(604) 685-3765   *SIC* 6411

MARSH CANADA LIMITED *p964*

120 BREMNER BLVD SUITE 800, TORONTO, ON, M5J 0A8

(416) 868-2600   *SIC* 6411

MARSH CANADA LIMITED *p964*

120 BREMNER BLVD SUITE 800, TORONTO, ON, M5J 0A8

(416) 868-2600   *SIC* 6411

MARSH CANADA LIMITED *p1198*

1981 AV MCGILL COLLEGE BUREAU 820, MONTREAL, QC, H3A 3T4

(514) 285-4700   *SIC* 6411

MARSH PRIVATE CLIENT SERVICES *p101*

17420 STONY PLAIN RD NW SUITE 100, EDMONTON, AB, T5S 1K6

SIC 6411

MARSHALL & WOODWARK INSURANCE BROKERS LTD *p579*

320 NORTH QUEEN ST SUITE 132, ETOBICOKE, ON, M9C 5K4

(416) 626-7831   *SIC* 6411

MARTIN MERRY & REID LIMITED *p942*

3 CHURCH ST SUITE 404, TORONTO, ON, M5E 1M2

(416) 366-3333   *SIC* 6411

MASS INSURANCE BROKER *p1206*

630 BOUL RENE-LEVESQUE O BUREAU 2500, MONTREAL, QC, H3B 1S6

(514) 925-3222   *SIC* 6411

MASTERS INSURANCE LIMITED *p555*

7501 KEELE ST SUITE 400, CONCORD, ON, L4K 1Y2

(905) 738-4164   *SIC* 6411

MASTERS LIFE INSURANCE AGENTS LIMITED *p555*

7501 KEELE ST SUITE 400, CONCORD, ON, L4K 1Y2

SIC 6411

MCAVOY BELAN & CAMPBELL INSURANCE AND FINANCIAL SERVICES LTD *p846*

350 KING ST, PORT COLBORNE, ON, L3K 4H3

(905) 834-3666   *SIC* 6411

MCCAM INSURANCE BROKERS LTD *p814*

292 KING ST W, OSHAWA, ON, L1J 2J9

(905) 579-0111   *SIC* 6411

MCDONALD & BYCHKOWSKI LTD *p125*

1430 91 ST SW SUITE 201, EDMONTON,

AB, T6X 1M5

(780) 424-2727   *SIC* 6411

MCDOUGALL INSURANCE BROKERS LIMITED *p491*

199 FRONT ST SUITE 401, BELLEVILLE, ON, K8N 5H5

(613) 966-7001   *SIC* 6411

MCFARLAN ROWLANDS INSURANCE BROKERS INC *p656*

503 YORK ST, LONDON, ON, N6B 1R4

(519) 679-5440   *SIC* 6411

MCLEAN & DICKEY LTD *p809*

390 LACLIE ST, ORILLIA, ON, L3V 4P5

(705) 325-4461   *SIC* 6411

MCLEAN & DICKEY LTD *p809*

174 WEST ST S, ORILLIA, ON, L3V 6L4

(705) 325-4461   *SIC* 6411

MCLEAN HALLMARK INSURANCE GROUP LTD *p672*

10 KONRAD CRES, MARKHAM, ON, L3R 8T7

(416) 364-4000   *SIC* 6411

MCLEAN HALLMARK INSURANCE GROUP LTD *p934*

184 FRONT ST E SUITE 601, TORONTO, ON, M5A 4N3

(416) 364-4000   *SIC* 6411

MCLEAN INSURANCE PROTECTION TEAM INC *p839*

58 FOSTER ST, PERTH, ON, K7H 1S1

(613) 267-5100   *SIC* 6411

MCTAVISH INSURANCE AGENCIES LTD *p337*

4430 CHATTERTON WAY, VICTORIA, BC, V8X 5J2

(905) 898-0361   *SIC* 6411

MDM INSURANCE SERVICES INC *p601*

834 GORDON ST, GUELPH, ON, N1G 1Y7

(519) 837-1531   *SIC* 6411

MEADWELL MOWAT FENNELL *p1014*

413 DUNDAS ST E, WHITBY, ON, L1N 2J2

(905) 668-3579   *SIC* 6411

MEDI-QUOTE INSURANCE BROKERS INC *p362*

505 PANDORA AVE W, WINNIPEG, MB, R2C 1M8

(204) 947-9210   *SIC* 6411

MEGSON FITZPATRICK INC *p333*

3561 SHELBOURNE ST, VICTORIA, BC, V8P 4G8

(250) 595-5212   *SIC* 6411

MEIER INSURANCE AGENCIES LTD *p237*

602 TWELFTH ST, NEW WESTMINSTER, BC, V3M 4J2

(604) 777-9999   *SIC* 6411

MELOCHE MONNEX FINANCIAL SERVICES INC *p90*

10115 100A ST NW SUITE 600, EDMONTON, AB, T5J 2W2

(780) 429-1112   *SIC* 6411

MELOCHE MONNEX FINANCIAL SERVICES INC *p672*

101 MCNABB ST, MARKHAM, ON, L3R 4H8

(416) 484-1112   *SIC* 6411

MERCER (CANADA) LIMITED *p964*

120 BREMNER BLVD SUITE 800, TORONTO, ON, M5J 0A8

(416) 868-2000   *SIC* 6411

MERIT INSURANCE BROKERS INC *p765*

111 GORDON BAKER RD SUITE 100, NORTH YORK, ON, M2H 3R1

(416) 497-5556   *SIC* 6411

METROPOLITAN LIFE INSURANCE COMPANY OF CANADA *p563*

55 WATER ST W SUITE 100, CORNWALL, ON, K6J 1A1

SIC 6411

MEYER, GENE INSURANCE AGENCIES LTD *p706*

315 OXBOW CRES, MISSISSAUGA, ON, L4Z 2S4

(905) 890-0998   *SIC* 6411

MFXCHANGE HOLDINGS INC *p777*

225 DUNCAN MILL RD SUITE 320, NORTH

YORK, ON, M3B 3K9

(416) 385-4800   *SIC* 6411

MHK INSURANCE INC *p96*

12316 107 AVE NW, EDMONTON, AB, T5M 1Z1

(780) 454-9363   *SIC* 6411

MILLENNIUM INSURANCE CORPORATION *p161*

340 SIOUX RD, SHERWOOD PARK, AB, T8A 3X6

(780) 467-1500   *SIC* 6411

MILLER INSURANCE BROKERS INC *p629*

1115 SUTTON ST, KINCARDINE, ON, N2Z 2C5

SIC 6411

MILNE, D. R. & COMPANY LTD *p379*

330 ST MARY AVE SUITE 210, WINNIPEG, MB, R3C 3Z5

(204) 949-7000   *SIC* 6411

MINET INC *p1206*

700 RUE DE LA GAUCHETIERE O BUREAU 1800, MONTREAL, QC, H3B 0A5

(514) 288-2273   *SIC* 6411

MISSISQUOI COMPAGNIE D'ASSURANCE, LA *p1273*

1175 AV LAVIGERIE BUREAU 30, QUEBEC, QC, G1V 4P1

SIC 6411

MITCHELL & ABBOTT GROUP INSURANCE BROKERS LIMITED, *p616*

2000 GARTH ST SUITE 101, HAMILTON, ON, L9B 0C1

(905) 385-6383   *SIC* 6411

MITCHELL MCCONNELL INSURANCE LIMITED *p412*

660 ROTHESAY AVE SUITE 344, SAINT JOHN, NB, E2H 2H4

(506) 634-7200   *SIC* 6411

MITCHELL SANDHAM INC *p946*

438 UNIVERSITY AVE SUITE 2000, TORONTO, ON, M5G 2K8

(416) 862-1750   *SIC* 6411

MLS INSURANCE BROKERS INC *p888*

4741 ST CATHERINE ST, ST ISIDORE, ON, K0C 2B0

(613) 524-2174   *SIC* 6411

MOBILE INSURANCE SERVICE LTD *p85*

11356 119 ST NW UNIT 201, EDMONTON, AB, T5G 2X4

(780) 477-8838   *SIC* 6411

MONKMAN GRACIE & JOHNSTON *p841*

261 GEORGE ST N, PETERBOROUGH, ON, K9J 3G9

(705) 742-8863   *SIC* 6411

MOONEY INSURANCE AGENCY LTD *p154*

4910 45 ST, RED DEER, AB, T4N 1K6

SIC 6411

MOTORCYCLE INSURANCE BROKERS INC *p853*

105 WEST BEAVER CREEK RD SUITE 1, RICHMOND HILL, ON, L4B 1C6

(905) 764-7868   *SIC* 6411

MP2B INC *p1084*

1600A BOUL SAINT-MARTIN E BUREAU 110, COTE SAINT-LUC, QC, H7G 4R8

(450) 668-5555   *SIC* 6411

MULTI-SECTOR NON PROFIT *p904*

105 COMMERCE VALLEY DR W UNIT 310, THORNHILL, ON, L3T 7W3

(905) 889-6200   *SIC* 6411

MUNICH COMPAGNIE DE REASSURANCE, LA *p1206*

630 BOUL RENE-LEVESQUE O BUREAU 2630, MONTREAL, QC, H3B 1S6

(514) 866-6825   *SIC* 6411

MUNN'S INSURANCE LIMITED *p430*

121 KELSEY DR SUITE 100, ST. JOHN'S, NL, A1B 0L2

(709) 726-8627   *SIC* 6411

MURRICK INSURANCE SERVICES LTD *p326*

1045 HOWE ST SUITE 925, VANCOUVER, BC, V6Z 2A9

(604) 688-5158   *SIC* 6411

MY INSURANCE BROKER HAMILTON CORP *p608*
163 CENTENNIAL PKY N SUITE 2, HAMILTON, ON, L8E 1H8
(905) 528-2886   *SIC* 6411

NACORA INSURANCE BROKERS LTD *p732*
77 FOSTER CRES, MISSISSAUGA, ON, L5R 0K1
(905) 507-1551   *SIC* 6411

NATIONAL BROKERS INSURANCE SERVICES INC *p741*
6725 EDWARDS BLVD, MISSISSAUGA, ON, L5T 2V9
SIC 6411

NAVIGATORS INSURANCE BROKERS LTD *p768*
4 LANSING SQ SUITE 100, NORTH YORK, ON, M2J 5A2
SIC 6411

NEWMAN, OLIVER & MCCARTEN INSURANCE BROKERS LTD *p539*
35 FRONT ST N, CAMPBELLFORD, ON, K0L 1L0
SIC 6411

NEZIOL INSURANCE BROKERS LTD *p514*
53 CHARING CROSS ST SUITE 1, BRANTFORD, ON, N3R 7K9
(519) 759-2110   *SIC* 6411

NORTHBRIDGE FINANCIAL CORPORATION *p955*
105 ADELAIDE ST W SUITE 700, TORONTO, ON, M5H 1P9
(416) 350-4400   *SIC* 6411

NORTHBRIDGE FINANCIAL CORPORATION *p1206*
1000 RUE DE LA GAUCHETIERE O, MONTREAL, QC, H3B 4W5
(514) 843-1111   *SIC* 6411

NORTHBRIDGE INDEMNITY INSURANCE CORPORATION *p329*
595 BURRARD ST SUITE 1500, VANCOUVER, BC, V7X 1G4
(604) 683-5511   *SIC* 6411

NORTHBRIDGE INDEMNITY INSURANCE CORPORATION *p955*
105 ADELAIDE ST W UNIT 700, TORONTO, ON, M5H 1P9
(855) 620-6262   *SIC* 6411

NTI INSURANCE BROKERS *p673*
800 DENISON ST SUITE 200, MARKHAM, ON, L3R 5M9
SIC 6411

OFFICE D'INVESTISSEMENT DES REGIMES DE PENSIONS DU SECTEUR PUBLIC *p1207*
1250 BOUL RENE-LEVESQUE O BUREAU 900, MONTREAL, QC, H3B 4W8
(514) 937-2772   *SIC* 6411

OGILVY & OGILVY INC *p1402*
4115 RUE SHERBROOKE O BUREAU 500, WESTMOUNT, QC, H3Z 1K9
(514) 932-8660   *SIC* 6411

OMNI INSURANCE BROKERS *p654*
560 WELLINGTON ST, LONDON, ON, N6A 3R4
(519) 667-1100   *SIC* 6411

ONLIA HOLDINGS INC *p934*
351 KING ST E SUITE 801, TORONTO, ON, M5A 1L1
(416) 479-2260   *SIC* 6411

ONTARIO EAST INSURANCE AGENCY/ BFG FINANCIAL *p769*
1210 SHEPPARD AVE E SUITE 401, NORTH YORK, ON, M2K 1E3
(416) 498-1444   *SIC* 6411

ONTARIO SCHOOL BOARDS' INSURANCE EXCHANGE *p604*
91 WESTMOUNT RD, GUELPH, ON, N1H 5J2
(519) 767-2182   *SIC* 6411

ONTARIO WEST INSURANCE BROKERS *p657*
1069 WELLINGTON RD SUITE 208, LONDON, ON, N6E 2H6

(519) 657-1400   *SIC* 6411

OPEN ACCESS LIMITED *p956*
1 RICHMOND ST W SUITE 800, TORONTO, ON, M5H 3W4
(416) 364-4444   *SIC* 6411

OPERATING ENGINEERS BENEFITS & PENSION PLANS *p189*
4333 LEDGER AVE SUITE 402, BURNABY, BC, V5G 4G9
(604) 299-8341   *SIC* 6411

OPTIMUM REASSURANCE INC *p1198*
425 BOUL DE MAISONNEUVE O BUREAU 1200, MONTREAL, QC, H3A 3G5
(514) 288-1900   *SIC* 6411

OPTIMUM SOCIETE D'ASSURANCE INC *p1198*
425 BOUL DE MAISONNEUVE O BUREAU 1500, MONTREAL, QC, H3A 3G5
(514) 288-8711   *SIC* 6411

ORACLE INSURANCE RISK MANAGEMENT SERVICES INC *p557*
100 DRUMLIN CIRCLE, CONCORD, ON, L4K 3E6
(905) 660-9740   *SIC* 6411

ORDRE DES DENTISTES DU QUEBEC *p1207*
800 BOUL RENE-LEVESQUE O BUREAU 1640, MONTREAL, QC, H3B 1X9
(514) 281-0300   *SIC* 6411

ORR INSURANCE BROKERS INC *p896*
50 COBOURG ST, STRATFORD, ON, N5A 3E5
(519) 271-4340   *SIC* 6411

OSBORN & LANGE INC *p1117*
17001 RTE TRANSCANADIENNE BUREAU 300, KIRKLAND, QC, H9H 0A7
(514) 694-4161   *SIC* 6411

OSTIC INSURANCE BROKERS LIMITED *p590*
210 ST PATRICK ST W, FERGUS, ON, N1M 1L7
(519) 843-2540   *SIC* 6411

P P I FINANCIAL GROUP (EASTERN) LTD *p982*
200 FRONT ST W SUITE 2400, TORONTO, ON, M5V 3K5
(416) 494-7707   *SIC* 6411

PACIFIC INSURANCE BROKER INC *p853*
120 EAST BEAVER CREEK RD SUITE 101, RICHMOND HILL, ON, L4B 4V1
(416) 494-1268   *SIC* 6411

PAFCO INSURANCE *p1052*
7100 RUE JEAN-TALON E BUREAU 300, ANJOU, QC, H1M 3S3
(514) 351-8711   *SIC* 6411

PAISLEY-MANOR INSURANCE BROKERS INC *p777*
1446 DON MILLS RD SUITE 110, NORTH YORK, ON, M3B 3N3
(416) 510-1177   *SIC* 6411

PALMER ATLANTIC INSURANCE LTD *p403*
538 MAIN ST UNIT 1, HARTLAND, NB, E7P 2N5
(506) 375-7500   *SIC* 6411

PARK GEORGIA INSURANCE AGENCIES LTD *p295*
180 PENDER ST E UNIT 200, VANCOUVER, BC, V6A 1T3
(604) 688-2323   *SIC* 6411

PARTNERS INDEMNITY INSURANCE BROKERS LTD *p940*
10 ADELAIDE ST E SUITE 400, TORONTO, ON, M5C 1J3
(416) 366-5243   *SIC* 6411

PBL INSURANCE LIMITED *p1021*
150 OUELLETTE PL SUITE 100, WINDSOR, ON, N8X 1L9
(519) 254-1633   *SIC* 6411

PEACE HILLS GENERAL INSURANCE COMPANY *p90*
10709 JASPER AVE NW SUITE 300, EDMONTON, AB, T5J 3N3
(780) 424-3986   *SIC* 6411

PEACOCK VANDERHOUT & VANDYK IN-

SURANCE BROKERS LTD *p882*
HWY 20 VILLAGE SQUARE MALL, SMITHVILLE, ON, L0R 2A0
(905) 957-2333   *SIC* 6411

PEAK REALTY LTD *p1009*
410 CONESTOGO RD SUITE 210, WATERLOO, ON, N2L 4E2
(519) 747-0231   *SIC* 6411

PEARSON DUNN INSURANCE INC *p893*
435 MCNEILLY RD SUITE 103, STONEY CREEK, ON, L8E 5E3
(905) 575-1122   *SIC* 6411

PENTAGON-RAYMOND INSURANCE BROKERS INC *p810*
3009 ST. JOSEPH BLVD UNIT 101, ORLEANS, ON, K1E 1E1
(613) 837-1060   *SIC* 6411

PERMA INSURANCE CONTINENTAL INC *p24*
901 CENTRE ST NW SUITE 200, CALGARY, AB, T2E 2P6
(403) 230-0808   *SIC* 6411

PERPETUAL INSURANCE SERVICES LTD *p290*
3479 FRASER ST SUITE 3473, VANCOUVER, BC, V5V 4C3
(604) 606-8118   *SIC* 6411

PETHEALTH INC *p802*
710 DORVAL DR SUITE 400, OAKVILLE, ON, L6K 3V7
(905) 842-2615   *SIC* 6411

PHILPOT & DELGATY LTD *p909*
800 VICTORIA AVE E, THUNDER BAY, ON, P7C 0A2
(807) 623-9022   *SIC* 6411

PIQUETTE, ROGER L. INSURANCE AGENCY INC *p899*
1210 LASALLE BLVD, SUDBURY, ON, P3A 1Y5
(705) 524-5755   *SIC* 6411

PLANDIRECT INSURANCE SERVICES INC *p768*
211 CONSUMERS RD SUITE 200, NORTH YORK, ON, M2J 4G8
(416) 490-0072   *SIC* 6411

PLANT HOPE ADJUSTERS LTD *p409*
16 CORONATION DR, MONCTON, NB, E1E 2X1
(506) 853-8500   *SIC* 6411

PLATFORM INSURANCE MANAGEMENT INC *p940*
20 TORONTO ST SUITE 440, TORONTO, ON, M5C 2B8
(416) 434-4322   *SIC* 6411

PMA ASSURANCES INC *p1112*
632 6E AV, GRAND-MERE, QC, G9T 2H5
(819) 538-8626   *SIC* 6411

PMA ASSURANCES INC *p1388*
6405 RUE CHRISTOPHE-PELISSIER, TROIS-RIVIERES, QC, G9A 5C9
(819) 379-3508   *SIC* 6411

PMT ROY ASSURANCE ET SERVICES FINANCIERS INC *p1262*
955 BOUL PIERRE-BERTRAND BUREAU 140, QUEBEC, QC, G1M 2E8
(418) 780-0808   *SIC* 6411

PORTAGE LA PRAIRIE MUTUAL INSURANCE CO, THE *p355*
749 SASKATCHEWAN AVE E, PORTAGE LA PRAIRIE, MB, R1N 0L3
(204) 857-3415   *SIC* 6411

PORTIA LEARNING CENTRE INC. *p831*
1770 COURTWOOD CRES SUITE 201, OTTAWA, ON, K2C 2B5
(613) 221-9777   *SIC* 6411

PREFERRED INSURANCE GROUP LIMITED *p659*
778 WHARNCLIFFE RD S, LONDON, ON, N6J 2N4
(519) 661-0200   *SIC* 6411

PRIMERICA FINANCIAL SERVICES LTD *p557*
8555 JANE ST SUITE 101, CONCORD, ON, L4K 5N9

(416) 495-0200   *SIC* 6411

PRIMERICA FINANCIAL SERVICES LTD *p887*
251 ST. PAUL ST W SUITE 1, ST CATHARINES, ON, L2S 2E4
(905) 687-9374   *SIC* 6411

PRIMERICA FINANCIAL SERVICES LTD *p1015*
1615 DUNDAS ST E SUITE 200, WHITBY, ON, L1N 2L1
(905) 436-8499   *SIC* 6411

PRINGLE INSURANCE BROKERS *p212*
380 TRUNK RD UNIT 1, DUNCAN, BC, V9L 2P6
(250) 748-3242   *SIC* 6411

PRO MUTUEL L'ABITIBIENNE, SOCIETE MUTUELLE D'ASSURANCE GENERALE *p1046*
282 1RE AV E, AMOS, QC, J9T 1H3
(819) 732-1531   *SIC* 6411

PRO-CLAIM RESTORATION LTD *p261*
5811 CEDARBRIDGE WAY UNIT 150, RICHMOND, BC, V6X 2A8
(604) 276-2483   *SIC* 6411

PROGRAMMED INSURANCE BROKERS INC *p568*
49 INDUSTRIAL DR, ELMIRA, ON, N3B 3B1
(519) 669-1631   *SIC* 6411

PROLINK BROKER NETWORK INC *p947*
480 UNIVERSITY AVE SUITE 800, TORONTO, ON, M5G 1V2
(416) 595-7484   *SIC* 6411

PROMUTUEL BEAUCE SOCIETE MUTUELLE D'ASSURANCE GENERALE *p1055*
650 BOUL RENAULT, BEAUCEVILLE, QC, G5X 3P2
(418) 774-3621   *SIC* 6411

PROMUTUEL BEAUCE-ETCHEMINS, SOCIETE MUTUELLE D'ASSURANCE GENERALE *p1055*
650 BOUL RENAULT, BEAUCEVILLE, QC, G5X 3P2
SIC 6411

PROMUTUEL DEUX-MONTAGNES, SOCIETE MUTUELLE D'ASSURANCE GENERALE *p1301*
200 RUE DUBOIS, SAINT-EUSTACHE, QC, J7P 4W9
(450) 623-5774   *SIC* 6411

PROMUTUEL DU LAC AU FJORD *p1045*
790 AV DU PONT S, ALMA, QC, G8B 2V4
(418) 662-6595   *SIC* 6411

PROMUTUEL DU LAC AU FJORD *p1113*
11 RUE COMMERCIALE, HEBERTVILLE, QC, G8N 1N3
(418) 344-1565   *SIC* 6411

PROMUTUEL DU LAC AU FLEUVE, SOCIETE MUTUELLE D'ASSURANCE GENERALE *p1054*
951 BOUL MONSEIGNEUR-DE LAVAL, BAIE-SAINT-PAUL, QC, G3Z 2W3
(418) 435-2793   *SIC* 6411

PROMUTUEL L'OUTAOUAIS SOCIETE MUTUELLE D'ASSURANCE GENERALE *p1291*
629 321 RTE N RR 3, SAINT-ANDRE-AVELLIN, QC, J0V 1W0
(819) 983-6141   *SIC* 6411

PROMUTUEL LOTNINIERE SOCIETE MUTUELLE D'ASSURANCE GENERALE *p1133*
175 BOUL LAURIER RR 1, LAURIER-STATION, QC, G0S 1N0
(418) 728-4110   *SIC* 6411

PROMUTUEL MONTMAGNY-L'ISLET, SOCIETE MUTUELLE D'ASSURANCE GENERALE *p1160*
124 BOUL TACHE O, MONTMAGNY, QC, G5V 3A5
(418) 248-7940   *SIC* 6411

PROMUTUEL MONTS ET RIVES, SOCIETE MUTUELLE D'ASSURANCE GENERALE

p1125
5240 BOUL DES VETERANS, LAC-MEGANTIC, QC, G6B 2G5
(819) 583-4555 *SIC* 6411

PROMUTUEL PORTNEUF-CHAMPLAIN SOCIETE, MUTUAL D'ASSURANCE GENERALE *p1294*
257 BOUL DU CENTENAIRE RR 1, SAINT-BASILE, QC, G0A 3G0
(418) 329-3330 *SIC* 6411

PROMUTUEL VAUDREUIL-SOULANGES, SOCIETE MUTUELLE D'ASSURANCE GENERALE *p1135*
245 338 RTE, LES COTEAUX, QC, J7X 1A2
(450) 267-9297 *SIC* 6411

PROTECTORS GROUP INSURANCE AGENCIES (1985) LTD, THE *p842*
215 GEORGE ST N, PETERBOROUGH, ON, K9J 3G7
(705) 748-5181 *SIC* 6411

PS TRAVEL INSURANCE BROKERS INC *p1033*
8001 WESTON RD SUITE 300, WOODBRIDGE, ON, L4L 9C8
(416) 798-8001 *SIC* 6411

PSHCP ADMINISTRATION AUTHORITY *p824*
100 SPARKS ST SUITE 1010, OTTAWA, ON, K1P 5B7
(613) 565-1762 *SIC* 6411

PURVES REDMOND LIMITED *p966*
70 UNIVERSITY AVE SUITE 400, TORONTO, ON, M5J 2M4
(416) 362-4246 *SIC* 6411

RACINE & CHAMBERLAND INC *p1170*
4001 BOUL CREMAZIE E BUREAU 100, MONTREAL, QC, H1Z 2L2
(514) 722-3501 *SIC* 6411

RAI INSURANCE BROKERS LTD *p674*
140 RENFREW DR SUITE 230, MARKHAM, ON, L3R 6B3
(905) 475-5800 *SIC* 6411

RAND & FOWLER INSURANCE LTD *p287*
2323 BOUNDARY RD SUITE 101, VANCOUVER, BC, V5M 4V8
(604) 298-4222 *SIC* 6411

RAND AND FOWLER INSURANCE COQUITLAM LTD *p198*
2918 GLEN DR UNIT 103, COQUITLAM, BC, V3B 2P5
(604) 941-3212 *SIC* 6411

RBC INSURANCE COMPANY OF CANADA *p726*
6880 FINANCIAL DR SUITE 200, MISSISSAUGA, ON, L5N 7Y5
(905) 949-3663 *SIC* 6411

RDA INC *p1033*
290 ROWNTREE DAIRY RD, WOODBRIDGE, ON, L4L 9J7
(905) 652-8680 *SIC* 6411

RE/MAX CENTRAL *p41*
2411 4 ST NW SUITE 206, CALGARY, AB, T2M 2Z8
(403) 241-8199 *SIC* 6411

RE/MAX QUEBEC INC *p1085*
1500 RUE CUNARD, COTE SAINT-LUC, QC, H7S 2B7
(450) 668-7743 *SIC* 6411

RED RIVER VALLEY MUTUAL INSURANCE COMPANY *p345*
245 CENTRE AVE E, ALTONA, MB, R0G 0B0
(204) 324-6434 *SIC* 6411

REIDER INSURANCE SERVICES *p370*
1399 MCPHILLIPS ST, WINNIPEG, MB, R2V 3C4
(204) 334-4319 *SIC* 6411

RELIANCE INSURANCE AGENCIES LTD *p186*
4853 HASTINGS ST SUITE 100, BURNABY, BC, V5C 2L1
(604) 255-4616 *SIC* 6411

RESIDENCE DU COLLEGE CRP (2014) INC *p1297*

1390 RUE NOTRE-DAME, SAINT-CESAIRE, QC, J0L 1T0
(450) 816-1390 *SIC* 6411

RHEAUME, MICHEL & ASSOCIES LTEE *p1177*
800-1611 BOUL CREMAZIE E, MONTREAL, QC, H2M 2P2
(514) 329-3333 *SIC* 6411

RHODES & WILLIAMS LIMITED *p832*
1050 MORRISON DR, OTTAWA, ON, K2H 8K7
(613) 226-6590 *SIC* 6411

RIEGER *p58*
808 4 AVE SW SUITE 600, CALGARY, AB, T2P 3E8
(403) 537-7642 *SIC* 6411

RISKTECH INSURANCE SERVICES INC *p98*
300-14727 87 AVE NW, EDMONTON, AB, T5R 4E5
(780) 732-7129 *SIC* 6411

RIVET, J. G. BROKERS LIMITED *p898*
229 MAIN ST SUITE 1, STURGEON FALLS, ON, P2B 1P5
(705) 753-0130 *SIC* 6411

ROBERTS, WALTER INSURANCE BROKERS INC *p853*
110 WEST BEAVER CREEK RD SUITE 22, RICHMOND HILL, ON, L4B 1J9
(905) 764-8061 *SIC* 6411

ROBERTSON EADIE & ASSOCIATES *p802*
41 MORDEN RD SUITE 210, OAKVILLE, ON, L6K 3W6
(905) 338-7002 *SIC* 6411

ROBERTSON INSURANCE AND FINANCIAL SERVICES INC *p655*
431 RICHMOND ST SUITE 300, LONDON, ON, N6A 6E2
(519) 680-3111 *SIC* 6411

ROCHEBANYAN *p596*
5310 CANOTEK RD SUITE 10, GLOUCESTER, ON, K1J 9N5
(613) 749-5027 *SIC* 6411

ROCHEFORT, PERRON, BILLETTE INC *p1365*
1000 BOUL MONSEIGNEUR-LANGLOIS BUREAU 300, SALABERRY-DE-VALLEYFIELD, QC, J6S 0J7
(514) 395-8703 *SIC* 6411

ROGERS INSURANCE LTD *p32*
1331 MACLEOD TRL SE SUITE 800, CALGARY, AB, T2G 0K3
(403) 296-2400 *SIC* 6411

ROMEO BESSETTE & FILS INC *p1317*
815 RUE PLANTE, SAINT-JEAN-SUR-RICHELIEU, QC, J3A 1M8
(450) 359-1471 *SIC* 6411

ROUGHLEY INSURANCE BROKERS LTD *p812*
1000 SIMCOE ST N SUITE 205, OSHAWA, ON, L1G 4W4
(905) 576-7770 *SIC* 6411

ROYAL & SUN ALLIANCE INSURANCE COMPANY OF CANADA *p1199*
1001 BOUL DE MAISONNEUVE O BUREAU 1004, MONTREAL, QC, H3A 3C8
(514) 844-1116 *SIC* 6411

ROYAL & SUN ALLIANCE INSURANCE COMPANY OF CANADA *p1271*
2475 BOUL LAURIER, QUEBEC, QC, G1T 1C4
(418) 622-2040 *SIC* 6411

ROZON INSURANCE BROKERS LTD *p643*
150 MAIN ST N, LANCASTER, ON, K0C 1N0
(613) 347-7600 *SIC* 6411

RRJ INSURANCE GROUP LIMITED *p768*
2450 VICTORIA PARK AVE SUITE 700, NORTH YORK, ON, M2J 4A1
(416) 636-4544 *SIC* 6411

RUSSELL INVESTMENTS CANADA LIMITED *p987*
100 KING ST W SUITE 5900, TORONTO, ON, M5X 2A1
(416) 362-8411 *SIC* 6411

SADERCOM INC *p1345*
4875 BOUL METROPOLITAIN E BUREAU 100, SAINT-LEONARD, QC, H1R 3J2
(514) 326-4100 *SIC* 6411

SAFETY INSURANCE SERVICE (1959) LTD *p674*
8300 WOODBINE AVE SUITE 200, MARKHAM, ON, L3R 9Y7
SIC 6411

SCHILL INSURANCE BROKERS LTD *p271*
15127 100 AVE UNIT 302, SURREY, BC, V3R 0N9
(604) 585-4445 *SIC* 6411

SCM ADJUSTERS CANADA LTD. *p392*
1479 BUFFALO PL SUITE 200, WINNIPEG, MB, R3T 1L7
(204) 985-1777 *SIC* 6411

SCM INSURANCE SERVICES INC *p125*
5083 WINDERMERE BLVD SW SUITE 101, EDMONTON, AB, T6W 0J5
(780) 430-9012 *SIC* 6411

SCM INSURANCE SERVICES INC *p1177*
255 BOUL CREMAZIE E BUREAU 1070, MONTREAL, QC, H2M 1L5
(514) 331-1030 *SIC* 6411

SCOTIA WEALTH INSURANCE SERVICES INC *p956*
40 KING ST W, TORONTO, ON, M5H 1H1
(416) 863-7272 *SIC* 6411

SEAFIRST INSURANCE BROKERS LTD *p268*
9769 FIFTH ST SUITE A2, SIDNEY, BC, V8L 2X1
(250) 656-9886 *SIC* 6411

SECURE INSURANCE SOLUTIONS GROUP INC *p665*
181 TORONTO ST, MARKDALE, ON, N0C 1H0
(519) 986-3250 *SIC* 6411

SEDGWICK CMS CANADA INC *p689*
5915 AIRPORT RD SUITE 200, MISSISSAUGA, ON, L4V 1T1
(905) 671-7800 *SIC* 6411

SENTINEL FINANCIAL MANAGEMENT CORP *p1430*
200-446 2ND AVE N, SASKATOON, SK, S7K 2C3
(306) 652-7225 *SIC* 6411

SENTINEL LIFE MANAGEMENT CORP *p1430*
446 2ND AVE N SUITE 200, SASKATOON, SK, S7K 2C3
(306) 652-7225 *SIC* 6411

SERVICEMASTER OF OWEN SOUND *p836*
107 JASON ST UNIT 1, OWEN SOUND, ON, N4K 5N7
SIC 6411

SERVICES FINANCIERS XN (CANADA) INC *p1199*
600 BOUL DE MAISONNEUVE O BUREAU 2310, MONTREAL, QC, H3A 3J2
(514) 908-1835 *SIC* 6411

SERVICES PROFESSIONNELS INC *p1283*
529 RUE NOTRE-DAME BUREAU 300, REPENTIGNY, QC, J6A 2T6
SIC 6411

SHAW SABEY & ASSOCIATES LTD *p329*
555 BURRARD ST SUITE 1275, VANCOUVER, BC, V7X 1M9
(604) 689-2441 *SIC* 6411

SHEEHAN & ROSIE LTD *p887*
70 ST. PAUL ST W, ST CATHARINES, ON, L2S 2C5
(905) 688-3713 *SIC* 6411

SHEFFAR, POTTER, MUCHAN INC *p655*
362 OXFORD ST E, LONDON, ON, N6A 1V7
(519) 432-6199 *SIC* 6411

SHOL DICE INSURANCE *p542*
300 GRAND AVE W, CHATHAM, ON, N7L 1C1
(519) 352-9016 *SIC* 6411

SIRIUS BENEFIT PLANS INC *p389*
1403 KENASTON BLVD, WINNIPEG, MB,

R3P 2T5
(204) 488-7600 *SIC* 6411

SMITH INSURANCE SERVICE *p130*
9902 102 ST, FORT SASKATCHEWAN, AB, T8L 2C3
(780) 998-2501 *SIC* 6411

SMITH PETRIE CARR & SCOTT INSURANCE BROKERS LTD *p834*
359 KENT ST SUITE 600, OTTAWA, ON, K2P 0R6
(613) 237-2871 *SIC* 6411

SOEURS FILLES DE JESUS *p1386*
1193 BOUL SAINT-LOUIS, TROIS-RIVIERES, QC, G8Z 2M8
(819) 376-3741 *SIC* 6411

SOPLEX SOLUTIONS D'ASSURANCE INC *p1087*
225 PROM DU CENTROPOLIS BUREAU 215, COTE SAINT-LUC, QC, H7T 0B3
(450) 781-6566 *SIC* 6411

SORRELL FINANCIAL INC *p91*
10111 104 AVE NW UNIT 2600, EDMONTON, AB, T5J 0J4
(780) 424-1424 *SIC* 6411

SOUND INSURANCE SERVICES INC *p777*
205 LESMILL RD, NORTH YORK, ON, M3B 2V1
(416) 756-3334 *SIC* 6411

SOUTH COAST INSURANCE AGENCY LIMITED *p425*
227 ATLANTIC ST, MARYSTOWN, NL, A0E 2M0
(709) 279-3200 *SIC* 6411

SOUTH EASTHOPE MUTUAL INSURANCE COMPANY *p902*
62 WOODSTOCK ST N, TAVISTOCK, ON, N0B 2R0
(519) 655-2011 *SIC* 6411

SOUTH WESTERN INSURANCE GROUP LIMITED *p580*
401 THE WEST MALL SUITE 700, ETOBICOKE, ON, M9C 5J4
(416) 620-6604 *SIC* 6411

SOVEREIGN GENERAL INSURANCE COMPANY, THE *p37*
6700 MACLEOD TRAIL SE UNIT 140, CALGARY, AB, T2H 0L3
(403) 298-4200 *SIC* 6411

SPRIGGS INSURANCE BROKERS LIMITED *p801*
159 CHURCH ST, OAKVILLE, ON, L6J 1N1
(905) 844-9232 *SIC* 6411

SSQ SOCIETE D'ASSURANCES GENERALES INC *p1273*
2515 BOUL LAURIER, QUEBEC, QC, G1V 2L2
(819) 538-4610 *SIC* 6411

ST-CLAIR INSURANCE BROKERS INC *p902*
13340 LANOUE ST, TECUMSEH, ON, N8N 5E1
(519) 259-1955 *SIC* 6411

STANDARD INSURANCE BROKERS LTD, THE *p628*
319 SECOND ST S, KENORA, ON, P9N 1G3
(807) 468-3333 *SIC* 6411

STANHOPE SIMPSON INSURANCE LIMITED *p457*
3845 JOSEPH HOWE DR SUITE 300, HALIFAX, NS, B3L 4H9
(902) 454-8641 *SIC* 6411

STATE FARM INSURANCE *p482*
333 FIRST COMMERCE DR, AURORA, ON, L4G 8A4
(905) 750-4100 *SIC* 6411

STATE FARM INSURANCE *p525*
5420 NORTH SERVICE RD SUITE 400, BURLINGTON, ON, L7L 6C7
(905) 315-3900 *SIC* 6411

STATE FARM INSURANCE COMPANIES *p9*
2611 37 AVE NE SUITE 3, CALGARY, AB, T1Y 5V7
(403) 291-1283 *SIC* 6411

STEERS INSURANCE LIMITED *p429*

▲ Public Company ■ Public Company Family Member **HQ** Headquarters **BR** Branch **SL** Single Location

99 AIRPORT RD UNIT 201, ST. JOHN'S, NL, A1A 4Y3

(709) 722-1532 *SIC 6411*

STRATEGIC UNDERWRITING MANAGERS INC *p940*

18 KING ST E SUITE 903, TORONTO, ON, M5C 1C4

(416) 603-7864 *SIC 6411*

SUN LIFE ASSURANCES (CANADA) LIMITEE *p1208*

1155 RUE METCALFE BUREAU 1024, MONTREAL, QC, H3B 2V9

(514) 866-6411 *SIC 6411*

SUN LIFE FINANCIAL INC *p967*

1 YORK ST, TORONTO, ON, M5J 0B6

(416) 979-9966 *SIC 6411*

SUREXDIRECT.COM LTD *p145*

6 SOUTH 1ST ST W, MAGRATH, AB, T0K 1J0

(403) 388-2387 *SIC 6411*

SURNET INSURANCE GROUP INC *p1015*

1621 MCEWEN DR SUITE 50, WHITBY, ON, L1N 9A5

(905) 433-2378 *SIC 6411*

SUSSEX FRANCHISE SYSTEMS INC. *p238*

173 FORESTER ST UNIT 108, NORTH VANCOUVER, BC, V7H 0A6

(604) 983-6955 *SIC 6411*

SUTHERLAND, JOHN & SONS LIMITED *p600*

240 VICTORIA RD N, GUELPH, ON, N1E 6L8

(519) 822-0160 *SIC 6411*

SWAN VALLEY AGENCIES LTD *p359*

922 MAIN ST E, SWAN RIVER, MB, R0L 1Z0

(204) 734-9421 *SIC 6411*

T K GROUP INC, THE *p829*

880 LADY ELLEN PL SUITE 100, OTTAWA, ON, K1Z 5L9

(613) 728-7030 *SIC 6411*

TEKSMED SERVICES INC *p197*

8635 YOUNG RD SUITE 7, CHILLIWACK, BC, V2P 4P3

(604) 702-3380 *SIC 6411*

THOMAS I. HULL INSURANCE LIMITED *p967*

220 BAY ST SUITE 600, TORONTO, ON, M5J 2W4

(416) 865-0131 *SIC 6411*

THOMSON SCHINDLE GREEN INSURANCE & FINANCIAL SERVICES LTD *p146*

623 4 ST SE SUITE 100, MEDICINE HAT, AB, T1A 0L1

(403) 526-3283 *SIC 6411*

THOUSAND ISLANDS INSURANCE & FINANCIAL GROUP LIMITED *p631*

1996 HIGHWAY 15, KINGSTON, ON, K7L 4V3

(613) 542-4440 *SIC 6411*

TOTTEN INSURANCE GROUP INC *p947*

20 DUNDAS ST W SUITE 910, TORONTO, ON, M5G 2C2

(416) 342-1159 *SIC 6411*

TOWERS WATSON CANADA INC *p711*

201 CITY CENTRE DR SUITE 1000, MISSISSAUGA, ON, L5B 4E4

(905) 272-6322 *SIC 6411*

TREDD INSURANCE BROKERS LTD *p958*

141 ADELAIDE ST W SUITE 1410, TORONTO, ON, M5H 3L5

(416) 306-6000 *SIC 6411*

TREMBLAY ASSURANCE LTEE *p1151*

15 RUE SAINT-ANTOINE, METABETCHOUAN-LAC-A-LA-CROIX, QC, G8G 1H2

(418) 349-2841 *SIC 6411*

TRILLIUM MUTUAL INSURANCE COMPANY *p647*

495 MITCHELL RD S, LISTOWEL, ON, N4W 0C8

(519) 291-9300 *SIC 6411*

TRIPEMCO BURLINGTON INSURANCE GROUP LIMITED *p894*

99 HIGHWAY 8, STONEY CREEK, ON, L8G 1C1

(905) 664-2266 *SIC 6411*

TURQUOISE, CABINET EN ASSURANCE DE DOMMAGES INC, LA *p1243*

481 131 RTE, NOTRE-DAME-DES-PRAIRIES, QC, J6E 0M1

(450) 759-6265 *SIC 6411*

UNDERWRITERS INSURANCE BROKERS (B.C.) LTD *p218*

310 NICOLA ST UNIT 103, KAMLOOPS, BC, V2C 2P5

(250) 374-2139 *SIC 6411*

UNDERWRITING COMPLIANCE SERVICES *p676*

25 VALLEYWOOD DR SUITE 7, MARKHAM, ON, L3R 5L9

(905) 754-6324 *SIC 6411*

UNIFUND ADJUSTING INC *p431*

68 PORTUGAL COVE RD, ST. JOHN'S, NL, A1B 2L9

(709) 737-1680 *SIC 6411*

UNITY MANAGING UNDERWRITERS HOLDCO LIMITED *p770*

5734 YONGE ST SUITE 605, NORTH YORK, ON, M2M 4E7

(416) 222-0676 *SIC 6411*

UNIVESTA ASSURANCES & SERVICES FINANCIERS INC *p1168*

3925 RUE RACHEL E BUREAU 100, MONTREAL, QC, H1X 3G8

(514) 899-5377 *SIC 6411*

UTTER-MORRIS INSURANCE BROKERS LIMITED *p527*

3070 MAINWAY UNIT 5, BURLINGTON, ON, L7M 3X1

(905) 332-7877 *SIC 6411*

VACHON, ENRIGHT & PETER INSURANCE LTD *p578*

5468 DUNDAS ST W UNIT 200, ETOBICOKE, ON, M9B 6E3

(416) 239-3373 *SIC 6411*

VALIDUS RESEARCH INC *p1007*

187 KING ST S SUITE 201, WATERLOO, ON, N2J 1R1

(519) 783-9100 *SIC 6411*

VAN ISLE INSURANCE SERVICES (1983) INC *p212*

471 TRANS CANADA HWY, DUNCAN, BC, V9L 3R7

SIC 6411

VAUGHAN ASSURANCE LIMITED *p471*

379 MAIN ST, YARMOUTH, NS, B5A 1G1

(902) 742-2000 *SIC 6411*

VERGE INSURANCE BROKERS LIMITED *p886*

131 ONTARIO ST, ST CATHARINES, ON, L2R 5J9

(905) 688-9170 *SIC 6411*

VERNON INSURANCE SERVICES INC *p332*

3118 32 AVE, VERNON, BC, V1T 2L9

(250) 549-3074 *SIC 6411*

VEZINA ASSURANCES INC *p1167*

4374 AV PIERRE-DE COUBERTIN BUREAU 220, MONTREAL, QC, H1V 1A6

(514) 253-5221 *SIC 6411*

VIAU, ROGER & FILS INC *p1181*

1100 BOUL CREMAZIE E BUREAU 500, MONTREAL, QC, H2P 2X2

(514) 374-9345 *SIC 6411*

W. B. WHITE INSURANCE LIMITED *p813*

110 KING ST E, OSHAWA, ON, L1H 1B6

(905) 576-6400 *SIC 6411*

W. H. SCRIVENS & SON LIMITED *p834*

270 MACLAREN ST, OTTAWA, ON, K2P 0M3

(613) 236-9101 *SIC 6411*

WAYPOINT INSURANCE SERVICES INC *p195*

1400 DOGWOOD ST UNIT 700, CAMPBELL RIVER, BC, V9W 3A6

(250) 287-9184 *SIC 6411*

WEDGWOOD INSURANCE LIMITED *p431*

85 THORBURN RD SUITE 102, ST.

JOHN'S, NL, A1B 3M2

(709) 753-3210 *SIC 6411*

WESTERN ASSURANCE COMPANY *p943*

10 WELLINGTON ST E, TORONTO, ON, M5E 1C5

(416) 366-7511 *SIC 6411*

WESTERN FINANCIAL GROUP (NETWORK) INC *p136*

1010 24 ST SE, HIGH RIVER, AB, T1V 2A7

(403) 652-2663 *SIC 6411*

WESTERN FINANCIAL GROUP INC *p382*

777 PORTAGE AVE, WINNIPEG, MB, R3G 0N3

(204) 943-0331 *SIC 6411*

WESTLAND INSURANCE GROUP LTD *p280*

2121 160 ST SUITE 200, SURREY, BC, V3Z 9N6

(604) 543-7788 *SIC 6411*

WESTLAND INSURANCE LIMITED PARTNERSHIP *p280*

2121 160 ST UNIT 200, SURREY, BC, V3Z 9N6

(604) 543-7788 *SIC 6411*

WILL INSURANCE BROKERS LTD *p645*

148 ERIE ST N, LEAMINGTON, ON, N8H 3A2

(519) 326-5746 *SIC 6411*

WILLIAM E. BURROWES INC *p1068*

1570B BOUL DE MONTARVILLE, BOUCHERVILLE, QC, J4B 5Y3

(450) 655-6023 *SIC 6411*

WILLIAMSON GROUP INC, THE *p515*

225 KING GEORGE RD, BRANTFORD, ON, N3R 7N7

(519) 756-9560 *SIC 6411*

WILLIS CANADA INC *p988*

100 KING ST W SUITE 4700, TORONTO, ON, M5X 1K7

(416) 368-9641 *SIC 6411*

WILSON INSURANCE LTD *p402*

404 QUEEN ST, FREDERICTON, NB, E3B 1B6

(506) 458-8505 *SIC 6411*

WORLD INSURANCE SERVICES LTD *p262*

7100 RIVER RD UNIT 2, RICHMOND, BC, V6X 1X5

SIC 6411

WORLD TRAVEL PROTECTION CANADA INC *p985*

901 KING ST W SUITE 300, TORONTO, ON, M5V 3H5

(416) 205-4618 *SIC 6411*

WOTHERSPOON, DON & ASSOCIATES LTD *p187*

4634 HASTINGS ST SUITE 101, BURNABY, BC, V5C 2K5

(604) 294-3242 *SIC 6411*

WYATT NU TREND INSURANCE AGENCY LTD *p363*

138 REGENT AVE W, WINNIPEG, MB, R2C 1P9

(204) 222-3221 *SIC 6411*

YORK FINANCIAL SERVICES INC. *p402*

440 YORK ST, FREDERICTON, NB, E3B 3P7

(506) 443-7776 *SIC 6411*

YOUNGS INSURANCE BROKERS INC *p1012*

55 EAST MAIN ST, WELLAND, ON, L3B 3W4

(905) 735-7212 *SIC 6411*

ZEHR INSURANCE BROKERS LIMITED *p753*

59 HURON ST, NEW HAMBURG, ON, N3A 1K1

(519) 662-1710 *SIC 6411*

ZLC FINANCIAL GROUP LTD *p311*

666 BURRARD ST SUITE 1200, VANCOUVER, BC, V6C 2X8

(604) 684-3863 *SIC 6411*

ZURICH INSURANCE COMPANY LTD *p988*

100 KING ST W SUITE 5500, TORONTO, ON, M5X 2A1

(416) 586-3000 *SIC 6411*

SIC 6512 Nonresidential building operators

1388688 ONTARIO LIMITED *p511*

499 MAIN ST S SUITE 56, BRAMPTON, ON, L6Y 1N7

(905) 459-1337 *SIC 6512*

2854-5150 QUEBEC INC *p1177*

9601 BOUL SAINT-LAURENT, MONTREAL, QC, H2N 1P6

(514) 385-1762 *SIC 6512*

9130-1093 QUEBEC INC *p1271*

2820 BOUL LAURIER BUREAU 850, QUEBEC, QC, G1V 0C1

(418) 681-8151 *SIC 6512*

9130-1093 QUEBEC INC *p1382*

805 BOUL FRONTENAC E, THETFORD MINES, QC, G6G 6L5

(418) 338-6388 *SIC 6512*

9130-1168 QUEBEC INC *p1285*

298 BOUL ARMAND-THERIAULT BUREAU 2, RIVIERE-DU-LOUP, QC, G5R 4C2

(418) 862-7848 *SIC 6512*

9161-5781 QUEBEC INC *p1230*

800 RUE DE LA GAUCHETIERE O BUREAU 1100, MONTREAL, QC, H5A 1M1

(514) 397-2222 *SIC 6512*

9167-0661 QUEBEC INC *p1380*

3205 BOUL DES ENTREPRISES, TERREBONNE, QC, J6X 4J9

(450) 477-2111 *SIC 6512*

9191-1263 QUEBEC INC *p1217*

7001 AV DU PARC, MONTREAL, QC, H3N 1X7

(514) 316-7457 *SIC 6512*

9343-0114 QUEBEC INC *p1311*

1325 RUE DANIEL-JOHNSON O, SAINT-HYACINTHE, QC, J2S 8S4

(450) 252-7988 *SIC 6512*

ACTION MANAGEMENT SERVICES INC *p438*

23 MAIN ST, ANTIGONISH, NS, B2G 2B3

(902) 863-3200 *SIC 6512*

ALLDRITT DEVELOPMENT LIMITED *p95*

14310 111 AVE NW SUITE 305, EDMONTON, AB, T5M 3Z7

(780) 453-5631 *SIC 6512*

ALTONE INVESTMENTS LIMITED *p785*

3625 DUFFERIN ST SUITE 503, NORTH YORK, ON, M3K 1N4

(416) 638-9902 *SIC 6512*

AQUILINI INVESTMENT GROUP INC *p296*

800 GRIFFITHS WAY, VANCOUVER, BC, V6B 6G1

(604) 687-8813 *SIC 6512*

AQUILINI PROPERTIES LIMITED PARTNERSHIP *p1187*

215 RUE SAINT-JACQUES UNITE 120, MONTREAL, QC, H2Y 1M6

(514) 847-9547 *SIC 6512*

ASSUMPTION PLACE LIMITED *p406*

770 MAIN ST, MONCTON, NB, E1C 1E7

(506) 853-5420 *SIC 6512*

BEAUWARD SHOPPING CENTRES LTD *p1301*

430 BOUL ARTHUR-SAUVE BUREAU 6010, SAINT-EUSTACHE, QC, J7R 6V7

(450) 473-6831 *SIC 6512*

BEAUWARD SHOPPING CENTRES LTD *p1311*

3200 BOUL LAFRAMBOISE BUREAU 1009, SAINT-HYACINTHE, QC, J2S 4Z5

(450) 773-8282 *SIC 6512*

BOUCHERIE COTE INC *p1320*

952A RUE LABELLE, SAINT-JEROME, QC, J7Z 5M8

(450) 438-4159 *SIC 6512*

BROOKFIELD ASSET MANAGEMENT INC *p960*

181 BAY ST SUITE 300, TORONTO, ON, M5J 2T3

(416) 363-9491 *SIC 6512*

BURMAC MANAGEMENT LIMITED *p468*

710 PRINCE ST, TRURO, NS, B2N 1G6

SIC 6512

CADILLAC FAIRVIEW CORPORATION LIMITED, THE *p935*
220 YONGE ST SUITE 110, TORONTO, ON, M5B 2H1
(416) 598-8700 *SIC 6512*

CADILLAC FAIRVIEW CORPORATION LIMITED, THE *p949*
20 QUEEN ST W SUITE 500, TORONTO, ON, M5H 3R4
(416) 598-8200 *SIC 6512*

CADOGAN HALL *p8*
GD, CADOGAN, AB, T0B 0T0
(780) 753-2963 *SIC 6512*

CANADA PLACE CORPORATION *p303*
999 CANADA PL SUITE 100, VANCOUVER, BC, V6C 3E1
(604) 775-7200 *SIC 6512*

CANAPEN INVESTMENTS LTD *p87*
10020 101A AVE NW SUITE 800, EDMONTON, AB, T5J 3G2
(780) 428-0511 *SIC 6512*

CB RICHARD ELLIS GLOBAL CORPORATE SERVICES LTD *p937*
18 KING ST E UNIT 1100, TORONTO, ON, M5C 1C4
(416) 775-3975 *SIC 6512*

CENTRE COMMERCIAL PROMENADES ST-NOEL *p1382*
100 1RE RUE BUREAU 12, THETFORD MINES, QC, G6G 4Y2
(418) 338-6066 *SIC 6512*

CENTRECORP MANAGEMENT SERVICES LIMITED *p668*
2851 JOHN ST SUITE 1, MARKHAM, ON, L3R 5R7
(905) 477-9200 *SIC 6512*

CENTURY HOLDINGS LTD *p237*
11 EIGHTH ST, NEW WESTMINSTER, BC, V3M 3N7
(604) 943-2203 *SIC 6512*

CHICO'S FAS CANADA, CO. *p452*
1959 UPPER WATER ST SUITE 900, HALIFAX, NS, B3J 3N2
(888) 855-4986 *SIC 6512*

COMPAGNIE FRANCE FILM INC *p1175*
505 RUE SHERBROOKE E BUREAU 2401, MONTREAL, QC, H2L 4N3
(514) 844-0680 *SIC 6512*

CONFEDERATION CENTRE BOX OFFICE *p1039*
145 RICHMOND ST, CHARLOTTETOWN, PE, C1A 1J1
(902) 628-1864 *SIC 6512*

CORPORATION DE LA SALLE ALBERT-ROUSSEAU, LA *p1272*
2410 CH SAINTE-FOY, QUEBEC, QC, G1V 1T3
(418) 659-6629 *SIC 6512*

CORPORATION DU THEATRE L'ETOILE *p1070*
6000 BOUL DE ROME BUREAU 240, BROSSARD, QC, J4Y 0B6
(450) 676-1030 *SIC 6512*

CORPORATION OF MASSEY HALL AND ROY THOMSON HALL, THE *p961*
60 SIMCOE ST, TORONTO, ON, M5J 2H5
(416) 593-4822 *SIC 6512*

CROMBIE DEVELOPMENTS LIMITED *p452*
2000 BARRINGTON ST SUITE 1210, HALIFAX, NS, B3J 3K1
SIC 6512

CROMBIE DEVELOPMENTS LIMITED *p466*
115 KING ST, STELLARTON, NS, B0K 1S0
(902) 755-4440 *SIC 6512*

DALFEN'S LIMITED *p1402*
4444 RUE SAINTE-CATHERINE O BUREAU 100, WESTMOUNT, QC, H3Z 1R2
(514) 938-1050 *SIC 6512*

DEL MANAGEMENT SOLUTIONS INC *p781*
4810 DUFFERIN ST SUITE E, NORTH YORK, ON, M3H 5S8
(416) 661-3070 *SIC 6512*

DEVELOPPEMENT OLYMBEC INC *p1325*

333 BOUL DECARIE BUREAU 500, SAINT-LAURENT, QC, H4N 3M9
(514) 344-3334 *SIC 6512*

DEVELOPPEMENTS GERARD BROUSSEAU INC *p1256*
7609 AV GRIGNON, QUEBEC, QC, G1H 6V7
(418) 626-6712 *SIC 6512*

DORAL HOLDINGS LIMITED *p1012*
800 NIAGARA ST, WELLAND, ON, L3C 5Z4
(905) 734-9900 *SIC 6512*

DOWNING STREET PROPERTY MANAGEMENT INC *p552*
668 MILLWAY AVE UNIT 7, CONCORD, ON, L4K 3V2
(905) 851-1717 *SIC 6512*

DRAGON CITY DEVELOPMENTS INC *p977*
131 BALDWIN ST, TORONTO, ON, M5T 1L7
(416) 596-8885 *SIC 6512*

EDMONTON CITY CENTRE *p88*
10025 102A AVE NW SUITE 1700, EDMONTON, AB, T5J 2Z2
(780) 426-8444 *SIC 6512*

EDON MANAGEMENT *p88*
10030 107 ST NW, EDMONTON, AB, T5J 3E4
(780) 428-1742 *SIC 6512*

ELGIN MALL *p890*
417 WELLINGTON ST SUITE 53, ST THOMAS, ON, N5R 5J5
(519) 633-4060 *SIC 6512*

EMBERS SERVICES LIMITED *p653*
80 DUFFERIN AVE, LONDON, ON, N6A 1K4
(519) 672-4510 *SIC 6512*

ENTERPRISE UNIVERSAL INC *p72*
4411 16 AVE NW, CALGARY, AB, T3B 0M3
(403) 209-4780 *SIC 6512*

ENTREPRISE DE CONSTRUCTION GASTON MORIN LTEE *p1090*
310 RUE DE QUEN, DOLBEAU-MISTASSINI, QC, G8L 5N1
(418) 276-4166 *SIC 6512*

EVENTS EAST GROUP *p453*
1800 ARGYLE ST P.O. BOX 955, HALIFAX, NS, B3J 3N8
(902) 421-8686 *SIC 6512*

FAIRMALL LEASEHOLDS INC *p767*
1800 SHEPPARD AVE E SUITE 330, NORTH YORK, ON, M2J 5A7
(416) 491-0151 *SIC 6512*

FATHERS OF CONFEDERATION BUILDINGS TRUST *p1039*
145 RICHMOND ST, CHARLOTTETOWN, PE, C1A 1J1
(902) 629-1166 *SIC 6512*

FENGATE PROPERTY MANAGEMENT LTD *p527*
3425 HARVESTER RD UNIT 105, BURLINGTON, ON, L7N 3N1
(289) 288-3822 *SIC 6512*

FIRST CAPITAL REALTY INC *p991*
85 HANNA AVE SUITE 400, TORONTO, ON, M6K 3S3
(416) 504-4114 *SIC 6512*

FIRST REAL PROPERTIES LIMITED *p612*
100 KING ST W SUITE 200, HAMILTON, ON, L8P 1A2
(905) 522-3501 *SIC 6512*

FORTIS PROPERTIES CORPORATION *p433*
5 SPRINGDALE ST SUITE 1100, ST. JOHN'S, NL, A1E 0E4
(709) 737-2800 *SIC 6512*

FRASTELL PROPERTY MANAGEMENT INC *p925*
22 ST CLAIR AVE E SUITE 1500, TORONTO, ON, M4T 2S3
(416) 499-3333 *SIC 6512*

GESTION H. DICKNER LTEE *p1284*
559 RUE DE LAUSANNE, RIMOUSKI, QC, G5L 4A7
(418) 723-7936 *SIC 6512*

GOTTARDO CONSTRUCTION LIMITED *p553*

277 PENNSYLVANIA AVE, CONCORD, ON, L4K 5R9
(905) 761-7707 *SIC 6512*

GREENBERG NAIMER GROUP *p834*
25 CARTIER ST, OTTAWA, ON, K2P 1J2
(613) 237-2111 *SIC 6512*

GREENWIN INC *p776*
19 LESMILL RD UNIT 100, NORTH YORK, ON, M3B 2T3
(416) 487-3883 *SIC 6512*

HUGH'S ROOM *p995*
2261 DUNDAS ST W, TORONTO, ON, M6R 1X6
(416) 533-5483 *SIC 6512*

IMMEUBLES CARREFOUR RICHELIEU LTEE, LES *p1197*
600 BOUL DE MAISONNEUVE O BUREAU 2600, MONTREAL, QC, H3A 3J2
(514) 499-8300 *SIC 6512*

IMMEUBLES FAIRWAY INC, LES *p1218*
5858 CH DE LA COTE-DES-NEIGES UNITE 612, MONTREAL, QC, H3S 2S1
(514) 342-2791 *SIC 6512*

IMMEUBLES GOYETTE INC, LES *p1313*
2825 BOUL CASAVANT O, SAINT-HYACINTHE, QC, J2S 7Y4
(450) 773-9615 *SIC 6512*

IMMEUBLES ROUSSIN LTEE, LES *p1279*
780 BOUL LEBOURGNEUF, QUEBEC, QC, G2J 1S1
(418) 623-5333 *SIC 6512*

IVANHOE CAMBRIDGE I INC. *p1191*
1001 RUE DU SQUARE-VICTORIA BUREAU 500, MONTREAL, QC, H2Z 2B5
(514) 841-7600 *SIC 6512*

IVANHOE CAMBRIDGE II INC. *p531*
900 MAPLE AVE, BURLINGTON, ON, L7S 2J8
(905) 681-2900 *SIC 6512*

IVANHOE CAMBRIDGE INC *p1191*
1001 RUE DU SQUARE-VICTORIA BUREAU 500, MONTREAL, QC, H2Z 2B5
(514) 841-7600 *SIC 6512*

KENPIER INVESTISSEMENTS LIMITEE *p1108*
1170 CH D'AYLMER, GATINEAU, QC, J9H 7L3
(819) 778-0000 *SIC 6512*

KOLTER PROPERTY MANAGEMENT LIMITED *p924*
2200 YONGE ST SUITE 1600, TORONTO, ON, M4S 2C6
SIC 6512

LANSDOWNE MALL INC *p841*
645 LANSDOWNE ST W, PETERBOROUGH, ON, K9J 7Y5
(705) 748-2961 *SIC 6512*

LINDSAY SQUARE MALL *p646*
401 KENT ST W SUITE 20, LINDSAY, ON, K9V 4Z1
(705) 324-1123 *SIC 6512*

LOBLAW PROPERTIES LIMITED *p511*
1 PRESIDENTS CHOICE CIR, BRAMPTON, ON, L6Y 5S5
(905) 459-2500 *SIC 6512*

MAGIL LAURENTIENNE GESTION IMMOBILIERE INC *p1229*
800 RUE DU SQUARE-VICTORIA BUREAU 4120, MONTREAL, QC, H4Z 1A1
(514) 875-6010 *SIC 6512*

MARKALTA DEVELOPMENTS LTD *p789*
1020 LAWRENCE AVE W SUITE 300, NORTH YORK, ON, M6A 1C8
(416) 787-1135 *SIC 6512*

MARQUISE FACILITIES CORPORATION *p255*
13351 COMMERCE PKY SUITE 1373, RICHMOND, BC, V6V 2X7
(604) 214-8525 *SIC 6512*

METRO LOGISTIQUE INC *p1198*
1002 RUE SHERBROOKE O BUREAU 2000, MONTREAL, QC, H3A 3L6
(514) 333-5500 *SIC 6512*

METROPOLIS *p1186*

59 RUE SAINTE-CATHERINE E, MONTREAL, QC, H2X 1K5
(514) 844-3500 *SIC 6512*

METRUS PROPERTIES LIMITED *p555*
30 FLORAL PKY SUITE 200, CONCORD, ON, L4K 4R1
(416) 798-7173 *SIC 6512*

MILMAN INDUSTRIES INC *p901*
2502 ELM ST, SUDBURY, ON, P3E 4R6
(705) 682-9277 *SIC 6512*

MINTO PROPERTIES INC *p823*
180 KENT ST SUITE 200, OTTAWA, ON, K1P 0B6
(613) 786-3000 *SIC 6512*

N.C.H. HOLDINGS LIMITED *p426*
14 CLYDE AVE, MOUNT PEARL, NL, A1N 4S1
(709) 368-2131 *SIC 6512*

NATIONAL DEVELOPMENTS LTD *p386*
220 SAULTEAUX CRES, WINNIPEG, MB, R3J 3W3
(204) 889-5430 *SIC 6512*

NUNASTAR PROPERTIES INC *p125*
1281 91 ST SW SUITE 200, EDMONTON, AB, T6X 1H1
(780) 452-4333 *SIC 6512*

OLD OAK PROPERTIES INC *p654*
465 RICHMOND ST SUITE 600, LONDON, ON, N6A 5P4
(519) 661-0215 *SIC 6512*

ONTARIO RACQUET SPORT ENTERPRISES LTD *p714*
884 SOUTHDOWN RD, MISSISSAUGA, ON, L5J 2Y4
(905) 822-5240 *SIC 6512*

ORCA BAY ARENA LIMITED PARTNERSHIP *p299*
800 GRIFFITHS WAY, VANCOUVER, BC, V6B 6G1
(604) 899-7400 *SIC 6512*

ORLANDO CORPORATION *p689*
6205 AIRPORT RD SUITE 500, MISSISSAUGA, ON, L4V 1E1
(905) 677-5480 *SIC 6512*

OXFORD PROPERTIES GROUP INC *p956*
100 ADELAIDE ST W SUITE 900, TORONTO, ON, M5H 0E2
(416) 865-8300 *SIC 6512*

PEKUAKAMIULNUATSH TAKUHIKAN *p1150*
65 RUE UAPAKALU, MASHTEUIATSH, QC, G0W 2H0
(418) 275-2473 *SIC 6512*

PIONEER FOOD COURTS INC *p1015*
1 PAISLEY CRT, WHITBY, ON, L1N 9L2
(905) 665-1217 *SIC 6512*

PODOLLAN'S CONSTRUCTION LTD *p332*
2201 11 AVE SUITE 205, VERNON, BC, V1T 8V7
(250) 545-7752 *SIC 6512*

POLARIS REALTY (CANADA) LIMITED *p699*
2605 SKYMARK AVE SUITE 105, MISSISSAUGA, ON, L4W 4L5
(905) 238-8363 *SIC 6512*

PREMIER OPERATING CORPORATION LIMITED *p777*
1262 DON MILLS RD SUITE 92, NORTH YORK, ON, M3B 2W7
(416) 443-1645 *SIC 6512*

PREMIERE EXECUTIVE SUITES ATLANTIC LIMITED *p448*
250 BROWNLOW AVE, DARTMOUTH, NS, B3B 1W9
(902) 420-1333 *SIC 6512*

PROMENADES DE L'OUTAOUAIS LTD, LES *p1105*
1100 BOUL MALONEY O, GATINEAU, QC, J8T 6G3
(819) 205-1340 *SIC 6512*

R.P. JOHNSON CONSTRUCTION LTD *p268*
360 TRANS CANADA HWY SW SUITE 317, SALMON ARM, BC, V1E 1B6
(250) 832-9731 *SIC 6512*

REGENCY MALL *p901*
469 BOUCHARD ST SUITE 203, SUD-

BURY, ON, P3E 2K8
(705) 522-4722 *SIC 6512*

REVENUE PROPERTIES COMPANY LIMITED *p710*
55 CITY CENTRE DR SUITE 1000, MISSISSAUGA, ON, L5B 1M3
(905) 281-5943 *SIC 6512*

ROBERT LEE LTD *p316*
1177 HASTINGS ST W SUITE 517, VANCOUVER, BC, V6E 2K3
(604) 669-7733 *SIC 6512*

ROSS VENTURES LTD *p401*
35 COLTER CRT, FREDERICTON, NB, E3B 1X7
(506) 453-1800 *SIC 6512*

ROYAL AND MCPHERSON THEATRES SOCIETY *p337*
1005 BROAD ST UNIT 302, VICTORIA, BC, V8W 2A1
(250) 361-0800 *SIC 6512*

SCARBOROUGH TOWN CENTRE HOLDINGS INC *p966*
200 BAY ST SUITE 900, TORONTO, ON, M5J 2J2
(416) 865-8300 *SIC 6512*

SECOND REAL PROPERTIES LIMITED *p613*
100 KING ST W, HAMILTON, ON, L8P 1A2
(905) 522-3501 *SIC 6512*

SHAWA ENTERPRISES CORP *p1208*
1250 BOUL ROBERT-BOURASSA UNITE 921, MONTREAL, QC, H3B 3B8
SIC 6512

SHERIDAN RETAIL INC *p715*
2225 ERIN MILLS PKY, MISSISSAUGA, ON, L5K 1T9
(905) 822-0344 *SIC 6512*

SKYLINE INVESTMENTS INC *p940*
36 KING ST E SUITE 700, TORONTO, ON, M5C 2L9
(416) 368-2565 *SIC 6512*

SLEEPING BAY BUILDING CORP *p147*
3292 DUNMORE RD SE SUITE F7, MEDICINE HAT, AB, T1B 2R4
(403) 526-4888 *SIC 6512*

SMARTCENTRES MANAGEMENT SERVICES INC *p558*
3200 HIGHWAY 7, CONCORD, ON, L4K 5Z5
(905) 326-6400 *SIC 6512*

SMARTCENTRES REAL ESTATE INVESTMENT TRUST *p1002*
3200 HIGHWAY 7, VAUGHAN, ON, L4K 5Z5
(905) 326-6400 *SIC 6512*

SOCIETE DE LA PLACE DES ARTS DE MONTREAL *p1186*
260 BOUL DE MAISONNEUVE O, MONTREAL, QC, H2X 1Y9
(514) 285-4200 *SIC 6512*

SOUTHWORS OUTLET MALL INC *p535*
64 GRAND AVE S, CAMBRIDGE, ON, N1S 2L8
(519) 740-0380 *SIC 6512*

ST LAWRENCE CENTRE FOR THE ARTS *p943*
27 FRONT ST E, TORONTO, ON, M5E 1B4
(416) 366-7723 *SIC 6512*

TRADE CENTRE LIMITED *p454*
1800 ARGYLE ST SUITE 801, HALIFAX, NS, B3J 3K5
(902) 421-8686 *SIC 6512*

UNION, THE *p117*
6240 99 ST NW, EDMONTON, AB, T6E 6C7
(780) 702-2562 *SIC 6512*

VENTURES ENTERPRISES LTD *p454*
1525 BIRMINGHAM ST, HALIFAX, NS, B3J 2J6
(902) 429-5680 *SIC 6512*

WESBILD HOLDINGS LTD *p317*
1055 W GEORGIA ST SUITE 2600, VANCOUVER, BC, V6E 3P3
(604) 694-8800 *SIC 6512*

WESGROUP PROPERTIES LIMITED PARTNERSHIP *p329*

1055 DUNSMUIR ST SUITE 910, VANCOUVER, BC, V7X 1J1
(604) 632-1727 *SIC 6512*

WEST EDMONTON MALL PROPERTY INC *p104*
8882 170 ST NW SUITE 3000, EDMONTON, AB, T5T 4M2
(780) 444-5200 *SIC 6512*

WESTCLIFF MANAGEMENT LTD *p1200*
600 BOUL DE MAISONNEUVE O BUREAU 2600, MONTREAL, QC, H3A 3J2
(514) 499-8300 *SIC 6512*

WITTINGTON INVESTMENTS, LIMITED *p926*
22 ST CLAIR AVE E SUITE 2001, TORONTO, ON, M4T 2S3
(416) 967-7990 *SIC 6512*

YONGE EGLINTON CENTRE MANAGEMENT SERVICES IN TRUST *p923*
20 EGLINTON AVE W SUITE 401, TORONTO, ON, M4R 1K8
(416) 489-2300 *SIC 6512*

YORKDALE SHOPPING CENTRE HOLDINGS INC *p790*
1 YORKDALE RD SUITE 500, NORTH YORK, ON, M6A 3A1
(416) 256-5066 *SIC 6512*

SIC 6513 Apartment building operators

1230172 ONTARIO INC *p830*
110 CENTRAL PARK DR SUITE 512, OTTAWA, ON, K2C 4G3
(613) 727-2773 *SIC 6513*

1716530 ONTARIO INC *p750*
22 BARNSTONE DR, NEPEAN, ON, K2G 2P9
(613) 843-9887 *SIC 6513*

488491 ONTARIO INC *p807*
355 BROADWAY SUITE 1, ORANGEVILLE, ON, L9W 3Y3
(519) 941-5161 *SIC 6513*

728567 ONTARIO LIMITED *p511*
400 RAY LAWSON BLVD, BRAMPTON, ON, L6Y 4G4
(905) 456-3334 *SIC 6513*

822188 ONTARIO INC *p490*
1023 COUNTY RD 22, BELLE RIVER, ON, N0R 1A0
(519) 727-5506 *SIC 6513*

9095-1302 QUEBEC INC *p1104*
60 RUE DE LA FUTAIE BUREAU 512, GATINEAU, QC, J8T 8P5
(819) 568-2355 *SIC 6513*

AIESEC CANADA INC *p612*
116 KING ST W, HAMILTON, ON, L8P 4V3
(905) 529-5515 *SIC 6513*

ALL SENIORS CARE HOLDINGS INC *p928*
175 BLOOR ST E SUITE 601, TORONTO, ON, M4W 3R8
(416) 323-3773 *SIC 6513*

ALL SENIORS CARE LIVING CENTRES LTD *p77*
21 AUBURN BAY ST SE SUITE 428, CALGARY, AB, T3M 2A9
(403) 234-9695 *SIC 6513*

ALL SENIORS CARE LIVING CENTRES LTD *p928*
175 BLOOR ST E SUITE 601, TORONTO, ON, M4W 3R8
(416) 323-3773 *SIC 6513*

ALLIANCE DU PERSONNEL PROFESSIONNEL ET TECHNIQUE DE LA SANTE ET DES SERVICES SOCIAUX *p1144*
1111 RUE SAINT-CHARLES O BUREAU 1050, LONGUEUIL, QC, J4K 5G4
(450) 670-2411 *SIC 6513*

AMICA AT WINDSOR *p1022*
4909 RIVERSIDE DR E SUITE 207, WINDSOR, ON, N8Y 0A4
(519) 948-5500 *SIC 6513*

ATLANTIC RETIREMENT CONCEPTS INC *p399*

10 BARTON CRES SUITE 504, FREDERICTON, NB, E3A 5S3
(506) 450-7088 *SIC 6513*

BARNEY RIVER INVESTMENTS LIMITED *p771*
4576 YONGE ST SUITE 300, NORTH YORK, ON, M2N 6N4
(416) 620-7200 *SIC 6513*

BARTON RETIREMENT INC *p615*
1430 UPPER WELLINGTON ST, HAMILTON, ON, L9A 5H3
(905) 385-2111 *SIC 6513*

BERKELEY HOLDINGS LIMITED *p455*
2633 GLADSTONE ST SUITE 312, HALIFAX, NS, B3K 4W3
(902) 492-3700 *SIC 6513*

BOARDWALK REIT LIMITED PARTNERSHIP *p64*
1501 1 ST SW SUITE 200, CALGARY, AB, T2R 0W1
(403) 531-9255 *SIC 6513*

BRANCH 133 LEGION VILLAGE INC *p544*
111 HIBERNIA ST SUITE 220, COBOURG, ON, K9A 4Y7
(905) 372-8705 *SIC 6513*

BRIARLANE RENTAL PROPERTY MANAGEMENT INC *p667*
85 SPY CRT SUITE 100, MARKHAM, ON, L3R 4Z4
(905) 944-9406 *SIC 6513*

CENTRE DE SANTE ET DE SERVICES SOCIAUX LUCILLE-TEASDALE *p1167*
3095 RUE SHERBROOKE E, MONTREAL, QC, H1W 1B2
(514) 523-0991 *SIC 6513*

CHARTWELL CLASSIC OAKVILLE *p796*
180 OAK PARK BLVD SUITE 221, OAKVILLE, ON, L6H 0A6
(905) 257-0095 *SIC 6513*

CHARTWELL COUNTRY COTTAGE RETIREMENT RESIDENCE *p162*
75 CRANFORD WAY, SHERWOOD PARK, AB, T8H 2B9
(780) 417-0757 *SIC 6513*

CHELSEY PARK RETIREMENT COMMUNITY *p658*
312 OXFORD ST W, LONDON, ON, N6H 4N7
(519) 434-3164 *SIC 6513*

COMMUNITY LIFECARE INC *p656*
81 GRAND AVE, LONDON, ON, N6C 1M2
(519) 432-1162 *SIC 6513*

COUNTY STETTLER HOUSING AUTHORITY, THE *p167*
620 47TH AVE SUITE 111, STETTLER, AB, T0C 2L1
(403) 742-2953 *SIC 6513*

COUNTY STETTLER HOUSING AUTHORITY, THE *p167*
611 50TH AVE, STETTLER, AB, T0C 2L1
(403) 742-9220 *SIC 6513*

CRAIGWIEL GARDENS *p473*
221 AILSA CRAIG MAIN ST, AILSA CRAIG, ON, N0M 1A0
(519) 293-3215 *SIC 6513*

CROSBY PROPERTY MANAGEMENT LTD *p326*
777 HORNBY ST SUITE 600, VANCOUVER, BC, V6Z 1S4
(604) 683-8900 *SIC 6513*

CSH DEVONSHIRE SENIORS INC *p1023*
901 RIVERSIDE DR W, WINDSOR, ON, N9A 7J6
(519) 252-2273 *SIC 6513*

CSH DOMAINE CASCADE *p1368*
695 7E RUE DE LA POINTE, SHAWINIGAN, QC, G9N 8K2
(819) 536-4463 *SIC 6513*

CSH FOUR TEDDINGTON PARK INC *p921*
4 TEDDINGTON PARK AVE, TORONTO, ON, M4N 2C3
(416) 481-2986 *SIC 6513*

CSH PARK PLACE MANOR INC *p480*
15055 YONGE ST, AURORA, ON, L4G 6T4

(905) 727-2952 *SIC 6513*

DEVON PROPERTIES LTD *p333*
2067 CADBORO BAY RD SUITE 201, VICTORIA, BC, V8R 5G4
(250) 595-7000 *SIC 6513*

DMS PROPERTY MANAGEMENT LTD *p781*
4810 DUFFERIN ST SUITE E, NORTH YORK, ON, M3H 5S8
(416) 661-3070 *SIC 6513*

DOUGLAS CAMPBELL LODGE *p354*
150 9TH ST SE, PORTAGE LA PRAIRIE, MB, R1N 3T6
(204) 239-6006 *SIC 6513*

DP IMMOBILIER QUEBEC INC *p1139*
8389 AV SOUS-LE-VENT BUREAU 300, LEVIS, QC, G6X 1K7
(418) 832-2222 *SIC 6513*

EMPIRE LIVING CENTRE INC *p763*
425 FRASER ST SUITE 505, NORTH BAY, ON, P1B 3X1
(705) 474-9555 *SIC 6513*

ESAM CONSTRUCTION LIMITED *p658*
301 OXFORD ST W, LONDON, ON, N6H 1S6
(519) 433-7291 *SIC 6513*

EVERGREENS FOUNDATION *p136*
102 GOVERNMENT RD, HINTON, AB, T7V 2A6
(780) 865-5444 *SIC 6513*

F. D. L. COMPAGNIE LTEE *p1218*
3600 AV BARCLAY BUREAU 200, MONTREAL, QC, H3S 1K5
(514) 737-2268 *SIC 6513*

FALOM *p542*
600 GRAND AVE W SUITE 10012, CHATHAM, ON, N7L 4E3
(519) 354-5842 *SIC 6513*

FERGUSLEA PROPERTIES LIMITED *p830*
98 WOODRIDGE CRES, OTTAWA, ON, K2B 7S9
(613) 366-5020 *SIC 6513*

FONDATION D'AMENAGEMENT ST-PATRICK *p1082*
6767 CH DE LA COTE-SAINT-LUC BUREAU 616, COTE SAINT-LUC, QC, H4V 2Z6
(514) 481-9609 *SIC 6513*

FRED VICTOR CENTRE *p938*
59 ADELAIDE ST E SUITE 600, TORONTO, ON, M5C 1K6
(416) 364-8228 *SIC 6513*

GESTION RESEAU SELECTION II INC *p1086*
2400 BOUL DANIEL-JOHNSON, COTE SAINT-LUC, QC, H7T 3A4
(450) 902-2000 *SIC 6513*

GOVERNOR'S WALK *p820*
150 STANLEY AVE, OTTAWA, ON, K1M 2J7
(613) 564-9255 *SIC 6513*

GREATER NORTH FOUNDATION *p4*
5210 47 AVE, ATHABASCA, AB, T9S 1K5
(780) 675-9660 *SIC 6513*

HEATH ST HOUSING CO-OP INC *p925*
232 HEATH ST E, TORONTO, ON, M4T 1S9
(416) 486-8169 *SIC 6513*

HOLLYBURN PROPERTIES (ALBERTA) LTD *p318*
1640 ALBERNI ST SUITE 300, VANCOUVER, BC, V6G 1A7
(604) 926-7345 *SIC 6513*

HOLLYBURN PROPERTIES LIMITED *p313*
1160 HARO ST SUITE 101, VANCOUVER, BC, V6E 1E2
(604) 685-8525 *SIC 6513*

HOLLYBURN PROPERTIES LIMITED *p342*
250 18TH ST, WEST VANCOUVER, BC, V7V 3V5
(604) 926-7345 *SIC 6513*

HOMESTEAD LAND HOLDINGS LIMITED *p630*
80 JOHNSON ST, KINGSTON, ON, K7L 1X7
(613) 546-3146 *SIC 6513*

ICORR PROPERTIES MANAGEMENT INC *p653*
700 RICHMOND ST SUITE 100, LONDON, ON, N6A 5C7

(519) 432-1888   *SIC 6513*

IDEA PARTNER MARKETING INC, THE *p322*
2799 YEW ST, VANCOUVER, BC, V6K 4W2
(604) 736-1640   *SIC 6513*

INVESTISSEMENT IMMOBILIER CCSM LTEE *p1169*
3200 RUE OMER-LAVALLEE, MONTREAL, QC, H1Y 3P5
(514) 523-1160   *SIC 6513*

IOOF SENIORS HOMES INC *p487*
10 BROOKS ST, BARRIE, ON, L4N 5L3
(705) 728-2389   *SIC 6513*

JARDINS INTERIEURS DE SAINT-LAMBERT INC, LES *p1323*
1705 AV VICTORIA BUREAU 904, SAINT-LAMBERT, QC, J4R 2T7
(450) 671-1314   *SIC 6513*

KBK NO 51 VENTURES LTD *p314*
1128 ALBERNI ST, VANCOUVER, BC, V6E 4R6
(604) 683-1399   *SIC 6513*

KENAIR APARTMENTS LIMITED *p927*
500 AVENUE RD, TORONTO, ON, M4V 2J6
(416) 923-7557   *SIC 6513*

KIDSINKS HOLDINGS INC *p823*
100 ELGIN ST, OTTAWA, ON, K1P 5K8
(613) 235-3333   *SIC 6513*

KILLAM PROPERTIES INC *p455*
3700 KEMPT RD SUITE 100, HALIFAX, NS, B3K 4X8
(902) 453-9000   *SIC 6513*

KINGSWAY ARMS MANAGEMENT (AT CARLETON PLACE) INC *p540*
6 ARTHUR ST, CARLETON PLACE, ON, K7C 4S4
(613) 253-7360   *SIC 6513*

KINGSWAY ARMS MANAGEMENT (AT ELGIN LODGE) INC *p847*
551 MARY ST, PORT ELGIN, ON, N0H 2C2
(519) 389-5457   *SIC 6513*

L'INDUSTRIELLE-ALLIANCE SERVICES IMMOBILIERS INC *p1275*
3810 RUE DE MARLY, QUEBEC, QC, G1X 4B1
(418) 651-7308   *SIC 6513*

LIFESTYLE OPERATIONS LP *p280*
15501 16 AVE, SURREY, BC, V4A 9M5
(604) 538-7227   *SIC 6513*

MACKENZIE HOUSING MANAGEMENT BOARD *p138*
9802 105 ST, LA CRETE, AB, T0H 2H0
(780) 928-3677   *SIC 6513*

MACLAB ENTERPRISES CORPORATION *p89*
10205 100 AVE NW SUITE 3400, EDMONTON, AB, T5J 4B5
(780) 420-4000   *SIC 6513*

MAINSTREET EQUITY CORP *p31*
305 10 AVE SE, CALGARY, AB, T2G 0W2
(403) 215-6060   *SIC 6513*

MAPLEWOOD NURSING HOME LIMITED *p881*
500 QUEENSWAY W SUITE 210, SIMCOE, ON, N3Y 4R4
(519) 426-8305   *SIC 6513*

MBS RESIDENCE INC *p364*
213 ST MARY'S RD SUITE 9, WINNIPEG, MB, R2H 1J2
(204) 233-5363   *SIC 6513*

MCCLURE PLACE ASSOCIATION INC *p1424*
1825 MCKERCHER DR SUITE 804, SASKATOON, SK, S7H 5N5
(306) 955-7677   *SIC 6513*

METROPOLITAIN REGIONAL HOUSING AUTHORITY *p455*
2131 GOTTINGEN ST, HALIFAX, NS, B3K 5Z7
(902) 420-6000   *SIC 6513*

MINTO GROUP INC *p825*
221 LYON ST N SUITE 806, OTTAWA, ON, K1R 7X5
SIC 6513

MINTO MANAGEMENT LIMITED *p823*

180 KENT ST UNIT 200, OTTAWA, ON, K1P 0B6
(613) 230-7051   *SIC 6513*

MOUNTAINVIEW RESIDENCE *p594*
222 MOUNTAINVIEW RD N SUITE 233, GEORGETOWN, ON, L7G 3R2
(905) 877-1800   *SIC 6513*

NACEL PROPERTIES LTD *p307*
925 GEORGIA ST W SUITE 800, VANCOUVER, BC, V6C 3L2
(604) 685-7789   *SIC 6513*

NANAIMO SENIORS VILLAGE VENTURES LTD *p235*
6085 UPLANDS DR, NANAIMO, BC, V9V 1T8
(250) 729-9524   *SIC 6513*

NEW VENTURES REALTY INC *p732*
20 KINGSBRIDGE GARDEN CIR SUITE 2004, MISSISSAUGA, ON, L5R 3K7
(905) 507-3030   *SIC 6513*

O'SHANTER DEVELOPMENT COMPANY LTD *p920*
245 CARLAW AVE SUITE 107, TORONTO, ON, M4M 2S1
(416) 466-2642   *SIC 6513*

OAKS RETIREMENT VILLAGE INC *p1005*
80 MCNAUGHTON AVE SUITE 114, WALLACEBURG, ON, N8A 1R9
(519) 627-9292   *SIC 6513*

PACIFICA RESORT LIVING RETIREMENT, THE *p283*
2525 KING GEORGE BLVD, SURREY, BC, V4P 0C8
(604) 535-9194   *SIC 6513*

PARK VIEW COLONY FARMS LTD *p355*
GD, RIDING MOUNTAIN, MB, R0J 1T0
(204) 967-2492   *SIC 6513*

PD KANCO LP *p689*
5945 AIRPORT RD SUITE 360, MISSISSAUGA, ON, L4V 1R9
(416) 234-8444   *SIC 6513*

PEOPLES PARK TOWER INC *p409*
960 ST GEORGE BLVD SUITE 144, MONCTON, NB, E1E 3Y3
(506) 857-8872   *SIC 6513*

PHC PROPERTY MANAGEMENT CORP *p988*
875 EGLINTON AVE W SUITE 300, TORONTO, ON, M6C 3Z9
(416) 789-2664   *SIC 6513*

PLACEMENTS ROCKHILL LTEE, LES *p1219*
4858 CH DE LA COTE-DES-NEIGES BUREAU 503, MONTREAL, QC, H3V 1G8
(514) 738-4704   *SIC 6513*

PMU OVL INC *p599*
1491 MANOTICK STATION RD, GREELY, ON, K4P 1P6
(613) 821-2233   *SIC 6513*

PRESTON PARK *p1425*
114 ARMISTICE WAY, SASKATOON, SK, S7J 3K9
(306) 933-0515   *SIC 6513*

REAL ESTATE INVESTMENT TRUST *p71*
80 EDENWOLD DR NW, CALGARY, AB, T3A 5R9
(403) 241-8990   *SIC 6513*

REVERA INC *p147*
223 PARK MEADOWS DR SE SUITE 127, MEDICINE HAT, AB, T1B 4K7
(403) 504-5123   *SIC 6513*

REVERA INC *p599*
85 MAIN ST E, GRIMSBY, ON, L3M 1N6
(905) 945-7044   *SIC 6513*

REVERA INC *p618*
101 10TH ST SUITE 2006, HANOVER, ON, N4N 1M9
(519) 364-4320   *SIC 6513*

REVERA INC *p700*
1500 RATHBURN RD E, MISSISSAUGA, ON, L4W 4L7
(905) 238-0800   *SIC 6513*

RIVERBEND RETIREMENT RESIDENCE *p123*
103 RABBIT HILL CRT NW, EDMONTON,

AB, T6R 2V3
(780) 438-2777   *SIC 6513*

RONKAY MANAGEMENT INC *p787*
2000 SHEPPARD AVE W SUITE 304, NORTH YORK, ON, M3N 1A2
(416) 740-4158   *SIC 6513*

ROYAL WEST COAST PENINSULA, THE *p280*
2088 152 ST SUITE 402, SURREY, BC, V4A 9Z4
(604) 538-2033   *SIC 6513*

SCHICKEDANZ BROS. LIMITED *p769*
3311 BAYVIEW AVE SUITE 105, NORTH YORK, ON, M2K 1G4
(416) 223-0710   *SIC 6513*

SCHLEGEL VILLAGES INC *p604*
60 WOODLAWN RD E, GUELPH, ON, N1H 8M8
(519) 822-5272   *SIC 6513*

SHELTER CANADIAN PROPERTIES LIMITED *p387*
7 EVERGREEN PL SUITE 2600, WINNIPEG, MB, R3L 2T3
(204) 474-5975   *SIC 6513*

SIFTON PROPERTIES LIMITED *p660*
600 LONGWORTH RD SUITE 118, LONDON, ON, N6K 4X9
(519) 472-1115   *SIC 6513*

SOCIETE DE GESTION COGIR INC *p1151*
701 CH DU RICHELIEU BUREAU 139, MCMASTERVILLE, QC, J3G 6T5
(450) 467-7667   *SIC 6513*

SOCIETE DE GESTION COGIR S.E.N.C. *p1145*
100 BOUL LA FAYETTE UNITE 426, LONGUEUIL, QC, J4K 5H6
(450) 674-8111   *SIC 6513*

SOCIETE EN COMMENDITE PLACE ALEXANDRA *p1256*
2475 RUE ALEXANDRA, QUEBEC, QC, G1E 7A8
(418) 666-7636   *SIC 6513*

ST ANDREWS HOUSING LIMITED *p97*
12720 111 AVE NW SUITE 345, EDMONTON, AB, T5M 3X3
(780) 452-4444   *SIC 6513*

ST. PAUL'S L'AMOREAUX CENTRE *p878*
3333 FINCH AVE E, SCARBOROUGH, ON, M1W 2R9
(416) 493-3333   *SIC 6513*

STURGEON CREEK RETIREMENT RESIDENCE II *p373*
707 SETTER ST SUITE 136, WINNIPEG, MB, R2Y 0A4
(204) 885-0303   *SIC 6513*

SUNSET MANSUNSET MANOR *p137*
3312 52 AVE SUITE 3402, INNISFAIL, AB, T4G 0C3
(403) 227-8200   *SIC 6513*

SYMPHONY SENIOR LIVING INC *p940*
20 TORONTO ST SUITE 440, TORONTO, ON, M5C 2B8
(416) 366-3888   *SIC 6513*

THOMAS HEALTH CARE CORPORATION, THE *p894*
490 HIGHWAY 8, STONEY CREEK, ON, L8G 1G6
(905) 573-4900   *SIC 6513*

TIDAN INC *p1200*
666 RUE SHERBROOKE O BUREAU 2300, MONTREAL, QC, H3A 1E7
(514) 845-6393   *SIC 6513*

UNIVERSAL PROPERTY MANAGEMENT LIMITED *p451*
1190 BARRINGTON ST 4TH FLOOR, HALIFAX, NS, B3H 2R4
(902) 425-8877   *SIC 6513*

URBANDALE CORPORATION *p819*
2193 ARCH ST, OTTAWA, ON, K1G 2H5
(613) 731-6331   *SIC 6513*

VALIANT RENTAL PROPERTIES LIMITED *p812*
177 NONQUON RD, OSHAWA, ON, L1G 3S2

(905) 579-1626   *SIC 6513*

VILLA COLOMBO VAUGHAN *p642*
10443 HWY 27, KLEINBURG, ON, L0J 1C0
(289) 202-2222   *SIC 6513*

WESTDALE CONSTRUCTION CO. LIMITED *p778*
35 LESMILL RD, NORTH YORK, ON, M3B 2T3
(416) 703-1877   *SIC 6513*

WINDSOR COURT RETIREMENT RESIDENCE LIMITED PARTNERSHIP *p400*
10 BARTON CRES SUITE 421, FREDERICTON, NB, E3A 5S3
(506) 450-7088   *SIC 6513*

WOODHALL PARK HOLDING CORP *p512*
10250 KENNEDY RD SUITE UNIT, BRAMPTON, ON, L6Z 4N7
(905) 846-1441   *SIC 6513*

YONGE-ROSEDALE CHARITABLE FOUNDATION *p931*
877 YONGE ST SUITE 1603, TORONTO, ON, M4W 3M2
(416) 923-8887   *SIC 6513*

Z REALTY COMPANY LIMITED *p652*
1135 ADELAIDE ST N SUITE 300, LONDON, ON, N5Y 5K7
(519) 673-1730   *SIC 6513*

SIC 6514 Dwelling operators, except apartments

CALHOME PROPERTIES LTD *p72*
820 PINE PL SW, CALGARY, AB, T3C 3N1
(403) 217-7933   *SIC 6514*

CHINOOK VILLAGE HOUSING SOCIETY *p145*
2801 13 AVE SE, MEDICINE HAT, AB, T1A 3R1
(403) 526-6951   *SIC 6514*

COOPERATIVE D'HABITATION LE TRAIT D'UNION DE GATINEAU *p1104*
29 RUE D'ORLEANS BUREAU 101, GATINEAU, QC, J8T 5T9
(819) 561-9702   *SIC 6514*

EMERALD MANAGEMENT & REALTY LTD *p64*
1036 10 AVE SW, CALGARY, AB, T2R 1M4
(403) 237-8600   *SIC 6514*

GESTION MAJEAU, MARCEL INC *p1120*
41 RUE DU COUVENT, L'EPIPHANIE, QC, J5X 0B6
(450) 938-0884   *SIC 6514*

GROUPE OPTIMUM INC *p1196*
425 BOUL DE MAISONNEUVE O BUREAU 1700, MONTREAL, QC, H3A 3G5
(514) 288-2010   *SIC 6514*

IMMEUBLES TURRET INC *p1155*
1320 BOUL GRAHAM BUREAU 330, MONT-ROYAL, QC, H3P 3C8
(514) 737-7132   *SIC 6514*

LARLYN PROPERTY MANAGEMENT LIMITED *p659*
540 WHARNCLIFFE RD S SUITE 200, LONDON, ON, N6J 2N4
(519) 690-0600   *SIC 6514*

MASTER AND FELLOWS OF MASSEY COLLEGE, THE *p976*
4 DEVONSHIRE PL, TORONTO, ON, M5S 2E1
(416) 978-2892   *SIC 6514*

REALSTAR PROPERTY MANAGEMENT LIMITED *p976*
77 BLOOR ST W SUITE 2000, TORONTO, ON, M5S 1M2
(416) 923-2950   *SIC 6514*

RESIDENCES COWANSVILLE (CRP) INC *p1088*
117 RUE PRINCIPALE, COWANSVILLE, QC, J2K 1J3
(450) 266-3757   *SIC 6514*

S. ROSSY INC *p1157*
5805 AV ROYALMOUNT, MONT-ROYAL, QC, H4P 0A1

(514) 737-1006   *SIC 6514*

VICTORIA PARK COMMUNITY HOMES INC *p614*

155 QUEEN ST N, HAMILTON, ON, L8R 2V6

(905) 527-0221   *SIC 6514*

SIC 6519 Real property lessors, nec

123179 CANADA INC *p1200*

1117 RUE SAINTE-CATHERINE O BUREAU 303, MONTREAL, QC, H3B 1H9

(514) 844-2612   *SIC 6519*

714638 ALBERTA LTD *p139*

4507 61 AVE, LEDUC, AB, T9E 7B5

(780) 986-0334   *SIC 6519*

ARTIS US HOLDINGS II GP, INC *p376*

360 MAIN ST SUITE 300, WINNIPEG, MB, R3C 3Z3

(204) 947-1250   *SIC 6519*

COBDEN AGRICULTURAL SOCIETY *p544*

43 ASTROLABE RD, COBDEN, ON, K0J 1K0

(613) 646-2426   *SIC 6519*

COOP FEDEREE, LA *p1225*

9001 BOUL DE L'ACADIE, MONTREAL, QC, H4N 3H7

(514) 384-6450   *SIC 6519*

CORPORATION MORGUARD *p824*

350 SPARKS ST SUITE 402, OTTAWA, ON, K1R 7S8

(613) 237-6373   *SIC 6519*

ENTERPRISE UNIVERSAL INC *p66*

2210 2 ST SW UNIT B250, CALGARY, AB, T2S 3C3

(403) 228-4431   *SIC 6519*

ERSKINE GREEN LIMITED *p776*

1 VALLEYBROOK DR SUITE 201, NORTH YORK, ON, M3B 2S7

(416) 487-3883   *SIC 6519*

FIRSTSERVICE CORPORATION *p974*

1140 BAY ST SUITE 4000, TORONTO, ON, M5S 2B4

(416) 960-9500   *SIC 6519*

FIRSTSERVICE RESIDENTIAL ALBERTA LTD *p49*

840 7 AVE SW SUITE 1100, CALGARY, AB, T2P 3G2

(403) 299-1810   *SIC 6519*

GALL CONSTRUCTION LIMITED *p635*

1550 VICTORIA ST N, KITCHENER, ON, N2B 3E2

(519) 743-6357   *SIC 6519*

INFORMATION SERVICES CORPORATION *p1421*

10 RESEARCH DR SUITE 300, REGINA, SK, S4S 7J7

(306) 787-8179   *SIC 6519*

RESSOURCES MSV INC *p1207*

1155 BOUL ROBERT-BOURASSA UNITE 1405, MONTREAL, QC, H3B 3A7

(418) 748-7691   *SIC 6519*

SASKATCHEWAN OPPORTUNITIES CORPORATION *p1433*

15 INNOVATION BLVD SUITE 114, SASKATOON, SK, S7N 2X8

(306) 933-6295   *SIC 6519*

T.C. ENTERPRISES LTD *p436*

5013 48 ST, YELLOWKNIFE, NT, X1A 1N4

(867) 669-8300   *SIC 6519*

VANCOUVER CONDOMINIUM SERVICES LTD *p317*

1281 GEORGIA ST W SUITE 400, VANCOUVER, BC, V6E 3J7

(604) 684-6291   *SIC 6519*

VARIETES LNJF INC *p1123*

84 5E AV E BUREAU 73, LA SARRE, QC, J9Z 1K9

(819) 333-5458   *SIC 6519*

WASAUKSING FIRST NATION *p764*

1508 LANE G PARRY ISLAND, NORTH BAY, ON, P2A 2X4

(705) 746-5519   *SIC 6519*

WHITE HILLS PROPERTY INC *p429*

251 EAST WHITE HILLS RD SUITE 100, ST. JOHN'S, NL, A1A 5X7

(709) 726-7596   *SIC 6519*

SIC 6531 Real estate agents and managers

0844212 BC LTD *p323*

7547 CAMBIE ST, VANCOUVER, BC, V6P 3H6

(604) 618-0646   *SIC 6531*

100% REALTY ASSOCIATES LTD *p1423*

1820 8TH ST E SUITE 250, SASKATOON, SK, S7H 0T6

(306) 242-6000   *SIC 6531*

10022441 MANITOBA LTD *p393*

15 SCURFIELD BLVD, WINNIPEG, MB, R3Y 1G3

(204) 615-7333   *SIC 6531*

101014233 SASKATCHEWAN LTD *p1416*

1874 SCARTH ST SUITE 2000, REGINA, SK, S4P 4B3

(306) 777-0600   *SIC 6531*

1140456 ALBERTA LTD *p119*

2852 CALGARY TRAIL NW, EDMONTON, AB, T6J 6V7

(780) 485-5005   *SIC 6531*

1906351 ONTARIO INC *p610*

1821 KING ST E, HAMILTON, ON, L8K 1V8

(905) 308-8333   *SIC 6531*

1ST LONDON REAL ESTATE SERVICES INC *p657*

1069 WELLINGTON RD, LONDON, ON, N6E 2H6

SIC 6531

2041098 ONTARIO LIMITED *p932*

260 RICHMOND ST E UNIT 300, TORONTO, ON, M5A 1P4

(416) 340-1600   *SIC 6531*

2615267 ONTARIO INC *p1010*

620 DAVENPORT RD UNIT 33, WATERLOO, ON, N2V 2C2

(226) 777-5833   *SIC 6531*

285 PEMBINA INC *p387*

285 PEMBINA HWY, WINNIPEG, MB, R3L 2E1

(204) 284-0802   *SIC 6531*

2945-9609 QUEBEC INC *p1236*

1850 BOUL LE CORBUSIER 200, MONTREAL, QC, H7S 2N5

(450) 682-4666   *SIC 6531*

3100477 NOVA SCOTIA LIMITED *p444*

110 GARLAND AVE UNIT 201, DARTMOUTH, NS, B3B 0A7

(902) 405-3948   *SIC 6531*

3500 STEELES AVENUE EAST LP *p665*

3500 STEELES AVE E UNIT 201, MARKHAM, ON, L3R 0X1

(905) 754-4826   *SIC 6531*

4395612 MANITOBA LTD *p388*

1450 CORYDON AVE SUITE 2, WINNIPEG, MB, R3N 0J3

(204) 989-5000   *SIC 6531*

462388 BC LTD *p311*

1095 PENDER ST W SUITE 1000, VANCOUVER, BC, V6E 2M6

(604) 662-3838   *SIC 6531*

501420 NB INC *p413*

71 PARADISE ROW, SAINT JOHN, NB, E2K 3H6

(506) 644-8095   *SIC 6531*

541823 BC LTD *p294*

51 PENDER ST E, VANCOUVER, BC, V6A 1S9

(604) 682-2088   *SIC 6531*

6036945 CANADA INC *p1401*

4150 RUE SHERBROOKE O BUREAU 400, WESTMOUNT, QC, H3Z 1C2

(514) 989-9909   *SIC 6531*

8961182 CANADA INC *p958*

181 BAY ST SUITE 330, TORONTO, ON, M5J 2T3

(416) 363-9491   *SIC 6531*

9046-6483 QUEBEC INC *p1216*

10314 BOUL SAINT-LAURENT, MONTREAL, QC, H3L 2P2

(514) 382-6789   *SIC 6531*

9049-8049 QUEBEC INC *p1261*

850 BOUL PIERRE-BERTRAND BUREAU 230, QUEBEC, QC, G1M 3K8

(418) 628-2223   *SIC 6531*

9065-0805 QUEBEC INC *p1274*

3075 CH DES QUATRE-BOURGEOIS BUREAU 430, QUEBEC, QC, G1W 4Y5

(418) 657-6060   *SIC 6531*

9085-3532 QUEBEC INC *p1078*

1212 BOUL TALBOT BUREAU 204, CHICOUTIMI, QC, G7H 4B7

(418) 543-5511   *SIC 6531*

921325 ALBERTA LTD *p118*

5620 104 ST NW, EDMONTON, AB, T6H 2K2

(780) 710-9112   *SIC 6531*

ACCENT CARE HOME & HOSPITAL HEALTH SERVICES INC *p374*

420 NOTRE DAME AVE, WINNIPEG, MB, R3B 1R1

(204) 783-9888   *SIC 6531*

ACCOR MANAGEMENT CANADA INC *p978*

155 WELLINGTON ST W SUITE 3300, TORONTO, ON, M5V 0C3

(416) 874-2600   *SIC 6531*

ACTION REALTY LTD *p515*

766 COLBORNE ST, BRANTFORD, ON, N3S 3S1

(519) 753-7311   *SIC 6531*

ADVANCE REALTY LTD *p194*

972 SHOPPERS ROW, CAMPBELL RIVER, BC, V9W 2C5

(250) 202-0160   *SIC 6531*

ADVANTAGE MANAGEMENT INC *p33*

6020 1A ST SW SUITE 10, CALGARY, AB, T2H 0G3

(403) 259-4141   *SIC 6531*

ALCOR HOLDINGS LTD *p127*

305 MACDONALD CRES UNIT 1, FORT MCMURRAY, AB, T9H 4B7

(780) 743-1343   *SIC 6531*

ALFID SERVICES IMMOBILIERS LTEE *p1187*

500 PLACE D'ARMES SUITE 1500, MONTREAL, QC, H2Y 2W2

(514) 282-7654   *SIC 6531*

ALGOMA CENTRAL PROPERTIES INC *p861*

293 BAY ST, SAULT STE. MARIE, ON, P6A 1X3

(705) 946-7220   *SIC 6531*

ALLEN, CENTURY 21 WENDA REALTY LTD *p870*

2025 MIDLAND AVE, SCARBOROUGH, ON, M1P 3E2

(416) 293-3900   *SIC 6531*

ALLIANCE REAL ESTATE CALGARY LTD *p41*

2003 14 ST NW SUITE 107, CALGARY, AB, T2M 3N4

(403) 270-7676   *SIC 6531*

ALTUS GROUP LIMITED *p1201*

1100 BOUL RENE-LEVESQUE O BUREAU 1600, MONTREAL, QC, H3B 4N4

(514) 392-7700   *SIC 6531*

AMENAGEMENT GRANRIVE INC *p1193*

600 BOUL DE MAISONNEUVE O BUREAU 2600, MONTREAL, QC, H3A 3J2

(514) 499-8300   *SIC 6531*

AMEX FRASERIDGE REALTY *p290*

6325 FRASER ST SUITE 200, VANCOUVER, BC, V5W 3A3

(604) 322-3272   *SIC 6531*

AMICA SENIOR LIFESTYLES INC *p948*

20 QUEEN ST W SUITE 3200, TORONTO, ON, M5H 3R3

(416) 487-2020   *SIC 6531*

ANDREWS REALTY LTD *p292*

650 41ST AVE W SUITE 410, VANCOUVER, BC, V5Z 2M9

(604) 263-2823   *SIC 6531*

ANGELL HASMAN & ASSOCIATES REALTY LTD *p342*

1544 MARINE DR SUITE 203, WEST VANCOUVER, BC, V7V 1H8

(604) 921-1188   *SIC 6531*

ANTHEM ACQUISITION LTD *p327*

SUITE 1100 BENTALL IV, 1055 DUNSMUIR ST, VANCOUVER, BC, V7X 1K8

(604) 689-3040   *SIC 6531*

APEX REALTY EXECUTIVES *p20*

1212 31 AVE NE SUITE 105, CALGARY, AB, T2E 7S8

(403) 250-5803   *SIC 6531*

APEX RESULTS REALTY INC *p526*

2465 WALKER'S LINE, BURLINGTON, ON, L7M 4K4

(905) 332-4111   *SIC 6531*

APOLLO MANAGEMENT SERVICES LTD *p830*

1200 PRINCE OF WALES DR SUITE D, OTTAWA, ON, K2C 3Y4

(613) 225-7969   *SIC 6531*

ARCTURUS REALTY CORPORATION *p578*

191 THE WEST MALL SUITE 400, ETOBICOKE, ON, M9C 5K8

(905) 943-4100   *SIC 6531*

ARNSBY, M. F. PROPERTY MANAGEMENT LTD *p651*

924 OXFORD ST E, LONDON, ON, N5Y 3J9

(519) 455-6080   *SIC 6531*

ASCENT REAL ESTATE MANAGEMENT CORPORATION *p184*

2176 WILLINGDON AVE, BURNABY, BC, V5C 5Z9

(604) 521-7653   *SIC 6531*

ASPEN PROPERTIES LTD *p43*

150 9 AVE SW UNIT 1510, CALGARY, AB, T2P 3H9

(403) 216-2660   *SIC 6531*

ASTOR & YORK RETAIL BC LTD *p918*

1721 BAYVIEW AVE UNIT 202, TORONTO, ON, M4G 3C1

(416) 434-2900   *SIC 6531*

AVISON YOUNG ADVISORS AND MANAGERS INC *p948*

257 ADELAIDE ST W SUITE 400, TORONTO, ON, M5H 1X9

(416) 343-0078   *SIC 6531*

AVISON YOUNG COMMERCIAL REAL ESTATE (ONTARIO) INC *p959*

18 YORK ST SUITE 400, TORONTO, ON, M5J 2T8

(416) 955-0000   *SIC 6531*

AYRE & OXFORD INC *p95*

13455 114 AVE NW UNIT 203, EDMONTON, AB, T5M 2E2

(780) 448-4984   *SIC 6531*

BANC PROPERTIES LIMITED *p439*

30 DAMASCUS RD SUITE 215, BEDFORD, NS, B4A 0C1

(902) 461-6450   *SIC 6531*

BANQUE NATIONALE DU CANADA *p1201*

1100 BOUL ROBERT-BOURASSA BUREAU 12E, MONTREAL, QC, H3B 3A5

(514) 866-6755   *SIC 6531*

BAY ST GEORGE RESIDENTIAL SUPPORT *p434*

30B ATLANTIC AVE, STEPHENVILLE, NL, A2N 2E9

(709) 643-9762   *SIC 6531*

BAYWEST MANAGEMENT CORPORATION *p275*

13468 77 AVE, SURREY, BC, V3W 6Y3

(604) 591-6060   *SIC 6531*

BCIMC REALTY CORPORATION *p334*

2950 JUTLAND RD UNIT 300, VICTORIA, BC, V8T 5K2

(778) 410-7100   *SIC 6531*

BENTALLGREENOAK (CANADA) LIMITED PARTNERSHIP *p328*

1055 DUNSMUIR ST SUITE 1800, VANCOUVER, BC, V7X 1B1

(604) 661-5000   *SIC 6531*

BENTALLGREENOAK (CANADA) LIMITED

PARTNERSHIP p328
1055 DUNSMUIR ST SUITE 1800, VANCOUVER, BC, V7X 1L3
(604) 646-2800 *SIC 6531*

BENTALLGREENOAK (CANADA) LIMITED PARTNERSHIP p582
10 CARLSON CRT SUITE 500, ETOBICOKE, ON, M9W 6L2
(416) 674-7707 *SIC 6531*

BENTALLGREENOAK (CANADA) LIMITED PARTNERSHIP p959
1 YORK ST SUITE 1100, TORONTO, ON, M5J 0B6
(416) 681-3400 *SIC 6531*

BGIS GLOBAL INTEGRATED SOLUTIONS CANADA LP p667
4175 14TH AVE SUITE 300, MARKHAM, ON, L3R 0J2
(905) 943-4100 *SIC 6531*

BGIS O&M SOLUTIONS INC p1185
87 RUE ONTARIO O BUREAU 200, MONTREAL, QC, H2X 0A7
(514) 840-8660 *SIC 6531*

BIRCHGROVE CAPITAL CORPORATION LTD p445
7 MELLOR AVE UNIT 1, DARTMOUTH, NS, B3B 0E8
(902) 453-9300 *SIC 6531*

BLACK, SHARON RE/MAX KELOWNA p221
1553 HARVEY AVE SUITE 100, KELOWNA, BC, V1Y 6G1
(250) 717-5040 *SIC 6531*

BLEEMAN HOLDINGS LIMITED p788
970 LAWRENCE AVE W SUITE 304, NORTH YORK, ON, M6A 3B6
(416) 256-3900 *SIC 6531*

BLUE ELEPHANT REALTY INC p979
548 KING ST W SUITE 202, TORONTO, ON, M5V 1M3
(416) 504-6133 *SIC 6531*

BOARDWALK REAL ESTATE INVESTMENT TRUST p64
1501 1 ST SW SUITE 200, CALGARY, AB, T2R 0W1
(403) 531-9255 *SIC 6531*

BOISE ST-FRANCIS INC, LE p1056
1981 RUE BERNARD-PILON, BELOEIL, QC, J3G 4S5
(450) 446-8221 *SIC 6531*

BOSA PROPERTIES INC p302
838 W HASTINGS ST, VANCOUVER, BC, V6C 2X1
(604) 412-0313 *SIC 6531*

BOSLEY REAL ESTATE LTD p923
290 MERTON ST, TORONTO, ON, M4S 1A9
(416) 322-8000 *SIC 6531*

BOUCHARD PARENT ASSOCIES INC p1244
1185 AV BERNARD, OUTREMONT, QC, H2V 1V5
(514) 271-4820 *SIC 6531*

BRAVO REALTY LIMITED p21
2116 27 AVE NE SUITE 122, CALGARY, AB, T2E 7A6
(403) 818-2020 *SIC 6531*

BROOKFIELD PROPERTIES MANAGEMENT CORPORATION p960
181 BAY ST SUITE 300, TORONTO, ON, M5J 2T3
(416) 369-2300 *SIC 6531*

BUCKINGHAM REALTY (WINDSOR) LTD p1019
4573 TECUMSEH RD E, WINDSOR, ON, N8W 1K6
(519) 948-8171 *SIC 6531*

CANADA LANDS COMPANY CLC LIMITED p960
1 UNIVERSITY AVE SUITE 1700, TORONTO, ON, M5J 2P1
(416) 214-1250 *SIC 6531*

CANADA LANDS COMPANY CLC LIMITED p979
301 FRONT ST W, TORONTO, ON, M5V 2T6
(416) 868-6937 *SIC 6531*

CANADIAN TIRE REAL ESTATE LIMITED p924
2180 YONGE ST, TORONTO, ON, M4S 2B9
(416) 480-3000 *SIC 6531*

CANADIAN TIRE REAL ESTATE LIMITED p1146
2211 BOUL ROLAND-THERRIEN BUREAU 256, LONGUEUIL, QC, J4N 1P2
(450) 448-1177 *SIC 6531*

CAPITAL REGION HOUSING CORPORATION p91
10232 112 ST NW, EDMONTON, AB, T5K 1M4
(780) 408-3301 *SIC 6531*

CAPITALE IMMOBILIERE MFQ INC, LA p1268
625 RUE JACQUES-PARIZEAU, QUEBEC, QC, G1R 2G5
(418) 644-4267 *SIC 6531*

CARVEST PROPERTIES LIMITED p662
3800 COLONEL TALBOT RD, LONDON, ON, N6P 1H5
(519) 653-4124 *SIC 6531*

CATHOLIC CEMETERIES OF THE DIOCESE OF HAMILTON p531
600 SPRING GARDENS RD, BURLINGTON, ON, L7T 1J1
(905) 522-7727 *SIC 6531*

CBRE LIMITEE p46
530 8 AVE SW SUITE 500, CALGARY, AB, T2P 3S8
(403) 536-1290 *SIC 6531*

CBRE LIMITEE p311
1021 HASTINGS ST W SUITE 2500, VANCOUVER, BC, V6E 0C3
(604) 319-1374 *SIC 6531*

CBRE LIMITEE p766
2001 SHEPPARD AVE E SUITE 300, NORTH YORK, ON, M2J 4Z8
(416) 494-0600 *SIC 6531*

CBRE LIMITEE p950
40 KING ST W SUITE 4100, TORONTO, ON, M5H 3Y2
(416) 947-7661 *SIC 6531*

CCL PROPERTIES LTD p297
475 GEORGIA ST W SUITE 800, VANCOUVER, BC, V6B 4M9
(604) 684-7117 *SIC 6531*

CENTRE CITY REAL ESTATE INC p249
1679 15TH AVE, PRINCE GEORGE, BC, V2L 3X2
(250) 552-2757 *SIC 6531*

CENTURION ASSET MANAGEMENT INC p771
25 SHEPPARD AVE W SUITE 710, NORTH YORK, ON, M2N 6S6
(416) 733-5600 *SIC 6531*

CENTURY 21 ASSOCIATES INC p705
5659 MCADAM RD UNIT C1, MISSISSAUGA, ON, L4Z 1N9
(905) 279-8888 *SIC 6531*

CENTURY 21 ASSURANCE REALTY LTD p221
251 HARVEY AVE, KELOWNA, BC, V1Y 6C2
(250) 869-0101 *SIC 6531*

CENTURY 21 ATRIA REALTY INC p851
1550 16TH AVE UNIT C SUITE 200 SOUTH, RICHMOND HILL, ON, L4B 3K9
(905) 883-1988 *SIC 6531*

CENTURY 21 B J ROTH REALTY LTD p484
355 BAYFIELD ST SUITE 5, BARRIE, ON, L4M 3C3
(705) 721-9111 *SIC 6531*

CENTURY 21 BAMBER REALTY LTD p67
1612 17 AVE SW, CALGARY, AB, T2T 0E3
(403) 875-4653 *SIC 6531*

CENTURY 21 BEST SELLERS LTD p705
4 ROBERT SPECK PKY SUITE 150, MISSISSAUGA, ON, L4Z 1S1
(905) 273-4211 *SIC 6531*

CENTURY 21 CAMDEC REAL ESTATE LTD p873
4544 SHEPPARD AVE E SUITE 100, SCAR-BOROUGH, ON, M1S 1V2
(416) 298-2800 *SIC 6531*

CENTURY 21 CARRIE REALTY LTD p368
1046 ST MARY'S RD, WINNIPEG, MB, R2M 5S6
(204) 987-2100 *SIC 6531*

CENTURY 21 COASTAL REALTY LTD p276
12837 76 AVE SUITE 217, SURREY, BC, V3W 2V3
(604) 599-4888 *SIC 6531*

CENTURY 21 COLONIAL REALTY INC p1038
111 ST. PETERS RD, CHARLOTTETOWN, PE, C1A 5P1
(902) 566-2121 *SIC 6531*

CENTURY 21 FIRST CANADIAN CORP p655
420 YORK ST SUITE 21, LONDON, ON, N6B 1R1
(519) 673-3390 *SIC 6531*

CENTURY 21 HERITAGE HOUSE LTD p1035
871 DUNDAS ST, WOODSTOCK, ON, N4S 1G8
(519) 539-5646 *SIC 6531*

CENTURY 21 KING'S QUAY REAL ESTATE INC p668
7300 WARDEN AVE SUITE 401, MARKHAM, ON, L3R 9Z6
(905) 940-3428 *SIC 6531*

CENTURY 21 LANTHORN REAL ESTATE LTD p491
266 FRONT ST UNIT 202, BELLEVILLE, ON, K8N 2Z2
(613) 967-2100 *SIC 6531*

CENTURY 21 MILLENNIUM INC p509
350 RUTHERFORD RD S SUITE 10, BRAMPTON, ON, L6W 4N6
(905) 450-8300 *SIC 6531*

CENTURY 21 NEW AGE REALTY INC p718
5618 TENTH LINE W UNIT 9, MISSISSAUGA, ON, L5M 7L9
(905) 567-1411 *SIC 6531*

CENTURY 21 NEW CONCEPT LTD p776
1993 LESLIE ST, NORTH YORK, ON, M3B 2M3
(416) 449-7600 *SIC 6531*

CENTURY 21 PEOPLE'S CHOICE REALTY INC p997
1780 ALBION RD SUITE 2, TORONTO, ON, M9V 1C1
(416) 742-8000 *SIC 6531*

CENTURY 21 PERCY FULTON LTD p876
2911 KENNEDY RD, SCARBOROUGH, ON, M1V 1S8
(416) 298-0465 *SIC 6531*

CENTURY 21 PROFESSIONAL GROUP INC p514
32 CHARING CROSS ST, BRANTFORD, ON, N3R 2H2
(519) 756-3900 *SIC 6531*

CENTURY 21 QUEENSWOOD REALTY LTD p332
2558 SINCLAIR RD, VICTORIA, BC, V8N 1B8
(250) 477-1100 *SIC 6531*

CENTURY 21 REGAL REALTY INC p873
4030 SHEPPARD AVE E SUITE 2, SCARBOROUGH, ON, M1S 1S6
(416) 291-0929 *SIC 6531*

CENTURY 21 SKYLARK REAL ESTATE LTD p734
1510 DREW RD UNIT 6, MISSISSAUGA, ON, L5S 1W7
(905) 673-3100 *SIC 6531*

CENTURY 21 TODAY REALTY LTD p591
225 GARRISON RD, FORT ERIE, ON, L2A 1M8
(905) 871-2121 *SIC 6531*

CENTURY 21 UNITED REALTY INC BROKAGE p840
387 GEORGE ST S, PETERBOROUGH, ON, K9J 3E1
(705) 743-4444 *SIC 6531*

CENTURY 21 VISION LTD p1221
5517 AV DE MONKLAND, MONTREAL, QC, H4A 1C8
(514) 481-2126 *SIC 6531*

CENTURY 21 WESTMAN REALTY LTD. p347
2915 VICTORIA AVE, BRANDON, MB, R7B 2N6
(204) 725-0555 *SIC 6531*

CENTURY 21 YOUR NUMBER ONE REALTY INC BROKERAGE p770
6400 YONGE ST SUITE 200, NORTH YORK, ON, M2M 3X4
SIC 6531

CENTURY 21-JOHN DEVRIES LTD p625
444 HAZELDEAN RD, KANATA, ON, K2L 1V2
(613) 836-2570 *SIC 6531*

CENTURY GROUP LANDS CORPORATION p237
11 EIGHTH ST 10TH FL, ANVIL CENTRE, NEW WESTMINSTER, BC, V3M 3N7
(604) 943-2203 *SIC 6531*

CIGM p1396
600 CH DU GOLF, VERDUN, QC, H3E 1A8
(514) 762-5264 *SIC 6531*

CIR COMMERCIAL REALTY INC p1417
2505 11TH AVE SUITE 200, REGINA, SK, S4P 0K6
(306) 789-8300 *SIC 6531*

CITYHOUSING FIRST PLACE HAMILTON p611
350 KING ST E SUITE 300, HAMILTON, ON, L8N 3Y3
(905) 525-9800 *SIC 6531*

CLV GROUP INC p833
485 BANK ST SUITE 200, OTTAWA, ON, K2P 1Z2
(613) 728-2000 *SIC 6531*

CMN CALGARY INC p46
335 8 AVE SW SUITE 1000, CALGARY, AB, T2P 1C9
(403) 266-5544 *SIC 6531*

COAST CAPITAL REAL ESTATE LTD p337
4460 CHATTERTON WAY SUITE 110, VICTORIA, BC, V8X 5J2
(250) 477-5353 *SIC 6531*

COAST REALTY GROUP (QUALICUM) LTD p252
689 MEMORIAL AVE, QUALICUM BEACH, BC, V9K 1S8
(250) 752-3375 *SIC 6531*

COBURN REALTY LTD p750
1415 WOODROFFE AVE, NEPEAN, ON, K2G 1V9
(613) 226-8790 *SIC 6531*

COGIR APARTMENTS REAL ESTATE INVESTMENT TRUST p1068
7250 BOUL TASCHEREAU BUREAU 200, BROSSARD, QC, J4W 1M9
(450) 672-5090 *SIC 6531*

COLDWELL BANKER FIRST OTTAWA REALTY LTD p828
1419 CARLING AVE SUITE 219, OTTAWA, ON, K1Z 7L6
(613) 728-2664 *SIC 6531*

COLDWELL BANKER HOME & FAMILY REALTY LTD p803
1515 REBECCA ST SUITE 25, OAKVILLE, ON, L6L 5G8
(905) 825-3305 *SIC 6531*

COLDWELL BANKER HORIZON REALTY LTD p221
1470 HARVEY AVE SUITE 14, KELOWNA, BC, V1Y 9K8
(250) 860-7500 *SIC 6531*

COLDWELL BANKER NATIONAL PREFERRED PROPERTIES p388
1530 TAYLOR AVE SUITE 6, WINNIPEG, MB, R3N 1Y1
(204) 985-4300 *SIC 6531*

COLDWELL BANKER NEUMANN HERB REAL ESTATE LTD p601
824 GORDON ST SUITE 201, GUELPH, ON, N1G 1Y7
(519) 821-3600 *SIC 6531*

COLDWELL BANKER NEUMANN REAL ES-

TATE *p601*
824 GORDON ST UNIT 201, GUELPH, ON, N1G 1Y7
(519) 821-3600 *SIC 6531*

COLDWELL BANKER PROPERTIES UN-LIMITED REALTY LTD *p918*
874 EGLINTON AVE E, TORONTO, ON, M4G 2L1
(416) 424-1300 *SIC 6531*

COLDWELL BANKER RHODES & COM-PANY LTD *p833*
100 ARGYLE AVE, OTTAWA, ON, K2P 1B6
(613) 236-9551 *SIC 6531*

COLDWELL CASE REALTY *p919*
836 DANFORTH AVE, TORONTO, ON, M4J 1L6
(416) 690-7771 *SIC 6531*

COLLIERS INTERNATIONAL (QUEBEC) INC *p1194*
1800 AV MCGILL COLLEGE BUREAU 400, MONTREAL, QC, H3A 3J6
(514) 866-1900 *SIC 6531*

COLLIERS INTERNATIONAL GROUP INC *p961*
181 BAY ST SUITE 1400, TORONTO, ON, M5J 2V1
(416) 777-2200 *SIC 6531*

COLLIERS INTERNATIONAL GROUP INC *p974*
1140 BAY ST SUITE 4000, TORONTO, ON, M5S 2B4
(416) 960-9500 *SIC 6531*

COLLIERS MACAULAY NICOLLS INC *p47*
335 8 AVE SW 900 ROYAL BANK BLDG, CALGARY, AB, T2P 1C9
(403) 265-9180 *SIC 6531*

COLLIERS MACAULAY NICOLLS INC *p303*
200 GRANVILLE ST UNIT 19, VANCOU-VER, BC, V6C 1S4
(604) 681-4111 *SIC 6531*

COLLIERS MCCLOCKLIN REAL ESTATE CORP *p1426*
728 SPADINA CRES E SUITE 101, SASKA-TOON, SK, S7K 3H2
(306) 653-4410 *SIC 6531*

COMENCO SERVICES AUX IMMEUBLES INC *p1051*
8150 BOUL METROPOLITAIN E BUREAU 310, ANJOU, QC, H1K 1A1
(514) 389-7233 *SIC 6531*

COMMERCIAL WELDING LTD *p361*
130 CANADA ST, WINKLER, MB, R6W 0J3
(204) 325-4195 *SIC 6531*

CONCEPT 2000 REAL ESTATE (1989) IN-CORPORATED *p270*
15127 100 AVE SUITE 103, SURREY, BC, V3R 0N9
(604) 583-2000 *SIC 6531*

CONCERT PROPERTIES LTD *p326*
1190 HORNBY ST, VANCOUVER, BC, V6Z 2K5
(604) 688-9460 *SIC 6531*

CONDOMINIUM FIRST MANAGEMENT SERVICES LTD *p47*
840 7 AVE SW SUITE 600, CALGARY, AB, T2P 3G2
(403) 299-1810 *SIC 6531*

CONDOR PROPERTIES LTD *p551*
1500 HIGHWAY 7, CONCORD, ON, L4K 5Y4
(905) 907-1500 *SIC 6531*

CONSTRUCTION J.C. LEPAGE LTEE *p1244*
254 132 RTE, PABOS MILLS, QC, G0C 2J0
(418) 689-0568 *SIC 6531*

CORPORATION DE DEVELOPMENT CUL-TUREL DE TROIS-RIVIERES *p1387*
1425 PLACE DE L'HOTEL-DE-VILLE, TROIS-RIVIERES, QC, G9A 4S7
(819) 372-4614 *SIC 6531*

CORPORATION DU FORT ST-JEAN *p1317*
15 RUE JACQUES-CARTIER N, SAINT-JEAN-SUR-RICHELIEU, QC, J3B 8R8
(450) 358-6900 *SIC 6531*

CORPORATION MORGUARD *p709*

55 CITY CENTRE DR SUITE 800, MISSIS-SAUGA, ON, L5B 1M3
(905) 281-3800 *SIC 6531*

COURTIERS INTER-QUEBEC INC, LES *p1254*
900 BOUL RAYMOND, QUEBEC, QC, G1B 3G3
SIC 6531

COURTIERS INTER-QUEBEC INC, LES *p1256*
805 RUE DE NEMOURS, QUEBEC, QC, G1H 6Z5
(418) 622-7537 *SIC 6531*

CREIT MANAGEMENT L.P. *p928*
175 BLOOR ST E SUITE 500N, TORONTO, ON, M4W 3R8
(416) 628-7771 *SIC 6531*

CREST REALTY LTD *p240*
2609 WESTVIEW DR SUITE 101, NORTH VANCOUVER, BC, V7N 4M2
(604) 985-1321 *SIC 6531*

CROWN PROPERTY MANAGEMENT INC *p944*
400 UNIVERSITY AVE SUITE 1900, TORONTO, ON, M5G 1S5
(416) 927-1851 *SIC 6531*

CUSHMAN & WAKEFIELD ASSET SER-VICES ULC *p937*
1 QUEEN ST E SUITE 300, TORONTO, ON, M5C 2W5
(416) 955-0595 *SIC 6531*

CUSHMAN & WAKEFIELD LTEE *p1195*
999 BOUL DE MAISONNEUVE O BUREAU 1500, MONTREAL, QC, H3A 3L4
(514) 841-5011 *SIC 6531*

CUSHMAN & WAKEFIELD ULC *p330*
700 GEORGIA ST W, VANCOUVER, BC, V7Y 1K8
(604) 683-3111 *SIC 6531*

CUSHMAN & WAKEFIELD ULC *p731*
5770 HURONTARIO ST SUITE 200, MIS-SISSAUGA, ON, L5R 3G5
(905) 568-9500 *SIC 6531*

CUSHMAN & WAKEFIELD ULC *p961*
161 BAY ST SUITE 1500, TORONTO, ON, M5J 2S1
(416) 862-0611 *SIC 6531*

CW EDMONTON INC *p88*
10088 102 AVE NW UNIT 2700, EDMON-TON, AB, T5J 2Z1
(780) 420-1177 *SIC 6531*

DANIELS GROUP INC, THE *p933*
130 QUEENS QUAY E 8 FL, TORONTO, ON, M5A 0P6
(416) 598-2129 *SIC 6531*

DAVPART INC *p771*
4576 YONGE ST UNIT 700, NORTH YORK, ON, M2N 6N4
(416) 222-3010 *SIC 6531*

DEERBROOK REALTY INC *p1021*
59 EUGENIE ST E, WINDSOR, ON, N8X 2X9
(519) 972-1000 *SIC 6531*

DEL PROPERTY MANAGEMENT INC *p781*
109-4800 DUFFERIN ST, NORTH YORK, ON, M3H 5S9
(416) 661-3151 *SIC 6531*

DEVENCORE INVESTMENTS INC *p1203*
800 BOUL RENE-LEVESQUE O BUREAU 900, MONTREAL, QC, H3B 1X9
(514) 392-1330 *SIC 6531*

DEVENCORE LTEE *p1203*
800 BOUL RENE-LEVESQUE O BUREAU 900, MONTREAL, QC, H3B 1X9
(514) 392-1330 *SIC 6531*

DFH REAL ESTATE LTD *p333*
3914 SHELBOURNE ST, VICTORIA, BC, V8P 4J1
(250) 477-7291 *SIC 6531*

DISTRICT REALTY CORPORATION *p828*
50 BAYSWATER AVE, OTTAWA, ON, K1Y 2E9
(613) 759-8383 *SIC 6531*

DORSET REALTY GROUP CANADA LTD

p260
10451 SHELLBRIDGE WAY SUITE 215, RICHMOND, BC, V6X 2W8
(604) 270-1711 *SIC 6531*

DOWNHOME SHOPPE AND GALLERY *p431*
303 WATER ST, ST. JOHN'S, NL, A1C 1B9
(709) 722-2970 *SIC 6531*

DOWNTOWN REALTY LTD *p331*
4007 32 ST, VERNON, BC, V1T 5P2
(250) 260-0453 *SIC 6531*

DREAM ASSET MANAGEMENT CORPO-RATION *p938*
30 ADELAIDE ST E SUITE 301, TORONTO, ON, M5C 3H1
(416) 365-3535 *SIC 6531*

DREAM INDUSTRIAL LP *p938*
30 ADELAIDE ST E SUITE 301, TORONTO, ON, M5C 3H1
(416) 365-3535 *SIC 6531*

DREAM OFFICE LP *p938*
30 ADELAIDE ST E SUITE 301, TORONTO, ON, M5C 3H1
(416) 365-3535 *SIC 6531*

DREAM OFFICE MANAGEMENT CORP *p938*
30 ADELAIDE ST E SUITE 301, TORONTO, ON, M5C 3H1
(416) 365-3535 *SIC 6531*

DUGGAN, PAT REAL ESTATE SERVICES LTD *p75*
156 CITADEL CLOSE NW, CALGARY, AB, T3G 4A6
(403) 547-8401 *SIC 6531*

DURHAM REGION NON PROFIT HOUSING CORPORATION *p812*
28 ALBERT ST, OSHAWA, ON, L1H 8S5
(905) 436-6609 *SIC 6531*

DYMON TECHNOLOGIES INC *p819*
1830 WALKLEY RD SUITE 2, OTTAWA, ON, K1H 8K3
(613) 247-0888 *SIC 6531*

ELITE PACIFIC REALTY INC *p194*
3010 BOUNDARY RD, BURNABY, BC, V5M 4A1
(604) 671-5259 *SIC 6531*

ELITE REALTY T. W. INC *p694*
5090 EXPLORER DR UNIT 7, MISSIS-SAUGA, ON, L4W 4X6
(905) 629-1515 *SIC 6531*

ENTERPRISE PROPERTY GROUP (MAN) INC *p377*
330 PORTAGE AVE UNIT 1000, WIN-NIPEG, MB, R3C 0C4
(204) 947-2242 *SIC 6531*

EPIC INVESTMENT SERVICES LIMITED PARTNERSHIP *p951*
141 ADELAIDE ST W SUITE 1201, TORONTO, ON, M5H 3L5
(416) 497-9332 *SIC 6531*

ESTATE REALTY LTD *p917*
1052 KINGSTON RD, TORONTO, ON, M4E 1T4
(416) 690-5100 *SIC 6531*

ESTIMATEURS PROFESSIONELS LER-OUX, BEAUDRY, PICARD & ASSOCIES INC, LES *p1176*
255 BOUL CREMAZIE E BUREAU 9E, MONTREAL, QC, H2M 1L5
(514) 384-4220 *SIC 6531*

EVERGREEN WEST REALTY *p198*
2963 GLEN DR SUITE 206, COQUITLAM, BC, V3B 2P7
(604) 782-7327 *SIC 6531*

EXIT REALTY ASSOCIATES *p397*
260 RUE CHAMPLAIN, DIEPPE, NB, E1A 1P3
(506) 382-3948 *SIC 6531*

EXIT REALTY CORP. INTERNATIONAL *p722*
2345 ARGENTIA RD SUITE 200, MISSIS-SAUGA, ON, L5N 8K4
(905) 363-4050 *SIC 6531*

EXIT REALTY GROUP BROKERAGE *p491*
5503 62 HWY, BELLEVILLE, ON, K8N 4Z7
(613) 966-9400 *SIC 6531*

EXIT REALTY HARE PEEL *p508*
134 QUEEN ST E SUITE 100, BRAMPTON, ON, L6V 1B2
(905) 451-2390 *SIC 6531*

EXIT REALTY OPTIMUM *p446*
1 GLOSTER CRT, DARTMOUTH, NS, B3B 1X9
(902) 444-3948 *SIC 6531*

EXP REALTY OF CANADA, INC *p771*
4711 YONGE ST 10 FL, NORTH YORK, ON, M2N 6K8
(866) 530-7737 *SIC 6531*

FARIS TEAM CORP, THE *p486*
431 BAYVIEW DR UNIT 14, BARRIE, ON, L4N 8Y2
(705) 797-8485 *SIC 6531*

FIRST CAPITAL ASSET MANAGEMENT LP *p991*
85 HANNA AVE SUITE 400, TORONTO, ON, M6K 3S3
(416) 504-4114 *SIC 6531*

FIRST CONTACT REALTY LTD *p487*
299 LAKESHORE DR SUITE 100, BARRIE, ON, L4N 7Y9
(705) 728-4067 *SIC 6531*

FIRST OTTAWA REALTY INC *p890*
2 HOBIN ST, STITTSVILLE, ON, K2S 1C3
(613) 831-9628 *SIC 6531*

FISHER, DEBBIE & LOCHHEAD, DAN *p331*
5603 27 ST, VERNON, BC, V1T 8Z5
(250) 549-4161 *SIC 6531*

FLAT FEE REALTY INC *p487*
21 PATTERSON RD UNIT 28, BARRIE, ON, L4N 7W6
SIC 6531

FOREST HILL REAL ESTATE INC *p771*
500 SHEPPARD AVE E SUITE 201, NORTH YORK, ON, M2N 6H7
(416) 226-1987 *SIC 6531*

FOREST HILL REAL ESTATE INC *p972*
441 SPADINA RD, TORONTO, ON, M5P 2W3
(416) 488-2875 *SIC 6531*

GEORGIA PACIFIC REALTY CORPORA-TION *p293*
601 BROADWAY W UNIT 200, VANCOU-VER, BC, V5Z 4C2
(604) 222-8585 *SIC 6531*

GESTIONS MONIT LTEE, LES *p1205*
1255 RUE UNIVERSITY, MONTREAL, QC, H3B 3X4
(514) 861-9772 *SIC 6531*

GLOBAL LINK REALTY GROUP INC *p670*
351 FERRIER ST UNIT 2351, MARKHAM, ON, L3R 2Z5
(905) 475-0028 *SIC 6531*

GM DEVELOPPEMENT INC *p1259*
520 BOUL CHAREST E BUREAU 233, QUEBEC, QC, G1K 3J3
(418) 692-7470 *SIC 6531*

GOLDEN LIFE MANAGEMENT CORP *p204*
1800 WILLOWBROOK DR, CRANBROOK, BC, V1C 7H9
(250) 489-0667 *SIC 6531*

GORDON'S STATE SERVICES LTD., BRO-KERAGE *p630*
490 DISCOVERY AVE UNIT 7, KINGSTON, ON, K7K 7E9
(613) 542-0963 *SIC 6531*

GRAND VALLEY REALTY INC *p641*
370 HIGHLAND RD W, KITCHENER, ON, N2M 5J9
(519) 745-7000 *SIC 6531*

GRANDE PRAIRIE ASSOCIATES REALTY LTD *p132*
10114 100 ST, GRANDE PRAIRIE, AB, T8V 2L9
(780) 538-4700 *SIC 6531*

GROUPE ALTUS *p1205*
1100 BOUL RENE-LEVESQUE O BUREAU 1600, MONTREAL, QC, H3B 4N4
SIC 6531

GROUPE SUTTON - ACTUEL INC *p1143*
115 RUE SAINT-CHARLES O, LONGUEUIL,

QC, J4H 1C7

(450) 651-1079   *SIC* 6531

GROUPE SUTTON EXCELLENCE INC *p*1237
1555 BOUL DE L'AVENIR BUREAU 100, MONTREAL, QC, H7S 2N5

(450) 662-3036   *SIC* 6531

GROUPE SUTTON SUR L'ILE INC   *p*1396
38 PLACE DU COMMERCE BUREAU 280, VERDUN, QC, H3E 1T8

(514) 769-7010   *SIC* 6531

GROUPE SUTTON SYNERGIE INC   *p*1114
635 RUE BEAUDRY N BUREAU 201, JOLI-ETTE, QC, J6E 8L7

(450) 585-0999   *SIC* 6531

GROUPE SUTTON-ACTION INC   *p*1068
2190 BOUL LAPINIERE, BROSSARD, QC, J4W 1M2

(450) 462-4414   *SIC* 6531

GROUPE SUTTON-CLODEM INC   *p*1132
9515 BOUL LASALLE, LASALLE, QC, H8R 2M9

(514) 364-3315   *SIC* 6531

GSL HOLDINGS LTD   *p*313
1177 W HASTINGS ST SUITE 2088, VAN-COUVER, BC, V6E 2K3

(604) 688-8999   *SIC* 6531

GWL REALTY ADVISORS INC   *p*709
1 CITY CENTRE DR SUITE 300, MISSIS-SAUGA, ON, L5B 1M2

(905) 275-6600   *SIC* 6531

GWL REALTY ADVISORS INC   *p*942
33 YONGE ST SUITE 1000, TORONTO, ON, M5E 1S9

(416) 507-2929   *SIC* 6531

H&R PROPERTY MANAGEMENT LTD *p*785
3625 DUFFERIN ST SUITE 409, NORTH YORK, ON, M3K 1Z2

(416) 635-0163   *SIC* 6531

HABITAT METIS DU NORD INC   *p*1102
213 RUE HERAULT, FORT-COULONGE, QC, J0X 1V0

(819) 683-1344   *SIC* 6531

HARVARD DEVELOPMENTS INC   *p*1418
1874 SCARTH ST SUITE 2000, REGINA, SK, S4P 4B3

(306) 777-0600   *SIC* 6531

HILL, NORMAN REALTY INC   *p*679
20 CACHET WOODS CRT SUITE 2, MARKHAM, ON, L6C 3G1

(416) 226-5515   *SIC* 6531

HOMEFRONT REALTY INC   *p*514
245 KING GEORGE RD, BRANTFORD, ON, N3R 7N7

(519) 756-8120   *SIC* 6531

HOMELIFE ATLANTIC   *p*457
233 BEDFORD HWY, HALIFAX, NS, B3M 2J9

(902) 457-4000   *SIC* 6531

HOMELIFE BAYVIEW REALTY INC   *p*904
505 HIGHWAY 7 E SUITE 201, THORN-HILL, ON, L3T 7T1

(416) 845-0000   *SIC* 6531

HOMELIFE BENCHMARK REALTY CORP *p*226
6323 197 ST, LANGLEY, BC, V2Y 1K8

(604) 530-4141   *SIC* 6531

HOMELIFE BENCHMARK TITUS REALTY *p*272
105-5477 152 ST, SURREY, BC, V3S 5A5

(604) 575-5262   *SIC* 6531

HOMELIFE CHOLKAN REALTY CORP *p*574
109 JUDGE RD, ETOBICOKE, ON, M8Z 5B5

(416) 236-7711   *SIC* 6531

HOMELIFE EXPERTS REALTY LTD   *p*499
50 COTTRELLE BLVD SUITE 29, BRAMP-TON, ON, L6S 0E1

SIC 6531

HOMELIFE FOUNDATION REALTY INC *p*769
648 FINCH AVE E SUITE 12, NORTH YORK, ON, M2K 2E6

(416) 229-0515   *SIC* 6531

HOMELIFE FRONTIER REALTY INC *p*906
7620 YONGE ST SUITE 400, THORNHILL,

ON, L4J 1V9

(416) 218-8800   *SIC* 6531

HOMELIFE GLENAYRE REALTY COMPANY LTD *p*175
3033 IMMEL ST UNIT 360, ABBOTSFORD, BC, V2S 6S2

(604) 520-6829   *SIC* 6531

HOMELIFE GOLD PACIFIC REALTY INC *p*877
3601 VICTORIA PARK AVE SUITE 401, SCARBOROUGH, ON, M1W 3Y3

(416) 490-1068   *SIC* 6531

HOMELIFE REALTY (GUELPH) LIMITED *p*601
1027 GORDON ST, GUELPH, ON, N1G 4X1

(519) 836-1072   *SIC* 6531

HOMELIFE SUPERSTARS REAL ESTATE LIMITED *p*503
2565 STEELES AVE E UNIT 11, BRAMP-TON, ON, L6T 4L6

(905) 792-7800   *SIC* 6531

HOMELIFE-KEMPENFELT KELLY REAL ESTATE LTD *p*622
7886 YONGE ST, INNISFIL, ON, L9S 1L4

(705) 436-5111   *SIC* 6531

HOMELIFE/ACES REALTY & INS. LTD *p*874
4002 SHEPPARD AVE E UNIT 216, SCAR-BOROUGH, ON, M1S 4R5

(416) 298-8880   *SIC* 6531

HOMELIFE/GOLDEN EAST REALTY INC *p*671
200 TOWN CENTRE BLVD SUITE 206, MARKHAM, ON, L3R 8G5

(905) 415-1331   *SIC* 6531

HOMELIFE/KEMPENFELT/KELLY REALTY LTD *p*487
284 DUNLOP ST W, BARRIE, ON, L4N 1B9

(705) 725-0000   *SIC* 6531

HOMELIFE/LEADER INC   *p*671
3636 STEELES AVE E UNIT 307, MARKHAM, ON, L3R 1K9

(416) 298-6633   *SIC* 6531

HOMELIFE/METROPARK REALTY INC *p*554
8700A DUFFERIN ST, CONCORD, ON, L4K 4S6

(416) 798-7705   *SIC* 6531

HOMELIFE/MIRACLE REALTY LTD   *p*580
5010 STEELES AVE W SUITE 11A, ETOBI-COKE, ON, M9V 5C6

(416) 747-9777   *SIC* 6531

HOMELIFE/RESPONSE REALTY INC *p*706
4312 VILLAGE CENTRE CRT, MISSIS-SAUGA, ON, L4Z 1S2

(905) 949-0070   *SIC* 6531

HOMELIFE/ROYALCORP REAL ESTATE INC *p*1031
4040 STEELES AVE W UNIT 12, WOOD-BRIDGE, ON, L4L 4Y5

(905) 856-6611   *SIC* 6531

HOMELIFE/VISION REALTY INC   *p*776
1945 LESLIE ST, NORTH YORK, ON, M3B 2M3

(416) 383-1828   *SIC* 6531

HOPEWELL RESIDENTIAL MANAGEMENT LP *p*67
2020 4 ST SW SUITE 410, CALGARY, AB, T2S 1W3

(403) 232-8821   *SIC* 6531

HUGH & MCKINNON REALTY LTD   *p*280
14007 16 AVE, SURREY, BC, V4A 1P9

(604) 531-1909   *SIC* 6531

HUMFORD MANAGEMENT INC   *p*92
10050 112 ST NW SUITE 300, EDMON-TON, AB, T5K 2J1

(780) 426-4960   *SIC* 6531

IMMEUBLES RICHELIEU N. REON INC, LES *p*1318
550 BOUL DU SEMINAIRE N, SAINT-JEAN-SUR-RICHELIEU, QC, J3B 5L6

(450) 349-5883   *SIC* 6531

IMMEUBLES VILLAGE D.D.O. INC, LES *p*1091
4000 BOUL SAINT-JEAN BUREAU 2000, DOLLARD-DES-ORMEAUX, QC, H9G 1X1

(514) 684-1141   *SIC* 6531

IMMEUBLES VILLAGE POINTE-CLAIRE INC *p*1250
263 BOUL SAINT-JEAN, POINTE-CLAIRE, QC, H9R 3J1

(514) 694-2121   *SIC* 6531

IMMIGRANT AND REFUGEE COMMUNITY ORGANIZATION OF MANITOBA INC *p*373
95 ELLEN ST, WINNIPEG, MB, R3A 1S8

(204) 943-8765   *SIC* 6531

INTERCITY REALTY INC   *p*554
163 BUTTERMILL AVE SUITE 15, CON-CORD, ON, L4K 3X8

(905) 738-6644   *SIC* 6531

INTERNET REALTY LTD   *p*222
1101 HARVEY AVE, KELOWNA, BC, V1Y 6E8

(250) 762-9979   *SIC* 6531

INVESTISSEMENTS   IMMOBILIERS KEVLAR INC *p*1197
1800 AV MCGILL COLLEGE BUREAU 1900, MONTREAL, QC, H3A 3J6

(514) 393-8858   *SIC* 6531

INVESTISSEMENTS KITZA INC   *p*1132
9515 BOUL LASALLE, LASALLE, QC, H8R 2M9

(514) 364-3315   *SIC* 6531

INVESTISSEMENTS MONIT INC, LES *p*1197
1000 RUE SHERBROOKE O UNITE 1800, MONTREAL, QC, H3A 3G4

(514) 933-3000   *SIC* 6531

INVESTISSEMENTS RAYPAUL LTEE, LES *p*1205
1258 RUE STANLEY, MONTREAL, QC, H3B 2S7

(514) 871-0057   *SIC* 6531

JON WOOD   *p*248
3137 ST JOHNS ST, PORT MOODY, BC, V3H 2C8

SIC 6531

JONES LANG LASALLE REAL ESTATE SERVICES, INC *p*953
22 ADELAIDE ST W 26TH FL EAST TOWER, TORONTO, ON, M5H 4E3

(416) 304-6000   *SIC* 6531

K & G APARTMENT HOLDINGS INC   *p*922
305 ROEHAMPTON AVE, TORONTO, ON, M4P 0B2

(416) 487-3050   *SIC* 6531

KALLES, HARVEY REAL ESTATE LTD *p*788
2145 AVENUE RD, NORTH YORK, ON, M5M 4B2

(416) 441-2888   *SIC* 6531

KAWARTHA PARTICIPATION PROJECTS *p*839
440 WATER ST, PETERBOROUGH, ON, K9H 7K6

(705) 745-9434   *SIC* 6531

KERR GROUP, THE   *p*243
886 WEMBLEY RD UNIT5, PARKSVILLE, BC, V9P 2E6

(250) 586-1100   *SIC* 6531

KILKENNY REAL ESTATE LTD   *p*387
663 STAFFORD ST, WINNIPEG, MB, R3M 2X7

(204) 475-9130   *SIC* 6531

L'EDIFICE 3333 BOUL GRAHAM   *p*1155
3333 BOUL GRAHAM BUREAU 100, MONT-ROYAL, QC, H3R 3L5

(514) 341-8182   *SIC* 6531

LAWMARK CAPITAL INC   *p*375
179 MCDERMOT AVE UNIT 301, WIN-NIPEG, MB, R3B 0S1

(204) 942-1138   *SIC* 6531

LE SYNDICAT DE LA COPROPRIETE LES JARDINS DU HAVRE *p*1256
25 RUE DES MOUETTES BUREAU 431, QUEBEC, QC, G1E 7G1

(418) 660-6599   *SIC* 6531

LEGEND REAL ESTATE GROUP LTD *p*290
4728 MAIN ST, VANCOUVER, BC, V5V 3R7

(604) 879-8989   *SIC* 6531

LEVIN, FISCHER LIMITED   *p*972
525 EGLINTON AVE W, TORONTO, ON,

M5N 1B1

(416) 487-5277   *SIC* 6531

LFM COURTIER IMMOBILIER AGREE INC *p*1104
130 AV GATINEAU, GATINEAU, QC, J8T 4J8

(819) 246-1118   *SIC* 6531

LIBERTY REALTY (1998) LTD   *p*1023
1125 MERCER ST, WINDSOR, ON, N9A 1N8

SIC 6531

LIN ROBERT SUTTON GROUP   *p*262
9100 BLUNDELL RD UNIT 550, RICH-MOND, BC, V6Y 3X9

(604) 727-0917   *SIC* 6531

LITTLE OAK REALTY LTD   *p*175
2630 BOURQUIN CRES W SUITE 9, AB-BOTSFORD, BC, V2S 5N7

(604) 309-5729   *SIC* 6531

LIVING GROUP OF COMPANIES INC *p*672
7030 WOODBINE AVE SUITE 300, MARKHAM, ON, L3R 6G2

(905) 474-0500   *SIC* 6531

LIVING REALTY INC   *p*672
7030 WOODBINE AVE SUITE 300, MARKHAM, ON, L3R 6G2

(905) 474-9856   *SIC* 6531

LIVING REALTY INC   *p*711
1177 CENTRAL PKY W UNIT 32, MISSIS-SAUGA, ON, L5C 4P3

(905) 896-0002   *SIC* 6531

LOCATIONS WEST REALTY INC   *p*243
484 MAIN ST, PENTICTON, BC, V2A 5C5

(250) 493-2244   *SIC* 6531

LOGISCO INC   *p*1138
950 RUE DE LA CONCORDE BUREAU 302, LEVIS, QC, G6W 8A8

(418) 834-4999   *SIC* 6531

LONDON & MIDDLESEX HOUSING COR-PORATION *p*652
1299 OXFORD ST E UNIT 5C5, LONDON, ON, N5Y 4W5

(519) 434-2765   *SIC* 6531

LOSANI HOMES (1998) LTD   *p*892
430 MCNEILLY RD, STONEY CREEK, ON, L8E 5E3

(905) 643-7386   *SIC* 6531

MACDONALD COMMECIAL REAL ESTATE SERVICES LTD *p*321
1827 5TH AVE W, VANCOUVER, BC, V6J 1P5

(604) 736-5611   *SIC* 6531

MACDONALD REALTY (1974) LTD   *p*322
2105 38TH AVE W SUITE 208, VANCOU-VER, BC, V6M 1R8

(604) 263-1911   *SIC* 6531

MAGIC REALTY INC   *p*846
805 CHRISTINA ST N, POINT EDWARD, ON, N7V 1X6

SIC 6531

MAGIC REALTY INC   *p*860
380 LONDON RD, SARNIA, ON, N7T 4W7

(519) 542-4005   *SIC* 6531

MANULIFE CANADIAN REAL ESTATE IN-VESTMENT FUND *p*929
250 BLOOR ST FL 15, TORONTO, ON, M4W 1E5

(416) 926-5500   *SIC* 6531

MAPLE RIDGE COMMUNITY MANAGE-MENT LTD *p*706
5753 COOPERS AVE UNIT A, MISSIS-SAUGA, ON, L4Z 1R9

(905) 507-6726   *SIC* 6531

MARK ANTHONY PROPERTIES LTD *p*242
7151 SIBCO LANDFILL, OLIVER, BC, V0H 1T0

SIC 6531

MAUREEN KLEIN   *p*226
19925 WILLOWBROOK DR UNIT 110, LAN-GLEY, BC, V2Y 1A7

(604) 530-0231   *SIC* 6531

MAX WRIGHT REAL ESTATE CORPORA-TION *p*321
1672 2ND AVE W, VANCOUVER, BC, V6J

1H4

(604) 632-3300   *SIC* 6531

MAXIMUM REALTY CORPORATION *p1032*
7694 ISLINGTON AVE, WOODBRIDGE, ON, L4L 1W3

(905) 856-7653   *SIC* 6531

MAXWELL WESTVIEW REALTY *p73*
1200 37 ST SW SUITE 41, CALGARY, AB, T3C 1S2

(403) 256-6015   *SIC* 6531

MCFADZEN HOLDINGS LIMITED *p403*
31 KINGSWOOD WAY, HANWELL, NB, E3C 2L4

(506) 443-3331   *SIC* 6531

MCINTEE , WILFRED & CO. LIMITED *p1004*
11 DURHAM ST, WALKERTON, ON, N0G 2V0

(519) 881-2270   *SIC* 6531

MEDALLION CORPORATION *p789*
970 LAWRENCE AVE W SUITE 304, NORTH YORK, ON, M6A 3B6

(416) 256-3900   *SIC* 6531

MEDALLION PROPERTIES INC *p789*
970 LAWRENCE AVE W SUITE 304, NORTH YORK, ON, M6A 3B6

(416) 256-3900   *SIC* 6531

METCALFE REALTY COMPANY LIMITED
p830
2700 QUEENSVIEW DR, OTTAWA, ON, K2B 8H6

(613) 820-6000   *SIC* 6531

METCAP LIVING INC *p934*
260 RICHMOND ST E SUITE 300, TORONTO, ON, M5A 1P4

(416) 340-1600   *SIC* 6531

METCAP LIVING MANAGEMENT INC *p934*
260 RICHMOND ST E SUITE 300, TORONTO, ON, M5A 1P4

(416) 340-1600   *SIC* 6531

METRO VANCOUVER HOUSING CORPO-RATION *p190*
4330 KINGSWAY SUITE 505, BURNABY, BC, V5H 4G7

(604) 432-6300   *SIC* 6531

METVIEW REALTY LIMITED *p823*
130 ALBERT ST SUITE 210, OTTAWA, ON, K1P 5G4

(613) 230-5174   *SIC* 6531

MID-LAND GROUP REALTY INC *p853*
330 HIGHWAY 7 E SUITE 502, RICHMOND HILL, ON, L4B 3P8

(905) 709-0828   *SIC* 6531

MIDAS REALTY CORPORATION OF CANADA INC *p874*
105 COMMANDER BLVD, SCARBOR-OUGH, ON, M1S 3M7

(416) 291-4261   *SIC* 6531

MILBORNE REAL ESTATE INC *p927*
385 MADISON AVE, TORONTO, ON, M4V 2W7

(416) 928-9998   *SIC* 6531

MINTO APARTMENTS LIMITED *p772*
90 SHEPPARD AVE E SUITE 500, NORTH YORK, ON, M2N 3A1

(416) 977-0777   *SIC* 6531

MOMENTUM REALTY INC *p884*
353 LAKE ST, ST CATHARINES, ON, L2N 7G4

(905) 935-8001   *SIC* 6531

MONTFORT RENAISSANCE INC *p821*
162 MURRAY ST, OTTAWA, ON, K1N 5M8

(613) 789-5144   *SIC* 6531

MORGUARD INVESTMENTS LIMITED *p710*
55 CITY CENTRE DR SUITE 800, MISSIS-SAUGA, ON, L5B 1M3

(905) 281-3800   *SIC* 6531

MULTIPLE REALTY LTD *p287*
2298 KINGSWAY, VANCOUVER, BC, V5N 5M9

(604) 434-8843   *SIC* 6531

MURPHY'S PHARMACIES INC *p1039*
41 ST. PETERS RD, CHARLOTTETOWN, PE, C1A 5N1

(902) 894-4447   *SIC* 6531

MURRAY HILL DEVELOPMENTS LTD *p92*
9833 110 ST NW, EDMONTON, AB, T5K 2P5

(780) 488-0287   *SIC* 6531

N R S WESTBURN REALTY LTD *p190*
5489 KINGSWAY, BURNABY, BC, V5H 2G1

(604) 209-1225   *SIC* 6531

NANAIMO DISTRICTY SENIOR CITIZENS HOUSING DEVELOPMENT SOCIETY *p234*
1233 KIWANIS CRES, NANAIMO, BC, V9S 5Y1

(250) 740-2815   *SIC* 6531

NANAIMO REALTY CO LTD *p234*
2000 ISLAND HWY N SUITE 275, NANAIMO, BC, V9S 5W3

(250) 713-0494   *SIC* 6531

NAPG EQUITIES INC *p673*
2851 JOHN ST SUITE 1, MARKHAM, ON, L3R 5R7

(905) 477-9200   *SIC* 6531

NECHAKO REAL ESTATE LTD *p326*
421 PACIFIC ST, VANCOUVER, BC, V6Z 2P5

(604) 685-5951   *SIC* 6531

NEW STAR REAL ESTATE LTD *p871*
1450 MIDLAND AVE UNIT 206, SCARBOR-OUGH, ON, M1P 4Z8

(416) 288-0800   *SIC* 6531

NEWFOUNDLAND AND LABRADOR HOUSING CORPORATION *p433*
2 CANADA DR, ST. JOHN'S, NL, A1E 0A1

(709) 724-3000   *SIC* 6531

NEWPORT REALTY LTD *p335*
1144 FORT ST, VICTORIA, BC, V8V 3K8

(250) 385-2033   *SIC* 6531

NEWTON, ALAN REAL ESTATE LTD *p906*
370 STEELES AVE W SUITE 102, THORN-HILL, ON, L4J 6X1

(905) 764-7200   *SIC* 6531

NEWTON-TRELAWNEY PROPERTY MAN-AGEMENT SERVICES INC *p474*
253 LAKE DRIVEWAY W, AJAX, ON, L1S 5B5

(905) 619-2886   *SIC* 6531

NIAGARA ACQUISITION GP INC *p970*
66 WELLINGTON ST W SUITE 4400, TORONTO, ON, M5K 1H6

(416) 687-6700   *SIC* 6531

NORTH HERITAGE REALTY INC *p898*
860 LASALLE BLVD, SUDBURY, ON, P3A 1X5

(705) 688-0007   *SIC* 6531

NORTH PEACE HOUSING FOUNDATION
p135
4918 49 AVE, GRIMSHAW, AB, T0H 1W0

SIC 6531

NORTHAM REALTY ADVISORS LIMITED
p935
2 CARLTON ST SUITE 909, TORONTO, ON, M5B 1J3

(416) 977-7151   *SIC* 6531

NORTHSTAR REALTY LTD *p279*
15272 CROYDON DR SUITE 118, SURREY, BC, V3Z 0Z5

(604) 597-1664   *SIC* 6531

NORTHWEST TERRITORIES NON-PROFIT HOUSING CORPORATION *p436*
GD LCD MAIN, YELLOWKNIFE, NT, X1A 2L8

(867) 873-7873   *SIC* 6531

NORTHWEST-ATLANTIC (CANADA) INC
p777
864 YORK MILLS RD, NORTH YORK, ON, M3B 1Y4

(416) 391-3900   *SIC* 6531

NORWEST REAL ESTATE LTD *p40*
3604 52 AVE NW SUITE 114, CALGARY, AB, T2L 1V9

(403) 282-7770   *SIC* 6531

NORWICH REAL ESTATE SERVICES INC
p222
1553 HARVEY AVE SUITE 100, KELOWNA, BC, V1Y 6G1

(250) 717-5000   *SIC* 6531

NPR LIMITED PARTNERSHIP *p36*
6131 6 ST SE SUITE 200, CALGARY, AB, T2H 1L9

(403) 531-0720   *SIC* 6531

OFFICE MUNICIPAL D'HABITATION DE MONTREAL *p1192*
415 RUE SAINT-ANTOINE O 2E ETAGE, MONTREAL, QC, H2Z 2B9

(514) 872-6442   *SIC* 6531

OFFICE MUNICIPAL D'HABITATION KA-TIVIK *p1119*
1105 RUE AKIANUT, KUUJJUAQ, QC, J0M 1C0

(819) 964-2000   *SIC* 6531

OLIVER & ASSOCIATES REAL ESTATE BROKERAGE INC *p659*
99 HORTON ST W, LONDON, ON, N6J 4Y6

(519) 657-2020   *SIC* 6531

ONE PROPERTIES CORPORATION *p90*
10111 104 AVE NW SUITE 2500, EDMON-TON, AB, T5J 0J4

(780) 423-5525   *SIC* 6531

ONTARIO REALTY CORPORATION *p947*
1 DUNDAS ST W SUITE 2000, TORONTO, ON, M5G 1Z3

(416) 327-3937   *SIC* 6531

ORION MANAGEMENT INC *p31*
4015 1 ST SE UNIT 3A, CALGARY, AB, T2G 4X7

(403) 243-8292   *SIC* 6531

OSGOODE PROPERTIES LTD *p828*
1284 WELLINGTON ST W, OTTAWA, ON, K1Y 3A9

(613) 729-0656   *SIC* 6531

OTTAWA COMMUNITY HOUSING CORPO-RATION *p749*
39 AURIGA DR, NEPEAN, ON, K2E 7Y8

(613) 731-1182   *SIC* 6531

OTTAWA COMMUNITY HOUSING CORPO-RATION *p749*
39 AURIGA DR, NEPEAN, ON, K2E 7Y8

(613) 731-7223   *SIC* 6531

OWENS, R S & COMPANY INCORPORATED
p680
271 YORKTECH DR, MARKHAM, ON, L6G 1A6

(905) 754-3355   *SIC* 6531

PACIFICA HOUSING ADVISORY ASSOCIA-TION *p336*
827 FISGARD ST, VICTORIA, BC, V8W 1R9

(250) 385-2131   *SIC* 6531

PARIS LADOUCEUR & ASSOCIES INC
p1234
63 RUE DE LA POINTE-LANGLOIS, MON-TREAL, QC, H7L 3J4

(450) 963-2777   *SIC* 6531

PARK GEORGIA REALTY LTD *p322*
5701 GRANVILLE ST SUITE 201, VAN-COUVER, BC, V6M 4J7

(604) 261-7275   *SIC* 6531

PARK PROPERTY MANAGEMENT INC *p673*
16 ESNA PARK DR SUITE 200, MARKHAM, ON, L3R 5X1

(905) 940-1718   *SIC* 6531

PARKER REALTY LTD *p1040*
535 NORTH RIVER RD SUITE 1, CHAR-LOTTETOWN, PE, C1E 1J6

(902) 566-4663   *SIC* 6531

PEAK REALTY LTD *p1009*
139 NORTHFIELD DR W SUITE 104, WA-TERLOO, ON, N2L 5A6

(519) 662-4900   *SIC* 6531

PEDLER, BOB REAL ESTATE LIMITED
p1021
280 EDINBOROUGH ST, WINDSOR, ON, N8X 3C4

(519) 966-3750   *SIC* 6531

PEEL HOUSING CORPORATION *p510*
5 WELLINGTON ST E, BRAMPTON, ON, L6W 1Y1

(905) 453-1300   *SIC* 6531

PEGGY HILL & ASSOCIATES REALTY INC
p488
11 VICTORIA ST UNIT B3, BARRIE, ON,

L4N 6T3

(705) 739-4455   *SIC* 6531

PERFORMANCE REALTY LTD *p819*
1500 BANK ST, OTTAWA, ON, K1H 1B8

(613) 733-9100   *SIC* 6531

PETER BENNINGER REALTY LTD *p640*
508 RIVERBEND DR SUITE 352, KITCH-ENER, ON, N2K 3S2

(519) 743-5211   *SIC* 6531

PETTIPIECE HELEN SUTTON GROUP *p262*
9100 BLUNDELL RD UNIT 550, RICH-MOND, BC, V6Y 3X9

(604) 341-7997   *SIC* 6531

PHOENIX ENTERPRISES LTD *p382*
500 ST JAMES ST, WINNIPEG, MB, R3G 3J4

(204) 956-2233   *SIC* 6531

PINEDALE PROPERTIES LTD *p789*
970 LAWRENCE AVE W SUITE 303, NORTH YORK, ON, M6A 3B6

(416) 256-2900   *SIC* 6531

PINO ALEJANDRO *p924*
1867 YONGE ST SUITE 100, TORONTO, ON, M4S 1Y5

(416) 960-9995   *SIC* 6531

PIONEER HOUSING FOUNDATION *p161*
495 WOODBRIDGE WAY, SHERWOOD PARK, AB, T8A 4P1

SIC 6531

PLACEMENTS CAMBRIDGE INC *p1252*
340 BOUL HYMUS BUREAU 640, POINTE-CLAIRE, QC, H9R 6B3

(514) 694-8383   *SIC* 6531

PMA BRETHOUR REAL ESTATE CORPO-RATION INC *p674*
250 SHIELDS CRT UNIT 1, MARKHAM, ON, L3R 9W7

(905) 415-2720   *SIC* 6531

PRATT MCGARRY INC *p379*
305 BROADWAY SUITE 500, WINNIPEG, MB, R3C 3J7

(204) 943-1600   *SIC* 6531

PRECISION PROPERTY MANAGEMENT INC *p587*
22 GOODMARK PL UNIT 22, ETOBICOKE, ON, M9W 6R2

(416) 675-2223   *SIC* 6531

PROALLIANCE REALTY CORPORATION
p491
357 FRONT ST, BELLEVILLE, ON, K8N 2Z9

(613) 966-6060   *SIC* 6531

PRODUITS BREATHER INC *p1183*
5605 AV DE GASPE BUREAU 610, MON-TREAL, QC, H2T 2A4

(514) 574-8059   *SIC* 6531

PROFESSIONAL GROUP INC, THE *p116*
9920 63 AVE NW SUITE 130, EDMONTON, AB, T6E 0G9

(780) 439-9818   *SIC* 6531

PROFESSIONAL GROUP INC, THE *p116*
9222 51 AVE NW, EDMONTON, AB, T6E 5L8

(780) 439-9818   *SIC* 6531

PROMPTON REAL ESTATE SERVICES INC
p327
179 DAVIE ST SUITE 201, VANCOUVER, BC, V6Z 2Y1

(604) 899-2333   *SIC* 6531

PROPERTIES TERRA INCOGNITA INC
p1186
3530 BOUL SAINT-LAURENT BUREAU 500, MONTREAL, QC, H2X 2V1

(514) 847-3536   *SIC* 6531

PRUDENTIAL SADIE MORANIS REALTY LIMITED *p777*
35 LESMILL RD, NORTH YORK, ON, M3B 2T3

(416) 960-9995   *SIC* 6531

PRUDENTIAL SUSSEX REALTY *p342*
2397 MARINE DR, WEST VANCOUVER, BC, V7V 1K9

(604) 913-4068   *SIC* 6531

PURE MULTI-FAMILY REIT LP *p308*
925 GEORGIA ST W SUITE 910, VANCOU-

VER, BC, V6C 3L2
(604) 681-5959   *SIC* 6531

QUADREAL PROPERTY GROUP LIMITED PARTNERSHIP   *p*308
666 BURRARD ST SUITE 800, VANCOUVER, BC, V6C 2X8
(604) 975-9500   *SIC* 6531

QUEENSWAY REAL ESTATE BROKERAGE INC   *p*996
8 HORNELL ST, TORONTO, ON, M8Z 1X2
(416) 259-4000   *SIC* 6531

QUINTAIN DEVELOPMENTS INC   *p*742
6720 COLUMBUS RD, MISSISSAUGA, ON, L5T 2G1
(905) 670-3599   *SIC* 6531

R.M.R REAL ESTATE LIMITED   *p*813
179 KING ST E, OSHAWA, ON, L1H 1C2
(905) 728-9414   *SIC* 6531

RE MAX CITE INC   *p*1247
13150 RUE SHERBROOKE E, POINTE-AUX-TREMBLES, QC, H1A 4B1
(514) 644-0000   *SIC* 6531

RE MAX QUINTE LTD   *p*492
308 NORTH FRONT ST, BELLEVILLE, ON, K8P 3C4
(613) 969-9907   *SIC* 6531

RE MAX WEST REALTY BROKERAGE INC
*p*994
1678 BLOOR ST W, TORONTO, ON, M6P 1A9
(416) 769-1616   *SIC* 6531

RE-MAX IMMO-CONTACT INC   *p*1232
2820 BOUL SAINT-MARTIN E BUREAU 201, MONTREAL, QC, H7E 5A1
(450) 661-6810   *SIC* 6531

RE-MAX MONTREAL METRO INC   *p*1166
5136 RUE DE BELLECHASSE, MONTREAL, QC, H1T 2A4
(514) 251-9000   *SIC* 6531

RE/MAX 2001 INC   *p*1241
360 BOUL CURE-LABELLE, MONTREAL-OUEST, QC, H7V 2S1
(450) 625-2001   *SIC* 6531

RE/MAX A-B REALTY LTD   *p*896
88 WELLINGTON ST, STRATFORD, ON, N5A 2L2
(519) 273-2821   *SIC* 6531

RE/MAX ACTION (1992) INC   *p*1131
8280 BOUL CHAMPLAIN, LASALLE, QC, H8P 1B5
(514) 364-3222   *SIC* 6531

RE/MAX ALL-STARS REALTY INC.   *p*1000
5071 HIGHWAY 7 E, UNIONVILLE, ON, L3R 1N3
(905) 477-0011   *SIC* 6531

RE/MAX BLUE SPRING REALTY (HALTON) CORP   *p*473
2 MILL ST E, ACTON, ON, L7J 1G9
(519) 853-2086   *SIC* 6531

RE/MAX CADIBEC INC   *p*1118
3535 BOUL SAINT-CHARLES BUREAU 304, KIRKLAND, QC, H9H 5B9
(514) 694-0840   *SIC* 6531

RE/MAX CAPITALE (1983) INC   *p*1257
7385 BOUL HENRI-BOURASSA, QUEBEC, QC, G1H 3E5
(418) 627-3120   *SIC* 6531

RE/MAX CENTRE CITY REALTY INC   *p*652
675 ADELAIDE ST N, LONDON, ON, N5Y 2L4
(519) 667-1800   *SIC* 6531

RE/MAX COLONIAL PACIFIC REALTY *p*280
15414 24 AVE, SURREY, BC, V4A 2J3
(604) 541-4850   *SIC* 6531

RE/MAX CONDOS PLUS CORPORATION
*p*966
45 HARBOUR SQ, TORONTO, ON, M5J 2G4
(416) 203-6636   *SIC* 6531

RE/MAX CROSSROADS REALTY INC *p*877
1055 MCNICOLL AVE, SCARBOROUGH, ON, M1W 3W6
(416) 491-4002   *SIC* 6531

RE/MAX CROWN REAL ESTATE LTD *p*1421

2350 2ND AVE, REGINA, SK, S4R 1A6
(306) 791-7666   *SIC* 6531

RE/MAX DE FRANCHEVILLE INC   *p*1368
1000 AV DES CEDRES BUREAU 5, SHAWINIGAN, QC, G9N 1P6
(819) 537-5000   *SIC* 6531

RE/MAX DE LA POINTE INC   *p*1247
13150 RUE SHERBROOKE E BUREAU 201, POINTE-AUX-TREMBLES, QC, H1A 4B1
(514) 644-0000   *SIC* 6531

RE/MAX EASTERN REALTY INC   *p*842
64 HASTINGS ST N, PETERBOROUGH, ON, K9J 3G3
(705) 743-9111   *SIC* 6531

RE/MAX ESCARPMENT REALTY INC *p*616
1595 UPPER JAMES ST UNIT 101, HAMILTON, ON, L9B 0H7
(905) 575-5478   *SIC* 6531

RE/MAX EXCELLENCE INC   *p*1052
7130 RUE BEAUBIEN E, ANJOU, QC, H1M 1B2
(514) 354-6240   *SIC* 6531

RE/MAX EXTRA INC   *p*1057
365 BOUL SIR-WILFRID-LAURIER BUREAU 202, BELOEIL, QC, J3G 4T2
(450) 464-1000   *SIC* 6531

RE/MAX FIRST CHOICE REALTY LTD *p*909
846 MACDONELL ST, THUNDER BAY, ON, P7B 5J1
(807) 344-5700   *SIC* 6531

RE/MAX FIRST REALTY LTD   *p*843
1154 KINGSTON RD, PICKERING, ON, L1V 1B4
(905) 831-3300   *SIC* 6531

RE/MAX FORTIN, DELAGE INC   *p*1274
3175 CH DES QUATRE-BOURGEOIS BUREAU 120, QUEBEC, QC, G1W 2K7
(418) 653-5353   *SIC* 6531

RE/MAX GARDEN CITY REALTY INC BROKERAGE   *p*886
161 CARLTON ST SUITE 123, ST CATHARINES, ON, L2R 1R5
(905) 641-1110   *SIC* 6531

RE/MAX GOLDENWAY REALTY INC *p*877
3390 MIDLAND AVE UNIT 7, SCARBOROUGH, ON, M1V 5K3
(416) 299-8199   *SIC* 6531

RE/MAX HALLMARK REALTY LTD   *p*915
1 DUNCAN MILL RD UNIT 101, TORONTO, ON, M3B 3J5
(416) 424-3170   *SIC* 6531

RE/MAX HALLMARK REALTY LTD   *p*917
2237 QUEEN ST E, TORONTO, ON, M4E 1G1
(416) 357-1059   *SIC* 6531

RE/MAX HARMONIE INC   *p*1168
3550 RUE RACHEL E BUREAU 201, MONTREAL, QC, H1W 1A7
(514) 259-8884   *SIC* 6531

RE/MAX IMPERIAL REALTY INC   *p*674
3000 STEELES AVE E SUITE 309, MARKHAM, ON, L3R 4T9
(905) 305-0033   *SIC* 6531

RE/MAX LONGUEUIL INC   *p*1143
50 RUE SAINT-CHARLES O BUREAU 100, LONGUEUIL, QC, J4H 1C6
(450) 651-8331   *SIC* 6531

RE/MAX METRO-CITY REALTY LTD *p*834
344 FRANK ST, OTTAWA, ON, K2P 0Y1
(613) 288-3300   *SIC* 6531

RE/MAX NIAGARA REALTY LTD   *p*759
5627 MAIN ST, NIAGARA FALLS, ON, L2G 5Z3
(905) 356-9600   *SIC* 6531

RE/MAX NOVA REAL ESTATE   *p*448
7 MELLOR AVE UNIT 1, DARTMOUTH, NS, B3B 0E8
(902) 478-0991   *SIC* 6531

RE/MAX ORILLIA REALTY (1996) LTD *p*810
97 NEYWASH ST, ORILLIA, ON, L3V 1X4
(705) 325-1373   *SIC* 6531

RE/MAX PERFORMANCE INC   *p*1322
15 RUE DU PRINCE-ARTHUR, SAINT-

LAMBERT, QC, J4P 1X1
(450) 466-4000   *SIC* 6531

RE/MAX PERFORMANCE REALTY   *p*368
942 ST MARY'S RD, WINNIPEG, MB, R2M 3R5
(204) 255-4204   *SIC* 6531

RE/MAX PERFORMANCE REALTY INC *p*712
1140 BURNHAMTHORPE RD W SUITE 141, MISSISSAUGA, ON, L5C 4E9
(905) 270-2000   *SIC* 6531

RE/MAX PERFORMANCE REALTY INC *p*712
141-1140 BURNHAMTHORPE RD W, MISSISSAUGA, ON, L5C 4E9
(905) 270-2000   *SIC* 6531

RE/MAX PREFERRED REALTY LTD *p*1018
6505 TECUMSEH RD E SUITE 1, WINDSOR, ON, N8T 1E7
(519) 944-5955   *SIC* 6531

RE/MAX PRIVILEGE INC   *p*1308
5920 BOUL COUSINEAU, SAINT-HUBERT, QC, J3Y 7R9
(450) 678-3150   *SIC* 6531

RE/MAX PROFESSIONALS INC   *p*576
270 THE KINGSWAY SUITE 200, ETOBICOKE, ON, M9A 3T7
(416) 236-1241   *SIC* 6531

RE/MAX PROFESSIONALS INC   *p*712
1645 DUNDAS ST W, MISSISSAUGA, ON, L5C 1E3
(905) 270-8840   *SIC* 6531

RE/MAX PROFESSIONEL INC   *p*1111
1050 RUE PRINCIPALE, GRANBY, QC, J2J 2N7
(450) 378-4120   *SIC* 6531

RE/MAX REAL ESTATE (EDMONTON) LTD
*p*116
4245 97 ST NW SUITE 102, EDMONTON, AB, T6E 5Y7
(780) 434-2323   *SIC* 6531

RE/MAX REAL ESTATE CENTRE INC *p*510
2 COUNTY COURT BLVD SUITE 150, BRAMPTON, ON, L6W 3W8
(905) 456-1177   *SIC* 6531

RE/MAX REAL ESTATE CENTRE INC *p*539
766 HESPELER RD SUITE 202, CAMBRIDGE, ON, N3H 5L8
(519) 623-6200   *SIC* 6531

RE/MAX REAL ESTATE CENTRE INC *p*539
766 HESPELER RD SUITE 202, CAMBRIDGE, ON, N3H 5L8
(519) 740-0001   *SIC* 6531

RE/MAX REALTRON REALTY INC   *p*674
88 KONRAD CRES SUITE 1, MARKHAM, ON, L3R 8T7
(905) 944-8800   *SIC* 6531

RE/MAX REALTRON REALTY INC   *p*773
183 WILLOWDALE AVE, NORTH YORK, ON, M2N 4Y9
(416) 222-8600   *SIC* 6531

RE/MAX REALTRON REALTY INC   *p*791
2815 BATHURST ST, NORTH YORK, ON, M6B 3A4
(416) 782-8882   *SIC* 6531

RE/MAX REALTRON REALTY INC   *p*906
7646 YONGE ST, THORNHILL, ON, L4J 1V9
(416) 802-0707   *SIC* 6531

RE/MAX REALTY ENTERPRISES INC *p*714
1697 LAKESHORE RD W, MISSISSAUGA, ON, L5J 1J4
(905) 823-3400   *SIC* 6531

RE/MAX REALTY ONE INC   *p*710
50 BURNHAMTHORPE RD W SUITE 102, MISSISSAUGA, ON, L5B 3C2
(905) 277-0771   *SIC* 6531

RE/MAX REALTY SERVICES INC   *p*510
295 QUEEN ST E SUITE 3, BRAMPTON, ON, L6W 3R1
(905) 456-1000   *SIC* 6531

RE/MAX REALTY SPECIALISTS INC *p*719
2691 CREDIT VALLEY RD SUITE 101, MISSISSAUGA, ON, L5M 7A1
(905) 828-3434   *SIC* 6531

RE/MAX REALTY SPECIALISTS INC *p*726

6850 MILLCREEK DR UNIT 200, MISSISSAUGA, ON, L5N 4J9
(905) 858-3434   *SIC* 6531

RE/MAX ROUGE RIVER REALTY LTD *p*865
6758 KINGSTON RD UNIT 1, SCARBOROUGH, ON, M1B 1G8
(416) 286-3993   *SIC* 6531

RE/MAX ROYAL (JORDAN) INC   *p*1253
201 AV CARTIER, POINTE-CLAIRE, QC, H9S 4S2
(514) 694-6900   *SIC* 6531

RE/MAX SASKATOON NORTH   *p*1429
227 PRIMROSE DR SUITE 200, SASKATOON, SK, S7K 5E4
(306) 934-0909   *SIC* 6531

RE/MAX SIGNATURE INC   *p*1067
130 BOUL DE MORTAGNE BUREAU 200, BOUCHERVILLE, QC, J4B 5M7
(450) 449-5730   *SIC* 6531

RE/MAX TMS INC   *p*1364
156 BOUL DU CURE-LABELLE, SAINTE-THERESE, QC, J7E 2X5
(450) 430-4207   *SIC* 6531

RE/MAX TREELAND REALTY (1992) LTD
*p*226
6337 198 ST SUITE 101, LANGLEY, BC, V2Y 2E3
(604) 533-3491   *SIC* 6531

RE/MAX TRENT VALLEY REALTY LTD *p*999
447 DUNDAS ST W, TRENTON, ON, K8V 3S4
(613) 243-2209   *SIC* 6531

RE/MAX TWIN CITY REALTY INC   *p*635
842 VICTORIA ST N SUITE 1, KITCHENER, ON, N2B 3C1
(519) 579-4110   *SIC* 6531

RE/MAX TWIN CITY REALTY INC   *p*1009
83 ERB ST W, WATERLOO, ON, N2L 6C2
(519) 885-0200   *SIC* 6531

RE/MAX UNIQUE INC   *p*926
1251 YONGE ST, TORONTO, ON, M4T 1W6
(416) 928-6833   *SIC* 6531

RE/MAX VISION (1990) INC   *p*1105
225 BOUL DE LA GAPPE BUREAU 102, GATINEAU, QC, J8T 7Y3
(819) 243-3111   *SIC* 6531

RE/MAX WEST REALTY INC   *p*587
96 REXDALE BLVD SUITE 1, ETOBICOKE, ON, M9W 1N7
(416) 745-2300   *SIC* 6531

RE/MAX YORK GROUP REALTY INC *p*481
15004 YONGE ST, AURORA, ON, L4G 1M6
(905) 727-1941   *SIC* 6531

REALTY EXECUTIVE SYNERGY INC *p*107
15341 97 ST NW, EDMONTON, AB, T5X 5V3
(780) 699-7347   *SIC* 6531

REALTY EXECUTIVES DEVONSHIRE *p*161
37 ATHABASCAN AVE SUITE 101, SHERWOOD PARK, AB, T8A 4H3
(780) 464-7700   *SIC* 6531

REALTY EXECUTIVES SASKATOON *p*1425
3032 LOUISE ST, SASKATOON, SK, S7J 3L8
(306) 373-7520   *SIC* 6531

REALTY EXECUTIVES TELOR   *p*161
37 ATHABASCAN AVE SUITE 101, SHERWOOD PARK, AB, T8A 4H3
(780) 464-7700   *SIC* 6531

REALTY NETWORK 100 INC   *p*599
263 MAIN ST E, GRIMSBY, ON, L3M 1P7
(905) 945-4555   *SIC* 6531

RED CARPET REAL WORLD REALTY INC
*p*674
340 FERRIER ST UNIT 218, MARKHAM, ON, L3R 2Z5
(905) 415-8855   *SIC* 6531

RED ROSE REALTY INC   *p*916
101 DUNCAN MILL RD UNIT G5, TORONTO, ON, M3B 1Z3
(416) 640-0512   *SIC* 6531

REFERRED REALTY INC   *p*777
156 DUNCAN MILL RD SUITE 1, NORTH YORK, ON, M3B 3N2

▲ Public Company   ■ Public Company Family Member   **HQ** Headquarters   **BR** Branch   **SL** Single Location

(416) 445-8855   *SIC* 6531

REGINA REALTY SALES LTD   *p1422*
3889 E ARCOLA AVE, REGINA, SK, S4V 1P5
(306) 359-1900   *SIC* 6531

REGIONAL GROUP OF COMPANIES INC, THE   *p831*
1737 WOODWARD DR SUITE 200, OTTAWA, ON, K2C 0P9
(613) 230-2100   *SIC* 6531

RELIANCE TRADE BROKERS INC   *p524*
4145 NORTH SERVICE RD, BURLINGTON, ON, L7L 6A3
(289) 201-7841   *SIC* 6531

REMAX ACTIF INC   *p1296*
1592 RUE MONTARVILLE BUREAU 102, SAINT-BRUNO, QC, J3V 3T7
(450) 461-1708   *SIC* 6531

REMAX ASSOCIATES   *p372*
1060 MCPHILLIPS ST, WINNIPEG, MB, R2X 2K9
(204) 989-9000   *SIC* 6531

REMAX DU CARTIER INC   *p1182*
7085 BOUL SAINT-LAURENT, MONTREAL, QC, H2S 3E3
(514) 278-7170   *SIC* 6531

REMAX EXCELLENCE REALTY INC   *p1033*
3700 STEELES AVE W, WOODBRIDGE, ON, L4L 8K8
(905) 856-1111   *SIC* 6531

REMAX FIRST REALTY   *p39*
9625 MACLEOD TRAIL SW, CALGARY, AB, T2J 0P6
(403) 938-4848   *SIC* 6531

REMAX GATEWAY REALTY LTD   *p830*
2255 CARLING AVE SUITE 101, OTTAWA, ON, K2B 7Z5
(613) 288-0090   *SIC* 6531

REMAX GEORGIAN BAY REALTY LTD *p682*
833 KING ST, MIDLAND, ON, L4R 0B7
(705) 526-9366   *SIC* 6531

REMAX MEDALTA REAL ESTATE (1989) LTD   *p147*
1235 SOUTHVIEW DR SE UNIT 109, MEDICINE HAT, AB, T1B 4K3
(403) 529-9393   *SIC* 6531

REMAX NORTH COUNTRY REALTY INC *p598*
405 MUSKOKA RD S UNIT B, GRAVENHURST, ON, P1P 1T1
(705) 687-2243   *SIC* 6531

REMAX REAL ESTATE 'MOUNTAIN VIEW' LTD   *p71*
4625 VARSITY DR NW SUITE 222, CALGARY, AB, T3A 0Z9
(403) 651-4400   *SIC* 6531

REMAX REAL ESTATE CALGARY SOUTH LTD   *p39*
8820 BLACKFOOT TRAIL SE SUITE 115, CALGARY, AB, T2J 3J1
(403) 278-2900   *SIC* 6531

REMAX REALTY SPECIALISTS INC   *p706*
4310 SHERWOODTOWNE BLVD UNIT 200, MISSISSAUGA, ON, L4Z 4C4
(905) 361-4663   *SIC* 6531

REMAX SABRE REAL ESTATE GROUP LTD *p246*
2748 LOUGHEED HWY SUITE 102, PORT COQUITLAM, BC, V3B 6P2
(604) 942-0606   *SIC* 6531

REMAX SOLID GOLD REALTY (II) LTD *p1007*
180 WEBER ST S, WATERLOO, ON, N2J 2B2
(519) 888-7110   *SIC* 6531

RESIDENCES AT ICON INC, THE   *p781*
4800 DUFFERIN ST, NORTH YORK, ON, M3H 5S9
(416) 661-9290   *SIC* 6531

RESIDENCES SELECTION S.E.C.- I, LES *p1087*
2400 BOUL DANIEL-JOHNSON, COTE SAINT-LUC, QC, H7T 3A4
(450) 902-2000   *SIC* 6531

RICHARDSON, ALISON REALTOR   *p156*
47 ROTH CRES, RED DEER, AB, T4P 2Y7
(403) 358-1557   *SIC* 6531

RIGHT AT HOME REALTY INC   *p853*
300 WEST BEAVER CREEK RD SUITE 202, RICHMOND HILL, ON, L4B 3B1
(905) 695-7888   *SIC* 6531

RIMOKA HOUSING FOUNDATION   *p152*
5608 57 AVE SUITE 101, PONOKA, AB, T4J 1P2
(403) 783-0128   *SIC* 6531

RIOCAN MANAGEMENT INC   *p923*
2300 YONGE ST SUITE 500, TORONTO, ON, M4P 1E4
(800) 465-2733   *SIC* 6531

RIOCAN PROPERTY SERVICES INC   *p790*
700 LAWRENCE AVE W SUITE 315, NORTH YORK, ON, M6A 3B4
(416) 256-0256   *SIC* 6531

RLK REALTY LTD   *p222*
1890 COOPER RD UNIT 1, KELOWNA, BC, V1Y 8B7
(250) 860-1100   *SIC* 6531

ROW, TED   *p421*
164 CONCEPTION BAY HWY, BAY ROBERTS, NL, A0A 1G0
(709) 786-2310   *SIC* 6531

ROYAL LE PAGE MAXIMUM REALTY *p1033*
7694 ISLINGTON AVE, WOODBRIDGE, ON, L4L 1W3
(416) 324-2626   *SIC* 6531

ROYAL LE PAGE REAL ESTATE   *p992*
905 KING ST W, TORONTO, ON, M6K 3G9
(416) 271-1569   *SIC* 6531

ROYAL LE PAGE SUPREME   *p990*
1245 DUPONT ST, TORONTO, ON, M6H 2A6
(416) 543-0979   *SIC* 6531

ROYAL LEPAGE (1598)   *p1155*
1301 CH CANORA, MONT-ROYAL, QC, H3P 2J5
(514) 735-2281   *SIC* 6531

ROYAL LEPAGE COMMUNITY REALTY LTD *p147*
1202 SOUTHVIEW DR SE, MEDICINE HAT, AB, T1B 4B6
(403) 528-4222   *SIC* 6531

ROYAL LEPAGE COMPLETE REALTY *p476*
7 VICTORIA ST W, ALLISTON, ON, L9R 1S9
(705) 435-3000   *SIC* 6531

ROYAL LEPAGE CROWN REALTY SERVICES INC   *p534*
471 HESPELER RD UNIT 4, CAMBRIDGE, ON, N1R 6J2
(519) 740-6400   *SIC* 6531

ROYAL LEPAGE GALE REAL ESTATE *p663*
5510 MANOTICK MAIN ST, MANOTICK, ON, K4M 0A1
(613) 692-2555   *SIC* 6531

ROYAL LEPAGE KAMLOOPS REALTY *p217*
322 SEYMOUR ST, KAMLOOPS, BC, V2C 2G2
(250) 374-3022   *SIC* 6531

ROYAL LEPAGE KAWARTHA LAKES REALTY INC   *p646*
261 KENT ST W, LINDSAY, ON, K9V 2Z3
(705) 878-3737   *SIC* 6531

ROYAL LEPAGE LIMITED   *p572*
3031 BLOOR ST W, ETOBICOKE, ON, M8X 1C5
(416) 236-1871   *SIC* 6531

ROYAL LEPAGE LIMITED   *p713*
1654 LAKESHORE RD E, MISSISSAUGA, ON, L5G 1E2
(905) 278-5273   *SIC* 6531

ROYAL LEPAGE LIMITED   *p719*
5055 PLANTATION PL UNIT 1, MISSISSAUGA, ON, L5M 6J3
(905) 828-1122   *SIC* 6531

ROYAL LEPAGE LIMITED   *p780*
39 WYNFORD DR, NORTH YORK, ON, M3C 3K5
(416) 510-5800   *SIC* 6531

ROYAL LEPAGE LIMITED   *p801*
326 LAKESHORE RD E, OAKVILLE, ON, L6J 1J6
(905) 845-4267   *SIC* 6531

ROYAL LEPAGE LIMITED   *p811*
250 CENTRUM BLVD SUITE 107, ORLEANS, ON, K1E 3J1
(613) 830-3350   *SIC* 6531

ROYAL LEPAGE LIMITED   *p921*
3080 YONGE ST SUITE 2060, TORONTO, ON, M4N 3N1
(416) 487-4311   *SIC* 6531

ROYAL LEPAGE LIMITED   *p924*
477 MOUNT PLEASANT RD, TORONTO, ON, M4S 2L9
(416) 489-2121   *SIC* 6531

ROYAL LEPAGE MARTIN-LIBERTY REALTY LTD   *p347*
920 VICTORIA AVE, BRANDON, MB, R7A 1A7
SIC 6531

ROYAL LEPAGE NIAGARA REAL ESTATE CENTRE   *p886*
33 MAYWOOD AVE, ST CATHARINES, ON, L2R 1C5
(905) 688-4561   *SIC* 6531

ROYAL LEPAGE PRIME REAL ESTATE *p364*
1877 HENDERSON HWY, WINNIPEG, MB, R2G 1P4
(204) 989-7900   *SIC* 6531

ROYAL LEPAGE PRINCE GEORGE   *p251*
3166 MASSEY DR, PRINCE GEORGE, BC, V2N 2S9
(250) 564-4488   *SIC* 6531

ROYAL LEPAGE PROALLIANCE REALTY *p545*
1111 ELGIN ST W, COBOURG, ON, K9A 5H7
(905) 377-8888   *SIC* 6531

ROYAL LEPAGE REAL ESTATE SERVICES LTD   *p719*
5055 PLANTATION PL UNIT 1, MISSISSAUGA, ON, L5M 6J3
(905) 828-1122   *SIC* 6531

ROYAL LEPAGE REAL ESTATE SERVICES LTD   *p819*
1500 BANK ST SUITE 201, OTTAWA, ON, K1H 7Z2
(613) 733-9100   *SIC* 6531

ROYAL LEPAGE REAL ESTATE SERVICES LTD   *p826*
165 PRETORIA AVE, OTTAWA, ON, K1S 1X1
(613) 238-2801   *SIC* 6531

ROYAL LEPAGE REAL ESTATE SERVICES LTD   *p916*
39 WYNFORD DR 3 FL, TORONTO, ON, M3C 3K5
(416) 510-5810   *SIC* 6531

ROYAL LEPAGE REAL ESTATE SERVICES LTD   *p927*
55 ST CLAIR AVE W, TORONTO, ON, M4V 2Y7
(416) 921-1112   *SIC* 6531

ROYAL LEPAGE REALTY PLUS LTD   *p715*
2575 DUNDAS ST W SUITE 3, MISSISSAUGA, ON, L5K 2M6
(905) 828-6550   *SIC* 6531

ROYAL LEPAGE ROYAL CITY REALTY LTD *p590*
840 TOWER ST S, FERGUS, ON, N1M 2R3
(519) 843-1365   *SIC* 6531

ROYAL LEPAGE SIGNATURE REALTY *p780*
49 THE DONWAY W, NORTH YORK, ON, M3C 3M9
(416) 443-0300   *SIC* 6531

ROYAL LEPAGE STERLING REALTY   *p248*
220 BREW ST SUITE 801, PORT MOODY, BC, V3H 0H6
(604) 421-1010   *SIC* 6531

ROYAL LEPAGE TEAM   *p625*
484 HAZELDEAN RD SUITE 1, KANATA, ON, K2L 1V4
(613) 867-2508   *SIC* 6531

ROYAL LEPAGE TEAM REALTY   *p829*
1335 CARLING AVE SUITE 200, OTTAWA, ON, K1Z 8N8
(613) 216-1198   *SIC* 6531

ROYAL LEPAGE TOP PRODUCERS   *p368*
1549 ST MARY'S RD SUITE 6, WINNIPEG, MB, R2M 5G9
(204) 989-6900   *SIC* 6531

ROYAL LEPAGE-WESTWIN REALTY LTD *p217*
800 SEYMOUR ST, KAMLOOPS, BC, V2C 2H5
(250) 819-3404   *SIC* 6531

ROYAL PACIFIC REALTY CORP   *p288*
3107 KINGSWAY, VANCOUVER, BC, V5R 5J9
(604) 439-0068   *SIC* 6531

S. A. M. (MANAGEMENT) INC   *p382*
200-1080 PORTAGE AVE, WINNIPEG, MB, R3G 3M3
(204) 942-0991   *SIC* 6531

SADIE MORANIS REALTY CORPORATION *p777*
35 LESMILL RD, NORTH YORK, ON, M3B 2T3
(416) 449-2020   *SIC* 6531

SARAZEN REALTY LTD   *p826*
80 ABERDEEN ST SUITE 300, OTTAWA, ON, K1S 5R5
(613) 831-4455   *SIC* 6531

SASK OPPORTUNITIES   *p1433*
1 ACCESS RD N, SASKATOON, SK, S7N 5A2
(306) 933-5485   *SIC* 6531

SASKATCHEWAN HOUSING CORPORATION   *p1419*
1920 BROAD ST SUITE 900, REGINA, SK, S4P 3V6
(306) 787-4177   *SIC* 6531

SAULT STE MARIE HOUSING CORPORATION   *p862*
180 BROCK ST, SAULT STE. MARIE, ON, P6A 3B7
(705) 946-2077   *SIC* 6531

SCHARF REALTY LTD   *p1009*
50 WESTMOUNT RD N, WATERLOO, ON, N2L 2R5
(519) 747-2040   *SIC* 6531

SEARCH REALTY CORP   *p707*
50 VILLAGE CENTRE PL UNIT 100, MISSISSAUGA, ON, L4Z 1V9
(416) 993-7653   *SIC* 6531

SEE REALTY INC   *p976*
991 BAY ST, TORONTO, ON, M5S 3C4
SIC 6531

SEVENTH LEVEL MANAGEMENT LTD *p39*
11012 MACLEOD TRAIL SE SUITE 600, CALGARY, AB, T2J 6A5
(403) 837-1195   *SIC* 6531

SHAPE MARKETING CORP   *p329*
505 BURRARD ST SUITE 2020, VANCOUVER, BC, V7X 1M6
(604) 681-2358   *SIC* 6531

SHAPE PROPERTIES (BTCR) CORP   *p329*
505 BURRARD ST SUITE 2020, VANCOUVER, BC, V7X 1M6
(604) 681-2358   *SIC* 6531

SIGNATURE SERVICE GMAC REAL ESTATE   *p707*
186 ROBERT SPECK PKY, MISSISSAUGA, ON, L4Z 3G1
(905) 896-4622   *SIC* 6531

SINCERE REALTY INC   *p877*
1033 MCNICOLL AVE, SCARBOROUGH, ON, M1W 3W6
(416) 497-8900   *SIC* 6531

SLAVENS ASSOCIATES   *p972*
435 EGLINTON AVE W, TORONTO, ON, M5N 1A4
(416) 483-4337   *SIC* 6531

SLEMON SPACE CORPORATION   *p1042*
30 AEROSPACE BLVD UNIT A, SLEMON PARK, PE, C0B 2A0
(902) 432-1700   *SIC* 6531

▲ Public Company   ■ Public Company Family Member   **HQ** Headquarters   **BR** Branch   **SL** Single Location

SMITH AGENCY LIMITED   p388
929 CORYDON AVE SUITE 3, WINNIPEG, MB, R3M 0W8
(204) 287-2872   SIC 6531

SNC-LAVALIN OPERATIONS & MAINTENANCE INC   p580
195 THE WEST MALL, ETOBICOKE, ON, M9C 5K8
(416) 207-4700   SIC 6531

SO, JAMES REALTY LTD   p921
259 BROADVIEW AVE, TORONTO, ON, M4M 2G6
(416) 465-2412   SIC 6531

SOCIETE DE GESTION COGIR INC   p1069
7250 BOUL TASCHEREAU BUREAU 200, BROSSARD, QC, J4W 1M9
(450) 671-6381   SIC 6531

SOCIETE DE GESTION COGIR S.E.N.C.   p1069
7250 BOUL TASCHEREAU BUREAU 200, BROSSARD, QC, J4W 1M9
(450) 671-6381   SIC 6531

SOCIETE IMMOBILIERE M.C.M. INC, LA   p1352
204 RUE PRINCIPALE, SAINT-SAUVEUR, QC, J0R 1R0
(450) 227-2611   SIC 6531

SOCIETE QUEBECOISE DES INFRASTRUCTURES   p1270
1075 RUE DE L'AMERIQUE-FRANCAISE, QUEBEC, QC, G1R 5P8
(418) 646-1766   SIC 6531

SOCIETE XYLEM CANADA   p1252
300 AV LABROSSE, POINTE-CLAIRE, QC, H9R 4V5
(514) 695-0133   SIC 6531

SONDER CANADA INC   p1184
15 RUE MARIE-ANNE O BUREAU 201, MONTREAL, QC, H2W 1B6
(800) 657-9859   SIC 6531

SRS VICTORIA REALTY   p291
7291 FRASER ST, VANCOUVER, BC, V5X 3V8
(604) 263-3033   SIC 6531

SSQ DISTRIBUTION INC   p1273
2525 BOUL LAURIER, QUEBEC, QC, G1V 4Z6
(418) 682-1245   SIC 6531

STARLIGHT INVESTMENTS   p572
3280 BLOOR ST W UNIT 1400, ETOBICOKE, ON, M8X 2X3
(416) 234-8444   SIC 6531

STATE REALTY LIMITED   p478
1122 WILSON ST W, ANCASTER, ON, L9G 3K9
(905) 648-4451   SIC 6531

STATE REALTY LIMITED   p615
987 RYMAL RD E, HAMILTON, ON, L8W 3M2
(905) 574-4600   SIC 6531

STATE REALTY LIMITED   p894
115 HIGHWAY 8, STONEY CREEK, ON, L8G 1C1
(905) 662-6666   SIC 6531

STATESMEN REALTY CORPORATION   p223
1980 COOPER RD SUITE 108, KELOWNA, BC, V1Y 8K5
(250) 861-5122   SIC 6531

STERN REALTY (1994) LTD   p323
6272 EAST BOULEVARD, VANCOUVER, BC, V6M 3V7
(604) 266-1364   SIC 6531

STEVENSON ADVISORS LTD   p379
260 ST MARY AVE UNIT 200, WINNIPEG, MB, R3C 0M6
(204) 956-1901   SIC 6531

STRACHAN, ALASTAIR   p733
5770 HURONTARIO ST SUITE 200, MISSISSAUGA, ON, L5R 3G5
(905) 568-9500   SIC 6531

STRATA CORPORATION # 962   p337
1234 WHARF ST SUITE 962, VICTORIA, BC, V8W 3H9
(250) 386-2211   SIC 6531

STRATEGIC REALTY MANAGEMENT CORP   p60
630 8 AVE SW SUITE 400, CALGARY, AB, T2P 1G6
(403) 770-2300   SIC 6531

SUTTON GRANITE HILL REALTY INC   p924
2010 YONGE ST SUITE 200, TORONTO, ON, M4S 1Z9
SIC 6531

SUTTON GROUP - TOWN AND COUNTRY REALTY LTD   p895
6209 MAIN ST, STOUFFVILLE, ON, L4A 4H8
(905) 640-0888   SIC 6531

SUTTON GROUP ADMIRAL REALTY INC   p781
1881 STEELES AVE W SUITE 12, NORTH YORK, ON, M3H 5Y4
(416) 739-7200   SIC 6531

SUTTON GROUP ELITE REALTY INC   p708
3643 CAWTHRA RD SUITE 201, MISSISSAUGA, ON, L5A 2Y4
(905) 848-9800   SIC 6531

SUTTON GROUP HERITAGE REALTY INC   p540
26 CAMERON ST W, CANNINGTON, ON, L0E 1E0
SIC 6531

SUTTON GROUP HERITAGE REALTY INC   p843
1755 PICKERING PKY UNIT 10, PICKERING, ON, L1V 6K5
(416) 678-9622   SIC 6531

SUTTON GROUP INCENTIVE REALTY INC   p488
241 MINET'S POINT RD, BARRIE, ON, L4N 4C4
(705) 739-1300   SIC 6531

SUTTON GROUP OLD MILL REALTY INC   p572
4237 DUNDAS ST W, ETOBICOKE, ON, M8X 1Y3
(416) 234-2424   SIC 6531

SUTTON GROUP PROFESSIONAL REALTY   p443
73 TACOMA DR SUITE 800, DARTMOUTH, NS, B2W 3Y6
(902) 223-1399   SIC 6531

SUTTON GROUP QUANTUM REALTY INC   p714
1673 LAKESHORE RD W, MISSISSAUGA, ON, L5J 1J4
(905) 822-5000   SIC 6531

SUTTON GROUP REALTY SYSTEMS INC   p712
1528 DUNDAS ST W UNIT 1, MISSISSAUGA, ON, L5C 1E4
(905) 896-3333   SIC 6531

SUTTON GROUP STATUS REALTY INC   p814
286 KING ST W, OSHAWA, ON, L1J 2J9
(905) 436-0990   SIC 6531

SUTTON GROUP-ASSOCIATES REALTY INC   p974
358 DAVENPORT RD, TORONTO, ON, M5R 1K6
(416) 966-0300   SIC 6531

SUTTON GROUP-CAPITAL REALTY LTD   p431
451 KENMOUNT RD, ST. JOHN'S, NL, A1B 3P9
(709) 726-6262   SIC 6531

SUTTON GROUP-NEW STANDARD REALTY INC   p854
360 HIGHWAY 7 E UNIT L 1, RICHMOND HILL, ON, L4B 3Y7
(905) 709-8000   SIC 6531

SUTTON GROUP-RIGHT WAY REAL ESTATE INC   p1035
28 PERRY ST, WOODSTOCK, ON, N4S 3C2
(519) 539-6194   SIC 6531

SUTTON GROUP-SECURITY REAL ESTATE INC   p989
1239 ST CLAIR AVE W, TORONTO, ON, M6E 1B5
(416) 654-1010   SIC 6531

SUTTON GROUP-SUMMIT REALTY INC   p712
1100 BURNHAMTHORPE RD W UNIT 27, MISSISSAUGA, ON, L5C 4G4
(905) 897-9555   SIC 6531

SUTTON WEST REALTY INC   p580
6 DIXON RD, ETOBICOKE, ON, M9P 2L1
(416) 240-1000   SIC 6531

TAPESTRY REALTY LTD   p278
13049 76 AVE SUITE 104, SURREY, BC, V3W 2V7
SIC 6531

TECHNOPARC MONTREAL   p1336
7150 RUE ALBERT-EINSTEIN BUREAU 200, SAINT-LAURENT, QC, H4S 2C1
(514) 956-2525   SIC 6531

TERREQUITY REALTY INC   p768
211 CONSUMERS RD UNIT 105, NORTH YORK, ON, M2J 4G8
(416) 496-9220   SIC 6531

TGS HARVARD PROPERTY MANAGEMENT INC   p1430
135 21ST ST E SUITE 21, SASKATOON, SK, S7K 0B4
(306) 668-8350   SIC 6531

THEREDPIN.COM REALTY INC., BROKERAGE   p943
5 CHURCH ST, TORONTO, ON, M5E 1M2
(416) 800-0812   SIC 6531

TOOLE PEET & CO LIMITED   p67
1135 17 AVE SW, CALGARY, AB, T2T 0B6
(403) 245-4366   SIC 6531

TORNGAT REGIONAL HOUSING ASSOCIATION   p424
436 HAMILTON RD, HAPPY VALLEY-GOOSE BAY, NL, A0P 1C0
(709) 896-8126   SIC 6531

TORONTO COMMUNITY HOUSING CORPORATION   p931
931 YONGE ST SUITE 400, TORONTO, ON, M4W 2H2
(416) 981-5500   SIC 6531

TOULON DEVELOPMENT CORPORATION   p1402
4060 RUE SAINTE-CATHERINE O BUREAU 700, WESTMOUNT, QC, H3Z 2Z3
(514) 931-5811   SIC 6531

TRANSGLOBE PROPERTY MANAGEMENT SERVICES LTD   p690
5935 AIRPORT RD UNIT 600, MISSISSAUGA, ON, L4V 1W5
SIC 6531

TREELAND REALTY LTD   p227
6337 198 ST SUITE 101, LANGLEY, BC, V2Y 2E3
(604) 533-3491   SIC 6531

TRILAND REALTY LTD   p651
235 NORTH CENTRE RD SUITE 1, LONDON, ON, N5X 4E7
(519) 661-0380   SIC 6531

TRILAND REALTY LTD   p656
240 WATERLOO ST UNIT 103, LONDON, ON, N6B 2N4
(519) 672-9880   SIC 6531

TRIOVEST REALTY ADVISORS INC   p968
40 UNIVERSITY AVE SUITE 1200, TORONTO, ON, M5J 1T1
(416) 362-0045   SIC 6531

TSYCCO LTD   p685
290 BRONTE ST S, MILTON, ON, L9T 1Y8
(905) 625-1234   SIC 6531

U OF T INNIS RESIDENCE   p976
111 ST. GEORGE ST, TORONTO, ON, M5S 2E8
(416) 978-2512   SIC 6531

UNIVERSITY OF WESTERN ONTARIO, THE   p655
1151 RICHMOND ST SUITE 3, LONDON, ON, N6A 5B9
(519) 661-2111   SIC 6531

UPG PROPERTY GROUP INC   p237
555 SIXTH ST UNIT 330, NEW WESTMINSTER, BC, V3L 5H1
(604) 525-8292   SIC 6531

URBAN REALTY INC   p920
840 PAPE AVE, TORONTO, ON, M4K 3T6
(416) 461-9900   SIC 6531

VALENTE, REMO REAL ESTATE (1990) LIMITED   p1025
2985 DOUGALL AVE, WINDSOR, ON, N9E 1S1
(519) 966-7777   SIC 6531

VANTAGE REALTY LTD   p604
214 SPEEDVALE AVE W SUITE 1, GUELPH, ON, N1H 1C4
(519) 822-7842   SIC 6531

VANTAGEONE FINANCIAL CORP   p332
3108 33 AVE, VERNON, BC, V1T 2N7
(250) 260-4513   SIC 6531

VENDEX REALTY INC   p512
4 MCLAUGHLIN RD S UNIT 10, BRAMPTON, ON, L6Y 3B2
(905) 452-7272   SIC 6531

VENTERRA REALTY (CANADA) INC   p854
1725 16TH AVE SUITE 201, RICHMOND HILL, ON, L4B 4C6
(905) 886-1059   SIC 6531

VERANOVA PROPERTIES LIMITED   p768
505 CONSUMERS RD SUITE 812, NORTH YORK, ON, M2J 4V8
(416) 701-9000   SIC 6531

VERTICA AU SERVICE DES RESIDENTS INC   p943
33 YONGE ST SUITE 1000, TORONTO, ON, M5E 1S9
(416) 507-2929   SIC 6531

VIA CAPITALE DU MONT ROYAL   p1173
1152 AV DU MONT-ROYAL E, MONTREAL, QC, H2J 1X8
(514) 597-2121   SIC 6531

VISTA PROPERTY MANAGEMENT INC   p580
380 DIXON RD SUITE 100, ETOBICOKE, ON, M9R 1T3
(416) 241-9171   SIC 6531

VPG REALTY INC   p239
1233 LYNN VALLEY RD SUITE 159, NORTH VANCOUVER, BC, V7J 0A1
(604) 770-4353   SIC 6531

W. CHAN INVESTMENTS LTD   p67
501 18 AVE SW SUITE 600, CALGARY, AB, T2S 0C7
(403) 229-3838   SIC 6531

WANG, JOHN C   p324
7547 CAMBIE ST, VANCOUVER, BC, V6P 3H6
(604) 322-3000   SIC 6531

WARRINGTON PROPERTY GROUP INCORPORATED, THE   p317
1030 GEORGIA ST W SUITE 1700, VANCOUVER, BC, V6E 2Y3
(604) 602-1887   SIC 6531

WEST COAST REALTY LTD   p242
889 HARBOURSIDE DR SUITE 100, NORTH VANCOUVER, BC, V7P 3S1
(604) 365-9120   SIC 6531

WESTCORP PROPERTIES INC   p118
8215 112 ST NW SUITE 200, EDMONTON, AB, T6G 2C8
(780) 431-3300   SIC 6531

WESTMAR REALTY LTD   p266
5188 WESTMINSTER HWY SUITE 203, RICHMOND, BC, V7C 5S7
(604) 506-5352   SIC 6531

WESTPOINT MANAGEMENT INC   p41
3604 52 AVE NW SUITE 114, CALGARY, AB, T2L 1V9
(403) 282-7770   SIC 6531

WHISTLER REAL ESTATE COMPANY LIMITED, THE   p343
4308 MAIN ST SUITE 17, WHISTLER, BC, V8E 1A9
(604) 932-5538   SIC 6531

WILLIAMS, KELLER REALTY   p728
7145 WEST CREDIT AVE BLDG 1 SUITE 201, MISSISSAUGA, ON, L5N 6J7
(905) 812-8123   SIC 6531

▲ Public Company   ■ Public Company Family Member   **HQ** Headquarters   **BR** Branch   **SL** Single Location

WINDMILL CROSSING LIMITED *p454*
1475 LOWER WATER ST SUITE 100, HAL-IFAX, NS, B3J 3Z2
(902) 422-6412   *SIC 6531*

WINDSOR-ESSEX COUNTY HOUSING CORPORATION *p1024*
945 MCDOUGALL ST, WINDSOR, ON, N9A 1L9
(519) 254-1681   *SIC 6531*

WOLLE REALTY INC *p636*
842 VICTORIA ST N SUITE 15, KITCH-ENER, ON, N2B 3C1
(519) 578-7300   *SIC 6531*

WOOD BUFFALO HOUSING & DEVELOP-MENT CORPORATION *p129*
9915 FRANKLIN AVE SUITE 9011, FORT MCMURRAY, AB, T9H 2K4
(780) 799-4050   *SIC 6531*

YORK CONDOMINIUM CORPORATION NO 382 *p571*
2045 LAKE SHORE BLVD W, ETOBICOKE, ON, M8V 2Z6
(416) 252-7701   *SIC 6531*

YORK CONDOMINIUM CORPORATION NO. 510 *p968*
55 HARBOUR SQ SUITE 3212, TORONTO, ON, M5J 2L1
(416) 362-1174   *SIC 6531*

YOUR COMMUNITY REALTY INC *p856*
9050 YONGE ST SUITE 100, RICHMOND HILL, ON, L4C 9S6
(905) 884-8700   *SIC 6531*

YUKON HOUSING CORPORATION *p1440*
410 JARVIS ST UNIT H, WHITEHORSE, YT, Y1A 2H5
(867) 667-5759   *SIC 6531*

Z69115 ALBERTA LTD *p74*
37 RICHARD WAY SW SUITE 200, CAL-GARY, AB, T3E 7M8
SIC 6531

SIC 6541 Title abstract offices

ESC CORPORATE SERVICES LTD *p980*
445 KING ST W SUITE 400, TORONTO, ON, M5V 1K4
(416) 595-7177   *SIC 6541*

WEST COAST TITLE SEARCH LTD *p237*
99 SIXTH ST, NEW WESTMINSTER, BC, V3L 5H8
(604) 659-8600   *SIC 6541*

SIC 6552 Subdividers and developers, nec

ALLDRITT DEVELOPMENT LIMITED *p280*
2055 152 ST SUITE 300, SURREY, BC, V4A 4N7
(604) 536-5525   *SIC 6552*

BAYWOOD HOMES PARTNERSHIP *p785*
1140 SHEPPARD AVE W UNIT 12, NORTH YORK, ON, M3K 2A2
(416) 633-7333   *SIC 6552*

FIRST GULF DEVELOPMENT CORPORA-TION *p933*
351 KING ST E 13TH FL, TORONTO, ON, M5A 0L6
(416) 773-7070   *SIC 6552*

MATTAMY HOMES LIMITED *p969*
66 WELLINGTON ST W, TORONTO, ON, M5K 1G8
(905) 829-2424   *SIC 6552*

NOVA BUILDERS INC *p94*
14020 128 AVE NW UNIT 200, EDMON-TON, AB, T5L 4M8
(780) 702-6682   *SIC 6552*

PACRIM DEVELOPMENTS INC *p457*
117 KEARNEY LAKE RD SUITE 11, HALI-FAX, NS, B3M 4N9
(902) 457-0144   *SIC 6552*

REID-WORLD WIDE CORPORATION *p102*
18140 107 AVE NW SUITE 200, EDMON-TON, AB, T5S 1K5

(780) 451-7778   *SIC 6552*
ROHIT COMMUNITIES INC *p125*
550 91 ST SW, EDMONTON, AB, T6X 0V1
(780) 436-9015   *SIC 6552*

STERLING CENTRECORP INC *p675*
2851 JOHN ST SUITE 1, MARKHAM, ON, L3R 5R7
(905) 477-9200   *SIC 6552*

SUN RIVERS LIMITED PARTNERSHIP *p218*
1000 CLUBHOUSE DR, KAMLOOPS, BC, V2H 1T9
(250) 828-9989   *SIC 6552*

YORK MAJOR HOLDINGS INC *p664*
10000 DUFFERIN ST, MAPLE, ON, L6A 1S3
(905) 417-2300   *SIC 6552*

SIC 6553 Cemetery subdividers and developers

1 KING WEST INC *p948*
1 KING ST W, TORONTO, ON, M5H 1A1
(416) 548-8100   *SIC 6553*

ACRES ENTERPRISES LTD *p216*
971 CAMOSUN CRES, KAMLOOPS, BC, V2C 6G1
(250) 372-7456   *SIC 6553*

ANTHEM RIVERFRONT LAND LIMITED PARTNERSHIP *p43*
104 2 ST SW, CALGARY, AB, T2P 0C7
(403) 536-8802   *SIC 6553*

ANTHEM WORKS LTD *p327*
1055 DUNSMUIR STREET, VANCOUVER, BC, V7X 1K8
(604) 689-3040   *SIC 6553*

AON INC *p840*
307 AYLMER ST N, PETERBOROUGH, ON, K9J 7M4
(705) 742-5445   *SIC 6553*

ARBOR MEMORIAL SERVICES INC *p995*
2 JANE ST SUITE 101, TORONTO, ON, M6S 4W8
(416) 763-3230   *SIC 6553*

ARNON DEVELOPMENT CORPORATION LIMITED *p830*
1801 WOODWARD DR, OTTAWA, ON, K2C 0R3
(613) 226-2000   *SIC 6553*

BATISE INVESTMENTS LIMITED *p785*
3625 DUFFERIN ST UNIT 503, NORTH YORK, ON, M3K 1N4
(416) 635-7520   *SIC 6553*

BROOKFIELD RESIDENTIAL PROPERTIES INC *p73*
4906 RICHARD RD SW, CALGARY, AB, T3E 6L1
(403) 231-8900   *SIC 6553*

BROOKLIN ESTATES GENERAL PARTNER INC. *p1030*
3700 STEELES AVE W SUITE 800, WOOD-BRIDGE, ON, L4L 8M9
(905) 850-8508   *SIC 6553*

CENTRE CITY CAPITAL LIMITED *p712*
1 PORT ST E SUITE 301, MISSISSAUGA, ON, L5G 4N1
(905) 274-5212   *SIC 6553*

CLARIDGE HOMES CORPORATION *p833*
210 GLADSTONE AVE SUITE 2001, OT-TAWA, ON, K2P 0Y6
(613) 233-6030   *SIC 6553*

CONCERT REAL ESTATE CORPORATION *p326*
1190 HORNBY ST, VANCOUVER, BC, V6Z 2K5
(604) 688-9460   *SIC 6553*

CONCORD ADEX DEVELOPMENTS CORP *p769*
1001 SHEPPARD AVE E, NORTH YORK, ON, M2K 1C2
(416) 813-0999   *SIC 6553*

DEVIMCO IMMOBILIER INC *p1071*
3400 RUE DE L'ECLIPSE BUREAU 310, BROSSARD, QC, J4Z 0P3

(450) 645-2525   *SIC 6553*
DREAM UNLIMITED CORP *p938*
30 ADELAIDE ST E SUITE 301, TORONTO, ON, M5C 3H1
(416) 365-3535   *SIC 6553*

EMBASSY DEVELOPMENT CORPORA-TION *p185*
2025 WILLINGDON AVE SUITE 1300, BURNABY, BC, V5C 0J3
(604) 294-0666   *SIC 6553*

FERCAN DEVELOPMENTS INC *p933*
193 KING ST E SUITE 200, TORONTO, ON, M5A 1J5
(416) 867-9899   *SIC 6553*

FIELDGATE DEVELOPMENT AND CON-STRUCTION LTD *p771*
5400 YONGE ST SUITE 2, NORTH YORK, ON, M2N 5R5
(416) 227-2220   *SIC 6553*

GENESIS LAND DEVELOPMENT CORP *p23*
7315 8 ST NE, CALGARY, AB, T2E 8A2
(403) 266-0746   *SIC 6553*

GESTION CANDEREL INC *p1196*
2000 RUE PEEL BUREAU 900, MON-TREAL, QC, H3A 2W5
(514) 842-8636   *SIC 6553*

HARDMAN GROUP LIMITED, THE *p453*
1226 HOLLIS ST, HALIFAX, NS, B3J 1T6
(902) 429-3743   *SIC 6553*

IMMEUBDES MOULINS INC., LES *p1379*
689 CH DU COTEAU, TERREBONNE, QC, J6W 5H2
SIC 6553

INNOVATIVE RESIDENTIAL INVESTMENTS INC *p1428*
101B ENGLISH CRES, SASKATOON, SK, S7K 8G4
(306) 979-7421   *SIC 6553*

IRONCLAD DEVELOPMENTS INC *p357*
57158 SYMINGTON ROAD 20E UNIT 101, SPRINGHILL, MB, R2J 4L6
(204) 777-1972   *SIC 6553*

KANEFF PROPERTIES LIMITED *p511*
8501 MISSISSAUGA RD SUITE 200, BRAMPTON, ON, L6Y 5G8
(905) 454-0221   *SIC 6553*

MELCOR DEVELOPMENTS LTD *p90*
10310 JASPER AVE NW SUITE 900, ED-MONTON, AB, T5J 1Y8
(780) 423-6931   *SIC 6553*

MENKES CONSTRUCTION LIMITED *p772*
4711 YONGE ST SUITE 1400, NORTH YORK, ON, M2N 7E4
(416) 491-2222   *SIC 6553*

MENKES HOLDINGS INC *p772*
4711 YONGE ST SUITE 1400, NORTH YORK, ON, M2N 7E4
(416) 491-2222   *SIC 6553*

MENKES PROPERTY MANAGEMENT SER-VICES LTD *p772*
4711 YONGE ST SUITE 1400, NORTH YORK, ON, M2N 7E4
(416) 491-2222   *SIC 6553*

MOSAIC SIMON FRASER HOLDINGS LTD *p319*
2609 GRANVILLE ST UNIT 500, VANCOU-VER, BC, V6H 3H3
(604) 685-3888   *SIC 6553*

MOUNT PLEASANT GROUP OF CEMETER-IES *p919*
65 OVERLEA BLVD SUITE 500, TORONTO, ON, M4H 1P1
(416) 696-7866   *SIC 6553*

ONE WEST HOLDINGS LTD *p315*
1095 PENDER ST W SUITE 900, VANCOU-VER, BC, V6E 2M6
(604) 681-8882   *SIC 6553*

PARKLANE VENTURES LTD *p329*
1055 DUNSMUIR ST SUITE 2000, VAN-COUVER, BC, V7X 1L5
(604) 648-1800   *SIC 6553*

PRINCETON DEVELOPMENTS LTD *p92*
9915 108 ST NW SUITE 1400, EDMON-TON, AB, T5K 2G8

(780) 423-7775   *SIC 6553*
QUALICO DEVELOPMENTS WEST LTD *p37*
5716 1 ST SE UNIT 100, CALGARY, AB, T2H 1H8
(403) 253-3311   *SIC 6553*

RANCHO REALTY (EDMONTON) LTD *p121*
3203 93 ST NW SUITE 300, EDMONTON, AB, T6N 0B2
(780) 463-2132   *SIC 6553*

RG PROPERTIES LTD *p316*
1177 HASTINGS ST W SUITE 2088, VAN-COUVER, BC, V6E 2K3
(604) 688-8999   *SIC 6553*

RICHCRAFT HOMES LTD *p818*
2280 ST. LAURENT BLVD SUITE 201, OT-TAWA, ON, K1G 4K1
(613) 739-7111   *SIC 6553*

SIFTON PROPERTIES LIMITED *p660*
1295 RIVERBEND RD SUITE 300, LON-DON, ON, N6K 0G2
(519) 434-1000   *SIC 6553*

SILVERADO LAND CORP *p203*
399 CLUBHOUSE DR, COURTENAY, BC, V9N 9G3
(250) 897-0233   *SIC 6553*

SLAVE LAKE EQUITIES INC *p94*
13920 YELLOWHEAD TRAIL NW SUITE 1000, EDMONTON, AB, T5L 3C2
(780) 702-6682   *SIC 6553*

STERLING SILVER DEVELOPMENT COR-PORATION *p774*
53 THE LINKS RD, NORTH YORK, ON, M2P 1T7
(416) 226-9400   *SIC 6553*

TIMBERCREEK INVESTMENTS INC *p931*
25 PRICE ST, TORONTO, ON, M4W 1Z1
(416) 923-9967   *SIC 6553*

TRICO HOMES INC *p66*
1005 11 AVE SW, CALGARY, AB, T2R 0G1
(403) 287-9300   *SIC 6553*

TRIDEL CORPORATION *p781*
4800 DUFFERIN ST SUITE 200, NORTH YORK, ON, M3H 5S9
(416) 661-9290   *SIC 6553*

UBC PROPERTIES INVESTMENTS LTD *p324*
3313 SHRUM LANE UNIT 200, VANCOU-VER, BC, V6S 0C8
(604) 731-3103   *SIC 6553*

VRANCOR PROPERTY MANAGEMENT INC *p613*
366 KING ST W, HAMILTON, ON, L8P 1B3
(905) 540-4800   *SIC 6553*

SIC 6712 Bank holding companies

1019728 ALBERTA LTD *p147*
8902 95 ST, MORINVILLE, AB, T8R 1K7
(780) 939-3000   *SIC 6712*

1055307 ONTARIO INC *p473*
403 CLEMENTS RD W, AJAX, ON, L1S 6N3
(905) 428-2002   *SIC 6712*

1059895 ONTARIO INC *p663*
GD, MABERLY, ON, K0H 2B0
(613) 268-2308   *SIC 6712*

1072667 ONTARIO LIMITED *p877*
3370 PHARMACY AVE, SCARBOROUGH, ON, M1W 3K4
(416) 494-1444   *SIC 6712*

1077947 ONTARIO INC *p482*
105 GUTHRIE ST SS 1, AYR, ON, N0B 1E0
(519) 632-9052   *SIC 6712*

1090349 ONTARIO INC *p879*
95 MAIN ST S, SEAFORTH, ON, N0K 1W0
(519) 527-1631   *SIC 6712*

1142024 ONTARIO INC *p648*
1425 CREAMERY RD, LONDON, ON, N5V 5B3
(519) 451-3748   *SIC 6712*

1168768 ONTARIO INC *p764*
6750 FOURTH LINE RD, NORTH GOWER, ON, K0A 2T0
(613) 489-0120   *SIC 6712*

119759 CANADA LTEE   *p1304*
8850 35E AV, SAINT-GEORGES, QC, G5Y
5C2
(418) 459-3423   *SIC 6712*

1220579 ONTARIO INC   *p665*
750 COCHRANE DR, MARKHAM, ON, L3R
8E1
(416) 293-8365   *SIC 6712*

1235052 ONTARIO LIMITED   *p485*
311 BRYNE DR, BARRIE, ON, L4N 8V4
(705) 728-5322   *SIC 6712*

1257391 ONTARIO LIMITED   *p1013*
80 WILLIAM SMITH DR, WHITBY, ON, L1N
9W1
(905) 668-5060   *SIC 6712*

1272227 ONTARIO INC   *p850*
21 EAST WILMOT ST SUITE 2, RICHMOND
HILL, ON, L4B 1A3
(905) 763-2929   *SIC 6712*

127901 CANADA INC   *p1175*
955 RUE AMHERST, MONTREAL, QC, H2L
3K4
(514) 523-1182   *SIC 6712*

131519 CANADA INC   *p1304*
4100 10E AV, SAINT-GEORGES, QC, G5Y
7S3
(418) 228-9458   *SIC 6712*

131638 CANADA INC   *p1307*
4605 AV THIBAULT, SAINT-HUBERT, QC,
J3Y 3S8
(450) 445-0550   *SIC 6712*

1324344 ONTARIO INC   *p850*
1725 16TH AVE SUITE 1, RICHMOND
HILL, ON, L4B 4C6
(905) 882-5563   *SIC 6712*

1340560 ONTARIO INC   *p1004*
7 INDUSTRIAL RD, WALKERTON, ON,
N0G 2V0
(519) 881-4055   *SIC 6712*

1367313 ONTARIO INC   *p968*
100 WELLINGTON ST SUITE 3200,
TORONTO, ON, M5K 1K7
(416) 304-1616   *SIC 6712*

137882 CANADA INC   *p1131*
9100 RUE ELMSLIE, LASALLE, QC, H8R
1V6
(514) 365-1642   *SIC 6712*

1392167 ONTARIO LIMITED   *p547*
248 BOWES RD, CONCORD, ON, L4K 1J9
(905) 660-5021   *SIC 6712*

1421239 ONTARIO INC   *p494*
124 COMMERCIAL RD, BOLTON, ON, L7E
1K4
(905) 951-6800   *SIC 6712*

1476399 ONTARIO LIMITED   *p589*
71301 LONDON RD, EXETER, ON, N0M
1S3
(519) 235-2121   *SIC 6712*

147755 CANADA INC   *p1063*
1501 RUE AMPERE BUREAU 200,
BOUCHERVILLE, QC, J4B 5Z5
(450) 655-2441   *SIC 6712*

151210 CANADA INC   *p1392*
245 RUE JEAN-COUTU, VARENNES, QC,
J3X 0E1
(450) 646-9760   *SIC 6712*

157341 CANADA INC   *p1181*
7236 RUE MARCONI, MONTREAL, QC,
H2R 2Z5
(514) 844-5050   *SIC 6712*

158473 CANADA INC   *p1192*
1555 RUE PEEL BUREAU 1100, MON-
TREAL, QC, H3A 3L8
(514) 846-4000   *SIC 6712*

159519 CANADA INC   *p1047*
9031 BOUL PARKWAY, ANJOU, QC, H1J
1N4
(514) 325-8700   *SIC 6712*

159585 CANADA INC   *p1401*
1 CAR WESTMOUNT BUREAU 1850,
WESTMOUNT, QC, H3Z 2P9
(514) 932-7422   *SIC 6712*

1596101 ONTARIO INC   *p911*
35 TOWNLINE RD, TILLSONBURG, ON,

N4G 2R5
(519) 688-5803   *SIC 6712*

160276 CANADA INC   *p1221*
6865 BOUL DE MAISONNEUVE O, MON-
TREAL, QC, H4B 1T1
SIC 6712

161251 CANADA INC   *p1055*
355 RUE DUPONT, BEAUPRE, QC, G0A
1E0
(418) 827-8347   *SIC 6712*

162583 CANADA INC   *p1224*
1625 RUE CHABANEL O BUREAU 801,
MONTREAL, QC, H4N 2S7
(514) 384-4776   *SIC 6712*

166260 CANADA INC   *p1331*
4747 BOUL DE LA COTE-VERTU, SAINT-
LAURENT, QC, H4S 1C9
(514) 336-8780   *SIC 6712*

1667779 ONTARIO LIMITED   *p778*
52 PRINCE ANDREW PL, NORTH YORK,
ON, M3C 2H4
(416) 391-5555   *SIC 6712*

1686943 ONTARIO LIMITED   *p597*
4726 BANK ST, GLOUCESTER, ON, K1T
3W7
(613) 822-7400   *SIC 6712*

173532 CANADA INC   *p1345*
7870 RUE FLEURICOURT, SAINT-
LEONARD, QC, H1R 2L3
(514) 274-2870   *SIC 6712*

174664 CANADA LTEE   *p1161*
7900 AV MARCO-POLO, MONTREAL, QC,
H1E 2S5
(514) 648-1015   *SIC 6712*

1788317 ONTARIO INC   *p1004*
18 INDUSTRIAL RD, WALKERTON, ON,
N0G 2V0
(519) 881-0187   *SIC 6712*

1797509 ALBERTA ULC   *p629*
1463 HIGHWAY 21, KINCARDINE, ON, N2Z
2X3
(519) 396-1324   *SIC 6712*

1939250 ONTARIO LTD   *p805*
251 NORTH SERVICE RD W, OAKVILLE,
ON, L6M 3E7
(905) 608-1999   *SIC 6712*

2153-1090 QUEBEC INC   *p1274*
3690 BOUL NEILSON, QUEBEC, QC, G1W
0A9
(418) 781-0471   *SIC 6712*

2163-2088 QUEBEC INC   *p1047*
10400 RUE RENAUDE-LAPOINTE, ANJOU,
QC, H1J 2V7
(514) 322-5300   *SIC 6712*

2224855 ONTARIO INC   *p691*
5450 EXPLORER DR UNIT 300, MISSIS-
SAUGA, ON, L4W 5M1
(416) 649-3939   *SIC 6712*

226138 ONTARIO INC   *p529*
2300 FAIRVIEW ST, BURLINGTON, ON,
L7R 2E4
(905) 681-2200   *SIC 6712*

2425-1761 QUEBEC INC   *p1307*
4355 BOUL SIR-WILFRID-LAURIER,
SAINT-HUBERT, QC, J3Y 3X3
(450) 443-6666   *SIC 6712*

2540-0417 QUEBEC INC   *p1353*
124 RUE DES ECOLIERS, SAINT-VICTOR,
QC, G0M 2B0
(418) 588-3913   *SIC 6712*

2618-1833 QUEBEC INC   *p1181*
274 RUE JEAN-TALON E, MONTREAL, QC,
H2R 1S7
(514) 273-3224   *SIC 6712*

2772981 CANADA INC   *p1084*
1 PLACE LAVAL BUREAU 400, COTE
SAINT-LUC, QC, H7N 1A1
(514) 335-3246   *SIC 6712*

2846-4436 QUEBEC INC   *p1265*
2440 AV DALTON, QUEBEC, QC, G1P 3X1
(418) 266-6600   *SIC 6712*

2850401 CANADA INC   *p1382*
189 BOUL HARWOOD, TERREBONNE,
QC, J7V 1Y3

(450) 964-9333   *SIC 6712*

2871149 CANADA INC   *p1393*
189 BOUL HARWOOD, VAUDREUIL-
DORION, QC, J7V 1Y3
(450) 455-2827   *SIC 6712*

2945-9708 QUEBEC INC   *p1063*
1175 RUE AMPERE, BOUCHERVILLE, QC,
J4B 7M6
(450) 655-2350   *SIC 6712*

302084 B.C. LTD   *p275*
8239 128 ST, SURREY, BC, V3W 4G1
(604) 596-9984   *SIC 6712*

3088-7061 QUEBEC INC   *p1351*
104 BOUL SAINT-REMI, SAINT-REMI, QC,
J0L 2L0
(450) 454-5171   *SIC 6712*

3101895 NOVA SCOTIA COMPANY   *p1092*
800 BOUL STUART-GRAHAM S BUREAU
315, DORVAL, QC, H4Y 1J6
(514) 422-1000   *SIC 6712*

324126 ALBERTA LTD   *p134*
10514 67 AVE UNIT 401, GRANDE
PRAIRIE, AB, T8W 0K8
(780) 532-7771   *SIC 6712*

3254160 CANADA INC   *p1342*
850 AV MUNCK, SAINT-LAURENT, QC,
H7S 1B1
(514) 384-5060   *SIC 6712*

3310485 CANADA INC   *p1224*
1625 RUE CHABANEL O BUREAU 201,
MONTREAL, QC, H4N 2S7
(514) 388-1700   *SIC 6712*

3346625 CANADA INC   *p1288*
54 RANG DE LA MONTAGNE, ROUGE-
MONT, QC, J0L 1M0
(450) 469-2912   *SIC 6712*

3358097 CANADA INC   *p1383*
4680 BOUL FRONTENAC E, THETFORD
MINES, QC, G6H 4G5
(418) 338-8588   *SIC 6712*

3378683 CANADA INC   *p1177*
9600 RUE MEILLEUR BUREAU 630, MON-
TREAL, QC, H2N 2E3
(514) 385-3629   *SIC 6712*

3379710 CANADA INC   *p1224*
1450 RUE DE LOUVAIN O, MONTREAL,
QC, H4N 1G5
(514) 495-1531   *SIC 6712*

3401987 CANADA INC.   *p1125*
900 RUE DU PACIFIQUE, LACHINE, QC,
H8S 1C4
(514) 367-3001   *SIC 6712*

347678 ALBERTA LTD   *p148*
1205 5 ST, NISKU, AB, T9E 7L6
(780) 955-7733   *SIC 6712*

3522997 CANADA INC   *p1337*
180 MONTEE DE LIESSE, SAINT-
LAURENT, QC, H4T 1N7
(450) 455-3963   *SIC 6712*

3645118 CANADA INC   *p1157*
8650 CH DARNLEY, MONT-ROYAL, QC,
H4T 1M4
(514) 345-0990   *SIC 6712*

3728099 CANADA INC   *p1295*
1370 RUE HOCQUART, SAINT-BRUNO,
QC, J3V 6E1
(450) 653-7868   *SIC 6712*

3731537 CANADA INC   *p1214*
2000 RUE SAINTE-CATHERINE O BU-
REAU 9000, MONTREAL, QC, H3H 2T2
(514) 939-4442   *SIC 6712*

3762971 CANADA INC   *p1222*
5080 RUE SAINT-AMBROISE, MONTREAL,
QC, H4C 2G1
(514) 939-3060   *SIC 6712*

3836185 CANADA INC   *p1133*
2850 AV JACQUES-BUREAU, LAVAL, QC,
H7P 0B7
(450) 688-6264   *SIC 6712*

3838731 CANADA INC   *p1182*
6885 BOUL SAINT-LAURENT, MONTREAL,
QC, H2S 3C9
(514) 284-4988   *SIC 6712*

3851401 CANADA INC   *p373*

555 LOGAN AVE, WINNIPEG, MB, R3A 0S4
(204) 788-4249   *SIC 6712*

386338 ONTARIO LIMITED   *p576*
39 POPLAR HEIGHTS DR, ETOBICOKE,
ON, M9A 5A1
(416) 247-2354   *SIC 6712*

3931714 CANADA INC   *p1380*
2215 CH COMTOIS, TERREBONNE, QC,
J6X 4H4
(450) 477-1002   *SIC 6712*

3958230 CANADA INC   *p1192*
600 BOUL DE MAISONNEUVE O BUREAU
2200, MONTREAL, QC, H3A 3J2
(450) 646-9760   *SIC 6712*

402424 ONTARIO LIMITED   *p895*
257 MONTEITH AVE, STRATFORD, ON,
N5A 2P6
(519) 271-4552   *SIC 6712*

4093879 CANADA LTD   *p371*
1771 INKSTER BLVD, WINNIPEG, MB, R2X
1R3
(204) 982-5783   *SIC 6712*

4116372 CANADA INC   *p978*
266 KING ST W SUITE 200, TORONTO,
ON, M5V 1H8
(416) 977-3238   *SIC 6712*

4129849 CANADA INC   *p1241*
807 BOUL CURE-LABELLE, MONTREAL-
OUEST, QC, H7V 2V2
(450) 781-8800   *SIC 6712*

4145151 CANADA INC   *p1038*
489 BRACKLEY POINT RD - RTE 15,
BRACKLEY, PE, C1E 1Z3
(902) 629-1500   *SIC 6712*

415329 ALBERTA LTD   *p145*
439 5 AVE SE, MEDICINE HAT, AB, T1A
2P9
(403) 529-2600   *SIC 6712*

4224795 CANADA INC   *p1153*
9200 RUE DESVOYAUX, MIRABEL, QC,
J7N 2H4
(450) 475-7924   *SIC 6712*

4366492 CANADA INC   *p1295*
1360 RUE MONTARVILLE, SAINT-BRUNO,
QC, J3V 3T5
(514) 498-7777   *SIC 6712*

4372727 CANADA INC   *p1343*
9275 RUE LE ROYER, SAINT-LEONARD,
QC, H1P 3H7
(514) 328-2772   *SIC 6712*

4384768 CANADA INC   *p985*
100 KING ST W SUITE 6600, TORONTO,
ON, M5X 2A1
(905) 624-7337   *SIC 6712*

4423038 CANADA INC   *p1216*
9850 RUE MEILLEUR, MONTREAL, QC,
H3L 3J4
(514) 385-5568   *SIC 6712*

4513380 CANADA INC   *p42*
450 1 ST SW SUITE 2500, CALGARY, AB,
T2P 5H1
SIC 6712

4834772 MANITOBA LTD   *p387*
600 PEMBINA HWY, WINNIPEG, MB, R3M
2M5
SIC 6712

512844 ALBERTA LTD   *p142*
3939 1 AVE S, LETHBRIDGE, AB, T1J 4P8
(403) 327-3154   *SIC 6712*

532551 ONTARIO LIMITED   *p485*
39 ANNE ST S, BARRIE, ON, L4N 2C7
(705) 726-1444   *SIC 6712*

553032 ONTARIO LIMITED   *p716*
4120 RIDGEWAY DR UNIT 28, MISSIS-
SAUGA, ON, L5L 5S9
(905) 607-8200   *SIC 6712*

561028 ONTARIO LIMITED   *p829*
890 BOYD AVE, OTTAWA, ON, K2A 2E3
(613) 798-8020   *SIC 6712*

564549 ALBERTA LTD   *p220*
1865 DILWORTH DR SUITE 335,
KELOWNA, BC, V1Y 9T1
(250) 215-1143   *SIC 6712*

564967 ALBERTA LTD   *p95*

11703 160 ST NW, EDMONTON, AB, T5M 3Z3
(780) 451-0060   *SIC* 6712

595140 ALBERTA LTD *p107*
5219 47 ST NW, EDMONTON, AB, T6B 3N4
(780) 444-7766   *SIC* 6712

601712 ONTARIO INC *p978*
315 ADELAIDE ST W, TORONTO, ON, M5V 1P8
(416) 977-2603   *SIC* 6712

6202667 CANADA INC *p1324*
3535 CH DE LA COTE-DE-LIESSE, SAINT-LAURENT, QC, H4N 2N5
(514) 356-7777   *SIC* 6712

6368174 CANADA INC *p1342*
6165 RUE DESSUREAUX, SAINT-LAURENT, QC, H7B 1B1
(450) 968-0880   *SIC* 6712

639809 BC LTD *p197*
45389 LUCKAKUCK WAY UNIT 100, CHILLIWACK, BC, V2R 3V1
(604) 858-5663   *SIC* 6712

6895051 CANADA INC *p1393*
135 RUE DU CHEMINOT, VAUDREUIL-DORION, QC, J7V 5V5
(450) 455-9877   *SIC* 6712

700635 ALBERTA LTD *p27*
1288 42 AVE SE UNIT 1, CALGARY, AB, T2G 5P1
(403) 287-5340   *SIC* 6712

722140 ONTARIO LIMITED *p686*
3160 CARAVELLE DR, MISSISSAUGA, ON, L4V 1K9
SIC 6712

7339101 CANADA INC *p1325*
387 RUE DESLAURIERS, SAINT-LAURENT, QC, H4N 1W2
(514) 344-5558   *SIC* 6712

762695 ONTARIO LIMITED *p691*
2770 MATHESON BLVD E, MISSISSAUGA, ON, L4W 4M5
(905) 238-3466   *SIC* 6712

792259 ALBERTA LTD *p95*
15377 117 AVE NW, EDMONTON, AB, T5M 3X4
(780) 454-4838   *SIC* 6712

8061076 CANADA INC *p1075*
217 BOUL INDUSTRIEL, CHATEAUGUAY, QC, J6J 4Z2
(514) 934-4684   *SIC* 6712

82212 CANADA LTD *p1420*
601 ALBERT ST, REGINA, SK, S4R 2P4
(306) 525-5411   *SIC* 6712

835799 ALBERTA LTD *p153*
4814 50 ST SUITE 300, RED DEER, AB, T4N 1X4
(403) 346-7555   *SIC* 6712

875647 ALBERTA LTD *p172*
GD STN MAIN, WHITECOURT, AB, T7S 1S1
(780) 778-6975   *SIC* 6712

87861 CANADA LTEE *p1387*
1000 RUE DU PERE-DANIEL BUREAU 728, TROIS-RIVIERES, QC, G9A 5R6
(819) 378-2747   *SIC* 6712

8959528 CANADA INC *p1107*
250 RUE DEVEAULT BUREAU A, GATINEAU, QC, J8Z 1S6
(819) 778-0114   *SIC* 6712

9001-6262 QUEBEC INC *p1292*
30 RUE DES GRANDS-LACS, SAINT-AUGUSTIN-DE-DESMAURES, QC, G3A 2E6
(418) 878-4135   *SIC* 6712

9023-4451 QUEBEC INC *p1271*
2700 BOUL LAURIER UNITE 3000, QUEBEC, QC, G1V 2L8
(418) 658-1820   *SIC* 6712

9027-3459 QUEBEC INC *p1397*
1171 RUE NOTRE-DAME O BUREAU 200, VICTORIAVILLE, QC, G6P 7L1
(819) 758-0313   *SIC* 6712

9029-5015 QUEBEC INC *p1097*
915 RUE HAINS, DRUMMONDVILLE, QC, J2C 3A1

(819) 478-4971   *SIC* 6712

90401 CANADA LTEE *p1328*
2255 RUE COHEN, SAINT-LAURENT, QC, H4R 2N7
(514) 334-5000   *SIC* 6712

9057-4245 QUEBEC INC *p1100*
3980 BOUL LEMAN, FABREVILLE, QC, H7E 1A1
(450) 661-6470   *SIC* 6712

9064-3792 QUEBEC INC *p1141*
2025 RUE DE LA METROPOLE, LONGUEUIL, QC, J4G 1S9
SIC 6712

9107-7081 QUEBEC INC *p1146*
351 RUE NOTRE-DAME N, LOUISEVILLE, QC, J5V 1X9
(819) 228-9497   *SIC* 6712

9109-5521 QUEBEC INC *p1255*
3261 RUE LOYOLA, QUEBEC, QC, G1E 2R9
(418) 660-2037   *SIC* 6712

9111-7523 QUEBEC INC *p1151*
12500 RUE DE L'AVENIR, MIRABEL, QC, J7J 2K3
(450) 435-9995   *SIC* 6712

9121-1128 QUEBEC INC *p1248*
188 AV ONEIDA, POINTE-CLAIRE, QC, H9R 1A8
(514) 694-3439   *SIC* 6712

9138-4438 QUEBEC INC *p1063*
1228 RUE NOBEL, BOUCHERVILLE, QC, J4B 5H1
(450) 655-9966   *SIC* 6712

9187-2853 QUEBEC INC *p1245*
2299 AV VALLEE, PLESSISVILLE, QC, G6L 2Y6
(819) 252-6315   *SIC* 6712

9262-4261 QUEBEC INC *p1159*
175 4E RUE, MONTMAGNY, QC, G5V 3L6
(418) 248-3089   *SIC* 6712

9303-6952 QUEBEC INC *p1044*
355 RUE BONIN, ACTON VALE, QC, J0H 1A0
(450) 546-3279   *SIC* 6712

9314-0887 QUEBEC INC *p1235*
4300 BOUL SAINT-ELZEAR O, MONTREAL, QC, H7P 4J4
(450) 622-5448   *SIC* 6712

932072 ONTARIO LIMITED *p493*
25 GRAHAM ST, BLENHEIM, ON, N0P 1A0
(519) 676-5198   *SIC* 6712

9353-0251 QUEBEC INC *p1119*
6150 BOUL SAINTE-ANNE, L'ANGE GARDIEN, QC, G0A 2K0
(418) 822-0643   *SIC* 6712

9368-9677 QUEBEC INC *p1078*
545 BOUL DU ROYAUME O, CHICOUTIMI, QC, G7H 5B1
(418) 968-4343   *SIC* 6712

9372-3575 QUEBEC INC *p1080*
1788 RUE MITIS, CHICOUTIMI, QC, G7K 1H5
(418) 543-1632   *SIC* 6712

94291 CANADA LTEE *p1397*
560 BOUL DES BOIS-FRANCS S, VICTORIAVILLE, QC, G6P 5X4
(819) 357-2241   *SIC* 6712

944128 ALBERTA LTD *p92*
14440 YELLOWHEAD TRAIL NW, EDMONTON, AB, T5L 3C5
(780) 413-0900   *SIC* 6712

960667 ONTARIO LIMITED *p990*
777 SAINT CLARENS AVE, TORONTO, ON, M6H 3X3
(416) 536-2194   *SIC* 6712

967003 ONTARIO LIMITED *p907*
581 RED RIVER RD, THUNDER BAY, ON, P7B 1H4
(807) 344-6666   *SIC* 6712

972683 ONTARIO INC *p1029*
150 CREDITVIEW RD, WOODBRIDGE, ON, L4L 9N4
(416) 798-7722   *SIC* 6712

974307 ALBERTA LTD *p112*

9850 41 AVE NW, EDMONTON, AB, T6E 5L6
(780) 414-0980   *SIC* 6712

9790446 CANADA INC *p1169*
9455 RUE J.-J.-GAGNIER, MONTREAL, QC, H1Z 3C8
(514) 384-0660   *SIC* 6712

A & M VENTURES LTD *p275*
12448 82 AVE SUITE 201, SURREY, BC, V3W 3E9
(604) 597-9058   *SIC* 6712

A.G. PENNER FARM SERVICES LTD *p346*
10 PENNER DR, BLUMENORT, MB, R0A 0C0
(204) 326-3781   *SIC* 6712

A.I.M. HOLDINGS INC *p171*
2300 PELLICAN DR, WABASCA, AB, T0G 2K0
(780) 891-1018   *SIC* 6712

A.J.M. MECHANICAL SERVICES LTD *p6*
5610 54 AVE, BONNYVILLE, AB, T9N 2N3
(780) 826-4412   *SIC* 6712

A.M. FISH HOLDINGS LTD *p1113*
26 RUE BRIARDALE, HAMPSTEAD, QC, H3X 3N6
(514) 788-0788   *SIC* 6712

ABC GROUP *p1029*
100 HANLAN RD SUITE 3, WOODBRIDGE, ON, L4L 4V8
(905) 392-0485   *SIC* 6712

ABC GROUP LIMITED *p792*
2 NORELCO DR, NORTH YORK, ON, M9L 2X6
(416) 246-1782   *SIC* 6712

ABITIBIBOWATER CANADA INC *p1209*
111 RUE DUKE BUREAU 5000, MONTREAL, QC, H3C 2M1
(514) 875-2160   *SIC* 6712

ABSOLUTE ENERGY LTD *p74*
600 CROWFOOT CRES NW SUITE 302, CALGARY, AB, T3G 0B4
(403) 509-4000   *SIC* 6712

ACCOR SERVICES CANADA INC *p978*
155 WELLINGTON ST W SUITE 3300, TORONTO, ON, M5V 0C3
(416) 874-2600   *SIC* 6712

ACCURCAST CORPORATION *p1004*
333 ARNOLD ST, WALLACEBURG, ON, N8A 3P3
(519) 627-2227   *SIC* 6712

ACE PHARMACY LTD *p198*
206 PORT AUGUSTA ST, COMOX, BC, V9M 3N1
(250) 339-2235   *SIC* 6712

ACI MANAGEMENT GROUP INC *p106*
12531 60 ST NW, EDMONTON, AB, T5W 5J5
(780) 476-3098   *SIC* 6712

ACROLAB TECHNOLOGIES INC *p1018*
7475 TRANBY AVE, WINDSOR, ON, N8S 2B7
(519) 944-5900   *SIC* 6712

ADI GROUP INC *p400*
1133 REGENT ST SUITE 300, FREDERICTON, NB, E3B 3Z2
(506) 452-9000   *SIC* 6712

ADMINISTRATION BEAULIEU INC *p1375*
6176 RUE BERTRAND-FABI, SHERBROOKE, QC, J1N 2P3
(819) 564-6161   *SIC* 6712

AFX HOLDINGS CORP *p231*
14301 256 ST SUITE 302, MAPLE RIDGE, BC, V4R 0B9
(604) 380-4458   *SIC* 6712

AGENCE COMEDIHAU INC *p1263*
214 AV SAINT-SACREMENT BUREAU 130, QUEBEC, QC, G1N 3X6
(418) 647-2525   *SIC* 6712

AGENCE DE VOYAGES D'AUTOMOBILE ET TOURING CLUB DU QUEBEC INC *p1278*
444 RUE BOUVIER, QUEBEC, QC, G2J 1E3
(418) 624-8222   *SIC* 6712

AIC GLOBAL HOLDINGS INC *p529*

1375 KERNS RD SUITE 100, BURLINGTON, ON, L7P 4V7
(905) 331-4242   *SIC* 6712

AIM HOLDING TRUST *p199*
2000 BRIGANTINE DR, COQUITLAM, BC, V3K 7B5
(604) 525-3900   *SIC* 6712

AIM METAUX & ALLIAGES INC *p1238*
9100 BOUL HENRI-BOURASSA E, MONTREAL-EST, QC, H1E 2S4
(514) 494-2000   *SIC* 6712

AIRIA LEASING INC *p650*
511 MCCORMICK BLVD, LONDON, ON, N5W 4C8
(519) 457-1904   *SIC* 6712

ALCATEL HOLDINGS CANADA CORP *p623*
600 MARCH RD, KANATA, ON, K2K 2T6
(613) 591-3600   *SIC* 6712

ALDON INVESTMENTS LTD *p891*
46 COMMUNITY AVE, STONEY CREEK, ON, L8E 2Y3
(905) 664-2126   *SIC* 6712

ALGONQUIN POWER & UTILITIES CORP *p800*
354 DAVIS RD, OAKVILLE, ON, L6J 2X1
(905) 465-4500   *SIC* 6712

ALIAXIS NORTH AMERICA INC *p796*
1425 NORTH SERVICE RD E SUITE 3, OAKVILLE, ON, L6H 1A7
(289) 881-0120   *SIC* 6712

ALIGN-TECH INDUSTRIES INC *p99*
18114 107 AVE NW, EDMONTON, AB, T5S 1K5
(780) 448-7303   *SIC* 6712

ALIMENTS KRISPY KERNELS INC *p1266*
2620 AV WATT, QUEBEC, QC, G1P 3T5
(418) 658-4640   *SIC* 6712

ALLEN-FELDMAN HOLDINGS LTD *p319*
1505 2ND AVE W SUITE 200, VANCOUVER, BC, V6H 3Y4
(604) 734-5945   *SIC* 6712

AMEC FOSTER WHEELER INC *p43*
801 6 AVE SW SUITE 900, CALGARY, AB, T2P 3W3
(403) 298-4170   *SIC* 6712

ANCASTER OLD MILL INC *p477*
548 OLD DUNDAS RD, ANCASTER, ON, L9G 3J4
(905) 648-1828   *SIC* 6712

ANDE CAPITAL CORP *p357*
2976 DAY ST, SPRINGFIELD, MB, R2C 2Z2
(204) 777-5345   *SIC* 6712

APOTEX INTERNATIONAL INC *p792*
150 SIGNET DR, NORTH YORK, ON, M9L 1T9
(416) 749-9300   *SIC* 6712

APPS TRANSPORT GROUP INC *p737*
6495 TOMKEN RD, MISSISSAUGA, ON, L5T 2X7
(905) 451-2720   *SIC* 6712

ARGO CANADA HOLDING ULC *p648*
3020 GORE RD, LONDON, ON, N5V 4T7
(519) 457-3400   *SIC* 6712

ARLBERG HOLDINGS INC *p1332*
4505 RUE COUSENS, SAINT-LAURENT, QC, H4S 1X5
SIC 6712

ARMOUR TRANSPORTATION SYSTEMS INC *p408*
689 EDINBURGH DR, MONCTON, NB, E1E 2L4
(506) 857-0205   *SIC* 6712

ARNO HOLDINGS LTD *p538*
201B PRESTON PKY, CAMBRIDGE, ON, N3H 5E8
(519) 653-3171   *SIC* 6712

ASDR CANADA INC *p1148*
691 RUE ROYALE, MALARTIC, QC, J0Y 1Z0
(819) 757-3039   *SIC* 6712

ASHMORE LIMITED *p419*
3307 ROUTE 101, TRACYVILLE, NB, E5L 1N7
(506) 459-7777   *SIC* 6712

ASKEW'S ENTERPRISES LTD p267
111 LAKESHORE DR NE, SALMON ARM, BC, V1E 4N3
(250) 832-2668 *SIC 6712*

ASPIN KEMP & ASSOCIATES HOLDING CORP p1041
23 BROOK ST, MONTAGUE, PE, C0A 1R0
(902) 361-3135 *SIC 6712*

ASSANTE WEALTH MANAGEMENT (CANADA) LTD p971
199 BAY ST SUITE 2700, TORONTO, ON, M5L 1E2
(416) 348-9994 *SIC 6712*

ATLANTIC BAPTIST SENIOR CITIZENS HOMES INC p408
35 ATLANTIC BAPTIST AVE, MONCTON, NB, E1E 4N3
(506) 858-7870 *SIC 6712*

AUGUST CORPORATE PARTNERS INC p184
4445 LOUGHEED HWY SUITE 1001, BURNABY, BC, V5C 0E4
(604) 731-0441 *SIC 6712*

AURUM CERAMIC DENTAL LABORATORIES LTD p66
115 17 AVE SW, CALGARY, AB, T2S 0A1
(403) 228-5120 *SIC 6712*

AUTOMOBILES F.M. INC p1311
5705 AV TRUDEAU, SAINT-HYACINTHE, QC, J2S 1H5
(450) 773-4736 *SIC 6712*

AY HOLDINGS ONTARIO INC p948
150 YORK ST SUITE 900, TORONTO, ON, M5H 3S5
(416) 955-0000 *SIC 6712*

AYRLINE LEASING INC p483
2558 CEDAR CREEK RD SS 2, AYR, ON, N0B 1E0
(519) 740-8209 *SIC 6712*

AZURITE HOLDINGS LTD p236
225 EDWORTHY WAY, NEW WESTMINSTER, BC, V3L 5G4
(604) 527-1120 *SIC 6712*

BABLAKE LTD p70
11800 40 ST SE, CALGARY, AB, T2Z 4T1
(403) 248-3559 *SIC 6712*

BAILLARGEON - MSA INC p1317
800 RUE DES CARRIERES, SAINT-JEAN-SUR-RICHELIEU, QC, J3B 2P2
(450) 346-4441 *SIC 6712*

BAINE JOHNSTON CORPORATION p428
410 EAST WHITE HILLS RD, ST. JOHN'S, NL, A1A 5J7
(709) 576-1780 *SIC 6712*

BALL CONSTRUCTION (CANADA) INC p635
5 SHIRLEY AVE, KITCHENER, ON, N2B 2E6
(519) 742-5851 *SIC 6712*

BANQUE LAURENTIENNE DU CANADA p1213
1360 BOUL RENE-LEVESQUE O BUREAU 600, MONTREAL, QC, H3G 0E5
(514) 284-4500 *SIC 6712*

BARLBOROUGH BUSINESS ENTERPRISES LTD p161
192 ORDZE AVE, SHERWOOD PARK, AB, T8B 1M6
(780) 449-1616 *SIC 6712*

BARRA HOLDINGS INC p907
285 MEMORIAL AVE, THUNDER BAY, ON, P7B 6H4
(807) 345-6564 *SIC 6712*

BAUER PARTNERSHIP p687
6490 VISCOUNT RD, MISSISSAUGA, ON, L4V 1H3
SIC 6712

BCC HOLDINGS INC p67
1912 13 ST SW, CALGARY, AB, T2T 3P6
(403) 617-0806 *SIC 6712*

BETON PROVINCIAL FINANCE LTEE p1150
1825 AV DU PHARE O, MATANE, QC, G4W 3M6
(418) 562-0074 *SIC 6712*

BETON PROVINCIAL LTEE p1150

1825 AV DU PHARE O, MATANE, QC, G4W 3M6
(418) 562-0074 *SIC 6712*

BILL GOSLING OUTSOURCING HOLDING CORP p754
16635 YONGE ST SUITE 26, NEWMARKET, ON, L3X 1V6
(905) 470-8181 *SIC 6712*

BLACKSTRAP HOSPITALITY CORPORATION p1424
1125 LOUISE AVE, SASKATOON, SK, S7H 2P8
(306) 931-1030 *SIC 6712*

BMML HOLDINGS p1417
2103 11TH AVE SUITE 700, REGINA, SK, S4P 4G1
(306) 347-8300 *SIC 6712*

BOCA BOYS HOLDINGS INC p1401
1 CAR WESTMOUNT BUREAU 1100, WESTMOUNT, QC, H3Z 2P9
(514) 341-5600 *SIC 6712*

BODTKER GROUP OF COMPANIES LTD p14
7905 46 ST SE, CALGARY, AB, T2C 2Y6
(403) 279-2191 *SIC 6712*

BOMBARDIER TRANSPORTATION CANADA HOLDING INC p1295
1101 RUE PARENT, SAINT-BRUNO, QC, J3V 6E6
(450) 441-2020 *SIC 6712*

BOSA ENTERPRISE CORPORATION p302
838 HASTINGS ST W SUITE 1100, VANCOUVER, BC, V6C 0A6
(604) 299-1363 *SIC 6712*

BOULDER CREEK GOLF COURSE LTD p139
333 BOULDER CREEK DR SUITE 3, LANGDON, AB, T0J 1X3
(403) 936-8777 *SIC 6712*

BOWEN MANUFACTURING LIMITED p546
188 KING ST E RR 2, COLBORNE, ON, K0K 1S0
(905) 355-3757 *SIC 6712*

BOYER HOLDINGS INC p907
391 OLIVER RD, THUNDER BAY, ON, P7B 2G2
(807) 344-8491 *SIC 6712*

BOZIKIS FOOD GROUP p788
216 YONGE BLVD, NORTH YORK, ON, M5M 3H8
SIC 6712

BPRE SAINT LOUIS HOLDINGS, LIMITED PARTNERSHIP p311
1075 GEORGIA ST W SUITE 2010, VANCOUVER, BC, V6E 3C9
(604) 806-3350 *SIC 6712*

BRENNER & ASSOCIATES INC p1010
630 SUPERIOR DR, WATERLOO, ON, N2V 2C6
(519) 746-0439 *SIC 6712*

BRICK WAREHOUSE LP, THE p95
16930 114 AVE NW, EDMONTON, AB, T5M 3S2
(780) 930-6000 *SIC 6712*

BRIDGE 8 INVESTMENTS INC p14
7805 46 ST SE, CALGARY, AB, T2C 2Y5
(403) 236-0305 *SIC 6712*

BRIS EQUITIES LTD p1426
75 24TH ST E, SASKATOON, SK, S7K 0K3
(306) 652-1660 *SIC 6712*

BRITISH CONFECTIONERY COMPANY (1982) LIMITED p426
7 PANTHER PL, MOUNT PEARL, NL, A1N 5B7
(709) 747-2377 *SIC 6712*

BRITISH PACIFIC TRANSPORT HOLDINGS LTD p224
9975 199B ST, LANGLEY, BC, V1M 3G4
(604) 882-5880 *SIC 6712*

BROCK SOLUTIONS HOLDINGS INC p636
88 ARDELT AVE, KITCHENER, ON, N2C 2C9
(519) 571-1522 *SIC 6712*

BROOKFIELD BRP CANADA CORP p1104

480 BOUL DE LA CITE BUREAU 200, GATINEAU, QC, J8T 8R3
(819) 561-2722 *SIC 6712*

BROWNSVILLE HOLDINGS INC p482
GD LCD MAIN, AYLMER, ON, N5H 2R7
(519) 866-3446 *SIC 6712*

BRULE HOLDINGS LTD p452
5686 SPRING GARDEN RD, HALIFAX, NS, B3J 1H5
(902) 423-6766 *SIC 6712*

BUNGE CANADA HOLDINGS 1 ULC p803
2190 SOUTH SERVICE RD W, OAKVILLE, ON, L6L 5N1
(905) 825-7900 *SIC 6712*

BURRELL OVERHEAD DOOR CO. LIMITED p549
1853 HIGHWAY 7, CONCORD, ON, L4K 1V4
(905) 669-1711 *SIC 6712*

C J I PROPERTIES INC p891
237 ARVIN AVE, STONEY CREEK, ON, L8E 5S6
(905) 664-8448 *SIC 6712*

CAE INTERNATIONAL HOLDINGS LIMITED p1338
8585 CH DE LA COTE-DE-LIESSE, SAINT-LAURENT, QC, H4T 1G6
(514) 341-6780 *SIC 6712*

CAFES VIENNE PRESS INC, LES p1210
1022 RUE NOTRE-DAME O, MONTREAL, QC, H3C 1K9
(514) 935-5553 *SIC 6712*

CANADIAN CAPITAL CORPORATION p990
1022 BLOOR ST W SUITE 300, TORONTO, ON, M6H 1M2
(416) 495-0909 *SIC 6712*

CANADIAN-BRITISH CONSULTING GROUP LIMITED p452
1489 HOLLIS ST, HALIFAX, NS, B3J 3M5
(902) 421-7241 *SIC 6712*

CANOPY GROWTH CORPORATION p881
1 HERSHEY DR, SMITHS FALLS, ON, K7A 0A8
(855) 558-9333 *SIC 6712*

CANTELON ENTERPRISES INC p73
2529 17 AVE SW, CALGARY, AB, T3E 0A2
(403) 246-1176 *SIC 6712*

CAPITALE GROUPE FINANCIER INC, LA p1268
625 RUE JACQUES-PARIZEAU, QUEBEC, QC, G1R 2G5
(418) 644-4229 *SIC 6712*

CARDEL CONSTRUCTION LTD p14
180 QUARRY PARK BLVD SE, CALGARY, AB, T2C 3G3
(403) 258-1511 *SIC 6712*

CAREY MANAGEMENT INC p40
5445 8 ST NE, CALGARY, AB, T2K 5R9
(403) 275-7360 *SIC 6712*

CARGOJET HOLDINGS LIMITED PARTNERSHIP p714
2281 NORTH SHERIDAN WAY, MISSISSAUGA, ON, L5K 2S3
(905) 501-7373 *SIC 6712*

CASCADES CANADA ULC p1117
404 BOUL MARIE-VICTORIN, KINGSEY FALLS, QC, J0A 1B0
(819) 363-5100 *SIC 6712*

CASLUMBER INC p1235
2885 BOUL DAGENAIS O, MONTREAL, QC, H7P 1T2
(450) 622-2420 *SIC 6712*

CAVALIER LAND LTD p22
1223 31 AVE NE SUITE 100, CALGARY, AB, T2E 7W1
(403) 264-5188 *SIC 6712*

CAWTHORN INVESTMENTS LTD p22
6700 9 ST NE, CALGARY, AB, T2E 8K6
(403) 295-5855 *SIC 6712*

CCD LIMITED PARTNERSHIP p734
1115 CARDIFF BLVD, MISSISSAUGA, ON, L5S 1L8
(905) 564-2115 *SIC 6712*

CCI ENTERTAINMENT LTD p926

210 ST CLAIR AVE W 4 FL, TORONTO, ON, M4V 1R2
(416) 964-8750 *SIC 6712*

CENTRAL ONTARIO HEALTHCARE PROCUREMENT ALLIANCE p851
95 MURAL ST SUITE 300, RICHMOND HILL, ON, L4B 3G2
(905) 886-5319 *SIC 6712*

CENTRIX ENVIRONNEMENT INC p1139
5314 AV DES BELLES-AMOURS BUREAU 104, LEVIS, QC, G6X 1P2
(418) 988-3888 *SIC 6712*

CERVUS CORPORATION p76
120 COUNTRY HILLS LANDNG NW SUITE 205, CALGARY, AB, T3K 5P3
(403) 567-0339 *SIC 6712*

CHANTALE'S BED & BREAKFAST INC p406
1234 MAIN ST, MONCTON, NB, E1C 1H7
SIC 6712

CHEROVAN HOLDINGS LTD p337
4400 CHATTERTON WAY SUITE 301, VICTORIA, BC, V8X 5J2
(250) 881-7878 *SIC 6712*

CIRION BIOPHARMA RECHERCHE INC p1233
3150 RUE DELAUNAY, MONTREAL, QC, H7L 5E1
(450) 688-6445 *SIC 6712*

CLEARTECH HOLDINGS LTD p1426
1500 QUEBEC AVE, SASKATOON, SK, S7K 1V7
(306) 664-2522 *SIC 6712*

CLOVERDALE INVESTMENTS LTD p279
2630 CROYDON DR STE 400, SURREY, BC, V3Z 6T3
(604) 594-6211 *SIC 6712*

CLUB DE GOLF TERREBONNE INC p1380
3555 CH MARTIN, TERREBONNE, QC, J6X 0B2
(450) 477-1817 *SIC 6712*

CLUETT HOLDINGS INC p445
629 WINDMILL RD, DARTMOUTH, NS, B3B 1B6
(902) 466-5328 *SIC 6712*

COBRA INTERNATIONAL SYSTEMES DE FIXATIONS CIE LTEE p1048
8051 BOUL METROPOLITAIN E, ANJOU, QC, H1J 1J8
(514) 354-2240 *SIC 6712*

COGECO MEDIA ACQUISITIONS INC p1202
5 PLACE VILLE-MARIE BUREAU 1700, MONTREAL, QC, H3B 0B3
(514) 764-4700 *SIC 6712*

COHENDAV INC p1338
153 RUE GRAVELINE, SAINT-LAURENT, QC, H4T 1R4
(514) 342-6700 *SIC 6712*

COLOR COMPASS CORPORATION p113
5308 97 ST NW, EDMONTON, AB, T6E 5W5
(780) 438-0808 *SIC 6712*

COMARK HOLDINGS INC p298
650 GEORGIA ST W SUITE 2900, VANCOUVER, BC, V6B 4N8
(604) 646-3790 *SIC 6712*

COMPAGNIE GESTIMET INC, LA p1384
3175 BOUL THIBEAU, TROIS-RIVIERES, QC, G8T 1G4
(819) 371-8456 *SIC 6712*

COMPUGEN SYSTEMS LTD p856
100 VIA RENZO DR, RICHMOND HILL, ON, L4S 0B8
(905) 707-2000 *SIC 6712*

COMPUTERSHARE CANADA INC p961
100 UNIVERSITY AVE SUITE 800, TORONTO, ON, M5J 2Y1
(416) 263-9200 *SIC 6712*

CONGEBEC LOGISTIQUE INC p1261
810 AV GODIN, QUEBEC, QC, G1M 2X9
(418) 683-3491 *SIC 6712*

CONNEX TELECOMMUNICATIONS CORPORATION p851
44 EAST BEAVER CREEK RD SUITE 16, RICHMOND HILL, ON, L4B 1G8
(905) 944-6500 *SIC 6712*

CONSEILLERS EN GESTION ET INFORMATIQUE CGI INC   p1213
1350 BOUL RENE-LEVESQUE O 15E ETAGE, MONTREAL, QC, H3G 1T4
(514) 841-3200   SIC 6712

CONTRANS CORP   p1036
1179 RIDGEWAY RD, WOODSTOCK, ON, N4V 1E3
(519) 421-4600   SIC 6712

CONTRANS HOLDING II LP   p1036
1179 RIDGEWAY RD, WOODSTOCK, ON, N4V 1E3
(519) 421-4600   SIC 6712

COONEY GROUP INC   p491
77 BELLEVUE DR, BELLEVILLE, ON, K8N 4Z5
(613) 962-6666   SIC 6712

COOPER INDUSTRIES (CANADA) INC p730
5925 MCLAUGHLIN RD, MISSISSAUGA, ON, L5R 1B8
(905) 501-3000   SIC 6712

COOPERATIVE DE L'UNIVERSITE LAVAL
p1272
2305 RUE DE L'UNIVERSITE BUREAU 1100, QUEBEC, QC, G1V 0B4
(418) 656-2600   SIC 6712

CORESLAB INTERNATIONAL INC   p891
332 JONES RD SUITE 8, STONEY CREEK, ON, L8E 5N2
(905) 643-0220   SIC 6712

CORIX INFRASTRUCTURE INC   p312
1188 GEORGIA ST W SUITE 1160, VANCOUVER, BC, V6E 4A2
(604) 697-6700   SIC 6712

CORPORATION ADFAST   p1333
2685 RUE DIAB, SAINT-LAURENT, QC, H4S 1E7
(514) 337-7307   SIC 6712

CORPORATION DE DEVELOPPEMENT CUIRS BENTLEY INC, LA   p1143
375 BOUL ROLAND-THERRIEN BUREAU 210, LONGUEUIL, QC, J4H 4A6
(450) 651-5000   SIC 6712

CORPORATION DE GESTION POSITRON CANADA   p1227
5101 RUE BUCHAN SUITE 220, MONTREAL, QC, H4P 2R9
(514) 345-2220   SIC 6712

CORPORATION DE SOINS DE LA SANTE HOSPIRA   p1118
17300 RTE TRANSCANADIENNE, KIRKLAND, QC, H9J 2M5
(514) 695-0500   SIC 6712

CORPORATION FINANCIERE J. DESCHAMPS INC   p1255
755 BOUL DES CHUTES, QUEBEC, QC, G1E 2C2
(418) 667-3322   SIC 6712

CORPORATION FINANCIERE QUEBECOISE INC   p1055
500 BOUL DU BEAU-PRE, BEAUPRE, QC, G0A 1E0
(418) 827-5211   SIC 6712

CORPORATION OPTIMUM   p1195
425 BOUL DE MAISONNEUVE O BUREAU 1700, MONTREAL, QC, H3A 3G5
(514) 288-2010   SIC 6712

CORPORATION STARLINK INC   p1093
9025 AV RYAN, DORVAL, QC, H9P 1A2
(514) 631-7500   SIC 6712

CORPORATION TRIBOSPEC, LA p1132
220 AV LAFLEUR, LASALLE, QC, H8R 4C9
(514) 595-7579   SIC 6712

COSTCO CANADA HOLDINGS INC p749
415 WEST HUNT CLUB RD, NEPEAN, ON, K2E 1C5
(613) 221-2000   SIC 6712

COUMELIN INC   p1264
2300 RUE CYRILLE-DUQUET, QUEBEC, QC, G1N 2G5
(418) 687-2700   SIC 6712

COURT GROUP OF COMPANIES LTD, THE
p530
490 ELIZABETH ST, BURLINGTON, ON,

L7R 2M2
(905) 333-5002   SIC 6712

COWS PRINCE EDWARD ISLAND INC
p1040
397 CAPITAL DR, CHARLOTTETOWN, PE, C1E 2E2
(902) 566-5558   SIC 6712

CPM FOODS LTD   p344
1324 BROADWAY AVE S, WILLIAMS LAKE, BC, V2G 4N2
(250) 392-4919   SIC 6712

CRI CANADA INC   p111
8925 82 AVE NW SUITE 207, EDMONTON, AB, T6C 0Z2
(780) 469-3808   SIC 6712

CROWN CAPITAL ENTERPRISES INC
p1415
1801 E TURVEY RD UNIT 7, REGINA, SK, S4N 3A4
(306) 546-8030   SIC 6712

CRYSTAL GROUP HOLDINGS INC.
165 MILNER AVE, SCARBOROUGH, ON, M1S 4G7
(416) 421-9299   SIC 6712

CYCLES LAMBERT INC   p1139
1000 RUE DES RIVEURS, LEVIS, QC, G6Y 9G3
(418) 835-1685   SIC 6712

CYPRESS MANAGEMENT LTD   p221
537 LEON AVE SUITE 200, KELOWNA, BC, V1Y 2A9
(250) 763-4323   SIC 6712

DAHL BROTHERS (CANADA) LIMITED p713
2600 SOUTH SHERIDAN WAY, MISSISSAUGA, ON, L5J 2M4
(905) 822-2330   SIC 6712

DAI TOKU HOLDINGS COMPANY LTD p294
1575 VERNON DR, VANCOUVER, BC, V6A 3P8
(604) 253-5111   SIC 6712

DANS UN JARDIN INC   p1064
240 BOUL INDUSTRIEL, BOUCHERVILLE, QC, J4B 2X4
(450) 449-2121   SIC 6712

DATA & AUDIO-VISUAL ENTERPRISES HOLDINGS INC   p962
161 BAY ST SUITE 2300, TORONTO, ON, M5J 2S1
(416) 361-1959   SIC 6712

DEHL HOLDINGS LTD   p221
1465 ELLIS ST SUITE 100, KELOWNA, BC, V1Y 2A3
(250) 762-5434   SIC 6712

DELGADO FOODS INTERNATIONAL LIMITED   p263
12031 NO. 5 RD, RICHMOND, BC, V7A 4E9
(604) 241-8175   SIC 6712

DENHAM HOLDINGS LTD   p137
4412 50 ST, INNISFAIL, AB, T4G 1P7
(403) 227-3311   SIC 6712

DENMAR INC   p1266
2365 AV WATT, QUEBEC, QC, G1P 3X2
(418) 654-2888   SIC 6712

DENTSU AEGIS NETWORK CANADA INC
p1195
400 BOUL DE MAISONNEUVE O BUREAU 250, MONTREAL, QC, H3A 1L4
(514) 284-4446   SIC 6712

DESJARDINS SOCIETE FINANCIERE INC
p1230
1 COMPLEXE DESJARDINS, MONTREAL, QC, H5B 1J1
(418) 838-7870   SIC 6712

DEVJO INDUSTRIES INC   p669
375 STEELCASE RD E, MARKHAM, ON, L3R 1G3
(905) 477-7689   SIC 6712

DEVRY CUSTOM WORK LTD   p196
49259 CASTLEMAN RD, CHILLIWACK, BC, V2P 6H4
(604) 794-3874   SIC 6712

DICK, JAMES HOLDINGS LIMITED   p494
14442 REGIONAL RD 50, BOLTON, ON, L7E 3E2

(905) 857-3500   SIC 6712

DICOM TRANSPORTATION GROUP CANADA PARENT, INC   p1093
10500 AV RYAN, DORVAL, QC, H9P 2T7
(514) 636-8033   SIC 6712

DIMPLEX NORTH AMERICA HOLDINGS LIMITED   p538
1367 INDUSTRIAL RD, CAMBRIDGE, ON, N3H 4W3
(519) 650-3630   SIC 6712

DIRK ENTERPRISES LTD   p88
10235 101 ST NW SUITE 800, EDMONTON, AB, T5J 3G1
(780) 944-9994   SIC 6712

DISTRI-CARR LTEE   p1264
214 AV SAINT-SACREMENT BUREAU 130, QUEBEC, QC, G1N 3X6
SIC 6712

DISTRIBUTION DENIS JALBERT INC p1266
2620 AV WATT, QUEBEC, QC, G1P 3T5
(418) 658-4640   SIC 6712

DIVERSE HOLDINGS LTD   p134
9610 62 AVE, GRANDE PRAIRIE, AB, T8W 2C3
(780) 539-6104   SIC 6712

DOW CANADA HOLDING LP   p48
450 1 ST SW SUITE 2100, CALGARY, AB, T2P 5H1
(403) 267-3500   SIC 6712

DSV SOLUTIONS INC   p502
8590 AIRPORT RD, BRAMPTON, ON, L6T 0C3
(905) 789-6211   SIC 6712

DUBOIS, ROGER INC   p1098
285 RUE SAINT-GEORGES, DRUMMONDVILLE, QC, J2C 4H3
(819) 477-1335   SIC 6712

DUFFIN FAMILY HOLDINGS LTD   p75
9 CROWFOOT CIR NW, CALGARY, AB, T3G 3J8
(403) 239-1115   SIC 6712

DURISOL MATERIALS LIMITED   p612
67 FRID ST, HAMILTON, ON, L8P 4M3
(905) 521-0999   SIC 6712

DUSTBANE HOLDINGS INC   p817
25 PICKERING PL, OTTAWA, ON, K1G 5P4
(613) 745-6861   SIC 6712

DUVALTEX INC   p1305
2805 90E RUE, SAINT-GEORGES, QC, G6A 1K1
(418) 227-9897   SIC 6712

E.B.C. HOLDINGS LTD   p124
12708 140 AVE NW, EDMONTON, AB, T6V 1K4
(780) 454-5258   SIC 6712

EBS CONTRACTING INC   p165
14 RAYBORN CRES SUITE 200, ST. ALBERT, AB, T8N 4B1
(780) 459-7110   SIC 6712

ECCO INVESTISSEMENT INC   p1286
54 RUE AMYOT, RIVIERE-DU-LOUP, QC, G5R 3E9
(418) 867-1695   SIC 6712

ECO-TEC LIMITED   p844
1145 SQUIRES BEACH RD, PICKERING, ON, L1W 3T9
(905) 427-0077   SIC 6712

ED. BRUNET ET ASSOCIES CANADA INC
p1106
9 RUE DUMAS, GATINEAU, QC, J8Y 2M4
(819) 777-3877   SIC 6712

EDJAR FOOD GROUP INC   p669
7650 BIRCHMOUNT RD, MARKHAM, ON, L3R 6B9
(905) 474-0710   SIC 6712

EHC GLOBAL INC   p813
1287 BOUNDARY RD, OSHAWA, ON, L1J 6Z7
(905) 432-3200   SIC 6712

ELSWOOD INVESTMENT CORPORATION
p328
1055 DUNSMUIR ST SUITE 3500, VANCOUVER, BC, V7X 1H3
(604) 691-9100   SIC 6712

EMPRESS TOWERS LTD   p326
1015 BURRARD ST SUITE 403, VANCOUVER, BC, V6Z 1Y5
(604) 682-4246   SIC 6712

ENDEVOR CORPORATION   p776
48 LESMILL RD, NORTH YORK, ON, M3B 2T5
(416) 445-5850   SIC 6712

ENERCARE INC   p669
7400 BIRCHMOUNT RD, MARKHAM, ON, L3R 5V4
(416) 649-1900   SIC 6712

ENERGERE INC   p1204
1200 AV MCGILL COLLEGE BUREAU 700, MONTREAL, QC, H3B 4G7
(514) 848-9199   SIC 6712

ENGLISH BAY ENTERPRISES INC   p205
904 CLIVEDEN AVE, DELTA, BC, V3M 5R5
(604) 540-0622   SIC 6712

ENS, PHILIPP R LTD   p361
301 ROBLIN BLVD, WINKLER, MB, R6W 4C4
(204) 325-4361   SIC 6712

ENTREPRISES CANDEREL INC   p1195
2000 RUE PEEL BUREAU 900, MONTREAL, QC, H3A 2W5
(514) 842-8636   SIC 6712

ENTREPRISES MIRCA INC, LES   p1170
3901 RUE JARRY E BUREAU 250, MONTREAL, QC, H1Z 2G1
(514) 253-3110   SIC 6712

ENTREPRISES S.J.M. INC, LES   p1048
8501 RUE JARRY, ANJOU, QC, H1J 1H7
(514) 321-2160   SIC 6712

ERB ENTERPRISES INC   p752
290 HAMILTON RD, NEW HAMBURG, ON, N3A 1A2
(519) 662-2710   SIC 6712

ERICKSON, DARYL HOLDINGS INC p1250
263 AV LABROSSE, POINTE-CLAIRE, QC, H9R 1A3
(514) 630-7484   SIC 6712

ERIE & MAIN CONSULTING INC   p543
62 KEIL DR S, CHATHAM, ON, N7M 3G8
(519) 351-2024   SIC 6712

EVANOV RADIO GROUP INC   p577
5312 DUNDAS ST W, ETOBICOKE, ON, M9B 1B3
(416) 213-1035   SIC 6712

FARMER INDUSTRIES GROUP INC   p339
360A HARBOUR RD, VICTORIA, BC, V9A 3S1
(250) 360-1511   SIC 6712

FARROW GROUP INC   p1025
2001 HURON CHURCH RD, WINDSOR, ON, N9C 2L6
(519) 252-4415   SIC 6712

FAYOLLE CANADA INC   p1225
1655 RUE DE BEAUHARNOIS O, MONTREAL, QC, H4N 1J6
(514) 381-6970   SIC 6712

FENGATE CORPORATION   p797
2275 UPPER MIDDLE ROAD EAST SUITE 700, OAKVILLE, ON, L6H 0C3
(289) 288-3822   SIC 6712

FERANO HOLDINGS LTD   p817
409 INDUSTRIAL AVE, OTTAWA, ON, K1G 0Z1
(613) 523-7731   SIC 6712

FERNANDO'S RESTAURANT LTD   p326
1277 HOWE ST, VANCOUVER, BC, V6Z 1R3
SIC 6712

FIRST CHATHAM CORPORATION LTD p543
615 RICHMOND ST, CHATHAM, ON, N7M 1R2
(519) 436-5506   SIC 6712

FIRSTONSITE CANADIAN HOLDINGS, INC.
p739
60 ADMIRAL BLVD, MISSISSAUGA, ON, L5T 2W1
(905) 696-2900   SIC 6712

FISHERCAST GLOBAL CORPORATION
p839

194 SOPHIA ST, PETERBOROUGH, ON, K9H 1E5
SIC 6712

FLEETWOOD PLACE HOLDINGS LTD *p281*
16011 83 AVE, SURREY, BC, V4N 0N2
(604) 590-6860 *SIC 6712*

FLUEVOG, JOHN VANCOUVER LTD *p326*
837 GRANVILLE ST, VANCOUVER, BC, V6Z 1K7
(604) 688-2828 *SIC 6712*

FORMGLAS HOLDINGS INC *p1031*
181 REGINA RD, WOODBRIDGE, ON, L4L 8M3
(416) 635-8030 *SIC 6712*

FORTIS GROUP INC *p1018*
3070 JEFFERSON BLVD, WINDSOR, ON, N8T 3G9
(519) 419-7828 *SIC 6712*

FOURNITURES INDUSTRIELLES PASCO INC, LES *p1246*
1124 RUE SAINT-CALIXTE, PLESSISVILLE, QC, G6L 1N8
(819) 362-7345 *SIC 6712*

FRASER VALLEY PACKERS HOLDINGS LTD *p174*
260 SHORT RD, ABBOTSFORD, BC, V2S 8A7
(604) 852-3525 *SIC 6712*

G & L GROUP LTD *p553*
401 BOWES RD, CONCORD, ON, L4K 1J4
(416) 798-7050 *SIC 6712*

G.S.K. MANAGEMENT INC *p771*
40 SHEPPARD AVE W SUITE 700, NORTH YORK, ON, M2N 6K9
(416) 225-9400 *SIC 6712*

GASTALDO CONCRETE HOLDINGS LTD *p206*
482 FRASERVIEW PL, DELTA, BC, V3M 6H4
(604) 525-3636 *SIC 6712*

GE BETZDEARBORN CANADA COMPANY *p722*
2300 MEADOWVALE BLVD, MISSISSAUGA, ON, L5N 5P9
(905) 465-3030 *SIC 6712*

GEEP HOLDINGS INC *p487*
220 JOHN ST, BARRIE, ON, L4N 2L2
(705) 725-1919 *SIC 6712*

GELLULE INC *p1266*
2300 BOUL PERE-LELIEVRE, QUEBEC, QC, G1P 2X5
(418) 681-6351 *SIC 6712*

GEM CAFE LTD *p1427*
401 21ST ST E, SASKATOON, SK, S7K 0C5
SIC 6712

GEM HEALTH CARE GROUP LIMITED *p458*
15 SHOREHAM LANE SUITE 101, HALIFAX, NS, B3P 2R3
(902) 429-6227 *SIC 6712*

GENUINE PARTS HOLDINGS LTD *p739*
1450 MEYERSIDE DR SUITE 305, MISSISSAUGA, ON, L5T 2N5
(905) 696-9301 *SIC 6712*

GESCLADO INC *p1362*
1400 BOUL DAGENAIS O, SAINTE-ROSE, QC, H7L 5C7
(450) 622-1600 *SIC 6712*

GESTION A.J.L.R. INC *p1285*
451 RUE DE L'EXPANSION, RIMOUSKI, QC, G5M 1B4
(418) 724-2243 *SIC 6712*

GESTION BELANGER, BERNARD LTEE *p1122*
1300 4E AV, LA POCATIERE, QC, G0R 1Z0
(418) 856-3858 *SIC 6712*

GESTION C.B.R. LASER INC *p1246*
340 RTE 116, PLESSISVILLE, QC, G6L 2Y2
(819) 362-2095 *SIC 6712*

GESTION C.T.M.A. INC *p1073*
435 CH AVILA-ARSENEAU, CAP-AUX-MEULES, QC, G4T 1J3
(418) 986-6600 *SIC 6712*

GESTION CARMINEX INC *p1358*
2255 RUE BOMBARDIER, SAINTE-JULIE,

QC, J3E 2J9
(450) 922-0900 *SIC 6712*

GESTION CENTRIA COMMERCE INC *p1086*
3131 BOUL SAINT-MARTIN O, COTE SAINT-LUC, QC, H7T 2Z5
(514) 874-0122 *SIC 6712*

GESTION D'INVESTISSEMENT 2300 INC *p1329*
2300 RUE EMILE-BELANGER, SAINT-LAURENT, QC, H4R 3J4
(514) 747-2536 *SIC 6712*

GESTION DAMIEN MORISSETTE INC *p1135*
333 CH DES SABLES, LEVIS, QC, G6C 1B5
(418) 838-7444 *SIC 6712*

GESTION FETIA INC *p1170*
8400 2E AV, MONTREAL, QC, H1Z 4M6
(514) 722-2324 *SIC 6712*

GESTION INDUSTRIES INC *p1305*
9095 25E AV, SAINT-GEORGES, QC, G6A 1A1
(418) 228-8934 *SIC 6712*

GESTION J.C. FAVREAU LTEE *p1059*
1083 BOUL DU CURE-LABELLE BUREAU 110, BLAINVILLE, QC, J7C 3M9
(450) 435-1981 *SIC 6712*

GESTION J.M.CLEMENT LTEE *p1278*
5830 BOUL PIERRE-BERTRAND BUREAU 400, QUEBEC, QC, G2J 1B7
(418) 626-0006 *SIC 6712*

GESTION L. FECTEAU LTEE *p1243*
3150 CH ROYAL, NOTRE-DAME-DES-PINS, QC, G0M 1K0
(418) 774-3324 *SIC 6712*

GESTION LABERGE INC *p1119*
6245 BOUL WILFRID-HAMEL, L'ANCIENNE-LORETTE, QC, G2E 5W2
(418) 667-1313 *SIC 6712*

GESTION M A S INC *p1310*
2890 BOUL LAURIER E, SAINT-HYACINTHE, QC, J2R 1P8
(450) 774-7511 *SIC 6712*

GESTION MARIO CHRISTIN INC *p1247*
12011 RUE SHERBROOKE E, POINTE-AUX-TREMBLES, QC, H1B 1C6
(514) 640-1050 *SIC 6712*

GESTION MARTIN BOUTET INC *p1303*
1180 RTE 243, SAINT-FELIX-DE-KINGSEY, QC, J0B 2T0
(819) 848-2521 *SIC 6712*

GESTION MICHEL JULIEN INC *p1065*
115 RUE DE LAUZON, BOUCHERVILLE, QC, J4B 1E7
(450) 641-3150 *SIC 6712*

GESTION PIERRE BEAUCHESNE INC *p1400*
17 RUE SAINTE-JEANNE-D'ARC, WARWICK, QC, J0A 1M0
(819) 358-3400 *SIC 6712*

GESTION POMERLEAU PAGE INC *p1159*
205 CH DES POIRIER, MONTMAGNY, QC, G5V 3X7
(418) 241-2102 *SIC 6712*

GESTION QUADRATEL INC *p1218*
6000 CH DEACON, MONTREAL, QC, H3S 2T9
(514) 731-5298 *SIC 6712*

GESTION RACAN INC *p1152*
18101 RUE J.A.BOMBARDIER, MIRABEL, QC, J7J 2H8
(450) 979-1212 *SIC 6712*

GESTION ROCECO INC *p1304*
2685 121E RUE, SAINT-GEORGES, QC, G5Y 5G2
(418) 227-4402 *SIC 6712*

GESTION RONALD HERTELEER INC *p1234*
3985 BOUL INDUSTRIEL, MONTREAL, QC, H7L 4S3
(514) 384-8300 *SIC 6712*

GESTION SIERA CAPITAL INC *p1196*
1501 AV MCGILL COLLEGE BUREAU 800, MONTREAL, QC, H3A 3M8
(514) 954-3300 *SIC 6712*

GESTION SINOMONDE INC *p1191*
99 AV VIGER O, MONTREAL, QC, H2Z 1E9

(514) 878-9888 *SIC 6712*

GESTION ST-H. INC *p1275*
1294 RUE ROLAND-DESMEULES, QUEBEC, QC, G1X 4Y3
(450) 836-7201 *SIC 6712*

GESTIONS ARDOVA LTEE, LES *p1178*
433 RUE CHABANEL O BUREAU 1000, MONTREAL, QC, H2N 2J8
(514) 381-5941 *SIC 6712*

GESTIONS AZURE INC., LES *p1342*
7909 BOUL ARTHUR-SAUVE, SAINT-LAURENT, QC, H7R 3X8
(450) 969-0150 *SIC 6712*

GESTIONS BAILLARGEON & OUELLET INC *p1299*
430 108 RTE O, SAINT-EPHREM-DE-BEAUCE, QC, G0M 1R0
(418) 484-5666 *SIC 6712*

GESTIONS LENALCO (CANADA) LTEE *p1326*
455 BOUL DE LA COTE-VERTU, SAINT-LAURENT, QC, H4N 1E8
(514) 334-1510 *SIC 6712*

GESTIONS MILLER CARMICHAEL INC *p1218*
3822 AV DE COURTRAI, MONTREAL, QC, H3S 1C1
(514) 735-4361 *SIC 6712*

GESTIONS MONK HERITAGE INC *p1339*
255 MONTEE DE LIESSE, SAINT-LAURENT, QC, H4T 1P5
(514) 345-0135 *SIC 6712*

GESTOLEX, SOCIETE EN COMMANDITE *p1229*
800 RUE DU SQUARE-VICTORIA BUREAU 4300, MONTREAL, QC, H4Z 1H1
(514) 686-8683 *SIC 6712*

GESTRUDO INC *p1283*
34 RUE BELMONT, RICHMOND, QC, J0B 2H0
(819) 826-5941 *SIC 6712*

GLENCO HOLDINGS LTD *p176*
2121 PEARDONVILLE RD, ABBOTSFORD, BC, V2T 6J7
(604) 850-1499 *SIC 6712*

GLOBAL RESSOURCES HUMAINES INC *p1170*
3737 BOUL CREMAZIE E BUREAU 400, MONTREAL, QC, H1Z 2K4
(514) 788-0599 *SIC 6712*

GOLF KENOSEE CAPITAL INC *p1408*
GD, KENOSEE LAKE, SK, S0C 2S0
(306) 577-2044 *SIC 6712*

GRAHAM CREATIVE DECAL INC *p1128*
1790 55E AV, LACHINE, QC, H8T 3J5
(514) 633-8800 *SIC 6712*

GRANDIN MEDICAL HOLDINGS LTD *p165*
1 ST ANNE ST, ST. ALBERT, AB, T8N 2E8
SIC 6712

GRANDVIEW BROKERAGE LIMITED *p200*
11 BURBIDGE ST SUITE 101, COQUITLAM, BC, V3K 7B2
(604) 461-6779 *SIC 6712*

GREGORY HERITAGE HOLDING INC *p1401*
23 AV WILLOW, WESTMOUNT, QC, H3Y 1Y3
SIC 6712

GROUPE AUTOBUS GIRARDIN LTEE *p1100*
4000 RUE GIRARDIN, DRUMMONDVILLE, QC, J2E 0A1
(819) 477-3222 *SIC 6712*

GROUPE AUTOMOBILES LAURUS LTEE *p1086*
3670 SUD LAVAL (A-440) O, COTE SAINT-LUC, QC, H7T 2H6
(450) 682-3670 *SIC 6712*

GROUPE BFL INC *p1358*
2121 RUE NOBEL BUREAU 101, SAINTE-JULIE, QC, J3E 1Z9
(514) 874-9050 *SIC 6712*

GROUPE BMTC INC *p1238*
8500 PLACE MARIEN, MONTREAL-EST, QC, H1B 5W8
(514) 648-5757 *SIC 6712*

GROUPE BONNET INC *p1298*
54 RUE PRINCIPALE, SAINT-DAMASE, QC, J0H 1J0
(450) 797-3301 *SIC 6712*

GROUPE BOUTIN INC *p1246*
1397 RUE SAVOIE, PLESSISVILLE, QC, G6L 1J8
(819) 362-7333 *SIC 6712*

GROUPE CANATAL INC *p1383*
2885 BOUL FRONTENAC E, THETFORD MINES, QC, G6G 6P6
(418) 338-6044 *SIC 6712*

GROUPE CD BEDARD INC *p1141*
753 RUE BERIAULT, LONGUEUIL, QC, J4G 1X7
(450) 679-7704 *SIC 6712*

GROUPE CONSEIL DFM INC, LE *p1272*
1175 AV LAVIGERIE BUREAU 580, QUEBEC, QC, G1V 4P1
(418) 650-2266 *SIC 6712*

GROUPE CONSEIL RES PUBLICA INC *p1205*
1155 RUE METCALFE BUREAU 800, MONTREAL, QC, H3B 0C1
(514) 843-2343 *SIC 6712*

GROUPE CONTROLE INC *p1305*
8800 25E AV, SAINT-GEORGES, QC, G6A 1K5
(418) 227-9141 *SIC 6712*

GROUPE CUISINE IDEALE INC *p1372*
980 RUE PANNETON, SHERBROOKE, QC, J1K 2B2
(819) 566-2401 *SIC 6712*

GROUPE DERIC INC *p1277*
5145 RUE RIDEAU, QUEBEC, QC, G2E 5H5
(418) 781-2228 *SIC 6712*

GROUPE DESCHENES INC *p1170*
3901 RUE JARRY E BUREAU 250, MONTREAL, QC, H1Z 2G1
(514) 253-3110 *SIC 6712*

GROUPE DESSAU INC *p1237*
1200 BOUL SAINT-MARTIN O BUREAU 300, MONTREAL, QC, H7S 2E4
(514) 281-1010 *SIC 6712*

GROUPE EQUICONCEPT INC *p1276*
2160 RUE DE CELLES, QUEBEC, QC, G2C 1X8
(418) 847-1480 *SIC 6712*

GROUPE FERTEK INC *p1362*
3000 AV FRAN?IS-HUGHES, SAINTE-ROSE, QC, H7L 3J5
(450) 663-8700 *SIC 6712*

GROUPE FILGO INC *p1360*
1133 BOUL VACHON N, SAINTE-MARIE, QC, G6E 1M9
(418) 387-5449 *SIC 6712*

GROUPE FOURNIER DIESEL INC *p1353*
5 CH DE LA COTE-SAINT-PAUL, SAINT-STANISLAS-DE-CHAMPLAIN, QC, G0X 3E0
(418) 668-5040 *SIC 6712*

GROUPE GAUDREAULT INC, LE *p1282*
1500 RUE RAYMOND-GAUDREAULT, REPENTIGNY, QC, J5Y 4E3
(450) 585-1210 *SIC 6712*

GROUPE GESTION NOR INC *p1157*
8550 CH DELMEADE, MONT-ROYAL, QC, H4T 1L7
(514) 342-2744 *SIC 6712*

GROUPE GOYETTE INC *p1312*
2825 BOUL CASAVANT O, SAINT-HYACINTHE, QC, J2S 7Y4
(450) 773-9615 *SIC 6712*

GROUPE GRAHAM INTERNATIONAL INC *p1128*
1455 32E AV, LACHINE, QC, H8T 3J1
(514) 631-6662 *SIC 6712*

GROUPE INDUSTRIES FOURNIER INC *p1383*
3787 BOUL FRONTENAC O, THETFORD MINES, QC, G6H 2B5
(418) 423-4241 *SIC 6712*

GROUPE KANWAL INC *p1147*
1426 BOUL INDUSTRIEL, MAGOG, QC.

J1X 4V9
(819) 868-4156   *SIC* 6712
GROUPE L.E.D. LAMARRE, EVANGE-LISTE, DELISLE INC   *p1167*
3006 RUE SAINTE-CATHERINE E, MONTREAL, QC, H1W 2B8
(514) 523-2831   *SIC* 6712
GROUPE LAUZON INC   *p1086*
2400 BOUL CHOMEDEY CARTE DES ENVIRONS, COTE SAINT-LUC, QC, H7T 2W3
(450) 434-1120   *SIC* 6712
GROUPE LEGARE LTEE   *p1351*
488 RUE SAINT-PIERRE, SAINT-RAYMOND, QC, G3L 1R5
(418) 337-2286   *SIC* 6712
GROUPE LOU-TEC INC   *p1049*
8500 RUE JULES-LEGER, ANJOU, QC, H1J 1A7
(514) 356-0047   *SIC* 6712
GROUPE M.G.B. INC   *p1350*
51 RUE SAINT-PIERRE, SAINT-PIE, QC, J0H 1W0
(450) 772-5608   *SIC* 6712
GROUPE MACHINEX INC   *p1246*
2121 RUE OLIVIER, PLESSISVILLE, QC, G6L 3G9
(819) 362-3281   *SIC* 6712
GROUPE MAILHOT INC   *p1380*
3330 BOUL DES ENTREPRISES, TERREBONNE, QC, J6X 4J8
(450) 477-6222   *SIC* 6712
GROUPE MARITIME VERREAULT INC   *p1135*
108 RUE DU COLLEGE, LES MECHINS, QC, G0J 1T0
(418) 729-3030   *SIC* 6712
GROUPE MECANITEC INC   *p1387*
2300 RUE JULES-VACHON, TROIS-RIVIERES, QC, G9A 5E1
(819) 374-4647   *SIC* 6712
GROUPE MEQUALTECH INC   *p1170*
8740 BOUL PIE-IX, MONTREAL, QC, H1Z 3V1
(514) 593-5755   *SIC* 6712
GROUPE MICHAUDVILLE INC   *p1158*
270 RUE BRUNET, MONT-SAINT-HILAIRE, QC, J3H 0M6
(450) 446-9933   *SIC* 6712
GROUPE MONTEL INC   *p1160*
225 4E AV, MONTMAGNY, QC, G5V 4N9
(418) 248-0235   *SIC* 6712
GROUPE MUNDIAL INC   *p1323*
12 RUE NAPOLEON-COUTURE, SAINT-LAMBERT-DE-LAUZON, QC, G0S 2W0
(418) 889-0502   *SIC* 6712
GROUPE PIXCOM INC   *p1188*
444 RUE SAINT-PAUL E, MONTREAL, QC, H2Y 3V1
(514) 931-1188   *SIC* 6712
GROUPE POMERLEAU INC   *p1305*
521 6E AV N, SAINT-GEORGES, QC, G5Y 0H1
(418) 228-6688   *SIC* 6712
GROUPE POSI-PLUS INC   *p1397*
10 RUE DE L'ARTISAN, VICTORIAVILLE, QC, G6P 7E4
(800) 758-5717   *SIC* 6712
GROUPE RATTE INC   *p1260*
103 3E AV, QUEBEC, QC, G1L 2V3
(418) 683-1518   *SIC* 6712
GROUPE ROUILLIER INC   *p1046*
824 AV DES FORESTIERS BUREAU 57, AMOS, QC, J9T 4L4
(819) 727-9269   *SIC* 6712
GROUPE S.M. TARDIF INC   *p1281*
15971 BOUL DE LA COLLINE, QUEBEC, QC, G3G 3A7
(418) 849-7104   *SIC* 6712
GROUPE SANFACON INC, LE   *p1138*
1980 5E RUE, LEVIS, QC, G6W 5M6
(418) 839-1370   *SIC* 6712
GROUPE ZOOM MEDIA INC   *p1197*
999 BOUL DE MAISONNEUVE O BUREAU 1000, MONTREAL, QC, H3A 3L4

(514) 842-1155   *SIC* 6712
GUNTHER'S BUILDING SUPPLIES LIMITED   *p72*
2100 10 AVE SW, CALGARY, AB, T3C 0K5
(403) 245-3311   *SIC* 6712
GVP HOLDIGS INC   *p305*
200 BURRARD ST SUITE 1200, VANCOUVER, BC, V6C 3L6
(604) 525-3900   *SIC* 6712
H. COLPRON INC   *p1298*
4061 GRAND RANG SAINTE-CATHERINE, SAINT-CUTHBERT, QC, J0K 2C0
(514) 593-5144   *SIC* 6712
HAILEY MANAGEMENT LTD   *p336*
1070 DOUGLAS ST SUITE 800, VICTORIA, BC, V8W 2C4
(250) 388-5421   *SIC* 6712
HALL TRANSPORTATION GROUP LIMITED   *p483*
552 PIPER ST, AYR, ON, N0B 1E0
(519) 632-7429   *SIC* 6712
HALLER GROUP INC   *p1021*
1537 MCDOUGALL ST, WINDSOR, ON, N8X 3M9
(519) 254-4635   *SIC* 6712
HAMILL CREEK TIMBERWRIGHTS INC   *p232*
13440 HWY 31, MEADOW CREEK, BC, V0G 1N0
(250) 366-4320   *SIC* 6712
HAMM HOLDINGS LTD   *p1408*
130 STEWART CRES, KINDERSLEY, SK, S0L 1S1
(306) 463-7112   *SIC* 6712
HAMPTON LUMBER MILLS - CANADA, LTD   *p194*
GD, BURNS LAKE, BC, V0J 1E0
(250) 692-7177   *SIC* 6712
HANCO MANAGEMENT LTD   *p211*
372 CORONATION AVE, DUNCAN, BC, V9L 2Z3
(250) 748-3761   *SIC* 6712
HAROLD E. SEEGMILLER HOLDINGS LIMITED   *p639*
305 ARNOLD ST, KITCHENER, ON, N2H 6G1
(519) 579-6460   *SIC* 6712
HARTCO INC   *p1402*
4120 RUE SAINTE-CATHERINE O, WESTMOUNT, QC, H3Z 1P4
(514) 354-0580   *SIC* 6712
HEERINGA, J.L. ENTERPRISES LTD   *p203*
278 OLD ISLAND HWY, COURTENAY, BC, V9N 3P1
(250) 338-6553   *SIC* 6712
HENRY SINGER LTD.   *p89*
10180 101 ST NW SUITE 160, EDMONTON, AB, T5J 3S4
(780) 420-0909   *SIC* 6712
HIGHLAND CATERERS LTD   *p249*
570 3RD AVE, PRINCE GEORGE, BC, V2L 3C3
(250) 563-5332   *SIC* 6712
HILBAR ENTERPRISES INC   *p341*
118 BRIDGE RD, WEST VANCOUVER, BC, V7P 3R2
(604) 983-2411   *SIC* 6712
HOLDBEST LTD   *p769*
24 MELLOWOOD DR, NORTH YORK, ON, M2L 2E3
(905) 831-0100   *SIC* 6712
HOLDECOM INC   *p1334*
1515 BOUL PITFIELD, SAINT-LAURENT, QC, H4S 1G3
(514) 956-7400   *SIC* 6712
HOLDING SECURITE C M LTEE, LE   *p1053*
19400 AV CRUICKSHANK, BAIE-D'URFE, QC, H9X 3P1
(514) 457-6650   *SIC* 6712
HOLDING SOPREMA CANADA INC   *p1099*
1688 RUE JEAN-BERCHMANS-MICHAUD, DRUMMONDVILLE, QC, J2C 8E9
(819) 478-8163   *SIC* 6712
HOSPITALITY FALLSVIEW HOLDINGS INC

p759
6361 FALLSVIEW BLVD, NIAGARA FALLS, ON, L2G 3V9
(905) 354-7887   *SIC* 6712
HUACHANGDA CANADA HOLDINGS INC   *p305*
2800 PARK PL 666 BURRARD ST, VANCOUVER, BC, V6C 2Z7
SIC 6712
HULL GROUP INC, THE   *p963*
181 BAY ST SUITE 4200, TORONTO, ON, M5J 2T3
(416) 865-0131   *SIC* 6712
HUSKY (U.S.A.), INC   *p51*
707 8 AVE SW, CALGARY, AB, T2P 1H5
(403) 298-6111   *SIC* 6712
HUSKY INJECTION MOLDING SYSTEMS LTD   *p495*
500 QUEEN ST S, BOLTON, ON, L7E 5S5
(905) 951-5000   *SIC* 6712
ICORR HOLDINGS INC   *p653*
700 RICHMOND ST SUITE 100, LONDON, ON, N6A 5C7
(519) 432-0120   *SIC* 6712
IDEAL DRAIN TILE LIMITED   *p903*
1100 IDEAL DR, THORNDALE, ON, N0M 2P0
(519) 473-2669   *SIC* 6712
IMMEUBLE M. & A. CONSTANTIN INC   *p1302*
1054 BOUL ARTHUR-SAUVE, SAINT-EUSTACHE, QC, J7R 4K3
(450) 473-2374   *SIC* 6712
IMPCO ECOTRANS TECHNOLOIGES, INC   *p640*
100 HOLLINGER CRES, KITCHENER, ON, N2K 2Z3
(519) 576-4270   *SIC* 6712
IMPERIA HOTEL ET SUITES INC   *p1380*
3215 BOUL DE LA PINIERE BUREAU 201, TERREBONNE, QC, J6X 4P7
(450) 492-3336   *SIC* 6712
INDUSTRIES GODDARD LTEE   *p1380*
2460 BOUL DES ENTREPRISES, TERREBONNE, QC, J6X 4J8
(514) 353-9141   *SIC* 6712
INDUSTRIES LASSONDE INC   *p1288*
755 RUE PRINCIPALE, ROUGEMONT, QC, J0L 1M0
(450) 469-4926   *SIC* 6712
INDUSTRIES SANIMAX INC   *p1161*
9900 BOUL MAURICE-DUPLESSIS, MONTREAL, QC, H1C 1G1
(514) 648-3000   *SIC* 6712
INEOS CANADA COMPANY   *p153*
HWY 815, RED DEER, AB, T4N 6A1
(403) 314-4500   *SIC* 6712
INNOVISION HOLDINGS CORPORATION   *p671*
55 RENFREW DR, MARKHAM, ON, L3R 8H3
(905) 940-2488   *SIC* 6712
INTERNATIONAL ASPHALT LEASING INC   *p109*
6105 76 AVE NW, EDMONTON, AB, T6B 0A7
(780) 469-7304   *SIC* 6712
INVESTISSEMENTS ALONIM INC, LES   *p1251*
237 BOUL HYMUS, POINTE-CLAIRE, QC, H9R 5C7
(514) 694-7710   *SIC* 6712
INVESTISSEMENTS BABE INC   *p1383*
374 RUE NOTRE-DAME E, THETFORD MINES, QC, G6G 2S4
SIC 6712
INVESTISSEMENTS ISAAM INC, LES   *p1330*
3100 BOUL DE LA COTE-VERTU BUREAU 210, SAINT-LAURENT, QC, H4R 2J8
(514) 335-6606   *SIC* 6712
INVESTISSEMENTS PELLERIN INC, LES   *p1217*
8600 AV DE L'EPEE, MONTREAL, QC, H3N 2G6
(514) 273-8855   *SIC* 6712

INVESTISSEMENTS PENTABEL LIMITEE, LES   *p1239*
6868 BOUL MAURICE-DUPLESSIS, MONTREAL-NORD, QC, H1G 1Z6
(514) 327-2800   *SIC* 6712
INVESTISSEMENTS SKYFOLD LTEE   *p1053*
325 AV LEE, BAIE-D'URFE, QC, H9X 3S3
(514) 735-5410   *SIC* 6712
INVESTISSEMENTS SYLNIC INC, LES   *p1172*
4351 RUE D'IBERVILLE, MONTREAL, QC, H2H 2L7
(514) 598-8130   *SIC* 6712
INVESTISSEMENTS TREVI INC   *p1152*
12775 RUE BRAULT, MIRABEL, QC, J7J 0C4
(450) 973-1249   *SIC* 6712
IOU FINANCIAL INC   *p1205*
1 PLACE VILLE-MARIE BUREAU 1670, MONTREAL, QC, H3B 2B6
(514) 789-0694   *SIC* 6712
IPPOLITO GROUP INC, THE   *p529*
201 NORTH SERVICE RD, BURLINGTON, ON, L7P 5C4
(905) 639-1174   *SIC* 6712
ISH EQUIPMENT LTD   *p52*
700 4 AVE SW UNIT 310, CALGARY, AB, T2P 3J4
SIC 6712
IT/NET GROUP INC   *p834*
150 ELGIN ST SUITE 1800, OTTAWA, ON, K2P 2P8
(613) 234-8638   *SIC* 6712
ITML HOLDINGS INC   *p516*
75 PLANT FARM BLVD, BRANTFORD, ON, N3S 7W2
(519) 753-2666   *SIC* 6712
J2 MANAGEMENT CORP   *p915*
200 YORKLAND BLVD SUITE 800, TORONTO, ON, M2J 5C1
(416) 438-6650   *SIC* 6712
JARDINE BROOK HOLDINGS LIMITED   *p415*
300 UNION ST, SAINT JOHN, NB, E2L 4Z2
(506) 632-5110   *SIC* 6712
JASTRAM HOLDINGS LTD   *p238*
135 RIVERSIDE DR, NORTH VANCOUVER, BC, V7H 1T6
(604) 986-0714   *SIC* 6712
JEEM HOLDINGS LTD   *p272*
19060 54 AVE, SURREY, BC, V3S 8E5
(604) 576-1808   *SIC* 6712
JENKINS, MALCOLM J. (HOLDINGS) LTD   *p1414*
3725 2ND AVE W, PRINCE ALBERT, SK, S6W 1A1
(306) 764-9000   *SIC* 6712
JESSEL, BRIAN HOLDINGS INC   *p286*
2311 BOUNDARY RD, VANCOUVER, BC, V5M 4W5
(604) 222-7788   *SIC* 6712
JO-AL DISTRIBUTING LTD   *p1161*
9900 6E RUE, MONTREAL, QC, H1C 1G2
(514) 643-3391   *SIC* 6712
JOINT INVESTMENT GROUP INC   *p1433*
118 VETERINARY RD, SASKATOON, SK, S7N 2R4
(306) 978-2800   *SIC* 6712
JOLINA CAPITAL INC   *p1344*
8000 BOUL LANGELIER BUREAU 200, SAINT-LEONARD, QC, H1P 3K2
(514) 328-3541   *SIC* 6712
JUST REWARDS MANAGEMENT LTD   *p332*
3009 28 ST SUITE B, VERNON, BC, V1T 4Z7
(250) 542-1177   *SIC* 6712
K.R.S. TECHNICAL SERVICES LIMITED   *p86*
10660 105 ST NW, EDMONTON, AB, T5H 2W9
(780) 426-7820   *SIC* 6712
KAMLOOPS PROFESSIONAL MANAGEMENT GROUP   *p217*
248 2ND AVE, KAMLOOPS, BC, V2C 2C9
(250) 372-5542   *SIC* 6712
KDA GROUP INC   *p1383*

1197 RUE NOTRE-DAME E, THETFORD MINES, QC, G6G 2V2
(418) 334-8767　*SIC 6712*

KELSON CANADA INC　　*p24*
2431 37 AVE NE SUITE 430, CALGARY, AB, T2E 6Y7
(403) 296-1500　*SIC 6712*

KEOLIS CANADA INC　　*p1211*
740 RUE NOTRE-DAME O BUREAU 1000, MONTREAL, QC, H3C 3X6
(514) 395-4000　*SIC 6712*

KERR INVESTMENT HOLDING CORP *p806*
381 NORTH SERVICE RD W, OAKVILLE, ON, L6M 0H4
(905) 678-3119　*SIC 6712*

KILLICK AEROSPACE HOLDING INC. *p52*
855 2 ST SW SUITE 3500, CALGARY, AB, T2P 4J8
SIC 6712

KINDERSTAR INC　　*p684*
690 AUGER TERR, MILTON, ON, L9T 5M2
(905) 864-4420　*SIC 6712*

KING-REED HOLDINGS LTD　*p776*
85 SCARSDALE RD SUITE 309, NORTH YORK, ON, M3B 2R2
(416) 449-8677　*SIC 6712*

KLEEN-FLO HOLDINGS INC　*p504*
75 ADVANCE BLVD, BRAMPTON, ON, L6T 4N1
(905) 793-4311　*SIC 6712*

KLOHN CRIPPEN BERGER HOLDINGS LTD *p286*
2955 VIRTUAL WAY SUITE 500, VANCOUVER, BC, V5M 4X6
(604) 669-3800　*SIC 6712*

KNELSON RECOVERY SYSTEMS INTERNATIONAL INC *p225*
19855 98 AVE, LANGLEY, BC, V1M 2X5
(604) 888-4015　*SIC 6712*

KNOWLTON DEVELOPMENT CORPORATION INC *p1143*
255 BOUL ROLAND-THERRIEN BUREAU 100, LONGUEUIL, QC, J4H 4A6
(450) 243-2000　*SIC 6712*

KNRV INVESTMENTS INC　*p767*
515 CONSUMERS RD UNIT 700, NORTH YORK, ON, M2J 4Z2
(416) 791-4200　*SIC 6712*

KORAB MARINE LTD　　*p1125*
255 RUE NORMAN, LACHINE, QC, H8R 1A3
(514) 489-5711　*SIC 6712*

KRUGER INC　　*p1218*
3285 CH DE BEDFORD, MONTREAL, QC, H3S 1G5
(514) 343-3100　*SIC 6712*

L & M ENTERPRISES LIMITED　*p447*
20 MACDONALD AVE, DARTMOUTH, NS, B3B 1C5
(902) 468-8040　*SIC 6712*

L.A. DALTON SYSTEMS LP　*p532*
1435 HIGHWAY 56, CALEDONIA, ON, N3W 1T1
SIC 6712

LAKERS GOLF CLUB INC, THE *p331*
7000 CUMMINS RD, VERNON, BC, V1H 1M2
(250) 260-1050　*SIC 6712*

LAKESHORE INC　　*p623*
2350 FOURTH AVE RR 1, JORDAN STATION, ON, L0R 1S0
(905) 562-4118　*SIC 6712*

LAMCORP MANAGEMENT LTD　*p115*
5708 75 ST NW, EDMONTON, AB, T6E 5X6
(780) 413-8388　*SIC 6712*

LAREN HOLDINGS INC　　*p752*
3228 MOODIE DR, NEPEAN, ON, K2J 4S8
(613) 838-2775　*SIC 6712*

LEBOVIC ENTERPRISES LIMITED *p894*
12045 MCCOWAN RD, STOUFFVILLE, ON, L4A 4C3
(905) 640-7361　*SIC 6712*

LEGGETT, H. & FILS INC　*p1242*
904 RUE DU CENTENAIRE, NAMUR, QC,

J0V 1N0
(819) 426-2176　*SIC 6712*

LEWIS-PATRICK INVESTMENTS LTD *p272*
6320 148 ST, SURREY, BC, V3S 3C4
(604) 598-9930　*SIC 6712*

LITERIES UNIVERSELLES PAGA INC *p1229*
6395 CH DE LA COTE-DE-LIESSE, MONTREAL, QC, H4T 1E5
(514) 376-7882　*SIC 6712*

LOCH LOMOND SKI AREA LIMITED *p910*
1800 LOCH LOMOND RD, THUNDER BAY, ON, P7J 1E9
(807) 475-7787　*SIC 6712*

LOGIC HOLDINGS LTD　　*p141*
1217 39 ST N, LETHBRIDGE, AB, T1H 6Y8
(403) 328-7755　*SIC 6712*

LONDON REINSURANCE GROUP INC *p654*
255 DUFFERIN AVE SUITE 540, LONDON, ON, N6A 4K1
(519) 432-2000　*SIC 6712*

LOOBY GROUP INCORPORATED　*p566*
10 MATILDA ST, DUBLIN, ON, N0K 1E0
(519) 345-2800　*SIC 6712*

LOWE'S HOLDING CANADA, ULC　*p697*
5150 SPECTRUM WAY SUITE 200, MISSISSAUGA, ON, L4W 5G2
(905) 219-1000　*SIC 6712*

MAC'S CONVENIENCE STORES INC *p914*
305 MILNER AVE SUITE 400, TORONTO, ON, M1B 0A5
(416) 291-4441　*SIC 6712*

MACHAN CONSULTING SERVICES LTD *p121*
9330 27 AVE NW, EDMONTON, AB, T6N 1B2
(780) 435-5722　*SIC 6712*

MACKIE TRANSPORTATION HOLDINGS INC *p814*
933 BLOOR ST W, OSHAWA, ON, L1J 5Y7
(905) 728-1603　*SIC 6712*

MAGELLAN AEROSPACE CORPORATION *p686*
3160 DERRY RD E, MISSISSAUGA, ON, L4T 1A9
(905) 677-1889　*SIC 6712*

MAGNASONIC INC.　　*p672*
300 ALDEN RD, MARKHAM, ON, L3R 4C1
SIC 6712

MAMMOET CANADA HOLDINGS INC *p849*
7504 MCLEAN RD E, PUSLINCH, ON, N0B 2J0
(519) 740-0550　*SIC 6712*

MANIOLI INVESTMENTS INC　*p1226*
1650 RUE CHABANEL O BUREAU 1205, MONTREAL, QC, H4N 3M8
(514) 384-0140　*SIC 6712*

MAPLE LODGE HOLDING CORPORATION *p511*
8301 WINSTON CHURCHILL BLVD, BRAMPTON, ON, L6Y 0A2
(905) 455-8340　*SIC 6712*

MAPLE REINDERS GROUP LTD　*p724*
2660 ARGENTIA RD, MISSISSAUGA, ON, L5N 5V4
(905) 821-4844　*SIC 6712*

MAR DEVELOPMENTS INC　*p555*
237 ROMINA DR UNIT 1, CONCORD, ON, L4K 4V3
(905) 738-2255　*SIC 6712*

MARINE HARVEST NORTH AMERICA INC *p195*
1334 ISLAND HWY SUITE 124, CAMPBELL RIVER, BC, V9W 8C9
(250) 850-3276　*SIC 6712*

MARKEL CANADA LIMITED　*p981*
200 WELLINGTON ST W UNIT 400, TORONTO, ON, M5V 3C7
(416) 601-1133　*SIC 6712*

MARTIN, IAN TECHNOLOGY STAFFING LIMITED *p801*
610 CHARTWELL RD SUITE 101, OAKVILLE, ON, L6J 4A5
(905) 815-1600　*SIC 6712*

MARWEST GROUP OF COMPANIES LTD

---

p379
360 MAIN ST SUITE 300, WINNIPEG, MB, R3C 3Z3
(204) 947-1200　*SIC 6712*

MASON GROUP OF COMPANIES LIMITED, THE　*p697*
1205 BRITANNIA RD E, MISSISSAUGA, ON, L4W 1C7
(905) 795-0122　*SIC 6712*

MASTERFEEDS INC　　*p657*
1020 HARGRIEVE RD SUITE 9, LONDON, ON, N6E 1P5
(519) 685-4300　*SIC 6712*

MAV BEAUTY BRANDS INC　*p555*
190 PIPPIN RD, CONCORD, ON, L4K 4X9
(905) 530-2500　*SIC 6712*

MAXRELCO INC　　*p1284*
90 201 RTE, RIGAUD, QC, J0P 1P0
(450) 458-5375　*SIC 6712*

MCMUNN & YATES BUILDING SUPPLIES LTD　*p348*
288 2 AVE NE, DAUPHIN, MB, R7N 0Z9
(204) 638-5303　*SIC 6712*

MEDIA5 CORPORATION　*p1374*
4229 RUE DE LA GARLOCK, SHERBROOKE, QC, J1L 2C8
(819) 829-8749　*SIC 6712*

MEDISYSTEM TECHNOLOGIES INC *p776*
75 LESMILL RD UNIT 3, NORTH YORK, ON, M3B 2T8
(416) 441-2293　*SIC 6712*

MELLOUL-BLAMEY ENTERPRISES INC *p1010*
700 RUPERT ST UNIT A, WATERLOO, ON, N2V 2B5
(519) 886-8850　*SIC 6712*

MELOCHE MONNEX INC　*p1180*
50 BOUL CREMAZIE O BUREAU 1200, MONTREAL, QC, H2P 1B6
(514) 382-6060　*SIC 6712*

MILTOM MANAGEMENT LP　*p954*
40 KING ST W SUITE 5800, TORONTO, ON, M5H 3S1
(416) 595-8500　*SIC 6712*

MINE AND MILL INSTALLATIONS LTD *p682*
524 6TH CONCESSION RD W, MILLGROVE, ON, L0R 1V0
SIC 6712

MINTO HOLDINGS INC　　*p823*
180 KENT ST SUITE 200, OTTAWA, ON, K1P 0B6
(613) 230-7051　*SIC 6712*

MISTAHIA REGIONAL HEALTH AUTHORITY　*p131*
10200 SHAND AVE, GRANDE CACHE, AB, T0E 0Y0
(780) 827-3701　*SIC 6712*

MIXCOR HOLDINGS INC　*p139*
6303 43 ST, LEDUC, AB, T9E 0G8
(780) 986-6721　*SIC 6712*

MLTH HOLDINGS INC　　*p897*
25 MCNAB ST, STRATHROY, ON, N7G 4H6
(519) 246-9600　*SIC 6712*

MONSTER WORLDWIDE CANADA INC *p1198*
2020 BOUL ROBERT-BOURASSA BUREAU 2000, MONTREAL, QC, H3A 2A5
(514) 284-0231　*SIC 6712*

MOORE CANADA CORPORATION　*p741*
6100 VIPOND DR, MISSISSAUGA, ON, L5T 2X1
(905) 362-3100　*SIC 6712*

MORRISON HERSHFIELD GROUP INC *p904*
125 COMMERCE VALLEY DR W SUITE 300, THORNHILL, ON, L3T 7W4
(416) 499-3110　*SIC 6712*

MOSAIC ESTERHAZY HOLDINGS ULC *p1406*
HWY 80 E, ESTERHAZY, SK, S0A 0X0
(306) 745-4200　*SIC 6712*

MOTT MANUFACTURING LIMITED　*p517*
452 HARDY RD, BRANTFORD, ON, N3T 5L8
(519) 752-7825　*SIC 6712*

MS ELITE HOLDINGS INC.　*p1087*
1811 BOUL CURE-LABELLE, COTE SAINT-LUC, QC, H7T 1L1
(450) 681-0060　*SIC 6712*

MT BECHER SKI RENTALS LTD　*p203*
267 6TH ST, COURTENAY, BC, V9N 1L9
(250) 334-2537　*SIC 6712*

MT-U OPERATING COMPANY INC　*p150*
31 SOUTHRIDGE DR SUITE 121A, OKOTOKS, AB, T1S 2N3
(403) 995-5217　*SIC 6712*

MUSTANG SURVIVAL HOLDINGS CORPORATION　*p255*
3810 JACOMBS RD, RICHMOND, BC, V6V 1Y6
(604) 270-8631　*SIC 6712*

MYRSA MANAGEMENT SERVICES LTD *p894*
3 ANDERSON BLVD SUITE 1, STOUFFVILLE, ON, L4A 7X4
(416) 291-9756　*SIC 6712*

NATION-WIDE HOME SERVICES CORP *p96*
11228 142 ST NW, EDMONTON, AB, T5M 1T9
(780) 454-1937　*SIC 6712*

NCSG HOLDINGS CANADA LTD　*p2*
28765 ACHESON RD, ACHESON, AB, T7X 6A8
(780) 960-6300　*SIC 6712*

NEWPARK CANADA INVESTMENTS LIMITED PARTNERSHIP　*p54*
635 6 AVE SW SUITE 300, CALGARY, AB, T2P 0T5
(403) 266-7383　*SIC 6712*

NEWTERRA GROUP LTD　　*p519*
1291 CALIFORNIA AVE, BROCKVILLE, ON, K6V 7N5
(613) 498-1876　*SIC 6712*

NICK'S WOODCRAFT INDUSTRIES LTD *p40*
112 SKYLINE CRES NE, CALGARY, AB, T2K 5X7
(403) 275-6432　*SIC 6712*

NIRADIA ENTERPRISES INC　*p206*
460 FRASERVIEW PL, DELTA, BC, V3M 6H4
(604) 523-6188　*SIC 6712*

NOR-SHAM HOLDINGS INC　*p715*
2125 NORTH SHERIDAN WAY, MISSISSAUGA, ON, L5K 1A3
(905) 305-5503　*SIC 6712*

NORMERICA CAPITAL CORPORATION *p713*
1599 HURONTARIO ST SUITE 300, MISSISSAUGA, ON, L5G 4S1
(416) 626-0556　*SIC 6712*

NORTH AMERICAN FUR PRODUCERS INC *p586*
65 SKYWAY AVE, ETOBICOKE, ON, M9W 6C7
(416) 675-9320　*SIC 6712*

NORTH WEST COMPANY LP, THE　*p379*
77 MAIN ST, WINNIPEG, MB, R3C 1A3
(204) 943-0881　*SIC 6712*

NORTHSIDE MARINE LTD　*p423*
300 MAIN ST N, GLOVERTOWN, NL, A0G 2L0
(709) 533-6792　*SIC 6712*

NORTHWATER CAPITAL INC　*p965*
181 BAY ST SUITE 4700, TORONTO, ON, M5J 2T3
(416) 360-5435　*SIC 6712*

NOVA METRIX GROUND MONITORING (CANADA) LTD　*p308*
666 BURRARD ST SUITE 1700, VANCOUVER, BC, V6C 2X8
(604) 430-4272　*SIC 6712*

NOVA PETROCHEMICALS LTD　*p55*
1000 7 AVE SW, CALGARY, AB, T2P 5L5
(403) 750-3600　*SIC 6712*

NOVERCO INC　　*p1192*
1000 PLACE JEAN-PAUL-RIOPELLE BUREAU A12, MONTREAL, QC, H2Z 2B3
(514) 847-2126　*SIC 6712*

NSM ACQUISITION COMPANY LIMITED

▲ Public Company　　■ Public Company Family Member　　**HQ** Headquarters　　**BR** Branch　　**SL** Single Location

p459
12575 HIGHWAY 4, HAVRE BOUCHER, NS, B0H 1P0
(902) 234-3202   *SIC 6712*

NUNAVIT TEST CASE 1 CANADA   p472
PO BOX 1211, IQALUIT, NU, X0A 0H0
(867) 979-1000   *SIC 6712*

NUTRINOR COOPERATIVE   p1296
425 RUE MELANCON, SAINT-BRUNO-LAC-SAINT-JEAN, QC, G0W 2L0
(418) 343-3636   *SIC 6712*

OAK-LANE PARK INVESTMENTS LIMITED
p801
570 TRAFALGAR RD, OAKVILLE, ON, L6J 3J2
(905) 844-3273   *SIC 6712*

ODYSSEY DISTRIBUTION GROUP INC p780
60 PRINCE ANDREW PL, NORTH YORK, ON, M3C 2H4
(647) 288-2222   *SIC 6712*

OMNI HEALTH INVESTMENTS INC   p841
2020 FISHER DR, PETERBOROUGH, ON, K9J 6X6
(705) 748-6631   *SIC 6712*

PAGEAU MOREL INC   p1180
210 BOUL CREMAZIE O BUREAU 110, MONTREAL, QC, H2P 1C6
(514) 382-5150   *SIC 6712*

PAJAR HOLDINGS INC   p1183
4509 AV COLONIALE, MONTREAL, QC, H2T 1V8
(514) 844-3067   *SIC 6712*

PALLISER FURNITURE HOLDINGS LTD
p363
70 LEXINGTON PK, WINNIPEG, MB, R2G 4H2
(866) 444-0777   *SIC 6712*

PANGEO HOLDINGS LTD   p1020
3000 TEMPLE DR, WINDSOR, ON, N8W 5J6
(519) 737-1678   *SIC 6712*

PAPERCON CANADA HOLDING CORP
p1238
200 AV MARIEN, MONTREAL-EST, QC, H1B 4V2
(514) 645-4571   *SIC 6712*

PAYNE TRANSPORTATION LTD   p369
435 LUCAS AVE, WINNIPEG, MB, R2R 2S9
(204) 953-1400   *SIC 6712*

PCL EMPLOYEES HOLDINGS LTD   p116
9915 56 AVE NW, EDMONTON, AB, T6E 5L7
(780) 733-5000   *SIC 6712*

PEAK PRODUCTS INTERNATIONAL INC
p263
11782 HAMMERSMITH WAY SUITE 203, RICHMOND, BC, V7A 5E2
(604) 448-8000   *SIC 6712*

PEER GROUP INC   p639
72 VICTORIA ST S SUITE 400, KITCH-ENER, ON, N2G 4Y9
(519) 749-9554   *SIC 6712*

PEKELES HOLDINGS INC   p1330
4045 BOUL POIRIER, SAINT-LAURENT, QC, H4R 2G9
(514) 735-6111   *SIC 6712*

PENN-CO CONSTRUCTION LTD   p346
24 CENTRE AVE, BLUMENORT, MB, R0A 0C0
(204) 326-1341   *SIC 6712*

PERLAW HOLDINGS LIMITED   p825
340 ALBERT ST, OTTAWA, ON, K1R 7Y6
(613) 238-2022   *SIC 6712*

PERMANENT SASH & DOOR COMPANY LTD   p662
1040 WILTON GROVE RD, LONDON, ON, N6N 1C7
(519) 686-6020   *SIC 6712*

PERPETUAL HOLDINGS LTD   p290
3473 FRASER ST, VANCOUVER, BC, V5V 4C3
(604) 874-4228   *SIC 6712*

PET VALU CANADA INC   p673
130 ROYAL CREST CRT, MARKHAM, ON,

L3R 0A1
(905) 946-1200   *SIC 6712*

PETRO ASSETS INC   p997
130 KING ST SUITE 2850, TORONTO, ON, M9N 1L5
(416) 364-8788   *SIC 6712*

PFEIFER HOLDINGS LTD   p1412
992 101ST ST, NORTH BATTLEFORD, SK, S9A 0Z3
(306) 445-9425   *SIC 6712*

PHILIPS CANADA LTD   p679
281 HILLMOUNT RD, MARKHAM, ON, L6C 2S3
(905) 201-4100   *SIC 6712*

PIC GROUP HOLDINGS LIMITED, THE p812
111 SIMCOE ST N, OSHAWA, ON, L1G 4S4
(905) 743-4600   *SIC 6712*

PIC INVESTMENT GROUP INC   p1429
70 24TH ST E, SASKATOON, SK, S7K 4B8
(306) 664-3955   *SIC 6712*

PIMM PRODUCTION SERVICES INC   p214
10924 ALASKA RD, FORT ST. JOHN, BC, V1J 5T5
(250) 787-0808   *SIC 6712*

PINE VIEW AUTO SALES INC   p1033
3790 HIGHWAY 7, WOODBRIDGE, ON, L4L 9C3
(905) 851-2851   *SIC 6712*

PIONEER ENVIRO GROUP LTD   p73
1711 10 AVE SW SUITE 200, CALGARY, AB, T3C 0K1
(403) 229-3969   *SIC 6712*

PL NOUVELLE FRANCE INC   p1393
1625 BOUL LIONEL-BOULET LOCAL 203, VARENNES, QC, J3X 1P7
(450) 809-0211   *SIC 6712*

PLACEMENTS A. LAJEUNESSE INC p1182
6500 RUE SAINT-HUBERT, MONTREAL, QC, H2S 2M3
(514) 272-8233   *SIC 6712*

PLACEMENTS BARAKAT INC, LES   p1335
5637 RUE KIERAN, SAINT-LAURENT, QC, H4S 0A3
(514) 335-0059   *SIC 6712*

PLACEMENTS CHRISTIAN BERGERON INC   p1280
655 RUE DE L'ARGON, QUEBEC, QC, G2N 2G7
(418) 849-7997   *SIC 6712*

PLACEMENTS CLAUDE GOSSELIN INC
p1383
680 RUE DES ERABLES, THETFORD MINES, QC, G6G 1H7
(418) 335-7552   *SIC 6712*

PLACEMENTS E.G.B. INC., LES   p1335
9000 BOUL HENRI-BOURASSA O, SAINT-LAURENT, QC, H4S 1L5
(514) 336-3213   *SIC 6712*

PLACEMENTS JEAN BEAUDRY INC, LES
p1248
12305 BOUL METROPOLITAIN E, POINTE-AUX-TREMBLES, QC, H1B 5R3
(514) 640-4440   *SIC 6712*

PLACEMENTS LAUZON INC   p1245
2101 COTE DES CASCADES, PAP-INEAUVILLE, QC, J0V 1R0
(819) 427-5144   *SIC 6712*

PLACEMENTS PLACEVIC LTEE, LES p1229
800 RUE DU SQUARE-VICTORIA BUREAU 4120, MONTREAL, QC, H4Z 1A1
(514) 875-6010   *SIC 6712*

PLACEMENTS ROBERT PHANEUF INC
p1158
270 RUE BRUNET, MONT-SAINT-HILAIRE, QC, J3H 0M6
(450) 446-9933   *SIC 6712*

PLACEMENTS ROLAND LAVOIE LTEE, LES
p1106
5 BOUL MONTCLAIR, GATINEAU, QC, J8Y 2E3
(819) 771-5841   *SIC 6712*

PLACEMENTS YVON GAREAU INC, LES
p1391
1100 3E AV, VAL-D'OR, QC, J9P 1T6

(819) 825-6880   *SIC 6712*

POLYGON HOMES LTD   p319
1333 BROADWAY W SUITE 900, VANCOU-VER, BC, V6H 4C2
(604) 877-1131   *SIC 6712*

PORTES GARAGA: STANDARD + INC p1306
8500 25E AV, SAINT-GEORGES, QC, G6A 1K5
(418) 227-2828   *SIC 6712*

POWER FINANCIAL CORPORATION p1190
751 RUE DU SQUARE-VICTORIA, MON-TREAL, QC, H2Y 2J3
(514) 286-7400   *SIC 6712*

PPHC NORTH LTD   p1025
1965 AMBASSADOR DR, WINDSOR, ON, N9C 3R5
(519) 969-4632   *SIC 6712*

PREMIER TECH LTEE   p1286
1 AV PREMIER BUREAU 101, RIVIERE-DU-LOUP, QC, G5R 6C1
(418) 867-8883   *SIC 6712*

PRISM MEDICAL LTD   p557
485 MILLWAY AVE UNIT 2, CONCORD, ON, L4K 3V4
(416) 260-2145   *SIC 6712*

PRODUITS DE SECURITE INDUSTRIELLE CHECKERS CANADA INC   p1132
990 RUE D'UPTON, LASALLE, QC, H8R 2T9
(514) 366-6116   *SIC 6712*

PRODUITS FORESTIERS ARBEC INC p1345
8000 BOUL LANGELIER BUREAU 210, SAINT-LEONARD, QC, H1P 3K2
(514) 327-3350   *SIC 6712*

PROLINE RESOURCES INC   p110
7141 67 ST NW, EDMONTON, AB, T6B 3L7
(780) 465-6161   *SIC 6712*

PROSPECT POINT HOLDINGS LTD   p318
2099 BEACH AVE, VANCOUVER, BC, V6G 1Z4
(604) 669-2737   *SIC 6712*

PTW ENERGY SERVICES LTD   p57
355 4 AVE SW SUITE 600 CALGARY PLACE II, CALGARY, AB, T2P 0J1
(403) 956-8600   *SIC 6712*

PURVIS HOLDINGS LTD   p86
11420 107 AVE NW, EDMONTON, AB, T5H 0Y5
(780) 423-4330   *SIC 6712*

QUALICO DEVELOPMENTS (WINNIPEG) LTD   p392
1 DR. DAVID FRIESEN DR, WINNIPEG, MB, R3X 0G8
(204) 233-2451   *SIC 6712*

QUALICO DEVELOPMENTS CANADA LTD
p392
1 DR. DAVID FRIESEN DR, WINNIPEG, MB, R3X 0G8
(204) 233-2451   *SIC 6712*

QUANTEC GEOSCIENCE LIMITED   p765
146 SPARKS AVE, NORTH YORK, ON, M2H 2S4
(416) 306-1941   *SIC 6712*

QUEBECOR INC   p1211
612 RUE SAINT-JACQUES BUREAU 700, MONTREAL, QC, H3C 4M8
(514) 380-1999   *SIC 6712*

QUEENSWAY CAWTHRA HOLDINGS LTD
p708
655 QUEENSWAY E, MISSISSAUGA, ON, L5A 3X6
(905) 273-9357   *SIC 6712*

QUIKRETE CANADA HOLDINGS, LIMITED
p183
8535 EASTLAKE DR, BURNABY, BC, V5A 4T7
(604) 444-3620   *SIC 6712*

R.C.R INVESTMENTS LIMITED   p456
6009 QUINPOOL RD SUITE 300, HALIFAX, NS, B3K 5J7
(902) 454-8533   *SIC 6712*

R.O.M CONTRACTORS LIMITED   p917
25 CURITY AVE UNIT 4, TORONTO, ON, M4B 3M2

(416) 285-0190   *SIC 6712*

RAM HERITAGE LTD   p468
29 GREENS POINT RD, TRENTON, NS, B0K 1X0
(902) 752-6934   *SIC 6712*

RED CARPET TRANSPORT LTD   p123
6303 18 ST NW, EDMONTON, AB, T6P 0B6
(780) 463-3936   *SIC 6712*

RED SUN FARMS CANADA INC   p634
2400 GRAHAM SIDERD, KINGSVILLE, ON, N9Y 2E5
(519) 733-3663   *SIC 6712*

REDFERN ENTERPRISES INC   p347
922 DOUGLAS ST, BRANDON, MB, R7A 7B2
(204) 725-8580   *SIC 6712*

REDLINE DRAFTING INC   p58
1000 7 AVE SW SUITE 600, CALGARY, AB, T2P 5L5
(403) 452-3810   *SIC 6712*

REIMER CONSOLIDATED CORP   p375
201 PORTAGE AVE SUITE 2900, WIN-NIPEG, MB, R3B 3K6
(204) 958-5300   *SIC 6712*

REIMER EXPRESS ENTERPRISES LTD
p375
201 PORTAGE AVE SUITE 2900, WIN-NIPEG, MB, R3B 3K6
(204) 958-5000   *SIC 6712*

RELIANCE INDUSTRIAL INVESTMENTS LTD   p149
606 19 AVE, NISKU, AB, T9E 7W1
(780) 955-7115   *SIC 6712*

RENNAT INC   p1341
4850 RUE BOURG, SAINT-LAURENT, QC, H4T 1J2
(514) 735-4255   *SIC 6712*

RENSERVALL LIMITED   p834
116 LISGAR ST SUITE 500, OTTAWA, ON, K2P 0C2
(613) 237-3444   *SIC 6712*

RETIREMENT LIVING CENTRES INC p658
1673 RICHMOND ST SUITE 147, LONDON, ON, N6G 2N3
(519) 858-9889   *SIC 6712*

REXEL AMERIQUE DU NORD INC   p1341
505 RUE LOCKE BUREAU 202, SAINT-LAURENT, QC, H4T 1X7
(514) 332-5331   *SIC 6712*

RGA INTERNATIONAL CORPORATION
p966
161 BAY ST SUITE 4600, TORONTO, ON, M5J 2S1
(416) 943-6770   *SIC 6712*

RICE DEVELOPMENT COMPANY INC p510
7735 KENNEDY RD, BRAMPTON, ON, L6W 0B9
(905) 796-3630   *SIC 6712*

ROBINSON SOLUTIONS (CANADA) INC
p633
1456 CENTENNIAL DR, KINGSTON, ON, K7P 0K4
(613) 389-7611   *SIC 6712*

ROBUCK CONTRACTING (1986) LIMITED
p651
2326 FANSHAWE PARK RD E, LONDON, ON, N5X 4A2
(519) 455-1108   *SIC 6712*

RODFAM HOLDINGS LIMITED   p1020
2575 AIRPORT RD, WINDSOR, ON, N8W 1Z4
(519) 969-3350   *SIC 6712*

ROGERS COMMUNICATIONS CANADA INC
p932
1 MOUNT PLEASANT RD SUITE 115, TORONTO, ON, M4Y 2Y5
(416) 764-2000   *SIC 6712*

ROMCO CORPORATION   p524
5575 NORTH SERVICE RD SUITE 401, BURLINGTON, ON, L7L 6M1
(905) 339-3555   *SIC 6712*

ROSEDALE ON ROBSON SUITE HOTEL (2018) INC   p300
838 HAMILTON ST, VANCOUVER, BC, V6B

6A2

(604) 689-8033 *SIC 6712*

ROSENEATH CAPITAL CORP *p853*
91 GRANTON DR, RICHMOND HILL, ON, L4B 2N5

(905) 882-4740 *SIC 6712*

ROTISSERIES AU COQ LTEE, LES *p1168*
3060 RUE HOCHELAGA, MONTREAL, QC, H1W 1G2

(514) 527-8833 *SIC 6712*

ROYAL CITY CHARTER COACH LINES LTD *p210*
8730 RIVER RD, DELTA, BC, V4G 1B5

(604) 940-1707 *SIC 6712*

S.B. SIMPSON HOLDINGS LIMITED *p526*
3210 MAINWAY, BURLINGTON, ON, L7M 1A5

(905) 335-6575 *SIC 6712*

SAEXPLORATION HOLDINGS INC *p13*
4860 25 ST SE, CALGARY, AB, T2B 3M2

(403) 776-1950 *SIC 6712*

SAKITAWAK DEVELOPMENT CORPORATION *p1407*
GD, ILE-A-LA-CROSSE, SK, S0M 1C0

(306) 833-2466 *SIC 6712*

SAMUEL, SON & CO., LIMITED *p704*
2360 DIXIE RD, MISSISSAUGA, ON, L4Y 1Z7

(905) 279-5460 *SIC 6712*

SAPPORO CANADA INC *p606*
551 CLAIR RD W, GUELPH, ON, N1L 1E9

(519) 822-1834 *SIC 6712*

SCHLAGER HOLDING LTD *p1182*
7070 RUE SAINT-URBAIN, MONTREAL, QC, H2S 3H6

(514) 276-2518 *SIC 6712*

SCHWAN'S CANADA CORPORATION *p1128*
2900 RUE LOUIS-A.-AMOS, LACHINE, QC, H8T 3K6

(514) 631-9275 *SIC 6712*

SCOTIA INVESTMENTS LIMITED *p440*
3 BEDFORD HILLS RD, BEDFORD, NS, B4A 1J5

(902) 835-7100 *SIC 6712*

SCOTLYNN INVESTMENTS INC *p1004*
1150 VITTORIA RD, VITTORIA, ON, N0E 1W0

(519) 426-2700 *SIC 6712*

SECURITE NATIONALE COMPAGNIE D'ASSURANCE *p1180*
50 BOUL CREMAZIE O BUREAU 1200, MONTREAL, QC, H2P 1B6

(514) 382-6060 *SIC 6712*

SELA INDUSTRIES INC *p1252*
755 BOUL SAINT-JEAN BUREAU 305, POINTE-CLAIRE, QC, H9R 5M9

(514) 693-9150 *SIC 6712*

SEPRACOR CANADA, INC *p727*
6790 CENTURY AVE SUITE 100, MISSISSAUGA, ON, L5N 2V8

(905) 814-9145 *SIC 6712*

SERVICES D'IMPRESSION ESSENCE DU PAPIER INC *p1190*
127 RUE SAINT-PIERRE BUREAU 200, MONTREAL, QC, H2Y 2L6

(514) 286-2880 *SIC 6712*

SERVICES MATREC INC *p1067*
4 CH DU TREMBLAY BUREAU 625, BOUCHERVILLE, QC, J4B 6Z5

(450) 641-3070 *SIC 6712*

SETAY HOLDINGS LIMITED *p610*
78 QUEENSTON RD, HAMILTON, ON, L8K 6R6

(905) 549-4656 *SIC 6712*

SG TRANSPORT ENERGIE INC *p1255*
520 RUE ADANAC, QUEBEC, QC, G1C 7B7

(418) 660-8888 *SIC 6712*

SHALABY ENTERPRISES LIMITED *p818*
2310 ST. LAURENT BLVD, OTTAWA, ON, K1G 5H9

(613) 526-5212 *SIC 6712*

SHAN INC *p1400*
4390 SUD LAVAL (A-440) O, VIMONT, QC,

H7T 2P7

(450) 687-7101 *SIC 6712*

SHATO HOLDINGS LTD *p293*
4088 CAMBIE ST SUITE 300, VANCOUVER, BC, V5Z 2X8

(604) 874-5533 *SIC 6712*

SHERGROUP INC *p1148*
205 RUE DU CENTRE, MAGOG, QC, J1X 5B6

(819) 843-4441 *SIC 6712*

SHERLOCK RESOURCES INC *p558*
289 BRADWICK DR, CONCORD, ON, L4K 1K5

(905) 669-5888 *SIC 6712*

SMITH GROUP HOLDINGS LTD *p7*
143040 TWP RD 191, BROOKS, AB, T1R 1B6

(403) 362-4071 *SIC 6712*

SMITHERS INTERNATIONAL LIMITED *p444*
1 CANAL ST, DARTMOUTH, NS, B2Y 2W1

(902) 465-3400 . *SIC 6712*

SNC-LAVALIN GTS INC *p1190*
360 RUE SAINT-JACQUES BUREAU 1600, MONTREAL, QC, H2Y 1P5

(514) 393-1000 *SIC 6712*

SOARING PHOENIX INC *p1364*
15 BOUL DU CURE-LABELLE, SAINTE-THERESE, QC, J7E 2X1

(450) 435-6541 *SIC 6712*

SOCIETE DE GESTION ALI INC *p1366*
760 BOUL DES ERABLES, SALABERRY-DE-VALLEYFIELD, QC, J6T 6G4

(450) 373-2010 *SIC 6712*

SOCIETE DE GESTION B3CG INTERCONNECT INC *p1302*
310 BOUL INDUSTRIEL, SAINT-EUSTACHE, QC, J7R 5R4

(450) 491-4040 *SIC 6712*

SOCIETE DE PLACEMENTS BERNFERST INC *p1402*
3 CAR WESTMOUNT, WESTMOUNT, QC, H3Z 2S5

(514) 384-7462 *SIC 6712*

SOCIETE DE PORTEFEUILLE ET D'ACQUISITION BANQUE NATIONAL INC *p1208*
600 RUE DE LA GAUCHETIERE O BUREAU 11E, MONTREAL, QC, H3B 4L2

(514) 394-4385 *SIC 6712*

SOCIETE GESTION LIBRAIRIE INC *p1260*
286 RUE SAINT-JOSEPH E, QUEBEC, QC, G1K 3A9

(418) 692-1175 *SIC 6712*

SOLCZ GROUP INC *p1019*
6555 HAWTHORNE DR, WINDSOR, ON, N8T 3G6

(519) 974-5200 *SIC 6712*

SOUP BONE ENTERPRISES INC *p203*
750 COMOX RD SUITE 121, COURTENAY, BC, V9N 3P6

(250) 897-1300 *SIC 6712*

SOUTH COUNTRY AG LTD *p1412*
40 MAIN ST, MOSSBANK, SK, S0H 3G0

SIC 6712

SOWA HOLDINGS LTD *p637*
500 MANITOU DR, KITCHENER, ON, N2C 1L3

(519) 748-5750 *SIC 6712*

SPCRC HOLDINGS INC *p1341*
850 MONT?E DE LIESSE, SAINT-LAURENT, QC, H4T 1P4

(514) 341-3550 *SIC 6712*

SPEQ LE DEVOIR INC *p1200*
2050 RUE DE BLEURY BUREAU 900, MONTREAL, QC, H3A 3M9

(514) 985-3333 *SIC 6712*

SPIN MASTER CORP *p983*
225 KING ST W SUITE 200, TORONTO, ON, M5V 3M2

(416) 364-6002 *SIC 6712*

SPINELLI TOYOTA (1981) INC *p1126*
561 BOUL SAINT-JOSEPH, LACHINE, QC, H8S 2K9

(514) 634-7171 *SIC 6712*

SPIRE GROUP LIMITED *p774*
4110 YONGE ST SUITE 602, NORTH YORK, ON, M2P 2B7

(416) 250-0090 *SIC 6712*

SPRUCE FALLS ACQUISITION CORP *p627*
1 GOVERNMENT RD, KAPUSKASING, ON, P5N 2Y2

(705) 337-1311 *SIC 6712*

SQI HOLDINGS II INC *p466*
115 KING ST, STELLARTON, NS, B0K 0A2

(902) 752-8371 *SIC 6712*

STAGELINE GROUPE INC *p1120*
827 BOUL DE L'ANGE-GARDIEN, L'ASSOMPTION, QC, J5W 1T3

(450) 589-1063 *SIC 6712*

STAMBAUGH HOLDINGS LTD *p130*
18 WESTPARK CRT, FORT SASKATCHEWAN, AB, T8L 3W9

(780) 992-1600 *SIC 6712*

STAR OFFICE INSTALLINS LTD *p917*
85 NORTHLINE RD, TORONTO, ON, M4B 3E9

(416) 750-1104 *SIC 6712*

STARCAN CORPORATION *p967*
211 QUEENS QUAY W SUITE 908, TORONTO, ON, M5J 2M6

(416) 361-0255 *SIC 6712*

STELCO HOLDINGS INC *p611*
386 WILCOX ST, HAMILTON, ON, L8L 8K5

(905) 528-2511 *SIC 6712*

STREAM-FLO RESOURCES LTD *p60*
202 6 AVE SW SUITE 400, CALGARY, AB, T2P 2R9

(403) 269-5531 *SIC 6712*

SUBURBAN CONSTRUCTION LTD *p1432*
2505 AVENUE C N, SASKATOON, SK, S7L 6A6

(306) 652-5322 *SIC 6712*

SUNNYHOLME INC *p604*
2 WYNDHAM ST N, GUELPH, ON, N1H 4E3

(519) 824-6664 *SIC 6712*

SUPERIOR CITY SERVICES LTD *p273*
15151 64 AVE, SURREY, BC, V3S 1X9

(604) 591-3434 *SIC 6712*

SUPREME GROUP INC *p2*
28169 96 AVE, ACHESON, AB, T7X 6J7

(780) 483-3278 *SIC 6712*

SYSTEMES D'AFFAIRES POUR PUBLICATION CANADA INC *p1084*
2012 BOUL RENE-LAENNEC BUREAU 275, COTE SAINT-LUC, QC, H7M 4J8

(450) 902-6000 *SIC 6712*

T.F. WARREN GROUP INC *p518*
57 OLD ONONDAGA RD W, BRANTFORD, ON, N3T 5M1

(519) 756-8222 *SIC 6712*

T.T.S. HOLDINGS INC *p913*
85 PINE ST S, TIMMINS, ON, P4N 2K1

(705) 264-7200 *SIC 6712*

TABOR VIEW HOLDINGS LTD *p249*
505 4TH AVE, PRINCE GEORGE, BC, V2L 3H2

(250) 563-8250 *SIC 6712*

TAKHAR INVESTMENTS INC *p534*
202 BEVERLY ST, CAMBRIDGE, ON, N1R 3Z8

(519) 622-3130 *SIC 6712*

TAMWIN HOLDINGS LIMITED *p1020*
3957 WALKER RD, WINDSOR, ON, N8W 3T4

(519) 969-7060 *SIC 6712*

TAO GROUP HOLDINGS CORP *p957*
11 KING ST W SUITE 1600, TORONTO, ON, M5H 4C7

(416) 309-7557 *SIC 6712*

TAT PROPERTIES LTD *p195*
GD STN A, CAMPBELL RIVER, BC, V9W 4Z8

(250) 287-7813 *SIC 6712*

TECHNILAB PHARMA INC *p1153*
17800 RUE LAPOINTE, MIRABEL, QC, J7J 0W8

(450) 433-7673 *SIC 6712*

TECSYS INC *p1221*
1 PLACE ALEXIS NIHON BUREAU 800, MONTREAL, QC, H3Z 3B8

(514) 866-0001 *SIC 6712*

TEKNION HOLDINGS (CANADA) INC *p784*
1150 FLINT RD, NORTH YORK, ON, M3J 2J5

(416) 661-1577 *SIC 6712*

TELECON INC *p1181*
7450 RUE DU MILE END, MONTREAL, QC, H2R 2Z6

(514) 644-2333 *SIC 6712*

TELUS COMMUNICATIONS (QUEBEC) INC *p1285*
6 RUE JULES-A.-BRILLANT BUREAU 20602, RIMOUSKI, QC, G5L 1W8

(418) 723-2271 *SIC 6712*

TERRAEX HOLDINGS INC *p416*
1942 MANAWAGONISH RD, SAINT JOHN, NB, E2M 5H5

(506) 672-4422 *SIC 6712*

TESHMONT CONSULTANTS INC *p392*
1190 WAVERLEY ST, WINNIPEG, MB, R3T 0P4

(204) 284-8100 *SIC 6712*

THE KITCHING GROUP (CANADA) INC. *p388*
747 CORYDON AVE SUITE B, WINNIPEG, MB, R3M 0W5

SIC 6712

THOMSON, A R LTD *p121*
10030 31 AVE NW, EDMONTON, AB, T6N 1G4

(780) 450-8080 *SIC 6712*

THOMSON, G. CAPITAL LIMITED *p525*
961 ZELCO DR, BURLINGTON, ON, L7L 4Y2

(905) 681-8832 *SIC 6712*

THOMSON-GORDON GROUP INC *p526*
3225 MAINWAY, BURLINGTON, ON, L7M 1A6

(905) 335-1440 *SIC 6712*

THORBURN INTERNATIONAL INC *p1252*
173 AV ONEIDA, POINTE-CLAIRE, QC, H9R 1A9

(514) 695-8710 *SIC 6712*

THORNTON STEAD ENTERPRISES INC *p207*
1223 DERWENT WAY, DELTA, BC, V3M 5V9

(604) 524-8000 *SIC 6712*

THORNVALE HOLDINGS LIMITED *p440*
757 BEDFORD HWY, BEDFORD, NS, B4A 3Z7

(902) 443-0550 *SIC 6712*

THUNDER BAY MARINE SERVICES (1998) LTD *p909*
100 MAIN ST SUITE 600, THUNDER BAY, ON, P7B 6R9

(807) 344-9221 *SIC 6712*

TI HOLDINGS INC *p919*
115 THORNCLIFFE PARK DR, TORONTO, ON, M4H 1M1

(416) 696-2853 *SIC 6712*

TICKETMASTER CANADA HOLDINGS ULC *p984*
1 BLUE JAYS WAY SUITE 3900, TORONTO, ON, M5V 1J3

(416) 345-9200 *SIC 6712*

TIGERCAT INTERNATIONAL INC *p535*
200 AVENUE RD, CAMBRIDGE, ON, N1R 8H5

(519) 620-0500 *SIC 6712*

TM CANADA ACQUISITION CORP *p256*
3831 NO. 6 RD, RICHMOND, BC, V6V 1P6

(604) 270-6899 *SIC 6712*

TMS TRANSPORTATION MANAGEMENT SERVICES LTD *p225*
9975 199B ST, LANGLEY, BC, V1M 3G4

(604) 882-2550 *SIC 6712*

TORQUEST PARTNERS INC *p968*
161 BAY ST SUITE 4240, TORONTO, ON, M5J 2S1

(416) 956-7022 *SIC 6712*

▲ Public Company   ■ Public Company Family Member   **HQ** Headquarters   **BR** Branch   **SL** Single Location

TRANSAT A.T. INC   *p1186*
300 RUE LEO-PARISEAU BUREAU 600, MONTREAL, QC, H2X 4C2
(514) 987-1616   *SIC* 6712

TRANSCONTINENTAL INC   *p1209*
1 PLACE VILLE-MARIE BUREAU 3240, MONTREAL, QC, H3B 0G1
(514) 954-4000   *SIC* 6712

TRANSDEV CANADA INC   *p1209*
1100 BOUL RENE-LEVESQUE O BUREAU 1305, MONTREAL, QC, H3B 4N4
(450) 970-8899   *SIC* 6712

TRANSPORT SCOLAIRE SOGESCO INC *p1099*
1125 BOUL SAINT-JOSEPH BUREAU 320, DRUMMONDVILLE, QC, J2C 2C8
(819) 472-1991   *SIC* 6712

TREASURY BOARD OF CANADA SECRETARIAT   *p824*
90 ELGIN ST FL 8, OTTAWA, ON, K1P 0C6
(613) 369-3200   *SIC* 6712

TRICAN WELL SERVICE LTD   *p62*
645 7 AVE SW SUITE 2900, CALGARY, AB, T2P 4G8
(403) 266-0202   *SIC* 6712

TRILOGY RETAIL ENTERPRISES L.P *p968*
161 BAY ST SUITE 4900, TORONTO, ON, M5J 2S1
(416) 943-4110   *SIC* 6712

TRIMAC TRANSPORTATION MANAGEMENT LTD   *p62*
800 5 AVE SW UNIT 2100, CALGARY, AB, T2P 3T6
(403) 298-5100   *SIC* 6712

TRIPLE DELTA HOLDINGS INC   *p690*
6205 AIRPORT RD SUITE 500, MISSISSAUGA, ON, L4V 1E1
(905) 677-5480   *SIC* 6712

TRIPLE FIVE CORPORATION INC   *p104*
8882 170 ST NW SUITE 3000, EDMONTON, AB, T5T 4M2
(780) 444-8100   *SIC* 6712

TURVEY FINANCIAL GROUP INC, THE *p264*
11388 NO. 5 RD SUITE 110, RICHMOND, BC, V7A 4E7
(604) 279-8484   *SIC* 6712

UNIVERSAL SYSTEMS LTD   *p401*
829 WOODSTOCK RD, FREDERICTON, NB, E3B 7R7
(506) 458-8533   *SIC* 6712

UPLAND EXCAVATING LTD   *p194*
7295 GOLD RIVER HWY, CAMPBELL RIVER, BC, V9H 1P1
(250) 286-1148   *SIC* 6712

USINES D'AUTRAY LTEE, LES   *p1303*
4581 RANG CASTLE-D'AUTRAY, SAINT-FELIX-DE-VALOIS, QC, J0K 2M0
(450) 889-5505   *SIC* 6712

VALENER INC   *p1174*
1717 RUE DU HAVRE, MONTREAL, QC, H2K 2X3
(514) 598-6220   *SIC* 6712

VALIANT CORPORATION   *p1019*
6555 HAWTHORNE DR, WINDSOR, ON, N8T 3G6
(519) 974-5200   *SIC* 6712

VALLEY COUNTER TOPS LTD   *p177*
30781 SIMPSON RD, ABBOTSFORD, BC, V2T 6X4
(604) 852-8125   *SIC* 6712

VANBREE, J HOLDINGS LTD   *p628*
9644 TOWNSEND LINE, KERWOOD, ON, N0M 2B0
(519) 247-3752   *SIC* 6712

VASTLON INVESTMENTS INC   *p560*
291 EDGELEY BLVD, CONCORD, ON, L4K 3Z4
(905) 660-9900   *SIC* 6712

VAUNTEK HOLDINGS INC.   *p906*
8707 DUFFERIN ST SUITE 10, THORNHILL, ON, L4J 0A6
SIC 6712

VESEY'S HOLDINGS LTD   *p1043*
411 YORK RD HWY SUITE 25, YORK, PE, C0A 1P0
(902) 368-7333   *SIC* 6712

VESPUCCI HOLDINGS INC   *p68*
8244 ELBOW DR SW, CALGARY, AB, T2V 1K4
(403) 252-9558   *SIC* 6712

VILLAGE FARMS INTERNATIONAL INC *p210*
4700 80 ST, DELTA, BC, V4K 3N3
(604) 940-6012   *SIC* 6712

VILLAGE MALL DELICATESSEN LTD *p41*
1921 20 AVE NW, CALGARY, AB, T2M 1H6
(403) 282-6600   *SIC* 6712

VILLAGE MANOR LTD   *p974*
14 MADISON AVE, TORONTO, ON, M5R 2S1
(416) 927-1722   *SIC* 6712

VISION 7 COMMUNICATIONS INC   *p1260*
300 RUE SAINT-PAUL BUREAU 300, QUEBEC, QC, G1K 7R1
(418) 647-2727   *SIC* 6712

VISION 7 INTERNATIONAL INC   *p1260*
300 RUE SAINT-PAUL BUREAU 300, QUEBEC, QC, G1K 7R1
(418) 647-2727   *SIC* 6712

VITRUM HOLDINGS LTD   *p226*
9739 201 ST, LANGLEY, BC, V1M 3E7
(604) 882-3513   *SIC* 6712

VIVANT GROUP INC, THE   *p26*
1820 30 AVE NE SUITE 3, CALGARY, AB, T2E 7M5
(403) 974-0370   *SIC* 6712

VOYAGEUR AVIATION CORP.   *p764*
1500 AIRPORT RD, NORTH BAY, ON, P1B 8G2
(705) 476-1750   *SIC* 6712

WAPPEL CONCRETE & CONSTRUCTION CO. LTD   *p1416*
230 E 10TH AVE, REGINA, SK, S4N 6G6
(306) 569-3000   *SIC* 6712

WARCO EQUIPMENT LTD   *p1342*
364 RUE MCARTHUR, SAINT-LAURENT, QC, H4T 1X8
(514) 685-7878   *SIC* 6712

WATERLOO NORTH HYDRO HOLDING CORPORATION   *p1007*
526 COUNTRY SQUIRE RD, WATERLOO, ON, N2J 4G8
(519) 886-5090   *SIC* 6712

WEATHERCRAFT HOLDINGS LIMITED *p794*
230 BARMAC DR, NORTH YORK, ON, M9L 2Z3
(416) 740-8020   *SIC* 6712

WEM HOLDINGS LTD   *p104*
8882 170 ST NW SUITE 3000, EDMONTON, AB, T5T 4M2
(780) 444-5200   *SIC* 6712

WEPAWAUG CANADA CORP   *p845*
870 BROCK RD, PICKERING, ON, L1W 1Z8
(905) 839-1138   *SIC* 6712

WESTCO INTERNATIONAL DEVELOPMENT CORP   *p38*
7245 12 ST SE, CALGARY, AB, T2H 2S6
SIC 6712

WESTHALL INVESTMENTS LTD   *p845*
1815 IRONSTONE MANOR UNIT 1, PICKERING, ON, L1W 3W9
(905) 839-3500   *SIC* 6712

WESTLAKE & ASSOCIATES HOLDINGS INC   *p527*
1149 NORTHSIDE RD, BURLINGTON, ON, L7M 1H5
(905) 336-5200   *SIC* 6712

WHITE POINT HOLDINGS LIMITED   *p459*
75 WHITE POINT RD SUITE 2, HUNTS POINT, NS, B0T 1G0
(902) 354-2711   *SIC* 6712

WHITE, GLEN INVESTMENTS LTD   *p482*
7825 SPRINGWATER RD RR 5, AYLMER, ON, N5H 2R4
(519) 765-2244   *SIC* 6712

WIELER ENTERPRISES LTD   *p359*
88 MILLWORK DR, STEINBACH, MB, R5G 1V9
(204) 326-4313   *SIC* 6712

WILSON BANWELL INTERNATIONAL INC *p311*
355 BURRARD ST SUITE 1600, VANCOUVER, BC, V6C 2G8
(604) 689-1717   *SIC* 6712

WILSON'S TRUCK LINES LIMITED   *p580*
111 THE WEST MALL, ETOBICOKE, ON, M9C 1C1
(416) 621-9020   *SIC* 6712

WOLSELEY HOLDINGS CANADA INC *p528*
880 LAURENTIAN DR SUITE 1, BURLINGTON, ON, L7N 3V6
(905) 335-7373   *SIC* 6712

WOODBRIDGE COMPANY LIMITED, THE *p958*
65 QUEEN ST W SUITE 2400, TORONTO, ON, M5H 2M8
(416) 364-8700   *SIC* 6712

WOODHAVEN CAPITAL CORP   *p141*
3125 24 AVE N, LETHBRIDGE, AB, T1H 5G2
(403) 320-7070   *SIC* 6712

WOODHOUSE INVESTMENTS INC   *p639*
207 MADISON AVE S SUITE 2, KITCHENER, ON, N2G 3M7
(519) 749-3790   *SIC* 6712

WORLD TECHNOLOGY GROUP INC   *p702*
1660 TECH AVE SUITE 2, MISSISSAUGA, ON, L4W 5S7
(905) 678-7588   *SIC* 6712

WSP CANADA INC   *p1215*
1600 BOUL RENE-LEVESQUE O 16E ETAGE, MONTREAL, QC, H3H 1P9
(514) 340-0046   *SIC* 6712

XE CORPORATION   *p757*
1145 NICHOLSON RD SUITE 200, NEWMARKET, ON, L3Y 9C3
(416) 214-5606   *SIC* 6712

YGGDRASIL HOLDINGS LTD.   *p324*
4550 LANGARA AVE, VANCOUVER, BC, V6R 1C8
SIC 6712

ZETON INTERNATIONAL INC   *p525*
740 OVAL CRT, BURLINGTON, ON, L7L 6A9
(905) 632-3123   *SIC* 6712

ZUBAR HOLDINGS LTD   *p26*
919 DRURY AVE NE, CALGARY, AB, T2E 0M3
(403) 813-1914   *SIC* 6712

ZUREIT HOLDINGS LIMITED   *p786*
620 WILSON AVE SUITE 401, NORTH YORK, ON, M3K 1Z3
(416) 630-6927   *SIC* 6712

ZURICH CANADIAN HOLDINGS LIMITED *p988*
100 KING ST W SUITE 5500, TORONTO, ON, M5X 1C9
(416) 586-3000   *SIC* 6712

SIC 6719 Holding companies, nec

10578959 CANADA INC   *p850*
155 EAST BEAVER CREEK RD, RICHMOND HILL, ON, L4B 2N1
(905) 904-0596   *SIC* 6719

1080414 ONTARIO LIMITED   *p990*
950 DUPONT ST, TORONTO, ON, M6H 1Z2
(416) 532-6700   *SIC* 6719

152163 CANADA INC   *p1156*
5591 RUE PARE, MONT-ROYAL, QC, H4P 1P7
(514) 735-5248   *SIC* 6719

1615517 ONTARIO INC   *p873*
5215 FINCH AVE E UNIT 203, SCARBOROUGH, ON, M1S 0C2
(416) 321-6969   *SIC* 6719

2945-2901 QUEBEC INC   *p1047*
10251 BOUL RAY-LAWSON, ANJOU, QC, H1J 1L6
(514) 493-6113   *SIC* 6719

300322 ONTARIO LIMITED   *p653*
150 DUFFERIN AVE SUITE 100, LONDON, ON, N6A 5N6
(519) 672-5272   *SIC* 6719

540806 BC LTD   *p296*
475 GEORGIA ST W SUITE 800, VANCOUVER, BC, V6B 4M9
(604) 684-7117   *SIC* 6719

595799 ONTARIO LTD   *p833*
180 MACLAREN ST SUITE 1112, OTTAWA, ON, K2P 0L3
(613) 232-1121   *SIC* 6719

609574 ONTARIO LIMITED   *p691*
2395 SKYMARK AVE, MISSISSAUGA, ON, L4W 4Y6
(905) 629-8999   *SIC* 6719

760496 ONTARIO LTD   *p837*
201 JOSEPH ST, PEMBROKE, ON, K8A 8J2
(613) 732-0077   *SIC* 6719

875578 ONTARIO LIMITED   *p581*
31 RACINE RD, ETOBICOKE, ON, M9W 2Z4
SIC 6719

995547 ONTARIO LTD   *p631*
1670 BATH RD, KINGSTON, ON, K7M 4X9
(613) 384-1000   *SIC* 6719

AGIORITIS HOLDINGS LTD   *p1433*
801 BROADWAY AVE, SASKATOON, SK, S7N 1B5
(306) 652-5374   *SIC* 6719

ALBERTA INVESTMENT MANAGEMENT CORPORATION   *p87*
10830 JASPER AVE NW SUITE 1100, EDMONTON, AB, T5J 2B3
(780) 392-3600   *SIC* 6719

AMEC FOSTER WHEELER INC   *p796*
2020 WINSTON PARK DR SUITE 700, OAKVILLE, ON, L6H 6X7
(905) 829-5400   *SIC* 6719

AMENAGEMENTS RICHARD LTEE, LES *p1108*
110 RUE COURT, GRANBY, QC, J2G 4Y9
(450) 372-3019   *SIC* 6719

AQUIFER INVESTMENTS LTD   *p1426*
227A VENTURE CRES, SASKATOON, SK, S7K 6N8
(306) 242-1567   *SIC* 6719

AUTOMOTIVE PROPERTIES REAL ESTATE INVESTMENT TRUST   *p936*
133 KING ST E SUITE 300, TORONTO, ON, M5C 1G6
(647) 789-2440   *SIC* 6719

BOREALIS INVESTMENTS INC   *p949*
100 ADELAIDE ST W SUITE 900, TORONTO, ON, M5H 0E2
(416) 361-1011   *SIC* 6719

BPO PROPERTIES LTD   *p960*
181 BAY ST SUITE 330, TORONTO, ON, M5J 2T3
(416) 363-9491   *SIC* 6719

BRIDGEMARQ REAL ESTATE SERVICES INC   *p779*
39 WYNFORD DR, NORTH YORK, ON, M3C 3K5
(416) 510-5800   *SIC* 6719

BROCK CONSTRUCTION LTD   *p147*
3735 8 ST, MEDICINE HAT, AB, T9E 8J8
(403) 526-8930   *SIC* 6719

BUCKLEY, W. K. INVESTMENTS LIMITED *p692*
5230 ORBITOR DR, MISSISSAUGA, ON, L4W 5G7
SIC 6719

C5 GROUP INC   *p972*
1329 BAY ST SUITE 300, TORONTO, ON, M5R 2C4
(416) 926-8200   *SIC* 6719

CANAC-MARQUIS GRENIER LTEE   *p1278*
5355 BOUL DES GRADINS, QUEBEC, QC, G2J 1C8
(418) 667-1313   *SIC* 6719

CANADA DEVELOPMENT INVESTMENT CORPORATION   *p972*

1240 BAY ST SUITE 302, TORONTO, ON, M5R 2A7

(416) 966-2221   *SIC* 6719

CANADA PENSION PLAN INVESTMENT BOARD   *p937*
1 QUEEN ST E, TORONTO, ON, M5C 2W5

(416) 868-4075   *SIC* 6719

CANADIAN AUSTIN GROUP HOLDINGS ULC   *p1396*
4 PLACE DU COMMERCE, VERDUN, QC, H3E 1J4

(514) 281-4040   *SIC* 6719

CANADIAN MARKETING TEST CASE 217   *p730*
5770 HURONTARIO ST, MISSISSAUGA, ON, L5R 3G5

SIC 6719

CANLIGHT MANAGEMENT INC   *p692*
5160 EXPLORER DR SUITE 17, MISSISSAUGA, ON, L4W 4T7

(905) 625-1522   *SIC* 6719

CANPRO KING-REED LP.   *p764*
155 GORDON BAKER RD SUITE 101, NORTH YORK, ON, M2H 3N5

(416) 449-8677   *SIC* 6719

CAPITAL PACKERS HOLDINGS INC   *p83*
12907 57 ST NW, EDMONTON, AB, T5A 0E7

(780) 476-1391   *SIC* 6719

CAPITAL REGIONAL ET COOPERATIF DESJARDINS   *p1230*
2 COMPLEXE DESJARDINS O BUREAU 1717, MONTREAL, QC, H5B 1B8

(514) 281-2322   *SIC* 6719

CENTRE BAY YACHT STATION LTD   *p239*
1103 HERITAGE BLVD, NORTH VANCOUVER, BC, V7J 3G8

(604) 986-0010   *SIC* 6719

CENTRE DES RECOLLETS-FOUCHER SOCIETE EN COMMANDITE   *p1194*
1555 RUE PEEL BUREAU 700, MONTREAL, QC, H3A 3L8

(514) 940-1555   *SIC* 6719

CHARTWELL RETIREMENT RESIDENCES   *p730*
100 MILVERTON DR SUITE 700, MISSISSAUGA, ON, L5R 4H1

(905) 501-9219   *SIC* 6719

COMMODITY IMPORT INC   *p1342*
845 AV MUNCK, SAINT-LAURENT, QC, H7S 1A9

(514) 384-4690   *SIC* 6719

COMPAGNIE IMMOBILIERE GUEYMARD & ASSOCIES LTEE   *p1299*
251 CH FUSEY, SAINT-DONAT-DE-MONTCALM, QC, J0T 2C0

(819) 424-1373   *SIC* 6719

CONALJAN INC   *p1174*
4045 RUE PARTHENAIS, MONTREAL, QC, H2K 3T8

(514) 522-2121   *SIC* 6719

CONGEBEC CAPITAL LTEE   *p1063*
5780 BOUL SAINTE-ANNE, BOISCHATEL, QC, G0A 1H0

(418) 822-4077   *SIC* 6719

CORIL HOLDINGS LTD   *p29*
1100 1 ST SE SUITE 600, CALGARY, AB, T2G 1B1

(403) 231-7700   *SIC* 6719

CPP INVESTMENT BOARD REAL ESTATE HOLDINGS INC   *p937*
1 QUEEN ST E SUITE 2500, TORONTO, ON, M5C 2W5

(416) 868-4075   *SIC* 6719

CRICH HOLDINGS AND BUILDINGS LIMITED   *p653*
560 WELLINGTON ST, LONDON, ON, N6A 3R4

(519) 434-1808   *SIC* 6719

CYTRONICS HOLDING CORPORATION LTD   *p1155*
3333 BOUL GRAHAM BUREAU 101, MONT-ROYAL, QC, H3R 3L5

(514) 382-0820   *SIC* 6719

DECISIVE DIVIDEND CORPORATION   *p221*
1674 BERTRAM ST UNIT 201, KELOWNA, BC, V1Y 9G4

(250) 870-9146   *SIC* 6719

DEVELOPPEMENTS REKERN INC, LES   *p1325*
333 BOUL DECARIE 5E ETAGE, SAINT-LAURENT, QC, H4N 3M9

(514) 344-3334   *SIC* 6719

DIONDE INC   *p1101*
1660 BOUL INDUSTRIEL, FARNHAM, QC, J2N 2X8

(450) 293-3909   *SIC* 6719

DOLEMO DEVELOPMENT CORPORATION   *p29*
128 2 AVE SE UNIT 200, CALGARY, AB, T2G 5J5

(403) 699-8830   *SIC* 6719

DREW-SMITH COMPANY LIMITED, THE   *p533*
42 AINSLIE ST N, CAMBRIDGE, ON, N1R 3J5

(519) 621-6988   *SIC* 6719

EFFORT CORPORATION   *p611*
242 MAIN ST E SUITE 240, HAMILTON, ON, L8N 1H5

(905) 528-8956   *SIC* 6719

ENERVEST DIVERSIFIED MANAGEMENT INC   *p48*
700 9 AVE SW SUITE 2800, CALGARY, AB, T2P 3V4

(403) 571-5550   *SIC* 6719

ENTREPRISES B. DURAND INC, LES   *p1241*
48 AV WOLSELEY N, MONTREAL-OUEST, QC, H4X 1V5

(514) 481-0368   *SIC* 6719

FAIRFAX INDIA HOLDINGS CORPORATION   *p962*
95 WELLINGTON ST W SUITE 800, TORONTO, ON, M5J 2N7

(416) 367-4755   *SIC* 6719

FALCON CAPITAL CORPORATION   *p384*
590 BERRY ST, WINNIPEG, MB, R3H 0R9

(204) 786-6451   *SIC* 6719

FALCON FASTENERS LIMITED   *p871*
251 NANTUCKET BLVD, SCARBOROUGH, ON, M1P 2P2

(416) 751-8284   *SIC* 6719

FLS INTERMEDIATE 2 ULC   *p1326*
400 AV SAINTE-CROIX, SAINT-LAURENT, QC, H4N 3L4

(514) 739-0939   *SIC* 6719

FRAM BUILDING GROUP LTD   *p712*
141 LAKESHORE RD E, MISSISSAUGA, ON, L5G 1E8

SIC 6719

GESTION DE PORTEFEUILLE NATCAN INC   *p1204*
1100 BOUL ROBERT-BOURASSA UNITE 400, MONTREAL, QC, H3B 3A5

SIC 6719

GESTION DESJARDINS CAPITAL INC   *p1230*
2 COMPLEXE DESJARDINS BUREAU 1717, MONTREAL, QC, H5B 1B8

(514) 281-7131   *SIC* 6719

GESTION DU GROUPE REDBOURNE INC   *p1196*
1555 RUE PEEL BUREAU 700, MONTREAL, QC, H3A 3L8

(514) 940-1555   *SIC* 6719

GESTION IMMOBILIERE LUC MAURICE INC   *p1329*
2400 RUE DES NATIONS BUREAU 137, SAINT-LAURENT, QC, H4R 3G4

(514) 331-2788   *SIC* 6719

GESTION L.L. LOZEAU LTEE   *p1182*
6229 RUE SAINT-HUBERT, MONTREAL, QC, H2S 2L9

(514) 274-6577   *SIC* 6719

GIAMPAOLO INVESTMENTS LIMITED   *p503*
471 INTERMODAL DR, BRAMPTON, ON, L6T 5G4

(905) 790-3095   *SIC* 6719

GIBRALTAR CONSOLIDATED CORPORATION   *p771*
4936 YONGE ST SUITE 508, NORTH YORK, ON, M2N 6S3

(416) 819-0644   *SIC* 6719

GISBORNE HOLDINGS LTD   *p187*
7476 HEDLEY AVE, BURNABY, BC, V5E 2P9

(604) 520-7300   *SIC* 6719

GLOBAL UPHOLSTERY CO LIMITED   *p783*
560 SUPERTEST RD, NORTH YORK, ON, M3J 2M6

(416) 661-3660   *SIC* 6719

GLOBAL UPHOLSTERY CO. INC   *p783*
1350 FLINT RD, NORTH YORK, ON, M3J 2J7

(416) 661-3660   *SIC* 6719

GREEN, DON HOLDINGS LTD   *p136*
702 11 AVE SE, HIGH RIVER, AB, T1V 1P2

(403) 652-2000   *SIC* 6719

GROUPE DESGAGNES INC   *p1259*
21 RUE DU MARCHE-CHAMPLAIN BUREAU 100, QUEBEC, QC, G1K 8Z8

(418) 692-1000   *SIC* 6719

HALTON INVESTMENTS INC   *p603*
166 WOOLWICH ST, GUELPH, ON, N1H 3V3

(519) 763-8024   *SIC* 6719

HEALTHCARE PROPERTIES HOLDINGS LTD   *p933*
284 KING ST E SUITE 100, TORONTO, ON, M5A 1K4

(416) 366-2000   *SIC* 6719

HOLLISWEALTH INC   *p942*
26 WELLINGTON ST E SUITE 700, TORONTO, ON, M5E 1S2

(416) 350-3250   *SIC* 6719

HYDRO-QUEBEC INTERNATIONAL INC   *p1191*
75 BOUL RENE-LEVESQUE O BUREAU 101, MONTREAL, QC, H2Z 1A4

(514) 289-2211   *SIC* 6719

IKO ENTERPRISES LTD   *p30*
1600 42 AVE SE, CALGARY, AB, T2G 5B5

(403) 265-6022   *SIC* 6719

IMMEUBLES JOSEPH PELLETIER INC, LES   *p1106*
116 RUE LOIS, GATINEAU, QC, J8Y 3R7

(819) 770-3038   *SIC* 6719

IMMEUBLES YALE LIMITEE, LES   *p1197*
2015 RUE PEEL BUREAU 1200, MONTREAL, QC, H3A 1T8

(514) 845-2265   *SIC* 6719

IMMOBILIER CARBONLEO INC   *p1070*
9160 BOUL LEDUC BUREAU 510, BROSSARD, QC, J4Y 0E3

(450) 550-8080   *SIC* 6719

INVESTISSEMENT IMMOBILIER GROUPE MAURICE INC   *p1329*
2400 RUE DES NATIONS BUREAU 137, SAINT-LAURENT, QC, H4R 3G4

(514) 331-2788   *SIC* 6719

INVESTISSEMENTS OLYMBEC INC   *p1326*
333 BOUL DECARIE ETAGE 5E, SAINT-LAURENT, QC, H4N 3M9

(514) 344-3334   *SIC* 6719

IQ SOQUIA INC   *p1272*
1195 AV LAVIGERIE BUREAU 060, QUEBEC, QC, G1V 4N3

(418) 643-5172   *SIC* 6719

JAFFSONS HOLDINGS LTD   *p341*
100 PARK ROYAL S SUITE 300, WEST VANCOUVER, BC, V7T 1A2

(604) 925-2700   *SIC* 6719

JODDES LIMITEE   *p1227*
6111 AV ROYALMOUNT BUREAU 100, MONTREAL, QC, H4P 2T4

(514) 340-1114   *SIC* 6719

JOSTEN DEVELOPMENTS LIMITED   *p789*
1020 LAWRENCE AVE W SUITE 300, NORTH YORK, ON, M6A 1C8

(416) 787-1135   *SIC* 6719

KIK HOLDCO COMPANY INC   *p554*
101 MACINTOSH BLVD, CONCORD, ON,

L4K 4R5

(905) 660-0444   *SIC* 6719

KINCORT BAKERY LIMITED   *p993*
8 KINCORT ST, TORONTO, ON, M6M 3E1

(416) 651-7671   *SIC* 6719

KODIAK GROUP HOLDINGS CO   *p536*
415 THOMPSON DR, CAMBRIDGE, ON, N1T 2K7

(519) 620-4000   *SIC* 6719

L'ART DE VIVRE A SON MEILLEUR   *p1402*
4152A RUE SAINTE-CATHERINE O, WESTMOUNT, QC, H3Z 1P4

SIC 6719

LABRADOR INUIT DEVELOPMENT CORPORATION   *p424*
6 ROYAL ST UNIT 2, HAPPY VALLEY-GOOSE BAY, NL, A0P 1E0

(709) 896-8505   *SIC* 6719

LAMBERT & GRENIER INC   *p1063*
1244 CH QUATRE-SAISONS, BON-CONSEIL, QC, J0C 1A0

(819) 336-2613   *SIC* 6719

LANSDOWNE EQUITY VENTURES LTD   *p69*
295 MIDPARK WAY SE SUITE 350, CALGARY, AB, T2X 2A8

(403) 254-6440   *SIC* 6719

LARCO INVESTMENTS LTD   *p342*
100 PARK ROYAL S SUITE 300, WEST VANCOUVER, BC, V7T 1A2

(604) 925-2700   *SIC* 6719

MACAULAY, SCOTT INVESTMENTS LIMITED   *p439*
368 SHORE RD, BADDECK, NS, B0E 1B0

(902) 295-3500   *SIC* 6719

MACKENZIE INC   *p378*
447 PORTAGE AVE, WINNIPEG, MB, R3C 3B6

(204) 943-0361   *SIC* 6719

MADISON PACIFIC PROPERTIES INC   *p292*
389 6 AVE W, VANCOUVER, BC, V5Y 1L1

(604) 732-6540   *SIC* 6719

MAGNUM PROJECTS LTD   *p299*
128 PENDER ST W SUITE 401, VANCOUVER, BC, V6B 1R8

(604) 569-3900   *SIC* 6719

MARK ANTHONY PROPERTIES LTD   *p289*
887 GREAT NORTHERN WAY SUITE 101, VANCOUVER, BC, V5T 4T5

(604) 263-9994   *SIC* 6719

MARWAL INVESTMENTS INC   *p724*
2875 ARGENTIA RD UNIT 2, MISSISSAUGA, ON, L5N 8G6

(905) 813-3005   *SIC* 6719

MCKERCHER HOLDINGS LIMITED   *p633*
2730 PRINCESS ST, KINGSTON, ON, K7P 2W6

(613) 384-2418   *SIC* 6719

MIDDLEFIELD GROUP LIMITED   *p987*
100 KING ST W SUITE 5855, TORONTO, ON, M5X 2A1

(416) 362-0714   *SIC* 6719

MOSAIC CAPITAL CORPORATION   *p67*
2424 4 ST SW SUITE 400, CALGARY, AB, T2S 2T4

(403) 218-6500   *SIC* 6719

NEWDALE HOLDINGS INC   *p326*
1335 HOWE ST, VANCOUVER, BC, V6Z 1R7

SIC 6719

NORTHERN METALIC SALES (ALTA) LTD   *p133*
10625 WEST SIDE DR UNIT 206, GRANDE PRAIRIE, AB, T8V 8E6

(780) 513-6095   *SIC* 6719

O'REGAN PROPERTIES LIMITED   *p443*
60 BAKER DR UNIT A, DARTMOUTH, NS, B2W 6L4

(902) 464-9550   *SIC* 6719

OMERS REALTY CORPORATION   *p955*
130 ADELAIDE ST W SUITE 1100, TORONTO, ON, M5H 3P5

(416) 369-2400   *SIC* 6719

ONCAP II L.P.   *p965*
161 BAY ST, TORONTO, ON, M5J 2S1

(416) 214-4300   *SIC 6719*
PACIFIC PAVING OF MARKHAM LIMITED
p698
5845 LUKE RD SUITE 204, MISSISSAUGA, ON, L4W 2K5
(905) 670-7730   *SIC 6719*
PARKBRIDGE LIFESTYLE COMMUNITIES INC   *p56*
500 4 AVE SW SUITE 1500, CALGARY, AB, T2P 2V6
(403) 215-2100   *SIC 6719*
PARTNERS VALUE INVESTMENTS LP *p965*
181 BAY ST SUITE 210, TORONTO, ON, M5J 2T3
(647) 503-6513   *SIC 6719*
PLACEMENTS MONTEVA INC   *p1207*
1134 RUE SAINTE-CATHERINE O BUREAU 800, MONTREAL, QC, H3B 1H4
(438) 796-8990   *SIC 6719*
PLAZACORP RETAIL PROPERTIES LTD
p400
98 MAIN ST, FREDERICTON, NB, E3A 9N6
(506) 451-1826   *SIC 6719*
POTTRUFF & SMITH INVESTMENTS INC
p1033
8001 WESTON RD SUITE 300, WOODBRIDGE, ON, L4L 9C8
(905) 265-7470   *SIC 6719*
PROPERTIES GROUP LTD, THE   *p834*
236 METCALFE ST, OTTAWA, ON, K2P 1R3
(613) 237-2425   *SIC 6719*
PROVINCIAL INVESTMENTS INC   *p431*
88 KENMOUNT RD, ST. JOHN'S, NL, A1B 3R1
(709) 758-0002   *SIC 6719*
RICHELIEU FINANCES LTEE   *p1336*
7900 BOUL HENRI-BOURASSA O BUREAU 200, SAINT-LAURENT, QC, H4S 1V4
(514) 336-4144   *SIC 6719*
ROLL'N OILFIELD INDUSTRIES LTD   *p154*
5208 53 AVE SUITE 305, RED DEER, AB, T4N 5K2
(403) 343-1710   *SIC 6719*
SENIOR CAPITAL CORP LTD   *p999*
21 ALBERT ST, TRENTON, ON, K8V 4S4
(613) 394-3317   *SIC 6719*
SHANAHAN FORD LINCOLN SALES   *p756*
567 DAVIS DR, NEWMARKET, ON, L3Y 2P5
(905) 853-5000   *SIC 6719*
SKYSERVICE INVESTMENTS INC   *p729*
6120 MIDFIELD RD, MISSISSAUGA, ON, L5P 1B1
(905) 678-5767   *SIC 6719*
SOCIETE EN COMMANDITE LE FELIX VAUDREUIL-DORION   *p1395*
3223 BOUL DE LA GARE, VAUDREUIL-DORION, QC, J7V 0L5
(514) 331-2788   *SIC 6719*
STOBER, AL CONSTRUCTION LTD   *p223*
1631 DICKSON AVE SUITE 1700, KELOWNA, BC, V1Y 0B5
(250) 763-2305   *SIC 6719*
STONE INVESTMENT GROUP LIMITED
p967
40 UNIVERSITY AVE SUITE 901, TORONTO, ON, M5J 1T1
(416) 364-9188   *SIC 6719*
STREET CAPITAL GROUP INC   *p943*
1 YONGE ST SUITE 2401, TORONTO, ON, M5E 1E5
(647) 259-7873   *SIC 6719*
TAR INVESTMENTS LIMITED   *p448*
30 TROOP AVE, DARTMOUTH, NS, B3B 1Z1
(902) 468-3200   *SIC 6719*
TARDIF, PIERRE INC   *p1265*
1595 BOUL WILFRID-HAMEL, QUEBEC, QC, G1N 3Y7
(418) 655-1521   *SIC 6719*
TERRASSES DE LA CHAUDIERE INC, LES
p1105
25 RUE EDDY BUREAU 203, GATINEAU, QC, J8X 4B5

(819) 997-7129   *SIC 6719*
TFORCE HOLDINGS INC   *p1336*
8801 RTE TRANSCANADIENNE BUREAU 500, SAINT-LAURENT, QC, H4S 1Z6
(514) 331-4000   *SIC 6719*
TRICON CAPITAL GROUP INC   *p976*
7 ST THOMAS ST SUITE 801, TORONTO, ON, M5S 2B7
(416) 925-7228   *SIC 6719*
TRUSTING INVESTMENT & CONSULTING CO., LTD   *p266*
10891 HOGARTH DR, RICHMOND, BC, V7E 3Z9
(778) 321-7399   *SIC 6719*
UNITEC INC   *p859*
1271 LOUGAR AVE, SARNIA, ON, N7S 5N5
(519) 332-0430   *SIC 6719*
WALTON INTERNATIONAL GROUP INC *p62*
215 2 ST SW SUITE 2500, CALGARY, AB, T2P 1M4
(403) 265-4255   *SIC 6719*
WHITECAP RESOURCES INC   *p63*
525 8 AVE SW UNIT 3800, CALGARY, AB, T2P 1G1
(403) 817-2209   *SIC 6719*
YCO CORPORATE INVESTMENTS LTD
p317
1040 GEORGIA ST W SUITE 1900, VANCOUVER, BC, V6E 4H3
(604) 689-1811   *SIC 6719*

SIC 6722 Management investment, open-end

A&W REVENUE ROYALTIES INCOME FUND   *p240*
171 ESPLANADE W SUITE 300, NORTH VANCOUVER, BC, V7M 3K9
(604) 988-2141   *SIC 6722*
ACKER FINLEY CANADA FOCUS FUND
p948
181 UNIVERSITY AVE SUITE 1400, TORONTO, ON, M5H 3M7
(416) 777-9005   *SIC 6722*
AGELLAN COMMERCIAL REAL ESTATE INVESTMENT TRUST   *p959*
156 FRONT ST W SUITE 303, TORONTO, ON, M5J 2L6
(416) 593-6800   *SIC 6722*
AGF EMERGING MARKETS BOND FUND
p968
66 WELLINGTON ST W SUITE 3100, TORONTO, ON, M5K 1E9
(905) 214-8204   *SIC 6722*
AGF GLOBAL MANAGEMENT LIMITED
p968
66 WELLINGTON ST W 31ST FL TORONTO DOMINION BANK TOWER, TORONTO, ON, M5K 1E6
(416) 367-1900   *SIC 6722*
AGF GLOBAL RESOURCES CLASS   *p968*
66 WELLINGTON ST W, TORONTO, ON, M5K 1E9
(905) 214-8203   *SIC 6722*
AGF INVESTMENTS INC   *p968*
66 WELLINGTON ST W SUITE 3100, TORONTO, ON, M5K 1E9
(416) 367-1900   *SIC 6722*
AGF U.S SMALL-MID CAP FUND   *p968*
66 WELLINGTON ST W, TORONTO, ON, M5K 1E9
(905) 214-8203   *SIC 6722*
AGFIQ ENHANCED CORE CANADIAN EQUITY ETF   *p968*
66 WELLINGTON ST W SUITE 3100, TORONTO, ON, M5K 1E9
(905) 214-8204   *SIC 6722*
AIC RSP AMERICAN FOCUSED FUND *p529*
1375 KERNS RD SUITE 100, BURLINGTON, ON, L7P 4V7
(905) 331-4250   *SIC 6722*
ALLSTATE LIFE INSURANCE COMPANY OF CANADA   *p666*

27 ALLSTATE PKY SUITE 100, MARKHAM, ON, L3R 5P8
(905) 477-6900   *SIC 6722*
ALPHAPRO MANAGEMENT INC   *p941*
26 WELLINGTON ST E SUITE 700, TORONTO, ON, M5E 1S2
(416) 933-5745   *SIC 6722*
ALTUS GROUP LIMITED   *p311*
1055 WEST GEORGIA ST SUITE 2500, VANCOUVER, BC, V6E 0B6
(604) 683-5591   *SIC 6722*
ALTUS GROUP LIMITED   *p941*
33 YONGE ST SUITE 500, TORONTO, ON, M5E 1G4
(416) 641-9500   *SIC 6722*
ARROW DIVERSIFIED FUND   *p936*
36 TORONTO ST SUITE 750, TORONTO, ON, M5C 2C5
(416) 323-0477   *SIC 6722*
ARTIS REAL ESTATE INVESTMENT TRUST
p376
220 PORTAGE AVE SUITE 600, WINNIPEG, MB, R3C 0A5
(204) 947-1250   *SIC 6722*
BLUE RIBBON INCOME FUND   *p959*
181 BAY ST SUITE 2930, TORONTO, ON, M5J 2T3
(416) 642-6000   *SIC 6722*
BMO INVESTMENTS INC   *p985*
100 KING ST W 43RD FLOOR, TORONTO, ON, M5X 1A1
(416) 359-5003   *SIC 6722*
BRITISH COLUMBIA INVESTMENT MANAGEMENT CORPORATION   *p336*
750 PANDORA AVE, VICTORIA, BC, V8W 0E4
(778) 410-7100   *SIC 6722*
BROMPTON FUNDS LIMITED   *p960*
181 BAY ST SUITE 2930, TORONTO, ON, M5J 2T3
(416) 642-9061   *SIC 6722*
BROMPTON GROUP LIMITED   *p960*
181 BAY ST SUITE 2930, TORONTO, ON, M5J 2T3
(416) 642-6000   *SIC 6722*
BROOKFIELD PRIVATE EQUITY INC   *p960*
181 BAY ST SUITE 300, TORONTO, ON, M5J 2T3
(416) 363-9491   *SIC 6722*
CAN-60 INCOME ETF   *p960*
95 WELLINGTON ST W SUITE 1400, TORONTO, ON, M5J 2N7
(416) 642-1289   *SIC 6722*
CANADIAN APARTMENT PROPERTIES REAL ESTATE INVESTMENT TRUST   *p941*
11 CHURCH ST SUITE 401, TORONTO, ON, M5E 1W1
(416) 861-9404   *SIC 6722*
CANADIAN BANC CORP   *p979*
200 FRONT ST W SUITE 2510, TORONTO, ON, M5V 3K2
(416) 304-4440   *SIC 6722*
CANADIAN SCIENCE AND TECHNOLOGY GROWTH FUND INC   *p986*
130 KING ST W SUITE 2200, TORONTO, ON, M5X 2A2
SIC 6722
CAPITAL DESJARDINS INC   *p1135*
100 AV DES COMMENDEURS, LEVIS, QC, G6V 7N5
(418) 835-8444   *SIC 6722*
CAPITAL INTERNATIONAL ASSET MANAGEMENT (CANADA), INC.   *p960*
181 BAY ST SUITE 3730, TORONTO, ON, M5J 2T3
(416) 815-2134   *SIC 6722*
CARFINCO INCOME FUND   *p113*
4245 97 ST NW SUITE 300, EDMONTON, AB, T6E 5Y7
(780) 413-7549   *SIC 6722*
CBRE CALEDON CAPITAL MANAGEMENT INC   *p950*
141 ADELAIDE ST W SUITE 1500, TORONTO, ON, M5H 3L5

(416) 861-0700   *SIC 6722*
CDP CAPITAL-CONSEIL IMMOBILIER INC
p1191
1000 PLACE JEAN-PAUL-RIOPELLE BUREAU A 300, MONTREAL, QC, H2Z 2B3
(514) 875-3360   *SIC 6722*
CIBC SECURITIES INC   *p950*
200 KING ST W SUITE 700, TORONTO, ON, M5H 4A8
(416) 980-2211   *SIC 6722*
CINRAM INTERNATIONAL INCOME FUND
p864
2255 MARKHAM RD, SCARBOROUGH, ON, M1B 2W3
(416) 298-8190   *SIC 6722*
CITIGROUP GLOBAL MARKETS CANADA INC   *p693*
2920 MATHESON BLVD E, MISSISSAUGA, ON, L4W 5R6
(905) 624-9889   *SIC 6722*
COMPASS FINANCIAL   *p377*
428 PORTAGE AVE SUITE 204, WINNIPEG, MB, R3C 0E2
(204) 940-3950   *SIC 6722*
CONNOR CLARK & LUNN PRIVATE CAPITAL LTD   *p986*
130 KING ST W UNIT 1400, TORONTO, ON, M5X 2A2
(416) 214-6325   *SIC 6722*
COUNSEL PORTFOLIO SERVICES INC
p693
2680 SKYMARK AVE SUITE 700, MISSISSAUGA, ON, L4W 5L6
(905) 625-9885   *SIC 6722*
COUNSEL SELECT SMALL CAP   *p693*
2680 SKYMARK AVE UNIT 700, MISSISSAUGA, ON, L4W 5L6
(905) 625-9885   *SIC 6722*
COVINGTON CAPITAL CORPORATION
p942
87 FRONT ST E SUITE 400, TORONTO, ON, M5E 1B8
(416) 504-5419   *SIC 6722*
DEANS KNIGHT CAPITAL MANAGEMENT LTD   *p303*
999 HASTINGS ST W SUITE 730, VANCOUVER, BC, V6C 2W2
(604) 669-0212   *SIC 6722*
DIF INFRA IV CANADA LTD   *p980*
100 WELLINGTON ST W, TORONTO, ON, M5V 1E3
(647) 748-2088   *SIC 6722*
DIVIDEND 15 SPLIT CORP   *p980*
200 FRONT ST W SUITE 2510, TORONTO, ON, M5V 3K2
(416) 304-4443   *SIC 6722*
DIVIDEND SELECT 15 CORP   *p980*
200 FRONT ST W SUITE 2510, TORONTO, ON, M5V 3K2
(416) 304-4443   *SIC 6722*
DREAM GLOBAL REAL ESTATE INVESTMENT TRUST   *p938*
30 ADELAIDE ST E SUITE 301, TORONTO, ON, M5C 3H1
(416) 365-3535   *SIC 6722*
DREAM HARD ASSET ALTERNATIVES TRUST   *p938*
30 ADELAIDE ST E SUITE 301, TORONTO, ON, M5C 3H1
(416) 365-3535   *SIC 6722*
ECHELON FINANCIAL CORP   *p118*
6328 104 ST NW 2ND FLR, EDMONTON, AB, T6H 2K9
(780) 989-2777   *SIC 6722*
EDGEPOINT CANADIAN PORTFOLIO *p974*
150 BLOOR ST W SUITE 200, TORONTO, ON, M5S 2X9
(416) 963-9353   *SIC 6722*
EDGEPOINT WEALTH MANAGEMENT INC
p974
150 BLOOR ST W SUITE 500, TORONTO, ON, M5S 2X9
(416) 963-9353   *SIC 6722*
EDGESTONE CAPITAL EQUITY PARTNERS

INC   p986
130 KING ST W SUITE 600, TORONTO,
ON, M5X 2A2
(416) 860-3740   SIC 6722

EDUCATOR'S FINANCIAL GROUP   p767
2225 SHEPPARD AVE E SUITE 1105,
NORTH YORK, ON, M2J 5C2
(416) 752-9410   SIC 6722

EMPIRE LIFE INVESTMENTS INC   p630
259 KING ST E, KINGSTON, ON, K7L 3A8
(613) 548-1881   SIC 6722

ENERVEST MANAGEMENT LTD   p49
350 7 AVE SW SUITE 3900, CALGARY, AB,
T2P 3N9
(403) 571-5550   SIC 6722

EXCEL LATIN AMERICA BOND FUND p694
2810 MATHESON BLVD E SUITE 800, MIS-
SISSAUGA, ON, L4W 4X7
SIC 6722

FA CAPITAL MANAGEMENT INC   p962
95 WELLINGTON ST W SUITE 1400,
TORONTO, ON, M5J 2N7
(416) 642-1289   SIC 6722

FIDELITY CLEARING CANADA ULC   p945
483 BAY ST SUITE 300, TORONTO, ON,
M5G 2N7
(416) 307-5200   SIC 6722

FIDELITY INVESTMENTS CANADA ULC
p935
250 YONGE ST SUITE 700, TORONTO,
ON, M5B 2L7
SIC 6722

FIDELITY INVESTMENTS CANADA ULC
p945
483 BAY ST SUITE 200, TORONTO, ON,
M5G 2N7
(416) 307-5200   SIC 6722

**FIDELITY RSP GLOBAL OPPORTUNITES
FUND**   p945
483 BAY ST SUITE 300, TORONTO, ON,
M5G 2N7
(416) 307-5200   SIC 6722

FINANCIAL 15 SPLIT CORP   p980
200 FRONT ST W SUITE 2510, TORONTO,
ON, M5V 3K2
(416) 304-4443   SIC 6722

FINANCIERE DES PROFESSIONNELS INC
p1230
2 COMPLEXE DESJARDINS E BUREAU
31, MONTREAL, QC, H5B 1C2
(514) 350-5054   SIC 6722

**FIRST ASSET CAN FINANCIALS COVERED
CALL ETF**   p962
95 WELLINGTON ST W SUITE 1400,
TORONTO, ON, M5J 2N7
(416) 642-1289   SIC 6722

**FIRST ASSET INVESTMENT GRADE BOND
ETF**   p938
2 QUEEN ST E SUITE 1200, TORONTO,
ON, M5C 3G7
(416) 642-1289   SIC 6722

**FIRSTASSET CANADIAN COVERTIBLE
DEBENTURE FUND**   p938
2 QUEEN ST E SUITE 1200, TORONTO,
ON, M5C 3G7
(416) 642-1289   SIC 6722

**FONDS DE SOLIDARITE DES TRA-
VAILLEURS DU QUEBEC (F.T.Q.)**   p1176
545 BOUL CREMAZIE E BUREAU 200,
MONTREAL, QC, H2M 2W4
(514) 383-8383   SIC 6722

**FONDS DE SOLIDARITE DES TRA-
VAILLEURS DU QUEBEC (F.T.Q.)**   p1176
8717 RUE BERRI, MONTREAL, QC, H2M
2T9
(514) 383-3663   SIC 6722

**FORESTERS FINANCIAL INVESTMENT
MANAGEMENT COMPANY OF CANADA
INC**   p771
5000 YONGE ST 8TH FLOOR, NORTH
YORK, ON, M2N 7J8
(416) 883-5800   SIC 6722

FOYSTON, GORDON & PAYNE INC   p938
1 ADELAIDE ST E SUITE 2600, TORONTO,

ON, M5C 2V9
(416) 362-4725   SIC 6722

FRONT STREET CAPITAL 2004   p942
33 YONGE ST SUITE 600, TORONTO, ON,
M5E 1G4
(416) 597-9595   SIC 6722

**FRONT STREET DIVERSIFIED INCOME
FUND**   p942
33 YONGE ST SUITE 600, TORONTO, ON,
M5E 1G4
(416) 597-9595   SIC 6722

**FRONT STREET SPECIAL OPPORTUNI-
TIES CANADIAN FUND**   p942
33 YONGE ST SUITE 600, TORONTO, ON,
M5E 1G4
(416) 597-9595   SIC 6722

**GESTION DE FONDS SENTIENT CANADA
LTEE**   p1196
1010 RUE SHERBROOKE O BUREAU
1512, MONTREAL, QC, H3A 2R7
SIC 6722

GESTION FERIQUE   p1204
1010 RUE DE LA GAUCHETIERE O, MON-
TREAL, QC, H3B 2N2
(514) 840-9206   SIC 6722

GESTION UNIVERSITAS INC   p1274
3005 AV MARICOURT BUREAU 250, QUE-
BEC, QC, G1W 4T8
(418) 651-8975   SIC 6722

GROUPE ACCISST INC, LE   p1277
5232 BOUL WILFRID-HAMEL, QUEBEC,
QC, G2E 2G9
(418) 864-7432   SIC 6722

HARMONY CANADIAN EQUITY POOL p969
66 WELLINGTON ST W, TORONTO, ON,
M5K 1E9
(905) 214-8203   SIC 6722

HARMONY FUNDS   p969
66 WELLINGTON ST W SUITE 3100,
TORONTO, ON, M5K 1E9
(905) 214-8204   SIC 6722

HARMONY GROWTH PLUS PORTFOLIO
p969
66 WELLINGTON ST W SUITE 3100,
TORONTO, ON, M5K 1E9
(905) 214-8204   SIC 6722

HARMONY MONEY MARKET POOL   p969
66 WELLINGTON ST W SUITE 3100,
TORONTO, ON, M5K 1E9
(905) 214-8204   SIC 6722

HARVEST PORTFOLIOS GROUP INC p802
710 DORVAL DR SUITE 200, OAKVILLE,
ON, L6K 3V7
(416) 649-4541   SIC 6722

**HEALTHCARE SPECIAL OPPURTUNITIES
FUND**   p986
130 KING ST W SUITE 2130, TORONTO,
ON, M5X 2A8
(416) 362-4141   SIC 6722

**HILLSDALE CANADIAN PERFORMANCE
EQUITY**   p969
100 WELLINGTON ST W SUITE 2100,
TORONTO, ON, M5K 1J3
(416) 913-3900   SIC 6722

**HORIZONS ACTIVE CORPORATE BOND
ETF**   p942
26 WELLINGTON ST E SUITE 700,
TORONTO, ON, M5E 1S2
(416) 933-5754   SIC 6722

HORIZONS ACTIVE HIGH YIELD BOND ETF
p942
26 WELLINGTON ST E SUITE 700,
TORONTO, ON, M5E 1S2
(416) 933-5745   SIC 6722

**IA CLARINGTON GLOBAL TACTICAL IN-
COME FUND INC**   p945
522 UNIVERSITY AVE SUITE 700,
TORONTO, ON, M5G 1Y7
(416) 860-9880   SIC 6722

IA CLARINGTON INVESTMENTS INC p946
522 UNIVERSITY AVE UNIT 700,
TORONTO, ON, M5G 1W7
(416) 860-9880   SIC 6722

IA CLERINGTON INVESTMENTS INC   p946

522 UNIVERSITY AVE SUITE 700,
TORONTO, ON, M5G 1W7
(416) 860-9880   SIC 6722

**INFO FINANCIAL CONSULTING GROUP
INC**   p852
350 HIGHWAY 7 E SUITE PH8, RICHMOND
HILL, ON, L4B 3N2
(905) 886-8811   SIC 6722

INVESCO CANDA LTD   p772
5140 YONGE ST SUITE 800, NORTH
YORK, ON, M2N 6X7
(416) 590-9855   SIC 6722

INVESTORS GROUP INC   p378
447 PORTAGE AVE, WINNIPEG, MB, R3C
3B6
(204) 943-0361   SIC 6722

**INVESTORS TACTICAL ASSET ALLOCA-
TION FUND**   p378
447 PORTAGE AVE, WINNIPEG, MB, R3C
3B6
(204) 957-7383   SIC 6722

**ISHARES U.S. HIGH YIELD BOND INDEX
ETF (CAD-HEDGED)**   p963
161 BAY ST SUITE 2500, TORONTO, ON,
M5J 2S1
(416) 643-4000   SIC 6722

KEG ROYALTIES INCOME FUND, THE p260
10100 SHELLBRIDGE WAY, RICHMOND,
BC, V6X 2W7
(604) 276-0242   SIC 6722

KINETIC CAPITAL PARTNERS   p319
1195 BROADWAY W SUITE 500, VANCOU-
VER, BC, V6H 3X5
(604) 692-2530   SIC 6722

LEITH WHEELER FIXED INCOME FUND
p306
400 BURRARD ST SUITE 1500, VANCOU-
VER, BC, V6C 3A6
(604) 683-3391   SIC 6722

LIFE & BANC SPLIT CORP   p964
181 BAY ST SUITE 2930, TORONTO, ON,
M5J 2T3
(416) 642-6000   SIC 6722

**LINCLUDEN INVESTMENT MANAGEMENT
LIMITED**   p806
1275 NORTH SERVICE RD W SUITE 607,
OAKVILLE, ON, L6M 3G4
(905) 825-9000   SIC 6722

MACKENZIE FINANCIAL CORPORATION
p981
180 QUEEN ST W SUITE 1600, TORONTO,
ON, M5V 3K1
(800) 387-0614   SIC 6722

MACKENZIE INVESTMENTS   p981
180 QUEEN ST W, TORONTO, ON, M5V
3K1
(416) 922-5322   SIC 6722

**MANULIFE ASSET MANAGEMENT LIM-
ITED**   p929
200 BLOOR ST E SUITE 1, TORONTO, ON,
M4W 1E5
(416) 581-8300   SIC 6722

**MANULIFE SECURITIES INVESTMENT
SERVICES INC**   p806
1235 NORTH SERVICE RD W SUITE 500,
OAKVILLE, ON, L6M 2W2
(905) 469-2100   SIC 6722

MANULIFE TRUST SERVICES LIMITED
p1213
1245 RUE SHERBROOKE O BUREAU
1500, MONTREAL, QC, H3G 1G3
(514) 499-7999   SIC 6722

**MARQUEST 2013-1 MINING SUPER FLOW-
THROUGH LIMITED PARTNERSHIP**   p964
161 BAY ST SUITE 4420, TORONTO, ON,
M5J 2S1
(416) 777-7350   SIC 6722

MARQUEST INVESTMENT COUNSEL INC
p964
161 BAY ST SUITE 4420, TORONTO, ON,
M5J 2S1
(416) 777-7350   SIC 6722

MAVRIX AMERICAN GROWTH FUND p939
36 LOMBARD ST SUITE 2200, TORONTO,

ON, M5C 2X3
(416) 362-3077   SIC 6722

MAVRIX GLOBAL FUND INC   p987
130 KING ST W SUITE 2200, TORONTO,
ON, M5X 2A2
(416) 362-3077   SIC 6722

MAWER GLOBAL SMALL CAP FUND LTD
p65
517 10 AVE SW SUITE 600, CALGARY, AB,
T2R 0A8
(403) 267-1988   SIC 6722

MAWER INVESTMENT MANAGEMENT LTD
p65
600-517 10 AVE SW, CALGARY, AB, T2R
0A8
(403) 262-4673   SIC 6722

**MCLEAN, BUDDEN CANADIAN EQUITY
GROWTH FUND**   p954
145 KING ST W SUITE 2525, TORONTO,
ON, M5H 1J8
(416) 862-9800   SIC 6722

MCLEAN, BUDDEN LIMITED   p954
145 KING ST W SUITE 2525, TORONTO,
ON, M5H 1J8
(416) 862-9800   SIC 6722

MD PRIVATE TRUST COMPANY   p818
1870 ALTA VISTA DR, OTTAWA, ON, K1G
6R7
(613) 731-8610   SIC 6722

**MELCOR REAL ESTATE INVESTMENT
TRUST**   p90
10310 JASPER AVE SUITE 900, EDMON-
TON, AB, T5J 1Y8
(780) 423-6931   SIC 6722

MENU FOODS INCOME FUND   p724
8 FALCONER DR UNIT 1, MISSISSAUGA,
ON, L5N 1B1
(905) 826-3870   SIC 6722

MONARCH WEALTH CORPORATION p697
5090 EXPLORER DR SUITE 200, MISSIS-
SAUGA, ON, L4W 4X6
(416) 640-2285   SIC 6722

MORNEAU SHEPELL INC   p780
895 DON MILLS RD SUITE 700, NORTH
YORK, ON, M3C 1W3
(416) 445-2700   SIC 6722

**NADG U.S. CORE PLUS ACQUISITION
FUND (CANADIAN) L.P.**   p673
2851 JOHN ST SUITE 1, MARKHAM, ON,
L3R 5R7
(905) 477-9200   SIC 6722

NATIONAL BANK SECURITIES INC. p1206
1100 BOUL ROBERT-BOURASSA UNITE
10 E, MONTREAL, QC, H3B 3A5
(514) 394-6282   SIC 6722

NBF INC   p987
130 KING ST W SUITE 3000, TORONTO,
ON, M5X 1J9
(416) 869-3707   SIC 6722

NEWPORT PARTNERS HOLDINGS LP p982
469 KING ST W, TORONTO, ON, M5V 3M4
(416) 867-7555   SIC 6722

NORANDA INCOME FUND   p987
100 KING ST W SUITE 6900, TORONTO,
ON, M5X 2A1
(416) 775-1500   SIC 6722

**NORTH AMERICAN FINANCIAL 15 SPLIT
CORP**   p982
200 FRONT ST WEST SUITE 2510,
TORONTO, ON, M5V 3K2
(416) 304-4440   SIC 6722

NORTHERN TRUST COMPANY, CANADA
p955
145 KING ST W SUITE 1910, TORONTO,
ON, M5H 1J8
(416) 365-7161   SIC 6722

**NORTHVIEW APARTMENT REAL ESTATE
INVESTMENT TRUST**   p36
6131 6 ST SE SUITE 200, CALGARY, AB,
T2H 1L9
(403) 531-0720   SIC 6722

**NORTHWEST MUTUAL FUNDS
INC/NORDOUEST FONDS MUTUELS INC**
p955

155 UNIVERSITY AVE SUITE 400, TORONTO, ON, M5H 3B7
(416) 594-6633 *SIC 6722*

OTG FINANCIAL *p787*
57 MOBILE DR, NORTH YORK, ON, M4A 1H5
(416) 752-9410 *SIC 6722*

PENEQUITY REALTY CORPORATION *p943*
33 YONGE ST SUITE 901, TORONTO, ON, M5E 1G4
(416) 408-3080 *SIC 6722*

PICTON MAHONEY LONG SHORT EQUITY FUND *p943*
33 YONGE ST SUITE 830, TORONTO, ON, M5E 1G4
(416) 955-4108 *SIC 6722*

PIZZA PIZZA ROYALTY CORP *p575*
500 KIPLING AVE, ETOBICOKE, ON, M8Z 5E5
(416) 967-1010 *SIC 6722*

PRESIMA INC *p1192*
1000 PLACE JEAN-PAUL-RIOPELLE UNITE 400, MONTREAL, QC, H2Z 2B6
(514) 673-1375 *SIC 6722*

PROMUTUEL CAPITAL, SOCIETE DE FIDUCIE INC *p1280*
2000 BOUL LEBOURGNEUF BUREAU 400, QUEBEC, QC, G2K 0B6
SIC 6722

PURE INDUSTRIAL REAL ESTATE TRUST *p956*
121 KING ST W SUITE 2100, TORONTO, ON, M5H 3T9
(416) 479-8590 *SIC 6722*

RBC O'SHAUGHNESSY U.S. VALUE FUND *p970*
77 KING ST W, TORONTO, ON, M5K 2A1
(800) 463-3863 *SIC 6722*

RETURN ON INNOVATION ADVISORS LTD *p943*
43 FRONT ST E SUITE 301, TORONTO, ON, M5E 1B3
(416) 361-6162 *SIC 6722*

RP DEBT OPPORTUNITIES FUND *p973*
39 HAZELTON AVE, TORONTO, ON, M5R 2E3
(647) 776-1777 *SIC 6722*

SAGIT INVESTMENT MANAGEMENT LTD *p309*
789 PENDER ST W SUITE 900, VANCOUVER, BC, V6C 1H2
SIC 6722

SCITI TRUST *p985*
40 KING ST W, TORONTO, ON, M5W 2X6
(416) 863-7411 *SIC 6722*

SENTRY ENHANCED CORPORATE BOND FUND *p971*
199 BAY ST SUITE 2700, TORONTO, ON, M5L 1E2
(416) 861-8729 *SIC 6722*

SPROTT BULL/BEAR RSP *p967*
200 BAY ST SUITE 2700, TORONTO, ON, M5J 2J1
(416) 943-6707 *SIC 6722*

SPROTT CANADIAN EQUITY FUND *p967*
200 BAY ST SUITE 2700, TORONTO, ON, M5J 2J1
(416) 362-7172 *SIC 6722*

STARLIGHT U.S. MULTI-FAMILY (NO.5) CORE FUND *p996*
3280 BLOOR ST W SUITE 1400, TORONTO, ON, M8X 2X3
(416) 234-8444 *SIC 6722*

STUART, W H MUTUALS LTD *p1000*
16 MAIN ST, UNIONVILLE, ON, L3R 2E4
(905) 305-0880 *SIC 6722*

SUMMIT INDUSTRIAL INCOME REIT *p506*
75 SUMMERLEA RD UNIT B, BRAMPTON, ON, L6T 4V2
(905) 791-1181 *SIC 6722*

SUN LIFE FINANCIAL INVESTMENT SERVICES (CANADA) INC *p1007*
227 KING ST S, WATERLOO, ON, N2J 1R2
(519) 888-2290 *SIC 6722*

TD ASSET MANAGEMENT INC *p967*
161 BAY ST SUITE 3200, TORONTO, ON, M5J 2T2
(416) 361-5400 *SIC 6722*

TD WATERHOUSE PRIVATE INVESTMENT COUNSEL INC *p970*
66 WELLINGTON ST W, TORONTO, ON, M5K 1A2
(416) 308-1933 *SIC 6722*

TDAM USA INC *p967*
161 BAY ST SUITE 3200, TORONTO, ON, M5J 2T2
(416) 982-6681 *SIC 6722*

TEMPLETON INTERNATIONAL STOCK FUND *p915*
5000 YONGE ST SUITE 900, TORONTO, ON, M2N 0A7
(416) 364-4672 *SIC 6722*

TERRAVEST INCOME FUND *p170*
4901 BRUCE RD, VEGREVILLE, AB, T9C 1C3
(780) 632-7774 *SIC 6722*

TETREM CAPITAL MANAGEMENT LTD *p376*
201 PORTAGE AVE SUITE 1910, WINNIPEG, MB, R3B 3K6
(204) 975-2865 *SIC 6722*

TRILOGY INTERNATIONAL PARTNERS INC *p987*
100 KING ST W SUITE 7050, TORONTO, ON, M5X 1C7
(416) 360-6390 *SIC 6722*

TRUE NORTH COMMERCIAL REIT *p996*
3280 BLOOR ST W SUITE 1400, TORONTO, ON, M8X 2X3
(416) 234-8444 *SIC 6722*

VANGUARD FTSE CANADA INDEX ETF *p984*
155 WELLINGTON ST W SUITE 3720, TORONTO, ON, M5V 3H1
(888) 293-6728 *SIC 6722*

WATEROUS ENERGY FUND *p62*
301 8 AVE SW SUITE 600, CALGARY, AB, T2P 1C5
(403) 930-6048 *SIC 6722*

WEST FACE CAPITAL INC *p931*
2 BLOOR ST E SUITE 3000, TORONTO, ON, M4W 1A8
(647) 724-8900 *SIC 6722*

WESTERNONE INC *p310*
925 GEORGIA ST W SUITE 910, VANCOUVER, BC, V6C 3L2
(604) 678-4042 *SIC 6722*

WESTSHORE TERMINALS INVESTMENT CORPORATION *p310*
1067 CORDOVA ST W SUITE 1800, VANCOUVER, BC, V6C 1C7
(604) 946-4491 *SIC 6722*

WORKING OPPORTUNITY FUND (EVCC) LTD *p317*
1055 GEORGIA ST W SUITE 260, VANCOUVER, BC, V6E 0B6
(604) 633-1418 *SIC 6722*

SIC 6726 Investment offices, nec

ABERDEEN ASIA-PACIFIC INCOME INVESTMENT COMPANY LIMITED *p958*
161 BAY ST, TORONTO, ON, M5J 2S1
SIC 6726

AURAY CAPITAL CANADA INC *p1201*
600 RUE DE LA GAUCHETIERE O BUREAU 2740, MONTREAL, QC, H3B 4L8
(514) 499-8440 *SIC 6726*

BIRCH HILL EQUITY PARTNERS MANAGEMENT INC *p969*
100 WELLINGTON ST W SUITE 2300, TORONTO, ON, M5K 1A1
(416) 775-3800 *SIC 6726*

BROMPTON SPLIT BANC CORP *p960*
181 BAY ST SUITE 2930, TORONTO, ON, M5J 2T3
(416) 642-9061 *SIC 6726*

CANADIAN GENERAL INVESTMENTS LIMITED *p937*
10 TORONTO ST, TORONTO, ON, M5C 2B7
(416) 366-2931 *SIC 6726*

CANADIAN NATIONAL RAILWAYS PENSION TRUST FUND *p1202*
5 PLACE VILLE-MARIE BUREAU 1100, MONTREAL, QC, H3B 2G2
(514) 399-5963 *SIC 6726*

CANOE EIT INCOME FUND *p45*
421 7 AVE SW SUITE 2750, CALGARY, AB, T2P 4K9
(403) 571-5554 *SIC 6726*

CANSO CREDIT INCOME FUND *p851*
100 YORK BLVD SUITE 501, RICHMOND HILL, ON, L4B 1J8
(416) 640-4275 *SIC 6726*

CATALYST CAPITAL GROUP INC, THE *p961*
181 BAY ST SUITE 4700, TORONTO, ON, M5J 2T3
(416) 945-3003 *SIC 6726*

CITADEL INCOME FUND *p925*
1300 YONGE ST SUITE 300, TORONTO, ON, M4T 1X3
(416) 361-9673 *SIC 6726*

CLAIRVEST GROUP INC *p925*
22 ST CLAIR AVE E SUITE 1700, TORONTO, ON, M4T 2S3
(416) 925-9270 *SIC 6726*

CYMBRIA CORPORATION *p974*
150 BLOOR ST W SUITE 500, TORONTO, ON, M5S 2X9
(416) 963-9353 *SIC 6726*

DIVISION D'ACTIFS DU CN *p1203*
5 PLACE VILLE-MARIE BUREAU 101, MONTREAL, QC, H3B 2G2
(514) 399-4811 *SIC 6726*

EAGLE ENERGY INC *p48*
500 4 AVE SW SUITE 2710, CALGARY, AB, T2P 2V6
(403) 531-1575 *SIC 6726*

FAS BENEFIT ADMINISTRATORS LTD *p89*
10154 108 ST NW, EDMONTON, AB, T5J 1L3
(780) 452-5161 *SIC 6726*

FIRM CAPITAL MORTGAGE INVESTMENT CORPORATION *p789*
163 CARTWRIGHT AVE, NORTH YORK, ON, M6A 1V5
(416) 635-0221 *SIC 6726*

GESTION D'ACTIFS CIBC INC *p1204*
1000 RUE DE LA GAUCHETIERE O BUREAU 3100, MONTREAL, QC, H3B 4W5
(514) 875-7040 *SIC 6726*

H&R FINANCE TRUST *p785*
3625 DUFFERIN ST UNIT 503, NORTH YORK, ON, M3K 1N4
(416) 635-7520 *SIC 6726*

INTERRENT REAL ESTATE INVESTMENT TRUST *p834*
485 BANK ST SUITE 207, OTTAWA, ON, K2P 1Z2
(613) 569-5699 *SIC 6726*

K2 & ASSOCIATES INVESTMENT MANAGEMENT INC *p929*
2 BLOOR ST W SUITE 801, TORONTO, ON, M4W 3E2
(416) 365-2155 *SIC 6726*

LAKEVIEW HOTEL INVESTMENT CORP *p378*
185 CARLTON ST SUITE 600, WINNIPEG, MB, R3C 3J1
(204) 947-1161 *SIC 6726*

MANULIFE US REGIONAL BANK TRUST *p929*
200 BLOOR ST E NORTH TOWER, TORONTO, ON, M4W 1E5
(416) 926-3000 *SIC 6726*

MARYNA (PRIVATE) LIMITED *p1003*
9926 KEELE ST UNIT 5444, VAUGHAN, ON, L6A 3Y4
SIC 6726

MORGAN MEIGHEN & ASSOCIATES LIM-

ITED *p939*
10 TORONTO ST, TORONTO, ON, M5C 2B7
(416) 366-2931 *SIC 6726*

MORGUARD REAL ESTATE INVESTMENT TRUST *p710*
55 CITY CENTRE DR SUITE 800, MISSISSAUGA, ON, L5B 1M3
(905) 281-3800 *SIC 6726*

NDX GROWTH & INCOME FUND *p955*
121 KING ST W SUITE 2600, TORONTO, ON, M5H 3T9
(416) 681-3966 *SIC 6726*

PRIMARIS RETAIL REAL ESTATE INVESTMENT TRUST *p940*
1 ADELAIDE ST E SUITE 900, TORONTO, ON, M5C 2V9
(416) 642-7800 *SIC 6726*

QUORUM FUNDING CORPORATION *p966*
70 YORK ST SUITE 1720, TORONTO, ON, M5J 1S9
SIC 6726

ROGERS SUGAR INC *p1168*
4026 RUE NOTRE-DAME E, MONTREAL, QC, H1W 2K3
(514) 940-4350 *SIC 6726*

SARONA ASSET MANAGEMENT INC *p640*
55 VICTORIA ST N UNIT K, KITCHENER, ON, N2H 5B7
(519) 883-7557 *SIC 6726*

SIR ROYALTY INCOME FUND *p525*
5360 SOUTH SERVICE RD SUITE 200, BURLINGTON, ON, L7L 5L1
(905) 681-2997 *SIC 6726*

SPROTT PHYSICAL GOLD & SILVER TRUST *p967*
200 BAY ST SUITE 2600, TORONTO, ON, M5J 2J1
(877) 403-2310 *SIC 6726*

TRIAX DIVERSIFIED HIGH-YIELD TRUST *p968*
95 WELLINGTON ST W SUITE 1400, TORONTO, ON, M5J 2N7
(416) 362-2929 *SIC 6726*

URBANA CORPORATION *p958*
150 KING ST W SUITE 1702, TORONTO, ON, M5H 1J9
(416) 595-9106 *SIC 6726*

VANGUARD FTSE DEVELOPED EX NORTH AMERICA INDEX ETF *p984*
155 WELLINGTON ST W SUITE 3720, TORONTO, ON, M5V 3H1
(888) 293-6728 *SIC 6726*

SIC 6732 Trusts: educational, religious, etc.

AGA KHAN FOUNDATION CANADA *p821*
199 SUSSEX DR, OTTAWA, ON, K1N 1K6
(613) 237-2532 *SIC 6732*

BEARDY'S & OKEMASIS WILLOW CREE FIRST NATION EDUCATION AUTHORITY *p1405*
GD, DUCK LAKE, SK, S0K 1J0
(306) 467-4441 *SIC 6732*

C.S.T. CONSULTANTS INC *p766*
2235 SHEPPARD AVE E UNIT 1600, NORTH YORK, ON, M2J 5B8
(416) 445-7377 *SIC 6732*

CANADA COUNCIL FOR THE ARTS *p822*
150 ELGIN ST, OTTAWA, ON, K1P 5V8
(613) 566-4414 *SIC 6732*

CANADIAN SCHOLARSHIP TRUST FOUNDATION *p766*
2225 SHEPPARD AVE E SUITE 600, NORTH YORK, ON, M2J 5C2
(416) 445-7377 *SIC 6732*

FONDATION UNIVERSITAS DU CANADA *p1274*
1035 AV WILFRID-PELLETIER BUREAU 500, QUEBEC, QC, G1W 0C5
(877) 410-7333 *SIC 6732*

GLOBAL RESP CORPORATION *p852*
100 MURAL ST SUITE 201, RICHMOND HILL, ON, L4B 1J3

(416) 741-7377   *SIC 6732*
HERITAGE EDUCATION FUNDS INC   *p767*
2005 SHEPPARD AVE E SUITE 700, NORTH YORK, ON, M2J 5B4
(416) 758-4400   *SIC 6732*
INDO CANADIAN CENTRE   *p23*
826 EDMONTON TRAIL NE, CALGARY, AB, T2E 3J6
(403) 277-1459   *SIC 6732*
KNOWLEDGE FIRST FINANCIAL INC   *p710*
50 BURNHAMTHORPE RD W SUITE 1000, MISSISSAUGA, ON, L5B 4A5
(905) 270-8777   *SIC 6732*
ST MICHAEL'S HOSPITAL FOUNDATION   *p936*
30 BOND ST, TORONTO, ON, M5B 1W8
(416) 864-5000   *SIC 6732*
TEMA CONTER MEMORIAL TRUST, THE   *p629*
175 PATRICIA DR, KING CITY, ON, L7B 1H3   *SIC 6732*
TERRY FOX FOUNDATION, THE   *p183*
8960 UNIVERSITY HIGH ST SUITE 150, BURNABY, BC, V5A 4Y6
(604) 200-0541   *SIC 6732*
UNITED JEWISH APPEAL OF GREATER TORONTO   *p775*
4600 BATHURST ST UNIT 5, NORTH YORK, ON, M2R 3V3
(416) 631-5716   *SIC 6732*
UNITED WAY/CENTRAIDE OTTAWA   *p820*
363 COVENTRY RD, OTTAWA, ON, K1K 2C5
(613) 228-6700   *SIC 6732*
VILLA CHARITIES INC   *p790*
901 LAWRENCE AVE W, NORTH YORK, ON, M6A 1C3
(416) 789-7011   *SIC 6732*
ZOOLOGICAL SOCIETY OF MANITOBA   *p389*
54 ZOO DR, WINNIPEG, MB, R3P 2N8
(204) 982-0660   *SIC 6732*

SIC 6733 Trusts, nec

ANNAPOLIS VALLEY WORK ACTIVITY SOCIETY   *p459*
11 OPPORTUNITY LANE, KENTVILLE, NS, B4N 3V7
(902) 679-2755   *SIC 6733*
ASTON HILL VIP INCOME FUND   *p968*
77 KING ST W SUITE 2110, TORONTO, ON, M5K 2A1
(416) 583-2300   *SIC 6733*
BANK OF NOVA SCOTIA, THE   *p948*
44 KING ST W SCOTIA PLAZA, TORONTO, ON, M5H 1H1
(416) 866-6161   *SIC 6733*
BOSA PROPERTIES INC   *p302*
838 HASTINGS ST W SUITE 1201, VANCOUVER, BC, V6C 0A6
(604) 299-1363   *SIC 6733*
CHILDREN'S EDUCATIONAL FOUNDATION OF CANADA, THE   *p738*
6705 TOMKEN RD UNIT 236, MISSISSAUGA, ON, L5T 2J6
    SIC 6733
COMPUTERSHARE TRUST COMPANY OF CANADA   *p961*
100 UNIVERSITY AVE SUITE 800, TORONTO, ON, M5J 2Y1
(416) 263-9200   *SIC 6733*
COMPUTERSHARE TRUST COMPANY OF CANADA   *p1194*
1500 BOUL ROBERT-BOURASSA BUREAU 700, MONTREAL, QC, H3A 3S8
(514) 982-7888   *SIC 6733*
D & D ASSOCIATES LTD   *p904*
8199 YONGE ST SUITE 401, THORNHILL, ON, L3T 2C6
(905) 881-5575   *SIC 6733*
DELOITTE LLP   *p1079*
901 BOUL TALBOT BUREAU 400,

CHICOUTIMI, QC, G7H 0A1
(418) 549-6650   *SIC 6733*
DURAND NEIGHBOURHOOD INVESTMENTS INC   *p612*
15 BOLD ST, HAMILTON, ON, L8P 1T3
    SIC 6733
ERNST & YOUNG INC   *p969*
222 BAY ST, TORONTO, ON, M5K 1J7
(416) 864-1234   *SIC 6733*
FIDUCIE DESJARDINS INC   *p1230*
1 COMPLEXE DESJARDINS TOUR S, MONTREAL, QC, H5B 1E4
(514) 286-9441   *SIC 6733*
MANCAL CORPORATION   *p53*
530 8 AVE SW SUITE 1600, CALGARY, AB, T2P 3S8
(403) 231-7580   *SIC 6733*
MENNONITE TRUST LTD   *p1437*
3005 CENTRAL AVE, WALDHEIM, SK, S0K 4R0
(306) 945-2080   *SIC 6733*
PROSPER CANADA   *p926*
60 ST CLAIR AVENUE E SUITE 700, TORONTO, ON, M4T 1N5
(416) 665-2828   *SIC 6733*
PUBLIC GUARDIAN AND TRUSTEE OF BRITISH COLUMBIA   *p308*
808 HASTINGS ST W SUITE 700, VANCOUVER, BC, V6C 3L3
(604) 660-4444   *SIC 6733*
PUBLIC TRUSTEE OFFICE   *p379*
155 CARLTON ST SUITE 500, WINNIPEG, MB, R3C 5R9
(204) 945-2700   *SIC 6733*
VESTCOR INVESTMENT MANAGEMENT CORPORATION, THE   *p402*
440 KING ST SUITE 581, FREDERICTON, NB, E3B 5H8
(506) 444-5800   *SIC 6733*

SIC 6792 Oil royalty traders

FREEHOLD ROYALTIES LTD   *p49*
144 4 AVE SW SUITE 400, CALGARY, AB, T2P 3N4
(403) 221-0802   *SIC 6792*
NORTHERN BLIZZARD   *p55*
440 2 AVE SW, CALGARY, AB, T2P 5E9
(403) 930-3000   *SIC 6792*

SIC 6794 Patent owners and lessors

1716871 ONTARIO INC   *p615*
1460 STONE CHURCH RD E, HAMILTON, ON, L8W 3V3
(905) 388-2264   *SIC 6794*
2281445 ONTARIO INC   *p870*
77 PROGRESS AVE, SCARBOROUGH, ON, M1P 2Y7
(416) 288-8515   *SIC 6794*
3 FOR 1 PIZZA & WINGS INC   *p958*
10 BAY ST SUITE 802, TORONTO, ON, M5J 2R8
(416) 360-0888   *SIC 6794*
709528 ONTARIO LTD   *p932*
246 PARLIAMENT ST, TORONTO, ON, M5A 3A4
    SIC 6794
9100-9647 QUEBEC INC   *p1277*
2800 AV SAINT-JEAN-BAPTISTE BUREAU 235, QUEBEC, QC, G2E 6J5
(418) 527-7775   *SIC 6794*
AQUARIUM SERVICES WAREHOUSE OUTLETS INC   *p1029*
441 CHRISLEA RD, WOODBRIDGE, ON, L4L 8N4
(905) 851-1858   *SIC 6794*
BIO PED FRANCHISING INC   *p796*
2150 WINSTON PARK DR UNIT 21, OAKVILLE, ON, L6H 5V1
(905) 829-0505   *SIC 6794*
BODY SHOP CANADA LIMITED, THE   *p788*

1 YORKDALE RD SUITE 510, NORTH YORK, ON, M6A 3A1
(416) 782-2948   *SIC 6794*
BOSTON PIZZA INTERNATIONAL INC   *p259*
10760 SHELLBRIDGE WAY UNIT 100, RICHMOND, BC, V6X 3H1
(604) 270-1108   *SIC 6794*
CAFE DEPOT INC, LE   *p1171*
2464 RUE JEAN-TALON E, MONTREAL, QC, H2E 1W2
(514) 281-2067   *SIC 6794*
CANADIAN COPYRIGHT LICENSING AGENCY   *p942*
1 YONGE ST SUITE 800, TORONTO, ON, M5E 1E5
(416) 868-1620   *SIC 6794*
CANADIAN MUSICAL REPRODUCTION RIGHTS AGENCY LIMITED, THE   *p974*
56 WELLESLEY ST W SUITE 320, TORONTO, ON, M5S 2S3
(416) 926-1966   *SIC 6794*
CHAIRMAN'S BRAND CORPORATION   *p870*
77 PROGRESS AVE, SCARBOROUGH, ON, M1P 2Y7
(416) 288-8515   *SIC 6794*
CHOICE HOTELS CANADA INC   *p693*
5015 SPECTRUM WAY SUITE 400, MISSISSAUGA, ON, L4W 0E4
(905) 602-2222   *SIC 6794*
CKRM NEWS   *p1417*
1900 ROSE ST, REGINA, SK, S4P 0A9
(306) 546-6200   *SIC 6794*
CLUB PISCINE PLUS QUEBEC C.P.P.Q. INC, LE   *p1060*
888 BOUL INDUSTRIEL, BOIS-DESFILION, QC, J6Z 4V1
(450) 965-9249   *SIC 6794*
COFFEE TIME DONUTS INCORPORATED   *p871*
77 PROGRESS AVE, SCARBOROUGH, ON, M1P 2Y7
(416) 288-8515   *SIC 6794*
CONREZ GROUP LTD, THE   *p919*
366 DANFORTH AVE SUITE A, TORONTO, ON, M4K 1N8
(416) 449-7444   *SIC 6794*
CORA FRANCHISE GROUP INC, THE   *p685*
2798 THAMESGATE DR UNIT 1, MISSISSAUGA, ON, L4T 4E8
(905) 673-2672   *SIC 6794*
CRUISESHIPCENTERS INTERNATIONAL INC   *p312*
1055 HASTINGS ST W SUITE 400, VANCOUVER, BC, V6E 2E9
(604) 685-1221   *SIC 6794*
D & L CRANSTON HOLDINGS LTD   *p145*
1601 DUNMORE RD SE SUITE 107, MEDICINE HAT, AB, T1A 1Z8
(800) 665-5122   *SIC 6794*
DAKIN NEWS SYSTEMS INC   *p718*
238 QUEEN ST S SUITE 2, MISSISSAUGA, ON, L5M 1L5
(905) 826-0862   *SIC 6794*
DE DUTCH PANNEKOEK HOUSE RESTAURANTS INC   *p281*
8484 162 ST SUITE 108, SURREY, BC, V4N 1B4
(604) 543-3101   *SIC 6794*
DOUBLE DOUBLE PIZZA CHICKEN LTD   *p584*
1 GREENSBORO DR SUITE 28, ETOBICOKE, ON, M9W 1C8
(416) 241-0088   *SIC 6794*
EDO INTERNATIONAL FOOD INC   *p12*
4838 32 ST SE, CALGARY, AB, T2B 2S6
(403) 215-8800   *SIC 6794*
ENTREPRISES MTY TIKI MING INC, LES   *p1333*
8210 RTE TRANSCANADIENNE, SAINTLAURENT, QC, H4S 1M5
(514) 368-8885   *SIC 6794*
EXTREME RETAIL CANADA INC   *p1031*
11 DIRECTOR CRT SUITE 554, WOODBRIDGE, ON, L4L 4S5

(905) 265-3160   *SIC 6794*
FABUTAN CORPORATION   *p35*
5925 3 ST SE, CALGARY, AB, T2H 1K3
(403) 640-2100   *SIC 6794*
FIRST CHOICE HAIRCUTTERS LTD   *p722*
6400 MILLCREEK DR, MISSISSAUGA, ON, L5N 3E7
(905) 858-8100   *SIC 6794*
FRANCHISES CORA INC   *p1364*
16 RUE SICARD BUREAU 50, SAINTETHERESE, QC, J7E 3W7
(450) 435-2426   *SIC 6794*
GLASWEGIAN ENTERPRISES INC   *p200*
1090 LOUGHEED HWY SUITE 214, COQUITLAM, BC, V3K 6G9
(604) 522-4000   *SIC 6794*
GRINNER'S FOOD SYSTEMS LIMITED   *p469*
105 WALKER ST, TRURO, NS, B2N 4B1
(902) 893-4141   *SIC 6794*
GROUPE CAFE VIENNE 1998 INC, LE   *p1210*
1422 RUE NOTRE-DAME O, MONTREAL, QC, H3C 1K9
(514) 935-5553   *SIC 6794*
GROUPE D'ALIMENTATION MTY INC   *p1334*
8210 RTE TRANSCANADIENNE, SAINTLAURENT, QC, H4S 1M5
(514) 336-8885   *SIC 6794*
GROUPE MAD SCIENCE INC   *p1227*
8360 RUE BOUGAINVILLE BUREAU 201, MONTREAL, QC, H4P 2G1
(514) 344-4181   *SIC 6794*
GROUPE RESTAURANTS IMVESCOR INC   *p1228*
8150 RTE TRANSCANADIENNE BUREAU 310, MONTREAL, QC, H4S 1M5
(514) 341-5544   *SIC 6794*
GROUPE RESTAURANTS IMVESCOR INC   *p1279*
1875 RUE BOUVIER, QUEBEC, QC, G2K 0B5
(418) 624-2525   *SIC 6794*
HIGHFIELD HOLDINGS INC   *p1031*
101 JEVLAN DR SUITE 1, WOODBRIDGE, ON, L4L 8C2
(905) 264-2799   *SIC 6794*
HUMPTY'S RESTAURANTS INTERNATIONAL INC   *p30*
2505 MACLEOD TRAIL SW, CALGARY, AB, T2G 5J4
(403) 269-4675   *SIC 6794*
INTEGRICO INC   *p491*
199 FRONT ST SUITE 215, BELLEVILLE, ON, K8N 5H5
(613) 966-6466   *SIC 6794*
JAN-PRO CANADA EST INC   *p1264*
2323 BOUL DU VERSANT-NORD BUREAU 114, QUEBEC, QC, G1N 4P4
(418) 527-1400   *SIC 6794*
JAN-PRO CANADA INC   *p1264*
2323 BOUL DU VERSANT-NORD BUREAU 114, QUEBEC, QC, G1N 4P4
(418) 527-1400   *SIC 6794*
KENTUCKY FRIED CHICKEN CANADA COMPANY   *p1003*
191 CREDITVIEW RD UNIT 100, VAUGHAN, ON, L4L 9T1
(416) 664-5200   *SIC 6794*
KEYCORP INC   *p430*
303 THORBURN RD, ST. JOHN'S, NL, A1B 4R1
(709) 753-2284   *SIC 6794*
L.A.M.M. INC   *p858*
1273 LONDON RD, SARNIA, ON, N7S 1P3
(519) 383-7727   *SIC 6794*
MADE IN JAPAN JAPANESE RESTAURANTS LIMITED   *p802*
700 KERR ST SUITE 100, OAKVILLE, ON, L6K 3W5
(905) 337-7777   *SIC 6794*
MBEC COMMUNICATIONS INC   *p806*
1115 NORTH SERVICE RD W UNIT 1, OAKVILLE, ON, L6M 2V9
(905) 338-9754   *SIC 6794*
MONDOFIX INC   *p1059*

▲ Public Company   ■ Public Company Family Member   **HQ** Headquarters   **BR** Branch   **SL** Single Location

99 RUE EMILIEN-MARCOUX BUREAU 101, BLAINVILLE, QC, J7C 0B4
(450) 433-1414   *SIC* 6794

MR. GREEK RESTAURANTS INC   *p780*
49 THE DONWAY W SUITE 402, NORTH YORK, ON, M3C 3M9
(416) 444-3266   *SIC* 6794

MR. LUBE CANADA LIMITED PARTNERSHIP   *p258*
6900 GRAYBAR RD SUITE 2330, RICHMOND, BC, V6W 0A5
(604) 759-4300   *SIC* 6794

MR. SUBMARINE LIMITED   *p772*
4576 YONGE ST SUITE 600, NORTH YORK, ON, M2N 6N4
(416) 225-5545   *SIC* 6794

NUTRITION HOUSE CANADA INC   *p853*
80 WEST BEAVER CREEK RD UNIT 12, RICHMOND HILL, ON, L4B 1H3
(905) 707-7633   *SIC* 6794

OBSIDIAN GROUP INC   *p725*
1770 ARGENTIA RD, MISSISSAUGA, ON, L5N 3S7
(905) 814-8030   *SIC* 6794

ORANGE JULIUS CANADA LIMITED   *p523*
5045 SOUTH SERVICE RD SUITE 3000, BURLINGTON, ON, L7L 5Y7
(905) 639-1492   *SIC* 6794

PANAGO PIZZA INC   *p175*
33149 MILL LAKE RD, ABBOTSFORD, BC, V2S 2A4
(604) 859-6621   *SIC* 6794

PHARMAPRIX INC   *p1226*
400 AV SAITE-CROIX BUREAU 200, MONTREAL, QC, H4N 3L4
(514) 933-9331   *SIC* 6794

PHARMASAVE DRUGS (NATIONAL) LTD   *p226*
8411 200 ST SUITE 201, LANGLEY, BC, V2Y 0E7
(604) 455-2400   *SIC* 6794

PIZZAVILLE INC   *p1033*
741 ROWNTREE DAIRY RD UNIT 1, WOODBRIDGE, ON, L4L 5T9
(905) 850-0070   *SIC* 6794

PREMIERE VAN LINES INC   *p699*
5800 AMBLER DR UNIT 210, MISSISSAUGA, ON, L4W 4J4
(905) 712-8960   *SIC* 6794

QUIZNO'S CANADA RESTAURANT CORPORATION   *p983*
355 KING ST W SUITE 300, TORONTO, ON, M5V 1J6
(647) 259-0333   *SIC* 6794

RDHR INVESTMENTS & HOLDINGS INC   *p717*
2187 DUNWIN DR, MISSISSAUGA, ON, L5L 1X2
(905) 820-7887   *SIC* 6794

RE:SOUND   *p973*
1235 BAY ST SUITE 900, TORONTO, ON, M5R 3K4
(416) 968-8870   *SIC* 6794

REDBERRY FRANCHISING CORP   *p579*
401 THE WEST MALL SUITE 700, ETOBICOKE, ON, M9C 5J4
(416) 626-6464   *SIC* 6794

RESEARCH AND MANAGEMENT CORPORATION   *p587*
20 CARLSON CRT SUITE 10, ETOBICOKE, ON, M9W 7K6
(905) 678-7588   *SIC* 6794

RESTAURANTS P & P INC, LES   *p1123*
170 BOUL TASCHEREAU BUREAU 300, LA PRAIRIE, QC, J5R 5H6
(450) 444-4749   *SIC* 6794

ROTISSERIES ST-HUBERT LTEE, LES   *p1087*
2500 BOUL DANIEL-JOHNSON BUREAU 700, COTE SAINT-LUC, QC, H7T 2P6
(450) 435-0674   *SIC* 6794

ROTISSERIES ST-HUBERT LTEE, LES   *p1219*
5235 CH DE LA COTE-DES-NEIGES, MON-

TREAL, QC, H3T 1Y1
(514) 342-9495   *SIC* 6794

SELECT FOOD SERVICES INC   *p765*
155 GORDON BAKER RD UNIT 214, NORTH YORK, ON, M2H 3N5
(416) 391-1244   *SIC* 6794

SERVICEMASTER OF CANADA LIMITED   *p700*
5462 TIMBERLEA BLVD, MISSISSAUGA, ON, L4W 2T7
(905) 670-0000   *SIC* 6794

SHAPIRO COHEN LLP   *p625*
555 LEGGET DR SUITE 830, KANATA, ON, K2K 2X3
(613) 232-5300   *SIC* 6794

SHOPPERS DRUG MART INC   *p745*
60 COURTNEYPARK DR W, MISSISSAUGA, ON, L5W 0B3
(416) 493-1220   *SIC* 6794

SHRED-IT AMERICA INC   *p801*
2794 SOUTH SHERIDAN WAY, OAKVILLE, ON, L6J 7T4
(905) 829-2794   *SIC* 6794

SODRAC (2003) INC   *p1199*
1470 RUE PEEL BUREAU 1010, MONTREAL, QC, H3A 1T1
(514) 845-3268   *SIC* 6794

SPEEDY CREEK (2011) LTD   *p123*
514 RONNING ST. NW, EDMONTON, AB, T6R 1B7
(780) 486-2882   *SIC* 6794

STOCKSY UNITED CO-OP   *p337*
560 JOHNSON ST SUITE 320, VICTORIA, BC, V8W 3C6
(250) 590-7308   *SIC* 6794

STONEWATER GROUP OF FRANCHISES   *p199*
2991 LOUGHEED HWY UNIT 32, COQUITLAM, BC, V3B 6J6
(604) 529-9220   *SIC* 6794

SUPERCLUB VIDEOTRON LTEE, LE   *p1173*
4545 RUE FRONTENAC BUREAU 101, MONTREAL, QC, H2H 2R7
(514) 259-6000   *SIC* 6794

SUTTON GROUP REALTY SERVICES LTD   *p300*
1080 MAINLAND ST SUITE 206, VANCOUVER, BC, V6B 2T4
(604) 568-1005   *SIC* 6794

T.F.G. (1987) LTD   *p388*
834 CORYDON AVE SUITE 1, WINNIPEG, MB, R3M 0Y2
SIC 6794

TDL GROUP CORP, THE   *p987*
130 KING ST SUITE 300, TORONTO, ON, M5X 1E1
(905) 845-6511   *SIC* 6794

TRADERS INTERNATIONAL FRANCHISE MANAGEMENT INC   *p335*
508 DISCOVERY ST, VICTORIA, BC, V8T 1G8
SIC 6794

ULTRACUTS LTD   *p364*
167 ST MARY'S RD, WINNIPEG, MB, R2H 1J1
(204) 231-0110   *SIC* 6794

UNIGLOBE TRAVEL (WESTERN CANADA) INC   *p320*
2695 GRANVILLE ST SUITE 600, VANCOUVER, BC, V6H 3H4
(604) 602-3470   *SIC* 6794

WALT DISNEY COMPANY (CANADA) LTD, THE   *p984*
200 FRONT ST W SUITE 2900, TORONTO, ON, M5V 3L4
(416) 596-7000   *SIC* 6794

WE CARE HEALTH SERVICES INC   *p572*
3300 BLOOR ST W SUITE 900, ETOBICOKE, ON, M8X 2X2
(416) 922-7601   *SIC* 6794

WINDSOR BUILDING SUPPLIES LTD   *p226*
20039 96 AVE, LANGLEY, BC, V1M 3C6
(604) 455-9663   *SIC* 6794

WINNERS HOME CENTRAL INC   *p894*

2105 RYMAL RD E, STONEY CREEK, ON, L8J 2R8
(905) 560-0800   *SIC* 6794

YOGEN FRUZ CANADA INC   *p677*
210 SHIELDS CRT SUITE 1, MARKHAM, ON, L3R 8V2
(905) 479-8762   *SIC* 6794

SIC 6798 Real estate investment trusts

AGELLAN COMMERCIAL REIT HOLDINGS INC   *p927*
890 YONGE ST STE 505, TORONTO, ON, M4W 3P4
(416) 593-6800   *SIC* 6798

ALLIED PROPERTIES REAL ESTATE INVESTMENT TRUST   *p978*
134 PETER ST SUITE 1700, TORONTO, ON, M5V 2H2
(416) 977-9002   *SIC* 6798

AMERICAN HOTEL INCOME PROPERTIES REIT LP   *p302*
925 GEORGIA ST W SUITE 800, VANCOUVER, BC, V6C 3L2
(604) 630-3134   *SIC* 6798

BROOKFIELD PROPERTY PARTNERS L.P.   *p960*
181 BAY ST SUITE 300, TORONTO, ON, M5J 2T3
(416) 363-9491   *SIC* 6798

CALLOWAY REIT (CARLETON) INC   *p549*
700 APPLEWOOD CRES SUITE 200, CONCORD, ON, L4K 5X3
(905) 326-6400   *SIC* 6798

CALLOWAY REIT (SOUTH KEYS) INC   *p549*
700 APPLEWOOD CRES SUITE 20, CONCORD, ON, L4K 5X3
(905) 326-6400   *SIC* 6798

CHOICE PROPERTIES REAL ESTATE INVESTMENT TRUST   *p928*
175 BLOOR ST E SUITE 1400N, TORONTO, ON, M4W 3R8
(416) 324-7840   *SIC* 6798

CITY OFFICE REIT, INC   *p312*
1075 GEORGIA ST W SUITE 2010, VANCOUVER, BC, V6E 3C9
(604) 806-3366   *SIC* 6798

CROMBIE REAL ESTATE INVESTMENT TRUST   *p463*
610 EAST RIVER RD SUITE 200, NEW GLASGOW, NS, B2H 3S2
(902) 755-8100   *SIC* 6798

CT REAL ESTATE INVESTMENT TRUST   *p922*
2180 YONGE ST, TORONTO, ON, M4P 2V8
(416) 480-2029   *SIC* 6798

DREAM INDUSTRIAL REAL ESTATE INVESTMENT TRUST   *p938*
30 ADELAIDE STREET E SUITE 301, TORONTO, ON, M5C 3H1
(416) 365-3535   *SIC* 6798

DREAM OFFICE REAL ESTATE INVESTMENT TRUST   *p938*
30 ADELAIDE ST E SUITE 301, TORONTO, ON, M5C 3H1
(416) 365-3535   *SIC* 6798

EDMONTON HOUSE REALTY LTD   *p88*
10205 100 AVE NW SUITE 3400, EDMONTON, AB, T5J 4B5
(780) 420-4040   *SIC* 6798

FIRST NATIONAL FINANCIAL CORPORATION   *p962*
100 UNIVERSITY AVE SUITE 700, TORONTO, ON, M5J 1V6
(416) 593-1100   *SIC* 6798

FONDS DE PLACEMENT IMMOBILIER BTB   *p1213*
1411 RUE CRESCENT BUREAU 300, MONTREAL, QC, H3G 2B3
(514) 286-0188   *SIC* 6798

GRANITE REIT INC   *p969*
77 KING ST W, TORONTO, ON, M5K 2A1
(647) 925-7500   *SIC* 6798

H & R (U.S.) HOLDINGS INC   *p785*
3625 DEUFFERIN ST SUITE 500, NORTH YORK, ON, M3K 1N4
(416) 635-7520   *SIC* 6798

H&R REAL ESTATE INVESTMENT TRUST   *p785*
3625 DUFFERIN ST SUITE 500, NORTH YORK, ON, M3K 1Z2
(416) 635-7520   *SIC* 6798

KILLAM APARTMENT REAL ESTATE INVESTMENT TRUST   *p455*
3700 KEMPT RD SUITE 100, HALIFAX, NS, B3K 4X8
(902) 453-9000   *SIC* 6798

KINGSETT CAPITAL INC   *p953*
40 KING ST W SUITE 3700, TORONTO, ON, M5H 3Y2
(416) 687-6700   *SIC* 6798

MCAN MORTGAGE CORPORATION   *p954*
200 KING ST W SUITE 600, TORONTO, ON, M5H 3T4
(416) 572-4880   *SIC* 6798

MEGAFORTUNE INTERNATIONAL INC   *p40*
3500 VARSITY DR NW UNIT 1608, CALGARY, AB, T2L 1Y3
(403) 261-8881   *SIC* 6798

MORGUARD INVESTMENTS LIMITED   *p710*
55 CITY CENTRE DR SUITE 800, MISSISSAUGA, ON, L5B 1M3
(905) 281-3800   *SIC* 6798

MORGUARD NORTH AMERICAN RESIDENTIAL REAL ESTATE INVESTMENT TRUST   *p710*
55 CITY CENTRE DR SUITE 1000, MISSISSAUGA, ON, L5B 1M3
(905) 281-3800   *SIC* 6798

MORTGAGE CENTRE (CANADA) INC, THE   *p954*
123 QUEEN ST W SUITE 403, TORONTO, ON, M5H 3M9
(416) 865-9750   *SIC* 6798

NEXUS REAL ESTATE INVESTMENT TRUST   *p801*
340 CHURCH ST, OAKVILLE, ON, L6J 1P1
(416) 613-1262   *SIC* 6798

NORTHWEST HEALTHCARE PROPERTIES REAL ESTATE INVESTMENT TRUST   *p946*
180 DUNDAS ST W SUITE 1100, TORONTO, ON, M5G 1Z8
(416) 366-2000   *SIC* 6798

PARTNERS REAL ESTATE INVESTMENT TRUST   *p488*
249 SAUNDERS RD UNIT 3, BARRIE, ON, L4N 9A3
(705) 725-6020   *SIC* 6798

R&R REAL ESTATE INVESTMENT TRUST   *p699*
5090 EXPLORER DR SUITE 700, MISSISSAUGA, ON, L4W 4X6
(905) 206-7100   *SIC* 6798

RIOCAN REAL ESTATE INVESTMENT TRUST   *p923*
2300 YONGE ST SUITE 500, TORONTO, ON, M4P 1E4
(416) 866-3033   *SIC* 6798

SITQ NATIONAL INC   *p1192*
1001 RUE DU SQUARE-VICTORIA BUREAU C 200, MONTREAL, QC, H2Z 2B1
(514) 287-1852   *SIC* 6798

SLATE OFFICE II L.P.   *p957*
121 KING ST W SUITE 200, TORONTO, ON, M5H 3T9
(416) 644-4264   *SIC* 6798

SLATE OFFICE REIT   *p957*
121 KING ST W SUITE 200, TORONTO, ON, M5H 3T9
(416) 644-4264   *SIC* 6798

SLATE RETAIL REAL ESTATE INVESTMENT TRUST   *p957*
121 KING ST W SUITE 200, TORONTO, ON, M5H 3T9
(416) 644-4264   *SIC* 6798

SNC-LAVALIN INC   *p396*
88 SR GREEN RD SUITE 101, CAMPBELL-

TON, NB, E3N 3Y6
(506) 759-6350   *SIC 6798*
TEMPLE HOTELS INC   *p711*
55 CITY CENTRE DR SUITE 1000, MISSIS-SAUGA, ON, L5B 1M3
(905) 281-4800   *SIC 6798*
TITLE & JONES INVESTMENTS LTD   *p707*
4230 SHERWOODTOWNE BLVD, MISSIS-SAUGA, ON, L4Z 2G6
(905) 281-3463   *SIC 6798*

SIC 6799 Investors, nec

ALL IN WESTU CAPITAL CORPORATION
p376
360 MAIN ST SUITE 400, WINNIPEG, MB, R3C 3Z3
(204) 947-1200   *SIC 6799*
BRANCH FINANCE CORPORATION LIM-ITED   *p881*
5 CHAMBERS ST, SMITHS FALLS, ON, K7A 2Y2
(613) 283-5555   *SIC 6799*
C.B. CONSTANTINI LTD   *p326*
910-980 HOWE ST, VANCOUVER, BC, V6Z 0C8
(604) 669-1212   *SIC 6799*
CANADA NATIONAL OWN COMPANY (CNOC)   *p919*
71 THORNCLIFFE PARK DR SUITE 403, TORONTO, ON, M4H 1L3
(647) 520-9004   *SIC 6799*
CHIEF ISAAC INCORPORATED   *p1440*
1371 2 AVE, DAWSON, YT, Y0B 1G0
(867) 993-5384   *SIC 6799*
CONSULATE GENERAL OF THE REPUB-LIC OF KOREA COMMERCIAL SECTION
p950
65 QUEEN ST W SUITE 600, TORONTO, ON, M5H 2M5
(416) 368-3399   *SIC 6799*
DANIELS CORPORATION, THE   *p933*
130 QUEENS QUAY E 8 FL, TORONTO, ON, M5A 0P6
(416) 598-2129   *SIC 6799*
DEQ SYSTEMS CORP   *p1138*
1840 1RE RUE BUREAU 103A, LEVIS, QC, G6W 5M6
(418) 839-3012   *SIC 6799*
DOMGEN INVESTMENTS INC   *p1333*
9500 BOUL HENRI-BOURASSA O, SAINT-LAURENT, QC, H4S 1N8
SIC 6799
DORCHESTER CORPORATION, THE   *p915*
4120 YONGE ST SUITE 215, TORONTO, ON, M2P 2C6
(416) 628-6238   *SIC 6799*
DORCHESTER OAKS CORPORATION   *p774*
120 YONGE ST SUITE 215, NORTH YORK, ON, M2P 2B8
(416) 628-6238   *SIC 6799*
ETG COMMODITIES INC   *p739*
6220 SHAWSON DR, MISSISSAUGA, ON, L5T 1J8
(416) 900-4148   *SIC 6799*
F.I.D. FUTUR INTERNATIONAL DIVERSIFIE INC   *p1060*
926 RUE JACQUES PASCHINI, BOIS-DES-FILION, QC, J6Z 4W4
(450) 621-4230   *SIC 6799*
FONDACTION, LE FONDS DE DEVEL-OPPEMENT DE LA CSN POUR LA COOP-ERATION ET L'EMPLOI   *p1174*
2175 BOUL DE MAISONNEUVE E BU-REAU 103, MONTREAL, QC, H2K 4S3
(514) 525-5505   *SIC 6799*
FONDS DE PLACEMENT IMMOBILIER COMINAR   *p1272*
2820 BOUL LAURIER BUREAU 850, QUE-BEC, QC, G1V 0C1
(418) 681-8151   *SIC 6799*
GLOBAL COMMERCIAL FINANCIAL INC
p852

45B WEST WILMOT ST SUITE 208, RICH-MOND HILL, ON, L4B 2P3
(905) 470-2127   *SIC 6799*
GP INTERNATIONAL INC   *p731*
796 FOUR WINDS WAY, MISSISSAUGA, ON, L5R 3W8
(416) 948-0336   *SIC 6799*
GREENERGY FUELS CANADA INC   *p415*
107 GERMAIN ST SUITE 300, SAINT JOHN, NB, E2L 2E9
(506) 632-1650   *SIC 6799*
GROUPE KDA INC   *p1383*
1351 RUE NOTRE-DAME E BUREAU 300, THETFORD MINES, QC, G6G 0G5
(514) 622-7370   *SIC 6799*
GROWTHWORKS CAPITAL LTD   *p313*
1055 GEORGIA ST W SUITE 2600, VAN-COUVER, BC, V6E 0B6
(604) 633-1418   *SIC 6799*
HURON COMMODITIES INC   *p544*
75 WELLINGTON ST, CLINTON, ON, N0M 1L0
(519) 482-8400   *SIC 6799*
ICE NGX CANADA INC   *p51*
300 5 AVE SW SUITE 1000, CALGARY, AB, T2P 3C4
(403) 974-1700   *SIC 6799*
IFABRIC CORP   *p671*
525 DENISON ST UNIT 2, MARKHAM, ON, L3R 1B8
(905) 752-0566   *SIC 6799*
IMPORT EXPORT SEAPASS INC   *p1149*
321 MONTEE MASSON BUREAU 301, MASCOUCHE, QC, J7K 2L6
(450) 918-4300   *SIC 6799*
JINZE (CANADA) CO., LTD   *p852*
9140 LESLIE ST SUITE 311 & 312, RICH-MOND HILL, ON, L4B 0A9
(905) 762-9300   *SIC 6799*
KELLER WILLIAMS INTEGRITY REALTY
p832
245 MENTEN PL UNIT 100, OTTAWA, ON, K2H 9E8
(613) 829-1818   *SIC 6799*
KIMATSU ENTERPRISES   *p772*
5334 YONGE ST, NORTH YORK, ON, M2N 6V1
SIC 6799
KTS TRADING INC   *p723*
3744 TRELAWNY CIR, MISSISSAUGA, ON, L5N 5J7
(905) 824-5679   *SIC 6799*
LASSER PRODUCE LTD   *p223*
601 KEREMEOS BYPASS RD, KERE-MEOS, BC, V0X 1N1
(250) 506-0707   *SIC 6799*
LONDON AGRICULTURAL COMMODITIES INC   *p658*
1615 NORTH ROUTLEDGE PK UNIT 43, LONDON, ON, N6H 5L6
(519) 473-9333   *SIC 6799*
M PRIVATE RESIDENCES INC   *p65*
322 11 AVE SW SUITE 205, CALGARY, AB, T2R 0C5
(403) 264-0993   *SIC 6799*
MAGRIS RESOURCES INC   *p954*
333 BAY ST SUITE 1101, TORONTO, ON, M5H 2R2
(416) 901-9877   *SIC 6799*
METFIN PROPERTIES LIMITED PARTNER-SHIP   *p982*
266 KING ST W SUITE 405, TORONTO, ON, M5V 1H8
(416) 360-0122   *SIC 6799*
OCEAN WAVE IMPORTS INC   *p689*
6295 NORTHAM DR UNIT 14, MISSIS-SAUGA, ON, L4V 1W8
(905) 672-5050   *SIC 6799*
OSMAN GLOBAL TRADING LTD   *p119*
3214 82 ST NW, EDMONTON, AB, T6K 3Y3
(780) 757-8100   *SIC 6799*
PACIFIC LINK MINING CORP   *p315*
1055 GEORGIA ST W SUITE 2772, VAN-COUVER, BC, V6E 0B6

SIC 6799
PERICHEM TRADING INC   *p915*
4711 YONGE ST 10F, TORONTO, ON, M2N 6K8
(416) 479-5498   *SIC 6799*
PLATINUM EQUITIES INC   *p65*
906 12 AVE SW SUITE 910, CALGARY, AB, T2R 1K7
(403) 228-4799   *SIC 6799*
PRODIGY VENTURES INC   *p966*
161 BAY ST SUITE 4420, TORONTO, ON, M5J 2S1
(416) 488-7700   *SIC 6799*
PS INTERNATIONAL CANADA CORP *p1422*
2595 E QUANCE ST SUITE 201, REGINA, SK, S4V 2Y8
(306) 565-3904   *SIC 6799*
RE/MAX REAL ESTATE CENTRAL AL-BERTA   *p152*
6000 48 AVE SUITE 2, PONOKA, AB, T4J 1K2
(403) 783-5007   *SIC 6799*
RESSOURCES FALCO LTEE   *p1207*
1100   AV   DES   CANADIENS-DE-MONTREAL BUREAU 300, MONTREAL, QC, H3B 2S2
(514) 905-3162   *SIC 6799*
RIOCAN RETAIL VALUE L.P.   *p923*
2300 YONGE ST SUITE 500, TORONTO, ON, M4P 1E4
(416) 866-3033   *SIC 6799*
SAMA RESOURCES INC   *p1155*
1320 BOUL GRAHAM BUREAU 132, MONT-ROYAL, QC, H3P 3C8
(514) 747-4653   *SIC 6799*
SAMMI INTERNATIONAL TRADING LTD
p266
6191 WESTMINSTER HWY UNIT 150, RICHMOND, BC, V7C 4V4
(778) 938-2277   *SIC 6799*
SCHWAB TRADING INC   *p799*
2391 CENTRAL PARK DR UNIT 608, OAKVILLE, ON, L6H 0E4
(905) 827-6298   *SIC 6799*
SCOULAR CANADA LTD   *p69*
10201 SOUTHPORT RD SW SUITE 1110, CALGARY, AB, T2W 4X9
(403) 720-9050   *SIC 6799*
STARLIGHT INVESTMENTS LTD   *p572*
3280 BLOOR ST W UNIT 1400, ETOBI-COKE, ON, M8X 2X3
(416) 234-8444   *SIC 6799*
SUMWA TRADING CO. LTD   *p11*
2710 5 AVE NE, CALGARY, AB, T2A 4V4
(403) 230-8823   *SIC 6799*
SUSTAINCO INC   *p1003*
1 ROYAL GATE BLVD, VAUGHAN, ON, L4L 8Z7
(905) 850-8686   *SIC 6799*
TALISKER CORPORATION   *p957*
145   ADELAIDE   ST   W   SUITE   500, TORONTO, ON, M5H 4E5
(416) 864-0213   *SIC 6799*
TRADEX INTERNATIONAL CORP   *p795*
809 ARROW RD, NORTH YORK, ON, M9M 2L4
SIC 6799
VENTURES WEST MANAGEMENT INC *p310*
999 HASTINGS ST W SUITE 400, VAN-COUVER, BC, V6C 2W2
SIC 6799
VOLAILLES MIRABEL LTEE   *p1154*
9051   RTE   SIR-WILFRID-LAURIER, MIRABEL, QC, J7N 1L6
(450) 258-0444   *SIC 6799*
WESLEY CLOVER CORPORATION   *p625*
390 MARCH RD SUITE 110, KANATA, ON, K2K 0G7
(613) 271-6305   *SIC 6799*
WINGSUM INTERNATIONAL TRADING INC
p259
21331 GORDON WAY UNIT 3110, RICH-MOND, BC, V6W 1J9
(604) 370-3610   *SIC 6799*

SIC 7011 Hotels and motels

10643645 CANADA INC   *p1212*
1440 RUE DE LA MONTAGNE, MON-TREAL, QC, H3G 1Z5
(514) 843-2500   *SIC 7011*
1090769 ONTARIO INC   *p1017*
2508 WINDERMERE RD, WINDERMERE, ON, P0B 1P0
(705) 769-3611   *SIC 7011*
1110 HOWE HOLDINGS INCORPORATED
p325
1110 HOWE ST, VANCOUVER, BC, V6Z 1R2
(604) 684-2151   *SIC 7011*
1212360 ONTARIO LIMITED   *p620*
42 DELAWANA RD, HONEY HARBOUR, ON, P0E 1E0
(705) 756-2424   *SIC 7011*
1264316 ONTARIO INC   *p884*
89 MEADOWVALE DR, ST CATHARINES, ON, L2N 3Z8
(905) 934-5400   *SIC 7011*
1265534 ONTARIO INC   *p581*
801 DIXON RD, ETOBICOKE, ON, M9W 1J5
(416) 675-6100   *SIC 7011*
1379025 ONTARIO LIMITED   *p376*
330 YORK AVE SUITE 508, WINNIPEG, MB, R3C 0N9
(204) 942-0101   *SIC 7011*
1406284 ONTARIO INC   *p547*
3201 HIGHWAY 7, CONCORD, ON, L4K 5Z7
(905) 660-4700   *SIC 7011*
1504953 ALBERTA LTD   *p63*
119 12 AVE SW, CALGARY, AB, T2R 0G8
(403) 206-9565   *SIC 7011*
1548383 ONTARIO INC   *p958*
249 QUEENS QUAY W SUITE 109, TORONTO, ON, M5J 2N5
(416) 203-3333   *SIC 7011*
1712093 ONTARIO LIMITED   *p758*
6455 FALLSVIEW BLVD, NIAGARA FALLS, ON, L2G 3V9
(905) 357-5200   *SIC 7011*
180 UNIVERSITY HOTEL LIMITED PART-NERSHIP   *p948*
188 UNIVERSITY AVE, TORONTO, ON, M5H 0A3
(647) 788-8888   *SIC 7011*
19959 YUKON INC   *p215*
3240 VILLAGE WAY, HEFFLEY CREEK, BC, V0E 1Z1
(250) 578-6000   *SIC 7011*
2095527 ONTARIO LIMITED   *p758*
6740 FALLSVIEW BLVD, NIAGARA FALLS, ON, L2G 3W6
(905) 356-3600   *SIC 7011*
2316-7240 QUEBEC INC   *p1097*
600   BOUL   SAINT-JOSEPH,   DRUM-MONDVILLE, QC, J2C 2C1
(819) 478-4141   *SIC 7011*
2318-7081 QUEBEC INC   *p1077*
1080 BOUL TALBOT, CHICOUTIMI, QC, G7H 4B6
(418) 543-1521   *SIC 7011*
2343-7393 QUEBEC INC   *p1387*
1620   RUE   NOTRE-DAME   CENTRE, TROIS-RIVIERES, QC, G9A 6E5
(819) 376-1991   *SIC 7011*
2735-3861 QUEBEC INC   *p1283*
321 CH DES ERABLES, RIGAUD, QC, J0P 1P0
(450) 451-0000   *SIC 7011*
287706 ALBERTA LTD   *p131*
11401 100 AVE, GRANDE PRAIRIE, AB, T8V 5M6
(780) 539-5678   *SIC 7011*
299 BURRARD HOTEL LIMITED PARTNER-SHIP   *p301*
1038 CANADA PL, VANCOUVER, BC, V6C 0B9

(604) 695-5300   *SIC* 7011
2990181 CANADA INC   *p1166*
5000 RUE SHERBROOKE E, MONTREAL, QC, H1V 1A1
(514) 253-3365   *SIC* 7011
3025235 NOVA SCOTIA ULC   *p1192*
1050 RUE SHERBROOKE O, MONTREAL, QC, H3A 2R6
(514) 985-6225   *SIC* 7011
3031632 MANITOBA INC   *p376*
222 BROADWAY, WINNIPEG, MB, R3C 0R3
(204) 942-8251   *SIC* 7011
3032948 NOVA SCOTIA LIMITED   *p468*
437 PRINCE ST, TRURO, NS, B2N 1E6
(902) 895-1651   *SIC* 7011
3072930 NOVA SCOTIA COMPANY   *p1257*
395 RUE DE LA COURONNE, QUEBEC, QC, G1K 7X4
(418) 647-2611   *SIC* 7011
3089-3242 QUEBEC INC   *p1271*
3031 BOUL LAURIER, QUEBEC, QC, G1V 2M2
(418) 658-2727   *SIC* 7011
35 LAURIER LIMITED PARTNERSHIP *p1105*
35 RUE LAURIER, GATINEAU, QC, J8X 4E9
(819) 778-6111   *SIC* 7011
357672 B.C. LTD   *p212*
742 HWY 3 RR 5, FERNIE, BC, V0B 1M5
(250) 423-6871   *SIC* 7011
464161 ALBERTA LTD   *p107*
4520 76 AVE NW, EDMONTON, AB, T6B 0A5
(780) 468-5400   *SIC* 7011
467935 ALBERTA LTD   *p131*
11633 CLAIRMONT RD, GRANDE PRAIRIE, AB, T8V 3Y4
(780) 532-5221   *SIC* 7011
541907 ONTARIO LIMITED   *p935*
30 CARLTON ST SUITE 1, TORONTO, ON, M5B 2E9
(416) 977-6655   *SIC* 7011
552653 ONTARIO INC   *p1036*
580 BRUIN BLVD, WOODSTOCK, ON, N4V 1E5
(519) 537-5586   *SIC* 7011
577793 ONTARIO INC   *p758*
6455 FALLSVIEW BLVD, NIAGARA FALLS, ON, L2G 3V9
(905) 357-1151   *SIC* 7011
598468 SASKATCHEWAN LTD   *p1431*
806 IDYLWYLD DR N, SASKATOON, SK, S7L 0Z6
(306) 665-6500   *SIC* 7011
607637 SASKATCHEWAN LTD   *p1417*
1818 VICTORIA AVE, REGINA, SK, S4P 0R1
(306) 569-1666   *SIC* 7011
6257 AIRPORT TORONTO HOSPITALITY INC   *p686*
6257 AIRPORT RD, MISSISSAUGA, ON, L4V 1E4
(905) 678-1400   *SIC* 7011
742718 ALBERTA LTD   *p119*
4235 GATEWAY BLVD NW, EDMONTON, AB, T6J 5H2
(780) 438-1222   *SIC* 7011
801 WEST GEORGIA LTD   *p301*
801 GEORGIA ST W, VANCOUVER, BC, V6C 1P7
(604) 682-5566   *SIC* 7011
9003-7755 QUEBEC INC   *p1142*
900 RUE SAINT-CHARLES E, LONGUEUIL, QC, J4H 3Y2
(450) 646-8100   *SIC* 7011
902776 N.W.T. LIMITED   *p85*
10835 120 ST NW, EDMONTON, AB, T5H 3P9
(780) 452-4333   *SIC* 7011
9055-8842 QUEBEC INC   *p1354*
1699 CH DU MONT-GABRIEL, SAINTE-ADELE, QC, J8B 1A5
(450) 229-3547   *SIC* 7011
9145-1971 QUEBEC INC   *p1214*
1808 RUE SHERBROOKE O, MONTREAL,

QC, H3H 1E5
(514) 933-8111   *SIC* 7011
9164-2033 QUEBEC INC   *p1063*
1228 RUE NOBEL, BOUCHERVILLE, QC, J4B 5H1
(450) 655-9966   *SIC* 7011
9187-7571 QUEBEC INC   *p1274*
3125 BOUL HOCHELAGA, QUEBEC, QC, G1W 2P9
(418) 653-7267   *SIC* 7011
9207-4616 QUEBEC INC   *p1093*
555 BOUL MCMILLAN, DORVAL, QC, H9P 1B7
(514) 631-2411   *SIC* 7011
9312-5581 QUEBEC INC   *p1345*
5250 RUE JARRY E, SAINT-LEONARD, QC, H1R 3A9
(514) 878-2332   *SIC* 7011
955 BAY STREET HOSPITALITY INC   *p86*
10235 101 ST NW, EDMONTON, AB, T5J 3E8
(780) 428-7111   *SIC* 7011
955 BAY STREET HOSPITALITY INC   *p325*
845 BURRARD ST, VANCOUVER, BC, V6Z 2K6
(604) 682-5511   *SIC* 7011
955 BAY STREET HOSPITALITY INC   *p974*
955 BAY ST, TORONTO, ON, M5S 2A2
SIC 7011
AB PALISADES LIMITED PARTNERSHIP *p311*
1277 ROBSON ST, VANCOUVER, BC, V6E 1C2
(604) 688-0461   *SIC* 7011
ACCENT INNS INC   *p337*
3233 MAPLE ST, VICTORIA, BC, V8X 4Y9
(250) 475-7500   *SIC* 7011
ACCOR CANADA INC   *p709*
3670 HURONTARIO ST, MISSISSAUGA, ON, L5B 1P3
(905) 896-1000   *SIC* 7011
ACCOR CANADA INC   *p820*
33 NICHOLAS ST, OTTAWA, ON, K1N 9M7
(613) 760-4771   *SIC* 7011
ACCOR CANADA INC   *p915*
3 PARK HOME AVE, TORONTO, ON, M2N 6L3
(416) 733-2929   *SIC* 7011
ACCOR MANAGEMENT CANADA INC *p1201*
900 BOUL RENE-LEVESQUE O, MONTREAL, QC, H3B 4A5
(514) 861-3511   *SIC* 7011
ACCOR SERVICES CANADA INC   *p42*
133 9 AVE SW, CALGARY, AB, T2P 2M3
(403) 262-1234   *SIC* 7011
AIRLINER MOTOR HOTEL (1972) LTD *p383*
1740 ELLICE AVE, WINNIPEG, MB, R3H 0B3
(204) 775-7131   *SIC* 7011
ALLIED DON VALLEY HOTEL INC   *p778*
175 WYNFORD DR, NORTH YORK, ON, M3C 1J3
(416) 449-4111   *SIC* 7011
ALLIED HOTEL PROPERTIES INC   *p296*
515 PENDER ST W SUITE 300, VANCOUVER, BC, V6B 6H5
(604) 669-5335   *SIC* 7011
ANGEL STAR HOLDINGS LTD   *p336*
740 BURDETT AVE SUITE 1901, VICTORIA, BC, V8W 1B2
(250) 382-4221   *SIC* 7011
APX HOSPITALITY MANAGEMENT INC *p99*
18335 105 AVE NW SUITE 101, EDMONTON, AB, T5S 2K9
(780) 484-1515   *SIC* 7011
AQUILINI INVESTMENT GROUP INC   *p406*
1005 MAIN ST, MONCTON, NB, E1C 1G9
(506) 854-6340   *SIC* 7011
AQUILNI GROUP PROPERTIES LP   *p400*
659 QUEEN ST, FREDERICTON, NB, E3B 1C3
(506) 455-3371   *SIC* 7011
ARSANDCO INVESTMENTS LIMITED *p935*

111 CARLTON ST, TORONTO, ON, M5B 2G3
(416) 977-8000   *SIC* 7011
ATCO FRONTEC LTD   *p63*
909 11 AVE SW SUITE 300, CALGARY, AB, T2R 1L7
(403) 245-7757   *SIC* 7011
ATLANTIC HOTELS PARTNERSHIP   *p297*
510 HASTINGS ST W, VANCOUVER, BC, V6B 1L8
(604) 687-8813   *SIC* 7011
ATLIFIC INC   *p138*
210 VILLAGE RD, LAKE LOUISE, AB, T0L 1E0
(403) 522-3791   *SIC* 7011
ATLIFIC INC   *p336*
728 HUMBOLDT ST, VICTORIA, BC, V8W 3Z5
(250) 480-3800   *SIC* 7011
ATLIFIC INC   *p390*
1330 PEMBINA HWY, WINNIPEG, MB, R3T 2B4
(204) 452-4747   *SIC* 7011
ATLIFIC INC   *p582*
231 CARLINGVIEW DR, ETOBICOKE, ON, M9W 5E8
(416) 675-0411   *SIC* 7011
ATLIFIC INC   *p758*
4960 CLIFTON HILL, NIAGARA FALLS, ON, L2G 3N4
(905) 358-3293   *SIC* 7011
ATLIFIC INC   *p1142*
900 RUE SAINT-CHARLES E, LONGUEUIL, QC, J4H 3Y2
(450) 646-8100   *SIC* 7011
AUBERGE DE LA POINTE INC   *p1285*
10 BOUL CARTIER, RIVIERE-DU-LOUP, QC, G5R 6A1
(418) 862-3514   *SIC* 7011
AUBERGE DE LA RIVE INC   *p1376*
165 CH SAINTE-ANNE, SOREL-TRACY, QC, J3P 6J7
(450) 742-5691   *SIC* 7011
AUBERGE DU LAC SACACOMIE INC *p1291*
4000 CH YVON-PLANTE, SAINT-ALEXIS-DES-MONTS, QC, J0K 1V0
(819) 265-4444   *SIC* 7011
AUBERGE DU PORTAGE LTEE   *p1243*
671 RTE DU FLEUVE, NOTRE-DAME-DU-PORTAGE, QC, G0L 1Y0
(418) 862-3601   *SIC* 7011
AUBERGE DU TRESOR INC   *p1268*
20 RUE SAINTE-ANNE, QUEBEC, QC, G1R 3X2
(418) 694-1876   *SIC* 7011
AUBERGE SAINT-ANTOINE INC   *p1257*
10 RUE SAINT-ANTOINE, QUEBEC, QC, G1K 4C9
(418) 692-2211   *SIC* 7011
BALMORAL INVESTMENTS LTD   *p267*
2476 MOUNT NEWTON CROSS RD, SAANICHTON, BC, V8M 2B8
(250) 652-1146   *SIC* 7011
BALMORAL INVESTMENTS LTD   *p340*
101 ISLAND HWY, VICTORIA, BC, V9B 1E8
(250) 388-7807   *SIC* 7011
BANFF CARIBOU PROPERTIES LTD   *p4*
229 BEAR ST SUITE 300, BANFF, AB, T1L 1H8
(403) 762-2642   *SIC* 7011
BATTERY MANAGEMENT INC   *p428*
100 SIGNAL HILL RD, ST. JOHN'S, NL, A1A 1B3
SIC 7011
BAYVIEW HOSPITALITY INC   *p944*
108 CHESTNUT ST, TORONTO, ON, M5G 1R3
(416) 977-5000   *SIC* 7011
BEST WESTERN SANDS HOTEL   *p318*
1755 DAVIE ST, VANCOUVER, BC, V6G 1W5
(604) 682-1831   *SIC* 7011
BEST WESTERN SANDS HOTEL   *p331*
3914 32 ST, VERNON, BC, V1T 5P1

(250) 545-3755   *SIC* 7011
BEVERLY CREST MOTOR INN LTD   *p106*
3414 118 AVE NW, EDMONTON, AB, T5W 0Z4
(780) 474-0456   *SIC* 7011
BIG WHITE SKI RESORT LTD   *p218*
5315 BIG WHITE RD, KELOWNA, BC, V1P 1P4
(250) 765-3101   *SIC* 7011
BLACK KNIGHT INN LTD   *p156*
2929 50 AVE, RED DEER, AB, T4R 1H1
(403) 343-6666   *SIC* 7011
BLACK SAXON III INC   *p762*
201 PINEWOOD PARK DR, NORTH BAY, ON, P1B 8Z4
(705) 472-0810   *SIC* 7011
BLACKCOMB SKIING ENTERPRISES LIMITED PARTNERSHIP   *p343*
4545 BLACKCOMB WAY, WHISTLER, BC, V8E 0X9
(604) 932-3141   *SIC* 7011
BLACKFOOT MOTOR INN LTD   *p33*
5940 BLACKFOOT TRAIL SE, CALGARY, AB, T2H 2B5
(403) 252-2253   *SIC* 7011
BLUE BOY MOTOR HOTEL LTD   *p290*
725 MARINE DR SE, VANCOUVER, BC, V5X 2T9
(604) 321-6611   *SIC* 7011
BLUE TREE HOTELS GP ULC   *p87*
10135 100 ST NW, EDMONTON, AB, T5J 0N7
(780) 426-3636   *SIC* 7011
BLUE TREE HOTELS INVESTMENT (CANADA), LTD   *p318*
1601 BAYSHORE DR, VANCOUVER, BC, V6G 2V4
(604) 682-3377   *SIC* 7011
BLUE TREE HOTELS INVESTMENT (CANADA), LTD   *p959*
WESTIN HARBOUR CASTLE, TORONTO, ON, M5J 1A6
(416) 869-1600   *SIC* 7011
BOND PLACE HOTEL LTD   *p935*
65 DUNDAS ST E, TORONTO, ON, M5B 2G8
(416) 362-6061   *SIC* 7011
BRAD-LEA MEADOWS LIMITED   *p542*
615 RICHMOND ST, CHATHAM, ON, N7M 1R2
(519) 436-5506   *SIC* 7011
BREWSTER INC   *p4*
GD STN MAIN, BANFF, AB, T1L 1H1
(403) 762-3331   *SIC* 7011
BRIARS ESTATES LIMITED   *p623*
55 HEDGE RD RR 1, JACKSONS POINT, ON, L0E 1L0
(800) 465-2376   *SIC* 7011
BRIDGE GAP CHATEAU INC   *p87*
10111 BELLAMY HILL NW, EDMONTON, AB, T5J 1N7
(780) 428-6611   *SIC* 7011
BROOKSTREET HOTEL CORPORATION *p623*
525 LEGGET DR, KANATA, ON, K2K 2W2
(613) 271-3582   *SIC* 7011
CABLE BRIDGE ENTERPRISES LIMITED *p476*
6015 HIGHWAY 89, ALLISTON, ON, L9R 1A4
(705) 435-5501   *SIC* 7011
CADE HOLDING INC   *p758*
6400 LUNDY'S LANE, NIAGARA FALLS, ON, L2G 1T6
(905) 356-1161   *SIC* 7011
CALGARY PLAZA HOTEL LTD   *p10*
1316 33 ST NE, CALGARY, AB, T2A 6B6
(403) 248-8888   *SIC* 7011
CALGARY RAMADA DOWNTOWN LIMITED PARTNERSHIP   *p45*
708 8 AVE SW, CALGARY, AB, T2P 1H2
(403) 263-7600   *SIC* 7011
CAMBRIDGE SUITES LIMITED, THE   *p452*
1601 LOWER WATER ST SUITE 700, HAL-

IFAX, NS, B3J 3P6
(902) 421-1601   SIC 7011
CANAD CORPORATION LTD   p354
2401 SASKATCHEWAN AVE W, PORTAGE
LA PRAIRIE, MB, R1N 4A6
(204) 857-9745   SIC 7011
CANAD CORPORATION OF CANADA INC
p370
2100 MCPHILLIPS ST, WINNIPEG, MB,
R2V 3T9
(204) 633-0024   SIC 7011
**CANAD CORPORATION OF MANITOBA
LTD**   p362
826 REGENT AVE W, WINNIPEG, MB, R2C
3A8
(204) 224-1681   SIC 7011
**CANAD CORPORATION OF MANITOBA
LTD**   p365
1034 ELIZABETH RD, WINNIPEG, MB, R2J
1B3
(204) 253-2641   SIC 7011
**CANAD CORPORATION OF MANITOBA
LTD**   p369
930 JEFFERSON AVE SUITE 3, WIN-
NIPEG, MB, R2P 1W1
(204) 697-1495   SIC 7011
**CANAD CORPORATION OF MANITOBA
LTD**   p390
1792 PEMBINA HWY, WINNIPEG, MB, R3T
2G2
(204) 269-6955   SIC 7011
**CANADIAN MOUNTAIN HOLIDAYS LIM-
ITED PARTNERSHIP**   p4
217 BEAR ST, BANFF, AB, T1L 1J6
(403) 762-7100   SIC 7011
CANADIAN NIAGARA HOTELS INC   p757
5685 FALLS AVE 3RD-5TH FL, NIAGARA
FALLS, ON, L2E 6W7
(905) 374-4444   SIC 7011
CANADIAN NIAGARA HOTELS INC   p758
5875 FALLS AVE, NIAGARA FALLS, ON,
L2G 3K7
(905) 374-4444   SIC 7011
**CANADIAN ROCKY MOUNTAIN RESORTS
LTD**   p66
332 17 AVE SW, CALGARY, AB, T2S 0A8
(403) 233-8066   SIC 7011
CARIBOO HELICOPTER SKIING (88) LTD
p180
1 HARRWOOD DR, BLUE RIVER, BC, V0E
1J0
(250) 673-8381   SIC 7011
**CARRIAGE HILLS RESORT CORPORA-
TION**   p484
1101 HORSESHOE VALLEY RD W, BAR-
RIE, ON, L4M 4Y8
(705) 835-0087   SIC 7011
**CARRIAGE HILLS VACATION OWNERS AS-
SOCIATION**   p880
90 HIGHLAND DR, SHANTY BAY, ON, L0L
2L0
(705) 835-5858   SIC 7011
CARRIAGE HOUSE MOTOR INN LTD   p34
9030 MACLEOD TRAIL SE, CALGARY, AB,
T2H 0M4
(403) 253-1101   SIC 7011
CASTLE MOUNTAIN RESORT INC   p152
GD, PINCHER CREEK, AB, T0K 1W0
(403) 627-5101   SIC 7011
CAVALIER ENTERPRISES LTD   p8
2620 32 AVE NE, CALGARY, AB, T1Y 6B8
(403) 291-0107   SIC 7011
CAVALIER ENTERPRISES LTD   p1426
620 SPADINA CRES E, SASKATOON, SK,
S7K 3T5
(306) 652-6770   SIC 7011
CENTENNIAL HOTELS LIMITED   p452
1515 SOUTH PARK ST, HALIFAX, NS, B3J
2L2
(902) 423-6331   SIC 7011
CENTENNIAL HOTELS LIMITED   p195
1583 BRUNSWICK ST, HALIFAX, NS, B3J
3P5
(902) 420-0555   SIC 7011

CENTRE CITY CAPITAL LIMITED   p712
15 STAVEBANK RD S SUITE 804, MISSIS-
SAUGA, ON, L5G 2T2
(905) 891-7770   SIC 7011
**CENTRE SHERATON LIMITED PARTNER-
SHIP, LE**   p1202
1201 BOUL RENE-LEVESQUE O BUREAU
217, MONTREAL, QC, H3B 2L7
(514) 878-2000   SIC 7011
CENTURY PLAZA LTD   p326
1015 BURRARD ST, VANCOUVER, BC,
V6Z 1Y5
(604) 687-0575   SIC 7011
CHATEAU BONNE ENTENTE INC   p1275
3400 CH SAINTE-FOY, QUEBEC, QC, G1X
1S6
(418) 650-4550   SIC 7011
CHATEAU BROMONT INC   p1068
90 RUE DE STANSTEAD, BROMONT, QC,
J2L 1K6
(450) 534-3433   SIC 7011
**CHATEAU CHAMPLAIN LIMITED PART-
NERSHIP**   p1202
1050 RUE DE LA GAUCHETIERE O, MON-
TREAL, QC, H3B 4C9
(514) 878-9000   SIC 7011
CHATEAU GRANVILLE INC   p326
1100 GRANVILLE ST, VANCOUVER, BC,
V6Z 2B6
(604) 669-7070   SIC 7011
CHATEAU LACOMBE HOTEL LTD   p88
10111 BELLAMY HILL NW, EDMONTON,
AB, T5J 1N7
(780) 428-6611   SIC 7011
CHATEAU LAURIER HOTEL GP INC   p821
1 RIDEAU ST, OTTAWA, ON, K1N 8S7
(613) 241-1414   SIC 7011
**CHATEAU LOUIS HOTEL & CONFERENCE
CENTRE LTD**   p84
11727 KINGSWAY NW, EDMONTON, AB,
T5G 3A1
(780) 452-7770   SIC 7011
CHATEAU M.T. INC   p1159
3045 CH DE LA CHAPELLE, MONT-
TREMBLANT, QC, J8E 1E1
(819) 681-7000   SIC 7011
CHATEAU OTTAWA HOTEL INC   p822
150 ALBERT ST, OTTAWA, ON, K1P 5G2
(613) 238-1500   SIC 7011
**CHIP REIT NO 16 OPERATIONS LIMITED
PARTNERSHIP**   p84
11830 KINGSWAY NW SUITE 906, ED-
MONTON, AB, T5G 0X5
(780) 454-9521   SIC 7011
**CHIP REIT NO 18 OPERATIONS LIMITED
PARTNERSHIP**   p142
320 SCENIC DR S, LETHBRIDGE, AB, T1J
4B4
(403) 328-1123   SIC 7011
**CHIP REIT NO 23 OPERATIONS LIMITED
PARTNERSHIP**   p693
5050 ORBITOR DR, MISSISSAUGA, ON,
L4W 4X2
(905) 238-9600   SIC 7011
CITY HOTELS LIMITED   p431
251 EMPIRE AVE SUITE 103, ST. JOHN'S,
NL, A1C 3H9
(709) 738-3989   SIC 7011
CLDH MEADOWVALE INC   p721
6750 MISSISSAUGA RD, MISSISSAUGA,
ON, L5N 2L3
(905) 826-0940   SIC 7011
CLUB TREMBLANT INC   p1159
121 RUE CUTTLE, MONT-TREMBLANT,
QC, J8E 1B9
SIC 7011
COAST HOTELS LIMITED   p88
10155 105 ST NW, EDMONTON, AB, T5J
1E2
(780) 423-4811   SIC 7011
COAST HOTELS LIMITED   p195
975 SHOPPERS ROW, CAMPBELL RIVER,
BC, V9W 2C4
(250) 287-9225   SIC 7011

COAST HOTELS LIMITED   p233
11 BASTION ST, NANAIMO, BC, V9R 6E4
(250) 753-6601   SIC 7011
COAST HOTELS LIMITED   p249
770 BRUNSWICK ST, PRINCE GEORGE,
BC, V2L 2C2
(250) 563-0121   SIC 7011
COAST HOTELS LIMITED   p312
1090 GEORGIA ST W SUITE 900, VAN-
COUVER, BC, V6E 3V7
(604) 682-7982   SIC 7011
COAST HOTELS LIMITED   p318
1763 COMOX ST, VANCOUVER, BC, V6G
1P6
(604) 688-7711   SIC 7011
COGIRES INC   p1269
1220 PLACE GEORGE-V O, QUEBEC, QC,
G1R 5B8
(418) 522-3848   SIC 7011
COMMONWEALTH HOSPITALITY LTD p451
1980 ROBIE ST, HALIFAX, NS, B3H 3G5
(902) 423-1161   SIC 7011
COMMONWEALTH HOSPITALITY LTD p527
3063 SOUTH SERVICE RD, BURLINGTON,
ON, L7N 3E9
(905) 639-4443   SIC 7011
COMMONWEALTH HOSPITALITY LTD p693
5090 EXPLORER DR SUITE 700, MISSIS-
SAUGA, ON, L4W 4T9
(905) 602-6224   SIC 7011
**COMPAGNIE DE VILLEGIATURE ET DE DE-
VELOPEMENT GRAND LODGE INC, LA**
p1159
2396 RUE LABELLE, MONT-TREMBLANT,
QC, J8E 1T8
(819) 425-2734   SIC 7011
**COMPAGNIE WW HOTELS (POINTE-
CLAIRE)**   p1249
6700 RTE TRANSCANADIENNE, POINTE-
CLAIRE, QC, H9R 1C2
(514) 697-7110   SIC 7011
CONKRISDA HOLDINGS LIMITED   p657
1150 WELLINGTON RD, LONDON, ON,
N6E 1M3
(519) 681-0600   SIC 7011
**CORPORATION DES HOTELS INTER-
CONTINENTAL (MONTREAL), LA**   p1187
360 RUE SAINT-ANTOINE O, MONTREAL,
QC, H2Y 3X4
(514) 987-9900   SIC 7011
COUPLES RESORT INC   p1016
139 GALEAIRY LAKE RD, WHITNEY, ON,
K0J 2M0
(613) 637-1179   SIC 7011
COURTENAY LODGE LTD   p203
1590 CLIFFE AVE, COURTENAY, BC, V9N
2K4
(250) 338-7741   SIC 7011
COUTURE, ARMAND & FILS INC   p1079
1080 BOUL TALBOT, CHICOUTIMI, QC,
G7H 4B6
(418) 543-1521   SIC 7011
CREST HOTEL LTD   p251
222 1ST AVE W, PRINCE RUPERT, BC, V8J
1A8
(250) 624-6771   SIC 7011
**CROWNE PLAZA MONCTON DOWNTOWN
HOTEL**   p406
1005 MAIN ST, MONCTON, NB, E1C 1G9
(506) 854-6340   SIC 7011
CRYSTAL MOUNTAIN RESORTS LTD p219
GD RPO BANKS CENTRE, KELOWNA, BC,
V1X 4K3
SIC 7011
D. L. PAGANI LIMITED   p601
716 GORDON ST, GUELPH, ON, N1G 1Y6
(519) 836-1240   SIC 7011
DAGMAR RESORT LIMITED   p479
1220 LAKERIDGE RD RR 1, ASHBURN,
ON, L0B 1A0
(905) 649-2002   SIC 7011
**DAVIE STREET MANAGEMENT SERVICES
LTD**   p298
322 DAVIE ST, VANCOUVER, BC, V6B 5Z6

(604) 642-6787   SIC 7011
DAYS INN & SUITES WEST EDMONTON
p100
10010 179A ST NW, EDMONTON, AB, T5S
2T1
(780) 444-4440   SIC 7011
DEER LODGE HOTELS LTD   p1431
106 CIRCLE DR W, SASKATOON, SK, S7L
4L6
(306) 242-8881   SIC 7011
DEER PARK HOLDINGS LTD   p153
7150 50 AVE, RED DEER, AB, T4N 6A5
(403) 343-8800   SIC 7011
DEERFOOT INN & CASINO INC   p70
11500 35 ST SE SUITE 1000, CALGARY,
AB, T2Z 3W4
(403) 236-7529   SIC 7011
DELTA HOTELS LIMITED   p118
4404 GATEWAY BLVD NW, EDMONTON,
AB, T6H 5C2
(780) 434-6415   SIC 7011
DELTA HOTELS LIMITED   p298
550 HASTINGS ST W, VANCOUVER, BC,
V6B 1L6
(604) 689-8188   SIC 7011
DELTA HOTELS LIMITED   p339
45 SONGHEES RD, VICTORIA, BC, V9A
6T3
(250) 360-2999   SIC 7011
DELTA HOTELS LIMITED   p377
350 ST MARY AVE, WINNIPEG, MB, R3C
3J2
(204) 944-7278   SIC 7011
**DELTA HOTELS NO. 12 LIMITED PARTNER-
SHIP**   p825
101 LYON ST N, OTTAWA, ON, K1R 5T9
(613) 237-1508   SIC 7011
**DELTA HOTELS NO. 12 LIMITED PARTNER-
SHIP**   p1312
1200 RUE JOHNSON O, SAINT-
HYACINTHE, QC, J2S 7K7
SIC 7011
**DELTA HOTELS NO. 2 LIMITED PARTNER-
SHIP**   p118
4404 GATEWAY BLVD NW, EDMONTON,
AB, T6H 5C2
(780) 434-6415   SIC 7011
**DELTA HOTELS NO. 32 LIMITED PARTNER-
SHIP**   p400
225 WOODSTOCK RD, FREDERICTON,
NB, E3B 2H8
(506) 451-7929   SIC 7011
DELTA SHERBROOKE   p1373
2685 RUE KING O, SHERBROOKE, QC,
J1L 1C1
(819) 822-1989   SIC 7011
**DIMENSION 3 HOSPITALITY CORPORA-
TION**   p1424
1139 8TH ST E, SASKATOON, SK, S7H 0S3
(306) 249-2882   SIC 7011
DJ WILL HOLDINGS LIMITED   p153
7150 50 AVE, RED DEER, AB, T4N 6A5
(403) 343-8800   SIC 7011
DOMAINE DU SKI MONT BRUNO INC p1295
550 RANG DES VINGT-CINQ E, SAINT-
BRUNO, QC, J3V 0G6
(450) 653-3441   SIC 7011
DRAKE HOTEL PROPERTIES (DHP) INC
p990
1150 QUEEN ST W, TORONTO, ON, M6J
1J3
(416) 531-5042   SIC 7011
EASTON'S GROUP OF HOTELS INC   p669
3100 STEELES AVE E SUITE 601,
MARKHAM, ON, L3R 8T3
(905) 940-9409   SIC 7011
**EASTON'S TORONTO AIRPORT HOTEL
(COROGA) LP**   p669
3100 STEELES AVE E, MARKHAM, ON,
L3R 8T3
(905) 940-9409   SIC 7011
EDGEWATER MANAGEMENT INC   p298
750 PACIFIC BLVD SUITE 311, VANCOU-
VER, BC, V6B 5E7

(604) 687-3343   *SIC 7011*
ELKHORN RANCH & RESORT LTD   p354
3 MOOSWA DR E, ONANOLE, MB, R0J
1N0
(204) 848-2802   *SIC 7011*
ELM HURST INN   p621
415 HARRIS ST, INGERSOLL, ON, N5C
3J8
(519) 485-5321   *SIC 7011*
EMBASSY WEST HOTEL   p829
1400 CARLING AVE SUITE 517, OTTAWA,
ON, K1Z 7L8
(613) 729-4321   *SIC 7011*
**EQUIPE JUNIOR DE SKI DU MONT ORIG-
NAL INC**   p1124
158 RANG DU MONT-ORIGNAL, LAC-
ETCHEMIN, QC, G0R 1S0
(418) 625-1551   *SIC 7011*
ERIE BEACH HOTEL LIMITED   p847
19 WALKER ST, PORT DOVER, ON, N0A
1N0
(519) 583-1391   *SIC 7011*
ESSAG CANADA INC   p502
30 PEEL CENTRE DR, BRAMPTON, ON,
L6T 4G3
SIC 7011
ESTHER'S INN LTD   p250
1151 COMMERCIAL CRES, PRINCE
GEORGE, BC, V2M 6W6
(250) 562-4131   *SIC 7011*
**EXECUTIVE HOTELS GENERAL PARTNER-
SHIP**   p185
4201 LOUGHEED HWY, BURNABY, BC,
V5C 3Y6
(604) 298-2010   *SIC 7011*
**EXECUTIVE HOTELS GENERAL PARTNER-
SHIP**   p200
405 NORTH RD, COQUITLAM, BC, V3K
3V9
(604) 936-9399   *SIC 7011*
**EXECUTIVE HOTELS GENERAL PARTNER-
SHIP**   p260
7311 WESTMINSTER HWY, RICHMOND,
BC, V6X 1A3
(604) 278-5555   *SIC 7011*
EXECUTIVE HOUSE LTD   p336
777 DOUGLAS ST, VICTORIA, BC, V8W
2B5
(250) 388-5111   *SIC 7011*
FAIRMONT HOT SPRINGS RESORT LTD
p212
5225 FAIRMONT RESORT RD RR 1, FAIR-
MONT HOT SPRINGS, BC, V0B 1L1
(250) 345-6070   *SIC 7011*
FAIRMONT HOTELS & RESORTS INC   p4
405 SPRAY AVE, BANFF, AB, T1L 1J4
(403) 762-6860   *SIC 7011*
FAIRMONT HOTELS & RESORTS INC   p49
255 BARCLAY PARADE SW, CALGARY,
AB, T2P 5C2
(403) 266-7200   *SIC 7011*
FAIRMONT HOTELS & RESORTS INC   p49
133 9 AVE SW, CALGARY, AB, T2P 2M3
(403) 262-1234   *SIC 7011*
FAIRMONT HOTELS & RESORTS INC   p49
133 9 AVE SW, CALGARY, AB, T2P 2M3
(403) 262-1234   *SIC 7011*
FAIRMONT HOTELS & RESORTS INC   p89
10065 100 ST NW, EDMONTON, AB, T5J
0N6
(780) 424-5181   *SIC 7011*
FAIRMONT HOTELS & RESORTS INC   p137
1 LODGE RD, JASPER, AB, T0E 1E0
(780) 852-3301   *SIC 7011*
FAIRMONT HOTELS & RESORTS INC   p138
111 LAKE LOUISE DR, LAKE LOUISE, AB,
T0L 1E0
(403) 522-3511   *SIC 7011*
FAIRMONT HOTELS & RESORTS INC   p264
3111 GRANT MCCONACHIE WAY, RICH-
MOND, BC, V7B 0A6
(604) 207-5200   *SIC 7011*
FAIRMONT HOTELS & RESORTS INC   p304
900 CANADA PL, VANCOUVER, BC, V6C

3L5
(604) 691-1991   *SIC 7011*
FAIRMONT HOTELS & RESORTS INC   p304
900 GEORGIA ST W, VANCOUVER, BC,
V6C 2W6
(604) 684-3131   *SIC 7011*
FAIRMONT HOTELS & RESORTS INC   p336
721 GOVERNMENT ST, VICTORIA, BC,
V8W 1W5
(250) 384-8111   *SIC 7011*
FAIRMONT HOTELS & RESORTS INC   p343
4599 CHATEAU BLVD, WHISTLER, BC,
V8E 0Z5
(604) 938-8000   *SIC 7011*
FAIRMONT HOTELS & RESORTS INC   p374
2 LOMBARD PL, WINNIPEG, MB, R3B 0Y3
(204) 957-1350   *SIC 7011*
FAIRMONT HOTELS & RESORTS INC   p418
184 ADOLPHUS ST, ST ANDREWS, NB,
E5B 1T7
(506) 529-8823   *SIC 7011*
FAIRMONT HOTELS & RESORTS INC   p821
1 RIDEAU ST, OTTAWA, ON, K1N 8S7
(613) 241-1414   *SIC 7011*
FAIRMONT HOTELS & RESORTS INC   p980
155 WELLINGTON ST W SUITE 3300,
TORONTO, ON, M5V 0C3
(416) 874-2600   *SIC 7011*
FAIRMONT HOTELS & RESORTS INCp1122
181 RUE RICHELIEU BUREAU 200, LA
MALBAIE, QC, G5A 1X7
(418) 665-3703   *SIC 7011*
FAIRMONT HOTELS & RESORTS INCp1159
392 RUE NOTRE-DAME, MONTEBELLO,
QC, J0V 1L0
(819) 423-6341   *SIC 7011*
FAIRMONT HOTELS & RESORTS INCp1204
900 BOUL RENE-LEVESQUE O, MON-
TREAL, QC, H3B 4A5
(514) 861-3511   *SIC 7011*
**FALLSVIEW NIAGARA LODGING COM-
PANY**   p758
6733 FALLSVIEW BLVD, NIAGARA FALLS,
ON, L2G 3W7
(905) 356-1944   *SIC 7011*
FELCOR CANADA CO   p584
970 DIXON RD, ETOBICOKE, ON, M9W
1J9
(416) 675-7611   *SIC 7011*
FIDELITAS HOLDING COMPANY LIMITED
p834
180 COOPER ST, OTTAWA, ON, K2P 2L5
(613) 236-5000   *SIC 7011*
FIRST CANADIAN MANAGEMENT CORP
p190
5945 KATHLEEN AVE SUITE 220, BURN-
ABY, BC, V5H 4J7
(604) 689-2467   *SIC 7011*
**FIVE BROTHERS HOSPITALITY PARTNER-
SHIP**   p884
2 NORTH SERVICE RD, ST CATHARINES,
ON, L2N 4G9
(905) 934-8000   *SIC 7011*
**FOUR POINTS BY SHERATON EDMONTON
GATEWAY**   p125
10010 12 AVE SW, EDMONTON, AB, T6X
0P9
(780) 801-4000   *SIC 7011*
**FOUR POINTS HOTEL SHERATON WIN-
NIPEG INTERNATIONAL AIRPORT**   p384
1999 WELLINGTON AVE, WINNIPEG, MB,
R3H 1H5
(204) 775-5222   *SIC 7011*
FOUR SEASONS HOLDINGS INC   p779
1165 LESLIE ST, NORTH YORK, ON, M3C
2K8
(416) 449-1750   *SIC 7011*
FOUR SEASONS HOTELS LIMITED   p304
791 GEORGIA ST W, VANCOUVER, BC,
V6C 2T4
(604) 689-9333   *SIC 7011*
FOUR SEASONS HOTELS LIMITED   p779
1165 LESLIE ST, NORTH YORK, ON, M3C
2K8

(416) 449-1750   *SIC 7011*
FOUR SEASONS HOTELS LIMITED   p928
60 YORKVILLE AVE, TORONTO, ON, M4W
0A4
(416) 964-0411   *SIC 7011*
FOX HARB'R DEVELOPMENT LIMITED
p470
1337 FOX HARBOUR RD, WALLACE, NS,
B0K 1Y0
(902) 257-1801   *SIC 7011*
FREDERICTON MOTOR INN LTD   p402
1315 REGENT ST, FREDERICTON, NB,
E3C 1A1
(506) 455-1430   *SIC 7011*
FRIENDSHIP DEVELOPMENTS LTD   p335
330 QUEBEC ST, VICTORIA, BC, V8V 1W3
(250) 381-3456   *SIC 7011*
FRONTENAC HOTEL GP INC   p1269
1 RUE DES CARRIERES, QUEBEC, QC,
G1R 5J5
(418) 692-3861   *SIC 7011*
FS WHISTLER HOLDINGS LIMITED   p343
4591 BLACKCOMB WAY, WHISTLER, BC,
V8E 0Y4
(604) 935-3400   *SIC 7011*
FS WHISTLER HOLDINGS LIMITED   p343
4591 BLACKCOMB WAY, WHISTLER, BC,
V8E 0Y4
(604) 935-3400   *SIC 7011*
FUJI STARLIGHT EXPRESS CO., LTD   p4
222 LYNX ST, BANFF, AB, T1L 1K5
(403) 762-4433   *SIC 7011*
GAMEHOST INC   p157
548 LAURA AVE SUITE 104, RED DEER
COUNTY, AB, T4E 0A5
(403) 346-4545   *SIC 7011*
**GATEWAY CASINOS & ENTERTAINMENT
INC**   p189
4331 DOMINION ST, BURNABY, BC, V5G
1C7
(604) 412-0166   *SIC 7011*
**GATEWAY CASINOS & ENTERTAINMENT
INC**   p237
350 GIFFORD ST SUITE 1, NEW WEST-
MINSTER, BC, V3M 7A3
(604) 777-2946   *SIC 7011*
**GATEWAY CASINOS & ENTERTAINMENT
LIMITED**   p189
4331 DOMINION ST, BURNABY, BC, V5G
1C7
(604) 412-0166   *SIC 7011*
GENESIS HOSPITALITY INC   p347
3550 VICTORIA AVE, BRANDON, MB, R7B
2R4
(204) 725-1532   *SIC 7011*
GESTION ESTEREL INC   p1100
39 CH FRIDOLIN-SIMARD, ESTEREL, QC,
J0T 1E0
(450) 228-2662   *SIC 7011*
GESTION J.L.T. UNIVERSELLE INC   p1098
915 RUE HAINS, DRUMMONDVILLE, QC,
J2C 3A1
(819) 472-2942   *SIC 7011*
**GLENGARRY MOTEL AND RESTAURANT
LIMITED**   p469
150 WILLOW ST, TRURO, NS, B2N 4Z6
(902) 893-4311   *SIC 7011*
GLENMORE INN HOLDINGS LTD   p16
2720 GLENMORE TRAIL SE, CALGARY,
AB, T2C 2E6
(403) 279-8611   *SIC 7011*
GLOBAL GATEWAY CORP   p318
1400 ROBSON ST, VANCOUVER, BC, V6G
1B9
(604) 566-2688   *SIC 7011*
GORDON HOTELS & MOTOR INNS LTD
p367
1011 HENDERSON HWY, WINNIPEG, MB,
R2K 2M2
(204) 334-4355   *SIC 7011*
GORDON HOTELS & MOTOR INNS LTD
p385
1975 PORTAGE AVE, WINNIPEG, MB, R3J
0J9

(204) 888-4806   *SIC 7011*
GOUVERNEUR INC   p1175
1415 RUE SAINT-HUBERT, MONTREAL,
QC, H2L 3Y9
(514) 842-4881   *SIC 7011*
GOUVERNEUR INC   p1196
1000 RUE SHERBROOKE O BUREAU
2300, MONTREAL, QC, H3A 3R3
(514) 875-8822   *SIC 7011*
GOUVERNEUR INC   p1289
41 6E RUE, ROUYN-NORANDA, QC, J9X
1Y8
(819) 762-2341   *SIC 7011*
GRAND CANADIAN RESORTS INC   p79
91 THREE SISTERS DR, CANMORE, AB,
T1W 3A1
(403) 678-0018   *SIC 7011*
GROUP FIVE INVESTORS LTD   p164
GD LCD MAIN, SPRUCE GROVE, AB, T7X
3A1
(780) 962-5000   *SIC 7011*
GROUPE GERMAIN INC   p1270
1200 RUE DES SOEURS-DU-BON-
PASTEUR BUREAU 500, QUEBEC, QC,
G1S 0B1
(418) 687-1123   *SIC 7011*
**GROUPE HOTELIER GRAND CHATEAU
INC**   p1085
2225 DES LAURENTIDES (A-15) E, COTE
SAINT-LUC, QC, H7S 1Z6
(450) 682-2225   *SIC 7011*
**GROUPE HOTELIER GRAND CHATEAU
INC**   p1086
2440 DES LAURENTIDES (A-15) O, COTE
SAINT-LUC, QC, H7T 1X5
(450) 687-2440   *SIC 7011*
**GROUPE HOTELIER GRAND CHATEAU
INC**   p1394
21700 RTE TRANSCANADIENNE,
VAUDREUIL-DORION, QC, J7V 8P7
(450) 455-0955   *SIC 7011*
**GROUPE LES MANOIRS DU QUEBEC INC,
LES**   p1269
44 COTE DU PALAIS, QUEBEC, QC, G1R
4H8
(418) 692-1030   *SIC 7011*
**GROUPE LES MANOIRS DU QUEBEC INC,
LES**   p1352
246 CH DU LAC-MILLETTE, SAINT-
SAUVEUR, QC, J0R 1R3
(450) 227-1811   *SIC 7011*
GUILDFORD VENTURES LTD   p270
15269 104 AVE, SURREY, BC, V3R 1N5
(604) 582-9288   *SIC 7011*
GUILDWOOD INN LIMITED, THE   p846
1400 VENETIAN BLVD, POINT EDWARD,
ON, N7T 7W6
(519) 337-7577   *SIC 7011*
**HARBOUR TOWERS LIMITED PARTNER-
SHIP**   p335
345 QUEBEC ST, VICTORIA, BC, V8V 1W4
(250) 385-2405   *SIC 7011*
**HARRISON HOT SPRINGS RESORT & SPA
CORP**   p215
100 ESPLANADE AVE, HARRISON HOT
SPRINGS, BC, V0M 1K0
(604) 796-2244   *SIC 7011*
HILTON CANADA CO.   p415
1 MARKET SQ, SAINT JOHN, NB, E2L 4Z6
(506) 693-8484   *SIC 7011*
HILTON CANADA CO.   p688
5875 AIRPORT RD, MISSISSAUGA, ON,
L4V 1N1
(905) 677-9900   *SIC 7011*
HILTON CANADA CO.   p952
145 RICHMOND ST W, TORONTO, ON,
M5H 2L2
(416) 869-3456   *SIC 7011*
HILTON CANADA CO.   p1269
1100 BOUL RENE-LEVESQUE E BUREAU
1797, QUEBEC, QC, G1R 5V2
(418) 647-2411   *SIC 7011*
HILTON VANCOUVER METROTOWN   p190
6083 MCKAY AVE, BURNABY, BC, V5H

2W7
(604) 438-1200   *SIC* 7011
HOCO LIMITED   *p759*
4960 CLIFTON HILL, NIAGARA FALLS, ON,
L2G 3N4
(905) 358-3293   *SIC* 7011
HOLIDAY INN (NIAGARA FALLS) LIMITED
p759
5339 MURRAY ST, NIAGARA FALLS, ON,
L2G 2J3
(905) 356-1333   *SIC* 7011
HOLIDAY INN TORONTO AIRPORT EAST
p585
600 DIXON RD, ETOBICOKE, ON, M9W
1J1
(416) 240-7511   *SIC* 7011
HOLLOWAY LODGING CORPORATION
p458
106-145 HOBSON LAKE DR, HALIFAX, NS,
B3S 0H9
(902) 404-3499   *SIC* 7011
HORSESHOE RESORT CORPORATION
p484
1101 HORSESHOE VALLEY RD W, BAR-
RIE, ON, L4M 4Y8
(705) 835-2790   *SIC* 7011
HORSESHOE VALLEY LIMITED PARTNER-
SHIP   *p484*
1101 HORSESHOE VALLEY RD W, BAR-
RIE, ON, L4M 4Y8
(705) 835-2790   *SIC* 7011
HOSPITALITY INNS LTD   *p39*
135 SOUTHLAND DR SE, CALGARY, AB,
T2J 5X5
(403) 278-5050   *SIC* 7011
HOSPITALITY MOTELS LIMITED   *p759*
6361 FALLSVIEW BLVD, NIAGARA FALLS,
ON, L2G 3V9
(905) 357-3184   *SIC* 7011
HOTEL & GOLF MARIGOT INC   *p1256*
7900 RUE DU MARIGOT, QUEBEC, QC,
G1G 6T8
(418) 627-8008   *SIC* 7011
HOTEL 550 WELLINGTON GP LTD   *p981*
550 WELLINGTON ST W, TORONTO, ON,
M5V 2V4
(416) 640-7778   *SIC* 7011
HOTEL BERNIERES INC   *p1140*
535 RUE DE BERNIERES, LEVIS, QC, G7A
1C9
(418) 831-3119   *SIC* 7011
HOTEL CHERIBOURG INC   *p1244*
2603 CH DU PARC, ORFORD, QC, J1X 8C8
(819) 843-3308   *SIC* 7011
HOTEL FORESTEL VAL-D'OR INC   *p1390*
1001 3E AV, VAL-D'OR, QC, J9P 1T4
(819) 825-5660   *SIC* 7011
HOTEL GEORGIA (OP) LIMITED PARTNER-
SHIP   *p305*
801 GEORGIA ST W, VANCOUVER, BC,
V6C 1P7
(604) 682-5566   *SIC* 7011
HOTEL N.S. OWNERSHIP LIMITED PART-
NERSHIP   *p451*
1181 HOLLIS ST SUITE 1, HALIFAX, NS,
B3H 2P6
(902) 421-1000   *SIC* 7011
HOTEL NEWFOUNDLAND (1982)   *p432*
CAVENDISH SQ, ST. JOHN'S, NL, A1C
5W8
(709) 726-4980   *SIC* 7011
HOTEL PALACE ROYAL INC   *p1269*
775 AV HONORE-MERCIER, QUEBEC,
QC, G1R 6A5
(418) 694-2000   *SIC* 7011
HOTEL SASKATCHEWAN (1990) LTD   *p298*
1118 HOMER ST SUITE 425, VANCOU-
VER, BC, V6B 6L5
SIC 7011
HOTEL SASKATCHEWAN (1990) LTD *p1418*
2125 VICTORIA AVE, REGINA, SK, S4P
0S3
(306) 522-7691   *SIC* 7011
HOTELLUS CANADA HOLDINGS INC *p1188*

360 RUE SAINT-ANTOINE O, MONTREAL,
QC, H2Y 3X4
(514) 987-9900   *SIC* 7011
HOTELS CANPRO INC, LES   *p1197*
1155 RUE SHERBROOKE O, MONTREAL,
QC, H3A 2N3
(514) 285-9000   *SIC* 7011
HOTELS COTE-DE-LIESSE INC   *p1339*
6500 CH DE LA COTE-DE-LIESSE, SAINT-
LAURENT, QC, H4T 1E3
(514) 739-6440   *SIC* 7011
HR OTTAWA, L.P.   *p597*
4837 ALBION RD, GLOUCESTER, ON, K1X
1A3
(613) 822-8668   *SIC* 7011
HUBER DEVELOPMENT LTD   *p235*
701 LAKESIDE DR, NELSON, BC, V1L 6G3
(250) 352-7222   *SIC* 7011
IMMEUBLES J.C. MILOT INC, LES   *p1099*
600 BOUL SAINT-JOSEPH, DRUM-
MONDVILLE, QC, J2C 2C1
(819) 478-4141   *SIC* 7011
INN AT THE FORKS LP   *p378*
75 FORKS MARKET RD, WINNIPEG, MB,
R3C 0A2
(204) 942-6555   *SIC* 7011
INN AT THE PARK INC   *p72*
8220 BOWRIDGE CRES NW, CALGARY,
AB, T3B 2V1
(403) 288-4441   *SIC* 7011
INNVEST HOTELS (LONDON) LTD   *p656*
325 DUNDAS ST, LONDON, ON, N6B 1T9
(519) 679-6111   *SIC* 7011
INNVEST HOTELS GP LTD   *p804*
2525 WYECROFT RD, OAKVILLE, ON, L6L
6P8
(905) 847-1000   *SIC* 7011
INNVEST HOTELS GP VIII LTD   *p626*
101 KANATA AVE, KANATA, ON, K2T 1E6
(613) 271-3057   *SIC* 7011
INNVEST HOTELS LP   *p823*
100 KENT ST, OTTAWA, ON, K1P 5R7
(613) 238-1122   *SIC* 7011
INNVEST HOTELS LP   *p963*
200 BAY ST SUITE 2200, TORONTO, ON,
M5J 2W4
(416) 607-7100   *SIC* 7011
INNVEST PROPERTIES CORP   *p939*
111 LOMBARD ST, TORONTO, ON, M5C
2T9
(416) 367-5555   *SIC* 7011
INNVEST PROPERTIES CORP   *p963*
200 BAY ST SUITE 2200, TORONTO, ON,
M5J 2J2
(416) 607-7100   *SIC* 7011
INNVEST PROPERTIES CORP   *p1023*
277 RIVERSIDE DR W, WINDSOR, ON,
N9A 5K4
(519) 973-5555   *SIC* 7011
INNVEST REAL ESTATE INVESTMENT
TRUST   *p407*
750 MAIN ST, MONCTON, NB, E1C 1E6
(506) 854-4344   *SIC* 7011
INNVEST REAL ESTATE INVESTMENT
TRUST   *p963*
200 BAY ST SUITE 3205, TORONTO, ON,
M5J 2J1
(416) 607-7100   *SIC* 7011
INTER-ALBERTA HOLDINGS CORPORA-
TION   *p149*
1101 4 ST, NISKU, AB, T9E 7N1
(780) 955-7744   *SIC* 7011
INTERCONTINENTAL TORONTO CENTRE,
THE   *p981*
225 FRONT ST W, TORONTO, ON, M5V
2X3
(416) 597-1400   *SIC* 7011
INTRAWEST RESORT CLUB GROUP *p343*
4580 CHATEAU BLVD, WHISTLER, BC,
V8E 0Z6
(604) 938-3030   *SIC* 7011
INTRAWEST ULC   *p298*
375 WATER ST SUITE 710, VANCOUVER,
BC, V6B 5C6

(604) 695-8200   *SIC* 7011
INTRAWEST ULC   *p493*
220 GORD CANNING DR, BLUE MOUN-
TAINS, ON, L9Y 0V9
(705) 443-8080   *SIC* 7011
INTRAWEST ULC   *p493*
108 JOZO WEIDER BLVD, BLUE MOUN-
TAINS, ON, L9Y 3Z2
(705) 445-0231   *SIC* 7011
INVEST REIT   *p762*
700 LAKESHORE DR, NORTH BAY, ON,
P1A 2G4
(705) 474-5800   *SIC* 7011
INVESTISSEMENTS RAMAN 'S.E.N.C.',
LES   *p1197*
1110 RUE SHERBROOKE O BUREAU 301,
MONTREAL, QC, H3A 1G8
(514) 844-3951   *SIC* 7011
IW RESORTS LIMITED PARTNERSHIP *p216*
2030 PANORAMA DR, INVERMERE, BC,
V0A 1K0
(250) 342-6941   *SIC* 7011
J.J.'S HOSPITALITY LIMITED   *p863*
360 GREAT NORTHERN RD, SAULT STE.
MARIE, ON, P6B 4Z7
(705) 949-8111   *SIC* 7011
J.J.'S HOSPITALITY LIMITED   *p863*
360 GREAT NORTHERN RD SUITE 787,
SAULT STE. MARIE, ON, P6B 4Z7
(705) 945-7614   *SIC* 7011
JAS DAY INVESTMENTS LTD   *p137*
96 GEIKIE ST, JASPER, AB, T0E 1E0
(780) 852-5644   *SIC* 7011
JAS DAY INVESTMENTS LTD   *p137*
94 GEIKIE ST, JASPER, AB, T0E 1E0
(780) 852-4431   *SIC* 7011
JORDAN ENTERPRISES LIMITED   *p213*
9830 100 AVE, FORT ST. JOHN, BC, V1J
1Y5
(250) 787-0521   *SIC* 7011
JORDAN ENTERPRISES LIMITED   *p225*
20111 93A AVE SUITE 200, LANGLEY, BC,
V1M 4A9
(604) 888-8677   *SIC* 7011
JOUVENCE, BASE DE PLEIN AIR INC *p1244*
131 CH DE JOUVENCE, ORFORD, QC, J1X
6R2
(450) 532-3134   *SIC* 7011
KING EDWARD REALTY INC   *p939*
37 KING ST E, TORONTO, ON, M5C 1E9
(416) 863-9700   *SIC* 7011
KSD ENTERPRISES LTD   *p585*
655 DIXON RD SUITE 1, ETOBICOKE, ON,
M9W 1J3
(416) 244-1711   *SIC* 7011
LAC LA BICHE INN LTD   *p138*
10030 101ST AVE, LAC LA BICHE, AB, T0A
2C0
(780) 623-4427   *SIC* 7011
LAC LA RONGE MOTOR HOTEL (1983) LTD
p1408
1120 LA RONGE AVE, LA RONGE, SK, S0J
1L0
(306) 425-2190   *SIC* 7011
LADCO COMPANY LIMITED   *p386*
2520 PORTAGE AVE, WINNIPEG, MB, R3J
3T6
(204) 885-4478   *SIC* 7011
LAIS HOTEL PROPERTIES LIMITED   *p761*
6 PINOT TRAIL, NIAGARA ON THE LAKE,
ON, L0S 1J0
(905) 468-3246   *SIC* 7011
LAIS HOTEL PROPERTIES LIMITED   *p761*
155 BYRON ST, NIAGARA ON THE LAKE,
ON, L0S 1J0
(905) 468-2195   *SIC* 7011
LAIS HOTEL PROPERTIES LIMITED   *p761*
48 JOHN ST, NIAGARA ON THE LAKE, ON,
L0S 1J0
(888) 669-5566   *SIC* 7011
LAKE LOUISE LIMITED PARTNERSHIP
p138
210 VILLAGE RD, LAKE LOUISE, AB, T0L
1E0

(403) 522-3791   *SIC* 7011
LAKE LOUISE SKI AREA LTD, THE   *p65*
1333 8 ST SW SUITE 908, CALGARY, AB,
T2R 1M6
(403) 244-4449   *SIC* 7011
LAKE LOUISE SKI AREA LTD, THE   *p138*
1 WHITEHORN RD, LAKE LOUISE, AB, T0L
1E0
(403) 522-3555   *SIC* 7011
LAKEVIEW MANAGEMENT INC   *p378*
185 CARLTON ST SUITE 600, WINNIPEG,
MB, R3C 3J1
(204) 947-1161   *SIC* 7011
LAMB PROPERTIES INC   *p178*
36035 NORTH PARALLEL RD, ABBOTS-
FORD, BC, V3G 2C6
(604) 870-1050   *SIC* 7011
LAMPLIGHTER INNS (LONDON) LIMITED
p654
100 PICCADILLY ST, LONDON, ON, N6A
1R8
(519) 681-7151   *SIC* 7011
LAMPLIGHTER INNS (LONDON) LIMITED
p656
591 WELLINGTON RD, LONDON, ON, N6C
4R3
(519) 681-7151   *SIC* 7011
LANGDON HALL LIMITED   *p539*
1 LANGDON DR SUITE 33, CAMBRIDGE,
ON, N3H 4R8
(519) 740-2100   *SIC* 7011
LARCO HOSPITALITY INC   *p342*
100 PARK ROYAL S UNIT 300, WEST VAN-
COUVER, BC, V7T 1A2
(604) 925-2700   *SIC* 7011
LARCO INVESTMENTS LTD   *p981*
1 BLUE JAYS WAY SUITE 1, TORONTO,
ON, M5V 1J4
(416) 341-7100   *SIC* 7011
LAW CRANBERRY RESORT LIMITED *p546*
19 KEITH AVE, COLLINGWOOD, ON, L9Y
4T9
(705) 445-6600   *SIC* 7011
LEADON (BARRINGTON) OPERATIONS LP
p453
1875 BARRINGTON ST, HALIFAX, NS, B3J
3L6
(902) 429-7410   *SIC* 7011
LEADON (HALIFAX) OPERATIONS LP *p453*
1990 BARRINGTON ST, HALIFAX, NS, B3J
1P2
(902) 425-6700   *SIC* 7011
LEADON (REGINA) OPERATIONS LP *p1418*
1975 BROAD ST, REGINA, SK, S4P 1Y2
(306) 525-6767   *SIC* 7011
LGL RESORTS COMPANY   *p1159*
2396 RUE LABELLE, MONT-TREMBLANT,
QC, J8E 1T8
(819) 425-2734   *SIC* 7011
LICKMAN TRAVEL CENTRE INC   *p197*
43971 INDUSTRIAL WAY SUITE 2, CHILLI-
WACK, BC, V2R 3A4
(604) 795-3828   *SIC* 7011
LIGHTHOUSE CAMP SERVICES LTD *p30*
714 1 ST SE UNIT 300, CALGARY, AB, T2G
2G8
(403) 265-5190   *SIC* 7011
LISTEL CANADA LTD   *p314*
1300 ROBSON ST, VANCOUVER, BC, V6E
1C5
(604) 684-8461   *SIC* 7011
LISTEL CANADA LTD   *p343*
4121 VILLAGE GREEN, WHISTLER, BC,
V8E 1H2
(604) 932-1133   *SIC* 7011
LIVERTON HOTELS INTERNATIONAL INC
p306
645 HOWE ST, VANCOUVER, BC, V6C 2Y9
(604) 687-1122   *SIC* 7011
LJC DEVELOPMENT CORPORATION *p1213*
1425 RUE DE LA MONTAGNE, MON-
TREAL, QC, H3G 1Z3
(514) 285-5555   *SIC* 7011
LONDON (KING ST.) PURCHASECO INC

---

p656
300 KING ST, LONDON, ON, N6B 1S2
(519) 439-1661   *SIC* 7011
LUXURY HOTELS INTERNATIONAL OF CANADA ULC   p30
110 9 AVE SE, CALGARY, AB, T2G 5A6
(403) 266-7331   *SIC* 7011
LUXURY HOTELS INTERNATIONAL OF CANADA ULC   p407
600 MAIN ST, MONCTON, NB, E1C 0M6
(506) 854-7100   *SIC* 7011
LUXURY HOTELS INTERNATIONAL OF CANADA ULC   p685
1050 PAIGNTON HOUSE RD, MINETT, ON, P0B 1G0
(705) 765-1900   *SIC* 7011
LUXURY HOTELS INTERNATIONAL OF CANADA ULC   p697
2425 MATHESON BLVD E SUITE 100, MISSISSAUGA, ON, L4W 5K4
(905) 366-5200   *SIC* 7011
LUXURY HOTELS INTERNATIONAL OF CANADA ULC   p946
525 BAY ST, TORONTO, ON, M5G 2L2
(416) 597-9200   *SIC* 7011
LUXURY HOTELS INTERNATIONAL OF CANADA ULC   p1092
800 PLACE LEIGH-CAPREOL, DORVAL, QC, H4Y 0A5
(514) 636-6700   *SIC* 7011
MACY HOLDINGS LIMITED   p825
435 ALBERT ST, OTTAWA, ON, K1R 7X4
(613) 238-8858   *SIC* 7011
MANGA HOTELS (DARTMOUTH) INC   p444
101 WYSE RD, DARTMOUTH, NS, B3A 1L9
(902) 463-1100   *SIC* 7011
MANOIR DES SABLES INC   p1244
90 AV DES JARDINS, ORFORD, QC, J1X 6M6
(819) 847-4747   *SIC* 7011
MANOIR DU LAC DELAGE INC   p1124
40 AV DU LAC, LAC-DELAGE, QC, G3C 5C4
(418) 848-0691   *SIC* 7011
MANOIR HOVEY (1985) INC   p1073
575 CH HOVEY, CANTON-DE-HATLEY, QC, J0B 2C0
(819) 842-2421   *SIC* 7011
MANTEO BEACH CLUB LTD   p219
3766 LAKESHORE RD, KELOWNA, BC, V1W 3L4
(250) 860-1031   *SIC* 7011
MARBOR HOLDINGS LTD   p236
422 VERNON ST, NELSON, BC, V1L 4E5
(250) 352-5331   *SIC* 7011
MARCHE AU CHALET (1978) INC   p1354
1300 BOUL DE SAINTE-ADELE, SAINTE-ADELE, QC, J8B 0K2
(450) 229-4256   *SIC* 7011
MARITIME INNS & RESORTS INCORPORATED   p463
174 ARCHIMEDES ST, NEW GLASGOW, NS, B2H 2T6
(902) 752-5644   *SIC* 7011
MARKET SQUARE LIMITED PARTNERSHIP   p821
350 DALHOUSIE ST, OTTAWA, ON, K1N 7E9
(613) 241-1000   *SIC* 7011
MARKHAM SUITES HOTEL LIMITED   p680
8500 WARDEN AVE, MARKHAM, ON, L6G 1A5
(905) 470-8500   *SIC* 7011
MARKHAM WOODBINE HOSPITALITY LTD   p672
3100 STEELES AVE E SUITE 601, MARKHAM, ON, L3R 8T3
(905) 940-9409   *SIC* 7011
MASSIF INC, LE   p1245
1350 RUE PRINCIPALE, PETITE-RIVIERE-SAINT-FRANCOIS, QC, G0A 2L0
(877) 536-2774   *SIC* 7011
MAYFAIR PROPERTIES LTD   p299
111 ROBSON ST, VANCOUVER, BC, V6B

6P5
(604) 681-0868   *SIC* 7011
MAYFIELD INVESTMENTS LTD   p90
10010 106 ST NW SUITE 1005, EDMONTON, AB, T5J 3L8
(780) 424-2921   *SIC* 7011
MAYFIELD INVESTMENTS LTD   p146
1051 ROSS GLEN DR SE, MEDICINE HAT, AB, T1B 3T8
(403) 502-8185   *SIC* 7011
MAYFIELD SUITES GENERAL PARTNER INC   p697
5400 DIXIE RD, MISSISSAUGA, ON, L4W 4T4
(905) 238-0159   *SIC* 7011
MELO, J.S. INC   p631
285 KING ST E, KINGSTON, ON, K7L 3B1
(613) 544-4434   *SIC* 7011
MITCHELL GROUP ALBERTA INC   p76
2500 48 AVE NE, CALGARY, AB, T3J 4V8
(403) 238-1000   *SIC* 7011
MONT SAINT-SAUVEUR INTERNATIONAL INC   p1352
350 AV SAINT-DENIS RR 3, SAINT-SAUVEUR, QC, J0R 1R3
(450) 227-4671   *SIC* 7011
MONTE CARLO HOTEL-MOTEL INTERNATIONAL INC   p735
7045 EDWARDS BLVD FL 5, MISSISSAUGA, ON, L5S 1X2
(905) 564-6194   *SIC* 7011
MR. SPORT HOTEL HOLDINGS LTD   p288
3484 KINGSWAY SUITE 101, VANCOUVER, BC, V5R 5L6
(604) 433-8255   *SIC* 7011
MT. WASHINGTON SKI RESORT LTD   p202
1 STRATHCONA PKY, COURTENAY, BC, V9J 1L0
(250) 338-1386   *SIC* 7011
NEW WORLD HOTELS LTD   p315
1133 HASTINGS ST W, VANCOUVER, BC, V6E 3T3
(604) 689-9211   *SIC* 7011
NIAGARA 21ST GROUP INC   p759
5950 VICTORIA AVE, NIAGARA FALLS, ON, L2G 3L7
(905) 353-4044   *SIC* 7011
NIAGARA 21ST GROUP INC   p759
6740 FALLSVIEW BLVD, NIAGARA FALLS, ON, L2G 3W6
(905) 357-7300   *SIC* 7011
NIAGARA HOSPITALITY HOTELS INC p759
6546 FALLSVIEW BLVD, NIAGARA FALLS, ON, L2G 3W2
(905) 358-4666   *SIC* 7011
NIPPON CABLE (CANADA) HOLDINGS LTD
p270
1280 ALPINE RD RR 1, SUN PEAKS, BC, V0E 5N0
(250) 578-7232   *SIC* 7011
NOR-SHAM HOTELS INC   p715
2125 NORTH SHERIDAN WAY, MISSISSAUGA, ON, L5K 1A3
(905) 855-2000   *SIC* 7011
NORBRO HOLDINGS LTD   p562
1515 VINCENT MASSEY DR, CORNWALL, ON, K6H 5R6
(613) 932-0451   *SIC* 7011
NORSEMEN INN CAMROSE CORPORATION   p78
6505 48 AVE, CAMROSE, AB, T4V 3K3
(780) 672-9171   *SIC* 7011
NORTHAMPTON GROUP INC   p698
2601 MATHESON BLVD E SUITE 212, MISSISSAUGA, ON, L4W 5A8
(905) 629-9992   *SIC* 7011
NORTHLAND PROPERTIES CORPORATION   p36
8001 11 ST SE, CALGARY, AB, T2H 0B8
(403) 252-7263   *SIC* 7011
NORTHLAND PROPERTIES CORPORATION   p222
2130 HARVEY AVE, KELOWNA, BC, V1Y 6G8

(250) 860-6409   *SIC* 7011
NORTHLAND PROPERTIES CORPORATION   p321
1755 BROADWAY W SUITE 310, VANCOUVER, BC, V6J 4S5
(604) 730-6610   *SIC* 7011
NORTHSTAR HOSPITALITY LIMITED PARTNERSHIP   p698
5090 EXPLORER DR SUITE 700, MISSISSAUGA, ON, L4W 4T9
(905) 629-3400   *SIC* 7011
NORTHSTAR HOSPITALITY LIMITED PARTNERSHIP   p955
145 RICHMOND ST W SUITE 212, TORONTO, ON, M5H 2L2
(416) 869-3456   *SIC* 7011
NORWOOD HOTEL CO LTD   p364
112 MARION ST, WINNIPEG, MB, R2H 0T1
(204) 233-4475   *SIC* 7011
NUNASTAR PROPERTIES INC   p436
4825 49TH AVE, YELLOWKNIFE, NT, X1A 2R3
(867) 873-3531   *SIC* 7011
NURMANN HOLDINGS LTD   p272
19500 LANGLEY BYPASS, SURREY, BC, V3S 7R2
(604) 530-6545   *SIC* 7011
OAK BAY BEACH HOTEL LIMITED   p333
1175 BEACH DR, VICTORIA, BC, V8S 2N2
(250) 598-4556   *SIC* 7011
OAK BAY MARINA LTD   p284
1943 PENINSULA RD, UCLUELET, BC, V0R 3A0
(250) 726-7771   *SIC* 7011
OCEAN PACIFIC HOTELS LTD   p308
999 CANADA PL SUITE 300, VANCOUVER, BC, V6C 3B5
(604) 662-8111   *SIC* 7011
OHR WHISTLER MANAGEMENT LTD p342
4090 WHISTLER WAY, WHISTLER, BC, V0N 1B4
(604) 905-5000   *SIC* 7011
OLD ORCHARD INN LIMITED   p471
153 GREENWICH RD S, WOLFVILLE, NS, B4P 2R2
(902) 542-5751   *SIC* 7011
OLDE YORKE ESPLANADE HOTELS LTD
p943
45 THE ESPLANADE, TORONTO, ON, M5E 1W2
(416) 367-8900   *SIC* 7011
OMT HOSPITALITY INC   p572
21 OLD MILL RD, ETOBICOKE, ON, M8X 1G5
(416) 236-2641   *SIC* 7011
P SUN'S ENTERPRISES (VANCOUVER) LTD   p308
885 GEORGIA ST W, VANCOUVER, BC, V6C 3E8
(604) 643-7939   *SIC* 7011
P SUN'S ENTERPRISES (VANCOUVER) LTD   p335
463 BELLEVILLE ST, VICTORIA, BC, V8V 1X3
(250) 386-0450   *SIC* 7011
P.G. HOTEL LTD   p454
1725 MARKET ST, HALIFAX, NS, B3J 3N9
(902) 425-1986   *SIC* 7011
P.R. DEVELOPMENTS LTD   p24
2828 23 ST NE, CALGARY, AB, T2E 8T4
(403) 291-2003   *SIC* 7011
PANORAMA MOUNTAIN VILLAGE INC p242
2000 PANORAMA DR, PANORAMA, BC, V0A 1T0
(250) 342-6941   *SIC* 7011
PARAMITA ENTERPRISES LIMITED   p902
538 BLANCHARD PK, TECUMSEH, ON, N8N 2L9
(519) 727-2323   *SIC* 7011
PARK PLACE CENTRE LIMITED   p447
240 BROWNLOW AVE, DARTMOUTH, NS, B3B 1X6
(902) 468-8888   *SIC* 7011
PARK TOWN ENTERPRISES LTD   p1429

924 SPADINA CRES E, SASKATOON, SK, S7K 3H5
(306) 244-5564   *SIC* 7011
PARKWAY HOTELS AND CONVENTION CENTRE INC   p853
600 HIGHWAY 7 E, RICHMOND HILL, ON, L4B 1B2
(905) 881-2121   *SIC* 7011
PASUTTO'S HOTELS (1984) LTD   p69
400 MIDPARK WAY SE, CALGARY, AB, T2X 3S4
(403) 514-0099   *SIC* 7011
PAUL'S RESTAURANTS LTD   p335
680 MONTREAL ST, VICTORIA, BC, V8V 1Z8
(250) 412-3194   *SIC* 7011
PEACE HILLS INVESTMENTS LTD   p139
5207 50 AVE, LEDUC, AB, T9E 6V3
(780) 986-2241   *SIC* 7011
PEACE HILLS INVESTMENTS LTD   p172
4103 56 ST, WETASKIWIN, AB, T9A 1V2
(780) 312-7300   *SIC* 7011
PENTICTON COURTYARD INN LTD   p244
1050 ECKHARDT AVE W, PENTICTON, BC, V2A 2C3
(250) 492-8926   *SIC* 7011
PIKE LAKE GOLF CENTRE LIMITED   p544
GD, CLIFFORD, ON, N0G 1M0
(519) 338-3010   *SIC* 7011
PINNACLE INTERNATIONAL MANAGEMENT INC   p299
911 HOMER ST SUITE 300, VANCOUVER, BC, V6B 2W6
(604) 602-7747   *SIC* 7011
PLACE MONTCALM HOTEL INC   p1269
1225 COURS DU GENERAL-DE-MONTCALM, QUEBEC, QC, G1R 4W6
(418) 647-2222   *SIC* 7011
PLATINUM INVESTMENTS LTD   p102
17610 STONY PLAIN RD NW, EDMONTON, AB, T5S 1A2
(780) 443-2233   *SIC* 7011
PLAZA 500 HOTELS LTD   p293
500 12TH AVE W, VANCOUVER, BC, V5Z 1M2
(604) 873-1811   *SIC* 7011
PLAZA II CORPORATION, THE   p930
90 BLOOR ST E, TORONTO, ON, M4W 1A7
(416) 922-9155   *SIC* 7011
POLEY MOUNTAIN RESORTS LTD   p419
69 POLEY MOUNTAIN RD, WATERFORD, NB, E4E 4Y2
(506) 433-7653   *SIC* 7011
POMEROY LODGING LP   p133
9820 100 AVE, GRANDE PRAIRIE, AB, T8V 0T8
(780) 814-5295   *SIC* 7011
PRETTY ESTATES LTD   p215
14282 MORRIS VALLEY RD, HARRISON MILLS, BC, V0M 1L0
(604) 796-1000   *SIC* 7011
PRINCE ALBERT DEVELOPMENT CORPORATION   p1414
67 13TH ST E, PRINCE ALBERT, SK, S6V 1C7
(306) 763-2643   *SIC* 7011
RADISSON HOTEL SASKATOON   p1429
405 20TH ST E, SASKATOON, SK, S7K 6X6
(306) 665-3322   *SIC* 7011
RED DEER LODGE LTD   p154
4311 49 AVE, RED DEER, AB, T4N 5Y7
(403) 754-5503   *SIC* 7011
REGINA TRAVELODGE LTD   p1422
4177 ALBERT ST, REGINA, SK, S4S 3R6
(306) 586-3443   *SIC* 7011
REMAI HOLDINGS LTD   p25
2828 23 ST NE, CALGARY, AB, T2E 8T4
(403) 291-2003   *SIC* 7011
REMAI INVESTMENT CORPORATION
p1429
500 SPADINA CRES E SUITE 101, SASKATOON, SK, S7K 4H9
(306) 244-1119   *SIC* 7011
REMAI VENTURES INC   p1432

143 CARDINAL CRES, SASKATOON, SK, S7L 6H5

(306) 934-2799 *SIC* 7011

RESORTS OF THE CANADIAN ROCKIES INC *p223*
301 NORTH STAR BLVD, KIMBERLEY, BC, V1A 2Y5

(250) 427-4881 *SIC* 7011

REVELSTOKE MOUNTAIN RESORT LIMITED PARTNERSHIP *p253*
2950 CAMOZZI RD, REVELSTOKE, BC, V0E 2S3

(250) 814-0087 *SIC* 7011

RICHMOND INN HOTEL LTD *p261*
7551 WESTMINSTER HWY, RICHMOND, BC, V6X 1A3

(604) 273-7878 *SIC* 7011

RITZ-CARLTON HOTEL COMPANY OF CANADA LIMITED, THE *p983*
181 WELLINGTON ST W, TORONTO, ON, M5V 3G7

(416) 585-2500 *SIC* 7011

RIVER CREE RESORT LIMITED PARTNERSHIP *p126*
300 E LAPOTAC BLVD, ENOCH, AB, T7X 3Y3

(780) 484-2121 *SIC* 7011

RODD MANAGEMENT LIMITED *p1038*
86 DEWARS LN, CARDIGAN, PE, C0A 1G0

(902) 652-2332 *SIC* 7011

ROYAL HOST INC *p41*
1804 CROWCHILD TRAIL NW, CALGARY, AB, T2M 3Y7

(403) 289-0241 *SIC* 7011

ROYAL HOST INC *p454*
1809 BARRINGTON ST SUITE 1108, HALIFAX, NS, B3J 3K8

(902) 470-4500 *SIC* 7011

ROYAL HOST INC *p587*
925 DIXON RD, ETOBICOKE, ON, M9W 1J8

(416) 674-2222 *SIC* 7011

ROYAL HOST INC *p801*
590 ARGUS RD, OAKVILLE, ON, L6J 3J3

(905) 842-5000 *SIC* 7011

ROYAL TOWERS HOTEL INC *p237*
140 SIXTH ST, NEW WESTMINSTER, BC, V3L 2Z9

(604) 524-4689 *SIC* 7011

ROYAL WEST EDMONTON INN LTD *p103*
10010 178 ST NW, EDMONTON, AB, T5S 1T3

(780) 484-6000 *SIC* 7011

ROYAL YORK OPERATIONS LP *p966*
100 FRONT ST W, TORONTO, ON, M5J 1E3

(416) 368-2511 *SIC* 7011

SANTEK INVESTMENTS (1991) INC *p578*
1 VALHALLA INN RD, ETOBICOKE, ON, M9B 1S9

(416) 233-5554 *SIC* 7011

SASCO DEVELOPMENTS LTD *p1411*
1590 MAIN ST N, MOOSE JAW, SK, S6J 1L3

(306) 693-7550 *SIC* 7011

SAWRIDGE ENTERPRISES LTD *p90*
10104 103 AVE NW UNIT 1910, EDMONTON, AB, T5J 0H8

(780) 428-3330 *SIC* 7011

SAYANI INVESTMENTS INC *p202*
405 NORTH RD, COQUITLAM, BC, V3K 3V9

(604) 936-9399 *SIC* 7011

SEARCHMONT SKI ASSOCIATION INC *p879*
103 SEARCHMONT RESORT RD, SEARCHMONT, ON, P0S 1J0

(705) 781-2340 *SIC* 7011

SEM RESORT LIMITED PARTNERSHIP *p204*
7777 MISSION RD, CRANBROOK, BC, V1C 7E5

(250) 420-2000 *SIC* 7011

SENATOR HOTELS LIMITED *p913*
14 MOUNTJOY ST S, TIMMINS, ON, P4N

1S4

(705) 267-6211 *SIC* 7011

SEVEN OAKS MOTOR INN LTD *p1421*
777 ALBERT ST, REGINA, SK, S4R 2P6

(306) 757-0121 *SIC* 7011

SHOREFAST SOCIAL ENTERPRISES INC *p425*
181 MAIN ST, JOE BATTS ARM, NL, A0G 2X0

(709) 658-3444 *SIC* 7011

SILVER HOTEL (AMBLER) INC *p727*
2501 ARGENTIA RD, MISSISSAUGA, ON, L5N 4G8

(905) 858-2424 *SIC* 7011

SILVERBIRCH NO. 38 OPERATIONS LIMITED PARTNERSHIP *p119*
4440 GATEWAY BLVD NW, EDMONTON, AB, T6H 5C2

(780) 437-6010 *SIC* 7011

SILVERBIRCH NO. 4 OPERATIONS LIMITED PARTNERSHIP *p25*
2120 16 AVE NE, CALGARY, AB, T2E 1L4

(403) 291-4666 *SIC* 7011

SIMDAR INC *p1291*
500 CH DU LAC-A-L'EAU-CLAIRE, SAINT-ALEXIS-DES-MONTS, QC, J0K 1V0

(819) 265-3185 *SIC* 7011

SKI CLUB OF THE CANADIAN ROCKIES LIMITED, THE *p139*
200 PIPESTONE RD, LAKE LOUISE, AB, T0L 1E0

(403) 522-3989 *SIC* 7011

SKI MARMOT BASIN LIMITED PARTNERSHIP *p137*
GD, JASPER, AB, T0E 1E0

(780) 852-3816 *SIC* 7011

SKI MARMOT GP CORP *p137*
GD, JASPER, AB, T0E 1E0

(780) 852-3816 *SIC* 7011

SKYLINE DEERHURST RESORT INC *p621*
1235 DEERHURST DR, HUNTSVILLE, ON, P1H 2E8

(705) 789-6411 *SIC* 7011

SOCIETE DE GESTION CAP-AUX-PIERRES INC *p1270*
57 RUE SAINTE-ANNE, QUEBEC, QC, G1R 3X4

(418) 692-2480 *SIC* 7011

SOCIETE EN COMMANDITE 901 SQUARE VICTORIA *p1192*
901 RUE DU SQUARE-VICTORIA BUREAU 1471, MONTREAL, QC, H2Z 1R1

(514) 395-3100 *SIC* 7011

SOCIETE EN COMMANDITE AUBERGE GODEFROY *p1056*
17575 BOUL BECANCOUR, BECANCOUR, QC, G9H 1A5

(819) 233-2200 *SIC* 7011

SOCIETE EN COMMANDITE MANOIR RICHELIEU *p1122*
181 RUE RICHELIEU BUREAU 200, LA MALBAIE, QC, G5A 1X7

(418) 665-3703 *SIC* 7011

SOMMETS DE LA VALLEE INC, LES *p1352*
350 AV SAINT-DENIS, SAINT-SAUVEUR, QC, J0R 1R3

(450) 227-4671 *SIC* 7011

SONCO GAMING NEW BRUNSWICK LIMITED PARTNERSHIP *p409*
21 CASINO DR, MONCTON, NB, E1G 0R7

(506) 859-7770 *SIC* 7011

SOUTH SURREY HOTEL LTD *p281*
1160 KING GEORGE BLVD, SURREY, BC, V4A 4Z2

(604) 535-1432 *SIC* 7011

STANLEY PARK INVESTMENTS LTD *p39*
12025 LAKE FRASER DR SE, CALGARY, AB, T2J 7G5

(403) 225-3000 *SIC* 7011

STARWOOD CANADA ULC *p60*
320 4 AVE SW, CALGARY, AB, T2P 2S6

(403) 266-1611 *SIC* 7011

STARWOOD CANADA ULC *p822*
11 COLONEL BY DR, OTTAWA, ON, K1N

9H4

(613) 560-7000 *SIC* 7011

STARWOOD CANADA ULC *p957*
123 QUEEN ST W SUITE 100, TORONTO, ON, M5H 2M9

(416) 947-4955 *SIC* 7011

STARWOOD HOTEL *p727*
2501 ARGENTIA RD, MISSISSAUGA, ON, L5N 4G8

(905) 858-2424 *SIC* 7011

STARWOOD HOTELS & RESORTS, INC *p1208*
1201 BOUL RENE-LEVESQUE O BUREAU 217, MONTREAL, QC, H3B 2L7

(514) 878-2046 *SIC* 7011

STATION MONT TREMBLANT INC *p1159*
1000 CH DES VOYAGEURS, MONT-TREMBLANT, QC, J8E 1T1

(819) 681-3000 *SIC* 7011

STATION MONT-SAINTE-ANNE INC *p1055*
2000 BOUL DU BEAU-PRE BUREAU 400, BEAUPRE, QC, G0A 1E0

(418) 827-4561 *SIC* 7011

STATION MONT-TREMBLANT SOCIETE EN COMMANDITE *p1159*
1000 CH DES VOYAGEURS, MONT-TREMBLANT, QC, J8E 1T1

(819) 681-2000 *SIC* 7011

STURGEON HOTEL LTD *p166*
156 ST ALBERT TRAIL SUITE 10, ST. ALBERT, AB, T8N 0P5

(780) 459-5551 *SIC* 7011

SUDBURY REGENT STREET INC *p901*
2270 REGENT ST, SUDBURY, ON, P3E 0B4

(705) 523-8100 *SIC* 7011

SUNSHINE VILLAGE CORPORATION *p65*
1037 11 AVE SW, CALGARY, AB, T2R 0G1

(403) 705-4000 *SIC* 7011

TALISMAN MOUNTAIN RESORT LTD *p628*
150 TALISMAN BLVD, KIMBERLEY, ON, N0C 1G0

SIC 7011

TEMPLE GARDENS MINERAL SPA INC *p1411*
24 FAIRFORD ST E, MOOSE JAW, SK, S6H 0C7

(306) 694-5055 *SIC* 7011

TIGH-NA-MARA RESORTS LTD *p243*
1155 RESORT DR, PARKSVILLE, BC, V9P 2E3

(250) 248-2072 *SIC* 7011

TOFINO RESORT + MARINA INC *p283*
634 CAMPBELL ST, TOFINO, BC, V0R 2Z0

(250) 725-3277 *SIC* 7011

TOKYU CANADA CORPORATION *p310*
999 CANADA PL SUITE 515, VANCOUVER, BC, V6C 3E1

SIC 7011

TORONTO AIRPORT MARRIOTT LTD, THE *p589*
901 DIXON RD, ETOBICOKE, ON, M9W 1J5

(416) 674-9400 *SIC* 7011

TREIT HOLDINGS 21 INC *p467*
380 ESPLANADE ST, SYDNEY, NS, B1P 1B1

(902) 562-6500 *SIC* 7011

UNITED ENTERPRISES LTD *p1413*
992 101ST ST, NORTH BATTLEFORD, SK, S9A 0Z3

(306) 445-9425 *SIC* 7011

VANCOUVER AIRPORT CENTRE LIMITED *p262*
5911 MINORU BLVD, RICHMOND, BC, V6X 4C7

(604) 273-6336 *SIC* 7011

VANCOUVER AIRPORT CENTRE LIMITED *p262*
7571 WESTMINSTER HWY, RICHMOND, BC, V6X 1A3

(604) 276-2112 *SIC* 7011

VICTORIA INN WINNIPEG INC *p385*
1808 WELLINGTON AVE, WINNIPEG, MB, R3H 0G3

(204) 786-4801 *SIC* 7011

VISCOUNT GORT MOTOR HOTEL LTD *p386*
1670 PORTAGE AVE, WINNIPEG, MB, R3J 0C9

(204) 775-0451 *SIC* 7011

VISTA SUDBURY HOTEL INC *p901*
85 STE ANNE RD, SUDBURY, ON, P3E 4S4

(705) 675-1123 *SIC* 7011

WALL FINANCIAL CORPORATION *p327*
1088 BURRARD ST, VANCOUVER, BC, V6Z 2R9

(604) 331-1000 *SIC* 7011

WALPER TERRACE HOTEL INC *p639*
1 KING ST W, KITCHENER, ON, N2G 1A1

(519) 745-4321 *SIC* 7011

WATERLOO MOTOR INN LIMITED *p1007*
475 KING ST N, WATERLOO, ON, N2J 2Z5

(519) 885-0721 *SIC* 7011

WAYSIDE MANAGEMENT LTD *p144*
5411 44 ST, LLOYDMINSTER, AB, T9V 0A9

(780) 875-4404 *SIC* 7011

WEDGEWOOD VILLAGE ESTATES LTD *p327*
845 HORNBY ST, VANCOUVER, BC, V6Z 1V1

(604) 689-7777 *SIC* 7011

WELLINGTON WINDSOR HOLDINGS LTD *p984*
255 WELLINGTON ST W, TORONTO, ON, M5V 3P9

(416) 581-1800 *SIC* 7011

WENTWORTH HOTELS LTD *p317*
1177 MELVILLE ST, VANCOUVER, BC, V6E 0A3

(604) 669-5060 *SIC* 7011

WEST ISLAND HOTELS INC *p1252*
6700 RTE TRANSCANADIENNE, POINTE-CLAIRE, QC, H9R 1C2

(514) 697-7110 *SIC* 7011

WESTBERG HOLDINGS INC *p327*
1176 GRANVILLE ST, VANCOUVER, BC, V6Z 1L8

(604) 688-8701 *SIC* 7011

WESTERN FIRST NATIONS HOSPITALITY LIMITED PARTNERSHIP *p1414*
914 CENTRAL AVE, PRINCE ALBERT, SK, S6V 4V3

(306) 922-0088 *SIC* 7011

WESTMARK HOTELS OF CANADA LTD *p1440*
2288 2ND AVE, WHITEHORSE, YT, Y1A 1C8

(867) 668-4747 *SIC* 7011

WESTMARK HOTELS OF CANADA LTD *p1440*
201 WOOD ST, WHITEHORSE, YT, Y1A 2E4

(867) 393-9700 *SIC* 7011

WESTMONT HOSPITALITY MANAGEMENT LIMITED *p589*
600 DIXON RD, ETOBICOKE, ON, M9W 1J1

(416) 240-7511 *SIC* 7011

WESTMONT HOSPITALITY MANAGEMENT LIMITED *p602*
601 SCOTTSDALE DR, GUELPH, ON, N1G 3E7

(519) 836-0231 *SIC* 7011

WESTVIEW INN LTD *p98*
16625 STONY PLAIN RD NW, EDMONTON, AB, T5P 4A8

(780) 484-7751 *SIC* 7011

WHISTLER & BLACKCOMB MOUNTAIN RESORTS LIMITED *p343*
4545 BLACKCOMB WAY RR 4, WHISTLER, BC, V0N 1B4

(604) 932-3141 *SIC* 7011

WHISTLER MOUNTAIN RESORT LIMITED PARTNERSHIP *p343*
4545 BLACKCOMB WAY, WHISTLER, BC, V8E 0X9

(604) 932-3141 *SIC* 7011

WHITEWATER SKI RESORT LTD *p236*
602 LAKE ST, NELSON, BC, V1L 4C8

(250) 354-4944   *SIC* 7011
WICKANINNISH INN LIMITED   *p283*
500 OSPREY LANE, TOFINO, BC, V0R 2Z0
(250) 725-3106   *SIC* 7011
WINDSOR ARMS DEVELOPMENT CORPORATION   *p976*
18 SAINT THOMAS ST, TORONTO, ON, M5S 3E7
(416) 971-9666   *SIC* 7011
WINDSOR CASINO LIMITED   *p1024*
377 RIVERSIDE DR E, WINDSOR, ON, N9A 7H7
(519) 258-7878   *SIC* 7011
WW HOTELS (WHISTLER) LIMITED PARTNERSHIP   *p343*
4050 WHISTLER WAY, WHISTLER, BC, V8E 1H9
(604) 932-1982   *SIC* 7011
WW HOTELS CORP   *p769*
55 HALLCROWN PL, NORTH YORK, ON, M2J 4R1
(416) 493-7000   *SIC* 7011
YELLOWHEAD MOTOR INN LTD   *p106*
15004 YELLOWHEAD TRAIL NW, EDMONTON, AB, T5V 1A1
(780) 447-2400   *SIC* 7011
YONGE STREET HOTEL LTD   *p932*
475 YONGE ST, TORONTO, ON, M4Y 1X7
(416) 924-0611   *SIC* 7011
YOUNG WOMEN'S CHRISTIAN ASSOCIATION   *p311*
535 HORNBY ST, VANCOUVER, BC, V6C 2E8
(604) 895-5800   *SIC* 7011
YOUNG WOMEN'S CHRISTIAN ASSOCIATION OF CANADA, THE   *p436*
5004 50TH AVE, YELLOWKNIFE, NT, X1A 2P3
(867) 920-2777   *SIC* 7011

SIC 7021 Rooming and boarding houses

CIVEO CORPORATION   *p113*
3790 98 ST NW, EDMONTON, AB, T6E 6B4
(780) 463-8872   *SIC* 7021
CSSS RICHELIEU-YAMASKA CH DE LA MRC D'ACTON   *p1312*
1955 AV PRATTE, SAINT-HYACINTHE, QC, J2S 7W5
(450) 771-4536   *SIC* 7021
MAISON BLANCHE DE NORTH HATLEY INC, LA   *p1243*
977 RUE MASSAWIPPI, NORTH HATLEY, QC, J0B 2C0
(450) 666-1567   *SIC* 7021
POMEROY HOTEL LTD   *p173*
4121 KEPLER ST, WHITECOURT, AB, T7S 0A3
(780) 778-8908   *SIC* 7021

SIC 7032 Sporting and recreational camps

1234121 ONTARIO LIMITED   *p716*
4069 PHEASANT RUN, MISSISSAUGA, ON, L5L 2C2
(905) 569-7595   *SIC* 7032
ASSOCIATION CHRETIENNE DES JEUNES FEMMES DE MONTREAL   *p1212*
1355 BOUL RENE-LEVESQUE O BUREAU 208, MONTREAL, QC, H3G 1T3
(514) 866-9941   *SIC* 7032
BIMINI UNITED CHURCH CAMP   *p757*
3180 113 RD, NEWTON, ON, N0K 1V0
(519) 271-4129   *SIC* 7032
CAMP AGUDAH   *p788*
129 MCGILLIVRAY AVE, NORTH YORK, ON, M5M 2Y7
(416) 781-7101   *SIC* 7032
CAMP B B-RIBACK   *p68*
1607 90 AVE SW, CALGARY, AB, T2V 4V7
SIC 7032
CAMP WAHANOWIN LIMITED   *p923*

227 EGLINTON AVE W, TORONTO, ON, M4R 1A9
(416) 482-2600   *SIC* 7032
CAMP WINNEBAGOE INC   *p972*
4 SILVERWOOD AVE, TORONTO, ON, M5P 1W4
(416) 486-1110   *SIC* 7032
MACMARMON FOUNDATION   *p776*
275 DUNCAN MILL RD, NORTH YORK, ON, M3B 3H9
(416) 443-1030   *SIC* 7032
PLEIN AIR BRUCHESI INC   *p1307*
50 365E AV, SAINT-HIPPOLYTE, QC, J8A 2Y6
(450) 563-3056   *SIC* 7032
RECREGESTION LE GROUPE INC   *p1084*
6010 RUE DE PRINCE-RUPERT, COTE SAINT-LUC, QC, H7H 1C4
(450) 625-0196   *SIC* 7032
SOCIETE DES CASINOS DU QUEBEC INC, LA   *p1122*
183 RUE RICHELIEU, LA MALBAIE, QC, G5A 1X8
(418) 665-5300   *SIC* 7032
SOCIETE DES ETABLISSEMENTS DE PLEIN AIR DU QUEBEC   *p1378*
140 MONTEE DE L'AUBERGE, STE-CATHERINE-DE-LA-J-CARTIE, QC, G3N 2Y6
(418) 875-2711   *SIC* 7032
SOCIETE POUR LES ENFANTS HANDICAPES DU QUEBEC   *p1291*
210 RUE PAPILLON, SAINT-ALPHONSE-RODRIGUEZ, QC, J0K 1W0
(450) 883-2915   *SIC* 7032
SPORTS MONTREAL INC   *p1177*
1000 AV EMILE-JOURNAULT, MONTREAL, QC, H2M 2E7
(514) 872-7177   *SIC* 7032
STATTEN, TAYLOR CAMP COMPANY, LIMITED   *p924*
59 HOYLE AVE, TORONTO, ON, M4S 2X5
(416) 486-6959   *SIC* 7032
TIM HORTON CHILDREN'S FOUNDATION, INC   *p137*
GD, KANANASKIS, AB, T0L 2H0
(403) 673-2494   *SIC* 7032
TIM HORTON CHILDREN'S FOUNDATION, INC   *p681*
550 LORIMER LAKE RD, MCDOUGALL, ON, P2A 2W7
(705) 389-2773   *SIC* 7032
TIM HORTON CHILDREN'S FOUNDATION, INC   *p888*
264 GLEN MORRIS RD, ST GEORGE BRANT, ON, N0E 1N0
(519) 448-1264   *SIC* 7032
TIM HORTON CHILDREN'S FOUNDATION, INC   *p888*
264 GLEN MORRIS RD SUITE 2, ST GEORGE BRANT, ON, N0E 1N0
(519) 448-1248   *SIC* 7032
YMCA OF GREATER TORONTO   *p998*
1090 GULLWING LAKE RD RR 1, TORRANCE, ON, P0C 1M0
(705) 762-3377   *SIC* 7032

SIC 7033 Trailer parks and campsites

CHRISTIE LAKE KIDS   *p820*
400 COVENTRY RD, OTTAWA, ON, K1K 2C7
(613) 742-6922   *SIC* 7033

SIC 7041 Membership-basis organization hotels

CENTRE DE SANTE ET DE SERVICE SOCIAUX DU HAUT SAINT-FRANCOIS, LE   *p1400*
245 RUE SAINT-JANVIER, WEEDON, QC, J0B 3J0
SIC 7041

CENTRE INTEGRE DE SANTE ET DE SERVICES SOCIAUX DES LAURENTIDES   *p1153*
9100 RUE DUMOUCHEL, MIRABEL, QC, J7N 5A1
(450) 258-2481   *SIC* 7041
CHATEAU WESTMOUNT INC   *p1401*
1860 BOUL DE MAISONNEUVE O, WESTMOUNT, QC, H3Z 3G2
(514) 369-3000   *SIC* 7041
LODGE AT VALLEY RIDGE, THE   *p72*
11479 VALLEY RIDGE DR NW SUITE 332, CALGARY, AB, T3B 5V5
(403) 286-4414   *SIC* 7041
NORALTA LODGE LTD   *p128*
7210 CLIFF AVE SUITE 7202, FORT MCMURRAY, AB, T9H 1A1
(780) 791-3334   *SIC* 7041

SIC 7211 Power laundries, family and commercial

ALSCO CANADA CORPORATION   *p92*
14710 123 AVE NW, EDMONTON, AB, T5L 2Y4
(780) 454-9641   *SIC* 7211
PERTH SERVICES LTD   *p381*
765 WELLINGTON AVE SUITE 1, WINNIPEG, MB, R3E 0J1
(204) 697-6100   *SIC* 7211

SIC 7212 Garment pressing and cleaners' agents

K-BRO LINEN INC   *p105*
14903 137 AVE NW, EDMONTON, AB, T5V 1R9
(780) 453-5218   *SIC* 7212

SIC 7213 Linen supply

ALSCO CANADA CORPORATION   *p92*
14630 123 AVE NW, EDMONTON, AB, T5L 2Y4
(780) 452-5955   *SIC* 7213
ALSCO CANADA CORPORATION   *p291*
5 4TH AVE W, VANCOUVER, BC, V5Y 1G2
(604) 876-3272   *SIC* 7213
CANADIAN LINEN AND UNIFORM SERVICE CO   *p28*
4525 MANILLA RD SE, CALGARY, AB, T2G 4B6
(403) 243-8080   *SIC* 7213
CANADIAN LINEN AND UNIFORM SERVICE CO   *p85*
8631 STADIUM RD NW, EDMONTON, AB, T5H 3W9
(780) 665-3905   *SIC* 7213
CANADIAN LINEN AND UNIFORM SERVICE CO   *p184*
2750 GILMORE AVE, BURNABY, BC, V5C 4T9
(778) 331-6200   *SIC* 7213
CANADIAN LINEN AND UNIFORM SERVICE CO   *p369*
1860 KING EDWARD ST, WINNIPEG, MB, R2R 0N2
(204) 633-7261   *SIC* 7213
CANADIAN LINEN AND UNIFORM SERVICE CO   *p445*
41 THORNHILL DR SUITE 136, DARTMOUTH, NS, B3B 1R9
(902) 468-2155   *SIC* 7213
CANADIAN LINEN AND UNIFORM SERVICE CO   *p486*
116 VICTORIA ST, BARRIE, ON, L4N 2J1
(705) 739-0573   *SIC* 7213
CANADIAN LINEN AND UNIFORM SERVICE CO   *p573*
20 ATOMIC AVE, ETOBICOKE, ON, M8Z 5L1
(416) 354-3100   *SIC* 7213

CANADIAN LINEN AND UNIFORM SERVICE CO   *p652*
155 ADELAIDE ST S, LONDON, ON, N5Z 3K8
(519) 686-5000   *SIC* 7213
CANADIAN LINEN AND UNIFORM SERVICE CO   *p817*
1695 RUSSELL RD, OTTAWA, ON, K1G 0N1
(613) 736-9975   *SIC* 7213
CANADIAN LINEN AND UNIFORM SERVICE CO   *p1415*
180 N LEONARD ST, REGINA, SK, S4N 5V7
(306) 721-4848   *SIC* 7213
CINTAS CANADA LIMITED   *p755*
255 HARRY WALKER PKY S SUITE 1, NEWMARKET, ON, L3Y 8Z5
(905) 853-4409   *SIC* 7213
FASTER LINEN SERVICE LIMITED   *p574*
89 TORLAKE CRES, ETOBICOKE, ON, M8Z 1B4
(416) 252-2030   *SIC* 7213
G&K SERVICES CANADA INC   *p688*
5935 AIRPORT RD, MISSISSAUGA, ON, L4V 1W5
(905) 677-6161   *SIC* 7213
G&K SERVICES CANADA INC   *p1017*
9085 TWIN OAKS DR, WINDSOR, ON, N8N 5B8
(519) 979-5913   *SIC* 7213
G&K SERVICES CANADA INC   *p1170*
8400 19E AV, MONTREAL, QC, H1Z 4J3
(514) 723-7666   *SIC* 7213
LOGISTIK UNICORP INC   *p1315*
820 CH DU GRAND-BERNIER N, SAINT-JEAN-SUR-RICHELIEU, QC, J2W 0A6
(450) 349-9700   *SIC* 7213
LONDON HOSPITAL LINEN SERVICE INCORPORATED   *p656*
11 MAITLAND ST, LONDON, ON, N6B 3K7
(519) 438-2925   *SIC* 7213
QUEBEC LINGE CO   *p1166*
4375 RUE DE ROUEN, MONTREAL, QC, H1V 1H2
(514) 670-2005   *SIC* 7213
QUINTEX SERVICES LTD   *p387*
332 NASSAU ST N, WINNIPEG, MB, R3L 0R8
(204) 477-6600   *SIC* 7213
UNIFIRST CANADA LTD   *p19*
5728 35 ST SE, CALGARY, AB, T2C 2G3
(403) 279-2800   *SIC* 7213
UNIFIRST CANADA LTD   *p117*
3691 98 ST NW, EDMONTON, AB, T6E 5N2
(780) 423-0384   *SIC* 7213
UNIFIRST CANADA LTD   *p225*
9189 196A ST, LANGLEY, BC, V1M 3B5
(604) 888-8119   *SIC* 7213
UNIFIRST CANADA LTD   *p701*
5250 ORBITOR DR, MISSISSAUGA, ON, L4W 5G7
(905) 624-8525   *SIC* 7213
UNIFIRST CANADA LTD   *p718*
2290 DUNWIN DR, MISSISSAUGA, ON, L5L 1C7
(905) 828-9621   *SIC* 7213

SIC 7215 Coin-operated laundries and cleaning

COINAMATIC CANADA INC   *p730*
301 MATHESON BLVD W, MISSISSAUGA, ON, L5R 3G3
(905) 755-1946   *SIC* 7215
STEPHEN GROUP INC., THE   *p381*
765 WELLINGTON AVE, WINNIPEG, MB, R3E 0J1
(204) 697-6100   *SIC* 7215

SIC 7216 Drycleaning plants, except rugs

1768652 ALBERTA LTD *p33*
402 53 AVE SE, CALGARY, AB, T2H 0N4
(403) 262-3791   *SIC 7216*

BROWN'S CLEANERS AND TAILORS LIMITED *p824*
270 CITY CENTRE AVE, OTTAWA, ON, K1R 7R7
(613) 235-5181   *SIC 7216*

G&K SERVICES CANADA INC *p536*
205 TURNBULL CRT, CAMBRIDGE, ON, N1T 1W1
(519) 623-7703   *SIC 7216*

SIC 7217 Carpet and upholstery cleaning

CORPORATE CLEANING SERVICES LTD *p231*
20285 STEWART CRES SUITE 402, MAPLE RIDGE, BC, V2X 8G1
(604) 465-4699   *SIC 7217*

GENTLE CARE DRAPERY & CARPET CLEANERS LTD *p189*
3755 WAYBURNE DR, BURNABY, BC, V5G 3L1
(604) 296-4000   *SIC 7217*

SIC 7218 Industrial launderers

ALSCO CANADA CORPORATION *p1130*
2500 RUE SENKUS, LASALLE, QC, H8N 2X9
(514) 595-7381   *SIC 7218*

BUANDERIE BLANCHELLE INC, LA *p1282*
94 RUE DE NORMANDIE, REPENTIGNY, QC, J6A 4W2
(450) 585-1218   *SIC 7218*

BUANDERIE BLANCHELLE INC, LA *p1316*
825 AV MONTRICHARD, SAINT-JEAN-SUR-RICHELIEU, QC, J2X 5K8
(450) 347-4390   *SIC 7218*

BUANDERIE CENTRALE DE MONTREAL INC *p1163*
7250 RUE JOSEPH-DAOUST, MONTREAL, QC, H1N 3N9
(514) 253-1635   *SIC 7218*

BUANDERIE VILLERAY LTEE *p1166*
4740 RUE DE ROUEN, MONTREAL, QC, H1V 3T7
(514) 259-4531   *SIC 7218*

CANADIAN LINEN AND UNIFORM SERVICE CO *p786*
75 NORFINCH DR SUITE 1, NORTH YORK, ON, M3N 1W8
(416) 849-5100   *SIC 7218*

CINTAS CANADA LIMITED *p28*
1235 23 AVE SE, CALGARY, AB, T2G 5S5
SIC 7218

CINTAS CANADA LIMITED *p229*
5293 272 ST, LANGLEY, BC, V4W 1P1
(604) 857-2281   *SIC 7218*

CINTAS CANADA LIMITED *p650*
30 CHARTERHOUSE CRES, LONDON, ON, N5W 5V5
(519) 453-5010   *SIC 7218*

CINTAS CANADA LIMITED *p716*
4170 SLADEVIEW CRES UNIT 2, MISSISSAUGA, ON, L5L 0A1
(416) 763-4400   *SIC 7218*

CINTAS CANADA LIMITED *p786*
149 EDDYSTONE AVE, NORTH YORK, ON, M3N 1H5
(416) 743-5070   *SIC 7218*

CINTAS CANADA LIMITED *p1064*
1470 RUE NOBEL, BOUCHERVILLE, QC, J4B 5H3
(450) 449-4747   *SIC 7218*

INDUSTRIES DE LAVAGE DENTEX INC, LES *p1247*
12480 RUE APRIL, POINTE-AUX-TREMBLES, QC, H1B 5N5
SIC 7218

JOLICOEUR LTEE *p1174*

4132 RUE PARTHENAIS, MONTREAL, QC, H2K 3T9
(514) 526-4444   *SIC 7218*

K-BRO LINEN SYSTEMS INC *p105*
14903 137 AVE NW, EDMONTON, AB, T5V 1R9
(780) 453-6855   *SIC 7218*

OTTAWA REGIONAL HOSPITAL LINEN SERVICES INCORPORATED *p750*
45 GURDWARA RD, NEPEAN, ON, K2E 7X6
(613) 842-3000   *SIC 7218*

PARTAGEC INC *p1255*
1299 RUE PAUL-EMILE-GIROUX, QUEBEC, QC, G1C 0K9
(418) 647-1428   *SIC 7218*

UNIFIRST CANADA LTD *p1132*
8951 RUE SALLEY, LASALLE, QC, H8R 2C8
(514) 365-8301   *SIC 7218*

SIC 7219 Laundry and garment services, nec

CROTHALL SERVICES CANADA INC *p443*
300 PLEASANT ST SUITE 10, DARTMOUTH, NS, B2Y 3S3
(902) 464-3115   *SIC 7219*

G&K SERVICES CANADA INC *p11*
2925 10 AVE NE SUITE 7, CALGARY, AB, T2A 5L4
(403) 272-4256   *SIC 7219*

K-BRO LINEN SYSTEMS INC *p105*
15253 121A AVE NW, EDMONTON, AB, T5V 1N1
(780) 451-3131   *SIC 7219*

K-BRO LINEN SYSTEMS INC *p577*
15 SHORNCLIFFE RD, ETOBICOKE, ON, M9B 3S4
(416) 233-5555   *SIC 7219*

MARTIN INC *p1318*
285 RUE SAINT-JACQUES BUREAU 2, SAINT-JEAN-SUR-RICHELIEU, QC, J3B 2L1
(450) 347-2373   *SIC 7219*

PARA-NET BUANDERIE & NETTOYAGE A SEC INC *p1265*
1105 RUE VINCENT-MASSEY, QUEBEC, QC, G1N 1N2
(418) 688-0889   *SIC 7219*

STITCH IT CANADA'S TAILOR INC *p528*
3221 NORTH SERVICE RD SUITE 101, BURLINGTON, ON, L7N 3G2
(905) 335-0922   *SIC 7219*

SUDBURY HOSPITAL SERVICES *p901*
363 YORK ST, SUDBURY, ON, P3E 2A8
(705) 674-2158   *SIC 7219*

SIC 7221 Photographic studios, portrait

DIGITAL ATTRACTIONS INC *p757*
6650 NIAGARA RIVER, NIAGARA FALLS, ON, L2E 6T2
(905) 371-2003   *SIC 7221*

STUDIO DE PHOTOS DES ECOLES QUEBECOISES INC *p1051*
8300 RUE DE L'INDUSTRIE, ANJOU, QC, H1J 1S7
(514) 351-8275   *SIC 7221*

SIC 7231 Beauty shops

ALTAVERO HAIRCARE LTD *p20*
1144 29 AVE NE SUITE 110W, CALGARY, AB, T2E 7P1
(403) 266-4595   *SIC 7231*

ANGLES SALON INC *p75*
555 STRATHCONA BLVD SW SUITE 420, CALGARY, AB, T3H 2Z9
(403) 242-6057   *SIC 7231*

BEAUTY EXPRESS CANADA INC *p679*
170 DUFFIELD DR SUITE 200, MARKHAM,

ON, L6G 1B5
(905) 258-0684   *SIC 7231*

CHATTERS LIMITED PARTNERSHIP *p158*
271 BURNT PARK DR, RED DEER COUNTY, AB, T4S 0K7
(403) 342-5055   *SIC 7231*

CORPORATION EPIDERMA INC *p1272*
2590 BOUL LAURIER BUREAU 330, QUEBEC, QC, G1V 4M6
(418) 651-8678   *SIC 7231*

CURLCO INDUSTRIES INC *p566*
85 LITTLE JOHN RD SUITE 1585, DUNDAS, ON, L9H 4H1
(905) 628-4287   *SIC 7231*

DONATO ACADEMY OF HAIRSTYLING AND AESTHETICS *p709*
100 CITY CENTRE DR, MISSISSAUGA, ON, L5B 2C9
(416) 252-8999   *SIC 7231*

EPIDERMA QUEBEC INC *p1272*
2590 BOUL LAURIER BUREAU 330, QUEBEC, QC, G1V 4M6
(418) 266-2027   *SIC 7231*

FAIRMONT HOTELS & RESORTS INC *p418*
184 ADOLPHUS ST, ST ANDREWS, NB, E5B 1T7
(506) 529-3004   *SIC 7231*

GISELLE'S PROFESSIONAL SKIN CARE LTD *p388*
1700 CORYDON AVE UNIT 13, WINNIPEG, MB, R3N 0K1
SIC 7231

GREAT CLIPS, INC *p1002*
3100 N RUTHERFORD RD SUITE 201, VAUGHAN, ON, L4K 0G6
SIC 7231

HEAD SHOPPE COMPANY LIMITED, THE *p446*
10 THORNE AVE, DARTMOUTH, NS, B3B 1Y5
(902) 455-1504   *SIC 7231*

KITTSON INVESTMENTS LTD *p381*
1450 WELLINGTON AVE, WINNIPEG, MB, R3E 0K5
(204) 772-3999   *SIC 7231*

LCI LASERCOM CLINICS INTERNATIONAL INC *p706*
4310 SHERWOODTOWNE BLVD, MISSISSAUGA, ON, L4Z 4C4
(905) 896-4000   *SIC 7231*

MACCHIA ENTERPRISES LTD *p389*
43 NEWBURY CRES, WINNIPEG, MB, R3P 0V6
(204) 255-7181   *SIC 7231*

MEGA HAIR GROUP INC, THE *p272*
6448 148 ST SUITE 107, SURREY, BC, V3S 7G7
(604) 599-6800   *SIC 7231*

NIKO COSMETICS INC *p998*
397 HUMBERLINE DR UNIT 7, TORONTO, ON, M9W 5T5
SIC 7231

SUKI'S BEAUTY BAZAAR LTD *p320*
3157 GRANVILLE ST, VANCOUVER, BC, V6H 3K1
(604) 738-2127   *SIC 7231*

TOWLE, RUSSELL L ENTERPRISES LTD *p931*
25 YORKVILLE AVE, TORONTO, ON, M4W 1L1
(416) 923-0993   *SIC 7231*

UNITES MOBILES DE COIFFURE DE MONTREAL INC, LES *p1224*
6226 BOUL MONK, MONTREAL, QC, H4E 3H7
(514) 766-3553   *SIC 7231*

WLB SERVICES LIMITED *p427*
4 O'FLAHERTY CRES, MOUNT PEARL, NL, A1N 4M1
(709) 747-2340   *SIC 7231*

SIC 7261 Funeral service and crematories

CATHOLIC CEMETERIES-ARCHDIOCESE OF TORONTO *p771*
4950 YONGE ST SUITE 206, NORTH YORK, ON, M2N 6K1
(416) 733-8544   *SIC 7261*

LEPINE-CLOUTIER LTEE *p1259*
715 RUE DE SAINT-VALLIER E, QUEBEC, QC, G1K 3P9
(418) 529-3371   *SIC 7261*

MAGNUS POIRIER INC *p1346*
7388 BOUL VIAU, SAINT-LEONARD, QC, H1S 2N9
(514) 727-2847   *SIC 7261*

PARK LAWN CORPORATION *p927*
2 ST CLAIR AVE W SUITE 1300, TORONTO, ON, M4V 1L5
(416) 231-1462   *SIC 7261*

SERVICE CORPORATION INTERNATIONAL (CANADA) LIMITED *p285*
1835 HASTINGS ST E, VANCOUVER, BC, V5L 1T3
(604) 806-4100   *SIC 7261*

SERVICES COMMEMORATIFS CELEBRIS INC *p1155*
160 BOUL GRAHAM, MONT-ROYAL, QC, H3P 3H9
(514) 735-2025   *SIC 7261*

TURNER & PORTER FUNERAL DIRECTORS LIMITED *p995*
380 WINDERMERE AVE, TORONTO, ON, M6S 3L4
(416) 767-7452   *SIC 7261*

SIC 7291 Tax return preparation services

FARM BUSINESS CONSULTANTS INC *p649*
2109 OXFORD ST E, LONDON, ON, N5V 2Z9
(519) 453-5040   *SIC 7291*

H & R BLOCK CANADA, INC *p50*
700 2 ST SW SUITE 2600, CALGARY, AB, T2P 2W2
(403) 254-8689   *SIC 7291*

THORSTEINSSONS *p329*
595 BURRARD ST SUITE 49123, VANCOUVER, BC, V7X 1J2
(604) 689-1261   *SIC 7291*

WOLTERS KLUWER CANADA LIMITED *p1372*
1120 RUE DE CHERBOURG, SHERBROOKE, QC, J1K 2N8
(819) 566-2000   *SIC 7291*

SIC 7299 Miscellaneous personal service

9052-9975 QUEBEC INC *p1337*
6600 CH DE LA COTE-DE-LIESSE, SAINT-LAURENT, QC, H4T 1E3
(514) 735-5150   *SIC 7299*

ASPLUNDH CANADA ULC *p450*
645 PRATT AND WHITNEY DR SUITE 1, GOFFS, NS, B2T 0H4
(902) 468-8733   *SIC 7299*

BELLIVO TRANSFORMATION INC *p1354*
1505 RTE LUPIEN, SAINTE-ANGELE-DE-PREMONT, QC, J0K 1R0
(819) 268-5199   *SIC 7299*

CANADIAN AUTOMOTIVE INSTITUTE, THE *p622*
3722 FAIRWAY RD, INNISFIL, ON, L9S 1A5
SIC 7299

CENTRE COMMUNAUTAIRE FRANCOPHONE WINDSOR-ESSEX-KENT INC *p1018*
7515 FOREST GLADE DR, WINDSOR, ON, N8T 3P5
(519) 948-5545   *SIC 7299*

CENTRE DE RECEPTION LE MADISON INC *p1345*
8750 BOUL PROVENCHER, SAINT-LEONARD, QC, H1R 3N7
(514) 374-7428   *SIC 7299*

CLUB ITALIA,NIAGARA, ORDER SONS OF

ITALY OF CANADA p760
2525 MONTROSE RD, NIAGARA FALLS, ON, L2H 0T9
(905) 374-7388   SIC 7299

CORPORATION OF THE CITY OF WATERLOO, THE p1008
101 FATHER DAVID BAUER DR, WATERLOO, ON, N2L 0B4
(519) 886-1177   SIC 7299

EF INTERNATIONAL LANGUAGE SCHOOLS (CANADA) LIMITED p980
127 PORTLAND ST, TORONTO, ON, M5V 2N4
(800) 387-1463   SIC 7299

ELLAS BANQUET HALL AND CONFERENCE CENTRE LTD p868
35 DANFORTH RD, SCARBOROUGH, ON, M1L 3W5
SIC 7299

EVAGELOU ENTERPRISES INC p916
39 CRANFIELD RD, TORONTO, ON, M4B 3H6
(416) 285-4774   SIC 7299

FREEMAN FORMALWEAR LIMITED p787
111 BERMONDSEY RD, NORTH YORK, ON, M4A 2T7
(416) 288-1222   SIC 7299

GATSBY VALET INC p688
6900 AIRPORT RD, MISSISSAUGA, ON, L4V 1E8
(416) 239-6998   SIC 7299

GOVERNMENT OF ONTARIO p995
900 BAY ST SUITE 200, TORONTO, ON, M7A 1L2
(866) 797-0000   SIC 7299

HAYS SPECIALIST RECRUITMENT (CANADA) INC p776
1500 DON MILLS RD SUITE 402, NORTH YORK, ON, M3B 3K4
(416) 203-1925   SIC 7299

HYDRO ONE NETWORKS INC p680
185 CLEGG RD, MARKHAM, ON, L6G 1B7
(800) 434-1235   SIC 7299

INDIGO PARC CANADA INC p1205
1 PLACE VILLE-MARIE BUREAU 1130, MONTREAL, QC, H3B 2A7
(514) 874-1208   SIC 7299

INFO-TECH RESEARCH GROUP INC p654
345 RIDOUT ST N, LONDON, ON, N6A 2N8
(519) 432-3550   SIC 7299

ISTOCKPHOTO L.P. p30
1240 20 AVE SE SUITE 200, CALGARY, AB, T2G 1M8
(403) 265-3062   SIC 7299

ISTOCKPHOTO ULC p30
1240 20 AVE SE SUITE 200, CALGARY, AB, T2G 1M8
(403) 265-3062   SIC 7299

JARDIN BANQUET & CONFERENCE CENTRE INC, LE p1032
8440 27 HWY, WOODBRIDGE, ON, L4L 1A5
(905) 851-2200   SIC 7299

LIUNA GARDENS LIMITED p611
360 JAMES ST N SUITE 201, HAMILTON, ON, L8L 1H5
(905) 525-2410   SIC 7299

NEWLANDS GOLF & COUNTRY CLUB LTD p228
21025 48 AVE, LANGLEY, BC, V3A 3M3
(604) 534-3205   SIC 7299

NIAGARA CONVENTION & CIVIC CENTER p759
6815 STANLEY AVE, NIAGARA FALLS, ON, L2G 3Y9
(905) 357-6222   SIC 7299

OLYMEL S.E.C. p1313
1425 AV ST-JACQUES, SAINT-HYACINTHE, QC, J2S 6M7
(450) 778-2211   SIC 7299

PALIN FOUNDATION, THE p936
63 GOULD ST, TORONTO, ON, M5B 1E9
(416) 979-5250   SIC 7299

POSTMEDIA NETWORK INC p375

300 CARLTON ST 6TH FL, WINNIPEG, MB, R3B 2K6
(204) 926-4600   SIC 7299

RENEX INC p443
73 TACOMA DR SUITE 800, DARTMOUTH, NS, B2W 3Y6
SIC 7299

RIVIERA PARQUE, BANQUET & CONVENTION CENTRE INC p558
2800 HIGHWAY 7 SUITE 301, CONCORD, ON, L4K 1W8
(905) 669-4933   SIC 7299

RUBY CORP p923
20 EGLINTON AVE W SUITE 1200, TORONTO, ON, M4R 1K8
(416) 480-2334   SIC 7299

S C RESTORATIONS LTD p223
1025 TRENCH PL, KELOWNA, BC, V1Y 9Y4
(250) 763-1556   SIC 7299

SILVERBIRCH NO. 15 OPERATIONS LIMITED PARTNERSHIP p454
1960 BRUNSWICK ST, HALIFAX, NS, B3J 2G7
(902) 422-1391   SIC 7299

SODEM INC p1073
4765 CH DE CAPELTON, CANTON-DE-HATLEY, QC, J0B 2C0
SIC 7299

THOMSON REUTERS CORPORATION p957
333 BAY ST, TORONTO, ON, M5H 2R2
(416) 687-7500   SIC 7299

TOULON DEVELOPMENT CORPORATION p471
76 STARRS RD, YARMOUTH, NS, B5A 2T5
(902) 742-9518   SIC 7299

TUXEDO ROYALE LIMITED p854
9078 LESLIE ST UNIT 5&6, RICHMOND HILL, ON, L4B 3L8
(416) 798-7617   SIC 7299

SIC 7311 Advertising agencies

1222010 ONTARIO INC p816
2000 THURSTON DR UNIT 12, OTTAWA, ON, K1G 4K7
(613) 739-4000   SIC 7311

1325931 CANADA INC p573
55 HORNER AVE UNIT 1, ETOBICOKE, ON, M8Z 4X6
(416) 620-1965   SIC 7311

1570707 ONTARIO INC p573
55 HORNER AVE UNIT 1, ETOBICOKE, ON, M8Z 4X6
(416) 620-1965   SIC 7311

ABSOLUTE RESULTS MARKETING SYSTEMS INC p278
2677 192 ST UNIT 104, SURREY, BC, V3Z 3X1
(888) 751-7171   SIC 7311

AGENCE MIRUM CANADA INC p1187
500 RUE SAINT-JACQUES BUREAU 1420, MONTREAL, QC, H2Y 1S1
(514) 987-9992   SIC 7311

ALSTOM CANADA INC p1191
1050 COTE DU BEAVER HALL, MONTREAL, QC, H2Z 0A5
(514) 333-0888   SIC 7311

ANIMAL SAFETY PUBLICATIONS p407
295 ENGLISH DR, MONCTON, NB, E1E 0J3
(506) 858-7807   SIC 7311

ARCANE DIGITAL INC p653
304 TALBOT ST, LONDON, ON, N6A 2R4
(226) 289-2445   SIC 7311

BBDO CANADA CORP p928
2 BLOOR ST W SUITE 3200, TORONTO, ON, M4W 3E2
(416) 972-1505   SIC 7311

BBDO CANADA CORP p928
2 BLOOR ST W SUITE 3200, TORONTO, ON, M4W 3R6
(416) 972-1505   SIC 7311

BCP LTEE p1185
3530 BOUL SAINT-LAURENT BUREAU 300, MONTREAL, QC, H2X 2V1
(514) 285-0077   SIC 7311

BENSIMON BYRNE INC p978
225 WELLINGTON ST W, TORONTO, ON, M5V 3G7
(416) 922-2211   SIC 7311

BURNETT, LEO COMPANY LTD p928
175 BLOOR ST E NORTH TOWER SUITE 1200, TORONTO, ON, M4W 3R9
(416) 925-5997   SIC 7311

BUSREL INC p1325
200 RUE DESLAURIERS, SAINT-LAURENT, QC, H4N 1V8
(514) 336-0000   SIC 7311

CALDWELL PARTNERS INTERNATIONAL INC, THE p972
165 AVENUE RD SUITE 600, TORONTO, ON, M5R 3S4
(416) 920-7702   SIC 7311

CARAT CANADA INC p979
276 KING ST W SUITE 400, TORONTO, ON, M5V 1J2
(416) 504-3965   SIC 7311

CARAT CANADA INC p1184
4446 BOUL SAINT-LAURENT BUREAU 500, MONTREAL, QC, H2W 1Z5
(514) 287-2555   SIC 7311

CARAT STRATEGEM INC p1194
400 BOUL DE MAISONNEUVE O BUREAU 250, MONTREAL, QC, H3A 1L4
(514) 284-4446   SIC 7311

CUNDARI GROUP LTD p979
26 DUNCAN ST, TORONTO, ON, M5V 2B9
(416) 510-1771   SIC 7311

DAC GROUP (HOLDINGS) LIMITED p769
1210 SHEPPARD AVE E SUITE 500, NORTH YORK, ON, M2K 1E3
(416) 492-4322   SIC 7311

DAC GROUP/CANADA LTD p769
1210 SHEPPARD AVE E SUITE 500, NORTH YORK, ON, M2K 1E3
(416) 492-4322   SIC 7311

DAN AGENCY INC p979
276 KING ST W SUITE 100, TORONTO, ON, M5V 1J2
(416) 929-9700   SIC 7311

DAN AGENCY INC p1222
3970 RUE SAINT-AMBROISE, MONTREAL, QC, H4C 2C7
(514) 848-0010   SIC 7311

DENTSU AEGIS NETWORK ENTERPRISE SOLUTIONS INC p962
1 UNIVERSITY AVE 10FL, TORONTO, ON, M5J 2P1
(416) 473-6287   SIC 7311

DISTRICT M INC p1183
5455 AV DE GASPE BUREAU 730, MONTREAL, QC, H2T 3B3
(888) 881-6930   SIC 7311

ENTREPRISE DE COMMUNICATIONS TANK INC p1210
55 RUE PRINCE, MONTREAL, QC, H3C 2M7
(514) 373-3333   SIC 7311

EPIC DEALS INC p715
2400 DUNDAS ST W SUITE 211, MISSISSAUGA, ON, L5K 2R8
(647) 478-9002   SIC 7311

EURO RSCG HEALTHCARE (CANADA) INC p980
473 ADELAIDE ST W SUITE 300, TORONTO, ON, M5V 1T1
(416) 925-9005   SIC 7311

FUM MEDIA CORP p313
1151 GEORGIA ST W SUITE 3205, VANCOUVER, BC, V6E 0B3
(778) 859-5882   SIC 7311

GREY ADVERTISING ULC p980
46 SPADINA AVE SUITE 500, TORONTO, ON, M5V 2H8
(416) 486-0700   SIC 7311

GRIP LIMITED p977

179 JOHN ST, TORONTO, ON, M5T 1X4
(416) 340-7111   SIC 7311

HAVAS CANADA HOLDINGS, INC p981
473 ADELAIDE ST W SUITE 300, TORONTO, ON, M5V 1T1
(416) 920-6864   SIC 7311

HOSPITALITY CAREERS ONLINE INC p190
4789 KINGSWAY SUITE 400, BURNABY, BC, V5H 0A3
(604) 435-8991   SIC 7311

I.M.S. INQUIRY MANAGEMENT SYSTEMS LTD p574
55 HORNER AVE UNIT 1, ETOBICOKE, ON, M8Z 4X6
(416) 620-1965   SIC 7311

INDEX EXCHANGE INC p791
74 WINGOLD AVE, NORTH YORK, ON, M6B 1P5
(416) 785-5908   SIC 7311

IPROSPECT CANADA INC p1223
3970 RUE SAINT-AMBROISE, MONTREAL, QC, H4C 2C7
(514) 524-7149   SIC 7311

ISOBAR CANADA INC p963
1 UNIVERSITY AVE FL 6, TORONTO, ON, M5J 2P1
(416) 646-2340   SIC 7311

J.W.T ENTERPRISES INC p929
160 BLOOR ST E SUITE 8TH, TORONTO, ON, M4W 3P7
(416) 926-7300   SIC 7311

JUNIPER PARK TBWA COMMUNICATIONS ULC p929
33 BLOOR ST E, TORONTO, ON, M4W 3H1
(416) 413-7301   SIC 7311

KBS+P CANADA INC p929
2 BLOOR ST E SUITE 137, TORONTO, ON, M4W 3J4
(416) 260-7000   SIC 7311

KBS+P CANADA LP KBS+P CANADA SEC p934
340 KING ST E 4TH FL SUITE 500, TORONTO, ON, M5A 1K8
(416) 260-7000   SIC 7311

KOGNITIVE MARKETING INC p922
150 EGLINTON AVE E SUITE 801, TORONTO, ON, M4P 1E8
(416) 534-5651   SIC 7311

LABARRE GAUTHIER INC p1186
3575 BOUL SAINT-LAURENT BUREAU 900, MONTREAL, QC, H2X 2T7
(514) 281-8901   SIC 7311

M5 MARKETING COMMUNICATIONS INC p430
42 O'LEARY AVE, ST. JOHN'S, NL, A1B 2C7
(709) 753-5559   SIC 7311

MARKETEL COMMUNICATIONS INC p1189
413 RUE SAINT-JACQUES 10E ETAGE, MONTREAL, QC, H2Y 1N9
(514) 935-9445   SIC 7311

MARKETEL/MCCANN-ERICKSON LTEE p1189
413 RUE SAINT-JACQUES BUREAU 10E, MONTREAL, QC, H2Y 1N9
(514) 935-9445   SIC 7311

MARTINI-VISPAK INC p1229
174 RUE MERIZZI, MONTREAL, QC, H4T 1S4
(514) 344-1551   SIC 7311

MCCANN WORLDGROUP CANADA INC p982
200 WELLINGTON ST W SUITE 1300, TORONTO, ON, M5V 0N6
(416) 594-6000   SIC 7311

MINDSHARE CANADA p930
160 BLOOR ST E SUITE 700, TORONTO, ON, M4W 0A2
(416) 987-5100   SIC 7311

MUNDO MEDIA LTD p853
120 EAST BEAVER CREEK RD SUITE 200, RICHMOND HILL, ON, L4B 4V1
(416) 342-5646   SIC 7311

NO FIXED ADDRESS INC p920

50 CARROLL ST, TORONTO, ON, M4M 3G3
(416) 947-8584 *SIC* 7311

OGILVY MONTREAL INC *p1190*
215 RUE SAINT-JACQUES BUREAU 333, MONTREAL, QC, H2Y 1M6
(514) 861-1811 *SIC* 7311

OMNICOM CANADA CORP *p326*
777 HORNBY ST SUITE 1600, VANCOUVER, BC, V6Z 2T3
(604) 687-7911 *SIC* 7311

OMNICOM CANADA CORP *p930*
33 BLOOR ST E SUITE 1300, TORONTO, ON, M4W 3H1
(416) 960-3830 *SIC* 7311

PALM COMMUNICATION MARKETING INC *p1207*
1253 AV MCGILL COLLEGE, MONTREAL, QC, H3B 2Y5
(514) 845-7256 *SIC* 7311

PROACTION GROUPE CONSEILS INC *p1186*
257 RUE SHERBROOKE E BUREAU 100, MONTREAL, QC, H2X 1E3
(514) 284-7447 *SIC* 7311

PUBLICIS CANADA INC *p940*
111 QUEEN ST E SUITE 200, TORONTO, ON, M5C 1S2
(416) 925-7733 *SIC* 7311

PUBLICIS CANADA INC *p1184*
358 RUE BEAUBIEN O BUREAU 500, MONTREAL, QC, H2V 4S6
(514) 285-1414 *SIC* 7311

PUBLICIS MEDIA CANADA INC *p930*
175 BLOOR ST E 9TH FLOOR, TORONTO, ON, M4W 3R8
(437) 222-5200 *SIC* 7311

PUBLICITE TAXI MONTREAL INC *p1215*
1600 BOUL RENE-LEVESQUE O BUREAU 1200, MONTREAL, QC, H3H 1P9
(514) 935-6375 *SIC* 7311

QUARRY INTEGRATED COMMUNICATIONS INC *p888*
1440 KING ST N UNIT 1, ST JACOBS, ON, N0B 2N0
(877) 723-2999 *SIC* 7311

QUARRY INTEGRATED COMMUNICATIONS INC *p888*
1440 KING ST N SUITE 1, ST JACOBS, ON, N0B 2N0
(877) 723-2999 *SIC* 7311

QUEBECOR MEDIA INC *p1207*
1100 BOUL RENE-LEVESQUE O SUITE 20E, MONTREAL, QC, H3B 4N4
(514) 380-1999 *SIC* 7311

RIVET CANADA *p992*
219 DUFFERIN ST SUITE 200A, TORONTO, ON, M6K 3J1
(416) 483-5024 *SIC* 7311

SAATCHI & SAATCHI ADVERTISING INC *p930*
2 BLOOR ST E SUITE 600, TORONTO, ON, M4W 1A8
(416) 359-9595 *SIC* 7311

SID LEE INC *p1212*
75 RUE QUEEN BUREAU 1400, MONTREAL, QC, H3C 2N6
(514) 282-2200 *SIC* 7311

SKIRON INC *p1260*
56 RUE SAINT-PIERRE BUREAU 101, QUEBEC, QC, G1K 4A1
(418) 694-0114 *SIC* 7311

SOCIETE DES CASINOS DU QUEBEC INC, LA *p1216*
325 RUE BRIDGE BUREAU 1178, MONTREAL, QC, H3K 2C7
(514) 409-3111 *SIC* 7311

STARCOM MEDIAVEST GROUP SMG *p930*
175 BLOOR ST E SUITE 1200N, TORONTO, ON, M4W 3R9
(416) 927-3300 *SIC* 7311

STIGAN MEDIA INC *p300*
55 WATER STREET, VANCOUVER, BC, V6B 1A1

(778) 379-0888 *SIC* 7311

T B W A CHIAT/DAY *p984*
10 LOWER SPADINA AVE, TORONTO, ON, M5V 2Z2
(416) 642-1380 *SIC* 7311

TAXI CANADA LTD *p984*
495 WELLINGTON ST W SUITE 102, TORONTO, ON, M5V 1E9
(416) 342-8294 *SIC* 7311

TAXI CANADA LTD *p1200*
1435 RUE SAINT-ALEXANDRE BUREAU 620, MONTREAL, QC, H3A 2G4
(514) 842-8294 *SIC* 7311

THOMPSON, J. WALTER COMPANY LIMITED *p930*
160 BLOOR ST E SUITE 1100, TORONTO, ON, M4W 3P7
(416) 926-7300 *SIC* 7311

TRANSCONTINENTAL INTERACTIF INC *p1209*
1 PLACE VILLE-MARIE BUREAU 3240, MONTREAL, QC, H3B 0G1
(514) 954-4000 *SIC* 7311

TRI-MEDIA INTEGRATED MARKETING TECHNOLOGIES INC *p887*
20 CORPORATE PARK DR SUITE 103, ST CATHARINES, ON, L2S 3W2
SIC 7311

UNION ADVERTISING CANADA LP *p984*
479 WELLINGTON ST W, TORONTO, ON, M5V 1E7
(416) 598-4944 *SIC* 7311

VENTURE COMMUNICATIONS LTD *p42*
2540 KENSINGTON RD NW, CALGARY, AB, T2N 3S3
(403) 265-4659 *SIC* 7311

VIZEUM CANADA INC *p1223*
3970 RUE SAINT-AMBROISE, MONTREAL, QC, H4C 2C7
(514) 270-1010 *SIC* 7311

WASSERMAN & PARTNERS ADVERTISING INC *p301*
1020 MAINLAND ST UNIT 160, VANCOUVER, BC, V6B 2T5
(604) 684-1111 *SIC* 7311

WAVEMAKER CANADA ULC *p931*
160 BLOOR ST E 5TH FL, TORONTO, ON, M4W 3S7
(416) 987-9100 *SIC* 7311

WPP GROUP CANADA COMMUNICATIONS LIMITED *p943*
33 YONGE ST SUITE 1100, TORONTO, ON, M5E 1X6
(416) 367-3573 *SIC* 7311

WPP GROUP CANADA COMMUNICATIONS LIMITED *p943*
33 YONGE ST, TORONTO, ON, M5E 1X6
(416) 367-3573 *SIC* 7311

XLR8 MEDIA INC *p1186*
3575 BOUL SAINT-LAURENT BUREAU 400, MONTREAL, QC, H2X 2T7
(514) 286-9000 *SIC* 7311

YOUNG & RUBICAM GROUP OF COMPANIES ULC, THE *p931*
160 BLOOR ST E SUITE 500, TORONTO, ON, M4W 1B9
(416) 987-9100 *SIC* 7311

YOUNG & RUBICAM GROUP OF COMPANIES ULC, THE *p931*
60 BLOOR ST W SUITE 8, TORONTO, ON, M4W 3B8
SIC 7311

YOUNG & RUBICAM GROUP OF COMPANIES ULC, THE *p985*
495 WELLINGTON ST W SUITE 102, TORONTO, ON, M5V 1E9

ZOMONGO.TV CORP *p78*
229 AVRO LANE, CALGARY, AB, T3Z 3S5
(403) 870-4951 *SIC* 7311

ZULU ALPHA KILO INC *p935*
260 KING ST E SUITE B 101, TORONTO, ON, M5A 4L5
(416) 777-9858 *SIC* 7311

SIC 7312 Outdoor advertising services

ACCESSOIRES POUR VELOS O.G.D. LTEE *p1332*
10555 BOUL HENRI-BOURASSA O, SAINT-LAURENT, QC, H4S 1A1
(514) 332-1320 *SIC* 7312

ASTRAL MEDIA AFFICHAGE, S.E.C. *p1193*
1800 AV MCGILL COLLEGE BUREAU 2700, MONTREAL, QC, H3A 3J6
(514) 939-5000 *SIC* 7312

BENCH PRESS LTD, THE *p598*
2402 STOUFFVILLE RD RR 1, GORMLEY, ON, L0H 1G0
(905) 887-3043 *SIC* 7312

NEWAD MEDIA INC *p1184*
4200 BOUL SAINT-LAURENT BUREAU 1440, MONTREAL, QC, H2W 2R2
(514) 278-3222 *SIC* 7312

OUTFRONT MEDIA CANADA LP *p571*
377 HORNER AVE, ETOBICOKE, ON, M8W 1Z6
(416) 255-1392 *SIC* 7312

PATTISON OUTDOOR ADVERTISING LIMITED PARTNERSHIP *p699*
2700 MATHESON BLVD E SUITE 500, MISSISSAUGA, ON, L4W 4V9
(905) 282-6800 *SIC* 7312

SIC 7313 Radio, television, publisher representatives

CFGO *p821*
87 GEORGE ST, OTTAWA, ON, K1N 9H7
(613) 789-2486 *SIC* 7313

CHUM SATELLITE SERVICES LIMITED *p678*
280 HILLMOUNT RD UNIT 6, MARKHAM, ON, L6C 3A1
(905) 475-1661 *SIC* 7313

SOCIETY OF COMPOSERS, AUTHORS AND MUSIC PUBLISHERS OF CANADA *p777*
41 VALLEYBROOK DR, NORTH YORK, ON, M3B 2S6
(416) 445-8700 *SIC* 7313

ZOOMERMEDIA LIMITED *p992*
70 JEFFERSON AVE, TORONTO, ON, M6K 1Y4
(416) 607-7735 *SIC* 7313

SIC 7319 Advertising, nec

ACT3 M.H.S. INC *p1181*
7236 RUE MARCONI, MONTREAL, QC, H2R 2Z5
(514) 844-5050 *SIC* 7319

AMERICA ONLINE CANADA INC *p978*
99 SPADINA AVE SUITE 200, TORONTO, ON, M5V 3P8
(416) 263-8100 *SIC* 7319

CAMERON ADVERTISING DISPLAYS LIMITED *p870*
12 NANTUCKET BLVD, SCARBOROUGH, ON, M1P 2N4
(416) 752-7220 *SIC* 7319

DIRECT WEST CORPORATION *p1415*
355 LONGMAN CRES, REGINA, SK, S4N 6G3
(306) 777-0333 *SIC* 7319

EYERETURN MARKETING INC *p922*
110 EGLINTON AVE E SUITE 701, TORONTO, ON, M4P 2Y1
(416) 929-4834 *SIC* 7319

GO BEE INDUSTRIES INC *p566*
1-334 A HATT ST, DUNDAS, ON, L9H 2H9
(289) 238-8829 *SIC* 7319

J. P. ABBOTT DISTRIBUTION SERVICE LTD *p600*
534 SPEEDVALE AVE E, GUELPH, ON, N1E 1P6
(519) 821-3206 *SIC* 7319

MEDIA BUYING SERVICES ULC *p946*
1 DUNDAS ST W SUITE 2800, TORONTO, ON, M5G 1Z3
(416) 961-1255 *SIC* 7319

MEDIACOM CANADA *p946*
1 DUNDAS ST W SUITE 2800, TORONTO, ON, M5G 1Z3
(416) 342-6500 *SIC* 7319

OMD CANADA *p955*
67 RICHMOND ST W SUITE 2, TORONTO, ON, M5H 1Z5
(416) 681-5600 *SIC* 7319

OMNICOM CANADA CORP *p982*
96 SPADINA AVE 7TH FLOOR, TORONTO, ON, M5V 2J6
(416) 922-0217 *SIC* 7319

PRESSE (2018) INC, LA *p1248*
12300 BOUL METROPOLITAIN E, POINTE-AUX-TREMBLES, QC, H1B 5Y2
(514) 640-1840 *SIC* 7319

QUALITY INSERTIONS LTD *p247*
1560 BROADWAY ST UNIT 2, PORT COQUITLAM, BC, V3C 2M8
(604) 941-1942 *SIC* 7319

QUEBECOR MEDIA INC *p934*
333 KING ST E SUITE 1, TORONTO, ON, M5A 3X5
(416) 947-2222 *SIC* 7319

RACING FORENSICS INC *p876*
3015 KENNEDY RD UNIT 2, SCARBOROUGH, ON, M1V 1E7
(416) 479-4489 *SIC* 7319

TVA VENTES ET MARKETING INC *p1176*
1600 BOUL DE MAISONNEUVE E, MONTREAL, QC, H2L 4P2
(514) 526-9251 *SIC* 7319

SIC 7322 Adjustment and collection services

(C.C.A.) COMMERCIAL CREDIT ADJUSTERS LTD *p374*
300-317 DONALD ST, WINNIPEG, MB, R3B 2H6
(204) 958-5850 *SIC* 7322

852515 ONTARIO LIMITED *p764*
716 GORDON BAKER RD SUITE 212, NORTH YORK, ON, M2H 3B4
(416) 503-9633 *SIC* 7322

ARM AGENCE DE RECOUVREMENT INC *p1387*
985 RUE ROYALE BUREAU 201, TROIS-RIVIERES, QC, G9A 4H7
(819) 375-3327 *SIC* 7322

ARO INC *p1175*
1001 RUE SHERBROOKE E BUREAU 700, MONTREAL, QC, H2L 1L3
(514) 322-1414 *SIC* 7322

CBV COLLECTION SERVICES LTD *p185*
4664 LOUGHEED HWY UNIT 20, BURNABY, BC, V5C 5T5
(604) 687-4559 *SIC* 7322

COLLECTCENTS INC *p738*
1450 MEYERSIDE DR UNIT 200, MISSISSAUGA, ON, L5T 2N5
(905) 670-7575 *SIC* 7322

COMMON COLLECTION AGENCY INC *p864*
5900 FINCH AVE E SUITE 200A, SCARBOROUGH, ON, M1B 5P8
(416) 297-7077 *SIC* 7322

CONTACT RESOURCE SERVICES INC *p715*
2225 ERIN MILLS PKWY, MISSISSAUGA, ON, L5K 2P0
(905) 855-8106 *SIC* 7322

CTL-WDW LTD *p851*
9130 LESLIE ST UNIT 204, RICHMOND HILL, ON, L4B 0B9
(416) 781-3635 *SIC* 7322

D & A COLLECTION CORPORATION *p705*
75 WATLINE AVE SUITE 142, MISSISSAUGA, ON, L4Z 3E5
(905) 507-1147 *SIC* 7322

DIXON COMMERCIAL INVESTIGATORS (1982) INC *p885*

91 GENEVA ST, ST CATHARINES, ON, L2R 4M9

(905) 688-0447   *SIC 7322*

EOS CANADA INC   *p864*

325 MILNER AVE SUITE 1111, SCARBOROUGH, ON, M1B 5N1

(647) 436-2605   *SIC 7322*

FINANCIAL DEBT RECOVERY LIMITED *p852*

40 WEST WILMOT ST UNIT 10, RICHMOND HILL, ON, L4B 1H8

(905) 771-6000   *SIC 7322*

FIRST RESOLUTION MANAGEMENT CORPORATION   *p188*

4585 CANADA WAY SUITE 320, BURNABY, BC, V5G 4L6

SIC 7322

GATESTONE & CO. INC   *p776*

180 DUNCAN MILL RD UNIT 300, NORTH YORK, ON, M3B 1Z6

(416) 961-9622   *SIC 7322*

GCQ CANADA INC   *p1379*

1450 GRANDE ALLEE, TERREBONNE, QC, J6W 6B7

(450) 471-0044   *SIC 7322*

GENERAL CREDIT SERVICES INC   *p313*

1201 WEST PENDER ST SUITE 400, VANCOUVER, BC, V6E 2V2

(604) 688-6097   *SIC 7322*

GLOBAL CREDIT & COLLECTION INC *p670*

1490 DENISON ST, MARKHAM, ON, L3R 9T7

(905) 479-2222   *SIC 7322*

GLOBAL CREDIT & COLLECTION INC *p1196*

2055 RUE PEEL BUREAU 100, MONTREAL, QC, H3A 1V4

(514) 284-5533   *SIC 7322*

GROUPE SOLUTION COLLECT SOLU INC *p1217*

560 BOUL HENRI-BOURASSA O BUREAU 202, MONTREAL, QC, H3L 1P4

(514) 331-1074   *SIC 7322*

METROPOLITAN CREDIT ADJUSTERS LTD *p90*

10310 JASPER AVE NW SUITE 400, EDMONTON, AB, T5J 2W4

(780) 423-2231   *SIC 7322*

PARTNERS IN CREDIT INC   *p905*

50 MINTHORN BLVD SUITE 700, THORNHILL, ON, L3T 7X8

(905) 886-0555   *SIC 7322*

PORTFOLIO MANAGEMENT SOLUTIONS INC   *p654*

200 QUEENS AVE SUITE 700, LONDON, ON, N6A 1J3

(519) 432-0075   *SIC 7322*

SERVICES FINANCIERS NCO, INC   *p492*

610 DUNDAS ST E, BELLEVILLE, ON, K8N 1G7

SIC 7322

SERVICES FINANCIERS NCO, INC   *p516*

33 SINCLAIR BLVD UNIT 4, BRANTFORD, ON, N3S 7X6

(519) 750-6000   *SIC 7322*

SERVICES FINANCIERS NCO, INC   *p1217*

75 RUE DE PORT-ROYAL E BUREAU 240, MONTREAL, QC, H3L 3T1

(514) 385-4444   *SIC 7322*

SOLUTIONS INHALOSTAT INC, LES *p1075*

1697 RUE FELIX-LECLERC, CHAMBLY, QC, J3L 5Z3

(450) 447-2112   *SIC 7322*

TECHNIGLOBE INC   *p1200*

666 RUE SHERBROOKE O UNITE 800, MONTREAL, QC, H3A 1E7

(514) 987-1815   *SIC 7322*

TOTAL CREDIT RECOVERY LIMITED *p768*

225 YORKLAND BLVD, NORTH YORK, ON, M2J 4Y7

(416) 774-4000   *SIC 7322*

WELLS FARGO FINANCIAL RETAIL SERVICES COMPANY OF CANADA   *p733*

55 STANDISH CRT SUITE 300, MISSIS-

SAUGA, ON, L5R 4B2

SIC 7322

SIC 7323 Credit reporting services

CREDIT BUREAU OF STRATFORD (1970) LTD   *p895*

61 LORNE AVE E SUITE 96, STRATFORD, ON, N5A 6S4

(519) 271-6211   *SIC 7323*

D&B COMPANIES OF CANADA ULC, THE *p406*

1234 MAIN ST SUITE 2001, MONCTON, NB, E1C 1H7

(506) 867-2000   *SIC 7323*

D&B COMPANIES OF CANADA ULC, THE *p721*

6750 CENTURY AVE SUITE 305, MISSISSAUGA, ON, L5N 2V8

SIC 7323

EQUIFAX CANADA CO.   *p770*

5700 YONGE ST SUITE 1700, NORTH YORK, ON, M2M 4K2

(800) 278-0278   *SIC 7323*

GROUPECHO CANADA INC   *p1084*

1 PLACE LAVAL BUREAU 400, COTE SAINT-LUC, QC, H7N 1A1

(514) 335-3246   *SIC 7323*

INCOHO   *p829*

1960 SCOTT ST SUITE 202C, OTTAWA, ON, K1Z 8L8

(613) 695-9800   *SIC 7323*

INTELYSIS CORP   *p922*

2619 YONGE ST SUITE 200, TORONTO, ON, M4P 2J1

(416) 216-6962   *SIC 7323*

QUALITY UNDERWRITING SERVICES LTD *p853*

111 GRANTON DR SUITE 105, RICHMOND HILL, ON, L4B 1L5

(905) 335-8783   *SIC 7323*

RAPIDE INVESTIGATION CANADA LTEE *p1123*

114 RUE SAINT-GEORGES, LA PRAIRIE, QC, J5R 2L9

(514) 879-1199   *SIC 7323*

TRANS UNION OF CANADA, INC   *p528*

3115 HARVESTER RD SUITE 201, BURLINGTON, ON, L7N 3N8

(800) 663-9980   *SIC 7323*

TRANS UNION OF CANADA, INC   *p528*

3115 HARVESTER RD SUITE 201, BURLINGTON, ON, L7N 3N8

(800) 663-9980   *SIC 7323*

SIC 7331 Direct mail advertising services

ANDREWS MAILING SERVICE LTD   *p480*

226 INDUSTRIAL PKY N UNIT 7, AURORA, ON, L4G 4C3

(905) 503-1700   *SIC 7331*

CANADIAN OVERSEAS MARKETING CORPORATION   *p291*

2020 YUKON ST, VANCOUVER, BC, V5Y 3N8

SIC 7331

DATA DIRECT GROUP INC   *p734*

2001 DREW RD UNIT 1, MISSISSAUGA, ON, L5S 1S4

(905) 564-0150   *SIC 7331*

DIRECT MULTI-PAK MAILING LTD   *p669*

20 TORBAY RD, MARKHAM, ON, L3R 1G6

(905) 415-1940   *SIC 7331*

EDITION LE TELEPHONE ROUGE INC *p1266*

2555 AV WATT BUREAU 6, QUEBEC, QC, G1P 3T2

(418) 658-8122   *SIC 7331*

G3 WORLDWIDE (CANADA) INC   *p688*

3198 ORLANDO DR, MISSISSAUGA, ON, L4V 1R5

(905) 405-8900   *SIC 7331*

MAIL-O-MATIC SERVICES LIMITED   *p193*

7550 LOWLAND DR, BURNABY, BC, V5J 5A4

(604) 439-9668   *SIC 7331*

PRINTLINX CORPORATION   *p868*

1170 BIRCHMOUNT RD SUITE 1, SCARBOROUGH, ON, M1K 5M1

(416) 752-8100   *SIC 7331*

SOMORICH MARKETING CORPORATION *p571*

324 HORNER AVE UNIT A, ETOBICOKE, ON, M8W 1Z3

(416) 461-9271   *SIC 7331*

TIGER NORTH AMERICA INC   *p872*

1170 BIRCHMOUNT RD, SCARBOROUGH, ON, M1P 5E3

(416) 752-8100   *SIC 7331*

SIC 7334 Photocopying and duplicating services

2016099 ONTARIO INC   *p581*

31 CONSTELLATION CRT, ETOBICOKE, ON, M9W 1K4

(905) 673-2000   *SIC 7334*

2853477 CANADA INC   *p1131*

790 RUE D'UPTON, LASALLE, QC, H8R 2T9

(514) 363-5511   *SIC 7334*

DOCU PLUS   *p1210*

980 RUE SAINT-ANTOINE O BUREAU 615, MONTREAL, QC, H3C 1A8

(514) 875-1616   *SIC 7334*

DOMINION BLUEPRINT & REPROGRAPHICS LTD   *p291*

99 6TH AVE W, VANCOUVER, BC, V5Y 1K2

(604) 681-7501   *SIC 7334*

DUPLIUM CORP   *p904*

35 MINTHORN BLVD, THORNHILL, ON, L3T 7N5

(905) 709-9930   *SIC 7334*

EARLY BIRD COMMUNICATORS INC *p639*

111 WATER ST N, KITCHENER, ON, N2H 5B1

SIC 7334

PACBLUE DIGITAL IMAGING INC   *p256*

3551 VIKING WAY UNIT 109, RICHMOND, BC, V6V 1W1

(604) 714-3288   *SIC 7334*

SISCA GESTION D'AFFAIRES INC   *p1132*

790 RUE D'UPTON, LASALLE, QC, H8R 2T9

(514) 363-5511   *SIC 7334*

SIC 7335 Commercial photography

MAGENTA STUDIO PHOTO INC   *p1211*

300 RUE DE LA MONTAGNE, MONTREAL, QC, H3C 2B1

(514) 935-2225   *SIC 7335*

MDA GEOSPATIAL SERVICES INC   *p255*

13800 COMMERCE PKWY, RICHMOND, BC, V6V 2J3

(604) 278-3411   *SIC 7335*

PROS DE LA PHOTO (QUEBEC) INC, LES *p1182*

90 RUE BEAUBIEN O BUREAU 101, MONTREAL, QC, H2S 1V6

(514) 322-7476   *SIC 7335*

SIC 7336 Commercial art and graphic design

ANIMATION SQUEEZE STUDIO INC *p1257*

520 BOUL CHAREST E BUREAU 340, QUEBEC, QC, G1K 3J3

(418) 476-1786   *SIC 7336*

BOLDER GRAPHICS INCORPORATED *p14*

10 SMED LANE SE UNIT 110, CALGARY, AB, T2C 4T5

(403) 259-0054   *SIC 7336*

DECO ADHESIVE PRODUCTS (1985) LIMITED   *p583*

28 GREENSBORO DR, ETOBICOKE, ON, M9W 1E1

(416) 247-7878   *SIC 7336*

FRIMA STUDIO INC   *p1259*

395 RUE VICTOR-REVILLON, QUEBEC, QC, G1K 3M8

(418) 529-9697   *SIC 7336*

GLENN DAVIS GROUP INC   *p709*

77 CITY CENTRE DR UNIT 2, MISSISSAUGA, ON, L5B 1M5

(905) 270-2501   *SIC 7336*

GREEN LIGHT GRAPHICS INC   *p802*

229 DEANE AVE, OAKVILLE, ON, L6K 1N6

(905) 469-8095   *SIC 7336*

ICON DIGITAL PRODUCTIONS INC   *p671*

7495 BIRCHMOUNT RD, MARKHAM, ON, L3R 5G2

(905) 889-2800   *SIC 7336*

INTERPUBLIC GROUP OF COMPANIES CANADA, INC, THE   *p963*

207 QUEENS QUAY W SUITE 2, TORONTO, ON, M5J 1A7

(647) 260-2116   *SIC 7336*

INTERPUBLIC GROUP OF COMPANIES CANADA, INC, THE   *p986*

100 KING ST W SUITE 6200, TORONTO, ON, M5X 1B8

(416) 545-5563   *SIC 7336*

M&T PRINTING GROUP LIMITED   *p1010*

675 DAVENPORT RD, WATERLOO, ON, N2V 2E2

(519) 804-0017   *SIC 7336*

PATENT PENDING IDEAS   *p343*

1200 ALPHA LAKE RD SUITE 205C, WHISTLER, BC, V0N 1B1

(604) 905-6485   *SIC 7336*

PERENNIAL INC   *p579*

15 WAULRON ST, ETOBICOKE, ON, M9C 1B4

(416) 251-2180   *SIC 7336*

PIGEON BRANDS INC   *p977*

179 JOHN ST 2ND FL, TORONTO, ON, M5T 1X4

(416) 532-9950   *SIC 7336*

SCHAWK CANADA INC   *p700*

1620 TECH AVE SUITE 3, MISSISSAUGA, ON, L4W 5P4

(905) 219-1600   *SIC 7336*

SOUTHERN GRAPHICS SYSTEMS-CANADA, CO.   *p576*

2 DORCHESTER AVE, ETOBICOKE, ON, M8Z 4W3

(416) 252-9331   *SIC 7336*

STUDIOS MOMENT FACTORY INC, LES *p1184*

6250 AV DU PARC, MONTREAL, QC, H2V 4H8

(514) 843-8433   *SIC 7336*

UBISOFT ARTS NUMERIQUES INC *p1183*

5505 BOUL SAINT-LAURENT BUREAU 2000, MONTREAL, QC, H2T 1S6

(514) 490-2000   *SIC 7336*

WEST CANADIAN INDUSTRIES GROUP LTD   *p32*

1601 9 AVE SE SUITE 200, CALGARY, AB, T2G 0H4

(403) 245-2555   *SIC 7336*

SIC 7338 Secretarial and court reporting

INFOROUTE SANTE DU CANADA INC *p953*

150 KING ST W SUITE 1308, TORONTO, ON, M5H 1J9

(416) 979-4606   *SIC 7338*

INFOROUTE SANTE DU CANADA INC *p1197*

1000 RUE SHERBROOKE O BUREAU 1200, MONTREAL, QC, H3A 3G4

(514) 868-0550   *SIC 7338*

PARTNERS YOUR SECRETARIAL SOLUTIONS   *p270*

14680 110 AVE, SURREY, BC, V3R 2A8
(604) 588-9926   *SIC* 7338

SIC 7342 Disinfecting and pest control services

1112308 ONTARIO INC   *p581*
246 ATTWELL DR, ETOBICOKE, ON, M9W 5B4
(416) 675-1635   *SIC* 7342

ABELL PEST CONTROL INC   *p581*
246 ATTWELL DR, ETOBICOKE, ON, M9W 5B4
(416) 675-1635   *SIC* 7342

ORKIN CANADA CORPORATION   *p732*
5840 FALBOURNE ST, MISSISSAUGA, ON, L5R 4B5
(905) 502-9700   *SIC* 7342

SIC 7349 Building maintenance services, nec

041216 NB LTD   *p397*
376 RUE CHAMPLAIN, DIEPPE, NB, E1A 1P3
(506) 858-5085   *SIC* 7349

1048536 ONTARIO LTD   *p748*
148 COLONNADE RD SUITE 13, NEPEAN, ON, K2E 7R4
(613) 727-0413   *SIC* 7349

1084408 ONTARIO INC   *p568*
8 YONGE ST S UNIT A, ELMVALE, ON, L0L 1P0
(705) 737-0480   *SIC* 7349

1200839 ONTARIO LIMITED   *p903*
2900 STEELES AVE E SUITE 210, THORN-HILL, ON, L3T 4X1
(905) 889-4224   *SIC* 7349

132405 CANADA INC   *p1092*
1484 BOUL HYMUS, DORVAL, QC, H9P 1J6
(514) 685-1425   *SIC* 7349

1434378 ONTARIO INC   *p883*
151 CUSHMAN RD, ST CATHARINES, ON, L2M 6T4
(905) 688-9220   *SIC* 7349

157971 CANADA INC   *p1172*
4315 RUE FRONTENAC BUREAU 200, MONTREAL, QC, H2H 2M4
(514) 527-1146   *SIC* 7349

1808963 ONTARIO INC   *p561*
1495 GERALD ST, CORNWALL, ON, K6H 7G8
(613) 932-5326   *SIC* 7349

188669 CANADA INC   *p1358*
1999 RUE NOBEL BUREAU 7A, SAINTE-JULIE, QC, J3E 1Z7
(450) 649-9400   *SIC* 7349

3933849 CANADA INC   *p1361*
1609 BOUL SAINT-ELZEAR O, SAINTE-ROSE, QC, H7L 3N6
(514) 744-6991   *SIC* 7349

4520556 CANADA INC   *p1337*
180 MONTEE DE LIESSE, SAINT-LAURENT, QC, H4T 1N7
(514) 904-1216   *SIC* 7349

469540 ONTARIO INC   *p648*
163 STRONACH CRES, LONDON, ON, N5V 3G5
(519) 679-8810   *SIC* 7349

550338 ALBERTA LIMITED   *p20*
3530 11A ST NE SUITE 1, CALGARY, AB, T2E 6M7
(403) 250-7878   *SIC* 7349

9119-5867 QUEBEC INC   *p1093*
657 AV MELOCHE, DORVAL, QC, H9P 2T1
(514) 363-5115   *SIC* 7349

9320-4048 QUEBEC INC   *p1361*
1611 BOUL SAINT-ELZEAR O, SAINTE-ROSE, QC, H7L 3N6
(438) 386-7886   *SIC* 7349

A LEADER BUILDING CLEANING SER-VICES OF CANADA LTD   *p368*

894 ST MARY'S RD, WINNIPEG, MB, R2M 3R1
(204) 255-4000   *SIC* 7349

ABCO MAINTENANCE SYSTEMS INC   *p20*
260 20 AVE NE, CALGARY, AB, T2E 1P9
(403) 293-5752   *SIC* 7349

ACOM BUILDING MAINTENANCE LTD *p191*
3871 NORTH FRASER WAY UNIT 23, BURNABY, BC, V5J 5G6
(604) 436-2121   *SIC* 7349

ACOUSTICAL CEILING & BUILDING MAIN-TENANCE LTD   *p112*
7940 CORONET RD NW, EDMONTON, AB, T6E 4N8
(780) 496-9035   *SIC* 7349

AINSWORTH MANAGEMENT SERVICES INC   *p1016*
56 CARLINDS DR, WHITBY, ON, L1R 3B9
(905) 666-9156   *SIC* 7349

ALBERTA JANITORIAL LTD   *p10*
2520 CENTRE AVE NE, CALGARY, AB, T2A 2L2
(403) 272-7801   *SIC* 7349

ALLIANCE BUILDING MAINTENANCE LTD *p99*
18823 111 AVE NW, EDMONTON, AB, T5S 2X4
(780) 447-2574   *SIC* 7349

AMBASSADOR BUILDING MAINTENANCE LIMITED   *p1022*
628 MONMOUTH RD, WINDSOR, ON, N8Y 3L1
(519) 255-1107   *SIC* 7349

AMPHORA MAINTENANCE SERVICES INC *p919*
707A DANFORTH AVE, TORONTO, ON, M4J 1L2
(416) 461-0401   *SIC* 7349

ANDORRA BUILDING MAINTENANCE LTD *p573*
46 CHAUNCEY AVE, ETOBICOKE, ON, M8Z 2Z4
(416) 537-7772   *SIC* 7349

ANGUS CONSULTING MANAGEMENT LIM-ITED   *p778*
1125 LESLIE ST, NORTH YORK, ON, M3C 2J6
(416) 443-8300   *SIC* 7349

AQUA-POWER CLEANERS (1979) LTD *p402*
65 ROYAL PARKWAY, FREDERICTON, NB, E3G 0J9
(506) 458-1113   *SIC* 7349

ARODAL SERVICES LTD   *p253*
2631 VIKING WAY SUITE 248, RICHMOND, BC, V6V 3B5
(604) 274-0477   *SIC* 7349

ARSENAL CLEANING SERVICES LTD *p876*
80 NASHDENE RD UNIT 7, SCARBOR-OUGH, ON, M1V 5E4
(416) 321-8777   *SIC* 7349

ASBURY BUILDING SERVICES INC   *p573*
323 EVANS AVE, ETOBICOKE, ON, M8Z 1K2
SIC 7349

ASSOCIATED PRO-CLEANING SERVICES CORP   *p666*
3400 14TH AVE SUITE 39, MARKHAM, ON, L3R 0H7
(905) 477-6966   *SIC* 7349

ATELIER DE READAPTATION AU TRAVAIL DE BEAUCE INC, L'   *p1321*
1280 AV DU PALAIS, SAINT-JOSEPH-DE-BEAUCE, QC, G0S 2V0
(418) 397-4341   *SIC* 7349

ATLANTIC BUILDING CLEANING LIMITED *p452*
1505 BARRINGTON ST SUITE 1310, HALI-FAX, NS, B3J 3K5
(902) 420-1497   *SIC* 7349

AURACLEAN BUILDING MAINTENANCE INC   *p990*
104 GREENLAW AVE, TORONTO, ON, M6H 3V5
(416) 561-6137   *SIC* 7349

AXIA SERVICES   *p1160*
13025 RUE JEAN-GROU, MONTREAL, QC, H1A 3N6
(514) 642-3250   *SIC* 7349

B. GINGRAS ENTERPRISES LTD   *p112*
4505 101 ST NW, EDMONTON, AB, T6E 5C6
(780) 435-3355   *SIC* 7349

BEE-CLEAN (TORONTO) LTD   *p918*
2 THORNCLIFFE PARK DR UNIT 22, TORONTO, ON, M4H 1H2
(416) 410-6181   *SIC* 7349

BEE-CLEAN BUILDING MAINTENANCE IN-CORPORATED   *p112*
4505 101 ST NW, EDMONTON, AB, T6E 5C6
(780) 435-3355   *SIC* 7349

BEE-CLEAN BUILDING MAINTENANCE IN-CORPORATED   *p1415*
1555 MCDONALD ST UNIT A, REGINA, SK, S4N 6H7
(306) 757-8020   *SIC* 7349

BI VIEW BUILDING SERVICES LTD   *p692*
5004 TIMBERLEA BLVD UNIT 26-29, MIS-SISSAUGA, ON, L4W 5C5
(905) 712-1831   *SIC* 7349

C & D CLEANING & SECURITY SERVICES LIMITED   *p458*
106 CHAIN LAKE DR UNIT 2A, HALIFAX, NS, B3S 1A8
(902) 450-5654   *SIC* 7349

CANADIAN CONTRACT CLEANING SPE-CIALISTS, INC   *p21*
1420 40 AVE NE SUITE 3, CALGARY, AB, T2E 6L1
(403) 259-5560   *SIC* 7349

CANADIAN CONTRACT CLEANING SPE-CIALISTS, INC   *p135*
603 10 AVE SE, HIGH RIVER, AB, T1V 1K2
SIC 7349

CANADIAN CONTRACT CLEANING SPE-CIALISTS, INC   *p155*
7550 40 AVE, RED DEER, AB, T4P 2H8
(403) 348-8440   *SIC* 7349

CANADIAN CONTRACT CLEANING SPE-CIALISTS, INC   *p851*
10 EAST WILMOT ST UNIT 25, RICHMOND HILL, ON, L4B 1G9
(905) 707-0410   *SIC* 7349

CAPABLE BUILDING CLEANING LTD *p399*
158 CLARK ST, FREDERICTON, NB, E3A 2W7
(506) 458-9343   *SIC* 7349

CARDINAL CARETAKERS CO LIMITED *p876*
80 DYNAMIC DR, SCARBOROUGH, ON, M1V 2V1
SIC 7349

CHD MAINTENANCE LIMITED   *p790*
274 VIEWMOUNT AVE, NORTH YORK, ON, M6B 1V2
(416) 782-5071   *SIC* 7349

CHEEMA CLEANING SERVICES LTD *p531*
12366 AIRPORT RD, CALEDON, ON, L7C 2W1
(905) 951-7156   *SIC* 7349

CLEAN HARBORS ENERGY AND INDUS-TRIAL SERVICES CORP   *p127*
26 AIRPORT RD, FORT MCMURRAY, AB, T9H 5B4
(780) 743-0222   *SIC* 7349

CLEAN HARBORS ENERGY AND INDUS-TRIAL SERVICES CORP   *p139*
3902 77 AVE, LEDUC, AB, T9E 0B6
(780) 980-1868   *SIC* 7349

CLEAN HARBORS ENERGY AND INDUS-TRIAL SERVICES CORP   *p159*
235133 RYAN RD, ROCKY VIEW COUNTY, AB, T1X 0K1
(403) 236-9891   *SIC* 7349

CLEAN-BRITE SERVICES OF REGINA LTD *p1420*
1201 OSLER ST, REGINA, SK, S4R 1W4
(306) 352-9953   *SIC* 7349

CLEANMARK GROUP INC   *p950*
141 ADELAIDE ST W SUITE 1000, TORONTO, ON, M5H 3L5
(416) 364-0677   *SIC* 7349

COLUMBIA BUILDING MAINTENANCE CO LTD   *p782*
65 MARTIN ROSS AVE UNIT 1, NORTH YORK, ON, M3J 2L6
(416) 663-5020   *SIC* 7349

COMMERCIAL BUILDING SERVICE LTD *p1415*
819 ARCOLA AVE, REGINA, SK, S4N 0S9
(306) 757-5332   *SIC* 7349

COMMERCIAL CLEANING SERVICES LIM-ITED   *p443*
166 BRAEMAR DR, DARTMOUTH, NS, B2X 2T3
(902) 435-9500   *SIC* 7349

CONCIERGERIE SPEICO INC   *p1130*
7651 RUE CORDNER, LASALLE, QC, H8N 2X2
(514) 364-0777   *SIC* 7349

CONCORDE BAGGAGE SERVICES INC *p22*
2000 AIRPORT RD NE, CALGARY, AB, T2E 6W5
(403) 735-5317   *SIC* 7349

CONMAR JANITORIAL CO. LTD   *p161*
50 RIDGEVIEW CRT, SHERWOOD PARK, AB, T8A 6B4
(780) 441-5459   *SIC* 7349

CORPORATION DE SECURITE GARDA CANADA   *p703*
2345 STANFIELD RD UNIT 400, MISSIS-SAUGA, ON, L4Y 3Y3
(416) 915-9500   *SIC* 7349

CORPORATION OF THE CITY OF BURLINGTON   *p527*
3330 HARVESTER RD, BURLINGTON, ON, L7N 3M8
(905) 333-6166   *SIC* 7349

CORREIA ENTERPRISES LTD   *p368*
375 NAIRN AVE, WINNIPEG, MB, R2L 0W8
(204) 668-4420   *SIC* 7349

DOMCLEAN LIMITED   *p514*
29 CRAIG ST, BRANTFORD, ON, N3R 7H8
(519) 752-3725   *SIC* 7349

DOMUS BUILDING CLEANING COMPANY LIMITED   *p815*
1366 TRIOLE ST SUITE 200, OTTAWA, ON, K1B 3M4
(613) 741-7722   *SIC* 7349

ENTRE-TIENS DE LA HAUTE-GASPESIE CORPORATION D'AIDE A DOMICILE *p1355*
378 BOUL SAINTE-ANNE O, SAINTE-ANNE-DES-MONTS, QC, G4V 1S8
(418) 763-7163   *SIC* 7349

ENTREPRISES DE NETTOYAGE M.P. INC *p1385*
1621 RUE DE LERY, TROIS-RIVIERES, QC, G8Y 7B3
SIC 7349

ENTREPRISES DE NETTOYAGE MARCEL LABBE INC   *p1264*
340 RUE JACKSON, QUEBEC, QC, G1N 4C5
(418) 523-9411   *SIC* 7349

ENTREPRISES PIERRE PICARD INC, LES *p1271*
1350 AV MAGUIRE BUREAU 103, QUE-BEC, QC, G1T 1Z3
(418) 683-4492   *SIC* 7349

ENTRETIEN 4M INC   *p1184*
6300 AV DU PARC BUREAU 202, MON-TREAL, QC, H2V 4H8
(514) 274-9933   *SIC* 7349

ENTRETIEN P.E.A.C.E. PLUS INC   *p1217*
950 AV OGILVY BUREAU 200, MONTREAL, QC, H3N 1P4
(514) 273-9764   *SIC* 7349

ENVIRO CLEAN (NFLD.) LIMITED   *p427*
155 MCNAMARA DR, PARADISE, NL, A1L 0A7
(709) 781-3264   *SIC* 7349

ENVIROCLEAN BUILDING MAINTENANCE

LTD   p100
  17233 109 AVE NW SUITE 101, EDMON-
  TON, AB, T5S 1H7
  (780) 489-0500   *SIC 7349*

ENVIROSYSTEMS INCORPORATED p416
  55 STINSON DR, SAINT JOHN, NB, E2M
  7E3
  (506) 652-9178   *SIC 7349*

ETD BUILDING MAINTENANCE LTD p323
  9001 SHAUGHNESSY ST, VANCOUVER,
  BC, V6P 6R9
  (604) 327-2555   *SIC 7349*

EVRIPOS JANITORIAL SERVICES LTD p825
  136 FLORA ST SUITE 1, OTTAWA, ON,
  K1R 5R5
  (613) 232-9069   *SIC 7349*

**FEDERATED BUILDING SERVICES LIM-
ITED**   p453
  1505 BARRINGTON ST SUITE 1310, HALI-
  FAX, NS, B3J 3K5
  SIC 7349

FOR-NET INC   p1260
  1875 AV DE LA NORMANDIE, QUEBEC,
  QC, G1L 3Y8
  (418) 529-6103   *SIC 7349*

GDI SERVICES (CANADA) LP   p30
  437 36 AVE SE, CALGARY, AB, T2G 1W5
  (403) 232-8402   *SIC 7349*

GDI SERVICES (CANADA) LP   p95
  14588 116 AVE NW, EDMONTON, AB, T5M
  3E9
  (780) 428-9508   *SIC 7349*

GDI SERVICES (CANADA) LP   p401
  475 WILSEY RD, FREDERICTON, NB, E3B
  7K1
  (506) 453-1404   *SIC 7349*

GDI SERVICES (CANADA) LP   p446
  202 BROWNLOW AVE, DARTMOUTH, NS,
  B3B 1T5
  (902) 468-3103   *SIC 7349*

GDI SERVICES (CANADA) LP   p584
  60 WORCESTER RD, ETOBICOKE, ON,
  M9W 5X2
  (416) 736-1144   *SIC 7349*

GDI SERVICES (CANADA) LP   p609
  39 DUNBAR AVE, HAMILTON, ON, L8H 3E3
  SIC 7349

GDI SERVICES (CANADA) LP   p639
  100 CAMPBELL AVE SUITE 12, KITCH-
  ENER, ON, N2H 4X8
  SIC 7349

GDI SERVICES (CANADA) LP   p652
  931 LEATHORNE ST UNIT E, LONDON,
  ON, N5Z 3M7
  (519) 681-3330   *SIC 7349*

GDI SERVICES (CANADA) LP   p818
  800 INDUSTRIAL AVE SUITE 12, OTTAWA,
  ON, K1G 4B8
  (613) 247-0065   *SIC 7349*

GDI SERVICES (CANADA) LP   p1420
  1319 HAMILTON ST, REGINA, SK, S4R 2B6
  SIC 7349

GDI SERVICES (QUEBEC) S.E.C.   p1132
  695 90E AV, LASALLE, QC, H8R 3A4
  (514) 368-1505   *SIC 7349*

GDI SERVICES AUX IMMEUBLES INC p1132
  695 90E AV, LASALLE, QC, H8R 3A4
  (514) 368-1504   *SIC 7349*

GDI SERVICES TECHNIQUES S.E.C. p1132
  695 90E AV, LASALLE, QC, H8R 3A4
  (514) 368-1504   *SIC 7349*

GRANDMOTHER'S TOUCH INC   p695
  5359 TIMBERLEA BLVD SUITE 20, MISSIS-
  SAUGA, ON, L4W 4N5
  (905) 361-0485   *SIC 7349*

GROUPE C.D.J. INC   p1293
  4740 RUE SAINT-FELIX, SAINT-
  AUGUSTIN-DE-DESMAURES, QC, G3A
  1B1
  SIC 7349

GROUPE POLY-M2 INC, LE   p1373
  4005A RUE DE LA GARLOCK, SHER-
  BROOKE, QC, J1L 1W9
  (819) 562-2161   *SIC 7349*

GSF CANADA INC   p1236
  4705 RUE LOUIS-B.-MAYER, MONTREAL,
  QC, H7P 6G5
  (450) 686-0555   *SIC 7349*

**HALLMARK HOUSEKEEPING SERVICES
INC**   p584
  34 RACINE RD, ETOBICOKE, ON, M9W
  2Z3
  (416) 748-0330   *SIC 7349*

HEARTLAND SERVICES GROUP LIMITED
p1031
  40 TROWERS RD UNIT 1, WOODBRIDGE,
  ON, L4L 7K6
  (905) 265-9667   *SIC 7349*

HELPING LIMITED   p885
  114 DUNKIRK RD UNIT 1, ST
  CATHARINES, ON, L2P 3H5
  (905) 646-9890   *SIC 7349*

**HINES INDUSTRIAL SITE SERVICES
GROUP INC**   p128
  8130 MANNING AVE, FORT MCMURRAY,
  AB, T9H 1V7
  (780) 790-3500   *SIC 7349*

HOODEX INDUSTRIES LIMITED   p696
  5650 TOMKEN RD UNIT 4, MISSISSAUGA,
  ON, L4W 4P1
  (905) 624-8668   *SIC 7349*

IMPACT CLEANING SERVICES LTD   p574
  21 GOODRICH RD SUITE 8, ETOBICOKE,
  ON, M8Z 6A3
  (416) 253-1234   *SIC 7349*

IN-PRO CLEANING SYSTEMS LTD   p671
  570 HOOD RD UNIT 24, MARKHAM, ON,
  L3R 4G7
  (905) 475-2020   *SIC 7349*

INTEGRAL PROPERTY SERVICES LTD p35
  343 FORGE RD SE SUITE 9, CALGARY,
  AB, T2H 0S9
  (403) 296-2206   *SIC 7349*

J&A CLEANING SOLUTIONS LTD   p795
  785 ARROW RD, NORTH YORK, ON, M9M
  2L4
  (416) 242-4151   *SIC 7349*

JACOBS INDUSTRIAL SERVICES   p122
  1104 70 AVE NW, EDMONTON, AB, T6P
  1P5
  (780) 468-2533   *SIC 7349*

JACOBS INDUSTRIAL SERVICES ULC p16
  205 QUARRY PARK BLVD SE SUITE 200,
  CALGARY, AB, T2C 3E7
  (403) 258-6899   *SIC 7349*

KELLOWAY CONSTRUCTION LIMITED p427
  1388 PORTUGAL COVE RD, PORTUGAL
  COVE-ST PHILIPS, NL, A1M 3J9
  (709) 895-6532   *SIC 7349*

KLEENZONE LTD   p599
  2489 SIXTH CONCESSION RD, GREEN-
  WOOD, ON, L0H 1H0
  (905) 686-6500   *SIC 7349*

LEADEC (CA) CORP   p476
  4700 INDUSTRIAL PKY, ALLISTON, ON,
  L9R 1A2
  (705) 435-5077   *SIC 7349*

MAGIC MAINTENANCE INC   p555
  25 EDILCAN DR UNIT 3, CONCORD, ON,
  L4K 3S4
  SIC 7349

MONTCALM SERVICES TECHNIQUES INC
p1132
  695 90E AV, LASALLE, QC, H8R 3A4
  SIC 7349

**NATIONAL CORPORATE HOUSEKEEPING
SERVICES INC**   p717
  3481 KELSO CRES, MISSISSAUGA, ON,
  L5L 4R3
  (905) 608-8004   *SIC 7349*

NOVACOS BUILDING CLEANING LTD p454
  1505 BARRINGTON ST SUITE 1310, HALI-
  FAX, NS, B3J 3K5
  SIC 7349

NUEST SERVICES LTD   p272
  17858 66 AVE, SURREY, BC, V3S 7X1
  (604) 888-1588   *SIC 7349*

P.R. ENTRETIEN D'EDIFICES INC   p1379

  1180 RUE LEVIS BUREAU 2, TERRE-
  BONNE, QC, J6W 5S6
  (450) 492-5999   *SIC 7349*

**PINKHAM & SONS BUILDING MAINTE-
NANCE INC**   p816
  1181 NEWMARKET ST UNIT M, OTTAWA,
  ON, K1B 3V1
  (613) 745-7753   *SIC 7349*

**PINKHAM & SONS BUILDING MAINTE-
NANCE INC**   p1330
  2449 RUE GUENETTE, SAINT-LAURENT,
  QC, H4R 2E9
  (514) 332-4522   *SIC 7349*

PRIME BUILDING MAINTENANCE LTD p256
  12800 BATHGATE WAY UNIT 13, RICH-
  MOND, BC, V6V 1Z4
  (604) 270-7766   *SIC 7349*

QUEEN'S UNIVERSITY AT KINGSTON p631
  207 STUART ST, KINGSTON, ON, K7L 2V9
  (613) 533-6075   *SIC 7349*

QUIET HARMONY INC   p505
  30 INTERMODAL DR UNIT 43, BRAMP-
  TON, ON, L6T 5K1
  (905) 794-0622   *SIC 7349*

**QUINTERRA PROPERTY MAINTENANCE
INC**   p321
  1681 CHESTNUT ST SUITE 400, VANCOU-
  VER, BC, V6J 4M6
  (604) 689-1800   *SIC 7349*

**QUINTERRA PROPERTY MAINTENANCE
INC**   p726
  6535 MILLCREEK DR UNIT 63, MISSIS-
  SAUGA, ON, L5N 2M2
  (905) 821-7171   *SIC 7349*

RELAMPING SERVICES CANADA LIMITED
p505
  48 WEST DR, BRAMPTON, ON, L6T 3T6
  (905) 457-1815   *SIC 7349*

ROSE BUILDING MAINTENANCE LTD p166
  7 ST ANNE ST SUITE 223, ST. ALBERT,
  AB, T8N 2X4
  (780) 459-4146   *SIC 7349*

S O S JANITORIAL SERVICES LTD   p1421
  2396 2ND AVE, REGINA, SK, S4R 1A6
  (306) 757-0027   *SIC 7349*

**SCANDINAVIAN BUILDING MAINTENANCE
LTD**   p242
  245 FELL AVE SUITE 101, NORTH VAN-
  COUVER, BC, V7P 2K1
  SIC 7349

SCANDINAVIAN BUILDING SERVICES LTD
p94
  14238 134 AVE NW, EDMONTON, AB, T5L
  5V8
  (780) 477-3311   *SIC 7349*

SCOT YOUNG (WESTERN) LIMITED   p37
  413 FORGE RD SE, CALGARY, AB, T2H
  0S9
  (403) 259-2293   *SIC 7349*

SERVANTAGE SERVICES INC   p42
  4 PARKDALE CRES NW, CALGARY, AB,
  T2N 3T8
  (403) 263-8170   *SIC 7349*

**SERVICE D'ENTRETIEN CLEAN INTERNA-
TIONAL INC**   p1140
  1006 RUE RENAULT, LEVIS, QC, G6Z 2Y8
  (418) 839-0928   *SIC 7349*

**SERVICES D'ENTRETIEN D'EDIFICES AL-
LIED (QUEBEC) INC**   p1184
  6585 RUE JEANNE-MANCE, MONTREAL,
  QC, H2V 4L1
  (514) 272-1137   *SIC 7349*

**SHANNON, BRENDA CONTRACTS LIM-
ITED**   p463
  130 GEORGE ST, NEW GLASGOW, NS,
  B2H 2K6
  SIC 7349

SIERRA VENTURES CORP   p1419
  1810 COLLEGE AVE, REGINA, SK, S4P
  1C1
  (306) 949-1510   *SIC 7349*

SIMCOE COUNTY CLEANING LIMITED p488
  49 MORROW RD UNIT 14, BARRIE, ON,
  L4N 3V7

  (705) 722-7203   *SIC 7349*

SODEXO CANADA LTD   p41
  1301 16 AVE NW, CALGARY, AB, T2M 0L4
  (403) 284-8536   *SIC 7349*

**SOLUTIONS DE MAINTENANCE AP-
PLIQUEES (AMS) INC**   p816
  1470 TRIOLE ST, OTTAWA, ON, K1B 3S6
  (613) 241-7794   *SIC 7349*

**SOLUTIONS DE MAINTENANCE AP-
PLIQUEES (AMS) INC**   p1182
  7075 RUE MARCONI, MONTREAL, QC,
  H2S 3K4
  (514) 272-8400   *SIC 7349*

SPECTRUM MANAGEMENT LTD   p316
  1166 ALBERNI ST SUITE 501, VANCOU-
  VER, BC, V6E 3Z3
  (604) 682-1388   *SIC 7349*

STATE BUILDING MAINTENANCE LIMITED
p580
  34 ASHMOUNT CRES, ETOBICOKE, ON,
  M9R 1C7
  (416) 247-1290   *SIC 7349*

STRONG, J.E. LIMITED   p713
  19 ANN ST, MISSISSAUGA, ON, L5G 3E9
  (905) 274-2327   *SIC 7349*

SUNSHINE BUILDING MAINTENANCE INC
p529
  2500 INDUSTRIAL ST, BURLINGTON, ON,
  L7P 1A5
  (905) 335-2020   *SIC 7349*

**SUPER SHINE JANITORIAL SERVICES
LIMITED**   p718
  4161 SLADEVIEW CRES UNIT 21, MISSIS-
  SAUGA, ON, L5L 5R3
  (905) 607-8200   *SIC 7349*

TBM SERVICE GROUP INC   p718
  2450 DUNWIN DR UNIT 6, MISSISSAUGA,
  ON, L5L 1J9
  (905) 608-8989   *SIC 7349*

**TORNADO BUILDING MAINTENANCE
CORPORATION**   p208
  9453 120 ST SUITE 201, DELTA, BC, V4C
  6S2
  (604) 930-6030   *SIC 7349*

ULTRA-TECH CLEANING SYSTEMS LTD
p285
  1420 ADANAC ST SUITE 201, VANCOU-
  VER, BC, V5L 2C3
  (604) 253-4698   *SIC 7349*

WATERFORD SERVICES INC   p677
  800 DENISON ST UNIT 7, MARKHAM, ON,
  L3R 5M9
  (905) 470-7766   *SIC 7349*

WEREK ENTERPRISES INC   p677
  164 TORBAY RD, MARKHAM, ON, L3R 1G6
  (905) 479-3131   *SIC 7349*

SIC 7352 Medical equipment rental

**GOUVERNEMENT DE LA PROVINCE DE
QUEBEC**   p1222
  7005 BOUL DE MAISONNEUVE O BU-
  REAU 620, MONTREAL, QC, H4B 1T3
  (514) 487-1770   *SIC 7352*

PRORESP INC   p649
  1909 OXFORD ST E SUITE 1, LONDON,
  ON, N5V 4L9
  (519) 686-2615   *SIC 7352*

---

*SIC 7353 Heavy construction equipment
rental*

175042 CANADA INC   p425
  2 FIRST AVE, LABRADOR CITY, NL, A2V
  2K5
  (709) 282-3910   *SIC 7353*

2122256 ALBERTA LTD   p78
  4613 41 ST, CAMROSE, AB, T4V 2Y8
  (780) 991-9997   *SIC 7353*

348461 ONTARIO LIMITED   p544
  30 ELGIN ST W, COBOURG, ON, K9A 5T4
  (905) 372-6131   *SIC 7353*

9020-4983 QUEBEC INC p1115
2035 RUE DESCHENES, JONQUIERE, QC, G7S 5E3
(418) 548-5000 *SIC 7353*

ALL CANADA CRANE RENTAL CORP p685
7215 TORBRAM RD, MISSISSAUGA, ON, L4T 1G7
(905) 795-1090 *SIC 7353*

ALUMA SYSTEMS INC p494
2 MANCHESTER CRT, BOLTON, ON, L7E 2J3
(905) 669-5282 *SIC 7353*

AMECO SERVICES INC p139
6909 42 ST UNIT 101, LEDUC, AB, T9E 0W1
(780) 440-6633 *SIC 7353*

APEX OILFIELD SERVICES (2000) INC p158
5402 BLINDMAN CRES, RED DEER COUNTY, AB, T4S 2M4
(403) 314-3385 *SIC 7353*

BLACK DIAMOND GROUP LIMITED p44
440 2 AVE SW SUITE 1000, CALGARY, AB, T2P 5E9
(403) 206-4747 *SIC 7353*

CAMEX EQUIPMENT SALES & RENTALS INC p148
1806 2 ST, NISKU, AB, T9E 0W8
(780) 955-2770 *SIC 7353*

CAPITAL CRANE LIMITED p426
20 SAGONA AVE, MOUNT PEARL, NL, A1N 4R2
(709) 748-8888 *SIC 7353*

COOPER EQUIPMENT RENTALS LIMITED p738
6335 EDWARDS BLVD, MISSISSAUGA, ON, L5T 2W7
(877) 329-6531 *SIC 7353*

COUGAR DRILLING SOLUTIONS INC p122
7319 17 ST NW, EDMONTON, AB, T6P 1P1
(780) 440-2400 *SIC 7353*

DOUGLAS LAKE EQUIPMENT LIMITED PARTNERSHIP p271
17924 56 AVE, SURREY, BC, V3S 1C7
(604) 576-7506 *SIC 7353*

DWIGHT CRANE LTD p474
131 DOWTY RD, AJAX, ON, L1S 2G3
(905) 686-3333 *SIC 7353*

EQUIPEMENT ST-GERMAIN INC p1358
1151 RUE NOBEL, SAINTE-JULIE, QC, J3E 1Z4
(450) 443-3290 *SIC 7353*

GREAT NORTH EQUIPMENT INC p114
8743 50 AVE NW, EDMONTON, AB, T6E 5H4
(780) 461-7400 *SIC 7353*

GROUPE AGF INC p1141
2270 RUE GARNEAU, LONGUEUIL, QC, J4G 1E7
(450) 442-9494 *SIC 7353*

GUAY INC p1049
10801 RUE COLBERT, ANJOU, QC, H1J 2G5
(514) 354-4420 *SIC 7353*

GUAY INC p1280
1160 RUE BOUVIER, QUEBEC, QC, G2K 1L9
(418) 628-8460 *SIC 7353*

GWIL INDUSTRIES INC p185
5337 REGENT ST, BURNABY, BC, V5C 4H4
(604) 291-9404 *SIC 7353*

IRVING, J. D. LIMITED p416
45 GIFFORD RD, SAINT JOHN, NB, E2M 5K7
(506) 635-5555 *SIC 7353*

LOCATION JEAN MILLER INC p1159
169 117 RTE, MONT-TREMBLANT, QC, J8E 2X2
(819) 425-3797 *SIC 7353*

MODU-LOC FENCE RENTALS LTD p219
240 NEAVE RD, KELOWNA, BC, V1V 2L9
(250) 491-4110 *SIC 7353*

NCSG CRANE & HEAVY HAUL SERVICES LTD p1
28765 ACHESON RD, ACHESON, AB, T7X 6A8
(780) 960-6300 *SIC 7353*

NORTHERN MAT & BRIDGE LIMITED PARTNERSHIP p80
8001 99 ST, CLAIRMONT, AB, T8X 5B1
(780) 538-4135 *SIC 7353*

PARTNERS CONSTRUCTION LIMITED p464
GD, PICTOU, NS, B0K 1H0
(902) 485-4576 *SIC 7353*

PERI FORMWORK SYSTEMS INC p495
45 NIXON RD, BOLTON, ON, L7E 1K1
(905) 951-5400 *SIC 7353*

PROCRANE INC p123
2440 76 AVE NW, EDMONTON, AB, T6P 1J5
(780) 440-4434 *SIC 7353*

PUMPCRETE CORPORATION p759
6000 PROGRESS ST, NIAGARA FALLS, ON, L2G 0C4
(905) 354-3855 *SIC 7353*

RAPID EQUIPMENT RENTAL LIMITED p784
5 SAINT REGIS CRES N UNIT 2, NORTH YORK, ON, M3J 1Y9
(416) 638-7007 *SIC 7353*

RAYDON RENTALS LTD p102
10235 180 ST NW, EDMONTON, AB, T5S 1C1
(780) 989-1301 *SIC 7353*

REDHEAD EQUIPMENT p1418
GD LCD MAIN, REGINA, SK, S4P 2Z4
(306) 721-2666 *SIC 7353*

REGIONAL CRANE RENTALS LTD p595
1409 CYRVILLE RD, GLOUCESTER, ON, K1B 3L7
(613) 748-7922 *SIC 7353*

RENTCO EQUIPMENT LTD p133
11437 97 AVE, GRANDE PRAIRIE, AB, T8V 5R8
(780) 539-7860 *SIC 7353*

ROYAL IRAQI HEAVY EQUIPMENT CORPORATION, THE p488
55 BROWNING TRAIL, BARRIE, ON, L4N 5A5
(705) 241-0082 *SIC 7353*

SARENS CANADA INC p140
6019 35 ST, LEDUC, AB, T9E 1E6
(780) 612-4400 *SIC 7353*

SELECT EQUIPMENT RENTALS LTD p166
4 RIEL DR, ST. ALBERT, AB, T8N 3Z7
(780) 419-6100 *SIC 7353*

STAMPEDE DRILLING INC p60
250 6 AVE SW 22ND FLR, CALGARY, AB, T2P 3H7
(403) 984-5042 *SIC 7353*

STRAD INC p60
440 2 AVE SW SUITE 1200, CALGARY, AB, T2P 5E9
(403) 232-6900 *SIC 7353*

STRATTY ENTERPRISES LTD p173
5116 59 ST, WHITECOURT, AB, T7S 1X7
(780) 706-4889 *SIC 7353*

STRONGCO CORPORATION p700
1640 ENTERPRISE RD, MISSISSAUGA, ON, L4W 4L4
(905) 670-5100 *SIC 7353*

TECHNICAL CONCRETE SOLUTIONS LTD p756
1341 KERRISDALE BLVD, NEWMARKET, ON, L3Y 8W8
(905) 761-9330 *SIC 7353*

TERRATEAM EQUIPMENT RENTALS INC p164
110 MANITOBA CRT, SPRUCE GROVE, AB, T7X 0V5
(780) 962-9598 *SIC 7353*

TESSIER LTEE p1260
21 RUE DU MARCHE-CHAMPLAIN, QUEBEC, QC, G1K 8Z8
(418) 569-3739 *SIC 7353*

TNT CRANE & RIGGING CANADA INC p177
2190 CARPENTER ST, ABBOTSFORD, BC, V2T 6B4
(800) 667-2215 *SIC 7353*

TORCAN LIFT EQUIPMENT LTD p795
115 RIVALDA RD, NORTH YORK, ON, M9M 2M6
(416) 743-2500 *SIC 7353*

VARCO CANADA ULC p111
7127 56 AVE NW, EDMONTON, AB, T6B 3L2
(780) 665-0200 *SIC 7353*

VARCO CANADA ULC p140
6621 45 ST, LEDUC, AB, T9E 7E3
(780) 986-6063 *SIC 7353*

VENETOR CRANE LTD p893
45 ORIOLE AVE, STONEY CREEK, ON, L8E 5C4
(905) 643-7943 *SIC 7353*

W.E. RENTALS 2K LTD p133
11489 95 AVE, GRANDE PRAIRIE, AB, T8V 5P7
(780) 539-1709 *SIC 7353*

ZEDCOR ENERGY SERVICES CORP p63
500 4 AVE SW UNIT 3000, CALGARY, AB, T2P 2V6
(403) 930-5430 *SIC 7353*

SIC 7359 Equipment rental and leasing, nec

2456317 ONTARIO LTD p932
431 RICHMOND ST E, TORONTO, ON, M5A 1R1
(647) 490-4839 *SIC 7359*

248276 ALBERTA LTD p130
100 1ST ST, FOX CREEK, AB, T0H 1P0
(780) 622-3566 *SIC 7359*

303567 SASKATCHEWAN LTD p1425
2636 MILLAR AVE, SASKATOON, SK, S7K 4C8
(306) 933-3020 *SIC 7359*

3161234 MANITOBA LIMITED p991
64 JEFFERSON AVE UNIT 3, TORONTO, ON, M6K 1Y4
(416) 589-6563 *SIC 7359*

3627730 CANADA INC p691
2365 MATHESON BLVD E, MISSISSAUGA, ON, L4W 5B3
(905) 366-9200 *SIC 7359*

3627730 CANADA INC p1126
1930 RUE ONESIME-GAGNON, LACHINE, QC, H8T 3M6
(514) 631-0710 *SIC 7359*

9363-9888 QUEBEC INC p1243
100 RUE HUOT, NOTRE-DAME-DE-L'ILE-PERROT, QC, J7V 7Z8
(514) 700-5319 *SIC 7359*

ALBERTA SPECIAL EVENT EQUIPMENT RENTALS & SALES LTD p112
6010 99 ST NW, EDMONTON, AB, T6E 3P2
(780) 435-2211 *SIC 7359*

AMHERST CRANE RENTALS LIMITED p870
105 NANTUCKET BLVD, SCARBOROUGH, ON, M1P 2N5
(416) 752-2602 *SIC 7359*

AMUSEMENTS AIRBOUNCE SENC, LES p1394
29 AV PASOLD, VAUDREUIL-DORION, QC, J7V 2W9
(450) 424-0214 *SIC 7359*

AUDIO VISUAL SERVICES (CANADA) CORPORATION p1029
180 TROWERS RD UNIT 28, WOODBRIDGE, ON, L4L 8A6
(647) 724-0880 *SIC 7359*

AV-CANADA INC p702
1655 QUEENSWAY E UNIT 2, MISSISSAUGA, ON, L4X 2Z5
(905) 566-5500 *SIC 7359*

AVW TELAV AUDIO VISUAL SERVICES p817
2295 ST. LAURENT BLVD, OTTAWA, ON, K1G 4H6
(613) 526-3121 *SIC 7359*

BEACON LITE LTD p817
4070 BELGREEN DR, OTTAWA, ON, K1G 3N2
(613) 737-7337 *SIC 7359*

BITUMINEX LIMITED p365
29 TERRACON PL, WINNIPEG, MB, R2J 4B3
(204) 237-6253 *SIC 7359*

BLACK DIAMOND LIMITED PARTNERSHIP p44
440 2 AVE SW SUITE 1000, CALGARY, AB, T2P 5E9
(403) 206-4747 *SIC 7359*

BRYJON ENTERPRISES LTD p381
925 MILT STEGALL DR, WINNIPEG, MB, R3G 3H7
(204) 786-8756 *SIC 7359*

CENTRE DE LOCATION G.M. INC p1152
12075 RUE ARTHUR-SICARD BUREAU 101, MIRABEL, QC, J7J 0E9
(450) 434-0505 *SIC 7359*

CHEP CANADA INC p721
7400 EAST DANBRO CRES, MISSISSAUGA, ON, L5N 8C6
(905) 790-2437 *SIC 7359*

COAST STORAGE & CONTAINERS LTD p268
5674 TEREDO ST SUITE 102, SECHELT, BC, V0N 3A0
(604) 883-2444 *SIC 7359*

CROFAM MANAGEMENT INC p915
501 CONSUMERS RD, TORONTO, ON, M2J 5E2
(416) 391-0400 *SIC 7359*

DAY, WILLIAM CONSTRUCTION LIMITED p483
2500 ELM ST, AZILDA, ON, P0M 1B0
(705) 682-1555 *SIC 7359*

EXPOSERVICE STANDARD INC p1130
2345 RUE LAPIERRE, LASALLE, QC, H8N 1B7
(514) 367-4848 *SIC 7359*

FR RENTALS LTD p203
2495 THEATRE RD, CRANBROOK, BC, V1C 7B8
(778) 517-8388 *SIC 7359*

FRISCHKORN AUDIO-VISUAL CORP p708
2360 TEDLO ST, MISSISSAUGA, ON, L5A 3V3
(905) 281-9000 *SIC 7359*

GAUDREAU ENVIRONNEMENT INC p1399
365 BOUL DE LA BONAVENTURE, VICTORIAVILLE, QC, G6T 1V5
(819) 758-8378 *SIC 7359*

GOEASY LTD p709
33 CITY CENTRE DR SUITE 510, MISSISSAUGA, ON, L5B 2N5
(905) 272-2788 *SIC 7359*

HIGGINS RENT-ALL LTD p571
389 HORNER AVE, ETOBICOKE, ON, M8W 2A2
(416) 252-4050 *SIC 7359*

HOPITEL INC p1227
8225 RUE LABARRE, MONTREAL, QC, H4P 2E6
(514) 739-2525 *SIC 7359*

LITZ, R. & SONS COMPANY LIMITED p381
277 MCPHILLIPS ST, WINNIPEG, MB, R3E 2K7
(204) 783-7979 *SIC 7359*

LOCATION BENCH & TABLE INC p1220
6999 AV VICTORIA, MONTREAL, QC, H3W 3E9
(514) 738-4755 *SIC 7359*

LOCATION D'OUTILS BROSSARD INC p1308
3905 MONTEE SAINT-HUBERT, SAINT-HUBERT, QC, J3Y 4K2
(450) 678-3385 *SIC 7359*

LONG & MCQUADE LIMITED p990
925 BLOOR ST W, TORONTO, ON, M6H 1L5
(416) 588-7886 *SIC 7359*

MASON LIFT LTD p206
1605 CLIVEDEN AVE, DELTA, BC, V3M 6P7
(604) 517-6500 *SIC 7359*

MATCOM INDUSTRIAL INSTALLATIONS INC p555

1531 CREDITSTONE RD, CONCORD, ON, L4K 5V6
(416) 667-0463   *SIC 7359*
MEDIACO THE PRESENTATION COMPANY INC   p193
4595 TILLICUM ST, BURNABY, BC, V5J 5K9
(604) 871-1000   *SIC 7359*
MYSHAK SALES & RENTALS LTD   p1
28527 ACHESON RD, ACHESON, AB, T7X 6A8
(780) 960-9255   *SIC 7359*
NORMAC EQUIPMENT/CONSTRUCTION LIMITED   p846
6855 HWY 101 E, PORCUPINE, ON, P0N 1C0
(705) 235-3277   *SIC 7359*
PHELPS APARTMENT LAUNDRIES LTD   p261
3640 NO. 4 RD SUITE 1, RICHMOND, BC, V6X 2L7
(604) 257-8200   *SIC 7359*
RAVEN CENTER HOLDINGS LTD   p214
49 ALASKA HWY, FORT ST. JOHN, BC, V1J 4H7
(250) 787-8474   *SIC 7359*
RED-D-ARC LIMITED   p599
667 SOUTH SERVICE RD, GRIMSBY, ON, L3M 4E8
(905) 643-4212   *SIC 7359*
RTO ASSET MANAGEMENT INC   p710
33 CITY CENTRE DR SUITE 510, MISSISSAUGA, ON, L5B 2N5
(905) 272-2788   *SIC 7359*
RUOFF & COMPANY INC   p708
2360 TEDLO ST, MISSISSAUGA, ON, L5A 3V3
(905) 281-9000   *SIC 7359*
SIGNALISATION COMO INC   p1345
4325 RUE J.-B.-MARTINEAU, SAINT-LEONARD, QC, H1R 3W9
(514) 327-2875   *SIC 7359*
SIGNALISATION DE L'ESTRIE INC   p1374
520 RUE PEPIN, SHERBROOKE, QC, J1L 2Y8
(819) 822-3828   *SIC 7359*
SIM VIDEO INTERNATIONAL INC   p992
1 ATLANTIC AVE SUITE 110, TORONTO, ON, M6K 3E7
(416) 979-9958   *SIC 7359*
SMITHRITE PORTABLE SERVICES LTD   p202
1650 HARTLEY AVE, COQUITLAM, BC, V3K 7A1
(604) 529-4028   *SIC 7359*
SOUND WAVES ENTERTAINMENT NETWORK LTD   p223
1-325 BAY AVE, KELOWNA, BC, V1Y 7S3
(250) 868-3333   *SIC 7359*
SOUTHERN MUSIC LTD   p9
3605 32 ST NE, CALGARY, AB, T1Y 5Y9
(403) 291-1666   *SIC 7359*
STEPHENSON'S RENTAL SERVICES INC   p743
6895 COLUMBUS RD SUITE 502, MISSISSAUGA, ON, L5T 2G9
(905) 507-3650   *SIC 7359*
SUNBELT RENTALS OF CANADA INC p202
93 NORTH BEND ST SUITE 838, COQUITLAM, BC, V3K 6N1
(604) 291-8001   *SIC 7359*
SUPERIOR EVENTS GROUP INC   p787
430 NORFINCH DR, NORTH YORK, ON, M3N 1Y4
(416) 249-4000   *SIC 7359*
SURERUS CONSTRUCTION & DEVELOPMENT LTD   p214
9312 109 ST, FORT ST. JOHN, BC, V1J 6G9
(250) 785-2423   *SIC 7359*
SWAN DUST CONTROL LIMITED   p1007
35 UNIVERSITY AVE E, WATERLOO, ON, N2J 2V9
(519) 885-4450   *SIC 7359*
TOROMONT INDUSTRIES LTD   p893

880 SOUTH SERVICE RD, STONEY CREEK, ON, L8E 5M7
(905) 643-9410   *SIC 7359*
TORQUIN CORPORATION LIMITED   p757
200 PONY DR, NEWMARKET, ON, L3Y 7B6
(905) 836-0988   *SIC 7359*
TUCKER'S TRAFFIC CONTROL   p174
5195 ODIAN ST, 108 MILE RANCH, BC, V0K 2Z0
(250) 791-5725   *SIC 7359*
UHAUL COMPANY OF EASTERN ONTARIO   p998
240 REXDALE BLVD, TORONTO, ON, M9W 1R2
(416) 335-1250   *SIC 7359*
VANCOUVER PARTYWORKS INTERACTIVE CO INC   p278
8473 124 ST UNIT 13, SURREY, BC, V3W 9G4
(604) 599-5541   *SIC 7359*
VENTURIS CAPITAL CORPORATION   p282
19433 96 AVE UNIT 102, SURREY, BC, V4N 4C4
(604) 607-8000   *SIC 7359*
WEST WIND AVIATION INC   p1432
3A HANGAR RD, SASKATOON, SK, S7L 5X4
(306) 652-9121   *SIC 7359*
WESTBURY NATIONAL SHOW SYSTEMS LTD   p869
772 WARDEN AVE, SCARBOROUGH, ON, M1L 4T7
(416) 752-1371   *SIC 7359*
WRANGLER RENTALS LTD   p140
3911 ALLARD AVE, LEDUC, AB, T9E 0R8
(780) 980-1331   *SIC 7359*

SIC 7361 Employment agencies

137077 CANADA INC   p824
203 ROCHESTER ST, OTTAWA, ON, K1R 7M5
(613) 232-1579   *SIC 7361*
1484558 ONTARIO INC   p770
2 SHEPPARD AVE E SUITE 700, NORTH YORK, ON, M2N 5Y7
(416) 203-1800   *SIC 7361*
162069 CANADA INC   p1063
1263 RUE VOLTA, BOUCHERVILLE, QC, J4B 7M7
(450) 670-1110   *SIC 7361*
1799795 ONTARIO LIMITED   p1001
171 MONTREAL RD, VANIER, ON, K1L 6E4
(613) 745-5720   *SIC 7361*
2059010 ONTARIO INC   p708
2515 HURONTARIO ST UNIT 2006, MISSISSAUGA, ON, L5A 4C8
(905) 281-9175   *SIC 7361*
2904357 CANADA INC   p1337
615 RUE MCCAFFREY, SAINT-LAURENT, QC, H4T 1N3
(514) 340-2844   *SIC 7361*
4386396 CANADA INC   p770
2 SHEPPARD AVE E SUITE 2000, NORTH YORK, ON, M2N 5Y7
(416) 225-9900   *SIC 7361*
4659551 MANITOBA LTD   p374
328 KING ST SUITE A, WINNIPEG, MB, R3B 3H4
(204) 989-5820   *SIC 7361*
500 STAFFING INC, THE   p991
67 MOWAT AVE SUITE 411, TORONTO, ON, M6K 3E3
SIC 7361
671061 ONTARIO LIMITED   p570
2913 LAKE SHORE BLVD W SUITE A, ETOBICOKE, ON, M8V 1J3
(416) 599-7232   *SIC 7361*
7251246 CANADA INC   p665
90C CENTURIAN DR UNIT 209, MARKHAM, ON, L3R 8C5
(416) 483-2200   *SIC 7361*
9778233 CANADA INC   p708

99 DUNDAS ST E 2ND FL, MISSISSAUGA, ON, L5A 1W7
(905) 232-5200   *SIC 7361*
ACHIEVERS SOLUTIONS INC   p991
190 LIBERTY ST SUITE 100, TORONTO, ON, M6K 3L5
(888) 622-3343   *SIC 7361*
ADECCO EMPLOYMENT SERVICES LIMITED   p374
228 NOTRE DAME AVE, WINNIPEG, MB, R3B 1N7
SIC 7361
ADECCO EMPLOYMENT SERVICES LIMITED   p959
20 BAY ST SUITE 800, TORONTO, ON, M5J 2N8
(416) 646-3322   *SIC 7361*
ADVANTAGE PERSONNEL LTD   p445
75 AKERLEY BLVD UNIT S, DARTMOUTH, NS, B3B 1R7
(902) 468-5624   *SIC 7361*
AEROTEK ULC   p253
13575 COMMERCE PKY SUITE 150, RICHMOND, BC, V6V 2L1
(604) 244-1007   *SIC 7361*
AEROTEK ULC   p709
350 BURNHAMTHORPE RD W SUITE 800, MISSISSAUGA, ON, L5B 3J1
(905) 283-1200   *SIC 7361*
AGENCE DE PLACEMENT SELECT INC p1319
96 RUE DE MARTIGNY O, SAINT-JEROME, QC, J7Y 2G1
(450) 431-6292   *SIC 7361*
AGENCE DE PLACEMENT TRESOR INC p1084
2A RUE GRENON O, COTE SAINT-LUC, QC, H7N 2G6
(450) 933-7090   *SIC 7361*
AIM GROUP INC, THE   p822
130 ALBERT ST SUITE 126, OTTAWA, ON, K1P 5G4
(613) 230-6991   *SIC 7361*
ALL HEALTH SERVICES INC   p927
66 COLLIER ST UNIT 9D, TORONTO, ON, M4W 1L9
(416) 515-1151   *SIC 7361*
ANCIA PERSONNEL INC   p1137
469 AV TANIATA BUREAU 400, LEVIS, QC, G6W 5M6
SIC 7361
ANT & BEE CORPORATION   p978
123 JOHN ST, TORONTO, ON, M5V 2E2
(416) 646-2811   *SIC 7361*
APLIN, DAVID & ASSOCIATES INC   p27
140 10 AVE SE STE 500, CALGARY, AB, T2G 0R1
(403) 261-9000   *SIC 7361*
APPLEONE SERVICES LTD   p578
50 PAXMAN RD SUITE 6, ETOBICOKE, ON, M9C 1B7
(416) 622-0100   *SIC 7361*
B&M EMPLOYMENT INC   p786
168 OAKDALE RD UNIT 8, NORTH YORK, ON, M3N 2S5
SIC 7361
B&N MANAGEMENT   p972
51 TRANBY AVE, TORONTO, ON, M5R 1N4
(613) 321-7401   *SIC 7361*
BARTECH TECHNICAL SERVICES OF CANADA, LTD   p704
160 TRADERS BLVD E SUITE 112, MISSISSAUGA, ON, L4Z 3K7
(905) 502-9914   *SIC 7361*
BLUEBIX SOLUTIONS INCORPORATED p916
1110 FINCH AVE W SUITE 612, TORONTO, ON, M3J 2T2
(416) 319-5486   *SIC 7361*
BRAUN ASSOCIATES LIMITED   p859
201 FRONT ST N SUITE 405, SARNIA, ON, N7T 7T9
(519) 336-4590   *SIC 7361*
C.T. CONSULTANTS INC   p1399

1696 BOUL DES LAURENTIDES, VIMONT, QC, H7M 2P4
(514) 375-0377   *SIC 7361*
CALIAN LTD   p1202
700 RUE DE LA GAUCHETIERE O BUREAU 26E, MONTREAL, QC, H3B 5M2
SIC 7361
CANADIAN EMPLOYMENT CONTRACTORS INC   p702
2077 DUNDAS ST E UNIT 101, MISSISSAUGA, ON, L4X 1M2
(905) 282-9578   *SIC 7361*
CAREY INDUSTRIAL SERVICES LTD p129
9918A 102 ST, FORT SASKATCHEWAN, AB, T8L 2C3
(780) 998-1919   *SIC 7361*
CERIDIAN CANADA LTD   p377
125 GARRY ST, WINNIPEG, MB, R3C 3P2
(204) 947-9400   *SIC 7361*
CHAUFFEUR EXPRESS LOCATION INC. p1387
3346 RUE BELLEFEUILLE, TROIS-RIVIERES, QC, G9A 3Z3
(819) 697-3555   *SIC 7361*
COLLABERA CANADA INC   p705
1 ROBERT SPECK PKY UNIT 900, MISSISSAUGA, ON, L4Z 3M3
(416) 639-6250   *SIC 7361*
COMMUNITY CONNECTIONS SOCIETY OF SOUTHEAST BC   p203
209 16TH AVE N, CRANBROOK, BC, V1C 5S8
(250) 426-2976   *SIC 7361*
COMMUNITY LIVING WALKERTON AND DISTRICT   p1004
19 DURHAM ST E, WALKERTON, ON, N0G 2V0
(519) 881-0233   *SIC 7361*
DBPC GROUP OF COMPANIES LTD   p767
250 CONSUMERS RD SUITE 605, NORTH YORK, ON, M2J 4V6
(416) 755-9198   *SIC 7361*
DESIGN GROUP STAFFING INC   p88
10012 JASPER AVE NW, EDMONTON, AB, T5J 1R2
(780) 448-5850   *SIC 7361*
DIALOG   p928
2 BLOOR ST E SUITE 1000, TORONTO, ON, M4W 1A8
(416) 966-0220   *SIC 7361*
DRAKE INTERNATIONAL INC   p950
320 BAY ST SUITE 1400, TORONTO, ON, M5H 4A6
(416) 216-1000   *SIC 7361*
DUKE MARINE TECHNICAL SERVICES CANADA INC   p527
3425 HARVESTER RD SUITE 213, BURLINGTON, ON, L7N 3N1
(800) 252-6027   *SIC 7361*
EAGLE PROFESSIONAL RESOURCES INC p823
170 LAURIER AVE W SUITE 902, OTTAWA, ON, K1P 5V5
SIC 7361
EAGLE PROFESSIONAL RESOURCES INC p942
67 YONGE ST SUITE 200, TORONTO, ON, M5E 1J8
(416) 861-1492   *SIC 7361*
ESPO BROTHERS MANAGEMENT I LTD p174
33780 KING RD, ABBOTSFORD, BC, V2S 7P2
(604) 859-2220   *SIC 7361*
EXECUTIVE WAITER RESOURCES INC p321
1975 16TH AVE W, VANCOUVER, BC, V6J 2M5
(604) 689-0640   *SIC 7361*
FIRST LINK LOGISTICS LTD   p722
7467 NINTH LINE, MISSISSAUGA, ON, L5N 7C3
(905) 565-1459   *SIC 7361*
GIRAFE SANTE INC   p1059

617 BOUL DU CURE-LABELLE BUREAU 100, BLAINVILLE, QC, J7C 2J1
SIC 7361

GLOBAL SKILLS INC *p951*
366 BAY ST 10TH FL, TORONTO, ON, M5H 4B2
(416) 907-8400 *SIC 7361*

GREAT CONNECTIONS EMPLOYMENT SERVICES INC *p781*
5050 DUFFERIN ST UNIT 109, NORTH YORK, ON, M3H 5T5
(416) 850-5060 *SIC 7361*

H R ASSOCIATES *p577*
302 THE EAST MALL SUITE 600, ETOBICOKE, ON, M9B 6C7
(416) 237-1500 *SIC 7361*

HALF, ROBERT CANADA INC *p963*
181 BAY ST SUITE 820, TORONTO, ON, M5J 2T3
(416) 203-7656 *SIC 7361*

HALF, ROBERT CANADA INC *p963*
181 BAY ST SUITE 820, TORONTO, ON, M5J 2T3
(416) 350-2010 *SIC 7361*

HALF, ROBERT INTERNATIONAL *p963*
181 BAY ST SUITE 820, TORONTO, ON, M5J 2T3
(416) 365-3153 *SIC 7361*

HCR PERSONNEL SOLUTIONS INC *p577*
19 FOUR SEASONS PL 2ND FL, ETOBICOKE, ON, M9B 6E7
(416) 622-1427 *SIC 7361*

HIRERIGHT CANADA CORPORATION *p963*
70 UNIVERSITY AVE SUITE 200, TORONTO, ON, M5J 2M4
(416) 956-5000 *SIC 7361*

HORIZON MARITIME SERVICES LTD *p444*
101 RESEARCH DR, DARTMOUTH, NS, B2Y 4T6
(902) 468-2341 *SIC 7361*

IAN MARTIN LIMITED *p800*
610 CHARTWELL RD SUITE 101, OAKVILLE, ON, L6J 4A5
(905) 815-1600 *SIC 7361*

IAN MARTIN LIMITED *p1329*
3333 BOUL DE LA COTE-VERTU BUREAU 202, SAINT-LAURENT, QC, H4R 2N1
(514) 338-3800 *SIC 7361*

IFG - INTERNATIONAL FINANCIAL GROUP (US) LTD *p986*
100 KING ST W SUITE 910, TORONTO, ON, M5X 1B1
(416) 645-2434 *SIC 7361*

INTERIM RESSOURCES HUMAINES INC *p1129*
50 RUE SIMON, LACHUTE, QC, J8H 3R8
SIC 7361

INTERIM RESSOURCES HUMAINES INC *p1132*
50 AV LABATT, LASALLE, QC, H8R 3E7
SIC 7361

IS2 WORKFORCE SOLUTIONS INC *p115*
8023 ROPER RD NW, EDMONTON, AB, T6E 6S4
(780) 420-9999 *SIC 7361*

ISG SEARCH INC *p935*
229 YONGE ST SUITE 408, TORONTO, ON, M5B 1N9
(416) 775-4800 *SIC 7361*

JOB SKILLS *p628*
155 RIVERGLEN DR SUITE 7, KESWICK, ON, L4P 3M3
(905) 476-8088 *SIC 7361*

K. A. S. PERSONNEL SERVICES INC *p534*
534 HESPELER RD SUITE A2, CAMBRIDGE, ON, N1R 6J7
(519) 622-7788 *SIC 7361*

K.A.S. GROUP OF COMPANIES INC, THE *p735*
7895 TRANMERE DR SUITE 18, MISSISSAUGA, ON, L5S 1V9
(905) 677-3368 *SIC 7361*

KELLY SERVICES (CANADA), LTD *p622*
70 DICKINSON DR, INGLESIDE, ON, K0C

1M0
(613) 537-8491 *SIC 7361*

LABOUR READY TEMPORARY SERVICES LTD *p841*
306 GEORGE ST N UNIT 6, PETERBOROUGH, ON, K9J 3H2
(705) 760-9111 *SIC 7361*

LANNICK GROUP INC *p969*
77 KING ST W SUITE 4110, TORONTO, ON, M5K 2A1
(416) 340-1500 *SIC 7361*

LEGACY PERSONNEL SOLUTIONS INC *p1022*
2480 SEMINOLE ST, WINDSOR, ON, N8Y 1X3
(519) 419-5073 *SIC 7361*

MACENNA BUSINESS SERVICES CORP *p213*
10139 101 AVE 2ND FL, FORT ST. JOHN, BC, V1J 2B4
(250) 785-8367 *SIC 7361*

MANDRAKE MANAGEMENT CONSULTANTS CORPORATION *p927*
55 ST CLAIR AVE W SUITE 401, TORONTO, ON, M4V 2Y7
(416) 922-5400 *SIC 7361*

MANPOWER PROFESSIONAL INC *p53*
734 7 AVE SW SUITE 120, CALGARY, AB, T2P 3P8
(403) 269-6936 *SIC 7361*

MATRIX LABOUR LEASING LTD *p71*
11420 27 ST SE SUITE 204, CALGARY, AB, T2Z 3R6
(403) 201-9520 *SIC 7361*

MAYFAIR PERSONNEL (NORTHERN) LTD *p134*
11039 78 AVE SUITE 102, GRANDE PRAIRIE, AB, T8W 2J7
(780) 539-5090 *SIC 7361*

MELCO CAPITAL INC *p1379*
1000 MONTEE DES PIONNIERS BUREAU 212, TERREBONNE, QC, J6V 1S8
(514) 564-7600 *SIC 7361*

METRO WIDE PERSONNEL INC *p504*
11 BLAIR DR, BRAMPTON, ON, L6T 2H4
SIC 7361

MNM INC *p795*
2473 FINCH AVE W, NORTH YORK, ON, M9M 2G1
(416) 744-9675 *SIC 7361*

MODIS CANADA INC *p965*
10 BAY ST SUITE 700, TORONTO, ON, M5J 2R8
(416) 367-2020 *SIC 7361*

NASCO SERVICES INC *p299*
128 PENDER ST W SUITE 205, VANCOUVER, BC, V6B 1R8
(604) 683-2512 *SIC 7361*

NORAMTEC CONSULTANTS INC *p750*
1400 CLYDE AVE SUITE 217, NEPEAN, ON, K2G 3J2
(613) 727-3997 *SIC 7361*

ONE SOURCE BUSINESS SERVICE *p784*
3991 CHESSWOOD DR, NORTH YORK, ON, M3J 2R8
(416) 398-0863 *SIC 7361*

PEO CANADA LTD *p56*
805 5 AVE SW SUITE 100, CALGARY, AB, T2P 0N6
(403) 237-5577 *SIC 7361*

PEOPLE PLACE, THE *p56*
805 5 AVE SW, CALGARY, AB, T2P 0N6
(403) 705-2353 *SIC 7361*

PEOPLESOURCE STAFFING SOLUTIONS INC *p991*
67 MOWAT AVE SUITE 411, TORONTO, ON, M6K 3E3
(905) 277-4455 *SIC 7361*

PERFORMANCE DRIVER SERVICES INC *p37*
5925 12 ST SE SUITE 220, CALGARY, AB, T2H 2M3
SIC 7361

PERM-A-TEM INC *p1145*

45 PLACE CHARLES-LE MOYNE BUREAU 100, LONGUEUIL, QC, J4K 5G5
SIC 7361

PERSONNEL DEPARTMENT LTD, THE *p90*
10665 JASPER AVE NW SUITE 850, EDMONTON, AB, T5J 3S9
(780) 421-1811 *SIC 7361*

PERSONNEL DEPARTMENT LTD, THE *p327*
980 HOWE ST UNIT 201, VANCOUVER, BC, V6Z 0C8
(604) 685-3530 *SIC 7361*

PERSONNEL OUTAOUAIS INC *p1106*
92 BOUL SAINT-RAYMOND BUREAU 400, GATINEAU, QC, J8Y 1S7
(819) 778-7020 *SIC 7361*

PERSONNEL SEARCH LTD *p407*
883 MAIN ST, MONCTON, NB, E1C 1G5
(506) 857-2156 *SIC 7361*

PINPOINT CAREERS INC *p510*
181 QUEEN ST E, BRAMPTON, ON, L6W 2B3
(905) 454-1144 *SIC 7361*

PLACEMENT POTENTIEL INC *p1252*
111 AV DONEGANI, POINTE-CLAIRE, QC, H9R 2W3
(514) 694-0315 *SIC 7361*

PRO COUNT STAFFING INC *p970*
77 KING ST W SUITE 4110, TORONTO, ON, M5K 2A1
(416) 340-1500 *SIC 7361*

PROTECH BUSINESS SOLUTIONS INC *p1241*
1200 BOUL CHOMEDEY BUREAU 720, MONTREAL-OUEST, QC, H7V 3Z3
(450) 934-9800 *SIC 7361*

PUGLISEVICH CREWS & SERVICES LIMITED *p429*
611 TORBAY RD UNIT 1, ST. JOHN'S, NL, A1A 5J1
(709) 722-2744 *SIC 7361*

RANDSTAD INTERIM INC *p534*
1315 BISHOP ST N, CAMBRIDGE, ON, N1R 6Z2
(519) 740-6944 *SIC 7361*

RANDSTAD INTERIM INC *p947*
777 BAY ST SUITE 2000, TORONTO, ON, M5G 2C8
(800) 540-3594 *SIC 7361*

RED BRANCH EXECUTIVE SEARCH & RECRUITMENT *p934*
232-366 ADELAIDE ST E, TORONTO, ON, M5A 3X9
(416) 862-2525 *SIC 7361*

RELIANCE OFFSHORE CANADA INC *p454*
1525 BIRMINGHAM ST, HALIFAX, NS, B3J 2J6
(902) 429-1255 *SIC 7361*

RESOLVE RECRUIT INC *p732*
30 EGLINTON AVE W SUITE 812, MISSISSAUGA, ON, L5R 3E7
(905) 568-8828 *SIC 7361*

RESSOURCES GLOBALES AERO INC *p1067*
333 CH DU TREMBLAY BUREAU J, BOUCHERVILLE, QC, J4B 7M1
(514) 667-9399 *SIC 7361*

SANTEREGIE INC *p1145*
3645 CH DE CHAMBLY, LONGUEUIL, QC, J4L 1N9
SIC 7361

SERVICES DE PERSONNEL S.M. INC. *p1179*
433, RUE CHABANEL OUEST 12E ETAGE, MONTREAL, QC, H2N 2J9
(514) 982-6001 *SIC 7361*

SERVICES DE PLACEMENT DE PERSONNEL DURAND & PRATT INC, LES *p1199*
666 RUE SHERBROOKE O BUREAU 800, MONTREAL, QC, H3A 1E7
(514) 987-1815 *SIC 7361*

SERVICES DE SECRETARIAT INTEGRALE ENR, LES *p1273*
2590 BOUL LAURIER BUREAU 1020, QUEBEC, QC, G1V 4M6

(418) 624-4989 *SIC 7361*

SERVICES DE SOINS A DOMICILE ROYAL TREATMENT INC *p1218*
5757 AV DECELLES, MONTREAL, QC, H3S 2C3
(514) 342-8293 *SIC 7361*

SOINS DIRECT INC *p1214*
1414 RUE DRUMMOND BUREAU 620, MONTREAL, QC, H3G 1W1
(514) 739-1919 *SIC 7361*

STAR LABOUR SUPPLY LTD *p291*
426E 59TH AVE E, VANCOUVER, BC, V5X 1Y1
(604) 325-1027 *SIC 7361*

STERLING IM INC *p801*
610 CHARTWELL RD SUITE 101, OAKVILLE, ON, L6J 4A5
(416) 979-6701 *SIC 7361*

SUTHERLAND GLOBAL SERVICES CANADA ULC *p1024*
500 OUELLETTE AVE, WINDSOR, ON, N9A 1B3
(800) 591-9395 *SIC 7361*

SYNERGIE HUNT INTERNATIONAL INC *p711*
50 BURNHAMTHORPE RD W SUITE 204, MISSISSAUGA, ON, L5B 3C2
(905) 273-3221 *SIC 7361*

TALENT EMPLOYMENT INC *p794*
5601 STEELES AVE W UNIT 5, NORTH YORK, ON, M9L 1S7
(416) 748-3982 *SIC 7361*

TEAMRECRUITER.COM INC *p675*
15 ALLSTATE PKY SUITE 600, MARKHAM, ON, L3R 5B4
(905) 889-8326 *SIC 7361*

TEK STAFF IT SOLUTIONS INC *p857*
30 VIA RENZO DR SUITE 200, RICHMOND HILL, ON, L4S 0B8
(416) 438-1099 *SIC 7361*

TEKSYSTEMS CANADA CORP *p711*
350 BURNHAMTHORPE RD W, MISSISSAUGA, ON, L5B 3J1
(905) 283-1300 *SIC 7361*

TRANS-OCEANIC HUMAN RESOURCES INC *p19*
5515 40 ST SE, CALGARY, AB, T2C 2A8
SIC 7361

TRANSPORT SOLUTIONS *p407*
883 MAIN ST, MONCTON, NB, E1C 1G5
(506) 857-1095 *SIC 7361*

TREBOR PERSONNEL INC *p704*
1090 DUNDAS ST E SUITE 203, MISSISSAUGA, ON, L4Y 2B8
(905) 566-0922 *SIC 7361*

VIA PERSONNEL SERVICES LTD *p1009*
105 BAUER PL, WATERLOO, ON, N2L 6B5
SIC 7361

VOLT CANADA INC *p707*
3 ROBERT SPECK PKY SUITE 260, MISSISSAUGA, ON, L4Z 2G5
(905) 306-1920 *SIC 7361*

WCG INTERNATIONAL CONSULTANTS LTD *p335*
915 FORT ST, VICTORIA, BC, V8V 3K3
(250) 389-0699 *SIC 7361*

WORKOPOLIS INC *p943*
1 YONGE ST SUITE 402, TORONTO, ON, M5E 1E6
(416) 957-8300 *SIC 7361*

SIC 7363 Help supply services

1453633 ONTARIO INC *p686*
6205 AIRPORT RD SUITE 500, MISSISSAUGA, ON, L4V 1E1
(416) 622-4766 *SIC 7363*

A-1 PERSONNEL RESOURCES INC *p736*
6685 TOMKEN RD SUITE 211, MISSISSAUGA, ON, L5T 2C5
(905) 564-1040 *SIC 7363*

BOMBARDIER TRANSPORTATION CANADA INC *p1295*

1101 RUE PARENT, SAINT-BRUNO, QC,
J3V 6E6
(450) 441-3193   *SIC 7363*

**CENTRE HOSPITALIER DU CENTRE LA
MAURICIE**   *p1368*
1265 RUE TRUDEL BUREAU 6, SHAWINI-
GAN, QC, G9N 8T3
(819) 539-8371   *SIC 7363*

CHOICE OFFICE PERSONNEL LTD   *p88*
10025 102A AVE NW SUITE 1102, EDMON-
TON, AB, T5J 2Z2
(780) 424-6816   *SIC 7363*

COMCARE (CANADA) LIMITED   *p406*
30 GORDON ST SUITE 105, MONCTON,
NB, E1C 1L8
(506) 853-9112   *SIC 7363*

COMCARE (CANADA) LIMITED   *p881*
52 ABBOTT ST N UNIT 3, SMITHS FALLS,
ON, K7A 1W3
SIC 7363

CRT - EBC, S.E.N.C.   *p1064*
95 RUE J.-A.-BOMBARDIER BUREAU 4,
BOUCHERVILLE, QC, J4B 8P1
SIC 7363

CRT - EBC, S.E.N.C.   *p1136*
870 RUE ARCHIMEDE, LEVIS, QC, G6V
7M5
(418) 833-8073   *SIC 7363*

DENAULT, BERGERON & ASSOCIES INC
p1203
1100 BOUL RENE-LEVESQUE O BUREAU
1520, MONTREAL, QC, H3B 4N4
SIC 7363

DODD DRIVER PERSONNEL INC   *p570*
2977E LAKE SHORE BLVD W SUITE L,
ETOBICOKE, ON, M8V 1J8
SIC 7363

ENTERRA HOLDINGS LTD   *p722*
6925 CENTURY AVE SUITE 100, MISSIS-
SAUGA, ON, L5N 7K2
(905) 567-4444   *SIC 7363*

EXTENDICARE (CANADA) INC   *p514*
325 WEST ST UNIT 201, BRANTFORD,
ON, N3R 3V6
(519) 756-4606   *SIC 7363*

FLEETWAY INC   *p416*
45 GIFFORD RD, SAINT JOHN, NB, E2M
5K7
(506) 635-7733   *SIC 7363*

**FOURNIER MAINTENANCE INDUS-
TRIELLE INC**   *p1383*
3787 BOUL FRONTENAC O, THETFORD
MINES, QC, G6H 2B5
(418) 423-4241   *SIC 7363*

GLOBAL DRIVER SERVICES INC   *p739*
1415 BONHILL RD SUITE 16, MISSIS-
SAUGA, ON, L5T 1R2
(905) 564-2309   *SIC 7363*

**HAMILTON COMMUNITY CARE ACCESS
CENTRE**   *p616*
310 LIMERIDGE RD W, HAMILTON, ON,
L9C 2V2
(905) 523-8600   *SIC 7363*

IMS SANTE CANADA INC   *p1117*
16720 RTE TRANSCANADIENNE, KIRK-
LAND, QC, H9H 5M3
(514) 428-6000   *SIC 7363*

KELLY SERVICES (CANADA), LTD   *p710*
77 CITY CENTRE DR, MISSISSAUGA, ON,
L5B 1M5
(416) 368-1058   *SIC 7363*

LIGHTHOUSE SUPPORTED LIVING   *p1428*
304 2ND AVE S, SASKATOON, SK, S7K 1L1
(306) 653-0538   *SIC 7363*

MANPOWER SERVICES (ALBERTA) LTD
p89
10201 JASPER AVE NW SUITE 102, ED-
MONTON, AB, T5J 3N7
(780) 420-0110   *SIC 7363*

MANPOWER SERVICES CANADA LIMITED
p772
4950 YONGE ST SUITE 700, NORTH
YORK, ON, M2N 6K1
(416) 225-4455   *SIC 7363*

MAVIRO CATALYST CANADA INC   *p110*
7805 34 ST NW, EDMONTON, AB, T6B 2V5
(780) 430-9696   *SIC 7363*

**MULTI-CAISSES ET MULTI-RESOURCES
INC**   *p1163*
5125 RUE DU TRIANON BUREAU 560,
MONTREAL, QC, H1M 2S5
(514) 848-1845   *SIC 7363*

NEWFOUNDLAND PERSONNEL INC   *p432*
3 QUEEN ST, ST. JOHN'S, NL, A1C 4K2
(709) 579-3400   *SIC 7363*

NORDA STELO INC   *p1206*
630 BOUL RENE-LEVESQUE O BUREAU
1500, MONTREAL, QC, H3B 1S6
(800) 463-2839   *SIC 7363*

ONEC CONSTRUCTION INC   *p110*
3811 78 AVE NW, EDMONTON, AB, T6B
3N8
(780) 440-0400   *SIC 7363*

ONTARIO TELEMEDICINE NETWORK   *p947*
438 UNIVERSITY AVE SUITE 200,
TORONTO, ON, M5G 2K8
(416) 446-4110   *SIC 7363*

P & A MANAGEMENT LTD   *p909*
1205 AMBER DR UNIT 106, THUNDER
BAY, ON, P7B 6M4
(807) 346-8367   *SIC 7363*

PEOPLETOGO INC   *p673*
201 WHITEHALL DR UNIT 4, MARKHAM,
ON, L3R 9Y3
(905) 940-9292   *SIC 7363*

PLANVIEW UTILITY SERVICES LIMITED
p674
7270 WOODBINE AVE SUITE 201,
MARKHAM, ON, L3R 4B9
(289) 800-7110   *SIC 7363*

SERVICE DE MANUTENTION D.B. INC
p1223
3971 RUE NOTRE-DAME O, MONTREAL,
QC, H4C 1R2
(514) 934-5681   *SIC 7363*

**SERVICES DE SANTE LES RAYONS DE
SOLEIL INC**   *p1171*
2055 RUE SAUVE E BUREAU 100, MON-
TREAL, QC, H2B 1A8
(514) 383-7555   *SIC 7363*

SKYSERVICE BUSINESS AVIATION INC *p25*
575 PALMER RD NE, CALGARY, AB, T2E
7G4
(403) 592-3700   *SIC 7363*

**SUDBURY MANAGEMENT SERVICES LIM-
ITED**   *p899*
1901 LASALLE BLVD, SUDBURY, ON, P3A
2A3
SIC 7363

TASK ENGINEERING LTD   *p338*
5141 CORDOVA BAY RD, VICTORIA, BC,
V8Y 2K1
(250) 590-2440   *SIC 7363*

TURN KEY STAFFING SOLUTIONS INC
p757
200 DAVIS DR SUITE 7, NEWMARKET, ON,
L3Y 2N4
(905) 953-9133   *SIC 7363*

WAPOSE MEDICAL SERVICES INC   *p129*
431 MACKENZIE BLVD SUITE 12, FORT
MCMURRAY, AB, T9H 4C5
(780) 714-6654   *SIC 7363*

WESTERN GLOVE WORKS LTD   *p373*
555 LOGAN AVE, WINNIPEG, MB, R3A 0S4
(204) 788-4249   *SIC 7363*

WSP CANADA INC   *p677*
600 COCHRANE DR FLOOR 5,
MARKHAM, ON, L3R 5K3
(905) 475-8727   *SIC 7363*

---

*SIC 7371 Custom computer programming
services*

10684651 CANADA INC   *p1278*
825 BOUL LEBOURGNEUF BUREAU 130,
QUEBEC, QC, G2J 0B9
(888) 523-1883   *SIC 7371*

1343929 ONTARIO LIMITED   *p527*

880 LAURENTIAN DR SUITE 1, BURLING-
TON, ON, L7N 3V6
(905) 632-0864   *SIC 7371*

2101440 ONTARIO INC   *p850*
30 EAST BEAVER CREEK RD SUITE 204,
RICHMOND HILL, ON, L4B 1J2
(416) 469-3131   *SIC 7371*

24/7 CUSTOMER CANADA, INC   *p936*
20 TORONTO ST SUITE 530, TORONTO,
ON, M5C 2B8
(416) 214-9337   *SIC 7371*

3517667 CANADA INC   *p623*
411 LEGGET DR SUITE 600, KANATA, ON,
K2K 3C9
(613) 599-9991   *SIC 7371*

3965546 CANADA LIMITEE   *p1224*
5995 BOUL GOUIN O BUREAU 308, MON-
TREAL, QC, H4J 2P8
(514) 337-7337   *SIC 7371*

3ES INNOVATION INC   *p42*
250 2 ST SW SUITE 800, CALGARY, AB,
T2P 0C1
(403) 270-3270   *SIC 7371*

9013-6573 QUEBEC INC   *p1169*
3565 RUE JARRY E BUREAU 650, MON-
TREAL, QC, H1Z 4K6
(514) 593-5012   *SIC 7371*

9022-5814 QUEBEC INC   *p1233*
1867 RUE BERLIER, MONTREAL, QC, H7L
3S4
(450) 663-6327   *SIC 7371*

9219-1568 QUEBEC INC   *p1227*
7777 BOUL DECARIE BUREAU 300, MON-
TREAL, QC, H4P 2H2
(514) 359-3555   *SIC 7371*

A THINKING APE ENTERTAINMENT LTD
p311
1132 ALBERNI ST UNIT 200, VANCOU-
VER, BC, V6E 1A5
(604) 682-7773   *SIC 7371*

ABELSOFT INC   *p527*
3310 SOUTH SERVICE RD SUITE 101,
BURLINGTON, ON, L7N 3M6
(905) 333-3200   *SIC 7371*

ABSOLUTE SOFTWARE CORPORATION
p327
1055 DUNSMUIR ST SUITE 1400, VAN-
COUVER, BC, V7X 1K8
(604) 730-9851   *SIC 7371*

ACCEO SOLUTIONS INC   *p1209*
75 RUE QUEEN BUREAU 5200, MON-
TREAL, QC, H3C 2N6
(514) 868-0333   *SIC 7371*

ACCULOGIC INC   *p666*
175 RIVIERA DR SUITE 1, MARKHAM, ON,
L3R 5J6
(905) 475-5907   *SIC 7371*

**ACHIEVO NETSTAR SOLUTIONS COM-
PANY**   *p775*
220 DUNCAN MILL RD SUITE 505, NORTH
YORK, ON, M3B 3J5
(416) 383-1818   *SIC 7371*

ACL SERVICES LTD   *p325*
980-HOWE ST SUITE 1500, VANCOUVER,
BC, V6Z 0C8
(604) 669-4225   *SIC 7371*

ACQUISIO WEB.COM, ULC   *p1071*
6300 AV AUTEUIL BUREAU 300,
BROSSARD, QC, J4Z 3P2
(450) 465-2631   *SIC 7371*

ACTIVE NETWORK   *p719*
2480 MEADOWVALE BLVD SUITE 1, MIS-
SISSAUGA, ON, L5N 8M6
(905) 286-6600   *SIC 7371*

ACTIVE NETWORK LTD, THE   *p286*
2925 VIRTUAL WAY SUITE 310, VANCOU-
VER, BC, V5M 4X5
(800) 661-1196   *SIC 7371*

ACUITYADS HOLDINGS INC   *p959*
181 BAY ST SUITE 320, TORONTO, ON,
M5J 2T3
(416) 218-9888   *SIC 7371*

ADASTRA CORPORATION   *p903*
8500 LESLIE ST SUITE 600, THORNHILL,

ON, L3T 7M8
(905) 881-7946   *SIC 7371*

ADVANCED MOBILE PAYMENT INC   *p850*
15 WERTHEIM CRT SUITE 401-403, RICH-
MOND HILL, ON, L4B 3H7
(905) 597-2333   *SIC 7371*

**ADVANCED UTILITY SYSTEMS CORPORA-
TION**   *p766*
2235 SHEPPARD AVE E SUITE 1400,
NORTH YORK, ON, M2J 5B5
(416) 496-0149   *SIC 7371*

AGFA HEALTHCARE INC   *p1008*
375 HAGEY BLVD, WATERLOO, ON, N2L
6R5
(519) 746-2900   *SIC 7371*

AJB SOFTWARE DESIGN INC   *p691*
5255 SOLAR DR, MISSISSAUGA, ON, L4W
5B8
(905) 282-1877   *SIC 7371*

**ALITHYA DIGITAL TECHNOLOGY CORPO-
RATION**   *p922*
2300 YONGE ST SUITE 1800, TORONTO,
ON, M4P 1E4
(416) 932-4700   *SIC 7371*

**AMDOCS CANADIAN MANAGED SER-
VICES INC**   *p1332*
2351 BOUL ALFRED-NOBEL BUREAU 200,
SAINT-LAURENT, QC, H4S 0B2
(514) 338-3100   *SIC 7371*

APPDIRECTE CANADA INC   *p1193*
2050 RUE DE BLEURY, MONTREAL, QC,
H3A 2J5
(514) 876-4449   *SIC 7371*

APTOS CANADA INC   *p1332*
9300 RTE TRANSCANADIENNE BUREAU
300, SAINT-LAURENT, QC, H4S 1K5
(514) 426-0822   *SIC 7371*

ARTECH DIGITAL ENTERTAINMENT INC
p828
6 HAMILTON AVE N, OTTAWA, ON, K1Y
4R1
(613) 728-4880   *SIC 7371*

ASIGRA INC   *p916*
79 BRISBANE ROAD, TORONTO, ON, M3J
2K3
(416) 736-8111   *SIC 7371*

ASSENT COMPLIANCE INC   *p820*
525 COVENTRY RD, OTTAWA, ON, K1K
2C5
(613) 369-8390   *SIC 7371*

AUTODATA SOLUTIONS COMPANY   *p653*
100 DUNDAS ST SUITE 500, LONDON,
ON, N6A 5B6
(519) 451-2323   *SIC 7371*

AUTODESK CANADA CIE   *p932*
210 KING ST E, TORONTO, ON, M5A 1J7
(416) 362-9181   *SIC 7371*

AUTODESK CANADA CIE   *p1210*
10 RUE DUKE, MONTREAL, QC, H3C 2L7
(514) 393-1616   *SIC 7371*

AVANADE CANADA INC   *p692*
5450 EXPLORER DR SUITE 400, MISSIS-
SAUGA, ON, L4W 5N1
(416) 641-5111   *SIC 7371*

AVID TECHNOLOGY CANADA CORP *p1185*
3510 BOUL SAINT-LAURENT BUREAU
300, MONTREAL, QC, H2X 2V2
(514) 845-1636   *SIC 7371*

AVOCETTE TECHNOLOGIES INC   *p236*
422 SIXTH ST 2ND FLR, NEW WESTMIN-
STER, BC, V3L 3B2
(604) 395-6000   *SIC 7371*

AXIOM REAL-TIME METRICS INC   *p997*
1 CITY VIEW DR, TORONTO, ON, M9W
5A5
(905) 845-9779   *SIC 7371*

AXIUM SOLUTIONS ULC   *p199*
1963 LOUGHEED HWY, COQUITLAM, BC,
V3K 3T8
(604) 468-6820   *SIC 7371*

BANCTEC (CANADA), INC   *p666*
100 ALLSTATE PKY SUITE 400,
MARKHAM, ON, L3R 6H3
(905) 475-6060   *SIC 7371*

BEENOX INC p1257
305 BOUL CHAREST E BUREAU 700, QUEBEC, QC, G1K 3H3
(418) 522-2468   SIC 7371

BEHAVIOUR INTERACTIF INC p1182
6666 RUE SAINT-URBAIN, MONTREAL, QC, H2S 3H1
(514) 843-4484   SIC 7371

BENEVITY, INC p21
611 MEREDITH RD NE UNIT 700, CALGARY, AB, T2E 2W5
(403) 237-7875   SIC 7371

BINARY STREAM SOFTWARE INC p182
4238 LOZELLS AVE UNIT 201, BURNABY, BC, V5A 0C4
(604) 522-6300   SIC 7371

BIOWARE CORP p118
4445 CALGARY TRAIL NW SUITE 200, EDMONTON, AB, T6H 5R7
(780) 430-0164   SIC 7371

BLACKBERRY LIMITED p1007
2200 UNIVERSITY AVE E, WATERLOO, ON, N2K 0A7
(519) 888-7465   SIC 7371

BOAT ROCKER RIGHTS INC p932
595 ADELAIDE ST E, TORONTO, ON, M5A 1N8
(416) 591-0065   SIC 7371

BORDERWARE TECHNOLOGIES INC p709
50 BURNHAMTHORPE RD W SUITE 502, MISSISSAUGA, ON, L5B 3C2
(905) 804-1855   SIC 7371

BROADCOM CANADA LTD p253
13711 INTERNATIONAL PL UNIT 200, RICHMOND, BC, V6V 2Z8
(604) 233-8500   SIC 7371

BROADRIDGE SOFTWARE LIMITED p949
4 KING ST W SUITE 500, TORONTO, ON, M5H 1B6
(416) 350-0999   SIC 7371

CAMILION SOLUTIONS, INC p904
123 COMMERCE VALLEY DR E SUITE 800, THORNHILL, ON, L3T 7W8
SIC 7371

CAMPANA SYSTEMS INC p1010
103 RANDALL DR UNIT 2, WATERLOO, ON, N2V 1C5
(226) 336-8085   SIC 7371

CGG SERVICES (CANADA) INC p75
3675 63 AVE NE, CALGARY, AB, T3J 5K1
(403) 291-1434   SIC 7371

CGI INC p1213
1350 BOUL RENE-LEVESQUE O SUITE 25E, MONTREAL, QC, H3G 1T4
(514) 841-3200   SIC 7371

CGTV GAMES LTD p311
1199 PENDER ST W SUITE 800, VANCOUVER, BC, V6E 2R1
SIC 7371

CHANGE HEALTHCARE CANADA COMPANY p259
10711 CAMBIE RD SUITE 130, RICHMOND, BC, V6X 3G5
(604) 279-5422   SIC 7371

CHANGEPOINT CANADA ULC p851
30 LEEK CRES SUITE 300, RICHMOND HILL, ON, L4B 4N4
(905) 886-7000   SIC 7371

CHELL GROUP CORPORATION p583
14 METEOR DR, ETOBICOKE, ON, M9W 1A4
(416) 675-3536   SIC 7371

CHROME DATA SOLUTIONS, LP p650
345 SASKATOON ST, LONDON, ON, N5W 4R4
(519) 451-2323   SIC 7371

CIRBA INC p680
179 ENTERPRISE BLVD UNIT 400, MARKHAM, ON, L6G 0E7
(905) 731-0090   SIC 7371

CLEVEST SOLUTIONS INC p254
13700 INTERNATIONAL PL SUITE 200, RICHMOND, BC, V6V 2X8
(604) 214-9700   SIC 7371

CLUB VIDEO SUTTON INC p1070
9160 BOUL LEDUC BUREAU 410, BROSSARD, QC, J4Y 0E3
(514) 251-8118   SIC 7371

COGSDALE CORPORATION p1040
3 LOWER MALPEQUE RD, CHARLOTTETOWN, PE, C1E 1R4
(902) 892-3101   SIC 7371

COMPAGNIE BROADSIGN CANADA p1203
1100 BOUL ROBERT-BOURASSA 12E ETAGE, MONTREAL, QC, H3B 3A5
(514) 399-1184   SIC 7371

COMPLETE INNOVATIONS HOLDINGS INC p961
88 QUEENS QUAY W SUITE 200, TORONTO, ON, M5J 0B8
(905) 944-0863   SIC 7371

COMPUSULT LIMITED p426
40 BANNISTER ST, MOUNT PEARL, NL, A1N 1W1
(709) 745-7914   SIC 7371

COMPUTER METHODS INTERNATIONAL CORP p782
4850 KEELE ST, NORTH YORK, ON, M3J 3K1
(416) 736-0123   SIC 7371

COMPUTER MODELLING GROUP LTD p40
3710 33 ST NW, CALGARY, AB, T2L 2M1
(403) 531-1300   SIC 7371

COMPUTER TALK TECHNOLOGY INC p904
150 COMMERCE VALLEY DR W UNIT 800, THORNHILL, ON, L3T 7Z3
(905) 882-5000   SIC 7371

COMPUTRONIX CORPORATION p97
10216 124 ST NW SUITE 200, EDMONTON, AB, T5N 4A3
(780) 454-3700   SIC 7371

CONCEPTWAVE SOFTWARE INC p687
5935 AIRPORT RD SUITE 1105, MISSISSAUGA, ON, L4V 1W5
SIC 7371

CONSTELLATION SOFTWARE INC p937
20 ADELAIDE ST E SUITE 1200, TORONTO, ON, M5C 2T6
(416) 861-2279   SIC 7371

CONVERGE TECHNOLOGY SOLUTIONS CORP. p961
161 BAY ST SUITE 2325, TORONTO, ON, M5J 2S1
(416) 360-3995   SIC 7371

COPERNIC INC p1258
400 BOUL JEAN-LESAGE BUREAU 345, QUEBEC, QC, G1K 8W1
(418) 524-4661   SIC 7371

COPPERLEAF TECHNOLOGIES INC p286
2920 VIRTUAL WAY SUITE 140, VANCOUVER, BC, V5M 0C4
(604) 639-9700   SIC 7371

COREL CORPORATION p828
1600 CARLING AVE SUITE 100, OTTAWA, ON, K1Z 8R7
(613) 728-8200   SIC 7371

CORITY SOFTWARE INC p928
250 BLOOR ST E 1ST FL, TORONTO, ON, M4W 1E6
(416) 863-6800   SIC 7371

CORPORATION INTERACTIVE EIDOS p1194
400 BOUL DE MAISONNEUVE O 6E ETAGE, MONTREAL, QC, H3A 1L4
(514) 670-6300   SIC 7371

COVEO SOLUTIONS INC p1274
3175 CH DES QUATRE-BOURGEOIS BUREAU 200, QUEBEC, QC, G1W 2K7
(418) 263-1111   SIC 7371

CPAS SYSTEMS INC p779
250 FERRAND DR 7TH FLOOR, NORTH YORK, ON, M3C 3G8
(416) 422-0563   SIC 7371

CRITICAL CONTROL ENERGY SERVICES CORP p29
140 10 AVE SE SUITE 800, CALGARY, AB, T2G 0R1
(403) 705-7500   SIC 7371

CRITICAL CONTROL ENERGY SERVICES CORP p88
10130 103 ST NW SUITE 1500, EDMONTON, AB, T5J 3N9
(780) 423-3100   SIC 7371

CROESUS FINANSOFT INC p1241
600 BOUL ARMAND-FRAPPIER BUREAU 200, MONTREAL-OUEST, QC, H7V 4B4
(450) 662-6101   SIC 7371

CROWDCARE CORPORATION p851
120 EAST BEAVER CREEK RD SUITE 202, RICHMOND HILL, ON, L4B 4V1
(647) 559-9190   SIC 7371

CRYSTAL INFOSOFT p933
186 FREDERICK ST, TORONTO, ON, M5A 4L4
SIC 7371

CYME INTERNATIONAL T & D INC p1295
1485 RUE ROBERVAL BUREAU 104, SAINT-BRUNO, QC, J3V 3P8
(450) 461-3655   SIC 7371

CYPHER SYSTEMS GROUP INC p1019
3600 RHODES DR, WINDSOR, ON, N8W 5A4
(519) 945-4943   SIC 7371

D.L.G.L. IMMOBILIERE LTEE p1058
850 BOUL MICHELE-BOHEC, BLAINVILLE, QC, J7C 5E2
(450) 979-4646   SIC 7371

D.L.G.L. LTEE p1058
850 BOUL MICHELE-BOHEC, BLAINVILLE, QC, J7C 5E2
(450) 979-4646   SIC 7371

DAPASOFT INC p914
111 GORDON BAKER SUITE 600, TORONTO, ON, M2H 3R1
(416) 847-4080   SIC 7371

DASSAULT SYSTEMES CANADA SOFTWARE INC p312
1066 HASTINGS ST W SUITE 1100, VANCOUVER, BC, V6E 3X1
(604) 684-6550   SIC 7371

DELTAWARE SYSTEMS INC p1039
176 GREAT GEORGE ST SUITE 300, CHARLOTTETOWN, PE, C1A 4K9
(902) 368-8122   SIC 7371

DENTAL WINGS INC p1166
2251 AV LETOURNEUX, MONTREAL, QC, H1V 2N9
(514) 807-8485   SIC 7371

DESCARTES SYSTEMS GROUP INC, THE p1010
120 RANDALL DR, WATERLOO, ON, N2V 1C6
(519) 746-8110   SIC 7371

DESTINY SOLUTIONS INC p924
40 HOLLY ST SUITE 800, TORONTO, ON, M4S 3C3
(416) 480-0500   SIC 7371

DEVELUS SYSTEMS INC p335
1112 FORT ST SUITE 600, VICTORIA, BC, V8V 3K8
(250) 388-0880   SIC 7371

DH CORPORATION p962
120 BREMNER BLVD 30 FLOOR, TORONTO, ON, M5J 0A8
(416) 696-7700   SIC 7371

DIALOGIC CORPORATION p1324
9800 CAVENDISH 5E ETAGE, SAINT-LAURENT, QC, H4M 2V9
(514) 745-5500   SIC 7371

DIVERTISSEMENTS GAMELOFT INC p1181
7250 RUE MARCONI, MONTREAL, QC, H2R 2Z5
(514) 798-1700   SIC 7371

DIVESTCO INC p22
1223 31 AVE NE, CALGARY, AB, T2E 7W1
(403) 237-9170   SIC 7371

DMT DEVELOPMENT SYSTEMS GROUP INC p390
1 RESEARCH RD UNIT 500, WINNIPEG, MB, R3T 6E3
(204) 927-1800   SIC 7371

DOXIM SOLUTIONS INC p669

EFFIGIS GEO SOLUTIONS INC p1169
4101 RUE MOLSON BUREAU 400, MONTREAL, QC, H1Y 3L1
(514) 495-6500   SIC 7371

ELASTIC PATH SOFTWARE INC p312
745 THURLOW ST UNIT 1400, VANCOUVER, BC, V6E 0C5
(604) 408-8078   SIC 7371

ELECTRONIC ARTS (CANADA) INC p188
4330 SANDERSON WAY, BURNABY, BC, V5G 4X1
(604) 456-3600   SIC 7371

ELECTRONIC ARTS (CANADA) INC p1203
3 PLACE VILLE-MARIE BUREAU 12350, MONTREAL, QC, H3B 0E7
(514) 448-8800   SIC 7371

ELEMENT AI INC p1182
6650 RUE SAINT-URBAIN BUREAU 500, MONTREAL, QC, H2S 3G9
(514) 379-3568   SIC 7371

EMERGIS INC p1158
505 BOUL SIR-WILFRID-LAURIER, MONT-SAINT-HILAIRE, QC, J3H 4X7
(800) 363-9398   SIC 7371

ENGHOUSE SYSTEMS LIMITED p669
80 TIVERTON CRT SUITE 800, MARKHAM, ON, L3R 0G4
(905) 946-3200   SIC 7371

ENTERO CORPORATION p49
1040 7 AVE SW SUITE 500, CALGARY, AB, T2P 3G9
(403) 261-1820   SIC 7371

ENTRUST DATACARD LIMITED p624
1000 INNOVATION DR, KANATA, ON, K2K 3E7
(613) 270-3400   SIC 7371

ENZYME TESTING LABS INC p1319
2031 BOUL DU CURE-LABELLE, SAINT-JEROME, QC, J7Y 1S5
(450) 995-2000   SIC 7371

EQUBE GAMING LIMITED p100
10493 184 ST NW SUITE 100, EDMONTON, AB, T5S 2L1
(780) 414-8890   SIC 7371

ESPIAL GROUP INC p834
200 ELGIN ST SUITE 1000, OTTAWA, ON, K2P 1L5
(613) 230-4770   SIC 7371

EVAULT CANADA INC p797
2315 BRISTOL CIR UNIT 200, OAKVILLE, ON, L6H 6P8
(905) 287-2600   SIC 7371

FARONICS CORPORATION p330
609 GRANVILLE ST SUITE 1400, VANCOUVER, BC, V7Y 1G5
(604) 637-3333   SIC 7371

FINGER FOOD STUDIOS INC p245
2755 LOUGHEED HWY SUITE 420, PORT COQUITLAM, BC, V3B 5Y9
(604) 475-0350   SIC 7371

FLEXTRONICS (CANADA) INC p527
3430 SOUTH SERVICE RD SUITE 101, BURLINGTON, ON, L7N 3T9
(905) 592-1443   SIC 7371

FLIPP CORPORATION p572
3250 BLOOR ST W SUITE 1200, ETOBICOKE, ON, M8X 2X9
(416) 626-7092   SIC 7371

FLOGEN TECHNOLOGIES INC p1155
1255 BOUL LAIRD BUREAU 388, MONT-ROYAL, QC, H3P 2T1
(514) 344-8786   SIC 7371

FUN TALKING SOFTWARE LTD p237
713 COLUMBIA ST SUITE 202, NEW WESTMINSTER, BC, V3M 1B2
(778) 999-1658   SIC 7371

G.D.G. INFORMATIQUE ET GESTION INC p1259
330 RUE DE SAINT-VALLIER E BUREAU 23, QUEBEC, QC, G1K 9C5
(418) 647-0006   SIC 7371

GARY JONAS COMPUTING LTD *p1000*
8133 WARDEN AVE SUITE 400, UNIONVILLE, ON, L6G 1B3
(905) 470-4600 *SIC 7371*

GENERAL DYNAMICS LAND SYSTEMS - CANADA CORPORATION *p23*
1020 68 AVE NE, CALGARY, AB, T2E 8P2
(403) 295-6700 *SIC 7371*

GENETEC INC *p1228*
2280 ALFRED-NOBEL BLVD, MONTREAL, QC, H4S 2A4
(514) 332-4000 *SIC 7371*

GENOLOGICS LIFE SCIENCES SOFTWARE INC *p338*
4464 MARKHAM ST SUITE 2302, VICTORIA, BC, V8Z 7X8
(250) 483-7011 *SIC 7371*

GEOLOGIC SYSTEMS LTD *p50*
401 9 AVE SW SUITE 1500, CALGARY, AB, T2P 3C5
(403) 262-1992 *SIC 7371*

GESCA NUMERIQUE INC *p1188*
750 BOUL SAINT-LAURENT, MONTREAL, QC, H2Y 2Z4
(514) 285-7000 *SIC 7371*

GILLILAND GOLD YOUNG CONSULTING INC *p771*
5001 YONGE ST SUITE 1300, NORTH YORK, ON, M2N 6P6
(416) 250-6777 *SIC 7371*

GIRO INC *p1217*
75 RUE DE PORT-ROYAL E BUREAU 500, MONTREAL, QC, H3L 3T1
(514) 383-0404 *SIC 7371*

GLOBAL IQX INC *p831*
1111 PRINCE OF WALES DR SUITE 500, OTTAWA, ON, K2C 3T2
(613) 723-8997 *SIC 7371*

GLOBAL RELAY COMMUNICATIONS INC *p298*
220 CAMBIE ST FL 2, VANCOUVER, BC, V6B 2M9
(604) 484-6630 *SIC 7371*

GOVIRAL INC *p653*
383 RICHMOND ST UNIT 1010, LONDON, ON, N6A 3C4
(519) 850-1991 *SIC 7371*

GPVTL CANADA INC *p939*
1 TORONTO ST SUITE 1100, TORONTO, ON, M5C 2V6
(416) 907-9470 *SIC 7371*

GROUPE ASKIDA INC *p1188*
410 RUE SAINT-NICOLAS BUREAU 101, MONTREAL, QC, H2Y 2P5
(514) 286-9366 *SIC 7371*

GROUPE DCM INC *p1059*
890 BOUL MICHELE-BOHEC, BLAINVILLE, QC, J7C 5E2
(450) 435-9210 *SIC 7371*

GROUPE DMD CONNEXIONS SANTE NUMERIQUES INC *p1396*
2 PLACE DU COMMERCE BUREAU 206, VERDUN, QC, H3E 1A1
(514) 783-1698 *SIC 7371*

GROUPE FACILITE INFORMATIQUE (GFI) INC *p1205*
5 PLACE VILLE-MARIE BUREAU 1045, MONTREAL, QC, H3B 2G2
(514) 284-5636 *SIC 7371*

GROUPE FACILITE INFORMATIQUE (GFI) INC *p1272*
1100-2875 BOUL LAURIER, QUEBEC, QC, G1V 5B1
(418) 780-3950 *SIC 7371*

HAEMONETICS CANADA LTD *p89*
10025 102A AVE NW SUITE 500, EDMONTON, AB, T5J 2Z2
(780) 425-6560 *SIC 7371*

HEALTHSPACE INFORMATICS LTD *p215*
417 WALLACE ST UNIT 7, HOPE, BC, V0X 1L0
SIC 7371

HERJAVEC GROUP INC, THE *p776*
180 DUNCAN MILL RD SUITE 700, NORTH YORK, ON, M3B 1Z6
(416) 639-2193 *SIC 7371*

HITACHI ID SYSTEMS HOLDING, INC *p30*
1401 1 ST SE SUITE 500, CALGARY, AB, T2G 2J3
(403) 233-0740 *SIC 7371*

HITACHI ID SYSTEMS, INC *p30*
1401 1 ST SE SUITE 500, CALGARY, AB, T2G 2J3
(403) 233-0740 *SIC 7371*

HONEYWELL LIMITED *p89*
10405 JASPER AVE NW SUITE 1800, EDMONTON, AB, T5J 3N4
(780) 448-1010 *SIC 7371*

HOPPER INC *p1182*
5795 AV DE GASPE BUREAU 100, MONTREAL, QC, H2S 2X3
(514) 276-0760 *SIC 7371*

IBM CANADA LIMITED *p51*
639 5 AVE SW SUITE 2100, CALGARY, AB, T2P 0M9
SIC 7371

IBM CANADA LIMITED *p626*
770 PALLADIUM DR, KANATA, ON, K2V 1C8
SIC 7371

IDEABYTES INC *p752*
142 GOLFLINKS DR, NEPEAN, ON, K2J 5N5
(613) 692-9908 *SIC 7371*

IFS AEROSPACE & DEFENSE LTD *p833*
175 TERENCE MATTHEWS CRES, OTTAWA, ON, K2M 1W8
(613) 576-2480 *SIC 7371*

INFINITE OUTSOURCING SOLUTIONS INC *p997*
2100 LAWRENCE AVE W UNIT 202A, TORONTO, ON, M9N 3W3
(647) 247-5490 *SIC 7371*

INFORMATIQUE COTE, COULOMBE INC *p1276*
3770 RUE JEAN-MARCHAND, QUEBEC, QC, G2C 1Y6
(418) 628-2100 *SIC 7371*

INFYNIA.COM INC *p1340*
170 MONTEE DE LIESSE, SAINT-LAURENT, QC, H4T 1N6
(514) 332-1999 *SIC 7371*

INSCRIBER TECHNOLOGY CORPORATION *p1006*
26 PEPPLER ST, WATERLOO, ON, N2J 3C4
(519) 570-9111 *SIC 7371*

INSURANCE SYSTEMS INC *p575*
170 EVANS AVE, ETOBICOKE, ON, M8Z 1J7
(416) 249-2260 *SIC 7371*

INTELEX CORPORATION *p963*
70 UNIVERSITY AVE SUITE 800, TORONTO, ON, M5J 2M4
(416) 599-6009 *SIC 7371*

INTELEX TECHNOLOGIES INC *p963*
70 UNIVERSITY AVE SUITE 800, TORONTO, ON, M5J 2M4
(416) 599-6009 *SIC 7371*

INTRINSYC TECHNOLOGIES CORPORATION *p306*
885 DUNSMUIR ST 3RD FL, VANCOUVER, BC, V6C 1N5
(604) 801-6461 *SIC 7371*

INTUIT CANADA ULC *p696*
5100 SPECTRUM WAY, MISSISSAUGA, ON, L4W 5S2
(888) 843-5449 *SIC 7371*

INVERA INC *p1402*
4333 RUE SAINTE-CATHERINE O BUREAU 201, WESTMOUNT, QC, H3Z 1P9
(514) 935-3535 *SIC 7371*

IQMETRIX SOFTWARE DEVELOPMENT CORP *p306*
250 HOWE ST SUITE 1210, VANCOUVER, BC, V6C 3R8
(866) 476-3874 *SIC 7371*

IRDETO CANADA CORPORATION *p624*
2500 SOLANDT RD SUITE 300, KANATA, ON, K2K 3G5
(613) 271-9446 *SIC 7371*

ISTUARY INNOVATION LABS INC *p326*
1125 HOWE ST 8TH FL, VANCOUVER, BC, V6Z 2K8
SIC 7371

IWN CONSULTING INC *p865*
10 MILNER BUSINESS CRT SUITE 300, SCARBOROUGH, ON, M1B 3C6
(416) 827-2727 *SIC 7371*

JAMES EVANS AND ASSOCIATES LTD *p338*
4464 MARKHAM ST SUITE 1205, VICTORIA, BC, V8Z 7X8
(250) 380-3811 *SIC 7371*

JATOM SYSTEMS INC *p626*
99 MICHAEL COWPLAND DR, KANATA, ON, K2M 1X3
(613) 591-5910 *SIC 7371*

JESTA I.S. INC *p1188*
755 RUE BERRI BUREAU 200, MONTREAL, QC, H2Y 3E5
(514) 925-5100 *SIC 7371*

JOSTLE CORPORATION *p314*
1090 WEST GEORGIA ST SUITE 1200, VANCOUVER, BC, V6E 3V7
(604) 566-9520 *SIC 7371*

KEAL COMPUTER SERVICES INC *p554*
55 ADMINISTRATION RD UNIT 21, CONCORD, ON, L4K 4G9
(905) 738-2112 *SIC 7371*

KIK INTERACTIVE INC. *p1008*
420 WEBER ST N SUITE I, WATERLOO, ON, N2L 4E7
(226) 868-0056 *SIC 7371*

KINAXIS INC *p626*
700 SILVER SEVEN RD SUITE 500, KANATA, ON, K2V 1C3
(613) 592-5780 *SIC 7371*

LATITUDE GEOGRAPHICS GROUP LTD *p336*
1117 WHARF ST UNIT 300, VICTORIA, BC, V8W 1T7
(250) 381-8130 *SIC 7371*

LAYER 7 TECHNOLOGIES INC *p306*
885 GEORGIA ST W SUITE 500, VANCOUVER, BC, V6C 3E8
(604) 681-9377 *SIC 7371*

LOGICIELS DTI INC *p1197*
1800 AV MCGILL COLLEGE UNITE 1800, MONTREAL, QC, H3A 3J6
(514) 499-0910 *SIC 7371*

LOGINRADIUS INC *p306*
815 HASTINGS ST W SUITE 801, VANCOUVER, BC, V6C 1B4
(844) 625-8889 *SIC 7371*

LOGISENSE CORPORATION *p536*
278 PINEBUSH RD SUITE 102, CAMBRIDGE, ON, N1T 1Z6
(519) 249-0508 *SIC 7371*

LOGITEK DATA SCIENCES LTD *p586*
155 REXDALE BLVD SUITE 801, ETOBICOKE, ON, M9W 5Z8
(416) 741-1595 *SIC 7371*

LOKI MANAGEMENT SYSTEMS INC *p255*
13351 COMMERCE PKY SUITE 1258, RICHMOND, BC, V6V 2X7
(604) 249-5050 *SIC 7371*

LPI LEVEL PLATFORMS INC *p624*
309 LEGGET DR SUITE 300, KANATA, ON, K2K 3A3
(613) 232-1000 *SIC 7371*

MACADAMIAN TECHNOLOGIES INC *p1105*
179 PROM DU PORTAGE UNITE 4, GATINEAU, QC, J8X 2K5
(819) 772-0300 *SIC 7371*

MAGMIC INC *p821*
126 YORK ST SUITE 400, OTTAWA, ON, K1N 5T5
(613) 241-3571 *SIC 7371*

MARINER PARTNERS INC *p415*
1 GERMAIN ST 18 FL, SAINT JOHN, NB, E2L 4V1
(506) 642-9000 *SIC 7371*

MASTERCARD TECHNOLOGIES CANADA ULC *p307*
475 HOWE ST SUITE 2000, VANCOUVER, BC, V6C 2B3
(604) 800-3711 *SIC 7371*

MATRIKON INC *p90*
10405 JASPER AVE NW SUITE 1800, EDMONTON, AB, T5J 3N4
(780) 448-1010 *SIC 7371*

MAXAR TECHNOLOGIES LTD *p307*
200 BURRARD ST SUITE 1570, VANCOUVER, BC, V6C 3L6
(604) 974-5275 *SIC 7371*

MERCATUS TECHNOLOGIES INC *p982*
545 KING ST W SUITE 500, TORONTO, ON, M5V 1M1
(416) 603-3406 *SIC 7371*

MERGE HEALTHCARE CANADA CORP *p688*
6303 AIRPORT RD SUITE 500, MISSISSAUGA, ON, L4V 1R8
(905) 672-2100 *SIC 7371*

METASOFT SYSTEMS INC *p299*
353 WATER ST SUITE 300, VANCOUVER, BC, V6B 1B8
(604) 683-6711 *SIC 7371*

MICROFLEX 2001 LLC *p1273*
2505 BOUL LAURIER BUREAU 300, QUEBEC, QC, G1V 2L2
(418) 694-2300 *SIC 7371*

MICROLAND TECHNICAL SERVICES INC *p672*
170 ALDEN RD UNIT 2, MARKHAM, ON, L3R 4C1
(905) 940-1982 *SIC 7371*

MICROSOFT CANADA INC *p54*
500 4 AVE SW SUITE 1900, CALGARY, AB, T2P 2V6
(403) 296-6500 *SIC 7371*

MIOVISION TECHNOLOGIES INCORPORATED *p638*
137 GLASGOW ST SUITE 110, KITCHENER, ON, N2G 4X8
(519) 513-2407 *SIC 7371*

MOBIFY RESEARCH AND DEVELOPMENT INC *p330*
725 GRANVILLE ST SUITE 420, VANCOUVER, BC, V7Y 1C6
(866) 502-5880 *SIC 7371*

N. HARRIS COMPUTER CORPORATION *p749*
1 ANTARES DR SUITE 400, NEPEAN, ON, K2E 8C4
(613) 226-5511 *SIC 7371*

NADINE INTERNATIONAL INC *p697*
2325 SKYMARK AVE, MISSISSAUGA, ON, L4W 5A9
(905) 602-1850 *SIC 7371*

NAKISA INC *p1206*
733 RUE CATHCART, MONTREAL, QC, H3B 1M6
(514) 228-2000 *SIC 7371*

NAVBLUE INC *p1008*
295 HAGEY BLVD SUITE 200, WATERLOO, ON, N2L 6R5
(519) 747-1170 *SIC 7371*

NOBUL CORPORATION *p982*
200 WELLINGTON ST W, TORONTO, ON, M5V 3C7
(416) 543-3710 *SIC 7371*

NORTH INC *p638*
27 GAUKEL ST, KITCHENER, ON, N2G 1Y6
(888) 777-2546 *SIC 7371*

NORTHFORGE INNOVATIONS INC *p1105*
72 RUE LAVAL, GATINEAU, QC, J8X 3H3
(819) 776-6066 *SIC 7371*

NTT DATA CANADA, INC *p853*
30 EAST BEAVER CREEK RD SUITE 206, RICHMOND HILL, ON, L4B 1J2
SIC 7371

NUCO NETWORKS INC *p982*
129 SPADINA AVE SUITE 200, TORONTO, ON, M5V 2L3

(647) 290-3419   *SIC 7371*
NURUN INC   *p1184*
358 RUE BEAUBIEN O, MONTREAL, QC, H2V 4S6
(514) 392-1900   *SIC 7371*
NURUN INC   *p1259*
330 RUE DE SAINT-VALLIER E BUREAU 120, QUEBEC, QC, G1K 9C5
(418) 627-2001   *SIC 7371*
NUUN DIGITAL INC   *p31*
1206 20 AVE SE, CALGARY, AB, T2G 1M8
(403) 907-0997   *SIC 7371*
NVENTIVE INC   *p1190*
215 RUE SAINT-JACQUES BUREAU 500, MONTREAL, QC, H2Y 1M6
(514) 312-4969   *SIC 7371*
OASIS TECHNOLOGY HOLDINGS LTD *p772*
90 SHEPPARD AVE E SUITE 100, NORTH YORK, ON, M2N 3A1
(416) 228-8000   *SIC 7371*
OCEANWIDE CANADA INC   *p1221*
3400 BOUL DE MAISONNEUVE O BUREAU 1450, MONTREAL, QC, H3Z 3B8
(514) 289-9090   *SIC 7371*
OKANAGAN COLLEGE   *p222*
1000 K.L.O. RD UNIT A108, KELOWNA, BC, V1Y 4X8
(250) 862-5480   *SIC 7371*
ONESPAN CANADA INC   *p1228*
8200 BOUL DECARIE BUREAU 300, MONTREAL, QC, H4P 2P5
(514) 337-5255   *SIC 7371*
ONLINE ENTERPRISES INC   *p375*
115 BANNATYNE AVE SUITE 200, WINNIPEG, MB, R3B 0R3
(204) 982-0200   *SIC 7371*
OPAL-RT TECHNOLOGIES INC   *p1216*
1751 RUE RICHARDSON BUREAU 2525, MONTREAL, QC, H3K 1G6
(514) 935-2323   *SIC 7371*
OPALIS SOFTWARE INC   *p698*
2680 MATHESON BLVD E SUITE 202, MISSISSAUGA, ON, L4W 0A5
(905) 670-8180   *SIC 7371*
OPTIVA CANADA INC   *p725*
2233 ARGENTIA RD SUITE 302, MISSISSAUGA, ON, L5N 2X7
(905) 625-2622   *SIC 7371*
OPTIVA INC   *p725*
2233 ARGENTIA RD SUITE 302, MISSISSAUGA, ON, L5N 2X7
(905) 625-2622   *SIC 7371*
ORACLE CANADA ULC   *p732*
100 MILVERTON DR SUITE 100, MISSISSAUGA, ON, L5R 4H1
(905) 890-8100   *SIC 7371*
ORACLE CANADA ULC   *p824*
45 O'CONNOR ST SUITE 400, OTTAWA, ON, K1P 1A4
(613) 569-0001   *SIC 7371*
P2 ENERGY SOLUTIONS ALBERTA ULC *p55*
639 5 AVE SW SUITE 2100, CALGARY, AB, T2P 0M9
(403) 774-1000   *SIC 7371*
PAYPROP CANADA LIMITED   *p956*
357 BAY ST UNIT 500, TORONTO, ON, M5H 2T7
(416) 735-7600   *SIC 7371*
PCI GEOMATICS ENTERPRISES INC *p673*
90 ALLSTATE PKY SUITE 501, MARKHAM, ON, L3R 6H3
(905) 764-0614   *SIC 7371*
PERLE SYSTEMS LIMITED   *p673*
60 RENFREW DR SUITE 100, MARKHAM, ON, L3R 0E1
(905) 475-8885   *SIC 7371*
PG SOLUTIONS INC   *p1285*
217 AV LEONIDAS S BUREAU 13, RIMOUSKI, QC, G5L 2T5
(418) 724-5037   *SIC 7371*
PICIS CLINICAL SOLUTIONS, INC   *p750*
1 ANTARES DR SUITE 400, NEPEAN, ON, K2E 8C4

(613) 226-5511   *SIC 7371*
PNI DIGITAL MEDIA ULC   *p299*
425 CARRALL ST SUITE 100, VANCOUVER, BC, V6B 6E3
(604) 893-8955   *SIC 7371*
POINT2 TECHNOLOGIES INC   *p1424*
3301 8TH ST E SUITE 500, SASKATOON, SK, S7H 5K5
(866) 977-1777   *SIC 7371*
POINTS.COM INC   *p977*
171 JOHN ST SUITE 500, TORONTO, ON, M5T 1X3
(416) 595-0000   *SIC 7371*
PONG GAME STUDIOS LIMITED   *p1033*
201 CREDITVIEW RD, WOODBRIDGE, ON, L4L 9T1
(905) 264-3555   *SIC 7371*
PRAXIS TECHNICAL GROUP, INC   *p234*
1618 NORTHFIELD RD, NANAIMO, BC, V9S 3A9
(250) 756-7971   *SIC 7371*
PREMIER ELECTION SOLUTIONS CANADA ULC   *p324*
1200 73RD AVE W SUITE 350, VANCOUVER, BC, V6P 6G5
(604) 261-6313   *SIC 7371*
PRONTOFORMS CORPORATION   *p832*
2500 SOLANDT SUITE 250, OTTAWA, ON, K2K 3G5
(613) 599-8288   *SIC 7371*
PROPHARM LIMITED   *p674*
131 MCNABB ST, MARKHAM, ON, L3R 5V7
(905) 943-9736   *SIC 7371*
PROPHIX SOFTWARE INC   *p710*
350 BURNHAMTHORPE RD W SUITE 1000, MISSISSAUGA, ON, L5B 3J1
(905) 279-8711   *SIC 7371*
PURE TECHNOLOGIES LTD   *p65*
705 11 AVE SW SUITE 300, CALGARY, AB, T2R 0E3
(403) 266-6794   *SIC 7371*
PYTHIAN GROUP INC, THE   *p829*
319 MCRAE AVE UNIT 700, OTTAWA, ON, K1Z 0B9
(613) 565-8696   *SIC 7371*
QUARTECH SYSTEMS LIMITED   *p287*
2889 12TH AVE E SUITE 650, VANCOUVER, BC, V5M 4T5
(604) 291-9686   *SIC 7371*
QUEST SOFTWARE CANADA INC   *p625*
515 LEGGET DR SUITE 1001, KANATA, ON, K2K 3G4
(613) 270-1500   *SIC 7371*
QUEST SOFTWARE CANADA INC   *p934*
260 KING ST E, TORONTO, ON, M5A 4L5
(416) 933-5000   *SIC 7371*
QUICKMOBILE INC   *p316*
1177 HASTINGS ST W SUITE 2600, VANCOUVER, BC, V6E 2K3
(604) 875-0403   *SIC 7371*
QUORUM INFORMATION SYSTEMS INC *p37*
7500 MACLEOD TRAIL SE SUITE 200, CALGARY, AB, T2H 0L9
(403) 777-0036   *SIC 7371*
QUORUM INFORMATION TECHNOLOGIES INC   *p37*
7500 MACLEOD TRAIL SE SUITE 200, CALGARY, AB, T2H 0L9
(403) 777-0036   *SIC 7371*
RADICAL ENTERTAINMENT INC   *p295*
369 TERMINAL AVE, VANCOUVER, BC, V6A 4C4
(604) 688-0606   *SIC 7371*
RAYMARK ULC   *p1157*
5460 CH DE LA COTE-DE-LIESSE, MONTROYAL, QC, H4P 1A5
(514) 737-0941   *SIC 7371*
RBC VENTURES INC   *p966*
20 BAY ST 17TH FL, TORONTO, ON, M5J 2N8
(416) 846-3465   *SIC 7371*
REAL MATTERS INC   *p905*
50 MINTHORN BLVD SUITE 401, THORN-

HILL, ON, L3T 7X8
(905) 739-1212   *SIC 7371*
REDSPACE INC   *p440*
1595 BEDFORD HWY SUITE 168, BEDFORD, NS, B4A 3Y4
(902) 444-3490   *SIC 7371*
REPLICON INC   *p58*
910 7 AVE SW SUITE 800, CALGARY, AB, T2P 3N8
(403) 262-6519   *SIC 7371*
RESERVEAMERICA ON INC   *p726*
2480 MEADOWVALE BLVD SUITE 1, MISSISSAUGA, ON, L5N 8M6
(905) 286-6600   *SIC 7371*
RESOLVER INC   *p983*
111 PETER ST SUITE 804, TORONTO, ON, M5V 2H1
(416) 622-2299   *SIC 7371*
ROOSTER ENERGY LTD   *p309*
666 BURRARD ST SUITE 1700, VANCOUVER, BC, V6C 2X8
(604) 574-7558   *SIC 7371*
ROSEVIEW FLC ELECTRIC INC   *p855*
51 ROSEVIEW AVE, RICHMOND HILL, ON, L4C 1C6
(647) 667-5618   *SIC 7371*
ROUTE1 INC   *p940*
8 KING ST E SUITE 600, TORONTO, ON, M5C 1B5
(416) 848-8391   *SIC 7371*
SAP CANADA INC   *p316*
1095 PENDER ST W SUITE 400, VANCOUVER, BC, V6E 2M6
(604) 647-8888   *SIC 7371*
SAP CANADA INC   *p1009*
445 WES GRAHAM WAY, WATERLOO, ON, N2L 6R2
(519) 886-3700   *SIC 7371*
SCARSIN CORPORATION   *p1001*
2 BROCK ST W SUITE 201, UXBRIDGE, ON, L9P 1P2
(905) 852-0086   *SIC 7371*
SCHNEIDER ELECTRIC SOFTWARE CANADA INC   *p18*
49 QUARRY PARK BLVD SE SUITE 100, CALGARY, AB, T2C 5H9
(403) 253-8848   *SIC 7371*
SCORE MEDIA VENTURES INC   *p983*
500 KING ST W, TORONTO, ON, M5V 1L9
(416) 479-8812   *SIC 7371*
SEARCHLIGHT SYSTEMS LTD   *p285*
1395 FRANCES ST, VANCOUVER, BC, V5L 1Z1
(604) 255-4620   *SIC 7371*
SECURITY COMPASS INC   *p956*
257 ADELAIDE ST W SUITE 500, TORONTO, ON, M5H 1X9
(888) 777-2211   *SIC 7371*
SECURITY COMPASS INC   *p983*
390 QUEENS QUAY W SUITE 209, TORONTO, ON, M5V 3A6
(888) 777-2211   *SIC 7371*
SEQUITER INC   *p116*
9644 54 AVE NW UNIT 209, EDMONTON, AB, T6E 5V1
(780) 437-2410   *SIC 7371*
SERVICES DE JEUX BABEL INC   *p1216*
1751 RUE RICHARDSON BUREAU 8400, MONTREAL, QC, H3K 1G6
(514) 904-3700   *SIC 7371*
SHOPLOGIX INC   *p524*
5100 SOUTH SERVICE RD SUITE 39, BURLINGTON, ON, L7L 6A5
(905) 469-9994   *SIC 7371*
SIEMENS CANADA LIMITED   *p905*
55 COMMERCE VALLEY DR W SUITE 400, THORNHILL, ON, L3T 7V9
SIC 7371
SIGMA BUSINESS SOLUTIONS INC   *p966*
55 YORK ST SUITE 900, TORONTO, ON, M5J 1R7
(416) 368-2000   *SIC 7371*
SIGMA SOFTWARE SOLUTIONS INC *p966*
55 YORK ST SUITE 1100, TORONTO, ON,

M5J 1R7
(416) 368-2000   *SIC 7371*
SIGMA SYSTEMS GROUP INC   *p966*
55 YORK ST SUITE 1100, TORONTO, ON, M5J 1R7
(416) 943-9696   *SIC 7371*
SIMBA TECHNOLOGIES INCORPORATED *p293*
938 8TH AVE W, VANCOUVER, BC, V5Z 1E5
(604) 633-0008   *SIC 7371*
SIMULATIONS CMLABS INC   *p1212*
645 RUE WELLINGTON BUREAU 301, MONTREAL, QC, H3C 1T2
(514) 287-1166   *SIC 7371*
SITA INFORMATION NETWORKING COMPUTING CANADA INC   *p528*
777 WALKER'S LINE, BURLINGTON, ON, L7N 2G1
(905) 681-6200   *SIC 7371*
SOFTCHOICE CORPORATION   *p992*
173 DUFFERIN ST SUITE 200, TORONTO, ON, M6K 3H7
(416) 588-9002   *SIC 7371*
SOFTCHOICE LP   *p992*
173 DUFFERIN ST SUITE 200, TORONTO, ON, M6K 3H7
(416) 588-9000   *SIC 7371*
SOLUTIONS MECANICA INC, LES   *p1336*
10000 BOUL HENRI-BOURASSA O, SAINT-LAURENT, QC, H4S 1R5
(514) 340-1818   *SIC 7371*
SOLUTIONS MEDIAS 360 INC   *p1212*
355 RUE PEEL BUREAU 901, MONTREAL, QC, H3C 2G9
(514) 717-9812   *SIC 7371*
SOPHOS INC   *p309*
580 GRANVILLE ST SUITE 400, VANCOUVER, BC, V6C 1W6
(604) 484-6400   *SIC 7371*
SOTI INC   *p733*
5770 HURONTARIO ST SUITE 1100, MISSISSAUGA, ON, L5R 3G5
(905) 624-9828   *SIC 7371*
SPERIDIAN TECHNOLOGIES CANADA INC *p957*
357 BAY ST SUITE 402, TORONTO, ON, M5H 2T7
(416) 613-1621   *SIC 7371*
SPHERE 3D CORP .   *p707*
240 MATHESON BLVD E, MISSISSAUGA, ON, L4Z 1X1
(416) 749-5999   *SIC 7371*
SQUIRREL SYSTEMS OF CANADA, LTD *p183*
8585 BAXTER PL, BURNABY, BC, V5A 4V7
(604) 412-3300   *SIC 7371*
SRB EDUCATION SOLUTIONS INC   *p675*
200 TOWN CENTRE BLVD SUITE 400, MARKHAM, ON, L3R 8G5
(877) 772-4685   *SIC 7371*
SS&C TECHNOLOGIES CANADA CORP *p700*
5255 ORBITOR DR UNIT 1, MISSISSAUGA, ON, L4W 5M6
(905) 629-8000   *SIC 7371*
STRADIGI INC   *p1200*
1470 RUE PEEL BUREAU A1050, MONTREAL, QC, H3A 1T1
(514) 395-9018   *SIC 7371*
SWEDA CANADA INC   *p774*
4101 YONGE ST SUITE 500, NORTH YORK, ON, M2P 1N6
(416) 614-0199   *SIC 7371*
SYMANTEC (CANADA) CORPORATION *p765*
3381 STEELES AVE E, NORTH YORK, ON, M2H 3S7
(416) 774-0000   *SIC 7371*
SYSCOR   *p1218*
6600 CH DE LA COTE-DES-NEIGES BUREAU 600, MONTREAL, QC, H3S 2A9
(514) 737-3201   *SIC 7371*
SYSTEMES CANADIEN KRONOS INC *p1219*

▲ Public Company   ■ Public Company Family Member   **HQ** Headquarters   **BR** Branch   **SL** Single Location

3535 CH QUEEN-MARY BUREAU 500, MONTREAL, QC, H3V 1H8
(514) 345-0580   *SIC 7371*

SYSTEMES MEDICAUX INTELERAD IN-CORPOREE, LES *p1176*
800 BOUL DE MAISONNEUVE E 12EME ETAGE, MONTREAL, QC, H2L 4L8
(514) 931-6222   *SIC 7371*

TECHNOLOGIES METAFORE INC *p1051*
9393 BOUL LOUIS-H.-LAFONTAINE, AN-JOU, QC, H1J 1Z1
(514) 354-3810   *SIC 7371*

TECHNOLOGY EVALUATION CENTERS INC *p1145*
1000 RUE DE SERIGNY BUREAU 300, LONGUEUIL, QC, J4K 5B1
(514) 954-3665   *SIC 7371*

TECHNOMEDIA FORMATION INC *p1200*
1001 BOUL DE MAISONNEUVE O, MON-TREAL, QC, H3A 3C8
(514) 287-1561   *SIC 7371*

TELEDYNE CARIS, INC. *p401*
115 WAGGONERS LANE, FREDERICTON, NB, E3B 2L4
(506) 458-8533   *SIC 7371*

TELEPIN SOFTWARE CORPORATION *p625*
411 LEGGET DR SUITE 100, KANATA, ON, K2K 3C9
(613) 366-1910   *SIC 7371*

TERANET ENTERPRISES INC *p967*
123 FRONT ST W SUITE 700, TORONTO, ON, M5J 2M2
(416) 360-5263   *SIC 7371*

TERANET INC *p941*
1 ADELAIDE ST E SUITE 600, TORONTO, ON, M5C 2V9
(416) 360-5263   *SIC 7371*

TERANET INC *p967*
123 FRONT ST W SUITE 700, TORONTO, ON, M5J 2M2
(416) 360-5263   *SIC 7371*

TERRALINK TECHNOLOGIES CANADA INC *p923*
181 EGLINTON AVE E SUITE 206, TORONTO, ON, M4P 1J4
(416) 593-0700   *SIC 7371*

THEMIS SOLUTIONS INC *p189*
4611 CANADA WAY SUITE 300, BURNABY, BC, V5G 4X3
(604) 210-2944   *SIC 7371*

THINK RESEARCH CORPORATION *p934*
351 KING ST E SUITE 500, TORONTO, ON, M5A 0L6
(416) 977-1955   *SIC 7371*

THINKWRAP SOLUTIONS INC *p625*
450 MARCH RD SUITE 500, KANATA, ON, K2K 3K2
(613) 751-4441   *SIC 7371*

TIM DEALER SERVICES INCORPORATED *p448*
250 BROWNLOW AVE SUITE 7, DART-MOUTH, NS, B3B 1W9
(902) 468-7177   *SIC 7371*

TINK PROFITABILITE NUMERIQUE INC *p1212*
87 RUE PRINCE BUREAU 140, MON-TREAL, QC, H3C 2M7
(514) 866-0995   *SIC 7371*

TRAPEZE SOFTWARE GROUP, INC *p701*
5800 EXPLORER DR UNIT 500, MISSIS-SAUGA, ON, L4W 5K9
(905) 629-8727   *SIC 7371*

TRUSTWAVE CANADA, INC *p537*
231 SHEARSON CRES SUITE 205, CAM-BRIDGE, ON, N1T 1J5
(519) 620-7227   *SIC 7371*

UBISOFT DIVERTISSEMENTS INC *p1183*
5505 BOUL SAINT-LAURENT BUREAU 5000, MONTREAL, QC, H2T 1S6
(514) 490-2000   *SIC 7371*

UBISOFT DIVERTISSEMENTS INC *p1191*
250 RUE SAINT-ANTOINE O BUREAU 700, MONTREAL, QC, H2Y 0A3
(514) 908-8100   *SIC 7371*

UNISYS CANADA INC *p454*
1809 BARRINGTON ST SUITE 600, HALI-FAX, NS, B3J 3K8
(902) 704-5340   *SIC 7371*

UNIVERIS CORPORATION *p934*
111 GEORGE ST 3RD FL, TORONTO, ON, M5A 2N4
(416) 979-3700   *SIC 7371*

UPLAND SOFTWARE INC *p1343*
275 BOUL ARMAND-FRAPPIER BUREAU 531, SAINT-LAURENT, QC, H7V 4A7
(450) 688-3444   *SIC 7371*

UPSTREAM WORKS SOFTWARE LTD *p1034*
777 WESTON RD SUITE 1000, WOOD-BRIDGE, ON, L4L 0G9
(905) 660-0969   *SIC 7371*

USTRI CANADA INC *p300*
1122 MAINLAND ST SUITE 470, VANCOU-VER, BC, V6B 5L1
SIC 7371

VERSATERM INC *p830*
2300 CARLING AVE, OTTAWA, ON, K2B 7G1
(613) 820-0311   *SIC 7371*

VISIER SOLUTIONS INC *p301*
858 BEATTY ST SUITE 400, VANCOUVER, BC, V6B 1C1
(778) 331-6950   *SIC 7371*

VISIONMAX SOLUTIONS INC *p701*
2680 SKYMARK AVE SUITE 600, MISSIS-SAUGA, ON, L4W 5L6
(905) 282-0503   *SIC 7371*

VOLARIS GROUP INC *p702*
5060 SPECTRUM WAY SUITE 110, MIS-SISSAUGA, ON, L4W 5N5
(905) 267-5400   *SIC 7371*

VOX INTEGRATED SOLUTIONS MODEL INC *p921*
36 GLENGOWAN RD, TORONTO, ON, M4N 1E8
(905) 840-7477   *SIC 7371*

WEBCT EDUCATIONAL TECHNOLOGIES CORPORATION *p325*
2389 HEALTH SCIENCES MALL SUITE 2, VANCOUVER, BC, V6T 1Z3
(604) 221-0558   *SIC 7371*

WENCO INTERNATIONAL MINING SYS-TEMS LTD *p257*
13777 COMMERCE PKY SUITE 100, RICH-MOND, BC, V6V 2X3
(604) 270-8277   *SIC 7371*

WHITEHILL TECHNOLOGIES INC *p410*
260 MACNAUGHTON AVE, MONCTON, NB, E1H 2J8
SIC 7371

WHITEHILL TECHNOLOGIES INC *p677*
19 ALLSTATE PKY SUITE 400, MARKHAM, ON, L3R 5A4
(905) 475-2112   *SIC 7371*

WINMAGIC CORP *p733*
5600A CANCROSS CRT, MISSISSAUGA, ON, L5R 3E9
(905) 502-7000   *SIC 7371*

XSTREAM SOFTWARE INC *p819*
2280 ST. LAURENT BLVD SUITE 101, OT-TAWA, ON, K1G 4K1
(613) 731-9443   *SIC 7371*

YOU I LABS INC *p625*
307 LEGGET DR, KANATA, ON, K2K 3C8
(613) 228-9107   *SIC 7371*

SIC 7372 Prepackaged software

3761258 CANADA INC *p86*
10180 101 ST NW SUITE 310, EDMON-TON, AB, T5J 3S4
(780) 702-1432   *SIC 7372*

ABB INC *p259*
10651 SHELLBRIDGE WAY, RICHMOND, BC, V6X 2W8
(604) 207-6000   *SIC 7372*

ACCEO SOLUTIONS INC *p1277*

7710 BOUL WILFRID-HAMEL, QUEBEC, QC, G2G 2J5
(418) 877-0088   *SIC 7372*

ACTIVESTATE SOFTWARE INC *p311*
1177 HASTINGS ST W UNIT 1000, VAN-COUVER, BC, V6E 2K3
(778) 786-1100   *SIC 7372*

ADOXIO BUSINESS SOLUTIONS LIMITED *p1415*
1445 PARK ST SUITE 200, REGINA, SK, S4N 4C5
(306) 569-6501   *SIC 7372*

ALLSCRIPTS CANADA CORPORATION *p253*
13888 WIRELESS WAY SUITE 110, RICH-MOND, BC, V6V 0A3
(604) 273-4900   *SIC 7372*

ALTERNATE HEALTH CORP. *p319*
1485 6TH AVE W SUITE 309, VANCOU-VER, BC, V6H 4G1
(604) 569-4969   *SIC 7372*

ANGUS SYSTEMS GROUP LIMITED *p778*
1125 LESLIE ST, NORTH YORK, ON, M3C 2J6
(416) 385-8550   *SIC 7372*

ARCURVE INC *p63*
902 11 AVE SW SUITE 300, CALGARY, AB, T2R 0E7
(403) 242-4361   *SIC 7372*

ARROW ECS CANADA LIMITED *p737*
171 SUPERIOR BLVD UNIT 2, MISSIS-SAUGA, ON, L5T 2L6
(905) 670-4699   *SIC 7372*

ATIMI SOFTWARE INC *p302*
800 PENDER ST W SUITE 800, VANCOU-VER, BC, V6C 2V6
(778) 372-2800   *SIC 7372*

BETTER SOFTWARE COMPANY INC, THE *p832*
303 TERRY FOX DR SUITE 101, OTTAWA, ON, K2K 3J1
(613) 627-3506   *SIC 7372*

BLUE CASTLE GAMES INC *p184*
4401 STILL CREEK DR UNIT 300, BURN-ABY, BC, V5C 6G9
(604) 299-5626   *SIC 7372*

BMC SOFTWARE CANADA INC *p903*
50 MINTHORN BLVD SUITE 200, THORN-HILL, ON, L3T 7X8
(905) 707-4600   *SIC 7372*

BOARDSUITE CORP *p949*
372 BAY ST SUITE 1800, TORONTO, ON, M5H 2W9
SIC 7372

BRIDGES TRANSITIONS INC *p221*
1726 DOLPHIN AVE UNIT 205, KELOWNA, BC, V1Y 9R9
(250) 869-4200   *SIC 7372*

BUILDSCALE, INC *p639*
8 QUEEN ST N UNIT 1, KITCHENER, ON, N2H 2G8
(800) 530-3878   *SIC 7372*

CENGEA SOLUTIONS INC *p311*
1188 GEORGIA ST W SUITE 560, VAN-COUVER, BC, V6E 4A2
(604) 697-6400   *SIC 7372*

CERTICOM CORP *p693*
4701 TAHOE BLVD, MISSISSAUGA, ON, L4W 0B5
(905) 507-4220   *SIC 7372*

CINEGROUPE INTERACTIF INC *p1175*
1010 RUE SAINTE-CATHERINE E, MON-TREAL, QC, H2L 2G3
(514) 524-7567   *SIC 7372*

CITADEL COMMERCE CORP *p192*
8610 GLENLYON PKY UNIT 130, BURN-ABY, BC, V5J 0B6
(604) 299-6924   *SIC 7372*

CONVERGE TECHNOLOGY PARTNERS INC *p961*
161 BAY ST SUITE 4420, TORONTO, ON, M5J 2S1
SIC 7372

COVER-ALL COMPUTER SERVICES CORP

p871
1170 BIRCHMOUNT RD, SCARBOROUGH, ON, M1P 5E3
(416) 752-8100   *SIC 7372*

DAISY INTELLIGENCE CORPORATION *p551*
2300 STEELES AVE W STE 250, CON-CORD, ON, L4K 5X6
(905) 642-2629   *SIC 7372*

DANA LOGIC INC *p1203*
1155 BOUL RENE-LEVESQUE O BUREAU 2500, MONTREAL, QC, H3B 2K4
(514) 845-5326   *SIC 7372*

DASH HUDSON INC *p452*
1668 BARRINGTON ST UNIT 600, HALI-FAX, NS, B3J 2A2
(902) 298-2795   *SIC 7372*

DEALERTRACK CANADA INC *p693*
2700 MATHESON BLVD E SUITE 702, MIS-SISSAUGA, ON, L4W 4V9
(905) 281-6200   *SIC 7372*

DEMAC MEDIA INC *p935*
211 YONGE ST SUITE 600, TORONTO, ON, M5B 1M4
(416) 670-1322   *SIC 7372*

DIGI117 LTD *p240*
145 CHADWICK CRT SUITE 220, NORTH VANCOUVER, BC, V7M 3K1
(778) 772-4770   *SIC 7372*

ELOQUA CORPORATION *p980*
553 RICHMOND ST W SUITE 214, TORONTO, ON, M5V 1Y6
(416) 864-0440   *SIC 7372*

ESENTIRE, INC *p536*
278 PINEBUSH RD SUITE 101, CAM-BRIDGE, ON, N1T 1Z6
(519) 651-2200   *SIC 7372*

ESRI CANADA LIMITED *p779*
12 CONCORDE PL SUITE 900, NORTH YORK, ON, M3C 3R8
(416) 441-6035   *SIC 7372*

EXPLORANCE INC *p1195*
1470 RUE PEEL BUREAU 500, MON-TREAL, QC, H3A 1T1
(514) 938-2111   *SIC 7372*

FORMING TECHNOLOGIES INCORPO-RATED *p527*
3370 SOUTH SERVICE RD SUITE 203, BURLINGTON, ON, L7N 3M6
(905) 340-3370   *SIC 7372*

GE FANUC AUTOMATION CANADA COM-PANY *p89*
10235 101 ST NW, EDMONTON, AB, T5J 3E9
(780) 420-2000   *SIC 7372*

GENESYS LABORATORIES CANADA INC *p415*
50 SMYTHE ST SUITE 2000, SAINT JOHN, NB, E2L 0B8
(506) 637-3900   *SIC 7372*

GOLDMONEY INC *p980*
334 ADELAIDE ST W UNIT 307, TORONTO, ON, M5V 0M1
(647) 499-6748   *SIC 7372*

HARTS SYSTEMS LTD *p240*
1200 LONSDALE AVE SUITE 304, NORTH VANCOUVER, BC, V7M 3H6
(604) 990-9101   *SIC 7372*

HCL AXON TECHNOLOGIES INC *p709*
77 CITY CENTRE DR, MISSISSAUGA, ON, L5B 1M5
(905) 603-4381   *SIC 7372*

HITACHI DATA SYSTEMS INC *p952*
11 KING ST W SUITE 1400, TORONTO, ON, M5H 4C7
(416) 494-4114   *SIC 7372*

HITACHI SOLUTIONS CANADA, LTD *p64*
550 11 AVE SW SUITE 1000, CALGARY, AB, T2R 1M7
(866) 231-4332   *SIC 7372*

HITACHI SOLUTIONS CANADA, LTD *p774*
36 YORK MILLS RD SUITE 502, NORTH YORK, ON, M2P 2E9
(416) 961-4332   *SIC 7372*

IBM CANADA LIMITED p1213
1360 BOUL RENE-LEVESQUE O BUREAU 400, MONTREAL, QC, H3G 2W6
(888) 245-5572 *SIC 7372*

IMAGINIT CANADA INC p744
151 COURTNEYPARK DR W SUITE 201, MISSISSAUGA, ON, L5W 1Y5
(905) 602-8783 *SIC 7372*

IMEX SYSTEMS INC p585
34 GREENSBORO DR 2ND FL, ETOBICOKE, ON, M9W 1E1
(647) 352-7520 *SIC 7372*

INCOGNITO SOFTWARE SYSTEMS INC p298
375 WATER ST SUITE 500, VANCOUVER, BC, V6B 5C6
(604) 688-4332 *SIC 7372*

INFOR (CANADA), LTD p779
250 FERRAND DR SUITE 1200, NORTH YORK, ON, M3C 3G8
(416) 421-6700 *SIC 7372*

INNOVAPOST INC p832
365 MARCH RD, OTTAWA, ON, K2K 3N5
(613) 270-6262 *SIC 7372*

INNOVMETRIC LOGICIELS INC p1264
2014 RUE CYRILLE-DUQUET BUREAU 310, QUEBEC, QC, G1N 4N6
(418) 688-2061 *SIC 7372*

KOGNITIV CORPORATION p1006
187 KING ST S, WATERLOO, ON, N2J 1R1
(226) 476-1124 *SIC 7372*

KONGSBERG GEOSPATIAL LTD p624
411 LEGGET DR SUITE 400, KANATA, ON, K2K 3C9
(613) 271-5500 *SIC 7372*

LIGHTSPEED POS INC p1189
700 RUE SAINT-ANTOINE E BUREAU 300, MONTREAL, QC, H2Y 1A6
(514) 907-1801 *SIC 7372*

LOGIBEC INC p1211
700 RUE WELLINGTON BUREAU 1500, MONTREAL, QC, H3C 3S4
(514) 766-0134 *SIC 7372*

LONE WOLF REAL ESTATE TECHNOLOGIES INC p536
231 SHEARSON CRES SUITE 310, CAMBRIDGE, ON, N1T 1J5
(866) 279-9653 *SIC 7372*

LONGVIEW SOLUTIONS INC p672
65 ALLSTATE PKY SUITE 200, MARKHAM, ON, L3R 9X1
(905) 940-1510 *SIC 7372*

LUMERICAL INC p314
1095 PENDER ST W SUITE 1700, VANCOUVER, BC, V6E 2M6
(604) 733-9006 *SIC 7372*

MAESTRO TECHNOLOGIES INC p1393
1625 BOUL LIONEL-BOULET BUREAU 300, VARENNES, QC, J3X 1P7
(450) 652-6200 *SIC 7372*

MAINTENANCE ASSISTANT INC p995
35 GOLDEN AVE SUITE A-201, TORONTO, ON, M6R 2J5
(647) 317-9055 *SIC 7372*

MANAGEMENT SYSTEMS RESOURCES INC p781
2 TIPPETT RD, NORTH YORK, ON, M3H 2V2
(416) 630-3000 *SIC 7372*

MAXIMIZER SOFTWARE INC p299
60 SMITHE ST UNIT 260, VANCOUVER, BC, V6B 0P5
(604) 601-8000 *SIC 7372*

MELTWATER NEWS CANADA INC p964
25 YORK ST SUITE 1200, TORONTO, ON, M5J 2V5
(416) 641-4902 *SIC 7372*

METALOGIX SOFTWARE CORP p295
55 CORDOVA ST E SUITE 604, VANCOUVER, BC, V6A 0A5
(604) 677-4636 *SIC 7372*

METEX INC p916
789 DON MILLS ROAD, SUITE 218, TORONTO, ON, M3C 1T5

(416) 203-8388 *SIC 7372*

MOMENTIS INFORMATIQUE INC p1157
5500 AV ROYALMOUNT BUREAU 250, MONT-ROYAL, QC, H4P 1H7
(514) 939-2306 *SIC 7372*

MOMENTUM HEALTHWARE, INC p364
131 PROVENCHER BLVD SUITE 308, WINNIPEG, MB, R2H 0G2
(204) 231-3836 *SIC 7372*

MUTUAL CONCEPT COMPUTER GROUP INC p660
785 WONDERLAND RD S SUITE 253, LONDON, ON, N6K 1M6
(519) 432-8553 *SIC 7372*

N-ABLE TECHNOLOGIES INTERNATIONAL INC p624
450 MARCH RD, KANATA, ON, K2K 3K2
(613) 592-6676 *SIC 7372*

NETGOVERN INC p1211
180 RUE PEEL BUREAU 333, MONTREAL, QC, H3C 2G7
(514) 392-9220 *SIC 7372*

NETGOVERN INC p1211
180 RUE PEEL BUREAU 333, MONTREAL, QC, H3C 2G7
(514) 392-9220 *SIC 7372*

NEXIA HEALTH TECHNOLOGIES INC p673
15 ALLSTATE PRKWY 6TH FL, MARKHAM, ON, L3R 5B4
(905) 415-3063 *SIC 7372*

OPEN SOLUTIONS DTS INC p321
1441 CREEKSIDE DR SUITE 300, VANCOUVER, BC, V6J 4S7
(604) 714-1848 *SIC 7372*

OPEN TEXT CORPORATION p1009
275 FRANK TOMPA DR, WATERLOO, ON, N2L 0A1
(519) 888-7111 *SIC 7372*

ORACLE CANADA ULC p1198
600 BOUL DE MAISONNEUVE O BUREAU 1900, MONTREAL, QC, H3A 3J2
(514) 843-6762 *SIC 7372*

ORACLE CORPORATION CANADA INC p732
100 MILVERTON DR SUITE 100, MISSISSAUGA, ON, L5R 4H1
SIC 7372

PATHFACTORY INC p977
174 SPADINA AVE SUITE 600, TORONTO, ON, M5T 2C2
(416) 304-9400 *SIC 7372*

PAYTM LABS INC p956
220 ADELAIDE ST W, TORONTO, ON, M5H 1W7
(647) 360-8331 *SIC 7372*

PEER GROUP INC, THE p639
72 VICTORIA ST S SUITE 400, KITCHENER, ON, N2G 4Y9
(519) 749-9554 *SIC 7372*

PERSE-TECHNOLOGIE INC p1370
2555 RUE DES FRENES BUREAU 100, SHERBROOKE, QC, J1G 4R3
SIC 7372

PLEXXIS SOFTWARE INC p505
14 ABACUS RD, BRAMPTON, ON, L6T 5B7
(905) 889-8979 *SIC 7372*

POINTCLICKCARE CORP p699
5570 EXPLORER DR, MISSISSAUGA, ON, L4W 0C4
(905) 858-8885 *SIC 7372*

POINTCLICKCARE TECHNOLOGIES INC p699
5570 EXPLORER DR, MISSISSAUGA, ON, L4W 0C4
(905) 858-8885 *SIC 7372*

POKA INC p1265
214 AV SAINT-SACREMENT BUREAU 240, QUEBEC, QC, G1N 3X6
(418) 476-2188 *SIC 7372*

QNX SOFTWARE SYSTEMS LIMITED p625
1001 FARRAR RD, KANATA, ON, K2K 0B3
(613) 591-0931 *SIC 7372*

QUEST SOFTWARE CANADA INC p454
5151 GEORGE ST, HALIFAX, NS, B3J 1M5

(902) 442-5800 *SIC 7372*

QUISITIVE TECHNOLOGY SOLUTIONS, INC p966
161 BAY ST SUITE 2325, TORONTO, ON, M5J 2S1
(519) 574-5520 *SIC 7372*

RELIC ENTERTAINMENT, INC p300
1040 HAMILTON ST SUITE 400, VANCOUVER, BC, V6B 2R9
(604) 801-6577 *SIC 7372*

RESPONSETEK NETWORKS CORP p327
969 ROBSON ST SUITE 320, VANCOUVER, BC, V6Z 2V7
(604) 484-2900 *SIC 7372*

ROCKWELL AUTOMATION CANADA LTD p1071
9975 RUE DE CHATEAUNEUF BUREAU U, BROSSARD, QC, J4Z 3V6
(450) 445-3353 *SIC 7372*

RPM TECHNOLOGIES CORPORATION p966
120 BREMNER BLVD SUITE 2300, TORONTO, ON, M5J 0A8
(416) 214-6232 *SIC 7372*

SABA SOFTWARE (CANADA) INC p625
345 MARCH RD SUITE 100, KANATA, ON, K2K 3G1
(613) 270-1011 *SIC 7372*

SAFE SOFTWARE INC p274
9639 137A ST SUITE 1200, SURREY, BC, V3T 0M1
(604) 501-9985 *SIC 7372*

SANGOMA TECHNOLOGIES CORPORATION p674
100 RENFREW DR SUITE 100, MARKHAM, ON, L3R 9R6
(905) 474-1990 *SIC 7372*

SAP CANADA INC p774
222 BAY ST SUITE 1800, 1900, 2000, NORTH YORK, ON, M2P 2B8
(416) 229-0574 *SIC 7372*

SAP CANADA INC p1190
380 RUE SAINT-ANTOINE O BUREAU 2000, MONTREAL, QC, H2Y 3X7
(514) 350-7300 *SIC 7372*

SAS INSTITUTE (CANADA) INC p934
280 KING ST E UNIT 500, TORONTO, ON, M5A 1K7
(416) 363-4424 *SIC 7372*

SCRIBBLE TECHNOLOGIES INC p983
49 SPADINA AVE UNIT 303, TORONTO, ON, M5V 2J1
(416) 364-8118 *SIC 7372*

SMART EMPLOYEE BENEFITS INC p700
5500 EXPLORER DR 4TH FLR, MISSISSAUGA, ON, L4W 5C7
(888) 939-8885 *SIC 7372*

SOLID XPERTS INC p1336
2650 AV MARIE-CURIE, SAINT-LAURENT, QC, H4S 2C3
(514) 343-9111 *SIC 7372*

STRATACACHE CANADA INC p689
5925 AIRPORT RD SUITE 200, MISSISSAUGA, ON, L4V 1W1
(905) 405-6208 *SIC 7372*

SUBNET SOLUTIONS INC p32
916 42 AVE SE UNIT 110, CALGARY, AB, T2G 1Z2
(403) 270-8885 *SIC 7372*

SURECOMP INC p790
1 YORKDALE RD SUITE 602, NORTH YORK, ON, M6A 3A1
(416) 781-5545 *SIC 7372*

SYLOGIST LTD p74
5 RICHARD WAY SW SUITE 102, CALGARY, AB, T3E 7M8
(403) 266-4808 *SIC 7372*

SYSCON JUSTICE SYSTEMS CANADA LTD p265
3600 LYSANDER LANE SUITE 300, RICHMOND, BC, V7B 1C3
(604) 606-7650 *SIC 7372*

SYSTEMES SYNTAX LTEE p1228
8000 BOUL DECARIE BUREAU 300, MON-

TREAL, QC, H4P 2S4
(514) 733-7777 *SIC 7372*

TECHNOLOGIES 20-20 INC p1241
400 BOUL ARMAND-FRAPPIER BUREAU 2020, MONTREAL-OUEST, QC, H7V 4B4
(514) 332-4110 *SIC 7372*

TECHNOLOGIES INTERACTIVES MEDIA-GRIF INC p1145
1111 RUE SAINT-CHARLES O BUREAU 255, LONGUEUIL, QC, J4K 5G4
(450) 449-0102 *SIC 7372*

TELUS SOLUTIONS EN SANTE INC p1209
22E ETAGE 630, BOUL RENE-LEVESQUE O, MONTREAL, QC, H3B 1S6
(514) 665-3050 *SIC 7372*

THESCORE INC p984
500 KING ST W 4TH FL, TORONTO, ON, M5V 1L9
(416) 479-8812 *SIC 7372*

THOMSON REUTERS DT IMPOT ET COMPTABILITE INC p1155
3333 BOUL GRAHAM BUREAU 222, MONT-ROYAL, QC, H3R 3L5
(514) 733-8355 *SIC 7372*

TITUS INC p826
343 PRESTON ST SUITE 800, OTTAWA, ON, K1S 1N4
(613) 820-5111 *SIC 7372*

UKEN STUDIOS INC p984
266 KING ST W 2ND FL, TORONTO, ON, M5V 1H8
(416) 616-8901 *SIC 7372*

VENDASTA TECHNOLOGIES INC p1430
220 3RD AVE S SUITE 405, SASKATOON, SK, S7K 1M1
(306) 955-5512 *SIC 7372*

VERSA SYSTEMS LTD p769
200 YORKLAND BLVD SUITE 200, NORTH YORK, ON, M2J 5C1
(416) 493-1833 *SIC 7372*

VISION33 CANADA INC p189
6400 ROBERTS ST SUITE 200, BURNABY, BC, V5G 4C9
(604) 473-2100 *SIC 7372*

VISUAL DEFENCE INC p854
9225 LESLIE ST SUITE 7, RICHMOND HILL, ON, L4B 3H6
(905) 731-1254 *SIC 7372*

VOLANTE SOFTWARE INC p778
49 COLDWATER RD, NORTH YORK, ON, M3B 1Y8
(416) 988-6333 *SIC 7372*

W MODE INC p41
3553 31 ST NW SUITE 201, CALGARY, AB, T2L 2K7
(403) 260-8690 *SIC 7372*

WATCHFIRE CORPORATION p625
1 HINES RD, KANATA, ON, K2K 3C7
SIC 7372

WATERLOO MAPLE INC p1011
615 KUMPF DR, WATERLOO, ON, N2V 1K8
(519) 747-2373 *SIC 7372*

WELLNESS LIVING SYSTEMS INC p854
30 FULTON WAY BLDG 8 SUITE 203, RICHMOND HILL, ON, L4B 1E6
(888) 668-7728 *SIC 7372*

WINMAGIC INC p733
5600 CANCROSS CRT, MISSISSAUGA, ON, L5R 3E9
(905) 502-7000 *SIC 7372*

YARDI SYSTEMS p690
5925 AIRPORT RD SUITE 605, MISSISSAUGA, ON, L4V 1W1
(905) 671-0315 *SIC 7372*

ZZEN DESIGN BUILD LIMITED p1029
100 ZENWAY BLVD, WOODBRIDGE, ON, L4H 2Y7
(905) 264-5962 *SIC 7372*

SIC 7373 Computer integrated systems design

1428427 ONTARIO LTD p527

3410 SOUTH SERVICE RD SUITE 203, BURLINGTON, ON, L7N 3T2
(905) 331-7207   SIC 7373

341234 B.C. LTD   p187
4400 DOMINION UNIT 280, BURNABY, BC, V5G 4G3
(604) 473-9889   SIC 7373

AGILIS NETWORKS   p900
500 REGENT ST SUITE 250, SUDBURY, ON, P3E 3Y2
(705) 675-0516   SIC 7373

AMEC FOSTER WHEELER INC   p429
133 CROSBIE RD, ST. JOHN'S, NL, A1B 1H3
(709) 724-1900   SIC 7373

AQUA DATA INC   p1245
95 5E AV, PINCOURT, QC, J7W 5K8
(514) 425-1010   SIC 7373

AVIYA TECHNOLOGIES INC   p719
2495 MEADOWPINE BLVD, MISSISSAUGA, ON, L5N 6C3
(905) 812-9995   SIC 7373

CALLISTO INTEGRATION LTD   p803
635 FOURTH LINE UNIT 16, OAKVILLE, ON, L6L 5W4
(905) 339-0059   SIC 7373

CCI INC   p99
17816 118 AVE NW, EDMONTON, AB, T5S 2W3
(780) 784-1990   SIC 7373

CIMTEK INC   p521
5328 JOHN LUCAS DR, BURLINGTON, ON, L7L 6A6
(905) 331-6338   SIC 7373

COMPUGEN INC   p856
100 VIA RENZO DR, RICHMOND HILL, ON, L4S 0B8
(905) 707-2000   SIC 7373

COMPUGEN SYSTEMS LTD   p10
1440 28 ST NE SUITE 3, CALGARY, AB, T2A 7W6
(403) 571-4400   SIC 7373

COMPUTER SCIENCES CANADA INC   p624
555 LEGGET DR, KANATA, ON, K2K 2X3
(613) 591-1810   SIC 7373

COMPUTER UPGRADING SPECIALISTS LTD   p77
232 MAHOGANY TERR SE, CALGARY, AB, T3M 0T5
(403) 271-3800   SIC 7373

CREAFORM INC   p1138
4700 RUE DE LA PASCALINE, LEVIS, QC, G6W 0L9
(418) 833-4446   SIC 7373

D2L CORPORATION   p638
151 CHARLES ST W SUITE 400, KITCHENER, ON, N2G 1H6
(519) 772-0325   SIC 7373

DASSAULT SYSTEMES CANADA INC p1188
393 RUE SAINT-JACQUES BUREAU 300, MONTREAL, QC, H2Y 1N9
(514) 940-2949   SIC 7373

GLOBAL MART INTERNATIONAL TECHNOLOGY INC   p826
2821 RIVERSIDE DR, OTTAWA, ON, K1V 8N4
      SIC 7373

GRANTEK SYSTEMS INTEGRATION INC p522
4480 HARVESTER RD, BURLINGTON, ON, L7L 4X2
(905) 634-0844   SIC 7373

GROUNDSWELL GROUP INC   p64
214 11 AVE SW SUITE 200, CALGARY, AB, T2R 0K1
(403) 262-2041   SIC 7373

GROUPE IN-RGY CONSULTATION INC p1188
390 RUE LE MOYNE, MONTREAL, QC, H2Y 1Y3
(514) 906-7767   SIC 7373

IVEDHA INC   p779
18 WYNFORD DR UNIT 306, NORTH YORK, ON, M3C 3S2

(416) 424-6614   SIC 7373

MDA SYSTEMS LTD   p255
13800 COMMERCE PKWY, RICHMOND, BC, V6V 2J3
(604) 278-3411   SIC 7373

MDA SYSTEMS LTD   p749
57 AURIGA DR UNIT 201, NEPEAN, ON, K2E 8B2
(613) 727-1087   SIC 7373

MDH ENGINEERED SOLUTIONS CORP p1428
216 1ST AVE S, SASKATOON, SK, S7K 1K3
(306) 934-7527   SIC 7373

NOVA NETWORKS INC   p831
1700 WOODWARD DR SUITE 100, OTTAWA, ON, K2C 3R8
(613) 563-6682   SIC 7373

QUALTECH INC   p1265
1880 RUE LEON-HARMEL, QUEBEC, QC, G1N 4K3
(418) 686-3802   SIC 7373

S TEAM 92 AUTOMATION TECHNOLOGY INC   p761
827 LINE 4 RR 2, NIAGARA ON THE LAKE, ON, L0S 1J0
      SIC 7373

SPG HYDRO INTERNATIONAL INC p1359
2161 RUE LEONARD-DE VINCI BUREAU 101, SAINTE-JULIE, QC, J3E 1Z3
(450) 922-3515   SIC 7373

TECHNOLOGIES DE TRANSFERT DE CHALEUR MAYA LTEE p1402
4999 RUE SAINTE-CATHERINE O BUREAU 400, WESTMOUNT, QC, H3Z 1T3
(514) 369-5706   SIC 7373

SIC 7374 Data processing and preparation

3043177 NOVA SCOTIA LIMITED   p444
61 RADDALL AVE, DARTMOUTH, NS, B3B 1T4
(902) 446-3940   SIC 7374

9209-5256 QUEBEC INC   p1227
4700 RUE DE LA SAVANE BUREAU 210, MONTREAL, QC, H4P 1T7
(514) 906-4713   SIC 7374

ADP CANADA CO   p1063
204   BOUL   DE   MONTARVILLE, BOUCHERVILLE, QC, J4B 6S2
      SIC 7374

APPNOVATION TECHNOLOGIES INC p294
190 ALEXANDER ST SUITE 600, VANCOUVER, BC, V6A 1B5
(604) 568-0313   SIC 7374

BIBLIOCOMMONS INC   p978
119   SPADINA   AVE   SUITE   1000, TORONTO, ON, M5V 2L1
(647) 436-6381   SIC 7374

BLAST RADIUS INC   p297
509 RICHARDS ST, VANCOUVER, BC, V6B 2Z6
(604) 647-6500   SIC 7374

BLAST RADIUS INC   p979
99 SPADINA AVE SUITE 200, TORONTO, ON, M5V 3P8
(416) 214-4220   SIC 7374

BONASOURCE INC   p960
144 FRONT ST W SUITE 725, TORONTO, ON, M5J 2L7
(416) 410-4059   SIC 7374

BROADRIDGE FINANCIAL SOLUTIONS (CANADA) INC p949
4 KING ST W SUITE 500, TORONTO, ON, M5H 1B6
(416) 350-0999   SIC 7374

BROADRIDGE SOFTWARE LIMITED p303
510 BURRARD ST SUITE 600, VANCOUVER, BC, V6C 3A8
(604) 687-2133   SIC 7374

CALGARY SCIENTIFIC INC   p28
1210 20 AVE SE SUITE 208, CALGARY, AB, T2G 1M8
(403) 270-7159   SIC 7374

CLAROCITY CORPORATION   p34
6940 FISHER RD SE SUITE 200, CALGARY, AB, T2H 0W3
(403) 984-9246   SIC 7374

CORPORATION XPRIMA.COM   p1241
420 BOUL ARMAND-FRAPPIER BUREAU 200, MONTREAL-OUEST, QC, H7V 4B4
(450) 681-5868   SIC 7374

CRITICAL MASS INC   p979
425 ADELAIDE ST W, TORONTO, ON, M5V 3C1
(416) 673-5275   SIC 7374

DISNEY CANADA INC   p221
1628   DICKSON   AVE   SUITE   500, KELOWNA, BC, V1Y 9X1
(250) 868-8622   SIC 7374

ELECTRONIC IMAGING SYSTEMS CORP p874
1361 HUNTINGWOOD DR UNIT 8, SCARBOROUGH, ON, M1S 3J1
(416) 292-0900   SIC 7374

GENERAL   DYNAMICS   INFORMATION TECHNOLOGY CANADA, LIMITED
30 CAMELOT DR, NEPEAN, ON, K2G 5X8
(613) 723-9500   SIC 7374

GIVEX CANADA CORP   p980
134 PETER ST SUITE 1400, TORONTO, ON, M5V 2H2
(416) 350-9660   SIC 7374

GLOBAL TRAVEL COMPUTER HOLDINGS LTD   p670
7550 BIRCHMOUNT RD, MARKHAM, ON, L3R 6C6
(905) 479-4949   SIC 7374

HOOTSUITE INC   p289
5 8TH AVE E, VANCOUVER, BC, V5T 1R6
(604) 681-4668   SIC 7374

HORTON TRADING LTD   p298
788 BEATTY ST SUITE 307, VANCOUVER, BC, V6B 2M1
(604) 688-8521   SIC 7374

INTRIA ITEMS INC   p731
5705 CANCROSS CT, MISSISSAUGA, ON, L5R 3E9
(905) 755-2400   SIC 7374

INTRIA ITEMS INC   p1131
8301 RUE ELMSLIE, LASALLE, QC, H8N 3H9
(514) 368-5222   SIC 7374

ISM INFORMATION SYSTEMS MANAGEMENT CANADA CORPORATION p1421
1 RESEARCH DR, REGINA, SK, S4S 7H1
(306) 337-5601   SIC 7374

KONRAD GROUP, INC   p627
1726 HENDERSON LINE, KEENE, ON, K9J 6X8
(416) 551-3684   SIC 7374

LEONARDO WORLDWIDE CORPORATION p981
111 PETER ST SUITE 530, TORONTO, ON, M5V 2H1
(416) 593-6634   SIC 7374

LIBEO INC   p1280
5700 BOUL DES GALERIES BUREAU 300, QUEBEC, QC, G2K 0H5
(418) 520-0739   SIC 7374

LIXAR I.T. INC   p820
373 COVENTRY RD, OTTAWA, ON, K1K 2C5
(613) 722-0688   SIC 7374

M.A.R.C. MANAGEMENT & ENTERTAINMENT INC   p755
1135 STELLAR DR, NEWMARKET, ON, L3Y 7B8
      SIC 7374

MATRIX GEOSERVICES LTD   p53
808 4 AVE SW SUITE 600, CALGARY, AB, T2P 3E8
(403) 294-0707   SIC 7374

METALAB DESIGN LTD   p336
524 YATES ST SUITE 101, VICTORIA, BC, V8W 1K8
      SIC 7374

METRO RICHELIEU INC   p1083

1600B BOUL SAINT-MARTIN E BUREAU 300, COTE SAINT-LUC, QC, H7G 4S7
(450) 662-3300   SIC 7374

NEW HORIZON SYSTEM SOLUTIONS INC p946
700   UNIVERSITY   AVE   SUITE   200, TORONTO, ON, M5G 1X6
      SIC 7374

NEXONIA TECHNOLOGIES INC   p925
2 ST CLAIR AVE E SUITE 750, TORONTO, ON, M4T 2T5
(416) 480-0688   SIC 7374

ORION FOUNDRY (CANADA), ULC   p604
503 IMPERIAL RD N, GUELPH, ON, N1H 6T9
(519) 827-1999   SIC 7374

POSTMEDIA NETWORK INC   p261
7280 RIVER RD SUITE 110, RICHMOND, BC, V6X 1X5
      SIC 7374

PRODUCTIONS TMV INC   p1223
642 RUE DE COURCELLE BUREAU 209, MONTREAL, QC, H4C 3C5
(514) 228-8740   SIC 7374

Q4 INC   p983
A-469 KING ST W, TORONTO, ON, M5V 1K4
(416) 626-7829   SIC 7374

RESOLVE CORPORATION   p818
2405 ST LAURENT BLVD, OTTAWA, ON, K1G 5B4
      SIC 7374

SALUMATICS INC.   p717
3250 RIDGEWAY DR UNIT 10, MISSISSAUGA, ON, L5L 5Y6
(905) 362-2230   SIC 7374

SHOPIFY INC   p834
150 ELGIN ST 8TH FLOOR, OTTAWA, ON, K2P 1L4
(613) 241-2828   SIC 7374

SYMCOR INC   p379
195 FORT ST, WINNIPEG, MB, R3C 3V1
(204) 924-5819   SIC 7374

SYMCOR INC   p707
1 ROBERT SPECK PKY SUITE 400, MISSISSAUGA, ON, L4Z 4E7
(905) 273-1000   SIC 7374

VALTECH DIGITAL CANADA INC   p984
49 SPADINA AVE SUITE 205, TORONTO, ON, M5V 2J1
(416) 203-2997   SIC 7374

VIDEOTRON   SERVICE   INFORMATIQUE LTEE   p1186
300 AV VIGER E BUREAU 6, MONTREAL, QC, H2X 3W4
(514) 281-1232   SIC 7374

WATERFRONT EMPLOYERS OF B.C. p296
349 RAILWAY ST SUITE 400, VANCOUVER, BC, V6A 1A4
(604) 689-7184   SIC 7374

XEROX CANADA LTD   p690
3060 CARAVELLE DR, MISSISSAUGA, ON, L4V 1L7
(905) 672-4700   SIC 7374

SIC 7375 Information retrieval services

CBL DATA RECOVERY TECHNOLOGIES INC   p668
590 ALDEN RD SUITE 105, MARKHAM, ON, L3R 8N2
(905) 479-9938   SIC 7375

ERIS INFORMATION LIMITED PARTNERSHIP   p776
38 LESMILL RD SUITE 2, NORTH YORK, ON, M3B 2T5
(416) 510-5204   SIC 7375

GOOGLE CANADA CORPORATION p1205
1253 AV MCGILL COLLEGE BUREAU 150, MONTREAL, QC, H3B 2Y5
(514) 670-8700   SIC 7375

SIC 7376 Computer facilities management

CENTRE D'INFORMATION RX LTEE *p1392*
245 RUE JEAN-COUTU, VARENNES, QC, J3X 0E1
(450) 646-9760   *SIC 7376*

CONTENT MANAGEMENT CORPORATION *p904*
50 MINTHORN BLVD SUITE 800, THORN-HILL, ON, L3T 7X8
(905) 889-6555   *SIC 7376*

ESIT CANADA ENTERPRISE SERVICES CO *p823*
50 O'CONNOR ST SUITE 500, OTTAWA, ON, K1P 6L2
(613) 266-9442   *SIC 7376*

FUJITSU CONSEIL (CANADA) INC *p89*
10020 101A AVE NW SUITE 1500, EDMON-TON, AB, T5J 3G2
(780) 423-2070   *SIC 7376*

GROUPE TECHNOLOGIES DESJARDINS INC *p1230*
ETAGE CP 1 SUCC PL-DESJARDINS, MONTREAL, QC, H5B 1B2
(514) 281-7000   *SIC 7376*

HITACHI SYSTEMS SECURITY INC *p1059*
955 BOUL MICHELE-BOHEC BUREAU 244, BLAINVILLE, QC, J7C 5J6
(450) 430-8166   *SIC 7376*

INTOUCH INSIGHT LTD *p624*
400 MARCH RD, KANATA, ON, K2K 3H4
(613) 270-7916   *SIC 7376*

NUVO NETWORK MANAGEMENT INC *p625*
400 MARCH RD SUITE 190, KANATA, ON, K2K 3H4
SIC 7376

SOCIETE DE GESTION DU RESEAU IN-FORMATIQUE DES COMMISSIONS SCO-LAIRES *p1167*
5100 RUE SHERBROOKE E BUREAU 300, MONTREAL, QC, H1V 3R9
(514) 251-3700   *SIC 7376*

SIC 7377 Computer rental and leasing

CENTRAL TECHNOLOGY SERVICES COR-PORATION *p800*
1400 CORNWALL RD UNIT 5, OAKVILLE, ON, L6J 7W5
(905) 829-9480   *SIC 7377*

SIC 7378 Computer maintenance and repair

BIGTECH CLI INC *p677*
5990 14TH AVE, MARKHAM, ON, L3S 4M4
(905) 695-0100   *SIC 7378*

CORPORATION SERVICES MONERIS *p687*
3190 ORLANDO DR, MISSISSAUGA, ON, L4V 1R5
SIC 7378

CPU SERVICE D'ORDINATEUR INC *p1264*
2323 BOUL DU VERSANT-NORD BUREAU 100, QUEBEC, QC, G1N 4P4
(418) 681-1234   *SIC 7378*

DECISIONONE CORPORATION *p851*
44 EAST BEAVER CREEK RD UNIT 19, RICHMOND HILL, ON, L4B 1G8
(905) 882-1555   *SIC 7378*

DECISIONONE CORPORATION *p1329*
2505 RUE COHEN, SAINT-LAURENT, QC, H4R 2N5
(514) 338-1927   *SIC 7378*

MAGIC TECHNOLOGY *p1166*
6635 39E AV, MONTREAL, QC, H1T 2W9
(438) 388-6512   *SIC 7378*

NORMAND NADEAU T.V. INC *p1360*
500 BOUL VACHON N, SAINTE-MARIE, QC, G6E 1M1
(418) 387-3242   *SIC 7378*

SOROC TECHNOLOGY INC *p1085*
1800 BOUL LE CORBUSIER BUREAU 132,

COTE SAINT-LUC, QC, H7S 2K1
(450) 682-5029   *SIC 7378*

SIC 7379 Computer related services, nec

2KEYS CORPORATION *p828*
300-1600 CARLING AVE, OTTAWA, ON, K1Z 1G3
(613) 860-1620   *SIC 7379*

6362222 CANADA INC *p1395*
1 CARREFOUR ALEXANDER-GRAHAM-BELL EDIFICE 4, VERDUN, QC, H3E 3B3
(514) 937-1188   *SIC 7379*

9152-2458 QUEBEC INC *p1200*
1000 RUE DE LA GAUCHETIERE O BU-REAU 2400, MONTREAL, QC, H3B 4W5
(514) 209-2665   *SIC 7379*

A.S.G. INC *p595*
1010 POLYTEK ST SUITE 8, GLOUCES-TER, ON, K1J 9H8
(613) 749-8353   *SIC 7379*

ACCENTURE INC *p822*
45 O'CONNOR ST SUITE 600, OTTAWA, ON, K1P 1A4
(613) 750-5000   *SIC 7379*

ALERTPAY INCORPORATED *p1215*
1610 RUE NOTRE-DAME O SUITE 175, MONTREAL, QC, H3J 1M1
(514) 748-5774   *SIC 7379*

ALITHYA CANADA INC *p1201*
700 RUE DE LA GAUCHETIERE O BU-REAU 2400, MONTREAL, QC, H3B 5M2
(514) 285-5552   *SIC 7379*

ALITHYA CANADA INC *p1212*
1350 BOUL RENE-LEVESQUE O BUREAU 200, MONTREAL, QC, H3G 1T4
(514) 285-5552   *SIC 7379*

ARC BUSINESS SOLUTIONS INC *p87*
10088 102 AVE NW SUITE 2507, EDMON-TON, AB, T5J 2Z1
(780) 702-5022   *SIC 7379*

ATOS INC *p737*
6375 SHAWSON DR, MISSISSAUGA, ON, L5T 1S7
(905) 819-5761   *SIC 7379*

AUTOLOG, GESTION DE LA PRODUCTION INC *p1058*
1240 BOUL MICHELE-BOHEC, BLAINVILLE, QC, J7C 5S4
(450) 434-8389   *SIC 7379*

BEVERTEC CST INC *p692*
5025 ORBITOR DR BLDG 6 UNIT 400, MIS-SISSAUGA, ON, L4W 4Y5
(416) 695-7525   *SIC 7379*

BIALIK, DON & ASSOCIATES *p44*
255 5 AVE SW SUITE 3100, CALGARY, AB, T2P 3G6
(403) 515-6900   *SIC 7379*

BLUECAT NETWORKS, INC *p773*
4100 YONGE ST SUITE 300, NORTH YORK, ON, M2P 2B5
(416) 646-8400   *SIC 7379*

BSM TECHNOLOGIES INC *p582*
75 INTERNATIONAL BLVD SUITE 100, ETOBICOKE, ON, M9W 6L9
(866) 768-4771   *SIC 7379*

CDSL CANADA LIMITED *p720*
2480 MEADOWVALE BLVD SUITE 100, MISSISSAUGA, ON, L5N 8M6
(905) 858-7100   *SIC 7379*

CDSL CANADA LIMITED *p1417*
1900 ALBERT ST UNIT 700, REGINA, SK, S4P 4K8
(306) 761-4000   *SIC 7379*

CHRIS DANIELLE MICRO SOLUTIONS (CDMS) INC *p1194*
550 RUE SHERBROOKE O BUREAU 250, MONTREAL, QC, H3A 1B9
(514) 286-2367   *SIC 7379*

COFOMO INC *p1202*
1000 RUE DE LA GAUCHETIERE O UNITE 1500, MONTREAL, QC, H3B 4X5
(514) 866-0039   *SIC 7379*

COGNIZANT TECHNOLOGY SOLUTIONS CANADA, INC *p977*
241 SPADINA AVE SUITE 500, TORONTO, ON, M5T 2E2
(647) 827-0412   *SIC 7379*

COMPAGNIE DE TELEPHONE BELL DU CANADA OU BELL CANADA, LA *p851*
9133 LESLIE ST, RICHMOND HILL, ON, L4B 4N1
(905) 762-9137   *SIC 7379*

COMPUTER SCIENCES CANADA INC *p1213*
1360 BOUL RENE-LEVESQUE O BUREAU 300, MONTREAL, QC, H3G 2W7
SIC 7379

COMPUVISION SYSTEMS INC *p105*
15511 123 AVE NW SUITE 101, EDMON-TON, AB, T5V 0C3
(587) 525-7600   *SIC 7379*

CONSEILLERS EN GESTION ET INFORMA-TIQUE CGI INC *p88*
10303 JASPER AVE NW SUITE 800, ED-MONTON, AB, T5J 3N6
(780) 409-2200   *SIC 7379*

CONSEILLERS EN GESTION ET INFORMA-TIQUE CGI INC *p596*
1410 BLAIR PL, GLOUCESTER, ON, K1J 9B9
(613) 740-5900   *SIC 7379*

CONSEILLERS EN GESTION ET INFORMA-TIQUE CGI INC *p1078*
930 RUE JACQUES-CARTIER E 3RD FLOOR, CHICOUTIMI, QC, G7H 7K9
(418) 696-6789   *SIC 7379*

CONSEILLERS EN GESTION ET INFORMA-TIQUE CGI INC *p1258*
410 BOUL CHAREST E BUREAU 700, QUEBEC, QC, G1K 8G3
(418) 623-0101   *SIC 7379*

CONSEILLERS LOGISIL INC, LES *p1213*
1440 RUE SAINTE-CATHERINE O BU-REAU 400, MONTREAL, QC, H3G 1R8
SIC 7379

COUNTERPATH CORPORATION *p328*
505 BURRARD ST SUITE 300, VANCOU-VER, BC, V7X 1M3
(604) 320-3344   *SIC 7379*

CW PROFESSIONAL SERVICES (CANADA) ULC *p1187*
500 RUE SAINT-JACQUES, MONTREAL, QC, H2Y 1S1
(514) 281-1888   *SIC 7379*

E.S. WILLIAMS & ASSOCIATES INC *p134*
10514 67 AVE SUITE 306, GRANDE PRAIRIE, AB, T8W 0K8
(780) 539-4544   *SIC 7379*

ENGAGE PEOPLE INC *p669*
1380 RODICK RD SUITE 300, MARKHAM, ON, L3R 4G5
(416) 775-9180   *SIC 7379*

EQUISOFT INC *p1204*
1250 BOUL RENE-LEVESQUE O 33E ETAGE, MONTREAL, QC, H3B 4W8
(514) 989-3141   *SIC 7379*

ESI TECHNOLOGIES DE L'INFORMATION INC *p1195*
1550 RUE METCALFE BUREAU 1100, MONTREAL, QC, H3A 1X6
(514) 745-3311   *SIC 7379*

ESIT CANADA ENTERPRISE SERVICES CO *p49*
240 4 AVE SW SUITE 500, CALGARY, AB, T2P 4H4
(403) 508-4500   *SIC 7379*

FACILITE INFORMATIQUE CANADA INC *p1204*
5 PLACE VILLE-MARIE BUREAU 1045, MONTREAL, QC, H3B 2G2
(514) 284-5636   *SIC 7379*

FORRESTALL GROUP INC, THE *p670*
201 WHITEHALL DR UNIT 4, MARKHAM, ON, L3R 9Y3
SIC 7379

FORTINET TECHNOLOGIES (CANADA)

ULC *p185*
4190 STILL CREEK DR UNIT 400, BURN-ABY, BC, V5C 6C6
(604) 430-1297   *SIC 7379*

FUJITSU CONSEIL (CANADA) INC *p50*
606 4 ST SW SUITE 1500, CALGARY, AB, T2P 1T1
(403) 265-6001   *SIC 7379*

FUJITSU CONSEIL (CANADA) INC *p980*
200 FRONT ST W SUITE 2300, TORONTO, ON, M5V 3K2
(416) 363-8661   *SIC 7379*

FUJITSU CONSEIL (CANADA) INC *p1217*
7101 AV DU PARC BUREAU 102, MON-TREAL, QC, H3N 1X9
(514) 877-3301   *SIC 7379*

FUJITSU CONSEIL (CANADA) INC *p1272*
2960 BOUL LAURIER BUREAU 400, QUE-BEC, QC, G1V 4S1
SIC 7379

GESTION ACCEO INC *p1210*
75 RUE QUEEN BUREAU 4700, MON-TREAL, QC, H3C 2N6
(514) 288-7161   *SIC 7379*

GROUPE NEXIO INC *p1196*
2050 RUE DE BLEURY BUREAU 500, MONTREAL, QC, H3A 2J5
(514) 798-3707   *SIC 7379*

HGS CANADA INC *p838*
100 CRANDALL ST SUITE 100, PEM-BROKE, ON, K8A 6X8
(613) 633-4600   *SIC 7379*

HGS CANADA INC *p1040*
82 HILLSTROM AVE, CHARLOTTETOWN, PE, C1E 2C6
(902) 370-3200   *SIC 7379*

I O T A INFORMATION MANAGEMENT LTD *p834*
150 METCALFE ST, OTTAWA, ON, K2P 1P1
SIC 7379

IBM CANADA LIMITED *p655*
275 DUNDAS ST, LONDON, ON, N6B 3L1
SIC 7379

INFORMATION BALANCE INC *p774*
4141 YONGE ST SUITE 205, NORTH YORK, ON, M2P 2A8
(416) 962-5235   *SIC 7379*

INFOSYS LIMITED *p51*
888 3 ST SW SUITE 1000, CALGARY, AB, T2P 5C5
(403) 444-6896   *SIC 7379*

INFOSYS LIMITED *p772*
5140 YONGE ST SUITE 1400, NORTH YORK, ON, M2N 6L7
(416) 224-7400   *SIC 7379*

INFOTEK CONSULTING SERVICES INC *p953*
80 RICHMOND ST W SUITE 400, TORONTO, ON, M5H 2A4
(416) 365-0337   *SIC 7379*

INFUSION DEVELOPMENT INC *p981*
200 WELLINGTON ST W, TORONTO, ON, M5V 3C7
(416) 593-6595   *SIC 7379*

INTERACTIVE TRACKING SYSTEMS INC *p1428*
820 51ST ST E SUITE 150, SASKATOON, SK, S7K 0X8
(306) 665-5026   *SIC 7379*

INVENTURE SOLUTIONS INC *p295*
183 TERMINAL AVE, VANCOUVER, BC, V6A 4G2
(604) 877-7000   *SIC 7379*

ISECURITY INC *p765*
111 GORDON BAKER RD 6TH FL, NORTH YORK, ON, M2H 3R1
(416) 843-6018   *SIC 7379*

KEYRUS CANADA INC *p1189*
759 RUE DU SQUARE-VICTORIA UNIT 420, MONTREAL, QC, H2Y 2J7
(514) 989-2000   *SIC 7379*

KLICK INC *p929*
175 BLOOR ST E SUITE 301, TORONTO, ON, M4W 3R8

(416) 214-4977   *SIC 7379*
KONICA MINOLTA BUSINESS SOLUTIONS (CANADA) LTD *p504*
7965 GOREWAY DR UNIT 1, BRAMPTON, ON, L6T 5T5
(905) 494-1040   *SIC 7379*
LEVIO CONSEILS INC *p1264*
1995 RUE FRANK-CARREL BUREAU 219, QUEBEC, QC, G1N 4H9
(418) 914-3623   *SIC 7379*
LONG VIEW SYSTEMS CORPORATION *p53*
250 2 ST SW SUITE 2100, CALGARY, AB, T2P 0C1
(403) 515-6900   *SIC 7379*
NAVANTIS INC *p994*
21 RANDOLPH AVE SUITE 200, TORONTO, ON, M6P 4G4
(416) 532-5554   *SIC 7379*
NEXJ SYSTEMS INC *p774*
10 YORK MILLS RD SUITE 700, NORTH YORK, ON, M2P 2G4
(416) 222-5611   *SIC 7379*
NORTAK SOFTWARE LTD *p596*
1105 CADBORO RD, GLOUCESTER, ON, K1J 7T8
(613) 234-7212   *SIC 7379*
NTT DATA CANADA, INC *p454*
2000 BARRINGTON ST SUITE 300, HALIFAX, NS, B3J 3K1
(902) 422-6036   *SIC 7379*
OKA COMPUTER SYSTEMS LTD *p1198*
2075 RUE UNIVERSITY BUREAU 750, MONTREAL, QC, H3A 2L1
SIC 7379
ONEPOINT CANADA INC *p1207*
606 RUE CATHCART BUREAU 400, MONTREAL, QC, H3B 1K9
(514) 989-3116   *SIC 7379*
ONLINE SUPPORT *p838*
1200 PEMBROKE ST W SUITE 25, PEMBROKE, ON, K8A 7T1
(613) 633-4200   *SIC 7379*
PECB GROUP INC *p1346*
6683 RUE JEAN-TALON E BUREAU 336, SAINT-LEONARD, QC, H1S 0A5
(514) 814-2548   *SIC 7379*
PIVOT FURNITURE TECHNOLOGIES INC *p1429*
142 ENGLISH CRES UNIT 20, SASKATOON, SK, S7K 8A5
(306) 220-4557   *SIC 7379*
PROFESSIONAL COMPUTER CONSULTANTS GROUP LTD *p923*
2323 YONGE ST SUITE 400, TORONTO, ON, M4P 2C9
(416) 483-0766   *SIC 7379*
SAPIENT CANADA INC *p983*
134 PETER ST SUITE 1200, TORONTO, ON, M5V 2H2
(416) 645-1500   *SIC 7379*
SCALAR DECISIONS INC *p940*
1 TORONTO ST 3RD FL, TORONTO, ON, M5C 2V6
(416) 202-0020   *SIC 7379*
SERVICES CONSEILS SYSTEMATIX INC, LES *p1273*
2600 BOUL LAURIER BUREAU 128, QUEBEC, QC, G1V 4Y4
(418) 681-0151   *SIC 7379*
SIERRA SYSTEMS GROUP INC *p91*
10104 103 AVE NW UNIT 1300, EDMONTON, AB, T5J 0H8
(780) 424-0852   *SIC 7379*
SIERRA SYSTEMS GROUP INC *p316*
1177 HASTINGS ST W SUITE 2500, VANCOUVER, BC, V6E 2K3
(604) 688-1371   *SIC 7379*
SIERRA SYSTEMS GROUP INC *p337*
737 COURTNEY ST, VICTORIA, BC, V8W 1C3
(250) 385-1535   *SIC 7379*
SIERRA SYSTEMS GROUP INC *p824*
220 LAURIER AVE W SUITE 800, OTTAWA, ON, K1P 5Z9

(613) 236-7888   *SIC 7379*
SIERRA SYSTEMS GROUP INC *p957*
150 YORK ST SUITE 1910, TORONTO, ON, M5H 3S5
(416) 777-1212   *SIC 7379*
SOLUTIONS ABILIS INC *p1199*
1010 RUE SHERBROOKE O BUREAU 1900, MONTREAL, QC, H3A 2R7
(514) 844-4888   *SIC 7379*
SOLUTIONS BEYOND TECHNOLOGIES INC *p1212*
111 BOUL ROBERT-BOURASSA BUREAU 3600, MONTREAL, QC, H3C 2M1
(514) 227-7323   *SIC 7379*
SOLUTIONS PROCESSIA INC *p1087*
3131 BOUL SAINT-MARTIN O BUREAU 220, COTE SAINT-LUC, QC, H7T 2Z5
(450) 786-0400   *SIC 7379*
SOLUTIONS VICTRIX INC, LES *p1199*
630 RUE SHERBROOKE O BUREAU 1100, MONTREAL, QC, H3A 1E4
(514) 879-1919   *SIC 7379*
SOLVERA SOLUTIONS *p1419*
1853 HAMILTON ST SUITE 201, REGINA, SK, S4P 2C1
(306) 757-3510   *SIC 7379*
SYSTEMATIX TECHNOLOGIES DE L'INFORMATION INC *p1208*
1 PLACE VILLE-MARIE UNITE 1601, MONTREAL, QC, H3B 3Y2
(514) 393-1313   *SIC 7379*
SYSTEMATIX TECHNOLOGY CONSULTANTS INC *p707*
5975 WHITTLE RD SUITE 120, MISSISSAUGA, ON, L4Z 3N1
(416) 650-9669   *SIC 7379*
T4G LIMITED *p934*
340 KING ST E SUITE 300, TORONTO, ON, M5A 1K8
(416) 462-4200   *SIC 7379*
TATA CONSULTANCY SERVICES CANADA INC *p947*
400 UNIVERSITY AVE 25TH FL, TORONTO, ON, M5G 1S5
(647) 790-7200   *SIC 7379*
THOUGHTCORP SYSTEMS INC *p773*
4950 YONGE ST SUITE 1700, NORTH YORK, ON, M2N 6K1
(416) 591-4004   *SIC 7379*
TOOLBOX SOLUTIONS INC *p507*
126 DEVON RD SUITE 2, BRAMPTON, ON, L6T 5B3
(905) 458-9262   *SIC 7379*
WILLIAMS, E. S. & ASSOCIATES INC *p134*
10514 67 AVE SUITE 306, GRANDE PRAIRIE, AB, T8W 0K8
(780) 539-4544   *SIC 7379*

SIC 7381 Detective and armored car services

1175469 ONTARIO LTD *p788*
1120 CALEDONIA RD UNIT 11, NORTH YORK, ON, M6A 2W5
(416) 256-3199   *SIC 7381*
2138894 ONTARIO INC *p873*
140 SHORTING RD, SCARBOROUGH, ON, M1S 3S6
(416) 240-0911   *SIC 7381*
2320610 ONTARIO INC *p511*
7900 HURONTARIO ST SUITE 303, BRAMPTON, ON, L6Y 0P6
(905) 782-4700   *SIC 7381*
2521153 ONTARIO INC *p903*
300 JOHN ST SUITE 310, THORNHILL, ON, L3T 5W4
(416) 222-7144   *SIC 7381*
295823 ONTARIO INC *p885*
31 RAYMOND ST, ST CATHARINES, ON, L2R 2T3
(905) 685-4279   *SIC 7381*
2969-9899 QUEBEC INC *p1240*
3905 BOUL INDUSTRIEL, MONTREAL-NORD, QC, H1H 2Z2

(514) 744-1010   *SIC 7381*
3 SIXTY RISK SOLUTIONS LTD *p476*
83 LITTLE BRIDGE ST SUITE 12, ALMONTE, ON, K0A 1A0
(866) 360-3360   *SIC 7381*
5126614 MANITOBA INC *p380*
857 SARGENT AVE UNIT 2, WINNIPEG, MB, R3E 0C5
(204) 772-4135   *SIC 7381*
9270-6258 QUEBEC INC *p1171*
5446 RUE CHAPLEAU BUREAU 201, MONTREAL, QC, H2G 2E4
(514) 444-9999   *SIC 7381*
9310-8405 QUEBEC INC *p1186*
239 RUE DU SAINT-SACREMENT BUREAU 304, MONTREAL, QC, H2Y 1W9
(514) 251-5050   *SIC 7381*
A.S.A.P. SECURED INC *p1200*
1255 RUE PEEL BUREAU 1101, MONTREAL, QC, H3B 2T9
(514) 868-0202   *SIC 7381*
A.S.P. INCORPORATED *p529*
460 BRANT ST SUITE 212, BURLINGTON, ON, L7R 4B6
(905) 333-4242   *SIC 7381*
ABBOTSFORD SECURITY SERVICES *p176*
2669 LANGDON ST SUITE 201, ABBOTSFORD, BC, V2T 3L3
(604) 870-4731   *SIC 7381*
AFIMAC CANADA INC *p682*
8160 PARKHILL DR, MILTON, ON, L9T 5V7
(905) 693-0746   *SIC 7381*
AGENCE DE SECURITE D'INVESTIGATION EXPO INC *p1173*
2335 RUE ONTARIO E, MONTREAL, QC, H2K 1W2
(514) 523-5333   *SIC 7381*
AGENCES DE SECURITE MIRADO 2002 INC *p1289*
121 8E RUE, ROUYN-NORANDA, QC, J9X 2A5
(819) 797-5184   *SIC 7381*
ALL PEACE PROTECTION LTD *p131*
11117 100 ST SUITE 202, GRANDE PRAIRIE, AB, T8V 2N2
(780) 538-1166   *SIC 7381*
APEX INVESTIGATION & SECURITY INC *p907*
391 OLIVER RD, THUNDER BAY, ON, P7B 2G2
(807) 344-8491   *SIC 7381*
ATLANTIC PRIVATE PROTECTION SERVICE *p445*
7 MELLOR AVE UNIT 12, DARTMOUTH, NS, B3B 0E8
(902) 468-9002   *SIC 7381*
AUTHENTIC CONCIERGE AND SECURITY SERVICES INC *p994*
2333 DUNDAS ST W SUITE 206, TORONTO, ON, M6R 3A6
(416) 777-1812   *SIC 7381*
AVION SERVICES CORP *p383*
2000 WELLINGTON AVE SUITE 503, WINNIPEG, MB, R3H 1C1
(204) 784-5800   *SIC 7381*
BARBER-COLLINS SECURITY SERVICES LTD *p1007*
245 LABRADOR DR UNIT 1, WATERLOO, ON, N2K 4M8
(519) 745-1111   *SIC 7381*
BEAUMARK PROTECTION SERVICES *p76*
20 COUNTRY HILLS MEWS NW, CALGARY, AB, T3K 4S4
(403) 803-1567   *SIC 7381*
BERETTA PROTECTIVE SERVICES INTERNATIONAL INC *p112*
9404 58 AVE NW, EDMONTON, AB, T6E 0B6
(780) 481-6348   *SIC 7381*
BRANDON, CITY OF *p346*
1020 VICTORIA AVE, BRANDON, MB, R7A 1A9
(204) 729-2345   *SIC 7381*
BRINK'S CANADA LIMITED *p10*

640 28 ST NE UNIT 8, CALGARY, AB, T2A 6R3
(403) 272-2259   *SIC 7381*
BRINK'S CANADA LIMITED *p93*
14680 134 AVE NW, EDMONTON, AB, T5L 4T4
(780) 453-5057   *SIC 7381*
BRINK'S CANADA LIMITED *p288*
247 1ST AVE E, VANCOUVER, BC, V5T 1A7
(604) 875-6221   *SIC 7381*
BRINK'S CANADA LIMITED *p445*
19 ILSLEY AVE, DARTMOUTH, NS, B3B 1L5
(902) 468-7124   *SIC 7381*
BRINK'S CANADA LIMITED *p571*
95 BROWNS LINE, ETOBICOKE, ON, M8W 3S2
(416) 461-0261   *SIC 7381*
BRINK'S CANADA LIMITED *p610*
75 LANSDOWNE AVE, HAMILTON, ON, L8L 8A3
(905) 549-5997   *SIC 7381*
BRINK'S CANADA LIMITED *p648*
1495 SPANNER ST, LONDON, ON, N5V 1Z1
(519) 659-3457   *SIC 7381*
BRINK'S CANADA LIMITED *p720*
2233 ARGENTIA RD SUITE 400, MISSISSAUGA, ON, L5N 2X7
(905) 306-9600   *SIC 7381*
BRINK'S CANADA LIMITED *p815*
2755 LANCASTER RD, OTTAWA, ON, K1B 4V8
(613) 521-8650   *SIC 7381*
BRITISH COLUMBIA CORPS OF COMMISSIONAIRES *p303*
595 HOWE ST UNIT 801, VANCOUVER, BC, V6C 2T5
(604) 646-3330   *SIC 7381*
C.R.A. COLLATERAL RECOVERY & ADMINISTRATION INC *p27*
1289 HIGHFIELD CRES SE UNIT 109, CALGARY, AB, T2G 5M2
(403) 240-3450   *SIC 7381*
CANADA SECURITY SERVICES LTD *p200*
91 GOLDEN DR SUITE 27, COQUITLAM, BC, V3K 6R2
SIC 7381
CANADIAN CORPS OF COMMISSIONAIRES (MANITOBA AND NORTHWESTERN ONTARIO DIVISION) *p381*
290 BURNELL ST, WINNIPEG, MB, R3G 2A7
(204) 942-5993   *SIC 7381*
CANADIAN CORPS OF COMMISSIONAIRES (NEWFOUNDLAND) *p429*
207A KENMOUNT RD, ST. JOHN'S, NL, A1B 3P9
(709) 754-0757   *SIC 7381*
CANADIAN CORPS OF COMMISSIONAIRES (NORTHERN ALBERTA) *p97*
10633 124 ST NW SUITE 101, EDMONTON, AB, T5N 1S5
(780) 451-1974   *SIC 7381*
CANADIAN CORPS OF COMMISSIONAIRES (OTTAWA DIVISION) *p748*
24 COLONNADE RD N, NEPEAN, ON, K2E 7J6
(613) 228-0715   *SIC 7381*
CANADIAN CORPS OF COMMISSIONAIRES (SOUTHERN ALBERTA) *p21*
1107 53 AVE NE, CALGARY, AB, T2E 6X9
(403) 244-4664   *SIC 7381*
CANADIAN CORPS OF COMMISSIONAIRES NATIONAL OFFICE, THE *p153*
4807 50 AVE SUITE 107, RED DEER, AB, T4N 4A5
(403) 314-4142   *SIC 7381*
CANADIAN CORPS OF COMMISSIONAIRES NATIONAL OFFICE, THE *p234*
711 NORTHUMBERLAND AVE, NANAIMO, BC, V9S 5C5
(250) 754-1042   *SIC 7381*

CANADIAN CORPS OF COMMISSION- AIRES NATIONAL OFFICE, THE p303
595 HOWE ST SUITE 801, VANCOUVER, BC, V6C 2T5
(604) 646-3330   SIC 7381

CANADIAN CORPS OF COMMISSION- AIRES NATIONAL OFFICE, THE p337
928 CLOVERDALE AVE, VICTORIA, BC, V8X 2T3
(250) 727-7755   SIC 7381

CANADIAN CORPS OF COMMISSION- AIRES NATIONAL OFFICE, THE p409
41 MECCA DR, MONCTON, NB, E1G 1B7
(506) 384-2020   SIC 7381

CANADIAN CORPS OF COMMISSION- AIRES NATIONAL OFFICE, THE p561
14 THIRD ST E, CORNWALL, ON, K6H 2C7
(613) 932-2594   SIC 7381

CANADIAN CORPS OF COMMISSION- AIRES NATIONAL OFFICE, THE p748
24 COLONNADE RD N, NEPEAN, ON, K2E 7J6
SIC 7381

CANADIAN CORPS OF COMMISSION- AIRES NATIONAL OFFICE, THE p1420
122 ALBERT ST, REGINA, SK, S4R 2N2
(306) 757-0998   SIC 7381

CANADIAN CORPS OF COMMISSION- AIRES NATIONAL OFFICE, THE p1426
493 2ND AVE N, SASKATOON, SK, S7K 2C1
(306) 244-6588   SIC 7381

CANADIAN CORRECTIONAL MANAGE- MENT INC p405
4 AIRPORT DR, MIRAMICHI, NB, E1N 3W4
(506) 624-2160   SIC 7381

CANCOM SECURITY INC p782
1183 FINCH AVE W UNIT 205, NORTH YORK, ON, M3J 2G2
(416) 763-0000   SIC 7381

CANNON SECURITY AND PATROL SER- VICES p812
23 SIMCOE ST S FL 2, OSHAWA, ON, L1H 4G1
(416) 742-9994   SIC 7381

CANTEC SECURITY SERVICES INC p885
140 WELLAND AVE UNIT 5, ST CATHARINES, ON, L2R 2N6
(905) 687-9500   SIC 7381

CAPITAL SECURITY & INVESTIGATIONS p562
504 PITT ST, CORNWALL, ON, K6J 3R5
(613) 937-4111   SIC 7381

CENTINEL SECURITY p8
3132 26 ST NE UNIT 335, CALGARY, AB, T1Y 6Z1
(403) 237-8485   SIC 7381

CENTRAL VICTORIA SECURITY LTD p334
612 GARBALLY RD, VICTORIA, BC, V8T 2K2
SIC 7381

CENTRALE ASHTON INC p1364
104B RUE TURGEON, SAINTE-THERESE, QC, J7E 3H9
(450) 435-6468   SIC 7381

CITIGUARD SECURITY SERVICES INC p870
1560 BRIMLEY RD SUITE 201, SCARBOR- OUGH, ON, M1P 3G9
(416) 431-6888   SIC 7381

COMMISSIONAIRES (GREAT LAKES) p657
1112 DEARNESS DR UNIT 14, LONDON, ON, N6E 1N9
(519) 433-6763   SIC 7381

COMMISSIONAIRES (GREAT LAKES) p796
2947 PORTLAND DR, OAKVILLE, ON, L6H 5S4
(416) 364-4496   SIC 7381

CONCORD SECURITY CORPORATION p190
4710 KINGSWAY SUITE 925, BURNABY, BC, V5H 4M2
(604) 689-4005   SIC 7381

CONDOR SECURITY p781
4610 DUFFERIN ST UNIT 1B, NORTH

YORK, ON, M3H 5S4
(416) 410-4035   SIC 7381

CONSOLIDATED MONITORING LTD p91
9707 110 ST NW SUITE 404, EDMONTON, AB, T5K 2L9
(780) 488-3777   SIC 7381

CONSULTANTS S.P.I. INC p1300
136C RUE SAINT-LAURENT, SAINT- EUSTACHE, QC, J7P 5G1
(514) 288-8868   SIC 7381

CORE SECURITY GROUP INC p274
13456 108 AVE, SURREY, BC, V3T 2K1
(604) 583-2673   SIC 7381

CORPORATE INVESTIGATIVE SERVICES LTD p650
544 EGERTON ST, LONDON, ON, N5W 3Z8
(519) 652-2163   SIC 7381

CORPORATION DE SECURITE GARDA CANADA p88
10250 101 ST NW SUITE 1010, EDMON- TON, AB, T5J 3P4
(780) 425-5000   SIC 7381

CORPORATION DE SECURITE GARDA WORLD p1210
1390 RUE BARRE, MONTREAL, QC, H3C 5X9
(514) 281-2811   SIC 7381

CORPORATION DE SECURITE GARDA WORLD p1426
316 2ND AVE N, SASKATOON, SK, S7K 2B9
(306) 242-3330   SIC 7381

CYPRESS SECURITY (2013) INC p276
7028 120 ST SUITE 203, SURREY, BC, V3W 3M8
(778) 564-4088   SIC 7381

DETECTEX SECURITY SERVICES CORP p181
8557 GOVERNMENT ST SUITE 102, BURNABY, BC, V3N 4S9
SIC 7381

DIAMOND SECURITY p660
377 GRAND VIEW AVE, LONDON, ON, N6K 2T1
(519) 471-8095   SIC 7381

DYNAMIC SECURITY AGENCY p1126
2366 RUE VICTORIA, LACHINE, QC, H8S 1Z3
(514) 898-3598   SIC 7381

EAGLE SURVEILLANCE GROUP LTD p657
1069 WELLINGTON RD SUITE 229, LON- DON, ON, N6E 2H6
(519) 680-3269   SIC 7381

EMPIRE INVESTIGATIONS AND PROTEC- TION SERVICES INC p844
940 BROCK RD UNIT 4, PICKERING, ON, L1W 2A1
(905) 426-3909   SIC 7381

FIRST ISLAND ARMOURED TRANSPORT (1998) LTD p334
612 GARBALLY RD, VICTORIA, BC, V8T 2K2
(250) 920-7114   SIC 7381

FIRST STRIKE SECURITY & INVESTIGA- TION LTD p466
2145 KINGS RD, SYDNEY, NS, B1L 1C2
(902) 539-9991   SIC 7381

G4S CASH SOLUTIONS (CANADA) LTD p23
5040 SKYLINE WAY NE, CALGARY, AB, T2E 6V1
(403) 974-8350   SIC 7381

G4S CASH SOLUTIONS (CANADA) LTD p286
2743 SKEENA ST SUITE 200, VANCOU- VER, BC, V5M 4T1
SIC 7381

G4S CASH SOLUTIONS (CANADA) LTD p286
2743 SKEENA ST, VANCOUVER, BC, V5M 4T1
SIC 7381

G4S CASH SOLUTIONS (CANADA) LTD p382

994 WALL ST, WINNIPEG, MB, R3G 2V3
(204) 774-6883   SIC 7381

G4S CASH SOLUTIONS (CANADA) LTD p639
108 AHRENS ST W, KITCHENER, ON, N2H 4C3
SIC 7381

G4S CASH SOLUTIONS (CANADA) LTD p779
150 FERRAND DR SUITE 600, NORTH YORK, ON, M3C 3E5
(416) 645-5555   SIC 7381

G4S SECURE SOLUTIONS (CANADA) LTD p114
9618 42 AVE NW SUITE 100, EDMONTON, AB, T6E 5Y4
(780) 423-4444   SIC 7381

G4S SECURE SOLUTIONS (CANADA) LTD p145
525 4 ST SE, MEDICINE HAT, AB, T1A 0K7
(403) 526-2001   SIC 7381

G4S SECURE SOLUTIONS (CANADA) LTD p384
530 CENTURY ST SUITE 231, WINNIPEG, MB, R3H 0Y4
(204) 774-0005   SIC 7381

G4S SECURE SOLUTIONS (CANADA) LTD p578
703 EVANS AVE UNIT 103, ETOBICOKE, ON, M9C 5E9
(416) 620-0762   SIC 7381

G4S SECURE SOLUTIONS (CANADA) LTD p632
2437 PRINCESS ST SUITE 204, KINGSTON, ON, K7M 3G1
(613) 389-1744   SIC 7381

G4S SECURE SOLUTIONS (CANADA) LTD p638
1448 KING ST E, KITCHENER, ON, N2G 2N7
SIC 7381

G4S SECURE SOLUTIONS (CANADA) LTD p653
383 RICHMOND ST SUITE 503, LONDON, ON, N6A 3C4
(647) 678-5111   SIC 7381

G4S SECURE SOLUTIONS (CANADA) LTD p767
2 LANSING SQ SUITE 204, NORTH YORK, ON, M2J 4P8
(416) 490-8329   SIC 7381

G4S SECURE SOLUTIONS (CANADA) LTD p812
214 KING ST E, OSHAWA, ON, L1H 1C7
(905) 579-8020   SIC 7381

G4S SECURE SOLUTIONS (CANADA) LTD p901
1351 D KELLY LAKE RD UNIT 9, SUD- BURY, ON, P3E 5P5
(705) 524-1519   SIC 7381

G4S SECURE SOLUTIONS (CANADA) LTD p913
211 CRAIG ST, TIMMINS, ON, P4N 4A2
(705) 268-7040   SIC 7381

G4S SECURE SOLUTIONS (CANADA) LTD p1019
3372 MANNHEIM WAY, WINDSOR, ON, N8W 5J9
(519) 255-1441   SIC 7381

GARDWELL SECURITY AGENCY INC p787
168 OAKDALE RD SUITE 6B, NORTH YORK, ON, M3N 2S5
(416) 746-6007   SIC 7381

GEMSTAR SECURITY SERVICE LTD p1031
4000 STEELES AVE W UNIT 29, WOOD- BRIDGE, ON, L4L 4V9
(905) 850-8517   SIC 7381

GFP LES HOTES DE MONTREAL INC p1182
6983 RUE DE LA ROCHE, MONTREAL, QC, H2S 2E6
(514) 274-6837   SIC 7381

GOVERNMENT OF ONTARIO p695
5090 COMMERCE BLVD UNIT 100, MIS- SISSAUGA, ON, L4W 5M4

(416) 622-0748   SIC 7381

GROUPE CAMBLI INC p1318
555 RUE SAINT-LOUIS, SAINT-JEAN-SUR- RICHELIEU, QC, J3B 8X7
(450) 358-4920   SIC 7381

GROUPE DE SECURITE GARDA INC, LE p35
8989 MACLEOD TRAIL SW SUITE 118, CALGARY, AB, T2H 0M2
(403) 517-5899   SIC 7381

GROUPE DE SECURITE GARDA INC, LE p1104
25 RUE DE VILLEBOIS, GATINEAU, QC, J8T 8J7
(819) 770-9438   SIC 7381

GROUPE DE SECURITE GARDA INC, LE p1119
1160 RUE VALETS, L'ANCIENNE- LORETTE, QC, G2E 5Y9
(418) 627-0088   SIC 7381

GROUPE DE SECURITE GARDA INC, LE p1210
1390 RUE BARRE, MONTREAL, QC, H3C 5X9
(514) 281-2811   SIC 7381

GROUPE DE SECURITE GARDA INC, LE p1367
456 AV ARNAUD BUREAU 218, SEPT-ILES, QC, G4R 3B1
(418) 968-8006   SIC 7381

GROUPE DE SECURITE GARDA INC, LE p1418
2505 11TH AVE SUITE 302, REGINA, SK, S4P 0K6
(306) 352-2099   SIC 7381

GROUPE S S E p1164
5948 RUE HOCHELAGA, MONTREAL, QC, H1N 1X1
(514) 254-9492   SIC 7381

GROUPE SOUCY INC p1385
1060 BOUL THIBEAU, TROIS-RIVIERES, QC, G8T 7B2
(819) 376-3111   SIC 7381

GSS SECURITY LTD p610
1219 MAIN ST E, HAMILTON, ON, L8K 1A5
(905) 547-5552   SIC 7381

GTA SECURITY GUARD SERVICES INC p553
150 SPINNAKER WAY UNIT 12, CON- CORD, ON, L4K 4M1
(905) 760-0838   SIC 7381

HALO SECURITY INC p920
1574 QUEEN ST E SUITE 1, TORONTO, ON, M4L 1G1
(416) 360-1902   SIC 7381

HIRE RITE PERSONNEL LTD p835
366 9TH ST E, OWEN SOUND, ON, N4K 1P1
(519) 376-6662   SIC 7381

I-CORP SECURITY SERVICES LTD p298
1040 HAMILTON ST SUITE 303, VANCOU- VER, BC, V6B 2R9
(604) 687-8645   SIC 7381

IMPACT SECURITY GROUP INC p374
456 MAIN ST 2ND FL, WINNIPEG, MB, R3B 1B6
(866) 385-7037   SIC 7381

INDEPENDENT ARMOURED TRANSPORT ATLANTIC INC p457
287 LACEWOOD DR UNIT 103, HALIFAX, NS, B3M 3Y7
(902) 450-1396   SIC 7381

INDEPENDENT SECURITY SERVICES AT- LANTIC (ISS) INC p457
287 LACEWOOD DR UNIT 103, HALIFAX, NS, B3M 3Y7
(902) 450-1396   SIC 7381

INDUSTRIAL SECURITY LIMITED p413
635 BAYSIDE DR, SAINT JOHN, NB, E2J 1B4
(506) 648-3060   SIC 7381

INNOVATIVE SECURITY MANAGEMENT (1998) INC p654
148 YORK ST SUITE 309, LONDON, ON,

N6A 1A9
(519) 858-4100　*SIC 7381*
INTELLIGARDE INTERNATIONAL INC p869
3090 KINGSTON RD SUITE 400, SCARBOROUGH, ON, M1M 1P2
(416) 760-0000　*SIC 7381*
INVESTIGATIONS RK INC p1224
2100 AV DE L'EGLISE, MONTREAL, QC, H4E 1H4
(514) 761-7121　*SIC 7381*
INVESTIGATIVE RESEARCH GROUP INC p487
49 TRUMAN RD SUITE 102, BARRIE, ON, L4N 8Y7
(705) 739-4800　*SIC 7381*
INVESTIGATORS GROUP INC, THE p874
2061 MCCOWAN RD SUITE 2, SCARBOROUGH, ON, M1S 3Y6
(416) 955-9450　*SIC 7381*
ISRA-GUARD (I.G.S.) SECURITE INC p1220
5165 CH QUEEN-MARY BUREAU 512, MONTREAL, QC, H3W 1X7
(514) 489-6336　*SIC 7381*
JARDINE SECURITY LTD p405
107 TARDY AVE, MIRAMICHI, NB, E1V 3Y8
(506) 622-2787　*SIC 7381*
KNIGHTS ON GUARD SECURITY SURVEILLANCE SYSTEMS CORPORATION p845
1048 TOY AVE SUITE 101, PICKERING, ON, L1W 3P1
(905) 427-7863　*SIC 7381*
LABRASH SECURITY SERVICES LTD p922
55 EGLINTON AVE E SUITE 403, TORONTO, ON, M4P 1G8
(416) 487-4864　*SIC 7381*
LIVE TO SECURE PROTECTIVE SERVICES INC p791
15 INGRAM DR UNITS 201-702, NORTH YORK, ON, M6M 2L7
(647) 560-4321　*SIC 7381*
LK PROTECTION INC p703
1590 DUNDAS ST E SUITE 220, MISSISSAUGA, ON, L4X 2Z2
(905) 566-7008　*SIC 7381*
LLEWELLYN SECURITY INCORPORATED p746
107 QUEEN ST, MORRISTON, ON, N0B 2C0
SIC 7381
MAGNUM PROTECTIVE SERVICES LIMITED p990
1043 BLOOR ST W, TORONTO, ON, M6H 1M4
(416) 591-1566　*SIC 7381*
MAXAMA PROTECTION INC p841
234 ROMAINE ST, PETERBOROUGH, ON, K9J 2C5
(705) 745-7500　*SIC 7381*
NEXUS PROTECTIVE SERVICES LIMITED p943
56 THE ESPLANADE SUITE 510, TORONTO, ON, M5E 1A7
(416) 815-7575　*SIC 7381*
NIGHT HAWK SECURITY LTD p331
9095 TRONSON RD, VERNON, BC, V1H 1E2
SIC 7381
NIPISSING TRANSITION HOUSE p763
547 JOHN ST, NORTH BAY, ON, P1B 2M9
(705) 476-2429　*SIC 7381*
NORTH STAR PATROL (1996) LTD p277
12981 80 AVE, SURREY, BC, V3W 3B1
SIC 7381
NORTHEASTERN INVESTIGATIONS INCORPORATED p447
202 BROWNLOW AVE SUITE 1, DARTMOUTH, NS, B3B 1T5
(902) 435-1336　*SIC 7381*
NORTHERN FORCE SECURITY p556
1750 STEELES AVE W, CONCORD, ON, L4K 2L7
(647) 982-1385　*SIC 7381*
NORTHWEST PROTECTION SERVICES LTD p989

1951 EGLINTON AVE W UNIT 201, TORONTO, ON, M6E 2J7
(416) 787-1448　*SIC 7381*
ORION SECURITY INCORPORATED p508
284 QUEEN ST E UNIT 229, BRAMPTON, ON, L6V 1C2
(905) 840-0400　*SIC 7381*
PALADIN TECHNOLOGIES INC p36
6455 MACLEOD TRAIL SW UNIT 701, CALGARY, AB, T2H 0K9
(403) 508-1888　*SIC 7381*
PALADIN TECHNOLOGIES INC p128
604 SIGNAL RD, FORT MCMURRAY, AB, T9H 4Z4
(780) 743-1422　*SIC 7381*
PALADIN TECHNOLOGIES INC p189
3001 WAYBURNE DR SUITE 201, BURNABY, BC, V5G 4W3
(604) 677-8700　*SIC 7381*
PATROLMAN SECURITY SERVICES INC p587
680 REXDALE BLVD SUITE 205, ETOBICOKE, ON, M9W 0B5
(416) 748-3202　*SIC 7381*
PENINSULA SECURITY SERVICES LTD p1012
50 DIVISION ST, WELLAND, ON, L3B 3Z6
(905) 732-2337　*SIC 7381*
POLO SECURITY SERVICES LTD p291
7251 FRASER ST, VANCOUVER, BC, V5X 3V8
(604) 321-4046　*SIC 7381*
PREMIER SECURITY INC p320
1055 BROADWAY W SUITE 603, VANCOUVER, BC, V6H 1E2
(604) 739-1893　*SIC 7381*
PROBE INVESTIGATION AND SECURITY SERVICES LTD p781
3995 BATHURST ST SUITE 301, NORTH YORK, ON, M3H 5V3
(416) 636-7000　*SIC 7381*
PRODUCTIVE SECURITY INC p990
940 LANSDOWNE AVE, TORONTO, ON, M6H 3Z4
(416) 535-9341　*SIC 7381*
PROTEC INVESTIGATION AND SECURITY INC p1222
3333 BOUL CAVENDISH BUREAU 200, MONTREAL, QC, H4B 2M5
(514) 485-3255　*SIC 7381*
PROTECTIVE TROOPS RESPONSE FORCE p879
15 WEAVER DR, SCARBOROUGH, ON, M1X 1V2
(905) 233-4873　*SIC 7381*
PROVIDENT SECURITY CORP p322
2309 41ST AVE W SUITE 400, VANCOUVER, BC, V6M 2A3
(604) 664-1087　*SIC 7381*
RBG SECURITY INC p729
6500 SILVER DART DR SUITE 228A, MISSISSAUGA, ON, L5P 1A2
(647) 729-2360　*SIC 7381*
REGAL SECURITY INC p790
1244 CALEDONIA RD, NORTH YORK, ON, M6A 2X5
(416) 633-8558　*SIC 7381*
REGIONAL SECURITY SERVICES LTD p249
190 VICTORIA ST, PRINCE GEORGE, BC, V2L 2J2
(250) 562-1215　*SIC 7381*
SECURED SECURITY GROUP (INTERNATIONAL) LIMITED p309
3555 BURRARD ST SUITE 1400, VANCOUVER, BC, V6C 2G8
(604) 385-1555　*SIC 7381*
SECURIGUARD SERVICES LIMITED p234
2520 BOWEN RD SUITE 205, NANAIMO, BC, V9T 3L3
(250) 756-4452　*SIC 7381*
SECURIGUARD SERVICES LIMITED p318
1445 GEORGIA ST W, VANCOUVER, BC, V6G 2T3
(604) 685-6011　*SIC 7381*

SECURITAS CANADA LIMITED p191
5172 KINGSWAY SUITE 270, BURNABY, BC, V5H 2E8
(604) 454-3600　*SIC 7381*
SECURITAS CANADA LIMITED p485
400 BAYFIELD ST SUITE 215, BARRIE, ON, L4M 5A1
(705) 728-7777　*SIC 7381*
SECURITAS CANADA LIMITED p534
1425 BISHOP ST N SUITE 14, CAMBRIDGE, ON, N1R 6J9
(519) 620-9864　*SIC 7381*
SECURITAS CANADA LIMITED p707
420 BRITANNIA RD E SUITE 100, MISSISSAUGA, ON, L4Z 3L5
(905) 272-0330　*SIC 7381*
SECURITAS CANADA LIMITED p768
400-235 YORKLAND BLVD, NORTH YORK, ON, M2J 4Y8
(416) 774-2500　*SIC 7381*
SECURITAS CANADA LIMITED p840
349A GEORGE ST N SUITE 206, PETERBOROUGH, ON, K9H 3P9
(705) 743-8026　*SIC 7381*
SECURITAS CANADA LIMITED p899
767 BARRYDOWNE RD SUITE 301, SUDBURY, ON, P3A 3T6
(705) 675-3654　*SIC 7381*
SECURITAS CANADA LIMITED p1018
11210 TECUMSEH RD E, WINDSOR, ON, N8R 1A8
(519) 979-1317　*SIC 7381*
SECURITAS CANADA LIMITED p1215
1980 RUE SHERBROOKE O BUREAU 300, MONTREAL, QC, H3H 1E8
(514) 935-2533　*SIC 7381*
SECURITAS CANADA LIMITED p1341
817 RUE MCCAFFREY, SAINT-LAURENT, QC, H4T 1N3
(514) 938-3433　*SIC 7381*
SECURITE KOLOSSAL INC p1262
325 RUE DU MARAIS BUREAU 220, QUEBEC, QC, G1M 3R3
(418) 683-1713　*SIC 7381*
SECURITE SIROIS EVENEMENTS SPECIAUX INC p1256
104 RUE SEIGNEURIALE, QUEBEC, QC, G1E 4Y5
(418) 692-4137　*SIC 7381*
SECURITY RESOURCE GROUP INC p274
10252 CITY PKY SUITE 301, SURREY, BC, V3T 4C2
(604) 951-3388　*SIC 7381*
SENTINEL PROTECTION SERVICES LTD p9
3132 26 ST NE SUITE 335, CALGARY, AB, T1Y 6Z1
(403) 237-8485　*SIC 7381*
SENTRY SECURITY AND INVESTIGATIONS INC p442
1225 COXHEATH RD, COXHEATH, NS, B1L 1B4
(902) 574-3276　*SIC 7381*
SHANNAHAN'S INVESTIGATION SECURITY LIMITED p470
30 BROOKFALLS CRT, WAVERLEY, NS, B2R 1J2
(902) 873-4536　*SIC 7381*
STAR SECURITY INCORPORATED p714
2351 ROYAL WINDSOR DR SUITE 205, MISSISSAUGA, ON, L5J 4S7
(905) 855-7827　*SIC 7381*
STEELE SECURITY & INVESTIGATION SERVICE DIVISION OF UNITED PROTECTIONS p116
8055 CORONET RD NW, EDMONTON, AB, T6E 4N7
SIC 7381
SUMMIT SECURITY GROUP LTD p218
GD STN MAIN, KAMLOOPS, BC, V2C 5K2
SIC 7381
SURETE CAVALERIE INC p1301
193A BOUL ARTHUR-SAUVE, SAINT-EUSTACHE, QC, J7P 2A7
(450) 983-7070　*SIC 7381*

TARGET INVESTIGATION & SECURITY LTD p559
2900 LANGSTAFF RD UNIT 3, CONCORD, ON, L4K 4R9
(905) 760-9090　*SIC 7381*
TUFF CONTROL SYSTEMS LIMITED p794
5145 STEELES AVE W SUITE 201, NORTH YORK, ON, M9L 1R5
SIC 7381
TYCO INTEGRATED FIRE & SECURITY CANADA, INC p781
5000 DUFFERIN ST, NORTH YORK, ON, M3H 5T5
SIC 7381
UNITED PROTECTION SERVICES p1432
2366 AVENUE C N, SASKATOON, SK, S7L 5X5
(306) 382-0002　*SIC 7381*
UNIVERSAL PROTECTION SERVICE OF CANADA CO p238
627 COLUMBIA ST SUITE 200A, NEW WESTMINSTER, BC, V3M 1A7
(604) 522-5550　*SIC 7381*
V.S.I. INC p513
18 REGAN RD UNIT 31, BRAMPTON, ON, L7A 1C2
SIC 7381
VP PROTECTION INC p769
259 YORKLAND RD 3RD FL, NORTH YORK, ON, M2J 5B2
(416) 218-3226　*SIC 7381*
WALKER INVESTIGATION BUREAU LTD p409
1765 MAIN ST, MONCTON, NB, E1E 1H3
(506) 857-8343　*SIC 7381*
WESTERN PROTECTION ALLIANCE INC p264
11771 HORSESHOE WAY UNIT 1, RICHMOND, BC, V7A 4V4
(604) 271-7475　*SIC 7381*
WIKWEMIKONG TRIBAL POLICE p1016
2074 WIKWEMIKONG WAY, WIKWEMIKONG, ON, P0P 2J0
(705) 859-3141　*SIC 7381*
WINDSOR SECURITY LIMITED p283
10833 160 ST SUITE 626, SURREY, BC, V4N 1P3
(604) 689-7588　*SIC 7381*
WISE OWL FRAUD PREVENTION p143
135 1 AVE S, LETHBRIDGE, AB, T1J 0A1
(403) 330-5020　*SIC 7381*

SIC 7382 Security systems services

1084999 ONTARIO INC p816
715 INDUSTRIAL AVE, OTTAWA, ON, K1G 0Z1
(613) 228-0073　*SIC 7382*
2733-8649 QUEBEC INC p1130
7351 RUE CHOUINARD, LASALLE, QC, H8N 2L6
(514) 768-6315　*SIC 7382*
ACCORD SPECIALIZED INVESTIGATIONS & SECURITY p917
1560 BAYVIEW AVE SUITE 300, TORONTO, ON, M4G 3B8
(416) 322-2013　*SIC 7382*
ALARMFORCE INDUSTRIES INC p792
675 GARYRAY DR, NORTH YORK, ON, M9L 1R2
(416) 445-2001　*SIC 7382*
ARMSTRONG'S COMMUNICATION LTD p397
380 SALMON RIVER MOUTH RD, COAL CREEK, NB, E4A 2T7
(506) 339-6066　*SIC 7382*
AVANTE SECURITY INC p775
1959 LESLIE ST, NORTH YORK, ON, M3B 2M3
(416) 923-2435　*SIC 7382*
COUNTERFORCE CORPORATION p408
1077 ST GEORGE BLVD, MONCTON, NB, E1E 4C9

(506) 862-5500   *SIC 7382*
COUNTERFORCE CORPORATION   *p693*
2740 MATHESON BLVD E UNIT 2A, MIS-SISSAUGA, ON, L4W 4X3
(905) 282-6200   *SIC 7382*
GUARDIAN ALARM COMPANY OF CANADA LTD   *p1018*
2885 LAUZON PKY SUITE 105, WINDSOR, ON, N8T 3H5
(519) 258-4646   *SIC 7382*
HALTON ALARM RESPONSE & PROTECTION LTD   *p803*
760 PACIFIC RD UNIT 21, OAKVILLE, ON, L6L 6M5
(905) 827-6655   *SIC 7382*
HOMME ET SA MAISON LTEE, L'   *p1238*
605 AV MARSHALL, MONTREAL, QC, H9P 1E1
(514) 737-1010   *SIC 7382*
K.O.P.S. SECURITY & INVESTIGATIONS INC   *p142*
1518 3 AVE S, LETHBRIDGE, AB, T1J 0K8
(403) 331-5677   *SIC 7382*
MASTER SECURITY LTD   *p266*
3580 MONCTON ST SUITE 212, RICH-MOND, BC, V7E 3A4
(604) 278-3024   *SIC 7382*
MAXGUARD ALARM AND SECURITY COMPANY LTD   *p555*
8700 DUFFERIN ST UNIT 17, CONCORD, ON, L4K 4S2
(416) 893-9082   *SIC 7382*
MICROCOM 'M' INC   *p1267*
3710 BOUL WILFRID-HAMEL, QUEBEC, QC, G1P 2J2
(418) 871-7676   *SIC 7382*
ONYX-FIRE PROTECTION SERVICES INC   *p586*
42 SHAFT RD, ETOBICOKE, ON, M9W 4M2
(416) 674-5633   *SIC 7382*
PALADIN VANCOUVER SECURITY SYSTEMS LTD   *p197*
4691 WILSON RD, CHILLIWACK, BC, V2R 5C4
(604) 823-2428   *SIC 7382*
PERPETUAL SECURITY CORPORATION   *p401*
880 HANWELL RD UNIT 203, FREDERICTON, NB, E3B 6A3
(506) 457-1458   *SIC 7382*
PREMIERE SOCIETE EN COMMANDITE NATIONALE ALARMCAP   *p1293*
4780 RUE SAINT-FELIX, SAINT-AUGUSTIN-DE-DESMAURES, QC, G3A 2J9
(418) 864-7924   *SIC 7382*
PROTELEC LTD   *p372*
1450 MOUNTAIN AVE UNIT 200, WINNIPEG, MB, R2X 3C4
(204) 949-1417   *SIC 7382*
SECURTEK MONITORING SOLUTIONS INC   *p1439*
70 FIRST AVE N, YORKTON, SK, S3N 1J6
(306) 786-4331   *SIC 7382*
SENSORMATIC CANADA INCORPORATED   *p506*
7 PAGET RD, BRAMPTON, ON, L6T 5S2
(905) 792-2858   *SIC 7382*
SIEMENS CANADA LIMITED   *p25*
1930 MAYNARD RD SE UNIT 24, CALGARY, AB, T2E 6J8
(403) 259-3404   *SIC 7382*
SMART-TEK COMMUNICATIONS INC   *p264*
130-11300 NO. 5 RD, RICHMOND, BC, V7A 5J7
(604) 718-1882   *SIC 7382*
STREAMLINE FIRE PROTECTION LTD   *p97*
15695 116 AVE NW, EDMONTON, AB, T5M 3W1
(780) 436-6911   *SIC 7382*
TYCO INTEGRATED FIRE & SECURITY CANADA, INC   *p1331*
5700 BOUL HENRI-BOURASSA O, SAINT-LAURENT, QC, H4R 1V9

(514) 737-5505   *SIC 7382*
UNIVERSITY OF NEW BRUNSWICK   *p401*
767 KINGS COLLEGE RD, FREDERICTON, NB, E3B 5A3
(506) 453-4889   *SIC 7382*
VANCOUVER FIRE PREVENTION SERVICE CO. LTD   *p259*
22131 FRASERWOOD WAY, RICHMOND, BC, V6W 1J5
(604) 232-3478   *SIC 7382*

SIC 7383 News syndicates

CANADIAN PRESS, THE   *p937*
36 KING ST E SUITE 301, TORONTO, ON, M5C 2L9
(416) 364-0321   *SIC 7383*
CANADIAN PRESS, THE   *p1187*
215 RUE SAINT-JACQUES UNITE 100, MONTREAL, QC, H2Y 1M6
(514) 849-3212   *SIC 7383*
CKWX NEWS   *p293*
2440 ASH ST SUITE 1130, VANCOUVER, BC, V5Z 4J6
(604) 873-2599   *SIC 7383*
HABENDUM HOLDING LTD   *p224*
365 DAVIS RD, LADYSMITH, BC, V9G 1V1
(250) 245-3212   *SIC 7383*
MS MEDIA GP HOLDING LIMITED   *p965*
25 YORK ST SUITE 900, TORONTO, ON, M5J 2V5
(416) 362-0885   *SIC 7383*
TORRES AVIATION INCORPORATED   *p676*
95 ROYAL CREST CRT UNIT 5, MARKHAM, ON, L3R 9X5
(905) 470-7655   *SIC 7383*

SIC 7384 Photofinish laboratories

1387208 ONTARIO LTD   *p873*
190 MILNER AVE, SCARBOROUGH, ON, M1S 5B6
(416) 293-9943   *SIC 7384*
24184863 QUEBEC INC   *p1265*
2717 AV WATT BUREAU 150, QUEBEC, QC, G1P 3X3
(418) 659-1560   *SIC 7384*
A B C PHOTOCOLOUR PRODUCTS LTD   *p320*
1618 4TH AVE W, VANCOUVER, BC, V6J 1L9
(604) 736-7017   *SIC 7384*
BEYOND DIGITAL IMAGING INC   *p667*
36 APPLE CREEK BLVD, MARKHAM, ON, L3R 4Y4
(905) 415-1888   *SIC 7384*
CAVALCADE COLOUR LAB INC   *p620*
34 KING WILLIAM ST, HUNTSVILLE, ON, P1H 1G5
(705) 789-9603   *SIC 7384*
COLORFAST CORPORATION   *p118*
6115 GATEWAY BLVD NW, EDMONTON, AB, T6H 2H3
SIC 7384
CUSTOM COLOUR LABS INC   *p792*
5703 STEELES AVE W, NORTH YORK, ON, M9L 1S7
(416) 630-2020   *SIC 7384*
IMAGE PLUS   *p176*
31935 SOUTH FRASER WAY UNIT 104, ABBOTSFORD, BC, V2T 5N7
(604) 504-7222   *SIC 7384*
LABOPRO P.S. INC   *p1277*
1405 AV SAINT-JEAN-BAPTISTE BUREAU 115, QUEBEC, QC, G2E 5K2
(418) 681-6128   *SIC 7384*
LABORATOIRE COULEUR UNIVERSEL INC   *p1237*
810 RUE SALABERRY, MONTREAL, QC, H7S 1H3
(514) 384-2251   *SIC 7384*
LIFETOUCH CANADA INC   *p372*

1410 MOUNTAIN AVE UNIT 1, WINNIPEG, MB, R2X 0A4
(204) 977-3475   *SIC 7384*
MP REPRODUCTIONS INC   *p1192*
1030 RUE CHENNEVILLE, MONTREAL, QC, H2Z 1V8
(514) 861-8541   *SIC 7384*
POST-PROD CMJ TECH INC   *p1322*
5000 RUE D'IBERVILLE BUREAU 332, SAINT-LAMBERT, QC, H2H 2S6
(514) 731-4242   *SIC 7384*
PROS DE LA PHOTO (QUEBEC) INC, LES   *p1182*
90 RUE BEAUBIEN O BUREAU 201, MONTREAL, QC, H2S 1V6
(514) 273-1588   *SIC 7384*
SILVANO COLOR LABORATORIES LIMITED   *p994*
355 WESTON RD, TORONTO, ON, M6N 4Y7
SIC 7384
TECHNICARE IMAGING LTD   *p86*
10924 119 ST NW, EDMONTON, AB, T5H 3P5
(780) 424-7161   *SIC 7384*
TORONTO IMAGE WORKS LIMITED   *p984*
80 SPADINA AVE SUITE 207, TORONTO, ON, M5V 2J4
(416) 703-1999   *SIC 7384*
TREND COLOUR LABS INC   *p790*
1194D CALEDONIA RD, NORTH YORK, ON, M6A 2W5
SIC 7384

SIC 7389 Business services, nec

0743398 B.C. LTD   *p334*
307 DAVID ST, VICTORIA, BC, V8T 5C1
(250) 381-5865   *SIC 7389*
1023248 ONTARIO INC   *p844*
870 MCKAY RD, PICKERING, ON, L1W 2Y4
(905) 426-8989   *SIC 7389*
1032396 ONTARIO LTD   *p781*
3858 CHESSWOOD DR, NORTH YORK, ON, M3J 2W6
(416) 398-5155   *SIC 7389*
1118528 ONTARIO INC   *p1022*
1172 GOYEAU ST, WINDSOR, ON, N9A 1J1
(519) 977-5757   *SIC 7389*
1132694 ONTARIO INC   *p547*
8001 KEELE ST, CONCORD, ON, L4K 1Y8
(905) 669-9855   *SIC 7389*
1132694 ONTARIO INC   *p733*
7550 KIMBEL ST, MISSISSAUGA, ON, L5S 1A2
(905) 677-1948   *SIC 7389*
1172895 ALBERTA LTD   *p127*
145 MACLEAN RD, FORT MCMURRAY, AB, T9H 4X2
(780) 790-9292   *SIC 7389*
1279317 ONTARIO LTD   *p790*
25 WINGOLD AVE, NORTH YORK, ON, M6B 1P8
(416) 588-1668   *SIC 7389*
1339022 ONTARIO LTD   *p998*
75 INDUSTRIAL RD, TOTTENHAM, ON, L0G 1W0
(800) 748-0277   *SIC 7389*
1391130 ALBERTA LTD   *p66*
333 24 AVE SW SUITE 300, CALGARY, AB, T2S 3E6
(403) 861-1556   *SIC 7389*
1430819 ONTARIO LIMITED   *p485*
112 SAUNDERS RD UNIT 11, BARRIE, ON, L4N 9A8
(705) 721-9809   *SIC 7389*
1484174 ALBERTA LTD   *p148*
1601 13 ST, NISKU, AB, T9E 0Y2
(780) 454-9231   *SIC 7389*
162013 CANADA INC   *p1191*
1080 COTE DU BEAVER HALL, MONTREAL, QC, H2Z 1S8

SIC 7389
1686416 ONTARIO INC   *p665*
10 ALDEN RD SUITE 6, MARKHAM, ON, L3R 2S1
(905) 305-0071   *SIC 7389*
1776963 ONTARIO INC   *p736*
1445 COURTNEYPARK DR E, MISSISSAUGA, ON, L5T 2E3
(905) 670-6683   *SIC 7389*
2161457 ONTARIO INC   *p990*
845 ADELAIDE ST W, TORONTO, ON, M6J 3X1
(416) 703-2022   *SIC 7389*
2179267 ONTARIO LTD   *p473*
655 FINLEY AVE SUITE 1, AJAX, ON, L1S 3V3
(905) 619-1477   *SIC 7389*
2182553 ONTARIO LTD   *p859*
750 ONTARIO ST UNIT 1, SARNIA, ON, N7T 1M6
(519) 383-8880   *SIC 7389*
239188 BC LTD   *p317*
1455 GEORGIA ST W SUITE 400, VANCOUVER, BC, V6G 2T3
(604) 669-7044   *SIC 7389*
24-7 INTOUCH INC   *p376*
240 KENNEDY ST 2ND FL, WINNIPEG, MB, R3C 1T1
(800) 530-1121   *SIC 7389*
2790173 CANADA INC   *p1047*
7900 RUE JARRY, ANJOU, QC, H1J 1H1
(514) 353-1710   *SIC 7389*
2895102 CANADA INC   *p1117*
16811 BOUL HYMUS, KIRKLAND, QC, H9H 3L4
(514) 426-1211   *SIC 7389*
2945-8171 QUEBEC INC   *p978*
296 RICHMOND ST W SUITE 401, TORONTO, ON, M5V 1X2
(416) 979-0000   *SIC 7389*
2948-4292 QUEBEC INC   *p1392*
9072 RUE DE LA MONTAGNE, VALCOURT, QC, J0E 2L0
(450) 532-2270   *SIC 7389*
3022528 CANADA INC   *p1141*
778 RUE JEAN-NEVEU, LONGUEUIL, QC, J4G 1P1
(450) 442-4087   *SIC 7389*
3119696 CANADA INC   *p978*
269 RICHMOND ST W SUITE 201, TORONTO, ON, M5V 1X1
(416) 368-1623   *SIC 7389*
324007 ALBERTA LTD   *p92*
13220 ST ALBERT TRAIL NW SUITE 303, EDMONTON, AB, T5L 4W1
(780) 477-2233   *SIC 7389*
338802 ALBERTA LTD   *p120*
2830 PARSONS RD NW, EDMONTON, AB, T6N 1H3
(780) 944-6922   *SIC 7389*
3627730 CANADA INC   *p816*
3020 HAWTHORNE RD SUITE 300, OTTAWA, ON, K1G 3J6
(613) 526-3121   *SIC 7389*
3812073 CANADA INC   *p1345*
4929 RUE JARRY E BUREAU 208, SAINT-LEONARD, QC, H1R 1Y1
(514) 324-1024   *SIC 7389*
3DS THREE DIMENSIONAL SERVICES INC   *p183*
2829 NORLAND AVE, BURNABY, BC, V5B 3A9
(604) 980-2450   *SIC 7389*
4166621 CANADA INC   *p733*
2244 DREW ROAD UNITS 4 & 5, MISSISSAUGA, ON, L5S 1B1
(905) 671-2244   *SIC 7389*
4211677 CANADA INC   *p1274*
5150 RUE JOHN-MOLSON, QUEBEC, QC, G1X 3X4
(514) 761-2345   *SIC 7389*
429400 ONTARIO LTD   *p494*
6 QUEEN ST N SUITE 207, BOLTON, ON, L7E 1C8

(905) 857-6949 *SIC 7389*
6091636 CANADA INC p1226
4700 RUE DE LA SAVANE BUREAU 310, MONTREAL, QC, H4P 1T7
(514) 448-6931 *SIC 7389*

620205 ALBERTA LIMITED p8
4321 84 ST NE, CALGARY, AB, T1Y 7H3
(403) 777-9393 *SIC 7389*

6232698 CANADA INC p581
397 HUMBERLINE DR UNIT 1, ETOBICOKE, ON, M9W 5T5
(416) 213-0088 *SIC 7389*

6875866 CANADA INC p866
40 PRODUCTION DR, SCARBOROUGH, ON, M1H 2X8
(905) 513-1097 *SIC 7389*

718009 ONTARIO INC p815
2617 EDINBURGH PL, OTTAWA, ON, K1B 5M1
(613) 742-7171 *SIC 7389*

718878 ONTARIO LIMITED p932
529 RICHMOND ST E UNIT 104, TORONTO, ON, M5A 1R4
(416) 365-0155 *SIC 7389*

744648 ALBERTA LTD p42
840 6 AVE SW SUITE 100, CALGARY, AB, T2P 3E5
(403) 265-6936 *SIC 7389*

87029 CANADA LTD p754
200 DAVIS DR, NEWMARKET, ON, L3Y 2N4
  SIC 7389

8948399 CANADA INC p380
1425 WHYTE AVE UNIT 200, WINNIPEG, MB, R3E 1V7
(204) 832-8001 *SIC 7389*

9029-2970 QUEBEC INC p1150
135 BOUL DION, MATANE, QC, G4W 3L8
(418) 562-3751 *SIC 7389*

9248-5523 QUEBEC INC p1337
4575 RUE HICKMORE, SAINT-LAURENT, QC, H4T 1S5
(514) 934-4545 *SIC 7389*

9274-4531 QUEBEC INC p1274
3000 AV WATT BUREAU 1, QUEBEC, QC, G1X 3Y8
(418) 659-9000 *SIC 7389*

9300-4901 QUEBEC INC p1263
356 RUE JACKSON, QUEBEC, QC, G1N 4C5
(581) 742-1222 *SIC 7389*

A WAY EXPRESS COURIER SERVICE p917
2168 DANFORTH AVE, TORONTO, ON, M4C 1K3
(416) 424-4471 *SIC 7389*

A. K. HOLDINGS INC p400
958 PROSPECT ST, FREDERICTON, NB, E3B 2T8
(506) 462-4444 *SIC 7389*

ABEILLES SERVICES DE CONDITIONNEMENT INC, LES p1246
12910 BOUL METROPOLITAIN E, POINTE-AUX-TREMBLES, QC, H1A 4A7
(514) 640-6941 *SIC 7389*

ABERCROMBIE VOLUNTEER FIRE DEPT p463
GD LCD MAIN, NEW GLASGOW, NS, B2H 5C9
(902) 752-4248 *SIC 7389*

ABLE TRANSLATIONS LTD p704
5749 COOPERS AVE, MISSISSAUGA, ON, L4Z 1R9
(905) 502-0000 *SIC 7389*

AC FINAL MILE INC p500
107 ALFRED KUEHNE BLVD, BRAMPTON, ON, L6T 4K3
(905) 362-2999 *SIC 7389*

ACCEL CONSTRUCTION MANAGEMENT INC p548
50 VICEROY RD UNIT 11, CONCORD, ON, L4K 3A7
(905) 660-6690 *SIC 7389*

ACCORD EXPOSITIONS INC p1127
1530 46E AV, LACHINE, QC, H8T 3J9

(514) 639-6998 *SIC 7389*
ADANAC RECOVERY LTD p337
3961 QUADRA ST, VICTORIA, BC, V8X 1J7
(250) 727-7480 *SIC 7389*

ADLER FIRESTOPPING LTD p1
53016 HWY 60 UNIT 23, ACHESON, AB, T7X 5A7
(780) 962-9495 *SIC 7389*

ADTEL INC p84
11630 KINGSWAY NW, EDMONTON, AB, T5G 0X5
(780) 424-7777 *SIC 7389*

ADVANTAGE COURIER SYSTEMS LIMITED p445
1 GURHOLT DR, DARTMOUTH, NS, B3B 1J8
(902) 444-1511 *SIC 7389*

ADVANTAGE DELIVERY SERVICE p1038
47 KENSINGTON RD, CHARLOTTETOWN, PE, C1A 5H6
(902) 940-3971 *SIC 7389*

AFFORDABLE PACKAGING LTD p473
225 MONARCH AVE, AJAX, ON, L1S 7M3
  SIC 7389

AFONSO GROUP LIMITED p428
14 ROBIN HOOD BAY RD, ST. JOHN'S, NL, A1A 5V3
(709) 576-6070 *SIC 7389*

AGROCROP EXPORTS LTD p494
100 AGROCROP RD, BOLTON, ON, L7E 4K4
(905) 458-4551 *SIC 7389*

AIR CANADA p413
1 AIR CANADA WAY, SAINT JOHN, NB, E2K 0B1
  SIC 7389

AL-PACK HOLDINGS LTD p409
60 COMMERCE ST, MONCTON, NB, E1H 0A5
(506) 852-4262 *SIC 7389*

ALBERTA BOILERS SAFETY ASSOCIATION (ABSA) p120
9410 20 AVE NW, EDMONTON, AB, T6N 0A4
(780) 437-9100 *SIC 7389*

ALBERTA SPRUCE INDUSTRIES LTD p164
26322 TWP RD SUITE 524, SPRUCE GROVE, AB, T7X 3H2
(780) 962-5118 *SIC 7389*

ALL LANGUAGES LTD p927
421 BLOOR ST E SUITE 306, TORONTO, ON, M4W 3T1
(647) 427-8308 *SIC 7389*

ALL SEA ATLANTIC LTD p414
9 LOWER COVE LOOP, SAINT JOHN, NB, E2L 1W7
(506) 632-3483 *SIC 7389*

ALLIANCE DE L'INDUSTRIE TOURISTIQUE DU QUEBEC p1236
1575 BOUL DE L'AVENIR BUREAU 330, MONTREAL, QC, H7S 2N5
(450) 686-8358 *SIC 7389*

ALLIANCE TRAFFIC GROUP INC p253
2600 VIKING WAY, RICHMOND, BC, V6V 1N2
(604) 273-5220 *SIC 7389*

ALLIED COFFEE CORP p648
775 INDUSTRIAL RD UNIT 2, LONDON, ON, N5V 3N5
(519) 451-8220 *SIC 7389*

ALTERNATURE INC p1169
9210 BOUL PIE-IX, MONTREAL, QC, H1Z 4H7
(514) 382-7520 *SIC 7389*

ALTIMAX COURIER (2006) LIMITED p397
274 BOUL DIEPPE, DIEPPE, NB, E1A 6P8
(866) 258-4629 *SIC 7389*

ALTIMAX COURIER (2006) LIMITED p445
132 TRIDER CRES, DARTMOUTH, NS, B3B 1R6
(902) 460-6006 *SIC 7389*

ALTO DESIGN INC p1168
2600 RUE WILLIAM-TREMBLAY BUREAU 220, MONTREAL, QC, H1Y 3J2

(514) 278-3050 *SIC 7389*
ALYKHAN VELJI DESIGNS INC p20
217 4 ST NE, CALGARY, AB, T2E 3S1
(403) 617-2406 *SIC 7389*

ALZAC HOLDINGS LTD p99
18011 105 AVE NW, EDMONTON, AB, T5S 2E1
(780) 447-4303 *SIC 7389*

ALZHEIMER SOCIETY OF B.C. p292
828 8TH AVE W SUITE 300, VANCOUVER, BC, V5Z 1E2
(604) 681-6530 *SIC 7389*

AM INSPECTION LTD p1405
501 RAILWAY ST N, CABRI, SK, S0N 0J0
(306) 587-2620 *SIC 7389*

AMITY-COOINDA PACKAGING SERVICES p241
1070 ROOSEVELT CRES, NORTH VANCOUVER, BC, V7P 1M3
(604) 985-7491 *SIC 7389*

AMSTERDAM PRODUCTS LTD p561
2 MONTREAL RD, CORNWALL, ON, K6H 6L4
(613) 933-7393 *SIC 7389*

ANARCHIST MOUNTAIN FIRE DEPARTMENT p242
115 GRIZZLY RD, OSOYOOS, BC, V0H 1V6
  SIC 7389

ANGLOCOM INC p1257
300 RUE SAINT-PAUL BUREAU 210, QUEBEC, QC, G1K 7R1
(418) 529-6928 *SIC 7389*

ANSWERPLUS COMMUNICATION SERVICES INC p233
235 BASTION ST SUITE 205, NANAIMO, BC, V9R 3A3
(250) 753-7587 *SIC 7389*

ANTLER EXPRESS LTD p104
16389 130 AVE NW, EDMONTON, AB, T5V 1K5
(780) 447-1639 *SIC 7389*

APPLE SECURITY INC p343
15216 NORTH BLUFF RD SUITE 604, WHITE ROCK, BC, V4B 0A7
(604) 507-9577 *SIC 7389*

ARCHIE'S SACKVILLE BOTTLE EXCHANGE LIMITED p461
446 SACKVILLE DR, LOWER SACKVILLE, NS, B4C 2R8
(902) 865-9010 *SIC 7389*

ARCTIC CRANE SERVICE LTD p134
14915 89 ST, GRANDE PRAIRIE, AB, T8X 0J2
(780) 814-6990 *SIC 7389*

ARMSTRONG TOP PACK LTD p644
500 COUNTY RD 18, LEAMINGTON, ON, N8H 3V5
(519) 326-3273 *SIC 7389*

ARSYSTEMS INTERNATIONAL INC p666
2770 14TH AVE SUITE 101, MARKHAM, ON, L3R 0J1
(905) 968-3096 *SIC 7389*

ARTHRITIS SOCIETY, THE p944
393 UNIVERSITY AVE SUITE 1700, TORONTO, ON, M5G 1E6
(416) 979-7228 *SIC 7389*

ARTSMARKETING SERVICES INC p932
260 KING ST E SUITE 500, TORONTO, ON, M5A 4L5
(416) 941-9000 *SIC 7389*

ASSOCIATED AUCTIONEERS INC p650
1881 SCANLAN ST, LONDON, ON, N5W 6C3
(519) 453-7182 *SIC 7389*

ASSOCIATION TOURISTIQUE REGIONALE DE CHARLEVOIX INC p1122
495 BOUL DE COMPORTE, LA MALBAIE, QC, G5A 3G3
(418) 665-4454 *SIC 7389*

ASTOUND GROUP INC, THE p805
1215 NORTH SERVICE RD W UNIT A, OAKVILLE, ON, L6M 2W2
(905) 465-0474 *SIC 7389*

ATCHELITZ THREHERMEN'S ASSOCIA-

TION p197
44146 LUCKAKUCK WAY, CHILLIWACK, BC, V2R 4A7
(604) 858-2119 *SIC 7389*

ATELIER ABACO INC p1047
9100 RUE CLAVEAU, ANJOU, QC, H1J 1Z4
(514) 355-6182 *SIC 7389*

ATELIER PEPIN INC p1242
1369 BOUL LOUIS-FRECHETTE, NICOLET, QC, J3T 1M3
(819) 293-5584 *SIC 7389*

ATELIERS FERROVIAIRES DE MONT-JOLI INC, LES p1357
125 RUE DE L'EXPANSION, SAINTE-FLAVIE, QC, G0J 2L0
(418) 775-7174 *SIC 7389*

ATELIERS LEOPOLD DESROSIERS INC p1150
60 RUE BRILLANT, MATANE, QC, G4W 0J9
(418) 562-2640 *SIC 7389*

ATELIERS T.A.Q. INC p1277
5255 RUE RIDEAU, QUEBEC, QC, G2E 5H5
(418) 871-4912 *SIC 7389*

ATELIERS TRANSITION INC, LES p1311
1255 RUE DELORME BUREAU 103, SAINT-HYACINTHE, QC, J2S 2J3
(450) 771-2747 *SIC 7389*

AUDIO ZONE INC p1187
444 RUE SAINT-PAUL E, MONTREAL, QC, H2Y 3V1
(514) 931-9466 *SIC 7389*

AUTOMATED STEEL DETAILING ASSOCIATES LTD p582
77 BELFIELD RD UNIT 100, ETOBICOKE, ON, M9W 1G6
(416) 241-6967 *SIC 7389*

AUXILIAIRE DE L'HOPITAL GENERAL JUIF SIR MORTIMER B. DAVIS INC, LES p1219
3755 CH DE LA COTE-SAINTE-CATHERINE BUREAU A018, MONTREAL, QC, H3T 1E2
(514) 340-8216 *SIC 7389*

AVOTUS INC p1249
116 AV PENDENNIS, POINTE-CLAIRE, QC, H9R 1H6
  SIC 7389

B+H CHIL DESIGN p320
1706 1ST AVE W SUITE 400, VANCOUVER, BC, V6J 0E4
(604) 688-8571 *SIC 7389*

BAILEY METAL PROCESSING LIMITED p521
1211 HERITAGE RD, BURLINGTON, ON, L7L 4Y1
(905) 336-5111 *SIC 7389*

BARRY, D F & ASSOCIATES INC p445
7 MELLOR AVE UNIT 12, DARTMOUTH, NS, B3B 0E8
(902) 468-9001 *SIC 7389*

BARTERPAY INC p891
102-1040 SOUTH SERVICE RD, STONEY CREEK, ON, L8E 6G3
(905) 777-0660 *SIC 7389*

BASE LINE DRAFTING SERVICES INC p549
30 PENNSYLVANIA AVE UNIT 3B, CONCORD, ON, L4K 4A5
(905) 660-7017 *SIC 7389*

BASQ INTERNATIONAL INC p1156
8515 PLACE DEVONSHIRE BUREAU 214, MONT-ROYAL, QC, H4P 2K1
(514) 733-0066 *SIC 7389*

BBO SERVICES LIMITED PARTNERSHIP p653
380 WELLINGTON ST SUITE 1600, LONDON, ON, N6A 5B5
(519) 679-0450 *SIC 7389*

BBW INTERNATIONAL INC p71
75 EDGEVALLEY CIR NW, CALGARY, AB, T3A 4Y9
  SIC 7389

BEAUSEJOUR TOWN FIRE HALL p380
1369 ERIN ST, WINNIPEG, MB, R3E 2S7
(204) 792-8627 *SIC 7389*

▲ Public Company   ■ Public Company Family Member   **HQ** Headquarters   **BR** Branch   **SL** Single Location

BEAUTYROCK HOLDINGS INC *p492*
3 APPLEWOOD DR SUITE 3, BELLEVILLE, ON, K8P 4E3
(613) 932-2525 *SIC 7389*

BEAVER FASHIONS LIMITED *p1169*
3565 RUE JARRY E BUREAU 109, MONTREAL, QC, H1Z 4K6
(514) 721-1180 *SIC 7389*

BELL CONFERENCING INC *p692*
5099 CREEKBANK RD SUITE B4, MISSISSAUGA, ON, L4W 5N2
(905) 602-3900 *SIC 7389*

BELLWYCK PACKAGING INC *p521*
977 CENTURY DR, BURLINGTON, ON, L7L 5J8
(905) 631-4475 *SIC 7389*

BELMONT PRESS LIMITED *p680*
5 BODRINGTON CRT, MARKHAM, ON, L6G 1A6
(905) 940-4900 *SIC 7389*

BELVIKA TRADE & PACKAGING LTD *p734*
A-450 EXPORT BLVD, MISSISSAUGA, ON, L5S 2A4
(905) 502-7444 *SIC 7389*

BENNETT DESIGN ASSOCIATES INC *p1001*
10 DOUGLAS RD UNIT 2, UXBRIDGE, ON, L9P 1S9
(905) 852-4617 *SIC 7389*

BGRS LIMITED *p778*
39 WYNFORD DR, NORTH YORK, ON, M3C 3K5
(416) 510-5600 *SIC 7389*

BISON FIRE PROTECTION INC *p362*
35 BOYS RD, WINNIPEG, MB, R2C 2Z2
(204) 237-3473 *SIC 7389*

BISON FIRE PROTECTION INC *p362*
35 BOYS RD, WINNIPEG, MB, R2C 2Z2
(204) 237-3473 *SIC 7389*

BLACKBURN SERVICE D'INVENTAIRE INC *p1078*
125 RUE DUBE, CHICOUTIMI, QC, G7H 2V3
(418) 543-4567 *SIC 7389*

BLIZZARD COURIER SERVICE LTD *p775*
1937 LESLIE ST, NORTH YORK, ON, M3B 2M3
(416) 444-0596 *SIC 7389*

BLUE OCEAN CONTACT CENTERS INC *p456*
7051 BAYERS RD SUITE 400, HALIFAX, NS, B3L 4V2
(902) 722-3300 *SIC 7389*

BONNYVILLE REGIONAL FIRE AUTHORITY *p6*
4407 50 AVE, BONNYVILLE, AB, T9N 2H3
(780) 826-4755 *SIC 7389*

BOUCHARD & BLANCHETTE MARINE LIMITEE *p1367*
60 RUE RETTY, SEPT-ILES, QC, G4R 3E1
(418) 968-2505 *SIC 7389*

BOUTEILLES RECYCLEES DU QUEBEC (B.R.Q) INC, LES *p1361*
1400 BOUL DAGENAIS O, SAINTE-ROSE, QC, H7L 5C7
(450) 622-1600 *SIC 7389*

BOW CITY DELIVERY (1989) LTD *p21*
1423 45 AVE NE BAY CTR, CALGARY, AB, T2E 2P3
(403) 250-5329 *SIC 7389*

BRIDGEMARK BRANDING & DESIGN *p709*
33 CITY CENTRE DR SUITE 380, MISSISSAUGA, ON, L5B 2N5
(905) 281-7240 *SIC 7389*

BRITACAN FACILITIES MANAGEMENT GROUP INC *p766*
505 CONSUMERS RD SUITE 1010, NORTH YORK, ON, M2J 4V8
(416) 494-2007 *SIC 7389*

BRITISH COLUMBIA'S WOMEN'S HOSPITAL AND HEALTH CENTRE FOUNDATION *p319*
4500 OAK ST RM D310, VANCOUVER, BC, V6H 3N1
(604) 875-2270 *SIC 7389*

BRONSKILL & CO. INC *p979*
662 KING ST W SUITE 101, TORONTO, ON, M5V 1M7
(416) 703-8689 *SIC 7389*

BROOKLYN VOLUNTEER FIRE DEPARTMENT *p441*
995 HWY 215, BROOKLYN, NS, B0J 1H0
(902) 757-2043 *SIC 7389*

BRYTOR INTERNATIONAL MOVING INC *p734*
275 EXPORT BLVD, MISSISSAUGA, ON, L5S 1Y4
(905) 564-8855 *SIC 7389*

BUFFALO PARCEL COURIER SERVICE LTD *p95*
11310 153 ST NW, EDMONTON, AB, T5M 1X6
(780) 455-9283 *SIC 7389*

BURDIFILEK INC *p977*
183 BATHURST ST SUITE 300, TORONTO, ON, M5T 2R7
(416) 703-4334 *SIC 7389*

BUREAU D'EVALUATION DE QUEBEC INC *p1261*
275 RUE METIVIER BUREAU 170, QUEBEC, QC, G1M 3X8
(418) 871-6777 *SIC 7389*

BURLINGTON CONVENTION CENTRE *p521*
1120 BURLOAK DR, BURLINGTON, ON, L7L 6P8
(905) 319-0319 *SIC 7389*

BURLINGTON MERCHANDISING & FIXTURES INC *p527*
3100 HARVESTER RD UNIT 8, BURLINGTON, ON, L7N 3W8
(905) 332-6652 *SIC 7389*

BYNG GROUP LTD, THE *p549*
511 EDGELEY BLVD UNIT 2, CONCORD, ON, L4K 4G4
(905) 660-5454 *SIC 7389*

C A S COMMUNICATIONS SERVICES LIMITED *p865*
503 CENTENNIAL RD N, SCARBOROUGH, ON, M1C 2A5
(416) 724-8333 *SIC 7389*

C S G BRODERIE & SOIE INTERNATIONALE INC *p1157*
8660 CH DARNLEY BUREAU 102, MONTROYAL, QC, H4T 1M4
(514) 738-3899 *SIC 7389*

C-LIVING INC *p779*
71 BARBER GREENE RD, NORTH YORK, ON, M3C 2A2
(416) 391-5777 *SIC 7389*

C.B.R. LASER INC *p1246*
340 RTE 116, PLESSISVILLE, QC, G6L 2Y2
(819) 362-9339 *SIC 7389*

CALGARY CONVENTION CENTRE AUTHORITY *p27*
120 9 AVE SE, CALGARY, AB, T2G 0P3
(403) 261-8500 *SIC 7389*

CALL CENTRE INC, THE *p429*
5 PIPPY PL SUITE 7, ST. JOHN'S, NL, A1B 3X2
(709) 722-3730 *SIC 7389*

CALL-US INFO LTD *p455*
6009 QUINPOOL RD, HALIFAX, NS, B3K 5J7
SIC 7389

CAMPUS TOWER SUITE HOTEL *p117*
11145 87 AVE NW, EDMONTON, AB, T6G 0Y1
(780) 439-6060 *SIC 7389*

CAMROSE REGIONAL EXHIBITION AND AGRICULTURAL SOCIETY *p78*
4250 EXHIBITION DR, CAMROSE, AB, T4V 4Z8
(780) 672-3640 *SIC 7389*

CANADA ROAD CARRIER LTD *p207*
11440 73 AVE, DELTA, BC, V4C 1B7
(604) 502-0240 *SIC 7389*

CANADA TAXES *p870*
200 TOWN CENTRE CRT SUITE 475, SCARBOROUGH, ON, M1P 4Y3

(800) 267-6999 *SIC 7389*

CANADA WORLDWIDE SERVICES INC *p501*
9 VAN DER GRAAF CRT, BRAMPTON, ON, L6T 5E5
(905) 671-1771 *SIC 7389*

CANADIAN ALPINE CENTRE *p138*
203 VILLAGE RD, LAKE LOUISE, AB, T0L 1E0
(403) 522-2200 *SIC 7389*

CANADIAN CANCER SOCIETY *p293*
565 10TH AVE W SUITE 44, VANCOUVER, BC, V5Z 4J4
(604) 879-9131 *SIC 7389*

CANADIAN NATIONAL SPORTSMEN'S SHOWS (1989) LIMITED *p705*
30 VILLAGE CENTRE PL, MISSISSAUGA, ON, L4Z 1V9
(905) 361-2677 *SIC 7389*

CANADIAN SOCIETY OF IMMIGRATION CONSULTANTS *p949*
390 BAY ST SUITE 1600, TORONTO, ON, M5H 2Y2
(416) 572-2800 *SIC 7389*

CANADIAN TEST CASE 11 *p730*
5770 HURONTARIO ST, MISSISSAUGA, ON, L5R 3G5
SIC 7389

CANADIAN TEST CASE 16 *p720*
6750 CENTURY AVE SUITE 305, MISSISSAUGA, ON, L5N 2V8
(905) 812-5920 *SIC 7389*

CANADIAN TEST CASE 167 *p730*
5770 HURONTARIO ST, MISSISSAUGA, ON, L5R 3G5
SIC 7389

CANADIAN TEST CASE 174 *p570*
123 FOURTH ST, ETOBICOKE, ON, M8V 2Y6
(905) 812-5920 *SIC 7389*

CANADIAN TEST CASE 22 *p730*
5770 HURONTARIO ST, MISSISSAUGA, ON, L5R 3G5
SIC 7389

CANADIAN TEST CASE 44 *p730*
5770 HURONTARIO ST, MISSISSAUGA, ON, L5R 3G5
SIC 7389

CANADIAN TEST CASE 74 *p730*
5770 HURONTARIO ST, MISSISSAUGA, ON, L5R 3G5
SIC 7389

CANOLA COUNCIL OF CANADA *p374*
167 LOMBARD AVE UNIT 400, WINNIPEG, MB, R3B 0T6
(204) 982-2100 *SIC 7389*

CANPAR TRANSPORT L.P. *p22*
707 BARLOW TRAIL SE UNIT D, CALGARY, AB, T2E 8C2
(800) 387-9335 *SIC 7389*

CANPAR TRANSPORT L.P. *p501*
201 WESTCREEK BLVD SUITE 102, BRAMPTON, ON, L6T 0G8
(905) 499-2699 *SIC 7389*

CARBON STEEL PROFILES LIMITED *p498*
2190 WILLIAMS PKY, BRAMPTON, ON, L6S 5X7
(905) 799-2427 *SIC 7389*

CARDINAL COURIERS LTD *p687*
6600 GOREWAY DR UNIT D, MISSISSAUGA, ON, L4V 1S6
(905) 507-4111 *SIC 7389*

CARON TRANSLATION CENTRE LTD *p822*
130 SLATER ST SUITE 700, OTTAWA, ON, K1P 6E2
(613) 230-4611 *SIC 7389*

CARTES, TIMBRES ET MONNAIE STE-FOY INC *p1271*
2740 BOUL LAURIER, QUEBEC, QC, G1V 4P7
(418) 658-5639 *SIC 7389*

CASCADES CANADA ULC *p734*
7830 TRANMERE DR SUITE UNIT, MISSISSAUGA, ON, L5S 1L9
(905) 678-8211 *SIC 7389*

CASTLE BUILDING CENTRES GROUP LTD *p730*
100 MILVERTON DR SUITE 400, MISSISSAUGA, ON, L5R 4H1
(905) 564-3307 *SIC 7389*

CECCONI SIMONE INC *p990*
1335 DUNDAS ST W, TORONTO, ON, M6J 1Y3
(416) 588-5900 *SIC 7389*

CENTRAIDE LAURENTIDES *p1058*
880 BOUL MICHELE-BOHEC BUREAU 107, BLAINVILLE, QC, J7C 5E2
(450) 436-1584 *SIC 7389*

CENTRE DE RESSOURCES EDUCATIVES ET COMMUNAUTAIRES POUR ADULTES *p1171*
10770 RUE CHAMBORD, MONTREAL, QC, H2C 2R8
(514) 596-7629 *SIC 7389*

CGTA GIFT SHOW *p583*
42 VOYAGER CRT S, ETOBICOKE, ON, M9W 5M7
(416) 679-0170 *SIC 7389*

CHASE PAYMENTECH SOLUTIONS *p866*
100 CONSILIUM PL SUITE 1400, SCARBOROUGH, ON, M1H 3E3
(416) 940-6300 *SIC 7389*

CHEMISES L. L. LESSARD INC *p1321*
1195 AV DU PALAIS, SAINT-JOSEPH-DE-BEAUCE, QC, G0S 2V0
(418) 397-5665 *SIC 7389*

CHESTER VOLUNTEER FIRE DEPARTMENT *p441*
149 CENTRAL ST, CHESTER, NS, B0J 1J0
(902) 275-5113 *SIC 7389*

CHILDREN'S WISH FOUNDATION OF CANADA, THE *p843*
1101 KINGSTON RD SUITE 350, PICKERING, ON, L1V 1B5
(905) 839-8882 *SIC 7389*

CHIPPAWA VOLUNTEER FIREFIGHTER ASSOCIATION *p758*
8696 BANTING AVE, NIAGARA FALLS, ON, L2G 6Z8
(905) 295-4398 *SIC 7389*

CIELO PRINT INC *p824*
250 CITY CENTRE AVE SUITE 138, OTTAWA, ON, K1R 6K7
(613) 232-1112 *SIC 7389*

CITILOGISTICS INC *p583*
22 HUDDERSFIELD RD, ETOBICOKE, ON, M9W 5Z6
(416) 251-5545 *SIC 7389*

CITITEL INC *p84*
11830 111 AVE NW SUITE 202, EDMONTON, AB, T5G 0E1
(780) 489-1212 *SIC 7389*

CITY OF ABBOTSFORD *p176*
32270 GEORGE FERGUSON WAY, ABBOTSFORD, BC, V2T 2L1
(604) 853-3566 *SIC 7389*

CITY-CORE MESSENGER SERVICES LTD *p294*
1185 GRANT ST, VANCOUVER, BC, V6A 2J7
(604) 254-9218 *SIC 7389*

CIVEO CANADA LIMITED PARTNERSHIP *p113*
3790 98 ST NW, EDMONTON, AB, T6E 6B4
(780) 463-8872 *SIC 7389*

CLASSIC FIRE PROTECTION INC *p792*
645 GARYRAY DR, NORTH YORK, ON, M9L 1P9
(416) 740-3000 *SIC 7389*

CLASSIC PACKAGING CORPORATION *p200*
1580 BRIGANTINE DR SUITE 100, COQUITLAM, BC, V3K 7C1
(604) 523-6700 *SIC 7389*

CLIMATE CHANGE EMISSIONS MANAGEMENT (CCEMC) CORPORATION *p162*
300 PALISADES WAY, SHERWOOD PARK, AB, T8H 2T9
(780) 417-1920 *SIC 7389*

CLSC-CHSLD D'AUTRAY p1357
2410 RUE PRINCIPALE, SAINTE-ELISABETH, QC, J0K 2J0
(450) 759-8355 *SIC* 7389

CO-PAK PACKAGING CORP p583
1231 MARTIN GROVE RD, ETOBICOKE, ON, M9W 4X2
(905) 799-0092 *SIC* 7389

COFFEE CONNECTION LTD, THE p10
401 33 ST NE UNIT 3, CALGARY, AB, T2A 7R3
(403) 269-5977 *SIC* 7389

COLISPRO INC p1307
3505 BOUL LOSCH, SAINT-HUBERT, QC, J3Y 5T7
(450) 445-7171 *SIC* 7389

COMMUNICATION DEMO INC p1187
407 RUE MCGILL BUREAU 311, MONTREAL, QC, H2Y 2G3
(514) 985-2523 *SIC* 7389

COMMUNICATION DEMO INC p1266
925 AV NEWTON BUREAU 220, QUEBEC, QC, G1P 4M2
(418) 877-0704 *SIC* 7389

COMMUNICATIONS METRO-MONTREAL INC p1218
3901 RUE JEAN-TALON O BUREAU 200, MONTREAL, QC, H3R 2G4
(514) 736-6767 *SIC* 7389

COMMUNICATIONS TRANSCRIPT INC p1194
625 AV DU PRESIDENT-KENNEDY BUREAU 800, MONTREAL, QC, H3A 1K2
(514) 874-9134 *SIC* 7389

COMMUNITY LIVING TORONTO p574
288 JUDSON ST UNIT 17, ETOBICOKE, ON, M8Z 5T6
(416) 252-1171 *SIC* 7389

COMPTEC S. G. INC p1381
1115 RUE ARMAND-BOMBARDIER, TERREBONNE, QC, J6Y 1S9
(450) 965-8166 *SIC* 7389

CONFECTION PAGAR INC p1109
451 RUE EDOUARD, GRANBY, QC, J2G 3Z4
(450) 375-5398 *SIC* 7389

CONFECTIONS STROMA INC., LES p1169
3565 RUE JARRY E BUREAU 501, MONTREAL, QC, H1Z 4K6
(514) 381-8422 *SIC* 7389

CONNECT NORTH AMERICA CORPORATION p394
275 MAIN ST SUITE 600, BATHURST, NB, E2A 1A9
(506) 545-9450 *SIC* 7389

CONSEJO DE PROMOCION TURISTICA DE MEXICO S.A. DE C.A. p303
999 HASTINGS ST W SUITE 1110, VANCOUVER, BC, V6C 2W2
SIC 7389

CONSTANT FIRE PROTECTION SYSTEMS LTD p15
5442 56 AVE SE, CALGARY, AB, T2C 4M6
(403) 279-7973 *SIC* 7389

CONSULAIR INC p1263
2022 RUE LAVOISIER BUREAU 125, QUEBEC, QC, G1N 4L5
(418) 650-5960 *SIC* 7389

CONSULTANTS DE L'ARCTIQUE INC, LES p1048
10200 RUE MIRABEAU, ANJOU, QC, H1J 1T6
(514) 353-3552 *SIC* 7389

CONSULTANTS LUPIEN ROULEAU INC p1064
1550 RUE AMPERE BUREAU 301, BOUCHERVILLE, QC, J4B 7L4
(450) 449-7333 *SIC* 7389

CONTINENTAL INVESTISSEMENTS CAPITAL INC p1338
7575 RTE TRANSCANADIENNE STE 100, SAINT-LAURENT, QC, H4T 1V6
(514) 875-6661 *SIC* 7389

CONVENTION CENTRE CORPORATION, THE p377
375 YORK AVE SUITE 243, WINNIPEG, MB, R3C 3J3
(204) 956-1720 *SIC* 7389

CORNERSTONE COURIER INC p637
219 SHOEMAKER ST, KITCHENER, ON, N2E 3B3
(519) 741-0446 *SIC* 7389

CORPORATE ASSETS INC p996
373 MUNSTER AVE, TORONTO, ON, M8Z 3C8
(416) 962-9600 *SIC* 7389

CORPORATE COURIERS LOGISTICS ULC p290
8350 PRINCE EDWARD ST, VANCOUVER, BC, V5X 3R9
SIC 7389

CORPORATION COMMERCIALE CRESCENT p1156
5430 AV ROYALMOUNT, MONT-ROYAL, QC, H4P 1H7
(514) 739-3355 *SIC* 7389

CORPORATION D'HABITATION JEANNE-MANCE, LA p1185
150 RUE ONTARIO E BUREAU 1, MONTREAL, QC, H2X 1H1
(514) 872-1221 *SIC* 7389

CORPORATION EFUNDRAISING.COM INC p1210
33 RUE PRINCE BUREAU 200, MONTREAL, QC, H3C 2M7
SIC 7389

CORPORATION OF THE CITY OF BRAMPTON, THE p509
8 RUTHERFORD RD S, BRAMPTON, ON, L6W 3J1
(905) 874-2700 *SIC* 7389

CORPORATION OF THE CITY OF CAMBRIDGE, THE p533
1625 BISHOP ST N, CAMBRIDGE, ON, N1R 7J4
(519) 621-6001 *SIC* 7389

CORPORATION OF THE CITY OF KAWARTHA LAKES, THE p645
9 CAMBRIDGE ST N, LINDSAY, ON, K9V 4C4
(705) 324-5731 *SIC* 7389

CORPORATION OF THE CITY OF NEW WESTMINSTER p236
1 SIXTH AVE E, NEW WESTMINSTER, BC, V3L 4G6
(604) 519-1000 *SIC* 7389

CORPORATION OF THE CITY OF NORTH BAY, THE p763
119 PRINCESS ST W, NORTH BAY, ON, P1B 6C2
(705) 474-5662 *SIC* 7389

CORPORATION OF THE CITY OF OSHAWA p813
199 ADELAIDE AVE W, OSHAWA, ON, L1J 7B1
(905) 433-1239 *SIC* 7389

CORPORATION OF THE CITY OF SAULT STE MARIE, THE p861
269 QUEEN ST E, SAULT STE. MARIE, ON, P6A 1Y9
(705) 759-5251 *SIC* 7389

CORPORATION OF THE CITY OF WATERLOO, THE p1007
265 LEXINGTON CRT, WATERLOO, ON, N2K 1W9
(519) 886-2310 *SIC* 7389

CORPORATION OF THE CITY OF WINDSOR p1023
815 GOYEAU ST, WINDSOR, ON, N9A 1H7
(519) 253-6573 *SIC* 7389

CORPORATION OF THE DISTRICT OF SAANICH, THE p337
760 VERNON AVE, VICTORIA, BC, V8X 2W6
(250) 475-5500 *SIC* 7389

CORPORATION OF THE TOWN OF AJAX, THE p473
435 MONARCH AVE, AJAX, ON, L1S 2G7

(905) 683-3050 *SIC* 7389

CORPORATION SERVICES MONERIS p1338
7350 RTE TRANSCANADIENNE, SAINT-LAURENT, QC, H4T 1A3
(514) 733-0443 *SIC* 7389

COSMOS I BOTTLE DEPOT p155
7428 49 AVE SUITE 1, RED DEER, AB, T4P 1M2
(403) 342-2034 *SIC* 7389

COTE OUELLET THIVIERGE NOTAIRES INC p1286
646 RUE LAFONTAINE BUREAU 100, RIVIERE-DU-LOUP, QC, G5R 3C8
(418) 863-5050 *SIC* 7389

COTE TASCHEREAU SAMSON DEMERS S.E.N.C.R.L p1270
871 GRANDE ALLEE O BUREAU 100, QUEBEC, QC, G1S 2L1
(418) 688-9375 *SIC* 7389

COUPE LASER ULTRA INC p1250
205 BOUL BRUNSWICK BUREAU 400, POINTE-CLAIRE, QC, H9R 1A5
(514) 333-8156 *SIC* 7389

COURIER COMPANY LTD, THE p989
1219 ST CLAIR AVE W, TORONTO, ON, M6E 1B5
(416) 504-7373 *SIC* 7389

COURRIER RAPIDE SERVICE p1126
640 RUE NOTRE-DAME, LACHINE, QC, H8S 2B3
(514) 866-8727 *SIC* 7389

COUTTS COURIER COMPANY LTD p1415
606 HENDERSON DR, REGINA, SK, S4N 5X3
(306) 569-9300 *SIC* 7389

COVERDELL CANADA CORPORATION p1195
1801 AV MCGILL COLLEGE BUREAU 800, MONTREAL, QC, H3A 2N4
(514) 847-7800 *SIC* 7389

COVILAC COOPERATIVE AGRICOLE p1054
40 RUE DE L'EGLISE, BAIE-DU-FEBVRE, QC, J0G 1A0
(450) 783-6491 *SIC* 7389

CRANE SERVICE SYSTEMS INC p891
419 MILLEN RD, STONEY CREEK, ON, L8E 2P6
(905) 664-9900 *SIC* 7389

CREATIONS SERGIO CANUTO INC p1169
3637 BOUL CREMAZIE E, MONTREAL, QC, H1Z 2J4
(514) 729-1116 *SIC* 7389

CREATIVE AVENUES INC p64
211 10 AVE SW, CALGARY, AB, T2R 0A4
(403) 292-0360 *SIC* 7389

CRITICAL PATH COURIERS LTD p693
1257 KAMATO RD, MISSISSAUGA, ON, L4W 2M2
(905) 212-8333 *SIC* 7389

CROSSFIELD ENVIRONMENTAL CONSULTANTS OF CANADA LIMITED p629
242 BURNS BLVD, KING CITY, ON, L7B 1E1
(905) 833-2108 *SIC* 7389

CUETS FINANCIAL LTD p1417
2055 ALBERT ST, REGINA, SK, S4P 2T8
(306) 566-1269 *SIC* 7389

CUMAF DU LAC p1045
5791 AV DU PONT N, ALMA, QC, G8E 1X1
SIC 7389

CUSTOM ALUMINUM, INC p551
40 ROMINA DR UNIT 2, CONCORD, ON, L4K 4Z7
(905) 669-8459 *SIC* 7389

CUSTOM COURIER CO. LTD p1431
501 PAKWA PL SUITE 2, SASKATOON, SK, S7L 6A3
(306) 653-8500 *SIC* 7389

CUSTOMIZED DELIVERY SERVICE INC p668
3075 14TH AVE SUITE 209, MARKHAM, ON, L3R 0G9
(905) 475-5908 *SIC* 7389

D & M LOCATING LTD p1437
4 2ND STREET W, TROSSACHS, SK, S0C 2N0
(306) 354-7907 *SIC* 7389

D.M. EXPRESS p95
11616 145 ST NW, EDMONTON, AB, T5M 1V8
(780) 454-1188 *SIC* 7389

DANGO INC p397
725 ROUTE 945 SUITE A, CORMIER-VILLAGE, NB, E4P 5Y4
(506) 533-6272 *SIC* 7389

DARTMOUTH CROSSING LIMITED p445
34 LOGIEALMOND CLOSE, DARTMOUTH, NS, B3B 0C8
(902) 445-8883 *SIC* 7389

DAWSCO COFFEE SERVICE LTD p29
4325 1 ST SE, CALGARY, AB, T2G 2L2
(403) 250-7494 *SIC* 7389

DCR STRATEGIES INC p693
2680 SKYMARK AVE SUITE 420, MISSISSAUGA, ON, L4W 5L6
(905) 212-9100 *SIC* 7389

DECOR & MORE INC p797
1171 INVICTA DR, OAKVILLE, ON, L6H 4M1
(905) 844-1300 *SIC* 7389

DEFENCE UNLIMITED INTERNATIONAL CORP p823
251 LAURIER AVE W SUITE 900, OTTAWA, ON, K1P 5J6
(613) 366-3677 *SIC* 7389

DELTA VIEW HABILITATION CENTRE LTD p210
9341 BURNS DR, DELTA, BC, V4K 3N3
(604) 501-6700 *SIC* 7389

DEPARTMENT OF COMMUNITY SERVICES CHILD WELFARE p463
161 TERRA COTTA DR, NEW GLASGOW, NS, B2H 6B6
(902) 755-5950 *SIC* 7389

DEPARTMENT OF NATIONAL DEFENCE AND THE CANADIAN ARMED FORCES p1132
9401 RUE WANKLYN, LASALLE, QC, H8R 1Z2
(514) 366-4310 *SIC* 7389

DESSINS DE STRUCTURE STELTEC INC, LES p1364
22 BOUL DESJARDINS E BUREAU 200, SAINTE-THERESE, QC, J7E 1C1
(450) 971-5995 *SIC* 7389

DESSINS DRUMMOND INC, LES p1098
455 BOUL SAINT-JOSEPH BUREAU 201, DRUMMONDVILLE, QC, J2C 7B5
(819) 477-3315 *SIC* 7389

DESTINATION WINNIPEG INC p374
259 PORTAGE AVE SUITE 300, WINNIPEG, MB, R3B 2A9
(204) 943-1970 *SIC* 7389

DGA FULFILLMENT SERVICES INC p678
80 TRAVAIL RD UNIT 1, MARKHAM, ON, L3S 3H9
SIC 7389

DHL EXPRESS (CANADA) LTD p100
10918 184 ST NW, EDMONTON, AB, T5S 2N9
(855) 345-7447 *SIC* 7389

DHL EXPRESS (CANADA) LTD p380
130 MIDLAND ST UNIT 2, WINNIPEG, MB, R3E 3R3
(855) 345-7447 *SIC* 7389

DIAMOND PLUS p544
56 ALLAN ST W, CLIFFORD, ON, N0G 1M0
(519) 327-4567 *SIC* 7389

DILL, W.C. & COMPANY INC p896
PERTH LINE SUITE 26, STRATFORD, ON, N5A 6S3
SIC 7389

DIRECT SOURCE INC p1130
2695 AV DOLLARD, LASALLE, QC, H8N 2J8
(514) 363-8882 *SIC* 7389

DIRECT TRAFFIC CONTROL INC p467

180 CHARLOTTE ST, SYDNEY, NS, B1P
1C5

(902) 564-8402 *SIC* 7389

DIRECT TRAFFIC MANAGEMENT INC *p*612
70 FRID ST SUITE 8, HAMILTON, ON, L8P
4M4

(905) 529-7000 *SIC* 7389

**DISTRIBUTIONS ALIMENTAIRES LE MAR-
QUIS INC** *p*1064
1630 RUE EIFFEL BUREAU 1,
BOUCHERVILLE, QC, J4B 7W1

(450) 645-1999 *SIC* 7389

**DISTRICT OF NORTH VANCOUVER MU-
NICIPAL PU** *p*239
165 13TH ST E, NORTH VANCOUVER, BC,
V7L 2L3

(604) 980-5021 *SIC* 7389

DISTRICT OF WEST KELOWNA *p*342
3651 OLD OKANAGAN HWY, WESTBANK,
BC, V4T 1P6

(250) 769-1640 *SIC* 7389

DMX MUSIC CANADA INC *p*35
7260 12 ST SE SUITE 120, CALGARY, AB,
T2H 2S5

(403) 640-8525 *SIC* 7389

DOCUMENS TRADUCTION INC *p*1181
7245 RUE ALEXANDRA BUREAU 301,
MONTREAL, QC, H2R 2Y9

(514) 868-9899 *SIC* 7389

DOLO INVESTIGATIONS LTD *p*270
10090 152 ST SUITE 408, SURREY, BC,
V3R 8X8

(604) 951-1600 *SIC* 7389

DOMINION DIVING LIMITED *p*443
7 CANAL ST, DARTMOUTH, NS, B2Y 2W1

(902) 434-5120 *SIC* 7389

DOVE CENTRE *p*6
6201 52 AVE, BONNYVILLE, AB, T9N 2L7

(780) 826-2552 *SIC* 7389

**DRIVE COURIER XPRESS LLC. CORPORA-
TION** *p*694
2680 MATHESON BLVD E, MISSISSAUGA,
ON, L4W 0A5

(905) 291-0888 *SIC* 7389

DUNRITE EXPRESS & HOTSHOT INC *p*109
9435 47 ST NW, EDMONTON, AB, T6B 2R7

(780) 463-8880 *SIC* 7389

DURE FOODS LIMITED *p*514
120 ROY BLVD, BRANTFORD, ON, N3R
7K2

(519) 753-5504 *SIC* 7389

DYLAN RYAN TELESERVICES *p*312
1177 HASTINGS ST W SUITE 411, VAN-
COUVER, BC, V6E 2K3

SIC 7389

DYNAMIC DIRECT COURIER *p*855
57 NEWKIRK RD, RICHMOND HILL, ON,
L4C 3G4

SIC 7389

E B M LASER INC *p*1292
109 RUE DES GRANDS-LACS, SAINT-
AUGUSTIN-DE-DESMAURES, QC, G3A 1V9

(418) 878-3616 *SIC* 7389

E CARE CONTACT CENTERS LTD *p*270
15225 104 AVE SUITE 400, SURREY, BC,
V3R 6Y8

(604) 587-6200 *SIC* 7389

E.R. PROBYN LTD *p*236
601 SIXTH ST UNIT 350, NEW WESTMIN-
STER, BC, V3L 3C1

(604) 526-8545 *SIC* 7389

EAST COAST CATERING LIMITED *p*431
30 QUEEN'S RD, ST. JOHN'S, NL, A1C 2A5

(709) 576-1741 *SIC* 7389

EASTERN EXPRESS LTD *p*427
21 ST. ANNE'S CRES, PARADISE, NL, A1L
3W1

(709) 754-8855 *SIC* 7389

EAZY EXPRESS INC *p*861
GD LCD MAIN, SAULT STE. MARIE, ON,
P6A 5L1

(705) 253-2222 *SIC* 7389

EBSCO CANADA LTD *p*678
110 COPPER CREEK DR SUITE 305,

MARKHAM, ON, L6B 0P9

(416) 297-8282 *SIC* 7389

ECON-O-PAC LIMITED *p*871
490 MIDWEST RD, SCARBOROUGH, ON,
M1P 3A9

(416) 750-7200 *SIC* 7389

EDGEWATER HOLDINGS LTD *p*250
8545 WILLOW CALE RD, PRINCE
GEORGE, BC, V2N 6Z9

(250) 561-7061 *SIC* 7389

**EDMONTON ECONOMIC DEVELOPMENT
CORPORATION** *p*88
9990 JASPER AVE NW 3RD FL, EDMON-
TON, AB, T5J 1P7

(780) 424-9191 *SIC* 7389

**EDMONTON ECONOMIC DEVELOPMENT
CORPORATION** *p*88
9797 JASPER AVE NW, EDMONTON, AB,
T5J 1N9

(780) 421-9797 *SIC* 7389

ELITE FLEET COURIER LTD *p*29
3615 MANCHESTER RD SE, CALGARY,
AB, T2G 3Z7

(403) 263-1247 *SIC* 7389

ELLIOT LAKE FIRE DEPARTMENT *p*568
55 HILLSIDE DR N, ELLIOT LAKE, ON, P5A
1X5

(705) 848-3232 *SIC* 7389

EMPIRE AUCTIONS INC *p*790
165 TYCOS DR, NORTH YORK, ON, M6B
1W6

(416) 784-4261 *SIC* 7389

ENSEIGNES INNOVA INC, LES *p*1048
9900 BOUL DU GOLF, ANJOU, QC, H1J
2Y7

(514) 323-6767 *SIC* 7389

ENTREC CORPORATION *p*1
28712 114 AVE, ACHESON, AB, T7X 6E6

(780) 962-1600 *SIC* 7389

ENTREPRISES LAMCOIL INC, LES *p*1236
2748 BOUL DANIEL-JOHNSON, MON-
TREAL, QC, H7P 5Z7

(450) 682-4444 *SIC* 7389

ENVIZION VENTURE CAPITAL CORP *p*669
3601 HIGHWAY 7 E, MARKHAM, ON, L3R
0M3

(289) 301-4485 *SIC* 7389

ERB INTERNATIONAL INC *p*752
290 HAMILTON RD, NEW HAMBURG, ON,
N3A 1A2

(519) 662-2710 *SIC* 7389

ESCAPE FIRE PROTECTION LTD *p*176
30465 PROGRESSIVE WAY UNIT 8, AB-
BOTSFORD, BC, V2T 6W3

(604) 864-0376 *SIC* 7389

EVENT RENTAL GROUP GP INC *p*918
210 WICKSTEED AVE, TORONTO, ON,
M4G 2C3

(416) 759-2611 *SIC* 7389

EVENT SCAPE INC *p*571
4 BESTOBELL RD, ETOBICOKE, ON, M8W
4H3

(416) 231-8855 *SIC* 7389

EXECUTIVE WOODWORK LTD *p*552
330 SPINNAKER WAY, CONCORD, ON,
L4K 4W1

(905) 669-6429 *SIC* 7389

EXPO SECURITE INVESTIGATIONS INC
*p*1174
1600 AV DE LORIMIER BUREAU 140,
MONTREAL, QC, H2K 3W5

SIC 7389

**EXPRESS-IT DELIVERY SERVICES (2002)
INC** *p*276
13350 COMBER WAY, SURREY, BC, V3W
5V9

(604) 543-7800 *SIC* 7389

EXTEND COMMUNICATIONS INC *p*517
49 CHARLOTTE ST, BRANTFORD, ON,
N3T 2W4

(416) 534-0477 *SIC* 7389

EXTERNAT SAINT-JEAN-EUDES *p*1144
2151 RUE SAINT-GEORGES, LONGUEUIL,
QC, J4K 4A7

(450) 677-2184 *SIC* 7389

FAIRMONT HOTELS & RESORTS INC *p*408
2081 MAIN ST, MONCTON, NB, E1E 1J2

(506) 877-3025 *SIC* 7389

FASTIK LABEL & SUPPLY INC *p*224
9703 199A ST, LANGLEY, BC, V1M 2X7

(604) 882-6853 *SIC* 7389

**FEDERAL EXPRESS CANADA CORPORA-
TION** *p*23
24 AERO DR NE, CALGARY, AB, T2E 8Z9

(800) 463-3339 *SIC* 7389

**FEDERAL EXPRESS CANADA CORPORA-
TION** *p*185
4270 DAWSON ST, BURNABY, BC, V5C
4B1

(800) 463-3339 *SIC* 7389

**FEDERAL EXPRESS CANADA CORPORA-
TION** *p*264
3151 AYLMER RD, RICHMOND, BC, V7B
1L5

(800) 463-3339 *SIC* 7389

**FEDERAL EXPRESS CANADA CORPORA-
TION** *p*702
1450 CATERPILLAR RD, MISSISSAUGA,
ON, L4X 2Y1

(800) 463-3339 *SIC* 7389

**FEDERAL EXPRESS CANADA CORPORA-
TION** *p*1309
5005 RUE J.-A.-BOMBARDIER BUREAU A,
SAINT-HUBERT, QC, J3Z 1G4

(800) 463-3339 *SIC* 7389

**FEDERAL EXPRESS CANADA CORPORA-
TION** *p*1339
4041 RUE SERE, SAINT-LAURENT, QC,
H4T 2A3

(800) 463-3339 *SIC* 7389

FEENEY R.A. LOGGING & TRUCKING LTD
*p*418
9 NEW MARKET BYE RD, SMITHFIELD,
NB, E6K 2T9

SIC 7389

**FENETY MARKETING SERVICES (AT-
LANTIC) LTD** *p*408
295 ENGLISH DR, MONCTON, NB, E1E
0J3

(800) 561-4422 *SIC* 7389

FERROTECH MENARD INC *p*1082
665 RUE AKHURST, COATICOOK, QC, K1A
0B4

(819) 849-9474 *SIC* 7389

FGG INSPECTIONS INC *p*162
140 PORTAGE CLOSE, SHERWOOD
PARK, AB, T8H 2W2

(780) 464-3444 *SIC* 7389

**FIELDING CHEMICAL TECHNOLOGIES
INC** *p*711
3575 MAVIS RD, MISSISSAUGA, ON, L5C
1T7

(905) 279-5122 *SIC* 7389

FIGURE 3 *p*951
200 UNIVERSITY AVE SUITE 200,
TORONTO, ON, M5H 3C6

(416) 363-6993 *SIC* 7389

FIRE EMERGENCY SERVICE *p*1004
510 NAPIER ST E, WALKERTON, ON, N0G
2V0

(519) 881-0642 *SIC* 7389

FIRE MONITORING OF CANADA INC *p*887
235 MARTINDALE RD UNIT 19, ST
CATHARINES, ON, L2W 1A5

(905) 688-0600 *SIC* 7389

FIRE PROTECTION INC *p*109
6748 59 ST NW, EDMONTON, AB, T6B 3N6

(780) 469-1454 *SIC* 7389

FIRE TECH FIRE PROTECTION INC *p*162
2210 PREMIER WAY UNIT 170, SHER-
WOOD PARK, AB, T8H 2L2

(780) 400-3473 *SIC* 7389

FIRE-PRO FIRE PROTECTION LTD *p*192
3871 NORTH FRASER WAY SUITE 15,
BURNABY, BC, V5J 5G6

(604) 299-1030 *SIC* 7389

**FIRST CANADIAN MESSENGER SERVICE
INC** *p*276

13350 COMBER WAY, SURREY, BC, V3W
5V9

(604) 590-3301 *SIC* 7389

**FIRST CHOICE COURIER & MESSENGER
LTD** *p*367
704 WATT ST, WINNIPEG, MB, R2K 2S7

(204) 661-3668 *SIC* 7389

**FIRST IMPRESSIONS SPORTSWEAR &
CRESTING INC** *p*35
6130 4 ST SE UNIT 7, CALGARY, AB, T2H
2B6

(403) 258-3212 *SIC* 7389

**FIRST INTERNATIONAL COURIER SYS-
TEMS INC** *p*584
33 INTERNATIONAL BLVD, ETOBICOKE,
ON, M9W 6H3

(416) 968-2000 *SIC* 7389

FLASH COURIER SERVICES INC *p*294
1213 FRANCES ST, VANCOUVER, BC,
V6A 1Z4

(604) 689-3278 *SIC* 7389

FLEX EXPORT *p*1086
2525 BOUL DANIEL-JOHNSON BUREAU
290, COTE SAINT-LUC, QC, H7T 1S9

(450) 687-3030 *SIC* 7389

FLEXTRONICS AUTOMOTIVE INC *p*670
450 HOOD RD, MARKHAM, ON, L3R 9Z3

(800) 668-5649 *SIC* 7389

**FONDATION DE L'HOPITAL DE MONTREAL
POUR ENFANTS, LA** *p*1220
3400 RUE DE MAISONNEUVE O BU-
REAU 1420, MONTREAL, QC, H3Z 3B8

(514) 934-4846 *SIC* 7389

**FONDATION DE L'HOPITAL SAINTE-ANNE-
DE-BEAUPRE INC** *p*1055
11000 RUE DES MONTAGNARDS,
BEAUPRE, QC, G0A 1E0

(418) 827-3726 *SIC* 7389

**FONDATION DE L'UNIVERSITE DU QUE-
BEC A MONTREAL** *p*1175
405 BOUL DE MAISONNEUVE E BUREAU
2300, MONTREAL, QC, H2L 4J5

(514) 987-3030 *SIC* 7389

FOOD ALLERGY CANADA *p*767
2005 SHEPPARD AVE E SUITE 800,
NORTH YORK, ON, M2J 5B4

(416) 785-5666 *SIC* 7389

FOOTPRINTS SECURITY PATROL INC *p*243
GD, PARKSVILLE, BC, V9P 2G2

(250) 248-9117 *SIC* 7389

FOR. PAR SODEPLAN INC *p*1188
388 RUE SAINT-JACQUES BUREAU 900,
MONTREAL, QC, H2Y 1S1

(514) 871-8833 *SIC* 7389

FORCE INSPECTION SERVICES INC *p*139
7500A 43 ST, LEDUC, AB, T9E 7E8

(780) 955-2370 *SIC* 7389

**FOREIGNEXCHANGE TRANSLATIONS
CANADA, INC** *p*446
10 MORRIS DR UNIT 40, DARTMOUTH,
NS, B3B 1K8

(902) 468-5553 *SIC* 7389

FREEMAN EXPOSITIONS, LTD *p*995
61 BROWNS LINE, TORONTO, ON, M8W
3S2

(416) 252-3361 *SIC* 7389

FUNDS FLOW CANADA INC *p*803
2201 SPEERS RD, OAKVILLE, ON, L6L 2X9

SIC 7389

FUSION BPO SERVICES LIMITED *p*1188
507 PLACE D'ARMES BUREAU 1000,
MONTREAL, QC, H2Y 2W8

(514) 227-3126 *SIC* 7389

FUSION SOLUTION INC *p*1111
700 RUE BERNARD, GRANBY, QC, J2J
0H6

(450) 372-4994 *SIC* 7389

FUTUREVAULT INC *p*980
441 KING ST W UNIT 200, TORONTO, ON,
M5V 1K4

(416) 560-7808 *SIC* 7389

GAGE-BABCOCK & ASSOCIATES LTD *p*319
1195 BROADWAY W SUITE 228, VANCOU-
VER, BC, V6H 3X5

(604) 732-3751 *SIC 7389*
GAGNE, ISABELLE, PATRY, LAFLAMME & ASSOCIES NOTAIRES INC *p1106*
188 RUE MONTCALM BUREAU 300, GATINEAU, QC, J8Y 3B5
(819) 771-3231 *SIC 7389*
GAGNON CANTIN LACHAPELLE & ASSOCIES (SENCRL) *p1359*
2484 RUE CARTIER, SAINTE-JULIENNE, QC, J0K 2T0
(450) 831-2171 *SIC 7389*
GAGNON SENECHAL COULOMBE & ASSOCIES *p1257*
800 BOUL DES CAPUCINS, QUEBEC, QC, G1J 3R8
(418) 648-1717 *SIC 7389*
GAGNON, CANTIN, LACHAPELLE, SASSEVILLE, ETHIER, RIOPEL, HEBERT, LORD (SENCRL) NOTAIRES *p1114*
37 PLACE BOURGET S BUREAU 301, JOLIETTE, QC, J6E 5G1
(450) 755-4535 *SIC 7389*
GEMALTO CANADA INC *p522*
5347 JOHN LUCAS DR, BURLINGTON, ON, L7L 6A8
(905) 335-9681 *SIC 7389*
GENERAL MOTORS OF CANADA COMPANY *p670*
101 MCNABB ST, MARKHAM, ON, L3R 4H8
(905) 644-5000 *SIC 7389*
GES EXPOSITION SERVICES (CANADA) LIMITED *p731*
5675 MCLAUGHLIN RD, MISSISSAUGA, ON, L5R 3K5
(905) 283-0500 *SIC 7389*
GESTION 357 DE LA COMMUNE INC *p1188*
357 RUE DE LA COMMUNE O, MONTREAL, QC, H2Y 2E2
(514) 499-0357 *SIC 7389*
GESTION D'ETUDE PPKF (1984) INC *p1188*
507 PLACE D'ARMES BUREAU 1300, MONTREAL, QC, H2Y 2W8
(514) 282-1287 *SIC 7389*
GILMAR CRANE SERVICE LTD *p142*
3216 3 AVE S, LETHBRIDGE, AB, T1J 4H5
(403) 327-6511 *SIC 7389*
GLENGARRY NEWS LIMITED, THE *p476*
3 MAIN ST S, ALEXANDRIA, ON, K0C 1A0
(613) 525-2020 *SIC 7389*
GLOBAL CONVENTION SERVICES LTD *p415*
48 BROAD ST, SAINT JOHN, NB, E2L 1Y5
(506) 658-0506 *SIC 7389*
GLOBAL NET TRADE *p1027*
50 PARISIENNE RD, WOODBRIDGE, ON, L4H 0V4
(905) 417-9470 *SIC 7389*
GLOBAL PAYMENT SYSTEMS OF CANADA, LTD *p765*
3381 STEELES AVE E SUITE 200, NORTH YORK, ON, M2H 3S7
(416) 644-5959 *SIC 7389*
GLOBAL TELESALES OF CANADA INC *p841*
1900 FISHER DR, PETERBOROUGH, ON, K9J 6X6
(705) 872-3021 *SIC 7389*
GOLDEN FOOD & MANUFACTURE LTD *p553*
241 SNIDERCROFT RD, CONCORD, ON, L4K 2J8
(905) 660-3233 *SIC 7389*
GOOD WATER COMPANY LTD, THE *p492*
163 COLLEGE ST W, BELLEVILLE, ON, K8P 2G7
(613) 707-8400 *SIC 7389*
GOODKEY SHOW SERVICES LTD *p109*
5506-48 ST NW, EDMONTON, AB, T6B 2Z1
(780) 426-2211 *SIC 7389*
GOUVERNEMENT DE LA PROVINCE DE QUEBEC *p1104*
1100 BOUL MALONEY O BUREAU 1600, GATINEAU, QC, J8T 6G3
(819) 994-7739 *SIC 7389*

GOUVERNEMENT DE LA PROVINCE DE QUEBEC *p1191*
159 RUE SAINT-ANTOINE O BUREAU 900, MONTREAL, QC, H2Z 1H2
(514) 871-8122 *SIC 7389*
GOUVERNEMENT DE LA PROVINCE DE QUEBEC *p1191*
159 RUE SAINT-ANTOINE O BUREAU 900, MONTREAL, QC, H2Z 1H2
(514) 871-8122 *SIC 7389*
GOVERNORS OF THE UNIVERSITY OF CALGARY, THE *p41*
2500 UNIVERSITY DR NW, CALGARY, AB, T2N 1N4
(403) 220-5110 *SIC 7389*
GRAPHISCAN QUEBEC INC *p1262*
210 RUE FORTIN BUREAU 100, QUEBEC, QC, G1M 0A4
(418) 266-0707 *SIC 7389*
GRAYMATTER DIRECT (CANADA) INC *p945*
600 BAY ST SUITE 400, TORONTO, ON, M5G 1M6
(416) 341-0623 *SIC 7389*
GREAT NORTHERN AUCTION COMPANY LTD *p409*
2131 ROUTE 128, MONCTON, NB, E1G 4K5
(506) 382-2777 *SIC 7389*
GREATER NAPANEE FIRE DEPARTMENT *p747*
66 ADVANCE AVE, NAPANEE, ON, K7R 3Y6
(613) 354-3415 *SIC 7389*
GREATER VANCOUVER CONVENTION AND VISITORS BUREAU *p305*
200 BURRARD ST SUITE 210, VANCOUVER, BC, V6C 3L6
(604) 682-2222 *SIC 7389*
GREEN LIGHT COURIER INC *p867*
705 PROGRESS AVE SUITE 26, SCARBOROUGH, ON, M1H 2X1
SIC 7389
GROOMBRIDGE, W. ENTERPRISES INC *p858*
1380 LONDON RD, SARNIA, ON, N7S 1P8
SIC 7389
GROUNDSTAR EXPRESS LTD *p206*
1260 CLIVEDEN AVE, DELTA, BC, V3M 6Y1
(604) 527-1038 *SIC 7389*
GROUPE CANTREX NATIONWIDE INC *p1324*
9900 BOUL CAVENDISH BUREAU 400, SAINT-LAURENT, QC, H4M 2V2
(514) 335-0260 *SIC 7389*
GROUPE CHAGALL INC *p1358*
2051 RUE LEONARD-DE VINCI, SAINTE-JULIE, QC, J3E 1Z2
(450) 649-1001 *SIC 7389*
GROUPE MARKETING INTERNATIONAL INC *p1083*
37 BOUL DES LAURENTIDES, COTE SAINT-LUC, QC, H7G 2S3
(450) 972-1540 *SIC 7389*
GROUPEX SYSTEMS CANADA INC *p105*
15102 128 AVE NW, EDMONTON, AB, T5V 1A8
(780) 454-3366 *SIC 7389*
GRUES J.M. FRANCOEUR INC *p1164*
6155 RUE LA FONTAINE, MONTREAL, QC, H1N 2B8
(514) 747-5700 *SIC 7389*
GSMPRJCT CREATION INC *p1205*
355 RUE SAINTE-CATHERINE O BUREAU 500, MONTREAL, QC, H3B 1A5
(514) 288-4233 *SIC 7389*
GUELPH PROFESSIONAL FIRE FIGHTERS ASSOCIATION *p603*
50 WYNDHAM ST S, GUELPH, ON, N1H 4E1
SIC 7389
GUELPH, CITY OF *p603*
50 WYNDHAM ST S, GUELPH, ON, N1H 4E1
(519) 824-6590 *SIC 7389*

HAMILTON ENTERTAINMENT AND CONVENTION FACILITIES INC, THE *p612*
1 SUMMERS LN, HAMILTON, ON, L8P 4Y2
(905) 546-3000 *SIC 7389*
HAMILTON HEALTH SCIENCES FOUNDATION *p613*
40 WELLINGTON ST N SUITE 203, HAMILTON, ON, L8R 1M8
(905) 522-3863 *SIC 7389*
HARDCASTLE DESIGNS LTD *p30*
1316 9 AVE SE SUITE 200, CALGARY, AB, T2G 0T3
(403) 250-7733 *SIC 7389*
HEALTHCONNECT INC *p407*
210 JOHN ST SUITE 200, MONCTON, NB, E1C 0B8
(506) 384-8020 *SIC 7389*
HEALTHPRO PROCUREMENT SERVICES INC *p731*
5770 HURONTARIO ST SUITE 902, MISSISSAUGA, ON, L5R 3G5
(905) 568-3478 *SIC 7389*
HEART AND STROKE FOUNDATION OF MANITOBA INC *p387*
6 DONALD ST SUITE 200, WINNIPEG, MB, R3L 0K6
(204) 949-2000 *SIC 7389*
HEARTLAND FRESH PAK INC *p361*
GD STN MAIN, WINKLER, MB, R6W 4A3
(204) 325-6948 *SIC 7389*
HEDLEY IMPROVEMENT DISTRICT *p215*
825 RUE SCOTT, HEDLEY, BC, V0X 1K0
(250) 292-8637 *SIC 7389*
HEFFEL GALLERY LIMITED *p319*
2247 GRANVILLE ST, VANCOUVER, BC, V6H 3G1
(604) 732-6505 *SIC 7389*
HGS CANADA INC *p446*
250 BROWNLOW AVE SUITE 11, DARTMOUTH, NS, B3B 1W9
(902) 481-9475 *SIC 7389*
HIGHTECH SALES COACH INC *p319*
1338 BROADWAY W SUITE 305, VANCOUVER, BC, V6H 1H2
(604) 731-1377 *SIC 7389*
HITE SERVICES LIMITED *p898*
790 LAPOINTE ST, SUDBURY, ON, P3A 5N8
(705) 524-5333 *SIC 7389*
HMC COMMUNICATIONS INC *p455*
2829 AGRICOLA ST, HALIFAX, NS, B3K 4E5
(902) 453-0700 *SIC 7389*
HMT CANADA LTD *p16*
11051 50 ST SE UNIT 130, CALGARY, AB, T2C 3E5
(403) 252-4487 *SIC 7389*
HOLMES & BRAKEL LIMITED *p844*
830 BROCK RD, PICKERING, ON, L1W 1Z8
(905) 831-6831 *SIC 7389*
HOME CAPITAL GROUP INC *p952*
145 KING ST W SUITE 2300, TORONTO, ON, M5H 1J8
(416) 360-4663 *SIC 7389*
HOMETOWN COMMUNICATIONS *p404*
97 PINE ST, LORNE, NB, E8G 1M6
SIC 7389
HORNBY ISLAND NEW HORIZONS *p284*
1765 SOLLANS, UNION BAY, BC, V0R 3B0
(250) 335-0385 *SIC 7389*
HOT SHOT TRUCKING (1990) LTD *p217*
937 LAVAL CRES, KAMLOOPS, BC, V2C 5P4
(250) 372-7651 *SIC 7389*
I-L SUCCESSOR CORP *p509*
31 HANSEN RD S, BRAMPTON, ON, L6W 3H7
SIC 7389
IBM CANADA LIMITED *p414*
400 MAIN ST SUITE 1000, SAINT JOHN, NB, E2K 4N5
(506) 646-4000 *SIC 7389*
ICT CANADA MARKETING INC *p405*
408 KING GEORGE HWY, MIRAMICHI, NB,

E1V 1L4
(506) 836-9050 *SIC 7389*
ICT CANADA MARKETING INC *p411*
720 COVERDALE RD UNIT 9, RIVERVIEW, NB, E1B 3L8
SIC 7389
ICT CANADA MARKETING INC *p414*
400 MAIN ST SUITE 2004, SAINT JOHN, NB, E2K 4N5
(506) 653-9050 *SIC 7389*
ICT CANADA MARKETING INC *p421*
80 POWELL DR, CARBONEAR, NL, A1Y 1A5
SIC 7389
ICT CANADA MARKETING INC *p461*
800 SACKVILLE DR, LOWER SACKVILLE, NS, B4E 1R8
(902) 869-9050 *SIC 7389*
ICT CANADA MARKETING INC *p463*
690 EAST RIVER RD, NEW GLASGOW, NS, B2H 3S1
(902) 755-9050 *SIC 7389*
ICT CANADA MARKETING INC *p467*
325 VULCAN AVE, SYDNEY, NS, B1P 5X1
SIC 7389
ICT CANADA MARKETING INC *p646*
370 KENT ST W UNIT 16, LINDSAY, ON, K9V 6G8
SIC 7389
IMAGEHOUSE LIMITED *p825*
275 BAY ST, OTTAWA, ON, K1R 5Z5
(613) 238-6232 *SIC 7389*
IMKT DIRECT SOLUTIONS CORPORATION *p923*
90 EGLINTON AVE W SUITE 300, TORONTO, ON, M4R 2E4
(416) 633-4646 *SIC 7389*
IMMEDIATE DELIVERY & COURIER SERVICE INC *p475*
255 SALEM RD N SUITE D2, AJAX, ON, L1Z 0B1
(905) 427-7733 *SIC 7389*
IMMOVEX INC *p1068*
2210 BOUL LAPINIERE, BROSSARD, QC, J4W 1M2
(450) 671-9205 *SIC 7389*
IMPACT AUTO AUCTIONS LTD *p710*
50 BURNHAMTHORPE RD W SUITE 800, MISSISSAUGA, ON, L5B 3C2
(905) 896-9727 *SIC 7389*
IMPRIMERIES TRANSCONTINENTAL 2005 S.E.N.C *p1146*
750 RUE DEVEAULT, LOUISEVILLE, QC, J5V 3C2
(819) 228-2766 *SIC 7389*
IN STORE FOCUS *p574*
50 QUEEN ELIZABETH BLVD, ETOBICOKE, ON, M8Z 1M1
SIC 7389
INDUSTRIES BONIMETAL INC, LES *p1344*
9225 RUE LE ROYER, SAINT-LEONARD, QC, H1P 3H7
(514) 325-6151 *SIC 7389*
INDUSTRIES HYPERSHELL INC *p1370*
740 RUE GALT O BUREAU 401, SHERBROOKE, QC, J1H 1Z3
(819) 822-3890 *SIC 7389*
INDUSTRIES LONGCHAMPS LTEE, LES *p1299*
25 BOUL SAINT-JOSEPH, SAINT-EPHREM-DE-BEAUCE, QC, G0M 1R0
(418) 484-2080 *SIC 7389*
INFINITY & ASSOCIATES LLP / INC *p991*
36 LISGAR ST SUITE 623W, TORONTO, ON, M6J 0C7
(888) 508-6277 *SIC 7389*
INFORMATION COMMUNICATION SERVICES (ICS) INC *p574*
288 JUDSON ST SUITE 1, ETOBICOKE, ON, M8Z 5T6
SIC 7389
INFORMATION COMMUNICATION SERVICES (ICS) INC *p874*
80 COWDRAY CRT, SCARBOROUGH, ON,

M1S 4N1

(416) 642-2477 *SIC* 7389

INMAR PROMOTIONS - CANADA INC. *p414*
661 MILLIDGE AVE, SAINT JOHN, NB, E2K
2N7

(506) 632-1400 *SIC* 7389

INNOVATION MARITIME *p1284*
53 RUE SAINT-GERMAIN O, RIMOUSKI,
QC, G5L 4B4

(418) 725-3525 *SIC* 7389

INNOVATIVE DETAILING SERVICES INC
p867
695 MARKHAM RD SUITE 29, SCARBOR-
OUGH, ON, M1H 2A5

(416) 438-6004 *SIC* 7389

INNOVATIVE INTERIOR SYSTEMS *p107*
2050 227 AVE NE, EDMONTON, AB, T5Y
6H5

(780) 414-0637 *SIC* 7389

INSERCO-QUEBEC INC *p1326*
674 RUE DESLAURIERS, SAINT-
LAURENT, QC, H4N 1W5

(514) 523-1551 *SIC* 7389

INSPECTIONS GROUP INC, THE *p85*
12010 111 AVE NW, EDMONTON, AB, T5G
0E6

(780) 454-5048 *SIC* 7389

INTEGRATED PROACTION CORP *p216*
1425 HUGH ALLAN DR, KAMLOOPS, BC,
V1S 1J3

(250) 828-7977 *SIC* 7389

INTELCOM COURRIER CANADA INC *p1211*
1380 RUE WILLIAM BUREAU 200, MON-
TREAL, QC, H3C 1R5

(514) 937-0430 *SIC* 7389

INTELCOM COURRIER CANADA INC *p1211*
1380 RUE WILLIAM, MONTREAL, QC, H3C
1R5

(514) 875-2778 *SIC* 7389

INTER CLOTURES INC *p1387*
9200 BOUL PARENT, TROIS-RIVIERES,
QC, G9A 5E1

(819) 377-5837 *SIC* 7389

INTERAXON INC *p981*
555 RICHMOND ST W, SUITE 900,
TORONTO, ON, M5V 3B1

(416) 598-8989 *SIC* 7389

INTERIOR IMAGES LIMITED *p346*
1440 ROSSER AVE UNIT 1, BRANDON,
MB, R7A 0M4

(204) 726-8282 *SIC* 7389

**INTERLAKES VOLUNTEER FIRE DEPART-
MENT** *p180*
7657 LITTLE FORT HWY SUITE 24,
BRIDGE LAKE, BC, V0K 1E0

(250) 593-4266 *SIC* 7389

**INTERMAP TECHNOLOGIES CORPORA-
TION** *p749*
2 GURDWARA RD SUITE 200, NEPEAN,
ON, K2E 1A2

SIC 7389

**INTERNATIONAL CONFERENCE SER-
VICES LTD** *p314*
1201 PENDER ST W SUITE 300, VANCOU-
VER, BC, V6E 2V2

(604) 681-2153 *SIC* 7389

**INTERNET COURIER MESSENGER SER-
VICES** *p362*
1137 PANDORA AVE W, WINNIPEG, MB,
R2C 1N4

SIC 7389

INTERPAC FOREST PRODUCTS LTD *p225*
9701 201 ST, LANGLEY, BC, V1M 3E7

(604) 881-2300 *SIC* 7389

INTERTEK INSPECTION SERVICES, LTD
p105
14920 135 AVE NW, EDMONTON, AB, T5V
1R9

(780) 482-5911 *SIC* 7389

INTERWORX PLANNING AND DESIGN *p314*
1140 PENDER ST W SUITE 600, VANCOU-
VER, BC, V6E 4G1

(604) 806-6255 *SIC* 7389

INVENTAIRES LAPARE INC *p1152*

11329 MONTEE SAINTE-MARIANNE,
MIRABEL, QC, J7J 2B2

(450) 435-2997 *SIC* 7389

**INVESTIGATION PROTECTION ACCES SE-
CURITE INC** *p1366*
283 RUE JACQUES-CARTIER BUREAU
6, SALABERRY-DE-VALLEYFIELD, QC, J6T
4S9

(450) 377-3008 *SIC* 7389

INVIS INC *p731*
5770 HURONTARIO ST SUITE 600, MIS-
SISSAUGA, ON, L5R 3G5

(905) 283-3300 *SIC* 7389

IQ OFFICE SUITES HOLDINGS INC *p953*
150 KING ST W SUITE 200, TORONTO,
ON, M5H 1J9

(888) 744-2292 *SIC* 7389

IQPC WORLDWIDE COMPANY *p925*
60 ST CLAIR AVE E SUITE 304, TORONTO,
ON, M4T 1N5

(416) 597-4700 *SIC* 7389

IRONHORSE CORPORATION *p749*
9 CAPELLA CRT UNIT 200, NEPEAN, ON,
K2E 8A7

(613) 228-2813 *SIC* 7389

**ISLAND TIMBERLANDS LIMITED PART-
NERSHIP** *p233*
65 FRONT ST, NANAIMO, BC, V9R 5H9

(250) 755-3500 *SIC* 7389

ISOTOPE MUSIC INC *p528*
3375 NORTH SERVICE RD UNIT B9-B11,
BURLINGTON, ON, L7N 3G2

(905) 333-3001 *SIC* 7389

IVEY BUSINESS SCHOOL FOUNDATION
p651
551 WINDERMERE RD, LONDON, ON,
N5X 2T1

(519) 679-4546 *SIC* 7389

J Y S ENTERPRISE INC *p740*
1081 MEYERSIDE DR UNIT 8, MISSIS-
SAUGA, ON, L5T 1M4

(905) 565-1472 *SIC* 7389

J.B. MERCHANDISE DESIGN INC *p681*
233 WHITFIELD CRES, MIDLAND, ON, L4R
5E3

(705) 361-2012 *SIC* 7389

**J.D. COLLINS FIRE PROTECTION COM-
PANY INC** *p1027*
101 INNOVATION DR UNIT 1, WOOD-
BRIDGE, ON, L4H 0S3

(905) 660-4535 *SIC* 7389

J.L. & SONS TRADING COMPANY LTD *p182*
6990 GREENWOOD ST, BURNABY, BC,
V5A 1X8

(604) 294-2331 *SIC* 7389

JARDINE AUCTIONEERS INC *p403*
1849 ROUTE 640, HANWELL, NB, E3C 2A7

(506) 454-4400 *SIC* 7389

JEWISH FEDERATION OF OTTAWA *p829*
21 NADOLNY SACHS PVT, OTTAWA, ON,
K2A 1R9

(613) 798-4696 *SIC* 7389

JOBS UNLIMITED INC *p401*
1079 YORK ST, FREDERICTON, NB, E3B
3S4

(506) 458-9380 *SIC* 7389

JONATHAN'S DONUTS LTD *p751*
250 GREENBANK RD, NEPEAN, ON, K2H
8X4

(613) 829-8691 *SIC* 7389

JONES PACKAGING INC *p504*
55 WALKER DR, BRAMPTON, ON, L6T 5K5

(800) 387-1188 *SIC* 7389

JPDL MULTI MANAGEMENT INC *p1197*
1555 RUE PEEL BUREAU 500, MON-
TREAL, QC, H3A 3L8

(514) 287-1070 *SIC* 7389

JSK TRAFFIC CONTROL SERVICES INC
p235
2005 WARING RD, NANAIMO, BC, V9X 1V1

(250) 618-0232 *SIC* 7389

**KAHNAWAKE FIRE BRIGADE AMBU-
LANCE SERVICE** *p1116*
520 RUE OLD MALONE, KAHNAWAKE,

QC, J0L 1B0

(450) 632-2010 *SIC* 7389

KARO DESIGN VANCOUVER INC *p295*
611 ALEXANDER ST SUITE 308, VANCOU-
VER, BC, V6A 1E1

(604) 255-6100 *SIC* 7389

KARO GROUP INC *p72*
1817 10 AVE SW, CALGARY, AB, T3C 0K2

(403) 266-4094 *SIC* 7389

KASTNER AUCTIONS LTD *p96*
11205 149 ST NW, EDMONTON, AB, T5M
1W6

(780) 447-0596 *SIC* 7389

KCLC PROPERTIES ULC *p629*
12750 JANE ST, KING CITY, ON, L7B 1A3

(905) 833-3086 *SIC* 7389

KEELE HOLDINGS INC *p554*
8001 KEELE ST, CONCORD, ON, L4K 1Y8

(905) 669-9855 *SIC* 7389

KELOWNA AMBASSADORS *p218*
680 VALLEY RD SUITE 25, KELOWNA, BC,
V1V 2J3

(250) 712-1634 *SIC* 7389

KENNEBECASIS VALLEY FIRE DEPT *p412*
7 CAMPBELL DR, ROTHESAY, NB, E2E
5B6

(506) 848-6601 *SIC* 7389

**KEYSTONE AGRICULTURE & RECRE-
ATION CENTRE INC** *p346*
1175 18TH ST UNIT 1, BRANDON, MB,
R7A 7C5

(204) 726-3500 *SIC* 7389

KHEERAN INSPECTION SERVICES INC
p149
702 23 AVE, NISKU, AB, T9E 7Y6

(780) 800-6295 *SIC* 7389

KING'S EMBROIDERY LTD *p874*
225 NUGGET AVE SUITE 6, SCARBOR-
OUGH, ON, M1S 3L2

(416) 292-7471 *SIC* 7389

KODIAK CALL CENTRE LTD *p1023*
525 WINDSOR AVE, WINDSOR, ON, N9A
1J4

SIC 7389

**KRUPP, MASHA TRANSLATION GROUP
LTD, THE** *p750*
1547 MERIVALE RD SUITE 500, NEPEAN,
ON, K2G 4V3

(613) 820-4566 *SIC* 7389

**L'ASSOCIATION TOURISTIQUE DE
L'OUTAOUAIS** *p1105*
103 RUE LAURIER, GATINEAU, QC, J8X
3V8

(819) 778-2222 *SIC* 7389

L'USINE TAC TIC INC *p1305*
2030 127E RUE, SAINT-GEORGES, QC,
G5Y 2W8

(418) 227-4279 *SIC* 7389

L.O.D.A INC *p1226*
1200 RUE DE LOUVAIN O, MONTREAL,
QC, H4N 1G5

(514) 382-0571 *SIC* 7389

LABELIX INC *p1109*
536 RUE GUY, GRANBY, QC, J2G 7J8

(450) 372-7777 *SIC* 7389

**LABORATOIRE D'ESSAIS MEQUALTECH
INC** *p1170*
8740 BOUL PIE-IX, MONTREAL, QC, H1Z
3V1

(514) 593-5755 *SIC* 7389

**LABORATOIRE DE CANALISATIONS
SOUTERRAINES (LCS) INC** *p1264*
255 AV SAINT-SACREMENT, QUEBEC,
QC, G1N 3X9

(418) 651-9306 *SIC* 7389

LAJOIE LEMIEUX NOTAIRES S.E.N.C.R.L
p1080
138 RUE PRICE O BUREAU 208,
CHICOUTIMI, QC, G7J 1G8

(418) 549-6464 *SIC* 7389

**LANGE TRANSPORTATION & STORAGE
LTD** *p688*
3965 NASHUA DR, MISSISSAUGA, ON,
L4V 1P3

(905) 362-1290 *SIC* 7389

**LANGLEY, CORPORATION OF THE TOWN-
SHIP OF** *p226*
22170 50 AVE, LANGLEY, BC, V2Y 2V4

(604) 532-7500 *SIC* 7389

LANGUAGES OF LIFE INC *p826*
99 FIFTH AVE SUITE 14, OTTAWA, ON,
K1S 5K4

(613) 232-9770 *SIC* 7389

LAPRAIRIE CRANE LTD *p284*
GD, TUMBLER RIDGE, BC, V0C 2W0

(250) 242-5561 *SIC* 7389

LASALLE CENTRE RECREATIF *p1132*
707 75E AV, LASALLE, QC, H8R 3Y2

(514) 367-1000 *SIC* 7389

LEADING EDGE GEOMATICS LTD *p404*
2398 ROUTE 102 HWY, LINCOLN, NB, E3B
7G1

(506) 446-4403 *SIC* 7389

LEDDARTECH INC *p1267*
4535 BOUL WILFRID-HAMEL BUREAU
240, QUEBEC, QC, G1P 2J7

(418) 653-9000 *SIC* 7389

LEMAY CO INC *p1223*
3500 RUE SAINT-JACQUES, MONTREAL,
QC, H4C 1H2

(514) 932-5101 *SIC* 7389

LEVEL 1 ACS INC *p1035*
225 MAIN ST, WOODSTOCK, ON, N4S 1T1

(519) 539-8519 *SIC* 7389

**LIFTSAFE ENGINEERING AND SERVICE
GROUP INC.** *p483*
306 DARRELL DR, AYR, ON, N0B 1E0

(519) 896-2430 *SIC* 7389

LION BRIDGE LTD *p398*
10 RUE DAWSON, DIEPPE, NB, E1A 6C8

(506) 859-5200 *SIC* 7389

LIONBRIDGE (CANADA) INC *p1069*
7900 BOUL TASCHEREAU BUREAU E204,
BROSSARD, QC, J4X 1C2

(514) 288-2243 *SIC* 7389

LNB INC *p853*
121 GRANTON DR SUITE 14, RICHMOND
HILL, ON, L4B 3N4

(905) 882-2500 *SIC* 7389

**LODGING COMPANY RESERVATIONS LTD,
THE** *p222*
510 BERNARD AVE SUITE 200,
KELOWNA, BC, V1Y 6P1

(250) 979-3939 *SIC* 7389

**LONDON CONVENTION CENTRE CORPO-
RATION, THE** *p656*
300 YORK ST, LONDON, ON, N6B 1P8

(519) 661-6200 *SIC* 7389

LOVEPAC INC *p1340*
140 RUE BARR, SAINT-LAURENT, QC, H4T
1Y4

(514) 904-4300 *SIC* 7389

LRI ENGINEERING INC *p954*
170 UNIVERSITY AVE 3RD FL, TORONTO,
ON, M5H 3B3

(416) 515-9331 *SIC* 7389

LUCIDIA STUDIOS LTD *p861*
123 MARCH ST SUITE 301, SAULT STE.
MARIE, ON, P6A 2Z5

(705) 941-9828 *SIC* 7389

**LUXURY HOTELS INTERNATIONAL OF
CANADA ULC** *p858*
1337 LONDON RD, SARNIA, ON, N7S 1P6

(519) 346-4551 *SIC* 7389

**LUXURY HOTELS INTERNATIONAL OF
CANADA, ULC** *p399*
102 MAIN ST UNIT 16, FREDERICTON,
NB, E3A 9N6

SIC 7389

M & D DRAFTING LTD *p110*
3604 76 AVE NW, EDMONTON, AB, T6B
2N8

(780) 465-1520 *SIC* 7389

M. E. T. UTILITIES MANAGEMENT LTD *p767*
2810 VICTORIA PARK AVE SUITE 105,
NORTH YORK, ON, M2J 4A9

(416) 495-9448 *SIC* 7389

MAILPORT COURIER (1986) INC *p688*

3405 AMERICAN DR UNIT 1, MISSISSAUGA, ON, L4V 1T6

(416) 679-1777 *SIC* 7389

MAIN ST. GROUP INC *p570*

2275 LAKE SHORE BLVD W SUITE 318, ETOBICOKE, ON, M8V 3Y3

(519) 537-3513 *SIC* 7389

MAISONEE D'EVELYNE, LA *p1079*

546 BOUL TALBOT, CHICOUTIMI, QC, G7H 4A5

(418) 543-5822 *SIC* 7389

MAKWA AVENTURES INC, LES *p1184*

4079 RUE SAINT-DENIS, MONTREAL, QC, H2W 2M7

(514) 285-2583 *SIC* 7389

MANHEIM AUTO AUCTIONS COMPANY *p684*

8277 LAWSON RD, MILTON, ON, L9T 5C7

(905) 275-3000 *SIC* 7389

MANITOBA HYDRO UTILITY SERVICES LIMITED *p371*

35 SUTHERLAND AVE, WINNIPEG, MB, R2W 3C5

(204) 360-5660 *SIC* 7389

MAPLECORE LTD *p981*

230 RICHMOND ST W SUITE 11, TORONTO, ON, M5V 3E5

(416) 961-1040 *SIC* 7389

MARCHE FLORAL INTER-PROVINCIAL LTEE *p1245*

3600 BOUL PITFIELD, PIERREFONDS, QC, H8Y 3L4

(514) 334-7733 *SIC* 7389

MARKO AUDIO POST PRODUCTION INC *p1175*

910 RUE DE LA GAUCHETIERE E BUREAU ENTREE, MONTREAL, QC, H2L 2N4

(514) 282-0961 *SIC* 7389

MAXIMUM EXPRESS & FREIGHT LTD *p334*

576 HILLSIDE AVE UNIT 3, VICTORIA, BC, V8T 1Y9

(250) 721-5170 *SIC* 7389

MAYNARDS LIQUIDATION GROUP INC *p255*

3331 JACOMBS RD, RICHMOND, BC, V6V 1Z6

(604) 876-6787 *SIC* 7389

MBW COURIER INCORPORATED *p469*

142 PARKWAY DR, TRURO HEIGHTS, NS, B6L 1N8

(902) 895-5120 *SIC* 7389

MCDONALD, D. SALES & MERCHANDISING LIMITED *p801*

2861 SHERWOOD HEIGHTS DR UNIT 28, OAKVILLE, ON, L6J 7K1

(905) 855-8550 *SIC* 7389

MCINNIS EXPRESS LTD *p1040*

2 MACALEER DR, CHARLOTTETOWN, PE, C1E 2A1

(902) 892-9333 *SIC* 7389

MCNICOL STEVENSON LIMITED *p878*

3640 MCNICOLL AVE SUITE B, SCARBOROUGH, ON, M1X 1G5

(416) 291-2933 *SIC* 7389

MEDI-TRAN SERVICES (1993) LTD *p193*

7125 CURRAGH AVE, BURNABY, BC, V5J 4V6

(604) 872-5293 *SIC* 7389

MEDIAS TRANSCONTINENTAL INC *p1206*

1155 BOUL RENE-LEVESQUE O UNITE 100, MONTREAL, QC, H3B 4R1

(514) 287-1717 *SIC* 7389

MEDLEY, LE *p1186*

1170 RUE SAINT-DENIS, MONTREAL, QC, H2X 3J5

SIC 7389

MEGA CRANES LTD *p272*

6330 148 ST, SURREY, BC, V3S 3C4

(604) 599-4200 *SIC* 7389

MEGALEXIS COMMUNICATION INC *p1198*

666 RUE SHERBROOKE O BUREAU 602, MONTREAL, QC, H3A 1F7

(514) 861-4999 *SIC* 7389

MESSAGER RAPIDE INC *p1110*

164 9E RANG E, GRANBY, QC, J2H 0T2

(450) 378-1298 *SIC* 7389

MESSAGERIES COURRIERTEL INC, LES *p1364*

148 AV DES MARQUISATS, SAINTE-THERESE, QC, J7E 5J7

(450) 437-9805 *SIC* 7389

METAL BERNARD INC *p1323*

12 RUE NAPOLEON-COUTURE, SAINT-LAMBERT-DE-LAUZON, QC, G0S 2W0

(418) 889-0502 *SIC* 7389

METALCARE GROUP INC *p128*

291 MACALPINE CRES UNIT A, FORT MCMURRAY, AB, T9H 4Y4

(780) 715-1889 *SIC* 7389

METALCARE GROUP INC *p128*

400 MACKENZIE BLVD SUITE 201, FORT MCMURRAY, AB, T9H 4C4

(780) 715-1889 *SIC* 7389

METALOGIC INSPECTION SERVICES INC *p110*

7211 68 AVE NW, EDMONTON, AB, T6B 3T6

(780) 469-6161 *SIC* 7389

METROPOLITAN TORONTO CONVENTION CENTRE CORPORATION *p982*

255 FRONT ST W, TORONTO, ON, M5V 2W6

(416) 585-8000 *SIC* 7389

MICHENER-ALLEN AUCTIONEERING LTD *p98*

HWY 16 A, EDMONTON, AB, T5P 4V8

(780) 470-5584 *SIC* 7389

MICRO COM SYSTEMS LTD *p289*

27 7TH AVE E, VANCOUVER, BC, V5T 1M4

(604) 872-6771 *SIC* 7389

MILL BAY FIRE DEPARTMENT *p232*

2675 LODGEPOLE RD, MILL BAY, BC, V0R 2P1

(250) 743-5563 *SIC* 7389

MILLIGANS FISHERIES LTD *p1042*

1968 CARDIGAN ROAD, ST-PETERS BAY, PE, C0A 2A0

(902) 961-2651 *SIC* 7389

MINTO FURNISHED SUITES *p973*

61 YORKVILLE AVE SUITE 200, TORONTO, ON, M5R 1B7

(416) 923-1000 *SIC* 7389

MIRATEL SOLUTIONS INC *p784*

2501 STEELES AVE W SUITE 200, NORTH YORK, ON, M3J 2P1

(416) 650-7850 *SIC* 7389

MISTER COFFEE & SERVICES INC *p871*

2045 MIDLAND AVE SUITE 1, SCARBOROUGH, ON, M1P 3E2

(416) 293-3333 *SIC* 7389

MISTRAS CANADA, INC *p156*

8109 EDGAR INDUSTRIAL DR, RED DEER, AB, T4P 3R2

(403) 556-1350 *SIC* 7389

MMCC SOLUTIONS CANADA COMPANY *p922*

75 EGLINTON AVE E, TORONTO, ON, M4P 3A4

(416) 922-3519 *SIC* 7389

MMCC SOLUTIONS CANADA COMPANY *p1166*

2030 BOUL PIE-IX BUREAU 330, MONTREAL, QC, H1V 2C8

(514) 287-1717 *SIC* 7389

MOBIL SHRED INC *p206*

588 ANNANCE CRT UNIT 4, DELTA, BC, V3M 6Y8

(604) 526-2622 *SIC* 7389

MOBILE 1 MESSENGERS INC *p186*

3737 NAPIER ST SUITE 200, BURNABY, BC, V5C 3E4

(604) 681-4227 *SIC* 7389

MODES J & X LTEE, LES *p1217*

7101 AV DU PARC BUREAU 301, MONTREAL, QC, H3N 1X9

SIC 7389

MOHWAK MEDBUY CORPORATION *p660*

4056 MEADOWBROOK DR UNIT 135, LONDON, ON, N6L 1E4

(519) 652-1688 *SIC* 7389

MONCTON, CITY OF *p408*

800 ST GEORGE BLVD, MONCTON, NB, E1E 2C7

(506) 857-8800 *SIC* 7389

MONERIS SOLUTIONS CORPORATION *p572*

3300 BLOOR ST W 10TH FLR, ETOBICOKE, ON, M8X 2X2

(416) 734-1000 *SIC* 7389

MONSTERCAT INC *p295*

380 RAILWAY ST, VANCOUVER, BC, V6A 4E3

(519) 729-2179 *SIC* 7389

MOOD MEDIA ENTERTAINMENT LTD *p556*

99 SANTE DR SUITE B, CONCORD, ON, L4K 3C4

(905) 761-4300 *SIC* 7389

MQN INTERIORS LTD *p332*

3313 32 AVE SUITE 100, VERNON, BC, V1T 2E1

(250) 542-1199 *SIC* 7389

MSC REHABILITATION INC *p1234*

2145 RUE MICHELIN, MONTREAL, QC, H7L 5B8

(450) 687-5610 *SIC* 7389

MULTILINGUAL COMMUNITY INTERPRETER SERVICES (ONTARIO) *p780*

789 DON MILLS RD SUITE 1010, NORTH YORK, ON, M3C 1T5

(416) 426-7051 *SIC* 7389

MUNICIPAL PROPERTY ASSESSMENT CORPORATION *p843*

1340 PICKERING PKY SUITE 101, PICKERING, ON, L1V 0C4

(905) 831-4433 *SIC* 7389

MYSHAK CRANE AND RIGGING LTD *p1*

53016 HWY 60 SUITE 42B, ACHESON, AB, T7X 5A7

(780) 960-9790 *SIC* 7389

NATIONEX INC *p1308*

3505 BOUL LOSCH, SAINT-HUBERT, QC, J3Y 5T7

(450) 445-7171 *SIC* 7389

NAV CANADA *p411*

222 OLD COACH RD, RIVERVIEW, NB, E1B 4G2

(613) 563-5588 *SIC* 7389

NCSG HAULING & RIGGING LTD *p160*

261106 WAGON WHEEL CRES SUITE 3, ROCKY VIEW COUNTY, AB, T4A 0E2

(403) 276-9955 *SIC* 7389

NETWORK MESSENGER INC *p995*

34 MAGWOOD CRT, TORONTO, ON, M6S 2M5

(416) 777-2278 *SIC* 7389

NETWORK SOUTH ENTERPRISES *p364*

188 GOULET ST, WINNIPEG, MB, R2H 0R8

(204) 474-1959 *SIC* 7389

NEUTRONICS COMPONENTS LTD *p751*

245 MENTEN PL SUITE 301, NEPEAN, ON, K2H 9E8

(613) 599-1263 *SIC* 7389

NIGHT SHIFT ANSWERING SERVICE LTD, THE *p414*

600 MAIN ST SUITE 201, SAINT JOHN, NB, E2K 1J5

(506) 637-7010 *SIC* 7389

NOR-MAR INDUSTRIES LTD *p243*

682 OKANAGAN AVE E, PENTICTON, BC, V2A 3K6

(250) 492-7866 *SIC* 7389

NORBEL METAL SERVICE LIMITED *p580*

100 GUIDED CRT, ETOBICOKE, ON, M9V 4K6

(416) 744-9988 *SIC* 7389

NORCARD ENTERPRISES LTD *p657*

444 NEWBOLD ST, LONDON, ON, N6E 1K3

(519) 690-1717 *SIC* 7389

NORDIA INC *p1177*

255 BOUL CREMAZIE E, MONTREAL, QC, H2M 1L5

(514) 387-1285 *SIC* 7389

NORDIA INC *p1236*

3020 AV JACQUES-BUREAU 2E ETAGE, MONTREAL, QC, H7P 6G2

(514) 415-7088 *SIC* 7389

NORMANDIN INC *p1377*

931 CH DE MILTON, ST-VALERIEN, QC, J0H 2B0

(450) 549-2949 *SIC* 7389

NORTH WEST CRANE ENTERPRISES LTD *p139*

7015 SPARROW DR, LEDUC, AB, T9E 7L1

(780) 980-2227 *SIC* 7389

NORTH WEST GEOMATICS LTD *p24*

245 AERO WAY NE, CALGARY, AB, T2E 6K2

(403) 295-0694 *SIC* 7389

NORTHERN AUTO AUCTIONS OF CANADA INC *p622*

3230 THOMAS ST, INNISFIL, ON, L9S 3W5

(705) 436-4111 *SIC* 7389

NORTHERN COMMUNICATION SERVICES INC *p900*

230 ALDER ST, SUDBURY, ON, P3C 4J2

(705) 677-6744 *SIC* 7389

NORTHERN TRANSPORT SERVICES INC *p913*

36 PINE ST S SUITE 200, TIMMINS, ON, P4N 2J8

(705) 268-6868 *SIC* 7389

NOTARIUS - TECHNOLGIES ET SYSTEMES D'INFORMATION NOTARIALE INC *p1190*

465 RUE MCGILL BUREAU 300, MONTREAL, QC, H2Y 2H1

(514) 281-1577 *SIC* 7389

NOVA EXPRESS MILLENNIUM INC *p255*

14271 KNOX WAY SUITE 105, RICHMOND, BC, V6V 2Z4

(604) 278-8044 *SIC* 7389

NUMBER EIGHTY-EIGHT HOLDINGS LTD *p249*

1922 1ST AVE, PRINCE GEORGE, BC, V2L 2Y9

(250) 562-3871 *SIC* 7389

NUTECH FIRE PROTECTION CO. LTD *p608*

2814 BARTON ST E, HAMILTON, ON, L8E 2J9

(905) 662-9991 *SIC* 7389

NUTRITION INTERNATIONAL *p834*

180 ELGIN ST 10 FL, OTTAWA, ON, K2P 2K3

(613) 782-6800 *SIC* 7389

O'CONNELL, ANN INTERIOR DESIGN LTD *p673*

7321 VICTORIA PARK AVE SUITE 2, MARKHAM, ON, L3R 2Z8

(905) 477-4695 *SIC* 7389

O.T.T. LEGAL SERVICES PROFESSIONAL CORPORATION *p865*

1504 MARKHAM RD, SCARBOROUGH, ON, M1B 2V9

(416) 292-2022 *SIC* 7389

OFFICE DU TOURISME DE LAVAL INC *p1087*

480 PROM DU CENTROPOLIS, COTE SAINT-LUC, QC, H7T 3C2

(450) 682-5522 *SIC* 7389

OII OWNERSHIP IDENTIFICATION INC *p217*

1402 MCGILL RD SUITE 102, KAMLOOPS, BC, V2C 1L3

(250) 314-9686 *SIC* 7389

OLAMETER INC *p1198*

2000 AV MCGILL COLLEGE BUREAU 500, MONTREAL, QC, H3A 3H3

(514) 982-6664 *SIC* 7389

OLDS AUCTION MART LTD *p151*

4613 54 ST, OLDS, AB, T4H 1E9

(403) 556-3655 *SIC* 7389

OMBUDSPERSON OF B C *p335*

947 FORT ST, VICTORIA, BC, V8V 3K3

(250) 387-5855 *SIC* 7389

OMNIPLAN DESIGN GROUP LIMITED *p564*

1748 BASELINE RD SUITE 200D, COURTICE, ON, L1E 2T1

(905) 421-9129 *SIC* 7389

ON CALL CENTRE INC p818
2405 ST. LAURENT BLVD UNIT B, OTTAWA, ON, K1G 5B4
(613) 238-3262 *SIC* 7389

ON TRACK SAFETY LTD p905
29 RUGGLES AVE, THORNHILL, ON, L3T 3S4
(905) 660-5969 *SIC* 7389

ONTARIO REGIONAL COMMON GROUND ALLIANCE p556
102-545 NORTH RIVERMEDE RD, CONCORD, ON, L4K 4H1
(905) 532-9836 *SIC* 7389

OTTAWA CONVENTION CENTRE CORPORATION p821
55 COLONEL BY DR, OTTAWA, ON, K1N 9J2
(613) 563-1984 *SIC* 7389

OTTAWA TOURISM p834
150 ELGIN ST SUITE 1405, OTTAWA, ON, K2P 1L4
(613) 237-5150 *SIC* 7389

OTTER POINT FIRE DEPARTMENT p269
3727 OTTER POINT RD, SOOKE, BC, V9Z 0K1
(250) 642-6211 *SIC* 7389

OUGHTRED COFFEE & TEA LTD p338
723B VANALMAN AVE, VICTORIA, BC, V8Z 3B6
(250) 384-7444 *SIC* 7389

OVER THE RAINBOW PACKAGING SERVICE INC p499
2165 WILLIAMS PKY, BRAMPTON, ON, L6S 6B8
SIC 7389

P & P PROJECTS INC p793
233 SIGNET DR SUITE 1, NORTH YORK, ON, M9L 1V3
(416) 398-6197 *SIC* 7389

P M L INSPECTION SERVICES LTD p130
11110 88 AVE SUITE 2, FORT SASKATCHEWAN, AB, T8L 3K8
(780) 992-9360 *SIC* 7389

PACIFIC DOCUMENT EXCHANGE LTD p299
111 SMITHE ST, VANCOUVER, BC, V6B 4Z8
(604) 684-3336 *SIC* 7389

PANTHER INDUSTRIES INC p1405
108 INTERNAL RD, DAVIDSON, SK, S0G 1A0
(306) 567-2814 *SIC* 7389

PAQUIN ENTERTAINMENT GROUP INC, THE p387
468 STRADBROOK AVE, WINNIPEG, MB, R3L 0J9
(204) 988-1120 *SIC* 7389

PARENTY REITMEIER INC p364
123B MARION ST, WINNIPEG, MB, R2H 0T3
(204) 237-3737 *SIC* 7389

PASWORD COMMUNICATIONS INC p612
122 HUGHSON ST S, HAMILTON, ON, L8N 2B2
(905) 974-1683 *SIC* 7389

PASWORD GROUP INC, THE p612
122 HUGHSON ST S, HAMILTON, ON, L8N 2B2
(905) 645-1162 *SIC* 7389

PEACHLAND FIRE & RESCUE SERVICE p243
4401 3RD ST, PEACHLAND, BC, V0H 1X7
(250) 767-2841 *SIC* 7389

PEMBINA COLONY FARMS LTD p348
GD, DARLINGFORD, MB, R0G 0L0
(204) 246-2182 *SIC* 7389

PERLICH BROS. AUCTION MARKET LTD p143
GD, LETHBRIDGE, AB, T1K 4P4
(403) 329-3101 *SIC* 7389

PERSONAL TOUCH INC p821
174 COBOURG ST SUITE 100, OTTAWA, ON, K1N 8H5
(613) 723-5891 *SIC* 7389

PESE PECHE INC p418

140 1RE RUE, SHIPPAGAN, NB, E8S 1A4
(506) 336-1400 *SIC* 7389

PF MEDIA GROUP INC p236
319 GOVERNORS CRT, NEW WESTMINSTER, BC, V3L 5S5
(604) 599-3876 *SIC* 7389

PHOENIX SERVICES ENVIRONNEMENTAUX INC. p1306
144 RTE DU PRESIDENT-KENNEDY, SAINT-HENRI-DE-LEVIS, QC, G0R 3E0
(418) 882-0014 *SIC* 7389

PII (CANADA) LIMITED p116
3575 97 ST NW, EDMONTON, AB, T6E 5S7
(780) 450-1031 *SIC* 7389

PINESTONE REGIONAL SALES OFFICE p607
4252 COUNTY RD 21, HALIBURTON, ON, K0M 1S0
SIC 7389

PIPETEK INFRASTRUCTURE SERVICES INC p529
2250 INDUSTRIAL ST, BURLINGTON, ON, L7P 1A1
(905) 319-0500 *SIC* 7389

PITNEY BOWES OF CANADA LTD p474
314 HARWOOD AVE S SUITE 200, AJAX, ON, L1S 2J1
(905) 619-7700 *SIC* 7389

PLACEMENTS C. D. F. G. INC p1393
59 RUE DE L'AQUEDUC, VARENNES, QC, J3X 2J3
SIC 7389

PME INTER NOTAIRES INC p1370
2140 RUE KING E UNITE 201, SHERBROOKE, QC, J1G 5G6
(819) 563-3344 *SIC* 7389

POMMES ENDERLE INC, LES p1113
514 CH JAMES-FISHER, HEMMINGFORD, QC, J0L 1H0
(450) 247-2463 *SIC* 7389

POSI-PLUS TECHNOLOGIES INC p1398
10 RUE DE L'ARTISAN, VICTORIAVILLE, QC, G6P 7E4
(819) 758-5717 *SIC* 7389

POST MODERN SOUND INC p321
1722 2ND AVE W, VANCOUVER, BC, V6J 1H6
(604) 736-7474 *SIC* 7389

POSTE EXPRESS INC p1267
2659 AV WATT BUREAU 5, QUEBEC, QC, G1P 3T2
(418) 653-1045 *SIC* 7389

POWER EXPRESS INC p116
4182 93 ST NW, EDMONTON, AB, T6E 5P5
(780) 461-4000 *SIC* 7389

PRC BOOKS OF LONDON LIMITED p657
1112 DEARNESS DR UNIT 15, LONDON, ON, N6E 1N9
SIC 7389

PREMIER CHOIX SOLUTIONS DE PAIEMENT S.E.N.C. p1211
1000 RUE SAINT-ANTOINE O BUREAU 333, MONTREAL, QC, H3C 3R7
(866) 437-3189 *SIC* 7389

PREMIER EVENT TENT RENTALS INC p505
10 CARSON CRT, BRAMPTON, ON, L6T 4P8
(416) 225-7500 *SIC* 7389

PRO DRAFT INC p270
14727 108 AVE UNIT 205, SURREY, BC, V3R 1V9
(604) 589-6425 *SIC* 7389

PRO PAK PACKAGING LIMITED p587
51 KELFIELD ST, ETOBICOKE, ON, M9W 5A3
(416) 246-0550 *SIC* 7389

PRO-X EXHIBIT INC p686
7621 BATH RD, MISSISSAUGA, ON, L4T 3T1
(905) 696-0993 *SIC* 7389

PROAX TECHNOLOGIES LTEE p1236
3505 RUE JOHN-PRATT, MONTREAL, QC, H7P 0C9
(450) 902-5900 *SIC* 7389

PROBYN LOG LTD p236
601 SIXTH ST UNIT 350, NEW WESTMINSTER, BC, V3L 3C1
(604) 526-8545 *SIC* 7389

PROCALL MARKETING INC p57
100 4 AVE SW UNIT 200, CALGARY, AB, T2P 3N2
(403) 265-4014 *SIC* 7389

PRODUCTIONS ARCHY'S INC, LES p1271
1457 AV OAK, QUEBEC, QC, G1T 1Z5
(418) 688-3553 *SIC* 7389

PRODUCTIVE SPACE INC p31
3632 BURNSLAND RD SE, CALGARY, AB, T2G 3Z2
SIC 7389

PROFESSIONAL WAREHOUSE DEMONSTRATIONS p143
3200 MAYOR MAGRATH DR S, LETHBRIDGE, AB, T1K 6Y6
SIC 7389

PROGRESS LUV2PAK INTERNATIONAL LTD p784
20 TANGIERS RD, NORTH YORK, ON, M3J 2B2
(416) 638-1221 *SIC* 7389

PROLINE PIPE EQUIPMENT INC p110
7141 67 ST NW, EDMONTON, AB, T6B 3L7
(780) 465-6161 *SIC* 7389

PROMOTIONAL PRODUCTS FULFILLMENT & DISTRIBUTION LT p1015
80 WILLIAM SMITH DR, WHITBY, ON, L1N 9W1
(905) 668-5060 *SIC* 7389

PROPERTY VALUATION SERVICES CORPORATION p448
238 BROWNLOW AVE SUITE 200, DARTMOUTH, NS, B3B 1Y2
(902) 476-2748 *SIC* 7389

PROTEKITE p557
380 SPINNAKER WAY, CONCORD, ON, L4K 4W1
(905) 738-1221 *SIC* 7389

PROVINCIAL PROTECTION INC p991
36 LISGAR ST SUITE 623W, TORONTO, ON, M6J 0C7
(888) 508-6277 *SIC* 7389

PROWEST SHIPPING & PACKAGING LTD p102
21635 115 AVE NW, EDMONTON, AB, T5S 2N6
(780) 455-5026 *SIC* 7389

PRT GROWING SERVICES LTD p308
355 BURRARD ST SUITE 410, VANCOUVER, BC, V6C 2G8
SIC 7389

PRUDENTIAL RELOCATION CANADA LTD p770
5700 YONGE ST SUITE 1110, NORTH YORK, ON, M2M 4K2
SIC 7389

PUBLIC OUTREACH CONSULTANCY INC p299
207 HASTINGS ST W SUITE 1005, VANCOUVER, BC, V6B 1H7
(604) 800-3730 *SIC* 7389

PUROLATOR INC p121
3104 97 ST NW, EDMONTON, AB, T6N 1K3
(780) 408-2420 *SIC* 7389

PUROLATOR INC p448
220 JOSEPH ZATZMAN DR, DARTMOUTH, NS, B3B 1P4
(902) 468-1611 *SIC* 7389

PUROLATOR INC p557
1550 CREDITSTONE RD, CONCORD, ON, L4K 5N1
(905) 660-6007 *SIC* 7389

PUROLATOR INC p608
21 WARRINGTON ST, HAMILTON, ON, L8E 3L1
(888) 744-7123 *SIC* 7389

PUROLATOR INC p742
6520 KESTREL RD, MISSISSAUGA, ON, L5T 1Z6
(905) 565-9306 *SIC* 7389

PUROLATOR INC p747
9300 AIRPORT RD, MOUNT HOPE, ON, L0R 1W0
(905) 679-5722 *SIC* 7389

PUROLATOR INC p1020
4520 NORTH SERVICE RD E, WINDSOR, ON, N8W 5X2
(519) 945-1363 *SIC* 7389

PUROLATOR INC p1116
3479 RUE DE L'ENERGIE, JONQUIERE, QC, G7X 0C1
(418) 695-1235 *SIC* 7389

PUROLATOR INC p1362
2005 BOUL DAGENAIS O, SAINTE-ROSE, QC, H7L 5V1
(450) 963-3050 *SIC* 7389

PUROLATOR INC p1420
702 TORONTO ST, REGINA, SK, S4R 8L1
(306) 359-0313 *SIC* 7389

Q CONTACTS p237
640 CLARKSON ST, NEW WESTMINSTER, BC, V3M 1C8
(604) 717-4500 *SIC* 7389

Q-PHARM INC p536
180 WERLICH DR, CAMBRIDGE, ON, N1T 1N6
(519) 650-9850 *SIC* 7389

QPS EVALUATION SERVICES INC p587
81 KELFIELD ST UNIT 8, ETOBICOKE, ON, M9W 5A3
(416) 241-8857 *SIC* 7389

QRC LOGISTICS (1978) LTD p594
8020 FIFTH LINE, GEORGETOWN, ON, L7G 0B8
(905) 791-9000 *SIC* 7389

QTRADE SECURITIES INC p329
505 BURRARD ST SUITE 1920, VANCOUVER, BC, V7X 1M6
(604) 605-4199 *SIC* 7389

QUADRA DESIGN STUDIOS INC p788
2171 AVENUE RD SUITE 302, NORTH YORK, ON, M5M 4B4
(416) 322-6334 *SIC* 7389

QUALITY MOVE MANAGEMENT INC p209
7979 82 ST, DELTA, BC, V4G 1L7
(604) 952-3650 *SIC* 7389

QUALITY PACKAGING SOLUTIONS INC p845
1420 BAYLY ST UNIT 7, PICKERING, ON, L1W 3R4
SIC 7389

QUEEN'S HOUSE RETREATS & RENEWAL CENTRE p1433
601 TAYLOR ST W, SASKATOON, SK, S7M 0C9
(306) 242-1916 *SIC* 7389

R HOME SECURITY LTD p913
28 COLUMBUS AVE, TIMMINS, ON, P4N 3H3
(705) 267-5547 *SIC* 7389

RAE ENGINEERING & INSPECTION LTD p116
4810 93 ST NW, EDMONTON, AB, T6E 5M4
(780) 469-2401 *SIC* 7389

RAVINE MUSHROOM FARMS INC p1033
131 MARYCROFT AVE UNIT 3, WOODBRIDGE, ON, L4L 5Y6
(905) 264-6173 *SIC* 7389

REBUTS SOLIDES CANADIENS INC p1170
2240 RUE MICHEL-JURDANT, MONTREAL, QC, H1Z 4N7
(514) 593-9211 *SIC* 7389

RED SEAL NOTARY INC p940
25 ADELAIDE ST E UNIT 100, TORONTO, ON, M5C 3A1
(416) 922-7325 *SIC* 7389

REDISHRED CAPITAL CORP p726
6505 MISSISSAUGA RD SUITE A, MISSISSAUGA, ON, L5N 1A6
(416) 490-8600 *SIC* 7389

REES N.D.T. INSPECTION SERVICES LTD p133
15612 89 ST, GRANDE PRAIRIE, AB, T8V 2N8

(780) 539-3594   *SIC 7389*

REFENDOIRS C. R. LTEE, LES *p1125*
300 RUE DE LA BERGE-DU-CANAL BUREAU 4, LACHINE, QC, H8R 1H3
(514) 366-2222   *SIC 7389*

REGAL AUCTIONS LTD *p11*
2600 7 AVE NE, CALGARY, AB, T2A 2L8
(403) 250-1995   *SIC 7389*

REGIE DU BATIMENT DU QUEBEC *p1145*
201 PLACE CHARLES-LE MOYNE BUREAU 310, LONGUEUIL, QC, J4K 2T5
(450) 928-7603   *SIC 7389*

REGIE INTERMUNICIPALE DE SECURITE PUBLIQUE DES CHUTES *p1089*
337 RUE PRINCIPALE, DAVELUYVILLE, QC, G0Z 1C0
(819) 367-3395   *SIC 7389*

REGUS BUSINESS CENTRE LTD *p966*
161 BAY ST, TORONTO, ON, M5J 2S1
(416) 572-2200   *SIC 7389*

REPROMATIC SYSTEMS INC *p558*
60 PIPPIN RD SUITE 34, CONCORD, ON, L4K 4M8
(905) 669-2900   *SIC 7389*

RES-MAR *p1102*
478 MONTEE DE WAKEHAM, GASPE, QC, G4X 1Y6
(418) 368-5373   *SIC 7389*

RESEAU ENCANS QUEBEC (S.E.C) *p1310*
5110 RUE MARTINEAU, SAINT-HYACINTHE, QC, J2R 1T9
(450) 796-2612   *SIC 7389*

RESOLVE CORPORATION *p1041*
50 WATTS AVE, CHARLOTTETOWN, PE, C1E 2B8
(902) 629-3000   *SIC 7389*

RESOLVE CORPORATION *p1043*
150 INDUSTRIAL CRES, SUMMERSIDE, PE, C1N 5N6
(902) 432-7500   *SIC 7389*

REX PAK LIMITED *p865*
85 THORNMOUNT DR, SCARBOROUGH, ON, M1B 5V3
(416) 755-3324   *SIC 7389*

RGIS CANADA ULC *p364*
196 TACHE AVE UNIT 5, WINNIPEG, MB, R2H 1Z6
(204) 774-0013   *SIC 7389*

RGIS CANADA ULC *p407*
236 ST GEORGE ST, MONCTON, NB, E1C 1W1
(506) 382-9146   *SIC 7389*

RGIS CANADA ULC *p478*
911 GOLF LINKS RD, ANCASTER, ON, L9K 1H9
(905) 304-9700   *SIC 7389*

RGIS CANADA ULC *p700*
2560 MATHESON BLVD E SUITE 224, MISSISSAUGA, ON, L4W 4Y9
(905) 206-1107   *SIC 7389*

RGIS CANADA ULC *p819*
2197 RIVERSIDE DR SUITE 305, OTTAWA, ON, K1H 7X3
(613) 226-4086   *SIC 7389*

RGIS CANADA ULC *p1228*
8300 RUE BOUGAINVILLE, MONTREAL, QC, H4P 2G1
(514) 521-5258   *SIC 7389*

RGIS CANADA ULC *p1237*
1882 BOUL SAINT-MARTIN O BUREAU 200, MONTREAL, QC, H7S 1M9
SIC 7389

RGIS INVENTORY SERVICES LLC *p610*
1889 KING ST E, HAMILTON, ON, L8K 1V9
(905) 527-8383   *SIC 7389*

RIDEAU AUCTIONS INC *p1016*
GD, WINCHESTER, ON, K0C 2K0
(613) 774-2735   *SIC 7389*

RITCHIE BROS. AUCTIONEERS INCORPORATED *p193*
9500 GLENLYON PKY, BURNABY, BC, V5J 0C6
(778) 331-5500   *SIC 7389*

RMR BONDING LTD *p102*

17413 107 AVE NW, EDMONTON, AB, T5S 1E5
(780) 465-4422   *SIC 7389*

ROBINSON SOLUTIONS (KINGSTON) INC *p633*
1456 CENTENNIAL DR, KINGSTON, ON, K7P 0K4
(613) 634-7552   *SIC 7389*

ROBOCUTS INC *p1226*
1625 RUE CHABANEL O BUREAU 729, MONTREAL, QC, H4N 2S7
(514) 388-8001   *SIC 7389*

ROKAN LAMINATING CO LTD *p742*
1660 TRINITY DR, MISSISSAUGA, ON, L5T 1L6
(905) 564-7525   *SIC 7389*

ROLTEK INTERNATIONAL INC *p576*
305 EVANS AVE, ETOBICOKE, ON, M8Z 1K2
(416) 252-1101   *SIC 7389*

ROME SALES INC *p640*
100 CAMPBELL AVE UNIT 2, KITCHENER, ON, N2H 4X8
(519) 883-4105   *SIC 7389*

ROSEHILL AUCTION SERVICE LTD *p151*
4613 54 ST, OLDS, AB, T4H 1E9
(403) 556-3655   *SIC 7389*

ROYAL LEPAGE LIMITED *p924*
477 MOUNT PLEASANT RD UNIT 210, TORONTO, ON, M4S 2L9
(416) 489-2121   *SIC 7389*

RSVP CUSTOMER CARE CENTRES INC *p327*
1265 HOWE ST SUITE 201, VANCOUVER, BC, V6Z 1R3
(604) 682-2001   *SIC 7389*

RTD QUALITY SERVICES INC *p110*
5504 36 ST NW, EDMONTON, AB, T6B 3P3
(780) 440-6600   *SIC 7389*

RTG PROTECH INC *p1222*
3333 BOUL CAVENDISH BUREAU 270, MONTREAL, QC, H4B 2M5
(514) 868-1919   *SIC 7389*

RUEL VENNE LEONARD ASSOCIES *p1321*
100 RUE DE LA GARE, SAINT-JEROME, QC, J7Z 2C1
(450) 432-2661   *SIC 7389*

RUNNERS LIGHT HAULING (2006) LTD *p110*
4320 82 AVE NW, EDMONTON, AB, T6B 2S4
(780) 465-5311   *SIC 7389*

S&P DATA CORP *p924*
1920 YONGE ST, TORONTO, ON, M4S 3E2
(844) 877-3282   *SIC 7389*

S.H.A.R.E. AGRICULTURE FOUNDATION *p622*
14110 KENNEDY RD, INGLEWOOD, ON, L7C 2G3
(905) 838-0897   *SIC 7389*

SAADCO EXPRESS INC *p674*
300 STEELCASE RD W UNIT 9, MARKHAM, ON, L3R 2W2
(905) 940-1680   *SIC 7389*

SAFETY FIRST ONTARIO INC *p1002*
41 COURTLAND AVE UNIT 1, VAUGHAN, ON, L4K 3T3
(905) 738-4999   *SIC 7389*

SAINT-HYACINTHE, VILLE DE *p1313*
935 RUE DESSAULLES, SAINT-HYACINTHE, QC, J2S 3C4
(450) 778-8550   *SIC 7389*

SANATORIUM BOARD OF MANITOBA *p373*
629 MCDERMOT AVE, WINNIPEG, MB, R3A 1P6
(204) 774-5501   *SIC 7389*

SAND LAKE HUTTERIAN BRETHREN INC *p1437*
GD, VAL MARIE, SK, S0N 2T0
(306) 298-2068   *SIC 7389*

SANI-GEAR INC *p642*
545 TRILLIUM DR UNIT 4, KITCHENER, ON, N2R 1J4
(519) 893-1235   *SIC 7389*

SASCOPACK INC *p1425*

106 MELVILLE ST, SASKATOON, SK, S7J 0R1
SIC 7389

SASKATOON PRIVATE INVESTIGATION INC *p1430*
333 25TH ST E SUITE 505, SASKATOON, SK, S7K 0L4
(306) 975-0999   *SIC 7389*

SAVE OUR LIVING ENVIRONMENT SOCIETY (S.O.L.E.) *p296*
39 HASTINGS ST E, VANCOUVER, BC, V6A 1M9
(604) 681-0001   *SIC 7389*

SCAN-TECH INSPECTION SERVICES LTD *p537*
221 HOLIDAY INN DR, CAMBRIDGE, ON, N3C 3T2
(519) 651-1656   *SIC 7389*

SCOTCHTOWN VOLUNTEER FIRE DEPARTMENT *p465*
11 CATHERINE ST, SCOTCHTOWN, NS, B1H 3B3
(902) 862-8362   *SIC 7389*

SCOTIAMCLEOD INC *p806*
1235 NORTH SERVICE RD W SUITE 200, OAKVILLE, ON, L6M 2W2
(905) 637-4962   *SIC 7389*

SDL INTERNATIONAL (CANADA) INC *p1208*
1155 RUE METCALFE BUREAU 1200, MONTREAL, QC, H3B 2V6
(514) 844-2577   *SIC 7389*

SEA TO SKY COURIER & FREIGHT LTD *p214*
38922 MID WAY SUITE 1, GARIBALDI HIGHLANDS, BC, V0N 1T0
(604) 892-8484   *SIC 7389*

SECURITAS TRANSPORT AVIATION SECURITY LTD *p1290*
100 AV DE L'AEROPORT UNITE 17, ROUYN-NORANDA, QC, J9Y 0G1
(819) 764-3507   *SIC 7389*

SELECT COMMUNICATIONS INC *p116*
10368 82 AVE NW SUITE 201, EDMONTON, AB, T6E 1Z8
(780) 917-5400   *SIC 7389*

SERVICE D'ENTRETIEN DES PLANTES ALPHA INC *p1212*
230 RUE PEEL, MONTREAL, QC, H3C 2G7
(514) 935-1812   *SIC 7389*

SERVICE DU DEVELOPPEMENT ECONOMIQUE *p1260*
295 BOUL CHAREST E, QUEBEC, QC, G1K 3G8
(418) 641-6186   *SIC 7389*

SERVICE REGIONAL D'INTERPRETARIAT DE L'EST DU QUEBEC INC *p1275*
9885 BOUL DE L'ORMIERE, QUEBEC, QC, G2B 3K9
(418) 622-1037   *SIC 7389*

SERVICE REGIONAL D'INTERPRETATION VISUELLE DE L'OUTAOUAIS *p1105*
115 BOUL SACRE-COEUR BUREAU 212, GATINEAU, QC, J8X 1C5
SIC 7389

SERVICES DAVID JONES INC, LES *p1118*
29 RUE DE BONDVILLE, KNOWLTON, QC, J0E 1V0
(450) 955-3600   *SIC 7389*

SERVICES DE CAFE VAN HOUTTE INC *p1170*
8215 17E AV, MONTREAL, QC, H1Z 4J9
(514) 728-2233   *SIC 7389*

SERVICES DE LOCALISATION GAT INTERNATIONAL INC *p1208*
1100 AV DES CANADIENS-DE-MONTREAL BUREAU C25, MONTREAL, QC, H3B 2S2
(514) 288-7818   *SIC 7389*

SERVICES INFRASPEC INC *p1133*
4585 BOUL LITE, LAVAL, QC, H7C 0B8
(450) 937-1508   *SIC 7389*

SERVICES LINGUISTIQUES VERSACOM INC *p1199*
1501 AV MCGILL COLLEGE 6E ETAGE,

MONTREAL, QC, H3A 3M8
(514) 397-1950   *SIC 7389*

SERVICES PARTAGES METSO LTEE *p1126*
795 AV GEORGE-V, LACHINE, QC, H8S 2R9
(877) 677-2005   *SIC 7389*

SERVICES PROFESSIONNELS DES ASSUREURS PLUS INC *p1051*
8290 BOUL METROPOLITAIN E, ANJOU, QC, H1K 1A2
SIC 7389

SERVICES TECHNIQUES LAURENTIDES INC *p1232*
3131 BOUL DE LA CONCORDE E BUREAU 410, MONTREAL, QC, H7E 4W4
SIC 7389

SERVOMAX INC *p1330*
1790 RUE BEAULAC, SAINT-LAURENT, QC, H4R 1W8
(514) 745-5757   *SIC 7389*

SHERWOOD YACHT SALES *p267*
6771 OLDFIELD RD, SAANICHTON, BC, V8M 2A2
(250) 652-5445   *SIC 7389*

SHOPPING WEB PLUS INC *p1385*
450 RUE DES ?RABLES, TROIS-RIVIERES, QC, G8T 5H9
SIC 7389

SHRED-IT INTERNATIONAL ULC *p799*
1383 NORTH SERVICE RD E, OAKVILLE, ON, L6H 1A7
(905) 829-2794   *SIC 7389*

SHRED-IT JV LP *p801*
2794 SOUTH SHERIDAN WAY, OAKVILLE, ON, L6J 7T4
(888) 750-6450   *SIC 7389*

SIERRA MESSENGER & COURIER SERVICE LTD *p370*
165 RYAN ST, WINNIPEG, MB, R2R 0N9
(204) 632-8920   *SIC 7389*

SIGMA ASSISTEL INC *p1208*
1100 BOUL RENE-LEVESQUE O BUREAU 514, MONTREAL, QC, H3B 4N4
(514) 875-9170   *SIC 7389*

SIGMAPAC ENGINEERED SERVICES INC *p865*
71 MELFORD DR UNIT 1, SCARBOROUGH, ON, M1B 2G6
(866) 805-4256   *SIC 7389*

SIGNA + INC *p1235*
975 RUE BERGAR, MONTREAL, QC, H7L 4Z6
(450) 668-0047   *SIC 7389*

SIGNATURE INTERPRETIVE & TRANSLATIVE SERVICES LTD *p9*
4608 26 AVE NE, CALGARY, AB, T1Y 2R8
(403) 590-6382   *SIC 7389*

SIGNATURES CRAFT SHOWS LTD *p920*
37 LANGLEY AVE, TORONTO, ON, M4K 1B4
(416) 465-8055   *SIC 7389*

SIMPRO SOLUTIONS INC *p867*
100 CONSILIUM PL UNIT 601, SCARBOROUGH, ON, M1H 3E3
(416) 915-9571   *SIC 7389*

SITEL CANADA CORPORATION *p409*
320C EDINBURGH DR, MONCTON, NB, E1E 2L1
SIC 7389

SIZELAND EVANS INTERIOR DESIGN INC *p59*
441 5 AVE SW SUITE 700, CALGARY, AB, T2P 2V1
SIC 7389

SMARTDESIGN GROUP (CANADA) LTD *p296*
1150 STATION ST SUITE 102, VANCOUVER, BC, V6A 4C7
(604) 662-7015   *SIC 7389*

SMARTDESIGN GROUP KTBS INC *p321*
1788 5TH AVF W SUITE 300, VANCOUVER, BC, V6J 1P2
(604) 662-7015   *SIC 7389*

SMITTY'S KIP IMPORTS *p515*

80 MORTON AVE E SUITE A, BRANT-FORD, ON, N3R 7J7
   SIC 7389

SOCAN FOUNDATION, THE   *p777*
41 VALLEYBROOK DR, NORTH YORK, ON, M3B 2S6
   (416) 445-8700   *SIC 7389*

SOCIETE D'ASSURANCES AUTOMOBILES DE QUEBEC   *p1336*
7575 BOUL HENRI-BOURASSA O BU-REAU 66, SAINT-LAURENT, QC, H4S 1Z2
   (514) 873-7620   *SIC 7389*

SOCIETE DU CENTRE DES CONGRES DE QUEBEC   *p1270*
1000 BOUL RENE-LEVESQUE E, QUE-BEC, QC, G1R 5T8
   (418) 644-4000   *SIC 7389*

SOCIETE GAMMA INC   *p834*
240 BANK ST SUITE 600, OTTAWA, ON, K2P 1X4
   (613) 233-4407   *SIC 7389*

SOLUTIONS CONTACT PHOCUS INC *p1190*
507 PLACE D'ARMES BUREAU 800, MON-TREAL, QC, H2Y 2W8
   (514) 788-5650   *SIC 7389*

SOLUTIONS D'EMBALLAGES PENTAFLEX INC   *p1050*
7905 RUE JARRY, ANJOU, QC, H1J 2C3
   (514) 353-4330   *SIC 7389*

SOUCY KOUTOU INC   *p1099*
1825 RUE POWER, DRUMMONDVILLE, QC, J2C 5X4
   (819) 478-9032   *SIC 7389*

SOURIS RIVER COLONY FARMS LTD *p349*
GD, ELGIN, MB, R0K 0T0
   SIC 7389

SP DATA CAPITAL ULC   *p613*
110 KING ST W SUITE 500, HAMILTON, ON, L8P 4S6
   (905) 645-5610   *SIC 7389*

SP DATA CAPITAL ULC   *p923*
1 EGLINTON AVE E 8TH FL, TORONTO, ON, M4P 3A1
   (416) 915-3300   *SIC 7389*

SPEAKERS' SPOTLIGHT INC   *p977*
179 JOHN ST SUITE 302, TORONTO, ON, M5T 1X4
   (416) 345-1559   *SIC 7389*

SPECIALIZED PROPERTY EVALUATION CONTROL SERVICES LIMITED   *p225*
9525 201 ST SUITE 303, LANGLEY, BC, V1M 4A5
   (604) 882-8930   *SIC 7389*

SPROUSE FIRE SAFETY LTD   *p18*
5329 72 AVE SE STE 38, CALGARY, AB, T2C 4X6
   SIC 7389

ST. ALBERT, CITY OF   *p166*
18 SIR WINSTON CHURCHILL AVE, ST. ALBERT, AB, T8N 2W5
   (780) 459-7021   *SIC 7389*

STAFF PERSONNEL EVENEMENTIEL INC *p1173*
5000 RUE D'IBERVILLE BUREAU 239, MONTREAL, QC, H2H 2S6
   (514) 899-8776   *SIC 7389*

STAGEVISION INC   *p707*
5915 COOPERS AVE, MISSISSAUGA, ON, L4Z 1R9
   (905) 890-8200   *SIC 7389*

STANDARD FIRE PROTECTION INC   *p998*
254 ATTWELL DR, TORONTO, ON, M9W 5B2
   (416) 240-7980   *SIC 7389*

STARLITE ILLUMINATION INC   *p341*
81 DEEP DENE RD, WEST VANCOUVER, BC, V7S 1A1
   (604) 926-4808   *SIC 7389*

STATION 50   *p620*
2 STATION, HILLSBURGH, ON, N0B 1Z0
   SIC 7389

STAX PACKAGING SERVICES INC   *p650*
575 INDUSTRIAL RD, LONDON, ON, N5V 1V2

(519) 455-0119   *SIC 7389*

STC STEEL TECHNOLOGIES CANADA LTD *p539*
16 CHERRY BLOSSOM RD, CAMBRIDGE, ON, N3H 4R7
   (519) 653-2880   *SIC 7389*

STOUGHTON FIRE PROTECTION LTD *p11*
620 MORAINE RD NE, CALGARY, AB, T2A 2P3
   (403) 291-0291   *SIC 7389*

STRATAPRIME SOLUTIONS, INC   *p987*
1 FIRST CANADIAN PLACE SUITE 350, TORONTO, ON, M5X 1C1
   (647) 693-7656   *SIC 7389*

STRATEGY INSTITUTE INC   *p983*
401 RICHMOND ST W SUITE 401, TORONTO, ON, M5V 3A8
   (416) 944-9200   *SIC 7389*

STRATICOM PLANNING ASSOCIATES INC *p983*
366 ADELAIDE ST W, TORONTO, ON, M5V 1R9
   (416) 362-7407   *SIC 7389*

STREAM INTERNATIONAL CANADA ULC *p197*
7955 EVANS RD, CHILLIWACK, BC, V2R 5R7
   (604) 702-5100   *SIC 7389*

STREAM INTERNATIONAL CANADA ULC *p450*
95 UNION ST, GLACE BAY, NS, B1A 2P6
   (902) 842-3800   *SIC 7389*

STREAMLINE INSPECTION LIMITED *p159*
240040 FRONTIER PL UNIT 5, ROCKY VIEW COUNTY, AB, T1X 0N2
   (403) 454-6630   *SIC 7389*

STRIKE FIRST CORPORATION   *p879*
777 TAPSCOTT RD, SCARBOROUGH, ON, M1X 1A2
   (416) 299-7767   *SIC 7389*

STRONCO DESIGNS INC   *p703*
1510 CATERPILLAR RD, MISSISSAUGA, ON, L4X 2Y1
   (905) 270-6767   *SIC 7389*

STUDIOS DESIGN GHA INC   *p1208*
1100 AV DES CANADIENS-DE-MONTREAL BUREAU 130, MONTREAL, QC, H3B 2S2
   (514) 843-5812   *SIC 7389*

STURDELL INDUSTRIES INC   *p588*
1907 ALBION RD, ETOBICOKE, ON, M9W 5S8
   (416) 675-2025   *SIC 7389*

SUNCORP VALUATIONS LTD   *p1430*
261 1ST AVE N SUITE 300, SASKATOON, SK, S7K 1X2
   (306) 652-0311   *SIC 7389*

SUPERIOR SAFETY CODES INC   *p94*
14613 134 AVE NW, EDMONTON, AB, T5L 4S9
   (780) 489-4777   *SIC 7389*

SYDNEY MINES FIRE DEPARTMENT *p468*
4 ELLIOT ST, SYDNEY MINES, NS, B1V 3G1
   (902) 736-2298   *SIC 7389*

SYM-CRC INC   *p1143*
174 BOUL SAINTE-FOY BUREAU 101, LONGUEUIL, QC, J4J 1W9
   (877) 565-6777   *SIC 7389*

SYMCOR INC   *p76*
3663 63 AVE NE, CALGARY, AB, T3J 0G6
   (905) 273-1000   *SIC 7389*

SYNERTEK INDUSTRIES INC   *p1140*
1044 RUE DU PARC-INDUSTRIEL, LEVIS, QC, G6Z 1C6
   (418) 835-6264   *SIC 7389*

T-BASE COMMUNICATIONS INC   *p831*
885 MEADOWLANDS DR SUITE 401, OT-TAWA, ON, K2C 3N2
   (613) 236-0866   *SIC 7389*

TECHNICO INC   *p413*
299 MCILVEEN DR, SAINT JOHN, NB, E2J 4Y6
   (506) 633-1300   *SIC 7389*

TECHNOLOGIES SYNERGX INC   *p1342*
2912 RUE JOSEPH-A.-BOMBARDIER, SAINT-LAURENT, QC, H7P 6E3
   (450) 978-1240   *SIC 7389*

TELEPARTNERS   *p996*
5407 EGLINTON AVE W SUITE 103, TORONTO, ON, M9C 5K6
   (416) 621-7600   *SIC 7389*

TELEPARTNERS CALL CENTRE INC *p578*
5429 DUNDAS ST W, ETOBICOKE, ON, M9B 1B5
   (416) 231-0520   *SIC 7389*

TELEXPRESS COURIER INC   *p500*
5 EDVAC DR UNIT 10, BRAMPTON, ON, L6S 5P3
   (905) 792-2222   *SIC 7389*

TEMPO DRAFTING SERVICES INC *p676*
260 TOWN CENTRE BLVD SUITE 300, MARKHAM, ON, L3R 8H8
   (905) 470-7000   *SIC 7389*

TESSIER TRANSLATIONS CORPORATION *p1107*
188 RUE MONTCALM BUREAU 100, GATINEAU, QC, J8Y 3B5
   (819) 776-6687   *SIC 7389*

TFORCE FINAL MILE CANADA INC *p507*
107 ALFRED KUEHNE BLVD, BRAMPTON, ON, L6T 4K3
   (905) 494-7600   *SIC 7389*

TFORCE FINAL MILE CANADA INC *p650*
2515 BLAIR BLVD SUITE B, LONDON, ON, N5V 3Z9
   (519) 659-8224   *SIC 7389*

TFORCE FINAL MILE CANADA INC *p1430*
3275 MINERS AVE, SASKATOON, SK, S7K 7Z1
   (306) 975-1010   *SIC 7389*

TG INDUSTRIES INC   *p289*
107 3RD AVE E, VANCOUVER, BC, V5T 1C7
   (604) 872-6676   *SIC 7389*

THERMI GROUP   *p727*
6745 FINANCIAL DR, MISSISSAUGA, ON, L5N 7J7
   (905) 813-9600   *SIC 7389*

THINK4D INC   *p345*
511 INDUSTRIAL DR, ALTONA, MB, R0G 0B0
   (204) 324-6401   *SIC 7389*

TIGER COURIER INC   *p1430*
705 47TH ST E, SASKATOON, SK, S7K 5G5
   (306) 242-7499   *SIC 7389*

TIGERTEL COMMUNICATIONS INC *p1200*
550 RUE SHERBROOKE O BUREAU 1650, MONTREAL, QC, H3A 1B9
   (514) 843-4313   *SIC 7389*

TIM HORTONS   *p999*
221 R.C.A.F. RD, TRENTON, ON, K8V 5P8
   (613) 965-0555   *SIC 7389*

TIM-BR MARTS LTD   *p26*
1601 AIRPORT RD NE SUITE 705, CAL-GARY, AB, T2E 6Z8
   (403) 717-1990   *SIC 7389*

TMS FULFILMENT INC   *p707*
5641 MCADAM RD, MISSISSAUGA, ON, L4Z 1N9
   (416) 706-9658   *SIC 7389*

TOR BAY FISHERIES LIMITED   *p460*
472 TOR BAY BRANCH RD, LARRYS RIVER, NS, B0H 1T0
   (902) 525-2423   *SIC 7389*

TORONTO CONGRESS CENTRE LTD *p589*
650 DIXON RD, ETOBICOKE, ON, M9W 1J1
   (416) 245-5000   *SIC 7389*

TORONTO GENERAL & WESTERN HOSPI-TAL FOUNDATION   *p947*
190 ELIZABETH ST, TORONTO, ON, M5G 2C4
   (416) 340-3935   *SIC 7389*

TOSHIBA BUSINESS SYSTEMS   *p19*
5329 72 AVE SE UNIT 62, CALGARY, AB, T2C 4X6

(403) 273-5200   *SIC 7389*

TOTAL DELIVERY SYSTEMS INC   *p339*
450 BANGA PL, VICTORIA, BC, V8Z 6X5
   (250) 382-9110   *SIC 7389*

TOTAL TECH POOLS INC   *p805*
1380 SPEERS RD SUITE 1, OAKVILLE, ON, L6L 5V3
   (905) 825-1389   *SIC 7389*

TOURISM CALGARY-CALGARY CONVEN-TION & VISITORS BUREAU   *p32*
238 11 AVE SE SUITE 200, CALGARY, AB, T2G 0X8
   (403) 263-8510   *SIC 7389*

TOWER EVENTS & SEATING RENTALS INC *p589*
365 ATTWELL DR, ETOBICOKE, ON, M9W 5C2
   (416) 213-1666   *SIC 7389*

TOY-SPORT AGENCIES LIMITED   *p877*
120 DYNAMIC DR SUITE 22, SCARBOR-OUGH, ON, M1V 5C8
   (905) 640-6598   *SIC 7389*

TRADUCTIONS HOULE INC   *p1105*
540 BOUL DE L'HOPITAL BUREAU 401, GATINEAU, QC, J8V 3T2
   (819) 568-1022   *SIC 7389*

TRADUCTIONS SERGE BELAIR INC *p1191*
276 RUE SAINT-JACQUES BUREAU 900, MONTREAL, QC, H2Y 1N3
   (514) 844-4682   *SIC 7389*

TRAFALGAR INDUSTRIES OF CANADA LIMITED   *p785*
333 RIMROCK RD, NORTH YORK, ON, M3J 3J9
   (416) 638-1111   *SIC 7389*

TRANS CANADA TRAIL   *p1191*
321 RUE DE LA COMMUNE O BUREAU 300, MONTREAL, QC, H2Y 2E1
   (514) 485-3959   *SIC 7389*

TRANSCRIPT HEROES TRANSCRIPTION SERVICES INC   *p943*
1 YONGE ST SUITE 1801, TORONTO, ON, M5E 1W7
   (647) 478-5188   *SIC 7389*

TRANSPERFECT TRANSLATION INC *p1200*
1010 RUE SHERBROOKE O BUREAU 811, MONTREAL, QC, H3A 2R7
   (514) 861-5177   *SIC 7389*

TRAVEL DISCOUNTERS   *p788*
1927 AVENUE RD, NORTH YORK, ON, M5M 4A2
   (416) 481-6701   *SIC 7389*

TRIATHLON   *p257*
13800 COMMERCE PKWY, RICHMOND, BC, V6V 2J3
   (604) 233-5000   *SIC 7389*

TRIMAX SECURITE INC   *p1237*
1965 BOUL INDUSTRIEL BUREAU 200, MONTREAL, QC, H7S 1P6
   (450) 934-5200   *SIC 7389*

TROISIEME DIVISION M.R. INC   *p1370*
880 RUE LONGPRE, SHERBROOKE, QC, J1G 5B9
   (819) 562-7772   *SIC 7389*

TWILIGHT HUTTERIAN BRETHREN *p127*
GD, FALHER, AB, T0H 1M0
   SIC 7389

TWO RIVERS TRANSPORT   *p251*
9408 PENN RD, PRINCE GEORGE, BC, V2N 5T6
   SIC 7389

TYCO INTEGRATED FIRE & SECURITY CANADA, INC   *p32*
431 MANITOU RD SE, CALGARY, AB, T2G 4C2
   (403) 287-3202   *SIC 7389*

TYCO INTEGRATED FIRE & SECURITY CANADA, INC   *p103*
17402 116 AVE NW, EDMONTON, AB, T5S 2X2
   (780) 452-5280   *SIC 7389*

TYCO INTEGRATED FIRE & SECURITY CANADA, INC   *p207*
1485 LINDSEY PL, DELTA, BC, V3M 6V1

---

(604) 515-8872   *SIC* 7389
TYCO INTEGRATED FIRE & SECURITY CANADA, INC   p1331
5800 BOUL HENRI-BOURASSA O, SAINT-LAURENT, QC, H4R 1V9
(514) 737-5505   *SIC* 7389
UNIONVILLE HOME SOCIETY FOUNDATION   p676
4300 HIGHWAY 7 E SUITE 1, MARKHAM, ON, L3R 1L8
(905) 477-2822   *SIC* 7389
UNITED FLORAL HOLDINGS INC   p194
4085 MARINE WAY, BURNABY, BC, V5J 5E2
(604) 438-3535   *SIC* 7389
UNITED PARCEL SERVICE CANADA LTD
p97
11204 151 ST NW, EDMONTON, AB, T5M 4A9
(800) 742-5877   *SIC* 7389
UNITED PARCEL SERVICE CANADA LTD
p207
790 BELGRAVE WAY, DELTA, BC, V3M 5R9
(800) 742-5877   *SIC* 7389
UNITED PARCEL SERVICE CANADA LTD
p407
1 FACTORY LANE SUITE 200, MONCTON, NB, E1C 9M3
(506) 877-4929   *SIC* 7389
UNITED PARCEL SERVICE CANADA LTD
p608
456 GRAYS RD, HAMILTON, ON, L8E 2Z4
(905) 578-2699   *SIC* 7389
UNITED PARCEL SERVICE CANADA LTD
p638
65 TRILLIUM PARK PL, KITCHENER, ON, N2E 1X1
(800) 742-5877   *SIC* 7389
UNITED PARCEL SERVICE CANADA LTD
p690
3195 AIRWAY DR, MISSISSAUGA, ON, L4V 1C2
(800) 742-5877   *SIC* 7389
UNITED PARCEL SERVICE CANADA LTD
p1017
5325 RHODES DR, WINDSOR, ON, N8N 2M1
(519) 251-7050   *SIC* 7389
UNITED PARCEL SERVICE CANADA LTD
p1071
3850 BOUL MATTE, BROSSARD, QC, J4Y 2Z2
(800) 742-5877   *SIC* 7389
UNITED PARCEL SERVICE CANADA LTD
p1129
1221 32E AV BUREAU 209, LACHINE, QC, H8T 3H2
(514) 633-0010   *SIC* 7389
UNITED PARCEL SERVICE CANADA LTD
p1277
625 RUE DES CANETONS, QUEBEC, QC, G2E 5X6
(418) 872-2686   *SIC* 7389
UPI GLASS INC   p332
1810 KOSMINA RD, VERNON, BC, V1T 8T2
(250) 549-1323   *SIC* 7389
UPS SCS INC   p560
777 CREDITSTONE RD, CONCORD, ON, L4K 5R5
(905) 660-6040   *SIC* 7389
VALE CANADA LIMITED   p847
187 DAVIS ST, PORT COLBORNE, ON, L3K 5W2
(905) 835-6000   *SIC* 7389
VALLEY TRAFFIC SYSTEMS INC   p225
19689 TELEGRAPH TRAIL, LANGLEY, BC, V1M 3E6
(604) 513-0210   *SIC* 7389
VANCOUVER EXTENDED STAY LTD   p317
1288 GEORGIA ST W UNIT 101, VANCOUVER, BC, V6E 4R3
(604) 891-6100   *SIC* 7389
VANCOUVER MARRIOTT PINNACLE DOWNTOWN HOTEL   p317

1128 HASTINGS ST W, VANCOUVER, BC, V6E 4R5
(604) 684-1128   *SIC* 7389
VANHOUTTE COFFEE SERVICES LTD p202
9 BURBIDGE ST SUITE 120, COQUITLAM, BC, V3K 7B2
(604) 552-5452   *SIC* 7389
VCS INVESTIGATION INC   p1129
10500 CH DE LA COTE-DE-LIESSE BUREAU 200, LACHINE, QC, H8T 1A4
(514) 737-1911   *SIC* 7389
VELOCITY EXPRESS CANADA LTD   p111
4424 55 AVE NW, EDMONTON, AB, T6B 3S2
(780) 465-3777   *SIC* 7389
VEOLIA ES CANADA SERVICES INDUSTRIELS INC   p595
4140 BELGREEN DR, GLOUCESTER, ON, K1G 3N2
(613) 739-1150   *SIC* 7389
VERTEX CUSTOMER MANAGEMENT (CANADA) LIMITED   p680
185 CLEGG RD, MARKHAM, ON, L6G 1B7
(905) 944-3200   *SIC* 7389
VETEMENTS PRESTIGIO INC, LES   p1345
6370 BOUL DES GRANDES-PRAIRIES, SAINT-LEONARD, QC, H1P 1A2
(514) 955-7131   *SIC* 7389
VIKING AUCTION MARKET LTD   p171
GD, VIKING, AB, T0B 4N0
(780) 688-2020   *SIC* 7389
VILLE DE MONTREAL   p1161
12001 BOUL MAURICE-DUPLESSIS, MONTREAL, QC, H1C 1V3
(514) 280-4359   *SIC* 7389
VINTECH DRAFTING INC   p181
7893 EDMONDS ST SUITE 203, BURNABY, BC, V3N 1B9
(604) 523-6439   *SIC* 7389
VOYSUS GROUP INC   p914
5900 FINCH AVE EAST UNIT 200B, TORONTO, ON, M1B 5P8
(416) 291-0224   *SIC* 7389
VRETTA INC   p941
120 ADELAIDE ST E, TORONTO, ON, M5C 1K9
(866) 522-9228   *SIC* 7389
VULSAY INDUSTRIES LTD   p513
35 REGAN RD, BRAMPTON, ON, L7A 1B2
(905) 846-2200   *SIC* 7389
W. H. ESCOTT COMPANY LIMITED   p376
95 ALEXANDER AVE, WINNIPEG, MB, R3B 2Y8
(204) 942-5127   *SIC* 7389
W.D. PACKAGING INC   p568
49 INDUSTRIAL DR, ELMIRA, ON, N3B 3B1
(519) 669-5486   *SIC* 7389
WADDINGTON MCLEAN & COMPANY LIMITED   p935
275 KING ST E, TORONTO, ON, M5A 1K2
(416) 504-9100   *SIC* 7389
WARE MALCOMB INC   p561
80 BASS PRO MILLS DR UNIT 1, CONCORD, ON, L4K 5W9
(905) 760-1221   *SIC* 7389
WARFIELD FIRE DEPARTMENT   p284
555 SCHOFIELD HWY, TRAIL, BC, V1R 2G7
(250) 368-9300   *SIC* 7389
WATT INTERNATIONAL INC   p984
590 KING ST W SUITE 300, TORONTO, ON, M5V 1M3
(416) 364-9384   *SIC* 7389
WAV INSPECTION LTD   p7
710 1 AVE E, BROOKS, AB, T1R 1E4
(403) 362-2008   *SIC* 7389
WAX PARTNERSHIP INCORPORATED p67
333 24 AVE SW SUITE 320, CALGARY, AB, T2S 3E6
(403) 262-9323   *SIC* 7389
WEAVERS ART INC   p988
1400 CASTLEFIELD AVE, TORONTO, ON, M6B 4N4

(416) 923-7929   *SIC* 7389
WEE-TOTE ENTERPRISES LTD   p194
7011 RANDOLPH AVE, BURNABY, BC, V5J 4W5
(604) 430-1411   *SIC* 7389
WEICHERT WORKFORCE MOBILITY CANADA ULC   p38
6700 MACLEOD TRAIL SE SUITE 210, CALGARY, AB, T2H 0L3
(888) 588-6664   *SIC* 7389
WENTWORTH TECH INC   p516
16 ADAMS BLVD, BRANTFORD, ON, N3S 7V5
(519) 754-5400   *SIC* 7389
WESTECH INTERIORS LTD   p81
21 PINEHURST RR 3, DE WINTON, AB, T0L 0X0
(403) 630-6768   *SIC* 7389
WESTERN INVENTORY SERVICE LTD   p12
720 28 ST NE SUITE 128, CALGARY, AB, T2A 6R3
(403) 272-3850   *SIC* 7389
WESTERN INVENTORY SERVICE LTD p364
73 GOULET ST, WINNIPEG, MB, R2H 0R5
(204) 669-6505   *SIC* 7389
WESTERN INVENTORY SERVICE LTD p690
3770 NASHUA DR SUITE 5, MISSISSAUGA, ON, L4V 1M5
(905) 677-1947   *SIC* 7389
WESTERN INVENTORY SERVICE LTD
p1402
4865 BOUL DE MAISONNEUVE O, WESTMOUNT, QC, H3Z 1M7
(514) 483-1337   *SIC* 7389
WESTERN MESSENGER & TRANSFER LIMITED   p383
839 ELLICE AVE, WINNIPEG, MB, R3G 0C3
(204) 987-7020   *SIC* 7389
WESTERN PACIFIC ACCEPTANCE CORPORATION   p317
1199 PENDER ST W SUITE 510, VANCOUVER, BC, V6E 2R1
(604) 678-3230   *SIC* 7389
WESTERN REPAIR & SALES INC   p374
500 HIGGINS AVE, WINNIPEG, MB, R3A 0B1
(204) 925-7900   *SIC* 7389
WG PRO-MANUFACTURING INC   p500
2110 WILLIAMS PKY SUITE 6, BRAMPTON, ON, L6S 5X6
(905) 790-3377   *SIC* 7389
WHITE OAKS TENNIS WORLD INC   p761
253 TAYLOR RD SS 4, NIAGARA ON THE LAKE, ON, L0S 1J0
(905) 688-2550   *SIC* 7389
WOLFVILLE VOLUNTEER FIRE DEPARTMENT   p471
355 MAIN ST, WOLFVILLE, NS, B4P 1A1
(902) 542-5635   *SIC* 7389
WORLD TRADE GROUP (NORTH AMERICA) INC   p936
211 YONGE ST, TORONTO, ON, M5B 1M4
(416) 214-3400   *SIC* 7389
WORLDMARK AT VICTORIA   p336
120 KINGSTON ST, VICTORIA, BC, V8V 1V4
(250) 386-8555   *SIC* 7389
WORLDWIDE EVANGELIZATION FOR CHRIST   p613
37 ABERDEEN AVE, HAMILTON, ON, L8P 2N6
(905) 529-0166   *SIC* 7389
WYCLIFFE BIBLE TRANSLATORS OF CANADA INC   p26
4316 10 ST NE, CALGARY, AB, T2E 6K3
(403) 250-5411   *SIC* 7389
YORK CONSULTING INC   p770
19 HENDON AVE, NORTH YORK, ON, M2M 4G8
(416) 410-2222   *SIC* 7389
ZEDD CUSTOMER SOLUTIONS L P INC
p764
180 SHIRREFF AVE SUITE 225, NORTH

BAY, ON, P1B 7K9
(705) 495-1333   *SIC* 7389
ZEDD CUSTOMER SOLUTIONS LP   p865
325 MILNER AVE, SCARBOROUGH, ON, M1B 5N1
(416) 745-1333   *SIC* 7389

SIC 7513 Truck rental and leasing, no drivers

BUDGET CAR & TRUCK RENTALS OF OTTAWA LTD   p817
851 INDUSTRIAL AVE, OTTAWA, ON, K1G 4L3
(613) 739-4231   *SIC* 7513
CALMONT LEASING LTD   p93
14610 YELLOWHEAD TRAIL NW, EDMONTON, AB, T5L 3C5
(780) 454-0491   *SIC* 7513
LOCATION BROSSARD INC   p1094
2190 BOUL HYMUS, DORVAL, QC, H9P 1J7
(514) 367-1343   *SIC* 7513
LOCATION V.A. INC   p1133
156 BOUL LAURIER RR 1, LAURIER-STATION, QC, G0S 1N0
(418) 728-2140   *SIC* 7513
PENSKE TRUCK LEASING CANADA INC
p725
7405 EAST DANBRO CRES, MISSISSAUGA, ON, L5N 6P8
(905) 819-7900   *SIC* 7513
PENSKE TRUCK LEASING CANADA INC
p1335
2500 BOUL PITFIELD, SAINT-LAURENT, QC, H4S 1Z7
(514) 333-4080   *SIC* 7513
RYDER TRUCK RENTAL CANADA LTD p662
2724 ROXBURGH RD SUITE 7, LONDON, ON, N6N 1K9
SIC 7513
RYDER TRUCK RENTAL CANADA LTD p726
6755 MISSISSAUGA RD SUITE 201, MISSISSAUGA, ON, L5N 7Y2
(905) 826-8777   *SIC* 7513

SIC 7514 Passenger car rental

ADVANTAGE CAR & TRUCK RENTALS LTD
p1002
110 JARDIN DR SUITE 13, VAUGHAN, ON, L4K 2T7
(416) 493-5250   *SIC* 7514
AVISCAR INC   p582
1 CONVAIR DR, ETOBICOKE, ON, M9W 6Z9
(416) 213-8400   *SIC* 7514
AVISCAR INC   p597
180 PAUL BENOIT DR, GLOUCESTER, ON, K1V 2E5
(613) 521-7541   *SIC* 7514
AVISCAR INC   p1092
975 BOUL ROMEO-VACHON N BUREAU 317, DORVAL, QC, H4Y 1H2
(514) 636-1902   *SIC* 7514
BUDGET RENT A CAR OF BC LTD   p259
7080 RIVER RD UNIT 203, RICHMOND, BC, V6X 1X5
(604) 678-1124   *SIC* 7514
BUDGET RENT-A-CAR OF EDMONTON LTD
p113
4612 95 ST NW, EDMONTON, AB, T6E 5Z6
(780) 448-2060   *SIC* 7514
BUDGET RENT-A-CAR OF VICTORIA LTD
p338
3657 HARRIET RD, VICTORIA, BC, V8Z 3T1
(250) 953-5300   *SIC* 7514
BUDGETAUTO INC   p583
1 CONVAIR DR, ETOBICOKE, ON, M9W 6Z9
(416) 213-8400   *SIC* 7514

DEVON TRANSPORT LTD   p234
2501 KENWORTH RD, NANAIMO, BC, V9T 3M4
(250) 729-2400   *SIC 7514*

ENTERPRISE RENT-A-CAR CANADA COMPANY   p23
2335 78 AVE NE, CALGARY, AB, T2E 7L2
(403) 250-1395   *SIC 7514*

ENTERPRISE RENT-A-CAR CANADA COMPANY   p29
114 5 AVE SE, CALGARY, AB, T2G 0E2
(403) 264-0424   *SIC 7514*

ENTERPRISE RENT-A-CAR CANADA COMPANY   p669
200-7390 WOODBINE AVE, MARKHAM, ON, L3R 1A5
(905) 477-1688   *SIC 7514*

ENTERPRISE RENT-A-CAR CANADA COMPANY   p1092
600 RUE ARTHUR-FECTEAU, DORVAL, QC, H4Y 1K5
(514) 422-1100   *SIC 7514*

HERTZ CANADA LIMITED   p585
2 CONVAIR DR, ETOBICOKE, ON, M9W 7A1
(416) 674-2020   *SIC 7514*

HOMES BY AVI (CANADA) INC   p35
245 FORGE RD SE, CALGARY, AB, T2H 0S9
(403) 536-7000   *SIC 7514*

LOCATION SAUVAGEAU INC   p1351
521 COTE JOYEUSE BUREAU 1, SAINT-RAYMOND, QC, G3L 4A9
(418) 692-1315   *SIC 7514*

MID CANADIAN INDUSTRIES   p381
1577 ERIN ST, WINNIPEG, MB, R3E 2T2
(204) 925-6600   *SIC 7514*

MONDART HOLDINGS LIMITED   p409
1543 MOUNTAIN RD, MONCTON, NB, E1G 1A3
(506) 857-2309   *SIC 7514*

PHELPS LEASING LTD   p261
3640 NO. 4 RD, RICHMOND, BC, V6X 2L7
(604) 257-8230   *SIC 7514*

PRAIRIE VIEW HOLDINGS LTD   p31
140 6 AVE SE, CALGARY, AB, T2G 0G2
(403) 232-4725   *SIC 7514*

R B D MARKETING INC   p910
230 WATERLOO ST S, THUNDER BAY, ON, P7E 2C3
(807) 622-3366   *SIC 7514*

STAR LIMOUSINE SERVICE LTD   p296
328 INDUSTRIAL AVE, VANCOUVER, BC, V6A 2P3
(604) 685-5600   *SIC 7514*

SIC 7515 Passenger car leasing

CANADIAN PREMIER AUTOMOTIVE LTD   p660
1065 WHARNCLIFFE RD S, LONDON, ON, N6L 1J9
(519) 680-1800   *SIC 7515*

CARTER, HOWARD LEASE LTD   p185
4550 LOUGHEED HWY, BURNABY, BC, V5C 3Z5
(604) 291-8899   *SIC 7515*

COMMUNAUTO INC   p1203
1117 RUE SAINTE-CATHERINE O BUREAU 806, MONTREAL, QC, H3B 1H9
(514) 842-4545   *SIC 7515*

DOLLAR THRIFTY AUTOMOTIVE GROUP CANADA INC   p709
3660 HURONTARIO ST, MISSISSAUGA, ON, L5B 3C4
(905) 612-1881   *SIC 7515*

ED LEARN FORD LINCOLN LTD   p885
375 ONTARIO ST, ST CATHARINES, ON, L2R 5L3
(905) 684-8791   *SIC 7515*

ELEMENT FLEET MANAGEMENT INC p705
4 ROBERT SPECK PKY SUITE 900, MISSISSAUGA, ON, L4Z 1S1

(905) 366-8900   *SIC 7515*

FINCH HYUNDAI   p656
300 SOUTHDALE RD E, LONDON, ON, N6C 5Y7
(519) 649-7779   *SIC 7515*

FOSS NATIONAL LEASING LTD.   p904
125 COMMERCE VALLEY DR W SUITE 801, THORNHILL, ON, L3T 7W4
(905) 886-2522   *SIC 7515*

GAUTHIER, JIM PONTIAC BUICK GMC LTD p370
2400 MCPHILLIPS ST, WINNIPEG, MB, R2V 4J6
(204) 633-8833   *SIC 7515*

HYUNDAI CAPITAL LEASE INC   p963
123 FRONT ST W SUITE 1000, TORONTO, ON, M5J 2M3
(647) 943-1887   *SIC 7515*

ONEIL MOTORS INC   p597
1493 SIEVERIGHT RD, GLOUCESTER, ON, K1T 1M5
SIC 7515

PARKWAY AUTOMOTIVE SALES LIMITED p787
1681 EGLINTON AVE E, NORTH YORK, ON, M4A 1J6
SIC 7515

SOMERVILLE NATIONAL LEASING & RENTALS LTD   p795
75 ARROW RD, NORTH YORK, ON, M9M 2L4
(416) 747-7576   *SIC 7515*

SURGENOR NATIONAL LEASING LIMITED p820
881 ST. LAURENT BLVD, OTTAWA, ON, K1K 3B1
(613) 706-4779   *SIC 7515*

WHITBY-OSHAWA IMPORTS LTD   p1015
300 THICKSON RD S, WHITBY, ON, L1N 9Z1
(905) 666-1772   *SIC 7515*

SIC 7519 Utility trailer rental

4452241 CANADA LTD   p540
6019 RUSSELL RD UNIT 2, CARLSBAD SPRINGS, ON, K0A 1K0
(613) 816-9917   *SIC 7519*

C. KEAY INVESTMENTS LTD   p208
9076 RIVER RD, DELTA, BC, V4G 1B5
(604) 940-0210   *SIC 7519*

CANADREAM CORPORATION   p160
292154 CROSSPOINTE DR, ROCKY VIEW COUNTY, AB, T4A 0V2
(403) 291-1000   *SIC 7519*

CANADREAM INC   p160
292154 CROSSPOINTE DR, ROCKY VIEW COUNTY, AB, T4A 0V2
SIC 7519

CRUISE CANADA INC   p8
2980 26 ST NE, CALGARY, AB, T1Y 6R7
(403) 291-4963   *SIC 7519*

DENILLE INDUSTRIES LTD   p93
14440 YELLOWHEAD TRAIL NW, EDMONTON, AB, T5L 3C5
(780) 413-0900   *SIC 7519*

MODSPACE FINANCIAL SERVICES CANADA, LTD   p499
2300 NORTH PARK DR, BRAMPTON, ON, L6S 6C6
(905) 794-3900   *SIC 7519*

PROVINCIAL CAPITAL CORP   p699
1611 BRITANNIA RD E, MISSISSAUGA, ON, L4W 1S5
(905) 670-7077   *SIC 7519*

TRAILCON LEASING INC   p500
15 SPAR DR, BRAMPTON, ON, L6S 6E1
(905) 670-9061   *SIC 7519*

TRAILER WIZARDS LTD   p187
4649 HASTINGS ST, BURNABY, BC, V5C 2K6
(604) 320-1666   *SIC 7519*

TRAILER WIZARDS LTD   p701

1880 BRITANNIA RD E, MISSISSAUGA, ON, L4W 1J3
(905) 670-7077   *SIC 7519*

TRAIN TRAILER RENTALS LIMITED   p743
400 ANNAGEM BLVD, MISSISSAUGA, ON, L5T 3A8
(905) 564-7247   *SIC 7519*

U-HAUL CO. (CANADA) LTD   p608
526 GRAYS RD, HAMILTON, ON, L8E 2Z4
(905) 560-0014   *SIC 7519*

WILLIAMS SCOTSMAN OF CANADA, INC p3
19 EAST LAKE AVE, AIRDRIE, AB, T4A 2G9
(403) 241-5357   *SIC 7519*

SIC 7521 Automobile parking

CALGARY PARKING AUTHORITY   p28
400 39 AVE SE, CALGARY, AB, T2G 5P8
(403) 537-7100   *SIC 7521*

CAPITAL PARKING INC   p824
400 SLATER ST SUITE 2102, OTTAWA, ON, K1R 7S7
(613) 593-8820   *SIC 7521*

CAR PARK MANAGEMENT SERVICES LIMITED   p931
40 ISABELLA ST, TORONTO, ON, M4Y 1N1
(416) 920-3382   *SIC 7521*

DIAMOND PARKING LTD   p318
817 DENMAN ST, VANCOUVER, BC, V6G 2L7
(604) 681-8797   *SIC 7521*

IMPERIAL PARKING CANADA CORPORATION   p89
10239 107 ST NW, EDMONTON, AB, T5J 1K1
(780) 420-1976   *SIC 7521*

IMPERIAL PARKING CANADA CORPORATION   p298
601 CORDOVA ST W SUITE 300, VANCOUVER, BC, V6B 1G1
(604) 681-7311   *SIC 7521*

IMPERIAL PARKING CANADA CORPORATION   p374
136 MARKET AVE SUITE 2, WINNIPEG, MB, R3B 0P4
(204) 943-3578   *SIC 7521*

IMPERIAL PARKING CANADA CORPORATION   p1211
640 RUE SAINT-PAUL O BUREAU 106, MONTREAL, QC, H3C 1L9
(514) 875-5626   *SIC 7521*

LOGIC-CONTROLE INC   p1049
8002 RUE JARRY, ANJOU, QC, H1J 1H5
(514) 493-1162   *SIC 7521*

METRO PARKING LTD   p315
1078 PENDER ST W, VANCOUVER, BC, V6E 2N7
(604) 682-6754   *SIC 7521*

MILLER ROAD HOLDINGS LTD   p265
6380 MILLER RD, RICHMOND, BC, V7B 1B3
(604) 270-9395   *SIC 7521*

PARKING CORPORATION OF VANCOUVER, THE   p308
700 PENDER ST W SUITE 209, VANCOUVER, BC, V6C 1G8
(604) 682-6744   *SIC 7521*

PNF HOLDINGS LIMITED   p689
5815 AIRPORT RD, MISSISSAUGA, ON, L4V 1C8
(905) 677-9143   *SIC 7521*

SOCIETE PARC-AUTO DU QUEBEC p1270
965 PLACE D'YOUVILLE, QUEBEC, QC, G1R 3P1
(418) 694-9662   *SIC 7521*

STATIONNEMENT & DEVELOPPEMENT INTERNATIONAL INC   p1212
544 RUE DE L'INSPECTEUR BUREAU 200, MONTREAL, QC, H3C 2K9
(514) 396-6421   *SIC 7521*

STEINBOCK DEVELOPMENT CORPORA-

TION LTD   p32
140 6 AVE SE, CALGARY, AB, T2G 0G2
(403) 232-4725   *SIC 7521*

TARGET PARK GROUP INC   p984
525 KING ST W SUITE 300, TORONTO, ON, M5V 1K4
(416) 425-7275   *SIC 7521*

TORONTO PARKING AUTHORITY, THE p941
33 QUEEN ST E, TORONTO, ON, M5C 1R5
(416) 393-7275   *SIC 7521*

U B C TRAFFIC OFFICE   p325
2075 WESBROOK MALL SUITE 204, VANCOUVER, BC, V6T 1Z1
(604) 822-6786   *SIC 7521*

UNIT PARK MANAGEMENT INC   p943
1 YONGE ST SUITE 1510, TORONTO, ON, M5E 1E5
(416) 366-7275   *SIC 7521*

WESTPARK PARKING SERVICES (2015) INC   p317
1140 PENDER ST W SUITE 1310, VANCOUVER, BC, V6E 4G1
(604) 669-7275   *SIC 7521*

SIC 7532 Top and body repair and paint shops

1555314 ONTARIO INC   p838
965 MACKAY ST, PEMBROKE, ON, K8B 1A2
(613) 735-4593   *SIC 7532*

402909 ALBERTA LTD   p118
5834 GATEWAY BLVD NW, EDMONTON, AB, T6H 2H6
(780) 434-7471   *SIC 7532*

427 AUTO COLLISION LIMITED   p573
395 EVANS AVE, ETOBICOKE, ON, M8Z 1K8
(416) 259-6344   *SIC 7532*

9071- 0575 QUEBEC INC   p1287
1638 BOUL MARCOTTE, ROBERVAL, QC, G8H 2P2
(418) 275-2724   *SIC 7532*

A-1 AUTO BODY LTD   p33
5304 1A ST SE, CALGARY, AB, T2H 1J2
(403) 253-7867   *SIC 7532*

A.P. PLASMAN INC   p911
24 INDUSTRIAL PARK RD, TILBURY, ON, N0P 2L0
(519) 682-1155   *SIC 7532*

ABOUGOUSH COLLISION INC   p220
1960 DAYTON ST, KELOWNA, BC, V1Y 7W6
(250) 868-2693   *SIC 7532*

AUTO CLEARING (1982) LTD   p1431
331 CIRCLE DR W, SASKATOON, SK, S7L 5S8
(306) 244-2186   *SIC 7532*

BIG RIG COLLISION AND PAINT LTD p174
933 COUTTS WAY, ABBOTSFORD, BC, V2S 7M2
(604) 857-4915   *SIC 7532*

BOYD GROUP INC, THE   p386
3570 PORTAGE AVE, WINNIPEG, MB, R3K 0Z8
(204) 895-1244   *SIC 7532*

BOYD GROUP INCOME FUND   p383
1745 ELLICE AVE, WINNIPEG, MB, R3H 1A6
(204) 895-1244   *SIC 7532*

BRIMELL AUTOMOTIVE SERVICES LIMITED   p873
5060 SHEPPARD AVE E, SCARBOROUGH, ON, M1S 4N3
(416) 292-2241   *SIC 7532*

CAM CLARK FORD LINCOLN LTD   p241
833 AUTOMALL DR, NORTH VANCOUVER, BC, V7P 3R8
(604) 980-3673   *SIC 7532*

CENTRE AUTO COLLISION LIMITED   p933
354 RICHMOND ST E, TORONTO, ON, M5A 1P7
(416) 364-1116   *SIC 7532*

CHABOT CARROSSERIE INC p1159
264 CH DES POIRIER, MONTMAGNY, QC, G5V 4S5
(418) 234-1525   *SIC 7532*

DARTMOUTH MOTORS LP p443
61 ATHORPE DR, DARTMOUTH, NS, B2W 1K9
(902) 469-9050   *SIC 7532*

DAVIS GMC BUICK LTD p146
1450 TRANS CANADA WAY SE, MEDICINE HAT, AB, T1B 4M2
(403) 527-1115   *SIC 7532*

FIX AUTO CANADA INC p1059
99 RUE EMILIEN-MARCOUX BUREAU 101, BLAINVILLE, QC, J7C 0B4
(450) 433-1414   *SIC 7532*

HERBERS AUTO BODY REPAIR LTD p120
2721 PARSONS RD NW, EDMONTON, AB, T6N 1B8
(780) 469-8888   *SIC 7532*

IMAGES TURBO INC, LES p1305
1225 107E RUE, SAINT-GEORGES, QC, G5Y 8C3
(418) 227-8872   *SIC 7532*

INTEVA PRODUCTS CANADA, ULC p1014
1555 WENTWORTH ST, WHITBY, ON, L1N 9T6
(905) 666-4600   *SIC 7532*

KEIZER'S COLLISION CENTRE p462
1682 SACKVILLE DR, MIDDLE SACKVILLE, NS, B4E 3A9
(902) 865-7311   *SIC 7532*

KIRMAC AUTOMOTIVE COLLISION SYSTEMS (CANADA) INC p198
2714 BARNET HWY SUITE 104, COQUITLAM, BC, V3B 1B8
(604) 461-4494   *SIC 7532*

L.M.B TRANSPORT LIMITED p491
209 PUTTMAN INDUSTRIAL RD, BELLEVILLE, ON, K8N 4Z6
(613) 968-7541   *SIC 7532*

LYONS AUTO BODY LIMITED p711
1020 BURNHAMTHORPE RD W, MISSISSAUGA, ON, L5C 2S4
(905) 277-1456   *SIC 7532*

MURRAY CHEVROLET OLDSMOBILE CADILLAC LTD p146
1270 TRANS CANADA WAY SE, MEDICINE HAT, AB, T1B 1J5
(403) 527-1141   *SIC 7532*

NEBRASKA COLLISION CENTRE INC p865
6511 KINGSTON RD, SCARBOROUGH, ON, M1C 1L5
(416) 282-5794   *SIC 7532*

NO 1 COLLISION (1993) INC p255
20 VULCAN WAY SUITE 124, RICHMOND, BC, V6V 1J8
(604) 231-9614   *SIC 7532*

RICHMOND AUTO BODY LTD p261
2691 NO. 5 RD, RICHMOND, BC, V6X 2S8
(604) 278-9158   *SIC 7532*

RM CLASSIC CARS INC p493
1 CLASSIC CAR DR RR 5, BLENHEIM, ON, N0P 1A0
(519) 352-4575   *SIC 7532*

SOLOMON COATINGS LTD p111
6382 50 ST NW, EDMONTON, AB, T6B 2N7
(780) 413-4545   *SIC 7532*

TUSKET SALES & SERVICE LIMITED p469
4143 GAVEL RD, TUSKET, NS, B0W 3M0
(902) 648-2600   *SIC 7532*

SIC 7533 Auto exhaust system repair shops

MUFFLERMAN INC, THE p657
3480 WHITE OAK RD, LONDON, ON, N6E 2Z9
(519) 685-0002   *SIC 7533*

WALTON ENTERPRISES LTD p814
460 TAUNTON RD E, OSHAWA, ON, L1K 1A8
(905) 404-1413   *SIC 7533*

SIC 7534 Tire retreading and repair shops

NEXXSOURCE RECYCLING INC p516
300 HENRY ST, BRANTFORD, ON, N3S 7R5
(519) 752-7696   *SIC 7534*

PROVINCIAL BANDAG TIRES LTD p399
410 RUE ST-FRANCOIS, EDMUNDSTON, NB, E3V 1G6
(506) 735-6136   *SIC 7534*

SIC 7536 Automotive glass replacement shops

BELRON CANADA INCORPOREE p1169
8288 BOUL PIE-IX, MONTREAL, QC, H1Z 3T6
(514) 593-7000   *SIC 7536*

CRYSTAL GLASS CANADA LTD p118
6424 GATEWAY BLVD NW, EDMONTON, AB, T6H 2H9
(780) 652-2512   *SIC 7536*

DECO WINDSHIELD REPAIR INC p72
1602 42 ST SW, CALGARY, AB, T3C 1Z5
(403) 829-6289   *SIC 7536*

TCG INTERNATIONAL INC p183
8658 COMMERCE CRT, BURNABY, BC, V5A 4N6
(604) 438-1000   *SIC 7536*

WINDSHIELD SURGEONS LTD p111
5203 82 AVE NW, EDMONTON, AB, T6B 2J6
(780) 466-9166   *SIC 7536*

SIC 7538 General automotive repair shops

3867359 MANITOBA INC p387
584 PEMBINA HWY SUITE 204, WINNIPEG, MB, R3M 3X7
(204) 925-3840   *SIC 7538*

884262 ONTARIO INC p563
1612 BASELINE RD, COURTICE, ON, L1E 2S5
(905) 435-1166   *SIC 7538*

893278 ALBERTA LTD p79
5501 50 AVE, CASTOR, AB, T0C 0X0
(403) 882-4040   *SIC 7538*

9056-6696 QUEBEC INC p1265
2700 AV WATT, QUEBEC, QC, G1P 3T6
(418) 654-1414   *SIC 7538*

BOYD GROUP HOLDINGS INC p386
3570 PORTAGE AVE, WINNIPEG, MB, R3K 0Z8
(204) 895-1244   *SIC 7538*

BUTCHER ENGINEERING ENTERPRISES LIMITED, THE p621
17 UNDERWOOD RD, INGERSOLL, ON, N5C 3K1
(519) 425-0999   *SIC 7538*

CAMIONS LAGUE INC p1064
205 CH DU TREMBLAY, BOUCHERVILLE, QC, J4B 6L6
(450) 655-6940   *SIC 7538*

CANADIAN BASE OPERATORS INC p546
101 PRETTY RIVER PKY S SUITE 6, COLLINGWOOD, ON, L9Y 4M8
(705) 446-9019   *SIC 7538*

CANADIAN STARTER DRIVES INC p792
176 MILVAN DR, NORTH YORK, ON, M9L 1Z9
(416) 748-1458   *SIC 7538*

CITY TIRE & AUTO CENTRE LIMITED p426
1123 TOPSAIL RD, MOUNT PEARL, NL, A1N 5G2
(709) 364-6808   *SIC 7538*

CMP - CLASSIC AUTOMOTIVE LTD p10
1313 36 ST NE, CALGARY, AB, T2A 6P9
(403) 207-1002   *SIC 7538*

CMP AUTOMOTIVE INC p10
1313 36 ST NE, CALGARY, AB, T2A 6P9
(403) 207-1000   *SIC 7538*

COOLEY, DEAN MOTORS LTD p348
1600 MAIN ST S, DAUPHIN, MB, R7N 3B3
(204) 638-4026   *SIC 7538*

CURRIE, DONALD TRUCKS INC p681
2 CURRIE DR, MIDHURST, ON, L9X 0N3
(705) 734-1953   *SIC 7538*

DANIELS SERVICE CENTRE LTD p857
21180 VICTORIA RD, RIDGETOWN, ON, N0P 2C0
(519) 674-5493   *SIC 7538*

DEVONIAN MOTOR INCORPORATION p100
17708 111 AVE NW, EDMONTON, AB, T5S 0A2
(780) 484-7733   *SIC 7538*

ENTREPRISES S.M.T.R. INC p1288
500 RTE 112, ROUGEMONT, QC, J0L 1M0
(450) 469-3153   *SIC 7538*

FLEET BRAKE PARTS & SERVICE LTD p16
7707 54 ST SE, CALGARY, AB, T2C 4R7
(403) 476-9011   *SIC 7538*

GARAGE DESHARNAIS & FILS LTEE p1279
6055 BOUL PIERRE-BERTRAND, QUEBEC, QC, G2K 1M1
(418) 628-0203   *SIC 7538*

GESTION F.D. DESHARNAIS INC p1279
6055 BOUL PIERRE-BERTRAND, QUEBEC, QC, G2K 1M1
(418) 628-0203   *SIC 7538*

JAYFER AUTOMOTIVE GROUP (MARKHAM) INC p665
5426 HIGHWAY 7 E, MARKHAM, ON, L3P 1B7
(905) 294-1210   *SIC 7538*

JENNER CHEVROLET BUICK GMC LTD p340
1730 ISLAND HWY, VICTORIA, BC, V9B 1H8
(250) 474-1211   *SIC 7538*

L.E.S. MECANIQUE INC p1335
1200 RUE SAINT-AMOUR, SAINT-LAURENT, QC, H4S 1J2
(514) 333-6968   *SIC 7538*

LAWLESS, M.J. HOLDINGS LTD p863
200 MCNABB ST, SAULT STE. MARIE, ON, P6B 1Y4
(705) 949-0770   *SIC 7538*

MACLEAN HOLDINGS LTD p36
7220 FISHER ST SE, CALGARY, AB, T2H 2H8
(403) 640-7400   *SIC 7538*

MCDONALD, GRANT P. HOLDINGS INC p595
2680 OVERTON DR, GLOUCESTER, ON, K1G 6T8
(613) 225-9588   *SIC 7538*

MISSISSAUGA BUS, COACH & TRUCK REPAIRS INC p741
6625 KESTREL RD, MISSISSAUGA, ON, L5T 1P4
(905) 696-8328   *SIC 7538*

MOPAC AUTO SUPPLY LTD p226
19950 84 AVE SUITE 596, LANGLEY, BC, V2Y 3C2
(604) 881-4900   *SIC 7538*

MTB TRUCK & BUS COLLISION INC p684
8170 LAWSON RD, MILTON, ON, L9T 5C4
(905) 876-0669   *SIC 7538*

NUMBER 7 HONDA SALES LIMITED p1032
5555 HIGHWAY 7, WOODBRIDGE, ON, L4L 1T5
(905) 851-2258   *SIC 7538*

O.E.M. REMANUFACTURING COMPANY INC p106
13315 156 ST NW, EDMONTON, AB, T5V 1V2
(780) 468-6220   *SIC 7538*

OAK POINT SERVICE p369
272 OAK POINT HWY, WINNIPEG, MB, R2R 1V1
(204) 633-9435   *SIC 7538*

P & R TRUCK CENTRE LTD p267
2005 KEATING CROSS RD, SAANICHTON, BC, V8M 2A5
(250) 652-9139   *SIC 7538*

PORTAGE TRANSPORT INC p355
1450 LORNE AVE E, PORTAGE LA PRAIRIE, MB, R1N 4A2
(204) 239-6451   *SIC 7538*

QUEENSWAY VOLKSWAGEN INC p576
1306 THE QUEENSWAY, ETOBICOKE, ON, M8Z 1S4
(416) 259-7656   *SIC 7538*

REGINA MOTOR PRODUCTS (1970) LTD p1418
ALBERT ST S HWY 1-6, REGINA, SK, S4P 3A8
(866) 273-5778   *SIC 7538*

SAFRAN MOTEURS D'HELICOPTERES CANADA INC p1153
11800 RUE HELEN-BRISTOL, MIRABEL, QC, J7N 3G8
(450) 476-2550   *SIC 7538*

SCHERER, STEVE PONTIAC BUICK GMC LTD p637
1225 COURTLAND AVE E, KITCHENER, ON, N2C 2N8
(519) 893-8888   *SIC 7538*

ST-BONIFACE MUNICIPAL GARAGE p1295
500 MUNICIPALE PL, SAINT-BONIFACE-DE-SHAWINIGAN, QC, G0X 2L0
(819) 535-5443   *SIC 7538*

STANDARD AERO LIMITED p385
33 ALLEN DYNE RD, WINNIPEG, MB, R3H 1A1
(204) 775-9711   *SIC 7538*

STANDARD AERO LIMITED p385
570 FERRY RD SUITE 4, WINNIPEG, MB, R3H 0T7
SIC 7538

STEVEN K. LEE AND CO. LTD p119
3803 CALGARY TRAIL NW SUITE 550, EDMONTON, AB, T6J 5M8
(780) 438-4921   *SIC 7538*

TECHNODIESEL INC p1115
1260 CH DES PRAIRIES, JOLIETTE, QC, J6E 0L4
(450) 759-3709   *SIC 7538*

TIGER MACHINING INC. p163
15 TURBO DR, SHERWOOD PARK, AB, T8H 2J6
SIC 7538

VILLE DE MONTREAL p1167
2269 RUE VIAU, MONTREAL, QC, H1V 3H8
(514) 872-4303   *SIC 7538*

ZANE HOLDINGS LTD p84
9525 127 AVE NW, EDMONTON, AB, T5E 6M7
(780) 474-7921   *SIC 7538*

SIC 7539 Automotive repair shops, nec

442527 ONTARIO LIMITED p762
40 EXETER ST, NORTH BAY, ON, P1B 8G5
(705) 474-7880   *SIC 7539*

ALL-WELD COMPANY LIMITED p875
14 PASSMORE AVE, SCARBOROUGH, ON, M1V 2R6
(416) 293-3638   *SIC 7539*

AUTOTEMP INC p21
3419 12 ST NE SUITE 3, CALGARY, AB, T2E 6S6
(403) 250-7837   *SIC 7539*

CXD MAINTENANCE SERVICE LTD p113
6276 92 ST NW, EDMONTON, AB, T6E 3A7
(780) 391-1565   *SIC 7539*

DIXIE ELECTRIC LTD p552
517 BASALTIC RD, CONCORD, ON, L4K 4W8
(905) 879-0533   *SIC 7539*

GATEWAY REPAIRS TRUCK & TRAILER LTD p124
14203 157 AVE NW, EDMONTON, AB, T6V 0K8
(780) 451-3343   *SIC 7539*

MAGNUM 2000 INC p798
1137 NORTH SERVICE RD E, OAKVILLE, ON, L6H 1A7

(905) 339-1104   *SIC 7539*
PEEL TRUCK & TRAILER EQUIPMENT INC
p699
1715 BRITANNIA RD E, MISSISSAUGA, ON, L4W 2A3
(905) 670-1780   *SIC 7539*
RESSORTS MASKA INC   *p1310*
2890 BOUL LAURIER E, SAINT-HYACINTHE, QC, J2R 1P8
(450) 774-7511   *SIC 7539*

SIC 7542 Carwashes

9101-7673 QUEBEC INC   *p1097*
620 RUE CORMIER, DRUMMONDVILLE, QC, J2C 5C4
(819) 472-1180   *SIC 7542*
CHAMOIS CAR WASH CORP, THE   *p362*
85 REENDERS DR, WINNIPEG, MB, R2C 5E8
(204) 669-9700   *SIC 7542*
HUGHES PETROLEUM LTD   *p101*
10330 178 ST NW, EDMONTON, AB, T5S 1J2
(780) 444-4040   *SIC 7542*
LAVE AUTO A LA MAIN STEVE INC   *p1092*
4216 BOUL SAINT-JEAN, DOLLARD-DES-ORMEAUX, QC, H9G 1X5
(514) 696-9274   *SIC 7542*
REENDERS CAR WASH LTD   *p363*
85 REENDERS DR, WINNIPEG, MB, R2C 5E8
(204) 669-9700   *SIC 7542*
SUDS EXPRESS INC   *p1007*
130 DEARBORN PL, WATERLOO, ON, N2J 4N5
(519) 886-0561   *SIC 7542*

SIC 7549 Automotive services, nec

1512081 ONTARIO LTD   *p916*
93 TORO RD, TORONTO, ON, M3J 2A4
(416) 398-2500   *SIC 7549*
470858 ALBERTA LTD   *p112*
5674 75 ST NW, EDMONTON, AB, T6E 5X6
(780) 485-9905   *SIC 7549*
9165-8021 QUEBEC INC   *p1080*
1690 RUE DE LA MANIC, CHICOUTIMI, QC, G7K 1J1
(418) 543-5111   *SIC 7549*
A TOWING SERVICE LTD   *p787*
185 BARTLEY DR, NORTH YORK, ON, M4A 1E6
(416) 656-4000   *SIC 7549*
ANTIROUILLE METROPOLITAIN INC   *p1384*
3175 BOUL THIBEAU, TROIS-RIVIERES, QC, G8T 1G4
(819) 378-8787   *SIC 7549*
AXIS SORTING INC   *p602*
300 WILLOW RD UNIT 102B, GUELPH, ON, N1H 7C6
(519) 212-4990   *SIC 7549*
BUSTERS TOWING 1987 LTD   *p289*
104 1ST AVE E, VANCOUVER, BC, V5T 1A4
(604) 685-8181   *SIC 7549*
CITY WIDE TOWING AND RECOVERY SERVICE LTD   *p14*
10885 84 ST SE, CALGARY, AB, T2C 5A6
(403) 798-0876   *SIC 7549*
CLUB AUTO ROADSIDE SERVICES LTD
p904
60 COMMERCE VALLEY DR E, THORNHILL, ON, L3T 7P9
(905) 771-4001   *SIC 7549*
CTS EQUIPMENT TRANSPORT LTD   *p95*
11480 156 ST NW, EDMONTON, AB, T5M 3N2
(780) 451-3900   *SIC 7549*
DRAKE TOWING LTD   *p285*
1553 POWELL ST, VANCOUVER, BC, V5L 5C3

(604) 251-3344   *SIC 7549*
ESCAPE PROOF INC   *p800*
1496 DURHAM ST, OAKVILLE, ON, L6J 2P3
(289) 837-0813   *SIC 7549*
FARMBRO ALL-TRAC LTD   *p716*
4200 SLADEVIEW CRES, MISSISSAUGA, ON, L5L 5Z2
(905) 569-0592   *SIC 7549*
GARAGE MONTPLAISIR LTEE   *p1098*
875 BOUL SAINT-JOSEPH, DRUMMONDVILLE, QC, J2C 2C4
(819) 477-2323   *SIC 7549*
GREELEY CONTAINMENT AND REWORK INC   *p496*
200 BASELINE RD E, BOWMANVILLE, ON, L1C 1A2
(905) 623-5678   *SIC 7549*
HARKEN TOWING CO. LTD   *p246*
1990 ARGUE ST, PORT COQUITLAM, BC, V3C 5K4
(604) 942-8511   *SIC 7549*
INDEPENDENT DOCKSIDE GRADING INC
p426
19 OLD PLACENTIA RD, MOUNT PEARL, NL, A1N 4P4
(709) 364-5473   *SIC 7549*
KERR INDUSTRIES LIMITED   *p812*
635 FAREWELL ST, OSHAWA, ON, L1H 6N2
(905) 725-6561   *SIC 7549*
PIC GROUP LTD, THE   *p843*
1305 PICKERING PKWY, PICKERING, ON, L1V 3P2
(905) 743-4600   *SIC 7549*
PIC GROUP LTD, THE   *p1021*
1303 MCDOUGALL ST, WINDSOR, ON, N8X 3M6
(519) 252-1611   *SIC 7549*
PRAIRIE LUBE LTD   *p31*
5040 12A ST SE UNIT B, CALGARY, AB, T2G 5K9
(403) 243-7800   *SIC 7549*
REMORQUAGE PROFESSIONNEL SAGUENAY INC   *p1116*
2386 RUE CANTIN, JONQUIERE, QC, G7X 8S6
(418) 695-1114   *SIC 7549*
REMORQUAGE ST-MICHEL INC   *p1349*
340 CH PIGEON, SAINT-MICHEL, QC, J0L 2J0
(450) 454-9973   *SIC 7549*
SUPER AUTO CENTRE INC   *p392*
2028 PEMBINA HWY, WINNIPEG, MB, R3T 2G8
(204) 269-8444   *SIC 7549*
SYKES ASSISTANCE SERVICES CORPORATION   *p655*
248 PALL MALL ST, LONDON, ON, N6A 5P6
(519) 434-3221   *SIC 7549*
TORA INVESTMENTS INC   *p884*
15 CUSHMAN RD, ST CATHARINES, ON, L2M 6S7
(905) 227-5088   *SIC 7549*
TORA INVESTMENTS INC   *p884*
453 EASTCHESTER AVE E, ST CATHARINES, ON, L2M 6S2
(905) 685-5409   *SIC 7549*
UNITOW SERVICES (1978) LTD   *p296*
1717 VERNON DR, VANCOUVER, BC, V6A 3P8
(604) 659-1225   *SIC 7549*
WEFF HOLDINGS LTD   *p1424*
1702 8TH ST E, SASKATOON, SK, S7H 0T5
(306) 952-4262   *SIC 7549*

SIC 7622 Radio and television repair

AVMAX GROUP INC   *p21*
275 PALMER RD NE, CALGARY, AB, T2E 7G4
(403) 250-2644   *SIC 7622*

DELPHI SOLUTIONS CORP   *p669*
7550 BIRCHMOUNT RD, MARKHAM, ON, L3R 6C6
    SIC 7622

SIC 7623 Refrigeration service and repair

619249 ALBERTA LTD   *p108*
4143 78 AVE NW, EDMONTON, AB, T6B 2N3
(780) 469-7799   *SIC 7623*
AIRCO LTD   *p898*
1510 OLD FALCONBRIDGE RD, SUDBURY, ON, P3A 4N8
(705) 673-2210   *SIC 7623*
FMR MECHANICAL ELECTRICAL INC *p128*
330 MACKENZIE BLVD, FORT MCMURRAY, AB, T9H 4C4
(780) 791-9283   *SIC 7623*
HIWAY REFRIGERATION LTD   *p246*
1462 MUSTANG PL, PORT COQUITLAM, BC, V3C 6L2
(604) 944-0119   *SIC 7623*
HUNT REFRIGERATION (CANADA) INC
p1164
6360 RUE NOTRE-DAME E, MONTREAL, QC, H1N 2E1
(514) 259-9041   *SIC 7623*
NORDIC MECHANICAL SERVICES LTD
p110
4143 78 AVE NW, EDMONTON, AB, T6B 2N3
(780) 469-7799   *SIC 7623*
REEFER SALES & SERVICE (TORONTO) INCORPORATED   *p742*
425 GIBRALTAR DR, MISSISSAUGA, ON, L5T 2S9
(905) 795-0234   *SIC 7623*
REFRIGERATION NOEL INC   *p1265*
1700 RUE LEON-HARMEL, QUEBEC, QC, G1N 4R9
(418) 663-0879   *SIC 7623*
REFRIGERATION, PLOMBERIE & CHAUFFAGE LONGUEUIL INC   *p1142*
800 RUE JEAN-NEVEU, LONGUEUIL, QC, J4G 2M1
(514) 789-0456   *SIC 7623*
THERMO KING OF BRITISH COLUMBIA INC   *p202*
68 FAWCETT RD, COQUITLAM, BC, V3K 6V5
(604) 526-4414   *SIC 7623*
VENTILABEC INC   *p1357*
1955 BOUL SAINT-ELZEAR O, SAINTE-DOROTHEE, QC, H7L 3N7
(514) 745-0230   *SIC 7623*

SIC 7629 Electrical repair shops

1378045 ONTARIO INC   *p1013*
220 WATER ST, WHITBY, ON, L1N 0G9
(905) 666-7669   *SIC 7629*
683949 ONTARIO LIMITED   *p875*
155 DYNAMIC DR, SCARBOROUGH, ON, M1V 5L8
(416) 366-6372   *SIC 7629*
9580166 CANADA INC   *p972*
15 PRINCE ARTHUR AVE, TORONTO, ON, M5R 1B2
(647) 282-2802   *SIC 7629*
A.M.P.M. SERVICE LTD   *p181*
6741 CARIBOO RD UNIT 101, BURNABY, BC, V3N 4A3
(604) 421-5677   *SIC 7629*
ATELIER LA FLECHE DE FER INC, L' *p1307*
3800 RUE RICHELIEU, SAINT-HUBERT, QC, J3Y 7B1
(450) 656-9150   *SIC 7629*
ATELIERS G. PAQUETTE INC   *p1282*
104 RUE LAROCHE, REPENTIGNY, QC, J6A 7M5
(450) 654-6744   *SIC 7629*

BELL AND HOWELL CANADA LTD   *p851*
30 MURAL ST UNIT 6, RICHMOND HILL, ON, L4B 1B5
(416) 747-2200   *SIC 7629*
CAMPBELL SCIENTIFIC (CANADA) CORP
p93
14532 131 AVE NW, EDMONTON, AB, T5L 4X4
(780) 454-2505   *SIC 7629*
ENCORE REPAIR SERVICES CANADA, ULC   *p552*
40 NORTH RIVERMEDE RD UNIT 10, CONCORD, ON, L4K 2H3
(905) 597-5972   *SIC 7629*
ERTH (HOLDINGS) INC   *p621*
180 WHITING ST, INGERSOLL, ON, N5C 3B5
(519) 485-6038   *SIC 7629*
FIXT WIRELESS INC   *p776*
1875 LESLIE ST UNIT 4, NORTH YORK, ON, M3B 2M5
(416) 441-3498   *SIC 7629*
KITCHENER AERO AVIONICS LIMITED
p518
4881 FOUNTAIN ST N SUITE 6, BRESLAU, ON, N0B 1M0
(519) 648-2921   *SIC 7629*
LANG'S VENTURES INC   *p341*
3099 SHANNON LAKE RD SUITE 105, WEST KELOWNA, BC, V4T 2M2
(250) 768-7055   *SIC 7629*
MEGLAB ELECTRONIQUE INC   *p1391*
281 19E RUE, VAL-D'OR, QC, J9P 0L7
(819) 824-7710   *SIC 7629*
NORALTA TECHNOLOGIES INC   *p55*
808 4 AVE SW UNIT 100, CALGARY, AB, T2P 3E8
(403) 269-4237   *SIC 7629*
PRONGHORN CONTROLS LTD   *p17*
4919 72 AVE SE SUITE 101, CALGARY, AB, T2C 3H3
(403) 720-2526   *SIC 7629*
PYLON ELECTRONICS INC   *p742*
6355 DANVILLE RD UNIT 10, MISSISSAUGA, ON, L5T 2L4
(905) 362-1395   *SIC 7629*
REV ENGINEERING LTD   *p13*
3236 50 AVE SE, CALGARY, AB, T2B 3A3
(403) 287-0156   *SIC 7629*
RONDAR INC   *p608*
333 CENTENNIAL PKY N, HAMILTON, ON, L8E 2X6
(905) 561-2808   *SIC 7629*
STRATUS ELECTRICAL & INSTRUMENTATION LTD   *p71*
12204 40 ST SE UNIT 12, CALGARY, AB, T2Z 4K6
(403) 775-7599   *SIC 7629*
TEKALIA AERONAUTIK (2010) INC *p1160*
3900 BOUL DU TRICENTENAIRE, MONTREAL, QC, H1B 5L6
(514) 640-2411   *SIC 7629*
TOTEM APPLIANCE & REFRIGERATION LTD   *p194*
5950 IMPERIAL ST, BURNABY, BC, V5J 4M2
(604) 437-5136   *SIC 7629*

SIC 7631 Watch, clock, and jewelry repair

FAR EAST WATCHCASES LTD   *p855*
120 NEWKIRK RD UNIT 5&6, RICHMOND HILL, ON, L4C 9S7
(905) 787-9919   *SIC 7631*
TIMECO WATCH & CLOCK REPAIRS LTD
p189
4459 CANADA WAY, BURNABY, BC, V5G 1J3
(604) 435-6383   *SIC 7631*

SIC 7641 Reupholstery and furniture repair

▲ Public Company   ■ Public Company Family Member   **HQ** Headquarters   **BR** Branch   **SL** Single Location

MAURICE SIGOUIN REPARATION DE MEUBLES LTEE p1107
142 CH FREEMAN BUREAU 8, GATINEAU, QC, J8Z 2B4
(819) 776-3522 *SIC* 7641

SIC 7692 Welding repair

1510610 ONTARIO INC p762
1811 SEYMOUR ST, NORTH BAY, ON, P1A 0C7
(705) 474-0350 *SIC* 7692

ADJ HOLDINGS INC p648
2068 PIPER LANE, LONDON, ON, N5V 3N6
(519) 455-4065 *SIC* 7692

AECOM CANADA LTD p171
1718 23RD AVE, WAINWRIGHT, AB, T9W 1T2
(780) 842-4220 *SIC* 7692

AUTOGENE INDUSTRIES NORTH BAY INC p762
1811 SEYMOUR ST, NORTH BAY, ON, P1A 0C7
(705) 474-0350 *SIC* 7692

DALKOTECH INC p1375
9330 BOUL BOURQUE, SHERBROOKE, QC, J1N 0G2
(819) 868-1997 *SIC* 7692

ENTREPRISES H.M. METAL INC, LES p1363
583 RANG SAINT-OVIDE, SAINTE-SOPHIE-DE-LEVRARD, QC, G0X 3C0
(819) 288-5287 *SIC* 7692

FABRICATION FRANSI INC p1052
32 AV BABIN, BAIE-COMEAU, QC, G4Z 3A6
(418) 296-6021 *SIC* 7692

G.T. SERVICE DE CONTENEURS INC p1161
10000 BOUL MAURICE-DUPLESSIS, MONTREAL, QC, H1C 2A2
(514) 648-4848 *SIC* 7692

GEMINI FIELD SOLUTIONS LTD p152
4100 67 ST, PONOKA, AB, T4J 1J8
SIC 7692

GENERAL METAL FABRICATION LTD p361
269 MANITOBA RD, WINKLER, MB, R6W 0J8
(204) 325-9374 *SIC* 7692

GROUPE G & G LTEE p1344
6245 BOUL DES GRANDES-PRAIRIES, SAINT-LEONARD, QC, H1P 1A5
(514) 325-3711 *SIC* 7692

HYDUKE DRILLING SOLUTIONS INC p149
2107 6 ST, NISKU, AB, T9E 7X8
(780) 955-0360 *SIC* 7692

INDUSTRIES FORESTEEL INC, LES p1162
9225 BOUL HENRI-BOURASSA E, MONTREAL, QC, H1E 1P6
(514) 645-9251 *SIC* 7692

MORSKATE MANUFACTURING LTD p152
431053 RANGE RD SUITE 261, PONOKA, AB, T4J 1R4
(403) 783-6140 *SIC* 7692

PEACE VALLEY INDUSTRIES (2016) LTD p196
4311 46TH ST, CHETWYND, BC, V0C 1J0
(250) 788-2922 *SIC* 7692

PLESSITECH INC p1246
2250 AV VALLEE, PLESSISVILLE, QC, G6L 2Y6
(819) 362-6315 *SIC* 7692

SOUDURES EXPRESS INC p1045
995 AV BOMBARDIER, ALMA, QC, G8B 6H2
(418) 669-1911 *SIC* 7692

SRW TECHNOLOGIES p116
4521 101 ST NW, EDMONTON, AB, T6E 5C6
(780) 413-4833 *SIC* 7692

STURGEON CREEK COLONY FARMS LTD p351
1069 ROAD 63, HEADINGLEY, MB, R4J 1C1
(204) 633-2196 *SIC* 7692

WHITFIELD WELDING INC p807
5425 ROSCON INDUSTRIAL DR, OLDCASTLE, ON, N0R 1L0
(519) 737-1814 *SIC* 7692

SIC 7694 Armature rewinding shops

BEAVER ELECTRICAL MACHINERY LTD p192
7440 LOWLAND DR, BURNABY, BC, V5J 5A4
(604) 431-5000 *SIC* 7694

CONTINENTAL ELECTRICAL MOTOR SERVICES (NORTHERN) LTD p122
8909 15 ST NW, EDMONTON, AB, T6P 0B8
(780) 410-8800 *SIC* 7694

CONTINENTAL ELECTRICAL MOTOR SERVICES LTD p29
4015 8 ST SE SUITE 201, CALGARY, AB, T2G 3A5
(403) 236-9428 *SIC* 7694

DELOM SERVICES INC p1160
13065 RUE JEAN-GROU, MONTREAL, QC, H1A 3N6
(514) 642-8220 *SIC* 7694

ELECTRIC MOTOR SERVICE LIMITED p114
8835 60 AVE NW, EDMONTON, AB, T6E 6L9
(780) 496-9300 *SIC* 7694

EVANS ENGINE SHOP LTD p174
33406 SOUTH FRASER WAY, ABBOTSFORD, BC, V2S 2B5
SIC 7694

MAGNETO ELECTRIC SERVICE CO. LIMITED p697
1150 EGLINTON AVE E, MISSISSAUGA, ON, L4W 2M6
(905) 625-9450 *SIC* 7694

NORTHPOINT TECHNICAL SERVICES ULC p12
4920 43 ST SE, CALGARY, AB, T2B 3N3
(403) 279-2211 *SIC* 7694

PENNECON TECHNICAL SERVICES LTD p433
650 WATER ST, ST. JOHN'S, NL, A1E 1B9
(709) 726-4554 *SIC* 7694

SHERWOOD ELECTROMOTION INC p558
20 BARNES CRT UNIT A-E, CONCORD, ON, L4K 4L4
(289) 695-5555 *SIC* 7694

SOLUTIONS TECHNIQUES INTELLIGENTES CB INC p1368
75 RUE DU PARC-INDUSTRIEL, SHAWINIGAN, QC, G9N 6T5
(819) 536-2609 *SIC* 7694

WORLD AVIATION CORP p561
45 CORSTATE AVE, CONCORD, ON, L4K 4Y2
(905) 660-4462 *SIC* 7694

SIC 7699 Repair services, nec

2985080 CANADA INC p1389
138 CH DES BOISES BUREAU 2, VAL-D'OR, QC, J9P 4N7
(819) 738-5289 *SIC* 7699

9356-3609 QUEBEC INC p1367
22C RUE LEMAIRE, SEPT-ILES, QC, G4S 1S3
(418) 960-1276 *SIC* 7699

965046 ONTARIO INC p679
80 CITIZEN CRT UNIT 11, MARKHAM, ON, L6G 1A7
(905) 305-0195 *SIC* 7699

A & D PRECISION LIMITED p548
289 BRADWICK DR, CONCORD, ON, L4K 1K5
(905) 669-5888 *SIC* 7699

ALBERTA EXCHANGER LTD p121
2210 70 AVE NW, EDMONTON, AB, T6P 1N6
(780) 440-1045 *SIC* 7699

ALSTOM CANADA INC p595
1430 BLAIR PL SUITE 600, GLOUCESTER, ON, K1J 9N2
(613) 747-5222 *SIC* 7699

AMNOR INDUSTRIES INC p1289
8 RUE DOYON, ROUYN-NORANDA, QC, J9X 7B4
(819) 762-9044 *SIC* 7699

ASKAN ARTS LIMITED p782
20 TORO RD, NORTH YORK, ON, M3J 2A7
(416) 398-2333 *SIC* 7699

CANADIAN ASSOCIATION OF TOKEN COLLECTORS p473
273 MILL ST E, ACTON, ON, L7J 1J7
(519) 853-3812 *SIC* 7699

CEDA FIELD SERVICES LP p108
6005 72A AVE NW, EDMONTON, AB, T6B 2J1
(780) 377-4306 *SIC* 7699

CGRIFF21 HOLDINGS INC p680
25 BODRINGTON CRT, MARKHAM, ON, L6G 1B6
(905) 940-9334 *SIC* 7699

COMPAGNIE DES CHEMINS DE FER NATIONAUX DU CANADA p650
363 EGERTON ST, LONDON, ON, N5W 6B1
SIC 7699

COMPRESSOR PRODUCTS INTERNATIONAL CANADA INC p113
6308 DAVIES RD NW, EDMONTON, AB, T6E 4M9
(780) 468-5145 *SIC* 7699

CONSULTANTS F. DRAPEAU INC p1348
2005 CH DE L'INDUSTRIE, SAINT-MATHIEU-DE-BELOEIL, QC, J3G 0S4
(450) 467-2642 *SIC* 7699

CSM COMPRESSOR INC p120
9330 27 AVE NW, EDMONTON, AB, T6N 1B2
(780) 435-5722 *SIC* 7699

DEFI POLYTECK p1371
1255 BOUL QUEEN-VICTORIA, SHERBROOKE, QC, J1J 4N6
(819) 348-1209 *SIC* 7699

DELSTAR ENERGIE INC p1160
12885 RUE JEAN-GROU, MONTREAL, QC, H1A 3N6
(514) 642-8222 *SIC* 7699

DELTA ELEVATOR COMPANY LIMITED p638
509 MILL ST, KITCHENER, ON, N2G 2Y5
(519) 745-5789 *SIC* 7699

DITECH PAINT CO. LTD p397
561 BOUL FERDINAND, DIEPPE, NB, E1A 7G1
(506) 384-8197 *SIC* 7699

DUTCHMEN EQUIPMENT LTD p78
4613 41 ST, CAMROSE, AB, T4V 2Y8
(780) 672-7946 *SIC* 7699

EDMONTON EXCHANGER & REFINERY SERVICES LTD p114
5545 89 ST NW, EDMONTON, AB, T6E 5W9
(780) 468-6722 *SIC* 7699

EGZATEK INC p1369
135 RUE OLIVA-TURGEON, SHERBROOKE, QC, J1C 0R3
(819) 846-6863 *SIC* 7699

ELLIOTT TURBOMACHINERY CANADA INC p530
955 MAPLE AVE, BURLINGTON, ON, L7S 2J4
(905) 333-4101 *SIC* 7699

ENTREPRISES A & R BROCHU CONSTRUCTION INC , LES p1295
1505 RUE MARIE-VICTORIN, SAINT-BRUNO, QC, J3V 6B7
(450) 441-7444 *SIC* 7699

ENTRETIEN PARAMEX INC p1389
3535 BOUL L.-P.-NORMAND, TROIS-RIVIERES, QC, G9B 0G8
(819) 377-5533 *SIC* 7699

FIVES SERVICES INC p1264
1580 RUE PROVINCIALE, QUEBEC, QC, G1N 4A2
(418) 656-9140 *SIC* 7699

FRAMEWORTH CUSTOM FRAMING INC p789
1198 CALEDONIA RD UNIT B, NORTH YORK, ON, M6A 2W5
(416) 781-1115 *SIC* 7699

FUJITSU FRONTECH CANADA INC p951
155 UNIVERSITY AVE SUITE 1600, TORONTO, ON, M5H 3B7
(800) 668-8325 *SIC* 7699

GAS DRIVE GLOBAL LP p12
4700 47 ST SE, CALGARY, AB, T2B 3R1
(403) 387-6300 *SIC* 7699

GAS DRIVE GLOBAL LP p1358
2091 RUE LEONARD-DE VINCI UNITE A, SAINTE-JULIE, QC, J3E 1Z2
(450) 649-3174 *SIC* 7699

GAZ METRO PLUS INC p1065
1350 RUE NOBEL BUREAU 100, BOUCHERVILLE, QC, J4B 5H3
(450) 641-6300 *SIC* 7699

GOODRICH AEROSPACE CANADA LTD p522
5415 NORTH SERVICE RD, BURLINGTON, ON, L7L 5H7
(905) 319-3006 *SIC* 7699

GRIF & GRAF INC p1070
9205 BOUL TASCHEREAU, BROSSARD, QC, J4Y 3B8
(450) 659-6999 *SIC* 7699

H.C. VIDAL LTEE p1223
5700 RUE PHILIPPE-TURCOT, MONTREAL, QC, H4C 1V6
(514) 937-6187 *SIC* 7699

HANSLER INDUSTRIES LTD p519
1385 CALIFORNIA AVE, BROCKVILLE, ON, K6V 5V5
(613) 342-4408 *SIC* 7699

HEAVY EQUIPMENT REPAIR LTD p163
404 BALSAM RD, SLAVE LAKE, AB, T0G 2A0
(780) 849-3768 *SIC* 7699

HELI-ONE CANADA ULC p264
4740 AGAR DR, RICHMOND, BC, V7B 1A3
(604) 276-7500 *SIC* 7699

INDUSTRIE DE PALETTES STANDARD (I.P.S.) INC p1083
2400 RUE DE LIERRE, COTE SAINT-LUC, QC, H7G 4Y4
(450) 661-4000 *SIC* 7699

INDUSTRY TRAINING AUTHORITY p262
8100 GRANVILLE AVE UNIT 800, RICHMOND, BC, V6Y 3T6
(604) 214-8700 *SIC* 7699

INSITUFORM TECHNOLOGIES LIMITED p122
7605 18 ST NW, EDMONTON, AB, T6P 1N9
(780) 413-0200 *SIC* 7699

INTERNATIONAL COOLING TOWER INC p120
3310 93 ST NW, EDMONTON, AB, T6N 1C7
(780) 469-4900 *SIC* 7699

IRONLINE COMPRESSION LIMITED PARTNERSHIP p149
700 15 AVE, NISKU, AB, T9E 7S2
(780) 955-0700 *SIC* 7699

JOHNSON MATTHEY MATERIAUX POUR BATTERIES LTEE p1073
280 AV LIBERTE, CANDIAC, QC, J5R 6X1
(514) 906-1359 *SIC* 7699

KONE INC p723
6696 FINANCIAL DR SUITE 2, MISSISSAUGA, ON, L5N 7J6
(905) 858-8383 *SIC* 7699

KONECRANES CANADA INC p523
5300 MAINWAY, BURLINGTON, ON, L7L 6A4
(905) 332-9494 *SIC* 7699

KONECRANES CANADA INC p523
5300 MAINWAY, BURLINGTON, ON, L7L 6A4
(905) 332-9494 *SIC* 7699

KRISTIAN ELECTRIC LTD p17

4215 64 AVE SE, CALGARY, AB, T2C 2C8

(403) 292-9111   *SIC 7699*

L. J. L. MECANIQUE INC   *p1358*
203 PARC INDUSTRIEL, SAINTE-GERMAINE-BOULE, QC, J0Z 1M0

(819) 787-6509   *SIC 7699*

L3 TECHNOLOGIES MAS INC   *p1153*
10000 RUE HELEN-BRISTOL, MIRABEL, QC, J7N 1H3

(450) 476-4000   *SIC 7699*

LIQUI-FORCE SERVICES (ONTARIO) INC   *p634*
2015 SPINKS DR SUITE 2, KINGSVILLE, ON, N9Y 2E5

(519) 322-4600   *SIC 7699*

LORTIE AVIATION INC   *p1378*
130 RUE TIBO, STE-CATHERINE-DE-LA-J-CARTIE, QC, G3N 2Y7

(418) 875-5111   *SIC 7699*

LOUNSBURY HEAVY-DUTY TRUCK LIMITED   *p408*
725 ST GEORGE BLVD, MONCTON, NB, E1E 2C2

(506) 857-4345   *SIC 7699*

MACHINERIES PROVINCIALES INC *p1280*
1160 RUE BOUVIER, QUEBEC, QC, G2K 1L9

(418) 628-8460   *SIC 7699*

MAGNETO, HYDRAULIQUE & PNEUMATIQUE INC   *p1066*
1375 RUE GAY-LUSSAC, BOUCHERVILLE, QC, J4B 7K1

(450) 655-2551   *SIC 7699*

MARITIME HYDRAULIC REPAIR CENTRE (1997) LTD   *p410*
355 MACNAUGHTON AVE, MONCTON, NB, E1H 2J9

(506) 858-0393   *SIC 7699*

MARITIME PRESSUREWORKS LIMITED *p444*
41 ESTATES RD, DARTMOUTH, NS, B2Y 4K3

(902) 468-8461   *SIC 7699*

METRO CHUTE SERVICE INC   *p586*
23 RACINE RD, ETOBICOKE, ON, M9W 2Z4

(416) 746-5547   *SIC 7699*

METRO COMPACTOR SERVICE INC   *p509*
145 HEART LAKE RD S, BRAMPTON, ON, L6W 3K3

(416) 743-8484   *SIC 7699*

MOORE'S INDUSTRIAL SERVICE LTD   *p24*
3333 23 ST NE, CALGARY, AB, T2E 6V8

(403) 219-7160   *SIC 7699*

MTU MAINTENANCE CANADA LTD   *p265*
6020 RUSS BAKER WAY, RICHMOND, BC, V7B 1B4

(604) 233-5700   *SIC 7699*

NORCAN FLUID POWER LTD   *p225*
19650 TELEGRAPH TRAIL, LANGLEY, BC, V1M 3E5

(604) 881-7877   *SIC 7699*

NORDMEC INDUSTRIELS & MINES INC *p1366*
850 BOUL DES ERABLES, SALABERRY-DE-VALLEYFIELD, QC, J6T 6G4

(450) 373-3739   *SIC 7699*

ONE WIND SERVICES INC   *p447*
4 MACDONALD AVE, DARTMOUTH, NS, B3B 1C5

(902) 482-8687   *SIC 7699*

OTIS CANADA, INC   *p36*
777 64 AVE SE SUITE 7, CALGARY, AB, T2H 2Q3

(403) 244-1040   *SIC 7699*

OTIS CANADA, INC   *p523*
4475 NORTH SERVICE RD SUITE 200, BURLINGTON, ON, L7L 4X7

(905) 332-9919   *SIC 7699*

OTIS CANADA, INC   *p1221*
5311 BOUL DE MAISONNEUVE O, MONTREAL, QC, H4A 1Z5

(514) 489-9781   *SIC 7699*

PALLET MANAGEMENT GROUP INC *p540*

9148 TWISS RD, CAMPBELLVILLE, ON, L0P 1B0

(905) 857-7939   *SIC 7699*

PAN-GLO CANADA PAN COATINGS INC *p513*
84 EASTON RD, BRANTFORD, ON, N3P 1J5

(519) 756-2800   *SIC 7699*

PENNECON ENERGY HYDRAULIC SYSTEMS LIMITED   *p427*
2 MAVERICK PL, PARADISE, NL, A1L 0H6

(709) 726-3490   *SIC 7699*

PERATON CANADA CORP   *p24*
6732 8 ST NE, CALGARY, AB, T2E 8M4

(403) 295-4770   *SIC 7699*

PGC SERVICES INC   *p598*
180 RAM FOREST RD, GORMLEY, ON, L0H 1G0

(905) 900-0010   *SIC 7699*

R.G. HENDERSON & SON LIMITED   *p919*
100 THORNCLIFFE PARK DR SUITE 416, TORONTO, ON, M4H 1L9

(416) 422-5580   *SIC 7699*

ROBERT K. BUZZELL LIMITED   *p409*
254 HORSMAN RD, MONCTON, NB, E1E 0E8

(506) 853-0936   *SIC 7699*

SANI-MANIC COTE-NORD INC   *p1246*
37 CH DE LA SCIERIE, POINTE-AUX-OUTARDES, QC, G5C 0B7

(418) 589-2376   *SIC 7699*

SKYCO INC   *p405*
734 KING GEORGE HWY, MIRAMICHI, NB, E1V 1P8

(506) 622-8890   *SIC 7699*

ST-FELICIEN DIESEL (1988) INC   *p1303*
981 BOUL HAMEL, SAINT-FELICIEN, QC, G8K 2E3

(418) 679-2474   *SIC 7699*

ST. FRANCIS ADVOCATES FOR THE AUTISTIC & DEVELOPMENTALLY DISABLED (SARNIA) INC   *p478*
7346 ARKONA RD, ARKONA, ON, N0M 1B0

(519) 828-3399   *SIC 7699*

STRAD COMPRESSION AND PRODUCTION SERVICES LTD   *p167*
HWY 12 W, STETTLER, AB, T0C 2L0

(403) 742-6900   *SIC 7699*

THYSSENKRUPP ELEVATOR (CANADA) LIMITED   *p19*
2419 52 AVE SE UNIT 5, CALGARY, AB, T2C 4X7

(403) 259-4183   *SIC 7699*

TOROMONT INDUSTRIES LTD   *p370*
140 INKSBROOK DR, WINNIPEG, MB, R2R 2W3

(204) 453-4343   *SIC 7699*

TOROMONT INDUSTRIES LTD   *p893*
460 SOUTH SERVICE RD, STONEY CREEK, ON, L8E 2P8

(905) 561-5901   *SIC 7699*

TRANSCANADA TURBINES LTD   *p3*
998 HAMILTON BLVD NE, AIRDRIE, AB, T4A 0K8

(403) 420-4200   *SIC 7699*

UNIFIED VALVE GROUP LTD   *p10*
3815 32 ST NE, CALGARY, AB, T1Y 7C1

(403) 215-7800   *SIC 7699*

UNION TRACTOR LTD   *p150*
3750 13 ST, NISKU, AB, T9E 1C6

(780) 979-8500   *SIC 7699*

WEATHERFORD CANADA LTD   *p1409*
3915 52 STREET CLOSE, LLOYDMINSTER, SK, S9V 2G9

(306) 820-5530   *SIC 7699*

WOODBRIDGE PALLET LTD   *p1034*
7200 MARTIN GROVE RD, WOODBRIDGE, ON, L4L 9J3

(905) 856-3332   *SIC 7699*

ZELUS MATERIAL HANDLING INC   *p893*
730 SOUTH SERVICE RD, STONEY CREEK, ON, L8E 5S7

(905) 643-4928   *SIC 7699*

SIC 7812 Motion picture and video production

3627730 CANADA INC   *p1126*
2056 32E AV, LACHINE, QC, H8T 3H7

(514) 631-1821   *SIC 7812*

BLACK STREET PRODUCTIONS LTD *p291*
2339 COLUMBIA ST SUITE 202, VANCOUVER, BC, V5Y 3Y3

(604) 257-4720   *SIC 7812*

BLACKSTONE PRODUCTIONS INC   *p291*
112 6TH AVE W, VANCOUVER, BC, V5Y 1K6

(604) 623-3369   *SIC 7812*

DELUXE VANCOUVER LTD   *p291*
50 2ND AVE W, VANCOUVER, BC, V5Y 1B3

(604) 872-7000   *SIC 7812*

DHX MEDIA (TORONTO PROD) LTD *p962*
207 QUEENS QUAY W SUITE 550, TORONTO, ON, M5J 1A7

(416) 363-8034   *SIC 7812*

DHX MEDIA LTD   *p452*
1478 QUEEN ST, HALIFAX, NS, B3J 2H7

(902) 423-0260   *SIC 7812*

ENTERTAINMENT ONE LTD   *p980*
134 PETER ST SUITE 700, TORONTO, ON, M5V 2H2

(416) 646-2400   *SIC 7812*

GEP PRODUCTIONS INC   *p785*
40 CARL HALL RD UNIT 3, NORTH YORK, ON, M3K 2C1

(416) 398-6869   *SIC 7812*

JAM FILLED ENTERTAINMENT INC *p831*
65 AURIGA DR SUITE 103, OTTAWA, ON, K2E 7W6

(613) 366-2550   *SIC 7812*

JAM FILLED ENTERTAINMENT INC *p981*
364 RICHMOND ST W SUITE 100, TORONTO, ON, M5V 1X6

(613) 366-2550   *SIC 7812*

KEW MEDIA GROUP INC   *p989*
672 DUPONT ST, TORONTO, ON, M6G 1Z6

(647) 956-1965   *SIC 7812*

LIONS GATE ENTERTAINMENT CORP *p306*
250 HOWE ST FL 20, VANCOUVER, BC, V6C 3R8

(877) 848-3866   *SIC 7812*

MAINFRAME ENTERTAINMENT INC *p321*
2025 BROADWAY W SUITE 200, VANCOUVER, BC, V6J 1Z6

(604) 714-2600   *SIC 7812*

MERCURY FILMWORKS EAST INC   *p749*
53 AURIGA DR, NEPEAN, ON, K2E 8C3

(613) 482-1814   *SIC 7812*

MONTREAL STUDIOS ET EQUIPMENTS S.E.N.C   *p1211*
1777 RUE CARRIE-DERICK, MONTREAL, QC, H3C 6G2

(514) 866-2170   *SIC 7812*

NATIONAL FILM BOARD OF CANADA *p1326*
3155 CH DE LA COTE-DE-LIESSE, SAINT-LAURENT, QC, H4N 2N4

(514) 283-9000   *SIC 7812*

NELVANA LIMITED   *p934*
25 DOCKSIDE DR, TORONTO, ON, M5A 0B5

(416) 479-7000   *SIC 7812*

OFFICE DES TELECOMMUNICATIONS EDUCATIVES DE LANGUE FRANCAISE DE L'ONTARIO   *p946*
21 COLLEGE ST SUITE 600, TORONTO, ON, M5G 2B3

(416) 968-3536   *SIC 7812*

PRODUCTIONS PIXCOM INC   *p1216*
1720 RUE DU CANAL, MONTREAL, QC, H3K 3E6

(514) 931-1188   *SIC 7812*

PRODUCTIONS VIC PELLETIER INC, LES *p1151*
296 RUE SAINT-PIERRE, MATANE, QC, G4W 2B9

(514) 667-0787   *SIC 7812*

SINKING SHIP ENTERTAINMENT INC *p992*

1179 KING ST W SUITE 302, TORONTO, ON, M6K 3C5

(416) 533-8172   *SIC 7812*

STUDIOS FRAMESTORE INC   *p1183*
5455 AV DE GASPE BUREAU 900, MONTREAL, QC, H2T 3B3

(514) 277-0004   *SIC 7812*

TOONBOX ENTERTAINMENT LTD   *p921*
100 BROADVIEW AVE UNIT 400, TORONTO, ON, M4M 3H3

(416) 362-8783   *SIC 7812*

VISION GLOBALE A.R. LTEE   *p1212*
80 RUE QUEEN BUREAU 201, MONTREAL, QC, H3C 2N5

(514) 879-0020   *SIC 7812*

WOW UNLIMITED MEDIA INC   *p322*
2025 BROADWAY W SUITE 200, VANCOUVER, BC, V6J 1Z6

(604) 714-2600   *SIC 7812*

ZONE3 INC   *p1176*
1055 BOUL RENE-LEVESQUE E BUREAU 300, MONTREAL, QC, H2L 4S5

(514) 284-5555   *SIC 7812*

SIC 7819 Services allied to motion pictures

ATOMIC FICTION CANADA, INC   *p1193*
2050 RUE DE BLEURY BUREAU 800, MONTREAL, QC, H3A 2J5

(514) 600-0399   *SIC 7819*

DELUXE TORONTO LTD   *p980*
901 KING ST W SUITE 700, TORONTO, ON, M5V 3H5

(416) 364-4321   *SIC 7819*

FRANTIC FILMS CORPORATION   *p378*
220 PORTAGE AVE SUITE 1300, WINNIPEG, MB, R3C 0A5

(204) 949-0070   *SIC 7819*

GENER8 MEDIA CORP   *p291*
177 7TH AVE W SUITE 200, VANCOUVER, BC, V5Y 1L8

(604) 669-8885   *SIC 7819*

METHOD STUDIOS   *p292*
50 2ND AVE W, VANCOUVER, BC, V5Y 1B3

(604) 874-8700   *SIC 7819*

RHYTHM & HUES STUDIOS   *p300*
401 GEORGIA ST W SUITE 500, VANCOUVER, BC, V6B 5A1

(604) 288-8745   *SIC 7819*

SCANLINE VFX INC   *p309*
580 GRANVILLE ST, VANCOUVER, BC, V6C 1W6

(604) 683-6822   *SIC 7819*

WHITE, WILLIAM F. INTERNATIONAL INC *p576*
800 ISLINGTON AVE, ETOBICOKE, ON, M8Z 6A1

(416) 239-5050   *SIC 7819*

SIC 7822 Motion picture and tape distribution

CINEPLEX INC   *p925*
1303 YONGE ST SUITE 300, TORONTO, ON, M4T 2Y9

(416) 323-6600   *SIC 7822*

CORUS MEDIA HOLDINGS INC   *p118*
5325 ALLARD WAY NW, EDMONTON, AB, T6H 5B8

(780) 436-1250   *SIC 7822*

UNIVERSAL STUDIOS CANADA INC *p768*
2450 VICTORIA PARK AVE SUITE 4, NORTH YORK, ON, M2J 4A2

(416) 491-3000   *SIC 7822*

SIC 7829 Motion picture distribution services

NEMO PRODUCTIONS - CAN, INC   *p181*
8035 GLENWOOD DR, BURNABY, BC, V3N 5C8

SIC 7829

SIC 7832 Motion picture theaters, except drive-in

CINEMAS GUZZO INC p1379
1055 CH DU COTEAU, TERREBONNE, QC, J6W 5Y8
(450) 961-2945　*SIC 7832*

CINEPLEX ENTERTAINMENT LIMITED PARTNERSHIP p925
1303 YONGE ST, TORONTO, ON, M4T 2Y9
(416) 323-6600　*SIC 7832*

CINEPLEX ODEON CORPORATION p104
8882 170 ST NW SUITE 3030, EDMONTON, AB, T5T 4M2
(780) 444-2400　*SIC 7832*

CINEPLEX ODEON CORPORATION p120
1525 99 ST NW, EDMONTON, AB, T6N 1K5
(780) 436-3675　*SIC 7832*

CINEPLEX ODEON CORPORATION p326
900 BURRARD ST, VANCOUVER, BC, V6Z 3G5
(604) 630-1407　*SIC 7832*

CINEPLEX ODEON CORPORATION p382
817 ST JAMES ST, WINNIPEG, MB, R3G 3L9
(204) 774-1001　*SIC 7832*

CINEPLEX ODEON CORPORATION p596
2385 CITY PARK DR, GLOUCESTER, ON, K1J 1G1
(613) 749-5861　*SIC 7832*

CINEPLEX ODEON CORPORATION p660
755 WONDERLAND RD S, LONDON, ON, N6K 1M6
(519) 474-2152　*SIC 7832*

CINEPLEX ODEON CORPORATION p709
309 RATHBURN RD W, MISSISSAUGA, ON, L5B 4C1
(905) 275-4969　*SIC 7832*

CINEPLEX ODEON CORPORATION p925
1303 YONGE ST, TORONTO, ON, M4T 2Y9
(416) 323-6600　*SIC 7832*

CINEPLEX ODEON CORPORATION p979
259 RICHMOND ST W, TORONTO, ON, M5V 3M6
(416) 368-5600　*SIC 7832*

CINEPLEX ODEON CORPORATION p1070
9350 BOUL LEDUC, BROSSARD, QC, J4Y 0B3
(450) 678-5542　*SIC 7832*

CINEPLEX ODEON CORPORATION p1086
2800 AV DU COSMODOME, COTE SAINT-LUC, QC, H7T 2X1
(450) 978-0212　*SIC 7832*

CINEPLEX ODEON CORPORATION p1202
977 RUE SAINTE-CATHERINE O, MONTREAL, QC, H3B 4W3
(514) 842-0549　*SIC 7832*

DRAYTON ENTERTAINMENT INC p535
46 GRAND AVE S, CAMBRIDGE, ON, N1S 2L8
(519) 621-8000　*SIC 7832*

GALAXY ENTERTAINMENT INC p925
1303 YONGE ST SUITE 100, TORONTO, ON, M4T 2Y9
(416) 323-6600　*SIC 7832*

ONTARIO CINEMAS INC p924
745 MOUNT PLEASANT RD SUITE 300, TORONTO, ON, M4S 2N4
(416) 481-1186　*SIC 7832*

OUTFRONT MEDIA CANADA LP p710
309 RATHBURN RD W, MISSISSAUGA, ON, L5B 4C1
(905) 275-4969　*SIC 7832*

SIC 7833 Drive-in motion picture theaters

CINE-PARC ST-EUSTACHE INC p1300
555 AV MATHERS, SAINT-EUSTACHE, QC, J7P 4C1
(514) 879-1707　*SIC 7833*

SIC 7841 Video tape rental

CLUB VIDEO ECLAIR INC p1281
1889 BOUL PIE-XI N, QUEBEC, QC, G3J 1P4
(418) 845-1212　*SIC 7841*

SIC 7911 Dance studios, schools, and halls

CANADA'S NATIONAL BALLET SCHOOL p931
400 JARVIS ST, TORONTO, ON, M4Y 2G6
(416) 964-3780　*SIC 7911*

SIC 7922 Theatrical producers and services

1607138 ONTARIO LIMITED p978
266 KING ST W SUITE 200, TORONTO, ON, M5V 1H8
(416) 977-3238　*SIC 7922*

ALBERTA BALLET COMPANY, THE p66
141 18 AVE SW, CALGARY, AB, T2S 0B8
(403) 228-4430　*SIC 7922*

ALUMNAE THEATRE COMPANY p932
70 BERKELEY ST, TORONTO, ON, M5A 2W6
(416) 364-4170　*SIC 7922*

ATTRACTION IMAGES PRODUCTIONS INC p1183
5455 AV DE GASPE BUREAU 804, MONTREAL, QC, H2T 3B3
(514) 285-7001　*SIC 7922*

BELFRY THEATRE SOCIETY, THE p334
1291 GLADSTONE AVE, VICTORIA, BC, V8T 1G5
(250) 385-6815　*SIC 7922*

BELL MEDIA INC p978
720 KING ST W SUITE 1000, TORONTO, ON, M5V 2T3
SIC 7922

CANADIAN OPERA COMPANY p932
227 FRONT ST E, TORONTO, ON, M5A 1E8
(416) 363-6671　*SIC 7922*

CARL SQUARED PRODUCTIONS INC p979
901 KING ST W SUITE 301, TORONTO, ON, M5V 3H5
(416) 483-9773　*SIC 7922*

CENTRE SEGAL DES ARTS DE LA SCENE p1219
5170 CH DE LA COTE-SAINTE-CATHERINE, MONTREAL, QC, H3W 1M7
(514) 739-7944　*SIC 7922*

COGECO MEDIA INC p1389
4141 BOUL SAINT-JEAN, TROIS-RIVIERES, QC, G9B 2M8
(819) 691-1001　*SIC 7922*

CORUS ENTERTAINMENT INC p1230
800 RUE DE LA GAUCHETIERE O BUREAU 1100, MONTREAL, QC, H5A 1M1
(514) 767-9250　*SIC 7922*

EDMONTON NORTHLANDS p83
7424 118 AVE NW, EDMONTON, AB, T5B 4M9
(780) 471-7210　*SIC 7922*

EKUMEN p1172
6616 AV DES ERABLES, MONTREAL, QC, H2G 2N1
(438) 764-7433　*SIC 7922*

EQUIPE SPECTRA INC, L' p1195
400 BOUL DE MAISONNEUVE O 9EME ETAGE, MONTREAL, QC, H3A 1L4
(514) 525-7732　*SIC 7922*

EXPERIENTIAL MARKETING LIMITED PARTNERSHIP p980
49 BATHURST ST SUITE 101, TORONTO, ON, M5V 2P2
(416) 703-3589　*SIC 7922*

FELDMAN AGENCY INC, THE p319
1505 2ND AVE W SUITE 200, VANCOUVER, BC, V6H 3Y4
(604) 734-5945　*SIC 7922*

HARBOURFRONT CORPORATION (1990) p963
235 QUEENS QUAY W, TORONTO, ON, M5J 2G8
(416) 973-4000　*SIC 7922*

LIVE NATION CANADA, INC p991
909 LAKE SHORE BLVD W SUITE 300, TORONTO, ON, M6K 3L3
(416) 260-5600　*SIC 7922*

MIRVISH PRODUCTIONS LTD p982
284 KING ST W SUITE 400, TORONTO, ON, M5V 1J2
(416) 593-0351　*SIC 7922*

MIRVISH, ED ENTERPRISES LIMITED p982
284 KING ST W SUITE 400, TORONTO, ON, M5V 1J2
(416) 593-0351　*SIC 7922*

MURDERS TASTEFULLY EXECUTED INC p761
128 WILLIAM ST, NIAGARA ON THE LAKE, ON, L0S 1J0
(905) 468-0007　*SIC 7922*

NATIONAL BALLET OF CANADA, THE p982
470 QUEENS QUAY W, TORONTO, ON, M5V 3K4
(416) 345-9686　*SIC 7922*

PRODUCTIONS VENDOME II INC, LES p1216
1751 RUE RICHARDSON BUREAU 5 105, MONTREAL, QC, H3K 1G6
(514) 369-4834　*SIC 7922*

ROYAL WINNIPEG BALLET, THE p379
380 GRAHAM AVE, WINNIPEG, MB, R3C 4K2
(204) 956-0183　*SIC 7922*

SASKATCHEWAN CENTRE OF THE ARTS FOUNDATION INC p1422
200A LAKESHORE DR, REGINA, SK, S4S 7L3
(306) 565-4500　*SIC 7922*

SASKATOON CENTENNIAL AUDITORIUM FOUNDATION p1429
35 22ND ST E, SASKATOON, SK, S7K 0C8
(306) 975-7777　*SIC 7922*

SHAW FESTIVAL THEATRE FOUNDATION CANADA p761
10 QUEENS PARADE, NIAGARA ON THE LAKE, ON, L0S 1J0
(905) 468-2172　*SIC 7922*

SOCIETE DU GRAND THEATRE DE QUEBEC, LA p1270
269 BOUL RENE-LEVESQUE E, QUEBEC, QC, G1R 2B3
(418) 643-8111　*SIC 7922*

SOCIETE SPECTRA SCENE INC, LA p1199
400 BOUL DE MAISONNEUVE O BUREAU 800, MONTREAL, QC, H3A 1L4
(514) 523-3378　*SIC 7922*

STRATFORD SHAKESPEAREAN FESTIVAL OF CANADA, THE p897
55 QUEEN ST, STRATFORD, ON, N5A 4M9
(519) 271-4040　*SIC 7922*

THEATRE DENISE PELLETIER INC p1167
4353 RUE SAINTE-CATHERINE E, MONTREAL, QC, H1V 1Y2
(514) 253-8974　*SIC 7922*

TICKETMASTER CANADA LP p1274
2505 BOUL LAURIER BUREAU 300, QUEBEC, QC, G1V 2L2
(418) 694-2300　*SIC 7922*

TICKETPRO INC p1200
1981 AV MCGILL COLLEGE BUREAU 1600, MONTREAL, QC, H3A 2Y1
(514) 849-0237　*SIC 7922*

SIC 7929 Entertainers and entertainment groups

9026-7139 QUEBEC INC p1378
630 MONTEE DES PIONNIERS, TERREBONNE, QC, J6V 1N9
(450) 585-0116　*SIC 7929*

CALGARY CENTRE FOR PERFORMING ARTS p27
205 8 AVE SE SUITE 1205, CALGARY, AB, T2G 0K9
(403) 294-7455　*SIC 7929*

CINEFLIX MEDIA INC p979
110 SPADINA AVE SUITE 400, TORONTO, ON, M5V 2K4
(416) 531-2500　*SIC 7929*

JAZZWORKS p827
1234 RIDGEMONT AVE, OTTAWA, ON, K1V 6E7
(613) 523-0316　*SIC 7929*

ORCHESTRE SYMPHONIQUE DE MONTREAL p1186
1600 RUE SAINT-URBAIN, MONTREAL, QC, H2X 0S1
(514) 842-9951　*SIC 7929*

ORCHESTRE SYMPHONIQUE DE QUEBEC, L' p1269
437 GRANDE ALLEE E BUREAU 250, QUEBEC, QC, G1R 2J5
(418) 643-8486　*SIC 7929*

VANCOUVER SYMPHONY SOCIETY p301
843 SEYMOUR ST SUITE 500, VANCOUVER, BC, V6B 3L4
(604) 684-9100　*SIC 7929*

VERSENT CORPORATION ULC p690
3415 AMERICAN DR, MISSISSAUGA, ON, L4V 1T4
(416) 613-4555　*SIC 7929*

WINNIPEG SYMPHONY ORCHESTRA INC p376
555 MAIN ST RM 1020, WINNIPEG, MB, R3B 1C3
(204) 949-3950　*SIC 7929*

SIC 7941 Sports clubs, managers, and promoters

8542732 CANADA INC p1361
2045 BOUL DAGENAIS O BUREAU 100, SAINTE-ROSE, QC, H7L 5V1
(514) 761-7373　*SIC 7941*

ADVANTAGE DISTRIBUTORS LTD p69
18011 SPRUCE MEADOWS WAY SW, CALGARY, AB, T2X 4B7
(403) 974-4200　*SIC 7941*

ARENA DES CANADIENS INC, L' p1209
1275 RUE SAINT-ANTOINE O, MONTREAL, QC, H3C 5L2
(514) 932-2582　*SIC 7941*

CALGARY FLAMES LIMITED PARTNERSHIP p28
555 SADDLEDOME RISE SE, CALGARY, AB, T2G 2W1
(403) 777-2177　*SIC 7941*

CANUCKS SPORTS & ENTERTAINMENT CORPORATION p297
800 GRIFFITHS WAY, VANCOUVER, BC, V6B 6G1
(604) 899-7400　*SIC 7941*

CLUB DE HOCKEY CANADIEN, INC p1210
1275 RUE SAINT-ANTOINE O, MONTREAL, QC, H3C 5L2
(514) 932-2582　*SIC 7941*

CLUB DE HOCKEY LES VOLTIGEURS p1098
300 RUE COCKBURN, DRUMMONDVILLE, QC, J2C 4L6
(819) 477-9400　*SIC 7941*

CLUB DE SOCCER LA PLAINE INC. p1382
6900 RUE GUERIN, TERREBONNE, QC, J7M 1L9
(450) 477-0372　*SIC 7941*

EDMONTON INVESTORS GROUP LTD p84
11230 110 ST NW, EDMONTON, AB, T5G 3H7
(780) 414-4000　*SIC 7941*

FITNESS KICKBOXING CANADA INC p808
10 SECOND ST, ORANGEVILLE, ON, L9W 2B5
(519) 942-1625　*SIC 7941*

HAMILTON HORNETS RUGBY FOOTBALL

CLUB INC   p616
1300 GARTH ST, HAMILTON, ON, L9C 4L7
(905) 575-3133   *SIC 7941*

INTERNATIONAL CHAMPIONSHIP MAN-
AGEMENT LIMITED   p939
20 TORONTO ST, TORONTO, ON, M5C 2B8
(416) 955-0375   *SIC 7941*

KELOWNA ROCKETS HOCKEY ENTER-
PRISES LTD   p222
1223 WATER ST SUITE 101, KELOWNA,
BC, V1Y 9V1
(250) 860-7825   *SIC 7941*

L'ARENA DES CANADIENS INC   p1211
1275 RUE SAINT-ANTOINE O, MON-
TREAL, QC, H3C 5L2
(514) 989-2814   *SIC 7941*

LANSDOWNE STADIUM LIMITED PART-
NERSHIP   p818
700 INDUSTRIAL AVE UNIT 220, OTTAWA,
ON, K1G 0Y9
(613) 232-6767   *SIC 7941*

LONDON CIVIC CENTRE CORPORATION
p654
99 DUNDAS ST, LONDON, ON, N6A 6K1
(519) 667-5700   *SIC 7941*

MAPLE LEAF SPORTS & ENTERTAINMENT
LTD   p964
50 BAY ST SUITE 500, TORONTO, ON, M5J
2L2
(416) 815-5400   *SIC 7941*

NIAGARA ICEDOGS HOCKEY CLUB INC
p886
35 QUEEN ST, ST CATHARINES, ON, L2R
5G4
(905) 687-3641   *SIC 7941*

O & O DEVELOPMENTS INC   p814
1401 PHILLIP MURRAY AVE, OSHAWA,
ON, L1J 8C4
(905) 725-6951   *SIC 7941*

OILERSNATION.COM LTD   p90
10020 100 ST NW, EDMONTON, AB, T5J
0N3
(780) 909-2445   *SIC 7941*

PEAK SPORTS MANAGEMENT INC   p772
2996 BAYVIEW AVE, NORTH YORK, ON,
M2N 5K9
SIC 7941

ROGERS BLUE JAYS BASEBALL PART-
NERSHIP   p983
1 BLUE JAYS WAY SUITE 3200,
TORONTO, ON, M5V 1J1
(416) 341-1000   *SIC 7941*

ROYAL CITY SOCCER CLUB   p531
336 PLAINS RD E SUITE 2, BURLINGTON,
ON, L7T 2C8
(905) 639-4178   *SIC 7941*

SIMPSON'S SPORTS LIMITED   p157
4847 19 ST SUITE C, RED DEER, AB, T4R
2N7
(403) 341-6000   *SIC 7941*

SOCIETE EN COMMANDITE FREE 2 PLAY
p1167
4750 RUE SHERBROOKE E, MONTREAL,
QC, H1V 3S8
(514) 328-3668   *SIC 7941*

SPRUCE MEADOWS LTD   p69
18011 SPRUCE MEADOWS WAY SW, CAL-
GARY, AB, T2X 4B7
(403) 974-4200   *SIC 7941*

SWSE ATHLETIC TEAMS LTD   p899
874 LAPOINTE ST, SUDBURY, ON, P3A
5N8
(705) 675-7973   *SIC 7941*

TITAN ACADIE BATHURST (2013) INC, LE
p395
14 SEAN COUTURIER AVE, BATHURST,
NB, E2A 6X2
(506) 549-3300   *SIC 7941*

TN ARENA LIMITED PARTNERSHIP   p379
345 GRAHAM AVE, WINNIPEG, MB, R3C
5S6
(204) 987-7825   *SIC 7941*

TORONTO ROCK LACROSSE INC   p799
1132 INVICTA DR, OAKVILLE, ON, L6H

6G1
TRUE NORTH SPORTS & ENTERTAIN-
MENT LIMITED   p380
345 GRAHAM AVE, WINNIPEG, MB, R3C
5S6
(204) 987-7825   *SIC 7941*

VANCOUVER HOCKEY LIMITED PARTNER-
SHIP   p301
800 GRIFFITHS WAY, VANCOUVER, BC,
V6B 6G1
(604) 899-4600   *SIC 7941*

VANCOUVER WHITECAPS FC L.P.   p301
375 WATER ST SUITE 550, VANCOUVER,
BC, V6B 5C6
(604) 669-9283   *SIC 7941*

WHITECAPS FOOTBALL CLUB LTD   p301
375 WATER ST SUITE 550, VANCOUVER,
BC, V6B 5C6
(604) 669-9283   *SIC 7941*

WINDSOR SPITFIRES INC   p1018
8787 MCHUGH ST, WINDSOR, ON, N8S
0A1
(519) 254-9256   *SIC 7941*

WINNIPEG JETS HOCKEY CLUB LIMITED
PARTNERSHIP   p380
345 GRAHAM AVE, WINNIPEG, MB, R3C
5S6
(204) 987-7825   *SIC 7941*

WORLD POND HOCKEY CHAMPIONSHIP
INC   p411
159 MAIN ST, PLASTER ROCK, NB, E7G
2H2
(506) 356-6070   *SIC 7941*

SIC 7948 Racing, including track operation

1233481 ONTARIO INC   p541
1040 KOHLER RD, CAYUGA, ON, N0A 1E0
(905) 772-0303   *SIC 7948*

1946328 ONTARIO LIMITED   p211
4063 COWICHAN VALLEY HWY, DUNCAN,
BC, V9L 6K4
(250) 856-0122   *SIC 7948*

4397291 CANADA INC   p1301
1016 BOUL ARTHUR-SAUVE, SAINT-
EUSTACHE, QC, J7R 4K3
(450) 472-6222   *SIC 7948*

ATTFIELD, ROGER INC   p762
GD, NOBLETON, ON, L0G 1N0
(416) 675-1231   *SIC 7948*

BRIDGE COUNTY RACEWAY LTD   p142
GD LCD MAIN, LETHBRIDGE, AB, T1J 3Y2
SIC 7948

DRESDEN AGRICULTURAL SOCIETY p565
255 PARK ST RR 5, DRESDEN, ON, N0P
1M0
(519) 683-1116   *SIC 7948*

FLAMBORO DOWNS HOLDINGS LIMITED
p566
967 5 HWY W, DUNDAS, ON, L9H 5E2
(905) 627-3561   *SIC 7948*

HANOVER, BENTINCK & BRANT AGRI-
CULTURAL SOCIETY   p617
265 5TH ST, HANOVER, ON, N4N 3X3
(519) 364-2860   *SIC 7948*

HASTINGS ENTERTAINMENT INC   p284
188 RENFREW ST N, VANCOUVER, BC,
V5K 3N8
(604) 254-1631   *SIC 7948*

KAWARTHA DOWNS LTD   p592
1382 COUNTY ROAD 28, FRASERVILLE,
ON, K0L 1V0
(705) 939-6316   *SIC 7948*

MANITOBA JOCKEY CLUB INC   p386
3975 PORTAGE AVE, WINNIPEG, MB, R3K
2E9
(204) 885-3330   *SIC 7948*

ONTARIO RACING COMMISSION   p586
10 CARLSON CRT SUITE 400, ETOBI-
COKE, ON, M9W 6L2
SIC 7948

PICOV DOWNS INC   p475

380 KINGSTON RD E, AJAX, ON, L1Z 1W4
(905) 686-8001   *SIC 7948*

PRINCE COUNTY HORSEMAN'S CLUB INC
p1043
477 NOTRE DAME ST, SUMMERSIDE, PE,
C1N 1T2
SIC 7948

ROCKY MOUNTAIN TURF CLUB INC   p142
3401 PARKSIDE DR S, LETHBRIDGE, AB,
T1J 4R3
(403) 380-1905   *SIC 7948*

SASKATCHEWAN DRAG RACING ASSOCI-
ATION INC   p1424
133 WESTERN CRES, SASKATOON, SK,
S7H 4J4
(306) 373-8148   *SIC 7948*

SASKATOON PRAIRIELAND PARK COR-
PORATION   p1424
2615 ST HENRY AVE, SASKATOON, SK,
S7H 0A1
(306) 242-6100   *SIC 7948*

WOODBINE ENTERTAINMENT GROUP
p998
555 REXDALE BLVD, TORONTO, ON, M9W
5L2
(416) 675-7223   *SIC 7948*

WOOLWICH AGRICULTURAL SOCIETY
p569
7445 WELLINGTON RD 21, ELORA, ON,
N0B 1S0
(519) 846-5455   *SIC 7948*

SIC 7991 Physical fitness facilities

802912 ONTARIO LIMITED   p766
2235 SHEPPARD AVE E SUITE 901,
NORTH YORK, ON, M2J 5B5
(416) 492-7611   *SIC 7991*

926715 ONTARIO INC   p598
384 ACADEMY HILL RD, GRAFTON, ON,
K0K 2G0
(905) 349-2493   *SIC 7991*

926715 ONTARIO INC   p598
1009 MASSEY RD, GRAFTON, ON, K0K
2G0
(905) 349-2493   *SIC 7991*

ASSOCIES SPORTIFS DE MONTREAL, SO-
CIETE EN COMMANDITE, LES   p1218
6105 AV DU BOISE, MONTREAL, QC, H3S
2V9
(514) 737-0000   *SIC 7991*

AUBERGE & SPA LE NORDIK INC   p1077
16 CH NORDIK, CHELSEA, QC, J9B 2P7
(819) 484-1112   *SIC 7991*

BRENTWOOD BAY LODGE LTD   p180
849 VERDIER AVE, BRENTWOOD BAY,
BC, V8M 1C5
(250) 544-2079   *SIC 7991*

BRYDSON GROUP LTD   p931
557 CHURCH ST, TORONTO, ON, M4Y 2E2
(416) 964-4525   *SIC 7991*

CAMBRIDGE GROUP OF CLUB   p949
100 RICHMOND ST W SUITE 444,
TORONTO, ON, M5H 3K6
(416) 862-1077   *SIC 7991*

CENTRE DE SANTE D'EASTMAN INCp1100
895 CH DES DILIGENCES, EASTMAN, QC,
J0E 1P0
(450) 297-3009   *SIC 7991*

CENTRE DE SANTE ET DE SERVICES
SOCIAUX DE DORVAL-LACHINE-LASALLE
p1126
1900 RUE NOTRE-DAME BUREAU 262,
LACHINE, QC, H8S 2G2
(514) 639-0650   *SIC 7991*

CENTRE DE SANTE ET DE SERVICES SO-
CIAUX DE PORTNEUF   p1348
1045 BOUL BONA-DUSSAULT, SAINT-
MARC-DES-CARRIERES, QC, G0A 4B0
(418) 268-3571   *SIC 7991*

CENTRE MONTEREGIEN DE READAPTA-
TION   p1307
5300 CH DE CHAMBLY, SAINT-HUBERT,

QC, J3Y 3N7
(450) 676-7447   *SIC 7991*

DELISLE CLUB   p925
1521 YONGE ST SUITE 303, TORONTO,
ON, M4T 1Z2
SIC 7991

EL BASIL GROUP INC   p84
13026 97 ST NW SUITE 203, EDMONTON,
AB, T5E 4C6
(780) 406-7272   *SIC 7991*

EXTREME FITNESS GROUP INC   p904
8281 YONGE ST, THORNHILL, ON, L3T
2C7
(905) 709-1248   *SIC 7991*

FITNESS INSTITUTE LIMITED, THE p969
79 WELIINGTON ST. W 36TH FL,
TORONTO, ON, M5K 1J5
(416) 865-0900   *SIC 7991*

GOODLIFE FITNESS CENTRES INC   p658
710 PROUDFOOT LANE, LONDON, ON,
N6H 5G5
(519) 661-0190   *SIC 7991*

GOODLIFE FITNESS CENTRES INC   p830
2655 QUEENSVIEW DR, OTTAWA, ON,
K2B 8K2
SIC 7991

GOODLIFE FITNESS CENTRES INC   p871
1911 KENNEDY RD, SCARBOROUGH, ON,
M1P 2L9
(416) 297-7279   *SIC 7991*

HALIBURTON KAWARTHA PINE RIDGE
DISTRICT HEALTH UNIT   p646
108 ANGELINE ST S, LINDSAY, ON, K9V
3L5
SIC 7991

INTERNATIONAL FITNESS HOLDINGS INC
p71
7222 EDGEMONT BLVD NW, CALGARY,
AB, T3A 2X7
(403) 278-2499   *SIC 7991*

LINDSAY PARK SPORTS SOCIETY   p30
2225 MACLEOD TRAIL SE, CALGARY, AB,
T2G 5B6
(403) 233-8393   *SIC 7991*

MAHOGANY SALON & SPA LTD   p891
1261 STITTSVILLE MAIN ST UNIT 1,
STITTSVILLE, ON, K2S 2E4
(613) 836-3334   *SIC 7991*

MOVATI ATHLETIC (BRANTFORD) INC.
p514
595 WEST ST, BRANTFORD, ON, N3R 7C5
(519) 756-0123   *SIC 7991*

MOVATI ATHLETIC (LONDON NORTH) INC.
p659
755 WONDERLAND RD N, LONDON, ON,
N6H 4L1
(519) 471-7181   *SIC 7991*

MOVATI ATHLETIC (LONDON SOUTH) INC.
p514
595 WEST ST, BRANTFORD, ON, N3R 7C5
(519) 756-0123   *SIC 7991*

MOVATI ATHLETIC (THUNDER BAY) INC.
p910
1185 ARTHUR ST W, THUNDER BAY, ON,
P7E 6E2
(807) 623-6223   *SIC 7991*

NUBODY'S FITNESS CENTRES INC   p447
51 RADDALL AVE, DARTMOUTH, NS, B3B
1T6
(902) 468-8920   *SIC 7991*

O A C HOLDINGS LIMITED   p816
2525 LANCASTER RD, OTTAWA, ON, K1B
4L5
(613) 523-1540   *SIC 7991*

SANI SPORT INC   p1069
7777 BOUL MARIE-VICTORIN,
BROSSARD, QC, J4W 1B3
(450) 465-7220   *SIC 7991*

SS STONEBRIDGE DEL FITNESS CORPO-
RATION   p1435
431 NELSON RD, SASKATOON, SK, S7S
1P2
(306) 975-1003   *SIC 7991*

STATION SKYSPA INC   p1070

▲ Public Company   ■ Public Company Family Member   **HQ** Headquarters   **BR** Branch   **SL** Single Location

6000 BOUL DE ROME BUREAU 400, BROSSARD, QC, J4Y 0B6
(450) 462-9111 *SIC 7991*

UTOPIA DAY SPAS & SALONS LTD *p227*
20486 64 AVE UNIT 106, LANGLEY, BC, V2Y 2V5
(604) 539-8772 *SIC 7991*

WINGBACK ENTERPRISES LIMITED *p921*
1 FIRST AVE, TORONTO, ON, M4M 1W7
(416) 367-9957 *SIC 7991*

YMCA DU QUEBEC, LES *p1184*
5550 AV DU PARC, MONTREAL, QC, H2V 4H1
(514) 271-3437 *SIC 7991*

YMCA OF GREATER TORONTO *p711*
325 BURNHAMTHORPE RD W, MISSISSAUGA, ON, L5B 3R2
(905) 897-6801 *SIC 7991*

SIC 7992 Public golf courses

1001432 B.C. LTD *p281*
7700 168 ST, SURREY, BC, V4N 0E1
(604) 576-8224 *SIC 7992*

351658 ONTARIO LIMITED *p511*
8525 MISSISSAUGA RD, BRAMPTON, ON, L6Y 0C1
(905) 455-8400 *SIC 7992*

4498411 MANITOBA LTD *p358*
GD, STEINBACH, MB, R5G 1L8
(204) 326-4653 *SIC 7992*

9175-2527 QUEBEC INC *p1129*
355 AV BETHANY, LACHUTE, QC, J8H 4G9
(450) 562-5228 *SIC 7992*

BOND HEAD GOLF RESORT INC *p490*
4805 7TH LINE RR 1, BEETON, ON, L0G 1A0
(905) 778-9400 *SIC 7992*

C A PIPPY PARK COMMISSION *p429*
460 ALLANDALE RD, ST. JOHN'S, NL, A1B 4E8
(709) 753-7110 *SIC 7992*

CALGARY ELKS LODGE #4 SOCIETY OF THE B.P.O.E. OF CANADA *p21*
2502 6 ST NE, CALGARY, AB, T2E 3Z3
(403) 250-7391 *SIC 7992*

CENTRE DE GOLF, LE VERSANT INC *p1381*
2075 COTE DE TERREBONNE, TERREBONNE, QC, J6Y 1H6
(450) 964-2251 *SIC 7992*

CLUB DE GOLF ACTON VALE INC *p1044*
1000 RTE 116, ACTON VALE, QC, J0H 1A0
(450) 549-5885 *SIC 7992*

CLUB LAVAL-SUR-LE-LAC, LE *p1236*
150 RUE LES PEUPLIERS, MONTREAL, QC, H7R 1G4
(450) 627-2643 *SIC 7992*

CLUBLINK CORPORATION ULC *p473*
13448 DUBLIN LINE SUITE 1, ACTON, ON, L7J 2L7
(519) 853-0904 *SIC 7992*

CLUBLINK CORPORATION ULC *p494*
15608 REGIONAL ROAD 50, BOLTON, ON, L7E 3E5
(905) 880-1400 *SIC 7992*

CLUBLINK CORPORATION ULC *p567*
109 ROYAL TROON LANE, DUNROBIN, ON, K0A 1T0
(613) 832-3804 *SIC 7992*

CLUBLINK CORPORATION ULC *p593*
11742 TENTH LINE SUITE 4, GEORGETOWN, ON, L7G 4S7
(905) 877-8468 *SIC 7992*

CLUBLINK CORPORATION ULC *p598*
12657 WOODBINE AVE S, GORMLEY, ON, L0H 1G0
(905) 888-1219 *SIC 7992*

CLUBLINK CORPORATION ULC *p622*
8165 10 SIDEROAD SUITE 11, INNISFIL, ON, L9S 4T3
(705) 431-7000 *SIC 7992*

CLUBLINK CORPORATION ULC *p629*
15675 DUFFERIN ST, KING CITY, ON, L7B

1K5
(905) 841-3730 *SIC 7992*

CLUBLINK CORPORATION ULC *p629*
14700 BATHURST ST, KING CITY, ON, L7B 1K5
(905) 713-6875 *SIC 7992*

CLUBLINK CORPORATION ULC *p748*
4999 BOUNDARY RD, NAVAN, ON, K4B 1P5
(613) 822-1454 *SIC 7992*

CLUBLINK CORPORATION ULC *p894*
14001 WARDEN AVE, STOUFFVILLE, ON, L4A 3T4
(905) 888-1100 *SIC 7992*

CLUBLINK CORPORATION ULC *p1058*
1 BOUL DE FONTAINEBLEAU, BLAINVILLE, QC, J7B 1L4
(450) 434-7569 *SIC 7992*

CLUBLINK CORPORATION ULC *p1248*
1199 CH DU BORD-DE-L'EAU, POINTE-CLAIRE, QC, H7Y 1A9
(450) 689-4130 *SIC 7992*

COPPER CREEK LIMITED PARTNERSHIP *p642*
11191 HWY 27, KLEINBURG, ON, L0J 1C0
(905) 893-3370 *SIC 7992*

CORDOVA BAY GOLF COURSE LTD *p338*
5333 CORDOVA BAY RD, VICTORIA, BC, V8Y 2L3
(250) 658-4445 *SIC 7992*

FURRY CREEK GOLF & COUNTRY CLUB INC *p230*
150 COUNTRY CLUB RD, LIONS BAY, BC, V0N 2E0
(604) 896-2216 *SIC 7992*

GOLDEN EAGLE GOLF COURSES INC *p244*
21770 LADNER RD, PITT MEADOWS, BC, V3Y 1Z1
(604) 460-1871 *SIC 7992*

GOLF DU GRAND PORTNEUF INC, LE *p1253*
2 RTE 365, PONT-ROUGE, QC, G3H 3R4
(418) 329-2238 *SIC 7992*

GOLFBC HOLDINGS INC *p313*
1030 GEORGIA ST W SUITE 1800, VANCOUVER, BC, V6E 2Y3
(604) 681-8700 *SIC 7992*

GROUPE BEAUDET INC, LE *p1061*
6455 RUE DORIS-LUSSIER BUREAU 110, BOISBRIAND, QC, J7H 0E8
(514) 990-5833 *SIC 7992*

HEATHERGLENEAGLES GOLF COMPANY LTD *p80*
100 GLENEAGLES DR, COCHRANE, AB, T4C 1P5
(403) 932-1100 *SIC 7992*

KNOLLWOOD GOLF LIMITED *p477*
1276 SHAVER RD, ANCASTER, ON, L9G 3L1
(905) 648-6687 *SIC 7992*

LINKS OF GLENEAGLES GOLF CORPORATION LTD, THE *p80*
100 GLENEAGLES DR, COCHRANE, AB, T4C 1P5
(403) 932-1100 *SIC 7992*

METCALFE REALTY COMPANY LIMITED *p832*
1755 OLD CARP RD, OTTAWA, ON, K2K 1X7
(613) 839-5401 *SIC 7992*

MUSKOKA BAY GOLF CORPORATION *p598*
1217 NORTH MULDREW LAKE RD, GRAVENHURST, ON, P1P 1T9
(705) 687-4900 *SIC 7992*

OSPREY VALLEY RESORTS INC *p477*
18821 MAIN ST SUITE 2, ALTON, ON, L7K 1R1
(905) 927-0586 *SIC 7992*

RADIUM RESORT INC *p253*
8100 GOLF COURSE RD, RADIUM HOT SPRINGS, BC, V0A 1M0
(250) 347-9311 *SIC 7992*

WILDS AT SALMONIER RIVER INC, THE *p432*

299 SALMONIER LINE, ST. JOHN'S, NL, A1C 5L7
(709) 229-5444 *SIC 7992*

SIC 7993 Coin-operated amusement devices

BRITISH COLUMBIA LOTTERY CORPORATION *p216*
74 SEYMOUR ST W, KAMLOOPS, BC, V2C 1E2
(250) 828-5500 *SIC 7993*

SASKATCHEWAN INDIAN GAMING AUTHORITY INC *p1438*
30 THIRD AVE N, YORKTON, SK, S3N 1B9
(306) 786-6777 *SIC 7993*

VANSHAW ENTERPRISES LTD *p147*
1051 ROSS GLEN DR SE, MEDICINE HAT, AB, T1B 3T8
(403) 504-4584 *SIC 7993*

SIC 7996 Amusement parks

BEASLEY, WILLIAM ENTERPRISES LIMITED *p959*
9 QUEENS QUAY W, TORONTO, ON, M5J 2H3
(416) 203-0405 *SIC 7996*

CANADA'S WONDERLAND COMPANY *p1003*
9580 JANE ST, VAUGHAN, ON, L6A 1S6
(905) 832-7000 *SIC 7996*

CANADIAN NATIONAL EXHIBITION ASSOCIATION *p991*
210 PRINCES BLVD, TORONTO, ON, M6K 3C3
(416) 263-3600 *SIC 7996*

GOUVERNEMENT DE LA PROVINCE DE QUEBEC *p1244*
2020 CH D'OKA, OKA, QC, J0N 1E0
(450) 479-8365 *SIC 7996*

HAMILTON REGION CONSERVATION AUTHORITY *p608*
585 VAN WAGNERS BEACH RD, HAMILTON, ON, L8E 3L8
(905) 561-2292 *SIC 7996*

PARC SIX FLAGS MONTREAL S.E.C. *p1211*
22 CH MACDONALD, MONTREAL, QC, H3C 6A3
(514) 397-0402 *SIC 7996*

SOCIETE DES ETABLISSEMENTS DE PLEIN AIR DU QUEBEC *p1067*
55 ILE-SAINTE-MARGUERITE, BOUCHERVILLE, QC, J4B 5J6
(450) 928-5089 *SIC 7996*

SIC 7997 Membership sports and recreation clubs

ARBUTUS CLUB, THE *p320*
2001 NANTON AVE, VANCOUVER, BC, V6J 4A1
(604) 266-7166 *SIC 7997*

BADMINTON AND RACQUET CLUB OF TORONTO, THE *p926*
25 ST CLAIR AVE W, TORONTO, ON, M4V 1K6
(416) 921-2159 *SIC 7997*

BARRIE NATIONAL PINES GOLF & COUNTRY CLUB *p484*
GD STN MAIN, BARRIE, ON, L4M 4S8
(705) 431-7000 *SIC 7997*

BELVEDERE GOLF & COUNTRY CLUB *p162*
51418 HWY 21 S, SHERWOOD PARK, AB, T8H 2T2
(780) 467-2025 *SIC 7997*

BOULEVARD CLUB LIMITED, THE *p991*
1491 LAKE SHORE BLVD W, TORONTO, ON, M6K 3C2
(416) 532-3341 *SIC 7997*

BUFFALO CANOE CLUB *p857*
4475 ERIE RD SUITE 1, RIDGEWAY, ON,

L0S 1N0
(905) 894-2750 *SIC 7997*

BURLINGTON GOLF AND COUNTRY CLUB LIMITED *p531*
422 NORTH SHORE BLVD E, BURLINGTON, ON, L7T 1W9
(905) 634-7726 *SIC 7997*

CANUCKS CENTRE FOR BC HOCKEY, THE *p297*
800 GRIFFITHS WAY SUITE 4, VANCOUVER, BC, V6B 6G1
(604) 899-7770 *SIC 7997*

CEDAR SPRINGS TENNIS LIMITED *p527*
960 CUMBERLAND AVE, BURLINGTON, ON, L7N 3J6
(905) 632-9758 *SIC 7997*

CENTRE DU GOLF U.F.O. INC *p1152*
9500 RANG SAINTE-HENRIETTE, MIRABEL, QC, J7J 2A1
(514) 990-8392 *SIC 7997*

CENTRE PERE SABLON *p1172*
4265 AV PAPINEAU, MONTREAL, QC, H2H 1T3
(514) 527-1256 *SIC 7997*

CHERRY HILL CLUB, LIMITED *p857*
912 CHERRY HILL BLVD, RIDGEWAY, ON, L0S 1N0
(905) 894-1122 *SIC 7997*

CLUB DE GOLF DE BELLE VUE (1984) INC *p1135*
880 BOUL DE LERY, LERY, QC, J6N 1B7
(450) 692-6793 *SIC 7997*

CLUB DE GOLF DE LA VALLEE DU RICHELIEU INC, LE *p1358*
100 CH DU GOLF, SAINTE-JULIE, QC, J3E 1Y1
(450) 649-1511 *SIC 7997*

CLUB DE GOLF DE ROSEMERE *p1287*
282 BOUL LABELLE, ROSEMERE, QC, J7A 2H6
(450) 437-7555 *SIC 7997*

CLUB DE GOLF LE BLAINVILLIER INC *p1058*
200 RUE DU BLAINVILLIER, BLAINVILLE, QC, J7C 4X6
(450) 433-1444 *SIC 7997*

CLUB DE GOLF SUMMERLEA INC *p1394*
1000 RTE DE LOTBINIERE, VAUDREUIL-DORION, QC, J7V 0H5
(450) 455-0921 *SIC 7997*

CLUB DE GOLF WHITLOCK *p1113*
128 COTE SAINT-CHARLES, HUDSON, QC, J0P 1H0
(450) 458-5305 *SIC 7997*

CLUB MAA INC *p1194*
2070 RUE PEEL, MONTREAL, QC, H3A 1W6
(514) 845-2233 *SIC 7997*

COMMUNITY BUILDERS INC *p443*
51 FOREST HILLS PKY SUITE 1, DARTMOUTH, NS, B2W 6C6
(902) 464-5100 *SIC 7997*

COTTONWOOD GOLF & COUNTRY CLUB *p127*
88008 226 AVE E, FOOTHILLS, AB, T1S 4A6
(403) 938-7216 *SIC 7997*

COUNTRY CLUB DE MONTREAL, LE *p1323*
5 RUE RIVERSIDE, SAINT-LAMBERT, QC, J4S 1B7
(450) 671-6181 *SIC 7997*

DARTMOUTH SPORTSPLEX COMMUNITY ASSOCIATION *p444*
110 WYSE RD, DARTMOUTH, NS, B3A 1M2
(902) 464-2600 *SIC 7997*

DERRICK GOLF AND WINTER CLUB *p119*
3500 119 ST NW, EDMONTON, AB, T6J 5P5
(780) 437-1833 *SIC 7997*

DONALDA CLUB *p775*
12 BUSHBURY DR, NORTH YORK, ON, M3A 2Z7
(416) 447-5575 *SIC 7997*

GEORGIAN MANOR RESORT & COUNTRY CLUB INC, THE p546
10 VACATION INN DR, COLLINGWOOD, ON, L9Y 5G4
(800) 696-5487   *SIC* 7997
GLENCOE CLUB, THE p67
636 29 AVE SW, CALGARY, AB, T2S 0P1
(403) 214-0032   *SIC* 7997
GLENDALE GOLF & COUNTRY CLUB LTD p105
12410 199 ST NW, EDMONTON, AB, T5V 1T8
(780) 447-3529   *SIC* 7997
GLENWAY COUNTRY CLUB LIMITED p754
470 CROSSLAND GATE, NEWMARKET, ON, L3X 1B8
(905) 235-5422   *SIC* 7997
GREEN LAKE PROJECTS INC p342
8080 NICKLAUS BLVD N, WHISTLER, BC, V0N 1B0
(604) 938-9898   *SIC* 7997
GTA GOLF p195
500 COLWYN ST SUITE 58, CAMPBELL RIVER, BC, V9W 5J2
(250) 255-8897   *SIC* 7997
GTA GOLF & COUNTRY CLUB p973
800 BATHURST ST UNIT 1, TORONTO, ON, M5R 3M8
(416) 762-2530   *SIC* 7997
GTA GOLF & COUNTRY CLUB p973
800 BATHURST ST UNIT 1, TORONTO, ON, M5R 3M8
(416) 762-2530   *SIC* 7997
GTA GOLF & COUNTRY CLUB p973
800 BATHURST ST UNIT 1, TORONTO, ON, M5R 3M8
(416) 762-2530   *SIC* 7997
GTA GOLF & COUNTRY CLUB p973
800 BATHURST ST UNIT 1, TORONTO, ON, M5R 3M8
(416) 762-2530   *SIC* 7997
GTA GOLF & COUNTRY CLUB p973
800 BATHURST ST UNIT 1, TORONTO, ON, M5R 3M8
(416) 762-2531   *SIC* 7997
GTA GOLF & COUNTRY CLUB p973
800 BATHURST ST UNIT 1, TORONTO, ON, M5R 3M8
(416) 762-2530   *SIC* 7997
GTA GOLF & COUNTRY CLUB p973
800 BATHURST ST UNIT 1, TORONTO, ON, M5R 3M8
(416) 762-2530   *SIC* 7997
GTA GOLF & COUNTRY CLUB p973
800 BATHURST ST UNIT 1, TORONTO, ON, M5R 3M8
(416) 762-2530   *SIC* 7997
GTA GOLF & COUNTRY CLUB p973
800 BATHURST ST UNIT 1, TORONTO, ON, M5R 3M8
(416) 762-2530   *SIC* 7997
GTA GOLF & COUNTRY CLUB p973
800 BATHURST ST UNIT 1, TORONTO, ON, M5R 3M8
(416) 762-2530   *SIC* 7997
GTA GOLF & COUNTRY CLUB p973
800 BATHURST ST UNIT 1, TORONTO, ON, M5R 3M8
(416) 762-2530   *SIC* 7997
GTA GOLF & COUNTRY CLUB p973
800 BATHURST ST UNIT 1, TORONTO, ON, M5R 3M8

GTA GOLF & COUNTRY CLUB p973
800 BATHURST ST UNIT 1, TORONTO, ON, M5R 3M8
(416) 762-2530   *SIC* 7997
GTA GOLF & COUNTRY CLUB p973
800 BATHURST ST UNIT 1, TORONTO, ON, M5R 3M8
(416) 762-2530   *SIC* 7997
GTA GOLF & COUNTRY CLUB p973
800 BATHURST ST UNIT 1, TORONTO, ON, M5R 3M8
(416) 762-2530   *SIC* 7997
GTA GOLF & COUNTRY CLUB p973
800 BATHURST ST UNIT 1, TORONTO, ON, M5R 3M8
(416) 762-2530   *SIC* 7997
HALIFAX GOLF & COUNTRY CLUB, LIMITED p457
3250 JOSEPH HOWE DR, HALIFAX, NS, B3L 4G1
(902) 443-8260   *SIC* 7997
HAMILTON EAST KIWANIS BOYS & GIRLS CLUB INCORPORATED p609
45 ELLIS AVE, HAMILTON, ON, L8H 4L8
(905) 543-9994   *SIC* 7997
HIGHLANDS GOLF CLUB p107
6603 ADA BLVD NW, EDMONTON, AB, T5W 4N5
(780) 474-4211   *SIC* 7997
HOLLYBURN COUNTRY CLUB p341
950 CROSS CREEK RD, WEST VANCOUVER, BC, V7S 2S5
(604) 922-0161   *SIC* 7997
HYLANDS GOLF CLUB p597
2101 ALERT RD, GLOUCESTER, ON, K1V 1J9
(613) 521-1842   *SIC* 7997
ISLINGTON GOLF CLUB, LIMITED p576
45 RIVERBANK DR, ETOBICOKE, ON, M9A 5B8
(416) 231-1114   *SIC* 7997
LETHBRIDGE COUNTRY CLUB p143
101 COUNTRY CLUB RD, LETHBRIDGE, AB, T1K 7N9
(403) 327-6900   *SIC* 7997
MAYFAIR TENNIS COURTS LIMITED p672
50 STEELCASE RD E, MARKHAM, ON, L3R 1E8
(905) 475-6668   *SIC* 7997
MAYFAIR TENNIS COURTS LIMITED p920
801 LAKE SHORE BLVD E, TORONTO, ON, M4M 1A9
(416) 466-3770   *SIC* 7997
MISSISSAUGUA GOLF AND COUNTRY CLUB, THE p713
1725 MISSISSAUGA RD, MISSISSAUGA, ON, L5H 2K4
(905) 278-4857   *SIC* 7997
QUILCHENA GOLF & COUNTRY CLUB p265
3551 GRANVILLE AVE, RICHMOND, BC, V7C 1C8
(604) 277-1101   *SIC* 7997
RECREATION ASSOCIATION OF THE PUBLIC SERVICE OF CANADA, THE p819
2451 RIVERSIDE DR, OTTAWA, ON, K1H 7X7
(613) 733-5100   *SIC* 7997
RHCC HOLDINGS LIMITED p855
8905 BATHURST ST, RICHMOND HILL, ON, L4C 0H4
(905) 731-2800   *SIC* 7997
RICHMOND COUNTRY CLUB p263
9100 STEVESTON HWY, RICHMOND, BC, V7A 1M5
(604) 277-3141   *SIC* 7997
ROSEDALE GOLF ASSOCIATION LIMITED, THE p921
1901 MOUNT PLEASANT RD, TORONTO, ON, M4N 2W3
(416) 485-9321   *SIC* 7997
ROYAL CANADIAN YACHT CLUB, THE p973
141 ST. GEORGE ST SUITE 218, TORONTO, ON, M5R 2L8

(416) 967-7245   *SIC* 7997
ROYAL GLENORA CLUB p90
11160 RIVER VALLEY RD, EDMONTON, AB, T5J 2G7
(780) 482-2371   *SIC* 7997
ROYAL MAYFAIR GOLF CLUB LTD p90
9450 GROAT RD NW, EDMONTON, AB, T5J 2G8
(780) 432-0066   *SIC* 7997
ROYAL VANCOUVER YACHT CLUB p324
3811 POINT GREY RD, VANCOUVER, BC, V6R 1B3
(604) 224-1344   *SIC* 7997
SHAUGHNESSY GOLF AND COUNTRY CLUB p323
4300 MARINE DR SW, VANCOUVER, BC, V6N 4A6
(604) 266-4141   *SIC* 7997
SILVER LAKES GOLF & COUNTRY CLUB INC p756
21114 YONGE ST, NEWMARKET, ON, L3Y 4V8
(905) 836-8070   *SIC* 7997
ST. CHARLES COUNTRY CLUB p387
100 COUNTRY CLUB BLVD, WINNIPEG, MB, R3K 1Z3
(204) 889-4444   *SIC* 7997
ST. GEORGE'S GOLF AND COUNTRY CLUB p577
1668 ISLINGTON AVE, ETOBICOKE, ON, M9A 3M9
(416) 231-3393   *SIC* 7997
STRATFORD-PERTH FAMILY YMCA p897
204 DOWNIE ST, STRATFORD, ON, N5A 1X4
(519) 271-0480   *SIC* 7997
SWAN-E-SET BAY RESORT LTD p244
16651 RANNIE RD, PITT MEADOWS, BC, V3Y 1Z1
(604) 465-9380   *SIC* 7997
TECHNOR DEVELOPMENTS LIMITED p777
85 SCARSDALE RD, NORTH YORK, ON, M3B 2R2
(905) 889-4653   *SIC* 7997
THORNHILL GOLF & COUNTRY CLUB p906
7994 YONGE ST, THORNHILL, ON, L4J 1W3
(905) 881-3000   *SIC* 7997
TORONTO CRICKET SKATING AND CURLING CLUB p788
141 WILSON AVE, NORTH YORK, ON, M5M 3A3
(416) 487-4581   *SIC* 7997
TORONTO GOLF CLUB LINKS, THE p712
1305 DIXIE RD, MISSISSAUGA, ON, L5E 2P5
(905) 278-5255   *SIC* 7997
U.G.C.C. HOLDINGS INC p325
5185 UNIVERSITY BLVD, VANCOUVER, BC, V6T 1X5
(604) 224-1018   *SIC* 7997
VANCOUVER GOLF CLUB p202
771 AUSTIN AVE, COQUITLAM, BC, V3K 3N2
(604) 936-3404   *SIC* 7997
VANCOUVER LAWN TENNIS AND BADMINTON CLUB p321
1630 15TH AVE W, VANCOUVER, BC, V6J 2K7
(604) 731-9411   *SIC* 7997
VICTORIA GOLF CLUB p334
1110 BEACH DR, VICTORIA, BC, V8S 2M9
(250) 598-4224   *SIC* 7997
WESBILD HOLDINGS LTD p199
3251 PLATEAU BLVD, COQUITLAM, BC, V3E 3B8
(604) 945-4007   *SIC* 7997
WESTMOUNT GOLF AND COUNTRY CLUB LIMITED p641
50 INVERNESS DR, KITCHENER, ON, N2M 4Z9
(519) 742-2323   *SIC* 7997
YMCA OF HAMILTON/BURLINGTON/BRANTFORD p530

500 DRURY LANE, BURLINGTON, ON, L7R 2X2
(905) 632-5000   *SIC* 7997
YMCA OF HAMILTON/BURLINGTON/BRANTFORD p613
79 JAMES ST S, HAMILTON, ON, L8P 2Z1
(905) 529-7102   *SIC* 7997
YMCA OF HAMILTON/BURLINGTON/BRANTFORD p1005
207 PARKSIDE DR, WATERDOWN, ON, L8B 1B9
(905) 690-3555   *SIC* 7997
YMCA-YWCA OF THE CENTRAL OKANAGAN p219
4075 GORDON DR, KELOWNA, BC, V1W 5J2
(250) 764-4040   *SIC* 7997

SIC 7999 Amusement and recreation, nec

301061 ONTARIO LIMITED p885
227 CHURCH ST, ST CATHARINES, ON, L2R 3E8
SIC 7999
4094468 CANADA INC p1073
448 CH DU MONT-DES-CASCADES, CANTLEY, QC, J8V 3B2
(819) 827-0301   *SIC* 7999
428675 BC LTD p275
7093 KING GEORGE BLVD SUITE 401A, SURREY, BC, V3W 5A2
(604) 590-3230   *SIC* 7999
9378-7471 QUEBEC INC p1261
945 AV GODIN, QUEBEC, QC, G1M 2X5
(418) 687-1988   *SIC* 7999
ADVENTURE VALLEY INC p903
7015 LESLIE ST, THORNHILL, ON, L3T 6L6
(905) 731-2267   *SIC* 7999
AFRICAN LION SAFARI & GAME FARM LTD p532
1386 COOPER RD RR 1, CAMBRIDGE, ON, N1R 5S2
(519) 623-2620   *SIC* 7999
ALIMENTATION LIGILICA LTEE p398
180 BOUL HEBERT, EDMUNDSTON, NB, E3V 2S7
(506) 735-3544   *SIC* 7999
APEX MOUNTAIN RESORT (1997) LTD p243
324 STRAYHORSE RD, PENTICTON, BC, V2A 6J9
(250) 292-8222   *SIC* 7999
ASENESKAK CASINO LIMITED PARTNERSHIP p359
GD STN MAIN, THE PAS, MB, R9A 1K2
(204) 627-2250   *SIC* 7999
ATLANTIC LOTTERY CORPORATION INC p406
922 MAIN ST, MONCTON, NB, E1C 8W6
(506) 867-5800   *SIC* 7999
B.C. LOTTOTECH INTERNATIONAL INC p216
74 SEYMOUR ST W, KAMLOOPS, BC, V2C 1E2
(250) 828-5500   *SIC* 7999
BAAGWATING COMMUNITY ASSOCIATION p848
22521 ISLAND RD, PORT PERRY, ON, L9L 1B6
(905) 985-3337   *SIC* 7999
BATHURST, CITY OF p394
14 SEAN COUTURIER AVE, BATHURST, NB, E2A 6X2
(506) 549-3300   *SIC* 7999
BEAUCE CARNAVAL INC p1304
1340 BOUL DIONNE, SAINT-GEORGES, QC, G5Y 3V6
(418) 228-8008   *SIC* 7999
BINGO KELOWNA CHANCES GAMING ENTERTAINMENT p221
1585 SPRINGFIELD RD, KELOWNA, BC, V1Y 5V5
(250) 860-9577   *SIC* 7999
BOARD OF GOVERNORS OF EXHIBITION

PLACE, THE *p991*
100 PRINCES BLVD SUITE 1, TORONTO, ON, M6K 3C3
(416) 263-3600   *SIC* 7999

BOARD OF MANAGEMENT OF THE TORONTO ZOO *p864*
361A OLD FINCH AVE, SCARBOROUGH, ON, M1B 5K7
(416) 392-5929   *SIC* 7999

BREAKAWAY GAMING CENTRE *p1023*
655 CRAWFORD AVE, WINDSOR, ON, N9A 5C7
(519) 256-0001   *SIC* 7999

BUCKLER AQUATICS LIMITED *p764*
562 MCNICOLL AVE, NORTH YORK, ON, M2H 2E1
(416) 499-0151   *SIC* 7999

CALGARY EXHIBITION AND STAMPEDE LIMITED *p28*
1410 OLYMPIC WAY SE, CALGARY, AB, T2G 2W1
(403) 261-0101   *SIC* 7999

CALGARY GYMNASTICS CENTRE *p72*
179 CANADA OLYMPIC RD SW, CALGARY, AB, T3B 5R5
(403) 242-1171   *SIC* 7999

CALGARY OLYMPIC DEVELOPMENT ASSOCIATION *p72*
88 CANADA OLYMPIC RD SW, CALGARY, AB, T3B 5R5
(403) 247-5452   *SIC* 7999

CALGARY ZOOLOGICAL SOCIETY, THE *p21*
1300 ZOO RD NE, CALGARY, AB, T2E 7V6
(403) 232-9300   *SIC* 7999

CANADIAN FITNESS PROFESSIONALS INC *p878*
225 SELECT AVE SUITE 110, SCARBOROUGH, ON, M1X 0B5
(416) 493-3515   *SIC* 7999

CANADIAN WESTERN AGRIBITION ASSOCIATION *p1417*
GD LCD MAIN, REGINA, SK, S4P 2Z4
(306) 565-0565   *SIC* 7999

CANLAN ICE SPORTS CORP *p184*
6501 SPROTT ST, BURNABY, BC, V5B 3B8
(604) 291-0626   *SIC* 7999

CANLAN ICE SPORTS CORP *p1068*
5880 BOUL TASCHEREAU, BROSSARD, QC, J4W 1M6
(450) 462-2113   *SIC* 7999

CARNAVAL DE QUEBEC INC *p1260*
205 BOUL DES CEDRES, QUEBEC, QC, G1L 1N8
(418) 626-3716   *SIC* 7999

CASINO NIAGARA LIMITED *p758*
5705 FALLS AVE, NIAGARA FALLS, ON, L2G 7M9
(905) 374-6928   *SIC* 7999

CASINO NIAGARA LIMITED *p758*
5705 FALLS AVE, NIAGARA FALLS, ON, L2G 3K6
(905) 374-3598   *SIC* 7999

CASINO RAMA INC *p849*
5899 RAMA RD, RAMA, ON, L3V 6H6
(705) 329-3325   *SIC* 7999

CENTRE SPORTIF PALADIUM INC *p1142*
475 BOUL ROLAND-THERRIEN, LONGUEUIL, QC, J4H 4A6
(450) 646-9995   *SIC* 7999

CINEPLEX ENTERTAINMENT LIMITED PARTNERSHIP *p120*
1725 99 ST NW, EDMONTON, AB, T6N 1K5
(587) 585-3760   *SIC* 7999

CIRQUE DU SOLEIL CANADA INC *p1169*
8400 2E AV, MONTREAL, QC, H1Z 4M6
(514) 722-2324   *SIC* 7999

CIRQUE DU SOLEIL INC *p1169*
CIRQUE DU SOLEIL, MONTREAL, QC, H1Z 4M6
(514) 722-2324   *SIC* 7999

CITY OF ABBOTSFORD *p176*
3106 CLEARBROOK RD, ABBOTSFORD, BC, V2T 4N6

CITY OF BURNABY *p185*
240 WILLINGDON AVE, BURNABY, BC, V5C 5E9
(604) 298-7946   *SIC* 7999

CITY OF DELTA *p207*
7815 112 ST, DELTA, BC, V4C 4V9
(604) 952-3075   *SIC* 7999

CITY OF OTTAWA *p810*
1490 YOUVILLE DR, ORLEANS, ON, K1C 2X8
(613) 580-9600   *SIC* 7999

COMOX VALLEY REGIONAL DISTRICT *p195*
225 DOGWOOD ST S, CAMPBELL RIVER, BC, V9W 8C8
(250) 287-9234   *SIC* 7999

COMPLEX SUPPLY INC *p757*
PO BOX 300 STN MAIN, NIAGARA FALLS, ON, L2E 6T3
(905) 374-6928   *SIC* 7999

CORPORATION DE FESTIVAL DE MONT-GOLFIERES DE SAINT-JEAN-SUR-RICHELIEU INC *p1317*
5 CH DE L'AEROPORT, SAINT-JEAN-SUR-RICHELIEU, QC, J3B 7B5
(450) 346-6000   *SIC* 7999

CORPORATION OF THE CITY OF BRAMPTON, THE *p508*
340 VODDEN ST E, BRAMPTON, ON, L6V 2N2
(905) 874-2814   *SIC* 7999

CORPORATION OF THE CITY OF COURTENAY, THE *p203*
489 OLD ISLAND HWY, COURTENAY, BC, V9N 3P5
(250) 338-5371   *SIC* 7999

CORPORATION OF THE CITY OF NEW WESTMINSTER *p236*
65 SIXTH AVE E, NEW WESTMINSTER, BC, V3L 4G6
(604) 526-4281   *SIC* 7999

CORPORATION OF THE TOWN OF WHITBY, THE *p1014*
500 VICTORIA ST W, WHITBY, ON, L1N 9G4
(905) 668-7765   *SIC* 7999

DAVEY TREE EXPERT CO. OF CANADA, LIMITED *p477*
611 TRADEWIND DR SUITE 500, ANCASTER, ON, L9G 4V5
(905) 333-1034   *SIC* 7999

EAGLE QUEST GOLF CENTERS INC *p200*
1001 UNITED BLVD, COQUITLAM, BC, V3K 4S8
(604) 523-6400   *SIC* 7999

EDMONTON NORTHLANDS *p83*
7410 BORDEN PARK RD NW, EDMONTON, AB, T5B 0H8
(780) 471-8174   *SIC* 7999

EDMONTON NORTHLANDS *p162*
2693 BROADMOOR BLVD SUITE 132, SHERWOOD PARK, AB, T8H 0G1
(780) 471-7210   *SIC* 7999

EDMONTON SCOTTISH SOCIETY *p125*
3105 101 ST SW, EDMONTON, AB, T6X 1A1
(780) 988-5357   *SIC* 7999

FAMILY LEISURE CENTRE ASSOCIATION OF SOUTHEAST CALGARY, THE *p39*
11150 BONAVENTURE DR SE, CALGARY, AB, T2J 6R9
(403) 278-7542   *SIC* 7999

FESTIVAL JUSTE POUR RIRE *p1185*
2101 BOUL SAINT-LAURENT, MONTREAL, QC, H2X 2T5
(514) 845-3155   *SIC* 7999

FESTIVAL MONDIAL DE FOLKLORE (DRUMMOND) *p1096*
226 RUE SAINT-MARCEL, DRUMMONDVILLE, QC, J2B 2E4
(819) 472-1184   *SIC* 7999

GAMEHOST INC *p128*
9825 HARDIN ST, FORT MCMURRAY, AB, T9H 4G9
(780) 790-9739   *SIC* 7999

GATEWAY CASINOS & ENTERTAINMENT LIMITED *p908*
50 CUMBERLAND ST S, THUNDER BAY, ON, P7B 5L4
(877) 656-4263   *SIC* 7999

GESTION JUSTE POUR RIRE INC *p1185*
2101 BOUL SAINT-LAURENT, MONTREAL, QC, H2X 2T5
(514) 845-3155   *SIC* 7999

GG BROADWAY INVESTMENTS LIMITED PARTNERSHIP *p185*
3823 HENNING DR UNIT 215, BURNABY, BC, V5C 6P3
(604) 293-0152   *SIC* 7999

GOFF FISHERIES LIMITED *p421*
5 BLUEBERRY CRES, CARBONEAR, NL, A1Y 1A6
(709) 596-7155   *SIC* 7999

GREAT CANADIAN CASINOS INC *p201*
2080 UNITED BLVD SUITE D, COQUITLAM, BC, V3K 6W3
(604) 523-6888   *SIC* 7999

GREAT CANADIAN CASINOS INC *p201*
95 SCHOONER ST, COQUITLAM, BC, V3K 7A8
(604) 303-1000   *SIC* 7999

GREAT CANADIAN CASINOS INC *p233*
620 TERMINAL AVE, NANAIMO, BC, V9R 5E2
(250) 753-3033   *SIC* 7999

GREAT CANADIAN CASINOS INC *p260*
8811 RIVER RD, RICHMOND, BC, V6X 3P8
(604) 247-8900   *SIC* 7999

GREAT CANADIAN GAMING CORPORATION *p201*
95 SCHOONER ST, COQUITLAM, BC, V3K 7A8
(604) 303-1000   *SIC* 7999

HAMPTONS GOLF COURSE LTD *p71*
69 HAMPTONS DR NW, CALGARY, AB, T3A 5H7
(403) 239-8088   *SIC* 7999

KAMLOOPS, THE CORPORATION OF THE CITY OF *p217*
910 MCGILL RD, KAMLOOPS, BC, V2C 6N6
(250) 828-3655   *SIC* 7999

LAURENTIAN SKI HILL SNOWBOARDING CLUB *p764*
15 JANEY AVE, NORTH BAY, ON, P1C 1N1
(705) 494-7463   *SIC* 7999

MEDICINE HAT EXHIBITION & STAMPEDE CO LTD *p146*
2055 21 AVE SE, MEDICINE HAT, AB, T1A 7N1
(403) 527-1234   *SIC* 7999

MERLIN ENTERTAINMENTS (CANADA) INC *p555*
1 BASS PRO MILLS DR, CONCORD, ON, L4K 5W4
(905) 761-7066   *SIC* 7999

MID-SCARBOROUGH COMMUNITY RECREATION CENTER *p868*
2467 EGLINTON AVE E, SCARBOROUGH, ON, M1K 2R1
(416) 267-0714   *SIC* 7999

NEWGIOCO GROUP INC *p955*
130 ADELAIDE ST W SUITE 701, TORONTO, ON, M5H 2K4
(647) 229-0136   *SIC* 7999

OAKVILLE GYMNASTIC CLUB *p806*
1415 THIRD LINE, OAKVILLE, ON, L6M 3G2
(905) 847-7747   *SIC* 7999

ONTARIO LOTTERY AND GAMING CORPORATION *p569*
7445 WELLINGTON RD 21, ELORA, ON, N0B 1S0
(519) 846-2022   *SIC* 7999

ONTARIO LOTTERY AND GAMING CORPORATION *p774*
4120 YONGE ST SUITE 500, NORTH YORK, ON, M2P 2B8
(416) 224-1772   *SIC* 7999

OTTAWA RIVER WHITE WATER RAFTING LIMITED *p489*
1260 GRANT SETTLEMENT RD, BEACHBURG, ON, K0J 1C0
(613) 646-2501   *SIC* 7999

OWL RAFTING INC *p826*
39 FIRST AVE, OTTAWA, ON, K1S 2G1
(613) 238-7238   *SIC* 7999

PACIFIC NATIONAL EXHIBITION *p284*
2901 HASTINGS ST E, VANCOUVER, BC, V5K 5J1
(604) 253-2311   *SIC* 7999

PAYS DE LA SAGOUINE INC, LE *p395*
57 RUE ACADIE, BOUCTOUCHE, NB, E4S 2T7
(506) 743-1400   *SIC* 7999

PLAYER ONE AMUSEMENT GROUP INC *p710*
99 RATHBURN RD W, MISSISSAUGA, ON, L5B 4C1
(905) 273-9000   *SIC* 7999

PLAYTIME COMMUNITY GAMING CENTRES INC *p277*
7445 132 ST SUITE 1001, SURREY, BC, V3W 1J8
(604) 590-2577   *SIC* 7999

POLLARD BANKNOTE INCOME FUND *p5*
6203 46 ST, BARRHEAD, AB, T7N 1A1
(780) 674-4750   *SIC* 7999

PRINCE GEORGE CASINO SUPPLY COMPANY INC *p251*
2003 HIGHWAY 97 S, PRINCE GEORGE, BC, V2N 7A3
(250) 564-7070   *SIC* 7999

PURE CANADIAN GAMING CORP *p106*
12464 153RD ST, EDMONTON, AB, T5V 3C5
(780) 424-9467   *SIC* 7999

PURE CANADIAN GAMING CORP *p112*
7055 ARGYLL RD NW, EDMONTON, AB, T6C 4A5
(780) 465-5377   *SIC* 7999

PURE CANADIAN GAMING CORP *p142*
1251 3 AVE S, LETHBRIDGE, AB, T1J 0K1
(403) 381-9467   *SIC* 7999

PURE FREEDOM YYOGA WELLNESS INC *p293*
575 8TH AVE W SUITE 500, VANCOUVER, BC, V5Z 0C4
(604) 736-6002   *SIC* 7999

QUATRE GLACES (1994) INC, LES *p1069*
5880 BOUL TASCHEREAU, BROSSARD, QC, J4W 1M6
(450) 462-2113   *SIC* 7999

RAY FRIEL RECREATION COMPLEX *p810*
1585 TENTH LINE RD, ORLEANS, ON, K1E 3E8
(613) 830-2747   *SIC* 7999

REAL ICE SPORTS FACILITY MANAGEMENT SERVICES LTD *p510*
7575 KENNEDY RD, BRAMPTON, ON, L6W 4T2
(905) 459-9340   *SIC* 7999

RECREATION OAK BAY *p333*
2291 CEDAR HILL CROSS RD, VICTORIA, BC, V8P 5H9
(250) 370-7200   *SIC* 7999

RESORTS OF THE CANADIAN ROCKIES INC *p67*
1505 17 AVE SW, CALGARY, AB, T2T 0E2
(403) 254-7669   *SIC* 7999

RESORTS OF THE CANADIAN ROCKIES INC *p139*
1 WHAIT HORN RD, LAKE LOUISE, AB, T0L 1E0
(403) 522-3555   *SIC* 7999

RG PROPERTIES LTD *p222*
1223 WATER ST SUITE 102, KELOWNA, BC, V1Y 9V1
(250) 979-0888   *SIC* 7999

RICHMOND OLYMPIC OVAL CORPORATION *p266*

6111 RIVER RD, RICHMOND, BC, V7C 0A2

(778) 296-1400   *SIC 7999*

SACKVILLE SPORTS STADIUM   *p461*

409 GLENDALE DR, LOWER SACKVILLE, NS, B4C 2T6

(902) 252-4000   *SIC 7999*

SAINT JOHN AQUATIC CENTRE COMMISSION

50 UNION ST, SAINT JOHN, NB, E2L 1A1

(506) 658-4715   *SIC 7999*

SASKATCHEWAN GAMING CORPORATION   *p1418*

1880 SASKATCHEWAN DR, REGINA, SK, S4P 0B2

(306) 565-3000   *SIC 7999*

SASKATCHEWAN INDIAN GAMING AUTHORITY INC   *p1405*

GD, CARLYLE, SK, S0C 0R0

(306) 577-4577   *SIC 7999*

SASKATCHEWAN INDIAN GAMING AUTHORITY INC   *p1413*

11906 RAILWAY AVE E, NORTH BATTLEFORD, SK, S9A 3K7

(306) 446-3833   *SIC 7999*

SASKATCHEWAN INDIAN GAMING AUTHORITY INC   *p1414*

44 MARQUIS RD W, PRINCE ALBERT, SK, S6V 7Y5

(306) 764-4777   *SIC 7999*

SASKATCHEWAN INDIAN GAMING AUTHORITY INC   *p1433*

103C PACKHAM AVE SUITE 250, SASKATOON, SK, S7N 4K4

(306) 477-7777   *SIC 7999*

SERVICES FORESTIERS ET TERRITORIAUX DE MANAWAN (SFTM) INC   *p1148*

180 RUE AMISKW, MANOUANE, QC, J0K 1M0

SIC 7999

SMG CANADA ULC   *p707*

5500 ROSE CHERRY PL, MISSISSAUGA, ON, L4Z 4B6

(905) 502-9100   *SIC 7999*

SOCIETE DES CASINOS DU QUEBEC INC, LA   *p1199*

500 RUE SHERBROOKE O BUREAU 1500, MONTREAL, QC, H3A 3C6

(514) 282-8000   *SIC 7999*

SOCIETE DES CASINOS DU QUEBEC INC, LA   *p1212*

1 AV DU CASINO, MONTREAL, QC, H3C 4W7

(514) 392-2756   *SIC 7999*

SOCIETE DES ETABLISSEMENTS DE PLEIN AIR DU QUEBEC   *p1081*

25 BOUL NOTRE-DAME, CLERMONT, QC, G4A 1C2

(418) 439-1227   *SIC 7999*

SOCIETE DES LOTERIES DU QUEBEC   *p1199*

500 RUE SHERBROOKE O, MONTREAL, QC, H3A 3C6

(514) 282-8000   *SIC 7999*

SODEM INC   *p1238*

11111 RUE NOTRE-DAME E, MONTREAL-EST, QC, H1B 2V7

(514) 640-2737   *SIC 7999*

SONCO GAMING LIMITED PARTNERSHIP   *p170*

377 GREY EAGLE DR, TSUU T'INA, AB, T3E 3X8

(403) 385-3777   *SIC 7999*

SPORTBALL LTD   *p905*

39 GLEN CAMERON RD UNIT 8, THORNHILL, ON, L3T 1P1

(905) 882-4473   *SIC 7999*

ST MARY'S ECONOMIC DEVELOPMENT CORPORATION   *p400*

185 GABRIEL DR, FREDERICTON, NB, E3A 5V9

(506) 462-9300   *SIC 7999*

ST. JOHN'S SPORTS & ENTERTAINMENT LTD   *p432*

50 NEW GOWER ST, ST. JOHN'S, NL, A1C

1J3

(709) 758-1111   *SIC 7999*

STRATHCONA COUNTY   *p163*

2000 PREMIER WAY, SHERWOOD PARK, AB, T8H 2G4

(780) 416-3300   *SIC 7999*

T.I.C.C. LIMITED   *p689*

6900 AIRPORT RD SUITE 120, MISSISSAUGA, ON, L4V 1E8

(905) 677-6131   *SIC 7999*

TICKETMASTER CANADA LP   *p984*

1 BLUE JAYS WAY SUITE 3900, TORONTO, ON, M5V 1J3

(416) 345-9200   *SIC 7999*

TN ICEPLEX LIMITED PARTNERSHIP   *p387*

3969 PORTAGE AVE, WINNIPEG, MB, R3K 1W4

SIC 7999

TOWN OF COMOX, THE   *p203*

377 LERWICK RD, COURTENAY, BC, V9N 9G4

(250) 334-2527   *SIC 7999*

TWC ENTERPRISES LIMITED   *p629*

15675 DUFFERIN ST, KING CITY, ON, L7B 1K5

(905) 841-5372   *SIC 7999*

VALLEE DU PARC DE SHAWINIGAN INC   *p1112*

10000 CH VALLEE-DU-PARC, GRAND-MERE, QC, G9T 5K5

(819) 538-1639   *SIC 7999*

VANCOUVER BAY CLUBS LTD   *p310*

610 GRANVILLE ST SUITE 201, VANCOUVER, BC, V6C 3T3

(604) 682-5213   *SIC 7999*

VILLAGE QUEBECOIS D'ANTAN INC   *p1100*

1425 RUE MONTPLAISIR, DRUMMONDVILLE, QC, J2C 0M2

(819) 478-1441   *SIC 7999*

VILLE DE MONTREAL   *p1397*

4110 BOUL LASALLE, VERDUN, QC, H4G 2A5

(514) 765-7130   *SIC 7999*

WATERMANIA   *p259*

14300 ENTERTAINMENT BLVD, RICHMOND, BC, V6W 1K3

(604) 448-9616   *SIC 7999*

WEST SHORE PARKS AND RECREATION SOCIETY   *p340*

1767 ISLAND HWY, VICTORIA, BC, V9B 1J1

(250) 478-8384   *SIC 7999*

WESTERN CANADA LOTTERY CORPORATION   *p380*

125 GARRY ST SUITE 1000, WINNIPEG, MB, R3C 4J1

(204) 942-8217   *SIC 7999*

WESTERN CANADA LOTTERY CORPORATION   *p1430*

1935 1ST AVE N, SASKATOON, SK, S7K 6W1

(306) 933-6850   *SIC 7999*

WINDSOR INTERNATIONAL FILM FESTIVAL   *p1024*

101 UNIVERSITY AVE W, WINDSOR, ON, N9A 5P4

(226) 826-9433   *SIC 7999*

YMCA OF GREATER SAINT JOHN INC, THE   *p414*

191 CHURCHILL BLVD, SAINT JOHN, NB, E2K 3E2

(506) 693-9622   *SIC 7999*

YMCA OF GREATER VANCOUVER, THE   *p197*

45844 HOCKING AVE, CHILLIWACK, BC, V2P 1B4

(604) 792-3371   *SIC 7999*

YMCA OF HAMILTON/BURLINGTON/BRANTFORD   *p607*

1883 KOSHLONG LAKE RD, HALIBURTON, ON, K0M 1S0

(705) 457-2132   *SIC 7999*

YORK COUNTY BOWMEN INC   *p757*

15887 MCCOWAN RD, NEWMARKET, ON,

L3Y 4W1

SIC 7999

SIC 8011 Offices and clinics of medical doctors

1246110 ONTARIO INC   *p754*

18120 YONGE ST, NEWMARKET, ON, L3Y 4V8

SIC 8011

2539393 ONTARIO INC   *p709*

71 KING ST W SUITE 102, MISSISSAUGA, ON, L5B 4A2

(905) 897-1144   *SIC 8011*

3887804 CANADA INC   *p1200*

1250 BOUL RENE-LEVESQUE O, MONTREAL, QC, H3B 4W8

(514) 845-1515   *SIC 8011*

924169 ONTARIO LIMITED   *p972*

66 AVENUE RD UNIT 4, TORONTO, ON, M5R 3N8

(416) 922-2868   *SIC 8011*

AFGHAN PHYSICIANS ASSOCIATION IN CANADA A.P.A.C.   *p1358*

108 RUE DU LISERON, SAINTE-JULIE, QC, J3E 3N9

SIC 8011

AIMHI-PRINCE GEORGE ASSOCIATION FOR COMMUNITY LIVING   *p250*

950 KERRY ST, PRINCE GEORGE, BC, V2M 5A3

(250) 564-6408   *SIC 8011*

ALBERTA HEALTH SERVICES   *p68*

10101 SOUTHPORT RD SW, CALGARY, AB, T2W 3N2

(403) 943-1111   *SIC 8011*

ALBERTA HEALTH SERVICES   *p86*

10030 107 ST NW SUITE 9, EDMONTON, AB, T5J 3E4

(403) 944-5705   *SIC 8011*

ALBERTA HEALTH SERVICES   *p91*

11111 JASPER AVE NW, EDMONTON, AB, T5K 0L4

(780) 482-8111   *SIC 8011*

ALEXANDRA COMMUNITY HEALTH CENTRE   *p10*

2840 2 AVE SE UNIT 101, CALGARY, AB, T2A 7X9

(403) 266-2622   *SIC 8011*

ATHLETE'S CARE SPORTS MEDICINE CENTRES INC   *p766*

505 CONSUMERS RD SUITE 809, NORTH YORK, ON, M2J 4V8

(416) 479-8562   *SIC 8011*

BANNESTER, DR LESLIE R   *p516*

221 BRANT AVE SUITE 1, BRANTFORD, ON, N3T 3J2

(519) 753-8666   *SIC 8011*

BIGELOW FOWLER CLINIC   *p142*

1605 9 AVE S, LETHBRIDGE, AB, T1J 1W2

(403) 327-3121   *SIC 8011*

BLACK CREEK COMMUNITY HEALTH CENTRE   *p786*

2202 JANE ST SUITE 5, NORTH YORK, ON, M3M 1A4

(416) 249-8000   *SIC 8011*

BOARD OF HEALTH FOR THE DISTRICT OF ALGOMA HEALTH UNIT   *p862*

294 WILLOW AVE, SAULT STE. MARIE, ON, P6B 0A9

(705) 942-4646   *SIC 8011*

BRANDON CLINIC MEDICAL CORPORATION   *p346*

620 DENNIS ST, BRANDON, MB, R7A 5E7

(204) 728-4440   *SIC 8011*

BRITISH COLUMBIA CENTRE FOR DISEASE CONTROL AND PREVENTION SOCIETY BRANCH   *p292*

655 12TH AVE W, VANCOUVER, BC, V5Z 4R4

(604) 660-0584   *SIC 8011*

CANADIAN CANNABIS CLINICS   *p885*

80 KING STREET, ST CATHARINES, ON, L2R 7G1

(289) 273-3851   *SIC 8011*

CANADIAN INSTITUTE FOR HEALTH INFORMATION   *p829*

495 RICHMOND RD SUITE 600, OTTAWA, ON, K2A 4B2

(613) 241-7860   *SIC 8011*

CANADIAN MENTAL HEALTH ASSOCIATION TORONTO BRANCH, THE   *p788*

700 LAWRENCE AVE W SUITE 480, NORTH YORK, ON, M6A 3B4

(416) 789-7957   *SIC 8011*

CANADIAN MENTAL HEALTH ASSOCIATION TORONTO BRANCH, THE   *p811*

60 BOND ST W, OSHAWA, ON, L1G 1A5

(905) 436-8760   *SIC 8011*

CANADIAN MENTAL HEALTH ASSOCIATION, NIAGARA BRANCH   *p885*

15 WELLINGTON ST, ST CATHARINES, ON, L2R 5P7

(905) 641-5222   *SIC 8011*

CANADIAN MENTAL HEALTH ASSOCIATION, PETERBOROUGH BRANCH   *p839*

466 GEORGE ST N, PETERBOROUGH, ON, K9H 3R7

(705) 748-6711   *SIC 8011*

CANADIAN MENTAL HEALTH ASSOCIATION, SIMCOE COUNTY BRANCH   *p486*

15 BRADFORD ST, BARRIE, ON, L4N 1W2

(705) 726-5033   *SIC 8011*

CANADIAN MENTAL HEALTH ASSOCIATION, WINDSOR-ESSEX COUNTY BRANCH   *p1021*

1400 WINDSOR AVE, WINDSOR, ON, N8X 3L9

(519) 255-7440   *SIC 8011*

CANADIAN MENTAL HEALTH ASSOCIATION-COCHRANE-TIMISKAMING BRANCH   *p912*

330 SECOND AVE SUITE 201, TIMMINS, ON, P4N 8A4

(705) 267-8100   *SIC 8011*

CANADIAN MENTAL HEALTH ASSOCIATION/PEEL BRANCH   *p511*

7700 HURONTARIO ST SUITE 314, BRAMPTON, ON, L6Y 4M3

(905) 451-1718   *SIC 8011*

CAREPARTNERS INC   *p642*

139 WASHBURN DR, KITCHENER, ON, N2R 1S1

(519) 748-5002   *SIC 8011*

CENTRAL COMMUNITY CARE ACCESS CENTRE   *p771*

45 SHEPPARD AVE E SUITE 700, NORTH YORK, ON, M2N 5W9

(416) 222-2241   *SIC 8011*

CENTRE DE READAPTATION EN DEFICIENCE PHYSIQUE LE BOUCLIER   *p1114*

1075 BOUL FIRESTONE BUREAU 1000, JOLIETTE, QC, J6E 6X6

(450) 755-2741   *SIC 8011*

CENTRE DE READAPTATION EN DEFICIENCE PHYSIQUE LE BOUCLIER   *p1320*

225 RUE DU PALAIS, SAINT-JEROME, QC, J7Z 1X7

(450) 560-9898   *SIC 8011*

CENTRE DE READAPTATION LA MAISON   *p1289*

7 9E RUE, ROUYN-NORANDA, QC, J9X 2A9

(819) 762-6592   *SIC 8011*

CENTRE DE SANTE ET DE SERVICES SOCIAUX DE CHICOUTIMI   *p1078*

305 RUE SAINT-VALLIER, CHICOUTIMI, QC, G7H 5H6

(418) 541-1046   *SIC 8011*

CENTRE DE SANTE ET DE SERVICES SOCIAUX DE LA VALLEE-DE-L'OR   *p1390*

1265 BOUL FOREST, VAL-D'OR, QC, J9P 5H3

(819) 825-5858   *SIC 8011*

CENTRE DE SANTE ET DE SERVICES SOCIAUX DE LA VIEILLE-CAPITALE   *p1268*

55 CH SAINTE-FOY, QUEBEC, QC, G1R 1S9

---

(418) 641-2572 *SIC 8011*
CENTRE DE SANTE ET DE SERVICES SO-CIAUX DE QUEBEC-NORD *p1254*
4E ETAGE 2915, AV DU BOURG-ROYAL, QUEBEC, QC, G1C 3S2
(418) 661-5666 *SIC 8011*
CENTRE DE SANTE ET DE SERVICES SO-CIAUX DE QUEBEC-NORD *p1256*
190 76E RUE E, QUEBEC, QC, G1H 7K4
(418) 628-6808 *SIC 8011*
CENTRE INTEGRE DE SANTE ET DE SERVICES SOCIAUX DE LANAUDIERE *p1379*
1317 BOUL DES SEIGNEURS, TERREBONNE, QC, J6W 5B1
(450) 471-2881 *SIC 8011*
CENTRE INTEGRE DE SANTE ET DE SERVICES SOCIAUX DES LAURENTIDES *p1321*
290 RUE DE MONTIGNY, SAINT-JEROME, QC, J7Z 5T3
(450) 432-2777 *SIC 8011*
CENTRE INTEGRE DE SANTE ET DE SERVICES SOCIAUX DES LAURENTIDES *p1321*
500 BOUL DES LAURENTIDES BUREAU 1010, SAINT-JEROME, QC, J7Z 4M2
(450) 436-8622 *SIC 8011*
CENTRE INTEGRE UNIVERSITAIRE SANTE ET SERVICES SOCIAUX DU CENTRE-SUD-DE-L'ILE-DE-MONTREAL *p1165*
4675 RUE BELANGER, MONTREAL, QC, H1T 1C2
(514) 593-3979 *SIC 8011*
CENTRE INTEGRE UNIVERSITAIRE SANTE ET SERVICES SOCIAUX DU CENTRE-SUD-DE-L'ILE-DE-MONTREAL *p1172*
2222 AV LAURIER E, MONTREAL, QC, H2H 1C4
(514) 527-4527 *SIC 8011*
CENTRE INTEGRE UNIVERSITAIRE SANTE ET SERVICES SOCIAUX DU CENTRE-SUD-DE-L'ILE-DE-MONTREAL *p1172*
2275 AV LAURIER E, MONTREAL, QC, H2H 2N8
(514) 527-4527 *SIC 8011*
CENTRE INTEGRE UNIVERSITAIRE SANTE ET SERVICES SOCIAUX DU CENTRE-SUD-DE-L'ILE-DE-MONTREAL *p1183*
155 BOUL SAINT-JOSEPH E, MONTREAL, QC, H2T 1H4
(514) 593-2044 *SIC 8011*
CENTRE INTEGRE UNIVERSITAIRE SANTE ET SERVICES SOCIAUX DU CENTRE-SUD-DE-L'ILE-DE-MONTREAL *p1185*
3430 RUE JEANNE-MANCE, MONTREAL, QC, H2X 2J9
(514) 842-1147 *SIC 8011*
CLINIQUE COMMUNAUTAIRE POINTE-ST-CHARLES *p1216*
500 AV ASH, MONTREAL, QC, H3K 2R4
(514) 937-9251 *SIC 8011*
CMN GLOBAL INC *p904*
150 COMMERCE VALLEY DR W SUITE 900, THORNHILL, ON, L3T 7Z3
(905) 669-4333 *SIC 8011*
COLLEGE OF PHYSICIANS & SURGEONS OF ALBERTA *p88*
10020 100 ST NW SUITE 2700, EDMONTON, AB, T5J 0N3
(780) 423-4764 *SIC 8011*
COMMUNITY HEALTH SERVICES (SASKATOON) ASSOCIATION LIMITED *p1426*
455 2ND AVE N, SASKATOON, SK, S7K 2C2
(306) 652-0300 *SIC 8011*
CSSS DE L'HEMATITE *p1102*
1 RUE ALEXANDRE, FERMONT, QC, G0G 1J0
(418) 287-5461 *SIC 8011*
EFW RADIOLOGY *p77*
3883 FRONT ST SE SUITE 312, CALGARY, AB, T3M 2J6
(403) 541-1200 *SIC 8011*
ETOBICOKE MEDICAL CENTRE FAMILY HEALTH TEAM *p574*
85 THE EAST MALL, ETOBICOKE, ON,

M8Z 5W4
(416) 621-2220 *SIC 8011*
FALSE CREEK SURGICAL CENTRE INC *p293*
555 8TH AVE W SUITE 600, VANCOUVER, BC, V5Z 1C6
(604) 739-9695 *SIC 8011*
FIRST NATIONS HEALTH AUTHORITY *p341*
100 PARK ROYAL S SUITE 501, WEST VANCOUVER, BC, V7T 1A2
(604) 693-6500 *SIC 8011*
FRASER HEALTH AUTHORITY *p196*
45470 MENHOLM RD, CHILLIWACK, BC, V2P 1M2
(604) 702-4900 *SIC 8011*
FRASER HEALTH AUTHORITY *p215*
1275 7TH AVE, HOPE, BC, V0X 1L4
(604) 869-5656 *SIC 8011*
GINEW WELLNESS CENTRE *p350*
GD, GINEW, MB, R0A 2R0
(204) 427-2384 *SIC 8011*
GOUVERNEMENT DE LA PROVINCE DE QUEBEC *p1106*
135 BOUL SAINT-RAYMOND, GATINEAU, QC, J8Y 6X7
(819) 777-6261 *SIC 8011*
GREIG ASSOCIATES X-RAY, ULTRASOUND AND MAMMOGRAPHY INC *p287*
5732 VICTORIA DR, VANCOUVER, BC, V5P 3W6
(604) 321-6769 *SIC 8011*
GROUP HEALTH CENTRE, THE *p862*
240 MCNABB ST, SAULT STE. MARIE, ON, P6B 1Y5
(705) 759-5521 *SIC 8011*
GROUPE SANTE PHYSIMED INC *p1339*
6363 RTE TRANSCANADIENNE BUREAU 121, SAINT-LAURENT, QC, H4T 1Z9
(514) 747-8888 *SIC 8011*
H.L.O. HEALTH SERVICES INC *p603*
341 WOOLWICH ST, GUELPH, ON, N1H 3W4
(519) 823-2784 *SIC 8011*
HASTINGS PRINCE EDWARD PUBLIC HEALTH *p492*
179 NORTH PARK ST, BELLEVILLE, ON, K8P 4P1
(613) 966-5500 *SIC 8011*
HEARTLAND REGIONAL HEALTH AUTHORITY *p1438*
GD, WILKIE, SK, S0K 4W0
(306) 843-2531 *SIC 8011*
HSG HEALTH SYSTEMS GROUP LIMITED *p718*
51 TANNERY ST, MISSISSAUGA, ON, L5M 1V3
(905) 858-0333 *SIC 8011*
I CARE SERVICE LTD *p71*
4935 40 AVE NW SUITE 450, CALGARY, AB, T3A 2N1
(403) 286-3022 *SIC 8011*
IMAGIX IMAGERIE MEDICALE INC *p1065*
600 BOUL DU FORT-SAINT-LOUIS UNITE 202, BOUCHERVILLE, QC, J4B 1S7
(450) 655-2430 *SIC 8011*
IMAGIX IMAGERIE MEDICALE INC *p1070*
F-4105 BOUL MATTE, BROSSARD, QC, J4Y 2P4
(514) 866-6622 *SIC 8011*
INSIGHT MEDICAL IMAGING *p98*
200 MEADOWLARK SHOPPING CTR NW, EDMONTON, AB, T5R 5W9
(780) 489-3391 *SIC 8011*
LAKERIDGE HEALTH *p812*
11 GIBB ST, OSHAWA, ON, L1H 2J9
(905) 579-1212 *SIC 8011*
LONDON HEALTH SCIENCES CENTRE *p654*
339 WINDERMERE RD, LONDON, ON, N6A 5A5
(519) 685-8500 *SIC 8011*
LONDON HEALTH SCIENCES CENTRE *p660*
790 COMMISSIONERS RD W, LONDON,

ON, N6K 1C2
(519) 685-8300 *SIC 8011*
MANITOBA CLINIC MEDICAL CORPORATION *p373*
790 SHERBROOK ST SUITE 503, WINNIPEG, MB, R3A 1M3
(204) 774-6541 *SIC 8011*
MEDCAN HEALTH MANAGEMENT INC *p954*
150 YORK ST SUITE 1500, TORONTO, ON, M5H 3S5
(416) 350-5900 *SIC 8011*
MEDICAL IMAGING CONSULTANTS *p86*
11010 101 ST NW SUITE 203, EDMONTON, AB, T5H 4B9
(780) 426-1121 *SIC 8011*
MEDICAL IMAGING CONSULTANTS *p118*
8215 112 ST NW SUITE 700, EDMONTON, AB, T6G 2C8
(780) 432-1121 *SIC 8011*
MEDICENTRES CANADA INC *p98*
10458 MAYFIELD RD NW SUITE 204, EDMONTON, AB, T5P 4P4
(780) 483-7115 *SIC 8011*
MISERICORDIA GENERAL HOSPITAL *p379*
99 CORNISH AVE SUITE 370, WINNIPEG, MB, R3C 1A2
(204) 774-6581 *SIC 8011*
MISSISSAUGA HALTON COMMUNITY CARE ACCESS CENTRE *p579*
401 THE WEST MALL SUITE 1001, ETOBICOKE, ON, M9C 5J5
(905) 855-9090 *SIC 8011*
MOUNT CARMEL CLINIC *p371*
886 MAIN ST, WINNIPEG, MB, R2W 5L4
(204) 582-2311 *SIC 8011*
NEWFOUNDLAND & LABRADOR CENTRE FOR HEALTH INFORMATION *p430*
70 O'LEARY AVE, ST. JOHN'S, NL, A1B 2C7
(709) 752-6000 *SIC 8011*
NOR'WEST CO-OP COMMUNITY HEALTH CENTRE, INC *p372*
785 KEEWATIN ST, WINNIPEG, MB, R2X 3B9
(204) 938-5900 *SIC 8011*
NORTH EASTMAN HEALTH ASSOCIATION INC *p354*
689 MAIN ST, OAKBANK, MB, R0E 1J2
(204) 444-2227 *SIC 8011*
NORTH HAMILTON COMMUNITY HEALTH CENTRE *p611*
438 HUGHSON ST N, HAMILTON, ON, L8L 4N5
(905) 523-1184 *SIC 8011*
NORTH OKANAGAN REGIONAL HEALTH BOARD *p331*
1440 14 AVE, VERNON, BC, V1B 2T1
(250) 549-5700 *SIC 8011*
NORTH YORK MEDICAL BUILDING INC *p786*
1017 WILSON AVE UNIT 304, NORTH YORK, ON, M3K 1Z1
(416) 783-5101 *SIC 8011*
OAK BAY KIWANIS HEALTH CARE SOCIETY *p334*
3034 CEDAR HILL RD, VICTORIA, BC, V8T 3J3
(250) 598-2022 *SIC 8011*
OSHAWA CLINIC *p813*
117 KING ST E, OSHAWA, ON, L1H 1B9
(905) 723-8551 *SIC 8011*
OTTAWA HOSPITAL, THE *p819*
501 SMYTH RD, OTTAWA, ON, K1H 8L6
(613) 737-8899 *SIC 8011*
PETERBOROUGH CLINIC, THE *p841*
26 HOSPITAL DR SUITE 204, PETERBOROUGH, ON, K9J 7C3
(705) 743-2040 *SIC 8011*
POLYCLINIC PROFESSIONAL CENTRE INC *p1039*
199 GRAFTON ST SUITE 307, CHARLOTTETOWN, PE, C1A 1L2
(902) 629-8810 *SIC 8011*
PORT ARTHUR HEALTH CENTRE INC, THE

p907
194 COURT ST N, THUNDER BAY, ON, P7A 4V7
(807) 345-2332 *SIC 8011*
PRAIRIE MOUNTAIN HEALTH *p357*
192 1ST AVE W, SOURIS, MB, R0K 2C0
(204) 483-5000 *SIC 8011*
PRINCE ALBERT CO-OPERATIVE HEALTH CENTRE/COMMUNITY CLINIC *p1414*
110 8TH ST E, PRINCE ALBERT, SK, S6V 0V7
(306) 763-6464 *SIC 8011*
RADIOLOGY CONSULTANTS ASSOCIATED *p68*
6707 ELBOW DR SW SUITE 120, CALGARY, AB, T2V 0E3
(403) 777-3007 *SIC 8011*
RIDEAU COMMUNITY HEALTH SERVICES *p681*
354 READ ST, MERRICKVILLE, ON, K0G 1N0
(613) 269-3400 *SIC 8011*
SASKATCHEWAN HEALTH AUTHORITY *p1407*
GD, ILE-A-LA-CROSSE, SK, S0M 1C0
(306) 833-2016 *SIC 8011*
SASKATCHEWAN HEALTH AUTHORITY *p1429*
701 QUEEN ST, SASKATOON, SK, S7K 0M7
(306) 655-0080 *SIC 8011*
SAULT STE MARIE & DISTRICT GROUP HEALTH ASSOCIATION *p863*
240 MCNABB ST, SAULT STE. MARIE, ON, P6B 1Y5
(705) 759-1234 *SIC 8011*
SCARBOROUGH CENTRE FOR HEALTHY COMMUNITIES *p867*
629 MARKHAM RD UNIT 2, SCARBOROUGH, ON, M1H 2A4
(416) 642-9445 *SIC 8011*
SEYMOUR MEDICAL CLINIC, THE *p321*
1530 7TH AVE W SUITE 200, VANCOUVER, BC, V6J 1S3
(604) 738-2151 *SIC 8011*
SIMCOE MUSKOKA DISTRICT HEALTH UNIT *p485*
15 SPERLING DR, BARRIE, ON, L4M 6K9
(705) 721-7520 *SIC 8011*
SOUTH CALGARY PRIMARY CARE NETWORK, THE *p69*
1800 194 AVE SE SUITE 4000, CALGARY, AB, T2X 0R3
(403) 256-3222 *SIC 8011*
SOUTH EAST COMMUNITY CARE ACCESS CENTRE *p632*
1471 JOHN COUNTER BLVD SUITE 200, KINGSTON, ON, K7M 8S8
(613) 544-7090 *SIC 8011*
SOUTH RIVERDALE COMMUNITY HEALTH CENTRE *p921*
955 QUEEN ST E, TORONTO, ON, M4M 3P3
(416) 461-1925 *SIC 8011*
ST. MARY'S GENERAL HOSPITAL *p641*
911 QUEENS BLVD SUITE 453, KITCHENER, ON, N2M 1B2
(519) 744-3311 *SIC 8011*
SURGICAL CENTRES INC *p72*
3125 BOWWOOD DR NW, CALGARY, AB, T3B 2E7
(403) 640-1188 *SIC 8011*
UNIVERSITY HEALTH NETWORK *p947*
200 ELIZABETH ST SUITE 224, TORONTO, ON, M5G 2C4
(416) 340-3111 *SIC 8011*
VANCOUVER COASTAL HEALTH AUTHORITY *p296*
569 POWELL ST, VANCOUVER, BC, V6A 1G8
(604) 255-3151 *SIC 8011*
VANCOUVER ISLAND HEALTH AUTHORITY *p204*
2696 WINDERMERE ST, CUMBERLAND,

BC, V0R 1S0
(250) 331-8505   *SIC 8011*
VANCOUVER ISLAND HEALTH AUTHOR-ITY   *p212*
3045 GIBBINS RD, DUNCAN, BC, V9L 1E5
(250) 737-2030   *SIC 8011*
VANCOUVER ISLAND HEALTH AUTHOR-ITY   *p243*
180 MCCARTER ST SUITE 100, PARKSVILLE, BC, V9P 2H3
(250) 731-1315   *SIC 8011*
VANCOUVER ISLAND HEALTH AUTHOR-ITY   *p243*
GD, PARKSVILLE, BC, V9P 2G2
(250) 947-8230   *SIC 8011*
VANCOUVER ISLAND HEALTH AUTHOR-ITY   *p252*
777 JONES ST, QUALICUM BEACH, BC, V9K 2L1
(250) 947-8220   *SIC 8011*
VANCOUVER ISLAND HEALTH AUTHOR-ITY   *p333*
1952 BAY ST, VICTORIA, BC, V8R 1J8
(250) 519-7700   *SIC 8011*
VANCOUVER ISLAND HEALTH AUTHOR-ITY   *p333*
2400 ARBUTUS RD, VICTORIA, BC, V8N 1V7
(250) 519-5390   *SIC 8011*
VANCOUVER ISLAND HEALTH AUTHOR-ITY   *p339*
1 HOSPITAL WAY, VICTORIA, BC, V8Z 6R5
(250) 370-8355   *SIC 8011*
WIEBE, DR. C.W. MEDICAL CORPORATION   *p361*
385 MAIN ST, WINKLER, MB, R6W 1J2
(204) 325-4312   *SIC 8011*
WINNIPEG CLINIC   *p380*
425 ST MARY AVE, WINNIPEG, MB, R3C 0N2
(204) 957-1900   *SIC 8011*
WORKPLACE HEALTH, SAFETY & COMPENSATION COMMISSION OF NEW BRUNSWICK   *p416*
3700 WESTFIELD RD, SAINT JOHN, NB, E2M 5Z4
(506) 738-8411   *SIC 8011*
YMCA-YWCA OF GREATER VICTORIA   *p337*
851 BROUGHTON ST, VICTORIA, BC, V8W 1E5
(250) 386-7511   *SIC 8011*

SIC 8021 Offices and clinics of dentists

ABBOTSFORD DENTAL GROUP INC   *p174*
33782 MARSHALL RD, ABBOTSFORD, BC, V2S 1L1
(604) 853-6441   *SIC 8021*
CENTRES DENTAIRES LAPOINTE INC   *p1142*
116 RUE GUILBAULT, LONGUEUIL, QC, J4H 2T2
(450) 679-2300   *SIC 8021*
ONION LAKE HEALTH BOARD INC   *p1413*
GD, ONION LAKE, SK, S0M 2E0
(306) 344-2330   *SIC 8021*

SIC 8041 Offices and clinics of chiropractors

GREY-SIMCOE SPORTS MEDICINE AND REHABILITATION CENTRES INC.   *p487*
480 HURONIA RD UNIT 104, BARRIE, ON, L4N 6M2
(705) 734-1588   *SIC 8041*

SIC 8042 Offices and clinics of optometrists

BISHOP, DONALD H. PROFESSIONAL CORPORATION   *p70*
11410 27 ST SE UNIT 6, CALGARY, AB,

T2Z 3R6
(403) 974-3937   *SIC 8042*
CENTRE DE VISION DELSON INC   *p1089*
70 132 RTE BUREAU 104, DELSON, QC, J5B 0A1
(450) 638-5212   *SIC 8042*
GROUPE MIOSIS, S.E.N.C.R.L.   *p1106*
425 BOUL SAINT-JOSEPH, GATINEAU, QC, J8Y 3Z8
(819) 771-5600   *SIC 8042*

SIC 8049 Offices of health practitioner

9006-5855 QUEBEC INC   *p1134*
300 RUE SAINT-ANTOINE N, LAVALTRIE, QC, J5T 2G4
(450) 586-0479   *SIC 8049*
ACTION SPORT PHYSIO VAUDREUIL-DORION INC   *p1394*
11 CITE DES JEUNES EST SUITE 101, VAUDREUIL-DORION, QC, J7V 8V9
(450) 455-0111   *SIC 8049*
ADVANCED PARAMEDIC LTD   *p152*
8703 75 ST W, PEACE RIVER, AB, T8S 0A5
(780) 624-4911   *SIC 8049*
BAYSHORE HEALTHCARE LTD.   *p385*
1700 NESS AVE, WINNIPEG, MB, R3J 3Y1
(204) 943-7124   *SIC 8049*
CANADIAN PARAMEDICAL SERVICES INC   *p34*
7053 FARRELL RD SE SUITE 5, CALGARY, AB, T2H 0T3
(403) 259-8399   *SIC 8049*
CBI LIMITED   *p64*
1400 1 ST SW SUITE 500, CALGARY, AB, T2R 0V8
(403) 232-8770   *SIC 8049*
CBI LIMITED   *p572*
3300 BLOOR ST W SUITE 900, ETOBICOKE, ON, M8X 2X2
(800) 463-2225   *SIC 8049*
CENTRAL WEST COMMUNITY CARE ACCESS CENTRE   *p509*
199 COUNTY COURT BLVD, BRAMPTON, ON, L6W 4P3
(905) 796-0040   *SIC 8049*
CENTRE D'EVALUATION & READAPTION PHYSIQUE C.E.R.P. INC   *p1235*
3095 NORD LAVAL (A-440) O, MONTREAL, QC, H7P 4W5
(450) 688-0445   *SIC 8049*
CENTRE DE PSYCHOLOGIE GOUIN INC   *p1216*
39 BOUL GOUIN O, MONTREAL, QC, H3L 1H9
(514) 331-5530   *SIC 8049*
CENTRE INTEGRE DE SANTE ET DE SERVICES SOCIAUX DE LANAUDIERE   *p1321*
11 RUE BOYER, SAINT-JEROME, QC, J7Z 2K5
(450) 432-7588   *SIC 8049*
COMCARE (CANADA) LIMITED   *p656*
339 WELLINGTON RD SUITE 200, LONDON, ON, N6C 5Z9
(800) 663-5775   *SIC 8049*
COMFORTING CARE LTD   *p199*
657 GATENSBURY ST, COQUITLAM, BC, V3J 5G9
    SIC 8049
COTA HEALTH   *p933*
550 QUEEN ST E SUITE 201, TORONTO, ON, M5A 1V2
(888) 785-2779   *SIC 8049*
DANIELS KIMBER PHYSIOTHERAPY CLINIC P.C. LTD   *p1424*
3907 8TH ST E SUITE 304, SASKATOON, SK, S7H 5M7
(306) 652-5151   *SIC 8049*
DIRECT SUPPORT CARE INC   *p755*
236 PARKVIEW CRES, NEWMARKET, ON, L3Y 2C8
(905) 895-5800   *SIC 8049*
EXTENDICARE (CANADA) INC   *p565*

40 GOODALL ST, DRYDEN, ON, P8N 1V8
(807) 223-5337   *SIC 8049*
EXTENDICARE (CANADA) INC   *p907*
3550 SCHMON PKY SUITE 4, THOROLD, ON, L2V 4Y6
(905) 685-6501   *SIC 8049*
FUNCTIONABILITY REHABILITATION SERVICES LP   *p553*
9135 KEELE ST UNIT B5, CONCORD, ON, L4K 0J4
(905) 764-2340   *SIC 8049*
IRIDIA MEDICAL INC   *p321*
1644 3RD AVE W, VANCOUVER, BC, V6J 1K2
(604) 685-4747   *SIC 8049*
KARDEL CONSULTING SERVICES INC   *p339*
2951 TILLICUM RD UNIT 209, VICTORIA, BC, V9A 2A6
(250) 382-5959   *SIC 8049*
PHYSIO-ERGO PLUS INC   *p1380*
3395 BOUL DE LA PINIERE BUREAU 200, TERREBONNE, QC, J6X 4N1
(450) 492-9999   *SIC 8049*
PROCARE HEALTH SERVICES INC   *p237*
624 COLUMBIA ST SUITE 201, NEW WESTMINSTER, BC, V3M 1A5
(604) 525-1234   *SIC 8049*
PT HEALTHCARE SOLUTIONS CORP   *p613*
70 FRID ST UNIT 2, HAMILTON, ON, L8P 4M4
(877) 734-9887   *SIC 8049*
RAINBOW NURSING REGISTRY LTD   *p973*
344 DUPONT ST SUITE 402C, TORONTO, ON, M5R 1V9
(416) 922-7616   *SIC 8049*
RJF HEALTHCARE SERVICES LTD   *p454*
5657 SPRING GARDEN RD UNIT 700, HALIFAX, NS, B3J 3R4
(902) 425-4031   *SIC 8049*
ROCKMAN PSYCHOLOGY PROFESSIONAL CORPORATION   *p905*
7191 YONGE ST SUITE 801, THORNHILL, ON, L3T 0C4
(416) 602-3230   *SIC 8049*
SHYLO NURSING SERVICES LTD   *p240*
1305 ST. GEORGES AVE, NORTH VANCOUVER, BC, V7L 3J2
(604) 985-6881   *SIC 8049*
SLIZEK INC   *p223*
1450 ST. PAUL ST, KELOWNA, BC, V1Y 2E6
(250) 861-3446   *SIC 8049*
SPB ORGANIZATIONNAL PSYCHOLOGY   *p1143*
555 BOUL ROLAND-THERRIEN UNITE 300, LONGUEUIL, QC, J4H 4E7
(450) 646-1022   *SIC 8049*

SIC 8051 Skilled nursing care facilities

1457271 ONTARIO LIMITED   *p478*
1217 OLD MOHAWK RD, ANCASTER, ON, L9K 1P6
(905) 304-6781   *SIC 8051*
2063412 INVESTMENT LP   *p564*
143 MARY ST, CREEMORE, ON, L0M 1G0
(705) 466-3437   *SIC 8051*
2063414 INVESTMENT LP   *p665*
302 TOWN CENTRE BLVD SUITE 200, MARKHAM, ON, L3R 0E8
(905) 477-4006   *SIC 8051*
2063414 ONTARIO LIMITED   *p514*
389 WEST ST, BRANTFORD, ON, N3R 3V9
(519) 759-4666   *SIC 8051*
2063414 ONTARIO LIMITED   *p564*
143 MARY ST, CREEMORE, ON, L0M 1G0
(705) 466-3437   *SIC 8051*
2063414 ONTARIO LIMITED   *p568*
120 BARNSWALLOW DR, ELMIRA, ON, N3B 2Y9
(519) 669-5777   *SIC 8051*
2063414 ONTARIO LIMITED   *p598*

200 KELLY DR, GRAVENHURST, ON, P1P 1P3
(705) 687-3444   *SIC 8051*
2063414 ONTARIO LIMITED   *p762*
401 WILLIAM ST, NORTH BAY, ON, P1A 1X5
(705) 476-2602   *SIC 8051*
2063414 ONTARIO LIMITED   *p786*
22 NORFINCH DR, NORTH YORK, ON, M3N 1X1
(416) 623-1120   *SIC 8051*
2063414 ONTARIO LIMITED   *p850*
170 RED MAPLE RD, RICHMOND HILL, ON, L4B 4T8
(905) 731-2273   *SIC 8051*
2063414 ONTARIO LIMITED   *p870*
1000 ELLESMERE RD SUITE 333, SCARBOROUGH, ON, M1P 5G2
(416) 291-0222   *SIC 8051*
2063414 ONTARIO LIMITED   *p972*
225 ST. GEORGE ST, TORONTO, ON, M5R 2M2
(416) 967-3985   *SIC 8051*
2063414 ONTARIO LIMITED   *p997*
2005 LAWRENCE AVE W SUITE 323, TORONTO, ON, M9N 3V4
(416) 243-8879   *SIC 8051*
2063414 ONTARIO LIMITED   *p1029*
5400 STEELES AVE W, WOODBRIDGE, ON, L4L 9S1
(905) 856-7200   *SIC 8051*
341822 ONTARIO INC   *p990*
28 HALTON ST, TORONTO, ON, M6J 1R3
(416) 533-5198   *SIC 8051*
3885136 MANITOBA ASSOCIATION INC   *p380*
1325 ERIN ST, WINNIPEG, MB, R3E 3R6
(204) 943-4424   *SIC 8051*
477281 ONTARIO LTD   *p485*
140 CUNDLES RD W, BARRIE, ON, L4N 9X8
    SIC 8051
601092 ONTARIO LIMITED   *p972*
914 BATHURST ST, TORONTO, ON, M5R 3G5
(416) 533-9473   *SIC 8051*
656955 ONTARIO LIMITED   *p846*
101 PARENT ST, PLANTAGENET, ON, K0B 1L0
(613) 673-4835   *SIC 8051*
913096 ONTARIO LIMITED   *p561*
1202 94 HWY, CORBEIL, ON, P0H 1K0
(705) 752-1100   *SIC 8051*
ALBERTA HEALTH SERVICES   *p143*
700 NURSING HOME RD, LINDEN, AB, T0M 1J0
(403) 546-3966   *SIC 8051*
ALDERGROVE LIONS SENIORS HOUSING SOCIETY   *p179*
27477 28 AVE, ALDERGROVE, BC, V4W 3L9
(604) 856-4161   *SIC 8051*
ARROWSMITH REST HOME SOCIETY   *p242*
266 MOILLIET ST S SUITE 1, PARKSVILLE, BC, V9P 1M9
(250) 947-9777   *SIC 8051*
BALLYCLIFFE LODGE LIMITED   *p473*
70 STATION ST, AJAX, ON, L1S 1R9
(905) 683-7321   *SIC 8051*
BANWELL GARDENS   *p1017*
3000 BANWELL RD, WINDSOR, ON, N8N 0B3
(519) 735-3204   *SIC 8051*
BAY HAVEN NURSING HOME INC   *p546*
499 HUME ST SUITE 18, COLLINGWOOD, ON, L9Y 4H8
(705) 445-6501   *SIC 8051*
BECKLEY FARM LODGE FOUNDATION   *p335*
530 SIMCOE ST, VICTORIA, BC, V8V 4W4
(250) 381-4421   *SIC 8051*
BELCREST NURSING HOMES LIMITED   *p492*
250 BRIDGE ST W SUITE 241,

BELLEVILLE, ON, K8P 5N3
(613) 968-4434 *SIC* 8051
BETEL HOME FOUNDATION *p350*
96 1ST AVE, GIMLI, MB, R0C 1B1
(204) 642-5556 *SIC* 8051
BETHANY CARE SOCIETY *p3*
1736 1 AVE NW SUITE 725, AIRDRIE, AB, T4B 2C4
(403) 948-6022 *SIC* 8051
BETHANY CARE SOCIETY *p41*
916 18A ST NW SUITE 3085, CALGARY, AB, T2N 1C6
(403) 284-0161 *SIC* 8051
BETHANY CARE SOCIETY *p76*
19 HARVEST GOLD MANOR NE, CALGARY, AB, T3K 4Y1
(403) 226-8200 *SIC* 8051
BETHANY CARE SOCIETY *p80*
32 QUIGLEY DR UNIT 1000, COCHRANE, AB, T4C 1X9
(403) 932-6422 *SIC* 8051
BRENDA STRAFFORD FOUNDATION LTD, THE *p72*
4628 MONTGOMERY BLVD NW, CALGARY, AB, T3B 0K7
(403) 288-1780 *SIC* 8051
BROADMEAD CARE SOCIETY *p337*
4579 CHATTERTON WAY, VICTORIA, BC, V8X 4Y7
(250) 656-0717 *SIC* 8051
BROADVIEW NURSING CENTRE LIMITED *p881*
210 BROCKVILLE ST, SMITHS FALLS, ON, K7A 3Z4
(613) 283-1845 *SIC* 8051
BROADWAY PENTECOSTAL CARE ASSOCIATION *p319*
1377 LAMEY'S MILL RD, VANCOUVER, BC, V6H 3S9
(604) 733-1441 *SIC* 8051
BURQUITLAM CARE SOCIETY *p200*
560 SYDNEY AVE, COQUITLAM, BC, V3K 6A4
SIC 8051
C.H.S.L.D. BAYVIEW INC *p1253*
27 CH DU BORD-DU-LAC LAKESHORE, POINTE-CLAIRE, QC, H9S 4H1
(514) 695-9384 *SIC* 8051
CAMA WOODLANDS NURSING HOME *p529*
159 PANIN RD, BURLINGTON, ON, L7P 5A6
(905) 681-6441 *SIC* 8051
CAMPBELLTON NURSING HOME INC *p396*
101 DOVER ST, CAMPBELLTON, NB, E3N 3K6
(506) 789-7350 *SIC* 8051
CANADIAN REFORMED SOCIETY FOR A HOME FOR THE AGED INC *p529*
4486 GUELPH LINE, BURLINGTON, ON, L7P 0N2
(905) 335-3636 *SIC* 8051
CAPITAL CARE GROUP INC *p91*
9925 109 ST NW SUITE 500, EDMONTON, AB, T5K 2J8
(780) 448-2400 *SIC* 8051
CARESSANT CARE NURSING HOME COBDEN *p544*
12 WREN DR, COBDEN, ON, K0J 1K0
(613) 646-2109 *SIC* 8051
CARESSANT-CARE NURSING AND RETIREMENT HOMES LIMITED *p538*
3680 SPEEDSVILLE RD SUITE 3, CAMBRIDGE, ON, N3H 4R6
(519) 650-0100 *SIC* 8051
CARESSANT-CARE NURSING AND RETIREMENT HOMES LIMITED *p618*
24 LOUISE ST, HARRISTON, ON, N0G 1Z0
(519) 338-3700 *SIC* 8051
CARESSANT-CARE NURSING AND RETIREMENT HOMES LIMITED *p645*
114 MCLAUGHLIN RD, LINDSAY, ON, K9V 6L1
(705) 324-0300 *SIC* 8051
CARESSANT-CARE NURSING AND RE-

TIREMENT HOMES LIMITED *p645*
240 MARY ST W, LINDSAY, ON, K9V 5K5
(705) 324-1913 *SIC* 8051
CARESSANT-CARE NURSING AND RETIREMENT HOMES LIMITED *p680*
58 BURSTHALL ST, MARMORA, ON, K0K 2M0
(613) 472-3130 *SIC* 8051
CARESSANT-CARE NURSING AND RETIREMENT HOMES LIMITED *p890*
15 BONNIE PL, ST THOMAS, ON, N5R 5T8
(519) 633-6493 *SIC* 8051
CARESSANT-CARE NURSING AND RETIREMENT HOMES LIMITED *p902*
94 WILLIAM ST S SUITE 202, TAVISTOCK, ON, N0B 2R0
(519) 655-2344 *SIC* 8051
CARESSANT-CARE NURSING AND RETIREMENT HOMES LIMITED *p1035*
264 NORWICH AVE, WOODSTOCK, ON, N4S 3V9
(519) 539-0408 *SIC* 8051
CARESSANT-CARE NURSING AND RETIREMENT HOMES LIMITED *p1035*
81 FYFE AVE, WOODSTOCK, ON, N4S 8Y2
(519) 539-6461 *SIC* 8051
CAREWEST *p75*
6363 SIMCOE RD SW, CALGARY, AB, T3H 4M3
(403) 240-7950 *SIC* 8051
CARLETON KIRK LODGE NURSING HOME *p416*
2 CARLETON KIRK PL, SAINT JOHN, NB, E2M 5B8
(506) 643-7040 *SIC* 8051
CARVETH NURSING HOME LIMITED *p592*
375 JAMES ST, GANANOQUE, ON, K7G 2Z1
(613) 382-4752 *SIC* 8051
CASE MANOR *p494*
28 BOYD ST, BOBCAYGEON, ON, K0M 1A0
(705) 738-2374 *SIC* 8051
CASEY HOUSE HOSPICE INC *p931*
119 ISABELLA ST, TORONTO, ON, M4Y 1P2
(416) 962-7600 *SIC* 8051
CENTENNIAL PLACE *p682*
2 CENTENNIAL LANE RR 3, MILLBROOK, ON, L0A 1G0
(705) 932-4464 *SIC* 8051
CENTRAL HAVEN SPECIAL CARE HOME *p1431*
1020 AVENUE I N, SASKATOON, SK, S7L 2H7
(306) 844-4040 *SIC* 8051
CENTRAL REGIONAL HEALTH AUTHORITY *p421*
25 PLEASANTVIEW RD, BOTWOOD, NL, A0H 1E0
(709) 257-2874 *SIC* 8051
CENTRE D'ACCUEIL SAINT-JOSEPH DE LEVIS INC *p1135*
107 RUE SAINT-LOUIS, LEVIS, QC, G6V 4G9
(418) 833-3414 *SIC* 8051
CENTRE D'HEBERGEMENT ET DE SOINS DE LONGUE DUREE BOURGET INC *p1247*
11570 RUE NOTRE-DAME E, POINTE-AUX-TREMBLES, QC, H1B 2X4
(514) 645-1673 *SIC* 8051
CENTRE D'HEBERGEMENT ST-JEAN-EUDES INC *p1256*
6000 3E AV O, QUEBEC, QC, G1H 7J5
(418) 627-1124 *SIC* 8051
CENTRE D'HEBERGEMENT ST-VINCENT DE MARIE INC *p1323*
1175 BOUL DE LA COTE-VERTU, SAINT-LAURENT, QC, H4L 5J1
(514) 744-1175 *SIC* 8051
CENTRE DE SANTE ET DE SERVICES SOCIAUX DE LA VALLEE-DE-LA-BATISCAN *p1355*
60 RUE DE LA FABRIQUE BUREAU 217,

SAINTE-ANNE-DE-LA-PERADE, QC, G0X 2J0
(418) 325-2313 *SIC* 8051
CENTRE DE SANTE ET DE SERVICES SOCIAUX DU PONTIAC *p1254*
2135 RUE DE LA TERRASSE-CADIEUX, QUEBEC, QC, G1C 1Z2
(418) 667-3910 *SIC* 8051
CENTRE DE SANTE TULATTAVIK DE L'UNGAVA *p1118*
GD, KUUJJUAQ, QC, J0M 1C0
(819) 964-2905 *SIC* 8051
CHANCELLOR PARK INC *p429*
270 PORTUGAL COVE RD SUITE 219, ST. JOHN'S, NL, A1B 4N6
(709) 754-1165 *SIC* 8051
CHANTELLE MANAGEMENT LTD *p142*
1255 5 AVE S, LETHBRIDGE, AB, T1J 0V6
(403) 328-6631 *SIC* 8051
CHARTWELL RETIREMENT RESIDENCES *p480*
32 MILL ST, AURORA, ON, L4G 2R9
(905) 727-1939 *SIC* 8051
CHARTWELL RETIREMENT RESIDENCES *p708*
590 LOLITA GDNS SUITE 355, MISSISSAUGA, ON, L5A 4N8
(905) 306-9984 *SIC* 8051
CHARTWELL RETIREMENT RESIDENCES *p760*
120 WELLNGTON ST, NIAGARA ON THE LAKE, ON, L0S 1J0
(905) 468-2111 *SIC* 8051
CHRISTIE GARDENS APARTMENTS AND CARE INC *p989*
600 MELITA CRES, TORONTO, ON, M6G 3Z4
(416) 530-1330 *SIC* 8051
CHSLD PROVIDENCE NOTRE-DAME DE LOURDES INC *p1166*
1870 BOUL PIE-IX, MONTREAL, QC, H1V 2C6
(514) 527-4595 *SIC* 8051
CHURCH OF ST. JOHN & ST. STEPHEN HOME INC, THE *p414*
130 UNIVERSITY AVE, SAINT JOHN, NB, E2K 4K3
(506) 643-6001 *SIC* 8051
CIRCLE DRIVE SPECIAL CARE HOME INC *p1435*
3055 PRESTON AVE, SASKATOON, SK, S7T 1C3
(306) 955-4800 *SIC* 8051
CITY CENTRE CARE SOCIETY *p297*
415 PENDER ST W, VANCOUVER, BC, V6B 1V2
(604) 681-9111 *SIC* 8051
CLARION NURSING HOMES LIMITED *p893*
337 HIGHWAY 8, STONEY CREEK, ON, L8G 1E7
(905) 664-2281 *SIC* 8051
COMCARE (CANADA) LIMITED *p456*
7071 BAYERS RD SUITE 1151, HALIFAX, NS, B3L 2C2
(902) 453-0838 *SIC* 8051
COMPLETE CARE INC *p370*
1801 MAIN ST, WINNIPEG, MB, R2V 2A2
(204) 949-5090 *SIC* 8051
CONMED DEVELOPMENTS INC *p591*
4 HAGEY AVE, FORT ERIE, ON, L2A 1W3
(905) 871-8330 *SIC* 8051
CONVALESCENT HOME OF WINNIPEG, THE *p387*
276 HUGO ST N, WINNIPEG, MB, R3M 2N6
(204) 453-4663 *SIC* 8051
COPPER TERRACE LIMITED *p542*
91 TECUMSEH RD, CHATHAM, ON, N7M 1B3
(519) 354-5442 *SIC* 8051
CORPORATION OF NORFOLK COUNTY *p880*
44 ROB BLAKE WAY, SIMCOE, ON, N3Y 0E3
(519) 426-0902 *SIC* 8051

CORPORATION OF THE CITY OF TORONTO *p578*
400 THE WEST MALL, ETOBICOKE, ON, M9C 5S1
(416) 394-3600 *SIC* 8051
CORPORATION OF THE COUNTY OF BRUCE, THE *p1016*
671 FRANK ST, WIARTON, ON, N0H 2T0
(519) 534-1113 *SIC* 8051
CORPORATION OF THE COUNTY OF GREY *p567*
575 SADDLER ST, DURHAM, ON, N0G 1R0
(519) 369-6035 *SIC* 8051
COUNTRY VILLAGE HEALTH CARE CENTRE *p882*
440 COUNTY RD 8 SUITE 8, SOUTH WOODSLEE, ON, N0R 1V0
(519) 839-4812 *SIC* 8051
CRESCENT PARK LODGE *p591*
4 HAGEY AVE, FORT ERIE, ON, L2A 1W3
(905) 871-8330 *SIC* 8051
CROWN RIDGE HEALTH CARE SERVICES INC *p492*
37 WILKIE ST, BELLEVILLE, ON, K8P 4E4
(613) 966-1323 *SIC* 8051
CROWN RIDGE HEALTH CARE SERVICES INC *p998*
106 CROWN ST, TRENTON, ON, K8V 6R3
(613) 392-1289 *SIC* 8051
DALHOUSIE NURSING HOME INC *p397*
296 VICTORIA ST UNIT 1, DALHOUSIE, NB, E8C 2R8
(506) 684-7800 *SIC* 8051
DALLOV HOLDINGS LIMITED *p530*
441 MAPLE AVE, BURLINGTON, ON, L7S 1L8
(905) 639-2264 *SIC* 8051
DARTMOUTH SENIOR CARE SOCIETY *p443*
10 MOUNT HOPE AVE, DARTMOUTH, NS, B2Y 4K1
(902) 469-3702 *SIC* 8051
DEEM MANAGEMENT SERVICES LIMITED *p848*
990 EDWARD ST, PRESCOTT, ON, K0E 1T0
(613) 925-2834 *SIC* 8051
DEEM MANAGEMENT SERVICES LIMITED *p1007*
229 LEXINGTON RD, WATERLOO, ON, N2K 2E1
(519) 772-1026 *SIC* 8051
DELHI NURSING HOME LIMITED *p564*
750 GIBRALTER ST, DELHI, ON, N4B 3B3
(519) 582-3400 *SIC* 8051
DISTRICT MUNICIPALITY OF MUSKOKA, THE *p496*
98 PINE ST SUITE 610, BRACEBRIDGE, ON, P1L 1N5
(705) 645-4488 *SIC* 8051
DIVERSICARE CANADA MANAGEMENT SERVICES CO., INC *p509*
133 KENNEDY RD S, BRAMPTON, ON, L6W 3G3
(905) 459-2324 *SIC* 8051
DIVERSICARE CANADA MANAGEMENT SERVICES CO., INC *p517*
612 MOUNT PLEASANT RD, BRANTFORD, ON, N3T 5L5
(519) 484-2431 *SIC* 8051
DIVERSICARE CANADA MANAGEMENT SERVICES CO., INC *p517*
612 MOUNT PLEASANT RD, BRANTFORD, ON, N3T 5L5
(519) 484-2500 *SIC* 8051
DIVERSICARE CANADA MANAGEMENT SERVICES CO., INC *p621*
263 WONHAM ST S, INGERSOLL, ON, N5C 3P6
(519) 485-3920 *SIC* 8051
DIVERSICARE CANADA MANAGEMENT SERVICES CO., INC *p658*
312 OXFORD ST W, LONDON, ON, N6H 4N7

(519) 432-1855   *SIC* 8051
DIVERSICARE CANADA MANAGEMENT SERVICES CO., INC   *p721*
2121 ARGENTIA RD SUITE 301, MISSISSAUGA, ON, L5N 2X4
(905) 821-1161   *SIC* 8051
DIVERSICARE CANADA MANAGEMENT SERVICES CO., INC   *p775*
5935 BATHURST ST, NORTH YORK, ON, M2R 1Y8
(416) 223-4050   *SIC* 8051
DONWOOD MANOR PERSONAL CARE HOME INC   *p363*
171 DONWOOD DR, WINNIPEG, MB, R2G 0V9
(204) 668-4410   *SIC* 8051
DOWNSVIEW LONG TERM CARE CENTRE *p783*
3595 KEELE ST, NORTH YORK, ON, M3J 1M7
(416) 633-3431   *SIC* 8051
DUNDAS MANOR LTD   *p1016*
533 CLARENCE ST SUITE 970, WINCHESTER, ON, K0C 2K0
(613) 774-2293   *SIC* 8051
EASTERN REGIONAL INTEGRATED HEALTH AUTHORITY   *p423*
1 SENIORS PL, GRAND BANK, NL, A0E 1W0
(709) 832-1660   *SIC* 8051
EASTERN REGIONAL INTEGRATED HEALTH AUTHORITY   *p427*
1 CORRIGAN PL, PLACENTIA, NL, A0B 2Y0
(709) 227-2061   *SIC* 8051
EDEN HOUSE CARE FACILITY INC   *p602*
5016 WELLINGTON ROAD 29, GUELPH, ON, N1H 6H8
(519) 856-4622   *SIC* 8051
EDGEWATER GARDENS LONG-TERM CARE CENTRE   *p567*
428 BROAD ST W, DUNNVILLE, ON, N1A 1T3
(905) 774-2503   *SIC* 8051
ELM GROVE LIVING CENTRE INC   *p991*
35 ELM GROVE AVE SUITE 209, TORONTO, ON, M6K 2J2
(416) 537-2465   *SIC* 8051
EVERGREEN BAPTIST HOME   *p343*
1550 OXFORD ST, WHITE ROCK, BC, V4B 3R5
(604) 536-3344   *SIC* 8051
EXTENDICARE (CANADA) INC   *p8*
2611 37 AVE NE UNIT 7, CALGARY, AB, T1Y 5V7
(403) 228-3877   *SIC* 8051
EXTENDICARE (CANADA) INC   *p41*
1512 8 AVE NW, CALGARY, AB, T2N 1C1
(403) 289-0236   *SIC* 8051
EXTENDICARE (CANADA) INC   *p112*
8008 95 AVE NW, EDMONTON, AB, T6C 2T1
(780) 469-1307   *SIC* 8051
EXTENDICARE (CANADA) INC   *p127*
654 29TH ST, FORT MACLEOD, AB, T0L 0Z0
(403) 553-3955   *SIC* 8051
EXTENDICARE (CANADA) INC   *p139*
4309 50 ST, LEDUC, AB, T9E 6K6
(780) 986-2245   *SIC* 8051
EXTENDICARE (CANADA) INC   *p388*
2060 CORYDON AVE, WINNIPEG, MB, R3P 0N3
(204) 889-2650   *SIC* 8051
EXTENDICARE (CANADA) INC   *p563*
812 PITT ST SUITE 16, CORNWALL, ON, K6J 5R1
(613) 932-4661   *SIC* 8051
EXTENDICARE (CANADA) INC   *p572*
56 ABERFOYLE CRES, ETOBICOKE, ON, M8X 2W4
(416) 236-1061   *SIC* 8051
EXTENDICARE (CANADA) INC   *p615*
883 UPPER WENTWORTH ST SUITE 301,

HAMILTON, ON, L9A 4Y6
(905) 318-8522   *SIC* 8051
EXTENDICARE (CANADA) INC   *p616*
90 CHEDMAC DR SUITE 2317, HAMILTON, ON, L9C 7W1
(905) 318-4472   *SIC* 8051
EXTENDICARE (CANADA) INC   *p632*
309 QUEEN MARY RD, KINGSTON, ON, K7M 6P4
(613) 549-5010   *SIC* 8051
EXTENDICARE (CANADA) INC   *p633*
786 BLACKBURN MEWS, KINGSTON, ON, K7P 2N7
(613) 549-0112   *SIC* 8051
EXTENDICARE (CANADA) INC   *p646*
108 ANGELINE ST S SUITE 1, LINDSAY, ON, K9V 3L5
(705) 328-2280   *SIC* 8051
EXTENDICARE (CANADA) INC   *p670*
3000 STEELES AVE E SUITE 700, MARKHAM, ON, L3R 9W2
(905) 470-1400   *SIC* 8051
EXTENDICARE (CANADA) INC   *p755*
320 HARRY WALKER PKY N SUITE 11, NEWMARKET, ON, L3Y 7B4
SIC 8051
EXTENDICARE (CANADA) INC   *p761*
509 GLENDALE AVE SUITE 200, NIAGARA ON THE LAKE, ON, L0S 1J0
(905) 682-6555   *SIC* 8051
EXTENDICARE (CANADA) INC   *p763*
222 MCINTYRE ST W SUITE 202, NORTH BAY, ON, P1B 2Y8
(705) 495-4391   *SIC* 8051
EXTENDICARE (CANADA) INC   *p769*
550 CUMMER AVE, NORTH YORK, ON, M2K 2M2
(416) 226-1331   *SIC* 8051
EXTENDICARE (CANADA) INC   *p796*
124 LLOYD ST RR 1, NORTHBROOK, ON, K0H 2G0
(613) 336-9120   *SIC* 8051
EXTENDICARE (CANADA) INC   *p802*
700 DORVAL DR SUITE 111, OAKVILLE, ON, L6K 3V3
(905) 847-1025   *SIC* 8051
EXTENDICARE (CANADA) INC   *p840*
80 ALEXANDER AVE, PETERBOROUGH, ON, K9J 6B4
(705) 743-7552   *SIC* 8051
EXTENDICARE (CANADA) INC   *p866*
3830 LAWRENCE AVE E SUITE 103, SCARBOROUGH, ON, M1G 1R6
(416) 439-1243   *SIC* 8051
EXTENDICARE (CANADA) INC   *p1425*
2225 PRESTON AVE, SASKATOON, SK, S7J 2E7
(306) 374-2242   *SIC* 8051
EXTENDICARE INC   *p72*
3330 8 AVE SW, CALGARY, AB, T3C 0E7
(403) 249-8915   *SIC* 8051
EXTENDICARE INC   *p143*
115 FAIRMONT BLVD S, LETHBRIDGE, AB, T1K 5V2
(403) 320-0120   *SIC* 8051
EXTENDICARE INC   *p145*
4706 54 ST, MAYERTHORPE, AB, T0E 1N0
(780) 786-2211   *SIC* 8051
EXTENDICARE INC   *p155*
12 MICHENER BLVD SUITE 3609, RED DEER, AB, T4P 0M1
(403) 348-0340   *SIC* 8051
EXTENDICARE INC   *p165*
4614 47 AVE, ST PAUL, AB, T0A 3A3
(780) 645-3375   *SIC* 8051
EXTENDICARE INC   *p171*
5020 57TH AVE, VIKING, AB, T0B 4N0
(780) 336-4790   *SIC* 8051
EXTENDICARE INC   *p385*
2395 NESS AVE, WINNIPEG, MB, R3J 1A5
(204) 888-3005   *SIC* 8051
EXTENDICARE INC   *p496*
98 PINE ST SUITE 610, BRACEBRIDGE, ON, P1L 1N5

(705) 645-4488   *SIC* 8051
EXTENDICARE INC   *p496*
264 KING ST E SUITE 306, BOWMANVILLE, ON, L1C 1P9
(905) 623-2553   *SIC* 8051
EXTENDICARE INC   *p545*
130 NEW DENSMORE RD, COBOURG, ON, K9A 5W2
(905) 372-0377   *SIC* 8051
EXTENDICARE INC   *p577*
420 THE EAST MALL, ETOBICOKE, ON, M9B 3Z9
(416) 621-8000   *SIC* 8051
EXTENDICARE INC   *p578*
140 SHERWAY DR, ETOBICOKE, ON, M9C 1A4
(416) 259-2573   *SIC* 8051
EXTENDICARE INC   *p596*
1715 MONTREAL RD, GLOUCESTER, ON, K1J 6N4
(613) 741-5122   *SIC* 8051
EXTENDICARE INC   *p632*
309 QUEEN MARY RD, KINGSTON, ON, K7M 6P4
(613) 549-5010   *SIC* 8051
EXTENDICARE INC   *p643*
19 FRASER ST, LAKEFIELD, ON, K0L 2H0
(705) 652-7112   *SIC* 8051
EXTENDICARE INC   *p646*
125 COLBORNE ST E, LINDSAY, ON, K9V 6J2
(705) 878-5392   *SIC* 8051
EXTENDICARE INC   *p653*
860 WATERLOO ST, LONDON, ON, N6A 3W6
(519) 433-6658   *SIC* 8051
EXTENDICARE INC   *p670*
3000 STEELES AVE E SUITE 103, MARKHAM, ON, L3R 4T9
(905) 470-4000   *SIC* 8051
EXTENDICARE INC   *p769*
550 CUMMER AVE, NORTH YORK, ON, M2K 2M2
(416) 226-1331   *SIC* 8051
EXTENDICARE INC   *p800*
291 REYNOLDS ST SUITE 128, OAKVILLE, ON, L6J 3L5
(905) 849-7766   *SIC* 8051
EXTENDICARE INC   *p831*
2179 ELMIRA DR, OTTAWA, ON, K2C 3S1
(613) 829-3501   *SIC* 8051
EXTENDICARE INC   *p847*
360 CROFT ST SUITE 1124, PORT HOPE, ON, L1A 4K8
(905) 885-1266   *SIC* 8051
EXTENDICARE INC   *p862*
39 VAN DAELE ST, SAULT STE. MARIE, ON, P6B 4V3
(705) 949-7934   *SIC* 8051
EXTENDICARE INC   *p866*
60 GUILDWOOD PKY SUITE 327, SCARBOROUGH, ON, M1E 1N9
(416) 266-7711   *SIC* 8051
EXTENDICARE INC   *p877*
1020 MCNICOLL AVE SUITE 547, SCARBOROUGH, ON, M1W 2J6
(416) 499-2020   *SIC* 8051
EXTENDICARE INC   *p887*
283 PELHAM RD, ST CATHARINES, ON, L2S 1X7
(905) 688-3311   *SIC* 8051
EXTENDICARE INC   *p892*
199 GLOVER RD, STONEY CREEK, ON, L8E 5J2
(905) 643-1795   *SIC* 8051
EXTENDICARE INC   *p898*
281 FALCONBRIDGE RD, SUDBURY, ON, P3A 5K4
(705) 566-7980   *SIC* 8051
EXTENDICARE INC   *p900*
333 YORK ST, SUDBURY, ON, P3E 5J3
(705) 674-4221   *SIC* 8051
EXTENDICARE INC   *p902*
2475 ST. ALPHONSE ST SUITE 1238,

TECUMSEH, ON, N8N 2X2
(519) 739-2998   *SIC* 8051
EXTENDICARE INC   *p1025*
1255 NORTH TALBOT RD, WINDSOR, ON, N9G 3A4
(519) 945-7249   *SIC* 8051
EXTENDICARE INC   *p1411*
1151 COTEAU ST W, MOOSE JAW, SK, S6H 5G5
(306) 693-5191   *SIC* 8051
EXTENDICARE INC   *p1421*
4125 RAE ST, REGINA, SK, S4S 3A5
(306) 586-1787   *SIC* 8051
EXTENDICARE INC   *p1421*
4540 RAE ST, REGINA, SK, S4S 3B4
(306) 586-0220   *SIC* 8051
EXTENDICARE INC   *p1421*
260 SUNSET DR, REGINA, SK, S4S 2S3
(306) 586-3355   *SIC* 8051
FAIRHAVEN HOME   *p839*
881 DUTTON RD, PETERBOROUGH, ON, K9H 7S4
(705) 743-4265   *SIC* 8051
FAIRHAVEN LONG TERM CARE   *p839*
881 DUTTON RD, PETERBOROUGH, ON, K9H 7S4
(705) 743-0881   *SIC* 8051
FENELON COURT LONG TERM CARE CENTRE   *p590*
44 WYCHWOOD CRES, FENELON FALLS, ON, K0M 1N0
(705) 887-2100   *SIC* 8051
FIDDICK'S NURSING HOME LIMITED *p843*
437 1ST AVE, PETROLIA, ON, N0N 1R0
(519) 882-0370   *SIC* 8051
FREDERICTON SOUTH NURSING HOME INC   *p401*
521 WOODSTOCK RD, FREDERICTON, NB, E3B 2J2
(506) 444-3400   *SIC* 8051
GARDEN HOME (1986) INCORPORATED *p1039*
310 NORTH RIVER RD, CHARLOTTETOWN, PE, C1A 3M4
(902) 892-4131   *SIC* 8051
GATEBY CARE FACILITY   *p332*
3000 GATEBY PL, VERNON, BC, V1T 8V8
(250) 545-4456   *SIC* 8051
GATEWAY LODGE INC   *p1405*
212 CENTRE AVE E, CANORA, SK, S0A 0L0
(306) 563-5685   *SIC* 8051
GEM HEALTH CARE GROUP LIMITED *p438*
260 CHURCH ST, AMHERST, NS, B4H 3C9
(902) 667-3501   *SIC* 8051
GEM HEALTH CARE GROUP LIMITED *p458*
15 SHOREHAM LANE SUITE 101, HALIFAX, NS, B3P 2R3
(902) 429-6227   *SIC* 8051
GEM HEALTH CARE GROUP LIMITED *p458*
25 ALTON DR, HALIFAX, NS, B3N 1M1
(902) 477-1777   *SIC* 8051
GEM HEALTH CARE GROUP LIMITED *p849*
470 RAGLAN ST N, RENFREW, ON, K7V 1P5
(613) 432-5823   *SIC* 8051
GENESIS GARDENS INC   *p645*
1003 LIMOGES RD, LIMOGES, ON, K0A 2M0
(613) 443-5751   *SIC* 8051
GEORGE DERBY CARE SOCIETY   *p181*
7550 CUMBERLAND ST, BURNABY, BC, V3N 3X5
(604) 521-2676   *SIC* 8051
GLACIER VIEW LODGE SOCIETY   *p203*
2450 BACK RD, COURTENAY, BC, V9N 8B5
(250) 338-1451   *SIC* 8051
GLEN HAVEN MANOR CORPORATION *p463*
739 EAST RIVER RD, NEW GLASGOW, NS, B2H 5E9
(902) 752-2588   *SIC* 8051
GOLDEN YEARS NURSING HOMES (CAMBRIDGE) INC   *p539*
704 EAGLE ST N, CAMBRIDGE, ON, N3H

1C3

(519) 653-5493   *SIC* 8051

GOUVERNEMENT DE LA PROVINCE DE QUEBEC

105 RUE HERMINE, QUEBEC, QC, G1K 1Y5

(418) 529-2501   *SIC* 8051

GOUVERNEMENT DE LA PROVINCE DE QUEBEC   *p1372*

375 RUE ARGYLL, SHERBROOKE, QC, J1J 3H5

(819) 821-1170   *SIC* 8051

GOVERNING COUNCIL OF THE SALVATION ARMY IN CANADA, THE   *p339*

952 ARM ST, VICTORIA, BC, V9A 4G7

(250) 385-3422   *SIC* 8051

GOVERNING COUNCIL OF THE SALVATION ARMY IN CANADA, THE   *p346*

510 6TH ST, BRANDON, MB, R7A 3N9

(204) 727-3636   *SIC* 8051

GOVERNING COUNCIL OF THE SALVATION ARMY IN CANADA, THE   *p757*

5050 JEPSON ST, NIAGARA FALLS, ON, L2E 1K5

(905) 356-1221   *SIC* 8051

GOVERNING COUNCIL OF THE SALVATION ARMY IN CANADA, THE   *p828*

1156 WELLINGTON ST W SUITE 613, OTTAWA, ON, K1Y 2Z3

(613) 722-8025   *SIC* 8051

GRAY HOUSE GUILD, THE   *p120*

5005 28 AVE NW, EDMONTON, AB, T6L 7G1

(780) 469-2371   *SIC* 8051

GREY GABLES   *p665*

206 TORONTO ST S, MARKDALE, ON, N0C 1H0

(519) 986-3010   *SIC* 8051

GROUPE ROY SANTE INC   *p1051*

7351 AV JEAN-DESPREZ BUREAU 103, ANJOU, QC, H1K 5A6

(514) 493-9397   *SIC* 8051

GROVE PARK HOME FOR SENIOR CITIZENS   *p484*

234 COOK ST SUITE 1274, BARRIE, ON, L4M 4H5

(705) 726-1003   *SIC* 8051

HANTS COUNTY RESIDENCE FOR SENIOR CITIZENS   *p470*

124 COTTAGE ST, WINDSOR, NS, B0N 2T0

(902) 798-8346   *SIC* 8051

HARDISTY NURSING HOME INC   *p107*

6420 101 AVE NW, EDMONTON, AB, T6A 0H5

(780) 466-9267   *SIC* 8051

HAVRE COMMUNAUTAIRE INC, LE   *p411*

17 COMMERCIALE, RICHIBUCTO, NB, E4W 3X5

(506) 523-6790   *SIC* 8051

HENLEY HOUSE LTD, THE   *p884*

20 ERNEST ST SUITE 2045, ST CATHARINES, ON, L2N 7T2

(905) 937-9703   *SIC* 8051

HERITAGE NURSING HOMES INC   *p920*

1195 QUEEN ST E SUITE 229, TORONTO, ON, M4M 1L6

SIC 8051

HIGH-CREST ENTERPRISES LIMITED *p466*

11 SPROUL ST, SPRINGHILL, NS, B0M 1X0

(902) 597-2797   *SIC* 8051

HILLCREST PLACE HOLDINGS LTD   *p347*

930 26TH ST SUITE 104, BRANDON, MB, R7B 2B8

(204) 728-6690   *SIC* 8051

HILLSIDE PINES HOME FOR SPECIAL CARE SOCIETY   *p441*

77 EXHIBITION DR, BRIDGEWATER, NS, B4V 3K6

(902) 543-1525   *SIC* 8051

HOLLAND CHRISTIAN HOMES INC   *p511*

7900 MCLAUGHLIN RD, BRAMPTON, ON, L6Y 5A7

(905) 463-7002   *SIC* 8051

HOPITAL CHINOIS DE MONTREAL (1963) INC, L'   *p1185*

189 AV VIGER E, MONTREAL, QC, H2X 3Y9

(514) 875-9120   *SIC* 8051

HUNTSVILLE DISTRICT NURSING HOME INC   *p620*

14 MILL ST SUITE 101, HUNTSVILLE, ON, P1H 2A4

(705) 789-4476   *SIC* 8051

HURONVIEW HOME FOR THE AGED   *p544*

77722A LONDON RD RR 5, CLINTON, ON, N0M 1L0

(519) 482-3451   *SIC* 8051

ICAN INDEPENDENCE CENTRE AND NETWORK   *p900*

765 BRENNAN RD, SUDBURY, ON, P3C 1C4

(705) 673-0655   *SIC* 8051

INTERIOR HEALTH AUTHORITY   *p222*

2255 ETHEL ST, KELOWNA, BC, V1Y 2Z9

(250) 862-4100   *SIC* 8051

INTERLAKE REGIONAL HEALTH AUTHORITY INC   *p345*

233 ST PHILLIPS DR, ARBORG, MB, R0C 0A0

(204) 376-5226   *SIC* 8051

INVERNESS MUNICIPAL HOUSING CORPORATION   *p442*

15092 CABOT TRAIL RD, CHETICAMP, NS, B0E 1H0

(902) 224-2087   *SIC* 8051

INVERNESS MUNICIPAL HOUSING CORPORATION   *p459*

72 MAPLE ST, INVERNESS, NS, B0E 1N0

(902) 258-2842   *SIC* 8051

JARLETTE LTD   *p542*

110 SANDYS ST, CHATHAM, ON, N7L 4X3

(519) 351-1330   *SIC* 8051

JARLETTE LTD   *p607*

100 BRUCE ST, HAILEYBURY, ON, P0J 1K0

(705) 672-2123   *SIC* 8051

JARLETTE LTD   *p620*

65 ROGERS COVE DR, HUNTSVILLE, ON, P1H 2L9

(705) 788-7713   *SIC* 8051

JARLETTE LTD   *p809*

25 MUSEUM DR SUITE 204, ORILLIA, ON, L3V 7T9

(705) 325-9181   *SIC* 8051

JARLETTE LTD   *p1005*

329 PARKSIDE DR E, WATERDOWN, ON, L0R 2H0

(905) 689-2662   *SIC* 8051

JBG MANAGEMENT INC   *p481*

28 MILL ST, AURORA, ON, L4G 2R9

SIC 8051

JEWISH HOME FOR THE AGED OF BRITISH COLUMBIA   *p322*

1055 41ST AVE W, VANCOUVER, BC, V6M 1W9

(604) 261-9376   *SIC* 8051

JUBILEE LODGE NURSING HOME LTD *p107*

10333 76 ST NW, EDMONTON, AB, T6A 3A8

(780) 469-4456   *SIC* 8051

JUBILEE RESIDENCES INC   *p1431*

833 AVENUE P N, SASKATOON, SK, S7L 2W5

(306) 382-2626   *SIC* 8051

KANNAMPUZHA HOLDINGS LTD   *p902*

160 HIGH ST, SUTTON WEST, ON, L0E 1R0

(905) 722-3631   *SIC* 8051

KELSEY TRAIL REGIONAL HEALTH AUTHORITY   *p1412*

400 6TH AVE E, NIPAWIN, SK, S0E 1E0

(306) 862-9828   *SIC* 8051

KENNEBEC MANOR INC   *p414*

475 WOODWARD AVE, SAINT JOHN, NB, E2K 4N1

(506) 632-9628   *SIC* 8051

KENNETH E. SPENCER MEMORIAL HOME INC, THE   *p408*

35 ATLANTIC BAPTIST AVE, MONCTON, NB, E1E 4N3

(506) 858-7870   *SIC* 8051

KING NURSING HOME LIMITED   *p495*

49 STERNE ST, BOLTON, ON, L7E 1B9

(905) 857-4117   *SIC* 8051

KINGS COUNTY SENIOR CITIZENS HOME CORP   *p441*

110A COMMERCIAL ST RR 1, BERWICK, NS, B0P 1E0

(902) 538-3118   *SIC* 8051

KINGSWAY LODGE ST. MARYS LTD   *p888*

310 QUEEN ST E, ST MARYS, ON, N4X 1C8

(519) 284-2921   *SIC* 8051

KIWANIS CARE SOCIETY (1979) OF NEW WESTMINSTER   *p236*

35 CLUTE ST, NEW WESTMINSTER, BC, V3L 1Z5

(604) 525-6471   *SIC* 8051

KIWANIS NURSING HOME INC   *p418*

11 BRYANT DR, SUSSEX, NB, E4E 2P3

(506) 432-3118   *SIC* 8051

KIWANIS VILLAGE LODGE   *p234*

1221 KIWANIS CRES, NANAIMO, BC, V9S 5Y1

(250) 753-6471   *SIC* 8051

KRISTUS DARZS LATVIAN HOME   *p1032*

11290 PINE VALLEY DR, WOODBRIDGE, ON, L4L 1A6

(905) 832-3300   *SIC* 8051

LABDARA LITHUANIAN NURSING HOME *p576*

5 RESURRECTION RD, ETOBICOKE, ON, M9A 5G1

(416) 232-2112   *SIC* 8051

LADY ISABELLE NURSING HOME LTD *p999*

102 CORKERY ST, TROUT CREEK, ON, P0H 2L0

(705) 723-5232   *SIC* 8051

LANGLEY CARE SOCIETY   *p228*

5451 204 ST, LANGLEY, BC, V3A 5M9

(604) 530-2305   *SIC* 8051

LAPOINTE-FISHER NURSING HOME, LIMITED   *p600*

271 METCALFE ST, GUELPH, ON, N1E 4Y8

(519) 821-9030   *SIC* 8051

LAPOINTE-FISHER NURSING HOME, LIMITED   *p1005*

1934 DUFFERIN AVE, WALLACEBURG, ON, N8A 4M2

(519) 627-1663   *SIC* 8051

LEE MANOR HOME FOR THE AGED *p835*

875 6TH ST E, OWEN SOUND, ON, N4K 5W5

(519) 376-4420   *SIC* 8051

LINCOURT MANOR INC   *p418*

1 CHIPMAN ST, ST STEPHEN, NB, E3L 2W9

(506) 466-7855   *SIC* 8051

LITTLE MOUNTAIN RESIDENTIAL CARE & HOUSING SOCIETY   *p284*

851 BOUNDARY RD, VANCOUVER, BC, V5K 4T2

(604) 299-7567   *SIC* 8051

LITTLE MOUNTAIN RESIDENTIAL CARE & HOUSING SOCIETY   *p290*

330 36TH AVE E, VANCOUVER, BC, V5W 3Z4

(604) 325-2298   *SIC* 8051

LOCH LOMOND VILLA INC   *p413*

185 LOCH LOMOND RD, SAINT JOHN, NB, E2J 3S3

(506) 643-7175   *SIC* 8051

LUNENBURG HOME FOR SPECIAL CARE CORP   *p462*

25 BLOCKHOUSE HILL RD, LUNENBURG, NS, B0J 2C0

(902) 634-8836   *SIC* 8051

LUTHER COURT SOCIETY   *p333*

1525 CEDAR HILL CROSS RD, VICTORIA,

BC, V8P 5M1

(250) 477-7241   *SIC* 8051

LUTHERAN HOMES KITCHENER-WATERLOO   *p636*

2727 KINGSWAY DR SUITE 227, KITCHENER, ON, N2C 1A7

(519) 893-6320   *SIC* 8051

LUTHERN SENIOR CITIZEN HOUSING SOCIETY   *p272*

5939 180 ST, SURREY, BC, V3S 4L2

(604) 576-2891   *SIC* 8051

MACGILLIVRAY, R.C. GUEST HOME SOCIETY   *p467*

25 XAVIER DR, SYDNEY, NS, B1S 2R9

(902) 539-6110   *SIC* 8051

MANITOBA BAPTIST HOME SOCIETY INC *p368*

577 ST ANNE'S RD, WINNIPEG, MB, R2M 3G5

(204) 257-2394   *SIC* 8051

MANORCARE PARTNERS   *p890*

218 EDWARD ST, STIRLING, ON, K0K 3E0

(613) 395-2596   *SIC* 8051

MAPLE HILL MANOR SOCIETY INC   *p464*

700 KING ST, NEW WATERFORD, NS, B1H 3Z5

(902) 862-6495   *SIC* 8051

MAPLES PERSONAL CARE HOME (1982) LTD   *p369*

500 MANDALAY DR, WINNIPEG, MB, R2P 1V4

(204) 632-8570   *SIC* 8051

MAPLEWOOD NURSING HOME LIMITED *p912*

73 BIDWELL ST, TILLSONBURG, ON, N4G 3T8

(519) 842-3563   *SIC* 8051

MARIANN NURSING HOME AND RESIDENCE   *p855*

9915 YONGE ST, RICHMOND HILL, ON, L4C 1V1

(905) 884-9276   *SIC* 8051

MARTINO NURSING CENTRES LIMITED *p614*

39 MARY ST, HAMILTON, ON, L8R 3L8

(905) 523-6427   *SIC* 8051

MAXVILLE MANOR   *p680*

80 MECHANIC ST W SUITE 620, MAXVILLE, ON, K0C 1T0

(613) 527-2170   *SIC* 8051

MEADOW PARK (LONDON) INC   *p657*

1210 SOUTHDALE RD E SUITE 9, LONDON, ON, N6E 1B4

(519) 686-0484   *SIC* 8051

MEAFORD NURSING HOME LTD   *p681*

135 WILLIAM ST, MEAFORD, ON, N4L 1T4

(519) 538-1010   *SIC* 8051

MELVILLE LODGE LIMITED PARTNERSHIP *p458*

50 SHOREHAM LANE, HALIFAX, NS, B3P 2R3

(902) 479-1030   *SIC* 8051

MENNONITE INTERMEDIATE CARE HOME SOCIETY OF RICHMOND   *p261*

11331 MELLIS DR, RICHMOND, BC, V6X 1L8

(604) 278-1296   *SIC* 8051

MENNONITE NURSING HOMES INCORPORATED   *p1423*

GD, ROSTHERN, SK, S0K 3R0

(306) 232-4861   *SIC* 8051

MIDDLECHURCH HOME OF WINNIPEG INC *p360*

280 BALDERSTONE RD, WEST ST PAUL, MB, R4A 4A6

(204) 339-1947   *SIC* 8051

MILL COVE NURSING HOME INC   *p405*

5647 ROUTE 105, MILL COVE, NB, E4C 3A5

SIC 8051

MIRAMICHI LODGE   *p838*

725 PEMBROKE ST W SUITE 735, PEMBROKE, ON, K8A 8S6

(613) 735-0175   *SIC* 8051

MIRAMICHI SENIOR CITIZENS HOME INC p405
1400 WATER ST, MIRAMICHI, NB, E1N 1A4
(506) 778-6810   *SIC* 8051
MON SHEONG FOUNDATION   p876
2030 MCNICOLL AVE, SCARBOROUGH, ON, M1V 5P4
(416) 291-3898   *SIC* 8051
MONT ST. JOSEPH HOME INC   p1414
777 28TH ST E, PRINCE ALBERT, SK, S6V 8C2
(306) 953-4500   *SIC* 8051
MOUNT SAINT JOSEPH NURSING HOME p405
51 LOBBAN AVE, MIRAMICHI, NB, E1N 2W8
(506) 622-5091   *SIC* 8051
NORTH CENTENNIAL MANOR INC   p627
2 KIMBERLY DR, KAPUSKASING, ON, P5N 1L5
(705) 335-6125   *SIC* 8051
NORTH PARK NURSING HOME LIMITED p791
450 RUSTIC RD, NORTH YORK, ON, M6L 1W9
(416) 247-0531   *SIC* 8051
NORTH SHORE PRIVATE HOSPITAL (1985) LTD   p239
1070 LYNN VALLEY RD SUITE 321, NORTH VANCOUVER, BC, V7J 1Z8
(604) 988-4181   *SIC* 8051
NORTHCREST CARE CENTRE LTD   p208
6771 120 ST, DELTA, BC, V4E 2A7
(604) 597-7878   *SIC* 8051
NORTHSIDE COMMUNITY GUEST HOME SOCIETY   p464
11 QUEEN ST, NORTH SYDNEY, NS, B2A 1A2
(902) 794-4733   *SIC* 8051
NUCLEUS INDEPENDENT LIVING   p798
3030 BRISTOL CIR SUITE 110, OAKVILLE, ON, L6H 0H2
(905) 829-0555   *SIC* 8051
OAKWOOD PARK LODGE   p759
6747 OAKWOOD DR, NIAGARA FALLS, ON, L2G 0J3
(905) 356-8732   *SIC* 8051
OCEAN VIEW MANOR SOCIETY   p449
1909 CALDWELL RD, EASTERN PASSAGE, NS, B3G 1M4
SIC 8051
ODD FELLOWS & REBEKAHS PERSONAL CARE HOMES INC   p368
2280 ST MARY'S RD, WINNIPEG, MB, R2N 3Z6
(204) 257-9947   *SIC* 8051
OMNI HEALTH CARE LIMITED PARTNERSHIP   p840
1155 WATER ST, PETERBOROUGH, ON, K9H 3P8
(705) 748-6706   *SIC* 8051
OMNI HEALTH CARE LTD   p481
13837 YONGE ST, AURORA, ON, L4G 0N9
(905) 727-0128   *SIC* 8051
OMNI HEALTH CARE LTD   p625
6501 CAMPEAU DR SUITE 353, KANATA, ON, K2K 3E9
(613) 599-1991   *SIC* 8051
OMNI HEALTH CARE LTD   p625
100 AIRD PL, KANATA, ON, K2L 4H8
(613) 254-9702   *SIC* 8051
OMNI HEALTH CARE LTD   p662
30 MILLE ROCHES RD SUITE 388, LONG SAULT, ON, K0C 1P0
(613) 534-2276   *SIC* 8051
OMNI HEALTH CARE LTD   p841
2020 FISHER DR, PETERBOROUGH, ON, K9J 6X6
(705) 742-8811   *SIC* 8051
OMNI HEALTH CARE LTD   p841
2020 FISHER DR SUITE 1, PETERBOROUGH, ON, K9J 6X6
(705) 748-6631   *SIC* 8051
OMNI HEALTH COUNTRY TERRACE NURS-

ING HOME   p643
10072 OXBOW DR, KOMOKA, ON, N0L 1R0
(519) 657-2955   *SIC* 8051
OUTLOOK & DISTRICT PIONEER HOME INC   p1413
500 SEMPLE ST, OUTLOOK, SK, S0L 2N0
(306) 867-8676   *SIC* 8051
PALMETER'S COUNTRY HOME (1986) LTD p460
655 PARK ST, KENTVILLE, NS, B4N 3V7
(902) 678-7355   *SIC* 8051
PARK LANE TERRACE LIMITED   p837
295 GRAND RIVER ST N, PARIS, ON, N3L 2N9
(519) 442-2753   *SIC* 8051
PARK PLACE SENIORS LIVING INC   p270
13525 HILTON RD, SURREY, BC, V3R 5J3
(604) 588-3424   *SIC* 8051
PARKVIEW HEALTH CARE PARTNERSHIP p613
545 KING ST W SUITE 412, HAMILTON, ON, L8P 1C1
(905) 525-5903   *SIC* 8051
PARKWOOD MENNONITE HOME INC p1007
726 NEW HAMPSHIRE ST, WATERLOO, ON, N2K 4M1
(519) 885-4810   *SIC* 8051
PEOPLE CARE CENTRES INC   p902
28 WILLIAM ST N, TAVISTOCK, ON, N0B 2R0
(519) 655-2031   *SIC* 8051
PICTON MANOR NURSING HOME LIMITED p845
9 HILL ST, PICTON, ON, K0K 2T0
SIC 8051
PLEASANT VIEW HOUSING SOCIETY 1980 p232
7540 HURD ST UNIT 101, MISSION, BC, V2V 3H9
(604) 826-2176   *SIC* 8051
POINTS WEST LIVING GP INC   p133
11460 104 AVE SUITE 403, GRANDE PRAIRIE, AB, T8V 3G9
(780) 357-5700   *SIC* 8051
PR SENIORS HOUSING MANAGEMENT LTD   p287
1880 RENFREW ST, VANCOUVER, BC, V5M 3H9
(604) 255-7723   *SIC* 8051
PROVIDENCE CARE CENTRE   p631
340 UNION ST, KINGSTON, ON, K7L 5A2
(613) 548-7222   *SIC* 8051
PROVINCE OF PEI   p1040
200 BEACH GROVE RD, CHARLOTTETOWN, PE, C1E 1L3
(902) 368-6750   *SIC* 8051
PROVINCE OF PEI   p1042
20 MACPHEE AVE, SOURIS, PE, C0A 2B0
(902) 687-7090   *SIC* 8051
PROVINCIAL LONG TERM CARE INC p620
100 QUEEN ST E, HENSALL, ON, N0M 1X0
(519) 262-2830   *SIC* 8051
PROVINCIAL NURSING HOME LIMITED PARTNERSHIP   p879
100 JAMES ST, SEAFORTH, ON, N0K 1W0
(519) 527-0030   *SIC* 8051
QUALICARE HEALTH SERVICES CORPORATION   p166
25 ERIN RIDGE RD, ST. ALBERT, AB, T8N 7K8
(780) 458-3044   *SIC* 8051
R.K. MACDONALD NURSING HOME CORPORATION   p438
64 PLEASANT ST, ANTIGONISH, NS, B2G 1W7
(902) 863-2578   *SIC* 8051
REGIONAL HEALTH AUTHORITY NB p401
700 PRIESTMAN ST, FREDERICTON, NB, E3B 3B7
(506) 452-5800   *SIC* 8051
REGIONAL MUNICIPALITY OF NIAGARA, THE   p760
6623 KALAR RD SUITE 312, NIAGARA

FALLS, ON, L2H 2T3
(905) 357-1911   *SIC* 8051
REGIONAL MUNICIPALITY OF PEEL, THE p714,
2460 TRUSCOTT DR, MISSISSAUGA, ON, L5J 3Z8
(905) 791-8668   *SIC* 8051
REGIONAL MUNICIPALITY OF YORK, THE p756
194 EAGLE ST SUITE 3011, NEWMARKET, ON, L3Y 1J6
(905) 895-2382   *SIC* 8051
RESIDENCE BERTHIAUME-DU TREMBLAY p1171
1635 BOUL GOUIN E, MONTREAL, QC, H2C 1C2
(514) 381-1841   *SIC* 8051
RESIDENCES MGR CHIASSON INC, LES p418
130J BOUL J D GAUTHIER, SHIPPAGAN, NB, E8S 1N8
(506) 336-3266   *SIC* 8051
REST HAVEN NURSING HOME OF STEINBACH INC   p358
185 WOODHAVEN AVE SUITE 175, STEINBACH, MB, R5G 1K7
(204) 326-2206   *SIC* 8051
REVERA INC   p71
80 PROMENADE WAY SE, CALGARY, AB, T2Z 4G4
(403) 508-9808   *SIC* 8051
REVERA INC   p72
5927 BOWNESS RD NW, CALGARY, AB, T3B 0C7
(403) 288-2373   *SIC* 8051
REVERA INC   p98
8903 168 ST NW, EDMONTON, AB, T5R 2V6
(780) 489-4931   *SIC* 8051
REVERA INC   p146
603 PROSPECT DR SW, MEDICINE HAT, AB, T1A 4C2
(403) 527-5531   *SIC* 8051
REVERA INC   p322
4505 VALLEY DR, VANCOUVER, BC, V6L 2L1
(604) 261-4292   *SIC* 8051
REVERA INC   p348
3015 VICTORIA AVE SUITE 219, BRANDON, MB, R7B 2K2
(204) 728-2030   *SIC* 8051
REVERA INC   p386
3555 PORTAGE AVE, WINNIPEG, MB, R3K 0X2
(204) 888-7940   *SIC* 8051
REVERA INC   p388
70 POSEIDON BAY SUITE 504, WINNIPEG, MB, R3M 3E5
(204) 452-6204   *SIC* 8051
REVERA INC   p534
614 CORONATION BLVD SUITE 200, CAMBRIDGE, ON, N1R 3E8
(519) 622-1840   *SIC* 8051
REVERA INC   p570
111 ILER AVE SUITE 1, ESSEX, ON, N8M 1T6
(519) 776-5243   *SIC* 8051
REVERA INC   p628
237 LAKEVIEW DR, KENORA, ON, P9N 4J7
(807) 468-9532   *SIC* 8051
REVERA INC   p700
5015 SPECTRUM WAY SUITE 600, MISSISSAUGA, ON, L4W 0E4
(289) 360-1252   *SIC* 8051
REVERA INC   p780
8 THE DONWAY E SUITE 557, NORTH YORK, ON, M3C 3R7
(416) 445-7555   *SIC* 8051
REVERA INC   p810
291 MISSISSAGA ST W SUITE 106, ORILLIA, ON, L3V 3B9
(705) 325-2289   *SIC* 8051
REVERA INC   p857

9 MYRTLE ST, RIDGETOWN, ON, N0P 2C0
(519) 674-5427   *SIC* 8051
REVERA INC   p905
7700 BAYVIEW AVE SUITE 518, THORNHILL, ON, L3T 5W1
(905) 881-9475   *SIC* 8051
REVERA INC   p972
645 CASTLEFIELD AVE SUITE 716, TORONTO, ON, M5N 3A5
(416) 785-1511   *SIC* 8051
REVERA INC   p993
1 NORTHWESTERN AVE, TORONTO, ON, M6M 2J7
(416) 654-2889   *SIC* 8051
REVERA INC   p1083
5885 BOUL CAVENDISH BUREAU 202, COTE SAINT-LUC, QC, H4W 3H4
(514) 485-5994   *SIC* 8051
REVERA INC   p1322
33 AV ARGYLE, SAINT-LAMBERT, QC, J4P 3P5
(450) 465-1401   *SIC* 8051
REVERA INC   p1397
GD SUCC BUREAU-CHEF, VERDUN, QC, H4G 3C9
SIC 8051
REVERA LONG TERM CARE INC   p83
14251 50 ST NW, EDMONTON, AB, T5A 5J4
(780) 478-9212   *SIC* 8051
REVERA LONG TERM CARE INC   p287
3490 PORTER ST, VANCOUVER, BC, V5N 5W4
(604) 874-2803   *SIC* 8051
REVERA LONG TERM CARE INC   p493
10 MARY ST, BLENHEIM, ON, N0P 1A0
(519) 676-8119   *SIC* 8051
REVERA LONG TERM CARE INC   p515
425 PARK RD N, BRANTFORD, ON, N3R 7G5
(519) 759-1040   *SIC* 8051
REVERA LONG TERM CARE INC   p534
650 CORONATION BLVD, CAMBRIDGE, ON, N1R 7S6
(519) 740-3820   *SIC* 8051
REVERA LONG TERM CARE INC   p535
200 STIRLING MACGREGOR DR, CAMBRIDGE, ON, N1S 5B7
(519) 622-3434   *SIC* 8051
REVERA LONG TERM CARE INC   p537
600 JAMIESON PKY, CAMBRIDGE, ON, N3C 0A6
(519) 622-1840   *SIC* 8051
REVERA LONG TERM CARE INC   p540
256 HIGH ST, CARLETON PLACE, ON, K7C 1X1
(613) 257-4355   *SIC* 8051
REVERA LONG TERM CARE INC   p612
330 MAIN ST E, HAMILTON, ON, L8N 3T9
(905) 523-1604   *SIC* 8051
REVERA LONG TERM CARE INC   p629
550 PHILIP PL, KINCARDINE, ON, N2Z 3A6
(519) 396-4400   *SIC* 8051
REVERA LONG TERM CARE INC   p641
60 WESTHEIGHTS DR, KITCHENER, ON, N2N 2A8
(519) 576-3320   *SIC* 8051
REVERA LONG TERM CARE INC   p659
46 ELMWOOD PL, LONDON, ON, N6J 1J2
(519) 433-7259   *SIC* 8051
REVERA LONG TERM CARE INC   p814
186 THORNTON RD S SUITE 1103, OSHAWA, ON, L1J 5Y2
(905) 576-5181   *SIC* 8051
REVERA LONG TERM CARE INC   p830
2330 CARLING AVE, OTTAWA, ON, K2B 7H1
(613) 820-9328   *SIC* 8051
REVERA LONG TERM CARE INC   p836
850 4TH ST E, OWEN SOUND, ON, N4K 6A3
(519) 376-3213   *SIC* 8051
REVERA LONG TERM CARE INC   p845
13628 LOYALIST PKY, PICTON, ON, K0K

2T0
(613) 476-4444   SIC 8051

REVERA LONG TERM CARE INC   p847
501 ST GEORGE ST, PORT DOVER, ON,
N0A 1N0
(519) 583-1422   SIC 8051

REVERA LONG TERM CARE INC   p857
182 YORKLAND ST SUITE 1, RICHMOND
HILL, ON, L4S 2M9
(905) 737-0858   SIC 8051

REVERA LONG TERM CARE INC   p858
1464 BLACKWELL RD, SARNIA, ON, N7S
5M4
(519) 542-3421   SIC 8051

REVERA LONG TERM CARE INC   p872
1400 KENNEDY RD, SCARBOROUGH, ON,
M1P 4V6
(416) 752-8282   SIC 8051

REVERA LONG TERM CARE INC   p884
168 SCOTT ST, ST CATHARINES, ON, L2N
1H2
(905) 934-3321   SIC 8051

REVERA LONG TERM CARE INC   p894
385 HIGHLAND RD W, STONEY CREEK,
ON, L8J 3X9
(905) 561-3332   SIC 8051

REVERA LONG TERM CARE INC   p896
5066 LINE 34 SUITE 8, STRATFORD, ON,
N5A 6S6
(519) 393-5132   SIC 8051

REVERA LONG TERM CARE INC   p917
77 MAIN ST, TORONTO, ON, M4E 2V6
(416) 690-3001   SIC 8051

REVERA LONG TERM CARE INC   p1001
130 REACH ST SUITE 25, UXBRIDGE, ON,
L9P 1L3
(905) 852-5191   SIC 8051

**RICHMOND INTERMEDIATE CARE SOCI-
ETY**   p266
6260 BLUNDELL RD, RICHMOND, BC, V7C
5C4
(604) 271-3590   SIC 8051

**RIVERCREST LODGE NURSING HOME
LTD**   p130
10104 101 AVE, FORT SASKATCHEWAN,
AB, T8L 2A5
(780) 998-2425   SIC 8051

RIVERVIEW HEALTH CENTRE INC   p387
1 MORLEY AVE, WINNIPEG, MB, R3L 2P4
(204) 478-6203   SIC 8051

ROYAL ARCH MASONIC HOMES SOCIETY   p288
7850 CHAMPLAIN CRES SUITE 252, VAN-
COUVER, BC, V5S 4C7
(604) 437-7343   SIC 8051

RUNNYMEDE HEALTHCARE CENTRE p995
625 RUNNYMEDE RD, TORONTO, ON,
M6S 3A3
(416) 762-7316   SIC 8051

SAINT LUKE'S PLACE   p537
1624 FRANKLIN BLVD, CAMBRIDGE, ON,
N3C 3P4
(519) 658-5183   SIC 8051

SALEM HOME INC   p361
165 15TH ST, WINKLER, MB, R6W 1T8
(204) 325-4316   SIC 8051

SALEM MANOR SOCIETY, THE   p139
4419 46 ST SUITE 612, LEDUC, AB, T9E
6L2
(780) 986-8654   SIC 8051

**SALVATION ARMY TORONTO GRACE
HEALTH CENTER, THE**   p932
650 CHURCH ST, TORONTO, ON, M4Y
2G5
(416) 925-2251   SIC 8051

SASKATCHEWAN HEALTH AUTHORITY
p1408
1003 1ST ST W RR 2, KINDERSLEY, SK,
S0L 1S2
SIC 8051

SASKATCHEWAN HEALTH AUTHORITY
p1411
1000 ALBERT ST, MOOSE JAW, SK, S6H
2Y2

(306) 693-4616   SIC 8051

SASKATOON CONVALESCENT HOME
p1432
101 31ST ST W, SASKATOON, SK, S7L 0P6
(306) 244-7155   SIC 8051

SAUGEEN VALLEY NURSING CENTER LTD
p746
465 DUBLIN ST, MOUNT FOREST, ON,
N0G 2L3
(519) 323-2140   SIC 8051

SCHLEGEL VILLAGES INC   p616
1620 UPPER WENTWORTH ST, HAMIL-
TON, ON, L9B 2W3
(905) 575-4735   SIC 8051

SEAVIEW MANOR CORPORATION   p450
275 SOUTH ST, GLACE BAY, NS, B1A 1W6
(902) 849-7300   SIC 8051

**SENIORS HEALTH CENTRE OF NORTH
YORK GENERAL HOSPITAL**   p768
2 BUCHAN CRT, NORTH YORK, ON, M2J
5A3
(416) 756-1040   SIC 8051

SEVEN OAKS HOMES INC   p866
9 NEILSON RD, SCARBOROUGH, ON,
M1E 5E1
(416) 392-3500   SIC 8051

**SHALOM MANOR LONG TERM CARE
HOME**   p600
12 BARTLETT AVE, GRIMSBY, ON, L3M
0A2
(905) 945-9631   SIC 8051

SHANNEX INCORPORATED   p457
245 MAIN AVE, HALIFAX, NS, B3M 1B7
(902) 443-1971   SIC 8051

SHANNEX INCORPORATED   p459
48 LOVETT LAKE CRT, HALIFAX, NS, B3S
1B8
(902) 454-7499   SIC 8051

SHANNEX INCORPORATED   p469
378 YOUNG ST, TRURO, NS, B2N 7H2
(902) 895-2891   SIC 8051

SHANTI ENTERPRISES LIMITED   p836
600 WHITES RD RR 3, PALMERSTON, ON,
N0G 2P0
(519) 343-2611   SIC 8051

SHARON FARMS & ENTERPRISES LTD
p650
1340 HURON ST, LONDON, ON, N5V 3R3
(519) 455-3910   SIC 8051

SHEPHERD'S CARE FOUNDATION   p120
6620 28 AVE NW, EDMONTON, AB, T6K
2R1
(780) 463-9810   SIC 8051

SHERWOOD CARE   p161
2020 BRENTWOOD BLVD, SHERWOOD
PARK, AB, T8A 0X1
(780) 467-2281   SIC 8051

SLOVENIAN LINDEN FOUNDATION   p580
52 NEILSON DR, ETOBICOKE, ON, M9C
1V7
(416) 621-3820   SIC 8051

SNOW, DR. V. A. CENTRE INC   p403
54 DEMILLE CRT SUITE 14, HAMPTON,
NB, E5N 5S7
(506) 832-6210   SIC 8051

SOUTHAMPTON CARE CENTRE INC p882
140 GREY ST S, SOUTHAMPTON, ON,
N0H 2L0
(519) 797-3220   SIC 8051

SPECIALTY CARE CASE MANOR INC p494
18 BOYD ST, BOBCAYGEON, ON, K0M 1A0
(705) 738-2374   SIC 8051

SPECIALTY CARE EAST INC   p632
800 EDGAR ST SUITE 114, KINGSTON,
ON, K7M 8S4
(613) 547-0040   SIC 8051

SPECIALTY CARE INC   p558
400 APPLEWOOD CRES SUITE 110, CON-
CORD, ON, L4K 0C3
SIC 8051

SPECIALTY CARE INC   p628
121 MORTON AVE SUITE 308, KESWICK,
ON, L4P 3T5
(905) 476-2656   SIC 8051

SPECIALTY CARE INC   p891
5501 ABBOTT ST E, STITTSVILLE, ON,
K2S 2C5
(613) 836-0331   SIC 8051

SPRUCEDALE CARE CENTRE INC   p897
96 KITTRIDGE AVE E SUITE 115,
STRATHROY, ON, N7G 2A8
(519) 245-2808   SIC 8051

**ST ANN'S SENIOR CITIZENS' VILLAGE
CORPORATION**   p1425
2910 LOUISE ST, SASKATOON, SK, S7J
3L8
(306) 374-8900   SIC 8051

**ST DEMETRIUS (UKRAINIAN CATHOLIC)
DEVELOPMENT CORPORATION, THE** p577
60 RICHVIEW RD, ETOBICOKE, ON, M9A
5E4
(416) 243-7653   SIC 8051

ST JOSEPH'S HEALTH CENTRE (GUELPH)
p604
100 WESTMOUNT RD, GUELPH, ON, N1H
5H8
(519) 824-6000   SIC 8051

ST JUDE'S ANGLICAN HOME SOCIETY
p293
810 27TH AVE W, VANCOUVER, BC, V5Z
2G7
(604) 874-3200   SIC 8051

**ST MICHAEL'S EXTENDED CARE CENTRE
SOCIETY**   p84
7404 139 AVE NW, EDMONTON, AB, T5C
3H7
(780) 473-5621   SIC 8051

**ST MICHAEL'S LONG TERM CARE CEN-
TRE**   p84
7404 139 AVE NW, EDMONTON, AB, T5C
3H7
(780) 473-5621   SIC 8051

ST NORBERT LODGES LTD   p392
50 ST PIERRE ST, WINNIPEG, MB, R3V
1J6
(204) 269-4538   SIC 8051

ST PATRICK'S HOME OF OTTAWA   p827
2865 RIVERSIDE DR, OTTAWA, ON, K1V
8N5
(613) 731-4660   SIC 8051

**ST. JOSEPH'S LIFECARE CENTRE,
BRANTFORD**   p516
99 WAYNE GRETZKY PKY, BRANTFORD,
ON, N3S 6T6
(519) 751-7096   SIC 8051

**ST. JOSEPH'S VILLA FOUNDATION, DUN-
DAS**   p566
56 GOVERNORS RD, DUNDAS, ON, L9H
5G7
(905) 627-3541   SIC 8051

**STEEVES & ROZEMA ENTERPRISES LIM-
ITED**   p859
1221 MICHIGAN AVE, SARNIA, ON, N7S
3Y3
(519) 542-5529   SIC 8051

**STEEVES & ROZEMA ENTERPRISES LIM-
ITED**   p861
265 FRONT ST N SUITE 200, SARNIA, ON,
N7T 7X1
(519) 344-8829   SIC 8051

SUMMIT CARE CORPORATION LTD   p77
10 COUNTRY VILLAGE COVE NE, CAL-
GARY, AB, T3K 6B4
(403) 567-0461   SIC 8051

**SUN COUNTRY REGIONAL HEALTH AU-
THORITY**   p1437
201 WILFRED ST, WAWOTA, SK, S0G 5A0
SIC 8051

SUNNYCREST NURSING HOMES LIMITED
p1015
1635 DUNDAS ST E, WHITBY, ON, L1N
2K9
(905) 576-0111   SIC 8051

**SUNNYSIDE ADVENTIST CARE CENTRE
LTD**   p1433
2200 ST HENRY AVE, SASKATOON, SK,
S7M 0P5
(306) 653-1267   SIC 8051

SUNRISE OF MARKHAM LIMITED   p1000
38 SWANSEA RD, UNIONVILLE, ON, L3R
5K2
(905) 947-4566   SIC 8051

SUTHERLAND HILLS REST HOME LTD
p219
3081 HALL RD, KELOWNA, BC, V1W 2R5
(250) 860-2330   SIC 8051

SWIFT CURRENT CARE CENTRE   p1436
700 ABERDEEN ST SUITE 22, SWIFT
CURRENT, SK, S9H 3E3
SIC 8051

TABOR HOME INC   p352
450 LOREN DR, MORDEN, MB, R6M 0E2
(204) 822-4848   SIC 8051

TENDERCARE NURSING HOMES LIMITED
p878
1020 MCNICOLL AVE SUITE 436, SCAR-
BOROUGH, ON, M1W 2J6
(416) 497-3639   SIC 8051

TIDAL VIEW MANOR   p471
64 VANCOUVER ST, YARMOUTH, NS, B5A
2P5
SIC 8051

TOWNSHIP OF OSGOODE CARE CENTRE
p681
7650 SNAKE ISLAND RD RR 3, MET-
CALFE, ON, K0A 2P0
SIC 8051

TRAVOIS HOLDINGS LTD   p68
8240 COLLICUTT ST SW, CALGARY, AB,
T2V 2X1
(403) 252-4445   SIC 8051

TUDOR HOUSE LTD   p356
800 MANITOBA AVE, SELKIRK, MB, R1A
2C9
(204) 482-6601   SIC 8051

TUFFORD NURSING HOME LTD   p885
312 QUEENSTON ST, ST CATHARINES,
ON, L2P 2X4
(905) 682-0411   SIC 8051

TYNDALL NURSING HOME LIMITED   p701
1060 EGLINTON AVE E SUITE 417, MIS-
SISSAUGA, ON, L4W 1K3
(905) 624-1511   SIC 8051

UNGER NURSING HOMES LIMITED   p531
75 PLAINS RD W SUITE 214, BURLING-
TON, ON, L7T 1E8
(905) 631-0700   SIC 8051

UNGER NURSING HOMES LIMITED   p885
312 QUEENSTON ST, ST CATHARINES,
ON, L2P 2X4
(905) 682-0503   SIC 8051

**UNITED CHURCH HOME FOR SENIOR CIT-
IZENS INC, THE**   p412
165 MAIN ST, SACKVILLE, NB, E4L 4S2
(506) 364-4900   SIC 8051

UNITED CHURCH OF CANADA, THE p1083
5790 AV PARKHAVEN, COTE SAINT-LUC,
QC, H4W 1X9
SIC 8051

VALLEY MANOR INC   p489
88 MINTHA ST, BARRYS BAY, ON, K0J 1B0
(613) 756-2643   SIC 8051

VALLEY PARK MANOR NURSING HOME
p154
5505 60 AVE, RED DEER, AB, T4N 4W2
SIC 8051

**VANCOUVER ISLAND HEALTH AUTHOR-
ITY**   p340
567 GOLDSTREAM AVE, VICTORIA, BC,
V9B 2W4
(250) 370-5790   SIC 8051

VENTA CARE CENTRE LTD   p84
13525 102 ST NW, EDMONTON, AB, T5E
4K3
(780) 476-6633   SIC 8051

VICTORIA GLEN MANOR INC   p404
30 BEECH GLEN RD, LOWER KINTORE,
NB, E7H 1J9
(506) 273-4885   SIC 8051

VICTORIA HOSPICE SOCIETY   p333
1952 BAY ST, VICTORIA, BC, V8R 1J8
(250) 370-8715   SIC 8051

VICTORIA VILLAGE INC   p488
78 ROSS ST, BARRIE, ON, L4N 1G3
(705) 728-3456   *SIC 8051*

VIGI SANTE LTEE   p1150
2893 AV DES ANCETRES, MASCOUCHE,
QC, J7K 1X6
(450) 474-6991   *SIC 8051*

VIGI SANTE LTEE   p1310
2042 BOUL MARIE, SAINT-HUBERT, QC,
J4T 2B4
(450) 671-5596   *SIC 8051*

VIGI SANTE LTEE   p1371
3220 12E AV N, SHERBROOKE, QC, J1H
5H3
(819) 820-8900   *SIC 8051*

VILLA ACADIENNE INC   p462
8403 HWY 1, METEGHAN, NS, B0W 2J0
(902) 645-2065   *SIC 8051*

VILLA FORUM   p707
175 FORUM DR, MISSISSAUGA, ON, L4Z
4E5
(905) 501-1443   *SIC 8051*

**VILLA MARCONI LONG TERM CARE CEN-
TRE**   p831
1026 BASELINE RD, OTTAWA, ON, K2C
0A6
(613) 727-6201   *SIC 8051*

VILLA MARIA INC   p417
19 RUE DU COLLEGE, SAINT-LOUIS-DE-
KENT, NB, E4X 1C2
(506) 876-3488   *SIC 8051*

VILLA PROVIDENCE SHEDIAC INC   p417
403 MAIN ST, SHEDIAC, NB, E4P 2B9
(506) 532-4484   *SIC 8051*

VISION '74 INC   p861
229 WELLINGTON ST, SARNIA, ON, N7T
1G9
(519) 336-6551   *SIC 8051*

WE CARE HEALTH SERVICES INC   p386
1661 PORTAGE AVE SUITE 209, WIN-
NIPEG, MB, R3J 3T7
(204) 987-3044   *SIC 8051*

WE CARE HEALTH SERVICES INC   p708
160 TRADERS BLVD E SUITE 208, MISSIS-
SAUGA, ON, L4Z 3K7
(905) 275-7250   *SIC 8051*

WELLESLEY CENTRAL PLACE   p932
160 WELLESLEY ST E SUITE 2044,
TORONTO, ON, M4Y 1J2
(416) 929-9385   *SIC 8051*

**WEST PARK MANOR PERSONAL CARE
HOME INC**   p389
3199 GRANT AVE, WINNIPEG, MB, R3R
1X2
(204) 889-3330   *SIC 8051*

WILLINGDON PARK HOSPITAL LTD   p191
4435 GRANGE ST, BURNABY, BC, V5H
1P4
(604) 433-2455   *SIC 8051*

**WINDSOR ELMS VILLAGE FOR CONTINU-
ING CARE SOCIETY**   p470
590 KING ST, WINDSOR, NS, B0N 2T0
(902) 798-2251   *SIC 8051*

WINSTON HALL NURSING HOME LTD p638
695 BLOCK LINE RD, KITCHENER, ON,
N2E 3K1
(519) 576-2430   *SIC 8051*

WOLFVILLE NURSING HOMES LIMITED
p471
601 MAIN ST SUITE 2, WOLFVILLE, NS,
B4P 1E9
(902) 542-2429   *SIC 8051*

YALETOWN HOUSE SOCIETY   p301
1099 CAMBIE ST, VANCOUVER, BC, V6B
5A8
(604) 689-0022   *SIC 8051*

**YEE HONG CENTRE FOR GERIATRIC
CARE**   p877
2311 MCNICOLL AVE, SCARBOROUGH,
ON, M1V 5L3
SIC 8051

YORK MANOR INC   p400
100 SUNSET DR SUITE 121, FREDERIC-
TON, NB, E3A 1A3

(506) 444-3880   *SIC 8051*

SIC 8052 Intermediate care facilities

CHARTWELL MASTER CARE LP   p714
2065 LEANNE BLVD, MISSISSAUGA, ON,
L5K 2L6
(905) 822-4663   *SIC 8052*

CHARTWELL MASTER CARE LP   p805
2140 BARONWOOD DR, OAKVILLE, ON,
L6M 4V6
(905) 827-2405   *SIC 8052*

**COCHRANE TEMISKAMING RESOURCE
CENTRE**   p912
600 TOKE ST, TIMMINS, ON, P4N 6W1
(705) 267-8181   *SIC 8052*

**DELTA VIEW LIFE ENRICHMENT CENTRES
LTD**   p210
9341 BURNS DR, DELTA, BC, V4K 3N3
(604) 501-6700   *SIC 8052*

**EDGEWELL PERSONAL CARE CANADA
ULC**   p722
6733 MISSISSAUGA RD SUITE 700, MIS-
SISSAUGA, ON, L5N 6J5
(905) 363-2720   *SIC 8052*

**FONDATION D'INSTITUT CANADIEN-
POLONAIS DU BIEN-ETRE INC**   p1165
5655 RUE BELANGER, MONTREAL, QC,
H1T 1G2
(514) 259-2551   *SIC 8052*

PROVINCE OF PEI   p1043
15 FRANK MELLISH ST, SUMMERSIDE,
PE, C1N 0H3
(902) 888-8310   *SIC 8052*

**SHERWOOD COURT LONG TERM CARE
CENTRE**   p664
300 RAVINEVIEW DR SUITE 1, MAPLE,
ON, L6A 3P8
(905) 303-3565   *SIC 8052*

SOUTHEAST PERSONAL CARE HOME INC
p392
1265 LEE BLVD, WINNIPEG, MB, R3T 2M3
(204) 269-7111   *SIC 8052*

SRIULLI LONG TERM CARE   p1033
40 FRIULI CRT, WOODBRIDGE, ON, L4L
9T3
(905) 856-3939   *SIC 8052*

SIC 8059 Nursing and personal care, nec

154644 CANADA INC   p926
40 ST CLAIR AVE W UNIT 102, TORONTO,
ON, M4V 1M2
(416) 481-2733   *SIC 8059*

2063414 ONTARIO LIMITED   p498
215 SUNNY MEADOW BLVD, BRAMPTON,
ON, L6R 3B5
(905) 458-7604   *SIC 8059*

9038-5477 QUEBEC INC   p1054
482 BOUL BEACONSFIELD BUREAU 204,
BEACONSFIELD, QC, H9W 4C4
(514) 695-3131   *SIC 8059*

ALBERTA HEALTH SERVICES   p162
2 BROWER DR, SHERWOOD PARK, AB,
T8H 1V4
(780) 342-4600   *SIC 8059*

ALERT BEST NURSING INCORPORATED
p612
290 CAROLINE ST S SUITE 4, HAMILTON,
ON, L8P 3L9
(905) 524-5990   *SIC 8059*

AVOKERIE HEALTHCARE INC   p582
10 HUMBERLINE DR UNIT 301, ETOBI-
COKE, ON, M9W 6J5
(416) 628-7151   *SIC 8059*

BAYSHORE HEALTHCARE LTD.   p456
7071 BAYERS RD SUITE 237, HALIFAX,
NS, B3L 2C2
(902) 425-7683   *SIC 8059*

BAYSHORE HEALTHCARE LTD.   p542
857 GRAND AVE W SUITE 206, CHATHAM,
ON, N7L 4T1

(519) 354-2019   *SIC 8059*

BIG HEARTS HOLDINGS LTD   p259
5760 MINORU BLVD SUITE 203, RICH-
MOND, BC, V6X 2A9
(604) 278-3318   *SIC 8059*

CANADIAN RED CROSS SOCIETY, THE
p445
133 TROOP AVE, DARTMOUTH, NS, B3B
2A7
(902) 496-0103   *SIC 8059*

CANADIAN RED CROSS SOCIETY, THE
p561
165 MONTREAL RD, CORNWALL, ON,
K6H 1B2
SIC 8059

**CAPE BRETON COUNTY HOMEMAKERS
AGENCY**   p466
5 DETHERIDGE DR SUITE 1, SYDNEY, NS,
B1L 1B8
(902) 562-5003   *SIC 8059*

CAPITAL CARE GROUP INC   p98
8740 165 ST NW SUITE 438, EDMONTON,
AB, T5R 2R8
(780) 341-2300   *SIC 8059*

CAREMED SERVICES INC   p1013
1450 HOPKINS ST SUITE 205, WHITBY,
ON, L1N 2C3
(905) 666-6656   *SIC 8059*

CAREWEST   p68
10301 SOUTHPORT LANE SW, CALGARY,
AB, T2W 1S7
(403) 943-8140   *SIC 8059*

**CENTRE D'HEBERGEMENT ET DE SOINS
DE LONGUE DUREE LOUISE-FAUBERT
INC**   p1319
300 RUE DU DOCTEUR-CHARLES-
LEONARD, SAINT-JEROME, QC, J7Y 0N2
(450) 710-1700   *SIC 8059*

**CENTRE DE SANTE ET DE SERVICES SO-
CIAUX DE RIVIERE-DU-LOUP**   p1286
28 RUE JOLY, RIVIERE-DU-LOUP, QC, G5R
3H2
(418) 862-6385   *SIC 8059*

CHARTWELL RETIREMENT RESIDENCES
p578
495 THE WEST MALL, ETOBICOKE, ON,
M9C 5S3
(416) 622-7094   *SIC 8059*

CHARTWELL RETIREMENT RESIDENCES
p678
380 CHURCH ST SUITE 421, MARKHAM,
ON, L6B 1E1
(905) 472-3320   *SIC 8059*

CHARTWELL RETIREMENT RESIDENCES
p805
2140 BARONWOOD DR SUITE 225,
OAKVILLE, ON, L6M 4V6
(905) 827-2405   *SIC 8059*

**CIRCLE OF HOME CARE SERVICES
(TORONTO)**   p773
4211 YONGE ST SUITE 401, NORTH
YORK, ON, M2P 2A9
(416) 635-2860   *SIC 8059*

CITY OF GREATER SUDBURY, THE   p898
960 NOTRE DAME AVE SUITE D, SUD-
BURY, ON, P3A 2T4
(705) 566-4270   *SIC 8059*

**CLOSING THE GAP HEALTHCARE GROUP
INC**   p693
2810 MATHESON BLVD E SUITE 100, MIS-
SISSAUGA, ON, L4W 4X7
(905) 306-0202   *SIC 8059*

COMCARE (CANADA) LIMITED   p400
168 BRUNSWICK ST, FREDERICTON, NB,
E3B 1G6
SIC 8059

COMCARE (CANADA) LIMITED   p880
8 QUEENSWAY E SUITE 4, SIMCOE, ON,
N3Y 4M3
(519) 426-5122   *SIC 8059*

**COMMUNITY LIVING BELLEVILLE AND
AREA**   p491
91 MILLENNIUM PKY, BELLEVILLE, ON,
K8N 4Z5

(613) 969-7407   *SIC 8059*

COMMUNITY LIVING WEST NIPISSING
p898
120 NIPISSING ST, STURGEON FALLS,
ON, P2B 1J6
(705) 753-3143   *SIC 8059*

COMMUNITY LIVING-STORMONT COUNTY
p563
280 NINTH ST W, CORNWALL, ON, K6J
3A6
(613) 938-9550   *SIC 8059*

**CORPORATION OF THE COUNTY OF
LAMBTON**   p591
39 MORRIS ST, FOREST, ON, N0N 1J0
(519) 786-2151   *SIC 8059*

COUNTY OF LENNOX & ADDINGTON   p747
309 BRIDGE ST W SUITE 113, NAPANEE,
ON, K7R 2G4
SIC 8059

CSH ROYAL OAK LTC INC   p633
1750 DIVISION RD N SUITE 415,
KINGSVILLE, ON, N9Y 4G7
(519) 733-9303   *SIC 8059*

DAUPHIN PERSONAL CARE HOME INC
p348
625 3RD ST SW, DAUPHIN, MB, R7N 1R7
(204) 638-3010   *SIC 8059*

**DIVERSICARE CANADA MANAGEMENT
SERVICES CO. INC**   p517
612 MOUNT PLEASANT RD, BRANTFORD,
ON, N3T 5L5
(519) 484-2431   *SIC 8059*

**DIVERSICARE CANADA MANAGEMENT
SERVICES CO., INC**   p911
16 FORT ST, TILBURY, ON, N0P 2L0
(519) 682-0243   *SIC 8059*

EQUINOXE, LIFE CARE SOLUTIONS INC
p1402
4060 RUE SAINTE-CATHERINE O BU-
REAU 201, WESTMOUNT, QC, H3Z 2Z3
(514) 935-2600   *SIC 8059*

EXTENDICARE (CANADA) INC   p838
595 PEMBROKE ST E, PEMBROKE, ON,
K8A 3L7
SIC 8059

EXTENDICARE (CANADA) INC   p879
15 HOLLINGER LANE, SCHUMACHER,
ON, P0N 1G0
SIC 8059

EXTENDICARE (CANADA) INC   p1021
880 NORTH SERVICE RD E SUITE 301,
WINDSOR, ON, N8X 3J5
(519) 966-5200   *SIC 8059*

FRASER HEALTH AUTHORITY   p274
13401 108TH AVE SUITE 1500, SURREY,
BC, V3T 5T3
(604) 953-4950   *SIC 8059*

FW GREEN HOME, THE   p203
1700 4TH ST S, CRANBROOK, BC, V1C
6E1
(250) 426-8016   *SIC 8059*

GEM HEALTH CARE GROUP LIMITED p469
426 YOUNG ST, TRURO, NS, B2N 7B1
(902) 895-8715   *SIC 8059*

GOLDEN LIFE MANAGEMENT CORP p212
55 COKATO RD SUITE 206, FERNIE, BC,
V0B 1M4
(250) 423-4214   *SIC 8059*

GOVERNMENT OF ONTARIO   p1014
920 CHAMPLAIN CRT, WHITBY, ON, L1N
6K9
(905) 430-3308   *SIC 8059*

**GREYSTOKE HOMES & SUPPORT SER-
VICES INC**   p142
701 2 AVE S, LETHBRIDGE, AB, T1J 0C4
(403) 320-0911   *SIC 8059*

**HAMILTON NIAGARA HALDIMAND BRANT
COMMUNITY CARE ACCESS CENTRE** p530
440 ELIZABETH ST, BURLINGTON, ON,
L7R 2M1
(905) 639-5228   *SIC 8059*

**HAMLETS AT PENTICTON RESIDENCE
INC, THE**   p243
103 DUNCAN AVE W, PENTICTON, BC,

▲ Public Company   ■ Public Company Family Member   **HQ** Headquarters   **BR** Branch   **SL** Single Location

V2A 2Y3
(250) 490-8503   *SIC* 8059
HERITAGE PLACE CARE FACILITY   p1004
GD, VIRGIL, ON, L0S 1T0
(905) 468-1111   *SIC* 8059
HOME SUPPORT CENTRAL SOCIETY p465
30 WATER ST, PORT HOOD, NS, B0E 2W0
(902) 787-3449   *SIC* 8059
**INTREPIDES DE ROUYN-NORANDA INC.,
LES**   p1289
380 AV RICHARD BUREAU 203, ROUYN-
NORANDA, QC, J9X 4L3
(819) 762-7217   *SIC* 8059
JARLETTE LTD   p1001
2100 MAIN ST, VAL CARON, ON, P3N 1S7
(705) 897-7695   *SIC* 8059
JOANS HOME SUPPORT CARE   p419
1815 ROUTE 860 SUITE 860, TITUSVILLE,
NB, E5N 3V6
(506) 832-0369   *SIC* 8059
MENNONITE BENEVOLENT SOCIETY p175
32910 BRUNDIGE AVE SUITE 257, AB-
BOTSFORD, BC, V2S 1N2
(604) 853-2411   *SIC* 8059
NIGHTINGALE NURSING REGISTRY LTD
p841
2948 LAKEFIELD RD, PETERBOROUGH,
ON, K9J 6X5
(705) 652-6118   *SIC* 8059
**NORTH EAST COMMUNITY CARE ACCESS
CENTRE**   p763
1164 DEVONSHIRE AVE, NORTH BAY, ON,
P1B 6X7
(705) 474-5885   *SIC* 8059
**NORTH EAST COMMUNITY CARE ACCESS
CENTRE**   p900
40 ELM ST SUITE 41-C, SUDBURY, ON,
P3C 1S8
(705) 522-3461   *SIC* 8059
NORTHRIDGE LONGTERM CARE CENTER
p798
496 POSTRIDGE DR, OAKVILLE, ON, L6H
7A2
(905) 257-9882   *SIC* 8059
NOVA LEAP HEALTH CORP   p457
7071 BAYERS RD SUITE 5003, HALIFAX,
NS, B3L 2C2
(902) 401-9480   *SIC* 8059
OSPREY CARE INC   p216
3255 OVERLANDER DR, KAMLOOPS, BC,
V2B 0A5
(250) 579-9061   *SIC* 8059
PEARL VILLA HOMES LTD   p94
14315 118 AVE NW SUITE 140, EDMON-
TON, AB, T5L 4S6
(780) 499-2337   *SIC* 8059
PRAIRIE MOUNTAIN HEALTH   p347
525 VICTORIA AVE E, BRANDON, MB, R7A
6S9
(204) 578-2670   *SIC* 8059
PROVIDENCE HEALTH CARE SOCIETY
p293
4950 HEATHER ST SUITE 321, VANCOU-
VER, BC, V5Z 3L9
(604) 261-9371   *SIC* 8059
PROVINCE OF PEI   p1040
165 JOHN YEO DR, CHARLOTTETOWN,
PE, C1E 3J3
(902) 368-4790   *SIC* 8059
QUALICARE INC   p781
3910 BATHURST ST SUITE 304, NORTH
YORK, ON, M3H 5Z3
(416) 630-0202   *SIC* 8059
**REGIE REGIONALE DE LA SANTE ET DES
SERVICES SOCIAUX NUNAVIK**   p1221
4039 RUE TUPPER BUREAU 7, MON-
TREAL, QC, H3Z 1T5
(514) 932-9047   *SIC* 8059
REVERA INC   p375
440 EDMONTON ST, WINNIPEG, MB, R3B
2M4
(204) 942-5291   *SIC* 8059
REVERA LONG TERM CARE INC   p475
1020 WESTNEY RD N, AJAX, ON, L1T 4K6

(905) 426-6296   *SIC* 8059
REVERA LONG TERM CARE INC   p756
52 GEORGE ST, NEWMARKET, ON, L3Y
4V3
(905) 853-3242   *SIC* 8059
REVERA LONG TERM CARE INC   p806
2370 THIRD LINE, OAKVILLE, ON, L6M
4E2
(905) 469-3294   *SIC* 8059
RICHMOND HOSPITAL, THE   p262
6111 MINORU BLVD, RICHMOND, BC, V6Y
1Y4
(604) 244-5300   *SIC* 8059
RIVER EAST PERSONAL CARE HOME LTD
p367
1375 MOLSON ST, WINNIPEG, MB, R2K
4K8
(204) 668-7460   *SIC* 8059
SAINT ELIZABETH HEALTH CARE   p750
30 COLONNADE RD N SUITE 225, NE-
PEAN, ON, K2E 7J6
(613) 738-9661   *SIC* 8059
**SERENITY NURSING AND HOME SUP-
PORT SERVICES LTD**   p426
2 GLENDALE AVE, MOUNT PEARL, NL,
A1N 1M9
(709) 364-9688   *SIC* 8059
SHERBROOKE COMMUNITY SOCIETY INC
p1424
401 ACADIA DR SUITE 330, SASKATOON,
SK, S7H 2E7
(306) 655-3600   *SIC* 8059
SIFTON PROPERTIES LIMITED   p715
2132 DUNDAS ST W, MISSISSAUGA, ON,
L5K 2K7
(905) 823-7273   *SIC* 8059
SIMON FRASER LODGE INC   p250
2410 LAURIER CRES, PRINCE GEORGE,
BC, V2M 2B3
(250) 563-3413   *SIC* 8059
SPECIALTY CARE INC   p497
2656 LINE 6, BRADFORD, ON, L3Z 2A1
(905) 952-2270   *SIC* 8059
SPECIALTY CARE INC   p512
10260 KENNEDY RD, BRAMPTON, ON,
L6Z 4N7
(905) 495-4695   *SIC* 8059
ST AMANT INC   p368
440 RIVER RD, WINNIPEG, MB, R2M 3Z9
(204) 256-4301   *SIC* 8059
ST. JOSEPH'S RESIDENCE INC   p369
1149 LEILA AVE, WINNIPEG, MB, R2P 1S6
(204) 697-8031   *SIC* 8059
ST. JOSEPH'S VILLA OF SUDBURY, INC
p901
1250 SOUTHBAY RD, SUDBURY, ON, P3E
6L9
    SIC 8059
**STEEVES & ROZEMA ENTERPRISES LIM-
ITED**   p859
1310 MURPHY RD SUITE 216, SARNIA,
ON, N7S 6K5
(519) 542-2939   *SIC* 8059
**STILLWATER CREEK LIMITED PARTNER-
SHIP**   p751
2018 ROBERTSON RD SUITE 353, NE-
PEAN, ON, K1H 1C6
(613) 828-7575   *SIC* 8059
SUNBEAM CENTRE   p637
595 GREENFIELD AVE SUITE 43, KITCH-
ENER, ON, N2C 2N7
(519) 894-2098   *SIC* 8059
SUNRISE NORTH SENIOR LIVING LTD
p1022
5065 RIVERSIDE DR E SUITE 203, WIND-
SOR, ON, N8Y 5B3
(519) 974-5858   *SIC* 8059
TABOR HOME SOCIETY   p177
31944 SUNRISE CRES, ABBOTSFORD,
BC, V2T 1N5
(604) 859-8718   *SIC* 8059
**TRI-COUNTY MENNONITE HOMES ASSO-
CIATION**   p897
90 GREENWOOD DR SUITE 117, STRAT-

FORD, ON, N5A 7W5
(519) 273-4662   *SIC* 8059
TRIPLE A LIVING COMMUNITIES INC   p70
14911 5 ST SW SUITE 115, CALGARY, AB,
T2Y 5B9
(403) 410-9155   *SIC* 8059
VHA HOME HEALTHCARE   p924
30 SOUDAN AVE SUITE 500, TORONTO,
ON, M4S 1V6
(416) 489-2500   *SIC* 8059
VILLA CATHAY CARE HOME SOCIETY p296
970 UNION ST, VANCOUVER, BC, V6A 3V1
(604) 254-5621   *SIC* 8059
WE CARE HOME HEALTH SERVICES   p39
10325 BONAVENTURE DR SE SUITE 100,
CALGARY, AB, T2J 7E4
(403) 225-1222   *SIC* 8059
**WHALLEY & DISTRICT SENIOR CITIZEN
HOUSING SOCIETY**   p274
13333 OLD YALE RD, SURREY, BC, V3T
5A2
(604) 588-0445   *SIC* 8059
WINDERMERE CARE CENTRE INC   p294
900 12TH AVE W SUITE 811, VANCOU-
VER, BC, V5Z 1N3
(604) 736-8676   *SIC* 8059
**YEE HONG CENTRE FOR GERIATRIC
CARE**   p678
2780 BUR OAK AVE, MARKHAM, ON, L6B
1C9
(905) 471-3232   *SIC* 8059
**YEE HONG CENTRE FOR GERIATRIC
CARE**   p875
60 SCOTTFIELD DR SUITE 428, SCAR-
BOROUGH, ON, M1S 5T7
(416) 321-3000   *SIC* 8059
**YOUVILLE HOME (GREY NUNS) OF ST AL-
BERT**   p166
9 ST VITAL AVE, ST. ALBERT, AB, T8N 1K1
(780) 460-6900   *SIC* 8059

---

*SIC 8062 General medical and surgical
hospitals*

100 MILE DISTRICT GENERAL HOSPITAL
p174
555 CEDAR AVE, 100 MILE HOUSE, BC,
V0K 2E0
(250) 395-7600   *SIC* 8062
ALBERTA HEALTH SERVICES   p4
305 LYNX ST, BANFF, AB, T1L 1H7
(403) 762-2222   *SIC* 8062
ALBERTA HEALTH SERVICES   p6
2001 107 ST, BLAIRMORE, AB, T0K 0E0
(403) 562-5011   *SIC* 8062
ALBERTA HEALTH SERVICES   p7
440 3 ST E SUITE 300, BROOKS, AB, T1R
0X8
(403) 501-3232   *SIC* 8062
ALBERTA HEALTH SERVICES   p81
5920 51 AVE, DAYSLAND, AB, T0B 1A0
(780) 374-3746   *SIC* 8062
ALBERTA HEALTH SERVICES   p82
1210 20E AVE, DIDSBURY, AB, T0M 0W0
(403) 335-9393   *SIC* 8062
ALBERTA HEALTH SERVICES   p83
14007 50 ST NW, EDMONTON, AB, T5A
5E4
(780) 342-4000   *SIC* 8062
ALBERTA HEALTH SERVICES   p85
10240 KINGSWAY NW, EDMONTON, AB,
T5H 3V9
(780) 735-4111   *SIC* 8062
ALBERTA HEALTH SERVICES   p91
9942 108 ST NW, EDMONTON, AB, T5K
2J5
(780) 342-7700   *SIC* 8062
ALBERTA HEALTH SERVICES   p119
10707 29 AVE NW, EDMONTON, AB, T6J
6W1
(780) 430-9110   *SIC* 8062
ALBERTA HEALTH SERVICES   p126
10628 100TH ST, FAIRVIEW, AB, T0H 1L0

(780) 835-6100   *SIC* 8062
ALBERTA HEALTH SERVICES   p129
9401 86 AVE, FORT SASKATCHEWAN, AB,
T8L 0C6
(780) 998-2256   *SIC* 8062
ALBERTA HEALTH SERVICES   p135
904 CENTRE ST N, HANNA, AB, T0J 1P0
(403) 854-3331   *SIC* 8062
ALBERTA HEALTH SERVICES   p135
560 9 AVE SW, HIGH RIVER, AB, T1V 1B3
(403) 652-2200   *SIC* 8062
ALBERTA HEALTH SERVICES   p137
518 ROBSON ST, JASPER, AB, T0E 1E0
(780) 852-3344   *SIC* 8062
ALBERTA HEALTH SERVICES   p142
960 19 ST S SUITE 110, LETHBRIDGE, AB,
T1J 1W5
(403) 388-6009   *SIC* 8062
ALBERTA HEALTH SERVICES   p145
600 2ND ST, MANNING, AB, T0H 2M0
(780) 836-3391   *SIC* 8062
ALBERTA HEALTH SERVICES   p145
350 3RD AVE NW, MCLENNAN, AB, T0H
2L0
(780) 324-3730   *SIC* 8062
ALBERTA HEALTH SERVICES   p151
3901 57 AVE, OLDS, AB, T4H 1T4
(403) 556-3381   *SIC* 8062
ALBERTA HEALTH SERVICES   p151
312 3 ST E, OYEN, AB, T0J 2J0
(403) 664-3528   *SIC* 8062
ALBERTA HEALTH SERVICES   p152
5800 57 AVE, PONOKA, AB, T4J 1P1
(403) 783-8135   *SIC* 8062
ALBERTA HEALTH SERVICES   p152
1222 BEV MCLACHLIN DR, PINCHER
CREEK, AB, T0K 1W0
(403) 627-1946   *SIC* 8062
ALBERTA HEALTH SERVICES   p153
5002 54 AVE, PROVOST, AB, T0B 3S0
(780) 753-2291   *SIC* 8062
ALBERTA HEALTH SERVICES   p164
4713 48 AVE, ST PAUL, AB, T0A 3A3
(780) 645-3331   *SIC* 8062
ALBERTA HEALTH SERVICES   p168
709 1 ST NE, SUNDRE, AB, T0M 1X0
(403) 638-3033   *SIC* 8062
ALBERTA HEALTH SERVICES   p170
5720 50 AVE, VERMILION, AB, T9X 1K7
(780) 853-5305   *SIC* 8062
ALBERTA HEALTH SERVICES   p171
10220 93 ST, WESTLOCK, AB, T7P 2G4
(780) 349-3301   *SIC* 8062
ALEXANDRA HOSPITAL INGERSOLL, THE
p621
29 NOXON ST, INGERSOLL, ON, N5C 1B8
(519) 485-1700   *SIC* 8062
ALMONTE GENERAL HOSPITAL   p477
75 SPRING ST SS 1, ALMONTE, ON, K0A
1A0
(613) 256-2500   *SIC* 8062
**ANNAPOLIS VALLEY DISTRICT HEALTH
AUTHORITY**   p459
150 EXHIBITION ST, KENTVILLE, NS, B4N
5E3
(902) 678-7381   *SIC* 8062
ARBORG & DISTRICT HEALTH CENTER
p345
GD, ARBORG, MB, R0C 0A0
(204) 376-5247   *SIC* 8062
ARNPRIOR REGIONAL HEALTH   p478
350 JOHN ST N, ARNPRIOR, ON, K7S 2P6
(613) 623-7962   *SIC* 8062
**ARTISTIC   DEVELOPMENT   SUPPORT
GROUP**   p856
27 NAPANEE ST, RICHMOND HILL, ON,
L4E 0X3
    SIC 8062
ATIKOKAN GENERAL HOSPITAL   p479
120 DOROTHY ST, ATIKOKAN, ON, P0T
1C1
(807) 597-4215   *SIC* 8062
AUDEAMUS   p858
1546   ROLLIN   RD,   SAINT-PASCAL-

BAYLON, ON, K0A 3N0
SIC 8062

BINGHAM MEMORIAL HOSPITAL *p680*
507 8TH AVE, MATHESON, ON, P0K 1N0
(705) 273-2424 SIC 8062

BLUEWATER HEALTH *p842*
450 BLANCHE ST, PETROLIA, ON, N0N 1R0
(519) 464-4400 SIC 8062

BLUEWATER HEALTH *p859*
89 NORMAN ST, SARNIA, ON, N7T 6S3
(519) 464-4400 SIC 8062

BOUNDARY HOSPITAL *p215*
7649 22ND ST, GRAND FORKS, BC, V0H 1H2
(250) 443-2100 SIC 8062

BROCKVILLE GENERAL HOSPITAL *p519*
75 CHARLES ST, BROCKVILLE, ON, K6V 1S8
(613) 345-5645 SIC 8062

BROCKVILLE GENERAL HOSPITAL *p519*
42 GARDEN ST, BROCKVILLE, ON, K6V 2C3
(613) 345-5649 SIC 8062

BULKLEY VALLEY HEALTH COUNCIL *p269*
3950 8 AVE, SMITHERS, BC, V0J 2N0
(250) 847-2611 SIC 8062

CALGARY SILVER LININGS FOUNDATION *p67*
2009 33 AVE SW SUITE 2, CALGARY, AB, T2T 1Z5
(403) 536-4025 SIC 8062

CAMBRIDGE MEMORIAL HOSPITAL *p532*
700 CORONATION BLVD, CAMBRIDGE, ON, N1R 3G2
(519) 621-2330 SIC 8062

CAMPBELLFORD MEMORIAL HOSPITAL *p539*
146 OLIVER RD, CAMPBELLFORD, ON, K0L 1L0
(705) 653-1140 SIC 8062

CANADIAN DENTAL RELIEF INTERNATIONAL *p994*
203 PARKSIDE DR, TORONTO, ON, M6R 2Z2
SIC 8062

CAPE BRETON DISTRICT HEALTH AUTHORITY *p467*
1482 GEORGE ST, SYDNEY, NS, B1P 1P3
(902) 567-8000 SIC 8062

CARIBOO MEMORIAL HOSPITAL *p344*
517 SIXTH AVE N SUITE 401, WILLIAMS LAKE, BC, V2G 2G8
(250) 392-4411 SIC 8062

CENTRAL PEACE HEALTH COMPLEX *p164*
5010 45TH AVE, SPIRIT RIVER, AB, T0H 3G0
(780) 864-3993 SIC 8062

CENTRAL REGIONAL HEALTH AUTHORITY *p423*
50 UNION ST, GRAND FALLS-WINDSOR, NL, A2A 2E1
(709) 292-2500 SIC 8062

CENTRE DE LA SANTE ET DU SERVICES SOCIAUX DE LA BASSE COTE-NORD *p1147*
1070 BOUL DOCTEUR-CAMILLE-MARCOUX, LOURDES-DE-BLANC-SABLON, QC, G0G 1W0
(418) 461-2144 SIC 8062

CENTRE DE SANTE DE TEMISCAMING INC *p1378*
180 RUE ANVIK, TEMISCAMING, QC, J0Z 3R0
SIC 8062

CENTRE DE SANTE ET DE SERVICE SOCIAUX LES ESKERS DE L'ABITIBI *p1046*
632 1RE RUE O, AMOS, QC, J9T 2N2
(819) 732-3271 SIC 8062

CENTRE DE SANTE ET DE SERVICES SOCIAUX DE DORVAL-LACHINE-LASALLE *p1131*
650 16E AV, LASALLE, QC, H8P 2S3
(514) 637-2351 SIC 8062

CENTRE DE SANTE ET DE SERVICES SOCIAUX DE GATINEAU *p1104*
85 RUE BELLEHUMEUR BUREAU 301, GATINEAU, QC, J8T 8B7
(819) 966-6016 SIC 8062

CENTRE DE SANTE ET DE SERVICES SOCIAUX DE GATINEAU *p1105*
273 RUE LAURIER, GATINEAU, QC, J8X 3W8
(819) 966-6420 SIC 8062

CENTRE DE SANTE ET DE SERVICES SOCIAUX DE L'OUEST-DE-L'ILE *p1249*
160 AV STILLVIEW, POINTE-CLAIRE, QC, H9R 2Y2
(514) 630-2225 SIC 8062

CENTRE DE SANTE ET DE SERVICES SOCIAUX DE LA MRC DE COATICOOK *p1081*
138 RUE JEANNE-MANCE, COATICOOK, QC, J1A 1W3
(819) 849-4876 SIC 8062

CENTRE DE SANTE ET DE SERVICES SOCIAUX DE LA VALLEE-DE-L'OR *p1148*
1141 RUE ROYALE, MALARTIC, QC, J0Y 1Z0
(819) 825-5858 SIC 8062

CENTRE DE SANTE ET DE SERVICES SOCIAUX DE LAVAL *p1092*
1515 BOUL CHOMEDEY, DORVAL, QC, H7V 3Y7
(450) 978-8300 SIC 8062

CENTRE DE SANTE ET DE SERVICES SOCIAUX DE PORTNEUF *p1351*
700 RUE SAINT-CYRILLE BUREAU 850, SAINT-RAYMOND, QC, G3L 1W1
(418) 337-4611 SIC 8062

CENTRE DE SANTE ET DE SERVICES SOCIAUX DE QUEBEC-NORD *p1055*
11000 RUE DES MONTAGNARDS, BEAUPRE, QC, G0A 1E0
(418) 827-3726 SIC 8062

CENTRE DE SANTE ET DE SERVICES SOCIAUX DU SUD-OUEST-VERDUN *p1223*
6161 RUE LAURENDEAU, MONTREAL, QC, H4E 3X6
(514) 762-2777 SIC 8062

CENTRE DE SANTE ET DE SERVICES SOCIAUX DU SUD-OUEST-VERDUN *p1396*
4000 BOUL LASALLE, VERDUN, QC, H4G 2A3
(514) 362-1000 SIC 8062

CENTRE DE SANTE ET DE SERVICES SOCIAUX PIERRE-BOUCHER *p1145*
1333 BOUL JACQUES-CARTIER E, LONGUEUIL, QC, J4M 2A5
(450) 468-8410 SIC 8062

CENTRE DE SANTE ET DES SERVICES SOCIAUX DE LA HAUTE-COTE-NORD *p1378*
162 RUE DES JESUITES, TADOUSSAC, QC, G0T 2A0
(418) 235-4588 SIC 8062

CENTRE DE SANTE ET SERVICES SOCIAUX DE MONTMAGNY - L'ISLET *p1159*
22 AV COTE, MONTMAGNY, QC, G5V 1Z9
(418) 248-0639 SIC 8062

CENTRE DE SANTE ET SERVICES SOCIAUX DE MONTMAGNY - L'ISLET *p1302*
10 RUE ALPHONSE, SAINT-FABIEN-DE-PANET, QC, G0R 2J0
(418) 249-2572 SIC 8062

CENTRE DE SANTE INUULITSIVIK *p1254*
GD, PUVIRNITUQ, QC, J0M 1P0
(819) 988-2957 SIC 8062

CENTRE HOSPITALIER AMBULATOIRE REGIONAL DE LAVAL *p1092*
1515 BOUL CHOMEDEY BUREAU 160, DORVAL, QC, H7V 3Y7
(450) 978-8300 SIC 8062

CENTRE HOSPITALIER DE L'UNIVERSITE DE MONTREAL *p1175*
1560 RUE SHERBROOKE E, MONTREAL, QC, H2L 4M1
(800) 224-7737 SIC 8062

CENTRE HOSPITALIER DE L'UNIVERSITE DE MONTREAL *p1185*
1058 RUE SAINT-DENIS, MONTREAL, QC, H2X 3J4
(514) 890-8000 SIC 8062

CENTRE HOSPITALIER DE L'UNIVERSITE DE MONTREAL *p1185*
850 RUE SAINT-DENIS, MONTREAL, QC, H2X 0A9
(514) 890-8000 SIC 8062

CENTRE HOSPITALIER DE ST. MARY'S *p1219*
3830 AV LACOMBE, MONTREAL, QC, H3T 1M5
(514) 345-3511 SIC 8062

CENTRE HOSPITALIER ET CENTRE DE READAPTATION ANTOINE-LABELLE *p1287*
1525 RUE L'ANNONCIATION N, RIVIERE-ROUGE, QC, J0T 1T0
(819) 275-2411 SIC 8062

CENTRE HOSPITALIER MONT-SINAI-MONTREAL *p1083*
5690 BOUL CAVENDISH, COTE SAINT-LUC, QC, H4W 1S7
(514) 369-2222 SIC 8062

CENTRE HOSPITALIER UNIVERSITAIRE DE QUEBEC *p1260*
10 RUE DE L'ESPINAY BUREAU 520, QUEBEC, QC, G1L 3L5
(418) 525-4444 SIC 8062

CENTRE HOSPITALIER UNIVERSITAIRE DE QUEBEC *p1268*
11 COTE DU PALAIS BUREAU 3431, QUEBEC, QC, G1R 2J6
(418) 525-4444 SIC 8062

CENTRE HOSPITALIER UNIVERSITAIRE DE QUEBEC *p1268*
11 COTE DU PALAIS, QUEBEC, QC, G1R 2J6
(418) 525-4444 SIC 8062

CENTRE HOSPITALIER UNIVERSITAIRE DE QUEBEC *p1271*
2705 BOUL LAURIER BUREAU 2211, QUEBEC, QC, G1V 4G2
(418) 525-4444 SIC 8062

CENTRE HOSPITALIER UNIVERSITAIRE DE QUEBEC *p1280*
775 RUE SAINT-VIATEUR UNITE 130A, QUEBEC, QC, G2L 2Z3
SIC 8062

CENTRE INTEGRE DE SANTE ET DE SERVICES SOCIAUX DES ILES *p1073*
430 CH PRINCIPAL, CAP-AUX-MEULES, QC, G4T 1R9
(418) 986-2121 SIC 8062

CENTRE INTEGRE DE SANTE ET DE SERVICES SOCIAUX DES LAURENTIDES *p1301*
29 CH D'OKA, SAINT-EUSTACHE, QC, J7R 1K6
(450) 491-1233 SIC 8062

CENTRE REGIONAL DE SANTE ET DE SERVICES SOCIAUX DE LA BAIE-JAMES *p1077*
51 3E RUE, CHIBOUGAMAU, QC, G8P 1N1
(418) 748-2676 SIC 8062

CENTRE UNIVERSITAIRE DE SANTE MCGILL *p1221*
1001 BOUL DECARIE, MONTREAL, QC, H4A 3J1
(514) 934-1934 SIC 8062

CHARLOTTE ELEANOR ENGLEHART HOSPITAL *p842*
450 BLANCHE ST, PETROLIA, ON, N0N 1R0
(519) 882-4325 SIC 8062

CHILLIWACK GENERAL HOSPITAL *p196*
45600 MENHOLM RD, CHILLIWACK, BC, V2P 1P7
(604) 795-4141 SIC 8062

CHURCHILL REGIONAL HEALTH AUTHORITY INC *p348*
162 LAVERENDRYE AVE, CHURCHILL, MB, R0B 0E0
(204) 675-8881 SIC 8062

COLLINGWOOD GENERAL AND MARINE HOSPITAL, THE *p546*
459 HUME ST, COLLINGWOOD, ON, L9Y 1W9
(705) 445-2550 SIC 8062

CONCORDIA HOSPITAL *p367*
1095 CONCORDIA AVE, WINNIPEG, MB, R2K 3S8
(204) 667-1560 SIC 8062

CONSEIL CRI DE LA SANTE ET DES SERVICES SOCIAUX DE LA BAIE JAMES *p1081*
GD, CHISASIBI, QC, J0M 1E0
(819) 855-9001 SIC 8062

CORNWALL COMMUNITY HOSPITAL *p562*
840 MCCONNELL AVE, CORNWALL, ON, K6H 5S5
(613) 938-4240 SIC 8062

COVENANT HEALTH *p119*
3033 66 ST NW, EDMONTON, AB, T6K 4B2
(780) 735-9000 SIC 8062

CROSS, DR G B MEMORIAL HOSPITAL *p421*
67 MANITOBA DR, CLARENVILLE, NL, A5A 1K3
(709) 466-3411 SIC 8062

CROSSROADS REGIONAL HEALTH AUTHORITY *p82*
4550 MADSEN AVE, DRAYTON VALLEY, AB, T7A 1N8
(780) 542-5321 SIC 8062

CSSS PIERRE-DE SAUREL *p1376*
400 AV DE L'HOTEL-DIEU, SOREL-TRACY, QC, J3P 1N5
(450) 746-6000 SIC 8062

DAUPHIN REGIONAL HEALTH CENTRE *p348*
625 3RD ST SW, DAUPHIN, MB, R7N 1R7
(204) 638-3010 SIC 8062

DEEP RIVER AND DISTRICT HOSPITAL CORPORATION *p564*
117 BANTING DR, DEEP RIVER, ON, K0J 1P0
(613) 584-2484 SIC 8062

DRYDEN REGIONAL HEALTH CENTRE *p565*
58 GOODALL ST, DRYDEN, ON, P8N 1V8
(807) 223-8200 SIC 8062

EASTERN REGIONAL INTEGRATED HEALTH AUTHORITY *p426*
760 TOPSAIL RD, MOUNT PEARL, NL, A1N 3J5
(709) 752-4534 SIC 8062

EASTERN REGIONAL INTEGRATED HEALTH AUTHORITY *p431*
154 LEMARCHANT RD, ST. JOHN'S, NL, A1C 5B8
(709) 777-6300 SIC 8062

ESPANOLA GENERAL HOSPITAL *p569*
825 MCKINNON DR SUITE 705, ESPANOLA, ON, P5E 1R4
(705) 869-1420 SIC 8062

FONDATION CENTRE HOSPITALIER REGIONAL DE TROIS-RIVIERES (RSTR) *p1387*
731 RUE SAINTE-JULIE, TROIS-RIVIERES, QC, G9A 1Y1
(819) 697-3333 SIC 8062

FONDATION DU CENTRE DE SANTE ET DE SERVICES SOCIAUX DE MANICOUAGAN *p1053*
635 BOUL JOLLIET, BAIE-COMEAU, QC, G5C 1P1
(418) 589-3701 SIC 8062

FONDATION DU CENTRE REGIONALE DE SANTE ET DE SERVICES SOCIAUX RIMOUSKI INC *p1284*
150 AV ROULEAU, RIMOUSKI, QC, G5L 5T1
(418) 724-8580 SIC 8062

FONDATION SANTE VALLEE-DE-LA-GATINEAU *p1148*
309 BOUL DESJARDINS, MANIWAKI, QC, J9E 2E7
(819) 449-4690 SIC 8062

FOUR COUNTIES HEALTH SERVICES CORPORATION, THE *p753*

1824 CONCESSION DR, NEWBURY, ON, N0L 1Z0

(519) 693-4441   *SIC* 8062

FRASER HEALTH AUTHORITY   *p189*
3935 KINCAID ST, BURNABY, BC, V5G 2X6

(604) 434-3992   *SIC* 8062

FRASER HEALTH AUTHORITY   *p207*
11245 84 AVE SUITE 101, DELTA, BC, V4C 2L9

(604) 507-5400   *SIC* 8062

FRASER HEALTH AUTHORITY   *p231*
11666 LAITY ST, MAPLE RIDGE, BC, V2X 5A3

(604) 463-4111   *SIC* 8062

FRASER HEALTH AUTHORITY   *p274*
13450 102 AVE SUITE 400, SURREY, BC, V3T 0H1

(604) 587-4600   *SIC* 8062

GEORGIAN BAY GENERAL HOSPITAL *p681*
1112 ST ANDREWS DR, MIDLAND, ON, L4R 4P4

(705) 526-1300   *SIC* 8062

GERALDTON DISTRICT HOSPITAL   *p594*
500 HOGARTH ST, GERALDTON, ON, P0T 1M0

(807) 854-1862   *SIC* 8062

GIMLI COMMUNITY HEALTH CENTRE *p350*
120 6TH AVE, GIMLI, MB, R0C 1B0

(204) 642-5116   *SIC* 8062

GLENGARRY MEMORIAL HOSPITAL *p476*
20260 COUNTY ROAD 43 RR 3, ALEXANDRIA, ON, K0C 1A0

(613) 525-2222   *SIC* 8062

GLOBAL RESEARCH EPICENTER AGAINST HUMAN TRAFFICKIN   *p1014*
301 SAINT JOHN ST W, WHITBY, ON, L1N 1N6

SIC 8062

GOUVERNEMENT DE LA PROVINCE DE QUEBEC   *p1106*
116 BOUL LIONEL-EMOND, GATINEAU, QC, J8Y 1W7

SIC 8062

GOUVERNEMENT DE LA PROVINCE DE QUEBEC   *p1147*
50 RUE SAINT-PATRICE E, MAGOG, QC, J1X 3X3

(819) 843-2572   *SIC* 8062

GOVERNMENT OF ONTARIO   *p580*
101 HUMBER COLLEGE BLVD, ETOBICOKE, ON, M9V 1R8

(416) 747-3400   *SIC* 8062

GOVERNMENT OF SASKATCHEWAN *p1412*
1092 107TH ST, NORTH BATTLEFORD, SK, S9A 1Z1

(306) 446-6600   *SIC* 8062

GOVERNMENT OF THE PROVINCE OF ALBERTA   *p5*
GD, BEAVERLODGE, AB, T0H 0C0

(780) 354-2136   *SIC* 8062

GOVERNMENT OF THE PROVINCE OF ALBERTA   *p127*
744 26TH ST, FORT MACLEOD, AB, T0L 0Z0

(403) 553-5300   *SIC* 8062

GOVERNMENT OF THE PROVINCE OF ALBERTA   *p153*
150 N 400 E, RAYMOND, AB, T0K 2S0

(403) 752-5411   *SIC* 8062

GOVERNMENT OF THE PROVINCE OF BRITISH COLUMBIA   *p210*
5800 MOUNTAIN VIEW BLVD, DELTA, BC, V4K 3V6

(604) 946-1121   *SIC* 8062

GRAND RIVER HOSPITAL CORPORATION *p638*
835 KING ST W, KITCHENER, ON, N2G 1G3

(519) 742-3611   *SIC* 8062

GREY BRUCE HEALTH SERVICES   *p835*
1800 8TH ST E, OWEN SOUND, ON, N4K 6M9

(519) 376-2121   *SIC* 8062

GROVES MEMORIAL COMMUNITY HOSPI-

TAL   *p590*
235 UNION ST E, FERGUS, ON, N1M 1W3

(519) 843-2010   *SIC* 8062

GUELPH GENERAL HOSPITAL   *p600*
115 DELHI ST, GUELPH, ON, N1E 4J4

(519) 822-5350   *SIC* 8062

GUYSBOROUGH ANTIGONISH STRAIT HEALTH AUTHORITY   *p442*
138 HOSPITAL RD, CLEVELAND, NS, B0E 1J0

(902) 625-3230   *SIC* 8062

HALDIMAND WAR MEMORIAL HOSPITAL *p567*
206 JOHN ST SUITE 101, DUNNVILLE, ON, N1A 2P7

(905) 774-7431   *SIC* 8062

HALIBURTON HIGHLANDS HEALTH SERVICES CORPORATION   *p607*
7199 GELERT RD, HALIBURTON, ON, K0M 1S0

(705) 457-1392   *SIC* 8062

HALIBURTON HIGHLANDS HEALTH SERVICES CORPORATION   *p607*
7199 GELERT RD RR 3, HALIBURTON, ON, K0M 1S0

(705) 457-1392   *SIC* 8062

HALTON HEALTHCARE SERVICES CORPORATION   *p806*
3001 HOSPITAL GATE, OAKVILLE, ON, L6M 0L8

(905) 845-2571   *SIC* 8062

HAMILTON HEALTH SCIENCES CORPORATION   *p612*
100 KING ST W SUITE 2300, HAMILTON, ON, L8P 1A2

(905) 521-2100   *SIC* 8062

HAMILTON HEALTH SCIENCES CORPORATION   *p614*
711 CONCESSION ST SUITE 201, HAMILTON, ON, L8V 1C3

(905) 389-4411   *SIC* 8062

HANOVER AND DISTRICT HOSPITAL *p617*
90 7TH AVE SUITE 1, HANOVER, ON, N4N 1N1

(519) 364-2340   *SIC* 8062

HEADWATERS HEALTH CARE CENTRE *p808*
100 ROLLING HILLS DR, ORANGEVILLE, ON, L9W 4X9

(519) 941-2410   *SIC* 8062

HEALTH SCIENCES NORTH   *p901*
41 RAMSEY LAKE RD, SUDBURY, ON, P3E 5J1

(705) 523-7100   *SIC* 8062

HOPITAL DU ST-SACREMENT DU CENTRE HOSPITALIER AFFILIE UQ   *p1270*
1050 CH SAINTE-FOY, QUEBEC, QC, G1S 4L8

(418) 682-7511   *SIC* 8062

HOPITAL GENERAL DE HAWKESBURY & DISTRICT GENERAL HOSPITAL INC *p619*
1111 GHISLAIN ST, HAWKESBURY, ON, K6A 3G5

(613) 632-1111   *SIC* 8062

HOPITAL MONTFORT   *p820*
713 MONTREAL RD, OTTAWA, ON, K1K 0T2

(613) 746-4621   *SIC* 8062

HOPITAL SANTA CABRINI   *p1165*
5655 RUE SAINT-ZOTIQUE E, MONTREAL, QC, H1T 1P7

(514) 252-1535   *SIC* 8062

HOSPITAL CHISASIBI   *p1081*
PR, CHISASIBI, QC, J0M 1E0

(819) 855-2844   *SIC* 8062

HOUSE OF HOPE SOCIETY INCORPORATED   *p1005*
87 BOUSFIELD RISE, WATERDOWN, ON, L8B 0T4

SIC 8062

HUMBER RIVER HOSPITAL   *p916*
1235 WILSON AVE, TORONTO, ON, M3M 0B2

(416) 242-1000   *SIC* 8062

HUMBER RIVER HOSPITAL   *p916*
2111 FINCH AVE W, TORONTO, ON, M3N 1N1

(416) 744-2500   *SIC* 8062

HURON PERTH HEALTHCARE ALLIANCE *p544*
98 SHIPLEY ST, CLINTON, ON, N0M 1L0

(519) 482-3447   *SIC* 8062

INFIRMIERES DE L'HUMANITE   *p1286*
4 RUE DES ORMES, RIVIERE-DU-LOUP, QC, G5R 4W7

SIC 8062

INSTITUT UNIVERSITAIRE EN SANTE MENTALE DOUGLAS   *p1397*
6875 BOUL LASALLE, VERDUN, QC, H4H 1R3

(514) 761-6131   *SIC* 8062

INTERIOR HEALTH   *p253*
1200 NEWLANDS RD SUITE 5000, REVELSTOKE, BC, V0E 2S1

(250) 837-2131   *SIC* 8062

INTERIOR HEALTH AUTHORITY   *p212*
1501 5 AVE, FERNIE, BC, V0B 1M0

(250) 423-4453   *SIC* 8062

INTERIOR HEALTH AUTHORITY   *p215*
835 9TH ST N, GOLDEN, BC, V0A 1H2

(250) 344-5271   *SIC* 8062

INTERIOR HEALTH AUTHORITY   *p222*
505 DOYLE AVE, KELOWNA, BC, V1Y 0C5

(250) 862-4200   *SIC* 8062

INTERIOR HEALTH AUTHORITY   *p230*
951 MURRAY ST, LILLOOET, BC, V0K 1V0

(250) 256-1300   *SIC* 8062

INTERIOR HEALTH AUTHORITY   *p235*
3 VIEW ST SUITE 426, NELSON, BC, V1L 2V1

(250) 352-3111   *SIC* 8062

INTERLAKE REGIONAL HEALTH AUTHORITY INC   *p345*
1 STEENSON DR, ASHERN, MB, R0C 0E0

(204) 768-2461   *SIC* 8062

INTERLAKE REGIONAL HEALTH AUTHORITY INC   *p356*
120 EASTON DRIVE, SELKIRK, MB, R1A 2M2

(204) 482-5800   *SIC* 8062

INTERLAKE REGIONAL HEALTH AUTHORITY INC   *p359*
68 MAIN ST, STONEWALL, MB, R0C 2Z0

(204) 378-2460   *SIC* 8062

INTERLAKE REGIONAL HEALTH AUTHORITY INC   *p359*
162 3 AVE SE, TEULON, MB, R0C 3B0

(204) 886-2108   *SIC* 8062

INTERNATIONAL VISION ORGANIZATION *p40*
44 COLERIDGE CRES NW, CALGARY, AB, T2K 1X9

SIC 8062

JAMES BAY GENERAL HOSPITAL   *p591*
GD, FORT ALBANY, ON, P0L 1H0

(705) 278-3330   *SIC* 8062

JAMES BAY GENERAL HOSPITAL   *p746*
78 FURGUSON RD, MOOSONEE, ON, P0L 1Y0

(705) 336-2947   *SIC* 8062

JOSEPH BRANT HOSPITAL   *p531*
1245 LAKESHORE RD, BURLINGTON, ON, L7S 0A2

(905) 632-3730   *SIC* 8062

KAMSACK UNION HOSPITAL DISTRICT *p1408*
341 STEWART ST, KAMSACK, SK, S0A 1S0

(306) 542-2635   *SIC* 8062

KELSEY TRAIL REGIONAL HEALTH AUTHORITY   *p1410*
505 BROADWAY AVE N, MELFORT, SK, S0E 1A0

(306) 752-8700   *SIC* 8062

KELSEY TRAIL REGIONAL HEALTH AUTHORITY   *p1437*
GD, TISDALE, SK, S0E 1T0

SIC 8062

KELSEY TRAIL REGIONAL HEALTH AUTHORITY   *p1437*
GD, TISDALE, SK, S0E 1T0

(306) 873-6600   *SIC* 8062

KEMPTVILLE DISTRICT HOSPITAL   *p627*
2675 CONCESSION RD, KEMPTVILLE, ON, K0G 1J0

(613) 258-3435   *SIC* 8062

KINGS COUNTY MEMORIAL HOSPITAL *p1041*
409 MCINTYRE AVE, MONTAGUE, PE, C0A 1R0

(902) 838-0777   *SIC* 8062

KINGSTON GENERAL HOSPITAL   *p631*
76 STUART ST, KINGSTON, ON, K7L 2V7

(613) 548-3232   *SIC* 8062

KINGSTON HEALTH SCIENCES CENTRE *p631*
76 STUART ST, KINGSTON, ON, K7L 2V7

(613) 549-6666   *SIC* 8062

LADY DUNN HEALTH CENTRE   *p1011*
17 GOVERNMENT RD, WAWA, ON, P0S 1K0

(705) 856-2335   *SIC* 8062

LADY MINTO HOSPITAL AT COCHRANE, THE   *p545*
241 EIGHTH ST, COCHRANE, ON, P0L 1C0

(705) 272-7200   *SIC* 8062

LAKE OF THE WOODS DISTRICT HOSPITAL   *p628*
21 SYLVAN ST, KENORA, ON, P9N 3W7

(807) 468-9861   *SIC* 8062

LAKERIDGE HEALTH   *p814*
850 1/4 CHAMPLAIN AVE, OSHAWA, ON, L1J 8R2

(905) 576-8711   *SIC* 8062

LAKERIDGE HEALTH   *p848*
451 PAXTON ST, PORT PERRY, ON, L9L 1L9

(905) 985-7321   *SIC* 8062

LEAMINGTON DISTRICT MEMORIAL HOSPITAL   *p644*
194 TALBOT ST W SUITE 167, LEAMINGTON, ON, N8H 1N9

(519) 326-2373   *SIC* 8062

LENNOX AND ADDINGTON COUNTY GENERAL HEALTH ASSOCIATION   *p747*
8 RICHMOND PARK DR, NAPANEE, ON, K7R 2Z4

(613) 354-3301   *SIC* 8062

LISTOWEL MEMORIAL HOSPITAL, THE *p647*
255 ELIZABETH ST E, LISTOWEL, ON, N4W 2P5

(519) 291-3120   *SIC* 8062

LONDON HEALTH SCIENCES CENTRE *p654*
375 SOUTH ST, LONDON, ON, N6A 4G5

(519) 685-8500   *SIC* 8062

LONDON HEALTH SCIENCES CENTRE *p654*
800 COMMISSIONERS RD E, LONDON, ON, N6A 5W9

(519) 685-8500   *SIC* 8062

MACKENZIE HEALTH   *p855*
10 TRENCH ST, RICHMOND HILL, ON, L4C 4Z3

(905) 883-1212   *SIC* 8062

MANITOULIN HEALTH CENTRE   *p647*
11 MERIDETH ST, LITTLE CURRENT, ON, P0P 1K0

(705) 368-2300   *SIC* 8062

MARKHAM STOUFFVILLE HOSPITAL *p665*
381 CHURCH ST, MARKHAM, ON, L3P 7P3

(905) 472-7000   *SIC* 8062

MARKHAM STOUFFVILLE HOSPITAL *p1001*
4 CAMPBELL DR, UXBRIDGE, ON, L9P 1S4

(905) 852-9771   *SIC* 8062

MCGILL UNIVERSITY HEALTH CENTRE *p1198*
3801 RUE UNIVERSITY BUREAU 548, MONTREAL, QC, H3A 2B4

(514) 398-6644 *SIC* 8062
MCGILL UNIVERSITY HEALTH CENTRE *p1198*
687 AV DES PINS O BUREAU 1408, MON-TREAL, QC, H3A 1A1
(514) 934-1934 *SIC* 8062
MCGILL UNIVERSITY HEALTH CENTRE *p1213*
1650 AV CEDAR, MONTREAL, QC, H3G 1A4
(514) 934-1934 *SIC* 8062
MEDICAL FACILITIES CORPORATION *p927*
45 ST CLAIR AVE W SUITE 200, TORONTO, ON, M4V 1K9
(416) 848-7380 *SIC* 8062
MK SAFETY NET CANADA *p1017*
1038 WINDHAM CENTRE RD, WINDHAM CENTRE, ON, N0E 2A0
SIC 8062
MUSKOKA ALGONQUIN HEALTHCARE *p620*
100 FRANK MILLER DR, HUNTSVILLE, ON, P1H 1H7
(705) 789-2311 *SIC* 8062
NEEPAWA HEALTH CENTRE *p353*
500 HOSPITAL ST, NEEPAWA, MB, R0J 1H0
(204) 476-2394 *SIC* 8062
NIAGARA HEALTH SYSTEM *p759*
5546 PORTAGE RD, NIAGARA FALLS, ON, L2G 5X8
(905) 378-4647 *SIC* 8062
NIAGARA HEALTH SYSTEM *p761*
176 WELLINGTON ST, NIAGARA ON THE LAKE, ON, L0S 1J0
(905) 378-4647 *SIC* 8062
NIAGARA HEALTH SYSTEM *p847*
260 SUGARLOAF ST, PORT COLBORNE, ON, L3K 2N7
(905) 834-4501 *SIC* 8062
NIAGARA HEALTH SYSTEM *p886*
142 QUEENSTON ST, ST CATHARINES, ON, L2R 2Z7
(905) 684-7271 *SIC* 8062
NIAGARA HEALTH SYSTEM *p887*
1200 FOURTH AVE, ST CATHARINES, ON, L2S 0A9
(905) 378-4647 *SIC* 8062
NIPIGON DISTRICT MEMORIAL HOSPITAL *p761*
125 HOGAN RD, NIPIGON, ON, P0T 2J0
(807) 887-3026 *SIC* 8062
NORFOLK GENERAL HOSPITAL *p881*
365 WEST ST, SIMCOE, ON, N3Y 1T7
(519) 426-0130 *SIC* 8062
NORTH EASTMAN HEALTH ASSOCIATION INC *p345*
151 1 ST S, BEAUSEJOUR, MB, R0E 0C0
(204) 268-1076 *SIC* 8062
NORTH SHORE HEALTH NETWORK *p493*
525 CAUSLEY ST, BLIND RIVER, ON, P0R 1B0
(705) 356-1220 *SIC* 8062
NORTH WELLINGTON HEALTH CARE CORPORATION *p746*
630 DUBLIN ST, MOUNT FOREST, ON, N0G 2L3
(519) 323-2210 *SIC* 8062
NORTH YORK GENERAL HOSPITAL *p769*
4001 LESLIE ST, NORTH YORK, ON, M2K 1E1
(416) 756-6000 *SIC* 8062
NORTH YORK GENERAL HOSPITAL *p775*
555 FINCH AVE W SUITE 262, NORTH YORK, ON, M2R 1N5
(416) 633-9420 *SIC* 8062
NORTHERN HEALTH AUTHORITY *p224*
920 LAHAKAS BLVD S, KITIMAT, BC, V8C 2S3
(250) 632-2121 *SIC* 8062
NORTHERN HEALTH AUTHORITY *p249*
299 VICTORIA ST SUITE 600, PRINCE GEORGE, BC, V2L 5B8
(250) 565-2649 *SIC* 8062

NORTHERN HEALTH AUTHORITY *p251*
1305 SUMMIT AVE, PRINCE RUPERT, BC, V8J 2A6
(250) 624-2171 *SIC* 8062
NORTHERN HEALTH AUTHORITY *p252*
543 FRONT ST, QUESNEL, BC, V2J 2K7
(250) 985-5600 *SIC* 8062
NORTHERN ONTARIO SCHOOL OF MEDICINE *p908*
955 OLIVER RD SUITE 2005, THUNDER BAY, ON, P7B 5E1
(807) 766-7300 *SIC* 8062
NORTHERN REGIONAL HEALTH AUTHORITY *p350*
84 CHURCH ST, FLIN FLON, MB, R8A 1L8
(204) 687-1300 *SIC* 8062
NORTHUMBERLAND HILLS HOSPITAL *p545*
1000 DEPALMA DR, COBOURG, ON, K9A 5W6
(905) 372-6811 *SIC* 8062
NORTHWEST TERRITORY HEALTH AND SOCIAL SERVICES AUTHORITY-BDR *p435*
285 MACKENZIE RD, INUVIK, NT, X0E 0T0
(867) 777-8000 *SIC* 8062
NOTRE DAME BAY MEMORIAL HEALTH CENTER *p434*
GD, TWILLINGATE, NL, A0G 4M0
(709) 884-2131 *SIC* 8062
NOVA SCOTIA HEALTH AUTHORITY *p438*
18 ALBION ST S, AMHERST, NS, B4H 2W3
(902) 661-1090 *SIC* 8062
NOVA SCOTIA HEALTH AUTHORITY *p442*
89 PAYZANT, CURRYS CORNER, NS, B0N 2T0
(902) 798-8351 *SIC* 8062
NOVA SCOTIA HEALTH AUTHORITY *p449*
75 WARWICK ST, DIGBY, NS, B0V 1A0
(902) 245-2501 *SIC* 8062
NOVA SCOTIA HEALTH AUTHORITY *p451*
1278 TOWER RD, HALIFAX, NS, B3H 2Y9
(902) 473-1787 *SIC* 8062
NOVA SCOTIA HEALTH AUTHORITY *p451*
1276 SOUTH PARK ST SUITE 1278, HALIFAX, NS, B3H 2Y9
(902) 473-5117 *SIC* 8062
NOVA SCOTIA HEALTH AUTHORITY *p460*
5 CHIPMAN DR, KENTVILLE, NS, B4N 3V7
(902) 365-1700 *SIC* 8062
NOVA SCOTIA HEALTH AUTHORITY *p465*
1606 LAKE RD, SHELBURNE, NS, B0T 1W0
(902) 875-3011 *SIC* 8062
OILFIELDS GENERAL HOSPITAL *p5*
717 GOVERNMENT RD, BLACK DIAMOND, AB, T0L 0H0
(403) 933-2222 *SIC* 8062
OTTAWA HOSPITAL, THE *p819*
1967 RIVERSIDE DR SUITE 323, OTTAWA, ON, K1H 7W9
(613) 798-5555 *SIC* 8062
OTTAWA HOSPITAL, THE *p828*
1053 CARLING AVE, OTTAWA, ON, K1Y 4E9
(613) 798-5555 *SIC* 8062
OTTAWA HOSPITAL, THE *p828*
1053 CARLING AVE SUITE 119, OTTAWA, ON, K1Y 4E9
(613) 722-7000 *SIC* 8062
OTTAWA NETWORK FOR BORDERLINE PERSONALITY DISORDER *p626*
412 ROSINGDALE ST, KANATA, ON, K2M 0L8
SIC 8062
PALEMERSTON AND DISTRICT HOSPITAL *p836*
500 WHITES RD RR 3, PALMERSTON, ON, N0G 2P0
(519) 343-2030 *SIC* 8062
PARKLAND REGIONAL HEALTH AUTHORITY INC *p349*
625 3RD ST SW, DAUPHIN, MB, R7N 1R7
(204) 638-2118 *SIC* 8062
PARKLAND REGIONAL HEALTH AUTHOR-

ITY INC *p355*
GD, ROBLIN, MB, R0L 1P0
(204) 937-2142 *SIC* 8062
PARKLAND REGIONAL HEALTH AUTHORITY INC *p359*
1011 MAIN ST E, SWAN RIVER, MB, R0L 1Z0
(204) 734-3441 *SIC* 8062
PAS HEALTH COMPLEX INC, THE *p360*
67 1ST ST W, THE PAS, MB, R9A 1K4
(204) 623-6431 *SIC* 8062
PEMBROKE REGIONAL HOSPITAL INC *p838*
705 MACKAY ST SUITE 732, PEMBROKE, ON, K8A 1G8
(613) 732-2811 *SIC* 8062
PENETANGUISHENE GENERAL HOSPITAL INC, THE *p838*
25 JEFFERY ST SUITE 670, PENETANGUISHENE, ON, L9M 1K6
(705) 549-7442 *SIC* 8062
PERTH AND SMITHS FALLS DISTRICT HOSPITAL *p839*
33 DRUMMOND ST W, PERTH, ON, K7H 2K1
(613) 267-1500 *SIC* 8062
PERTH AND SMITHS FALLS DISTRICT HOSPITAL *p882*
60 CORNELIA ST W, SMITHS FALLS, ON, K7A 2H9
(613) 283-2330 *SIC* 8062
PRAIRIE MOUNTAIN HEALTH *p351*
86 ELLICE DR, KILLARNEY, MB, R0K 1G0
(204) 523-4661 *SIC* 8062
PRAIRIE MOUNTAIN HEALTH *p352*
334 1ST ST SW, MINNEDOSA, MB, R0J 1E0
(204) 867-2701 *SIC* 8062
PRAIRIE MOUNTAIN HEALTH *p352*
147 SUMMIT ST, MELITA, MB, R0M 1L0
(204) 522-8197 *SIC* 8062
PRAIRIE MOUNTAIN HEALTH *p360*
480 KING ST E, VIRDEN, MB, R0M 2C0
(204) 748-1230 *SIC* 8062
PRAIRIE NORTH REGIONAL HEALTH AUTHORITY *p1410*
711 CENTRE ST SUITE 7, MEADOW LAKE, SK, S9X 1E6
(306) 236-1550 *SIC* 8062
PRAIRIE NORTH REGIONAL HEALTH AUTHORITY *p1412*
1092 107TH ST, NORTH BATTLEFORD, SK, S9A 1Z1
(306) 446-6600 *SIC* 8062
PRINCE COUNTY HOSPITAL *p1043*
65 ROY BOATES AVE, SUMMERSIDE, PE, C1N 6M8
(902) 438-4200 *SIC* 8062
PROVIDENCE HEALTH CARE SOCIETY *p288*
7801 ARGYLE ST, VANCOUVER, BC, V5P 3L6
(604) 321-2661 *SIC* 8062
PROVIDENCE HEALTH CARE SOCIETY *p289*
3080 PRINCE EDWARD ST, VANCOUVER, BC, V5T 3N4
(604) 877-8302 *SIC* 8062
PROVIDENCE HEALTH CARE SOCIETY *p327*
1081 BURRARD ST, VANCOUVER, BC, V6Z 1Y6
(604) 682-2344 *SIC* 8062
PROVINCE OF PEI *p1039*
60 RIVERSIDE DR, CHARLOTTETOWN, PE, C1A 8T5
(902) 894-2111 *SIC* 8062
PUBLIC GENERAL HOSPITAL SOCIETY OF CHATHAM, THE *p542*
80 GRAND AVE W SUITE 301, CHATHAM, ON, N7L 1B7
(519) 352-6400 *SIC* 8062
QUEENSWAY-CARLETON HOSPITAL *p751*
QUEENSWAY-CARLETON HOSPITAL, NE-

PEAN, ON, K2H 8P4
(613) 721-2000 *SIC* 8062
QUINTE HEALTHCARE CORPORATION *p491*
265 DUNDAS ST E, BELLEVILLE, ON, K8N 5A9
(613) 969-7400 *SIC* 8062
QUINTE HEALTHCARE CORPORATION *p999*
242 KING ST, TRENTON, ON, K8V 5S6
(613) 392-2540 *SIC* 8062
R H A CENTRAL MANITOBA INC. *p353*
215 RAILROAD AVE E, MORRIS, MB, R0G 1K0
(204) 746-2301 *SIC* 8062
RED LAKE MARGARET COCHENOUR MEMORIAL HOSPITAL CORPORATION, THE *p849*
51 HWY 105, RED LAKE, ON, P0V 2M0
(807) 727-2231 *SIC* 8062
REGIONAL HEALTH AUTHORITY - CENTRAL MANITOBA INC *p350*
24 MILL ST, GLADSTONE, MB, R0J 0T0
(204) 385-2968 *SIC* 8062
REGIONAL HEALTH AUTHORITY - CENTRAL MANITOBA INC *p355*
524 5TH ST SE, PORTAGE LA PRAIRIE, MB, R1N 3A8
(204) 239-2211 *SIC* 8062
REGIONAL HEALTH AUTHORITY - CENTRAL MANITOBA INC *p357*
180 CENTENNAIRE DR, SOUTHPORT, MB, R0H 1N1
(204) 428-2720 *SIC* 8062
REGIONAL HEALTH AUTHORITY A *p394*
1750 SUNSET DR, BATHURST, NB, E2A 4L7
(506) 544-3000 *SIC* 8062
REGIONAL HEALTH AUTHORITY A *p394*
275 MAIN ST SUITE 600, BATHURST, NB, E2A 1A9
(506) 544-2188 *SIC* 8062
REGIONAL HEALTH AUTHORITY A *p404*
29 RUE DE L'HOPITAL, LAMEQUE, NB, E8T 1C5
(506) 344-2261 *SIC* 8062
REGIONAL HEALTH AUTHORITY A *p419*
400 RUE DES HOSPITALIERES, TRACADIE-SHEILA, NB, E1X 1G5
(506) 394-3000 *SIC* 8062
REGIONAL HEALTH AUTHORITY NB *p401*
180 WOODBRIDGE ST, FREDERICTON, NB, E3B 4R3
(506) 623-5500 *SIC* 8062
REGIONAL HEALTH AUTHORITY NB *p412*
8 MAIN ST, SACKVILLE, NB, E4L 4A3
(506) 364-4100 *SIC* 8062
RELIGIOUS HOSPITALLERS OF SAINT JOSEPH OF THE HOTEL DIEU OF KINGSTON *p631*
166 BROCK ST SUITE 262D, KINGSTON, ON, K7L 5G2
(613) 544-3310 *SIC* 8062
RENFREW VICTORIA HOSPITAL *p849*
499 RAGLAN ST N, RENFREW, ON, K7V 1P6
(613) 432-4851 *SIC* 8062
RESTIGOUCHE HEALTH AUTHORITY *p396*
189 LILY LAKE RD, CAMPBELLTON, NB, E3N 3H3
(506) 789-5000 *SIC* 8062
RICHMOND HOSPITAL, THE *p261*
7000 WESTMINSTER HWY, RICHMOND, BC, V6X 1A2
(604) 278-9711 *SIC* 8062
RIVERDALE HEALTH SERVICES DISTRICT FOUNDATION INC *p355*
512 QUEBEC ST, RIVERS, MB, R0K 1X0
(204) 328-5321 *SIC* 8062
RIVERSIDE HEALTH CARE FACILITIES INC *p592*
110 VICTORIA AVE, FORT FRANCES, ON, P9A 2B7
(807) 274-3266 *SIC* 8062

ROSS MEMORIAL HOSPITAL, THE   *p646*
10 ANGELINE ST N, LINDSAY, ON, K9V 4M8
(705) 324-6111   *SIC 8062*

SASKATCHEWAN CATHOLIC HEALTH CORPORATION, THE   *p1410*
200 HERITAGE DR, MELVILLE, SK, S0A 2P0
(306) 728-5407   *SIC 8062*

SASKATCHEWAN HEALTH AUTHORITY   *p1407*
1210 NINTH ST N, HUMBOLDT, SK, S0K 2A1
(306) 682-2603   *SIC 8062*

SASKATCHEWAN HEALTH AUTHORITY   *p1409*
3820 43 AVE, LLOYDMINSTER, SK, S9V 1Y5
(306) 820-6000   *SIC 8062*

SASKATCHEWAN HEALTH AUTHORITY   *p1433*
1319 COLONY ST, SASKATOON, SK, S7N 2Z1
(306) 655-1070   *SIC 8062*

SASKATCHEWAN HEALTH AUTHORITY   *p1436*
2004 SASKATCHEWAN DR, SWIFT CURRENT, SK, S9H 5M8
(306) 778-9400   *SIC 8062*

SASKATCHEWAN HEALTH AUTHORITY   *p1438*
304 7TH ST E, WILKIE, SK, S0K 4W0
(306) 843-2644   *SIC 8062*

SAULT AREA HOSPITAL   *p863*
750 GREAT NORTHERN RD SUITE 1, SAULT STE. MARIE, ON, P6B 0A8
(705) 759-3434   *SIC 8062*

SCARBOROUGH AND ROUGE HOSPITAL   *p872*
3050 LAWRENCE AVE E, SCARBOROUGH, ON, M1P 2V5
(416) 438-2911   *SIC 8062*

SEA TO SKY COMMUNITY HEALTH COUNCIL   *p269*
38140 BEHRNER DR, SQUAMISH, BC, V8B 0J3
(604) 892-9337   *SIC 8062*

SENSENBRENNER HOSPITAL   *p627*
101 PROGRESS CRES, KAPUSKASING, ON, P5N 3H5
(705) 337-6111   *SIC 8062*

SEVEN OAKS GENERAL HOSPITAL   *p370*
2300 MCPHILLIPS ST, WINNIPEG, MB, R2V 3M3
(204) 632-7133   *SIC 8062*

SHOAL LAKE-STRATHCLAIR HEALTH CENTRE   *p356*
524 MARY ST, SHOAL LAKE, MB, R0J 1Z0
(204) 759-2336   *SIC 8062*

SINAI HEALTH SYSTEM   *p947*
600 UNIVERSITY AVE, TORONTO, ON, M5G 1X5
(416) 596-4200   *SIC 8062*

SIOUX LOOKOUT MENO-YA-WIN HEALTH CENTRE PLANNING CORPORATION   *p881*
1 MENO YA WIN WAY, SIOUX LOOKOUT, ON, P8T 1B4
(807) 737-3030   *SIC 8062*

SMOOTH ROCK FALLS HOSPITAL CORPORATION   *p882*
107 KELLY RD, SMOOTH ROCK FALLS, ON, P0L 2B0
(705) 338-2781   *SIC 8062*

SOURIS DISTRICT HOSPITAL & AMBULANCE SERVICE   *p357*
155 BRINDLE AVE E, SOURIS, MB, R0K 2C0
(204) 483-2121   *SIC 8062*

SOUTH BRUCE GREY HEALTH CENTRE   *p1004*
21 MCGIVERN ST, WALKERTON, ON, N0G 2V0
(519) 881-1220   *SIC 8062*

SOUTH HURON HOSPITAL ASSOCIATION   *p590*
24 HURON ST W, EXETER, ON, N0M 1S2
(519) 235-2700   *SIC 8062*

SOUTH OKANAGAN GENERAL HOSPITAL   *p242*
7139 362 AVE, OLIVER, BC, V0H 1T0
(250) 498-5000   *SIC 8062*

SOUTHERN HEALTH-SANTE SUD   *p357*
354 PREFONTAINE AVE, ST PIERRE JOLYS, MB, R0A 1V0
(204) 433-7611   *SIC 8062*

SOUTHERN HEALTH-SANTE SUD   *p358*
316 HENRY ST, STEINBACH, MB, R5G 0P9
(204) 326-6411   *SIC 8062*

SOUTHERN HEALTH-SANTE SUD   *p360*
217 1ST AVE, VITA, MB, R0A 2K0
(204) 425-3325   *SIC 8062*

SOUTHLAKE REGIONAL HEALTH CENTRE   *p756*
596 DAVIS DR, NEWMARKET, ON, L3Y 2P9
(905) 895-4521   *SIC 8062*

ST JOSEPH'S GENERAL HOSPITAL   *p170*
5241 43RD ST, VEGREVILLE, AB, T9C 1R5
(780) 632-2811   *SIC 8062*

ST JOSEPH'S GENERAL HOSPITAL   *p198*
2137 COMOX AVE, COMOX, BC, V9M 1P2
(250) 339-1451   *SIC 8062*

ST MARY'S HOSPITAL CAMROSE   *p78*
4607 53 ST, CAMROSE, AB, T4V 1Y5
(780) 679-6100   *SIC 8062*

ST MARYS MEMORIAL HOSPITAL   *p888*
267 QUEEN ST W, ST MARYS, ON, N4X 1B6
(519) 284-1330   *SIC 8062*

ST. JOSEPH'S GENERAL HOSPITAL ELLIOT LAKE   *p568*
70 SPINE RD, ELLIOT LAKE, ON, P5A 1X2
(705) 848-7181   *SIC 8062*

ST. BONIFACE GENERAL HOSPITAL   *p364*
409 TACHE AVE, WINNIPEG, MB, R2H 2A6
(204) 233-8563   *SIC 8062*

ST. FRANCIS MEMORIAL HOSPITAL ASSOCIATION   *p489*
7 ST FRANCIS MEMORIAL DR, BARRYS BAY, ON, K0J 1B0
(613) 756-3044   *SIC 8062*

ST. JOSEPH'S (GREY NUN'S) OF GRAVELBOURG   *p1407*
216 BETTEZ ST, GRAVELBOURG, SK, S0H 1X0
(306) 648-3185   *SIC 8062*

ST. JOSEPH'S CONTINUING CARE CENTRE OF SUDBURY   *p901*
1140 SOUTH BAY RD, SUDBURY, ON, P3E 0B6
(705) 674-2846   *SIC 8062*

ST. JOSEPH'S HEALTH CENTRE   *p995*
30 THE QUEENSWAY, TORONTO, ON, M6R 1B5
(416) 530-6000   *SIC 8062*

ST. JOSEPH'S HOSPITAL OF ESTEVAN   *p1406*
1176 NICHOLSON RD SUITE 203, ESTEVAN, SK, S4A 0H3
(306) 637-2400   *SIC 8062*

ST. THOMAS-ELGIN GENERAL HOSPITAL, THE   *p890*
189 ELM ST, ST THOMAS, ON, N5R 5C4
(519) 631-2030   *SIC 8062*

STANTON TERRITORIAL HEALTH AUTHORITY   *p436*
550 BYRNE RD, YELLOWKNIFE, NT, X1A 2N1
(867) 669-4111   *SIC 8062*

STE ROSE GENERAL HOSPITAL   *p358*
540 3RD AVE E, STE ROSE DU LAC, MB, R0L 1S0
(204) 447-2131   *SIC 8062*

STEVENSON MEMORIAL HOSPITAL, THE   *p476*
200 FLETCHER CRES, ALLISTON, ON, L9R 1M1
(705) 435-6281   *SIC 8062*

STRATHROY MIDDLESEX GENERAL HOSPITAL   *p897*
395 CARRIE ST SUITE 360, STRATHROY, ON, N7G 3C9
(519) 245-5295   *SIC 8062*

SUN COUNTRY REGIONAL HEALTH AUTHORITY   *p1415*
18 EICHHORST ST, REDVERS, SK, S0C 2H0
(306) 452-3553   *SIC 8062*

SUN COUNTRY REGIONAL HEALTH AUTHORITY   *p1438*
201 1ST AVE NE, WEYBURN, SK, S4H 0N1
(306) 842-8400   *SIC 8062*

SUNNYBROOK HEALTH SCIENCES CENTRE   *p921*
2075 BAYVIEW AVE, TORONTO, ON, M4N 3M5
(416) 480-6100   *SIC 8062*

SYNDICAT DES PROFESSIONNELLES DE LA SANTE DU RESEAU PAPNEAU, SPSRP-FIQ   *p1102*
617 AV DE BUCKINGHAM, GATINEAU, QC, J8L 2H4
(819) 986-3359   *SIC 8062*

SYNDICAT DES PROFESSIONNELLES EN SOINS DU CENTRE DE SANTE ET SERVICES SOCIAUX DU COEUR DE   *p1171*
1385 RUE JEAN-TALON E, MONTREAL, QC, H2E 1S6
(514) 495-6767   *SIC 8062*

THUNDER BAY REGIONAL HEALTH SCIENCES CENTRE   *p909*
980 OLIVER RD RM 1480, THUNDER BAY, ON, P7B 6V4
(807) 684-6500   *SIC 8062*

TILLSONBURG DISTRICT MEMORIAL HOSPITAL TRUST   *p912*
167 ROLPH ST SUITE 3100, TILLSONBURG, ON, N4G 3Y9
(519) 842-3611   *SIC 8062*

TIMMINS AND DISTRICT HOSPITAL   *p913*
700 ROSS AVE E SUITE 1559, TIMMINS, ON, P4N 8P2
(705) 267-2131   *SIC 8062*

TOFIELD HEALTH CENTER   *p170*
5543 44 ST, TOFIELD, AB, T0B 4J0
(780) 662-3263   *SIC 8062*

TORONTO EAST HEALTH NETWORK   *p917*
825 COXWELL AVE, TORONTO, ON, M4C 3E7
(416) 461-8272   *SIC 8062*

TRENTON MEMORIAL HOSPITAL   *p999*
242 KING ST, TRENTON, ON, K8V 3X1
(613) 392-2541   *SIC 8062*

TRILLIUM HEALTH PARTNERS   *p711*
100 QUEENSWAY W, MISSISSAUGA, ON, L5B 1B8
(905) 848-7580   *SIC 8062*

TRILLIUM HEALTH PARTNERS   *p719*
2200 EGLINTON AVE W SUITE 905, MISSISSAUGA, ON, L5M 2N1
(905) 813-2200   *SIC 8062*

TRILLIUM HEALTH PARTNERS   *p996*
150 SHERWAY DR, TORONTO, ON, M9C 1A5
(416) 259-6671   *SIC 8062*

UNITY & DISTRICT HEALTH CENTRE   *p1437*
100 1ST AVE W UNIT 1, UNITY, SK, S0K 4L0
(306) 228-2666   *SIC 8062*

UNIVERSITY HEALTH NETWORK   *p947*
200 ELIZABETH ST, TORONTO, ON, M5G 2C4
(416) 340-3111   *SIC 8062*

UNIVERSITY OF WESTERN ONTARIO, THE   *p655*
1151 RICHMOND ST RM 4, LONDON, ON, N6A 5C1
(519) 661-2111   *SIC 8062*

VANCOUVER COASTAL HEALTH   *p240*
231 15TH ST E, NORTH VANCOUVER, BC, V7L 2L7
(604) 988-3131   *SIC 8062*

VANCOUVER COASTAL HEALTH   *p240*
231 15TH ST E, NORTH VANCOUVER, BC, V7L 2L7
(604) 988-3131   *SIC 8062*

VANCOUVER COASTAL HEALTH AUTHORITY   *p289*
377 2ND AVE E, VANCOUVER, BC, V5T 1B9
(604) 658-1253   *SIC 8062*

VANCOUVER COASTAL HEALTH AUTHORITY   *p294*
855 12TH AVE W SUITE 101, VANCOUVER, BC, V5Z 1M9
(604) 875-4111   *SIC 8062*

VANCOUVER COASTAL HEALTH AUTHORITY   *p325*
2211 WESBROOK MALL, VANCOUVER, BC, V6T 2B5
(604) 822-7121   *SIC 8062*

VICTORIA GENERAL HOSPITAL   *p392*
2340 PEMBINA HWY, WINNIPEG, MB, R3T 2E8
(204) 269-3570   *SIC 8062*

VITALITE HEALTH NETWORK   *p395*
275 MAIN ST SUITE 600, BATHURST, NB, E2A 1A9
(506) 544-2133   *SIC 8062*

VITALITE HEALTH NETWORK   *p403*
625 BOUL EVERARD H DAIGLE, GRAND-SAULT/GRAND FALLS, NB, E3Z 2R9
(506) 473-7555   *SIC 8062*

VITALITE HEALTH NETWORK   *p407*
330 AV UNIVERSITE, MONCTON, NB, E1C 2Z3
(506) 862-4000   *SIC 8062*

WEENEEBAYKO HEALTH AHTUSKAYWIN   *p746*
19 HOSPITAL DR, MOOSE FACTORY, ON, P0L 1W0
(705) 658-4544   *SIC 8062*

WEST COAST GENERAL HOSPITAL   *p245*
3949 PORT ALBERNI HWY, PORT ALBERNI, BC, V9Y 4S1
(250) 731-1370   *SIC 8062*

WEST HALDIMAND GENERAL HOSPITAL   *p607*
75 PARKVIEW RD, HAGERSVILLE, ON, N0A 1H0
(905) 768-3311   *SIC 8062*

WEST NIPISSING GENERAL HOSPITAL, THE   *p898*
725 COURSOL RD SUITE 427, STURGEON FALLS, ON, P2B 2Y6
(705) 753-3110   *SIC 8062*

WEST PARRY SOUND HEALTH CENTRE   *p837*
6 ALBERT ST, PARRY SOUND, ON, P2A 3A4
(705) 746-9321   *SIC 8062*

WESTERN HOSPITAL   *p1038*
148 POPULAR ST, ALBERTON, PE, C0B 1B0
(902) 853-8650   *SIC 8062*

WESTERN REGIONAL INTEGRATED HEALTH AUTHORITY, THE   *p423*
1 BROOKFIELD AVE, CORNER BROOK, NL, A2H 6J7
(709) 637-5000   *SIC 8062*

WESTERN REGIONAL INTEGRATED HEALTH AUTHORITY, THE   *p427*
GD, NORRIS POINT, NL, A0K 3V0
(709) 458-2211   *SIC 8062*

WESTERN REGIONAL INTEGRATED HEALTH AUTHORITY, THE   *p434*
142 MINNESOTA DR, STEPHENVILLE, NL, A2N 3X9
(709) 643-5111   *SIC 8062*

WILLIAM OSLER HEALTH SYSTEM   *p498*
2100 BOVAIRD DR E, BRAMPTON, ON, L6R 3J7
(905) 494-2120   *SIC 8062*

WILLIAM OSLER HEALTH SYSTEM   *p498*
2100 BOVAIRD DR E, BRAMPTON, ON, L6R 3J7

(905) 494-2120   *SIC 8062*
WILLIAM OSLER HEALTH SYSTEM   *p581*
101 HUMBER COLLEGE BLVD, ETOBI-
COKE, ON, M9V 1R8
(416) 494-2120   *SIC 8062*
WILSON MEMORIAL GENERAL HOSPITAL
p664
26 PENINSULA RD, MARATHON, ON, P0T
2E0
(807) 229-1740   *SIC 8062*
**WINCHESTER DISTRICT MEMORIAL HOS-
PITAL**   *p1016*
566 LOUISE ST RR 4, WINCHESTER, ON,
K0C 2K0
(613) 774-2420   *SIC 8062*
WINDSOR REGIONAL HOSPITAL   *p1020*
1995 LENS AVE, WINDSOR, ON, N8W 1L9
(519) 254-5577   *SIC 8062*
WINGHAM AND DISTRICT HOSPITALp1026
270 CARLING TERR, WINGHAM, ON, N0G
2W0
(519) 357-3210   *SIC 8062*
**WINNIPEG REGIONAL HEALTH AUTHOR-
ITY, THE**   *p374*
820 SHERBROOK ST SUITE 543, WIN-
NIPEG, MB, R3A 1R9
(204) 774-6511   *SIC 8062*
**WINNIPEG REGIONAL HEALTH AUTHOR-
ITY, THE**   *p376*
650 MAIN ST 4TH FL, WINNIPEG, MB, R3B
1E2
(204) 926-7000   *SIC 8062*
**WINNIPEG REGIONAL HEALTH AUTHOR-
ITY, THE**   *p381*
720 MCDERMOT AVE RM AD301, WIN-
NIPEG, MB, R3E 0T3
(204) 787-1165   *SIC 8062*
WOMEN'S COLLEGE HOSPITAL   *p976*
76 GRENVILLE ST, TORONTO, ON, M5S
1B2
(416) 323-6400   *SIC 8062*
**WOODSTOCK GENERAL HOSPITAL
TRUST**   *p1036*
310 JULIANA DR, WOODSTOCK, ON, N4V
0A4
(519) 421-4211   *SIC 8062*
WYNYARD HOSPITAL   *p1438*
300 10 ST E, WYNYARD, SK, S0A 4T0
(306) 554-2586   *SIC 8062*
YUKON HOSPITAL CORPORATION   *p1440*
5 HOSPITAL RD, WHITEHORSE, YT, Y1A
3H7
(867) 393-8930   *SIC 8062*

SIC 8063 Psychiatric hospitals

ALBERTA HEALTH SERVICES   *p107*
17480 FORT RD NW SUITE 175, EDMON-
TON, AB, T5Y 6A8
(780) 342-5555   *SIC 8063*
**BRITISH COLUMBIA MENTAL HEALTH SO-
CIETY**   *p199*
2601 LOUGHEED HWY, COQUITLAM, BC,
V3C 4J2
(604) 524-7000   *SIC 8063*
CENTRACARE   *p416*
414 BAY ST, SAINT JOHN, NB, E2M 7L4
(506) 649-2550   *SIC 8063*
**FONDATION DE L'INSTITUT UNIVERSI-
TAIRE EN SANTE MENTALE DE MON-
TREAL**   *p1164*
7401 RUE HOCHELAGA, MONTREAL, QC,
H1N 3M5
(514) 251-4000   *SIC 8063*
**FORENSIC PSYCHIATRIC SERVICES COM-
MISSION**   *p199*
70 COLONY FARM RD, COQUITLAM, BC,
V3C 5X9
(604) 524-7700   *SIC 8063*
HOMEWOOD HEALTH CENTRE INC   *p600*
150 DELHI ST, GUELPH, ON, N1E 6K9
(519) 824-1010   *SIC 8063*
ONTARIO SHORES CENTRE FOR MENTAL

HEALTH SCIENCES   *p1015*
700 GORDON ST, WHITBY, ON, L1N 5S9
(905) 668-5881   *SIC 8063*
PROVIDENCE CARE CENTRE   *p631*
752 KING ST W, KINGSTON, ON, K7L 4X3
(613) 548-5567   *SIC 8063*
PROVINCE OF PEI   *p1039*
115 DACON GROVE LANE, CHARLOTTE-
TOWN, PE, C1A 7N5
(902) 368-5400   *SIC 8063*
**SISTERS OF ST. JOSEPH OF SAULT STE.
MARIE, THE**   *p907*
580 ALGOMA ST N, THUNDER BAY, ON,
P7A 8C5
(807) 343-4300   *SIC 8063*
**ST. JOSEPH'S HEALTHCARE FOUNDA-
TION, HAMILTON**   *p617*
100 WEST 5TH ST, HAMILTON, ON, L9C
0E3
(905) 388-2511   *SIC 8063*
**WAYPOINT CENTRE FOR MENTAL
HEALTH CARE**   *p838*
500 CHURCH ST, PENETANGUISHENE,
ON, L9M 1G3
(705) 549-3181   *SIC 8063*

---

*SIC 8069 Specialty hospitals, except
psychiatric*

ARCAN DEVELOPMENTS LTD   *p342*
1675 27TH ST, WEST VANCOUVER, BC,
V7V 4K9
(604) 925-1247   *SIC 8069*
**BAYCREST CENTRE FOR GERIATRIC
CARE**   *p988*
3560 BATHURST ST, TORONTO, ON, M6A
2E1
(416) 785-2500   *SIC 8069*
BC CANCER FOUNDATION   *p221*
399 ROYAL AVE, KELOWNA, BC, V1Y 5L3
(250) 712-3900   *SIC 8069*
**BRITISH COLUMBIA'S CHILDRENS HOSPI-
TAL**   *p319*
4480 OAK ST SUITE B321, VANCOUVER,
BC, V6H 3V4
(604) 875-2345   *SIC 8069*
CANCER CARE ONTARIO   *p630*
25 KING ST W, KINGSTON, ON, K7L 5P9
(613) 544-2630   *SIC 8069*
CANCERCARE MANITOBA   *p380*
675 MCDERMOT AVE UNIT 4025, WIN-
NIPEG, MB, R3E 0V9
(204) 787-2197   *SIC 8069*
**CANCERCARE MANITOBA FOUNDATION
INC**   *p380*
675 MCDERMOT AVE SUITE 1160, WIN-
NIPEG, MB, R3E 0V9
(204) 787-4142   *SIC 8069*
**CARLETON PLACE & DISTRICT MEMO-
RIAL HOSPITAL**   *p540*
211 LAKE AVE E, CARLETON PLACE, ON,
K7C 1J4
(613) 257-2200   *SIC 8069*
CENTRE DE SANTE PAUL GILBERT   *p1139*
9330 BOUL DU CENTRE-HOSPITALIER,
LEVIS, QC, G6X 1L6
(418) 380-8993   *SIC 8069*
CENTRE HOSPITALIER DE BEDFORD
p1056
34 RUE SAINT-JOSEPH, BEDFORD, QC,
J0J 1A0
(450) 248-4304   *SIC 8069*
**CENTRE HOSPITALIER DE TROIS-
PISTOLES**   *p1384*
550 RUE NOTRE-DAME E, TROIS-
PISTOLES, QC, G0L 4K0
(418) 851-1111   *SIC 8069*
**CENTRE HOSPITALIER REGIONAL DE
TROIS-RIVIERES**   *p1386*
1991 BOUL DU CARMEL, TROIS-
RIVIERES, QC, G8Z 3R9
(819) 697-3333   *SIC 8069*
CENTRE HOSPITALIER UNIVERSITAIRE

SAINTE-JUSTINE   *p1219*
3175 CH DE LA COTE-SAINTE-
CATHERINE, MONTREAL, QC, H3T 1C5
(514) 345-4931   *SIC 8069*
CENTRE LE CARDINAL INC   *p1247*
12900 RUE NOTRE-DAME E, POINTE-
AUX-TREMBLES, QC, H1A 1R9
(514) 645-0095   *SIC 8069*
CHEMAINUS HEALTH CARE CENTRE *p196*
9909 ESPLANADE ST, CHEMAINUS, BC,
V0R 1K1
(250) 737-2040   *SIC 8069*
**CHILDREN'S & WOMEN'S HEALTH CEN-
TRE OF BRITISH COLUMBIA BRANCH**p319
4500 OAK ST, VANCOUVER, BC, V6H 3N1
(604) 875-2424   *SIC 8069*
**CHILDRENS HOSPITAL OF EASTERN ON-
TARIO**   *p819*
401 SMYTH RD, OTTAWA, ON, K1H 8L1
(613) 737-7600   *SIC 8069*
**CIUSSS DE LA MAURICIE-ET-DU-CENTRE-
DU-QUEBEC**   *p1389*
11931 RUE NOTRE-DAME O, TROIS-
RIVIERES, QC, G9B 6W9
(819) 377-2441   *SIC 8069*
DONWOOD INSTITUTE, THE   *p918*
175 BRENTCLIFFE RD, TORONTO, ON,
M4G 0C5
(416) 425-3930   *SIC 8069*
**GOOD SAMARITAN SOCIETY, THE (A
LUTHERAN SOCIAL SERVICE ORGANIZA-
TION)**   *p112*
8861 75 ST NW, EDMONTON, AB, T6C 4G8
(780) 431-3600   *SIC 8069*
GOVERNMENT OF ONTARIO   *p490*
29 MAIN ST W, BEETON, ON, L0G 1A0
(905) 729-4004   *SIC 8069*
**HOLLAND BLOORVIEW KIDS REHABILI-
TATION HOSPITAL**   *p918*
150 KILGOUR RD, TORONTO, ON, M4G
1R8
(416) 425-6220   *SIC 8069*
**HOPITAL MARIE-CLARAC DES SOEURS
DE CHARITE DE STE-MARIE (1995) INC**
p1240
3530 BOUL GOUIN E, MONTREAL-NORD,
QC, H1H 1B7
(514) 321-8800   *SIC 8069*
HOPITAL ST-JOSEPH   *p1286*
28 RUE JOLY, RIVIERE-DU-LOUP, QC, G5R
3H2
(418) 862-6385   *SIC 8069*
HOSPITAL FOR SICK CHILDREN, THEp945
555 UNIVERSITY AVE, TORONTO, ON,
M5G 1X8
(416) 813-1500   *SIC 8069*
**INSTITUT DE CARDIOLOGIE DE MON-
TREAL**   *p1165*
5000 RUE BELANGER, MONTREAL, QC,
H1T 1C8
(514) 376-3330   *SIC 8069*
**IZAAK WALTON KILLAM HEALTH CENTRE,
THE**   *p455*
5980 UNIVERSITY AVE, HALIFAX, NS, B3K
6R8
(902) 470-8888   *SIC 8069*
KATERI MEMORIAL HOSPITAL CENTRE
p1117
GD, KAHNAWAKE, QC, J0L 1B0
(450) 638-3930   *SIC 8069*
**KINGS REGIONAL REHABILITATION CEN-
TRE**   *p470*
1349 COUNTY RD, WATERVILLE, NS, B0P
1V0
(902) 538-3103   *SIC 8069*
**L'INSTITUT DE READAPTATION GINGRAS-
LINDSAY-DE-MONTREAL**   *p1218*
6300 AV DE DARLINGTON, MONTREAL,
QC, H3S 2J4
(514) 340-2085   *SIC 8069*
LABORATOIRE VICTHOM INC   *p1237*
2101 BOUL LE CARREFOUR BUREAU
102, MONTREAL, QC, H7S 2J7
(450) 239-6162   *SIC 8069*

LAKERIDGE HEALTH   *p1014*
300 GORDON ST SUITE 779, WHITBY, ON,
L1N 5T2
(905) 668-6831   *SIC 8069*
MARIE ESTHER SOCIETY, THE   *p335*
861 FAIRFIELD RD SUITE 317, VICTORIA,
BC, V8V 5A9
(250) 480-3100   *SIC 8069*
MCGILL UNIVERSITY HEALTH CENTRE
p1215
2300 RUE TUPPER BUREAU F372, MON-
TREAL, QC, H3H 1P3
(514) 412-4307   *SIC 8069*
**NIAGARA PENINSULA CHILDREN'S CEN-
TRE**   *p887*
567 GLENRIDGE AVE, ST CATHARINES,
ON, L2T 4C2
(905) 688-3553   *SIC 8069*
OTTAWA HOSPITAL, THE   *p828*
200 MELROSE AVE S, OTTAWA, ON, K1Y
4K7
(613) 737-7700   *SIC 8069*
**PRINCESS MARGARET CANCER FOUN-
DATION, THE**   *p947*
610 UNIVERSITY AVE, TORONTO, ON,
M5G 2M9
(416) 946-6560   *SIC 8069*
**PROGRAMME DE PORTAGE RELATIF A LA
DEPENDENCE DE LA DROGUE INC, LE**
p1215
865 PLACE RICHMOND, MONTREAL, QC,
H3J 1V8
(514) 939-0202   *SIC 8069*
PROVIDENCE HEALTHCARE   *p869*
3276 ST CLAIR AVE E, SCARBOROUGH,
ON, M1L 1W1
(416) 285-3666   *SIC 8069*
**PROVINCIAL HEALTH SERVICES AUTHOR-
ITY**   *p275*
13750 96 AVE, SURREY, BC, V3V 1Z2
(604) 930-2098   *SIC 8069*
**PROVINCIAL HEALTH SERVICES AUTHOR-
ITY**   *p293*
600 10TH AVE W, VANCOUVER, BC, V5Z
4E6
(604) 675-8251   *SIC 8069*
QUINTE HEALTHCARE CORPORATION
p484
1H MANOR LANE, BANCROFT, ON, K0L
1C0
(613) 332-2825   *SIC 8069*
**RELIGIOUS HOSPITALLERS OF SAINT
JOSEPH OF THE HOTEL DIEU OF
KINGSTON**   *p631*
166 BROCK ST, KINGSTON, ON, K7L 5G2
(613) 549-2680   *SIC 8069*
RESIDENCE RIVIERA INC   *p1241*
2999 BOUL NOTRE-DAME, MONTREAL-
OUEST, QC, H7V 4C4
(450) 682-0111   *SIC 8069*
SASKATCHEWAN HEALTH AUTHORITY
p1425
2003 ARLINGTON AVE, SASKATOON, SK,
S7J 2H6
(306) 655-4500   *SIC 8069*
SHOULDICE HOSPITAL LIMITED   *p905*
7750 BAYVIEW AVE SUITE 370, THORN-
HILL, ON, L3T 4A3
(905) 889-1125   *SIC 8069*
**SOUTH SHORE DISTRICT HEALTH AU-
THORITY**   *p461*
175 SCHOOL ST, LIVERPOOL, NS, B0T
1K0
(902) 354-5785   *SIC 8069*
**ST MICHAEL'S CENTRE HOSPITAL SOCI-
ETY**   *p193*
7451 SUSSEX AVE, BURNABY, BC, V5J
5C2
(604) 434-1323   *SIC 8069*
**SUNNYBROOK HEALTH SCIENCES CEN-
TRE**   *p932*
43 WELLESLEY ST E SUITE 327,
TORONTO, ON, M4Y 1H1
(416) 967-8500   *SIC 8069*

▲ Public Company   ■ Public Company Family Member   **HQ** Headquarters   **BR** Branch   **SL** Single Location

VILLA MEDICA INC *p1186*
225 RUE SHERBROOKE E, MONTREAL, QC, H2X 1C9
(514) 288-8201   *SIC 8069*
WEST PARK HEALTHCARE CENTRE *p993*
82 BUTTONWOOD AVE SUITE 1121, TORONTO, ON, M6M 2J5
(416) 243-3600   *SIC 8069*
WOODVIEW CHILDREN'S CENTRE *p529*
69 FLATT RD, BURLINGTON, ON, L7P 0T3
(905) 689-4727   *SIC 8069*

SIC 8071 Medical laboratories

ALS CANADA LTD *p181*
8081 LOUGHEED HWY SUITE 100, BURNABY, BC, V5A 1W9
(778) 370-3150   *SIC 8071*
BC BIOMEDICAL LABORATORIES LTD *p275*
7455 130 ST, SURREY, BC, V3W 1H8
(604) 507-5000   *SIC 8071*
BIRON LABORATOIRE MEDICAL INC *p1069*
4105 BOUL MATTE, BROSSARD, QC, J4Y 2P4
(514) 866-6146   *SIC 8071*
CML HEALTHCARE INC *p744*
60 COURTNEYPARK DR W UNIT 1, MISSISSAUGA, ON, L5W 0B3
(905) 565-0043   *SIC 8071*
DYNACARE-GAMMA LABORATORY PARTNERSHIP *p502*
115 MIDAIR CRT, BRAMPTON, ON, L6T 5M3
(905) 790-3515   *SIC 8071*
DYNACARE-GAMMA LABORATORY PARTNERSHIP *p817*
750 PETER MORAND CRES, OTTAWA, ON, K1G 6S4
(613) 729-0200   *SIC 8071*
DYNALIFEDX *p88*
10150 102 ST NW SUITE 200, EDMONTON, AB, T5J 5E2
(780) 451-3702   *SIC 8071*
EFW RADIOLOGY *p8*
2851 SUNRIDGE BLVD NE SUITE 130, CALGARY, AB, T1Y 0B7
(403) 541-1200   *SIC 8071*
INSIGHT MEDICAL HOLDINGS LTD *p98*
200 MEADOWLARK SHOPPING CTR NW, EDMONTON, AB, T5R 5W9
(780) 489-8430   *SIC 8071*
INSTITUT DE RECHERCHE DU CENTRE UNIVERSITAIRE DE SANTE MCGILL, L' *p1215*
2155 RUE GUY BUREAU 500, MONTREAL, QC, H3H 2R9
(514) 934-8354   *SIC 8071*
LIFELABS INC *p585*
100 INTERNATIONAL BLVD, ETOBICOKE, ON, M9W 6J6
(416) 675-4530   *SIC 8071*
LIFELABS LP *p871*
1290 ELLESMERE RD, SCARBOROUGH, ON, M1P 2X9
(416) 291-1464   *SIC 8071*
LONDON X-RAY ASSOCIATES *p656*
450 CENTRAL AVE UNIT 104, LONDON, ON, N6B 2E8
(519) 672-7900   *SIC 8071*
MIDDLESEX LONDON HEALTH UNIT *p654*
50 KING ST SUITE 101, LONDON, ON, N6A 5L7
(519) 663-5317   *SIC 8071*
NORDION (CANADA) INC *p189*
3680 GILMORE WAY, BURNABY, BC, V5G 4V8
(604) 431-5005   *SIC 8071*
NORDION (CANADA) INC *p656*
746 BASE LINE RD E SUITE 11, LONDON, ON, N6C 5Z2
(877) 849-3637   *SIC 8071*
NORDION (CANADA) INC *p698*

1980 MATHESON BLVD E SUITE 1, MISSISSAUGA, ON, L4W 5R7
(905) 206-8887   *SIC 8071*
PROVINCIAL LAB FOR PUBLIC HEALTH *p42*
3030 HOSPITAL DR NW, CALGARY, AB, T2N 4W4
(403) 944-1200   *SIC 8071*
SYNEOS HEALTH CLINIQUE INC *p1268*
2500 RUE EINSTEIN, QUEBEC, QC, G1P 0A2
(418) 527-4000   *SIC 8071*
TRILLIUM THERAPEUTICS INC *p718*
2488 DUNWIN DR, MISSISSAUGA, ON, L5L 1J9
(416) 595-0627   *SIC 8071*
TRUE NORTH IMAGING INC *p906*
7330 YONGE ST SUITE 120, THORNHILL, ON, L4J 7Y7
(905) 889-5926   *SIC 8071*
WENTWORTH-HALTON X-RAY AND ULTRASOUND INC *p612*
1 YOUNG ST SUITE 218, HAMILTON, ON, L8N 1T8
(905) 522-2344   *SIC 8071*
WESTMAN REGIONAL LABORATORY SERVICES INC *p347*
150 MCTAVISH AVE E SUITE 1, BRANDON, MB, R7A 7H8
(204) 578-4440   *SIC 8071*

SIC 8072 Dental laboratories

CLASSIC DENTAL LABORATORIES LTD *p66*
115 17 AVE SW, CALGARY, AB, T2S 0A1
(403) 228-5120   *SIC 8072*
PROTEC DENTAL LABORATORIES LTD *p289*
38 1ST AVE E, VANCOUVER, BC, V5T 1A1
(604) 873-8000   *SIC 8072*
PROTEC ORTHODONTIC LABORATORIES LTD *p289*
38 1ST AVE E, VANCOUVER, BC, V5T 1A1
(604) 734-8966   *SIC 8072*
ROTSAERT DENTAL LABORATORY SERVICES INC *p612*
71 EMERALD ST S, HAMILTON, ON, L8N 2V4
(905) 527-1422   *SIC 8072*
SPACE MAINTAINERS LAB CANADA LTD *p67*
115 17 AVE SW, CALGARY, AB, T2S 0A1
(403) 228-7001   *SIC 8072*
TGM HOLDINGS LTD *p67*
115 17 AVE SW, CALGARY, AB, T2S 0A1
(403) 228-5120   *SIC 8072*

SIC 8082 Home health care services

1207715 ONTARIO INC *p856*
11685 YONGE ST SUITE 205, RICHMOND HILL, ON, L4E 0K7
(905) 770-9450   *SIC 8082*
ACCLAIM HEALTH COMMUNITY CARE SERVICES *p803*
2370 SPEERS RD, OAKVILLE, ON, L6L 5M2
(905) 827-8800   *SIC 8082*
BAYSHORE HEALTHCARE LTD. *p292*
555 12TH AVE W UNIT 410, VANCOUVER, BC, V5Z 3X7
(604) 873-2545   *SIC 8082*
BAYSHORE HEALTHCARE LTD. *p333*
1512 FORT ST, VICTORIA, BC, V8S 5J2
(250) 370-2253   *SIC 8082*
BAYSHORE HEALTHCARE LTD. *p408*
50 DRISCOLL CRES SUITE 201, MONCTON, NB, E1E 3R8
(506) 857-9992   *SIC 8082*
BAYSHORE HEALTHCARE LTD. *p413*
600 MAIN ST SUITE C150, SAINT JOHN,

NB, E2K 1J5
(506) 633-9588   *SIC 8082*
BAYSHORE HEALTHCARE LTD. *p562*
112 SECOND ST W, CORNWALL, ON, K6J 1G5
(613) 938-1691   *SIC 8082*
BAYSHORE HEALTHCARE LTD. *p614*
755 CONCESSION ST SUITE 100, HAMILTON, ON, L8V 1C4
(905) 523-5999   *SIC 8082*
BAYSHORE HEALTHCARE LTD. *p714*
2101 HADWEN RD, MISSISSAUGA, ON, L5K 2L3
(905) 822-8075   *SIC 8082*
BAYSHORE HEALTHCARE LTD. *p826*
310 HUNT CLUB RD SUITE 202, OTTAWA, ON, K1V 1C1
(613) 733-4408   *SIC 8082*
BAYSHORE HEALTHCARE LTD. *p881*
94 BECKWITH ST N, SMITHS FALLS, ON, K7A 2C1
(613) 283-1400   *SIC 8082*
BAYSHORE HEALTHCARE LTD. *p900*
2120 REGENT ST SUITE 8, SUDBURY, ON, P3E 3Z9
(705) 523-6668   *SIC 8082*
BAYSHORE HEALTHCARE LTD. *p1022*
1275 WALKER RD SUITE 10, WINDSOR, ON, N8Y 4X9
(519) 973-5411   *SIC 8082*
C L S C OLIVIER-GUIMOND *p1164*
5810 RUE SHERBROOKE E, MONTREAL, QC, H1N 1B2
(514) 255-2365   *SIC 8082*
CAN-CARE HEALTH SERVICES INC *p771*
45 SHEPPARD AVE E SUITE 204, NORTH YORK, ON, M2N 5W9
(647) 725-1048   *SIC 8082*
CAREFOR HEALTH & COMMUNITY SERVICES *p838*
425 CECELIA ST, PEMBROKE, ON, K8A 1S7
(613) 732-9993   *SIC 8082*
CAREMED SERVICES INC *p866*
1200 MARKHAM RD SUITE 220, SCARBOROUGH, ON, M1H 3C3
(416) 438-4577   *SIC 8082*
COMMUNITY CARE ACCESS CENTRE - OXFORD *p1035*
1147 DUNDAS ST, WOODSTOCK, ON, N4S 8W3
(519) 539-1284   *SIC 8082*
COMMUNITY CARE ACCESS CENTRE NIAGARA *p884*
149 HARTZEL RD, ST CATHARINES, ON, L2P 1N6
(905) 684-9441   *SIC 8082*
COMMUNITY HOMEMAKERS LTD *p705*
160 TRADERS BLVD E SUITE 103, MISSISSAUGA, ON, L4Z 3K7
(905) 275-0544   *SIC 8082*
NORTHWOOD HOMECARE LTD *p447*
130 EILEEN STUBBS AVE SUITE 19N, DARTMOUTH, NS, B3B 2C4
(902) 425-2273   *SIC 8082*
PRO WELLNESS HEALTH SERVICES INC *p887*
110 HANNOVER DR SUITE B107, ST CATHARINES, ON, L2W 1A4
(905) 682-1059   *SIC 8082*
SAINT ELIZABETH HEALTH CARE *p674*
90 ALLSTATE PKY SUITE 300, MARKHAM, ON, L3R 6H3
(905) 940-9655   *SIC 8082*
SPECTRUM HEALTH CARE LTD *p930*
2 BLOOR ST E SUITE 1200, TORONTO, ON, M4W 1A8
(416) 964-0322   *SIC 8082*
ST. JOSEPH'S HOME CARE *p616*
1550 UPPER JAMES ST SUITE 201, HAMILTON, ON, L9B 2L6
(905) 522-6887   *SIC 8082*
VICTORIAN ORDER OF NURSES FOR CANADA *p68*

9705 HORTON RD SW SUITE 100, CALGARY, AB, T2V 2X5
(403) 640-4765   *SIC 8082*
VICTORIAN ORDER OF NURSES FOR CANADA *p438*
43 PRINCE ARTHUR ST, AMHERST, NS, B4H 1V8
(902) 667-8796   *SIC 8082*
VICTORIAN ORDER OF NURSES FOR CANADA *p469*
30 DUKE ST SUITE 5, TRURO, NS, B2N 2A1
(902) 893-3803   *SIC 8082*
VICTORIAN ORDER OF NURSES FOR CANADA *p611*
414 VICTORIA AVE N SUITE M2, HAMILTON, ON, L8L 5G8
(905) 529-0700   *SIC 8082*
VICTORIAN ORDER OF NURSES FOR CANADA *p651*
1151 FLORENCE ST SUITE 100, LONDON, ON, N5W 2M7
(519) 659-2273   *SIC 8082*
VICTORIAN ORDER OF NURSES FOR CANADA *p676*
7100 WOODBINE AVE SUITE 402, MARKHAM, ON, L3R 5J2
(905) 479-3201   *SIC 8082*
VICTORIAN ORDER OF NURSES FOR CANADA *p819*
2315 ST. LAURENT BLVD SUITE 100, OTTAWA, ON, K1G 4J8
(613) 233-5694   *SIC 8082*
VICTORIAN ORDER OF NURSES FOR CANADA *p840*
360 GEORGE ST N SUITE 25, PETERBOROUGH, ON, K9H 7E7
(705) 745-9155   *SIC 8082*
VICTORIAN ORDER OF NURSES FOR CANADA *p861*
1705 LONDON LINE, SARNIA, ON, N7W 1B2
(519) 542-2310   *SIC 8082*
VICTORIAN ORDER OF NURSES FOR CANADA *p999*
80 DIVISION ST SUITE 14, TRENTON, ON, K8V 5S5
(613) 392-4181   *SIC 8082*
VICTORIAN ORDER OF NURSES NEW BRUNSWICK BRANCH INC *p409*
1077 ST GEORGE BLVD SUITE 310, MONCTON, NB, E1E 4C9
SIC 8082
VON CANADA FOUNDATION *p909*
214 RED RIVER RD SUITE 200, THUNDER BAY, ON, P7B 1A6
(807) 344-0012   *SIC 8082*
WATERLOO WELLINGTON LOCAL HEALTH INTEGRATION NETWORK *p604*
450 SPEEDVALE AVE W SUITE 201, GUELPH, ON, N1H 7G7
(519) 823-2550   *SIC 8082*
WE CARE HEALTH SERVICES INC *p757*
1124 STELLAR DR, NEWMARKET, ON, L3Y 7B7
(905) 715-7950   *SIC 8082*

SIC 8093 Specialty outpatient clinics, nec

ACCES SERVICES SANTE GSS INC *p1122*
1650 CH DE SAINT-JEAN BUREAU 101, LA PRAIRIE, QC, J5R 0J1
SIC 8093
ALBERTA HEALTH SERVICES *p150*
11 CIMARRON COMMON, OKOTOKS, AB, T1S 2E9
(403) 995-2600   *SIC 8093*
AUXILIAIRES BENEVOLES DU CENTRE D'HEBERGEMENT DE BEAUCEVILLE (CBH) *p1055*
253 108 RTE, BEAUCEVILLE, QC, G5X 2Z3
(418) 774-3304   *SIC 8093*
BRITISH COLUMBIA CENTRE FOR ABIL-

ITY ASSOCIATION *p288*
2805 KINGSWAY, VANCOUVER, BC, V5R 5H9
(604) 451-5511 *SIC 8093*

C L S C SAINT-LEONARD *p1343*
5540 RUE JARRY E, SAINT-LEONARD, QC, H1P 1T9
(514) 328-3460 *SIC 8093*

C.L.S.C. DU HAVRE *p1376*
30 RUE FERLAND, SOREL-TRACY, QC, J3P 3C7
(450) 746-4545 *SIC 8093*

CALGARY URBAN PROJECT SOCIETY *p64*
1001 10 AVE SW, CALGARY, AB, T2R 0B7
(403) 221-8780 *SIC 8093*

CEDARS DISCOVERY CENTRE LTD *p198*
3741 HOLLAND AVE, COBBLE HILL, BC, V0R 1L0
(250) 733-2006 *SIC 8093*

CENTRE D'INSEMINATION ARTIFICIELLE DU QUEBEC (C.I.A.Q.) SOCIETE EN COMMANDITE *p1311*
3450 RUE SICOTTE, SAINT-HYACINTHE, QC, J2S 2M2
(450) 774-1141 *SIC 8093*

CENTRE DE READAPTATION CONSTANCE LETHBRIDGE, LE *p1221*
7005 BOUL DE MAISONNEUVE O, MONTREAL, QC, H4B 1T3
(514) 487-1770 *SIC 8093*

CENTRE DE READAPTATION MAB-MACKAY *p1222*
7000 RUE SHERBROOKE O, MONTREAL, QC, H4B 1R3
(514) 489-8201 *SIC 8093*

CENTRE DE SANTE ET DE SERVICES SOCIAUX DE LA MAINGANIE *p1113*
1035 PROM DES ANCIENS, HAVRE-SAINT-PIERRE, QC, G0G 1P0
(418) 538-2212 *SIC 8093*

CENTRE FOR ADDICTION AND MENTAL HEALTH *p918*
175 BRENTCLIFFE RD, TORONTO, ON, M4G 0C5
(416) 425-3930 *SIC 8093*

CENTRE FOR ADDICTION AND MENTAL HEALTH *p974*
33 RUSSELL ST, TORONTO, ON, M5S 2S1
(416) 535-8501 *SIC 8093*

CENTRE FOR ADDICTION AND MENTAL HEALTH *p990*
1001 QUEEN ST W SUITE 301, TORONTO, ON, M6J 1H4
(416) 535-8501 *SIC 8093*

CENTRE HOSPITALIER UNIVERSITAIRE SAINTE-JUSTINE *p1165*
5200 RUE BELANGER, MONTREAL, QC, H1T 1C9
(514) 374-1710 *SIC 8093*

CENTRE READAPTATION DE GASPESIE *p1102*
150 RUE MGR-ROSS BUREAU 550, GASPE, QC, G4X 2R8
(418) 368-2306 *SIC 8093*

CENTRETOWN COMMUNITY HEALTH CENTRE *p833*
420 COOPER ST, OTTAWA, ON, K2P 2N6
(613) 233-4443 *SIC 8093*

EDGEWOOD CHEMICAL DEPENDENCY TREATMENT CENTRE *p234*
2121 BOXWOOD RD, NANAIMO, BC, V9S 4L2
(250) 751-0111 *SIC 8093*

ERINOAKKIDS CENTRE FOR TREATMENT AND DEVELOPMENT *p716*
2277 SOUTH MILLWAY, MISSISSAUGA, ON, L5L 2M5
(905) 855-2690 *SIC 8093*

GOUVERNEMENT DE LA PROVINCE DE QUEBEC *p1177*
950 RUE DE LOUVAIN E, MONTREAL, QC, H2M 2E8
(514) 385-1232 *SIC 8093*

GOUVERNEMENT DE LA PROVINCE DE

QUEBEC *p1262*
525 BOUL WILFRID-HAMEL, QUEBEC, QC, G1M 2S8
(418) 649-3700 *SIC 8093*

GROUPE SANTE MEDISYS INC *p1197*
600 BOUL DE MAISONNEUVE O 22E ETAGE, MONTREAL, QC, H3A 3J2
(514) 845-1211 *SIC 8093*

HAMILTON HEALTH SCIENCES CORPORATION *p614*
699 CONCESSION ST, HAMILTON, ON, L8V 5C2
(905) 387-9495 *SIC 8093*

HASTON, NANCY & ASSOCIATES INC *p929*
175 BLOOR ST E SUITE 807, TORONTO, ON, M4W 3R8
SIC 8093

HEARINGLIFE CANADA LTD *p926*
1 ST CLAIR AVE W SUITE 800, TORONTO, ON, M4V 1K7
(416) 925-9223 *SIC 8093*

HINCKS-DELLCREST TREATMENT CENTRE, THE *p786*
1645 SHEPPARD AVE W, NORTH YORK, ON, M3M 2X4
(416) 633-0515 *SIC 8093*

HOMEWOOD HEALTH INC *p600*
49 EMMA ST SUITE 100, GUELPH, ON, N1E 6X1
(519) 821-9258 *SIC 8093*

I HAVE A CHANCE SUPPORT SERVICES LTD *p167*
990 BOULDER BLVD, STONY PLAIN, AB, T7Z 0E5
(780) 962-0433 *SIC 8093*

INSTITUT DE READAPTATION EN DEFICIENCE PHYSIQUE DE QUEBEC *p1262*
525 BOUL WILFRID-HAMEL, QUEBEC, QC, G1M 2S8
(418) 529-9141 *SIC 8093*

INSTITUT NAZARETH ET LOUIS-BRAILLE *p1144*
1111 RUE SAINT-CHARLES O BUREAU 200, LONGUEUIL, QC, J4K 5G4
(450) 463-1710 *SIC 8093*

KING'S HEALTH CENTRE CORPORATION THE *p953*
250 UNIVERSITY AVE, TORONTO, ON, M5H 3E5
SIC 8093

LANSDOWNE CHILDREN'S CENTRE *p517*
39 MOUNT PLEASANT ST, BRANTFORD, ON, N3T 1S7
(519) 753-3153 *SIC 8093*

LIFEMARK HEALTH CORP *p923*
20 EGLINTON AVE W SUITE 600, TORONTO, ON, M4R 1K8
(416) 485-1344 *SIC 8093*

LOBE RESEAU INC *p1293*
3520 RUE DE L'HETRIERE BUREAU 103, SAINT-AUGUSTIN-DE-DESMAURES, QC, G3A 0B4
(418) 877-7222 *SIC 8093*

MADAME VANIER CHILDREN'S SERVICES *p652*
871 TRAFALGAR ST, LONDON, ON, N5Z 1E6
(519) 433-3101 *SIC 8093*

MCI MEDICAL CLINICS INC *p789*
1 YORKDALE RD SUITE 209, NORTH YORK, ON, M6A 3A1
(416) 440-4040 *SIC 8093*

MEDISYS CORPORATE HEALTH LP *p1198*
500 RUE SHERBROOKE O BUREAU 1100, MONTREAL, QC, H3A 3C6
(514) 499-2778 *SIC 8093*

MENTAL HEALTH SERVICES *p154*
4733 49 ST, RED DEER, AB, T4N 1T6
(403) 340-5466 *SIC 8093*

MINCAVI (1986) INC *p1089*
88 CH DU PINACLE, DANVILLE, QC, J0A 1A0
(819) 839-2747 *SIC 8093*

NRCS INC *p901*

31 LARCH ST SUITE 200, SUDBURY, ON, P3E 1B7
(705) 688-1288 *SIC 8093*

OPTIONS FOR SEXUAL HEALTH *p284*
3550 HASTINGS ST E, VANCOUVER, BC, V5K 2A7
(604) 731-4252 *SIC 8093*

PEEL HALTON ACQUIRED BRAIN INJURIES SERVICES *p713*
1048 CAWTHRA RD, MISSISSAUGA, ON, L5G 4K2
(905) 891-8384 *SIC 8093*

POST ROAD HEALTH & DIET INC *p777*
21 KERN RD, NORTH YORK, ON, M3B 1S9
(416) 447-3438 *SIC 8093*

RECONNECT COMMUNITY HEALTH SERVICES *p989*
1281 ST. CLAIR AVE W, TORONTO, ON, M6E 1B8
(416) 248-2050 *SIC 8093*

SANDY HILL COMMUNITY HEALTH CENTRE INC *p821*
221 NELSON ST, OTTAWA, ON, K1N 1C7
(613) 789-6309 *SIC 8093*

SASKATCHEWAN CANCER AGENCY *p1422*
4101 DEWDNEY AVE SUITE 300, REGINA, SK, S4T 7T1
(306) 766-2213 *SIC 8093*

SOCIETY FOR MANITOBANS WITH DISABILITIES INC *p373*
825 SHERBROOK ST, WINNIPEG, MB, R3A 1M5
(204) 975-3010 *SIC 8093*

ST JOHN'S REHABILITATION HOSPITAL *p770*
285 CUMMER AVE, NORTH YORK, ON, M2M 2G1
(416) 226-6780 *SIC 8093*

ST. JOSEPH'S HEALTH CARE, LONDON *p652*
850 HIGHBURY AVE N, LONDON, ON, N5Y 1A4
(519) 455-5110 *SIC 8093*

ST. JOSEPH'S HEALTH CARE, LONDON *p655*
268 GROSVENOR ST, LONDON, ON, N6A 4V2
(519) 646-6100 *SIC 8093*

ST. JOSEPH'S HEALTH CARE, LONDON *p889*
GD, ST THOMAS, ON, N5P 3T4
(519) 631-8510 *SIC 8093*

ST. JOSEPH'S HEALTHCARE FOUNDATION, HAMILTON *p609*
2757 KING ST E, HAMILTON, ON, L8G 5E4
(905) 573-7777 *SIC 8093*

STRATFORD CHILDREN'S SERVICES INC *p896*
508 ERIE ST, STRATFORD, ON, N5A 2N6
(519) 273-3623 *SIC 8093*

THAMES VALLEY CHILDREN'S CENTRE *p656*
779 BASE LINE RD E, LONDON, ON, N6C 5Y6
(519) 685-8680 *SIC 8093*

TORONTO REHABILITATION INSTITUTE *p918*
520 SUTHERLAND DR, TORONTO, ON, M4G 3V9
(416) 597-3422 *SIC 8093*

TORONTO REHABILITATION INSTITUTE *p947*
550 UNIVERSITY AVE, TORONTO, ON, M5G 2A2
(416) 597-3422 *SIC 8093*

VANCOUVER COASTAL HEALTH AUTHORITY *p294*
4255 LAUREL ST, VANCOUVER, BC, V5Z 2G9
(604) 734-1313 *SIC 8093*

WE CARE HEALTH SERVICES INC *p407*
236 ST GEORGE ST SUITE 110, MONCTON, NB, E1C 1W1
(506) 384-2273 *SIC 8093*

WINDSOR REGIONAL HOSPITAL *p1025*
3901 CONNAUGHT AVE, WINDSOR, ON, N9C 4H4
(519) 257-5215 *SIC 8093*

WINNIPEG REGIONAL HEALTH AUTHORITY, THE *p367*
975 HENDERSON HWY, WINNIPEG, MB, R2K 4L7
(204) 938-5000 *SIC 8093*

WINNIPEG REGIONAL HEALTH AUTHORITY, THE *p374*
490 HARGRAVE ST, WINNIPEG, MB, R3A 0X7
(204) 940-2665 *SIC 8093*

SIC 8099 Health and allied services, nec

1185985 ONTARIO INC *p919*
1573 DANFORTH AVE, TORONTO, ON, M4J 1N8
(905) 607-1322 *SIC 8099*

BLOOD TRIBE DEPARTMENT OF HEALTH INC *p167*
GD, STAND OFF, AB, T0L 1Y0
(403) 737-2102 *SIC 8099*

BOARD OF HEALTH FOR THE TIMISKAMING HEALTH UNIT *p753*
421 SHEPHERDSON RD, NEW LISKEARD, ON, P0J 1P0
(705) 647-4305 *SIC 8099*

BTC INDIAN HEALTH SERVICE INC *p1412*
1192 101ST ST SUITE 103, NORTH BATTLEFORD, SK, S9A 0Z6
(306) 937-6700 *SIC 8099*

CANADIAN BLOOD SERVICES *p45*
200 BARCLAY PARADE SW UNIT 10, CALGARY, AB, T2P 4R5
SIC 8099

CANADIAN BLOOD SERVICES *p817*
1800 ALTA VISTA DR, OTTAWA, ON, K1G 4J5
(613) 739-2300 *SIC 8099*

CANADIAN BLOOD SERVICES *p928*
2 BLOOR ST W, TORONTO, ON, M4W 3E2
(613) 739-2300 *SIC 8099*

CENTRE DE SANTE ET DE SERVICES SOCIAUX - INSTITUT UNIVERSITAIRE DE GERIATRIE DE SHERBROOKE *p1371*
375 RUE ARGYLL, SHERBROOKE, QC, J1J 3H5
(819) 780-2222 *SIC 8099*

CENTRE DE SANTE ET DE SERVICES SOCIAUX DE LAVAL *p1084*
1755 BOUL RENE-LAENNEC, COTE SAINT-LUC, QC, H7M 3L9
(450) 668-1010 *SIC 8099*

CENTRE DE SANTE ET SERVICES SOCIAUX DU PONTIAC *p1369*
200 RUE ARGUE, SHAWVILLE, QC, J0X 2Y0
(819) 647-2211 *SIC 8099*

EMERGENCY AND HEALTH SERVICES COMMISSION *p224*
9440 202 ST, LANGLEY, BC, V1M 4A6
(604) 215-8103 *SIC 8099*

HEMA-QUEBEC *p1272*
1070 AV DES SCIENCES-DE-LA-VIE, QUEBEC, QC, G1V 5C3
(418) 780-4362 *SIC 8099*

HEMA-QUEBEC *p1329*
4045 BOUL DE LA COTE-VERTU, SAINT-LAURENT, QC, H4R 2W7
(514) 832-5000 *SIC 8099*

MCCREARY ALONSA HEALTH CENTRE *p352*
613 GOVERNMENT RD, MCCREARY, MB, R0J 1B0
(204) 835-2482 *SIC 8099*

MEDICAL MERCY CANADA SOCIETY *p24*
1216 34 AVE NE SUITE 6, CALGARY, AB, T2E 6L9
(403) 717-0933 *SIC 8099*

MR IMAGING CORP *p36*

5920 1A ST SW UNIT 301, CALGARY, AB, T2H 0G3

(403) 253-4666   *SIC 8099*

MUSKOKA ALGONQUIN HEALTHCARE *p620*
8 CRESCENT RD, HUNTSVILLE, ON, P1H 0B3

(705) 789-6451   *SIC 8099*

NOVA SCOTIA HEARING AND SPEECH CENTRES *p453*
5657 SPRING GARDEN RD SUITE 401, HALIFAX, NS, B3J 3R4

(902) 492-8289   *SIC 8099*

PROTEM HEALTH SERVICES INC *p409*
2069 MOUNTAIN RD, MONCTON, NB, E1G 1B1

(506) 852-9652   *SIC 8099*

PROVINCIAL HEALTH SERVICES AUTHORITY *p327*
1380 BURRARD ST SUITE 700, VANCOUVER, BC, V6Z 2H3

(604) 675-7400   *SIC 8099*

PUBLIC SERVICES HEALTH AND SAFETY ASSOCIATION *p773*
4950 YONGE ST SUITE 1800, NORTH YORK, ON, M2N 6K1

(416) 250-2131   *SIC 8099*

RUDD SERVICES LTD *p947*
123 EDWARD ST SUITE 825, TORONTO, ON, M5G 1E2

(416) 597-6995   *SIC 8099*

SYKES ASSISTANCE SERVICES CORPORATION *p764*
555 OAK ST E, NORTH BAY, ON, P1B 8E3
SIC 8099

TRILLIUM GIFT OF LIFE NETWORK *p947*
483 BAY ST SOUTH TOWER 4TH FLOOR, TORONTO, ON, M5G 2C9

(416) 363-4001   *SIC 8099*

WINNIPEG REGIONAL HEALTH AUTHORITY, THE *p367*
345 DE BAETS ST, WINNIPEG, MB, R2J 3V6

(204) 654-5100   *SIC 8099*

WW CANADA LTD *p799*
1415 JOSHUAS CREEK DR UNIT 200, OAKVILLE, ON, L6H 7G4

(800) 387-8227   *SIC 8099*

SIC 8111 Legal services

885 PROFESSIONAL MANAGEMENT LIMITED PARTNERSHIP *p301*
885 GEORGIA ST W SUITE 900, VANCOUVER, BC, V6C 3H1

(604) 687-5700   *SIC 8111*

AIRD & BERLIS LLP *p959*
181 BAY ST SUITE 1800, TORONTO, ON, M5J 2T9

(416) 863-1500   *SIC 8111*

ALEXANDER HOLBURN BEAUDIN & LANG LLP *p329*
700 GEORGIA ST W SUITE 2700, VANCOUVER, BC, V7Y 1B8

(604) 484-1700   *SIC 8111*

ANDERSON, RHONDA MPA KPMG LLP LAWYER *p87*
10175 101 ST NW UNIT 2200, EDMONTON, AB, T5J 0H3

(780) 429-7300   *SIC 8111*

BCF CAPITAL S.E.N.C *p1201*
1100 BOUL RENE-LEVESQUE O BUREAU 2500, MONTREAL, QC, H3B 5C9

(514) 397-8500   *SIC 8111*

BDO CANADA LIMITED *p527*
3115 HARVESTER RD SUITE 400, BURLINGTON, ON, L7N 3N8

(905) 639-9500   *SIC 8111*

BDO CANADA LIMITED *p959*
123 FRONT ST W SUITE 1200, TORONTO, ON, M5J 2M2

(416) 865-0210   *SIC 8111*

BEARD WINTER LLP *p948*

130 ADELAIDE ST W SUITE 701, TORONTO, ON, M5H 2K4

(416) 593-5555   *SIC 8111*

BELANGER SAUVE S.E.N.C.R.L. *p1201*
5 PLACE VILLE-MARIE BUREAU 900, MONTREAL, QC, H3B 2G2

(514) 878-3081   *SIC 8111*

BELL, TEMPLE *p944*
393 UNIVERSITY AVE SUITE 1300, TORONTO, ON, M5G 1E6

(416) 581-8200   *SIC 8111*

BENNETT JONES LLP *p44*
855 2 ST SW SUITE 4500, CALGARY, AB, T2P 4K7

(403) 298-3100   *SIC 8111*

BENNETT JONES LLP *p985*
3400 ONE FIRST CANADIAN PL, TORONTO, ON, M5X 1A4

(416) 863-1200   *SIC 8111*

BERESKIN & PARR LLP *p949*
40 KING ST W 4TH FL, TORONTO, ON, M5H 3Y2

(416) 364-7311   *SIC 8111*

BISHOP & MCKENZIE LLP *p87*
10180 101 ST SUITE 2300, EDMONTON, AB, T5J 1V3

(780) 426-5550   *SIC 8111*

BLAKE, CASSELS & GRAYDON LLP *p44*
855 2 ST SW SUITE 3500, CALGARY, AB, T2P 4J8

(403) 260-9600   *SIC 8111*

BLAKE, CASSELS & GRAYDON LLP *p328*
595 BURRARD ST SUITE 2600, VANCOUVER, BC, V7X 1L3

(604) 631-3300   *SIC 8111*

BLAKE, CASSELS & GRAYDON LLP *p971*
199 BAY ST SUITE 4000, TORONTO, ON, M5L 1A9

(416) 863-2400   *SIC 8111*

BLAKE, CASSELS & GRAYDON LLP *p1202*
1 PLACE VILLE-MARIE BUREAU 3000, MONTREAL, QC, H3B 4N8

(514) 982-4000   *SIC 8111*

BLANEY MCMURTRY LLP *p937*
2 QUEEN ST E SUITE 1500, TORONTO, ON, M5C 3G5

(416) 593-1221   *SIC 8111*

BORDEN LADNER GERVAIS LLP *p44*
520 3 AVE SW SUITE 1900, CALGARY, AB, T2P 0R3

(403) 232-9500   *SIC 8111*

BORDEN LADNER GERVAIS LLP *p302*
200 BURRARD ST SUITE 1200, VANCOUVER, BC, V6C 3L6

(604) 687-5744   *SIC 8111*

BORDEN LADNER GERVAIS LLP *p822*
100 QUEEN ST SUITE 1100, OTTAWA, ON, K1P 1J9

(613) 237-5160   *SIC 8111*

BORDEN LADNER GERVAIS LLP *p949*
22 ADELAIDE ST W SUITE 3400, TORONTO, ON, M5H 4E3

(416) 367-6000   *SIC 8111*

BORDEN LADNER GERVAIS LLP *p1202*
1000 RUE DE LA GAUCHETIERE O BUREAU 900, MONTREAL, QC, H3B 5H4

(514) 879-1212   *SIC 8111*

BOYNECLARKE LLP *p444*
99 WYSE RD SUITE 600, DARTMOUTH, NS, B3A 4S5

(902) 469-9500   *SIC 8111*

BRATTYS LLP *p549*
7501 KEELE ST SUITE 200, CONCORD, ON, L4K 1Y2

(905) 760-2600   *SIC 8111*

BROMWICH & SMITH INC *p45*
1000 9 AVE SW SUITE 201, CALGARY, AB, T2P 2Y6

(855) 884-9243   *SIC 8111*

BROWNLEE LLP *p87*
10155 102 ST NW SUITE 2200, EDMONTON, AB, T5J 4G8

(780) 497-4800   *SIC 8111*

BRYAN & COMPANY LLP *p87*

10180 101 ST NW SUITE 2600, EDMONTON, AB, T5J 3Y2

(780) 423-5730   *SIC 8111*

BULL, HOUSSER & TUPPER LLP *p297*
510 GEORGIA ST W SUITE 1800, VANCOUVER, BC, V6B 0M3

(604) 687-6575   *SIC 8111*

CAIN LAMARRE CASGRAIN WELLS, S.E.N.C.R.L. *p1078*
255 RUE RACINE E BUREAU 600, CHICOUTIMI, QC, G7H 7L2

(418) 545-4580   *SIC 8111*

CAIN LAMARRE CASGRAIN WELLS, S.E.N.C.R.L. *p1202*
630 BOUL RENE-LEVESQUE O BUREAU 2780, MONTREAL, QC, H3B 1S6

(514) 393-4580   *SIC 8111*

CARTHOS SERVICES LP *p1202*
1000 RUE DE LA GAUCHETIERE O BUREAU 2100, MONTREAL, QC, H3B 4W5

(514) 904-8100   *SIC 8111*

CASSELS BROCK & BLACKWELL LLP *p950*
40 KING ST W SUITE 2100, TORONTO, ON, M5H 3C2

(416) 869-5300   *SIC 8111*

CENTRE COMMUNAUTAIRE JURIDIQUE DE LA RIVE-SUD *p1142*
101 RUE ROLAND-THERRIEN BUREAU 301, LONGUEUIL, QC, J4H 4B9

(450) 928-7655   *SIC 8111*

CENTRE COMMUNAUTAIRE JURIDIQUE DE MONTREAL *p1194*
425 BOUL DE MAISONNEUVE O BUREAU 600, MONTREAL, QC, H3A 3K5

(514) 864-2111   *SIC 8111*

CHAITON MANAGEMENT LTD *p771*
185 SHEPPARD AVE W, NORTH YORK, ON, M2N 1M9

(416) 222-8888   *SIC 8111*

CHSM & C MANAGEMENT *p977*
474 BATHURST ST SUITE 300, TORONTO, ON, M5T 2S6

(416) 964-1115   *SIC 8111*

COMMONWEALTH LEGAL INC *p961*
145 WELLINGTON ST W SUITE 901, TORONTO, ON, M5J 1H8

(416) 703-3755   *SIC 8111*

COX & PALMER *p452*
1959 UPPER WATER ST SUITE 1100, HALIFAX, NS, B3J 3N2

(902) 491-4118   *SIC 8111*

DAVIES WARD PHILLIPS & VINEBERG LLP *p979*
155 WELLINGTON ST W, TORONTO, ON, M5V 3J7

(416) 863-0900   *SIC 8111*

DAVIES WARD PHILLIPS & VINEBERG LLP *p1195*
1501 AV MCGILL COLLEGE BUREAU 2600, MONTREAL, QC, H3A 3N9

(514) 841-6400   *SIC 8111*

DAVIS LLP *p47*
250 2 ST SW SUITE 1000, CALGARY, AB, T2P 0C1

(403) 296-4470   *SIC 8111*

DAVIS LLP *p303*
666 BURRARD ST SUITE 2800, VANCOUVER, BC, V6C 2Z7

(604) 687-9444   *SIC 8111*

DAVIS MANAGEMENT LTD *p986*
100 KING ST W UNIT 60, TORONTO, ON, M5X 2A1

(416) 365-3500   *SIC 8111*

DE GRANDPRE CHAIT S.E.N.C.R.L. *p1203*
1000 RUE DE LA GAUCHETIERE O BUREAU 2900, MONTREAL, QC, H3B 4W5

(514) 878-4311   *SIC 8111*

DELOITTE & TOUCHE MANAGEMENT CONSULTANTS *p779*
1 CONCORDE GATE SUITE 200, NORTH YORK, ON, M3C 3N6

(416) 601-6150   *SIC 8111*

DELOITTE LLP *p1371*

1802 RUE KING O BUREAU 300, SHERBROOKE, QC, J1J 0A2

(819) 823-1616   *SIC 8111*

DENTONS CANADA LLP *p47*
850 2 ST SW SUITE 1500, CALGARY, AB, T2P 0R8

(403) 268-7000   *SIC 8111*

DENTONS CANADA LLP *p88*
10180 101 ST NW SUITE 2900, EDMONTON, AB, T5J 3V5

(780) 423-7100   *SIC 8111*

DENTONS CANADA LLP *p303*
250 HOWE ST SUITE 2000, VANCOUVER, BC, V6C 3R8

(604) 687-4460   *SIC 8111*

DENTONS CANADA LLP *p823*
99 BANK ST SUITE 1420, OTTAWA, ON, K1P 1H4

(613) 783-9600   *SIC 8111*

DENTONS CANADA LLP *p969*
77 KING ST W SUITE 400, TORONTO, ON, M5K 2A1

(416) 863-4511   *SIC 8111*

DENTONS CANADA LLP *p1203*
1 PLACE VILLE-MARIE BUREAU 3900, MONTREAL, QC, H3B 4M7

(514) 878-8800   *SIC 8111*

DEVEAU, BOURGEOIS, GAGNE, HEBERT ET ASSOCIES S.E.N.C.R.L *p1120*
1210 CH DE LA VERNIERE BUREAU 2, L'ETANG-DU-NORD, QC, G4T 3E6

(418) 986-4782   *SIC 8111*

DICKINSON WRIGHT LLP *p969*
222 BAY ST 18TH FL, TORONTO, ON, M5K 1H1

(416) 777-0101   *SIC 8111*

DUNCAN CRAIG LLP *p88*
10060 JASPER AVE NW SUITE 2800, EDMONTON, AB, T5J 3V9

(780) 428-6036   *SIC 8111*

DUNCAN CRAIG LLP *p172*
4725 56 ST SUITE 103, WETASKIWIN, AB, T9A 3M2

(780) 352-1662   *SIC 8111*

DUNTON RAINVILLE SENC *p1229*
800 RUE DU SQUARE-VICTORIA BUREAU 43, MONTREAL, QC, H4Z 1A1

(514) 866-6743   *SIC 8111*

EPSTEIN COLE LLP *p944*
393 UNIVERSITY AVE SUITE 2200, TORONTO, ON, M5G 1E6

(416) 862-9888   *SIC 8111*

EWASIUK RICK W QC *p89*
10180 101 ST NW SUITE 3200, EDMONTON, AB, T5J 3W8

(780) 497-3384   *SIC 8111*

FARRIS, VAUGHAN, WILLS & MURPHY LLP *p330*
700 GEORGIA ST W SUITE 25, VANCOUVER, BC, V7Y 1K8

(604) 684-9151   *SIC 8111*

FASKEN MARTINEAU DUMOULIN LLP *p304*
550 BURRARD ST SUITE 2900, VANCOUVER, BC, V6C 0A3

(604) 631-3131   *SIC 8111*

FASKEN MARTINEAU DUMOULIN LLP *p951*
333 BAY ST SUITE 2400, TORONTO, ON, M5H 2T6

(416) 366-8381   *SIC 8111*

FASKEN MARTINEAU DUMOULIN LLP *p1229*
800 RUE DU SQUARE-VICTORIA BUREAU 3700, MONTREAL, QC, H4Z 1A1

(514) 397-7400   *SIC 8111*

FASKEN MARTINEAU DUMOULIN LLP *p1269*
140 GRANDE ALLEE E BUREAU 800, QUEBEC, QC, G1R 5M8

(418) 640-2000   *SIC 8111*

FETHERSTONHAUGH & CO. *p823*
55 METCALFE ST SUITE 900, OTTAWA, ON, K1P 6L5

(613) 235-4373   *SIC 8111*

FETHERSTONHAUGH & CO. *p945*

438 UNIVERSITY AVE SUITE 1500, TORONTO, ON, M5G 2K8
(416) 598-4209 *SIC* 8111

FIELD LLP *p49*
444 7 AVE SW SUITE 400, CALGARY, AB, T2P 0X8
(403) 260-8500 *SIC* 8111

FIELD LLP *p89*
10175 101 ST NW SUITE 2500, EDMONTON, AB, T5J 0H3
(780) 423-3003 *SIC* 8111

FILLMORE RILEY LLP *p377*
360 MAIN ST SUITE 1700, WINNIPEG, MB, R3C 3Z3
(204) 956-2970 *SIC* 8111

FOGLER, RUBINOFF LLP *p969*
77 KING ST W SUITE 3000, TORONTO, ON, M5K 2A1
(416) 864-9700 *SIC* 8111

FORTIN, JEAN & ASSOCIES SYNDICS INC *p1141*
2360 BOUL MARIE-VICTORIN, LONGUEUIL, QC, J4G 1B5
(450) 442-3260 *SIC* 8111

FOSTER, TOWNSEND, GRAHAM & ASSOCIATES LLP *p653*
150 DUFFERIN AVE SUITE 900, LONDON, ON, N6A 5N6
(519) 672-5272 *SIC* 8111

G-WLG LP *p612*
1 MAIN ST W, HAMILTON, ON, L8P 4Z5
(905) 540-8208 *SIC* 8111

GARDINER ROBERTS LLP *p951*
22 ADELAIDE ST W UNIT 3600, TORONTO, ON, M5H 4E3
(416) 865-6600 *SIC* 8111

GINSBERG, GINGRAS & ASSOCIES INC *p1105*
145 PROM DU PORTAGE, GATINEAU, QC, J8X 2K4
(819) 776-0283 *SIC* 8111

GOODLAW SERVICES INC *p935*
250 YONGE ST SUITE 2400, TORONTO, ON, M5B 2L7
(416) 979-2211 *SIC* 8111

GOODMAN & GRIFFIN BARRISTERS & SOLICITORS *p705*
44 VILLAGE CENTRE PL 3RD FL SUITE 300, MISSISSAUGA, ON, L4Z 1V9
(905) 276-5050 *SIC* 8111

GOODMANS LLP *p952*
333 BAY ST SUITE 3400, TORONTO, ON, M5H 2S7
(416) 979-2211 *SIC* 8111

GOUVERNEMENT DE LA PROVINCE DE QUEBEC *p1188*
1 RUE NOTRE-DAME E BUREAU 4.100, MONTREAL, QC, H2Y 1B6
(514) 393-2703 *SIC* 8111

GOUVERNEMENT DE LA PROVINCE DE QUEBEC *p1269*
525 BOUL RENE-LEVESQUE E BUREAU 125, QUEBEC, QC, G1R 5Y4
(418) 643-2688 *SIC* 8111

GOUVERNEMENT DE LA PROVINCE DE QUEBEC *p1320*
25 RUE DE MARTIGNY O, SAINT-JEROME, QC, J7Y 4Z1
(450) 431-4406 *SIC* 8111

GOVERNMENT OF ONTARIO *p995*
400 UNIVERSITY AVE 14TH FLR, TORONTO, ON, M7A 1T7
(416) 326-7600 *SIC* 8111

GOWLING WLG (CANADA) LLP *p50*
421 7 AVE SW UNIT 1600, CALGARY, AB, T2P 4K9
(403) 298-1000 *SIC* 8111

GOWLING WLG (CANADA) LLP *p305*
550 BURRARD ST SUITE 2300, VANCOUVER, BC, V6C 2B5
(604) 683-6498 *SIC* 8111

GOWLING WLG (CANADA) LLP *p612*
1 MAIN ST W, HAMILTON, ON, L8P 4Z5
(905) 540-8208 *SIC* 8111

GOWLING WLG (CANADA) LLP *p639*
50 QUEEN ST N SUITE 1020, KITCHENER, ON, N2H 6P4
(519) 576-6910 *SIC* 8111

GOWLING WLG (CANADA) LLP *p639*
50 QUEEN ST N SUITE 1020, KITCHENER, ON, N2H 6P4
(519) 576-6910 *SIC* 8111

GOWLING WLG (CANADA) LLP *p639*
50 QUEEN ST N UNIT 1020, KITCHENER, ON, N2H 6P4
(519) 576-6910 *SIC* 8111

GOWLING WLG (CANADA) LLP *p639*
50 QUEEN ST N SUITE 1020, KITCHENER, ON, N2H 6P4
(519) 575-7506 *SIC* 8111

GOWLING WLG (CANADA) LLP *p823*
160 ELGIN ST SUITE 2600, OTTAWA, ON, K1P 1C3
(613) 233-1781 *SIC* 8111

GOWLING WLG (CANADA) LLP *p986*
1 FIRST CANADIAN PL 100 KING ST W SUITE 1600, TORONTO, ON, M5X 1G5
(416) 862-7525 *SIC* 8111

GOWLING WLG (CANADA) LLP *p1205*
1 PLACE VILLE-MARIE BUREAU 3700, MONTREAL, QC, H3B 3P4
(514) 878-9641 *SIC* 8111

GOWLINGS CANADA INC *p834*
160 ELGIN ST SUITE 200, OTTAWA, ON, K2P 2C4
(613) 233-1781 *SIC* 8111

GOWLINGS CANADA INC *p1205*
1 PLACE VILLE-MARIE BUREAU 3700, MONTREAL, QC, H3B 3P4
(514) 878-9641 *SIC* 8111

GREEN AND SPIEGEL, LLP *p952*
150 YORK ST 5TH FL, TORONTO, ON, M5H 3S5
(416) 862-7880 *SIC* 8111

GRILLO BARRISTERS PROFESSIONAL CORPORATION *p988*
38 APEX RD UNIT A, TORONTO, ON, M6A 2V2
(416) 614-6000 *SIC* 8111

HARPER GREY LLP *p298*
650 GEORGIA ST W SUITE 3200, VANCOUVER, BC, V6B 4P7
(604) 687-0411 *SIC* 8111

HARRISON PENSA LLP *p653*
450 TALBOT ST, LONDON, ON, N6A 5J6
(519) 679-9660 *SIC* 8111

HEENAN BLAIKIE S.E.N.C.R.L. *p963*
200 BAY ST, TORONTO, ON, M5J 2J4
(514) 898-5398 *SIC* 8111

HICKS MORLEY HAMILTON STEWART STORIE LLP *p969*
77 KING ST W 39TH FL TD CENTRE, TORONTO, ON, M5K 2A1
(416) 362-1011 *SIC* 8111

JOLI-COEUR LACASSE S.E.N.C.R.L *p1270*
1134 GRANDE ALLEE O BUREAU 600, QUEBEC, QC, G1S 1E5
(418) 681-7007 *SIC* 8111

KOSKIE MINSKY LLP *p953*
20 QUEEN ST W UNIT 900, TORONTO, ON, M5H 3R3
(416) 977-8353 *SIC* 8111

KRONIS, ROTSZTAIN, MARGLES, CAPPEL LLP *p772*
25 SHEPPARD AVE W SUITE 700, NORTH YORK, ON, M2N 6S6
(416) 225-8750 *SIC* 8111

LANGLOIS AVOCATS S.E.N.C.R.L. *p1272*
2820 BOUL LAURIER BUREAU 1300, QUEBEC, QC, G1V 0C1
(418) 650-7000 *SIC* 8111

LANGLOIS GAUDREAU S.E.N.C. *p1197*
1002 RUE SHERBROOKE O BUREAU 27, MONTREAL, QC, H3A 3L6
(514) 842-9512 *SIC* 8111

LANGLOIS KRONSTROM DESJARDINS S.E.N.C. *p1197*
1002 RUE SHERBROOKE O BUREAU

2800, MONTREAL, QC, H3A 3L6
(514) 842-9512 *SIC* 8111

LAVERY DE BILLY, SOCIETE EN NOM COLLECTIF A RESPONSABILITE LIMITEE *p1205*
1 PLACE VILLE-MARIE BUREAU 4000, MONTREAL, QC, H3B 4M4
(514) 871-1522 *SIC* 8111

LAW SOCIETY OF UPPER CANADA, THE *p953*
130 QUEEN ST W SUITE 100, TORONTO, ON, M5H 2N6
(416) 644-4886 *SIC* 8111

LAW SOCIETY OF UPPER CANADA, THE *p953*
130 QUEEN ST W SUITE 100, TORONTO, ON, M5H 2N6
(416) 947-3315 *SIC* 8111

LAWSON LUNDELL LLP *p306*
925 GEORGIA ST W SUITE 1600, VANCOUVER, BC, V6C 3L2
(604) 685-3456 *SIC* 8111

LEGAL AID ONTARIO *p946*
LEGAL AID ONTARIO, TORONTO, ON, M5G 2H1
(416) 979-1446 *SIC* 8111

LEGAL AID SERVICES SOCIETY OF MANITOBA *p378*
294 PORTAGE AVE UNIT 402, WINNIPEG, MB, R3C 0B9
(204) 985-8500 *SIC* 8111

LEGAL AID SOCIETY OF ALBERTA *p89*
10320 102 AVE NW SUITE 300, EDMONTON, AB, T5J 4A1
(780) 427-7575 *SIC* 8111

LEGAL SERVICES SOCIETY *p306*
510 BURRARD ST SUITE 400, VANCOUVER, BC, V6C 3A8
(604) 601-6200 *SIC* 8111

LERNERS LLP *p654*
80 DUFFERIN AVE, LONDON, ON, N6A 1K4
(519) 672-4510 *SIC* 8111

LERNERS LLP *p954*
130 ADELAIDE ST W SUITE 2400, TORONTO, ON, M5H 3P5
(416) 867-3076 *SIC* 8111

LINDSAY KENNEY LLP *p299*
401 GEORGIA ST W SUITE 1800, VANCOUVER, BC, V6B 5A1
(604) 687-1323 *SIC* 8111

MACKIMMIE MATTHEWS *p53*
401 9 AVE SW SUITE 700, CALGARY, AB, T2P 3C5
SIC 8111

MCCAGUE BORLACK LLP *p987*
130 KING ST W SUITE 2700, TORONTO, ON, M5X 2A2
(416) 860-0001 *SIC* 8111

MCCARTHY TETRAULT LLP *p53*
421 7 AVE SW SUITE 4000, CALGARY, AB, T2P 4K9
(403) 260-3500 *SIC* 8111

MCCARTHY TETRAULT LLP *p969*
66 WELLINGTON ST W SUITE 5300, TORONTO, ON, M5K 1E6
(416) 362-1812 *SIC* 8111

MCCARTHY TETRAULT LLP *p1206*
1000 RUE DE LA GAUCHETIERE O BUREAU 2500, MONTREAL, QC, H3B 0A2
SIC 8111

MCDOUGALL GAULEY LLP *p1418*
1881 SCARTH ST SUITE 1500, REGINA, SK, S4P 4K9
(306) 757-1641 *SIC* 8111

MCDOUGALL GAULEY LLP *p1424*
500-616 MAIN ST, SASKATOON, SK, S7H 0J6
(306) 653-1212 *SIC* 8111

MCDOUGALL GAULEY LLP *p1424*
616 MAIN ST SUITE 500, SASKATOON, SK, S7H 0J6
(306) 653-1212 *SIC* 8111

MCINNES COOPER *p453*

1969 UPPER WATER ST SUITE 1300, HALIFAX, NS, B3J 3R7
(902) 425-6500 *SIC* 8111

MCKERCHER LLP *p1428*
374 3RD AVE S, SASKATOON, SK, S7K 1M5
(306) 653-2000 *SIC* 8111

MCLENNAN ROSS LLP *p97*
12220 STONY PLAIN RD NW SUITE 600, EDMONTON, AB, T5N 3Y4
(780) 482-9200 *SIC* 8111

MCLEOD & COMPANY LLP *p69*
14505 BANNISTER RD SE SUITE 300, CALGARY, AB, T2X 3J3
(403) 225-6400 *SIC* 8111

MCMILLAN LLP *p315*
1055 GEORGIA ST W SUITE 1500, VANCOUVER, BC, V6E 4N7
(604) 689-9111 *SIC* 8111

MCMILLAN LLP *p964*
181 BAY ST SUITE 4400, TORONTO, ON, M5J 2T3
(416) 865-7000 *SIC* 8111

MCMILLAN LLP *p1198*
1000 RUE SHERBROOKE O BUREAU 2700, MONTREAL, QC, H3A 3G4
(514) 987-5000 *SIC* 8111

MILLER THOMSON LLP *p54*
700 9 AVE SW SUITE 3000, CALGARY, AB, T2P 3V4
(403) 298-2400 *SIC* 8111

MILLER THOMSON LLP *p90*
10155 102 ST NW SUITE 2700, EDMONTON, AB, T5J 4G8
(780) 429-1751 *SIC* 8111

MILLER THOMSON LLP *p326*
840 HOWE ST SUITE 1000, VANCOUVER, BC, V6Z 2M1
(604) 687-2242 *SIC* 8111

MILLER THOMSON LLP *p672*
60 COLUMBIA WAY SUITE 600, MARKHAM, ON, L3R 0C9
(905) 415-6700 *SIC* 8111

MILLER THOMSON LLP *p954*
40 KING ST W UNIT 5800, TORONTO, ON, M5H 3S1
(416) 595-8500 *SIC* 8111

MILLER THOMSON LLP *p1008*
295 HAGEY BLVD SUITE 300, WATERLOO, ON, N2L 6R5
(519) 579-3660 *SIC* 8111

MILLER THOMSON LLP *p1206*
1000 RUE DE LA GAUCHETIERE O BUREAU 3700, MONTREAL, QC, H3B 4W5
(514) 875-5210 *SIC* 8111

MINDEN GROSS LLP *p954*
145 KING ST W SUITE 2200, TORONTO, ON, M5H 4G2
(416) 362-3711 *SIC* 8111

MLT AIKINS LLP *p1418*
1874 SCARTH ST SUITE 1500, REGINA, SK, S4P 4E9
(306) 347-8000 *SIC* 8111

MLT AIKINS LLP *p1428*
410 22ND ST E SUITE 1500, SASKATOON, SK, S7K 5T6
(306) 975-7100 *SIC* 8111

MONTY COULOMBE S.E.N.C *p1371*
234 RUE DUFFERIN BUREAU 200, SHERBROOKE, QC, J1H 4M2
(819) 566-4466 *SIC* 8111

MT SERVICES LIMITED PARTNERSHIP *p315*
745 THURLOW ST UNIT 2400, VANCOUVER, BC, V6E 0C5
(604) 643-7100 *SIC* 8111

MT SERVICES LIMITED PARTNERSHIP *p970*
66 WELLINGTON ST W RD SUITE 5300, TORONTO, ON, M5K 1E6
(416) 601-8200 *SIC* 8111

NEWFOUNDLAND & LABRADOR LEGAL AID COMMISSION *p432*
251 EMPIRE AVE SUITE 200, ST. JOHN'S,

NL, A1C 3H9

(709) 753-7860   *SIC* 8111

NIXON WENGER LLP p332
2706 30 AVE SUITE 301, VERNON, BC,
V1T 2B6

(250) 542-5353   *SIC* 8111

NORTON ROSE FULBRIGHT CANADA LLP
p55
400 3 AVE SW SUITE 3700, CALGARY, AB,
T2P 4H2

(403) 267-8222   *SIC* 8111

NORTON ROSE FULBRIGHT CANADA S.E.N.C.R.L. S.R.L. p1273
2828 BOUL LAURIER BUREAU 1500, QUE-
BEC, QC, G1V 0B9

(418) 640-7414   *SIC* 8111

NORTON ROSE FULBRIGHT CANADA S.E.N.C.R.L., S.R.L. p824
45 O'CONNOR ST SUITE 1600, OTTAWA,
ON, K1P 1A4

(613) 780-8661   *SIC* 8111

NORTON ROSE FULBRIGHT CANADA S.E.N.C.R.L., S.R.L. p965
200 BAY ST SUITE 3800, TORONTO, ON,
M5J 2Z4

(416) 216-4000   *SIC* 8111

NORTON ROSE FULBRIGHT CANADA S.E.N.C.R.L., S.R.L. p1206
1 PLACE VILLE-MARIE BUREAU 2500,
MONTREAL, QC, H3B 4S2

(514) 847-4747   *SIC* 8111

NORTON ROSE FULBRIGHT CANADA S.E.N.C.R.L., S.R.L. p1273
2828 BOUL LAURIER BUREAU 1500, QUE-
BEC, QC, G1V 0B9

(418) 640-5000   *SIC* 8111

ONTARIO SECURITIES COMMISSION p955
20 QUEEN ST W 22 FLR, TORONTO, ON,
M5H 3R3

(416) 593-8314   *SIC* 8111

OSLER, HOSKIN & HARCOURT LLP   p55
450 1 ST SW SUITE 2500, CALGARY, AB,
T2P 5H1

(403) 260-7000   *SIC* 8111

OSLER, HOSKIN & HARCOURT LLP p825
340 ALBERT ST SUITE 1900, OTTAWA,
ON, K1R 7Y6

(613) 235-7234   *SIC* 8111

OSLER, HOSKIN & HARCOURT LLP p987
100 KING ST W SUITE 4600 FIRST CANA-
DIAN PLACE, TORONTO, ON, M5X 1B8

(416) 362-2111   *SIC* 8111

OSLER, HOSKIN & HARCOURT LLP p1207
1000 RUE DE LA GAUCHETIERE O BU-
REAU 2100, MONTREAL, QC, H3B 4W5

(514) 904-8100   *SIC* 8111

OWEN BIRD LAW CORPORATION   p329
595 BURRARD ST SUITE 2900, VANCOU-
VER, BC, V7X 1J5

(604) 688-0401   *SIC* 8111

**PACE LAW FIRM PROFESSIONAL CORPO-
RATION** p578
300 THE EAST MALL UNIT 500, ETOBI-
COKE, ON, M9B 6B7

(416) 236-3060   *SIC* 8111

**PAQUETTE ET ASSOCIES HUISSIERS DE
JUSTICE S.E.N.C.R.L.** p1190
511 PLACE D'ARMES BUREAU 800, MON-
TREAL, QC, H2Y 2W7

(514) 937-5500   *SIC* 8111

PARLEE MCLAWS LLP   p56
421 7 AVE SW UNIT 3300, CALGARY, AB,
T2P 4K9

(403) 294-7000   *SIC* 8111

PARLEE MCLAWS LLP   p90
10175 101 ST NW, EDMONTON, AB, T5J
0H3

(780) 423-8500   *SIC* 8111

PENSA AND ASSOCIATES   p654
450 TALBOT ST, LONDON, ON, N6A 5J6

(519) 679-9660   *SIC* 8111

**PERLEY-ROBERTSON, HILL & MC-
DOUGALL LLP/S.R.L.** p825
340 ALBERT ST SUITE 1400, OTTAWA,

ON, K1R 0A5

(613) 238-2022   *SIC* 8111

PITBLADO LLP p379
360 MAIN ST SUITE 2500, WINNIPEG, MB,
R3C 4H6

(204) 956-0560   *SIC* 8111

PUSHOR MITCHELL LLP p222
1665 ELLIS ST SUITE 301, KELOWNA, BC,
V1Y 2B3

(250) 869-1100   *SIC* 8111

RAYMOND CHABOT INC p1207
600 RUE DE LA GAUCHETIERE O BU-
REAU 2000, MONTREAL, QC, H3B 4L8

(514) 879-1385   *SIC* 8111

**REYNOLDS MIRTH RICHARDS & FARMER
LLP** p90
10180 101 ST NW SUITE 3200, EDMON-
TON, AB, T5J 3W8

(780) 425-9510   *SIC* 8111

RICHARDS BUELL SUTTON LLP p300
401 GEORGIA ST W SUITE 700, VANCOU-
VER, BC, V6B 5A1

(604) 682-3664   *SIC* 8111

RIDOUT & MAYBEE LLP p956
250 UNIVERSITY AVE 5TH FL, TORONTO,
ON, M5H 3E5

(416) 868-1482   *SIC* 8111

ROBIC, S.E.N.C.R.L. p1208
630 BOUL RENE-LEVESQUE O 20E
ETAGE, MONTREAL, QC, H3B 1S6

(514) 987-6242   *SIC* 8111

**ROBINSON, SHEPPARD, SHAPIRO,
S.E.N.C.R.L.** p1229
800 RUE DU SQUARE-VICTORIA BUREAU
4600, MONTREAL, QC, H4Z 1H6

(514) 878-2631   *SIC* 8111

ROYAL LEGAL SOLUTIONS P.C. INC p943
1 YONGE ST SUITE 1801, TORONTO, ON,
M5E 1W7

SIC 8111

S & E LIMITED PARTNERSHIP p309
666 BURRARD ST SUITE 1700, VANCOU-
VER, BC, V6C 2X8

(604) 631-1300   *SIC* 8111

**SASKATCHEWAN LEGAL AID COMMIS-
SION, THE** p1429
201 21ST ST E SUITE 502, SASKATOON,
SK, S7K 0B8

(306) 933-5300   *SIC* 8111

SERVICES CONSEILS ARBITREX INC, LES
p1273
2875 BOUL LAURIER UNITE 200, QUE-
BEC, QC, G1V 5B1

(418) 651-9900   *SIC* 8111

SHIBLEY RIGHTON LLP p957
250 UNIVERSITY AVE SUITE 700,
TORONTO, ON, M5H 3E5

(416) 214-5200   *SIC* 8111

SIMBAS LIMITED p947
330 UNIVERSITY AVE SUITE 504,
TORONTO, ON, M5G 1R7

(416) 595-1155   *SIC* 8111

SINGLETON URQUHART LLP p309
925 GEORGIA ST W SUITE 1200, VAN-
COUVER, BC, V6C 3L2

(604) 682-7474   *SIC* 8111

SISKINDS LLP p655
680 WATERLOO ST, LONDON, ON, N6A
0B3

(519) 672-2121   *SIC* 8111

SMART & BIGGAR p824
55 METCALFE ST SUITE 900, OTTAWA,
ON, K1P 6L5

(613) 232-2486   *SIC* 8111

SPIEGEL SOHMER INC p1208
1255 RUE PEEL BUREAU 1000, MON-
TREAL, QC, H3B 2T9

(514) 875-2100   *SIC* 8111

STEIN MONAST S.E.N.C.R.L. p1260
70 RUE DALHOUSIE BUREAU 300, QUE-
BEC, QC, G1K 4B2

(418) 529-6531   *SIC* 8111

STEWART MCKELVEY STIRLING SCALES
p415

44 CHIPMAN HILL SUITE 1000, SAINT
JOHN, NB, E2L 2A9

(506) 632-1970   *SIC* 8111

STEWART MCKELVEY STIRLING SCALES
p454
1959 UPPER WATER ST SUITE 900, HALI-
FAX, NS, B3J 3N2

(902) 420-3200   *SIC* 8111

**STEWART, JAMIE D MCLEOD & COMPANY
LLP LAWYERS** p69
14505 BANNISTER RD SE, CALGARY, AB,
T2X 3J3

(403) 225-6412   *SIC* 8111

STIKEMAN ELLIOTT LLP p971
5300 COMMERCE CRT W SUITE 199,
TORONTO, ON, M5L 1B9

(416) 869-5500   *SIC* 8111

STIKEMAN ELLIOTT LLP p1208
1155 BOUL RENE-LEVESQUE O BUREAU
B01, MONTREAL, QC, H3B 4R1

(514) 397-3000   *SIC* 8111

**THERRIEN COUTURE AVOCATS
S.E.N.C.R.L.** p1313
1200 RUE DANIEL-JOHNSON O # 7000,
SAINT-HYACINTHE, QC, J2S 7K7

(450) 773-6326   *SIC* 8111

THOMSON ROGERS p957
390 BAY ST SUITE 3100, TORONTO, ON,
M5H 1W2

(416) 868-3100   *SIC* 8111

TORKIN MANES LLP p941
151 YONGE ST SUITE 1500, TORONTO,
ON, M5C 2W7

(416) 863-1188   *SIC* 8111

TORYS LLP p970
79 WELLINGTON ST W SUITE 3000,
TORONTO, ON, M5K 1N2

(416) 865-0040   *SIC* 8111

**TREMBLAY BOIS MIGNAULT LEMAY & AS-
SOCIES INC** p1274
1195 AV LAVIGERIE BUREAU 200, QUE-
BEC, QC, G1V 4N3

(418) 658-9966   *SIC* 8111

UNIFOR LEGAL SERVICES PLAN p927
1 ST CLAIR AVE W SUITE 600, TORONTO,
ON, M4V 3C3

(416) 960-2410   *SIC* 8111

WEIRFOULDS LLP p970
66 WELLINGTON ST W SUITE 4100,
TORONTO, ON, M5K 1B7

(416) 365-1110   *SIC* 8111

WITTEN LLP p91
10303 JASPER AVE NW SUITE 2500, ED-
MONTON, AB, T5J 3N6

(780) 428-0501   *SIC* 8111

YEUNG, GAYNOR C. LAW CORPORATION
p311
200 GRANVILLE ST SUITE 2400, VAN-
COUVER, BC, V6C 1S4

(604) 682-5466   *SIC* 8111

---

*SIC 8211 Elementary and secondary
schools*

ACADEMIE LAFONTAINE INC p1319
2171 BOUL MAURICE, SAINT-JEROME,
QC, J7Y 4M7

(450) 431-3733   *SIC* 8211

ACADEMIE MICHELE-PROVOST INC p1212
1517 AV DES PINS O, MONTREAL, QC,
H3G 1B3

(514) 935-2344   *SIC* 8211

ACADEMIE STE-THERESE INC, L' p1287
1 CH DES ECOLIERS, ROSEMERE, QC,
J7A 4Y1

(450) 434-1130   *SIC* 8211

**AHKWESAHSNE MOHAWK BOARD OF ED-
UCATION** p475
169 AKWESASNE INTERNATIONAL RD,
AKWESASNE, ON, K6H 0G5

(613) 933-0409   *SIC* 8211

ALBERTA DISTANCE LEARNING CENTRE
p86
10055 106 ST NW SUITE 300, EDMON-

TON, AB, T5J 2Y2

(780) 452-4655   *SIC* 8211

ALGOMA DISTRICT SCHOOL BOARD p861
644 ALBERT ST E, SAULT STE. MARIE,
ON, P6A 2K7

(705) 945-7111   *SIC* 8211

ALGOMA DISTRICT SCHOOL BOARD p861
1601 WELLINGTON ST E, SAULT STE.
MARIE, ON, P6A 2R8

(705) 945-7177   *SIC* 8211

ALGOMA DISTRICT SCHOOL BOARD p862
750 NORTH ST, SAULT STE. MARIE, ON,
P6B 2C5

(705) 945-7177   *SIC* 8211

ALGOMA DISTRICT SCHOOL BOARD p863
636 GOULAIS AVE, SAULT STE. MARIE,
ON, P6C 5A7

(705) 945-7180   *SIC* 8211

**ALGONQUIN & LAKESHORE CATHOLIC
DISTRICT SCHOOL BOARD** p490
301 CHURCH ST, BELLEVILLE, ON, K8N
3C7

(613) 967-0404   *SIC* 8211

**ALGONQUIN & LAKESHORE CATHOLIC
DISTRICT SCHOOL BOARD** p629
130 RUSSELL ST, KINGSTON, ON, K7K
2E9

(613) 545-1902   *SIC* 8211

**ALGONQUIN & LAKESHORE CATHOLIC
DISTRICT SCHOOL BOARD** p632
1085 WOODBINE RD, KINGSTON, ON,
K7P 2V9

(613) 384-1919   *SIC* 8211

**ANGLOPHONE SOUTH SCHOOL DISTRICT
(ASD-S)** p411
398 HAMPTON RD, QUISPAMSIS, NB, E2E
4V5

(506) 847-6200   *SIC* 8211

**ANGLOPHONE SOUTH SCHOOL DISTRICT
(ASD-S)** p413
490 WOODWARD AVE, SAINT JOHN, NB,
E2K 5N3

(506) 658-5300   *SIC* 8211

**ANGLOPHONE SOUTH SCHOOL DISTRICT
(ASD-S)** p418
55 LEONARD DR, SUSSEX, NB, E4E 2P8

(506) 432-2017   *SIC* 8211

ANGLOPHONE WEST SCHOOL DISTRICT
p399
499 CLIFFE ST, FREDERICTON, NB, E3A
9P5

(506) 457-6898   *SIC* 8211

ANGLOPHONE WEST SCHOOL DISTRICT
p400
300 PRIESTMAN ST, FREDERICTON, NB,
E3B 6J8

(506) 453-5435   *SIC* 8211

ANGLOPHONE WEST SCHOOL DISTRICT
p400
1135 PROSPECT ST, FREDERICTON, NB,
E3B 3B9

(506) 453-5454   *SIC* 8211

**ANNAPOLIS VALLEY REGIONAL SCHOOL
BOARD** p439
1941 HWY 1, AUBURN, NS, B0P 1A0

(902) 847-4440   *SIC* 8211

**ANNAPOLIS VALLEY REGIONAL SCHOOL
BOARD** p441
121 ORCHARD ST RR 3, BERWICK, NS,
B0P 1E0

(902) 538-4600   *SIC* 8211

**ANNAPOLIS VALLEY REGIONAL SCHOOL
BOARD** p470
225 PAYZANT DR, WINDSOR, NS, B0N 2T0

(902) 792-6740   *SIC* 8211

**ANNAPOLIS VALLEY REGIONAL SCHOOL
BOARD** p471
75 GREENWICH RD S, WOLFVILLE, NS,
B4P 2R2

(902) 542-6060   *SIC* 8211

**ANNE & MAX TANENBAUM COMMUNITY
HEBREW ACADEMY OF TORONTO** p664
9600 BATHURST ST, MAPLE, ON, L6A 3Z8

SIC 8211

APPLEBY COLLEGE p802
540 LAKESHORE RD W, OAKVILLE, ON, L6K 3P1
(905) 845-4681   *SIC* 8211

ASHBURY COLLEGE INCORPORATED p820
362 MARIPOSA AVE, OTTAWA, ON, K1M 0T3
(613) 749-5954   *SIC* 8211

ASPEN VIEW PUBLIC SCHOOL DIVISION NO. 78 p4
3600 48 AVE SUITE 19, ATHABASCA, AB, T9S 1M8
(780) 675-7080   *SIC* 8211

ASSOCIATED HEBREW SCHOOLS OF TORONTO p775
252 FINCH AVE W, NORTH YORK, ON, M2R 1M9
(416) 494-7666   *SIC* 8211

ASSOCIATION B.C.S p1374
80 CH MOULTON HILL, SHERBROOKE, QC, J1M 2K4
(819) 566-0227   *SIC* 8211

ASSOCIATION DES ETUDIANTS DU COLLEGE REGIONAL CHAMPLAIN L' p1271
790 AV NEREE-TREMBLAY, QUEBEC, QC, G1V 4K2
(418) 656-6921   *SIC* 8211

ATHOL MURRAY COLLEGE OF NOTRE DAME p1438
49 MAIN ST, WILCOX, SK, S0G 5E0
(306) 732-2080   *SIC* 8211

ATLANTIC PROVINCES SPECIAL EDUCATION AUTHORITY p451
5940 SOUTH ST, HALIFAX, NS, B3H 1S6
(902) 423-8469   *SIC* 8211

AVON MAITLAND DISTRICT SCHOOL BOARD p589
92 GIDLEY E, EXETER, ON, N0M 1S0
(519) 235-0880   *SIC* 8211

AVON MAITLAND DISTRICT SCHOOL BOARD p646
155 MAITLAND AVE S, LISTOWEL, ON, N4W 2M4
(519) 291-1880   *SIC* 8211

AVON MAITLAND DISTRICT SCHOOL BOARD p895
428 FORMAN AVE, STRATFORD, ON, N5A 6R7
(519) 271-9740   *SIC* 8211

AVON MAITLAND DISTRICT SCHOOL BOARD p1026
231 MADILL DR E, WINGHAM, ON, N0G 2W0
(519) 357-1800   *SIC* 8211

BALMORAL HALL - SCHOOL FOR GIRLS p376
630 WESTMINSTER AVE, WINNIPEG, MB, R3C 3S1
(204) 784-1600   *SIC* 8211

BATTLE RIVER REGIONAL DIVISION 31 p78
5402 48A AVE, CAMROSE, AB, T4V 0L3
(780) 672-6131   *SIC* 8211

BEAUTIFUL PLAINS SCHOOL DIVISION p353
213 MOUNTAIN AVE, NEEPAWA, MB, R0J 1H0
(204) 476-2387   *SIC* 8211

BIALIK HEBREW DAY SCHOOL p790
2760 BATHURST ST, NORTH YORK, ON, M6B 3A1
(416) 783-3346   *SIC* 8211

BISHOP STRACHAN SCHOOL, THE p926
298 LONSDALE RD, TORONTO, ON, M4V 1X2
(416) 483-4325   *SIC* 8211

BLACK GOLD REGIONAL DIVISION #18 p5
5417 43 AVE, BEAUMONT, AB, T4X 1K1
(780) 929-6282   *SIC* 8211

BLACK GOLD REGIONAL DIVISION #18 p81
105 ATHABASCA AVE, DEVON, AB, T9G 1A4
(780) 987-3709   *SIC* 8211

BLACK GOLD REGIONAL DIVISION #18 p148
1101 5 ST SUITE 301, NISKU, AB, T9E 7N3
(780) 955-6025   *SIC* 8211

BLUEWATER DISTRICT SCHOOL BOARD p835
1550 8TH ST E, OWEN SOUND, ON, N4K 0A2
(519) 376-2010   *SIC* 8211

BLUEWATER DISTRICT SCHOOL BOARD p847
780 GUSTAVUS ST SS 4, PORT ELGIN, ON, N0H 2C4
(519) 832-2091   *SIC* 8211

BOARD OF EDUCATION OF SASKATOON SCHOOL DIVISION NO. 13 OF SASKATCHEWAN, THE p1424
1905 PRESTON AVE, SASKATOON, SK, S7J 2E7
(306) 683-7850   *SIC* 8211

BOARD OF EDUCATION OF SASKATOON SCHOOL DIVISION NO. 13 OF SASKATCHEWAN, THE p1426
310 21ST ST E, SASKATOON, SK, S7K 1M7
(306) 683-8200   *SIC* 8211

BOARD OF EDUCATION OF SASKATOON SCHOOL DIVISION NO. 13 OF SASKATCHEWAN, THE p1426
310 21ST ST E, SASKATOON, SK, S7K 1M7
(306) 683-8200   *SIC* 8211

BOARD OF EDUCATION OF SASKATOON SCHOOL DIVISION NO. 13 OF SASKATCHEWAN, THE p1431
2220 RUSHOLME RD, SASKATOON, SK, S7L 4A4
(306) 683-7800   *SIC* 8211

BOARD OF EDUCATION OF SCHOOL DISTRICT #82 (COAST M p223
1491 KINGFISHER AVE N, KITIMAT, BC, V8C 1E9
(250) 632-6174   *SIC* 8211

BOARD OF EDUCATION OF SCHOOL DISTRICT #82 (COAST M p283
3430 SPARKS ST, TERRACE, BC, V8G 2V3
(250) 638-0306   *SIC* 8211

BOARD OF EDUCATION OF SCHOOL DISTRICT NO. 06 (ROCKY MOUNTAIN), THE p216
1535 14TH ST SUITE 4, INVERMERE, BC, V0A 1K4
(250) 342-9213   *SIC* 8211

BOARD OF EDUCATION OF SCHOOL DISTRICT NO. 23 (CENTRAL OKANAGAN), THE p219
705 RUTLAND RD N, KELOWNA, BC, V1X 3B6
(250) 870-5134   *SIC* 8211

BOARD OF EDUCATION OF SCHOOL DISTRICT NO. 23 (CENTRAL OKANAGAN), THE p219
1040 HOLLYWOOD RD S, KELOWNA, BC, V1X 4N2
(250) 860-8888   *SIC* 8211

BOARD OF EDUCATION OF SCHOOL DISTRICT NO. 23 (CENTRAL OKANAGAN), THE p219
3130 GORDON DR, KELOWNA, BC, V1W 3M4
(250) 870-5106   *SIC* 8211

BOARD OF EDUCATION OF SCHOOL DISTRICT NO. 23 (CENTRAL OKANAGAN), THE p221
1079 RAYMER AVE, KELOWNA, BC, V1Y 4Z7
(250) 870-5105   *SIC* 8211

BOARD OF EDUCATION OF SCHOOL DISTRICT NO. 35 (LANGLEY) p227
4875 222 ST, LANGLEY, BC, V3A 3Z7
(604) 534-7891   *SIC* 8211

BOARD OF EDUCATION OF SCHOOL DISTRICT NO. 39 (VANCOUVER), THE p286
2600 BROADWAY E, VANCOUVER, BC, V5M 1Y5

(604) 713-8215   *SIC* 8211
BOARD OF EDUCATION OF SCHOOL DISTRICT NO. 39 (VANCOUVER), THE p287
1755 55TH AVE E, VANCOUVER, BC, V5P 1Z7
(604) 713-8278   *SIC* 8211

BOARD OF EDUCATION OF SCHOOL DISTRICT NO. 39 (VANCOUVER), THE p288
6454 KILLARNEY ST, VANCOUVER, BC, V5S 2X7
(604) 713-8950   *SIC* 8211

BOARD OF EDUCATION OF SCHOOL DISTRICT NO. 39 (VANCOUVER), THE p292
5025 WILLOW ST SUITE 39, VANCOUVER, BC, V5Z 3S1
(604) 713-8927   *SIC* 8211

BOARD OF EDUCATION OF SCHOOL DISTRICT NO. 39 (VANCOUVER), THE p320
1580 BROADWAY W, VANCOUVER, BC, V6J 5K8
(604) 713-5000   *SIC* 8211

BOARD OF EDUCATION OF SCHOOL DISTRICT NO. 39 (VANCOUVER), THE p322
6360 MAPLE ST, VANCOUVER, BC, V6M 4M2
(604) 713-8200   *SIC* 8211

BOARD OF EDUCATION OF SCHOOL DISTRICT NO. 39 (VANCOUVER), THE p322
2250 EDDINGTON DR, VANCOUVER, BC, V6L 2E7
(604) 713-8974   *SIC* 8211

BOARD OF EDUCATION OF SCHOOL DISTRICT NO. 39 (VANCOUVER), THE p322
2706 TRAFALGAR ST, VANCOUVER, BC, V6K 2J6
(604) 713-8961   *SIC* 8211

BOARD OF EDUCATION OF SCHOOL DISTRICT NO. 39 (VANCOUVER), THE p323
7055 HEATHER ST, VANCOUVER, BC, V6P 3P7
(604) 713-8189   *SIC* 8211

BOARD OF EDUCATION OF SCHOOL DISTRICT NO. 39 (VANCOUVER), THE p324
3939 16TH AVE W, VANCOUVER, BC, V6R 3C9
(604) 713-8171   *SIC* 8211

BOARD OF EDUCATION OF SCHOOL DISTRICT NO. 57 (PRINCE GEORGE), THE p248
4540 HANDLEN RD, PRINCE GEORGE, BC, V2K 2J8
(250) 962-9271   *SIC* 8211

BOARD OF EDUCATION OF SCHOOL DISTRICT NO. 57 (PRINCE GEORGE), THE p249
2100 FERRY AVE, PRINCE GEORGE, BC, V2L 4R5
(250) 561-6800   *SIC* 8211

BOARD OF EDUCATION OF SCHOOL DISTRICT NO. 57 (PRINCE GEORGE), THE p249
747 WINNIPEG ST, PRINCE GEORGE, BC, V2L 2V3
(250) 563-7124   *SIC* 8211

BOARD OF EDUCATION OF SCHOOL DISTRICT NO. 57 (PRINCE GEORGE), THE p250
2901 GRIFFITHS AVE, PRINCE GEORGE, BC, V2M 2S7
(250) 562-6441   *SIC* 8211

BOARD OF EDUCATION OF SCHOOL DISTRICT NO. 61 (GREATER VICTORIA) p332
3970 GORDON HEAD RD, VICTORIA, BC, V8N 3X3
(250) 477-6977   *SIC* 8211

BOARD OF EDUCATION OF SCHOOL DISTRICT NO. 61 (GREATER VICTORIA) p333
3963 BORDEN ST, VICTORIA, BC, V8P 3H9
(250) 479-1696   *SIC* 8211

BOARD OF EDUCATION OF SCHOOL DISTRICT NO. 61 (GREATER VICTORIA) p334
1260 GRANT ST, VICTORIA, BC, V8T 1C2
(250) 388-5456   *SIC* 8211

BOARD OF EDUCATION OF SCHOOL DISTRICT NO. 61 (GREATER VICTORIA) p338
957 BURNSIDE RD W, VICTORIA, BC, V8Z 6E9

(250) 479-8271   *SIC* 8211
BOARD OF EDUCATION OF SCHOOL DISTRICT NO. 61 (GREATER VICTORIA) p338
556 BOLESKINE RD, VICTORIA, BC, V8Z 1E8
(250) 475-3212   *SIC* 8211

BOARD OF EDUCATION OF SCHOOL DISTRICT NO. 61 (GREATER VICTORIA) p339
847 COLVILLE RD, VICTORIA, BC, V9A 4N9
(250) 382-9226   *SIC* 8211

BOARD OF EDUCATION OF SCHOOL DISTRICT NO. 91 (NECHAKO LAKE), THE p330
153 CONNAUGHT ST E, VANDERHOOF, BC, V0J 3A0
(250) 567-2284   *SIC* 8211

BOARD OF EDUCATION OF THE CHINOOK SCHOOL DIVISION NO. 211 OF SASKATCHEWAN p1436
2100 GLADSTONE ST E, SWIFT CURRENT, SK, S9H 3W7
(306) 778-9200   *SIC* 8211

BOARD OF EDUCATION OF THE GOOD SPIRIT SCHOOL DIVISION NO. 204 OF SASKATCHEWAN p1438
150 GLADSTONE AVE N, YORKTON, SK, S3N 2A8
(306) 786-5560   *SIC* 8211

BOARD OF EDUCATION OF THE LIVING SKY SCHOOL DIVISION NO. 202 SASKATCHEWAN p1412
509 PIONEER AVE, NORTH BATTLEFORD, SK, S9A 4A5
(306) 937-7702   *SIC* 8211

BOARD OF EDUCATION OF THE LIVING SKY SCHOOL DIVISION NO. 202 SASKATCHEWAN p1412
1791 110TH ST, NORTH BATTLEFORD, SK, S9A 2Y2
(306) 445-6101   *SIC* 8211

BOARD OF EDUCATION OF THE REGINA ROMAN CATHOLIC SEPARATE SCHOOL DIVISION NO. 81 p1417
1027 COLLEGE AVE, REGINA, SK, S4P 1A7
(306) 791-7230   *SIC* 8211

BOARD OF EDUCATION OF THE REGINA ROMAN CATHOLIC SEPARATE SCHOOL DIVISION NO. 81 p1420
134 ARGYLE ST, REGINA, SK, S4R 4C3
(306) 791-7240   *SIC* 8211

BOARD OF EDUCATION REGINA SCHOOL DIVISION NO. 4 OF SASKATCHEWAN p1422
3838 E BUCKINGHAM DR, REGINA, SK, S4V 3A1
(306) 791-8585   *SIC* 8211

BOARD OF EDUCATION REGINA SCHOOL DIVISION NO. 4 OF SASKATCHEWAN p1423
5255 ROCHDALE BLVD, REGINA, SK, S4X 4M8
(306) 523-3400   *SIC* 8211

BOARD OF EDUCATION SCHOOL DISTRICT #38 (RICHMOND) p253
4151 JACOMBS RD, RICHMOND, BC, V6V 1N7
(604) 668-6430   *SIC* 8211

BOARD OF EDUCATION SCHOOL DISTRICT #38 (RICHMOND) p262
9500 NO. 4 RD, RICHMOND, BC, V7A 2Y9
(604) 668-6575   *SIC* 8211

BOARD OF EDUCATION SCHOOL DISTRICT #38 (RICHMOND) p262
7811 GRANVILLE AVE, RICHMOND, BC, V6Y 3E3
(604) 668-6000   *SIC* 8211

BOARD OF EDUCATION SCHOOL DISTRICT #38 (RICHMOND) p262
7171 MINORU BLVD, RICHMOND, BC, V6Y 1Z3
(604) 668-6400   *SIC* 8211

BOARD OF EDUCATION SCHOOL DISTRICT #38 (RICHMOND) p266
9200 NO. 1 RD, RICHMOND, BC, V7E 6L5
(604) 668-6615   *SIC* 8211

BOARD OF EDUCATION SCHOOL DISTRICT #38 (RICHMOND)   p266
6600 WILLIAMS RD, RICHMOND, BC, V7E 1K5
(604) 668-6668   *SIC* 8211

BOARD OF EDUCATION SCHOOL DISTRICT #38 (RICHMOND)   p266
4251 GARRY ST, RICHMOND, BC, V7E 2T9
(604) 718-4050   *SIC* 8211

BOARD OF SCHOOL TRUSTEES   p320
1580 BROADWAY W, VANCOUVER, BC, V6J 5K8
(604) 713-5000   *SIC* 8211

BOARD OF SCHOOL TRUSTEES OF SCHOOL DISTRICT #40 (NEW WESTMINSTER), THE   p237
1001 COLUMBIA ST, NEW WESTMINSTER, BC, V3M 1C4
(604) 517-6240   *SIC* 8211

BOARD OF SCHOOL TRUSTEES OF SCHOOL DISTRICT NO. 45   p341
1250 CHARTWELL DR, WEST VANCOUVER, BC, V7S 2R2
(604) 981-1130   *SIC* 8211

BOARD OF TRUSTEES OF HORIZON SCHOOL DIVISION NO 67   p169
6302 56 ST, TABER, AB, T1G 1Z9
(403) 223-3547   *SIC* 8211

BOARD OF TRUSTEES OF THE RED DEER PUBLIC SCHOOL DISTRICT NO. 104, THE   p153
4204 58 ST, RED DEER, AB, T4N 2L6
(403) 347-1171   *SIC* 8211

BOARD OF TRUSTEES OF THE RED DEER PUBLIC SCHOOL DISTRICT NO. 104, THE   p156
150 LOCKWOOD AVE, RED DEER, AB, T4R 2M4
(403) 342-6655   *SIC* 8211

BRANDON SCHOOL DIVISION, THE   p346
1031 6TH ST, BRANDON, MB, R7A 4K5
(204) 729-3100   *SIC* 8211

BRANDON SCHOOL DIVISION, THE   p346
1930 1ST ST, BRANDON, MB, R7A 6Y6
(204) 729-3900   *SIC* 8211

BRANDON SCHOOL DIVISION, THE   p347
715 MCDIARMID DR, BRANDON, MB, R7B 2H7
(204) 729-3170   *SIC* 8211

BRANKSOME HALL   p928
10 ELM AVE, TORONTO, ON, M4W 1N4
(416) 920-9741   *SIC* 8211

BRANT HALDIMAND NORFOLK CATHOLIC DISTRICT SCHOOL BOARD   p514
322 FAIRVIEW DR, BRANTFORD, ON, N3R 2X6
(519) 756-6369   *SIC* 8211

BRANT HALDIMAND NORFOLK CATHOLIC DISTRICT SCHOOL BOARD   p514
80 PARIS RD, BRANTFORD, ON, N3R 1H9
(519) 759-2318   *SIC* 8211

BRANT HALDIMAND NORFOLK CATHOLIC DISTRICT SCHOOL BOARD   p516
257 SHELLARD'S LANE, BRANTFORD, ON, N3T 5L5
(519) 751-2030   *SIC* 8211

BRANT HALDIMAND NORFOLK CATHOLIC DISTRICT SCHOOL BOARD   p516
257 SHELLARD'S LANE, BRANTFORD, ON, N3T 5L5
(519) 751-2030   *SIC* 8211

BRANT HALDIMAND NORFOLK CATHOLIC DISTRICT SCHOOL BOARD   p880
128 EVERGREEN HILL RD, SIMCOE, ON, N3Y 4K1
(519) 429-3600   *SIC* 8211

BRENTWOOD COLLEGE ASSOCIATION   p232
2735 MT BAKER RD, MILL BAY, BC, V0R 2P1
(250) 743-5521   *SIC* 8211

BRUCE-GREY CATHOLIC DISTRICT SCHOOL BOARD   p617
799 16TH AVE, HANOVER, ON, N4N 3A1

(519) 364-5820   *SIC* 8211

BRUCE-GREY CATHOLIC DISTRICT SCHOOL BOARD   p1004
450 ROBINSON ST, WALKERTON, ON, N0G 2V0
(519) 881-1900   *SIC* 8211

BUFFALO TRAIL PUBLIC SCHOOLS REGIONAL DIVISION NO. 28   p171
1041 10A ST, WAINWRIGHT, AB, T9W 2R4
(780) 842-6144   *SIC* 8211

BURNABY SCHOOL BOARD DISTRICT 41   p180
8800 EASTLAKE DR, BURNABY, BC, V3J 7X5
(604) 296-6870   *SIC* 8211

BURNABY SCHOOL BOARD DISTRICT 41   p181
8580 16TH AVE, BURNABY, BC, V3N 1S6
(604) 296-6890   *SIC* 8211

BURNABY SCHOOL BOARD DISTRICT 41   p181
7777 18TH ST, BURNABY, BC, V3N 5E5
(604) 296-6885   *SIC* 8211

BURNABY SCHOOL BOARD DISTRICT 41   p184
751 HAMMARSKJOLD DR RM 115, BURNABY, BC, V5B 4A1
SIC 8211

BURNABY SCHOOL BOARD DISTRICT 41   p184
4600 PARKER ST, BURNABY, BC, V5C 3E2
(604) 296-6865   *SIC* 8211

BURNABY SCHOOL BOARD DISTRICT 41   p188
5325 KINCAID ST, BURNABY, BC, V5G 1W2
(604) 296-6900   *SIC* 8211

BURNABY SCHOOL BOARD DISTRICT 41   p189
4404 SARDIS ST, BURNABY, BC, V5H 1K7
SIC 8211

BURNABY SCHOOL BOARD DISTRICT 41   p189
6060 MARLBOROUGH AVE, BURNABY, BC, V5H 3L7
(604) 296-9021   *SIC* 8211

BURNABY SCHOOL BOARD DISTRICT 41   p192
5455 RUMBLE ST, BURNABY, BC, V5J 2B7
(604) 296-6880   *SIC* 8211

CALGARY BOARD OF EDUCATION   p8
3020 52 ST NE, CALGARY, AB, T1Y 5P4
(403) 280-6565   *SIC* 8211

CALGARY BOARD OF EDUCATION   p10
1304 44 ST SE, CALGARY, AB, T2A 1M8
(403) 272-6665   *SIC* 8211

CALGARY BOARD OF EDUCATION   p34
9019 FAIRMOUNT DR SE, CALGARY, AB, T2H 0Z4
(403) 259-5585   *SIC* 8211

CALGARY BOARD OF EDUCATION   p34
47 FYFFE RD SE, CALGARY, AB, T2H 1B9
(403) 777-6420   *SIC* 8211

CALGARY BOARD OF EDUCATION   p40
6620 4 ST NW, CALGARY, AB, T2K 1C2
(403) 274-2240   *SIC* 8211

CALGARY BOARD OF EDUCATION   p40
5220 NORTHLAND DR NW, CALGARY, AB, T2L 2J6
(403) 289-9241   *SIC* 8211

CALGARY BOARD OF EDUCATION   p41
3009 MORLEY TRAIL NW, CALGARY, AB, T2M 4G9
(403) 289-2551   *SIC* 8211

CALGARY BOARD OF EDUCATION   p41
512 18 ST NW, CALGARY, AB, T2N 2G5
(403) 777-6380   *SIC* 8211

CALGARY BOARD OF EDUCATION   p41
1019 1 ST NW, CALGARY, AB, T2M 2S2
(403) 276-5521   *SIC* 8211

CALGARY BOARD OF EDUCATION   p64
1221 8 ST SW, CALGARY, AB, T2R 0L4
(403) 817-4000   *SIC* 8211

CALGARY BOARD OF EDUCATION   p66

641 17 AVE SW, CALGARY, AB, T2S 0B5
(403) 228-5363   *SIC* 8211

CALGARY BOARD OF EDUCATION   p68
2266 WOODPARK AVE SW, CALGARY, AB, T2W 2Z8
(403) 251-8022   *SIC* 8211

CALGARY BOARD OF EDUCATION   p68
910 75 AVE SW, CALGARY, AB, T2V 0S6
(403) 253-2261   *SIC* 8211

CALGARY BOARD OF EDUCATION   p72
4627 77 ST NW, CALGARY, AB, T3B 2N6
(403) 286-5092   *SIC* 8211

CALGARY BOARD OF EDUCATION   p73
2336 53 AVE SW, CALGARY, AB, T3E 1L2
(403) 243-4500   *SIC* 8211

CALGARY BOARD OF EDUCATION   p73
5111 21 ST SW, CALGARY, AB, T3E 1R9
(403) 243-8880   *SIC* 8211

CALGARY ROMAN CATHOLIC SEPARATE SCHOOL DISTRICT #1   p40
877 NORTHMOUNT DR NW, CALGARY, AB, T2L 0A3
(403) 500-2026   *SIC* 8211

CALGARY ROMAN CATHOLIC SEPARATE SCHOOL DISTRICT #1   p45
1000 5 AVE SW SUITE 1, CALGARY, AB, T2P 4T9
(403) 500-2000   *SIC* 8211

CALGARY ROMAN CATHOLIC SEPARATE SCHOOL DISTRICT #1   p66
111 18 AVE SW SUITE 1, CALGARY, AB, T2S 0B8
(403) 500-2024   *SIC* 8211

CALGARY ROMAN CATHOLIC SEPARATE SCHOOL DISTRICT #1   p68
111 HADDON RD SW, CALGARY, AB, T2V 2Y2
(403) 500-2047   *SIC* 8211

CALGARY ROMAN CATHOLIC SEPARATE SCHOOL DISTRICT #1   p73
4624 RICHARD RD SW, CALGARY, AB, T3E 6L1
(403) 500-2056   *SIC* 8211

CANADIAN TAMIL ACADEMY   p873
8 MILNER AVE, SCARBOROUGH, ON, M1S 3P8
(416) 757-2006   *SIC* 8211

CAPE BRETON-VICTORIA REGIONAL SCHOOL BOARD   p465
999 GABARUS HWY, PRIME BROOK, NS, B1L 1E5
(902) 562-4595   *SIC* 8211

CAPE BRETON-VICTORIA REGIONAL SCHOOL BOARD   p467
275 GEORGE ST, SYDNEY, NS, B1P 1J7
(902) 564-8293   *SIC* 8211

CATHOLIC DISTRICT SCHOOL BOARD OF EASTERN ONTARIO   p519
40 CENTRAL AVE W, BROCKVILLE, ON, K6V 4N5
(613) 342-4911   *SIC* 8211

CATHOLIC DISTRICT SCHOOL BOARD OF EASTERN ONTARIO   p562
1500A CUMBERLAND ST, CORNWALL, ON, K6J 5V9
(613) 932-0349   *SIC* 8211

CATHOLIC INDEPENDENT SCHOOLS OF NELSON DIOCESE, THE   p219
3665 BENVOULIN RD, KELOWNA, BC, V1W 4M7
(250) 762-2905   *SIC* 8211

CATHOLIC INDEPENDENT SCHOOLS, DIOCESE OF VICTORIA   p337
4044 NELTHORPE ST SUITE 1, VICTORIA, BC, V8X 2A1
(250) 727-6893   *SIC* 8211

CDI EDUCATION (ALBERTA) LIMITED PARTNERSHIP   p273
13401 108 AVE SUITE 360, SURREY, BC, V3T 5T3
(604) 915-7288   *SIC* 8211

CENTRAL MONTESSORI SCHOOLS INC   p771
200 SHEPPARD AVE E, NORTH YORK,

ON, M2N 3A9
(416) 222-5940   *SIC* 8211

CENTRE DE FORMATION PROFESSIONNELLE PIERRE DUPUY   p1146
1150 CH DU TREMBLAY, LONGUEUIL, QC, J4N 1A2
(450) 468-4000   *SIC* 8211

CENTRE SCOLAIRE COMMUNAUTAIRE LA FONTAINE   p410
700 RUE PRINCIPALE, NEGUAC, NB, E9G 1N4
(506) 776-3808   *SIC* 8211

CHIGNECTO CENTRAL REGIONAL SCHOOL BOARD   p468
60 LORNE ST, TRURO, NS, B2N 3K3
(902) 897-8900   *SIC* 8211

CHIGNECTO CENTRAL REGIONAL SCHOOL BOARD   p468
34 LORNE ST, TRURO, NS, B2N 3K3
(902) 896-5700   *SIC* 8211

CHINOOKS EDGE SCHOOL DIVISION NO. 73   p136
4904 50 ST, INNISFAIL, AB, T4G 1W4
(403) 227-7070   *SIC* 8211

CHRIST THE TEACHER CATHOLIC SCHOOLS DIVISION 212   p1438
45A PALLISER WAY, YORKTON, SK, S3N 4C5
(306) 783-8787   *SIC* 8211

COLLEGE BEAUBOIS   p1245
4901 RUE DU COLLEGE-BEAUBOIS, PIERREFONDS, QC, H8Y 3T4
(514) 684-7642   *SIC* 8211

COLLEGE CHARLES-LEMOYNE DE LONGUEUIL INC   p1144
1430 RUE PATENAUDE, LONGUEUIL, QC, J4K 5H4
(450) 463-1592   *SIC* 8211

COLLEGE ESTHER-BLONDIN   p1314
101 RUE SAINTE-ANNE, SAINT-JACQUES, QC, J0K 2R0
(450) 839-7652   *SIC* 8211

COLLEGE FRANCAIS (1965) INC   p1144
1391 RUE BEAUREGARD, LONGUEUIL, QC, J4K 2M3
(450) 670-7391   *SIC* 8211

COLLEGE FRANCOIS-DE-LAVAL   p1269
6 RUE DE LA VIEILLE-UNIVERSITE BUREAU 70, QUEBEC, QC, G1R 5X8
(418) 694-1020   *SIC* 8211

COLLEGE INTERNATIONAL MARIE DE FRANCE   p1219
4635 CH QUEEN-MARY, MONTREAL, QC, H3W 1W3
(514) 737-1177   *SIC* 8211

COLLEGE JEAN DE LA MENNAIS   p1123
870 CH DE SAINT-JEAN, LA PRAIRIE, QC, J5R 2L5
(450) 659-7657   *SIC* 8211

COLLEGE JEAN-EUDES INC   p1168
3535 BOUL ROSEMONT, MONTREAL, QC, H1X 1K7
(514) 376-5740   *SIC* 8211

COLLEGE JESUS MARIE DE SILLERY   p1271
2047 CH SAINT-LOUIS, QUEBEC, QC, G1T 1P3
(418) 687-9250   *SIC* 8211

COLLEGE LAVAL   p1231
1275 AV DU COLLEGE, MONTREAL, QC, H7C 1W8
(450) 661-7714   *SIC* 8211

COLLEGE MARIE-DE-L'INCARNATION   p1387
725 RUE HART, TROIS-RIVIERES, QC, G9A 4R9
(819) 379-3223   *SIC* 8211

COLLEGE MONT-SAINT-LOUIS   p1171
1700 BOUL HENRI-BOURASSA E, MONTREAL, QC, H2C 1J3
(514) 382-1560   *SIC* 8211

COLLEGE NOTRE-DAME-DE-LOURDES   p1146
845 CH TIFFIN, LONGUEUIL, QC, J4P 3G5

(450) 670-4740 *SIC* 8211
COLLEGE REGINA ASSUMPTA (1995)
p1171
1750 RUE SAURIOL E, MONTREAL, QC,
H2C 1X4
(514) 382-9998 *SIC* 8211
COLLEGE SAINT-BERNARD *p1096*
25 AV DES FRERES-DE-LA-CHARITE,
DRUMMONDVILLE, QC, J2B 6A2
(819) 478-3330 *SIC* 8211
COLLEGE SAINT-SACREMENT *p1379*
901 RUE SAINT-LOUIS, TERREBONNE,
QC, J6W 1K1
(450) 471-6615 *SIC* 8211
COLLEGE SAINTE MARCELLAINE *p1224*
9155 BOUL GOUIN O, MONTREAL, QC,
H4K 1C3
(514) 334-9651 *SIC* 8211
COLLEGE STANISLAS INCORPORE *p1244*
780 BOUL DOLLARD, OUTREMONT, QC,
H2V 3G5
(514) 273-9521 *SIC* 8211
COLLINGWOOD SCHOOL SOCIETY *p341*
70 MORVEN DR, WEST VANCOUVER, BC,
V7S 1B2
(604) 925-3331 *SIC* 8211
COLLINGWOOD SCHOOL SOCIETY *p341*
2605 WENTWORTH AVE, WEST VANCOU-
VER, BC, V7S 3H4
(604) 925-8375 *SIC* 8211
**COLUMBIA PRIVATE SECONDARY
SCHOOL INC** *p614*
1003 MAIN ST W SUITE 163, HAMILTON,
ON, L8S 4P3
(905) 572-7883 *SIC* 8211
**COMISSION SCOLAIRE DE LANGUE
FRANCAISE, LA** *p1043*
1596 124 RTE, WELLINGTON STATION,
PE, C0B 2E0
(902) 854-2975 *SIC* 8211
COMMISSION SCOLAIRE ABITIBI *p1123*
24 5E AV E, LA SARRE, QC, J9Z 1K8
(819) 333-5591 *SIC* 8211
**COMMISSION SCOLAIRE AU COEUR DES
VALLEES** *p1102*
582 RUE MACLAREN E, GATINEAU, QC,
J8L 2W2
(819) 986-8511 *SIC* 8211
COMMISSION SCOLAIRE CRIE (LA) *p1081*
11 MAAMUU, CHISASIBI, QC, J0M 1E0
(819) 855-2833 *SIC* 8211
COMMISSION SCOLAIRE CRIE (LA) *p1154*
203 MAIN ST, MISTISSINI, QC, G0W 1C0
(418) 923-2764 *SIC* 8211
**COMMISSION SCOLAIRE DE
CHARLEVOIX, LA** *p1054*
200 RUE SAINT-AUBIN, BAIE-SAINT-PAUL,
QC, G3Z 2R2
(418) 435-2824 *SIC* 8211
**COMMISSION SCOLAIRE DE
CHARLEVOIX, LA** *p1054*
200 RUE SAINT-AUBIN UNITE 102, BAIE-
SAINT-PAUL, QC, G3Z 2R2
(418) 435-2824 *SIC* 8211
**COMMISSION SCOLAIRE DE
CHARLEVOIX, LA** *p1122*
88 RUE DES CIMES, LA MALBAIE, QC,
G5A 1T3
(418) 665-3791 *SIC* 8211
**COMMISSION SCOLAIRE DE
KAMOURASKA RIVIERE-DU-LOUP** *p1286*
320 RUE SAINT-PIERRE, RIVIERE-DU-
LOUP, QC, G5R 3V3
(418) 862-8203 *SIC* 8211
**COMMISSION SCOLAIRE DE
KAMOURASKA RIVIERE-DU-LOUP** *p1349*
525 AV DE L'EGLISE, SAINT-PASCAL, QC,
G0L 3Y0
(418) 856-7030 *SIC* 8211
COMMISSION SCOLAIRE DE L'ENERGIE
p1353
405 BOUL SAINT-JOSEPH RR 1, SAINT-
TITE, QC, G0X 3H0
(418) 365-5191 *SIC* 8211

COMMISSION SCOLAIRE DE L'ENERGIE
p1368
5285 AV ALBERT TESSIER, SHAWINIGAN,
QC, G9N 6T9
(819) 539-2285 *SIC* 8211
COMMISSION SCOLAIRE DE L'ENERGIE
p1368
5105 AV ALBERT-TESSIER BUREAU 840,
SHAWINIGAN, QC, G9N 7A3
(819) 539-2265 *SIC* 8211
COMMISSION SCOLAIRE DE L'ENERGIE
p1369
1200 RUE DE VAL-MAURICIE, SHAWINI-
GAN, QC, G9P 2L9
(819) 536-5675 *SIC* 8211
COMMISSION SCOLAIRE DE L'ESTUAIRE
p1053
620 RUE JALBERT, BAIE-COMEAU, QC,
G5C 0B8
(418) 589-0806 *SIC* 8211
**COMMISSION SCOLAIRE DE L'OR-ET-DES-
BOIS** *p1390*
799 BOUL FOREST, VAL-D'OR, QC, J9P
2L4
(819) 825-4220 *SIC* 8211
**COMMISSION SCOLAIRE DE L'OR-ET-DES-
BOIS** *p1390*
125 RUE SELF, VAL-D'OR, QC, J9P 3N2
(819) 825-4670 *SIC* 8211
**COMMISSION SCOLAIRE DE L'OR-ET-DES-
BOIS** *p1390*
125 RUE SELF, VAL-D'OR, QC, J9P 3N2
(819) 825-6366 *SIC* 8211
**COMMISSION SCOLAIRE DE LA BAIE
JAMES** *p1077*
596 4E RUE, CHIBOUGAMAU, QC, G8P
1S3
(418) 748-7621 *SIC* 8211
**COMMISSION SCOLAIRE DE LA BEAUCE-
ETCHEMIN** *p1304*
1925 118E RUE, SAINT-GEORGES, QC,
G5Y 7R7
(418) 228-5541 *SIC* 8211
**COMMISSION SCOLAIRE DE LA BEAUCE-
ETCHEMIN** *p1304*
2121 119E RUE, SAINT-GEORGES, QC,
G5Y 5S1
(418) 228-8964 *SIC* 8211
**COMMISSION SCOLAIRE DE LA BEAUCE-
ETCHEMIN** *p1304*
11700 25E AV, SAINT-GEORGES, QC, G5Y
8B8
(418) 228-1993 *SIC* 8211
**COMMISSION SCOLAIRE DE LA BEAUCE-
ETCHEMIN** *p1321*
695 AV ROBERT-CLICHE, SAINT-JOSEPH-
DE-BEAUCE, QC, G0S 2V0
(418) 397-6841 *SIC* 8211
**COMMISSION SCOLAIRE DE LA BEAUCE-
ETCHEMIN** *p1348*
30A CH DE LA POLYVALENTE BUREAU
3033, SAINT-MARTIN, QC, G0M 1B0
(418) 228-5541 *SIC* 8211
**COMMISSION SCOLAIRE DE LA BEAUCE-
ETCHEMIN** *p1350*
2105 25E AV, SAINT-PROSPER-DE-
DORCHESTER, QC, G0M 1Y0
(418) 594-8231 *SIC* 8211
**COMMISSION SCOLAIRE DE LA CAPI-
TALE, LA** *p1257*
1640 8E AV, QUEBEC, QC, G1J 3N5
(418) 686-4040 *SIC* 8211
**COMMISSION SCOLAIRE DE LA CAPI-
TALE, LA** *p1258*
50 RUE DU CARDINAL-MAURICE-ROY,
QUEBEC, QC, G1K 8S9
(418) 686-4040 *SIC* 8211
**COMMISSION SCOLAIRE DE LA CAPI-
TALE, LA** *p1260*
1625 BOUL BENOIT-XV, QUEBEC, QC, G1L
2Z3
(418) 686-4040 *SIC* 8211
**COMMISSION SCOLAIRE DE LA CAPI-
TALE, LA** *p1260*

1201 RUE DE LA POINTE-AUX-LIEVRES,
QUEBEC, QC, G1L 4M1
(418) 686-4040 *SIC* 8211
**COMMISSION SCOLAIRE DE LA CAPI-
TALE, LA** *p1270*
555 CH SAINTE-FOY, QUEBEC, QC, G1S
2J9
(418) 686-4040 *SIC* 8211
**COMMISSION SCOLAIRE DE LA CAPI-
TALE, LA** *p1275*
158 BOUL DES ETUDIANTS, QUEBEC,
QC, G2A 1N8
(418) 686-4040 *SIC* 8211
**COMMISSION SCOLAIRE DE LA CAPI-
TALE, LA** *p1276*
3600 AV CHAUVEAU, QUEBEC, QC, G2C
1A1
(418) 686-4040 *SIC* 8211
**COMMISSION SCOLAIRE DE LA COTE-DU-
SUD, LA** *p1159*
141 BOUL TACHE E, MONTMAGNY, QC,
G5V 1B9
(418) 248-2370 *SIC* 8211
**COMMISSION SCOLAIRE DE LA COTE-DU-
SUD, LA** *p1291*
825 RTE BEGIN, SAINT-ANSELME, QC,
G0R 2N0
(418) 885-4431 *SIC* 8211
**COMMISSION SCOLAIRE DE LA COTE-DU-
SUD, LA** *p1299*
70 RTE SAINT-GERARD, SAINT-DAMIEN-
DE-BUCKLAND, QC, G0R 2Y0
(418) 789-1001 *SIC* 8211
**COMMISSION SCOLAIRE DE LA JON-
QUIERE** *p1115*
3450 BOUL DU ROYAUME, JONQUIERE,
QC, G7S 5T2
(418) 547-5781 *SIC* 8211
**COMMISSION SCOLAIRE DE LA JON-
QUIERE** *p1115*
2215 BOUL MELLON BUREAU 101, JON-
QUIERE, QC, G7S 3G4
(418) 548-3113 *SIC* 8211
**COMMISSION SCOLAIRE DE LA JON-
QUIERE** *p1116*
1954 RUE DES ETUDIANTS, JONQUIERE,
QC, G7X 4B1
(418) 542-3571 *SIC* 8211
**COMMISSION SCOLAIRE DE LA
MOYENNE-COTE-NORD, LA** *p1113*
1235 RUE DE LA DIGUE, HAVRE-SAINT-
PIERRE, QC, G0G 1P0
(418) 538-3044 *SIC* 8211
**COMMISSION SCOLAIRE DE LA POINTE-
DE-L'ILE** *p1163*
8205 RUE FONTENEAU, MONTREAL, QC,
H1K 4E1
(514) 353-9970 *SIC* 8211
**COMMISSION SCOLAIRE DE LA POINTE-
DE-L'ILE** *p1239*
11480 BOUL ROLLAND, MONTREAL-
NORD, QC, H1G 3T9
(514) 328-3570 *SIC* 8211
**COMMISSION SCOLAIRE DE LA POINTE-
DE-L'ILE** *p1239*
6051 BOUL MAURICE-DUPLESSIS,
MONTREAL-NORD, QC, H1G 1Y6
(514) 328-3200 *SIC* 8211
**COMMISSION SCOLAIRE DE LA POINTE-
DE-L'ILE** *p1240*
11411 AV PELLETIER, MONTREAL-NORD,
QC, H1H 3S3
(514) 328-3250 *SIC* 8211
**COMMISSION SCOLAIRE DE LA POINTE-
DE-L'ILE** *p1240*
10748 BOUL SAINT-VITAL, MONTREAL-
NORD, QC, H1H 4T3
(514) 328-3272 *SIC* 8211
**COMMISSION SCOLAIRE DE LA POINTE-
DE-L'ILE** *p1247*
550 53E AV, POINTE-AUX-TREMBLES, QC,
H1A 2T7
(514) 642-9520 *SIC* 8211
COMMISSION SCOLAIRE DE LA POINTE-

DE-L'ILE *p1343*
5950 RUE HONORE-MERCIER, SAINT-
LEONARD, QC, H1P 3E4
(514) 321-8475 *SIC* 8211
**COMMISSION SCOLAIRE DE LA REGION-
DE-SHERBROOKE** *p1370*
135 RUE KING O, SHERBROOKE, QC, J1H
1P4
(819) 822-5520 *SIC* 8211
**COMMISSION SCOLAIRE DE LA REGION-
DE-SHERBROOKE** *p1370*
405 RUE SARA, SHERBROOKE, QC, J1H
5S6
(819) 822-5455 *SIC* 8211
**COMMISSION SCOLAIRE DE LA REGION-
DE-SHERBROOKE** *p1370*
825 RUE BOWEN S, SHERBROOKE, QC,
J1G 2G2
(819) 822-5444 *SIC* 8211
**COMMISSION SCOLAIRE DE LA REGION-
DE-SHERBROOKE** *p1370*
955 RUE DE CAMBRIDGE, SHER-
BROOKE, QC, J1H 1E2
(819) 822-5400 *SIC* 8211
**COMMISSION SCOLAIRE DE LA REGION-
DE-SHERBROOKE** *p1372*
2965 BOUL DE L'UNIVERSITE, SHER-
BROOKE, QC, J1K 2X6
(819) 822-5540 *SIC* 8211
**COMMISSION SCOLAIRE DE LA REGION-
DE-SHERBROOKE** *p1372*
2955 BOUL DE L'UNIVERSITE BUREAU
822, SHERBROOKE, QC, J1K 2Y3
(819) 822-5540 *SIC* 8211
**COMMISSION SCOLAIRE DE LA REGION-
DE-SHERBROOKE** *p1375*
4076 BOUL DE L'UNIVERSITE, SHER-
BROOKE, QC, J1N 2Y1
(819) 822-5577 *SIC* 8211
**COMMISSION SCOLAIRE DE LA
RIVERAINE** *p1242*
375 RUE DE MONSEIGNEUR-BRUNAULT,
NICOLET, QC, J3T 1Y6
(819) 293-5821 *SIC* 8211
**COMMISSION SCOLAIRE DE LA
RIVERAINE** *p1347*
401 RUE GERMAIN, SAINT-LEONARD-
D'ASTON, QC, J0C 1M0
(819) 399-2122 *SIC* 8211
**COMMISSION SCOLAIRE DE LA
RIVERAINE** *p1350*
165 218 RTE, SAINT-PIERRE-LES-
BECQUETS, QC, G0X 2Z0
(819) 263-2323 *SIC* 8211
**COMMISSION SCOLAIRE DE LA RIVIERE-
DU-NORD** *p1129*
452 AV D'ARGENTEUIL BUREAU 103,
LACHUTE, QC, J8H 1W9
(450) 562-8841 *SIC* 8211
**COMMISSION SCOLAIRE DE LA RIVIERE-
DU-NORD** *p1321*
1155 AV DU PARC, SAINT-JEROME, QC,
J7Z 6X6
(450) 438-1296 *SIC* 8211
**COMMISSION SCOLAIRE DE LA RIVIERE-
DU-NORD** *p1321*
535 RUE FILION, SAINT-JEROME, QC, J7Z
1J6
(450) 436-1560 *SIC* 8211
**COMMISSION SCOLAIRE DE LA RIVIERE-
DU-NORD** *p1321*
600 36E AV, SAINT-JEROME, QC, J7Z 5W2
(450) 436-1858 *SIC* 8211
**COMMISSION SCOLAIRE DE LA
SEIGNEURIE-DES-MILLE-ILES** *p1061*
2700 RUE JEAN-CHARLES-BONENFANT,
BOISBRIAND, QC, J7H 1P1
(450) 433-5455 *SIC* 8211
**COMMISSION SCOLAIRE DE LA
SEIGNEURIE-DES-MILLE-ILES** *p1301*
430 BOUL ARTHUR-SAUVE BUREAU
3050, SAINT-EUSTACHE, QC, J7R 6V7
(450) 974-7000 *SIC* 8211
COMMISSION SCOLAIRE DE LA

SEIGNEURIE-DES-MILLE-ILES   *p*1364
8 RUE TASSE, SAINTE-THERESE, QC, J7E 1V3
(450) 433-5445   *SIC* 8211

COMMISSION SCOLAIRE DE LA SEIGNEURIE-DES-MILLE-ILES   *p*1364
401 BOUL DU DOMAINE, SAINTE-THERESE, QC, J7E 4S4
(450) 433-5400   *SIC* 8211

COMMISSION SCOLAIRE DE LA VALLEE-DES-TISSERANDS, LA   *p*1055
250 RUE GAGNON, BEAUHARNOIS, QC, J6N 2W8
(450) 225-2260   *SIC* 8211

COMMISSION SCOLAIRE DE LA VALLEE-DES-TISSERANDS, LA   *p*1366
70 RUE LOUIS VI-MAJOR, SALABERRY-DE-VALLEYFIELD, QC, J6T 3G2
(450) 371-2004   *SIC* 8211

COMMISSION SCOLAIRE DE LAVAL *p*1085
955 BOUL SAINT-MARTIN O BUREAU 144, COTE SAINT-LUC, QC, H7S 1M5
(450) 662-7000   *SIC* 8211

COMMISSION SCOLAIRE DE MONTREAL *p*1163
2800 BOUL LAPOINTE, MONTREAL, QC, H1L 5M1
(514) 596-5035   *SIC* 8211

COMMISSION SCOLAIRE DE MONTREAL *p*1163
5850 AV DE CARIGNAN, MONTREAL, QC, H1M 2V4
(514) 596-4134   *SIC* 8211

COMMISSION SCOLAIRE DE MONTREAL *p*1164
5555 RUE SHERBROOKE E, MONTREAL, QC, H1N 1A2
(514) 596-5100   *SIC* 8211

COMMISSION SCOLAIRE DE MONTREAL *p*1164
6200 AV PIERRE-DE COUBERTIN, MONTREAL, QC, H1N 1S4
(514) 596-4140   *SIC* 8211

COMMISSION SCOLAIRE DE MONTREAL *p*1166
2455 AV LETOURNEUX, MONTREAL, QC, H1V 2N9
(514) 596-4949   *SIC* 8211

COMMISSION SCOLAIRE DE MONTREAL *p*1166
1860 AV MORGAN, MONTREAL, QC, H1V 2R2
(514) 596-4844   *SIC* 8211

COMMISSION SCOLAIRE DE MONTREAL *p*1168
3737 RUE SHERBROOKE E, MONTREAL, QC, H1X 3B3
(514) 596-6000   *SIC* 8211

COMMISSION SCOLAIRE DE MONTREAL *p*1168
6855 16E AV, MONTREAL, QC, H1X 2T5
(514) 596-4166   *SIC* 8211

COMMISSION SCOLAIRE DE MONTREAL *p*1169
2901 RUE DE LOUVAIN E, MONTREAL, QC, H1Z 1J7
(514) 596-5353   *SIC* 8211

COMMISSION SCOLAIRE DE MONTREAL *p*1171
8200 RUE ROUSSELOT, MONTREAL, QC, H2E 1Z6
(514) 596-4350   *SIC* 8211

COMMISSION SCOLAIRE DE MONTREAL *p*1171
1350 BOUL CREMAZIE E, MONTREAL, QC, H2E 1A1
(514) 596-4300   *SIC* 8211

COMMISSION SCOLAIRE DE MONTREAL *p*1172
2110 BOUL SAINT-JOSEPH E, MONTREAL, QC, H2H 1E7
(514) 596-5700   *SIC* 8211

COMMISSION SCOLAIRE DE MONTREAL *p*1180

1205 RUE JARRY E, MONTREAL, QC, H2P 1W9
(514) 596-4160   *SIC* 8211

COMMISSION SCOLAIRE DE MONTREAL *p*1180
8200 BOUL SAINT-LAURENT, MONTREAL, QC, H2P 2L8
(514) 596-5400   *SIC* 8211

COMMISSION SCOLAIRE DE MONTREAL *p*1182
6555 RUE DE NORMANVILLE, MONTREAL, QC, H2S 2B8
(514) 596-4940   *SIC* 8211

COMMISSION SCOLAIRE DE MONTREAL *p*1183
6080 AV DE L'ESPLANADE, MONTREAL, QC, H2T 3A3
(514) 596-4800   *SIC* 8211

COMMISSION SCOLAIRE DE MONTREAL *p*1217
11845 BOUL DE L'ACADIE BUREAU 281, MONTREAL, QC, H3M 2T4
(514) 596-5280   *SIC* 8211

COMMISSION SCOLAIRE DE MONTREAL *p*1220
6300 CH DE LA COTE-SAINT-LUC, MONTREAL, QC, H3X 2H4
(514) 596-5920   *SIC* 8211

COMMISSION SCOLAIRE DE MONTREAL *p*1222
717 RUE SAINT-FERDINAND, MONTREAL, QC, H4C 2T3
(514) 596-5960   *SIC* 8211

COMMISSION SCOLAIRE DE MONTREAL *p*1224
12055 RUE DEPATIE, MONTREAL, QC, H4J 1W9
(514) 596-5565   *SIC* 8211

COMMISSION SCOLAIRE DE PORTNEUF *p*1351
400 BOUL CLOUTIER, SAINT-RAYMOND, QC, G3L 3M8
(418) 337-6721   *SIC* 8211

COMMISSION SCOLAIRE DE ROUYN-NORANDA *p*1289
70 RUE DES OBLATS E, ROUYN-NORANDA, QC, J9X 3N6
(819) 762-8161   *SIC* 8211

COMMISSION SCOLAIRE DE SAINT-HYACINTHE, LA *p*1044
1450 3E AV, ACTON VALE, QC, J0H 1A0
(450) 546-5575   *SIC* 8211

COMMISSION SCOLAIRE DE SAINT-HYACINTHE, LA *p*1312
2255 AV SAINTE-ANNE, SAINT-HYACINTHE, QC, J2S 5H7
(450) 773-8401   *SIC* 8211

COMMISSION SCOLAIRE DE SAINT-HYACINTHE, LA *p*1312
2700 AV T.-D.-BOUCHARD, SAINT-HYACINTHE, QC, J2S 7G2
(450) 773-8408   *SIC* 8211

COMMISSION SCOLAIRE DE SOREL-TRACY *p*1376
265 RUE DE RAMEZAY, SOREL-TRACY, QC, J3P 4A5
(450) 742-5901   *SIC* 8211

COMMISSION SCOLAIRE DE SOREL-TRACY *p*1377
2800 BOUL DES ERABLES, SOREL-TRACY, QC, J3R 2W4
(450) 746-3510   *SIC* 8211

COMMISSION SCOLAIRE DES AFFLUENTS *p*1281
250 BOUL LOUIS-PHILIPPE-PICARD, REPENTIGNY, QC, J5Y 3W9
(450) 492-3578   *SIC* 8211

COMMISSION SCOLAIRE DES AFFLUENTS *p*1379
400 MONTEE DUMAIS, TERREBONNE, QC, J6W 5W9
(450) 492-3613   *SIC* 8211

COMMISSION SCOLAIRE DES AFFLUENTS *p*1380

1659 BOUL DES SEIGNEURS, TERREBONNE, QC, J6X 3E3
(450) 492-3622   *SIC* 8211

COMMISSION SCOLAIRE DES APPALACHES *p*1382
561 RUE SAINT-PATRICK, THETFORD MINES, QC, G6G 5W1
(418) 338-7831   *SIC* 8211

COMMISSION SCOLAIRE DES APPALACHES *p*1382
650 RUE LAPIERRE, THETFORD MINES, QC, G6G 7P1
(418) 338-7800   *SIC* 8211

COMMISSION SCOLAIRE DES APPALACHES *p*1383
499 RUE SAINT-DESIRE, THETFORD MINES, QC, G6H 1L7
(418) 423-4291   *SIC* 8211

COMMISSION SCOLAIRE DES BOIS-FRANCS *p*1246
1159 RUE SAINT-JEAN, PLESSISVILLE, QC, G6L 1E1
(819) 362-3226   *SIC* 8211

COMMISSION SCOLAIRE DES BOIS-FRANCS *p*1397
40 BOUL DES BOIS-FRANCS N, VICTORIAVILLE, QC, G6P 1E5
(819) 758-6453   *SIC* 8211

COMMISSION SCOLAIRE DES BOIS-FRANCS *p*1397
40 BOUL DES BOIS-FRANCS N, VICTORIAVILLE, QC, G6P 1E5
(819) 758-6453   *SIC* 8211

COMMISSION SCOLAIRE DES BOIS-FRANCS *p*1397
20 RUE DE L'ERMITAGE, VICTORIAVILLE, QC, G6P 1J5
(819) 752-4591   *SIC* 8211

COMMISSION SCOLAIRE DES CHENES *p*1096
457 RUE DES ECOLES BUREAU 846, DRUMMONDVILLE, QC, J2B 1J3
(819) 478-6700   *SIC* 8211

COMMISSION SCOLAIRE DES CHENES *p*1098
265 RUE SAINT-FELIX, DRUMMONDVILLE, QC, J2C 5M1
(819) 478-6600   *SIC* 8211

COMMISSION SCOLAIRE DES CHENES *p*1098
175 RUE PELLETIER, DRUMMONDVILLE, QC, J2C 2W1
(819) 474-0750   *SIC* 8211

COMMISSION SCOLAIRE DES CHICCHOCS *p*1355
170 BOUL SAINTE-ANNE O, SAINTE-ANNE-DES-MONTS, QC, G4V 1R8
(418) 763-2206   *SIC* 8211

COMMISSION SCOLAIRE DES DECOUVREURS *p*1270
1255 AV DU CHANOINE-MOREL, QUEBEC, QC, G1S 4B1
(418) 684-0064   *SIC* 8211

COMMISSION SCOLAIRE DES DECOUVREURS *p*1271
3000 BOUL HOCHELAGA, QUEBEC, QC, G1V 3Y4
(418) 652-2159   *SIC* 8211

COMMISSION SCOLAIRE DES DECOUVREURS *p*1271
945 AV WOLFE BUREAU 100, QUEBEC, QC, G1V 4E2
(418) 652-2121   *SIC* 8211

COMMISSION SCOLAIRE DES DECOUVREURS *p*1275
1505 RUE DES GRANDES-MAREES, QUEBEC, QC, G1Y 2T3
(418) 652-2196   *SIC* 8211

COMMISSION SCOLAIRE DES DECOUVREURS *p*1275
3643 AV DES COMPAGNONS, QUEBEC, QC, G1X 3Z6
(418) 652-2170   *SIC* 8211

COMMISSION SCOLAIRE DES DRAVEURS

*p*1103
360 BOUL LA VERENDRYE E, GATINEAU, QC, J8P 6K7
(819) 663-9241   *SIC* 8211

COMMISSION SCOLAIRE DES DRAVEURS *p*1104
9 RUE SAINTE-YVONNE BUREAU 253, GATINEAU, QC, J8T 1X6
(819) 568-0233   *SIC* 8211

COMMISSION SCOLAIRE DES GRANDES-SEIGNEURIES *p*1072
4 AV DE CHAMPAGNE, CANDIAC, QC, J5R 4W3
(514) 380-8899   *SIC* 8211

COMMISSION SCOLAIRE DES GRANDES-SEIGNEURIES *p*1089
35 RUE BOARDMAN, DELSON, QC, J5B 2C3
(514) 380-8899   *SIC* 8211

COMMISSION SCOLAIRE DES GRANDES-SEIGNEURIES *p*1123
1100 BOUL TASCHEREAU, LA PRAIRIE, QC, J5R 1W8
(514) 380-8899   *SIC* 8211

COMMISSION SCOLAIRE DES GRANDES-SEIGNEURIES *p*1123
50 BOUL TASCHEREAU BUREAU 310, LA PRAIRIE, QC, J5R 4V3
(514) 380-8899   *SIC* 8211

COMMISSION SCOLAIRE DES HAUTES-RIVIERES *p*1149
677 RUE DESJARDINS, MARIEVILLE, QC, J3M 1R1
(450) 460-4491   *SIC* 8211

COMMISSION SCOLAIRE DES HAUTES-RIVIERES *p*1297
1881 AV SAINT-PAUL, SAINT-CESAIRE, QC, J0L 1T0
(450) 469-3187   *SIC* 8211

COMMISSION SCOLAIRE DES HAUTES-RIVIERES *p*1316
940 BOUL DE NORMANDIE, SAINT-JEAN-SUR-RICHELIEU, QC, J3A 1A7
(450) 348-0413   *SIC* 8211

COMMISSION SCOLAIRE DES HAUTES-RIVIERES *p*1316
365 AV LANDRY, SAINT-JEAN-SUR-RICHELIEU, QC, J2X 2P6
(450) 347-1225   *SIC* 8211

COMMISSION SCOLAIRE DES HAUTES-RIVIERES *p*1316
511 RUE PIERRE-CAISSE, SAINT-JEAN-SUR-RICHELIEU, QC, J3A 1N5
(450) 348-0958   *SIC* 8211

COMMISSION SCOLAIRE DES HAUTES-RIVIERES *p*1317
151 RUE NOTRE-DAME, SAINT-JEAN-SUR-RICHELIEU, QC, J3B 6M9
(450) 348-4747   *SIC* 8211

COMMISSION SCOLAIRE DES HAUTES-RIVIERES *p*1317
210 RUE NOTRE-DAME, SAINT-JEAN-SUR-RICHELIEU, QC, J3B 6N3
(450) 359-6411   *SIC* 8211

COMMISSION SCOLAIRE DES HAUTS-CANTONS *p*1081
311 RUE SAINT-PAUL E, COATICOOK, QC, J1A 1G1
(819) 849-4825   *SIC* 8211

COMMISSION SCOLAIRE DES HAUTS-CANTONS *p*1100
308 RUE PALMER, EAST ANGUS, QC, J0B 1R0
(819) 832-4953   *SIC* 8211

COMMISSION SCOLAIRE DES HAUTS-CANTONS *p*1125
3409 RUE LAVAL, LAC-MEGANTIC, QC, G6B 1A5
(819) 583-3023   *SIC* 8211

COMMISSION SCOLAIRE DES ILES *p*1120
1419 CH DE L'ETANG-DU-NORD, L'ETANG-DU-NORD, QC, G4T 3B9
(418) 986-5511   *SIC* 8211

COMMISSION SCOLAIRE DES LAUREN-

TIDES *p1159*
700 BOUL DU DOCTEUR-GERVAIS, MONT-TREMBLANT, QC, J8E 2T3
(819) 425-3743 *SIC* 8211

COMMISSION SCOLAIRE DES LAUREN-TIDES *p1354*
13 RUE SAINT-ANTOINE, SAINTE-AGATHE-DES-MONTS, QC, J8C 2C3
(819) 324-8670 *SIC* 8211

COMMISSION SCOLAIRE DES LAUREN-TIDES *p1354*
258 BOUL DE SAINTE-ADELE, SAINTE-ADELE, QC, J8B 0K6
(450) 240-6220 *SIC* 8211

COMMISSION SCOLAIRE DES MONTS-ET-MAREES *p1046*
93 AV DU PARC BUREAU 3, AMQUI, QC, G5J 2L8
(418) 629-6200 *SIC* 8211

COMMISSION SCOLAIRE DES MONTS-ET-MAREES *p1046*
93 AV DU PARC BUREAU 3, AMQUI, QC, G5J 2L8
(418) 629-6200 *SIC* 8211

COMMISSION SCOLAIRE DES MONTS-ET-MAREES *p1046*
95 AV DU PARC, AMQUI, QC, G5J 2L8
(418) 629-6200 *SIC* 8211

COMMISSION SCOLAIRE DES NAVIGA-TEURS *p1136*
55 RUE DES COMMANDEURS, LEVIS, QC, G6V 6P5
(418) 838-8402 *SIC* 8211

COMMISSION SCOLAIRE DES NAVIGA-TEURS *p1136*
6045 RUE SAINT-GEORGES, LEVIS, QC, G6V 4K6
(418) 838-8548 *SIC* 8211

COMMISSION SCOLAIRE DES NAVIGA-TEURS *p1137*
1860 1RE RUE BUREAU 90, LEVIS, QC, G6W 5M6
(418) 839-0500 *SIC* 8211

COMMISSION SCOLAIRE DES NAVIGA-TEURS *p1139*
3724 AV DES EGLISES, LEVIS, QC, G6X 1X4
(418) 839-0500 *SIC* 8211

COMMISSION SCOLAIRE DES NAVIGA-TEURS *p1291*
1134 RUE DU CENTENAIRE, SAINT-AGAPIT, QC, G0S 1Z0
(418) 888-3961 *SIC* 8211

COMMISSION SCOLAIRE DES NAVIGA-TEURS *p1349*
368 RTE DU PONT, SAINT-NICOLAS, QC, G7A 2V3
(418) 834-2461 *SIC* 8211

COMMISSION SCOLAIRE DES NAVIGA-TEURS *p1357*
6380 RUE GARNEAU, SAINTE-CROIX, QC, G0S 2H0
(418) 796-0503 *SIC* 8211

COMMISSION SCOLAIRE DES PATRIOTES *p1056*
225 RUE HUBERT, BELOEIL, QC, J3G 2S8
(450) 467-9309 *SIC* 8211

COMMISSION SCOLAIRE DES PATRIOTES *p1056*
725 RUE DE LEVIS, BELOEIL, QC, J3G 2M1
(450) 467-0262 *SIC* 8211

COMMISSION SCOLAIRE DES PATRIOTES *p1074*
535 BOUL BRASSARD, CHAMBLY, QC, J3L 6H3
(450) 461-5908 *SIC* 8211

COMMISSION SCOLAIRE DES PATRIOTES *p1158*
525 RUE JOLLIET, MONT-SAINT-HILAIRE, QC, J3H 3N2
(450) 467-0261 *SIC* 8211

COMMISSION SCOLAIRE DES PATRIOTES *p1295*

1740 RUE ROBERVAL, SAINT-BRUNO, QC, J3V 3R3
(450) 441-2919 *SIC* 8211

COMMISSION SCOLAIRE DES PATRIOTES *p1295*
221 BOUL CLAIREVUE E, SAINT-BRUNO, QC, J3V 5J3
(450) 653-1541 *SIC* 8211

COMMISSION SCOLAIRE DES PHARES *p1284*
250 BOUL ARTHUR-BUIES O, RIMOUSKI, QC, G5L 7A7
(418) 724-3439 *SIC* 8211

COMMISSION SCOLAIRE DES PREMIERES-SEIGNEURIES *p1055*
10975 BOUL SAINTE-ANNE, BEAUPRE, QC, G0A 1E0
(418) 821-8053 *SIC* 8211

COMMISSION SCOLAIRE DES PREMIERES-SEIGNEURIES *p1254*
2265 AV LARUE, QUEBEC, QC, G1C 1J9
(418) 821-4220 *SIC* 8211

COMMISSION SCOLAIRE DES PREMIERES-SEIGNEURIES *p1254*
2233 AV ROYALE, QUEBEC, QC, G1C 1P3
(418) 821-8988 *SIC* 8211

COMMISSION SCOLAIRE DES PREMIERES-SEIGNEURIES *p1255*
645 AV DU CENACLE, QUEBEC, QC, G1E 1B3
(418) 666-4666 *SIC* 8211

COMMISSION SCOLAIRE DES PREMIERES-SEIGNEURIES *p1255*
643 AV DU CENACLE, QUEBEC, QC, G1E 1B3
(418) 666-4666 *SIC* 8211

COMMISSION SCOLAIRE DES PREMIERES-SEIGNEURIES *p1255*
2740 AV SAINT-DAVID, QUEBEC, QC, G1E 4K7
(418) 666-4500 *SIC* 8211

COMMISSION SCOLAIRE DES RIVES-DU-SAGUENAY *p1077*
350 RUE SAINT-GERARD, CHICOUTIMI, QC, G7G 1J2
(418) 541-4343 *SIC* 8211

COMMISSION SCOLAIRE DES RIVES-DU-SAGUENAY *p1078*
36 RUE JACQUES-CARTIER E, CHICOUTIMI, QC, G7H 1W2
(418) 698-5000 *SIC* 8211

COMMISSION SCOLAIRE DES RIVES-DU-SAGUENAY *p1078*
847 RUE GEORGES-VANIER, CHICOUTIMI, QC, G7H 4M1
(418) 698-5170 *SIC* 8211

COMMISSION SCOLAIRE DES RIVES-DU-SAGUENAY *p1078*
985 RUE BEGIN, CHICOUTIMI, QC, G7H 4P1
(418) 698-5185 *SIC* 8211

COMMISSION SCOLAIRE DES RIVES-DU-SAGUENAY *p1121*
1802 AV JOHN-KANE, LA BAIE, QC, G7B 1K2
(418) 544-2843 *SIC* 8211

COMMISSION SCOLAIRE DES SAMARES *p1057*
881 RUE PIERRE-DE-LESTAGE, BERTHIERVILLE, QC, J0K 1A0
(450) 758-3599 *SIC* 8211

COMMISSION SCOLAIRE DES SAMARES *p1281*
3144 18E AV BUREAU 760, RAWDON, QC, J0K 1S0
(450) 758-3749 *SIC* 8211

COMMISSION SCOLAIRE DES SAMARES *p1303*
4671 RUE PRINCIPALE BUREAU 190, SAINT-FELIX-DE-VALOIS, QC, J0K 2M0
(450) 439-6046 *SIC* 8211

COMMISSION SCOLAIRE DES SAMARES *p1352*
60 MONTEE REMI-HENRI, SAINT-ROCH-

DE-L'ACHIGAN, QC, J0K 3H0
(450) 588-7410 *SIC* 8211

COMMISSION SCOLAIRE DES SOMMETS *p1052*
430 5E AV, ASBESTOS, QC, J1T 1X2
(819) 879-5413 *SIC* 8211

COMMISSION SCOLAIRE DES SOMMETS *p1403*
250 RUE SAINT-GEORGES, WINDSOR, QC, J1S 1K4
(819) 845-2728 *SIC* 8211

COMMISSION SCOLAIRE DU CHEMIN-DU-ROY *p1384*
500 RUE DES ERABLES, TROIS-RIVIERES, QC, G8T 9S4
(819) 373-1422 *SIC* 8211

COMMISSION SCOLAIRE DU CHEMIN-DU-ROY *p1384*
501 RUE DES ERABLES, TROIS-RIVIERES, QC, G8T 5J2
(819) 375-8931 *SIC* 8211

COMMISSION SCOLAIRE DU CHEMIN-DU-ROY *p1385*
3750 RUE JEAN-BOURDON, TROIS-RIVIERES, QC, G8Y 2A5
(819) 691-3366 *SIC* 8211

COMMISSION SCOLAIRE DU CHEMIN-DU-ROY *p1385*
3750 RUE JEAN-BOURDON, TROIS-RIVIERES, QC, G8Y 2A5
(819) 379-8714 *SIC* 8211

COMMISSION SCOLAIRE DU CHEMIN-DU-ROY *p1386*
1725 BOUL DU CARMEL, TROIS-RIVIERES, QC, G8Z 3R8
(819) 379-5822 *SIC* 8211

COMMISSION SCOLAIRE DU CHEMIN-DU-ROY *p1389*
365 RUE CHAVIGNY, TROIS-RIVIERES, QC, G9B 1A7
(819) 377-4391 *SIC* 8211

COMMISSION SCOLAIRE DU FER *p1367*
110 RUE COMEAU, SEPT-ILES, QC, G4R 1J4
(418) 964-2811 *SIC* 8211

COMMISSION SCOLAIRE DU FLEUVE ET DES LACS *p1378*
14 RUE DU VIEUX-CHEMIN, TEMISCOUATA-SUR-LE-LAC, QC, G0L 1E0
(418) 854-2370 *SIC* 8211

COMMISSION SCOLAIRE DU FLEUVE ET DES LACS *p1384*
455 RUE JENKIN, TROIS-PISTOLES, QC, G0L 4K0
SIC 8211

COMMISSION SCOLAIRE DU LAC-ST-JEAN *p1045*
850 AV B?GIN, ALMA, QC, G8B 2X6
(418) 669-6063 *SIC* 8211

COMMISSION SCOLAIRE DU LITTORAL *p1367*
789 RUE BEAULIEU, SEPT-ILES, QC, G4R 1P8
(418) 962-5558 *SIC* 8211

COMMISSION SCOLAIRE DU PAYS-DES-BLEUETS *p1090*
300 AV JEAN-DOLBEAU, DOLBEAU-MISTASSINI, QC, G8L 2T7
(418) 276-0984 *SIC* 8211

COMMISSION SCOLAIRE DU PAYS-DES-BLEUETS *p1287*
171 BOUL DE LA JEUNESSE, ROBERVAL, QC, G8H 2N9
(418) 275-3110 *SIC* 8211

COMMISSION SCOLAIRE DU VAL-DES-CERFS *p1088*
222 RUE MERCIER, COWANSVILLE, QC, J2K 3R9
(450) 263-6660 *SIC* 8211

COMMISSION SCOLAIRE DU VAL-DES-CERFS *p1109*
1111 RUE SIMONDS S, GRANBY, QC, J2G 9H7

(450) 378-9981 *SIC* 8211

COMMISSION SCOLAIRE DU VAL-DES-CERFS *p1109*
55 RUE COURT, GRANBY, QC, J2G 9N6
(450) 372-0221 *SIC* 8211

COMMISSION SCOLAIRE DU VAL-DES-CERFS *p1110*
549 RUE FOURNIER, GRANBY, QC, J2J 2K5
(450) 777-7536 *SIC* 8211

COMMISSION SCOLAIRE EASTERN TOWNSHIPS *p1088*
224 RUE MERCIER, COWANSVILLE, QC, J2K 5C3
(450) 263-3772 *SIC* 8211

COMMISSION SCOLAIRE EASTERN TOWNSHIPS *p1147*
340 RUE SAINT-JEAN-BOSCO, MAGOG, QC, J1X 1K9
(819) 868-3100 *SIC* 8211

COMMISSION SCOLAIRE HARRICANA *p1046*
850 1RE RUE E, AMOS, QC, J9T 2H8
(819) 732-3221 *SIC* 8211

COMMISSION SCOLAIRE HARRICANA *p1046*
800 1RE RUE E, AMOS, QC, J9T 2H8
(819) 732-3221 *SIC* 8211

COMMISSION SCOLAIRE KATIVIK *p1113*
PR, INUKJUAK, QC, J0M 1M0
(819) 254-8211 *SIC* 8211

COMMISSION SCOLAIRE KATIVIK *p1254*
GD, PUVIRNITUQ, QC, J0M 1P0
(819) 988-2960 *SIC* 8211

COMMISSION SCOLAIRE KATIVIK *p1324*
9800 BOUL CAVENDISH BUREAU 400, SAINT-LAURENT, QC, H4M 2V9
(514) 482-8220 *SIC* 8211

COMMISSION SCOLAIRE MARGUERITE-BOURGEOYS *p1127*
50 34E AV, LACHINE, QC, H8T 1Z2
(514) 748-4662 *SIC* 8211

COMMISSION SCOLAIRE MARGUERITE-BOURGEOYS *p1131*
8585 RUE GEORGE, LASALLE, QC, H8P 1G5
(514) 595-2052 *SIC* 8211

COMMISSION SCOLAIRE MARGUERITE-BOURGEOYS *p1132*
9199 RUE CENTRALE, LASALLE, QC, H8R 2J9
(514) 595-2044 *SIC* 8211

COMMISSION SCOLAIRE MARGUERITE-BOURGEOYS *p1155*
1101 CH ROCKLAND, MONT-ROYAL, QC, H3P 2X8
(514) 739-6311 *SIC* 8211

COMMISSION SCOLAIRE MARGUERITE-BOURGEOYS *p1155*
50 AV MONTGOMERY, MONT-ROYAL, QC, H3R 2B3
(514) 731-2761 *SIC* 8211

COMMISSION SCOLAIRE MARGUERITE-BOURGEOYS *p1249*
311 AV INGLEWOOD, POINTE-CLAIRE, QC, H9R 2Z8
(514) 855-4225 *SIC* 8211

COMMISSION SCOLAIRE MARGUERITE-BOURGEOYS *p1253*
3 AV SAINTE-ANNE, POINTE-CLAIRE, QC, H9S 4P6
(514) 855-4236 *SIC* 8211

COMMISSION SCOLAIRE MARGUERITE-BOURGEOYS *p1323*
1100 BOUL DE LA COTE-VERTU, SAINT-LAURENT, QC, H4L 4V1
(514) 855-4500 *SIC* 8211

COMMISSION SCOLAIRE MARGUERITE-BOURGEOYS *p1325*
235 RUE BLEIGNIER, SAINT-LAURENT, QC, H4N 1B1
(514) 332-0742 *SIC* 8211

COMMISSION SCOLAIRE MARGUERITE-BOURGEOYS *p1328*

2395 BOUL THIMENS, SAINT-LAURENT, QC, H4R 1T4

(514) 332-3190 *SIC* 8211

COMMISSION SCOLAIRE MARIE-VICTORIN *p1069*
8350 BOUL PELLETIER, BROSSARD, QC, J4X 1M8

(450) 465-6290 *SIC* 8211

COMMISSION SCOLAIRE MARIE-VICTORIN *p1070*
3055 BOUL DE ROME, BROSSARD, QC, J4Y 1S9

(450) 443-0010 *SIC* 8211

COMMISSION SCOLAIRE MARIE-VICTORIN *p1143*
13 RUE SAINT-LAURENT E, LONGUEUIL, QC, J4H 4B7

(450) 670-0730 *SIC* 8211

COMMISSION SCOLAIRE MARIE-VICTORIN *p1143*
444 RUE DE GENTILLY E, LONGUEUIL, QC, J4H 3X7

(450) 651-6800 *SIC* 8211

COMMISSION SCOLAIRE MARIE-VICTORIN *p1146*
1250 CH DU TREMBLAY, LONGUEUIL, QC, J4N 1A2

(450) 468-0833 *SIC* 8211

COMMISSION SCOLAIRE MARIE-VICTORIN *p1308*
7450 BOUL COUSINEAU, SAINT-HUBERT, QC, J3Y 3L4

(450) 678-2080 *SIC* 8211

COMMISSION SCOLAIRE MARIE-VICTORIN *p1308*
5095 RUE AURELE, SAINT-HUBERT, QC, J3Y 2E6

(450) 678-0145 *SIC* 8211

COMMISSION SCOLAIRE MARIE-VICTORIN *p1309*
1600 RUE DE MONACO, SAINT-HUBERT, QC, J3Z 1B7

(450) 462-3844 *SIC* 8211

COMMISSION SCOLAIRE MARIE-VICTORIN *p1310*
3875 GRANDE ALLEE, SAINT-HUBERT, QC, J4T 2V8

(450) 676-0261 *SIC* 8211

COMMISSION SCOLAIRE MARIE-VICTORIN *p1310*
3855 GRANDE ALLEE, SAINT-HUBERT, QC, J4T 2V8

(450) 678-2781 *SIC* 8211

COMMISSION SCOLAIRE NEW FRONTIER *p1076*
210 RUE MCLEOD, CHATEAUGUAY, QC, J6J 2H4

(450) 691-3230 *SIC* 8211

COMMISSION SCOLAIRE NEW FRONTIER *p1076*
214 RUE MCLEOD, CHATEAUGUAY, QC, J6J 2H4

(450) 691-1440 *SIC* 8211

COMMISSION SCOLAIRE PIERRE-NEVEU, LA *p1154*
525 RUE DE LA MADONE, MONT-LAURIER, QC, J9L 1S4

(819) 623-4310 *SIC* 8211

CONSEIL DES ECOLES CATHOLIQUES DE LANGUE FRANCAISE DU CENTRE-EST *p596*
4000 LABELLE ST, GLOUCESTER, ON, K1J 1A1

(613) 744-2555 *SIC* 8211

CONSEIL DES ECOLES CATHOLIQUES DE LANGUE FRANCAISE DU CENTRE-EST *p596*
4000 LABELLE ST, GLOUCESTER, ON, K1J 1A1

(613) 744-2555 *SIC* 8211

CONSEIL DES ECOLES CATHOLIQUES DE LANGUE FRANCAISE DU CENTRE-EST *p820*
704 CARSON'S RD, OTTAWA, ON, K1K

2H3

(613) 744-8344 *SIC* 8211

CONSEIL DES ECOLES CATHOLIQUES DE LANGUE FRANCAISE DU CENTRE-EST *p832*
2675 DRAPER AVE, OTTAWA, ON, K2H 7A1

SIC 8211

CONSEIL DES ECOLES PUBLIQUES DE L'EST DE L'ONTARIO *p811*
500 MILLENNIUM BLVD, ORLEANS, ON, K4A 4X3

(613) 833-0018 *SIC* 8211

CONSEIL DES ECOLES PUBLIQUES DE L'EST DE L'ONTARIO *p817*
2445 ST. LAURENT BLVD, OTTAWA, ON, K1G 6C3

(613) 742-8960 *SIC* 8211

CONSEIL SCOLAIRE ACADIEN PROVINCIAL *p462*
9248 ROUTE 1, METEGHAN RIVER, NS, B0W 2L0

(902) 769-5458 *SIC* 8211

CONSEIL SCOLAIRE ACADIEN PROVINCIAL *p464*
3435 RTE 206, PETIT DE GRAT, NS, B0E 2L0

(902) 226-5232 *SIC* 8211

CONSEIL SCOLAIRE CATHOLIQUE DE DISTRICT DES GRANDES RIVIERES, LE *p627*
75 QUEEN ST, KAPUSKASING, ON, P5N 1H5

(705) 335-6091 *SIC* 8211

CONSEIL SCOLAIRE CATHOLIQUE DE DISTRICT DES GRANDES RIVIERES, LE *p912*
896 RIVERSIDE DR, TIMMINS, ON, P4N 3W2

(705) 267-1421 *SIC* 8211

CONSEIL SCOLAIRE CATHOLIQUE MON-AVENIR *p770*
110 DREWRY AVE, NORTH YORK, ON, M2M 1C8

(416) 397-6564 *SIC* 8211

CONSEIL SCOLAIRE CATHOLIQUE PROVIDENCE *p1018*
7515 FOREST GLADE DR, WINDSOR, ON, N8T 3P5

(519) 948-9227 *SIC* 8211

CONSEIL SCOLAIRE CENTRE-NORD *p111*
8627 91 ST NW SUITE 322, EDMONTON, AB, T6C 3N1

(780) 468-5250 *SIC* 8211

CONSEIL SCOLAIRE DE DISTRICT CATHOLIQUE CENTRE-SUD *p770*
110 DREWRY AVE, NORTH YORK, ON, M2M 1C8

(416) 250-1754 *SIC* 8211

CONSEIL SCOLAIRE DE DISTRICT CATHOLIQUE DE L'EST ONTARIEN *p562*
510 MCCONNELL AVE, CORNWALL, ON, K6H 4M1

(613) 933-0172 *SIC* 8211

CONSEIL SCOLAIRE DE DISTRICT CATHOLIQUE DE L'EST ONTARIEN *p619*
572 KITCHENER ST SUITE 8E, HAWKESBURY, ON, K6A 2P3

(613) 632-7055 *SIC* 8211

CONSEIL SCOLAIRE DE DISTRICT CATHOLIQUE DE L'EST ONTARIEN *p643*
875 COUNTY ROAD 17, L'ORIGNAL, ON, K0B 1K0

(613) 675-4691 *SIC* 8211

CONSEIL SCOLAIRE DE DISTRICT CATHOLIQUE DE L'EST ONTARIEN *p857*
1535 DU PARC AVE, ROCKLAND, ON, K4K 1C3

(613) 446-5169 *SIC* 8211

CONSEIL SCOLAIRE DE DISTRICT CATHOLIQUE DU NOUVEL-ONTARIO, LE *p899*
100 LEVIS ST, SUDBURY, ON, P3C 2H1

(705) 674-7484 *SIC* 8211

CONSEIL SCOLAIRE DE DISTRICT CATHOLIQUE DU NOUVEL-ONTARIO, LE *p899*
201 JOGUES ST, SUDBURY, ON, P3C 5L7

(705) 673-5626 *SIC* 8211

CONSEIL SCOLAIRE DE DISTRICT CATHOLIQUE DU NOUVEL-ONTARIO, LE *p899*
201 JOGUES ST, SUDBURY, ON, P3C 5L7

(705) 673-5626 *SIC* 8211

CONSEIL SCOLAIRE DE DISTRICT CATHOLIQUE DU GRAND NORD DE L'ONTARIO *p899*
296 VAN HORNE ST, SUDBURY, ON, P3B 1H9

(705) 671-1533 *SIC* 8211

CONSEIL SCOLAIRE DISTRICT NO 5 *p394*
915 ST. ANNE ST, BATHURST, NB, E2A 6X1

(506) 547-2785 *SIC* 8211

CONSEIL SCOLAIRE DISTRICT NO 5 *p396*
45A RUE DU VILLAGE, CAMPBELLTON, NB, E3N 3G4

(506) 789-2250 *SIC* 8211

CONSEIL SCOLAIRE DU DISTRICT DU NORD-EST DE L'ONTARIO *p763*
2345 CONNAUGHT AVE, NORTH BAY, ON, P1B 0A3

(705) 497-8700 *SIC* 8211

CONSEIL SCOLAIRE FRANCOPHONE DE LA COLOMBIE-BRITANNIQUE *p254*
13511 COMMERCE PKY UNIT 100, RICHMOND, BC, V6V 2J8

(604) 214-2600 *SIC* 8211

CONSEIL SCOLAIRE VIAMONDE *p791*
116 CORNELIUS PKY, NORTH YORK, ON, M6L 2K5

(416) 614-0844 *SIC* 8211

CORPORATION OF TRINITY COLLEGE SCHOOL, THE *p847*
55 DEBLAQUIRE ST N, PORT HOPE, ON, L1A 4K7

(905) 885-4565 *SIC* 8211

COUNTRY DAY SCHOOL, THE *p629*
13415 DUFFERIN ST, KING CITY, ON, L7B 1K5

(905) 833-5366 *SIC* 8211

CROSS LAKE EDUCATION AUTHORITY *p348*
GD, CROSS LAKE, MB, R0B 0J0

(204) 676-3030 *SIC* 8211

DELTA SCHOOL DISTRICT NO.37 *p207*
9115 116 ST, DELTA, BC, V4C 5W8

(604) 594-6100 *SIC* 8211

DELTA SCHOOL DISTRICT NO.37 *p207*
11447 82 AVE, DELTA, BC, V4C 5J6

(604) 596-7471 *SIC* 8211

DELTA SCHOOL DISTRICT NO.37 *p208*
11584 LYON RD, DELTA, BC, V4E 2K4

(604) 946-4101 *SIC* 8211

DELTA SCHOOL DISTRICT NO.37 *p210*
4615 51 ST, DELTA, BC, V4K 2V8

(604) 946-4194 *SIC* 8211

DELTA SCHOOL DISTRICT NO.37 *p211*
750 53 ST, DELTA, BC, V4M 3B7

(604) 943-7407 *SIC* 8211

DISTRICT SCHOOL BOARD OF NIAGARA *p591*
350 HWY 20 W, FONTHILL, ON, L0S 1E0

(905) 892-2635 *SIC* 8211

DISTRICT SCHOOL BOARD OF NIAGARA *p599*
5 BOULTON AVE, GRIMSBY, ON, L3M 1H6

(905) 945-5416 *SIC* 8211

DISTRICT SCHOOL BOARD OF NIAGARA *p760*
5960 PITTON RD, NIAGARA FALLS, ON, L2H 1T5

(905) 356-2401 *SIC* 8211

DISTRICT SCHOOL BOARD OF NIAGARA *p846*
255 OMER AVE, PORT COLBORNE, ON, L3K 3Z1

(905) 834-9732 *SIC* 8211

DISTRICT SCHOOL BOARD OF NIAGARA *p885*
91 BUNTING RD, ST CATHARINES, ON, L2P 3G8

(905) 684-9461 *SIC* 8211

DISTRICT SCHOOL BOARD OF NIAGARA *p885*
34 CATHERINE ST, ST CATHARINES, ON, L2R 5E7

(905) 687-7301 *SIC* 8211

DISTRICT SCHOOL BOARD ONTARIO NORTH EAST *p634*
GD, KIRKLAND LAKE, ON, P2N 3P4

(705) 567-4981 *SIC* 8211

DISTRICT SCHOOL BOARD ONTARIO NORTH EAST *p753*
90 NIVEN ST, NEW LISKEARD, ON, P0J 1P0

(705) 647-7336 *SIC* 8211

DISTRICT SCHOOL BOARD ONTARIO NORTH EAST *p879*
153 CROATIA AVE, SCHUMACHER, ON, P0N 1G0

(705) 360-1151 *SIC* 8211

DISTRICT SCOLAIRE 11 *p395*
37 AV RICHARD, BOUCTOUCHE, NB, E4S 3T5

(506) 743-7200 *SIC* 8211

DISTRICT SCOLAIRE 3 *p398*
298 RUE MARTIN SUITE 3, EDMUNDSTON, NB, E3V 5E5

(506) 737-4567 *SIC* 8211

DISTRICT SCOLAIRE 3 *p398*
300 RUE MARTIN, EDMUNDSTON, NB, E3V 0G9

(506) 735-2008 *SIC* 8211

DISTRICT SCOLAIRE FRANCOPHONE NORD-EST *p419*
3376 RUE PRINCIPALE, TRACADIE-SHEILA, NB, E1X 1A4

(506) 394-3400 *SIC* 8211

DISTRICT SCOLAIRE FRANCOPHONE NORD-EST *p419*
585 RUE DE L'EGLISE, TRACADIE-SHEILA, NB, E1X 1B1

(506) 394-3508 *SIC* 8211

DISTRICT SCOLAIRE FRANCOPHONE NORD-EST *p419*
585 CHURCH ST, TRACADIE-SHEILA, NB, E1X 1G5

(506) 394-3500 *SIC* 8211

DISTRICT SCOLAIRE FRANCOPHONE SUD *p397*
425 RUE CHAMPLAIN, DIEPPE, NB, E1A 1P2

(506) 856-3333 *SIC* 8211

DIVISION SCOLAIRE FRANCO-MANITOBAINE *p351*
1263 DAWSON RD, LORETTE, MB, R0A 0Y0

(204) 878-9399 *SIC* 8211

DRYDEN BOARD OF EDUCATION *p565*
79 CASIMIR AVE, DRYDEN, ON, P8N 2H4

(807) 223-2316 *SIC* 8211

DUFFERIN-PEEL CATHOLIC DISTRICT SCHOOL BOARD *p499*
25 CORPORATION DR, BRAMPTON, ON, L6S 6A2

(905) 791-1195 *SIC* 8211

DUFFERIN-PEEL CATHOLIC DISTRICT SCHOOL BOARD *p499*
950 NORTH PARK DR, BRAMPTON, ON, L6S 3L5

(905) 792-2282 *SIC* 8211

DUFFERIN-PEEL CATHOLIC DISTRICT SCHOOL BOARD *p512*
2 NOTRE DAME AVE, BRAMPTON, ON, L6Z 4L5

(905) 840-2802 *SIC* 8211

DUFFERIN-PEEL CATHOLIC DISTRICT SCHOOL BOARD *p532*
6500 OLD CHURCH RD, CALEDON EAST, ON, L7C 0H3

(905) 584-1670 *SIC* 8211

DUFFERIN-PEEL CATHOLIC DISTRICT

SCHOOL BOARD p694
635 WILLOWBANK TRAIL, MISSISSAUGA, ON, L4W 3L6
(905) 279-1554 *SIC* 8211

DUFFERIN-PEEL CATHOLIC DISTRICT SCHOOL BOARD p694
4235 GOLDEN ORCHARD DR, MISSISSAUGA, ON, L4W 3G1
(905) 624-4529 *SIC* 8211

DUFFERIN-PEEL CATHOLIC DISTRICT SCHOOL BOARD p709
330 CENTRAL PKY W, MISSISSAUGA, ON, L5B 3K6
(905) 277-0326 *SIC* 8211

DUFFERIN-PEEL CATHOLIC DISTRICT SCHOOL BOARD p718
2800 ERIN CENTRE BLVD, MISSISSAUGA, ON, L5M 6R5
(905) 820-3900 *SIC* 8211

DUFFERIN-PEEL CATHOLIC DISTRICT SCHOOL BOARD p718
3801 THOMAS ST, MISSISSAUGA, ON, L5M 7G2
(905) 285-0050 *SIC* 8211

DUFFERIN-PEEL CATHOLIC DISTRICT SCHOOL BOARD p731
40 MATHESON BLVD W, MISSISSAUGA, ON, L5R 1C5
(905) 890-1221 *SIC* 8211

DUFFERIN-PEEL CATHOLIC DISTRICT SCHOOL BOARD p744
5555 CREDITVIEW RD, MISSISSAUGA, ON, L5V 2B9
(905) 812-1376 *SIC* 8211

DURHAM CATHOLIC DISTRICT SCHOOL BOARD p474
80 MANDRAKE ST, AJAX, ON, L1S 5H4
(905) 427-6667 *SIC* 8211

DURHAM CATHOLIC DISTRICT SCHOOL BOARD p475
1375 HARWOOD AVE N, AJAX, ON, L1T 4G8
(905) 686-4300 *SIC* 8211

DURHAM CATHOLIC DISTRICT SCHOOL BOARD p813
650 ROSSLAND RD W, OSHAWA, ON, L1J 7C4
(905) 576-6150 *SIC* 8211

DURHAM CATHOLIC DISTRICT SCHOOL BOARD p1015
3001 COUNTRY LANE, WHITBY, ON, L1P 1M1
(905) 666-7753 *SIC* 8211

DURHAM CATHOLIC DISTRICT SCHOOL BOARD p1016
1020 DRYDEN BLVD, WHITBY, ON, L1R 2A2
(905) 666-2010 *SIC* 8211

DURHAM DISTRICT SCHOOL BOARD p474
105 BAYLY ST E, AJAX, ON, L1S 1P2
(905) 683-1610 *SIC* 8211

DURHAM DISTRICT SCHOOL BOARD p811
265 HARMONY RD N, OSHAWA, ON, L1G 6L4
(905) 723-8157 *SIC* 8211

DURHAM DISTRICT SCHOOL BOARD p811
301 SIMCOE ST N, OSHAWA, ON, L1G 4T2
(905) 728-7531 *SIC* 8211

DURHAM DISTRICT SCHOOL BOARD p812
1356 SIMCOE ST S, OSHAWA, ON, L1H 4M4
(905) 725-7042 *SIC* 8211

DURHAM DISTRICT SCHOOL BOARD p813
570 STEVENSON RD N, OSHAWA, ON, L1J 5P1
(905) 728-9407 *SIC* 8211

DURHAM DISTRICT SCHOOL BOARD p813
155 GIBB ST, OSHAWA, ON, L1J 1Y4
SIC 8211

DURHAM DISTRICT SCHOOL BOARD p843
655 SHEPPARD AVE, PICKERING, ON, L1V 1G2
(905) 839-1125 *SIC* 8211

DURHAM DISTRICT SCHOOL BOARD p845

2155 LIVERPOOL RD, PICKERING, ON, L1X 1V4
(905) 420-1885 *SIC* 8211

DURHAM DISTRICT SCHOOL BOARD p848
160 ROSA ST, PORT PERRY, ON, L9L 1L7
(905) 985-7337 *SIC* 8211

DURHAM DISTRICT SCHOOL BOARD p1014
400 ANDERSON ST, WHITBY, ON, L1N 3V6
(905) 668-5809 *SIC* 8211

DURHAM DISTRICT SCHOOL BOARD p1014
600 HENRY ST, WHITBY, ON, L1N 5C7
(905) 666-5500 *SIC* 8211

DURHAM DISTRICT SCHOOL BOARD p1015
681 ROSSLAND RD W, WHITBY, ON, L1P 1Y1
(905) 665-5057 *SIC* 8211

DURHAM DISTRICT SCHOOL BOARD p1016
400 TAUNTON RD E, WHITBY, ON, L1R 2K6
(905) 686-2711 *SIC* 8211

EAST CENTRAL ALBERTA CATHOLIC SEPERATE SCHOOLS REGIONAL DIVISION NO 16 p171
1018 1 AVE, WAINWRIGHT, AB, T9W 1G9
(780) 842-3992 *SIC* 8211

EASTERN SCHOOL DISTRICT p1041
274 VALLEYFIELD RD, MONTAGUE, PE, C0A 1R0
(902) 838-0835 *SIC* 8211

EASTERN SCHOOL DISTRICT p1042
234 SHAKESPEARE DR, STRATFORD, PE, C1B 2V8
(902) 368-6990 *SIC* 8211

EASTERN SHORES SCHOOL BOARD p1242
40 RUE MOUNT-SORREL, NEW CARLISLE, QC, G0C 1Z0
(418) 752-2247 *SIC* 8211

EBB AND FLOW FIRST NATION EDUCATION AUTHORITY p349
GD, EBB AND FLOW, MB, R0L 0R0
(204) 448-2012 *SIC* 8211

EBB AND FLOW FIRST NATION EDUCATION AUTHORITY p349
PO BOX 160, EBB AND FLOW, MB, R0L 0R0
(204) 448-2438 *SIC* 8211

ECOLE ARMENIENNE SOURP HAGOP, L' p1224
3400 RUE NADON, MONTREAL, QC, H4J 1P5
(514) 332-1373 *SIC* 8211

ECOLE BETH JACOB DE RAV HIRSCHPRUNG p1244
1750 AV GLENDALE, OUTREMONT, QC, H2V 1B3
(514) 731-6607 *SIC* 8211

ECOLE HORIZON JEUNESSE p1241
155 BOUL SAINTE-ROSE E, MONTREAL-OUEST, QC, H7H 1P2
(450) 662-6720 *SIC* 8211

ECOLE NATIONALE DE CIRQUE p1170
8181 2E AV, MONTREAL, QC, H1Z 4N9
(514) 982-0859 *SIC* 8211

ECOLE SECONDAIRE LOYOLA p1222
7272 RUE SHERBROOKE O, MONTREAL, QC, H4B 1R2
(514) 486-1101 *SIC* 8211

ECOLE SECONDAIRE MARCELLIN-CHAMPAGNAT p1316
14 CH DES PATRIOTES E, SAINT-JEAN-SUR-RICHELIEU, QC, J2X 5P9
(450) 347-5343 *SIC* 8211

ECOLE SECONDAIRE SAINT-JOSEPH DE ST-HYACINTHE p1312
2875 AV BOURDAGES N, SAINT-HYACINTHE, QC, J2S 5S3
(450) 774-7087 *SIC* 8211

EDMONTON CATHOLIC SCHOOLS p84
8760 132 AVE NW, EDMONTON, AB, T5E

0X8
(780) 476-6251 *SIC* 8211

EDMONTON CATHOLIC SEPARATE SCHOOL DISTRICT NO.7 p85
10830 109 ST NW, EDMONTON, AB, T5H 3C1
(780) 426-2010 *SIC* 8211

EDMONTON CATHOLIC SEPARATE SCHOOL DISTRICT NO.7 p92
106 ST NW SUITE SUITE 9807, EDMONTON, AB, T5K 1C2
(780) 441-6000 *SIC* 8211

EDMONTON CATHOLIC SEPARATE SCHOOL DISTRICT NO.7 p98
9250 163 ST NW, EDMONTON, AB, T5R 0A7
(780) 489-2571 *SIC* 8211

EDMONTON CATHOLIC SEPARATE SCHOOL DISTRICT NO.7 p109
6110 95 AVE NW, EDMONTON, AB, T6B 1A5
(780) 466-3161 *SIC* 8211

EDMONTON CATHOLIC SEPARATE SCHOOL DISTRICT NO.7 p119
11230 43 AVE NW, EDMONTON, AB, T6J 0X8
(780) 435-3964 *SIC* 8211

EDMONTON SCHOOL DISTRICT NO. 7 p84
6804 144 AVE NW, EDMONTON, AB, T5C 3C7
(780) 408-9800 *SIC* 8211

EDMONTON SCHOOL DISTRICT NO. 7 p86
1 KINGSWAY NW, EDMONTON, AB, T5H 4G9
(780) 429-8000 *SIC* 8211

EDMONTON SCHOOL DISTRICT NO. 7 p111
7835 76 AVE NW, EDMONTON, AB, T6C 2N1
(780) 428-1111 *SIC* 8211

EDMONTON SCHOOL DISTRICT NO. 7 p114
10450 72 AVE NW, EDMONTON, AB, T6E 0Z6
(780) 439-3957 *SIC* 8211

EITZ CHAIM DAY SCHOOL p790
1 VIEWMOUNT AVE, NORTH YORK, ON, M6B 1T2
(416) 789-4366 *SIC* 8211

ELK ISLAND PUBLIC SCHOOLS REGIONAL DIVISION NO. 14 p4
53129 RANGE ROAD 222, ARDROSSAN, AB, T8E 2M8
(780) 922-2228 *SIC* 8211

ELK ISLAND PUBLIC SCHOOLS REGIONAL DIVISION NO. 14 p161
20 FESTIVAL WAY, SHERWOOD PARK, AB, T8A 4Y1
(780) 467-8816 *SIC* 8211

ELK ISLAND PUBLIC SCHOOLS REGIONAL DIVISION NO. 14 p162
683 WYE RD, SHERWOOD PARK, AB, T8B 1N2
(780) 464-3477 *SIC* 8211

ELMWOOD SCHOOL INCORPORATED p857
261 BUENA VISTA RD, ROCKCLIFFE, ON, K1M 0V9
(613) 749-6761 *SIC* 8211

ELVES SPECIAL NEEDS SOCIETY p97
10825 142 ST NW, EDMONTON, AB, T5N 3Y7
(780) 454-5310 *SIC* 8211

ESKASONI SCHOOL BOARD p450
4645 SHORE RD, ESKASONI, NS, B1W 1K3
(902) 379-2825 *SIC* 8211

ESKASONI SCHOOL BOARD p450
4645 SHORE RD, ESKASONI, NS, B1W 1K3
(902) 379-2507 *SIC* 8211

EVERGREEN CATHOLIC SEPARATE REGIONAL DIVISION 2 p164
381 GROVE DR UNIT 110, SPRUCE GROVE, AB, T7X 2Y9
(780) 962-5627 *SIC* 8211

EVERGREEN SCHOOL DIVISION p350
140 CENTRE AVE W, GIMLI, MB, R0C 1B1
(204) 642-6260 *SIC* 8211

EXTERNAT SACRE-COEUR p1287
535 RUE LEFRANCOIS, ROSEMERE, QC, J7A 4R5
(450) 621-6720 *SIC* 8211

FFCA CHARTER SCHOOL SOCIETY p35
7000 RAILWAY ST SE, CALGARY, AB, T2H 3A8
(403) 520-3206 *SIC* 8211

FONDATION DE LA COMMISSION SCOLAIRE DES PORTAGES-DE-L'OUTAOUAIS p1105
255 RUE SAINT-REDEMPTEUR, GATINEAU, QC, J8X 2T4
(819) 771-4548 *SIC* 8211

FONDATION ECOLE MONTCALM INC p1372
2050 BOUL DE PORTLAND, SHERBROOKE, QC, J1J 1T9
(819) 822-5633 *SIC* 8211

FONDATION EDUCATIVE DE LA COMMISSION SCOLAIRE ENGLISH-MONTREAL, LA p1220
6000 AV FIELDING, MONTREAL, QC, H3X 1T4
(514) 483-7200 *SIC* 8211

FONDATION EDUCATIVE DE LA COMMISSION SCOLAIRE ENGLISH-MONTREAL, LA p1239
11575 AV P.-M.-FAVIER, MONTREAL-NORD, QC, H1G 6E5
(514) 328-4442 *SIC* 8211

FONDATION EDUCATIVE DE LA COMMISSION SCOLAIRE ENGLISH-MONTREAL, LA p1329
2505 BOUL DE LA COTE-VERTU, SAINT-LAURENT, QC, H4R 1P3
(514) 331-8781 *SIC* 8211

FONDATION EDUCATIVE DE LA COMMISSION SCOLAIRE ENGLISH-MONTREAL, LA p1346
7355 BOUL VIAU, SAINT-LEONARD, QC, H1S 3C2
(514) 374-6000 *SIC* 8211

FOOTHILLS SCHOOL DIVISION NO. 38 p136
120 5 AVE SE SUITE 38, HIGH RIVER, AB, T1V 1G2
(403) 652-3001 *SIC* 8211

FOOTHILLS SCHOOL DIVISION NO. 38 p150
229 WOODHAVEN DR, OKOTOKS, AB, T1S 2A7
(403) 938-6116 *SIC* 8211

FOREST HILL LEARNING CENTRE LIMITED p779
411 LAWRENCE AVE E, NORTH YORK, ON, M3C 1N9
(416) 444-5858 *SIC* 8211

FORT LA BOSSE SCHOOL DIVISION p360
523 9TH AVE, VIRDEN, MB, R0M 2C0
(204) 748-2692 *SIC* 8211

FORT MCMURRAY PUBLIC SCHOOL DISTRICT #2833 p128
231 HARDIN ST SUITE 2833, FORT MCMURRAY, AB, T9H 2G2
(780) 799-7900 *SIC* 8211

FORT MCMURRAY PUBLIC SCHOOL DISTRICT #2833 p128
8453 FRANKLIN AVE, FORT MCMURRAY, AB, T9H 2J2
(780) 743-2444 *SIC* 8211

FORT MCMURRAY PUBLIC SCHOOL DISTRICT #2833 p129
107 BRETT DR, FORT MCMURRAY, AB, T9K 1V1
(780) 743-1079 *SIC* 8211

FORT VERMILION SCHOOL DIVISON NO. 52 p130
5213 RIVER RD, FORT VERMILION, AB, T0H 1N0
(780) 927-3766 *SIC* 8211

FRONTIER SCHOOL DIVISION p353
1 ROSSVILLE RD, NORWAY HOUSE, MB, R0B 1B0

(204) 359-4100   *SIC* 8211
FRONTIER SCHOOL DIVISION   *p365*
30 SPEERS RD, WINNIPEG, MB, R2J 1L9
(204) 775-9741   *SIC* 8211
FRONTIER SCHOOL DIVISION   *p365*
30 SPEERS RD, WINNIPEG, MB, R2J 1L9
(204) 775-9741   *SIC* 8211
GARDEN VALLEY SCHOOL DIVISION *p361*
GARDEN VALLEY COLLEGIATE, WIN-KLER, MB, R6W 4C8
(204) 325-8008   *SIC* 8211
GARDEN VALLEY SCHOOL DIVISION *p361*
750 TRIPLE E BLVD, WINKLER, MB, R6W 0M7
(204) 325-8335   *SIC* 8211
GLENLYON-NORFOLK SCHOOL SOCIETY
p333
801 BANK ST, VICTORIA, BC, V8S 4A8
(250) 370-6801   *SIC* 8211
GOUVERNEMENT DE LA PROVINCE DE QUEBEC   *p1113*
1235 RUE DE LA DIGUE, HAVRE-SAINT-PIERRE, QC, G0G 1P0
(418) 538-2662   *SIC* 8211
GPRC FAIRVIEW CAMPUS   *p126*
11235 98TH AVE, FAIRVIEW, AB, T0H 1L0
(780) 835-6600   *SIC* 8211
GRAND ERIE DISTRICT SCHOOL BOARD
p516
627 COLBORNE ST, BRANTFORD, ON, N3S 3M8
(519) 756-1320   *SIC* 8211
GRAND ERIE DISTRICT SCHOOL BOARD
p516
349 ERIE AVE, BRANTFORD, ON, N3S 2H7
(519) 756-6301   *SIC* 8211
GRAND ERIE DISTRICT SCHOOL BOARD
p607
70 PARKVIEW RD, HAGERSVILLE, ON, N0A 1H0
(905) 768-3318   *SIC* 8211
GRAND ERIE DISTRICT SCHOOL BOARD
p880
40 WILSON AVE, SIMCOE, ON, N3Y 2E5
(519) 426-4664   *SIC* 8211
GRANDE PRAIRIE CATHOLIC SCHOOL DISTRICT 28   *p132*
9902 101 ST SUITE 28, GRANDE PRAIRIE, AB, T8V 2P4
(780) 532-3013   *SIC* 8211
GRANDE PRAIRIE PUBLIC SCHOOL DIS-TRICT #2357   *p132*
9351 116 AVE, GRANDE PRAIRIE, AB, T8V 6L5
(780) 830-3384   *SIC* 8211
GRANDE PRAIRIE PUBLIC SCHOOL DIS-TRICT #2357   *p132*
11202 104 ST SUITE 2357, GRANDE PRAIRIE, AB, T8V 2Z1
(780) 532-7721   *SIC* 8211
GRANDE PRAIRIE PUBLIC SCHOOL DIS-TRICT #2357   *p132*
10127 120 AVE, GRANDE PRAIRIE, AB, T8V 8H8
(780) 532-4491   *SIC* 8211
GRANDE YELLOWHEAD PUBLIC SCHOOL DIVISION 77   *p126*
3656 1 AVE SUITE 35, EDSON, AB, T7E 1N9
(780) 723-4471   *SIC* 8211
GRASSLANDS REGIONAL DIVISION 6 *p7*
745 2 AVE E SUITE 1, BROOKS, AB, T1R 1L2
(403) 793-6700   *SIC* 8211
GREATER ESSEX COUNTY DISTRICT SCHOOL BOARD   *p490*
333 SOUTH ST, BELLE RIVER, ON, N0R 1A0
(519) 728-1212   *SIC* 8211
GREATER ESSEX COUNTY DISTRICT SCHOOL BOARD   *p1018*
8465 JEROME ST, WINDSOR, ON, N8S 1W8
(519) 948-4116   *SIC* 8211

GREATER ESSEX COUNTY DISTRICT SCHOOL BOARD   *p1020*
1930 ROSSINI BLVD, WINDSOR, ON, N8W 4P5
(519) 944-4700   *SIC* 8211
GREATER ESSEX COUNTY DISTRICT SCHOOL BOARD   *p1021*
245 TECUMSEH RD E, WINDSOR, ON, N8X 2R2
(519) 254-6475   *SIC* 8211
GREATER ESSEX COUNTY DISTRICT SCHOOL BOARD   *p1022*
2100 RICHMOND ST, WINDSOR, ON, N8Y 1L4
(519) 252-6514   *SIC* 8211
GREATER ESSEX COUNTY DISTRICT SCHOOL BOARD   *p1023*
451 PARK ST W, WINDSOR, ON, N9A 5V4
(519) 255-3200   *SIC* 8211
GREATER ESSEX COUNTY DISTRICT SCHOOL BOARD   *p1024*
1375 CALIFORNIA AVE, WINDSOR, ON, N9B 2Z8
(519) 253-2481   *SIC* 8211
GREATER ESSEX COUNTY DISTRICT SCHOOL BOARD   *p1025*
1800 LIBERTY ST, WINDSOR, ON, N9E 1J2
(519) 969-2530   *SIC* 8211
GREATER ST. ALBERT ROMAN CATHOLIC SEPARATE SCHOOL DISTRICT NO. 734
p165
6 ST VITAL AVE, ST. ALBERT, AB, T8N 1K2
(780) 459-7711   *SIC* 8211
GREENWOOD COLLEGE SCHOOL   *p924*
443 MOUNT PLEASANT RD, TORONTO, ON, M4S 2L8
(416) 482-9811   *SIC* 8211
HALIFAX REGIONAL SCHOOL BOARD
p440
200 INNOVATION DR, BEDFORD, NS, B4B 0G4
(902) 832-8964   *SIC* 8211
HALIFAX REGIONAL SCHOOL BOARD
p444
95 VICTORIA RD, DARTMOUTH, NS, B3A 1V2
(902) 464-2457   *SIC* 8211
HALIFAX REGIONAL SCHOOL BOARD
p446
33 SPECTACLE LAKE DR, DARTMOUTH, NS, B3B 1X7
(902) 464-2000   *SIC* 8211
HALIFAX REGIONAL SCHOOL BOARD
p450
148 LOCKVIEW RD, FALL RIVER, NS, B2T 1J1
(902) 860-6000   *SIC* 8211
HALIFAX REGIONAL SCHOOL BOARD
p451
1855 TROLLOPE ST, HALIFAX, NS, B3H 0A4
(902) 491-4444   *SIC* 8211
HALIFAX REGIONAL SCHOOL BOARD
p458
283 THOMAS RADDALL DR, HALIFAX, NS, B3S 1R1
(902) 457-8900   *SIC* 8211
HALTON CATHOLIC DISTRICT SCHOOL BOARD   *p526*
2333 HEADON FOREST DR, BURLING-TON, ON, L7M 3X6
(905) 335-1544   *SIC* 8211
HALTON CATHOLIC DISTRICT SCHOOL BOARD   *p530*
802 DRURY LANE, BURLINGTON, ON, L7R 2Y2
(905) 632-6300   *SIC* 8211
HALTON CATHOLIC DISTRICT SCHOOL BOARD   *p593*
70 GUELPH ST, GEORGETOWN, ON, L7G 3Z5
(905) 877-6966   *SIC* 8211
HALTON CATHOLIC DISTRICT SCHOOL BOARD   *p593*

161 GUELPH ST, GEORGETOWN, ON, L7G 4A1
(905) 702-8838   *SIC* 8211
HALTON CATHOLIC DISTRICT SCHOOL BOARD   *p683*
1120 MAIN ST E, MILTON, ON, L9T 6H7
(905) 875-0124   *SIC* 8211
HALTON CATHOLIC DISTRICT SCHOOL BOARD   *p802*
124 DORVAL DR, OAKVILLE, ON, L6K 2W1
(905) 842-9494   *SIC* 8211
HALTON DISTRICT SCHOOL BOARD *p473*
69 ACTON BLVD, ACTON, ON, L7J 2H4
(519) 853-3800   *SIC* 8211
HALTON DISTRICT SCHOOL BOARD *p522*
4181 NEW ST, BURLINGTON, ON, L7L 1T3
(905) 637-3825   *SIC* 8211
HALTON DISTRICT SCHOOL BOARD *p522*
5151 NEW ST, BURLINGTON, ON, L7L 1V3
(905) 632-5151   *SIC* 8211
HALTON DISTRICT SCHOOL BOARD *p526*
3290 STEEPLECHASE DR, BURLINGTON, ON, L7M 0W1
(905) 332-4206   *SIC* 8211
HALTON DISTRICT SCHOOL BOARD *p526*
1433 HEADON RD, BURLINGTON, ON, L7M 1V7
(905) 335-0961   *SIC* 8211
HALTON DISTRICT SCHOOL BOARD *p529*
2425 UPPER MIDDLE RD, BURLINGTON, ON, L7P 3N9
(905) 335-5588   *SIC* 8211
HALTON DISTRICT SCHOOL BOARD *p529*
2050 GUELPH LINE, BURLINGTON, ON, L7P 5A8
(905) 335-3663   *SIC* 8211
HALTON DISTRICT SCHOOL BOARD *p529*
2399 MOUNTAINSIDE DR, BURLINGTON, ON, L7P 1C6
(905) 335-5605   *SIC* 8211
HALTON DISTRICT SCHOOL BOARD *p593*
170 EATON ST, GEORGETOWN, ON, L7G 5V6
(905) 877-0151   *SIC* 8211
HALTON DISTRICT SCHOOL BOARD *p682*
1110 FARMSTEAD DR, MILTON, ON, L9E 0B5
(905) 864-9641   *SIC* 8211
HALTON DISTRICT SCHOOL BOARD *p683*
820 FARMSTEAD DR, MILTON, ON, L9T 8J6
(905) 878-2076   *SIC* 8211
HALTON DISTRICT SCHOOL BOARD *p683*
396 WILLIAMS AVE, MILTON, ON, L9T 2G4
(905) 878-2839   *SIC* 8211
HALTON DISTRICT SCHOOL BOARD *p683*
1151 FERGUSON DR, MILTON, ON, L9T 7V8
(905) 878-0575   *SIC* 8211
HALTON DISTRICT SCHOOL BOARD *p683*
625 SAUVE ST, MILTON, ON, L9T 8M4
(905) 693-0712   *SIC* 8211
HALTON DISTRICT SCHOOL BOARD *p683*
650 YATES DR, MILTON, ON, L9T 7P6
(905) 878-2255   *SIC* 8211
HALTON DISTRICT SCHOOL BOARD *p797*
1330 MONTCLAIR DR, OAKVILLE, ON, L6H 1Z5
(905) 845-5200   *SIC* 8211
HALTON DISTRICT SCHOOL BOARD *p797*
1123 GLENASHTON DR, OAKVILLE, ON, L6H 5M1
(905) 845-0012   *SIC* 8211
HALTON DISTRICT SCHOOL BOARD *p800*
1460 DEVON RD, OAKVILLE, ON, L6J 3L6
(905) 845-2875   *SIC* 8211
HALTON DISTRICT SCHOOL BOARD *p803*
1160 REBECCA ST, OAKVILLE, ON, L6L 1Y9
(905) 827-1158   *SIC* 8211
HALTON DISTRICT SCHOOL BOARD *p803*
1160 REBECCA ST, OAKVILLE, ON, L6L 1Y9
(905) 827-1158   *SIC* 8211

HALTON DISTRICT SCHOOL BOARD *p805*
2561 VALLEYRIDGE DR, OAKVILLE, ON, L6M 5H4
(905) 469-1138   *SIC* 8211
HALTON DISTRICT SCHOOL BOARD *p805*
2071 FOURTH LINE, OAKVILLE, ON, L6M 3K1
(905) 469-6119   *SIC* 8211
HALTON DISTRICT SCHOOL BOARD *p805*
2820 WESTOAK TRAILS BLVD, OAKVILLE, ON, L6M 4W2
(905) 847-6875   *SIC* 8211
HALTON DISTRICT SCHOOL BOARD *p805*
1455 GLEN ABBEY GATE, OAKVILLE, ON, L6M 2G5
(905) 827-4101   *SIC* 8211
HAMILTON-WENTWORTH CATHOLIC SCHOOL BOARD   *p493*
200 WINDWOOD DR, BINBROOK, ON, L0R 1C0
(905) 523-2316   *SIC* 8211
HAMILTON-WENTWORTH CATHOLIC SCHOOL BOARD   *p614*
90 MULBERRY ST, HAMILTON, ON, L8R 2C8
SIC 8211
HAMILTON-WENTWORTH CATHOLIC SCHOOL BOARD   *p614*
90 MULBERRY ST, HAMILTON, ON, L8R 2C8
(905) 525-2930   *SIC* 8211
HAMILTON-WENTWORTH CATHOLIC SCHOOL BOARD   *p614*
200 WHITNEY AVE, HAMILTON, ON, L8S 2G7
(905) 528-0214   *SIC* 8211
HAMILTON-WENTWORTH CATHOLIC SCHOOL BOARD   *p615*
150 EAST 5TH ST, HAMILTON, ON, L9A 2Z8
(905) 575-5202   *SIC* 8211
HAMILTON-WENTWORTH CATHOLIC SCHOOL BOARD   *p615*
200 ACADIA DR, HAMILTON, ON, L8W 1B8
(905) 388-7020   *SIC* 8211
HAMILTON-WENTWORTH CATHOLIC SCHOOL BOARD   *p616*
1045 UPPER PARADISE RD, HAMILTON, ON, L9B 2N4
(905) 388-1178   *SIC* 8211
HAMILTON-WENTWORTH CATHOLIC SCHOOL BOARD   *p617*
1824 RYMAL RD, HANNON, ON, L0R 1P0
(905) 573-2151   *SIC* 8211
HAMILTON-WENTWORTH CATHOLIC SCHOOL BOARD   *p894*
127 GRAY RD, STONEY CREEK, ON, L8G 3V3
(905) 523-2314   *SIC* 8211
HAMILTON-WENTWORTH DISTRICT SCHOOL BOARD, THE   *p477*
374 JERSEYVILLE RD W, ANCASTER, ON, L9G 3K8
(905) 648-4468   *SIC* 8211
HAMILTON-WENTWORTH DISTRICT SCHOOL BOARD, THE   *p566*
310 GOVERNORS RD, DUNDAS, ON, L9H 5P8
(905) 628-2203   *SIC* 8211
HAMILTON-WENTWORTH DISTRICT SCHOOL BOARD, THE   *p614*
700 MAIN ST W, HAMILTON, ON, L8S 1A5
(905) 522-1387   *SIC* 8211
HAMILTON-WENTWORTH DISTRICT SCHOOL BOARD, THE   *p614*
130 YORK BLVD, HAMILTON, ON, L8R 1Y5
(905) 528-8363   *SIC* 8211
HAMILTON-WENTWORTH DISTRICT SCHOOL BOARD, THE   *p614*
75 PALMER RD, HAMILTON, ON, L8T 3G1
(905) 389-2234   *SIC* 8211
HAMILTON-WENTWORTH DISTRICT SCHOOL BOARD, THE   *p616*
39 MONTCALM DR, HAMILTON, ON, L9C

4B1

(905) 385-5395 *SIC* 8211
HAMILTON-WENTWORTH DISTRICT SCHOOL BOARD, THE *p616*
20 EDUCATION CRT, HAMILTON, ON, L9A 0B9

(905) 527-5092 *SIC* 8211
HAMILTON-WENTWORTH DISTRICT SCHOOL BOARD, THE *p616*
465 EAST 16TH ST, HAMILTON, ON, L9A 4K6

(905) 318-1291 *SIC* 8211
HAMILTON-WENTWORTH DISTRICT SCHOOL BOARD, THE *p616*
145 MAGNOLIA DR, HAMILTON, ON, L9C 5P4

(905) 383-3337 *SIC* 8211
HAMILTON-WENTWORTH DISTRICT SCHOOL BOARD, THE *p892*
200 DEWITT RD, STONEY CREEK, ON, L8E 4M5

(905) 573-3550 *SIC* 8211
HAMILTON-WENTWORTH DISTRICT SCHOOL BOARD, THE *p894*
108 HIGHLAND RD W, STONEY CREEK, ON, L8J 2T2

(905) 573-3000 *SIC* 8211
HAMILTON-WENTWORTH DISTRICT SCHOOL BOARD, THE *p1005*
215 PARKSIDE DR, WATERDOWN, ON, L8B 1B9

(905) 689-6692 *SIC* 8211
HANOVER SCHOOL DIVISION *p358*
190 MCKENZIE AVE, STEINBACH, MB, R5G 0P1

(204) 326-6426 *SIC* 8211
HANOVER SCHOOL DIVISION *p358*
5 CHRYSLER GATE, STEINBACH, MB, R5G 0E2

(204) 326-6471 *SIC* 8211
HASTINGS AND PRINCE EDWARD DISTRICT SCHOOL BOARD *p484*
16 MONCK ST SUITE 14, BANCROFT, ON, K0L 1C0

(613) 332-1220 *SIC* 8211
HASTINGS AND PRINCE EDWARD DISTRICT SCHOOL BOARD *p492*
160 PALMER RD, BELLEVILLE, ON, K8P 4E1

(613) 962-9233 *SIC* 8211
HASTINGS AND PRINCE EDWARD DISTRICT SCHOOL BOARD *p492*
45 COLLEGE ST W, BELLEVILLE, ON, K8P 2G3

(613) 962-9295 *SIC* 8211
HASTINGS AND PRINCE EDWARD DISTRICT SCHOOL BOARD *p492*
224 PALMER RD, BELLEVILLE, ON, K8P 4E1

(613) 962-2516 *SIC* 8211
HASTINGS AND PRINCE EDWARD DISTRICT SCHOOL BOARD *p845*
41 BARKER ST, PICTON, ON, K0K 2T0
(613) 476-2196 *SIC* 8211
HASTINGS AND PRINCE EDWARD DISTRICT SCHOOL BOARD *p999*
15 FOURTH AVE, TRENTON, ON, K8V 5N4
(613) 392-1227 *SIC* 8211
HAVERGAL COLLEGE *p788*
1451 AVENUE RD, NORTH YORK, ON, M5N 2H9

(416) 483-3519 *SIC* 8211
HEBREW ACADEMY INC *p1083*
5700 AV KELLERT, COTE SAINT-LUC, QC, H4W 1T4

(514) 489-5321 *SIC* 8211
HEBREW FOUNDATION SCHOOL OF CONGREGATION BETH TIKVAH *p1090*
2 RUE HOPE, DOLLARD-DES-ORMEAUX, QC, H9A 2V5

(514) 684-6270 *SIC* 8211
HIGH PRAIRIE SCHOOL DIVISION NO 48 *p135*
16532 TOWNSHIP RD 744, HIGH PRAIRIE,

AB, T0G 1E0

(780) 523-3337 *SIC* 8211
HILLFIELD-STRATHALLAN COLLEGE *p617*
299 FENNELL AVE W, HAMILTON, ON, L9C 1G3

(905) 389-1367 *SIC* 8211
HOLY FAMILY CATHOLIC REGIONAL DIVISION 37 *p152*
10307 99 ST, PEACE RIVER, AB, T8S 1K1

(780) 624-3956 *SIC* 8211
HOLY FAMILY ROMAN CATHOLIC SEPARATE SCHOOL DIVISION 140 *p1406*
1118 2ND ST, ESTEVAN, SK, S4A 0L9
(306) 634-5995 *SIC* 8211
HOLY FAMILY ROMAN CATHOLIC SEPARATE SCHOOL DIVISION 140 *p1437*
110 SOURIS AVE SUITE 3, WEYBURN, SK, S4H 2Z8

(306) 842-7025 *SIC* 8211
HOLY TRINITY ROMAN CATHOLIC SEPARATE SCHOOL DIVISION #22 *p1411*
502 6TH AVE NE, MOOSE JAW, SK, S6H 6B8

(306) 694-5333 *SIC* 8211
HOLY TRINITY SCHOOL (CO-EDUCATIONAL) RICHMOND HILL *p856*
11300 BAYVIEW AVE, RICHMOND HILL, ON, L4S 1L4

(905) 737-1114 *SIC* 8211
HORIZON SCHOOL DIVISION NO 205 *p1407*
10333 8TH AVE, HUMBOLDT, SK, S0K 2A0
(306) 682-2558 *SIC* 8211
HURON PERTH CATHOLIC DISTRICT SCHOOL BOARD *p566*
87 MILL ST, DUBLIN, ON, N0K 1E0
(519) 345-2440 *SIC* 8211
HURON-SUPERIOR CATHOLIC DISTRICT SCHOOL BOARD *p863*
90 ONTARIO AVE, SAULT STE. MARIE, ON, P6B 6G7

(705) 945-5400 *SIC* 8211
HUTTERIAN BRETHREN *p171*
GD, WARNER, AB, T0K 2L0
(403) 642-2407 *SIC* 8211
INSTITUT CANADIEN POUR DEVELOPPEMENT NEURO-INTEGRATIF, L *p1229*
5460 AV CONNAUGHT, MONTREAL, QC, H4V 1X7

(514) 935-1911 *SIC* 8211
INTERLAKE SCHOOL DIVISION *p359*
192 2ND AVE N, STONEWALL, MB, R0C 2Z0

(204) 467-5100 *SIC* 8211
JEWISH PEOPLE'S SCHOOLS AND PERETZ SCHOOLS INC *p1083*
6500 CH KILDARE, COTE SAINT-LUC, QC, H4W 3B8

SIC 8211
JEWISH PEOPLE'S SCHOOLS AND PERETZ SCHOOLS INC *p1083*
6500 CH KILDARE, COTE SAINT-LUC, QC, H4W 3B8

(514) 731-3841 *SIC* 8211
K R T CHRISTIAN SCHOOLS *p508*
141 KENNEDY RD N, BRAMPTON, ON, L6V 1X9

(905) 459-2300 *SIC* 8211
KAWARTHA PINE RIDGE DISTRICT SCHOOL BOARD *p496*
200 CLARINGTON BLVD, BOWMANVILLE, ON, L1C 5N8

(905) 697-9857 *SIC* 8211
KAWARTHA PINE RIDGE DISTRICT SCHOOL BOARD *p518*
71 DUNDAS ST, BRIGHTON, ON, K0K 1H0
(613) 475-0540 *SIC* 8211
KAWARTHA PINE RIDGE DISTRICT SCHOOL BOARD *p539*
119 RANNEY ST N UNIT 960, CAMPBELLFORD, ON, K0L 1L0

(705) 653-3060 *SIC* 8211
KAWARTHA PINE RIDGE DISTRICT SCHOOL BOARD *p545*
335 KING ST E, COBOURG, ON, K9A 1M2

(905) 372-2271 *SIC* 8211
KAWARTHA PINE RIDGE DISTRICT SCHOOL BOARD *p563*
1717 NASH RD, COURTICE, ON, L1E 2L8
(905) 436-2074 *SIC* 8211
KAWARTHA PINE RIDGE DISTRICT SCHOOL BOARD *p841*
633 MONAGHAN RD, PETERBOROUGH, ON, K9J 5J2

(705) 743-2181 *SIC* 8211
KEEWATIN PATRICIA DISTRICT SCHOOL BOARD *p628*
1400 NINTH ST N, KENORA, ON, P9N 2T7
(807) 468-6401 *SIC* 8211
KEEWATIN PATRICIA DISTRICT SCHOOL BOARD *p628*
240 VETERANS DR 4TH FL, KENORA, ON, P9N 3Y5

(807) 468-5571 *SIC* 8211
KELSEY SCHOOL DIVISION *p359*
322 EDWARDS AVE, THE PAS, MB, R9A 1R4

(204) 623-6421 *SIC* 8211
LABRADOR SCHOOL BOARD *p424*
16 STRATHCONA ST, HAPPY VALLEY-GOOSE BAY, NL, A0P 1E0
(709) 896-7220 *SIC* 8211
LAKEHEAD DISTRICT SCHOOL BOARD *p908*
174 MARLBOROUGH ST, THUNDER BAY, ON, P7B 4G4

(807) 345-1468 *SIC* 8211
LAKEHEAD DISTRICT SCHOOL BOARD *p908*
80 CLARKSON ST S, THUNDER BAY, ON, P7B 4W8

(807) 767-1631 *SIC* 8211
LAKEHEAD DISTRICT SCHOOL BOARD *p909*
130 CHURCHILL DR W, THUNDER BAY, ON, P7C 1V5

SIC 8211
LAKELAND ROMAN CATHOLIC SEPARATE SCHOOL DISTRICT NO. 150 *p6*
4810 46 ST, BONNYVILLE, AB, T9N 2R2
(780) 826-3764 *SIC* 8211
LAKESHORE SCHOOL DIVISION *p349*
23 SECOND AVE, ERIKSDALE, MB, R0C 0W0

(204) 739-2101 *SIC* 8211
LAMBTON KENT DISTRICT SCHOOL BOARD *p542*
285 MCNAUGHTON AVE E, CHATHAM, ON, N7L 2G7

(519) 352-2870 *SIC* 8211
LAMBTON KENT DISTRICT SCHOOL BOARD *p543*
300 CECILE AVE, CHATHAM, ON, N7M 2C6

(519) 354-1740 *SIC* 8211
LAMBTON KENT DISTRICT SCHOOL BOARD *p843*
4141 DUFFERIN AVE, PETROLIA, ON, N0N 1R0

(519) 882-1910 *SIC* 8211
LAMBTON KENT DISTRICT SCHOOL BOARD *p858*
1257 MICHIGAN AVE, SARNIA, ON, N7S 3Y3

(519) 542-5505 *SIC* 8211
LAMBTON KENT DISTRICT SCHOOL BOARD *p858*
340 MURPHY RD, SARNIA, ON, N7S 2X1
(519) 332-1140 *SIC* 8211
LAMBTON KENT DISTRICT SCHOOL BOARD *p860*
275 WELLINGTON ST, SARNIA, ON, N7T 1H1

(519) 336-6131 *SIC* 8211
LAMBTON KENT DISTRICT SCHOOL BOARD *p860*
200 WELLINGTON ST SUITE 2019, SARNIA, ON, N7T 7L2

(519) 336-1500 *SIC* 8211

LAMBTON KENT DISTRICT SCHOOL BOARD *p1005*
920 ELGIN ST, WALLACEBURG, ON, N8A 3E1

(519) 627-3368 *SIC* 8211
LESTER B. PEARSON SCHOOL BOARD *p1054*
250 BEAUREPAIRE DR, BEACONSFIELD, QC, H9W 5G7

(514) 697-7220 *SIC* 8211
LESTER B. PEARSON SCHOOL BOARD *p1128*
5050 RUE SHERBROOKE, LACHINE, QC, H8T 1H8

(514) 637-2505 *SIC* 8211
LESTER B. PEARSON SCHOOL BOARD *p1131*
2241 RUE MENARD, LASALLE, QC, H8N 1J4

(514) 595-2043 *SIC* 8211
LESTER B. PEARSON SCHOOL BOARD *p1131*
8310 RUE GEORGE, LASALLE, QC, H8P 1E5

(514) 363-6213 *SIC* 8211
LESTER B. PEARSON SCHOOL BOARD *p1245*
5060 BOUL DES SOURCES, PIERREFONDS, QC, H8Y 3E4

(514) 684-2337 *SIC* 8211
LESTER B. PEARSON SCHOOL BOARD *p1251*
111 AV BROADVIEW, POINTE-CLAIRE, QC, H9R 3Z3

(514) 694-2760 *SIC* 8211
LESTER B. PEARSON SCHOOL BOARD *p1251*
120 AV AMBASSADOR, POINTE-CLAIRE, QC, H9R 1S8

(514) 694-3770 *SIC* 8211
LESTER B. PEARSON SCHOOL BOARD *p1251*
501 BOUL SAINT-JEAN, POINTE-CLAIRE, QC, H9R 3J5

(514) 697-3210 *SIC* 8211
LESTER B. PEARSON SCHOOL BOARD *p1355*
17 RUE MAPLE, SAINTE-ANNE-DE-BELLEVUE, QC, H9X 2E5

(514) 457-3770 *SIC* 8211
LESTER B. PEARSON SCHOOL BOARD *p1397*
6100 BOUL CHAMPLAIN, VERDUN, QC, H4H 1A5

(514) 766-2357 *SIC* 8211
LETHBRIDGE SCHOOL DISTRICT NO. 51 *p141*
1605 15 AVE N, LETHBRIDGE, AB, T1H 1W4

(403) 328-4723 *SIC* 8211
LETHBRIDGE SCHOOL DISTRICT NO. 51 *p141*
2003 9 AVE N, LETHBRIDGE, AB, T1H 1J3
(403) 329-3144 *SIC* 8211
LETHBRIDGE SCHOOL DISTRICT NO. 51 *p142*
433 15 ST S, LETHBRIDGE, AB, T1J 2Z4
(403) 380-5321 *SIC* 8211
LIGHT OF CHRIST RCSSD *p1412*
9301 19TH AVE, NORTH BATTLEFORD, SK, S9A 3N5

(306) 445-6158 *SIC* 8211
LIGHT OF CHRIST RCSSD *p1412*
1491 97TH ST, NORTH BATTLEFORD, SK, S9A 0K1

(306) 446-2232 *SIC* 8211
LIMESTONE DISTRICT SCHOOL BOARD *p630*
145 KIRKPATRICK ST, KINGSTON, ON, K7K 2P4

SIC 8211
LIMESTONE DISTRICT SCHOOL BOARD *p631*
773 HIGHWAY 15, KINGSTON, ON, K7L

5H6

(613) 546-1737   *SIC* 8211
LIMESTONE DISTRICT SCHOOL BOARD
p632
1789 BATH RD, KINGSTON, ON, K7M 4Y3
(613) 389-2130   *SIC* 8211
LIMESTONE DISTRICT SCHOOL BOARD
p632
153 VAN ORDER DR, KINGSTON, ON, K7M 1B9
(613) 546-5575   *SIC* 8211
LIMESTONE DISTRICT SCHOOL BOARD
p632
153 VAN ORDER DR, KINGSTON, ON, K7M 1B9
(613) 542-9871   *SIC* 8211
LIMESTONE DISTRICT SCHOOL BOARD
p632
1059 TAYLOR-KIDD BLVD, KINGSTON, ON, K7M 6J9
(613) 389-8932   *SIC* 8211
LIMESTONE DISTRICT SCHOOL BOARD
p747
245 BELLEVILLE RD, NAPANEE, ON, K7R 3M7
(613) 354-3381   *SIC* 8211
LIMESTONE DISTRICT SCHOOL BOARD
p902
2860 RUTLEDGE RD, SYDENHAM, ON, K0H 2T0
(613) 376-3612   *SIC* 8211
LINDEN CHRISTIAN SCHOOL INC   *p389*
877 WILKES AVE, WINNIPEG, MB, R3P 1B8
(204) 989-6730   *SIC* 8211
LITTLE RED RIVER CREE NATION BOARD OF EDUCATION   *p130*
GD, FOX LAKE, AB, T0H 1R0
(780) 759-3912   *SIC* 8211
LIVING WATERS CATHOLIC REGIONAL DIVISION NO.42   *p173*
4204 KEPLER ST UNIT 1, WHITECOURT, AB, T7S 0A3
(780) 778-5044   *SIC* 8211
LLOYDMINSTER SCHOOL DIVISION NO 99
p144
5017 46 ST SUITE 99, LLOYDMINSTER, AB, T9V 1R4
(780) 875-5541   *SIC* 8211
LORD SELKIRK SCHOOL DIVISION, THE
p356
205 MERCY ST, SELKIRK, MB, R1A 2C8
(204) 482-5942   *SIC* 8211
LORD SELKIRK SCHOOL DIVISION, THE
p356
221 MERCY ST, SELKIRK, MB, R1A 2C8
(204) 482-6926   *SIC* 8211
LOUIS RIEL SCHOOL DIVISION   *p366*
831 BEAVERHILL BLVD, WINNIPEG, MB, R2J 3K1
(204) 257-0637   *SIC* 8211
LOUIS RIEL SCHOOL DIVISION   *p368*
661 DAKOTA ST, WINNIPEG, MB, R2M 3K3
(204) 256-4366   *SIC* 8211
LOUIS RIEL SCHOOL DIVISION   *p368*
770 ST MARY'S RD, WINNIPEG, MB, R2M 3N7
(204) 233-3263   *SIC* 8211
LOUIS RIEL SCHOOL DIVISION   *p368*
900 ST MARY'S RD, WINNIPEG, MB, R2M 3R3
(204) 257-7827   *SIC* 8211
LOWER CANADA COLLEGE   *p1221*
4090 AV ROYAL, MONTREAL, QC, H4A 2M5
(514) 482-9916   *SIC* 8211
LYCEE CLAUDEL   *p818*
1635 RIVERSIDE DR, OTTAWA, ON, K1G 0E5
(613) 733-8522   *SIC* 8211
MEDICINE HAT CATHOLIC BOARD OF EDUCATION   *p145*
1251 1 AVE SW SUITE 20, MEDICINE HAT, AB, T1A 8B4

(403) 527-2292   *SIC* 8211
MEDICINE HAT SCHOOL DISTRICT NO. 76
p146
601 1 AVE SW, MEDICINE HAT, AB, T1A 4Y7
(403) 528-6700   *SIC* 8211
MEDICINE HAT SCHOOL DISTRICT NO. 76
p146
1201 DIVISION AVE N, MEDICINE HAT, AB, T1A 5Y8
(403) 527-6641   *SIC* 8211
MENNONITE EDUCATIONAL INSTITUTE SOCIETY   *p178*
4081 CLEARBROOK RD, ABBOTSFORD, BC, V4X 2M8
(604) 859-3700   *SIC* 8211
MIALTA HUTTERIAN BRETHREN   *p171*
GD, VULCAN, AB, T0L 2B0
SIC 8211
MIYO WAHKOHTOWIN COMMUNITY EDUCATION AUTHORITY   *p136*
GD, HOBBEMA, AB, T0C 1N0
(780) 585-2118   *SIC* 8211
MOHAWK COUNCIL OF AKWESASNE   *p475*
169 AKWESASNE INTERNATIONAL RD, AKWESASNE, ON, K6H 0G5
(613) 933-0409   *SIC* 8211
MOUNTAIN VIEW SCHOOL DIVISION   *p348*
182519 SW, DAUPHIN, MB, R7N 3B3
(204) 638-3001   *SIC* 8211
MOUNTAIN VIEW SCHOOL DIVISION   *p349*
330 MOUNTAIN RD, DAUPHIN, MB, R7N 2V6
(204) 638-4629   *SIC* 8211
MULGRAVE INDEPENDENT SCHOOL SOCIETY   *p341*
2330 CYPRESS BOWL LANE, WEST VANCOUVER, BC, V7S 3H9
(604) 922-3223   *SIC* 8211
NEAR NORTH DISTRICT SCHOOL BOARD
p764
963 AIRPORT RD, NORTH BAY, ON, P1C 1A5
(705) 472-8170   *SIC* 8211
NELSON HOUSE EDUCATION AUTHORITY, INC   *p353*
8 BAY RD, NELSON HOUSE, MB, R0B 1A0
(204) 484-2095   *SIC* 8211
NEWFOUNDLAND AND LABRADOR ENGLISH SCHOOL DISTRICT   *p423*
55 FRASER RD, GANDER, NL, A1V 1K8
(709) 256-8531   *SIC* 8211
NIAGARA CATHOLIC DISTRICT SCHOOL BOARD   *p760*
3834 WINDERMERE RD, NIAGARA FALLS, ON, L2J 2Y5
(905) 356-4313   *SIC* 8211
NIAGARA CATHOLIC DISTRICT SCHOOL BOARD   *p760*
8699 MCLEOD RD, NIAGARA FALLS, ON, L2H 0Z2
(905) 356-5155   *SIC* 8211
NIAGARA CATHOLIC DISTRICT SCHOOL BOARD   *p846*
150 JANET ST, PORT COLBORNE, ON, L3K 2E7
(905) 835-2451   *SIC* 8211
NIAGARA CATHOLIC DISTRICT SCHOOL BOARD   *p883*
460 LINWELL RD, ST CATHARINES, ON, L2M 2P9
(905) 937-6446   *SIC* 8211
NIAGARA CATHOLIC DISTRICT SCHOOL BOARD   *p887*
40 GLEN MORRIS DR, ST CATHARINES, ON, L2T 2M9
(905) 684-8731   *SIC* 8211
NIAGARA CATHOLIC DISTRICT SCHOOL BOARD   *p1012*
64 SMITH ST, WELLAND, ON, L3C 4H4
(905) 788-3060   *SIC* 8211
NIAGARA CATHOLIC DISTRICT SCHOOL BOARD   *p1012*
427 RICE RD, WELLAND, ON, L3C 7C1

(905) 562-1321   *SIC* 8211
NORTH EAST SCHOOL DIVISION   *p1410*
402 MAIN ST, MELFORT, SK, S0E 1A0
(306) 752-5741   *SIC* 8211
NORTH OKANAGAN SHUSWAP SCHOOL DISTRICT 83   *p179*
2365 PLEASANT VALLEY RD, ARMSTRONG, BC, V0E 1B2
(250) 546-3114   *SIC* 8211
NORTHEASTERN CATHOLIC DISTRICT SCHOOL BOARD   *p913*
383 BIRCH ST N, TIMMINS, ON, P4N 6E8
(705) 268-7443   *SIC* 8211
NORTHERN GATEWAY REGIONAL DIVISION #10   *p173*
4816 49 AVE, WHITECOURT, AB, T7S 0E8
(780) 778-2800   *SIC* 8211
NORTHERN LIGHTS SCHOOL DIVISION 113   *p1408*
108 FINLAYSON ST, LA RONGE, SK, S0J 1L0
(306) 425-3302   *SIC* 8211
NORTHERN LIGHTS SCHOOL DIVISION NO. 69   *p6*
6005 50 AVE, BONNYVILLE, AB, T9N 2L4
(780) 826-3145   *SIC* 8211
NORTHLAND SCHOOL DIVISION 61   *p152*
9809 77 AVE, PEACE RIVER, AB, T8S 1C9
(780) 624-2060   *SIC* 8211
NORTHWEST CATHOLIC DISTRICT SCHOOL BOARD, THE   *p592*
555 FLINDERS AVE, FORT FRANCES, ON, P9A 3L2
(807) 274-2931   *SIC* 8211
NUNAVUT ARCTIC COLLEGE   *p472*
GD, IQALUIT, NU, X0A 0H0
(867) 979-7200   *SIC* 8211
OPAWIKOSCIKEN SCHOOL   *p1413*
GD, PELICAN NARROWS, SK, S0P 0E0
(306) 632-2161   *SIC* 8211
OTTAWA CATHOLIC DISTRICT SCHOOL BOARD   *p596*
2072 JASMINE CRES, GLOUCESTER, ON, K1J 8M5
(613) 741-4525   *SIC* 8211
OTTAWA CATHOLIC DISTRICT SCHOOL BOARD   *p625*
5115 KANATA AVE, KANATA, ON, K2K 3K5
(613) 271-4254   *SIC* 8211
OTTAWA CATHOLIC DISTRICT SCHOOL BOARD   *p663*
1040 DOZOIS RD, MANOTICK, ON, K4M 1B2
(613) 692-2551   *SIC* 8211
OTTAWA CATHOLIC DISTRICT SCHOOL BOARD   *p750*
570 WEST HUNT CLUB RD, NEPEAN, ON, K2G 3R4
(613) 224-2222   *SIC* 8211
OTTAWA CATHOLIC DISTRICT SCHOOL BOARD   *p752*
3333 GREENBANK RD, NEPEAN, ON, K2J 4J1
(613) 823-4797   *SIC* 8211
OTTAWA CATHOLIC DISTRICT SCHOOL BOARD   *p752*
440 LONGFIELDS DR, NEPEAN, ON, K2J 4T1
(613) 823-1663   *SIC* 8211
OTTAWA CATHOLIC DISTRICT SCHOOL BOARD   *p810*
6550 BILBERRY DR, ORLEANS, ON, K1C 2S9
(613) 837-3161   *SIC* 8211
OTTAWA CATHOLIC DISTRICT SCHOOL BOARD   *p811*
750 CHARLEMAGNE BLVD, ORLEANS, ON, K4A 3M4
(613) 837-9377   *SIC* 8211
OTTAWA CATHOLIC DISTRICT SCHOOL BOARD   *p826*
140 MAIN ST, OTTAWA, ON, K1S 5P4
(613) 237-2001   *SIC* 8211
OTTAWA CATHOLIC DISTRICT SCHOOL

BOARD   *p829*
710 BROADVIEW AVE, OTTAWA, ON, K2A 2M2
(613) 722-6565   *SIC* 8211
OTTAWA CATHOLIC DISTRICT SCHOOL BOARD   *p831*
1481 FISHER AVE, OTTAWA, ON, K2C 1X4
(613) 225-8105   *SIC* 8211
OTTAWA CATHOLIC DISTRICT SCHOOL BOARD   *p832*
2675 DRAPER AVE, OTTAWA, ON, K2H 7A1
(613) 820-9705   *SIC* 8211
OTTAWA CATHOLIC DISTRICT SCHOOL BOARD   *p891*
SACRED HEART CATHOLIC HIGH SCHOOL, STITTSVILLE, ON, K2S 1X4
(613) 831-6643   *SIC* 8211
OTTAWA-CARLETON DISTRICT SCHOOL BOARD   *p567*
3088 DUNROBIN RD, DUNROBIN, ON, K0A 1T0
(613) 832-0126   *SIC* 8211
OTTAWA-CARLETON DISTRICT SCHOOL BOARD   *p596*
2060 OGILVIE RD, GLOUCESTER, ON, K1J 7N8
(613) 745-7176   *SIC* 8211
OTTAWA-CARLETON DISTRICT SCHOOL BOARD   *p625*
150 ABBEYHILL DR, KANATA, ON, K2L 1H7
(613) 836-2527   *SIC* 8211
OTTAWA-CARLETON DISTRICT SCHOOL BOARD   *p625*
4 PARKWAY THE, KANATA, ON, K2K 1Y4
(613) 592-3361   *SIC* 8211
OTTAWA-CARLETON DISTRICT SCHOOL BOARD   *p681*
2800 8TH LINE RD, METCALFE, ON, K0A 2P0
(613) 821-2241   *SIC* 8211
OTTAWA-CARLETON DISTRICT SCHOOL BOARD   *p750*
1755 MERIVALE RD, NEPEAN, ON, K2G 1E2
(613) 224-1807   *SIC* 8211
OTTAWA-CARLETON DISTRICT SCHOOL BOARD   *p751*
131 GREENBANK RD, NEPEAN, ON, K2H 8R1
(613) 721-1820   *SIC* 8211
OTTAWA-CARLETON DISTRICT SCHOOL BOARD   *p751*
40 CASSIDY RD, NEPEAN, ON, K2H 6K1
(613) 828-9101   *SIC* 8211
OTTAWA-CARLETON DISTRICT SCHOOL BOARD   *p751*
133 GREENBANK RD, NEPEAN, ON, K2H 6L3
(613) 721-1820   *SIC* 8211
OTTAWA-CARLETON DISTRICT SCHOOL BOARD   *p752*
103 MALVERN DR, NEPEAN, ON, K2J 4T2
(613) 823-0367   *SIC* 8211
OTTAWA-CARLETON DISTRICT SCHOOL BOARD   *p818*
900 CANTERBURY AVE, OTTAWA, ON, K1G 3A7
(613) 731-1191   *SIC* 8211
OTTAWA-CARLETON DISTRICT SCHOOL BOARD   *p818*
1900 DAUPHIN RD, OTTAWA, ON, K1G 2L7
(613) 733-1755   *SIC* 8211
OTTAWA-CARLETON DISTRICT SCHOOL BOARD   *p820*
815 ST. LAURENT BLVD, OTTAWA, ON, K1K 3A7
SIC 8211
OTTAWA-CARLETON DISTRICT SCHOOL BOARD   *p825*
300 ROCHESTER ST SUITE 302, OTTAWA, ON, K1R 7N4
(613) 239-2416   *SIC* 8211

OTTAWA-CARLETON DISTRICT SCHOOL BOARD p826
212 GLEBE AVE, OTTAWA, ON, K1S 2C9
(613) 239-2424   SIC 8211

OTTAWA-CARLETON DISTRICT SCHOOL BOARD p827
824 BROOKFIELD RD, OTTAWA, ON, K1V 6J3
(613) 733-0610   SIC 8211

OTTAWA-CARLETON DISTRICT SCHOOL BOARD p827
2597 ALTA VISTA DR, OTTAWA, ON, K1V 7T3
(613) 733-4860   SIC 8211

OTTAWA-CARLETON DISTRICT SCHOOL BOARD p829
574 BROADVIEW AVE, OTTAWA, ON, K2A 3V8
(613) 722-6551   SIC 8211

OTTAWA-CARLETON DISTRICT SCHOOL BOARD p829
590 BROADVIEW AVE, OTTAWA, ON, K2A 2L8
(613) 728-1721   SIC 8211

OTTAWA-CARLETON DISTRICT SCHOOL BOARD p830
2410 GEORGINA DR, OTTAWA, ON, K2B 7M8
(613) 820-7186   SIC 8211

OTTAWA-CARLETON DISTRICT SCHOOL BOARD p831
55 CENTREPOINTE DR, OTTAWA, ON, K2G 5L4
(613) 723-5136   SIC 8211

OTTAWA-CARLETON DISTRICT SCHOOL BOARD p834
29 LISGAR ST, OTTAWA, ON, K2P 0B9
(613) 239-2696   SIC 8211

OTTAWA-CARLETON DISTRICT SCHOOL BOARD p850
3673 MCBEAN ST, RICHMOND, ON, K0A 2Z0
(613) 838-2212   SIC 8211

PACIFIC PENTECOSTAL EDUCATION AND COMMUNICATION SOCIETY p282
10238 168 ST, SURREY, BC, V4N 1Z4
(604) 581-0132   SIC 8211

PARK WEST SCHOOL DIVISION p345
1161 ST CLARE ST N, BIRTLE, MB, R0M 0C0
(204) 842-2100   SIC 8211

PARKLAND SCHOOL DIVISION NO. 70 p164
1000 CALAHOO RD, SPRUCE GROVE, AB, T7X 2T7
(780) 962-0800   SIC 8211

PARKLAND SCHOOL DIVISION NO. 70 p164
505 MCLEOD AVE SUITE 505, SPRUCE GROVE, AB, T7X 2Y5
(780) 962-0212   SIC 8211

PARKLAND SCHOOL DIVISION NO. 70 p167
4603 48 ST, STONY PLAIN, AB, T7Z 2A8
(780) 963-4010   SIC 8211

PATHWAYS TO EDUCATION CANADA p947
439 UNIVERSITY AVE SUITE 1600, TORONTO, ON, M5G 1Y8
(416) 646-0123   SIC 8211

PEACE RIVER SCHOOL DIVISION 10 p152
10018 101 ST SUITE 10, PEACE RIVER, AB, T8S 2A5
(780) 624-3601   SIC 8211

PEACE WAPITI SCHOOL DIVISION NO.76 p133
8611A 108 ST, GRANDE PRAIRIE, AB, T8V 4C5
(780) 532-8133   SIC 8211

PEEL DISTRICT SCHOOL BOARD p498
275 FERNFOREST DR, BRAMPTON, ON, L6R 1L9
(905) 793-6157   SIC 8211

PEEL DISTRICT SCHOOL BOARD p499
10 NORTH PARK DR, BRAMPTON, ON, L6S 3M1
(905) 456-1906   SIC 8211

PEEL DISTRICT SCHOOL BOARD p499

1305 WILLIAMS PKY, BRAMPTON, ON, L6S 3J8
(905) 791-6770   SIC 8211

PEEL DISTRICT SCHOOL BOARD p499
1370 WILLIAMS PKY, BRAMPTON, ON, L6S 1V3
(905) 791-2400   SIC 8211

PEEL DISTRICT SCHOOL BOARD p505
5000 MAYFIELD RD RR 4, BRAMPTON, ON, L6T 3S1
(905) 846-6060   SIC 8211

PEEL DISTRICT SCHOOL BOARD p505
215 ORENDA RD, BRAMPTON, ON, L6T 5L1
(905) 451-2862   SIC 8211

PEEL DISTRICT SCHOOL BOARD p508
32 KENNEDY RD N, BRAMPTON, ON, L6V 1X4
(905) 451-0432   SIC 8211

PEEL DISTRICT SCHOOL BOARD p510
7935 KENNEDY RD, BRAMPTON, ON, L6W 0A2
(905) 453-9220   SIC 8211

PEEL DISTRICT SCHOOL BOARD p512
251 MCMURCHY AVE S, BRAMPTON, ON, L6Y 1Z4
(905) 451-2860   SIC 8211

PEEL DISTRICT SCHOOL BOARD p512
296 CONESTOGA DR, BRAMPTON, ON, L6Z 3M1
(905) 840-2328   SIC 8211

PEEL DISTRICT SCHOOL BOARD p513
370 BRISDALE DR, BRAMPTON, ON, L7A 3K7
(905) 840-2135   SIC 8211

PEEL DISTRICT SCHOOL BOARD p513
10750 CHINGUACOUSY RD, BRAMPTON, ON, L7A 2Z7
(905) 495-2675   SIC 8211

PEEL DISTRICT SCHOOL BOARD p513
10750 CHINGUACOUSY RD, BRAMPTON, ON, L7A 2Z7
(905) 451-1263   SIC 8211

PEEL DISTRICT SCHOOL BOARD p686
3545 MORNING STAR DR, MISSISSAUGA, ON, L4T 1Y3
(905) 676-1191   SIC 8211

PEEL DISTRICT SCHOOL BOARD p703
3575 FIELDGATE DR, MISSISSAUGA, ON, L4X 2J6
(905) 625-7731   SIC 8211

PEEL DISTRICT SCHOOL BOARD p712
1490 OGDEN AVE, MISSISSAUGA, ON, L5E 2H8
(905) 274-2391   SIC 8211

PEEL DISTRICT SCHOOL BOARD p712
3225 ERINDALE STATION RD, MISSISSAUGA, ON, L5C 1Y5
(905) 279-0575   SIC 8211

PEEL DISTRICT SCHOOL BOARD p713
1305 CAWTHRA RD, MISSISSAUGA, ON, L5G 4L1
(905) 274-1271   SIC 8211

PEEL DISTRICT SCHOOL BOARD p713
1324 LORNE PARK RD, MISSISSAUGA, ON, L5H 3B1
(905) 278-6177   SIC 8211

PEEL DISTRICT SCHOOL BOARD p714
2524 BROMSGROVE RD, MISSISSAUGA, ON, L5J 1L8
(905) 822-6700   SIC 8211

PEEL DISTRICT SCHOOL BOARD p715
2021 DUNDAS ST W, MISSISSAUGA, ON, L5K 1R2
(905) 828-7206   SIC 8211

PEEL DISTRICT SCHOOL BOARD p719
72 JOYMAR DR, MISSISSAUGA, ON, L5M 1G3
(905) 826-1195   SIC 8211

PEEL DISTRICT SCHOOL BOARD p719
2665 ERIN CENTRE BLVD, MISSISSAUGA, ON, L5M 5H6
(905) 858-5910   SIC 8211

PEEL DISTRICT SCHOOL BOARD p725

6325 MONTEVIDEO RD, MISSISSAUGA, ON, L5N 4G7
(905) 858-3087   SIC 8211

PEEL DISTRICT SCHOOL BOARD p725
6700 EDENWOOD DR, MISSISSAUGA, ON, L5N 3B2
(905) 824-1790   SIC 8211

PEEL DISTRICT SCHOOL BOARD p732
5650 HURONTARIO ST SUITE 106, MISSISSAUGA, ON, L5R 1C6
(905) 890-1099   SIC 8211

PEEL DISTRICT SCHOOL BOARD p744
1150 DREAM CREST RD, MISSISSAUGA, ON, L5V 1N6
(905) 567-4260   SIC 8211

PEEL DISTRICT SCHOOL BOARD p745
550 COURTNEYPARK DR W, MISSISSAUGA, ON, L5W 1L9
(905) 564-1033   SIC 8211

PEGUIS SCHOOL BOARD p354
GD, PEGUIS, MB, R0C 3J0
(204) 645-2648   SIC 8211

PEMBINA HILLS REGIONAL DIVISION 7 p4
5307 53 AVE, BARRHEAD, AB, T7N 1P2
(780) 674-8521   SIC 8211

PEMBINA HILLS REGIONAL DIVISION 7 p4
5310 49 ST, BARRHEAD, AB, T7N 1P3
(780) 674-8500   SIC 8211

PEMBINA TRAILS SCHOOL DIVISION, THE p389
2240 GRANT AVE, WINNIPEG, MB, R3P 0P7
(204) 888-5898   SIC 8211

PEMBINA TRAILS SCHOOL DIVISION, THE p391
175 KILLARNEY AVE, WINNIPEG, MB, R3T 3B3
(204) 269-6210   SIC 8211

PEMBINA TRAILS SCHOOL DIVISION, THE p393
181 HENLOW BAY, WINNIPEG, MB, R3Y 1M7
(204) 488-1757   SIC 8211

PETERBOROUGH VICTORIA NORTHUMBERLAND AND CLARINGTON CATHOLIC DISTRICT SCHOOL BOARD p496
300 SCUGOG ST, BOWMANVILLE, ON, L1C 6Y8
(905) 623-3990   SIC 8211

PETERBOROUGH VICTORIA NORTHUMBERLAND AND CLARINGTON CATHOLIC DISTRICT SCHOOL BOARD p545
1050 BIRCHWOOD TRAIL, COBOURG, ON, K9A 5S9
(905) 372-4339   SIC 8211

PETERBOROUGH VICTORIA NORTHUMBERLAND AND CLARINGTON CATHOLIC DISTRICT SCHOOL BOARD p564
2260 COURTICE RD, COURTICE, ON, L1E 2M8
(905) 404-9349   SIC 8211

PETERBOROUGH VICTORIA NORTHUMBERLAND AND CLARINGTON CATHOLIC DISTRICT SCHOOL BOARD p841
1355 LANSDOWNE ST W, PETERBOROUGH, ON, K9J 7M3
(705) 748-4861   SIC 8211

PICKERING COLLEGE p756
16945 BAYVIEW AVE, NEWMARKET, ON, L3Y 4X2
(905) 895-1700   SIC 8211

PIKANGIKUM EDUCATION AUTHORITY p846
1 SCHOOL RD, PIKANGIKUM, ON, P0V 2L0
(807) 773-1093   SIC 8211

PINE CREEK SCHOOL DIVISION p350
25 BROWN ST, GLADSTONE, MB, R0J 0T0
(204) 385-2216   SIC 8211

PORTER CREEK SECONDARY SCHOOL p1440
1405 HICKORY ST, WHITEHORSE, YT, Y1A 4M4
(867) 667-8044   SIC 8211

PRAIRIE SOUTH SCHOOL DIVISION NO 210 p1411
145 ROSS ST E, MOOSE JAW, SK, S6H 0S3
(306) 693-4626   SIC 8211

PRAIRIE SOUTH SCHOOL DIVISION NO 210 p1411
1075 9TH AVE NW, MOOSE JAW, SK, S6H 1V7
(306) 694-1200   SIC 8211

PRAIRIE VALLEY SCHOOL DIVISION NO 208 p1418
3080 ALBERT ST N, REGINA, SK, S4P 3E1
(306) 949-3366   SIC 8211

PRINCE RUPERT SCHOOL DISTRICT 52 p251
634 6TH AVE E, PRINCE RUPERT, BC, V8J 1X1
(250) 624-6717   SIC 8211

PRINCE RUPERT SCHOOL DISTRICT 52 p251
634 6TH AVE E, PRINCE RUPERT, BC, V8J 1X1
(250) 624-6717   SIC 8211

QUEEN MARGARET'S SCHOOL p212
660 BROWNSEY AVE, DUNCAN, BC, V9L 1C2
(250) 746-4185   SIC 8211

QUEEN OF ANGELS ACADEMY INC p1096
100 BOUL BOUCHARD, DORVAL, QC, H9S 1A7
(514) 636-0900   SIC 8211

RAINBOW DISTRICT SCHOOL BOARD p899
1545 KENNEDY ST, SUDBURY, ON, P3A 2G1
(705) 566-2280   SIC 8211

RAINBOW DISTRICT SCHOOL BOARD p901
69 YOUNG ST, SUDBURY, ON, P3E 3G5
(705) 377-4615   SIC 8211

RED DEER CATHOLIC REGIONAL DIVISION NO. 39 p154
5210 61 ST, RED DEER, AB, T4N 6N8
(403) 343-1055   SIC 8211

RED RIVER VALLEY SCHOOL DIVISION p353
233 MAIN ST, MORRIS, MB, R0G 1K0
(204) 746-2317   SIC 8211

REGIONAL AUTHORITY OF THE EAST CENTRAL FRANCOPHONE EDUCATION REGION NO.3, THE p165
4617 50 AVE, ST PAUL, AB, T0A 3A3
(780) 645-3888   SIC 8211

RENFREW COUNTY DISTRICT SCHOOL BOARD p838
420 BELL ST, PEMBROKE, ON, K8A 2K5
(613) 735-6858   SIC 8211

RENFREW EDUCATIONAL SERVICES SOCIETY p69
75 SUNPARK DR SE, CALGARY, AB, T2X 3V4
(403) 291-5038   SIC 8211

RICHMOND CHRISTIAN SCHOOL ASSOCIATION p263
10200 NO. 5 RD, RICHMOND, BC, V7A 4E5
(604) 272-5720   SIC 8211

RIVER EAST TRANSCONA SCHOOL DIVISION p363
260 REDONDA ST, WINNIPEG, MB, R2C 1L6
(204) 958-6460   SIC 8211

RIVER EAST TRANSCONA SCHOOL DIVISION p364
295 SUTTON AVE, WINNIPEG, MB, R2G 0T1
(204) 338-4611   SIC 8211

RIVER EAST TRANSCONA SCHOOL DIVISION p367
589 ROCH ST, WINNIPEG, MB, R2K 2P7
(204) 667-7130   SIC 8211

RIVER EAST TRANSCONA SCHOOL DIVISION p367
757 ROCH ST, WINNIPEG, MB, R2K 2R1
(204) 667-1103   SIC 8211

RIVER EAST TRANSCONA SCHOOL DIVI-

SION *p367*
845 CONCORDIA AVE, WINNIPEG, MB, R2K 2M6
(204) 667-2960 *SIC 8211*
RIVER EAST TRANSCONA SCHOOL DIVISION *p367*
795 PRINCE RUPERT AVE, WINNIPEG, MB, R2K 1W6
(204) 668-9304 *SIC 8211*
RIVERSIDE SCHOOL BOARD *p1112*
776 RUE CAMPBELL, GREENFIELD PARK, QC, J4V 1Y7
(450) 672-0042 *SIC 8211*
RIVERSIDE SCHOOL BOARD *p1112*
880 RUE HUDSON, GREENFIELD PARK, QC, J4V 1H1
(450) 656-6100 *SIC 8211*
RIVERSIDE SCHOOL BOARD *p1308*
7445 CH DE CHAMBLY, SAINT-HUBERT, QC, J3Y 3S3
(450) 678-1070 *SIC 8211*
ROBERT THIRSK HIGH SCHOOL *p75*
8777 NOSE HILL DR NW, CALGARY, AB, T3G 5T3
(403) 817-3400 *SIC 8211*
ROCKY VIEW SCHOOL DIVISION NO. 41, THE *p3*
2651 CHINOOK WINDS DR SW, AIRDRIE, AB, T4B 0B4
(403) 945-4000 *SIC 8211*
ROTHESAY COLLEGIATE SCHOOL, THE *p412*
40 COLLEGE HILL RD, ROTHESAY, NB, E2E 5H1
(506) 847-8224 *SIC 8211*
ROYAL ST GEORGE'S COLLEGE *p973*
120 HOWLAND AVE, TORONTO, ON, M5R 3B5
(416) 533-9481 *SIC 8211*
SANDY BAY SCHOOL *p352*
GD, MARIUS, MB, R0H 0T0
(204) 843-2407 *SIC 8211*
SASKATCHEWAN RIVER SCHOOL DIVISION #119 *p1414*
665 28TH ST E, PRINCE ALBERT, SK, S6V 6E9
(306) 922-3115 *SIC 8211*
SCHECHTER, SOLOMON ACADEMY INC *p1220*
5555 CH DE LA COTE-SAINT-LUC, MONTREAL, QC, H3X 2C9
(514) 485-0866 *SIC 8211*
SCHOOL BOARD DISTRICT 01 *p401*
715 PRIESTMAN ST, FREDERICTON, NB, E3B 5W7
(506) 453-3991 *SIC 8211*
SCHOOL DISTRICT #28 *p252*
401 NORTH STAR RD SUITE 28, QUESNEL, BC, V2J 5K2
(250) 992-8802 *SIC 8211*
SCHOOL DISTRICT #28 *p252*
850 ANDERSON DR, QUESNEL, BC, V2J 1G4
(250) 992-7007 *SIC 8211*
SCHOOL DISTRICT #28 *p252*
585 CALLANAN ST, QUESNEL, BC, V2J 2V3
(250) 992-2131 *SIC 8211*
SCHOOL DISTRICT #59 PEACE RIVER SOUTH *p205*
11600 7 ST, DAWSON CREEK, BC, V1G 4R8
(250) 782-2106 *SIC 8211*
SCHOOL DISTRICT #70 (ALBERNI) SCHOOL BOARD *p245*
4000 BURDE ST, PORT ALBERNI, BC, V9Y 3L6
(250) 724-3284 *SIC 8211*
SCHOOL DISTRICT #74 (GOLD TRAIL) *p180*
400 HOLLIS RD, ASHCROFT, BC, V0K 1A0
(250) 453-9101 *SIC 8211*
SCHOOL DISTRICT #75 (MISSION) *p232*
32939 7TH AVE, MISSION, BC, V2V 2C5
(604) 826-7191 *SIC 8211*

SCHOOL DISTRICT #75 (MISSION) *p232*
34800 DEWDNEY TRUNK RD SUITE 1, MISSION, BC, V2V 5V6
(604) 826-3651 *SIC 8211*
SCHOOL DISTRICT #75 (MISSION) *p232*
33046 4TH AVE SUITE 75, MISSION, BC, V2V 1S5
(604) 826-6286 *SIC 8211*
SCHOOL DISTRICT #81 (FORT NELSON) *p213*
5104 AIRPORT DR, FORT NELSON, BC, V0C 1R0
(250) 774-2591 *SIC 8211*
SCHOOL DISTRICT 14 *p403*
217 ROCKLAND RD, HARTLAND, NB, E7P 0A2
(506) 375-3000 *SIC 8211*
SCHOOL DISTRICT 17 *p410*
25 MACKENZIE AVE, OROMOCTO, NB, E2V 1K4
(506) 357-4015 *SIC 8211*
SCHOOL DISTRICT 2 *p407*
207 CHURCH ST, MONCTON, NB, E1C 5A3
(506) 856-3439 *SIC 8211*
SCHOOL DISTRICT 2 *p409*
1077 ST GEORGE BLVD, MONCTON, NB, E1E 4C9
(506) 856-3222 *SIC 8211*
SCHOOL DISTRICT 51 BOUNDARY *p215*
1021 CENTRAL AVE, GRAND FORKS, BC, V0H 1H0
(250) 442-8258 *SIC 8211*
SCHOOL DISTRICT 63 (SAANICH) *p180*
1101 NEWTON PL, BRENTWOOD BAY, BC, V8M 1G3
(250) 652-1135 *SIC 8211*
SCHOOL DISTRICT 63 (SAANICH) *p267*
1627 STELLYS CROSS RD, SAANICHTON, BC, V8M 1S8
(250) 652-4401 *SIC 8211*
SCHOOL DISTRICT 63 (SAANICH) *p338*
4980 WESLEY RD, VICTORIA, BC, V8Y 1Y9
(250) 686-5221 *SIC 8211*
SCHOOL DISTRICT 73 (KAMLOOPS/THOMPSON) *p217*
821 MUNRO ST, KAMLOOPS, BC, V2C 3E9
(250) 374-1405 *SIC 8211*
SCHOOL DISTRICT 73 (KAMLOOPS/THOMPSON) *p218*
1383 9TH AVE, KAMLOOPS, BC, V2C 3X7
(250) 374-0679 *SIC 8211*
SCHOOL DISTRICT 8 *p413*
1490 HICKEY RD, SAINT JOHN, NB, E2J 4E7
(506) 658-5367 *SIC 8211*
SCHOOL DISTRICT 8 *p414*
305 DOUGLAS AVE, SAINT JOHN, NB, E2K 1E5
(506) 658-5359 *SIC 8211*
SCHOOL DISTRICT NO 22 (VERNON) *p331*
2301 FULTON RD, VERNON, BC, V1H 1Y1
(250) 545-1348 *SIC 8211*
SCHOOL DISTRICT NO 22 (VERNON) *p332*
2701 41 AVE, VERNON, BC, V1T 6X3
(250) 542-3361 *SIC 8211*
SCHOOL DISTRICT NO 22 (VERNON) *p332*
2303 18 ST, VERNON, BC, V1T 3Z9
(250) 545-0701 *SIC 8211*
SCHOOL DISTRICT NO 22 (VERNON) *p332*
1401 15 ST, VERNON, BC, V1T 8S8
(250) 542-3331 *SIC 8211*
SCHOOL DISTRICT NO 27 (CARIBOO-CHILCOTIN) *p344*
350 SECOND AVE N, WILLIAMS LAKE, BC, V2G 1Z9
(250) 398-3800 *SIC 8211*
SCHOOL DISTRICT NO 33 CHILLIWACK *p196*
8430 CESSNA DR, CHILLIWACK, BC, V2P 7K4
(604) 792-1321 *SIC 8211*
SCHOOL DISTRICT NO 33 CHILLIWACK *p197*

45460 STEVENSON RD, CHILLIWACK, BC, V2R 2Z6
(604) 858-9424 *SIC 8211*
SCHOOL DISTRICT NO 33 CHILLIWACK *p197*
46363 YALE RD, CHILLIWACK, BC, V2P 2P8
(604) 795-7295 *SIC 8211*
SCHOOL DISTRICT NO 34 (ABBOTSFORD) *p175*
35045 EXBURY AVE, ABBOTSFORD, BC, V2S 7L1
(604) 864-0220 *SIC 8211*
SCHOOL DISTRICT NO 34 (ABBOTSFORD) *p175*
34620 OLD YALE RD, ABBOTSFORD, BC, V2S 7S6
(604) 853-0778 *SIC 8211*
SCHOOL DISTRICT NO 34 (ABBOTSFORD) *p177*
32355 MOUAT DR, ABBOTSFORD, BC, V2T 4E9
(604) 853-7191 *SIC 8211*
SCHOOL DISTRICT NO 34 (ABBOTSFORD) *p177*
31150 BLUERIDGE DR, ABBOTSFORD, BC, V2T 5R2
(604) 864-0011 *SIC 8211*
SCHOOL DISTRICT NO 42 (MAPLE RIDGE-PITT MEADOWS) *p230*
10445 245 ST SUITE 10445, MAPLE RIDGE, BC, V2W 2G4
(604) 466-8409 *SIC 8211*
SCHOOL DISTRICT NO 42 (MAPLE RIDGE-PITT MEADOWS) *p231*
24789 DEWDNEY TRUNK RD, MAPLE RIDGE, BC, V4R 1X2
(604) 463-3500 *SIC 8211*
SCHOOL DISTRICT NO 42 (MAPLE RIDGE-PITT MEADOWS) *p231*
22225 BROWN AVE, MAPLE RIDGE, BC, V2X 8N6
(604) 463-4200 *SIC 8211*
SCHOOL DISTRICT NO 42 (MAPLE RIDGE-PITT MEADOWS) *p231*
21911 122 AVE, MAPLE RIDGE, BC, V2X 3X2
(604) 463-4175 *SIC 8211*
SCHOOL DISTRICT NO 42 (MAPLE RIDGE-PITT MEADOWS) *p231*
20905 WICKLUND AVE, MAPLE RIDGE, BC, V2X 8E8
(604) 467-3481 *SIC 8211*
SCHOOL DISTRICT NO 42 (MAPLE RIDGE-PITT MEADOWS) *p244*
19438 116B AVE, PITT MEADOWS, BC, V3Y 1G1
(604) 465-7141 *SIC 8211*
SCHOOL DISTRICT NO 5 (SOUTHEAST KOOTENAY) *p204*
940 INDUSTRIAL ROAD 1 SUITE 1, CRANBROOK, BC, V1C 4C6
(250) 426-4201 *SIC 8211*
SCHOOL DISTRICT NO 58 (NICOLA-SIMILKAMEEN) *p232*
1550 CHAPMAN ST, MERRITT, BC, V1K 1B0
(250) 378-5161 *SIC 8211*
SCHOOL DISTRICT NO 62 (SOOKE) *p340*
3341 PAINTER RD, VICTORIA, BC, V9C 2J1
(250) 478-5548 *SIC 8211*
SCHOOL DISTRICT NO 62 (SOOKE) *p340*
3143 JACKLIN RD, VICTORIA, BC, V9B 5R1
(250) 474-9800 *SIC 8211*
SCHOOL DISTRICT NO 62 (SOOKE) *p340*
3067 JACKLIN RD, VICTORIA, BC, V9B 3Y7
(250) 478-5501 *SIC 8211*
SCHOOL DISTRICT NO 67 (OKANAGAN SKAHA) *p244*
425 JERMYN AVE, PENTICTON, BC, V2A 174
(250) 770-7700 *SIC 8211*
SCHOOL DISTRICT NO 69 (QUALICUM)

p243
135 N PYM RD, PARKSVILLE, BC, V9P 2H4
(250) 248-5721 *SIC 8211*
SCHOOL DISTRICT NO. 20 (KOOTENAY-COLUMBIA) *p284*
2001 THIRD AVE, TRAIL, BC, V1R 1R6
(250) 368-6434 *SIC 8211*
SCHOOL DISTRICT NO. 35 (LANGLEY) *p179*
26850 29 AVE, ALDERGROVE, BC, V4W 3C1
(604) 856-2521 *SIC 8211*
SCHOOL DISTRICT NO. 35 (LANGLEY) *p225*
8919 WALNUT GROVE DR, LANGLEY, BC, V1M 2N7
(604) 882-0220 *SIC 8211*
SCHOOL DISTRICT NO. 35 (LANGLEY) *p227*
21405 56 AVE, LANGLEY, BC, V2Y 2N1
(604) 534-7155 *SIC 8211*
SCHOOL DISTRICT NO. 35 (LANGLEY) *p227*
23752 52 AVE, LANGLEY, BC, V2Z 2P3
(604) 530-2151 *SIC 8211*
SCHOOL DISTRICT NO. 36 (SURREY) *p271*
15350 99 AVE, SURREY, BC, V3R 0R9
(604) 581-5500 *SIC 8211*
SCHOOL DISTRICT NO. 36 (SURREY) *p271*
10719 150 ST, SURREY, BC, V3R 4C8
(604) 585-2566 *SIC 8211*
SCHOOL DISTRICT NO. 36 (SURREY) *p273*
6151 180 ST, SURREY, BC, V3S 4L5
(604) 574-7407 *SIC 8211*
SCHOOL DISTRICT NO. 36 (SURREY) *p273*
7940 156 ST, SURREY, BC, V3S 3R3
(604) 597-2301 *SIC 8211*
SCHOOL DISTRICT NO. 36 (SURREY) *p274*
10441 132 ST, SURREY, BC, V3T 3V3
(604) 588-6934 *SIC 8211*
SCHOOL DISTRICT NO. 36 (SURREY) *p275*
14033 92 AVE, SURREY, BC, V3V 0B7
(604) 596-7733 *SIC 8211*
SCHOOL DISTRICT NO. 36 (SURREY) *p277*
12600 66 AVE, SURREY, BC, V3W 2A8
(604) 597-5234 *SIC 8211*
SCHOOL DISTRICT NO. 36 (SURREY) *p277*
12772 88 AVE, SURREY, BC, V3W 3J9
(604) 502-5710 *SIC 8211*
SCHOOL DISTRICT NO. 36 (SURREY) *p277*
12870 72 AVE, SURREY, BC, V3W 2M9
(604) 594-5458 *SIC 8211*
SCHOOL DISTRICT NO. 36 (SURREY) *p278*
6248 144 ST, SURREY, BC, V3X 1A1
(604) 543-8749 *SIC 8211*
SCHOOL DISTRICT NO. 36 (SURREY) *p280*
1785 148 ST, SURREY, BC, V4A 4M6
(604) 536-2131 *SIC 8211*
SCHOOL DISTRICT NO. 36 (SURREY) *p280*
15751 16 AVE, SURREY, BC, V4A 1S1
(604) 531-8354 *SIC 8211*
SCHOOL DISTRICT NO. 36 (SURREY) *p281*
13484 24 AVE, SURREY, BC, V4A 2G5
(604) 538-6678 *SIC 8211*
SCHOOL DISTRICT NO. 36 (SURREY) *p282*
15945 96 AVE, SURREY, BC, V4N 2R8
(604) 581-4433 *SIC 8211*
SCHOOL DISTRICT NO. 36 (SURREY) *p282*
16060 108 AVE, SURREY, BC, V4N 1M1
(604) 582-9231 *SIC 8211*
SCHOOL DISTRICT NO. 43 (COQUITLAM) *p198*
1195 LANSDOWNE DR, COQUITLAM, BC, V3B 7Y8
(604) 464-5793 *SIC 8211*
SCHOOL DISTRICT NO. 43 (COQUITLAM) *p199*
2525 COMO LAKE AVE, COQUITLAM, BC, V3J 3R8
(604) 461-5581 *SIC 8211*
SCHOOL DISTRICT NO. 43 (COQUITLAM) *p199*
570 POIRIER ST, COQUITLAM, BC, V3J 6A8

(604) 939-9201   *SIC* 8211
SCHOOL DISTRICT NO. 43 (COQUITLAM)
p199
550 POIRIER ST, COQUITLAM, BC, V3J
6A7
(604) 939-9201   *SIC* 8211
SCHOOL DISTRICT NO. 43 (COQUITLAM)
p246
1260 RIVERWOOD GATE, PORT COQUIT-
LAM, BC, V3B 7Z5
(604) 941-5401   *SIC* 8211
SCHOOL DISTRICT NO. 43 (COQUITLAM)
p247
1982 KINGSWAY AVE, PORT COQUITLAM,
BC, V3C 1S5
(604) 941-5643   *SIC* 8211
SCHOOL DISTRICT NO. 43 (COQUITLAM)
p247
2215 REEVE ST, PORT COQUITLAM, BC,
V3C 6K8
(604) 941-6053   *SIC* 8211
SCHOOL DISTRICT NO. 43 (COQUITLAM)
p248
300 ALBERT ST, PORT MOODY, BC, V3H
2M5
(604) 939-6656   *SIC* 8211
SCHOOL DISTRICT NO. 43 (COQUITLAM)
p248
1300 DAVID AVE, PORT MOODY, BC, V3H
5K6
(604) 461-8679   *SIC* 8211
**SCHOOL DISTRICT NO. 44 (NORTH VAN-
COUVER)**
p238
931 BROADVIEW DR, NORTH VANCOU-
VER, BC, V7H 2E9
(604) 903-3700   *SIC* 8211
**SCHOOL DISTRICT NO. 44 (NORTH VAN-
COUVER)**
p239
1131 FREDERICK RD, NORTH VANCOU-
VER, BC, V7K 1J3
(604) 903-3300   *SIC* 8211
**SCHOOL DISTRICT NO. 44 (NORTH VAN-
COUVER)**
p240
1860 SUTHERLAND AVE, NORTH VAN-
COUVER, BC, V7L 4C2
(604) 903-3500   *SIC* 8211
**SCHOOL DISTRICT NO. 44 (NORTH VAN-
COUVER)**
p240
2121 LONSDALE AVE, NORTH VANCOU-
VER, BC, V7M 2K6
(604) 903-3444   *SIC* 8211
**SCHOOL DISTRICT NO. 44 (NORTH VAN-
COUVER)**
p242
1044 EDGEWOOD RD, NORTH VANCOU-
VER, BC, V7R 1Y7
(604) 903-3600   *SIC* 8211
**SCHOOL DISTRICT NO. 45 (WEST VAN-
COUVER)**
p342
1075 21ST ST SUITE 45, WEST VANCOU-
VER, BC, V7V 4A9
(604) 981-1000   *SIC* 8211
**SCHOOL DISTRICT NO. 45 (WEST VAN-
COUVER)**
p342
1750 MATHERS AVE, WEST VANCOUVER,
BC, V7V 2G7
(604) 981-1100   *SIC* 8211
**SCHOOL DISTRICT NO. 46 (SUNSHINE
COAST)**
p214
494 SOUTH FLETCHER RD, GIBSONS,
BC, V0N 1V0
(604) 886-8811   *SIC* 8211
SCHOOL DISTRICT NO. 48 (HOWE SOUND)
p269
37866 2ND AVE, SQUAMISH, BC, V8B 0A2
(604) 892-3421   *SIC* 8211
**SCHOOL DISTRICT NO. 54 (BULKLEY VAL-
LEY)**
p269
3377 THIRD AVE, SMITHERS, BC, V0J 2N3
(250) 847-4846   *SIC* 8211
**SCHOOL DISTRICT NO. 60 (PEACE RIVER
NORTH)**
p214
9304 86 ST, FORT ST. JOHN, BC, V1J 6L9
(250) 785-4429   *SIC* 8211
SCHOOL DISTRICT NO. 60 (PEACE RIVER

NORTH)
p214
10112 105 AVE, FORT ST. JOHN, BC, V1J
4S4
(250) 262-6000   *SIC* 8211
**SCHOOL DISTRICT NO. 68 (NANAIMO-
LADYSMITH)**
p224
710 6TH AVE, LADYSMITH, BC, V9G 1A1
(250) 245-3043   *SIC* 8211
**SCHOOL DISTRICT NO. 68 (NANAIMO-
LADYSMITH)**
p233
395 WAKESIAH AVE, NANAIMO, BC, V9R
3K6
(250) 754-5521   *SIC* 8211
**SCHOOL DISTRICT NO. 68 (NANAIMO-
LADYSMITH)**
p234
1270 STRATHMORE ST, NANAIMO, BC,
V9S 2L9
(250) 753-2271   *SIC* 8211
**SCHOOL DISTRICT NO. 68 (NANAIMO-
LADYSMITH)**
p234
3135 MEXICANA RD, NANAIMO, BC, V9T
2W8
(250) 758-9191   *SIC* 8211
**SCHOOL DISTRICT NO. 68 (NANAIMO-
LADYSMITH)**
p235
6135 MCGIRR RD, NANAIMO, BC, V9V
1M1
(250) 756-4595   *SIC* 8211
**SCHOOL DISTRICT NO. 71 (COMOX VAL-
LEY)**
p203
1551 LERWICK RD, COURTENAY, BC, V9N
9B5
(250) 334-2428   *SIC* 8211
**SCHOOL DISTRICT NO. 79 (COWICHAN
VALLEY)**
p232
953 SHAWNIGAN-MILL BAY RD, MILL BAY,
BC, V0R 2P2
(250) 743-6916   *SIC* 8211
SCHOOL DISTRICT NO. 92 (NISGA'A) *p179*
5002 SKATEEN AVE, AIYANSH, BC, V0J
1A0
(250) 633-2228   *SIC* 8211
SELWYN HOUSE ASSOCIATION   *p1401*
95 CH DE LA COTE-SAINT-ANTOINE,
WESTMOUNT, QC, H3Y 2H8
(514) 931-9481   *SIC* 8211
SEMINAIRE DES TROIS-RIVIERES   *p1388*
858 RUE LAVIOLETTE BUREAU 553,
TROIS-RIVIERES, QC, G9A 5J1
(819) 376-4459   *SIC* 8211
SEMINAIRE DES TROIS-RIVIERES   *p1388*
858 RUE LAVIOLETTE, TROIS-RIVIERES,
QC, G9A 5J1
(819) 376-4459   *SIC* 8211
SEMINAIRE SAINT-FRANCOIS   *p1293*
4900   RUE   SAINT-FELIX,   SAINT-
AUGUSTIN-DE-DESMAURES,   QC,   G3A
0L4
(418) 872-0611   *SIC* 8211
**SEMINAIRE SALESIEN DE SHERBROOKE,
LE**   *p1374*
135 RUE DON-BOSCO N, SHERBROOKE,
QC, J1L 1E5
(819) 566-2222   *SIC* 8211
SEVEN OAKS SCHOOL DIVISION   *p369*
1330 JEFFERSON AVE, WINNIPEG, MB,
R2P 1L3
(204) 632-6641   *SIC* 8211
SEVEN OAKS SCHOOL DIVISION   *p370*
830 POWERS ST, WINNIPEG, MB, R2V
4E7
(204) 586-8061   *SIC* 8211
SEVEN OAKS SCHOOL DIVISION   *p370*
711 JEFFERSON AVE, WINNIPEG, MB,
R2V 0P7
(204) 336-5050   *SIC* 8211
SIKSIKA BOARD OF EDUCATION   *p163*
PO BOX 1099, SIKSIKA, AB, T0J 3W0
(403) 734-5400   *SIC* 8211
**SIMCOE COUNTY DISTRICT SCHOOL
BOARD, THE**   *p476*
203 VICTORIA ST E, ALLISTON, ON, L9R
1G5
(705) 435-6288   *SIC* 8211

**SIMCOE COUNTY DISTRICT SCHOOL
BOARD, THE**   *p485*
110 GROVE ST E, BARRIE, ON, L4M 2P3
(705) 726-6541   *SIC* 8211
**SIMCOE COUNTY DISTRICT SCHOOL
BOARD, THE**   *p485*
421 GROVE ST E, BARRIE, ON, L4M 5S1
(705) 728-1321   *SIC* 8211
**SIMCOE COUNTY DISTRICT SCHOOL
BOARD, THE**   *p488*
125 DUNLOP ST W, BARRIE, ON, L4N 1A9
SIC 8211
**SIMCOE COUNTY DISTRICT SCHOOL
BOARD, THE**   *p497*
70 PROFESSOR DAY DR, BRADFORD,
ON, L3Z 3B9
(905) 775-2262   *SIC* 8211
**SIMCOE COUNTY DISTRICT SCHOOL
BOARD, THE**   *p547*
6 CAMERON ST, COLLINGWOOD, ON, L9Y
2J2
(705) 445-3161   *SIC* 8211
**SIMCOE COUNTY DISTRICT SCHOOL
BOARD, THE**   *p681*
1170 HWY 26, MIDHURST, ON, L0L 1X0
(705) 734-6363   *SIC* 8211
**SIMCOE COUNTY DISTRICT SCHOOL
BOARD, THE**   *p682*
865 HUGEL AVE, MIDLAND, ON, L4R 1X8
(705) 526-7817   *SIC* 8211
**SIMCOE COUNTY DISTRICT SCHOOL
BOARD, THE**   *p810*
233 PARK ST, ORILLIA, ON, L3V 5W1
SIC 8211
**SIMCOE COUNTY DISTRICT SCHOOL
BOARD, THE**   *p810*
381 BIRCH ST, ORILLIA, ON, L3V 2P5
(705) 325-1318   *SIC* 8211
**SIMCOE COUNTY DISTRICT SCHOOL
BOARD, THE**   *p810*
2 BORLAND ST E, ORILLIA, ON, L3V 2B4
(705) 728-7570   *SIC* 8211
**SIMCOE MUSKOKA CATHOLIC DISTRICT
SCHOOL BOARD**   *p485*
243 CUNDLES RD E, BARRIE, ON, L4M
6L1
(705) 728-3120   *SIC* 8211
**SIMCOE MUSKOKA CATHOLIC DISTRICT
SCHOOL BOARD**   *p485*
46 ALLIANCE BLVD, BARRIE, ON, L4M 5K3
(705) 722-3555   *SIC* 8211
**SIMCOE MUSKOKA CATHOLIC DISTRICT
SCHOOL BOARD**   *p488*
201 ASHFORD DR, BARRIE, ON, L4N 6A3
(705) 734-0168   *SIC* 8211
**SIMCOE MUSKOKA CATHOLIC DISTRICT
SCHOOL BOARD**   *p998*
2 NOLAN RD, TOTTENHAM, ON, L0G 1W0
(905) 936-4743   *SIC* 8211
**SIR JAMES WHITNEY SCHOOL FOR THE
DEAF**   *p492*
350 DUNDAS ST W, BELLEVILLE, ON, K8P
1B2
(613) 967-2823   *SIC* 8211
SIR WILFRID LAURIER SCHOOL BOARD
p1087
2323 BOUL DANIEL-JOHNSON, COTE
SAINT-LUC, QC, H7T 1H8
(450) 686-6300   *SIC* 8211
SIR WILFRID LAURIER SCHOOL BOARD
p1129
448 AV D'ARGENTEUIL, LACHUTE, QC,
J8H 1W9
(450) 562-8571   *SIC* 8211
SIR WILFRID LAURIER SCHOOL BOARD
p1288
530 RUE NORTHCOTE, ROSEMERE, QC,
J7A 1Y2
(450) 621-5900   *SIC* 8211
**SMITHERS SCHOOL BOARD DISTRICT #54
(BULKLEY VALLEY)**   *p269*
4408 THIRD AVE, SMITHERS, BC, V0J 2N3
(250) 847-2231   *SIC* 8211
SOUTH   SHORE   REGIONAL   SCHOOL

BOARD   *p441*
69 WENTZELL DR, BRIDGEWATER, NS,
B4V 0A2
(902) 543-2468   *SIC* 8211
**SOUTHWEST HORIZON SCHOOL DIVI-
SION**   *p352*
GD, MELITA, MB, R0M 1L0
(204) 483-6292   *SIC* 8211
**SPRINGS OF LIVING WATER CHRISTIAN
ACADEMY INC**   *p364*
261 YOUVILLE ST, WINNIPEG, MB, R2H
2S7
(204) 231-3640   *SIC* 8211
ST JOHN'S-RAVENSCOURT SCHOOL *p392*
400 SOUTH DR, WINNIPEG, MB, R3T 3K5
(204) 504-3110   *SIC* 8211
**ST. ALBERT PUBLIC SCHOOL DISTRICT
NO. 5565**   *p166*
12 CUNNINGHAM RD, ST. ALBERT, AB,
T8N 2E9
(780) 459-4405   *SIC* 8211
**ST. ALBERT PUBLIC SCHOOL DISTRICT
NO. 5565**   *p166*
49 GIROUX RD, ST. ALBERT, AB, T8N 6N4
(780) 460-8490   *SIC* 8211
**ST. ALBERT PUBLIC SCHOOL DISTRICT
NO. 5565**   *p166*
60 SIR WINSTON CHURCHILL AVE, ST.
ALBERT, AB, T8N 0G4
(780) 460-3712   *SIC* 8211
ST. ANDREW'S COLLEGE   *p481*
15800 YONGE ST, AURORA, ON, L4G 3H7
(905) 727-3178   *SIC* 8211
**ST. CLAIR CATHOLIC DISTRICT SCHOOL
BOARD**   *p1005*
420 CREEK ST, WALLACEBURG, ON, N8A
4C4
(519) 627-6762   *SIC* 8211
ST. CLEMENT'S SCHOOL   *p923*
21 ST CLEMENTS AVE, TORONTO, ON,
M4R 1G8
(416) 483-4835   *SIC* 8211
ST. FRANCIS XAVIER UNIVERSITY   *p438*
5005 CHAPEL SQ, ANTIGONISH, NS, B2G
2W5
(902) 863-3300   *SIC* 8211
**ST.   JAMES-ASSINIBOIA SCHOOL DIVI-
SION**   *p386*
2574 PORTAGE AVE, WINNIPEG, MB, R3J
0H8
(204) 888-7951   *SIC* 8211
**ST. JOAN OF ARC CATHOLIC HIGH
SCHOOL**   *p488*
460 MAPLETON AVE, BARRIE, ON, L4N
9C2
(705) 721-0398   *SIC* 8211
ST. JOHN'S SCHOOL SOCIETY   *p322*
2215 10TH AVE W, VANCOUVER, BC, V6K
2J1
(604) 732-4434   *SIC* 8211
**ST. JOSEPH-SCOLLARD HALL CATHOLIC
SECONDARY SCHOOL**   *p764*
675 O'BRIEN ST, NORTH BAY, ON, P1B
9R3
(705) 494-8600   *SIC* 8211
ST. MARGARET'S SCHOOL   *p338*
1080 LUCAS AVE, VICTORIA, BC, V8X 3P7
(250) 479-7171   *SIC* 8211
ST. MICHAEL'S COLLEGE SCHOOL *p972*
1515 BATHURST ST, TORONTO, ON, M5P
3H4
(416) 653-4483   *SIC* 8211
**ST. MICHAELS UNIVERSITY SCHOOL SO-
CIETY**   *p333*
3400 RICHMOND RD, VICTORIA, BC, V8P
4P5
(250) 592-2411   *SIC* 8211
ST. MILDRED'S-LIGHTBOURN SCHOOL
p801
1080 LINBROOK RD, OAKVILLE, ON, L6J
2L1
(905) 845-2386   *SIC* 8211
**ST. PAUL EDUCATION REGIONAL DIVI-
SION NO 1**   *p165*

▲ Public Company   ■ Public Company Family Member   **HQ** Headquarters   **BR** Branch   **SL** Single Location

5201 50 AVE, ST PAUL, AB, T0A 3A0
(780) 645-3237   SIC 8211
ST. PAUL EDUCATION REGIONAL DIVISION NO 1   p165
4313 48 AVE SUITE 1, ST PAUL, AB, T0A 3A3
(780) 645-3323   SIC 8211
ST. PAUL'S ROMAN CATHOLIC SEPARATE SCHOOL DIVISION NO 20   p1432
411 AVENUE M N, SASKATOON, SK, S7L 2S7
(306) 659-7550   SIC 8211
ST. PAUL'S ROMAN CATHOLIC SEPARATE SCHOOL DIVISION NO 20   p1435
115 NELSON RD, SASKATOON, SK, S7S 1H1
(306) 659-7650   SIC 8211
STRAIT REGIONAL CENTRE FOR EDUCATION, THE   p438
105 BRAEMORE AVE, ANTIGONISH, NS, B2G 1L3
(902) 863-1620   SIC 8211
STRAIT REGIONAL CENTRE FOR EDUCATION, THE   p465
304 PITT ST UNIT 2, PORT HAWKESBURY, NS, B9A 2T9
(902) 625-2191   SIC 8211
STRATHCONA-TWEEDSMUIR   SCHOOL
p151
GD, OKOTOKS, AB, T1S 1A3
(403) 938-4431   SIC 8211
STURGEON SCHOOL DIVISION #24 p147
9820 104 ST, MORINVILLE, AB, T8R 1L8
(780) 939-4341   SIC 8211
SUDBURY CATHOLIC DISTRICT SCHOOL BOARD   p900
165A D'YOUVILLE ST, SUDBURY, ON, P3C 5E7
(705) 674-4231   SIC 8211
SUN WEST SCHOOL DIVISION NO 207 SASKATCHEWAN   p1423
501 FIRST ST W, ROSETOWN, SK, S0L 2V0
(306) 882-2677   SIC 8211
SUNRISE SCHOOL DIVISION   p345
85 5TH ST S, BEAUSEJOUR, MB, R0E 0C0
(204) 268-2423   SIC 8211
SUNRISE SCHOOL DIVISION   p345
344 2ND ST N, BEAUSEJOUR, MB, R0E 0C0
(204) 268-6500   SIC 8211
SUPERIOR   GREENSTONE   DISTRICT SCHOOL BOARD   p664
12 HEMLO DR BAG A, MARATHON, ON, P0T 2E0
(807) 229-0436   SIC 8211
SWAN VALLEY SCHOOL DIVISION   p359
1483 3RD ST N, SWAN RIVER, MB, R0L 1Z0
(204) 734-4511   SIC 8211
TALL PINES SCHOOL INC   p506
8525 TORBRAM RD, BRAMPTON, ON, L6T 5K4
(905) 458-6770   SIC 8211
THAMES VALLEY DISTRICT SCHOOL BOARD   p479
14405 MEDWAY RD, ARVA, ON, N0M 1C0
(519) 660-8418   SIC 8211
THAMES VALLEY DISTRICT SCHOOL BOARD   p482
362 TALBOT ST W, AYLMER, ON, N5H 1K6
(519) 773-3174   SIC 8211
THAMES VALLEY DISTRICT SCHOOL BOARD   p622
37 ALMA ST, INGERSOLL, ON, N5C 1N1
(519) 485-1200   SIC 8211
THAMES VALLEY DISTRICT SCHOOL BOARD   p651
656 TENNENT AVE, LONDON, ON, N5X 1L8
(519) 452-2600   SIC 8211
THAMES VALLEY DISTRICT SCHOOL BOARD   p651
1250 DUNDAS ST, LONDON, ON, N5W 5P2

(519) 452-2000   SIC 8211
THAMES VALLEY DISTRICT SCHOOL BOARD   p652
951 LEATHORNE ST SUITE 1, LONDON, ON, N5Z 3M7
(519) 452-2444   SIC 8211
THAMES VALLEY DISTRICT SCHOOL BOARD   p652
1350 HIGHBURY AVE N, LONDON, ON, N5Y 1B5
(519) 452-2730   SIC 8211
THAMES VALLEY DISTRICT SCHOOL BOARD   p656
371 TECUMSEH AVE E, LONDON, ON, N6C 1T4
(519) 452-2860   SIC 8211
THAMES VALLEY DISTRICT SCHOOL BOARD   p656
509 WATERLOO ST, LONDON, ON, N6B 2P8
(519) 452-2620   SIC 8211
THAMES VALLEY DISTRICT SCHOOL BOARD   p656
450 MILLBANK DR, LONDON, ON, N6C 4W7
(519) 452-2840   SIC 8211
THAMES VALLEY DISTRICT SCHOOL BOARD   p657
565 BRADLEY AVE, LONDON, ON, N6E 3Z8
(519) 452-8680   SIC 8211
THAMES VALLEY DISTRICT SCHOOL BOARD   p658
950 LAWSON RD, LONDON, ON, N6G 3M2
(519) 452-8690   SIC 8211
THAMES VALLEY DISTRICT SCHOOL BOARD   p659
230 BASE LINE RD W, LONDON, ON, N6J 1W1
(519) 452-2900   SIC 8211
THAMES VALLEY DISTRICT SCHOOL BOARD   p659
1040 OXFORD ST W, LONDON, ON, N6H 1V4
(519) 452-2750   SIC 8211
THAMES VALLEY DISTRICT SCHOOL BOARD   p660
941 VISCOUNT RD, LONDON, ON, N6K 1H5
(519) 452-2770   SIC 8211
THAMES VALLEY DISTRICT SCHOOL BOARD   p890
41 FLORA ST, ST THOMAS, ON, N5P 2X5
(519) 631-3770   SIC 8211
THAMES VALLEY DISTRICT SCHOOL BOARD   p890
241 SUNSET DR, ST THOMAS, ON, N5R 3C2
(519) 633-0090   SIC 8211
THAMES VALLEY DISTRICT SCHOOL BOARD   p912
37 GLENDALE DR SUITE 16, TILLSONBURG, ON, N4G 1J6
(519) 842-4207   SIC 8211
THAMES VALLEY DISTRICT SCHOOL BOARD   p1035
700 COLLEGE AVE, WOODSTOCK, ON, N4S 2C8
(519) 539-0020   SIC 8211
THAMES VALLEY DISTRICT SCHOOL BOARD   p1035
900 CROMWELL ST, WOODSTOCK, ON, N4S 5B5
(519) 537-2347   SIC 8211
THIRD ACADEMY INTERNATIONAL LTD, THE   p74
2452 BATTLEFORD AVE SW, CALGARY, AB, T3E 7K9
(403) 288-5335   SIC 8211
THUNDER BAY CATHOLIC DISTRICT SCHOOL BOARD   p907
285 GIBSON ST, THUNDER BAY, ON, P7A 2J6
(807) 344-8433   SIC 8211

THUNDER BAY CATHOLIC DISTRICT SCHOOL BOARD   p909
459 VICTORIA AVE W, THUNDER BAY, ON, P7C 0A4
(807) 625-1555   SIC 8211
THUNDER BAY CATHOLIC DISTRICT SCHOOL BOARD   p910
621 SELKIRK ST S, THUNDER BAY, ON, P7E 1T9
(807) 623-5218   SIC 8211
TORONTO CATHOLIC DISTRICT SCHOOL BOARD   p573
721 ROYAL YORK RD, ETOBICOKE, ON, M8Y 2T3
(416) 393-5549   SIC 8211
TORONTO CATHOLIC DISTRICT SCHOOL BOARD   p770
3379 BAYVIEW AVE, NORTH YORK, ON, M2M 3S4
(416) 393-5516   SIC 8211
TORONTO CATHOLIC DISTRICT SCHOOL BOARD   p770
211 STEELES AVE E, NORTH YORK, ON, M2M 3Y6
(416) 393-5508   SIC 8211
TORONTO CATHOLIC DISTRICT SCHOOL BOARD   p773
80 SHEPPARD AVE E SUITE 222, NORTH YORK, ON, M2N 6E8
(416) 222-8282   SIC 8211
TORONTO CATHOLIC DISTRICT SCHOOL BOARD   p773
80 SHEPPARD AVE E, NORTH YORK, ON, M2N 6E8
(416) 222-8282   SIC 8211
TORONTO CATHOLIC DISTRICT SCHOOL BOARD   p785
1440 FINCH AVE W, NORTH YORK, ON, M3J 3G3
(416) 393-5527   SIC 8211
TORONTO CATHOLIC DISTRICT SCHOOL BOARD   p788
101 MASON BLVD, NORTH YORK, ON, M5M 3E2
(416) 393-5510   SIC 8211
TORONTO CATHOLIC DISTRICT SCHOOL BOARD   p866
685 MILITARY TRAIL, SCARBOROUGH, ON, M1E 4P6
(416) 393-5531   SIC 8211
TORONTO CATHOLIC DISTRICT SCHOOL BOARD   p869
100 BRIMLEY RD S, SCARBOROUGH, ON, M1M 3X4
(416) 393-5519   SIC 8211
TORONTO CATHOLIC DISTRICT SCHOOL BOARD   p877
3200 KENNEDY RD, SCARBOROUGH, ON, M1V 3S8
(416) 393-5544   SIC 8211
TORONTO CATHOLIC DISTRICT SCHOOL BOARD   p919
49 FELSTEAD AVE, TORONTO, ON, M4J 1G3
(416) 393-5546   SIC 8211
TORONTO CATHOLIC DISTRICT SCHOOL BOARD   p990
270 BARTON AVE, TORONTO, ON, M6G 1R4
(416) 393-5293   SIC 8211
TORONTO CATHOLIC DISTRICT SCHOOL BOARD   p994
99 HUMBER BLVD, TORONTO, ON, M6N 2H4
(416) 393-5555   SIC 8211
TORONTO CATHOLIC DISTRICT SCHOOL BOARD   p994
70 GUESTVILLE AVE, TORONTO, ON, M6N 4N3
(416) 393-5247   SIC 8211
TORONTO DISTRICT SCHOOL BOARD p573
675 ROYAL YORK RD, ETOBICOKE, ON, M8Y 2T1

(416) 394-6910   SIC 8211
TORONTO DISTRICT SCHOOL BOARD
p577
86 MONTGOMERY RD, ETOBICOKE, ON, M9A 3N5
(416) 394-7840   SIC 8211
TORONTO DISTRICT SCHOOL BOARD
p578
50 WINTERTON DR, ETOBICOKE, ON, M9B 3G7
(416) 394-7110   SIC 8211
TORONTO DISTRICT SCHOOL BOARD
p581
2580 KIPLING AVE, ETOBICOKE, ON, M9V 3B2
(416) 394-7550   SIC 8211
TORONTO DISTRICT SCHOOL BOARD
p581
1675 MARTIN GROVE RD, ETOBICOKE, ON, M9V 3S3
(416) 394-7570   SIC 8211
TORONTO DISTRICT SCHOOL BOARD
p766
50 FRANCINE DR, NORTH YORK, ON, M2H 2G6
(416) 395-3140   SIC 8211
TORONTO DISTRICT SCHOOL BOARD
p770
155 HILDA AVE, NORTH YORK, ON, M2M 1V6
(416) 395-3280   SIC 8211
TORONTO DISTRICT SCHOOL BOARD
p773
100 PRINCESS AVE, NORTH YORK, ON, M2N 3R7
(416) 395-3210   SIC 8211
TORONTO DISTRICT SCHOOL BOARD
p773
5050 YONGE ST 5TH FL, NORTH YORK, ON, M2N 5N8
(416) 397-3000   SIC 8211
TORONTO DISTRICT SCHOOL BOARD
p775
15 WALLINGFORD RD, NORTH YORK, ON, M3A 2V1
(416) 395-3310   SIC 8211
TORONTO DISTRICT SCHOOL BOARD
p778
490 YORK MILLS RD, NORTH YORK, ON, M3B 1W6
(416) 395-3340   SIC 8211
TORONTO DISTRICT SCHOOL BOARD
p780
55 OVERLAND DR, NORTH YORK, ON, M3C 2C3
(416) 395-5080   SIC 8211
TORONTO DISTRICT SCHOOL BOARD
p780
9 GRENOBLE DR, NORTH YORK, ON, M3C 1C3
(416) 397-2900   SIC 8211
TORONTO DISTRICT SCHOOL BOARD
p780
130 OVERLEA BLVD, NORTH YORK, ON, M3C 1B2
(416) 396-2465   SIC 8211
TORONTO DISTRICT SCHOOL BOARD
p786
7 HAWKSDALE RD, NORTH YORK, ON, M3K 1W3
(416) 395-3200   SIC 8211
TORONTO DISTRICT SCHOOL BOARD
p787
450 BLYTHWOOD RD, NORTH YORK, ON, M4N 1A9
(416) 393-9275   SIC 8211
TORONTO DISTRICT SCHOOL BOARD
p790
38 ORFUS RD, NORTH YORK, ON, M6A 1L6
(416) 395-3350   SIC 8211
TORONTO DISTRICT SCHOOL BOARD
p790
640 LAWRENCE AVE W, NORTH YORK,

ON, M6A 1B1

(416) 395-3303   *SIC* 8211

TORONTO DISTRICT SCHOOL BOARD p865

150 TAPSCOTT RD, SCARBOROUGH, ON, M1B 2L2

(416) 396-5892   *SIC* 8211

TORONTO DISTRICT SCHOOL BOARD p865

5400 LAWRENCE AVE E, SCARBOROUGH, ON, M1C 2C6

(416) 396-6802   *SIC* 8211

TORONTO DISTRICT SCHOOL BOARD p866

145 GUILDWOOD PKY, SCARBOROUGH, ON, M1E 1P5

(416) 396-6820   *SIC* 8211

TORONTO DISTRICT SCHOOL BOARD p866

350 MORNINGSIDE AVE, SCARBOROUGH, ON, M1E 3G3

(416) 396-6864   *SIC* 8211

TORONTO DISTRICT SCHOOL BOARD p866

2222 ELLESMERE RD, SCARBOROUGH, ON, M1G 3M3

(416) 396-4575   *SIC* 8211

TORONTO DISTRICT SCHOOL BOARD p866

120 GALLOWAY RD, SCARBOROUGH, ON, M1E 1W7

(416) 396-6765   *SIC* 8211

TORONTO DISTRICT SCHOOL BOARD p867

21 GATESVIEW AVE, SCARBOROUGH, ON, M1J 3G4

(416) 396-6120   *SIC* 8211

TORONTO DISTRICT SCHOOL BOARD p867

550 MARKHAM RD, SCARBOROUGH, ON, M1H 2A2

(416) 396-4400   *SIC* 8211

TORONTO DISTRICT SCHOOL BOARD p869

3800 ST CLAIR AVE E, SCARBOROUGH, ON, M1M 1V3

(416) 396-5550   *SIC* 8211

TORONTO DISTRICT SCHOOL BOARD p872

1555 MIDLAND AVE, SCARBOROUGH, ON, M1P 3C1

(416) 396-6695   *SIC* 8211

TORONTO DISTRICT SCHOOL BOARD p875

2621 MIDLAND AVE, SCARBOROUGH, ON, M1S 1R6

(416) 396-6675   *SIC* 8211

TORONTO DISTRICT SCHOOL BOARD p875

1050 HUNTINGWOOD DR, SCARBOROUGH, ON, M1S 3H5

(416) 396-6830   *SIC* 8211

TORONTO DISTRICT SCHOOL BOARD p875

52 MCGRISKIN RD, SCARBOROUGH, ON, M1S 5C5

(416) 396-7610   *SIC* 8211

TORONTO DISTRICT SCHOOL BOARD p875

2450 BIRCHMOUNT RD, SCARBOROUGH, ON, M1T 2M5

(416) 396-8000   *SIC* 8211

TORONTO DISTRICT SCHOOL BOARD p877

1550 SANDHURST CIR, SCARBOROUGH, ON, M1V 1S6

(416) 396-6684   *SIC* 8211

TORONTO DISTRICT SCHOOL BOARD p878

2501 BRIDLETOWNE CIR, SCARBOROUGH, ON, M1W 2K1

(416) 396-6745   *SIC* 8211

TORONTO DISTRICT SCHOOL BOARD p917

650 COSBURN AVE, TORONTO, ON, M4C 2V2

(416) 396-2355   *SIC* 8211

TORONTO DISTRICT SCHOOL BOARD p918

305 RUMSEY RD, TORONTO, ON, M4G 1R4

(416) 396-2395   *SIC* 8211

TORONTO DISTRICT SCHOOL BOARD p919

80 THORNCLIFFE PARK DR, TORONTO, ON, M4H 1K3

(416) 396-2460   *SIC* 8211

TORONTO DISTRICT SCHOOL BOARD p919

1 HANSON ST, TORONTO, ON, M4J 1G6

(416) 393-0190   *SIC* 8211

TORONTO DISTRICT SCHOOL BOARD p920

1 DANFORTH AVE, TORONTO, ON, M4K 1M8

(416) 393-9740   *SIC* 8211

TORONTO DISTRICT SCHOOL BOARD p921

1094 GERRARD ST E, TORONTO, ON, M4M 2A1

(416) 393-9820   *SIC* 8211

TORONTO DISTRICT SCHOOL BOARD p923

17 BROADWAY AVE, TORONTO, ON, M4P 1T7

(416) 393-9180   *SIC* 8211

TORONTO DISTRICT SCHOOL BOARD p923

851 MOUNT PLEASANT RD, TORONTO, ON, M4P 2L5

(416) 393-0270   *SIC* 8211

TORONTO DISTRICT SCHOOL BOARD p931

711 BLOOR ST E, TORONTO, ON, M4W 1J4

(416) 393-1580   *SIC* 8211

TORONTO DISTRICT SCHOOL BOARD p932

495 JARVIS ST, TORONTO, ON, M4Y 2G8

(416) 393-0140   *SIC* 8211

TORONTO DISTRICT SCHOOL BOARD p976

725 BATHURST ST, TORONTO, ON, M5S 2R5

(416) 393-0060   *SIC* 8211

TORONTO DISTRICT SCHOOL BOARD p989

991 ST CLAIR AVE W, TORONTO, ON, M6E 1A3

(416) 393-1780   *SIC* 8211

TORONTO DISTRICT SCHOOL BOARD p990

286 HARBORD ST, TORONTO, ON, M6G 1G5

(416) 393-1650   *SIC* 8211

TORONTO DISTRICT SCHOOL BOARD p990

570 SHAW ST, TORONTO, ON, M6G 3L6

(416) 393-0030   *SIC* 8211

TORONTO DISTRICT SCHOOL BOARD p992

100 CLOSE AVE, TORONTO, ON, M6K 2V3

(416) 530-0683   *SIC* 8211

TORONTO DISTRICT SCHOOL BOARD p992

209 JAMESON AVE, TORONTO, ON, M6K 2Y3

(416) 393-9000   *SIC* 8211

TORONTO DISTRICT SCHOOL BOARD p993

100 EMMETT AVE, TORONTO, ON, M6M 2E6

(416) 394-3280   *SIC* 8211

TORONTO DISTRICT SCHOOL BOARD p993

2690 EGLINTON AVE W, TORONTO, ON, M6M 1T9

(416) 394-3000   *SIC* 8211

TORONTO DISTRICT SCHOOL BOARD p994

69 PRITCHARD AVE, TORONTO, ON, M6N 1T6

(416) 394-2340   *SIC* 8211

TORONTO DISTRICT SCHOOL BOARD p997

100 PINE ST, TORONTO, ON, M9N 2Y9

(416) 394-3250   *SIC* 8211

TORONTO FRENCH SCHOOL p787

306 LAWRENCE AVE E, NORTH YORK, ON, M4N 1T7

(416) 484-6980   *SIC* 8211

TORONTO MONTESSORI SCHOOLS p854

8569 BAYVIEW AVE, RICHMOND HILL, ON, L4B 3M7

(905) 889-6882   *SIC* 8211

TRI-COUNTY REGIONAL SCHOOL BOARD p471

79 WATER ST, YARMOUTH, NS, B5A 1L4

(902) 749-5696   *SIC* 8211

TRILLIUM LAKELANDS DISTRICT SCHOOL BOARD p590

66 LINDSAY ST, FENELON FALLS, ON, K0M 1N0

(705) 887-2018   *SIC* 8211

TRILLIUM LAKELANDS DISTRICT SCHOOL BOARD p646

300 COUNTY RD 36, LINDSAY, ON, K9V 4R4

(705) 324-6776   *SIC* 8211

TRILLIUM LAKELANDS DISTRICT SCHOOL BOARD p646

260 KENT ST W, LINDSAY, ON, K9V 2Z5

(705) 324-3556   *SIC* 8211

TRILLIUM LAKELANDS DISTRICT SCHOOL BOARD p646

24 WELDON RD, LINDSAY, ON, K9V 4R4

(705) 324-3585   *SIC* 8211

TRIOS CORPORATION p728

6755 MISSISSAUGA RD SUITE 103, MISSISSAUGA, ON, L5N 7Y2

(905) 814-7212   *SIC* 8211

TURTLE MOUNTAIN SCHOOL DIVISION p351

435 WILLIAMS AVE, KILLARNEY, MB, R0K 1G0

(204) 523-7531   *SIC* 8211

TURTLE RIVER SCHOOL DIVISION p352

808 BURROWS RD, MCCREARY, MB, R0J 1B0

(204) 835-2067   *SIC* 8211

UPPER CANADA COLLEGE p927

200 LONSDALE RD, TORONTO, ON, M4V 1W6

(416) 488-1125   *SIC* 8211

UPPER CANADA DISTRICT SCHOOL BOARD, THE p520

225 CENTRAL AVE W, BROCKVILLE, ON, K6V 5X1

(613) 342-0371   *SIC* 8211

UPPER CANADA DISTRICT SCHOOL BOARD, THE p520

2510 PARKEDALE AVE, BROCKVILLE, ON, K6V 3H1

(613) 342-1100   *SIC* 8211

UPPER GRAND DISTRICT SCHOOL BOARD, THE p600

500 VICTORIA RD N, GUELPH, ON, N1E 6K2

(519) 822-4420   *SIC* 8211

UPPER GRAND DISTRICT SCHOOL BOARD, THE p604

155 PAISLEY ST SUITE UPPER, GUELPH, ON, N1H 2P3

(519) 824-9800   *SIC* 8211

UPPER GRAND DISTRICT SCHOOL BOARD, THE p607

1428 GORDON ST, GUELPH, ON, N1L 1C8

(519) 836-7280   *SIC* 8211

UPPER GRAND DISTRICT SCHOOL BOARD, THE p809

300 ALDER ST, ORANGEVILLE, ON, L9W 5A2

(519) 938-9355   *SIC* 8211

UPPER GRAND DISTRICT SCHOOL BOARD, THE p836

GD, PALMERSTON, ON, N0G 2P0

(519) 343-3107   *SIC* 8211

UPPER GRAND DISTRICT SCHOOL BOARD, THE p880

150 FOURTH AVE, SHELBURNE, ON, L9V 3R5

(519) 925-3834   *SIC* 8211

VANCOUVER CAREER COLLEGE (BURNABY) INC p310

400 BURRARD ST SUITE 1800, VANCOUVER, BC, V6C 3A6

(604) 915-7288   *SIC* 8211

VANCOUVER COLLEGE LIMITED p323

5400 CARTIER ST, VANCOUVER, BC, V6M 3A5

(604) 261-4285   *SIC* 8211

VILLA SAINTE MARCELLINE p1401

815 AV UPPER BELMONT, WESTMOUNT, QC, H3Y 1K5

(514) 488-2528   *SIC* 8211

WATERLOO CATHOLIC DISTRICT SCHOOL BOARD p532

50 SAGINAW PKY, CAMBRIDGE, ON, N1P 1A1

(519) 621-4050   *SIC* 8211

WATERLOO CATHOLIC DISTRICT SCHOOL BOARD p535

185 MYERS RD, CAMBRIDGE, ON, N1R 7H2

(519) 622-1290   *SIC* 8211

WATERLOO CATHOLIC DISTRICT SCHOOL BOARD p637

1500 BLOCK LINE RD, KITCHENER, ON, N2C 2S2

(519) 745-6891   *SIC* 8211

WATERLOO CATHOLIC DISTRICT SCHOOL BOARD p640

35A WEBER ST W, KITCHENER, ON, N2H 3Z1

(519) 578-3660   *SIC* 8211

WATERLOO CATHOLIC DISTRICT SCHOOL BOARD p641

560 PIONEER DR, KITCHENER, ON, N2P 1P2

(519) 895-1716   *SIC* 8211

WATERLOO CATHOLIC DISTRICT SCHOOL BOARD p641

455 UNIVERSITY AVE W, KITCHENER, ON, N2N 3B9

(519) 741-1990   *SIC* 8211

WATERLOO REGION DISTRICT SCHOOL BOARD p484

1206 SNYDER'S RD W, BADEN, ON, N3A 1A4

(519) 634-5441   *SIC* 8211

WATERLOO REGION DISTRICT SCHOOL BOARD p535

30 SOUTHWOOD DR, CAMBRIDGE, ON, N1S 4K3

(519) 621-5920   *SIC* 8211

WATERLOO REGION DISTRICT SCHOOL BOARD p535

200 WATER ST N, CAMBRIDGE, ON, N1R 6V2

(519) 623-3600   *SIC* 8211

WATERLOO REGION DISTRICT SCHOOL BOARD p535

55 MCKAY ST, CAMBRIDGE, ON, N1R 4G6

(519) 621-9510   *SIC* 8211

WATERLOO REGION DISTRICT SCHOOL BOARD p537

355 HOLIDAY INN DR, CAMBRIDGE, ON, N3C 1Z2

(519) 658-4910   *SIC* 8211

WATERLOO REGION DISTRICT SCHOOL BOARD p539

550 ROSE ST, CAMBRIDGE, ON, N3H 2E6

(519) 653-2367   *SIC* 8211

WATERLOO REGION DISTRICT SCHOOL BOARD p568

4 UNIVERSITY AVE W, ELMIRA, ON, N3B

1K2
(519) 669-5414   *SIC* 8211
WATERLOO REGION DISTRICT SCHOOL BOARD   p637
51 ARDELT AVE, KITCHENER, ON, N2C 2R5
(519) 570-0300   *SIC* 8211
WATERLOO REGION DISTRICT SCHOOL BOARD   p638
245 ACTIVA AVE, KITCHENER, ON, N2E 4A3
(519) 579-1160   *SIC* 8211
WATERLOO REGION DISTRICT SCHOOL BOARD   p639
301 CHARLES ST E, KITCHENER, ON, N2G 2P8
(519) 578-8330   *SIC* 8211
WATERLOO REGION DISTRICT SCHOOL BOARD   p640
760 WEBER ST E, KITCHENER, ON, N2H 1H6
(519) 742-1848   *SIC* 8211
WATERLOO REGION DISTRICT SCHOOL BOARD   p641
255 FISCHER HALLMAN RD, KITCHENER, ON, N2M 4X8
(519) 744-6567   *SIC* 8211
WATERLOO REGION DISTRICT SCHOOL BOARD   p1007
80 BLUEVALE ST N, WATERLOO, ON, N2J 3R5
(519) 885-4620   *SIC* 8211
WATERLOO REGION DISTRICT SCHOOL BOARD   p1008
520 CHESAPEAKE DR, WATERLOO, ON, N2K 4G5
(519) 880-0300   *SIC* 8211
WATERLOO REGION DISTRICT SCHOOL BOARD   p1009
300 HAZEL ST, WATERLOO, ON, N2L 3P2
(519) 884-9590   *SIC* 8211
WEBBER ACADEMY FOUNDATION   p75
1515 93 ST SW, CALGARY, AB, T3H 4A8
(403) 277-4700   *SIC* 8211
WELLINGTON CATHOLIC DISTRICT SCHOOL BOARD   p600
57 VICTORIA RD N, GUELPH, ON, N1E 5G9
(519) 822-4290   *SIC* 8211
WELLINGTON CATHOLIC DISTRICT SCHOOL BOARD   p605
54 WESTMOUNT RD, GUELPH, ON, N1H 5H7
(519) 836-2170   *SIC* 8211
WELLINGTON CATHOLIC DISTRICT SCHOOL BOARD   p607
200 CLAIR RD W, GUELPH, ON, N1L 1G1
(519) 822-8502   *SIC* 8211
WEST POINT GREY INDEPENDENT SCHOOL SOCIETY   p324
4125 8TH AVE W, VANCOUVER, BC, V6R 4P9
(604) 222-8750   *SIC* 8211
WESTERN QUEBEC SCHOOL BOARD   p1108
15 RUE KATIMAVIK, GATINEAU, QC, J9J 0E9
(819) 684-1313   *SIC* 8211
WESTERN SCHOOL DIVISION   p352
75 THORNHILL ST UNIT 4, MORDEN, MB, R6M 1P2
(204) 822-4448   *SIC* 8211
WESTMOUNT CHARTER SCHOOL SOCIETY   p74
2519 RICHMOND RD SW, CALGARY, AB, T3E 4M2
(403) 217-0426   *SIC* 8211
WESTWIND SCHOOL DIVISION #74   p79
730 4TH AVE W, CARDSTON, AB, T0K 0K0
(403) 653-4955   *SIC* 8211
WESTWIND SCHOOL DIVISION #74   p153
145 N 200 W, RAYMOND, AB, T0K 2S0
(403) 752-3004   *SIC* 8211
WETASKIWIN REGIONAL PUBLIC

SCHOOLS   p172
4619 50 AVE, WETASKIWIN, AB, T9A 0R6
(780) 352-2295   *SIC* 8211
WETASKIWIN REGIONAL PUBLIC SCHOOLS   p172
5515 47A AVE, WETASKIWIN, AB, T9A 3S3
(780) 352-6018   *SIC* 8211
WILD ROSE SCHOOL DIVISION NO. 66p159
4912 43 ST, ROCKY MOUNTAIN HOUSE, AB, T4T 1P4
(403) 845-3376   *SIC* 8211
WINDSOR-ESSEX CATHOLIC DISTRICT SCHOOL BOARD, THE   p643
2555 SANDWICH WEST PKY, LASALLE, ON, N9H 2P7
(519) 972-6050   *SIC* 8211
WINDSOR-ESSEX CATHOLIC DISTRICT SCHOOL BOARD, THE   p1022
441 TECUMSEH RD E, WINDSOR, ON, N8X 2R7
(519) 256-3171   *SIC* 8211
WINDSOR-ESSEX CATHOLIC DISTRICT SCHOOL BOARD, THE   p1024
1325 CALIFORNIA AVE, WINDSOR, ON, N9B 3Y6
(519) 253-2481   *SIC* 8211
WINDSOR-ESSEX CATHOLIC DISTRICT SCHOOL BOARD, THE   p1024
2800 NORTH TOWN LINE RD, WINDSOR, ON, N9A 6Z6
(519) 734-6444   *SIC* 8211
WINDSOR-ESSEX CATHOLIC DISTRICT SCHOOL BOARD, THE   p1025
1400 NORTHWOOD ST, WINDSOR, ON, N9E 1A4
(519) 966-2504   *SIC* 8211
WINDSOR-ESSEX CATHOLIC DISTRICT SCHOOL BOARD, THE   p1025
1100 HURON CHURCH RD, WINDSOR, ON, N9C 2K7
(519) 256-7801   *SIC* 8211
WINNIPEG SCHOOL DIVISION   p370
2424 KING EDWARD ST, WINNIPEG, MB, R2R 2R2
(204) 694-0483   *SIC* 8211
WINNIPEG SCHOOL DIVISION   p371
401 CHURCH AVE, WINNIPEG, MB, R2W 1C4
(204) 589-4374   *SIC* 8211
WINNIPEG SCHOOL DIVISION   p373
1360 REDWOOD AVE, WINNIPEG, MB, R2X 0Z1
(204) 589-8321   *SIC* 8211
WINNIPEG SCHOOL DIVISION   p381
720 ALVERSTONE ST, WINNIPEG, MB, R3E 2H1
(204) 783-7131   *SIC* 8211
WINNIPEG SCHOOL DIVISION   p381
1555 WALL ST, WINNIPEG, MB, R3E 2S2
(204) 786-1401   *SIC* 8211
WINNIPEG SCHOOL DIVISION   p381
1577 WALL ST E, WINNIPEG, MB, R3E 2S5
(204) 775-0231   *SIC* 8211
WINNIPEG SCHOOL DIVISION   p381
2 SARGENT PARK PL, WINNIPEG, MB, R3E 0V8
(204) 775-8985   *SIC* 8211
WINNIPEG SCHOOL DIVISION   p381
1395 SPRUCE ST SUITE 1, WINNIPEG, MB, R3E 2V8
(204) 786-0344   *SIC* 8211
WINNIPEG SCHOOL DIVISION   p383
3 BORROWMAN PL, WINNIPEG, MB, R3G 1M6
(204) 774-5401   *SIC* 8211
WINNIPEG SCHOOL DIVISION   p387
510 HAY ST, WINNIPEG, MB, R3L 2L6
(204) 474-1301   *SIC* 8211
WINNIPEG SCHOOL DIVISION   p388
450 NATHANIEL ST, WINNIPEG, MB, R3M 3E3
(204) 452-3112   *SIC* 8211
WINNIPEG SCHOOL DIVISION   p388
155 KINGSWAY, WINNIPEG, MB, R3M 0G3

(204) 474-1492   *SIC* 8211
WOLF CREEK SCHOOL DIVISION NO.72   p153
6000 HIGHWAY 2A, PONOKA, AB, T4J 1P6
(403) 783-5441   *SIC* 8211
YELLOWKNIFE PUBLIC DENOMINATIONAL DISTRICT EDUCATION AUTHORITY   p436
5124 49 ST, YELLOWKNIFE, NT, X1A 1P8
(867) 766-7400   *SIC* 8211
YESHIVA YESODEI HATORAH   p788
77 GLEN RUSH BLVD, NORTH YORK, ON, M5N 2T8
(416) 787-1101   *SIC* 8211
YORK CATHOLIC DISTRICT SCHOOL BOARD   p482
210 BLOOMINGTON RD SUITE SIDE, AURORA, ON, L4G 0P9
(905) 727-2455   *SIC* 8211
YORK CATHOLIC DISTRICT SCHOOL BOARD   p482
320 BLOOMINGTON RD, AURORA, ON, L4G 0M1
(905) 713-1211   *SIC* 8211
YORK CATHOLIC DISTRICT SCHOOL BOARD   p628
185 GLENWOODS AVE, KESWICK, ON, L4P 2W6
(905) 656-9140   *SIC* 8211
YORK CATHOLIC DISTRICT SCHOOL BOARD   p664
400 ST. JOAN OF ARC AVE, MAPLE, ON, L6A 2S8
(905) 303-6121   *SIC* 8211
YORK CATHOLIC DISTRICT SCHOOL BOARD   p678
5300 14TH AVE, MARKHAM, ON, L3S 3K8
(905) 472-4961   *SIC* 8211
YORK CATHOLIC DISTRICT SCHOOL BOARD   p679
2188 RODICK RD, MARKHAM, ON, L6C 1S3
(905) 887-6171   *SIC* 8211
YORK CATHOLIC DISTRICT SCHOOL BOARD   p757
1 CRUSADER WAY, NEWMARKET, ON, L3Y 6R2
(905) 895-3340   *SIC* 8211
YORK CATHOLIC DISTRICT SCHOOL BOARD   p905
8101 LESLIE ST, THORNHILL, ON, L3T 7P4
(905) 889-4982   *SIC* 8211
YORK CATHOLIC DISTRICT SCHOOL BOARD   p1029
120 LA ROCCA AVE, WOODBRIDGE, ON, L4H 2A9
(905) 303-4646   *SIC* 8211
YORK CATHOLIC DISTRICT SCHOOL BOARD   p1034
250 ANSLEY GROVE RD, WOODBRIDGE, ON, L4L 3W4
(905) 851-6643   *SIC* 8211
YORK CATHOLIC DISTRICT SCHOOL BOARD   p1034
7501 MARTIN GROVE RD, WOODBRIDGE, ON, L4L 1A5
(905) 851-6699   *SIC* 8211
YORK REGION DISTRICT SCHOOL BOARD   p482
60 WELLINGTON ST W, AURORA, ON, L4G 3H2
(905) 727-3141   *SIC* 8211
YORK REGION DISTRICT SCHOOL BOARD   p628
100 BISCAYNE BLVD, KESWICK, ON, L4P 3S2
(905) 476-0933   *SIC* 8211
YORK REGION DISTRICT SCHOOL BOARD   p629
2001 KING RD, KING CITY, ON, L7B 1K2
(905) 833-5332   *SIC* 8211
YORK REGION DISTRICT SCHOOL BOARD   p664

50 SPRINGSIDE RD, MAPLE, ON, L6A 2W5
(905) 417-9444   *SIC* 8211
YORK REGION DISTRICT SCHOOL BOARD   p665
89 CHURCH ST, MARKHAM, ON, L3P 2M3
(905) 294-1886   *SIC* 8211
YORK REGION DISTRICT SCHOOL BOARD   p678
525 HIGHGLEN AVE, MARKHAM, ON, L3S 3L5
(905) 472-8900   *SIC* 8211
YORK REGION DISTRICT SCHOOL BOARD   p679
90 BUR OAK AVE, MARKHAM, ON, L6C 2E6
(905) 887-2216   *SIC* 8211
YORK REGION DISTRICT SCHOOL BOARD   p754
705 COLUMBUS WAY, NEWMARKET, ON, L3X 2M7
(905) 967-1045   *SIC* 8211
YORK REGION DISTRICT SCHOOL BOARD   p757
135 BRISTOL RD, NEWMARKET, ON, L3Y 8J7
(905) 836-0021   *SIC* 8211
YORK REGION DISTRICT SCHOOL BOARD   p757
505 PICKERING CRES, NEWMARKET, ON, L3Y 8H1
(905) 895-5159   *SIC* 8211
YORK REGION DISTRICT SCHOOL BOARD   p757
40 HURON HEIGHTS DR, NEWMARKET, ON, L3Y 3J9
(905) 895-2384   *SIC* 8211
YORK REGION DISTRICT SCHOOL BOARD   p854
81 STRATHEARN AVE, RICHMOND HILL, ON, L4B 2J5
(905) 508-0806   *SIC* 8211
YORK REGION DISTRICT SCHOOL BOARD   p856
10077 BAYVIEW AVE, RICHMOND HILL, ON, L4C 2L4
(905) 884-4453   *SIC* 8211
YORK REGION DISTRICT SCHOOL BOARD   p856
106 GARDEN AVE, RICHMOND HILL, ON, L4C 6M1
(905) 889-6266   *SIC* 8211
YORK REGION DISTRICT SCHOOL BOARD   p856
300 MAJOR MACKENZIE DR W, RICHMOND HILL, ON, L4C 3S3
(905) 884-0554   *SIC* 8211
YORK REGION DISTRICT SCHOOL BOARD   p895
801 HOOVER PARK DR, STOUFFVILLE, ON, L4A 0A4
(905) 640-1433   *SIC* 8211
YORK REGION DISTRICT SCHOOL BOARD   p902
20798 DALTON RD, SUTTON WEST, ON, L0E 1R0
(905) 722-3281   *SIC* 8211
YORK REGION DISTRICT SCHOOL BOARD   p905
8075 BAYVIEW AVE, THORNHILL, ON, L3T 4N4
(905) 889-9696   *SIC* 8211
YORK REGION DISTRICT SCHOOL BOARD   p906
1401 CLARK AVE W, THORNHILL, ON, L4J 7R4
(905) 660-1397   *SIC* 8211
YORK REGION DISTRICT SCHOOL BOARD   p1000
1000 CARLTON RD, UNIONVILLE, ON, L3P 7P5
(905) 940-8840   *SIC* 8211
YORK REGION DISTRICT SCHOOL BOARD   p1029
4901 RUTHERFORD RD, WOODBRIDGE,

ON, L4H 3C2

(905) 850-5012   *SIC* 8211
YORK SCHOOL, THE   *p926*
1320 YONGE ST, TORONTO, ON, M4T 1X2
(416) 926-1325   *SIC* 8211
YORKTON ROMAN CATHOLIC SEPERATE SCHOOL DIVISION NO. 86   *p1439*
259 CIRCLEBROOKE DR, YORKTON, SK, S3N 2S8

SIC 8211

SIC 8221 Colleges and universities

131427 CANADA INC   *p1214*
2000 RUE SAINTE-CATHERINE O BUREAU 2, MONTREAL, QC, H3H 2T2
(514) 939-4444   *SIC* 8221
ALBERTA COLLEGE OF PARAMEDICS   *p162*
2755 BROADMOOR BLVD UNIT 220, SHERWOOD PARK, AB, T8H 2W7
(780) 449-3114   *SIC* 8221
ALGOMA UNIVERSITY   *p508*
24 QUEEN ST E SUITE 102, BRAMPTON, ON, L6V 1A3
(905) 451-0100   *SIC* 8221
ALGOMA UNIVERSITY   *p861*
1520 QUEEN ST E, SAULT STE. MARIE, ON, P6A 2G4
(705) 949-2301   *SIC* 8221
AMBROSE UNIVERSITY COLLEGE   *p75*
150 AMBROSE CIR SW, CALGARY, AB, T3H 0L5
(403) 410-2000   *SIC* 8221
ART INSTITUTE OF VANCOUVER INC, THE   *p286*
2665 RENFREW ST, VANCOUVER, BC, V5M 0A7
(604) 683-9200   *SIC* 8221
ATHABASCA UNIVERSITY   *p4*
1 UNIVERSITY DR, ATHABASCA, AB, T9S 3A3
(780) 675-6100   *SIC* 8221
AURORA COLLEGE   *p435*
50 CONIBEAR CRES, FORT SMITH, NT, X0E 0P0
(867) 872-7000   *SIC* 8221
BOARD OF GOVERNERS OF BOW VALLEY COLLEGE, THE   *p27*
345 6 AVE SE, CALGARY, AB, T2G 4V1
(403) 410-1400   *SIC* 8221
BRIERCREST COLLEGE AND SEMINARY   *p1405*
510 COLLEGE DR, CARONPORT, SK, S0H 0S0
(306) 756-3200   *SIC* 8221
BRITISH COLUMBIA INSTITUTE OF TECHNOLOGY, THE   *p188*
3700 WILLINGDON AVE, BURNABY, BC, V5G 3H2
(604) 434-5734   *SIC* 8221
BROCK UNIVERSITY   *p886*
1812 SIR ISAAC BROCK WAY, ST CATHARINES, ON, L2S 3A1
(905) 688-5550   *SIC* 8221
BURMAN UNIVERSITY   *p138*
6730 UNIVERSITY DR ROOM A104, LACOMBE, AB, T4L 2E5
(403) 782-3381   *SIC* 8221
CALGARY BOARD OF EDUCATION   *p73*
2519 RICHMOND RD SW SUITE 168, CALGARY, AB, T3E 4M2
(403) 777-7200   *SIC* 8221
CAMOSUN COLLEGE   *p333*
3100 FOUL BAY RD, VICTORIA, BC, V8P 5J2
(250) 370-3550   *SIC* 8221
CAMPUS NOTRE-DAME-DE-FOY   *p1292*
5000 RUE CLEMENT-LOCKQUELL, SAINT-AUGUSTIN-DE-DESMAURES, QC, G3A 1B3
(418) 872-8041   *SIC* 8221
CANADIAN BIBLE COLLEGE   *p1422*
4400 4TH AVE, REGINA, SK, S4T 0H8

(306) 545-0210   *SIC* 8221
CANADIAN MEMORIAL CHIROPRACTIC COLLEGE   *p764*
6100 LESLIE ST, NORTH YORK, ON, M2H 3J1
(416) 482-2340   *SIC* 8221
CANADIAN MENNONITE UNIVERSITY *p388*
500 SHAFTESBURY BLVD, WINNIPEG, MB, R3P 2N2
(204) 487-3300   *SIC* 8221
CAPE BRETON UNIVERSITY   *p466*
1250 GRAND LAKE RD, SYDNEY, NS, B1M 1A2
(902) 539-5300   *SIC* 8221
CAPILANO UNIVERSITY   *p239*
2055 PURCELL WAY SUITE 284, NORTH VANCOUVER, BC, V7J 3H5
(604) 986-1911   *SIC* 8221
CARLETON UNIVERSITY   *p825*
1125 COLONEL BY DR, OTTAWA, ON, K1S 5B6
(613) 520-2600   *SIC* 8221
CEGEP DE BAIE-COMEAU   *p1053*
537 BOUL BLANCHE, BAIE-COMEAU, QC, G5C 2B2
(418) 589-5707   *SIC* 8221
CEGEP DE GRANBY HAUTE-YAMASKA *p1109*
235 RUE SAINT-JACQUES, GRANBY, QC, J2G 3N1
(450) 372-6614   *SIC* 8221
CEGEP DE THETFORD   *p1382*
671 BOUL FRONTENAC O, THETFORD MINES, QC, G6G 1N1
(418) 338-8591   *SIC* 8221
CEGEP HERITAGE COLLEGE   *p1106*
325 BOUL DE LA CITE-DES-JEUNES, GATINEAU, QC, J8Y 6T3
(819) 778-2270   *SIC* 8221
CHOEUR DU CEGEP DE SHERBROOKE *p1370*
475 RUE DU CEGEP, SHERBROOKE, QC, J1E 4K1
(819) 564-6350   *SIC* 8221
COAST MOUNTAIN COLLEGE   *p283*
5331 MCCONNELL AVE, TERRACE, BC, V8G 4X2
(250) 635-6511   *SIC* 8221
COLLEGE AHUNTSIC   *p1176*
9155 RUE SAINT HUBERT, MONTREAL, QC, H2M 1Y8
(514) 389-5921   *SIC* 8221
COLLEGE ANTOINE-GIROUARD   *p1312*
700 RUE GIROUARD E, SAINT-HYACINTHE, QC, J2S 2Y2
SIC 8221
COLLEGE BOURGET   *p1283*
65 RUE SAINT-PIERRE, RIGAUD, QC, J0P 1P0
(450) 451-0815   *SIC* 8221
COLLEGE CHARLEMAGNE INC   *p1245*
5000 RUE PILON, PIERREFONDS, QC, H9K 1G4
(514) 626-7060   *SIC* 8221
COLLEGE CHARLES-LEMOYNE DE LONGUEUIL INC   *p1146*
901 CH TIFFIN, LONGUEUIL, QC, J4P 3G6
(514) 875-0505   *SIC* 8221
COLLEGE D'AFFAIRES ELLIS (1974) INC *p1098*
235 RUE MOISAN, DRUMMONDVILLE, QC, J2C 1W9
(819) 477-3113   *SIC* 8221
COLLEGE D'ENSEIGNEMENT GENERAL & PROFESSIONEL DE LA POCATIERE *p1122*
140 4E AV, LA POCATIERE, QC, G0R 1Z0
(418) 856-1525   *SIC* 8221
COLLEGE D'ENSEIGNEMENT GENERAL & PROFESSIONNEL DE MATANE   *p1150*
616 AV SAINT-REDEMPTEUR, MATANE, QC, G4W 1L1
(418) 562-1240   *SIC* 8221
COLLEGE D'ENSEIGNEMENT GENERAL ET PROFESSIONEL MARIE-VICTORIN

p1163
7000 RUE MARIE-VICTORIN, MONTREAL, QC, H1G 2J6
(514) 325-0150   *SIC* 8221
COLLEGE D'ENSEIGNEMENT GENERAL ET PROFESSIONNEL DE RIVIERE-DU-LOUP   *p1286*
80 RUE FRONTENAC, RIVIERE-DU-LOUP, QC, G5R 1R1
(418) 862-6903   *SIC* 8221
COLLEGE D'ENSEIGNEMENT GENERAL ET PROFESSIONNEL DE VICTORIAVILLE *p1397*
475 RUE NOTRE-DAME E, VICTORIAVILLE, QC, G6P 4B3
(819) 758-6401   *SIC* 8221
COLLEGE D'ENSEIGNEMENT GENERAL ET PROFESSIONNEL GERALD-GODIN *p1358*
15615 BOUL GOUIN O, SAINTE-GENEVIEVE, QC, H9H 5K8
(514) 626-2666   *SIC* 8221
COLLEGE D'ENSEIGNEMENT GENERAL ET PROFESSIONNEL JOHN ABBOTT*p1355*
21275 RUE LAKESHORE, SAINTE-ANNE-DE-BELLEVUE, QC, H9X 3L9
(514) 457-6610   *SIC* 8221
COLLEGE D'ENSEIGNEMENT GENERAL ET PROFESSIONNEL SOREL-TRACY*p1377*
3000 BOUL DE TRACY, SOREL-TRACY, QC, J3R 5B9
(450) 742-6651   *SIC* 8221
COLLEGE D'ENSEIGNEMENT GENERALE & PROFESSIONNEL DE LA GASPESIE & DES ILES   *p1102*
96 RUE JACQUES-CARTIER, GASPE, QC, G4X 2S8
(418) 368-2201   *SIC* 8221
COLLEGE DE LEVIS   *p1136*
9 RUE MONSEIGNEUR-GOSSELIN BUREAU 109, LEVIS, QC, G6V 5K1
(418) 833-1249   *SIC* 8221
COLLEGE DE MONT-ROYAL   *p1163*
2165 RUE BALDWIN, MONTREAL, QC, H1L 5A7
(514) 351-7851   *SIC* 8221
COLLEGE DE MONTREAL   *p1214*
1931 RUE SHERBROOKE O, MONTREAL, QC, H3H 1E3
(514) 933-7397   *SIC* 8221
COLLEGE DE SAINT-BONIFACE   *p364*
200 DE LA CATHEDRALE AVE, WINNIPEG, MB, R2H 0H7
(204) 233-0210   *SIC* 8221
COLLEGE LAFLECHE   *p1386*
1687 BOUL DU CARMEL, TROIS-RIVIERES, QC, G8Z 3R8
(819) 375-7346   *SIC* 8221
COLLEGE LETENDRE   *p1235*
1000 BOUL DE L'AVENIR, MONTREAL, QC, H7N 6J6
(450) 688-9933   *SIC* 8221
COLLEGE MERICI   *p1270*
755 GRANDE ALLEE O BUREAU 683, QUEBEC, QC, G1S 1C1
(418) 683-1591   *SIC* 8221
COLLEGE OF NEW CALEDONIA, THE*p250*
3330 22ND AVE, PRINCE GEORGE, BC, V2N 1P8
(250) 562-2131   *SIC* 8221
COLLEGE SAINT-ALEXANDRE DE LA GATINEAU   *p1105*
2425 RUE SAINT-LOUIS, GATINEAU, QC, J8V 1E7
(819) 561-3812   *SIC* 8221
COLLEGE SAINT-CHARLES-GARNIER, LE *p1270*
1150 BOUL RENE-LEVESQUE O, QUEBEC, QC, G1S 1V7
(418) 681-0107   *SIC* 8221
COLLEGE SAINT-MAURICE   *p1312*
630 RUE GIROUARD O, SAINT-HYACINTHE, QC, J2S 2Y3
(450) 773-7478   *SIC* 8221

COLLEGE SAINTE-ANNE   *p1126*
1250 BOUL SAINT-JOSEPH, LACHINE, QC, H8S 2M8
(514) 637-3571   *SIC* 8221
COLLEGE SHAWINIGAN   *p1368*
2263 AV DU COLLEGE, SHAWINIGAN, QC, G9N 6V8
(819) 539-6401   *SIC* 8221
COLLEGE STE-ANNE-DE-LA POCATIERE *p1122*
100 4E AV, LA POCATIERE, QC, G0R 1Z0
(418) 856-3012   *SIC* 8221
COLUMBIA COLLEGE   *p297*
555 SEYMOUR ST SUITE 500, VANCOUVER, BC, V6B 3H6
(604) 683-8360   *SIC* 8221
COMMISSION SCOLAIRE DES NAVIGATEURS   *p1136*
30 RUE VINCENT-CHAGNON, LEVIS, QC, G6V 4V6
(418) 838-8400   *SIC* 8221
CONCORDIA UNIVERSITY COLLEGE OF ALBERTA   *p83*
7128 ADA BLVD NW, EDMONTON, AB, T5B 4E4
(780) 479-8481   *SIC* 8221
COOPERATIVE ETUDIANTE DU CEGEP DE SEPT-ILES   *p1367*
175 RUE DE LA VERENDRYE, SEPT-ILES, QC, G4R 5B7
(418) 962-9848   *SIC* 8221
CORPORATION DE CEGEP ANDRE-LAURENDEAU   *p1130*
1111 RUE LAPIERRE BUREAU 300, LASALLE, QC, H8N 2J4
(514) 364-3320   *SIC* 8221
CORPORATION DE L'ECOLE DES HAUTES ETUDES COMMERCIALES DE MONTREAL *p1219*
3000 CH DE LA COTE-SAINTE-CATHERINE, MONTREAL, QC, H3T 2A7
(514) 340-6000   *SIC* 8221
CORPORATION DE L'ECOLE POLYTECHNIQUE DE MONTREAL   *p1219*
2900 BOUL EDOUARD-MONTPETIT, MONTREAL, QC, H3T 1J4
(514) 340-4711   *SIC* 8221
CORPORATION DU COLLEGE DE L'ASSOMPTION, LA   *p1120*
270 BOUL DE L'ANGE-GARDIEN, L'ASSOMPTION, QC, J5W 1R7
(450) 589-5621   *SIC* 8221
DALHOUSIE UNIVERSITY   *p451*
1276 SOUTH PARK ST RM 225, HALIFAX, NS, B3H 2Y9
(902) 473-7736   *SIC* 8221
DALHOUSIE UNIVERSITY   *p451*
6135 UNIVERSITY AVE RM 3030, HALIFAX, NS, B3H 4P9
(902) 494-1440   *SIC* 8221
DALHOUSIE UNIVERSITY   *p451*
5850 COLLEGE ST UNIT 13B, HALIFAX, NS, B3H 1X5
(902) 494-6850   *SIC* 8221
DALHOUSIE UNIVERSITY   *p451*
6299 SOUTH ST, HALIFAX, NS, B3H 4J1
(902) 494-2211   *SIC* 8221
DALHOUSIE UNIVERSITY   *p468*
62 CUMMING DR, TRURO, NS, B2N 5E3
(902) 893-6600   *SIC* 8221
DIVISION SCOLAIRE FRANCO-MANITOBAINE   *p364*
585 RUE ST JEAN BAPTISTE, WINNIPEG, MB, R2H 2Y2
(204) 237-8927   *SIC* 8221
FIRST NATIONS UNIVERSITY OF CANADA *p1421*
1 FIRST NATIONS WAY, REGINA, SK, S4S 7K2
(306) 790-5950   *SIC* 8221
FONDATION DE L'UNIVERSITE DU QUEBEC EN OUTAOUAIS   *p1105*
283 BOUL ALEXANDRE-TACHE BUREAU F-0239, GATINEAU, QC, J8X 3X7

---

(819) 595-3900   *SIC* 8221
FONDATION DU CEGEP DU VIEUX MONTREAL, LA *p1185*
255 RUE ONTARIO E, MONTREAL, QC, H2X 1X6
(514) 982-3437   *SIC* 8221
FONDATION DU CEGEP REGIONAL DE LANAUDIERE *p1282*
781 RUE NOTRE-DAME, REPENTIGNY, QC, J5Y 1B4
(450) 470-0911   *SIC* 8221
FONDATION DU CEGEP REGIONAL DE LANAUDIERE *p1380*
2505 BOUL DES ENTREPRISES, TERREBONNE, QC, J6X 5S5
(450) 470-0933   *SIC* 8221
FONDATION UNIVERSITE DU QUEBEC *p1175*
405 RUE SAINTE-CATHERINE E, MONTREAL, QC, H2L 2C4
SIC 8221
GEORGE BROWN COLLEGE OF APPLIED ARTS AND TECHNOLOGY, THE *p977*
160 KENDAL AVE SUITE 126A, TORONTO, ON, M5T 2T9
(416) 415-5000   *SIC* 8221
GOVERNING COUNCIL OF THE UNIVERSITY OF TORONTO, THE *p570*
80 QUEENS AVE, ETOBICOKE, ON, M8V 2N3
(416) 978-0414   *SIC* 8221
GOVERNING COUNCIL OF THE UNIVERSITY OF TORONTO, THE *p570*
84 QUEENS AVE, ETOBICOKE, ON, M8V 2N3
(416) 978-8789   *SIC* 8221
GOVERNING COUNCIL OF THE UNIVERSITY OF TORONTO, THE *p570*
78 QUEENS AVE, ETOBICOKE, ON, M8V 2N3
(416) 978-0210   *SIC* 8221
GOVERNING COUNCIL OF THE UNIVERSITY OF TORONTO, THE *p865*
1265 MILITARY TRAIL SUITE 303, SCARBOROUGH, ON, M1C 1A4
(416) 287-7033   *SIC* 8221
GOVERNING COUNCIL OF THE UNIVERSITY OF TORONTO, THE *p932*
10 ST MARY ST SUITE 700, TORONTO, ON, M4Y 2W8
(416) 978-1000   *SIC* 8221
GOVERNING COUNCIL OF THE UNIVERSITY OF TORONTO, THE *p945*
190 ELIZABETH ST, TORONTO, ON, M5G 2C4
(416) 978-8383   *SIC* 8221
GOVERNING COUNCIL OF THE UNIVERSITY OF TORONTO, THE *p945*
101 COLLEGE ST RM 15-701, TORONTO, ON, M5G 1L7
(416) 634-8755   *SIC* 8221
GOVERNING COUNCIL OF THE UNIVERSITY OF TORONTO, THE *p945*
123 EDWARD ST SUITE 1200, TORONTO, ON, M5G 1E2
(416) 978-2668   *SIC* 8221
GOVERNING COUNCIL OF THE UNIVERSITY OF TORONTO, THE *p945*
500 UNIVERSITY AVE SUITE 160, TORONTO, ON, M5G 1V7
(416) 946-8554   *SIC* 8221
GOVERNING COUNCIL OF THE UNIVERSITY OF TORONTO, THE *p945*
124 EDWARD ST, TORONTO, ON, M5G 1G6
(416) 979-4927   *SIC* 8221
GOVERNING COUNCIL OF THE UNIVERSITY OF TORONTO, THE *p945*
100 COLLEGE ST RM 110, TORONTO, ON, M5G 1L5
(416) 978-4059   *SIC* 8221
GOVERNING COUNCIL OF THE UNIVERSITY OF TORONTO, THE *p945*
555 UNIVERSITY AVE RM 1436D,

TORONTO, ON, M5G 1X8
(416) 813-6122   *SIC* 8221
GOVERNING COUNCIL OF THE UNIVERSITY OF TORONTO, THE *p972*
170 ST. GEORGE ST, TORONTO, ON, M5R 2M8
(416) 978-3190   *SIC* 8221
GOVERNING COUNCIL OF THE UNIVERSITY OF TORONTO, THE *p972*
170 ST. GEORGE ST 4 FL, TORONTO, ON, M5R 2M8
(416) 978-3311   *SIC* 8221
GOVERNING COUNCIL OF THE UNIVERSITY OF TORONTO, THE *p974*
35 ST. GEORGE ST SUITE 173, TORONTO, ON, M5S 1A4
(416) 978-3099   *SIC* 8221
GOVERNING COUNCIL OF THE UNIVERSITY OF TORONTO, THE *p974*
40 ST. GEORGE ST RM 4113, TORONTO, ON, M5S 2E4
(416) 978-1655   *SIC* 8221
GOVERNING COUNCIL OF THE UNIVERSITY OF TORONTO, THE *p975*
40 ST. GEORGE ST RM 6290, TORONTO, ON, M5S 2E4
(416) 978-3323   *SIC* 8221
GOVERNING COUNCIL OF THE UNIVERSITY OF TORONTO, THE *p975*
1 KING'S COLLEGE CIR RM 4396, TORONTO, ON, M5S 1A8
(416) 978-3730   *SIC* 8221
GOVERNING COUNCIL OF THE UNIVERSITY OF TORONTO, THE *p975*
100 ST. GEORGE ST, TORONTO, ON, M5S 3G3
(416) 978-3383   *SIC* 8221
GOVERNING COUNCIL OF THE UNIVERSITY OF TORONTO, THE *p975*
1 KING'S COLLEGE CIR RM 4207, TORONTO, ON, M5S 1A8
(416) 978-2728   *SIC* 8221
GOVERNING COUNCIL OF THE UNIVERSITY OF TORONTO, THE *p975*
725 SPADINA AVE, TORONTO, ON, M5S 2J4
(416) 946-4058   *SIC* 8221
GOVERNING COUNCIL OF THE UNIVERSITY OF TORONTO, THE *p975*
27 KING'S COLLEGE CIR, TORONTO, ON, M5S 1A1
(416) 978-2196   *SIC* 8221
GOVERNING COUNCIL OF THE UNIVERSITY OF TORONTO, THE *p975*
144 COLLEGE ST, TORONTO, ON, M5S 3M2
(416) 978-2889   *SIC* 8221
GOVERNING COUNCIL OF THE UNIVERSITY OF TORONTO, THE *p975*
1 DEVONSHIRE PL, TORONTO, ON, M5S 3K7
(416) 946-8900   *SIC* 8221
GOVERNING COUNCIL OF THE UNIVERSITY OF TORONTO, THE *p975*
1 KING'S COLLEGE CIRCLE 3RD FL, TORONTO, ON, M5S 1A8
SIC 8221
GOVERNING COUNCIL OF THE UNIVERSITY OF TORONTO, THE *p975*
1 KING'S COLLEGE CIR SUITE 2109, TORONTO, ON, M5S 1A8
(416) 978-6585   *SIC* 8221
GOVERNING COUNCIL OF THE UNIVERSITY OF TORONTO, THE *p975*
10 KING'S COLLEGE RD SUITE 3302, TORONTO, ON, M5S 3G4
(416) 978-6025   *SIC* 8221
GOVERNING COUNCIL OF THE UNIVERSITY OF TORONTO, THE *p975*
1 SPADINA CRES, TORONTO, ON, M5S 2J5
(416) 978-5038   *SIC* 8221
GOVERNING COUNCIL OF THE UNIVERSITY OF TORONTO, THE *p975*

1 KING'S COLLEGE CIRCLE RM 7207, TORONTO, ON, M5S 1A8
SIC 8221
GOVERNING COUNCIL OF THE UNIVERSITY OF TORONTO, THE *p975*
55 HARBORD ST SUITE 1048, TORONTO, ON, M5S 2W6
(416) 978-7375   *SIC* 8221
GOVERNING COUNCIL OF THE UNIVERSITY OF TORONTO, THE *p975*
105 ST. GEORGE ST, TORONTO, ON, M5S 3E6
(416) 978-5703   *SIC* 8221
GOVERNING COUNCIL OF THE UNIVERSITY OF TORONTO, THE *p975*
80 ST. GEORGE ST, TORONTO, ON, M5S 3H6
(416) 978-3564   *SIC* 8221
GOVERNING COUNCIL OF THE UNIVERSITY OF TORONTO, THE *p975*
105 ST. GEORGE ST SUITE 275, TORONTO, ON, M5S 3E6
(416) 978-4574   *SIC* 8221
GOVERNING COUNCIL OF THE UNIVERSITY OF TORONTO, THE *p975*
25 WILLCOCKS STREET, TORONTO, ON, M5S 3B2
SIC 8221
GOVERNING COUNCIL OF THE UNIVERSITY OF TORONTO, THE *p975*
150 ST. GEORGE ST, TORONTO, ON, M5S 3G7
(416) 978-4622   *SIC* 8221
GOVERNING COUNCIL OF THE UNIVERSITY OF TORONTO, THE *p975*
100 ST. GEORGE ST RM 5047, TORONTO, ON, M5S 3G3
(416) 978-3375   *SIC* 8221
GOVERNING COUNCIL OF THE UNIVERSITY OF TORONTO, THE *p975*
200 COLLEGE ST UNIT 217, TORONTO, ON, M5S 3E5
(416) 978-6204   *SIC* 8221
GOVERNING COUNCIL OF THE UNIVERSITY OF TORONTO, THE *p975*
40 ST. GEORGE ST RM BA 5165, TORONTO, ON, M5S 2E4
SIC 8221
GOVERNING COUNCIL OF THE UNIVERSITY OF TORONTO, THE *p975*
10 KING'S COLLEGE RD RM 1024, TORONTO, ON, M5S 3H5
(416) 978-3112   *SIC* 8221
GOVERNING COUNCIL OF THE UNIVERSITY OF TORONTO, THE *p977*
263 MCCAUL ST 3 FL, TORONTO, ON, M5T 1W7
(416) 978-5938   *SIC* 8221
GOVERNING COUNCIL OF THE UNIVERSITY OF TORONTO, THE *p977*
155 COLLEGE ST SUITE 130, TORONTO, ON, M5T 1P8
(416) 978-2392   *SIC* 8221
GOVERNING COUNCIL OF THE UNIVERSITY OF TORONTO, THE *p977*
263 MCCAUL ST, TORONTO, ON, M5T 1W7
(416) 978-6801   *SIC* 8221
GOVERNING COUNCIL OF THE UNIVERSITY OF TORONTO, THE *p977*
250 COLLEGE ST 8 FL, TORONTO, ON, M5T 1R8
(416) 979-6948   *SIC* 8221
GOVERNING COUNCIL OF THE UNIVERSITY OF TORONTO, THE *p977*
340 COLLEGE ST SUITE 400, TORONTO, ON, M5T 3A9
(416) 978-4321   *SIC* 8221
GOVERNMENT OF ONTARIO *p861*
1520 QUEEN ST E, SAULT STE. MARIE, ON, P6A 2G4
(705) 949-2301   *SIC* 8221
GOVERNORS OF ST FRANCIS XAVIER UNIVERSITY *p438*
1 WEST ST, ANTIGONISH, NS, B2G 2W5

(902) 863-3300   *SIC* 8221
GOVERNORS OF THE UNIVERSITY OF ALBERTA, THE *p117*
116 ST & 85 AVE, EDMONTON, AB, T6G 2R3
(780) 492-3111   *SIC* 8221
GOVERNORS OF THE UNIVERSITY OF ALBERTA, THE *p117*
5 HUMANITIES CTR UNIT 6, EDMONTON, AB, T6G 2E5
(780) 492-2787   *SIC* 8221
GOVERNORS OF THE UNIVERSITY OF ALBERTA, THE *p117*
11405 87 AVE 5TH FL, EDMONTON, AB, T6G 1C9
(780) 492-5391   *SIC* 8221
GOVERNORS OF THE UNIVERSITY OF ALBERTA, THE *p117*
111 89 AVE, EDMONTON, AB, T6G 2H5
(780) 492-3111   *SIC* 8221
GOVERNORS OF THE UNIVERSITY OF ALBERTA, THE *p117*
51 UNIVERSITY CAMPUS NW SUITE 632, EDMONTON, AB, T6G 2G1
(780) 492-3396   *SIC* 8221
GOVERNORS OF THE UNIVERSITY OF ALBERTA, THE *p118*
26 EARTH SCIENCES BLDG UNIT 1, EDMONTON, AB, T6G 2E3
(780) 492-3265   *SIC* 8221
GOVERNORS OF THE UNIVERSITY OF ALBERTA, THE *p118*
302 GENERAL SERVICES BLDG, EDMONTON, AB, T6G 2E1
(780) 492-9400   *SIC* 8221
GRANDE PRAIRIE REGIONAL COLLEGE *p132*
10726 106 AVE, GRANDE PRAIRIE, AB, T8V 4C4
(780) 539-2911   *SIC* 8221
GRANT MACEWAN UNIVERSITY *p89*
10700 104 AVE NW, EDMONTON, AB, T5J 4S2
(780) 497-5168   *SIC* 8221
HOLLAND COLLEGE *p1039*
140 WEYMOUTH ST, CHARLOTTETOWN, PE, C1A 4Z1
(902) 629-4217   *SIC* 8221
HOLLAND COLLEGE *p1039*
4 SYDNEY ST, CHARLOTTETOWN, PE, C1A 1E9
(902) 894-6805   *SIC* 8221
HUMBER COLLEGE INSTITUTE OF TECHNOLOGY AND ADVANCE LEARNING, THE *p570*
3199 LAKE SHORE BLVD W, ETOBICOKE, ON, M8V 1K8
(416) 675-6622   *SIC* 8221
HURON UNIVERSITY COLLEGE *p658*
1349 WESTERN RD, LONDON, ON, N6G 1H3
(519) 679-7905   *SIC* 8221
INSTITUTE NATIONAL DE LA RECHERCHE SCIENTIFIQUE *p1087*
531 BOUL DES PRAIRIES BUREAU 26, COTE SAINT-LUC, QC, H7V 1B7
(450) 687-5010   *SIC* 8221
INSTITUTE OF NATUROPATHIC EDUCATION AND RESEARCH *p769*
1255 SHEPPARD AVE E, NORTH YORK, ON, M2K 1E2
(416) 498-1255   *SIC* 8221
JUSTICE INSTITUTE OF BRITISH COLUMBIA *p236*
715 MCBRIDE BLVD, NEW WESTMINSTER, BC, V3L 5T4
(604) 525-5422   *SIC* 8221
KEYANO COLLEGE *p128*
8115 FRANKLIN AVE, FORT MCMURRAY, AB, T9H 2H7
(780) 791-4800   *SIC* 8221
KING'S UNIVERSITY COLLEGE AT THE UNIVERSITY OF WESTERN ONTARIO *p654*
266 EPWORTH AVE, LONDON, ON, N6A

2M3
(519) 433-3491   SIC 8221
KING'S UNIVERSITY COLLEGE, THE p109
9125 50 ST NW, EDMONTON, AB, T6B 2H3
(780) 465-3500   SIC 8221
KWANTLEN POLYTECHNIC UNIVERSITY FOUNDATION p277
12666 72 AVE, SURREY, BC, V3W 2M8
(604) 599-2000   SIC 8221
LAKEHEAD UNIVERSITY p908
955 OLIVER RD SUITE 2008, THUNDER BAY, ON, P7B 5E1
(807) 343-8500   SIC 8221
LAKEHEAD UNIVERSITY p908
955 OLIVER RD, THUNDER BAY, ON, P7B 5E1
(807) 343-8110   SIC 8221
LAKELAND COLLEGE p1409
2602 59TH AVE, LLOYDMINSTER, SK, S9V 1Z3
(780) 871-5700   SIC 8221
LANGARA COLLEGE p292
100 49TH AVE W, VANCOUVER, BC, V5Y 2Z6
(604) 323-5511   SIC 8221
LONDON DISTRICT CATHOLIC SCHOOL BOARD p657
5250 WELLINGTON RD S, LONDON, ON, N6E 3X8
(519) 663-2088   SIC 8221
LUTHER COLLEGE p1422
1500 ROYAL ST, REGINA, SK, S4T 5A5
(306) 791-9150   SIC 8221
MARIANOPOLIS COLLEGE p1401
4873 AV WESTMOUNT, WESTMOUNT, QC, H3Y 1X9
(514) 931-8792   SIC 8221
MCMASTER UNIVERSITY p612
GD, HAMILTON, ON, L8N 3Z5
(905) 521-2100   SIC 8221
MCMASTER UNIVERSITY p614
1280 MAIN ST W GH209, HAMILTON, ON, L8S 4L8
(905) 525-9140   SIC 8221
MEMORIAL UNIVERSITY OF NEWFOUND-LAND p432
208 ELIZABETH AVE, ST. JOHN'S, NL, A1C 5S7
(709) 637-6298   SIC 8221
MICHENER INSTITUTE OF EDUCATION AT UHN, THE p977
222 SAINT PATRICK ST SUITE 414, TORONTO, ON, M5T 1V4
(416) 596-3101   SIC 8221
MOUNT ALLISON UNIVERSITY p412
65 YORK ST, SACKVILLE, NB, E4L 1E4
(506) 364-2269   SIC 8221
MOUNT SAINT VINCENT UNIVERSITY p457
166 BEDFORD HWY, HALIFAX, NS, B3M 2J6
(902) 457-6788   SIC 8221
NEW BRUNSWICK COMMUNITY COLLEGE (NBCC) p401
284 SMYTHE ST, FREDERICTON, NB, E3B 3C9
(888) 796-6222   SIC 8221
NIAGARA COLLEGE OF APPLIED ARTS & TECHNOLOGY p759
5881 DUNN ST, NIAGARA FALLS, ON, L2G 2N9
(905) 735-2211   SIC 8221
NIPISSING UNIVERSITY p763
100 COLLEGE DR, NORTH BAY, ON, P1B 8L7
(705) 474-3450   SIC 8221
NORQUEST COLLEGE FOUNDATION, THE p90
10215 108 ST NW, EDMONTON, AB, T5J 1L6
(780) 644-6300   SIC 8221
NORQUEST COLLEGE FOUNDATION, THE p167
3201 43 AVE, STONY PLAIN, AB, T7Z 1L1
(780) 968-6489   SIC 8221

NORTH ISLAND COLLEGE p195
1685 DOGWOOD ST S, CAMPBELL RIVER, BC, V9W 8C1
(250) 923-9700   SIC 8221
NORTHERN COLLEGE OF APPLIED ARTS & TECHNOLOGY p634
140 GOVERNMENT RD W, KIRKLAND LAKE, ON, P2N 2E9
(705) 567-9291   SIC 8221
NORTHERN ONTARIO SCHOOL OF MEDICINE p901
935 RAMSEY LAKE RD, SUDBURY, ON, P3E 2C6
(705) 675-4883   SIC 8221
NOVA SCOTIA COLLEGE OF ART AND DE-SIGN p453
5163 DUKE ST, HALIFAX, NS, B3J 3J6
(902) 444-9600   SIC 8221
NOVA SCOTIA COMMUNITY COLLEGE p455
5685 LEEDS ST, HALIFAX, NS, B3K 2T3
(902) 491-3387   SIC 8221
NOVA SCOTIA COMMUNITY COLLEGE MARCONI CAMPUS p466
1240 GRAND LAKE RD, SYDNEY, NS, B1M 1A2
(902) 563-2450   SIC 8221
NOVA SCOTIA, PROVINCE OF p441
75 HIGH ST, BRIDGEWATER, NS, B4V 1V8
(902) 543-4608   SIC 8221
NUNAVUT ARCTIC COLLEGE p472
GD, ARVIAT, NU, X0C 0E0
(867) 857-8600   SIC 8221
OKANAGAN COLLEGE p222
1000 K.L.O. RD, KELOWNA, BC, V1Y 4X8
(250) 762-5445   SIC 8221
ONTARIO COLLEGE OF ART & DESIGN UNIVERSITY p977
100 MCCAUL ST SUITE 500, TORONTO, ON, M5T 1W1
(416) 977-6000   SIC 8221
ONTARIO POLICE COLLEGE p482
10716 HACIENDA RD, AYLMER, ON, N5H 2T2
(519) 773-5361   SIC 8221
PARKLAND REGIONAL COLLEGE p1410
200 BLOCK 9 AVE E, MELVILLE, SK, S0A 2P0
(306) 728-4471   SIC 8221
PORTAGE COLLEGE p138
9531 94 AVE, LAC LA BICHE, AB, T0A 2C0
(780) 623-5511   SIC 8221
PORTAGE COLLEGE p170
5005 50 AVE, VEGREVILLE, AB, T9C 1T1
SIC 8221
PROVIDENCE UNIVERSITY COLLEGE AND THEOLOGICAL SEMINARY p354
10 COLLEGE CRES, OTTERBURNE, MB, R0A 1G0
(204) 433-7488   SIC 8221
PROVINCE OF NEW BRUNSWICK p398
505 RUE DU COLLEGE, DIEPPE, NB, E1A 6X2
(506) 856-2200   SIC 8221
PROVINCE OF NEW BRUNSWICK p405
80 UNIVERSITY AVE, MIRAMICHI, NB, E1N 0C6
(506) 778-6000   SIC 8221
QUEEN'S SCHOOL OF BUSINESS p534
355 HESPELER RD, CAMBRIDGE, ON, N1R 6B3
(613) 533-2330   SIC 8221
QUEEN'S UNIVERSITY AT KINGSTON p631
75 BADER LANE RM D015, KINGSTON, ON, K7L 3N8
(613) 533-2529   SIC 8221
QUEEN'S UNIVERSITY AT KINGSTON p631
25 UNION ST, KINGSTON, ON, K7L 3N5
(613) 533-6050   SIC 8221
QUEEN'S UNIVERSITY AT KINGSTON p631
99 UNIVERSITY AVE, KINGSTON, ON, K7L 3N5
(613) 533-2000   SIC 8221
REGENT COLLEGE p325

5800 UNIVERSITY BLVD, VANCOUVER, BC, V6T 2E4
(604) 224-3245   SIC 8221
REGIE DES CLUBS D'EXCELLENCE COL-LEGE D'ENSEIGNEMENT GENERAL ET PROFESSIONNEL DE LIMOILOU p1257
1300 8E AV BUREAU 1400, QUEBEC, QC, G1J 5L5
(418) 647-6600   SIC 8221
RENISON UNIVERSITY COLLEGE p1009
265 WESTMOUNT RD N, WATERLOO, ON, N2L 3G7
(519) 884-4404   SIC 8221
RIDLEY COLLEGE p886
2 RIDLEY RD, ST CATHARINES, ON, L2R 7C3
(905) 684-1889   SIC 8221
ROYAL INSTITUTE FOR ADVANCEMENT OF LEARNING MCGILL p1199
845 SHERBROOKE STREET WEST, MON-TREAL, QC, H3A 0G4
(514) 398-8120   SIC 8221
ROYAL INSTITUTE FOR ADVANCEMENT OF LEARNING MCGILL p1199
817 RUE SHERBROOKE O BUREAU 382, MONTREAL, QC, H3A 0C3
(514) 398-7251   SIC 8221
ROYAL ROADS UNIVERSITY p340
2005 SOOKE RD, VICTORIA, BC, V9B 5Y2
(250) 391-2511   SIC 8221
RYERSON UNIVERSITY p936
350 VICTORIA ST, TORONTO, ON, M5B 2K3
(416) 979-5000   SIC 8221
SAINT MARY'S UNIVERSITY p451
923 ROBIE ST SUITE 210, HALIFAX, NS, B3H 3C3
(902) 420-5400   SIC 8221
SAINT PAUL UNIVERSITY p826
223 MAIN ST SUITE 267, OTTAWA, ON, K1S 1C4
(613) 236-1393   SIC 8221
SAULT COLLEGE OF APPLIED ARTS & TECHNOLOGY, THE p863
443 NORTHERN AVE E, SAULT STE. MARIE, ON, P6B 4J3
(705) 759-2554   SIC 8221
SELKIRK COLLEGE p195
301 FRANK BEINDER WAY, CASTLEGAR, BC, V1N 4L3
(250) 365-7292   SIC 8221
SIMON FRASER UNIVERSITY p183
8888 UNIVERSITY DR SUITE 1200, BURN-ABY, BC, V5A 1S6
(778) 782-3111   SIC 8221
ST MARY'S UNIVERSITY p69
14500 BANNISTER RD SE 4TH FL, CAL-GARY, AB, T2X 1Z4
(403) 531-9130   SIC 8221
ST. CLAIR CATHOLIC DISTRICT SCHOOL BOARD p542
85 GRAND AVE W, CHATHAM, ON, N7L 1B6
(519) 351-2987   SIC 8221
ST. LAWRENCE COLLEGE OF APPLIED ARTS AND TECHNOLOGY, THE p562
2 ST LAWRENCE DR, CORNWALL, ON, K6H 4Z1
(613) 933-6080   SIC 8221
ST. LAWRENCE COLLEGE OF APPLIED ARTS AND TECHNOLOGY, THE p632
100 PORTSMOUTH AVE, KINGSTON, ON, K7M 1G2
(613) 544-5400   SIC 8221
ST. THOMAS UNIVERSITY p401
51 DINEEN DR COLLEGE HILL, FREDER-ICTON, NB, E3B 5G3
(506) 452-0640   SIC 8221
THOMPSON RIVERS UNIVERSITY p218
805 TRU WAY, KAMLOOPS, BC, V2C 0C8
(250) 828-5000   SIC 8221
TORONTO DISTRICT SCHOOL BOARD p872
2740 LAWRENCE AVE E, SCARBOR-

OUGH, ON, M1P 2S7
(416) 396-5525   SIC 8221
TREBAS INSTITUTE ONTARIO INC p994
2340 DUNDAS ST W SUITE 2, TORONTO, ON, M6P 4A9
(416) 966-3066   SIC 8221
TRINITY WESTERN UNIVERSITY p227
7600 GLOVER RD, LANGLEY, BC, V2Y 1Y1
(604) 888-7511   SIC 8221
TYNDALE UNIVERSITY COLLEGE & SEMI-NARY p915
3377 BAYVIEW AVE, TORONTO, ON, M2M 3S4
(416) 226-6380   SIC 8221
UNIVERSITE BISHOP'S p1375
2600 RUE COLLEGE, SHERBROOKE, QC, J1M 1Z7
(819) 822-9600   SIC 8221
UNIVERSITE CONCORDIA p1214
1600 RUE SAINTE-CATHERINE O 1ER ETAGE FB-117, MONTREAL, QC, H3G 1M8
(514) 848-3600   SIC 8221
UNIVERSITE CONCORDIA p1214
1455 BOUL DE MAISONNEUVE O, MON-TREAL, QC, H3G 1M8
(514) 848-2424   SIC 8221
UNIVERSITE DE MONCTON p406
18 AV ANTONINE-MAILLET, MONCTON, NB, E1A 3E9
(506) 858-4000   SIC 8221
UNIVERSITE DE MONTREAL p1219
3744 RUE JEAN-BRILLANT, MONTREAL, QC, H3T 1P1
(514) 343-6090   SIC 8221
UNIVERSITE DE MONTREAL p1219
2900 BOUL EDOUARD-MONTPETIT, MON-TREAL, QC, H3T 1J4
(514) 343-6111   SIC 8221
UNIVERSITE DE SHERBROOKE p1145
150 PLACE CHARLES-LE MOYNE BU-REAU 200, LONGUEUIL, QC, J4K 0A8
(450) 463-1835   SIC 8221
UNIVERSITE DE SHERBROOKE p1372
2500 BOUL DE L'UNIVERSITE, SHER-BROOKE, QC, J1K 2R1
(819) 821-7000   SIC 8221
UNIVERSITE DU QUEBEC p1087
531 BOUL DES PRAIRIES, COTE SAINT-LUC, QC, H7V 1B7
(450) 687-5010   SIC 8221
UNIVERSITE DU QUEBEC p1108
283 BOUL ALEXANDRE-TACHE, GATINEAU, QC, J9A 1L8
(819) 595-3900   SIC 8221
UNIVERSITE DU QUEBEC p1123
500 RUE PRINCIPALE BUREAU AR60, LA SARRE, QC, J9Z 2A2
(819) 333-2624   SIC 8221
UNIVERSITE DU QUEBEC p1137
1595 BOUL ALPHONSE-DESJARDINS, LEVIS, QC, G6V 0A6
(418) 833-8800   SIC 8221
UNIVERSITE DU QUEBEC p1186
315 RUE SAINTE-CATHERINE E BUREAU 3570, MONTREAL, QC, H2X 3X2
(514) 987-3000   SIC 8221
UNIVERSITE DU QUEBEC p1212
1440 RUE SAINT-DENIS, MONTREAL, QC, H3C 3P8
(514) 987-3092   SIC 8221
UNIVERSITE DU QUEBEC p1260
475 RUE DU PARVIS, QUEBEC, QC, G1K 9H7
(418) 657-3551   SIC 8221
UNIVERSITE DU QUEBEC p1260
490 RUE DE LA COURONNE, QUEBEC, QC, G1K 9A9
(418) 687-6400   SIC 8221
UNIVERSITE DU QUEBEC p1260
455 RUE DU PARVIS BUREAU 2140, QUE-BEC, QC, G1K 9H6
(418) 657-2262   SIC 8221
UNIVERSITE DU QUEBEC p1285
300 ALLEE DES URSULINES, RIMOUSKI.

QC, G5L 3A1
(418) 723-1986   *SIC* 8221

UNIVERSITE DU QUEBEC   *p1290*
445 BOUL DE L'UNIVERSITE, ROUYN-NORANDA, QC, J9X 5E4
(819) 762-0971   *SIC* 8221

UNIVERSITE DU QUEBEC   *p1386*
3351 BOUL DES FORGES, TROIS-RIVIERES, QC, G8Z 4M3
(819) 376-5011   *SIC* 8221

UNIVERSITE LAVAL   *p1274*
2345 ALLEE DES BIBLIOTHEQUES, QUEBEC, QC, G1V 0A6
(418) 656-3530   *SIC* 8221

UNIVERSITE LAVAL   *p1274*
1030 AV DES SCIENCES HUMAINES, QUEBEC, QC, G1V 0A6
(418) 656-2131   *SIC* 8221

UNIVERSITE LAVAL   *p1274*
1065 AV DE LA MEDECINE PAVILLON ADRIEN-POULIOT, QUEBEC, QC, G1V 0A6
(418) 656-3474   *SIC* 8221

UNIVERSITE MCGILL   *p1200*
845 RUE SHERBROOKE O BUREAU 310, MONTREAL, QC, H3A 0G4
(514) 398-4455   *SIC* 8221

UNIVERSITE SAINTE-ANNE   *p442*
1695 RTE 1, CHURCH POINT, NS, B0W 1M0
(902) 769-2114   *SIC* 8221

UNIVERSITY COLLEGE OF THE NORTH
p360
436 7TH ST E, THE PAS, MB, R9A 1M7
(204) 627-8500   *SIC* 8221

UNIVERSITY OF BRITISH COLUMBIA, THE
p289
950 10TH AVE E RM 3350, VANCOUVER, BC, V5T 2B2
SIC 8221

UNIVERSITY OF BRITISH COLUMBIA, THE
p294
2775 LAUREL ST 11 FL, VANCOUVER, BC, V5Z 1M9
(604) 875-4192   *SIC* 8221

UNIVERSITY OF BRITISH COLUMBIA, THE
p325
2121 WEST MALL, VANCOUVER, BC, V6T 1Z4
(604) 822-1555   *SIC* 8221

UNIVERSITY OF BRITISH COLUMBIA, THE
p325
5959 STUDENT UNION BLVD, VANCOUVER, BC, V6T 1K2
(604) 822-1000   *SIC* 8221

UNIVERSITY OF BRITISH COLUMBIA, THE
p325
1984 MATHEMATICS RD RM 121, VANCOUVER, BC, V6T 1Z2
(604) 822-2666   *SIC* 8221

UNIVERSITY OF BRITISH COLUMBIA, THE
p325
6270 UNIVERSITY BLVD RM 3200, VANCOUVER, BC, V6T 1Z4
(604) 822-2133   *SIC* 8221

UNIVERSITY OF BRITISH COLUMBIA, THE
p325
2194 HEALTH SCIENCES MALL UNIT 317, VANCOUVER, BC, V6T 1Z6
(604) 822-2421   *SIC* 8221

UNIVERSITY OF BRITISH COLUMBIA, THE
p325
2215 WESBROOK MALL 3RD FL, VANCOUVER, BC, V6T 1Z3
(604) 822-1388   *SIC* 8221

UNIVERSITY OF BRITISH COLUMBIA, THE
p325
1873 EAST MALL RM 1097, VANCOUVER, BC, V6T 1Z1
(604) 822-9171   *SIC* 8221

UNIVERSITY OF BRITISH COLUMBIA, THE
p325
2194 HEALTH SCIENCES MALL, VANCOUVER, BC, V6T 1Z6
(604) 822-5773   *SIC* 8221

UNIVERSITY OF BRITISH COLUMBIA, THE
p325
2366 MAIN MALL UNIT 289, VANCOUVER, BC, V6T 1Z4
(604) 822-6894   *SIC* 8221

UNIVERSITY OF BRITISH COLUMBIA, THE
p325
2053 MAIN MALL SUITE 247, VANCOUVER, BC, V6T 1Z2
(604) 822-8500   *SIC* 8221

UNIVERSITY OF BRITISH COLUMBIA, THE
p325
6081 UNIVERSITY BLVD RM 210, VANCOUVER, BC, V6T 1Z1
(604) 822-9192   *SIC* 8221

UNIVERSITY OF BRITISH COLUMBIA, THE
p325
2211 WESBROOK MALL RM T201, VANCOUVER, BC, V6T 2B5
(604) 822-7417   *SIC* 8221

UNIVERSITY OF BRITISH COLUMBIA, THE
p325
2332 MAIN MALL SUITE 5000, VANCOUVER, BC, V6T 1Z4
(604) 822-0895   *SIC* 8221

UNIVERSITY OF BRITISH COLUMBIA, THE
p325
2366 MAIN MALL SUITE 201, VANCOUVER, BC, V6T 1Z4
(604) 822-3061   *SIC* 8221

UNIVERSITY OF BRITISH COLUMBIA, THE
p325
1871 WEST MALL UNIT 607, VANCOUVER, BC, V6T 1Z2
(604) 822-0019   *SIC* 8221

UNIVERSITY OF BRITISH COLUMBIA, THE
p325
1822 EAST MALL, VANCOUVER, BC, V6T 1Y1
(604) 822-2275   *SIC* 8221

UNIVERSITY OF BRITISH COLUMBIA, THE
p325
2329 WEST MALL, VANCOUVER, BC, V6T 1Z4
(604) 822-2211   *SIC* 8221

UNIVERSITY OF GUELPH   *p602*
50 STONE RD E, GUELPH, ON, N1G 2W1
(519) 824-4120   *SIC* 8221

UNIVERSITY OF GUELPH   *p602*
95 STONE RD W, GUELPH, ON, N1G 2Z4
(519) 767-6299   *SIC* 8221

UNIVERSITY OF GUELPH   *p627*
830 PRESCOTT ST, KEMPTVILLE, ON, K0G 1J0
(613) 258-8336   *SIC* 8221

UNIVERSITY OF GUELPH   *p857*
120 MAIN ST, RIDGETOWN, ON, N0P 2C0
(519) 674-1500   *SIC* 8221

UNIVERSITY OF KING'S COLLEGE   *p451*
6350 COBURG RD, HALIFAX, NS, B3H 2A1
(902) 422-1271   *SIC* 8221

UNIVERSITY OF LETHBRIDGE, THE   *p91*
10707 100 AVE NW SUITE 1100, EDMONTON, AB, T5J 3M1
SIC 8221

UNIVERSITY OF LETHBRIDGE, THE   *p143*
4401 UNIVERSITY DR W, LETHBRIDGE, AB, T1K 3M4
(403) 329-2244   *SIC* 8221

UNIVERSITY OF MANITOBA THE   *p381*
675 MCDERMOT AVE SUITE 5008, WINNIPEG, MB, R3E 0V9
(204) 787-2137   *SIC* 8221

UNIVERSITY OF MANITOBA THE   *p392*
181 FREEDMAN CRES SUITE 121, WINNIPEG, MB, R3T 5V4
(204) 474-6200   *SIC* 8221

UNIVERSITY OF MANITOBA,THE   *p381*
727 MCDERMOT AVE SUITE 408, WINNIPEG, MB, R3E 3P5
(204) 474-9668   *SIC* 8221

UNIVERSITY OF NEW BRUNSWICK   *p402*
3 BAILEY DR, FREDERICTON, NB, E3B 5A3

(506) 453-4666   *SIC* 8221

UNIVERSITY OF NEW BRUNSWICK   *p415*
100 TUCKER PARK RD, SAINT JOHN, NB, E2L 4L5
(506) 648-5500   *SIC* 8221

UNIVERSITY OF ONTARIO INSTITUTE OF TECHNOLOGY   *p812*
2000 SIMCOE ST N, OSHAWA, ON, L1G 0C5
(905) 721-8668   *SIC* 8221

UNIVERSITY OF OTTAWA   *p819*
451 SMYTH RD SUITE RGN, OTTAWA, ON, K1H 8M5
(613) 562-5800   *SIC* 8221

UNIVERSITY OF OTTAWA   *p822*
75 LAURIER AVE E, OTTAWA, ON, K1N 6N5
(613) 562-5700   *SIC* 8221

UNIVERSITY OF OTTAWA   *p822*
55 LAURIER AVE E SUITE 5105, OTTAWA, ON, K1N 6N5
(613) 562-5731   *SIC* 8221

UNIVERSITY OF OTTAWA   *p822*
800 KING EDWARD AVE SUITE 2002, OTTAWA, ON, K1N 6N5
(613) 562-5800   *SIC* 8221

UNIVERSITY OF OTTAWA   *p822*
120 UNIVERSITE PVT UNIT 3010, OTTAWA, ON, K1N 6N5
(613) 562-5800   *SIC* 8221

UNIVERSITY OF PRINCE EDWARD ISLAND
p1040
550 UNIVERSITY AVE, CHARLOTTETOWN, PE, C1A 4P3
(902) 628-4353   *SIC* 8221

UNIVERSITY OF REGINA   *p1422*
3737 WASCANA PKY, REGINA, SK, S4S 0A2
(306) 584-1255   *SIC* 8221

UNIVERSITY OF REGINA   *p1422*
3737 WASCANA PKY SUITE 148, REGINA, SK, S4S 0A2
(306) 585-4111   *SIC* 8221

UNIVERSITY OF SASKATCHEWAN   *p1434*
107 WIGGINS RD 4TH FL SUITE B419, SASKATOON, SK, S7N 5E5
(306) 966-8641   *SIC* 8221

UNIVERSITY OF SASKATCHEWAN   *p1434*
104 CLINIC PLACE, SASKATOON, SK, S7N 2Z4
(306) 966-6221   *SIC* 8221

UNIVERSITY OF SASKATCHEWAN   *p1434*
51 CAMPUS DR RM 5D34, SASKATOON, SK, S7N 5A8
(306) 966-6829   *SIC* 8221

UNIVERSITY OF SASKATCHEWAN   *p1434*
117 SCIENCE PL RM 323, SASKATOON, SK, S7N 5C8
(306) 966-1985   *SIC* 8221

UNIVERSITY OF SASKATCHEWAN   *p1434*
103 HOSPITAL DR, SASKATOON, SK, S7N 0W8
(306) 844-1132   *SIC* 8221

UNIVERSITY OF SASKATCHEWAN   *p1434*
28 CAMPUS DR SUITE 3079, SASKATOON, SK, S7N 0X1
(306) 966-7619   *SIC* 8221

UNIVERSITY OF SASKATCHEWAN   *p1434*
57 CAMPUS DR RM 3B48, SASKATOON, SK, S7N 5A9
(306) 966-5273   *SIC* 8221

UNIVERSITY OF SASKATCHEWAN   *p1434*
52 CAMPUS DR RM 3101, SASKATOON, SK, S7N 5B4
(306) 966-7477   *SIC* 8221

UNIVERSITY OF SASKATCHEWAN   *p1434*
103 HOSPITAL DR, SASKATOON, SK, S7N 0W8
(306) 844-1068   *SIC* 8221

UNIVERSITY OF SASKATCHEWAN   *p1434*
107 ADMINISTRATION PL SUITE 201, SASKATOON, SK, S7N 5A2
(306) 966-8514   *SIC* 8221

UNIVERSITY OF SASKATCHEWAN   *p1434*

105 ADMINISTRATION PL SUITE E, SASKATOON, SK, S7N 5A2
(306) 966-4343   *SIC* 8221

UNIVERSITY OF SASKATCHEWAN   *p1434*
107 WIGGINS RD SUITE B103, SASKATOON, SK, S7N 5E5
(306) 966-6135   *SIC* 8221

UNIVERSITY OF ST MICHAEL'S COLLEGE, THE   *p976*
81 ST MARY ST, TORONTO, ON, M5S 1J4
(416) 926-1300   *SIC* 8221

UNIVERSITY OF THE FRASER VALLEY
p175
33844 KING RD, ABBOTSFORD, BC, V2S 7M8
(604) 504-7441   *SIC* 8221

UNIVERSITY OF THE FRASER VALLEY
p198
45190 CAEN AVE, CHILLIWACK, BC, V2R 0N3
(604) 792-0025   *SIC* 8221

UNIVERSITY OF VICTORIA   *p333*
3800 FINNERTY RD, VICTORIA, BC, V8P 5C2
(250) 721-7211   *SIC* 8221

UNIVERSITY OF VICTORIA   *p333*
3800A FINNERTY RD SUITE 168, VICTORIA, BC, V8P 5C2
(250) 721-6673   *SIC* 8221

UNIVERSITY OF WATERLOO   *p1009*
200 UNIVERSITY AVE W, WATERLOO, ON, N2L 3G1
(519) 888-4567   *SIC* 8221

UNIVERSITY OF WESTERN ONTARIO, THE
p655
1151 RICHMOND ST SUITE 2, LONDON, ON, N6A 5B8
(519) 661-2111   *SIC* 8221

UNIVERSITY OF WESTERN ONTARIO, THE
p658
1137 WESTERN RD SUITE 1118, LONDON, ON, N6G 1G7
(519) 661-3182   *SIC* 8221

UNIVERSITY OF WINDSOR   *p1024*
401 SUNSET AVE SUITE G07, WINDSOR, ON, N9B 3P4
(519) 253-3000   *SIC* 8221

UNIVERSITY OF WINNIPEG, THE   *p376*
515 PORTAGE AVE, WINNIPEG, MB, R3B 2E9
(204) 786-7811   *SIC* 8221

URSULINE RELIGIOUS OF THE DIOCESE OF LONDON IN ONTARIO   *p658*
1285 WESTERN RD, LONDON, ON, N6G 1H2
(519) 432-8353   *SIC* 8221

VANCOUVER COMMUNITY COLLEGE *p289*
1155 BROADWAY E SUITE 2713, VANCOUVER, BC, V5T 4V5
(604) 871-7000   *SIC* 8221

VANCOUVER COMMUNITY COLLEGE *p301*
250 PENDER ST W SUITE 358, VANCOUVER, BC, V6B 1S9
(604) 443-8484   *SIC* 8221

VANCOUVER ISLAND UNIVERSITY   *p233*
90 FIFTH ST, NANAIMO, BC, V9R 1N1
(250) 753-3245   *SIC* 8221

VICTORIA UNIVERSITY   *p976*
140 CHARLES ST W, TORONTO, ON, M5S 1K9
(416) 585-4524   *SIC* 8221

WILFRID LAURIER UNIVERSITY   *p1009*
75 UNIVERSITY AVE W, WATERLOO, ON, N2L 3C5
(519) 884-1970   *SIC* 8221

YORK UNIVERSITY   *p785*
4700 KEELE ST RM 428, NORTH YORK, ON, M3J 1P3
(416) 736-5113   *SIC* 8221

YORK UNIVERSITY   *p785*
4700 KEELE ST, NORTH YORK, ON, M3J 1P3
(416) 736-2100   *SIC* 8221

YUKON COLLEGE   *p1440*

500 COLLEGE DR, WHITEHORSE, YT, Y1A 5K4
(867) 668-8800   *SIC 8221*

SIC 8222 Junior colleges

ALGONQUIN COLLEGE OF APPLIED ARTS AND TECHNOLOGY   p750
1385 WOODROFFE AVE, NEPEAN, ON, K2G 1V8
(613) 727-4723   *SIC 8222*
BOARD OF GOVERNOR'S OF RED RIVER COLLEGE, THE   p383
2055 NOTRE DAME AVE, WINNIPEG, MB, R3H 0J9
(204) 632-3960   *SIC 8222*
CAMBRIAN COLLEGE OF APPLIED ARTS & TECHNOLOGY, THE   p898
1400 BARRYDOWNE RD, SUDBURY, ON, P3A 3V8
(705) 566-8101   *SIC 8222*
CANADORE COLLEGE OF APPLIED ARTS AND TECHNOLOGY   p762
100 COLLEGE DR, NORTH BAY, ON, P1B 8K9
(705) 474-7600   *SIC 8222*
CEGEP DE TROIS-RIVIERES   p1386
3500 RUE DE COURVAL, TROIS-RIVIERES, QC, G8Z 1T2
(819) 376-1721   *SIC 8222*
CENTENNIAL COLLEGE OF APPLIED ARTS & TECHNOLOGY, THE   p866
941 PROGRESS AVE, SCARBOROUGH, ON, M1G 3T8
(416) 289-5000   *SIC 8222*
CITE COLLEGIALE, LA   p820
801 AVIATION PKY, OTTAWA, ON, K1K 4R3
(613) 742-2483   *SIC 8222*
COLLEGE D'ENSEIGNEMENT GENERAL ET PROFESSIONEL DE SAINT-HYACINTHE   p1312
3000 AV BOULLE, SAINT-HYACINTHE, QC, J2S 1H9
(450) 773-6800   *SIC 8222*
COLLEGE D'ENSEIGNEMENT GENERAL ET PROFESSIONEL FRANCOIS-XAVIER-GARNEAU   p1270
1640 BOUL DE L'ENTENTE, QUEBEC, QC, G1S 4S7
(418) 688-8310   *SIC 8222*
COLLEGE D'ENSEIGNEMENT GENERAL ET PROFESSIONNEL EDOUARD-MONTPETIT   p1143
945 CH DE CHAMBLY, LONGUEUIL, QC, J4H 3M6
(450) 679-2631   *SIC 8222*
COLLEGE DAWSON   p1220
3040 RUE SHERBROOKE O, MONTREAL, QC, H3Z 1A4
(514) 931-8731   *SIC 8222*
COLLEGE DE ROSEMONT   p1168
6400 16E AV, MONTREAL, QC, H1X 2S9
(514) 376-1620   *SIC 8222*
COLLEGE MONT SACRE-COEUR   p1110
210 RUE DENISON E, GRANBY, QC, J2H 2R6
(450) 372-6882   *SIC 8222*
COLLEGE OF NEW CALEDONIA, THE p252
100 CAMPUS WAY, QUESNEL, BC, V2J 7K1
(250) 991-7500   *SIC 8222*
COLLEGE OF THE NORTH ATLANTIC p434
432 MASSACHUSETTS DR, STEPHENVILLE, NL, A2N 3C1
(709) 643-7868   *SIC 8222*
COLLEGE OF THE ROCKIES   p203
2700 COLLEGE WAY, CRANBROOK, BC, V1C 5L7
(250) 489-2751   *SIC 8222*
CONESTOGA COLLEGE COMMUNICATIONS CORPORATION   p638
299 DOON VALLEY DR, KITCHENER, ON, N2G 4M4

(519) 748-5220   *SIC 8222*
CONESTOGA COLLEGE INSTITUTE OF TECHNOLOGY AND ADVANCED LEARNING   p638
299 DOON VALLEY DR, KITCHENER, ON, N2G 4M4
(519) 748-5220   *SIC 8222*
CONFEDERATION COLLEGE OF APPLIED ARTS AND TECHNOLOGY, THE   p909
1450 NAKINA DR, THUNDER BAY, ON, P7C 4W1
(807) 475-6110   *SIC 8222*
COOPSCO SAINT-HYACINTHE   p1312
3230 RUE SICOTTE, SAINT-HYACINTHE, QC, J2S 2M2
(450) 778-6504   *SIC 8222*
DOUGLAS COLLEGE   p237
700 ROYAL AVE UNIT 2814, NEW WESTMINSTER, BC, V3M 5Z5
(604) 527-5400   *SIC 8222*
DURHAM COLLEGE OF APPLIED ARTS AND TECHNOLOGY, THE   p812
2000 SIMCOE ST N, OSHAWA, ON, L1H 7K4
(905) 721-2000   *SIC 8222*
FANSHAWE COLLEGE OF APPLIED ARTS AND TECHNOLOGY, T   p652
1001 BOUL FANSHAWE COLLEGE, LONDON, ON, N5Y 5R6
(519) 452-4277   *SIC 8222*
GEORGE BROWN COLLEGE OF APPLIED ARTS & TECHNOLOGY, THE   p972
500 MACPHERSON AVE, TORONTO, ON, M5R 1M3
(416) 415-2000   *SIC 8222*
GEORGIAN COLLEGE OF APPLIED ARTS AND TECHNOLOGY, THE   p484
1 GEORGIAN DR, BARRIE, ON, L4M 3X9
(705) 728-1968   *SIC 8222*
GRAND ERIE DISTRICT SCHOOL BOARD p517
120 BRANT AVE, BRANTFORD, ON, N3T 3H3
(519) 759-3210   *SIC 8222*
HUMBER COLLEGE INSTITUTE OF TECHNOLOGY AND ADVANCE LEARNING, THE p585
205 HUMBER COLLEGE BLVD, ETOBICOKE, ON, M9W 5L7
(416) 675-3111   *SIC 8222*
KWANTLEN POLYTECHNIC UNIVERSITY FOUNDATION   p228
20901 LANGLEY BYPASS, LANGLEY, BC, V3A 8G9
(604) 599-2100   *SIC 8222*
LAKELAND COLLEGE   p171
5707 COLLEGE DR, VERMILION, AB, T9X 1K5
(780) 853-8400   *SIC 8222*
LAMBTON COLLEGE OF APPLIED ARTS & TECHNOLOGY, THE   p858
1457 LONDON RD, SARNIA, ON, N7S 6K4
(519) 542-7751   *SIC 8222*
LETHBRIDGE COLLEGE   p143
3000 COLLEGE DR S, LETHBRIDGE, AB, T1K 1L6
(403) 320-3200   *SIC 8222*
MEMORIAL UNIVERSITY OF NEWFOUNDLAND   p432
155 RIDGE ROAD, ST. JOHN'S, NL, A1C 5R3
(709) 778-0483   *SIC 8222*
MOHAWK COLLEGE OF APPLIED ARTS AND TECHNOLOGY, THE   p617
135 FENNELL AVE W, HAMILTON, ON, L9C 0E5
(905) 575-1212   *SIC 8222*
MOHAWK COLLEGE OF APPLIED ARTS AND TECHNOLOGY, THE   p617
135 FENNELL AVE W, HAMILTON, ON, L9C 0E5
(905) 575-1212   *SIC 8222*
MOHAWK COLLEGE OF APPLIED ARTS AND TECHNOLOGY, THE   p892

481 BARTON ST, STONEY CREEK, ON, L8E 2L7
(905) 662-9796   *SIC 8222*
MOUNT ROYAL UNIVERSITY   p74
4825 MOUNT ROYAL GATE SW, CALGARY, AB, T3E 6K6
(403) 440-6111   *SIC 8222*
NIAGARA COLLEGE OF APPLIED ARTS & TECHNOLOGY   p1012
100 NIAGARA COLLEGE BLVD, WELLAND, ON, L3C 7L3
(905) 735-2211   *SIC 8222*
NORTHERN ALBERTA INSTITUTE OF TECHNOLOGY   p85
10504 PRINCESS ELIZABETH AVE NW, EDMONTON, AB, T5G 3K4
(780) 471-6248   *SIC 8222*
NORTHERN ALBERTA INSTITUTE OF TECHNOLOGY   p85
11762 106 ST NW UNIT 108, EDMONTON, AB, T5G 3H2
(780) 471-6248   *SIC 8222*
NORTHERN ALBERTA INSTITUTE OF TECHNOLOGY   p106
12204 149 ST NW, EDMONTON, AB, T5V 1A2
(780) 378-7200   *SIC 8222*
NORTHERN LIGHTS COLLEGE   p204
11401 8 ST, DAWSON CREEK, BC, V1G 4G2
(250) 782-5251   *SIC 8222*
NOVA SCOTIA COMMUNITY COLLEGE p456
5685 LEEDS ST, HALIFAX, NS, B3K 2T3
(902) 491-6701   *SIC 8222*
NOVA SCOTIA COMMUNITY COLLEGE p466
39 ACADIA AVE, STELLARTON, NS, B0K 1S0
(902) 752-2002   *SIC 8222*
NOVA SCOTIA, PROVINCE OF   p460
50 ELLIOTT RD SUITE 1, LAWRENCETOWN., NS, B0S 1M0
(902) 584-2226   *SIC 8222*
RED DEER COLLEGE   p154
100 COLLEGE BLVD, RED DEER, AB, T4N 5H5
(403) 342-3300   *SIC 8222*
SASKATCHEWAN POLYTECHNIC   p1429
119 4TH AVE S SUITE 400, SASKATOON, SK, S7K 5X2
(866) 467-4278   *SIC 8222*
SEMINAIRE DE SHERBROOKE   p1371
195 RUE MARQUETTE BUREAU 116, SHERBROOKE, QC, J1H 1L6
(819) 563-2050   *SIC 8222*
SENECA COLLEGE OF APPLIED ARTS & TECHNOLOGY   p768
1750 FINCH AVE E, NORTH YORK, ON, M2J 2X5
(416) 491-5050   *SIC 8222*
SHERIDAN COLLEGE INSTITUTE OF TECHNOLOGY AND ADVANCED LEARNING   p512
7899 MCLAUGHLIN RD, BRAMPTON, ON, L6Y 5H9
(647) 309-6634   *SIC 8222*
SHERIDAN COLLEGE INSTITUTE OF TECHNOLOGY AND ADVANCED LEARNING   p710
4180 DUKE OF YORK BLVD, MISSISSAUGA, ON, L5B 0G5
(905) 845-9430   *SIC 8222*
SHERIDAN COLLEGE INSTITUTE OF TECHNOLOGY AND ADVANCED LEARNING   p799
1430 TRAFALGAR RD, OAKVILLE, ON, L6H 2L1
(905) 845-9430   *SIC 8222*
SIR SANDFORD FLEMING COLLEGE OF APPLIED ARTS AND TECHNOLOGY p842
599 BREALEY DR, PETERBOROUGH, ON, K9J 7B1
(705) 749-5530   *SIC 8222*

ST. LAWRENCE COLLEGE OF APPLIED ARTS AND TECHNOLOGY, THE   p520
2288 PARKEDALE AVE, BROCKVILLE, ON, K6V 5X3
(613) 345-0660   *SIC 8222*
TEC THE EDUCATION COMPANY INC p223
1632 DICKSON AVE SUITE 100, KELOWNA, BC, V1Y 7T2
(250) 860-2787   *SIC 8222*
VANIER COLLEGE OF GENERAL AND VOCATIONAL EDUCATION   p1323
821 AV SAINTE-CROIX, SAINT-LAURENT, QC, H4L 3X9
(514) 744-7500   *SIC 8222*
VILLA-MARIA   p1221
4245 BOUL DECARIE, MONTREAL, QC, H4A 3K4
(514) 484-4950   *SIC 8222*
WINNIPEG TECHNICAL COLLEGE   p393
130 HENLOW BAY, WINNIPEG, MB, R3Y 1G4
(204) 989-6500   *SIC 8222*

SIC 8231 Libraries

BIBLIOTHEQUE ET ARCHIVES NATIONALES DU QUEBEC   p1175
475 BOUL DE MAISONNEUVE E, MONTREAL, QC, H2L 5C4
(514) 873-1100   *SIC 8231*
BIBLIOTHEQUE ET ARCHIVES NATIONALES DU QUEBEC   p1284
337 RUE MOREAULT, RIMOUSKI, QC, G5L 1P4
(418) 727-3500   *SIC 8231*
BRAMPTON PUBLIC LIBRARY BOARD, THE   p508
65 QUEEN ST E, BRAMPTON, ON, L6W 3L6
(905) 793-4636   *SIC 8231*
BURNABY PUBLIC LIBRARY   p189
6100 WILLINGDON AVE, BURNABY, BC, V5H 4N5
(604) 436-5400   *SIC 8231*
CALGARY PUBLIC LIBRARY   p28
800 3 ST SE, CALGARY, AB, T2G 2E7
(403) 260-2712   *SIC 8231*
CAMBRIDGE PUBLIC LIBRARY BOARD, THE   p535
1 NORTH SQUARE, CAMBRIDGE, ON, N1S 2K6
(519) 621-0460   *SIC 8231*
EDMONTON PUBLIC LIBRARY   p88
7 SIR WINSTON CHURCHILL SQ NW SUITE 5, EDMONTON, AB, T5J 2V4
(780) 496-7050   *SIC 8231*
EDMONTON PUBLIC LIBRARY   p88
7 SIR WINSTON CHURCHILL SQ NW, EDMONTON, AB, T5J 2V4
(780) 496-7000   *SIC 8231*
FRASER VALLEY REGIONAL LIBRARY DISTRICT   p174
34589 DELAIR RD, ABBOTSFORD, BC, V2S 5Y1
(604) 859-7141   *SIC 8231*
GOUVERNEMENT DE LA PROVINCE DE QUEBEC   p1175
475 BOUL DE MAISONNEUVE E, MONTREAL, QC, H2L 5C4
(514) 873-1100   *SIC 8231*
GOVERNORS OF THE UNIVERSITY OF ALBERTA, THE   p117
52 UNIVERSITY CAMPUS NW, EDMONTON, AB, T6G 2J8
(780) 492-3790   *SIC 8231*
GUELPH, CITY OF   p603
100 NORFOLK ST, GUELPH, ON, N1H 4J6
(519) 824-6220   *SIC 8231*
HAMILTON PUBLIC LIBRARY BOARD, THE p614
55 YORK BLVD, HAMILTON, ON, L8R 3K1
(905) 546-3200   *SIC 8231*
INSTITUT CANADIEN DE QUEBEC, L'p1259

350 RUE SAINT-JOSEPH E 4E ETAGE, QUEBEC, QC, G1K 3B2
(418) 529-0924   *SIC* 8231
KITCHENER PUBLIC LIBRARY BOARD
p640
85 QUEEN ST N, KITCHENER, ON, N2H 2H1
(519) 743-0271   *SIC* 8231
MEMORIAL UNIVERSITY OF NEWFOUND-LAND   *p430*
234 ELIZABETH AVE, ST. JOHN'S, NL, A1B 3Y1
(709) 864-8000   *SIC* 8231
MONERIS SOLUTIONS CORPORATION
p412
2 CHARLOTTE ST, SACKVILLE, NB, E4L 3S8
(506) 364-1920   *SIC* 8231
OKANAGAN REGIONAL LIBRARY DISTRICT   *p219*
1430 K.L.O. RD, KELOWNA, BC, V1W 3P6
(250) 860-4652   *SIC* 8231
OTTAWA PUBLIC LIBRARY BOARD   *p824*
120 METCALFE ST, OTTAWA, ON, K1P 5M2
(613) 580-2940   *SIC* 8231
RICHMOND PUBLIC LIBRARY BOARD *p262*
7700 MINORU GATE SUITE 100, RICHMOND, BC, V6Y 1R8
(604) 231-6422   *SIC* 8231
SASKATOON PUBLIC LIBRARY   *p1430*
311 23RD ST E, SASKATOON, SK, S7K 0J6
(306) 975-7558   *SIC* 8231
SURREY PUBLIC LIBRARY   *p274*
10350 UNIVERSITY DR 3RD FLOOR, SURREY, BC, V3T 4B8
(604) 598-7300   *SIC* 8231
TORONTO PUBLIC LIBRARY BOARD *p931*
789 YONGE ST, TORONTO, ON, M4W 2G8
(416) 397-5946   *SIC* 8231
VANCOUVER ISLAND REGIONAL LIBRARY   *p235*
6250 HAMMOND BAY RD, NANAIMO, BC, V9T 6M9
(250) 758-4697   *SIC* 8231
VANCOUVER PUBLIC LIBRARY FOUNDATION   *p301*
350 GEORGIA ST W, VANCOUVER, BC, V6B 6B1
(604) 331-3603   *SIC* 8231
VANCOUVER, CITY OF   *p342*
1950 MARINE DR, WEST VANCOUVER, BC, V7V 1J8
(604) 925-7400   *SIC* 8231
VAUGHAN PUBLIC LIBRARIES   *p663*
2191 MAJOR MACKENZIE DR, MAPLE, ON, L4A 4W2
(905) 653-7323   *SIC* 8231
WAPITI REGIONAL LIBRARY   *p1414*
145 12TH ST E, PRINCE ALBERT, SK, S6V 1B7
(306) 764-0712   *SIC* 8231

SIC 8244 Business and secretarial schools

ACADEMY CANADA INC   *p422*
25 PARK DR, CORNER BROOK, NL, A2H 7H8
(709) 637-2130   *SIC* 8244
COLLEGE O'SULLIVAN DE MONTREAL INC   *p1213*
1191 RUE DE LA MONTAGNE, MONTREAL, QC, H3G 1Z2
(514) 866-4622   *SIC* 8244
FIRST NATIONS TECHNICAL INSTITUTE
p564
3 OLD YORK RD, DESERONTO, ON, K0K 1X0
(613) 396-2122   *SIC* 8244
HERZING INSTITUTES OF CANADA INC
p935
220 YONGE ST SUITE 202, TORONTO, ON, M5B 2H1

(416) 599-6996   *SIC* 8244
SIMON FRASER UNIVERSITY   *p309*
500 GRANVILLE ST, VANCOUVER, BC, V6C 1W6
(778) 782-5013   *SIC* 8244

SIC 8249 Vocational schools, nec

BOMBARDIER INC   *p1338*
8575 CH DE LA COTE-DE-LIESSE, SAINT-LAURENT, QC, H4T 1G5
(514) 344-6620   *SIC* 8249
CAE FORMATION POUR L'AVIATION MILITAIRE INC   *p1405*
15 WING MOOSE JAW BLDG 160, BUSHELL PARK, SK, S0H 0N0
(306) 694-2719   *SIC* 8249
COLLEGE LASALLE   *p1214*
2120 RUE SAINTE-CATHERINE O, MONTREAL, QC, H3H 1M7
(514) 939-2006   *SIC* 8249
COMMISSION SCOLAIRE DU VAL-DES-CERFS   *p1109*
700 RUE DENISON O, GRANBY, QC, J2G 4G3
(450) 378-8544   *SIC* 8249
EXCALIBUR LEARNING RESOURCE CENTRE, CANADA CORP   *p630*
25 MARKLAND ST, KINGSTON, ON, K7K 1S2
SIC 8249
EXCHANGE INCOME CORPORATION *p384*
1067 SHERWIN RD, WINNIPEG, MB, R3H 0T8
(204) 982-1857   *SIC* 8249
GOUVERNEMENT DE LA PROVINCE DE QUEBEC   *p1185*
3535 RUE SAINT-DENIS, MONTREAL, QC, H2X 3P1
(514) 282-5111   *SIC* 8249
HARRIS INSTITUTE FOR THE ARTS INCORPORATED, THE   *p933*
118 SHERBOURNE ST, TORONTO, ON, M5A 2R2
(416) 367-0162   *SIC* 8249
NAV CANADA   *p562*
1950 MONTREAL RD, CORNWALL, ON, K6H 6L2
(613) 936-5050   *SIC* 8249

SIC 8299 Schools and educational services, nec

1057206 ONTARIO LTD   *p796*
2359 BRISTOL CIR, OAKVILLE, ON, L6H 6P8
SIC 8299
7226438 CANADA INC   *p932*
80 SACKVILLE ST RM 315, TORONTO, ON, M5A 3E5
(416) 834-5951   *SIC* 8299
BEARSKIN LAKE AIR SERVICE LP   *p359*
585 6TH AVE S, STONEWALL, MB, R0C 2Z0
SIC 8299
BERLITZ CANADA INC   *p709*
3660 HURONTARIO ST SUITE 302, MISSISSAUGA, ON, L5B 3C4
(905) 896-0215   *SIC* 8299
BOMBARDIER INC   *p1410*
GD, MOOSE JAW, SK, S6H 7Z8
(306) 694-2222   *SIC* 8299
BRAMPTON FLYING CLUB   *p544*
13691 MCLAUGHLIN RD, CHELTENHAM, ON, L7C 2B2
(416) 798-7928   *SIC* 8299
BRIGHTPATH EARLY LEARNING INC   *p14*
200 RIVERCREST DR SE SUITE 201, CALGARY, AB, T2C 2X5
(403) 705-0362   *SIC* 8299
BURNSTEIN, DR. & ASSOCIATES   *p800*
1484 CORNWALL RD, OAKVILLE, ON, L6J

7W5
(905) 844-3240   *SIC* 8299
CALGARY FRENCH & INTERNATIONAL SCHOOL SOCIETY, THE   *p75*
700 77 ST SW, CALGARY, AB, T3H 5R1
(403) 240-1500   *SIC* 8299
CENTRE DE LANGUES INTERNATIONALES CHARPENTIER   *p1371*
20 RUE BRYANT, SHERBROOKE, QC, J1J 3E4
(819) 822-2542   *SIC* 8299
CENTRE FOR SKILLS DEVELOPMENT & TRAINING, THE   *p521*
5151 NEW ST, BURLINGTON, ON, L7L 1V3
(905) 637-3393   *SIC* 8299
CHILDREN'S ARTS UMBRELLA ASSOCIATION   *p319*
1286 CARTWRIGHT ST, VANCOUVER, BC, V6H 3R8
(604) 681-5268   *SIC* 8299
CHINESE ACADEMY FOUNDATION, THE
p40
6600 4 ST NW, CALGARY, AB, T2K 1C2
(403) 777-7663   *SIC* 8299
CHUNG DAHM IMMERSION SCHOOL, VANCOUVER INC   *p238*
2420 DOLLARTON HWY, NORTH VANCOUVER, BC, V7H 2Y1
SIC 8299
CMI INTERLANGUES INC   *p833*
412 MACLAREN ST, OTTAWA, ON, K2P 0M8
(613) 236-3763   *SIC* 8299
COLUMBIA COLLEGE CORP   *p22*
802 MANNING RD NE, CALGARY, AB, T2E 7N8
(403) 235-9300   *SIC* 8299
COMMISSION SCOLAIRE DE LA RIVIERE-DU-NORD   *p1152*
17000 RUE AUBIN, MIRABEL, QC, J7J 1B1
(450) 435-0167   *SIC* 8299
COMMISSION SCOLAIRE DES PREMIERES-SEIGNEURIES   *p1280*
700 RUE DE L'ARGON, QUEBEC, QC, G2N 2G5
(418) 634-5580   *SIC* 8299
COMMUNITY LIVING GUELPH WELLINGTON   *p602*
8 ROYAL RD, GUELPH, ON, N1H 1G3
(519) 824-2480   *SIC* 8299
COQUITLAM, CITY OF   *p200*
1120 BRUNETTE AVE, COQUITLAM, BC, V3K 1G2
(604) 664-1636   *SIC* 8299
CSI GLOBAL EDUCATION INC   *p979*
200 WELLINGTON ST W SUITE 1200, TORONTO, ON, M5V 3G2
(416) 364-9130   *SIC* 8299
DISTRICT SCOLAIRE FRANCOPHONE NORD-EST   *p410*
700 RUE PRINCIPALE, NEGUAC, NB, E9G 1N4
(506) 776-3808   *SIC* 8299
DOLCE INTERNATIONAL (ONTARIO) CO.
p986
130 KING ST W, TORONTO, ON, M5X 2A2
(416) 861-9600   *SIC* 8299
ECOLE DE CONDUITE TECNIC RIVE SUD INC   *p1308*
3285 MONTEE SAINT-HUBERT, SAINT-HUBERT, QC, J3Y 4J4
(450) 443-4104   *SIC* 8299
ECOLE DE LANGUES DE LA CITE, L' *p823*
280 ALBERT ST SUITE 500, OTTAWA, ON, K1P 5G8
(613) 569-6260   *SIC* 8299
EMILY CARR UNIVERSITY OF ART & DESIGN   *p289*
520 1ST AVE E, VANCOUVER, BC, V5T 0H2
(604) 844-3800   *SIC* 8299
ENTERPHASE CHILD AND FAMILY SERVICES INC   *p812*
250 HARMONY RD S, OSHAWA, ON, L1H

6T9
SIC 8299
EXCELLENTE GESTION INC   *p1261*
550 BOUL PERE-LELIEVRE BUREAU 100, QUEBEC, QC, G1M 3R2
(418) 529-3868   *SIC* 8299
FLIGHTSAFETY CANADA LTD   *p785*
95 GARRATT BLVD, NORTH YORK, ON, M3K 2A5
(416) 638-9313   *SIC* 8299
FLIGHTSAFETY CANADA LTD   *p1094*
9555 AV RYAN, DORVAL, QC, H9P 1A2
(514) 631-2084   *SIC* 8299
GRANT MACEWAN UNIVERSITY   *p98*
10045 156 ST NW RM 402, EDMONTON, AB, T5P 2P7
(780) 497-4310   *SIC* 8299
ILSC (VANCOUVER) INC   *p298*
555 RICHARDS ST, VANCOUVER, BC, V6B 2Z5
(604) 689-9095   *SIC* 8299
JEWISH VOCATIONAL SERVICE OF METROPOLITAN TORONTO   *p791*
74 TYCOS DR, NORTH YORK, ON, M6B 1V9
(416) 785-0515   *SIC* 8299
JUNIOR ACHIEVEMENT OF CANADA *p579*
1 EVA RD SUITE 218, ETOBICOKE, ON, M9C 4Z5
(416) 622-4602   *SIC* 8299
KHALSA SCHOOL   *p276*
6933 124 ST, SURREY, BC, V3W 3W6
(604) 591-2248   *SIC* 8299
KUMON CANADA INC   *p1027*
6240 HIGHWAY 7 SUITE 300, WOODBRIDGE, ON, L4H 4G3
(416) 490-1434   *SIC* 8299
LA FONDATION DE L'INSTITUT MARITIME DU QUEBEC INC   *p1284*
53 RUE SAINT-GERMAIN O, RIMOUSKI, QC, G5L 4B4
(418) 724-2822   *SIC* 8299
MERRITHEW INTERNATIONAL INC   *p924*
2200 YONGE ST SUITE 500, TORONTO, ON, M4S 2C6
(416) 482-4050   *SIC* 8299
MOODY'S ANALYTICS GLOBAL EDUCATION (CANADA), INC   *p982*
200 WELLINGTON ST W, TORONTO, ON, M5V 3C7
(416) 364-9130   *SIC* 8299
NORTHERN NISHNAWBE EDUCATION COUNCIL   *p881*
21 KING ST, SIOUX LOOKOUT, ON, P8T 1B9
(807) 737-2002   *SIC* 8299
ONTARIO CONSERVATORY OF MUSIC INC
p725
2915 ARGENTIA RD UNIT 3, MISSISSAUGA, ON, L5N 8G6
(905) 286-1133   *SIC* 8299
SASKATCHEWAN INDIAN INSTITUTE OF TECHNOLOGIES   *p1429*
229 4TH AVE S SUITE 201, SASKATOON, SK, S7K 4K3
(306) 373-4777   *SIC* 8299
SATNAM EDUCATION SOCIETY OF BRITISH COLUMBIA   *p277*
6933 124 ST, SURREY, BC, V3W 3W6
SIC 8299
SEABIRD ISLAND INDIAN BAND   *p179*
2895 CHOWAT RD RR 2, AGASSIZ, BC, V0M 1A2
(604) 796-2177   *SIC* 8299
SYLVAN LEARNING CENTRE INC   *p628*
205 SECOND ST S, KENORA, ON, P9N 1G1
(807) 467-8374   *SIC* 8299
TOP ACES INC   *p1091*
79B BOUL BRUNSWICK, DOLLARD-DES-ORMEAUX, QC, H9B 2J5
(514) 694-5565   *SIC* 8299
TOP ACES INC   *p1095*
1675 RTE TRANSCANADIENNE BUREAU

201, DORVAL, QC, H9P 1J1

(514) 694-5565   *SIC* 8299

VANCOUVER ENGLISH CENTRE INC *p301*

250 SMITHE ST, VANCOUVER, BC, V6B 1E7

SIC 8299

VANCOUVER FILM SCHOOL LIMITED *p301*

198 HASTINGS ST W SUITE 200, VANCOUVER, BC, V6B 1H2

(604) 685-5808   *SIC* 8299

WESTCOAST ENGLISH LANGUAGE CENTER LIMITED *p301*

888 CAMBIE ST, VANCOUVER, BC, V6B 2P6

(604) 684-1010   *SIC* 8299

SIC 8322 Individual and family services

446784 B.C. LTD *p174*

2291 WEST RAILWAY ST SUITE B, ABBOTSFORD, BC, V2S 2E3

(604) 864-9682   *SIC* 8322

ACCREDITED SUPPORTS TO THE COMMUNITY *p82*

1709 15TH AVE, DIDSBURY, AB, T0M 0W0

(403) 335-8671   *SIC* 8322

ACCREDITED SUPPORTS TO THE COMMUNITY *p151*

4322 50 AVE, OLDS, AB, T4H 1A5

(403) 556-4110   *SIC* 8322

AGE LINK PERSONNEL SERVICES INC *p609*

400 PARKDALE AVE N UNIT 2A, HAMILTON, ON, L8H 5Y2

(905) 572-6162   *SIC* 8322

AIDE-MAISON VALLEE DE LA MATAPEDIA *p1046*

20A RUE DESBIENS BUREAU 100, AMQUI, QC, G5J 3P1

(418) 629-5812   *SIC* 8322

ALBRIGHT GARDENS HOMES INCORPORATED *p489*

5050 HILLSIDE DR, BEAMSVILLE, ON, L0R 1B2

(905) 563-8252   *SIC* 8322

ASSOCIATION D'ENTRAIDE LE CHAINON INC, L' *p1184*

4373 AV DE L'ESPLANADE, MONTREAL, QC, H2W 1T2

(514) 845-0151   *SIC* 8322

ATELIER LA FLECHE DE FER INC, L' *p1063*

1730 RUE EIFFEL, BOUCHERVILLE, QC, J4B 7W1

(450) 552-9150   *SIC* 8322

AZGA SERVICE CANADA INC *p641*

4273 KING ST E, KITCHENER, ON, N2P 2E9

(519) 742-2800   *SIC* 8322

BARRIE MEMORIAL HOSPITAL FOUNDATION *p1113*

10 RUE KING BUREAU 200, HUNTINGDON, QC, J0S 1H0

(450) 829-3877   *SIC* 8322

BAYSHORE HEALTHCARE LTD. *p884*

282 LINWELL RD SUITE 205, ST CATHARINES, ON, L2N 6N5

(905) 688-5214   *SIC* 8322

BEA FISHER CENTRE INC, THE *p143*

3514 51 AVE, LLOYDMINSTER, AB, T9V 1C8

(780) 875-3633   *SIC* 8322

BEHAVIOURAL HEALTH FOUNDATION INC, THE *p392*

35 DE LA DIGUE AVE, WINNIPEG, MB, R3V 1M7

(204) 269-3430   *SIC* 8322

BEN CALF ROBE SOCIETY OF EDMONTON *p83*

12046 77 ST NW, EDMONTON, AB, T5B 2G7

(780) 477-6648   *SIC* 8322

BETHANY CARE SOCIETY *p12*

2915 26 AVE SE UNIT 100, CALGARY, AB,

T2B 2W6

(403) 210-4600   SIC 8322

BETHANY CARE SOCIETY *p156*

99 COLLEGE CIR, RED DEER, AB, T4R 0M3

(403) 357-3700   *SIC* 8322

BOYS & GIRLS CLUBS OF EDMONTON, THE *p85*

9425 109A AVE NW, EDMONTON, AB, T5H 1G1

(780) 424-8181   *SIC* 8322

BOYS' AND GIRLS' CLUBS OF GREATER VANCOUVER *p288*

2875 ST. GEORGE ST, VANCOUVER, BC, V5T 3R8

(604) 879-9118   *SIC* 8322

BRADLEY AIR SERVICES LIMITED *p826*

100 THAD JOHNSON PVT, OTTAWA, ON, K1V 0R1

(613) 254-6200   *SIC* 8322

BRAMPTON CALEDON COMMUNITY LIVING *p510*

34 CHURCH ST W, BRAMPTON, ON, L6X 1H3

(905) 453-8841   *SIC* 8322

BRANDON COMMUNITY OPTIONS INC *p346*

136 11TH ST, BRANDON, MB, R7A 4J4

(204) 571-5770   *SIC* 8322

BROCKVILLE & AREA COMMUNITY LIVING ASSOCIATION *p519*

6 GLENN WOOD PL SUITE 100, BROCKVILLE, ON, K6V 2T3

(613) 342-2953   *SIC* 8322

BROCKVILLE AREA CENTRE FOR DEVELOPMENTALLY HANDICAPPED PERSONS INC *p519*

61 KING ST E, BROCKVILLE, ON, K6V 1B2

SIC 8322

C L S C PLATEAU MONT-ROYAL *p1172*

4689 AV PAPINEAU, MONTREAL, QC, H2H 1V4

(514) 521-7663   *SIC* 8322

CALGARY ALTERNATIVE SUPPORT SERVICES INC *p41*

1240 KENSINGTON RD NW SUITE 408, CALGARY, AB, T2N 3P7

(403) 283-0611   *SIC* 8322

CALGARY CATHOLIC IMMIGRATION SOCIETY *p64*

1111 11 AVE SW UNIT 111, CALGARY, AB, T2R 0G5

(403) 262-2006   *SIC* 8322

CALGARY CATHOLIC IMMIGRATION SOCIETY *p64*

1111 11 AVE SW SUITE 103, CALGARY, AB, T2R 0G5

(403) 262-5692   *SIC* 8322

CALGARY COUNSELLING CENTRE *p28*

105 12 AVE SE SUITE 100, CALGARY, AB, T2G 1A1

(403) 265-4980   *SIC* 8322

CALGARY HANDI-BUS ASSOCIATION *p21*

231 37 AVE NE, CALGARY, AB, T2E 8J2

(403) 276-8028   *SIC* 8322

CALGARY SCOPE SOCIETY *p21*

219 18 ST SE, CALGARY, AB, T2E 6J5

(403) 509-0200   *SIC* 8322

CALGARY YOUNG MEN'S CHRISTIAN ASSOCIATION, THE *p69*

333 SHAWVILLE BLVD SE SUITE 400, CALGARY, AB, T2Y 4H3

(403) 256-5533   *SIC* 8322

CALGARY YOUNG WOMEN'S CHRISTIAN ASSOCIATION, THE *p28*

320 5 AVE SE, CALGARY, AB, T2G 0E5

(403) 263-1550   *SIC* 8322

CANADIAN INDUSTRIAL PARAMEDICS *p122*

8917 13 ST NW, EDMONTON, AB, T6P 0C7

(780) 467-4262   *SIC* 8322

CANADIAN RED CROSS SOCIETY, THE *p833*

400 COOPER ST SUITE 8000, OTTAWA,

ON, K2P 2H8

(613) 740-1900   *SIC* 8322

CANADIAN RED CROSS SOCIETY, THE *p1396*

6 PLACE DU COMMERCE, VERDUN, QC, H3E 1P4

(514) 362-2930   *SIC* 8322

CAREFIRST SENIORS AND COMMUNITY SERVICES ASSOCIATION *p876*

300 SILVER STAR BLVD, SCARBOROUGH, ON, M1V 0G2

(416) 502-2323   *SIC* 8322

CATHOLIC CHILDREN'S AID SOCIETY OF HAMILTON-WENTWORTH *p611*

735 KING ST E, HAMILTON, ON, L8M 1A1

(905) 525-2012   *SIC* 8322

CATHOLIC CHILDREN'S AID SOCIETY OF TORONTO, THE *p931*

26 MAITLAND ST, TORONTO, ON, M4Y 1C6

(416) 395-1500   *SIC* 8322

CATHOLIC CHILDREN'S AID SOCIETY OF TORONTO, THE *p990*

900 DUFFERIN ST SUITE 219, TORONTO, ON, M6H 4A9

(416) 395-1500   *SIC* 8322

CATHOLIC FAMILY SERVICE OF CALGARY, THE *p64*

707 10 AVE SW SUITE 250, CALGARY, AB, T2R 0B3

(403) 233-2360   *SIC* 8322

CENTRAL WEST SPECIALIZED DEVELOPMENTAL SERVICES *p526*

3782 STAR LANE, BURLINGTON, ON, L7M 5A0

(905) 336-4248   *SIC* 8322

CENTRAL WEST SPECIALIZED DEVELOPMENTAL SERVICES *p802*

53 BOND ST, OAKVILLE, ON, L6K 1L8

(905) 844-7864   *SIC* 8322

CENTRE COMMUNAUTAIRE DE LOISIR DE LA COTE-DES-NEIGES *p1219*

5347 CH DE LA COTE-DES-NEIGES, MONTREAL, QC, H3T 1Y4

(514) 733-1478   *SIC* 8322

CENTRE COMMUNAUTAIRE LEONARDO DA VINCI *p1345*

8370 BOUL LACORDAIRE, SAINT-LEONARD, QC, H1R 3Y6

(514) 955-8350   *SIC* 8322

CENTRE D'ETUDE ET DE COOPERATION INTERNATIONALE *p1168*

3000 RUE OMER-LAVALLEE, MONTREAL, QC, H1Y 3R8

(514) 875-9911   *SIC* 8322

CENTRE DE BENEVOLAT DE LA TUQUE INC *p1124*

497 RUE SAINT-ANTOINE, LA TUQUE, QC, G9X 2Y3

SIC 8322

CENTRE DE SANTE ET DE SERVICES SOCIAUX CHAMPLAIN *p1069*

5050 PLACE NOGENT, BROSSARD, QC, J4Y 2K3

(450) 672-3328   *SIC* 8322

CENTRE DE SANTE ET DE SERVICES SOCIAUX DE LA VIEILLE-CAPITALE *p1258*

50 RUE SAINT-JOSEPH E, QUEBEC, QC, G1K 3A5

(418) 529-2572   *SIC* 8322

CENTRE DE SANTE ET DE SERVICES SOCIAUX DE THERESE-DE-BLAINVILLE *p1364*

125 RUE DUQUET, SAINTE-THERESE, QC, J7E 0A5

(450) 430-4553   *SIC* 8322

CENTRE DE SANTE ET DE SERVICES SOCIAUX LUCILLE-TEASDALE *p1164*

7445 RUE HOCHELAGA, MONTREAL, QC, H1N 3V2

(514) 251-6000   *SIC* 8322

CENTRE DE SANTE ET DE SERVICES SOCIAUX LUCILLE-TEASDALE *p1164*

5810 RUE SHERBROOKE E, MONTREAL, QC, H1N 1B2

(514) 255-2365   *SIC* 8322

CENTRE FOR CHILD DEVELOPMENT OF THE LOWER MAINLAND, THE *p274*

9460 140 ST, SURREY, BC, V3V 5Z4

(604) 584-1361   *SIC* 8322

CENTRE INTEGRE DE SANTE ET DE SERVICES SOCIAUX DE LA MONTEREGIE-OUEST *p1076*

95 CH DE LA HAUTE-RIVIERE, CHATEAUGUAY, QC, J6K 3P1

(450) 692-8231   *SIC* 8322

CENTRE INTEGRE UNIVERSITAIRE SANTE ET SERVICES SOCIAUX DU CENTRE-SUD-DE-L'ILE-DE-MONTREAL *p1163*

8147 RUE SHERBROOKE E, MONTREAL, QC, H1L 1A7

(514) 356-4500   *SIC* 8322

CENTRE JEUNESSE DE L'ESTRIE *p1370*

340 RUE DUFFERIN, SHERBROOKE, QC, J1H 4M7

(819) 822-2727   *SIC* 8322

CENTRE JEUNESSE DE LA MAURICIE ET DU CENTRE-DU-QUEBEC, LE *p1386*

2735 RUE PAPINEAU, TROIS-RIVIERES, QC, G8Z 1N8

(819) 378-8635   *SIC* 8322

CENTRE JEUNESSE DE LA MAURICIE ET DU CENTRE-DU-QUEBEC, LE *p1386*

1455 BOUL DU CARMEL, TROIS-RIVIERES, QC, G8Z 3R7

(819) 378-5481   *SIC* 8322

CENTRE JEUNESSE DE LA MAURICIE ET DU CENTRE-DU-QUEBEC, LE *p1386*

1455 BOUL DU CARMEL, TROIS-RIVIERES, QC, G8Z 3R7

(819) 378-5481   *SIC* 8322

CENTRE JEUNESSE DES LAURENTIDES *p1319*

358 RUE LAVIOLETTE, SAINT-JEROME, QC, J7Y 2T1

(450) 432-9753   *SIC* 8322

CENTRES DE LA JEUNESSE ET DE LA FAMILLE BATSHAW, L *p1253*

3065 BOUL DU CURE-LABELLE, PREVOST, QC, J0R 1T0

(450) 224-8234   *SIC* 8322

CENTRES DE LA JEUNESSE ET DE LA FAMILLE BATSHAW, L *p1401*

5 RUE WEREDALE PARK, WESTMOUNT, QC, H3Z 1Y5

(514) 989-1885   *SIC* 8322

CENTRES JEUNESSE CHAUDIERE-APPALACHES, LES *p1135*

100 RTE MONSEIGNEUR-BOURGET BUREAU 300, LEVIS, QC, G6V 2Y9

(418) 837-9331   *SIC* 8322

CENTRES JEUNESSE DE L'OUTAOUAIS, LES *p1105*

105 BOUL SACRE-COEUR BUREAU 1, GATINEAU, QC, J8X 1C5

(819) 771-6631   *SIC* 8322

CHARTWELL MASTER CARE LP *p730*

100 MILVERTON DR SUITE 700, MISSISSAUGA, ON, L5R 4H1

(905) 501-9219   *SIC* 8322

CHATHAM-KENT CHILDREN'S SERVICES *p542*

495 GRAND AVE W, CHATHAM, ON, N7L 1C5

(519) 352-0440   *SIC* 8322

CHILD & FAMILY SERVICES OF WESTERN MANITOBA *p346*

800 MCTAVISH AVE, BRANDON, MB, R7A 7L4

(204) 726-6030   *SIC* 8322

CHILDREN AND FAMILY SERVICES FOR YORK REGION *p755*

16915 LESLIE ST, NEWMARKET, ON, L3Y 9A1

(905) 895-2318   *SIC* 8322

CHILDREN'S AID SOCIETY OF ALGOMA *p862*

191 NORTHERN AVE E, SAULT STE. MARIE, ON, P6B 4H8

▲ Public Company   ■ Public Company Family Member   **HQ** Headquarters   **BR** Branch   **SL** Single Location

(705) 949-0162   *SIC* 8322
CHILDREN'S AID SOCIETY OF HALDIMAND AND NORFOLK, THE   *p998*
70 TOWN CENTRE DR, TOWNSEND, ON, N0A 1S0
(519) 587-5437   *SIC* 8322
CHILDREN'S AID SOCIETY OF HAMILTON, THE   *p608*
26 ARROWSMITH RD, HAMILTON, ON, L8E 4H8
(905) 522-1121   *SIC* 8322
CHILDREN'S AID SOCIETY OF OXFORD COUNTY   *p1035*
712 PEEL ST, WOODSTOCK, ON, N4S 0B4
(519) 539-6176   *SIC* 8322
CHILDREN'S AID SOCIETY OF THE CITY OF SARNIA AND THE COUNTY OF LAMBTON   *p861*
161 KENDALL ST, SARNIA, ON, N7V 4G6
(519) 336-0623   *SIC* 8322
CHILDREN'S AID SOCIETY OF THE COUNTY OF RENFREW   *p838*
77 MARY ST SUITE 100, PEMBROKE, ON, K8A 5V4
(613) 735-6866   *SIC* 8322
CHILDREN'S AID SOCIETY OF THE DISTRICT OF NIPISSING & PARRY SOUND, THE   *p763*
433 MCINTYRE ST W, NORTH BAY, ON, P1B 2Z3
(705) 472-0910   *SIC* 8322
CHILDREN'S AID SOCIETY OF THE DISTRICTS OF SUDBURY AND MANITOULIN, THE   *p898*
319 LASALLE BLVD UNIT 3, SUDBURY, ON, P3A 1W7
(705) 566-3113   *SIC* 8322
CHILDREN'S AID SOCIETY OF THE NIAGARA REGION, THE   *p887*
82 HANNOVER DR, ST CATHARINES, ON, L2W 1A4
(905) 937-7731   *SIC* 8322
CHILDREN'S AID SOCIETY OF THE REGION OF PEEL, THE   *p721*
6860 CENTURY AVE, MISSISSAUGA, ON, L5N 2W5
(905) 363-6131   *SIC* 8322
CHILDREN'S AID SOCIETY OF THE REGIONAL MUNICIPALITY OF HALTON   *p521*
1445 NORJOHN CRT, BURLINGTON, ON, L7L 0E6
(905) 333-4441   *SIC* 8322
CHILDREN'S AID SOCIETY OF THE REGIONAL MUNICIPALITY OF WATERLOO, THE   *p636*
200 ARDELT AVE, KITCHENER, ON, N2C 2L9
(519) 576-0540   *SIC* 8322
CHILDREN'S AID SOCIETY OF THE REGIONAL MUNICIPALITY OF WATERLOO, THE   *p636*
200 ARDELT AVE, KITCHENER, ON, N2C 2L9
(519) 576-0540   *SIC* 8322
CHILDREN'S AID SOCIETY OF TORONTO   *p782*
20 DE BOERS DR SUITE 250, NORTH YORK, ON, M3J 0H1
(416) 924-4646   *SIC* 8322
CHILDREN'S AID SOCIETY OF TORONTO   *p931*
30 ISABELLA ST, TORONTO, ON, M4Y 1N1
(416) 924-4646   *SIC* 8322
CHILDRENS AID SOCIETY UNITED COUNTIES STORMONT, DUNDAS & GLENGARRY   *p562*
150 BOUNDARY RD, CORNWALL, ON, K6H 6J5
(613) 933-2292   *SIC* 8322
CHIMO YOUTH RETREAT CENTRE   *p85*
10585 111 ST NW SUITE 103, EDMONTON, AB, T5H 3E8
(780) 420-0324   *SIC* 8322
CITY OF BURNABY   *p190*

6533 NELSON AVE, BURNABY, BC, V5H 0C2
SIC 8322
COLCHESTER RESIDENTIAL SERVICES SOCIETY   *p468*
35 COMMERCIAL ST SUITE 201, TRURO, NS, B2N 3H9
(902) 893-4273   *SIC* 8322
COLUMBUS CENTRE OF TORONTO   *p788*
901 LAWRENCE AVE W SUITE 306, NORTH YORK, ON, M6A 1C3
(416) 789-7011   *SIC* 8322
COMMUNITY LIVING - FORT ERIE   *p591*
615 INDUSTRIAL DR, FORT ERIE, ON, L2A 5M4
(905) 871-6770   *SIC* 8322
COMMUNITY LIVING ALGOMA   *p862*
99 NORTHERN AVE E, SAULT STE. MARIE, ON, P6B 4H5
(705) 253-1700   *SIC* 8322
COMMUNITY LIVING BRANT   *p515*
366 DALHOUSIE ST, BRANTFORD, ON, N3S 3W2
(519) 756-2662   *SIC* 8322
COMMUNITY LIVING BURLINGTON   *p526*
3057 MAINWAY, BURLINGTON, ON, L7M 1A1
(905) 335-6711   *SIC* 8322
COMMUNITY LIVING ESSEX COUNTY   *p1017*
13158 TECUMSEH RD E, WINDSOR, ON, N8N 3T6
(519) 979-0057   *SIC* 8322
COMMUNITY LIVING GUELPH WELLINGTON   *p602*
8 ROYAL RD, GUELPH, ON, N1H 1G3
(519) 824-2480   *SIC* 8322
COMMUNITY LIVING GUELPH WELLINGTON   *p746*
135 FERGUS ST S, MOUNT FOREST, ON, N0G 2L2
(519) 323-4050   *SIC* 8322
COMMUNITY LIVING HALDIMAND   *p541*
2256 RIVER RD E, CAYUGA, ON, N0A 1E0
(905) 772-3344   *SIC* 8322
COMMUNITY LIVING KINGSTON AND DISTRICT   *p631*
541 DAYS RD UNIT 6, KINGSTON, ON, K7M 3R8
(613) 546-6613   *SIC* 8322
COMMUNITY LIVING LONDON INC   *p652*
180 ADELAIDE ST S SUITE 4, LONDON, ON, N5Z 3L1
(519) 686-3000   *SIC* 8322
COMMUNITY LIVING LONDON INC   *p652*
190 ADELAIDE ST S, LONDON, ON, N5Z 3L1
(519) 686-3000   *SIC* 8322
COMMUNITY LIVING NORTH BAY   *p763*
161 MAIN ST E, NORTH BAY, ON, P1B 1A9
(705) 476-3288   *SIC* 8322
COMMUNITY LIVING NORTH HALTON *p683*
917 NIPISSING RD, MILTON, ON, L9T 5E3
(905) 878-2337   *SIC* 8322
COMMUNITY LIVING NORTH HALTON *p683*
500 VALLEYVIEW CRES, MILTON, ON, L9T 3L2
(905) 693-0528   *SIC* 8322
COMMUNITY LIVING ONTARIO   *p776*
240 DUNCAN MILL RD SUITE 403, NORTH YORK, ON, M3B 3S6
(416) 447-4348   *SIC* 8322
COMMUNITY LIVING TIMMINS INTERGRATION COMMUNAUTAIRE   *p912*
166 BROUSSEAU AVE, TIMMINS, ON, P4N 5Y4
(705) 268-8811   *SIC* 8322
COMMUNITY LIVING TORONTO   *p782*
1122 FINCH AVE W UNIT 18, NORTH YORK, ON, M3J 3J5
(416) 225-7166   *SIC* 8322
COMMUNITY LIVING TORONTO   *p972*
20 SPADINA RD, TORONTO, ON, M5R 2S7
(416) 968-0650   *SIC* 8322

COMMUNITY LIVING WINDSOR   *p1019*
2840 TEMPLE DR, WINDSOR, ON, N8W 5J5
(519) 944-2464   *SIC* 8322
COMMUNITY LIVING-GRIMSBY, LINCOLN AND WEST LINCOLN   *p489*
5041 KING ST, BEAMSVILLE, ON, L0R 1B0
(905) 563-4115   *SIC* 8322
COMPASSION HOME CARE INC   *p421*
GD, BAY ROBERTS, NL, A0A 1G0
(709) 786-8677   *SIC* 8322
CORE(CLIENT ONGOING REHABILITATION AND EQUALITY) ASSOCIATION   *p145*
412 3 ST SE, MEDICINE HAT, AB, T1A 0H1
(403) 527-3302   *SIC* 8322
CORPORATION DU CENTRE DU SABLON INC   *p1237*
755 CH DU SABLON, MONTREAL, QC, H7W 4H5
(450) 688-8961   *SIC* 8322
CORPORATION OF THE CITY OF KITCHENER   *p639*
350 MARGARET AVE, KITCHENER, ON, N2H 4J8
(519) 741-2502   *SIC* 8322
CORPORATION OF THE CITY OF PETERBOROUGH, THE   *p840*
151 LANSDOWNE ST W, PETERBOROUGH, ON, K9J 1Y4
(705) 743-3561   *SIC* 8322
CORPORATION OF THE CITY OF VAUGHAN, THE   *p1030*
9201 ISLINGTON AVE, WOODBRIDGE, ON, L4L 1A6
(905) 832-8564   *SIC* 8322
CORPORATION OF THE COUNTY OF DUFFERIN, THE   *p880*
151 CENTRE ST, SHELBURNE, ON, L9V 3R7
(519) 925-2140   *SIC* 8322
COSTI IMMIGRANT SERVICES   *p989*
1710 DUFFERIN ST, TORONTO, ON, M6E 3P2
(416) 658-1600   *SIC* 8322
COVENANT HOUSE TORONTO   *p935*
20 GERRARD ST E, TORONTO, ON, M5B 2P3
(416) 598-4898   *SIC* 8322
CRAIGWOOD YOUTH SERVICES   *p473*
26996 NEW ONTARIO RD, AILSA CRAIG, ON, N0M 1A0
(519) 232-4301   *SIC* 8322
CRANBROOK SOCIETY FOR COMMUNITY LIVING   *p203*
1629 BAKER ST SUITE 100, CRANBROOK, BC, V1C 1B4
(250) 426-7588   *SIC* 8322
CRIDGE CENTRE FOR THE FAMILY, THE *p334*
1307 HILLSIDE AVE SUITE 414, VICTORIA, BC, V8T 0A2
(250) 384-8058   *SIC* 8322
DEVELOPMENTAL DISABILITIES ASSOCIATION OF VANCOUVER-RICHMOND *p260*
3851 SHELL RD SUITE 100, RICHMOND, BC, V6X 2W2
(604) 273-9778   *SIC* 8322
DIXON HALL   *p933*
58 SUMACH ST, TORONTO, ON, M5A 3J7
(416) 863-0499   *SIC* 8322
DRUMHELLER AND REGION TRANSITION SOCIETY   *p82*
105 3RD AVE E, DRUMHELLER, AB, T0J 0Y0
(403) 823-6690   *SIC* 8322
EPIC OPPORTUNITIES INC   *p384*
1644 DUBLIN AVE, WINNIPEG, MB, R3H 0X5
(204) 982-4673   *SIC* 8322
FAMILY DYNAMICS   *p374*
393 PORTAGE AVE SUITE 401, WINNIPEG, MB, R3B 3H6
(204) 947-1401   *SIC* 8322
FAMILY SERVICE TORONTO   *p994*

202-128A STERLING RD, TORONTO, ON, M6R 2B7
(416) 595-9230   *SIC* 8322
FEDERATION CJA   *p1219*
5151 CH DE LA COTE-SAINTE-CATHERINE, MONTREAL, QC, H3W 1M6
(514) 345-2645   *SIC* 8322
FEDERATION CJA   *p1219*
5151 CH DE LA COTE-SAINTE-CATHERINE, MONTREAL, QC, H3W 1M6
(514) 735-3541   *SIC* 8322
FONDATION D'ENTRAIDE EN SANTE DES BENEVOLES DE STE-ANNE   *p1355*
43 RUE SAINTE-ANNE BUREAU 3, SAINTE-ANNE-DE-BELLEVUE, QC, H9X 1L4
(514) 457-1642   *SIC* 8322
FONDATION DU CENTRE DE SANTE ET DE SERVICES SOCIAUX DE TROIS-RIVIERES *p1387*
731 RUE SAINTE-JULIE, TROIS-RIVIERES, QC, G9A 1Y1
(819) 370-2100   *SIC* 8322
FONDATION DU CENTRE JEUNESSE DE LA MONTEREGIE   *p1141*
575 RUE ADONCOUR, LONGUEUIL, QC, J4G 2M6
(450) 679-0140   *SIC* 8322
FONDATION DU CENTRE JEUNESSE DE LA MONTEREGIE   *p1318*
145 BOUL SAINT-JOSEPH BUREAU 200, SAINT-JEAN-SUR-RICHELIEU, QC, J3B 1W5
(450) 359-7525   *SIC* 8322
FONDATION DU CENTRE JEUNESSE DE QUEBEC   *p1255*
3510 RUE CAMBRONNE, QUEBEC, QC, G1E 7H2
(418) 661-3700   *SIC* 8322
FONDATION DU CENTRE JEUNESSE DE QUEBEC   *p1258*
540 BOUL CHAREST E, QUEBEC, QC, G1K 8L1
(418) 529-7351   *SIC* 8322
FORT ERIE NATIVE CULTURAL CENTRE INC   *p591*
796 BUFFALO RD, FORT ERIE, ON, L2A 5H2
(905) 871-6592   *SIC* 8322
GOOD SHEPHERD CENTRE HAMILTON, THE   *p612*
143 WENTWORTH ST S SUITE 302, HAMILTON, ON, L8N 2Z1
(905) 528-5877   *SIC* 8322
GOODFOOD MARKET CORP   *p1339*
4600 RUE HICKMORE, SAINT-LAURENT, QC, H4T 1K2
(514) 730-9530   *SIC* 8322
GOUVERNEMENT DE LA PROVINCE DE QUEBEC   *p1084*
308 BOUL CARTIER O, COTE SAINT-LUC, QC, H7N 2J2
(450) 975-4150   *SIC* 8322
GOUVERNEMENT DE LA PROVINCE DE QUEBEC   *p1191*
1080 COTE DU BEAVER HALL BUREAU 1000, MONTREAL, QC, H2Z 1S8
(514) 873-2032   *SIC* 8322
GOUVERNEMENT DE LA PROVINCE DE QUEBEC   *p1351*
110 RUE DU COLLEGE, SAINT-REMI, QC, J0L 2L0
(450) 454-4694   *SIC* 8322
GOVERNING COUNCIL OF THE SALVATION ARMY IN CANADA, THE   *p86*
9611 102 AVE NW, EDMONTON, AB, T5H 0E5
(780) 429-4274   *SIC* 8322
GOVERNING COUNCIL OF THE SALVATION ARMY IN CANADA, THE   *p298*
555 HOMER ST SUITE 703, VANCOUVER, BC, V6B 1K8
(604) 681-3405   *SIC* 8322
GOVERNING COUNCIL OF THE SALVATION ARMY IN CANADA, THE   *p373*

811 SCHOOL RD, WINNIPEG, MB, R2Y 0S8

(204) 888-3311   SIC 8322

GOVERNMENT OF SASKATCHEWAN p1412
123 JERSEY ST, NORTH BATTLEFORD, SK, S9A 4B4

(306) 446-7819   SIC 8322

GOVERNMENT OF THE PROVINCE OF ALBERTA   p140
3305 18 AVE N SUITE 107, LETHBRIDGE, AB, T1H 5S1

(403) 381-5543   SIC 8322

GRANDE PRAIRIE AND DISTRICT ASSOCIATION FOR PERSONS WITH DEVELOPMENTAL DISABILITIES   p132
8702 113 ST, GRANDE PRAIRIE, AB, T8V 6K5

(780) 532-0236   SIC 8322

GROUPE EDIFIO INC   p1380
3205 BOUL DES ENTREPRISES, TERREBONNE, QC, J6X 4J9

(514) 284-7070   SIC 8322

HERITAGE FAMILY SERVICES LTD   p153
4825 47 ST SUITE 300, RED DEER, AB, T4N 1R3

(403) 343-3428   SIC 8322

HIGHLAND SHORES CHILDREN'S AID SOCIETY   p492
363 DUNDAS ST W, BELLEVILLE, ON, K8P 1B3

(613) 962-9291   SIC 8322

HURON-PERTH CHILDREN'S AID SOCIETY p896
639 LORNE AVE E, STRATFORD, ON, N5A 6S4

(519) 271-5290   SIC 8322

IMMIGRANT SERVICES CALGARY SOCIETY   p51
910 7 AVE SW SUITE 1200, CALGARY, AB, T2P 3N8

(403) 265-1120   SIC 8322

INDEPENDENT COUNSELLING ENTERPRISES INC   p16
4888 72 AVE SE SUITE 200E, CALGARY, AB, T2C 3Z2

(403) 219-0503   SIC 8322

INTEGRATION RE SOURCE   p1103
312 RUE SAINT-LOUIS, GATINEAU, QC, J8P 8B3

(819) 770-2018   SIC 8322

JEWISH COMMUNITY CENTRE OF GREATER VANCOUVER   p293
950 41ST AVE W, VANCOUVER, BC, V5Z 2N7

(604) 257-5111   SIC 8322

KAMLOOPS HOME SUPPORT SERVICES ASSOCIATION   p216
396 TRANQUILLE RD, KAMLOOPS, BC, V2B 3G7

(250) 851-7550   SIC 8322

KAWARTHA-HALIBURTON CHILDREN'S AID SOCIETY, THE   p839
1100 CHEMONG RD, PETERBOROUGH, ON, K9H 7S2

(705) 743-9751   SIC 8322

KIDS HELP PHONE   p946
439 UNIVERSITY AVE SUITE 300, TORONTO, ON, M5G 1Y8

(416) 586-5437   SIC 8322

KINARK CHILD AND FAMILY SERVICES p487
34 SIMCOE ST SUITE 3, BARRIE, ON, L4N 6T4

(888) 454-6275   SIC 8322

KINARK CHILD AND FAMILY SERVICES p671
500 HOOD RD SUITE 200, MARKHAM, ON, L3R 9Z3

(905) 474-9595   SIC 8322

KINARK CHILD AND FAMILY SERVICES p798
475 IROQUOIS SHORE RD, OAKVILLE, ON, L6H 1M3

(905) 844-4110   SIC 8322

KITCHENER-WATERLOO YWCA   p640
84 FREDERICK ST, KITCHENER, ON, N2H 2L7

(519) 576-8856   SIC 8322

KLINIC INC   p382
870 PORTAGE AVE, WINNIPEG, MB, R3G 0P1

(204) 784-4090   SIC 8322

LACOMBE ACTION GROUP FOR THE HANDICAPPED   p138
4 IRON WOLF BLVD, LACOMBE, AB, T4L 2K6

(403) 782-5531   SIC 8322

LO-SE-CA FOUNDATION - A CHRISTIAN SOCIETY FOR PERSONS WITH DISABILITIES   p166
215 CARNEGIE DR SUITE 1, ST. ALBERT, AB, T8N 5B1

(780) 460-1400   SIC 8322

LOFT COMMUNITY SERVICES   p939
15 TORONTO ST SUITE 9, TORONTO, ON, M5C 2E3

SIC 8322

LYY LIFE INC   p906
147 NER ISRAEL DR, THORNHILL, ON, L4J 8Z7

(647) 673-8888   SIC 8322

M.O.S.A.I.C. MULTI-LINGUAL ORIENTATION SERVICE ASSOCIATION FOR IMMIGRANT COMMUNITIES   p287
2555 COMMERCIAL DR SUITE 312, VANCOUVER, BC, V5N 4C1

(604) 708-3905   SIC 8322

MARKHAM CENTENNIAL CENTRE   p1000
8600 MCCOWAN RD, UNIONVILLE, ON, L3P 3M2

(905) 294-6111   SIC 8322

MASONIC PARK INC   p426
100 MASONIC DR, MOUNT PEARL, NL, A1N 3K5

SIC 8322

MCMAN YOUTH, FAMILY AND COMMUNITY SERVICES ASSOCIATION   p96
11016 127 ST NW, EDMONTON, AB, T5M 0T2

(780) 482-4461   SIC 8322

MILES NADAL JEWISH COMMUNITY CENTRE   p976
750 SPADINA AVE, TORONTO, ON, M5S 2J2

(416) 944-8002   SIC 8322

NATIONAL ASSOCIATION OF FRIENDSHIP CENTRES   p212
5462 TRANS CANADA HWY UNIT 205, DUNCAN, BC, V9L 6W4

(250) 748-2242   SIC 8322

NATIVE COUNSELLING SERVICES OF ALBERTA   p106
14904 121A AVE NW, EDMONTON, AB, T5V 1A3

(780) 451-4002   SIC 8322

NEIGHBOURHOOD GROUP COMMUNITY SERVICES, THE   p917
11 COATSWORTH CRES, TORONTO, ON, M4C 5P8

(416) 691-7407   SIC 8322

NEIGHBOURHOOD GROUP COMMUNITY SERVICES, THE   p917
3036 DANFORTH AVE, TORONTO, ON, M4C 1N2

(416) 691-7407   SIC 8322

NORTH EAST COMMUNITY CARE ACCESS CENTRE   p862
390 BAY ST, SAULT STE. MARIE, ON, P6A 1X2

(705) 949-1650   SIC 8322

ONE KID'S PLACE   p621
100 FRANK MILLER DR SUITE 2, HUNTSVILLE, ON, P1H 1H7

(705) 789-9985   SIC 8322

ONTARIO FEDERATION FOR CEREBRAL PALSY   p791
1630 LAWRENCE AVE W UNIT 104, NORTH YORK, ON, M6L 1C5

(416) 244-0899   SIC 8322

ONTARIO FINNISH RESTHOME ASSOCIATION, THE   p863
725 NORTH ST SUITE 209, SAULT STE. MARIE, ON, P6B 5Z3

(705) 945-9987   SIC 8322

OPERATION SPRINGBOARD   p936
2 CARLTON ST SUITE 800, TORONTO, ON, M5B 1J3

(416) 977-0089   SIC 8322

OTTAWA CHILDREN'S TREATMENT CENTRE   p818
2211 THURSTON DR, OTTAWA, ON, K1G 6C9

(613) 688-2126   SIC 8322

OTTAWA-CARLETON ASSOCIATION FOR PERSONS WITH DEVELOPMENTAL DISABILITIES   p562
1141 SYDNEY ST UNIT 1, CORNWALL, ON, K6H 7C2

(613) 933-9520   SIC 8322

OTTAWA-CARLETON ASSOCIATION FOR PERSONS WITH DEVELOPMENTAL DISABILITIES   p825
250 CITY CENTRE AVE SUITE 200, OTTAWA, ON, K1R 6K7

(613) 569-8993   SIC 8322

P D G (MILLWOODS GOOD SAMARITAN) p120
101 YOUVILLE DRIVE EAST NW, EDMONTON, AB, T6L 7A4

(780) 485-0816   SIC 8322

PACEKIDS SOCIETY FOR CHILDREN WITH SPECIAL NEEDS   p24
808 55 AVE NE, CALGARY, AB, T2E 6Y4

(403) 234-7876   SIC 8322

PACIFIC COMMUNITY RESOURCES SOCIETY   p287
2830 GRANDVIEW HWY SUITE 201, VANCOUVER, BC, V5M 2C9

(604) 412-7950   SIC 8322

PARKLAND COMMUNITY LIVING AND SUPPORTS SOCIETY   p154
6010 45 AVE, RED DEER, AB, T4N 3M4

(403) 347-3333   SIC 8322

PATHWAYS HEALTH CENTRE FOR CHILDREN   p858
1240 MURPHY RD, SARNIA, ON, N7S 2Y6

(519) 542-3471   SIC 8322

PATRO DE LEVIS INC, LE   p1137
6150 RUE SAINT-GEORGES, LEVIS, QC, G6V 4J8

(418) 833-4477   SIC 8322

PATRO LE PREVOST INC   p1181
7355 AV CHRISTOPHE-COLOMB, MONTREAL, QC, H2R 2S5

(514) 273-8535   SIC 8322

PAVILLON SAINT-DOMINIQUE   p1271
1045 BOUL RENE-LEVESQUE O, QUEBEC, QC, G1S 1V3

(418) 681-3561   SIC 8322

PENTICTON AND DISTRICT SOCIETY FOR COMMUNITY LIVING   p244
180 INDUSTRIAL AVE W, PENTICTON, BC, V2A 6X9

(250) 493-0312   SIC 8322

PHARE DES SERVICES COMMUNAUTAIRES INC, LE   p395
68 AV DE LA RIVIERE, BOUCTOUCHE, NB, E4S 3A7

(506) 743-7377   SIC 8322

PR SENIORS HOUSING MANAGEMENT LTD   p203
4640 HEADQUARTERS RD SUITE 227, COURTENAY, BC, V9N 7J3

(250) 331-1183   SIC 8322

PROGRAM DE PORTAGE INC, LE   p1215
2455 AV LIONEL-GROULX, MONTREAL, QC, H3J 1J6

(514) 935-3431   SIC 8322

PROVINCE OF NEWFOUNDLAND & LABRADOR   p434
BOND RD, WHITBOURNE, NL, A0B 3K0

(709) 759-2471   SIC 8322

RED RIVER MANOR INC   p356
133 MANCHESTER AVE, SELKIRK, MB, R1A 0B5

(204) 482-3036   SIC 8322

RENFREW PARK COMMUNITY ASSOCIATION   p287
2929 22ND AVE E, VANCOUVER, BC, V5M 2Y3

(604) 257-8388   SIC 8322

REPIT-RESSOURCE DE L'EST DE MONTREAL   p1163
7707 RUE HOCHELAGA BUREAU 100, MONTREAL, QC, H1L 2K4

(514) 353-1479   SIC 8322

RESSOURCES SANTE L M INC   p1352
21 RUE FORGET, SAINT-SAUVEUR, QC, J0R 1R0

(450) 227-6663   SIC 8322

REVERA INC   p77
150 SCOTIA LANDNG NW, CALGARY, AB, T3L 2K1

(403) 208-0338   SIC 8322

REVERA INC   p478
12 TRANQUILITY AVE SUITE 1, ANCASTER, ON, L9G 5C2

(905) 304-1993   SIC 8322

REVERA INC   p658
355 MCGARRELL DR, LONDON, ON, N6G 0B1

(519) 672-0500   SIC 8322

RICHMOND, CITY OF   p256
12800 CAMBIE RD, RICHMOND, BC, V6V 0A9

(604) 233-8399   SIC 8322

RICHMOND, CITY OF   p266
9180 NO. 1 RD, RICHMOND, BC, V7E 6L5

(604) 238-8400   SIC 8322

SARNIA AND DISTRICT ASSOCIATION FOR COMMUNITY LIVING   p860
551 EXMOUTH ST SUITE 202, SARNIA, ON, N7T 5P6

(519) 332-0560   SIC 8322

SEMIAHMOO HOUSE SOCIETY   p281
15306 24 AVE, SURREY, BC, V4A 2J1

(604) 536-1242   SIC 8322

SENIOR PEOPLES' RESOURCES IN NORTH TORONTO INCORPORATED   p924
140 MERTON ST, TORONTO, ON, M4S 1A1

(416) 481-6411   SIC 8322

SHEPHERD'S CARE FOUNDATION   p94
12603 135 AVE NW, EDMONTON, AB, T5L 5B2

(780) 447-3840   SIC 8322

SHEPHERDS OF GOOD HOPE   p822
256 KING EDWARD AVE, OTTAWA, ON, K1N 7M1

(613) 789-8210   SIC 8322

SHOREHAM VILLAGE SENIOR CITIZENS ASSOCIATION   p442
50 SHOREHAM VILLAGE CRES, CHESTER, NS, B0J 1J0

(902) 275-5631   SIC 8322

SIMON FRASER SOCIETY FOR COMMUNITY LIVING, THE   p202
218 BLUE MOUNTAIN ST SUITE 300, COQUITLAM, BC, V3K 4H2

(604) 525-9494   SIC 8322

SOMERSET WEST COMMUNITY HEALTH CENTRE   p825
55 ECCLES ST, OTTAWA, ON, K1R 6S3

(613) 238-8210   SIC 8322

SOUTHERN FIRST NATIONS NETWORK OF CARE   p382
835 PORTAGE AVE, WINNIPEG, MB, R3G 0N6

(204) 944-4200   SIC 8322

STRATHCONA COMMUNITY CENTRE ASSOCIATION (1972)   p296
601 KEEFER ST, VANCOUVER, BC, V6A 3V8

(604) 713-1838   SIC 8322

SUNDRIDGE HAPPY GANG, THE   p902
110 MAIN ST E, SUNDRIDGE, ON, P0A 1Z0

(705) 384-7351   *SIC 8322*
SUNRISE NORTH SENIOR LIVING LTD*p717*
4046 ERIN MILLS PKY, MISSISSAUGA, ON, L5L 2W7
(905) 569-0004   *SIC 8322*
SUPPORTED LIFESTYLES LTD   *p11*
495 36 ST NE SUITE 210, CALGARY, AB, T2A 6K3
(403) 207-5115   *SIC 8322*
SYNDICAT DES PROFESSIONNELLES EN SOINS DU CENTRE DE SANTE ET SERVICES SOCIAUX DU COEUR DE   *p1182*
6910 RUE BOYER, MONTREAL, QC, H2S 2J7
(514) 272-3011   *SIC 8322*
THOMPSON COMMUNITY ASSOCIATION, THE   *p266*
5151 GRANVILLE AVE, RICHMOND, BC, V7C 1E6
(604) 238-8422   *SIC 8322*
TIKINAGAN CHILD & FAMILY SERVICES   *p881*
63 KING ST, SIOUX LOOKOUT, ON, P8T 1B1
(807) 737-3466   *SIC 8322*
TIMISKAMING CHILD AND FAMILY SERVICES   *p753*
25 PAGET ST, NEW LISKEARD, ON, P0J 1P0
(705) 647-1200   *SIC 8322*
TURNING POINT YOUTH SERVICES   *p932*
95 WELLESLEY ST E, TORONTO, ON, M4Y 2X9
(416) 925-9250   *SIC 8322*
UNLIMITED POTENTIAL COMMUNITY SERVICES SOCIETY   *p103*
10403 172 ST NW SUITE 145, EDMONTON, AB, T5S 1K9
(780) 440-0708   *SIC 8322*
VANCOUVER COASTAL HEALTH AUTHORITY   *p288*
3425 CROWLEY DR, VANCOUVER, BC, V5R 6G3
(604) 872-2511   *SIC 8322*
VILLE DE MONTREAL   *p1177*
9335 RUE SAINT-HUBERT, MONTREAL, QC, H2M 1Y7
(514) 385-2893   *SIC 8322*
VISTA PARK LODGE   *p368*
144 NOVAVISTA DR, WINNIPEG, MB, R2N 1P8
(204) 257-6688   *SIC 8322*
WAUKLEHEGAN MANOR INC   *p404*
11 SAUNDERS RD, MCADAM, NB, E6J 1K9
(506) 784-6303   *SIC 8322*
WE CARE HEALTH SERVICES INC   *p656*
190 WORTLEY RD SUITE 100F, LONDON, ON, N6C 4Y7
(519) 642-1208   *SIC 8322*
WINDSOR ESSEX COMMUNITY HEALTH CENTRE   *p1022*
1361 OUELLETTE AVE UNIT 101, WINDSOR, ON, N8X 1J6
(519) 253-8481   *SIC 8322*
WINDSOR-ESSEX CHILDREN'S AID SOCIETY   *p1022*
1671 RIVERSIDE DR E, WINDSOR, ON, N8Y 5B5
(519) 252-1171   *SIC 8322*
WINNIFRED STEWART ASSOCIATION FOR THE MENTALLY HANDICAPPED   *p97*
11130 131 ST NW, EDMONTON, AB, T5M 1C1
(780) 453-6707   *SIC 8322*
WOOD HOMES FOUNDATION   *p42*
805 37 ST NW, CALGARY, AB, T2N 4N8
(403) 270-1718   *SIC 8322*
WORLD VISION CANADA   *p744*
1 WORLD DR SUITE 2500, MISSISSAUGA, ON, L5T 2Y4
(905) 565-6100   *SIC 8322*
YARMOUTH ASSOCIATION FOR COMMUNITY RESIDENTIAL OPTIONS   *p449*
1 GLOSTER CRT, DARTMOUTH, NS, B3B

1X9
(902) 832-0433   *SIC 8322*
YONGE STREET MISSION, THE   *p978*
365 SPADINA AVE, TORONTO, ON, M5T 2G3
(416) 929-9614   *SIC 8322*
YOUNG WOMEN'S CHRISTIAN ASSOCIATION OF CANADA, THE   *p33*
2003 16 ST SE, CALGARY, AB, T2G 5B7
(403) 266-0707   *SIC 8322*
YOUNG WOMEN'S CHRISTIAN ASSOCIATION OF SASKATOON   *p1430*
510 25TH ST E, SASKATOON, SK, S7K 4A7
(306) 244-0944   *SIC 8322*
YOUTH SERVICES BUREAU OF OTTAWA   *p819*
3000 HAWTHORNE RD, OTTAWA, ON, K1G 5Y3
(613) 738-7776   *SIC 8322*
YOUTH SERVICES BUREAU OF OTTAWA   *p830*
2675 QUEENSVIEW DR, OTTAWA, ON, K2B 8K2
(613) 729-1000   *SIC 8322*

SIC 8331 Job training and related services

(S.P.A.N.) ST PAUL ABILITIES NETWORK (SOCIETY)   *p164*
4637 45 AVE, ST PAUL, AB, T0A 3A3
(780) 645-3405   *SIC 8331*
ARC INDUSTRIES   *p532*
466 FRANKLIN BLVD, CAMBRIDGE, ON, N1R 8G6
(519) 621-0680   *SIC 8331*
CANADIAN NATIONAL INSTITUTE FOR THE BLIND, THE   *p918*
1929 BAYVIEW AVE, TORONTO, ON, M4G 3E8
(416) 486-2500   *SIC 8331*
CARPENTERS LOCAL UNION 27 JOINT APPRENTICESHIP AND TRAINING TRUST FUND INC   *p1030*
222 ROWNTREE DAIRY RD, WOODBRIDGE, ON, L4L 9T2
(905) 652-5507   *SIC 8331*
CATHOLIC IMMIGRATION CENTRE OTTAWA   *p368*
219 ARGYLE AVE SUITE 500, OTTAWA, ON, K2P 2H4
(613) 232-9634   *SIC 8331*
CHRYSALIS: AN ALBERTA SOCIETY FOR CITIZENS WITH DISABILITIES   *p93*
13325 ST ALBERT TRAIL NW, EDMONTON, AB, T5L 4R3
(780) 454-9656   *SIC 8331*
COMMISSION SCOLAIRE DE LA CAPITALE, LA   *p1263*
1060 RUE BORNE, QUEBEC, QC, G1N 1L9
(418) 686-4040   *SIC 8331*
COMMISSION SCOLAIRE DE LA CAPITALE, LA   *p1276*
3400 AV CHAUVEAU, QUEBEC, QC, G2C 1A1
(418) 686-4040   *SIC 8331*
COMMISSION SCOLAIRE DE LAVAL   *p1232*
1740 MONTEE MASSON, MONTREAL, QC, H7E 4P2
(450) 662-7000   *SIC 8331*
COMMISSION SCOLAIRE DES PREMIERES-SEIGNEURIES   *p1256*
800 RUE DE LA SORBONNE, QUEBEC, QC, G1H 1H1
(418) 622-7821   *SIC 8331*
COMMUNITY LIVING CAMBRIDGE   *p533*
466 FRANKLIN BLVD, CAMBRIDGE, ON, N1R 8G6
(519) 621-0680   *SIC 8331*
GOODWILL INDUSTRIES OF ALBERTA (REGISTERED SOCIETY)   *p114*
8761 51 AVE NW, EDMONTON, AB, T6E 5H1
(780) 944-1414   *SIC 8331*

GOODWILL INDUSTRIES, ONTARIO GREAT LAKES   *p655*
390 KING ST, LONDON, ON, N6B 1S3
(519) 850-9675   *SIC 8331*
GOUVERNEMENT DE LA PROVINCE DE QUEBEC   *p1188*
276 RUE SAINT-JACQUES, MONTREAL, QC, H2Y 1N3
(514) 725-5221   *SIC 8331*
MARCH OF DIMES CANADA   *p919*
10 OVERLEA BLVD, TORONTO, ON, M4H 1A4
(416) 425-3463   *SIC 8331*
QUALITY CONTINUOUS IMPROVEMENT CENTRE FOR COMMUNITY EDUCATION AND TRAINING   *p710*
90 BURNHAMTHORPE RD W SUITE 210, MISSISSAUGA, ON, L5B 3C3
(905) 949-0049   *SIC 8331*
REHOBOTH A CHRISTIAN ASSOCIATION FOR THE MENTALLY HANDICAPPED OF ALBERTA   *p9*
3505 29 ST NE SUITE 106, CALGARY, AB, T1Y 5W4
(403) 250-7333   *SIC 8331*
SASKATCHEWAN ABILITIES COUNCIL INC   *p1425*
2310 LOUISE AVE, SASKATOON, SK, S7J 2C7
(306) 374-4448   *SIC 8331*
SASKATCHEWAN ABILITIES COUNCIL INC   *p1436*
1551 NORTH RAILWAY ST W, SWIFT CURRENT, SK, S9H 5G3
(306) 773-2076   *SIC 8331*
SKILLS FOR CHANGE OF METRO TORONTO   *p989*
791 ST CLAIR AVE W, TORONTO, ON, M6C 1B7
(416) 658-3101   *SIC 8331*
SUMMER STREET INDUSTRIES INC   *p463*
72 PARK ST, NEW GLASGOW, NS, B2H 5B8
(902) 755-1745   *SIC 8331*
VANCOUVER COASTAL HEALTH AUTHORITY   *p324*
700 57TH AVE W SUITE 909, VANCOUVER, BC, V6P 1S1
(604) 321-3231   *SIC 8331*

SIC 8351 Child day care services

A CHILD'S WORLD FAMILY CHILD CARE SERVICES OF NIAGARA   *p1011*
344 AVON ST, WELLAND, ON, L3B 6E5
(905) 735-1162   *SIC 8351*
CENTRE DE LA PETITE ENFANCE LA GIBOULEE   *p1238*
531 RUE HUBERDEAU, MONTREAL, QC, H7X 1P6
(450) 689-6442   *SIC 8351*
CENTRE DE LA PETITE ENFANCE PARC-EN-CIEL   *p1090*
888 RUE SAINT-ANTOINE, DISRAELI, QC, G0N 1E0
(418) 449-3004   *SIC 8351*
CHILDREN'S HOUSE MONTESSORI, THE   *p1025*
2611 LABELLE ST, WINDSOR, ON, N9E 4G4
(519) 969-5278   *SIC 8351*
E3 (EDUCATE, ENABLE, EMPOWER) COMMUNITY SERVICES INC   *p546*
100 PRETTY RIVER PKY N, COLLINGWOOD, ON, L9Y 4X2
(705) 445-6351   *SIC 8351*
GETTING READY FOR INCLUSION TODAY (THE GRIT PROGRAM) SOCIETY OF EDMONTON   *p95*
14930 114 AVE NW, EDMONTON, AB, T5M 4G4
(780) 454-9910   *SIC 8351*
GOVERNING COUNCIL OF THE SALVA-

TION ARMY IN CANADA, THE   *p651*
1340 DUNDAS ST, LONDON, ON, N5W 3B6
(519) 455-4810   *SIC 8351*
GROWING TYKES CHILD CARE   *p867*
910 MARKHAM RD, SCARBOROUGH, ON, M1H 2Y2
(416) 438-4088   *SIC 8351*
LONDON CHILDREN'S CONNECTION INC   *p660*
346 WONDERLAND RD S, LONDON, ON, N6K 1L3
(519) 471-4300   *SIC 8351*
MINI-SKOOL A CHILD'S PLACE INC   *p712*
1100 CENTRAL PKY W SUITE 17, MISSISSAUGA, ON, L5C 4E5
(905) 275-2378   *SIC 8351*
OAKVILLE FAMILY YMCA   *p802*
410 REBECCA ST, OAKVILLE, ON, L6K 1K7
(905) 845-3417   *SIC 8351*
OUR CHILDREN, OUR FUTURE   *p569*
273 MEAD BLVD, ESPANOLA, ON, P5E 1B3
(705) 869-5545   *SIC 8351*
PLASP CHILD CARE SERVICES   *p745*
60 COURTNEYPARK DR W UNIT 5, MISSISSAUGA, ON, L5W 0B3
(905) 890-1711   *SIC 8351*
RAINBOW DAY NURSERY INC   *p392*
445 ISLAND SHORE BLVD UNIT 11, WINNIPEG, MB, R3X 2B4
(204) 256-0672   *SIC 8351*
RED DEER CHILD CARE SOCIETY   *p154*
5571 45 ST UNIT 2, RED DEER, AB, T4N 1L2
(403) 347-7973   *SIC 8351*
UMBRELLA FAMILY AND CHILD CENTRES OF HAMILTON   *p617*
310 LIMERIDGE RD W UNIT 9, HAMILTON, ON, L9C 2V2
(905) 312-9836   *SIC 8351*
UPPER CANADA CREATIVE CHILD CARE CENTRES OF ONTARIO   *p854*
30 FULTON WAY UNIT 4, RICHMOND HILL, ON, L4B 1E6
(289) 982-1113   *SIC 8351*
YMCA OF GREATER TORONTO   *p769*
567 SHEPPARD AVE E, NORTH YORK, ON, M2K 1B2
(416) 225-9622   *SIC 8351*

SIC 8361 Residential care

126074 ONTARIO INC   *p809*
6 KITCHENER ST, ORILLIA, ON, L3V 6Z9
(705) 327-2232   *SIC 8361*
2550-7856 QUEBEC INC   *p1316*
1050 RUE STEFONI, SAINT-JEAN-SUR-RICHELIEU, QC, J3A 1T5
(450) 349-5861   *SIC 8361*
4489161 CANADA INC   *p1131*
400 RUE LOUIS-FORTIER BUREAU 100A, LASALLE, QC, H8R 0A8
(514) 370-8000   *SIC 8361*
6423264 CANADA INC   *p1241*
3055 BOUL NOTRE-DAME BUREAU 1700, MONTREAL-OUEST, QC, H7V 4C6
(450) 681-3055   *SIC 8361*
ACCESS COMMUNITY SERVICES INC *p847*
160 WALTON ST, PORT HOPE, ON, L1A 1N6
(905) 885-6358   *SIC 8361*
ACTION LINE HOUSING SOCIETY   *p184*
3755 MCGILL ST, BURNABY, BC, V5C 1M2
(604) 291-0607   *SIC 8361*
ALDERWOOD CORPORATION   *p439*
42 JONES ST, BADDECK, NS, B0E 1B0
(902) 295-2644   *SIC 8361*
ALGOMA MANOR NURSING HOME   *p903*
145 DAWSON ST, THESSALON, ON, P0R 1L0
(705) 842-2840   *SIC 8361*
ALL SENIORS CARE LIVING CENTRES

LTD *p373*
10 HALLONQUIST DR SUITE 318, WIN-
NIPEG, MB, R2Y 2M5
(204) 885-1415 *SIC 8361*

AMICA MATURE LIFESTYLES INC *p594*
2645 INNES RD SUITE 342, GLOUCES-
TER, ON, K1B 3J7
(613) 837-8720 *SIC 8361*

AMICA MATURE LIFESTYLES INC *p665*
6360 16TH AVE SUITE 336, MARKHAM,
ON, L3P 7Y6
(905) 201-6058 *SIC 8361*

AMICA MATURE LIFESTYLES INC *p718*
4620 KIMBERMOUNT AVE, MISSIS-
SAUGA, ON, L5M 5W5
(905) 816-9163 *SIC 8361*

AMICA MATURE LIFESTYLES INC *p948*
20 QUEEN ST W SUITE 2700, TORONTO,
ON, M5H 3R3
(416) 487-2020 *SIC 8361*

**ANAGO (NON) RESIDENTIAL RESOURCES
INC** *p837*
252 DELAWARE ST, PARKHILL, ON, N0M
2K0
(519) 294-6238 *SIC 8361*

ARCHE DAYBREAK, L' *p856*
11339 YONGE ST, RICHMOND HILL, ON,
L4S 1L1
(905) 884-3454 *SIC 8361*

**ASSOCIATION DES RESIDENTS ET RESI-
DENTES DU CENTRE D'ACCEUIL DE
GATINEAU, L'** *p1103*
134 RUE JEAN-RENE-MONETTE,
GATINEAU, QC, J8P 7C3
(819) 966-6450 *SIC 8361*

**BAPTIST HOUSING MINISTRIES SOCIETY,
THE** *p335*
1002 VANCOUVER ST SUITE 112, VICTO-
RIA, BC, V8V 3V8
(250) 384-1313 *SIC 8361*

**BELLWOODS CENTRES FOR COMMUNITY
LIVING INC** *p778*
789 DON MILLS RD SUITE 701, NORTH
YORK, ON, M3C 1T5
(416) 696-9663 *SIC 8361*

**BENEVOLES DE LA RESIDENCE YVON-
BRUNET INC, LES** *p1223*
6250 AV NEWMAN, MONTREAL, QC, H4E
4K4
(514) 765-8000 *SIC 8361*

**BERWICK RETIREMENT COMMUNITIES
LTD** *p198*
1700 COMOX AVE, COMOX, BC, V9M 4H4
(250) 339-1690 *SIC 8361*

**BETHANIA MENNONITE PERSONAL CARE
HOME INC** *p367*
1045 CONCORDIA AVE, WINNIPEG, MB,
R2K 3S7
(204) 667-0795 *SIC 8361*

**BLUE HERON SUPPORT SERVICES ASSO-
CIATION** *p4*
GD STN MAIN, BARRHEAD, AB, T7N 1B8
(780) 674-4944 *SIC 8361*

**BOYNE VALLEY HOSTEL CORPORATION,
THE** *p348*
120 4TH AVE SW RR 3, CARMAN, MB, R0G
0J0
(204) 745-6715 *SIC 8361*

**BRANTWOOD RESIDENTIAL DEVELOP-
MENT CENTRE** *p517*
25 BELL LANE, BRANTFORD, ON, N3T
1E1
(519) 753-2658 *SIC 8361*

BROADVIEW FOUNDATION *p868*
3555 DANFORTH AVE, SCARBOROUGH,
ON, M1L 1E3
(416) 466-2173 *SIC 8361*

C.L.S.C. MONTREAL-NORD *p1176*
1615 AV EMILE-JOURNAULT, MONTREAL,
QC, H2M 2G3
(514) 384-2000 *SIC 8361*

**CAMROSE ASSOCIATION FOR COMMU-
NITY LIVING** *p78*
4604 57 ST, CAMROSE, AB, T4V 2E7

(780) 672-0257 *SIC 8361*

**CANADIAN INSTITUTE FOR HEALTH IN-
FORMATION** *p922*
90 EGLINTON AVE E SUITE 300,
TORONTO, ON, M4P 2Y3
(416) 481-2002 *SIC 8361*

CANTERBURY FOUNDATION *p98*
8403 142 ST NW SUITE 125, EDMONTON,
AB, T5R 4L3
(780) 483-5361 *SIC 8361*

**CARPE DIEM RESIDENTIAL TREATMENT
HOMES FOR CHILDREN INC** *p499*
9355 DIXIE RD, BRAMPTON, ON, L6S 1J7
(905) 799-2947 *SIC 8361*

**CARREFOUR DE LA SANTE ET DES SER-
VICES SOCIAUX DU VAL-SAINT-FRANCOIS**
p1403
79 RUE ALLEN BUREAU 501, WINDSOR,
QC, J1S 2P8
(819) 542-2777 *SIC 8361*

CARTIER HOUSE CARE CENTRE LTD *p200*
1419 CARTIER AVE, COQUITLAM, BC,
V3K 2C6
(604) 939-4654 *SIC 8361*

CASSELLHOLME HOME FOR THE AGED
p762
400 OLIVE ST, NORTH BAY, ON, P1B 6J4
(705) 474-4250 *SIC 8361*

CATHOLIC SOCIAL SERVICES *p113*
8815 99 ST NW, EDMONTON, AB, T6E 3V3
(780) 432-1137 *SIC 8361*

CATHOLIC SOCIAL SERVICES *p153*
5104 48 AVE, RED DEER, AB, T4N 3T8
(403) 347-8844 *SIC 8361*

CATHOLIC SOCIAL SERVICES *p172*
5206 51 AVE, WETASKIWIN, AB, T9A 0V4
(780) 352-5535 *SIC 8361*

CENTRE ACCEUIL HENRIETTE CERE
p1307
6435 CH DE CHAMBLY, SAINT-HUBERT,
QC, J3Y 3R6
(450) 678-3291 *SIC 8361*

**CENTRE D' HEBERGEMENT ET DE SOINS
DE LONGUE DUREE HEATHER INC** *p1281*
3931 RUE LAKESHORE DRIVE, RAWDON,
QC, J0K 1S0
(450) 834-3070 *SIC 8361*

CENTRE D'ACCEUIL JEANNE CREVIER
p1064
151 RUE DE MUY, BOUCHERVILLE, QC,
J4B 4W7
SIC 8361

CENTRE D'ACCUEIL PONTIAC *p1369*
290 RUE MARION, SHAWVILLE, QC, J0X
2Y0
(450) 647-5755 *SIC 8361*

**CENTRE D'ACCUEIL DU HAUT-ST LAU-
RENT (CHSLD)** *p1244*
65 RUE HECTOR, ORMSTOWN, QC, J0S
1K0
(450) 829-2346 *SIC 8361*

CENTRE D'ACCUEIL FATHER DOWD *p1218*
6565 CH HUDSON BUREAU 217, MON-
TREAL, QC, H3S 2T7
SIC 8361

CENTRE D'ACCUEIL MARCELLE FERRON
p1069
8600 BOUL MARIE-VICTORIN,
BROSSARD, QC, J4X 1A1
(450) 923-1430 *SIC 8361*

CENTRE D'ACCUEIL ROGER SEGUIN *p544*
435 LEMAY ST RR 1, CLARENCE CREEK,
ON, K0A 1N0
(613) 488-2053 *SIC 8361*

**CENTRE D'ENTRAINEMENT A LA VIE DE
CHICOUTIMI INC** *p1078*
766 RUE DU CENACLE, CHICOUTIMI, QC,
G7H 2J2
(418) 549-4003 *SIC 8361*

**CENTRE D'HEBERGEMENT DE NAZAIRE
PICHE** *p1126*
150 15E AV BUREAU 319, LACHINE, QC,
H8S 3L9
(514) 637-2326 *SIC 8361*

**CENTRE D'HEBERGEMENT DU BOISE
LTEE** *p1274*
3690 BOUL NEILSON, QUEBEC, QC, G1W
0A9
(418) 781-0471 *SIC 8361*

**CENTRE D'HEBERGEMENT SOIN LONGUE
DUREE MRC DE MASKINONGE, LE** *p1146*
181 6E AV, LOUISEVILLE, QC, J5V 1V2
(819) 228-2706 *SIC 8361*

**CENTRE DE PROTECTION ET DE READAP-
TATION DE LA COTE-NORD** *p1053*
835 BOUL JOLLIET, BAIE-COMEAU, QC,
G5C 1P5
(418) 589-9927 *SIC 8361*

**CENTRE DE READAPTATION EN DEFI-
CIENCE INTELLECTUELLE ET TED** *p1135*
55 RUE DU MONT-MARIE, LEVIS, QC, G6V
0B8
(418) 833-3218 *SIC 8361*

**CENTRE DE READAPTATION EN DEFI-
CIENCE INTELLECTUELLE ET TED** *p1159*
20 AV COTE, MONTMAGNY, QC, G5V 1Z9
(418) 248-4970 *SIC 8361*

**CENTRE DE READAPTATION LA MYRI-
ADE, LE** *p1149*
1280 CH SAINT-HENRI, MASCOUCHE,
QC, J7K 2N1
(450) 474-4175 *SIC 8361*

**CENTRE DE SANTE ET DE SERVICES SO-
CIAUX DE CHICOUTIMI** *p1078*
1236 RUE D'ANGOULEME, CHICOUTIMI,
QC, G7H 6P9
(418) 698-3907 *SIC 8361*

**CENTRE DE SANTE ET DE SERVICES
SOCIAUX DE DORVAL-LACHINE-LASALLE**
p1126
650 PLACE D'ACCUEIL, LACHINE, QC,
H8S 3Z5
(514) 634-7161 *SIC 8361*

**CENTRE DE SANTE ET DE SERVICES SO-
CIAUX DE LA POINTE-DE-L'ILE** *p1163*
4900 BOUL LAPOINTE, MONTREAL, QC,
H1K 4W9
(514) 353-1227 *SIC 8361*

**CENTRE DE SANTE ET DE SERVICES SO-
CIAUX DE LA POMMERAIE, LE** *p1378*
50 RUE WESTERN, SUTTON, QC, J0E 2K0
(450) 538-3332 *SIC 8361*

**CENTRE DE SANTE ET DE SERVICES SO-
CIAUX DE LA VIEILLE-CAPITALE** *p1261*
1451 BOUL PERE-LELIEVRE BUREAU
363, QUEBEC, QC, G1M 1N8
(418) 683-2516 *SIC 8361*

**CENTRE DE SANTE ET DE SERVICES SO-
CIAUX DE LAVAL** *p1231*
4895 RUE SAINT-JOSEPH, MONTREAL,
QC, H7C 1H6
(450) 661-3305 *SIC 8361*

**CENTRE DE SANTE ET DE SERVICES SO-
CIAUX DE LAVAL** *p1238*
350 BOUL SAMSON O, MONTREAL, QC,
H7X 1J4
(450) 689-0933 *SIC 8361*

**CENTRE DE SANTE ET DE SERVICES SO-
CIAUX DE PORTNEUF** *p1092*
250 BOUL GAUDREAU BUREAU 370,
DONNACONA, QC, G3M 1L7
(418) 285-3025 *SIC 8361*

**CENTRE DE SANTE ET DE SERVICES SO-
CIAUX DE PORTNEUF** *p1347*
444 RUE BEAUCHAMP, SAINT-MARC-
DES-CARRIERES, QC, G0A 4B0
(418) 268-3511 *SIC 8361*

**CENTRE DE SANTE ET DE SERVICES SO-
CIAUX DE QUEBEC-NORD** *p1255*
3365 RUE GUIMONT, QUEBEC, QC, G1E
2H1
(418) 663-8171 *SIC 8361*

**CENTRE DE SANTE ET DE SERVICES SO-
CIAUX JEANNE-MANCE** *p1174*
1440 RUE DUFRESNE, MONTREAL, QC,
H2K 3J3
(514) 527-8921 *SIC 8361*

CENTRE DE SANTE ET DE SERVICES SO-

CIAUX LA POMMERAIE *p1101*
800 RUE SAINT-PAUL, FARNHAM, QC, J2N
2K6
(450) 293-3167 *SIC 8361*

**CENTRE DE SANTE ET DE SERVICES SO-
CIAUX PIERRE-BOUCHER** *p1082*
4700 RTE MARIE-VICTORIN, CONTRE-
COEUR, QC, J0L 1C0
(450) 468-8410 *SIC 8361*

**CENTRE DE SANTE ET SERVICES SOCI-
AUX DE PAPINEAU** *p1291*
14 RUE SAINT-ANDRE, SAINT-ANDRE-
AVELLIN, QC, J0V 1W0
(819) 983-7341 *SIC 8361*

**CENTRE HOSPITALIER DU CENTRE LA
MAURICIE** *p1368*
243 1RE RUE DE LA POINTE, SHAWINI-
GAN, QC, G9N 1K2
SIC 8361

**CENTRE HOSPITALIER ET CENTRE DE
READAPTATION ANTOINE-LABELLE** *p1154*
411 RUE DE LA MADONE, MONT-
LAURIER, QC, J9L 1S1
(819) 623-5940 *SIC 8361*

**CENTRE INTEGRE DE SANTE ET DE SER-
VICES SOCIAUX DE LA MONTEREGIE-
OUEST** *p1123*
500 AV DE BALMORAL, LA PRAIRIE, QC,
J5R 4N5
(450) 659-9148 *SIC 8361*

**CENTRE INTEGRE DE SANTE ET DE SER-
VICES SOCIAUX DE LA MONTEREGIE-
OUEST** *p1317*
315 RUE MACDONALD BUREAU 105,
SAINT-JEAN-SUR-RICHELIEU, QC, J3B 8J3
(450) 348-6121 *SIC 8361*

**CENTRE INTEGRE DE SANTE ET DE SER-
VICES SOCIAUX DES LAURENTIDES** *p1354*
125 CH DU TOUR-DU-LAC, SAINTE-
AGATHE-DES-MONTS, QC, J8C 1B4
(819) 326-6221 *SIC 8361*

**CENTRE INTEGRE UNIVERSITAIRE DE
SANTE ET DE SERVICES SOCIAUX DE LA
CAPITALE-NATIONALE, LE** *p1255*
700 BOUL DES CHUTES, QUEBEC, QC,
G1E 2B7
(418) 663-9934 *SIC 8361*

CENTRE JEUNESSE DE L'ESTRIE *p1375*
8475 CH BLANCHETTE, SHERBROOKE,
QC, J1N 3A3
(819) 864-4221 *SIC 8361*

**CENTRE JEUNESSE DE LA MAURICIE ET
DU CENTRE-DU-QUEBEC, LE** *p1096*
3100 BOUL LEMIRE, DRUMMONDVILLE,
QC, J2B 7R2
(819) 477-5115 *SIC 8361*

CENTRE LA TRAVERSEE *p1171*
1460 BOUL CREMAZIE E, MONTREAL,
QC, H2E 1A2
(514) 321-4984 *SIC 8361*

CENTRE LAFLECHE GRAND-MERE *p1368*
555 AV DE LA STATION, SHAWINIGAN,
QC, G9N 1V9
(819) 536-0071 *SIC 8361*

**CHARTWELL QUEBEC (MEL) HOLDINGS
INC** *p1232*
3245 BOUL SAINT-MARTIN E, MONTREAL,
QC, H7E 4T6
(450) 661-0911 *SIC 8361*

CHRISTIAN HORIZONS *p641*
4278 KING ST E, KITCHENER, ON, N2P
2G5
(519) 650-0966 *SIC 8361*

**CHSLD LACHINE, NAZAIRE PICHE ET
FOYER DORVAL, LES** *p1096*
225 AV DE LA PRESENTATION, DORVAL,
QC, H9S 3L7
(514) 631-9090 *SIC 8361*

CHSLD MARIE-CLARET INC *p1240*
3345 BOUL HENRI-BOURASSA E,
MONTREAL-NORD, QC, H1H 1H6
(514) 322-4380 *SIC 8361*

CLAIR FOYER INC *p1046*
841 3E RUE O, AMOS, QC, J9T 2T4

(819) 732-6511   *SIC* 8361
CLSC-CHSLD THERESE DE BLAINVILLE *p1287*
365 CH DE LA GRANDE-COTE, ROSE-MERE, QC, J7A 1K4
(450) 621-3760   *SIC* 8361
COFORCE INC   *p1048*
11301 RUE MIRABEAU, ANJOU, QC, H1J 2S2
(514) 354-3430   *SIC* 8361
COLUMBUS LONG TERM CARE SOCIETY *p323*
704 69TH AVE W, VANCOUVER, BC, V6P 2W3
(604) 321-4405   *SIC* 8361
COMMUNITY LIVING CAMBRIDGE   *p538*
1124 VALENTINE DR, CAMBRIDGE, ON, N3H 2N8
(519) 650-5091   *SIC* 8361
COMMUNITY LIVING DURHAM NORTH *p848*
60 VANEDWARD DR UNIT 2, PORT PERRY, ON, L9L 1G3
(905) 985-8511   *SIC* 8361
COMMUNITY LIVING ELGIN   *p889*
400 TALBOT ST, ST THOMAS, ON, N5P 1B8
(519) 631-9222   *SIC* 8361
COMMUNITY LIVING OS-HAWA/CLARINGTON   *p812*
39 WELLINGTON AVE E, OSHAWA, ON, L1H 3Y1
(905) 576-3011   *SIC* 8361
COMMUNITY LIVING YORK SOUTH   *p855*
101 EDWARD AVE, RICHMOND HILL, ON, L4C 5E5
(905) 884-9110   *SIC* 8361
COMMUNITY LODGE INCORPORATED *p467*
320 ALEXANDRA ST, SYDNEY, NS, B1S 2G1
(902) 539-5267   *SIC* 8361
CONSTRUCTIONS MAXERA INC, LES *p1346*
7675 RUE LESPINAY, SAINT-LEONARD, QC, H1S 3C6
(514) 254-9002   *SIC* 8361
CORPORATION NOTRE-DAME DE BON-SECOURS, LA   *p1270*
990 RUE GERARD-MORISSET, QUEBEC, QC, G1S 1X6
(418) 681-4637   *SIC* 8361
CORPORATION OF HALDIMAND COUNTY, THE   *p567*
657 LOCK ST W SUITE A, DUNNVILLE, ON, N1A 1V9
(800) 265-2818   *SIC* 8361
CORPORATION OF THE CITY OF KAWARTHA LAKES, THE   *p645*
220 ANGELINE ST S, LINDSAY, ON, K9V 0J8
(705) 324-3558   *SIC* 8361
CORPORATION OF THE CITY OF KINGSTON, THE   *p630*
175 RIDEAU ST SUITE 416, KINGSTON, ON, K7K 3H6
(613) 530-2818   *SIC* 8361
CORPORATION OF THE CITY OF THUN-DER BAY, THE   *p907*
523 ALGOMA ST N, THUNDER BAY, ON, P7A 5C2
SIC 8361
CORPORATION OF THE CITY OF WIND-SOR   *p1025*
1881 CABANA RD W, WINDSOR, ON, N9G 1C7
(519) 253-6060   *SIC* 8361
CORPORATION OF THE COUNTY OF EL-GIN   *p482*
475 TALBOT ST E, AYLMER, ON, N5H 3A5
(519) 773-9205   *SIC* 8361
CORPORATION OF THE COUNTY OF EL-GIN   *p889*
39232 FINGAL LINE, ST THOMAS, ON,

N5P 3S5
(519) 631-0620   *SIC* 8361
CORPORATION OF THE COUNTY OF ES-SEX, THE   *p644*
175 TALBOT ST E, LEAMINGTON, ON, N8H 1L9
(519) 326-5731   *SIC* 8361
CORPORATION OF THE COUNTY OF LAMBTON   *p859*
749 DEVINE ST, SARNIA, ON, N7T 1X3
(519) 336-3720   *SIC* 8361
CORPORATION OF THE COUNTY OF MID-DLESEX   *p897*
599 ALBERT ST, STRATHROY, ON, N7G 1X1
(519) 245-2520   *SIC* 8361
CORPORATION OF THE COUNTY OF NORTHUMBERLAND   *p545*
983 BURNHAM ST SUITE 1321, COBOURG, ON, K9A 5J6
(905) 372-8759   *SIC* 8361
CORPORATION OF THE COUNTY OF REN-FREW   *p849*
470 ALBERT ST, RENFREW, ON, K7V 4L5
(613) 432-4873   *SIC* 8361
CORPORATION OF THE COUNTY OF SIM-COE   *p809*
12 GRACE AVE, ORILLIA, ON, L3V 2K2
(705) 325-1504   *SIC* 8361
CORPORATION OF THE REGIONAL MU-NICIPALITY OF DURHAM, THE   *p1014*
632 DUNDAS ST W, WHITBY, ON, L1N 5S3
(905) 668-5851   *SIC* 8361
CORPORATION OF THE TOWN OF GEORGINA, THE   *p902*
26943 48 HWY RR 2, SUTTON WEST, ON, L0E 1R0
(905) 722-8947   *SIC* 8361
CSH CASTEL ROYAL INC   *p1083*
5740 BOUL CAVENDISH BUREAU 2006, COTE SAINT-LUC, QC, H4W 2T8
SIC 8361
CSH L'OASIS ST. JEAN INC   *p1316*
1050 RUE STEFONI, SAINT-JEAN-SUR-RICHELIEU, QC, J3A 1T5
(450) 349-5861   *SIC* 8361
CSH WOODHAVEN LTC INC   *p678*
380 CHURCH ST, MARKHAM, ON, L6B 1E1
(905) 472-3320   *SIC* 8361
CUMBERLAND SENIOR CARE CORPORA-TION   *p465*
262 CHURCH ST, PUGWASH, NS, B0K 1L0
(902) 243-2504   *SIC* 8361
CYPRESS HEALTH REGION   *p1436*
440 CENTRAL AVE S, SWIFT CURRENT, SK, S9H 3G6
SIC 8361
DANIA HOME SOCIETY   *p188*
4279 NORLAND AVE, BURNABY, BC, V5G 3Z6
(604) 299-1370   *SIC* 8361
DIAMOND LODGE CO LTD   *p1404*
402 2ND AVE W, BIGGAR, SK, S0K 0M0
SIC 8361
DIRECT ACTION IN SUPPORT OF COMMU-NITY HOMES INCORPORATED   *p388*
117 VICTOR LEWIS DR UNIT 1, WIN-NIPEG, MB, R3P 1J6
(204) 987-1550   *SIC* 8361
DISTRICT OF PARRY SOUND (WEST) BELVEDERE HEIGHTS HOME FOR THE AGED   *p837*
21 BELVEDERE AVE, PARRY SOUND, ON, P2A 2A2
(705) 746-5871   *SIC* 8361
DIVERSICARE CANADA MANAGEMENT SERVICES CO., INC   *p221*
867 K.L.O. RD, KELOWNA, BC, V1Y 9G5
(250) 861-6636   *SIC* 8361
DIVERSICARE REALTY INVESTMENTS LIMITED   *p221*
867 K.L.O. RD, KELOWNA, BC, V1Y 9G5
(250) 861-6636   *SIC* 8361
DOVERCOURT BAPTIST FOUNDATION

p990
1140 BLOOR ST W, TORONTO, ON, M6H 4E6
(416) 536-6111   *SIC* 8361
EASTHOLME HOME FOR THE AGED *p848*
62 BIG BEND AVE, POWASSAN, ON, P0H 1Z0
(705) 724-2005   *SIC* 8361
ECHO VILLAGE FOUNDATION   *p245*
4200 10TH AVE, PORT ALBERNI, BC, V9Y 4X3
(250) 724-1090   *SIC* 8361
ELGIN MANOR HOME FOR SR CITIZENS *p889*
39262 FINGAL LINE, ST THOMAS, ON, N5P 3S5
(519) 631-0620   *SIC* 8361
FAIR HAVEN UNITED CHURCH HOMES, THE   *p288*
2720 48TH AVE E, VANCOUVER, BC, V5S 1G7
(604) 433-2939   *SIC* 8361
FAIRMOUNT HOME FOR THE AGED *p594*
2069 BATTERSEA RD, GLENBURNIE, ON, K0H 1S0
(613) 548-9400   *SIC* 8361
FAIRVIEW MENNONITE HOMES   *p539*
515 LANGS DR SUITE D, CAMBRIDGE, ON, N3H 5E4
(519) 653-2222   *SIC* 8361
FAIRWAY MANAGEMENT CORPORATION LTD   *p1402*
4430 RUE SAINTE-CATHERINE O BU-REAU 505, WESTMOUNT, QC, H3Z 3E4
(514) 935-1212   *SIC* 8361
FONDATION DE LA MAISON DU PERE *p1175*
545 RUE DE LA GAUCHETIERE E BU-REAU 296, MONTREAL, QC, H2L 5E1
(514) 843-3739   *SIC* 8361
FONDATION LE PILIER   *p1224*
23 AV DU RUISSEAU, MONTREAL, QC, H4K 2C8
(450) 624-9922   *SIC* 8361
FONDATION SANTE VALLEE-DE-LA-GATINEAU   *p1148*
177 RUE DES OBLATS, MANIWAKI, QC, J9E 1G5
(819) 449-2513   *SIC* 8361
FOYER DE CHARLESBOURG INC   *p1256*
7150 BOUL CLOUTIER, QUEBEC, QC, G1H 5V5
(418) 628-0456   *SIC* 8361
FOYER NOTRE-DAME DE LOURDES INC, LE   *p394*
2055 VALLEE LOURDES DR, BATHURST, NB, E2A 4P8
(506) 549-5085   *SIC* 8361
FOYER NOTRE-DAME DE SAINT-LEONARD INC   *p417*
604 RUE PRINCIPALE, SAINT-LEONARD, NB, E7E 2H5
SIC 8361
FOYER RICHELIEU WELLAND   *p1011*
655 TANGUAY AVE, WELLAND, ON, L3B 6A1
(905) 734-1400   *SIC* 8361
FOYER ST-FRANCOIS INC   *p1079*
912 RUE JACQUES-CARTIER E, CHICOUTIMI, QC, G7H 2A9
(418) 549-3727   *SIC* 8361
GESTION VALLIERES ET PELLETIER INC, LES   *p1098*
275 RUE COCKBURN, DRUMMONDVILLE, QC, J2C 4L5
(819) 475-0545   *SIC* 8361
GLEBE CENTRE INCORPORATED, THE *p825*
950 BANK ST, OTTAWA, ON, K1S 5G6
(613) 230-5730   *SIC* 8361
GLEN STOR DUN LODGE FOUNDATION *p562*
1900 MONTREAL RD, CORNWALL, ON, K6H 7L1

(613) 933-3384   *SIC* 8361
GOUVERNEMENT DE LA PROVINCE DE QUEBEC   *p1055*
11000 RUE DES MONTAGNARDS RR 1, BEAUPRE, QC, G0A 1E0
(418) 661-5666   *SIC* 8361
GOUVERNEMENT DE LA PROVINCE DE QUEBEC   *p1146*
450 2E RUE, LOUISEVILLE, QC, J5V 1V3
(819) 228-2700   *SIC* 8361
GOUVERNEMENT DE LA PROVINCE DE QUEBEC   *p1168*
3730 RUE DE BELLECHASSE, MON-TREAL, QC, H1X 3E5
(514) 374-8665   *SIC* 8361
GOUVERNEMENT DE LA PROVINCE DE QUEBEC   *p1256*
7843 RUE DES SANTOLINES, QUEBEC, QC, G1G 0G3
(418) 683-2511   *SIC* 8361
GOUVERNEMENT DE LA PROVINCE DE QUEBEC   *p1347*
521 RUE SAINT-ANTOINE, SAINT-LIN-LAURENTIDES, QC, J5M 3A3
(450) 439-2609   *SIC* 8361
GOUVERNEMENT DE LA PROVINCE DE QUEBEC   *p1357*
5436 BOUL LEVESQUE E, SAINTE-DOROTHEE, QC, H7C 1N7
(450) 661-5440   *SIC* 8361
GOVERNING COUNCIL OF THE SALVA-TION ARMY IN CANADA, THE   *p236*
409 BLAIR AVE, NEW WESTMINSTER, BC, V3L 4A4
(604) 522-7033   *SIC* 8361
GOVERNING COUNCIL OF THE SALVA-TION ARMY IN CANADA, THE   *p1420*
50 ANGUS RD, REGINA, SK, S4R 8P6
(306) 543-0655   *SIC* 8361
GRANDVIEW LODGE HOME FOR THE AGED   *p909*
200 LILLIE ST N, THUNDER BAY, ON, P7C 5Y2
SIC 8361
GREATER EDMONTON FOUNDATION *p97*
14220 109 AVE NW, EDMONTON, AB, T5N 4B3
(780) 482-6561   *SIC* 8361
GRIFFIN CENTRE MENTAL HEALTH SER-VICES   *p916*
1126 FINCH AVE W UNIT 16, TORONTO, ON, M3J 3J6
(416) 222-1153   *SIC* 8361
GROUPE CHAMPLAIN INC   *p1057*
1231 RUE DR OLIVIER-M.-GENDRON PR, BERTHIERVILLE, QC, J0K 1A0
(450) 836-6241   *SIC* 8361
GROUPE CHAMPLAIN INC   *p1280*
791 RUE DE SHERWOOD, QUEBEC, QC, G2N 1X7
(418) 849-1891   *SIC* 8361
GROUPE CHAMPLAIN INC   *p1298*
199 RUE SAINT-PIERRE, SAINT-CONSTANT, QC, J5A 2N8
(450) 632-4451   *SIC* 8361
GROUPE SANTE VALEO INC   *p1301*
495 RUE BIBEAU, SAINT-EUSTACHE, QC, J7R 0B9
(450) 472-6115   *SIC* 8361
HAMILTON JEWISH HOME FOR THE AGED *p614*
70 MACKLIN ST N, HAMILTON, ON, L8S 3S1
(905) 528-5377   *SIC* 8361
HARO PARK CENTRE SOCIETY   *p313*
1233 HARO ST, VANCOUVER, BC, V6E 3Y5
(604) 687-5584   *SIC* 8361
HELLENIC HOME FOR THE AGE INC *p989*
33 WINONA DR, TORONTO, ON, M6G 3Z7
(416) 654-7700   *SIC* 8361
IDLEWYLD MANOR   *p617*
449 SANATORIUM RD, HAMILTON, ON, L9C 2A7

(905) 574-2000   *SIC* 8361
INGERSOLL SUPPORT SERVICES INCp621
148 THAMES ST S, INGERSOLL, ON, N5C 2T4
(519) 425-0005   *SIC* 8361
INSTITUT RAYMOND-DEWAR   p1175
3600 RUE BERRI BUREAU 469, MONTREAL, QC, H2L 4G9
(514) 284-2214   *SIC* 8361
INTERIOR HEALTH KIMBERLY SPECIAL CARE HOME   p223
386 2ND AVE, KIMBERLEY, BC, V1A 2Z8
(250) 427-4807   *SIC* 8361
INVESQUE INC   p953
333 BAY ST SUITE 3400, TORONTO, ON, M5H 2S7
SIC 8361
INVESTISSEMENTS DU HAUT-ST-LAURENT INC, LES   p1293
4770 RUE SAINT-FELIX, SAINT-AUGUSTIN-DE-DESMAURES, QC, G3A 0K9
(418) 872-4936   *SIC* 8361
K-W HABILITATION SERVICES   p638
99 OTTAWA ST S, KITCHENER, ON, N2G 3S8
(519) 744-6307   *SIC* 8361
KINSMEN RETIREMENT CENTRE ASSOCIATION   p211
5410 10 AVE, DELTA, BC, V4M 3X8
(604) 943-0155   *SIC* 8361
KNOLLCREST LODGE   p685
50 WILLIAM ST SUITE 221, MILVERTON, ON, N0K 1M0
(519) 595-8121   *SIC* 8361
LAMBTON MEADOWVIEW VILLA   p843
3958 PETROLIA LINE SUITE 499, PETROLIA, ON, N0N 1R0
(519) 882-1470   *SIC* 8361
LANARK LODGE   p839
115 CHRISTIE LAKE RD SUITE 223, PERTH, ON, K7H 3C6
(613) 267-4225   *SIC* 8361
LETHBRIDGE FAMILY SERVICES   p143
1410 MAYOR MAGRATH DR S SUITE 106, LETHBRIDGE, AB, T1K 2R3
(403) 317-4624   *SIC* 8361
LIONS CLUB OF WINNIPEG HOUSING CENTRES   p375
320 SHERBROOK ST, WINNIPEG, MB, R3B 2W6
(204) 784-1240   *SIC* 8361
LIONS CLUB OF WINNIPEG PLACE FOR SENIOR CITIZENS INC   p378
610 PORTAGE AVE SUITE 1214, WINNIPEG, MB, R3C 0G5
(204) 784-1236   *SIC* 8361
LIONS CLUB OF WINNIPEG SENIOR CITIZENS HOME   p375
320 SHERBROOK ST, WINNIPEG, MB, R3B 2W6
(204) 784-1240   *SIC* 8361
LOOKOUT THE EMERGENCY AID SOCIETY   p295
429 ALEXANDER ST, VANCOUVER, BC, V6A 1C6
(604) 255-2347   *SIC* 8361
M. KOPERNIK (NICOLAUS COPERNICUS) FOUNDATION   p288
3150 ROSEMONT DR, VANCOUVER, BC, V5S 2C9
(604) 438-2474   *SIC* 8361
MANOIR ET COURS DE L'ATRIUM INC
p1256
545 RUE FRANCIS-BYRNE, QUEBEC, QC, G1H 7L3
(418) 626-6060   *SIC* 8361
MANOIR SAINT-JEAN BAPTISTE INC p395
5 AV RICHARD, BOUCTOUCHE, NB, E4S 3T2
(506) 743-7344   *SIC* 8361
MANOIR ST-PATRICE INC   p1087
3615 BOUL PERRON, COTE SAINT-LUC, QC, H7V 1P4

(450) 681-1621   *SIC* 8361
MAPLE GROVE CARE COMMUNITY   p498
215 SUNNY MEADOW BLVD, BRAMPTON, ON, L6R 3B5
(905) 458-7604   *SIC* 8361
MARYVALE ADOLESCENT FAMILY SERVICE   p1025
3640 WELLS ST, WINDSOR, ON, N9C 1T9
(519) 258-0484   *SIC* 8361
MENNO HOME FOR THE AGED   p350
235 PARK ST, GRUNTHAL, MB, R0A 0R0
(204) 434-6496   *SIC* 8361
METROPOLITAN CALGARY FOUNDATION
p36
7015 MACLEOD TRAIL SW SUITE 804, CALGARY, AB, T2H 2K6
(403) 276-5541   *SIC* 8361
MISSION ASSOCIATION FOR COMMUNITY LIVING   p232
33345 2ND AVE, MISSION, BC, V2V 1K4
(604) 826-9080   *SIC* 8361
MISSION OLD BREWERY   p1192
902 BOUL SAINT-LAURENT, MONTREAL, QC, H2Z 1J2
(514) 866-6591   *SIC* 8361
MOUNTAIN VIEW SENIORS HOUSING p82
1100A 20 AVE, DIDSBURY, AB, T0M 0W0
(403) 335-8404   *SIC* 8361
NANAIMO TRAVELLERS LODGE SOCIETY
p234
1917 NORTHFIELD RD, NANAIMO, BC, V9S 3B6
(250) 758-4676   *SIC* 8361
NEW VISTA SOCIETY, THE   p187
7550 ROSEWOOD ST SUITE 235, BURNABY, BC, V5E 3Z3
(604) 521-7764   *SIC* 8361
NIAGARA INA GRAFTON GAGE HOME OF THE UNITED CHURCH   p883
413 LINWELL RD SUITE 4212, ST CATHARINES, ON, L2M 7Y2
(905) 935-6822   *SIC* 8361
NISBET LODGE   p920
740 PAPE AVE, TORONTO, ON, M4K 3S7
(416) 469-1105   *SIC* 8361
NORTH QUEENS NURSING HOME INCp441
9565 HIGHWAY 8, CALEDONIA, NS, B0T 1B0
(902) 682-2553   *SIC* 8361
NORWEGIAN OLD PEOPLE'S HOME ASSOCIATION   p181
7725 4TH ST, BURNABY, BC, V3N 5B6
(604) 522-5812   *SIC* 8361
NUCLEUS INDEPENDENT LIVING   p993
30 DENARDA ST SUITE 309, TORONTO, ON, M6M 5C3
(416) 244-1234   *SIC* 8361
OLIVER LODGE   p1431
1405 FAULKNER CRES, SASKATOON, SK, S7L 3R5
(306) 382-4111   *SIC* 8361
OMNI HEALTH CARE LTD   p646
225 MARY ST W, LINDSAY, ON, K9V 5K3
(705) 324-8333   *SIC* 8361
ONGWANADA HOSPITAL   p632
191 PORTSMOUTH AVE, KINGSTON, ON, K7M 8A6
(613) 548-4417   *SIC* 8361
ONTARIO FAMILY GROUP HOMES INCp995
146 WESTMINSTER AVE, TORONTO, ON, M6R 1N7
(416) 532-6234   *SIC* 8361
ONTARIO MISSION FOR THE DEAF, THE
p769
2395 BAYVIEW AVE, NORTH YORK, ON, M2L 1A2
(416) 449-9651   *SIC* 8361
ORCHIDEE BLANCHE CENTRE D'HEBERGEMENT SOINS LONGUE DUREE INC, L   p1232
2577 BOUL RENE-LAENNEC, MONTREAL, QC, H7K 3V4
(450) 629-1200   *SIC* 8361
OTTAWA JEWISH HOME FOR THE AGED

p829
10 NADOLNY SACHS PVT, OTTAWA, ON, K2A 4G7
(613) 728-3900   *SIC* 8361
OUR NEIGHBOURHOOD LIVING SOCIETY
p440
15 DARTMOUTH RD SUITE 210, BEDFORD, NS, B4A 3X6
(902) 835-8826   *SIC* 8361
PARAGON HEALTH CARE INC   p784
3595 KEELE ST, NORTH YORK, ON, M3J 1M7
(416) 633-3431   *SIC* 8361
PEMBINA CARE SERVICES LTD   p391
1679 PEMBINA HWY, WINNIPEG, MB, R3T 2G6
(204) 269-6308   *SIC* 8361
PHOENIX HUMAN SERVICES ASSOCIATION   p335
1824 STORE ST, VICTORIA, BC, V8T 4R4
(250) 383-4821   *SIC* 8361
PINES LONG TERM CARE RESIDENCE, THE   p497
98 PINE ST SUITE 610, BRACEBRIDGE, ON, P1L 1N5
(705) 645-4488   *SIC* 8361
PIONEER RIDGE HOME FOR THE AGED
p909
750 TUNGSTEN ST, THUNDER BAY, ON, P7B 6R1
(807) 684-3910   *SIC* 8361
PORT COQUITLAM SENIOR CITIZENS HOUSING SOCIETY   p247
2111 HAWTHORNE AVE SUITE 406, PORT COQUITLAM, BC, V3C 1W3
(604) 941-4051   *SIC* 8361
PRESCOTT & RUSSEL RESIDENCE   p619
1020 CARTIER BLVD, HAWKESBURY, ON, K6A 1W7
(613) 632-2755   *SIC* 8361
PRODIMAX INC   p1399
1050 15E AV, VIMONT, QC, H7R 4N9
(450) 627-6068   *SIC* 8361
QUEENS HOME FOR SPECIAL CARE SOCIETY   p460
20 HOLLANDS DR, LIVERPOOL, NS, B0T 1K0
(902) 354-3451   *SIC* 8361
QUEST - A SOCIETY FOR ADULT SUPPORT AND REHABILITATION   p456
2131 GOTTINGEN ST SUITE 101, HALIFAX, NS, B3K 5Z7
(902) 490-7200   *SIC* 8361
RANCH EHRLO SOCIETY   p1413
GD, PILOT BUTTE, SK, S0G 3Z0
(306) 781-1800   *SIC* 8361
REGENCY INTERMEDIATE CARE FACILITIES INC   p277
13855 68 AVE, SURREY, BC, V3W 2G9
(604) 597-9333   *SIC* 8361
REGIONAL MUNICIPALITY OF NIAGARA, THE   p1012
277 PLYMOUTH RD, WELLAND, ON, L3B 6E3
(905) 714-7428   *SIC* 8361
REGIONAL RESIDENTIAL SERVICES SOCIETY   p448
202 BROWNLOW AVE SUITE LKD1, DARTMOUTH, NS, B3B 1T5
(902) 465-4022   *SIC* 8361
REHABILITATION CENTRE FOR CHILDREN INC   p381
1155 NOTRE DAME AVE, WINNIPEG, MB, R3E 3G1
(204) 452-4311   *SIC* 8361
RESIDENCE COTE JARDINS INC   p1271
880 AV PAINCHAUD, QUEBEC, QC, G1S 0A3
(418) 688-1221   *SIC* 8361
RESIDENCE LE GIBRALTAR INC   p1271
1300 CH SAINTE-FOY BUREAU 610, QUEBEC, QC, G1S 0A6
(418) 681-2777   *SIC* 8361
RESIDENCE SEPHARADE SALOMON

(COMMUNAUTE SEPHARADE UNIFIEE DU QUEBEC)   p1220
5900 BOUL DECARIE, MONTREAL, QC, H3X 2J7
(514) 733-2157   *SIC* 8361
RESIDENCE SOREL-TRACY INC   p1377
4025 RUE FRONTENAC, SOREL-TRACY, QC, J3R 4G8
(450) 742-9427   *SIC* 8361
REVERA INC   p68
9229 16 ST SW, CALGARY, AB, T2V 5H3
(403) 255-2105   *SIC* 8361
REVERA INC   p90
10015 103 AVE NW SUITE 1208, EDMONTON, AB, T5J 0H1
(780) 420-1222   *SIC* 8361
REVERA INC   p323
2803 41ST AVE W SUITE 110, VANCOUVER, BC, V6N 4B4
(604) 263-0921   *SIC* 8361
REVERA INC   p597
290 SOUTH ST, GODERICH, ON, N7A 4G6
(519) 524-7324   *SIC* 8361
REVERA INC   p857
980 ELGIN MILLS RD E, RICHMOND HILL, ON, L4S 1M4
(905) 884-9248   *SIC* 8361
REVERA LONG TERM CARE INC   p910
2625 WALSH ST E SUITE 1127, THUNDER BAY, ON, P7E 2E5
(807) 577-1127   *SIC* 8361
RIVERPARK PLACE LIMITED PARTNERSHIP   p751
1 CORKSTOWN RD, NEPEAN, ON, K2H 1B6
(613) 828-8882   *SIC* 8361
RIVERSIDE RETIREMENT CENTRE LTD
p242
4315 SKYLINE DR, NORTH VANCOUVER, BC, V7R 3G9
(604) 307-1104   *SIC* 8361
RIVERVIEW HOME CORPORATION   p466
24 RIVERVIEW LANE, STELLARTON, NS, B0K 0A2
(902) 755-4884   *SIC* 8361
ROCK LAKE HEALTH DISTRICT FOUNDATION INC   p354
115 BROWN ST APT 27, PILOT MOUND, MB, R0G 1P0
(204) 825-2246   *SIC* 8361
ROSEWAY MANOR INCORPORATED p465
1604 LAKE RD, SHELBURNE, NS, B0T 1W0
(902) 875-4707   *SIC* 8361
ROYAL CITY MANOR LTD   p236
77 JAMIESON CRT, NEW WESTMINSTER, BC, V3L 5P8
(604) 522-6699   *SIC* 8361
RYGIEL SUPPORTS FOR COMMUNITY LIVING   p616
930 UPPER PARADISE RD UNIT 11, HAMILTON, ON, L9B 2N1
(905) 525-4311   *SIC* 8361
SAINT BRIGID'S HOME INC   p1271
1645 CH SAINT-LOUIS, QUEBEC, QC, G1S 4M3
(418) 681-4687   *SIC* 8361
SAINT ELIZABETH HEALTH CARE   p1015
420 GREEN ST SUITE 202, WHITBY, ON, L1N 8R1
(905) 430-6997   *SIC* 8361
SAINT VINCENT'S NURSING HOME   p456
2080 WINDSOR ST SUITE 509, HALIFAX, NS, B3K 5B2
(902) 429-0550   *SIC* 8361
SANTE COURVILLE INC   p1342
5200 80E RUE, SAINT-LAURENT, QC, H7R 5T6
(450) 627-7990   *SIC* 8361
SASKATCHEWAN HEALTH AUTHORITY
p1406
300 JAMES ST, ESTERHAZY, SK, S0A 0X0
(306) 745-6444   *SIC* 8361
SERVICES DE READAPTATION SUD

OUEST ET DU RENFORT, LES   p1318
315 RUE MACDONALD BUREAU 105, SAINT-JEAN-SUR-RICHELIEU, QC, J3B 8J3
(450) 348-6121   SIC 8361
SERVICES DE READAPTATION SUD OUEST ET DU RENFORT, LES   p1366
30 RUE SAINT-THOMAS BUREAU 200, SALABERRY-DE-VALLEYFIELD, QC, J6T 4J2
(450) 371-4816   SIC 8361
SHEPHERD VILLAGE INC   p875
3760 SHEPPARD AVE E, SCARBOROUGH, ON, M1T 3K9
(416) 609-5700   SIC 8361
SIENNA SENIOR LIVING INC   p675
302 TOWN CENTRE BLVD SUITE 300, MARKHAM, ON, L3R 0E8
(905) 477-4006   SIC 8361
SIMCOE MANOR HOME FOR THE AGED   p490
5988 8TH LINE, BEETON, ON, L0G 1A0
(905) 729-2267   SIC 8361
SNR NURSING HOMES LTD   p1017
11550 MCNORTON ST, WINDSOR, ON, N8P 1T9
(519) 979-6730   SIC 8361
SOEURS DE LA CHARITE D'OTTAWA, LES   p810
879 HIAWATHA PARK RD, ORLEANS, ON, K1C 2Z6
(613) 562-6262   SIC 8361
SPRUCE LODGE HOME FOR THE AGED   p896
643 WEST GORE ST, STRATFORD, ON, N5A 1L4
(519) 271-4090   SIC 8361
ST THOMAS CENTRE DE SANTE   p112
8411 91 ST NW SUITE 234, EDMONTON, AB, T6C 1Z9
(780) 450-2987   SIC 8361
ST. CLAIR O'CONNOR COMMUNITY INC   p917
2701 ST CLAIR AVE E SUITE 211, TORONTO, ON, M4B 1M5
(416) 757-8757   SIC 8361
ST. HILDA'S TOWERS, INC   p989
2339 DUFFERIN ST, TORONTO, ON, M6E 4Z5
(416) 781-6621   SIC 8361
ST. JOSEPH'S HEALTH CARE, LONDON   p655
268 GROSVENOR ST, LONDON, ON, N6A 4V2
(519) 646-6100   SIC 8361
ST. JOSEPH'S HEALTH CARE, LONDON   p655
268 GROSVENOR ST, LONDON, ON, N6A 4V2
(519) 646-6100   SIC 8361
ST. LAWRENCE LODGE   p520
1803 HIGHWAY 2 E, BROCKVILLE, ON, K6V 5T1
(613) 345-0255   SIC 8361
ST. LEONARD'S COMMUNITY SERVICES   p516
133 ELGIN ST, BRANTFORD, ON, N3S 5A4
(519) 759-8830   SIC 8361
SUDBURY DEVELOPMENTAL SERVICES   p899
245 MOUNTAIN ST, SUDBURY, ON, P3B 2T8
(705) 674-1451   SIC 8361
SUMMIT CARE CORPORATION (EDMONTON) LTD   p124
1808 RABBIT HILL RD NW, EDMONTON, AB, T6R 3H2
(780) 665-8050   SIC 8361
SUN PARLOR HOME   p645
175 TALBOT ST E, LEAMINGTON, ON, N8H 1L9
(519) 326-5731   SIC 8361
SUNRISE NORTH ASSISTED LIVING LTD   p704
1279 BURNHAMTHORPE RD E SUITE 220, MISSISSAUGA, ON, L4Y 3V7

(905) 625-1344   SIC 8361
SUNRISE NORTH ASSISTED LIVING LTD   p856
9800 YONGE ST SUITE 101, RICHMOND HILL, ON, L4C 0P5
(905) 883-6963   SIC 8361
SUNRISE NORTH SENIOR LIVING LTD   p239
980 LYNN VALLEY RD, NORTH VANCOUVER, BC, V7J 3V7
(604) 904-1226   SIC 8361
SUNRISE NORTH SENIOR LIVING LTD   p324
999 57TH AVE W, VANCOUVER, BC, V6P 6Y9
(604) 261-5799   SIC 8361
SUNRISE NORTH SENIOR LIVING LTD   p482
3 GOLF LINKS DR SUITE 2, AURORA, ON, L4G 7Y4
(905) 841-0022   SIC 8361
SUNRISE NORTH SENIOR LIVING LTD   p525
5401 LAKESHORE RD, BURLINGTON, ON, L7L 6S5
(905) 333-9969   SIC 8361
SUNRISE NORTH SENIOR LIVING LTD   p801
456 TRAFALGAR RD SUITE 312, OAKVILLE, ON, L6J 7X1
(905) 337-1145   SIC 8361
SUNRISE NORTH SENIOR LIVING LTD   p1058
50 BOUL DES CHATEAUX, BLAINVILLE, QC, J7B 0A3
(450) 420-2727   SIC 8361
SUNSET RESIDENTIAL & REHABILITATION SERVICES INCORPORATED   p465
140 SUNSET LANE, PUGWASH, NS, B0K 1L0
(902) 243-2571   SIC 8361
SYMPHONY SENIOR LIVING INC   p70
2220 162 AVE SW SUITE 210, CALGARY, AB, T2Y 5E3
(403) 201-3555   SIC 8361
TEN TEN SINCLAIR HOUSING INC   p370
1010 SINCLAIR ST, WINNIPEG, MB, R2V 3H7
(204) 339-9268   SIC 8361
TORONTO AGED MEN'S AND WOMEN'S HOMES, THE   p974
55 BELMONT ST SUITE 403, TORONTO, ON, M5R 1R1
(416) 964-9231   SIC 8361
TREATMENT CENTRE OF WATERLOO REGION, THE   p1007
500 HALLMARK DR, WATERLOO, ON, N2K 3P5
(519) 886-8886   SIC 8361
TWIN OAKS SENIOR CITIZENS ASSOCIATION   p463
7702 # 7 HWY, MUSQUODOBOIT HARBOUR, NS, B0J 2L0
(902) 889-3474   SIC 8361
UKRAINIAN HOME FOR THE AGED   p718
3058 WINSTON CHURCHILL BLVD SUITE 1, MISSISSAUGA, ON, L5L 3J1
(905) 820-0573   SIC 8361
UNIONVILLE HOME SOCIETY   p676
4300 HIGHWAY 7 E SUITE 1, MARKHAM, ON, L3R 1L8
(905) 477-2822   SIC 8361
UNITED COUNTIES OF LEEDS AND GRENVILLE   p479
746 COUNTY RD 42, ATHENS, ON, K0E 1B0
(613) 924-2696   SIC 8361
UNITED MENNONITE HOME FOR THE AGED   p1003
4024 23RD ST, VINELAND, ON, L0R 2C0
(905) 562-7385   SIC 8361
UNIVERSAL REHABILITATION SERVICE AGENCY   p26
808 MANNING RD NE, CALGARY, AB, T2E 7N8
(403) 272-7722   SIC 8361
VANCOUVER COASTAL HEALTH AUTHORITY   p248
7105 KEMANO ST, POWELL RIVER, BC,

V8A 1L8
(604) 485-9868   SIC 8361
VIGI SANTE LTEE   p1071
5955 GRANDE-ALLEE, BROSSARD, QC, J4Z 3S3
(450) 656-8500   SIC 8361
VIGI SANTE LTEE   p1155
275 AV BRITTANY, MONT-ROYAL, QC, H3P 3C2
(514) 739-5593   SIC 8361
VIGI SANTE LTEE   p1221
2055 AV NORTHCLIFFE BUREAU 412, MONTREAL, QC, H4A 3K6
(514) 788-2085   SIC 8361
VIGI SANTE LTEE   p1245
14775 BOUL DE PIERREFONDS BUREAU 229, PIERREFONDS, QC, H9H 4Y1
(514) 620-1220   SIC 8361
VIGI SANTE LTEE   p1294
4954 RUE CLEMENT-LOCKQUELL, SAINT-AUGUSTIN-DE-DESMAURES, QC, G3A 1V5
(418) 871-1232   SIC 8361
VIGI SANTE LTEE   p1369
5000 AV ALBERT-TESSIER, SHAWINIGAN, QC, G9N 8P9
(819) 539-5408   SIC 8361
VILLA BEAUSEJOUR INC   p396
253 BOUL ST-PIERRE O, CARAQUET, NB, E1W 1A4
(506) 726-2744   SIC 8361
VILLA COLOMBO HOMES FOR THE AGED INC   p791
40 PLAYFAIR AVE, NORTH YORK, ON, M6B 2P9
(416) 789-2113   SIC 8361
VILLA DU REPOS INC   p406
125 MURPHY AVE, MONCTON, NB, E1A 8V2
(506) 857-3560   SIC 8361
VILLA ST-GEORGES INC   p1398
185 RUE SAINT-GEORGES, VICTORIAVILLE, QC, G6P 9H6
(819) 758-6760   SIC 8361
WALES HOME, THE   p1081
506 RTE 243, CLEVELAND, QC, J0B 2H0
(819) 826-3266   SIC 8361
WAYS MENTAL HEALTH SUPPORT   p651
714 YORK ST, LONDON, ON, N5W 2S8
(519) 432-2209   SIC 8361
WELLS GORDON LIMITED   p925
720 MOUNT PLEASANT RD, TORONTO, ON, M4S 2N6
(416) 487-3392   SIC 8361
WESTBANK FIRST NATION PINE ACRES HOME   p342
1902 PHEASANT LANE, WESTBANK, BC, V4T 2H4
(250) 768-7676   SIC 8361
WEXFORD RESIDENCE INC, THE   p873
1860 LAWRENCE AVE E, SCARBOROUGH, ON, M1R 5B1
(416) 752-8877   SIC 8361
WINNIPEG REGIONAL HEALTH AUTHORITY, THE   p368
735 ST ANNE'S RD, WINNIPEG, MB, R2N 0C4
(204) 255-9073   SIC 8361
WOMEN'S CHRISTIAN ASSOCIATION OF LONDON   p660
2022 KAINS RD SUITE 2105, LONDON, ON, N6K 0A8
(519) 432-2648   SIC 8361
WOOD'S HOMES SOCIETY   p72
9400 48 AVE NW, CALGARY, AB, T3B 2B2
(403) 247-6751   SIC 8361
WYNN PARK VILLA LIMITED   p469
32 WINDSOR WAY, TRURO, NS, B2N 0B4
(902) 843-3939   SIC 8361

SIC 8399 Social services, nec

ABBOTSFORD COMMUNITY SERVICES   p174

2420 MONTROSE AVE, ABBOTSFORD, BC, V2S 3S9
(604) 859-7681   SIC 8399
ACCREDITATION CANADA   p595
1150 CYRVILLE RD SUITE 759, GLOUCESTER, ON, K1J 7S9
(613) 738-3800   SIC 8399
ACT II CHILD & FAMILY SERVICES SOCIETY   p199
1034 AUSTIN AVE, COQUITLAM, BC, V3K 3P3
(604) 937-7776   SIC 8399
AGE D'OR SACRE-COEUR TORONTO, L'   p931
474 ONTARIO ST, TORONTO, ON, M4X 1M7
(416) 923-3724   SIC 8399
AGENCE DE LA SANTE ET DES SERVICES SOCIAUX DES LAURENTIDES, L'   p1320
500 BOUL DES LAURENTIDES BUREAU 1010, SAINT-JEROME, QC, J7Z 4M2
(450) 436-8622   SIC 8399
AGENCE POUR VIVRE CHEZ SOI INC   p1122
502 RUE SAINT-ETIENNE, LA MALBAIE, QC, G5A 1H5
(418) 665-1067   SIC 8399
ALZHEIMER SOCIETY OF CANADA   p923
20 EGLINTON AVE W SUITE 1200, TORONTO, ON, M4R 1K8
(416) 488-8772   SIC 8399
ANGELS THERE FOR YOU   p266
12031 2ND AVE SUITE 100, RICHMOND, BC, V7E 3L6
(604) 271-4427   SIC 8399
ANIMIKII OZOSON CHILD AND FAMILY SERVICES INC   p373
313 PACIFIC AVE UNIT 3, WINNIPEG, MB, R3A 0M2
(204) 944-0040   SIC 8399
ARROW AND SLOCAN LAKES COMMUNITY SERVICES   p233
205 6 AVE NW, NAKUSP, BC, V0G 1R0
(250) 265-3674   SIC 8399
ARROWSMITH POTTERS GUILD   p242
600 ALBERNI HWY, PARKSVILLE, BC, V9P 1J9
(250) 954-1872   SIC 8399
ASSOCIATION OF NEIGHBOURHOOD HOUSES OF BRITISH COLUMBIA   p288
3102 MAIN ST SUITE 203, VANCOUVER, BC, V5T 3G7
(604) 875-9111   SIC 8399
ASSOCIATION QUEBECOISE D'ETABLISSEMENT DE SANTE & DES SERVICES SOCIAUX   p1193
505 BOUL DE MAISONNEUVE O BUREAU 400, MONTREAL, QC, H3A 3C2
(514) 842-4861   SIC 8399
AXIS FAMILY RESOURCES LTD   p344
321 SECOND AVE N, WILLIAMS LAKE, BC, V2G 2A1
(250) 392-1000   SIC 8399
B & L HOMES FOR CHILDREN LTD   p374
470 NOTRE DAME AVE SUITE 200, WINNIPEG, MB, R3B 1R5
(204) 774-6089   SIC 8399
BETHESDA COMMUNITY SERVICES INC   p906
3280 SCHMON PKY, THOROLD, ON, L2V 4Y6
(905) 684-6918   SIC 8399
BETHESDA HOME FOR THE MENTALLY HANDICAPPED INC   p906
3280 SCHMON PKY, THOROLD, ON, L2V 4Y6
(905) 684-6918   SIC 8399
BETHESDA HOME FOR THE MENTALLY HANDICAPPED INC   p1003
3950 FLY RD RR 1, VINELAND, ON, L0R 2C0
(905) 562-4184   SIC 8399
BIRTHRIGHT   p917
777 COXWELL AVE, TORONTO, ON, M4C 3C6

(416) 469-1111 *SIC* 8399
BLOOD TRIBE DEPARTMENT OF HEALTH INC *p166*
MAIN ST, STAND OFF, AB, T0L 1Y0
(403) 737-3888 *SIC* 8399
BOYS AND GIRLS CLUBS FOUNDATION OF SOUTH COAST BC *p288*
2875 ST. GEORGE ST, VANCOUVER, BC, V5T 3R8
(604) 879-6554 *SIC* 8399
BRAIN INJURY COMMUNITY RE-ENTRY (NIAGARA) INC *p907*
3340 SCHMON PKWY UNIT 2, THOROLD, ON, L2V 4Y6
(905) 687-6788 *SIC* 8399
C L S C DU VIEUX LACHINE *p1126*
1900 RUE NOTRE-DAME, LACHINE, QC, H8S 2G2
(514) 639-0650 *SIC* 8399
C L S C LA PETITE PATRIE *p1182*
6520 RUE DE SAINT-VALLIER, MONTREAL, QC, H2S 2P7
(514) 273-4508 *SIC* 8399
CALGARY DROP-IN & REHAB CENTRE SOCIETY *p28*
1 DERMOT BALDWIN WAY SE, CALGARY, AB, T2G 0P8
(403) 266-3600 *SIC* 8399
CALGARY IMMIGRANT WOMEN'S ASSOCIATION *p28*
138 4 AVE SE SUITE 200, CALGARY, AB, T2G 4Z6
(403) 517-8830 *SIC* 8399
CALGARY YOUNG MEN'S CHRISTIAN ASSOCIATION *p68*
11 HADDON RD SW, CALGARY, AB, T2V 2X8
SIC 8399
CALGARY YOUNG MEN'S CHRISTIAN ASSOCIATION, THE *p45*
101 3 ST SW, CALGARY, AB, T2P 4G6
(403) 269-6701 *SIC* 8399
CALGARY YOUNG MEN'S CHRISTIAN ASSOCIATION, THE *p74*
8100 JOHN LAURIE BLVD NW, CALGARY, AB, T3G 3S3
(403) 547-6576 *SIC* 8399
CALGARY YOUNG WOMEN'S CHRISTIAN ASSOCIATION *p28*
1715 17 AVE SE, CALGARY, AB, T2G 5J1
(403) 262-0498 *SIC* 8399
CAMPBELL RIVER AND DISTRICT ASSOCIATION FOR COMMUNITY LIVING *p194*
1153 GREENWOOD ST, CAMPBELL RIVER, BC, V9W 3C5
(250) 287-9731 *SIC* 8399
CANADIAN ASSOCIATES OF THE BEN-GURION UNIVERSITY OF NEGEV INC, THE *p782*
1000 FINCH AVE W SUITE 506, NORTH YORK, ON, M3J 2V5
(416) 665-8054 *SIC* 8399
CANADIAN ASSOCIATION FOR COMMUNITY LIVING *p813*
850 KING ST W UNIT 20, OSHAWA, ON, L1J 8N5
(905) 436-2500 *SIC* 8399
CANADIAN CANCER SOCIETY *p252*
172 2 AVE W, QUALICUM BEACH, BC, V9K 1T7
SIC 8399
CANADIAN CANCER SOCIETY *p926*
55 ST CLAIR AVE W SUITE 500, TORONTO, ON, M4V 2Y7
(416) 961-7223 *SIC* 8399
CANADIAN CANCER SOCIETY *p926*
55 ST CLAIR AVE W SUITE 300, TORONTO, ON, M4V 2Y7
(416) 961-7223 *SIC* 8399
CANADIAN CANCER SOCIETY *p1165*
5151 BOUL DE L'ASSOMPTION, MONTREAL, QC, H1T 4A9
(514) 255-5151 *SIC* 8399
CANADIAN DEAFBLIND ASSOCIATION

ONTARIO CHAPTER *p517*
54 BRANT AVE FL 3, BRANTFORD, ON, N3T 3G8
SIC 8399
CANADIAN FEDERATION OF UNIVERSITY WOMEN *p268*
GD, SALT SPRING ISLAND, BC, V8K 2W1
SIC 8399
CANADIAN MEDIA FUND *p942*
50 WELLINGTON ST E, TORONTO, ON, M5E 1C8
(416) 214-4400 *SIC* 8399
CANADIAN UNICEF COMMITTEE *p924*
2200 YONGE ST SUITE 1100, TORONTO, ON, M4S 2C6
(416) 482-4444 *SIC* 8399
CAPE BRETON ISLAND HOUSING AUTHORITY *p467*
18 DOLBIN ST, SYDNEY, NS, B1P 1S5
(902) 539-8520 *SIC* 8399
CAPE CARE SERVICES (1996) LTD *p466*
4 DRYDEN AVE, SYDNEY, NS, B1N 3K4
(902) 562-2444 *SIC* 8399
CAPITOL HILL COMMUNITY ASSOCIATION *p41*
1531 21 AVE NW, CALGARY, AB, T2M 1L9
(403) 289-0859 *SIC* 8399
CARRIER SEKANI FAMILY SERVICES SOCIETY *p249*
987 4TH AVE, PRINCE GEORGE, BC, V2L 3H7
(250) 562-3591 *SIC* 8399
CATHOLIC FAMILY SERVICES OF HAMILTON *p614*
2B-688 QUEENSDALE AVE E, HAMILTON, ON, L8V 1M1
(905) 527-3823 *SIC* 8399
CATHOLIC SOCIAL SERVICES *p85*
10709 105 ST NW, EDMONTON, AB, T5H 2X3
(780) 424-3545 *SIC* 8399
CENTRAIDE DU GRAND MONTREAL *p1194*
493 RUE SHERBROOKE O, MONTREAL, QC, H3A 1B6
(514) 288-1261 *SIC* 8399
CENTRE D'ACTION DE DEVELOPPEMENT ET DE RECHERCHE EN EMPLOYABILITE *p1132*
1005 RUE D'UPTON, LASALLE, QC, H8R 2V2
(514) 367-3576 *SIC* 8399
CENTRE DE SANTE ET DE SERVICE SOCIAUX DE LA REGION DE THETFORD *p1382*
1717 RUE NOTRE-DAME E, THETFORD MINES, QC, G6G 2V4
(418) 338-7777 *SIC* 8399
CENTRE DE SANTE ET DE SERVICES SOCIAUX DE BEAUCE *p1304*
12523 25E AV, SAINT-GEORGES, QC, G5Y 5N6
(418) 228-2244 *SIC* 8399
CENTRE DE SANTE ET DE SERVICES SOCIAUX DE LA VALLEE-DE-LA-BATISCAN *p1358*
90 RANG RIVIERE VEILLETTE, SAINTE-GENEVIEVE-DE-BATISCAN, QC, G0X 2R0
(418) 362-2727 *SIC* 8399
CENTRE DE SANTE ET DE SERVICES SOCIAUX DE LAVAL *p1241*
800 BOUL CHOMEDEY BUREAU 200, MONTREAL-OUEST, QC, H7V 3Y4
(450) 682-2952 *SIC* 8399
CENTRE DE SANTE ET DE SERVICES SOCIAUX DE QUEBEC-NORD *p1275*
11999 RUE DE L'HOPITAL BUREAU 217, QUEBEC, QC, G2A 2T7
(418) 843-2572 *SIC* 8399
CENTRE FOR AFFORDABLE WATER AND SANITATION TECHNOLOGY (CAWST) *p34*
6020 2 ST SE UNIT B12, CALGARY, AB, T2H 2L8
(403) 243-3285 *SIC* 8399
CENTRE INTEGRE DE SANTE ET DE SERVICES SOCIAUX DU BAS-SAINT-LAURENT

p1284
355 BOUL SAINT-GERMAIN, RIMOUSKI, QC, G5L 3N2
(418) 724-3000 *SIC* 8399
CENTRE LOCAL DES SERVICES COMMUNAUTAIRES KATERI INC *p1072*
90 BOUL MARIE-VICTORIN, CANDIAC, QC, J5R 1C1
(450) 659-7661 *SIC* 8399
CENTRE LOCAL DES SERVICES COMMUNAUTAIRES LE NOROIS *p1045*
100 RUE SAINT-JOSEPH, ALMA, QC, G8B 7A6
(418) 668-4563 *SIC* 8399
CEREBRAL PALSY PARENT COUNCIL OF TORONTO *p678*
379 CHURCH ST SUITE 402, MARKHAM, ON, L6B 0T1
(905) 513-2756 *SIC* 8399
CFB ESQUIMALT MILITARY FAMILY RESOURCE CENTRE *p339*
1505 ESQUIMALT RD, VICTORIA, BC, V9A 7N2
(250) 363-8628 *SIC* 8399
CHILDREN'S AID SOCIETY OF THE COUNTY OF LANARK AND THE TOWN OF SMITHS FALLS, THE *p839*
8 HERRIOTT ST, PERTH, ON, K7H 1S9
(613) 264-9991 *SIC* 8399
CHILDREN'S AID SOCIETY OF THE REGION OF PEEL, THE *p709*
101 QUEENSWAY W SUITE 500, MISSISSAUGA, ON, L5B 2P7
SIC 8399
CHILDREN'S FOUNDATION, THE *p286*
2750 18TH AVE E, VANCOUVER, BC, V5M 4W8
(604) 434-9101 *SIC* 8399
CITY OF CALGARY, THE *p28*
315 10 AVE SE SUITE 101, CALGARY, AB, T2G 0W2
(403) 268-5153 *SIC* 8399
CLSC DE BELLECHASSE SOCIAL *p1343*
100A RUE MONSEIGNEUR-BILODEAU, SAINT-LAZARE-DE-BELLECHASSE, QC, G0R 3J0
(418) 883-2227 *SIC* 8399
CLSC DE SAINT-MICHEL *p1169*
3355 RUE JARRY E, MONTREAL, QC, H1Z 2E5
(514) 374-8223 *SIC* 8399
CLSC SIMONNE-MONET-CHARTRAND *p1145*
1303 BOUL JACQUES-CARTIER E, LONGUEUIL, QC, J4M 2Y8
(450) 463-2850 *SIC* 8399
COCHRANE DISTRICT SOCIAL SERVICES ADMINISTRATION BOARD *p912*
500 ALGONQUIN BLVD E, TIMMINS, ON, P4N 1B7
(705) 268-7722 *SIC* 8399
COLLINGWOOD NEIGHBOURHOOD HOUSE SOCIETY *p288*
5288 JOYCE ST, VANCOUVER, BC, V5R 6C9
(604) 435-0323 *SIC* 8399
COMMISSION DE LA SANTE ET DES SERVICES SOCIAUX PREMIERE NATION DU QUEBEC ET DU LABRADOR *p1401*
250 RUE CHEF-MICHEL-LAVEAU, WENDAKE, QC, G0A 4V0
(418) 842-1540 *SIC* 8399
COMMUNITY & PRIMARY HEALTH CARE-LANARK, LEEDS & GRENVILLE *p519*
2235 PARKEDALE AVE, BROCKVILLE, ON, K6V 6B2
(613) 342-1747 *SIC* 8399
COMMUNITY EDUCATION NETWORK INC *p434*
31 GALLANT ST, STEPHENVILLE, NL, A2N 2B5
(709) 643-4891 *SIC* 8399
COMMUNITY LIVING ACCESS SUPPORT SERVICES *p880*

89 CULVER ST, SIMCOE, ON, N3Y 2V5
(519) 426-0007 *SIC* 8399
COMMUNITY LIVING KIRKLAND LAKE *p634*
51 GOVERNMENT RD W, KIRKLAND LAKE, ON, P2N 2E5
(705) 567-9331 *SIC* 8399
COMMUNITY LIVING NEWMARKET/AURORA DISTRICT *p755*
195 HARRY WALKER PKY N, NEWMARKET, ON, L3Y 7B3
(905) 773-6346 *SIC* 8399
COMMUNITY LIVING OAKVILLE *p802*
301 WYECROFT RD, OAKVILLE, ON, L6K 2H2
(905) 844-0146 *SIC* 8399
COMMUNITY LIVING OWEN SOUND AND DISTRICT *p835*
769 4TH AVE E, OWEN SOUND, ON, N4K 2N5
(519) 371-9251 *SIC* 8399
COMMUNITY LIVING PARRY SOUND *p837*
38 JOSEPH ST, PARRY SOUND, ON, P2A 2G5
(705) 746-9330 *SIC* 8399
COMMUNITY LIVING RENFREW COUNTY SOUTH *p849*
326 RAGLAN ST S, RENFREW, ON, K7V 1R5
(613) 432-6763 *SIC* 8399
COMMUNITY RESPITE SERVICE *p380*
1155 NOTRE DAME AVE, WINNIPEG, MB, R3E 3G1
(204) 953-2400 *SIC* 8399
CONSUMER/SURVIVOR BUSINESS COUNCIL OF ONTARIO *p994*
1499 QUEEN ST W SUITE 203, TORONTO, ON, M6R 1A3
(416) 504-1693 *SIC* 8399
COOPERATIVE DE SERVICES A DOMICILE BEAUCE-NORD *p1321*
700 AV ROBERT-CLICHE, SAINT-JOSEPH-DE-BEAUCE, QC, G0S 2V0
(418) 397-8283 *SIC* 8399
CORPORATION COMPAGNONS DE MONTREAL *p1168*
2602 BEAUBIEN E, MONTREAL, QC, H1Y 1G5
(514) 727-4444 *SIC* 8399
CORPORATION LEEDS GRENVILLE & LANARK DISTRICT HEALTH UNIT, THE *p519*
458 LAURIER BLVD SUITE 200, BROCKVILLE, ON, K6V 7K5
(613) 345-5685 *SIC* 8399
COVENANT HOUSE VANCOUVER *p298*
326 PENDER ST W, VANCOUVER, BC, V6B 1T1
(604) 647-4480 *SIC* 8399
CRESTON VALLEY GLEANERS SOCIETY *p204*
807 CANYON ST, CRESTON, BC, V0B 1G3
(250) 428-4106 *SIC* 8399
CRISIS CENTRE NORTH BAY *p763*
198 SECOND AVE W, NORTH BAY, ON, P1B 3K9
SIC 8399
CROHN'S AND COLITIS CANADA *p925*
60 ST CLAIR AVE E SUITE 600, TORONTO, ON, M4T 1N5
(416) 920-5035 *SIC* 8399
DILICO ANISHINABEK FAMILY CARE *p592*
200 ANEMKI PL SUITE 1, FORT WILLIAM FIRST NATION, ON, P7J 1L6
(807) 623-8511 *SIC* 8399
DISTRICT OF NIPPISSING SOCIAL SERVICES ADMINISTRATION BOARD *p763*
200 MCINTYRE ST E, NORTH BAY, ON, P1B 8V6
(705) 474-2151 *SIC* 8399
DIVERSECITY COMMUNITY RESOURCES SOCIETY *p276*
13455 76 AVE, SURREY, BC, V3W 2W3
(604) 597-0205 *SIC* 8399
DURHAM MENTAL HEALTH SERVICES

921 QUEEN ELIZABETH WAY II SUITE 301, IQALUIT, NU, X0A 0H0

(867) 975-4900   *SIC 8399*

NURSING & HOMEMAKERS INC   *p875*
2347 KENNEDY RD SUITE 204, SCARBOROUGH, ON, M1T 3T8

(416) 754-0700   *SIC 8399*

ONTARIO LUNG ASSOCIATION   *p916*
18 WYNFORD DR SUITE 401, TORONTO, ON, M3C 0K8

(416) 864-9911   *SIC 8399*

OPTIONS NORTHWEST PERSONAL SUPPORT SERVICES   *p907*
95 CUMBERLAND ST N, THUNDER BAY, ON, P7A 4M1

(807) 344-4994   *SIC 8399*

OSBORNE HOUSE INC   *p379*
GD, WINNIPEG, MB, R3C 2H6

(204) 942-7373   *SIC 8399*

OTTAWA FOOD BANK, THE   *p595*
1317 MICHAEL ST, GLOUCESTER, ON, K1B 3M9

(613) 745-7001   *SIC 8399*

OXFAM CANADA   *p820*
39 MCARTHUR AVE, OTTAWA, ON, K1L 8L7

(613) 237-5236   *SIC 8399*

PACE INDEPENDENT LIVING   *p789*
970 LAWRENCE AVE W SUITE 210, NORTH YORK, ON, M6A 3B6

(416) 789-7806   *SIC 8399*

PACIFIC LEGAL EDUCATION ASSOCIATION   *p287*
3894 COMMERCIAL ST, VANCOUVER, BC, V5N 4G2

(604) 871-0450   *SIC 8399*

PARENTS FOR COMMUNITY LIVING KITCHENER WATERLOO INC   *p640*
82 WEBER ST E, KITCHENER, ON, N2H 1C7

(519) 742-5849   *SIC 8399*

PARRY SOUND DISTRICT SOCIAL SERVICES ADMINISTRATION BOARD, THE   *p837*
1 BEECHWOOD DR, PARRY SOUND, ON, P2A 1J2

(705) 746-7777   *SIC 8399*

PARTAGE VANIER FOOD BANK   *p1001*
161 MARIER AVE, VANIER, ON, K1L 5R8

(613) 747-2839   *SIC 8399*

PARTICIPATION HOUSE PROJECT (DURHAM REGION), THE   *p814*
1255 TERWILLEGAR AVE UNIT 9, OSHAWA, ON, L1J 7A4

(905) 579-5267   *SIC 8399*

PARTICIPATION HOUSE SUPPORT SERVICES - LONDON AND AREA   *p656*
633 COLBORNE ST SUITE 101, LONDON, ON, N6B 2V3

(519) 660-6635   *SIC 8399*

PATHWAYS TO INDEPENDENCE   *p491*
289 PINNACLE ST, BELLEVILLE, ON, K8N 3B3

(613) 962-2541   *SIC 8399*

PENTICTON & DISTRICT COMMUNITY RESOURCES SOCIETY   *p244*
330 ELLIS ST, PENTICTON, BC, V2A 4L7

(250) 492-5814   *SIC 8399*

PRINCESS MARGARET CANCER FOUNDATION, THE   *p947*
700 UNIVERSITY AVE 10TH FLOOR, TORONTO, ON, M5G 1Z5

(416) 946-6560   *SIC 8399*

PROGRESSIVE ALTERNATIVES SOCIETY OF CALGARY   *p31*
4014 MACLEOD TRAIL SE SUITE 211, CALGARY, AB, T2G 2R7

(403) 262-8515   *SIC 8399*

PROVINCIAL HEALTH SERVICES AUTHORITY   *p333*
2410 LEE AVE, VICTORIA, BC, V8R 6V5

(250) 519-5500   *SIC 8399*

PULAARVIK KABLU FRIENDSHIP CENTRE   *p472*

GD, RANKIN INLET, NU, X0C 0G0

(867) 645-2600   *SIC 8399*

QUEBEC EN FORME   *p1322*
668 AV VICTORIA, SAINT-LAMBERT, QC, J4P 2J6

SIC 8399

QUEEN ELIZABETH II HEALTH SCIENCES CENTRE FOUNDATION   *p454*
5657 SPRING GARDEN RD SUITE 3005, HALIFAX, NS, B3J 3R4

(902) 334-1546   *SIC 8399*

REGINA RESIDENTIAL RESOURCE CENTRE   *p1416*
1047 WADEY DR, REGINA, SK, S4N 7J6

(306) 352-3223   *SIC 8399*

RELANCE OUTAOUAIS INC, LA   *p1105*
45 BOUL SACRE-COEUR, GATINEAU, QC, J8X 1C6

(819) 776-5870   *SIC 8399*

RELANCE OUTAOUAIS INC, LA   *p1105*
270 BOUL DES ALLUMETTIERES, GATINEAU, QC, J8X 1N3

(819) 770-5325   *SIC 8399*

ROCKLAND HELP CENTRE   *p857*
2815 CHAMBERLAND ST, ROCKLAND, ON, K4K 1M7

(613) 446-7594   *SIC 8399*

ROCKY SUPPORT SERVICES SOCIETY   *p159*
4940 50 AVE, ROCKY MOUNTAIN HOUSE, AB, T4T 1A8

(403) 845-4080   *SIC 8399*

ROSALIE HALL   *p872*
3020 LAWRENCE AVE E, SCARBOROUGH, ON, M1P 2T7

(416) 438-6880   *SIC 8399*

ROTARY CLUB OF VANCOUVER   *p309*
475 HOWE ST SUITE 315, VANCOUVER, BC, V6C 2B3

(604) 685-0481   *SIC 8399*

S O S CHILDREN'S VILLAGE SOCIETY *p266*
3800 MONCTON ST, RICHMOND, BC, V7E 3A6

(604) 274-8866   *SIC 8399*

S.O.S. DEPANNAGE GRANBY ET REGION INC   *p1109*
327 RUE MATTON, GRANBY, QC, J2G 7R1

(450) 378-4208   *SIC 8399*

S.U.C.C.E.S.S. (ALSO KNOWN AS UNITED CHINESE COMMUNITY ENRICHMENT SERVICES SOCIETY)   *p300*
28 PENDER ST W, VANCOUVER, BC, V6B 1R6

(604) 684-1628   *SIC 8399*

SAVE THE CHILDREN CANADA   *p774*
4141 YONGE ST SUITE 300, NORTH YORK, ON, M2P 2A8

(416) 221-5501   *SIC 8399*

SCOUTS FRANCOPHONES DIST. DE   *p900*
30 STE. ANNE RD, SUDBURY, ON, P3C 5E1

(705) 560-4499   *SIC 8399*

SOCIETE DE GESTION DU FONDS POUR LE DEVELOPPEMENT DES JEUNES ENFANTS   *p1223*
4720 RUE DAGENAIS BUREAU 117, MONTREAL, QC, H4C 1L7

(514) 526-2187   *SIC 8399*

SOUTH COCHRANE CHILD AND YOUTH SERVICE INCORPORATED   *p680*
507 EIGTH AVE SUITE 15, MATHESON, ON, P0K 1N0

(705) 273-3041   *SIC 8399*

SOUTH PEACE COMMUNITY RESOURCES SOCIETY   *p205*
10110 13 ST, DAWSON CREEK, BC, V1G 3W2

(250) 782-9174   *SIC 8399*

SOUTHEAST RESOURCE DEVELOPMENT COUNCIL CORP   *p379*
360 BROADWAY, WINNIPEG, MB, R3C 0T6

(204) 956-7500   *SIC 8399*

ST CLAIR WEST SERVICES FOR SENIORS *p993*

2562 EGLINTON AVE W SUITE 202, TORONTO, ON, M6M 1T4

(416) 787-2114   *SIC 8399*

ST JOHN'S NATIVE FRIENDSHIP CENTRE ASSOCIATION   *p433*
716 WATER ST, ST. JOHN'S, NL, A1E 1C1

(709) 726-5902   *SIC 8399*

ST STEPHENS COMMUNITY HOUSE   *p977*
91 BELLEVUE AVE, TORONTO, ON, M5T 2N8

(416) 925-2103   *SIC 8399*

ST VINCENT DE PAUL SOCIETY   *p936*
240 CHURCH ST, TORONTO, ON, M5B 1Z2

(416) 364-5577   *SIC 8399*

STAFF OF THE NON-PUBLIC FUNDS, CANADIAN FORCES   *p815*
101 COLONEL BY DR, OTTAWA, ON, K1A 0K2

(613) 995-8509   *SIC 8399*

STELMASCHUK, W. J. AND ASSOCIATES LTD   *p231*
22470 DEWDNEY TRUNK RD SUITE 510, MAPLE RIDGE, BC, V2X 5Z6

SIC 8399

STOREFRONT HUMBER INCORPORATED *p571*
2445 LAKE SHORE BLVD W, ETOBICOKE, ON, M8V 1C5

(416) 259-4207   *SIC 8399*

SURREY PLACE CENTRE   *p976*
2 SURREY PL, TORONTO, ON, M5S 2C2

(416) 925-5141   *SIC 8399*

TILLSONBURG & DISTRICT MULTISERVICE CENTRE INC   *p912*
96 TILLSON AVE, TILLSONBURG, ON, N4G 3A1

(519) 842-9000   *SIC 8399*

TORONTO ARTSCAPE INC   *p992*
171 EAST LIBERTY ST SUITE 224, TORONTO, ON, M6K 3P6

(416) 392-1038   *SIC 8399*

TRI-COUNTY COMMUNITY SUPPORT SERVICES   *p840*
349A GEORGE ST N UNIT 303, PETERBOROUGH, ON, K9H 3P9

(705) 876-9245   *SIC 8399*

UNION MISSION FOR MEN, THE   *p822*
35 WALLER ST, OTTAWA, ON, K1N 7G4

(613) 234-1144   *SIC 8399*

UNION OF ONTARIO INDIANS   *p564*
1024 MISSISSAUGA RD, CURVE LAKE, ON, K0L 1R0

(705) 657-9383   *SIC 8399*

UNITED WAY OF WINNIPEG   *p376*
580 MAIN ST, WINNIPEG, MB, R3B 1C7

(204) 477-5360   *SIC 8399*

UNIVERSITY OF VICTORIA STUDENTS' SOCIETY   *p333*
3800 FINNERTY RD RM B128, VICTORIA, BC, V8P 5C2

(250) 472-4317   *SIC 8399*

VENTUREKIDS TECH ORGANIZATION *p971*
30 WELLINGTON ST W 5TH FL, TORONTO, ON, M5L 1E2

(416) 985-6839   *SIC 8399*

VICTORIA COOL AID SOCIETY, THE   *p337*
749 PANDORA AVE SUITE 102, VICTORIA, BC, V8W 1N9

(250) 380-2663   *SIC 8399*

VICTORIA WOMEN IN NEED SOCIETY *p337*
785 PANDORA AVE, VICTORIA, BC, V8W 1N9

(250) 480-4006   *SIC 8399*

VON CANADA FOUNDATION   *p611*
414 VICTORIA AVE N SUITE 568, HAMILTON, ON, L8L 5G8

(905) 529-0700   *SIC 8399*

WATERLOO WELLINGTON LOCAL HEALTH INTEGRATION NETWORK *p1007*
141 WEBER ST S, WATERLOO, ON, N2J 2A9

(519) 748-2222   *SIC 8399*

WEECHI - IT - TE - WIN FAMILY SERVICES INC   *p592*

1450 IDYLWYLD DR, FORT FRANCES, ON, P9A 3M3

(807) 274-3201   *SIC 8399*

WELLAND ASSOCIATION FOR COMMUNITY LIVING   *p1012*
535 SUTHERLAND AVE, WELLAND, ON, L3B 5A4

(905) 735-0081   *SIC 8399*

WEST REGION CHILD AND FAMILY SERVICES COMMITTEE INCORPORATED *p349*
GD, ERICKSON, MB, R0J 0P0

(204) 636-6100   *SIC 8399*

WINDSOR-ESSEX CHILDREN'S AID SOCIETY   *p861*
161 KENDALL ST, SARNIA, ON, N7V 4G6

(519) 336-0623   *SIC 8399*

WOODGREEN COMMUNITY SERVICES *p919*
815 DANFORTH AVE SUITE 100, TORONTO, ON, M4J 1L2

(416) 645-6000   *SIC 8399*

YMCA DU QUEBEC, LES   *p1214*
1435 RUE DRUMMOND BUREAU 4E, MONTREAL, QC, H3G 1W4

(514) 849-5331   *SIC 8399*

YMCA DU QUEBEC, LES   *p1253*
230 BOUL BRUNSWICK, POINTE-CLAIRE, QC, H9R 5N5

(514) 630-9622   *SIC 8399*

YMCA OF GREATER VANCOUVER, THE *p288*
5055 JOYCE ST SUITE 300, VANCOUVER, BC, V5R 6B2

(604) 681-9622   *SIC 8399*

YOR-SUP-NET SUPPORT SERVICE NETWORK   *p757*
102 MAIN ST S UNIT 3, NEWMARKET, ON, L3Y 3Y7

(905) 898-3721   *SIC 8399*

YOUNG WOMEN'S CHRISTIAN ASSOCIATION OF CANADA, THE   *p91*
10080 JASPER AVE NW SUITE 400, EDMONTON, AB, T5J 1V9

(780) 423-9922   *SIC 8399*

YOUNG WOMEN'S CHRISTIAN ASSOCIATION OF GREATER TORONTO   *p926*
80 WOODLAWN AVE E, TORONTO, ON, M4T 1C1

(416) 923-8454   *SIC 8399*

YOUNG WOMEN'S CHRISTIAN ASSOCIATION OF PETERBOROUGH, VICTORIA & HALIBURTON   *p840*
216 SIMCOE ST, PETERBOROUGH, ON, K9H 2H7

(705) 743-3526   *SIC 8399*

YOUTH PROTECTION   *p1391*
700 BOUL FOREST, VAL-D'OR, QC, J9P 2L3

(819) 825-0002   *SIC 8399*

SIC 8412 Museums and art galleries

ART GALLERY OF ONTARIO   *p977*
317 DUNDAS ST W SUITE 535, TORONTO, ON, M5T 1G4

(416) 977-0414   *SIC 8412*

CALGARY SCIENCE CENTRE SOCIETY *p21*
220 ST GEORGES DR NE, CALGARY, AB, T2E 5T2

(403) 817-6800   *SIC 8412*

CANADA SCIENCE AND TECHNOLOGY MUSEUMS CORPORATION   *p817*
2421 LANCASTER RD, OTTAWA, ON, K1G 5A3

(613) 991-3044   *SIC 8412*

CANADIAN MUSEUM OF NATURE   *p833*
240 MCLEOD ST, OTTAWA, ON, K2P 2R1

(613) 566-4700   *SIC 8412*

CENTENNIAL CENTRE OF SCIENCE AND TECHNOLOGY   *p779*
770 DON MILLS RD, NORTH YORK, ON, M3C 1T3

(416) 429-4100   *SIC 8412*

CENTRE CANADIEN D'ARCHITECURE *p1214*
1920 RUE BAILE, MONTREAL, QC, H3H 2S6
(514) 939-7028   *SIC 8412*

CORPORATION DU PARC REGIONAL DE VAL-JALBERT
95 RUE SAINT-GEORGES, CHAMBORD, QC, G0W 1G0
(418) 275-3132   *SIC 8412*

EDMONTON SPACE & SCIENCE FOUNDATION *p95*
11211 142 ST NW, EDMONTON, AB, T5M 4A1
(780) 452-9100   *SIC 8412*

GLENBOW-ALBERTA INSTITUTE *p30*
130 9 AVE SE, CALGARY, AB, T2G 0P3
(403) 268-4100   *SIC 8412*

GOUVERNEMENT DE LA PROVINCE DE QUEBEC *p1108*
100 RUE LAURIER, GATINEAU, QC, K1A 0M8
(819) 776-7000   *SIC 8412*

GOUVERNEMENT DE LA PROVINCE DE QUEBEC *p1269*
179 RUE GRANDE ALLEE O, QUEBEC, QC, G1R 2H1
(418) 643-2150   *SIC 8412*

HERITAGE PARK SOCIETY *p68*
1900 HERITAGE DR SW, CALGARY, AB, T2V 2X3
(403) 268-8526   *SIC 8412*

HOCKEY HALL OF FAME AND MUSEUM *p942*
30 YONGE ST, TORONTO, ON, M5E 1X8
(416) 360-7735   *SIC 8412*

MCMICHAEL CANADIAN ART COLLECTION *p642*
10365 ISLINGTON AVE, KLEINBURG, ON, L0J 1C0
(905) 893-1121   *SIC 8412*

MUSEE CANADIEN DE L'HISTOIRE *p1108*
100 RUE LAURIER, GATINEAU, QC, K1A 0M8
(819) 776-7000   *SIC 8412*

MUSEE D'ART CONTEMPORAIN DE MONTREAL *p1186*
185 RUE SAINTE-CATHERINE O, MONTREAL, QC, H2X 3X5
(514) 847-6226   *SIC 8412*

MUSEE DE LA CIVILISATION *p1259*
85 RUE DALHOUSIE, QUEBEC, QC, G1K 8R2
(418) 643-2158   *SIC 8412*

MUSEE DES BEAUX-ARTS DE MONTREAL *p1213*
1380 RUE SHERBROOKE O, MONTREAL, QC, H3G 1J5
(514) 285-2000   *SIC 8412*

MUSEE DES BEAUX-ARTS DE MONTREAL *p1214*
1379 RUE SHERBROOKE O, MONTREAL, QC, H3G 1J5
(514) 285-1600   *SIC 8412*

NATIONAL GALLERY OF CANADA *p821*
380 SUSSEX DR, OTTAWA, ON, K1N 9N4
(613) 990-1985   *SIC 8412*

PATTISON, JIM ENTERTAINMENT LTD *p308*
1067 CORDOVA ST W SUITE 1800, VANCOUVER, BC, V6C 1C7
(604) 688-6764   *SIC 8412*

ROYAL ONTARIO MUSEUM, THE *p976*
100 QUEEN'S PK, TORONTO, ON, M5S 2C6
(416) 586-8000   *SIC 8412*

SHERBROOKE RESTORATION COMMISSION *p466*
42 MAIN ST, SHERBROOKE, NS, B0J 3C0
(902) 522-2400   *SIC 8412*

TORONTO AND REGION CONSERVATION AUTHORITY *p784*
1000 MURRAY ROSS PKY, NORTH YORK, ON, M3J 2P3
(416) 736-1740   *SIC 8412*

VANCOUVER ART GALLERY ASSOCIATION, THE *p327*
750 HORNBY ST, VANCOUVER, BC, V6Z 2H7
(604) 662-4700   *SIC 8412*

VILLAGE QUEBECOIS D'ANTAN, LE *p1100*
1425 RUE MONTPLAISIR, DRUMMONDVILLE, QC, J2C 0M2
(819) 478-1441   *SIC 8412*

SIC 8422 Botanical and zoological gardens

BUTCHART GARDENS LTD, THE *p180*
800 BENVENUTO AVE, BRENTWOOD BAY, BC, V8M 1J8
(250) 652-5256   *SIC 8422*

OCEAN WISE CONSERVATION ASSOCIATION *p318*
845 STANLEY PARK DR, VANCOUVER, BC, V6G 3E2
(604) 659-3400   *SIC 8422*

VANCOUVER, CITY OF *p323*
5251 OAK ST, VANCOUVER, BC, V6M 4H1
(604) 257-8666   *SIC 8422*

ZENABIS GLOBAL INC *p281*
1688 152 ST SUITE 205, SURREY, BC, V4A 4N2
(604) 888-0420   *SIC 8422*

SIC 8611 Business associations

9102-7045 QUEBEC INC *p1142*
365 RUE SAINT-JEAN BUREAU 212, LONGUEUIL, QC, J4H 2X7
(450) 465-0441   *SIC 8611*

ACHIEVING EXCELLENCE *p7*
120 3 ST W, BROOKS, AB, T1R 0S3
(403) 362-6661   *SIC 8611*

ALBERTA CONSERVATION ASSOCIATION *p161*
9 CHIPPEWA RD SUITE 101, SHERWOOD PARK, AB, T8A 6J7
(780) 410-1999   *SIC 8611*

ALBERTA HOTEL & LODGING ASSOCIATION *p125*
2707 ELLWOOD DR SW, EDMONTON, AB, T6X 0P7
(780) 436-6112   *SIC 8611*

ALBERTA MILK *p125*
1303 91 ST SW, EDMONTON, AB, T6X 1H1
(780) 453-5942   *SIC 8611*

ALLIANCES DES MANUFACTURIERS ET DES EXPORTATEURS DU CANADA *p729*
55 STANDISH CRT SUITE 620, MISSISSAUGA, ON, L5R 4B2
(905) 672-3466   *SIC 8611*

ARCANE HORIZON INC *p383*
1313 BORDER ST UNIT 62, WINNIPEG, MB, R3H 0X4
(204) 897-5482   *SIC 8611*

ASSOCIATION DU TRANSPORT AERIEN INTERNATIONAL (IATA) *p1229*
800 RUE DU SQUARE-VICTORIA BUREAU 1538, MONTREAL, QC, H4Z 1A1
(514) 874-0202   *SIC 8611*

ASSOCIATION PROVINCIALE DES CONSTRUCTEURS D'HABITATIONS DU QUEBEC INC *p1051*
5930 BOUL LOUIS-H.-LAFONTAINE, ANJOU, QC, H1M 1S7
(514) 353-9960   *SIC 8611*

AUTISME ET TROUBLES ENVAHISSANTS DU DEVELOPPEMENT MONTR AL *p1173*
4450 RUE SAINT-HUBERT BUREAU 320, MONTREAL, QC, H2J 2W9
(514) 524-6114   *SIC 8611*

AZ GROUP *p1035*
847 BERKSHIRE DR, WOODSTOCK, ON, N4S 8R6
(519) 421-2423   *SIC 8611*

BUILDING INDUSTRY AND LAND DEVELOPMENT ASSOCIATION *p775*

20 UPJOHN RD SUITE 100, NORTH YORK, ON, M3B 2V9
(416) 391-3445   *SIC 8611*

CALGARY CHAMBER OF COMMERCE *p27*
237 8 AVE SE SUITE 600, CALGARY, AB, T2G 5C3
(403) 750-0400   *SIC 8611*

CALGARY REAL ESTATE BOARD CO-OPERATIVE LIMITED *p21*
300 MANNING RD NE, CALGARY, AB, T2E 8K4
(403) 263-4940   *SIC 8611*

CANADA GREEN BUILDING COUNCIL *p821*
47 CLARENCE ST SUITE 202, OTTAWA, ON, K1N 9K1
(613) 288-8097   *SIC 8611*

CANADIAN ASSOCIATION OF PETROLEUM PRODUCERS *p45*
350 7 AVE SW SUITE 2100, CALGARY, AB, T2P 3N9
(403) 267-1100   *SIC 8611*

CANADIAN BANKERS ASSOCIATION, THE *p971*
199 BAY ST 30TH FL, TORONTO, ON, M5L 1G2
(416) 362-6092   *SIC 8611*

CANADIAN CANOLA GROWERS ASSOCIATION *p385*
1661 PORTAGE AVE SUITE 400, WINNIPEG, MB, R3J 3T7
(204) 788-0090   *SIC 8611*

CANADIAN FEDERATION OF INDEPENDENT BUSINESS *p773*
4141 YONGE ST SUITE 401, NORTH YORK, ON, M2P 2A8
(416) 222-8022   *SIC 8611*

CANADIAN LIFE AND HEALTH INSURANCE ASSOCIATION INC *p969*
79 WELLINGTON ST W SUITE 2300, TORONTO, ON, M5K 1G8
(416) 777-2221   *SIC 8611*

CANADIAN MARKETING ASSOCIATION *p960*
55 UNIVERSITY AVE SUITE 603, TORONTO, ON, M5J 2H7
(416) 391-2362   *SIC 8611*

CANADIAN PAYROLL ASSOCIATION, THE *p928*
250 BLOOR ST E SUITE 1600, TORONTO, ON, M4W 1E6
(416) 487-3380   *SIC 8611*

CANADIAN REAL ESTATE ASSOCIATION, THE *p833*
200 CATHERINE ST 6H FL, OTTAWA, ON, K2P 2K9
(613) 237-7111   *SIC 8611*

CAW COMMUNITY CHILD CARE AND DEVELOPMENTAL SERVICES INC *p1019*
3450 YPRES AVE SUITE 100, WINDSOR, ON, N8W 5K9
SIC 8611

CAW LOCAL 542 *p486*
26 LORENA ST, BARRIE, ON, L4N 4P4
(705) 739-3532   *SIC 8611*

CENTRAL NOVA SCOTIA CIVIC CENTER SOCIETY *p468*
625 ABENAKI RD, TRURO, NS, B2N 0G6
(902) 893-2224   *SIC 8611*

CENTRE DE SANTE & DE SERVICES SOCIAUX DE MATANE *p1150*
349 AV SAINT-JEROME, MATANE, QC, G4W 3A8
(418) 562-5741   *SIC 8611*

CHAMBRE DE COMMERCE DU MONTREAL METROPOLITAIN *p1187*
380 RUE SAINT-ANTOINE O BUREAU 6000, MONTREAL, QC, H2Y 3X7
(514) 871-4000   *SIC 8611*

CHAMBRE IMMOBILIERE DU GRAND MONTREAL *p1396*
600 CH DU GOLF, VERDUN, QC, H3E 1A8
(514) 762-2440   *SIC 8611*

CHRISTIAN LABOUR ASSOCIATION OF CANADA *p105*

14920 118 AVE NW, EDMONTON, AB, T5V 1B8
(780) 454-6181   *SIC 8611*

COLLIERS MACAULAY NICOLLS INC *p961*
181 BAY ST UNIT 1400, TORONTO, ON, M5J 2V1
(416) 777-2200   *SIC 8611*

COMMISSION DE LA CONSTRUCTION DU QUEBEC *p1176*
1201 BOUL CREMAZIE E, MONTREAL, QC, H2M 0A6
(514) 593-3121   *SIC 8611*

COMMISSION DE LA CONSTRUCTION DU QUEBEC *p1176*
8485 AV CHRISTOPHE-COLOMB, MONTREAL, QC, H2M 0A7
(514) 341-7740   *SIC 8611*

COMMUNITECH CORPORATION *p638*
151 CHARLES ST W SUITE 100, KITCHENER, ON, N2G 1H6
(519) 888-9944   *SIC 8611*

CONSTRUCTION SAFETY ASSOCIATION OF ONTARIO *p583*
21 VOYAGER CRT S, ETOBICOKE, ON, M9W 5M7
SIC 8611

CREDIT UNION CENTRAL OF MANITOBA LIMITED *p374*
317 DONALD ST SUITE 400, WINNIPEG, MB, R3B 2H6
(204) 985-4700   *SIC 8611*

DAIRY FARMERS OF CANADA *p833*
21 FLORENCE ST, OTTAWA, ON, K2P 0W6
(613) 236-9997   *SIC 8611*

DAIRY FARMERS OF ONTARIO *p721*
6780 CAMPOBELLO RD, MISSISSAUGA, ON, L5N 2L8
(905) 821-8970   *SIC 8611*

DISTRICT OF TIMISKAMING SOCIAL SERVICES ADMINISTRATION BOARD *p634*
29 DUNCAN AVE S, KIRKLAND LAKE, ON, P2N 1X5
(705) 567-9366   *SIC 8611*

DOWNTOWN WATCH *p377*
426 PORTAGE AVE SUITE 101, WINNIPEG, MB, R3C 0C9
(204) 958-4620   *SIC 8611*

EDMONTON REAL ESTATE BOARD CO-OPERATIVE LISTING BUREAU LIMITED *p95*
14220 112 AVE NW, EDMONTON, AB, T5M 2T8
(780) 451-6666   *SIC 8611*

ELECTRICITY DISTRIBUTORS ASSOCIATION *p1031*
3700 STEELES AVE W SUITE 1100, WOODBRIDGE, ON, L4L 8K8
(905) 265-5300   *SIC 8611*

ENERCARE CONNECTIONS INC *p765*
4000 VICTORIA PARK AVE, NORTH YORK, ON, M2H 3P4
(416) 649-1900   *SIC 8611*

FEDERATION OF CANADIAN MUNICIPALITIES *p821*
24 CLARENCE ST SUITE 2, OTTAWA, ON, K1N 5P3
(613) 482-8004   *SIC 8611*

FINANCIAL ADVISORS ASSOCIATION OF CANADA, THE *p980*
10 LOWER SPADINA AVE SUITE 600, TORONTO, ON, M5V 2Z2
(416) 444-5251   *SIC 8611*

GLENDALE GLENDALE MEADOWS COMMUNITY ASSOCIATION *p73*
2405 GLENMOUNT DR SW, CALGARY, AB, T3E 4C1
(403) 242-2110   *SIC 8611*

GOLDEN TEACHERS ASSOCIATION *p215*
912 11TH AVE S, GOLDEN, BC, V0A 1H0
SIC 8611

GREATER VICTORIA VISITORS & CONVENTION BUREAU *p336*
31 BASTION SQ, VICTORIA, BC, V8W 1J1
(250) 414-6999   *SIC 8611*

GS1 CANADA *p776*

1500 DON MILLS RD SUITE 800, NORTH YORK, ON, M3B 3K4

(416) 510-8039 *SIC 8611*

GUELPH, CITY OF *p603*
19 NORTHUMBERLAND ST, GUELPH, ON, N1H 3A6

(519) 837-5618 *SIC 8611*

HALDIMAND-NORFOLK COMMUNITY SENIOR SUPPORT SERVICES INC *p881*
230 VICTORIA ST, SIMCOE, ON, N3Y 4K2

(519) 426-6060 *SIC 8611*

HAMLET OF RANKIN *p472*
GD, RANKIN INLET, NU, X0C 0G0

(867) 645-2895 *SIC 8611*

HOLSTEIN ASSOCIATION OF CANADA, THE *p514*
20 CORPORATE PL, BRANTFORD, ON, N3R 8A6

(519) 756-8300 *SIC 8611*

INFRASTRUCTURE HEALTH AND SAFETY ASSOCIATION *p696*
5110 CREEKBANK RD SUITE 400, MISSISSAUGA, ON, L4W 0A1

(416) 674-2726 *SIC 8611*

INVESTMENT INDUSTRY REGULATORY ORGANIZATION OF CANADA *p953*
121 KING ST W SUITE 1600, TORONTO, ON, M5H 3T9

(416) 364-0604 *SIC 8611*

KENORA DISTRICT SERVICES BOARD *p565*
211 PRINCESS ST SUITE 2, DRYDEN, ON, P8N 3L5

(807) 223-2100 *SIC 8611*

MANITOBA CHAMBERS OF COMMERCE, THE *p375*
227 PORTAGE AVE, WINNIPEG, MB, R3B 2A6

(204) 948-0100 *SIC 8611*

MINING ASSOCIATION OF CANADA, THE *p823*
275 SLATER ST SUITE 1100, OTTAWA, ON, K1P 5H9

(613) 233-9391 *SIC 8611*

NATIONAL INDIAN BROTHERHOOD *p825*
473 ALBERT ST SUITE 810, OTTAWA, ON, K1R 5B4

(613) 241-6789 *SIC 8611*

NORBULK SHIPPING NB LTD *p413*
120 MCDONALD ST UNIT 135, SAINT JOHN, NB, E2J 1M5

(506) 657-7555 *SIC 8611*

ONTARIO ASSOCIATION OF CHILDREN'S AID SOCIETIES *p943*
75 FRONT ST E SUITE 308, TORONTO, ON, M5E 1V9

(416) 987-7725 *SIC 8611*

ONTARIO DAIRY HERD IMPROVEMENT CORPORATION *p606*
660 SPEEDVALE AVE W SUITE 101, GUELPH, ON, N1K 1E5

(519) 824-2320 *SIC 8611*

ONTARIO FLOWER GROWERS CO-OPERATIVE LIMITED *p741*
910 MID-WAY BLVD, MISSISSAUGA, ON, L5T 1T9

(905) 670-9556 *SIC 8611*

ONTARIO REAL ESTATE ASSOCIATION *p777*
99 DUNCAN MILL RD, NORTH YORK, ON, M3B 1Z2

(416) 445-9910 *SIC 8611*

ORGANISME D'AUTOREGLEMENTATION DU COUTAGE IMMOBILERS DU QUEBEC, L' *p1071*
4905 BOUL LAPINIERE BUREAU 2200, BROSSARD, QC, J4Z 0G2

(450) 676-4800 *SIC 8611*

PARA-MED HEALTH SERVICES INC *p947*
480 UNIVERSITY AVE SUITE 708, TORONTO, ON, M5G 1V2

(416) 977-5008 *SIC 8611*

REAL ESTATE BOARD OF GREATER VANCOUVER *p320*

2433 SPRUCE ST, VANCOUVER, BC, V6H 4C8

(604) 730-3000 *SIC 8611*

REGROUPEMENT DES CENTRE DE LA PETITE ENFANCE DE L' *p1173*
4321 AV PAPINEAU, MONTREAL, QC, H2H 1T3

(514) 528-1442 *SIC 8611*

RESTAURANTS CANADA *p991*
1155 QUEEN ST W, TORONTO, ON, M6J 1J4

(416) 923-8416 *SIC 8611*

SASKATCHEWAN ASSOCIATION OF RURAL MUNICIPALITIES, THE *p1422*
2301 WINDSOR PARK RD, REGINA, SK, S4V 3A4

(306) 757-3577 *SIC 8611*

SIMARIL INC *p373*
321 MCDERMOT AVE SUITE 402, WINNIPEG, MB, R3A 0A3

(204) 788-4366 *SIC 8611*

ST. JOHN COUNCIL FOR ONTARIO *p940*
15 TORONTO ST SUITE 800, TORONTO, ON, M5C 2E3

(416) 923-8411 *SIC 8611*

STANDARDBRED CANADA *p727*
2150 MEADOWVALE BLVD SUITE 1, MISSISSAUGA, ON, L5N 6R6

(905) 858-3060 *SIC 8611*

TORONTO CONVENTION & VISITORS ASSOCIATION *p967*
207 QUEENS QUAY W SUITE 405, TORONTO, ON, M5J 1A7

(416) 203-2600 *SIC 8611*

TORONTO REAL ESTATE BOARD, THE *p778*
1400 DON MILLS RD SUITE 1, NORTH YORK, ON, M3B 3N1

(416) 443-8100 *SIC 8611*

UNITED ASSOCIATION OF JOURNEYMEN AND APPRENTICES OF THE PLUMBING AND PIPEFITTING INDUSTRY *p859*
1151 CONFEDERATION ST, SARNIA, ON, N7S 3Y5

(519) 337-6261 *SIC 8611*

UNIVERSITY OF SASKATCHEWAN STUDENTS' UNION *p1434*
1 CAMPUS DR RM 65, SASKATOON, SK, S7N 5A3

(306) 966-6960 *SIC 8611*

VICTORIA FIREFIGHTERS SOCIETY *p335*
1234 YATES ST, VICTORIA, BC, V8V 3M8

(250) 384-1122 *SIC 8611*

VICTORIAN ORDER OF NURSES FOR CANADA *p836*
1280 20TH ST E, OWEN SOUND, ON, N4K 6H6

(519) 376-5895 *SIC 8611*

WINDSOR UTILITIES COMMISSION *p1024*
787 OUELLETTE AVE, WINDSOR, ON, N9A 4J4

(519) 255-2727 *SIC 8611*

SIC 8621 Professional organizations

ACCESS CENTRE FOR HASTINGS AND PRINCE EDWARD COUNTIES, THE *p490*
470 DUNDAS ST E, BELLEVILLE, ON, K8N 1G1

(613) 962-7272 *SIC 8621*

ASPEN REGIONAL HEALTH *p138*
9503 BEAVER HILL RD, LAC LA BICHE, AB, T0A 2C0

(780) 623-4472 *SIC 8621*

ASSOCIATION ETUDIANTE DE L'UNIVERSITE MCGILL *p1193*
3600 RUE MCTAVISH BUREAU 1200, MONTREAL, QC, H3A 0G3

(514) 398-6800 *SIC 8621*

ASSOCIATION INTERNATIONALE DES ETUDIANTS EN SCIENCES ECONOMIQUES ET COMMERCIALES *p1185*

315 RUE SAINTE-CATHERINE E BUREAU 213, MONTREAL, QC, H2X 3X2

(514) 987-3288 *SIC 8621*

ASSOCIATION OF PROFESSIONAL ENGINEERS AND GEOSCIENTISTS OF ALBERTA, THE *p87*
10060 JASPER AVE NW SUITE 1500, EDMONTON, AB, T5J 4A2

(780) 426-3990 *SIC 8621*

ASSOCIATION QUEBECOISE DES TRANSPORTS *p1201*
1255 RUE UNIVERSITY BUREAU 200, MONTREAL, QC, H3B 3X4

(514) 523-6444 *SIC 8621*

BARREAU DU QUEBEC, LE *p1187*
445 BOUL SAINT-LAURENT BUREAU 100, MONTREAL, QC, H2Y 3T8

(514) 954-3400 *SIC 8621*

BC CANCER FOUNDATION *p274*
13750 96 AVE, SURREY, BC, V3V 1Z2

(604) 930-2098 *SIC 8621*

BRITISH COLUMBIA COLLEGE OF NURSING PROFESSIONALS *p302*
200 GRANVILLE ST SUITE 900, VANCOUVER, BC, V6C 1S4

(604) 742-6200 *SIC 8621*

BRITISH COLUMBIA MEDICAL ASSOCIATION (CANADIAN MEDICAL ASSOCIATION - B.C. DIVISION) *p320*
1665 BROADWAY W SUITE 115, VANCOUVER, BC, V6J 5A4

(604) 736-5551 *SIC 8621*

BRITISH COLUMBIA TEACHER'S FEDERATION *p292*
550 6TH AVE W SUITE 100, VANCOUVER, BC, V5Z 4P2

(604) 871-2283 *SIC 8621*

CALGARY YOUNG MEN'S CHRISTIAN ASSOCIATION *p126*
GD, EXSHAW, AB, T0L 2C0

(403) 673-3858 *SIC 8621*

CANADIAN ASSOCIATION FOR CO-OPERATIVE EDUCATION *p974*
720 SPADINA AVE SUITE 202, TORONTO, ON, M5S 2T9

(416) 483-3311 *SIC 8621*

CANADIAN ASSOCIATION OF CLERGY *p614*
114 ARKELL ST, HAMILTON, ON, L8S 1N7

(905) 522-3775 *SIC 8621*

CANADIAN BAR ASSOCIATION, THE *p822*
66 SLATER ST SUITE 1200, OTTAWA, ON, K1P 5H1

(613) 237-2925 *SIC 8621*

CANADIAN CORPS OF COMMISSION-AIRES NATIONAL OFFICE, THE *p142*
1222 3 AVE S, LETHBRIDGE, AB, T1J 0J9

(403) 327-1222 *SIC 8621*

CANADIAN CORPS OF COMMISSION-AIRES NATIONAL OFFICE, THE *p1038*
15 ST. PETERS RD, CHARLOTTETOWN, PE, C1A 5N1

(902) 894-7026 *SIC 8621*

CANADIAN FOUNDATION FOR HEALTH-CARE IMPROVEMENT (CFHI) *p822*
150 KENT ST SUITE 200, OTTAWA, ON, K1P 0E4

(613) 728-2238 *SIC 8621*

CANADIAN HOME BUILDERS' ASSOCIATION OF BRITISH COLUMBIA *p188*
3700 WILLINGDON AVE, BURNABY, BC, V5G 3H2

(604) 432-7112 *SIC 8621*

CANADIAN INSTITUTE OF TRAVEL COUNSELLORS OF ONTARIO *p766*
505 CONSUMERS RD SUITE 406, NORTH YORK, ON, M2J 4V8

(416) 484-4450 *SIC 8621*

CANADIAN KENNEL CLUB, THE *p583*
200 RONSON DR SUITE 400, ETOBICOKE, ON, M9W 5Z9

(416) 675-5511 *SIC 8621*

CANADIAN MEDICAL ASSOCIATION *p817*
1867 ALTA VISTA DR, OTTAWA, ON, K1G

5W8

(613) 731-9331 *SIC 8621*

CANADIAN MEDICAL PROTECTIVE ASSOCIATION, THE *p825*
875 CARLING AVE SUITE 928, OTTAWA, ON, K1S 5P1

(613) 725-2000 *SIC 8621*

CANADIAN MENTAL HEALTH ASSOCIATION, MIDDLESEX *p655*
534 QUEENS AVE, LONDON, ON, N6B 1Y6

(519) 668-0624 *SIC 8621*

CANADIAN MENTAL HEALTH ASSOCIATION, THUNDER BAY BRANCH *p907*
200 VAN NORMAN ST, THUNDER BAY, ON, P7A 4B8

(807) 345-5564 *SIC 8621*

CANADIAN MENTAL HEALTH ASSOCIATION/PEEL BRANCH *p511*
7700 HURONTARIO ST SUITE 601, BRAMPTON, ON, L6Y 4M3

(905) 451-2123 *SIC 8621*

CANADIAN POSTMASTERS AND ASSISTANTS ASSOCIATION *p820*
281 QUEEN MARY ST, OTTAWA, ON, K1K 1X1

(613) 745-2095 *SIC 8621*

CANADIAN PUBLIC HEALTH ASSOCIATION *p828*
1565 CARLING AVE SUITE 300, OTTAWA, ON, K1Z 8R1

(613) 725-3769 *SIC 8621*

CAREFOR HEALTH & COMMUNITY SERVICES *p817*
760 BELFAST RD, OTTAWA, ON, K1G 6M8

(613) 749-7557 *SIC 8621*

CEGERTEC INC *p1071*
4805 BOUL LAPINIERE BUREAU 4300, BROSSARD, QC, J4Z 0G2

(450) 656-3356 *SIC 8621*

CENTRAL TORONTO COMMUNITY HEALTH CENTRES *p979*
168 BATHURST ST SUITE 3199, TORONTO, ON, M5V 2R4

(416) 703-8480 *SIC 8621*

CENTRE DE SANTE ET DE SERVICES SOCIAUX DE LA HAUTE-GASPESIE *p1355*
50 RUE DU BELVEDERE, SAINTE-ANNE-DES-MONTS, QC, G4V 1X4

(418) 797-2744 *SIC 8621*

CENTRE DE SANTE ET DE SERVICES SOCIAUX LA POMMERAIE *p1056*
34 RUE SAINT-JOSEPH, BEDFORD, QC, J0J 1A0

(450) 248-4304 *SIC 8621*

CENTRE HOSPITALIER UNIVERSITAIRE DE SHERBROOKE *p1370*
3001 12E AV N, SHERBROOKE, QC, J1H 5N4

(819) 346-1110 *SIC 8621*

CENTRE INTEGRE UNIVERSITAIRE DE SANTE ET DE SERVICES SOCIAUX DE L'ESTRIE *p1371*
375 RUE ARGYLL, SHERBROOKE, QC, J1J 3H5

(819) 780-2222 *SIC 8621*

CERTIFIED GENERAL ACCOUNTANTS ASSOCIATION OF BRITISH COLUMBIA *p297*
555 HASTINGS ST W SUITE 800, VANCOUVER, BC, V6B 4N6

(604) 872-7222 *SIC 8621*

CERTIFIED GENERAL ACCOUNTANTS ASSOCIATION OF CANADA *p192*
4200 NORTH FRASER WAY SUITE 100, BURNABY, BC, V5J 5K7

(604) 408-6660 *SIC 8621*

CHARTERED PROFESSIONAL ACCOUNTANTS OF ALBERTA *p46*
444 7 AVE SW SUITE 800, CALGARY, AB, T2P 0X8

(403) 299-1300 *SIC 8621*

CHARTERED PROFESSIONAL ACCOUNTANTS OF BRITISH COLUMBIA *p297*
555 HASTINGS ST W UNIT 800, VANCOUVER, BC, V6B 4N5

(604) 872-7222   *SIC 8621*

CHARTERED PROFESSIONAL ACCOUNTANTS OF CANADA   *p979*
277 WELLINGTON ST W SUITE 600, TORONTO, ON, M5V 3H2
(416) 977-3222   *SIC 8621*

CHARTERED PROFESSIONAL ACCOUNTANTS OF ONTARIO   *p928*
69 BLOOR ST E, TORONTO, ON, M4W 1B3
(416) 962-1841   *SIC 8621*

CHIPMAN OUTREACH INC   *p396*
12 CIVIC CRT, CHIPMAN, NB, E4A 2H9
(506) 339-5639   *SIC 8621*

CLUB NAUTIQUE DE LA BAIE DE BEAUPORT   *p1257*
1 BOUL HENRI-BOURASSA, QUEBEC, QC, G1J 1W8
(418) 266-0722   *SIC 8621*

COLLEGE AND ASSOCIATION OF REGISTERED NURSES OF ALBERTA   *p95*
11620 168 ST NW, EDMONTON, AB, T5M 4A6
(780) 451-0043   *SIC 8621*

COLLEGE DES MEDECINS DU QUEBEC   *p1202*
1250 BOUL RENE-LEVESQUE O BUREAU 3500, MONTREAL, QC, H3B 0G2
(514) 933-4441   *SIC 8621*

COLLEGE OF NURSES OF ONTARIO   *p972*
101 DAVENPORT RD, TORONTO, ON, M5R 3P1
(416) 928-0900   *SIC 8621*

COLLEGE OF PHYSICIANS AND SURGEONS OF ONTARIO   *p944*
80 COLLEGE ST, TORONTO, ON, M5G 2E2
(416) 967-2600   *SIC 8621*

COLLEGE OF REGISTERED NURSES OF BC   *p320*
2855 ARBUTUS ST, VANCOUVER, BC, V6J 3Y8
(604) 736-7331   *SIC 8621*

COMITE PARITAIRE DE L'INDUSTRIE DES SERVICES AUTOMOBILES DE LA REGION DE MONTREAL   *p1182*
509 RUE BELANGER BUREAU 165, MONTREAL, QC, H2S 1G5
(514) 288-3003   *SIC 8621*

CONTINUING LEGAL EDUC, THE   *p298*
845 CAMBIE ST SUITE 500, VANCOUVER, BC, V6B 4Z9
(604) 669-3544   *SIC 8621*

CORPORATION DE SERVICE DE LA CHAMBRE DES NOTAIRES DU QUEBEC, LA   *p1194*
1801 AV MCGILL COLLEGE BUREAU 600, MONTREAL, QC, H3A 0A7
(514) 879-1793   *SIC 8621*

CORPORATION DES MAITRES MECANICIENS EN TUYAUTERIE DU QUEBEC   *p1180*
8175 BOUL SAINT-LAURENT, MONTREAL, QC, H2P 2M1
(514) 382-2668   *SIC 8621*

CORPORATION OF COUNCIL OF MINISTERS OF EDUCATION CANADA, THE   *p926*
95 ST CLAIR AVE W SUITE 1106, TORONTO, ON, M4V 1N6
(416) 962-8100   *SIC 8621*

COU HOLDING ASSOCIATION INC   *p944*
180 DUNDAS ST W SUITE 1100, TORONTO, ON, M5G 1Z8
(416) 979-2165   *SIC 8621*

CWB GROUP - INDUSTRY SERVICES CORP   *p683*
8260 PARKHILL DR, MILTON, ON, L9T 5V7
(905) 542-1312   *SIC 8621*

DENTALCORP HEALTH SERVICES ULC   *p962*
181 BAY ST STE 2600, TORONTO, ON, M5J 2T3
(416) 558-8338   *SIC 8621*

DHS (OSHAWA) LTD   *p811*
88 CENTRE ST N SUITE 1, OSHAWA, ON, L1G 4B6
(905) 571-1511   *SIC 8621*

DRAKE MEDOX HEALTH SERVICES (VANCOUVER) INC   *p312*
1166 ALBERNI ST SUITE 802, VANCOUVER, BC, V6E 3Z3
(604) 682-2801   *SIC 8621*

EABAMETOONG EDUCATION AUTHORITY   *p567*
GD, EABAMET LAKE, ON, P0T 1L0
(807) 242-1305   *SIC 8621*

EAST CENTRAL HEALTH AND PUBLIC HEATH HOMECARE AND REHABILITATION   *p170*
4701 52 ST SUITE 11, VERMILION, AB, T9X 1J9
(780) 853-5270   *SIC 8621*

EASTERN ONTARIO HEALTH UNIT   *p563*
1000 PITT ST, CORNWALL, ON, K6J 5T1
(613) 933-1375   *SIC 8621*

EDMONTON PETROLEUM CLUB   *p85*
11110 108 ST NW SUITE 1, EDMONTON, AB, T5G 2T2
(780) 474-3411   *SIC 8621*

ELEVEURS DE PORCS DU QUEBEC, LES   *p1143*
555 BOUL ROLAND-THERRIEN BUREAU 120, LONGUEUIL, QC, J4H 4E9
(450) 679-0540   *SIC 8621*

ELGIN ST. THOMAS HEALTH UNIT   *p889*
1230 TALBOT ST, ST THOMAS, ON, N5P 1G9
(519) 631-9900   *SIC 8621*

FARMS AND FAMILIES OF NORTH AMERICA INCORPORATED   *p1427*
320 22ND ST E, SASKATOON, SK, S7K 0H1
(306) 665-2294   *SIC 8621*

FEDERATION DES MEDECINS OMNIPRACTICIENS DU QUEBEC, LA   *p1402*
3500 BOUL DE MAISONNEUVE O BUREAU 2000, WESTMOUNT, QC, H3Z 3C1
(514) 878-1911   *SIC 8621*

FEDERATION DES MEDECINS SPECIALISTES DU QUEBEC   *p1230*
2 COMPLEXE DESJARDINS BUREAU 3000, MONTREAL, QC, H5B 1G8
(514) 350-5000   *SIC 8621*

FEDERATION QUEBECOISE DES COOPERATIVES EN MILIEU SCOLAIRE   *p1275*
3188 CH SAINTE-FOY BUREAU 200, QUEBEC, QC, G1X 1R4
(418) 650-3333   *SIC 8621*

GCT REPRESENTITIVE SERVICES   *p628*
237 AIRPORT RD, KENORA, ON, P9N 0A2
(807) 548-4214   *SIC 8621*

GHD CONSULTANTS LTEE   *p1277*
445 AV SAINT-JEAN-BAPTISTE BUREAU 390, QUEBEC, QC, G2E 5N7
(418) 658-0112   *SIC 8621*

GHD CONSULTANTS LTEE   *p1334*
4600 BOUL DE LA COTE-VERTU BUREAU 200, SAINT-LAURENT, QC, H4S 1C7
(514) 333-5151   *SIC 8621*

GILBERT PLAINS HEALTH CENTRE INC   *p350*
100 CUTFORTH ST N, GILBERT PLAINS, MB, R0L 0X0
(204) 548-2161   *SIC 8621*

GLENCOE AGRICULTURAL SOCIETY   *p594*
268 CURRIE ST, GLENCOE, ON, N0L 1M0
(519) 287-2836   *SIC 8621*

GOLDER ASSOCIES LTEE   *p1367*
690 BOUL LAURE BUREAU 112, SEPT-ILES, QC, G4R 4N8
(418) 968-6111   *SIC 8621*

GUELPH COMMUNITY HEALTH CENTRE   *p603*
176 WYNDHAM ST N SUITE 1, GUELPH, ON, N1H 8N9
(519) 821-6638   *SIC 8621*

HALIBURTON KAWARTHA PINE RIDGE DISTRICT HEALTH UNIT   *p847*
200 ROSEGLEN RD, PORT HOPE, ON, L1A 3V6
(905) 885-9100   *SIC 8621*

HARMONY HEALTH CARE   *p211*
2753 CHARLOTTE RD SUITE 2A, DUNCAN, BC, V9L 5J2
(250) 701-9990   *SIC 8621*

HEALTH ASSOCIATION OF NOVA SCOTIA   *p439*
2 DARTMOUTH RD, BEDFORD, NS, B4A 2K7
(902) 832-8500   *SIC 8621*

HEALTH EMPLOYERS ASSOCIATION OF BRITISH COLUMBIA   *p286*
2889 12TH AVE E SUITE 300, VANCOUVER, BC, V5M 4T5
(604) 736-5909   *SIC 8621*

HEALTH INTEGRATION NETWORK OF WATERLOO WELLINGTON   *p1006*
141 WEBER ST S, WATERLOO, ON, N2J 2A9
(519) 748-2222   *SIC 8621*

HENRIQUEZ PARTNERS   *p298*
598 GEORGIA ST W, VANCOUVER, BC, V6B 2A3
(604) 687-5681   *SIC 8621*

INSPECTEUR EN BATIMENT   *p1076*
110 RUE ALBERT-SEERS, CHATEAUGUAY, QC, J6K 5E5
(514) 515-2334   *SIC 8621*

INSTITUTE OF CHARTERED ACCOUNTANTS OF ALBERTA   *p89*
10088 102 AVE NW UNIT 1900 TD TOWER, EDMONTON, AB, T5J 2Z1
(780) 424-7391   *SIC 8621*

INSURANCE INSTITUTE OF CANADA, THE   *p939*
18 KING ST E SUITE 600, TORONTO, ON, M5C 1C4
(416) 362-8586   *SIC 8621*

JOULE INC   *p826*
1031 BANK ST, OTTAWA, ON, K1S 3W7
(888) 855-2555   *SIC 8621*

KIMBERLEY TEACHER'S ASSOCIATION   *p223*
144 DEER PARK AVE SUITE 201, KIMBERLEY, BC, V1A 2J4
(250) 427-3113   *SIC 8621*

L B C D INGENIEURS CONSEILS INC   *p1366*
40 RUE SAINTE-CECILE, SALABERRY-DE-VALLEYFIELD, QC, J6T 1L7
(450) 371-5722   *SIC 8621*

LAW SOCIETY OF ALBERTA   *p65*
919 11 AVE SW SUITE 500, CALGARY, AB, T2R 1P3
(403) 229-4700   *SIC 8621*

MANITOBA TEACHERS' SOCIETY, THE   *p386*
191 HARCOURT ST, WINNIPEG, MB, R3J 3H2
(204) 888-7961   *SIC 8621*

MUTUAL FUND DEALERS ASSOCIATION OF CANADA   *p955*
121 KING ST W SUITE 1000, TORONTO, ON, M5H 3T9
(416) 361-6332   *SIC 8621*

NATIONAL CLUB, THE   *p955*
303 BAY ST, TORONTO, ON, M5H 2R1
(416) 364-3247   *SIC 8621*

NATIONAL HOCKEY LEAGUE PLAYERS ASSOCIATION, THE   *p965*
20 BAY ST SUITE 1700, TORONTO, ON, M5J 2N8
(416) 313-2300   *SIC 8621*

NORTH BAY PARRY SOUND DISTRICT HEALTH UNIT   *p763*
345 OAK ST W, NORTH BAY, ON, P1B 2T2
(705) 474-1400   *SIC 8621*

NUMERIS   *p777*
1500 DON MILLS RD SUITE 305, NORTH YORK, ON, M3B 3L7
(416) 445-9800   *SIC 8621*

ONTARIO COLLEGE OF PHARMACISTS ORDRE DES PHARMACIENS DE L'ONTARIO   *p973*
483 HURON ST, TORONTO, ON, M5R 2R4
(416) 962-4861   *SIC 8621*

ONTARIO DENTAL ASSOCIATION, THE   *p973*
4 NEW ST, TORONTO, ON, M5R 1P6
(416) 922-3900   *SIC 8621*

ONTARIO ENGLISH CATHOLIC TEACHERS' ASSOCIATION, THE   *p926*
65 ST CLAIR AVE E SUITE 400, TORONTO, ON, M4T 2Y8
(416) 925-2493   *SIC 8621*

ONTARIO HIV TREATMENT NETWORK, THE   *p926*
1300 YONGE ST SUITE 600, TORONTO, ON, M4T 1X3
(416) 642-6486   *SIC 8621*

ONTARIO MEDICAL ASSOCIATION   *p976*
150 BLOOR ST W SUITE 900, TORONTO, ON, M5S 3C1
(416) 599-2580   *SIC 8621*

ONTARIO PHARMACISTS' ASSOCIATION   *p955*
155 UNIVERSITY AVE SUITE 600, TORONTO, ON, M5H 3B7
(416) 441-0788   *SIC 8621*

ONTARIO PODIATRIC MEDICAL ASSOCIATION   *p772*
45 SHEPPARD AVE E SUITE 900, NORTH YORK, ON, M2N 5W9
(416) 927-9111   *SIC 8621*

ONTARIO SECONDARY SCHOOL TEACHERS' FEDERATION, THE   *p787*
60 MOBILE DR SUITE 100, NORTH YORK, ON, M4A 2P3
(416) 751-8300   *SIC 8621*

ORDRE DES INGENIEURS DU QUEBEC   *p1207*
1100 AV DES CANADIENS-DE-MONTREAL BUREAU 350, MONTREAL, QC, H3B 2S2
(514) 845-6141   *SIC 8621*

ORDRE DES TRAVAILLEURS SOCIAUX ET DES THERAPEUTES CONJUGAUX ET FAMILIAUX DU QUEBEC   *p1177*
255 BOUL CREMAZIE E BUREAU 520, MONTREAL, QC, H2M 1L5
(514) 731-3925   *SIC 8621*

OTTAWA YOUNG MEN'S AND YOUNG WOMEN'S CHRISTIAN ASSOCIATION   *p834*
180 ARGYLE AVE SUITE 1622, OTTAWA, ON, K2P 1B7
(613) 237-1320   *SIC 8621*

OXFORD SEMINARS   *p90*
162221-10405 JASPER AVE NW, EDMONTON, AB, T5J 3N4
(780) 428-8700   *SIC 8621*

PROFESSIONNEL(LE)S EN SOINS DE SANTE UNIS LES   *p1165*
5630 RUE HOCHELAGA, MONTREAL, QC, H1N 3L7
(514) 932-4417   *SIC 8621*

PROVENCHER ROY + ASSOCIES ARCHITECTES INC   *p1190*
276 RUE SAINT-JACQUES BUREAU 700, MONTREAL, QC, H2Y 1N3
(514) 844-3938   *SIC 8621*

QUINTE HEALTHCARE CORPORATION   *p845*
403 PICTON MAIN ST, PICTON, ON, K0K 2T0
(613) 476-1008   *SIC 8621*

REGISTERED NURSES ASSOCIATION OF ONTARIO   *p956*
158 PEARL ST, TORONTO, ON, M5H 1L3
(416) 599-1925   *SIC 8621*

ROYAL CANADIAN GOLF ASSOCIATION   *p806*
1333 DORVAL DR UNIT 1, OAKVILLE, ON, L6M 4X6
(905) 849-9700   *SIC 8621*

ROYAL COLLEGE OF DENTAL SURGEONS OF ONTARIO   *p930*
6 CRESCENT RD, TORONTO, ON, M4W 1T1
(416) 961-6555   *SIC 8621*

ROYAL COLLEGE OF PHYSICIANS AND

SURGEONS OF CANADA, THE   p826
774 ECHO DR, OTTAWA, ON, K1S 5N8
(613) 730-8177   SIC 8621
SAGKEENG EDUCATION AUTHORITY p354
GD, PINE FALLS, MB, R0E 1M0
(204) 367-4109   SIC 8621
SALERS ASSOCIATION OF CANADA   p25
5160 SKYLINE WAY NE, CALGARY, AB,
T2E 6V1
(403) 264-5850   SIC 8621
**SARNIA/LAMBTON COMMUNITY CARE
ACCESS CENTRE**   p859
1150 PONTIAC DR, SARNIA, ON, N7S 3A7
(519) 337-1000   SIC 8621
**SASKATCHEWAN BAND ASSOCIATION
INC**   p1438
34 SUNSET DR N, YORKTON, SK, S3N
3K9
(306) 783-2263   SIC 8621
**SASKATCHEWAN TEACHERS' FEDERA-
TION**   p1425
2317 ARLINGTON AVE, SASKATOON, SK,
S7J 2H8
(306) 373-1660   SIC 8621
**SOUTH WEST LOCAL HEALTH INTEGRA-
TION NETWORK**   p659
356 OXFORD ST W, LONDON, ON, N6H
1T3
(519) 672-0445   SIC 8621
**STAFF RELIEF HEALTH CARE SERVICES
INC**   p854
350 HIGHWAY 7 E UNIT PH4, RICHMOND
HILL, ON, L4B 3N2
(905) 709-1767   SIC 8621
TEXTURES FINE CRAFTS   p613
236 LOCKE ST S, HAMILTON, ON, L8P 4B7
(905) 523-0636   SIC 8621
THUNDER BAY DISTRICT HEALTH UNIT
p909
999 BALMORAL ST, THUNDER BAY, ON,
P7B 6E7
(807) 625-5900   SIC 8621
**TRIAL LAWYERS ASSOCIATION OF
BRITISH COLUMBIA**   p317
1100 MELVILLE ST SUITE 1111, VANCOU-
VER, BC, V6E 4A6
(604) 682-5343   SIC 8621
TRUESTAR HEALTH INC   p927
55 ST CLAIR AVE W SUITE 600,
TORONTO, ON, M4V 2Y7
SIC 8621
UNION CLUB OF BRITISH COLUMBIA p337
805 GORDON ST, VICTORIA, BC, V8W 1Z6
(250) 384-1151   SIC 8621
UNION DES ARTISTES   p1214
1441 BOUL RENE-LEVESQUE O BUREAU
400, MONTREAL, QC, H3G 1T7
(514) 288-6682   SIC 8621
UNITED NURSES OF ALBERTA   p92
11150 JASPER AVE NW SUITE 700, ED-
MONTON, AB, T5K 0C7
(780) 425-1025   SIC 8621
UNIVERSITIES CANADA   p825
350 ALBERT ST SUITE 1710, OTTAWA,
ON, K1R 1B1
(613) 563-1236   SIC 8621
VON CANADA FOUNDATION   p460
46 CHIPMAN DR SUITE 1, KENTVILLE,
NS, B4N 3V7
(902) 678-1733   SIC 8621
**WESTERN REGIONAL INTERGREATED
HEALTH AUTHORITY**   p434
149 MONTANA DR, STEPHENVILLE, NL,
A2N 2T4
(709) 643-8608   SIC 8621

SIC 8631 Labor organizations

AIR CANADA PILOTS ASSOCIATION p687
6299 AIRPORT RD SUITE 205, MISSIS-
SAUGA, ON, L4V 1N3
(905) 678-9008   SIC 8631
ALBERTA REGL COUNCIL CARPENTERS

CORP   p104
15210 123 AVE NW SUITE 176, EDMON-
TON, AB, T5V 0A3
(780) 474-8599   SIC 8631
ALBERTA TEACHERS' ASSOCIATION, THE
p97
11010 142 ST NW, EDMONTON, AB, T5N
2R1
(780) 447-9400   SIC 8631
**ALBERTA UNION OF PROVINCIAL EM-
PLOYEES, THE**   p97
10451 170 ST NW SUITE 200, EDMON-
TON, AB, T5P 4S7
(780) 930-3300   SIC 8631
**ALLIANCE OF CANADIAN CINEMA, TELE-
VISION & RADIO ARTISTS**   p931
625 CHURCH ST, TORONTO, ON, M4Y
2G1
(416) 489-1311   SIC 8631
**ALLIANCE PERSONNELLE PROFES-
SIONELLE ET TECHNIQUE DE LA SANTE
ET DES SERVICES SOCIAUX**   p1279
1305 BOUL LEBOURGNEUF BUREAU 200,
QUEBEC, QC, G2K 2E4
(418) 622-2541   SIC 8631
**ALLIANCE QUEBECOISE DES TECHNI-
CIENS DE L'IMAGE ET DU SON (AQTIS)**
p1175
533 RUE ONTARIO E BUREAU 300, MON-
TREAL, QC, H2L 1N8
(514) 844-2113   SIC 8631
**ASSOCIATION DES EMPLOYEURS MAR-
ITIME, L'**   p1209
2100 AV PIERRE-DUPUY, MONTREAL,
QC, H3C 3R5
(514) 878-3721   SIC 8631
**ASSOCIATION DES MANOEUVRES INTER-
PROVINCIAUX (AMI), L'**   p1176
565 BOUL CREMAZIE E BUREAU 3800,
MONTREAL, QC, H2M 2V6
(514) 381-8780   SIC 8631
**ASSOCIATION DES POMPIERS DE MON-
TREAL INC**   p1168
2655 PLACE CHASSE 2E ETAGE, MON-
TREAL, QC, H1Y 2C3
(514) 527-9691   SIC 8631
**ASSOCIATION PARITAIRE POUR LA
SANTE ET LA SECURITE DU TRAVAIL
DU SECTEUR AFFAIRES SOCIALES** p1166
5100 RUE SHERBROOKE E BUREAU 950,
MONTREAL, QC, H1V 3R9
(514) 253-6871   SIC 8631
**BC GOVERNMENT AND SERVICE EM-
PLOYEES' UNION**   p188
4925 CANADA WAY, BURNABY, BC, V5G
1M1
(604) 291-9611   SIC 8631
**BC GOVERNMENT AND SERVICE EM-
PLOYEES' UNION**   p188
4911 CANADA WAY SUITE 101, BURNABY,
BC, V5G 3W3
(604) 291-9611   SIC 8631
**BRITISH COLUMBIA MARITIME EMPLOY-
ERS ASSOCIATION**   p294
349 RAILWAY ST SUITE 500, VANCOU-
VER, BC, V6A 1A4
(604) 688-1155   SIC 8631
BRITISH COLUMBIA NURSES UNION p184
4060 REGENT ST, BURNABY, BC, V5C 6P5
(604) 433-2268   SIC 8631
BROCKVILLE POLICE ASSOCIATION p519
2269 PARKEDALE AVE W, BROCKVILLE,
ON, K6V 3G9
(613) 342-0127   SIC 8631
C E P LOCAL 30   p416
1216 SAND COVE RD UNIT 15, SAINT
JOHN, NB, E2M 5V8
(506) 635-5786   SIC 8631
**CANADA EMPLOYMENT & IMMIGRATION
UNION**   p822
275 SLATER ST UNIT 1204, OTTAWA, ON,
K1P 5H9
(613) 236-9634   SIC 8631
CANADIAN ASSOCIATION OF PROFES-

SIONAL EMPLOYEES   p822
100 QUEEN ST SUITE 400, OTTAWA, ON,
K1P 1J9
(613) 236-9181   SIC 8631
CANADIAN LABOUR CONGRESS   p826
2841 RIVERSIDE DR, OTTAWA, ON, K1V
8X7
(613) 521-3400   SIC 8631
**CANADIAN UNION OF BREWERY AND
GENERAL WORKERS LOCAL 325**   p583
1 CARLINGVIEW DR, ETOBICOKE, ON,
M9W 5E5
(416) 675-2648   SIC 8631
CANADIAN UNION OF POSTAL WORKERS
p833
377 BANK ST, OTTAWA, ON, K2P 1Y3
(613) 236-7238   SIC 8631
**CANADIAN UNION OF PUBLIC EMPLOY-
EES**   p188
4940 CANADA WAY SUITE 500, BURNABY,
BC, V5G 4T3
(604) 291-1940   SIC 8631
**CANADIAN UNION OF PUBLIC EMPLOY-
EES**   p377
275 BROADWAY SUITE 403B, WINNIPEG,
MB, R3C 4M6
(204) 942-6524   SIC 8631
**CANADIAN UNION OF PUBLIC EMPLOY-
EES**   p817
1375 ST. LAURENT BLVD, OTTAWA, ON,
K1G 0Z7
(613) 237-1590   SIC 8631
**CENTRALE DES SYNDICATS DEMOCRA-
TIQUES**   p1274
990 AV DE BOURGOGNE BUREAU 600,
QUEBEC, QC, G1W 0E8
(418) 529-2956   SIC 8631
**CENTRALE DES SYNDICATS DU QUEBEC
(CSQ), LA**   p1163
9405 RUE SHERBROOKE E, MONTREAL,
QC, H1L 6P3
(514) 356-8888   SIC 8631
**CENTRALE DES SYNDICATS DU QUEBEC
(CSQ), LA**   p1258
320 RUE SAINT-JOSEPH E BUREAU 100,
QUEBEC, QC, G1K 9E7
(514) 356-8888   SIC 8631
CENTRE DE MATERIAUX COMPOSITES
p1321
170 RUE DU PARC, SAINT-JOSEPH-DE-
BEAUCE, QC, G0S 2V0
(418) 397-6514   SIC 8631
**CENTRES D'EVALUATION DE LA TECH-
NOLOGIE INC**   p1210
740 RUE SAINT-MAURICE, MONTREAL,
QC, H3C 1L5
(514) 954-3665   SIC 8631
**CHRISTIAN LABOUR ASSOCIATION OF
CANADA**   p721
2335 ARGENTIA RD, MISSISSAUGA, ON,
L5N 0A3
(905) 812-2855   SIC 8631
**COMITE PARITAIRE DES AGENTS DE SE-
CURITE**   p1051
7450 BOUL DES GALERIES D'ANJOU
UNITE 490, ANJOU, QC, H1M 3M3
(514) 493-9105   SIC 8631
**CONFEDERATION DES SYNDICATS NA-
TIONAUX (C.S.N.)**   p1174
1601 AV DE LORIMIER, MONTREAL, QC,
H2K 4M5
(514) 529-4993   SIC 8631
**CONSEIL CENTRAL DES SYNDICATS NA-
TIANAUX DE L'ESTRIE**   p1370
180 COTE DE L'ACADIE, SHERBROOKE,
QC, J1H 2T3
(819) 563-6515   SIC 8631
**CONSEIL REGIONAL MAURICIE ET CEN-
TRE DU QUEBEC (FTQ)**   p1387
7080 RUE MARION BUREAU 101, TROIS-
RIVIERES, QC, G9A 6G4
(819) 378-4049   SIC 8631
**CONSTRUCTION & GENERAL WORKERS
UNION LOCAL NO. 92**   p85

10319 106 AVE NW SUITE 104, EDMON-
TON, AB, T5H 0P4
(780) 426-6630   SIC 8631
**EDIFICE DES ROUTIERS LOCAL 1999
CANADA INC.**   p1048
9393 RUE EDISON BUREAU 100, ANJOU,
QC, H1J 1T4
(514) 355-1110   SIC 8631
**ELEMENTARY TEACHERS FEDERATION
OF ONTARIO**   p931
136 ISABELLA ST, TORONTO, ON, M4Y
0B5
(416) 962-3836   SIC 8631
**ELEMENTARY TEACHERS FEDERATION
OF ONTARIO**   p932
136 ISABELLA ST, TORONTO, ON, M4Y
0B5
(416) 962-3836   SIC 8631
**FEDERATION AUTONOME DE
L'ENSEIGNEMENT**   p1170
400-8550 BOUL PIE-IX, MONTREAL, QC,
H1Z 4G2
(514) 666-7763   SIC 8631
**FEDERATION DE L'UPA DU BAS-SAINT-
LAURENT**   p1284
284 RUE POTVIN, RIMOUSKI, QC, G5L
7P5
(418) 723-2424   SIC 8631
FEDERATION DE LA CSN-CONSTRUCTION
p1312
2000 RUE GIROUARD O BUREAU 201,
SAINT-HYACINTHE, QC, J2S 3A6
(450) 261-8053   SIC 8631
**FEDERATION DES EMPLOYES ET EM-
PLOYEES DE SERVICES PUBLICS (CSN)
INC**   p1174
1601 AV DE LORIMIER BUREAU 150,
MONTREAL, QC, H2K 4M5
(514) 598-2360   SIC 8631
**FEDERATION DES TRAVAILLEURS ET
TRAVAILLEUSES DU QUEBEC (FTQ)** p1176
565 BOUL CREMAZIE E BUREAU 12100,
MONTREAL, QC, H2M 2W3
(514) 383-8000   SIC 8631
**FEDERATION INTERPROFESSIONNELLE
DE LA SANTE DU QUEBEC-FIQ**   p1195
2050 RUE DE BLEURY, MONTREAL, QC,
H3A 2J5
(514) 987-1141   SIC 8631
FISH FOOD & ALLIED WORKERS   p433
368 HAMILTON AVE, ST. JOHN'S, NL, A1E
1K2
(709) 576-7276   SIC 8631
**FRATERNITE DES POLICIERS ET
POLICIERES DE MONTREAL INC**   p1173
480 RUE GILFORD BUREAU 300, MON-
TREAL, QC, H2J 1N3
(514) 527-4161   SIC 8631
**FRATERNITE NATIONALE DES
CHARPENTIERS-MENUISIERS (SECTION
LOCALE 9)**   p1051
9100 BOUL METROPOLITAIN E, ANJOU,
QC, H1K 4L2
(514) 374-5871   SIC 8631
**HEALTH SCIENCES ASSOCIATION OF
BRITISH COLUMBIA**   p236
180 COLUMBIA ST E, NEW WESTMIN-
STER, BC, V3L 0G7
(604) 517-0994   SIC 8631
HYDRO-QUEBEC   p1279
5050 BOUL DES GRADINS BUREAU 200,
QUEBEC, QC, G2J 1P8
(418) 624-2811   SIC 8631
**I.A.T.S.E. LOCAL 891 MOTION PICTURE
STUDIO PRODUCTION TECHTIONS** p194
1640 BOUNDARY RD SUITE 891, BURN-
ABY, BC, V5K 4V4
(604) 664-8910   SIC 8631
**INTERNATIONAL ASSOCIATION OF HEAT
& FROST INSULATORS & ALLIED WORK-
ERS**   p381
946 ELGIN AVE SUITE 99, WINNIPEG, MB,
R3E 1B4
(204) 694-0726   SIC 8631

▲ Public Company   ■ Public Company Family Member   **HQ** Headquarters   **BR** Branch   **SL** Single Location

INTERNATIONAL UNION OF OPERATING ENGINEERS LOCAL 793   *p804*
2245 SPEERS RD, OAKVILLE, ON, L6L 6X8
(905) 469-9299   *SIC* 8631

INTERNATIONAL UNION OF OPERATING ENGINEERS LOCAL 955   *p101*
17603 114 AVE NW, EDMONTON, AB, T5S 2R9
(780) 483-8955   *SIC* 8631

LABOURERS INTERNATIONAL UNION OF NORTH AMERICA-LOCAL 183   *p786*
1263 WILSON AVE SUITE 200, NORTH YORK, ON, M3M 3G2
(416) 241-1183   *SIC* 8631

MANITOBA GOVERNMENT AND GENERAL EMPLOYEES UNION   *p378*
275 BROADWAY SUITE 601, WINNIPEG, MB, R3C 4M6
(204) 982-6438   *SIC* 8631

MANITOBA NURSES' UNION   *p379*
275 BROADWAY UNIT 301, WINNIPEG, MB, R3C 4M6
(204) 942-1320   *SIC* 8631

MAPLE TERRAZZO MARBLE & TILE INCORPORATED   *p555*
200 EDGELEY BLVD UNIT 9, CONCORD, ON, L4K 3Y8
(905) 760-1776   *SIC* 8631

MCMASTER STUDENTS UNION INCORPORATED   *p614*
1280 MAIN ST W RM 1, HAMILTON, ON, L8S 4K1
(905) 525-9140   *SIC* 8631

O S S T F DISTRICT 1   *p913*
111 WILSON AVE SUITE E, TIMMINS, ON, P4N 2S8
SIC 8631

OFFICE AND PROFESSIONAL EMPLOYEES INTERNATIONAL UNION   *p190*
4501 KINGSWAY UNIT 301, BURNABY, BC, V5H 0E5
(604) 299-0378   *SIC* 8631

OFFICE MUNICIPAL D'HABITATION DE QUEBEC   *p1265*
110 RUE DE COURCELETTE, QUEBEC, QC, G1N 4T4
(418) 780-5200   *SIC* 8631

ONTARIO NURSES' ASSOCIATION   *p976*
85 GRENVILLE ST SUITE 400, TORONTO, ON, M5S 3A2
(416) 964-8833   *SIC* 8631

ONTARIO PUBLIC SERVICE EMPLOYEES UNION   *p777*
100 LESMILL RD, NORTH YORK, ON, M3B 3P8
(416) 443-8888   *SIC* 8631

ORDRE PROFESSIONEL DES TECHNOLOGISTES MEDICAUX DU QUEBEC, L'   *p1183*
281 AV LAURIER E BUREAU 162, MONTREAL, QC, H2T 1G2
(514) 527-9811   *SIC* 8631

PLUMBERS AND STEAMFITTERS UNION LOCAL 46   *p869*
936 WARDEN AVE SUITE 46, SCARBOROUGH, ON, M1L 4C9
(416) 759-6791   *SIC* 8631

POWER WORKERS UNION   *p922*
244 EGLINTON AVE E, TORONTO, ON, M4P 1K2
(416) 481-4491   *SIC* 8631

PRINCE EDWARD ISLAND UNION OF PUBLIC SECTOR EMPLOYEES   *p1040*
4 ENMAN CRES, CHARLOTTETOWN, PE, C1E 1E6
(902) 892-5335   *SIC* 8631

PRODUCTEURS DE LAIT DU QUEBEC, LES   *p1143*
555 BOUL ROLAND-THERRIEN BUREAU 415, LONGUEUIL, QC, J4H 4G3
(450) 679-0530   *SIC* 8631

PROFESSIONAL INSTITUTE OF THE PUBLIC SERVICE OF CANADA, THE   *p818*
250 TREMBLAY RD, OTTAWA, ON, K1G 3J8

(613) 228-6310   *SIC* 8631
PUBLIC SERVICE ALLIANCE OF CANADA   *p834*
233 GILMOUR ST SUITE 402, OTTAWA, ON, K2P 0P2
(613) 560-2560   *SIC* 8631

S C. F P SECTION LOCALE 1500   *p1290*
75 AV QUEBEC, ROUYN-NORANDA, QC, J9X 7A2
(819) 762-4422   *SIC* 8631

SASKATCHEWAN GOVERNMENT & GENERAL EMPLOYEES' UNION   *p1423*
1011 N DEVONSHIRE DR, REGINA, SK, S4X 2X4
(306) 522-8571   *SIC* 8631

SASKATCHEWAN UNION OF NURSES   *p1421*
2330 2ND AVE, REGINA, SK, S4R 1A6
(306) 525-1666   *SIC* 8631

SERVICE EMPLOYEES INTERNATIONAL UNION LOCAL 204   *p558*
2180 STEELES AVE W SUITE 200, CONCORD, ON, L4K 2Z5
(905) 660-1800   *SIC* 8631

SYNDICAT CANADIEN DES COMMUNICATIONS DE L'ENERGIE ET DU PAPIER *p1051*
8290 BOUL METROPOLITAIN E, ANJOU, QC, H1K 1A2
(514) 259-7237   *SIC* 8631

SYNDICAT CANADIEN DES EMPLOYES DU METIER D'HYDRO-QUEBEC   *p1388*
7080 RUE MARION BUREAU 207, TROIS-RIVIERES, QC, G9A 6G4
(819) 693-1500   *SIC* 8631

SYNDICAT DE LA FONCTION PUBLIQUE ET PARAPUBLIQUE DU QUEBEC INC *p1279*
5100 BOUL DES GRADINS, QUEBEC, QC, G2J 1N4
(418) 623-2424   *SIC* 8631

SYNDICAT DE PROFESSIONNELLES ET PROFESSIONNELS DU GOUVERNEMENT DU QUEBEC   *p1176*
1001 RUE SHERBROOKE E BUREAU 300, MONTREAL, QC, H2L 1L3
(514) 849-1103   *SIC* 8631

SYNDICAT DES EMPLOYE-E-S DE TECHNIQUES PROFFESSION   *p1180*
2E ETAGE 1010, RUE DE LIEGE E, MONTREAL, QC, H2P 1L2
(514) 381-2000   *SIC* 8631

SYNDICAT DES EMPLOYEES COLS BLANCS DE VILLE DE SAGUENAY *p1376*
3760 RTE SAINT-LEONARD, SHIPSHAW, QC, G7P 1G9
SIC 8631

SYNDICAT DES EMPLOYEES ET EMPLOYES PROFESIONNELS-LES ET DE BUREAU-QUEBEC (SEPB-QUEBEC) *p1177*
565 BOUL CREMAZIE E BUREAU 11100, MONTREAL, QC, H2M 2W2
(514) 522-6511   *SIC* 8631

SYNDICAT DES EMPLOYES EN RADIO TELEDIFFUSION DE TELE-QUEBEC *p1174*
1000 RUE FULLUM BUREAU 231, MONTREAL, QC, H2K 3L7
(514) 529-2805   *SIC* 8631

SYNDICAT DES METALLOS SECTION LOCAL 9153   *p1305*
11780 1RE AV BUREAU 204, SAINT-GEORGES, QC, G5Y 2C8
SIC 8631

SYNDICAT DES SALARIES DE PINTENDRE AUTO   *p1135*
914 RTE DU PRESIDENT-KENNEDY, LEVIS, QC, G6C 1A5
(418) 833-8111   *SIC* 8631

SYNDICAT DES TRAVAILLEUSES & TRAVAILLEURS DE LA CSN DU CSSS DU AM-N *p1171*
2180 RUE FLEURY E, MONTREAL, QC, H2B 1K3
(514) 383-5054   *SIC* 8631

SYNDICAT DES TRAVAILLEUSES ET TRAVAILLEURS DE SYLVANIA   *p1099*

1 RUE SYLVAN, DRUMMONDVILLE, QC, J2C 2S8
(819) 477-8541   *SIC* 8631
SYNDICAT EMPLOYEE-ES DE METIERS D'HYDRO-QUEBEC SECTION LOCALE 1500 SCFP (F.T.Q.)   *p1180*
1010 RUE DE LIEGE E BUREAU 1500, MONTREAL, QC, H2P 1L2
(514) 387-1500   *SIC* 8631

SYNDICAT NATIONAL DES EMPLOYES DE L'ALUMINUM D'ARVIDA INC, LE *p1116*
1932 BOUL MELLON, JONQUIERE, QC, G7S 3H3
(418) 548-4667   *SIC* 8631

SYNDICAT NATIONAL DES TRAVAILLEURS ET TRAVAILLEUSES DE L'AUTOMOBILE DU CANADA INC *p1364*
49 RUE SAINT-LAMBERT BUREAU 728, SAINTE-THERESE, QC, J7E 3J9
(450) 434-9664   *SIC* 8631

SYNDICAT NATIONAL TCA   *p1303*
155 RTE MARIE-VICTORIN, SAINT-FRANCOIS-DU-LAC, QC, J0G 1M0
(514) 531-5362   *SIC* 8631

SYNDICAT QUEBECOIS DES EMPLOYES & EMPLOYES DE SERVICE SECTION LOCAL 298 (FTQ)   *p1177*
565 BOUL CREMAZIE E BUREAU 4300, MONTREAL, QC, H2M 2V6
(514) 727-1696   *SIC* 8631

SYNDICAT REGIONAL DES EMPLOYES DE SOUTIEN (C S Q) ENR   *p1079*
895 RUE BEGIN, CHICOUTIMI, QC, G7H 4P1
(418) 698-5271   *SIC* 8631

SYNDICAT SCFP DU CSSSRDL   *p1287*
28 RUE JOLY, RIVIERE-DU-LOUP, QC, G5R 3H2
SIC 8631

TEAMSTERS CANADA   *p1087*
2540 BOUL DANIEL-JOHNSON, COTE SAINT-LUC, QC, H7T 2S3
(450) 682-5521   *SIC* 8631

TEAMSTERS LOCAL UNION 938   *p707*
275 MATHESON BLVD E, MISSISSAUGA, ON, L4Z 1X8
(905) 502-0062   *SIC* 8631

TEAMSTERS UNION LOCAL NO. 213   *p289*
490 BROADWAY E SUITE 464, VANCOUVER, BC, V5T 1X3
(604) 874-3654   *SIC* 8631

TORONTO PROFESSIONAL FIREFIGHTERS ASSOCIATION LOCAL 3888   *p872*
14 COSENTINO DR, SCARBOROUGH, ON, M1P 3A2
(416) 466-1167   *SIC* 8631

TRAVAILLEURS & TRAVAILLEUSES UNIS DE L'ALIMENTATION ET DU COMMERCE T U A C LOCAL 501   *p1346*
4850 BOUL METROPOLITAIN E BUREAU 501, SAINT-LEONARD, QC, H1S 2Z7
(514) 725-9525   *SIC* 8631

TRAVAILLEURS ET TRAVAILLEUSES UNIS DE L'ALIMENTATION ET DU COMMERCE LOCAL-500   *p1181*
1200 BOUL CREMAZIE E BUREAU 100, MONTREAL, QC, H2P 3A7
(514) 332-5825   *SIC* 8631

UNIFOR   *p215*
1045 GIBSONS WAY, GIBSONS, BC, V0N 1V4
(604) 886-2722   *SIC* 8631

UNIFOR   *p477*
110 ST. ARNAUD ST, AMHERSTBURG, ON, N9V 2N8
(519) 730-0099   *SIC* 8631

UNIFOR   *p492*
160 CATHARINE ST, BELLEVILLE, ON, K8P 1M8
(613) 962-8122   *SIC* 8631

UNIFOR   *p507*
15 WESTCREEK BLVD SUITE 1, BRAMPTON, ON, L6T 5T4
(905) 874-4026   *SIC* 8631

UNIFOR   *p565*
34 QUEEN ST, DRYDEN, ON, P8N 1A3
(807) 223-8146   *SIC* 8631

UNIFOR   *p632*
728 ARLINGTON PARK PL, KINGSTON, ON, K7M 8H9
(613) 542-7368   *SIC* 8631

UNIFOR   *p637*
1111 HOMER WATSON BLVD, KITCHENER, ON, N2C 2P7
SIC 8631

UNIFOR   *p766*
205 PLACER CRT, NORTH YORK, ON, M2H 3H9
(416) 497-4110   *SIC* 8631

UNIFOR   *p847*
115 AV SHIPLEY, PORT ELGIN, ON, N0H 2C5
(519) 389-3200   *SIC* 8631

UNIFOR   *p887*
20 WALNUT ST, ST CATHARINES, ON, L2T 1H5
(905) 227-7717   *SIC* 8631

UNION DES EMPLOYES ET EMPLOYEES DE SERVICE, SECTION LOCALE 800 *p1171*
920 RUE DE PORT-ROYAL E, MONTREAL, QC, H2C 2B3
(514) 385-1717   *SIC* 8631

UNION DES PRODUCTEURS AGRICOLE, L'   *p1143*
555 BOUL ROLAND-THERRIEN BUREAU 100, LONGUEUIL, QC, J4H 3Y9
(450) 679-0530   *SIC* 8631

UNION OF BC PERFORMERS   *p292*
380 2ND AVE W UNIT 300, VANCOUVER, BC, V5Y 1C8
(604) 689-0727   *SIC* 8631

UNION OF NATIONAL DEFENCE EMPLOYEES   *p630*
17 PRINCESS MARY, KINGSTON, ON, K7K 7B4
SIC 8631

UNITED BROTHERHOOD OF CARPENTERS JOINERS AMERICA LOCAL 83 *p1034*
222 ROWNTREE DAIRY RD SUITE 598, WOODBRIDGE, ON, L4L 9T2
(416) 749-0675   *SIC* 8631

UNITED BROTHERHOOD OF CARPENTERS JOINERS AMERICA LOCAL 83 *p1041*
22 ENMAN CRES, CHARLOTTETOWN, PE, C1E 1E6
(902) 566-1414   *SIC* 8631

UNITED FOOD & COMMERCIAL WORKER CANADA   *p728*
2200 ARGENTIA RD SUITE 175, MISSISSAUGA, ON, L5N 2K7
(905) 821-8329   *SIC* 8631

UNITED FOOD & COMMERCIAL WORKERS LOCAL NO. 832   *p382*
1412 PORTAGE AVE, WINNIPEG, MB, R3G 0V5
(204) 786-5055   *SIC* 8631

UNITED FOOD & COMMERCIAL WORKERS UNION LOCAL 1518   *p191*
4021 KINGSWAY, BURNABY, BC, V5H 1Y9
(604) 434-3101   *SIC* 8631

UNITED FOOD AND COMMERCIAL WORKERS CANADA UNION   *p589*
61 INTERNATIONAL BLVD UNIT 300, ETOBICOKE, ON, M9W 6K4
(416) 675-1104   *SIC* 8631

UNITED STEELWORKERS OF AMERICA *p438*
10 TANTRAMAR PL, AMHERST, NS, B4H 2A1
(902) 667-0727   *SIC* 8631

UNITED STEELWORKERS OF AMERICA *p468*
1 DIAMOND ST, TRENTON, NS, B0K 1X0
SIC 8631

UNITED STEELWORKERS OF AMERICA *p547*
1000 26 HWY, COLLINGWOOD, ON, L9Y 4V8

SIC 8631

UNITED STEELWORKERS OF AMERICA *p923*
234 EGLINTON AVE E SUITE 800, TORONTO, ON, M4P 1K7
(416) 487-1571   *SIC 8631*

YORK REGIONAL POLICE ASSOCIATION, THE *p754*
600 STONEHAVEN AVE, NEWMARKET, ON, L3X 2M4
(905) 830-4947   *SIC 8631*

SIC 8641 Civic and social associations

1527 UPPER JAMES ST.,HAMILTON, IN-CORPORATED *p616*
1527 UPPER JAMES ST, HAMILTON, ON, L9B 1K2
(905) 385-1523   *SIC 8641*

AGENCE UNIVERSITAIRE DE LA FRANCO-PHONIE *p1219*
3034 BOUL EDOUARD-MONTPETIT, MON-TREAL, QC, H3T 1J7
(514) 343-6630   *SIC 8641*

AIR CANADA PILOTS ASSOCIATION *p383*
2000 WELLINGTON AVE SUITE 124A, WINNIPEG, MB, R3H 1C1
(204) 779-0736   *SIC 8641*

BOYS & GIRLS CLUB OF OTTAWA *p830*
2825 DUMAURIER AVE, OTTAWA, ON, K2B 7W3
(613) 828-0428   *SIC 8641*

BOYS AND GIRLS CLUB OF NIAGARA *p758*
6681 CULP ST, NIAGARA FALLS, ON, L2G 2C5
(905) 357-2444   *SIC 8641*

CALGARY PETROLEUM CLUB *p45*
319 5 AVE SW, CALGARY, AB, T2P 0L5
(403) 269-7981   *SIC 8641*

CANADA WORLD YOUTH INC *p1215*
2330 RUE NOTRE-DAME O BUREAU 300, MONTREAL, QC, H3J 1N4
(514) 931-3526   *SIC 8641*

CENTRE SOCIAL DES FONCTIONNAIRES MUNICIPAUX DE MONTREAL *p1178*
8790 AV DU PARC, MONTREAL, QC, H2N 1Y6
(514) 842-9463   *SIC 8641*

CENTRES JEUNESSE DE LANAUDIERE, LES *p1114*
1170 RUE LADOUCEUR, JOLIETTE, QC, J6E 3W7
(450) 759-0755   *SIC 8641*

CHATHAM KENT FAMILY YOUNG MEN'S CHRISTIAN ASSOCIATION, THE *p542*
101 COURTHOUSE LANE, CHATHAM, ON, N7L 0B5
SIC 8641

CIOCIARO CLUB OF WINDSOR INC *p807*
3745 NORTH TALBOT RD, OLDCASTLE, ON, N0R 1L0
(519) 737-6153   *SIC 8641*

COMMUNITY CLUB *p882*
219 5TH ST, SMOOTH ROCK FALLS, ON, P0L 2B0
(705) 338-2336   *SIC 8641*

CONESTOGA STUDENTS INCORPORATED *p638*
299 DOON VALLEY DR, KITCHENER, ON, N2G 4M4
(519) 748-5131   *SIC 8641*

CONFEDERATION DES ASSOCIATIONS D'ETUDIANTS ET D'ETUDIANTES DE L'UNIVERSITE LAVAL (CADEU *p1258*
PAVILLON MAURICE-POLLACK BUREAU 2265, QUEBEC, QC, G1K 7P4
(418) 656-7931   *SIC 8641*

DAUPHIN GENERAL HOSPITAL FOUNDA-TION, THE *p348*
625 3RD ST SW, DAUPHIN, MB, R7N 1R7
(204) 638-3010   *SIC 8641*

FOGOLAR FURLAN WINDSOR *p1019*
1800 NORTH SERVICE RD E, WINDSOR,

ON, N8W 1Y3
(519) 966-2230   *SIC 8641*

FRATERNITE DES POLICIERS DE LA REGIE INTERMUNICIPALE ROUSSILLON INC *p1072*
90 CH SAINT-FRANCOIS-XAVIER, CAN-DIAC, QC, J5R 6M6
(450) 635-9911   *SIC 8641*

GIRL GUIDES OF CANADA *p924*
50 MERTON ST, TORONTO, ON, M4S 1A3
(416) 487-5281   *SIC 8641*

GRAND RIVER CONSERVATION AUTHOR-ITY *p541*
GD, CAYUGA, ON, N0A 1E0
(905) 768-3288   *SIC 8641*

GRANITE CLUB *p915*
2350 BAYVIEW AVE, TORONTO, ON, M2L 1E4
(416) 449-8713   *SIC 8641*

HAMILTON YOUNG WOMEN'S CHRISTIAN ASSOCIATION, THE *p613*
75 MACNAB ST S, HAMILTON, ON, L8P 3C1
(905) 522-9922   *SIC 8641*

IMMIGRANT SERVICES ASSOCIATION OF NOVA SCOTIA *p457*
6960 MUMFORD RD SUITE 2120, HALI-FAX, NS, B3L 4P1
(902) 423-3607   *SIC 8641*

ITALIAN FOLK SOCIETY OF BC, THE *p286*
3075 SLOCAN ST, VANCOUVER, BC, V5M 3E4
(604) 430-3337   *SIC 8641*

KIPNESS CENTRE FOR VETERANS INC *p84*
4470 MCCRAE AVE NW, EDMONTON, AB, T5E 6M8
(780) 442-5700   *SIC 8641*

MCMAN YOUTH, FAMILY AND COMMUNITY SERVICES ASSOCIATION *p36*
6712 FISHER ST SE UNIT 80, CALGARY, AB, T2H 2A7
(403) 508-7742   *SIC 8641*

MEMORIAL UNIVERSITY OF NEWFOUND-LAND STUDENTS UNION *p432*
1 ARCTIC PL, ST. JOHN'S, NL, A1C 5S7
SIC 8641

MONCTON YOUTH RESIDENCES INC *p407*
536 MOUNTAIN RD, MONCTON, NB, E1C 2N5
(506) 869-6333   *SIC 8641*

ONTARIO ENGLISH CATHOLIC TEACH-ERS' ASSOCIATION, THE *p860*
281 EAST ST N, SARNIA, ON, N7T 6X8
(519) 332-4550   *SIC 8641*

ORDRE FRATERNEL DES AIGLES DE MONT-LAURIER INC *p1154*
742 RUE DE LA MADONE, MONT-LAURIER, QC, J9L 1S9
SIC 8641

POLISH WAR VETERAN'S SOCIETY *p1186*
63 RUE PRINCE-ARTHUR E, MONTREAL, QC, H2X 1B4
(514) 842-7551   *SIC 8641*

POLYCULTURAL IMMIGRANT AND COM-MUNITY SERVICES *p578*
17 FOUR SEASONS PL SUITE 102, ETO-BICOKE, ON, M9B 6E6
(416) 233-1655   *SIC 8641*

REAL ESTATE COUNCIL OF ONTARIO *p572*
3300 BLOOR ST W UNIT 1200, ETOBI-COKE, ON, M8X 2X2
(416) 207-4800   *SIC 8641*

RIDEAU COUNCIL 2444 *p896*
93 MORGAN ST, STRATFORD, ON, N5A 7V2
(519) 272-9700   *SIC 8641*

ROYAL CANADIAN AIR FORCE ASSOCIA-TION *p860*
415 EXMOUTH ST, SARNIA, ON, N7T 8A4
(519) 344-8050   *SIC 8641*

ROYAL CANADIAN LEGION ONTARIO COMMAND,THE *p865*
45 LAWSON RD, SCARBOROUGH, ON,

M1C 2J1
(416) 281-2992   *SIC 8641*

ROYAL CANADIAN LEGION, THE *p479*
49 DANIEL ST N, ARNPRIOR, ON, K7S 2K6
(613) 623-4722   *SIC 8641*

SASKATOON FAMILY YOUNG MEN'S CHRISTIAN ASSOCIATION *p1429*
25 22ND ST E, SASKATOON, SK, S7K 0C7
(306) 652-7515   *SIC 8641*

SCOUTS CANADA *p831*
1345 BASELINE RD SUITE 200, OTTAWA, ON, K2C 0A7
(613) 224-0139   *SIC 8641*

SECRETARIAT DE LA CONVENTION SUR LA DIVERSITE BIOLOGIQUE *p1190*
413 RUE SAINT-JACQUES BUREAU 500, MONTREAL, QC, H2Y 1N9
(514) 288-2220   *SIC 8641*

SIMON FRASER STUDENT SOCIETY *p183*
8888 UNIVERSITY DR SUITE 2250, BURN-ABY, BC, V5A 1S6
(778) 782-3111   *SIC 8641*

SIRCOM LODGE #66 *p470*
GD, WHYCOCOMAGH, NS, B0E 3M0
(902) 756-3262   *SIC 8641*

SOCIETE DE GESTION DE LA ZONE POR-TUAIRE DE CHICOUTIMI INC *p1079*
49 RUE LA FONTAINE, CHICOUTIMI, QC, G7H 7Y7
(418) 698-3025   *SIC 8641*

SOCIETY CARUSO CLUB OF SUDBURY *p900*
385 HAIG ST, SUDBURY, ON, P3C 1C5
(705) 675-1357   *SIC 8641*

ST. JOHN'S YOUNG MEN'S AND YOUNG WOMEN'S CHRISTIAN ASSOCIATION *p429*
34 NEW COVE RD, ST. JOHN'S, NL, A1A 2B8
(709) 754-2960   *SIC 8641*

UNIVERSITY OF MANITOBA STUDENTS UNION *p392*
81 UNIVERSITY CRES SUITE 101, WIN-NIPEG, MB, R3T 4W9
(204) 474-8678   *SIC 8641*

UNIVERSITY OF TORONTO ENGINEERING SOCIETY, THE *p976*
10 KING'S COLLEGE RD SUITE B740, TORONTO, ON, M5S 3G4
(416) 978-2917   *SIC 8641*

VANCOUVER CLUB, THE *p310*
915 HASTINGS ST W, VANCOUVER, BC, V6C 1C6
(604) 685-9321   *SIC 8641*

WAR AMPUTATIONS OF CANADA, THE *p828*
2827 RIVERSIDE DR SUITE 101, OTTAWA, ON, K1V 0C4
(613) 731-3821   *SIC 8641*

WOOD'S HOMES SOCIETY *p42*
805 37 ST NW, CALGARY, AB, T2N 4N8
(403) 220-0349   *SIC 8641*

YMCA OF NIAGARA *p1012*
310 WOODLAND RD, WELLAND, ON, L3C 7N3
(905) 735-9622   *SIC 8641*

YMCA-YWCA OF BROCKVILLE AND AREA *p520*
345 PARK ST, BROCKVILLE, ON, K6V 5Y7
(613) 342-7961   *SIC 8641*

YOUNG MEN'S AND YOUNG WOMEN'S CHRISTIAN ASSOCIATION OF WINNIPEG INCORPORATED, THE *p376*
301 VAUGHAN ST, WINNIPEG, MB, R3B 2N7
(204) 661-9474   *SIC 8641*

YOUNG MEN'S AND YOUNG WOMEN'S CHRISTIAN ASSOCIATION OF WINNIPEG INCORPORATED, THE *p387*
3550 PORTAGE AVE, WINNIPEG, MB, R3K 0Z8
(204) 889-8052   *SIC 8641*

YOUNG MEN'S CHRISTIAN ASSOCIATION OF CAMBRIDGE *p535*
250 HESPELER RD, CAMBRIDGE, ON,

N1R 3H3
(519) 623-9622   *SIC 8641*

YOUNG MEN'S CHRISTIAN ASSOCIATION OF NORTH BAY AND DISTRICT *p764*
186 CHIPPEWA ST W, NORTH BAY, ON, P1B 6G2
(705) 497-9622   *SIC 8641*

YOUNG MENS CHRISTIAN ASSOCIATION *p901*
140 DURHAM ST, SUDBURY, ON, P3E 3M7
(705) 673-9136   *SIC 8641*

YOUNG MENS CHRISTIAN ASSOCIATION OF REGINA *p1419*
2400 13TH AVE, REGINA, SK, S4P 0V9
(306) 757-9622   *SIC 8641*

YOUNG WOMEN'S CHRISTIAN ASSOCIA-TION *p311*
535 HORNBY ST SUITE 100, VANCOU-VER, BC, V6C 2E8
(604) 895-5777   *SIC 8641*

SIC 8651 Political organizations

ASSEMBLY OF MANITOBA CHIEFS SEC-RETARIAT INC *p374*
275 PORTAGE AVE SUITE 200, WIN-NIPEG, MB, R3B 2B3
(204) 956-0610   *SIC 8651*

CROATION CLUB KARLOVAC *p683*
1880 THOMPSON RD S, MILTON, ON, L9T 2X5
(905) 878-6185   *SIC 8651*

DASONG ZAO CAMPAIGN, THE *p914*
3469 SHEPPARD AVE E, TORONTO, ON, M1T 3K5
(647) 641-7292   *SIC 8651*

DIANNE WATTS CAMPAIGN, THE *p276*
7327 137 ST UNIT 307, SURREY, BC, V3W 1A4
SIC 8651

ERINDALE COLLEGE STUDENT UNION *p716*
3359 MISSISSAUGA RD, MISSISSAUGA, ON, L5L 1C6
(905) 828-5249   *SIC 8651*

FEDERATION OF SASKATCHEWAN INDI-ANS, INC *p1433*
103A PACKHAM AVE SUITE 100, SASKA-TOON, SK, S7N 4K4
(306) 665-1215   *SIC 8651*

KINGSTON AND THE ISLANDS POLITICAL PARTY *p631*
15 ALAMEIN DR, KINGSTON, ON, K7L 4R5
(613) 546-6081   *SIC 8651*

MANITOBA METIS FEDERATION INC *p375*
150 HENRY AVE SUITE 300, WINNIPEG, MB, R3B 0J7
(204) 586-8474   *SIC 8651*

METIS EDUCATION FOUNDATION OF THE METIS NATION OF ALBERTA ASSOCIA-TION, THE *p85*
11738 KINGSWAY NW SUITE 100, ED-MONTON, AB, T5G 0X5
(780) 455-2200   *SIC 8651*

MULRONEY, CAROLINE LEADERSHIP CAMPAIGN *p925*
1491 YONGE ST SUITE 201, TORONTO, ON, M4T 1Z4
(416) 922-0573   *SIC 8651*

NATIVE COUNCIL OF NOVA SCOTIA *p469*
129 TRURO HEIGHTS RD, TRURO HEIGHTS, NS, B6L 1X2
(902) 895-1523   *SIC 8651*

NEW DEMOCRATIC PARTY OF B.C. *p186*
4180 LOUGHEED HWY UNIT 301, BURN-ABY, BC, V5C 6A7
(604) 430-8600   *SIC 8651*

ONTARIO PC PARTY *p996*
56 ABERFOYLE CRES UNIT 400, TORONTO, ON, M8X 2W4
(416) 861-0020   *SIC 8651*

SASKATCHEWAN LIBERAL ASSOCIATION *p1419*

2054 BROAD ST, REGINA, SK, S4P 1Y3
SIC 8651
STUDENTS ASSOCIATION OF MOUNT ROYAL COLLEGE   *p74*
4825 MOUNT ROYAL GATE SW, CALGARY, AB, T3E 6K6
(403) 440-6077   *SIC* 8651

SIC 8661 Religious organizations

ABBOTSFORD CHRISTIAN SCHOOL SOCIETY   *p174*
35011 OLD CLAYBURN RD, ABBOTSFORD, BC, V2S 7L7
(604) 755-1891   *SIC* 8661
ALBERTA CONFERENCE OF THE SEVENTH-DAY ADVENTISTS CHURCH, THE   *p138*
5816 HIGHWAY 2A, LACOMBE, AB, T4L 2G5
(403) 342-5044   *SIC* 8661
ANGLICAN CHURCH OF CANADA   *p931*
80 HAYDEN ST SUITE 400, TORONTO, ON, M4Y 3G2
(416) 924-9192   *SIC* 8661
APOTRES DE L'AMOUR INFINI CANADA, LES   *p1159*
290 7E RANG, MONT-TREMBLANT, QC, J8E 1Y4
(819) 425-7257   *SIC* 8661
ARCHDIOCESE OF ST BONIFACE, THE   *p364*
151 DE LA CATHEDRALE AVE, WINNIPEG, MB, R2H 0H6
(204) 237-9851   *SIC* 8661
ARCHEVEQUE CATHOLIQUE ROMAIN DE QUEBEC, L'   *p1270*
1073 BOUL RENE-LEVESQUE O, QUEBEC, QC, G1S 4R5
(418) 688-1211   *SIC* 8661
ARCHIDIOCESE DE MONCTON   *p397*
452 RUE AMIRAULT, DIEPPE, NB, E1A 1G3
(506) 857-9531   *SIC* 8661
BASILIQUE SAINTE-ANNE-DE-BEAUPRE   *p1354*
10018 AV ROYALE, SAINTE-ANNE-DE-BEAUPRE, QC, G0A 3C0
(418) 827-3781   *SIC* 8661
BETH TZEDEC CONGREGATION INC *p972*
1700 BATHURST ST, TORONTO, ON, M5P 3K3
(416) 781-3511   *SIC* 8661
BISHOP OF VICTORIA CORPORATION SOLE   *p337*
4044 NELTHORPE ST SUITE 1, VICTORIA, BC, V8X 2A1
(250) 479-1331   *SIC* 8661
CANADA TORONTO EAST MISSION   *p867*
30 SEMINOLE AVE, SCARBOROUGH, ON, M1J 1N1
SIC 8661
CANADA TORONTO EAST MISSION   *p989*
851 OSSINGTON AVE, TORONTO, ON, M6G 3V2
(416) 531-0535   *SIC* 8661
CATHOLIC INDEPENDENT SCHOOLS OF VANCOUVER ARCHDIOCESE, THE   *p293*
4885 SAINT JOHN PAUL II WAY, VANCOUVER, BC, V5Z 0G3
(604) 683-9331   *SIC* 8661
CENTRE D'HEBERGEMENT ET DE SOINS DE LONGUE DUREE PROVIDENCE SAINT-JOSEPH INC   *p1165*
5605 RUE BEAUBIEN E BUREAU 114, MONTREAL, QC, H1T 1X4
(514) 254-4991   *SIC* 8661
CENTRE STREET CHURCH   *p22*
3900 2 ST NE, CALGARY, AB, T2E 9C1
(403) 293-3900   *SIC* 8661
CHRISTIAN & MISSIONARY ALLIANCE - CANADIAN PACIFIC DISTRICT   *p276*
7565 132 ST SUITE 107, SURREY, BC, V3W 1K5

SIC 8661
CHRISTIAN AND MISSIONARY ALLIANCE IN CANADA, THE   *p685*
7560 AIRPORT RD UNIT 1, MISSISSAUGA, ON, L4T 4H4
(416) 674-7878   *SIC* 8661
CHRISTIAN BLIND MISSION INTERNATIONAL   *p894*
GD, STOUFFVILLE, ON, L4A 7Z9
(905) 640-6464   *SIC* 8661
CONGREGATION DES SOEURS DE NOTRE-DAME DU PERPETUEL SECOURS *p1299*
159 RUE COMMERCIALE, SAINT-DAMIEN-DE-BUCKLAND, QC, G0R 2Y0
(418) 789-2112   *SIC* 8661
CORPORATION ARCHIEPISCOPALE CATHOLIQUE ROMAINE DE MONTREAL, LA   *p1215*
2000 RUE SHERBROOKE O, MONTREAL, QC, H3H 1G4
(514) 931-7311   *SIC* 8661
CORPORATION MAURICE-RATTE   *p1397*
905 BOUL DES BOIS-FRANCS S, VICTORIAVILLE, QC, G6P 5W1
(819) 357-8217   *SIC* 8661
EVANGELICAL LUTHERAN CHURCH IN CANADA   *p293*
585 41ST AVE W, VANCOUVER, BC, V5Z 2M7
(604) 261-2442   *SIC* 8661
FABRIQUE DE LA PAROISSE NOTRE-DAME DE MONTREAL, LA   *p1188*
424 RUE SAINT-SULPICE, MONTREAL, QC, H2Y 2V5
(514) 842-2925   *SIC* 8661
FILLES DE JESUS, (RIMOUKI)   *p1284*
949 BOUL SAINT-GERMAIN, RIMOUSKI, QC, G5L 8Y9
(418) 723-4346   *SIC* 8661
FILLES DE LA CHARITE DU SACRE-COEUR DE JESUS, LES   *p1370*
575 RUE ALLEN, SHERBROOKE, QC, J1G 1Z1
(819) 569-9617   *SIC* 8661
FRERES MARISTES, LES   *p1075*
7141 AV ROYALE, CHATEAU-RICHER, QC, G0A 1N0
(418) 824-4215   *SIC* 8661
HUTTERIAN BRETHEREN CHURCH OF STAHLVILLE   *p160*
GD, ROCKYFORD, AB, T0J 2R0
(403) 533-2102   *SIC* 8661
HUTTERIAN BRETHREN CHURCH OF DOWNIE LAKE INC   *p1409*
GD, MAPLE CREEK, SK, S0N 1N0
(306) 662-3462   *SIC* 8661
HUTTERIAN BRETHREN CHURCH OF HILLVIEW COLONY   *p160*
GD, ROSEBUD, AB, T0J 2T0
(403) 677-2360   *SIC* 8661
HUTTERIAN BRETHERN OF SOVEREIGN *p1423*
GD, ROSETOWN, SK, S0L 2V0
(306) 882-2447   *SIC* 8661
HUTTERIAN BRETHRAN CHURCH OF BEISEKER   *p5*
GD, BEISEKER, AB, T0M 0G0
(403) 947-2181   *SIC* 8661
HUTTERIAN BRETHREN CHURCH OF CAMROSE   *p78*
GD LCD MAIN, CAMROSE, AB, T4V 1X1
(780) 672-1553   *SIC* 8661
HUTTERIAN BRETHREN CHURCH OF CASTOR   *p79*
GD, CASTOR, AB, T0C 0X0
(403) 882-3305   *SIC* 8661
HUTTERIAN BRETHREN CHURCH OF CLEARDALE   *p80*
GD, CLEARDALE, AB, T0H 3Y0
(780) 685-2870   *SIC* 8661
HUTTERIAN BRETHREN CHURCH OF EWELME COLONY   *p127*
GD, FORT MACLEOD, AB, T0L 0Z0

(403) 553-2606   *SIC* 8661
HUTTERIAN BRETHREN CHURCH OF FERRYBANK   *p152*
GD, PONOKA, AB, T4J 1R9
(403) 783-2259   *SIC* 8661
HUTTERIAN BRETHREN CHURCH OF GRANDVIEW   *p134*
723042A RANGE ROAD 74, GRANDE PRAIRIE, AB, T8X 4L1
(780) 532-6500   *SIC* 8661
HUTTERIAN BRETHREN CHURCH OF HOLT   *p137*
GD, IRMA, AB, T0B 2H0
(780) 754-2175   *SIC* 8661
HUTTERIAN BRETHREN CHURCH OF MOUNTAINVIEW, THE   *p168*
GD STN MAIN, STRATHMORE, AB, T1P 1J5
(403) 935-4210   *SIC* 8661
HUTTERIAN BRETHREN CHURCH OF SIMMIE INC   *p1436*
GD, SIMMIE, SK, S0N 2N0
(306) 297-6304   *SIC* 8661
HUTTERIAN BRETHREN CHURCH OF THE LITTLE BOW   *p79*
GD, CHAMPION, AB, T0L 0R0
(403) 897-3838   *SIC* 8661
HUTTERIAN BRETHREN CHURCH OF TSCHETTER   *p137*
GD, IRRICANA, AB, T0M 1B0
(403) 935-2362   *SIC* 8661
HUTTERIAN BRETHREN CHURCH OF VALLEYVIEW RANCH   *p170*
GD, TORRINGTON, AB, T0M 2B0
(403) 631-2372   *SIC* 8661
HUTTERIAN BRETHREN CHURCH OF VETERAN   *p171*
GD, VETERAN, AB, T0C 2S0
(403) 575-2169   *SIC* 8661
HUTTERIAN BRETHREN OF KYLE INC *p1408*
GD, KYLE, SK, S0L 1T0
(306) 375-2910   *SIC* 8661
HUTTERIAN BRETHREN OF PENNANT INC *p1413*
GD, PENNANT STATION, SK, S0N 1X0
(306) 626-3369   *SIC* 8661
HUTTERIAN BRETHREN SPRING CREEK COLONY   *p171*
GD, WALSH, AB, T0J 3L0
(403) 937-2524   ·*SIC* 8661
INCORPORATED SYNOD OF THE DIOCESE OF TORONTO, THE   *p939*
135 ADELAIDE ST E, TORONTO, ON, M5C 1L8
(416) 363-6021   *SIC* 8661
INCORPORATION SYNOD DIOCESE OF OTTAWA   *p825*
71 BRONSON AVE, OTTAWA, ON, K1R 6G6
(613) 232-7124   *SIC* 8661
INTER-VARSITY CHRISTIAN FELLOWSHIP OF CANADA   *p585*
1 INTERNATIONAL BLVD, ETOBICOKE, ON, M9W 6H3
(416) 443-1170   *SIC* 8661
JEHOVAH'S WITNESSES EAST ST PAUL CONGREGATION   *p363*
3760 ANDREWS RD, WINNIPEG, MB, R2E 1C2
(204) 654-1829   *SIC* 8661
JEWISH COMMUNITY COUNCIL OF MONTREAL   *p1220*
6819 BOUL DECARIE, MONTREAL, QC, H3W 3E4
(514) 739-6363   *SIC* 8661
KELOWNA CHRISTIAN CENTER SOCIETY *p220*
907 BADKE RD, KELOWNA, BC, V1X 5Z5
(250) 862-2376   *SIC* 8661
L'ORATOIRE SAINT-JOSEPH DU MONT-ROYAL   *p1219*
3800 CH QUEEN-MARY, MONTREAL, QC, H3V 1H6

(514) 733-8211   *SIC* 8661
LUTHERAN CHURCH-CANADA   *p386*
3074 PORTAGE AVE, WINNIPEG, MB, R3K 0Y2
(204) 895-3433   *SIC* 8661
MACMILLAN HUTTERIAN BRETHREN *p79*
658 32 ST SW, CAYLEY, AB, T0L 0P0
(403) 395-2221   *SIC* 8661
MB MISSION   *p178*
32040 DOWNES RD SUITE 300, ABBOTSFORD, BC, V4X 1X5
(604) 859-6267   *SIC* 8661
MENNONITE BRETHREN CHURCH OF MANITOBA, THE   *p388*
1310 TAYLOR AVE, WINNIPEG, MB, R3M 3Z6
(204) 415-0670   *SIC* 8661
NEW HAVEN COLONY FARMS LTD   *p345*
82080 RD 1 E, ARGYLE, MB, R0C 0B0
(204) 467-8790   *SIC* 8661
NOTRE DAME HIGH SCHOOL   *p76*
11900 COUNTRY VILLAGE LINK NE, CALGARY, AB, T3K 6E4
(403) 500-2109   *SIC* 8661
ONTARIO CONFERENCE OF THE SEVENTH-DAY ADVENTISTS CHURCH *p813*
1110 KING ST E, OSHAWA, ON, L1H 1H8
(905) 571-1022   *SIC* 8661
OVERSEAS MISSIONARY FELLOWSHIP *p877*
10 HUNTINGDALE BLVD, SCARBOROUGH, ON, M1W 2S5
(905) 568-9971   *SIC* 8661
PENTECOSTAL ASSEMBLIES OF CANADA, THE   *p725*
2450 MILLTOWER CRT, MISSISSAUGA, ON, L5N 5Z6
(905) 542-7400   *SIC* 8661
PENTECOSTAL ASSEMBLIES OF NEWFOUNDLAND AND LABRADOR CORPORATION   *p431*
57 THORBURN RD, ST. JOHN'S, NL, A1B 3M2
(709) 753-6314   *SIC* 8661
PEOPLES MINISTRIES INC   *p772*
374 SHEPPARD AVE E, NORTH YORK, ON, M2N 3B6
(416) 222-3341   *SIC* 8661
PETITE SOEURS DE LA SAINTE-FAMILLE, LES   *p1372*
1820 RUE GALT O, SHERBROOKE, QC, J1K 1H9
(819) 823-0345   *SIC* 8661
POWER TO CHANGE MINISTRIES   *p226*
20385 64 AVE, LANGLEY, BC, V2Y 1N5
(604) 514-2000   *SIC* 8661
PRESBYTERIAN CHURCH IN CANADA, THE   *p780*
50 WYNFORD DR, NORTH YORK, ON, M3C 1J7
(416) 441-1111   *SIC* 8661
PROVINCE DU QUEBEC DE L'UNION CANADIENNE DES MONIALES DE L'ORDRE DE SAINTE-URSULE   *p1275*
20 RUE DES DAMES-URSULINES, QUEBEC, QC, G2B 2V1
(418) 692-2523   *SIC* 8661
RAINBOW COLONY FARMING CO LTD *p158*
26052 TOWNSHIP ROAD 350, RED DEER COUNTY, AB, T4G 0M4
(403) 227-6465   *SIC* 8661
RELIGIEUSES DE JESUS-MARIE, LES *p1271*
2049 CH SAINT-LOUIS, QUEBEC, QC, G1T 1P2
(418) 687-9260   *SIC* 8661
ROMAN CATHOLIC ARCHDIOCESE OF VANCOUVER, THE   *p293*
4885 SAINT JOHN PAUL II WAY, VANCOUVER, BC, V5Z 0G3
(604) 683-0281   *SIC* 8661
ROMAN CATHOLIC EPISCOPAL CORP OF THE DIOCESE OF PETERBOROUGH *p840*

350 HUNTER ST W, PETERBOROUGH, ON, K9H 2M4

(705) 745-5123   *SIC* 8661

ROMAN CATHOLIC EPISCOPAL CORP OF THE DIOCESE OF SAULT STE MARIE, IN ONTARIO CANADA   *p*900

30 STE. ANNE RD, SUDBURY, ON, P3C 5E1

(705) 674-2727   *SIC* 8661

ROMAN CATHOLIC EPISCOPAL CORPORATION FOR THE DIOCESE OF TORONTO, IN CANADA   *p*926

1155 YONGE ST, TORONTO, ON, M4T 1W2

(416) 934-3400   *SIC* 8661

ROMAN CATHOLIC EPISCOPAL CORPORATION FOR THE DIOCESE OF TORONTO, IN CANADA   *p*926

1155 YONGE ST SUITE 603, TORONTO, ON, M4T 1W2

(416) 934-0606   *SIC* 8661

ROMAN CATHOLIC EPISCOPAL CORPORATION OF THE DIOCESE OF LONDON IN ONTARIO, THE   *p*655

1070 WATERLOO ST, LONDON, ON, N6A 3Y2

(519) 433-0658   *SIC* 8661

SANCTUAIRE NOTRE-DAME-DU-CAP   *p*1385

626 RUE NOTRE-DAME E, TROIS-RIVIERES, QC, G8T 4G9

(819) 374-2441   *SIC* 8661

SHAMROCK HUTTERIAN BRETHREN   *p*6

GD, BOW ISLAND, AB, T0K 0G0

(403) 545-6190   *SIC* 8661

SISTERS OF CHARITY   *p*457

215 SETON RD, HALIFAX, NS, B3M 0C9

(902) 406-8100   *SIC* 8661

SISTERS OF CHARITY OF OTTAWA, THE   *p*820

50 MAPLE LANE, OTTAWA, ON, K1M 1G8

(613) 745-1584   *SIC* 8661

SISTERS OF CHARITY OF PROVIDENCE OF WESTERN CANADA, THE   *p*119

3005 119 ST NW, EDMONTON, AB, T6J 5R5

(780) 430-9491   *SIC* 8661

SISTERS OF ST. JOSEPHS OF HAMILTON   *p*566

574 NORTHCLIFFE AVE, DUNDAS, ON, L9H 7L9

(905) 528-0138   *SIC* 8661

SOCIETE DES MISSIONNAIRES D'AFRIQUE (PERES BLANCS) PROVINCE DE L'AMERIQUE DU NORD   *p*1176

1640 RUE SAINT-HUBERT, MONTREAL, QC, H2L 3Z3

(514) 849-1167   *SIC* 8661

SOEURS DE CHARITE DE SAINT-HYACINTHE, LES   *p*1314

16470 AV BOURDAGES S, SAINT-HYACINTHE, QC, J2T 4J8

(450) 773-9785   *SIC* 8661

SOEURS DE LA CHARITE (SOEURS GRISES) DE MONTREAL, LES   *p*1190

138 RUE SAINT-PIERRE, MONTREAL, QC, H2Y 2L7

(514) 842-9411   *SIC* 8661

SOEURS DE LA CHARITE D'OTTAWA, LES   *p*822

27 BRUYERE ST, OTTAWA, ON, K1N 5C9

(613) 241-2710   *SIC* 8661

SOEURS DE LA CHARITE D'OTTAWA, LES   *p*822

43 BRUYERE ST, OTTAWA, ON, K1N 5C8

(613) 562-0050   *SIC* 8661

SOEURS DE LA CONGREGATION DE NOTRE-DAME, LES   *p*1115

393 RUE DE LANAUDIERE, JOLIETTE, QC, J6E 3L9

(450) 752-1481   *SIC* 8661

SOEURS DE LA CONGREGATION DE NOTRE-DAME, LES   *p*1215

2330 RUE SHERBROOKE O, MONTREAL, QC, H3H 1G8

(514) 931-5891   *SIC* 8661

SOEURS DE LA CONGREGATION DE NOTRE-DAME, LES   *p*1221

5015 AV NOTRE-DAME-DE-GRACE, MONTREAL, QC, H4A 1K2

(514) 485-1461   *SIC* 8661

SOEURS DE LA PRESENTATION DE MARIE DU QUEBEC   *p*1168

3600 RUE BELANGER, MONTREAL, QC, H1X 1B1

(514) 721-4979   *SIC* 8661

SOEURS DE SAINT-FRANCOIS D'ASSISE, LES   *p*1257

600 60E RUE E, QUEBEC, QC, G1H 3A9

(418) 623-1515   *SIC* 8661

SOEURS DE SAINTE-ANNE DU QUEBEC, LES   *p*1126

1950 RUE PROVOST, LACHINE, QC, H8S 1P7

(514) 637-3783   *SIC* 8661

SOEURS DE SAINTE-CROIX   *p*1323

900 BOUL DE LA COTE-VERTU, SAINT-LAURENT, QC, H4L 4T9

SIC 8661

SOEURS DES SAINTS NOMS DE JESUS ET DE MARIE DU QUEBEC, LES   *p*1143

82 RUE SAINT-CHARLES E, LONGUEUIL, QC, J4H 1A9

(450) 651-3744   *SIC* 8661

SOEURS DES SAINTS NOMS DE JESUS ET DE MARIE DU QUEBEC, LES   *p*1143

86 RUE SAINT-CHARLES E, LONGUEUIL, QC, J4H 1A9

(450) 651-0179   *SIC* 8661

SOEURS GRISES DE MONTREAL, LES   *p*1215

1190 RUE GUY, MONTREAL, QC, H3H 2L4

SIC 8661

SOUTHDOWN INSTITUTE, THE   *p*481

1335 ST. JOHN'S SIDEROAD SUITE 2, AURORA, ON, L4G 0P8

(905) 727-4214   *SIC* 8661

SPRINGS OF LIVING WATER CENTRE INC   *p*366

595 LAGIMODIERE BLVD SUITE 1, WINNIPEG, MB, R2J 3X2

(204) 233-7003   *SIC* 8661

SPRINT-PIONEERS MINISTRIES INC   *p*565

51 BYRON AVE SS 2, DORCHESTER, ON, N0L 1G2

(519) 268-8778   *SIC* 8661

TALMUD TORAHS UNIS DE MONTREAL INC   *p*1220

4840 AV SAINT-KEVIN BUREAU 210, MONTREAL, QC, H3W 1P2

(514) 739-2294   *SIC* 8661

TORONTO AIRPORT CHRISTIAN FELLOWSHIP   *p*589

272 ATTWELL DR, ETOBICOKE, ON, M9W 6M3

(416) 674-8463   *SIC* 8661

UKRANIAN CATHOLIC ARCHEPARCHY OF WINNIPEG   *p*370

233 SCOTIA ST, WINNIPEG, MB, R2V 1V7

(204) 338-7801   *SIC* 8661

UNITED CHURCH OF CANADA, THE   *p*572

3250 BLOOR ST W SUITE 300, ETOBICOKE, ON, M8X 2Y4

(416) 231-5931   *SIC* 8661

WATCH TOWER BIBLE AND TRACT SOCIETY OF CANADA   *p*594

13893 HIGHWAY 7, GEORGETOWN, ON, L7G 4S4

(905) 873-4100   *SIC* 8661

WATCH TOWER BIBLE AND TRACT SOCIETY OF CANADA   *p*1012

390 CLARE AVE, WELLAND, ON, L3C 5R2

SIC 8661

WESLEYAN CHURCH OF CANADA   *p*663

3545 CENTENNIAL RD, LYN, ON, K0E 1M0

(613) 345-3424   *SIC* 8661

———————————

SIC 8699 Membership organizations, nec

———————————

2637-5808 QUEBEC INC   *p*1140

2091 RTE MARIE-VICTORIN, LEVIS, QC, G7A 4H4

(418) 831-9967   *SIC* 8699

360 KIDS SUPPORT SERVICES   *p*855

10415 YONGE ST SUITE C, RICHMOND HILL, ON, L4C 0Z3

(905) 475-6694   *SIC* 8699

6038263 CANADA INC   *p*1185

3575 AV DU PARC, MONTREAL, QC, H2X 3P9

(514) 288-8221   *SIC* 8699

ACCEUIL BONNEAU INC   *p*1187

427 RUE DE LA COMMUNE E, MONTREAL, QC, H2Y 1J4

(514) 845-3906   *SIC* 8699

ACL SELKIRK INC   *p*356

306 JEMIMA ST, SELKIRK, MB, R1A 1X1

(204) 482-5435   *SIC* 8699

ADVENT HEALTH CARE CORPORATION   *p*775

541 FINCH AVE W, NORTH YORK, ON, M2R 3Y3

(416) 636-5800   *SIC* 8699

AGAPE STREET MINISTRY   *p*294

887 KEEFER ST, VANCOUVER, BC, V6A 1Y8

(604) 215-4115   *SIC* 8699

AIESEC SASKATOON   *p*1433

25 CAMPUS DR SUITE 248, SASKATOON, SK, S7N 5A7

(306) 966-7767   *SIC* 8699

ALBERTA CHILDREN'S HOSPITAL FOUNDATION   *p*72

2888 SHAGANAPPI TRAIL NW, CALGARY, AB, T3B 6A8

(403) 955-8818   *SIC* 8699

ALBERTA EASTER SEALS SOCIETY   *p*86

10025 106 ST NW SUITE 1408, EDMONTON, AB, T5J 1G4

(780) 429-0137   *SIC* 8699

ALBERTA MOTOR ASSOCIATION   *p*112

9520 42 AVE NW, EDMONTON, AB, T6E 5Y4

(780) 989-6230   *SIC* 8699

ALBERTA MOTOR ASSOCIATION   *p*119

10310A G A MACDONALD AVE NW, EDMONTON, AB, T6J 6R7

(780) 430-5555   *SIC* 8699

ALICE SADDY ASSOCIATION   *p*655

111 WATERLOO ST SUITE 401, LONDON, ON, N6B 2M4

(519) 433-2801   *SIC* 8699

ALPINE CANADA ALPIN   *p*72

151 CANADA OLYMPIC RD SW SUITE 302, CALGARY, AB, T3B 6B7

(403) 777-3200   *SIC* 8699

AMITY GOODWILL INDUSTRIES   *p*613

225 KING WILLIAM ST, HAMILTON, ON, L8R 1B1

(905) 526-8482   *SIC* 8699

ANOVA: A FUTURE WITHOUT VIOLENCE   *p*655

255 HORTON ST E FL 3, LONDON, ON, N6B 1L1

(519) 642-3003   *SIC* 8699

ASPEN FAMILY AND COMMUNITY NETWORK SOCIETY   *p*20

2609 15 ST NE SUITE 200, CALGARY, AB, T2E 8Y4

(403) 219-3477   *SIC* 8699

ASSINIBOINE PARK CONSERVANCY INC   *p*388

55 PAVILION CRES, WINNIPEG, MB, R3P 2N6

(204) 927-6002   *SIC* 8699

ASSOCIATION DES ETUDIANTS DU CEGEP ST-LAURENT INC   *p*1323

625 AV SAINTE-CROIX, SAINT-LAURENT, QC, H4L 3X7

(514) 747-4026   *SIC* 8699

ASSOCIATION FOR COMMUNITY LIVING-STEINBACH BRANCH INC   *p*358

395 MAIN ST, STEINBACH, MB, R5G 1Z4

(204) 326-7539   *SIC* 8699

ASSOCIATION YWCA DE QUEBEC, L'   *p*1270

855 AV HOLLAND, QUEBEC, QC, G1S 3S5

(418) 683-2155   *SIC* 8699

ATHABASCA TRIBAL COUNCIL LTD   *p*127

9206 MCCORMICK DR, FORT MCMURRAY, AB, T9H 1C7

(780) 791-6538   *SIC* 8699

ATTIC, THE   *p*245

4760 JOHNSTON RD, PORT ALBERNI, BC, V9Y 5M3

(250) 723-2143   *SIC* 8699

AUTOMOBILE ET TOURING CLUB DU QUEBEC (A.T.C.Q.)   *p*1278

444 RUE BOUVIER, QUEBEC, QC, G2J 1E3

(418) 624-2424   *SIC* 8699

AVALANCHE CANADA   *p*253

1596 ILLECILLEWAET RD, REVELSTOKE, BC, V0E 2S1

(250) 837-2141   *SIC* 8699

B C FUNDRAISERS   *p*290

8278 MANITOBA ST, VANCOUVER, BC, V5X 3A2

SIC 8699

B.C. CUSTOM CAR ASSOCIATION   *p*232

32670 DYKE RD, MISSION, BC, V2V 4J5

(604) 826-6315   *SIC* 8699

BANYAN COMMUNITY SERVICES INC   *p*614

688 QUEENSDALE AVE E UNIT 2B, HAMILTON, ON, L8V 1M1

(905) 545-0133   *SIC* 8699

BARBOUR LIVING HERITAGE VILLAGE   *p*427

GD, NEWTOWN, NL, A0G 3L0

(709) 536-3220   *SIC* 8699

BARRIE MINOR BASEBALL ASSOCIATION   *p*486

14 BROADMOOR AVE, BARRIE, ON, L4N 3M9

(705) 726-1441   *SIC* 8699

BEACON COMMUNITY SERVICES   *p*268

9860 THIRD ST, SIDNEY, BC, V8L 4R2

(250) 658-6407   *SIC* 8699

BEDDINGTON HEIGHTS COMMUNITY ASSOCIATION   *p*76

375 BERMUDA DR NW, CALGARY, AB, T3K 2J5

(403) 295-8837   *SIC* 8699

BEDFORD LIONS CLUB   *p*439

36 HOLLAND AVE, BEDFORD, NS, B4A 1L9

(902) 835-0862   *SIC* 8699

BERGER BLANC INC, LE   *p*1160

9825 BOUL HENRI-BOURASSA E, MONTREAL, QC, H1C 1G5

(514) 494-2002   *SIC* 8699

BIG TROUT LAKE BAND PERSONNEL OFFICE   *p*493

GD, BIG TROUT LAKE, ON, P0V 1G0

SIC 8699

BLEAK HOUSE SENIOR'S CENTRE   *p*370

1637 MAIN ST, WINNIPEG, MB, R2V 1Y8

(204) 338-4723   *SIC* 8699

BOULOT VERS..., LE   *p*1166

4447 RUE DE ROUEN, MONTREAL, QC, H1V 1H1

(514) 259-2312   *SIC* 8699

BOUNDLESS ADVENTURES INC   *p*836

7513 RIVER RD, PALMER RAPIDS, ON, K0J 2E0

(613) 758-2702   *SIC* 8699

BRAIN INJURED GROUP SOCIETY   *p*249

1070 4TH AVE, PRINCE GEORGE, BC, V2L 3J1

(250) 564-2447   *SIC* 8699

BRENTWOOD FOUNDATION   *p*1021

2335 DOUGALL AVE SUITE 42, WINDSOR, ON, N8X 1S9

(519) 946-3115   *SIC* 8699

BRIGGS, GEORGE L. AERIE 4269 FRATERNAL ORDER OF EAGLES   *p*1011

3 CENTRE ST, WEBBWOOD, ON, P0P 2G0

(705) 869-4269   *SIC* 8699
BRITISH COLUMBIA AUTOMOBILE ASSO-CIATION   *p*188
4567 CANADA WAY, BURNABY, BC, V5G 4T1
(604) 268-5500   *SIC* 8699
BRITISH COLUMBIA SOCIETY FOR THE PREVENTION OF CRUELTY TO ANIMALS, THE   *p*288
1245 7TH AVE E, VANCOUVER, BC, V5T 1R1
(604) 681-7271   *SIC* 8699
BRITISH COLUMBIA'S CHILDREN'S HOS-PITAL FOUNDATION   *p*292
938 28TH AVE W, VANCOUVER, BC, V5Z 4H4
(604) 875-2444   *SIC* 8699
CAA ATLANTIC LIMITED   *p*412
378 WESTMORLAND RD, SAINT JOHN, NB, E2J 2G4
(506) 634-1400   *SIC* 8699
CAA CLUB GROUP   *p*903
60 COMMERCE VALLEY DR E, THORN-HILL, ON, L3T 7P9
(905) 771-3000   *SIC* 8699
CAA NIAGARA   *p*907
3271 SCHMON PKY, THOROLD, ON, L2V 4Y6
(905) 984-8585   *SIC* 8699
CAA NORTH & EAST ONTARIO   *p*817
2151 THURSTON DR, OTTAWA, ON, K1G 6C9
(613) 820-1890   *SIC* 8699
CALGARY HOMELESS FOUNDATION   *p*28
615 MACLEOD TRAIL SE SUITE 1500, CALGARY, AB, T2G 4T8
(403) 237-6456   *SIC* 8699
CALGARY HUMANE SOCIETY FOR PRE-VENTION OF CRUELTY TO ANIMALS   *p*14
4455 110 AVE SE, CALGARY, AB, T2C 2T7
(403) 205-4455   *SIC* 8699
CAMBODIA SUPPORT GROUP SOCIETY   *p*223
135 THOMPSON ST, KIMBERLEY, BC, V1A 1T9
(250) 427-2159   *SIC* 8699
CAMP KINTAIL   *p*597
85153 BLUEWATER HWY, GODERICH, ON, N7A 3X9
(519) 529-7317   *SIC* 8699
CAMP WINSTON FOUNDATION   *p*922
55 EGLINTON AVE E SUITE 312, TORONTO, ON, M4P 1G8
(416) 487-6229   *SIC* 8699
CANADA MILLENNIUM SCHOLARSHIP FOUNDATION   *p*1194
1000 RUE SHERBROOKE O UNITE 800, MONTREAL, QC, H3A 3G4
SIC 8699
CANADA UKRAINE FOUNDATION   *p*573
145 EVANS AVE UNIT 300, ETOBICOKE, ON, M8Z 5X8
(416) 966-9700   *SIC* 8699
CANADIAN ARTISTS' REPRESENTATION (MANITOBA) INC   *p*374
100 ARTHUR ST SUITE 407, WINNIPEG, MB, R3B 1H3
(204) 943-7211   *SIC* 8699
CANADIAN AUTOMOBILE ASSOCIATION   *p*828
1545 CARLING AVE SUITE 500, OTTAWA, ON, K1Z 8P9
(613) 247-0117   *SIC* 8699
CANADIAN CENTER FOR CHILD PROTEC-TION INC   *p*388
615 ACADEMY RD, WINNIPEG, MB, R3N 0E7
(204) 945-5735   *SIC* 8699
CANADIAN CHAMBER OF COMMERCE, THE   *p*822
275 SLATER ST SUITE 1700, OTTAWA, ON, K1P 5H9
(613) 238-4000   *SIC* 8699
CANADIAN EXECUTIVE SERVICE ORGA-

NIZATION   *p*944
700 BAY ST SUITE 800, TORONTO, ON, M5G 1Z6
(416) 961-2376   *SIC* 8699
CANADIAN FOOTBALL LEAGUE   *p*942
50 WELLINGTON ST E 3RD FL, TORONTO, ON, M5E 1C8
(416) 322-9650   *SIC* 8699
CANADIAN FOUNDATION FOR THE AMER-ICAS   *p*821
1 NICHOLAS ST SUITE 720, OTTAWA, ON, K1N 7B7
(613) 562-0005   *SIC* 8699
CANADIAN GOODWILL INDUSTRIES CORP   *p*374
70 PRINCESS ST, WINNIPEG, MB, R3B 1K2
(204) 943-6435   *SIC* 8699
CANADIAN INTERNATIONAL MILITARY GAMES CORPORATION   *p*949
357 BAY ST SUITE 300, TORONTO, ON, M5H 2T7
(416) 364-0001   *SIC* 8699
CANADIAN OLYMPIC COMMITTEE   *p*925
21 ST CLAIR AVE E SUITE 900, TORONTO, ON, M4T 1L9
(416) 962-0262   *SIC* 8699
CANADIAN PARALYMPIC COMMITTEE   *p*833
225 METCALFE ST SUITE 310, OTTAWA, ON, K2P 1P9
(613) 569-4333   *SIC* 8699
CANADIAN SOCCER ASSOCIATION IN-CORPORATED, THE   *p*833
237 METCALFE ST, OTTAWA, ON, K2P 1R2
(613) 237-7678   *SIC* 8699
CANADIAN SPECIAL OLYMPICS INC   *p*925
60 ST CLAIR AVE E SUITE 700, TORONTO, ON, M4T 1N5
(416) 927-9050   *SIC* 8699
CANADIAN TENNIS ASSOCIATION   *p*786
1 SHOREHAM DR SUITE 200, NORTH YORK, ON, M3N 3A7
(416) 665-9777   *SIC* 8699
CANADIAN TOURISM HUMAN RESOURCE COUNCIL   *p*822
151 SLATER ST SUITE 608, OTTAWA, ON, K1P 5H3
(613) 231-6949   *SIC* 8699
CANADIAN WARPLANE HERITAGE INC   *p*747
9280 AIRPORT RD, MOUNT HOPE, ON, L0R 1W0
(905) 679-4183   *SIC* 8699
CARPENTERS DISTRICT COUNCIL OF ON-TARIO TRAINING TRUST FUND, THE   *p*1030
222 ROWNTREE DAIRY RD, WOOD-BRIDGE, ON, L4L 9T2
SIC 8699
CARREFOUR JEUNESSE-EMPLOI TROIS-RIVIERES/MRC DES CHENAUX   *p*1384
580 RUE BARKOFF BUREAU 300, TROIS-RIVIERES, QC, G8T 9T7
(819) 376-0179   *SIC* 8699
CARROT RIVER CO-OPERATIVE LIMITED, THE   *p*1405
1002 MAIN ST, CARROT RIVER, SK, S0E 0L0
(306) 768-2622   *SIC* 8699
CATHOLIC FAMILY SERVICES OF PEEL-DUFFERIN   *p*501
60 WEST DR SUITE 201, BRAMPTON, ON, L6T 3T6
(905) 450-1608   *SIC* 8699
CENTRAL ALBERTA RESIDENCE SOCI-ETY   *p*153
5000 50 AVE SUITE 300, RED DEER, AB, T4N 6C2
(403) 342-4550   *SIC* 8699
CENTRAL OKANAGAN BOYS & GIRLS CLUB   *p*221
1434 GRAHAM ST, KELOWNA, BC, V1Y 3A8
(250) 762-3914   *SIC* 8699

CENTRAL OKANAGAN CHILD DEVELOP-MENT ASSOCIATION   *p*221
1546 BERNARD AVE, KELOWNA, BC, V1Y 6R9
(250) 763-5100   *SIC* 8699
CENTRE DE REFERENCE EN AGRICUL-TURE ET AGROALIMENTAIRE DU QUEBEC   *p*1271
2875 BOUL LAURIER UNITE 900, QUE-BEC, QC, G1V 5B1
(418) 523-5411   *SIC* 8699
CENTRE DE SANTE ET DE SERVICES SO-CIAUX DE QUEBEC-NORD-CLSC DE LA JACQUES-CARTIER -VAL-BELA   *p*1281
1465 RUE DE L'ETNA, QUEBEC, QC, G3K 2S2
(418) 843-2572   *SIC* 8699
CENTRE FOR ADDICTION AND MENTAL HEALTH FOUNDATION   *p*990
100 STOKES ST FL 5, TORONTO, ON, M6J 1H4
(416) 979-6909   *SIC* 8699
CENTRE FOR AUTISM SERVICES AL-BERTA   *p*113
4752 99 ST NW, EDMONTON, AB, T6E 5H5
(780) 488-6600   *SIC* 8699
CENTRE FOR GLOBAL STUDIES, THE *p*333
3800 FINNERTY RD SUITE 3800, VICTO-RIA, BC, V8P 5C2
(250) 472-4990   *SIC* 8699
CENTRE INTERNATIONAL DE COURSE AUTOMOBILE (ICAR) INC   *p*1153
12800 BOUL HENRI-FABRE, MIRABEL, QC, J7N 0A6
(514) 955-4227   *SIC* 8699
CENTRETOWN CITIZENS OTTAWA COR-PORATION   *p*833
415 GILMOUR ST UNIT 200, OTTAWA, ON, K2P 2M8
(613) 234-4065   *SIC* 8699
CHEDER CHABAD   *p*782
900 ALNESS ST UNIT 203, NORTH YORK, ON, M3J 2H6
(416) 663-1972   *SIC* 8699
CHEER SPORT SHARKS LIMITED   *p*538
600 BOXWOOD DR, CAMBRIDGE, ON, N3E 1A5
(519) 653-1221   *SIC* 8699
CHEO-AUTISM PROGRAM EASTERN ON-TARIO   *p*819
401 SMYTH RD, OTTAWA, ON, K1H 8L1
(613) 745-5963   *SIC* 8699
CHEVALIERS DE COLOMB THETFORD-MINES, LES   *p*1382
95 9E RUE N, THETFORD MINES, QC, G6G 5J1
(418) 335-6444   *SIC* 8699
CHRISTIAN CHILDREN'S FUND OF CANADA   *p*668
1200 DENISON ST, MARKHAM, ON, L3R 8G6
(905) 754-1001   *SIC* 8699
CLARENDON FOUNDATION (CHESHIRE HOMES) INC   *p*933
25 HENRY LANE TERR SUITE 442, TORONTO, ON, M5A 4B6
SIC 8699
CLOSE TO HOME   *p*73
3507 17 AVE SW SUITE A, CALGARY, AB, T3E 0B6
(403) 543-0550   *SIC* 8699
CO-OPERATIVE DEVELOPMENT FOUNDA-TION OF CANADA   *p*833
275 BANK ST SUITE 400, OTTAWA, ON, K2P 2L6
(613) 238-6711   *SIC* 8699
COMMUNITY LIVING PRINCE EDWARD   *p*845
67 KING ST UNIT 1, PICTON, ON, K0K 2T0
(613) 476-6038   *SIC* 8699
COMMUNITY LIVING WALLACEBURG   *p*1004
1100 DUFFERIN AVE, WALLACEBURG, ON, N8A 2W1

(519) 627-0776   *SIC* 8699
COMMUNITY THERAPY SERVICES INC   *p*383
1555 ST JAMES ST UNIT 201, WINNIPEG, MB, R3H 1B5
(204) 949-0533   *SIC* 8699
COMOX VALLEY TRANSITION SOCIETY   *p*203
625 ENGLAND AVE, COURTENAY, BC, V9N 2N5
(250) 897-0511   *SIC* 8699
COMPASSIONATE RESOURCE WARE-HOUSE   *p*339
831 DEVONSHIRE RD SUITE 2, VICTORIA, BC, V9A 4T5
(250) 381-4483   *SIC* 8699
CONNECT SOCIETY   *p*118
6240 113 ST NW, EDMONTON, AB, T6H 3L2
(780) 454-9581   *SIC* 8699
CONSEIL SANTA MARIA 2267   *p*1134
173 RUE RENE-PHILIPPE, LEMOYNE, QC, J4R 2J9
(450) 671-1580   *SIC* 8699
COOP NOVAGO, LA   *p*1114
839 RUE PAPINEAU, JOLIETTE, QC, J6E 2L6
(418) 873-2535   *SIC* 8699
COOPERATIVE AGRICOLE-APPALACHE   *p*1147
120 RUE SAINT-PIERRE, LYSTER, QC, G0S 1V0
(819) 389-5553   *SIC* 8699
COOPERATIVE FORESTIERE DU BAS ST-MAURICE   *p*1294
1410 BOUL TRUDEL E, SAINT-BONIFACE-DE-SHAWINIGAN, QC, G0X 2L0
(819) 535-6262   *SIC* 8699
CORPORATION CULTURELLE DE SHAW-INIGAN   *p*1368
2100 BOUL DES HETRES, SHAWINIGAN, QC, G9N 8R8
(819) 539-1888   *SIC* 8699
COWICHAN VALLEY INDEPENDENT LIV-ING RESOURCES CENTRE SOCIETY   *p*211
121 FIRST ST UNIT 103, DUNCAN, BC, V9L 1R1
(250) 746-3930   *SIC* 8699
CRESTON PET ADOPTION & WELFARE SOCIETY   *p*204
2805 LOWER WYNNDEL RD, CRESTON, BC, V0B 1G8
(250) 428-7297   *SIC* 8699
DAVID SUZUKI FOUNDATION, THE   *p*322
2211 4TH AVE W UNIT 219, VANCOUVER, BC, V6K 4S2
(604) 732-4228   *SIC* 8699
DEAFBLIND SERVICES SOCIETY OF BRITISH COLUMBIA   *p*290
3369 FRASER ST SUITE 212, VANCOU-VER, BC, V5V 4C2
SIC 8699
DIABETES ASSOCIATION (BROOKS & DIS-TRICT)   *p*7
215 3 ST W, BROOKS, AB, T1R 0S3
SIC 8699
DIABETES CANADA   *p*944
522 UNIVERSITY AVE SUITE 1400, TORONTO, ON, M5G 2R5
(416) 363-3373   *SIC* 8699
DOMINION HAWKS CLUB   *p*449
28 LOWER MITCHELL AVE, DOMINION, NS, B1G 1L2
(902) 849-0414   *SIC* 8699
EASTSIDE FAMILY CENTRE   *p*11
495 36 ST NE SUITE 255, CALGARY, AB, T2A 6K3
(403) 299-9696   *SIC* 8699
ECUHOME CORPORATION   *p*962
73 SIMCOE ST SUITE 308, TORONTO, ON, M5J 1W9
(416) 593-9313   *SIC* 8699
EDMONTON HUMANE SOCIETY FOR THE PREVENTION OF CRUELTY TO ANIMALS

p105
13620 163 ST NW, EDMONTON, AB, T5V 0B2
(780) 471-1774   *SIC* 8699
EDMONTON NORTHSTARS ATHLETIC CLUB   p83
7308 112 AVE NW, EDMONTON, AB, T5B 0E3
(780) 471-0010   *SIC* 8699
EGALE CANADA HUMAN RIGHTS TRUST p933
185 CARLTON ST, TORONTO, ON, M5A 2K7
(888) 204-7777   *SIC* 8699
ELIZABETH FRY SOC. OF HAMILTON p611
85 HOLTON AVE S, HAMILTON, ON, L8M 2L4
(905) 527-3097   *SIC* 8699
ELLERSLIE ROAD BAPTIST CHURCH SOCIETY   p124
10603 ELLERSLIE RD SW, EDMONTON, AB, T6W 1A1
(780) 437-5433   *SIC* 8699
ENTRAIDE AGAPE   p1255
3148 CH ROYAL, QUEBEC, QC, G1E 1V2
(418) 661-7485   *SIC* 8699
ERINOAK KIDS CENTRE FOR TREATMENT p715
2655 NORTH SHERIDAN WAY SUITE N, MISSISSAUGA, ON, L5K 2P8
(905) 855-2690   *SIC* 8699
ESTONIAN RELIEF COMMITTEE IN CANADA   p866
40 OLD KINGSTON RD, SCARBOROUGH, ON, M1E 3J5
(416) 724-6144   *SIC* 8699
ETOBICOKE CAMERA CLUB   p576
76 ANGLESEY BLVD, ETOBICOKE, ON, M9A 3C1
(416) 234-2014   *SIC* 8699
ETOBICOKE HUMANE SOCIETY   p574
67 SIX POINT RD, ETOBICOKE, ON, M8Z 2X3
(416) 249-6100   *SIC* 8699
EXPLOS-NATURE   p1112
302 RUE DE LA RIVIERE, GRANDES-BERGERONNES, QC, G0T 1G0
(418) 232-6249   *SIC* 8699
FEDERATION MONDIALE DE L'HEMOPHILIE   p1213
1425 BOUL RENE-LEVESQUE O BUREAU 1010, MONTREAL, QC, H3G 1T7
(514) 875-7944   *SIC* 8699
FEDERATION OF ONTARIO NATURALISTS p951
214 KING ST W SUITE 612, TORONTO, ON, M5H 3S6
(416) 444-8419   *SIC* 8699
FIRE FIGHTERS ASSOCIATION LOCAL 510 p1413
76 15TH ST E, PRINCE ALBERT, SK, S6V 1E8
SIC 8699
FONDATION CENTRAIDE DU GRAND MONTREAL   p1196
493 RUE SHERBROOKE O, MONTREAL, QC, H3A 1B6
(514) 288-1261   *SIC* 8699
FONDATION CHAMPLAIN ET MANOIR-DE-VERDUN   p1397
1325 RUE CRAWFORD, VERDUN, QC, H4H 2N6
(514) 766-8513   *SIC* 8699
FONDATION D'ENTRAIDE BOUDDHISTE TZU CHI DU CANADA   p1397
3988 RUE WELLINGTON BUREAU 1, VERDUN, QC, H4G 1V3
(514) 844-2074   *SIC* 8699
FONDATION DU MOUVEMENT DU GRAAL-CANADA INC   p1077
470 CH DES HAUTEURS, CHENEVILLE, QC, J0V 1E0
(819) 428-7001   *SIC* 8699
FONDATION JULES & PAUL-EMILE LEGER

p1244
130 AV DE L'EPEE, OUTREMONT, QC, H2V 3T2
(514) 495-2409   *SIC* 8699
FONDATION LUCIE & ANDRE CHAGNON p1196
2001 AV MCGILL COLLEGE BUREAU 1000, MONTREAL, QC, H3A 1G1
(514) 380-2001   *SIC* 8699
FONDATION SOURCE BLEU   p1065
1130 RUE DE MONTBRUN, BOUCHERVILLE, QC, J4B 8W6
(450) 641-3165   *SIC* 8699
FOOD BANK   p170
4615 60 ST, VEGREVILLE, AB, T9C 1N4
(780) 632-6002   *SIC* 8699
FOOD BANKS CANADA   p695
5090 EXPLORER DR SUITE 203, MISSISSAUGA, ON, L4W 4T9
(905) 602-5234   *SIC* 8699
FOOTHILLS COWBOYS ASSOCIATION, THE   p136
609 CENTRE ST SW UNIT 7, HIGH RIVER, AB, T1V 2C2
(403) 652-1405   *SIC* 8699
FORT CALGARY PRESERVATION SOCIETY   p29
750 9 AVE SE, CALGARY, AB, T2G 5E1
(403) 290-1875   *SIC* 8699
FORUM NATIONAL INVESTMENTS LTD p266
13040 NO. 2 RD SUITE 180A, RICHMOND, BC, V7E 2G1
(604) 275-2170   *SIC* 8699
FURNITURE BANK   p574
25 CONNELL CRT UNIT 1, ETOBICOKE, ON, M8Z 1E8
(416) 934-1229   *SIC* 8699
GANOHKWA SRA FAMILY ASSAULT SUPPORT SERVICES   p806
1781 CHIEFSWOOD RD, OHSWEKEN, ON, N0A 1M0
(519) 445-4324   *SIC* 8699
GOOD SAMARITAN SOCIETY, THE (A LUTHERAN SOCIAL SERVICE ORGANIZATION)   p146
550 SPRUCE WAY SE, MEDICINE HAT, AB, T1B 4P1
(403) 528-5050   *SIC* 8699
GROUPE CHINOOK AVENTURE INC p1312
990 AV DE L'H?TEL-DE-VILLE, SAINT-HYACINTHE, QC, J2S 5B2
(514) 773-1911   *SIC* 8699
GUELPH SERVICES FOR THE AUTISTIC p600
16 CARIBOU CRES, GUELPH, ON, N1E 1C9
(519) 823-9232   *SIC* 8699
GYMN-EAU LAVAL   p1234
2465 RUE HONORE-MERCIER, MONTREAL, QC, H7L 2S9
(450) 625-2674   *SIC* 8699
GYMNASTICS MISSISSAUGA   p705
5600 ROSE CHERRY PL, MISSISSAUGA, ON, L4Z 4B6
(905) 270-6161   *SIC* 8699
HALIFAX STUDENT HOUSING SOCIETY p451
1094 WELLINGTON ST, HALIFAX, NS, B3H 2Z9
(902) 494-6888   *SIC* 8699
HAMILTON HEALTH SCIENCES CORPORATION   p612
1200 MAIN ST W RM 2, HAMILTON, ON, L8N 3Z5
(905) 521-2100   *SIC* 8699
HAMILTON-WENTWORTH CATHOLIC CHILD CARE CENTRES INC   p609
785 BRITANNIA AVE, HAMILTON, ON, L8H 2B6
(905) 523-2349   *SIC* 8699
HAVEN SOCIETYTRANSITION HOUSEp234
3200 ISLAND HWY UNIT 38, NANAIMO, BC, V9T 6N4

(250) 756-2452   *SIC* 8699
HIGH PRAIRIE & DISTRICT REGIONAL RECREATION BOARD   p135
5209 50TH ST, HIGH PRAIRIE, AB, T0G 1E0
(780) 536-2630   *SIC* 8699
HIGHLANDS SUMMER FESTIVAL, THE p607
5358 COUNTY RD 21, HALIBURTON, ON, K0M 1S0
(705) 457-9933   *SIC* 8699
HIROC FOUNDATION, THE   p772
4711 YONGE ST SUITE 1600, NORTH YORK, ON, M2N 6K8
(416) 733-2773   *SIC* 8699
HISTORIC SITES ASSOCIATION OF NEWFOUNDLAND AND LABRADOR INC   p433
10 FORBES ST SUITE 204, ST. JOHN'S, NL, A1E 3L5
(709) 753-5515   *SIC* 8699
HOCKEY CANADA   p72
151 CANADA OLYMPIC RD SW SUITE 201, CALGARY, AB, T3B 6B7
(403) 777-3636   *SIC* 8699
HOCKEY CANADA   p821
801 KING EDWARD AVE SUITE N204, OTTAWA, ON, K1N 6N5
(613) 696-0211   *SIC* 8699
HOLLAND BLOORVIEW KIDS REHABILITATION HOSPITAL FOUNDATION   p918
150 KILGOUR RD, TORONTO, ON, M4G 1R8
(416) 424-3809   *SIC* 8699
HOMES FIRST SOCIETY   p935
90 SHUTER ST, TORONTO, ON, M5B 2K6
(416) 214-1870   *SIC* 8699
HOSPITAL FOR SICK CHILDREN FOUNDATION INC, THE   p945
525 UNIVERSITY AVE 14TH FL, TORONTO, ON, M5G 2L3
(416) 813-5320   *SIC* 8699
HOUSE OF FRIENDSHIP   p638
51 CHARLES ST E, KITCHENER, ON, N2G 2P3
(519) 742-8327   *SIC* 8699
INTERIOR PROVINCIAL EXHIBITION, THE p179
3371 PEASANT VALLEY RD, ARMSTRONG, BC, V0E 1B0
(250) 546-9406   *SIC* 8699
IODE BARGAIN SHOP   p64
1320 1 ST SW, CALGARY, AB, T2R 0V7
(403) 266-6855   *SIC* 8699
IONA HOLDINGS CORPORATION   p67
120 17 AVE SW, CALGARY, AB, T2S 2T2
(403) 218-5500   *SIC* 8699
IWK HEALTH CENTRE CHARITABLE FOUNDATIONS   p451
5855 SPRING GARDEN RD SUITE B220, HALIFAX, NS, B3H 4S2
(902) 470-8085   *SIC* 8699
JOHN VOLKEN ACADEMY SOCIETY p276
6911 KING GEORGE BLVD, SURREY, BC, V3W 5A1
(604) 594-1700   *SIC* 8699
JORDAN LION PARK   p1003
2769 4 AVE, VINELAND, ON, L0R 2C0
SIC 8699
JOURNALISTS FOR HUMAN RIGHTS (JHR) p981
147 SPADINA AVE SUITE 206, TORONTO, ON, M5V 2L7
(416) 413-0240   *SIC* 8699
KARE FOR KIDS INTERNATIONAL   p770
7 BISHOP AVE SUITE 2107, NORTH YORK, ON, M2M 4J4
(416) 226-4111   *SIC* 8699
KARIS SUPPORT SOCIETY   p222
1849 ETHEL ST, KELOWNA, BC, V1Y 2Z3
(250) 860-9507   *SIC* 8699
KENORA-RAINY RIVER DISTRICTS CHILD AND FAMILY SERVICES   p628
820 LAKEVIEW DR, KENORA, ON, P9N 3P7

(807) 467-5437   *SIC* 8699
KETTLE FRIENDSHIP SOCIETY   p285
1725 VENABLES ST, VANCOUVER, BC, V5L 2H3
(604) 251-2856   *SIC* 8699
KIDS LINK/ NDSA   p883
1855 NOTRE DAME DR, ST AGATHA, ON, N0B 2L0
(519) 746-5437   *SIC* 8699
KIDZINC SCHOOL AGE CARE SOCIETY OF ALBERTA   p73
4411 10 AVE SW, CALGARY, AB, T3C 0L9
(403) 240-2059   *SIC* 8699
KIMBERLEY SEARCH & RESCUE SOCIETY p223
340 SPOKANE ST, KIMBERLEY, BC, V1A 2E8
(250) 427-5998   *SIC* 8699
KITCHENER WATERLOO YOUNG MENS CHRISTIAN ASSOCIATION, THE   p640
460 FREDERICK ST SUITE 203, KITCHENER, ON, N2H 2P5
(519) 584-7479   *SIC* 8699
KITCHENER-WATERLOO AND NORTH WATERLOO HUMANE SOCIETY   p635
250 RIVERBEND DR, KITCHENER, ON, N2B 2E9
(519) 745-5615   *SIC* 8699
KNIGHTS OF COLUMBUS   p490
1303 COUNTY RD 22, BELLE RIVER, ON, N0R 1A0
SIC 8699
L'ARCHE ASSOCIATION OF CALGARY p36
307 57 AVE SW, CALGARY, AB, T2H 2T6
(403) 571-0155   *SIC* 8699
L'ARCHE TORONTO HOMES INC   p919
186 FLOYD AVE, TORONTO, ON, M4J 2J1
(416) 406-2869   *SIC* 8699
LAKELAND FETAL ALCOHOL SPECTRUM DISORDER SOCIETY   p81
4823 50 AVE, COLD LAKE, AB, T9M 1Y2
(780) 594-9905   *SIC* 8699
LAROCHE PARK COMMUNITY (SPORTS) ASSOCIATION   p828
42 STONEHURST AVE, OTTAWA, ON, K1Y 1R4
(613) 722-3944   *SIC* 8699
LEARNING PARTNERSHIP CANADA, THE p915
45 SHEPPARD AVE E SUITE 400, TORONTO, ON, M2N 5W9
(416) 440-5100   *SIC* 8699
LETHBRIDGE YOUNG MEN'S CHRISTIAN ASSOCIATION, THE   p142
74 MAURETANIA RD W UNIT 140, LETHBRIDGE, AB, T1J 5L4
(403) 942-5757   *SIC* 8699
LIMESTONE ADVISORY FOR CHILD CARE PROGRAMS   p633
930 WOODBINE RD, KINGSTON, ON, K7P 2X4
(613) 384-5188   *SIC* 8699
LIVE DIFFERENT   p610
1429 MAIN ST E SUITE 111, HAMILTON, ON, L8K 1C2
(905) 777-1662   *SIC* 8699
LIVING HOPE NATIVE MINISTRIES   p849
23 HWY 105 SUITE 1, RED LAKE, ON, P0V 2M0
SIC 8699
LUNG ASSOCIATION OF NOVA SCOTIA p455
6331 LADY HAMMOND RD SUITE 200, HALIFAX, NS, B3K 2S2
(902) 443-8141   *SIC* 8699
MA MAWI-WI-CHI-ITATA CENTRE INC p375
443 SPENCE ST, WINNIPEG, MB, R3B 2R8
(204) 925-0348   *SIC* 8699
MAISON DES PARENTS DE BORDEAUX-CARTIERVILLE INC   p1224
5680 RUE DE SALABERRY, MONTREAL, QC, H4J 1J7
(514) 745-1144   *SIC* 8699
MAISON ELIZABETH INC   p1221

2131 AV DE MARLOWE, MONTREAL, QC, H4A 3L4

(514) 482-2488   *SIC* 8699

MAKE-A-WISH FOUNDATION (OF THE) AT-LANTIC PROVINCES   *p451*

5991 SPRING GARDEN RD SUITE 705, HALIFAX, NS, B3H 1Y6

(902) 464-9474   *SIC* 8699

MAKE-A-WISH FOUNDATION OF CANADA   *p774*

4211 YONGE ST SUITE 520, NORTH YORK, ON, M2P 2A9

(416) 224-9474   *SIC* 8699

MALTON NEIGHBOURHOOD SERVICES   *p686*

3540 MORNING STAR DR, MISSISSAUGA, ON, L4T 1Y2

(905) 677-6270   *SIC* 8699

MANITOBA MOTOR LEAGUE, THE   *p382*

870 EMPRESS ST, WINNIPEG, MB, R3G 3H3

(204) 262-6115   *SIC* 8699

MANY RIVERS COUNSELLING & SUP-PORT SERVICES   *p1440*

4071 4TH AVE, WHITEHORSE, YT, Y1A 1H3

(867) 667-2970   *SIC* 8699

MAPLE RIDGE/PITT MEADOWS COMMU-NITY SERVICES   *p231*

11907 228 ST, MAPLE RIDGE, BC, V2X 8G8

(604) 467-6911   *SIC* 8699

MAY COURT CLUB OF OTTAWA, THE   *p821*

228 LAURIER AVE E, OTTAWA, ON, K1N 6P2

(613) 235-0333   *SIC* 8699

MAYTREE FOUNDATION, THE   *p976*

170 BLOOR ST W SUITE 804, TORONTO, ON, M5S 1T9

(416) 944-1101   *SIC* 8699

MECHET CHARITIES LIMITED   *p101*

18216 102 AVE NW SUITE 200, EDMON-TON, AB, T5S 1S7

(780) 442-3640   *SIC* 8699

MEDICINE HAT FAMILY YOUNG MEN'S CHRISTIAN ASSOCIATION   *p146*

150 ASH AVE SE, MEDICINE HAT, AB, T1A 3A9

(403) 529-8115   *SIC* 8699

MENAGEZ-VOUS TERRITOIRE LES FORGES   *p1388*

749 BOUL DU SAINT-MAURICE, TROIS-RIVIERES, QC, G9A 3P5

SIC 8699

MENNONITE ECONOMIC DEVELOPMENT ASSOCIATES OF CANADA   *p1010*

155 FROBISHER DR SUITE I-106, WATER-LOO, ON, N2V 2E1

(519) 725-1633   *SIC* 8699

MENTAL HEALTH COMMISSION OF CANADA   *p17*

110 QUARRY PARK BLVD SE SUITE 320, CALGARY, AB, T2C 3G3

(403) 255-5808   *SIC* 8699

METIS CHILD, FAMILY AND COMMUNITY SERVICES AGENCY INC   *p386*

2000 PORTAGE AVE, WINNIPEG, MB, R3J 0K1

(204) 927-6960   *SIC* 8699

MISSION COMMUNITY FOUNDATION   *p232*

GD LCD MAIN, MISSION, BC, V2V 4J2

(604) 826-5322   *SIC* 8699

MNAASGED CHILD AND FAMILY SER-VICES   *p747*

311 JUBILEE DR, MUNCEY, ON, N0L 1Y0

(519) 289-1117   *SIC* 8699

MONUMENT COMMUNITY ECONOMIC DE-VELOPMENT SOCIETY   *p11*

2936 RADCLIFFE DR SE SUITE 16, CAL-GARY, AB, T2A 6M8

(403) 272-9323   *SIC* 8699

MOTOR DEALER COUNCIL OF BRITISH COLUMBIA   *p226*

8029 199 ST SUITE 280, LANGLEY, BC,

V2Y 0E2

(604) 574-5050   *SIC* 8699

MUTUAL SUPPORT SYSTEMS OF THE NI-AGARA REGION   *p590*

792 CANBORO RD, FENWICK, ON, L0S 1C0

(905) 892-4332   *SIC* 8699

NORTH EAST OUTREACH AND SUPPORT SERVICES, INC   *p1410*

128 MCKENDRY AVE W, MELFORT, SK, S0E 1A0

(306) 752-9464   *SIC* 8699

NORTH TORONTO BASEBALL ASSOCIA-TION   *p922*

2708 YONGE ST, TORONTO, ON, M4P 3J4

(519) 740-3900   *SIC* 8699

NORTHERN DIABETES HEALTH NET-WORK INC   *p908*

1204 ROLAND ST UNIT A, THUNDER BAY, ON, P7B 5M4

(807) 624-1720   *SIC* 8699

NOVA SCOTIA SOCIETY FOR THE PRE-VENTION OF CRUELTY   *p440*

1600 BEDFORD HWY SUITE 422, BED-FORD, NS, B4A 1E8

(902) 835-4798   *SIC* 8699

OCASI - ONTARIO COUNCIL OF AGENCIES SERVING IMMIGRANTS   *p923*

110 EGLINTON AVE W SUITE 200, TORONTO, ON, M4R 1A3

(416) 322-4950   *SIC* 8699

ONTARIO ASSOCIATION OF CHILDREN'S AID SOCIETIES   *p546*

187 2ND AVE, COCHRANE, ON, P0L 1C0

(705) 272-2449   *SIC* 8699

ONTARIO FEDERATION OF ANGLERS AND HUNTERS, THE   *p841*

4601 GUTHRIE DR, PETERBOROUGH, ON, K9J 0C9

(705) 748-6324   *SIC* 8699

ONTARIO HEALTHY COMMUNITY COALI-TION   *p936*

2 CARLTON ST SUITE 1810, TORONTO, ON, M5B 1J3

SIC 8699

ONTARIO SOCCER ASSOCIATION INCOR-PORATED, THE   *p1032*

7601 MARTIN GROVE RD, WOODBRIDGE, ON, L4L 9E4

(905) 264-9390   *SIC* 8699

ONTARIO SOCIETY FOR THE PREVEN-TION OF CRUELTY TO ANIMALS, THE   *p756*

16586 WOODBINE AVE SUITE 3, NEW-MARKET, ON, L3Y 4W1

(905) 898-7122   *SIC* 8699

OOLAGEN COMMUNITY SERVICES   *p932*

65 WELLESLEY ST E SUITE 500, TORONTO, ON, M4Y 1G7

(416) 395-0660   *SIC* 8699

ORGANISATION CATHOLIQUE CANADI-ENNE POUR LE DEVELOPPEMENT ET LA PAIX   *p1214*

1425 BOUL RENE-LEVESQUE O BUREAU 300, MONTREAL, QC, H3G 1T7

(514) 257-8711   *SIC* 8699

OTTAWA COMMUNITY IMMIGRANT SER-VICES ORGANIZATION   *p828*

959 WELLINGTON ST W, OTTAWA, ON, K1Y 2X5

(613) 725-5671   *SIC* 8699

OTTAWA HUMANE SOCIETY   *p750*

245 WEST HUNT CLUB RD, NEPEAN, ON, K2E 1A6

(613) 725-3166   *SIC* 8699

OUR PLACE FAMILY RESOURCE AND EARLY YEARS CENTRE   *p641*

154 GATEWOOD RD, KITCHENER, ON, N2M 4E4

(519) 571-1626   *SIC* 8699

PARACHUTE LEADERS IN INJURY PRE-VENTION   *p922*

150 EGLINTON AVE E SUITE 300, TORONTO, ON, M4P 1E8

(647) 776-5100   *SIC* 8699

PARKINSON SOCIETY CANADA   *p774*

4211 YONGE ST SUITE 316, NORTH YORK, ON, M2P 2A9

(416) 227-9700   *SIC* 8699

PARLIAMENTARY CENTRE   *p824*

255 ALBERT ST SUITE 802, OTTAWA, ON, K1P 6A9

(613) 237-0143   *SIC* 8699

PAUKTUUTIT INUIT WOMEN OF CANADA   *p821*

1 NICHOLAS ST SUITE 520, OTTAWA, ON, K1N 7B7

(613) 238-3977   *SIC* 8699

PEGASUS COMMUNITY PROJECT   *p917*

931 KINGSTON RD, TORONTO, ON, M4E 1S6

(416) 691-5651   *SIC* 8699

PEMBROKE OLD TIME FIDDLING ASSOCI-ATION INCORPORATED   *p564*

GD, DEEP RIVER, ON, K0J 1P0

(613) 635-7200   *SIC* 8699

PEOPLE PLAYERS INC   *p575*

343 EVANS AVE, ETOBICOKE, ON, M8Z 1K2

(416) 532-1137   *SIC* 8699

PEROGY - POLISH HALL   *p909*

818 SPRING ST, THUNDER BAY, ON, P7C 3L6

SIC 8699

PIVOT CENTRE-DU-QUEBEC   *p1099*

795 RUE CORMIER, DRUMMONDVILLE, QC, J2C 6P7

(819) 478-3134   *SIC* 8699

PORT ALBERNI ASSOCIATION FOR COM-MUNITY LIVING   *p245*

3008 2ND AVE, PORT ALBERNI, BC, V9Y 1Y9

(250) 724-7155   *SIC* 8699

POWELL RIVER ASSOCIATION FOR COM-MUNITY LIVING   *p248*

4675 MARINE AVE UNIT 201, POWELL RIVER, BC, V8A 2L2

(604) 485-4628   *SIC* 8699

PRIME QUADRANT FOUNDATION   *p926*

2 ST CLAIR AVE E SUITE 800, TORONTO, ON, M4T 2T5

(647) 749-4118   *SIC* 8699

PRINCE GEORGE HOSPICE SOCIETY   *p249*

3089 CLAPPERTON ST, PRINCE GEORGE, BC, V2L 5N4

(250) 563-2551   *SIC* 8699

PRINCE GEORGE SEARCH AND RESCUE SOCIETY   *p249*

4057 HART HWY, PRINCE GEORGE, BC, V2K 2Z5

(250) 962-5544   *SIC* 8699

QIKIQTANI INUIT ASSOCIATION   *p472*

GD, IQALUIT, NU, X0A 0H0

(867) 975-8400   *SIC* 8699

RADICALS CAR CLUB INC   *p594*

14 TODD RD, GEORGETOWN, ON, L7G 4R7

(905) 877-9937   *SIC* 8699

RAINCITY HOUSING AND SUPPORT SOCI-ETY   *p295*

191 ALEXANDER ST, VANCOUVER, BC, V6A 1B8

(604) 662-7023   *SIC* 8699

RED DEER GYMNASTIC ASSOCIATION   *p157*

3031 30 AVE, RED DEER, AB, T4R 2Z7

(403) 342-4940   *SIC* 8699

REGINA HUMANE SOCIETY INC   *p1418*

GD LCD MAIN, REGINA, SK, S4P 2Z4

(306) 543-6363   *SIC* 8699

REGROUPEMENT DES ORGANISMES NA-TIONAUX DE LOISIRS DU QUEBEC   *p1166*

4545 AV PIERRE-DE COUBERTIN, MON-TREAL, QC, H1V 0B2

(514) 252-3126   *SIC* 8699

RENE GOUPIL JESUITS   *p845*

2315 LIVERPOOL RD, PICKERING, ON, L1X 1V4

(905) 839-5155   *SIC* 8699

REPITS DE GABY, LES   *p1089*

51 19E RUE, CRABTREE, QC, J0K 1B0

(450) 754-2782   *SIC* 8699

RICK HANSEN FOUNDATION   *p265*

3820 CESSNA DR SUITE 300, RICHMOND, BC, V7B 0A2

(604) 295-8149   *SIC* 8699

RIDEAU CLUB LIMITED   *p824*

99 BANK ST SUITE 1500, OTTAWA, ON, K1P 6B9

(613) 233-7787   *SIC* 8699

RIGHT TO LIFE ASSOCIATION OF WIND-SOR AND AREA   *p1025*

3021 DOUGALL AVE, WINDSOR, ON, N9E 1S3

(519) 969-7555   *SIC* 8699

ROOTS OF EMPATHY   *p780*

250 FERRAND DR SUITE 1501, NORTH YORK, ON, M3C 3G8

(416) 944-3001   *SIC* 8699

ROYAL ONTARIO MUSEUM FOUNDATION, THE   *p976*

100 QUEEN'S PK, TORONTO, ON, M5S 2C6

(416) 586-5660   *SIC* 8699

S.I.T. (SERVICE D'INTEGRATION AU TRA-VAIL)   *p1388*

1090 RUE LA VERENDRYE, TROIS-RIVIERES, QC, G9A 2S8

(819) 694-9971   *SIC* 8699

SAINT JOHN'S SCHOOL OF ALBERTA   *p167*

GD, STONY PLAIN, AB, T7Z 1X5

(780) 701-5625   *SIC* 8699

SAINT LEONARD'S SOCIETY OF NOVA SCOTIA   *p456*

5506 CUNARD ST SUITE 101, HALIFAX, NS, B3K 1C2

(902) 406-3631   *SIC* 8699

SASK SPORT INC   *p1418*

1870 LORNE ST, REGINA, SK, S4P 2L7

(306) 780-9340   *SIC* 8699

SASKATCHEWAN   *p149*

2510 SPARROW DR, NISKU, AB, T9E 8N5

(780) 955-3639   *SIC* 8699

SASKATCHEWAN MOTOR CLUB   *p1421*

200 ALBERT ST N, REGINA, SK, S4R 2N4

(306) 791-4321   *SIC* 8699

SASKATCHEWAN PLAYWRIGHTS' CEN-TRE   *p1429*

601 SPADINA CRES E SUITE 700, SASKA-TOON, SK, S7K 3G8

(306) 665-7707   *SIC* 8699

SASKATOON RINGETTE ASSOCIATION   *p1432*

510 CYNTHIA ST SUITE 128, SASKA-TOON, SK, S7L 7K7

(306) 975-0839   *SIC* 8699

SAT SOCIETE DES ARTS TECH-NOLOGIQUES   *p1186*

1201 BOUL SAINT-LAURENT, MONTREAL, QC, H2X 2S6

(514) 844-2033   *SIC* 8699

SCANDINAVIAN HERITAGE SOCIETY OF EDMONTON   *p94*

12336 ST ALBERT TRAIL NW, EDMON-TON, AB, T5L 4G8

(780) 451-3868   *SIC* 8699

SEED WINNIPEG INC   *p371*

80 SALTER ST, WINNIPEG, MB, R2W 4J6

(204) 927-9935   *SIC* 8699

SEMINAIRE DE CHICOUTIMI   *p1079*

602 RUE RACINE E BUREAU 102, CHICOUTIMI, QC, G7H 1V1

(418) 693-8448   *SIC* 8699

SERVUS CREDIT UNION PLACE   *p166*

400 CAMPBELL RD, ST. ALBERT, AB, T8N 0R8

(780) 418-6088   *SIC* 8699

SIMCOE MUSKOKA CHILD, YOUTH AND FAMILY SERVICES   *p485*

60 BELL FARM RD SUITE 7, BARRIE, ON, L4M 5G6

(800) 461-4236   *SIC* 8699

SKATE CANADA   *p820*

1200 ST. LAURENT BLVD SUITE 261, OTTAWA, ON, K1K 3B8

(613) 747-1007   SIC 8699

SOCIAL ENTERPRISE FOR CANADA p756

17705A LESLIE ST SUITE 202, NEWMARKET, ON, L3Y 3E3

(905) 895-0809   SIC 8699

SOCIETE DE QUEBEC POUR PREVENIR LES CRUAUTES CONTRE LES ANIMAUX, LA p1268

1130 AV GALILEE BUREAU 487, QUEBEC, QC, G1P 4B7

(418) 527-9104   SIC 8699

SOCIETE DE SAINT-VINCENT DE PAUL DE MONTREAL, LA p1176

1930 RUE DE CHAMPLAIN, MONTREAL, QC, H2L 2S8

(514) 526-5937   SIC 8699

SOCIETE POUR LA PREVENTION DE LA CRUAUTE ENVERS LES ANIMAUX (CANADIENNE), LA p1228

5215 RUE JEAN-TALON O, MONTREAL, QC, H4P 1X4

(514) 735-2711   SIC 8699

SOCIETE PROTECTRICE DES ANIMAUX DE L'ESTRIE p1374

145 RUE SAUVE, SHERBROOKE, QC, J1L 1L6

(819) 821-4727   SIC 8699

SOCIETY FOR THE INVOLVEMENT OF GOOD NEIGHBOURS p1439

83 NORTH ST, YORKTON, SK, S3N 0G9

(306) 783-9409   SIC 8699

SOCIETY OF SAINT VINCENT DE PAUL p426

110 ASHFORD DR, MOUNT PEARL, NL, A1N 3L6

(709) 747-3320   SIC 8699

SON'S OF ITALY CHARITABLE CORPORATION p617

530 UPPER PARADISE RD, HAMILTON, ON, L9C 7W2

(905) 388-4552   SIC 8699

SOUTHDOWN INSTITUTE, THE p620

18798 OLD YONGE ST, HOLLAND LANDING, ON, L9N 0L1

(905) 727-4214   SIC 8699

SOUTHERN ALBERTA COMMUNITY LIVING ASSOCIATION p141

401 21A ST N, LETHBRIDGE, AB, T1H 6L6

(403) 329-1525   SIC 8699

SPECIAL ABILITY RIDING INSTITUTE p479

12659 MEDWAY RD, ARVA, ON, N0M 1C0

(519) 666-1123   SIC 8699

SPECIAL OLYMPICS MANITOBA, INC p375

145 PACIFIC AVE SUITE 304, WINNIPEG, MB, R3B 2Z6

(204) 925-5628   SIC 8699

SPECIAL OLYMPICS ONTARIO INC p919

65 OVERLEA BLVD SUITE 200, TORONTO, ON, M4H 1P1

(416) 447-8326   SIC 8699

SPORT BY ABILITY NIAGARA p886

8 NAPIER ST, ST CATHARINES, ON, L2R 6B4

SIC 8699

ST CATHARINES MAINSTREAM NON PROFIT HOUSING PROJECT p887

263 PELHAM RD, ST CATHARINES, ON, L2S 1X7

(905) 934-3924   SIC 8699

ST COLUMBIA CATHOLIC WOMEN LEAGUE FAIRFIELD p1041

3849 EAST POINT RD -RTE 16, ELMIRA, PE, C0A 1K0

(902) 357-2695   SIC 8699

ST LEONARDS SOCIETY OF TORONTO p919

779 DANFORTH AVE, TORONTO, ON, M4J 1L2

(416) 462-1596   SIC 8699

ST. JOSEPH'S HEALTH SYSTEM p612

50 CHARLTON AVE E, HAMILTON, ON, L8N 4A6

(905) 522-4941   SIC 8699

ST. JOSEPH'S HOSPICE RESOURCE CENTRE OF SARNIA LAMBTON p861

475 CHRISTINA ST N, SARNIA, ON, N7T 5W3

(519) 337-0537   SIC 8699

ST. JOSEPH'S PROVINCE HOUSE INC p995

419 PARKSIDE DR, TORONTO, ON, M6R 2Z7

(416) 604-7992   SIC 8699

STUDENT ASSOCIATION OF GEORGE BROWN COLLEGE p974

142 KENDAL AVE RM E100, TORONTO, ON, M5R 1M3

(416) 415-5000   SIC 8699

SUDANESE CANADIAN COMMUNITY ASSOCIATION OF LONDON p659

360 SPRINGBANK DR SUITE 9, LONDON, ON, N6J 1G5

(519) 681-6719   SIC 8699

SUMMERSIDE LIONS CENTRE p422

19 PARK DR, CORNER BROOK, NL, A2H 4T4

(709) 783-2616   SIC 8699

SUNSHINE COAST ASSOCIATION FOR COMMUNITY LIVING p268

5711 MERMAID ST SUITE 105, SECHELT, BC, V0N 3A3

(604) 885-7455   SIC 8699

SURREY GYMNASTIC SOCIETY p278

13940 77 AVE, SURREY, BC, V3W 5Z4

(604) 594-2442   SIC 8699

SWAN RIVER FRIENDSHIP CENTRE INC p359

1413 MAIN ST, SWAN RIVER, MB, R0L 1Z0

(204) 734-9301   SIC 8699

TABER SPECIAL NEEDS SOCIETY p169

6005 60 AVE, TABER, AB, T1G 2C1

(403) 223-4941   SIC 8699

TAGGEL AUTOMOBILE INC p528

805 WALKER'S LINE, BURLINGTON, ON, L7N 2G1

(905) 333-0595   SIC 8699

TAMARACK FOUNDATION p1432

510 CYNTHIA ST SUITE 136, SASKATOON, SK, S7L 7K7

(306) 975-0855   SIC 8699

TAOIST TAI CHI SOCIETY OF CANADA p978

134 D'ARCY ST, TORONTO, ON, M5T 1K3

(416) 656-2110   SIC 8699

TEAM FUTURES SCHOOL OF GYMNASTICS INC p727

6991 MILLCREEK DR, MISSISSAUGA, ON, L5N 6B9

SIC 8699

TEEN CHALLENGE OF CENTRAL CANADA INC p376

414 EDMONTON ST, WINNIPEG, MB, R3B 2M2

(204) 949-9484   SIC 8699

TERMINAL CITY CLUB INC p310

837 HASTINGS ST W SUITE 100, VANCOUVER, BC, V6C 1B6

(604) 488-8970   SIC 8699

THINKING IN PICTURES EDUCATIONAL SERVICE p626

160 TERENCE MATTHEWS CRES SUITE B2, KANATA, ON, K2M 0B2

(613) 592-8800   SIC 8699

THORNHILL VOLUNTEER FIREFIGHTERS ASSOCIATION p283

3128 16 HWY E, THORNHILL, BC, V8G 4N8

(250) 638-1466   SIC 8699

TIDES CANADA INITIATIVES SOCIETY p300

163 HASTINGS ST W SUITE 400, VANCOUVER, BC, V6B 1H5

(604) 647-6611   SIC 8699

TILLICUM HAUS SOCIETY p233

602 HALIBURTON ST, NANAIMO, BC, V9R 4W5

(250) 753-6578   SIC 8699

TORONTO CENTRAL COMMUNITY CARE ACCESS CENTRE p978

250 DUNDAS ST W SUITE 305, TORONTO, ON, M5T 2Z5

(416) 506-9888   SIC 8699

TORONTO HUMANE SOCIETY, THE p934

11 RIVER ST, TORONTO, ON, M5A 4C2

(416) 392-2273   SIC 8699

TORONTO INTERNATIONAL FILM FESTIVAL INC p984

350 KING ST W SUITE 477, TORONTO, ON, M5V 3X5

(416) 967-7371   SIC 8699

TRI-CITY TRANSITIONS SOCIETY p247

2540 SHAUGHNESSY ST SUITE 200, PORT COQUITLAM, BC, V3C 3W4

(604) 941-7111   SIC 8699

TRURO AND DISTRICT LIONS CLUB p469

1100 PRINCE ST, TRURO, NS, B2N 1J1

(902) 893-4773   SIC 8699

TULA FOUNDATION p215

1713 HYACINTHE BAY RD, HERIOT BAY, BC, V0P 1H0

(250) 285-2628   SIC 8699

TUMBLERS GYMNASTIC CENTRE p811

330 VANTAGE DR, ORLEANS, ON, K4A 3W1

(613) 834-4334   SIC 8699

UNITED WAY OF GREATER TORONTO p943

26 WELLINGTON ST E FL 12, TORONTO, ON, M5E 1S2

(416) 777-2001   SIC 8699

USASK SMALL ANIMAL CLINICAL STUD p1434

52 CAMPUS DR, SASKATOON, SK, S7N 5B4

(306) 966-7126   SIC 8699

VALLEY INTEGRATION TO ACTIVE LIVING SOCIETY p212

80 STATION ST SUITE 217, DUNCAN, BC, V9L 1M4

(250) 748-5899   SIC 8699

VANCOUVER DODGEBALL LEAGUE SOCIETY p288

5695 ABERDEEN ST, VANCOUVER, BC, V5R 4M5

(604) 353-7892   SIC 8699

VILLAG HISTORIQUE ACADIEN p396

14311 ROUTE 11, CARAQUET, NB, E1W 1B7

(506) 726-2600   SIC 8699

VISIONS OF INDEPENDENCE INC. p355

20 SASKATCHEWAN AVE W, PORTAGE LA PRAIRIE, MB, R1N 0L9

(204) 239-6698   SIC 8699

VITA COMMUNITY LIVING SERVICES OF TORONTO p794

4301 WESTON RD, NORTH YORK, ON, M9L 2Y3

(416) 783-6227   SIC 8699

WALDORF EDUCATION SOCIETY OF EDMONTON p117

7114 98 ST NW, EDMONTON, AB, T6E 3M1

(780) 466-3312   SIC 8699

WALRUS FOUNDATION, THE p935

411 RICHMOND ST E SUITE B15, TORONTO, ON, M5A 3S5

(416) 971-5004   SIC 8699

WAR AMPUTATIONS OF CANADA, THE p914

1 MAYBROOK DR, TORONTO, ON, M1V 5K9

(416) 412-0600   SIC 8699

WATERLOO CONSERVATIVE EDA p1009

420 ERB ST W UNIT 5 STE 424, WATERLOO, ON, N2L 6K6

(519) 888-8300   SIC 8699

WATERLOO POTTERS' WORKSHOP p1007

75 KING ST S, WATERLOO, ON, N2J 1P2

(519) 885-5570   SIC 8699

WE CHARITY p935

339 QUEEN ST E, TORONTO, ON, M5A 1S9

(416) 925-5894   SIC 8699

WELLAND & DISTRICT SOCIETY FOR THE PREVENTION OF CRUELTY TO ANIMALS p1012

60 PROVINCIAL ST, WELLAND, ON, L3B 5W7

(905) 735-1552   SIC 8699

WELLESLEY INSTITUTE p927

10 ALCORN AVE SUITE 300, TORONTO, ON, M4V 3A9

(416) 972-1010   SIC 8699

WESTMINSTER HOUSE SOCIETY p238

228 SEVENTH ST, NEW WESTMINSTER, BC, V3M 3K3

(604) 524-5633   SIC 8699

WET'SUWET'EN TREATY OFFICE p269

3873 1ST AVE, SMITHERS, BC, V0J 2N0

(250) 847-3630   SIC 8699

WHITE ROCK CHRISTIAN ACADEMY SOCIETY p281

2265 152 ST, SURREY, BC, V4A 4P1

(604) 531-9186   SIC 8699

WINDIGO AVENTURE INC p1244

400 AV ATLANTIC BUREAU 802, OUTREMONT, QC, H2V 1A5

(514) 948-4145   SIC 8699

WINDSOR ESSEX COUNTY HUMANE SOCIETY p1020

1375 PROVINCIAL RD, WINDSOR, ON, N8W 5V8

(519) 966-5751   SIC 8699

WINDSPEAR CENTRE p91

9720 102 AVE NW, EDMONTON, AB, T5J 4B2

(780) 401-2520   SIC 8699

WINNIPEG HUMANE SOCIETY FOR THE PREVENTION CRUELTY TO ANIMALS p392

45 HURST WAY, WINNIPEG, MB, R3T 0R3

(204) 982-2021   SIC 8699

WOODSTOCK FLYING CLUB p1036

GD LCD MAIN, WOODSTOCK, ON, N4S 7W4

(519) 539-3303   SIC 8699

WORLD WILDLIFE FUND CANADA p985

410 ADELAIDE ST W SUITE 400, TORONTO, ON, M5V 1S8

(416) 489-8800   SIC 8699

YMCA OF GREATER TORONTO p489

22 GROVE ST W, BARRIE, ON, L4N 1M7

(705) 726-6421   SIC 8699

YMCA OF GREATER TORONTO p925

2200 YONGE ST SUITE 300, TORONTO, ON, M4S 2C6

(416) 928-9622   SIC 8699

YMCA OF NIAGARA p884

25 YMCA DR, ST CATHARINES, ON, L2N 7P9

(905) 646-9622   SIC 8699

YMCA OF NORTHERN ALBERTA p91

10030 102A AVE NW SUITE 300, EDMONTON, AB, T5J 0G5

(780) 421-9622   SIC 8699

YMCA OF WOOD BUFFALO p91

10030 102A AVE NW SUITE 300, EDMONTON, AB, T5J 0G5

(780) 423-9609   SIC 8699

YMCA OF WOOD BUFFALO p129

221 TUNDRA DR, FORT MCMURRAY, AB, T9H 4Z7

(780) 790-9622   SIC 8699

YOUNG ENTREPRENEUR LEADERSHIP LAUNCHPAD (YELL) p319

1500 GEORGIA ST W UNIT 1250, VANCOUVER, BC, V6G 2Z6

(778) 808-4641   SIC 8699

YOUNG MEN'S CHRISTIAN ASSOCIATION OF BRANDON, THE p347

231 8TH ST, BRANDON, MB, R7A 3X2

(204) 727-5456   SIC 8699

YOUNG MEN'S CHRISTIAN ASSOCIATION OF EDMONTON, THE p91

10211 105 ST NW, EDMONTON, AB, T5J 1E3

(780) 429-9622   SIC 8699

YOUNG MEN'S CHRISTIAN ASSOCIATION OF EDMONTON, THE p104

7121 178 ST NW, EDMONTON, AB, T5T 5T9

(780) 930-2311 *SIC 8699*

YOUNG MEN'S CHRISTIAN ASSOCIATION OF WINDSOR AND ESSEX COUNTY *p1024*
500 VICTORIA AVE, WINDSOR, ON, N9A 4M8
(519) 258-3881 *SIC 8699*

YOUNG MENS CHRISTIAN ASSOCIATION *p760*
7150 MONTROSE RD, NIAGARA FALLS, ON, L2H 3N3
(905) 358-9622 *SIC 8699*

YOUNG WOMEN'S CHRISTIAN ASSOCIA-TION *p454*
1239 BARRINGTON ST, HALIFAX, NS, B3J 1Y3
(902) 423-6162 *SIC 8699*

YOUTH FOR CHRIST CANADA *p228*
19705 FRASER HWY UNIT 135, LANGLEY, BC, V3A 7E9
SIC 8699

SIC 8711 Engineering services

30 FORENSIC ENGINEERING INC *p958*
40 UNIVERSITY AVE SUITE 800, TORONTO, ON, M5J 1T1
(416) 368-1700 *SIC 8711*

9051-8127 QUEBEC INC *p1243*
1144 RUE LYDORIC-DOUCET, NOR-MANDIN, QC, G8M 5A6
(418) 274-5525 *SIC 8711*

ABB INC *p27*
4411 6 ST SE UNIT 110, CALGARY, AB, T2G 4E8
(403) 253-0271 *SIC 8711*

ABSOLUTE COMPLETION TECHNOLO-GIES LTD *p74*
302-600 CROWFOOT CRES NW, CAL-GARY, AB, T3G 0B4
(403) 266-5027 *SIC 8711*

ACERO ENGINEERING INC *p42*
600 6 AVE SW SUITE 900, CALGARY, AB, T2P 0S5
(403) 237-7388 *SIC 8711*

ACUREN GROUP INC *p129*
240 TAIGANOVA CRES UNIT 2, FORT MC-MURRAY, AB, T9K 0T4
(780) 790-1776 *SIC 8711*

ADELARD SOUCY (1975) INC *p1285*
217 RUE TEMISCOUATA, RIVIERE-DU-LOUP, QC, G5R 2Y6
(418) 862-2355 *SIC 8711*

ADI LIMITED *p400*
1133 REGENT ST SUITE 300, FREDERIC-TON, NB, E3B 3Z2
(506) 452-9000 *SIC 8711*

AECOM CANADA LTD *p33*
6807 RAILWAY ST SE SUITE 200, CAL-GARY, AB, T2H 2V6
(403) 270-9200 *SIC 8711*

AECOM CANADA LTD *p69*
340 MIDPARK WAY SE SUITE 300, CAL-GARY, AB, T2X 1P1
(403) 270-9200 *SIC 8711*

AECOM CANADA LTD *p99*
17203 103 AVE NW, EDMONTON, AB, T5S 1J4
(780) 488-2121 *SIC 8711*

AECOM CANADA LTD *p181*
3292 PRODUCTION WAY, BURNABY, BC, V5A 4R4
(604) 444-6400 *SIC 8711*

AECOM CANADA LTD *p388*
99 COMMERCE DR, WINNIPEG, MB, R3P 0Y7
(204) 477-5381 *SIC 8711*

AECOM CANADA LTD *p691*
5080 COMMERCE BLVD, MISSISSAUGA, ON, L4W 4P2
(905) 238-0007 *SIC 8711*

AECOM CANADA LTD *p1013*
300 WATER ST SUITE 1, WHITBY, ON, L1N 9J2

(905) 668-9363 *SIC 8711*

AINLEY & ASSOCIATES LIMITED *p546*
280 PRETTY RIVER PKY N, COLLING-WOOD, ON, L9Y 4J5
(705) 445-3451 *SIC 8711*

AIOLOS INC *p581*
135 QUEEN'S PLATE DR SUITE 300, ETO-BICOKE, ON, M9W 6V1
(416) 674-3017 *SIC 8711*

AIRBORNE ENGINES LTD *p208*
7762 PROGRESS WAY, DELTA, BC, V4G 1A4
(604) 244-1668 *SIC 8711*

AMEC BDR LIMITED *p43*
401 9 AVE SW SUITE 1300, CALGARY, AB, T2P 3C5
(403) 283-0060 *SIC 8711*

AMEC FOSTER WHEELER INC *p796*
2020 WINSTON PARK DR SUITE 700, OAKVILLE, ON, L6H 6X7
(905) 829-5400 *SIC 8711*

AMTEK ENGINEERING SERVICES LTD *p595*
1900 CITY PARK DR SUITE 510, GLOUCESTER, ON, K1J 1A3
(613) 749-3990 *SIC 8711*

ANDRITZ AUTOMATION LTD *p253*
13700 INTERNATIONAL PL SUITE 100, RICHMOND, BC, V6V 2X8
(604) 214-9248 *SIC 8711*

ANDRITZ HYDRO CANADA INC *p1074*
7920 RUE SAMUEL-HATT BUREAU 7902, CHAMBLY, QC, J3L 6W4
(450) 658-5554 *SIC 8711*

ANDRITZ HYDRO CANADA INC *p1249*
6100 RTE TRANSCANADIENNE, POINTE-CLAIRE, QC, H9R 1B9
(514) 428-6700 *SIC 8711*

ANGUS, H.H. AND ASSOCIATES LIMITED *p778*
1127 LESLIE ST, NORTH YORK, ON, M3C 2J6
(416) 443-8200 *SIC 8711*

APLIN & MARTIN CONSULTANTS LTD *p275*
12448 82 AVE SUITE 201, SURREY, BC, V3W 3E9
(604) 597-9189 *SIC 8711*

APTIM SERVICES CANADA CORP *p162*
15 TURBO DR UNIT 1, SHERWOOD PARK, AB, T8H 2J6
(780) 467-2411 *SIC 8711*

ARROW ENGINEERING INC *p92*
13167 146 ST NW SUITE 202, EDMON-TON, AB, T5L 4S8
(780) 801-6100 *SIC 8711*

ASPIN KEMP & ASSOCIATES INC *p1041*
23 BROOK ST, MONTAGUE, PE, C0A 1R0
(902) 361-3135 *SIC 8711*

ASSOCIATED ENGINEERING (B.C.) LTD *p286*
2889 12TH AVE E SUITE 500, VANCOU-VER, BC, V5M 4T5
(604) 293-1411 *SIC 8711*

ASSOCIATED ENGINEERING (ONT.) LTD *p577*
304 THE EAST MALL SUITE 800, ETOBI-COKE, ON, M9B 6E2
(416) 622-9502 *SIC 8711*

ASSOCIATED ENGINEERING (SASK) LTD *p1431*
2225 NORTHRIDGE DR SUITE 1, SASKA-TOON, SK, S7L 6X6
(306) 653-4969 *SIC 8711*

ASSOCIATED ENGINEERING ALBERTA LTD *p74*
600 CROWFOOT CRES NW SUITE 400, CALGARY, AB, T3G 0B4
(403) 262-4500 *SIC 8711*

ASSOCIATED ENGINEERING ALBERTA LTD *p87*
9888 JASPER AVE NW SUITE 500, ED-MONTON, AB, T5J 5C6
(780) 451-7666 *SIC 8711*

ASSOCIATED ENGINEERING GROUP LTD

p87
9888 JASPER AVE NW SUITE 500, ED-MONTON, AB, T5J 5C6
(780) 451-7666 *SIC 8711*

ASSOCIATED ENGINEERING GROUP LTD *p187*
4940 CANADA WAY SUITE 300, BURNABY, BC, V5G 4K6
(604) 293-1411 *SIC 8711*

AUSENCO ENGINEERING CANADA INC *p297*
855 HOMER ST, VANCOUVER, BC, V6B 2W2
(604) 684-9311 *SIC 8711*

AUTOPRO AUTOMATION CONSULTANTS LTD *p10*
525 28 ST SE SUITE 360, CALGARY, AB, T2A 6W9
(403) 569-6480 *SIC 8711*

AUTOPRO AUTOMATION CONSULTANTS LTD *p134*
11039 78 AVE SUITE 103, GRANDE PRAIRIE, AB, T8W 2J7
(780) 539-2450 *SIC 8711*

AVERSAN INC *p729*
30 EGLINTON AVE W SUITE 500, MISSIS-SAUGA, ON, L5R 3E7
(416) 289-1554 *SIC 8711*

AVL MANUFACTURING INC *p613*
243 QUEEN ST N, HAMILTON, ON, L8R 3N6
(905) 545-7660 *SIC 8711*

BAE-NEWPLAN GROUP LIMITED *p425*
1133 TOPSAIL RD, MOUNT PEARL, NL, A1N 5G2
(709) 368-0118 *SIC 8711*

BANTREL CO. *p67*
1201 GLENMORE TRAIL SW SUITE 1061, CALGARY, AB, T2V 4Y8
(403) 290-5000 *SIC 8711*

BANTREL CO. *p67*
600-1201 GLENMORE TRAIL SW, CAL-GARY, AB, T2V 4Y8
(403) 290-5000 *SIC 8711*

BANTREL CO. *p108*
4999 98 AVE NW UNIT 401, EDMONTON, AB, T6B 2X3
(780) 462-5600 *SIC 8711*

BBA INC *p582*
10 CARLSON CRT SUITE 420, ETOBI-COKE, ON, M9W 6L2
(416) 585-2115 *SIC 8711*

BBA INC *p1158*
375 BOUL SIR-WILFRID-LAURIER, MONT-SAINT-HILAIRE, QC, J3H 6C3
(450) 464-2111 *SIC 8711*

BBA INC *p1193*
2020 BOUL ROBERT-BOURASSA, MON-TREAL, QC, H3A 2A5
(514) 866-2111 *SIC 8711*

BEAIRSTO & ASSOCIATES ENGINEERING LTD *p131*
10940 92 AVE, GRANDE PRAIRIE, AB, T8V 6B5
(780) 532-4919 *SIC 8711*

BECHTEL QUEBEC LIMITEE *p1193*
1500 BOUL ROBERT-BOURASSA BU-REAU 910, MONTREAL, QC, H3A 3S7
SIC 8711

BELCAN CANADA INC *p1249*
1000 BOUL SAINT-JEAN BUREAU 715, POINTE-CLAIRE, QC, H9R 5P1
(514) 697-9212 *SIC 8711*

BINNIE, R.F. & ASSOCIATES LTD *p188*
300-4940 CANADA WAY, BURNABY, BC, V5G 4K6
(604) 420-1721 *SIC 8711*

BMT CANADA LTD *p623*
311 LEGGET DR, KANATA, ON, K2K 1Z8
(613) 592-2830 *SIC 8711*

BOMBARDIER INC *p762*
1500 AIRPORT RD, NORTH BAY, ON, P1B 8G2
SIC 8711

BOMBARDIER INC *p1093*
9501 AV RYAN, DORVAL, QC, H9P 1A2
(514) 855-5000 *SIC 8711*

BOUDREAU-ESPLEY-PITRE CORPORA-TION *p899*
1040 LORNE ST UNIT 3, SUDBURY, ON, P3C 4R9
(705) 675-7720 *SIC 8711*

BOUTHILLETTE PARIZEAU INC *p1216*
9825 RUE VERVILLE, MONTREAL, QC, H3L 3E1
(514) 383-3747 *SIC 8711*

BPR INC *p1266*
4655 BOUL WILFRID-HAMEL, QUEBEC, QC, G1P 2J7
(418) 871-8151 *SIC 8711*

BROOKFIELD INFRASTRUCTURE PART-NERS L.P. *p960*
181 BAY ST SUITE 300, TORONTO, ON, M5J 2T3
(416) 363-9491 *SIC 8711*

BUILT BY ENGINEERS CONSTRUCTION INC *p532*
520 COLLIER MACMILLAN DR SUITE 8, CAMBRIDGE, ON, N1R 6R6
(519) 620-8886 *SIC 8711*

BURLOAK TOOL & DIE LTD *p526*
3121 MAINWAY, BURLINGTON, ON, L7M 1A4
(905) 331-6838 *SIC 8711*

C-CORE *p429*
1 MORRISSEY RD, ST. JOHN'S, NL, A1B 3X5
(709) 864-8354 *SIC 8711*

C.O.M. RESOURCES LTD *p34*
6223 2 ST SE SUITE 165, CALGARY, AB, T2H 1J5
(403) 299-9400 *SIC 8711*

CALIAN GROUP LTD *p835*
770 PALLADIUM DR, OTTAWA, ON, K2V 1C8
(613) 599-8600 *SIC 8711*

CANA HIGH VOLTAGE LTD *p34*
5720 4 ST SE UNIT 100, CALGARY, AB, T2H 1K7
(403) 247-3121 *SIC 8711*

CANADIAN TEST CASE 95 INC *p730*
5770 HURONTARIO ST, MISSISSAUGA, ON, L5R 3G5
SIC 8711

CAPITAL ENGINEERING *p99*
17187 114 AVE NW SUITE 101, EDMON-TON, AB, T5S 2N5
(780) 488-2504 *SIC 8711*

CARMICHAEL ENGINEERING LTD *p1218*
3822 AV DE COURTRAI, MONTREAL, QC, H3S 1C1
(514) 735-4361 *SIC 8711*

CASCADES CS+ INC *p1069*
9500 AV ILLINOIS, BROSSARD, QC, J4Y 3B7
(450) 923-3300 *SIC 8711*

CASCADES CS+ INC *p1117*
471 BOUL MARIE-VICTORIN, KINGSEY FALLS, QC, J0A 1B0
(819) 363-5700 *SIC 8711*

CASCADES CS+ INC *p1117*
15 RUE LAMONTAGNE, KINGSEY FALLS, QC, J0A 1B0
(819) 363-5971 *SIC 8711*

CBCL LIMITED *p452*
1489 HOLLIS ST, HALIFAX, NS, B3J 3M5
(902) 421-7241 *SIC 8711*

CH2M HILL CANADA LIMITED *p190*
4720 KINGSWAY SUITE 2100, BURNABY, BC, V5H 4N2
(604) 684-3282 *SIC 8711*

CH2M HILL CANADA LIMITED *p766*
245 CONSUMERS RD SUITE 400, NORTH YORK, ON, M2J 1R3
(416) 499-9000 *SIC 8711*

CHEMETICS INC *p286*
2930 VIRTUAL WAY SUITE 200, VANCOU-VER, BC, V5M 0A5

(604) 734-1200 *SIC* 8711
CHRISTOFFERSEN, READ JONES LTD
p319
1285 BROADWAY W UNIT 300, VANCOUVER, BC, V6H 3X8
(604) 738-0048 *SIC* 8711
CIMA+ S.E.N.C. *p1103*
420 BOUL MALONEY E BUREAU 201, GATINEAU, QC, J8P 7N8
(819) 663-9294 *SIC* 8711
CIMA+ S.E.N.C. *p1210*
740 RUE NOTRE-DAME O UNITE 900, MONTREAL, QC, H3C 3X6
(514) 337-2462 *SIC* 8711
CIMA+ S.E.N.C. *p1279*
1145 BOUL LEBOURGNEUF BUREAU 300, QUEBEC, QC, G2K 2K8
(418) 623-3373 *SIC* 8711
CIMA+ S.E.N.C. *p1343*
3400 BOUL DU SOUVENIR BUREAU 600, SAINT-LAURENT, QC, H7V 3Z2
(514) 337-2462 *SIC* 8711
CIMA+ S.E.N.C. *p1373*
3385 RUE KING O, SHERBROOKE, QC, J1L 1P8
(819) 565-3385 *SIC* 8711
CIMARRON PROJECTS LTD *p34*
6025 11 ST SE SUITE 300, CALGARY, AB, T2H 2Z2
(403) 252-3436 *SIC* 8711
CITY OF SURREY, THE *p271*
6651 148 ST FL 3, SURREY, BC, V3S 3C7
(604) 591-4152 *SIC* 8711
CLEARESULT CANADA INC *p944*
393 UNIVERSITY AVE SUITE 1622, TORONTO, ON, M5G 1E6
(416) 504-3400 *SIC* 8711
CLIFTON ASSOCIATES LTD *p1415*
340 MAXWELL CRES, REGINA, SK, S4N 5Y5
(306) 721-7611 *SIC* 8711
CMC ELECTRONIQUE INC *p832*
415 LEGGET DR, OTTAWA, ON, K2K 2B2
(613) 592-6500 *SIC* 8711
CMC ELECTRONIQUE INC *p1324*
600 BOUL DR.-FREDERIK-PHILIPS, SAINT-LAURENT, QC, H4M 2S9
(514) 748-3148 *SIC* 8711
COCHRANE GROUP INC *p66*
320 23 AVE SW SUITE 104, CALGARY, AB, T2S 0J2
(403) 262-3638 *SIC* 8711
COLE ENGINEERING GROUP LTD *p668*
70 VALLEYWOOD DR, MARKHAM, ON, L3R 4T5
(905) 940-6161 *SIC* 8711
COMPAGNIE GE AVIATION CANADA, LA *p1068*
2 BOUL DE L'AEROPORT, BROMONT, QC, J2L 1S6
(450) 534-0917 *SIC* 8711
CONCEPTROMEC EXPORTATION INC *p1147*
1780 BOUL INDUSTRIEL, MAGOG, QC, J1X 4V9
(819) 847-3627 *SIC* 8711
CONSTRUCTION KIEWIT CIE *p1133*
3055 BOUL SAINT-MARTIN O BUREAU 200, LAVAL, QC, H7T 0J3
(450) 435-5756 *SIC* 8711
CONSTRUCTIONS LOUISBOURG LTEE *p1301*
699 BOUL INDUSTRIEL, SAINT-EUSTACHE, QC, J7R 6C3
(450) 623-7100 *SIC* 8711
CONSULTANTS AECOM INC *p1084*
1 PLACE LAVAL BUREAU 200, COTE SAINT-LUC, QC, H7N 1A1
(450) 967-1260 *SIC* 8711
CONSULTANTS AECOM INC *p1185*
85 RUE SAINTE-CATHERINE O, MONTREAL, QC, H2X 3P4
(514) 287-8500 *SIC* 8711
CONSULTANTS AECOM INC *p1266*

4700 BOUL WILFRID-HAMEL, QUEBEC, QC, G1P 2J9
(418) 871-2444 *SIC* 8711
CONSULTANTS MESAR INC *p1389*
4500 RUE CHARLES-MALHIOT, TROIS-RIVIERES, QC, G9B 0V4
(819) 537-5771 *SIC* 8711
CONSULTANTS VFP INC *p1387*
1455 RUE CHAMPLAIN, TROIS-RIVIERES, QC, G9A 5X4
(819) 378-6159 *SIC* 8711
CONSULTEC LTD *p993*
139 MULOCK AVE, TORONTO, ON, M6N 1G9
(416) 236-2426 *SIC* 8711
CONVERGINT TECHNOLOGIES LTD *p34*
6020 11 ST SE SUITE 2, CALGARY, AB, T2H 2L7
(403) 291-3241 *SIC* 8711
CORRPRO CANADA, INC *p100*
10848 214 ST NW, EDMONTON, AB, T5S 2A7
(780) 447-4565 *SIC* 8711
CORRPRO CANADA, INC *p213*
8607 101 ST, FORT ST. JOHN, BC, V1J 5K4
(250) 787-9100 *SIC* 8711
CP ENERGY MARKETING INC *p47*
505 2 ST SW SUITE 84, CALGARY, AB, T2P 1N8
(403) 717-4600 *SIC* 8711
CRH CANADA GROUP INC *p802*
690 DORVAL DR SUITE 200, OAKVILLE, ON, L6K 3W7
(905) 842-2741 *SIC* 8711
CROSSEY ENGINEERING LTD *p766*
2255 SHEPPARD AVE E, NORTH YORK, ON, M2J 4Y1
(416) 497-3111 *SIC* 8711
DELCAN INTERNATIONAL CORPORATION *p669*
625 COCHRANE DR SUITE 500, MARKHAM, ON, L3R 9R9
(905) 943-0500 *SIC* 8711
DESSAU INC *p1279*
1260 BOUL LEBOURGNEUF BUREAU 250, QUEBEC, QC, G2K 2G2
(418) 626-1688 *SIC* 8711
DIGICO FABRICATION ELECTRONIQUE INC *p1101*
950 RUE BERGAR, FABREVILLE, QC, H7L 5A1
(450) 967-7100 *SIC* 8711
DILLON CONSULTING LIMITED *p390*
1558 WILLSON PL, WINNIPEG, MB, R3T 0Y4
(204) 453-2301 *SIC* 8711
DILLON CONSULTING LIMITED *p653*
130 DUFFERIN AVE SUITE 1400, LONDON, ON, N6A 5R2
(519) 438-6192 *SIC* 8711
DILLON CONSULTING LIMITED *p767*
235 YORKLAND BLVD SUITE 800, NORTH YORK, ON, M2J 4Y8
(416) 229-4646 *SIC* 8711
DST CONSULTING ENGINEERS INC *p908*
605 HEWITSON ST, THUNDER BAY, ON, P7B 5V5
(807) 623-2929 *SIC* 8711
EMERSON ELECTRIC CANADA LIMITED *p15*
110 QUARRY PARK BLVD SE SUITE 200, CALGARY, AB, T2C 3G3
(403) 258-6200 *SIC* 8711
EMS-TECH INC *p491*
699 DUNDAS ST W, BELLEVILLE, ON, K8N 4Z2
(613) 966-6611 *SIC* 8711
ENTEGRUS INC *p542*
320 QUEEN ST, CHATHAM, ON, N7M 2H6
(519) 352-6300 *SIC* 8711
ENTREPRISES MICHAUDVILLE INC, LES *p1158*
270 RUE BRUNET, MONT-SAINT-HILAIRE, QC, J3H 0M6

(450) 446-9933 *SIC* 8711
ENTUITIVE CORPORATION *p49*
150 9 AVE SW SUITE 1610, CALGARY, AB, T2P 3H9
(403) 879-1270 *SIC* 8711
ENTUITIVE CORPORATION *p951*
200 UNIVERSITY AVE 7TH FL, TORONTO, ON, M5H 3C6
(416) 477-5832 *SIC* 8711
EQUINOX ENGINEERING LTD *p49*
940 6 AVE SW UNIT 400, CALGARY, AB, T2P 3T1
(587) 390-1000 *SIC* 8711
EXP GLOBAL INC *p508*
56 QUEEN ST E SUITE 301, BRAMPTON, ON, L6V 4M8
(855) 225-5397 *SIC* 8711
EXP SERVICES INC *p188*
3001 WAYBURNE DR SUITE 275, BURNABY, BC, V5G 4W3
(604) 874-1245 *SIC* 8711
EXP SERVICES INC *p401*
1133 REGENT ST SUITE 300, FREDERICTON, NB, E3B 3Z2
(506) 452-9000 *SIC* 8711
EXP SERVICES INC *p502*
1595 CLARK BLVD, BRAMPTON, ON, L6T 4V1
(905) 793-9800 *SIC* 8711
EXP SERVICES INC *p508*
56 QUEEN ST E SUITE 301, BRAMPTON, ON, L6V 4M8
(905) 796-3200 *SIC* 8711
EXP SERVICES INC *p749*
154 COLONNADE RD S, NEPEAN, ON, K2E 7J5
(613) 225-9940 *SIC* 8711
EXP SERVICES INC *p1195*
1001 BOUL DE MAISONNEUVE O BUREAU 800B, MONTREAL, QC, H3A 3C8
(514) 788-6158 *SIC* 8711
FIDUS SYSTEMS INC *p832*
375 TERRY FOX DR, OTTAWA, ON, K2K 0J8
(613) 595-0507 *SIC* 8711
FLEETWAY INC *p458*
84 CHAIN LAKE DR SUITE 200, HALIFAX, NS, B3S 1A2
(902) 494-5700 *SIC* 8711
FLEETWAY INC *p823*
141 LAURIER AVE W SUITE 800, OTTAWA, ON, K1P 5J3
(613) 236-6048 *SIC* 8711
FLEXTRONICS CANADA DESIGN SERVICES INC *p624*
1280 TERON RD, KANATA, ON, K2K 2C1
(613) 895-2050 *SIC* 8711
FLEXTRONICS EMS CANADA INC *p832*
1280 TERON RD, OTTAWA, ON, K2K 2C1
(613) 895-2056 *SIC* 8711
FLUOR CANADA LTD *p69*
55 SUNPARK PLAZA SE, CALGARY, AB, T2X 3R4
(403) 537-4000 *SIC* 8711
FLUOR CANADA LTD *p313*
1075 GEORGIA ST W SUITE 700, VANCOUVER, BC, V6E 4M7
(604) 488-2000 *SIC* 8711
FRIENDEFI INC *p1184*
6750 AV DE L'ESPLANADE BUREAU 320, MONTREAL, QC, H2V 4M1
(514) 397-0415 *SIC* 8711
G.C.M. CONSULTANTS INC *p1049*
9496 BOUL DU GOLF, ANJOU, QC, H1J 3A1
(514) 351-8350 *SIC* 8711
GAMSBY AND MANNEROW LIMITED *p603*
255 WOODLAWN RD W SUITE 210, GUELPH, ON, N1H 8J1
(519) 824-8150 *SIC* 8711
GASTOPS LTD *p596*
1011 POLYTEK ST, GLOUCESTER, ON, K1J 9J3
(613) 744-3530 *SIC* 8711

GEMINI ENGINEERING LIMITED *p50*
839 5 AVE SW SUITE 400, CALGARY, AB, T2P 3C8
(403) 255-2916 *SIC* 8711
GEMTEC LIMITED *p402*
191 DOAK RD, FREDERICTON, NB, E3C 2E6
(506) 453-1025 *SIC* 8711
GENERAL ELECTRIC CANADA INTERNATIONAL INC *p722*
2300 MEADOWVALE BLVD SUITE 100, MISSISSAUGA, ON, L5N 5P9
(905) 858-5100 *SIC* 8711
GENERAL MOTORS OF CANADA COMPANY *p812*
500 WENTWORTH ST E SUITE 1, OSHAWA, ON, L1H 3V9
(905) 644-4716 *SIC* 8711
GENIVAR INC *p1215*
EDIFICE NORTHERN 1600 RENE-LEVESQUE BLVD W, MONTREAL, QC, H3H 1P9
(514) 340-0046 *SIC* 8711
GENOA DESIGN INTERNATIONAL LTD *p426*
117 GLENCOE DR SUITE 201, MOUNT PEARL, NL, A1N 4S7
(709) 368-0669 *SIC* 8711
GHD INC *p722*
6705 MILLCREEK DR SUITE 1, MISSISSAUGA, ON, L5N 5M4
(416) 213-7121 *SIC* 8711
GHD LIMITED *p1008*
455 PHILLIP ST, WATERLOO, ON, N2L 3X2
(519) 884-0510 *SIC* 8711
GOLDER ASSOCIATES CORPORATION *p723*
6925 CENTURY AVE SUITE 100, MISSISSAUGA, ON, L5N 7K2
(905) 567-4444 *SIC* 8711
GOLDER ASSOCIATES LTD *p98*
16820 107 AVE NW, EDMONTON, AB, T5P 4C3
(780) 483-3499 *SIC* 8711
GOLDER ASSOCIATES LTD *p338*
3795 CAREY RD FL 2, VICTORIA, BC, V8Z 6T8
(250) 881-7372 *SIC* 8711
GOLDER ASSOCIATES LTD *p723*
6925 CENTURY AVE, MISSISSAUGA, ON, L5N 0E3
(905) 567-4444 *SIC* 8711
GOLDER ASSOCIATES LTD *p751*
1931 ROBERTSON RD, NEPEAN, ON, K2H 5B7
(613) 592-9600 *SIC* 8711
GOLDER ASSOCIATES LTD *p900*
33 MACKENZIE ST SUITE 100, SUDBURY, ON, P3C 4Y1
(705) 524-6861 *SIC* 8711
GOLDER ASSOCIATES LTD *p1424*
1721 8TH ST E, SASKATOON, SK, S7H 0T4
(306) 665-7989 *SIC* 8711
GOLDER CONSTRUCTION INC *p1226*
9200 BOUL DE L'ACADIE BUREAU 10, MONTREAL, QC, H4N 2T2
(514) 389-1631 *SIC* 8711
GOUVERNEMENT DE LA PROVINCE DE QUEBEC *p1278*
700 7E RUE DE L'AEROPORT, QUEBEC, QC, G2G 2S8
(418) 528-8686 *SIC* 8711
GROUPE ABS INC *p1351*
17 RUE DE L'INDUSTRIE, SAINT-REMI, QC, J0L 2L0
(450) 454-5644 *SIC* 8711
GROUPE ADF INC *p1381*
300 RUE HENRY-BESSEMER, TERREBONNE, QC, J6Y 1T3
(450) 965-1911 *SIC* 8711
GROUPE ALPHARD INC *p1183*
5570 AV CASGRAIN BUREAU 101, MONTREAL, QC, H2T 1X9
(514) 543-6580 *SIC* 8711
GROUPE BBA INC *p1158*

375 BOUL SIR-WILFRID-LAURIER, MONT-SAINT-HILAIRE, QC, J3H 6C3
(450) 464-2111   SIC 8711
GROUPE CONSEIL TDA INC p1052
26 BOUL COMEAU, BAIE-COMEAU, QC, G4Z 3A8
(418) 296-6711   SIC 8711
GROUPE MANUFACTURIER D'ASCENSEURS GLOBAL TARDIF INC, LE p1293
120 RUE DE NAPLES, SAINT-AUGUSTIN-DE-DESMAURES, QC, G3A 2Y2
(418) 878-4116   SIC 8711
GROUPE S.M. INC, LE p1178
433 RUE CHABANEL O 12E ETAGE, MON-TREAL, QC, H2N 2J8
(514) 982-6001   SIC 8711
GROUPE S.M. INTERNATIONAL INC, LE p1178
433 RUE CHABANEL O BUREAU 1200, MONTREAL, QC, H2N 2J8
(514) 982-6001   SIC 8711
GROUPE SNC-LAVALIN INC p1191
455 BOUL RENE-LEVESQUE O BUREAU 202, MONTREAL, QC, H2Z 1Z3
(514) 393-1000   SIC 8711
GROUPE ULTRAGEN LTEE, LE p1065
50 RUE DE LAUZON, BOUCHERVILLE, QC, J4B 1E6
(450) 650-0770   SIC 8711
HAMEL CONSTRUCTION INC p1299
2106 RTE PRINCIPALE, SAINT-EDOUARD-DE-LOTBINIERE, QC, G0S 1Y0
(418) 796-2074   SIC 8711
HATCH CORPORATION p522
5035 SOUTH SERVICE RD, BURLINGTON, ON, L7L 6M9
(905) 315-3500   SIC 8711
HATCH CORPORATION p715
2800 SPEAKMAN DR, MISSISSAUGA, ON, L5K 2R7
(905) 855-2010   SIC 8711
HATCH CORPORATION p1205
5 PLACE VILLE-MARIE BUREAU 1400, MONTREAL, QC, H3B 2G2
(514) 861-0583   SIC 8711
HATCH LTD p313
1066 HASTINGS ST W SUITE 400, VAN-COUVER, BC, V6E 3X1
(604) 689-5767   SIC 8711
HATCH LTD p378
500 PORTAGE AVE SUITE 600, WIN-NIPEG, MB, R3C 3Y8
(204) 786-8751   SIC 8711
HATCH LTD p715
2800 SPEAKMAN DR, MISSISSAUGA, ON, L5K 2R7
(905) 855-7600   SIC 8711
HATCH LTD p758
4342 QUEEN ST SUITE 500, NIAGARA FALLS, ON, L2E 7J7
(905) 374-5200   SIC 8711
HATCH LTD p797
2265 UPPER MIDDLE RD E SUITE 300, OAKVILLE, ON, L6H 0G5
(905) 855-7600   SIC 8711
HATCH LTD p1205
5 PLACE VILLE-MARIE BUREAU 1400, MONTREAL, QC, H3B 2G2
(514) 861-0583   SIC 8711
HATCHCOS HOLDINGS LTD p715
2800 SPEAKMAN DR, MISSISSAUGA, ON, L5K 2R7
(905) 855-7600   SIC 8711
IBI GROUP INC p927
55 ST CLAIR AVE W SUITE 700, TORONTO, ON, M4V 2Y7
(416) 596-1930   SIC 8711
ILF CONSULTANTS INC p51
833 4 AVE SW SUITE 600, CALGARY, AB, T2P 3T5
(587) 288-2600   SIC 8711
INDUSTRIAL ROOF CONSULTANTS (IRC) GROUP INC p723

2121 ARGENTIA RD SUITE 401, MISSIS-SAUGA, ON, L5N 2X4
(905) 607-7244   SIC 8711
INDUSTRIES FOURNIER INC, LES p1383
3787 BOUL FRONTENAC O, THETFORD MINES, QC, G6H 2B5
(418) 423-4241   SIC 8711
INVODANE ENGINEERING LTD p914
44 METROPOLITAN RD, TORONTO, ON, M1R 2T6
(416) 443-8049   SIC 8711
IRC BUILDING SCIENCES GROUP p723
2121 ARGENTIA RD SUITE 401, MISSIS-SAUGA, ON, L5N 2X4
(905) 607-7244   SIC 8711
ISL ENGINEERING AND LAND SERVICES LTD p115
7909 51 AVE NW SUITE 100, EDMONTON, AB, T6E 5L9
(780) 438-9000   SIC 8711
ISL HOLDINGS INC p115
7909 51 AVE NW, EDMONTON, AB, T6E 5L9
(780) 438-9000   SIC 8711
J & B ENGINEERING INC p770
5734 YONGE ST SUITE 501, NORTH YORK, ON, M2M 4E7
(416) 229-2636   SIC 8711
J.L. RICHARDS & ASSOCIATES LIMITED p829
864 LADY ELLEN PL, OTTAWA, ON, K1Z 5M2
(613) 728-3571   SIC 8711
JABLONSKY AST AND PARTNERS p779
1129 LESLIE ST, NORTH YORK, ON, M3C 2K5
(416) 447-7405   SIC 8711
JACOBS CANADA INC p16
205 QUARRY PARK BLVD SE, CALGARY, AB, T2C 3E7
(403) 258-6411   SIC 8711
JENSEN HUGHES CONSULTING CANADA LTD p255
13900 MAYCREST WAY UNIT 135, RICH-MOND, BC, V6V 3E2
(604) 295-4000   SIC 8711
JMP ENGINEERING INC p533
1425 BISHOP ST N UNIT 8, CAMBRIDGE, ON, N1R 6J9
(519) 622-2505   SIC 8711
JMP ENGINEERING INC p660
4026 MEADOWBROOK DR UNIT 143, LONDON, ON, N6L 1C9
(519) 652-2741   SIC 8711
JNE CONSULTING LTD p611
121 SHAW ST, HAMILTON, ON, L8L 3P6
(905) 529-5122   SIC 8711
JNE CONSULTING LTD p611
176 SHAW ST, HAMILTON, ON, L8L 3P7
(905) 529-5122   SIC 8711
JOHNSON CONTROLS CANADA LP p852
56 LEEK CRES, RICHMOND HILL, ON, L4B 1H1
(866) 468-1484   SIC 8711
JOHNSTON-VERMETTE GROUPE CON-SEIL INC p1388
6110 RUE CHRISTOPHE-PELISSIER, TROIS-RIVIERES, QC, G9A 5C9
(819) 373-3550   SIC 8711
JP2G CONSULTANTS INC p838
12 INTERNATIONAL DR, PEMBROKE, ON, K8A 6W5
(613) 735-2507   SIC 8711
KB COMPONENTS CANADA INC p1020
2900 ST ETIENNE BLVD, WINDSOR, ON, N8W 5E6
(519) 974-6596   SIC 8711
KENAIDAN CONTRACTING LTD p745
7080 DERRYCREST DR, MISSISSAUGA, ON, L5W 0G5
(905) 670-2660   SIC 8711
KLOHN CRIPPEN BERGER LTD p9
2618 HOPEWELL PL NE SUITE 500, CAL-GARY, AB, T1Y 7J7

(403) 274-3424   SIC 8711
KLOHN CRIPPEN BERGER LTD p286
2955 VIRTUAL WAY SUITE 500, VANCOU-VER, BC, V5M 4X6
(604) 669-3800   SIC 8711
KNIGHT PIESOLD LTD p306
750 PENDER ST W SUITE 1400, VANCOU-VER, BC, V6C 2T8
(604) 685-0543   SIC 8711
KONTZAMANIS GRAUMANN SMITH MACMILLAN INC p391
865 WAVERLEY ST SUITE 300, WIN-NIPEG, MB, R3T 5P4
(204) 896-1209   SIC 8711
KSH SOLUTIONS INC p1220
3400 BOUL DE MAISONNEUVE O BU-REAU 1600, MONTREAL, QC, H3Z 3B8
(514) 932-4611   SIC 8711
L.A. HEBERT LTEE p1070
9700 PLACE JADE, BROSSARD, QC, J4Y 3C1
(450) 444-4847   SIC 8711
LAUREN ENGINEERS & CONSTRUCTORS, ULC p53
736 6 AVE SW UNIT 800, CALGARY, AB, T2P 3T7
(403) 237-7160   SIC 8711
LEA CONSULTING LTD p671
625 COCHRANE DR 9TH FLR, MARKHAM, ON, L3R 9R9
(905) 470-0015   SIC 8711
LEA GROUP HOLDINGS INC p671
625 COCHRANE DR SUITE 900, MARKHAM, ON, L3R 9R9
(905) 470-0015   SIC 8711
LEVELTON CONSULTANTS LTD p255
12791 CLARKE PL SUITE 150, RICH-MOND, BC, V6V 2H9
(604) 278-1411   SIC 8711
LOTEK WIRELESS INC p755
115 PONY DR, NEWMARKET, ON, L3Y 7B5
(905) 836-5329   SIC 8711
LVM / MARITIME TESTING LIMITED p447
97 TROOP AVE, DARTMOUTH, NS, B3B 2A7
(902) 468-6486   SIC 8711
MAGEST INC p895
25 WRIGHT BLVD, STRATFORD, ON, N4Z 1H3
(519) 272-1001   SIC 8711
MAPLE REINDERS CONSTRUCTORS LTD p724
2660 ARGENTIA RD, MISSISSAUGA, ON, L5N 5V4
(905) 821-4844   SIC 8711
MARCH CONSULTING ASSOCIATES INC p1428
201 21ST ST E SUITE 200, SASKATOON, SK, S7K 0B8
(306) 651-6330   SIC 8711
MATSU MANUFACTURING INC p594
71 TODD RD, GEORGETOWN, ON, L7G 4R8
SIC 8711
MCCORMICK RANKIN CORPORATION p715
2655 NORTH SHERIDAN WAY SUITE 300, MISSISSAUGA, ON, L5K 2P8
(905) 823-8500   SIC 8711
MCINTOSH PERRY CONSULTING ENGI-NEERS LTD p541
115 WALGREEN RD RR 3, CARP, ON, K0A 1L0
(613) 836-2184   SIC 8711
MCMILLAN-MCGEE CORP p12
4895 35B ST SE, CALGARY, AB, T2B 3M9
(403) 569-5100   SIC 8711
MCW CONSULTANTS LTD p964
207 QUEENS QUAY W SUITE 615, TORONTO, ON, M5J 1A7
(416) 598-2920   SIC 8711
MCW CUSTOM ENERGY SOLUTIONS LTD p964
207 QUEENS QUAY W SUITE 615,

TORONTO, ON, M5J 1A7
(416) 598-2920   SIC 8711
MDS AERO SUPPORT CORPORATION p816
1220 OLD INNES RD SUITE 200, OTTAWA, ON, K1B 3V3
(613) 744-7257   SIC 8711
MDS AERO SUPPORT CORPORATION p816
1220 OLD INNES RD SUITE 200, OTTAWA, ON, K1B 3V3
(613) 744-5794   SIC 8711
MEDA LIMITED p1018
1575 LAUZON RD, WINDSOR, ON, N8S 3N4
(519) 944-7221   SIC 8711
MILLENIA RESOURCE CONSULTING p65
628 11 AVE SW SUITE 200, CALGARY, AB, T2R 0E2
(403) 571-0510   SIC 8711
MITCHELL PARTNERSHIP INC, THE p768
285 YORKLAND BLVD, NORTH YORK, ON, M2J 1S5
(416) 499-8000   SIC 8711
MORRISON HERSHFIELD LIMITED p36
6807 RAILWAY ST SE SUITE 300, CAL-GARY, AB, T2H 2V6
(403) 246-4500   SIC 8711
MORRISON HERSHFIELD LIMITED p904
125 COMMERCE VALLEY DR W UNIT 300, THORNHILL, ON, L3T 7W4
(416) 499-3110   SIC 8711
MPE ENGINEERING LTD p142
714 5 AVE S SUITE 300, LETHBRIDGE, AB, T1J 0V1
(403) 329-3442   SIC 8711
MTE CONSULTANTS INC p635
520 BINGEMANS CENTRE DR, KITCH-ENER, ON, N2B 3X9
(519) 743-6500   SIC 8711
MULVEY & BANANI INTERNATIONAL INC p787
44 MOBILE DR, NORTH YORK, ON, M4A 2P2
(416) 751-2520   SIC 8711
NAVTECH INC p1008
295 HAGEY BLVD SUITE 200, WATERLOO, ON, N2L 6R5
(519) 747-1170   SIC 8711
NEMETZ, ARNOLD & ASSOCIATES LTD p321
2009 4TH AVE W, VANCOUVER, BC, V6J 1N3
(604) 736-6562   SIC 8711
NEPTEC DESIGN GROUP LTD p625
302 LEGGET DR UNIT 202, KANATA, ON, K2K 1Y5
(613) 599-7602   SIC 8711
NORDA STELO INC p1079
159 RUE SALABERRY, CHICOUTIMI, QC, G7H 4K2
(418) 549-6471   SIC 8711
NORDA STELO INC p1189
33 RUE SAINT-JACQUES BUREAU 400, MONTREAL, QC, H2Y 1K9
(514) 282-4181   SIC 8711
NORDA STELO INC p1274
1015 AV WILFRID-PELLETIER, QUEBEC, QC, G1W 0C4
(418) 654-9600   SIC 8711
NORTHWEST HYDRAULIC CONSULTANTS LTD p125
9819 12 AVE SW, EDMONTON, AB, T6X 0E3
(780) 436-5868   SIC 8711
NOVATECH ENGINEERING CONSULTANTS LTD p626
240 MICHAEL COWPLAND DR SUITE 200, KANATA, ON, K2M 1P6
(613) 254-9643   SIC 8711
O'ROURKE ENGINEERING LTD p9
2711 39 AVE NE, CALGARY, AB, T1Y 4T8
(403) 261-4991   SIC 8711
OCEANEERING CANADA LIMITED p426
23 DUNDEE AVE, MOUNT PEARL, NL, A1N 4R6

(709) 570-7072 *SIC 8711*
OFFICE OF THE FIRE COMMISSIONER
p379
401 YORK AVE UNIT 508, WINNIPEG, MB, R3C 0P8
(204) 945-3322 *SIC 8711*
ONEC ENGINEERING INC *p110*
3821 78 AVE NW, EDMONTON, AB, T6B 3N8
(780) 485-5375 *SIC 8711*
PARSONS INC *p673*
625 COCHRANE DR SUITE 500, MARKHAM, ON, L3R 9R9
(905) 943-0500 *SIC 8711*
PCO INNOVATION CANADA INC *p1190*
384 RUE SAINT-JACQUES, MONTREAL, QC, H2Y 1S1
(514) 866-3000 *SIC 8711*
PELLEMON INC *p1192*
455 BOUL RENE-LEVESQUE O, MONTREAL, QC, H2Z 1Z3
(514) 735-5651 *SIC 8711*
PETO MACCALLUM LTD *p789*
165 CARTWRIGHT AVE, NORTH YORK, ON, M6A 1V5
(416) 785-5110 *SIC 8711*
PLACEMENTS HEBDEN INC *p1070*
9700 PLACE JADE, BROSSARD, QC, J4Y 3C1
(450) 444-4847 *SIC 8711*
PLURITEC CIVIL LTEE *p1368*
585 AV DES CEDRES, SHAWINIGAN, QC, G9N 1N6
(819) 537-1882 *SIC 8711*
POYRY (MONTREAL) INC *p1228*
5250 RUE FERRIER BUREAU 700, MONTREAL, QC, H4P 1L4
(514) 341-3221 *SIC 8711*
PRIMARY ENGINEERING AND CONSTRUCTION CORPORATION *p25*
207 39 AVE NE, CALGARY, AB, T2E 7E3
(403) 873-0400 *SIC 8711*
R. V. ANDERSON ASSOCIATES LIMITED *p768*
2001 SHEPPARD AVE E SUITE 400, NORTH YORK, ON, M2J 4Z8
(416) 497-8600 *SIC 8711*
R.J. BURNSIDE & ASSOCIATES LIMITED *p808*
15 TOWN LINE, ORANGEVILLE, ON, L9W 3R4
(519) 941-5331 *SIC 8711*
RANGELAND ENGINEERING LTD *p65*
1520 4 ST SW SUITE 1000, CALGARY, AB, T2R 1H5
(403) 265-5130 *SIC 8711*
RDH BUILDING SCIENCE INC *p186*
4333 STILL CREEK DR SUITE 400, BURNABY, BC, V5C 6S6
(604) 873-1181 *SIC 8711*
REID CROWTHER & PARTNERS LIMITED *p69*
340 MIDPARK WAY SE SUITE 300, CALGARY, AB, T2X 1P1
SIC 8711
REINDERS GROUP LTD *p726*
2660 ARGENTIA RD, MISSISSAUGA, ON, L5N 5V4
(905) 821-4844 *SIC 8711*
RICE ENGINEERING & OPERATING LTD *p116*
9333 41 AVE NW, EDMONTON, AB, T6E 6R5
(780) 469-1356 *SIC 8711*
ROCTEST LTEE *p1322*
680 AV BIRCH, SAINT-LAMBERT, QC, J4P 2N3
(450) 465-1113 *SIC 8711*
ROLLS-ROYCE CIVIL NUCLEAR CANADA LTD *p842*
678 NEAL DR, PETERBOROUGH, ON, K9J 6X7
(705) 743-2708 *SIC 8711*
ROWAN WILLIAMS DAVIES & IRWIN INC

p601
600 SOUTHGATE DR, GUELPH, ON, N1G 4P6
(519) 823-1311 *SIC 8711*
ROY CONSULTANTS GROUP LTD *p394*
548 KING AVE, BATHURST, NB, E2A 1P7
(506) 546-4484 *SIC 8711*
RPS ENERGY CANADA LTD *p58*
800 5 AVE SW SUITE 1400, CALGARY, AB, T2P 3T6
(403) 265-7226 *SIC 8711*
RSW INC *p1208*
1010 RUE DE LA GAUCHETIERE O BUREAU 1400, MONTREAL, QC, H3B 2N2
(514) 287-8500 *SIC 8711*
RWDI AIR INC *p601*
600 SOUTHGATE DR, GUELPH, ON, N1G 4P6
(519) 823-1311 *SIC 8711*
RWDI GROUP INC *p601*
600 SOUTHGATE DR, GUELPH, ON, N1G 4P6
(519) 823-1311 *SIC 8711*
SACRE CONSULTANTS LTD *p239*
315 MOUNTAIN HWY, NORTH VANCOUVER, BC, V7J 2K7
(604) 983-0305 *SIC 8711*
SAFRAN CABIN CANADA CO. *p1118*
18107 RTE TRANSCANADIENNE, KIRKLAND, QC, H9J 3K1
(514) 697-5555 *SIC 8711*
SCHEFFER ANDREW LTD *p94*
12204 145 ST NW, EDMONTON, AB, T5L 4V7
(780) 732-7800 *SIC 8711*
SCHNEIDER ELECTRIC CANADA INC *p1070*
4100 PLACE JAVA, BROSSARD, QC, J4Y 0C4
(450) 444-0143 *SIC 8711*
SERNAS GROUP INC, THE *p1015*
110 SCOTIA CRT UNIT 41, WHITBY, ON, L1N 8Y7
(905) 432-7878 *SIC 8711*
SERVICES EXP INC., LES *p1372*
150 RUE DE VIMY, SHERBROOKE, QC, J1J 3M7
(819) 780-1868 *SIC 8711*
SINTRA INC *p1290*
240 AV MARCEL-BARIL, ROUYN-NORANDA, QC, J9X 7C1
(819) 762-6505 *SIC 8711*
SMITH AND ANDERSEN CONSULTING ENGINEERING *p774*
4211 YONGE ST SUITE 500, NORTH YORK, ON, M2P 2A9
(416) 487-8151 *SIC 8711*
SNC-LAVALIN ATP INC *p59*
640 5 AVE SW UNIT 300, CALGARY, AB, T2P 3G4
(403) 539-4550 *SIC 8711*
SNC-LAVALIN INC *p59*
605 5 AVE SW SUITE 1400, CALGARY, AB, T2P 3H5
(403) 294-2100 *SIC 8711*
SNC-LAVALIN INC *p91*
10235 101 ST NW SUITE 608, EDMONTON, AB, T5J 3G1
(780) 426-1000 *SIC 8711*
SNC-LAVALIN INC *p316*
745 THURLOW ST SUITE 500, VANCOUVER, BC, V6E 0C5
(604) 662-3555 *SIC 8711*
SNC-LAVALIN INC *p426*
1090 TOPSAIL RD, MOUNT PEARL, NL, A1N 5E7
(709) 368-0118 *SIC 8711*
SNC-LAVALIN INC *p454*
5657 SPRING GARDEN RD SUITE 200, HALIFAX, NS, B3J 3R4
(902) 424-4544 *SIC 8711*
SNC-LAVALIN INC *p580*
195 THE WEST MALL, ETOBICOKE, ON, M9C 5K1

(416) 252-5315 *SIC 8711*
SNC-LAVALIN INC *p1192*
455 BOUL RENE-LEVESQUE O, MONTREAL, QC, H2Z 1Z3
(514) 393-1000 *SIC 8711*
SNC-LAVALIN INC *p1280*
5500 BOUL DES GALERIES BUREAU 200, QUEBEC, QC, G2K 2E2
(418) 621-5500 *SIC 8711*
SNC-LAVALIN INTERNATIONAL INC *p59*
605 5 AVE SW SUITE 1400, CALGARY, AB, T2P 3H5
(403) 294-2100 *SIC 8711*
SNC-LAVALIN INTERNATIONAL INC *p799*
2275 UPPER MIDDLE RD E, OAKVILLE, ON, L6H 0C3
(905) 829-8808 *SIC 8711*
SNC-LAVALIN INTERNATIONAL INC *p861*
265 FRONT ST N SUITE 301, SARNIA, ON, N7T 7X1
(519) 336-0201 *SIC 8711*
SNC-LAVALIN PHARMA INC *p1228*
8000 BOUL DECARIE 3EME ETAGE, MONTREAL, QC, H4P 2S4
(514) 735-5651 *SIC 8711*
SNC-LAVALIN STAVIBEL INC *p1290*
1375 AV LARIVIERE, ROUYN-NORANDA, QC, J9X 6M6
(819) 764-5181 *SIC 8711*
SNC-LAVALIN STAVIBEL INC *p1391*
1271 7E RUE, VAL-D'OR, QC, J9P 3S1
(819) 825-2233 *SIC 8711*
SPROULE ASSOCIATES LIMITED *p60*
140 4 AVE SW UNIT 900, CALGARY, AB, T2P 3N3
(403) 294-5500 *SIC 8711*
SPROULE HOLDINGS LIMITED *p60*
140 4 AVE SW SUITE 900, CALGARY, AB, T2P 3N3
(403) 294-5500 *SIC 8711*
SPROULE INTERNATIONAL LIMITED *p60*
140 4 AVE SW SUITE 900, CALGARY, AB, T2P 3N3
(403) 294-5500 *SIC 8711*
STANTEC ARCHITECTURE LTD *p11*
325 25 ST SE SUITE 200, CALGARY, AB, T2A 7H8
(403) 716-8000 *SIC 8711*
STANTEC CONSULTING INTERNATIONAL LTD *p91*
10220 103 AVE NW SUITE 400, EDMONTON, AB, T5J 0K4
(780) 917-7000 *SIC 8711*
STANTEC CONSULTING INTERNATIONAL LTD *p764*
147 MCINTYRE ST W SUITE 200, NORTH BAY, ON, P1B 2Y5
(705) 494-8255 *SIC 8711*
STANTEC CONSULTING LTD *p91*
10220 103 AVE NW SUITE 400, EDMONTON, AB, T5J 0K4
(780) 917-7000 *SIC 8711*
STANTEC CONSULTING LTD *p375*
311 PORTAGE AVE UNIT 500, WINNIPEG, MB, R3B 2B9
(204) 489-5900 *SIC 8711*
STANTEC CONSULTING LTD *p431*
141 KELSEY DR, ST. JOHN'S, NL, A1B 0L2
(709) 576-1458 *SIC 8711*
STANTEC CONSULTING LTD *p655*
171 QUEENS AVE 6TH FLOOR, LONDON, ON, N6A 5J7
(519) 645-2007 *SIC 8711*
STANTEC CONSULTING LTD *p675*
675 COCHRANE DR SUITE 300 W, MARKHAM, ON, L3R 0B8
(905) 944-7777 *SIC 8711*
STANTEC CONSULTING LTD *p1009*
300 HAGEY BLVD SUITE 100, WATERLOO, ON, N2L 0A4
(519) 579-4410 *SIC 8711*
STANTEC CONSULTING LTD *p1079*
255 RUE RACINE E, CHICOUTIMI, QC, G7H 7L2

(418) 549-6680 *SIC 8711*
STANTEC CONSULTING LTD *p1208*
1060 BOUL ROBERT-BOURASSA UNITE 600, MONTREAL, QC, H3B 4V3
(514) 281-1033 *SIC 8711*
STANTEC INC *p91*
10220 103 AVE NW SUITE 400, EDMONTON, AB, T5J 0K4
(780) 917-7000 *SIC 8711*
STORAGE & TRANSFER TECHNOLOGIES, INC *p684*
8485 PARKHILL DR, MILTON, ON, L9T 5E9
(905) 693-9301 *SIC 8711*
SUPERHEAT FGH CANADA INC *p629*
1463 HIGHWAY 21, KINCARDINE, ON, N2Z 2X3
(519) 396-1324 *SIC 8711*
SYMBOTIC CANADA ULC *p1051*
10925 BOUL LOUIS-H.-LAFONTAINE, ANJOU, QC, H1J 2E8
(514) 352-0500 *SIC 8711*
SYSTRA CANADA INC *p1209*
1100 BOUL RENE-LEVESQUE O ETAGE 10E, MONTREAL, QC, H3B 4N4
(514) 985-0930 *SIC 8711*
TATHAM, C.C. & ASSOCIATES LTD *p547*
115 SANDFORD FLEMING RD SUITE 200, COLLINGWOOD, ON, L9Y 5A6
(705) 444-2565 *SIC 8711*
TECHINSIGHTS INC *p832*
1891 ROBERTSON RD SUITE 500, OTTAWA, ON, K2H 5B7
(613) 599-6500 *SIC 8711*
TECHNI-AIR 2000 INC *p1252*
97 BOUL HYMUS, POINTE-CLAIRE, QC, H9R 1E2
(514) 918-0299 *SIC 8711*
TELECON DESIGN INC *p1181*
7450 RUE DU MILE END, MONTREAL, QC, H2R 2Z6
(514) 644-2333 *SIC 8711*
TERRACON GEOTECHNIQUE LTD *p129*
8212 MANNING AVE, FORT MCMURRAY, AB, T9H 1V9
(780) 743-9343 *SIC 8711*
TERRAPROBE INC *p507*
11 INDELL LANE, BRAMPTON, ON, L6T 3Y3
(905) 796-2650 *SIC 8711*
TESHMONT CONSULTANTS LP *p392*
1190 WAVERLEY ST, WINNIPEG, MB, R3T 0P4
(204) 284-8100 *SIC 8711*
TETRA TECH CANADA INC *p19*
200 RIVERCREST DR SE SUITE 115, CALGARY, AB, T2C 2X5
(403) 203-3355 *SIC 8711*
TETRA TECH CANADA INC *p106*
14940 123 AVE NW, EDMONTON, AB, T5V 1B4
(780) 451-2121 *SIC 8711*
TETRA TECH CANADA INC *p376*
161 PORTAGE AVE E SUITE 400, WINNIPEG, MB, R3B 0Y4
(204) 954-6800 *SIC 8711*
TETRA TECH CANADA INC *p727*
6835 CENTURY AVE UNIT A, MISSISSAUGA, ON, L5N 7K2
(905) 369-3000 *SIC 8711*
TETRA TECH CANADA INC *p909*
725 HEWITSON ST, THUNDER BAY, ON, P7B 6B5
(807) 345-5453 *SIC 8711*
TETRA TECH CANADA INC *p957*
330 BAY ST SUITE 900, TORONTO, ON, M5H 2S8
(416) 368-9080 *SIC 8711*
TETRA TECH CANADA INC *p1430*
410 22ND ST E SUITE 1400, SASKATOON, SK, S7K 5T6
(306) 244-4888 *SIC 8711*
TETRA TECH INDUSTRIES INC *p1167*
5100 RUE SHERBROOKE E, MONTREAL, QC, H1V 3R9

(514) 257-1112　*SIC 8711*
TETRA TECH INDUSTRIES INC　*p1167*
5100 RUE SHERBROOKE E BUREAU 400, MONTREAL, QC, H1V 3R9
(514) 257-0707　*SIC 8711*
TETRA TECH OGD INC　*p262*
10851 SHELLBRIDGE WAY SUITE 100, RICHMOND, BC, V6X 2W8
(604) 270-7728　*SIC 8711*
TETRA TECH QE INC　*p1167*
5100 RUE SHERBROOKE E BUREAU 900, MONTREAL, QC, H1V 3R9
(514) 257-0707　*SIC 8711*
THALES CANADA INC　*p778*
105 MOATFIELD DR SUITE 100, NORTH YORK, ON, M3B 0A4
(416) 742-3900　*SIC 8711*
THE HIDI GROUP INC　*p915*
155 GORDON BAKER RD SUITE 200, TORONTO, ON, M2H 3N5
(416) 364-2100　*SIC 8711*
THURBER ENGINEERING LTD　*p38*
7330 FISHER ST SE SUITE 180, CALGARY, AB, T2H 2H8
(403) 253-9217　*SIC 8711*
THURBER ENGINEERING LTD　*p117*
9636 51 AVE NW SUITE 200, EDMONTON, AB, T6E 6A5
(780) 438-1460　*SIC 8711*
THYSSENKRUPP INDUSTRIAL SOLUTIONS (CANADA) INC　*p74*
4838 RICHARD RD SW SUITE 400, CALGARY, AB, T3E 6L1
(403) 245-2866　*SIC 8711*
TOYO ENGINEERING CANADA LTD　*p61*
727 7 AVE SW SUITE 1400, CALGARY, AB, T2P 0Z5
(403) 266-4400　*SIC 8711*
TWD TECHNOLOGIES LTD　*p525*
905 CENTURY DR, BURLINGTON, ON, L7L 5J8
(905) 634-3324　*SIC 8711*
UPSIDE ENGINEERING LTD　*p32*
409 10 AVE SE, CALGARY, AB, T2G 0W3
(403) 290-4650　*SIC 8711*
URBAN SYSTEMS LTD　*p218*
286 ST PAUL ST SUITE 200, KAMLOOPS, BC, V2C 6G4
(250) 374-8311　*SIC 8711*
URBAN SYSTEMS LTD　*p223*
1353 ELLIS ST UNIT 304, KELOWNA, BC, V1Y 1Z9
(250) 762-2517　*SIC 8711*
URS CANADA INC　*p854*
30 LEEK CRES 4TH FL, RICHMOND HILL, ON, L4B 4N4
(905) 882-9190　*SIC 8711*
VALCOM CONSULTING GROUP INC　*p824*
85 ALBERT ST SUITE 300, OTTAWA, ON, K1P 6A4
(613) 594-5200　*SIC 8711*
VANDERWESTEN & RUTHERFORD ASSOCIATES, INC　*p661*
7242 COLONEL TALBOT RD, LONDON, ON, N6L 1H8
(519) 652-5047　*SIC 8711*
VARD MARINE INC　*p287*
2930 VIRTUAL WAY SUITE 180, VANCOUVER, BC, V5M 0A5
(604) 216-3360　*SIC 8711*
VISTA PROJECTS LIMITED　*p32*
4000 4 ST SE SUITE 330, CALGARY, AB, T2G 2W3
(403) 255-3455　*SIC 8711*
VTECH ENGINEERING CANADA LTD　*p262*
7671 ALDERBRIDGE WAY SUITE 200, RICHMOND, BC, V6X 1Z9
(604) 273-5131　*SIC 8711*
W.F.M.H. ENGINEERING LIMITED　*p641*
546 BELMONT AVE W, KITCHENER, ON, N2M 5E3
SIC 8711
WALTER FEDY PARTNERSHIP, THE　*p641*
675 QUEEN ST S SUITE 111, KITCHENER,

ON, N2M 1A1
(519) 576-2150　*SIC 8711*
WATT CONSULTING GROUP LTD　*p12*
3016 5 AVE NE SUITE 310, CALGARY, AB, T2A 6K4
(403) 273-9001　*SIC 8711*
WOOD CANADA LIMITED　*p63*
801 6 AVE SW SUITE 900, CALGARY, AB, T2P 3W3
(403) 298-4170　*SIC 8711*
WOOD CANADA LIMITED　*p111*
5681 70 ST NW, EDMONTON, AB, T6B 3P6
(780) 436-2152　*SIC 8711*
WOOD CANADA LIMITED　*p187*
4445 LOUGHEED HWY SUITE 600, BURNABY, BC, V5C 0E4
(604) 294-3811　*SIC 8711*
WOOD CANADA LIMITED　*p284*
1385 CEDAR AVE, TRAIL, BC, V1R 4C3
(250) 368-2400　*SIC 8711*
WOOD CANADA LIMITED　*p301*
111 DUNSMUIR ST SUITE 400, VANCOUVER, BC, V6B 5W3
(604) 664-4315　*SIC 8711*
WOOD CANADA LIMITED　*p528*
3215 NORTH SERVICE RD, BURLINGTON, ON, L7N 3G2
(905) 335-2353　*SIC 8711*
WOOD CANADA LIMITED　*p873*
104 CROCKFORD BLVD, SCARBOROUGH, ON, M1R 3C3
(416) 751-6565　*SIC 8711*
WOOD GROUP ASSET INTEGRITY SOLUTIONS, INC　*p33*
4242 7 ST SE SUITE 118, CALGARY, AB, T2G 2Y8
(403) 245-5666　*SIC 8711*
WOOD GROUP PSN CANADA INC　*p432*
277 WATER ST, ST. JOHN'S, NL, A1C 6L3
(709) 778-4400　*SIC 8711*
WORLEY CANADA SERVICES LTD　*p38*
8500 MACLEOD TRAIL SE, CALGARY, AB, T2H 2N1
(403) 258-8000　*SIC 8711*
WORLEYPARSONSCORD LP　*p66*
540 12 AVE SW, CALGARY, AB, T2R 0H4
SIC 8711
WORLEYPARSONSCORD LP　*p111*
9405 50 ST NW SUITE 101, EDMONTON, AB, T6B 2T4
(780) 440-8100　*SIC 8711*
WORLEYPARSONSCORD LP　*p117*
5008 86 ST NW SUITE 120, EDMONTON, AB, T6E 5S2
(780) 440-5300　*SIC 8711*
WORLEYPARSONSCORD LP　*p187*
4321 STILL CREEK DR SUITE 600, BURNABY, BC, V5C 6S7
(604) 298-1616　*SIC 8711*
WORLEYPARSONSCORD LP　*p240*
233 1ST ST W, NORTH VANCOUVER, BC, V7M 1B3
SIC 8711
WORLEYPARSONSCORD LP　*p702*
2645 SKYMARK AVE, MISSISSAUGA, ON, L4W 4H2
(905) 940-4774　*SIC 8711*
WORLEYPARSONSCORD LP　*p1000*
8133 WARDEN AVE, UNIONVILLE, ON, L6G 1B3
(905) 940-4774　*SIC 8711*
WSP CANADA GROUP LIMITED　*p327*
1000-840 HOWE ST, VANCOUVER, BC, V6Z 2M1
(604) 685-9381　*SIC 8711*
WSP CANADA GROUP LIMITED　*p905*
100 COMMERCE VALLEY DR W, THORNHILL, ON, L3T 0A1
(905) 882-1100　*SIC 8711*
WSP CANADA INC　*p163*
2693 BROADMOOR BLVD SUITE 132, SHERWOOD PARK, AB, T8H 0G1
(780) 410-6740　*SIC 8711*
WSP CANADA INC　*p677*

600 COCHRANE DR SUITE 500, MARKHAM, ON, L3R 5K3
(905) 475-7270　*SIC 8711*
WSP CANADA INC　*p830*
2611 QUEENSVIEW DR SUITE 300, OTTAWA, ON, K2B 8K2
(613) 829-2800　*SIC 8711*
WSP CANADA INC　*p909*
1269 PREMIER WAY, THUNDER BAY, ON, P7B 0A3
(807) 625-6700　*SIC 8711*
WSP CANADA INC　*p1087*
2525 BOUL DANIEL-JOHNSON BUREAU 525, COTE SAINT-LUC, QC, H7T 1S9
(450) 686-0980　*SIC 8711*
WSP CANADA INC　*p1389*
3450 BOUL GENE-H.-KRUGER BUREAU 300, TROIS-RIVIERES, QC, G9A 4M3
(819) 375-1292　*SIC 8711*

SIC 8712 Architectural services

3102597 NOVA SCOTIA LIMITED　*p444*
109 ILSLEY AVE UNIT 1, DARTMOUTH, NS, B3B 1S8
(902) 429-5002　*SIC 8712*
ABBARCH ARCHITECTURE INC　*p327*
505 BURRARD ST SUITE 1830, VANCOUVER, BC, V7X 1M6
(604) 669-4041　*SIC 8712*
ABCP ARCHITECTURE ET URBANISME LTEE　*p1257*
300 RUE SAINT-PAUL BUREAU 412, QUEBEC, QC, G1K 7R1
(418) 649-7369　*SIC 8712*
ADAMSON ASSOCIATES　*p978*
401 WELLINGTON ST W 3RD FLR, TORONTO, ON, M5V 1E7
(416) 967-1500　*SIC 8712*
AEDIFICA INC　*p1201*
606 RUE CATHCART BUREAU 800, MONTREAL, QC, H3B 1K9
(514) 844-6611　*SIC 8712*
ALLIED TECHNICAL SALES INC　*p913*
885 MILNER AVE, TORONTO, ON, M1B 5V8
(416) 282-1010　*SIC 8712*
ARCHITECTURE49 INC　*p390*
1600 BUFFALO PL, WINNIPEG, MB, R3T 6B8
(204) 477-1260　*SIC 8712*
BGLA INC　*p1258*
50 COTE DINAN, QUEBEC, QC, G1K 8N6
(418) 694-9041　*SIC 8712*
BLEU TECH MONTREAL INC　*p1342*
4150 CHOMEDEY (A-13) O, SAINT-LAURENT, QC, H7R 6E9
(450) 767-2890　*SIC 8712*
BRISBIN BROOK BEYNON, ARCHITECTS　*p949*
14 DUNCAN ST SUITE 400, TORONTO, ON, M5H 3G8
(416) 591-8999　*SIC 8712*
CANNON DESIGN ARCHITECTURE INC　*p318*
1500 GEORGIA ST W SUITE 710, VANCOUVER, BC, V6G 2Z6
(250) 388-0115　*SIC 8712*
CEI - ARCHITECTURE PLANNING INTERIORS　*p318*
1500 GEORGIA ST W SUITE 500, VANCOUVER, BC, V6G 2Z6
(604) 687-1898　*SIC 8712*
CORE ARCHITECTS INC　*p933*
130 QUEENS QUAY E SUITE 700, TORONTO, ON, M5A 0P6
(416) 343-0400　*SIC 8712*
COTE, REGIS ET ASSOCIES ARCHITECTES　*p1086*
2990 AV PIERRE-PELADEAU BUREAU 200, COTE SAINT-LUC, QC, H7T 0B1
SIC 8712
COWI NORTH AMERICA LTD　*p239*

400-138 13TH ST E, NORTH VANCOUVER, BC, V7L 0E5
(604) 986-1222　*SIC 8712*
DANIELS LR CORPORATION　*p933*
130 QUEENS QUAY E 8 FL, TORONTO, ON, M5A 0P6
(416) 598-2129　*SIC 8712*
DIALOG　*p29*
134 11 AVE SE SUITE 300, CALGARY, AB, T2G 0X5
(403) 541-5501　*SIC 8712*
DIALOG　*p88*
10237 104 ST NW SUITE 100, EDMONTON, AB, T5J 1B1
(780) 429-1580　*SIC 8712*
DIAMOND AND SCHMITT ARCHITECTS INCORPORATED　*p980*
384 ADELAIDE ST W SUITE 300, TORONTO, ON, M5V 1R7
(416) 862-8800　*SIC 8712*
FEATURE WALTERS INC　*p615*
1318 RYMAL RD E, HAMILTON, ON, L8W 3N1
(905) 388-7111　*SIC 8712*
GENSLER ARCHITECTURE & DESIGN CANDA, INC　*p951*
150 KING ST W SUITE 1400, TORONTO, ON, M5H 1J9
(416) 601-3890　*SIC 8712*
GESTION NEUF ASSOCIES INC　*p1204*
630 BOUL RENE-LEVESQUE O BUREAU 3200, MONTREAL, QC, H3B 1S6
(514) 847-1117　*SIC 8712*
GIBBS GAGE ARCHITECTS　*p30*
350-140 10 AVE SE, CALGARY, AB, T2G 0R1
(403) 233-2000　*SIC 8712*
GROUPE ARCOP S.E.N.C., LE　*p1213*
1244 RUE SAINTE-CATHERINE O BUREAU 3E, MONTREAL, QC, H3G 1P1
(514) 878-3941　*SIC 8712*
GROUPE COTE REGIS INC　*p1210*
682 RUE WILLIAM BUREAU 200, MONTREAL, QC, H3C 1N9
(514) 871-8595　*SIC 8712*
HARIRI PONTARINI ARCHITECTS LLP*p920*
235 CARLAW AVE SUITE 301, TORONTO, ON, M4M 2S1
(416) 929-4901　*SIC 8712*
HDR ARCHITECTURE ASSOCIATES, INC　*p952*
255 ADELAIDE ST W, TORONTO, ON, M5H 1X9
(647) 777-4900　*SIC 8712*
HDR CORPORATION　*p829*
300 RICHMOND DR SUITE 200, OTTAWA, ON, K1Z 6X6
(613) 233-6799　*SIC 8712*
IBI GROUP　*p23*
611 MEREDITH RD NE SUITE 500, CALGARY, AB, T2E 2W5
(403) 270-5600　*SIC 8712*
IBI GROUP　*p89*
10830 JASPER AVE NW SUITE 300, EDMONTON, AB, T5J 2B3
(780) 428-4000　*SIC 8712*
IBI GROUP　*p313*
1285 PENDER ST W SUITE 700, VANCOUVER, BC, V6E 4B1
(604) 683-8797　*SIC 8712*
IBI GROUP INC　*p927*
95 ST CLAIR AVE W SUITE 200, TORONTO, ON, M4V 1N6
(416) 596-1930　*SIC 8712*
INDUSTRIES SHOW CANADA INC, LES　*p1231*
5555 RUE MAURICE-CULLEN, MONTREAL, QC, H7C 2T8
(450) 664-5155　*SIC 8712*
INGENIUM GROUP INC　*p585*
2 INTERNATIONAL BLVD, ETOBICOKE, ON, M9W 1A2
(416) 675-5950　*SIC 8712*
JODOIN LAMARRE PRATTE ARCHI-

TECTES INC p1167
3200 RUE RACHEL E, MONTREAL, QC,
H1W 1A4
(514) 527-8821   *SIC 8712*

**KASIAN ARCHITECTURE INTERIOR DE-
SIGN AND PLANNING LTD** p52
1011 9 AVE SW, CALGARY, AB, T2P 1L3
(403) 265-2440   *SIC 8712*

**KASIAN ARCHITECTURE INTERIOR DE-
SIGN AND PLANNING LTD** p318
1500 GEORGIA ST W SUITE 1685, VAN-
COUVER, BC, V6G 2Z6
(604) 683-4145   *SIC 8712*

KEITH PANEL SYSTEMS CO., LTD p240
40 GOSTICK PL SUITE 2, NORTH VAN-
COUVER, BC, V7M 3G3
(604) 987-4499   *SIC 8712*

KENAR CONSULTANTS INC p1189
511 PLACE D'ARMES BUREAU 100, MON-
TREAL, QC, H2Y 2W7
(514) 397-2616   *SIC 8712*

KPMB ARCHITECTS p981
322 KING ST W, TORONTO, ON, M5V 1J2
(416) 977-5104   *SIC 8712*

MORIYAMA & TESHIMA ARCHITECTS p934
117 GEORGE ST, TORONTO, ON, M5A
2N4
(416) 925-4484   *SIC 8712*

N F O E & ASSOCIES ARCHITECTS p1189
511 PLACE D'ARMES BUREAU 100, MON-
TREAL, QC, H2Y 2W7
(514) 397-2616   *SIC 8712*

NFOE INC p1189
511 PLACE D'ARMES BUREAU 100, MON-
TREAL, QC, H2Y 2W7
(514) 397-2616   *SIC 8712*

NORR LIMITED p930
175 BLOOR ST E, TORONTO, ON, M4W
3R8
(416) 929-0200   *SIC 8712*

**OMICRON ARCHITECTURE ENGINEERING
CONSTRUCTION LTD** p329
595 BURRARD ST, VANCOUVER, BC, V7X
1M7
(604) 632-3350   *SIC 8712*

OMICRON CANADA INC p329
595 BURRARD ST, VANCOUVER, BC, V7X
1M7
(604) 632-3350   *SIC 8712*

PERKINS + WILL ARCHITECTS CO p299
1220 HOMER ST, VANCOUVER, BC, V6B
2Y5
(604) 684-5446   *SIC 8712*

PETROFF PARTNERSHIP ARCHITECTS
p674
260 TOWN CENTRE BLVD SUITE 300,
MARKHAM, ON, L3R 8H8
(905) 470-7000   *SIC 8712*

PLANNING ALLIANCE INC p983
317 ADELAIDE ST W SUITE 205,
TORONTO, ON, M5V 1P9
(416) 593-6499   *SIC 8712*

STANTEC ARCHITECTURE LTD p91
10220 103 AVE NW SUITE 400, EDMON-
TON, AB, T5J 0K4
(780) 917-7000   *SIC 8712*

STANTEC ARCHITECTURE LTD p375
500 / 311 PORTAGE AVE, WINNIPEG, MB,
R3B 2B9
(204) 489-5900   *SIC 8712*

STANTEC ARCHITECTURE LTD p748
1331 CLYDE AVE SUITE 400, NEPEAN,
ON, K2C 3G4
(613) 722-4420   *SIC 8712*

STANTEC ARCHITECTURE QUEBEC LTD
p1324
100 BOUL ALEXIS-NIHON BUREAU 110,
SAINT-LAURENT, QC, H4M 2N6
(514) 739-0708   *SIC 8712*

TELECOR INC p743
6205 KESTREL RD, MISSISSAUGA, ON,
L5T 2A1
(905) 564-0801   *SIC 8712*

TURNER FLEISCHER ARCHITECTS INC
p778
67 LESMILL RD SUITE A, NORTH YORK,
ON, M3B 2T8
(416) 425-2222   *SIC 8712*

WHITE HOUSE DESIGN COMPANY INC
p183
3676 BAINBRIDGE AVE UNIT 100, BURN-
ABY, BC, V5A 2T4
(604) 451-1539   *SIC 8712*

WZMH ARCHITECTS p927
95 ST CLAIR AVE W SUITE 1500,
TORONTO, ON, M4V 1N6
(416) 961-4111   *SIC 8712*

ZEIDLER PARTNERSHIP ARCHITECTS
p985
315 QUEEN ST W UNIT 200, TORONTO,
ON, M5V 2X2
(416) 596-8300   *SIC 8712*

SIC 8713 Surveying services

ABACUS DATAGRAPHICS LTD p153
4814 50 ST SUITE 300, RED DEER, AB,
T4N 1X4
(403) 346-7555   *SIC 8713*

**ALTUS GEOMATICS LIMITED PARTNER-
SHIP** p66
2020 4TH ST SW UNIT 310, CALGARY, AB,
T2S 1W3
(403) 508-7770   *SIC 8713*

**ALTUS GEOMATICS LIMITED PARTNER-
SHIP** p99
17327 106A AVE NW, EDMONTON, AB,
T5S 1M7
(780) 481-3399   *SIC 8713*

**ALTUS GEOMATICS LIMITED PARTNER-
SHIP** p941
33 YONGE ST SUITE 500, TORONTO, ON,
M5E 1G4
(416) 641-9500   *SIC 8713*

BARNES J.D., LIMITED p667
140 RENFREW DR SUITE 100, MARKHAM,
ON, L3R 6B3
(905) 477-3600   *SIC 8713*

CALTECH GROUP LTD p64
1011 1 ST SW SUITE 520, CALGARY, AB,
T2R 1J2
(403) 263-8055   *SIC 8713*

CAN-AM GEOMATICS CORP p64
340 12 AVE SW SUITE 900, CALGARY, AB,
T2R 1L5
(403) 269-8887   *SIC 8713*

CENTERLINE GEOMATICS LTD p127
GD LCD MAIN, FORT MCMURRAY, AB,
T9H 3E2
(780) 881-4696   *SIC 8713*

CHALLENGER GEOMATICS LTD p107
9945 50 ST NW SUITE 200, EDMONTON,
AB, T6A 0L4
(780) 424-5511   *SIC 8713*

GEODIGITAL INTERNATIONAL INC p831
1 ANTARES DR UNIT 140, OTTAWA, ON,
K2E 8C4
(613) 820-4545   *SIC 8713*

GLOBAL RAYMAC SURVEYS INC p30
4000 4 ST SE SUITE 312, CALGARY, AB,
T2G 2W3
(403) 283-5455   *SIC 8713*

ISC SASKATCHEWAN INC p1421
10 RESEARCH DR SUITE 300, REGINA,
SK, S4S 7J7
(306) 787-8179   *SIC 8713*

**IVAN B. WALLACE ONTARIO LAND SUR-
VEYOR LTD** p496
71 MEARNS CRT UNIT 16, BOW-
MANVILLE, ON, L1C 4N4
(905) 623-2205   *SIC 8713*

**LN LAND DEVELOPMENT TECHNOLO-
GIES INC** p128
9908 FRANKLIN AVE UNIT 4, FORT MC-
MURRAY, AB, T9H 2K5
(780) 791-0075   *SIC 8713*

MCELHANNEY ASSOCIATES LAND SUR-

VEYING LTD p214
8808 72 ST, FORT ST. JOHN, BC, V1J 6M2
(250) 787-0356   *SIC 8713*

**MCELHANNEY ASSOCIATES LAND SUR-
VEYING LTD** p299
858 BEATTY ST SUITE 200, VANCOUVER,
BC, V6B 1C1
(604) 683-8521   *SIC 8713*

MCELHANNEY LAND SURVEYS LTD p31
100-402 11 AVE SE, CALGARY, AB, T2G
0Y4
(403) 245-4711   *SIC 8713*

MCELHANNEY LAND SURVEYS LTD p94
14315 118 AVE NW SUITE 138, EDMON-
TON, AB, T5L 4S6
(780) 451-3420   *SIC 8713*

MERIDIAN SURVEYS LTD p1428
3111 MILLAR AVE SUITE 1, SASKATOON,
SK, S7K 6N3
(306) 934-1818   *SIC 8713*

MIDWEST SURVEYS INC p9
2827 SUNRIDGE BLVD NE, CALGARY, AB,
T1Y 6G1
(403) 244-7471   *SIC 8713*

PALS GEOMATICS CORP p102
10704 176 ST NW, EDMONTON, AB, T5S
1G7
(780) 455-3177   *SIC 8713*

PRECISION GEOMATICS INC p102
17403 105 AVE NW, EDMONTON, AB, T5S
2G8
(780) 470-4000   *SIC 8713*

**RIDEAU VALLEY CONSERVATION AU-
THORITY** p663
3889 RIDEAU VALLEY DR, MANOTICK,
ON, K4M 1A5
(613) 692-3571   *SIC 8713*

SEISLAND SURVEYS LTD p37
7235 FLINT RD SE, CALGARY, AB, T2H
1G2
(403) 255-2770   *SIC 8713*

STANTEC GEOMATICS LTD p11
325 25 ST SE SUITE 200, CALGARY, AB,
T2A 7H8
(403) 716-8000   *SIC 8713*

STANTEC GEOMATICS LTD p91
10220 103 AVE NW SUITE 400, EDMON-
TON, AB, T5J 0K4
(780) 917-7000   *SIC 8713*

STANTEC GEOMATICS LTD p1009
300 HAGEY BLVD SUITE 100, WATERLOO,
ON, N2L 0A4
(519) 579-4410   *SIC 8713*

STANTEC LAND SURVEYING LTD. p191
4730 KINGSWAY SUITE 500, BURNABY,
BC, V5H 0C6
(604) 436-3014   *SIC 8713*

TOMKINSON, D.N. INVESTMENTS LTD p65
340 12 AVE SW SUITE 900, CALGARY, AB,
T2R 1L5
(403) 269-8887   *SIC 8713*

TURNER & TOWNSEND CM2R INC p927
2 ST CLAIR AVE W 12TH FL, TORONTO,
ON, M4V 1L5
(416) 925-1424   *SIC 8713*

**UNIVERSAL GEOMATICS SOLUTIONS
CORP.** p106
15111 123 AVE NW, EDMONTON, AB, T5V
1J7
(780) 454-3030   *SIC 8713*

URTHECAST CORP p310
1055 CANADA PL UNIT 33, VANCOUVER,
BC, V6C 0C3
(604) 265-6266   *SIC 8713*

WSP CANADA INC p63
717 7 AVE SW SUITE 1800, CALGARY, AB,
T2P 0Z3
(403) 263-8200   *SIC 8713*

WSP CANADA INC p92
9925 109 ST NW SUITE 1000, EDMON-
TON, AB, T5K 2J8
(780) 466-6555   *SIC 8713*

WSP CANADA INC p214
10716 100 AVE, FORT ST. JOHN, BC, V1J

1Z3
(250) 787-0300   *SIC 8713*

---

*SIC 8721 Accounting, auditing, and
bookkeeping*

10SHEET SERVICES INC p301
717 PENDER ST W UNIT 200, VANCOU-
VER, BC, V6C 1G9
(888) 760-1940   *SIC 8721*

1924345 ONTARIO INC p994
1655 DUPONT ST SUITE 250, TORONTO,
ON, M6P 3T1
(416) 481-6946   *SIC 8721*

ADP CANADA CO p33
6025 11 ST SE SUITE 100, CALGARY, AB,
T2H 2Z2
(888) 901-7402   *SIC 8721*

ADP CANADA CO p189
4720 KINGSWAY SUITE 500, BURNABY,
BC, V5H 4N2
(604) 431-2700   *SIC 8721*

ADP CANADA CO p444
130 EILEEN STUBBS AVE UNIT 22, DART-
MOUTH, NS, B3B 2C4
(800) 668-8441   *SIC 8721*

ADP CANADA CO p571
3250 BLOOR ST W 6TH FL SUITE 1600,
ETOBICOKE, ON, M8X 2X9
(416) 207-2900   *SIC 8721*

**AUDICO SERVICES LIMITED PARTNER-
SHIP** p948
390 BAY ST SUITE 1900, TORONTO, ON,
M5H 2Y2
(416) 361-1622   *SIC 8721*

BDO CANADA & ASSOCIATES LTD p937
36 TORONTO ST SUITE 600, TORONTO,
ON, M5C 2C5
(416) 369-3100   *SIC 8721*

BDO CANADA LIMITED p302
925 GEORGIA ST W SUITE 600, VANCOU-
VER, BC, V6C 3L2
(604) 688-5421   *SIC 8721*

BDO CANADA LLP p44
903 8 AVE SW SUITE 620, CALGARY, AB,
T2P 0P7
(403) 266-5608   *SIC 8721*

BDO CANADA LLP p302
925 GEORGIA ST W SUITE 600, VANCOU-
VER, BC, V6C 3L2
(604) 688-5421   *SIC 8721*

BDO CANADA LLP p377
200 GRAHAM AVE SUITE 700, WINNIPEG,
MB, R3C 4L5
(204) 956-7200   *SIC 8721*

BDO CANADA LLP p527
3115 HARVESTER RD SUITE 400,
BURLINGTON, ON, L7N 3N8
(905) 639-9500   *SIC 8721*

BDO CANADA LLP p667
60 COLUMBIA WAY SUITE 300,
MARKHAM, ON, L3R 0C9
(905) 946-1066   *SIC 8721*

BDO CANADA LLP p709
1 CITY CENTRE DR SUITE 1700, MISSIS-
SAUGA, ON, L5B 1M2
(905) 270-7700   *SIC 8721*

BDO CANADA LLP p941
20 WELLINGTON ST E SUITE 500,
TORONTO, ON, M5E 1C5
(416) 865-0111   *SIC 8721*

BDO CANADA LLP p1112
289 RUE PRINCIPALE, GRENVILLE, QC,
J0V 1J0
SIC 8721

BDO CANADA LLP p1201
1000 RUE DE LA GAUCHETIERE O BU-
REAU 200, MONTREAL, QC, H3B 4W5
(514) 931-0841   *SIC 8721*

**BERRIS MANGAN CHARTERED ACCOUN-
TANTS** p320
1827 5TH AVE W, VANCOUVER, BC, V6J
1P5

SIC 8721

BESSNER GALLAY KREISMAN   *p*1401
4150 RUE SAINTE-CATHERINE O BU-
REAU 600, WESTMOUNT, QC, H3Z 2Y5
(514) 908-3600   *SIC* 8721

**BLANCHETTE VACHON ET ASSOCIES CA
SENCRL**   *p*1139
8149 RUE DU MISTRAL BUREAU 202,
LEVIS, QC, G6X 1G5
(418) 387-3636   *SIC* 8721

**BLANCHETTE VACHON ET ASSOCIES CA
SENCRL**   *p*1359
266 AV DU COLLEGE, SAINTE-MARIE,
QC, G6E 3Y4
(418) 387-3636   *SIC* 8721

CANADA REVENUE AGENCY   *p*414
126 PRINCE WILLIAM ST, SAINT JOHN,
NB, E2L 2B6
(506) 636-4623   *SIC* 8721

**CANADIAN PUBLIC ACCOUNTABILITY
BOARD**   *p*949
150 YORK ST SUITE 900, TORONTO, ON,
M5H 3S5
(416) 913-8260   *SIC* 8721

CAPSERVCO LIMITED PARTNERSHIP *p*452
2000 BARRINGTON ST SUITE 1100, HALI-
FAX, NS, B3J 3K1
(902) 421-1734   *SIC* 8721

CAPSERVCO LIMITED PARTNERSHIP *p*960
50 BAY ST SUITE 1200, TORONTO, ON,
M5J 3A5
(416) 366-4240   *SIC* 8721

CATALYST LLP   *p*14
200 QUARRY PARK BLVD SE SUITE 250,
CALGARY, AB, T2C 5E3
(403) 296-0082   *SIC* 8721

CCTF CORPORATION   *p*521
4151 NORTH SERVICE RD UNIT 2,
BURLINGTON, ON, L7L 4X6
(905) 335-5320   *SIC* 8721

CENTRE DE SERVICES DE PAIE CGI INC
*p*1176
1611 BOUL CREMAZIE E 7TH FLOOR,
MONTREAL, QC, H2M 2P2
(514) 850-6300   *SIC* 8721

CERIDIAN CANADA LTD   *p*8
2618 HOPEWELL PL NE SUITE 310, CAL-
GARY, AB, T1Y 7J7
(403) 262-6035   *SIC* 8721

CERIDIAN CANADA LTD   *p*323
1200 73RD AVE W SUITE 1400, VANCOU-
VER, BC, V6P 6G5
(604) 267-6200   *SIC* 8721

CERIDIAN CANADA LTD   *p*668
675 COCHRANE DR SUITE 515N,
MARKHAM, ON, L3R 0B8
(905) 947-7000   *SIC* 8721

CERIDIAN CANADA LTD   *p*693
5600 EXPLORER DR SUITE 400, MISSIS-
SAUGA, ON, L4W 4Y2
(905) 282-8100   *SIC* 8721

CERIDIAN CANADA LTD   *p*1333
8777 RTE TRANSCANADIENNE, SAINT-
LAURENT, QC, H4S 1Z6
(514) 908-3000   *SIC* 8721

**CHILDREN'S & WOMEN'S HEALTH CEN-
TRE OF BRITISH COLUMBIA BRANCH***p*320
1770 7TH AVE W SUITE 260, VANCOU-
VER, BC, V6J 4Y6
(604) 733-6721   *SIC* 8721

**CLARKSON CONSTRUCTION COMPANY
LIMITED**   *p*803
1224 SPEERS RD, OAKVILLE, ON, L6L 5B6
(905) 827-4167   *SIC* 8721

COLLINS BARROW KAWARTHAS LLP*p*840
272 CHARLOTTE ST, PETERBOROUGH,
ON, K9J 2V4
(705) 742-3418   *SIC* 8721

COLLINS BARROW MONTREAL   *p*1203
625 BOUL RENE-LEVESQUE O BUREAU
1100, MONTREAL, QC, H3B 1R2
(514) 866-8553   *SIC* 8721

COLLINS BARROW OTTAWA LLP   *p*751
301 MOODIE DR SUITE 400, NEPEAN, ON,
K2H 9C4
(613) 820-8010   *SIC* 8721

COLLINS BARROW TORONTO LLP   *p*950
11 KING ST W SUITE 700, TORONTO, ON,
M5H 4C7
(416) 480-0160   *SIC* 8721

COLLINS BARROW VICTORIA LTD   *p*336
645 FORT ST SUITE 540, VICTORIA, BC,
V8W 1G2
(250) 386-0500   *SIC* 8721

**COLLINS BARROW, SUDBURY - NIPISSING
LLP**   *p*898
1174 ST. JEROME ST, SUDBURY, ON, P3A
2V9
(705) 560-5592   *SIC* 8721

**CONCENTRIX TECHNOLOGIES SERVICES
(CANADA) LIMITED**   *p*687
6725 AIRPORT RD 6TH FL, MISSIS-
SAUGA, ON, L4V 1V2
(416) 380-3800   *SIC* 8721

**CRAWFORD SMITH & SWALLOW CHAR-
TERED ACCOUNTANTS LLP**   *p*757
4741 QUEEN ST, NIAGARA FALLS, ON,
L2E 2M2
(905) 356-4200   *SIC* 8721

CROWE SOBERMAN LLP   *p*925
2 ST CLAIR AVE E SUITE 1100, TORONTO,
ON, M4T 2T5
(416) 964-7633   *SIC* 8721

**D & H GROUP CHARTERED ACCOUN-
TANTS**   *p*319
1333 BROADWAY W, VANCOUVER, BC,
V6H 4C1
(604) 731-5881   *SIC* 8721

**DALE MATHESON CARR-HILTON
LABONTE LLP**   *p*312
1140 PENDER ST W SUITE 1500, VAN-
COUVER, BC, V6E 4G1
(604) 687-4747   *SIC* 8721

**DALLAIRE FOREST KIROUAC, COMPT-
ABLES PROFESSIONNELS AGRES,
S.E.N.C.R.L.**   *p*1272
1175 AV LAVIGERIE BUREAU 580, QUE-
BEC, QC, G1V 4P1
(418) 650-2266   *SIC* 8721

**DAVIDSON & COMPANY CHARTERED AC-
COUNTANTS LLP**   *p*330
609 GRANVILLE ST SUITE 1200, VAN-
COUVER, BC, V7Y 1G6
(604) 687-0947   *SIC* 8721

DELOITTE ERS INC   *p*1210
1190 AV DES CANADIENS-DE-
MONTREAL BUREAU 500, MONTREAL,
QC, H3C 0M7
(514) 393-7115   *SIC* 8721

DELOITTE LLP   *p*47
850 2 ST SW SUITE 700, CALGARY, AB,
T2P 0R8
(403) 267-1700   *SIC* 8721

DELOITTE LLP   *p*88
10180 101 ST NW SUITE 2000, EDMON-
TON, AB, T5J 4E4
(780) 421-3611   *SIC* 8721

DELOITTE LLP   *p*328
1055 DUNSMUIR ST SUITE 2800, VAN-
COUVER, BC, V7X 1P4
(604) 669-4466   *SIC* 8721

DELOITTE LLP   *p*452
1969 UPPER WATER ST SUITE 1500, HAL-
IFAX, NS, B3J 3R7
(902) 422-8541   *SIC* 8721

DELOITTE LLP   *p*529
1005 SKYVIEW DR SUITE 202, BURLING-
TON, ON, L7P 5B1
(905) 315-6770   *SIC* 8721

DELOITTE LLP   *p*638
195 JOSEPH ST, KITCHENER, ON, N2G
1J6
(519) 650-7600   *SIC* 8721

DELOITTE LLP   *p*771
5140 YONGE ST SUITE 1700, NORTH
YORK, ON, M2N 6L7
(416) 601-6150   *SIC* 8721

DELOITTE LLP   *p*823

100 QUEEN ST SUITE 1600, OTTAWA, ON,
K1P 5T8
(613) 236-2442   *SIC* 8721

DELOITTE LLP   *p*950
8 ADELAIDE ST W SUITE 200, TORONTO,
ON, M5H 0A9
(416) 601-6150   *SIC* 8721

DELOITTE LLP   *p*950
22 ADELAIDE ST W SUITE 200,
TORONTO, ON, M5H 0A9
(416) 601-6150   *SIC* 8721

DELOITTE LLP   *p*1427
122 1ST AVE S SUITE 400, SASKATOON,
SK, S7K 7E5
(306) 343-4400   *SIC* 8721

DELOITTE MANAGEMENT SERVICES LP
*p*950
121 KING ST W SUITE 300, TORONTO,
ON, M5H 3T9
(416) 775-2364   *SIC* 8721

DELOITTE RESTRUCTURING INC   *p*1086
2540 BOUL DANIEL-JOHNSON BUREAU
210, COTE SAINT-LUC, QC, H7T 2S3
(450) 978-3500   *SIC* 8721

DELOITTE RESTRUCTURING INC   *p*1270
925 GRANDE ALLEE O BUREAU 400,
QUEBEC, QC, G1S 4Z4
(418) 624-3333   *SIC* 8721

DELOITTE RESTRUCTURING INC   *p*1387
1500 RUE ROYALE BUREAU 250, TROIS-
RIVIERES, QC, G9A 6E6
(819) 691-1212   *SIC* 8721

DEMERS BEAULNE S.E.N.C.R.L.   *p*1195
1800 AV MCGILL COLLEGE BUREAU 600,
MONTREAL, QC, H3A 3J6
(514) 878-9631   *SIC* 8721

DESSUREAULT LEBLANC LEFEBVRE C.A.
*p*1387
950 RUE ROYALE BUREAU 104, TROIS-
RIVIERES, QC, G9A 4H8
(819) 379-0133   *SIC* 8721

DIGIFACTS SYNDICATE   *p*190
4720 KINGSWAY SUITE 900, BURNABY,
BC, V5H 4N2
(604) 435-4317   *SIC* 8721

**DURWARD JONES BARKWELL & COM-
PANY LLP**   *p*886
20 CORPORATE PARK DR SUITE 300, ST
CATHARINES, ON, L2S 3W2
(905) 684-9221   *SIC* 8721

**EASTERN ONTARIO TACCX SERVICES
LLP**   *p*832
301 MOODY DR SUITE 400, OTTAWA, ON,
K2H 9C4
(613) 820-8010   *SIC* 8721

ENABIL SOLUTIONS LTD   *p*29
438 11 AVE SE SUITE 500, CALGARY, AB,
T2G 0Y4
(403) 398-1600   *SIC* 8721

ERNST & YOUNG INC   *p*377
360 MAIN ST SUITE 2700, WINNIPEG, MB,
R3C 4G9
(204) 947-6519   *SIC* 8721

ERNST & YOUNG INC   *p*453
1871 HOLLIS ST UNIT 500, HALIFAX, NS,
B3J 0C3
(902) 420-1080   *SIC* 8721

ERNST & YOUNG INC   *p*640
515 RIVERBEND DR, KITCHENER, ON,
N2K 3S3
(519) 744-1171   *SIC* 8721

ERNST & YOUNG INC   *p*653
255 QUEENS AVE SUITE 1800, LONDON,
ON, N6A 5R8
(519) 672-6100   *SIC* 8721

ERNST & YOUNG INC   *p*1195
900 BOUL DE MAISONNEUVE O, MON-
TREAL, QC, H3A 0A8
(514) 875-6060   *SIC* 8721

ERNST & YOUNG LLP   *p*49
215 2 ST SW SUITE 2200, CALGARY, AB,
T2P 1M4
(403) 290-4100   *SIC* 8721

ERNST & YOUNG LLP   *p*823

700 GEORGIA ST W SUITE 2200, VAN-
COUVER, BC, V7Y 1K8
(604) 891-8200   *SIC* 8721

ERNST & YOUNG LLP   *p*653
1800-255 QUEENS AVE, LONDON, ON,
N6A 5S8
(519) 744-1171   *SIC* 8721

ERNST & YOUNG LLP   *p*823
99 BANK ST SUITE 1600, OTTAWA, ON,
K1P 6B9
(613) 232-1511   *SIC* 8721

ERNST & YOUNG LLP   *p*904
175 COMMERCE VALLEY DR W SUITE
600, THORNHILL, ON, L3T 7P6
SIC 8721

ERNST & YOUNG LLP   *p*951
100 ADELAIDE ST W SUITE 3100,
TORONTO, ON, M5H 0B3
(416) 864-1234   *SIC* 8721

ERNST & YOUNG LLP   *p*969
222 BAY ST 16TH FLR, TORONTO, ON,
M5K 1J7
(416) 943-2040   *SIC* 8721

ERNST & YOUNG LLP   *p*1204
1 PLACE VILLE-MARIE BUREAU 1900,
MONTREAL, QC, H3B 1X9
(514) 875-6060   *SIC* 8721

ERNST & YOUNG LLP   *p*1269
90 RUE DE MAISONNEUVE, QUEBEC, QC,
G1R 2C3
(514) 875-6060   *SIC* 8721

ERNST & YOUNG LLP   *p*1272
2875 BOUL LAURIER UNITE 410, QUE-
BEC, QC, G1V 0C7
(418) 524-5151   *SIC* 8721

**FAMME & CO. PROFESSIONAL CORPORA-
TION**   *p*896
125 ONTARIO ST, STRATFORD, ON, N5A
3H1
(519) 271-7581   *SIC* 8721

**FAUTEUX, BRUNO, BUSSIERE, LEEWAR-
DEN, CPA, S.E.N.C.R.L.**   *p*1180
1100 BOUL CREMAZIE E BUREAU 805,
MONTREAL, QC, H2P 2X2
(514) 729-3221   *SIC* 8721

**FEDERATION DES CAISSES DESJARDINS
DU QUEBEC**   *p*1176
1611 BOUL CREMAZIE E BUREAU 300,
MONTREAL, QC, H2M 2P2
(514) 356-5000   *SIC* 8721

FULLER LANDAU LLP   *p*974
151 BLOOR ST W, TORONTO, ON, M5S
1S4
(416) 645-6500   *SIC* 8721

FULLER LANDAU SENCRL   *p*1204
1010 RUE DE LA GAUCHETIERE O BU-
REAU 200, MONTREAL, QC, H3B 2S1
(514) 875-2865   *SIC* 8721

GAVILLER & COMPANY LLP   *p*835
945 3RD AVE E SUITE 201, OWEN
SOUND, ON, N4K 2K8
(519) 376-5850   *SIC* 8721

**GINSBERG GLUZMAN FAGE & LEVITZ,
LLP**   *p*829
287 RICHMOND RD, OTTAWA, ON, K1Z
6X4
(613) 728-5831   *SIC* 8721

GOLDFARB SHULMAN PATEL & CO LLP
*p*553
400 BRADWICK DR SUITE 100, CON-
CORD, ON, L4K 5V9
(416) 226-6800   *SIC* 8721

GRANT THORNTON LLP   *p*89
10060 JASPER AVE NW SUITE 1701, ED-
MONTON, AB, T5J 3R8
(780) 422-7114   *SIC* 8721

GRANT THORNTON LLP   *p*222
1633 ELLIS ST SUITE 200, KELOWNA, BC,
V1Y 2A8
(250) 712-6800   *SIC* 8721

GRANT THORNTON LLP   *p*298
333 SEYMOUR ST SUITE 1600, VANCOU-
VER, BC, V6B 0A4
(604) 687-2711   *SIC* 8721

▲ Public Company   ■ Public Company Family Member   **HQ** Headquarters   **BR** Branch   **SL** Single Location

GRANT THORNTON LLP *p453*
2000 BARRINGTON ST SUITE 1100, HALI-FAX, NS, B3J 3K1
(902) 421-1734 *SIC* 8721

GRANT THORNTON LLP *p670*
15 ALLSTATE PKY SUITE 200, MARKHAM, ON, L3R 5B4
(416) 607-2656 *SIC* 8721

GRANT THORNTON LLP *p709*
201 CITY CENTRE DR SUITE 501, MISSIS-SAUGA, ON, L5B 2T4
(416) 369-7076 *SIC* 8721

GRANT THORNTON LLP *p963*
12TH-50 BAY ST, TORONTO, ON, M5J 2Z8
(416) 366-4240 *SIC* 8721

GRANT THORTON *p908*
979 ALLOY DR SUITE 300, THUNDER BAY, ON, P7B 5Z8
(807) 346-7302 *SIC* 8721

GRECO MANAGEMENT INC *p892*
21 TEAL AVE, STONEY CREEK, ON, L8E 2P1
(905) 560-0661 *SIC* 8721

GROUPE NORMANDIN INC *p1275*
2335 BOUL BASTIEN, QUEBEC, QC, G2B 1B3
(418) 842-9160 *SIC* 8721

HARDY, NORMAND & ASSOCIES S.E.N.C.R.L. *p1051*
7875 BOUL LOUIS-H.-LAFONTAINE BU-REAU 200, ANJOU, QC, H1K 4E4
(514) 355-1550 *SIC* 8721

HARTEL FINANCIAL MANAGEMENT COR-PORATION *p811*
540 LACOLLE WAY, ORLEANS, ON, K4A 0N9
(613) 837-8282 *SIC* 8721

HERGOTT DUVAL STACK LLP *p1427*
410 22ND ST E SUITE 1200, SASKATOON, SK, S7K 5T6
(306) 934-8000 *SIC* 8721

HOGG SHAIN & SCHECK PROFESSIONAL CORPORATION *p767*
2235 SHEPPARD AVE E UNIT 800, NORTH YORK, ON, M2J 5B5
(416) 499-3100 *SIC* 8721

HUDSON & CO *p64*
625 11 AVE SW SUITE 300, CALGARY, AB, T2R 0E1
(403) 265-4357 *SIC* 8721

IFG - INTERNATIONAL FINANCIAL GROUP LTD *p986*
100 KING ST W SUITE 910, TORONTO, ON, M5X 1B1
(416) 645-2434 *SIC* 8721

IRVING TRANSPORTATION SERVICES LIM-ITED *p402*
71 ALISON BLVD, FREDERICTON, NB, E3C 2N5
SIC 8721

KINGSTON ROSS PASNAK LLP *p89*
9888 JASPER AVE NW SUITE 1500, ED-MONTON, AB, T5J 5C6
(780) 424-3000 *SIC* 8721

KPMG INC *p89*
10125 102 ST NW, EDMONTON, AB, T5J 3V8
(780) 429-7300 *SIC* 8721

KPMG INC *p554*
100 NEW PARK PL SUITE 1400, CON-CORD, ON, L4K 0J3
(905) 265-5900 *SIC* 8721

KPMG LLP *p52*
205 5 AVENUE SW SUITE 3100, CALGARY, AB, T2P 4B9
(403) 691-8000 *SIC* 8721

KPMG LLP *p89*
2200-10175 101 ST NW, EDMONTON, AB, T5J 3V8
(780) 429-7300 *SIC* 8721

KPMG LLP *p190*
4720 KINGSWAY SUITE 2400, BURNABY, BC, V5H 4N2
(604) 527-3600 *SIC* 8721

KPMG LLP *p217*
206 SEYMOUR ST SUITE 200, KAM-LOOPS, BC, V2C 6P5
(250) 372-5581 *SIC* 8721

KPMG LLP *p330*
777 DUNSMUIR ST SUITE 900, VANCOU-VER, BC, V7Y 1K3
(604) 691-3000 *SIC* 8721

KPMG LLP *p336*
730 VIEW ST SUITE 800, VICTORIA, BC, V8W 3Y7
(250) 480-3500 *SIC* 8721

KPMG LLP *p375*
1 LOMBARD PL UNIT 2000, WINNIPEG, MB, R3B 0X3
(204) 957-1770 *SIC* 8721

KPMG LLP *p613*
21 KING ST W SUITE 700, HAMILTON, ON, L8P 4W7
(905) 523-2259 *SIC* 8721

KPMG LLP *p774*
4100 YONGE ST UNIT 200, NORTH YORK, ON, M2P 2B5
(416) 228-7000 *SIC* 8721

KPMG LLP *p834*
160 ELGIN ST SUITE 2000, OTTAWA, ON, K2P 2P7
(613) 212-5764 *SIC* 8721

KPMG LLP *p953*
333 BAY ST SUITE 4600, TORONTO, ON, M5H 2S5
(416) 777-8500 *SIC* 8721

KPMG LLP *p1006*
115 KING ST S SUITE 201, WATERLOO, ON, N2J 5A3
(519) 747-8800 *SIC* 8721

KPMG LLP *p1197*
600 BOUL DE MAISONNEUVE O UNITE1500, MONTREAL, QC, H3A 0A3
(514) 840-2100 *SIC* 8721

KPMG-SECOUR *p1192*
555 BOUL RENE-LEVESQUE O BUREAU 1700, MONTREAL, QC, H2Z 1B1
SIC 8721

LEMIEUX NOLET, COMPTABLES AGREES S.E.N.C.R.L. *p1137*
1610 BOUL ALPHONSE-DESJARDINS BU-REAU 400, LEVIS, QC, G6V 0H1
(418) 833-2114 *SIC* 8721

LEVY PILOTTE S.E.N.C.R.L. *p1220*
5250 BOUL DECARIE BUREAU 700, MON-TREAL, QC, H3X 3Z6
(514) 487-1566 *SIC* 8721

LIPTON CHARTERED ACCOUNTANTS LLP *p767*
245 FAIRVIEW MALL DR SUITE 600, NORTH YORK, ON, M2J 4T1
(416) 496-2900 *SIC* 8721

M2 SOLUTIONS INC *p812*
628 BEECHWOOD ST, OSHAWA, ON, L1G 2R9
(905) 436-1784 *SIC* 8721

MALENFANT DALLAIRE, S.E.N.C.R.L. *p1273*
2600 BOUL LAURIER BUREAU 872, QUE-BEC, QC, G1V 4W2
(418) 654-0636 *SIC* 8721

MALLETTE S.E.N.C.R.L. *p1274*
3075 CH DES QUATRE-BOURGEOIS BU-REAU 200, QUEBEC, QC, G1W 5C4
(418) 653-4431 *SIC* 8721

MANNING ELLIOTT LLP *p314*
1050 PENDER ST W 11TH FL, VANCOU-VER, BC, V6E 3S7
(604) 714-3600 *SIC* 8721

MARCIL LAVALLEE *p596*
1420 BLAIR PL SUITE 400, GLOUCESTER, ON, K1J 9L8
(613) 745-8387 *SIC* 8721

MAZARS HAREL DROUIN, S.E.N.C.R.L. *p1189*
215 RUE SAINT-JACQUES BUREAU 1200, MONTREAL, QC, H2Y 1M6
(514) 845-9253 *SIC* 8721

MAZARS, S.E.N.C.R.L *p1189*
215 RUE SAINT-JACQUES, BUREAU 1200, MONTREAL, QC, H2Y 1M6
(514) 878-2600 *SIC* 8721

MILLARD, ROUSE & ROSEBRUGH LLP *p517*
96 NELSON ST, BRANTFORD, ON, N3T 2N1
(519) 759-3511 *SIC* 8721

MNP LLP *p54*
330 5 AVE SW SUITE 2000, CALGARY, AB, T2P 0L4
(403) 444-0150 *SIC* 8721

MNP LLP *p90*
10235 101 ST NW SUITE 1600, EDMON-TON, AB, T5J 3G1
(780) 451-4406 *SIC* 8721

MNP LLP *p142*
3425 2 AVE S SUITE 1, LETHBRIDGE, AB, T1J 4V1
(403) 380-1600 *SIC* 8721

MNP LLP *p328*
1055 DUNSMUIR SUITE 2300, VANCOU-VER, BC, V7X 1J1
(604) 639-0001 *SIC* 8721

MNP LLP *p347*
1401 PRINCESS AVE, BRANDON, MB, R7A 7L7
(204) 727-0661 *SIC* 8721

MNP LLP *p954*
111 RICHMOND ST W SUITE 300, TORONTO, ON, M5H 2G4
(416) 596-1711 *SIC* 8721

MNP LLP *p1206*
1155 BOUL RENE-LEVESQUE O BUREAU 2300, MONTREAL, QC, H3B 2K2
(514) 932-4115 *SIC* 8721

MNP LLP *p1418*
2010 11TH AVE SUITE 900, REGINA, SK, S4P 0J3
(306) 790-7900 *SIC* 8721

MSCM LLP *p579*
701 EVANS AVE SUITE 800, ETOBICOKE, ON, M9C 1A3
(416) 626-6000 *SIC* 8721

NEXIA FRIEDMAN S.E.N.C.R.L. *p1228*
8000 BOUL DECARIE BUREAU 500, MON-TREAL, QC, H4P 2S4
(514) 731-7901 *SIC* 8721

NORTON MCMULLEN & CO. LLP *p673*
1 VALLEYWOOD DR SUITE 200, MARKHAM, ON, L3R 5L9
(905) 479-7001 *SIC* 8721

OAKRIDGE ACCOUNTING SERVICES LTD *p220*
2604 ENTERPRISE WAY UNIT 1, KELOWNA, BC, V1X 7Y5
(250) 712-3800 *SIC* 8721

PATMAN LTD *p347*
927 DOUGLAS ST, BRANDON, MB, R7A 7B3
(204) 728-1188 *SIC* 8721

PAYWORKS INC *p391*
1565 WILLSON PL, WINNIPEG, MB, R3T 4H1
(204) 779-0537 *SIC* 8721

PEO CANADA LTD *p56*
805 5 AVE SW SUITE 100, CALGARY, AB, T2P 0N6
(403) 237-5577 *SIC* 8721

PETRIE RAYMOND S.E.N.C.R.L *p1177*
255 BOUL CREMAZIE E BUREAU 1000, MONTREAL, QC, H2M 1L5
(514) 342-4740 *SIC* 8721

PRGX CANADA CORP *p745*
60 COURTNEY PARK DR W UNIT 4, MIS-SISSAUGA, ON, N5W 0B3
(905) 670-7879 *SIC* 8721

PRICEWATERHOUSECOOPERS LLP *p90*
10088 102 AVE NW SUITE 1501, EDMON-TON, AB, T5J 3N5
(780) 441-6700 *SIC* 8721

PRICEWATERHOUSECOOPERS LLP *p308*
250 HOWE ST SUITE 700, VANCOUVER, BC, V6C 3S7
(604) 806-7000 *SIC* 8721

PRICEWATERHOUSECOOPERS LLP *p375*
1 LOMBARD PL SUITE 2300, WINNIPEG, MB, R3B 0X6
(204) 926-2400 *SIC* 8721

PRICEWATERHOUSECOOPERS LLP *p454*
1601 LOWER WATER ST SUITE 400, HAL-IFAX, NS, B3J 3P6
(902) 491-7400 *SIC* 8721

PRICEWATERHOUSECOOPERS LLP *p613*
21 KING ST W SUITE 100, HAMILTON, ON, L8P 4W7
SIC 8721

PRICEWATERHOUSECOOPERS LLP *p655*
465 RICHMOND ST SUITE 300, LONDON, ON, N6A 5P4
(519) 640-8000 *SIC* 8721

PRICEWATERHOUSECOOPERS LLP *p824*
99 BANK ST SUITE 800, OTTAWA, ON, K1P 1E4
(613) 237-3702 *SIC* 8721

PRICEWATERHOUSECOOPERS LLP *p966*
18 YORK ST SUITE 2600, TORONTO, ON, M5J 0B2
(416) 863-1133 *SIC* 8721

PRICEWATERHOUSECOOPERS LLP *p1207*
1250 BOUL RENE-LEVESQUE O BUREAU 2800, MONTREAL, QC, H3B 4W8
(514) 866-8409 *SIC* 8721

PRICEWATERHOUSECOOPERS LLP *p1273*
2640 BOUL LAURIER BUREAU 1700, QUE-BEC, QC, G1V 5C2
(418) 522-7001 *SIC* 8721

PSB BOISJOLI S.E.N.R.C.L *p1155*
3333 BOUL GRAHAM BUREAU 400, MONT-ROYAL, QC, H3R 3L5
(514) 341-5511 *SIC* 8721

PWC MANAGEMENT SERVICES LP *p270*
10190 152A ST 3 FL, SURREY, BC, V3R 1J7
(604) 806-7000 *SIC* 8721

RAYMOND CHABOT GRANT THORNTON S.E.N.C.R.L. *p1207*
600 RUE DE LA GAUCHETIERE O BU-REAU 2000, MONTREAL, QC, H3B 4L8
(514) 878-2691 *SIC* 8721

RAYMOND CHABOT GRANT THORNTON S.E.N.C.R.L. *p1371*
455 RUE KING O BUREAU 500, SHER-BROOKE, QC, J1H 6G4
(819) 822-4000 *SIC* 8721

RDL LEGARE MC NICOLL INC *p1280*
1305 BOUL LEBOURGNEUF BUREAU 401, QUEBEC, QC, G2K 2E4
(418) 622-6666 *SIC* 8721

RICHTER S.E.N.C.R.L. *p1199*
1981 AV MCGILL COLLEGE SUITE 11E, MONTREAL, QC, H3A 2W9
(514) 934-3400 *SIC* 8721

RLB LLP *p604*
15 LEWIS RD SUITE 1, GUELPH, ON, N1H 1E9
(519) 822-9933 *SIC* 8721

ROSENBERG SMITH & PARTNERS LLP *p558*
2000 STEELES AVE W UNIT 200, CON-CORD, ON, L4K 3E9
(905) 660-3800 *SIC* 8721

ROY DESROCHERS LAMBERT S.E.N.C.R.L *p1398*
450 BOUL DES BOIS-FRANCS N, VICTO-RIAVILLE, QC, G6P 1H3
(819) 758-1544 *SIC* 8721

RSM US LLP *p713*
81 LAKESHORE ROAD E, MISSISSAUGA, ON, L5G 4S7
SIC 8721

RYDER TRUCK RENTAL CANADA LTD *p506*
30 PEDIGREE CRT SUITE 1, BRAMPTON, ON, L6T 5T8
(905) 759-2000 *SIC* 8721

S. F. PARTNERSHIP LLP *p773*
4950 YONGE ST SUITE 400, NORTH

YORK, ON, M2N 6K1
(416) 250-1212   *SIC 8721*
SCHWARTZ LEVITSKY FELDMAN LLP *p923*
2300 YONGE ST SUITE 1500, TORONTO,
ON, M4P 1E4
(416) 785-5353   *SIC 8721*
SCHWARTZ LEVITSKY FELDMAN LLP
p1215
1980 RUE SHERBROOKE O ETAGE 10,
MONTREAL, QC, H3H 1E8
(514) 937-6392   *SIC 8721*
SEGAL LLP *p915*
502-4101 YONGE ST, TORONTO, ON, M2P
1N6
(416) 391-4499   *SIC 8721*
SGGG FUND SERVICES INC. *p957*
121 KING ST W UNIT 300, TORONTO, ON,
M5H 3T9
(416) 967-0038   *SIC 8721*
SHIMMERMAN PENN LLP *p957*
111 RICHMOND ST W SUITE 300,
TORONTO, ON, M5H 2G4
(416) 964-7200   *SIC 8721*
SMYTHE RATCLIFFE LLP *p309*
355 BURRARD ST SUITE 700, VANCOU-
VER, BC, V6C 2G8
(604) 687-1231   *SIC 8721*
SOLBAKKEN AND ASSOCIATES *p335*
990 HILLSIDE AVE SUITE 201, VICTORIA,
BC, V8T 2A1
(250) 590-5211   *SIC 8721*
TAUB, BERNARD & COMPANY *p790*
1167 CALEDONIA RD, NORTH YORK, ON,
M6A 2X1
(416) 785-5353   *SIC 8721*
TAYLOR, LEIBOW LLP *p612*
105 MAIN ST E SUITE 700, HAMILTON,
ON, L8N 1G6
(905) 523-0003   *SIC 8721*
**VIRTUS GROUP CHARTERED ACCOUN-
TANTS & BUSINESS ADVISORS LLP** *p1430*
157 2ND AVE N SUITE 200, SASKATOON,
SK, S7K 2A9
(306) 653-6100   *SIC 8721*
WELCH LLP *p815*
123 SLATER ST, OTTAWA, ON, K1A 1B9
(613) 236-9191   *SIC 8721*
WHITE BURGESS LANGILLE INMAN *p440*
26 UNION ST 2ND FLR, BEDFORD, NS,
B4A 2B5
(902) 835-7333   *SIC 8721*
WILKINSON & COMPANY LLP *p999*
71 DUNDAS ST W, TRENTON, ON, K8V
3P4
(888) 713-7283   *SIC 8721*
ZEIFMANS LLP *p790*
201 BRIDGELAND AVE SUITE 1, NORTH
YORK, ON, M6A 1Y7
(416) 256-4000   *SIC 8721*

SIC 8731 Commercial physical research

8867038 CANADA INC *p859*
1609 LENA CRT, SARNIA, ON, N7T 7H4
(519) 704-1317   *SIC 8731*
A.U.G. SIGNALS LTD *p948*
73 RICHMOND ST W SUITE 103,
TORONTO, ON, M5H 4E8
(416) 923-4425   *SIC 8731*
ABATTIS BIOCEUTICALS CORP *p301*
625 HOWE ST SUITE 1200, VANCOUVER,
BC, V6C 2T6
SIC 8731
ACRODEX INC *p98*
11420 170 ST NW, EDMONTON, AB, T5S
1L7
(780) 426-4444   *SIC 8731*
AFILIAS CANADA, CORP *p773*
4141 YONGE ST SUITE 204, NORTH
YORK, ON, M2P 2A8
(416) 646-3304   *SIC 8731*
AGAT LABORATORIES LTD *p20*
2905 12 ST NE, CALGARY, AB, T2E 7J2

(403) 736-2000   *SIC 8731*
AGAT LABORATORIES LTD *p704*
5835 COOPERS AVE, MISSISSAUGA, ON,
L4Z 1Y2
(905) 712-5100   *SIC 8731*
ALPHORA RESEARCH INC *p714*
2395 SPEAKMAN DR SUITE 2001, MISSIS-
SAUGA, ON, L5K 1B3
(905) 403-0477   *SIC 8731*
ALPHORA RESEARCH INC *p796*
2884 PORTLAND DR, OAKVILLE, ON, L6H
5W8
(905) 829-9704   *SIC 8731*
ALTASCIENCES COMPAGNIE INC *p1155*
1200 AV BEAUMONT, MONT-ROYAL, QC,
H3P 3P1
(514) 858-6077   *SIC 8731*
ALTASCIENCES COMPAGNIE INC *p1241*
575 BOUL ARMAND-FRAPPIER,
MONTREAL-OUEST, QC, H7V 4B3
(450) 973-6077   *SIC 8731*
ALTER NRG CORP *p63*
227 11 AVE SW SUITE 460, CALGARY, AB,
T2R 1R9
(403) 806-3875   *SIC 8731*
ANALOGIC CANADA CORPORATION *p1328*
4950 RUE LEVY, SAINT-LAURENT, QC,
H4R 2P1
(514) 856-6920   *SIC 8731*
ANGIOTECH PHARMACEUTICALS, INC
p302
355 BURRARD ST SUITE 1100, VANCOU-
VER, BC, V6C 2G8
(604) 221-7676   *SIC 8731*
**APOTEX PHARMACEUTICAL HOLDINGS
INC** *p792*
150 SIGNET DR, NORTH YORK, ON, M9L
1T9
(416) 749-9300   *SIC 8731*
APPLIED BIOLOGICAL MATERIALS INC
p253
1-3671 VIKING WAY, RICHMOND, BC, V6V
2J5
(604) 247-2416   *SIC 8731*
**APPLIED CONSUMER & CLINICAL EVALU-
ATIONS INC** *p716*
2575B DUNWIN DR, MISSISSAUGA, ON,
L5L 3N9
(905) 828-0493   *SIC 8731*
AURORA BIOMED INC *p294*
1001 PENDER ST E, VANCOUVER, BC,
V6A 1W2
(604) 215-8700   *SIC 8731*
BOEHRINGER INGELHEIM (CANADA) LTD
p1084
2100 RUE CUNARD, COTE SAINT-LUC,
QC, H7S 2G5
SIC 8731
**BROOKFIELD RENEWABLE ENERGY
PARTNERS L.P.** *p1105*
41 RUE VICTORIA, GATINEAU, QC, J8X
2A1
(819) 561-2722   *SIC 8731*
BUREAU VERITAS CANADA (2019) INC
p440
200 BLUEWATER RD SUITE 201, BED-
FORD, NS, B4B 1G9
(902) 420-0203   *SIC 8731*
CAMSO INC *p1147*
2675 RUE MACPHERSON, MAGOG, QC,
J1X 0E6
(819) 868-1500   *SIC 8731*
**CANADIAN AGENCY FOR DRUGS AND
TECHNOLOGIES IN HEALTH (CADTH)** *p825*
865 CARLING AVE SUITE 600, OTTAWA,
ON, K1S 5S8
(613) 226-2553   *SIC 8731*
CANADIAN HEART RESEARCH CENTRE
p766
259 YORKLAND RD SUITE 200, NORTH
YORK, ON, M2J 0B5
(416) 977-8010   *SIC 8731*
CANCER CARE ONTARIO *p908*
980 OLIVER RD, THUNDER BAY, ON, P7B

6V4
(807) 343-1610   *SIC 8731*
**CENTRE DE RECHERCHE INDUSTRIELLE
DU QUEBEC** *p1266*
333 RUE FRANQUET, QUEBEC, QC, G1P
4C7
(418) 659-1550   *SIC 8731*
**CENTRE DE RECHERCHE INFORMATIQUE
DE MONTREAL INC** *p1217*
405 AV OGILVY BUREAU 101, MONTREAL,
QC, H3N 1M3
(514) 840-1234   *SIC 8731*
CESL LIMITED *p323*
8898 HEATHER ST UNIT 107, VANCOU-
VER, BC, V6P 3S8
SIC 8731
CITOXLAB AMERIQUE DU NORD INC *p1241*
445 BOUL ARMAND-FRAPPIER,
MONTREAL-OUEST, QC, H7V 4B3
(450) 973-2240   *SIC 8731*
**CORE ENERGY RECOVERY SOLUTIONS
INC** *p285*
1455 GEORGIA ST E, VANCOUVER, BC,
V5L 2A9
(604) 488-1132   *SIC 8731*
CORREVIO PHARMA CORP *p320*
1441 CREEKSIDE DR 6 FL, VANCOUVER,
BC, V6J 4S7
(604) 677-6905   *SIC 8731*
COVALON TECHNOLOGIES LTD *p693*
1660 TECH AVE UNIT 5, MISSISSAUGA,
ON, L4W 5S7
(905) 568-8400   *SIC 8731*
CRESCITA THERAPEUTICS INC *p721*
6733 MISSISSAUGA RD SUITE 610, MIS-
SISSAUGA, ON, L5N 6J5
(905) 673-4295   *SIC 8731*
EMERGENT BIOSOLUTIONS CANADA INC
p393
26 HENLOW BAY, WINNIPEG, MB, R3Y
1G4
(204) 275-4200   *SIC 8731*
ENDOCEUTICS INC *p1272*
2795 BOUL LAURIER BUREAU 500, QUE-
BEC, QC, G1V 4M7
(418) 653-0033   *SIC 8731*
EPOCAL INC *p817*
2060 WALKLEY RD, OTTAWA, ON, K1G
3P5
(613) 738-6192   *SIC 8731*
FPINNOVATIONS *p324*
2665 EAST MALL, VANCOUVER, BC, V6T
1Z4
(604) 224-3221   *SIC 8731*
FPINNOVATIONS *p1250*
570 BOUL SAINT-JEAN, POINTE-CLAIRE,
QC, H9R 3J9
(514) 630-4100   *SIC 8731*
FPINNOVATIONS *p1264*
300 RUE DE DIEPPE, QUEBEC, QC, G1N
3M8
(418) 659-2647   *SIC 8731*
GARMIN CANADA INC *p80*
30 BOW ST COMMON UNIT 124,
COCHRANE, AB, T4C 2N1
(403) 932-9292   *SIC 8731*
GENERAL FUSION INC *p181*
3680 BONNEVILLE PL SUITE 106, BURN-
ABY, BC, V3N 4T5
(604) 420-0920   *SIC 8731*
GENOME QUEBEC *p1204*
630 BOUL RENE-LEVESQUE O BUREAU
2660, MONTREAL, QC, H3B 1S6
(514) 398-0668   *SIC 8731*
**GOUVERNEMENT DE LA PROVINCE DE
QUEBEC** *p1267*
2700 RUE EINSTEIN BUREAU C2105,
QUEBEC, QC, G1P 3W8
(418) 643-1632   *SIC 8731*
GRAPHIQUES MATROX INC *p1094*
1055 BOUL SAINT-REGIS, DORVAL, QC,
H9P 2T4
(514) 822-6000   *SIC 8731*
HEWLETT PACKARD ENTERPRISE

CANADA CO *p696*
5150 SPECTRUM WAY SUITE 400, MIS-
SISSAUGA, ON, L4W 5G2
(905) 206-4725   *SIC 8731*
HP CANADA CO *p696*
5150 SPECTRUM WAY 6 FL, MISSIS-
SAUGA, ON, L4W 5G2
(888) 206-0289   *SIC 8731*
HVE HEALTHCARE ASSESSMENTS INC
p554
260 EDGELEY BLVD UNIT 22, CONCORD,
ON, L4K 3Y4
(905) 264-2020   *SIC 8731*
HYDRO-QUEBEC *p1180*
140 BOUL CREMAZIE O, MONTREAL, QC,
H2P 1C3
(514) 858-8000   *SIC 8731*
HYDRO-QUEBEC *p1393*
1800 BOUL LIONEL-BOULET, VARENNES,
QC, J3X 1P7
(450) 925-2008   *SIC 8731*
**ID BIOMEDICAL CORPORATION OF QUE-
BEC** *p1267*
2323 BOUL DU PARC-TECHNOLOGIQUE,
QUEBEC, QC, G1P 4R8
(450) 978-4599   *SIC 8731*
INFLAMAX RESEARCH LIMITED *p696*
1310 FEWSTER DR, MISSISSAUGA, ON,
L4W 1A4
(905) 282-1808   *SIC 8731*
INNOVADERM RECHERCHES INC *p1174*
1851 RUE SHERBROOKE E UNITE 502,
MONTREAL, QC, H2K 4L5
(514) 521-3111   *SIC 8731*
**INSTITUT DE RECHERCHE ET DEVEL-
OPPEMENT EN AGROENVIRONEMENT
INC** *p1267*
2700 RUE EINSTEIN BUREAU D1110,
QUEBEC, QC, G1P 3W8
(418) 643-2380   *SIC 8731*
**INSTITUT DE RECHERCHE ROBERT
SAUVE EN SANTE ET EN SECURITE
DU TRAVAIL** *p1197*
505 BOUL DE MAISONNEUVE O, MON-
TREAL, QC, H3A 3C2
(514) 288-1551   *SIC 8731*
INSTITUT NATIONAL D'OPTIQUE *p1267*
2740 RUE EINSTEIN, QUEBEC, QC, G1P
4S4
(418) 657-7006   *SIC 8731*
**INSTITUT NATIONALE DE SANTE
PUBLIQUE DU QUEBEC** *p1272*
945 AV WOLFE BUREAU 4, QUEBEC, QC,
G1V 5B3
(418) 650-5115   *SIC 8731*
**INSTITUT NATIONALE DE SANTE
PUBLIQUE DU QUEBEC** *p1355*
20045 CH SAINTE-MARIE, SAINTE-ANNE-
DE-BELLEVUE, QC, H9X 3R5
(514) 457-2070   *SIC 8731*
**INTERNATIONAL NEWTECH DEVELOP-
MENT INCORPORATED** *p206*
1629 FOSTER'S WAY, DELTA, BC, V3M 6S7
SIC 8731
**INTERTEK TESTING SERVICES (ITS)
CANADA LTD** *p1239*
2561 AV GEORGES-V, MONTREAL-EST,
QC, H1L 6S4
(514) 640-6332   *SIC 8731*
IQVIA RDS CANADA ULC *p1324*
100 BOUL ALEXIS-NIHON 8E ETAGE,
SAINT-LAURENT, QC, H4M 2P4
(514) 855-0888   *SIC 8731*
ISKIN INC *p779*
3 CONCORDE GATE UNIT 311, NORTH
YORK, ON, M3C 3N7
(416) 924-9607   *SIC 8731*
**IZAAK WALTON KILLAM HEALTH CENTRE,
THE** *p455*
GD, HALIFAX, NS, B3K 6R8
(902) 470-6682   *SIC 8731*
JAPAN CANADA OIL SANDS LIMITED *p52*
639 5 AVE SW SUITE 2300, CALGARY, AB,
T2P 0M9

(403) 264-9046   *SIC 8731*
KARDIUM INC   p192
8518 GLENLYON PKY SUITE 155, BURN-ABY, BC, V5J 0B6
(604) 248-8891   *SIC 8731*
KONTRON CANADA INC   p1062
4555 RUE AMBROISE-LAFORTUNE, BOISBRIAND, QC, J7H 0A4
(450) 437-5682   *SIC 8731*
KS CIRCUITS INC   p987
100 KING ST W SUITE 5600, TORONTO, ON, M5X 1C9
(416) 913-5438   *SIC 8731*
LABORATOIRES CHARLES RIVER MON-TREAL ULC   p1366
22022 AUT FELIX-LECLERC, SEN-NEVILLE, QC, H9X 3R3
(514) 630-8200   *SIC 8731*
LABORATOIRES CHARLES RIVER MON-TREAL ULC   p1370
1580 RUE IDA-METIVIER, SHERBROOKE, QC, J1E 0B5
(819) 346-8200   *SIC 8731*
LABORATOIRES D'ANALYSES S.M. INC   p1393
1471 BOUL LIONEL-BOULET, VARENNES, QC, J3X 1P7
(514) 332-6001   *SIC 8731*
LABORATOIRES ITR CANADA INC, LES   p1053
19601 AV CLARK-GRAHAM, BAIE-D'URFE, QC, H9X 3T1
(514) 457-7400   *SIC 8731*
LABORATOIRES KABS INC   p1308
4500 RUE DE TONNANCOUR, SAINT-HUBERT, QC, J3Y 9G2
(450) 656-4404   *SIC 8731*
LIFE SCIENCE NUTRITIONALS INCORPO-RATED   p1044
575 RUE DE ROXTON, ACTON VALE, QC, J0H 1A0
(866) 942-2429   *SIC 8731*
MARINE CANADA ACQUISITION INC   p255
3831 NO. 6 RD SUITE 100, RICHMOND, BC, V6V 1P6
(604) 270-6899   *SIC 8731*
MEDI-SHARE INC   p534
1986 CEDAR CREEK RD, CAMBRIDGE, ON, N1R 5S5
(519) 740-3336   *SIC 8731*
MEDICAGO INC   p1273
1020 RTE DE L'EGLISE BUREAU 600, QUEBEC, QC, G1V 3V9
(418) 658-9393   *SIC 8731*
MEDICAGO R&D INC   p1273
1020 RTE DE L'EGLISE BUREAU 600, QUEBEC, QC, G1V 3V9
(418) 658-9393   *SIC 8731*
MICHAEL SMITH LABORATORIES   p324
2185 EAST MALL SUITE 301, VANCOU-VER, BC, V6T 1Z4
(604) 822-4838   *SIC 8731*
MILLIPORE (CANADA) LTD   p586
109 WOODBINE DOWNS BLVD UNIT 5, ETOBICOKE, ON, M9W 6Y1
(416) 675-1598   *SIC 8731*
MORGAN SOLAR INC   p993
100 SYMES RD UNIT 100A, TORONTO, ON, M6N 0A8
(416) 203-1655   *SIC 8731*
MPB COMMUNICATIONS INC   p1251
147 BOUL HYMUS, POINTE-CLAIRE, QC, H9R 1E9
(514) 694-8751   *SIC 8731*
NATIONAL HEARING SERVICES INC   p637
20 BEASLEY DR, KITCHENER, ON, N2E 1Y6
(519) 895-0100   *SIC 8731*
NATUR+L XTD INC   p1313
2905 AV JOSE-MARIA-ROSELL, SAINT-HYACINTHE, QC, J2S 0J9
(450) 250-4981   *SIC 8731*
NEPTUNE TECHNOLOGIES & BIORES-SOURCES INC   p1087

545 PROM DU CENTROPOLIS SUITE 100, COTE SAINT-LUC, QC, H7T 0A3
(450) 687-2262   *SIC 8731*
NERIUM BIOTECHNOLOGY, INC   p965
220 BAY ST UNIT 500, TORONTO, ON, M5J 2W4
(416) 862-7330   *SIC 8731*
NEURORX RESEARCH INC   p1186
3575 AV DU PARC BUREAU 5322, MON-TREAL, QC, H2X 3P9
(514) 906-0062   *SIC 8731*
NEW B INNOVATION LIMITED   p193
8508 GLENLYON PKY UNIT 168, BURN-ABY, BC, V5J 0B6
(604) 421-7308   *SIC 8731*
NIGHT HAWK TECHNOLOGIESTM INCp818
25 GREAT OAK PVT, OTTAWA, ON, K1G 6P7
(613) 795-8262   *SIC 8731*
NOVOZYMES BIOAG LIMITED   p1435
3935 THATCHER AVE, SASKATOON, SK, S7R 1A3
(306) 657-8200   *SIC 8731*
NSF CANADA   p601
125 CHANCELLORS WAY, GUELPH, ON, N1G 0E7
(519) 821-1246   *SIC 8731*
PANASONIC ECO SOLUTIONS CANADA INC   p699
5770 AMBLER DR UNIT 70, MISSIS-SAUGA, ON, L4W 2T3
(905) 624-5010   *SIC 8731*
PEI BUSINESS DEVELOPMENT INCp1039
94 EUSTON ST, CHARLOTTETOWN, PE, C1A 1W4
(902) 368-5800   *SIC 8731*
PHARMA MEDICA RESEARCH INC   p732
6100 BELGRAVE RD, MISSISSAUGA, ON, L5R 0B7
(905) 624-9115   *SIC 8731*
PHARMA MEDICA RESEARCH INC   p874
4770 SHEPPARD AVE E SUITE 2, SCAR-BOROUGH, ON, M1S 3V6
(416) 759-5554   *SIC 8731*
PIVOT TECHNOLOGY SOLUTIONS INCp674
55 RENFREW DR SUITE 200, MARKHAM, ON, L3R 8H3
(416) 360-4777   *SIC 8731*
PLUG CANADA INC   p256
13120 VANIER PL, RICHMOND, BC, V6V 2J2
(604) 303-0050   *SIC 8731*
POS MANAGEMENT CORP   p1433
118 VETERINARY RD, SASKATOON, SK, S7N 2R4
(306) 978-2800   *SIC 8731*
PROFOUND MEDICAL INC   p699
2400 SKYMARK AVE UNIT 6, MISSIS-SAUGA, ON, L4W 5K5
(647) 476-1350   *SIC 8731*
PROTECT-YU SECURITY & TECHNOLO-GIES INC   p1133
3055 BOUL SAINT-MARTIN O BUREAU 5, LAVAL, QC, H7T 0J3
(514) 916-7280   *SIC 8731*
PROVINCIAL HEALTH SERVICES AUTHOR-ITY   p293
570 7TH AVE W SUITE 100, VANCOUVER, BC, V5Z 4S6
(604) 707-5800   *SIC 8731*
QVELLA CORPORATION   p853
9133 LESLIE ST UNIT 110, RICHMOND HILL, ON, L4B 4N1
(289) 317-0414   *SIC 8731*
RESEARCH NOW INC   p921
3080 YONGE ST SUITE 2000, TORONTO, ON, M4N 3N1
(800) 599-7938   *SIC 8731*
RIO TINTO ALCAN INTERNATIONAL LTEEp1208
1190 AV DES CANADIENS-DE-MONTREAL BUREAU 400, MONTREAL, QC, H3B 0E3

(514) 848-8000   *SIC 8731*
SERVICES BIOANALYTIQUES BIOTRIAL INC   p1235
3885 BOUL INDUSTRIEL, MONTREAL, QC, H7L 4S3
(450) 663-6724   *SIC 8731*
SIERRA ONCOLOGY, INC   p309
885 WEST GEORGIA ST SUITE 2150, VANCOUVER, BC, V6C 3E8
(604) 558-6536   *SIC 8731*
SO CANADA INC   p768
2005 SHEPPARD AVE E SUITE 100, NORTH YORK, ON, M2J 5B4
SIC 8731
SOGEMA TECHNOLOGIES INC   p1145
1111 RUE SAINT-CHARLES O BUREAU 700, LONGUEUIL, QC, J4K 5G4
(450) 651-2800   *SIC 8731*
SOLARWINDS MSP CANADA ULC   p832
450 MARCH RD 2ND FL, OTTAWA, ON, K2K 3K2
(613) 592-6676   *SIC 8731*
SOLUTIONS MUNVO INC   p1199
1400 RUE METCALFE SUITE 300, MON-TREAL, QC, H3A 1X2
(514) 392-9822   *SIC 8731*
SONAVOX CANADA INC   p1028
100-261 MILANI BLVD, WOODBRIDGE, ON, L4H 4E3
(905) 265-2060   *SIC 8731*
STRYKER CANADA HOLDING COMPANYp183
8329 EASTLAKE DR UNIT 101, BURNABY, BC, V5A 4W2
(604) 232-9861   *SIC 8731*
SYNCRUDE CANADA LTD   p121
9421 17 AVE NW, EDMONTON, AB, T6N 1H4
(780) 970-6800   *SIC 8731*
TAMARACK GEOGRAPHIC TECHNOLO-GIES LTD   p431
303 THORBURN RD SUITE 302, ST. JOHN'S, NL, A1B 4R1
(709) 726-1046   *SIC 8731*
TECK RESOURCES LIMITED   p264
12380 HORSESHOE WAY, RICHMOND, BC, V7A 4Z1
(778) 296-4900   *SIC 8731*
THERATECHNOLOGIES INC   p1200
2015 RUE PEEL SUITE 1100, MONTREAL, QC, H3A 1T8
(514) 336-7800   *SIC 8731*
TRANS BIOTECH   p1137
201 MGR BOURGET, LEVIS, QC, G6V 9V6
(418) 833-8876   *SIC 8731*
UNIVERSITY OF OTTAWA HEART INSTI-TUTE   p828
40 RUSKIN ST, OTTAWA, ON, K1Y 4W7
(613) 696-7000   *SIC 8731*
VECIMA NETWORKS INC   p1432
150 CARDINAL PL, SASKATOON, SK, S7L 6H7
(306) 955-7075   *SIC 8731*
VIMY RIDGE GROUP LTD, THE   p867
2000 ELLESMERE RD UNIT 16, SCAR-BOROUGH, ON, M1H 2W4
(416) 438-6727   *SIC 8731*
WEATHERFORD LABORATORIES (CANADA) LTD   p26
1620 27 AVE NE, CALGARY, AB, T2E 8W4
(403) 736-3500   *SIC 8731*
WORKSHOPX INC   p828
6 HAMILTON AVE N SUITE 004, OTTAWA, ON, K1Y 4R1
(613) 860-7000   *SIC 8731*
XENON PHARMACEUTICALS INC   p189
3650 GILMORE WAY, BURNABY, BC, V5G 4W8
(604) 484-3300   *SIC 8731*
XEROX CANADA INC   p715
2660 SPEAKMAN DR, MISSISSAUGA, ON, L5K 2L1
(905) 823-7091   *SIC 8731*
YESUP ECOMMERCE SOLUTIONS INC

p915
200 CONSUMERS RD SUITE 308, TORONTO, ON, M2J 4R4
(416) 499-8009   *SIC 8731*

SIC 8732 Commercial nonphysical research

411 LOCAL SEARCH CORP   p778
1200 EGLINTON AVE E SUITE 200, NORTH YORK, ON, M3C 1H9
(416) 840-2566   *SIC 8732*
4665181 MANITOBA LTD   p390
2855 PEMBINA HWY SUITE 35, WIN-NIPEG, MB, R3T 2H5
(800) 710-2713   *SIC 8732*
7503083 CANADA INC   p1193
2000 RUE PEEL BUREAU 400, MON-TREAL, QC, H3A 2W5
(514) 384-1570   *SIC 8732*
9182-9978 QUEBEC INC   p1209
774 RUE SAINT PAUL O, MONTREAL, QC, H3C 1M4
(514) 876-4101   *SIC 8732*
A & A MERCHANDISING LTD   p570
3250 LAKE SHORE BLVD W, ETOBICOKE, ON, M8V 1M1
(416) 503-3341   *SIC 8732*
A.C. NIELSEN COMPANY OF CANADA LIM-ITED   p666
160 MCNABB ST, MARKHAM, ON, L3R 4B8
(905) 475-3344   *SIC 8732*
ACASTA ENTERPRISES INC   p916
1 APOLLO PL, TORONTO, ON, M3J 0H2
SIC 8732
ACCESS RESEARCH INC   p974
180 BLOOR ST W SUITE 1402, TORONTO, ON, M5S 2V6
(416) 960-9603   *SIC 8732*
ACROBAT RESEARCH LTD   p540
GD, CAPREOL, ON, P0M 1H0
(705) 858-4343   *SIC 8732*
ACROBAT RESEARCH LTD   p704
170 ROBERT SPECK PKY SUITE 201, MIS-SISSAUGA, ON, L4Z 3G1
(416) 503-4343   *SIC 8732*
AD HOC RECHERCHE INC   p1193
400 BOUL DE MAISONNEUVE O BUREAU 1200, MONTREAL, QC, H3A 1L4
(514) 937-4040   *SIC 8732*
ADEASE MEDIA RESEARCH INC   p778
150 FERRAND DR SUITE 800, NORTH YORK, ON, M3C 3E5
(416) 423-2010   *SIC 8732*
AERIC INC   p819
255 SMYTH RD, OTTAWA, ON, K1H 8M7
(613) 526-3280   *SIC 8732*
AIMIA INC   p1191
525 AV VIGER O BUREAU 1000, MON-TREAL, QC, H2Z 0B2
(514) 897-6800   *SIC 8732*
ALBERTA MILK   p125
1303 91 ST SW, EDMONTON, AB, T6X 1H1
(780) 453-5942   *SIC 8732*
ALLO PROF   p1173
1000 RUE FULLUM, MONTREAL, QC, H2K 3L7
(514) 509-2025   *SIC 8732*
AND AGENCY INC   p769
1220 SHEPPARD AVE E SUITE 100, NORTH YORK, ON, M2K 2S5
(416) 493-6111   *SIC 8732*
ARCHIPELAGO MARINE RESEARCH LTDp339
525 HEAD ST SUITE 1, VICTORIA, BC, V9A 5S1
(250) 383-4535   *SIC 8732*
AXIS DATABASE MARKETING GROUP INCp692
1331 CRESTLAWN DR UNIT A, MISSIS-SAUGA, ON, L4W 2P9
(416) 503-3210   *SIC 8732*
B3INTELLIGENCE LTD   p915
100 SHEPPARD AVE E SUITE 503,

TORONTO, ON, M2N 6N5
(416) 549-8000 *SIC 8732*
BANISTER RESEARCH & CONSULTING INC *p91*
11223 99 AVE NW, EDMONTON, AB, T5K 0G9
(780) 451-4444 *SIC 8732*
BC CENTRE FOR EXCELLENCE IN HIV AIDS *p326*
1081 BURRARD ST SUITE 608, VANCOUVER, BC, V6Z 1Y6
(604) 806-8477 *SIC 8732*
BUREAU DES INTERVIEWEURS PROFESSIONNELS (B.I.P.) (1988) INC *p1193*
2021 AV UNION BUREAU 1221, MONTREAL, QC, H3A 2S9
(514) 288-1980 *SIC 8732*
C-W AGENCIES INC *p291*
2020 YUKON ST, VANCOUVER, BC, V5Y 3N8
(604) 879-9080 *SIC 8732*
CANADIAN CENTRE ON SUBSTANCE ABUSE *p822*
75 ALBERT ST SUITE 500, OTTAWA, ON, K1P 5E7
(613) 235-4048 *SIC 8732*
CANADIAN DEVELOPMENT CONSULTANTS INTERNATIONAL INC *p303*
541 HOWE ST UNIT 200, VANCOUVER, BC, V6C 2C2
(604) 633-1849 *SIC 8732*
CANADIAN RESEARCH DATA CENTER NETWORK *p614*
1280 MAIN ST W, HAMILTON, ON, L8S 4M1
(905) 525-9140 *SIC 8732*
CANADIAN VIEWPOINT INC *p855*
9350 YONGE ST SUITE 206, RICHMOND HILL, ON, L4C 5G2
(905) 770-1770 *SIC 8732*
CCI RESEARCH INC *p808*
71 BROADWAY, ORANGEVILLE, ON, L9W 1K1
(519) 938-9552 *SIC 8732*
CENTRE FOR MOLECULAR MEDICINE AND THERAPEUTIC *p293*
950 28TH AVE W SUITE 3109, VANCOUVER, BC, V5Z 4H4
(604) 875-3535 *SIC 8732*
CENTRE HOSPITALIER UNIVERSITAIRE DE QUEBEC *p1269*
9 RUE MCMAHON, QUEBEC, QC, G1R 3S3
(418) 691-5281 *SIC 8732*
COMPUSTAT CONSULTANTS INC *p808*
67 FIRST ST, ORANGEVILLE, ON, L9W 2E6
(519) 938-9552 *SIC 8732*
COMWAVE TELECOM INC *p781*
4884 DUFFERIN ST UNIT 1, NORTH YORK, ON, M3H 5S8
(416) 663-9700 *SIC 8732*
CONNOR, CLARK & LUNN FINANCIAL GROUP *p312*
1111 GEORGIA ST W SUITE 2200, VANCOUVER, BC, V6E 4M3
(604) 685-4465 *SIC 8732*
COREM *p1263*
1180 RUE DE LA MINERALOGIE, QUEBEC, QC, G1N 1X7
(418) 527-8211 *SIC 8732*
CROP INC *p1195*
550 RUE SHERBROOKE O BUREAU 900, MONTREAL, QC, H3A 1B9
(514) 807-9431 *SIC 8732*
DATA PROBE INC *p364*
297 ST MARY'S RD, WINNIPEG, MB, R2H 1J5
SIC 8732
DECIMA INC *p922*
2345 YONGE ST SUITE 704, TORONTO, ON, M4P 2E5
(416) 962-9109 *SIC 8732*
ELEMENTAL DATA COLLECTION INC *p823*
170 LAURIER AVE W SUITE 400, OTTAWA, ON, K1P 5V5

(613) 667-9352 *SIC 8732*
ENVIRONICS ANALYTICS GROUP LTD *p928*
33 BLOOR ST E SUITE 400, TORONTO, ON, M4W 3H1
(416) 969-2733 *SIC 8732*
EVEREST CLINICAL RESEARCH CORPORATION *p670*
675 COCHRANE DR SUITE 408, MARKHAM, ON, L3R 0B8
(905) 752-5222 *SIC 8732*
FAST, DOUG & ASSOCIATES LTD *p1433*
112 RESEARCH DR SUITE 112, SASKATOON, SK, S7N 3R3
(306) 956-3070 *SIC 8732*
FIRST AVENUE CLEARING CORPORATION *p574*
47 JUTLAND RD, ETOBICOKE, ON, M8Z 2G6
(416) 259-3600 *SIC 8732*
GENERATION 5 MATHEMATICAL TECHNOLOGIES INC *p767*
515 CONSUMERS RD SUITE 600, NORTH YORK, ON, M2J 4Z2
SIC 8732
GESTION CANADADIRECT INC *p1094*
743 AV RENAUD, DORVAL, QC, H9P 2N1
(514) 422-8557 *SIC 8732*
GEXEL TELECOM INTERNATIONAL INC *p1188*
507 PLACE D'ARMES BUREAU 1503, MONTREAL, QC, H2Y 2W8
(514) 935-9300 *SIC 8732*
GOLD LINE SOLUTIONS *p527*
3228 SOUTH SERVICE RD SUITE 102, BURLINGTON, ON, L7N 3H8
(905) 633-3835 *SIC 8732*
GREG KELLY WOOLSTEN CROFT *p821*
60 GEORGE ST SUITE 205, OTTAWA, ON, K1N 1J4
(613) 236-0296 *SIC 8732*
GROUPE SECOR INC *p1191*
555 BOUL RENE-LEVESQUE O BUREAU 900, MONTREAL, QC, H2Z 1B1
SIC 8732
HARRIS/DECIMA *p922*
2345 YONGE ST SUITE 405, TORONTO, ON, M4P 2E5
(416) 716-4903 *SIC 8732*
HJ LINNEN ASSOCIATES *p1418*
2161 SCARTH ST SUITE 200, REGINA, SK, S4P 2H8
(306) 586-9611 *SIC 8732*
HOLINSHED RESEARCH GROUP INC *p834*
200 ELGIN ST SUITE 1102, OTTAWA, ON, K2P 1L5
SIC 8732
HOTSPEX INC *p922*
40 EGLINTON AVE E SUITE 801, TORONTO, ON, M4P 3A2
(416) 487-5439 *SIC 8732*
ICOM INFORMATION & COMMUNICATIONS L.P. *p914*
111 GORDON BAKER RD SUITE 300, TORONTO, ON, M2H 3R1
(647) 795-9600 *SIC 8732*
ICT CANADA MARKETING INC *p405*
459 ELMWOOD DR, MONCTON, NB, E1A 2X2
SIC 8732
IMPACT RESEARCH INC *p1259*
300 RUE SAINT-PAUL BUREAU 300, QUEBEC, QC, G1K 7R1
(418) 647-2727 *SIC 8732*
IN-SYNC CONSUMER INSIGHT CORP *p922*
90 EGLINTON AVE E SUITE 403, TORONTO, ON, M4P 2Y3
(416) 932-0921 *SIC 8732*
INGENIO, FILALE DE LOTO-QUEBEC INC *p1197*
500 RUE SHERBROOKE O BUREAU 2000, MONTREAL, QC, H3A 3G6
(514) 282-0210 *SIC 8732*
INTERHEALTH CANADA LIMITED *p953*
357 BAY ST SUITE 600, TORONTO, ON,

M5H 2T7
(416) 362-4681 *SIC 8732*
INTERNATIONAL DATA CORPORATION (CANADA) LTD *p942*
33 YONGE ST SUITE 420, TORONTO, ON, M5E 1G4
(416) 369-0033 *SIC 8732*
INTERNATIONAL DEVELOPMENT RESEARCH CENTRE *p823*
150 KENT ST, OTTAWA, ON, K1P 0B2
(613) 236-6163 *SIC 8732*
INTOUCH INSIGHT INC *p624*
400 MARCH RD, KANATA, ON, K2K 3H4
(613) 270-7900 *SIC 8732*
IOGEN BIO-PRODUCTS CORPORATION *p827*
310 HUNT CLUB RD, OTTAWA, ON, K1V 1C1
(613) 733-9830 *SIC 8732*
IPERCEPTIONS INC *p1205*
606 RUE CATHCART SUITE 1007, MONTREAL, QC, H3B 1K9
(514) 488-3600 *SIC 8732*
IPSOS CORP *p314*
1285 PENDER ST W SUITE 200, VANCOUVER, BC, V6E 4B1
(778) 373-5000 *SIC 8732*
IPSOS LIMITED PARTNERSHIP *p314*
1700-1075 GEORGIA ST W, VANCOUVER, BC, V6E 3C9
(778) 373-5000 *SIC 8732*
IPSOS LIMITED PARTNERSHIP *p378*
185 CARLTON ST FL 4, WINNIPEG, MB, R3C 3J1
(204) 949-3100 *SIC 8732*
IPSOS LIMITED PARTNERSHIP *p929*
160 BLOOR ST E SUITE 300, TORONTO, ON, M4W 1B9
(416) 925-4444 *SIC 8732*
IPSOS-ASI, LTD *p929*
160 BLOOR ST E SUITE 300, TORONTO, ON, M4W 1B9
(416) 925-4444 *SIC 8732*
IPSOS-ASI, LTD *p929*
160 BLOOR ST E SUITE 300, TORONTO, ON, M4W 1B9
(416) 324-2900 *SIC 8732*
IPSOS-INSIGHT CORPORATION *p314*
1075 GEORGIA ST W UNIT 1700, VANCOUVER, BC, V6E 3C9
(778) 373-5000 *SIC 8732*
KANTAR CANADA INC *p929*
2 BLOOR ST E SUITE 900, TORONTO, ON, M4W 3H8
(416) 924-5751 *SIC 8732*
KISQUARED CORPORATION *p374*
388 DONALD ST SUITE 226, WINNIPEG, MB, R3B 2J4
(204) 989-8002 *SIC 8732*
LAMBDA THERAPEUTIC RESEARCH INC *p869*
460 COMSTOCK RD, SCARBOROUGH, ON, M1L 4S4
(416) 752-3636 *SIC 8732*
LEGAL LINK CORPORATION, THE *p953*
333 BAY ST SUITE 400, TORONTO, ON, M5H 2R2
(416) 348-0432 *SIC 8732*
LEGER MARKETING INC *p375*
35 KING ST SUITE 5, WINNIPEG, MB, R3B 1H4
(204) 885-7570 *SIC 8732*
LEGER MARKETING INC *p1189*
507 PLACE D'ARMES BUREAU 700, MONTREAL, QC, H2Y 2W8
(514) 845-5660 *SIC 8732*
LOGIT GROUP INC, THE *p996*
302 THE EAST MALL SUITE 400, TORONTO, ON, M9B 6C7
(416) 236-4770 *SIC 8732*
MALATEST, R. A. & ASSOCIATES LTD *p336*
858 PANDORA AVE, VICTORIA, BC, V8W 1P4
(250) 384-2770 *SIC 8732*

MARITZ INC *p1431*
2318 NORTHRIDGE DR, SASKATOON, SK, S7L 1B9
SIC 8732
MARKET PROBE CANADA COMPANY *p572*
1243 ISLINGTON AVE SUITE 200, ETOBICOKE, ON, M8X 1Y9
(416) 233-1555 *SIC 8732*
MARU GROUP CANADA INC *p929*
2 BLOOR ST E SUITE 1600, TORONTO, ON, M4W 1A8
(647) 258-1416 *SIC 8732*
MATRIX RESEARCH LIMITED *p904*
55 DONCASTER AVE SUITE 280, THORNHILL, ON, L3T 1L7
(905) 707-1300 *SIC 8732*
MBA RECHERCHE INC *p1198*
1470 RUE PEEL BUREAU 800, MONTREAL, QC, H3A 1T1
(514) 284-9644 *SIC 8732*
MINTZ GLOBAL SCREENING INC *p1211*
1303 RUE WILLIAM BUREAU 200, MONTREAL, QC, H3C 1R4
(514) 587-6200 *SIC 8732*
MUSTEL RESEARCH GROUP LTD *p319*
1505 2ND AVE W UNIT 402, VANCOUVER, BC, V6H 3Y4
(604) 733-4213 *SIC 8732*
NATIONAL RESEARCH COUNCIL CANADA *p430*
GD, ST. JOHN'S, NL, A1B 3T5
(709) 772-4939 *SIC 8732*
NCSG ACQUISITION LTD *p1*
53016 HWY 60 UNIT 817, ACHESON, AB, T7X 5A7
(780) 960-6300 *SIC 8732*
NIELSEN MEDIA RESEARCH LIMITED *p673*
160 MCNABB ST, MARKHAM, ON, L3R 4B8
(905) 475-1131 *SIC 8732*
NORTHSTAR RESEARCH PARTNERS INC *p940*
18 KING ST E SUITE 1500, TORONTO, ON, M5C 1C4
(416) 907-7100 *SIC 8732*
NPD GROUP CANADA INC, THE *p777*
1500 DON MILLS RD SUITE 502, NORTH YORK, ON, M3B 3K4
(647) 723-7700 *SIC 8732*
NPD INTELECT CANADA INC *p777*
1500 DON MILLS RD SUITE 502, NORTH YORK, ON, M3B 3K4
(647) 723-7700 *SIC 8732*
NRG RESEARCH GROUP INC *p315*
1100 MELVILLE ST SUITE 1380, VANCOUVER, BC, V6E 4A6
(604) 681-0381 *SIC 8732*
NRG RESEARCH GROUP INC *p379*
360 MAIN ST SUITE 1910, WINNIPEG, MB, R3C 3Z3
(204) 989-8999 *SIC 8732*
NUMERIS *p407*
1234 MAIN ST SUITE 600, MONCTON, NB, E1C 1H7
(506) 859-7700 *SIC 8732*
ONE10 CANADA HOLDINGS ULC *p1190*
759 RUE DU SQUARE-VICTORIA BUREAU 105, MONTREAL, QC, H2Y 2J7
(514) 288-9889 *SIC 8732*
ONEMETHOD INC *p982*
225 WELLINGTON ST W, TORONTO, ON, M5V 3G7
(416) 649-0180 *SIC 8732*
ONTARIO CENTRES OF EXCELLENCE INC *p982*
325 FRONT ST SUITE 300, TORONTO, ON, M5V 2Y1
(416) 861-1092 *SIC 8732*
OPINION SEARCH INC *p1198*
1080 RUE BEAVERHALL BUREAU 400, MONTREAL, QC, H3A 1E4
(514) 288-0199 *SIC 8732*
ORACLEPOLL RESEARCH LTD *p900*
130 ELM ST SUITE 102, SUDBURY, ON, P3C 1T6

(705) 674-9591   SIC 8732
PASKWAYAK BUSINESS DEVELOMENT CORPORATION LTD   p354
HWY 10 N, OPASKWAYAK, MB, R0B 2J0
(204) 627-7200   SIC 8732
PRAIRIE RESEARCH ASSOCIATES PRA INC   p379
363 BROADWAY UNIT 500, WINNIPEG, MB, R3C 3N9
(204) 987-2030   SIC 8732
PUBLIC HISTORY INC   p834
331 COOPER ST SUITE 500, OTTAWA, ON, K2P 0G5
(613) 236-0713   SIC 8732
RESEARCH & DEVELOPMENT CORPORATION OF NEWFOUNDLAND AND LABRADOR   p431
68 PORTUGAL COVE RD, ST. JOHN'S, NL, A1B 2L9
(709) 758-0913   SIC 8732
RESEARCH HOUSE INC   p1169
2953 RUE BELANGER BUREAU 214, MONTREAL, QC, H1Y 3G4
SIC 8732
SAINE MARKETING INC   p1215
2222 BOUL RENE-LEVESQUE O BUREAU 220, MONTREAL, QC, H3H 1R6
(514) 931-8233   SIC 8732
SAULT STE. MARIE INNOVATION CENTRE   p862
1520 QUEEN ST E SUITE 307, SAULT STE. MARIE, ON, P6A 2G4
(705) 942-7927   SIC 8732
SERVICE QUALITY MEASUREMENT GROUP INC   p332
3126 31 AVE SUITE 301, VERNON, BC, V1T 2H1
(800) 446-2095   SIC 8732
SMT DIRECT MARKETING INC   p773
5255 YONGE ST SUITE 1400, NORTH YORK, ON, M2N 6P4
SIC 8732
SOCIAL SCIENCES AND HUMANITIES RESEARCH COUNCIL OF CANADA   p825
350 ALBERT ST SUITE 1610, OTTAWA, ON, K1R 1A4
(613) 992-0691   SIC 8732
SPECTRA ENERGY EMPRESS L.P.   p60
425 1 ST SW SUITE 2600, CALGARY, AB, T2P 3L8
(403) 699-1999   SIC 8732
SUNNYBROOK RESEARCH INSTITUTE   p921
2075 BAYVIEW AVE, TORONTO, ON, M4N 3M5
(416) 480-6100   SIC 8732
TELE-SONDAGES PLUS INC   p1192
505 BOUL RENE-LEVESQUE O BUREAU 1400, MONTREAL, QC, H2Z 1Y7
(514) 392-4702   SIC 8732
TRANSALTA ENERGY MARKETING CORP   p66
110 12 AVE SW, CALGARY, AB, T2R 0G7
(403) 267-7987   SIC 8732
UNIVERSITE DU QUEBEC   p1260
490 RUE DE LA COURONNE, QUEBEC, QC, G1K 9A9
(418) 654-2665   SIC 8732
VIEWPOINTS RESEARCH LTD   p376
115 BANNATYNE AVE SUITE 404, WINNIPEG, MB, R3B 0R3
(204) 988-9253   SIC 8732
ZOOMER MEDIA LIMITED   p992
70 JEFFERSON AVE, TORONTO, ON, M6K 1Y4
(416) 367-5353   SIC 8732

SIC 8733 Noncommercial research organizations

ARTHRITIS RESEARCH CENTRE SOCIETY OF CANADA, THE   p259
5591 NO. 3 RD, RICHMOND, BC, V6X 2C7

(604) 879-7511   SIC 8733
CANADIAN LIGHT SOURCE INC   p1433
44 INNOVATION BLVD, SASKATOON, SK, S7N 2V3
(306) 657-3500   SIC 8733
CANADIAN PARTNERSHIP AGAINST CANCER CORPORATION   p949
145 KING ST W STE 900, TORONTO, ON, M5H 1J8
(416) 915-9222   SIC 8733
CANADIAN SCIENCE CENTRE FOR HUMAN AND ANIMAL HEALTH   p380
1015 ARLINGTON ST SUITE A1010, WINNIPEG, MB, R3E 3P6
(204) 789-6001   SIC 8733
CANCER CARE ONTARIO   p944
620 UNIVERSITY AVE SUITE 1500, TORONTO, ON, M5G 2L7
(416) 971-9800   SIC 8733
CENTRE FOR PHENOGENOMICS INC, THE   p977
25 ORDE ST, TORONTO, ON, M5T 3H7
(647) 837-5811   SIC 8733
CENTRE FOR RESEARCH IN EARTH AND SPACE TECHNOLOGY   p782
4850 KEELE ST, NORTH YORK, ON, M3J 3K1
(416) 736-5247   SIC 8733
CHILDREN'S HOSPITAL FOUNDATION OF MANITOBA, TH   p380
715 MCDERMOT AVE SUITE 513, WINNIPEG, MB, R3E 3P4
(204) 789-3968   SIC 8733
CHU DE QUEBEC - UNIVERSITE LAVAL   p1269
11 COTE DU PALAIS, QUEBEC, QC, G1R 2J6
(418) 525-4444   SIC 8733
COASTAL ZONE RESEARCH INSTITUTE INC   p417
232B AV DE L'EGLISE, SHIPPAGAN, NB, E8S 1J2
(506) 336-6600   SIC 8733
FOREST ENGINEERING RESEARCH INSTITUTE   p324
2601 EAST MALL, VANCOUVER, BC, V6T 1Z4
(604) 228-1555   SIC 8733
FPINNOVATIONS   p1250
570 BOUL SAINT-JEAN, POINTE-CLAIRE, QC, H9R 3J9
(514) 630-4100   SIC 8733
GOVERNORS OF THE UNIVERSITY OF ALBERTA, THE   p117
8625 112 ST NW SUITE 222, EDMONTON, AB, T6G 1K8
(780) 492-5787   SIC 8733
GOVERNORS OF THE UNIVERSITY OF CALGARY, THE   p41
3330 HOSPITAL DR NW SUITE 3330, CALGARY, AB, T2N 4N1
SIC 8733
HEALTH SCIENCES NORTH RESEARCH INSTITUTE   p901
41 RAMSEY LAKE RD, SUDBURY, ON, P3E 5J1
(705) 523-7300   SIC 8733
INC RESEARCH TORONTO, INC   p981
720 KING ST W 7TH FL, TORONTO, ON, M5V 2T3
(416) 963-9338   SIC 8733
INNOTECH ALBERTA INC   p120
250 KARL CLARK RD, EDMONTON, AB, T6N 1E4
(780) 450-5111   SIC 8733
INSTITUT DE RECHERCHES CLINIQUES DE MONTREAL   p1184
110 AV DES PINS O, MONTREAL, QC, H2W 1R7
(514) 987-5500   SIC 8733
INSTITUT NATIONAL DE LA RECHERCHE SCIENTIFIQUE   p1259
490 RUE DE LA COURONNE, QUEBEC, QC, G1K 9A9

(418) 654-4677   SIC 8733
INSTITUTE FOR CLINICAL EVALUATIVE SCIENCES   p921
2075 BAYVIEW AVE SUITE G106, TORONTO, ON, M4N 3M5
(416) 480-4055   SIC 8733
INSTITUTE OF PUBLIC ADMINISTRATION OF CANADA, THE   p975
1075 BAY ST SUITE 401, TORONTO, ON, M5S 2B1
(416) 924-8787   SIC 8733
INTERNATIONAL INSTITUTE FOR SUSTAINABLE DEVELOPMENT   p374
111 LOMBARD AVE SUITE 325, WINNIPEG, MB, R3B 0T4
(204) 958-7700   SIC 8733
LAWSON RESEARCH INSTITUTE   p656
750 BASE LINE RD E SUITE 300, LONDON, ON, N6C 5Z2
(519) 646-6100   SIC 8733
LEADING ENGLISH AND EDUCATION RESOURCE NETWORK (LEARN)   p1134
2030 BOUL DAGENAIS O BUREAU 2, LAVAL-OUEST, QC, H7L 5W2
(450) 622-2212   SIC 8733
LUNENFELD RESEARCH INSTITUTE   p946
600 UNIVERSITY AVE RM 850, TORONTO, ON, M5G 1X5
(416) 586-8811   SIC 8733
MEDICAL COUNCIL OF CANADA   p818
1021 THOMAS SPRATT PL, OTTAWA, ON, K1G 5L5
SIC 8733
NATIONAL CANCER INSTITUTE OF CANADA   p927
10 ALCORN AVE SUITE 200, TORONTO, ON, M4V 3B1
(416) 961-7223   SIC 8733
NCIC CLINICAL TRIALS GROUP   p631
10 STUART ST, KINGSTON, ON, K7L 2V5
(613) 533-6410   SIC 8733
ONTARIO EDUCATIONAL COMMUNICATIONS AUTHORITY, THE   p924
2180 YONGE ST, TORONTO, ON, M4S 2B9
(416) 484-2600   SIC 8733
ONTARIO INSTITUTE FOR CANCER RESEARCH   p947
661 UNIVERSITY AVE SUITE 510, TORONTO, ON, M5G 0A3
(416) 977-7599   SIC 8733
ONTARIO INSTITUTE FOR STUDIES IN EDUCATION OF THE UNIVERSITY OF TORONTO   p976
252 BLOOR ST W SUITE 100, TORONTO, ON, M5S 1V6
(416) 978-0005   SIC 8733
OTTAWA HEART INSTITUTE RESEARCH CORPORATION   p828
40 RUSKIN ST, OTTAWA, ON, K1Y 4W7
SIC 8733
OTTAWA HOSPITAL, THE   p828
725 PARKDALE AVE, OTTAWA, ON, K1Y 4E9
(613) 761-4395   SIC 8733
PERIMETER INSTITUTE   p1009
31 CAROLINE ST N, WATERLOO, ON, N2L 2Y5
(519) 569-7600   SIC 8733
PRAIRIE SWINE CENTRE INC   p1424
2105 8TH ST E, SASKATOON, SK, S7H 0T8
(306) 373-9922   SIC 8733
SASKATCHEWAN RESEARCH COUNCIL, THE   p1433
15 INNOVATION BLVD SUITE 125, SASKATOON, SK, S7N 2X8
(306) 933-5400   SIC 8733
STEMCELL TECHNOLOGIES CANADA INC   p293
570 7TH AVE W SUITE 400, VANCOUVER, BC, V5Z 1B3
(604) 877-0713   SIC 8733
STRONGEST FAMILIES INSTITUTE   p461
267 COBEQUID RD SUITE 200, LOWER SACKVILLE, NS, B4C 4E6

(902) 442-9520   SIC 8733
SUDBURY NEUTRINO OBSERVATORY   p647
1039 REGIONAL RD 24, LIVELY, ON, P3Y 1N2
(705) 692-7000   SIC 8733
TECHNICAL STANDARDS AND SAFETY AUTHORITY   p588
345 CARLINGVIEW DR, ETOBICOKE, ON, M9W 6N9
(416) 734-3300   SIC 8733
THORNHILL RESEARCH INC   p947
210 DUNDAS ST W SUITE 200, TORONTO, ON, M5G 2E8
(416) 597-1325   SIC 8733
TRIUMF   p325
4004 WESBROOK MALL, VANCOUVER, BC, V6T 2A3
(604) 222-1047   SIC 8733
UNIVERSITE DU QUEBEC   p1393
1650 BOUL LIONEL-BOULET, VARENNES, QC, J3X 1P7
(450) 929-8100   SIC 8733
UNIVERSITY HEALTH NETWORK   p947
620 UNIVERSITY AVE SUITE 706, TORONTO, ON, M5G 2C1
(416) 946-2294   SIC 8733
VANCOUVER COASTAL HEALTH AUTHORITY   p294
2647 WILLOW ST RM 100, VANCOUVER, BC, V5Z 1M9
(604) 875-4372   SIC 8733
VANCOUVER COASTAL HEALTH AUTHORITY   p294
2635 LAUREL ST, VANCOUVER, BC, V5Z 1M9
(604) 675-2575   SIC 8733
VISION RESEARCH INC   p1041
94 WATTS AVE, CHARLOTTETOWN, PE, C1E 2C1
(902) 569-7300   SIC 8733
WORKERS HEALTH AND SAFETY CENTRE FEDERATION OF ONTARIO   p677
710-675 COCHRANE DR, MARKHAM, ON, L3R 0B8
(416) 441-1939   SIC 8733
ZYMEWORKS INC   p320
1385 8TH AVE W SUITE 540, VANCOUVER, BC, V6H 3V9
(604) 678-1388   SIC 8733

SIC 8734 Testing laboratories

ACUREN GROUP INC   p121
7450 18 ST NW, EDMONTON, AB, T6P 1N8
(780) 440-2131   SIC 8734
AGAT LABORATORIES LTD   p20
3801 21 ST NE, CALGARY, AB, T2E 6T5
(403) 216-2077   SIC 8734
ALS CANADA LTD   p238
2103 DOLLARTON HWY, NORTH VANCOUVER, BC, V7H 0A7
(604) 984-0221   SIC 8734
BUFFALO INSPECTION SERVICES (2005) INC   p108
3867 ROPER RD NW, EDMONTON, AB, T6B 3S5
(780) 486-7344   SIC 8734
BUREAU VERITAS CANADA (2019) INC   p21
2021 41 AVE NE, CALGARY, AB, T2E 6P2
(403) 291-3077   SIC 8734
BUREAU VERITAS CANADA (2019) INC   p108
6744 50 ST NW, EDMONTON, AB, T6B 3M9
(780) 378-8500   SIC 8734
BUREAU VERITAS CANADA (2019) INC   p188
4606 CANADA WAY, BURNABY, BC, V5G 1K5
(604) 734-7276   SIC 8734
BUREAU VERITAS CANADA (2019) INC   p720
1919 MINNESOTA CRT SUITE 500, MISSISSAUGA, ON, L5N 0C9

(905) 288-2150   *SIC 8734*

BUREAU VERITAS COMMODITIES CANADA LTD   p323
9050 SHAUGHNESSY ST, VANCOUVER, BC, V6P 6E5
(604) 253-3158   *SIC 8734*

CANADIAN ANALYTICAL LABORATORIES INC   p720
6733 KITIMAT RD, MISSISSAUGA, ON, L5N 1W3
(416) 286-3332   *SIC 8734*

CANADIAN CONSTRUCTION MATERIALS ENGINEERING & TESTING INC   p192
6991 CURRAGH AVE, BURNABY, BC, V5J 4V6
(604) 436-9111   *SIC 8734*

CANADIAN STANDARDS ASSOCIATION   p254
13799 COMMERCE PKY, RICHMOND, BC, V6V 2N9
(604) 273-4581   *SIC 8734*

CANADIAN STANDARDS ASSOCIATION   p583
178 REXDALE BLVD, ETOBICOKE, ON, M9W 1R3
(416) 747-4000   *SIC 8734*

CANADIAN STANDARDS ASSOCIATION   p583
178 REXDALE BLVD, ETOBICOKE, ON, M9W 1R3
(416) 747-4000   *SIC 8734*

CAR-BER TESTING SERVICES INC   p846
911 MICHIGAN AVE, POINT EDWARD, ON, N7V 1H2
(519) 336-7775   *SIC 8734*

CARDIOLOGY PLUS (CALGARY) INC   p22
803 1 AVE NE SUITE 306, CALGARY, AB, T2E 7C5
(403) 571-8600   *SIC 8734*

CARO ANALYTICAL SERVICES LTD   p254
4011 VIKING WAY UNIT 110, RICHMOND, BC, V6V 2K9
(604) 279-1499   *SIC 8734*

CGL-GRS SWISS CANADIAN GEM LAB INC   p303
409 GRANVILLE ST SUITE 510, VANCOUVER, BC, V6C 1T2
(604) 687-0091   *SIC 8734*

CORE LABORATORIES CANADA LTD   p22
2810 12 ST NE, CALGARY, AB, T2E 7P7
(403) 250-4000   *SIC 8734*

CORE LABORATORIES CANADA LTD   p22
2810 12 ST NE, CALGARY, AB, T2E 7P7
(403) 250-4000   *SIC 8734*

DAVROC TESTING LABORATORIES INC   p499
2051 WILLIAMS PKY UNIT 21, BRAMPTON, ON, L6S 5T3
(905) 792-7792   *SIC 8734*

ELECTRONIC WARFARE ASSOCIATES - CANADA, LTD   p596
1223 MICHAEL ST N SUITE 200, GLOUCESTER, ON, K1J 7T2
(613) 230-6067   *SIC 8734*

ELEMENT MATERIALS TECHNOLOGY CANADA INC   p715
2395 SPEAKMAN DR SUITE 583, MISSISSAUGA, ON, L5K 1B3
(905) 822-4111   *SIC 8734*

EUROFINS BIOPHARMA PRODUCT TESTING TORONTO, INC   p783
1111 FLINT RD UNIT 36, NORTH YORK, ON, M3J 3C7
(416) 665-2134   *SIC 8734*

EUROFINS ENVIRONMENT TESTING CANADA, INC   p783
1111 FLINT RD UNIT 36, NORTH YORK, ON, M3J 3C7
(416) 665-2134   *SIC 8734*

EUROFINS ENVIRONMENT TESTING CANADA, INC   p1295
1390 RUE HOCQUART, SAINT-BRUNO, QC, J3V 6E1
(450) 441-5880   *SIC 8734*

EXOVA   p1250
121 BOUL HYMUS, POINTE-CLAIRE, QC, H9R 1E6
(514) 697-3400   *SIC 8734*

FINE ANALYSIS LABORATORIES LTD   p615
236 PRITCHARD RD, HAMILTON, ON, L8W 3P7
SIC 8734

GENTOX LABORATORIES INC   p670
1345 DENISON ST, MARKHAM, ON, L3R 5V2
(416) 798-4988   *SIC 8734*

INTERTEK TESTING SERVICES NA LTD   p1128
1829 32E AV, LACHINE, QC, H8T 3J1
(514) 631-3100   *SIC 8734*

IOTRON INDUSTRIES CANADA INC   p246
1425 KEBET WAY, PORT COQUITLAM, BC, V3C 6L3
(604) 945-8838   *SIC 8734*

IRISNDT CORP   p115
5311 86 ST NW, EDMONTON, AB, T6E 5T8
(780) 437-2022   *SIC 8734*

KASHRUTH COUNCIL OF CANADA   p789
3200 DUFFERIN ST SUITE 308, NORTH YORK, ON, M6A 3B2
(416) 635-9550   *SIC 8734*

LABSTAT INTERNATIONAL INC   p636
262 MANITOU DR, KITCHENER, ON, N2C 1L3
(519) 748-5409   *SIC 8734*

LINEMAN'S TESTING LABORATORIES OF CANADA LIMITED   p586
46 MERIDIAN RD, ETOBICOKE, ON, M9W 4Z7
(416) 742-6911   *SIC 8734*

MISTRAS SERVICES INC   p1138
765 RUE DE SAINT-ROMUALD, LEVIS, QC, G6W 5M6
(418) 837-4664   *SIC 8734*

MISTRAS SERVICES INC   p1359
2161 RUE LEONARD-DE VINCI, SAINTE-JULIE, QC, J3E 1Z3
(450) 922-3515   *SIC 8734*

MORGAN SCHAFFER LTEE   p1131
8300 RUE SAINT-PATRICK BUREAU 150, LASALLE, QC, H8N 2H1
(514) 739-1967   *SIC 8734*

NEOPHARM LABS INC   p1059
865 BOUL MICHELE-BOHEC, BLAINVILLE, QC, J7C 5J6
(450) 435-8864   *SIC 8734*

ONTARIO NUTRI LAB INC   p590
6589 FIRST LINE SUITE 3, FERGUS, ON, N1M 2W4
(519) 843-5669   *SIC 8734*

PAINE, J. R. & ASSOCIATES LTD   p102
17505 106 AVE NW, EDMONTON, AB, T5S 1E7
(780) 489-0700   *SIC 8734*

POWERTECH LABS INC   p277
12388 88 AVE, SURREY, BC, V3W 7R7
(604) 590-7500   *SIC 8734*

PRAIRIE AGRICULTURAL MACHINERY INSTITUTE   p1407
2215 8 AVE, HUMBOLDT, SK, S0K 2A1
(306) 682-2555   *SIC 8734*

QSL QUEBEC INC   p1138
765 RUE DE SAINT-ROMUALD, LEVIS, QC, G6W 5M6
(418) 837-4664   *SIC 8734*

SERVICES EXP INC, LES   p1236
4500 RUE LOUIS-B.-MAYER, MONTREAL, QC, H7P 6E4
(450) 682-8013   *SIC 8734*

SGS AXYS ANALYTICAL SERVICES LTD   p268
2045 MILLS RD W, SIDNEY, BC, V8L 5X2
(250) 655-5800   *SIC 8734*

SGS CANADA INC   p129
235 MACDONALD CRES, FORT MCMURRAY, AB, T9H 4B5
(780) 791-6454   *SIC 8734*

SGS CANADA INC   p643

3347 LAKEFIELD RD RR 3, LAKEFIELD, ON, K0L 2H0
(705) 652-2000   *SIC 8734*

SGS CANADA INC   p700
5825 EXPLORER DR, MISSISSAUGA, ON, L4W 5P6
(905) 364-3757   *SIC 8734*

SGS CANADA INC   p743
6490 VIPOND DR, MISSISSAUGA, ON, L5T 1W8
(905) 364-3757   *SIC 8734*

SGS CANADA INC   p777
1885 LESLIE ST, NORTH YORK, ON, M3B 2M3
(416) 736-2782   *SIC 8734*

SILLIKER CANADA CO   p675
90 GOUGH RD UNIT 4, MARKHAM, ON, L3R 5V5
(905) 479-5255   *SIC 8734*

SILLIKER JR LABORATORIES, ULC   p193
3871 NORTH FRASER WAY UNIT 12, BURNABY, BC, V5J 5G6
(604) 432-9311   *SIC 8734*

SUREPOINT SERVICES INC   p133
11004 96 AVE, GRANDE PRAIRIE, AB, T8V 3J5
(780) 832-0551   *SIC 8734*

TECHNOLOGIES MPB INC, LES   p1252
151 BOUL HYMUS, POINTE-CLAIRE, QC, H9R 1E9
(514) 694-8751   *SIC 8734*

TRIQUEST NONDESTRUCTIVE TESTING CORP   p19
7425 107 AVE SE, CALGARY, AB, T2C 5N6
(403) 263-2216   *SIC 8734*

VETERINARY REFERRAL CLINIC   p931
920 YONGE ST SUITE 117, TORONTO, ON, M4W 3C7
(416) 920-2002   *SIC 8734*

VOLT CANADA INC   p1209
1155 RUE METCALFE BUREAU 2002, MONTREAL, QC, H3B 2V6
(514) 787-3175   *SIC 8734*

WATERS LTEE   p1072
9935 RUE DE CHATEAUNEUF UNITE 330, BROSSARD, QC, J4Z 3V4
(450) 656-0120   *SIC 8734*

SIC 8741 Management services

/N SPRO INC   p1186
465 RUE SAINT-JEAN BUREAU 601, MONTREAL, QC, H2Y 2R6
(514) 907-2505   *SIC 8741*

10647802 CANADA LIMITED   p686
5915 AIRPORT RD SUITE 425, MISSISSAUGA, ON, L4V 1T1
(416) 483-5152   *SIC 8741*

1451805 ONTARIO LTD   p872
2 PRINCIPAL RD UNIT 10, SCARBOROUGH, ON, M1R 4Z3
(416) 497-4363   *SIC 8741*

1576640 ONTARIO LTD   p948
157 ADELAIDE ST W SUITE 207, TORONTO, ON, M5H 4E7
SIC 8741

1700 MANAGEMENT CORPORATION   p376
360 MAIN ST SUITE 1700, WINNIPEG, MB, R3C 3Z3
(204) 956-2970   *SIC 8741*

1719094 ONTARIO INC   p917
953 WOODBINE AVE, TORONTO, ON, M4C 4B6
(416) 698-1384   *SIC 8741*

2020 BUSINESS ADVISORY CORPORATION   p1422
4032 WASCANA RIDGE BAY, REGINA, SK, S4V 2L6
(306) 790-2020   *SIC 8741*

2985420 CANADA INC   p1192
420 RUE SHERBROOKE O, MONTREAL, QC, H3A 1B2
SIC 8741

373813 ONTARIO LIMITED   p968
GD, TORONTO, ON, M5K 1N2
(416) 865-0040   *SIC 8741*

3798143 CANADA INC   p978
155 WELLINGTON ST W SUITE 2901, TORONTO, ON, M5V 3H6
(416) 955-0514   *SIC 8741*

3MC INVESTMENTS LTD   p311
1030 GEORGIA ST W SUITE 1700, VANCOUVER, BC, V6E 2Y3
(604) 602-1887   *SIC 8741*

459324 ONTARIO INC   p850
40 EAST PEARCE ST, RICHMOND HILL, ON, L4B 1B7
(905) 764-9533   *SIC 8741*

582219 ONTARIO INC   p948
214 KING ST W SUITE 508, TORONTO, ON, M5H 3S6
(416) 340-9710   *SIC 8741*

678925 ONTARIO INC   p944
14 COLLEGE ST, TORONTO, ON, M5G 1K2
(416) 962-7500   *SIC 8741*

7093373 CANADA INC   p600
4 FOXWOOD CRES, GUELPH, ON, N1C 1A6
(519) 400-9587   *SIC 8741*

8056323 CANADA INC   p86
10665 JASPER AVE NW SUITE 900, EDMONTON, AB, T5J 3S9
(587) 206-8611   *SIC 8741*

806040 ONTARIO LTD   p782
4496 CHESSWOOD DR, NORTH YORK, ON, M3J 2B9
(416) 665-6400   *SIC 8741*

8262900 CANADA INC   p642
139 WASHBURN DR, KITCHENER, ON, N2R 1S1
(519) 748-5002   *SIC 8741*

834 HUTTERIEN BRETHERN OF WHITELAKE   p150
GD, NOBLEFORD, AB, T0L 1S0
(403) 824-3688   *SIC 8741*

9155-3164 QUEBEC INC   p1108
386 RUE DORCHESTER, GRANBY, QC, J2G 3Z7
(450) 372-5826   *SIC 8741*

9178-8562 QUEBEC INC   p1359
266 AV DU COLLEGE, SAINTE-MARIE, QC, G6E 3Y4
(418) 387-3636   *SIC 8741*

A. FARBER & PARTNERS INC   p769
1220 SHEPPARD AVE E SUITE 300, NORTH YORK, ON, M2K 2S5
(416) 496-1200   *SIC 8741*

ACCENTURE BUSINESS SERVICES FOR UTILITIES INC   p296
510 GEORGIA ST W SUITE 2075, VANCOUVER, BC, V6B 0M3
(604) 646-5000   *SIC 8741*

ACCENTURE BUSINESS SERVICES FOR UTILITIES INC   p903
123 COMMERCE VALLEY DR E SUITE 500, THORNHILL, ON, L3T 7W8
SIC 8741

ACCENTURE INC   p296
401 GEORGIA ST W SUITE 1500, VANCOUVER, BC, V6B 5A1
(604) 646-5000   *SIC 8741*

ACCENTURE INC   p691
5450 EXPLORER DR SUITE 400, MISSISSAUGA, ON, L4W 5N1
(416) 641-5000   *SIC 8741*

ACCENTURE INC   p948
40 KING ST W SUITE 4800, TORONTO, ON, M5H 3Y2
(416) 641-5220   *SIC 8741*

ACCENTURE INC   p1193
1800 AV MCGILL COLLEGE BUREAU 800, MONTREAL, QC, H3A 3J6
(514) 848-1648   *SIC 8741*

ACCLAIM ABILITY MANAGEMENT INC   p978
82 PETER ST, TORONTO, ON, M5V 2G5
(416) 486-9706   *SIC 8741*

ACCORD FINANCIAL LTD p922
40 EGLINTON AVE E SUITE 602, TORONTO, ON, M4P 3A2
(416) 961-0007   SIC 8741

ACTUS MANAGEMENT (VAUGHAN) INC p548
7501 KEELE ST, CONCORD, ON, L4K 1Y2
(905) 760-2700   SIC 8741

ADGA GROUP CONSULTANTS INC p833
110 ARGYLE AVE, OTTAWA, ON, K2P 1B4
(613) 237-3022   SIC 8741

ADVANIS INC p86
10123 99 ST NW SUITE 1600, EDMONTON, AB, T5J 3H1
(780) 944-9212   SIC 8741

AECOM MAINTENANCE SERVICES LTD p33
6025 11 ST SE SUITE 240, CALGARY, AB, T2H 2Z2
(403) 265-9033   SIC 8741

AGROPUR COOPERATIVE p1309
4700 RUE ARMAND-FRAPPIER, SAINT-HUBERT, QC, J3Z 1G5
(450) 443-5662   SIC 8741

AGTA HOME HEALTH CARE AND NURSING INC p785
795 WILSON AVE SUITE 102, NORTH YORK, ON, M3K 1E4
(416) 630-0737   SIC 8741

AHBL MANAGEMENT LIMITED PARTNERSHIP p329
700 GEORGIA ST W SUITE 2700, VANCOUVER, BC, V7Y 1K8
(604) 688-1351   SIC 8741

AIR PARTNERS CORP p20
263 AERO WAY NE, CALGARY, AB, T2E 6K2
(403) 275-3930   SIC 8741

ALCOR FACILITIES MANAGEMENT INC p99
10470 176 ST NW SUITE 206, EDMONTON, AB, T5S 1L3
(780) 483-1213   SIC 8741

ALIGNED CAPITAL PARTNERS INC p520
1001 CHAMPLAIN AVENUE, SUITE 300, BURLINGTON, ON, L7L 5Z4
SIC 8741

ALLIANCE PIPELINE LTD p43
605 5 AVE SW SUITE 800, CALGARY, AB, T2P 3H5
(403) 266-4464   SIC 8741

ALTIMA DENTAL CANADA INC p788
1 YORKDALE RD SUITE 320, NORTH YORK, ON, M6A 3A1
(416) 785-1828   SIC 8741

APPLESHORE RESTAURANTS INC p1017
11865 COUNTY RD 42, WINDSOR, ON, N8N 2M1
(519) 979-7800   SIC 8741

ARI FINANCIAL SERVICES INC p711
1270 CENTRAL PKY W SUITE 500, MISSISSAUGA, ON, L5C 4P4
(905) 803-8000   SIC 8741

ASENTUS CONSULTING GROUP LTD p296
1286 HOMER ST SUITE 200, VANCOUVER, BC, V6B 2Y5
(604) 609-9993   SIC 8741

ASL ENTERPRISES INC p582
155 REXDALE BLVD SUITE 800, ETOBICOKE, ON, M9W 5Z8
(416) 740-6996   SIC 8741

ASSANTE FINANCIAL MANAGEMENT LTD p1010
855 BIRCHMOUNT DR, WATERLOO, ON, N2V 2R7
(519) 886-3257   SIC 8741

ASSEMBLE-RITE, LTD p1018
2755 LAUZON PKY, WINDSOR, ON, N8T 3H5
(519) 945-8464   SIC 8741

AST TRUST COMPANY (CANADA) p936
1 TORONTO ST SUITE 1200, TORONTO, ON, M5C 2V6
(416) 682-3800   SIC 8741

ATIRA PROPERTY MANAGEMENT INC p294

405 POWELL ST, VANCOUVER, BC, V6A 1G7
(604) 439-8848   SIC 8741

ATLIFIC INC p1187
250 RUE SAINT-ANTOINE O BUREAU 400, MONTREAL, QC, H2Y 0A3
(514) 509-5500   SIC 8741

AVISINA PROPERTIES LTD p187
3787 CANADA WAY UNIT 200, BURNABY, BC, V5G 1G5
(604) 419-6000   SIC 8741

AVOGESCO INC p1201
1 PLACE VILLE-MARIE BUREAU 1300, MONTREAL, QC, H3B 0E6
(514) 925-6300   SIC 8741

AWG NORTHERN INDUSTRIES INC p269
3424 16 HWY E RR 6, SMITHERS, BC, V0J 2N6
(250) 847-9211   SIC 8741

BAMBORA INC p334
2659 DOUGLAS ST SUITE 302, VICTORIA, BC, V8T 4M3
(250) 472-2326   SIC 8741

BANQUE NATIONALE DU CANADA p44
450 1 ST SW SUITE 2800, CALGARY, AB, T2P 5H1
(403) 266-1116   SIC 8741

BARRINGTON CONSULTING GROUP INCORPORATED, THE p452
1326 BARRINGTON ST, HALIFAX, NS, B3J 1Z1
(902) 491-4462   SIC 8741

BAST, PAUL & ASSOCIATES p636
625 WABANAKI DR UNIT 4, KITCHENER, ON, N2C 2G3
(519) 893-3500   SIC 8741

BCB CORPORATE SERVICES LTD p241
1000 14TH ST W UNIT 100, NORTH VANCOUVER, BC, V7P 3P3
(778) 340-1060   SIC 8741

BEEDIE CONSTRUCTION CO LTD p188
3030 GILMORE DIVERS, BURNABY, BC, V5G 3B4
(604) 435-3321   SIC 8741

BEST ADVICE FINANCIAL SERVICES INC p766
250 CONSUMERS RD SUITE 1111, NORTH YORK, ON, M2J 4V6
(416) 490-1474   SIC 8741

BGI BENCHMARK GROUP INTERNATIONAL INC p667
207-30 CENTURIAN DR, MARKHAM, ON, L3R 8B8
(905) 305-8900   SIC 8741

BLAKES SERVICES INC p971
199 BAY ST, TORONTO, ON, M5L 1A9
(416) 863-2603   SIC 8741

BOND BRAND LOYALTY INC p744
6900 MARITZ DR, MISSISSAUGA, ON, L5W 1L8
(905) 696-9400   SIC 8741

BOSTON CONSULTING GROUP OF CANADA LIMITED, THE p960
181 BAY ST SUITE 2400, TORONTO, ON, M5J 2T3
(416) 955-4200   SIC 8741

BOUYGUES ENERGIES AND SERVICES CANADA LIMITED p273
9801 KING GEORGE BLVD UNIT 125, SURREY, BC, V3T 5H5
(604) 585-3358   SIC 8741

BRASSARD GOULET YARGEAU SERVICES FINANCIERS INTEGRES INC p1268
686 GRANDE ALLEE E BUREAU 100, QUEBEC, QC, G1R 2K5
(418) 682-5853   SIC 8741

BRETON AGRI-MANAGEMENT INC p1294
1312 RUE SAINT-GEORGES, SAINT-BERNARD, QC, G0S 2G0
(418) 475-6601   SIC 8741

BROCK CANADA MANAGEMENT CORPORATION p113
8925 62 AVE NW, EDMONTON, AB, T6E 5L2

(780) 465-9016   SIC 8741

BROOKFIELD CAPITAL PARTNERS LTD p960
181 BAY ST SUITE 300, TORONTO, ON, M5J 2T3
(416) 363-9491   SIC 8741

BSI GROUP CANADA INC p687
6205B AIRPORT RD SUITE 108, MISSISSAUGA, ON, L4V 1E3
(416) 620-9991   SIC 8741

BT LAW LIMITED PARTNERSHIP p944
393 UNIVERSITY AVE SUITE 1300, TORONTO, ON, M5G 1E6
(416) 581-8200   SIC 8741

BURGUNDY ASSET MANAGEMENT LTD p1194
1501 AV MCGILL COLLEGE BUREAU 2090, MONTREAL, QC, H3A 3M8
(514) 844-8091   SIC 8741

BUTTE COLONY p1404
GD, BRACKEN, SK, S0N 0G0
(306) 298-4445   SIC 8741

C MAR SERVICES (CANADA) LTD p434
20 BEAR COVE RD, WITLESS BAY, NL, A0A 4K0
(709) 334-2033   SIC 8741

C. WALKER GROUP INC p341
1455 BELLEVUE AVE SUITE 300, WEST VANCOUVER, BC, V7T 1C3
(604) 922-6563   SIC 8741

CACEIS (CANADA) LIMITED p705
1 ROBERT SPECK PKY SUITE 1510, MISSISSAUGA, ON, L4Z 3M3
(905) 281-4145   SIC 8741

CAISSE DESJARDINS DU NORD DE LANAUDIERE p1114
275 RUE BEAUDRY N, JOLIETTE, QC, J6E 6A7
(450) 756-0999   SIC 8741

CAISSE DESJARDINS DU SUD DE LA CHAUDIERE p1304
1275 BOUL DIONNE, SAINT-GEORGES, QC, G5Y 0R4
(418) 227-7000   SIC 8741

CALCON MANAGEMENT, L.P. p27
700 CENTRE ST SE, CALGARY, AB, T2G 5P6
(403) 537-4426   SIC 8741

CALLIDUS CAPITAL CORPORATION p960
181 BAY ST UNIT 4620, TORONTO, ON, M5J 2T3
(416) 945-3016   SIC 8741

CANA PROJECT MANAGEMENT LTD p34
5720 4 ST SE UNIT 100, CALGARY, AB, T2H 1K7
(403) 255-5521   SIC 8741

CANA SERVICES LTD p34
5720 4 ST SE SUITE 100, CALGARY, AB, T2H 1K7
(403) 255-5521   SIC 8741

CANADIAN PAYMENTS ASSOCIATION p824
350 ALBERT ST UNIT 800, OTTAWA, ON, K1R 1A4
(613) 238-4173   SIC 8741

CANADIAN TEST CASE 20 p720
6750 CENTURY AVE SUITE 305, MISSISSAUGA, ON, L5N 0B7
(905) 812-5920   SIC 8741

CANADIENNE DE CROISSANCE p1168
3795 RUE MASSON BUREAU 108, MONTREAL, QC, H1X 1S7
SIC 8741

CANASSISTANCE INC p1194
550 RUE SHERBROOKE O, MONTREAL, QC, H3A 3S3
(800) 264-1852   SIC 8741

CANFIN CAPITAL GROUP INC p800
2829 SHERWOOD HEIGHTS DR SUITE 102, OAKVILLE, ON, L6J 7R7
(905) 829-0020   SIC 8741

CANTRAV SERVICES INC p291
22 2ND AVE W, VANCOUVER, BC, V5Y 1B3
(604) 708-2500   SIC 8741

CARDTRONICS CANADA OPERATIONS

INC p10
1420 28 ST NE SUITE 6, CALGARY, AB, T2A 7W6
(403) 207-1500   SIC 8741

CARIBOO FOREST CONSULTANTS LTD p252
335 VAUGHAN ST, QUESNEL, BC, V2J 2T1
SIC 8741

CARILLION CANADA INC p828
1145 CARLING AVE SUITE 1317, OTTAWA, ON, K1Z 7K4
(613) 722-6521   SIC 8741

CARILLION CONSTRUCTION INC p550
7077 KEELE ST, CONCORD, ON, L4K 0B6
(905) 532-5200   SIC 8741

CARLISLE GROUP p8
2891 SUNRIDGE WAY NE UNIT 230, CALGARY, AB, T1Y 7K7
(403) 571-8400   SIC 8741

CARLSUN ENERGY SOLUTIONS INC p847
1606 BRUCE-SAUGEEN TLINE, PORT ELGIN, ON, N0H 2C5
(519) 832-4075   SIC 8741

CARTHOS SERVICES LP p986
1 1ST CANADIAN PL, TORONTO, ON, M5X 1B8
(416) 362-2111   SIC 8741

CBI LIMITED p492
11 BAY BRIDGE RD, BELLEVILLE, ON, K8P 3P6
(613) 962-3426   SIC 8741

CBI LIMITED p608
45 GODERICH RD, HAMILTON, ON, L8E 4W8
(905) 777-1255   SIC 8741

CENTRE DE SOINS DE LONGUE DUREE MONTFORT p820
705 MONTREAL RD, OTTAWA, ON, K1K 0M9
(613) 746-8602   SIC 8741

CENTRE FINANCIER AUX ENTREPRISES - QUEBEC-CAPITALE p1254
3333 RUE DU CARREFOUR BUREAU 280, QUEBEC, QC, G1C 5R9
(418) 660-2229   SIC 8741

CENTRE FINANCIER AUX ENTREPRISES DESJARDINS LEVIS LOTBINIERE p1135
1610 BOUL ALPHONSE-DESJARDINS BUREAU 600, LEVIS, QC, G6V 0H1
(418) 834-4343   SIC 8741

CENTRE FINANCIER AUX ENTREPRISES DESJARDINS TROIS-RIVIERES p1386
2000 BOUL DES RECOLLETS, TROIS-RIVIERES, QC, G8Z 3X4
(819) 376-4000   SIC 8741

CHARLOTTE COUNTY HUMANE RESOURCES INC p418
15 MARKS ST, ST STEPHEN, NB, E3L 2A9
(506) 466-5081   SIC 8741

CHESSWOOD GROUP LIMITED p776
156 DUNCAN MILL RD SUITE 15, NORTH YORK, ON, M3B 3N2
(416) 386-3099   SIC 8741

CIM-CONSEIL EN IMMOBILISATION ET MANAGEMENT INC p1191
440 BOUL RENE-LEVESQUE O BUREAU 1700, MONTREAL, QC, H2Z 1V7
(514) 393-4563   SIC 8741

CIMA CANADA INC p1343
3400 BOUL DU SOUVENIR SUITE 600, SAINT-LAURENT, QC, H7V 3Z2
(514) 337-2462   SIC 8741

CITCO (CANADA) INC p452
5151 GEORGE ST SUITE 700, HALIFAX, NS, B3J 1M5
(902) 442-4242   SIC 8741

CLEARSTREAM ENERGY SERVICES INC p46
311 6 AVE SW SUITE 415, CALGARY, AB, T2P 3H2
(587) 318-0997   SIC 8741

CMS CREATIVE MANAGEMENT SERVICES LIMITED p377
330 ST MARY AVE SUITE 750, WINNIPEG,

MB, R3C 3Z5

(204) 944-0789   *SIC* 8741

COFACE SERVICES CANADA COMPANY
p766

251 CONSUMERS RD SUITE 910, NORTH YORK, ON, M2J 4R3

(647) 426-4730   *SIC* 8741

COGNERA   *p46*

530 8 AVE SW SUITE 920, CALGARY, AB, T2P 3S8

(403) 218-2010   *SIC* 8741

COLLIERS PROJECT LEADERS INC *p831*

2720 IRIS ST, OTTAWA, ON, K2C 1E6

(613) 820-6610   *SIC* 8741

CONFIDENCE MANAGEMENT LTD   *p388*

275 COMMERCE DR, WINNIPEG, MB, R3P 1B3

(204) 487-2500   *SIC* 8741

CONSEILLERS EN GESTION ET INFORMATIQUE CGI INC
p935

250 YONGE ST SUITE 2000, TORONTO, ON, M5B 2L7

(416) 363-7827   *SIC* 8741

CONSULTATION EN TECHNOLOGIE DE L'INFORMATION ET DES COMUNICATIONS DACSYS INC   *p1145*

612 RUE DU CAPRICORNE, LONGUEUIL, QC, J4L 4X2

(514) 260-1616   *SIC* 8741

CONTAX INC   *p928*

893 YONGE ST, TORONTO, ON, M4W 2H2

(416) 927-1913   *SIC* 8741

CORPA HOLDINGS INC   *p521*

2000 APPLEBY LINE SUITE G3, BURLINGTON, ON, L7L 7H7

(905) 331-1333   *SIC* 8741

CORPORATION MAGIL CONSTRUCTION
p1225

1655 RUE DE BEAUHARNOIS O BUREAU 16, MONTREAL, QC, H4N 1J6

(514) 341-9899   *SIC* 8741

CORPORATION OF THE COUNTY OF LAMBTON   *p1037*

789 BROADWAY ST, WYOMING, ON, N0N 1T0

(519) 845-0801   *SIC* 8741

CORPORATION OF THE REGIONAL MUNICIPALITY OF DURHAM, THE   *p811*

600 OSHAWA BLVD N SUITE 208, OSHAWA, ON, L1G 5T9

(905) 579-3313   *SIC* 8741

COWATERSOGEMA INTERNATIONAL INC
p822

275 SLATER ST SUITE 1600, OTTAWA, ON, K1P 5H9

(613) 722-6434   *SIC* 8741

CREDENTIAL FINANCIAL INC   *p312*

1111 GEORGIA ST W SUITE 800, VANCOUVER, BC, V6E 4T6

(604) 714-3800   *SIC* 8741

CROWN CAPITAL PARTNERS INC   *p47*

888 3 ST SW FL 10, CALGARY, AB, T2P 5C5

(403) 775-2554   *SIC* 8741

CUSTOMPLAN FINANCIAL ADVISORS INC
p318

1500 GEORGIA ST W SUITE 1900, VANCOUVER, BC, V6G 2Z6

(604) 687-7773   *SIC* 8741

DAVIS MANAGEMENT LTD   *p303*

666 BURRARD ST SUITE 2800, VANCOUVER, BC, V6C 2Z7

(604) 687-9444   *SIC* 8741

DEFENCE CONSTRUCTION (1951) LIMITED
p824

350 ALBERT ST SUITE 1900, OTTAWA, ON, K1R 1A4

(613) 998-9548   *SIC* 8741

DELOITTE & TOUCHE MANAGEMENT CONSULTANTS   *p452*

1969 UPPER WATER ST SUITE 1500, HALIFAX, NS, B3J 3R7

(902) 422-8541   *SIC* 8741

DELOITTE & TOUCHE MANAGEMENT

CONSULTANTS   *p962*

181 BAY ST SUITE 1400, TORONTO, ON, M5J 2V1

(416) 601-6150   *SIC* 8741

DELOITTE LLP   *p823*

100 QUEEN ST SUITE 800, OTTAWA, ON, K1P 5T8

(613) 236-2442   *SIC* 8741

DELTA HOTELS LIMITED   *p22*

2001 AIRPORT RD NE, CALGARY, AB, T2E 6Z8

(403) 291-2600   *SIC* 8741

DELTA HOTELS LIMITED   *p29*

209 4 AVE SE, CALGARY, AB, T2G 0C6

(403) 266-1980   *SIC* 8741

DELTA HOTELS LIMITED   *p88*

10222 102 ST NW, EDMONTON, AB, T5J 4C5

(780) 429-3900   *SIC* 8741

DELTA HOTELS LIMITED   *p264*

3500 CESSNA DR, RICHMOND, BC, V7B 1C7

(604) 278-1241   *SIC* 8741

DELTA HOTELS LIMITED   *p400*

1133 REGENT ST, FREDERICTON, NB, E3B 3Z2

SIC 8741

DELTA HOTELS LIMITED   *p415*

39 KING ST, SAINT JOHN, NB, E2L 4W3

(506) 648-1981   *SIC* 8741

DELTA HOTELS LIMITED   *p467*

300 ESPLANADE ST, SYDNEY, NS, B1P 1A7

(902) 562-7500   *SIC* 8741

DELTA HOTELS LIMITED   *p620*

939 60 HWY, HUNTSVILLE, ON, P1H 1B2

(705) 789-4417   *SIC* 8741

DELTA HOTELS LIMITED   *p638*

105 KING ST E, KITCHENER, ON, N2G 2K8

(519) 569-4588   *SIC* 8741

DELTA HOTELS LIMITED   *p655*

325 DUNDAS ST, LONDON, ON, N6B 1T9

(519) 679-6111   *SIC* 8741

DELTA HOTELS LIMITED   *p694*

5444 DIXIE RD SUITE 47, MISSISSAUGA, ON, L4W 2L2

(905) 624-1144   *SIC* 8741

DELTA HOTELS LIMITED   *p721*

6750 MISSISSAUGA RD, MISSISSAUGA, ON, L5N 2L3

(905) 821-1981   *SIC* 8741

DELTA HOTELS LIMITED   *p824*

361 QUEEN ST, OTTAWA, ON, K1R 0C7

SIC 8741

DELTA HOTELS LIMITED   *p969*

77 KING ST W SUITE 2300, TORONTO, ON, M5K 2A1

SIC 8741

DELTA HOTELS LIMITED   *p1039*

18 QUEEN ST, CHARLOTTETOWN, PE, C1A 4A1

(902) 566-2222   *SIC* 8741

DELTA HOTELS LIMITED   *p1373*

2685 RUE KING O, SHERBROOKE, QC, J1L 1C1

(819) 822-1989   *SIC* 8741

DELTA HOTELS LIMITED   *p1417*

1919 SASKATCHEWAN DR SUITE 100, REGINA, SK, S4P 4H2

(306) 525-5255   *SIC* 8741

DESJARDINS GESTION INTERNATIONALE D'ACTIFS INC   *p1230*

1 COMPLEXE DESJARDINS, MONTREAL, QC, H5B 1B3

(514) 281-2859   *SIC* 8741

DEVELOPEMENT CYREX INC   *p1073*

455 CH PRINCIPAL, CAP-AUX-MEULES, QC, G4T 1E4

(418) 986-2871   *SIC* 8741

DEVELOPPEMENT INTERNATIONAL DESJARDINS INC   *p1136*

150 RUE DES COMMANDEURS, LEVIS, QC, G6V 6P8

(418) 835-2400   *SIC* 8741

DEVELOPPEMENT PIEKUAKAMI ILNU-ATSH   *p1150*

1425 RUE OUIATCHOUAN, MASH-TEUIATSH, QC, G0W 2H0

(418) 275-8181   *SIC* 8741

DEVIMCO INC   *p1070*

6000 BOUL DE ROME BUREAU 410, BROSSARD, QC, J4Y 0B6

(450) 645-2525   *SIC* 8741

DIAGNOSTIC SERVICES OF MANITOBA INC   *p377*

155 CARLTON ST SUITE 1502, WINNIPEG, MB, R3C 3H8

(204) 926-8005   *SIC* 8741

DIGBY TOWN AND MUNICIPAL HOUSING CORPORATION, THE   *p449*

74 PLEASANT ST, DIGBY, NS, B0V 1A0

(902) 245-4718   *SIC* 8741

DOME PRODUCTIONS INC   *p980*

1 BLUE JAYS WAY SUITE 3400, TORONTO, ON, M5V 1J3

(416) 341-2001   *SIC* 8741

DRAKKAR & ASSOCIES INC   *p1222*

780 AV BREWSTER BUREAU 200, MONTREAL, QC, H4C 2K1

(514) 733-6655   *SIC* 8741

DUCARTOR HOLDINGS LTD   *p950*

130 ADELAIDE ST W SUITE 701, TORONTO, ON, M5H 2K4

(416) 593-5555   *SIC* 8741

DURWEST HOLDINGS LTD   *p337*

4400 CHATTERTON WAY SUITE 301, VICTORIA, BC, V8X 5J2

(250) 881-7878   *SIC* 8741

DYNAVENTURE CORP   *p1431*

2100 AIRPORT DR SUITE 202, SASKATOON, SK, S7L 6M6

SIC 8741

EARL'S RESTAURANTS CARRELL LTD
p298

425 CARRALL ST UNIT 200, VANCOUVER, BC, V6B 6E3

(604) 646-4880   *SIC* 8741

EDON PROPERTIES INC   *p29*

1441 HASTINGS CRES SE, CALGARY, AB, T2G 4C8

(403) 245-1941   *SIC* 8741

ELITE CONSTRUCTION INC   *p552*

35 ROMINA DR SUITE 100, CONCORD, ON, L4K 4Z9

(905) 660-1663   *SIC* 8741

ENBRIDGE COMMERCIAL SERVICES INC
p767

500 CONSUMERS RD, NORTH YORK, ON, M2J 1P8

(416) 492-5000   *SIC* 8741

ENERPLUS GLOBAL ENERGY MANAGEMENT CO   *p48*

333 7 AVE SW SUITE 3000, CALGARY, AB, T2P 2Z1

(403) 298-2200   *SIC* 8741

EXCHANGE SOLUTIONS INC   *p938*

36 TORONTO ST SUITE 1200, TORONTO, ON, M5C 2C5

(416) 646-7000   *SIC* 8741

EXIT CERTIFIED CORPORATION   *p823*

220 LAURIER AVE W SUITE 1000, OTTAWA, ON, K1P 5Z9

(613) 232-3948   *SIC* 8741

FAIRMONT VILLA MANAGEMENT   *p212*

5247 FAIRMONT CREEK RD RR 1, FAIRMONT HOT SPRINGS, BC, V0B 1L1

(250) 345-6341   *SIC* 8741

FARM BUSINESS CONSULTANTS LTD *p11*

3015 5 AVE NE SUITE 150, CALGARY, AB, T2A 6T8

(403) 735-6105   *SIC* 8741

FEDERAL LIBERAL AGENCY OF CANADA, THE   *p823*

350 ALBERT ST SUITE 920, OTTAWA, ON, K1P 6M8

(613) 237-0740   *SIC* 8741

FINANCES & INDEMNISATIONS INC *p1277*

540 RUE MICHEL-FRAGASSO, QUEBEC,

QC, G2E 5N4

(418) 861-9506   *SIC* 8741

FIRST CAPITAL REALTY CORP   *p819*

1980 OGILVIE RD SUITE 149, OTTAWA, ON, K1J 9L3

SIC 8741

FIRST GULF GROUP INC   *p722*

6860 CENTURY AVE SUITE 1000, MISSISSAUGA, ON, L5N 2W5

(905) 812-8030   *SIC* 8741

FLEXTRACK INC   *p924*

2200 YONGE ST SUITE 801, TORONTO, ON, M4S 2C6

(416) 545-5288   *SIC* 8741

FORREST GREEN CONSULTING CORPORATION   *p855*

10520 YONGE ST UNIT 35B, RICHMOND HILL, ON, L4C 3C7

(905) 884-3103   *SIC* 8741

FOSSIL EPC LTD   *p148*

1805 8 ST, NISKU, AB, T9E 7S8

(780) 449-0773   *SIC* 8741

FRANMED CONSULTANTS (1993) INC *p951*

150 YORK ST SUITE 1500, TORONTO, ON, M5H 3S5

(416) 350-7700   *SIC* 8741

FUJITSU CONSEIL (CANADA) INC   *p823*

55 METCALFE ST SUITE 530, OTTAWA, ON, K1P 6L5

(613) 238-2697   *SIC* 8741

FUNDSERV INC   *p997*

130 KING ST UNIT 1700, TORONTO, ON, M9N 1L5

(416) 362-2400   *SIC* 8741

FUSEPOINT INC   *p722*

6800 MILLCREEK DR, MISSISSAUGA, ON, L5N 4J9

(905) 363-3737   *SIC* 8741

G-WLG LP   *p834*

160 ELGIN ST SUITE 2600, OTTAWA, ON, K2P 3C3

(613) 233-1781   *SIC* 8741

GATEWAY PROPERTY MANAGEMENT CORPORATION   *p207*

11950 80 AVE SUITE 400, DELTA, BC, V4C 1Y2

(604) 635-5000   *SIC* 8741

GERICO FOREST PRODUCTS LTD   *p218*

666 ATHABASCA ST W, KAMLOOPS, BC, V2H 1C4

(250) 374-0333   *SIC* 8741

GESTION G.S.F. INC   *p1283*

581 RUE NOTRE-DAME BUREAU 302, REPENTIGNY, QC, J6A 2V1

(450) 654-5226   *SIC* 8741

GESTION GEORGES SZARAZ INC. *p1301*

311 RUE BOILEAU, SAINT-EUSTACHE, QC, J7R 2V5

SIC 8741

GESTION LJT INC   *p1188*

380 RUE SAINT-ANTOINE O BUREAU 7100, MONTREAL, QC, H2Y 3X7

(514) 842-8891   *SIC* 8741

GESTION MAJERO INC   *p1339*

8180 COTE-DE-LIESSE ROAD, SAINT-LAURENT, QC, H4T 1G8

SIC 8741

GESTION MD MANAGEMENT   *p1204*

1000 RUE DE LA GAUCHETIERE O BUREAU 650, MONTREAL, QC, H3B 4W5

(514) 392-1434   *SIC* 8741

GESTION ORION LTEE   *p1229*

800 RUE DU SQUARE-VICTORIA BUREAU 3700, MONTREAL, QC, H4Z 1A1

(514) 871-9167   *SIC* 8741

GESTION PLACE VICTORIA INC   *p1229*

800 RUE DU SQUARE-VICTORIA BUREAU 4120, MONTREAL, QC, H4Z 1A1

(514) 875-6010   *SIC* 8741

GESTION RAPID INC.   *p1149*

321 MONTEE MASSON BUREAU 301, MASCOUCHE, QC, J7K 2L6

SIC 8741

GESTION THERRIEN COUTURE INC *p1312*

1200 RUE DANIEL-JOHNSON O UNITE 7000, SAINT-HYACINTHE, QC, J2S 7K7
(450) 773-6326   *SIC* 8741

GESTIONS G H P (1986) INC, LES   *p1304*
521 6E AV N, SAINT-GEORGES, QC, G5Y 0H1
(418) 228-6688   *SIC* 8741

GIBSON HOLDINGS (ONTARIO) LTD   *p477*
343 AMHERST DR SUITE 133, AMHERSTVIEW, ON, K7N 1X3
(613) 384-4585   *SIC* 8741

GIBSON, R. W. CONSULTING SERVICES LTD   *p96*
14713 116 AVE NW, EDMONTON, AB, T5M 3E8
(780) 452-8800   *SIC* 8741

GIFFELS CORPORATION   *p584*
2 INTERNATIONAL BLVD, ETOBICOKE, ON, M9W 1A2
(416) 798-5500   *SIC* 8741

GILLIS, JOHN M MEMORIAL LODGE *p1038*
3134 GARFIELD RD, BELFAST, PE, C0A 1A0
(902) 659-2337   *SIC* 8741

GILMORE GLOBAL LOGISTICS SERVICES INC   *p624*
120 HERZBERG RD, KANATA, ON, K2K 3B7
(613) 599-6065   *SIC* 8741

GLOBAL KNOWLEDGE NETWORK (CANADA) INC   *p928*
2 BLOOR ST E UNIT 3100, TORONTO, ON, M4W 1A8
(613) 254-6530   *SIC* 8741

GLOBAL MINING MANAGEMENT CORPORATION   *p304*
999 CANADA PL SUITE 654, VANCOUVER, BC, V6C 3E1
(604) 689-8765   *SIC* 8741

GOUVERNEMENT DE LA PROVINCE DE QUEBEC   *p1229*
800 SQ VICTORIA 22E ETAGE, MONTREAL, QC, H4Z 1G3
(514) 395-0337   *SIC* 8741

GOVAN BROWN & ASSOCIATES LIMITED *p994*
108 VINE AVE, TORONTO, ON, M6P 1V7
(416) 703-5100   *SIC* 8741

GOVERNMENT OF THE PROVINCE OF ALBERTA   *p165*
5025 49 AVE, ST PAUL, AB, T0A 3A4
(780) 645-6210   *SIC* 8741

GROUPE ALERTE SANTE INC   *p1143*
440 BOUL SAINTE-FOY, LONGUEUIL, QC, J4J 5G5
(450) 670-0911   *SIC* 8741

GROUPE CONSEIL PARISELLA VINCELLI, ASSOCIES INC   *p1060*
20865 CH DE LA COTE N UNITE 200, BOISBRIAND, QC, J7E 4H5
(450) 970-1970   *SIC* 8741

GROUPE EDGENDA INC   *p1262*
1751 RUE DU MARAIS BUREAU 300, QUEBEC, QC, G1M 0A2
(418) 626-2344   *SIC* 8741

GROUPE HELIOS, GESTION D'INFRASTRUCTURES ET DE SERVICES URBAINS INC   *p1141*
2099 BOUL FERNAND-LAFONTAINE, LONGUEUIL, QC, J4G 2J4
(450) 646-1903   *SIC* 8741

GROUPE LE MASSIF INC   *p1272*
2505 BOUL LAURIER BUREAU 200, QUEBEC, QC, G1V 2L2
(418) 948-1725   *SIC* 8741

GROUPE WSP GLOBAL INC   *p1215*
1600 BOUL RENE-LEVESQUE O BUREAU 16, MONTREAL, QC, H3H 1P9
(514) 340-0046   *SIC* 8741

GROWTHWORKS CAPITAL LTD   *p986*
130 KING ST W SUITE 2200, TORONTO, ON, M5X 2A2
SIC 8741

HALDIMAND-NORFOLK COMMUNITY

CARE ACCESS CENTRE   *p880*
76 VICTORIA ST, SIMCOE, ON, N3Y 1L5
(519) 426-7400   *SIC* 8741

HALIFAX DEVELOPMENTS   *p453*
2000 BARRINGTON ST SUITE 1210, HALIFAX, NS, B3J 3K1
(902) 429-3660   *SIC* 8741

HAMPTON FINANCIAL CORPORATION *p952*
141 ADELAIDE ST W SUITE 1800, TORONTO, ON, M5H 3L5
(416) 862-7800   *SIC* 8741

HANSCOMB LIMITED   *p924*
40 HOLLY ST SUITE 900, TORONTO, ON, M4S 3C3
(416) 487-3811   *SIC* 8741

HAY GROUP LIMITED   *p952*
121 KING ST W SUITE 700, TORONTO, ON, M5H 3T9
(416) 868-1371   *SIC* 8741

HITACHI CAPITAL CANADA CORP   *p528*
3390 SOUTH SERVICE RD SUITE 301, BURLINGTON, ON, L7N 3J5
(866) 241-9021   *SIC* 8741

HOMELAND HOUSING   *p147*
9922 103 ST, MORINVILLE, AB, T8R 1R7
(780) 939-5116   *SIC* 8741

IDEACA LIMITED   *p774*
36 YORK MILLS RD, NORTH YORK, ON, M2P 2E9
(416) 961-4332   *SIC* 8741

IHS ENERGY (CANADA) LTD   *p30*
1331 MACLEOD TRAIL SE SUITE 200, CALGARY, AB, T2G 0K3
(403) 532-8175   *SIC* 8741

INA GRAFTON GAGE HOME OF TORONTO *p868*
40 BELL ESTATE RD SUITE 402, SCARBOROUGH, ON, M1L 0E2
(416) 422-4890   *SIC* 8741

INDUSTRIES KINGSTON LTEE, LES *p1132*
9100 RUE ELMSLIE, LASALLE, QC, H8R 1V6
(514) 365-1642   *SIC* 8741

INNOMAR STRATEGIES INC   *p804*
3470 SUPERIOR CRT SUITE 2, OAKVILLE, ON, L6L 0C4
(905) 847-4310   *SIC* 8741

INSIGHTU.COM INC   *p755*
350 HARRY WALKER PKY N SUITE 14, NEWMARKET, ON, L3Y 8L3
(905) 883-9620   *SIC* 8741

INTEGRATED ASSET MANAGEMENT CORP   *p963*
70 UNIVERSITY AVE SUITE 1200, TORONTO, ON, M5J 2M4
(416) 360-7667   *SIC* 8741

INUVIALUIT DEVELOPMENT CORPORATION   *p435*
107 MACKENZIE RD 3RD FL, INUVIK, NT, X0E 0T0
(867) 777-7000   *SIC* 8741

INVENTIV CANADA ULC   *p779*
895 DON MILLS RD SUITE 700, NORTH YORK, ON, M3C 1W3
(416) 391-5166   *SIC* 8741

INVESTMENT PLANNING COUNSEL INC *p696*
5015 SPECTRUM WAY SUITE 200, MISSISSAUGA, ON, L4W 0E4
(905) 212-9799   *SIC* 8741

INVESTMENT PLANNING COUNSEL OF CANADA LIMITED   *p696*
2680 SKYMARK AVE SUITE 700, MISSISSAUGA, ON, L4W 5L6
SIC 8741

INVESTORS GROUP FINANCIAL SERVICES INC   *p89*
10060 JASPER AVE NW SUITE 2400, EDMONTON, AB, T5J 3R8
(780) 448-1988   *SIC* 8741

INVESTORS GROUP FINANCIAL SERVICES INC   *p378*
447 PORTAGE AVE, WINNIPEG, MB, R3C

3B6
(204) 943-0361   *SIC* 8741

INVESTORS GROUP FINANCIAL SERVICES INC   *p386*
1661 PORTAGE AVE SUITE 702, WINNIPEG, MB, R3J 3T7
(204) 786-2708   *SIC* 8741

INVESTORS GROUP FINANCIAL SERVICES INC   *p509*
208 COUNTY COURT BLVD, BRAMPTON, ON, L6W 4S9
(905) 450-1500   *SIC* 8741

INVESTORS GROUP FINANCIAL SERVICES INC   *p767*
200 YORKLAND BLVD SUITE 300, NORTH YORK, ON, M2J 5C1
(416) 491-7400   *SIC* 8741

INVESTORS GROUP FINANCIAL SERVICES INC   *p1014*
1614 DUNDAS ST E UNIT 111, WHITBY, ON, L1N 8Y8
(905) 434-8400   *SIC* 8741

INVESTORS GROUP FINANCIAL SERVICES INC   *p1251*
6500 RTE TRANSCANADIENNE UNITE 600, POINTE-CLAIRE, QC, H9R 0A5
(514) 426-0886   *SIC* 8741

IPEX GESTION INC   *p1396*
3 PLACE DU COMMERCE BUREAU 101, VERDUN, QC, H3E 1H7
(514) 769-2200   *SIC* 8741

JCS NURSING & HOME CARE SERVICES INC   *p869*
3464 KINGSTON RD SUITE 207A, SCARBOROUGH, ON, M1M 1R5
(416) 265-1687   *SIC* 8741

JDS ENERGY & MINING INC   *p219*
3200 RICHTER ST UNIT 206, KELOWNA, BC, V1W 5K9
(250) 763-6369   *SIC* 8741

JMC MARKETING COMMUNICATIONS CORPORATION   *p779*
789 DON MILLS RD, NORTH YORK, ON, M3C 1T5
(416) 424-6644   *SIC* 8741

KBR CANADA LTD   *p149*
1302 10 S, NISKU, AB, T9E 8K2
(780) 468-1341   *SIC* 8741

KEATING TECHNOLOGIES INC   *p671*
25 ROYAL CREST CRT SUITE 120, MARKHAM, ON, L3R 9X4
(905) 479-0230   *SIC* 8741

KEYBASE FINANCIAL GROUP INC   *p852*
1725 16TH AVE SUITE 101, RICHMOND HILL, ON, L4B 0B3
(905) 709-7911   *SIC* 8741

KHOWUTZUN DEVELOPMENT CORP *p212*
200 COWICHAN WAY, DUNCAN, BC, V9L 6P4
SIC 8741

KINDRED CONSTRUCTION LTD   *p322*
2150 BROADWAY W UNIT 308, VANCOUVER, BC, V6K 4L9
(604) 736-4847   *SIC* 8741

KPMG INC   *p837*
84 JAMES ST, PARRY SOUND, ON, P2A 1T9
(705) 746-9346   *SIC* 8741

KPMG INC   *p953*
333 BAY ST SUITE 4600, TORONTO, ON, M5H 2S5
(416) 777-8500   *SIC* 8741

LEISUREWORLD SENIOR CARE LP *p672*
302 TOWN CENTRE BLVD SUITE 200, MARKHAM, ON, L3R 0E8
(905) 477-4006   *SIC* 8741

LM SERVICES LIMITED PARTNERSHIP *p964*
181 BAY ST SUITE 2500, TORONTO, ON, M5J 2T3
SIC 8741

LODGING OVATIONS CORP   *p299*
375 WATER ST SUITE 326, VANCOUVER, BC, V6B 5C6

(604) 938-9999   *SIC* 8741

LOGIHEDRON INC   *p798*
2320 BRISTOL CIR UNIT 1, OAKVILLE, ON, L6H 5S3
(905) 823-5767   *SIC* 8741

LOSS PREVENTION SERVICES LIMITED *p791*
2221 KEELE ST SUITE 308, NORTH YORK, ON, M6M 3Z5
(416) 248-1261   *SIC* 8741

LUXURY RETREATS INTERNATIONAL ULC *p1224*
5530 RUE SAINT-PATRICK BUREAU 2210, MONTREAL, QC, H4E 1A8
(514) 400-5109   *SIC* 8741

MACDONALD MAINTENANCE INC   *p1335*
6037 CH SAINT-FRANCOIS, SAINT-LAURENT, QC, H4S 1B6
(514) 637-6453   *SIC* 8741

MANITOBA HYDRO INTERNATIONAL LTD *p389*
211 COMMERCE DR, WINNIPEG, MB, R3P 1A3
(204) 480-5200   *SIC* 8741

MANOIR DE LA ROSELIERE   *p1243*
3055 1E AV BUREAU 259, NOTRE-DAME-DES-PINS, QC, G0M 1K0
(418) 774-6700   *SIC* 8741

MANTRALOGIX INC   *p706*
267 MATHESON BLVD E SUITE 5, MISSISAUGA, ON, L4Z 1X8
(905) 629-3200   *SIC* 8741

MAPLE LEAF INTERNATIONAL CONSULTING INC   *p925*
27 ST CLAIR AVE E SUITE 1145, TORONTO, ON, M4T 1L8
(416) 724-6475   *SIC* 8741

MARQUE CONSTRUCTION LIMITED   *p414*
400 CHESLEY DR, SAINT JOHN, NB, E2K 5L6
(506) 634-1144   *SIC* 8741

MATTAMY (MONARCH) LIMITED   *p767*
2550 VICTORIA PARK AVE SUITE 200, NORTH YORK, ON, M2J 5A9
(416) 491-7440   *SIC* 8741

MCBRIDE CAREER GROUP INC   *p92*
10045 111 ST NW SUITE 910, EDMONTON, AB, T5K 2M5
(780) 448-1380   *SIC* 8741

MCDANIEL GROUP HOLDING CORPORATION, THE   *p53*
255 5 AVE SW SUITE 2200, CALGARY, AB, T2P 3G6
(403) 262-5506   *SIC* 8741

MCPORT CITY FOOD SERVICES LIMITED *p414*
399 MAIN ST, SAINT JOHN, NB, E2K 1J3
(506) 657-4381   *SIC* 8741

MD FINANCIAL MANAGEMENT INC   *p818*
1870 ALTA VISTA DR SUITE 1, OTTAWA, ON, K1G 6R7
(613) 731-4552   *SIC* 8741

MD MANAGEMENT LIMITED   *p818*
1870 ALTA VISTA DR, OTTAWA, ON, K1G 6R7
(613) 731-4552   *SIC* 8741

MEANEY, B. CONSULTING LTD   *p101*
21110 108 AVE NW, EDMONTON, AB, T5S 1X4
SIC 8741

MEDIA PROFILE INC   *p982*
579 RICHMOND ST W SUITE 500, TORONTO, ON, M5V 1Y6
(416) 504-8464   *SIC* 8741

MELLOY MANAGEMENT LIMITED   *p970*
77 KING ST W SUITE 3000, TORONTO, ON, M5K 1G8
(416) 864-9700   *SIC* 8741

MERCEDES-BENZ FINANCIAL SERVICES CANADA CORPORATION   *p697*
2680 MATHESON BLVD E SUITE 500, MISSISSAUGA, ON, L4W 0A5
(800) 532-7362   *SIC* 8741

MERITAS CARE CORPORATION   *p1023*

567 VICTORIA AVE, WINDSOR, ON, N9A
4N1
(519) 254-1141   *SIC* 8741

MIDLAND GARDENS INC   *p*870
130 MIDLAND AVE SUITE 1006, SCAR-
BOROUGH, ON, M1N 4E6
(416) 264-2301   *SIC* 8741

MILLENNIUM PROCESS GROUP, INC *p*586
251 ATTWELL DR, ETOBICOKE, ON, M9W
7G2
(416) 503-1800   *SIC* 8741

MIMERI INVESTMENTS LTD   *p*925
1220 YONGE ST, TORONTO, ON, M4T 1W1
(416) 961-3700   *SIC* 8741

MINES OPINACA LTEE, LES   *p*1290
853 BOUL RIDEAU BUREAU 764, ROUYN-
NORANDA, QC, J9Y 0G3
(819) 764-6400   *SIC* 8741

MLG BLOCKCHAIN CONSULTING LTD*p*954
214 KING ST W SUITE 210, TORONTO,
ON, M5H 3S6
(647) 377-3489   *SIC* 8741

MLT MANAGEMENT INC   *p*1418
1874 SCARTH ST SUITE 1500, REGINA,
SK, S4P 4E9
(306) 347-8000   *SIC* 8741

MONITOR COMPANY CANADA   *p*954
8 ADELAIDE ST W STE 20, TORONTO, ON,
M5H 0A9
(416) 408-4800   *SIC* 8741

MONTAGE TECHNOLOGIES INC   *p*54
GD LCD 1, CALGARY, AB, T2P 2G8
(403) 263-4089   *SIC* 8741

MORRIS, ALWIN   *p*1117
1470 RTE 138, KAHNAWAKE, QC, J0L 1B0
(450) 633-5100   *SIC* 8741

**MULTIPLEX CANADA HSP HOLDINGS LIM-
ITED**   *p*987
130 KING ST W SUITE 2350, TORONTO,
ON, M5X 2A2
(416) 359-8559   *SIC* 8741

**MULTIPLEX CONSTRUCTION CANADA
LIMITED**   *p*987
130 KING ST W SUITE 2350, TORONTO,
ON, M5X 2A2
(416) 359-8559   *SIC* 8741

MURSKA MANAGEMENT (1969) LTD   *p*90
10180 101 ST NW SUITE 3200, EDMON-
TON, AB, T5J 3W8
(780) 425-9510   *SIC* 8741

NAL RESOURCES MANAGEMENT LIMITED
*p*54
550 6 AVE SW SUITE 600, CALGARY, AB,
T2P 0S2
(403) 294-3600   *SIC* 8741

NASITTUQ CORPORATION   *p*825
360 ALBERT ST UNIT 1830, OTTAWA, ON,
K1R 7X7
(613) 234-9033   *SIC* 8741

NATIONAL RESEARCH COUNCIL CANADA
*p*815
1200 MONTREAL RD BUILDING M-58, OT-
TAWA, ON, K1A 0R6
(613) 993-9200   *SIC* 8741

NEW HORIZON SYSTEM SOLUTIONS INC
*p*575
800 KIPLING AVE SUITE 8, ETOBICOKE,
ON, M8Z 5G5
(416) 207-6800   *SIC* 8741

NICOLA TRIBAL ASSOCIATION INC *p*232
2090 COUTLEE AVE UNIT 202, MERRITT,
BC, V1K 1B8
(250) 378-4235   *SIC* 8741

NORREP CAPITAL MANAGEMENT LTD*p*55
333 7 AVE SW SUITE 1850, CALGARY, AB,
T2P 2Z1
(403) 531-2650   *SIC* 8741

**NOVITEX ENTERPRISE SOLUTIONS
CANADA, INC**   *p*915
2225 SHEPPARD AVE E SUITE 1008,
TORONTO, ON, M2J 5C2
(416) 886-2540   *SIC* 8741

NUNASI CORPORATION   *p*472
1104 INUKSUGAIT PLAZA SUITE 210,

IQALUIT, NU, X0A 0H0
(867) 979-8920   *SIC* 8741

**OAKWOOD CONSTRUCTION SERVICES
LTD**   *p*363
20 BURNETT AVE, WINNIPEG, MB, R2G
1C1
(204) 661-8415   *SIC* 8741

OLIVER, WYMAN LIMITED   *p*965
120 BREMNER BLVD SUITE 800,
TORONTO, ON, M5J 0A8
(416) 868-2200   *SIC* 8741

ONE10 CANADA HOLDINGS ULC   *p*987
130 KING ST W SUITE 1600, TORONTO,
ON, M5X 2A2
(905) 214-8699   *SIC* 8741

OPEN SOLUTIONS CANADA INC   *p*802
700 DORVAL DR SUITE 202, OAKVILLE,
ON, L6K 3V3
(905) 849-1390   *SIC* 8741

**OPSIS GESTION D'INFRASTRUCTURES
INC**   *p*1142
2099 BOUL FERNAND-LAFONTAINE,
LONGUEUIL, QC, J4G 2J4
(514) 982-6774   *SIC* 8741

OPTIMUS SBR INC   *p*940
30 ADELAIDE ST E SUITE 600, TORONTO,
ON, M5C 3G8
(416) 962-7500   *SIC* 8741

ORGANIZATIONAL SOLUTIONS INC *p*523
5360 SOUTH SERVICE RD, BURLINGTON,
ON, L7L 5L1
(905) 315-7179   *SIC* 8741

ORXESTRA INC   *p*576
5 HEATHROW CRT, ETOBICOKE, ON, M9A
3A2
(416) 233-9318   *SIC* 8741

PACRIM HOSPITALITY SERVICES INC*p*440
30 DAMASCUS RD SUITE 201, BEDFORD,
NS, B4A 0C1
(902) 404-7474   *SIC* 8741

PARTNERS IN COMMUNITY NURSING
*p*1015
1001 BURNS ST E UNIT 2, WHITBY, ON,
L1N 6A6
(905) 665-1711   *SIC* 8741

PAVILION FINANCIAL CORPORATION*p*388
1001 CORYDON AVE SUITE 300, WIN-
NIPEG, MB, R3M 0B6
(204) 954-5103   *SIC* 8741

PCL CONSTRUCTION MANAGEMENT INC
*p*24
2882 11 ST NE, CALGARY, AB, T2E 7S7
(403) 250-4800   *SIC* 8741

PCL CONSTRUCTION MANAGEMENT INC
*p*115
5400 99 ST NW, EDMONTON, AB, T6E 3P4
(780) 733-6000   *SIC* 8741

PENNECON ENERGY LTD   *p*433
650 WATER ST, ST. JOHN'S, NL, A1E 1B9
(709) 726-5888   *SIC* 8741

PERSONNEL UNIQUE CANADA INC *p*1096
455 BOUL FENELON BUREAU 210, DOR-
VAL, QC, H9S 5T8
(514) 633-6220   *SIC* 8741

PINK ELEPHANT INC   *p*524
5575 NORTH SERVICE RD SUITE 200,
BURLINGTON, ON, L7L 6M1
(905) 331-5060   *SIC* 8741

PLUSONE INC   *p*956
347 BAY ST SUITE 506, TORONTO, ON,
M5H 2R7
(416) 861-1662   *SIC* 8741

**PONTEIX COLONY OF HUTTERIAN
BRETHREN**   *p*1413
GD, PONTEIX, SK, S0N 1Z0
(306) 625-3652   *SIC* 8741

PRIMA ENTERPRISES LTD   *p*216
1103 12TH ST UNIT 102, KAMLOOPS, BC,
V2B 8A6
(250) 376-9554   *SIC* 8741

PRIMARIS MANAGEMENT INC   *p*940
1 ADELAIDE ST E SUITE 900, TORONTO,
ON, M5C 2V9
(416) 642-7800   *SIC* 8741

**PRIMERICA LIFE INSURANCE COMPANY
OF CANADA**   *p*154
5580 45 ST UNIT C 8, RED DEER, AB, T4N
1L1
(403) 347-2829   *SIC* 8741

PROCASE CONSULTING INC   *p*1033
180 CASTER AVE SUITE 55, WOOD-
BRIDGE, ON, L4L 5Y7
(905) 856-7479   *SIC* 8741

PROCEPT ASSOCIATES LTD   *p*936
250 YONGE ST SUITE 2201-49,
TORONTO, ON, M5B 2L7
(416) 693-5559   *SIC* 8741

PROLOGIC SYSTEMS LIMITED   *p*818
2255 ST LAURENT BLVD SUITE 320, OT-
TAWA, ON, K1G 4K3
(613) 238-1376   *SIC* 8741

PROPHIT MANAGEMENT LTD   *p*18
4540 54 AVE SE UNIT 200, CALGARY, AB,
T2C 2Y8
(403) 640-0200   *SIC* 8741

PROTEGRA INC   *p*84
12031 76 ST NW, EDMONTON, AB, T5B
2C9

SIC 8741

QWINSTAR CANADA INC   *p*736
1040 CARDIFF BLVD, MISSISSAUGA, ON,
L5S 1P3
(905) 696-8102   *SIC* 8741

**R.D.M. MANAGEMENT COMPANY (1987)
LTD**   *p*175
33695 SOUTH FRASER WAY, ABBOTS-
FORD, BC, V2S 2C1
SIC 8741

RAND A TECHNOLOGY CORPORATION
*p*745
151 COURTNEYPARK DR W SUITE 201,
MISSISSAUGA, ON, L5W 1Y5
(905) 565-2929   *SIC* 8741

REALSTAR MANAGEMENT PARTNERSHIP
*p*976
77 BLOOR ST W SUITE 2000, TORONTO,
ON, M5S 1M2
(416) 923-2950   *SIC* 8741

REIMER WORLD CORP   *p*375
201 PORTAGE AVE SUITE 2900, WIN-
NIPEG, MB, R3B 3K6
(204) 958-5300   *SIC* 8741

REM TEK ENTERPRISES LTD   *p*320
3195 GRANVILLE ST SUITE 218, VAN-
COUVER, BC, V6H 3K2
(604) 733-6345   *SIC* 8741

REPRODUCTIONS-PHOTOS M.P. LTEE
*p*1226
222 BOUL LEBEAU, MONTREAL, QC, H4N
1R4
(514) 383-4313   *SIC* 8741

RESCOM INC   *p*96
12704 110 AVE NW, EDMONTON, AB, T5M
2L7
(780) 454-6500   *SIC* 8741

RESMAN MANAGEMENT LIMITED   *p*37
1209 59 AVE SE SUITE 245, CALGARY, AB,
T2H 2P6
(403) 259-8826   *SIC* 8741

REVAY ET ASSOCIES LIMITEE   *p*1402
4333 RUE SAINTE-CATHERINE O BU-
REAU 500, WESTMOUNT, QC, H3Z 1P9
(514) 932-2188   *SIC* 8741

RICHTER GROUPE CONSEIL SENC *p*1402
3500 BOUL DE MAISONNEUVE O UNITE
1800, WESTMOUNT, QC, H3Z 3C1
(514) 934-3497   *SIC* 8741

RIMANESA PROPERTIES INC   *p*1230
800 RUE DE LA GAUCHETIERE O BU-
REAU 240, MONTREAL, QC, H5A 1K6
(514) 397-2211   *SIC* 8741

RIVER BUTTE MANAGEMENT LTD   *p*180
2866 BRISCO RD, BRISCO, BC, V0A 1B0
(250) 346-3315   *SIC* 8741

ROBERTA PLACE   *p*488
503 ESSA RD, BARRIE, ON, L4N 9E4
(705) 733-3231   *SIC* 8741

ROBINSON SOLUTIONS INC   *p*956

390 BAY ST SUITE 1520, TORONTO, ON,
M5H 2Y2
(416) 479-7440   *SIC* 8741

ROBINSON SOLUTIONS INC   *p*1035
715106 OXFORD RD SUITE 4, WOOD-
STOCK, ON, N4S 7V9
(519) 653-1111   *SIC* 8741

ROGERS WEST GROUP INCORPORATED
*p*375
201 PORTAGE AVE SUITE 1800, WIN-
NIPEG, MB, R3B 3K6
(204) 800-0202   *SIC* 8741

ROYAL LEPAGE FACILITY   *p*652
955 HIGHBURY AVE N, LONDON, ON, N5Y
1A3
(519) 659-9058   *SIC* 8741

**RWAM INSURANCE ADMINISTRATORS
INC**   *p*568
49 INDUSTRIAL DR, ELMIRA, ON, N3B
3B1
(519) 669-1632   *SIC* 8741

S.I. SYSTEMS LTD   *p*58
401 9 AVE SW SUITE 309, CALGARY, AB,
T2P 3C5
(403) 263-1200   *SIC* 8741

S.I. SYSTEMS PARTNERSHIP   *p*58
401 9 AVE SW SUITE 309, CALGARY, AB,
T2P 3C5
(403) 286-1200   *SIC* 8741

SAFEHAVEN NURSING & SERVICES INC
*p*340
3700 RIDGE POND DR, VICTORIA, BC,
V9C 4M8
(250) 477-8339   *SIC* 8741

**SALESFORCE.COM CANADA CORPORA-
TION**   *p*966
20 BAY ST SUITE 800, TORONTO, ON, M5J
2N8
(647) 258-3800   *SIC* 8741

SANOOR INVESTMENT LTD   *p*186
4201 LOUGHEED HWY, BURNABY, BC,
V5C 3Y6
(604) 298-2010   *SIC* 8741

**SASKATOON PRAIRIELAND PARK COR-
PORATION**   *p*1429
503 RUTH ST W, SASKATOON, SK, S7K
4E4
(306) 931-7149   *SIC* 8741

SAVVIS COMMUNICATIONS CANADA, INC
*p*727
6800 MILLCREEK DR, MISSISSAUGA, ON,
L5N 4J9
(905) 363-3737   *SIC* 8741

SEASPAN SHIP MANAGEMENT LTD *p*309
200 GRANVILLE ST SUITE 2600, VAN-
COUVER, BC, V6C 1S4
(604) 638-2575   *SIC* 8741

SERCO CANADA INC   *p*424
271 CANADIAN FORCES, HAPPY VALLEY-
GOOSE BAY, NL, A0P 1C0
(709) 896-6946   *SIC* 8741

SERCO CANADA INC   *p*957
330 BAY ST SUITE 400, TORONTO, ON,
M5H 2S8
(416) 225-3788   *SIC* 8741

**SERVICE D'AIDE A LA FAMILLE EDMUND-
STON GRAND SAULT INC**   *p*399
13 RUE DUGAL, EDMUNDSTON, NB, E3V
1X4
(506) 737-8000   *SIC* 8741

**SERVICES DE GESTION QUANTUM LIMI-
TEE, LES**   *p*1199
2000 AV MCGILL COLLEGE BUREAU
1800, MONTREAL, QC, H3A 3H3
(514) 842-5555   *SIC* 8741

SERVICES FERROVIAIRES CANAC INC
*p*1341
6505 RTE TRANSCANADIENNE BUREAU
405, SAINT-LAURENT, QC, H4T 1S3
(514) 734-4700   *SIC* 8741

SERVICES INFIRMIERS PRO-SOIN INC
*p*1273
2750 CH SAINTE-FOY BUREAU 240, QUE-
BEC, QC, G1V 1V6

▲ Public Company   ■ Public Company Family Member   **HQ** Headquarters   **BR** Branch   **SL** Single Location

(418) 653-4471 *SIC* 8741
SERVICES OR LP/SEC p1208
1 PLACE VILLE-MARIE UNITE 2500, MON-
TREAL, QC, H3B 1R1
(514) 847-4747 *SIC* 8741
**SEYEM' QWANTLEN BUSINESS MANAGE-
MENT LTD** p225
23684 GABRIEL LANE, LANGLEY, BC, V1M
2S4
(604) 888-5556 *SIC* 8741
SHAW MANAGEMENT CONSULTANTS INC
p579
145 THE WEST MALL, ETOBICOKE, ON,
M9C 5P5
(416) 767-4200 *SIC* 8741
**SHAWN & ASSOCIATES MANAGEMENT
LTD** p37
1209 59 AVE SE SUITE 100, CALGARY, AB,
T2H 2P6
(403) 255-5017 *SIC* 8741
SILVACOM LTD p116
3912 91 ST NW, EDMONTON, AB, T6E 5K7
(780) 462-3238 *SIC* 8741
SIMERRA PROPERTY MANAGEMENT INC
p588
89 SKYWAY AVE SUITE 200, ETOBICOKE,
ON, M9W 6R4
(416) 293-5900 *SIC* 8741
SITQ INTERNATIONAL INC p1192
1001 RUE DU SQUARE-VICTORIA BU-
REAU 500, MONTREAL, QC, H2Z 2B5
(514) 287-1852 *SIC* 8741
**SIX NATIONS OF THE GRAND RIVER DE-
VELOPMENT CORPORATION** p806
2498 CHIEFSWOOD, OHSWEKEN, ON,
N0A 1M0
(519) 753-1950 *SIC* 8741
SMH MANAGEMENT INC p82
545 HWY 10 E, DRUMHELLER, AB, T0J
0Y0
(403) 823-2030 *SIC* 8741
SOCIETE CONSEIL GROUPE LGS p1208
1 PLACE VILLE-MARIE BUREAU 2200,
MONTREAL, QC, H3B 2B2
(514) 964-0939 *SIC* 8741
SOCIETE D'ENERGIE DE LA BAIE JAMES
p1176
800 BOUL DE MAISONNEUVE E BUREAU
1100, MONTREAL, QC, H2L 4L8
(514) 286-2020 *SIC* 8741
**SOCIETE D'HABITATION DE ST-ANTOINE
INC** p416
7 DE L'EGLISE AVE, SAINT-ANTOINE, NB,
E4V 1L6
(506) 525-4040 *SIC* 8741
SODEM INC p1183
4750 AV HENRI-JULIEN BUREAU RC 050,
MONTREAL, QC, H2T 2C8
(514) 527-9546 *SIC* 8741
SOGEP INC p1142
2099 BOUL FERNAND-LAFONTAINE,
LONGUEUIL, QC, J4G 2J4
(514) 527-9546 *SIC* 8741
SORBARA SERVICES LIMITED p1033
3700 STEELES AVE W SUITE 800, WOOD-
BRIDGE, ON, L4L 8M9
(905) 850-6154 *SIC* 8741
SOURCE SANTE ACTION INC p1297
100 RUE JOHANNE, SAINT-COLOMBAN,
QC, J5K 2A5
(450) 560-4980 *SIC* 8741
SOUTHBRIDGE HEALTH CARE LP p539
766 HESPELER RD SUITE 301, CAM-
BRIDGE, ON, N3H 5L8
(519) 621-8886 *SIC* 8741
SPECTRUM HEALTH CARE LTD p712
1290 CENTRAL PKY W SUITE 302, MIS-
SISSAUGA, ON, L5C 4R3
(905) 272-2271 *SIC* 8741
**SPENCER STUART & ASSOCIATES
(CANADA) LTD** p967
1 UNIVERSITY AVE UNIT 1900,
TORONTO, ON, M5J 2P1
(416) 361-0311 *SIC* 8741

SPRINGSIDE HUTTERIAN BRETHREN LTD
p83
GD, DUCHESS, AB, T0J 0Z0
(403) 378-4734 *SIC* 8741
STANDARD LAND COMPANY INC p60
734 7 AVE SW SUITE 1400, CALGARY, AB,
T2P 3P8
(403) 269-3931 *SIC* 8741
**STELMASCHUK, W.J. AND ASSOCIATES
LTD** p231
11491 KINGSTON ST SUITE 2, MAPLE
RIDGE, BC, V2X 0Y6
(604) 465-5515 *SIC* 8741
STERLING HEALTH SERVICES CORP p296
1188 QUEBEC ST SUITE 1402, VANCOU-
VER, BC, V6A 4B3
(604) 261-2616 *SIC* 8741
STI MAINTENANCE INC p1115
1946 RUE DAVIS, JONQUIERE, QC, G7S
3B6
(418) 699-5101 *SIC* 8741
STRATEGIC COACH INC, THE p992
33 FRASER AVE SUITE 201, TORONTO,
ON, M6K 3J9
(416) 531-7399 *SIC* 8741
STURGEON FOUNDATION p147
9922 103 ST, MORINVILLE, AB, T8R 1R7
(780) 939-5116 *SIC* 8741
SUNDER GROUP OF COMPANIES LTD p770
5650 YONGE ST, NORTH YORK, ON, M2M
4G3
(416) 226-1809 *SIC* 8741
SUNRISE NORTH SENIOR LIVING LTD p906
484 STEELES AVE W, THORNHILL, ON,
L4J 0C7
(905) 731-4300 *SIC* 8741
SYMCOR INC p780
8 PRINCE ANDREW PL, NORTH YORK,
ON, M3C 2H4
(905) 273-1000 *SIC* 8741
TEACH AWAY INC p300
896 CAMBIE ST SUITE 301, VANCOUVER,
BC, V6B 2P6
(604) 628-1822 *SIC* 8741
TELIGENCE (CANADA) LTD p300
303 PENDER ST W UNIT 300, VANCOU-
VER, BC, V6B 1T3
(604) 629-6055 *SIC* 8741
THE PERSONNEL DEPARTMENT LTD p327
980 HOWE ST UNIT 201, VANCOUVER,
BC, V6Z 0C8
(604) 685-3530 *SIC* 8741
THE&PARTNERSHIP INC p984
99 SPADINA AVE UNIT 100, TORONTO,
ON, M5V 3P8
(647) 252-6801 *SIC* 8741
THINKMAX CONSULTING INC p1324
1111 BOUL DR.-FREDERIK-PHILIPS BU-
REAU 500, SAINT-LAURENT, QC, H4M 2X6
(514) 316-8959 *SIC* 8741
**THOMPSON, ROACH & HUGHES CON-
SULTING INC** p559
261 MILLWAY AVE UNIT 1, CONCORD, ON,
L4K 4K9
(905) 669-9517 *SIC* 8741
THURBER MANAGEMENT LTD p339
4396 WEST SAANICH RD SUITE 100, VIC-
TORIA, BC, V8Z 3E9
(250) 727-2201 *SIC* 8741
**TLC NURSING AND HOME CARE SER-
VICES LIMITED** p431
25 ANDERSON AVE, ST. JOHN'S, NL, A1B
3E4
(709) 726-3473 *SIC* 8741
TODDGLEN MANAGEMENT LIMITED p768
2225 SHEPPARD AVE E SUITE 1100,
NORTH YORK, ON, M2J 5C2
(416) 492-2450 *SIC* 8741
**TOP RANK BUSINESS ASSOCIATES
GROUP OF COMPANY INC** p917
2863 ST CLAIR AVE E, TORONTO, ON,
M4B 1N4
SIC 8741
TORCE FINANCIAL GROUPE INC p1324

575 RUE DORAIS, SAINT-LAURENT, QC,
H4M 1Z7
SIC 8741
TOWERS WATSON CANADA INC p61
111 5 AVE SW SUITE 1600, CALGARY, AB,
T2P 3Y6
(403) 261-1400 *SIC* 8741
TOWERS WATSON ULC p958
20 QUEEN ST W SUITE 2800, TORONTO,
ON, M5H 3R3
(416) 960-2700 *SIC* 8741
TOWERS WATSON ULC p1200
600 BOUL DE MAISONNEUVE O BUREAU
2400, MONTREAL, QC, H3A 3J2
SIC 8741
TRACTION SALES AND MARKETING INC
p183
2700 PRODUCTION WAY SUITE 500,
BURNABY, BC, V5A 0C2
(604) 917-0274 *SIC* 8741
TRILLIUM PRACTICE MANAGEMENT LTD
p856
9625 YONGE ST SUITE F, RICHMOND
HILL, ON, L4C 5T2
(905) 918-9573 *SIC* 8741
TRIMARK HEALTHCARE SERVICES LTD
p318
1500 GEORGIA ST W SUITE 1300, VAN-
COUVER, BC, V6G 2Z6
(604) 425-2208 *SIC* 8741
TROTTER AND MORTON LIMITED p38
5711 1 ST SE, CALGARY, AB, T2H 1H9
(403) 255-7535 *SIC* 8741
UNITED RENTALS OF CANADA, INC p515
150 ROY BLVD, BRANTFORD, ON, N3R
7K2
(519) 756-0700 *SIC* 8741
UNIVEX MANAGEMENT LIMITED p597
303 RIVER RD SUITE 3, GLOUCESTER,
ON, K1V 1H2
(613) 526-1500 *SIC* 8741
URBACON BUILDINGS GROUP CORP p921
750 LAKE SHORE BLVD E, TORONTO, ON,
M4M 3M3
(416) 865-9405 *SIC* 8741
USC CONSULTING GROUP (CANADA), LP
p690
5925 AIRPORT RD SUITE 730, MISSIS-
SAUGA, ON, L4V 1W1
(905) 673-2600 *SIC* 8741
VALLEY PERSONNEL LTD p247
2509 KINGSWAY AVE, PORT COQUITLAM,
BC, V3C 1T5
SIC 8741
VAULT CREDIT CORPORATION p916
41 SCARSDALE RD SUITE 5, TORONTO,
ON, M3B 2R2
(416) 499-8466 *SIC* 8741
VEA GROUP INC, THE p75
150 CROWFOOT CRES NW SUITE 105,
CALGARY, AB, T3G 3T2
(403) 547-7727 *SIC* 8741
VENGROWTH ASSET MANAGEMENT INC
p958
105 ADELAIDE ST W SUITE 1000,
TORONTO, ON, M5H 1P9
(416) 971-6656 *SIC* 8741
VIKING LIMITED PARTNERSHIP p958
333 BAY ST SUITE 2500, TORONTO, ON,
M5H 2R2
(416) 408-3221 *SIC* 8741
VISA CANADA INC p958
40 KING ST W SUITE 3710, TORONTO,
ON, M5H 3Y2
(416) 367-8472 *SIC* 8741
VISIONS PERSONNEL SERVICES INC p795
2300 FINCH AVE W UNIT 30, NORTH
YORK, ON, M9M 2Y3
(416) 740-3319 *SIC* 8741
W.O.W. HOSPITALITY CONCEPTS INC p388
529 WELLINGTON CRES 3RD FL, WIN-
NIPEG, MB, R3M 0A1
(204) 942-1090 *SIC* 8741
WE CARE HOME HEALTH SERVICES p233

2349 EAST WELLINGTON RD, NANAIMO,
BC, V9R 6V7
(250) 740-0035 *SIC* 8741
WESTSIDE NURSING SERVICES LTD p321
1892 BROADWAY W SUITE 200, VANCOU-
VER, BC, V6J 1Y9
(604) 261-9161 *SIC* 8741
WOOD CANADA LIMITED p799
2020 WINSTON PARK DR SUITE 700,
OAKVILLE, ON, L6H 6X7
(905) 829-5400 *SIC* 8741
WOOD, BRENDAN INTERNATIONAL LTD
p974
17 PRINCE ARTHUR AVE, TORONTO, ON,
M5R 1B2
(416) 924-8110 *SIC* 8741
**WORLDSOURCE WEALTH MANAGEMENT
INC** p677
625 COCHRANE DR SUITE 700,
MARKHAM, ON, L3R 9R9
(905) 940-5500 *SIC* 8741
WORTH PERSONNEL LTD p813
219 WENTWORTH ST E, OSHAWA, ON,
L1H 3V7
(905) 725-5544 *SIC* 8741
WSB TITAN INC p1029
50 ROYAL GROUP CRES UNIT 2, WOOD-
BRIDGE, ON, L4H 1X9
(905) 669-1898 *SIC* 8741
WW HOTELS CORP p702
5090 EXPLORER DR SUITE 700, MISSIS-
SAUGA, ON, L4W 4T9
(905) 624-9720 *SIC* 8741
**XPERA RISK MITIGATION & INVESTIGA-
TION LP** p766
155 GORDON BAKER RD SUITE 101,
NORTH YORK, ON, M2H 3N5
(416) 449-8677 *SIC* 8741
Y FIRM MANAGEMENT INC p997
2700-130 KING ST, TORONTO, ON, M9N
1L5
(416) 860-8370 *SIC* 8741
YOUNGHUSBAND RESOURCES LTD p247
1628 KEBET WAY UNIT 100, PORT CO-
QUITLAM, BC, V3C 5W9
(604) 466-1220 *SIC* 8741
ZE POWERGROUP INC p266
5920 NO. 2 RD SUITE 130, RICHMOND,
BC, V7C 4R9
(604) 244-1469 *SIC* 8741

SIC 8742 Management consulting services

1221271 ONTARIO INC p754
200 DAVIS DR SUITE 1, NEWMARKET, ON,
L3Y 2N4
SIC 8742
1496803 ALBERTA INC p95
15849 116 AVE NW, EDMONTON, AB, T5M
3W1
(780) 463-7787 *SIC* 8742
2384309 ONTARIO INC p665
7357 WOODBINE AVE SUITE 619,
MARKHAM, ON, L3R 6L3
(905) 944-0700 *SIC* 8742
9003-9306 QUEBEC INC p1275
9115 BOUL DE L'ORMIERE, QUEBEC, QC,
G2B 3K2
(418) 407-4400 *SIC* 8742
9186-5758 QUEBEC INC p1227
5000 RUE BUCHAN BUREAU 1000, MON-
TREAL, QC, H4P 1T2
(514) 342-4151 *SIC* 8742
A HUNDRED ANSWERS INC p623
340 MARCH RD SUITE 500, KANATA, ON,
K2K 2E4
(613) 271-3700 *SIC* 8742
A.X.C. CONSTRUCTION INC p1227
5101 RUE BUCHAN BUREAU 400, MON-
TREAL, QC, H4P 1S4
(514) 937-3737 *SIC* 8742
ACCULOGIX DISTRIBUTION SERVICES p13
4747 68 AVE SE, CALGARY, AB, T2C 4Z4

(403) 236-1555   *SIC 8742*
AECOM CANADA LTD   *p641*
50 SPORTSWORLD CROSSING RD SUITE 290, KITCHENER, ON, N2P 0A4
(519) 650-5313   *SIC 8742*
AECOM CANADA LTD   *p666*
300 TOWN CENTRE BLVD SUITE 300, MARKHAM, ON, L3R 5Z6
SIC 8742
AECOM CANADA LTD   *p1266*
4700 BOUL WILFRID-HAMEL, QUEBEC, QC, G1P 2J9
(418) 871-2444   *SIC 8742*
AECOM ENERGY SERVICES LTD   *p158*
1901 HIGHWAY AVE SE, REDCLIFF, AB, T0J 2P0
SIC 8742
ALIZENT CANADA INC   *p1209*
740 RUE NOTRE-DAME O BUREAU 600, MONTREAL, QC, H3C 3X6
(514) 876-2855   *SIC 8742*
ALLSTAR CONSTRUCTION LTD   *p99*
11130 199 ST, EDMONTON, AB, T5S 2C6
(780) 452-6330   *SIC 8742*
ALMA MATER SOCIETY OF QUEEN'S UNIVERSITY INCORPORATED   *p630*
99 UNIVERSITY AVE, KINGSTON, ON, K7L 3N5
(613) 533-2725   *SIC 8742*
ALPHA TRADING SYSTEMS INC   *p959*
70 YORK ST SUITE 1501, TORONTO, ON, M5J 1S9
(416) 563-5896   *SIC 8742*
AMDOCS CANADIAN MANAGED SERVICES INC   *p691*
1705 TECH AVE UNIT 2, MISSISSAUGA, ON, L4W 0A2
(905) 614-4000   *SIC 8742*
AMT MANAGEMENT SERVICES   *p376*
360 MAIN ST SUITE 3000, WINNIPEG, MB, R3C 4G1
(204) 957-4868   *SIC 8742*
ANNEX CONSULTING GROUP INC   *p327*
555 BURRARD ST SUITE 950, VANCOUVER, BC, V7X 1M8
(604) 638-8878   *SIC 8742*
ARAMARK ENTERTAINMENT SERVICES (CANADA) INC
1223 WATER ST, KELOWNA, BC, V1Y 9V1
(250) 979-0878   *SIC 8742*
ARAMARK ENTERTAINMENT SERVICES (CANADA) INC   *p296*
800 GRIFFITHS WAY, VANCOUVER, BC, V6B 6G1
(604) 780-7623   *SIC 8742*
ARAMARK ENTERTAINMENT SERVICES (CANADA) INC   *p626*
1000 PALLADIUM DR SUITE 107, KANATA, ON, K2V 1A4
(613) 599-0230   *SIC 8742*
ATTABOTICS INC   *p20*
7944 10 ST NE, CALGARY, AB, T2E 8W1
(403) 909-8230   *SIC 8742*
AV & R VISION & ROBOTIQUES INC   *p1210*
269 RUE PRINCE, MONTREAL, QC, H3C 2N4
(514) 788-1420   *SIC 8742*
AVC INSURANCE SERVICES INC   *p297*
650 GEORGIA ST W SUITE 11588, VANCOUVER, BC, V6B 4N8
(604) 685-6431   *SIC 8742*
AVISON YOUNG (CANADA) INC   *p959*
18 YORK ST SUITE 400, TORONTO, ON, M5J 2T8
(416) 955-0000   *SIC 8742*
B WYZE INC   *p666*
20 VALLEYWOOD DR UNIT 100, MARKHAM, ON, L3R 6G1
(905) 780-0444   *SIC 8742*
B.P.D.L. INC   *p1044*
890 RUE DES PINS O, ALMA, QC, G8B 7R3
(418) 668-6161   *SIC 8742*
BAIN & COMPANY CANADA, INC   *p928*
2 BLOOR ST E, TORONTO, ON, M4W 1A8

(416) 929-1888   *SIC 8742*
BENEFIT PLAN ADMINISTRATORS LIMITED   *p576*
90 BURNHAMTHORPE RD, ETOBICOKE, ON, M9A 1H2
(905) 275-6466   *SIC 8742*
BENEFIT PLAN ADMINISTRATORS LIMITED   *p709*
90 BURNHAMTHORPE RD W SUITE 300, MISSISSAUGA, ON, L5B 3C3
(905) 275-6466   *SIC 8742*
BEWORKS INC   *p990*
946 QUEEN ST W, TORONTO, ON, M6J 1G8
(416) 920-1921   *SIC 8742*
BREVITAS CONSULTING INC   *p851*
70 EAST BEAVER CREEK RD SUITE 24, RICHMOND HILL, ON, L4B 3B2
(289) 819-1339   *SIC 8742*
BTY CONSULTANCY GROUP INC   *p291*
2288 MANITOBA ST, VANCOUVER, BC, V5Y 4B5
(604) 734-3126   *SIC 8742*
CAISSE POPULAIRE DE SAINT-BONIFACE LIMITEE, LA   *p364*
205 PROVENCHER BLVD SUITE 100, WINNIPEG, MB, R2H 0G4
(204) 237-8874   *SIC 8742*
CANADIAN LOCATORS INC   *p10*
525 28 ST SE SUITE 201, CALGARY, AB, T2A 6W9
(403) 263-6310   *SIC 8742*
CANADIAN URBAN LIMITED   *p85*
10572-105 ST NW, EDMONTON, AB, T5H 2W7
(780) 424-7722   *SIC 8742*
CAPCO   *p986*
100 KING ST W SUITE 5010, TORONTO, ON, M5X 1C7
(416) 923-4570   *SIC 8742*
CAPGEMINI CANADA INC   *p949*
200 UNIVERSITY AVE SUITE 1100, TORONTO, ON, M5H 3C6
(416) 365-4400   *SIC 8742*
CAPITAL DESSAU INC   *p1236*
1200 BOUL SAINT-MARTIN O BUREAU 300, MONTREAL, QC, H7S 2E4
(514) 281-1010   *SIC 8742*
CARLTON ONE ENGAGEMENT ULC   *p851*
38 LEEK CRES 4TH FL, RICHMOND HILL, ON, L4B 4N8
(905) 477-3971   *SIC 8742*
CARPEDIA GROUP INTERNATIONAL INC *p800*
75 NAVY ST, OAKVILLE, ON, L6J 2Z1
(905) 337-3407   *SIC 8742*
CELERO SOLUTIONS INC   *p34*
8500 MACLEOD TRAIL SE SUITE 350N, CALGARY, AB, T2H 2N1
(403) 258-5900   *SIC 8742*
CENTRIA COMMERCE INC   *p1086*
3131 BOUL SAINT-MARTIN O BUREAU 500, COTE SAINT-LUC, QC, H7T 2Z5
(514) 874-0122   *SIC 8742*
CENTRIC HEALTH CORPORATION   *p923*
20 EGLINTON AVE W SUITE 2100, TORONTO, ON, M4R 1K8
(416) 927-8400   *SIC 8742*
CHARTRIGHT AIR INC   *p734*
2450 DERRY RD E, MISSISSAUGA, ON, L5S 1B2
(905) 671-4674   *SIC 8742*
CITCO (CANADA) INC   *p928*
2 BLOOR ST E SUITE 2700, TORONTO, ON, M4W 1A8
(416) 966-9200   *SIC 8742*
CLEARPATH ROBOTICS INC   *p642*
1425 STRASBURG RD UNIT 2A, KITCHENER, ON, N2R 1H2
(519) 513-2416   *SIC 8742*
COMMUNITY FIRST DEVELOPMENTS INC *p788*
2171 AVENUE RD SUITE 303, NORTH YORK, ON, M5M 4B4

(416) 932-9249   *SIC 8742*
COMMUNITY LIVING TORONTO   *p972*
20 SPADINA RD SUITE 257, TORONTO, ON, M5R 2S7
(416) 968-0650   *SIC 8742*
COMPLYWORKS LTD   *p73*
4838 RICHARD RD SW SUITE 600, CALGARY, AB, T3E 6L1
(403) 219-4792   *SIC 8742*
COMPREHENSIVE CARE INTERNATIONAL INC   *p991*
173 DUFFERIN ST SUITE 200, TORONTO, ON, M6K 3H7
(416) 531-5950   *SIC 8742*
CONNECTRA TECHNOLOGIES INC   *p125*
1803 91 ST SUITE 102, EDMONTON, AB, T6X 0W8
(888) 731-5210   *SIC 8742*
CONTACT NORTH/CONTACT NORD   *p908*
1139 ALLOY DR SUITE 104, THUNDER BAY, ON, P7B 6M8
(807) 344-1616   *SIC 8742*
CORNERSTONE GROUP OF COMPANIES LIMITED   *p923*
20 EGLINTON AVE W 4TH FLOOR, TORONTO, ON, M4R 1K8
(416) 932-9555   *SIC 8742*
CPT GLOBAL CONSULTING CORPORATION   *p986*
100 KING ST W SUITE 5600, TORONTO, ON, M5X 1C9
(416) 642-2886   *SIC 8742*
CRC SOGEMA INC   *p1144*
1111 RUE SAINT-CHARLES O BUREAU 454, LONGUEUIL, QC, J4K 5G4
(450) 651-2800   *SIC 8742*
CREDENTIAL FINANCIAL STRATEGIES INC   *p312*
1111 GEORGIA ST W SUITE 800, VANCOUVER, BC, V6E 4T6
(604) 742-8259   *SIC 8742*
CRITICAL CONTROL ENERGY SERVICES CORP   *p91*
10045 111 ST NW, EDMONTON, AB, T5K 2M5
(780) 423-3100   *SIC 8742*
CROSSLINX TRANSIT SOLUTIONS CONSTRUCTORS GP   *p771*
4711 YONGE ST UNIT 1500, NORTH YORK, ON, M2N 6K8
(416) 679-6116   *SIC 8742*
CYGNUS MARKETING INC   *p1188*
507 PLACE D'ARMES BUREAU 1519, MONTREAL, QC, H2Y 2W8
(514) 284-5569   *SIC 8742*
DAIRY QUEEN CANADA INC   *p530*
1111 INTERNATIONAL BLVD, BURLINGTON, ON, L7R 3Y3
(905) 639-1492   *SIC 8742*
DELOITTE LLP   *p669*
15 ALLSTATE PKY SUITE 400, MARKHAM, ON, L3R 5B4
SIC 8742
DESSAU INC   *p1237*
1200 BOUL SAINT-MARTIN O BUREAU 300, MONTREAL, QC, H7S 2E4
(514) 281-1010   *SIC 8742*
DET NORSKE VERITAS CANADA LTD   *p8*
2618 HOPEWELL PL NE SUITE 150, CALGARY, AB, T1Y 7J7
(403) 250-9041   *SIC 8742*
DRA AMERICAS INC   *p938*
44 VICTORIA ST SUITE 300, TORONTO, ON, M5C 1Y2
(416) 800-8797   *SIC 8742*
DRW CANADA CO   *p1213*
1360 BOUL RENE-LEVESQUE O BUREAU 1700, MONTREAL, QC, H3G 2W4
(514) 940-4040   *SIC 8742*
DURHAM REGION PLANNING   *p1014*
1615 DUNDAS ST E SUITE 4, WHITBY, ON, L1N 2L1
(905) 723-1365   *SIC 8742*
EASTERN DOOR LOGISTICS INC   *p422*

3 CHURCH ST, CORNER BROOK, NL, A2H 2Z4
(709) 639-2479   *SIC 8742*
EDT GCV CIVIL S.E.P.   *p1119*
1095 RUE VALETS, L'ANCIENNE-LORETTE, QC, G2E 4M7
(418) 872-0600   *SIC 8742*
ELEMENT FLEET MANAGEMENT CORP
p962
161 BAY ST SUITE 3600, TORONTO, ON, M5J 2S1
(416) 386-1067   *SIC 8742*
ENGIE SERVICES INC   *p1195*
1001 BOUL DE MAISONNEUVE O BUREAU 1000, MONTREAL, QC, H3A 3C8
(514) 876-8748   *SIC 8742*
EPCOR TECHNOLOGIES INC   *p93*
13410 ST ALBERT TRAIL NW, EDMONTON, AB, T5L 4P2
(780) 412-3414   *SIC 8742*
EPIC REALTY PARTNERS INC   *p767*
2225 SHEPPARD AVE E SUITE 900, NORTH YORK, ON, M2J 5C2
(416) 497-9332   *SIC 8742*
ERIE ST. CLAIR COMMUNITY CARE ACCESS CENTRE   *p543*
712 RICHMOND ST, CHATHAM, ON, N7M 5J5
(519) 436-2222   *SIC 8742*
EVERWORKS INC   *p1005*
64 SPRING CREEK DR, WATERDOWN, ON, L8B 0X4
(905) 208-1668   *SIC 8742*
EVIMBEC LTEE   *p1138*
1175 BOUL GUILLAUME-COUTURE BUREAU 200, LEVIS, QC, G6W 0S2
(418) 834-7000   *SIC 8742*
EVOLOCITY FINANCIAL GROUP INC *p1204*
1100 BOUL RENE-LEVESQUE O BUREAU 1825, MONTREAL, QC, H3B 4N4
(877) 781-0148   *SIC 8742*
FAIRSTONE FINANCIERE INC   *p552*
1750 STEELES AVE W, CONCORD, ON, L4K 2L7
(905) 761-4538   *SIC 8742*
FELIX GLOBAL CORP   *p951*
80 RICHMOND ST W SUITE 1000, TORONTO, ON, M5H 2A4
(416) 512-7244   *SIC 8742*
FINE LINE COMMUNICATIONS LTD   *p378*
290 GARRY ST, WINNIPEG, MB, R3C 1H3
(204) 947-9520   *SIC 8742*
FIRST NATIONS FINANCIAL MANAGEMENT BOARD   *p341*
100 PARK ROYAL S SUITE 905, WEST VANCOUVER, BC, V7T 1A2
(604) 925-6665   *SIC 8742*
FORD CREDIT CANADA LIMITED   *p100*
10335 172 ST NW SUITE 300, EDMONTON, AB, T5S 1K9
SIC 8742
FRANCO FOLIES DE MONTREAL   *p1196*
400 BOUL DE MAISONNEUVE O, MONTREAL, QC, H3A 1L4
(514) 288-1040   *SIC 8742*
FRASER HEALTH AUTHORITY   *p226*
8521 198A ST, LANGLEY, BC, V2Y 0A1
(604) 455-1300   *SIC 8742*
FRASER HEALTH AUTHORITY   *p248*
220 BREW ST SUITE 700, PORT MOODY, BC, V3H 0H6
(604) 777-7300   *SIC 8742*
FREEDOM FINANCIAL SERVICES INCORPORATED   *p442*
115 COLDBROOK VILLAGE PARK DR, COLDBROOK, NS, B4R 1B9
(902) 681-1100   *SIC 8742*
FUGRO CANADA CORP   *p722*
2505 MEADOWVALE BLVD, MISSISSAUGA, ON, L5N 5S2
(905) 567-2870   *SIC 8742*
GESTION DELOITTE S.E.C   *p1312*
850 BOUL CASAVANT O, SAINT-HYACINTHE, QC, J2S 7S3

(450) 774-4000   *SIC 8742*
GESTION FRP INC   *p1272*
2960 BOUL LAURIER BUREAU 214, QUE-BEC, QC, G1V 4S1
(418) 652-1737   *SIC 8742*
GESTION SOROMA (MONT ORFORD) INC
p1210
640 RUE SAINT-PAUL O, MONTREAL, QC, H3C 1L9
(514) 527-9546   *SIC 8742*
GILLAM GROUP INC   *p916*
36 NORTHLINE RD, TORONTO, ON, M4B 3E2
(416) 486-6776   *SIC 8742*
GLOBAL REWARD SOLUTIONS INC   *p852*
38 LEEK CRES 4TH FL, RICHMOND HILL, ON, L4B 4N8
(905) 477-3971   *SIC 8742*
GOUVERNEMENT DE LA PROVINCE DE QUEBEC   *p1269*
150 BOUL RENE-LEVESQUE E, QUEBEC, QC, G1R 2B2
(418) 646-4646   *SIC 8742*
GOVERNORS OF THE UNIVERSITY OF AL-BERTA, THE   *p117*
8900 114 ST NW, EDMONTON, AB, T6G 2V2
(780) 492-4241   *SIC 8742*
GP WEALTH MANAGEMENT CORPORA-TION   *p695*
5045 ORBITOR DR SUITE 400 BUILDING 11, MISSISSAUGA, ON, L4W 4Y4
(416) 622-9969   *SIC 8742*
GROUP GSOFT INC   *p1216*
1751 RUE RICHARDSON BUREAU 5400, MONTREAL, QC, H3K 1G6
(514) 303-8203   *SIC 8742*
GROUPE CONSEIL FXINNOVATION INC
p1196
400 BOUL DE MAISONNEUVE O BUREAU 1100, MONTREAL, QC, H3A 1L4
(514) 525-5777   *SIC 8742*
GROUPE D.R.I. INC   *p1163*
5125 RUE DU TRIANON BUREAU 510, MONTREAL, QC, H1M 2S5
SIC 8742
GROUPE MTA CONSEILS EN GESTION D'EVENEMENTS PUBLIQUES INC, LE
p1211
80 RUE QUEEN BUREAU 601, MON-TREAL, QC, H3C 2N5
(514) 982-0835   *SIC 8742*
GROUPE PICHE CONSTRUCTION (2005) INC   *p1061*
755 BOUL DU CURE-BOIVIN BUREAU 100, BOISBRIAND, QC, J7G 2J2
(450) 433-0783   *SIC 8742*
HEALTHCARE MATERIALS MANAGEMENT SERVICES   *p649*
188 STRONACH CRES SUITE 519, LON-DON, ON, N5V 3A1
(519) 453-7888   *SIC 8742*
HEXAVEST INC   *p1205*
1250 BOUL RENE-LEVESQUE O BUREAU 4200, MONTREAL, QC, H3B 4W8
(514) 390-8484   *SIC 8742*
HOGG ROBINSON CANADA INC   *p981*
370 KING ST W SUITE 700, TORONTO, ON, M5V 1J9
(416) 593-8866   *SIC 8742*
HOLLISWEALTH INC   *p875*
2075 KENNEDY RD SUITE 500, SCAR-BOROUGH, ON, M1T 3V3
(416) 292-0869   *SIC 8742*
HOME AND COMMUNITY CARE ACCESS
p334
1947 COOK ST, VICTORIA, BC, V8T 3P7
(250) 388-2273   *SIC 8742*
HORIZONS ACTIVE DIVERSIFIED INCOME ETF INC   *p942*
26 WELLINGTON ST E SUITE 700, TORONTO, ON, M5E 1S2
(416) 933-5745   *SIC 8742*
HSBC BANK CANADA   *p298*

401 GEORGIA ST W SUITE 1300, VAN-COUVER, BC, V6B 5A1
(604) 668-4682   *SIC 8742*
HUDSON'S BAY COMPANY   *p1128*
2105 23E AV, LACHINE, QC, H8T 1X3
SIC 8742
HURON PERTH HEALTHCARE ALLIANCE
p896
46 GENERAL HOSPITAL DR, STRATFORD, ON, N5A 2Y6
(519) 271-2120   *SIC 8742*
HUTCHINSON SMILEY LIMITED   *p929*
890 YONGE ST SUITE 1002, TORONTO, ON, M4W 3P4
SIC 8742
I-CAR CANADA   *p585*
110 WOODBINE DOWNS BLVD UNIT 4, ETOBICOKE, ON, M9W 5S6
SIC 8742
IBI GROUP   *p927*
55 ST CLAIR AVE W SUITE 700, TORONTO, ON, M4V 2Y7
(416) 596-1930   *SIC 8742*
IC AXON INC   *p1185*
3575 BOUL SAINT-LAURENT BUREAU 650, MONTREAL, QC, H2X 2T7
(514) 940-1142   *SIC 8742*
INKAS FINANCE CORP   *p917*
2192 GERRARD ST E, TORONTO, ON, M4E 2C7
(416) 686-4587   *SIC 8742*
INNOVATION INSTITUTE OF ONTARIO*p946*
101 COLLEGE ST SUITE HL20, TORONTO, ON, M5G 1L7
SIC 8742
INSIGHT DIRECT CANADA, INC   *p1220*
5410 BOUL DECARIE, MONTREAL, QC, H3X 4B2
(514) 344-3500   *SIC 8742*
INTEGRATED BUSINESS ANALYSIS, INC
p997
130 KING ST, TORONTO, ON, M9N 1L5
(800) 531-7100   *SIC 8742*
INTEGRATED FINANCIAL TECHNOLOGIES INC   *p186*
4180 LOUGHEED HWY UNIT 400, BURN-ABY, BC, V5C 6A7
(844) 303-4899   *SIC 8742*
INTERAC CORP   *p963*
200 BAY ST SUITE 2400, TORONTO, ON, M5J 2J1
(416) 362-8550   *SIC 8742*
INTERNATIONAL ECONOMY SERVICES INC   *p775*
1057 STEELES AVE W SUITE 1, NORTH YORK, ON, M2R 2S9
(416) 725-1294   *SIC 8742*
INTERNATIONAL UNION OF OPERATING ENGINEERS LOCAL 115   *p189*
4333 LEDGER AVE SUITE 115, BURNABY, BC, V5G 4G9
(604) 291-8831   *SIC 8742*
INTERVISTAS CONSULTING INC   *p323*
1200 73RD AVE W SUITE 550, VANCOU-VER, BC, V6P 6G5
(604) 717-1800   *SIC 8742*
INVESTORS GROUP FINANCIAL SER-VICES INC   *p74*
37 RICHARD WAY SW UNIT 100, CAL-GARY, AB, T3E 7M8
(403) 253-4840   *SIC 8742*
INVESTORS GROUP FINANCIAL SER-VICES INC   *p222*
1628 DICKSON AVE SUITE 100, KELOWNA, BC, V1Y 9X1
(250) 762-3329   *SIC 8742*
INVESTORS GROUP FINANCIAL SER-VICES INC   *p579*
295 THE WEST MALL SUITE 700, ETOBI-COKE, ON, M9C 4Z4
(416) 695-8600   *SIC 8742*
INVESTORS GROUP FINANCIAL SER-VICES INC   *p706*
1 ROBERT SPECK PKWY 10 FL, MISSIS-

SAUGA, ON, L4Z 3M3
(905) 306-0031   *SIC 8742*
INVESTORS GROUP FINANCIAL SER-VICES INC   *p1227*
8250 BOUL DECARIE BUREAU 200, MON-TREAL, QC, H4P 2P5
(514) 733-3950   *SIC 8742*
IRVING FOREST SERVICES LIMITED   *p415*
300 UNION ST 11TH FL, SAINT JOHN, NB, E2L 4Z2
(506) 634-4242   *SIC 8742*
J & M GROUP INC   *p696*
5225 ORBITOR DR UNIT 8, MISSIS-SAUGA, ON, L4W 4Y8
(905) 766-2157   *SIC 8742*
JACOBS CONSULTANCY CANADA INC
p823
220 LAURIER AVE W SUITE 500, OTTAWA, ON, K1P 5Z9
SIC 8742
KENDRAKYLE INVESTMENTS INC   *p1086*
2540 BOUL DANIEL-JOHNSON BUREAU 207, COTE SAINT-LUC, QC, H7T 2S3
(450) 682-6227   *SIC 8742*
KERR WOOD LEIDAL ASSOCIATES LTD
p186
4185A STILL CREEK DR SUITE 200, BURNABY, BC, V5C 6G9
(604) 294-2088   *SIC 8742*
KEYBASE FINANCIAL GROUP INC   *p852*
1725 16TH AVE SUIT1 101, RICHMOND HILL, ON, L4B 0B3
(905) 709-7911   *SIC 8742*
KING MARKETING INC   *p263*
11121 HORSESHOE WAY SUITE 148, RICHMOND, BC, V7A 5G7
(604) 271-3455   *SIC 8742*
KPH TURCOT, UN PARTENARIAT S.E.N.C
p1062
4333 BOUL DE LA GRANDE-ALLEE, BOIS-BRIAND, QC, J7H 1M7
(450) 435-5756   *SIC 8742*
LABORATOIRES BUG TRACKER INC*p1166*
2030 BOUL PIE-IX BUREAU 307, MON-TREAL, QC, H1V 2C8
(514) 496-0093   *SIC 8742*
LAROCHELLE GROUPE CONSEIL INC
p1205
1010 RUE DE LA GAUCHETIERE O BU-REAU 650, MONTREAL, QC, H3B 2N2
(514) 848-1881   *SIC 8742*
LEE HECHT HARRISON-CANADA CORP
p935
250 YONGE ST SUITE 2800, TORONTO, ON, M5B 2L7
(416) 922-7561   *SIC 8742*
LIFEPLAN FINANCIAL SERVICES GROUP INC   *p337*
3960 QUADRA ST SUITE 101, VICTORIA, BC, V8X 4A3
(250) 727-7197   *SIC 8742*
LINKAGE GROUP INC, THE   *p672*
30 CENTURIAN DR SUITE 200, MARKHAM, ON, L3R 8B8
(905) 415-2300   *SIC 8742*
LIQUOR SOURCE CORPORATION   *p5*
4916 50 AVE, BEAUMONT, AB, T4X 1J9
(780) 851-7336   *SIC 8742*
LOGICIELS TANGERINE INC   *p1324*
555 BOUL DR.-FREDERIK-PHILIPS BU-REAU 450, SAINT-LAURENT, QC, H4M 2X4
(514) 748-9309   *SIC 8742*
LVM INC   *p1237*
1200 BOUL SAINT-MARTIN O BUREAU 300, MONTREAL, QC, H7S 2E4
(514) 281-1010   *SIC 8742*
M30 RETAIL SERVICES INC   *p67*
332 20 ST W UNIT 415, CALGARY, AB, T2T 6S1
(403) 313-9105   *SIC 8742*
MACDONALD REALTY LTD   *p321*
1827 5TH AVE W, VANCOUVER, BC, V6J 1P5
(604) 736-5611   *SIC 8742*

MACNAUGHTON HERMSEN BRITTON CLARKSON PLANNING LIMITED   *p635*
540 BINGEMANS CENTRE DR SUITE 200, KITCHENER, ON, N2B 3X9
(519) 576-3650   *SIC 8742*
MACQUARIE NORTH AMERICA LTD   *p964*
181 BAY ST SUITE 3100, TORONTO, ON, M5J 2T3
(416) 607-5000   *SIC 8742*
MANULIFE CANADA LTD   *p1198*
2000 RUE MANSFIELD UNITE 200, MON-TREAL, QC, H3A 2Z4
(514) 845-1612   *SIC 8742*
MANULIFE FINANCIAL SERVICES INC*p929*
200 BLOOR ST E SUITE 1, TORONTO, ON, M4W 1E5
(416) 926-3000   *SIC 8742*
MANUS INC   *p53*
350 7 AVE SW SUITE 1400, CALGARY, AB, T2P 3N9
(403) 299-9600   *SIC 8742*
MARCON CONSTRUCTION LTD   *p228*
5645 199 ST, LANGLEY, BC, V3A 1H9
(604) 530-5646   *SIC 8742*
MARKET REGULATION SERVICES INC
p954
145 KING ST W UNIT 900, TORONTO, ON, M5H 1J8
(416) 646-7204   *SIC 8742*
MASK MANAGEMENT CONSULTANTS LIM-ITED   *p816*
2571 LANCASTER RD, OTTAWA, ON, K1B 4L5
(613) 733-7800   *SIC 8742*
MAXPRO MANAGEMENT SERVICES LTD
p504
170 WILKINSON RD UNIT 3, BRAMPTON, ON, L6T 4Z5
(905) 452-9669   *SIC 8742*
MCINTOSH PERRY LIMITED   *p555*
7900 KEELE ST SUITE 200, CONCORD, ON, L4K 2A3
(905) 856-5200   *SIC 8742*
MCRAE INTEGRATION LTD   *p586*
34 MERIDIAN RD, ETOBICOKE, ON, M9W 4Z7
(416) 252-8833   *SIC 8742*
MD FINANCIAL MANAGEMENT LIMITED
p946
522 UNIVERSITY AVE SUITE 1100, TORONTO, ON, M5G 1W7
(416) 598-1442   *SIC 8742*
MDINA ENTERPRISES LTD   *p442*
121 DUKE ST SUITE 49, CHESTER, NS, B0J 1J0
(855) 855-3180   *SIC 8742*
MERCER (CANADA) LIMITED   *p964*
70 UNIVERSITY AVE SUITE 900, TORONTO, ON, M5J 2M4
(416) 868-2000   *SIC 8742*
MONTRIUM HOSTED SOLUTIONS INC
p1189
507 PLACE D'ARMES BUREAU 1050, MONTREAL, QC, H2Y 2W8
(514) 223-9153   *SIC 8742*
N.K.S. PHARMACY LIMITED   *p708*
130 DUNDAS ST E SUITE 500, MISSIS-SAUGA, ON, L5A 3V8
(905) 232-2322   *SIC 8742*
NATIONAL ARTS CENTRE CORPORATION
p824
1 ELGIN ST, OTTAWA, ON, K1P 5W1
(613) 947-7000   *SIC 8742*
NATIONAL UTILITY SERVICE (CANADA) LIMITED   *p765*
111 GORDON BAKER RD SUITE 500, NORTH YORK, ON, M2H 3R2
(416) 490-9922   *SIC 8742*
NAVIGANT CONSULTING LTD   *p940*
1 ADELAIDE ST E SUITE 1250, TORONTO, ON, M5C 2V9
(416) 777-2440   *SIC 8742*
NIIT LEARNING SOLUTIONS (CANADA) LTD   *p698*

5045 ORBITOR DR UNIT 100, MISSISSAUGA, ON, L4W 4Y4
(905) 572-1664   *SIC* 8742

NORTHERN HEALTH AUTHORITY   p250
1000 LIARD DR, PRINCE GEORGE, BC, V2M 3Z3
(250) 649-7293   *SIC* 8742

NORTHRIDGE ENERGY DEVELOPMENT GROUP INC   p31
1509 CENTRE ST SW SUITE 500, CALGARY, AB, T2G 2E6
SIC 8742

NOXENT INC   p1069
6400 BOUL TASCHEREAU BUREAU 200, BROSSARD, QC, J4W 3J2
(450) 926-0662   *SIC* 8742

NULOGX INC   p725
2233 ARGENTIA RD SUITE 202, MISSISSAUGA, ON, L5N 2X7
(905) 486-1162   *SIC* 8742

ONTARIO HOSPITAL ASSOCIATION   p982
200 FRONT ST W SUITE 2800, TORONTO, ON, M5V 3L1
(416) 205-1300   *SIC* 8742

OPEN SOLUTIONS DATAWEST INC   p321
1770 BURRARD ST SUITE 300, VANCOUVER, BC, V6J 3G7
(604) 734-7494   *SIC* 8742

PARADIGM CONSULTING GROUP INC   p1418
1881 SCARTH ST UNIT 1200, REGINA, SK, S4P 4K9
(306) 522-8588   *SIC* 8742

PEAK POTENTIALS TRAINING INC   p238
2155 DOLLARTON HWY SUITE 130, NORTH VANCOUVER, BC, V7H 3B2
(604) 083-3344   *SIC* 8742

PEMCO CONSTRUCTION LTD   p85
50 AIRPORT RD NW, EDMONTON, AB, T5G 0W7
(780) 414-5410   *SIC* 8742

PEOPLE CORPORATION   p389
1403 KENASTON BLVD, WINNIPEG, MB, R3P 2T5
(204) 940-3933   *SIC* 8742

PLAZA CONSULTING INC   p770
5700 YONGE ST SUITE 1400, NORTH YORK, ON, M2M 4K2
(416) 238-5333   *SIC* 8742

POINTS INTERNATIONAL LTD   p956
111 RICHMOND ST W SUITE 700, TORONTO, ON, M5H 2G4
(416) 595-0000   *SIC* 8742

PORCHLIGHT DEVELOPMENTS LTD   p170
414 MAIN ST NW, TURNER VALLEY, AB, T0L 2A0
(403) 933-3440   *SIC* 8742

PRESIDENT'S CHOICE BANK   p965
25 YORK ST SUITE 7FL, TORONTO, ON, M5J 2V5
(416) 204-2600   *SIC* 8742

PROFESSIONAL ABORIGINAL TESTING ORGANIZATION INC   p401
231 REGENT ST SUITE 301, FREDERICTON, NB, E3B 3W8
(506) 455-7725   *SIC* 8742

PROFESSIONAL QUALITY ASSURANCE LTD   p401
231 REGENT ST SUITE 104, FREDERICTON, NB, E3B 3W8
(506) 455-7725   *SIC* 8742

PROGESYS INC   p1235
4020 BOUL LE CORBUSIER BUREAU 201, MONTREAL, QC, H7L 5R2
(450) 667-7646   *SIC* 8742

PROGISTIX-SOLUTIONS INC   p997
99 SIGNET DR SUITE 300, TORONTO, ON, M9L 0A2
(416) 401-7000   *SIC* 8742

PROMAXIS SYSTEMS INC   p818
2385 ST. LAURENT BLVD, OTTAWA, ON, K1G 6C3
(613) 737-2112   *SIC* 8742

QUALICOM INNOVATIONS INC   p765

3389 STEELES AVE E SUITE 401, NORTH YORK, ON, M2H 3S8
(416) 492-3833   *SIC* 8742

QUALITY SERVICES INC   p604
497 WOOLWICH ST UNIT 2, GUELPH, ON, N1H 3X9
(519) 827-1147   *SIC* 8742

QUEEN ELIZABETH TWO HOSPITAL   p133
10409 98 ST, GRANDE PRAIRIE, AB, T8V 2E8
(780) 538-7100   *SIC* 8742

R3D CONSEIL INC   p1190
485 RUE MCGILL BUREAU 1110, MONTREAL, QC, H2Y 2H4
(514) 879-9000   *SIC* 8742

RESEARCH UNIVERSITIES' COUNCIL OF BRITISH COLUMBIA, THE   p336
880 DOUGLAS ST SUITE 400, VICTORIA, BC, V8W 2B7
(250) 480-4859   *SIC* 8742

RESOLVE CORPORATION   p441
197 DUFFERIN ST SUITE 100, BRIDGEWATER, NS, B4V 2G9
(902) 541-3600   *SIC* 8742

RESOLVE CORPORATION   p700
2400 SKYMARK AVE UNIT 6, MISSISSAUGA, ON, L4W 5K5
SIC 8742

RICHARDSON GMP LIMITED   p58
525 8 AVE SW SUITE 4700, CALGARY, AB, T2P 1G1
(403) 355-7735   *SIC* 8742

RITCHIE BROS. FINANCIAL SERVICES LTD   p193
9500 GLENLYON PKY, BURNABY, BC, V5J 0C6
(778) 331-5500   *SIC* 8742

ROYAL JUBILEE HOSPITAL AUXILIARY   p333
1952 BAY ST, VICTORIA, BC, V8R 1J8
(250) 370-8496   *SIC* 8742

RUSSELL HEALTH CENTRE   p356
426 ALEXANDRIA AVE, RUSSELL, MB, R0J 1W0
(204) 773-2125   *SIC* 8742

RYAN ULC   p726
6775 FINANCIAL DR SUITE 102, MISSISSAUGA, ON, L5N 0A4
(905) 567-7926   *SIC* 8742

SAI GLOBAL INC   p587
20 CARLSON CRT SUITE 200, ETOBICOKE, ON, M9W 7K6
(416) 401-8700   *SIC* 8742

SARNIA CARE-A-VAN   p859
1169 MICHENER RD, SARNIA, ON, N7S 4W3
(519) 336-3789   *SIC* 8742

SAUDER SCHOOL OF BUSINESS   p325
2053 MAIN MALL SUITE 402, VANCOUVER, BC, V6T 1Z2
(604) 822-8391   *SIC* 8742

SAVAGE CANAC INTERNATIONAL INC   p1341
6505 RTE TRANSCANADIENNE BUREAU 405, SAINT-LAURENT, QC, H4T 1S3
(514) 734-4700   *SIC* 8742

SCHAEFFER & ASSOCIATES LTD   p558
6 RONROSE DR SUITE 100, CONCORD, ON, L4K 4R3
SIC 8742

SERVICES S & E SOCIETE EN COMMANDITE   p1208
1155 BOUL RENE-LEVESQUE O BUREAU 4100, MONTREAL, QC, H3B 3V2
(514) 397-3318   *SIC* 8742

SHERWOOD FORD   p163
2540 BROADMOOR BLVD, SHERWOOD PARK, AB, T8H 1B4
(780) 449-3673   *SIC* 8742

SIEMENS CANADA LIMITED   p111
6652 50 ST NW, EDMONTON, AB, T6B 2N7
(780) 450-6762   *SIC* 8742

SIEMENS CANADA LIMITED   p743
6375 SHAWSON DR, MISSISSAUGA, ON,

L5T 1S7
(905) 212-4500   *SIC* 8742

SIGNATURE SUR LE SAINT-LAURENT CONSTRUCTION S.E.N.C.   p1396
8 PLACE DU COMMERCE UNITE 300, VERDUN, QC, H3E 1N3
(514) 876-1020   *SIC* 8742

SILVERBIRCH HOTELS AND RESORTS LIMITED PARTNERSHIP   p316
1188 GEORGIA ST W UNIT 1640, VANCOUVER, BC, V6E 4A2
(604) 646-2447   *SIC* 8742

SMG ADVISORS INC   p191
4250 KINGSWAY SUITE 213, BURNABY, BC, V5H 4T7
(604) 419-0455   *SIC* 8742

SNAP HOME FINANCE CORP   p300
538 CAMBIE ST, VANCOUVER, BC, V6B 2N7
(866) 282-2384   *SIC* 8742

SNC-LAVALIN GEM QUEBEC INC   p1116
3306 BOUL SAINT-FRANCOIS, JONQUIERE, QC, G7X 2W9
(418) 547-5716   *SIC* 8742

SNC-LAVALIN GEM QUEBEC INC   p1192
455 BOUL RENE-LEVESQUE O, MONTREAL, QC, H2Z 1Z3
(514) 393-8000   *SIC* 8742

SOLUTIA SDO LTD   p983
30 DUNCAN ST UNIT 202, TORONTO, ON, M5V 2C3
(416) 204-9797   *SIC* 8742

STADIUM CONSULTANTS INTERNATIONAL INC   p957
14 DUNCAN ST, TORONTO, ON, M5H 3G8
(416) 591-6777   *SIC* 8742

STERIPRO CANADA INC   p689
6580 NORTHWEST DR UNIT B, MISSISSAUGA, ON, L4V 1L5
(905) 766-4051   *SIC* 8742

STIRIS RESEARCH INC   p660
1650 BIRCHWOOD PL, LONDON, ON, N6K 4X3
(519) 471-6211   *SIC* 8742

SUN LIFE FINANCIAL AND DEPATIE FINANCIAL SERVICES INC   p138
4906 50 AVE, LACOMBE, AB, T4L 1Y1
(403) 782-3555   *SIC* 8742

TECHNI-DATA PERFORMANCE INC   p1248
12305 BOUL METROPOLITAIN E, POINTE-AUX-TREMBLES, QC, H1B 5R3
(514) 640-1666   *SIC* 8742

TECHNOLOGIES GLOBALSTEP INC   p1167
2030 BOUL PIE-IX BUREAU 307, MONTREAL, QC, H1V 2C8
(514) 496-0093   *SIC* 8742

THERMO CRS LTD   p525
5250 MAINWAY, BURLINGTON, ON, L7L 5Z1
(905) 332-2000   *SIC* 8742

THIINC LOGISTICS INC   p957
120 ADELAIDE ST W SUITE 2150, TORONTO, ON, M5H 1T1
(416) 862-5552   *SIC* 8742

TLI CHO LOGISTICS INC   p436
25 STANTON PLAZA, YELLOWKNIFE, NT, X1A 2N6
(867) 920-7288   *SIC* 8742

TODDGLEN WINDERMERE LIMITED   p768
2225 SHEPPARD AVE E SUITE 1100, NORTH YORK, ON, M2J 5C2
(416) 492-2450   *SIC* 8742

TRADEGECKO SOFTWARE CANADA LTD   p984
409 KING ST W SUITE 201, TORONTO, ON, M5V 1K1
(647) 621-5456   *SIC* 8742

TRANSPLANT QUEBEC   p1169
4100 RUE MOLSON BUREAU 200, MONTREAL, QC, H1Y 3N1
(514) 286-1414   *SIC* 8742

TROJAN CONSOLIDATED INVESTMENTS LIMITED   p780
18 WYNFORD DR SUITE 516, NORTH

YORK, ON, M3C 3S2
SIC 8742

TRUE NORTH AUTOMATION INC   p38
7180 11 ST SE, CALGARY, AB, T2H 2S9
(403) 984-2000   *SIC* 8742

TST OVERLAND EXPRESS   p701
5200 MAINGATE DR, MISSISSAUGA, ON, L4W 1G5
(905) 625-7500   *SIC* 8742

TUNDRA INTERNATIONAL INC   p890
1393 CENTRE LINE RD, STAYNER, ON, L0M 1S0
(705) 428-0544   *SIC* 8742

TUNDRA STRATEGIES, INC   p890
1393 CENTRE LINE RD, STAYNER, ON, L0M 1S0
(705) 734-7700   *SIC* 8742

UNITE DE SANTE INTERNATIONALE p1186
850 RUE SAINT-DENIS BUREAU S03, MONTREAL, QC, H2X 0A9
(514) 890-8156   *SIC* 8742

UTOURS INC   p984
345 ADELAIDE ST W SUITE 400, TORONTO, ON, M5V 1R5
(416) 479-3972   *SIC* 8742

VALACTA, SOCIETE EN COMMANDITE p1355
555 BOUL DES ANCIENS-COMBATTANTS, SAINTE-ANNE-DE-BELLEVUE, QC, H9X 3R4
(514) 459-3030   *SIC* 8742

VEREQUEST INCORPORATED   p984
370 QUEENS QUAY W SUITE 301, TORONTO, ON, M5V 3J3
(416) 362-6777   *SIC* 8742

VICTORIA UNIVERSITY   p976
75 QUEEN'S PARK CRES E, TORONTO, ON, M5S 1K7
(416) 585-4467   *SIC* 8742

VINCENT ASSOCIATES INC   p778
38 LESMILL RD, NORTH YORK, ON, M3B 2T5
(416) 445-5443   *SIC* 8742

WELLINGTON-ALTUS PRIVATE WEALTH INC   p376
201 PORTAGE AVEE 3RD FL, WINNIPEG, MB, R3B 3K6
(888) 315-8729   *SIC* 8742

WESTON CONSULTING GROUP INC   p561
201 MILLWAY AVE UNIT 19, CONCORD, ON, L4K 5K8
(905) 738-8080   *SIC* 8742

WILCO CONTRACTORS NORTHWEST INC p124
14420 154 AVE NW SUITE 107, EDMONTON, AB, T6V 0K8
(780) 447-1199   *SIC* 8742

WINDLEY ELY LEGAL SERVICES PROFESSIONAL CORPORATION   p656
275 COLBORNE ST, LONDON, ON, N6B 2S7
(519) 657-4242   *SIC* 8742

WIPRO SOLUTIONS CANADA LIMITED p91
10040 104 ST NW SUITE 100, EDMONTON, AB, T5J 0Z2
(780) 420-7875   *SIC* 8742

WITRON CANADA CORPORATION   p948
480 UNIVERSITY AVE SUITE 1500, TORONTO, ON, M5G 1V2
(416) 598-7096   *SIC* 8742

WOLVERTON SECURITIES LTD   p330
777 DUNSMUIR ST SUITE 1700, VANCOUVER, BC, V7Y 1J5
(604) 622-1000   *SIC* 8742

WORLEYPARSONSCORD LP   p859
1086 MODELAND RD BLDG 1050, SARNIA, ON, N7S 6L2
(519) 332-0160   *SIC* 8742

YOKOGAWA CANADA INC   p20
11133 40 ST SE SUITE 4, CALGARY, AB, T2C 2Z4
(403) 258-2681   *SIC* 8742

YUKON OCCUPATIONAL HEALTH   p1440
401 STRICKLAND ST, WHITEHORSE, YT,

Y1A 5N8
(867) 667-5450   *SIC 8742*

SIC 8743 Public relations services

1120423 ONTARIO LIMITED   *p791*
15 DENSLEY AVE, NORTH YORK, ON, M6M 2P5
(416) 429-2257   *SIC 8743*

2040830 ONTARIO INC   *p1186*
460 RUE SAINT-PAUL E SUITE 330, MONTREAL, QC, H2Y 3V1
SIC 8743

2842-3861 QUEBEC INC   *p1224*
1201 RUE DE LOUVAIN O, MONTREAL, QC, H4N 1G6
(514) 858-0066   *SIC 8743*

ACCUMARK PARTNERS INC   *p927*
2 BLOOR ST E SUITE 2600, TORONTO, ON, M4W 1A8
(416) 446-7758   *SIC 8743*

AIMIA INC   *p985*
130 KING ST W SUITE 1600, TORONTO, ON, M5X 2A2
(905) 214-8699   *SIC 8743*

AIMIA PROPRIETARY LOYALTY CANADA INC   *p985*
130 KING ST W SUITE 1600, TORONTO, ON, M5X 2A2
(905) 214-8699   *SIC 8743*

ARMSTRONG PARTNERSHIP LP   *p778*
23 PRINCE ANDREW PL, NORTH YORK, ON, M3C 2H2
(416) 444-3050   *SIC 8743*

BURLINGTON BUSINESS FORMS INC *p530*
2289 FAIRVIEW ST UNIT 208, BURLINGTON, ON, L7R 2E3
(905) 632-4611   *SIC 8743*

C F & R SERVICES INC   *p844*
1920 CLEMENTS RD, PICKERING, ON, L1W 3V6
(905) 426-3891   *SIC 8743*

CABINET DE RELATIONS PUBLIQUES NATIONAL INC, LE   *p979*
320 FRONT ST W SUITE 1600, TORONTO, ON, M5V 3B5
(416) 586-0180   *SIC 8743*

CABINET DE RELATIONS PUBLIQUES NATIONAL INC, LE   *p1202*
1155 RUE METCALFE SUITE 800, MONTREAL, QC, H3B 0C1
(514) 843-7171   *SIC 8743*

CANADIAN INTERNATIONAL GRAINS INSTITUTE   *p377*
303 MAIN ST SUITE 1000, WINNIPEG, MB, R3C 3G7
(204) 983-5344   *SIC 8743*

CENTRIC GROUP, THE   *p668*
161 ALDEN RD UNIT 9, MARKHAM, ON, L3R 3W7
(905) 415-9577   *SIC 8743*

COMMISSION DE LA CAPITALE NATIONALE DU QUEBEC   *p1269*
525 BOUL RENE-LEVESQUE E BUREAU RC, QUEBEC, QC, G1R 5S9
(418) 528-0773   *SIC 8743*

CROSSMARK CANADA INC   *p693*
5580 EXPLORER DR SUITE 300, MISSISSAUGA, ON, L4W 4Y1
SIC 8743

DIRECT FOCUS MARKETING COMMUNICATIONS INC   *p373*
315 PACIFIC AVE, WINNIPEG, MB, R3A 0M2
(204) 947-6912   *SIC 8743*

EDELMAN PUBLIC RELATIONS WORLDWIDE CANADA INC   *p974*
150 BLOOR ST W SUITE 300, TORONTO, ON, M5S 2X9
(416) 979-1120   *SIC 8743*

EPERNAY TASTING & PROMOTIONAL COMPANY LTD, THE   *p746*
4 CLEVERDON BLVD, MOUNT ALBERT,

ON, L0G 1M0
(905) 473-5905   *SIC 8743*

GORRIE ADVERTISING MANAGEMENT LIMITED   *p695*
2770 MATHESON BLVD E, MISSISSAUGA, ON, L4W 4M5
(905) 238-3466   *SIC 8743*

H K STRATEGIES CANADA   *p929*
160 BLOOR ST E SUITE 700, TORONTO, ON, M4W 0A2
(416) 413-1218   *SIC 8743*

HARDING GROUP LIMITED, THE   *p876*
150 DYNAMIC DR, SCARBOROUGH, ON, M1V 5A5
(416) 754-3215   *SIC 8743*

HIVE STRATEGIC MARKETING INC, THE *p981*
544 KING ST W, TORONTO, ON, M5V 1M3
(416) 923-3800   *SIC 8743*

IC GROUP INC   *p393*
383 DOVERCOURT DR, WINNIPEG, MB, R3Y 1G4
(204) 487-5000   *SIC 8743*

INVENTA SALES & PROMOTIONS INC *p319*
1401 8TH AVE W SUITE 210, VANCOUVER, BC, V6H 1C9
(604) 687-0544   *SIC 8743*

LAC LA RONGE INDIAN BAND   *p1404*
54 FAR RESERVE RD, AIR RONGE, SK, S0J 3G0
(306) 425-2884   *SIC 8743*

LPI COMMUNICATIONS GROUP INC   *p36*
253 62 AVE SE SUITE 101, CALGARY, AB, T2H 0R5
(403) 735-0655   *SIC 8743*

MANITOBA PUBLIC INSURANCE CORPORATION, THE   *p379*
234 DONALD ST SUITE 912, WINNIPEG, MB, R3C 4A4
(204) 985-7000   *SIC 8743*

MARCO CORPORATION, THE   *p518*
470 HARDY RD, BRANTFORD, ON, N3V 6T1
(519) 751-2227   *SIC 8743*

MARKETING STORE WORLDWIDE (CANADA) L.P., THE   *p991*
1209 KING ST W, TORONTO, ON, M6K 1G2
(416) 583-3931   *SIC 8743*

MARTINI-VISPAK INC   *p1117*
3535 BOUL SAINT-CHARLES BUREAU 600, KIRKLAND, QC, H9H 5B9
(514) 739-4666   *SIC 8743*

MATCH MG CANADA INC   *p697*
5225 SATELLITE DR, MISSISSAUGA, ON, L4W 5P9
(905) 566-2824   *SIC 8743*

MOSAIC SALES SOLUTIONS   *p1087*
2500 BOUL DANIEL-JOHNSON BUREAU 203, COTE SAINT-LUC, QC, H7T 2P6
(450) 686-1013   *SIC 8743*

MOSAIC SALES SOLUTIONS CANADA OPERATING CO.   *p697*
2700 MATHESON BLVD E UNIT 101, MISSISSAUGA, ON, L4W 4V9
(905) 238-8058   *SIC 8743*

NEWS MARKETING CANADA CORP *p987*
100 KING ST W SUITE 7000, TORONTO, ON, M5X 1A4
(416) 775-3000   *SIC 8743*

NOWPAC INC   *p878*
780 TAPSCOTT RD UNIT 5, SCARBOROUGH, ON, M1X 1A3
(416) 321-5799   *SIC 8743*

OFFICE DES CONGRES ET DU TOURISME DU GRAND MONTREAL INC, L'   *p1207*
800 BOUL RENE-LEVESQUE O BUREAU 2450, MONTREAL, QC, H3B 1X9
(514) 844-5400   *SIC 8743*

OGILVYONE WORLDWIDE LTD   *p943*
33 YONGE ST SUITE 1100, TORONTO, ON, M5E 1X6
(416) 363-9514   *SIC 8743*

OMNICOM CANADA CORP   *p930*
2 BLOOR ST W SUITE 2900, TORONTO,

ON, M4W 3E2
(416) 972-7571   *SIC 8743*

OP PROMOTIONS INC   *p917*
1017 WOODBINE AVE UNIT 408, TORONTO, ON, M4C 4C3
(416) 425-0363   *SIC 8743*

PROOF INC   *p930*
33 BLOOR ST E SUITE 900, TORONTO, ON, M4W 3H1
(416) 920-9000   *SIC 8743*

PULP & FIBER INC   *p991*
822 RICHMOND ST W SUITE 400, TORONTO, ON, M6J 1C9
(416) 361-0030   *SIC 8743*

QUINTINMANUS MARKETING GROUP INC *p934*
258 ADELAIDE ST E SUITE 400, TORONTO, ON, M5A 1N1
SIC 8743

RESOLVE CORPORATION   *p918*
210 WICKSTEED AVE, TORONTO, ON, M4G 2C3
SIC 8743

SECOND DIMENSION INTERNATIONAL LIMITED   *p588*
175 GALAXY BLVD UNIT 202, ETOBICOKE, ON, M9W 0C9
(416) 674-9010   *SIC 8743*

SOCIETE DU VIEUX-PORT DE MONTREAL INC   *p1190*
333 RUE DE LA COMMUNE O, MONTREAL, QC, H2Y 2E2
(514) 283-5256   *SIC 8743*

STAPLES PROMOTIONAL PRODUCTS CANADA, LTD   *p559*
55 INTERCHANGE WAY UNIT 4, CONCORD, ON, L4K 5W3
(905) 660-0685   *SIC 8743*

T & L FOOD MERCHANDISING SERVICES LTD   *p878*
78 PINEMEADOW BLVD, SCARBOROUGH, ON, M1W 1P2
(416) 497-6573   *SIC 8743*

THORNBURY FINANCIAL LTD   *p780*
23 PRINCE ANDREW PL, NORTH YORK, ON, M3C 2H2
(416) 444-3050   *SIC 8743*

VERIDAY INC   *p701*
5520 EXPLORER DR UNIT 400, MISSISSAUGA, ON, L4W 5L1
(905) 273-4399   *SIC 8743*

VILLE DE RIMOUSKI   *p1285*
475 2E RUE E, RIMOUSKI, QC, G5M 0A1
(418) 724-3142   *SIC 8743*

VILLE DE SALABERRY DE VALLEYFIELD *p1365*
275 RUE HEBERT, SALABERRY-DE-VALLEYFIELD, QC, J6S 5Y9
(450) 370-4820   *SIC 8743*

VISION 7 COMMUNICATIONS INC   *p1214*
2100 RUE DRUMMOND, MONTREAL, QC, H3G 1X1
(514) 845-2727   *SIC 8743*

VISION 7 COMMUNICATIONS INC   *p1214*
2100 RUE DRUMMOND, MONTREAL, QC, H3G 1X1
(514) 845-4040   *SIC 8743*

WEBER SHANDWICK WORLDWIDE (CANADA) INC   *p935*
351 KING ST E SUITE 800, TORONTO, ON, M5A 0L6
(416) 964-6444   *SIC 8743*

WHISTLER RESORT ASSOCIATION   *p343*
4010 WHISTLER WAY, WHISTLER, BC, V8E 1J2
(604) 664-5625   *SIC 8743*

WPP GROUP CANADA COMMUNICATIONS LIMITED   *p931*
160 BLOOR ST E SUITE 800, TORONTO, ON, M4W 1B9
(416) 987-5121   *SIC 8743*

SIC 8748 Business consulting, nec

1087338 ONTARIO LIMITED   *p527*
3320 SOUTH SERVICE RD SUITE 200, BURLINGTON, ON, L7N 3M6
(905) 681-1113   *SIC 8748*

2207544 ONTARIO INC   *p744*
1250 EGLINTON AVE W SUITE 138, MISSISSAUGA, ON, L5V 1N3
(905) 795-7781   *SIC 8748*

ABSOLUTE RESULTS PRODUCTIONS LTD *p278*
2677 192 ST UNIT 104, SURREY, BC, V3Z 3X1
(888) 751-7171   *SIC 8748*

ACCREON INC   *p400*
414 YORK ST, FREDERICTON, NB, E3B 3P7
(506) 452-0551   *SIC 8748*

AFCC AUTOMOTIVE FUEL CELL COOPERATION CORP   *p191*
9000 GLENLYON PKY, BURNABY, BC, V5J 5J8
(604) 415-7290   *SIC 8748*

AGRITEAM CANADA CONSULTING LTD *p69*
14707 BANNISTER RD SE UNIT 200, CALGARY, AB, T2X 1Z2
(403) 253-5298   *SIC 8748*

AGS INTERNATIONAL   *p99*
17942 105 AVE NW SUITE 200, EDMONTON, AB, T5S 2H5
(780) 455-0199   *SIC 8748*

ALBERTA SAFETY COUNCIL, THE   *p108*
4831 93 AVE NW, EDMONTON, AB, T6B 3A2
(780) 462-7300   *SIC 8748*

ALLEN & ASSOCIATES INC   *p484*
60 COLLIER ST UNIT 217, BARRIE, ON, L4M 1G8
SIC 8748

ALLNORTH CONSULTANTS LIMITED *p248*
2011 PRINCE GEORGE PULPMILL RD, PRINCE GEORGE, BC, V2K 5P5
(250) 614-7291   *SIC 8748*

AMA NSG INC   *p719*
6699 CAMPOBELLO RD, MISSISSAUGA, ON, L5N 2L7
(905) 826-3922   *SIC 8748*

AND 07 CONSULTING   *p608*
674 QUEENSTON RD, HAMILTON, ON, L8G 1A3
(905) 561-8960   *SIC 8748*

ANGUS GEOSOLUTIONS INC   *p620*
13029 STEELES AVE, HORNBY, ON, L0P 1E0
(905) 876-0700   *SIC 8748*

AON BENFIELD CANADA ULC   *p978*
225 KING ST W SUITE 1000, TORONTO, ON, M5V 3M2
(416) 979-3300   *SIC 8748*

APEX REFORESTATION LTD   *p296*
GD STN TERMINAL, VANCOUVER, BC, V6B 3P7
(604) 736-0063   *SIC 8748*

APPSONTIME TECHNOLOGIES LTD *p330*
320-645 FORT ST, VANCOUVER, BC, V8W 1G2
(778) 433-1268   *SIC 8748*

AQUACULTURE DEVELOPMENT BRANCH *p336*
3RD FL, VICTORIA, BC, V8W 2Z7
SIC 8748

ARCADIS CANADA INC   *p691*
4005 HICKORY DR, MISSISSAUGA, ON, L4W 1L1
(905) 614-1978   *SIC 8748*

ARCADIS CANADA INC   *p850*
121 GRANTON DR UNIT 12, RICHMOND HILL, ON, L4B 3N4
(905) 764-9380   *SIC 8748*

ASL ENVIRONMENTAL SCIENCES INC *p266*
6703 RAJPUR PL UNIT 1, SAANICHTON, BC, V8M 1Z5

---

(250) 656-0177   *SIC* 8748
AUDIENCEVIEW *p978*
2ND FLOOR, TORONTO, ON, M5V 3C7
(416) 687-2100   *SIC* 8748

AVIZO EXPERTS-CONSEILS INC *p1372*
1125 RUE DE CHERBOURG, SHER-
BROOKE, QC, J1K 0A8
(819) 346-4342   *SIC* 8748

AXYS TECHNOLOGIES INC *p268*
2035 MILLS RD W, SIDNEY, BC, V8L 5X2
(250) 655-5850   *SIC* 8748

BARROW SAFETY SERVICES INC *p136*
889 SWITZER DR, HINTON, AB, T7V 1V1
(780) 865-7763   *SIC* 8748

BC2 GROUPE CONSEIL INC *p1187*
85 RUE SAINT-PAUL O BUREAU 300,
MONTREAL, QC, H2Y 3V4
(514) 507-3600   *SIC* 8748

BDO CANADA LLP *p969*
66 WELLINGTON ST W SUITE 3600,
TORONTO, ON, M5K 1H1
(416) 865-0200   *SIC* 8748

BEAR SCARE LTD *p5*
5905 44 AVE, BEAUMONT, AB, T4X 0J1
(780) 717-0139   *SIC* 8748

BEDFORD BIOFUELS INC *p44*
510 5 ST SW SUITE 1500, CALGARY, AB,
T2P 3S2
(403) 648-6100   *SIC* 8748

BELL - GRASSLANDS *p1422*
4609 GORDON RD, REGINA, SK, S4W 0B7
(306) 779-1910   *SIC* 8748

BIOREX INC *p1268*
295 CH SAINTE-FOY, QUEBEC, QC, G1R
1T5
(418) 522-4945   *SIC* 8748

BLYTH EDUCATIONAL GROUP INC *p972*
160 AVENUE RD, TORONTO, ON, M5R 2H8
(416) 960-3552   *SIC* 8748

BOURASSA BOYER SOLUTION INC *p1394*
3323 BOUL DE LA GARE, VAUDREUIL-
DORION, QC, J7V 8W5
(450) 424-7000   *SIC* 8748

**BROADRIDGE INVESTOR COMMUNICA-
TIONS CORPORATION** *p730*
5970 CHEDWORTH WAY, MISSISSAUGA,
ON, L5R 4G5
(905) 507-5100   *SIC* 8748

BROCK SOLUTIONS INC *p636*
88 ARDELT AVE, KITCHENER, ON, N2C
2C9
(519) 571-1522   *SIC* 8748

**BROWN & ASSOCIATES PLANNING
GROUP LTD** *p45*
215 9 AVE SW SUITE 600, CALGARY, AB,
T2P 1K3
(403) 269-4733   *SIC* 8748

BUCK CONSULTANTS LIMITED *p979*
155 WELLINGTON ST W SUITE 3000,
TORONTO, ON, M5V 3L3
(416) 865-0060   *SIC* 8748

BUREAU VERITAS CANADA (2019) INC
p1338
889 MONTEE DE LIESSE, SAINT-
LAURENT, QC, H4T 1P5
(514) 448-9001   *SIC* 8748

BUSINESS IMPROVEMENT GROUP INC
p605
400 MICHENER RD SUITE 3, GUELPH,
ON, N1K 1E4
(519) 823-1110   *SIC* 8748

C T M GATINEAU *p1107*
73 RUE JEAN-PROULX, GATINEAU, QC,
J8Z 1W2
(819) 777-0999   *SIC* 8748

C-FER TECHNOLOGIES (1999) INC *p120*
200 KARL CLARK RD NW, EDMONTON,
AB, T6N 1H2
(780) 450-3300   *SIC* 8748

C4MEDIA INC *p570*
2267 LAKE SHORE BLVD W, ETOBICOKE,
ON, M8V 3X2
(647) 917-4470   *SIC* 8748

CAMBIUM INC *p839*

52 HUNTER ST E, PETERBOROUGH, ON,
K9H 1G5
(705) 742-7900   *SIC* 8748

CAMBIUM INC *p839*
52 HUNTER ST E, PETERBOROUGH, ON,
K9H 1G5
(705) 742-7900   *SIC* 8748

CANADA HEALTH INFOWAY *p949*
150 KING ST W SUITE 1300, TORONTO,
ON, M5H 1J9
(416) 979-4606   *SIC* 8748

**CANADIAN COUNCIL ON REHABILITA-
TION AND WORK, THE** *p923*
477 MOUNT PLEASANT RD SUITE 105,
TORONTO, ON, M4S 2L9
(416) 260-3060   *SIC* 8748

CANADIAN NURSES ASSOCIATION *p833*
50 DRIVEWAY, OTTAWA, ON, K2P 1E2
(613) 232-6424   *SIC* 8748

CANADIAN TEST CASE 62 *p720*
6750 CENTURY AVE SUITE 305, MISSIS-
SAUGA, ON, L5N 2V8
(437) 999-9999   *SIC* 8748

**CARIBOO PRESS PRINTING & PUBLISH-
ING LTD** *p219*
2495 ENTERPRISE WAY, KELOWNA, BC,
V1X 7K2
(250) 763-3212   *SIC* 8748

CBRE LIMITEE *p950*
145 KING ST W SUITE 1100, TORONTO,
ON, M5H 1J8
(416) 362-2244   *SIC* 8748

**CENTRE DE RECHERCHE EN INFECTI-
OLOGIE (CRI)** *p1271*
2705 BOUL LAURIER BUREAU RC 709,
QUEBEC, QC, G1V 4G2
(418) 654-2705   *SIC* 8748

CH2M HILL ENERGY CANADA LTD *p14*
205 QUARRY PARK BLVD SE, CALGARY,
AB, T2C 3E7
(403) 407-6000   *SIC* 8748

CHECKWELL SOLUTIONS CORPORATION
p281
19433 96 AVE SUITE 200, SURREY, BC,
V4N 4C4
(604) 506-4663   *SIC* 8748

**COMMISSION FOR ENVIRONMENTAL CO-
OPERATION** *p1187*
393 RUE SAINT-JACQUES BUREAU 200,
MONTREAL, QC, H2Y 1N9
(514) 350-4300   *SIC* 8748

COMMUNICATIONS MEDPLAN INC *p1223*
2077 RUE CABOT, MONTREAL, QC, H4E
1E2
(514) 767-6166   *SIC* 8748

CONTACT SERVICES INC *p298*
128 PENDER ST W FLR 6-7, VANCOUVER,
BC, V6B 1R8
(604) 688-5523   *SIC* 8748

CONTROL TECH 2011 LTD *p134*
11001 78 AVE, GRANDE PRAIRIE, AB,
T8W 2J7
(780) 539-7114   *SIC* 8748

CONTROLES I.S.I. INC, LES *p1333*
4030 CH DU BOIS-FRANC, SAINT-
LAURENT, QC, H4S 1A7
(514) 338-1562   *SIC* 8748

CREATION STRATEGIQUE ABSOLUE INC
p1397
1097 RUE NOTRE-DAME O BUREAU 100,
VICTORIAVILLE, QC, G6P 7L1
(819) 752-8888   *SIC* 8748

CRESTVIEW STRATEGY INC *p823*
222 QUEEN ST SUITE 1201, OTTAWA, ON,
K1P 5V9
(613) 232-3192   *SIC* 8748

**CUNNINGHAM LINDSEY CANADA CLAIMS
SERVICES LTD** *p709*
50 BURNHAMTHORPE RD W SUITE 1102,
MISSISSAUGA, ON, L5B 3C2
(905) 896-8181   *SIC* 8748

D DENISON CONSULTANTS *p921*
1535 MOUNT PLEASANT RD, TORONTO,
ON, M4N 2V1

(416) 484-1893   *SIC* 8748
**DAVIS MARTINDALE PROFESSIONAL
CORPORATION** *p659*
373 COMMISSIONERS RD W, LONDON,
ON, N6J 1Y4
(519) 673-3141   *SIC* 8748

DIABSOLUT INC *p1250*
181 BOUL HYMUS BUREAU 100, POINTE-
CLAIRE, QC, H9R 5P4
(514) 461-3314   *SIC* 8748

**DIVERSIFIED TECHNOLOGY SYSTEMS
INC** *p920*
1043 GERRARD ST E, TORONTO, ON,
M4M 1Z7
(416) 486-6587   *SIC* 8748

DWB CONSULTING SERVICES LTD *p224*
3361 HELENA LAKE RD, LAC LA HACHE,
BC, V0K 1T1
(250) 396-7208   *SIC* 8748

ECOFISH RESEARCH LTD *p203*
450 8TH ST SUITE F, COURTENAY, BC,
V9N 1N5
(250) 334-3042   *SIC* 8748

ECOFOR CONSULTING LTD *p213*
9940 104 AVE, FORT ST. JOHN, BC, V1J
2K3
(250) 787-6009   *SIC* 8748

ECONOLER INC *p1258*
160 RUE SAINT-PAUL BUREAU 200, QUE-
BEC, QC, G1K 3W1
(418) 692-2592   *SIC* 8748

EFFICIENCY NOVA SCOTIA CORP *p446*
230 BROWNLOW AVE SUITE 300, DART-
MOUTH, NS, B3B 0G5
(902) 470-3500   *SIC* 8748

EHS CANADA INC *p882*
2964 SOUTH GRIMSBY RD 18 RR 1,
SMITHVILLE, ON, L0R 2A0
(905) 643-3343   *SIC* 8748

ELECTROLAB LIMITED *p491*
631 COLLEGE ST E, BELLEVILLE, ON,
K8N 0A3
(613) 962-9577   *SIC* 8748

ENERCON CANADA INC *p1204*
700 RUE DE LA GAUCHETIERE O BU-
REAU 1200, MONTREAL, QC, H3B 5M2
(514) 363-7266   *SIC* 8748

ENERGY ADVANTAGE INC *p522*
5515 NORTH SERVICE RD UNIT 303,
BURLINGTON, ON, L7L 6G4
(905) 319-1717   *SIC* 8748

ENERGY SAFETY CANADA *p22*
5055 11 ST NE, CALGARY, AB, T2E 8N4
(403) 516-8000   *SIC* 8748

ESIT ADVANCED SOLUTIONS INC *p338*
4464 MARKHAM ST SUITE 2200, VICTO-
RIA, BC, V8Z 7X8
(250) 405-4500   *SIC* 8748

**EVERGREEN ENVIROMENTAL FOUNDA-
TION** *p928*
550 BAYVIEW AVE SUITE 300, TORONTO,
ON, M4W 3X8
(416) 596-1495   *SIC* 8748

**FALCK SAFETY SERVICES CANADA IN-
CORPORATED** *p443*
20 ORION CRT SUITE 1, DARTMOUTH,
NS, B2Y 4W6
(902) 466-7878   *SIC* 8748

**FAMILY CENTRED PRACTICES GROUP
INC** *p321*
1820 FIR ST UNIT 210, VANCOUVER, BC,
V6J 3B1
(604) 736-0094   *SIC* 8748

FARMERS EDGE INC *p388*
25 ROTHWELL RD, WINNIPEG, MB, R3P
2M5
(204) 452-3131   *SIC* 8748

FARMLINK MARKETING SOLUTIONS *p374*
93 LOMBARD AVE SUITE 110, WINNIPEG,
MB, R3B 3B1
(877) 376-5465   *SIC* 8748

FIREMASTER OILFIELD SERVICES INC
p155
4728 78A ST CLOSE, RED DEER, AB, T4P

2J2
(403) 342-7500   *SIC* 8748

FTI CONSULTING CANADA ULC *p969*
79 WELLINGTON ST W SUITE 2010,
TORONTO, ON, M5K 1B1
(416) 649-8100   *SIC* 8748

G-TEL ENGINEERING INC *p651*
1150 FRANCES ST 2ND FL, LONDON, ON,
N5W 5N5
(519) 439-0763   *SIC* 8748

G-TEL ENGINEERING INC *p1031*
200 HANLAN RD, WOODBRIDGE, ON, L4L
3P6
(905) 856-1162   *SIC* 8748

G.D.G. ENVIRONNEMENT LTEE *p1384*
430 RUE SAINT-LAURENT, TROIS-
RIVIERES, QC, G8T 6H3
(819) 373-3097   *SIC* 8748

**GEOSYNTEC CONSULTANTS INTERNA-
TIONAL INC** *p601*
130 STONE RD W, GUELPH, ON, N1G 3Z2
(519) 822-2230   *SIC* 8748

GEVITY CONSULTING INC *p298*
375 WATER ST SUITE 350, VANCOUVER,
BC, V6B 5C6
(604) 608-1779   *SIC* 8748

GLOBAL INTERNATIONAL INC *p168*
GD STN MAIN, STRATHMORE, AB, T1P
1J5
(403) 934-5046   *SIC* 8748

GOLDER ASSOCIATES LTD *p11*
2535 3 AVE SE SUITE 102, CALGARY, AB,
T2A 7W5
(403) 299-5600   *SIC* 8748

GOLDER ASSOCIATES LTD *p1181*
7250 RUE DU MILE END 3E ETAGE, MON-
TREAL, QC, H2R 3A4
(514) 383-0990   *SIC* 8748

**GOUVERNEMENT DE LA PROVINCE DE
QUEBEC** *p1138*
1400 BOUL GUILLAUME-COUTURE
UNITE RC, LEVIS, QC, G6W 8K7
(418) 838-5615   *SIC* 8748

**GRANT PRODUCTION TESTING SERVICES
LTD** *p155*
6750 GOLDEN WEST AVE, RED DEER,
AB, T4P 1A8
(403) 314-0042   *SIC* 8748

GROUPE CONSEIL FXINNOVATION INC
p1143
125 BOUL SAINTE-FOY, LONGUEUIL, QC,
J4J 1W7
SIC 8748

GROUPE IBI/DAA INC *p1211*
100 RUE PEEL 4E ETAGE, MONTREAL,
QC, H3C 0L8
(514) 316-1010   *SIC* 8748

GROUPEX INC *p929*
3 ROWANWOOD AVE, TORONTO, ON,
M4W 1Y5
(416) 968-0000   *SIC* 8748

GROUPEX LIMITED *p929*
3 ROWANWOOD AVE, TORONTO, ON,
M4W 1Y5
(416) 968-0000   *SIC* 8748

GSI ENVIRONNEMENT INC *p1267*
4495 BOUL WILFRID-HAMEL BUREAU
100, QUEBEC, QC, G1P 2J7
(418) 872-4227   *SIC* 8748

GUIDELITE FINANCIAL NETWORKS LTD
p553
1600 STEELES AVE W SUITE 231, CON-
CORD, ON, L4K 4M2
SIC 8748

HARRIS SECURITY AGENCY *p830*
2720 QUEENSVIEW DR SUITE 1140, OT-
TAWA, ON, K2B 1A5
(613) 726-6713   *SIC* 8748

HEALTHCARE BENEFIT TRUST *p286*
350-2889 12TH AVE E, VANCOUVER, BC,
V5M 4T5
(604) 736-2087   *SIC* 8748

HEARTSAFE EMS INC *p495*
159 VICTORIA ST, BOLTON, ON, L7E 3G9

(416) 410-4911 *SIC* 8748
HEMMERA ENVIROCHEM INC p190
4730 KINGSWAY 18 FL, BURNABY, BC,
V5H 0C6
(604) 669-0424 *SIC* 8748
HEWITT ASSOCIATES CORP p772
2 SHEPPARD AVE E SUITE 1500, NORTH
YORK, ON, M2N 7A4
(416) 225-5001 *SIC* 8748
HISHKOONIKUN EDUCATION AUTHORITY
p627
GD, KASHECHEWAN, ON, P0L 1S0
(705) 275-4111 *SIC* 8748
HOMESTARTS INCORPORATED p723
6537 MISSISSAUGA RD UNIT B, MISSIS-
SAUGA, ON, L5N 1A6
(905) 858-1110 *SIC* 8748
**HORTICULTURAL SOCIETIES OF PARK-
DALE & TORONTO** p994
1938 BLOOR ST W, TORONTO, ON, M6P
3K8
(416) 486-0898 *SIC* 8748
HSE INTEGRATED LTD p6
5503 50 AVE, BONNYVILLE, AB, T9N 2K9
(780) 826-5300 *SIC* 8748
HSE INTEGRATED LTD p51
630 6 AVE SW SUITE 1000, CALGARY, AB,
T2P 0S8
(403) 266-1833 *SIC* 8748
**I.W.A. FOREST INDUSTRY PENSION &
PLAN** p190
3777 KINGSWAY SUITE 2100, BURNABY,
BC, V5H 3Z7
(604) 433-6310 *SIC* 8748
ICOM PRODUCTIONS INC p51
140 8 AVE SW SUITE 400, CALGARY, AB,
T2P 1B3
(403) 539-9276 *SIC* 8748
IGF AXIOM INC p1134
4125 DES LAURENTIDES (A-15) E, LAVAL-
OUEST, QC, H7L 5W5
(514) 645-3443 *SIC* 8748
ILLUMITI INC p904
123 COMMERCE VALLEY DR E SUITE
500, THORNHILL, ON, L3T 7W8
(905) 737-1066 *SIC* 8748
IMMEDIATE RESPONSE FORCE INC p920
1127 BROADVIEW AVE UNIT B,
TORONTO, ON, M4K 2S6
(647) 987-0002 *SIC* 8748
INNOVATIA INC p415
1 GERMAIN ST, SAINT JOHN, NB, E2L 4V1
(506) 640-4000 *SIC* 8748
**INSIGHTS LEARNING & DEVELOPMENT
LTD** p35
5824 2 ST SW SUITE 302, CALGARY, AB,
T2H 0H2
(403) 233-7263 *SIC* 8748
INSTEAD ROBOTIC CORP p1296
1370 RUE HOCQUART, SAINT-BRUNO,
QC, J3V 6E1
(450) 653-7868 *SIC* 8748
**INTEGRATED SUSTAINABILITY CONSUL-
TANTS LTD** p52
1600-400 3 AVE SW, CALGARY, AB, T2P
4H2
SIC 8748
**INTERNATIONAL ORNITHOLOGICAL
CONGRESS 2018 ORGANIZING SOCIETY**
p287
7190 DUFF ST, VANCOUVER, BC, V5P 4B3
(604) 218-9138 *SIC* 8748
INTERTEK HEALTH SCIENCES INC. p723
2233 ARGENTIA RD SUITE 201, MISSIS-
SAUGA, ON, L5N 2X7
(905) 542-2900 *SIC* 8748
INVESTISSEMENT QUEBEC p1188
413 RUE SAINT-JACQUES BUREAU 500,
MONTREAL, QC, H2Y 1N9
(514) 873-4375 *SIC* 8748
IQ PARTNERS INC p963
144 FRONT ST W SUITE 600, TORONTO,
ON, M5J 2L7
(416) 599-4700 *SIC* 8748

**JENSEN HUGHES CONSULTING CANADA
LTD** p997
2150 ISLINGTON AVE SUITE 100,
TORONTO, ON, M9P 3V4
(647) 559-1251 *SIC* 8748
JKL PROPERTIES LTD p793
32 PENN DR, NORTH YORK, ON, M9L 2A9
(416) 740-5671 *SIC* 8748
JOHNSTON GROUP INC p384
1051 KING EDWARD ST, WINNIPEG, MB,
R3H 0R4
(204) 774-6677 *SIC* 8748
KARABUS MANAGEMENT INC p789
1 YORKDALE RD SUITE 412, NORTH
YORK, ON, M6A 3A1
SIC 8748
KEYSTONE ENVIRONMENTAL LTD p189
4400 DOMINION ST SUITE 320, BURN-
ABY, BC, V5G 4G3
(604) 430-0671 *SIC* 8748
KNEBEL WATTERS & ASSOCIATES INC
p964
10 BAY ST SUITE 605, TORONTO, ON, M5J
2R8
(416) 362-4300 *SIC* 8748
KORPACH CONSULTING LTD p11
611 MALVERN DR NE, CALGARY, AB, T2A
5G8
(403) 219-7481 *SIC* 8748
L3 MAPPS INC p1340
8565 CH DE LA COTE-DE-LIESSE, SAINT-
LAURENT, QC, H4T 1G5
(514) 787-5000 *SIC* 8748
LGL LIMITED p629
22 FISHER ST, KING CITY, ON, L7B 1G3
(905) 833-1244 *SIC* 8748
LIFEWORKS CANADA LTD p672
675 COCHRANE DR 5TH FL, MARKHAM,
ON, L3R 0B8
(905) 947-7214 *SIC* 8748
M I C A p935
229 YONGE ST SUITE 400, TORONTO,
ON, M5B 1N9
SIC 8748
MACHIBRODA, P. ENGINEERING LTD p1428
806 48TH ST E, SASKATOON, SK, S7K 3Y4
(306) 665-8444 *SIC* 8748
MANHAL AL HABBOBI CONSULTANTS
p684
6541 DERRY RD, MILTON, ON, L9T 7W1
(905) 491-6864 *SIC* 8748
MANION WILKINS & ASSOCIATES LTD
p577
21 FOUR SEASONS PL SUITE 500, ETO-
BICOKE, ON, M9B 0A5
(416) 234-5044 *SIC* 8748
**MANITOBA FIRST NATIONS EDUCATION
RESOURCE CENTRE INC** p351
4820 PORTAGE AVE, HEADINGLEY, MB,
R4H 1C8
(204) 831-1224 *SIC* 8748
MAPLEBRAINS TECHNOLOGIES INC p398
842 GAUVIN RD, DIEPPE, NB, E1A 1N1
(506) 899-1526 *SIC* 8748
MARTEC LIMITED p453
1888 BRUNSWICK ST SUITE 400, HALI-
FAX, NS, B3J 3J8
(902) 425-5101 *SIC* 8748
MATRIX SOLUTIONS INC p65
214 11 AVE SW SUITE 600, CALGARY, AB,
T2R 0K1
(403) 237-0606 *SIC* 8748
MAXSYS STAFFING & CONSULTING INC
p821
173 DALHOUSIE ST SUITE A, OTTAWA,
ON, K1N 7C7
(613) 562-9943 *SIC* 8748
MCC INDUSTRIAL SERVICES LTD p538
125 VONDRAU DR SUITE 1, CAMBRIDGE,
ON, N3E 1A8
(519) 650-9886 *SIC* 8748
**MCELHANNEY CONSULTING SERVICES
LTD** p274
13450 102 AVE SUITE 2300, SURREY, BC,

V3T 5X3
(604) 596-0391 *SIC* 8748
**MCELHANNEY CONSULTING SERVICES
LTD** p299
858 BEATTY ST SUITE 200, VANCOUVER,
BC, V6B 1C1
(604) 683-8521 *SIC* 8748
MDA SYSTEMS HOLDINGS LTD p255
13800 COMMERCE PKWY, RICHMOND,
BC, V6V 2J3
(604) 278-3411 *SIC* 8748
MESSAGEPOINT INC p965
207 QUEENS QUAY W SUITE 802,
TORONTO, ON, M5J 1A7
(416) 410-8956 *SIC* 8748
**METIS PROVINCIAL COUNCIL OF BRITISH
COLUMBIA** p272
103-5668 192 ST, SURREY, BC, V3S 2V7
(604) 557-5851 *SIC* 8748
MILLENNIUM EMS SOLUTIONS LTD p163
2257 PREMIER WAY UNIT 148, SHER-
WOOD PARK, AB, T8H 2M8
(780) 496-9048 *SIC* 8748
MILLENNIUM RESEARCH GROUP INC p930
175 BLOOR ST E SUITE 400, TORONTO,
ON, M4W 3R8
(416) 364-7776 *SIC* 8748
MILLS, BRYAN IRODESSO CORP p779
1129 LESLIE ST, NORTH YORK, ON, M3C
2K5
(416) 447-4740 *SIC* 8748
MONT-ROYAL DEVELOPPEMENT p1155
20 AV ROOSEVELT, MONT-ROYAL, QC,
H3R 1Z4
(514) 734-3034 *SIC* 8748
MONTREAL INTERNATIONAL p1189
380 RUE SAINT-ANTOINE O BUREAU
8000, MONTREAL, QC, H2Y 3X7
(514) 987-8191 *SIC* 8748
MORINVILLE COLONY LTD p147
GD, MORINVILLE, AB, T8R 1A1
(780) 939-2118 *SIC* 8748
MULTI-HEALTH SYSTEMS INC p765
3770 VICTORIA PARK AVE, NORTH YORK,
ON, M2H 3M6
(416) 492-2627 *SIC* 8748
**NATIONAL INCOME PROTECTION PLAN
INC** p698
2595 SKYMARK AVE UNIT 206, MISSIS-
SAUGA, ON, L4W 4L5
(905) 219-0096 *SIC* 8748
**NATIONAL MERCHANDISING CORPORA-
TION** p1244
400 AV ATLANTIC BUREAU 705, OUT-
REMONT, QC, H2V 1A5
(514) 764-0141 *SIC* 8748
**NATIONAL PORT SECURITY SERVICES
INC** p1039
379 QUEEN ST, CHARLOTTETOWN, PE,
C1A 4C9
(902) 892-9977 *SIC* 8748
**NEWFOUNDLAND & LABRADOR SAFETY
COUNCIL INC** p426
3 MOFFATT RD, MOUNT PEARL, NL, A1N
5B9
(709) 754-0210 *SIC* 8748
NORTH/SOUTH CONSULTANTS INC p393
83 SCURFIELD BLVD, WINNIPEG, MB,
R3Y 1G4
(204) 284-3366 *SIC* 8748
NORTHERN LIGHTS AVIATION LTD p134
3795 56 AVE E, GRANDE PRAIRIE, AB,
T9E 0V4
(780) 890-1300 *SIC* 8748
NORWEST CORPORATION p31
411 1 ST SE SUITE 2700, CALGARY, AB,
T2G 4Y5
(403) 237-7763 *SIC* 8748
NOTRA INC p830
2725 QUEENSVIEW DR SUITE 200, OT-
TAWA, ON, K2B 0A1
(613) 738-0887 *SIC* 8748
**NUCOR ENVIRONMENTAL SOLUTIONS
LTD** p272

5250 185A ST SUITE 2, SURREY, BC, V3S
7A4
(604) 575-4721 *SIC* 8748
O.B.N. CONSULTANTS INC p575
78 QUEEN ELIZABETH BLVD, ETOBI-
COKE, ON, M8Z 1M3
(416) 253-7416 *SIC* 8748
OH ENVIRONMENTAL INC p706
311 MATHESON BLVD E, MISSISSAUGA,
ON, L4Z 1X8
(905) 890-9000 *SIC* 8748
OKANAGAN COLLEGE p243
583 DUNCAN AVE W, PENTICTON, BC,
V2A 8E1
(250) 492-4305 *SIC* 8748
OLYMPE CONSULTANTS p1280
1500 RUE MIGNERON, QUEBEC, QC, G2K
1X5
SIC 8748
ONACTUATE CONSULTING INC. p327
777 HORNBY ST SUITE 600, VANCOU-
VER, BC, V6Z 2H7
(604) 506-3435 *SIC* 8748
**ONTARIO INFRASTRUCTURE AND LANDS
CORPORATION** p946
1 DUNDAS ST W SUITE 2000, TORONTO,
ON, M5G 2L5
(416) 327-3937 *SIC* 8748
OPTIONS NON TRADITIONNELLES INC.
p1143
125 BOUL SAINTE-FOY BUREAU 300,
LONGUEUIL, QC, J4J 1W7
(450) 646-1030 *SIC* 8748
OPTUMINSIGHT (CANADA) INC p566
4 INNOVATION DR, DUNDAS, ON, L9H 7P3
(905) 689-3980 *SIC* 8748
**PINCHIN LEBLANC ENVIRONMENTAL LIM-
ITED** p448
42 DOREY AVE, DARTMOUTH, NS, B3B
0B1
(902) 461-9999 *SIC* 8748
PINCHIN LTD p725
2470 MILLTOWER CRT, MISSISSAUGA,
ON, L5N 7W5
(905) 363-0678 *SIC* 8748
PLANET ENERGY CORP p772
5525 YONGE ST SUITE 1500, NORTH
YORK, ON, M2N 5S3
SIC 8748
PORTSMOUTH ATLANTIC LIMITED p1039
20 GREAT GEORGE ST SUITE 103, CHAR-
LOTTETOWN, PE, C1A 4J6
(902) 978-1400 *SIC* 8748
POTENTIA RENEWABLES INC p983
200 WELLINGTON ST W SUITE 1102,
TORONTO, ON, M5V 3G2
(416) 703-1911 *SIC* 8748
**POTTINGER GAHERTY ENVIRONMENTAL
CONSULTANTS LTD** p315
1185 GEORGIA ST W SUITE 1200, VAN-
COUVER, BC, V6E 4E6
(604) 682-3707 *SIC* 8748
**PRECISiON COMMUNICATION SERVICES
CORP** p793
99 SIGNET DR UNIT 200, NORTH YORK,
ON, M9L 1T6
(416) 749-0110 *SIC* 8748
PRECISIONERP INCORPORATED p821
12 YORK ST 4TH FL, OTTAWA, ON, K1N
5S6
(613) 226-9900 *SIC* 8748
PRINCETON REVIEW CANADA INC, THE
p973
1255 BAY ST SUITE 550, TORONTO, ON,
M5R 2A9
(416) 944-8001 *SIC* 8748
PROCEED SOLUTIONS INC p65
906 12 AVE SW SUITE 600, CALGARY, AB,
T2R 1K7
(403) 685-8390 *SIC* 8748
PROCOM CONSULTANTS GROUP LTD p924
2200 YONGE ST SUITE 700, TORONTO,
ON, M4S 2C6
(416) 483-0766 *SIC* 8748

▲ Public Company   ■ Public Company Family Member   **HQ** Headquarters   **BR** Branch   **SL** Single Location

PROTECT AIR CO *p674*
2751 JOHN ST, MARKHAM, ON, L3R 2Y8
(905) 944-8877   *SIC 8748*

PRUDENT BENEFITS ADMINISTRATION SERVICES INC *p587*
61 INTERNATIONAL BLVD SUITE 110, ETOBICOKE, ON, M9W 6K4
(416) 674-8581   *SIC 8748*

PUBLIC GUARDIAN TRUSTEE OF SASKATCHEWAN *p1418*
1871 SMITH ST SUITE 100, REGINA, SK, S4P 4W4
(306) 787-5424   *SIC 8748*

R'OHAN RIG SERVICES LTD *p144*
GD, LLOYDMINSTER, AB, T9V 3C1
(780) 872-7887   *SIC 8748*

RADIOLOGY CONSULTANTS ASSOCIATED *p3*
110 MAYFAIR CLOSE SE, AIRDRIE, AB, T4A 1T6
(403) 777-3040   *SIC 8748*

RAYMOND CHABOT GRANT THORTON CONSULTING INC. *p824*
116 ALBERT ST, OTTAWA, ON, K1P 5G3
(613) 760-3500   *SIC 8748*

RESEAUX ACCEDIAN INC, LES *p1336*
2351 BOUL ALFRED-NOBEL SUITE N-410, SAINT-LAURENT, QC, H4S 0B2
(514) 331-6181   *SIC 8748*

RESOLUTE TECHNOLOGY SOLUTIONS INC *p375*
433 MAIN ST SUITE 600, WINNIPEG, MB, R3B 1B3
(204) 927-3520   *SIC 8748*

RIDGELINE CANADA INC *p25*
3016 19 ST NE SUITE 101, CALGARY, AB, T2E 6Y9
(403) 806-2380   *SIC 8748*

RIVERSIDE HUTTERIAN MUTUAL CORPORATION *p345*
GD, ARDEN, MB, R0J 0B0
(204) 368-2444   *SIC 8748*

ROY NORTHERN LAND SERVICE LTD *p126*
10912-100F, FAIRVIEW, AB, T0H 1L0
(780) 835-2682   *SIC 8748*

SAFEMAP INTERNATIONAL INC *p309*
666 BURRARD ST SUITE 500, VANCOUVER, BC, V6C 3P6
(604) 642-6110   *SIC 8748*

SAFETY SERVICES NOVA SCOTIA *p448*
201 BROWNLOW AVE UNIT 1, DARTMOUTH, NS, B3B 1W2
(902) 454-9621   *SIC 8748*

SALTWORKS TECHNOLOGIES INC *p258*
13800 STEVESTON HWY, RICHMOND, BC, V6W 1A8
(604) 628-6508   *SIC 8748*

SANTINEL INC *p1145*
1061 BOUL SAINTE-FOY, LONGUEUIL, QC, J4K 1W5
(450) 679-7801   *SIC 8748*

SC 360 INC *p1336*
2425 BOUL PITFIELD, SAINT-LAURENT, QC, H4S 1W8
(514) 735-8557   *SIC 8748*

SCOTT AND STEWART FORESTRY CONSULTANTS LTD *p466*
2267 ANTIGONISH GUYSBOROUGH RD, ST ANDREWS, NS, B0H 1X0
(902) 863-5508   *SIC 8748*

SENES HOLDINGS CORP *p854*
121 GRANTON DR UNIT 12, RICHMOND HILL, ON, L4B 3N4
(905) 764-9380   *SIC 8748*

SLALOM CONSULTING ULC *p940*
8 KING ST E UNIT 2000, TORONTO, ON, M5C 1B5
(416) 366-5390   *SIC 8748*

SLR CONSULTING (CANADA) LTD *p321*
1620 8TH AVE W SUITE 200, VANCOUVER, BC, V6J 1V4
(604) 738-2500   *SIC 8748*

SOCIETE DE DEVELOPPEMENT INTERNATIONAL (SDI) INC *p1273*

2006 RUE RICHER, QUEBEC, QC, G1V 1P1
(418) 264-8188   *SIC 8748*

SOFTLANDING SOLUTIONS INC *p300*
555 HASTINGS ST W SUITE 1605, VANCOUVER, BC, V6B 4N6
(604) 633-1410   *SIC 8748*

SOLUTIONS DE RECONNAISSANCE RIDEAU INC *p1327*
473 RUE DESLAURIERS, SAINT-LAURENT, QC, H4N 1W2
(514) 336-9200   *SIC 8748*

SOUTH EAST CONSTRUCTION *p1406*
600 MAIN ST, ESTERHAZY, SK, S0A 0X0
(306) 745-4830   *SIC 8748*

SPECTRUM RESOURCE GROUP INC *p251*
3810 18TH AVE, PRINCE GEORGE, BC, V2N 4V5
(250) 564-0383   *SIC 8748*

SPRINGFIELD HUTTERIAN BRETHREN INC *p1408*
GD, KINDERSLEY, SK, S0L 1S0
(306) 463-4255   *SIC 8748*

STRATEGIC COMMUNICATIONS INC *p992*
1179 KING ST W SUITE 202, TORONTO, ON, M6K 3C5
(416) 537-6100   *SIC 8748*

SUNRISE HUTTERIAN BRETHREN *p126*
GD, ETZIKOM, AB, T0K 0W0
(403) 666-3787   *SIC 8748*

SYNCHRONICA INC *p1208*
1100 AV DES CANADIENS-DE-MONTREAL, MONTREAL, QC, H3B 2S2
(514) 390-1333   *SIC 8748*

SYSTEMES RAILTERM INC, LES *p1095*
10765 CH COTE-DE-LIESSE BUREAU 201, DORVAL, QC, H9P 2R9
(514) 420-1200   *SIC 8748*

TBS CANADA INC *p736*
7090 EDWARDS BLVD, MISSISSAUGA, ON, L5S 1Z1
(905) 362-5206   *SIC 8748*

TECH INCENTIVES INC *p41*
1816 CROWCHILD TRAIL NW UNIT 700, CALGARY, AB, T2M 3Y7
(403) 713-1050   *SIC 8748*

TERRAPEX ENVIRONMENTAL LTD *p777*
90 SCARSDALE RD, NORTH YORK, ON, M3B 2R7
(416) 245-0011   *SIC 8748*

TERRAPEX ENVIRONNEMENT LTEE *p1071*
3615 RUE ISABELLE BUREAU A, BROSSARD, QC, J4Y 2R2
(450) 444-3255   *SIC 8748*

TERRAPROBE LIMITED *p510*
10 BRAM CRT, BRAMPTON, ON, L6W 3R6
(905) 796-2650   *SIC 8748*

TERVITA CORPORATION *p32*
140 10 AVE SE SUITE 1600, CALGARY, AB, T2G 0R1
(855) 837-8482   *SIC 8748*

THOMAS, J.O. & ASSOCIATES LTD *p285*
1370 KOOTENAY ST, VANCOUVER, BC, V5K 4R1
(604) 291-6340   *SIC 8748*

TORONTO WATERFRONT REVITALIZATION CORPORATION *p968*
20 BAY ST SUITE 1310, TORONTO, ON, M5J 2N8
(416) 214-1344   *SIC 8748*

TOTAL SAFETY SERVICES INC *p239*
1336 MAIN ST, NORTH VANCOUVER, BC, V7J 1C3
SIC 8748

TYCO INTEGRATED FIRE & SECURITY CANADA, INC *p38*
401 FORGE RD SE, CALGARY, AB, T2H 0S9
SIC 8748

U P A CENTRE DU QUEBEC *p1243*
1940 RUE DES PINS, NICOLET, QC, J3T 1Z9
(819) 293-5838   *SIC 8748*

UNIVERSITY OF WESTERN ONTARIO, THE

p655
1151 RICHMOND ST SUITE 3140, LONDON, ON, N6A 3K7
(519) 661-2111   *SIC 8748*

URBAN ENVIRONMENT CENTRE (TORONTO), THE *p576*
74 SIX POINT RD, ETOBICOKE, ON, M8Z 2X2
(416) 203-3106   *SIC 8748*

URBAN STRATEGIES INC *p978*
197 SPADINA AVE SUITE 600, TORONTO, ON, M5T 2C8
(416) 340-9004   *SIC 8748*

VALCOM CONSULTING GROUP INC *p411*
281 RESTIGOUCHE RD SUITE 204, OROMOCTO, NB, E2V 2H2
(506) 357-5835   *SIC 8748*

VEOLIA SERVICE A L'ENVIRONNEMENT *p1139*
2800 RUE DE L'ETCHEMIN, LEVIS, QC, G6W 7X6
(418) 833-6840   *SIC 8748*

VERAX SOLUTIONS CORPORATION *p958*
120 ADELAIDE ST W SUITE 1501, TORONTO, ON, M5H 1T1
(416) 363-3030   *SIC 8748*

VERITAS COMMUNICATIONS INC *p984*
370 KING ST W SUITE 800, TORONTO, ON, M5V 1J9
(416) 482-2248   *SIC 8748*

VERTEX *p134*
705079 RANGE ROAD 61, GRANDE PRAIRIE, AB, T8W 5A8
(780) 532-7707   *SIC 8748*

VF SERVICES (CANADA) INC *p834*
280 METCALFE ST SUITE 200, OTTAWA, ON, K2P 1R7
(613) 686-9911   *SIC 8748*

VFA CANADA CORPORATION *p191*
4211 KINGSWAY SUITE 400, BURNABY, BC, V5H 1Z6
(604) 685-3757   *SIC 8748*

VTRAC CONSULTING CORPORATION *p773*
4950 YONGE ST SUITE 1005, NORTH YORK, ON, M2N 6K1
(416) 366-2600   *SIC 8748*

W.O.H.A HOLDINGS LIMITED *p71*
11505 35 ST SE SUITE 111, CALGARY, AB, T2Z 4B1
(403) 250-5722   *SIC 8748*

WESTPORT POWER INC *p324*
1750 75TH AVE W SUITE 101, VANCOUVER, BC, V6P 6G2
(604) 718-2000   *SIC 8748*

WHITE CLARKE NORTH AMERICA INC *p985*
901 KING ST W SUITE 202, TORONTO, ON, M5V 3H5
(416) 467-1900   *SIC 8748*

WHOLISTIC CHILD AND FAMILY SERVICES INC *p785*
601 MAGNETIC DR UNIT 39, NORTH YORK, ON, M3J 3J2
(416) 531-5616   *SIC 8748*

WIKITOR *p857*
129 ROSE BRANCH DR, RICHMOND HILL, ON, L4S 1H6
(647) 498-8773   *SIC 8748*

WILSON CONTINGENT TALENT SOLUTIONS, INC *p941*
44 VICTORIA ST SUITE 2000, TORONTO, ON, M5C 1Y2
(416) 440-0097   *SIC 8748*

WIND POWER MEDIA INC *p866*
49 FEAGAN DR, SCARBOROUGH, ON, M1C 3B6
(416) 471-4420   *SIC 8748*

WOOD CANADA LIMITED *p1095*
1425 RTE TRANSCANADIENNE BUREAU 400, DORVAL, QC, H9P 2W9
(514) 684-5555   *SIC 8748*

WORKPLACE SAFETY & PREVENTION SERVICES *p702*
5110 CREEKBANK RD SUITE 300, MISSIS-

SAUGA, ON, L4W 0A1
(905) 614-1400   *SIC 8748*

WORLDSOURCE SECURITIES INC *p677*
625 COCHRANE DR SUITE 700, MARKHAM, ON, L3R 9R9
(905) 940-0094   *SIC 8748*

WSP *p242*
889 HARBOURSIDE DR SUITE 210, NORTH VANCOUVER, BC, V7P 3S1
(604) 990-4800   *SIC 8748*

XCG CONSULTING LIMITED *p800*
2620 BRISTOL CIR SUITE 300, OAKVILLE, ON, L6H 6Z7
(905) 829-8880   *SIC 8748*

SIC 8811 Private households

TWIN CREEK HUTTERIAN BRETHREN *p167*
GD, STANDARD, AB, T0J 3G0
(403) 644-2283   *SIC 8811*

SIC 8999 Services, nec

9117-9077 QUEBEC INC *p1390*
560B 3E AV, VAL-D'OR, QC, J9P 1S4
(819) 874-0447   *SIC 8999*

AMEC FOSTER WHEELER NCL LIMITED *p944*
700 UNIVERSITY AVE SUITE 200, TORONTO, ON, M5G 1X6
(416) 592-2102   *SIC 8999*

AON HEWITT INC *p978*
225 KING ST W SUITE 1600, TORONTO, ON, M5V 3M2
(416) 542-5500   *SIC 8999*

AON HEWITT INC *p1201*
700 RUE DE LA GAUCHETIERE O BUREAU 1900, MONTREAL, QC, H3B 0A7
(514) 845-6231   *SIC 8999*

AON HEWITT INC *p1271*
2600 BOUL LAURIER BUREAU 750, QUEBEC, QC, G1V 4W2
(418) 650-1119   *SIC 8999*

ARROWSMITH SEARCH & RESCUE *p252*
3241 ALBERNI HWY, QUALICUM BEACH, BC, V9K 1Y6
(250) 752-7774   *SIC 8999*

BEHAVIOUR INSTITUTE *p611*
57 YOUNG ST, HAMILTON, ON, L8N 1V1
(905) 570-0777   *SIC 8999*

BRAIN MATTERS *p884*
314 LAKE ST SUITE 2, ST CATHARINES, ON, L2N 4H4
SIC 8999

C L CONSULTANTS LIMITED *p21*
3601 21 ST NE SUITE A, CALGARY, AB, T2E 6T5
(403) 250-3982   *SIC 8999*

CANADA MANITOBA BUSINESS SERVICE CENTRE *p377*
240 GRAHAM AVE SUITE 250, WINNIPEG, MB, R3C 0J7
(204) 984-2272   *SIC 8999*

CANADIAN NUCLEAR SOCIETY *p944*
655 BAY ST, TORONTO, ON, M5G 2K4
(416) 977-7620   *SIC 8999*

CANADIAN PARKS & WILDERNESS SOCIETY *p824*
250 CITY CENTRE AVE SUITE 506, OTTAWA, ON, K1R 6K7
(613) 569-7226   *SIC 8999*

CANADIAN WILDLIFE FEDERATION *p626*
350 MICHAEL COWPLAND DR, KANATA, ON, K2M 2W1
(613) 599-9594   *SIC 8999*

CENTRAL FRASER VALLEY SEARCH & RESCUE SOCIETY *p174*
1594 RIVERSIDE RD, ABBOTSFORD, BC, V2S 8J2
(604) 852-7271   *SIC 8999*

CENTRE DE LA NATURE DU MONT-SAINT-HILAIRE *p1158*

▲ Public Company   ■ Public Company Family Member   **HQ** Headquarters   **BR** Branch   **SL** Single Location

422 CH DES MOULINS, MONT-SAINT-HILAIRE, QC, J3G 4S6

(450) 467-1755   *SIC* 8999

CENTRE DE PREVENTION DU SUICIDE: ACCALMIE   *p*1387
1905 RUE ROYALE, TROIS-RIVIERES, QC, G9A 4K8

(819) 378-8585   *SIC* 8999

CENTRES DE DONNEES ESTRUXTURE INC   *p*1229
800 RUE DU SQUARE-VICTORIA BUREAU 1, MONTREAL, QC, H4Z 1B7

(514) 369-2209   *SIC* 8999

COAST MOUNTAIN GEOLOGICAL LTD*p*303
625 HOWE ST SUITE 488, VANCOUVER, BC, V6C 2T6

(604) 681-0209   *SIC* 8999

COPERNICUS STUDIOS INC   *p*452
1226 HOLLIS ST SUITE 100, HALIFAX, NS, B3J 1T6

(902) 474-5194   *SIC* 8999

CORBEILLE - BORDEAUX - CARTIERVILLE, LA   *p*1224
5080 RUE DUDEMAINE, MONTREAL, QC, H4J 1N6

(514) 856-0838   *SIC* 8999

DAVIS, ANN TRANSITION SOCIETY   *p*196
9046 YOUNG RD, CHILLIWACK, BC, V2P 4R6

(604) 792-2760   *SIC* 8999

DION, DURRELL & ASSOCIATES INC *p*935
250 YONGE ST SUITE 2, TORONTO, ON, M5B 2L7

(416) 408-2626   *SIC* 8999

DUCKS UNLIMITED CANADA   *p*250
7813 RENISON PL, PRINCE GEORGE, BC, V2N 3J2

(250) 964-3825   *SIC* 8999

DUCKS UNLIMITED CANADA   *p*359
1 MALLARD BAY HWY SUITE 220, STONEWALL, MB, R0C 2Z0

(204) 467-3000   *SIC* 8999

DYNAMIC RESCUE SYSTEMS INC   *p*200
63A CLIPPER ST, COQUITLAM, BC, V3K 6X2

(604) 522-0228   *SIC* 8999

ECKLER LTD   *p*915
5140 YONGE ST SUITE 1700, TORONTO, ON, M2N 6L7

(416) 429-3330   *SIC* 8999

EDITIONS BLAIS, YVON INC, LES   *p*1210
75 RUE QUEEN BUREAU 4700, MONTREAL, QC, H3C 2N6

(514) 842-3937   *SIC* 8999

FESTIVAL JUSTE POUR RIRE   *p*1344
8375 RUE PASCAL-GAGNON, SAINT-LEONARD, QC, H1P 1Y5

SIC 8999

FIRST MEDIA GROUP INC   *p*574
536 KIPLING AVE, ETOBICOKE, ON, M8Z 5E3

(416) 252-2424   *SIC* 8999

FUNKTIONAL SLEEP SOLUTIONS LTD *p*173
4920 51ST AVE, WHITECOURT, AB, T7S 1W2

(780) 778-6461   *SIC* 8999

GEOLOGICAL INDUSTRY RESEARCH INC *p*939
140 YONGE ST, TORONTO, ON, M5C 1X6

(416) 477-1164   *SIC* 8999

GEOPHYSICAL EXPLORATION & DEVELOPMENT CORPORATION   *p*30
125 9 AVE SE UNIT 200, CALGARY, AB, T2G 0P6

(403) 262-5780   *SIC* 8999

GEOPHYSIQUE G.P.R. INTERNATIONAL INC   *p*1144
2545 RUE DE LORIMIER BUREAU 100, LONGUEUIL, QC, J4K 3P7

(450) 679-2400   *SIC* 8999

GEOTECH LTD   *p*480
245 INDUSTRIAL PKY N, AURORA, ON, L4G 4C4

(905) 841-5004   *SIC* 8999

HELIX IT INC   *p*101
18211 105 AVE NW UNIT 101, EDMONTON, AB, T5S 2L5

(780) 454-3549   *SIC* 8999

HRDOWNLOADS INC   *p*653
195 DUFFERIN AVE SUITE 500, LONDON, ON, N6A 1K7

(519) 438-9763   *SIC* 8999

JOURNAL PREMIERE EDITION   *p*1394
469 AV SAINT-CHARLES, VAUDREUIL-DORION, QC, J7V 2N4

(450) 455-7955   *SIC* 8999

KEY SEISMIC SOLUTIONS LTD   *p*52
205 5 AVE SW SUITE 700, CALGARY, AB, T2P 2V7

(403) 232-6557   *SIC* 8999

KINECTRICS NSS INC   *p*946
393 UNIVERSITY AVE 4TH FLR, TORONTO, ON, M5G 1E6

(416) 592-7000   *SIC* 8999

LAKE SIMCOE REGION CONSERVATION AUTHORITY   *p*755
120 BAYVIEW PKY, NEWMARKET, ON, L3Y 3W3

(905) 895-1281   *SIC* 8999

LEMERVEIL, LAURA   *p*1092
160 AV DU COUVENT, DONNACONA, QC, G3M 1P5

(418) 462-3325   *SIC* 8999

MARITIME RESCUE & MEDICAL ACADEMY INC   *p*414
7 FOSTER THURSTON DR, SAINT JOHN, NB, E2K 5J4

(506) 672-3389   *SIC* 8999

MERCER (CANADA) LIMITED   *p*54
222 3 AVE SW SUITE 1200, CALGARY, AB, T2P 0B4

(403) 269-4945   *SIC* 8999

MERCER (CANADA) LIMITED   *p*307
550 BURRARD ST SUITE 900, VANCOUVER, BC, V6C 3S8

(604) 683-6761   *SIC* 8999

MERCER (CANADA) LIMITED   *p*1198
1981 AV MCGILL COLLEGE BUREAU 800, MONTREAL, QC, H3A 3T5

(514) 285-1802   *SIC* 8999

MORNEAU SHEPELL LTD   *p*328
505 BURRARD ST UNIT 1070, VANCOUVER, BC, V7X 1M5

(604) 642-5200   *SIC* 8999

MORNEAU SHEPELL LTD   *p*780
895 DON MILLS RD, NORTH YORK, ON, M3C 1W3

(416) 445-2700   *SIC* 8999

MORNEAU SHEPELL LTD   *p*1229
800 SQUARE VICTORIA BUREAU 4000, MONTREAL, QC, H4Z 0A4

(514) 878-9090   *SIC* 8999

NATURE CONSERVANCY OF CANADA, THE   *p*922
245 EGLINTON AVE E SUITE 410, TORONTO, ON, M4P 3J1

(416) 932-3202   *SIC* 8999

NATURE TRUST OF BRITISH COLUMBIA, THE   *p*307
888 DUNSMUIR ST SUITE 500, VANCOUVER, BC, V6C 3K4

(604) 924-9771   *SIC* 8999

NORMANDIN BEAUDRY, ACTUAIRES CONSEIL INC   *p*1206
630 BOUL RENE-LEVESQUE O SUITE 30E, MONTREAL, QC, H3B 1S6

(514) 285-1122   *SIC* 8999

NUCLEAR WASTE MANAGEMENT ORGANIZATION (NWMO)   *p*925
22 ST CLAIR AVE E 6TH FL, TORONTO, ON, M4T 2S3

(416) 934-9814   *SIC* 8999

NUVIA CANADA INC   *p*556
222 SNIDERCROFT RD, CONCORD, ON, L4K 2K1

(647) 800-1319   *SIC* 8999

OPTIMUM ACTUAIRES & CONSEILLERS

INC   *p*1198
425 BOUL DE MAISONNEUVE O BUREAU 1120, MONTREAL, QC, H3A 3G5

(514) 288-1620   *SIC* 8999

PEEL CHILDREN'S CENTRE   *p*741
85 AVENTURA CRT UNIT A, MISSISSAUGA, ON, L5T 2Y6

(905) 795-3500   *SIC* 8999

PELMOREX CORP   *p*798
2655 BRISTOL CIR, OAKVILLE, ON, L6H 7W1

(905) 829-1159   *SIC* 8999

PELMOREX WEATHER NETWORKS (TELEVISION) INC   *p*1174
1205 AV PAPINEAU BUREAU 251, MONTREAL, QC, H2K 4R2

(514) 597-0232   *SIC* 8999

PIRATE GROUP INC   *p*934
260 KING ST E SUITE 507, TORONTO, ON, M5A 4L5

(416) 594-3784   *SIC* 8999

PITEAU ASSOCIATES ENGINEERING LTD   *p*240
788 COPPING ST SUITE 300, NORTH VANCOUVER, BC, V7M 3G6

(604) 986-8551   *SIC* 8999

RCM TECHNOLOGIES CANADA CORP *p*845
895 BROCK RD, PICKERING, ON, L1W 3C1

(905) 837-8333   *SIC* 8999

RECYCLING COUNCIL OF BRITISH COLUMBIA   *p*300
119 PENDER ST W SUITE 10, VANCOUVER, BC, V6B 1S5

(604) 683-6009   *SIC* 8999

ROSCOE POSTLE ASSOCIATES INC *p*966
55 UNIVERSITY AVE SUITE 501, TORONTO, ON, M5J 2H7

(416) 947-0907   *SIC* 8999

RPS CANADA LIMITED   *p*58
555 4 AVE SW SUITE 700, CALGARY, AB, T2P 3E7

(403) 691-9717   *SIC* 8999

SAUVETAGE L'ARANEA INC   *p*1350
2351 RANG RENVERSY, SAINT-PAULIN, QC, J0K 3G0

(819) 268-3369   *SIC* 8999

SNC-LAVALIN NUCLEAR INC   *p*715
2251 SPEAKMAN DR, MISSISSAUGA, ON, L5K 1B2

(905) 829-8808   *SIC* 8999

SPB PSYCHOLOGIE ORGANISATION-NELLE INC.   *p*1143
555 BOUL ROLAND-THERRIEN BUREAU 300, LONGUEUIL, QC, J4H 4E7

(450) 646-1022   *SIC* 8999

SPRINGHILL GROUND SEARCH AND RESCUE (EMO)   *p*466
GD, SPRINGHILL, NS, B0M 1X0

(902) 597-3866   *SIC* 8999

TEKNICA OVERSEAS LTD   *p*61
350 7 AVE SW SUITE 2700, CALGARY, AB, T2P 3N9

SIC 8999

THOMSON REUTERS CANADA LIMITED *p*957
333 BAY ST SUITE 400, TORONTO, ON, M5H 2R2

(416) 687-7500   *SIC* 8999

TOWERS WATSON CANADA INC   *p*931
175 BLOOR ST E SUITE 1701, TORONTO, ON, M4W 3T6

(416) 960-2700   *SIC* 8999

TOWERS WATSON CANADA INC   *p*1200
1800 AV MCGILL COLLEGE BUREAU 2200, MONTREAL, QC, H3A 3J6

(514) 982-9411   *SIC* 8999

VALLEY SEARCH & RESCUE   *p*441
5876 HWY 1 BLDG 2, CAMBRIDGE, NS, B0P 1G0

SIC 8999

W.B.C. CORPORATION   *p*1209
1000 RUE DE LA GAUCHETIERE O, MON-

TREAL, QC, H3B 4W5

SIC 8999

WESTERN CANADA WILDERNESS COMMITTEE   *p*301
341 WATER ST, VANCOUVER, BC, V6B 1B8

(604) 609-3752   *SIC* 8999

XYZ TECHNOLOGIE CULTURELLE INC *p*1172
5700 RUE FULLUM, MONTREAL, QC, H2G 2H7

(514) 340-7717   *SIC* 8999

▲ Public Company   ■ Public Company Family Member   **HQ** Headquarters   **BR** Branch   **SL** Single Location

2019 Canadian Key Business Directory
Répertoire des principales entreprises Canadiennes 2019

Section III

Central Information Source
Alphabetic Listing

Source d'information
centrale—inscriptions
dans l'ordre alphabétique

O

0092584 B.C. LTD *p 219*
1200 LEATHEAD RD, KELOWNA, BC, V1X 2K4
(250) 491-2475 *SIC 5511*

011810 N.B. LIMITED *p 412*
435 BAYSIDE DR, SAINT JOHN, NB, E2J 1B2
(506) 633-3333 *SIC 2679*

0127494 B.C. LTD *p 331*
4608 27 ST, VERNON, BC, V1T 4Y6
(250) 275-4004 *SIC 5511*

0319637 B.C. LTD *p 317*
8901 STANLEY PARK DR, VANCOUVER, BC, V6G 3E2
SIC 5812

041216 NB LTD *p 397*
376 RUE CHAMPLAIN, DIEPPE, NB, E1A 1P3
(506) 858-5085 *SIC 7349*

0429746 B.C. LTD *p 205*
1345 CLIVEDEN AVE, DELTA, BC, V3M 6C7
(604) 515-4555 *SIC 5142*

0429746 B.C. LTD *p 661*
2825 INNOVATION DR, LONDON, ON, N6M 0B6
(519) 937-7777 *SIC 5142*

045502 N. B. LTD *p 412*
312 ROTHESAY AVE, SAINT JOHN, NB, E2J 2B9
(506) 634-6060 *SIC 5511*

050537 N.B. LTEE *p 398*
475 RUE VICTORIA, EDMUNDSTON, NB, E3V 2K7
(506) 739-7716 *SIC 5511*

053944 NB INC *p 400*
546 KING ST SUITE A, FREDERICTON, NB, E3B 1E6
(506) 459-0067 *SIC 5461*

055841 NB LTD *p 397*
1170 AV AVIATION, DIEPPE, NB, E1A 9A3
(506) 853-1116 *SIC 5511*

0561768 B.C. LTD *p 322*
3080 BROADWAY W, VANCOUVER, BC, V6K 2H1
(604) 733-4191 *SIC 5141*

056186 N.B. INC *p 396*
101 WATER ST, CAMPBELLTON, NB, E3N 1B2
(506) 759-8547 *SIC 5912*

056729 N.B. LTD *p 403*
18 DIVOT DR, HANWELL, NB, E3C 0L2
(506) 457-0305 *SIC 5148*

059884 N.B. INC *p 412*
1360 ROTHESAY RD, SAINT JOHN, NB, E2H 2J1
(506) 633-1200 *SIC 5032*

0695602 BC LTD *p 241*
998 HARBOURSIDE DR SUITE 211, NORTH VANCOUVER, BC, V7P 3T2
(604) 988-3833 *SIC 5153*

0705507 BC LTD *p 219*
3260 HIGHWAY 97 N, KELOWNA, BC, V1X 5C1
(250) 491-9467 *SIC 5511*

0743398 B.C. LTD *p 334*
307 DAVID ST, VICTORIA, BC, V8T 5C1
(250) 381-5865 *SIC 7389*

0756271 B.C. LTD *p 275*
13412 72 AVE, SURREY, BC, V3W 2N8
(604) 591-6064 *SIC 5531*

0769510 B.C. LTD *p 243*
510 DUNCAN AVE W, PENTICTON, BC, V2A 7N1
(250) 492-0100 *SIC 5511*

0781337 B.C. LTD *p 291*
380 2ND AVE W SUITE 300, VANCOUVER, BC, V5Y 1C8
(604) 699-2328 *SIC 4832*

0794856 B.C. LTD *p 243*
448 DUNCAN AVE W, PENTICTON, BC, V2A 7N1
(250) 492-0205 *SIC 5511*

0809021 B.C. LTD *p 331*

6417 HWY 97, VERNON, BC, V1B 3R4
(250) 542-0371 *SIC 5511*

0844212 BC LTD *p 323*
7547 CAMBIE ST, VANCOUVER, BC, V6P 3H6
(604) 618-0646 *SIC 6531*

0859291 B.C. LTD *p 334*
780 KINGS RD, VICTORIA, BC, V8T 5A2
(250) 480-3732 *SIC 4833*

0859710 B.C. LTD *p 219*
2767 HIGHWAY 97 N, KELOWNA, BC, V1X 4J8
(250) 448-0990 *SIC 5511*

0889541 BC LTD *p 203*
1027 VICTORIA AVE N, CRANBROOK, BC, V1C 3Y6
(250) 489-4311 *SIC 5511*

0962358 B.C. LTD *p 178*
29898 MACLURE RD, ABBOTSFORD, BC, V4X 1G5
(604) 825-5060 *SIC 5065*

0998236 B.C. LTD *p 259*
4151 HAZELBRIDGE WAY SUITE 1700, RICHMOND, BC, V6X 4J7
(604) 288-1002 *SIC 5137*

1

1 *p 1289*
See *J.Y. MOREAU ELECTRIQUE INC*

1 KING WEST INC *p 948*
1 KING ST W, TORONTO, ON, M5H 1A1
(416) 548-8100 *SIC 6553*

1 UP INSURANCE INC *p 76*
36 PANATELLA LINK NW, CALGARY, AB, T3K 0T6
(403) 910-2442 *SIC 6411*

1-800-GOT-JUNK ? *p 289*
See *RBDS RUBBISH BOYS DISPOSAL SERVICE INC*

1-800-GOT-JUNK? *p 921*
See *P. G. DISPOSAL SERVICE LTD*

1-800-USEBLUE *p 1194*
See *CANASSISTANCE INC*

10 ACRE TRUCK STOP *p 491*
See *HANNAFIN, E.J. ENTERPRISES LIMITED*

10 X LESS MORTGAGE (MC) *p 1213*
See *BANQUE LAURENTIENNE DU CANADA*

100 MILE DISTRICT GENERAL HOSPITAL *p 174*
555 CEDAR AVE, 100 MILE HOUSE, BC, V0K 2E0
(250) 395-7600 *SIC 8062*

100 MILE LUMBER *p 174*
See *WEST FRASER TIMBER CO. LTD*

100 PLANS *p 1244*
See *TVA PUBLICATIONS INC*

100% REALTY ASSOCIATES LTD *p 1423*
1820 8TH ST E SUITE 250, SASKATOON, SK, S7H 0T6
(306) 242-6000 *SIC 6531*

1000 DE LA GAUCHETIERE *p 1191*
See *IVANHOE CAMBRIDGE INC*

1000 ISLAND R.V., POWER SPORTS AND MARINE *p 592*
See *1000 ISLANDS R.V. CENTRE INC*

1000 ISLANDS R.V. CENTRE INC *p 592*
409 COUNTY ROAD 2 E, GANANOQUE, ON, K7G 2V4
(613) 382-4400 *SIC 5561*

1000 ISLANDS TOYOTA *p 518*
See *734393 ONTARIO LIMITED*

1000 RUE SHERBROOKE OUEST *p 1197*
See *INVESTISSEMENTS MONIT INC, LES*

10013340 CANADA INC *p 1088*
75 BOUL DUPONT, COTEAU-DU-LAC, QC, J0P 1B0
(450) 455-0961 *SIC 3086*

1001432 B.C. LTD *p 281*
7700 168 ST, SURREY, BC, V4N 0E1
(604) 576-8224 *SIC 7992*

1001511 ALBERTA LTD *p 153*
GD, PROVOST, AB, T0B 3S0

(780) 753-6404 *SIC 1389*

1001943 ONTARIO LIMITED *p 473*
725 WESTNEY RD S UNIT 1, AJAX, ON, L1S 7J7
(905) 686-1212 *SIC 5999*

10022441 MANITOBA LTD *p 393*
15 SCURFIELD BLVD, WINNIPEG, MB, R3Y 1G3
(204) 615-7333 *SIC 6531*

1002495 B.C. LTD *p 246*
2060 OXFORD CONNECTOR, PORT CO-QUITLAM, BC, V3C 0A4
(604) 464-3330 *SIC 5511*

10033618 CANADA INC *p 1337*
4930 RUE COURVAL, SAINT-LAURENT, QC, H4T 1L1
(514) 343-0220 *SIC 5021*

1004839 ONTARIO LIMITED *p 715*
3105 DUNDAS ST W SUITE 101, MISSIS-SAUGA, ON, L5L 3R8
(905) 569-7000 *SIC 5812*

1004907 ALBERTA LTD *p 33*
22 HERITAGE MEADOWS RD SE, CAL-GARY, AB, T2H 3C1
(403) 250-4930 *SIC 5511*

1005199 B.C. LTD *p 327*
555 BURRARD ST SUITE 600, VANCOU-VER, BC, V7X 1M8
(604) 559-4322 *SIC 6141*

10079952 CANADA INC *p 1327*
2431 RUE GUENETTE, SAINT-LAURENT, QC, H4R 2E9
(514) 337-0566 *SIC 5084*

1008648 ONTARIO INC *p 736*
6243 NETHERHART RD, MISSISSAUGA, ON, L5T 1G5
(905) 564-2800 *SIC 1711*

10087408 CANADA INC *p 1200*
1280 AVE DES CANADIENS-DE-MONTREAL, MONTREAL, QC, H3B 3B3
(514) 261-7661 *SIC 5812*

1008803 ONTARIO LTD *p 1000*
4780 HIGHWAY 7 E, UNIONVILLE, ON, L3R 1M8
(905) 477-2003 *SIC 5541*

1009833 ALBERTA LTD *p 160*
261116 WAGON WHEEL WAY, ROCKY VIEW COUNTY, AB, T4A 0E3
(403) 250-8484 *SIC 5999*

1009931 ALBERTA LTD *p 75*
20 FREEPORT LANDNG NE, CALGARY, AB, T3J 5H6
(403) 290-1111 *SIC 5511*

101 - TRANSPORTS - REGION DE LA CAP-ITALE *p 1279*
See *SYNDICAT DE LA FONCTION PUBLIQUE ET PARAPUBLIQUE DU QUE-BEC INC*

101013121 SASKATCHEWAN LTD *p 1424*
730 BRAND RD, SASKATOON, SK, S7J 5J3
(306) 955-5080 *SIC 5511*

101014233 SASKATCHEWAN LTD *p 1416*
1874 SCARTH ST SUITE 2000, REGINA, SK, S4P 4B3
(306) 777-0600 *SIC 6531*

101055401 SASKATCHEWAN LTD *p 1423*
2404 8TH ST E, SASKATOON, SK, S7H 0V6
SIC 5812

101105464 SASKATCHEWAN LTD *p 1425*
635 CIRCLE DR E, SASKATOON, SK, S7K 7Y2
(306) 955-8877 *SIC 5511*

1011191 ONTARIO INC *p 1001*
3140 OLD HWY 69 N SUITE 28, VAL CARON, ON, P3N 1G3
(705) 897-4958 *SIC 5411*

1015605 SALES LIMITED *p 467*
1124 KINGS RD, SYDNEY, NS, B1S 1C8
(902) 562-1298 *SIC 5511*

10167819 CANADA INC *p 1381*
460 RUE FERNAND-POITRAS, TERRE-BONNE, QC, J6Y 1Y4
(514) 493-9423 *SIC 5149*

1019728 ALBERTA LTD *p 147*
8902 95 ST, MORINVILLE, AB, T8R 1K7
(780) 939-3000 *SIC 6712*

1019884 ONTARIO INC *p 596*
1913 KINGSDALE AVE, GLOUCESTER, ON, K1T 1H9
SIC 0139

1020012 ONTARIO INC *p 617*
580 24TH AVE SUITE 1, HANOVER, ON, N4N 3B8
(519) 364-3410 *SIC 5211*

1021076 ONTARIO INC *p 1393*
434 RUE AIME-VINCENT, VAUDREUIL-DORION, QC, J7V 5V5
(450) 510-0560 *SIC 5044*

1022013 ONTARIO LIMITED *p 863*
1231 PEOPLES RD, SAULT STE. MARIE, ON, P6C 3W7
(705) 759-5148 *SIC 1711*

1022481 ONTARIO INC *p 813*
419 KING ST W SUITE 2482, OSHAWA, ON, L1J 2K5
(905) 576-1600 *SIC 6099*

1023248 ONTARIO INC *p 844*
870 MCKAY RD, PICKERING, ON, L1W 2Y4
(905) 426-8989 *SIC 7389*

1023714 ONTARIO LTD *p 855*
10488 YONGE ST, RICHMOND HILL, ON, L4C 3G7
(905) 884-2600 *SIC 5411*

1025091 ONTARIO LIMITED *p 659*
585 SPRINGBANK DR SUITE 204, LON-DON, ON, N6J 1H3
(519) 641-1178 *SIC 5812*

1028918 ONTARIO INC *p 528*
1249 GUELPH LINE, BURLINGTON, ON, L7P 2T1
(905) 335-0223 *SIC 5511*

1031647 ONTARIO LTD *p 682*
575 ONTARIO ST S UNIT 9, MILTON, ON, L9T 2N2
SIC 5411

103190 ONTARIO INC *p 567*
2452 YORKS CORNERS RD, EDWARDS, ON, K0A 1V0
(613) 821-2751 *SIC 0831*

1032002 ONTARIO INC *p 520*
4025 NEW ST, BURLINGTON, ON, L7L 1S8
(905) 639-0319 *SIC 5411*

1032396 ONTARIO LTD *p 781*
3858 CHESSWOOD DR, NORTH YORK, ON, M3J 2W6
(416) 398-5155 *SIC 7389*

1032451 B.C. LTD *p 20*
2615 12 ST NE SUITE 1, CALGARY, AB, T2E 7W9
(403) 250-4192 *SIC 2711*

1032451 B.C. LTD *p 107*
4990 92 AVE NW SUITE 350, EDMONTON, AB, T6B 3A1
(780) 468-0100 *SIC 2711*

1032451 B.C. LTD *p 107*
9300 47 ST NW, EDMONTON, AB, T6B 2P6
(780) 468-0506 *SIC 2711*

1032451 B.C. LTD *p 131*
10604 100 ST, GRANDE PRAIRIE, AB, T8V 2M5
(780) 532-1110 *SIC 2711*

1032451 B.C. LTD *p 139*
4504 61 AVE, LEDUC, AB, T9E 3Z1
(780) 986-2271 *SIC 2711*

1032451 B.C. LTD *p 518*
1600 CALIFORNIA AVE, BROCKVILLE, ON, K6V 5T6
(613) 342-4441 *SIC 2711*

1032451 B.C. LTD *p 655*
369 YORK ST SUITE 2A, LONDON, ON, N6B 3R4
(519) 679-1111 *SIC 2711*

1032451 B.C. LTD *p 748*
6 ANTARES DR SUITE 3, NEPEAN, ON, K2E 8A9
SIC 2711

1032451 B.C. LTD *p 895*

16 PACKHAM RD, STRATFORD, ON, N5A
6T6
(519) 271-2220   SIC 2711

1032451 B.C. LTD   p 911
25 TOWNLINE RD SUITE 190, TILLSON-
BURG, ON, N4G 2R5
(519) 688-6397   SIC 2711

1032451 B.C. LTD   p 932
333 KING ST E UNIT 1, TORONTO, ON,
M5A 0E1
(416) 947-2222   SIC 2711

1034250 ONTARIO LTD   p 631
401 BATH RD, KINGSTON, ON, K7M 7C9
(613) 634-4000   SIC 5511

1035312 ONTARIO LIMITED   p 512
190 CANAM CRES, BRAMPTON, ON, L7A
1A9
(905) 459-1810   SIC 5511

10365289 CANADA INC   p 1029
7777 WESTON RD 8TH FL, WOOD-
BRIDGE, ON, L4L 0G9
(905) 695-1700   SIC 1731

10373532 CANADA LTD   p 171
10851 100 ST, WESTLOCK, AB, T7P 2R5
(780) 349-7040   SIC 5141

10393266 CANADA INC   p 1192
925 BOUL DE MAISONNEUVE O BUREAU
247, MONTREAL, QC, H3A 0A5
   SIC 2521

1039658 ONTARIO INC   p 825
1123 BANK ST, OTTAWA, ON, K1S 3X4
   SIC 5731

1042735 ONTARIO INC   p 512
15 VAN KIRK DR, BRAMPTON, ON, L7A
1W4
(905) 459-0290   SIC 5511

1043133 ONTARIO INC   p 830
1825 WOODWARD DR, OTTAWA, ON, K2C
0P9
(613) 228-6557   SIC 4899

1044912 ONTARIO LIMITED   p 843
2215 BROCK RD N, PICKERING, ON, L1V
2R4
(905) 683-5952   SIC 5261

1045761 ONTARIO LIMITED   p 573
289 HORNER AVE, ETOBICOKE, ON, M8Z
4Y4
(416) 259-1113   SIC 3312

1046809 ALBERTA INC   p 41
2112 CROWCHILD TRAIL NW, CALGARY,
AB, T2M 3Y7
(403) 338-1268   SIC 5921

1048271 ONTARIO INC   p 837
1200 PEMBROKE ST W, PEMBROKE, ON,
K8A 7T1
(613) 735-5335   SIC 5411

1048536 ONTARIO LTD   p 748
148 COLONNADE RD SUITE 13, NEPEAN,
ON, K2E 7R4
(613) 727-0413   SIC 7349

1048547 ONTARIO INC   p 888
185 COUNTY RD 10, ST EUGENE, ON,
K0B 1P0
(613) 674-3183   SIC 2022

1049054 B.C. LTD.   p 234
3612 ISLAND HWY N, NANAIMO, BC, V9T
1W2
(250) 756-1515   SIC 5511

1051107 ONTARIO LTD   p 843
1725 KINGSTON RD SUITE 25, PICKER-
ING, ON, L1V 4L9
(905) 619-1000   SIC 5812

105262 CANADA INC   p 1218
3500 RUE JEAN-TALON O, MONTREAL,
QC, H3R 2E8
(514) 739-3175   SIC 5511

1053038 ONTARIO LIMITED   p 616
1495 UPPER JAMES ST, HAMILTON, ON,
L9B 1K2
(905) 574-8200   SIC 5511

1055307 ONTARIO INC   p 473
403 CLEMENTS RD W, AJAX, ON, L1S 6N3
(905) 428-2002   SIC 6712

1055551 ONTARIO INC   p 618

341 TUPPER ST, HAWKESBURY, ON, K6A
3T6
(613) 632-6598   SIC 5511

105675 ONTARIO LIMITED   p 686
6577 NORTHWEST DR, MISSISSAUGA,
ON, L4V 1L1
(905) 293-9900   SIC 3471

1057206 ONTARIO LTD   p 796
2359 BRISTOL CIR, OAKVILLE, ON, L6H
6P8
   SIC 8299

1057362 ONTARIO LTD   p 578
460 RENFORTH DR SUITE 1, ETOBI-
COKE, ON, M9C 2N2
(416) 622-1840   SIC 5411

10578959 CANADA INC   p 850
155 EAST BEAVER CREEK RD, RICH-
MOND HILL, ON, L4B 2N1
(905) 904-0596   SIC 6719

1059895 ONTARIO INC   p 663
GD, MABERLY, ON, K0H 2B0
(613) 268-2308   SIC 6712

106203 CANADA LTD   p 545
158 SECOND AVE, COCHRANE, ON, P0L
1C0
(705) 272-4305   SIC 5149

10643645 CANADA INC   p 1212
1440 RUE DE LA MONTAGNE, MON-
TREAL, QC, H3G 1Z5
(514) 843-2500   SIC 7011

10647802 CANADA LIMITED   p 686
5915 AIRPORT RD SUITE 425, MISSIS-
SAUGA, ON, L4V 1T1
(416) 483-5152   SIC 8741

1067863 ALBERTA LTD   p 86
10250 101 ST NW SUITE 1550, EDMON-
TON, AB, T5J 3P4
(780) 428-1522   SIC 6211

1068409 ONTARIO LIMITED   p 633
2237 COUNTY RD 31, KINGSVILLE, ON,
N9Y 2E5
(519) 326-5919   SIC 5148

10684210 CANADA INC   p 1224
101 BOUL MARCEL-LAURIN BUREAU 320,
MONTREAL, QC, H4N 2M3
(514) 286-1066   SIC 2721

10684651 CANADA INC   p 1278
825 BOUL LEBOURGNEUF BUREAU 130,
QUEBEC, QC, G2J 0B9
(888) 523-1883   SIC 7371

1068827 ONTARIO INC   p 564
11211   LONGWOODS   RD   RR   1,
DELAWARE, ON, N0L 1E0
(519) 652-9766   SIC 5521

1072667 ONTARIO LIMITED   p 877
3370 PHARMACY AVE, SCARBOROUGH,
ON, M1W 3K4
(416) 494-1444   SIC 6712

1073849 ONTARIO LIMITED   p 485
75 DYMENT RD, BARRIE, ON, L4N 3H6
(705) 733-0022   SIC 3841

1075177 ONTARIO LTD   p 858
1129 VANIER RD, SARNIA, ON, N7S 3Y6
   SIC 1541

1076528 ALBERTA LTD   p 155
6720 JOHNSTONE DR, RED DEER, AB,
T4P 3Y2
(403) 347-7777   SIC 5521

1076634 ONTARIO INC   p 788
3080 DUFFERIN ST, NORTH YORK, ON,
M6A 2S6
(416) 243-1550   SIC 5521

1077947 ONTARIO LTD   p 482
105 GUTHRIE ST SS 1, AYR, ON, N0B 1E0
(519) 632-9052   SIC 6712

1079259 B.C. LTD   p 246
2060 OXFORD CONNECTOR, PORT CO-
QUITLAM, BC, V3C 0A4
(604) 464-3330   SIC 5511

1079746 ONTARIO LIMITED   p 781
1021 FINCH AVE W, NORTH YORK, ON,
M3J 2C7
(416) 650-9996   SIC 5131

1080414 ONTARIO LIMITED   p 990

950 DUPONT ST, TORONTO, ON, M6H 1Z2
(416) 532-6700   SIC 6719

1083153 ONTARIO LTD   p 715
2400 MOTORWAY BLVD, MISSISSAUGA,
ON, L5L 1X3
(905) 828-0070   SIC 5511

1083211 ONTARIO LTD   p 591
19 WARREN ST, FORT ERIE, ON, L2A 2N4
(905) 994-0800   SIC 5051

1084408 ONTARIO INC   p 568
8 YONGE ST S UNIT A, ELMVALE, ON, L0L
1P0
(705) 737-0480   SIC 7349

1084999 ONTARIO INC   p 816
715 INDUSTRIAL AVE, OTTAWA, ON, K1G
0Z1
(613) 228-0073   SIC 7382

1085453 ONTARIO LTD   p 623
2054 JOYCEVILLE RD, JOYCEVILLE, ON,
K0H 1Y0
(613) 546-5025   SIC 5541

1087299 ONTARIO LTD   p 1004
10 MCNAB ST, WALKERTON, ON, N0G
2V0
(519) 881-2794   SIC 5461

1087338 ONTARIO LIMITED   p 527
3320 SOUTH SERVICE RD SUITE 200,
BURLINGTON, ON, L7N 3M6
(905) 681-1113   SIC 8748

108786 CANADA INC   p 1331
4775 RUE COUSENS, SAINT-LAURENT,
QC, H4S 1X5
(514) 383-0042   SIC 5049

1089243 ALBERTA LTD   p 131
9625 144 AVE, GRANDE PRAIRIE, AB, T8V
7V4
(780) 830-0955   SIC 3533

1090349 ONTARIO INC   p 879
95 MAIN ST S, SEAFORTH, ON, N0K 1W0
(519) 527-1631   SIC 6712

1090769 ONTARIO INC   p 1017
2508 WINDERMERE RD, WINDERMERE,
ON, P0B 1P0
(705) 769-3611   SIC 7011

1092072 ONTARIO INC   p 1327
4500 BOUL THIMENS, SAINT-LAURENT,
QC, H4R 2P2
(514) 344-3533   SIC 5021

1092072 ONTARIO INC   p 1331
2520 AV MARIE-CURIE, SAINT-LAURENT,
QC, H4S 1N1
(800) 511-1100   SIC 4731

1094285 ONTARIO LIMITED   p 931
112 ISABELLA ST, TORONTO, ON, M4Y
1P1
(416) 920-9410   SIC 5812

1095086 ONTARIO INC   p 921
3080 YONGE ST SUITE 4054, TORONTO,
ON, M4N 3N1
   SIC 5072

1095141 ONTARIO LIMITED   p 665
7225   WOODBINE   AVE   SUITE   119,
MARKHAM, ON, L3R 1A3
(905) 940-2199   SIC 5812

109578 CANADA LTEE   p 1156
5790 RUE FERRIER, MONT-ROYAL, QC,
H4P 1M7
(514) 937-0044   SIC 3993

109652 CANADA LTD/LTEE   p 1337
8750 CH DE LA COTE-DE-LIESSE BU-
REAU 100, SAINT-LAURENT, QC, H4T 1H2
(514) 344-9660   SIC 5136

10SHEET SERVICES INC   p 301
717 PENDER ST W UNIT 200, VANCOU-
VER, BC, V6C 1G9
(888) 760-1940   SIC 8721

1100378 ONTARIO LIMITED   p 792
805 FENMAR DR, NORTH YORK, ON, M9L
1C8
   SIC 3694

1100833 ONTARIO LIMITED   p 989
672 DUPONT ST SUITE 201, TORONTO,
ON, M6G 1Z6
(416) 535-1555   SIC 5722

1107078 ONTARIO INC   p 773
4021 YONGE ST, NORTH YORK, ON, M2P
1N6
(416) 223-0837   SIC 5541

1084836 CANADA INC.   p 1103
1205 RUE ODILE-DAOUST, GATINEAU,
QC, J8M 1Y7
(819) 986-2224   SIC 5511

1110 HOWE HOLDINGS INCORPORATEDp
325
1110 HOWE ST, VANCOUVER, BC, V6Z
1R2
(604) 684-2151   SIC 7011

11108204 CANADA INC   p 547
235 RAYETTE RD UNIT 1A, CONCORD,
ON, L4K 2G1
(437) 218-3702   SIC 5146

1112308 ONTARIO INC   p 581
246 ATTWELL DR, ETOBICOKE, ON, M9W
5B4
(416) 675-1635   SIC 7342

111616 OPERATIONS (CANADA) INC   p
1200
1 PLACE VILLE-MARIE UNITE 3900, MON-
TREAL, QC, H3B 4M7
(800) 465-6325   SIC 3861

1118528 ONTARIO INC   p 1022
1172 GOYEAU ST, WINDSOR, ON, N9A
1J1
(519) 977-5757   SIC 7389

1118741 ONTARIO LTD   p 855
278 NEWKIRK RD, RICHMOND HILL, ON,
L4C 3G7
(905) 780-7722   SIC 2434

11198173 CANADA INC   p 850
155 EAST BEAVER CREEK RD UNIT 24,
RICHMOND HILL, ON, L4B 2N1
(905) 904-0612   SIC 4212

1120423 ONTARIO LIMITED   p 791
15 DENSLEY AVE, NORTH YORK, ON,
M6M 2P5
(416) 429-2257   SIC 8743

1120919 ONTARIO LTD   p 748
18 BENTLEY AVE SUITE A, NEPEAN, ON,
K2E 6T8
(613) 723-9227   SIC 1521

1121121 ONTARIO INC   p 762
240 LAKESHORE DR, NORTH BAY, ON,
P1A 2B6
(705) 476-5100   SIC 5511

1122630 ONTARIO LIMITED   p 718
5399 DURIE RD, MISSISSAUGA, ON, L5M
2C8
(905) 567-6457   SIC 5499

1123932 ONTARIO INC   p 872
2124 LAWRENCE AVE E, SCARBOR-
OUGH, ON, M1R 3A3
(416) 752-0970   SIC 5511

1124029 ONTARIO INC   p 664
217 TORONTO ST S, MARKDALE, ON,
N0C 1H0
(519) 986-3683   SIC 5411

1124178 ONTARIO INC   p 809
351 WEST ST S, ORILLIA, ON, L3V 5H1
(705) 327-1300   SIC 5051

1124965 ONTARIO LTD   p 489
800 ESSA RD, BARRIE, ON, L9J 0A8
(705) 728-9211   SIC 5084

1124980 ONTARIO INC   p 898
1276 LASALLE BLVD SUITE 683, SUD-
BURY, ON, P3A 1Y8
(705) 566-5551   SIC 5912

1125151 ONTARIO LIMITED   p 581
6931 STEELES AVE W, ETOBICOKE, ON,
M9W 6K7
(416) 675-9235   SIC 5661

1125278 ONTARIO LTD   p 788
3180 DUFFERIN ST, NORTH YORK, ON,
M6A 2T1
(416) 256-1405   SIC 5511

1126194 ONTARIO LIMITED   p 528
1150 GUELPH LINE, BURLINGTON, ON,
L7P 2S8
(905) 335-5595   SIC 5541

▲ Public Company   ■ Public Company Family Member   **HQ** Headquarters   **BR** Branch   **SL** Single Location

1127770 B.C. LTD   *p 292*
777 BROADWAY W, VANCOUVER, BC, V5Z
4J7
  SIC 5047
1127919 ONTARIO LIMITED   *p 598*
290 FIRST ST N, GRAVENHURST, ON,
P1P 1H3
  (705) 687-0554   *SIC 5411*
112792 CANADA INC   *p 208*
9924 RIVER RD, DELTA, BC, V4G 1B5
  (604) 940-4208   *SIC 4212*
11292580 ONTARIO LIMITED   *p 652*
649 RICHMOND ST, LONDON, ON, N6A
3G7
  (519) 238-2720   *SIC 5136*
1129822 ONTARIO INC   *p 618*
1000 MCGILL ST, HAWKESBURY, ON, K6A
1R6
  (613) 632-8278   *SIC 5461*
1131898 ALBERTA LTD   *p 146*
1450 STRACHAN RD SE, MEDICINE HAT,
AB, T1B 4V2
  (403) 526-3633   *SIC 5511*
1132145 ONTARIO LIMITED   *p 631*
1030 COVERDALE DR, KINGSTON, ON,
K7M 9E1
  (613) 389-0090   *SIC 5411*
1132694 ONTARIO INC   *p 547*
8001 KEELE ST, CONCORD, ON, L4K 1Y8
  (905) 669-9855   *SIC 7389*
1132694 ONTARIO INC   *p 733*
7550 KIMBEL ST, MISSISSAUGA, ON, L5S
1A2
  (905) 677-1948   *SIC 7389*
1133571 ALBERTA LTD   *p 172*
4120 56 ST, WETASKIWIN, AB, T9A 1V3
  (780) 352-2225   *SIC 5511*
1336 NEWFOUNDLAND INC   *p 429*
73 KENMOUNT RD, ST. JOHN'S, NL, A1B
3P8
  (709) 753-4051   *SIC 5511*
113514 CANADA INC   *p 1303*
262 RUE MARCEL RR 2, SAINT-GABRIEL-
DE-BRANDON, QC, J0K 2N0
  (450) 835-2066   *SIC 5031*
113559 ONTARIO LIMITED   *p 837*
425 PEMBROKE ST E, PEMBROKE, ON,
K8A 3L1
  (613) 735-4136   *SIC 5411*
113712 CANADA INC   *p 1061*
3780 RUE LA VERENDRYE, BOISBRIAND,
QC, J7H 1R5
  (450) 437-7077   *SIC 5149*
1137283 ONTARIO LTD   *p 867*
2594 EGLINTON AVE E SUITE 2592,
SCARBOROUGH, ON, M1K 2R5
  (416) 266-4594   *SIC 5411*
11375644 CANADA INC   *p 1323*
1935 BOUL KELLER, SAINT-LAURENT,
QC, H4K 2V6
  (514) 727-9999   *SIC 5411*
1140456 ALBERTA LTD   *p 119*
2852 CALGARY TRAIL NW, EDMONTON,
AB, T6J 6V7
  (780) 485-5005   *SIC 6531*
1142024 ONTARIO INC   *p 648*
1425 CREAMERY RD, LONDON, ON, N5V
5B3
  (519) 451-3748   *SIC 6712*
1144257 ONTARIO LIMITED   *p 477*
181 SANDWICH ST S, AMHERSTBURG,
ON, N9V 1Z9
  (519) 736-7378   *SIC 5411*
1144259 ONTARIO LIMITED   *p 647*
65 REGIONAL RD 24, LIVELY, ON, P3Y 1H3
  (705) 692-3514   *SIC 5411*
1145678 ONTARIO LIMITED   *p 616*
1221 UPPER JAMES ST, HAMILTON, ON,
L9C 3B2
  (905) 574-8989   *SIC 5511*
1146490 ONTARIO INC   *p 628*
1229 HIGHWAY 17 E SUITE 1, KENORA,
ON, P9N 1L9
  (807) 468-3014   *SIC 5531*

1146898 ONTARIO INC   *p 1029*
101 WESTCREEK DR, WOODBRIDGE,
ON, L4L 9N6
  (905) 850-2212   *SIC 5039*
1147048 ONTARIO LIMITED   *p 807*
5000 REGAL DR, OLDCASTLE, ON, N0R
1L0
  (519) 737-7535   *SIC 3089*
1148044 ONTARIO LTD   *p 754*
1250 JOURNEY'S END CIR SUITE 1, NEW-
MARKET, ON, L3Y 0B9
  (905) 830-6026   *SIC 1542*
1148290 ONTARIO INC   *p 535*
95 SAGINAW PKY SUITE A, CAMBRIDGE,
ON, N1T 1W2
  (519) 623-1856   *SIC 5499*
1148956 ONTARIO LTD   *p 569*
745 CENTRE ST, ESPANOLA, ON, P5E 1S8
  (705) 869-0284   *SIC 5411*
1149318 ONTARIO INC   *p 733*
6900 TRANMERE DR, MISSISSAUGA, ON,
L5S 1L9
  (866) 576-4228   *SIC 4214*
1150018 ONTARIO INC   *p 831*
15 CAPELLA CRT UNIT 115, OTTAWA, ON,
K2E 7X1
  (613) 225-5044   *SIC 3679*
1151377 ONTARIO INC   *p 518*
14 MAIN ST, BRIGHTON, ON, K0K 1H0
  (613) 475-0200   *SIC 5411*
115161 CANADA INC   *p 1126*
5203 RUE FAIRWAY, LACHINE, QC, H8T
3K8
  (514) 635-1088   *SIC 4226*
1152174 ONTARIO LIMITED   *p 769*
6464 YONGE ST, NORTH YORK, ON, M2M
3X4
  SIC 5999
115419 ALBERTA LTD   *p 158*
28042 HWY 11 UNIT 231, RED DEER
COUNTY, AB, T4S 2L4
  (403) 347-6222   *SIC 1629*
1155760 ONTARIO LIMITED   *p 873*
5500 FINCH AVE E, SCARBOROUGH, ON,
M1S 0C7
  (416) 283-7100   *SIC 5511*
1161396 ONTARIO INC   *p 796*
2965 BRISTOL CIR BLDG C, OAKVILLE,
ON, L6H 6P9
  (905) 829-2229   *SIC 5145*
1162095 ALBERTA LTD   *p 5*
5204 50 ST, BEAUMONT, AB, T4X 1E5
  (780) 929-6466   *SIC 5541*
116260 CANADA INC   *p 1354*
350 RUE PRINCIPALE, SAINT-ZOTIQUE,
QC, J0P 1Z0
  (450) 267-3343   *SIC 5411*
116278 CANADA INC   *p 1183*
365 RUE BEAUBIEN O, MONTREAL, QC,
H2V 1C8
  (514) 495-2435   *SIC 5144*
1166709 ONTARIO LIMITED   *p 498*
2250 QUEEN ST E SUITE 2000, BRAMP-
TON, ON, L6S 5X9
  (905) 458-7100   *SIC 5511*
1168170 ONTARIO LTD   *p 647*
10 DUHAMEL RD, LIVELY, ON, P3Y 1L4
  (705) 692-4746   *SIC 5511*
1168768 ONTARIO INC   *p 764*
6750 FOURTH LINE RD, NORTH GOWER,
ON, K0A 2T0
  (613) 489-0120   *SIC 6712*
1170760 ONTARIO LTD   *p 788*
1 YORKDALE RD UNIT 402, NORTH YORK,
ON, M6A 3A1
  (416) 785-8801   *SIC 5944*
1172413 ONTARIO INC   *p 625*
651 TERRY FOX DR SUITE SIDE, KANATA,
ON, K2L 4E7
  (613) 836-3680   *SIC 5812*
1172895 ALBERTA LTD   *p 127*
145 MACLEAN RD, FORT MCMURRAY, AB,
T9H 4X2
  (780) 790-9292   *SIC 7389*

1174976 ONTARIO INC   *p 936*
19 TORONTO ST, TORONTO, ON, M5C
2R1
  (416) 214-5888   *SIC 5812*
1175469 ONTARIO LTD   *p 788*
1120 CALEDONIA RD UNIT 11, NORTH
YORK, ON, M6A 2W5
  (416) 256-3199   *SIC 7381*
1175648 ONTARIO LIMITED   *p 736*
1190 MEYERSIDE DR, MISSISSAUGA,
ON, L5T 1R7
  (905) 564-8784   *SIC 4213*
1176356 ONTARIO INC   *p 809*
385 WEST ST S, ORILLIA, ON, L3V 5H2
  (705) 329-4277   *SIC 5511*
1179131 ONTARIO LIMITED   *p 493*
101 EAST ST S SUITE 7, BOBCAYGEON,
ON, K0M 1A0
  (705) 738-9811   *SIC 5411*
1179132 ONTARIO LIMITED   *p 826*
2681 ALTA VISTA DR, OTTAWA, ON, K1V
7T5
  (613) 733-2311   *SIC 5411*
1184038 ONTARIO LIMITED   *p 778*
747 DON MILLS RD SUITE 60, NORTH
YORK, ON, M3C 1T2
  (416) 239-7171   *SIC 5411*
1184892 ALBERTA LTD   *p 26*
115 9 AVE SE SUITE 294, CALGARY, AB,
T2G 0P5
  (403) 246-3636   *SIC 5812*
1185140 ALBERTA LTD   *p 162*
31 AUTOMALL RD, SHERWOOD PARK,
AB, T8H 0C7
  (780) 410-2455   *SIC 5511*
1185985 ONTARIO INC   *p 919*
1573 DANFORTH AVE, TORONTO, ON,
M4J 1N8
  (905) 607-1322   *SIC 8099*
1191460 ONTARIO INC   *p 907*
545 THIRTEENTH AVE, THUNDER BAY,
ON, P7B 7B4
  (807) 345-2552   *SIC 5511*
119155 CANADA LIMITED   *p 831*
159 CLEOPATRA DR SUITE 100, OTTAWA,
ON, K2G 5X4
  (613) 226-8680   *SIC 5136*
1192901 ONTARIO LTD   *p 498*
14 AUTOMATIC RD SUITE 38, BRAMP-
TON, ON, L6S 5N5
  (905) 458-1400   *SIC 6411*
1195149 ONTARIO INC   *p 632*
1586 CENTENNIAL DR, KINGSTON, ON,
K7P 0C7
  (613) 389-8010   *SIC 5411*
119678 CANADA INC   *p 1239*
11600   BOUL   ALBERT-HUDON,
MONTREAL-NORD, QC, H1G 3K2
  (514) 328-4230   *SIC 3089*
1196977 ONTARIO LTD   *p 643*
1002 MERSEA ROAD 7, LEAMINGTON,
ON, N8H 3V8
  (519) 324-0631   *SIC 0182*
1197243 ONTARIO LTD   *p 1037*
425 BROADWAY ST, WYOMING, ON, N0N
1T0
  (519) 845-3352   *SIC 5511*
1197283 ONTARIO LIMITED   *p 858*
1030 CONFEDERATION ST UNIT 2, SAR-
NIA, ON, N7S 6H1
  (519) 383-8837   *SIC 5147*
119759 CANADA LTEE   *p 1304*
8850 35E AV, SAINT-GEORGES, QC, G5Y
5C2
  (418) 459-3423   *SIC 6712*
1197767 ONTARIO LTD   *p 597*
2536 BANK ST, GLOUCESTER, ON, K1T
1M9
  (613) 260-7331   *SIC 5541*
1199893 ONTARIO LIMITED   *p 581*
1850 ALBION RD UNIT 6, ETOBICOKE,
ON, M9W 6J9
  (416) 213-1165   *SIC 5441*
12 M MOIS   *p 1131*

See GUERLAIN (CANADA) LTD
12 OUNCES   *p 1325*
See 6356036 CANADA INC
120033 CANADA INC   *p 1103*
581 BOUL SAINT-REN? E, GATINEAU, QC,
J8P 8A6
  (819) 663-5868   *SIC 5983*
1200839 ONTARIO LIMITED   *p 903*
2900 STEELES AVE E SUITE 210, THORN-
HILL, ON, L3T 4X1
  (905) 889-4224   *SIC 7349*
1203130 ONTARIO INC   *p 490*
391 COLLEGE ST E, BELLEVILLE, ON,
K8N 5S7
  (613) 962-9003   *SIC 1796*
120348 CANADA INC   *p 1331*
4600 CH DU BOIS-FRANC, SAINT-
LAURENT, QC, H4S 1A7
  (514) 331-3130   *SIC 5199*
1204626 ONTARIO INC   *p 907*
570 SQUIER PL, THUNDER BAY, ON, P7B
6M2
  (807) 935-2792   *SIC 1794*
120601 CANADA INC   *p 1040*
26 FOURTH ST, CHARLOTTETOWN, PE,
C1E 2B3
  (902) 566-1220   *SIC 5084*
1207273 ALBERTA ULC   *p 704*
570 MATHESON BLVD E UNIT 8, MISSIS-
SAUGA, ON, L4Z 4G4
  (905) 890-8300   *SIC 5047*
1207715 ONTARIO INC   *p 856*
11685 YONGE ST SUITE 205, RICHMOND
HILL, ON, L4E 0K7
  (905) 770-9450   *SIC 8082*
1210670 ONTARIO INC   *p 866*
1940 ELLESMERE RD UNIT 18, SCAR-
BOROUGH, ON, M1H 2V7
  (416) 438-5151   *SIC 4121*
1211084 ONTARIO LTD   *p 490*
6521 HWY 62, BELLEVILLE, ON, K8N 4Z5
  (613) 968-6811   *SIC 5541*
1212360 ONTARIO LIMITED   *p 620*
42 DELAWANA RD, HONEY HARBOUR,
ON, P0E 1E0
  (705) 756-2224   *SIC 7011*
1212551 ONTARIO INC   *p 652*
95 POND MILLS RD, LONDON, ON, N5Z
3X3
  (519) 645-1917   *SIC 5812*
1213475 ONTARIO INC   *p 811*
4358 INNES RD, ORLEANS, ON, K4A 3W3
  (613) 834-6533   *SIC 5541*
121352 CANADA INC   *p 1288*
1156 AV LARIVIERE, ROUYN-NORANDA,
QC, J9X 4K8
  (819) 797-3300   *SIC 5084*
121409 CANADA INC   *p 848*
3425 HANDS RD, PRESCOTT, ON, K0E
1T0
  (613) 925-4502   *SIC 5199*
1214288 ONTARIO LIMITED   *p 482*
125 JOHN ST N, AYLMER, ON, N5H 2A7
  (519) 773-9219   *SIC 5411*
1216037 ONTARIO INC   *p 870*
170 MIDWEST RD, SCARBOROUGH, ON,
M1P 3A9
  (416) 751-9445   *SIC 3089*
1216809 ONTARIO LIMITED   *p 868*
1897 EGLINTON AVE E, SCARBOROUGH,
ON, M1L 2L6
  (416) 751-4892   *SIC 5511*
1220579 ONTARIO INC   *p 665*
750 COCHRANE DR, MARKHAM, ON, L3R
8E1
  (416) 293-8365   *SIC 6712*
1221271 ONTARIO INC   *p 754*
200 DAVIS DR SUITE 1, NEWMARKET, ON,
L3Y 2N4
  SIC 8742
1222010 ONTARIO INC   *p 816*
2000 THURSTON DR UNIT 12, OTTAWA,
ON, K1G 4K7
  (613) 739-4000   *SIC 7311*

▲ Public Company   ■ Public Company Family Member   **HQ** Headquarters   **BR** Branch   **SL** Single Location

1222433 ONTARIO INC   p 993
144 UNION ST, TORONTO, ON, M6N 3M9
(416) 654-3464   *SIC* 5093

123 ENTERPRISES LTD   p 268
374 LOWER GANGES RD, SALT SPRING ISLAND, BC, V8K 2V7
(250) 537-4144   *SIC* 5411

1230172 ONTARIO INC   p 830
110 CENTRAL PARK DR SUITE 512, OTTAWA, ON, K2C 4G3
(613) 727-2773   *SIC* 6513

123179 CANADA INC   p 1200
1117 RUE SAINTE-CATHERINE O BUREAU 303, MONTREAL, QC, H3B 1H9
(514) 844-2612   *SIC* 6519

123273 CANADA INC   p 1319
298 RUE DE MARTIGNY O UNITE 101, SAINT-JEROME, QC, J7Y 4C9
(450) 436-1022   *SIC* 5912

1233481 ONTARIO INC   p 541
1040 KOHLER RD, CAYUGA, ON, N0A 1E0
(905) 772-0303   *SIC* 7948

1234121 ONTARIO LIMITED   p 716
4069 PHEASANT RUN, MISSISSAUGA, ON, L5L 2C2
(905) 569-7595   *SIC* 7032

1235052 ONTARIO LIMITED   p 485
311 BRYNE DR, BARRIE, ON, L4N 8V4
(705) 728-5322   *SIC* 6712

1235054 ONTARIO LIMITED   p 485
311 BRYNE DR, BARRIE, ON, L4N 8V4
(705) 728-5322   *SIC* 5571

1238902 ALBERTA CORP   p 13
200 RIVERCREST DR SE SUITE 160, CALGARY, AB, T2C 2X5
(403) 203-4747   *SIC* 1629

123INKCARTRIDGES.CA   p 1128
See SHOPPER+ INC

1246110 ONTARIO INC   p 754
18120 YONGE ST, NEWMARKET, ON, L3Y 4V8
  SIC 8011

1246607 ALBERTA LTD   p 155
8080 EDGAR INDUSTRIAL CRES, RED DEER, AB, T4P 3R3
(403) 347-9727   *SIC* 1381

1248671 ONTARIO INC   p 594
1481 MICHAEL ST UNIT C, GLOUCESTER, ON, K1B 3R5
(613) 742-9999   *SIC* 5148

1249413 ALBERTA LTD   p 41
1632 14 AVE NW SUITE 1774, CALGARY, AB, T2N 1M7
(403) 289-4441   *SIC* 5941

1249592 ONTARIO LTD   p 872
2110 LAWRENCE AVE E, SCARBOROUGH, ON, M1R 3A3
(416) 750-8885   *SIC* 5511

1249762 ONTARIO INC   p 547
390 EDGELEY BLVD UNIT 8, CONCORD, ON, L4K 3Z6
(905) 761-9009   *SIC* 1743

1249932 ONTARIO INC   p 547
1514 STEELES AVE W, CONCORD, ON, L4K 2P7
(905) 738-0338   *SIC* 5541

125173 CANADA INC   p 1232
2380 MONTEE MASSON, MONTREAL, QC, H7E 4P2
(450) 666-2444   *SIC* 5561

1253207 ALBERTA LTD   p 27
4040 BLACKFOOT TRAIL SE SUITE 120, CALGARY, AB, T2G 4E6
(403) 252-5366   *SIC* 5084

125382 CANADA INC   p 1181
5800 RUE SAINT-DENIS BUREAU 402, MONTREAL, QC, H2S 3L5
(514) 274-2407   *SIC* 5137

1254561 ONTARIO INC   p 479
67 INDUSTRIAL PKY N UNIT 1, AURORA, ON, L4G 4C4
(905) 726-9404   *SIC* 1623

1254613 ONTARIO LIMITED   p 645
207 KENT ST W, LINDSAY, ON, K9V 2Y9

(705) 324-4611   *SIC* 5072

1254711 ONTARIO LIMITED   p 539
437 MARK RD SUITE 1, CAMERON, ON, K0M 1G0
(705) 374-4700   *SIC* 5193

125668 CANADA INC   p 1389
292 RUE PRINCIPALE, UPTON, QC, J0H 2E0
(450) 549-5811   *SIC* 5083

1257391 ONTARIO LIMITED   p 1013
80 WILLIAM SMITH DR, WHITBY, ON, L1N 9W1
(905) 668-5060   *SIC* 6712

1260261 ONTARIO INC   p 541
GD, CHAPLEAU, ON, P0M 1K0
(705) 864-1974   *SIC* 2411

126074 ONTARIO INC   p 809
6 KITCHENER ST, ORILLIA, ON, L3V 6Z9
(705) 327-2232   *SIC* 8361

1262510 ONTARIO LIMITED   p 563
1414 HIGHWAY 2 UNIT 8, COURTICE, ON, L1E 3B4
(905) 433-7735   *SIC* 5411

1263528 ONTARIO LIMITED   p 932
132 QUEENS QUAY E, TORONTO, ON, M5A 0S1
  SIC 5813

1263815 ONTARIO INC   p 903
7079 YONGE ST, THORNHILL, ON, L3T 2A7
(905) 763-3688   *SIC* 5511

1264316 ONTARIO INC   p 884
89 MEADOWVALE DR, ST CATHARINES, ON, L2N 3Z8
(905) 934-5400   *SIC* 7011

1265534 ONTARIO INC   p 581
801 DIXON RD, ETOBICOKE, ON, M9W 1J5
(416) 675-6100   *SIC* 7011

1265767 ONTARIO LIMITED   p 857
311 GORHAM RD, RIDGEWAY, ON, L0S 1N0
(905) 894-5266   *SIC* 5411

1265768 ONTARIO LTD   p 769
3259 BAYVIEW AVE, NORTH YORK, ON, M2K 1G4
(416) 221-6702   *SIC* 5411

1266093 ONTARIO LIMITED   p 643
614 HIGHWAY 77, LEAMINGTON, ON, N8H 3V8
(519) 326-9878   *SIC* 0182

1266192 ONTARIO INC   p 902
302 PATILLO RD SUITE 1, TECUMSEH, ON, N8N 2L9
(519) 727-4578   *SIC* 4212

1266304 ONTARIO INC   p 600
500 HANLON CREEK BLVD, GUELPH, ON, N1C 0A1
(519) 826-6700   *SIC* 1521

126677 CANADA LIMITED   p 815
1620 MICHAEL ST, OTTAWA, ON, K1B 3T7
(613) 741-2800   *SIC* 5812

1268558 ONTARIO LIMITED   p 813
880 CHAMPLAIN AVE, OSHAWA, ON, L1J 7A6
(905) 434-6550   *SIC* 5571

1270477 ONTARIO INC   p 815
1556 MICHAEL ST, OTTAWA, ON, K1B 3T7
(613) 741-0337   *SIC* 5511

127113 CANADA INC   p 1096
960 CH HERRON, DORVAL, QC, H9S 1B3
  SIC 5411

1271591 ONTARIO INC   p 887
261 MARTINDALE RD UNIT 14, ST CATHARINES, ON, L2W 1A2
(905) 688-7755   *SIC* 5092

1272227 ONTARIO INC   p 850
21 EAST WILMOT ST SUITE 2, RICHMOND HILL, ON, L4B 1A3
(905) 763-2929   *SIC* 6712

1277487 ONTARIO INC   p 513
20 SAGE CRT, BRANTFORD, ON, N3R 7T4
(519) 752-4937   *SIC* 5149

127897 CANADA LTD   p 629

295 DALTON AVE, KINGSTON, ON, K7K 6Z1
(613) 544-4600   *SIC* 5571

127901 CANADA INC   p 1175
955 RUE AMHERST, MONTREAL, QC, H2L 3K4
(514) 523-1182   *SIC* 6712

1279028 ONTARIO LIMITED   p 658
755 WONDERLAND RD N, LONDON, ON, N6H 4L1
(519) 473-7772   *SIC* 5461

1279317 ONTARIO LTD   p 790
25 WINGOLD AVE, NORTH YORK, ON, M6B 1P8
(416) 588-1668   *SIC* 7389

128388 CANADA INC   p 1140
1100 RUE HERELLE BUREAU 4, LONGUEUIL, QC, J4G 2M8
(450) 646-3949   *SIC* 5962

1290357 ONTARIO LIMITED   p 905
1054 CENTRE ST, THORNHILL, ON, L4J 3M8
(905) 882-2240   *SIC* 5411

1290685 ONTARIO INC   p 610
135 BARTON ST E, HAMILTON, ON, L8L 8A8
(905) 523-0641   *SIC* 5411

1291292 ONTARIO LIMITED   p 809
43 ONTARIO ST, ORILLIA, ON, L3V 0T7
(705) 326-3586   *SIC* 5411

129157 CANADA INC   p 1263
1831 BOUL WILFRID-HAMEL, QUEBEC, QC, G1N 3Z1
(418) 527-4489   *SIC* 5571

1294711 ALBERTA LTD   p 8
3515 27 ST NE SUITE 8, CALGARY, AB, T1Y 5E4
(403) 250-8222   *SIC* 5146

1300323 ONTARIO INC   p 678
176 HILLMOUNT RD, MARKHAM, ON, L6C 1Z9
(905) 887-5557   *SIC* 4214

130355 CANADA INC   p 1301
225 RUE ROY, SAINT-EUSTACHE, QC, J7R 5R5
(450) 472-0024   *SIC* 3088

130395 CANADA INC   p 1044
200 RUE DES PINS O BUREAU 201, ALMA, QC, G8B 6P9
(418) 668-0420   *SIC* 1794

1307299 ONTARIO INC.   p 840
1200 LANSDOWNE ST W, PETERBOROUGH, ON, K9J 2A1
(705) 748-5655   *SIC* 5411

13089980 ONTARIO LTD   p 881
1 BLACK BEAR RD, SIOUX LOOKOUT, ON, P8T 1B3
(807) 737-2250   *SIC* 5171

1309497 ALBERTA LTD   p 136
4923 50 ST, INNISFAIL, AB, T4G 1T1
(403) 227-2774   *SIC* 5153

1312983 ONTARIO INC   p 648
2016 OXFORD ST E, LONDON, ON, N5V 2Z8
(519) 659-2711   *SIC* 2439

131427 CANADA INC   p 1214
2000 RUE SAINTE-CATHERINE O BUREAU 2, MONTREAL, QC, H3H 2T2
(514) 939-4444   *SIC* 8221

131519 CANADA INC   p 1304
4100 10E AV, SAINT-GEORGES, QC, G5Y 7S3
(418) 228-9458   *SIC* 6712

131638 CANADA INC   p 1307
4605 AV THIBAULT, SAINT-HUBERT, QC, J3Y 3S8
(450) 445-0550   *SIC* 6712

1319691 ONTARIO INCORPORATED p 651
1845 ADELAIDE ST N, LONDON, ON, N5X 0E3
(519) 660-1205   *SIC* 5541

132082 CANADA INC   p 1294
250 CH BELLA-VISTA, SAINT-BASILE-LE-GRAND, QC, J3N 1L1

(450) 461-1988   *SIC* 0161

132087 CANADA INC   p 1223
6675 BOUL MONK, MONTREAL, QC, H4E 3J2
(514) 767-5323   *SIC* 5411

1323339 ONTARIO LIMITED   p 902
20954 DALTON RD, SUTTON WEST, ON, L0E 1R0
(905) 722-5671   *SIC* 5411

132405 CANADA INC   p 1092
1484 BOUL HYMUS, DORVAL, QC, H9P 1J6
(514) 685-1425   *SIC* 7349

1324344 ONTARIO INC   p 850
1725 16TH AVE SUITE 1, RICHMOND HILL, ON, L4B 4C6
(905) 882-5563   *SIC* 6712

1325931 CANADA INC   p 573
55 HORNER AVE UNIT 1, ETOBICOKE, ON, M8Z 4X6
(416) 620-1965   *SIC* 7311

1327187 ONTARIO INC   p 484
2 7 ST, BALMERTOWN, ON, P0V 1C0
(807) 735-2132   *SIC* 5411

1327601 ONTARIO INC   p 736
50 COURTNEYPARK DR E, MISSISSAUGA, ON, L5T 2Y3
(905) 565-6225   *SIC* 5812

1329481 ONTARIO INC   p 564
2930 FRENCH HILL RD, CUMBERLAND, ON, K4C 1K7
(613) 833-1917   *SIC* 4212

1334130 ALBERTA LTD   p 42
550 6 AVE SW SUITE 1000, CALGARY, AB, T2P 0S2
(403) 515-2800   *SIC* 1382

1334869 ONTARIO LIMITED   p 736
6575 KESTREL RD, MISSISSAUGA, ON, L5T 1P4
(905) 670-9100   *SIC* 3714

1335270 ONTARIO INC   p 704
87 MATHESON BLVD E, MISSISSAUGA, ON, L4Z 2Y5
(905) 502-8000   *SIC* 5812

133876 CANADA INC   p 1075
800 BOUL FORD BUREAU 104, CHATEAUGUAY, QC, J6J 4Z2
(450) 692-5570   *SIC* 3999

1339022 ONTARIO LTD   p 998
75 INDUSTRIAL RD, TOTTENHAM, ON, L0G 1W0
(800) 748-0277   *SIC* 7389

1340123 ONTARIO LTD   p 754
869 MULOCK DR SUITE 6, NEWMARKET, ON, L3Y 8S3
(905) 853-3356   *SIC* 5411

1340560 ONTARIO INC   p 1004
7 INDUSTRIAL RD, WALKERTON, ON, N0G 2V0
(519) 881-4055   *SIC* 6712

1341611 ONTARIO INC   p 736
6975 PACIFIC CIR UNIT D, MISSISSAUGA, ON, L5T 2H3
(905) 362-1111   *SIC* 4731

1341805 ONTARIO INC   p 682
1245 STEELES AVE E, MILTON, ON, L9T 0K2
(905) 875-1700   *SIC* 5511

1342205 ONTARIO LIMITED   p 485
90 ANNE STREET S, BARRIE, ON, L4N 2E3
(613) 247-3300   *SIC* 5712

1343080 ALBERTA LTD   p 1438
2 RAMM AVE, WHITE CITY, SK, S4L 5B1
(306) 757-2403   *SIC* 3444

1343929 ONTARIO LIMITED   p 527
880 LAURENTIAN DR SUITE 1, BURLINGTON, ON, L7N 3V6
(905) 632-0864   *SIC* 7371

1348441 ONTARIO INC   p 690
1775 SISMET RD, MISSISSAUGA, ON, L4W 1P9
(905) 282-9371   *SIC* 5719

1350950 ONTARIO LTD   p 750

1558 MERIVALE RD, NEPEAN, ON, K2G 3J9
(613) 225-3470   *SIC* 5149

135456 CANADA INC   *p* 1052
5547 RTE 112, ASCOT CORNER, QC, J0B 1A0
(819) 822-1833   *SIC* 5199

1356594 ONTARIO LTD   *p* 682
1516 CARMEL LINE, MILLBROOK, ON, L0A 1G0
(705) 932-2996   *SIC* 1521

1357000 ALBERTA ULC   *p* 1126
2409 46E AV, LACHINE, QC, H8T 3C9
SIC 4899

135770 CANADA LTEE   *p* 1084
2037 AV FRANCIS-HUGHES, COTE SAINT-LUC, QC, H7S 2G2
(450) 669-3002   *SIC* 2521

1359238 ONTARIO INC.   *p* 1029
643 CHRISLEA RD UNIT 3, WOOD-BRIDGE, ON, L4L 8A3
(905) 669-3882   *SIC* 4813

1359470 ONTARIO INC.   *p* 679
138 ANDERSON AVE UNIT 6, MARKHAM, ON, L6E 1A4
(905) 472-7773   *SIC* 2631

13601 YUKON INC.   *p* 1440
4220 4TH AVE, WHITEHORSE, YT, Y1A 1K1
(867) 667-2527   *SIC* 5411

1360548 ONTARIO LIMITED   *p* 547
370 NORTH RIVERMEDE RD UNIT 1, CONCORD, ON, L4K 3N2
(905) 669-5883   *SIC* 5461

1362385 ONTARIO LIMITED   *p* 633
1932 SETTERINGTON DR, KINGSVILLE, ON, N9Y 2E5
SIC 5148

1363199 ONTARIO LIMITED   *p* 1018
5923 TECUMSEH RD E SUITE 1, WIND-SOR, ON, N8T 1E4
(519) 252-2011   *SIC* 5047

1364279 ONTARIO INC   *p* 597
2559 BANK ST, GLOUCESTER, ON, K1T 1M8
(613) 736-7022   *SIC* 5511

136562 CANADA INC   *p* 1221
6695 RUE SAINT-JACQUES BUREAU 514, MONTREAL, QC, H4B 1V3
(514) 483-6686   *SIC* 5571

1365992 ONTARIO LTD   *p* 923
710 MOUNT PLEASANT RD, TORONTO, ON, M4S 2N6
(416) 483-1290   *SIC* 5411

1367313 ONTARIO INC   *p* 968
100 WELLINGTON ST SUITE 3200, TORONTO, ON, M5K 1K7
(416) 304-1616   *SIC* 6712

137077 CANADA INC   *p* 824
203 ROCHESTER ST, OTTAWA, ON, K1R 7M5
(613) 232-1579   *SIC* 7361

1371185 ONTARIO INC   *p* 665
4011 14TH AVE, MARKHAM, ON, L3R 0Z9
(905) 415-1166   *SIC* 5045

1371500 ONTARIO INC   *p* 690
1770 BRITANNIA RD E, MISSISSAUGA, ON, L4W 1J3
(905) 565-8406   *SIC* 5531

1373744 ONTARIO INC   *p* 500
155 HEDGEDALE RD, BRAMPTON, ON, L6T 5P3
(905) 672-1300   *SIC* 5051

137448 CANADA INC   *p* 1241
734 BOUL CURE-LABELLE, MONTREAL-OUEST, QC, H7V 2T9
(450) 978-5638   *SIC* 5944

1376302 ONTARIO INC   *p* 661
329 SOVEREIGN RD, LONDON, ON, N6M 1A6
(519) 859-5056   *SIC* 2434

1376371 ONTARIO INC   *p* 702
3066 JARROW AVE, MISSISSAUGA, ON, L4X 2C7

(905) 238-9818   *SIC* 5147

1378045 ONTARIO INC   *p* 1013
220 WATER ST, WHITBY, ON, L1N 0G9
(905) 666-7669   *SIC* 7629

137882 CANADA INC   *p* 1131
9100 RUE ELMSLIE, LASALLE, QC, H8R 1V6
(514) 365-1642   *SIC* 6712

1379025 ONTARIO LIMITED   *p* 376
330 YORK AVE SUITE 508, WINNIPEG, MB, R3C 0N9
(204) 942-0101   *SIC* 7011

1383791 ONTARIO INC   *p* 621
952 HUMPHREY RD, IGNACE, ON, P0T 1T0
(807) 934-6500   *SIC* 2411

1387208 ONTARIO LTD   *p* 873
190 MILNER AVE, SCARBOROUGH, ON, M1S 5B6
(416) 293-9943   *SIC* 7384

13876 ENTERPRISES LTD   *p* 213
10020 93 AVE, FORT ST. JOHN, BC, V1J 1E2
(250) 785-6679   *SIC* 5074

1388688 ONTARIO LIMITED   *p* 511
499 MAIN ST S SUITE 56, BRAMPTON, ON, L6Y 1N7
(905) 459-1337   *SIC* 6512

1389773 ONTARIO INC   *p* 610
399 GREENHILL AVE, HAMILTON, ON, L8K 6N5
(905) 561-2221   *SIC* 5411

138984 CANADA LTEE   *p* 1217
6744 RUE HUTCHISON, MONTREAL, QC, H3N 1Y4
(514) 270-3024   *SIC* 2051

1389984 ONTARIO INC   *p* 690
5525 AMBLER DR, MISSISSAUGA, ON, L4W 3Z1
(905) 602-0884   *SIC* 5511

1390835 ONTARIO LIMITED   *p* 978
528 FRONT ST W SUITE 325, TORONTO, ON, M5V 1B8
(416) 703-7700   *SIC* 5511

1391130 ALBERTA LTD   *p* 66
333 24 AVE SW SUITE 300, CALGARY, AB, T2S 3E6
(403) 861-1556   *SIC* 7389

1392167 ONTARIO LIMITED   *p* 547
248 BOWES RD, CONCORD, ON, L4K 1J9
(905) 660-5021   *SIC* 6712

139273 CANADA INC   *p* 1083
5800 BOUL CAVENDISH, COTE SAINT-LUC, QC, H4W 2T5
(514) 482-6340   *SIC* 5912

139464 CANADA LIMITED   *p* 476
4920 COUNTY ROAD 17, ALFRED, ON, K0B 1A0
(613) 679-2252   *SIC* 5211

139670 CANADA LTEE   *p* 1103
1885 RUE SAINT-LOUIS BUREAU 100, GATINEAU, QC, J8T 6G4
(819) 568-1723   *SIC* 5812

1401911 ONTARIO LIMITED   *p* 842
4136 PETROLIA LINE, PETROLIA, ON, N0N 1R0
(519) 882-2211   *SIC* 5411

1404136 ONTARIO LIMITED   *p* 925
1510 YONGE ST, TORONTO, ON, M4T 1Z6
(416) 962-8662   *SIC* 5651

1406284 ONTARIO INC   *p* 547
3201 HIGHWAY 7, CONCORD, ON, L4K 5Z7
(905) 660-4700   *SIC* 7011

1408939 ONTARIO LIMITED   *p* 510
345 MAIN ST N, BRAMPTON, ON, L6X 1N6
(905) 452-9122   *SIC* 5411

141187 VENTURES LTD   *p* 283
5720 16 HWY W, TERRACE, BC, V8G 0C6
(250) 638-1881   *SIC* 1611

1412873 ALBERTA LTD   *p* 125
1205 101 ST SW, EDMONTON, AB, T6X 1A1
(780) 486-5100   *SIC* 5511

1413249 ONTARIO INC   *p* 1013
75 CONSUMERS DR SUITE 17, WHITBY, ON, L1N 9S2
(905) 665-6575   *SIC* 5812

141517 CANADA LTEE   *p* 1075
270 BOUL INDUSTRIEL, CHATEAUGUAY, QC, J6J 4Z2
(450) 692-5527   *SIC* 1761

1416018 ONTARIO LIMITED   *p* 993
853 JANE ST, TORONTO, ON, M6N 4C4
(416) 762-7975   *SIC* 5411

1416720 ONTARIO LIMITED   *p* 570
260 NEW TORONTO ST, ETOBICOKE, ON, M8V 2E8
(416) 243-7000   *SIC* 4953

141793 CANADA INC   *p* 1144
869 BOUL CURE-POIRIER O, LONGUEUIL, QC, J4K 2C3
(450) 674-1521   *SIC* 5063

1421239 ONTARIO INC   *p* 494
124 COMMERCIAL RD, BOLTON, ON, L7E 1K4
(905) 951-6800   *SIC* 6712

1422545 ONTARIO INC   *p* 547
74 EDILCAN DR UNIT 1, CONCORD, ON, L4K 3S5
(905) 660-3357   *SIC* 5137

1422718 ONTARIO INC   *p* 485
125 MAPLEVIEW DR W, BARRIE, ON, L4N 9H7
(705) 727-0000   *SIC* 5511

1426159 ONTARIO LIMITED   *p* 842
400 LANSDOWNE ST E SUITE 1, PETER-BOROUGH, ON, K9L 0B2
(705) 740-9365   *SIC* 5411

1426195 ONTARIO LIMITED   *p* 690
1257 EGLINTON AVE E, MISSISSAUGA, ON, L4W 1K7
(905) 629-4044   *SIC* 5511

1426420 ONTARIO INC   *p* 566
161 HWY 8, DUNDAS, ON, L9H 5E1
(905) 627-2228   *SIC* 5144

1428309 ONTARIO LTD   *p* 1029
5585 HIGHWAY 7, WOODBRIDGE, ON, L4L 1T5
(877) 694-8654   *SIC* 5511

1428427 ONTARIO LTD   *p* 527
3410 SOUTH SERVICE RD SUITE 203, BURLINGTON, ON, L7N 3T2
(905) 331-7207   *SIC* 7373

1428508 ONTARIO LIMITED   *p* 547
407 BASALTIC RD, CONCORD, ON, L4K 4W8
(905) 303-8010   *SIC* 1521

1429634 ONTARIO INC   *p* 496
51 PORT DARLINGTON RD SUITE 1, BOW-MANVILLE, ON, L1C 3K3
(905) 697-0503   *SIC* 4151

1430819 ONTARIO INC   *p* 485
112 SAUNDERS RD UNIT 11, BARRIE, ON, L4N 9A8
(705) 721-9809   *SIC* 7389

1434378 ONTARIO INC   *p* 883
151 CUSHMAN RD, ST CATHARINES, ON, L2M 6T4
(905) 688-9220   *SIC* 7349

1435207 ONTARIO INC   *p* 496
2305 HIGHWAY 2, BOWMANVILLE, ON, L1C 3K7
(905) 623-8521   *SIC* 5541

1437384 ONTARIO LIMITED   *p* 917
1500 BAYVIEW AVE, TORONTO, ON, M4G 3B4
(416) 486-8294   *SIC* 5411

1437716 ONTARIO LIMITED   *p* 820
596 MONTREAL RD, OTTAWA, ON, K1K 0T9
(613) 745-0778   *SIC* 5411

1437782 ONTARIO INC   *p* 690
2810 MATHESON BLVD E SUITE 300, MIS-SISSAUGA, ON, L4W 4X7
(905) 694-2650   *SIC* 4724

1439037 ONTARIO LTD   *p* 645
220 LINDSAY ST S, LINDSAY, ON, K9V 2N3

(705) 324-3516   *SIC* 5251

1441246 ONTARIO INC   *p* 895
3010 LINE 34, STRATFORD, ON, N5A 6S5
(519) 271-4370   *SIC* 5251

1441571 ONTARIO INC   *p* 839
501 TOWERHILL RD, PETERBOROUGH, ON, K9H 7S3
(705) 740-9026   *SIC* 5411

1442503 ONTARIO INC   *p* 581
18 NAMCO RD, ETOBICOKE, ON, M9W 1M5
(416) 741-4498   *SIC* 3251

1443190 ONTARIO INC   *p* 643
605 COUNTY RD 18, LEAMINGTON, ON, N8H 3V5
(519) 322-2264   *SIC* 3469

1443237 ONTARIO,INC   *p* 807
713003 1ST LINE, ORANGEVILLE, ON, L9W 2Z2
(519) 941-9291   *SIC* 5511

1443635 ONTARIO INC   *p* 618
3235 FRONT RD, HAWKESBURY, ON, K6A 2R2
(613) 632-6256   *SIC* 5172

1443803 ALBERTA LTD   *p* 162
30 AUTOMALL RD, SHERWOOD PARK, AB, T8H 2N1
(780) 417-0005   *SIC* 5511

144503 CANADA INC   *p* 1248
6361 RTE TRANSCANADIENNE BUREAU 119, POINTE-CLAIRE, QC, H9R 5A5
(514) 694-6843   *SIC* 5999

1449132 ONTARIO LIMITED   *p* 1006
343 WEBER ST N, WATERLOO, ON, N2J 3H8
(519) 579-8243   *SIC* 5736

1451805 ONTARIO INC   *p* 872
2 PRINCIPAL RD UNIT 10, SCARBOR-OUGH, ON, M1R 4Z3
(416) 497-4363   *SIC* 8741

1453633 ONTARIO INC   *p* 686
6205 AIRPORT RD SUITE 500, MISSIS-SAUGA, ON, L4V 1E1
(416) 622-4766   *SIC* 7363

1454615 ALBERTA LTD   *p* 125
830 100 ST SW, EDMONTON, AB, T6X 0S8
(780) 989-2222   *SIC* 5511

1456661 ONTARIO INCORPORATED   *p* 903
300 JOHN ST SUITE 87552, THORNHILL, ON, L3T 5W4
(905) 669-1103   *SIC* 4212

1456882 ONTARIO LTD   *p* 788
3401 DUFFERIN ST, NORTH YORK, ON, M6A 2T9
(416) 789-3533   *SIC* 5461

1457271 ONTARIO LIMITED   *p* 478
1217 OLD MOHAWK RD, ANCASTER, ON, L9K 1P6
(905) 304-6781   *SIC* 8051

1459243 ONTARIO INC   *p* 690
2180 MATHESON BLVD E UNIT 1, MISSIS-SAUGA, ON, L4W 5E1
(905) 206-5500   *SIC* 5087

1459564 ONTARIO LTD   *p* 568
68 YONGE ST S, ELMVALE, ON, L0L 1P0
(705) 322-5504   *SIC* 5461

1460932 ONTARIO LIMITED   *p* 832
2577 BASELINE RD, OTTAWA, ON, K2H 7B3
(613) 726-9513   *SIC* 5411

1461148 ONTARIO CORP   *p* 918
8 THORNCLIFFE PARK DR, TORONTO, ON, M4H 1H4
(416) 421-3723   *SIC* 5541

1461616 ONTARIO INC   *p* 1017
10280 TECUMSEH RD E, WINDSOR, ON, N8R 1A2
(519) 735-7706   *SIC* 5511

1468792 ONTARIO INC   *p* 647
206 FIELDING RD, LIVELY, ON, P3Y 1L6
(705) 682-4471   *SIC* 1611

1470341 ONTARIO INC   *p* 751
1581 GREENBANK RD SUITE 16, NE-PEAN, ON, K2J 4Y6

(613) 825-5495 *SIC* 5411
1470754 ONTARIO INC *p* 498
2280 QUEEN ST E, BRAMPTON, ON, L6S
5X9
(905) 494-1000 *SIC* 5511
1471899 ALBERTA LTD *p* 92
13040 148 ST, EDMONTON, AB, T5L 2H8
(780) 460-2399 *SIC* 1542
1475541 ONTARIO LTD *p* 547
2651 RUTHERFORD RD, CONCORD, ON,
L4K 2N6
(905) 856-0662 *SIC* 5541
1476182 ONTARIO LIMITED *p* 990
22 NORTHCOTE AVE, TORONTO, ON, M6J
3K3
(416) 537-4124 *SIC* 5411
1476399 ONTARIO LIMITED *p* 589
71301 LONDON RD, EXETER, ON, N0M
1S3
(519) 235-2121 *SIC* 6712
1476482 ONTARIO INC *p* 618
323 FRONT RD, HAWKESBURY, ON, K6A
2T1
(613) 632-1816 *SIC* 4731
147755 CANADA INC *p* 1063
1501 RUE AMPERE BUREAU 200,
BOUCHERVILLE, QC, J4B 5Z5
(450) 655-2441 *SIC* 6712
147766 CANADA INC *p* 1018
7180 TECUMSEH RD E, WINDSOR, ON,
N8T 1E6
(519) 945-8100 *SIC* 5511
1478575 ONTARIO LIMITED *p* 690
5505 AMBLER DR, MISSISSAUGA, ON,
L4W 3Z1
(905) 206-8886 *SIC* 5511
148274 CANADA INC *p* 1092
100 AV JENKINS BUREAU 100, DORVAL,
QC, H9P 2R1
(514) 631-5058 *SIC* 4512
1484174 ALBERTA LTD *p* 148
1601 13 ST, NISKU, AB, T9E 0Y2
(780) 454-9231 *SIC* 7389
1484558 ONTARIO INC *p* 770
2 SHEPPARD AVE E SUITE 700, NORTH
YORK, ON, M2N 5Y7
(416) 203-1800 *SIC* 7361
1491222 ONTARIO LTD *p* 796
450 DUNDAS ST E, OAKVILLE, ON, L6H
7L4
(905) 257-5185 *SIC* 5541
1496201 ONTARIO INC *p* 750
1963 MERIVALE RD, NEPEAN, ON, K2G
1G1
(613) 736-8899 *SIC* 5571
1496519 ONTARIO INC *p* 815
2675 BLACKWELL ST UNIT 8, OTTAWA,
ON, K1B 4E4
(613) 747-6660 *SIC* 5141
149667 CANADA INC *p* 1346
6925 RUE JEAN-TALON E, SAINT-
LEONARD, QC, H1S 1N2
(514) 254-2153 *SIC* 5731
1496803 ALBERTA INC *p* 95
15849 116 AVE NW, EDMONTON, AB, T5M
3W1
(780) 463-7787 *SIC* 8742
1497665 ONTARIO INC *p* 562
1107 BROOKDALE AVE, CORNWALL, ON,
K6J 4P6
(613) 933-7555 *SIC* 5511
1498403 ONTARIO INC *p* 1018
7400 TECUMSEH RD E, WINDSOR, ON,
N8T 1E9
(519) 974-7116 *SIC* 5541
1498882 ONTARIO INC *p* 648
1915 DUNDAS ST SUITE SIDE, LONDON,
ON, N5V 5J9
(519) 451-5737 *SIC* 5812
149942 CANADA INC *p* 1233
1955 RUE MONTEREY, MONTREAL, QC,
H7L 3T6
(450) 688-7660 *SIC* 5144
1500451 ONTARIO LIMITED *p* 484

165 WELLINGTON ST E, BARRIE, ON, L4M
2C7
(705) 737-0389 *SIC* 5411
150147 CANADA INC *p* 1173
4284 RUE DE LA ROCHE BUREAU 220,
MONTREAL, QC, H2J 3H9
(438) 380-3516 *SIC* 4731
150157 CANADA INC *p* 1327
2320 RUE COHEN, SAINT-LAURENT, QC,
H4R 2N8
(514) 745-1080 *SIC* 5074
1502026 ONTARIO LTD *p* 864
80 AUTO MALL DR, SCARBOROUGH, ON,
M1B 5N5
(416) 291-2929 *SIC* 5511
1503647 ONTARIO LIMITED *p* 690
1173 MATHESON BLVD E, MISSISSAUGA,
ON, L4W 1B6
(416) 255-7370 *SIC* 5075
1504953 ALBERTA LTD *p* 63
119 12 AVE SW, CALGARY, AB, T2R 0G8
(403) 206-9565 *SIC* 7011
1506369 ALBERTA ULC *p* 1328
6635 BOUL HENRI-BOURASSA O, SAINT-
LAURENT, QC, H4R 1E1
SIC 5122
1508235 ONTARIO INC *p* 992
1 WOODBOROUGH AVE, TORONTO, ON,
M6M 5A1
(416) 654-8008 *SIC* 3651
1509611 ONTARIO INC *p* 547
577 EDGELEY BLVD SUITE 1, CONCORD,
ON, L4K 4B2
(905) 660-4200 *SIC* 5084
1510610 ONTARIO INC *p* 762
1811 SEYMOUR ST, NORTH BAY, ON, P1A
0C7
(705) 474-0350 *SIC* 7692
1511905 ONTARIO INC *p* 602
359 WOODLAWN RD W, GUELPH, ON,
N1H 7K9
(519) 824-9150 *SIC* 5511
1512081 ONTARIO LTD *p* 916
93 TORO RD, TORONTO, ON, M3J 2A4
(416) 398-2500 *SIC* 7549
151210 CANADA INC *p* 1392
245 RUE JEAN-COUTU, VARENNES, QC,
J3X 0E1
(450) 646-9760 *SIC* 6712
1512804 ONTARIO INC *p* 510
47 BOVAIRD DR W, BRAMPTON, ON, L6X
0G9
(905) 459-2600 *SIC* 5511
1514498 ONTARIO INC *p* 815
2445 SHEFFIELD RD, OTTAWA, ON, K1B
3V6
(613) 749-5611 *SIC* 1711
1514505 ONTARIO INC *p* 625
240 TERENCE MATTHEWS CRES SUITE
101, KANATA, ON, K2M 2C4
(613) 592-1114 *SIC* 1542
1514660 ONTARIO INC *p* 826
2498 BANK ST, OTTAWA, ON, K1V 8S2
(613) 523-2027 *SIC* 5541
1519418 ONTARIO INC *p* 733
265 EXPORT BLVD, MISSISSAUGA, ON,
L5S 1Y4
(905) 670-9300 *SIC* 4731
1519694 ONTARIO INC *p* 875
135 SELECT AVE UNIT 8-9, SCARBOR-
OUGH, ON, M1V 4A5
(416) 754-0483 *SIC* 2015
1519950 ONTARIO INC *p* 508
25 CLARK BLVD, BRAMPTON, ON, L6W
1X4
(905) 452-0111 *SIC* 5531
1520202 ONTARIO LTD *p* 493
286 CHATHAM ST N RR 5, BLENHEIM, ON,
N0P 1A0
(519) 676-0353 *SIC* 5411
1520940 ONTARIO INC *p* 747
9196 DICKENSON RD, MOUNT HOPE, ON,
L0R 1W0
(905) 679-6066 *SIC* 5051

152163 CANADA INC *p* 1156
5591 RUE PARE, MONT-ROYAL, QC, H4P
1P7
(514) 735-5248 *SIC* 6719
152258 CANADA INC *p* 1177
555 RUE CHABANEL O BUREAU M53B,
MONTREAL, QC, H2N 2H7
SIC 5137
152429 CANADA INC *p* 1319
298 RUE DE MARTIGNY O BUREAU 10,
SAINT-JEROME, QC, J7Y 4C9
(450) 438-1263 *SIC* 5063
152610 CANADA INC *p* 748
43 AURIGA DR, NEPEAN, ON, K2E 7Y8
(800) 565-2874 *SIC* 1542
**1527 UPPER JAMES ST.,HAMILTON, IN-
CORPORATED** *p*
616
1527 UPPER JAMES ST, HAMILTON, ON,
L9B 1K2
(905) 385-1523 *SIC* 8641
1527619 ONTARIO INC *p* 1013
5 SUNRAY ST, WHITBY, ON, L1N 8Y3
(905) 668-6881 *SIC* 5511
1528593 ONTARIO INC *p* 1004
6941 BASE LINE, WALLACEBURG, ON,
N8A 4L3
(519) 627-7885 *SIC* 3479
1529295 ONTARIO INC *p* 770
386 SHEPPARD AVE E UNIT 2, NORTH
YORK, ON, M2N 3B7
(416) 226-6667 *SIC* 4724
1529813 ALBERTA LTD *p* 165
5 GIROUX RD SUITE 420, ST. ALBERT, AB,
T8N 6J8
(780) 460-7499 *SIC* 5499
1530431 ONTARIO LIMITED *p* 677
7075 MARKHAM RD, MARKHAM, ON, L3S
3J9
(905) 471-0089 *SIC* 5411
1530460 ONTARIO INC *p* 762
390 LAKESHORE DR SUITE 7, NORTH
BAY, ON, P1A 2C7
(705) 476-1230 *SIC* 5541
1531011 ONTARIO INC *p* 581
185 CARLINGVIEW DR SUITE 1, ETOBI-
COKE, ON, M9W 5E8
(416) 285-0041 *SIC* 5199
1535477 ONTARIO LIMITED *p* 619
GD, HEARST, ON, P0L 1N0
(705) 362-4085 *SIC* 5541
153924 CANADA INC *p* 1396
4061 RUE WELLINGTON, VERDUN, QC,
H4G 1V6
(514) 761-4591 *SIC* 5912
153927 CANADA INC *p* 1106
15 BOUL MONTCLAIR BUREAU 203,
GATINEAU, QC, J8Y 2E2
(819) 770-4232 *SIC* 5912
1540886 ONTARIO INC *p* 526
2180 ITABASHI WAY SUITE 1A, BURLING-
TON, ON, L7M 5A5
(905) 319-7272 *SIC* 5411
1541094 ONTARIO INC *p* 996
1581 THE QUEENSWAY SUITE 2,
TORONTO, ON, M8Z 1T8
(416) 253-5001 *SIC* 5561
1542053 ONTARIO LIMITED *p* 520
1175 CORPORATE DR UNIT 8, BURLING-
TON, ON, L7L 5V5
(905) 332-7755 *SIC* 5065
1543738 ONTARIO LIMITED *p* 905
222 STEELES AVE W, THORNHILL, ON,
L4J 1A1
(416) 221-8876 *SIC* 5511
1543892 ONTARIO LTD *p* 645
42 RUSSELL ST W, LINDSAY, ON, K9V
2W9
(705) 328-0622 *SIC* 5411
1544982 ONTARIO INC *p* 643
50 VICTORIA AVE N, LEAMINGTON, ON,
N8H 2W1
(519) 776-9153 *SIC* 3471
154644 CANADA INC *p* 926

40 ST CLAIR AVE W UNIT 102, TORONTO,
ON, M4V 1M2
(416) 481-2733 *SIC* 8059
1548383 ONTARIO INC *p* 958
249 QUEENS QUAY W SUITE 109,
TORONTO, ON, M5J 2N5
(416) 203-3333 *SIC* 7011
1548732 ONTARIO LIMITED *p* 907
640 RIVER ST, THUNDER BAY, ON, P7A
3S4
(807) 345-8012 *SIC* 5912
1551121 ONTARIO INC *p* 815
1427 MICHAEL ST, OTTAWA, ON, K1B 3R3
(613) 749-4858 *SIC* 5013
1553690 ONTARIO INC *p* 652
277 HIGHBURY AVE N, LONDON, ON, N5Z
2W8
(519) 455-0329 *SIC* 5541
1555314 ONTARIO INC *p* 838
965 MACKAY ST, PEMBROKE, ON, K8B
1A2
(613) 735-4593 *SIC* 7532
1555965 ONTARIO INC *p* 615
473 CONCESSION ST, HAMILTON, ON,
L9A 1C1
(905) 383-7160 *SIC* 5461
1556890 ONTARIO LTD *p* 788
1 YORKDALE RD SUITE 404, NORTH
YORK, ON, M6A 3A1
(416) 787-1612 *SIC* 6282
1557483 ONTARIO INC *p* 988
2471 DUFFERIN ST, TORONTO, ON, M6B
3P6
SIC 5531
1558775 ONTARIO LIMITED *p* 901
80 NATIONAL ST, SUDBURY, ON, P3L 1M5
(705) 673-8218 *SIC* 5087
156023 CANADA INC *p* 1151
20900 CH DE LA COTE N, MIRABEL, QC,
J7J 0E5
(450) 437-8000 *SIC* 5511
1561109 ONTARIO INC *p* 972
40 BERNARD AVE, TORONTO, ON, M5R
1R2
(416) 460-0980 *SIC* 5122
1561716 ONTARIO LTD *p* 581
930 DIXON RD, ETOBICOKE, ON, M9W
1J9
(416) 674-7777 *SIC* 5812
1561716 ONTARIO LTD *p* 843
705 KINGSTON RD, PICKERING, ON, L1V
6K3
(905) 420-3334 *SIC* 5812
1562067 ONTARIO INC *p* 826
1720 BANK ST, OTTAWA, ON, K1V 7Y6
SIC 5531
1562246 ONTARIO INC *p* 912
108 THIRD AVE, TIMMINS, ON, P4N 1C3
(705) 264-2274 *SIC* 5712
156560 CANADA INC *p* 1233
1123 NORD LAVAL (A-440) O, MONTREAL,
QC, H7L 3W3
(514) 337-1222 *SIC* 0782
156861 CANADA INC *p* 1091
64 BOUL BRUNSWICK, DOLLARD-DES-
ORMEAUX, QC, H9B 2L3
(514) 421-4445 *SIC* 3625
1569243 ONTARIO INC *p* 485
316 BAYVIEW DR, BARRIE, ON, L4N 8X9
(705) 719-4870 *SIC* 5712
1570707 ONTARIO INC *p* 573
55 HORNER AVE UNIT 1, ETOBICOKE,
ON, M8Z 4X6
(416) 620-1965 *SIC* 7311
1571921 ONTARIO LIMITED *p* 864
51 TAPSCOTT RD, SCARBOROUGH, ON,
M1B 4Y7
SIC 5411
1572900 ONTARIO INC *p* 728
6301 SILVER DART DR, MISSISSAUGA,
ON, L5P 1B2
(416) 776-2247 *SIC* 4724
157341 CANADA INC *p* 1181
7236 RUE MARCONI, MONTREAL, QC,

H2R 2Z5

(514) 844-5050 *SIC* 6712

1574942 ONTARIO LIMITED *p* 811
1802 SIMCOE ST N, OSHAWA, ON, L1G 4X9

(905) 576-2092 *SIC* 5499

157503 CANADA INC *p* 1155
4360 CH DE LA COTE-DE-LIESSE, MONT-ROYAL, QC, H4N 2P7

(514) 344-5140 *SIC* 5621

1576610 ONTARIO LTD *p* 870
2471 KINGSTON RD, SCARBOROUGH, ON, M1N 1V4

(416) 261-4569 *SIC* 5411

1576640 ONTARIO LTD *p* 948
157 ADELAIDE ST W SUITE 207, TORONTO, ON, M5H 4E7

SIC 8741

1579149 ONTARIO LTD *p* 1006
106 BRIDGEPORT RD E, WATERLOO, ON, N2J 2J9

(519) 746-0139 *SIC* 5541

157971 CANADA INC *p* 1172
4315 RUE FRONTENAC BUREAU 200, MONTREAL, QC, H2H 2M4

(514) 527-1146 *SIC* 7349

1579901 ONTARIO INC *p* 498
27 AUTOMATIC RD, BRAMPTON, ON, L6S 5N8

(416) 741-5454 *SIC* 4731

1583647 ALBERTA LTD *p* 98
10220 184 ST NW, EDMONTON, AB, T5S 0B9

(780) 483-4024 *SIC* 5511

158473 CANADA INC *p* 1192
1555 RUE PEEL BUREAU 1100, MON-TREAL, QC, H3A 3L8

(514) 846-4000 *SIC* 6712

1588545 ALBERTA LTD *p* 8
3825 34 ST NE SUITE 113B, CALGARY, AB, T1Y 6Z8

(403) 272-3032 *SIC* 5065

1589711 ONTARIO INC *p* 515
156 ADAMS BLVD, BRANTFORD, ON, N3S 7V5

(905) 643-9044 *SIC* 3544

1589711 ONTARIO INC *p* 891
566 ARVIN AVE UNIT 3, STONEY CREEK, ON, L8E 5P1

SIC 3544

1594058 ONTARIO LTD *p* 658
1190 OXFORD ST W, LONDON, ON, N6H 4N2

(519) 474-2561 *SIC* 5411

1594414 ONTARIO LIMITED *p* 866
4473 KINGSTON RD, SCARBOROUGH, ON, M1E 2N7

(416) 281-9140 *SIC* 5411

159519 CANADA INC *p* 1047
9031 BOUL PARKWAY, ANJOU, QC, H1J 1N4

(514) 325-8700 *SIC* 6712

159585 CANADA INC *p* 1401
1 CAR WESTMOUNT BUREAU 1850, WESTMOUNT, QC, H3Z 2P9

(514) 932-7422 *SIC* 6712

1596101 ONTARIO INC *p* 911
35 TOWNLINE RD, TILLSONBURG, ON, N4G 2R5

(519) 688-5803 *SIC* 6712

160276 CANADA INC *p* 1221
6865 BOUL DE MAISONNEUVE O, MON-TREAL, QC, H4B 1T1

SIC 6712

1607138 ONTARIO LIMITED *p* 978
266 KING ST W SUITE 200, TORONTO, ON, M5V 1H8

(416) 977-3238 *SIC* 7922

1607408 ONTARIO INC *p* 490
720 DUNDAS ST W, BELLEVILLE, ON, K8N 4Z2

(613) 969-1166 *SIC* 5511

160841 CANADA INC *p* 1239
10671 AV BRUNET, MONTREAL-NORD,

QC, H1G 5E1

(514) 325-3680 *SIC* 5149

161251 CANADA INC *p* 1055
355 RUE DUPONT, BEAUPRE, QC, G0A 1E0

(418) 827-8347 *SIC* 6712

1615517 ONTARIO INC *p* 873
5215 FINCH AVE E UNIT 203, SCARBOR-OUGH, ON, M1S 0C2

(416) 321-6969 *SIC* 6719

1619214 ONTARIO LIMITED *p* 921
2552 YONGE ST, TORONTO, ON, M4P 2J2

(416) 485-0303 *SIC* 5719

162013 CANADA INC *p* 1191
1080 COTE DU BEAVER HALL, MON-TREAL, QC, H2Z 1S8

SIC 7389

162069 CANADA INC *p* 1063
1263 RUE VOLTA, BOUCHERVILLE, QC, J4B 7M7

(450) 670-1110 *SIC* 7361

1625443 ONTARIO INC *p* 535
75 LINGARD RD, CAMBRIDGE, ON, N1T 2A8

(519) 624-9914 *SIC* 4731

162583 CANADA INC *p* 1224
1625 RUE CHABANEL O BUREAU 801, MONTREAL, QC, H4N 2S7

(514) 384-4776 *SIC* 6712

1627198 ONTARIO INC *p* 633
1956 SETTERINGTON DR, KINGSVILLE, ON, N9Y 2E5

(519) 326-1333 *SIC* 3312

1627880 ONTARIO INC *p* 500
100 PARKSHORE DR, BRAMPTON, ON, L6T 5M1

SIC 2752

1630389 ONTARIO LTD *p* 485
11 KING ST UNIT 4, BARRIE, ON, L4N 6B5

(705) 721-1600 *SIC* 5075

163288 CANADA INC *p* 1244
47 AV COURCELETTE, OUTREMONT, QC, H2V 3A5

(514) 277-0880 *SIC* 5137

1633578 ONTARIO LIMITED *p* 906
434 STEELES AVE W, THORNHILL, ON, L4J 6X6

(905) 889-0080 *SIC* 5511

1633936 ONTARIO INC *p* 599
1349 MEADOW DR, GREELY, ON, K4P 1N3

(613) 821-3016 *SIC* 5411

163453 CANADA INC *p* 1248
6800 RTE TRANSCANADIENNE, POINTE-CLAIRE, QC, H9R 1C2

(514) 956-7482 *SIC* 5099

1637136 ONTARIO INC *p* 485
82 WELHAM RD, BARRIE, ON, L4N 8Y4

(705) 733-1349 *SIC* 2752

1638-2723 QUEBEC INC. *p* 1307
2805 BOUL LOSCH, SAINT-HUBERT, QC, J3Y 3V6

(514) 866-8683 *SIC* 5087

163972 CANADA INC *p* 1177
9600 RUE MEILLEUR BUREAU 730, MON-TREAL, QC, H2N 2E3

(514) 385-3629 *SIC* 5621

1642852 ONTARIO INC *p* 547
30 MACINTOSH BLVD UNIT 7, CONCORD, ON, L4K 4P1

(416) 252-5907 *SIC* 5065

1649313 ONTARIO INC *p* 888
5552 RUE ST CATHARINE, ST ISIDORE, ON, K0C 2B0

(613) 524-2079 *SIC* 5984

1649338 ONTARIO INC *p* 540
266 WESTBROOK RD, CARP, ON, K0A 1L0

(613) 831-4446 *SIC* 5149

1650473 ONTARIO INC *p* 610
10 HILLYARD ST, HAMILTON, ON, L8L 8J9

SIC 5093

1652472 ONTARIO INC *p* 747
24 ADVANCE AVE, NAPANEE, ON, K7R 3Y6

(613) 354-7653 *SIC* 1611

1661899 ONTARIO LIMITED *p* 719
6980 CREDITVIEW RD, MISSISSAUGA, ON, L5N 8E2

(905) 812-7300 *SIC* 2043

166260 CANADA INC *p* 1331
4747 BOUL DE LA COTE-VERTU, SAINT-LAURENT, QC, H4S 1C9

(514) 336-8780 *SIC* 6712

166606 CANADA INC *p* 1324
3333 CH DE LA COTE-DE-LIESSE, SAINT-LAURENT, QC, H4N 3C2

(514) 748-7777 *SIC* 5511

1667779 ONTARIO LIMITED *p* 778
52 PRINCE ANDREW PL, NORTH YORK, ON, M3C 2H4

(416) 391-5555 *SIC* 6712

1669051 NOVA SCOTIA LIMITED *p* 781
680 STEEPROCK DR, NORTH YORK, ON, M3J 2X1

(416) 635-6500 *SIC* 5085

1670747 ONTARIO INC *p* 907
720 HEWITSON ST, THUNDER BAY, ON, P7B 5Z1

(807) 623-3996 *SIC* 5172

1673594 ALBERTA LTD *p* 79
10702 79 AVE, CLAIRMONT, AB, T8X 5G9

(780) 538-2445 *SIC* 5172

1673612 ONTARIO INC *p* 788
3400 DUFFERIN ST, NORTH YORK, ON, M6A 2V1

(416) 789-4101 *SIC* 5511

167395 CANADA INC *p* 1183
5242 AV DU PARC, MONTREAL, QC, H2V 4G7

(514) 273-8782 *SIC* 5411

1675001 ONTARIO LIMITED *p* 856
11188 YONGE ST, RICHMOND HILL, ON, L4S 1K9

(905) 884-5100 *SIC* 5511

167986 CANADA INC *p* 1093
1901 RTE TRANSCANADIENNE, DORVAL, QC, H9P 1J1

(514) 685-2202 *SIC* 5099

1681230 ONTARIO INC *p* 1018
10380 TECUMSEH RD E, WINDSOR, ON, N8R 1A7

(519) 979-9900 *SIC* 5511

168287 CANADA INC *p* 1284
217 AV LEONIDAS S BUREAU 3B, RI-MOUSKI, QC, G5L 2T5

(418) 722-9257 *SIC* 1541

168360 CANADA INC *p* 1281
845 RUE NOTRE-DAME BUREAU 1989, REPENTIGNY, QC, J5Y 1C4

(450) 582-3182 *SIC* 5511

168406 CANADA INC *p* 1393
135 RUE DU CHEMINOT, VAUDREUIL-DORION, QC, J7V 5V5

(450) 455-9877 *SIC* 5013

1685300 ONTARIO INC *p* 680
1835 DIAMOND RD, MATHESON, ON, P0K 1N0

(705) 273-3219 *SIC* 1629

1686416 ONTARIO INC *p* 665
10 ALDEN RD SUITE 6, MARKHAM, ON, L3R 2S1

(905) 305-0071 *SIC* 7389

168662 CANADA INC *p* 1177
333 RUE CHABANEL O BUREAU 800, MONTREAL, QC, H2N 2E7

(514) 384-7691 *SIC* 5632

168662 CANADA INC *p* 1181
260 RUE GARY-CARTER, MONTREAL, QC, H2R 2V7

(514) 384-7691 *SIC* 5632

1686943 ONTARIO LIMITED *p* 597
4726 BANK ST, GLOUCESTER, ON, K1T 3W7

(613) 822-7400 *SIC* 6712

1688150 ALBERTA LTD *p* 121
2004 80 AVE NW, EDMONTON, AB, T6P 1N2

(780) 462-4430 *SIC* 5087

1690651 ONTARIO INC *p* 577

5559 DUNDAS ST W, ETOBICOKE, ON, M9B 1B9

(416) 239-7171 *SIC* 5411

1692038 ONTARIO LTD *p* 788
1811 AVENUE RD, NORTH YORK, ON, M5M 3Z3

(416) 781-3917 *SIC* 5411

1692246 ONTARIO INC *p* 665
91 ESNA PARK DR UNIT 8, MARKHAM, ON, L3R 2S2

(905) 845-6556 *SIC* 5712

169727 CANADA INC *p* 1103
720 MONTEE PAIEMENT BUREAU 100, GATINEAU, QC, J8R 4A3

(819) 643-4233 *SIC* 5411

1700 MANAGEMENT CORPORATION *p* 376
360 MAIN ST SUITE 1700, WINNIPEG, MB, R3C 3Z3

(204) 956-2970 *SIC* 8741

170260 CANADA INC *p* 862
773 GREAT NORTHERN RD, SAULT STE. MARIE, ON, P6B 0B7

(705) 946-0876 *SIC* 5734

1702660 ONTARIO INC *p* 748
2013 PRINCE OF WALES DR, NEPEAN, ON, K2C 3J7

(613) 913-5539 *SIC* 1761

1708828 ONTARIO LIMITED *p* 646
8082 ROAD 129, LISTOWEL, ON, N4W 3G8

(519) 291-4162 *SIC* 3523

1712093 ONTARIO LIMITED *p* 758
6455 FALLSVIEW BLVD, NIAGARA FALLS, ON, L2G 3V9

(905) 357-5200 *SIC* 7011

1712318 ONTARIO LIMITED *p* 334
2546 GOVERNMENT ST, VICTORIA, BC, V8T 4P7

(250) 385-1408 *SIC* 5511

1716530 ONTARIO INC *p* 750
22 BARNSTONE DR, NEPEAN, ON, K2G 2P9

(613) 843-9887 *SIC* 6513

1716871 ONTARIO INC *p* 615
1460 STONE CHURCH RD E, HAMILTON, ON, L8W 3V3

(905) 388-2264 *SIC* 6794

1719094 ONTARIO INC *p* 917
953 WOODBINE AVE, TORONTO, ON, M4C 4B6

(416) 698-1384 *SIC* 8741

1719108 ONTARIO INC *p* 547
368 FOUR VALLEY DR, CONCORD, ON, L4K 5Z1

(416) 749-5665 *SIC* 5039

1721502 ONTARIO INC *p* 729
5880 FALBOURNE ST, MISSISSAUGA, ON, L5R 0E6

(905) 238-8328 *SIC* 2051

1726837 ONTARIO INC *p* 577
10 FOUR SEASONS PL SUITE 601, ETO-BICOKE, ON, M9B 6H7

(416) 695-8900 *SIC* 2051

1729787 ONTARIO LIMITED *p* 906
133 FRONT ST N SUITE 1, THOROLD, ON, L2V 0A3

(905) 227-2015 *SIC* 5144

173532 CANADA INC *p* 1345
7870 RUE FLEURICOURT, SAINT-LEONARD, QC, H1R 2L3

(514) 274-2870 *SIC* 6712

1737868 ONTARIO INC. *p* 625
200 TERENCE MATTHEWS CRES, KANATA, ON, K2M 2C6

(613) 591-0044 *SIC* 5122

1742009 ALBERTA INC *p* 167
28007 HIGHWAY 16, STONY PLAIN, AB, T7Z 1S5

(780) 963-2251 *SIC* 3523

174664 CANADA LTEE *p* 1161
7900 AV MARCO-POLO, MONTREAL, QC, H1E 2S5

(514) 648-1015 *SIC* 6712

174761 CANADA INC *p* 1107
961 BOUL SAINT-JOSEPH, GATINEAU,

QC, J8Z 1W8
(819) 776-6700   *SIC* 5511
174762 CANADA INC   *p* 1107
961 BOUL SAINT-JOSEPH, GATINEAU, QC, J8Z 1W8
(819) 776-6700   *SIC* 5511
1748271 ONTARIO INC   *p* 880
36 MAPLEHYRN AVE, SHARON, ON, L0G 1V0
(519) 457-2863   *SIC* 5963
175042 CANADA INC   *p* 425
2 FIRST AVE, LABRADOR CITY, NL, A2V 2K5
(709) 282-3910   *SIC* 7353
1750769 ONTARIO INC   *p* 833
504A KENT ST, OTTAWA, ON, K2P 2B9
(613) 231-3474   *SIC* 5146
175246 CANADA INC   *p* 1245
4928 BOUL DES SOURCES BUREAU 2545, PIERREFONDS, QC, H8Y 3E1
(514) 684-0779   *SIC* 5812
175784 CANADA INC   *p* 1295
585 RUE SAGARD, SAINT-BRUNO, QC, J3V 6C1
(450) 461-3310   *SIC* 4212
1758691 ONTARIO INC   *p* 620
21360 BATHURST ST, HOLLAND LANDING, ON, L9N 1P6
(905) 830-0333   *SIC* 5148
1759800 ONTARIO INC   *p* 590
804 COUNTY ROAD 8, FENELON FALLS, ON, K0M 1N0
(705) 887-9458   *SIC* 5032
1760   *p* 1101
See BROUE-ALLIANCE INC
176026 CANADA INC   *p* 1001
134 SAINT PAUL ST UNIT 2A, VANIER, ON, K1L 6A3
(613) 742-7550   *SIC* 1542
176061 CANADA INC   *p* 1217
6915 AV QUERBES, MONTREAL, QC, H3N 2B3
(514) 270-5567   *SIC* 2051
1767388 ONTARIO INC   *p* 657
1020 ADELAIDE ST S, LONDON, ON, N6E 1R6
(519) 963-4010   *SIC* 5047
1768652 ALBERTA LTD   *p* 33
402 53 AVE SE, CALGARY, AB, T2H 0N4
(403) 262-3791   *SIC* 7216
1770918 ONTARIO INC   *p* 748
92 BENTLEY AVE, NEPEAN, ON, K2E 6T9
(613) 225-9111   *SIC* 1795
1772887 ONTARIO LIMITED   *p* 791
15 BENTON RD, NORTH YORK, ON, M6M 3G2
(416) 364-3333   *SIC* 2721
1776963 ONTARIO INC   *p* 736
1445 COURTNEYPARK DR E, MISSISSAUGA, ON, L5T 2E3
(905) 670-6683   *SIC* 7389
1777621 ONTARIO INC   *p* 594
73 MAIN ST, GLENCOE, ON, N0L 1M0
(519) 913-5420   *SIC* 5083
177786 CANADA INC   *p* 1104
850 BOUL MALONEY O, GATINEAU, QC, J8T 3R6
(819) 568-0066   *SIC* 5511
178011 CANADA INC   *p* 386
3636 PORTAGE AVE, WINNIPEG, MB, R3K 0Z8
(204) 837-3636   *SIC* 5511
178023 CANADA LTD   *p* 386
3965 PORTAGE AVE SUITE 100, WINNIPEG, MB, R3K 2H4
(204) 837-4000   *SIC* 5511
1784007 ONTARIO LTD   *p* 932
200 FRONT ST E SUITE 3458, TORONTO, ON, M5A 4T9
(416) 368-8484   *SIC* 5411
1787930 ONTARIO INC   *p* 889
150 DENNIS RD, ST THOMAS, ON, N5P 0B6
(519) 631-9604   *SIC* 4731

1788317 ONTARIO INC   *p* 1004
18 INDUSTRIAL RD, WALKERTON, ON, N0G 2V0
(519) 881-0187   *SIC* 6712
1788741 ONTARIO INC   *p* 760
6161 THOROLD STONE RD SUITE 3, NIAGARA FALLS, ON, L2J 1A4
(905) 357-5600   *SIC* 5461
1791884 ONTARIO LIMITED   *p* 781
3685 KEELE ST SUITE 5, NORTH YORK, ON, M3J 3H6
(866) 987-6453   *SIC* 5411
1794318 ONTARIO INC   *p* 580
1701 MARTIN GROVE RD SUITE 1, ETOBICOKE, ON, M9V 4N4
(416) 742-8688   *SIC* 5411
1794342 ONTARIO INC   *p* 1372
2745 RUE DE LA SHERWOOD, SHERBROOKE, QC, J1K 1E1
(819) 563-2202   *SIC* 3949
1796640 ONTARIO LIMITED   *p* 910
920 COMMERCE ST, THUNDER BAY, ON, P7E 6E9
(807) 475-9555   *SIC* 5172
1797509 ALBERTA ULC   *p* 629
1463 HIGHWAY 21, KINCARDINE, ON, N2Z 2X3
(519) 396-1324   *SIC* 6712
1799795 ONTARIO LIMITED   *p* 1001
171 MONTREAL RD, VANIER, ON, K1L 6E4
(613) 745-5720   *SIC* 7361
18 WHEELS LOGISTICS LTD   *p* 180
7185 11TH AVE, BURNABY, BC, V3N 2M5
(604) 439-8938   *SIC* 4731
180 UNIVERSITY HOTEL LIMITED PARTNERSHIP   *p* 948
188 UNIVERSITY AVE, TORONTO, ON, M5H 0A3
(647) 788-8888   *SIC* 7011
1801794 ONTARIO INC   *p* 1337
935 RUE REVERCHON, SAINT-LAURENT, QC, H4T 4L2
(514) 733-3515   *SIC* 5992
1808963 ONTARIO INC   *p* 561
1495 GERALD ST, CORNWALL, ON, K6H 7G8
(613) 932-5326   *SIC* 7349
1815264 ONTARIO INC   *p* 718
251 QUEEN ST S UNIT 252, MISSISSAUGA, ON, L5M 1L7
(905) 593-4204   *SIC* 5153
1827212 ONTARIO LIMITED   *p* 648
1925 DUNDAS ST SUITE 3453, LONDON, ON, N5V 1P7
(519) 453-8226   *SIC* 5411
1835755 ONTARIO LIMITED   *p* 545
227 HWY 11 S, COCHRANE, ON, P0L 1C0
(705) 272-2090   *SIC* 1611
1840807 ALBERTA LTD   *p* 27
1208 3 ST SE UNIT 11, CALGARY, AB, T2G 2S9
(403) 460-1401   *SIC* 4212
1847674 ONTARIO INC   *p* 1012
609 SOUTH PELHAM RD, WELLAND, ON, L3C 3C7
(905) 735-7467   *SIC* 5411
1850178 ONTARIO LIMITED   *p* 906
7064 YONGE ST, THORNHILL, ON, L4J 1V7
(905) 882-9660   *SIC* 5511
1853865 ONTARIO INC   *p* 840
1699 CHEMONG RD, PETERBOROUGH, ON, K9J 6X2
(705) 748-9111   *SIC* 5211
1857-2123 QUEBEC INC   *p* 1354
2330 117 RTE, SAINTE-AGATHE-NORD, QC, J8C 2Z8
(819) 326-1044   *SIC* 5511
1882540 ONTARIO INC   *p* 994
1444 DUPONT ST UNIT 11, TORONTO, ON, M6P 4H3
(416) 516-1569   *SIC* 5193
188461 CANADA INC   *p* 1221

7100 RUE SAINT-JACQUES, MONTREAL, QC, H4B 1V2
(514) 487-7777   *SIC* 5511
188669 CANADA INC   *p* 1358
1999 RUE NOBEL BUREAU 7A, SAINTE-JULIE, QC, J3E 1Z7
(450) 649-9400   *SIC* 7349
1894359 ONTARIO INC   *p* 485
455 WELHAM RD, BARRIE, ON, L4N 8Z6
(705) 726-5841   *SIC* 3569
190394 CANADA INC   *p* 1248
5977 RTE TRANSCANADIENNE, POINTE-CLAIRE, QC, H9R 1C1
(514) 630-2800   *SIC* 5085
1905405 ONTARIO LIMITED   *p* 870
300 BOROUGH DR UNIT 267, SCARBOROUGH, ON, M1P 4P5
(416) 290-6863   *SIC* 5651
1906351 ONTARIO INC   *p* 610
1821 KING ST E, HAMILTON, ON, L8K 1V8
(905) 308-8333   *SIC* 6531
190712 CANADA INC   *p* 1177
270 RUE DE LOUVAIN O, MONTREAL, QC, H2N 1B6
(514) 389-8221   *SIC* 2297
1909203 ONTARIO INC   *p* 795
35 OAK ST, NORTH YORK, ON, M9N 1A1
(416) 245-7991   *SIC* 3646
190937 CANADA LTEE   *p* 1139
6000 RUE DES MOISSONS, LEVIS, QC, G6Y 0Z6
(418) 830-2834   *SIC* 5511
191017 CANADA INC   *p* 1331
4747 BOUL DE LA COTE-VERTU, SAINT-LAURENT, QC, H4S 1C9
(514) 336-8780   *SIC* 5023
1911661 ONTARIO INC   *p* 498
5 COACHWORKS CRES, BRAMPTON, ON, L6R 3Y2
(416) 981-9400   *SIC* 5511
191191 CANADA LTD   *p* 383
670 CENTURY ST, WINNIPEG, MB, R3H 0A1
(204) 788-1100   *SIC* 5511
191609 CANADA INC   *p* 1337
4125 RUE GRIFFITH, SAINT-LAURENT, QC, H4T 1A9
(514) 731-9466   *SIC* 2673
191837 CANADA INC   *p* 1218
3901 RUE JEAN-TALON O BUREAU 301, MONTREAL, QC, H3R 2G4
(514) 373-3131   *SIC* 5999
1923921 ONTARIO INC   *p* 547
200 SPINNAKER WAY, CONCORD, ON, L4K 5E5
(905) 738-3682   *SIC* 3542
1924345 ONTARIO INC   *p* 994
1655 DUPONT ST SUITE 250, TORONTO, ON, M6P 3T1
(416) 481-6946   *SIC* 8721
1928321 ONTARIO INC   *p* 1006
23 KING ST N, WATERLOO, ON, N2J 2W6
(519) 954-6622   *SIC* 5149
1936100 ONTARIO INC   *p* 483
1457 GINGERICH RD, BADEN, ON, N3A 3J7
(519) 634-5708   *SIC* 5049
1937225 NOVA SCOTIA LIMITED   *p* 444
224 WYSE RD, DARTMOUTH, NS, B3A 1M9
(902) 466-0086   *SIC* 5511
1939243 ONTARIO INC   *p* 500
316 ORENDA RD, BRAMPTON, ON, L6T 1G3
(905) 793-7100   *SIC* 3089
1939250 ONTARIO LTD   *p* 805
251 NORTH SERVICE RD W, OAKVILLE, ON, L6M 3E7
(905) 608-1999   *SIC* 6712
1942675 ALBERTA LTD   *p* 13
7905 46 ST SE, CALGARY, AB, T2C 2Y6
(403) 279-2090   *SIC* 3412
1946328 ONTARIO LIMITED   *p* 211
4063 COWICHAN VALLEY HWY, DUNCAN,

BC, V9L 6K4
(250) 856-0122   *SIC* 7948
1957444 ONTARIO INC   *p* 498
40 MARBLESEED CRES, BRAMPTON, ON, L6R 2J7
(905) 795-1101   *SIC* 4213
1959197 ONTARIO INC   *p* 527
875 LAURENTIAN DR SUITE 12, BURLINGTON, ON, L7N 3W7
(905) 634-1900   *SIC* 2752
1959612 ONTARIO INC   *p* 480
194 EARL STEWART DR, AURORA, ON, L4G 6V7
(905) 726-4933   *SIC* 5211
1971041 ONTARIO LTD   *p* 778
1155 LESLIE ST, NORTH YORK, ON, M3C 2J6
(416) 444-4269   *SIC* 5511
1986114 ALBERTA INC   *p* 42
605 5 AVE SW SUITE 3200, CALGARY, AB, T2P 3H5
(403) 269-4400   *SIC* 1311
1987 THE TRAVEL GROUP LTD   *p* 301
890 PENDER ST W SUITE 330, VANCOUVER, BC, V6C 1J9
(604) 681-6345   *SIC* 4724
1991943 ONTARIO INC   *p* 884
155 SCOTT ST, ST CATHARINES, ON, L2N 1H3
(888) 511-2862   *SIC* 5511
1992013 ONTARIO LTD   *p* 868
1880 EGLINTON AVE E, SCARBOROUGH, ON, M1L 2L1
(416) 750-4400   *SIC* 5411
19959 YUKON INC   *p* 215
3240 VILLAGE WAY, HEFFLEY CREEK, BC, V0E 1Z1
(250) 578-6000   *SIC* 7011
1ST CHOICE SAVINGS AND CREDIT UNION LTD   *p* 143
45 FAIRMONT BLVD S, LETHBRIDGE, AB, T1K 1T1
(403) 320-4600   *SIC* 6062
1ST LONDON REAL ESTATE SERVICES INC   *p* 657
1069 WELLINGTON RD, LONDON, ON, N6E 2H6
SIC 6531
1ST SECURE   *p* 176
See ABBOTSFORD SECURITY SERVICES
1ST STUDENT CANADA   *p* 904
See FIRSTCANADA ULC

2

2 SISTERS POULTRY & MEAT LTD   *p* 191
5791 SIDLEY ST, BURNABY, BC, V5J 5E6
(604) 327-5526   *SIC* 5142
20 BEES WINERY   *p* 761
See LAKEVIEW CELLARS ESTATE WINERY LIMITED
20/20 PROPERTIES INC   *p* 292
638 MILLBANK, VANCOUVER, BC, V5Z 4B7
(604) 620-3130   *SIC* 6211
2000007 ONTARIO INC   *p* 792
3605 WESTON RD, NORTH YORK, ON, M9L 1V7
(416) 744-3322   *SIC* 3711
2004104 ONTARIO LIMITED   *p* 618
857 CECILE BLVD, HAWKESBURY, ON, K6A 1P4
(613) 632-5994   *SIC* 5411
2008788 ONTARIO LIMITED   *p* 888
580 JAMES ST S, ST MARYS, ON, N4X 1B3
(519) 349-2850   *SIC* 3317
2010162 ONTARIO LTD   *p* 759
6868 KINSMEN CRT, NIAGARA FALLS, ON, L2H 0Y5
(905) 358-3674   *SIC* 5199
2012865 ONTARIO INC   *p* 1029
71 SILTON RD UNIT 8, WOODBRIDGE, ON, L4L 7Z8
(905) 856-8252   *SIC* 5141
2014767 ONTARIO LIMITED   *p* 547

96 PLANCHET RD, CONCORD, ON, L4K 2C7

(905) 738-0583   *SIC* 2653

2016099 ONTARIO INC   *p* 581
31 CONSTELLATION CRT, ETOBICOKE, ON, M9W 1K4

(905) 673-2000   *SIC* 7334

2018775 ONTARIO LIMITED   *p* 652
234 OXFORD ST E, LONDON, ON, N6A 1T7

(519) 432-1127   *SIC* 5411

2020 BUSINESS ADVISORY CORPORATION   *p* 1422
4032 WASCANA RIDGE BAY, REGINA, SK, S4V 2L6

(306) 790-2020   *SIC* 8741

2020 MC   *p* 1241
See *TECHNOLOGIES 20-20 INC*

2020455 ONTARIO INC   *p* 805
1525 NORTH SERVICE RD W, OAKVILLE, ON, L6M 2W2

(905) 825-8777   *SIC* 5511

2022839 ONTARIO INC   *p* 1002
8500 KEELE ST, VAUGHAN, ON, L4K 2A6

(905) 532-1455   *SIC* 5141

2023225 ONTARIO LTD   *p* 766
259 YORKLAND RD SUITE 300, NORTH YORK, ON, M2J 5B2

(416) 733-9500   *SIC* 5051

2023649 ONTARIO LIMITED   *p* 906
9 PINE ST N, THOROLD, ON, L2V 3Z9

(905) 227-0533   *SIC* 5411

2024232 ONTARIO LIMITED   *p* 906
7040 YONGE ST UNIT B1, THORNHILL, ON, L4J 1V7

(905) 882-0040   *SIC* 5411

2026798 ONTARIO LIMITED   *p* 745
120 ONTARIO RD, MITCHELL, ON, N0K 1N0

(519) 348-8446   *SIC* 5411

2027844 ONTARIO INC   *p* 493
325 CHATHAM ST N, BLENHEIM, ON, N0P 1A0

(519) 676-8161   *SIC* 3714

2030413 ONTARIO LIMITED   *p* 514
10 KING GEORGE RD, BRANTFORD, ON, N3R 5J7

(519) 751-3333   *SIC* 5251

2031113 ONTARIO LIMITED   *p* 785
600 WILSON AVE, NORTH YORK, ON, M3K 1C9

(416) 741-7480   *SIC* 5511

2032244 ONTARIO LIMITED   *p* 746
121 MAIN ST S, MOUNT FOREST, ON, N0G 2L0

(519) 323-1390   *SIC* 5411

2037247 ONTARIO LIMITED   *p* 618
52 BRIDGE ST, HASTINGS, ON, K0L 1Y0

(705) 696-3504   *SIC* 5411

2037247 ONTARIO LIMITED   *p* 1077
1155 BOUL TALBOT, CHICOUTIMI, QC, G7H 4B5

(418) 690-0063   *SIC* 5411

2040830 ONTARIO INC   *p* 1186
460 RUE SAINT-PAUL E SUITE 330, MONTREAL, QC, H2Y 3V1

SIC 8743

2041098 ONTARIO LIMITED   *p* 932
260 RICHMOND ST E UNIT 300, TORONTO, ON, M5A 1P4

(416) 340-1600   *SIC* 6531

2041188 ONTARIO INC   *p* 718
2632 CREDIT VALLEY RD, MISSISSAUGA, ON, L5M 4J6

(647) 986-0000   *SIC* 5541

2043665 ONTARIO LIMITED   *p* 620
131 HOWLAND DR, HUNTSVILLE, ON, P1H 2P7

(705) 789-6972   *SIC* 5411

2051183 ONTARIO LIMITED   *p* 875
2555 VICTORIA PARK AVE SUITE 19, SCARBOROUGH, ON, M1T 1A3

(416) 773-1166   *SIC* 5411

2058658 ONTARIO INC   *p* 618
1275 TUPPER ST, HAWKESBURY, ON, K6A 3T5

(613) 675-1515   *SIC* 5912

2059010 ONTARIO INC   *p* 708
2515 HURONTARIO ST UNIT 2006, MISSISSAUGA, ON, L5A 4C8

(905) 281-9175   *SIC* 7361

2063412 INVESTMENT LP   *p* 564
143 MARY ST, CREEMORE, ON, L0M 1G0

(705) 466-3437   *SIC* 8051

2063414 INVESTMENT LP   *p* 665
302 TOWN CENTRE BLVD SUITE 200, MARKHAM, ON, L3R 0E8

(905) 477-4006   *SIC* 8051

2063414 ONTARIO LIMITED   *p* 498
215 SUNNY MEADOW BLVD, BRAMPTON, ON, L6R 3B5

(905) 458-7604   *SIC* 8059

2063414 ONTARIO LIMITED   *p* 514
389 WEST ST, BRANTFORD, ON, N3R 3V9

(519) 759-4666   *SIC* 8051

2063414 ONTARIO LIMITED   *p* 564
143 MARY ST, CREEMORE, ON, L0M 1G0

(705) 466-3437   *SIC* 8051

2063414 ONTARIO LIMITED   *p* 568
120 BARNSWALLOW DR, ELMIRA, ON, N3B 2Y9

(519) 669-5777   *SIC* 8051

2063414 ONTARIO LIMITED   *p* 598
200 KELLY DR, GRAVENHURST, ON, P1P 1P3

(705) 687-3444   *SIC* 8051

2063414 ONTARIO LIMITED   *p* 762
401 WILLIAM ST, NORTH BAY, ON, P1A 1X5

(705) 476-2602   *SIC* 8051

2063414 ONTARIO LIMITED   *p* 786
22 NORFINCH DR, NORTH YORK, ON, M3N 1X1

(416) 623-1120   *SIC* 8051

2063414 ONTARIO LIMITED   *p* 850
170 RED MAPLE RD, RICHMOND HILL, ON, L4B 4T8

(905) 731-2273   *SIC* 8051

2063414 ONTARIO LIMITED   *p* 870
1000 ELLESMERE RD SUITE 333, SCARBOROUGH, ON, M1P 5G2

(416) 291-0222   *SIC* 8051

2063414 ONTARIO LIMITED   *p* 972
225 ST. GEORGE ST, TORONTO, ON, M5R 2M2

(416) 967-3985   *SIC* 8051

2063414 ONTARIO LIMITED   *p* 997
2005 LAWRENCE AVE W SUITE 323, TORONTO, ON, M9N 3V4

(416) 243-8879   *SIC* 8051

2063414 ONTARIO LIMITED   *p* 1029
5400 STEELES AVE W, WOODBRIDGE, ON, L4L 9S1

(905) 856-7200   *SIC* 8051

2069718 ONTARIO LIMITED   *p* 785
1140 SHEPPARD AVE W UNIT 13, NORTH YORK, ON, M3K 2A2

SIC 1521

2071848 ALBERTA LTD   *p* 125
1235 101 ST SW, EDMONTON, AB, T6X 1A1

(780) 462-2834   *SIC* 5511

2072223 ONTARIO LIMITED   *p* 473
274 MACKENZIE AVE SUITE 2, AJAX, ON, L1S 2E9

(905) 686-7000   *SIC* 2542

2075894 ONTARIO INC   *p* 665
170 ESNA PARK DR UNIT 14, MARKHAM, ON, L3R 1E3

(905) 752-0460   *SIC* 5149

2076631 ONTARIO LIMITED   *p* 581
151 CARLINGVIEW DR UNIT 6, ETOBICOKE, ON, M9W 5S4

(416) 679-8884   *SIC* 5661

2079421 ONTARIO LIMITED   *p* 1003
1551 NIAGARA STONE RD, VIRGIL, ON, L0S 1T0

(905) 468-3286   *SIC* 5411

2079608 ONTARIO INC   *p* 1034
1455 DUNDAS ST, WOODSTOCK, ON, N4S 7V9

(519) 537-5614   *SIC* 5511

2080613 ONTARIO INC   *p* 795
See *MCDONALD'S RESTAURANTS OF CANADA LIMITED*

2088847 ONTARIO INC   *p* 547
155 DRUMLIN CIR UNIT 2, CONCORD, ON, L4K 3E7

(905) 761-9999   *SIC* 4731

2088941 CANADA INC   *p* 1107
1235 BOUL SAINT-JOSEPH, GATINEAU, QC, J8Z 3J6

(819) 776-0077   *SIC* 5511

2095008 ONTARIO INC   *p* 682
170 STEELES AVE E, MILTON, ON, L9T 2Y5

(905) 864-8588   *SIC* 5511

2095527 ONTARIO LIMITED   *p* 758
6740 FALLSVIEW BLVD, NIAGARA FALLS, ON, L2G 3W6

(905) 356-3600   *SIC* 7011

2097738 ONTARIO INC   *p* 591
1637 PETTIT RD, FORT ERIE, ON, L2A 5M4

SIC 5541

21 CENTURY TRADING INC   *p* 208
6951 72 ST UNIT 110, DELTA, BC, V4G 0A2

(604) 952-4565   *SIC* 5141

2100050 ONTARIO INC   *p* 766
3030 DON MILLS RD SUITE 26, NORTH YORK, ON, M2J 3C1

(416) 756-1668   *SIC* 5411

2101440 ONTARIO INC   *p* 850
30 EAST BEAVER CREEK RD SUITE 204, RICHMOND HILL, ON, L4B 1J2

(416) 469-3131   *SIC* 7371

2104225 ONTARIO LTD   *p* 389
23 CHEVRIER BLVD, WINNIPEG, MB, R3T 1Y7

(416) 252-7323   *SIC* 2051

2104225 ONTARIO LTD   *p* 389
See *2104225 ONTARIO LTD*

2104225 ONTARIO LTD   *p* 573
1425 THE QUEENSWAY, ETOBICOKE, ON, M8Z 1T3

(416) 252-7323   *SIC* 2051

2104225 ONTARIO LTD   *p* 629
83 RAILWAY ST, KINGSTON, ON, K7K 2L7

(613) 548-4434   *SIC* 2051

2104225 ONTARIO LTD   *p* 1103
255 CH INDUSTRIEL, GATINEAU, QC, J8R 3V8

(819) 669-7246   *SIC* 5461

2104225 ONTARIO LTD   *p* 1145
2700 BOUL JACQUES-CARTIER E BUREAU 67, LONGUEUIL, QC, J4N 1L5

(450) 448-7246   *SIC* 2051

2104225 ONTARIO LTD   *p* 1242
150 BOUL INDUSTRIEL, NAPIERVILLE, QC, J0J 1L0

(450) 245-7542   *SIC* 2051

2104225 ONTARIO LTD   *p* 1417
GD LCD MAIN, REGINA, SK, S4P 2Z4

(306) 359-7400   *SIC* 2045

2104225 ONTARIO LTD   *p* 1419
1310 OTTAWA ST, REGINA, SK, S4R 1P4

(306) 359-3096   *SIC* 2051

2116160 ONTARIO INC   *p* 685
7355 GOREWAY DR, MISSISSAUGA, ON, L4T 2T8

(905) 405-0881   *SIC* 5541

2119485 ALBERTA LTD   *p* 547
301 MILLWAY AVE, CONCORD, ON, L4K 4T3

(905) 761-0808   *SIC* 3429

2121361 ONTARIO INC   *p* 847
6829 DALE RD, PORT HOPE, ON, L1A 3V6

(905) 885-9237   *SIC* 2064

2122256 ALBERTA LTD   *p* 78
4613 41 ST, CAMROSE, AB, T4V 2Y8

(780) 991-9997   *SIC* 7353

2124688 ONTARIO LIMITED   *p* 781
3975 KEELE ST, NORTH YORK, ON, M3J 1P1

(416) 665-7594   *SIC* 5172

2124964 ONTARIO INC   *p* 511
471 MAIN ST S, BRAMPTON, ON, L6Y 1N6

(905) 451-6489   *SIC* 5541

2125341 ALBERTA LTD   *p* 172
4802 51 ST SUITE 1, WHITECOURT, AB, T7S 1R9

(780) 778-5900   *SIC* 5411

2136284 ONTARIO INC   *p* 535
55 FLEMING DR UNIT 2, CAMBRIDGE, ON, N1T 2A9

(905) 696-1977   *SIC* 4731

2138894 ONTARIO INC   *p* 873
140 SHORTING RD, SCARBOROUGH, ON, M1S 3S6

(416) 240-0911   *SIC* 7381

2142064 ONTARIO INC   *p* 704
5570 KENNEDY RD, MISSISSAUGA, ON, L4Z 2A9

(905) 238-1777   *SIC* 3674

2142242 ONTARIO INC   *p* 635
1800 VICTORIA ST N, KITCHENER, ON, N2B 3E5

(519) 747-0269   *SIC* 5511

2144011 ONTARIO INC   *p* 628
443 THE QUEENSWAY S SUITE 26, KESWICK, ON, L4P 3J4

(905) 476-7773   *SIC* 5411

2144205 ONTARIO INC   *p* 703
3415 DIXIE RD SUITE 113, MISSISSAUGA, ON, L4Y 2B1

(905) 670-7677   *SIC* 5961

2145150 ONTARIO INC   *p* 617
150 7TH AVE, HANOVER, ON, N4N 2G9

(519) 364-1010   *SIC* 5511

215 REDFERN   *p* 1402
See *L'ART DE VIVRE A SON MEILLEUR*

2153-1090 QUEBEC INC   *p* 1274
3690 BOUL NEILSON, QUEBEC, QC, G1W 0A9

(418) 781-0471   *SIC* 6712

2154781 CANADA LTD   *p* 581
25 VICE REGENT BLVD, ETOBICOKE, ON, M9W 6N2

(416) 748-2900   *SIC* 5511

2156110 ONTARIO LIMITED   *p* 1005
115 HAMILTON ST N SUITE 81, WATERDOWN, ON, L8B 1A8

(905) 690-6446   *SIC* 5411

2156775 ONTARIO INC   *p* 691
4544 EASTGATE PKY, MISSISSAUGA, ON, L4W 3W6

(905) 238-6300   *SIC* 2086

2158124 ONTARIO INC   *p* 477
1336 SANDHILL DR UNIT 3, ANCASTER, ON, L9G 4V5

(905) 648-6767   *SIC* 6411

2161-1298 QUEBEC INC   *p* 1402
1031 7E RANG, WICKHAM, QC, J0C 1S0

(819) 398-6303   *SIC* 2491

2161457 ONTARIO INC   *p* 990
845 ADELAIDE ST W, TORONTO, ON, M6J 3X1

(416) 703-2022   *SIC* 7389

2163-2088 QUEBEC INC   *p* 1047
10400 RUE RENAUDE-LAPOINTE, ANJOU, QC, H1J 2V7

(514) 322-5300   *SIC* 6712

2164-1204 QUEBEC INC   *p* 1216
9795 RUE WAVERLY, MONTREAL, QC, H3L 2V7

(514) 381-8524   *SIC* 5198

2166-2440 QUEBEC INC   *p* 1397
19 BOUL DES BOIS-FRANCS S, VICTORIAVILLE, QC, G6P 4S2

(819) 758-7176   *SIC* 5813

2168587 ONTARIO LTD   *p* 781
55 CANARCTIC DR SUITE UPPER, NORTH YORK, ON, M3J 2N7

(416) 661-9455   *SIC* 2053

2168587 ONTARIO LTD   *p* 794

50 MARMORA ST, NORTH YORK, ON, M9M 2X5
(416) 661-7744   SIC 2053

2169-5762 QUEBEC INC   p 1378
281 RUE EDWARD-ASSH, STE-CATHERINE-DE-LA-J-CARTIE, QC, G3N 1A3
(418) 875-1839   SIC 5661

2169319 ONTARIO INC   p 778
747 DON MILLS RD UNIT 60, NORTH YORK, ON, M3C 1T2
(416) 900-1699   SIC 5411

2171-0751 QUEBEC INC   p 1377
74A 132 RTE O, ST-ADELME-DE-MATANE, QC, G0L 2R0
(418) 498-2405   SIC 5211

2172004 ONTARIO INC   p 547
200 CONNIE CRES UNIT 4, CONCORD, ON, L4K 1M1
(905) 738-1688   SIC 5112

2173-4108 QUEBEC INC   p 1363
640 CHOMEDEY (A-13) O, SAINTE-ROSE, QC, H7X 3S9
    SIC 5941

2176069 ONTARIO LIMITED   p 475
100 ACHILLES RD, AJAX, ON, L1Z 0C5
(905) 619-5522   SIC 5511

2176542 ONTARIO LTD   p 920
11 SUNLIGHT PARK RD, TORONTO, ON, M4M 1B5
(416) 623-4269   SIC 5521

2177761 ONTARIO INC   p 716
2477 MOTORWAY BLVD SUITE 3, MISSISSAUGA, ON, L5L 3R2
(905) 828-8488   SIC 5511

2178320 CANADA LTD   p 458
12 LAKELANDS BLVD, HALIFAX, NS, B3S 1S8
(902) 454-2369   SIC 5511

2179267 ONTARIO LTD   p 473
655 FINLEY AVE SUITE 1, AJAX, ON, L1S 3V3
(905) 619-1477   SIC 7389

2179321 ONTARIO LIMITED   p 775
27 LARABEE CRES, NORTH YORK, ON, M3A 3E6
(416) 219-1050   SIC 5074

2182553 ONTARIO LTD   p 859
750 ONTARIO ST UNIT 1, SARNIA, ON, N7T 1M6
(519) 383-8880   SIC 7389

2187878 NOVA SCOTIA LIMITED   p 454
2672 ROBIE ST, HALIFAX, NS, B3K 4N8
(902) 453-4115   SIC 5511

2188262 ONTARIO LTD   p 921
586 EGLINTON AVE E UNIT 208, TORONTO, ON, M4P 1P2
(416) 802-2382   SIC 5047

2188652 ONTARIO LTD   p 760
337 FOUR MILE CREEK RD, NIAGARA ON THE LAKE, ON, L0S 1J0
(905) 262-8200   SIC 2034

219 AUTOMOTIVE INC   p 442
580 PORTLAND ST, DARTMOUTH, NS, B2W 2M3
(902) 434-7700   SIC 5511

2194747 ONTARIO INC   p 894
1288 MILLARD ST, STOUFFVILLE, ON, L4A 0W7
(416) 921-1288   SIC 5511

22 ENTERPRISES LTD   p 262
11131 NO. 5 RD, RICHMOND, BC, V7A 4E8
(604) 204-0047   SIC 5541

2207412 NOVA SCOTIA LTD   p 442
580 PORTLAND ST, DARTMOUTH, NS, B2W 2M3
(902) 434-4000   SIC 5511

2207544 ONTARIO INC   p 744
1250 EGLINTON AVE W SUITE 138, MISSISSAUGA, ON, L5V 1N3
(905) 795-7781   SIC 8748

2210961 ONTARIO LIMITED   p 542
135 BOTHWELL ST, CHATHAM, ON, N7M 5K5

(519) 354-4600   SIC 5146

2213802 ONTARIO INC   p 736
964 WESTPORT CRES SUITE 6, MISSISSAUGA, ON, L5T 1S3
(905) 696-6932   SIC 5045

2214264 ONTARIO INC   p 702
1550 CATERPILLAR RD, MISSISSAUGA, ON, L4X 1E7
(905) 848-1550   SIC 2752

2224855 ONTARIO INC   p 691
5450 EXPLORER DR UNIT 300, MISSISSAUGA, ON, L4W 5M1
(416) 649-3939   SIC 6712

2231737 NOVA SCOTIA LIMITED   p 471
45 STARRS RD, YARMOUTH, NS, B5A 2T2
(902) 742-7191   SIC 5511

2232556 ONTARIO INC   p 920
11 SUNLIGHT PARK RD, TORONTO, ON, M4M 1B5
(416) 623-6464   SIC 5511

2233451 ONTARIO INC   p 773
See SECOND CUP LTD, THE

2242974 CANADA INC   p 1288
1300 RUE SAGUENAY, ROUYN-NORANDA, QC, J9X 7C3
(819) 797-7500   SIC 1731

2248085 ONTARIO INC   p 691
5500 DIXIE RD, MISSISSAUGA, ON, L4W 4N3
(905) 238-7188   SIC 5511

2261079 ONTARIO LTD   p 1029
100 HAIST AVE UNIT B, WOODBRIDGE, ON, L4L 5V4
(905) 851-0173   SIC 5051

226138 ONTARIO INC   p 529
2300 FAIRVIEW ST, BURLINGTON, ON, L7R 2E4
(905) 681-2200   SIC 6712

2275510 ONTARIO LTD   p 656
35 SOUTHDALE RD E, LONDON, ON, N6C 4X5
(519) 668-0600   SIC 5511

227835 ALBERTA LTD   p 107
9211 48 ST NW, EDMONTON, AB, T6B 2R9
(780) 465-9321   SIC 1623

2281445 ONTARIO INC   p 870
77 PROGRESS AVE, SCARBOROUGH, ON, M1P 2Y7
(416) 288-8515   SIC 6794

2302659 MANITOBA LTD   p 393
59 SCURFIELD BLVD SUITE 9, WINNIPEG, MB, R3Y 1V2
(204) 925-6880   SIC 5661

2308061 ONTARIO LIMITED   p 792
239 TORYORK DR, NORTH YORK, ON, M9L 1Y2
(416) 640-1790   SIC 2015

2310-3393 QUEBEC INC   p 1097
520 BOUL SAINT-JOSEPH BUREAU 10, DRUMMONDVILLE, QC, J2C 2B8
(819) 472-3003   SIC 5912

2310884 ONTARIO INC   p 831
350 WEST HUNT CLUB RD, OTTAWA, ON, K2E 1A5
(613) 688-6000   SIC 5511

2311390 ONTARIO INC   p 622
2484 DORAL DR, INNISFIL, ON, L9S 0A3
(705) 431-9393   SIC 5511

2313-3606 QUEBEC INC   p 1171
2251 RUE JEAN-TALON E, MONTREAL, QC, H2E 1V6
(514) 325-0966   SIC 1521

2316-7240 QUEBEC INC   p 1097
600 BOUL SAINT-JOSEPH, DRUMMONDVILLE, QC, J2C 2C1
(819) 478-4141   SIC 7011

2318-4211 QUEBEC INC   p 1299
413 RUE PRINCIPALE, SAINT-DONAT-DE-MONTCALM, QC, J0T 2C0
(819) 424-2220   SIC 5461

2318-7081 QUEBEC INC   p 1077
1080 BOUL TALBOT, CHICOUTIMI, QC, G7H 4B6
(418) 543-1521   SIC 7011

2319793 ONTARIO INC   p 547
350 CREDITSTONE RD UNIT 103, CONCORD, ON, L4K 3Z2
(905) 760-0000   SIC 2098

2320610 ONTARIO INC   p 511
7900 HURONTARIO ST SUITE 303, BRAMPTON, ON, L6Y 0P6
(905) 782-4700   SIC 7381

2321-1998 QUEBEC INC   p 1231
1070 MONTEE MASSON, MONTREAL, QC, H7C 2R2
(450) 661-1515   SIC 5211

2326236 ONTARIO INC   p 508
31 SELBY RD, BRAMPTON, ON, L6W 1K5
(905) 455-9100   SIC 4731

2330-2029 QUEBEC INC   p 1168
5135 10E AV, MONTREAL, QC, H1Y 2G5
(514) 525-3757   SIC 5999

2333-2224 QUEBEC INC   p 1265
2400 AV DALTON, QUEBEC, QC, G1P 3X1
(418) 654-9292   SIC 5511

2343-7393 QUEBEC INC   p 1387
1620 RUE NOTRE-DAME CENTRE, TROIS-RIVIERES, QC, G9A 6E5
(819) 376-1991   SIC 7011

2350936 ONTARIO INC   p 691
1080 FEWSTER DR UNIT 10, MISSISSAUGA, ON, L4W 2T2
(905) 282-6000   SIC 4213

2355291 ONTARIO INC   p 912
92 BALSAM ST S SUITE 1, TIMMINS, ON, P4N 2C8
(705) 268-7956   SIC 1081

2360083 ONTARIO LIMITED   p 780
4750 DUFFERIN ST, NORTH YORK, ON, M3H 5S7
(416) 736-6606   SIC 5411

2365927 ONTARIO LIMITED   p 657
90 BESSEMER RD UNIT 2, LONDON, ON, N6E 1R1
(519) 668-7331   SIC 5031

2384309 ONTARIO INC   p 665
7357 WOODBINE AVE SUITE 619, MARKHAM, ON, L3R 6L3
(905) 944-0700   SIC 8742

2389807 ONTARIO INC   p 787
3885 YONGE ST, NORTH YORK, ON, M4N 2P2
(416) 322-5544   SIC 5812

239188 BC LTD   p 317
1455 GEORGIA ST W SUITE 400, VANCOUVER, BC, V6G 2T3
(604) 669-7044   SIC 7389

2394748 ONTARIO INC   p 855
9144 YONGE ST, RICHMOND HILL, ON, L4C 7A1
(905) 763-3688   SIC 5511

24 HEURES   p 1211
See MEDIAQMI INC

24 HOUR THERMAL GLASS INSULATION LTD   p 547
250 BOWES RD, CONCORD, ON, L4K 1J9
(905) 738-7585   SIC 5039

24-7 INTOUCH INC   p 376
240 KENNEDY ST 2ND FL, WINNIPEG, MB, R3C 1T1
(800) 530-1121   SIC 7389

24/7 CUSTOMER CANADA, INC   p 936
20 TORONTO ST SUITE 530, TORONTO, ON, M5C 2B8
(416) 214-9337   SIC 7371

2408234 ONTARIO INC   p 882
239 ST CATHARINES ST, SMITHVILLE, ON, L0R 2A0
(905) 957-3374   SIC 5411

2410147 ONTARIO INC   p 691
4505 DIXIE RD, MISSISSAUGA, ON, L4W 5K3
(905) 625-7533   SIC 5511

2412-8779 QUEBEC INC   p 1077
121 RUE DUBUC, CHIBOUGAMAU, QC, G8P 2H4
(418) 748-4785   SIC 1542

2417821 CANADA INC   p 592

210 JAMES A. BRENNAN RD, GANANOQUE, ON, K7G 1N7
(613) 549-3221   SIC 2865

24184863 CANADA INC   p 1265
2717 AV WATT BUREAU 150, QUEBEC, QC, G1P 3X3
(418) 659-1560   SIC 7384

2421593 CANADA INC   p 602
130 MACDONELL ST, GUELPH, ON, N1H 2Z6
(519) 824-4400   SIC 6411

242408 STEEL FABRICATION LIMITED   p 844
1625 FELDSPAR CRT, PICKERING, ON, L1W 3R7
(905) 831-6172   SIC 3589

2425-1761 QUEBEC INC   p 1307
4355 BOUL SIR-WILFRID-LAURIER, SAINT-HUBERT, QC, J3Y 3X3
(450) 443-6666   SIC 6712

2427-9028 QUEBEC INC   p 1279
5401 BOUL DES GALERIES BUREAU 240, QUEBEC, QC, G2K 1N4
(418) 627-0062   SIC 5941

242747 ONTARIO LIMITED   p 658
680 OXFORD ST W, LONDON, ON, N6H 1T9
(519) 472-4890   SIC 5511

2428391 ONTARIO INC   p 477
1430 CORMORANT RD, ANCASTER, ON, L9G 4V5
(905) 304-1010   SIC 5736

2436-3392 QUEBEC INC   p 1301
807 BOUL ARTHUR-SAUVE, SAINT-EUSTACHE, QC, J7R 4K3
(450) 472-8400   SIC 5193

2437-0223 QUEBEC INC   p 1282
364 RUE NOTRE-DAME, REPENTIGNY, QC, J6A 2S5
(450) 581-7071   SIC 4493

2437090 ONTARIO LTD   p 485
75 DYMENT RD, BARRIE, ON, L4N 3H6
(705) 733-0022   SIC 3841

2443499 ONTARIO INC   p 1029
48 CASTER AVE, WOODBRIDGE, ON, L4L 5Z1
(905) 771-0637   SIC 5149

2445120 ONTARIO INC   p 631
1412 BATH RD, KINGSTON, ON, K7M 4X6
(613) 817-1808   SIC 5511

2447496 ONTARIO INC   p 769
See WW HOTELS CORP

2449616 ONTARIO INC   p 894
35 AUTOMALL BLVD, STOUFFVILLE, ON, L4A 0W7
(289) 451-0087   SIC 5511

2456317 ONTARIO LTD   p 932
431 RICHMOND ST E, TORONTO, ON, M5A 1R1
(647) 490-4854   SIC 7359

2463103 NOVA SCOTIA LTD   p 442
7181 HIGHWAY 1, COLDBROOK, NS, B4R 1A2
(902) 678-2155   SIC 5511

2469447 ONTARIO LIMITED   p 782
14 ASHWARREN RD, NORTH YORK, ON, M3J 1Z5
(416) 636-7772   SIC 2033

2474761 MANITOBA LTD   p 364
1272 DUGALD RD, WINNIPEG, MB, R2J 0H2
(204) 987-5640   SIC 5561

248276 ALBERTA LTD   p 130
100 1ST ST, FOX CREEK, AB, T0H 1P0
(780) 622-3566   SIC 7359

2486535 ONTARIO LTD   p 578
2000 THE QUEENSWAY, ETOBICOKE, ON, M9C 5H5
(416) 913-5780   SIC 5511

2489736 ONTARIO LIMITED   p 855
10414 YONGE ST, RICHMOND HILL, ON, L4C 3C3
(905) 780-9999   SIC 5511

2494719 ONTARIO INC   p 1018

▲ Public Company   ■ Public Company Family Member   **HQ** Headquarters   **BR** Branch   **SL** Single Location

10980 TECUMSEH RD E, WINDSOR, ON, N8R 1A8

(519) 956-7700   *SIC* 5511

2507246 ONTARIO INC   *p* 802
2270 SOUTH SERVICE RD W, OAKVILLE, ON, L6L 5M9

(905) 827-7191   *SIC* 5511

2508046 ONTARIO LTD   *p* 847
50 BENSON CRT, PORT HOPE, ON, L1A 3V6

(905) 885-6421   *SIC* 5511

2518879 ONTARIO INC   *p* 650
1712 DUNDAS ST, LONDON, ON, N5W 3C9

(519) 659-8725   *SIC* 5621

2521153 ONTARIO INC   *p* 903
300 JOHN ST SUITE 310, THORNHILL, ON, L3T 5W4

(416) 222-7144   *SIC* 7381

2525-7577 QUEBEC INC.   *p* 1233
3050 BOUL INDUSTRIEL, MONTREAL, QC, H7L 4P7

SIC 2821

2527-9829 QUEBEC INC   *p* 1375
4367 BOUL BOURQUE, SHERBROOKE, QC, J1N 1S4

(819) 564-1600   *SIC* 5511

2529-0032 QUEBEC INC   *p* 1122
3005 BOUL TASCHEREAU, LA PRAIRIE, QC, J5R 5S6

(450) 444-3112   *SIC* 5051

2531-7504 QUEBEC INC   *p* 1104
850 BOUL MALONEY O, GATINEAU, QC, J8T 3R6

(819) 568-0066   *SIC* 5511

2539393 ONTARIO INC   *p* 709
71 KING ST W SUITE 102, MISSISSAUGA, ON, L5B 4A2

(905) 897-1144   *SIC* 8011

2540-0417 QUEBEC INC   *p* 1353
124 RUE DES ECOLIERS, SAINT-VICTOR, QC, G0M 2B0

(418) 588-3913   *SIC* 6712

2549204 ONTARIO INC   *p* 870
1 WILLIAM KITCHEN RD SUITE 1, SCARBOROUGH, ON, M1P 5B7

(416) 293-1010   *SIC* 5461

2550-7856 QUEBEC INC   *p* 1316
1050 RUE STEFONI, SAINT-JEAN-SUR-RICHELIEU, QC, J3A 1T5

(450) 349-5861   *SIC* 8361

2551194 ONTARIO INC   *p* 625
74 OSPREY CRES, KANATA, ON, K2M 2Z8

(613) 567-7100   *SIC* 5461

2552-4018 QUEBEC INC   *p* 1085
2480 BOUL CURE-LABELLE, COTE SAINT-LUC, QC, H7T 1R1

(450) 682-6000   *SIC* 5511

2553-4330 QUEBEC INC   *p* 1277
714 7E AVENUE DE L'AEROPORT, QUEBEC, QC, G2G 2T6

(418) 877-2808   *SIC* 4512

2553-4330 QUEBEC INC   *p* 1367
18 AVIATION GENERAL E, SEPT-ILES, QC, G4R 4K2

(418) 961-2808   *SIC* 4512

2585693 ONTARIO INC   *p* 787
1681 EGLINTON AVE E SUITE 1671, NORTH YORK, ON, M4A 1J6

(416) 752-6666   *SIC* 5511

2595385 ONTARIO INC   *p* 542
650 RIVERVIEW DR, CHATHAM, ON, N7M 0N2

(519) 380-9265   *SIC* 2952

260304 BC LTD   *p* 334
2120 QUADRA ST, VICTORIA, BC, V8T 4C5

(250) 382-7722   *SIC* 5088

2615267 ONTARIO INC   *p* 1010
620 DAVENPORT RD UNIT 33, WATERLOO, ON, N2V 2C2

(226) 777-5833   *SIC* 6531

2618-1833 QUEBEC INC   *p* 1181
274 RUE JEAN-TALON E, MONTREAL, QC, H2R 1S7

(514) 273-3224   *SIC* 6712

2618-7922 QUEBEC INC   *p* 1343
8055 BOUL LANGELIER, SAINT-LEONARD, QC, H1P 2B7

(514) 852-9181   *SIC* 5172

2619-0645 QUEBEC INC   *p* 1365
1658 BOUL SAINTE-MARIE, SALABERRY-DE-VALLEYFIELD, QC, J6T 6M2

(450) 373-0690   *SIC* 5148

2619473 ONTARIO INC   *p* 758
8481 EARL THOMAS AVE, NIAGARA FALLS, ON, L2G 0B5

(905) 358-0699   *SIC* 2761

2621-9634 QUEBEC INC   *p* 1291
37 204 RTE E, SAINT-ADALBERT, QC, G0R 2M0

(418) 356-5591   *SIC* 2491

2623-4419 QUEBEC INC   *p* 1131
9615 RUE CLEMENT, LASALLE, QC, H8R 4B4

(514) 363-0276   *SIC* 5154

2625-2106 QUEBEC INC   *p* 1354
155 BOUL NORBERT-MORIN, SAINTE-AGATHE-DES-MONTS, QC, J8C 3M2

(819) 326-1600   *SIC* 5511

2625-8368 QUEBEC INC   *p* 1304
16850 BOUL LACROIX, SAINT-GEORGES, QC, G5Y 8G9

(418) 228-8661   *SIC* 5411

2627 W 16TH AVENUE HOLDINGS LTD   *p* 322
2627 16TH AVE W, VANCOUVER, BC, V6K 3C2

(604) 736-0009   *SIC* 5411

2630-6241 QUEBEC INC   *p* 1052
305 BOUL LA SALLE, BAIE-COMEAU, QC, G4Z 2L5

(418) 296-9191   *SIC* 5571

2634912 ONTARIO INC   *p* 856
11262 YONGE ST, RICHMOND HILL, ON, L4S 1K9

(905) 770-0005   *SIC* 5511

2635-8762 QUEBEC INC   *p* 1129
922 GRANDE COTE O, LANORAIE, QC, J0K 1E0

(450) 887-7446   *SIC* 4213

2637-5808 QUEBEC INC   *p* 1140
2091 RTE MARIE-VICTORIN, LEVIS, QC, G7A 4H4

(418) 831-9967   *SIC* 8699

2639-1862 QUEBEC INC   *p* 1402
1031 7E RANG, WICKHAM, QC, J0C 1S0

(819) 398-6303   *SIC* 1752

2699001 CANADA LIMITED   *p* 565
509 GOVERNMENT ST, DRYDEN, ON, P8N 2P6

(807) 223-3381   *SIC* 5211

27 DOLLAR BUSINESS CARD CO   *p* 86
See EXCEL RESOURCES SOCIETY

2701545 CANADA INC   *p* 1125
300 RUE DE LA BERGE-DU-CANAL BUREAU 312, LACHINE, QC, H8R 1H3

(514) 367-0000   *SIC* 4213

2704242 CANADA INC   *p* 1161
9025 BOUL MAURICE-DUPLESSIS, MONTREAL, QC, H1E 6M3

(514) 648-1883   *SIC* 5411

2709970 CANADA INC   *p* 1147
2500 RUE SHERBROOKE, MAGOG, QC, J1X 4E8

(819) 843-9883   *SIC* 5511

2714159 CANADA INC   *p* 850
44 EAST BEAVER CREEK RD UNIT 16, RICHMOND HILL, ON, L4B 1G8

(905) 886-5432   *SIC* 5541

2730-8303 QUEBEC INC   *p* 1350
239 RTE 230 O, SAINT-PHILIPPE-DE-NERI, QC, G0L 4A0

(418) 498-2100   *SIC* 5031

2732-2304 QUEBEC INC   *p* 1288
1225 AV LARIVIERE, ROUYN-NORANDA, QC, J9X 6M6

(819) 762-6565   *SIC* 5511

2732-3930 QUEBEC INC   *p* 1315
950 RUE BERNIER, SAINT-JEAN-SUR-RICHELIEU, QC, J2W 2H1

(450) 359-1311   *SIC* 5039

2733-8649 QUEBEC INC   *p* 1130
7351 RUE CHOUINARD, LASALLE, QC, H8N 2L6

(514) 768-6315   *SIC* 7382

2734-7681 QUEBEC INC   *p* 1104
850 BOUL MALONEY O, GATINEAU, QC, J8T 3R6

(819) 568-0066   *SIC* 5511

2735-3861 QUEBEC INC   *p* 1283
321 CH DES ERABLES, RIGAUD, QC, J0P 1P0

(450) 451-0000   *SIC* 7011

2737-1822 QUEBEC INC   *p* 1260
3417 1RE AV, QUEBEC, QC, G1L 3R4

(418) 622-1237   *SIC* 5912

2737-2895 QUEBEC INC   *p* 1121
2152 CH SAINT-JOSEPH, LA BAIE, QC, G7B 3N9

(418) 544-2622   *SIC* 5143

2739-0988 QUEBEC INC   *p* 1346
4675 RUE JEAN-TALON E, SAINT-LEONARD, QC, H1S 1K3

(514) 722-4664   *SIC* 5912

2739-9708 QUEBEC INC   *p* 1218
5192 CH DE LA COTE-DES-NEIGES, MONTREAL, QC, H3T 1X8

(514) 738-1384   *SIC* 5431

2741-3327 QUEBEC INC   *p* 1184
5692 AV DU PARC, MONTREAL, QC, H2V 4H1

(514) 270-6500   *SIC* 5912

2742-7608 QUEBEC INC   *p* 1044
225 AV DU PONT S, ALMA, QC, G8B 2T7

(418) 668-3061   *SIC* 5531

2747-6035 QUEBEC INC   *p* 1126
2302 52E AV, LACHINE, QC, H8T 2Y3

(514) 631-1988   *SIC* 5084

2747-6761 QUEBEC INC   *p* 1317
400 BOUL DU SEMINAIRE N BUREAU 2747, SAINT-JEAN-SUR-RICHELIEU, QC, J3B 5L2

(450) 349-2878   *SIC* 5411

2747-8353 QUEBEC INC   *p* 1235
530 PLACE FORAND, MONTREAL, QC, H7P 5L9

(450) 622-0070   *SIC* 5143

2755-4609 QUEBEC INC   *p* 1061
4243 RUE MARCEL-LACASSE, BOIS-BRIAND, QC, J7H 1N4

(450) 435-8899   *SIC* 4131

2757-5158 QUEBEC INC   *p* 1134
4589 AUT 440 O BUREAU 103, LAVAL, QC, H7W 0J7

(450) 688-9050   *SIC* 5211

2757-5158 QUEBEC INC   *p* 1316
1050 BOUL DU SEMINAIRE N BUREAU 210, SAINT-JEAN-SUR-RICHELIEU, QC, J3A 1S7

(450) 359-7980   *SIC* 2434

2757-5158 QUEBEC INC   *p* 1363
2854 RTE 235, SAINTE-SABINE, QC, J0J 2B0

(450) 293-5037   *SIC* 2514

2758792 CANADA INC   *p* 1091
3352 BOUL DES SOURCES, DOLLARD-DES-ORMEAUX, QC, H9B 1Z9

(514) 684-6846   *SIC* 5999

2759-1106 QUEBEC INC   *p* 1119
1415 RUE NOTRE-DAME, L'ANCIENNE-LORETTE, QC, G2E 3A8

(418) 872-2864   *SIC* 5912

2759-9687 QUEBEC INC.   *p* 1143
1516 CH DE CHAMBLY, LONGUEUIL, QC, J4J 3X5

(450) 670-1235   *SIC* 4724

2772981 CANADA INC   *p* 1084
1 PLACE LAVAL BUREAU 400, COTE SAINT-LUC, QC, H7N 1A1

(514) 335-3246   *SIC* 6712

2778751 CANADA INC   *p* 1354
220 RUE PRINCIPALE, SAINT-ZOTIQUE, QC, J0P 1Z0

(450) 267-5955   *SIC* 5084

2782677 CANADA INC   *p* 1058
1053 BOUL DU CURE-LABELLE, BLAINVILLE, QC, J7C 2M2

(450) 434-5484   *SIC* 5511

2786591 CANADA INC   *p* 1395
14 PLACE DU COMMERCE BUREAU 600, VERDUN, QC, H3E 1T5

(514) 287-1211   *SIC* 6163

2788331 CANADA INC   *p* 1306
701 AV SAINT-GEORGES, SAINT-GEORGES-DE-CHAMPLAIN, QC, G9T 5K4

(819) 533-5445   *SIC* 5411

2790173 CANADA INC   *p* 1047
7900 RUE JARRY, ANJOU, QC, H1J 1H1

(514) 353-1710   *SIC* 7389

2792924 MANITOBA LTD   *p* 373
228 ISABEL ST, WINNIPEG, MB, R3A 1G9

SIC 5541

28 AUGUSTA FUND LTD   *p* 33
6920 MACLEOD TRAIL SE, CALGARY, AB, T2H 0L3

(403) 259-3119   *SIC* 5812

2809664 CANADA INC   *p* 1117
16711 RTE TRANSCANADIENNE, KIRKLAND, QC, H9H 3L1

(514) 343-0044   *SIC* 4731

2810221 CANADA INC   *p* 1177
9500 RUE MEILLEUR BUREAU 800, MONTREAL, QC, H2N 2B7

(514) 388-0284   *SIC* 5136

2842-3861 QUEBEC INC   *p* 1224
1201 RUE DE LOUVAIN O, MONTREAL, QC, H4N 1G6

(514) 858-0066   *SIC* 8743

2843-5816 QUEBEC INC   *p* 1129
235 2E AV, LAMBTON, QC, G0M 1H0

(418) 486-7401   *SIC* 2431

2846-3826 QUEBEC INC   *p* 1284
210 AV LEONIDAS S, RIMOUSKI, QC, G5L 2T2

(418) 722-6633   *SIC* 5511

2846-4436 QUEBEC INC   *p* 1265
2440 AV DALTON, QUEBEC, QC, G1P 3X1

(418) 266-6600   *SIC* 6712

2846-6589 QUEBEC INC   *p* 1300
509 BOUL ARTHUR-SAUVE, SAINT-EUSTACHE, QC, J7P 4X4

(450) 473-4169   *SIC* 5912

2848-7403 QUEBEC INC   *p* 1058
700 BOUL DU CURE-LABELLE, BLAINVILLE, QC, J7C 2J6

(450) 435-1122   *SIC* 5511

285 PEMBINA INC   *p* 387
285 PEMBINA HWY, WINNIPEG, MB, R3L 2E1

(204) 284-0802   *SIC* 6531

2850401 CANADA INC   *p* 1382
189 BOUL HARWOOD, TERREBONNE, QC, J7V 1Y3

(450) 964-9333   *SIC* 6712

2851262 MANITOBA LTD   *p* 364
393 DAWSON RD N, WINNIPEG, MB, R2J 0S8

(204) 988-3278   *SIC* 4212

2853167 CANADA INC   *p* 529
2016 PLAINS RD E, BURLINGTON, ON, L7R 5B3

(905) 633-8811   *SIC* 5511

2853477 CANADA INC   *p* 1131
790 RUE D'UPTON, LASALLE, QC, H8R 2T9

(514) 363-5511   *SIC* 7334

2854-5150 QUEBEC INC   *p* 1177
9601 BOUL SAINT-LAURENT, MONTREAL, QC, H2N 1P6

(514) 385-1762   *SIC* 6512

2857-4077 QUEBEC INC   *p* 1369
850 7E AV, SHAWINIGAN, QC, G9T 2B8

(819) 533-4553   *SIC* 5411

2858-6691 QUEBEC INC   *p* 1282
305 BOUL IBERVILLE, REPENTIGNY, QC, J6A 2A6

(450) 581-2630   *SIC* 5411

2864-4920 QUEBEC INC   p 1364
120 BOUL DESJARDINS E, SAINTE-THERESE, QC, J7E 1C8
(450) 435-3685   SIC 5511

2865-8169 QUEBEC INC   p 1222
4700 RUE SAINT-AMBROISE BUREAU 100, MONTREAL, QC, H4C 2C7
(514) 937-1117   SIC 5021

2871149 CANADA INC   p 1393
189 BOUL HARWOOD, VAUDREUIL-DORION, QC, J7V 1Y3
(450) 455-2827   SIC 6712

2875446 CANADA INC   p 1384
266 RUE VICTORIA, THURSO, QC, J0X 3B0
(819) 985-3259   SIC 5411

2875448 CANADA INC   p 1105
2505 RUE SAINT-LOUIS, GATINEAU, QC, J8V 1A4
(819) 561-3772   SIC 5411

287706 ALBERTA LTD   p 131
11401 100 AVE, GRANDE PRAIRIE, AB, T8V 5M6
(780) 539-5678   SIC 7011

2891379 CANADA INC   p 468
90 ROBIE ST, TRURO, NS, B2N 1L1
(902) 897-4466   SIC 5531

2895102 CANADA INC   p 1117
16811 BOUL HYMUS, KIRKLAND, QC, H9H 3L4
(514) 426-1211   SIC 7389

2900319 CANADA INC   p 1240
146 PROM RONALD, MONTREAL-OUEST, QC, H4X 1M8
(514) 489-9159   SIC 5137

2904357 CANADA INC   p 1337
615 RUE MCCAFFREY, SAINT-LAURENT, QC, H4T 1N3
(514) 340-2844   SIC 7361

2913097 CANADA INC   p 1392
650 RUE LIONEL-BOULET, VARENNES, QC, J3X 1P7
(450) 652-5400   SIC 1629

2920409 CANADA INC   p 1169
8575 8E AV, MONTREAL, QC, H1Z 2X2
(514) 374-2700   SIC 5149

2920654 CANADA INC   p 1156
5785 RUE PARE, MONT-ROYAL, QC, H4P 1S1
(514) 736-0810   SIC 5199

2931028 CANADA INC   p 1331
6405 RUE VANDEN-ABEELE, SAINT-LAURENT, QC, H4S 1S1
(514) 335-6161   SIC 4813

2931621 CANADA INC   p 795
2625B WESTON RD, NORTH YORK, ON, M9N 3W1
(416) 247-2196   SIC 5531

293564 ALBERTA LTD   p 165
15 INGLEWOOD DR SUITE 2, ST. ALBERT, AB, T8N 5E2
(780) 458-7227   SIC 5571

2938286 CANADA INC   p 1142
60 BOUL ROLAND-THERRIEN, LONGUEUIL, QC, J4H 3V8
(450) 928-2000   SIC 5511

293967 ALBERTA LTD   p 92
13080 ST ALBERT TRAIL NW, EDMONTON, AB, T5L 4Y6
(780) 482-5696   SIC 5812

2941881 CANADA INC   p 686
6415 NORTHWEST DR UNIT 11, MISSISSAUGA, ON, L4V 1X1
(905) 612-1170   SIC 3841

2941902 CANADA INC   p 1346
6852A RUE JEAN-TALON E, SAINT-LEONARD, QC, H1S 1N1
(514) 252-8277   SIC 5411

2944715 CANADA INC   p 1224
9150 RUE CHARLES-DE LA TOUR, MONTREAL, QC, H4N 1M2
(514) 389-3815   SIC 5148

2945-2901 QUEBEC INC   p 1047
10251 BOUL RAY-LAWSON, ANJOU, QC, H1J 1L6
(514) 493-6113   SIC 6719

2945-8171 QUEBEC INC   p 978
296 RICHMOND ST W SUITE 401, TORONTO, ON, M5V 1X2
(416) 979-0000   SIC 7389

2945-9344 QUEBEC INC   p 1063
1540 RUE AMPERE, BOUCHERVILLE, QC, J4B 7L4
(450) 449-7929   SIC 5511

2945-9609 QUEBEC INC   p 1236
1850 BOUL LE CORBUSIER 200, MONTREAL, QC, H7S 2N5
(450) 682-4666   SIC 6531

2945-9708 QUEBEC INC   p 1063
1175 RUE AMPERE, BOUCHERVILLE, QC, J4B 7M6
(450) 655-2350   SIC 6712

294557 ALBERTA LTD   p 6
GD STN MAIN, BONNYVILLE, AB, T9N 2J6
(780) 826-3278   SIC 5511

2946-4617 QUEBEC INC   p 1324
393A AV SAINTE-CROIX, SAINT-LAURENT, QC, H4N 2L3
SIC 2816

2946-5440 QUEBEC INC   p 1331
4850 CH DU BOIS-FRANC BUREAU 100, SAINT-LAURENT, QC, H4S 1A7
(514) 335-3433   SIC 5047

2948-4292 QUEBEC INC   p 1392
9072 RUE DE LA MONTAGNE, VALCOURT, QC, J0E 2L0
(450) 532-2270   SIC 7389

2948-7659 QUEBEC INC   p 1075
411 BOUL SAINT-FRANCIS, CHATEAUGUAY, QC, J6J 1Z6
(450) 699-8555   SIC 5511

2950-0519 QUEBEC INC   p 1289
160 BOUL INDUSTRIEL, ROUYN-NORANDA, QC, J9X 6T3
(819) 797-0088   SIC 1731

2950-4602 QUEBEC INC   p 1347
435 RUE SAINT-ISIDORE, SAINT-LIN-LAURENTIDES, QC, J5M 2V1
(450) 439-2000   SIC 5251

2953-6778 QUEBEC INC   p 1063
549 RUE DE VERRAZANO BUREAU 3000, BOUCHERVILLE, QC, J4B 7W2
(450) 449-1516   SIC 1711

2954-8682 QUEBEC INC   p 1256
475 BOUL DE L'ATRIUM BUREAU 104, QUEBEC, QC, G1H 7H9
SIC 5812

2955-4201 QUEBEC INC   p 1375
4620 BOUL BOURQUE, SHERBROOKE, QC, J1N 2A8
(819) 821-9272   SIC 5511

2956-1198 QUEBEC INC   p 1222
3974 RUE NOTRE-DAME O BUREAU 101, MONTREAL, QC, H4C 1R1
(514) 573-2850   SIC 5099

2956-2584 QUEBEC INC   p 1046
98 235 RTE, ANGE-GARDIEN, QC, J0E 1E0
(450) 293-6115   SIC 5411

295823 ONTARIO INC   p 885
31 RAYMOND ST, ST CATHARINES, ON, L2R 2T3
(905) 685-4279   SIC 7381

2960-2778 QUEBEC INC   p 1337
7300 RTE TRANSCANADIENNE, SAINT-LAURENT, QC, H4T 1A3
(514) 448-9455   SIC 5131

2960-7082 QUEBEC INC   p 1393
115 RUE JOSEPH-CARRIER, VAUDREUIL-DORION, QC, J7V 5V5
(450) 455-5555   SIC 5511

2961-4765 QUEBEC INC   p 1261
595 BOUL PIERRE-BERTRAND BUREAU 125, QUEBEC, QC, G1M 3T8
(418) 622-5126   SIC 5092

2962-9060 QUEBEC INC   p 1151
12770 RUE BRAULT, MIRABEL, QC, J7J 0W3

(450) 420-1839   SIC 5085

2965-6311 QUEBEC INC   p 1084
2065 BOUL DES LAURENTIDES BUREAU 84, COTE SAINT-LUC, QC, H7M 4M2
(450) 663-0672   SIC 5912

2967-3183 QUEBEC INC   p 1002
300 RUE UNIVERSELLE SS 4, VARS, ON, K0A 3H0
(613) 443-0044   SIC 3713

2968-4305 QUEBEC INC   p 1246
12800 RUE SHERBROOKE E BUREAU 61, POINTE-AUX-TREMBLES, QC, H1A 4Y3
(514) 498-4840   SIC 5912

2969-9477 QUEBEC INC   p 1319
11 RUE JOHN-F.-KENNEDY BUREAU 2, SAINT-JEROME, QC, J7Y 4B4
(450) 436-9390   SIC 5051

2969-9899 QUEBEC INC   p 1240
3905 BOUL INDUSTRIEL, MONTREAL-NORD, QC, H1H 2Z2
(514) 744-1010   SIC 7381

2970-7528 QUEBEC INC   p 1300
625 RUE DUBOIS, SAINT-EUSTACHE, QC, J7P 3W1
(450) 472-7272   SIC 5511

2970-9177 QUEBEC INC   p 1323
1051 RUE DECARIE, SAINT-LAURENT, QC, H4L 3M8
(514) 748-7725   SIC 5912

2971038 QUEBEC INC   p 1231
5535 RUE ERNEST-CORMIER, MONTREAL, QC, H7C 2S9
(450) 665-8780   SIC 5084

2972-6924 QUEBEC INC   p 1263
2150 RUE LEON-HARMEL, QUEBEC, QC, G1N 4L2
(418) 683-2431   SIC 3442

2972344 CANADA INC   p 1144
900 RUE SAINT-LAURENT O, LONGUEUIL, QC, J4K 1C5
(450) 674-7474   SIC 5511

2982651 MANITOBA LIMITED   p 359
333 MAIN ST SUITE 17, STONEWALL, MB, R0C 2Z0
(204) 467-8113   SIC 5947

2982897 CANADA INC   p 1233
2425 RUE MICHELIN, MONTREAL, QC, H7L 5B9
(514) 332-4830   SIC 1711

2985080 CANADA INC   p 1389
138 CH DES BOISES BUREAU 2, VAL-D'OR, QC, J9P 4N7
(819) 738-5289   SIC 7699

2985420 CANADA INC   p 1192
420 RUE SHERBROOKE O, MONTREAL, QC, H3A 1B2
SIC 8741

299 BURRARD HOTEL LIMITED PARTNERSHIP   p 301
1038 CANADA PL, VANCOUVER, BC, V6C 0B9
(604) 695-5300   SIC 7011

2990181 CANADA INC   p 1166
5000 RUE SHERBROOKE E, MONTREAL, QC, H1V 1A1
(514) 253-3365   SIC 7011

2993821 CANADA INC   p 1382
1591 CH SAINTE-CLAIRE, TERREBONNE, QC, J7M 1M2
(450) 478-2055   SIC 2011

2KEYS CORPORATION   p 828
300-1600 CARLING AVE, OTTAWA, ON, K1Z 1G3
(613) 860-1620   SIC 7379

2KEYS SECURITY SOLUTIONS   p 828
See 2KEYS CORPORATION

2XPOSE   p 1179
See RUDSAK INC

3

3 D S   p 183
See 3DS THREE DIMENSIONAL SERVICES INC

3 FOR 1 PIZZA & WINGS INC   p 958
10 BAY ST SUITE 802, TORONTO, ON, M5J 2R8
(416) 360-0888   SIC 6794

3 POINTS AVIATION CORP   p 1040
91 WATTS AVE, CHARLOTTETOWN, PE, C1E 2B7
(902) 628-8846   SIC 5088

3 SIXTY   p 476
See 3 SIXTY RISK SOLUTIONS LTD

3 SIXTY RISK SOLUTIONS LTD   p 476
83 LITTLE BRIDGE ST SUITE 12, ALMONTE, ON, K0A 1A0
(866) 360-3360   SIC 7381

3-D AUTO PARTS LTD   p 466
17 BRIDGE AVE, STELLARTON, NS, B0K 0A2
(902) 752-9370   SIC 5531

30 FORENSIC ENGINEERING INC   p 958
40 UNIVERSITY AVE SUITE 800, TORONTO, ON, M5J 1T1
(416) 368-1700   SIC 8711

300322 ONTARIO LIMITED   p 653
150 DUFFERIN AVE SUITE 100, LONDON, ON, N6A 5N6
(519) 672-5272   SIC 6719

301061 ONTARIO LIMITED   p 885
227 CHURCH ST, ST CATHARINES, ON, L2R 3E8
SIC 7999

3011933 CANADA INC   p 1082
80 CH DES ETANGS, COOKSHIRE-EATON, QC, J0B 1M0
(819) 875-5559   SIC 3069

301726 ALBERTA LTD   p 129
8751 94 ST, FORT SASKATCHEWAN, AB, T8L 4P7
(780) 998-9999   SIC 5812

301776 ALBERTA LTD   p 84
10611 KINGSWAY NW SUITE 114, EDMONTON, AB, T5G 3C8
(780) 424-6094   SIC 5047

302084 B.C. LTD   p 275
8239 128 ST, SURREY, BC, V3W 4G1
(604) 596-9984   SIC 6712

3022528 CANADA INC   p 1141
778 RUE JEAN-NEVEU, LONGUEUIL, QC, J4G 1P1
(450) 442-4087   SIC 7389

3025052 NOVA SCOTIA LIMITED   p 454
3363 KEMPT RD, HALIFAX, NS, B3K 4X5
(902) 453-2110   SIC 5012

3025235 NOVA SCOTIA ULC   p 1192
1050 RUE SHERBROOKE O, MONTREAL, QC, H3A 2R6
(514) 985-6225   SIC 7011

3025906 NOVA SCOTIA LIMITED   p 456
6389 QUINPOOL RD, HALIFAX, NS, B3L 1A6
(902) 424-1397   SIC 5541

3031632 MANITOBA INC   p 376
222 BROADWAY, WINNIPEG, MB, R3C 0R3
(204) 942-8251   SIC 7011

3032948 NOVA SCOTIA LIMITED   p 468
437 PRINCE ST, TRURO, NS, B2N 1E6
(902) 895-1651   SIC 7011

3033441 NOVA SCOTIA COMPANY   p 162
172 TURBO DR, SHERWOOD PARK, AB, T8H 2J6
(780) 464-7774   SIC 5085

303567 SASKATCHEWAN LTD   p 1425
2636 MILLAR AVE, SASKATOON, SK, S7K 4C8
(306) 933-3020   SIC 7359

3039214 NOVA SCOTIA LIMITED   p 454
3625 KEMPT RD, HALIFAX, NS, B3K 4X6
(902) 454-1000   SIC 5511

3041000 CANADA INC   p 1107
951 BOUL SAINT-JOSEPH, GATINEAU, QC, J8Z 1S8
(819) 777-2611   SIC 5511

3041518 NOVA SCOTIA LIMITED   p 454
3773 WINDSOR ST, HALIFAX, NS, B3K 0A2
(902) 453-1130   SIC 5511

3043177 NOVA SCOTIA LIMITED *p 444*
61 RADDALL AVE, DARTMOUTH, NS, B3B
1T4
(902) 446-3940 *SIC 7374*

305466 B.C. LTD *p 191*
8155 NORTH FRASER WAY UNIT 100,
BURNABY, BC, V5J 5M8
(604) 435-1220 *SIC 1542*

3059714 NOVA SCOTIA COMPANY *p 539*
103 SECOND ST, CAMPBELLFORD, ON,
K0L 1L0
(705) 653-3590 *SIC 5149*

3067419 NOVA SCOTIA LIMITED *p 442*
15 LANSING CRT, DARTMOUTH, NS, B2W
0K3
(902) 462-6600 *SIC 5511*

3072930 NOVA SCOTIA COMPANY *p 1257*
395 RUE DE LA COURONNE, QUEBEC,
QC, G1K 7X4
(418) 647-2611 *SIC 7011*

3075109 CANADA INC *p 1072*
47 BOUL MARIE-VICTORIN, CANDIAC,
QC, J5R 1B6
(450) 444-4405 *SIC 3443*

3075487 MANITOBA LTD *p 380*
1124 SANFORD ST, WINNIPEG, MB, R3E
2Z9
(204) 788-4117 *SIC 1711*

307711 ALBERTA LTD *p 156*
1824 49 AVE, RED DEER, AB, T4R 2N7
(403) 347-7700 *SIC 5511*

3081354 CANADA INC *p 1091*
2001 RUE SAINT-REGIS, DOLLARD-DES-
ORMEAUX, QC, H9B 2M9
SIC 5045

3084761 MANITOBA LTD *p 353*
262 MAIN ST, NIVERVILLE, MB, R0A 1E0
(204) 883-2327 *SIC 5211*

3088-7061 QUEBEC INC *p 1351*
104 BOUL SAINT-REMI, SAINT-REMI, QC,
J0L 2L0
(450) 454-5171 *SIC 6712*

3089-3242 QUEBEC INC *p 1271*
3031 BOUL LAURIER, QUEBEC, QC, G1V
2M2
(418) 658-2727 *SIC 7011*

3089554 NOVA SCOTIA ULC *p 1263*
875 BOUL CHAREST O BUREAU 100,
QUEBEC, QC, G1N 2C9
(418) 266-3020 *SIC 3829*

3092983 NOVA SCOTIA LIMITED *p 459*
877 HIGHWAY 203, KEMPTVILLE, NS, B5A
5R3
(902) 761-2334 *SIC 5146*

3093-6975 QUEBEC INC *p 1233*
1780 PLACE MARTENOT BUREAU 17,
MONTREAL, QC, H7L 5B5
(450) 668-4888 *SIC 3993*

3093-9920 QUEBEC INC *p 1116*
2350 RUE SAINT-HUBERT, JONQUIERE,
QC, G7X 5N4
(418) 547-6611 *SIC 5411*

3095-0497 QUEBEC INC *p 1311*
1340 BOUL CHOQUETTE, SAINT-
HYACINTHE, QC, J2S 6G1
(450) 778-5558 *SIC 5411*

3095-6395 QUEBEC INC *p 1097*
1175 BOUL LEMIRE, DRUMMONDVILLE,
QC, J2C 7X8
(819) 474-7281 *SIC 5148*

3096-3227 QUEBEC INC *p 1226*
8270 RUE MAYRAND, MONTREAL, QC,
H4P 2C5
(514) 288-6000 *SIC 5045*

3097-8217 QUEBEC INC *p 1235*
3475 BOUL DAGENAIS O BUREAU 119,
MONTREAL, QC, H7P 4V9
(450) 963-0846 *SIC 5912*

3099-3562 QUEBEC INC *p 1081*
1021 RUE CHILD, COATICOOK, QC, J1A
2S5
(819) 849-0532 *SIC 5075*

30TH STREET LIQUOR STORE LTD *p 331*
2901 30 ST, VERNON, BC, V1T 5C9

(250) 545-5800 *SIC 5921*

310 DUMP *p 101*
See KASH VENTURES LTD

3100-2504 QUEBEC INC *p 1077*
1401 BOUL TALBOT BUREAU 3,
CHICOUTIMI, QC, G7H 5N6
(418) 545-4945 *SIC 5941*

3100-6588 QUEBEC INC *p 1114*
920 BOUL FIRESTONE, JOLIETTE, QC,
J6E 2W5
(450) 756-4545 *SIC 5251*

3100-7669 QUEBEC INC *p 1101*
1989 RUE MICHELIN, FABREVILLE, QC,
H7L 5B7
(450) 973-7765 *SIC 5063*

3100-8410 QUEBEC INC *p 1110*
1165 RUE PRINCIPALE, GRANBY, QC, J2J
0M3
(450) 994-4220 *SIC 5511*

3100477 NOVA SCOTIA LIMITED *p 444*
110 GARLAND AVE UNIT 201, DART-
MOUTH, NS, B3B 0A7
(902) 405-3948 *SIC 6531*

3101-2883 QUEBEC INC *p 1370*
760 RUE CHALIFOUX, SHERBROOKE,
QC, J1G 1R6
(819) 820-0808 *SIC 3069*

310104 ALBERTA LTD *p 161*
278 CREE RD, SHERWOOD PARK, AB,
T8A 4G2
(780) 449-3710 *SIC 5146*

3101895 NOVA SCOTIA COMPANY *p 1092*
800 BOUL STUART-GRAHAM S BUREAU
315, DORVAL, QC, H4Y 1J6
(514) 422-1000 *SIC 6712*

3102597 NOVA SCOTIA LIMITED *p 444*
109 ILSLEY AVE UNIT 1, DARTMOUTH,
NS, B3B 1S8
(902) 429-5002 *SIC 8712*

3105-4521 QUEBEC INC *p 1302*
1200 BOUL SAINT-FELICIEN, SAINT-
FELICIEN, QC, G8K 2N6
(418) 679-1431 *SIC 5411*

3111326 CANADA INC *p 1077*
1611 BOUL TALBOT, CHICOUTIMI, QC,
G7H 4C3
(418) 698-8611 *SIC 5812*

3116506 CANADA INC *p 1145*
2479 CH DE CHAMBLY, LONGUEUIL, QC,
J4L 1M2
(450) 468-4406 *SIC 5461*

3119696 CANADA INC *p 978*
269 RICHMOND ST W SUITE 201,
TORONTO, ON, M5V 1X1
(416) 368-1623 *SIC 7389*

3120772 NOVA SCOTIA COMPANY *p 1103*
2 CH DE MONTREAL E, GATINEAU, QC,
J8M 1E9
(819) 986-4300 *SIC 2621*

3122298 CANADA INC *p 1166*
4445 RUE ONTARIO E BUREAU 4, MON-
TREAL, QC, H1V 3V3
(514) 259-5929 *SIC 5461*

312407 ALBERTA LTD *p 92*
14728 119 AVE NW, EDMONTON, AB, T5L
2P2
(780) 454-5797 *SIC 2051*

3135772 CANADA INC *p 412*
73 LORNE ST, SACKVILLE, NB, E4L 4A2
SIC 3322

3161234 MANITOBA LIMITED *p 991*
64 JEFFERSON AVE UNIT 3, TORONTO,
ON, M6K 1Y4
(416) 589-6563 *SIC 7359*

316291 ALBERTA LTD *p 107*
4315 92 AVE NW, EDMONTON, AB, T6B
3M7
(780) 465-9771 *SIC 2439*

3169693 CANADA INC *p 1200*
895 RUE DE LA GAUCHETIERE O BU-
REAU 401, MONTREAL, QC, H3B 4G1
(514) 393-1247 *SIC 5461*

3174891 CANADA INC *p 1093*
2945 AV ANDRE, DORVAL, QC, H9P 1K7

(514) 685-9505 *SIC 4783*

3175120 CANADA INC *p 1379*
1887 CH SAINT-CHARLES, TERRE-
BONNE, QC, J6W 5W5
(450) 964-5696 *SIC 1731*

3177743 MANITOBA LTD *p 356*
1018 MANITOBA AVE, SELKIRK, MB, R1A
4M2
(204) 785-7777 *SIC 5812*

3183441 CANADA INC *p 1245*
4957 BOUL SAINT-JEAN, PIERREFONDS,
QC, H9H 2A9
SIC 5411

3188192 NOVA SCOTIA INCORPORATED *p 459*
971 PARK ST, KENTVILLE, NS, B4N 3X1
(902) 678-3323 *SIC 5511*

3197786 CANADA INC *p 1106*
13 RUE DUMAS, GATINEAU, QC, J8Y 2M4
(819) 775-9844 *SIC 1521*

320114 ALBERTA INC *p 27*
328 CENTRE ST SE SUITE 202, CALGARY,
AB, T2G 4X6
(403) 777-0777 *SIC 4724*

320114 ALBERTA INC *p 42*
400 4 AVE SW SUITE 230, CALGARY, AB,
T2P 0J4
SIC 4724

320364 ALBERTA LTD *p 80*
5411 55 ST, COLD LAKE, AB, T9M 1R6
(780) 594-3311 *SIC 5411*

321124 B.C. LTD *p 213*
9820 108 ST, FORT ST. JOHN, BC, V1J 0A7
(250) 787-0371 *SIC 5251*

3213463 CANADA INC *p 1047*
7545 AV M.-B.-JODOIN, ANJOU, QC, H1J
2H9
(514) 528-1150 *SIC 5149*

3213695 NOVA SCOTIA LIMITED *p 463*
300 WESTVILLE RD, NEW GLASGOW, NS,
B2H 2J5
(902) 752-8321 *SIC 5511*

3223701 CANADA INC *p 1106*
98 RUE LOIS BUREAU 205, GATINEAU,
QC, J8Y 3R7
(819) 243-7392 *SIC 1521*

3225518 CANADA INC *p 1171*
2590 RUE JEAN-TALON E, MONTREAL,
QC, H2A 1T9
(514) 847-1287 *SIC 4724*

3225537 NOVA SCOTIA LIMITED *p 371*
90 HUTCHINGS ST UNIT B, WINNIPEG,
MB, R2X 2X1
(204) 272-2880 *SIC 5013*

3235 ONTARIO INC *p 540*
9184 TWISS RD RR 2, CAMPBELLVILLE,
ON, L0P 1B0
(416) 233-1227 *SIC 5031*

3235149 CANADA INC *p 1393*
1033 RUE VALOIS, VAUDREUIL-DORION,
QC, J7V 8P2
(450) 455-4545 *SIC 4731*

3237681 CANADA INC *p 1038*
489 BRACKLEY POINT RD -RTE 15,
BRACKLEY, PE, C1E 1Z3
(902) 629-1500 *SIC 5719*

324007 ALBERTA LTD *p 92*
13220 ST ALBERT TRAIL NW SUITE 303,
EDMONTON, AB, T5L 4W1
(780) 477-2233 *SIC 7389*

324007 ALBERTA LTD *p 1437*
GD LCD MAIN, WEYBURN, SK, S4H 2J7
SIC 5154

324126 ALBERTA LTD *p 134*
10514 67 AVE UNIT 401, GRANDE
PRAIRIE, AB, T8W 0K8
(780) 532-7771 *SIC 6712*

3248 KING GEORGE HWY HOLDINGS LTD *p 283*
3248 KING GEORGE BLVD, SURREY, BC,
V4P 1A5
(604) 541-3902 *SIC 5499*

3248224 CANADA INC *p 1104*
1255 BOUL LA VERENDRYE O,

GATINEAU, QC, J8T 8K2
(819) 568-4646 *SIC 5511*

3254160 CANADA INC *p 1342*
850 AV MUNCK, SAINT-LAURENT, QC,
H7S 1B1
(514) 384-5060 *SIC 6712*

3274876 NOVA SCOTIA LIMITED *p 442*
55 ORION WHARF RD, CLARKS HAR-
BOUR, NS, B0W 1P0
(902) 745-2943 *SIC 5146*

327494 B.C. LTD *p 208*
7763 PROGRESS WAY, DELTA, BC, V4G
1A3
(604) 420-3511 *SIC 5149*

3278724 NOVA SCOTIA LIMITED *p 468*
126 MAIN ST, TRURO, NS, B2N 4G9
(902) 897-1700 *SIC 5511*

327989 BC LTD *p 218*
1271 SALISH RD, KAMLOOPS, BC, V2H
1P6
(250) 828-1515 *SIC 5541*

328633 BC LTD *p 271*
19265 LANGLEY BYPASS, SURREY, BC,
V3S 6K1
(604) 534-0181 *SIC 5511*

3286509 CANADA INC *p 1311*
450 RUE DANIEL-JOHNSON E, SAINT-
HYACINTHE, QC, J2S 8W5
(450) 774-1679 *SIC 5511*

3294269 CANADA INC *p 1337*
7020 CH DE LA C?TE-DE-LIESSE, SAINT-
LAURENT, QC, H4T 1E7
(514) 344-8883 *SIC 5999*

329985 ONTARIO LIMITED *p 1026*
50 ROYAL GROUP CRES UNIT 1, WOOD-
BRIDGE, ON, L4H 1X9
(905) 652-2363 *SIC 2024*

3302775 NOVA SCOTIA LTD *p 441*
15133 HEBBVILLE RD, BRIDGEWATER,
NS, B4V 2W4
(902) 543-2493 *SIC 5511*

330542 BC LTD *p 252*
259 MCLEAN ST, QUESNEL, BC, V2J 2N8
(250) 992-9293 *SIC 5511*

330558 ALBERTA LTD *p 3*
GD, ALTARIO, AB, T0C 0E0
(403) 552-2477 *SIC 1611*

3307862 NOVA SCOTIA LIMITED *p 444*
132 TRIDER CRES SUITE 2, DART-
MOUTH, NS, B3B 1R6
(800) 371-8022 *SIC 4731*

3310485 CANADA INC *p 1224*
1625 RUE CHABANEL O BUREAU 201,
MONTREAL, QC, H4N 2S7
(514) 388-1700 *SIC 6712*

331265 CANADA INC *p 762*
1872 SEYMOUR ST SUITE 3, NORTH BAY,
ON, P1A 0E2
(705) 472-5454 *SIC 3441*

3320235 CANADA INC *p 1120*
175 MONTEE DE SAINT-SULPICE,
L'ASSOMPTION, QC, J5W 2T3
(450) 589-5718 *SIC 5561*

3323501 CANADA INC *p 1238*
8201 PLACE MARIEN, MONTREAL-EST,
QC, H1B 5W6
(514) 322-9120 *SIC 3479*

3330389 CANADA INC *p 1248*
125 BOUL HYMUS, POINTE-CLAIRE, QC,
H9R 1E6
(514) 428-8898 *SIC 3679*

333111 ONTARIO LIMITED *p 733*
7805 TRANMERE DR, MISSISSAUGA, ON,
L5S 1V5
(905) 364-5000 *SIC 3728*

333308 ONTARIO LTD *p 927*
55 BLOOR ST W SUITE 506, TORONTO,
ON, M4W 1A5
(416) 964-2900 *SIC 5719*

3346625 CANADA INC *p 1288*
54 RANG DE LA MONTAGNE, ROUGE-
MONT, QC, J0L 1M0
(450) 469-2912 *SIC 6712*

3347818 CANADA INC *p 1120*

12 BOUL DON-QUICHOTTE, L'ILE-PERROT, QC, J7V 6N5

(514) 425-2255   *SIC* 5511

3358097 CANADA INC   *p* 1383
4680 BOUL FRONTENAC E, THETFORD MINES, QC, G6H 4G5

(418) 338-8588   *SIC* 6712

3367771 CANADA INC   *p* 1393
189 BOUL HARWOOD, VAUDREUIL-DORION, QC, J7V 1Y3

(450) 455-2827   *SIC* 5149

3370160 CANADA INC   *p* 1281
839 RUE NOTRE-DAME, REPENTIGNY, QC, J5Y 1C4

(450) 654-7111   *SIC* 5511

3374840 CANADA INC   *p* 1093
565 AV EDWARD VII, DORVAL, QC, H9P 1E7

SIC 5141

3378683 CANADA INC   *p* 1177
9600 RUE MEILLEUR BUREAU 630, MONTREAL, QC, H2N 2E3

(514) 385-3629   *SIC* 6712

3379710 CANADA INC   *p* 1224
1450 RUE DE LOUVAIN O, MONTREAL, QC, H4N 1G5

(514) 495-1531   *SIC* 6712

338802 ALBERTA LTD   *p* 120
2830 PARSONS RD NW, EDMONTON, AB, T6N 1H3

(780) 944-6922   *SIC* 7389

3394603 CANADA INC   *p* 531
34 PERDUE CRT, CALEDON, ON, L7C 3M6

(905) 840-4300   *SIC* 4213

340107 ALBERTA LTD   *p* 85
10665 109 ST NW, EDMONTON, AB, T5H 3B5

(780) 474-6466   *SIC* 5812

3401987 CANADA INC.   *p* 1125
900 RUE DU PACIFIQUE, LACHINE, QC, H8S 1C4

(514) 367-3001   *SIC* 6712

340532 ONTARIO LIMITED   *p* 548
565 EDGELEY BLVD, CONCORD, ON, L4K 4G4

(905) 669-9930   *SIC* 5149

341-7777 TAXI LTD   *p* 153
4819 48 AVE UNIT 280, RED DEER, AB, T4N 3T2

(403) 341-7777   *SIC* 4121

341234 B.C. LTD   *p* 187
4400 DOMINION UNIT 280, BURNABY, BC, V5G 4G3

(604) 473-9889   *SIC* 7373

341822 ONTARIO INC   *p* 990
28 HALTON ST, TORONTO, ON, M6J 1R3

(416) 533-5198   *SIC* 8051

3424626 CANADA INC   *p* 1323
1855 AV O'BRIEN, SAINT-LAURENT, QC, H4L 3W6

(450) 681-4100   *SIC* 5411

3427277 CANADA INC   *p* 1393
887 RTE HARWOOD BUREAU 53, VAUDREUIL-DORION, QC, J7V 8P2

(450) 424-2323   *SIC* 5111

3427951 CANADA INC   *p* 1134
180 BOUL BELLEROSE O, LAVAL-OUEST, QC, H7L 6A2

(450) 628-4835   *SIC* 1623

343315 ONTARIO LTD   *p* 898
916 LAPOINTE ST, SUDBURY, ON, P3A 5N8

(705) 521-1575   *SIC* 1541

3469051 CANADA INC   *p* 1216
9680 BOUL SAINT-LAURENT, MONTREAL, QC, H3L 2M9

(514) 388-8080   *SIC* 1542

3471250 CANADA INC   *p* 1367
440 RUE HOLLIDAY, SEPT-ILES, QC, G4R 4X6

(418) 962-1234   *SIC* 1794

3474534 CANADA INC   *p* 1241
800 BOUL CHOMEDEY BUREAU 160, MONTREAL-OUEST, QC, H7V 3Y4

(450) 682-7711   *SIC* 5999

347678 ALBERTA LTD   *p* 148
1205 5 ST, NISKU, AB, T9E 7L6

(780) 955-7733   *SIC* 6712

347942 B. C. LTD   *p* 285
57 LAKEWOOD DR, VANCOUVER, BC, V5L 4W4

(604) 251-9168   *SIC* 5421

348461 ONTARIO LIMITED   *p* 544
30 ELGIN ST W, COBOURG, ON, K9A 5T4

(905) 372-6131   *SIC* 7353

3490051 MANITOBA LTD   *p* 361
880 MEMORIAL DR, WINKLER, MB, R6W 0M6

(204) 325-9133   *SIC* 5211

3496252 CANADA INC   *p* 1282
340 RUE SAINT-PAUL, REPENTIGNY, QC, J5Z 4H9

(450) 585-0308   *SIC* 5021

3499481 CANADA INC   *p* 578
25 THE WEST MALL, ETOBICOKE, ON, M9C 1B8

(905) 593-3179   *SIC* 5999

3499481 CANADA INC   *p* 716
4161 SLADEVIEW CRES UNIT 12, MISSISSAUGA, ON, L5L 5R3

(905) 593-3177   *SIC* 5999

35 LAURIER LIMITED PARTNERSHIP   *p* 1105
35 RUE LAURIER, GATINEAU, QC, J8X 4E9

(819) 778-6111   *SIC* 7011

3500 STEELES AVENUE EAST LP   *p* 665
3500 STEELES AVE E UNIT 201, MARKHAM, ON, L3R 0X1

(905) 754-4826   *SIC* 6531

351658 ONTARIO LIMITED   *p* 511
8525 MISSISSAUGA RD, BRAMPTON, ON, L6Y 0C1

(905) 455-8400   *SIC* 7992

351684 BC LTD   *p* 331
6425 HWY 97, VERNON, BC, V1B 3R4

(250) 545-0531   *SIC* 5511

3517667 CANADA INC   *p* 623
411 LEGGET DR SUITE 600, KANATA, ON, K2K 3C9

(613) 599-9991   *SIC* 7371

3522920 CANADA INC   *p* 1242
80 RUE CAMPBELL RR 2, MORIN-HEIGHTS, QC, J0R 1H0

(450) 226-2314   *SIC* 2032

3522997 CANADA INC   *p* 1337
180 MONTEE DE LIESSE, SAINT-LAURENT, QC, H4T 1N7

(450) 455-3963   *SIC* 6712

3523462 CANADA INC   *p* 1307
3400 BOUL LOSCH BUREAU 35, SAINT-HUBERT, QC, J3Y 5T6

(450) 443-0060   *SIC* 5141

353903 ONTARIO LTD.   *p* 444
161 JOSEPH ZATZMAN DR, DARTMOUTH, NS, B3B 1M7

(902) 463-0101   *SIC* 5082

3539491 CANADA INC   *p* 1125
500 RUE NOTRE-DAME, LACHINE, QC, H8S 2B2

(514) 634-2287   *SIC* 3441

3552047 CANADA INC   *p* 1092
545 BOUL STUART-GRAHAM N BUREAU 201, DORVAL, QC, H4Y 1E2

(514) 633-1118   *SIC* 4581

3566072 CANADA INC   *p* 1214
1920 RUE SAINTE-CATHERINE O, MONTREAL, QC, H3H 1M4

(514) 937-7777   *SIC* 5511

357672 B.C. LTD   *p* 212
742 HWY 3 RR 5, FERNIE, BC, V0B 1M5

(250) 423-6871   *SIC* 7011

35790 MANITOBA LTD   *p* 347
1836 BRANDON AVE, BRANDON, MB, R7B 3G8

(204) 725-4223   *SIC* 5812

357C, LE   *p* 1188
See GESTION 357 DE LA COMMUNE INC

3580768 CANADA INC   *p* 736

6505 VIPOND DR, MISSISSAUGA, ON, L5T 1J9

(905) 670-6613   *SIC* 4212

3588025 CANADA INC   *p* 1093
2291 PLACE TRANSCANADIENNE, DORVAL, QC, H9P 2X7

(514) 683-3880   *SIC* 5511

3592898 CANADA INC   *p* 1108
1706 CH PINK BUREAU F, GATINEAU, QC, J9J 3N7

(819) 771-3969   *SIC* 1752

3595650 CANADA INC   *p* 1107
1135 BOUL SAINT-JOSEPH, GATINEAU, QC, J8Z 1W8

(819) 770-7768   *SIC* 5511

360 KIDS SUPPORT SERVICES   *p* 855
10415 YONGE ST SUITE C, RICHMOND HILL, ON, L4C 0Z3

(905) 475-6694   *SIC* 8699

360 STEEL INC   *p* 117
11050 UNIVERSITY AVE NW, EDMONTON, AB, T6G 1Y3

(780) 429-0360   *SIC* 5051

3600106 MANITOBA INC   *p* 381
660 WALL ST SUITE 843, WINNIPEG, MB, R3G 2T3

(204) 783-0816   *SIC* 5013

360641 BC LTD   *p* 292
555 12TH AVE W UNIT 201, VANCOUVER, BC, V5Z 3X7

(604) 879-8038   *SIC* 5812

3609022 CANADA INC   *p* 1235
4155 CHOMEDEY (A-13) E, MONTREAL, QC, H7P 0A8

(450) 628-4488   *SIC* 5021

360I CANADA   *p* 979
See DAN AGENCY INC

3611981 CANADA INC   *p* 1307
6200 RTE DE L'A?ROPORT, SAINT-HUBERT, QC, J3Y 8Y9

(450) 443-0500   *SIC* 4512

3617581 CANADA INC   *p* 1104
346 BOUL GREBER, GATINEAU, QC, J8T 5R6

(819) 561-6669   *SIC* 5511

3618358 CANADA INC   *p* 13
2680 61 AVE SE, CALGARY, AB, T2C 4V2

(403) 279-5208   *SIC* 4212

3618358 CANADA INC   *p* 581
96 DISCO RD, ETOBICOKE, ON, M9W 0A3

(416) 679-7979   *SIC* 4731

3619842 CANADA INC   *p* 1192
666 RUE SHERBROOKE O STE 801, MONTREAL, QC, H3A 1E7

SIC 5961

3627730 CANADA INC   *p* 691
2365 MATHESON BLVD E, MISSISSAUGA, ON, L4W 5B3

(905) 366-9200   *SIC* 7359

3627730 CANADA INC   *p* 816
3020 HAWTHORNE RD SUITE 300, OTTAWA, ON, K1G 3J6

(613) 526-3121   *SIC* 7389

3627730 CANADA INC   *p* 1125
1930 RUE ONESIME-GAGNON, LACHINE, QC, H8T 3M6

(514) 631-0710   *SIC* 7359

3627730 CANADA INC   *p* 1126
2056 32E AV, LACHINE, QC, H8T 3H7

(514) 631-1821   *SIC* 7812

3635112 CANADA INC   *p* 622
14935 COUNTY RD 2, INGLESIDE, ON, K0C 1M0

(613) 537-9559   *SIC* 5087

3645118 CANADA INC   *p* 1157
8650 CH DARNLEY, MONT-ROYAL, QC, H4T 1M4

(514) 345-0990   *SIC* 6712

3652548 CANADA INC   *p* 1311
3400 AV CUSSON, SAINT-HYACINTHE, QC, J2S 8N9

(450) 774-1332   *SIC* 5511

3653340 CANADA INC   *p* 1324
9800 BOUL CAVENDISH BUREAU 200,

SAINT-LAURENT, QC, H4M 2V9

SIC 6211

3680215 CANADA INC   *p* 1343
6660 RUE P.-E.-LAMARCHE, SAINT-LEONARD, QC, H1P 1J7

(514) 325-4488   *SIC* 3312

3680258 CANADA INC   *p* 1108
795 BOUL INDUSTRIEL, GRANBY, QC, J2G 9A1

(450) 378-3617   *SIC* 3612

370071 ALBERTA LTD   *p* 80
5609 55 ST, COLD LAKE, AB, T9M 1R6

(780) 594-4666   *SIC* 5013

370271 ONTARIO LIMITED   *p* 548
1600 STEELES AVE W SUITE 426, CONCORD, ON, L4K 4M2

(905) 660-4006   *SIC* 6411

3705391 CANADA LIMITED   *p* 595
5370 CANOTEK RD UNIT 1, GLOUCESTER, ON, K1J 9E6

(613) 742-7555   *SIC* 4214

3717291 CANADA INC   *p* 1084
2205 RUE INDUSTRIEL, COTE SAINT-LUC, QC, H7S 1P8

(450) 669-2323   *SIC* 5712

372103 ONTARIO LTD   *p* 548
33 CORSTATE AVE, CONCORD, ON, L4K 4Y2

(905) 669-5712   *SIC* 1731

3725766 CANADA INC   *p* 1047
7050 BOUL HENRI-BOURASSA E, ANJOU, QC, H1E 7K7

(514) 354-7901   *SIC* 5511

3725839 CANADA INC   *p* 1092
4600B BOUL SAINT-JEAN, DOLLARD-DES-ORMEAUX, QC, H9H 2A6

(514) 624-7777   *SIC* 5511

3727513 CANADA INC   *p* 1169
8920 BOUL PIE-IX BUREAU 300, MONTREAL, QC, H1Z 4H9

(514) 328-9220   *SIC* 5136

3727513 CANADA INC   *p* 1169
8920 BOUL PIE-IX BUREAU 300, MONTREAL, QC, H1Z 4H9

(514) 328-7212   *SIC* 5131

3728099 CANADA INC   *p* 1295
1370 RUE HOCQUART, SAINT-BRUNO, QC, J3V 6E1

(450) 653-7868   *SIC* 6712

3728111 MANITOBA LTD   *p* 357
2262 SPRINGFIELD RD BLDG A, SPRINGFIELD, MB, R2C 2Z2

(204) 654-1955   *SIC* 1721

3729451 CANADA INC   *p* 1125
230 BOUL MONTREAL-TORONTO, LACHINE, QC, H8S 1B8

(514) 637-1153   *SIC* 5511

3731537 CANADA INC   *p* 1214
2000 RUE SAINTE-CATHERINE O BUREAU 9000, MONTREAL, QC, H3H 2T2

(514) 939-4442   *SIC* 6712

373813 ONTARIO LIMITED   *p* 968
GD, TORONTO, ON, M5K 1N2

(416) 865-0040   *SIC* 8741

374872 ONTARIO LIMITED   *p* 532
21 INDUSTRIAL DR SUITE 6, CALEDONIA, ON, N3W 1H8

(905) 765-5424   *SIC* 4213

375414 ONTARIO LIMITED   *p* 900
2240 LONG LAKE RD, SUDBURY, ON, P3E 5H4

(705) 682-4463   *SIC* 5599

375645 ONTARIO LIMITED   *p* 548
8800 DUFFERIN ST UNIT 101, CONCORD, ON, L4K 0C5

(416) 736-6010   *SIC* 4724

3761045 CANADA INC   *p* 1085
2888 AV DU COSMODOME BUREAU 2, COTE SAINT-LUC, QC, H7T 2X1

(450) 682-1800   *SIC* 5461

3761258 CANADA INC   *p* 86
10180 101 ST NW SUITE 310, EDMONTON, AB, T5J 3S4

(780) 702-1432   *SIC* 7372

3762530 CANADA INC   *p 1157*
5775 AV ANDOVER, MONT-ROYAL, QC, H4T 1H6
(514) 739-3633   *SIC 5122*

3762971 CANADA INC   *p 1222*
5080 RUE SAINT-AMBROISE, MONTREAL, QC, H4C 2G1
(514) 939-3060   *SIC 6712*

3764605 CANADA INC   *p 1069*
9600 RUE IGNACE BUREAU G, BROSSARD, QC, J4Y 2R4
(450) 444-2956   *SIC 5141*

376599 ALBERTA INC   *p 27*
4630 MACLEOD TRAIL SW, CALGARY, AB, T2G 5E8
(403) 287-2500   *SIC 5813*

3798143 CANADA INC   *p 978*
155 WELLINGTON ST W SUITE 2901, TORONTO, ON, M5V 3H6
(416) 955-0514   *SIC 8741*

3812073 CANADA INC   *p 1345*
4929 RUE JARRY E BUREAU 208, SAINT-LEONARD, QC, H1R 1Y1
(514) 324-1024   *SIC 7389*

381572 ONTARIO LIMITED   *p 645*
2 FLEETWOOD RD, LINDSAY, ON, K9V 6H4
(705) 324-3762   *SIC 3553*

381611 ONTARIO LTD   *p 490*
60 DUNDAS ST E, BELLEVILLE, ON, K8N 1B8
   SIC 5063

381616 ALBERTA LTD   *p 158*
4315 44 ST, ROCKY MOUNTAIN HOUSE, AB, T4T 1A4
(403) 845-3633   *SIC 5531*

3823202 CANADA INC   *p 653*
130 DUFFERIN AVE SUITE 204, LONDON, ON, N6A 5R2
(519) 675-1415   *SIC 6411*

3834310 CANADA INC   *p 1077*
1051 BOUL TALBOT, CHICOUTIMI, QC, G7H 5C1
(418) 545-4474   *SIC 2711*

3834310 CANADA INC   *p 1257*
410 BOUL CHAREST E BUREAU 300, QUEBEC, QC, G1K 8G3
(418) 686-3233   *SIC 2711*

383565 ONTARIO INC   *p 719*
2660 MEADOWVALE BLVD UNIT 17, MISSISSAUGA, ON, L5N 6M6
(905) 670-8700   *SIC 3599*

3836185 CANADA INC   *p 1133*
2850 AV JACQUES-BUREAU, LAVAL, QC, H7P 0B7
(450) 688-6264   *SIC 6712*

3838731 CANADA INC   *p 1182*
6885 BOUL SAINT-LAURENT, MONTREAL, QC, H2S 3C9
(514) 284-4988   *SIC 6712*

3851401 CANADA INC   *p 373*
555 LOGAN AVE, WINNIPEG, MB, R3A 0S4
(204) 788-4249   *SIC 6712*

3855155 CANADA INC   *p 1184*
5029 AV DU PARC, MONTREAL, QC, H2V 4E9
(514) 271-8788   *SIC 5411*

3855155 CANADA INC   *p 1214*
1420 RUE DU FORT, MONTREAL, QC, H3H 2C4
   SIC 5411

3856011 CANADA INC   *p 691*
4800 EASTGATE PKY UNIT 4, MISSISSAUGA, ON, L4W 3W6
(905) 366-0800   *SIC 5193*

386140 ONTARIO LIMITED   *p 611*
191 VICTORIA AVE S, HAMILTON, ON, L8N 0A4
(905) 522-2730   *SIC 5149*

386338 ONTARIO LIMITED   *p 576*
39 POPLAR HEIGHTS DR, ETOBICOKE, ON, M9A 5A1
(416) 247-2354   *SIC 6712*

3867359 MANITOBA INC   *p 387*

584 PEMBINA HWY SUITE 204, WINNIPEG, MB, R3M 3X7
(204) 925-3840   *SIC 7538*

388010 ALBERTA LTD   *p 157*
142 LEVA AVE, RED DEER COUNTY, AB, T4E 1B9
(403) 342-2923   *SIC 5511*

3881793 MANITOBA LTD   *p 370*
2575 MAIN ST, WINNIPEG, MB, R2V 4W3
(204) 334-1211   *SIC 5411*

3885136 MANITOBA ASSOCIATION INC *p 380*
1325 ERIN ST, WINNIPEG, MB, R3E 3R6
(204) 943-4424   *SIC 8051*

3887804 CANADA INC   *p 1200*
1250 BOUL RENE-LEVESQUE O, MONTREAL, QC, H3B 4W8
(514) 845-1515   *SIC 8011*

3887952 CANADA INC   *p 1367*
440 HOLIDAY, SEPT-ILES, QC, G4R 4X6
(418) 962-1234   *SIC 1442*

389259 ONTARIO LIMITED   *p 508*
236 RUTHERFORD RD S, BRAMPTON, ON, L6W 3J6
(905) 451-6470   *SIC 5013*

389987 ALBERTA LTD   *p 136*
120 NORTH ST, HINTON, AB, T7V 1S8
(780) 865-8800   *SIC 5531*

392268 ALBERTA LTD   *p 118*
5305 ALLARD WAY NW SUITE 310, EDMONTON, AB, T6H 5X8
(780) 777-7776   *SIC 5561*

3931714 CANADA INC   *p 1380*
2215 CH COMTOIS, TERREBONNE, QC, J6X 4H4
(450) 477-1002   *SIC 6712*

393346 ALBERTA LTD   *p 165*
15 INGLEWOOD DR UNIT 2, ST. ALBERT, AB, T8N 5E2
(780) 458-7227   *SIC 5571*

3933849 CANADA INC   *p 1361*
1609 BOUL SAINT-ELZEAR O, SAINTE-ROSE, QC, H7L 3N6
(514) 744-6991   *SIC 7349*

394045 ALBERTA LTD   *p 84*
8007 127 AVE NW, EDMONTON, AB, T5C 1R9
(780) 473-6567   *SIC 5141*

3958230 CANADA INC   *p 1192*
600 BOUL DE MAISONNEUVE O BUREAU 2200, MONTREAL, QC, H3A 3J2
(450) 646-9760   *SIC 6712*

3965546 CANADA LIMITEE   *p 1224*
5995 BOUL GOUIN O BUREAU 308, MONTREAL, QC, H4J 2P8
(514) 337-7337   *SIC 7371*

399837 BC LTD   *p 212*
4823 50TH AVE S, FORT NELSON, BC, V0C 1R0
(250) 774-2791   *SIC 5411*

3B HOCKEY   *p 1314*
See INVESTISSEURS 3 B INC

3D DISTRIBUTION CANADA INC   *p 184*
5045 STILL CREEK AVE, BURNABY, BC, V5C 5V1
(604) 299-5045   *SIC 5149*

3DS THREE DIMENSIONAL SERVICES INC
p 183
2829 NORLAND AVE, BURNABY, BC, V5B 3A9
(604) 980-2450   *SIC 7389*

3ES INNOVATION INC   *p 42*
250 2 ST SW SUITE 800, CALGARY, AB, T2P 0C1
(403) 270-3270   *SIC 7371*

3GMETALWORX INC   *p 548*
90 SNOW BLVD UNIT 2, CONCORD, ON, L4K 4A2
(905) 738-7973   *SIC 3679*

3M CANADA   *p 741*
See MTI POLYFAB INC

3M CANADA COMPANY   *p 352*
400 ROUTE 100, MORDEN, MB, R6M 1Z9
(204) 822-6284   *SIC 2821*

3M CANADA COMPANY   *p 518*
1360 CALIFORNIA AVE, BROCKVILLE, ON, K6V 5V8
(613) 345-0111   *SIC 2891*

3M CANADA COMPANY   *p 518*
60 CALIFORNIA AVE, BROCKVILLE, ON, K6V 7N5
(613) 498-5900   *SIC 2672*

3M CANADA COMPANY   *p 648*
300 TARTAN DR, LONDON, ON, N5V 4M9
(519) 451-2500   *SIC 2891*

3M CANADA COMPANY   *p 682*
2751 PEDDIE RD, MILTON, ON, L9T 0K1
(905) 875-2568   *SIC 4225*

3M CANADA COMPANY   *p 839*
2 CRAIG ST, PERTH, ON, K7H 3E2
(613) 267-5300   *SIC 2672*

3MC INVESTMENTS LTD   *p 311*
1030 GEORGIA ST W SUITE 1700, VANCOUVER, BC, V6E 2Y3
(604) 602-1887   *SIC 8741*

3RETC   *p 1063*
See BAU-VAL INC

3TWENTY MODULAR   *p 1435*
See 3TWENTY SOLUTIONS INC

3TWENTY SOLUTIONS INC   *p 1435*
36 CAPITAL CIR, SASKATOON, SK, S7R 0H4
(306) 382-3320   *SIC 1542*

4

4 CORNERS PHARMACYSTEMS INC *p 900*
1935 PARIS ST SUITE 69, SUDBURY, ON, P3E 3C6
(705) 523-3730   *SIC 5912*

4 EVERGREEN RESOURCES INC.   *p 233*
1717 BOUCHER LAKE RD, MOBERLY LAKE, BC, V0C 1X0
(250) 788-7916   *SIC 1389*

4 GLACES, LES   *p 1068*
See CANLAN ICE SPORTS CORP

4 OFFICE AUTOMATION LTD   *p 736*
425 SUPERIOR BLVD UNIT 1, MISSISSAUGA, ON, L5T 2W5
(905) 564-0522   *SIC 5044*

4 ON THE FLOOR SEATING COMPANY LIMITED   *p 932*
13 POLSON ST, TORONTO, ON, M5A 1A4
(416) 466-3376   *SIC 5021*

4 SAISONS CHEVROLET OLDSMOBILE (1988)   *p 1286*
See PLACEMENTS BERIVES INC, LES

4 SEASON KING MUSHROOM LTD   *p 178*
28345 KING RD, ABBOTSFORD, BC, V4X 1C9
(604) 857-2790   *SIC 0182*

4 STAR DRYWALL (99) LTD   *p 1029*
115 SHARER RD UNIT 1, WOODBRIDGE, ON, L4L 8Z3
(905) 660-9676   *SIC 1742*

4-HOWELL BROTHERS INC   *p 718*
3030 ARTESIAN DR, MISSISSAUGA, ON, L5M 7P5
(905) 828-5926   *SIC 5541*

4-M MAINTENANCE   *p 1184*
See ENTRETIEN 4M INC

4001966 MANITOBA LTD   *p 360*
176 HAYES RD, THOMPSON, MB, R8N 1M4
(204) 677-4548   *SIC 1541*

401 AUTO DEALERS EXCHANGE   *p 629*
60 RIGNEY ST, KINGSTON, ON, K7K 6Z2
(613) 536-0401   *SIC 5012*

401 DIXIE HYUNDAI   *p 694*
See DIXIE MOTORS LP

401 DIXIE KIA   *p 690*
See 1478575 ONTARIO LIMITED

401 DIXIE NISSAN LTD   *p 691*
5500 DIXIE RD UNIT B, MISSISSAUGA, ON, L4W 4N3
(905) 238-5500   *SIC 5511*

401 DIXIE VOLKSWAGEN   *p 691*
See 2248085 ONTARIO INC

401 MACK   *p 663*

See 401 TRUCKSOURCE INC

401 PAVING LTD   *p 775*
1260 DON MILLS RD, NORTH YORK, ON, M3B 2W6
(416) 441-0401   *SIC 1611*

401 TRUCKSOURCE INC   *p 663*
4293 COUNTY RD 46, MAIDSTONE, ON, N0R 1K0
(519) 737-6956   *SIC 5511*

401919 ALBERTA LTD   *p 107*
3740 73 AVE NW, EDMONTON, AB, T6B 2Z2
(780) 440-1414   *SIC 3441*

4019636 CANADA INC   *p 1169*
3733 RUE JARRY E BUREAU A, MONTREAL, QC, H1Z 2G1
(514) 727-8919   *SIC 5141*

402424 ONTARIO LIMITED   *p 895*
257 MONTEITH AVE, STRATFORD, ON, N5A 2P6
(519) 271-4552   *SIC 6712*

402909 ALBERTA LTD   *p 118*
5834 GATEWAY BLVD NW, EDMONTON, AB, T6H 2H6
(780) 434-7471   *SIC 7532*

4048873 CANADA INC   *p 1173*
860 AV DU MONT-ROYAL E, MONTREAL, QC, H2J 1X1
(514) 523-2751   *SIC 5461*

405 AUTO SALES INC   *p 532*
227 HESPELER RD, CAMBRIDGE, ON, N1R 3H8
(519) 623-5991   *SIC 5511*

405-4547 CANADA INC   *p 1220*
6100 BOUL DECARIE, MONTREAL, QC, H3X 2J8
(514) 342-2222   *SIC 5511*

406106 ALBERTA INC   *p 180*
6741 CARIBOO RD SUITE 101, BURNABY, BC, V3N 4A3
(604) 421-5677   *SIC 5044*

406421 ALBERTA LTD   *p 155*
8133 EDGAR INDUSTRIAL CLOSE, RED DEER, AB, T4P 3R4
(403) 340-9825   *SIC 1381*

4069838 CANADA INC   *p 1235*
2750 AV JACQUES-BUREAU, MONTREAL, QC, H7P 6B3
(450) 681-0400   *SIC 5141*

407 ETR   *p 1027*
See CANADIAN TOLLING COMPANY INTERNATIONAL INC

407 ETR CONCESSION COMPANY LIMITED   *p 1026*
6300 STEELES AVE W, WOODBRIDGE, ON, L4H 1J1
(905) 265-4070   *SIC 4785*

407 INTERNATIONAL INC   *p 1026*
6300 STEELES AVE W, WOODBRIDGE, ON, L4H 1J1
(905) 265-4070   *SIC 4785*

407994 ONTARIO LIMITED   *p 885*
417 LAKESHORE RD, ST CATHARINES, ON, L2R 7K6
(905) 646-6247   *SIC 2754*

4089171 CANADA INC   *p 833*
207 BANK ST SUITE 405, OTTAWA, ON, K2P 2N2
(613) 235-2126   *SIC 1541*

4093640 CANADA INC   *p 1085*
2350 BOUL CHOMEDEY, COTE SAINT-LUC, QC, H7T 2W3
(450) 682-3336   *SIC 5511*

4093879 CANADA LTD   *p 371*
1771 INKSTER BLVD, WINNIPEG, MB, R2X 1R3
(204) 982-5783   *SIC 6712*

4094468 CANADA INC   *p 1073*
448 CH DU MONT-DES-CASCADES, CANTLEY, QC, J8V 3B2
(819) 827-0301   *SIC 7999*

4094590 CANADA INC   *p 1069*
9550 BOUL LEDUC BUREAU 15,

BROSSARD, QC, J4Y 0B3
SIC 5941

4094590 CANADA INC *p* 1278
200 RUE BOUVIER UNITE 100, QUEBEC,
QC, G2J 1R8
(418) 627-6665 *SIC* 5941

41 DIXIE SUZUKI *p* 690
See 1389984 ONTARIO INC

410648 ONTARIO LIMITED *p* 879
225 HURON RD, SEBRINGVILLE, ON, N0K
1X0
(519) 393-6194 *SIC* 4213

41068 TORONTO HYUNDAI *p* 989
2460 DUFFERIN ST, TORONTO, ON, M6E
3T3
(416) 787-9789 *SIC* 5511

411 LOCAL SEARCH CORP *p* 778
1200 EGLINTON AVE E SUITE 200,
NORTH YORK, ON, M3C 1H9
(416) 840-2566 *SIC* 8732

411.CA *p* 778
See 411 LOCAL SEARCH CORP

4113993 CANADA INC *p* 1177
555 RUE CHABANEL O BUREAU 707,
MONTREAL, QC, H2N 2H8
(514) 382-7066 *SIC* 5137

4116372 CANADA INC *p* 978
266 KING ST W SUITE 200, TORONTO,
ON, M5V 1H8
(416) 977-3238 *SIC* 6712

4117638 MANITOBA LTD *p* 346
94 PENNER DR S, BLUMENORT, MB, R0A
0C0
(204) 346-9314 *SIC* 2448

4128001 CANADA INC *p* 1237
4919 BOUL NOTRE-DAME, MONTREAL,
QC, H7W 1V3
(450) 681-4300 *SIC* 5411

4129849 CANADA INC *p* 1241
807 BOUL CURE-LABELLE, MONTREAL-
OUEST, QC, H7V 2V2
(450) 781-8800 *SIC* 6712

4131827 MANITOBA LTD *p* 369
75 MERIDIAN DR UNIT 3, WINNIPEG, MB,
R2R 2V9
(204) 786-1604 *SIC* 5074

4134320 CANADA INC *p* 1285
379 RUE ARTHUR-BUIES E, RIMOUSKI,
QC, G5M 0C7
(418) 724-5180 *SIC* 5511

4137566 CANADA LTD *p* 807
99 FIRST ST, ORANGEVILLE, ON, L9W
2E8
(519) 941-1090 *SIC* 5531

413877 ALBERTA LTD *p* 134
4703 50 AVE UNIT A, GRASSLAND, AB,
T0A 1V0
(780) 525-2295 *SIC* 5541

414067 B.C. LTD *p* 227
20622 LANGLEY BYPASS, LANGLEY, BC,
V3A 6K8
(604) 530-3156 *SIC* 5511

4145151 CANADA INC *p* 1038
489 BRACKLEY POINT RD - RTE 15,
BRACKLEY, PE, C1E 1Z3
(902) 629-1500 *SIC* 6712

415329 ALBERTA LTD *p* 145
439 5 AVE SE, MEDICINE HAT, AB, T1A
2P9
(403) 529-2600 *SIC* 6712

415841 ONTARIO LIMITED *p* 989
2000 EGLINTON AVE W, TORONTO, ON,
M6E 2J9
(416) 751-1530 *SIC* 5511

4166621 CANADA INC *p* 733
2244 DREW ROAD UNITS 4 & 5, MISSIS-
SAUGA, ON, L5S 1B1
(905) 671-2244 *SIC* 7389

416818 ALBERTA LTD *p* 86
10012 JASPER AVE NW, EDMONTON, AB,
T5J 1R2
(780) 428-1505 *SIC* 1542

417 BUS LINE LIMITED *p* 541
50 INDUSTRIAL ST, CASSELMAN, ON,

K0A 1M0
(613) 764-2192 *SIC* 4151

417 COLLISION CENTER *p* 594
1599 STAR TOP RD, GLOUCESTER, ON,
K1B 5P5
(613) 749-8382 *SIC* 5511

417 INFINITI NISSAN LTD *p* 594
1599 STAR TOP RD, GLOUCESTER, ON,
K1B 5P5
(613) 749-9417 *SIC* 5511

417 NISSAN INFINITI *p* 595
See OTWA N MOTORS LTD

4170083 CANADA INC *p* 1245
2250 RUE SAINT-JEAN, PLESSISVILLE,
QC, G6L 2Y4
(819) 362-6317 *SIC* 3553

4174071 CANADA INC *p* 1126
4905 RUE FAIRWAY, LACHINE, QC, H8T
1B7
(514) 633-7455 *SIC* 5499

4178963 CANADA INC *p* 1328
11200 BOUL CAVENDISH, SAINT-
LAURENT, QC, H4R 2J7
(514) 337-4862 *SIC* 5531

4207602 CANADA INC *p* 1192
2024 RUE PEEL BUREAU 400, MON-
TREAL, QC, H3A 1W5
(514) 881-2525 *SIC* 5136

420877 B.C. LTD *p* 264
5200 MILLER RD UNIT 2170, RICHMOND,
BC, V7B 1L1
(604) 233-1377 *SIC* 4512

421042 BC LTD *p* 331
887 FAIRWEATHER RD, VERNON, BC, V1T
8T8
(250) 542-5481 *SIC* 1731

4211596 CANADA INC *p* 63
326 11 AVE SW SUITE 500, CALGARY, AB,
T2R 0C5
(403) 262-8868 *SIC* 6411

4211677 CANADA INC *p* 1093
10315 CH COTE-DE-LIESSE, DORVAL,
QC, H9P 1A6
(514) 636-8033 *SIC* 4212

4211677 CANADA INC *p* 1274
5150 RUE JOHN-MOLSON, QUEBEC, QC,
G1X 3X4
(514) 761-2345 *SIC* 7389

421229 ONTARIO LIMITED *p* 736
7255 PACIFIC CIR, MISSISSAUGA, ON,
L5T 1V1
(905) 564-5581 *SIC* 5992

421342 ONTARIO LIMITED *p* 631
775 GARDINERS RD, KINGSTON, ON,
K7M 7H8
(613) 384-2531 *SIC* 5511

4213424 CANADA INC *p* 733
7885 TRANMERE DR UNIT 1, MISSIS-
SAUGA, ON, L5S 1V8
(905) 677-7299 *SIC* 5013

4223373 CANADA INC *p* 1311
3003 RUE PICARD, SAINT-HYACINTHE,
QC, J2S 1H2
(450) 252-4488 *SIC* 5571

4224795 CANADA INC *p* 1153
9200 RUE DESVOYAUX, MIRABEL, QC,
J7N 2H4
(450) 475-7924 *SIC* 6712

4233964 CANADA INC *p* 1331
2575 RUE PITFIELD, SAINT-LAURENT,
QC, H4S 1T2
(514) 383-4442 *SIC* 5621

4236009 MANITOBA LTD *p* 348
1445 18TH ST N SUITE 1445, BRANDON,
MB, R7C 1A6
(204) 728-8554 *SIC* 5511

4247728 CANADA INC *p* 691
1600 TOYO CIRCLE, MISSISSAUGA, ON,
L4W 0E7
(905) 238-6000 *SIC* 5511

4247744 CANADA INC *p* 691
1700 TOYO CIR, MISSISSAUGA, ON, L4W
0E7
(905) 816-4200 *SIC* 5511

425480 B.C. LTD *p* 224
9440 202 ST UNIT 117, LANGLEY, BC, V1M
4A6
(604) 882-2550 *SIC* 4213

425507 ALBERTA LTD *p* 150
100 NORTHGATE BLVD, OKOTOKS, AB,
T1S 0H9
(403) 842-1100 *SIC* 5511

425579 ALBERTA LTD *p* 72
130 BOWNESS CTR NW, CALGARY, AB,
T3B 5M5
(403) 242-1020 *SIC* 5169

4256344 CANADA INC *p* 1212
1245 RUE SHERBROOKE O BUREAU
2100, MONTREAL, QC, H3G 1G3
(877) 499-9555 *SIC* 6311

4259238 CANADA INC *p* 1346
5915 RUE BELANGER, SAINT-LEONARD,
QC, H1T 1G8
(514) 259-4216 *SIC* 5411

4259891 CANADA LTD *p* 617
2260 RYMAL RD E, HANNON, ON, L0R 1P0
(905) 528-7001 *SIC* 5511

427 AUTO COLLISION LIMITED *p* 573
395 EVANS AVE, ETOBICOKE, ON, M8Z
1K8
(416) 259-6344 *SIC* 7532

427 QEW KIA *p* 996
See 1541094 ONTARIO INC

4270797 CANADA INC *p* 1063
1270 RUE NOBEL, BOUCHERVILLE, QC,
J4B 5H1
(450) 645-0296 *SIC* 2899

4271815 CANADA INC *p* 1248
61 BOUL HYMUS, POINTE-CLAIRE, QC,
H9R 1E2
(514) 428-0848 *SIC* 5093

428675 BC LTD *p* 275
7093 KING GEORGE BLVD SUITE 401A,
SURREY, BC, V3W 5A2
(604) 590-3230 *SIC* 7999

429149 B.C. LTD *p* 180
8168 GLENWOOD DR, BURNABY, BC, V3N
5E9
(604) 549-2000 *SIC* 5719

429400 ONTARIO LTD *p* 494
6 QUEEN ST N SUITE 207, BOLTON, ON,
L7E 1C8
(905) 857-6949 *SIC* 7389

4318200 CANADA INC *p* 1377
3295 RUE JOSEPH-SIMARD, SOREL-
TRACY, QC, J3R 0E4
(450) 742-5663 *SIC* 4911

4335325 CANADA INC *p* 1241
1530 BOUL CHOMEDEY, MONTREAL-
OUEST, QC, H7V 3N8
(450) 680-1000 *SIC* 5511

4345240 CANADA INC *p* 1076
147 RUE PRINCIPALE, CHATEAUGUAY,
QC, J6K 1G2
(450) 691-1654 *SIC* 4213

434870 B.C. LTD *p* 233
262 SOUTHSIDE DR, NANAIMO, BC, V9R
6Z5
(250) 753-4135 *SIC* 2092

4355768 CANADA INC *p* 1257
410 BOUL CHAREST E BUREAU 500,
QUEBEC, QC, G1K 8G3
(418) 977-3169 *SIC* 3993

435682 ONTARIO LIMITED *p* 497
19990 11 HWY S, BRADFORD, ON, L3Z
2B6
(905) 775-6497 *SIC* 5521

435809 B.C. LTD *p* 219
2580 ENTERPRISE WAY, KELOWNA, BC,
V1X 7X5
(250) 712-0505 *SIC* 5511

4358376 CANADA INC *p* 691
400-5450 EXPLORER DR, MISSISSAUGA,
ON, L4W 5N1
(905) 238-3399 *SIC* 4724

4359241 MANITOBA INC *p* 72
1002 37 ST SW, CALGARY, AB, T3C 1S1
(403) 249-7799 *SIC* 5812

4361806 CANADA INC *p* 1147
205 RUE DU CENTRE, MAGOG, QC, J1X
5B6
(819) 843-4441 *SIC* 5072

4366492 CANADA INC *p* 1295
1360 RUE MONTARVILLE, SAINT-BRUNO,
QC, J3V 3T5
(514) 498-7777 *SIC* 6712

4372727 CANADA INC *p* 1343
9275 RUE LE ROYER, SAINT-LEONARD,
QC, H1P 3H7
(514) 328-2772 *SIC* 6712

4384768 CANADA INC *p* 985
100 KING ST W SUITE 6600, TORONTO,
ON, M5X 2A1
(905) 624-7337 *SIC* 6712

4386396 CANADA INC *p* 770
2 SHEPPARD AVE E SUITE 2000, NORTH
YORK, ON, M2N 5Y7
(416) 225-9900 *SIC* 7361

4395612 MANITOBA LTD *p* 388
1450 CORYDON AVE SUITE 2, WINNIPEG,
MB, R3N 0J3
(204) 989-5000 *SIC* 6531

4397291 CANADA INC *p* 1301
1016 BOUL ARTHUR-SAUVE, SAINT-
EUSTACHE, QC, J7R 4K3
(450) 472-6222 *SIC* 7948

440 CHEVROLET BUICK GMC LTEE *p* 1085
3670 SUD LAVAL (A-440) O, COTE SAINT-
LUC, QC, H7T 2H6
(450) 682-3670 *SIC* 5511

440 FORD LINCOLN *p* 1235
*See CHOMEDEY/DESLAURIERS FORD
LINCOLN INC*

441861 ONTARIO LTD *p* 479
8035 LINE 2 W, ARTHUR, ON, N0G 1A0
(519) 848-2575 *SIC* 4213

4423038 CANADA INC *p* 1216
9850 RUE MEILLEUR, MONTREAL, QC,
H3L 3J4
(514) 385-5568 *SIC* 6712

442527 ONTARIO LIMITED *p* 762
40 EXETER ST, NORTH BAY, ON, P1B 8G5
(705) 474-7880 *SIC* 7539

4427378 CANADA INC *p* 1074
830 BOUL DE PERIGNY, CHAMBLY, QC,
J3L 1W3
(450) 658-6623 *SIC* 5511

443696 B.C. LTD *p* 334
1856 QUADRA ST, VICTORIA, BC, V8T 4B9
(250) 384-8000 *SIC* 5047

4452241 CANADA LTD *p* 540
6019 RUSSELL RD UNIT 2, CARLSBAD
SPRINGS, ON, K0A 1K0
(613) 816-9917 *SIC* 7519

4453166 CANADA INC *p* 1328
1420 RUE BEAULAC, SAINT-LAURENT,
QC, H4R 1R7
(514) 744-5559 *SIC* 5136

4453760 CANADA INC *p* 1179
225 RUE DE LIEGE O BUREAU 200, MON-
TREAL, QC, H2P 1H4
(514) 385-3515 *SIC* 3645

446784 B.C. LTD *p* 174
2291 WEST RAILWAY ST SUITE B, AB-
BOTSFORD, BC, V2S 2E3
(604) 864-9682 *SIC* 8322

446987 ONTARIO INC *p* 500
3389 STEELES AVE E, BRAMPTON, ON,
L6T 5W4
(905) 494-1118 *SIC* 5712

4475470 CANADA INC *p* 131
12803 100 ST SUITE 100, GRANDE
PRAIRIE, AB, T8V 4H3
(780) 532-4488 *SIC* 5013

4475518 CANADA INC *p* 618
455 COUNTY RD 17, HAWKESBURY, ON,
K6A 3R4
(613) 632-5222 *SIC* 5511

4486404 CANADA INC *p* 1300
312 RUE DUBOIS, SAINT-EUSTACHE, QC,
J7P 4W9
(450) 623-8977 *SIC* 5511

4486404 CANADA INC.   *p 1074*
840 BOUL DE PERIGNY, CHAMBLY, QC, J3L 1W3
(450) 447-6699   *SIC* 5511

4488601 CANADA INC   *p 1261*
120 RUE DU MARAIS, QUEBEC, QC, G1M 3G2
(418) 683-6565   *SIC* 5012

4489161 CANADA INC   *p 1131*
400 RUE LOUIS-FORTIER BUREAU 100A, LASALLE, QC, H8R 0A8
(514) 370-8000   *SIC* 8361

4498411 MANITOBA LTD   *p 358*
GD, STEINBACH, MB, R5G 1L8
(204) 326-4653   *SIC* 7992

4499034 CANADA INC   *p 278*
19275 25 AVE, SURREY, BC, V3Z 3X1
(604) 542-4773   *SIC* 5063

45 DRIVES   *p 467*
See PROTOCASE INCORPORATED

4501403 CANADA INC   *p 1246*
3478 32E AV, POINTE-AUX-TREMBLES, QC, H1A 3M1
(514) 498-7227   *SIC* 5411

4501403 CANADA INC   *p 1248*
230 BOUL HYMUS, POINTE-CLAIRE, QC, H9R 5P5
(514) 694-3747   *SIC* 5411

450252 ONTARIO LTD   *p 879*
95 MAIN ST S, SEAFORTH, ON, N0K 1W0
(519) 527-1631   *SIC* 5411

4507525 CANADA INC   *p 1343*
8755 BOUL LANGELIER, SAINT-LEONARD, QC, H1P 2C6
(514) 356-0677   *SIC* 5712

4513380 CANADA INC   *p 42*
450 1 ST SW SUITE 2500, CALGARY, AB, T2P 5H1
SIC 6712

4513380 CANADA INC   *p 686*
6725 AIRPORT RD SUITE 400, MISSISSAUGA, ON, L4V 1V2
(905) 676-3700   *SIC* 4731

4513380 CANADA INC   *p 686*
6725 AIRPORT RD UNIT 500, MISSISSAUGA, ON, L4V 1V2
(905) 676-3700   *SIC* 4731

4520556 CANADA INC   *p 1337*
180 MONTEE DE LIESSE, SAINT-LAURENT, QC, H4T 1N7
(514) 904-1216   *SIC* 7349

452056 ONTARIO LTD   *p 618*
3191 COUNTY ROAD 11, HARROW, ON, N0R 1G0
(519) 738-6885   *SIC* 4213

4525663 CANADA INC   *p 1060*
87 RUE PREVOST, BOISBRIAND, QC, J7G 3A1
(450) 437-7182   *SIC* 2013

4542410 CANADA INC   *p 1261*
550 AV GODIN, QUEBEC, QC, G1M 2K2
(418) 687-5320   *SIC* 5441

4544391 CANADA INC   *p 1104*
1299 BOUL LA VERENDRYE O, GATINEAU, QC, J8T 8K2
(819) 243-5454   *SIC* 5511

4549440 MANITOBA LTD   *p 393*
99 SCURFIELD BLVD UNIT 100, WINNIPEG, MB, R3Y 1Y1
(204) 954-7620   *SIC* 6162

4577 NUNAVUT LIMITED   *p 748*
69 JAMIE AVE, NEPEAN, ON, K2E 7Y6
SIC 5039

458890 B.C. LTD   *p 211*
101 TRANS CANADA HWY, DUNCAN, BC, V9L 3P8
(250) 748-5151   *SIC* 5812

459324 ONTARIO INC   *p 850*
40 EAST PEARCE ST, RICHMOND HILL, ON, L4B 1B7
(905) 764-9533   *SIC* 8741

45TH STREET LIMITED PARTNERSHIP   *p 1431*
701 45TH ST W, SASKATOON, SK, S7L 5W5
(306) 934-0600   *SIC* 5039

462388 BC LTD   *p 311*
1095 PENDER ST W SUITE 1000, VANCOUVER, BC, V6E 2M6
(604) 662-3838   *SIC* 6531

462673 ONTARIO INC   *p 567*
3315 67 HWY, EARLTON, ON, P0J 1E0
(705) 563-2656   *SIC* 3441

464161 ALBERTA LTD   *p 107*
4520 76 AVE NW, EDMONTON, AB, T6B 0A5
(780) 468-5400   *SIC* 7011

464290 ONTARIO LIMITED   *p 548*
3300 STEELES AVE W SUITE 202, CONCORD, ON, L4K 2Y4
(416) 445-1999   *SIC* 4111

465439 ONTARIO INC   *p 530*
1200 PLAINS RD E, BURLINGTON, ON, L7S 1W6
(905) 632-8010   *SIC* 4214

465912 ONTARIO INC   *p 760*
343 AIRPORT RD, NIAGARA ON THE LAKE, ON, L0S 1J0
(905) 682-1711   *SIC* 5511

4659555 MANITOBA LTD   *p 374*
328 KING ST SUITE A, WINNIPEG, MB, R3B 3H4
(204) 989-5820   *SIC* 7361

4665181 MANITOBA LTD   *p 390*
2855 PEMBINA HWY SUITE 35, WINNIPEG, MB, R3T 2H5
(800) 710-2713   *SIC* 8732

467935 ALBERTA LTD   *p 131*
11633 CLAIRMONT RD, GRANDE PRAIRIE, AB, T8V 3Y4
(780) 532-5221   *SIC* 7011

469006 ONTARIO INC   *p 648*
163 STRONACH CRES, LONDON, ON, N5V 3G5
(519) 679-8810   *SIC* 7349

4695900 MANITOBA LTD   *p 386*
3777 PORTAGE AVE, WINNIPEG, MB, R3K 0X6
(204) 895-3777   *SIC* 5521

470695 BC LTD   *p 252*
2712 ISLAND HWY W, QUALICUM BEACH, BC, V9K 2C4
(250) 752-3111   *SIC* 5541

470858 ALBERTA LTD   *p 112*
5674 75 ST NW, EDMONTON, AB, T6E 5X6
(780) 485-9905   *SIC* 7549

473464 ONTARIO LIMITED   *p 548*
380 SPINNAKER WAY, CONCORD, ON, L4K 4W1
(905) 669-6464   *SIC* 4783

473980 ONTARIO LTD   *p 812*
485 WATERLOO CRT, OSHAWA, ON, L1H 3X2
(905) 433-1392   *SIC* 4151

476982 BRITISH COLUMBIA LTD   *p 1013*
75 CONSUMERS DR, WHITBY, ON, L1N 9S2
SIC 5812

477281 ONTARIO LTD   *p 485*
140 CUNDLES RD W, BARRIE, ON, L4N 9X8
SIC 8051

480412 B.C. LTD   *p 294*
645 MALKIN AVE, VANCOUVER, BC, V6A 3V7
(604) 255-6684   *SIC* 5148

4834772 MANITOBA LTD   *p 387*
600 PEMBINA HWY, WINNIPEG, MB, R3M 2M5
SIC 6712

483696 ALBERTA LTD   *p 112*
7921 CORONET RD NW, EDMONTON, AB, T6E 4N7
SIC 5812

488491 ONTARIO INC   *p 807*
355 BROADWAY SUITE 1, ORANGEVILLE, ON, L9W 3Y3
(519) 941-5161   *SIC* 6513

489425 ALBERTA LTD   *p 20*
1204 EDMONTON TRAIL NE UNIT 1, CALGARY, AB, T2E 3K5
(403) 276-5156   *SIC* 5191

49 NORTH MECHANICAL LTD   *p 324*
3641 29TH AVE W SUITE 201, VANCOUVER, BC, V6S 1T5
(604) 224-7604   *SIC* 1711

492632 BC LTD   *p 341*
1412 SANDHURST PL, WEST VANCOUVER, BC, V7S 2P3
(604) 451-1600   *SIC* 4725

498326 ONTARIO LIMITED   *p 920*
677 QUEEN ST E, TORONTO, ON, M4M 1G6
(416) 465-5471   *SIC* 5511

49TH PARALLEL GROCERY   *p 224*
See 49TH PARALLEL GROCERY LIMITED

49TH PARALLEL GROCERY LIMITED   *p 224*
1020 1ST AVE, LADYSMITH, BC, V9G 1A5
(250) 245-3221   *SIC* 5411

4L COMMUNICATIONS INC   *p 361*
1555 REGENT AVE W SUITE T58, WINNIPEG, MB, R2C 4J2
(204) 927-6363   *SIC* 5999

4REFUEL CANADA LP   *p 224*
9440 202 ST SUITE 215, LANGLEY, BC, V1M 4A6
(604) 513-0386   *SIC* 5172

4TH & BURRARD ESSO SERVICE   *p 320*
1790 4TH AVE W, VANCOUVER, BC, V6J 1M1
SIC 5541

4TRACKS LTD   *p 356*
374 EAGLE DR, ROSSER, MB, R0H 1E0
SIC 4212

5

5 D INFORMATION MANAGEMENT   *p 89*
See HAEMONETICS CANADA LTD

5 MILLION ADVANTAGE   *p 668*
See COMPAGNIE D'ASSURANCE HABITATION ET AUTO TD

5 SAISONS INC   *p 1401*
1250 AV GREENE, WESTMOUNT, QC, H3Z 2A3
(514) 931-0249   *SIC* 5149

5 STAR DEALERS   *p 650*
See 5 STAR DEALERS INC

5 STAR DEALERS INC   *p 650*
1500 DUNDAS ST, LONDON, ON, N5W 3B9
(519) 455-4227   *SIC* 5521

500 PLANCHERS DESIGN   *p 1149*
See 9240-9770 QUEBEC INC

500 STAFFING INC, THE   *p 991*
67 MOWAT AVE SUITE 411, TORONTO, ON, M6K 3E3
SIC 7361

500323 (N.B.) LTD   *p 412*
60 GRANDVIEW AVE, SAINT JOHN, NB, E2J 4N1
(506) 642-6683   *SIC* 4225

500PX, INC   *p 948*
20 DUNCAN ST UNIT 100, TORONTO, ON, M5H 3G8
(647) 465-1033   *SIC* 4813

501420 NB INC   *p 413*
71 PARADISE ROW, SAINT JOHN, NB, E2K 3H6
(506) 644-8095   *SIC* 6531

501479 NB LTD   *p 406*
48 BONACCORD ST, MONCTON, NB, E1C 5K7
(506) 857-0000   *SIC* 5736

501548 ONTARIO LTD   *p 830*
955 RICHMOND RD, OTTAWA, ON, K2B 6R1
(613) 726-0333   *SIC* 5511

502386 ALBERTA LTD   *p 10*
888 MERIDIAN RD NE, CALGARY, AB, T2A 2N8
(403) 291-1444   *SIC* 5511

504147 ALBERTA LTD   *p 33*
34 HERITAGE MEADOWS RD SE, CALGARY, AB, T2H 3C1
(403) 253-0338   *SIC* 5511

504148 ALBERTA INC   *p 38*
11700 LAKE FRASER DR SE, CALGARY, AB, T2J 7J5
(403) 253-6531   *SIC* 5511

5043680 MANITOBA INC   *p 360*
17 SELKIRK AVE SUITE 549, THOMPSON, MB, R8N 0M5
(204) 778-8391   *SIC* 5912

506165 ONTARIO LIMITED   *p 637*
50 STECKLE PL, KITCHENER, ON, N2E 2C3
(519) 748-5295   *SIC* 3469

509334 ONTARIO INC   *p 861*
1141 LAKESHORE RD, SARNIA, ON, N7V 2V5
(519) 542-1241   *SIC* 5431

510127 ONTARIO INC   *p 861*
219 TRUNK RD, SAULT STE. MARIE, ON, P6A 3S7
(705) 254-7466   *SIC* 5411

510172 ONTARIO LTD   *p 898*
100 FOUNDRY ST, SUDBURY, ON, P3A 4R7
(705) 674-5626   *SIC* 3743

511670 ALBERTA LTD   *p 112*
4220 98 ST NW SUITE 201, EDMONTON, AB, T6E 6A1
(780) 466-1262   *SIC* 1542

511670 ALBERTA LTD   *p 1419*
845 BROAD ST SUITE 205, REGINA, SK, S4R 8G9
(306) 525-1644   *SIC* 1542

5126614 MANITOBA INC   *p 380*
857 SARGENT AVE UNIT 2, WINNIPEG, MB, R3E 0C5
(204) 772-4135   *SIC* 7381

512844 ALBERTA LTD   *p 142*
3939 1 AVE S, LETHBRIDGE, AB, T1J 4P8
(403) 327-1333   *SIC* 6712

5177007 MANITOBA LTD   *p 364*
24 TERRACON PL SUITE 467, WINNIPEG, MB, R2J 4G7
(204) 654-5194   *SIC* 5961

518162 ALBERTA INC   *p 98*
11104 180 ST NW, EDMONTON, AB, T5S 2X5
(780) 452-7410   *SIC* 5033

5195684 MANITOBA LTD   *p 392*
3357 PEMBINA HWY, WINNIPEG, MB, R3V 1A2
(204) 261-3014   *SIC* 5541

519728 ONTARIO LTD   *p 839*
38 LANARK RD, PERTH, ON, K7H 3C9
(613) 267-5880   *SIC* 5085

526293 BC LTD   *p 195*
1502 COLUMBIA AVE UNIT 1, CASTLEGAR, BC, V1N 4G5
(250) 304-2470   *SIC* 5411

5274398 MANITOBA LTD   *p 352*
418 SOUTH RAILWAY ST SUITE 2, MORDEN, MB, R6M 2G2
(204) 822-9509   *SIC* 3715

527758 B.C. LTD   *p 343*
14995 MARINE DR SUITE 6, WHITE ROCK, BC, V4B 1C3
SIC 5921

530664 ALBERTA LTD   *p 131*
13116 100 ST SUITE 780, GRANDE PRAIRIE, AB, T8V 4H9
(780) 532-8010   *SIC* 5511

531442 ONTARIO INC   *p 591*
1031 HELENA ST, FORT ERIE, ON, L2A 4K3
(905) 871-3358   *SIC* 4731

532551 ONTARIO INC   *p 485*
39 ANNE ST S, BARRIE, ON, L4N 2C7
(705) 726-1444   *SIC* 6712

533438 ONTARIO LIMITED   *p 589*
165 THAMES RD W SS 3 SUITE 83, EXETER, ON, N0M 1S3
(519) 235-1530   *SIC* 2451

534422 B.C. LTD   *p 286*

▲ Public Company   ■ Public Company Family Member   **HQ** Headquarters   **BR** Branch   **SL** Single Location

1988 KOOTENAY ST, VANCOUVER, BC, V5M 4Y3

(604) 294-2629　*SIC* 0742

539290 ONTARIO LTD　*p 907*
940 COBALT CRES, THUNDER BAY, ON, P7B 5W3

(807) 346-9399　*SIC* 5561

540731 ONTARIO LIMITED　*p 736*
7105 PACIFIC CIR, MISSISSAUGA, ON, L5T 2A8

(905) 564-5620　*SIC* 1721

540806 BC LTD　*p 296*
475 GEORGIA ST W SUITE 800, VANCOUVER, BC, V6B 4M9

(604) 684-7117　*SIC* 6719

541823 BC LTD　*p 294*
51 PENDER ST E, VANCOUVER, BC, V6A 1S9

(604) 682-2088　*SIC* 6531

541907 ONTARIO LIMITED　*p 935*
30 CARLTON ST SUITE 1, TORONTO, ON, M5B 2E9

(416) 977-6655　*SIC* 7011

542144 ONTARIO LTD　*p 760*
1695 NIAGARA STONE RD, NIAGARA ON THE LAKE, ON, L0S 1J0

(905) 468-3217　*SIC* 5193

543077 ALBERTA LTD　*p 124*
305 116 AVE NW, EDMONTON, AB, T6S 1G3

(780) 440-2121　*SIC* 5032

546073 ONTARIO LIMITED　*p 919*
348 DANFORTH AVE SUITE 8, TORONTO, ON, M4K 1N8

(416) 466-2129　*SIC* 5499

5465461 MANITOBA INC　*p 362*
28 CHRISTOPHER ST, WINNIPEG, MB, R2C 2Z2

(204) 989-7696　*SIC* 5153

547121 ONTARIO LTD　*p 496*
380 ECCLESTONE DR, BRACEBRIDGE, ON, P1L 1R1

(705) 645-8763　*SIC* 5511

548050 ONTARIO INC　*p 631*
1388 BATH RD, KINGSTON, ON, K7M 4X6

(613) 546-2211　*SIC* 5511

550338 ALBERTA LIMITED　*p 20*
3530 11A ST NE SUITE 1, CALGARY, AB, T2E 6M7

(403) 250-7878　*SIC* 7349

551546 ALBERTA LTD　*p 151*
6207 46 ST, OLDS, AB, T4H 1L7

(403) 556-7332　*SIC* 5511

5517509 MANITOBA LTD　*p 346*
1329 ROSSER AVE E, BRANDON, MB, R7A 7J2

(204) 728-7540　*SIC* 5261

552653 ONTARIO INC　*p 1036*
580 BRUIN BLVD, WOODSTOCK, ON, N4V 1E5

(519) 537-5586　*SIC* 7011

553032 ONTARIO INC　*p 716*
4120 RIDGEWAY DR UNIT 28, MISSISSAUGA, ON, L5L 5S9

(905) 607-8200　*SIC* 6712

553562 ONTARIO INC　*p 640*
7 GRAND AVE, KITCHENER, ON, N2K 1B2

(519) 744-3597　*SIC* 4213

561028 ONTARIO LIMITED　*p 829*
890 BOYD AVE, OTTAWA, ON, K2A 2E3

(613) 798-8020　*SIC* 6712

561861 ONTARIO LTD　*p 569*
1482 ST JACQUES RD, EMBRUN, ON, K0A 1W0

(613) 443-2311　*SIC* 1794

563737 SASKATCHEWAN LTD　*p 1423*
3502 TAYLOR ST E SUITE 103, SASKATOON, SK, S7H 5H9

(306) 955-1330　*SIC* 6331

563769 B.C. LTD　*p 214*
1900 GARIBALDI WAY, GARIBALDI HIGHLANDS, BC, V0N 1T0

(604) 898-6810　*SIC* 5411

564205 ONTARIO INC　*p 839*

1370 CHEMONG RD, PETERBOROUGH, ON, K9H 0E7

(705) 876-6591　*SIC* 5511

564242 ONTARIO LIMITED　*p 840*
728 RYE ST, PETERBOROUGH, ON, K9J 6W9

(705) 745-1666　*SIC* 4141

564549 ALBERTA LTD　*p 220*
1865 DILWORTH DR SUITE 335, KELOWNA, BC, V1Y 9T1

(250) 215-1143　*SIC* 6712

564967 ALBERTA LTD　*p 95*
11703 160 ST NW, EDMONTON, AB, T5M 3Z3

(780) 451-0060　*SIC* 6712

566735 ONTARIO INC　*p 567*
GD LCD MAIN, DUNNVILLE, ON, N1A 2W9

(905) 774-5900　*SIC* 5147

567945 ALBERTA LTD　*p 4*
116 EAGLE CRES, BANFF, AB, T1L 1A3

(403) 762-3287　*SIC* 1731

569398 ALBERTA LTD　*p 98*
17311 103 AVE NW UNIT 100, EDMONTON, AB, T5S 1J4

(780) 454-5864　*SIC* 5065

570026 ONTARIO LIMITED　*p 994*
26 ERNEST AVE, TORONTO, ON, M6P 3M7

(416) 531-1131　*SIC* 5051

570230 ONTARIO INC　*p 656*
387 WELLINGTON RD, LONDON, ON, N6C 4P9

(519) 680-1830　*SIC* 5812

573349 ONTARIO LIMITED　*p 573*
121 SHORNCLIFFE RD, ETOBICOKE, ON, M8Z 5K7

(416) 234-2290　*SIC* 5147

574852 ALBERTA LIMITED　*p 20*
2202 CENTRE ST NE, CALGARY, AB, T2E 2T5

(403) 277-9166　*SIC* 5411

575636 ONTARIO LIMITED　*p 498*
1 LASCELLES BLVD, BRAMPTON, ON, L6S 3T1

SIC 4731

576195 ONTARIO LIMITED　*p 792*
500 BARMAC DR SUITE 2, NORTH YORK, ON, M9L 2X8

(416) 789-1477　*SIC* 5137

576794 ONTARIO LTD　*p 978*
69 SPADINA AVE, TORONTO, ON, M5V 3P8

(416) 979-8155　*SIC* 5411

577793 ONTARIO INC　*p 758*
6455 FALLSVIEW BLVD, NIAGARA FALLS, ON, L2G 3V9

(905) 357-1151　*SIC* 7011

581917 ONTARIO INC　*p 906*
1108 BEAVER DAM RD, THOROLD, ON, L2V 3Y7

(905) 227-4118　*SIC* 5531

581976 SASKATCHEWAN LTD　*p 1409*
802 1ST ST W, MEADOW LAKE, SK, S9X 1E2

(306) 236-4467　*SIC* 5211

582219 ONTARIO LTD　*p 948*
214 KING ST W SUITE 508, TORONTO, ON, M5H 3S6

(416) 340-9710　*SIC* 8741

583455 SASKATCHEWAN LTD　*p 1419*
700 BROAD ST, REGINA, SK, S4R 8H7

(306) 522-2222　*SIC* 5511

586307 ALBERTA LTD　*p 74*
7422 CROWFOOT RD NW UNIT 201, CALGARY, AB, T3G 3N7

(403) 296-2200　*SIC* 5921

587577 ALBERTA LIMITED　*p 72*
909 15 ST SW, CALGARY, AB, T3C 1E5

(403) 232-6400　*SIC* 5511

588388 ALBERTA LTD　*p 40*
4849 NORTHLAND DR NW, CALGARY, AB, T2L 2K3

(403) 286-4849　*SIC* 5511

591182 ONTARIO LIMITED　*p 1019*

2500 AIRPORT RD, WINDSOR, ON, N8W 5E7

(519) 966-8970　*SIC* 4212

591226 SASKATCHEWAN LTD　*p 1425*
110A CIRCLE DR E, SASKATOON, SK, S7K 4K1

(306) 373-7477　*SIC* 5511

593130 BC LTD　*p 283*
1200 SECOND AVE, TRAIL, BC, V1R 1L6

(250) 364-2253　*SIC* 1731

593631 ONTARIO LIMITED　*p 788*
3522 BATHURST ST, NORTH YORK, ON, M6A 2C6

SIC 5461

594827 SASKATCHEWAN LTD　*p 1431*
715 46TH ST W SUITE E, SASKATOON, SK, S7L 6A1

(306) 249-3515　*SIC* 4731

595028 ALBERTA LTD　*p 85*
11825 105 AVE NW, EDMONTON, AB, T5H 0L9

(780) 421-7361　*SIC* 5621

595140 ALBERTA LTD　*p 107*
5219 47 ST NW, EDMONTON, AB, T6B 3N4

(780) 444-7766　*SIC* 6712

595799 ONTARIO LTD　*p 833*
180 MACLAREN ST SUITE 1112, OTTAWA, ON, K2P 0L3

(613) 232-1121　*SIC* 6719

596042 ONTARIO LIMITED　*p 711*
720 BURNHAMTHORPE RD W UNIT 28, MISSISSAUGA, ON, L5C 3G1

(905) 270-9840　*SIC* 5149

598468 SASKATCHEWAN LTD　*p 1431*
806 IDYLWYLD DR N, SASKATOON, SK, S7L 0Z6

(306) 665-6500　*SIC* 7011

598755 B.C. LTD　*p 227*
20257 LANGLEY BYPASS, LANGLEY, BC, V3A 6K9

(604) 539-2111　*SIC* 5511

598840 SASKATCHEWAN LTD　*p 1411*
1788 MAIN ST N, MOOSE JAW, SK, S6J 1L4

(306) 692-1808　*SIC* 5511

599515 ALBERTA LTD　*p 66*
730 17 AVE SW, CALGARY, AB, T2S 0B7

(403) 228-3566　*SIC* 5813

599681 SASKATCHEWAN LTD　*p 1417*
HWY 1 E, REGINA, SK, S4P 3R8

(306) 791-7777　*SIC* 5084

5BLUE PROCESS EQUIPMENT INC　*p 148*
2303 8 ST, NISKU, AB, T9E 7Z3

(780) 955-2040　*SIC* 5085

5CROWD　*p 576*
See SOUTHERN GRAPHIC SYSTEMS-CANADA LTD

5N PLUS INC　*p 1328*
4385 RUE GARAND, SAINT-LAURENT, QC, H4R 2B4

(514) 856-0644　*SIC* 3339

6

6 MILE BAKERY & DELI LTD　*p 338*
3950 CAREY RD, VICTORIA, BC, V8Z 4E2

(250) 727-7737　*SIC* 5149

600038 SASKATCHEWAN LTD　*p 350*
557 SOUTH HUDSON ST, FLIN FLON, MB, R8A 1E1

(306) 688-3426　*SIC* 5411

600956 ONTARIO LTD　*p 609*
469 WOODWARD AVE, HAMILTON, ON, L8H 6N6

(905) 549-4572　*SIC* 3089

601092 ONTARIO LIMITED　*p 972*
914 BATHURST ST, TORONTO, ON, M5R 3G5

(416) 533-9473　*SIC* 8051

601712 ONTARIO INC　*p 978*
315 ADELAIDE ST W, TORONTO, ON, M5V 1P8

(416) 977-2603　*SIC* 6712

601861 SASKATCHEWAN LTD　*p 1425*
855 60TH ST E, SASKATOON, SK, S7K 5Z7

(306) 934-3383　*SIC* 4213

602390 ONTARIO LIMITED　*p 873*
81 SCOTTFIELD DR, SCARBOROUGH, ON, M1S 5R4

(416) 740-9000　*SIC* 5146

602667 ONTARIO LTD　*p 526*
4551 PALLADIUM WAY, BURLINGTON, ON, L7M 0W9

(905) 335-9951　*SIC* 5139

602726 ONTARIO LTD　*p 919*
623 DANFORTH AVE, TORONTO, ON, M4K 1R2

(416) 466-5371　*SIC* 5411

6036945 CANADA INC　*p 1401*
4150 RUE SHERBROOKE O BUREAU 400, WESTMOUNT, QC, H3Z 1C2

(514) 989-9909　*SIC* 6531

6038263 CANADA INC　*p 1185*
3575 AV DU PARC, MONTREAL, QC, H2X 3P9

(514) 288-8221　*SIC* 8699

604329 SASKATCHEWAN LTD　*p 1420*
444 BROAD ST, REGINA, SK, S4R 1X3

(306) 525-8848　*SIC* 5511

605494 ALBERTA LTD　*p 104*
15462 131 AVE NW, EDMONTON, AB, T5V 0A1

(780) 454-4321　*SIC* 5112

6074961 CANADA INC　*p 748*
20 GURDWARA RD UNIT 16, NEPEAN, ON, K2E 8B3

(613) 225-5500　*SIC* 1799

607637 SASKATCHEWAN LTD　*p 1417*
1818 VICTORIA AVE, REGINA, SK, S4P 0R1

(306) 569-1666　*SIC* 7011

6089585 CANADA LTD　*p 364*
500 CAMIEL SYS ST, WINNIPEG, MB, R2J 4K2

(204) 663-2866　*SIC* 1542

6091636 CANADA INC　*p 1226*
4700 RUE DE LA SAVANE BUREAU 310, MONTREAL, QC, H4P 1T7

(514) 448-6931　*SIC* 7389

609173 N.B. LTD　*p 402*
1165 HANWELL RD, FREDERICTON, NB, E3C 1A5

(506) 450-0800　*SIC* 5511

6094376 CANADA INC　*p 162*
117 PEMBINA RD SUITE 109, SHERWOOD PARK, AB, T8H 0J4

(780) 467-4118　*SIC* 3679

609574 ONTARIO LIMITED　*p 691*
2395 SKYMARK AVE, MISSISSAUGA, ON, L4W 4Y6

(905) 629-8999　*SIC* 6719

609905 SASKATCHEWAN LTD　*p 1408*
30 HIGHWAY 3, KINISTINO, SK, S0J 1H0

(306) 864-2200　*SIC* 5083

611421 ONTARIO INC.　*p 762*
119 PROGRESS CRT, NORTH BAY, ON, P1A 0C1

(705) 476-4222　*SIC* 3799

6119701 MANITOBA LTD　*p 380*
1574 ERIN ST, WINNIPEG, MB, R3E 2T1

(204) 255-5005　*SIC* 1521

612031-376964 ONTARIO LTD　*p 859*
1275 PLANK RD, SARNIA, ON, N7T 7H3

(519) 344-5532　*SIC* 5051

612111 NB LTD　*p 402*
505 BISHOP DR, FREDERICTON, NB, E3C 2M6

(506) 454-3634　*SIC* 5511

612337 ALBERTA LTD.　*p 140*
3042 2 AVE N, LETHBRIDGE, AB, T1H 0C6

(403) 328-9621　*SIC* 5013

6131646 CANADA INC　*p 548*
120 INTERCHANGE WAY, CONCORD, ON, L4K 5C3

(905) 760-7600　*SIC* 5812

6132511 CANADA INC　*p 1405*
GD, DAVIDSON, SK, S0G 1A0

(306) 567-3222　*SIC* 5541

6138144 CANADA LTEE　*p 1315*

60 RUE DES GEAIS-BLEUS, SAINT-JEAN-SUR-RICHELIEU, QC, J2W 3E5
SIC 1521

61401 MANITOBA LTD *p 370*
1650 MAIN ST, WINNIPEG, MB, R2V 1Y9
(204) 339-0213 *SIC* 5411

614128 ONTARIO LTD *p 879*
5878 HIGHWAY 9, SCHOMBERG, ON, L0G 1T0
(416) 410-3839 *SIC* 1611

6142974 CANADA INC *p 927*
175 BLOOR ST E SUITE 606, TORONTO, ON, M4W 3R8
(416) 934-1436 *SIC* 6282

6143580 CANADA INC. *p 1257*
10 RUE SAINT-ANTOINE, QUEBEC, QC, G1K 4C9
(418) 692-1022 *SIC* 5812

614568 ALBERTA LTD *p 10*
1100 MERIDIAN RD NE, CALGARY, AB, T2A 2N9
(403) 571-3077 *SIC* 5511

615315 SASKATCHEWAN LTD *p 1425*
875 58TH ST E, SASKATOON, SK, S7K 6X5
(306) 653-5400 *SIC* 4213

615317 NB INC *p 395*
891 ROUTE 880, BERWICK, NB, E5P 3H5
(506) 433-6168 *SIC* 5193

616536 B.C. LTD *p 331*
4601 27 ST, VERNON, BC, V1T 4Y8
(250) 545-5384 *SIC* 5211

616813 N.B. LTD *p 412*
1350 HICKEY RD, SAINT JOHN, NB, E2J 5C9
(506) 657-8463 *SIC* 5411

617274 SASKATCHEWAN LTD *p 1411*
1743 MAIN ST N, MOOSE JAW, SK, S6J 1L6
(306) 694-1355 *SIC* 5511

617885 ONTARIO LTD *p 858*
1581 COUNTY ROAD 34, RUTHVEN, ON, N0P 2G0
(519) 326-4907 *SIC* 0182

618382 ALBERTA LTD *p 135*
102 24 ST SE, HIGH RIVER, AB, T1V 0B3
(403) 652-3171 *SIC* 5561

618717 ONTARIO INC *p 762*
348 BIRCHS RD, NORTH BAY, ON, P1A 4A9
(705) 476-4411 *SIC* 4213

619020 SASKATCHEWAN LTD *p 1415*
HWY 6 N, RAYMORE, SK, S0A 3J0
(306) 746-2911 *SIC* 5999

619249 ALBERTA LTD *p 108*
4143 78 AVE NW, EDMONTON, AB, T6B 2N3
(780) 469-7799 *SIC* 7623

620126 ALBERTA LTD *p 108*
6803 72 AVE NW, EDMONTON, AB, T6B 3A5
(780) 465-3499 *SIC* 5145

620205 ALBERTA LIMITED *p 8*
4321 84 ST NE, CALGARY, AB, T1Y 7H3
(403) 777-9393 *SIC* 7389

6202667 CANADA INC *p 1324*
3535 CH DE LA COTE-DE-LIESSE, SAINT-LAURENT, QC, H4N 2N5
(514) 356-7777 *SIC* 6712

621189 ONTARIO INC *p 485*
85 ELLIS DR, BARRIE, ON, L4N 8Z3
(705) 739-1551 *SIC* 4213

621509 ONTARIO INC *p 490*
658 DUNDAS ST W, BELLEVILLE, ON, K8N 4Z2
(613) 966-9936 *SIC* 5511

6232698 CANADA INC *p 581*
397 HUMBERLINE DR UNIT 1, ETOBI-COKE, ON, M9W 5T5
(416) 213-0088 *SIC* 7389

625056 SASKATCHEWAN LTD *p 369*
1050 KEEWATIN ST, WINNIPEG, MB, R2R 2E2
(204) 694-0085 *SIC* 5411

6257 AIRPORT TORONTO HOSPITALITY

INC *p 686*
6257 AIRPORT RD, MISSISSAUGA, ON, L4V 1E4
(905) 678-1400 *SIC* 7011

625974 SASKATCHEWAN LTD *p 1431*
2035 IDYLWYLD DR N, SASKATOON, SK, S7L 4R3
(306) 664-6767 *SIC* 5511

629112 SASKATCHEWAN LTD *p 1425*
366 3RD AVE S, SASKATOON, SK, S7K 1M5
(306) 244-1975 *SIC* 4832

629728 ONTARIO LIMITED *p 858*
1271 LOUGAR AVE, SARNIA, ON, N7S 5N5
(519) 332-0430 *SIC* 5162

6304966 CANADA INC *p 1085*
3475 BOUL LE CARREFOUR, COTE SAINT-LUC, QC, H7T 3A3
(450) 688-1880 *SIC* 5511

6318703 CANADA INC *p 1150*
1460 RUE DE MATANE-SUR-MER, MATANE, QC, G4W 3M6
(418) 562-0911 *SIC* 3731

633569 ONTARIO LIMITED *p 906*
206 RICHMOND ST, THOROLD, ON, L2V 4L8
(905) 227-1575 *SIC* 5141

6356036 CANADA INC *p 1325*
590 RUE HODGE, SAINT-LAURENT, QC, H4N 2A4
(514) 389-8885 *SIC* 5137

6358101 CANADA INC *p 1106*
7 BOUL DU CASINO, GATINEAU, QC, J8Y 6V7
(819) 777-1771 *SIC* 5511

636066 ALBERTA LTD *p 146*
16 STRACHAN CRT SE, MEDICINE HAT, AB, T1B 4R7
(403) 526-0626 *SIC* 5511

6362222 CANADA INC *p 1395*
1 CARREFOUR ALEXANDER-GRAHAM-BELL EDIFICE 4, VERDUN, QC, H3E 3B3
(514) 937-1188 *SIC* 7379

6368174 CANADA INC *p 1342*
6165 RUE DESSUREAUX, SAINT-LAURENT, QC, H7B 1B1
(450) 968-0880 *SIC* 6712

6368425 CANADA LTD *p 1104*
47 RUE LE BARON, GATINEAU, QC, J8T 4C3
SIC 5051

638691 ONTARIO LIMITED *p 846*
658 MAIN ST W, PORT COLBORNE, ON, L3K 5V4
(905) 835-8120 *SIC* 5511

639809 BC LTD *p 197*
45389 LUCKAKUCK WAY UNIT 100, CHILLIWACK, BC, V2R 3V1
(604) 858-5663 *SIC* 6712

640039 BC LTD *p 292*
885 BROADWAY W SUITE 263, VANCOU-VER, BC, V5Z 1J9
(604) 708-1135 *SIC* 5912

641100 ALBERTA LTD *p 80*
544 RAILWAY ST W, COCHRANE, AB, T4C 2E2
(403) 932-4072 *SIC* 5511

6423264 CANADA INC *p 1241*
3055 BOUL NOTRE-DAME BUREAU 1700, MONTREAL-OUEST, QC, H7V 4C6
(450) 681-3055 *SIC* 8361

643487 ONTARIO LIMITED *p 1001*
1 PARRATT RD, UXBRIDGE, ON, L9P 1R1
(905) 862-0830 *SIC* 3086

645373 ALBERTA LTD *p 151*
6307 46 ST, OLDS, AB, T4H 1L7
(403) 556-2550 *SIC* 5251

646371 B.C. LTD *p 216*
1355 CARIBOO PL, KAMLOOPS, BC, V2C 5Z3
(250) 828-7966 *SIC* 5511

647802 ONTARIO LIMITED *p 757*
4199 RIVER RD, NIAGARA FALLS, ON, L2E 3E7

(905) 357-1133 *SIC* 5947

6482066 CANADA INC *p 1121*
905 RUE DE L'INNOVATION, LA BAIE, QC, G7B 3N8
(418) 677-3939 *SIC* 3354

648781 ALBERTA LTD *p 98*
17109 109 AVE NW, EDMONTON, AB, T5S 2H8
(780) 481-7800 *SIC* 5712

650124 ONTARIO LIMITED *p 485*
261 MAPLEVIEW DR W, BARRIE, ON, L4N 9E8
(705) 737-3440 *SIC* 5511

651233 ONTARIO INC *p 616*
630 STONE CHURCH RD W, HAMILTON, ON, L9B 1A7
(905) 389-3487 *SIC* 5461

653457 B.C. LTD *p 211*
1215C 56 ST UNIT C, DELTA, BC, V4L 2A6
(604) 943-1144 *SIC* 5912

6535577 CANADA INC *p 1282*
47 RUE DE LYON, REPENTIGNY, QC, J5Z 4Z3
(450) 582-2442 *SIC* 5571

65548 MANITOBA LTD *p 355*
GD, ROBLIN, MB, R0L 1P0
(204) 937-2106 *SIC* 5154

656706 ONTARIO INC *p 665*
2701 JOHN ST, MARKHAM, ON, L3R 2W5
(905) 479-9515 *SIC* 3672

656955 ONTARIO LIMITED *p 846*
101 PARENT ST, PLANTAGENET, ON, K0B 1L0
(613) 673-4835 *SIC* 8051

657720 ONTARIO LTD *p 658*
1260 GAINSBOROUGH RD, LONDON, ON, N6H 5K8
(519) 473-2273 *SIC* 5431

658612 ONTARIO LTD *p 633*
215 INDUSTRY RD, KINGSVILLE, ON, N9Y 1K9
(519) 733-9100 *SIC* 5146

658771 ONTARIO LTD *p 1020*
2727 HOWARD AVE, WINDSOR, ON, N8X 3X4
(519) 972-1440 *SIC* 5431

662117 ONTARIO INC *p 807*
17 SHANNON CRT, ORANGEVILLE, ON, L9W 5L8
(519) 941-2950 *SIC* 4212

662942 BC LTD *p 232*
32530 LOUGHEED HWY SUITE 206, MIS-SION, BC, V2V 1A5
(604) 826-1244 *SIC* 5912

663353 B.C. LTD *p 259*
11800 CAMBIE RD, RICHMOND, BC, V6X 1L5
(604) 278-9105 *SIC* 5912

6648215 CANADA LTD *p 566*
115 5 HWY W, DUNDAS, ON, L9H 7L6
(905) 689-4774 *SIC* 5051

6654100 CANADA INC *p 1116*
2400 RUE ALEXIS-LE-TROTTEUR, JON-QUIERE, QC, G7X 0J7
(418) 542-6164 *SIC* 5084

6669409 CANADA INC *p 1233*
3504 AV FRANCIS-HUGHES, MONTREAL, QC, H7L 5A9
(450) 696-1090 *SIC* 5199

668824 ALBERTA LTD *p 33*
6009 1A ST SW SUITE 1, CALGARY, AB, T2H 0G5
(403) 255-2270 *SIC* 5731

668977 ALBERTA INC *p 69*
235 SHAWVILLE BLVD SE, CALGARY, AB, T2Y 3H9
(403) 256-6999 *SIC* 5812

669021 ALBERTA LTD *p 108*
5104 55 AVE NW, EDMONTON, AB, T6B 3C6
(780) 865-4183 *SIC* 5211

669779 ONTARIO LTD *p 571*
355 HORNER AVE SUITE 416, ETOBI-COKE, ON, M8W 1Z7

(416) 754-0999 *SIC* 4213

6702601 CANADA INC *p 1292*
4919 RUE SAINT-FELIX, SAINT-AUGUSTIN-DE-DESMAURES, QC, G3A 1B4
(418) 571-0705 *SIC* 5149

671061 ONTARIO LIMITED *p 570*
2913 LAKE SHORE BLVD W SUITE A, ETO-BICOKE, ON, M8V 1J3
(416) 599-7232 *SIC* 7361

673753 ONTARIO LIMITED *p 682*
375 WHEELABRATOR WAY SUITE 1, MIL-TON, ON, L9T 3C1
(905) 875-0708 *SIC* 4731

673753 ONTARIO LIMITED *p 800*
104-610 CHARTWELL RD, OAKVILLE, ON, L6J 4A5
(905) 875-0708 *SIC* 4731

673927 ONTARIO INC *p 665*
3175 14TH AVE UNIT 2, MARKHAM, ON, L3R 0H1
(905) 479-8444 *SIC* 5172

675122 ALBERTA LTD *p 112*
4207 98 ST NW SUITE 102, EDMONTON, AB, T6E 5R7
SIC 5921

677957 ONTARIO INC *p 880*
19101 LESLIE ST, SHARON, ON, L0G 1V0
(905) 478-8241 *SIC* 5411

678925 ONTARIO INC *p 944*
14 COLLEGE ST, TORONTO, ON, M5G 1K2
(416) 962-7500 *SIC* 8741

679475 ONTARIO INC *p 665*
4440 STEELES AVE E UNIT 3, MARKHAM, ON, L3R 0L4
SIC 4724

680061 ONTARIO LIMITED *p 648*
44 BELLEISLE CRT, LONDON, ON, N5V 4L2
(519) 659-2696 *SIC* 5085

68235 MANITOBA LTD *p 351*
5461 PORTAGE AVE UNIT B, HEADING-LEY, MB, R4H 1H8
(204) 885-8120 *SIC* 5191

682439 ONTARIO INC *p 762*
348 BIRCHS RD SUITE 824, NORTH BAY, ON, P1A 4A9
(705) 476-0444 *SIC* 4213

682770 ONTARIO INC *p 915*
49 RAILSIDE RD, TORONTO, ON, M3A 1B3
(416) 289-2344 *SIC* 3089

682880 B.C. LTD *p 243*
7338 INDUSTRIAL WAY, PEMBERTON, BC, V0N 2L0
(604) 894-6220 *SIC* 5172

683060 ALBERTA LTD *p 86*
8 EDMONTON CITY CENTRE NW, ED-MONTON, AB, T5J 2Y7
(780) 477-6853 *SIC* 5461

683949 ONTARIO LIMITED *p 875*
155 DYNAMIC DR, SCARBOROUGH, ON, M1V 5L8
(416) 366-6372 *SIC* 7629

6842071 CANADA INC *p 168*
436 RIDGE RD SUITE 1, STRATHMORE, AB, T1P 1B5
SIC 5541

6861083 CANADA INC *p 1107*
53 RUE DU BLIZZARD, GATINEAU, QC, J9A 0C8
(819) 777-2222 *SIC* 5091

6875866 CANADA INC *p 866*
40 PRODUCTION DR, SCARBOROUGH, ON, M1H 2X8
(905) 513-1097 *SIC* 7389

6894658 CANADA INC *p 1160*
10660 BOUL HENRI-BOURASSA E, MON-TREAL, QC, H1C 1G9
(514) 881-1234 *SIC* 3081

6895051 CANADA INC *p 1393*
135 RUE DU CHEMINOT, VAUDREUIL-DORION, QC, J7V 5V5
(450) 455-9877 *SIC* 6712

689803 ALBERTA LTD *p 1*

25245 111 AVE, ACHESON, AB, T7X 6C8
(780) 452-9414   *SIC* 4213

6929818 CANADA INC   *p* 729
10 KINGSBRIDGE GARDEN CIR SUITE 704, MISSISSAUGA, ON, L5R 3K6
    SIC 2421

6938001 CANADA INC   *p* 1177
433 RUE CHABANEL O UNITE 801, MONTREAL, QC, H2N 2J7
(514) 383-0026   *SIC* 5621

697739 ONTARIO INC   *p* 849
555 O'BRIEN RD, RENFREW, ON, K7V 3Z3
(613) 432-5138   *SIC* 5251

698004 ALBERTA LTD   *p* 13
8338 18 ST SE SUITE 100, CALGARY, AB, T2C 4E4
(403) 279-9070   *SIC* 0742

699215 ONTARIO LIMITED   *p* 605
949 WOODLAWN RD W, GUELPH, ON, N1K 1C9
(519) 837-3020   *SIC* 5511

6I SOLUTION   *p* 1201
See *ALITHYA CANADA INC*

7

7 DAYS GROUP   *p* 1325
See *7339101 CANADA INC*

7 SEAS   *p* 256
See *SEVEN SEAS FISH CO. LTD*

7-ELEVEN CANADA, INC   *p* 253
3531 VIKING WAY UNIT 7, RICHMOND, BC, V6V 1W1
(604) 273-2008   *SIC* 5411

7-ELEVEN CANADA, INC   *p* 273
13450 102 AVE SUITE 2400, SURREY, BC, V3T 0C3
(604) 586-0711   *SIC* 5411

7-ELEVEN FOOD CENTER   *p* 253
See *7-ELEVEN CANADA, INC*

700635 ALBERTA LTD   *p* 27
1288 42 AVE SE UNIT 1, CALGARY, AB, T2G 5P1
(403) 287-5340   *SIC* 6712

701 GOLD BOOK   *p* 611
See *INTERINFORMA INC*

7013990 CANADA INC   *p* 602
367 SPEEDVALE AVE W, GUELPH, ON, N1H 1C7
(519) 265-5161   *SIC* 4213

701466 ONTARIO LIMITED   *p* 733
7195 TRANMERE DR SUITE 4, MISSISSAUGA, ON, L5S 1N4
(905) 672-6370   *SIC* 5051

701671 ALBERTA LTD   *p* 42
450 1 ST SW, CALGARY, AB, T2P 5H1
(403) 920-2000   *SIC* 4911

702856 ALBERTA LTD   *p* 63
940A 11 AVE SW, CALGARY, AB, T2R 0E7
(403) 262-7224   *SIC* 5044

706017 ONTARIO CORP   *p* 1029
101 CASTER AVE, WOODBRIDGE, ON, L4L 5Z2
(905) 851-3189   *SIC* 1521

7062001 CANADA LIMITED   *p* 371
1180 FIFE ST, WINNIPEG, MB, R2X 2N6
(204) 633-8161   *SIC* 4212

7073674 CANADA LTD   *p* 822
77 BANK ST, OTTAWA, ON, K1P 5N2
(613) 831-2235   *SIC* 5812

709226 ONTARIO LIMITED   *p* 748
370 WEST HUNT CLUB RD, NEPEAN, ON, K2E 1A5
(613) 523-9951   *SIC* 5511

7093373 CANADA INC   *p* 600
4 FOXWOOD CRES, GUELPH, ON, N1C 1A6
(519) 400-9587   *SIC* 8741

709528 ONTARIO LTD   *p* 932
246 PARLIAMENT ST, TORONTO, ON, M5A 3A4
    SIC 6794

7098961 CANADA INC   *p* 1337
4600 RUE HICKMORE, SAINT-LAURENT, QC, H4T 1K2

(514) 733-4666   *SIC* 5621

711620 ONTARIO LIMITED   *p* 769
20 MANGO DR, NORTH YORK, ON, M2K 2G1
(416) 733-8285   *SIC* 5122

714638 ALBERTA LTD   *p* 139
4507 61 AVE, LEDUC, AB, T9E 7B5
(780) 986-0334   *SIC* 6519

715137 ONTARIO LTD   *p* 830
1071 RICHMOND RD, OTTAWA, ON, K2B 6R2
    SIC 5521

715837 ONTARIO INC   *p* 1013
1520 DUNDAS ST E, WHITBY, ON, L1N 2K7
(905) 430-2351   *SIC* 5511

7169311 MANITOBA LTD   *p* 383
975 SHERWIN RD UNIT 1, WINNIPEG, MB, R3H 0T8
(855) 838-7852   *SIC* 5193

717940 ONTARIO LIMITED   *p* 611
435 MAIN ST E, HAMILTON, ON, L8N 1K1
(905) 528-5493   *SIC* 5411

718009 ONTARIO INC   *p* 815
2617 EDINBURGH PL, OTTAWA, ON, K1B 5M1
(613) 742-7171   *SIC* 7389

718695 ONTARIO INC   *p* 616
1170 UPPER JAMES ST, HAMILTON, ON, L9C 3B1
(905) 574-7880   *SIC* 5812

718878 ONTARIO LIMITED   *p* 932
529 RICHMOND ST E UNIT 104, TORONTO, ON, M5A 1R4
(416) 365-0155   *SIC* 7389

7190891 CANADA INC   *p* 1337
4200 RUE HICKMORE, SAINT-LAURENT, QC, H4T 1K2
(514) 488-2525   *SIC* 1623

722140 ONTARIO LIMITED   *p* 686
3160 CARAVELLE DR, MISSISSAUGA, ON, L4V 1K9
    SIC 6712

7226438 CANADA INC   *p* 932
80 SACKVILLE ST RM 315, TORONTO, ON, M5A 3E5
(416) 834-5951   *SIC* 8299

723926 ONTARIO LIMITED   *p* 812
880 FAREWELL ST SUITE 1, OSHAWA, ON, L1H 6N6
(905) 436-2554   *SIC* 1541

724053 ALBERTA LIMITED   *p* 74
125 CROWFOOT WAY NW, CALGARY, AB, T3G 2R2
(403) 239-6677   *SIC* 5511

724412 ONTARIO LIMITED   *p* 597
2555 BANK ST, GLOUCESTER, ON, K1T 1M8
(613) 526-5202   *SIC* 5511

7251246 CANADA INC   *p* 665
90C CENTURIAN DR UNIT 209, MARKHAM, ON, L3R 8C5
(416) 483-2200   *SIC* 7361

7255721 CANADA INC   *p* 1395
1003 BOUL RENE-LEVESQUE, VERDUN, QC, H3E 0B2
(514) 769-3555   *SIC* 5511

727432 ONTARIO LIMITED   *p* 758
6460 LUNDY'S LANE, NIAGARA FALLS, ON, L2G 1T6
(905) 357-4623   *SIC* 5411

727849 ONTARIO LIMITED   *p* 599
1357 BARFIELD RD, GREELY, ON, K4P 1A1
(613) 821-0166   *SIC* 5211

728567 ONTARIO LIMITED   *p* 511
400 RAY LAWSON BLVD, BRAMPTON, ON, L6Y 4G4
(905) 456-3334   *SIC* 6513

7339101 CANADA INC   *p* 1325
387 RUE DESLAURIERS, SAINT-LAURENT, QC, H4N 1W2
(514) 344-5558   *SIC* 6712

734046 ONTARIO LIMITED   *p* 1017

1613 LESPERANCE RD, WINDSOR, ON, N8N 1Y2
(519) 735-3400   *SIC* 5251

734393 ONTARIO LIMITED   *p* 518
555 STEWART BLVD, BROCKVILLE, ON, K6V 7H2
(613) 342-9111   *SIC* 5511

734758 ONTARIO LIMITED   *p* 716
3100 RIDGEWAY DR UNIT 16, MISSISSAUGA, ON, L5L 5M5
(905) 820-2266   *SIC* 4724

73502 MANITOBA LIMITED   *p* 348
1873 1ST ST N, BRANDON, MB, R7C 1A9
(204) 728-4554   *SIC* 5171

742718 ONTARIO LTD   *p* 119
4235 GATEWAY BLVD NW, EDMONTON, AB, T6J 5H2
(780) 438-1222   *SIC* 7011

742906 ONTARIO INC   *p* 535
300 SHELDON DR, CAMBRIDGE, ON, N1T 1A8
(519) 740-7797   *SIC* 3599

744648 ALBERTA LTD   *p* 42
840 6 AVE SW SUITE 100, CALGARY, AB, T2P 3E5
(403) 265-6936   *SIC* 7389

745926 ONTARIO LIMITED   *p* 643
159 FRASER RD, LEAMINGTON, ON, N8H 4E6
(519) 322-2769   *SIC* 1521

746746 ONTARIO LIMITED   *p* 826
400 HUNT CLUB RD, OTTAWA, ON, K1V 1C1
(613) 741-0962   *SIC* 2752

747395 ALBERTA LTD   *p* 172
GD LCD MAIN, WETASKIWIN, AB, T9A 1W7
(780) 352-6041   *SIC* 1389

74829 MANITOBA LTD   *p* 359
945 GARDEN AVE. THE PAS, MB, R9A 1L6
(204) 623-2581   *SIC* 5171

749416 ONTARIO INC   *p* 568
40 HILLSIDE DR S, ELLIOT LAKE, ON, P5A 1M7
(705) 848-9790   *SIC* 5411

7503083 CANADA INC   *p* 1193
2000 RUE PEEL BUREAU 400, MONTREAL, QC, H3A 2W5
(514) 384-1570   *SIC* 8732

75040 MANITOBA LTD   *p* 390
1717 WAVERLEY ST UNIT 900, WINNIPEG, MB, R3T 6A9
(204) 261-9580   *SIC* 5511

7506406 CANADA INC   *p* 691
5310 EXPLORER DR, MISSISSAUGA, ON, L4W 5H8
(647) 428-2005   *SIC* 4522

7513283 CANADA INC   *p* 1328
3333 BOUL DE LA COTE-VERTU BUREAU 600, SAINT-LAURENT, QC, H4R 2N1
(514) 570-7741   *SIC* 4813

753146 ALBERTA LTD   *p* 118
10755 69 AVE NW, EDMONTON, AB, T6H 2C9
(780) 432-6535   *SIC* 5963

7531877 CANADA LTEE   *p* 1103
1265 RUE ODILE-DAOUST, GATINEAU, QC, J8M 1Y7
(819) 281-7788   *SIC* 5511

7577010 CANADA INC   *p* 1063
1501 RUE AMPERE BUREAU 200, BOUCHERVILLE, QC, J4B 5Z5
(450) 655-2441   *SIC* 5211

760496 ONTARIO LTD   *p* 837
201 JOSEPH ST, PEMBROKE, ON, K8A 8J2
(613) 732-0077   *SIC* 6719

7618280 CANADA INC   *p* 1103
1255 RUE ODILE-DAOUST, GATINEAU, QC, J8M 1Y7
(819) 281-1110   *SIC* 5511

762695 ONTARIO LIMITED   *p* 691
2770 MATHESON BLVD E, MISSISSAUGA, ON, L4W 4M5

(905) 238-3466   *SIC* 6712

7643454 CANADA INC   *p* 1108
35 RUE DUFFERIN BUREAU 204, GRANBY, QC, J2G 4W5
(450) 776-3930   *SIC* 5963

7648243 CANADA LIMITED   *p* 33
5730 BURBANK RD SE, CALGARY, AB, T2H 1Z4
(403) 255-0202   *SIC* 1799

765620 ONTARIO INC   *p* 691
5500 DIXIE RD UNIT F, MISSISSAUGA, ON, L4W 4N3
(905) 238-9888   *SIC* 5511

765620 ONTARIO INC   *p* 830
955 RICHMOND RD, OTTAWA, ON, K2B 6R1
(613) 726-0333   *SIC* 5511

765865 ONTARIO INC   *p* 511
8501 MISSISSAUGA RD SUITE 302, BRAMPTON, ON, L6Y 5G8
(905) 497-4114   *SIC* 4581

7660715 CANADA INC   *p* 1212
2100 DRUMMOND ST, MONTREAL, QC, H3G 1X1
(514) 845-2727   *SIC* 4899

7667965 CANADA INC   *p* 771
2942 BAYVIEW AVE, NORTH YORK, ON, M2N 5K5
(416) 388-2806   *SIC* 1521

767405 ALBERTA LTD   *p* 98
10220 170 ST NW, EDMONTON, AB, T5S 1N9
(780) 420-1111   *SIC* 5511

768308 ONTARIO INC   *p* 903
30043 JANE RD, THAMESVILLE, ON, N0P 2K0
(519) 692-4416   *SIC* 2035

770976 ONTARIO LIMITED   *p* 1029
100 WHITMORE RD, WOODBRIDGE, ON, L4L 7K4
(905) 850-1477   *SIC* 5461

771922 ALBERTA INC   *p* 20
1211 CENTRE ST NW, CALGARY, AB, T2E 2R3
(403) 930-0610   *SIC* 5511

775757 ONTARIO INC   *p* 602
55473 HIGHWAY 6 N, GUELPH, ON, N1H 6J2
(519) 836-1957   *SIC* 5571

777603 ONTARIO INC   *p* 621
952 HUMPHREY RD, IGNACE, ON, P0T 1T0
(807) 934-6500   *SIC* 4212

7786395 CANADA INC   *p* 832
1120 MORRISON DR UNIT 1, OTTAWA, ON, K2H 8M7
(613) 736-8288   *SIC* 5136

779173 ONTARIO LIMITED   *p* 564
75 DEEP RIVER ROAD, DEEP RIVER, ON, K0J 1P0
(613) 584-3893   *SIC* 5411

7818696 CANADA INC   *p* 1222
642 RUE DE COURCELLE BUREAU 101, MONTREAL, QC, H4C 3C5
(514) 659-1681   *SIC* 5912

782659 ONTARIO LTD   *p* 1018
2910 JEFFERSON BLVD, WINDSOR, ON, N8T 3J2
(519) 944-1212   *SIC* 1521

783312 ONTARIO LIMITED   *p* 708
2281 CAMILLA RD, MISSISSAUGA, ON, L5A 2K2
(905) 848-4840   *SIC* 5411

783814 ALBERTA LTD   *p* 146
1960 STRACHAN RD SE, MEDICINE HAT, AB, T1B 4K4
(403) 504-5400   *SIC* 5411

784704 ONTARIO LTD   *p* 617
832 10TH ST, HANOVER, ON, N4N 1S3
(519) 364-4661   *SIC* 5411

7853807 CANADA INC   *p* 1348
3126 RUE BERNARD-PILON, SAINT-MATHIEU-DE-BELOEIL, QC, J3G 4S5
(450) 467-7352   *SIC* 4213

7868774 CANADA INC   p 616
762 UPPER JAMES ST UNIT 287, HAMIL-TON, ON, L9C 3A2
(866) 635-6918   *SIC* 4899

788265 ONTARIO LIMITED   p 665
250 SHIELDS CRT UNIT 1, MARKHAM, ON, L3R 9W7
(905) 415-8020   *SIC* 5199

7902476 CANADA INC   p 594
1750 CYRVILLE RD, GLOUCESTER, ON, K1B 3L8
(613) 749-0001   *SIC* 5712

7912854 CANADA INC   p 1380
3530 BOUL DES ENTREPRISES, TERRE-BONNE, QC, J6X 4J8
(450) 968-0880   *SIC* 2591

792259 ALBERTA LTD   p 95
15377 117 AVE NW, EDMONTON, AB, T5M 3X4
(780) 454-4838   *SIC* 6712

792716 ONTARIO LTD   p 1024
735 PRINCE RD, WINDSOR, ON, N9C 2Z2
(519) 256-6700   *SIC* 3714

793337 ONTARIO INC   p 1006
341 MARSLAND DR, WATERLOO, ON, N2J 3Z2
(519) 886-7730   *SIC* 5813

7979134 CANADA INC   p 1182
7075 AV CASGRAIN, MONTREAL, QC, H2S 3A3
   SIC 2051

798826 ONTARIO INC   p 605
91 MONARCH RD, GUELPH, ON, N1K 1S4
(519) 767-9628   *SIC* 1611

798983 ONTARIO INC   p 639
663 VICTORIA ST N, KITCHENER, ON, N2H 5G3
   SIC 5511

7SEEDS   p 802
See MIN-CHEM CANADA LTD

8

8-RINK ICE SPORTS CENTRE   p 184
See CANLAN ICE SPORTS CORP

800743 ALBERTA LTD   p 20
1225 34 AVE NE, CALGARY, AB, T2E 6N4
(403) 291-4239   *SIC* 3944

8008655 CANADA INC.   p 573
409 EVANS AVE, ETOBICOKE, ON, M8Z 1K8
(416) 521-6100   *SIC* 2426

801 WEST GEORGIA LTD   p 301
801 GEORGIA ST W, VANCOUVER, BC, V6C 1P7
(604) 682-5566   *SIC* 7011

8027722 CANADA INC   p 1093
9500 AV RYAN, DORVAL, QC, H9P 3A1
(514) 634-7655   *SIC* 4731

802912 ONTARIO LIMITED   p 766
2235 SHEPPARD AVE E SUITE 901, NORTH YORK, ON, M2J 5B5
(416) 492-7611   *SIC* 7991

804652 ALBERTA LTD   p 155
7703 EDGAR INDUSTRIAL DR SUITE 1, RED DEER, AB, T4P 3R2
(403) 343-1316   *SIC* 5031

8056323 CANADA INC   p 86
10665 JASPER AVE NW SUITE 900, ED-MONTON, AB, T5J 3S9
(587) 206-8611   *SIC* 8741

805658 ONTARIO INC   p 520
4100 HARVESTER RD SUITE 1, BURLING-TON, ON, L7L 0C1
(905) 632-5371   *SIC* 5511

806040 ONTARIO LTD   p 782
4496 CHESSWOOD DR, NORTH YORK, ON, M3J 2B9
(416) 665-6400   *SIC* 8741

8061076 CANADA INC   p 1075
217 BOUL INDUSTRIEL, CHATEAUGUAY, QC, J6J 4Z2
(514) 934-4684   *SIC* 6712

808269 ONTARIO INC   p 890
20 WILLIAM ST, ST THOMAS, ON, N5R 3G9
(519) 633-9370   *SIC* 5411

817936 ALBERTA LTD   p 42
513 8 AVE SW SUITE 126, CALGARY, AB, T2P 1G1
(403) 508-9999   *SIC* 5812

81918 ONTARIO LTD   p 800
125 CROSS AVE SUITE 1, OAKVILLE, ON, L6J 2W8
(905) 844-7493   *SIC* 5411

821373 ONTARIO LTD   p 500
3 BREWSTER RD SUITE 5, BRAMPTON, ON, L6T 5G9
(905) 794-2074   *SIC* 5087

822099 ONTARIO LIMITED   p 573
12 LOCKPORT AVE, ETOBICOKE, ON, M8Z 2R7
(416) 236-1277   *SIC* 5531

82212 CANADA LTD   p 1420
601 ALBERT ST, REGINA, SK, S4R 2P4
(306) 525-5411   *SIC* 6712

822188 ONTARIO INC   p 490
1023 COUNTY RD 22, BELLE RIVER, ON, N0R 1A0
(519) 727-5506   *SIC* 6513

825209 ALBERTA LTD   p 169
121 - 17 AVE NE, THREE HILLS, AB, T0M 2A0
(403) 443-2601   *SIC* 1521

8262900 CANADA INC   p 642
139 WASHBURN DR, KITCHENER, ON, N2R 1S1
(519) 748-5002   *SIC* 8741

8268533 CANADA INC   p 1225
155 BOUL MONTPELLIER, MONTREAL, QC, H4N 2G3
(514) 385-2509   *SIC* 5194

8273537 CANADA LIMITED   p 155
3 CLEARVIEW MARKET WAY, RED DEER, AB, T4P 0M9
(403) 342-1265   *SIC* 5411

828324 ONTARIO LIMITED   p 757
6913 OAKWOOD DR, NIAGARA FALLS, ON, L2E 6S5
(905) 646-3333   *SIC* 5065

828590 ONTARIO INC   p 1006
94 BRIDGEPORT RD E, WATERLOO, ON, N2J 2J9
(519) 746-6804   *SIC* 5461

8313784 CANADA   p 1211
See MINTZ GLOBAL SCREENING INC

834 HUTTERIEN BRETHERN OF WHITE-LAKE   p 150
GD, NOBLEFORD, AB, T0L 1S0
(403) 824-3688   *SIC* 8741

835799 ALBERTA LTD   p 153
4814 50 ST SUITE 300, RED DEER, AB, T4N 1X4
(403) 346-7555   *SIC* 6712

837705 ONTARIO LTD   p 561
5 NINTH ST E, CORNWALL, ON, K6H 6R3
(613) 938-7339   *SIC* 5912

838116 ONTARIO INC   p 548
35 ADESSO DR SUITE 18, CONCORD, ON, L4K 3C7
(905) 760-0850   *SIC* 2051

8388059 CANADA INC   p 679
210 DUFFIELD DR, MARKHAM, ON, L6G 1C9
(416) 848-8500   *SIC* 2752

8421722 CANADA INC   p 1112
4844 BOUL TASCHEREAU, GREENFIELD PARK, QC, J4V 2J2
(450) 672-2720   *SIC* 5511

845453 ONTARIO LTD   p 618
959 MCGILL ST, HAWKESBURY, ON, K6A 3K8
(613) 632-4125   *SIC* 5511

8463859 CANADA INC   p 829
416 RICHMOND RD, OTTAWA, ON, K2A 0G2
(613) 695-3416   *SIC* 5137

846840 ALBERTA LTD   p 165

174 ST ALBERT TRAIL, ST. ALBERT, AB, T8N 0P7
(780) 418-1165   *SIC* 5541

849432 ONTARIO LIMITED   p 531
29 PLAINS RD W UNIT 1, BURLINGTON, ON, L7T 1E8
(905) 634-2669   *SIC* 5461

852515 ONTARIO LIMITED   p 764
716 GORDON BAKER RD SUITE 212, NORTH YORK, ON, M2H 3B4
(416) 503-9633   *SIC* 7322

853569 ONTARIO LIMITED   p 480
33 ERIC T SMITH WAY, AURORA, ON, L4G 0Z6
(905) 726-9669   *SIC* 5032

8542732 CANADA INC   p 1361
2045 BOUL DAGENAIS O BUREAU 100, SAINTE-ROSE, QC, H7L 5V1
(514) 761-7373   *SIC* 7941

8561567 CANADA INC   p 1114
585 RUE SAINT-PIERRE S, JOLIETTE, QC, J6E 8R8
(450) 759-6361   *SIC* 2053

859689 ONTARIO INC   p 884
158 SCOTT ST, ST CATHARINES, ON, L2N 1H1
   SIC 5511

8603600 CANADA INC   p 751
27 NORTHSIDE RD UNIT 2710, NEPEAN, ON, K2H 8S1
(613) 265-4095   *SIC* 5947

862390 ONTARIO INC   p 898
1035 FALCONBRIDGE RD, SUDBURY, ON, P3A 4M9
(705) 560-6625   *SIC* 5511

864475 ALBERTA LTD   p 98
10151 179 ST NW, EDMONTON, AB, T5S 1P9
(780) 444-8645   *SIC* 5511

864773 ONTARIO INC   p 520
4480 PALETTA CRT, BURLINGTON, ON, L7L 5R2
(905) 825-1856   *SIC* 2011

864884 ONTARIO INC   p 1026
180 NEW HUNTINGTON RD UNIT 1, WOODBRIDGE, ON, L4H 0P5
(905) 264-6670   *SIC* 5112

868971 ONTARIO INC   p 837
1751 PAUL MARTIN DR, PEMBROKE, ON, K8A 6W5
(613) 735-7066   *SIC* 5411

87029 CANADA LTD   p 754
200 DAVIS DR, NEWMARKET, ON, L3Y 2N4
   SIC 7389

870892 ALBERTA LTD   p 38
11435 WILKES RD SE, CALGARY, AB, T2J 2E5
(403) 452-3122   *SIC* 1541

871442 ONTARIO INC   p 748
18 BENTLEY AVE SUITE A, NEPEAN, ON, K2E 6T8
(613) 723-9227   *SIC* 1521

875578 ONTARIO LIMITED   p 581
31 RACINE RD, ETOBICOKE, ON, M9W 2Z4
   SIC 6719

8756074 CANADA INC   p 1325
828 RUE DESLAURIERS, SAINT-LAURENT, QC, H4N 1X1
(514) 336-0445   *SIC* 2258

875647 ALBERTA LTD   p 172
GD STN MAIN, WHITECOURT, AB, T7S 1S1
(780) 778-6975   *SIC* 6712

878175 ALBERTA LTD   p 172
3365 33 ST, WHITECOURT, AB, T7S 0A2
   SIC 1389

8782601 CANADA INC   p 1172
4293 RUE HOGAN, MONTREAL, QC, H2H 2N2
(514) 931-7228   *SIC* 5082

87861 CANADA LTEE   p 1387
1000 RUE DU PERE-DANIEL BUREAU 728,

TROIS-RIVIERES, QC, G9A 5R6
(819) 378-2747   *SIC* 6712

882547 ONTARIO INC   p 530
1235 FAIRVIEW ST SUITE 1, BURLING-TON, ON, L7S 2H9
(905) 632-6000   *SIC* 5812

882819 ONTARIO LTD   p 1021
3049 DEVON DR, WINDSOR, ON, N8X 4L3
(519) 250-8008   *SIC* 4213

883481 ONTARIO INC   p 839
17100 HIGHWAY 7 RR 6, PERTH, ON, K7H 3C8
   SIC 5571

884262 ONTARIO INC   p 563
1612 BASELINE RD, COURTICE, ON, L1E 2S5
(905) 435-1166   *SIC* 7538

885 PROFESSIONAL MANAGEMENT LIM-ITED PARTNERSHIP   p 301
885 GEORGIA ST W SUITE 900, VANCOU-VER, BC, V6C 3H1
(604) 687-5700   *SIC* 8111

8863377 CANADA INC   p 1247
12277 BOUL METROPOLITAIN E, POINTE-AUX-TREMBLES, QC, H1B 5R3
(514) 645-1694   *SIC* 5511

8867038 CANADA INC   p 859
1609 LENA CRT, SARNIA, ON, N7T 7H4
(519) 704-1317   *SIC* 8731

887252 ONTARIO LIMITED   p 990
1042 BLOOR ST W, TORONTO, ON, M6H 1M3
(416) 531-7462   *SIC* 5421

887804 ONTARIO INC   p 691
5580 AMBLER DR, MISSISSAUGA, ON, L4W 2K9
(905) 629-2990   *SIC* 5045

8885168 CANADA INC   p 1248
215 RUE VOYAGEUR, POINTE-CLAIRE, QC, H9R 6B2
(819) 294-4484   *SIC* 1799

888930 ONTARIO INC   p 691
1290 FEWSTER DR, MISSISSAUGA, ON, L4W 1A4
(905) 625-4447   *SIC* 5963

891934 ONTARIO LIMITED   p 808
60 FOURTH AVE SUITE 1, ORANGEVILLE, ON, L9W 3Z7
(519) 941-5407   *SIC* 5211

892316 ONTARIO LIMITED   p 665
4476 16TH AVE, MARKHAM, ON, L3R 0M1
(905) 940-0655   *SIC* 5411

893278 ALBERTA LTD   p 79
5501 50 AVE, CASTOR, AB, T0C 0X0
(403) 882-4040   *SIC* 7538

894812 ONTARIO INC   p 681
806 KING ST, MIDLAND, ON, L4R 0B8
(705) 526-6640   *SIC* 5511

8948399 CANADA INC   p 380
1425 WHYTE AVE UNIT 200, WINNIPEG, MB, R3E 1V7
(204) 832-8001   *SIC* 7389

89536 BC LTD   p 240
132 ESPLANADE W SUITE 200, NORTH VANCOUVER, BC, V7M 1A2
(604) 982-3100   *SIC* 6411

8956642 CANADA CORP   p 868
757 WARDEN AVE UNIT 4, SCARBOR-OUGH, ON, M1L 4B5
(416) 759-2000   *SIC* 2051

8956995 CANADA INC   p 1116
3450 RUE SAINT-DOMINIQUE BUREAU 100, JONQUIERE, QC, G8A 2M3
(514) 374-1315   *SIC* 5153

8959528 CANADA INC   p 1107
250 RUE DEVEAULT BUREAU A, GATINEAU, QC, J8Z 1S6
(819) 778-0114   *SIC* 6712

8961182 CANADA INC   p 958
181 BAY ST SUITE 330, TORONTO, ON, M5J 2T3
(416) 363-9491   *SIC* 6531

898984 ONTARIO INC   p 855

▲ Public Company   ■ Public Company Family Member   **HQ** Headquarters   **BR** Branch   **SL** Single Location

10427 YONGE ST SUITE 2, RICHMOND HILL, ON, L4C 3C2
SIC 5511

9

9001-6262 QUEBEC INC *p 1292*
30 RUE DES GRANDS-LACS, SAINT-AUGUSTIN-DE-DESMAURES, QC, G3A 2E6
(418) 878-4135 *SIC* 6712

900261 ONTARIO LTD *p 913*
670 AIRPORT RD SUITE 200, TIMMINS, ON, P4P 1J2
(705) 268-5020 *SIC* 5411

9003-2723 QUEBEC INC *p 1243*
576 131 RTE, NOTRE-DAME-DES-PRAIRIES, QC, J6E 0M2
(450) 752-1224 *SIC* 5551

9003-4406 QUEBEC INC *p 1285*
169 BOUL SAINTE-ANNE, RIMOUSKI, QC, G5M 1C3
(418) 725-0911 *SIC* 5511

9003-7755 QUEBEC INC *p 1142*
900 RUE SAINT-CHARLES E, LONGUEUIL, QC, J4H 3Y2
(450) 646-8100 *SIC* 7011

9003-9306 QUEBEC INC *p 1275*
9115 BOUL DE L'ORMIERE, QUEBEC, QC, G2B 3K2
(418) 407-4400 *SIC* 8742

9006-5855 QUEBEC INC *p 1134*
300 RUE SAINT-ANTOINE N, LAVALTRIE, QC, J5T 2G4
(450) 586-0479 *SIC* 8049

9007-6720 QUEBEC INC *p 1116*
3495 RUE DE LA RECHERCHE, JONQUIERE, QC, G7X 0H5
(418) 695-4181 *SIC* 4213

9007-8361 QUEBEC INC *p 1054*
50 BOUL SAINT-CHARLES, BEACONS-FIELD, QC, H9W 2X3
(514) 697-4550 *SIC* 5912

9008-4013 QUEBEC INC *p 1394*
585 AV SAINT-CHARLES BUREAU 500, VAUDREUIL-DORION, QC, J7V 8P9
(450) 424-3550 *SIC* 5411

9008-6398 QUEBEC INC *p 1357*
80 RUE DE L'HOTEL-DE-VILLE, SAINTE-ELIZABETH-DE-WARWICK, QC, J0A 1M0
(819) 358-9008 *SIC* 5651

9010-5826 QUEBEC INC *p 1212*
1459 RUE CRESCENT, MONTREAL, QC, H3G 2B2
(514) 288-3814 *SIC* 5812

901089 ONTARIO LIMITED *p 665*
90 ROYAL CREST CRT SUITE 1, MARKHAM, ON, L3R 9X6
(905) 513-7733 *SIC* 5043

9013-5617 QUEBEC INC *p 1221*
6411 RUE SHERBROOKE O, MONTREAL, QC, H4B 1N3
(819) 823-2295 *SIC* 5912

9013-6573 QUEBEC INC *p 1169*
3565 RUE JARRY E BUREAU 650, MONTREAL, QC, H1Z 4K6
(514) 593-5012 *SIC* 7371

9014-5467 QUEBEC INC *p 1080*
2315 BOUL SAINT-PAUL, CHICOUTIMI, QC, G7K 1E5
(418) 543-6477 *SIC* 5511

9015-0178 QUEBEC INC *p 1093*
1405 RTE TRANS-CANADA BUREAU 100, DORVAL, QC, H9P 2V9
SIC 5045

9015-6472 QUEBEC INC *p 1290*
140 RUE JACQUES-BIBEAU, ROUYN-NORANDA, QC, J9Y 0A3
(819) 764-4666 *SIC* 1629

9015-9492 QUEBEC INC *p 1222*
3025 RUE SAINT-AMBROISE, MONTREAL, QC, H4C 2C2
(514) 932-0328 *SIC* 5461

9016-0003 QUEBEC INC *p 1360*
1315 BOUL SAINT-JEAN-BAPTISTE O, SAINTE-MARTINE, QC, J0S 1V0

(450) 427-1999 *SIC* 5172

9019-4002 QUEBEC INC *p 1047*
9601 BOUL PARKWAY, ANJOU, QC, H1J 1P3
(514) 352-0858 *SIC* 5112

9020-2292 QUEBEC INC *p 1140*
1060 CH OLIVIER, LEVIS, QC, G7A 2M7
(418) 853-6265 *SIC* 2099

9020-2516 QUEBEC INC *p 1239*
5671 BOUL INDUSTRIEL, MONTREAL-NORD, QC, H1G 3Z9
(514) 321-8376 *SIC* 2015

9020-4983 QUEBEC INC *p 1115*
2035 RUE DESCHENES, JONQUIERE, QC, G7S 5E3
(418) 548-5000 *SIC* 7353

9020-5758 QUEBEC INC *p 1108*
11 RUE EVANGELINE, GRANBY, QC, J2G 6N3
(450) 994-4794 *SIC* 5499

9020-7424 QUEBEC INC *p 1280*
3373 RUE DE L'HETRIERE, QUEBEC, QC, G3A 0M2
(418) 872-4113 *SIC* 5411

9020-7697 QUEBEC INC *p 1361*
250 BOUL CURE-LABELLE, SAINTE-ROSE, QC, H7L 3A2
SIC 5511

9022-5814 QUEBEC INC *p 1233*
1867 RUE BERLIER, MONTREAL, QC, H7L 3S4
(450) 663-6327 *SIC* 7371

9022-9097 QUEBEC INC *p 1260*
103 3E AV, QUEBEC, QC, G1L 2V3
(418) 529-5378 *SIC* 5014

9023-4436 QUEBEC INC *p 1271*
2700 BOUL LAURIER, QUEBEC, QC, G1V 2L8
(418) 658-1820 *SIC* 5941

9023-4451 QUEBEC INC *p 1271*
2700 BOUL LAURIER UNITE 3000, QUEBEC, QC, G1V 2L8
(418) 658-1820 *SIC* 6712

9023-4683 QUEBEC INC *p 1319*
2012 RUE SAINT-GEORGES, SAINT-JEROME, QC, J7Y 1M8
(450) 565-8890 *SIC* 5411

9026-2437 QUEBEC INC *p 1167*
3845 RUE ONTARIO E, MONTREAL, QC, H1W 1S5
(514) 524-7727 *SIC* 5912

9026-4979 QUEBEC INC *p 1313*
2260 RUE SAINT-CHARLES, SAINT-HYACINTHE, QC, J2T 1V5
(450) 774-4189 *SIC* 5411

9026-7139 QUEBEC INC *p 1378*
630 MONTEE DES PIONNIERS, TERREBONNE, QC, J6V 1N9
(450) 585-0116 *SIC* 7929

9027-0653 QUEBEC INC *p 1149*
175 MONTEE MASSON, MASCOUCHE, QC, J7K 3B4
(450) 474-6181 *SIC* 5251

9027-3459 QUEBEC INC *p 1397*
1171 RUE NOTRE-DAME O BUREAU 200, VICTORIAVILLE, QC, G6P 7L1
(819) 758-0313 *SIC* 6712

9027-9118 QUEBEC INC *p 1389*
3115 BOUL SAINT-JEAN, TROIS-RIVIERES, QC, G9B 2M3
(819) 377-7500 *SIC* 5511

902776 N.W.T. LIMITED *p 85*
10835 120 ST NW, EDMONTON, AB, T5H 3P9
(780) 452-4333 *SIC* 7011

9028-3409 QUEBEC INC *p 1400*
210 RUE SAINT-LOUIS, WARWICK, QC, J0A 1M0
(819) 559-8484 *SIC* 5651

9028-7939 QUEBEC INC *p 1093*
117 AV LINDSAY, DORVAL, QC, H9P 2S6
(514) 636-1676 *SIC* 1542

9029-0917 QUEBEC INC *p 1092*
4301 BOUL SAINT-JEAN BUREAU 77,

DOLLARD-DES-ORMEAUX, QC, H9H 2A4
(514) 626-4477 *SIC* 5912

9029-2970 QUEBEC INC *p 1150*
135 BOUL DION, MATANE, QC, G4W 3L8
(418) 562-3751 *SIC* 7389

9029-5015 QUEBEC INC *p 1097*
915 RUE HAINS, DRUMMONDVILLE, QC, J2C 3A1
(819) 478-4971 *SIC* 6712

9030-5418 QUEBEC INC *p 1319*
801 MONTEE SAINT-NICOLAS, SAINT-JEROME, QC, J7Y 4C7
(450) 569-8001 *SIC* 2099

9030-5582 QUEBEC INC *p 1380*
1460 CH GASCON BUREAU 101, TERREBONNE, QC, J6X 2Z5
(450) 492-5225 *SIC* 5812

9032-8402 QUEBEC INC *p 1078*
1257 BOUL TALBOT BUREAU 268, CHICOUTIMI, QC, G7H 4C1
(418) 549-5014 *SIC* 5531

9035-2022 QUEBEC INC *p 1358*
546 3E RANG BUREAU 3, SAINTE-HELENE-DE-BAGOT, QC, J0H 1M0
(450) 791-2304 *SIC* 5541

9036-4514 QUEBEC INC *p 1287*
45 RUE WHITELEY, RIVIERE-SAINT-PAUL, QC, G0G 2P0
(418) 379-2087 *SIC* 5146

9038-5477 QUEBEC INC *p 1054*
482 BOUL BEACONSFIELD BUREAU 204, BEACONSFIELD, QC, H9W 4C4
(514) 695-3131 *SIC* 8059

9038-7200 QUEBEC INC *p 1300*
255 25E AV BUREAU 926, SAINT-EUSTACHE, QC, J7P 4Y1
(450) 974-3493 *SIC* 5461

9039-4735 QUEBEC INC *p 1069*
9100 BOUL TASCHEREAU, BROSSARD, QC, J4X 1C3
(450) 659-1616 *SIC* 5511

9039-7571 QUEBEC INC *p 1069*
9425 BOUL TASCHEREAU, BROSSARD, QC, J4Y 2J3
(450) 659-6688 *SIC* 5511

9039-8082 QUEBEC INC *p 1247*
12150 RUE SHERBROOKE E, POINTE-AUX-TREMBLES, QC, H1B 1C7
(514) 645-6700 *SIC* 5511

90401 CANADA LTEE *p 1328*
2255 RUE COHEN, SAINT-LAURENT, QC, H4R 2N7
(514) 334-5000 *SIC* 6712

9042-0209 QUEBEC INC *p 1343*
5625 BOUL METROPOLITAIN E, SAINT-LEONARD, QC, H1P 1X3
(514) 362-2872 *SIC* 5511

9044-4928 QUEBEC INC *p 1372*
2980 RUE KING O, SHERBROOKE, QC, J1L 1Y7
(819) 566-5555 *SIC* 5999

9045-1410 QUEBEC INC *p 1093*
1620 CROIS NEWMAN, DORVAL, QC, H9P 2R8
(514) 631-1888 *SIC* 1794

9045-4604 QUEBEC INC *p 1097*
1200 BOUL RENE-LEVESQUE, DRUMMONDVILLE, QC, J2C 5W4
(819) 474-3930 *SIC* 5511

9045-9827 QUEBEC INC *p 1385*
6060 BOUL JEAN-XXIII, TROIS-RIVIERES, QC, G8Z 4B5
(819) 374-6060 *SIC* 5411

9046-6483 QUEBEC INC *p 1216*
10314 BOUL SAINT-LAURENT, MONTREAL, QC, H3L 2P2
(514) 382-6789 *SIC* 6531

9047-6334 QUEBEC INC *p 1370*
1597 RUE GALT E, SHERBROOKE, QC, J1G 3H4
(819) 566-8558 *SIC* 5999

9048-9493 QUEBEC INC *p 1294*
27 RUE INDUSTRIELLE, SAINT-BENOIT-LABRE, QC, G0M 1P0

(418) 228-6979 *SIC* 4213

9049-1135 QUEBEC INC *p 1360*
1325 BOUL SAINT-JEAN-BAPTISTE O, SAINTE-MARTINE, QC, J0S 1V0
(450) 427-1706 *SIC* 5984

9049-3347 QUEBEC INC *p 1398*
383 BOUL DE LA BONAVENTURE, VICTORIAVILLE, QC, G6T 1V5
(819) 758-0667 *SIC* 2752

9049-8049 QUEBEC INC *p 1261*
850 BOUL PIERRE-BERTRAND BUREAU 230, QUEBEC, QC, G1M 3K8
(418) 628-2223 *SIC* 6531

9050-4283 QUEBEC INC *p 1159*
488 AV SAINT-DAVID, MONTMAGNY, QC, G5V 4P9
(418) 248-2602 *SIC* 5531

9050-6015 QUEBEC INC *p 1083*
500 BOUL DES LAURENTIDES, COTE SAINT-LUC, QC, H7G 2V1
SIC 5541

9050-7641 QUEBEC INC *p 1137*
4457 BOUL GUILLAUME-COUTURE, LEVIS, QC, G6W 6M9
(418) 838-4464 *SIC* 5039

9051-1916 QUEBEC INC *p 1384*
65 BOUL SAINTE-MADELEINE, TROIS-RIVIERES, QC, G8T 3K8
(819) 694-9050 *SIC* 5122

9051-4076 QUEBEC INC *p 1307*
3500 BOUL SIR-WILFRID-LAURIER, SAINT-HUBERT, QC, J3Y 6T1
(450) 321-2446 *SIC* 1622

9051-8051 QUEBEC INC *p 1130*
8371 BOUL NEWMAN BUREAU 79, LASALLE, QC, H8N 1Y4
(514) 595-8550 *SIC* 5912

9051-8127 QUEBEC INC *p 1243*
1144 RUE LYDORIC-DOUCET, NORMANDIN, QC, G8M 5A6
(418) 274-5525 *SIC* 8711

9052-9025 QUEBEC INC *p 1337*
700 MONTEE DE LIESSE, SAINT-LAURENT, QC, H4T 1N8
(514) 631-6669 *SIC* 4213

9052-9975 QUEBEC INC *p 1337*
6600 CH DE LA COTE-DE-LIESSE, SAINT-LAURENT, QC, H4T 1E3
(514) 735-5150 *SIC* 7299

905364 ONTARIO LIMITED *p 663*
3817 COUNTY RD 46 RR 3, MAIDSTONE, ON, N0R 1K0
(519) 737-2630 *SIC* 5531

9055-5749 QUEBEC INC *p 1110*
1060 RUE ANDRE-LINE, GRANBY, QC, J2J 1J9
(450) 772-1112 *SIC* 4212

9055-8842 QUEBEC INC *p 1354*
1699 CH DU MONT-GABRIEL, SAINTE-ADELE, QC, J8B 1A5
(450) 229-3547 *SIC* 7011

9056-4725 QUEBEC INC *p 1045*
1151 111 RTE E, AMOS, QC, J9T 1N2
(819) 732-7000 *SIC* 5511

9056-6696 QUEBEC INC *p 1265*
2700 AV WATT, QUEBEC, QC, G1P 3T6
(418) 654-1414 *SIC* 7538

9057-4245 QUEBEC INC *p 1100*
3980 BOUL LEMAN, FABREVILLE, QC, H7E 1A1
(450) 661-6470 *SIC* 6712

9058-7239 QUEBEC INC *p 1169*
9250 BOUL PIE-IX, MONTREAL, QC, H1Z 4H7
(514) 850-0020 *SIC* 5148

9060-1899 QUEBEC INC *p 1097*
126 RUE HERIOT, DRUMMONDVILLE, QC, J2C 1J8
(819) 472-1121 *SIC* 5999

9060-5015 QUEBEC INC *p 1300*
440 RUE DUBOIS, SAINT-EUSTACHE, QC, J7P 4W9
(450) 623-1438 *SIC* 5211

9064-3792 QUEBEC INC *p 1141*

2025 RUE DE LA METROPOLE, LONGUEUIL, QC, J4G 1S9
SIC 6712

9064-4048 QUEBEC INC *p* 1114
1505 RUE BASE-DE-ROC, JOLIETTE, QC, J6E 0L1
(450) 759-6900 *SIC* 5812

9064-4287 QUEBEC INC *p* 1289
543 BOUL TEMISCAMINGUE, ROUYN-NORANDA, QC, J9X 7C8
(819) 762-2620 *SIC* 4212

9064-6795 QUEBEC INC *p* 1300
497 CH DE LA GRANDE-COTE, SAINT-EUSTACHE, QC, J7P 1K3
(450) 473-2934 *SIC* 4724

9065-0805 QUEBEC INC *p* 1274
3075 CH DES QUATRE-BOURGEOIS BUREAU 430, QUEBEC, QC, G1W 4Y5
(418) 657-6060 *SIC* 6531

9065-1837 QUEBEC INC *p* 1387
300 RUE DES FORGES, TROIS-RIVIERES, QC, G9A 2G8
(819) 370-2005 *SIC* 5813

9067-3385 QUEBEC INC *p* 1101
190 RUE COMEAU, FARNHAM, QC, J2N 2N4
(450) 293-3106 *SIC* 2011

9067-3476 QUEBEC INC *p* 1287
348 CH DE LA GRANDE-COTE, ROSE-MERE, QC, J7A 1K3
(450) 621-3510 *SIC* 5411

9067-6628 QUEBEC INC *p* 1083
164 BOUL DES LAURENTIDES, COTE SAINT-LUC, QC, H7G 4P6
(450) 667-0255 *SIC* 5211

9067-7246 QUEBEC INC *p* 1097
1355 BOUL SAINT-JOSEPH, DRUMMONDVILLE, QC, J2C 2E4
(819) 477-1414 *SIC* 5521

9069-5057 QUEBEC INC *p* 1209
1000 RUE SAINT-ANTOINE O STE 509, MONTREAL, QC, H3C 3R7
SIC 2711

9069-7897 QUEBEC INC *p* 1291
790 343 RTE, SAINT-ALPHONSE-RODRIGUEZ, QC, J0K 1W0
(450) 883-2963 *SIC* 5411

9070-4701 QUEBEC INC *p* 1218
2635 AV VAN HORNE, MONTREAL, QC, H3S 1P6
(514) 731-3366 *SIC* 5912

9070-5245 QUEBEC INC *p* 1257
272 RUE SAINT-JOSEPH E, QUEBEC, QC, G1K 3A9
(418) 648-2805 *SIC* 5411

9070-9734 QUEBEC INC *p* 1356
1580 BOUL DES ECLUSES, SAINTE-CATHERINE, QC, J5C 2B4
(450) 638-9018 *SIC* 5812

9071- 0575 QUEBEC INC *p* 1287
1638 BOUL MARCOTTE, ROBERVAL, QC, G8H 2P2
(418) 275-2724 *SIC* 7532

9071-2670 QUEBEC INC *p* 1145
2400 CH DU LAC, LONGUEUIL, QC, J4N 1G8
(450) 670-5445 *SIC* 5084

9071-3975 QUEBEC INC *p* 1186
410 RUE SAINT-NICOLAS BUREAU 5, MONTREAL, QC, H2Y 2P5
(514) 286-1754 *SIC* 2011

9071-3975 QUEBEC INC *p* 1403
212 CH DU CANTON S, YAMACHICHE, QC, G0X 3L0
(819) 296-1754 *SIC* 2011

9071-7851 QUEBEC INC *p* 1325
200 BOUL LEBEAU, SAINT-LAURENT, QC, H4N 1R4
(514) 332-5437 *SIC* 5137

9072-3917 QUEBEC INC *p* 1117
3790 BOUL SAINT-CHARLES BUREAU 69, KIRKLAND, QC, H9H 3C3
(514) 426-1011 *SIC* 5912

9075-5125 QUEBEC INC *p* 1044

2625 AV DU PONT S BUREAU 1, ALMA, QC, G8B 5V2
(418) 480-4776 *SIC* 5511

9075-6602 QUEBEC INC *p* 1276
6275 BOUL DE L'ORMIERE, QUEBEC, QC, G2C 1B9
(418) 842-3232 *SIC* 1541

9076-5223 QUEBEC INC *p* 1177
9200 RUE MEILLEUR STE 501, MONTREAL, QC, H2N 2A5
(514) 274-5677 *SIC* 5023

9080-0822 QUEBEC INC *p* 1161
8222 BOUL MAURICE-DUPLESSIS, MONTREAL, QC, H1E 2Y5
(514) 494-8888 *SIC* 5912

9080-3404 QUEBEC INC *p* 1239
6464 BOUL HENRI-BOURASSA E, MONTREAL-NORD, QC, H1G 5W9
(514) 256-1010 *SIC* 5511

9081-9012 QUEBEC INC *p* 1403
4 RUE SAINTE-ANNE, YAMACHICHE, QC, G0X 3L0
(819) 228-5620 *SIC* 5541

9084-2733 QUEBEC INC *p* 1254
2650 CH DU PETIT-VILLAGE, QUEBEC, QC, G1C 1V9
(418) 624-1301 *SIC* 4841

9084-4622 QUEBEC INC *p* 1103
1205 RUE DE NEUVILLE, GATINEAU, QC, J8M 2E7
(819) 986-7579 *SIC* 5411

9085-1379 QUEBEC INC *p* 1261
1035 BOUL WILFRID-HAMEL, QUEBEC, QC, G1M 2R7
(418) 683-4775 *SIC* 5411

9085-3532 QUEBEC INC *p* 1078
1212 BOUL TALBOT BUREAU 204, CHICOUTIMI, QC, G7H 4B7
(418) 543-5511 *SIC* 6531

9085-7160 QUEBEC INC *p* 1289
75 RUE MONSEIGNEUR-TESSIER O, ROUYN-NORANDA, QC, J9X 2S5
(819) 764-4747 *SIC* 5995

9085327 CANADA INC *p* 1282
225 BOUL BRIEN, REPENTIGNY, QC, J6A 6M4
(450) 585-5824 *SIC* 5511

908593 ONTARIO LIMITED *p* 911
3613 QUEEN'S LINE, TILBURY, ON, N0P 2L0
(519) 682-3235 *SIC* 5541

9088-3570 QUEBEC INC *p* 1058
40 RUE EMILIEN-MARCOUX BUREAU 109, BLAINVILLE, QC, J7C 0B5
(450) 420-9814 *SIC* 4789

9089-3470 QUEBEC INC *p* 1280
290 RUE BERNIER E, QUEBEC, QC, G2M 1K7
(418) 849-6246 *SIC* 1731

9089-8131 QUEBEC INC *p* 1389
2888 CH SULLIVAN BUREAU 3, VAL-D'OR, QC, J9P 0B9
(819) 874-3435 *SIC* 3548

9090-5092 QUEBEC INC *p* 1134
56 CH DE LAVALTRIE, LAVALTRIE, QC, J5T 2H1
(450) 586-1400 *SIC* 3272

9091-4532 QUEBEC INC *p* 1121
89 RUE VILLERAY, L'ISLE-VERTE, QC, G0L 1L0
(418) 898-3330 *SIC* 3599

9091-9101 QUEBEC INC *p* 1151
14495 RUE JOSEPH-MARC-VERMETTE, MIRABEL, QC, J7J 1X2
(450) 434-5858 *SIC* 1522

9093-3789 QUEBEC INC *p* 1389
1801 3E AV BUREAU 180, VAL-D'OR, QC, J9P 5K1
(819) 874-7741 *SIC* 5411

9093-6907 QUEBEC INC *p* 1246
13155 RUE SHERBROOKE E, POINTE-AUX-TREMBLES, QC, H1A 1B9
(514) 498-2220 *SIC* 5411

9093451 CANADA INC *p* 1093

10475 CH COTE-DE-LIESSE, DORVAL, QC, H9P 1A7
(514) 685-9444 *SIC* 5084

9094-0594 QUEBEC INC *p* 1130
1255 BOUL SHEVCHENKO, LASALLE, QC, H8N 1N8
(514) 595-9111 *SIC* 5411

9095-1302 QUEBEC INC *p* 1104
60 RUE DE LA FUTAIE BUREAU 512, GATINEAU, QC, J8T 8P5
(819) 568-2355 *SIC* 6513

9095-6988 QUEBEC INC *p* 1348
3120 RUE BERNARD-PILON, SAINT-MATHIEU-DE-BELOEIL, QC, J3G 4S5
(450) 467-8181 *SIC* 5211

9096-9080 QUEBEC INC *p* 1069
8450 BOUL TASCHEREAU, BROSSARD, QC, J4X 1C2
(450) 466-0999 *SIC* 5511

9097-4775 QUEBEC INC *p* 1161
9100 BOUL MAURICE-DUPLESSIS, MONTREAL, QC, H1E 7C2
(514) 494-4798 *SIC* 5099

9097-8875 QUEBEC INC *p* 1355
671 RUE PRINCIPALE, SAINTE-ANNE-DE-LA-PERADE, QC, G0X 2J0
(418) 325-2444 *SIC* 5511

9098-0145 QUEBEC INC *p* 1375
4701 BOUL BOURQUE, SHERBROOKE, QC, J1N 2G6
(819) 564-2257 *SIC* 3272

9098-2067 QUEBEC INC *p* 1319
1 RUE JOHN-F.-KENNEDY, SAINT-JEROME, QC, J7Y 4B4
(450) 660-6200 *SIC* 5812

9098-2067 QUEBEC INC *p* 1319
2001 BOUL DU CURE-LABELLE, SAINT-JEROME, QC, J7Y 1S2
(450) 431-6411 *SIC* 5812

9098-8585 QUEBEC INC *p* 1397
59 RUE GIROUARD, VICTORIAVILLE, QC, G6P 5T2
(819) 357-8395 *SIC* 5149

9099-7768 QUEBEC INC *p* 1292
109 RUE DES GRANDS-LACS, SAINT-AUGUSTIN-DE-DESMAURES, QC, G3A 1V9
(418) 878-3616 *SIC* 3444

9099-9012 QUEBEC INC *p* 1081
709 RUE MERRILL, COATICOOK, QC, J1A 2S2
SIC 5699

9100-9647 QUEBEC INC *p* 1277
2800 AV SAINT-JEAN-BAPTISTE BUREAU 235, QUEBEC, QC, G2E 6J5
(418) 527-7775 *SIC* 6794

9100-9720 QUEBEC INC *p* 1395
38 PLACE DU COMMERCE BUREAU 7, VERDUN, QC, H3E 1T8
(514) 762-6666 *SIC* 5912

9101-2468 QUEBEC INC *p* 1375
5119 BOUL BOURQUE, SHERBROOKE, QC, J1N 2K6
(819) 564-8664 *SIC* 5511

9101-7673 QUEBEC INC *p* 1097
620 RUE CORMIER, DRUMMONDVILLE, QC, J2C 5C4
(819) 472-1180 *SIC* 7542

9102-7045 QUEBEC INC *p* 1142
365 RUE SAINT-JEAN BUREAU 212, LONGUEUIL, QC, J4H 2X7
(450) 465-0441 *SIC* 8611

910259 ONTARIO INC *p* 748
100 BAYSHORE DR UNIT 301, NEPEAN, ON, K2B 8C1
(819) 829-7680 *SIC* 5941

9104-7332 QUEBEC INC *p* 1185
351 RUE EMERY, MONTREAL, QC, H2X 1J2
(514) 286-4002 *SIC* 5149

9105-6705 QUEBEC INC *p* 1116
2485 RUE ALEXIS-LE-TROTTEUR, JONQUIERE, QC, G7X 0E4
(418) 820-6647 *SIC* 1521

9106-3644 QUEBEC INC *p* 1110

1289 RUE PRINCIPALE, GRANBY, QC, J2J 0M3
(450) 372-2007 *SIC* 5511

9106-5235 QUEBEC INC *p* 1058
1044 BOUL DU CURE-LABELLE, BLAINVILLE, QC, J7C 2M5
(450) 939-4799 *SIC* 5094

9107-7081 QUEBEC INC *p* 1146
351 RUE NOTRE-DAME N, LOUISEVILLE, QC, J5V 1X9
(819) 228-9497 *SIC* 6712

9108-1950 QUEBEC INC *p* 1179
8355 RUE JEANNE-MANCE, MONTREAL, QC, H2P 2Y1
SIC 4731

9109-5521 QUEBEC INC *p* 1255
3261 RUE LOYOLA, QUEBEC, QC, G1E 2R9
(418) 660-2037 *SIC* 6712

9109-9861 QUEBEC INC *p* 1061
2525 BOUL DE LA GRANDE-ALLEE, BOISBRIAND, QC, J7H 1E3
(450) 430-4475 *SIC* 5541

911 RESTORATION OF DURHAM REGION *p* 812
500 RALEIGH AVE UNIT 11, OSHAWA, ON, L1H 3T2
(905) 436-9911 *SIC* 6331

9111-7523 QUEBEC INC *p* 1151
12500 RUE DE L'AVENIR, MIRABEL, QC, J7J 2K3
(450) 435-9995 *SIC* 6712

9111735 CANADA INC *p* 816
1730 ST. LAURENT BLVD SUITE 800, OTTAWA, ON, K1G 5L1
(343) 996-8101 *SIC* 5084

9113-0476 QUEBEC INC *p* 1121
2152 CH SAINT-JOSEPH, LA BAIE, QC, G7B 3N9
(418) 544-2622 *SIC* 2022

9114-9534 QUEBEC INC *p* 1371
2424 RUE KING O BUREAU 200, SHERBROOKE, QC, J1J 2E8
(819) 780-9505 *SIC* 5731

9115-7776 QUEBEC INC *p* 1361
580 BOUL CURE-LABELLE, SAINTE-ROSE, QC, H7L 4V6
(450) 963-9507 *SIC* 5912

9117-4227 QUEBEC INC *p* 1169
8018 20E AV, MONTREAL, QC, H1Z 3S7
(514) 376-1740 *SIC* 5065

9117-9077 QUEBEC INC *p* 1390
560B 3E AV, VAL-D'OR, QC, J9P 1S4
(819) 874-0447 *SIC* 8999

9118-8706 QUEBEC INC *p* 1254
585 RUE CLEMENCEAU, QUEBEC, QC, G1C 7Z9
(418) 667-3131 *SIC* 5511

911803 ONTARIO INC *p* 594
370 WILLIAM ST, GEORGIAN BLUFFS, ON, N0H 2T0
(519) 534-0760 *SIC* 5411

9119-5867 QUEBEC INC *p* 1093
657 AV MELOCHE, DORVAL, QC, H9P 2T1
(514) 363-5115 *SIC* 7349

9119-6188 QUEBEC INC *p* 1145
2786 CH DU LAC BUREAU 1, LONGUEUIL, QC, J4N 1B8
(450) 646-2888 *SIC* 5699

9119-8523 QUEBEC INC *p* 1069
9200 BOUL TASCHEREAU, BROSSARD, QC, J4X 1C3
(450) 465-3200 *SIC* 5511

9120-9734 QUEBEC INC *p* 1256
4250 1RE AV BUREAU 95, QUEBEC, QC, G1H 2S5
(418) 627-0660 *SIC* 5411

9121-1128 QUEBEC INC *p* 1248
188 AV ONEIDA, POINTE-CLAIRE, QC, H9R 1A8
(514) 694-3439 *SIC* 6712

9121-2936 QUEBEC INC *p* 1092
167 RUE ARMAND-BOMBARDIER, DONNACONA, QC, G3M 1V4

(418) 285-4499　*SIC* 3441

9121196 CANADA INC　*p* 1395
14 PLACE DU COMMERCE, VERDUN, QC, H3E 1T5
(514) 287-1211　*SIC* 6162

9122-4568 QUEBEC INC　*p* 1097
10 RUE CORMIER, DRUMMONDVILLE, QC, J2C 0L4
(819) 477-1777　*SIC* 5511

9122-6910 QUEBEC INC　*p* 1387
4520 BOUL DES RECOLLETS, TROIS-RIVIERES, QC, G9A 4N2
(819) 370-1099　*SIC* 5812

9122-8171 QUEBEC INC　*p* 1088
165 RUE DE SALABERRY, COWANSVILLE, QC, J2K 5G9
(450) 263-8888　*SIC* 5511

9123-1878 QUEBEC INC　*p* 1140
1190 CH INDUSTRIEL, LEVIS, QC, G7A 1B1
(418) 831-2245　*SIC* 1541

9123-2165 QUEBEC INC　*p* 1072
185 BOUL DE L'INDUSTRIE, CANDIAC, QC, J5R 1J4
(450) 659-6511　*SIC* 5511

9124-4269 QUEBEC INC　*p* 1044
1049 AV DU PONT S, ALMA, QC, G8B 0E8
(418) 662-1178　*SIC* 5812

9124-4905 QUEBEC INC　*p* 1140
1019 CH INDUSTRIEL, LEVIS, QC, G7A 1B3
(418) 831-1019　*SIC* 1542

9125-9051 QUEBEC INC.　*p* 1242
120 BOUL PERRON O, NEW RICHMOND, QC, G0C 2B0
(418) 392-4237　*SIC* 5411

9127-2021 QUEBEC INC　*p* 1225
1350 RUE MAZURETTE BUREAU 314, MONTREAL, QC, H4N 1H2
(514) 739-9112　*SIC* 5182

9127-7509 QUEBEC INC　*p* 1081
151 116 RTE, CLEVELAND, QC, J0B 2H0
(819) 826-5923　*SIC* 5511

9128-0453 QUEBEC INC　*p* 1360
2950 BOUL DES PROMENADES, SAINTE-MARTHE-SUR-LE-LAC, QC, J0N 1P0
(450) 623-3010　*SIC* 5411

9128-3820 QUEBEC INC　*p* 1147
1526 RUE SHERBROOKE, MAGOG, QC, J1X 2T3
(819) 868-1122　*SIC* 5411

9130-1093 QUEBEC INC　*p* 1271
2820 BOUL LAURIER BUREAU 850, QUEBEC, QC, G1V 0C1
(418) 681-8151　*SIC* 6512

9130-1093 QUEBEC INC　*p* 1382
805 BOUL FRONTENAC E, THETFORD MINES, QC, G6G 6L5
(418) 338-6388　*SIC* 6512

9130-1168 QUEBEC INC　*p* 1285
298 BOUL ARMAND-THERIAULT BUREAU 2, RIVIERE-DU-LOUP, QC, G5R 4C2
(418) 862-7848　*SIC* 6512

9130-6381 QUEBEC INC　*p* 1077
971 3E RUE, CHIBOUGAMAU, QC, G8P 1R4
(418) 748-3682　*SIC* 1521

913096 ONTARIO LIMITED　*p* 561
1202 94 HWY, CORBEIL, ON, P0H 1K0
(705) 752-1100　*SIC* 8051

9131-1050 QUEBEC INC　*p* 1355
65 CH DE LA PINERAIE BUREAU 121, SAINTE-ANNE-DES-LACS, QC, J0R 1B0
SIC 1521

9132-1604 QUEBEC INC　*p* 1125
1600 CROIS CLAIRE, LACHINE, QC, H8S 1A2
(514) 485-1121　*SIC* 3993

9132-8997 QUEBEC INC　*p* 1349
700 RUE NOTRE-DAME, SAINT-NARCISSE, QC, G0X 2Y0
(418) 328-3200　*SIC* 1521

9132-9326 QUEBEC INC　*p* 1398
1111 BOUL JUTRAS E BUREAU 20, VIC-

TORIAVILLE, QC, G6S 1C1
(819) 357-4748　*SIC* 5912

9135-3904 QUEBEC INC　*p* 1061
2515 AV DE LA RENAISSANCE, BOIS-BRIAND, QC, J7H 1T9
(514) 667-0623　*SIC* 5092

9136-3283 QUEBEC INC　*p* 1307
5335 RUE ALBERT-MILLICHAMP BUREAU 1, SAINT-HUBERT, QC, J3Y 8Z8
(450) 350-0420　*SIC* 5045

9137-0080 QUEBEC INC　*p* 1135
5500 BOUL GUILLAUME-COUTURE BUREAU 140, LEVIS, QC, G6V 4Z2
(418) 830-8800　*SIC* 3842

9138-1616 QUEBEC INC　*p* 1168
4600 RUE MOLSON, MONTREAL, QC, H1Y 0A3
(514) 223-2600　*SIC* 5149

9138-4438 QUEBEC INC　*p* 1063
1228 RUE NOBEL, BOUCHERVILLE, QC, J4B 5H1
(450) 655-9966　*SIC* 6712

9138-4529 QUEBEC INC　*p* 1398
330 RUE DE LA JACQUES-CARTIER, VICTORIAVILLE, QC, G6T 1Y3
(514) 868-1811　*SIC* 3699

9138-7472 QUEBEC INC　*p* 1381
1060 RUE ARMAND-BOMBARDIER, TERREBONNE, QC, J6Y 1R9
(450) 477-9996　*SIC* 4213

9138-9494 QUEBEC INC　*p* 1403
212 CH DU CANTON S, YAMACHICHE, QC, G0X 3L0
(819) 296-1754　*SIC* 2011

9139-6317 QUEBEC INC　*p* 1322
3765 CH D'OKA, SAINT-JOSEPH-DU-LAC, QC, J0N 1M0
(450) 413-2789　*SIC* 5411

9140-5621 QUEBEC INC　*p* 1357
222 RUE PRINCIPALE, SAINTE-ELIZABETH-DE-WARWICK, QC, J0A 1M0
(819) 358-6555　*SIC* 5143

9141-1967 QUEBEC INC　*p* 1345
4815 BOUL COUTURE, SAINT-LEONARD, QC, H1R 3H7
(514) 326-0185　*SIC* 5149

9141-9721 QUEBEC INC　*p* 1287
401 BOUL LABELLE, ROSEMERE, QC, J7A 3T2
(450) 971-4664　*SIC* 5912

9142-5454 QUEBEC INC　*p* 1078
2000 BOUL TALBOT, CHICOUTIMI, QC, G7H 7Y2
(418) 698-9556　*SIC* 5411

9144-1923 QUEBEC INC　*p* 1284
192 RUE SAINT-GERMAIN E, RIMOUSKI, QC, G5L 1A8
(418) 723-0606　*SIC* 5045

9144-8720 QUEBEC INC　*p* 1154
1092 RUE LACHAPELLE, MONT-LAURIER, QC, J9L 3T9
(819) 623-6745　*SIC* 1799

9145-1971 QUEBEC INC　*p* 1214
1808 RUE SHERBROOKE O, MONTREAL, QC, H3H 1E5
(514) 933-8111　*SIC* 7011

9146-3000 QUEBEC INC　*p* 1364
120 BOUL DESJARDINS E, SAINTE-THERESE, QC, J7E 1C8
(450) 435-3685　*SIC* 5511

9147-8453 QUEBEC INC　*p* 1371
2325 RUE KING O, SHERBROOKE, QC, J1J 2G2
(819) 566-6882　*SIC* 5551

9149-5077 QUEBEC INC　*p* 1177
333 RUE CHABANEL O BUREAU 504, MONTREAL, QC, H2N 2E7
(514) 381-2886　*SIC* 5137

9149-8980 QUEBEC INC　*p* 1233
1683 RUE TAILLEFER, MONTREAL, QC, H7L 1T9
(514) 467-9555　*SIC* 1542

9151-8100 QUEBEC INC　*p* 1294
141 BOUL SIR-WILFRID-LAURIER, SAINT-

BASILE-LE-GRAND, QC, J3N 1M2
(450) 653-1003　*SIC* 5511

9152-2458 QUEBEC INC　*p* 1200
1000 RUE DE LA GAUCHETIERE O BUREAU 2400, MONTREAL, QC, H3B 4W5
(514) 209-2665　*SIC* 7379

9153-7639 QUEBEC INC　*p* 1263
1600 RUE CYRILLE-DUQUET, QUEBEC, QC, G1N 2E5
(418) 654-2929　*SIC* 5511

9154-4742 QUEBEC INC　*p* 1084
2000 BOUL RENE-LAENNEC, COTE SAINT-LUC, QC, H7M 4J8
(450) 629-5115　*SIC* 5461

9155- 5714 QUEBEC INC　*p* 1304
17850 BOUL LACROIX, SAINT-GEORGES, QC, G5Y 5B8
(418) 228-8661　*SIC* 5141

9155-3164 QUEBEC INC　*p* 1108
386 RUE DORCHESTER, GRANBY, QC, J2G 3Z7
(450) 372-5826　*SIC* 8741

9155-8593 QUEBEC INC　*p* 1226
5015 RUE BUCHAN, MONTREAL, QC, H4P 1S4
SIC 5012

9156-0763 QUEBEC INC　*p* 1248
6500 RTE TRANSCANADIENNE UNITE 400, POINTE-CLAIRE, QC, H9R 0A5
(514) 695-9192　*SIC* 5065

9156-4302 QUEBEC INC　*p* 1226
7881 BOUL DECARIE BUREAU 300, MONTREAL, QC, H4P 2H2
(514) 733-5828　*SIC* 5045

9157-5548 QUEBEC INC　*p* 1075
40 RUE EMILE-DESPINS, CHARLEMAGNE, QC, J5Z 3L6
(450) 581-6611　*SIC* 5411

9158-7022 QUEBEC INC　*p* 1361
3595 BOUL DE LA CONCORDE E, SAINTE-ROSE, QC, H7E 2E1
(450) 661-2525　*SIC* 5411

9158-9093 QUEBEC INC　*p* 1319
1005 BOUL DU GRAND-HERON, SAINT-JEROME, QC, J7Y 3P2
(450) 438-5214　*SIC* 5411

9158-9325 QUEBEC INC　*p* 1139
1015 RUE DU BASILIC, LEVIS, QC, G6Z 3K4
(418) 834-8077　*SIC* 5411

9159-9159 QUEBEC INC　*p* 1248
6815 RTE TRANSCANADIENNE, POINTE-CLAIRE, QC, H9R 5J1
(514) 695-4211　*SIC* 5912

9161-5781 QUEBEC INC　*p* 1230
800 RUE DE LA GAUCHETIERE O BUREAU 1100, MONTREAL, QC, H5A 1M1
(514) 397-2222　*SIC* 6512

9162-7331 QUEBEC INC　*p* 1331
7420 RUE VERITE, SAINT-LAURENT, QC, H4S 1C5
(877) 353-7683　*SIC* 4731

9164-2033 QUEBEC INC　*p* 1063
1228 RUE NOBEL, BOUCHERVILLE, QC, J4B 5H1
(450) 655-9966　*SIC* 7011

9165-1588 QUEBEC INC　*p* 1311
5445 BOUL LAURIER O, SAINT-HYACINTHE, QC, J2S 3V6
(450) 773-0333　*SIC* 5411

9165-2214 QUEBEC INC　*p* 1044
130 RUE NOTRE-DAME O, ALMA, QC, G8B 2K1
(450) 964-0057　*SIC* 1541

9165-8021 QUEBEC INC　*p* 1080
1690 RUE DE LA MANIC, CHICOUTIMI, QC, G7K 1J1
(418) 543-5111　*SIC* 7549

9167-0661 QUEBEC INC　*p* 1380
3205 BOUL DES ENTREPRISES, TERREBONNE, QC, J6X 4J9
(450) 477-2111　*SIC* 6512

9168-1924 QUEBEC INC　*p* 1154
1351 BOUL ALBINY-PAQUETTE, MONT-

LAURIER, QC, J9L 1M8
(819) 623-1767　*SIC* 5039

9168-8820 QUEBEC INC　*p* 1156
5771 RUE FERRIER, MONT-ROYAL, QC, H4P 1N3
(514) 735-6622　*SIC* 5136

9168-9406 QUEBEC INC　*p* 1237
1033 CHOMEDEY (A-13) E, MONTREAL, QC, H7W 4V3
(450) 668-5888　*SIC* 5147

9170-7570 QUEBEC INC　*p* 1077
949 3E RUE, CHIBOUGAMAU, QC, G8P 1R4
(418) 748-2691　*SIC* 1711

9171-1440 QUEBEC INC.　*p* 1090
42 RUE SAINT-MICHEL, DOLBEAU-MISTASSINI, QC, G8L 5J3
(418) 276-6511　*SIC* 5511

9171-2802 QUEBEC INC　*p* 1243
450 BOUL DON-QUICHOTTE, NOTRE-DAME-DE-L'ILE-PERROT, QC, J7V 0J9
(514) 425-6111　*SIC* 5411

9173-1307 QUEBEC INC　*p* 1152
13448 BOUL DU CURE-LABELLE, MIRABEL, QC, J7J 1G9
(450) 939-3255　*SIC* 5032

9175-2527 QUEBEC INC　*p* 1129
355 AV BETHANY, LACHUTE, QC, J8H 4G9
(450) 562-5228　*SIC* 7992

9175-6429 QUEBEC INC　*p* 1364
214 BOUL RENE-A.-ROBERT, SAINTE-THERESE, QC, J7E 4L2
(450) 971-0458　*SIC* 5411

9178-8562 QUEBEC INC　*p* 1359
266 AV DU COLLEGE, SAINTE-MARIE, QC, G6E 3Y4
(418) 387-3636　*SIC* 8741

9180-2710 QUEBEC INC　*p* 1161
7364 BOUL HENRI-BOURASSA E, MONTREAL, QC, H1E 1P2
(514) 351-4000　*SIC* 4924

9180-6166 QUEBEC INC　*p* 1281
1507 BOUL PIE-XI S, QUEBEC, QC, G3K 1Y1
(418) 845-6060　*SIC* 5511

9180-9582 QUEBEC INC　*p* 1090
2500 BOUL DES PROMENADES, DEUX-MONTAGNES, QC, J7R 6L2
(450) 472-6444　*SIC* 5122

9181-2958 QUEBEC INC　*p* 1154
2443 CH DU 5E-RANG S, MONT-LAURIER, QC, J9L 3G7
(819) 623-5672　*SIC* 5144

9181-8153 QUEBEC INC　*p* 1242
680 CH DU VILLAGE, MORIN-HEIGHTS, QC, J0R 1H0
(450) 226-5769　*SIC* 5411

9182-2452 QUEBEC INC　*p* 1261
215 RUE ETIENNE-DUBREUIL, QUEBEC, QC, G1M 4A6
(418) 681-5000　*SIC* 5511

9182-9978 QUEBEC INC　*p* 1209
774 RUE SAINT PAUL O, MONTREAL, QC, H3C 1M4
(514) 876-4101　*SIC* 8732

9183-7252 QUEBEC INC　*p* 1058
730 BOUL INDUSTRIEL, BLAINVILLE, QC, J7C 3V4
(450) 979-8700　*SIC* 3567

9183-9530 QUEBEC INC　*p* 1284
401 RUE SAINT-JEAN-BAPTISTE E, RIMOUSKI, QC, G5L 1Z2
(418) 723-1156　*SIC* 5531

9184-2518 QUEBEC INC　*p* 1265
2511 BOUL DU PARC-TECHNOLOGIQUE, QUEBEC, QC, G1P 4S5
(418) 656-9917　*SIC* 3544

9185-9322 QUEBEC INC　*p* 1316
1000 RUE DOUGLAS, SAINT-JEAN-SUR-RICHELIEU, QC, J3A 1V1
(450) 348-6816　*SIC* 5571

9186-5758 QUEBEC INC　*p* 1227
5000 RUE BUCHAN BUREAU 1000, MONTREAL, QC, H4P 1T2

(514) 342-4151　*SIC* 8742

9187-2853 QUEBEC INC　*p 1245*
2299 AV VALLEE, PLESSISVILLE, QC, G6L 2Y6
(819) 252-6315　*SIC* 6712

9187-7571 QUEBEC INC　*p 1274*
3125 BOUL HOCHELAGA, QUEBEC, QC, G1W 2P9
(418) 653-7267　*SIC* 7011

9189-8718 QUEBEC INC　*p 1177*
350 RUE DE LOUVAIN O BUREAU 310, MONTREAL, QC, H2N 2E8
(514) 389-7297　*SIC* 5137

9190-4144 QUEBEC INC.　*p 1349*
400 AV CHAPLEAU, SAINT-PASCAL, QC, G0L 3Y0
(418) 492-2902　*SIC* 5411

9190-5730 QUEBEC INC　*p 1263*
1175 RUE LOMER-GOUIN, QUEBEC, QC, G1N 1T3
(418) 687-4711　*SIC* 5031

9191-0174 QUEBEC INC　*p 1184*
5600 AV DU PARC, MONTREAL, QC, H2V 4H1
(514) 272-5258　*SIC* 5411

9191-1263 QUEBEC INC　*p 1217*
7001 AV DU PARC, MONTREAL, QC, H3N 1X7
(514) 316-7457　*SIC* 6512

9191-1404 QUEBEC INC　*p 1193*
420 RUE SHERBROOKE O, MONTREAL, QC, H3A 1B2
(514) 499-7777　*SIC* 5921

9191-7906 QUEBEC INC　*p 1072*
200 RUE STRASBOURG, CANDIAC, QC, J5R 0B4
(450) 659-3434　*SIC* 5099

9192-2773 QUEBEC INC　*p 1147*
2620 RUE MACPHERSON, MAGOG, QC, J1X 0E6
(819) 868-4215　*SIC* 5084

9192-4548 QUEBEC INC　*p 1390*
539 CH DE LA BAIE-DOREE, VAL-D'OR, QC, J9P 7B3
(819) 637-2444　*SIC* 5149

91933614 QUEBEC INC　*p 1141*
844 RUE JEAN-NEVEU, LONGUEUIL, QC, J4G 2M1
(579) 721-3016　*SIC* 5149

9195-4750 QUEBEC INC　*p 1227*
8255 AV MOUNTAIN SIGHTS BUREAU 408, MONTREAL, QC, H4P 2B5
(514) 340-7737　*SIC* 5149

9195-7639 QUEBEC INC　*p 1302*
780 BOUL HAMEL, SAINT-FELICIEN, QC, G8K 1X9
(418) 679-4533　*SIC* 1422

9196-5905 QUEBEC INC　*p 1154*
395 BOUL DES RUISSEAUX, MONT-LAURIER, QC, J9L 0H6
(819) 623-4422　*SIC* 2411

9199-4467 QUEBEC INC　*p 1225*
1350 RUE MAZURETTE BUREAU 228, MONTREAL, QC, H4N 1H2
(514) 316-2404　*SIC* 5199

9204-6424 QUEBEC INC　*p 1367*
5570 BOUL ROYAL, SHAWINIGAN, QC, G9N 4R8
(819) 539-8333　*SIC* 5511

9205-2976 QUEBEC INC　*p 1075*
1200 RUE DES CASCADES, CHATEAU-GUAY, QC, J6J 4Z2
(450) 699-9300　*SIC* 3465

9206-5580 QUEBEC INC　*p 1287*
1221 BOUL MARCOTTE, ROBERVAL, QC, G8H 3B8
(418) 275-5288　*SIC* 5912

9207-4616 QUEBEC INC　*p 1093*
555 BOUL MCMILLAN, DORVAL, QC, H9P 1B7
(514) 631-2411　*SIC* 7011

9207-8922 QUEBEC INC　*p 1394*
29 BOUL DE LA CITE-DES-JEUNES, VAUDREUIL-DORION, QC, J7V 0N3

(450) 455-7941　*SIC* 5511

9208-3179 QUEBEC INC　*p 1240*
10240 AV ARMAND-LAVERGNE, MONTREAL-NORD, QC, H1H 3N4
(514) 664-4646　*SIC* 5961

9208-4144 QUEBEC INC　*p 1369*
561 RUE JOSEPH-LATOUR, SHER-BROOKE, QC, J1C 0W2
(819) 846-3338　*SIC* 1799

9209-5256 QUEBEC INC　*p 1227*
4700 RUE DE LA SAVANE BUREAU 210, MONTREAL, QC, H4P 1T7
(514) 906-4713　*SIC* 7374

9210-7556 QUEBEC INC　*p 1100*
3954D BOUL LEMAN, FABREVILLE, QC, H7E 1A1
SIC 5099

9210-7580 QUEBEC INC　*p 1282*
29 RUE DE LYON, REPENTIGNY, QC, J5Z 4Z3
(450) 585-9909　*SIC* 5942

9211-6409 QUEBEC INC　*p 1075*
33 BOUL SAINT-JEAN-BAPTISTE, CHATEAUGUAY, QC, J6J 3H5
(450) 699-9000　*SIC* 5511

9213-0699 QUEBEC INC　*p 1084*
2555 BOUL LE CORBUSIER BUREAU 090, COTE SAINT-LUC, QC, H7S 1Z4
(450) 686-6767　*SIC* 5137

921325 ALBERTA LTD　*p 118*
5620 104 ST NW, EDMONTON, AB, T6H 2K2
(780) 710-9112　*SIC* 6531

9214-1142 QUEBEC INC　*p 1354*
10459 BOUL SAINTE-ANNE, SAINTE-ANNE-DE-BEAUPRE, QC, G0A 3C0
(418) 827-3714　*SIC* 5912

9214-6489 QUEBEC INC　*p 1116*
3590 RUE DE L'ENERGIE, JONQUIERE, QC, G7X 9H3
(418) 695-1793　*SIC* 5211

9215-0770 QUEBEC INC　*p 1357*
2650 RUE ETIENNE-LENOIR, SAINTE-DOROTHEE, QC, H7R 0A3
(450) 504-9866　*SIC* 5531

9215-5936 QUEBEC INC　*p 1315*
860 RUE LUCIEN-BEAUDIN, SAINT-JEAN-SUR-RICHELIEU, QC, J2X 5V5
(450) 346-6363　*SIC* 3612

9215-9516 QUEBEC INC　*p 1071*
3260 BOUL LAPINIERE, BROSSARD, QC, J4Z 3L8
(450) 445-1224　*SIC* 5411

9217-5041 QUEBEC INC　*p 1263*
1095 RUE EUGENE-CHINIC, QUEBEC, QC, G1N 4N2
(581) 741-3233　*SIC* 5094

9218-4118 QUEBEC INC　*p 1395*
507 RTE MARIE-VICTORIN, VERCHERES, QC, J0L 2R0
(450) 583-3513　*SIC* 6282

9218-8069 QUEBEC INC　*p 1139*
5990 BOUL WILFRID-CARRIER, LEVIS, QC, G6Y 9X9
(418) 837-9199　*SIC* 5511

9219-1568 QUEBEC INC　*p 1227*
7777 BOUL DECARIE BUREAU 300, MON-TREAL, QC, H4P 2H2
(514) 359-3555　*SIC* 7371

921983 ONTARIO INC　*p 1013*
119 CONSUMERS DR, WHITBY, ON, L1N 1C4
(905) 665-9565　*SIC* 5211

9220-3785 QUEBEC INC　*p 1279*
4901 BOUL DES GALERIES, QUEBEC, QC, G2K 1X1
(418) 622-8180　*SIC* 5511

9220-9147 QUEBEC INC　*p 1381*
355 RUE GEORGE-VI, TERREBONNE, QC, J6Y 1N9
(450) 621-4856　*SIC* 2759

9221-7017 QUEBEC INC　*p 1161*
See CONSTRUCTION DIMCO INC.

9222-0201 QUEBEC INC　*p 1148*

890 RUE LA SALLE, MALARTIC, QC, J0Y 1Z0
(819) 757-4868　*SIC* 1794

9222-0524 QUEBEC INC　*p 1287*
1395 RUE L'ANNONCIATION S, RIVIERE-ROUGE, QC, J0T 1T0
SIC 5411

9223-0846 QUEBEC INC　*p 1155*
1365 AV BEAUMONT, MONT-ROYAL, QC, H3P 2H7
(514) 738-2401　*SIC* 5912

9223-3196 QUEBEC INC　*p 1150*
9 RUE NOTTAWAY, MATAGAMI, QC, J0Y 2A0
SIC 5039

9223-4202 QUEBEC INC　*p 1281*
15369 RUE DU PETIT-VALLON, QUEBEC, QC, G3K 0E6
(418) 840-2406　*SIC* 2038

9227-6898 QUEBEC INC　*p 1233*
1527 NORD LAVAL (A-440) O BUREAU 230, MONTREAL, QC, H7L 3W3
SIC 5136

9228-5329 QUEBEC INC　*p 1346*
100 RUE CARTER, SAINT-LEONARD-D'ASTON, QC, J0C 1M0
(819) 399-3400　*SIC* 3564

9229-3786 QUEBEC INC　*p 1355*
671 RUE PRINCIPALE, SAINTE-ANNE-DE-LA-PERADE, QC, G0X 2J0
(418) 325-2444　*SIC* 5411

9230-9970 QUEBEC INC　*p 1276*
2295 AV CHAUVEAU BUREAU 200, QUE-BEC, QC, G2C 0G7
(418) 842-3381　*SIC* 5411

9231-4897 QUEBEC INC　*p 1280*
625 RUE DE L'ARGON, QUEBEC, QC, G2N 2G7
(418) 841-2001　*SIC* 5082

923416 ALBERTA LTD　*p 73*
25 RICHARD WAY SW, CALGARY, AB, T3E 7M8
(403) 568-2834　*SIC* 5012

9240-9770 QUEBEC INC　*p 1149*
500 RUE SICARD, MASCOUCHE, QC, J7K 3G5
(450) 474-5002　*SIC* 5713

924169 ONTARIO LIMITED　*p 972*
AVENUE RD UNIT 4, TORONTO, ON, M5R 3N8
(416) 922-2868　*SIC* 8011

9248-5523 QUEBEC INC　*p 1337*
4575 RUE HICKMORE, SAINT-LAURENT, QC, H4T 1S5
(514) 934-4545　*SIC* 7389

9248-9202 QUEBEC INC　*p 1337*
235 RUE NESS, SAINT-LAURENT, QC, H4T 1S1
(514) 508-2529　*SIC* 5963

9252-9064 QUEBEC INC　*p 1358*
2090 RUE BOMBARDIER, SAINTE-JULIE, QC, J3E 2J9
(450) 649-1331　*SIC* 5145

9255-8097 QUEBEC INC.　*p 1112*
185 GRANDE ALLEE E, GRANDE-RIVIERE, QC, G0C 1V0
(418) 385-2121　*SIC* 5912

9256-5589 QUEBEC INC　*p 1157*
8593 CH DELMEADE, MONT-ROYAL, QC, H4T 1M1
(514) 522-1196　*SIC* 5147

9256-8971 QUEBEC INC　*p 1093*
22 AV LINDSAY, DORVAL, QC, H9P 2T8
SIC 5149

9258-0547 QUEBEC INC　*p 1261*
215 RUE ETIENNE-DUBREUIL, QUEBEC, QC, G1M 4A6
(418) 681-5000　*SIC* 5599

9260-8553 QUEBEC INC　*p 1119*
6029 BOUL WILFRID-HAMEL, L'ANCIENNE-LORETTE, QC, G2E 2H3
(418) 872-9705　*SIC* 5261

9262-4261 QUEBEC INC　*p 1159*
175 4E RUE, MONTMAGNY, QC, G5V 3L6

(418) 248-3089　*SIC* 6712

9264 0085 QUEBEC INC　*p 1221*
6080 RUE SHERBROOKE O, MONTREAL, QC, H4A 1Y1
SIC 2879

9264-1711 QUEBEC INC　*p 1151*
179 BOUL SAINT-JEAN-BAPTISTE, MERCIER, QC, J6R 2C1
(450) 844-7888　*SIC* 5511

9264-6231 QUEBEC INC　*p 1378*
281 RUE EDWARD-ASSH, STE-CATHERINE-DE-LA-J-CARTIE, QC, G3N 1A3
(418) 875-1839　*SIC* 5621

9267-8010 QUEBEC INC　*p 1108*
338 RUE SAINT-JACQUES, GRANBY, QC, J2G 3N2
(450) 372-4447　*SIC* 5961

926715 ONTARIO INC　*p 598*
1009 MASSEY RD, GRAFTON, ON, K0K 2G0
(905) 349-2493　*SIC* 7991

926715 ONTARIO INC　*p 598*
384 ACADEMY HILL RD, GRAFTON, ON, K0K 2G0
(905) 349-2493　*SIC* 7991

9268-8241 QUEBEC INC　*p 1158*
230 RUE DE SAINT-JOVITE BUREAU 229, MONT-TREMBLANT, QC, J8E 2Z9
(819) 425-3711　*SIC* 5511

9270-6258 QUEBEC INC　*p 1171*
5446 RUE CHAPLEAU BUREAU 201, MON-TREAL, QC, H2G 2E4
(514) 444-9999　*SIC* 7381

9272-8781 QUEBEC INC　*p 1047*
11020 BOUL PARKWAY, ANJOU, QC, H1J 1R6
(514) 270-7181　*SIC* 5078

9273-9127 QUEBEC INC　*p 1231*
575 MONTEE SAINT-FRANCOIS, MON-TREAL, QC, H7C 2S8
(514) 935-5446　*SIC* 5147

9273743 CANADA INC　*p 1235*
4141 NORD LAVAL (A-440) O BUREAU 200, MONTREAL, QC, H7P 4W6
(450) 973-8808　*SIC* 4899

9274-4531 QUEBEC INC　*p 1274*
3000 AV WATT BUREAU 1, QUEBEC, QC, G1X 3Y8
(418) 659-9000　*SIC* 7389

9274-8706 QUEBEC INC　*p 1063*
5740 BOUL SAINTE-ANNE, BOISCHATEL, QC, G0A 1H0
(418) 822-2424　*SIC* 5511

9275-0181 QUEBEC INC　*p 1284*
290 RUE MICHAUD UNITE 101, RI-MOUSKI, QC, G5L 6A4
(418) 722-9257　*SIC* 1542

9277-8091 QUEBEC INC　*p 1257*
105 COTE DE LA MONTAGNE SUITE 105, QUEBEC, QC, G1K 4E4
(418) 692-3621　*SIC* 4724

9278-3455 QUEBEC INC　*p 1215*
2715 RUE DE READING, MONTREAL, QC, H3K 1P7
(514) 937-8571　*SIC* 5147

927912 ONTARIO LIMITED　*p 816*
3150 HAWTHORNE RD SUITE B-1, OT-TAWA, ON, K1G 5H5
(613) 247-0099　*SIC* 5148

9283-9034 QUEBEC INC　*p 1045*
2185 BOUL EUGENE-ROBITAILLE, ALMA, QC, G8C 0H5
(418) 769-3113　*SIC* 3354

9292-1394 QUEBEC INC　*p 1179*
225 RUE DE LIEGE O BUREAU A, MON-TREAL, QC, H2P 1H4
(514) 381-4392　*SIC* 5136

9297-6232 QUEBEC INC　*p 1338*
361 RUE LOCKE, SAINT-LAURENT, QC, H4T 1X7
(514) 389-5757　*SIC* 5947

9300-4901 QUEBEC INC　*p 1263*
356 RUE JACKSON, QUEBEC, QC, G1N

4C5

(581) 742-1222   *SIC* 7389

9303-6952 QUEBEC INC   p 1044
355 RUE BONIN, ACTON VALE, QC, J0H 1A0

(450) 546-3279   *SIC* 6712

9306-8906 QUEBEC INC   p 1058
1083 BOUL DU CURE-LABELLE BUREAU 110, BLAINVILLE, QC, J7C 3M9

(450) 435-1981   *SIC* 5912

9306609 CANADA INC   p 511
2 BERKWOOD HOLLOW, BRAMPTON, ON, L6Y 0X6

(647) 993-1968   *SIC* 5012

9308-3152 QUEBEC INC   p 1367
10303 BOUL DES HETRES, SHAWINIGAN, QC, G9N 4Y2

(819) 539-5457   *SIC* 5511

9308-5934 QUEBEC INC   p 1384
300 RUE VACHON, TROIS-RIVIERES, QC, G8T 8Y2

(819) 691-3025   *SIC* 5511

9309-6774 QUEBEC INC   p 1387
9300 BOUL INDUSTRIEL, TROIS-RIVIERES, QC, G9A 5E1

(819) 539-8058   *SIC* 5142

9310-6607 QUEBEC INC   p 1294
771 RUE PRINCIPALE BUREAU 396, SAINT-BONAVENTURE, QC, J0C 1C0

(819) 396-2293   *SIC* 2875

9310-8405 QUEBEC INC   p 1186
239 RUE DU SAINT-SACREMENT BUREAU 304, MONTREAL, QC, H2Y 1W9

(514) 251-5050   *SIC* 7381

9311-9089 QUEBEC INC   p 1281
1459 BOUL PIE-XI S, QUEBEC, QC, G3K 0P8

(418) 767-2500   *SIC* 5511

9312-5581 QUEBEC INC   p 1345
5250 RUE JARRY E, SAINT-LEONARD, QC, H1R 3A9

(514) 878-2332   *SIC* 7011

9314-0887 QUEBEC INC   p 1235
4300 BOUL SAINT-ELZEAR O, MONTREAL, QC, H7P 4J4

(450) 622-5448   *SIC* 6712

9314-8591 QUEBEC INC   p 1063
1250 RUE NOBEL BUREAU 200, BOUCHERVILLE, QC, J4B 5H1

(450) 645-2211   *SIC* 5143

9317-3649 QUEBEC INC   p 1370
31 RUE KING O BUREAU 203, SHERBROOKE, QC, J1H 1N5

(819) 791-3123   *SIC* 5812

9320-4048 QUEBEC INC   p 1361
1611 BOUL SAINT-ELZEAR O, SAINTE-ROSE, QC, H7L 3N6

(438) 386-7886   *SIC* 7349

932072 ONTARIO LIMITED   p 493
25 GRAHAM ST, BLENHEIM, ON, N0P 1A0

(519) 676-5198   *SIC* 6712

9323-7055 QUEBEC INC   p 1058
1190 BOUL MICHELE-BOHEC, BLAINVILLE, QC, J7C 5S4

(450) 433-2210   *SIC* 5074

9327-0197 QUEBEC INC   p 1247
12321 BOUL METROPOLITAIN E, POINTE-AUX-TREMBLES, QC, H1B 5R3

(514) 645-7184   *SIC* 4213

9327-0197 QUEBEC INC   p 1331
8801 RTE TRANSCANADIENNE BUREAU 500, SAINT-LAURENT, QC, H4S 1Z6

(514) 331-4000   *SIC* 4213

9329-5558 QUEBEC INC   p 1357
1596 1ER RANG, SAINTE-CLOTILDE-DE-CHATEAUGUAY, QC, J0L 1W0

(514) 807-0707   *SIC* 0161

9330-4855 QUEBEC INC   p 1047
7900 RUE JARRY, ANJOU, QC, H1J 1H1

(514) 353-1710   *SIC* 2673

9332-3301 QUEBEC INC   p 1392
84 RUE RIENDEAU, VARENNES, QC, J3X 1P7

(450) 652-9871   *SIC* 1794

9338-4337 QUEBEC INC   p 1307
6600 GRANDE ALLEE, SAINT-HUBERT, QC, J3Y 1B7

(450) 656-5121   *SIC* 3273

9341-6246 QUEBEC INC   p 1101
523 BOUL CURE-LABELLE, FABREVILLE, QC, H7P 2P5

(450) 628-9901   *SIC* 5092

9342-6484 QUEBEC INC   p 1187
425 RUE SAINT-NICOLAS, MONTREAL, QC, H2Y 2P4

(514) 619-9649   *SIC* 5812

9342-7490 QUEBEC INC   p 1101
3980 BOUL LEMAN, FABREVILLE, QC, H7E 1A1

(514) 209-1750   *SIC* 4212

9343-0114 QUEBEC INC   p 1311
1325 RUE DANIEL-JOHNSON O, SAINT-HYACINTHE, QC, J2S 8S4

(450) 252-7988   *SIC* 6512

9343-8919 QUEBEC INC   p 1072
300 AV LIBERTE, CANDIAC, QC, J5R 6X1

(450) 633-9303   *SIC* 2869

9349-6446 QUEBEC INC   p 1068
6 RUE DE LA PLACE-DU-COMMERCE BUREAU 100, BROSSARD, QC, J4W 3J9

(450) 923-3000   *SIC* 1731

9351-8371 QUEBEC INC   p 1295
1905 BOUL SIR-WILFRID-LAURIER, SAINT-BRUNO, QC, J3V 0G8

(450) 653-1553   *SIC* 5511

9353-0251 QUEBEC INC   p 1119
6150 BOUL SAINTE-ANNE, L'ANGE GARDIEN, QC, G0A 2K0

(418) 822-0643   *SIC* 6712

9356-1405 QUEBEC INC.   p 1225
9050, RUE CHARLES-DE LA TOUR, MONTREAL, QC, H4N 1M2

SIC 0273

9356-3609 QUEBEC INC   p 1367
22C RUE LEMAIRE, SEPT-ILES, QC, G4S 1S3

(418) 960-1276   *SIC* 7699

9363-9888 QUEBEC INC   p 1243
100 RUE HUOT, NOTRE-DAME-DE-L'ILE-PERROT, QC, J7V 7Z8

(514) 700-5319   *SIC* 7359

9368-1476 QUEBEC INC   p 1397
575 BOUL DES BOIS-FRANCS S, VICTORIAVILLE, QC, G6P 5X5

(819) 357-2055   *SIC* 5651

9368-7952 QUEBEC INC   p 1300
497 CH DE LA GRANDE-COTE, SAINT-EUSTACHE, QC, J7P 1K3

(450) 473-2934   *SIC* 4724

9368-9607 QUEBEC INC   p 1078
545 BOUL DU ROYAUME O, CHICOUTIMI, QC, G7H 5B1

(418) 968-4343   *SIC* 6712

9372-3575 QUEBEC INC   p 1080
1788 RUE MITIS, CHICOUTIMI, QC, G7K 1H5

(418) 543-1632   *SIC* 6712

9378-7471 QUEBEC INC   p 1261
945 AV GODIN, QUEBEC, QC, G1M 2X5

(418) 687-1988   *SIC* 7999

9378-7471 QUEBEC INC   p 1261
909 BOUL PIERRE-BERTRAND BUREAU 150, QUEBEC, QC, G1M 3R8

(418) 687-1988   *SIC* 5999

9381-0455 QUEBEC INC   p 1275
1450 RUE ESTHER-BLONDIN BUREAU 100, QUEBEC, QC, G1Y 3N7

(418) 524-6464   *SIC* 5137

9381-0596 QUEBEC INC   p 1265
2530 BOUL WILFRID-HAMEL BUREAU 101, QUEBEC, QC, G1P 2J1

(418) 524-6464   *SIC* 5651

9387-0616 QUEBEC INC   p 1240
10035 AV PLAZA, MONTREAL-NORD, QC, H1H 4L5

(514) 321-8260   *SIC* 5147

9387-0616 QUEBEC INC   p 1361
6625 RUE ERNEST-CORMIER, SAINTE-

ROSE, QC, H7C 2V2

(450) 665-6100   *SIC* 5147

9391134 CANADA LTD   p 199
91 GOLDEN DR UNIT 18, COQUITLAM, BC, V3K 6R2

(604) 428-9644   *SIC* 5021

9395-8098 QUEBEC INC   p 1047
9595 BOUL METROPOLITAIN E, ANJOU, QC, H1J 3C1

(514) 744-6641   *SIC* 5147

939927 ONTARIO LIMITED   p 581
200 QUEEN'S PLATE DR, ETOBICOKE, ON, M9W 6Y9

(416) 746-6000   *SIC* 5812

940734 ONTARIO LIMITED   p 636
670 FAIRWAY RD S, KITCHENER, ON, N2C 1X3

(519) 894-0811   *SIC* 5812

941-2401 HEATING LTD   p 808
400 RICHARDSON RD, ORANGEVILLE, ON, L9W 4W8

(519) 941-2401   *SIC* 5983

942599 ONTARIO LIMITED   p 593
316 GUELPH ST, GEORGETOWN, ON, L7G 4B5

(905) 873-1818   *SIC* 5511

94291 CANADA LTEE   p 1397
560 BOUL DES BOIS-FRANCS S, VICTORIAVILLE, QC, G6P 5X4

(819) 357-2241   *SIC* 6712

944128 ALBERTA LTD   p 92
14440 YELLOWHEAD TRAIL NW, EDMONTON, AB, T5L 3C5

(780) 413-0900   *SIC* 6712

944622 ONTARIO LIMITED   p 617
175 SWAYZE RD, HANNON, ON, L0R 1P0

(905) 692-4488   *SIC* 4151

944743 ONTARIO INC   p 643
477 HIGHWAY 77, LEAMINGTON, ON, N8H 3V6

(519) 325-1005   *SIC* 1761

944746 ONTARIO INC   p 1021
2594 HOWARD AVE, WINDSOR, ON, N8X 3W5

(519) 966-2006   *SIC* 5531

945575 ALBERTA LTD   p 150
10 SOUTHRIDGE DR, OKOTOKS, AB, T1S 1N1

(403) 995-0224   *SIC* 5812

9458778 CANADA LIMITED   p 1295
1917 BOUL SIR-WILFRID-LAURIER, SAINT-BRUNO, QC, J3V 0G8

(514) 443-5648   *SIC* 5812

9462287 CANADA INC   p 1232
2000 RUE LEOPOLD-HAMELIN, MONTREAL, QC, H7E 4P2

(450) 720-1331   *SIC* 3341

947465 ONTARIO LTD   p 648
573 ADMIRAL CRT, LONDON, ON, N5V 4L3

(519) 455-1390   *SIC* 4151

947786 ALBERTA LTD   p 1404
BUFFALO NARROWS AIRPORT, BUFFALO NARROWS, SK, S0M 0J0

(306) 235-4373   *SIC* 4522

949043 ONTARIO INC   p 473
500 BAYLY ST W, AJAX, ON, L1S 4G6

(905) 686-0555   *SIC* 5511

9517154 CANADA LTD   p 691
5300 SATELLITE DR, MISSISSAUGA, ON, L4W 5J2

(905) 602-1225   *SIC* 4226

953866 ONTARIO LIMITED   p 754
17735 LESLIE ST, NEWMARKET, ON, L3Y 3E3

(905) 898-2721   *SIC* 5511

955 BAY STREET HOSPITALITY INC p 86
10235 101 ST NW, EDMONTON, AB, T5J 3E8

(780) 428-7111   *SIC* 7011

955 BAY STREET HOSPITALITY INC p 325
845 BURRARD ST, VANCOUVER, BC, V6Z 2K6

(604) 682-5511   *SIC* 7011

955 BAY STREET HOSPITALITY INC p 974

955 BAY ST, TORONTO, ON, M5S 2A2

SIC 7011

9580166 CANADA INC   p 972
15 PRINCE ARTHUR AVE, TORONTO, ON, M5R 1B2

(647) 282-2802   *SIC* 7629

959009 ONTARIO INC   p 492
390 NORTH FRONT ST, BELLEVILLE, ON, K8P 3E1

(613) 962-8440   *SIC* 5812

960667 ONTARIO LIMITED   p 990
777 SAINT CLARENS AVE, TORONTO, ON, M6H 3X3

(416) 536-2194   *SIC* 6712

961945 ALBERTA LTD   p 92
12240 142 ST NW, EDMONTON, AB, T5L 2G9

(780) 443-4338   *SIC* 1799

963488 ONTARIO LIMITED   p 537
255 HOLIDAY INN DR SUITE 312, CAMBRIDGE, ON, N3C 3T2

(519) 220-1151   *SIC* 5191

963618 ALBERTA LTD   p 84
13205 97 ST NW, EDMONTON, AB, T5E 4C7

(780) 478-7833   *SIC* 5541

964211 ONTARIO INC   p 1104
215 RUE BELLEHUMEUR, GATINEAU, QC, J8T 8H3

SIC 5431

965046 ONTARIO INC   p 679
80 CITIZEN CRT UNIT 11, MARKHAM, ON, L6G 1A7

(905) 305-0195   *SIC* 7699

965515 ALBERTA LTD   p 98
17920 100 AVE NW SUITE SIDE, EDMONTON, AB, T5S 2T6

(780) 481-0924   *SIC* 5511

965591 ALBERTA LTD   p 92
14721 123 AVE NW, EDMONTON, AB, T5L 2Y6

(780) 455-3000   *SIC* 1731

966850 ONTARIO INC   p 571
100 CARSON ST UNIT A, ETOBICOKE, ON, M8W 3R9

(416) 259-0282   *SIC* 5049

967003 ONTARIO LIMITED   p 907
581 RED RIVER RD, THUNDER BAY, ON, P7B 1H4

(807) 344-6666   *SIC* 6712

967210 ALBERTA LTD   p 20
2256 23 ST NE, CALGARY, AB, T2E 8N3

(403) 250-2502   *SIC* 5511

967530 ALBERTA LTD   p 112
9820 34 AVE NW, EDMONTON, AB, T6E 6L1

(780) 989-8888   *SIC* 5511

967961 ONTARIO LIMITED   p 754
349 MULOCK DR, NEWMARKET, ON, L3Y 5W2

(416) 798-7877   *SIC* 5511

968502 ONTARIO INC   p 590
1050 CANBORO RD, FENWICK, ON, L0S 1C0

(905) 892-4766   *SIC* 5193

969642 ALBERTA LIMITED   p 69
14750 5 ST SW, CALGARY, AB, T2Y 2E7

(403) 256-4788   *SIC* 5511

969774 ONTARIO LIMITED   p 889
140 BURWELL RD, ST THOMAS, ON, N5P 3R8

(519) 631-5041   *SIC* 1611

970207 ONTARIO LIMITED   p 815
851 HIGHWAY 7, OTONABEE, ON, K9J 6X7

(705) 748-2777   *SIC* 5521

970426 ALBERTA LTD   p 98
11754 170 ST NW, EDMONTON, AB, T5S 1J7

(780) 452-0220   *SIC* 5531

970910 ONTARIO INC   p 988
147 BENTWORTH AVE, TORONTO, ON, M6A 1P6

SIC 5521

971016 ONTARIO LIMITED   p 858

1621 ROAD 3, RUTHVEN, ON, N0P 2G0
SIC 5148

972683 ONTARIO INC p 1029
150 CREDITVIEW RD, WOODBRIDGE,
ON, L4L 9N4
(416) 798-7722 SIC 6712

9736140 CANADA INC p 1307
6200 RTE DE L'AEROPORT, SAINT-
HUBERT, QC, J3Y 8Y9
(450) 443-0500 SIC 4512

974307 ALBERTA LTD p 112
9850 41 AVE NW, EDMONTON, AB, T6E
5L6
(780) 414-0980 SIC 6712

974475 ONTARIO LIMITED p 748
200 GRANT CARMAN DR, NEPEAN, ON,
K2E 7Z8
(613) 727-1672 SIC 5411

974479 ONTARIO LIMITED p 762
1 LAURENTIAN AVE, NORTH BAY, ON,
P1B 9T2
(705) 472-8866 SIC 5411

975002 ALBERTA INC p 33
161 GLENDEER CIR SE, CALGARY, AB,
T2H 2S8
(403) 275-6464 SIC 5521

975445 ONTARIO INC p 529
2084 OLD LAKESHORE RD, BURLING-
TON, ON, L7R 1A3
(905) 634-2084 SIC 5812

976576 ALBERTA LTD p 146
1433 30 ST SW, MEDICINE HAT, AB, T1B
3N4
(403) 529-9099 SIC 5172

976736 ONTARIO LIMITED p 477
7 MANITOU CRES W, AMHERSTVIEW,
ON, K7N 1B7
(613) 389-4184 SIC 5411

9778233 CANADA INC p 708
99 DUNDAS ST E 2ND FL, MISSISSAUGA,
ON, L5A 1W7
(905) 232-5200 SIC 7361

9790446 CANADA INC p 1169
9455 RUE J.-J.-GAGNIER, MONTREAL,
QC, H1Z 3C8
(514) 384-0660 SIC 6712

979094 ALBERTA LTD p 112
9605 34 AVE NW, EDMONTON, AB, T6E
5W8
(780) 465-5252 SIC 5511

97971 CANADA INC p 1156
5405 AV ROYALMOUNT, MONT-ROYAL,
QC, H4P 1H6
(514) 731-7736 SIC 1521

979786 ONTARIO LIMITED p 958
146 FRONT ST W, TORONTO, ON, M5J
1G2
(416) 977-8840 SIC 5812

979861 ONTARIO INC p 687
3220 CARAVELLE DR, MISSISSAUGA, ON,
L4V 1K9
(905) 362-8877 SIC 4731

982874 ONTARIO LIMITED p 716
3045 GLEN ERIN DR, MISSISSAUGA, ON,
L5L 1J3
(905) 828-5923 SIC 5511

982875 ONTARIO LIMITED p 637
44 ALPINE RD, KITCHENER, ON, N2E 1A1
(519) 749-1314 SIC 5511

984379 ONTARIO INC p 1003
3620 MOYER RD, VINELAND, ON, L0R 2C0
(905) 562-7088 SIC 2084

985178 ONTARIO INC p 512
30 VAN KIRK DR, BRAMPTON, ON, L7A
2Y4
(905) 454-1434 SIC 5511

985907 ONTARIO LIMITED p 862
389 GREAT NORTHERN RD, SAULT STE.
MARIE, ON, P6B 4Z8
(705) 941-9999 SIC 5812

98599 CANADA LTD p 444
30 AKERLEY BLVD, DARTMOUTH, NS,
B3B 1N1
(902) 481-1010 SIC 5713

987112 ONTARIO INC p 607
32 KING ST E, HAGERSVILLE, ON, N0A
1H0
(905) 768-3571 SIC 5411

987217 ONTARIO LIMITED p 666
168 KONRAD CRES UNIT 2, MARKHAM,
ON, L3R 9T9
(905) 474-9304 SIC 5199

988690 ALBERTA INC p 146
1771 30 ST SW SUITE 8, MEDICINE HAT,
AB, T1B 3N5
(403) 529-6559 SIC 1382

989116 ONTARIO LIMITED p 865
503 CENTENNIAL RD N, SCARBOROUGH,
ON, M1C 2A5
(416) 208-5441 SIC 5112

98946 CANADA INC p 1375
6185 CH DE SAINT-ELIE, SHERBROOKE,
QC, J1R 0L1
(819) 566-8555 SIC 5411

**99 TRUCK PARTS & INDUSTRIAL EQUIP-
MENT LTD** p
273
12905 KING GEORGE BLVD, SURREY, BC,
V3T 2T1
(604) 580-1677 SIC 5531

990550 ONTARIO INC p 659
766 WHARNCLIFFE RD S, LONDON, ON,
N6J 2N4
(519) 685-2277 SIC 5511

990731 ONTARIO INC p 1034
1401 DUNDAS ST, WOODSTOCK, ON, N4S
7V9
(519) 537-8095 SIC 5084

991909 ONTARIO INC p 514
595 WEST ST UNIT 5, BRANTFORD, ON,
N3R 7C5
(519) 754-4775 SIC 5661

993106 ALBERTA LTD p 121
1444 78 AVE NW, EDMONTON, AB, T6P
1L7
(780) 438-5930 SIC 5172

994421 N.W.T. LTD p 435
353A OLD AIRPORT RD, YELLOWKNIFE,
NT, X1A 3T4
(867) 873-5338 SIC 5141

994486 N.W.T LTD p 435
GD LCD MAIN, YELLOWKNIFE, NT, X1A
2L8
(867) 873-5600 SIC 5812

994731 ONTARIO LTD p 894
5710 MAIN ST, STOUFFVILLE, ON, L4A
8B1
(866) 987-6453 SIC 5411

994794 ONTARIO INC p 1001
4 BANFF RD SUITE 3, UXBRIDGE, ON,
L9P 1S9
(905) 852-6977 SIC 5999

995451 ONTARIO INC p 490
1806 CASEY RD SUITE 6, BELLEVILLE,
ON, K8N 4Z6
(613) 969-7403 SIC 1711

995547 ONTARIO INC p 631
1670 BATH RD, KINGSTON, ON, K7M 4X9
(613) 384-1000 SIC 6719

995843 ONTARIO LTD p 736
6691 EDWARDS BLVD SUITE 1, MISSIS-
SAUGA, ON, L5T 2H8
(905) 795-2610 SIC 5084

996660 ONTARIO LIMITED p 792
63 SIGNET DR, NORTH YORK, ON, M9L
2W5
(416) 747-8707 SIC 5141

99702 CANADA LTEE p 594
1750 CYRVILLE RD, GLOUCESTER, ON,
K1B 3L8
(613) 749-0001 SIC 5712

99767 CANADA p 1401
See 99767 CANADA LTEE

99767 CANADA LTEE p 1401
4795 RUE SAINTE-CATHERINE O, WEST-
MOUNT, QC, H3Z 1S8
(514) 731-5654 SIC 5194

998699 ALBERTA LTD p 33

168 GLENDEER CIR SE, CALGARY, AB,
T2H 2V4
(403) 253-6800 SIC 5511

A

**A & A CONTRACT CUSTOMS BROKERS
LTD** p 278
120 176 ST SUITE 101, SURREY, BC, V3Z
9S2
(604) 538-1042 SIC 4731

A & A ENTERPRISES INC p 1034
354 DUNDAS ST, WOODSTOCK, ON, N4S
1B4
SIC 5199

A & A MERCHANDISING LTD p 570
3250 LAKE SHORE BLVD W, ETOBICOKE,
ON, M8V 1M1
(416) 503-3343 SIC 8732

A & A NATURAL STONE p 594
See ASHCROFT & ASSOCIATES NATU-
RAL STONE LTD

A & B RAIL SERVICES LTD p 162
50 STRATHMOOR DR SUITE 200, SHER-
WOOD PARK, AB, T8H 2B6
(780) 449-7699 SIC 1629

A & B RAIL SERVICES LTD p 480
325 INDUSTRIAL PKY S, AURORA, ON,
L4G 3V8
SIC 1629

A & D PRECISION LIMITED p 548
289 BRADWICK DR, CONCORD, ON, L4K
1K5
(905) 669-5888 SIC 7699

A & E WARDELL LTD p 450
130 RESERVE ST, GLACE BAY, NS, B1A
4W5
(902) 842-0077 SIC 5531

A & F GALATI LIMITED p 764
5845 LESLIE ST, NORTH YORK, ON, M2H
1J8
(416) 756-2000 SIC 5411

A & H STEEL LTD p 108
4710 82 AVE NW, EDMONTON, AB, T6B
0E4
(780) 465-6425 SIC 3441

A & L SEAFOODS LIMITED p 461
20 MINTO ST, LOUISBOURG, NS, B1C 1L1
(902) 733-2900 SIC 5146

A & M VENTURES LTD p 275
12448 82 AVE SUITE 201, SURREY, BC,
V3W 3E9
(604) 597-9058 SIC 6712

A & O AUTO PARTS p 479
See ROWMONT HOLDINGS LIMITED

A & P p 760
See METRO ONTARIO INC

A & P FOOD STORES p 644
See METRO ONTARIO INC

A & P FOOD STORES p 814
See METRO ONTARIO INC

A & P FRUIT GROWERS LTD p 178
1794 PEARDONVILLE RD, ABBOTSFORD,
BC, V4X 2M4
(604) 864-4900 SIC 2033

A & P STORES p 1018
See METRO ONTARIO INC

A & R DECORATIONS p 1242
166 RTE 299, NEW RICHMOND, QC, G0C
2B0
(418) 392-4686 SIC 5199

A & W p 240
See A & W FOOD SERVICES OF CANADA
INC

A & W p 331
See LAWDAN INVESTMENTS LTD

A & W p 456
See BOONE FOOD SERVICES LIMITED

A & W FOOD SERVICES OF CANADA INC
p 240
171 ESPLANADE W SUITE 300, NORTH
VANCOUVER, BC, V7M 3K9
(604) 988-2141 SIC 5812

A & W RESTAURANT p 11
See ELECTRIC FOODS INC

A & W RESTAURANT p 1412
See AWNBCO FOODS LTD

A & W RESTAURANTS p 118
See CHIRO FOODS LIMITED

A - 1 BUILDING SUPPLIES LTD p 275
8683 132 ST, SURREY, BC, V3W 4P1
(604) 599-3822 SIC 5032

A 1 MEDICAL CENTRE INC p 751
3161 STRANDHERD DR UNIT 305, NE-
PEAN, ON, K2J 5N1
(613) 823-7766 SIC 6324

A 1 SHIPPING SUPPLIES, A DIV OF p 552
See EXAGON MARKETING INC

A 52 WAREHOUSE INC p 224
20146 100A AVE SUITE 2, LANGLEY, BC,
V1M 3G2
(604) 881-0251 SIC 4225

A A A ALARM SYSTEMS LTD p 388
180 NATURE PARK WAY, WINNIPEG, MB,
R3P 0X7
(204) 949-0078 SIC 1731

A A A ALARM SYSTEMS WINNIPEG p 388
See A A A ALARM SYSTEMS LTD

A AB ACTION ADMINISTRATION p 1239
See TRANSPORT LYON INC

A AND P FOOD STORES 083 p 498
See METRO ONTARIO INC

A AND W RESTAURANT p 463
689 WESTVILLE RD, NEW GLASGOW, NS,
B2H 2J6
SIC 5812

A B C COMPANY LIMITED p 570
123 FOURTH ST, ETOBICOKE, ON, M8V
2Y6
(905) 812-5941 SIC 5311

A B C PHOTOCOLOUR PRODUCTS LTD p
320
1618 4TH AVE W, VANCOUVER, BC, V6J
1L9
(604) 736-7017 SIC 7384

A B S PRODUCTS & DESIGN p 540
See ABSOPULSE ELECTRONICS LTD

A BUCK OR TWO p 769
See 1152174 ONTARIO LIMITED

A C & D INSURANCE SERVICES LTD p 241
1196 MARINE DR, NORTH VANCOUVER,
BC, V7P 1S8
(604) 985-0581 SIC 6411

A C PRODUCTS LTD p 174
3422 MCCALLUM RD, ABBOTSFORD, BC,
V2S 7W6
(604) 852-4967 SIC 3272

A C T R A NATIONAL p 931
See ALLIANCE OF CANADIAN CINEMA,
TELEVISION & RADIO ARTISTS

A C TAXI LTD p 233
835 OLD VICTORIA RD, NANAIMO, BC,
V9R 5Z9
(250) 754-9555 SIC 4111

**A CHILD'S WORLD FAMILY CHILD CARE
SERVICES OF NIAGARA** p 1011
344 AVON ST, WELLAND, ON, L3B 6E5
(905) 735-1162 SIC 8351

A COUNTY OF ELGIN p 889
See ELGIN MANOR HOME FOR SR CITI-
ZENS

A D P DATAPHIE p 949
See BROADRIDGE SOFTWARE LIMITED

A E PEACOCK COLLEGIATE p 1411
See PRAIRIE SOUTH SCHOOL DIVISION
NO 210

A E S WAREHOUSE DISTRIBUTORS p
1420
See AUTO ELECTRIC SERVICE LTD

A F A C 403 WING p 860
See ROYAL CANADIAN AIR FORCE ASSO-
CIATION

A G S AUTOMOTIVE p 532
See A.G. SIMPSON AUTOMOTIVE INC

A HIGH RISK p 800
349 DAVIS RD, OAKVILLE, ON, L6J 2X2
(905) 845-5252 SIC 6411

A HUNDRED ANSWERS INC p 623
340 MARCH RD SUITE 500, KANATA, ON,

K2K 2E4
(613) 271-3700　SIC 8742
A I INDUSTRIES　p 274
12349 104 AVE, SURREY, BC, V3V 3H2
(604) 583-2171　SIC 3441
A I M QUEBEC　p 1238
9100 BOUL HENRI-BOURASSA E, MONTREAL-EST, QC, H1E 2S4
(514) 648-3883　SIC 3471
A I T　p 1434
See APPLIED INDUSTRIAL TECHNOLO-GIES, LP
A L MANAGEMENT GROUP　p 1422
See 2020 BUSINESS ADVISORY CORPO-RATION
A L NEILSON FAMILY PHARMACY LTD　p 998
90 DUNDAS ST W, TRENTON, ON, K8V 3P3
(613) 392-1212　SIC 5912
A LA CARTE EXPRESS INC　p 1222
4700 RUE SAINT-AMBROISE BUREAU 44, MONTREAL, QC, H4C 2C7
(514) 933-7000　SIC 4212
A LA CARTE REWARDS TRAVEL　p 1186
See TRANSAT DISTRIBUTION CANADA INC
A LEADER BUILDING CLEANING SER-VICES OF CANADA LTD　p 368
894 ST MARY'S RD, WINNIPEG, MB, R2M 3R1
(204) 255-4000　SIC 7349
A M A　p 73
See ALBERTA MOTOR ASSOCIATION
A M A　p 112
See ALBERTA MOTOR ASSOCIATION
A P M PROPERTIES　p 1040
See A.P.M. LANDMARK INC
A PLEIN GAZ　p 511
See LOBLAWS INC
A POWER INTERNATIONAL TRADING COMPANY　p 318
1575 ROBSON ST, VANCOUVER, BC, V6G 1C3
(604) 872-0712　SIC 5812
A PROPOS　p 1136
See FEDERATION DES CAISSES DES-JARDINS DU QUEBEC
A R G　p 872
See APPAREL RESOURCE GROUP INC
A S D A　p 582
See AUTOMATED STEEL DETAILING AS-SOCIATES LTD
A S L PAVING LTD　p 1425
1840 ONTARIO AVE, SASKATOON, SK, S7K 1T4
(306) 652-5525　SIC 1611
A S M INDUSTRIES　p 14
See BRAZZO CONTRACTORS (CALGARY) LTD
A TASTE OF MONTREAL SINCE 1928　p 1310
See YOPLAIT LIBERTE CANADA CIE
A THINKING APE ENTERTAINMENT LTD　p 311
1132 ALBERNI ST UNIT 200, VANCOU-VER, BC, V6E 1A5
(604) 682-7773　SIC 7371
A TOWING SERVICE LTD　p 787
185 BARTLEY DR, NORTH YORK, ON, M4A 1E6
(416) 656-4000　SIC 7549
A V GAUGE & FIXTURE INC　p 807
4000 DELDUCA DR, OLDCASTLE, ON, N0R 1L0
(519) 737-7677　SIC 3544
A WAY EXPRESS COURIER SERVICE　p 917
2168 DANFORTH AVE, TORONTO, ON, M4C 1K3
(416) 424-4471　SIC 7389
A Y JACKSON SECONDARY SCHOOL　p 766

See TORONTO DISTRICT SCHOOL BOARD
A&W　p 463
See A AND W RESTAURANT
A&W REVENUE ROYALTIES INCOME FUND　p 240
171 ESPLANADE W SUITE 300, NORTH VANCOUVER, BC, V7M 3K9
(604) 988-2141　SIC 6722
A+ ENTREPRENEURS GENERAUX　p 1171
See AVANTAGE PLUS INC
A-1 AUTO BODY LTD　p 33
5304 1A ST SE, CALGARY, AB, T2H 1J2
(403) 253-7867　SIC 7532
A-1 AUTO RENTAL & LEASING　p 842
See TRANS CANADA MOTORS (PETER-BOROUGH) LIMITED
A-1 BAGS & SUPPLIES INC　p 736
6400 KENNEDY RD, MISSISSAUGA, ON, L5T 2Z5
(905) 676-9950　SIC 5087
A-1 CASH & CARRY　p 736
See A-1 BAGS & SUPPLIES INC
A-1 PERSONNEL RESOURCES INC　p 736
6685 TOMKEN RD SUITE 211, MISSIS-SAUGA, ON, L5T 2C5
(905) 564-1040　SIC 7363
A-A-A BATTERIES LTD　p 757
5559 GEORGE ST, NIAGARA FALLS, ON, L2E 7K9
(905) 371-0666　SIC 5531
A-BUDGET CAR AND TRUCK RENTALS　p 583
See BUDGETAUTO INC
A-FIRE BURNER SYSTEMS　p 144
See GRIT INDUSTRIES INC
A-LA-CARTE ESTATES　p 1206
See NATIONAL BANK TRUST INC
A-LINE ATLANTIC INC　p 422
43 MAPLE VALLEY RD SUITE 6, CORNER BROOK, NL, A2H 6T3
(709) 634-1280　SIC 5112
A-LINE GREETING CARDS　p 422
See A-LINE ATLANTIC INC
A-SCOTT DISCOUNT USED AUTO PARTS　p 256
See RALPH'S AUTO SUPPLY (B.C.) LTD
A-WIN INSURANCE LTD　p 38
10325 BONAVENTURE DR SE SUITE 100, CALGARY, AB, T2J 7E4
(403) 278-1050　SIC 6411
A-Z FOAM LTD　p 205
811 CUNDY AVE, DELTA, BC, V3M 5P6
(604) 525-1665　SIC 3086
A. & D. PREVOST INC　p 1283
305 12E AV, RICHELIEU, QC, J3L 3T2
(450) 658-8771　SIC 3449
A. & J.L. BOURGEOIS LTEE　p 1082
1745 RTE MARIE-VICTORIN, CONTRE-COEUR, QC, J0L 1C0
(450) 587-2724　SIC 1794
A. & R. BELLEY INC　p 1372
1035 RUE PANNETON, SHERBROOKE, QC, J1K 2B3
(819) 823-1843　SIC 5113
A. & R. METAL INDUSTRIES LTD　p 253
2020 NO. 6 RD, RICHMOND, BC, V6V 1P1
(604) 276-2838　SIC 3441
A. B. LUCAS SECONDARY SCHOOL　p 651
See THAMES VALLEY DISTRICT SCHOOL BOARD
A. BEAUMONT TRANSPORT INC　p 1292
280 RTE DE FOSSAMBAULT, SAINT-AUGUSTIN-DE-DESMAURES, QC, G3A 2P9
(418) 878-4888　SIC 4213
A. BERGER PRECISION LTD　p 512
28 REGAN RD SUITE 1, BRAMPTON, ON, L7A 1A7
(905) 840-4207　SIC 3451
A. BISSON ET FILS LTEE　p 1382
410 BOUL FRONTENAC O, THETFORD MINES, QC, G6G 6N7
(418) 335-2928　SIC 5015
A. BOSA & CO. LTD　p 284

1465 KOOTENAY ST, VANCOUVER, BC, V5K 4Y3
(604) 253-5578　SIC 5141
A. C. T. EQUIPMENT SALES LTD　p 184
4455 ALASKA ST, BURNABY, BC, V5C 5T3
(604) 294-6271　SIC 5085
A. D. WELDING & FABRICATION INC　p 500
21 MELANIE DR, BRAMPTON, ON, L6T 4K8
(905) 791-2914　SIC 5046
A. FARBER & PARTNERS INC　p 769
320 SHEPPARD AVE E SUITE 300, NORTH YORK, ON, M2K 2S5
(416) 496-1200　SIC 8741
A. GIRARDIN INC　p 1100
4000 RUE GIRARDIN, DRUMMONDVILLE, QC, J2E 0A1
(819) 477-3222　SIC 4151
A. JAFFER PHARMACY LTD　p 778
946 LAWRENCE AVE E SUITE 1330, NORTH YORK, ON, M3C 1R1
(416) 444-4445　SIC 5912
A. K. HOLDINGS INC　p 400
958 PROSPECT ST, FREDERICTON, NB, E3B 2T8
(506) 462-4444　SIC 7389
A. LACROIX & FILS GRANIT LTEE　p 1352
450 RUE PRINCIPALE, SAINT-SEBASTIEN-DE-FRONTENAC, QC, G0Y 1M0
(819) 652-2828　SIC 1411
A. LASSONDE INC　p 581
95 VULCAN ST, ETOBICOKE, ON, M9W 1L4
(416) 244-4224　SIC 2086
A. LASSONDE INC　p 1288
170 5E AV, ROUGEMONT, QC, J0L 1M0
(450) 469-4926　SIC 2033
A. LASSONDE INC　p 1343
9420 BOUL LANGELIER, SAINT-LEONARD, QC, H1P 3H8
(514) 351-4010　SIC 5499
A. M. CASTLE & CO. (CANADA) INC　p 719
2150 ARGENTIA RD, MISSISSAUGA, ON, L5N 2K7
(905) 858-3888　SIC 5051
A. M. G. MEDICAL　p 1157
See A.M.G. MEDICALE INC
A. P. C. H. Q.　p 1051
See ASSOCIATION PROVINCIALE DES CONSTRUCTEURS D'HABITATIONS DU QUEBEC INC
A. RAYMOND TINNERMAN MANUFACTUR-ING HAMILTON, INC　p 609
686 PARKDALE AVE N, HAMILTON, ON, L8H 5Z4
(905) 549-4661　SIC 3429
A. SETLAKWE LIMITEE　p 1382
188 RUE NOTRE-DAME O, THETFORD MINES, QC, G6G 1J6
(418) 335-9121　SIC 5311
A. T. DESIGNS INSIGNIA LTD　p 866
70 PRODUCTION DR, SCARBOROUGH, ON, M1H 2X8
(800) 288-0111　SIC 3961
A.A. MUNRO INSURANCE BROKERS INC　p 470
9492 TRANS CANADA HWY, WHYCOCO-MAGH, NS, B0E 3M0
(902) 756-2700　SIC 6411
A.B. IMAGE OPTICS INC　p 198
2764 BARNET HWY SUITE 101, COQUIT-LAM, BC, V3B 1B9
(604) 942-1642　SIC 5995
A.B. MECHANICAL LIMITED　p 464
35 RUDDERHAM RD, POINT EDWARD, NS, B2A 4V4
(902) 567-3897　SIC 1711
A.B.C. HOLDINGS LTD　p 180
8081 MEADOW AVE, BURNABY, BC, V3N 2V9
SIC 5093
A.B.C. RECYCLING LTD　p 180

8081 MEADOW AVE, BURNABY, BC, V3N 2V9
(604) 522-9727　SIC 5093
A.B.F. MINES　p 1389
See 2985080 CANADA INC
A.B.M. TOOL & DIE CO. LTD　p 500
80 WALKER DR, BRAMPTON, ON, L6T 4H6
(905) 458-2203　SIC 3544
A.B.P. & DEESIN　p 1292
See LAFLAMME PORTES ET FENETRES CORP
A.C. DISPENSING EQUIPMENT INCORPO-RATED　p 461
100 DISPENSING WAY, LOWER SACKVILLE, NS, B4C 4H2
(902) 865-9602　SIC 3585
A.C. NIELSEN COMPANY OF CANADA LIMITED　p 666
160 MCNABB ST, MARKHAM, ON, L3R 4B8
(905) 475-3344　SIC 8732
A.C. PLASTICS CANADA　p 1135
See PLASTICON CANADA INC
A.C.D. WHOLESALE MEATS LTD　p 993
140 RYDING AVE, TORONTO, ON, M6N 1H2
(416) 766-2200　SIC 5147
A.C.I　p 1114
See ACTION CONSTRUCTION INFRAS-TRUCTURE ACI INC
A.D. DISPLAYS　p 1075
See 133876 CANADA INC
A.D. RUTHERFORD INTERNATIONAL INC　p 371
1355 MOUNTAIN AVE SUITE 301, WIN-NIPEG, MB, R2X 3B6
(204) 633-7207　SIC 4731
A.D.H. DRUGS LIMITED　p 971
550 EGLINTON AVE W SUITE 506, TORONTO, ON, M5N 1B6
(416) 485-3093　SIC 5912
A.D.L. TOBACO　p 1150
See GESTION A.D.L. SENC
A.G. HAIR COSMETICS　p 199
See A.G. PROFESSIONAL HAIR CARE PRODUCTS LTD
A.G. PENNER FARM SERVICES LTD　p 346
10 PENNER DR, BLUMENORT, MB, R0A 0C0
(204) 326-3781　SIC 6712
A.G. PROFESSIONAL HAIR CARE PROD-UCTS LTD　p 199
14 KING EDWARD ST, COQUITLAM, BC, V3K 0E7
(604) 294-8870　SIC 2844
A.G. SIMPSON AUTOMOTIVE INC　p 532
560 CONESTOGA BLVD, CAMBRIDGE, ON, N1R 7P7
(519) 621-7953　SIC 3465
A.G. SIMPSON AUTOMOTIVE INC　p 812
901 SIMCOE ST S, OSHAWA, ON, L1H 4L1
(905) 571-2121　SIC 3465
A.G. SIMPSON AUTOMOTIVE INC　p 915
200 YORKLAND BLVD SUITE 800, TORONTO, ON, M2J 5C1
(416) 438-6650　SIC 3714
A.I.E.S.E.C. CANADA INC　p 612
See AIESEC CANADA INC
A.I.M　p 593
See AERODROME INTERNATIONAL MAINTENANCE INC
A.I.M. HOLDINGS INC　p 171
2300 PELLICAN DR, WABASCA, AB, T0G 2K0
(780) 891-1018　SIC 6712
A.J. BUS LINES LIMITED　p 568
2 CHARLES WALK, ELLIOT LAKE, ON, P5A 2A3
(705) 848-3013　SIC 5943
A.J. FORSYTH, A DIVISION OF RUSSEL METALS　p 207
See RUSSEL METALS INC
A.J. LANZAROTTA WHOLESALE FRUIT &

VEGETABLES LTD p 712
1000 LAKESHORE RD E, MISSISSAUGA, ON, L5E 1E4
(905) 891-0510 *SIC* 5148

A.J.M. MECHANICAL SERVICES LTD p 6
5610 54 AVE, BONNYVILLE, AB, T9N 2N3
(780) 826-4412 *SIC* 6712

A.J.M. PROMOTIONS SPORTIVES INTER-NATIONALES LTEE p
1338
350 RUE MCCAFFREY, SAINT-LAURENT, QC, H4T 1N1
(514) 344-6767 *SIC* 5136

A.K. DRAFT SEAL LTD p 229
100-4825 275 ST, LANGLEY, BC, V4W 0C7
(604) 451-1080 *SIC* 3442

A.K.D. TRADING INC p 878
10 NEWGALE GATE SUITE 5, SCARBOR-OUGH, ON, M1X 1C5
(416) 299-7384 *SIC* 5141

A.M. FISH HOLDINGS LTD p 1113
26 RUE BRIARDALE, HAMPSTEAD, QC, H3X 3N6
(514) 788-0788 *SIC* 6712

A.M. GUY MEMORIAL HEALTH CENTRE p
423
See CENTRAL REGIONAL HEALTH AU-THORITY

A.M.A. HOLICULTURE INC p 633
2011 SPINKS DR, KINGSVILLE, ON, N9Y 2E5
(519) 322-1397 *SIC* 5193

A.M.A. INSURANCE AGENCY LTD p 118
10310 39A AVE, EDMONTON, AB, T6H 5X9
(780) 430-5555 *SIC* 6411

A.M.D. RITMED p 1248
See AMD MEDICOM INC

A.M.G. MEDICALE INC p 1157
8505 CH DALTON, MONT-ROYAL, QC, H4T 1V5
(514) 737-5251 *SIC* 5047

A.M.I. MECANIQUE INC p 1116
2455 RUE CANTIN, JONQUIERE, QC, G7X 8S7
(418) 542-3531 *SIC* 1796

A.M.P.M. SERVICE LTD p 181
6741 CARIBOO RD UNIT 101, BURNABY, BC, V3N 4A3
(604) 421-5677 *SIC* 7629

A.O. SMITH ENTERPRISES LTD p 590
599 HILL ST W, FERGUS, ON, N1M 2X1
(519) 843-1610 *SIC* 3639

A.O. SMITH GSW WATER HEATING p 590
See A.O. SMITH ENTERPRISES LTD

A.P. PLASMAN INC p 911
24 INDUSTRIAL PARK RD, TILBURY, ON, N0P 2L0
(519) 682-1155 *SIC* 7532

A.P. PLASMAN INC p 1017
418 SILVER CREEK INDUSTRIAL DR, WINDSOR, ON, N8N 4Y3
(519) 727-4545 *SIC* 3089

A.P. PLASMAN INC p 1022
5245 BURKE ST, WINDSOR, ON, N9A 6J6
(519) 737-6984 *SIC* 3089

A.P. PLASMAN INC p 1022
5265 OUTER DR, WINDSOR, ON, N9A 6J3
(519) 737-9602 *SIC* 3089

A.P. PLASMAN INC p 1022
5265 OUTER DR SUITE 2, WINDSOR, ON, N9A 6J3
(519) 737-9602 *SIC* 3089

A.P. PLASMAN INC p 1024
635 SPRUCEWOOD AVE, WINDSOR, ON, N9C 0B3
(519) 791-9119 *SIC* 3089

A.P. PLASMAN INC. p 911
See A.P. PLASMAN INC

A.P. PLASMAN INC. p 1017
See A.P. PLASMAN INC

A.P. PLASMAN INC. p 1022
See A.P. PLASMAN INC

A.P. PLASMAN INC. p 1024
See A.P. PLASMAN INC

A.P.A p 1325
See AGENCES W PELLETIER (1980) INC

A.P.I. ALARM INC p 770
700-5775 YONGE ST, NORTH YORK, ON, M2M 4J1
(416) 661-5566 *SIC* 1731

A.P.M. DIESEL p 1088
See A.P.M. DIESEL (1992) INC.

A.P.M. DIESEL (1992) INC. p 1088
135 RUE MINER, COWANSVILLE, QC, J2K 3Y5
(450) 260-1999 *SIC* 3519

A.P.M. LANDMARK INC p 1040
16 MCCARVILLE ST, CHARLOTTETOWN, PE, C1E 2A6
(902) 569-8400 *SIC* 1542

A.P.M. LIMITED p 406
96 KING ST, MONCTON, NB, E1C 4M6
(506) 857-3838 *SIC* 5013

A.P.S. METAL INDUSTRIES INC p 844
895 SANDY BEACH RD UNIT 4, PICKER-ING, ON, L1W 3N7
(905) 831-7698 *SIC* 3444

A.P.T. AUTO PARTS TRADING CO. LTD p
181
7342 WINSTON ST UNIT 10, BURNABY, BC, V5A 2H1
(604) 421-2781 *SIC* 5531

A.R. CONSTRUCTION p 1116
See 9105-6705 QUEBEC INC

A.R. THOMSON GROUP p 120
10030 31 AVE NW, EDMONTON, AB, T6N 1G4
(780) 450-8080 *SIC* 3053

A.R. THOMSON GROUP p 278
3420 189 ST, SURREY, BC, V3Z 1A7
(604) 507-6050 *SIC* 3053

A.R.G GROUP INC p 548
111 CREDITSTONE RD, CONCORD, ON, L4K 1N3
(905) 669-4133 *SIC* 1541

A.R.P. AUTO-AUXILIARIES INC p 1125
2300 RUE VICTORIA, LACHINE, QC, H8S 1Z3
(514) 634-7000 *SIC* 5962

A.R.T.B. p 1321
See ATELIER DE READAPTATION AU TRA-VAIL DE BEAUCE INC, L'

A.S. MAY POWELL CORPORATION p 691
2475 SKYMARK AVE UNIT 1, MISSIS-SAUGA, ON, L4W 4Y6
(905) 625-9306 *SIC* 5141

A.S.A. ALLOYS, DIV OF p 583
See CANADIAN SPECIALTY METALS ULC

A.S.A.P. SECURED INC p 1200
1255 RUE PEEL BUREAU 1101, MON-TREAL, QC, H3B 2T9
(514) 868-0202 *SIC* 7381

A.S.G. INC p 595
1010 POLYTEK ST SUITE 8, GLOUCES-TER, ON, K1J 9H8
(613) 749-8353 *SIC* 7379

A.S.P. INCORPORATED p 529
460 BRANT ST SUITE 212, BURLINGTON, ON, L7R 4B6
(905) 333-4242 *SIC* 7381

A.T. STORRS LTD p 285
1353 PENDER ST E, VANCOUVER, BC, V5L 1V7
(800) 561-5800 *SIC* 5094

A.T.L.A.S. AERONAUTIQUE INC p 1108
420 RUE EDOUARD, GRANBY, QC, J2G 3Z3
(450) 378-8107 *SIC* 5084

A.T.S. SECURITE p 1293
See PREMIERE SOCIETE EN COMMAN-DITE NATIONALE ALARMCAP

A.U.G. SIGNALS LTD p 948
73 RICHMOND ST W SUITE 103, TORONTO, ON, M5H 4E8
(416) 923-4425 *SIC* 8731

A.V.K. NURSERY HOLDINGS INC p 857
1724 CONCESSION 4, ROCKTON, ON, L0R 1X0

(905) 659-1518 *SIC* 5193

A.X.C. CONSTRUCTION INC p 1227
5101 RUE BUCHAN BUREAU 400, MON-TREAL, QC, H4P 1S4
(514) 937-3737 *SIC* 8742

A.Y. JACKSON SECONDARY SCHOOL p
625
See OTTAWA-CARLETON DISTRICT SCHOOL BOARD

A.Y.K. INTERNATIONAL INC p 1047
8250 RUE EDISON, ANJOU, QC, H1J 1S8
(514) 279-4648 *SIC* 5136

A/D FIRE PROTECTION SYSTEMS INC p
864
420 TAPSCOTT RD UNIT 5, SCARBOR-OUGH, ON, M1B 1Y4
(416) 292-2361 *SIC* 3479

A1 AIR CONDITIONING & HEATING SER-VICES p
801
See MESSENGER MECHANICAL INCOR-PORATED

A2M p 1182
See BEHAVIOUR INTERACTIF INC

A2Z p 1334
See GROUPE ALGO INC

A7 INTEGRATION INC p 1110
884 RUE COWIE, GRANBY, QC, J2J 1A8
(450) 305-6218 *SIC* 3499

AA MUNRO INSURANCE p 461
209 COBEQUID RD, LOWER SACKVILLE, NS, B4C 3P3
(902) 864-2510 *SIC* 6311

AAA CANADA INC p 1222
780 AV BREWSTER BUREAU 03-200, MONTREAL, QC, H4C 2K1
(514) 733-6655 *SIC* 4581

AAA ENTERPRISES INC p 184
3918 KITCHENER ST, BURNABY, BC, V5C 3M2
(604) 558-2250 *SIC* 5719

AAA PRECISION TIRE AND AUTOMOTIVE p 425
86 CLYDE AVE, MOUNT PEARL, NL, A1N 4S2
(709) 747-9595 *SIC* 5511

AAAAAA S.P. RADIAL SERVICE p 1179
See GROUPE TOUCHETTE INC

AACE FINANCIAL SERVICES LTD p 500
5 MELANIE DR UNIT 10, BRAMPTON, ON, L6T 4K8
(905) 799-8004 *SIC* 6311

AADA CAR LEASING p 750
See GRAHAM, TONY MOTORS (1980) LIM-ITED

AAER p 1110
See ELECTROGROUPE PIONEER CANADA INC

AAF CANADA INC p 1328
3233 RUE SARTELON, SAINT-LAURENT, QC, H4R 1E6
(514) 333-9048 *SIC* 5075

AAF INTERNATIONAL p 1328
See AAF CANADA INC

AALBERS TOOL & MOLD INC p 807
5390 BRENDAN LANE, OLDCASTLE, ON, N0R 1L0
(519) 737-1369 *SIC* 3544

AALTO'S FAMILY DINING p 354
See CANAD CORPORATION LTD

AALTO'S FAMILY DINING p 369
See CANAD CORPORATION LTD

AAR AIRCRAFT SERVICES - TROIS RIV-IERES ULC p
1387
3750 RUE DE L'AEROPORT, TROIS-RIVIERES, QC, G9A 5E1
(819) 377-4500 *SIC* 4581

AARDVARK p 1218
See MODES DO-GREE LTEE, LES

AARKEL TOOL AND DIE INC p 1004
17 ELM DR S, WALLACEBURG, ON, N8A 5E8
(519) 627-6078 *SIC* 3544

AARKEL TOOL AND DIE INC p 1004
760 LOWE AVE, WALLACEBURG, ON, N8A 5H5
(519) 627-9601 *SIC* 3544

AARKEL TOOL AND DIE INC p 1004
740 LOWE AVE, WALLACEBURG, ON, N8A 5H5
(519) 627-9601 *SIC* 3544

AAROC EQUIPMENT p 649
See J-AAR EXCAVATING LIMITED

AAS CO OF NFLD ULC p 423
1000 JAMES BLVD, GANDER, NL, A1V 2V4
(709) 256-8043 *SIC* 4581

AATEL COMMUNICATIONS INC p 610
413 VICTORIA AVE N, HAMILTON, ON, L8L 8G4
(905) 523-5451 *SIC* 1731

AB COX AUTOMOTIVE LTD p 480
305 WELLINGTON ST E, AURORA, ON, L4G 6C3
(905) 841-2121 *SIC* 5511

AB MAURI (CANADA) LIMITEE p 1131
31 RUE AIRLIE, LASALLE, QC, H8R 1Z8
(514) 366-1053 *SIC* 2099

AB NOTE NORTH AMERICA p 870
See ABCORP CA LTD

AB PALISADES LIMITED PARTNERSHIP p
311
1277 ROBSON ST, VANCOUVER, BC, V6E 1C2
(604) 688-0461 *SIC* 7011

ABACO PHARMA p 1047
See ATELIER ABACO INC

ABACUS DATAGRAPHICS LTD p 153
4814 50 ST SUITE 300, RED DEER, AB, T4N 1X4
(403) 346-7555 *SIC* 8713

ABALONE CONSTRUCTION (WESTERN) INC p 104
15531 131 AVE NW, EDMONTON, AB, T5V 0A4
(780) 451-3681 *SIC* 1629

ABANDONRITE ENVIRO SERVICES p 54
See NABORS DRILLING CANADA LIM-ITED

ABATTIS BIOCEUTICALS CORP p 301
625 HOWE ST SUITE 1200, VANCOUVER, BC, V6C 2T6

SIC 8731

ABATTOIR COLBEX INC p 1298
455 4E RANG DE SIMPSON, SAINT-CYRILLE-DE-WENDOVER, QC, J1Z 1T8
SIC 2011

ABATTOIR DES VOLTIGEURS p 1100
See FERME DES VOLTIGEURS INC

ABATTOIR DUBREUIL ENR p 1358
See VIANDE DUBREUIL INC

ABATTOIR DUCHARME INC p 1108
110 RUE AUTHIER, GRANBY, QC, J2G 7X2
(450) 375-4620 *SIC* 2011

ABB BOMEM p 1332
See ABB INC

ABB INC p 13
2 SMED LANE SE SUITE 110, CALGARY, AB, T2C 4T5
(403) 806-1700 *SIC* 5063

ABB INC p 27
4411 6 ST SE UNIT 110, CALGARY, AB, T2G 4E8
(403) 253-0271 *SIC* 8711

ABB INC p 77
9800 ENDEAVOR DR SE, CALGARY, AB, T3S 0A1
(403) 252-7551 *SIC* 3621

ABB INC p 259
10651 SHELLBRIDGE WAY, RICHMOND, BC, V6X 2W8
(604) 207-6000 *SIC* 7372

ABB INC p 500
201 WESTCREEK BLVD, BRAMPTON, ON, L6T 0G8
(905) 460-3000 *SIC* 5065

ABB INC p 527
3450 HARVESTER RD, BURLINGTON, ON,

L7N 3W5
(905) 639-8840   *SIC* 3823
ABB INC   *p* 1126
2117 32E AV, LACHINE, QC, H8T 3J1
SIC 5211
ABB INC   *p* 1257
585 BOUL CHAREST E BUREAU 300,
QUEBEC, QC, G1K 9H4
(418) 877-2944   *SIC* 3823
ABB INC   *p* 1332
800 BOUL HYMUS, SAINT-LAURENT, QC,
H4S 0B5
(514) 710-1203   *SIC* 3612
ABB INC   *p* 1332
800 BOUL HYMUS, SAINT-LAURENT, QC,
H4S 0B5
(438) 843-6000   *SIC* 3621
ABB INC   *p* 1392
1600 BOUL LIONEL-BOULET, VARENNES,
QC, J3X 1P7
(450) 652-1500   *SIC* 3612
ABB PRODUITS D'INSTALLATION LTEE *p*
1093
1811 BOUL HYMUS, DORVAL, QC, H9P
1J5
(514) 685-2277   *SIC* 3648
ABB PRODUITS D'INSTALLATION LTEE *p*
1248
4025 RTE TRANSCANADIENNE, POINTE-
CLAIRE, QC, H9R 1B4
(514) 694-6800   *SIC* 3699
ABB PRODUITS D'INSTALLATION LTEE *p*
1248
180 AV LABROSSE, POINTE-CLAIRE, QC,
H9R 1A1
(514) 630-4877   *SIC* 3699
ABB PRODUITS D'INSTALLATION LTEE *p*
1316
700 AV THOMAS, SAINT-JEAN-SUR-
RICHELIEU, QC, J2X 2M9
(450) 347-5318   *SIC* 3699
ABB PRODUITS D'INSTALLATION LTEE *p*
1317
100 RUE LONGTIN, SAINT-JEAN-SUR-
RICHELIEU, QC, J3B 3G5
(450) 347-2304   *SIC* 3644
**ABB SOLUTIONS INDUSTRIELLES
(CANADA) INC**   *p* 1332
800 BOUL HYMUS, SAINT-LAURENT, QC,
H4S 0B5
(450) 688-8690   *SIC* 4911
ABBARCH ARCHITECTURE INC   *p* 327
505 BURRARD ST SUITE 1830, VANCOU-
VER, BC, V7X 1M6
(604) 669-4041   *SIC* 8712
ABBEY CARDS & GIFTS LIMITED, THE   *p*
762
126 MAIN ST W, NORTH BAY, ON, P1B 2T5
(705) 472-2760   *SIC* 5947
ABBEY PARK HIGH SCHOOL   *p* 805
See HALTON DISTRICT SCHOOL BOARD
ABBEYWOOD MOVING & STORAGE INC *p*
878
480 FINCHDENE SQ, SCARBOROUGH,
ON, M1X 1C2
(416) 292-1107   *SIC* 4213
**ABBOTSFORD CHRISTIAN SCHOOL SO-
CIETY**   *p*
174
35011 OLD CLAYBURN RD, ABBOTS-
FORD, BC, V2S 7L7
(604) 755-1891   *SIC* 8661
**ABBOTSFORD CHRYSLER DODGE JEEP
RAM LTD**   *p* 176
30285 AUTOMALL DR, ABBOTSFORD, BC,
V2T 5M1
(604) 857-1000   *SIC* 5511
ABBOTSFORD COMMUNITY SERVICES *p*
174
2420 MONTROSE AVE, ABBOTSFORD,
BC, V2S 3S9
(604) 859-7681   *SIC* 8399
**ABBOTSFORD CONCRETE PRODUCTS
LTD**   *p* 174

3422 MCCALLUM RD, ABBOTSFORD, BC,
V2S 7W6
(604) 852-4967   *SIC* 3271
ABBOTSFORD DENTAL GROUP INC *p* 174
33782 MARSHALL RD, ABBOTSFORD, BC,
V2S 1L1
(604) 853-6441   *SIC* 8021
ABBOTSFORD FIRE RESCUE SERVICE *p*
176
See CITY OF ABBOTSFORD
ABBOTSFORD NEWS, THE   *p* 174
See BLACK PRESS GROUP LTD
ABBOTSFORD NISSAN LTD   *p* 176
30180 AUTOMALL DR, ABBOTSFORD, BC,
V2T 5M1
(604) 857-7755   *SIC* 5511
ABBOTSFORD RESTAURANTS LTD *p* 174
2142 WEST RAILWAY ST, ABBOTSFORD,
BC, V2S 2E2
(604) 855-9893   *SIC* 5812
ABBOTSFORD SECURITY SERVICES   *p*
176
2669 LANGDON ST SUITE 201, ABBOTS-
FORD, BC, V2T 3L3
(604) 870-4731   *SIC* 7381
ABBOTT   *p* 791
See ABBOTT OF ENGLAND 1981 LIMITED
ABBOTT DIAGNOSTICS, DIV OF   *p* 723
See LABORATOIRES ABBOTT, LIMITEE
ABBOTT MEDICAL OPTICAL INC *p* 666
80 WHITEHALL DR, MARKHAM, ON, L3R
0P3
(905) 305-3305   *SIC* 5995
ABBOTT OF ENGLAND 1981 LIMITED *p*
791
545 TRETHEWEY DR, NORTH YORK, ON,
M6M 2J4
(416) 789-7663   *SIC* 5199
**ABBOTT POINT OF CARE CANADA LIM-
ITED**   *p*
751
185 CORKSTOWN RD, NEPEAN, ON, K2H
8V4
(613) 688-5949   *SIC* 3841
ABBOTTSFORD HOUSE SENIOR CITIZ *p*
825
*See GLEBE CENTRE INCORPORATED,
THE*
ABBSRY NEW & USED TIRES   *p* 176
See ABBSRY USED TIRES LTD
ABBSRY USED TIRES LTD   *p* 176
31088 PEARDONVILLE RD UNIT 1, AB-
BOTSFORD, BC, V2T 6K5
(604) 870-0490   *SIC* 5531
ABC   *p* 1291
*See ASPHALTE, BETON, CARRIERES
RIVE-NORD INC*
ABC AIR MANAGEMENT SYSTEMS INC *p*
581
110 RONSON DR, ETOBICOKE, ON, M9W
1B6
(416) 744-3113   *SIC* 3089
ABC BENEFITS CORPORATION   *p* 86
10009 108 ST NW, EDMONTON, AB, T5J
3C5
(780) 498-8000   *SIC* 6321
ABC CANADA TECHNOLOGY GROUP LTD
p 1425
1802 QUEBEC AVE, SASKATOON, SK,
S7K 1W2
(306) 653-4303   *SIC* 2822
ABC CLIMATE CONTROL SYSTEMS INC *p*
581
54 BETHRIDGE RD, ETOBICOKE, ON,
M9W 1N1
(416) 744-3113   *SIC* 3089
ABC GROUP   *p* 1029
100 HANLAN RD SUITE 3, WOODBRIDGE,
ON, L4L 4V8
(905) 392-0485   *SIC* 6712
ABC GROUP LIMITED   *p* 792
2 NORELCO DR, NORTH YORK, ON, M9L
2X6
(416) 246-1782   *SIC* 6712

**ABC GROUP PRODUCT DEVELOPMENT,
DIV. OF**   *p* 500
See ABC TECHNOLOGIES INC
ABC GROUP TECH CENTRE   *p* 792
See ABC TECHNOLOGIES INC
ABC GROUP TRANSPORTATION   *p* 1029
See ABC GROUP
ABC INOAC EXTERIOR SYSTEMS INC *p*
581
220 BROCKPORT DR, ETOBICOKE, ON,
M9W 5S1
(416) 675-7480   *SIC* 3089
ABC INTERIOR SYSTEMS INC   *p* 581
10 DISCO RD, ETOBICOKE, ON, M9W 1L7
(416) 675-2220   *SIC* 3089
ABC OPERATIONS   *p* 764
See 1168768 ONTARIO INC
ABC PLASTIC MOULDING   *p* 687
See ABC TECHNOLOGIES INC
ABC PLASTICS LIMITED   *p* 792
2 NORELCO DR, NORTH YORK, ON, M9L
2X6
(416) 742-9600   *SIC* 3465
ABC PLASTICS MOULDING, A DIV OF *p*
581
See ABC TECHNOLOGIES INC
ABC TECHNOLOGIES INC   *p* 500
303 ORENDA RD SUITE B, BRAMPTON,
ON, L6T 5C3
(905) 450-3600   *SIC* 3089
ABC TECHNOLOGIES INC   *p* 581
20 BRYDON DR, ETOBICOKE, ON, M9W
5R6
SIC 3089
ABC TECHNOLOGIES INC   *p* 687
3325 ORLANDO DR, MISSISSAUGA, ON,
L4V 1C5
(905) 671-0310   *SIC* 3089
ABC TECHNOLOGIES INC   *p* 792
2 NORELCO DR, NORTH YORK, ON, M9L
2X6
(416) 246-1782   *SIC* 3089
ABC VENTILATION   *p* 1425
*See ABC CANADA TECHNOLOGY GROUP
LTD*
ABCANN MEDICINALS INC   *p* 747
126 VANLUVEN RD, NAPANEE, ON, K7R
3L2
(613) 354-6384   *SIC* 5122
ABCO   *p* 687
See ABCO INTERNATIONAL FREIGHT INC
ABCO INDUSTRIES INC   *p* 461
81 TANNERY RD, LUNENBURG, NS, B0J
2C0
(902) 634-8821   *SIC* 3569
ABCO INDUSTRIES LIMITED   *p* 461
81 TANNERY RD, LUNENBURG, NS, B0J
2C0
(902) 634-8821   *SIC* 3556
ABCO INTERNATIONAL FREIGHT INC *p*
687
5945 AIRPORT RD SUITE 338, MISSIS-
SAUGA, ON, L4V 1R9
(905) 405-8088   *SIC* 4731
ABCO MAINTENANCE SYSTEMS INC *p* 20
260 20 AVE NE, CALGARY, AB, T2E 1P9
(403) 293-5752   *SIC* 7349
ABCO MOVING SERVICES INC   *p* 870
2480 LAWRENCE AVE E SUITE 1, SCAR-
BOROUGH, ON, M1P 2R7
(416) 750-0118   *SIC* 1799
ABCO OFFICE INSTALLATION   *p* 870
See ABCO MOVING SERVICES INC
ABCO STC INC   *p* 1377
75 RUE PRINCIPALE, STANSTEAD, QC,
J0B 3E5
(819) 876-7281   *SIC* 3069
ABCO SUPPLY & SERVICE LTD   *p* 380
1346 SPRUCE ST, WINNIPEG, MB, R3E
2V7
(204) 633-8071   *SIC* 1711
ABCOR FILTERS INC   *p* 581
41 CITY VIEW DR, ETOBICOKE, ON, M9W
5A5

(416) 245-6886   *SIC* 3714
ABCORP CA LTD   *p* 870
15 GOLDEN GATE CRT, SCARBOROUGH,
ON, M1P 3A4
(416) 293-3842   *SIC* 3089
ABCOTT CONSTRUCTION LTD   *p* 515
124 GARDEN AVE, BRANTFORD, ON, N3S
7W4
(519) 756-4350   *SIC* 1542
ABCOURT SILVER MINE   *p* 1158
See MINES ABCOURT INC
**ABCP ARCHITECTURE ET URBANISME
LTEE**   *p* 1257
300 RUE SAINT-PAUL BUREAU 412, QUE-
BEC, QC, G1K 7R1
(418) 649-7369   *SIC* 8712
ABCRC   *p* 20
*See ALBERTA BEVERAGE CONTAINER
RECYCLING CORPORATION*
ABEBOOKS EUROPE GMBH   *p* 339
See ABEBOOKS INC
ABEBOOKS INC   *p* 339
655 TYEE RD SUITE 500, VICTORIA, BC,
V9A 6X5
(250) 412-3200   *SIC* 5192
ABEILLES BUSY BEES   *p* 1246
*See ABEILLES SERVICES DE CONDI-
TIONNEMENT INC, LES*
**ABEILLES SERVICES DE CONDITION-
NEMENT INC, LES**   *p*
1246
12910 BOUL METROPOLITAIN E, POINTE-
AUX-TREMBLES, QC, H1A 4A7
(514) 640-6941   *SIC* 7389
ABELL PEST CONTROL INC   *p* 581
246 ATTWELL DR, ETOBICOKE, ON, M9W
5B4
(416) 675-1635   *SIC* 7342
ABELSOFT INC   *p* 527
3310 SOUTH SERVICE RD SUITE 101,
BURLINGTON, ON, L7N 3M6
(905) 333-3200   *SIC* 7371
ABERCROMBI FIRE HALL   *p* 463
*See ABERCROMBIE VOLUNTEER FIRE
DEPT*
ABERCROMBIE VOLUNTEER FIRE DEPT *p*
463
GD LCD MAIN, NEW GLASGOW, NS, B2H
5C9
(902) 752-4248   *SIC* 7389
**ABERDEEN ASIA-PACIFIC INCOME IN-
VESTMENT COMPANY LIMITED**   *p*
958
161 BAY ST, TORONTO, ON, M5J 2S1
SIC 6726
ABERNETHY FOODS (ORILLIA) INC *p* 809
80 FITTONS RD W, ORILLIA, ON, L3V 7A1
(705) 325-9072   *SIC* 5411
ABF CUSTOM MFG. LTD   *p* 687
6750 PROFESSIONAL CRT, MISSIS-
SAUGA, ON, L4V 1X6
(905) 612-0743   *SIC* 3469
ABHAY ENTERPRISES LTD   *p* 199
1401 JOHNSON ST, COQUITLAM, BC, V3E
3J3
(604) 464-1347   *SIC* 5541
**ABI/ADVANCED BUSINESS INTERIORS
INC**   *p* 816
2355 ST. LAURENT BLVD, OTTAWA, ON,
K1G 4L2
(613) 738-1003   *SIC* 5712
ABILITY FABRICATORS INC   *p* 548
187 ROMINA DR, CONCORD, ON, L4K 4V3
(905) 761-1401   *SIC* 3312
ABILITY HAULING DIV OF   *p* 43
*See AVEDA TRANSPORTATION AND EN-
ERGY SERVICES INC*
ABIPA CANADA INC   *p* 1061
3700 AV DES GRANDES TOURELLES,
BOISBRIAND, QC, J7H 0A1
(450) 963-6888   *SIC* 3721
ABITIBI BOWATER   *p* 887
See PF RESOLU CANADA INC
ABITIBI GEOPHYSIQUE INC   *p* 1390

1746 CH SULLIVAN, VAL-D'OR, QC, J9P 7H1

(819) 874-8800   *SIC* 1382

ABITIBI-CONSOLIDATED, DIVISION BAIE-COMEAU *p* 1052

See PF RESOLU CANADA INC

ABITIBIBOWATER *p* 1148

See PF RESOLU CANADA INC

ABITIBIBOWATER CANADA INC *p* 1209

111 RUE DUKE BUREAU 5000, MONTREAL, QC, H3C 2M1

(514) 875-2160   *SIC* 6712

ABLE COPIERS LTD *p* 238

12 ORWELL ST, NORTH VANCOUVER, BC, V7J 2G1

(604) 904-9858   *SIC* 5999

ABLE INSURANCE BROKERS LTD *p* 691

2560 MATHESON BLVD E SUITE 400, MISSISSAUGA, ON, L4W 4Y9

(905) 629-2253   *SIC* 6411

ABLE TRANSLATIONS LTD *p* 704

5749 COOPERS AVE, MISSISSAUGA, ON, L4Z 1R9

(905) 502-0000   *SIC* 7389

ABLE-ONE SYSTEMS INC *p* 638

127 VICTORIA ST S SUITE 101, KITCHENER, ON, N2G 2B4

(519) 570-9100   *SIC* 5045

ABM *p* 253

See APPLIED BIOLOGICAL MATERIALS INC

ABOND CORPORATION INC *p* 1126

10050 CH DE LA COTE-DE-LIESSE, LACHINE, QC, H8T 1A3

(514) 636-7979   *SIC* 5099

ABONNEMENT CANADA *p* 1269

See GROUPE SOMITEL INC

ABONNEMENT QUEBEC & DESSIN *p* 1205

See IMPRIMERIES TRANSCONTINENTAL INC

ABORIGINAL PEOPLE'S TELEVISION NETWORK INCORPORATED *p* 374

339 PORTAGE AVE, WINNIPEG, MB, R3B 2C3

(204) 947-9331   *SIC* 4833

ABOUGOUCHE BROS ENTERPRISES LTD *p* 138

10114 101 ST, LAC LA BICHE, AB, T0A 2C0

(780) 623-4234   *SIC* 5411

ABOUGOUSH COLLISION INC *p* 220

1960 DAYTON ST, KELOWNA, BC, V1Y 7W6

(250) 868-2693   *SIC* 7532

ABOVE BOARD CONSTRUCTION INC *p* 844

1731 ORANGEBROOK CRT, PICKERING, ON, L1W 3G8

(905) 420-0656   *SIC* 1542

ABRAHAM, R.J. DRUGS LTD *p* 658

1186 OXFORD ST W, LONDON, ON, N6H 4N2

(519) 471-7151   *SIC* 5912

ABRAMS *p* 916

See 1512081 ONTARIO LTD

ABRASIFS J.J.S. INC *p* 1140

900 CH OLIVIER, LEVIS, QC, G7A 2N1

(418) 836-0557   *SIC* 5085

ABRASIVE BLAST & PAINT INC *p* 148

1207 16 AVE, NISKU, AB, T9E 0A8

(780) 955-3616   *SIC* 5085

ABRASIVE TECHNOLOGY NA, INC *p* 1093

2250 BOUL HYMUS, DORVAL, QC, H9P 1J9

(514) 421-7396   *SIC* 5085

ABREY ENTERPRISES INC *p* 236

815 MCBRIDE BLVD, NEW WESTMINSTER, BC, V3L 2B9

(604) 718-1189   *SIC* 5812

ABRPPVM *p* 1173

See ASSOCIATION DE BIENFAISSANCE ET DE RETRAITE DES POLICIERS DE LA VILLE DE MONTREAL

ABS EQUIPMENT LEASING LTD *p* 702

1495 SEDLESCOMB DR, MISSISSAUGA, ON, L4X 1M4

(905) 625-5941   *SIC* 3545

ABS FRICTION INC *p* 606

55 TAGGART ST, GUELPH, ON, N1L 1M6

(519) 763-9000   *SIC* 3714

ABS GROUP OF COMPANIES *p* 647

See ABS MANUFACTURING AND DISTRIBUTING LIMITED

ABS MACHINING INC *p* 702

1495 SEDLESCOMB DR, MISSISSAUGA, ON, L4X 1M4

(905) 625-5941   *SIC* 3499

ABS MANUFACTURING AND DISTRIBUTING LIMITED *p* 647

185 MAGILL ST, LIVELY, ON, P3Y 1K6

(705) 692-5445   *SIC* 3569

ABSA THE PRESSURE EQUIPMENT SAFETY AUTHORITY *p* 120

See ALBERTA BOILERS SAFETY ASSOCIATION (ABSA)

ABSOLU COMMUNICATION MARKETING *p* 1397

See CREATION STRATEGIQUE ABSOLUE INC

ABSOLUTE *p* 327

See ABSOLUTE SOFTWARE CORPORATION

ABSOLUTE COMPLETION TECHNOLOGIES LTD *p* 74

302-600 CROWFOOT CRES NW, CALGARY, AB, T3G 0B4

(403) 266-5027   *SIC* 8711

ABSOLUTE ENERGY LTD *p* 74

600 CROWFOOT CRES NW SUITE 302, CALGARY, AB, T3G 0B4

(403) 509-4000   *SIC* 6712

ABSOLUTE ENERGY SOLUTIONS INC *p* 108

5710 36 ST NW, EDMONTON, AB, T6B 3T2

(780) 440-9058   *SIC* 3545

ABSOLUTE METALS *p* 1152

See METAUX ABSOLUS INC

ABSOLUTE PALLET & CRATE INC *p* 884

104 DUNKIRK RD, ST CATHARINES, ON, L2P 3H5

SIC 4953

ABSOLUTE RESULTS *p* 278

See ABSOLUTE RESULTS PRODUCTIONS LTD

ABSOLUTE RESULTS MARKETING SYSTEMS INC *p* 278

2677 192 ST UNIT 104, SURREY, BC, V3Z 3X1

(888) 751-7171   *SIC* 7311

ABSOLUTE RESULTS PRODUCTIONS LTD *p* 278

2677 192 ST UNIT 104, SURREY, BC, V3Z 3X1

(888) 751-7171   *SIC* 8748

ABSOLUTE SOFTWARE CORPORATION *p* 327

1055 DUNSMUIR ST SUITE 1400, VANCOUVER, BC, V7X 1K8

(604) 730-9851   *SIC* 7371

ABSOLUTE TOOL TECHNOLOGIES INC *p* 1022

5455 OUTER DR, WINDSOR, ON, N9A 6J3

(519) 737-9428   *SIC* 3544

ABSOPULSE ELECTRONICS LTD *p* 540

110 WALGREEN RD, CARP, ON, K0A 1L0

(613) 836-3511   *SIC* 3679

ABSORBENT PRODUCTS LTD *p* 218

724 SARCEE ST E, KAMLOOPS, BC, V2H 1E7

(250) 372-1600   *SIC* 2048

ABSOLUTE COMPLETION TECHNOLOGIES *p* 108

See ABSOLUTE ENERGY SOLUTIONS INC

ABZAC AMERIQUE *p* 1096

See ABZAC CANADA INC

ABZAC CANADA INC *p* 1096

2945 BOUL LEMIRE, DRUMMONDVILLE, QC, J2B 6Y8

(514) 866-3488   *SIC* 2655

AC CUISINES *p* 1267

See JULIEN INC

AC FINAL MILE INC *p* 500

107 ALFRED KUEHNE BLVD, BRAMPTON, ON, L6T 4K3

(905) 362-2999   *SIC* 7389

AC OMEX *p* 896

See OMEX MANUFACTURING ULC

AC PETROLEUM *p* 243

See 682880 B.C. LTD

ACA *p* 161

See ALBERTA CONSERVATION ASSOCIATION

ACA TMETRIX INC *p* 716

3585 LAIRD RD UNIT 15-16, MISSISSAUGA, ON, L5L 5Y4

(905) 890-2010   *SIC* 5065

ACADEMIE CULINAIRE ROLAND & FRERES *p* 1349

See ROLAND & FRERES LIMITEE

ACADEMIE DU SACRE-COEUR *p* 1372

See COMMISSION SCOLAIRE DE LA REGION-DE-SHERBROOKE

ACADEMIE HEBRAIQUE *p* 1083

See HEBREW ACADEMY INC

ACADEMIE INTERNATIONALE CHARLES-LEMOYNE *p* 1146

See COLLEGE CHARLES-LEMOYNE DE LONGUEUIL INC

ACADEMIE LAFONTAINE INC *p* 1319

2171 BOUL MAURICE, SAINT-JEROME, QC, J7Y 4M7

(450) 431-3733   *SIC* 8211

ACADEMIE LES ESTACADES *p* 1384

See COMMISSION SCOLAIRE DU CHEMIN-DU-ROY

ACADEMIE MICHELE-PROVOST INC *p* 1212

1517 AV DES PINS O, MONTREAL, QC, H3G 1B3

(514) 935-2344   *SIC* 8211

ACADEMIE SAINTE-ANNE *p* 1126

See COLLEGE SAINTE-ANNE

ACADEMIE STE-THERESE INC, L' *p* 1287

1 CH DES ECOLIERS, ROSEMERE, QC, J7A 4Y1

(450) 434-1130   *SIC* 8211

ACADEMY CANADA INC *p* 422

25 PARK DR, CORNER BROOK, NL, A2H 7H8

(709) 637-2130   *SIC* 8244

ACADEMY CONSTRUCTION & MAINTENANCE LIMITED PARTNERSHIP *p* 108

4066 78 AVE NW, EDMONTON, AB, T6B 3M8

(780) 395-4914   *SIC* 3498

ACADEMY CONSTRUCTION & MAINTENANCE LTD *p* 108

4066 78 AVE NW, EDMONTON, AB, T6B 3M8

(780) 466-6360   *SIC* 3498

ACADEMY FABRICATORS GROUP LIMITED PARTNERSHIP *p* 108

4066-78 AVE, EDMONTON, AB, T6B 3M8

(780) 395-4914   *SIC* 6211

ACADEMY FABRICATORS LIMITED PARTNERSHIP *p* 151

5208 LAC STE ANNE TR N, ONOWAY, AB, T0E 1V0

(780) 967-3111   *SIC* 3498

ACADEMY GROUP, THE *p* 151

See ACADEMY FABRICATORS LIMITED PARTNERSHIP

ACADEX IMPORTS *p* 1177

See 9189-8718 QUEBEC INC

ACADIA DRYWALL SUPPLIES LTD *p* 397

521 BOUL FERDINAND, DIEPPE, NB, E1A 7G1

(506) 858-1319   *SIC* 5032

ACADIA JUNIOR HIGH SCHOOL *p* 391

See PEMBINA TRAILS SCHOOL DIVISION, THE

ACADIA MOTORS LTD *p* 407

22 BAIG BLVD, MONCTON, NB, E1E 1C8

(506) 857-8611   *SIC* 5511

ACADIA PAVING LTD. *p* 1433

121 105TH ST E, SASKATOON, SK, S7N 1Z2

(306) 374-4738   *SIC* 1611

ACADIA STUDENTS' UNION INC *p* 471

30 HIGHLAND AVE, WOLFVILLE, NS, B4P 1Y7

(902) 585-2110   *SIC* 6321

ACADIA TOYOTA *p* 407

See ACADIA MOTORS LTD

ACADIAN COACH LINES LP *p* 406

300 MAIN ST UNIT B2-2, MONCTON, NB, E1C 1B9

SIC 4142

ACADIAN CONSTRUCTION (1991) LTD *p* 397

671 BOUL MALENFANT SUITE 2, DIEPPE, NB, E1A 5T8

(506) 857-1909   *SIC* 1542

ACADIAN GROUP *p* 738

See COATINGS 85 LTD

ACADIAN SEAPLANTS LIMITED *p* 444

30 BROWN AVE, DARTMOUTH, NS, B3B 1X8

(902) 468-2840   *SIC* 2875

ACADIAN SUPREME INC *p* 1043

8323 11 RTE, WELLINGTON STATION, PE, C0B 2E0

(902) 854-2675   *SIC* 5146

ACADIAN TIMBER CORP *p* 311

1055 GEORGIA ST W SUITE 1800, VANCOUVER, BC, V6E 0B6

(604) 661-9143   *SIC* 5082

ACADIAN TIMBER EDMUNDSTON DIV OF *p* 398

See AT LIMITED PARTNERSHIP

ACADIE NOUVELLE *p* 396

See EDITIONS DE L'ACADIE NOUVELLE (1984) LTEE, LES

ACAN WINDOWS AND DOORS *p* 427

See ACAN WINDOWS INC

ACAN WINDOWS INC *p* 427

1641 TOPSAIL RD, PARADISE, NL, A1L 1V1

SIC 3089

ACANA CAPITAL CORP *p* 275

8338 120 ST SUITE 200, SURREY, BC, V3W 3N4

(604) 592-6881   *SIC* 1521

ACAPULCO POOLS LIMITED *p* 635

1550 VICTORIA ST N, KITCHENER, ON, N2B 3E2

(519) 743-6357   *SIC* 5091

ACASTA *p* 916

See ACASTA ENTERPRISES INC

ACASTA ENTERPRISES INC *p* 916

1 APOLLO PL, TORONTO, ON, M3J 0H2

SIC 8732

ACC S COMMUNICATION *p* 1156

See 152163 CANADA INC

ACC CABLES *p* 20

See ALBERTA COMPUTER CABLE INC

ACCEL CONSTRUCTION MANAGEMENT INC *p* 548

50 VICEROY RD UNIT 11, CONCORD, ON, L4K 3A7

(905) 660-6690   *SIC* 7389

ACCEL HIGH RISE CONSTRUCTION LTD *p* 978

66 PORTLAND ST SUITE 801, TORONTO, ON, M5V 2M6

SIC 1542
ACCELERATED CONNECTIONS INC p 978
155 WELLINGTON ST W SUITE 3740,
TORONTO, ON, M5V 3H1
(416) 637-3432 SIC 4899
ACCENT p 1249
See AMEUBLEMENTS EL RAN LTEE
**ACCENT CARE HOME & HOSPITAL
HEALTH SERVICES INC** p 374
420 NOTRE DAME AVE, WINNIPEG, MB,
R3B 1R1
(204) 783-9888 SIC 6531
ACCENT CRUISES.CA p 319
1676 DURANLEAU ST SUITE 100, VAN-
COUVER, BC, V6H 3S4
(604) 688-8072 SIC 4725
ACCENT HOME PRODUCTS p 1329
See GROUPE ACCENT-FAIRCHILD INC
ACCENT IMPORTS p 680
See CANDYM ENTERPRISES LTD
ACCENT INNS INC p 337
3233 MAPLE ST, VICTORIA, BC, V8X 4Y9
(250) 475-7500 SIC 7011
**ACCENTURE BUSINESS SERVICES FOR
UTILITIES INC** p 296
510 GEORGIA ST W SUITE 2075, VAN-
COUVER, BC, V6B 0M3
(604) 646-5000 SIC 8741
**ACCENTURE BUSINESS SERVICES FOR
UTILITIES INC** p 903
123 COMMERCE VALLEY DR E SUITE
500, THORNHILL, ON, L3T 7W8
SIC 8741
ACCENTURE INC p 296
401 GEORGIA ST W SUITE 1500, VAN-
COUVER, BC, V6B 5A1
(604) 646-5000 SIC 8741
ACCENTURE INC p 691
5450 EXPLORER DR SUITE 400, MISSIS-
SAUGA, ON, L4W 5N1
(416) 641-5000 SIC 8741
ACCENTURE INC p 822
45 O'CONNOR ST SUITE 600, OTTAWA,
ON, K1P 1A4
(613) 750-5000 SIC 7379
ACCENTURE INC p 948
40 KING ST W SUITE 4800, TORONTO,
ON, M5H 3Y2
(416) 641-5220 SIC 8741
ACCENTURE INC p 1193
1800 AV MCGILL COLLEGE BUREAU 800,
MONTREAL, QC, H3A 3J6
(514) 848-1648 SIC 8741
ACCEO SOLUTIONS INC p 1209
75 RUE QUEEN BUREAU 5200, MON-
TREAL, QC, H3C 2N6
(514) 868-0333 SIC 7371
ACCEO SOLUTIONS INC p 1277
7710 BOUL WILFRID-HAMEL, QUEBEC,
QC, G2G 2J5
(418) 877-0088 SIC 7372
ACCES JEUX p 1173
See SUPERCLUB VIDEOTRON LTEE, LE
ACCES PHARMA CHEZ WALMART p 1148
See WAL-MART CANADA CORP
ACCES PHARMA CHEZ WALMART p 1363
See WAL-MART CANADA CORP
ACCES PHARMA CHEZ WALMART p 1365
See WAL-MART CANADA CORP
ACCES QUEEN SANTE GSS INC p 1122
1650 CH DE SAINT-JEAN BUREAU 101, LA
PRAIRIE, QC, J5R 0J1
SIC 8093
ACCES TOYOTA p 1289
See AU CARROSSIER INC
ACCES VACANCES p 1278
See AGENCE DE VOYAGES
D'AUTOMOBILE ET TOURING CLUB DU
QUEBEC INC
ACCESS p 1201
See AIR LIQUIDE CANADA INC
ACCESS p 1329
See GROUPE ALDO INC, LE
ACCESS p 1338

See CUIRS BENTLEY INC
ACCESS CASH GENERAL PARTNERSHIP
p 581
191 ATTWELL DR UNIT 4, ETOBICOKE,
ON, M9W 5Z2
(416) 247-0200 SIC 6099
**ACCESS CENTRE FOR HASTINGS AND
PRINCE EDWARD COUNTIES, THE** p 490
470 DUNDAS ST E, BELLEVILLE, ON, K8N
1G1
(613) 962-7272 SIC 8621
ACCESS COMMUNICATIONS p 1415
See ACCESS COMMUNICATIONS CO-
OPERATIVE LIMITED
**ACCESS COMMUNICATIONS CO-
OPERATIVE LIMITED** p
1415
2250 PARK ST, REGINA, SK, S4N 7K7
(306) 569-2225 SIC 4813
ACCESS COMMUNITY SERVICES INC p
847
160 WALTON ST, PORT HOPE, ON, L1A
1N6
(905) 885-6358 SIC 8361
ACCESS COPYRIGHT p 942
See CANADIAN COPYRIGHT LICENSING
AGENCY
ACCESS CREDIT UNION LIMITED p 361
23111 PTH 14 UNIT 2, WINKLER, MB, R6W
4B4
(204) 331-1612 SIC 6062
ACCESS FLOWER TRADING INC p 802
700 DORVAL DR SUITE 405, OAKVILLE,
ON, L6K 3V3
(905) 849-1343 SIC 5193
ACCESS INSURANCE GROUP LTD p 112
4435 99 ST NW, EDMONTON, AB, T6E 5B6
(780) 435-2400 SIC 6411
ACCESS METAL SERVICE INC p 737
1035 MID-WAY BLVD, MISSISSAUGA, ON,
L5T 2C1
(905) 670-3151 SIC 5051
ACCESS PIPELINE INC p 42
520 3 AVE SW SUITE 1500, CALGARY, AB,
T2P 0R3
(403) 264-6514 SIC 4619
ACCESS PLUMBING & HEATING LTD p 165
215 CARNEGIE DR UNIT 5, ST. ALBERT,
AB, T8N 5B1
(780) 459-5999 SIC 1711
ACCESS RESEARCH INC p 974
180 BLOOR ST W SUITE 1402, TORONTO,
ON, M5S 2V6
(416) 960-9603 SIC 8732
ACCESS RIVER EAST p 367
See WINNIPEG REGIONAL HEALTH AU-
THORITY, THE
ACCESS SECURITY PROFESSIONALS p
529
See A.S.P. INCORPORATED
ACCESSOIRES BY/PAR RAE p 1109
See LANDES CANADA INC
ACCESSOIRES CAPELLI p 1340
See IMPORTATIONS INTERNATIONALES
BOCHITEX INC, LES
ACCESSOIRES D'AUTO LEBLANC LTEE p
1387
3125 BOUL GENE-H.-KRUGER BUREAU
1624, TROIS-RIVIERES, QC, G9A 4M2
(819) 378-2871 SIC 5013
ACCESSOIRES DE JARDIN p 1320
See MATERIAUX LAURENTIENS INC
ACCESSOIRES DE MOTO ADM p 1311
See 4223373 CANADA INC
ACCESSOIRES DE MOTOS A. D. M. p 1263
See 129157 CANADA INC
ACCESSOIRES OUTILLAGE LIMITEE p
1177
8755 BOUL SAINT-LAURENT, MONTREAL,
QC, H2N 1M2
(514) 387-6466 SIC 5082
ACCESSOIRES POUR VELOS O.G.D. LTEE
p 1332
10555 BOUL HENRI-BOURASSA O, SAINT-

LAURENT, QC, H4S 1A1
(514) 332-1320 SIC 7312
ACCESSOIRES SEPT-ILES p 1367
See DISTRIBUTIONS J.R.V. INC
ACCESSORY WAREHOUSE p 119
See TRUCK OUTFITTERS INC, THE
ACCEUIL BONNEAU INC p 1187
427 RUE DE LA COMMUNE E, MON-
TREAL, QC, H2Y 1J4
(514) 845-3906 SIC 8699
ACCIDENT BENEFIT SOLUTION p 719
6300 PRAIRIE CIR, MISSISSAUGA, ON,
L5N 5Y9
(905) 824-4476 SIC 6321
**ACCIDENT INJURY MEDICAL ASSESS-
MENT** p
782
1280 FINCH AVE W SUITE 507, NORTH
YORK, ON, M3J 3K6
(416) 665-4010 SIC 6321
**ACCIONA INFRASTRUCTURE CANADA
INC** p 327
595 BURRARD ST SUITE 2000, VANCOU-
VER, BC, V7X 1J1
(604) 622-6550 SIC 1541
ACCLAIM ABILITY MANAGEMENT INC p
978
82 PETER ST, TORONTO, ON, M5V 2G5
(416) 486-9706 SIC 8741
ACCLAIM HEALTH p 803
See ACCLAIM HEALTH COMMUNITY
CARE SERVICES
**ACCLAIM HEALTH COMMUNITY CARE
SERVICES** p 803
2370 SPEERS RD, OAKVILLE, ON, L6L
5M2
(905) 827-8800 SIC 8082
ACCO BRANDS CANADA INC p 733
7381 BRAMALEA RD, MISSISSAUGA, ON,
L5S 1C4
(905) 364-2600 SIC 3579
ACCO BRANDS CANADA LP p 733
7381 BRAMALEA RD, MISSISSAUGA, ON,
L5S 1C4
(905) 364-2600 SIC 2678
ACCOLADE GROUP p 850
See ACCOLADE GROUP INC
ACCOLADE GROUP INC p 850
66 WEST BEAVER CREEK RD, RICH-
MOND HILL, ON, L4B 1G5
(416) 465-7211 SIC 2329
ACCOR CANADA INC p 709
3670 HURONTARIO ST, MISSISSAUGA,
ON, L5B 1P3
(905) 896-1000 SIC 7011
ACCOR CANADA INC p 820
33 NICHOLAS ST, OTTAWA, ON, K1N 9M7
(613) 760-4771 SIC 7011
ACCOR CANADA INC p 915
3 PARK HOME AVE, TORONTO, ON, M2N
6L3
(416) 733-2929 SIC 7011
ACCOR MANAGEMENT CANADA INC p
978
155 WELLINGTON ST W SUITE 3300,
TORONTO, ON, M5V 0C3
(416) 874-2600 SIC 6531
ACCOR MANAGEMENT CANADA INC p
1201
900 BOUL RENE-LEVESQUE O, MON-
TREAL, QC, H3B 4A5
(514) 861-3511 SIC 7011
ACCOR SERVICES CANADA INC p 42
133 9 AVE SW, CALGARY, AB, T2P 2M3
(403) 262-1234 SIC 7011
ACCOR SERVICES CANADA INC p 978
155 WELLINGTON ST W SUITE 3300,
TORONTO, ON, M5V 0C3
(416) 874-2600 SIC 6712
ACCORA VILLAGE p 830
See FERGUSLEA PROPERTIES LIMITED
ACCORD EXPOSITIONS INC p 1127
1530 46E AV, LACHINE, QC, H8T 3J9
(514) 639-6998 SIC 7389

ACCORD FINANCIAL CORP p 974
77 BLOOR ST W 18 FL, TORONTO, ON,
M5S 1M2
(416) 961-0007 SIC 6159
ACCORD FINANCIAL LTD p 922
40 EGLINTON AVE E' SUITE 602,
TORONTO, ON, M4P 3A2
(416) 961-0007 SIC 8741
ACCORD INTERNATIONAL LEAF INC p
1249
193 AV LABROSSE, POINTE-CLAIRE, QC,
H9R 1A3
SIC 5159
ACCORD LOGISTICS LTD p 271
17660 65A AVE UNIT 207, SURREY, BC,
V3S 5N4
(604) 331-9515 SIC 4731
ACCORD PLASTICS CORP p 548
60 COURTLAND AVE, CONCORD, ON, L4K
5B3
SIC 3089
**ACCORD SPECIALIZED INVESTIGATIONS
& SECURITY** p 917
1560 BAYVIEW AVE SUITE 300,
TORONTO, ON, M4G 3B8
(416) 322-2013 SIC 7382
ACCORD TRANSPORTATION LTD p 271
17665 66A AVE SUITE 801, SURREY, BC,
V3S 2A7
(604) 575-7500 SIC 4213
ACCOUNTEMPS, DIV OF p 963
See HALF, ROBERT CANADA INC
**ACCREDITATION ASSISTANCE ACCESS
CENTRE** p 756
See SOCIAL ENTERPRISE FOR CANADA
ACCREDITATION CANADA p 595
1150 CYRVILLE RD SUITE 759,
GLOUCESTER, ON, K1J 7S9
(613) 738-3800 SIC 8399
ACCREDITED SUPPORTS p 151
See ACCREDITED SUPPORTS TO THE
COMMUNITY
**ACCREDITED SUPPORTS TO THE COM-
MUNITY** p
82
1709 15TH AVE, DIDSBURY, AB, T0M 0W0
(403) 335-8671 SIC 8322
**ACCREDITED SUPPORTS TO THE COM-
MUNITY** p
151
4322 50 AVE, OLDS, AB, T4H 1A5
(403) 556-4110 SIC 8322
ACCREON INC p 400
414 YORK ST, FREDERICTON, NB, E3B
3P7
(506) 452-0551 SIC 8748
ACCU-FLO METER SERVICE LTD p 27
4024 7 ST SE, CALGARY, AB, T2G 2Y8
(403) 243-1425 SIC 5084
ACCUCAM MACHINING p 535
See 742906 ONTARIO INC
ACCUCUT PROFILE & GRINDING LIMITED
p 548
300 CONNIE CRES, CONCORD, ON, L4K
5W6
(416) 798-7716 SIC 5051
ACCUFLEX INDUSTRIAL HOSE LTD p 605
760 IMPERIAL RD N, GUELPH, ON, N1K
1Z3
(519) 836-5460 SIC 3052
ACCULOGIC INC p 666
175 RIVIERA DR SUITE 1, MARKHAM, ON,
L3R 5J6
(905) 475-5907 SIC 7371
ACCULOGIX DISTRIBUTION SERVICES p
13
4747 68 AVE SE, CALGARY, AB, T2C 4Z4
(403) 236-1555 SIC 8742
ACCUMARK PARTNERS INC p 927
2 BLOOR ST E SUITE 2600, TORONTO,
ON, M4W 1A8
(416) 446-7758 SIC 8743
ACCURATE ARCHERY p 3
See ECKO MARINE LTD

ACCURATE DORWIN INC   p 390
1535 SEEL AVE, WINNIPEG, MB, R3T 1C6
(204) 982-4640   SIC 3229

ACCURATE FASTENERS LTD   p 548
550 APPLEWOOD CRES SUITE 1, CONCORD, ON, L4K 4B4
(416) 798-7887   SIC 5085

ACCURATE GROUP OF COMPANIES, THE   p 548
See ACCURATE FASTENERS LTD

ACCURATE MACHINE & TOOL LIMITED   p 794
1844 WILSON AVE, NORTH YORK, ON, M9M 1A1
(416) 742-8301   SIC 3469

ACCURATE SCREEN LTD   p 13
7571 57 ST SE, CALGARY, AB, T2C 5M2
(403) 723-0323   SIC 5051

ACCURCAST CORPORATION   p 1004
333 ARNOLD ST, WALLACEBURG, ON, N8A 3P3
(519) 627-2227   SIC 6712

ACCURCAST INC   p 1004
333 ARNOLD ST, WALLACEBURG, ON, N8A 3P3
(519) 627-2227   SIC 3365

ACCURETTE DESSIN   p 1158
See APTALIS PHARMA CANADA ULC

ACCURIDE CANADA INC   p 650
31 FIRESTONE BLVD, LONDON, ON, N5W 6E6
(519) 453-0880   SIC 3714

ACCURISTIX   p 1026
122 STONE RIDGE RD, WOODBRIDGE, ON, L4H 0A5
(905) 829-9927   SIC 4225

ACCURISTIX ADVANCING HEALTHCARE LOGISTIC   p 1026
See ACCURISTIX

ACD   p 452
See ATLANTIC CATCH DATA LIMITED

ACE BAKERY LIMITED   p 733
580 SECRETARIAT CRT, MISSISSAUGA, ON, L5S 2A5
(905) 565-8138   SIC 5461

ACE CANADA   p 392
See RONA INC

ACE COM CANADA CORPORATION p 1193
1981 AV MCGILL COLLEGE BUREAU 500, MONTREAL, QC, H3A 2X1
SIC 4899

ACE COURIER SERVICES   p 183
See ALL-CAN EXPRESS LTD

ACE INA INSURANCE   p 959
25 YORK ST SUITE 1400, TORONTO, ON, M5J 2V5
(416) 368-2911   SIC 6331

ACE INSTRUMENTS LTD   p 213
11207 TAHLTAN RD, FORT ST. JOHN, BC, V1J 6G8
(250) 785-1207   SIC 5084

ACE MANUFACTURING METALS LTD p 5
GD, BITTERN LAKE, AB, T0C 0L0
(780) 352-7145   SIC 3644

ACE PHARMACY LTD   p 198
206 PORT AUGUSTA ST, COMOX, BC, V9M 3N1
(250) 339-2235   SIC 6712

ACE PLUMBING   p 219
See BRICOR MECHANICAL LTD

ACE VEGETATION CONTROL SERVICE LTD   p 148
2001 8 ST, NISKU, AB, T9E 7Z1
(780) 955-8980   SIC 1629

ACE VEGETATION SERVICE   p 148
See ACE VEGETATION CONTROL SERVICE LTD

ACEMA IMPORTATIONS INC   p 1145
2616 BOUL JACQUES-CARTIER E, LONGUEUIL, QC, J4N 1P8
(450) 646-2591   SIC 5141

ACER AMERICA CORPORATION CANADA   p 704
5540 MCADAM RD, MISSISSAUGA, ON,
L4Z 1P1
(905) 755-7570   SIC 5065

ACERO ENGINEERING INC   p 42
600 6 AVE SW SUITE 900, CALGARY, AB, T2P 0S5
(403) 237-7388   SIC 8711

ACETAMINOPHENE-ODAN 325 MG COMPRIMES   p 1251
See LABORATOIRES ODAN LTEE, LES

ACF   p 737
See ADVANCED COPPER FOIL INC

ACF/TRANSPORTAIDE   p 1337
See 2904357 CANADA INC

ACGI SHIPPING INC   p 301
900 HASTINGS ST W SUITE 1100, VANCOUVER, BC, V6C 1E5
(604) 683-4221   SIC 4731

ACHAT SURPLUS MONTREAL INC p 1332
2800 RUE DE MINIAC, SAINT-LAURENT, QC, H4S 1K9
(438) 995-2650   SIC 5065

ACHESON, A.J. SALES LIMITED   p 444
30 LAMONT TERR, DARTMOUTH, NS, B3B 0B5
(902) 434-2823   SIC 5531

ACHESON, ALAN J. LIMITED   p 444
30 LAMONT TERR, DARTMOUTH, NS, B3B 0B5
(902) 434-2823   SIC 5014

ACHIEVA FINANCIAL DIV OF   p 377
See CAMBRIAN CREDIT UNION LIMITED

ACHIEVERS SOLUTIONS INC   p 991
190 LIBERTY ST SUITE 100, TORONTO, ON, M6K 3L5
(888) 622-3343   SIC 7361

ACHIEVING EXCELLENCE   p 7
120 3 ST W, BROOKS, AB, T1R 0S3
(403) 362-6661   SIC 8611

ACHIEVO NETSTAR SOLUTIONS COMPANY   p 775
220 DUNCAN MILL RD SUITE 505, NORTH YORK, ON, M3B 3J5
(416) 383-1818   SIC 7371

ACHOO TISSU   p 1117
See MARTINI-VISPAK INC

ACHOO TISSU   p 1229
See MARTINI-VISPAK INC

ACI BRANDS INC   p 800
2616 SHERIDAN GARDEN DR, OAKVILLE, ON, L6J 7Z2
(905) 829-1566   SIC 5137

ACI MANAGEMENT GROUP INC   p 106
12531 60 ST NW, EDMONTON, AB, T5W 5J5
(780) 476-3098   SIC 6712

ACI TECTNOLOGY   p 27
See AKINAI CANADA INC

ACI WORLDWIDE (CANADA) INC   p 978
200 WELLINGTON ST W SUITE 700, TORONTO, ON, M5V 3C7
(416) 813-3000   SIC 5045

ACIC PHARMACEUTICALS INC   p 515
81 SINCLAIR BLVD, BRANTFORD, ON, N3S 7X6
(519) 751-3668   SIC 5122

ACIER ADF / ADF STEEL   p 1381
See GROUPE ADF INC

ACIER AGF INC   p 1141
2270 RUE GARNEAU, LONGUEUIL, QC, J4G 1E7
(450) 442-9494   SIC 1791

ACIER AGF INC   p 1265
595 AV NEWTON, QUEBEC, QC, G1P 4C4
(418) 877-7715   SIC 2499

ACIER ANICA   p 1053
See DISTRIBUTIONS D'ACIER ANICA INC, LES

ACIER ATR   p 1141
See ACIER AGF INC

ACIER BRETON   p 1296
See STRUCTURES BRETON INC, LES

ACIER CAMPI   p 1364
See ACIER OUELLETTE INC

ACIER CENTURY INC   p 1125
600 RUE DE LA BERGE-DU-CANAL, LACHINE, QC, H8R 1H4
(514) 364-1505   SIC 5093

ACIER DE FONDATIONS SKYLINE (PHP) CANADA   p 1069
See SKYLINE (PHP) CANADA ULC

ACIER DM   p 1104
See 6368425 CANADA LTD

ACIER DRUMMOND INC   p 1097
1750 RUE JANELLE, DRUMMONDVILLE, QC, J2C 3E5
(819) 477-4418   SIC 5051

ACIER ECAN   p 1265
See ACIER AGF INC

ACIER FASTECH INC   p 1124
652 RUE DU PARC, LAC-DROLET, QC, G0Y 1C0
(819) 549-1010   SIC 1541

ACIER GENDRON LTEE   p 1141
2270 RUE GARNEAU, LONGUEUIL, QC, J4G 1E7
(450) 442-9494   SIC 5051

ACIER HYDRAULIQUE INC   p 1292
173 RUE DE LIVERPOOL, SAINT-AUGUSTIN-DE-DESMAURES, QC, G3A 2C8
(418) 878-5711   SIC 5051

ACIER INOXYDABLE FAFARD INC   p 1063
21 RUE DE MONTGOLFIER, BOUCHERVILLE, QC, J4B 8C4
(450) 641-4349   SIC 3312

ACIER INOXYDABLE PINACLE INC   p 737
455 AMBASSADOR DR, MISSISSAUGA, ON, L5T 2J3
(905) 795-2882   SIC 5051

ACIER LACHINE INC   p 1125
1520 CROIS CLAIRE, LACHINE, QC, H8S 4E6
(514) 634-2252   SIC 5051

ACIER LEROUX   p 726
See RUSSEL METALS INC

ACIER MARTIN BASTILLE   p 1285
See BASTILLE, MARTIN INC

ACIER METOSTEEL   p 1162
See GROUPE J.S.V. INC, LE

ACIER METROPOLITAN   p 1308
See METROBEC INC

ACIER NOVA INC   p 891
830 SOUTH SERVICE RD, STONEY CREEK, ON, L8E 5M7
(905) 643-3300   SIC 3312

ACIER NOVA INC   p 1034
807 PATTULLO AVE, WOODSTOCK, ON, N4S 7W3
(519) 537-6639   SIC 3312

ACIER NOVA INC   p 1130
6001 RUE IRWIN, LASALLE, QC, H8N 1A1
(514) 789-0511   SIC 5051

ACIER OUELLETTE INC   p 1319
22 RUE JOHN-F.-KENNEDY, SAINT-JEROME, QC, J7Y 4B6
(514) 876-1414   SIC 5051

ACIER OUELLETTE INC   p 1364
935 BOUL DU HAVRE, SALABERRY-DE-VALLEYFIELD, QC, J6S 5L1
(450) 377-4248   SIC 3312

ACIER OUELLETTE SAINT-JEROME p 1319
See ACIER OUELLETTE INC

ACIER PACIFIQUE INC   p 1342
845 AV MUNCK, SAINT-LAURENT, QC, H7S 1A9
(514) 384-4690   SIC 5051

ACIER PICARD INC   p 1137
3000 RUE DE L'ETCHEMIN, LEVIS, QC, G6W 7X6
(418) 834-8300   SIC 5051

ACIER PICARD INC   p 1392
1951 CH DE L'ENERGIE, VARENNES, QC, J3X 1P7
(450) 652-7000   SIC 5051

ACIER PROFILE S.B.B. INC   p 1058
10 RUE EMILIEN-MARCOUX, BLAINVILLE,
QC, J7C 0B5
(450) 970-3055   SIC 5063

ACIER QUEBEC-MARITIMES INC   p 1285
396 RUE TEMISCOUATA, RIVIERE-DU-LOUP, QC, G5R 2Z2
(418) 862-1320   SIC 5051

ACIER STRUCTURAL LAINCO   p 1381
See LAINCO INC

ACIER TRIMAX INC   p 1359
1440 3E AV DU PARC-INDUSTRIEL, SAINTE-MARIE, QC, G6E 3T9
(418) 387-7798   SIC 3441

ACIER VALLEYFIELD   p 1097
See ACIER DRUMMOND INC

ACIER VALLEYFIELD   p 1317
See ACIERS H & H INC, LES

ACIER VALLEYFIELD INC   p 1365
480 BOUL DES ERABLES, SALABERRY-DE-VALLEYFIELD, QC, J6T 6G4
(450) 373-4350   SIC 5051

ACIER VICTORIA LTEE   p 1398
900 RUE DE L'ACADIE, VICTORIAVILLE, QC, G6T 1V1
(819) 758-7575   SIC 5051

ACIERS DYMIN ALBERTA, LES   p 1309
See TUYAUX ET MATERIEL DE FONDATION LTEE

ACIERS H & H INC, LES   p 1317
920 RUE PIERRE-CAISSE, SAINT-JEAN-SUR-RICHELIEU, QC, J3B 7Y5
(450) 349-5801   SIC 5051

ACIERS INOXYDABLES   p 1332
See ACIERS INOXYDABLES C.F.F. (QUEBEC) INC

ACIERS INOXYDABLES C.F.F. (QUEBEC) INC   p 1332
4900 CH DU BOIS-FRANC, SAINT-LAURENT, QC, H4S 1A7
(514) 337-7700   SIC 5085

ACIERS J.P. INC, LES   p 1123
15 3E AV E, LA REINE, QC, J0Z 2L0
(819) 947-8291   SIC 5084

ACIERS REMI LATULIPPE INC, LES p 1392
481 112 RTE E, VALLEE-JONCTION, QC, G0S 3J0
(418) 253-5521   SIC 5093

ACIERS RICHELIEU INC, LES   p 1376
190 RUE DU ROI, SOREL-TRACY, QC, J3P 4N5
(450) 743-1265   SIC 3499

ACIERS SOFATEC INC, LES   p 1355
867 5E AV BUREAU A, SAINTE-ANNE-DES-PLAINES, QC, J0N 1H0
(450) 478-3365   SIC 3441

ACIERS SOLIDER INC, LES   p 1398
300 RUE DE LA JACQUES-CARTIER, VICTORIAVILLE, QC, G6T 1Y3
(819) 758-2897   SIC 1791

ACIERS TECHFORM MONTAL INC p 1380
3139 BOUL DES ENTREPRISES, TERREBONNE, QC, J6X 4J9
(450) 477-5705   SIC 3312

ACKER FINLEY CANADA FOCUS FUND p 948
181 UNIVERSITY AVE SUITE 1400, TORONTO, ON, M5H 3M7
(416) 777-9005   SIC 6722

ACKLANDS - GRAINGER INC   p 92
14360 123 AVE NW, EDMONTON, AB, T5L 2Y3
SIC 5085

ACKLANDS - GRAINGER INC   p 95
11708 167 ST NW, EDMONTON, AB, T5M 3Z2
(780) 453-0300   SIC 5085

ACKLANDS - GRAINGER INC   p 903
123 COMMERCE VALLEY DR E SUITE 700, THORNHILL, ON, L3T 7W8
(905) 731-5516   SIC 5085

ACKLANDS - GRAINGER INC   p 903
50 MINTHORN BLVD, THORNHILL, ON, L3T 7X8
(905) 763-3474   SIC 5084

ACKLANDS - GRAINGER INC   p 1434

3602 MILLAR AVE, SASKATOON, SK, S7P 0B1
(306) 664-5500   SIC 5085

ACL   p 356
See ACL SELKIRK INC

ACL SELKIRK INC   p 356
306 JEMIMA ST, SELKIRK, MB, R1A 1X1
(204) 482-5435   SIC 8699

ACL SERVICES LTD   p 325
980 HOWE ST SUITE 1500, VANCOUVER, BC, V6Z 0C8
(604) 669-4225   SIC 7371

ACL STEEL LTD   p 635
2255 SHIRLEY DR, KITCHENER, ON, N2B 3X4
(519) 568-8822   SIC 3441

ACM PANELWORX INC   p 1017
357 CROFT DR, WINDSOR, ON, N8N 2L9
(519) 739-2380   SIC 5051

ACME   p 808
See ACME UNITED LIMITED

ACME ANALYTICAL LABORATORIES   p 323
See BUREAU VERITAS COMMODITIES CANADA LTD

ACME AWNINGS PRESTIGE   p 1163
5598 RUE HOCHELAGA BUREAU 101, MONTREAL, QC, H1N 3L7
(514) 252-1998   SIC 5039

ACME FOOD CO, THE   p 233
14 COMMERCIAL ST, NANAIMO, BC, V9R 5G2
(250) 753-0042   SIC 5411

ACME GLASS LTD   p 275
8335 129 ST, SURREY, BC, V3W 0A6
(604) 543-8777   SIC 1521

ACME SUPPLIES LTD   p 334
2311 GOVERNMENT ST, VICTORIA, BC, V8T 4P4
(250) 383-8822   SIC 5087

ACME UNITED LIMITED   p 808
210 BROADWAY SUITE 204, ORANGEVILLE, ON, L9W 5G4
(519) 940-8755   SIC 5112

ACML   p 778
See ANGUS CONSULTING MANAGEMENT LIMITED

ACOM BUILDING MAINTENANCE LTD   p 191
3871 NORTH FRASER WAY UNIT 23, BURNABY, BC, V5J 5G6
(604) 436-2121   SIC 7349

ACORN CONTINENTAL HARDWOODS   p 361
See ELIAS WOODWORKING AND MANUFACTURING LTD

ACORN PACKAGING INC   p 708
563 QUEENSWAY E UNIT B, MISSISSAUGA, ON, L5A 3X6
(905) 279-5256   SIC 2759

ACOSTA CANADA   p 1029
See ACOSTA CANADA CORPORATION

ACOSTA CANADA CORP   p 1029
250 ROWNTREE DAIRY RD, WOODBRIDGE, ON, L4L 9J7
(905) 264-0466   SIC 5141

ACOUSTICAL & TOTAL CLEANING SERVICES   p 112
See ACOUSTICAL CEILING & BUILDING MAINTENANCE LTD

ACOUSTICAL CEILING & BUILDING MAINTENANCE LTD   p 112
7940 CORONET RD NW, EDMONTON, AB, T6E 4N8
(780) 496-9035   SIC 7349

ACOUSTIQUE ISOLATION QUATRE SAISONS INC   p 1282
525 RUE LANAUDIERE, REPENTIGNY, QC, J6A 7N1
(450) 657-5000   SIC 5033

ACOUSTIQUE S. MAYER   p 1106
See 3197786 CANADA INC

ACP MARKETING CANADA INC   p 1227
8375 RUE BOUGAINVILLE BUREAU 100, MONTREAL, QC, H4P 2G5
(514) 733-5247   SIC 4725

ACP RAIL INTERNATIONAL   p 1227
See ACP MARKETING CANADA INC

ACPI   p 520
See ALIGNED CAPITAL PARTNERS INC

ACQUISIO WEB.COM, ULC   p 1071
6300 AV AUTEUIL BUREAU 300, BROSSARD, QC, J4Z 3P2
(450) 465-2631   SIC 7371

ACQUISITION GMP   p 952
See GRIFFITHS MCBURNEY CANADA CORP

ACR CANADA CORPORATION   p 364
122 PAQUIN RD, WINNIPEG, MB, R2J 3V4
(204) 669-2345   SIC 2821

ACR FULLER GROUP   p 148
511 12 AVE, NISKU, AB, T9E 7N8
(780) 955-2802   SIC 3069

ACRES ENTERPRISES LTD   p 216
971 CAMOSUN CRES, KAMLOOPS, BC, V2C 6G1
(250) 372-7456   SIC 6553

ACRES MANITOBA   p 378
See HATCH LTD

ACROBAT RESEARCH LTD   p 540
GD, CAPREOL, ON, P0M 1H0
(705) 858-4343   SIC 8732

ACROBAT RESEARCH LTD   p 704
170 ROBERT SPECK PKY SUITE 201, MISSISSAUGA, ON, L4Z 3G1
(416) 503-4343   SIC 8732

ACROBAT RESULT MARKETING   p 540
See ACROBAT RESEARCH LTD

ACROBAT RESULT MARKETING   p 704
See ACROBAT RESEARCH LTD

ACRODEX INC   p 98
11420 170 ST NW, EDMONTON, AB, T5S 1L7
(780) 426-4444   SIC 8731

ACROLAB TECHNOLOGIES INC   p 1018
7475 TRANBY AVE, WINDSOR, ON, N8S 2B7
(519) 944-5900   SIC 6712

ACROSS CANADA CONSTRUCTION LTD   p 1029
220 REGINA RD, WOODBRIDGE, ON, L4L 8L6
(905) 264-9500   SIC 1542

ACRYLCO MFG. LTD   p 205
711 DERWENT WAY, DELTA, BC, V3M 5P9
(604) 524-9441   SIC 5162

ACRYLIC FABRICATORS LIMITED   p 548
89A CONNIE CRES UNIT 4, CONCORD, ON, L4K 1L3
(905) 660-6666   SIC 2542

ACRYLIQUE WEEDON (1995) INC   p 1383
591 RUE DES ENTREPRISES, THETFORD MINES, QC, G6H 4B2
(418) 332-4224   SIC 3089

ACRYLON PLASTICS INC   p 357
2954 DAY ST, SPRINGFIELD, MB, R2C 2Z2
(204) 669-2224   SIC 3089

ACRYLON PLASTICS MB (1983) INC   p 361
355 AIRPORT DR, WINKLER, MB, R6W 0J9
(204) 325-9569   SIC 3089

ACT II CHILD & FAMILY SERVICES SOCIETY   p 199
1034 AUSTIN AVE, COQUITLAM, BC, V3K 3P3
(604) 937-7776   SIC 8399

ACT3 M.H.S. INC   p 1181
7236 RUE MARCONI, MONTREAL, QC, H2R 2Z5
(514) 844-5050   SIC 7319

ACTAVIS PHARMA COMPANY   p 719
6500 KITIMAT RD, MISSISSAUGA, ON, L5N 2B8
(905) 814-1820   SIC 2834

ACTE3 M.H.S.   p 1181
See ACT3 M.H.S. INC

ACTELION PHARMACEUTIQUES CANADA INC   p 1133
3111 BOUL SAINT-MARTIN O BUREAU 300, LAVAL, QC, H7T 0K2
(450) 681-1664   SIC 5122

ACTION CAR AND TRUCK ACCESSORIES   p 407
See ACTION CAR AND TRUCK ACCESSORIES INC

ACTION CAR AND TRUCK ACCESSORIES INC   p 407
200 HORSMAN RD, MONCTON, NB, E1E 0E8
(506) 857-8786   SIC 5013

ACTION CHEVROLET INC   p 1307
7955 CH DE CHAMBLY, SAINT-HUBERT, QC, J3Y 5K2
(450) 445-7333   SIC 5511

ACTION COLLECTIONS AND RECEIVABLES MANAGEMENT   p 764
See 852515 ONTARIO LIMITED

ACTION CONSTRUCTION INFRASTRUCTURE ACI INC   p 1114
1095 RUE SAMUEL-RACINE, JOLIETTE, QC, J6E 0E8
(450) 755-6887   SIC 1611

ACTION D'AUTRAY   p 1309
See GROUPE LEXIS MEDIA INC

ACTION ELECTRIC LTD   p 294
1277 GEORGIA ST E, VANCOUVER, BC, V6A 2A9
(604) 734-9146   SIC 1731

ACTION ELECTRICAL LTD   p 121
2333 91 AVE, EDMONTON, AB, T6P 1L1
(780) 465-0792   SIC 1731

ACTION EXPRESS & HOTSHOT   p 148
See 1484174 ALBERTA LTD

ACTION GROUP   p 138
See LACOMBE ACTION GROUP FOR THE HANDICAPPED

ACTION HONDA   p 866
See CHEVALIER AUTOMOBILES INC

ACTION IMPORTS   p 737
See ARANA GARDENING SUPPLIES LIMITED

ACTION LINE HOUSING SOCIETY   p 184
3755 MCGILL ST, BURNABY, BC, V5C 1M2
(604) 291-0607   SIC 8361

ACTION MANAGEMENT SERVICES INC   p 438
23 MAIN ST, ANTIGONISH, NS, B2G 2B3
(902) 863-3200   SIC 6512

ACTION REALTY LTD   p 515
766 COLBORNE ST, BRANTFORD, ON, N3S 3S1
(519) 753-7311   SIC 6531

ACTION REBAR, DIV OF   p 243
See ACTION STEEL SALES (OKANAGAN) LTD

ACTION SPORT PHYSIO VAUDREUIL-DORION INC   p 1394
11 CITE DES JEUNES EST SUITE 101, VAUDREUIL-DORION, QC, J7V 8V9
(450) 455-0111   SIC 8049

ACTION STEEL SALES (OKANAGAN) LTD   p 243
2365 BARNES ST, PENTICTON, BC, V2A 7K6
(250) 492-7822   SIC 5051

ACTION TQS   p 1209
See V INTERACTIONS INC

ACTION TRAILER SALES INC   p 734
2332 DREW RD, MISSISSAUGA, ON, L5S 1B8
(905) 678-1444   SIC 5012

ACTIONWEAR SASKATOON INC   p 1424
114 MELVILLE ST, SASKATOON, SK, S7J 0R1
(306) 933-3088   SIC 3842

ACTIONWEST   p 1424
See ACTIONWEAR SASKATOON INC

ACTIVA CONSTRUCTION INC   p 1006
55 COLUMBIA ST E SUITE 1, WATERLOO, ON, N2J 4N7
(519) 886-9400   SIC 1521

ACTIVATION MARKETING   p 1205
See IMPRIMERIES TRANSCONTINENTAL 2005 S.E.N.C.

ACTIVATION MARKETING   p 1209
See TRANSCONTINENTAL INTERACTIF INC

ACTIVATION MARKETING   p 1209
See TRANSCONTINENTAL INC

ACTIVATION PRODUCTS (CAN) INC   p 544
975A ELGIN ST W SUITE 357, COBOURG, ON, K9A 5J3
(416) 702-2962   SIC 5169

ACTIVE BURGESS MOULD & DESIGN   p 1023
See ACTIVE INDUSTRIAL SOLUTIONS INC

ACTIVE ENERGY   p 529
See ACTIVE ENERGY CORP

ACTIVE ENERGY CORP   p 529
390 BRANT ST SUITE 402, BURLINGTON, ON, L7R 4J4
(416) 238-5540   SIC 4924

ACTIVE EXHAUST CORP   p 870
1865 BIRCHMOUNT RD, SCARBOROUGH, ON, M1P 2J5
(416) 445-9610   SIC 5084

ACTIVE FIRE & SAFETY SERVICES LTD   p 275
12110 86 AVE, SURREY, BC, V3W 3H7
(604) 590-0149   SIC 5099

ACTIVE GEAR COMPANY OF CANADA LIMITED   p 548
201R SNIDERCROFT RD SUITE 1, CONCORD, ON, L4K 2J9
(905) 669-2292   SIC 5013

ACTIVE GREEN + ROSS   p 571
See ACTIVE TIRE & AUTO CENTRE INC

ACTIVE INDUSTRIAL SOLUTIONS INC   p 1023
5250 PULLEYBLANK ST, WINDSOR, ON, N9A 6J3
SIC 3544

ACTIVE INDUSTRIAL SOLUTIONS INC   p 1023
2155 NORTH TALBOT RD SUITE 3, WINDSOR, ON, N9A 6J3
(519) 737-1341   SIC 3544

ACTIVE MARBLE & TILE LTD   p 39
5355 8 ST NE, CALGARY, AB, T2K 5R9
(403) 274-2111   SIC 5211

ACTIVE NETWORK   p 719
2480 MEADOWVALE BLVD SUITE 1, MISSISSAUGA, ON, L5N 8M6
(905) 286-6600   SIC 7371

ACTIVE NETWORK LTD, THE   p 286
2925 VIRTUAL WAY SUITE 310, VANCOUVER, BC, V5M 4X5
(800) 661-1196   SIC 7371

ACTIVE OPTICAL SUPPLY   p 485
125 ANNE ST S SUITE 207, BARRIE, ON, L4N 7B6
(705) 812-2602   SIC 5049

ACTIVE SECURITY ENTERPRISE   p 511
See 2320610 ONTARIO INC

ACTIVE TIRE & AUTO CENTRE INC   p 571
580 EVANS AVE, ETOBICOKE, ON, M8W 2W1
(416) 255-5581   SIC 5531

ACTIVE TRANSPORT INC   p 682
245 BRONTE ST N, MILTON, ON, L9T 3N7
(905) 878-8167   SIC 4212

ACTIVESTATE SOFTWARE INC   p 311
1177 HASTINGS ST W UNIT 1000, VANCOUVER, BC, V6E 2K3
(778) 786-1100   SIC 7372

ACTO   p 1172
See XYZ TECHNOLOGIE CULTURELLE INC

ACTTON SUPER-SAVE GAS STATIONS LTD   p 271

19395 LANGLEY BYPASS, SURREY, BC, V3S 6K1

(604) 533-4423   SIC 5541

ACTTON TRANSPORT LTD   p 271
19395 LANGLEY BYPASS, SURREY, BC, V3S 6K1

(604) 533-4423   SIC 4213

ACTUS MANAGEMENT (VAUGHAN) INC p 548
7501 KEELE ST, CONCORD, ON, L4K 1Y2

(905) 760-2700   SIC 8741

ACUITY HOLDINGS, INC   p 99
11627 178 ST NW, EDMONTON, AB, T5S 1N6

(780) 453-5800   SIC 2844

ACUITYADS HOLDINGS INC   p 959
181 BAY ST SUITE 320, TORONTO, ON, M5J 2T3

(416) 218-9888   SIC 7371

ACUMEN CAPITAL FINANCE PARTNERS LIMITED   p 42
404 6 AVE SW UNIT 700, CALGARY, AB, T2P 0R9

(403) 571-0300   SIC 6211

ACUMEN CAPITAL PARTNERS   p 42
See ACUMEN CAPITAL FINANCE PARTNERS LIMITED

ACUMEN INSURANCE GROUP INC p 894
835 PARAMOUNT DR SUITE 301, STONEY CREEK, ON, L8J 0B4

(905) 574-7000   SIC 6411

ACURA   p 1065
See HONDA CANADA INC

ACURA 2000   p 498
See 1166709 ONTARIO LIMITED

ACURA BROSSARD   p 1069
See 9039-4735 QUEBEC INC

ACURA CENTRE OF SASKATOON p 1425
See KELLY & BELL HOLDINGS LTD

ACURA GABRIEL   p 1092
See FADY AUTO INC

ACURA IN MARKHAM   p 1000
See TRANSASIAN FINE CARS LTD

ACURA LAVAL   p 1086
See LAVAL AUTOS HAMEL INC

ACURA OF BARRIE   p 485
See 1422718 ONTARIO INC

ACURA OF LANGLEY   p 227
See 598755 B.C. LTD

ACURA OF MONCTON   p 397
See 055841 NB LTD

ACURA OF NORTH TORONTO   p 906
See 1850178 ONTARIO LIMITED

ACURA OF OAKVILLE   p 805
See 2020455 ONTARIO INC

ACURA ON BRANT   p 530
See TRIUS AUTOMOBILE INC

ACURA PLUS   p 1058
See AUTO PLUS J.F. HAMEL INC

ACURA SHERWAY   p 578
See 2486535 ONTARIO LTD

ACUREN GROUP INC   p 121
7450 18 ST NW, EDMONTON, AB, T6P 1N8

(780) 440-2131   SIC 8734

ACUREN GROUP INC   p 129
240 TAIGANOVA CRES UNIT 2, FORT MCMURRAY, AB, T9K 0T4

(780) 790-1776   SIC 8711

ACUREN GROUP INC   p 262
12271 HORSESHOE WAY, RICHMOND, BC, V7A 4V4

(604) 275-3800   SIC 3821

ACUREX HEALTH CARE MANUFACTURING   p 513
See 1277487 ONTARIO LIMITED

ACUSHNET CANADA INC   p 754
500 HARRY WALKER PKY NE, NEWMARKET, ON, L3Y 8T6

(905) 898-7575   SIC 5091

ACUTE NETWORK SOLUTIONS   p 859
See 8867038 CANADA INC

ACUTRUSS INDUSTRIES (1996) LTD p 331
2003 43 ST, VERNON, BC, V1T 6K7

(250) 545-3215   SIC 2439

AD HOC MARKETING   p 1193
See AD HOC RECHERCHE INC

AD HOC RECHERCHE INC   p 1193
400 BOUL DE MAISONNEUVE O BUREAU 1200, MONTREAL, QC, H3A 1L4

(514) 937-4040   SIC 8732

AD-BAG   p 1206
See MEDIAS TRANSCONTINENTAL S.E.N.C.

AD-LIB FORMATION   p 1202
See CABINET DE RELATIONS PUBLIQUES NATIONAL INC, LE

ADACEL INC   p 1201
895 RUE DE LA GAUCHETIERE O BUREAU 300, MONTREAL, QC, H3B 4G1

(450) 444-2687   SIC 3812

ADACEL TECHNOLOGIES   p 1201
See ADACEL INC

ADAGIO   p 1364
See CONVECTAIR-NMT INC

ADAM   p 845
See WEPAWAUG CANADA CORP

ADAM INTERNATIONAL   p 1192
See 10393266 CANADA INC

ADAM'S   p 1335
See OLD DUTCH FOODS LTD

ADAMO ESTATE WINERY   p 808
See LJP CORPORATION

ADAMS 22 HOLDINGS LTD   p 211
2628 BEVERLY ST, DUNCAN, BC, V9L 5C7

(250) 709-2205   SIC 5461

ADAMS LAKE LUMBER   p 195
See INTERFOR CORPORATION

ADAMS PHARMACY LTD   p 630
797 PRINCESS ST, KINGSTON, ON, K7L 1G1

(613) 544-2500   SIC 5912

ADAMSON & DOBBIN LIMITED   p 840
407 PIDO RD, PETERBOROUGH, ON, K9J 6X7

(705) 745-5751   SIC 1711

ADAMSON ASSOCIATES   p 978
401 WELLINGTON ST W 3RD FLR, TORONTO, ON, M5V 1E7

(416) 967-1500   SIC 8712

ADAMSON SYSTEMS ENGINEERING INCp 848
1401 SCUGOG LINE 6, PORT PERRY, ON, L9L 1B2

(905) 982-0520   SIC 3651

ADANAC PARK LODGE   p 284
See LITTLE MOUNTAIN RESIDENTIAL CARE & HOUSING SOCIETY

ADANAC RECOVERY LTD   p 337
3961 QUADRA ST, VICTORIA, BC, V8X 1J7

(250) 727-7480   SIC 7389

ADARE PHARMACEUTICALS, ULC p 1158
597 BOUL SIR-WILFRID-LAURIER, MONT-SAINT-HILAIRE, QC, J3H 6C4

(514) 774-2973   SIC 2834

ADARE PHARMATECH CANADA   p 1158
See ADARE PHARMACEUTICALS, ULC

ADASTRA CORPORATION   p 903
8500 LESLIE ST SUITE 600, THORNHILL, ON, L3T 7M8

(905) 881-7946   SIC 7371

ADC   p 130
See ASENIWUCHE DEVELOPEMENT CORPORATION

ADC ASSURANCES ABITIBI   p 1390
See HARMONIA ASSURANCE INC

ADCO LOGISTICS   p 736
See 1175648 ONTARIO LIMITED

ADD INK   p 876
See ATLANTIC PACKAGING PRODUCTS LTD

ADDENDA CAPITAL INC   p 1201
800 BOUL RENE-LEVESQUE O BUREAU 2750, MONTREAL, QC, H3B 1X9

(514) 287-0223   SIC 6282

ADDENERGIE   p 1266
See ADDENERGIE TECHNOLOGIES INC

ADDENERGIE TECHNOLOGIES INCp 1266

2800 RUE LOUIS-LUMIERE STE 100, QUEBEC, QC, G1P 0A4

(877) 505-2674   SIC 3629

ADDIK.TV   p 1175
See GROUPE TVA INC

ADDISON CHEVROLET BUICK GMC (WEST)   p 719
6600 TURNER VALLEY RD, MISSISSAUGA, ON, L5N 5Z1

(866) 980-6928   SIC 5511

ADDITIFS DE PERFORMANCE ELITE p 1063
See AZELIS CANADA INC

ADDITION ELLE   p 1217
See REITMANS (CANADA) LIMITEE

ADEASE MEDIA INTELLIGENCE   p 778
See ADEASE MEDIA RESEARCH INC

ADEASE MEDIA RESEARCH INC   p 778
150 FERRAND DR SUITE 800, NORTH YORK, ON, M3C 3E5

(416) 423-2010   SIC 8732

ADECCO   p 374
See ADECCO EMPLOYMENT SERVICES LIMITED

ADECCO EMPLOYMENT SERVICES LIMITED   p 374
228 NOTRE DAME AVE, WINNIPEG, MB, R3B 1N7

SIC 7361

ADECCO EMPLOYMENT SERVICES LIMITED   p 959
20 BAY ST SUITE 800, TORONTO, ON, M5J 2N8

(416) 646-3322   SIC 7361

ADELAIDE CLUB, THE   p 921
See WINGBACK ENTERPRISES LIMITED

ADELARD SOUCY (1975) INC   p 1285
217 RUE TEMISCOUATA, RIVIERE-DU-LOUP, QC, G5R 2Y6

(418) 862-2355   SIC 8711

ADELCO   p 1342
See VERITIV CANADA, INC

ADEN BOWMAN COLLEGIATE   p 1426
See BOARD OF EDUCATION OF SASKATOON SCHOOL DIVISION NO. 13 OF SASKATCHEWAN, THE

ADENA SPRINGS NORTH   p 480
See ALPEN HOUSE ULC, THE

ADENAT INC   p 500
3 BREWSTER RD UNIT 1, BRAMPTON, ON, L6T 5G9

(905) 794-2808   SIC 5122

ADESA AUCTIONS CANADA CORPORATION   p 2
1621 VETERANS BLVD NW, AIRDRIE, AB, T4A 2G7

(403) 912-4400   SIC 5012

ADESA AUCTIONS CANADA CORPORATION   p 148
1701 9 ST, NISKU, AB, T9E 8M8

(780) 955-4400   SIC 5012

ADESA AUCTIONS CANADA CORPORATION   p 257
7111 NO. 8 RD, RICHMOND, BC, V6W 1L9

(604) 232-4403   SIC 5012

ADESA AUCTIONS CANADA CORPORATION   p 376
HWY 7 N, WINNIPEG, MB, R3C 2E6

(204) 697-4400   SIC 5012

ADESA AUCTIONS CANADA CORPORATION   p 482
55 WAYDOM DR SUITE 1, AYR, ON, N0B 1E0

(519) 622-9500   SIC 5012

ADESA AUCTIONS CANADA CORPORATION   p 500

55 AUCTION LANE, BRAMPTON, ON, L6T 5P4

(905) 790-7653   SIC 5012

ADESA AUCTIONS CANADA CORPORATION   p 500
55 AUCTION LANE 2ND FLOOR, BRAMPTON, ON, L6T 5P4

(905) 790-7653   SIC 5012

ADESA AUCTIONS CANADA CORPORATION   p 1002
1717 BURTON RD, VARS, ON, K0A 3H0

(613) 443-4400   SIC 5012

ADESA AUCTIONS CANADA CORPORATION   p 1425
37507 HWY 12, SASKATOON, SK, S7K 3J7

(306) 242-8711   SIC 5012

ADESA CALGARY   p 2
See ADESA AUCTIONS CANADA CORPORATION

ADESA CANADA   p 500
See ADESA AUCTIONS CANADA CORPORATION

ADESA EDMONTON   p 148
See ADESA AUCTIONS CANADA CORPORATION

ADESA KITCHENER   p 482
See ADESA AUCTIONS CANADA CORPORATION

ADESA MONTREAL   p 1301
See ADESA MONTREAL CORPORATION

ADESA MONTREAL CORPORATION   p 1301
300 BOUL ALBERT-MONDOU, SAINT-EUSTACHE, QC, J7R 7A7

(450) 472-4400   SIC 5511

ADESA OTTAWA   p 1002
See ADESA AUCTIONS CANADA CORPORATION

ADESA SASKATOON   p 1425
See ADESA AUCTIONS CANADA CORPORATION

ADESA TORONTO   p 500
See ADESA AUCTIONS CANADA CORPORATION

ADESA VANCOUVER   p 257
See ADESA AUCTIONS CANADA CORPORATION

ADESA WINNIPEG   p 376
See ADESA AUCTIONS CANADA CORPORATION

ADEXMAT   p 1113
See SYSTEMES ADEX INC, LES

ADF DIESEL MONTREAL INC   p 1353
5 CH DE LA COTE-SAINT-PAUL, SAINT-STANISLAS-DE-CHAMPLAIN, QC, G0X 3E0

(418) 328-8713   SIC 5084

ADF DIESEL SAINT-STANISLAS INCp 1353
5 CH DE LA COTE-SAINT-PAUL, SAINT-STANISLAS-DE-CHAMPLAIN, QC, G0X 3E0

(418) 328-8713   SIC 5084

ADF INDUSTRIES LOURDES   p 1125
See 3539491 CANADA INC

ADGA GROUP CONSULTANTS INC p 833
110 ARGYLE AVE, OTTAWA, ON, K2P 1B4

(613) 237-3022   SIC 8741

ADHESIFS PROMA INC   p 1047
9801 BOUL PARKWAY, ANJOU, QC, H1J 1P3

(514) 852-8585   SIC 5169

ADI GROUP INC   p 400
1133 REGENT ST SUITE 300, FREDERICTON, NB, E3B 3Z2

(506) 452-9000   SIC 6712

ADI LIMITED   p 400
1133 REGENT ST SUITE 300, FREDERICTON, NB, E3B 3Z2

(506) 452-9000   SIC 8711

ADI-QC   p 10
See BW TECHNOLOGIES LTD

ADIDAS CANADA LIMITED   p 1026
8100 27 HWY SUITE 1, WOODBRIDGE,

ON, L4H 3N2
(905) 266-4200   *SIC* 5091
ADIDAS CANADA LIMITED   *p* 1026
8100 27 HWY SUITE 1, WOODBRIDGE, ON, L4H 3N2
(905) 266-4200   *SIC* 5139
ADIDAS GROUP   *p* 1026
See ADIDAS CANADA LIMITED
ADJ HOLDINGS INC   *p* 648
2068 PIPER LANE, LONDON, ON, N5V 3N6
(519) 455-4065   *SIC* 7692
ADJ INDUSTRIES INC   *p* 648
2068 PIPER LANE, LONDON, ON, N5V 3N6
(519) 455-4065   *SIC* 3441
ADJUVANTS EUCLID CANADA INC *p* 1310
2835 GRANDE ALLEE BUREAU 300, SAINT-HUBERT, QC, J4T 3K3
(450) 465-2233   *SIC* 5169
ADJUVANTZ   *p* 1328
See CORPORATION MCKESSON CANADA, LA
ADL QUALITY PRODUCTS   *p* 1042
See AMALGAMATED DAIRIES LIMITED
ADLER FIRESTOPPING LTD   *p* 1
53016 HWY 60 UNIT 23, ACHESON, AB, T7X 5A7
(780) 962-9495   *SIC* 7389
ADLER INTERNATIONAL, LTD   *p* 864
5610 FINCH AVE E, SCARBOROUGH, ON, M1B 6A6
(416) 291-9000   *SIC* 5199
ADLI LOGISTICS   *p* 737
See ADVANCE DISTRIBUTION LOGISTICS INTERNATIONAL INC
ADLYS HOTELS INC   *p* 1006
59 KING ST N, WATERLOO, ON, N2J 2X2
(519) 886-3350   *SIC* 5812
ADM AGRI-INDUSTRIES COMPANY   *p* 27
4002 BONNYBROOK RD SE, CALGARY, AB, T2G 4M9
(403) 267-5600   *SIC* 2045
ADM AGRI-INDUSTRIES COMPANY   *p* 846
1 KING ST SW, PORT COLBORNE, ON, L3K 5W1
(905) 835-4218   *SIC* 0723
ADM AGRI-INDUSTRIES COMPANY *p* 1024
5550 MAPLEWOOD DR, WINDSOR, ON, N9C 0B9
(519) 972-8100   *SIC* 2079
ADM AGRI-INDUSTRIES COMPANY *p* 1072
155 AV D'IBERIA, CANDIAC, QC, J5R 3H1
(450) 659-1911   *SIC* 2046
ADM COCOA, DIV OF   *p* 1024
See ADM AGRI-INDUSTRIES COMPANY
ADM MILLING DIV OF   *p* 27
See ADM AGRI-INDUSTRIES COMPANY
ADM MILLING CO   *p* 846
See ADM AGRI-INDUSTRIES COMPANY
ADMINISTRATION BEAULIEU INC   *p* 1375
6176 RUE BERTRAND-FABI, SHER-BROOKE, QC, J1N 2P3
SIC 6712
ADMINISTRATION PORTUAIRE DU QUE-BEC   *p* 1257
150 RUE DALHOUSIE BUREAU 2268, QUEBEC, QC, G1K 4C4
(418) 648-3640   *SIC* 4491
ADMIRAL'S GREEN CLUB HOUSE, THE   *p* 429
See C A PIPPY PARK COMMISSION
ADMISSION OFFICE   *p* 1039
See HOLLAND COLLEGE
ADMIT ONE   *p* 1342
See VETEMENTS NTD INC, LES
ADONIS   *p* 1086
See GROUPE ADONIS INC
ADONIS   *p* 1226
See GROUPE ADONIS INC
ADOX/OKI BERING   *p* 739
See ESSANDANT CANADA, INC
ADOXIO BUSINESS SOLUTIONS LIMITED *p* 1415
1445 PARK ST SUITE 200, REGINA, SK,

S4N 4C5
(306) 569-6501   *SIC* 7372
ADP   *p* 33
See ADP CANADA CO
ADP CANADA CO   *p* 33
6025 11 ST SE SUITE 100, CALGARY, AB, T2H 2Z2
(888) 901-7402   *SIC* 8721
ADP CANADA CO   *p* 189
4720 KINGSWAY SUITE 500, BURNABY, BC, V5H 4N2
(604) 431-2700   *SIC* 8721
ADP CANADA CO   *p* 444
130 EILEEN STUBBS AVE UNIT 22, DART-MOUTH, NS, B3B 2C4
(800) 668-8441   *SIC* 8721
ADP CANADA CO   *p* 571
3250 BLOOR ST W 6TH FL SUITE 1600, ETOBICOKE, ON, M8X 2X9
(416) 207-2900   *SIC* 8721
ADP CANADA CO   *p* 1063
204 BOUL DE MONTARVILLE, BOUCHERVILLE, QC, J4B 6S2
SIC 7374
ADP DEALER SERVICES   *p* 189
See ADP CANADA CO
ADP DEALER SERVICES   *p* 444
See ADP CANADA CO
ADP DIRECT POULTRY LTD   *p* 573
34 VANSCO RD, ETOBICOKE, ON, M8Z 5J4
(416) 658-0911   *SIC* 5144
ADP DISTRIBUTORS INC   *p* 281
18940 94 AVE SUITE 100, SURREY, BC, V4N 4X5
(604) 888-3726   *SIC* 5084
ADPM   *p* 1168
See ASSOCIATION DES POMPIERS DE MONTREAL INC
ADRA SALES INC   *p* 412
400 WESTMORLAND RD SUITE 254, SAINT JOHN, NB, E2J 2G4
(506) 634-2606   *SIC* 5014
ADRENALINE SPORTS   *p* 1119
See ADRENALINE SPORTS INC
ADRENALINE SPORTS INC   *p* 1119
6280 BOUL WILFRID-HAMEL, L'ANCIENNE-LORETTE, QC, G2E 2H8
(418) 687-0383   *SIC* 5571
ADRESSE BARS SYMPHONIQUE, L'   *p* 580
See SNC-LAVALIN OPERATIONS & MAIN-TENANCE INC
ADRESSE IMMOBILIERE HOMA   *p* 1244
See BOUCHARD PARENT ASSOCIES INC
ADRIAN'S NO FRILLS   *p* 648
See 1827212 ONTARIO LIMITED
ADRIATIC INSURANCE BROKERS LTD   *p* 1029
10 DIRECTOR CRT SUITE 100, WOOD-BRIDGE, ON, L4L 7E8
(905) 851-8555   *SIC* 6411
ADRICO MACHINE WORKS LTD   *p* 27
1165J 44 AVE SE, CALGARY, AB, T2G 4X4
(403) 243-7930   *SIC* 3599
ADT   *p* 1309
See AXSUN INC
ADT CANADA INC   *p* 1343
8481 BOUL LANGELIER, SAINT-LEONARD, QC, H1P 2C3
(514) 323-5000   *SIC* 1731
ADT RETAIL   *p* 506
See SENSORMATIC CANADA INCORPO-RATED
ADT SECURITY SERVICES CANADA, INC *p* 691
2815 MATHESON BLVD E, MISSISSAUGA, ON, L4W 5J8
(416) 218-1000   *SIC* 5063
ADTEL INC   *p* 84
11630 KINGSWAY NW, EDMONTON, AB, T5G 0X5
(780) 424-7777   *SIC* 7389
ADTS   *p* 421
See ATLANTICA DIVERSIFIED TRANS-

PORTATION SYSTEMS
ADTS   *p* 445
See ATLANTICA DIVERSIFIED TRANS-PORTATION SYSTEMS INC
ADULT COMMUNITY ALTERNATIVE MEA-SURES PROGRAM   *p* 231
See STELMASCHUK, W. J. AND ASSO-CIATES LTD
ADULT HIGH SCHOOL   *p* 825
See OTTAWA-CARLETON DISTRICT SCHOOL BOARD
ADULT RESIDENTIAL CENTRE   *p* 466
See RIVERVIEW HOME CORPORATION
ADVANCE   *p* 76
See NOVATEL INC
ADVANCE AUTOMOTIVE INDUSTRIES INC *p* 687
6520 VISCOUNT RD, MISSISSAUGA, ON, L4V 1H3
(905) 677-0912   *SIC* 5511
ADVANCE BEAUTY & ESTHETICS SUPPLY   *p* 1019
See ADVANCE BEAUTY SUPPLY LIMITED
ADVANCE BEAUTY SUPPLY LIMITED   *p* 1019
2979 TECUMSEH RD E, WINDSOR, ON, N8W 1G6
(519) 944-0904   *SIC* 5087
ADVANCE DISTRIBUTION LOGISTICS IN-TERNATIONAL INC   *p* 737
7391 PACIFIC CIR, MISSISSAUGA, ON, L5T 2A4
(905) 362-0548   *SIC* 4731
ADVANCE DOOR SYSTEMS LTD   *p* 1417
GD, REGINA, SK, S4P 2Z4
(306) 781-0207   *SIC* 5031
ADVANCE DRAINAGE SYSTEM INC *p* 1306
250A BOUL INDUSTRIEL, SAINT-GERMAIN-DE-GRANTHAM, QC, J0C 1K0
(800) 733-7473   *SIC* 1711
ADVANCE DRILLING LTD   *p* 42
100 4 AVE SW SUITE 706, CALGARY, AB, T2P 3N2
SIC 1781
ADVANCE ELECTRONICS LTD   *p* 381
1300 PORTAGE AVE, WINNIPEG, MB, R3G 0V1
(204) 786-6541   *SIC* 5999
ADVANCE ENGINEERED PRODUCTS LTD *p* 1415
144 HENDERSON DR, REGINA, SK, S4N 5P7
(306) 721-5678   *SIC* 3069
ADVANCE FOODS LTD   *p* 98
9106 142 ST NW, EDMONTON, AB, T5R 0M7
(780) 483-1525   *SIC* 5411
ADVANCE PALLET & CRATE LTD   *p* 274
12184 OLD YALE RD, SURREY, BC, V3V 3X5
(888) 791-2323   *SIC* 2448
ADVANCE REALTY LTD   *p* 194
972 SHOPPERS ROW, CAMPBELL RIVER, BC, V9W 2C5
(250) 202-0160   *SIC* 6531
ADVANCE RENTALS DIV OF   *p* 1042
See CURRAN & BRIGGS LIMITED
ADVANCE SHEET METAL LTD   *p* 205
1546 DERWENT WAY SUITE 311C, DELTA, BC, V3M 6M4
(604) 540-4955   *SIC* 1711
ADVANCE WIRE PRODUCTS LTD   *p* 278
19095 24 AVE SUITE 19095, SURREY, BC, V3Z 3S9
(604) 541-4666   *SIC* 2599
ADVANCED 2000 SYSTEMS INC   *p* 1425
718 CIRCLE DR E, SASKATOON, SK, S7K 3T7
(306) 955-2355   *SIC* 5999
ADVANCED AUDIO & VIDEO   *p* 381
See ADVANCE ELECTRONICS LTD
ADVANCED BENDING TECHNOLOGIES

INC   *p* 229
27372 GLOUCESTER WAY, LANGLEY, BC, V4W 4A1
(604) 856-6220   *SIC* 5051
ADVANCED COPPER FOIL INC   *p* 737
1116 MID-WAY BLVD UNIT 5, MISSIS-SAUGA, ON, L5T 2H2
(905) 362-8404   *SIC* 5051
ADVANCED DESIGN SOLUTIONS INC   *p* 895
533 ROMEO ST S SUITE 1, STRATFORD, ON, N5A 4V3
(519) 271-7810   *SIC* 3499
ADVANCED ENERGY MANAGEMENT LTD *p* 445
60 DOREY AVE SUITE 103, DARTMOUTH, NS, B3B 0B1
(902) 453-4498   *SIC* 5084
ADVANCED FLOW SYSTEMS INC   *p* 230
27222 LOUGHEED HWY, MAPLE RIDGE, BC, V2W 1M4
(604) 462-1514   *SIC* 3569
ADVANCED MEDICAL DISCOVERIES IN-STITUTE   *p* 947
See UNIVERSITY HEALTH NETWORK
ADVANCED MEDICAL GROUP   *p* 75
See STATESMAN CORPORATION
ADVANCED MEDICAL SOLUTIONS INC   *p* 435
233 UTSINGI DR, YELLOWKNIFE, NT, X1A 0E7
(866) 578-9111   *SIC* 5047
ADVANCED MILLWRIGHT SERVICES LTD *p* 330
971 HWY 16, VANDERHOOF, BC, V0J 3A1
(250) 567-5756   *SIC* 1796
ADVANCED MOBILE PAYMENT INC   *p* 850
15 WERTHEIM CRT SUITE 401-403, RICH-MOND HILL, ON, L4B 3H7
(905) 597-2333   *SIC* 7371
ADVANCED MOBILITY PRODUCTS LTD   *p* 191
8620 GLENLYON PKY SUITE 101, BURN-ABY, BC, V5J 0B6
(604) 293-0002   *SIC* 5999
ADVANCED MOTION & CONTROLS LTD   *p* 485
26 SAUNDERS RD, BARRIE, ON, L4N 9A8
(705) 726-2260   *SIC* 5065
ADVANCED NUTRIENTS LTD   *p* 176
32526 GEORGE FERGUSON WAY SUITE 102, ABBOTSFORD, BC, V2T 4Y1
(604) 854-6793   *SIC* 2873
ADVANCED ORTHOMOLECULAR RE-SEARCH INC   *p* 20
3900 12 ST NE, CALGARY, AB, T2E 8H9
(403) 250-9997   *SIC* 5122
ADVANCED PARAMEDIC LTD   *p* 152
8703 75 ST W, PEACE RIVER, AB, T8S 0A5
(780) 624-4911   *SIC* 8049
ADVANCED PRECAST INC   *p* 494
6 NIXON RD, BOLTON, ON, L7E 1K3
(905) 857-6111   *SIC* 3272
ADVANCED PRECISION MACHINING AND FABRICATION LIMITED   *p* 445
70 THORNHILL DR, DARTMOUTH, NS, B3B 1S3
(902) 468-5653   *SIC* 3599
ADVANCED PREFABS LIMITED   *p* 829
1722 CARLING AVE, OTTAWA, ON, K2A 1C7
(613) 728-1775   *SIC* 5719
ADVANCED PRESENTATION PRODUCTS INC   *p* 716
4180 SLADEVIEW CRES UNIT 4, MISSIS-SAUGA, ON, L5L 0A1
(905) 502-1110   *SIC* 5999
ADVANCED SECURITY AND INVESTIGA-TION SERVICES   *p* 913
See R HOME SECURITY LTD
ADVANCED STEEL STRUCTURES INC   *p*

229
5250 272 ST, LANGLEY, BC, V4W 1S3
(604) 626-4211   *SIC* 1791
ADVANCED TECHNOLOGY & ASSEMBLY*p*
1091
See 156861 CANADA INC
ADVANCED TOWER SERVICES (2007) LTD
p 685
54 MILL ST W, MILVERTON, ON, N0K 1M0
(519) 595-3500   *SIC* 3441
ADVANCED UTILITY SYSTEMS CORPO-RATION   *p*
766
2235 SHEPPARD AVE E SUITE 1400,
NORTH YORK, ON, M2J 5B5
(416) 496-0149   *SIC* 7371
**ADVANCED UVALUX SUN TANNING
EQUIPMENT**   *p* 1036
See UVALUX INTERNATIONAL INC
ADVANCEMENT SERVICES   *p* 333
See UNIVERSITY OF VICTORIA
ADVANIS INC   *p* 86
10123 99 ST NW SUITE 1600, EDMON-TON, AB, T5J 3H1
(780) 944-9212   *SIC* 8741
ADVANTA BY MAAX   *p* 1126
See MAAX BATH INC
ADVANTAGE CAR & TRUCK RENTALS   *p*
1002
*See ADVANTAGE CAR & TRUCK RENTALS
LTD*
ADVANTAGE CAR & TRUCK RENTALS LTD
p 1002
110 JARDIN DR SUITE 13, VAUGHAN, ON,
L4K 2T7
(416) 493-5250   *SIC* 7514
ADVANTAGE CO-OPERATIVE ASSOCIA-TION LTD   *p*
1415
3 BROADWAY ST S, REDVERS, SK, S0C
2H0
(306) 452-3513   *SIC* 5171
ADVANTAGE COMMUNICATIONS INC   *p*
1040
265 BRACKLEY POINT RD, CHARLOTTE-TOWN, PE, C1E 2A3
(902) 892-1585   *SIC* 4899
ADVANTAGE COURIER SYSTEMS LIM-ITED   *p*
445
1 GURHOLT DR, DARTMOUTH, NS, B3B
1J8
(902) 444-1511   *SIC* 7389
ADVANTAGE CREDIT UNION   *p* 1410
114 MAIN ST, MELFORT, SK, S0E 1A0
(306) 752-2744   *SIC* 6062
ADVANTAGE DATASYSTEMS CORPORA-TION   *p*
181
8061 LOUGHEED HWY SUITE 110, BURN-ABY, BC, V5A 1W9
(604) 415-3950   *SIC* 5963
ADVANTAGE DELIVERY SERVICE   *p* 1038
47 KENSINGTON RD, CHARLOTTETOWN,
PE, C1A 5H6
(902) 940-3971   *SIC* 7389
ADVANTAGE DISTRIBUTORS LTD   *p* 69
18011 SPRUCE MEADOWS WAY SW, CAL-GARY, AB, T2X 4B7
(403) 974-4200   *SIC* 7941
ADVANTAGE ENGINEERING INC   *p* 807
5000 REGAL DR, OLDCASTLE, ON, N0R
1L0
(519) 737-7535   *SIC* 3089
ADVANTAGE ENGINEERING INC   *p* 1023
2030 NORTH TALBOT RD, WINDSOR, ON,
N9A 6J3
(519) 737-7535   *SIC* 3089
ADVANTAGE FARM EQUIPMENT LTD   *p*
1037
392 BROADWAY ST, WYOMING, ON, N0N
1T0
(519) 845-3346   *SIC* 5999
ADVANTAGE FORD SALES LTD   *p* 39

12800 MACLEOD TRAIL SE, CALGARY,
AB, T2J 7E5
(403) 225-3636   *SIC* 5511
ADVANTAGE LIFE SCIENCE FUND II   *p* 308
*See PENDER NDI LIFE SCIENCES FUND
(VCC) INC*
ADVANTAGE LOSS PREVENTION SER-VICES (ALPS)   *p*
40
See T.F. LYNN AND ASSOCIATES INC
ADVANTAGE MACHINE & TOOL INC   *p* 745
155 HURON RD SS 1, MITCHELL, ON, N0K
1N0
(519) 348-4414   *SIC* 3541
**ADVANTAGE MAINTENANCE PRODUCTS
LTD**   *p* 836
105 SCOTT AVE, PARIS, ON, N3L 3K4
(519) 442-7881   *SIC* 5087
ADVANTAGE MANAGEMENT INC   *p* 33
6020 1A ST SW SUITE 10, CALGARY, AB,
T2H 0G3
(403) 259-4141   *SIC* 6531
ADVANTAGE OIL & GAS LTD   *p* 42
440 2 AVE SW SUITE 2200, CALGARY, AB,
T2P 5E9
(403) 718-8000   *SIC* 1382
ADVANTAGE PARTS SOULTION   *p* 181
See ADVANTAGE DATASYSTEMS CORPO-RATION
ADVANTAGE PERSONNEL LTD   *p* 445
75 AKERLEY BLVD UNIT S, DARTMOUTH,
NS, B3B 1R7
(902) 468-5624   *SIC* 7361
ADVANTAGE RESTAURANT SUPPLY INC *p*
759
4529 KENT AVE, NIAGARA FALLS, ON,
L2H 1J1
(905) 356-1152   *SIC* 5046
**ADVANTAGE SALES AND MARKETING
CANADA**   *p* 666
See ASM CANADA, INC
ADVANTECH SANS FIL INC   *p* 1095
See SPACEBRIDGE INC
ADVANTECH TECHNOLOGIES SANS FIL *p*
1117
See ADVANTECH WIRELESS TECHNOLO-GIES INC
**ADVANTECH WIRELESS TECHNOLOGIES
INC**   *p* 1117
16715 BOUL HYMUS, KIRKLAND, QC, H9H
5M8
(514) 694-8666   *SIC* 3679
ADVANTECHAMT   *p* 1095
See SPACEBRIDGE INC
ADVANTEX EXPRESS INC   *p* 687
6725 AIRPORT RD SUITE 101, MISSIS-SAUGA, ON, L4V 1V2
(905) 677-0340   *SIC* 4731
ADVANZ PHARMA CORP   *p* 729
5770 HURONTARIO ST SUITE 310, MIS-SISSAUGA, ON, L5R 3G5
(905) 842-5150   *SIC* 5122
ADVENT HEALTH CARE CORPORATION *p*
775
541 FINCH AVE W, NORTH YORK, ON,
M2R 3Y3
(416) 636-5800   *SIC* 8699
ADVENTEC MANUFACTURING INC   *p* 566
55 INNOVATION DR, DUNDAS, ON, L9H
7L8
(289) 895-7909   *SIC* 3089
ADVENTURE DESTINATIONS INTERNA-TIONAL   *p*
1429
See PIC INVESTMENT GROUP INC
ADVENTURE VALLEY   *p* 903
See ADVENTURE VALLEY INC
ADVENTURE VALLEY INC   *p* 903
7015 LESLIE ST, THORNHILL, ON, L3T 6L6
(905) 731-2267   *SIC* 7999
ADVISOR'S ADVANTAGE TRUST   *p* 1208
See SOCIETE DE FIDUCIE BMO
ADVOCATE HEALTH SERVICES   *p* 223
See SLIZEK INC

**ADVOCATE PRINTING AND PUBLISHING
COMPANY LIMITED**   *p* 464
GD, PICTOU, NS, B0K 1H0
(902) 485-1990   *SIC* 2731
ADVOCATE SIGNS AND BANNERS   *p* 464
See ADVOCATE PRINTING AND PUBLISH-ING COMPANY LIMITED
ADVOCIS   *p* 980
*See FINANCIAL ADVISORS ASSOCIATION
OF CANADA, THE*
AE CONCRETE PRODUCTS INC   *p* 271
19060 54 AVE, SURREY, BC, V3S 8E5
(604) 576-1808   *SIC* 3272
AECL   *p* 541
See ATOMIC ENERGY OF CANADA LIM-ITED
AECL   *p* 913
See ATOMIC ENERGY OF CANADA LIM-ITED
AECL WHITE SHELL LABORATORY   *p* 354
See ATOMIC ENERGY OF CANADA LIM-ITED
AECO GAS STORAGE PARTNERSHIP *p* 42
607 8 AVE SW SUITE 400, CALGARY, AB,
T2P 0A7
(403) 513-8600   *SIC* 4922
AECOM CANADA LTD   *p* 33
6807 RAILWAY ST SE SUITE 200, CAL-GARY, AB, T2H 2V6
(403) 270-9200   *SIC* 8711
AECOM CANADA LTD   *p* 69
340 MIDPARK WAY SE SUITE 300, CAL-GARY, AB, T2X 1P1
(403) 270-9200   *SIC* 8711
AECOM CANADA LTD   *p* 99
17203 103 AVE NW, EDMONTON, AB, T5S
1J4
(780) 488-2121   *SIC* 8711
AECOM CANADA LTD   *p* 171
1718 23RD AVE, WAINWRIGHT, AB, T9W
1T2
(780) 842-4220   *SIC* 7692
AECOM CANADA LTD   *p* 181
3292 PRODUCTION WAY, BURNABY, BC,
V5A 4R4
(604) 444-6400   *SIC* 8711
AECOM CANADA LTD   *p* 388
99 COMMERCE DR, WINNIPEG, MB, R3P
0Y7
(204) 477-5381   *SIC* 8711
AECOM CANADA LTD   *p* 641
50 SPORTSWORLD CROSSING RD SUITE
290, KITCHENER, ON, N2P 0A4
(519) 650-5313   *SIC* 8742
AECOM CANADA LTD   *p* 666
300 TOWN CENTRE BLVD SUITE 300,
MARKHAM, ON, L3R 5Z6
SIC 8742
AECOM CANADA LTD   *p* 691
5080 COMMERCE BLVD, MISSISSAUGA,
ON, L4W 4P2
(905) 238-0007   *SIC* 8711
AECOM CANADA LTD   *p* 1013
300 WATER ST SUITE 1, WHITBY, ON, L1N
9J2
(905) 668-9363   *SIC* 8711
AECOM CANADA LTD   *p* 1266
4700 BOUL WILFRID-HAMEL, QUEBEC,
QC, G1P 2J9
(418) 871-2444   *SIC* 8742
AECOM CANADA LTD   *p* 1438
HIGHWAY 1 EAST 3 NORTH SERVICE RD,
WHITE CITY, SK, S4L 5B1
(306) 779-2200   *SIC* 1389
AECOM CANADIAN OPERATIONS LTD *p*
627
GD LCD MAIN, KAPUSKASING, ON, P5N
2X9
(705) 335-3800   *SIC* 1475
AECOM CONSULTANTS   *p* 1266
See AECOM CANADA LTD
AECOM ENERGY SERVICES LTD   *p* 33
6025 11 ST SE SUITE 240, CALGARY, AB,
T2H 2Z2

(403) 218-7100   *SIC* 1389
AECOM ENERGY SERVICES LTD   *p* 80
See AECOM ENERGY SERVICES LTD
AECOM ENERGY SERVICES LTD   *p* 80
HWY 55 W, COLD LAKE, AB, T9M 1P7
(780) 639-6034   *SIC* 1799
AECOM ENERGY SERVICES LTD   *p* 126
10211 98 ST, FAIRVIEW, AB, T0H 1L0
(403) 218-7100   *SIC* 1389
AECOM ENERGY SERVICES LTD   *p* 158
See AECOM ENERGY SERVICES LTD
AECOM ENERGY SERVICES LTD   *p* 158
1901 HIGHWAY AVE SE, REDCLIFF, AB,
T0J 2P0
SIC 8742
AECOM FACILITY CONSTRUCTION LTD *p*
33
1209 59 AVE SE SUITE 205, CALGARY, AB,
T2H 2P6
(403) 218-7113   *SIC* 1623
AECOM MAINTENANCE SERVICES LTD *p*
33
6025 11 ST SE SUITE 240, CALGARY, AB,
T2H 2Z2
(403) 265-9033   *SIC* 8741
AECOM PRODUCTION SERVICES LTD*p* 13
9727 40 ST SE, CALGARY, AB, T2C 2P4
(403) 236-5611   *SIC* 3494
AECOM PRODUCTION SERVICES LTD*p* 33
6025 11 ST SE UNIT 240, CALGARY, AB,
T2H 2Z2
(403) 386-1000   *SIC* 1389
AECOM PRODUCTION SERVICES LTD*p* 79
10414 84 AVE, CLAIRMONT, AB, T8X 5B2
(780) 539-0069   *SIC* 1731
AECOM TECSULT   *p* 1084
See CONSULTANTS AECOM INC
AECOM TECSULT   *p* 1266
See CONSULTANTS AECOM INC
AECOM-GRAHAM JOINT VENTURE   *p* 70
See GRAHAM GROUP LTD
AECON   *p* 1196
See GROUPE AECON QUEBEC LTEE
AECON CONSTRUCTION AND MATERI-ALS LIMITED   *p*
581
20 CARLSON CRT SUITE 800, ETOBI-COKE, ON, M9W 7K6
(905) 454-1078   *SIC* 1629
AECON CONSTRUCTION GROUP INC   *p*
997
20 CARLSON CRT SUITE 800, TORONTO,
ON, M9W 7K6
(416) 293-7004   *SIC* 1541
AECON GROUP INC   *p* 581
20 CARLSON CRT SUITE 800, ETOBI-COKE, ON, M9W 7K6
(416) 297-2600   *SIC* 1541
AECON INDUSTRIAL WESTERN INC *p* 104
14940 121A AVE NW, EDMONTON, AB,
T5V 1A3
(780) 452-1250   *SIC* 1542
AECON MATERIALS ENGINEERING CORP
p 581
20 CARLSON CRT SUITE 800, ETOBI-COKE, ON, M9W 7K6
(416) 293-7004   *SIC* 1481
AECON MINING, DIV OF   *p* 581
See AECON GROUP INC
AECON TRANSPORTATION WEST LTD *p*
158
590 HIGHWAY AVE NE, REDCLIFF, AB, T0J
2P0
(403) 548-3961   *SIC* 1611
AECON UTILITIES   *p* 997
*See AECON CONSTRUCTION GROUP
INC*
AECON UTILITIES INC   *p* 597
2495 DEL ZOTTO AVE, GLOUCESTER,
ON, K1T 3V6
(613) 822-6193   *SIC* 1623
AEDIFICA INC   *p* 1201
606 RUE CATHCART BUREAU 800, MON-TREAL, QC, H3B 1K9

(514) 844-6611 *SIC 8712*
AEGIS TRADE *p 979*
See CARAT CANADA INC
AEM *p 445*
See ADVANCED ENERGY MANAGEMENT LTD
AENOS FOOD SERVICES INC *p 826*
2455 KALADAR AVE, OTTAWA, ON, K1V 8B9
(613) 736-0310 *SIC 5148*
AERCO INDUSTRIES LTD *p 246*
201-1952 KINGSWAY AVE, PORT COQUIT-LAM, BC, V3C 6C2
(604) 431-6883 *SIC 1711*
AERIAL SURVEY *p 404*
See LEADING EDGE GEOMATICS LTD
AERIC INC *p 819*
255 SMYTH RD, OTTAWA, ON, K1H 8M7
(613) 526-3280 *SIC 8732*
AERIS *p 1401*
See ATRIUM INNOVATIONS INC
AERLOC INDUSTRIES LTD *p 566*
64 HEAD ST, DUNDAS, ON, L9H 3H7
(905) 628-6061 *SIC 5211*
AERO *p 1170*
See INDUSTRIES MIDWAY LTEE
AERO *p 1183*
See GROUPE YELLOW INC
AERO AVIATION INC *p 20*
2139 PEGASUS WAY NE SUITE 13, CAL-GARY, AB, T2E 8T2
(403) 250-7553 *SIC 4581*
AERO AVIATION INC *p 20*
393 PALMER RD NE SUITE 59, CALGARY, AB, T2E 7G4
(403) 250-3663 *SIC 4581*
AERO DERIVATIVE GAS TURBINES *p 1095*
See SIEMENS CANADA LIMITED
AERO MAG 2000 (YEG) INC *p 134*
4123 39 ST E, GRANDE PRAIRIE, AB, T9E 0V4
(780) 890-7273 *SIC 4581*
AERO MAG 2000 (YUL) INC *p 1332*
8181 RUE HERVE-SAINT-MARTIN, SAINT-LAURENT, QC, H4S 2A5
(514) 636-1930 *SIC 3728*
AERO MECANIQUE TURCOTTE INC *p 1361*
1289 BOUL DAGENAIS O, SAINTE-ROSE, QC, H7L 5Z9
(450) 625-2627 *SIC 1711*
AERO RECIP. (CANADA) LTD *p 383*
540 MARJORIE ST, WINNIPEG, MB, R3H 0S9
(204) 788-4765 *SIC 4581*
AERO TRADING CO LTD *p 290*
8592 FRASER ST SUITE 200, VANCOU-VER, BC, V5X 3Y3
(604) 327-6331 *SIC 5146*
AERODET *p 1066*
See MAGCHEM INC
AERODROME INTERNATIONAL MAINTE-NANCE INC *p 593*
330 GUELPH ST UNIT 4, GEORGETOWN, ON, L7G 4B5
(905) 873-8777 *SIC 4212*
AEROGARE DE BAGOTVILLE *p 1079*
See PROMOTION SAGUENAY INC
AEROPORT DE QUEBEC INC *p 1278*
505 RUE PRINCIPALE, QUEBEC, QC, G2G 0J4
(418) 640-2700 *SIC 4581*
AEROPORT INTERNATIONALE JEAN LESAGE DE QUEBEC *p 1278*
See AEROPORT DE QUEBEC INC
AEROPORT REGIONAL DE ROUYN NO-RANDA *p 1290*
80 AV DE L'AEROPORT BUREAU 82, ROUYN-NORANDA, QC, J9Y 0G1
(819) 762-8171 *SIC 4581*
AEROPORTS DE MONTREAL *p 1092*
580 BOUL STUART-GRAHAM S, DORVAL, QC, H4Y 1G4

(514) 633-2811 *SIC 4581*
AEROPORTS DE MONTREAL *p 1092*
800 PLACE LEIGH-CAPREOL BUREAU 1000, DORVAL, QC, H4Y 0A5
(514) 394-7200 *SIC 4581*
AEROPORTS DE MONTREAL *p 1153*
12655 BOUL HENRI-FABRE O UNITE A4, MIRABEL, QC, J7N 1E1
(514) 394-7377 *SIC 4581*
AEROPRO *p 1277*
See 2553-4330 QUEBEC INC
AEROPRO *p 1367*
See 2553-4330 QUEBEC INC
AEROSPATIAL ROCKLAND *p 1355*
See MHD - ROCKLAND INC
AEROSPATIALE HEMMINGFORD INC *p 1113*
447 RTE 202 O, HEMMINGFORD, QC, J0L 1H0
(450) 247-2722 *SIC 3728*
AEROSPATIALE HOCHELAGA *p 641*
See DEVTEK AEROSPACE INC
AEROSPATIALE SARGENT CANADA *p 1050*
See RBC BEARINGS CANADA, INC
AEROSTRUCTURES PCC DORVAL *p 1094*
See PCC AEROSTRUCTURES DORVAL INC
AEROTEK AVIATION *p 709*
See AEROTEK ULC
AEROTEK ULC *p 253*
13575 COMMERCE PKY SUITE 150, RICH-MOND, BC, V6V 2L1
(604) 244-1007 *SIC 7361*
AEROTEK ULC *p 709*
350 BURNHAMTHORPE RD W SUITE 800, MISSISSAUGA, ON, L5B 3J1
(905) 283-1200 *SIC 7361*
AEROTERM RIVE-SUD *p 1092*
See 3101895 NOVA SCOTIA COMPANY
AEROTV & DESSIN *p 1193*
See ASTRAL MEDIA AFFICHAGE, S.E.C.
AERRIANTA INTERNATIONAL (AMERIQUE DU NORD) INC *p 1332*
6400 RUE ABRAMS, SAINT-LAURENT, QC, H4S 1Y2
(514) 335-0254 *SIC 5399*
AERYON LABS INC *p 1010*
575 KUMPF DR, WATERLOO, ON, N2V 1K3
(519) 489-6726 *SIC 3861*
AES DRILLING FLUIDS *p 46*
See CES ENERGY SOLUTIONS CORP
AES DRILLING FLUIDS *p 1405*
See CES ENERGY SOLUTIONS CORP
AES WAREHOUSE & DISTRIBUTION *p 687*
See CORE LOGISTICS INTERNATIONAL INC
AESHU PROPANE *p 389*
See STERLING O&G INTERNATIONAL CORPORATION
AESO *p 42*
See ALBERTA ELECTRIC SYSTEM OPER-ATOR
AESTHETICS LANDSCAPE CONTRAC-TORS *p 891*
1092 HIGHWAY 8, STONEY CREEK, ON, L8E 5H8
(905) 643-9933 *SIC 5083*
AEVITAS INC *p 482*
75 WANLESS CRT, AYR, ON, N0B 1E0
(519) 740-1333 *SIC 4953*
AFA FOREST PRODUCTS INC *p 494*
244 ELLWOOD DR W, BOLTON, ON, L7E 4W4
(905) 857-6423 *SIC 5039*
AFA NORDALE PACKAGING SYSTEMS *p 500*
See AFA SYSTEMS LTD
AFA SYSTEMS LTD *p 500*
8 TILBURY CRT, BRAMPTON, ON, L6T 3T4
(905) 456-8700 *SIC 3565*
AFCC *p 191*
See AFCC AUTOMOTIVE FUEL CELL CO-

OPERATION CORP
AFCC AUTOMOTIVE FUEL CELL COOPER-ATION CORP *p 191*
9000 GLENLYON PKY, BURNABY, BC, V5J 5J8
(604) 415-7290 *SIC 8748*
AFD PETROLEUM LTD *p 121*
1444 78 AVE NW, EDMONTON, AB, T6P 1L7
(780) 438-5930 *SIC 5172*
AFD PROCESSING LTD *p 229*
5292 272 ST, LANGLEY, BC, V4W 1S3
(604) 856-3886 *SIC 2034*
AFEXA *p 1363*
See VALEANT CANADA S.E.C.
AFFI *p 1063*
See ATELIER LA FLECHE DE FER INC, L'
AFFI *p 1307*
See ATELIER LA FLECHE DE FER INC, L'
AFFILIATED ANIMAL SERVICES *p 829*
900 BOYD AVE, OTTAWA, ON, K2A 2E3
(613) 725-1182 *SIC 0742*
AFFILIATED: BELL CANADA *p 638*
See CTV SPECIALTY TELEVISION INC
AFFINIO INC *p 456*
2717 JOSEPH HOWE DR SUITE 300, HAL-IFAX, NS, B3L 4T9
(866) 991-3263 *SIC 5734*
AFFINITY FOOD GROUP INC *p 661*
480 SOVEREIGN RD UNIT 3, LONDON, ON, N6M 1A4
(519) 453-6873 *SIC 5812*
AFFIRMATIVE DYNAMIC INDUSTRY INC *p 762*
1765 JANE ST, NORTH BAY, ON, P1B 3K3
(705) 476-8809 *SIC 5199*
AFFORDABLE FUELS *p 468*
362 WILLOW ST, TRURO, NS, B2N 5A5
(902) 895-4328 *SIC 4924*
AFFORDABLE PACKAGING LTD *p 473*
225 MONARCH AVE, AJAX, ON, L1S 7M3
SIC 7389
AFG GLASS *p 1253*
See AGC FLAT GLASS NORTH AMERICA LTD
AFGHAN PHYSICIANS ASSOCIATION IN CANADA A.P.A.C. *p 1358*
108 RUE DU LISERON, SAINTE-JULIE, QC, J3E 3N9
SIC 8011
AFI *p 1262*
See GROUPE EDGENDA INC
AFILIAS CANADA, CORP *p 773*
4141 YONGE ST SUITE 204, NORTH YORK, ON, M2P 2A8
(416) 646-3304 *SIC 8731*
AFIMAC CANADA INC *p 682*
8160 PARKHILL DR, MILTON, ON, L9T 5V7
(905) 693-0746 *SIC 7381*
AFL DISPLAY GROUP *p 548*
See ACRYLIC FABRICATORS LIMITED
AFL GROUP FINANCES *p 1135*
See ASSURANCES FONTAINE LEMAY & ASS INC, LES
AFM *p 1357*
See ATELIERS FERROVIAIRES DE MONT-JOLI INC, LES
AFONSO GROUP LIMITED *p 428*
14 ROBIN HOOD BAY RD, ST. JOHN'S, NL, A1A 5V3
(709) 576-6070 *SIC 7389*
AFRICA OIL CORP *p 301*
885 GEORGIA ST W SUITE 2000, VAN-COUVER, BC, V6C 3E8
(604) 689-7842 *SIC 1382*
AFRICAN GOLD GROUP, INC *p 936*
151 YONGE ST 11TH FL, TORONTO, ON, M5C 2W7
(647) 775-8538 *SIC 1041*
AFRICAN LION SAFARI & GAME FARM LTD *p 532*
1386 COOPER RD RR 1, CAMBRIDGE, ON, N1R 5S2

(519) 623-2620 *SIC 7999*
AFSC *p 138*
See AGRICULTURE FINANCIAL SER-VICES CORPORATION
AFTERMARKET PARTS COMPANY LLC, THE *p 362*
630 KERNAGHAN AVE DOOR 76, WIN-NIPEG, MB, R2C 5G1
(800) 665-2637 *SIC 3711*
AFTON OPERATING CORPORATION *p 301*
3300 BURRARD ST, VANCOUVER, BC, V6C 0B3
(604) 699-4000 *SIC 1021*
AFX HOLDINGS CORP *p 231*
14301 256 ST SUITE 302, MAPLE RIDGE, BC, V4R 0B9
(604) 380-4458 *SIC 6712*
AG ALFAGOMMA DESIGN *p 1332*
See ALFAGOMMA CANADA INC
AG ENERGY CO-OPERATIVE LTD *p 602*
45 SPEEDVALE AVE E SUITE 2, GUELPH, ON, N1H 1J2
(519) 763-3026 *SIC 4924*
AG GROWTH INTERNATIONAL INC *p 150*
215 BARONS ST, NOBLEFORD, AB, T0L 1S0
(403) 320-5585 *SIC 3523*
AG GROWTH INTERNATIONAL INC *p 364*
450 RUE DESAUTELS, WINNIPEG, MB, R2H 3E6
(204) 233-7133 *SIC 3443*
AG GROWTH INTERNATIONAL INC *p 388*
198 COMMERCE DR, WINNIPEG, MB, R3P 0Z6
(204) 489-1855 *SIC 3496*
AG HAIR LTD *p 199*
14 KING EDWARD ST, COQUITLAM, BC, V3K 0E7
(604) 294-8870 *SIC 2844*
AGA ASSURANCES COLLECTIVES *p 1402*
See GROUPE FINANCIER AGA INC
AGA KHAN FOUNDATION CANADA *p 821*
199 SUSSEX DR, OTTAWA, ON, K1N 1K6
(613) 237-2532 *SIC 6732*
AGAPE STREET MINISTRY *p 294*
887 KEEFER ST, VANCOUVER, BC, V6A 1Y8
(604) 215-4115 *SIC 8699*
AGAT *p 20*
See AGAT LABORATORIES LTD
AGAT *p 704*
See AGAT LABORATORIES LTD
AGAT LABORATORIES LTD *p 20*
2905 12 ST NE, CALGARY, AB, T2E 7J2
(403) 736-2000 *SIC 8731*
AGAT LABORATORIES LTD *p 20*
3801 21 ST NE, CALGARY, AB, T2E 6T5
(403) 216-2077 *SIC 8734*
AGAT LABORATORIES LTD *p 704*
5835 COOPERS AVE, MISSISSAUGA, ON, L4Z 1Y2
(905) 712-5100 *SIC 8731*
AGC AUTOMOTIVE CANADA, INC *p 497*
120 ARTESIAN INDUSTRIAL PKY, BRAD-FORD, ON, L3Z 3G3
(905) 778-8224 *SIC 3231*
AGC FLAT GLASS NORTH AMERICA LTD *p 1253*
250 RUE DE COPENHAGUE, PORTNEUF, QC, G0A 2Y0
SIC 3211
AGCO CANADA, LTD *p 1415*
515 DEWDNEY AVE, REGINA, SK, S4N 6S1
(306) 757-2681 *SIC 5083*
AGCOM LTD *p 140*
3240 2 AVE N, LETHBRIDGE, AB, T1H 0C6
(403) 328-9228 *SIC 5172*
AGCOM PETROLEUM SALES *p 140*
See AGCOM LTD
AGCOM PETROLEUM SALES LTD *p 7*
600 INDUSTRIAL RD, BROOKS, AB, T1R 1B6
(403) 362-5700 *SIC 5171*

AGE D'OR SACRE-COEUR TORONTO, L' *p* 931
474 ONTARIO ST, TORONTO, ON, M4X 1M7
(416) 923-3724   *SIC* 8399

AGE LINK PERSONNEL SERVICES INC *p* 609
400 PARKDALE AVE N UNIT 2A, HAMILTON, ON, L8H 5Y2
(905) 572-6162   *SIC* 8322

AGELLAN COMMERCIAL REAL ESTATE INVESTMENT TRUST *p* 959
156 FRONT ST W SUITE 303, TORONTO, ON, M5J 2L6
(416) 593-6800   *SIC* 6722

AGELLAN COMMERCIAL REIT HOLDINGS INC *p* 927
890 YONGE ST STE 505, TORONTO, ON, M4W 3P4
(416) 593-6800   *SIC* 6798

AGENCE ANDRE BEAULNE LTEE *p* 1345
5055 BOUL METROPOLITAIN E BUREAU 200, SAINT-LEONARD, QC, H1R 1Z7
(514) 329-3333   *SIC* 6411

AGENCE COMEDIHAU INC *p* 1263
214 AV SAINT-SACREMENT BUREAU 130, QUEBEC, QC, G1N 3X6
(418) 647-2525   *SIC* 6712

AGENCE D'ASSURANCE NFIA *p* 1278
See HOLLIS INSURANCE INC

AGENCE D'ASSURANCE VIE MANUEL SMITH LTEE *p* 1328
3333 BOUL DE LA COTE-VERTU STE 450, SAINT-LAURENT, QC, H4R 2N1
(514) 343-0200   *SIC* 6311

AGENCE D'ASSURANCES ANDRE DUFRESNE *p* 1167
4061 RUE HOCHELAGA, MONTREAL, QC, H1W 1K4
(514) 256-3626   *SIC* 6411

AGENCE D'ASSURANCES RANDLE (2000) *p* 1117
See OSBORN & LANGE INC

AGENCE DE LA SANTE ET DES SERVICES SOCIAUX DE L'ESTRIE *p* 1370
See GOUVERNEMENT DE LA PROVINCE DE QUEBEC

AGENCE DE LA SANTE ET DES SERVICES SOCIAUX DES LAURENTIDES, L' *p* 1320
500 BOUL DES LAURENTIDES BUREAU 1010, SAINT-JEROME, QC, J7Z 4M2
(450) 436-8622   *SIC* 8399

AGENCE DE PLACEMENT SELECT INC *p* 1319
96 RUE DE MARTIGNY O, SAINT-JEROME, QC, J7Y 2G1
(450) 431-6292   *SIC* 7361

AGENCE DE PLACEMENT TRESOR *p* 1084
See AGENCE DE PLACEMENT TRESOR INC

AGENCE DE PLACEMENT TRESOR INC *p* 1084
2A RUE GRENON O, COTE SAINT-LUC, QC, H7N 2G6
(450) 933-7090   *SIC* 7361

AGENCE DE PUBLICITE D.I.K. *p* 1276
See JOUET K.I.D. INC

AGENCE DE RECOUVREMENT NCO *p* 1217
See SERVICES FINANCIERS NCO, INC

AGENCE DE REVENUE DU CANADA *p* 1104
See GOUVERNEMENT DE LA PROVINCE DE QUEBEC

AGENCE DE SANTE ET DES SEVICES SOCIAUX DE LA MONTEREGIE *p* 1144
See GOUVERNEMENT DE LA PROVINCE DE QUEBEC

AGENCE DE SECURITE BELLEY *p* 1210
See GROUPE DE SECURITE GARDA INC, LE

AGENCE DE SECURITE D'INVESTIGATION EXPO INC *p* 1173

2335 RUE ONTARIO E, MONTREAL, QC, H2K 1W2
(514) 523-5333   *SIC* 7381

AGENCE DE SECURITE MIRADO 2002, LES *p* 1289
See AGENCES DE SECURITE MIRADO 2002 INC

AGENCE DE SECURITE REGIONALE *p* 1212
See SECURITE KOLOSSAL INC

AGENCE DE VOYAGE ESCAPADE 2000 *p* 1374
See VOYAGES ESCAPADE INC

AGENCE DE VOYAGES D'AUTOMOBILE ET TOURING CLUB DU QUEBEC INC *p* 1278
444 RUE BOUVIER, QUEBEC, QC, G2J 1E3
(418) 624-8222   *SIC* 6712

AGENCE DE VOYAGES DE L'AUTOMOBILE ET TOURING CLUB DU QUEBEC INC *p* 1278
444 RUE BOUVIER, QUEBEC, QC, G2J 1E3
(418) 624-2424   *SIC* 4724

AGENCE DE VOYAGES SEARS *p* 701
See TRAVELBRANDS INC

AGENCE DU LIVRE *p* 1371
See BIBLAIRIE G.G.C. LTEE

AGENCE IMPORT ET EXPORT *p* 1177
See 152258 CANADA INC

AGENCE INTERNATIONALE TRADE-BRIDGE INC *p* 1209
620 RUE SAINT-JACQUES BUREAU 500, MONTREAL, QC, H3C 1C7
(514) 393-9100   *SIC* 4731

AGENCE MEDIA EQUATION HUMAINE *p* 1190
See NVENTIVE INC

AGENCE MIRUM CANADA INC *p* 1187
500 RUE SAINT-JACQUES BUREAU 1420, MONTREAL, QC, H2Y 1S1
(514) 987-9992   *SIC* 7311

AGENCE NEWS *p* 1259
See GENEX COMMUNICATIONS INC

AGENCE POUR VIVRE CHEZ SOI INC *p* 1122
502 RUE SAINT-ETIENNE, LA MALBAIE, QC, G5A 1H5
(418) 665-1067   *SIC* 8399

AGENCE QMI *p* 1212
See QUEBECOR MEDIA INC

AGENCE QUEBEC PLUS *p* 1370
See CORPORATION ASICS CANADA

AGENCE UNIVERSITAIRE DE LA FRANCOPHONIE *p* 1219
3034 BOUL EDOUARD-MONTPETIT, MONTREAL, QC, H3T 1J7
(514) 343-6630   *SIC* 8641

AGENCES D'ASSURANCE COPOLOFF INC, LES *p* 1227
5500 AV ROYALMOUNT BUREAU 325, MONTREAL, QC, H4P 1H7
(514) 731-9605   *SIC* 6351

AGENCES D'ASSURANCE RANDLE INC *p* 1117
17001 RTE TRANSCANADIENNE, KIRKLAND, QC, H9H 0A7
(514) 694-4161   *SIC* 6411

AGENCES DE SECURITE MIRADO 2002 INC *p* 1289
121 8E RUE, ROUYN-NORANDA, QC, J9X 2A5
(819) 797-5184   *SIC* 7381

AGENCES KYOTO LTEE, LES *p* 1152
16500 MONTEE GUENETTE, MIRABEL, QC, J7J 2E2
(450) 438-1255   *SIC* 5511

AGENCES LISETTE LIMOGES INC, LES *p* 1177
9250 AV DU PARC BUREAU 300, MONTREAL, QC, H2N 1Z2
(514) 385-1222   *SIC* 5137

AGENCES W PELLETIER (1980) INC *p* 1325
1400 BOUL JULES-POITRAS, SAINT-LAURENT, QC, H4N 1X7
(514) 276-6700   *SIC* 5087

AGENCES WANT INC, LES *p* 1180
8480 RUE JEANNE-MANCE, MONTREAL, QC, H2P 2S3
(514) 868-9268   *SIC* 5137

AGF *p* 969
See HARMONY GROWTH PLUS PORTFOLIO

AGF - REBAR INC *p* 666
2800 14TH AVE SUITE 204, MARKHAM, ON, L3R 0E4
(416) 862-5015   *SIC* 3449

AGF ACCES *p* 1120
See GROUPE AGF ACCES INC

AGF EMERGING MARKETS BOND FUND *p* 968
66 WELLINGTON ST W SUITE 3100, TORONTO, ON, M5K 1E9
(905) 214-8204   *SIC* 6722

AGF GLOBAL MANAGEMENT LIMITED *p* 968
66 WELLINGTON ST W 31ST FL TORONTO DOMINION BANK TOWER, TORONTO, ON, M5K 1E6
(416) 367-1900   *SIC* 6722

AGF GLOBAL RESOURCES CLASS *p* 968
66 WELLINGTON ST W, TORONTO, ON, M5K 1E9
(905) 214-8203   *SIC* 6722

AGF HARMONY FUNDS *p* 969
See HARMONY FUNDS

AGF INVESTMENTS INC *p* 968
66 WELLINGTON ST W SUITE 3100, TORONTO, ON, M5K 1E9
(416) 367-1900   *SIC* 6722

AGF MANAGEMENT LIMITED *p* 968
66 WELLINGTON ST W FL 31, TORONTO, ON, M5K 1E9
(800) 268-8583   *SIC* 6282

AGF MANAGEMENT LIMITED *p* 968
66 WELLINGTON ST W SUITE 3300, TORONTO, ON, M5K 1E9
(416) 367-1900   *SIC* 6211

AGF U.S SMALL-MID CAP FUND *p* 968
66 WELLINGTON ST W, TORONTO, ON, M5K 1E9
(905) 214-8203   *SIC* 6722

AGFA HEALTHCARE INC *p* 729
5975 FALBOURNE ST SUITE 2, MISSISSAUGA, ON, L5R 3V8
(416) 241-1110   *SIC* 5047

AGFA HEALTHCARE INC *p* 1008
375 HAGEY BLVD, WATERLOO, ON, N2L 6R5
(519) 746-2900   *SIC* 7371

AGFA INC *p* 729
5975 FALBOURNE ST SUITE 2, MISSISSAUGA, ON, L5R 3V8
(905) 361-6982   *SIC* 2752

AGFIQ ENHANCED CORE CANADIAN EQUITY ETF *p* 968
66 WELLINGTON ST W SUITE 3100, TORONTO, ON, M5K 1E9
(905) 214-8204   *SIC* 6722

AGGRESSIVE TRANSPORT LTD *p* 229
5111 272 ST, LANGLEY, BC, V4W 3Z2
(604) 626-4511   *SIC* 4213

AGGRESSIVE TUBE BENDING INC *p* 281
9750 188 ST, SURREY, BC, V4N 3M2
(604) 882-4872   *SIC* 3498

AGI *p* 95
See ACKLANDS - GRAINGER INC

AGI *p* 903
See ACKLANDS - GRAINGER INC

AGI CCAA INC *p* 373
625 HENRY AVE, WINNIPEG, MB, R3A 0V1
(204) 772-2473   *SIC* 2097

AGI ENVIROTANK LTD *p* 1404
401 HWY 4, BIGGAR, SK, S0K 0M0

(306) 948-5262   *SIC* 3443

AGI SHOREWOOD *p* 872
See SHOREWOOD PACKAGING CORP. OF CANADA LIMITED

AGI-METAL FAB *p* 388
198 COMMERCE DR, WINNIPEG, MB, R3P 0Z6
(204) 489-1855   *SIC* 3441

AGILENT TECHNOLOGIES CANADA INC *p* 719
6705 MILLCREEK DR UNIT 5, MISSISSAUGA, ON, L5N 5M4
(289) 290-3859   *SIC* 5084

AGILIS NETWORKS *p* 900
500 REGENT ST SUITE 250, SUDBURY, ON, P3E 3Y2
(705) 675-0516   *SIC* 7373

AGILITY FUEL SYSTEMS *p* 221
See ENVIROMECH INDUSTRIES INC

AGILITY LOGISTICS, CO *p* 737
185 COURTNEYPARK DR E SUITE B, MISSISSAUGA, ON, L5T 2T6
(905) 612-7500   *SIC* 4731

AGINCOURT COLLEGIATE INSTITUTE *p* 875
See TORONTO DISTRICT SCHOOL BOARD

AGINCOURT HYUNDAI *p* 864
See 1502026 ONTARIO LTD

AGINCOURT MAZDA *p* 873
See 1155760 ONTARIO LIMITED

AGINCOURT NISSAN *p* 873
See AGINCOURT NISSAN LIMITED

AGINCOURT NISSAN LIMITED *p* 873
1871 MCCOWAN RD, SCARBOROUGH, ON, M1S 4L4
(416) 291-1188   *SIC* 5511

AGIORITIS HOLDINGS LTD *p* 1433
801 BROADWAY AVE, SASKATOON, SK, S7N 1B5
(306) 652-5374   *SIC* 6719

AGLAND CORP *p* 143
HWY 16, LLOYDMINSTER, AB, T9V 3A2
(780) 874-4154   *SIC* 5083

AGM BEEF FARMS LTD *p* 278
5175 184 ST, SURREY, BC, V3Z 1B5
(604) 576-8318   *SIC* 0212

AGM SURVEYING ENGINEERING *p* 657
See ARCHIBALD, GRAY & MCKAY LTD

AGNEW, J. E. FOOD SERVICES LTD *p* 631
83 TERRY FOX DR SUITE A, KINGSTON, ON, K7M 8N4
(613) 544-9400   *SIC* 5812

AGNICO EAGLE MINES LIMITED *p* 936
145 KING ST E SUITE 400, TORONTO, ON, M5C 2Y7
(416) 947-1212   *SIC* 1041

AGNICO EAGLE MINES LIMITED *p* 1288
10200 RTE DE PREISSAC, ROUYN-NORANDA, QC, J0Y 1C0
(819) 759-3700   *SIC* 1041

AGNICO EAGLE MINES LIMITED *p* 1390
1953 3RD AV O, VAL-D'OR, QC, J9P 4N9
(819) 874-7822   *SIC* 1041

AGNICO EAGLE MINES, DIVISION GOLDEX *p* 1390
See AGNICO EAGLE MINES LIMITED

AGNICO EAGLE MINES, DIVISION LARONDE *p* 1288
See AGNICO EAGLE MINES LIMITED

AGO INDUSTRIES INC *p* 661
500 SOVEREIGN RD, LONDON, ON, N6M 1A4
(519) 452-3780   *SIC* 3842

AGORA MANUFACTURING INC *p* 734
7770 TRANMERE DR, MISSISSAUGA, ON, L5S 1L9
(905) 362-1700   *SIC* 3499

AGOSTINO & NANCY'S NO FRILLS *p* 812
151 BLOOR ST E, OSHAWA, ON, L1H 3M3
(905) 571-6488   *SIC* 5411

AGRACITY CROP & NUTRITION LTD *p* 1426
320 22ND ST E, SASKATOON, SK, S7K

0H1
(306) 665-2294　*SIC* 5191
AGRATURF EQUIPMENT SERVICES INC *p* 564
170 COUNTY ROAD 13, COURTLAND, ON, N0J 1E0
(519) 688-1011　*SIC* 5999
AGRAWEST FOODS　*p* 1042
See AGRAWEST INVESTMENTS LIMITED
AGRAWEST INVESTMENTS LIMITED *p* 1042
30 HOPE ST, SOURIS, PE, C0A 2B0
(902) 687-1400　*SIC* 2034
AGRI TRANS SERVICES INC　*p* 179
2200 KIRTON AVE, ARMSTRONG, BC, V0E 1B0
(250) 546-8898　*SIC* 4731
AGRI-MARCHE INC　*p* 1314
236 RUE SAINTE-GENEVIEVE, SAINT-ISIDORE, QC, G0S 2S0
(418) 882-5656　*SIC* 2041
AGRIBRANDS PURINA CANADA *p* 1035
See CARGILL LIMITED
AGRICO　*p* 685
See AGRICO CANADA LIMITED
AGRICO CANADA LIMITED　*p* 685
7420 AIRPORT RD UNIT 202, MISSISSAUGA, ON, L4T 4E5
(905) 672-5700　*SIC* 5191
AGRICOM INTERNATIONAL INC　*p* 241
828 HARBOURSIDE DR SUITE 213, NORTH VANCOUVER, BC, V7P 3R9
(604) 983-6922　*SIC* 5153
AGRICORE UNITED　*p* 1422
See VITERRA INC
AGRICORP　*p* 601
1 STONE RD W, GUELPH, ON, N1G 4Y2
(888) 247-4999　*SIC* 6331
AGRICOTECH　*p* 1296
See GROUPE AGRITEX INC, LE
AGRICREDIT ACCEPTANCE CANADA, A DIV OF　*p* 803
See DE LAGE LANDEN FINANCIAL SERVICES CANADA INC
AGRICULTURE FINANCIAL SERVICES CORPORATION　*p* 138
5718 56 AVE, LACOMBE, AB, T4L 1B1
(403) 782-8200　*SIC* 6159
AGRIFOODS INTERNATIONAL COOPERATIVE LTD　*p* 20
4215 12 ST NE, CALGARY, AB, T2E 4P9
(403) 571-6400　*SIC* 2026
AGRIFOODS INTERNATIONAL COOPERATIVE LTD　*p* 95
11671 160 ST NW, EDMONTON, AB, T5M 3Z3
(780) 962-5787　*SIC* 4212
AGRIFOODS INTERNATIONAL COOPERATIVE LTD　*p* 153
5410 50 AVE, RED DEER, AB, T4N 4B5
SIC 2021
AGRILAIT, COOPERATIVE AGRICOLE *p* 1306
83 RANG DE L'EGLISE, SAINT-GUILLAUME, QC, J0C 1L0
(819) 396-2022　*SIC* 2022
AGRINOR　*p* 1296
See NUTRINOR COOPERATIVE
AGRINOVE　*p* 1036
See KERRY (CANADA) INC
AGRIS CO-OPERATIVE LTD　*p* 542
835 PARK AVE W, CHATHAM, ON, N7M 0N1
(519) 354-7178　*SIC* 5999
AGRISTAR INC　*p* 10
720 28 ST NE SUITE 208, CALGARY, AB, T2A 6R3
(403) 873-5177　*SIC* 5148
AGRITEAM CANADA CONSULTING LTD *p* 69
14707 BANNISTER RD SE UNIT 200, CAL-

GARY, AB, T2X 1Z2
(403) 253-5298　*SIC* 8748
AGRITEC　*p* 208
See EVERGRO CANADA INC
AGRITERRA EQUIPMENT　*p* 167
See 1742009 ALBERTA INC
AGRITIBI R.H. INC　*p* 1045
2711 RTE 111 E BUREAU 2, AMOS, QC, J9T 3A1
(819) 732-6296　*SIC* 5083
AGRIUM INC　*p* 39
13131 LAKE FRASER DR SE, CALGARY, AB, T2J 7E8
(403) 225-7000　*SIC* 2873
AGRIVERT, COOPERATIVE AGRICOLE REGIONALE　*p* 1114
See COOP NOVAGO, LA
AGROCENTRE　*p* 1353
See AGROCENTRE LANAUDIERE INC
AGROCENTRE BELCAN INC　*p* 1360
180 MONT E SAINTE-MARIE, SAINTE-MARTHE, QC, J0P 1W0
(450) 459-4288　*SIC* 2874
AGROCENTRE LANAUDIERE INC　*p* 1353
531 RANG SUD, SAINT-THOMAS, QC, J0K 3L0
(450) 759-1520　*SIC* 2874
AGROCENTRE ST-PIE　*p* 1242
See AGROCENTRE TECHNOVA INC
AGROCENTRE TECHNOVA INC　*p* 1242
515 RUE DE MONSEIGNEUR-COURCHESNE, NICOLET, QC, J3T 1C8
(819) 293-5851　*SIC* 5191
AGROCROP EXPORTS LTD　*p* 494
100 AGROCROP RD, BOLTON, ON, L7E 4K4
(905) 458-4551　*SIC* 7389
AGROMART GROUP　*p* 903
See AGRONOMY COMPANY OF CANADA LTD
AGROMEX INC　*p* 1047
251 235 RTE, ANGE-GARDIEN, QC, J0E 1E0
(450) 293-3694　*SIC* 2011
AGRONOMY COMPANY OF CANADA LTD *p* 903
17554 PLOVER MILLS RD, THORNDALE, ON, N0M 2P0
(519) 461-9057　*SIC* 5191
AGROPUR　*p* 1129
See ALIMENTS LEBEL INC, LES
AGROPUR　*p* 1245
See AGROPUR COOPERATIVE
AGROPUR　*p* 1309
See PRODUITS ALIMENTAIRES ANCO LTEE, LES
AGROPUR COOPERATIVE　*p* 92
13944 YELLOWHEAD TRAIL NW, EDMONTON, AB, T5L 3C2
(780) 488-2214　*SIC* 2024
AGROPUR COOPERATIVE　*p* 181
7650 18TH ST, BURNABY, BC, V3N 4K3
(604) 524-4491　*SIC* 0241
AGROPUR COOPERATIVE　*p* 334
2220 DOWLER PL, VICTORIA, BC, V8T 4H3
(250) 360-5200　*SIC* 5143
AGROPUR COOPERATIVE　*p* 405
256 LAWLOR LANE, MIRAMICHI, NB, E1V 3Z9
(506) 627-7720　*SIC* 5143
AGROPUR COOPERATIVE　*p* 811
1001 DAIRY DR, ORLEANS, ON, K4A 3N3
(613) 834-5700　*SIC* 5143
AGROPUR COOPERATIVE　*p* 1046
466 132 RTE O BUREAU 1320, AMQUI, QC, G5J 2G7
(418) 629-3133　*SIC* 2026
AGROPUR COOPERATIVE　*p* 1055
75 AV LAMBERT, BEAUCEVILLE, QC, G5X 3N5
(418) 774-9848　*SIC* 2022
AGROPUR COOPERATIVE　*p* 1063
81 RUE SAINT-FELIX, BON-CONSEIL, QC,

J0C 1A0
(819) 336-2727　*SIC* 5143
AGROPUR COOPERATIVE　*p* 1108
510 RUE PRINCIPALE, GRANBY, QC, J2G 2X2
(450) 375-1991　*SIC* 2022
AGROPUR COOPERATIVE　*p* 1110
1100 RUE OMER-DESLAURIERS, GRANBY, QC, J2J 0S7
(450) 777-5300　*SIC* 2022
AGROPUR COOPERATIVE　*p* 1129
724 RUE PRINCIPALE, LACHUTE, QC, J8H 1Z4
(450) 562-5500　*SIC* 2024
AGROPUR COOPERATIVE　*p* 1244
See AGROPUR COOPERATIVE
AGROPUR COOPERATIVE　*p* 1244
1400 CH D'OKA, OKA, QC, J0N 1E0
(450) 479-6396　*SIC* 2022
AGROPUR COOPERATIVE　*p* 1245
2400 RUE DE LA COOPERATIVE, PLESSISVILLE, QC, G6L 3G8
(819) 362-7338　*SIC* 2023
AGROPUR COOPERATIVE　*p* 1260
2465 1RE AV, QUEBEC, QC, G1L 3M9
(418) 641-0857　*SIC* 2026
AGROPUR COOPERATIVE　*p* 1309
4600 RUE ARMAND-FRAPPIER, SAINT-HUBERT, QC, J3Z 1G5
(450) 878-2333　*SIC* 5143
AGROPUR COOPERATIVE　*p* 1309
4700 RUE ARMAND-FRAPPIER, SAINT-HUBERT, QC, J3Z 1G5
(450) 443-5662　*SIC* 8741
AGROPUR COOPERATIVE　*p* 1311
995 RUE DANIEL-JOHNSON E, SAINT-HYACINTHE, QC, J2S 7V6
(450) 773-6493　*SIC* 5143
AGROPUR COOPERATIVE　*p* 1325
333 BOUL LEBEAU, SAINT-LAURENT, QC, H4N 1S3
(800) 501-1150　*SIC* 3556
AGROPUR DIV. NATREL　*p* 1046
See AGROPUR COOPERATIVE
AGROPUR DIVISION FROMAGE ET PRODUITS FONCTIONNELS　*p* 1055
See AGROPUR COOPERATIVE
AGROPUR DIVISION NATREL　*p* 1260
See AGROPUR COOPERATIVE
AGROPUR DIVISION NATREL　*p* 1309
See AGROPUR COOPERATIVE
AGROPUR FINE CHEESE DIVISION *p* 1309
See AGROPUR COOPERATIVE
AGROPUR, DIV FROMAGES FIN　*p* 1311
See AGROPUR COOPERATIVE
AGS AUTOMOTIVE SYSTEMS　*p* 915
See A.G. SIMPSON AUTOMOTIVE INC
AGS INTERNATIONAL　*p* 99
17942 105 AVE NW SUITE 200, EDMONTON, AB, T5S 2H5
(780) 455-0199　*SIC* 8748
AGSI　*p* 620
See ANGUS GEOSOLUTIONS INC
AGT　*p* 1238
See ORUS INTEGRATION INC
AGT CLIC FOODS INC　*p* 1084
2185 AV FRANCIS-HUGHES, COTE SAINT-LUC, QC, H7S 1N5
(450) 669-2663　*SIC* 5099
AGT FOOD AND INGREDIENTS INC *p* 1422
6200 E PRIMROSE GREEN DR, REGINA, SK, S4V 3L7
(306) 525-4490　*SIC* 0723
AGT FOODS　*p* 1084
See AGT CLIC FOODS INC
AGTA HOME HEALTH CARE AND NURSING INC　*p* 785
795 WILSON AVE SUITE 102, NORTH YORK, ON, M3K 1E4
(416) 630-0737　*SIC* 8741
AGWORLD EQUIPMENT　*p* 1408
See 609905 SASKATCHEWAN LTD

AHBL MANAGEMENT　*p* 329
See ALEXANDER HOLBURN BEAUDIN & LANG LLP
AHBL MANAGEMENT LIMITED PARTNERSHIP　*p* 329
700 GEORGIA ST W SUITE 2700, VANCOUVER, BC, V7Y 1K8
(604) 688-1351　*SIC* 8741
AHEARN & SOPER INC　*p* 581
100 WOODBINE DOWNS BLVD, ETOBICOKE, ON, M9W 5S6
(416) 675-3999　*SIC* 5044
AHEARN RESIDENCE　*p* 825
See OTTAWA-CARLETON ASSOCIATION FOR PERSONS WITH DEVELOPMENTAL DISABILITIES
AHIP　*p* 302
See AMERICAN HOTEL INCOME PROPERTIES REIT LP
AHKWESAHSNE MOHAWK BOARD OF EDUCATION　*p* 475
See MOHAWK COUNCIL OF AKWESASNE
AHKWESAHSNE MOHAWK BOARD OF EDUCATION　*p* 475
169 AKWESASNE INTERNATIONAL RD, AKWESASNE, ON, K6H 0G5
(613) 933-0409　*SIC* 8211
AHLA　*p* 125
See ALBERTA HOTEL & LODGING ASSOCIATION
AHMAD, J DRUGS LTD　*p* 770
6428 YONGE ST, NORTH YORK, ON, M2M 3X4
(416) 223-6250　*SIC* 5912
AHS　*p* 275
See ASSOCIATED HEALTH SYSTEMS INC
AIC　*p* 753
See ALLIED INTERNATIONAL CREDIT CORP
AIC GLOBAL COMMUNICATIONS INC *p* 187
3707 WAYBURNE DR, BURNABY, BC, V5G 3L1
(604) 708-3899　*SIC* 4899
AIC GLOBAL HOLDINGS INC　*p* 529
1375 KERNS RD SUITE 100, BURLINGTON, ON, L7P 4V7
(905) 331-4242　*SIC* 6712
AIC RSP AMERICAN FOCUSED FUND *p* 529
1375 KERNS RD SUITE 100, BURLINGTON, ON, L7P 4V7
(905) 331-4250　*SIC* 6722
AIDE JURIDIQUE　*p* 1194
See CENTRE COMMUNAUTAIRE JURIDIQUE DE MONTREAL
AIDE-MAISON VALLEE DE LA MATAPEDIA *p* 1046
20A RUE DESBIENS BUREAU 100, AMQUI, QC, G5J 3P1
(418) 629-5812　*SIC* 8322
AIDUS INTERNATIONAL　*p* 259
2560 SHELL RD UNIT 1048, RICHMOND, BC, V6X 0B8
(604) 304-7889　*SIC* 5149
AIESEC　*p* 1185
See ASSOCIATION INTERNATIONALE DES ETUDIANTS EN SCIENCES ECONOMIQUES ET COMMERCIALES
AIESEC CANADA INC　*p* 612
116 KING ST W, HAMILTON, ON, L8P 4V3
(905) 529-5515　*SIC* 6513
AIESEC SASKATOON　*p* 1433
25 CAMPUS DR SUITE 248, SASKATOON, SK, S7N 5A7
(306) 966-7767　*SIC* 8699
AIG INSURANCE CANADA　*p* 959
See AIG INSURANCE COMPANY OF CANADA
AIG INSURANCE COMPANY OF CANADA *p* 959
145 WELLINGTON ST W SUITE 1400, TORONTO, ON, M5J 1H8

(416) 596-3000 *SIC* 6331

AIG INSURANCE COMPANY OF CANADA*p*
1193
2000 AV MCGILL COLLEGE BUREAU
1200, MONTREAL, QC, H3A 3H3
(514) 842-0603 *SIC* 6411

AIKAWA FIBER TECHNOLOGIES INC *p*
1374
72 RUE QUEEN, SHERBROOKE, QC, J1M
2C3
(819) 562-4754 *SIC* 3554

AIKAWA GROUP *p* 1374
*See FIDUCIE TECHNOLOGIES DE FI-
BRES AIKAWA*

AIL CANADA *p* 368
1549 ST MARY'S RD SUITE 101, WIN-
NIPEG, MB, R2M 5G9
(204) 942-9477 *SIC* 6311

AILE D'ARGENT MOYEN ORIENT *p* 1266
See EDDYFI NDT INC

AIM *p* 1257
*See COMPAGNIE AMERICAINE DE FER &
METAUX INC, LA*

AIM DELSAN *p* 1162
*See SERVICES ENVIRONNEMENTAUX
DELSAN-A.I.M. INC, LES*

AIM GROUP INC, THE *p* 822
130 ALBERT ST SUITE 126, OTTAWA, ON,
K1P 5G4
(613) 230-6991 *SIC* 7361

AIM HOLDING TRUST *p* 199
2000 BRIGANTINE DR, COQUITLAM, BC,
V3K 7B5
(604) 525-3900 *SIC* 6712

AIM INDUSTRIAL INC *p* 538
29 CHERRY BLOSSOM RD, CAMBRIDGE,
ON, N3H 4R7
(519) 747-2255 *SIC* 1796

AIM METAUX & ALLIAGES INC *p* 1238
9100 BOUL HENRI-BOURASSA E,
MONTREAL-EST, QC, H1E 2S4
(514) 494-2000 *SIC* 6712

AIM METAUX & ALLIAGES S.E.C. *p* 1238
9100 BOUL HENRI-BOURASSA E,
MONTREAL-EST, QC, H1E 2S4
(514) 494-2000 *SIC* 3399

AIM OILFIELD SERVICES *p* 171
See A.I.M. HOLDINGS INC

AIM RECYCLAGE *p* 1238
*See COMPAGNIE AMERICAINE DE FER &
METAUX INC, LA*

AIM RECYCLING HAMILTON *p* 609
See AMERICAN IRON & METAL LP

AIMCO *p* 87
*See ALBERTA INVESTMENT MANAGE-
MENT CORPORATION*

**AIMHI-PRINCE GEORGE ASSOCIATION
FOR COMMUNITY LIVING** *p* 250
950 KERRY ST, PRINCE GEORGE, BC,
V2M 5A3
(250) 564-6408 *SIC* 8011

AIMIA INC *p* 985
130 KING ST W SUITE 1600, TORONTO,
ON, M5X 2A2
(905) 214-8699 *SIC* 8743

AIMIA INC *p* 1191
525 AV VIGER O BUREAU 1000, MON-
TREAL, QC, H2Z 0B2
(514) 897-6800 *SIC* 8732

**AIMIA PROPRIETARY LOYALTY CANADA
INC** *p* 985
130 KING ST W SUITE 1600, TORONTO,
ON, M5X 2A2
(905) 214-8699 *SIC* 8743

AINLEY & ASSOCIATES LIMITED *p* 546
280 PRETTY RIVER PKY N, COLLING-
WOOD, ON, L9Y 4J5
(705) 445-3451 *SIC* 8711

**AINSWORTH ENGINEERED CANADA LIM-
ITED PARTNERSHIP** *p*
327
1055 DUNSMUIR ST SUITE 3194, VAN-
COUVER, BC, V7X 1L3
(604) 661-3200 *SIC* 3491

AINSWORTH INC *p* 787
131 BERMONDSEY RD, NORTH YORK,
ON, M4A 1X4
(416) 751-4420 *SIC* 1731

**AINSWORTH MANAGEMENT SERVICES
INC** *p* 1016
56 CARLINDS DR, WHITBY, ON, L1R 3B9
(905) 666-9156 *SIC* 7349

AIOLOS INC *p* 581
135 QUEEN'S PLATE DR SUITE 300, ETO-
BICOKE, ON, M9W 6V1
(416) 674-3017 *SIC* 8711

AION FOUNDATION *p* 982
See NUCO NETWORKS INC

AIR BOREALIS LIMITED PARTNERSHIP *p*
424
1 CENTRALIA DR, HAPPY VALLEY-
GOOSE BAY, NL, A0P 1C0
(709) 576-1800 *SIC* 4512

AIR CAB LIMOUSINE (1985) LIMITED*p* 548
7733 KEELE ST, CONCORD, ON, L4K 1Y5
(416) 225-1555 *SIC* 4119

AIR CANADA *p* 374
355 PORTAGE AVE SUITE 3850, WIN-
NIPEG, MB, R3B 0J6
(204) 941-2684 *SIC* 4512

AIR CANADA *p* 383
2000 WELLINGTON AVE RM 222, WIN-
NIPEG, MB, R3H 1C1
(204) 788-6953 *SIC* 4581

AIR CANADA *p* 383
2020 SARGENT AVE, WINNIPEG, MB, R3H
0E1
(204) 788-7871 *SIC* 4581

AIR CANADA *p* 413
1 AIR CANADA WAY, SAINT JOHN, NB,
E2K 0B1
SIC 7389

AIR CANADA *p* 450
1 BELL BLVD SUITE 7, ENFIELD, NS, B2T
1K2
(902) 873-2350 *SIC* 4581

AIR CANADA *p* 1229
735 STUART GRAHAM N, MONTREAL,
QC, H4Y 1C3
SIC 4512

AIR CANADA *p* 1332
7373 BOUL DE LA COTE-VERTU BUREAU
1290, SAINT-LAURENT, QC, H4S 1Z3
(514) 393-3333 *SIC* 4512

AIR CANADA CARGO *p* 1229
See AIR CANADA

AIR CANADA CARGO *p* 1332
See AIR CANADA

AIR CANADA CENTRE *p* 964
*See MAPLE LEAF SPORTS & ENTERTAIN-
MENT LTD*

AIR CANADA EXPRESS *p* 447
See JAZZ AVIATION LP

AIR CANADA EXPRESS *p* 734
See AIR GEORGIAN LIMITED

AIR CANADA PILOTS ASSOCIATION *p* 383
2000 WELLINGTON AVE SUITE 124A,
WINNIPEG, MB, R3H 1C1
(204) 779-0736 *SIC* 8641

AIR CANADA PILOTS ASSOCIATION *p* 687
6299 AIRPORT RD SUITE 205, MISSIS-
SAUGA, ON, L4V 1N3
(905) 678-9008 *SIC* 8631

AIR CANADA VACATION *p* 690
See TOURAM LIMITED PARTNERSHIP

AIR CANADA VACATIONS *p* 1214
See TOURAM LIMITED PARTNERSHIP

AIR CONTROL AVIATION *p* 423
See AAS CO OF NFLD ULC

AIR CREEBEC INC *p* 912
GD LCD MAIN, TIMMINS, ON, P4N 7C4
(705) 264-9521 *SIC* 4512

AIR CREEBEC INC *p* 1400
18 RUE WASKAGANISH, WASKAGANISH,
QC, J0M 1R0
(819) 895-8355 *SIC* 4512

AIR GEORGIAN LIMITED *p* 734
2450 DERRY RD E SUITE 3, MISSIS-

SAUGA, ON, L5S 1B2
(905) 676-1221 *SIC* 4522

AIR INUIT LTEE *p* 1332
6005 BOUL DE LA COTE-VERTU, SAINT-
LAURENT, QC, H4S 0B1
(514) 905-9445 *SIC* 4512

AIR INUIT SERVICE D'ENTRETIEN *p* 1332
See AIR INUIT LTEE

AIR LIQUIDE CANADA INC *p* 13
3004 54 AVE SE, CALGARY, AB, T2C 0A7
(403) 310-9353 *SIC* 5169

AIR LIQUIDE CANADA INC *p* 112
10020 56 AVE NW, EDMONTON, AB, T6E
5Z2
(780) 434-2060 *SIC* 2813

AIR LIQUIDE CANADA INC *p* 1201
1250 BOUL RENE-LEVESQUE O BUREAU
1700, MONTREAL, QC, H3B 5E6
(514) 933-0303 *SIC* 2813

**AIR LIQUIDE GLOBAL E&C SOLUTIONS
CANADA INC** *p* 42
140 4 AVE SW SUITE 550, CALGARY, AB,
T2P 3N3
(403) 774-4300 *SIC* 5169

**AIR LIQUIDE GLOBAL E&C SOLUTIONS
CANADA LP** *p* 42
140 4 AVE SW SUITE 550, CALGARY, AB,
T2P 3N3
(403) 774-4300 *SIC* 5169

AIR NORTH PARTNERSHIP *p* 264
1 3RD SUITE 3135, RICHMOND, BC, V7B
1Y7
(604) 207-1165 *SIC* 4512

AIR NORTH PARTNERSHIP *p* 1440
150 CONDOR RD, WHITEHORSE, YT, Y1A
6E6
(867) 668-2228 *SIC* 4512

AIR NORTH, YUKON'S AIRLINE *p* 1440
See AIR NORTH PARTNERSHIP

AIR PARTNERS CORP *p* 20
263 AERO WAY NE, CALGARY, AB, T2E
6K2
(403) 275-3930 *SIC* 8741

AIR PRODUCTS CANADA LTD *p* 719
2233 ARGENTIA RD, MISSISSAUGA, ON,
L5N 2X7
(905) 816-6670 *SIC* 5169

AIR TINDI LTD *p* 435
28 MITCHELL DR, YELLOWKNIFE, NT,
X1A 2H5
(867) 669-8200 *SIC* 4522

AIR TRANSAT *p* 1186
See TRANSAT TOURS CANADA INC

AIR TRANSAT A.T. INC *p* 1332
5959 BOUL DE LA COTE-VERTU, SAINT-
LAURENT, QC, H4S 2E6
(514) 906-0330 *SIC* 4512

AIR TRANSAT CARGO *p* 1332
See AIR TRANSAT A.T. INC

AIR-KING LIMITED *p* 498
8 EDVAC DR, BRAMPTON, ON, L6S 5P2
(905) 456-2033 *SIC* 5064

AIR-SERV CANADA INC. *p* 501
80 DEVON RD UNIT 4, BRAMPTON, ON,
L6T 5B3
SIC 5084

AIR-SERVICE CANADA *p* 501
See AIR-SERV CANADA INC.

AIR-TERRE EQUIPEMENT *p* 1108
See A.T.L.A.S. AERONAUTIQUE INC

AIRBORN FLEXIBLE CIRCUITS INC *p* 916
11 DOHME AVE, TORONTO, ON, M4B 1Y7
(416) 752-2224 *SIC* 3672

AIRBORNE ENGINES LTD *p* 208
7762 PROGRESS WAY, DELTA, BC, V4G
1A4
(604) 244-1668 *SIC* 8711

AIRBOSS & DESING (TMA494,030) *p* 1044
*See AIRBOSS ENGINEERED PRODUCTS
INC*

AIRBOSS ENGINEERED PRODUCTS INC*p*
1044
970 RUE LANDRY, ACTON VALE, QC, J0H
1A0

(450) 546-2776 *SIC* 3069

AIRBOSS OF AMERICA CORP *p* 638
101 GLASGOW ST, KITCHENER, ON, N2G
4X8
(519) 576-5565 *SIC* 3069

AIRBOSS OF AMERICA CORP *p* 753
16441 YONGE ST, NEWMARKET, ON, L3X
2G8
(905) 751-1188 *SIC* 3069

AIRBOSS RUBBER COMPOUNDING *p* 638
See AIRBOSS OF AMERICA CORP

**AIRBOSS RUBBER COMPOUNDING, DIV
OF** *p* 753
See AIRBOSS OF AMERICA CORP

AIRBUS *p* 591
*See AIRBUS HELICOPTERS CANADA LIM-
ITED*

AIRBUS HELICOPTERS CANADA LIMITED
p 591
1100 GILMORE RD, FORT ERIE, ON, L2A
5M4
(905) 871-7772 *SIC* 3721

AIRCO *p* 1170
See DESCAIR INC

AIRCO LTD *p* 898
1510 OLD FALCONBRIDGE RD, SUD-
BURY, ON, P3A 4N8
(705) 673-2210 *SIC* 7623

AIRCONSOL AVIATION SERVICES ULC *p*
423
GD LCD MAIN, GANDER, NL, A1V 1W4
(709) 256-3042 *SIC* 5172

**AIRCRAFT APPLIANCES AND EQUIP-
MENT LIMITED** *p*
501
150 EAST DR, BRAMPTON, ON, L6T 1C1
(905) 791-1666 *SIC* 3677

AIRD & BERLIS LLP *p* 959
181 BAY ST SUITE 1800, TORONTO, ON,
M5J 2T9
(416) 863-1500 *SIC* 8111

AIRDEX CORP *p* 485
230 SAUNDERS RD, BARRIE, ON, L4N 9A2
SIC 5084

AIRDRIE CHRYSLER DODGE JEEP *p* 3
See NORTH HILL MOTORS (1975) LTD

AIRDRIE MOTORS (1986) LTD *p* 2
149 EAST LAKE CRES NE, AIRDRIE, AB,
T4A 2H7
(403) 948-6912 *SIC* 5531

AIRDRIE PONTIAC BUICK GMC *p* 2
See AIRDRIE MOTORS (1986) LTD

AIRDRY *p* 1293
See LOUIS GARNEAU SPORTS INC

AIRE ONE HEATING AND COOLING INC *p*
616
1065 UPPER JAMES ST, HAMILTON, ON,
L9C 3A6
(905) 385-2800 *SIC* 1711

AIREAU QUALITE CONTROLE INC *p* 1060
660 RUE DE LA SABLIERE, BOIS-DES-
FILION, QC, J6Z 4T7
(450) 621-6661 *SIC* 5075

AIREX CONTROLE *p* 1231
See AIREX INDUSTRIES INC

AIREX INC *p* 501
5 SANDHILL CRT UNIT C, BRAMPTON,
ON, L6T 5J5
(905) 790-8667 *SIC* 5075

AIREX INDUSTRIES INC *p* 1231
2500 RUE BERNARD-LEFEBVRE, MON-
TREAL, QC, H7C 0A5
(514) 351-2303 *SIC* 3564

AIRFLEX SYSTEM & DESSIN *p* 1124
See L.P. ROYER INC

AIRFLIGHT SERVICES *p* 548
See 464290 ONTARIO LIMITED

AIRGAS CANADA INC *p* 205
634 DERWENT WAY, DELTA, BC, V3M 5P8
SIC 5169

AIRIA LEASING INC *p* 650
511 MCCORMICK BLVD, LONDON, ON,
N5W 4C8
(519) 457-1904 *SIC* 6712

AIRIA RESIDENTIAL SYSTEMS INC *p* 650
511 MCCORMICK BLVD, LONDON, ON,
N5W 4C8
(519) 457-1904   *SIC* 5084
AIRLINE EXPRESS SERVICES INC *p* 687
3133 ORLANDO DR, MISSISSAUGA, ON,
L4V 1C5
(905) 670-2000   *SIC* 4731
AIRLINER MOTOR HOTEL (1972) LTD *p* 320
2233 BURRARD ST SUITE 309, VANCOU-
VER, BC, V6J 3H9
SIC 5813
AIRLINER MOTOR HOTEL (1972) LTD *p* 383
1740 ELLICE AVE, WINNIPEG, MB, R3H
0B3
(204) 775-7131   *SIC* 7011
AIRLINERS, DIV OF *p* 923
See CREATIVE TRAVEL SOLUTIONS INC
AIRMEDIC AMBULANCE AERIENNE *p*
1307
See AIRMEDIC INC
AIRMEDIC INC *p* 1307
4980 RTE DE L'AEROPORT, SAINT-
HUBERT, QC, J3Y 8Y9
(450) 766-0770   *SIC* 4522
**AIRPORT COLONY OF HUTTERIAN
BRETHREN TRUST** *p* 354
GD LCD MAIN, PORTAGE LA PRAIRIE, MB,
R1N 3A7
(204) 274-2422   *SIC* 0191
AIRPORT FORD LINCOLN SALES LIMITED
p 616
49 RYMAL RD E, HAMILTON, ON, L9B 1B9
(905) 388-6665   *SIC* 5511
AIRPORT STEEL & TUBING LTD *p* 501
155 HEDGEDALE RD, BRAMPTON, ON,
L6T 5P3
SIC 5051
**AIRPORT TERMINAL SERVICE INC CANA-
DIAN** *p*
728
6500 SILVER DART DR UNIT 211, MISSIS-
SAUGA, ON, L5P 1B1
(905) 405-9550   *SIC* 4581
**AIRPORT TERMINAL SERVICES CANA-
DIAN COMPANY** *p*
20
8075 22 ST NE, CALGARY, AB, T2E 7Z6
(403) 291-0965   *SIC* 4581
**AIRPORT TERMINAL SERVICES CANA-
DIAN COMPANY** *p*
383
2000 WELLINGTON AVE SUITE 221, WIN-
NIPEG, MB, R3H 1C1
SIC 4581
AIRPORTER, SERVICE, DIV OF *p* 775
See FIRSTCANADA ULC
AIRSPRAY (1967) LTD *p* 97
10141 122 ST NW, EDMONTON, AB, T5N
1L7
(780) 453-1737   *SIC* 0851
AIRSPRINT INC *p* 20
1910 MCCALL LANDNG NE, CALGARY,
AB, T2E 9B5
(403) 730-2344   *SIC* 4522
AIRSTART INC *p* 691
2680 SKYMARK AVE SUITE 901, MISSIS-
SAUGA, ON, L4W 5L6
(905) 366-8730   *SIC* 5088
AIRSTART REGIONAL SPARES *p* 691
See AIRSTART INC
AIRTEX MANUFACTURING PARTNERSHIP
p 27
1401 HASTINGS CRES SE SUITE 1421,
CALGARY, AB, T2G 4C8
(403) 287-2590   *SIC* 3433
AIRTEX MANUFACTURING PARTNERSHIP
p 754
1175 TWINNEY DR, NEWMARKET, ON,
L3Y 9C8
(905) 898-1114   *SIC* 3585
AIRWAY SURGICAL APPLIANCES LTD *p*
831
189 COLONNADE RD, OTTAWA, ON, K2E

7J4
(613) 723-4790   *SIC* 3842
AIRWAYS TRANSIT SERVICE LIMITED *p*
566
35 5 HWY W, DUNDAS, ON, L9H 7L5
(905) 333-3113   *SIC* 4131
AIRWAYS TRANSIT SERVICE LIMITED *p*
1010
99 NORTHLAND RD UNIT A, WATERLOO,
ON, N2V 1Y8
(519) 658-5521   *SIC* 4131
AIRWORLD *p* 16
See IMPERIAL OIL LIMITED
AISIN *p* 895
See AISIN CANADA INC
AISIN CANADA INC *p* 895
180 WRIGHT BLVD, STRATFORD, ON, N4Z
1H3
(519) 271-1575   *SIC* 3465
**AIT WORLDWIDE LOGISTICS (CANADA),
INC** *p* 450
588 BARNES DR, GOFFS, NS, B2T 1K3
(902) 873-5285   *SIC* 4512
AITKEN CHEVROLET *p* 880
See AITKEN MOTORS LTD
AITKEN MOTORS LTD *p* 880
51 QUEENSWAY E, SIMCOE, ON, N3Y
4M5
(519) 426-1793   *SIC* 5511
AITON DRUG COMPANY, LIMITED *p* 403
20 AITON CRES, HARTLAND, NB, E7P 2H2
(506) 375-4469   *SIC* 5122
AJAX DOWN SIMULCAST *p* 475
See PICOV DOWNS INC
AJAX FIRE AND EMERGENCY SERVICES
p 473
*See CORPORATION OF THE TOWN OF
AJAX, THE*
AJAX HIGH SCHOOL *p* 474
See DURHAM DISTRICT SCHOOL BOARD
AJAX JEEP EAGLE LTD *p* 1013
1602 CHAMPLAIN AVE, WHITBY, ON, L1N
6A7
(905) 683-4100   *SIC* 5511
**AJAX MAINTENANCE & SHIPPING SUP-
PLIES CO LTD** *p*
873
100 COMMANDER BLVD, SCARBOR-
OUGH, ON, M1S 3H7
(416) 291-7601   *SIC* 5087
AJAX MAZDA *p* 473
See AJAX SALES & SERVICE INC
AJAX NISSAN *p* 473
See 949043 ONTARIO INC
AJAX SALES & SERVICE INC *p* 473
301 BAYLY ST W, AJAX, ON, L1S 6M2
(905) 428-0088   *SIC* 5511
AJAX TEXTILE CORPORATION *p* 473
170 COMMERCIAL AVE, AJAX, ON, L1S
2H5
(905) 683-6800   *SIC* 2257
AJB SOFTWARE DESIGN INC *p* 691
5255 SOLAR DR, MISSISSAUGA, ON, L4W
5B8
(905) 282-1877   *SIC* 7371
AJPRO DISTRIBUTION INC *p* 1233
2047 NORD LAVAL (A-440) O, MONTREAL,
QC, H7L 3W3
(450) 681-0666   *SIC* 5137
AJRAM'S, ANNY PHARMACY LTD *p* 592
615 KING ST E, GANANOQUE, ON, K7G
1H4
(613) 382-2303   *SIC* 5912
AJW TECHNIQUE INC *p* 1332
7055 RUE ALEXANDER-FLEMING BU-
REAU 100, SAINT-LAURENT, QC, H4S 2B7
(514) 339-5100   *SIC* 4581
AKA GROUP OF COMPANIES *p* 1041
*See ASPIN KEMP & ASSOCIATES HOLD-
ING CORP*
AKHURST HOLDINGS LIMITED *p* 205
1669 FOSTER'S WAY, DELTA, BC, V3M 6S7
(604) 540-1430   *SIC* 5084
AKHURST MACHINERY LIMITED *p* 112

9615 63 AVE NW, EDMONTON, AB, T6E
0G2
(780) 435-3936   *SIC* 5084
AKHURST MACHINERY LIMITED *p* 205
1669 FOSTER'S WAY, DELTA, BC, V3M 6S7
(604) 540-1430   *SIC* 5084
AKINAI CANADA INC *p* 27
2600 PORTLAND ST SE SUITE 1010, CAL-
GARY, AB, T2G 4M6
(403) 280-6482   *SIC* 5044
AKITA DRILLING LTD *p* 42
333 7 AVE SW UNIT 1000, CALGARY, AB,
T2P 2Z1
(403) 292-7979   *SIC* 1382
AKITA DRILLING LTD *p* 148
See AKITA DRILLING LTD
AKITA DRILLING LTD *p* 148
2302 8 ST, NISKU, AB, T9E 7Z2
(780) 955-6700   *SIC* 1381
AKRAN MARKETING *p* 816
See 1222010 ONTARIO INC
AKTELUX CORPORATION *p* 719
2145 MEADOWPINE BLVD, MISSIS-
SAUGA, ON, L5N 6R8
SIC 3812
AKUNA CANADA INC *p* 691
5115 SATELLITE DR, MISSISSAUGA, ON,
L4W 5B6
(905) 290-0326   *SIC* 5499
AKUNA INTERNATIONAL CORP *p* 691
5115 SATELLITE DR, MISSISSAUGA, ON,
L4W 5B6
(905) 848-0428   *SIC* 5122
AKZO NOBEL COATINGS LTD *p* 582
110 WOODBINE DOWNS BLVD UNIT 4,
ETOBICOKE, ON, M9W 5S6
(416) 674-6633   *SIC* 2851
AKZO NOBEL COATINGS LTD *p* 1319
1001 BOUL ROLAND-GODARD, SAINT-
JEROME, QC, J7Y 4C2
SIC 2851
AKZO NOBEL PEINTURES *p* 1319
See AKZO NOBEL COATINGS LTD
AKZO NOBEL WOOD COATINGS LTD *p*
847
155 ROSE GLEN RD, PORT HOPE, ON,
L1A 3V6
(905) 885-6388   *SIC* 2851
AKZO NOBEL WOOD COATINGS LTD *p*
1400
274 RUE SAINT-LOUIS BUREAU 6, WAR-
WICK, QC, J0A 1M0
(819) 358-7500   *SIC* 5198
AL BARNIM INC *p* 621
90 SAMNAH CRES, INGERSOLL, ON, N5C
3J7
(519) 424-3402   *SIC* 5014
AL PALLADINI COMMUNITY CENTRE *p*
1030
*See CORPORATION OF THE CITY OF
VAUGHAN, THE*
AL SAFA HALAL *p* 704
See ALSAFA FOODS CANADA LIMITED
AL'S POWER PLUS *p* 214
921 GIBSONS WAY, GIBSONS, BC, V0N
1V8
(604) 886-3700   *SIC* 5251
AL'S TIRE CRAFT *p* 621
See AL BARNIM INC
AL'S TIRE SERVICE *p* 520
See BARNIM HOLDINGS INC
AL-PAC *p* 7
*See ALBERTA-PACIFIC FOREST INDUS-
TRIES INC*
AL-PACK ENTERPRISES LTD *p* 409
60 COMMERCE ST, MONCTON, NB, E1H
0A5
(506) 852-4262   *SIC* 2653
AL-PACK HOLDINGS LTD *p* 409
60 COMMERCE ST, MONCTON, NB, E1H
0A5
(506) 852-4262   *SIC* 7389
ALACER GOLD CORP *p* 1440
3081 3RD AVE, WHITEHORSE, YT, Y1A

4Z7
(800) 387-0825   *SIC* 1041
ALAGASH INVESTMENTS LIMITED *p* 861
73 BROCK ST, SAULT STE. MARIE, ON,
P6A 3B4
SIC 4119
ALAM DRUGS LIMITED *p* 601
615 SCOTTSDALE DR SUITE 1089,
GUELPH, ON, N1G 3P4
(519) 823-8000   *SIC* 5912
ALAMOS GOLD INC *p* 680
259 MATHESON ST, MATACHEWAN, ON,
P0K 1M0
(705) 565-9800   *SIC* 1041
ALAMOS GOLD INC *p* 959
181 BAY ST SUITE 3910, TORONTO, ON,
M5J 2T3
(416) 368-9932   *SIC* 1041
ALARIS ROYALTY CORP *p* 66
333 24TH AVE SW SUITE 250, CALGARY,
AB, T2S 3E6
(403) 228-0873   *SIC* 6159
ALARM CAP *p* 1048
See ENTREPRISES MICROTEC INC, LES
ALARMCAP *p* 1293
See ENTREPRISES MICROTEC INC, LES
ALARME ALTEC *p* 1233
See ALTEL INC
ALARME DIGITECH *p* 1343
See ADT CANADA INC
ALARME MICROCOM *p* 1267
See MICROCOM 'M' INC
ALARMFORCE INDUSTRIES INC *p* 792
675 GARYRAY DR, NORTH YORK, ON,
M9L 1R2
(416) 445-2001   *SIC* 7382
ALASKA GOLD *p* 308
See NOVAGOLD RESOURCES INC
**ALASKAN COPPER & BRASS CANADA
INC** *p* 199
225 NORTH RD, COQUITLAM, BC, V3K
3V7
(604) 937-6620   *SIC* 5051
ALASKAN COPPER & BRASS COMPANY *p*
199
*See ALASKAN COPPER & BRASS
CANADA INC*
ALASKAN TECHNOLOGIES CORP *p* 104
11810 152 ST NW, EDMONTON, AB, T5V
1E3
(780) 447-2660   *SIC* 1711
ALBANY INTERNATIONAL CANADA CORP
p 839
2947 RIDEAU FERRY RD, PERTH, ON,
K7H 3E3
(613) 267-6600   *SIC* 2231
ALBANY INTERNATIONAL CANADA CORP
p 1088
300 RUE DE WESTMOUNT, COW-
ANSVILLE, QC, J2K 1S9
(450) 263-2880   *SIC* 2231
ALBARRIE CANADA LIMITED *p* 486
85 MORROW RD, BARRIE, ON, L4N 3V7
(705) 737-0551   *SIC* 2297
ALBARRIE GEOCOMPOSITES LIMITED *p*
486
85 MORROW RD, BARRIE, ON, L4N 3V7
(705) 737-0551   *SIC* 1389
ALBERICI CONSTRUCTORS, LTD *p* 529
1005 SKYVIEW DR SUITE 300, BURLING-
TON, ON, L7P 5B1
(905) 315-3000   *SIC* 1542
ALBERNI CHRYSLER DODGE JEEP *p* 245
See ALBERNI CHRYSLER LTD
ALBERNI CHRYSLER LTD *p* 245
2611 PORT ALBERNI HWY, PORT AL-
BERNI, BC, V9Y 8P2
(250) 723-5331   *SIC* 5521
**ALBERNI DISTRICT CO-OPERATIVE AS-
SOCIATION** *p*
245
4006 JOHNSTON RD, PORT ALBERNI, BC,
V9Y 5N3
(250) 724-0008   *SIC* 4925

ALBERNI DISTRICT SECONDARY SCHOOL *p 245*
See SCHOOL DISTRICT #70 (ALBERNI) SCHOOL BOARD

ALBERNI ECHO TOYOTA *p 245*
2555 PORT ALBERNI HWY, PORT ALBERNI, BC, V9Y 8P2
(250) 723-9448 *SIC 5511*

ALBERNI PACIFIC SAWMILL *p 245*
See WESTERN FOREST PRODUCTS INC

ALBERO RIDGE HOMES LTD *p 548*
29 FLORAL PKY, CONCORD, ON, L4K 5C5
(905) 669-9292 *SIC 1521*

ALBERT CAMPBELL C.I. *p 877*
See TORONTO DISTRICT SCHOOL BOARD

ALBERT PERRON INC *p 1350*
156 AV ALBERT-PERRON, SAINT-PRIME, QC, G8J 1L4
(418) 251-3164 *SIC 5143*

ALBERT, PAUL CHEVROLET BUICK CADILLAC GMC LTEE *p 1078*
870 BOUL TALBOT, CHICOUTIMI, QC, G7H 4B4
(418) 696-4444 *SIC 5511*

ALBERTA BALLET COMPANY, THE *p 66*
141 18 AVE SW, CALGARY, AB, T2S 0B8
(403) 228-4430 *SIC 7922*

ALBERTA BEVERAGE CONTAINER RECYCLING CORPORATION *p 20*
901 57 AVE NE, CALGARY, AB, T2E 8X9
(403) 264-0170 *SIC 4953*

ALBERTA BLUE CROSS *p 86*
See ABC BENEFITS CORPORATION

ALBERTA BOILERS SAFETY ASSOCIATION (ABSA) *p 120*
9410 20 AVE NW, EDMONTON, AB, T6N 0A4
(780) 437-9100 *SIC 7389*

ALBERTA BUILDING CONTRACTORS LTD *p 67*
9232 HORTON RD SW, CALGARY, AB, T2V 2X4
(403) 888-1960 *SIC 5193*

ALBERTA CENTRAL *p 35*
See CREDIT UNION CENTRAL ALBERTA LIMITED

ALBERTA CHILDREN'S HOSPITAL FOUNDATION *p 72*
2888 SHAGANAPPI TRAIL NW, CALGARY, AB, T3B 6A8
(403) 955-8818 *SIC 8699*

ALBERTA COLLEGE OF PARAMEDICS *p 162*
2755 BROADMOOR BLVD UNIT 220, SHERWOOD PARK, AB, T8H 2W7
(780) 449-3114 *SIC 8221*

ALBERTA COMPUTER CABLE INC *p 20*
1816 25 AVE NE, CALGARY, AB, T2E 7K1
(403) 291-5560 *SIC 5065*

ALBERTA CONFERENCE OF THE SEVENTH-DAY ADVENTISTS CHURCH, THE *p 138*
5816 HIGHWAY 2A, LACOMBE, AB, T4L 2G5
(403) 342-5044 *SIC 8661*

ALBERTA CONSERVATION ASSOCIATION *p 161*
9 CHIPPEWA RD SUITE 101, SHERWOOD PARK, AB, T8A 6J7
(780) 410-1999 *SIC 8611*

ALBERTA CONSTRUCTION GROUP CORP *p 13*
6565 40 ST SE UNIT 11, CALGARY, AB, T2C 2J4
(587) 349-3000 *SIC 1542*

ALBERTA DISTANCE LEARNING CENTRE *p 86*
10055 106 ST NW SUITE 300, EDMONTON, AB, T5J 2Y2
(780) 452-4655 *SIC 8211*

ALBERTA DISTILLERS LIMITED *p 27*
1521 34 AVE SE, CALGARY, AB, T2G 1V9
(403) 265-2541 *SIC 2085*

ALBERTA EASTER SEALS MCQUEEN RESIDENCE *p 86*
See ALBERTA EASTER SEALS SOCIETY

ALBERTA EASTER SEALS SOCIETY *p 86*
10025 106 ST NW SUITE 1408, EDMONTON, AB, T5J 1G4
(780) 429-0137 *SIC 8699*

ALBERTA ELECTRIC SYSTEM OPERATOR *p 42*
330 5 AVE SW SUITE 2500, CALGARY, AB, T2P 0L4
(403) 539-2450 *SIC 4911*

ALBERTA ENVIROFUELS INC *p 121*
9511 17 ST NW, EDMONTON, AB, T6P 1Y3
(780) 449-7800 *SIC 2911*

ALBERTA ENVIRONMENTAL RUBBER PRODUCTS INC *p 104*
13520 170 ST NW, EDMONTON, AB, T5V 1M7
(780) 447-1994 *SIC 4953*

ALBERTA EXCHANGER LTD *p 121*
2210 70 AVE NW, EDMONTON, AB, T6P 1N6
(780) 440-1045 *SIC 7699*

ALBERTA FUEL *p 121*
See AFD PETROLEUM LTD

ALBERTA GLASS COMPANY INC *p 8*
2820 37 AVE NE, CALGARY, AB, T1Y 5T3
(403) 219-7466 *SIC 1793*

ALBERTA GOLD TAXI *p 153*
See 341-7777 TAXI LTD

ALBERTA HEALTH SERVICES *p 4*
305 LYNX ST, BANFF, AB, T1L 1H7
(403) 762-2222 *SIC 8062*

ALBERTA HEALTH SERVICES *p 6*
2001 107 ST, BLAIRMORE, AB, T0K 0E0
(403) 562-5011 *SIC 8062*

ALBERTA HEALTH SERVICES *p 7*
440 3 ST E SUITE 300, BROOKS, AB, T1R 0X8
(403) 501-3232 *SIC 8062*

ALBERTA HEALTH SERVICES *p 68*
10101 SOUTHPORT RD SW, CALGARY, AB, T2W 3N2
(403) 943-1111 *SIC 8011*

ALBERTA HEALTH SERVICES *p 78*
1100 HOSPITAL PL, CANMORE, AB, T1W 1N2
(403) 678-3769 *SIC 6324*

ALBERTA HEALTH SERVICES *p 81*
5920 51 AVE, DAYSLAND, AB, T0B 1A0
(780) 374-3746 *SIC 8062*

ALBERTA HEALTH SERVICES *p 82*
1210 20E AVE, DIDSBURY, AB, T0M 0W0
(403) 335-9393 *SIC 8062*

ALBERTA HEALTH SERVICES *p 83*
14007 50 ST NW, EDMONTON, AB, T5A 5E4
(780) 342-4000 *SIC 8062*

ALBERTA HEALTH SERVICES *p 85*
10240 KINGSWAY NW, EDMONTON, AB, T5H 3V9
(780) 735-4111 *SIC 8062*

ALBERTA HEALTH SERVICES *p 86*
10030 107 ST NW SUITE 9, EDMONTON, AB, T5J 3E4
(403) 944-5705 *SIC 8011*

ALBERTA HEALTH SERVICES *p 91*
11111 JASPER AVE NW, EDMONTON, AB, T5K 0L4
(780) 482-8111 *SIC 8011*

ALBERTA HEALTH SERVICES *p 91*
9942 108 ST NW, EDMONTON, AB, T5K 2J5
(780) 342-7700 *SIC 8062*

ALBERTA HEALTH SERVICES *p 107*
17480 FORT RD NW SUITE 175, EDMONTON, AB, T5Y 6A8
(780) 342-5555 *SIC 8063*

ALBERTA HEALTH SERVICES *p 119*
10707 29 AVE NW, EDMONTON, AB, T6J 6W1
(780) 430-9110 *SIC 8062*

ALBERTA HEALTH SERVICES *p 126*
10628 100TH ST, FAIRVIEW, AB, T0H 1L0
(780) 835-6100 *SIC 8062*

ALBERTA HEALTH SERVICES *p 129*
9401 86 AVE, FORT SASKATCHEWAN, AB, T8L 0C6
(780) 998-2256 *SIC 8062*

ALBERTA HEALTH SERVICES *p 135*
560 9 AVE SW, HIGH RIVER, AB, T1V 1B3
(403) 652-2200 *SIC 8062*

ALBERTA HEALTH SERVICES *p 135*
904 CENTRE ST N, HANNA, AB, T0J 1P0
(403) 854-3331 *SIC 8062*

ALBERTA HEALTH SERVICES *p 137*
518 ROBSON ST, JASPER, AB, T0E 1E0
(780) 852-3344 *SIC 8062*

ALBERTA HEALTH SERVICES *p 142*
960 19 ST S SUITE 110, LETHBRIDGE, AB, T1J 1W5
(403) 388-6009 *SIC 8062*

ALBERTA HEALTH SERVICES *p 143*
700 NURSING HOME RD, LINDEN, AB, T0M 1J0
(403) 546-3966 *SIC 8051*

ALBERTA HEALTH SERVICES *p 145*
350 3RD AVE NW, MCLENNAN, AB, T0H 2L0
(780) 324-3730 *SIC 8062*

ALBERTA HEALTH SERVICES *p 145*
600 2ND ST, MANNING, AB, T0H 2M0
(780) 836-3391 *SIC 8062*

ALBERTA HEALTH SERVICES *p 150*
11 CIMARRON COMMON, OKOTOKS, AB, T1S 2E9
(403) 995-2600 *SIC 8093*

ALBERTA HEALTH SERVICES *p 151*
312 3 ST E, OYEN, AB, T0J 2J0
(403) 664-3528 *SIC 8062*

ALBERTA HEALTH SERVICES *p 151*
3901 57 AVE, OLDS, AB, T4H 1T4
(403) 556-3381 *SIC 8062*

ALBERTA HEALTH SERVICES *p 152*
5800 57 AVE, PONOKA, AB, T4J 1P1
(403) 783-8135 *SIC 8062*

ALBERTA HEALTH SERVICES *p 152*
1222 BEV MCLACHLIN DR, PINCHER CREEK, AB, T0K 1W0
(403) 627-1946 *SIC 8062*

ALBERTA HEALTH SERVICES *p 153*
5002 54 AVE, PROVOST, AB, T0B 3S0
(780) 753-2291 *SIC 8062*

ALBERTA HEALTH SERVICES *p 162*
2 BROWER DR, SHERWOOD PARK, AB, T8H 1V4
(780) 342-4600 *SIC 8059*

ALBERTA HEALTH SERVICES *p 164*
4713 48 AVE, ST PAUL, AB, T0A 3A3
(780) 645-3331 *SIC 8062*

ALBERTA HEALTH SERVICES *p 168*
709 1 ST NE, SUNDRE, AB, T0M 1X0
(403) 638-3033 *SIC 8062*

ALBERTA HEALTH SERVICES *p 170*
5720 50 AVE, VERMILION, AB, T9X 1K7
(780) 853-5305 *SIC 8062*

ALBERTA HEALTH SERVICES *p 171*
10220 93 ST, WESTLOCK, AB, T7P 2G4
(780) 349-3301 *SIC 8062*

ALBERTA HIGHWAY SERVICES LTD *p 99*
11010 178 ST NW SUITE 200, EDMONTON, AB, T5S 1R7
(780) 701-8668 *SIC 1611*

ALBERTA HONDA *p 84*
See ZANE HOLDINGS LTD

ALBERTA HOSPITAL EDMONTON *p 107*
See ALBERTA HEALTH SERVICES

ALBERTA HOTEL & LODGING ASSOCIATION *p 125*
2707 ELLWOOD DR SW, EDMONTON, AB, T6X 0P7
(780) 436-6112 *SIC 8611*

ALBERTA INSURANCE COUNCIL *p 87*

10104 103 AVE NW SUITE 600, EDMONTON, AB, T5J 0H8
(780) 421-4148 *SIC 6411*

ALBERTA INVESTMENT MANAGEMENT CORPORATION *p 87*
10830 JASPER AVE NW SUITE 1100, EDMONTON, AB, T5J 2B3
(780) 392-3600 *SIC 6719*

ALBERTA JANITORIAL LTD *p 10*
2520 CENTRE AVE NE, CALGARY, AB, T2A 2L2
(780) 272-7801 *SIC 7349*

ALBERTA LAWYERS INSURANCE ASSOCIATION, THE *p 65*
See LAW SOCIETY OF ALBERTA

ALBERTA LEGAL & SERVICES DIRECTORY *p 290*
See B. & C. LIST (1982) LTD

ALBERTA MILK *p 125*
1303 91 ST SW, EDMONTON, AB, T6X 1H1
(780) 453-5942 *SIC 8732*

ALBERTA MILK *p 125*
1303 91 ST SW, EDMONTON, AB, T6X 1H1
(780) 453-5942 *SIC 8611*

ALBERTA MOTOR ASSOCIATION *p 73*
4700 17 AVE SW, CALGARY, AB, T3E 0E3
(403) 240-5300 *SIC 4724*

ALBERTA MOTOR ASSOCIATION *p 112*
9520 42 AVE NW, EDMONTON, AB, T6E 5Y4
(780) 989-6230 *SIC 8699*

ALBERTA MOTOR ASSOCIATION *p 119*
10310A G A MACDONALD AVE NW, EDMONTON, AB, T6J 6R7
(780) 430-5555 *SIC 8699*

ALBERTA MOTOR ASSOCIATION TRAVEL AGENCY LTD *p 118*
10310 39A AVE, EDMONTON, AB, T6H 5X9
(780) 430-5555 *SIC 4724*

ALBERTA NEW HOME WARRANTY PROGRAM, THE *p 75*
30 SPRINGBOROUGH BLVD SW SUITE 301, CALGARY, AB, T3H 0N9
(403) 253-3636 *SIC 6351*

ALBERTA NEWSPRINT *p 173*
See WEST FRASER TIMBER CO. LTD

ALBERTA NURSERIES & SEEDS LTD *p 6*
GD, BOWDEN, AB, T0M 0K0
SIC 5191

ALBERTA OPERATIONS, PRENTISS SITE *p 153*
See DOW CHEMICAL CANADA ULC

ALBERTA PETROLEUM INDUSTRIES LTD *p 108*
6607 59 ST NW, EDMONTON, AB, T6B 3P8
(780) 436-9693 *SIC 5082*

ALBERTA PLYWOOD *p 164*
See WEST FRASER MILLS LTD

ALBERTA POWER (2000) LTD *p 63*
919 11 AVE SW SUITE 400, CALGARY, AB, T2R 1P3
(403) 209-6900 *SIC 4911*

ALBERTA PRAIRIE STEAM TOURS LTD *p 167*
4611 47TH AVE, STETTLER, AB, T0C 2L0
(403) 742-2811 *SIC 4725*

ALBERTA PROCESSING *p 19*
See WEST COAST REDUCTION LTD

ALBERTA PROCESSING CO. *p 296*
See WEST COAST REDUCTION LTD

ALBERTA REGL COUNCIL CARPENTERS CORP *p 104*
15210 123 AVE NW SUITE 176, EDMONTON, AB, T5V 0A3
(780) 474-8599 *SIC 8631*

ALBERTA SAFETY COUNCIL, THE *p 108*
4831 93 AVE NW, EDMONTON, AB, T6B 3A2
(780) 462-7300 *SIC 8748*

ALBERTA SCHOOL EMPLOYEE BENEFIT PLAN, THE *p 118*

6104 104 ST NW SUITE 301, EDMONTON, AB, T6H 2K7

(780) 438-5300   *SIC* 6371

ALBERTA SPECIAL EVENT EQUIPMENT RENTALS & SALES LTD   *p* 112

6010 99 ST NW, EDMONTON, AB, T6E 3P2

(780) 435-2211   *SIC* 7359

ALBERTA SPRUCE INDUSTRIES LTD *p* 164

26322 TWP RD SUITE 524, SPRUCE GROVE, AB, T7X 3H2

(780) 962-5118   *SIC* 7389

ALBERTA SYSTEM, THE   *p* 55

See NOVA GAS TRANSMISSION LTD

ALBERTA TEACHERS' ASSOCIATION, THE   *p* 97

11010 142 ST NW, EDMONTON, AB, T5N 2R1

(780) 447-9400   *SIC* 8631

ALBERTA TEACHERS' RETIREMENT FUND BOARD   *p* 97

11010 142 ST NW SUITE 600, EDMONTON, AB, T5N 2R1

(780) 451-4166   *SIC* 6371

ALBERTA TREASURY BOARD   *p* 92

See GOVERNMENT OF THE PROVINCE OF ALBERTA

ALBERTA TRUSS LTD   *p* 121

2140 RAILWAY ST NW, EDMONTON, AB, T6P 1X3

(780) 464-5551   *SIC* 5031

ALBERTA TUBULAR PRODUCTS LTD *p* 42

500 4 AVE SW SUITE 1100, CALGARY, AB, T2P 2V6

(403) 264-2136   *SIC* 5051

ALBERTA UNION OF PROVINCIAL EMPLOYEES, THE   *p* 97

10451 170 ST NW SUITE 200, EDMONTON, AB, T5P 4S7

(780) 930-3300   *SIC* 8631

ALBERTA WILBERT SALES LTD   *p* 104

16910 129 AVE NW SUITE 1, EDMONTON, AB, T5V 1L1

(780) 447-2222   *SIC* 5032

ALBERTA-PACIFIC FOREST INDUSTRIES INC   *p* 7

P.O. BOX 8000, BOYLE, AB, T0A 0M0

(780) 525-8000   *SIC* 2611

ALBERTS FAMILY RESTAURANT   *p* 85

See ALBERTS RESTAURANTS LTD

ALBERTS FAMILY RESTAURANT   *p* 118

See ALBERTS RESTAURANTS LTD

ALBERTS RESTAURANTS LTD   *p* 85

10550 115 ST NW, EDMONTON, AB, T5H 3K6

(780) 429-1259   *SIC* 5812

ALBERTS RESTAURANTS LTD   *p* 104

1640 BURLINGTON AVE, EDMONTON, AB, T5T 3J7

(780) 444-3105   *SIC* 5812

ALBERTS RESTAURANTS LTD   *p* 118

10362 51 AVE NW, EDMONTON, AB, T6H 5X6

(780) 437-7081   *SIC* 5812

ALBI   *p* 1149

See ALBI LE GEANT INC

ALBI BEVERAGES LIMITED   *p* 284

3440 BRIDGEWAY, VANCOUVER, BC, V5K 1B6

SIC 5149

ALBI CORP   *p* 13

4770 110 AVE SE, CALGARY, AB, T2C 2T8

(403) 236-4032   *SIC* 1521

ALBI FORD LINCOLN JOLIETTE INC *p* 1243

525 131 RTE, NOTRE-DAME-DES-PRAIRIES, QC, J6E 0M1

(450) 759-7750   *SIC* 5511

ALBI LE GEANT INC   *p* 1149

3550 AV DE LA GARE, MASCOUCHE, QC, J7K 3C1

(450) 474-7000   *SIC* 5511

ALBI LE GEANT INC   *p* 1149

3550 AV DE LA GARE, MASCOUCHE, QC,

J7K 3C1

(450) 474-5555   *SIC* 5511

ALBI NISSAN DE REPENTIGNY   *p* 1282

See 9085327 CANADA INC

ALBION FARMS AND FISHERIES   *p* 255

See INTERCITY PACKERS LTD

ALBION FERRY, THE   *p* 230

See FRASER RIVER MARINE TRANSPORTATION LTD

ALBRIGHT GARDENS HOMES INCORPORATED   *p* 489

5050 HILLSIDE DR, BEAMSVILLE, ON, L0R 1B2

(905) 563-8252   *SIC* 8322

ALC - AUTO LIST OF CANADA INC   *p* 362

823 REGENT AVE W, WINNIPEG, MB, R2C 3A7

(204) 224-0636   *SIC* 5521

ALC MICRO   *p* 850

See ASIA LINK COMPUTER INC

ALCA DISTRIBUTION INC   *p* 278

2153 192 ST UNIT 4, SURREY, BC, V3Z 3X2

(604) 635-3901   *SIC* 5137

ALCAN AUTOMOTIVE STRUCTURES   *p* 1208

See RIO TINTO ALCAN INC

ALCAN PACKAGING CANADA LIMITED   *p* 794

130 ARROW RD, NORTH YORK, ON, M9M 2M1

SIC 2657

ALCAN PRIMARY METAL GROUP, DIV OF *p* 224

See RIO TINTO ALCAN INC

ALCAN USINE SHAWINIGAN   *p* 1368

See RIO TINTO ALCAN INC

ALCANNA INC   *p* 99

17220 STONY PLAIN RD SUITE 101, EDMONTON, AB, T5S 1K6

(780) 944-9994   *SIC* 5921

ALCATEL HOLDINGS CANADA CORP   *p* 623

600 MARCH RD, KANATA, ON, K2K 2T6

(613) 591-3600   *SIC* 6712

ALCATEL-LUCENT CANADA INC   *p* 832

600 MARCH RD, OTTAWA, ON, K2K 2T6

(613) 591-3600   *SIC* 4899

ALCE   *p* 1222

See A LA CARTE EXPRESS INC

ALCO ELECTRONICS INC   *p* 666

725 DENISON ST, MARKHAM, ON, L3R 1B8

(905) 477-7878   *SIC* 5099

ALCO GAS & OIL PRODUCTION EQUIPMENT LTD   *p* 112

5203 75 ST NW, EDMONTON, AB, T6E 5S5

(780) 465-9061   *SIC* 3533

ALCO INC   *p* 118

6925 104 ST NW, EDMONTON, AB, T6H 2L5

(780) 435-3502   *SIC* 3541

ALCO SPORTS   *p* 1232

See 125173 CANADA INC

ALCO-TMI INC   *p* 1044

995 AV BOMBARDIER, ALMA, QC, G8B 6H2

(418) 669-1911   *SIC* 1711

ALCOA CANADA CIE   *p* 1052

100 RTE MARITIME, BAIE-COMEAU, QC, G4Z 2L6

(418) 296-3311   *SIC* 3354

ALCOA CANADA CIE   *p* 1090

1 BOUL DES SOURCES, DESCHAMBAULT, QC, G0A 1S0

(418) 286-5287   *SIC* 3334

ALCOA CANADA CIE   *p* 1201

1 PLACE VILLE-MARIE BUREAU 2310, MONTREAL, QC, H3B 3M5

(514) 904-5030   *SIC* 3334

ALCOA CANADA CIE   *p* 1233

4001 DES LAURENTIDES (A-15) E, MON-

TREAL, QC, H7L 3H7

(450) 680-2500   *SIC* 3334

ALCOA DESCHAMBAULT LTEE   *p* 1090

1 BOUL DES SOURCES, DESCHAMBAULT, QC, G0A 1S0

(418) 286-5287   *SIC* 3334

ALCOA-ALUMINERIE DE DESCHAMBAULT S.E.C.   *p* 1090

1 BOUL DES SOURCES, DESCHAMBAULT, QC, G0A 1S0

(418) 286-5287   *SIC* 3334

ALCOHOL COUNTERMEASURE SYSTEMS CORP   *p* 582

60 INTERNATIONAL BLVD, ETOBICOKE, ON, M9W 6J2

(416) 619-3500   *SIC* 3829

ALCON CANADA INC   *p* 719

2665 MEADOWPINE BLVD, MISSISSAUGA, ON, L5N 8C7

(905) 826-6700   *SIC* 5122

ALCOOL GLOBAL   *p* 1066

See MAISON DES FUTAILLES, S.E.C.

ALCOOL GLOBAL (MC)   *p* 1164

See MAISON DES FUTAILLES, S.E.C.

ALCOOL NB LIQUOR   *p* 401

See NEW BRUNSWICK LIQUOR CORPORATION

ALCOR COMMERCIAL REALTY   *p* 127

See ALCOR HOLDINGS LTD

ALCOR FACILITIES MANAGEMENT INC   *p* 99

10470 176 ST NW SUITE 206, EDMONTON, AB, T5S 1L3

(780) 483-1213   *SIC* 8741

ALCOR HOLDINGS LTD   *p* 127

305 MACDONALD CRES UNIT 1, FORT MCMURRAY, AB, T9H 4B7

(780) 743-1343   *SIC* 6531

ALCOS MACHINERY INC   *p* 754

190 HARRY WALKER PKY N, NEWMARKET, ON, L3Y 7B4

(905) 836-6030   *SIC* 5084

ALDACO INDUSTRIES INC   *p* 850

25B EAST PEARCE ST SUITE 1, RICHMOND HILL, ON, L4B 2M9

(905) 764-7736   *SIC* 3841

ALDER AUTO PARTS LTD   *p* 281

19414 96 AVE SUITE 3, SURREY, BC, V4N 4C2

(604) 888-3722   *SIC* 5531

ALDERGROVE COMMUNITY SECONDARY SCHOOL   *p* 179

See SCHOOL DISTRICT NO. 35 (LANGLEY)

ALDERGROVE CREDIT UNION   *p* 179

See CREDIT UNION CENTRAL OF CANADA

ALDERGROVE LIONS SENIORS HOUSING SOCIETY   *p* 179

27477 28 AVE, ALDERGROVE, BC, V4W 3L9

(604) 856-4161   *SIC* 8051

ALDERSHOT GREENHOUSES LIMITED   *p* 531

1135 GALLAGHER RD, BURLINGTON, ON, L7T 2M7

(905) 632-9272   *SIC* 0181

ALDERSHOT LANDSCAPE CONTRACTORS LP   *p* 529

166 FLATT RD, BURLINGTON, ON, L7P 0T3

(905) 689-7321   *SIC* 0781

ALDERWOOD CORPORATION   *p* 439

42 JONES ST, BADDECK, NS, B0E 1B0

(902) 295-2644   *SIC* 8361

ALDERWOOD REST HOME   *p* 439

See ALDERWOOD CORPORATION

ALDES CANADA   *p* 1346

See 9228-5329 QUEBEC INC

ALDILA BOUTIQUE   *p* 263

See EUROPEAN CREATIONS LTD

ALDON INVESTMENTS LTD   *p* 891

46 COMMUNITY AVE, STONEY CREEK, ON, L8E 2Y3

(905) 664-2126   *SIC* 6712

ALDRICH PEARS ASSOCIATES   *p* 317

See 239188 BC LTD

ALDRIDGE MINERALS INC   *p* 936

10 KING ST E SUITE 300, TORONTO, ON, M5C 1C3

SIC 1041

ALDUS CAPITAL CORP   *p* 748

28 CONCOURSE GATE SUITE 105, NEPEAN, ON, K2E 7T7

(613) 723-4567   *SIC* 5172

ALEAFIA HEALTH INC   *p* 548

8810 JANE ST 2ND FL, CONCORD, ON, L4K 2M9

(416) 860-5665   *SIC* 5122

ALECTRA INC   *p* 719

2185 DERRY RD W, MISSISSAUGA, ON, L5N 7A6

(905) 273-7425   *SIC* 4911

ALECTRA UTILITIES CORPORATION *p* 613

55 JOHN ST N, HAMILTON, ON, L8R 3M8

(905) 522-6611   *SIC* 4911

ALECTRA UTILITIES CORPORATION *p* 613

55 JOHN ST N, HAMILTON, ON, L8R 3M8

(905) 522-9200   *SIC* 4911

ALENDEL FABRICS LIMITED   *p* 548

274 EDGELEY BLVD, CONCORD, ON, L4K 3Y4

(905) 669-1998   *SIC* 5131

ALERT BEST NURSING INCORPORATED *p* 612

290 CAROLINE ST S SUITE 4, HAMILTON, ON, L8P 3L9

(905) 524-5990   *SIC* 8059

ALERT PAY   *p* 1227

See ALERT SERVICES INC

ALERT SERVICES INC   *p* 1227

8255 AV MOUNTAIN SIGHTS BUREAU 100, MONTREAL, QC, H4P 2B5

SIC 4813

ALERTPAY INCORPORATED   *p* 1215

1610 RUE NOTRE-DAME O SUITE 175, MONTREAL, QC, H3J 1M1

(514) 748-5774   *SIC* 7379

ALES GROUPE CANADA INC   *p* 1187

420 RUE NOTRE-DAME O BUREAU 500, MONTREAL, QC, H2Y 1V3

(514) 932-3636   *SIC* 5131

ALEX COMMUNITY HEALTH CENTRE, THE *p* 10

See ALEXANDRA COMMUNITY HEALTH CENTRE

ALEX MACINTYRE & ASSOCIATES LIMITED   *p* 634

1390 GOVERNMENT RD W, KIRKLAND LAKE, ON, P2N 3J5

(705) 567-3266   *SIC* 1081

ALEX MARION RESTAURANTS LTD *p* 1415

940 E VICTORIA AVE, REGINA, SK, S4N 7A9

SIC 5812

ALEX WILLIAMSON MOTOR SALES LIMITED   *p* 1001

259 TORONTO ST S, UXBRIDGE, ON, L9P 1R1

(905) 852-3332   *SIC* 5511

ALEXANDER CENTRE INDUSTRIES LIMITED   *p* 900

1297 KELLY LAKE RD, SUDBURY, ON, P3E 5P5

(705) 674-4291   *SIC* 3273

ALEXANDER HOLBURN BEAUDIN & LANG   *p* 329

See AHBL MANAGEMENT LIMITED PARTNERSHIP

ALEXANDER HOLBURN BEAUDIN & LANG LLP   *p* 329

700 GEORGIA ST W SUITE 2700, VAN-

COUVER, BC, V7Y 1B8
(604) 484-1700   *SIC* 8111
ALEXANDER MACKENZIE HIGH SCHOOL
p 856
See YORK REGION DISTRICT SCHOOL BOARD
ALEXANDER MACKENZIE SECONDARY SCHOOL   *p* 858
See LAMBTON KENT DISTRICT SCHOOL BOARD
ALEXANDER PLACE LONG TERM CARE *p* 1005
See JARLETTE LTD
ALEXANDRA COMMUNITY HEALTH CENTRE   *p* 10
2840 2 AVE SE UNIT 101, CALGARY, AB, T2A 7X9
(403) 266-2622   *SIC* 8011
ALEXANDRA HOSPITAL INGERSOLL, THE *p* 621
29 NOXON ST, INGERSOLL, ON, N5C 1B8
(519) 485-1700   *SIC* 8062
ALEXANDRE GAUDET   *p* 1052
See METRO INC
ALEXANDRIA FORD SALES   *p* 563
See MILLER-HUGHES FORD SALES LIMITED
ALEXANIAN CARPET & FLOORING *p* 612
See ALEXANIAN FLOORING LIMITED
ALEXANIAN FLOORING LIMITED *p* 612
601 MAIN ST W, HAMILTON, ON, L8P 1K9
(905) 527-2857   *SIC* 5713
ALEXCO RESOURCE CORP   *p* 327
555 BURRARD ST TWO BENTALL CENTRE SUITE 1225, VANCOUVER, BC, V7X 1M9
(604) 633-4888   *SIC* 1041
ALEXION PHARMA CANADA CORP   *p* 548
3100 RUTHERFORD RD, CONCORD, ON, L4K 0G6
(866) 393-1188   *SIC* 5122
ALF CURTIS HOME IMPROVEMENTS INC*p* 842
370 PARKHILL RD E, PETERBOROUGH, ON, K9L 1C3
(705) 742-4690   *SIC* 5211
ALFA LAVAL INC   *p* 873
101 MILNER AVE, SCARBOROUGH, ON, M1S 4S6
(416) 299-6101   *SIC* 5085
ALFAGOMMA CANADA INC   *p* 1332
6550 RUE ABRAMS BUREAU 6540, SAINT-LAURENT, QC, H4S 1Y2
(514) 333-5577   *SIC* 5085
ALFID SERVICES IMMOBILIERS LTEE   *p* 1187
500 PLACE D'ARMES SUITE 1500, MONTREAL, QC, H2Y 2W2
(514) 282-7654   *SIC* 6531
ALFIELD INDUSTRIES   *p* 1032
See MARTINREA INTERNATIONAL INC
ALFINITI   *p* 1081
See SPECTUBE INC
ALFINITI INC   *p* 1080
1152 RUE DE LA MANIC, CHICOUTIMI, QC, G7K 1A2
(418) 696-2545   *SIC* 3354
ALFRED CLOUTIER LIMITEE   *p* 1280
1737 RUE WILLIAM-MARSH, QUEBEC, QC, G3E 1K9
(418) 842-4390   *SIC* 3144
ALFRED HOME HARDWARE   *p* 476
See 139464 CANADA LIMITED
ALFRED HORIE CONSTRUCTION CO. LTD *p* 184
3830 1ST AVE, BURNABY, BC, V5C 3W1
(604) 291-8156   *SIC* 1542
ALGGIN METAL INDUSTRIES LTD   *p* 12
4540 46 AVE SE, CALGARY, AB, T2B 3N7
(403) 252-0132   *SIC* 3444
ALGO COMMUNICATION PRODUCTS LTD *p* 191
4500 BEEDIE ST, BURNABY, BC, V5J 5L2

(604) 438-3333   *SIC* 4899
ALGOMA CENTRAL CORPORATION *p* 846
1 CHESTNUT ST, PORT COLBORNE, ON, L3K 1R3
(905) 834-4549   *SIC* 3731
ALGOMA CENTRAL CORPORATION *p* 885
63 CHURCH ST SUITE 600, ST CATHARINES, ON, L2R 3C4
(905) 687-7888   *SIC* 4432
ALGOMA CENTRAL CORPORATION *p* 885
63 CHURCH ST SUITE 600, ST CATHARINES, ON, L2R 3C4
SIC 4432
ALGOMA CENTRAL MARINE   *p* 885
See ALGOMA CENTRAL CORPORATION
ALGOMA CENTRAL PROPERTIES INC   *p* 861
293 BAY ST, SAULT STE. MARIE, ON, P6A 1X3
(705) 946-7220   *SIC* 6531
ALGOMA CENTRAL RAILWAY INC   *p* 861
129 BAY ST, SAULT STE. MARIE, ON, P6A 1W7
(705) 541-2900   *SIC* 4011
ALGOMA DISTRICT SCHOOL BOARD   *p* 861
1601 WELLINGTON ST E, SAULT STE. MARIE, ON, P6A 2R8
(705) 945-7177   *SIC* 8211
ALGOMA DISTRICT SCHOOL BOARD   *p* 861
644 ALBERT ST E, SAULT STE. MARIE, ON, P6A 2K7
(705) 945-7111   *SIC* 8211
ALGOMA DISTRICT SCHOOL BOARD   *p* 862
750 NORTH ST, SAULT STE. MARIE, ON, P6B 2C5
(705) 945-7177   *SIC* 8211
ALGOMA DISTRICT SCHOOL BOARD   *p* 863
636 GOULAIS AVE, SAULT STE. MARIE, ON, P6C 5A7
(705) 945-7180   *SIC* 8211
ALGOMA MANOR   *p* 903
See ALGOMA MANOR NURSING HOME
ALGOMA MANOR NURSING HOME   *p* 903
145 DAWSON ST, THESSALON, ON, P0R 1L0
(705) 842-2840   *SIC* 8361
ALGOMA MUTUAL INSURANCE COMPANY   *p* 903
131 MAIN ST, THESSALON, ON, P0R 1L0
(705) 842-3345   *SIC* 6331
ALGOMA POWER INC   *p* 862
2 SACKVILLE RD SUITE A, SAULT STE. MARIE, ON, P6B 6J6
(705) 256-3850   *SIC* 4911
ALGOMA PUBLIC HEALTH   *p* 862
See BOARD OF HEALTH FOR THE DISTRICT OF ALGOMA HEALTH UNIT
ALGOMA STEEL INC   *p* 861
105 WEST ST, SAULT STE. MARIE, ON, P6A 7B4
(705) 945-2351   *SIC* 3312
ALGOMA TUBES INC   *p* 863
547 WALLACE TERR, SAULT STE. MARIE, ON, P6C 1L9
(705) 946-8130   *SIC* 3317
ALGOMA UNIVERSITY   *p* 508
24 QUEEN ST E SUITE 102, BRAMPTON, ON, L6V 1A3
(905) 451-0100   *SIC* 8221
ALGOMA UNIVERSITY   *p* 861
See GOVERNMENT OF ONTARIO
ALGOMA UNIVERSITY   *p* 861
1520 QUEEN ST E, SAULT STE. MARIE, ON, P6A 2G4
(705) 949-2301   *SIC* 8221
ALGOMA WATERTOWER INN   *p* 863
See J.J.'S HOSPITALITY LIMITED
ALGONQUIN & LAKESHORE CATHOLIC DISTRICT SCHOOL BOARD   *p* 490

301 CHURCH ST, BELLEVILLE, ON, K8N 3C7
(613) 967-0404   *SIC* 8211
ALGONQUIN & LAKESHORE CATHOLIC DISTRICT SCHOOL BOARD   *p* 629
130 RUSSELL ST, KINGSTON, ON, K7K 2E9
(613) 545-1902   *SIC* 8211
ALGONQUIN & LAKESHORE CATHOLIC DISTRICT SCHOOL BOARD   *p* 632
1085 WOODBINE RD, KINGSTON, ON, K7P 2V9
(613) 384-1919   *SIC* 8211
ALGONQUIN COLLEGE OF APPLIED ARTS AND TECHNOLOGY   *p* 750
1385 WOODROFFE AVE, NEPEAN, ON, K2G 1V8
(613) 727-4723   *SIC* 8222
ALGONQUIN POWER & UTILITIES CORP *p* 800
354 DAVIS RD, OAKVILLE, ON, L6J 2X1
(905) 465-4500   *SIC* 6712
ALGONQUIN POWER ENERGY FROM WASTE INC   *p* 501
7656 BRAMALEA RD, BRAMPTON, ON, L6T 5M5
(905) 791-2777   *SIC* 4953
ALGONQUIN POWER SERVICES CANADA INC   *p* 796
2845 BRISTOL CIR, OAKVILLE, ON, L6H 6X5
(905) 465-4500   *SIC* 4911
ALGONQUIN POWER SYSTEMS INC *p* 800
354 DAVIS RD, OAKVILLE, ON, L6J 0C5
(905) 465-4500   *SIC* 4911
ALGORITHME PHARMA   *p* 1155
See ALTASCIENCES COMPAGNIE INC
ALGORITHME PHARMA   *p* 1241
See ALTASCIENCES COMPAGNIE INC
ALI ARC INDUSTRIES LP   *p* 364
155 ELAN BLVD, WINNIPEG, MB, R2J 4H1
(204) 253-6080   *SIC* 3714
ALI EXCAVATION INC   *p* 1365
760 BOUL DES ERABLES, SALABERRY-DE-VALLEYFIELD, QC, J6T 6G4
(450) 373-2010   *SIC* 1794
ALI'S NO FRILLS   *p* 868
See 1992013 ONTARIO LTD
ALI-PRET   *p* 1103
See ALIMENTS MARTEL INC
ALIA CONSEIL INC   *p* 1193
550 RUE SHERBROOKE O, MONTREAL, QC, H3A 1B9
(418) 652-1737   *SIC* 6411
ALIA CONSULTING   *p* 1193
See ALIA CONSEIL INC
ALIANZA MINERALS LTD   *p* 302
325 HOWE ST SUITE 410, VANCOUVER, BC, V6C 1Z7
(604) 687-3520   *SIC* 1041
ALIAXIS NORTH AMERICA INC   *p* 796
1425 NORTH SERVICE RD E SUITE 3, OAKVILLE, ON, L6H 1A7
(289) 881-0120   *SIC* 6712
ALICE SADDY ASSOCIATION   *p* 655
111 WATERLOO ST SUITE 401, LONDON, ON, N6B 2M4
(519) 433-2801   *SIC* 8699
ALICE-ALIYA (CANADA) INC   *p* 850
92 SPRINGBROOK DR, RICHMOND HILL, ON, L4B 3P9
(905) 886-1172   *SIC* 5085
ALIGN-TECH INDUSTRIES INC   *p* 99
18114 107 AVE NW, EDMONTON, AB, T5S 1K5
(780) 448-7303   *SIC* 6712
ALIGNED CAPITAL PARTNERS INC   *p* 520
1001 CHAMPLAIN AVENUE, SUITE 300, BURLINGTON, ON, L7L 5Z4
SIC 8741
ALIK ENTERPRISES LTD   *p* 342
4222 VILLAGE SQ, WHISTLER, BC, V0N 1B4
(604) 932-4540   *SIC* 5812

ALIM JOHNVINCE   *p* 1066
See JOHNVINCE FOODS
ALIMENT ENCORE GOURMET   *p* 1052
See ALTIUS EPICES ET ASSAISONNEMENTS INC
ALIMENTATION A.D.R. INC   *p* 1280
795 BOUL DU LAC BUREAU 264, QUEBEC, QC, G2M 0E4
(418) 849-3674   *SIC* 5411
ALIMENTATION ANDREA JOLICOEUR INC *p* 1246
3000 BOUL DE LA ROUSSELIERE, POINTE-AUX-TREMBLES, QC, H1A 4G3
(514) 498-7117   *SIC* 5411
ALIMENTATION ASIE-MONTREAL INC   *p* 1381
3010A RUE ANDERSON, TERREBONNE, QC, J6Y 1W1
(450) 621-3288   *SIC* 5147
ALIMENTATION BENOIT ROBERT INC   *p* 1385
1375 RUE AUBUCHON, TROIS-RIVIERES, QC, G8Y 5K4
(819) 373-5166   *SIC* 5411
ALIMENTATION BLANCHETTE & CYRENNE INC   *p* 1163
9280 RUE SHERBROOKE E, MONTREAL, QC, H1L 1E5
(514) 351-1252   *SIC* 5411
ALIMENTATION CHRISTIAN VERREAULT INC   *p* 1121
150 6E RUE, LA BAIE, QC, G7B 4V9
(418) 544-8251   *SIC* 5411
ALIMENTATION COATICOOK (1986) INC   *p* 1081
265 RUE CHILD, COATICOOK, QC, J1A 2B5
(819) 849-6226   *SIC* 5411
ALIMENTATION COUCHE-TARD INC*p* 1233
4204 BOUL INDUSTRIEL, MONTREAL, QC, H7L 0E3
(450) 662-3272   *SIC* 5411
ALIMENTATION D.M. ST-GEORGES INC   *p* 1349
110 RUE BRASSARD, SAINT-MICHEL-DES-SAINTS, QC, J0K 3B0
(450) 833-1313   *SIC* 5411
ALIMENTATION DANIEL BRUYERE INC   *p* 1173
1955 RUE SAINTE-CATHERINE E, MONTREAL, QC, H2K 2H6
(514) 525-5090   *SIC* 5411
ALIMENTATION DANIEL INC   *p* 1245
13057 BOUL GOUIN O, PIERREFONDS, QC, H8Z 1X1
(514) 620-7370   *SIC* 5411
ALIMENTATION DANIEL LAROUCHE INC *p* 1369
1100 13E AV N, SHERBROOKE, QC, J1E 3J7
(819) 562-6788   *SIC* 5411
ALIMENTATION DE LA MITIS INC   *p* 1154
1330 BOUL BENOIT-GABOURY, MONT-JOLI, QC, G5H 4B2
(418) 775-8915   *SIC* 5411
ALIMENTATION DENIS GODIN INC   *p* 1166
4405 RUE SAINTE-CATHERINE E, MONTREAL, QC, H1V 1Y4
(514) 254-0126   *SIC* 5411
ALIMENTATION DOMINIC POTVIN INC   *p* 1163
6550 RUE SHERBROOKE E, MONTREAL, QC, H1N 1C6
(514) 259-8403   *SIC* 5411
ALIMENTATION DUPLESSIS, MARTIN INC *p* 1219
5150 CH DE LA COTE-DES-NEIGES, MONTREAL, QC, H3T 1X8
(514) 738-7377   *SIC* 5411
ALIMENTATION ERIC DA PONTE INC   *p* 1167
3800 RUE ONTARIO E, MONTREAL, QC, H1W 1S4
(514) 524-8850   *SIC* 5411

ALIMENTATION FRANCIS LAMONTAGNE INC p 1104
1100 BOUL MALONEY O, GATINEAU, QC, J8T 6G3
SIC 5411

ALIMENTATION GAETAN PLANTE INC p 1134
53 PLACE QUEVILLON, LEBEL-SUR-QUEVILLON, QC, J0Y 1X0
(819) 755-4803   SIC 5411

ALIMENTATION GAUTHIER & FRERES ENR p 1369
See 2857-4077 QUEBEC INC

ALIMENTATION HOCHELAGA G.S. INC p 1163
7975 RUE HOCHELAGA, MONTREAL, QC, H1L 2K9
(514) 351-7340   SIC 5411

ALIMENTATION IGA p 1270
See ALIMENTATION RAYMOND ROUSSEAU INC

ALIMENTATION J. G. D. INC p 1122
975 BOUL TASCHEREAU BUREAU 302, LA PRAIRIE, QC, J5R 1W7
(450) 659-1611   SIC 5411

ALIMENTATION L'EPICIER INC p 1161
11460 BOUL ARMAND-BOMBARDIER, MONTREAL, QC, H1E 2W9
(514) 351-1991   SIC 5411

ALIMENTATION LAPOINTE & FRERES INC p 1122
25 BOUL KANE, LA MALBAIE, QC, G5A 1J2
(418) 665-3954   SIC 5411

ALIMENTATION LAROCHE & FILS INC p 1135
3045 RTE LAGUEUX BUREAU 100, LEVIS, QC, G6J 1K6
(418) 831-7987   SIC 5411

ALIMENTATION LE SIEUR ENR p 1379
1415 GRANDE ALLEE, TERREBONNE, QC, J6W 5M9
(450) 492-7272   SIC 5411

ALIMENTATION LEBEL INC p 1122
615 RUE 1 RE, LA POCATIERE, QC, G0R 1Z0
(418) 856-3827   SIC 5411

ALIMENTATION LIGILICA LTEE p 398
180 BOUL HEBERT, EDMUNDSTON, NB, E3V 2S7
(506) 735-3544   SIC 7999

ALIMENTATION MARC BOUGIE INC p 1168
3185 RUE BEAUBIEN E, MONTREAL, QC, H1Y 1H5
(514) 721-2433   SIC 5411

ALIMENTATION MARIE GIGNAC INC p 1271
2450 BOUL LAURIER BUREAU 418, QUEBEC, QC, G1V 2L1
(418) 651-8150   SIC 5411

ALIMENTATION MARQUIS, YVES INC p 1359
1116 BOUL VACHON N, SAINTE-MARIE, QC, G6E 1N7
(418) 387-3120   SIC 5411

ALIMENTATION MARTIN CLOUTIER p 1073
See METRO RICHELIEU CANDIAC INC

ALIMENTATION NONNI'S p 1327
See THINADDICTIVES INC

ALIMENTATION OLIVIER,GUY INC p 1292
3525 RUE DE L'HETRIERE, SAINT-AUGUSTIN-DE-DESMAURES, QC, G3A 0C1
(418) 872-4444   SIC 5411

ALIMENTATION POIVRE ET SEL LA CHARCUTIERE INC p 1168
3245 RUE MASSON, MONTREAL, QC, H1Y 1Y4
(514) 374-3611   SIC 5149

ALIMENTATION POIVRE ET SEL LA PATISSIERE p 1168
See ALIMENTATION POIVRE ET SEL LA CHARCUTIERE INC

ALIMENTATION R DENIS INC p 1235

255 BOUL DE LA CONCORDE O, MONTREAL, QC, H7N 5T1
(450) 668-0793   SIC 5411

ALIMENTATION RAYMOND DROUIN INC p 1142
369 RUE SAINT-JEAN O, LONGUEUIL, QC, J4H 2X7
(450) 679-4570   SIC 5411

ALIMENTATION RAYMOND ROUSSEAU INC p 1270
1580 CH SAINT-LOUIS, QUEBEC, QC, G1S 1G6
(418) 527-7758   SIC 5411

ALIMENTATION RICHARD GAGNON S C INC p 1322
1461 AV VICTORIA, SAINT-LAMBERT, QC, J4R 1R5
(450) 671-6205   SIC 5411

ALIMENTATION ROBERT DESROCHER INC p 1135
44 RTE DU PRESIDENT-KENNEDY, LEVIS, QC, G6V 6C5
(418) 835-6313   SIC 5411

ALIMENTATION ROBERT DUFOUR INC p 1122
375 BOUL DE COMPORTE BUREAU 129, LA MALBAIE, QC, G5A 1H9
(418) 665-4473   SIC 5411

ALIMENTATION SERRO INC p 1263
707 BOUL CHAREST O, QUEBEC, QC, G1N 4P6
(418) 681-7385   SIC 5411

ALIMENTATION SOGESCO INC p 1311
3000 BOUL LAFRAMBOISE, SAINT-HYACINTHE, QC, J2S 4Z4
(450) 773-7582   SIC 5411

ALIMENTATION ST-DENIS INC p 1084
307 BOUL CARTIER O, COTE SAINT-LUC, QC, H7N 2J1
(450) 669-7501   SIC 5411

ALIMENTATION ST-ONGE INC p 1307
972 CH DES HAUTEURS, SAINT-HIPPOLYTE, QC, J8A 1L2
(450) 224-5179   SIC 5411

ALIMENTATION ST-RAYMOND INC p 1351
333 COTE JOYEUSE BUREAU 100, SAINT-RAYMOND, QC, G3L 4A8
(418) 337-6781   SIC 5411

ALIMENTATION SYLVAIN BRIERE INC p 1377
7000 AV DE LA PLAZA BUREAU 2036, SOREL-TRACY, QC, J3R 4L8
(450) 742-8227   SIC 5411

ALIMENTATION THOMASSIN, STEPHANE INC p 1271
815 AV MYRAND, QUEBEC, QC, G1V 2V7
(418) 683-1981   SIC 5411

ALIMENTATION TRACY p 1172
See NEPCO INC

ALIMENTATION TRACY INC p 1168
4900 RUE MOLSON, MONTREAL, QC, H1Y 3J8
(450) 743-0644   SIC 5146

ALIMENTATIONS BECHAR INC p 1104
455 BOUL GREBER, GATINEAU, QC, J8T 5T7
(819) 243-0011   SIC 5411

ALIMENTATIONS GAREAU INC p 1281
3450 RUE QUEEN, RAWDON, QC, J0K 1S0
(450) 834-2633   SIC 5411

ALIMENTATIONS GOVANNI ROUSSO 2004 INC p 1229
6645 AV SOMERLED, MONTREAL, QC, H4V 1T3
(514) 486-3042   SIC 5411

ALIMENTATIONS SHNAIDMAN PAGANO INC, LES p 1083
5800 BOUL CAVENDISH BUREAU 111, COTE SAINT-LUC, QC, H4W 2T5
(514) 482-4710   SIC 5411

ALIMENTS ALASKO INC p 1165
6810 BOUL DES GRANDES-PRAIRIES, MONTREAL, QC, H1P 3P3
(514) 328-6661   SIC 5142

ALIMENTS ASTA INC p 1291
767 RTE 289, SAINT-ALEXANDRE-DE-KAMOURASKA, QC, G0L 2G0
(418) 495-2728   SIC 2011

ALIMENTS AULT p 579
See PARMALAT CANADA INC

ALIMENTS BARI INC, LES p 1347
297 155 RTE, SAINT-LEONARD-D'ASTON, QC, J0C 1M0
(819) 399-2277   SIC 2099

ALIMENTS BCI INC, LES p 1311
4800 AV PINARD, SAINT-HYACINTHE, QC, J2S 8E1
(888) 797-3210   SIC 2032

ALIMENTS BERCY INC, LES p 1169
9210 BOUL PIE-IX, MONTREAL, QC, H1Z 4H7
(514) 528-6262   SIC 0723

ALIMENTS BRETON INC p 1294
1312 RUE SAINT-GEORGES, SAINT-BERNARD, QC, G0S 2G0
(418) 475-6601   SIC 5149

ALIMENTS CHATEL INC, LES p 1231
575 MONTEE ST FRANCOIS, MONTREAL, QC, H7C 2S8
(514) 935-5446   SIC 5147

ALIMENTS CHATEL, LES p 1231
See 9273-9127 QUEBEC INC

ALIMENTS CHEVREFILS INC, LES p 1354
555 BOUL DE SAINTE-ADELE BUREAU 205, SAINTE-ADELE, QC, J8B 1A7
(450) 227-2712   SIC 5411

ALIMENTS CONAN INC, LES p 1332
7007 BOUL HENRI-BOURASSA O, SAINT-LAURENT, QC, H4S 2E2
(514) 334-7977   SIC 5141

ALIMENTS CONGELES MOOV INC p 1343
6810 BOUL DES GRANDES-PRAIRIES, SAINT-LEONARD, QC, H1P 3P3
(514) 328-6661   SIC 5142

ALIMENTS DA VINCI LTEE, LES p 1223
5655 RUE BEAULIEU, MONTREAL, QC, H4E 3E4
(514) 769-1234   SIC 2045

ALIMENTS DAINTY FOODS INC, LES p 1401
2 PLACE ALEXIS NIHON NO1777 3500 DE MAISONNEUVE O, WESTMOUNT, QC, H3Z 3C1
(514) 908-7777   SIC 5149

ALIMENTS DARE p 1322
See DARE FOODS LIMITED

ALIMENTS DELIHAM p 1313
See SUPRALIMENT S.E.C.

ALIMENTS E.D. p 1249
See ALIMENTS LUDA FOODS INC

ALIMENTS ESPOSITO (ST-MICHEL) LTEE, LES p 1171
7030 BOUL SAINT-MICHEL, MONTREAL, QC, H2A 2Z4
(514) 722-1069   SIC 5411

ALIMENTS EXCEL S.E.C., LES p 1295
1081 RUE PARENT, SAINT-BRUNO, QC, J3V 6L7
(450) 441-6111   SIC 2015

ALIMENTS EXPRESCO INC p 1332
8205 RTE TRANSCANADIENNE, SAINT-LAURENT, QC, H4S 1S4
(514) 344-9499   SIC 2013

ALIMENTS F. LECLERC p 1292
See BISCUITS LECLERC LTEE

ALIMENTS FIDAS LTEE, LES p 1343
6575 BOUL DES GRANDES-PRAIRIES, SAINT-LEONARD, QC, H1P 3G8
(514) 322-7575   SIC 5146

ALIMENTS FINS DE L'USINE DE LA FOURCHETTE GRASSE, LES p 1182
See BRUNO & NICK INC

ALIMENTS FLAMINGO p 1225
See BEXEL INC

ALIMENTS FONTAINE SANTE INC p 1325
450 RUE DESLAURIERS, SAINT-LAURENT, QC, H4N 1V8
(514) 745-3085   SIC 2099

ALIMENTS FOO LAY FOODS, LES p 1069
See 3764605 CANADA INC

ALIMENTS G DION, LES p 1319
See 9030-5418 QUEBEC INC

ALIMENTS GARNIE p 1068
See FRUITS DORES INC

ALIMENTS IMEX INC p 1225
1605 RUE DE BEAUHARNOIS O BUREAU 100, MONTREAL, QC, H4N 1J6
SIC 5141

ALIMENTS JARDI INC, LES p 1372
4650 BOUL DE PORTLAND, SHERBROOKE, QC, J1L 0H6
(819) 820-1003   SIC 2064

ALIMENTS KIM PHAT (JARRY), LES p 1169
See 4019636 CANADA INC

ALIMENTS KIM PHAT (ST-LAURENT), LES p 1323
See 11375644 CANADA INC

ALIMENTS KOYO INC p 1338
4605 RUE HICKMORE, SAINT-LAURENT, QC, H4T 1S5
(514) 744-1299   SIC 5149

ALIMENTS KRISPY KERNELS p 1266
See DISTRIBUTION DENIS JALBERT INC

ALIMENTS KRISPY KERNELS INC p 1266
2620 AV WATT, QUEBEC, QC, G1P 3T5
(418) 658-4640   SIC 6712

ALIMENTS KRISPY KERNELS INC p 1400
40 RUE DU MOULIN, WARWICK, QC, J0A 1M0
(819) 358-3600   SIC 2096

ALIMENTS LA BROCHETTE INC, LES p 1158
404 RTE 104, MONT-SAINT-GREGOIRE, QC, J0J 1K0
(450) 346-4144   SIC 5144

ALIMENTS LEBEL INC, LES p 1129
724 RUE PRINCIPALE, LACHUTE, QC, J8H 1Z4
(450) 562-5500   SIC 2024

ALIMENTS LESTERS LIMITEE, LES p 1084
2105 BOUL INDUSTRIEL, COTE SAINT-LUC, QC, H7S 1P7
(450) 629-1100   SIC 2011

ALIMENTS LEVITTS (CANADA) INC, LES p 1130
7070 RUE SAINT-PATRICK, LASALLE, QC, H8N 1V2
(514) 367-1654   SIC 2011

ALIMENTS LUCY PORC/PORK p 1403
See OLY-ROBI TRANSFORMATION S.E.C.

ALIMENTS LUCYPORC p 1186
See 9071-3975 QUEBEC INC

ALIMENTS LUDA FOODS INC p 1249
6200 RTE TRANSCANADIENNE, POINTE-CLAIRE, QC, H9R 1B9
(514) 695-3333   SIC 2034

ALIMENTS MARTEL INC p 1103
212 BOUL DE L'AEROPORT, GATINEAU, QC, J8R 3X3
(819) 663-0835   SIC 5963

ALIMENTS MARTEL INC p 1125
2387 RUE REMEMBRANCE, LACHINE, QC, H8S 1X4
SIC 2099

ALIMENTS MARTEL INC p 1381
460 RUE FERNAND-POITRAS, TERREBONNE, QC, J6Y 1Y4
(514) 493-9423   SIC 2099

ALIMENTS MARTEL INC p 1381
460 RUE FERNAND-POITRAS, TERREBONNE, QC, J6Y 1Y4
(514) 493-9423   SIC 5149

ALIMENTS MATRIX INC, LES p 618
896 CECILE BLVD, HAWKESBURY, ON, K6A 3R5
(613) 632-8623   SIC 5143

ALIMENTS MEJIVANO +, LES p 1047
See 3213463 CANADA INC

ALIMENTS MIA, LES p 1047
See ALIMENTS RUSTICA INC, LES

ALIMENTS MOUKAS p 1183
See 116278 CANADA INC

ALIMENTS MULTIBAR INC, LES p 1047
9000 BOUL DES SCIENCES, ANJOU, QC, H1J 3A9
(514) 355-1151 SIC 5142

ALIMENTS NEWLY WEDS, LES p 1066
See NEWLY WEDS FOODS CO.

ALIMENTS NOBLE INC p 1249
250 AV AVRO, POINTE-CLAIRE, QC, H9R 6B1
(514) 426-0680 SIC 2064

ALIMENTS NONNA ROSA, LES p 1061
See ALIMENTS O SOLE MIO INC, LES

ALIMENTS NOVALI p 1066
See NOVALI GOURMET INC

ALIMENTS NUTRIK p 1059
See LABORATOIRES NICAR INC, LES

ALIMENTS O SOLE MIO INC, LES p 1061
4600 RUE AMBROISE-LAFORTUNE, BOISBRIAND, QC, J7H 0G1
(450) 435-4111 SIC 2098

ALIMENTS OATBOX p 1116
See 8956995 CANADA INC

ALIMENTS ORGANIQUES NATURE'S TOUCH p 1340
See NATURE'S TOUCH FROZEN FOODS INC

ALIMENTS ORIGINAL, DIVISION CANTIN INC p 1255
1910 AV DU SANCTUAIRE, QUEBEC, QC, G1E 3L2
(418) 663-3523 SIC 2033

ALIMENTS OUIMET-CORDON BLEU INC p 1047
8383 RUE J.-RENE-OUIMET, ANJOU, QC, H1J 2P8
(514) 352-3000 SIC 2032

ALIMENTS PASTA ROMANA INC p 1239
11430 BOUL ALBERT-HUDON, MONTREAL-NORD, QC, H1G 3J8
(514) 494-4767 SIC 2098

ALIMENTS PHILIPS p 1045
See CHARCUTERIE L. FORTIN LIMITEE

ALIMENTS PREMONT INC p 1354
1505 RTE LUPIEN, SAINTE-ANGELE-DE-PREMONT, QC, J0K 1R0
(819) 268-2820 SIC 5147

ALIMENTS PRINCE, S.E.C. p 1097
255 RUE ROCHELEAU, DRUM-MONDVILLE, QC, J2C 7G2
(819) 475-3030 SIC 2013

ALIMENTS PRINCE, S.E.C. p 1311
2200 AV PRATTE BUREAU 400, SAINT-HYACINTHE, QC, J2S 4B6
(450) 771-7060 SIC 2013

ALIMENTS PRO-LACTO INC, LES p 1399
303 RTE 265, VILLEROY, QC, G0S 3K0
(819) 385-1232 SIC 5191

ALIMENTS PROLIMER INC p 1261
650 BOUL PERE-LELIEVRE BUREAU 200, QUEBEC, QC, G1M 3T2
SIC 5141

ALIMENTS RELIANCE INTERNATIONAL, LES p 1120
See RELIANCE FOODS INTERNATIONAL INC

ALIMENTS ROMA LTEE, LES p 1325
660 RUE WRIGHT, SAINT-LAURENT, QC, H4N 1M6
(514) 332-0340 SIC 2032

ALIMENTS ROSE HILL p 1335
See PRODUITS & BASES DE SOUPE MAJOR DU CANADA INC, LES

ALIMENTS ROSEHILL INC, LES p 1332
7171 BOUL THIMENS, SAINT-LAURENT, QC, H4S 2A2
(514) 745-1153 SIC 5149

ALIMENTS RUSTICA INC, LES p 1047
10301 RUE COLBERT, ANJOU, QC, H1J 2G5
(514) 325-9009 SIC 5149

ALIMENTS S.R.C. INC, LES p 1345
4617 BOUL DES GRANDES-PRAIRIES, SAINT-LEONARD, QC, H1R 1A5
(514) 721-2421 SIC 5411

ALIMENTS SAPUTO LIMITEE p 593
279 GUELPH ST, GEORGETOWN, ON, L7G 4B3
(905) 702-7200 SIC 2026

ALIMENTS SAPUTO LIMITEE p 902
284 HOPE ST W, TAVISTOCK, ON, N0B 2R0
(519) 655-2337 SIC 2022

ALIMENTS SAPUTO LIMITEE p 1343
6869 BOUL METROPOLITAIN E, SAINT-LEONARD, QC, H1P 1X8
(514) 328-6662 SIC 5141

ALIMENTS SARDO INC., LES p 494
99 PILLSWORTH RD, BOLTON, ON, L7E 4E4
(905) 951-9096 SIC 2079

ALIMENTS SERVAL CANADA LTEE, LES p 1146
303 RUE SAINT-MARC, LOUISEVILLE, QC, J5V 2G2
(819) 228-5551 SIC 5085

ALIMENTS SUNCHEF INC p 1047
9750 BOUL DES SCIENCES, ANJOU, QC, H1J 0A1
(514) 272-3238 SIC 2015

ALIMENTS TOUSAIN INC p 1325
95 RUE STINSON, SAINT-LAURENT, QC, H4N 2E1
(514) 748-7353 SIC 5141

ALIMENTS TRANS GRAS INC, LES p 1097
2825 RUE POWER, DRUMMONDVILLE, QC, J2C 6Z6
(819) 472-1125 SIC 2011

ALIMENTS TRIOVA INC, LES p 1114
696 RUE MARION, JOLIETTE, QC, J6E 8S2
(450) 756-6322 SIC 2034

ALIMENTS ULTIMA FOODS & DESSIN p 1309
See ALIMENTS ULTIMA INC

ALIMENTS ULTIMA INC p 1309
4600 RUE ARMAND-FRAPPIER, SAINT-HUBERT, QC, J3Z 1G5
(450) 651-3737 SIC 2026

ALIMENTS UNI INC, LES p 1338
6100 CH DE LA COTE-DE-LIESSE BUREAU 200, SAINT-LAURENT, QC, H4T 1E3
(514) 731-3401 SIC 5147

ALIMENTS V-H p 693
See CONAGRA FOODS CANADA INC

ALIMENTS VALLI INC., LES p 1307
3400 BOUL LOSCH BUREAU 35, SAINT-HUBERT, QC, J3Y 5T6
(450) 443-0060 SIC 5141

ALIMENTS VERMONT FOODS INC p 1253
210 RUE SAINT-JEAN-BAPTISTE N, PRINCEVILLE, QC, G6L 5E1
SIC 2011

ALIMENTS VIVI p 1307
See ALIMENTS VALLI INC., LES

ALIMENTS VLM INC, LES p 1091
1651 RUE SAINT-REGIS, DOLLARD-DES-ORMEAUX, QC, H9B 3H7
(514) 426-4100 SIC 5142

ALIMENTS WHYTE'S INC, LES p 1233
1540 RUE DES PATRIOTES, MONTREAL, QC, H7L 2N6
(450) 625-1976 SIC 5141

ALIMEX INC p 1172
4425 RUE D'IBERVILLE, MONTREAL, QC, H2H 2L7
(514) 522-5700 SIC 5046

ALIMPLUS INC p 1047
9777 RUE COLBERT, ANJOU, QC, H1J 1Z9
(514) 274-5662 SIC 5141

ALIMPLUS INC p 1047
340 235 RTE, ANGE-GARDIEN, QC, J0E 1E0
(450) 293-3626 SIC 5141

ALIO p 1200
See TOURS NEW YORK INC

ALIO GOLD INC p 302
700 WEST PENDER ST SUITE 507, VANCOUVER, BC, V6C 1G8
(604) 682-4002 SIC 1041

ALISON SHERI p 1177
See 4113993 CANADA INC

ALITHYA CANADA INC p 1201
700 RUE DE LA GAUCHETIERE O BUREAU 2400, MONTREAL, QC, H3B 5M2
(514) 285-5552 SIC 7379

ALITHYA CANADA INC p 1212
1350 BOUL RENE-LEVESQUE O BUREAU 200, MONTREAL, QC, H3G 1T4
(514) 285-5552 SIC 7379

ALITHYA DIGITAL TECHNOLOGY CORPORATION p 922
2300 YONGE ST SUITE 1800, TORONTO, ON, M4P 1E4
(416) 932-4700 SIC 7371

ALIVE HEALTH CENTRE LTD p 259
2680 SHELL RD SUITE 228, RICHMOND, BC, V6X 4C9
(604) 273-6266 SIC 5499

ALIYA'S FOODS LIMITED p 108
6364 ROPER RD NW, EDMONTON, AB, T6B 3P9
(780) 467-4600 SIC 2038

ALIZENT CANADA INC p 1209
740 RUE NOTRE-DAME O BUREAU 600, MONTREAL, QC, H3C 3X6
(514) 876-2855 SIC 8742

ALL 4 WATER CORP p 108
7115 GIRARD RD NW, EDMONTON, AB, T6B 2C5
SIC 2086

ALL CANADA CRANE RENTAL CORP p 685
7215 TORBRAM RD, MISSISSAUGA, ON, L4T 1G7
(905) 795-1090 SIC 7353

ALL CITY IMPORTERS LTD p 285
1290 ODLUM DR, VANCOUVER, BC, V5L 3L9
(604) 251-1045 SIC 5141

ALL CONNECT p 803
See ALL-CONNECT LOGISTICAL SERVICES INC

ALL GOLD IMPORTS INC p 666
4255 14TH AVE, MARKHAM, ON, L3R 0J2
(416) 740-4653 SIC 5149

ALL GRAPHICS SUPPLIES p 736
See 995843 ONTARIO LTD

ALL HEALTH SERVICES INC p 927
66 COLLIER ST UNIT 9D, TORONTO, ON, M4W 1L9
(416) 515-1151 SIC 7361

ALL IN WESTU CAPITAL CORPORATION p 376
360 MAIN ST SUITE 400, WINNIPEG, MB, R3C 3Z3
(204) 947-1200 SIC 6799

ALL LANGUAGES LTD p 927
421 BLOOR ST E SUITE 306, TORONTO, ON, M4W 3T1
(647) 427-8308 SIC 7389

ALL NATIONS COORDINATED RESPONSE NETWORK (ANCR) p 382
See SOUTHERN FIRST NATIONS NETWORK OF CARE

ALL NORTH TRUCK CENTRE p 647
See 1168170 ONTARIO LTD

ALL PARTS AUTOMOTIVE LIMITED p 582
66 RONSON DR, ETOBICOKE, ON, M9W 1B6
(416) 743-1200 SIC 5013

ALL PEACE PROTECTION LTD p 131
11117 100 ST SUITE 202, GRANDE PRAIRIE, AB, T8V 2N2
(780) 538-1166 SIC 7381

ALL SAINT CATHOLIC SECONDARY SCHOOL p 1015
See DURHAM CATHOLIC DISTRICT SCHOOL BOARD

ALL SAINTS HIGH SCHOOL p 625
See OTTAWA CATHOLIC DISTRICT SCHOOL BOARD

ALL SEA ATLANTIC LTD p 414
9 LOWER COVE LOOP, SAINT JOHN, NB, E2L 1W7
(506) 632-3483 SIC 7389

ALL SEASONS p 1333
See ENTREPRISE COMMERCIALE SHAH LIMITEE, L'

ALL SENIORS CARE HOLDINGS INC p 928
175 BLOOR ST E SUITE 601, TORONTO, ON, M4W 3R8
(416) 323-3773 SIC 6513

ALL SENIORS CARE LIVING CENTRES LTD p 77
21 AUBURN BAY ST SE SUITE 428, CALGARY, AB, T3M 2A9
(403) 234-9695 SIC 6513

ALL SENIORS CARE LIVING CENTRES LTD p 373
10 HALLONQUIST DR SUITE 318, WINNIPEG, MB, R2Y 2M5
(204) 885-1415 SIC 8361

ALL SENIORS CARE LIVING CENTRES LTD p 928
175 BLOOR ST E SUITE 601, TORONTO, ON, M4W 3R8
(416) 323-3773 SIC 6513

ALL SPAN BUILDING SYSTEMS LTD p 80
424 GRIFFIN RD W, COCHRANE, AB, T4C 2E1
(403) 932-7878 SIC 2439

ALL STAR MOVING IN NEW MARKET p 474
See ROCKBRUNE BROTHERS LIMITED

ALL TEAM GLASS & MIRROR LTD p 1029
281 HANLAN RD, WOODBRIDGE, ON, L4L 3R7
(905) 851-7711 SIC 3231

ALL TEMP FOODS LTD p 644
15 INDUSTRIAL RD, LEAMINGTON, ON, N8H 4W4
(519) 326-8611 SIC 5146

ALL THERM SERVICES INC p 191
8528 GLENLYON PKY UNIT 141, BURNABY, BC, V5J 0B6
(604) 559-4331 SIC 5033

ALL TRADE COMPUTER FORMS INC p 737
60 ADMIRAL BLVD, MISSISSAUGA, ON, L5T 2W1
SIC 2761

ALL TREAT FARMS LIMITED p 479
7963 WELLINGTON ROAD 109 RR 4, ARTHUR, ON, N0G 1A0
(519) 848-3145 SIC 2048

ALL TYPE TRANSPORTS p 1127
See COHEN, JERRY FORWARDERS LTD

ALL WEATHER PRODUCTS LTD p 275
12510 82 AVE, SURREY, BC, V3W 3E9
(604) 572-8088 SIC 5033

ALL WEATHER WINDOWS LTD p 99
18550 118A AVE NW, EDMONTON, AB, T5S 2K7
(780) 468-2989 SIC 3442

ALL-CAN EXPRESS LTD p 183
2830 NORLAND AVE, BURNABY, BC, V5B 3A7
(604) 294-8631 SIC 4212

ALL-CAN MEDICAL INC p 734
7575 KIMBEL ST UNIT 5, MISSISSAUGA, ON, L5S 1C8
(905) 677-9410 SIC 4925

ALL-CANADIAN SELF STORAGE p 982
See METFIN PROPERTIES LIMITED PARTNERSHIP

ALL-CARE HOME HEALTH & STAFFING p 856
See 1207715 ONTARIO INC

ALL-CONNECT LOGISTICAL SERVICES INC p 803
2070 WYECROFT RD, OAKVILLE, ON, L6L 5V6
(905) 847-6555 SIC 4731

ALL-FAB BUILDING COMPONENTS INC p 364
1755 DUGALD RD, WINNIPEG, MB, R2J 0H3
(204) 661-8880 SIC 2431

ALL-FAB BUILDING COMPONENTS INC *p*
1415
610 HENDERSON DR, REGINA, SK, S4N
5X3
(306) 721-8131   *SIC* 5039
ALL-LIFT LTD *p* 508
320 CLARENCE ST SUITE 7-10, BRAMP-
TON, ON, L6W 1T5
(905) 459-5348   *SIC* 5084
**ALL-RISKS INSURANCE BROKERS LIM-
ITED** *p*
1021
1591 OUELLETTE AVE, WINDSOR, ON,
N8X 1K5
(519) 253-6376   *SIC* 6411
ALL-SEA UNDERWATER SOLUTIONS *p*
414
See ALL SEA ATLANTIC LTD
ALL-WELD COMPANY LIMITED *p* 875
14 PASSMORE AVE, SCARBOROUGH,
ON, M1V 2R6
(416) 293-3638   *SIC* 7539
ALL-WELD COMPANY LIMITED *p* 875
49 PASSMORE AVE, SCARBOROUGH,
ON, M1V 4T1
(416) 299-3311   *SIC* 3499
**ALLAIN EQUIPMENT MANUFACTURING
LTD** *p* 410
577 ROUTE 535, NOTRE-DAME, NB, E4V
2K4
(506) 576-6436   *SIC* 3599
ALLAN BLAIR CANCER CENTER *p* 1422
See SASKATCHEWAN CANCER AGENCY
ALLAN CANDY COMPANY LIMITED, THE *p*
704
3 ROBERT SPECK PKY SUITE 250, MIS-
SISSAUGA, ON, L4Z 2G5
(905) 270-2221   *SIC* 2064
ALLAN CANDY COMPANY LIMITED, THE *p*
1110
850 BOUL INDUSTRIEL, GRANBY, QC, J2J
1B8
(450) 372-1080   *SIC* 2064
ALLAN CONSTRUCTION *p* 1433
317 103 ST E, SASKATOON, SK, S7N 1Y9
(306) 477-5520   *SIC* 1542
ALLAN CONSTRUCTION CO. LTD *p* 1433
317 103RD ST E, SASKATOON, SK, S7N
1Y9
(306) 477-5520   *SIC* 1542
ALLAN FRANCIS & PRINGLE *p* 332
See JUST REWARDS MANAGEMENT LTD
ALLAN RAMSAY ET COMPAGNIE LIMITEE
p 1222
3711 RUE SAINT-ANTOINE O, MON-
TREAL, QC, H4C 3P6
(514) 932-6161   *SIC* 2111
ALLANA POTASH CORP *p* 948
65 QUEEN ST W SUITE 805, TORONTO,
ON, M5H 2M5
(416) 861-5800   *SIC* 1474
ALLANDALE SCHOOL TRANSIT LIMITED *p*
486
137 BROCK ST, BARRIE, ON, L4N 2M3
(705) 728-1100   *SIC* 4151
ALLANSON INTERNATIONAL INC *p* 678
83 COMMERCE VALLEY DR E,
MARKHAM, ON, L3T 7T3
(416) 755-1191   *SIC* 1731
ALLANSON INTERNATIONAL INC *p* 678
83 COMMERCE VALLEY DR E,
MARKHAM, ON, L3T 7T3
(800) 668-9162   *SIC* 3612
ALLARD *p* 425
See ALLARD DISTRIBUTING LIMITED
ALLARD CONTRACTORS LTD *p* 199
1520 PIPELINE RD, COQUITLAM, BC, V3E
3P6
(604) 944-2556   *SIC* 5032
ALLARD DISTRIBUTING LIMITED *p* 425
208 HUMPHRY RD, LABRADOR CITY, NL,
A2V 2K7
(709) 944-5144   *SIC* 5172
ALLCARD LIMITED *p* 537

765 BOXWOOD DR SUITE 650, CAM-
BRIDGE, ON, N3E 1A4
(519) 650-9515   *SIC* 3089
ALLCO ELECTRICAL LTD *p* 383
930 BRADFORD ST, WINNIPEG, MB, R3H
0N5
(204) 697-1000   *SIC* 1731
ALLCOLOUR HOLLOWAY, DIV OF *p* 803
See ALLCOLOUR PAINT LIMITED
ALLCOLOUR PAINT LIMITED *p* 803
1257 SPEERS RD, OAKVILLE, ON, L6L 2X5
(905) 827-4173   *SIC* 2851
ALLDRITT DEVELOPMENT LIMITED *p* 95
14310 111 AVE NW SUITE 305, EDMON-
TON, AB, T5M 3Z7
(780) 453-5631   *SIC* 6512
ALLDRITT DEVELOPMENT LIMITED *p* 95
15035 114 AVE NW, EDMONTON, AB, T5M
2Z1
(780) 451-2732   *SIC* 1711
ALLDRITT DEVELOPMENT LIMITED *p* 280
2055 152 ST SUITE 300, SURREY, BC, V4A
4N7
(604) 536-5525   *SIC* 6552
ALLEGION CANADA INC *p* 582
51 WORCESTER RD, ETOBICOKE, ON,
M9W 4K2
(800) 900-1434   *SIC* 5084
ALLEGION CANADA INC *p* 712
1076 LAKESHORE RD E, MISSISSAUGA,
ON, L5E 1E4
(905) 403-1800   *SIC* 5072
ALLEGRA *p* 1087
See SANOFI-AVENTIS CANADA INC
ALLEN & ASSOCIATES INC *p* 484
60 COLLIER ST UNIT 217, BARRIE, ON,
L4M 1G8
SIC 8748
ALLEN ENTREPRENEUR GENERAL INC *p*
1306
118 RUE DE LA GARE, SAINT-HENRI-DE-
LEVIS, QC, G0R 3E0
(418) 882-2277   *SIC* 1611
**ALLEN GRAY CONTINUING CARE CEN-
TRE** *p*
120
See GRAY HOUSE GUILD, THE
ALLEN INSURANCE *p* 1005
*See ALLEN, G & B INSURANCE BROKERS
LIMITED*
ALLEN MAINTENANCE *p* 816
*See SOLUTIONS DE MAINTENANCE AP-
PLIQUEES (AMS) INC*
ALLEN VANGUARD CORP *p* 837
421 UPPER VALLEY DR, PEMBROKE, ON,
K8A 6W5
(613) 735-3996   *SIC* 3842
ALLEN'S FISHERIES LIMITED *p* 421
151 MAIN RD, BENOITS COVE, NL, A0L
1A0
(709) 789-3139   *SIC* 2092
ALLEN, A.W. HOMES LIMITED *p* 462
166 COMMERCIAL ST, MIDDLETON, NS,
B0S 1P0
(902) 825-4854   *SIC* 5072
**ALLEN, CENTURY 21 WENDA REALTY
LTD** *p* 870
2025 MIDLAND AVE, SCARBOROUGH,
ON, M1P 3E2
(416) 293-3900   *SIC* 6531
**ALLEN, G & B INSURANCE BROKERS
LIMITED** *p* 1005
45 DOMINION ST, WARKWORTH, ON, K0K
3K0
(705) 924-2632   *SIC* 6411
ALLEN-BRADLEY *p* 534
*See ROCKWELL AUTOMATION CANADA
INC*
ALLEN-FELDMAN HOLDINGS LTD *p* 319
1505 2ND AVE W SUITE 200, VANCOU-
VER, BC, V6H 3Y4
(604) 734-5945   *SIC* 6712
ALLEN-VANGUARD CORPORATION *p* 817
2405 ST. LAURENT BLVD, OTTAWA, ON,

K1G 5B4
(613) 739-9646   *SIC* 5065
ALLGARD SECURITY SERVICES *p* 283
See 593130 BC LTD
ALLIAGES ZABO INC *p* 1322
201 RUE MONTCALM BUREAU 213,
SAINT-JOSEPH-DE-SOREL, QC, J3R 1B9
(450) 746-1126   *SIC* 5051
ALLIANCE *p* 1211
See MUSIQUE SELECT INC
ALLIANCE *p* 1236
*See ALLIANCE DE L'INDUSTRIE TOURIS-
TIQUE DU QUEBEC*
ALLIANCE 9000 *p* 1046
See IMPRESSION ALLIANCE 9000 INC
ALLIANCE AGRI-TURF INC *p* 494
8112 KING ST, BOLTON, ON, L7E 0T8
(905) 857-2000   *SIC* 3523
ALLIANCE ASSURANCE INC *p* 403
166 BOUL BROADWAY SUITE 200,
GRAND-SAULT/GRAND FALLS, NB, E3Z
2J9
(506) 473-9400   *SIC* 6411
**ALLIANCE ATLANTIS COMMUNICATIONS
INC** *p* 928
121 BLOOR ST E SUITE 1500, TORONTO,
ON, M4W 3M5
(416) 967-1174   *SIC* 4899
ALLIANCE BEAUTY COMPANY *p* 339
*See THREE AMIGO'S BEAUTY SUPPLY
CO LTD*
ALLIANCE BUILDING MAINTENANCE LTD
p 99
18823 111 AVE NW, EDMONTON, AB, T5S
2X4
(780) 447-2574   *SIC* 7349
ALLIANCE CENTER *p* 119
See EYEWEAR PLACE LTD, THE
ALLIANCE COMMUNICATION *p* 632
See JACK FRENCH LIMITED
ALLIANCE CONCRETE PUMPS INC *p* 179
26162 30A AVE, ALDERGROVE, BC, V4W
2W5
(604) 607-0908   *SIC* 3561
ALLIANCE CORPORATION *p* 719
2395 MEADOWPINE BLVD, MISSIS-
SAUGA, ON, L5N 7W6
(905) 821-4797   *SIC* 5065
**ALLIANCE DE L'INDUSTRIE TOURISTIQUE
DU QUEBEC** *p* 1236
1575 BOUL DE L'AVENIR BUREAU 330,
MONTREAL, QC, H7S 2N5
(450) 686-8358   *SIC* 7389
**ALLIANCE DU PERSONNEL PROFES-
SIONNEL ET TECHNIQUE DE LA SANTE ET
DES SERVICES SOCIAUX** *p* 1144
1111 RUE SAINT-CHARLES O BUREAU
1050, LONGUEUIL, QC, J4K 5G4
(450) 670-2411   *SIC* 6513
ALLIANCE ENERGY LIMITED *p* 1415
504 HENDERSON DR, REGINA, SK, S4N
5X2
(306) 721-6484   *SIC* 1731
**ALLIANCE ENVIRONMENTAL & ABATE-
MENT CONTRACTORS INC** *p*
876
589 MIDDLEFIELD RD UNIT 14, SCAR-
BOROUGH, ON, M1V 4Y6
(416) 298-4500   *SIC* 4953
ALLIANCE FABRICATING LTD *p* 858
763 CHESTER ST, SARNIA, ON, N7S 5N2
(519) 336-4328   *SIC* 3499
ALLIANCE FORD INC *p* 1354
90 BOUL NORBERT-MORIN, SAINTE-
AGATHE-DES-MONTS, QC, J8C 3K8
(819) 326-8944   *SIC* 5511
ALLIANCE FORMING LTD *p* 494
91 PARR BLVD, BOLTON, ON, L7E 4E3
(416) 749-5030   *SIC* 1623
ALLIANCE GRAIN TERMINAL LTD *p* 294
1155 STEWART ST, VANCOUVER, BC,
V6A 4H4
(604) 254-4414   *SIC* 4221
ALLIANCE HANGER INC *p* 1328

2500 RUE GUENETTE, SAINT-LAURENT,
QC, H4R 2H2
(514) 339-9600   *SIC* 3496
ALLIANCE MERCANTILE INC *p* 187
3451 WAYBURNE DR, BURNABY, BC, V5G
3L1
(604) 299-3566   *SIC* 5023
**ALLIANCE OCCIDENTALE LOGISTIQUES
INC** *p* 1117
16766 RTE TRANSCANADIENNE BUREAU
400, KIRKLAND, QC, H9H 4M7
(514) 534-0114   *SIC* 4731
**ALLIANCE OF CANADIAN CINEMA, TELE-
VISION & RADIO ARTISTS** *p*
931
625 CHURCH ST, TORONTO, ON, M4Y
2G1
(416) 489-1311   *SIC* 8631
**ALLIANCE PERSONNELLE PROFES-
SIONELLE ET TECHNIQUE DE LA SANTE
ET DES SERVICES SOCIAUX** *p* 1279
1305 BOUL LEBOURGNEUF BUREAU 200,
QUEBEC, QC, G2K 2E4
(418) 622-2541   *SIC* 8631
**ALLIANCE PIPELINE LIMITED PARTNER-
SHIP** *p*
42
605 5 AVE SW SUITE 800, CALGARY, AB,
T2P 3H5
(403) 266-4464   *SIC* 4922
ALLIANCE PIPELINE LTD *p* 43
605 5 AVE SW SUITE 800, CALGARY, AB,
T2P 3H5
(403) 266-4464   *SIC* 8741
**ALLIANCE POUR LA SANTE ETUDIANTE
AU QUEBEC INC** *p* 1201
1200 AV MCGILL COLLEGE BUREAU
2200, MONTREAL, QC, H3B 4G7
(514) 844-4423   *SIC* 6324
**ALLIANCE QUEBECOISE DES TECHNI-
CIENS DE L'IMAGE ET DU SON (AQTIS)** *p*
1175
533 RUE ONTARIO E BUREAU 300, MON-
TREAL, QC, H2L 1N8
(514) 844-2113   *SIC* 8631
ALLIANCE READY MIX LTD *p* 165
47 ELLIOT ST, ST. ALBERT, AB, T8N 5S5
(780) 459-1090   *SIC* 5211
ALLIANCE REAL ESTATE CALGARY LTD *p*
41
2003 14 ST NW SUITE 107, CALGARY, AB,
T2M 3N4
(403) 270-7676   *SIC* 6531
ALLIANCE ROOFING & SHEET METAL LTD
p 605
25 COPE CRT, GUELPH, ON, N1K 0A4
(519) 763-1442   *SIC* 1761
ALLIANCE SEAFOOD INCORPORATED *p*
397
621 CH GAUVIN, DIEPPE, NB, E1A 1M7
(506) 854-5800   *SIC* 2092
ALLIANCE STORE FIXTURES INC *p* 1027
370 NEW HUNTINGTON RD, WOOD-
BRIDGE, ON, L4H 0R4
(905) 660-5944   *SIC* 2542
ALLIANCE SUPPLY LTD *p* 246
1585 BROADWAY ST SUITE 104, PORT
COQUITLAM, BC, V3C 2M7
(604) 944-4081   *SIC* 5051
ALLIANCE TRAFFIC GROUP INC *p* 253
2600 VIKING WAY, RICHMOND, BC, V6V
1N2
(604) 273-5220   *SIC* 7389
**ALLIANCES DES MANUFACTURIERS ET
DES EXPORTATEURS DU CANADA** *p* 729
55 STANDISH CRT SUITE 620, MISSIS-
SAUGA, ON, L5R 4B2
(905) 672-3466   *SIC* 8611
ALLIANZ GLOBAL ASSISTANCE *p* 641
See AZGA SERVICE CANADA INC
ALLIBERT-TREKKING *p* 1192
See UNIKTOUR INC
ALLIED BLOWER & SHEET METAL LTD *p*
274

12224 103A AVE, SURREY, BC, V3V 3G9
(604) 930-7000 *SIC* 1796
ALLIED BUILDING SERVICES *p* 1184
See SERVICES D'ENTRETIEN D'EDIFICES ALLIED (QUEBEC) INC
ALLIED COFFEE CORP *p* 648
775 INDUSTRIAL RD UNIT 2, LONDON, ON, N5V 5N5
(519) 451-8220 *SIC* 7389
ALLIED CONTRACTORS INC. *p* 13
7003 30 ST SE BAY 26, CALGARY, AB, T2C 1N6
(403) 243-3311 *SIC* 1742
ALLIED DON VALLEY HOTEL INC *p* 778
175 WYNFORD DR, NORTH YORK, ON, M3C 1J3
(416) 449-4111 *SIC* 7011
ALLIED FITTING CANADA *p* 162
See 3033441 NOVA SCOTIA COMPANY
ALLIED FOOD DISTRIBUTORS *p* 1093
See COMPAGNIE REGITAN LTEE, LA
ALLIED HOTEL PROPERTIES INC *p* 296
515 PENDER ST W SUITE 300, VANCOUVER, BC, V6B 6H5
(604) 669-5335 *SIC* 7011
ALLIED INTERNATIONAL CREDIT CORP *p* 753
16635 YONGE ST SUITE 26, NEWMARKET, ON, L3X 1V6
(905) 470-8181 *SIC* 4899
ALLIED INTERNATIONAL OF VANCOUVER *p* 209
See QUALITY MOVE MANAGEMENT INC
ALLIED LUMBERLAND LTD *p* 1410
240 5TH AVE NW, MOOSE JAW, SK, S6H 4R3
(306) 694-4000 *SIC* 5211
ALLIED PLASTIC GROUP OF COMPANIES LTD *p* 794
707 ARROW RD, NORTH YORK, ON, M9M 2L4
(416) 749-7070 *SIC* 5162
ALLIED PROJECTS LTD *p* 33
7017 FARRELL RD SE, CALGARY, AB, T2H 0T3
(403) 543-4530 *SIC* 1731
ALLIED PROPERTIES REAL ESTATE INVESTMENT TRUST *p* 978
134 PETER ST SUITE 1700, TORONTO, ON, M5V 2H2
(416) 977-9002 *SIC* 6798
ALLIED SHIPBUILDERS LTD *p* 238
1870 HARBOUR RD, NORTH VANCOUVER, BC, V7H 1A1
(604) 929-2365 *SIC* 3731
ALLIED SYSTEMS (CANADA) COMPANY *p* 498
2000 WILLIAMS PKY, BRAMPTON, ON, L6S 6B3
(905) 458-0900 *SIC* 4213
ALLIED SYSTEMS (CANADA) COMPANY *p* 662
6151 COLONEL TALBOT RD, LONDON, ON, N6P 1J2
SIC 4213
ALLIED SYSTEMS (CANADA) COMPANY *p* 1019
1790 PROVINCIAL RD, WINDSOR, ON, N8W 5W3
SIC 4213
ALLIED SYSTEMS (CANADA) COMPANY *p* 1083
5901 AV WESTMINSTER, COTE SAINT-LUC, QC, H4W 2J9
SIC 4213
ALLIED TECHNICAL SALES INC *p* 913
885 MILNER AVE, TORONTO, ON, M1B 5V8
(416) 282-1010 *SIC* 8712
ALLIED TEXTILES & REFUSE INC *p* 1223
3700 RUE SAINT-PATRICK BUREAU 200, MONTREAL, QC, H4E 1A2
(514) 932-5962 *SIC* 5093

ALLIED TRACK SERVICES INC *p* 599
169A SOUTH SERVICE RD, GRIMSBY, ON, L3M 4H6
(905) 769-1317 *SIC* 1629
ALLIED VISION TECHNOLOGIES CANADA INC *p* 187
4621 CANADA WAY SUITE 300, BURNABY, BC, V5G 4X8
(604) 875-8855 *SIC* 3861
ALLIED WORLD SPECIALTY INSURANCE COMPANY *p* 948
200 KING ST W SUITE 1600, TORONTO, ON, M5H 3T4
(647) 558-1120 *SIC* 6331
ALLIED-HALO INDUSTRIES INC *p* 870
345 NANTUCKET BLVD, SCARBOROUGH, ON, M1P 2P2
(416) 751-2042 *SIC* 2673
ALLMAR INC *p* 368
287 RIVERTON AVE, WINNIPEG, MB, R2L 0N2
(204) 668-1000 *SIC* 5039
ALLMAR INTERNATIONAL *p* 368
See ALLMAR INC
ALLNORTH CONSULTANTS LIMITED*p* 248
2011 PRINCE GEORGE PULPMILL RD, PRINCE GEORGE, BC, V2K 5P5
(250) 614-7291 *SIC* 8748
ALLO PROF *p* 1173
1000 RUE FULLUM, MONTREAL, QC, H2K 3L7
(514) 509-2025 *SIC* 8732
ALLOY CASTING INDUSTRIES LIMITED *p* 752
374 HAMILTON RD UNIT 1, NEW HAMBURG, ON, N3A 2K2
(519) 662-3111 *SIC* 3325
ALLOY FAB *p* 858
See ALLIANCE FABRICATING LTD
ALLOYCORP MINING INC *p* 941
67 YONGE ST SUITE 501, TORONTO, ON, M5E 1J8
(416) 847-0376 *SIC* 1061
ALLSCO WINDOWS AND DOORS *p* 408
See ATIS LP
ALLSCRIPTS CANADA CORPORATION *p* 253
13888 WIRELESS WAY SUITE 110, RICHMOND, BC, V6V 0A3
(604) 273-4900 *SIC* 7372
ALLSEAS FISHERIES INC *p* 573
55 VANSCO RD, ETOBICOKE, ON, M8Z 5Z8
(416) 255-3474 *SIC* 5146
ALLSEATING CORPORATION *p* 729
5800 AVEBURY RD UNIT 3, MISSISSAUGA, ON, L5R 3M3
(905) 502-7200 *SIC* 2522
ALLSTAR CONSTRUCTION LTD *p* 99
11130 199 ST, EDMONTON, AB, T5S 2C6
(780) 452-6330 *SIC* 8742
ALLSTAR RV *p* 162
See LAZY DAYS RV CENTRE INC
ALLSTATE INSURANCE COMPANY OF CANADA *p* 666
27 ALLSTATE PKY SUITE 100, MARKHAM, ON, L3R 5P8
(905) 477-6900 *SIC* 6331
ALLSTATE INSURANCE COMPANY OF CANADA *p* 1278
1150 AUT DUPLESSIS UNIT 600, QUEBEC, QC, G2G 2B5
(819) 569-5911 *SIC* 6411
ALLSTATE LIFE INSURANCE COMPANY OF CANADA *p* 666
27 ALLSTATE PKY SUITE 100, MARKHAM, ON, L3R 5P8
(905) 477-6900 *SIC* 6722
ALLSTONE QUARRY PRODUCTS INC *p* 879
16105 HIGHWAY 27 RR 1, SCHOMBERG, ON, L0G 1T0
(905) 939-8491 *SIC* 5032
ALLSTREAM *p* 985

See ZAYO CANADA INC
ALLSTREAM BUSINESS INC *p* 346
517 18TH ST, BRANDON, MB, R7A 5Y9
(204) 225-5687 *SIC* 4899
ALLSTREAM BUSINESS INC *p* 666
7550 BIRCHMOUNT RD, MARKHAM, ON, L3R 6C6
(905) 513-4600 *SIC* 1731
ALLSTREAM BUSINESS INC *p* 691
5160 ORBITOR DR, MISSISSAUGA, ON, L4W 5H2
(888) 288-2273 *SIC* 4899
ALLTECH CANADA INC *p* 601
20 CUTTEN PL, GUELPH, ON, N1G 4Z7
(519) 763-3331 *SIC* 5191
ALLTECH, DIV OF *p* 657
See MASTERFEEDS INC
ALLTECK LINE CONTRACTORS INC *p* 184
4333 STILL CREEK DR SUITE 300, BURNABY, BC, V5C 6S6
(604) 857-6600 *SIC* 1623
ALLTEMP PRODUCTS COMPANY LIMITED *p* 844
827 BROCK RD, PICKERING, ON, L1W 3J2
(905) 831-3311 *SIC* 5075
ALLTERRA CONSTRUCTION LTD *p* 340
2158 MILLSTREAM RD, VICTORIA, BC, V9B 6H4
(250) 658-3772 *SIC* 1794
ALLTRADE INDUSTRIAL CONTRACTORS INC *p* 532
1477 BISHOP ST N, CAMBRIDGE, ON, N1R 7J4
(519) 740-1090 *SIC* 1731
ALLUMINEK *p* 1360
See GROUPE APTAS INC
ALLWEST ELECTRIC LTD *p* 245
55 FREMONT ST, PORT COQUITLAM, BC, V3B 0M3
(604) 464-6200 *SIC* 1731
ALLWEST FURNISHINGS LTD *p* 95
14325 112 AVE NW, EDMONTON, AB, T5M 2V3
(780) 452-8212 *SIC* 5021
ALLWEST INSURANCE SERVICES LTD *p* 320
2-1855 BURRARD ST, VANCOUVER, BC, V6J 3G9
(604) 736-1969 *SIC* 6411
ALLWOOD CARPENTRY MANUFACTURING *p* 573
See ALLWOOD INDUSTRIES LTD
ALLWOOD INDUSTRIES LTD *p* 573
33 ATOMIC AVE UNIT 1, ETOBICOKE, ON, M8Z 5K8
(416) 398-1460 *SIC* 2431
ALMA FORD INC *p* 1044
1570 AV DU PONT S, ALMA, QC, G8B 6N1
(418) 662-6695 *SIC* 5511
ALMA HONDA *p* 1044
See 9075-5125 QUEBEC INC
ALMA MATER SOCIETY OF QUEEN'S UNIVERSITY INCORPORATED *p* 630
99 UNIVERSITY AVE, KINGSTON, ON, K7L 3N5
(613) 533-2725 *SIC* 8742
ALMAG ALUMINUM INC *p* 501
22 FINLEY RD, BRAMPTON, ON, L6T 1A9
(905) 457-9000 *SIC* 3354
ALMETCO BUILDING PRODUCTS LTD *p* 205
620 AUDLEY BLVD, DELTA, BC, V3M 5P2
SIC 3442
ALMIQ CONTRACTING LTD *p* 472
1340 ULU LANE, IQALUIT, NU, X0A 0H0
(867) 975-2225 *SIC* 1521
ALMITA PILING INC *p* 125
1603 91 ST SW SUITE 200, EDMONTON, AB, T6X 0W8
(800) 363-4868 *SIC* 3312
ALMON ENVIRONMENTAL LTD *p* 582
45 RACINE RD, ETOBICOKE, ON, M9W

2Z4
(416) 743-1364 *SIC* 1611
ALMON EQUIPMENT LTD *p* 582
45 RACINE RD, ETOBICOKE, ON, M9W 2Z4
(416) 743-1771 *SIC* 1611
ALMONTE GENERAL HOSPITAL *p* 477
75 SPRING ST SS 1, ALMONTE, ON, K0A 1A0
(613) 256-2500 *SIC* 8062
ALMONTE GENERAL HOSPITAL *p* 540
37 NEELIN ST, CARLETON PLACE, ON, K7C 2J6
(613) 205-1021 *SIC* 4119
ALMONTY INDUSTRIES INC *p* 985
100 KING ST W SUITE 5700, TORONTO, ON, M5X 1C7
(647) 438-9766 *SIC* 1061
ALO CANADA INC *p* 760
8485 MONTROSE RD, NIAGARA FALLS, ON, L2H 3L7
(800) 361-7563 *SIC* 5082
ALOUETTE BUS LINES LTD *p* 898
194 FRONT ST SUITE FRONT, STURGEON FALLS, ON, P2B 2J3
(705) 753-3911 *SIC* 4151
ALPA EQUIPMENT *p* 394
See ALPA EQUIPMENT COMPANY LIMITED
ALPA EQUIPMENT COMPANY LIMITED *p* 394
258 DRAPEAU ST, BALMORAL, NB, E8E 1H3
(506) 826-2717 *SIC* 5082
ALPA LUMBER INC *p* 685
7630 AIRPORT RD, MISSISSAUGA, ON, L4T 4G6
(905) 612-1222 *SIC* 5031
ALPA ROOF TRUSSES *p* 664
See ALPA ROOF TRUSSES INC
ALPA ROOF TRUSSES *p* 894
See ALPA ROOF TRUSSES INC
ALPA ROOF TRUSSES INC *p* 664
10311 KEELE ST, MAPLE, ON, L6A 3Y9
(905) 832-2250 *SIC* 2439
ALPA ROOF TRUSSES INC *p* 894
5532 SLATERS RD, STOUFFVILLE, ON, L4A 2G7
(905) 713-6616 *SIC* 2439
ALPA STAIRS & RAILINGS INC. *p* 687
3770 NASHUA DR UNIT 3, MISSISSAUGA, ON, L4V 1M5
(905) 694-9556 *SIC* 2431
ALPATECH VINYL INC *p* 498
100 EXCHANGE DR, BRAMPTON, ON, L6S 0C8
(905) 678-4695 *SIC* 5162
ALPEN HOUSE ULC, THE *p* 480
14875 BAYVIEW AVE, AURORA, ON, L4G 0K8
(905) 841-0336 *SIC* 0272
ALPER, SEYMOUR INC *p* 1156
5520 RUE PARE BUREAU 1, MONT-ROYAL, QC, H4P 2M1
(514) 737-3434 *SIC* 6411
ALPHA BETTER LANDSCAPING LTD *p* 70
11800 40 ST SE, CALGARY, AB, T2Z 4T1
(403) 248-3559 *SIC* 0782
ALPHA COMMODITIES CORP *p* 691
5750 TIMBERLEA BLVD UNIT 17, MISSISSAUGA, ON, L4W 5G9
(416) 907-5505 *SIC* 5153
ALPHA COMPAGNIE D'ASSURANCE INC, L' *p* 1097
430 RUE SAINT-GEORGES UNITE 119, DRUMMONDVILLE, QC, J2C 4H4
(819) 474-7958 *SIC* 6411
ALPHA FIELD PRODUCTS CO *p* 691
See ALPHA COMMODITIES CORP
ALPHA OIL INC *p* 792
490 GARYRAY DR, NORTH YORK, ON, M9L 1P8
(416) 745-6131 *SIC* 5983
ALPHA PLANTES *p* 1212

See SERVICE D'ENTRETIEN DES PLANTES ALPHA INC

ALPHA POLY CORPORATION p 501
296 WALKER DR, BRAMPTON, ON, L6T 4B3
(905) 789-6770 *SIC* 2673

ALPHA PRO TECH p 666
See ALPHA PRO TECH, LTD

ALPHA PRO TECH, LTD p 666
60 CENTURIAN DR SUITE 112, MARKHAM, ON, L3R 9R2
(800) 749-1363 *SIC* 3842

ALPHA SECONDARY SCHOOL p 184
See BURNABY SCHOOL BOARD DISTRICT 41

ALPHA SPORTSWEAR LIMITED p 288
112 6TH AVE E, VANCOUVER, BC, V5T 1J5
(604) 873-2621 *SIC* 5137

ALPHA TECHNOLOGIES LTD p 191
7700 RIVERFRONT GATE, BURNABY, BC, V5J 5M4
(604) 436-5900 *SIC* 3669

ALPHA TRADING SYSTEMS INC p 959
70 YORK ST SUITE 1501, TORONTO, ON, M5J 1S9
(416) 563-5896 *SIC* 8742

ALPHACASTING INC p 1325
391 AV SAINTE-CROIX, SAINT-LAURENT, QC, H4N 2L3
(514) 748-7511 *SIC* 3324

ALPHAPRO MANAGEMENT INC p 941
26 WELLINGTON ST E SUITE 700, TORONTO, ON, M5E 1S2
(416) 933-5745 *SIC* 6722

ALPHORA RESEARCH INC p 714
2395 SPEAKMAN DR SUITE 2001, MISSISSAUGA, ON, L5K 1B3
(905) 403-0477 *SIC* 8731

ALPHORA RESEARCH INC p 796
2884 PORTLAND DR, OAKVILLE, ON, L6H 5W8
(905) 829-9704 *SIC* 8731

ALPINE AEROTECH LIMITED PARTNERSHIP p 341
1260 INDUSTRIAL RD, WEST KELOWNA, BC, V1Z 1G5
(250) 769-6344 *SIC* 4581

ALPINE CANADA ALPIN p 72
151 CANADA OLYMPIC RD SW SUITE 302, CALGARY, AB, T3B 6B7
(403) 777-3200 *SIC* 8699

ALPINE DISPOSAL & RECYCLING p 340
See EVERGREEN INDUSTRIES LTD

ALPINE ELECTRIC LTD p 342
1085 MILLAR CREEK RD SUITE 3, WHISTLER, BC, V0N 1B1
SIC 1731

ALPINE HEATING LTD p 99
10333 174 ST NW, EDMONTON, AB, T5S 1H1
(780) 469-0491 *SIC* 1711

ALPINE HELICOPTERS INC p 341
1295 INDUSTRIAL RD, WEST KELOWNA, BC, V1Z 1G4
(250) 769-4111 *SIC* 4522

ALPINE INSURANCE & FINANCIAL INC p 39
8820 BLACKFOOT TRAIL SE SUITE 123, CALGARY, AB, T2J 3J1
(403) 270-8822 *SIC* 6411

ALPINE INT'L TRANSPORTATION INC p 482
480 WAYDOM DR, AYR, ON, N0B 1E0
(519) 624-6776 *SIC* 4731

ALPNET CANADA p 1208
See SDL INTERNATIONAL (CANADA) INC

ALROS PRODUCTS LIMITED p 782
350 WILDCAT RD, NORTH YORK, ON, M3J 2N5
(416) 661-1750 *SIC* 3081

ALS CANADA LTD p 181
8081 LOUGHEED HWY SUITE 100, BURN-ABY, BC, V5A 1W9
(778) 370-3150 *SIC* 8071

ALS CANADA LTD p 238
2103 DOLLARTON HWY, NORTH VANCOUVER, BC, V7H 0A7
(604) 984-0221 *SIC* 8734

ALS ENVIRONMENTAL p 181
See ALS CANADA LTD

ALS GROUP p 238
See ALS CANADA LTD

ALSAFA FOODS CANADA LIMITED p 704
57 VILLAGE CENTRE PL SUITE 302, MISSISSAUGA, ON, L4Z 1V9
(800) 268-8174 *SIC* 5142

ALSCO CANADA CORPORATION p 92
14630 123 AVE NW, EDMONTON, AB, T5L 2Y4
(780) 452-5955 *SIC* 7213

ALSCO CANADA CORPORATION p 92
14710 123 AVE NW, EDMONTON, AB, T5L 2Y4
(780) 454-9641 *SIC* 7211

ALSCO CANADA CORPORATION p 291
5 4TH AVE W, VANCOUVER, BC, V5Y 1G2
(604) 876-3272 *SIC* 7213

ALSCO CANADA CORPORATION p 1130
2500 RUE SENKUS, LASALLE, QC, H8N 2X9
(514) 595-7381 *SIC* 7218

ALSCO UNIFORM & LINEN SERVICE p 291
See ALSCO CANADA CORPORATION

ALSCO UNIFORM & LINEN SERVICES p 92
See ALSCO CANADA CORPORATION

ALSCOTT AIR SYSTEMS LIMITED p 663
1127 RIVER RD, MANOTICK, ON, K4M 1B4
(613) 692-9517 *SIC* 1711

ALSIP'S INDUSTRIAL PRODUCTS LTD p 368
1 COLE AVE, WINNIPEG, MB, R2L 1J3
(204) 667-3330 *SIC* 5039

ALSTAR OILFIELD CONTRACTORS LTD p 136
310 RIVER RD E, HINTON, AB, T7V 1X5
(780) 865-5938 *SIC* 1389

ALSTOM p 1191
See ALSTOM TRANSPORT CANADA INC

ALSTOM CANADA INC p 13
7550 OGDEN DALE RD SE SUITE 200, CALGARY, AB, T2C 4X9
SIC 4789

ALSTOM CANADA INC p 595
1430 BLAIR PL SUITE 600, GLOUCESTER, ON, K1J 9N2
(613) 747-5222 *SIC* 7699

ALSTOM CANADA INC p 1191
1050 COTE DU BEAVER HALL, MONTREAL, QC, H2Z 0A5
(514) 333-0888 *SIC* 7311

ALSTOM CANADA INC p 1193
1010 RUE SHERBROOKE O BUREAU 2320, MONTREAL, QC, H3A 2R7
(514) 281-6200 *SIC* 3511

ALSTOM CANADA INC p 1377
1350 CH SAINT-ROCH, SOREL-TRACY, QC, J3R 5P9
(450) 746-6500 *SIC* 4911

ALSTOM RESEAU CANADA p 1123
See RESEAU SOLUTIONS CANADA ULC

ALSTOM TELECITE MONTREAL p 1191
See ALSTOM CANADA INC

ALSTOM TRANSPORT CANADA INC p 1191
1050 COTE DU BEAVER HALL BUREAU 1840, MONTREAL, QC, H2Z 0A4
(514) 333-0888 *SIC* 3743

ALSTOM TRANSPORT, DIV OF p 13
See ALSTOM CANADA INC

ALTA - OCI CONSTRUCTION p 1225
See ALTA CONSTRUCTION (2011) LTEE

ALTA CONSTRUCTION (2011) LTEE p 1225
1655 RUE DE BEAUHARNOIS O, MONTREAL, QC, H4N 1J6
(514) 748-8881 *SIC* 1611

ALTA E-SOLUTIONS p 737
1145 WESTPORT CRES, MISSISSAUGA, ON, L5T 1E8
(905) 564-5539 *SIC* 5045

ALTA GENETICS INC p 160
263090 RGE RD 11, ROCKY VIEW COUNTY, AB, T4B 2T3
(403) 226-0666 *SIC* 5159

ALTA INFINITI p 1029
See 1428309 ONTARIO LTD

ALTA MODA TM p 1325
See CIE D'IMPORTATION DE NOUVEAUTES STEIN INC, LA

ALTA NISSAN p 1031
See ISLINGTON MOTOR SALES LIMITED

ALTA PRAIRIE RAILWAY EXCURSION p 167
See ALBERTA PRAIRIE STEAM TOURS LTD

ALTA PRECISION INC p 1047
11120 RUE COLBERT, ANJOU, QC, H1J 2X4
(514) 353-0919 *SIC* 3599

ALTA PRO ELECTRIC LTD p 92
13415 149 ST NW, EDMONTON, AB, T5L 2T3
(780) 444-6510 *SIC* 1731

ALTA PROCESSING CO p 13
7030 OGDEN DALE PL SE, CALGARY, AB, T2C 2A3
(403) 279-4441 *SIC* 2077

ALTA STEEL p 110
See MOLY-COP ALTASTEEL LTD

ALTA TELECOM p 112
See ATI TELECOM INTERNATIONAL, COMPANY

ALTA WEST INDUSTRIES p 136
141 HAMPSHIRE RD, HINTON, AB, T7V 1G8
(780) 865-2930 *SIC* 5085

ALTA-FAB STRUCTURES p 148
See 347678 ALBERTA LTD

ALTA-FAB STRUCTURES LTD p 148
1205 5 ST, NISKU, AB, T9E 7L6
(780) 955-7733 *SIC* 2452

ALTACORP CAPITAL INC p 43
585 8 AVE SW UNIT 410, CALGARY, AB, T2P 1G1
(403) 539-8600 *SIC* 6282

ALTADORE QUALITY HOTEL & SUITES p 1036
See 552653 ONTARIO INC

ALTAGAS EXTRACTION AND TRANSMISSION LIMITED PARTNERSHIP p 43
355 4 AVE SW UNIT 1700, CALGARY, AB, T2P 0J1
(403) 691-7575 *SIC* 4923

ALTAGAS LPG LIMITED PARTNERSHIP p 43
355 4 AVE SW SUITE 1700, CALGARY, AB, T2P 0J1
(403) 691-7196 *SIC* 4924

ALTAGAS LTD p 43
355 4 AVE SW SUITE 1700, CALGARY, AB, T2P 0J1
(403) 691-7575 *SIC* 1311

ALTAGAS NORTHWEST PROCESSING LIMITED PARTNERSHIP p 43
55 4 AVE SW SUITE 1700, CALGARY, AB, T2P 0J1
(403) 691-7196 *SIC* 4924

ALTAGAS UTILITIES INC p 139
5509 45 ST, LEDUC, AB, T9E 6T6
(780) 986-5215 *SIC* 4923

ALTALINK MANAGEMENT LTD p 10
2611 3 AVE SE, CALGARY, AB, T2A 7W7
(403) 267-3400 *SIC* 4911

ALTALINK, L.P. p 10
2611 3 AVE SE, CALGARY, AB, T2A 7W7
(403) 267-3400 *SIC* 4911

ALTANIRA SECURITIES p 1201
See BANQUE NATIONALE DU CANADA

ALTAS PARTNERS p 968
See AP FOUNDERS LP

ALTASCIENCES COMPAGNIE INC p 1155
1200 AV BEAUMONT, MONT-ROYAL, QC, H3P 3P1
(514) 858-6077 *SIC* 8731

ALTASCIENCES COMPAGNIE INC p 1241
575 BOUL ARMAND-FRAPPIER, MONTREAL-OUEST, QC, H7V 4B3
(450) 973-6077 *SIC* 8731

ALTAVERO HAIRCARE LTD p 20
1144 29 AVE NE SUITE 110W, CALGARY, AB, T2E 7P1
(403) 266-4595 *SIC* 7231

ALTE-REGO CORPORATION p 582
36 TIDEMORE AVE, ETOBICOKE, ON, M9W 5H4
(416) 740-3397 *SIC* 2821

ALTEC INDUSTRIES LTD p 682
831 NIPISSING RD, MILTON, ON, L9T 4Z4
(905) 875-2000 *SIC* 5084

ALTEL INC p 1233
3150 BOUL LE CORBUSIER, MONTREAL, QC, H7L 4S8
(450) 682-9788 *SIC* 5999

ALTER NRG CORP p 63
227 11 AVE SW SUITE 460, CALGARY, AB, T2R 1R9
(403) 806-3875 *SIC* 8731

ALTERNA SAVINGS p 582
165 ATTWELL DR, ETOBICOKE, ON, M9W 5Y5
(416) 213-7900 *SIC* 6062

ALTERNA SAVINGS p 828
See ALTERNA SAVINGS AND CREDIT UNION LIMITED

ALTERNA SAVINGS AND CREDIT UNION LIMITED p 828
319 MCRAE AVE, OTTAWA, ON, K1Z 0B9
(613) 560-0150 *SIC* 6062

ALTERNATE CHOICE INC p 527
3325 NORTH SERVICE RD UNIT 1, BURLINGTON, ON, L7N 3G2
(905) 336-8818 *SIC* 5021

ALTERNATE CHOICING p 527
See ALTERNATE CHOICE INC

ALTERNATE HEALTH CORP. p 319
1485 6TH AVE W SUITE 309, VANCOUVER, BC, V6H 4G1
(604) 569-4969 *SIC* 7372

ALTERNATIVE BEAUTY SERVICES LTD p 737
1680 COURTNEYPARK DR E UNIT 9, MISSISSAUGA, ON, L5T 1R4
(905) 670-0611 *SIC* 5087

ALTERNATIVE BENEFIT SOLUTIONS INC p 486
556 BRYNE DR UNIT 19 & 20, BARRIE, ON, L4N 9P6
(705) 726-6100 *SIC* 6324

ALTERNATIVE PROCESSING SYSTEMS INC p 790
60 WINGOLD AVE, NORTH YORK, ON, M6B 1P5
(416) 256-2010 *SIC* 4212

ALTERNATURE INC p 1169
9210 BOUL PIE-IX, MONTREAL, QC, H1Z 4H7
(514) 382-7520 *SIC* 7389

ALTEX ENERGY LTD p 43
700 9 AVE SW SUITE 1100, CALGARY, AB, T2P 3V4
(403) 508-7525 *SIC* 1389

ALTEX FIELD SERVICES p 108
See ALTEX INDUSTRIES INC

ALTEX INC p 1380
3530 BOUL DES ENTREPRISES, TERREBONNE, QC, J6X 4J8
(450) 968-0880 *SIC* 5023

ALTEX INDUSTRIES INC p 108
6831 42 ST NW, EDMONTON, AB, T6B 2X1
(780) 468-6862 *SIC* 3443

ALTHON INC p 666
140 SHIELDS CRT, MARKHAM, ON, L3R 9T5
(905) 513-1221 *SIC* 5045

ALTIMA CONTRACTING LTD   p 290
8029 FRASER ST, VANCOUVER, BC, V5X 3X5
(604) 327-5977   *SIC* 1742

ALTIMA DENTAL CANADA INC   p 788
1 YORKDALE RD SUITE 320, NORTH YORK, ON, M6A 3A1
(416) 785-1828   *SIC* 8741

ALTIMA DENTAL CENTRE   p 788
See ALTIMA DENTAL CANADA INC

ALTIMATE AUTOMOBILES   p 660
See HULLY GULLY AUTOMOBILES INC

ALTIMAX COURIER (2006) LIMITED   p 397
274 BOUL DIEPPE, DIEPPE, NB, E1A 6P8
(866) 258-4629   *SIC* 7389

ALTIMAX COURIER (2006) LIMITED   p 445
132 TRIDER CRES, DARTMOUTH, NS, B3B 1R6
(902) 460-6006   *SIC* 7389

ALTIUM PACKAGING CANADA INC   p 971
199 BAY ST SUITE 4000, TORONTO, ON, M5L 1A9
SIC 5199

ALTIUS EPICES ET ASSAISONNEMENTS INC   p 1052
19000 AUT TRANSCANADIENNE, BAIE D URFE, QC, H9X 3S4
(514) 457-2200   *SIC* 2099

ALTIUS MINERALS CORPORATION   p 429
38 DUFFY PL 2ND FL, ST. JOHN'S, NL, A1B 4M5
(709) 576-3440   *SIC* 1081

ALTO CONSTRUCTION LTD   p 1433
307 103RD ST E, SASKATOON, SK, S7N 1Y9
(306) 955-0554   *SIC* 1629

ALTO DESIGN INC   p 1168
2600 RUE WILLIAM-TREMBLAY BUREAU 220, MONTREAL, QC, H1Y 3J2
(514) 278-3050   *SIC* 7389

ALTON VILLAGE PUBLIC SCHOOL   p 526
See HALTON DISTRICT SCHOOL BOARD

ALTONE INVESTMENTS LIMITED   p 785
3625 DUFFERIN ST SUITE 503, NORTH YORK, ON, M3K 1N4
(416) 638-9902   *SIC* 6512

ALTROM AUTO GROUP LTD   p 182
4242 PHILLIPS AVE UNIT C, BURNABY, BC, V5A 2X2
(604) 294-2311   *SIC* 5015

ALTROM GROUP   p 182
See ALTROM AUTO GROUP LTD

ALTRUCK INTERNATIONAL TRUCK CENTRES, DIV OF   p 636
See KIRBY INTERNATIONAL TRUCKS LTD

ALTRUM   p 1348
See GESTION BC-A INC

ALTURA ENERGY INC   p 43
640 5 AVE SW SUITE 2500, CALGARY, AB, T2P 3G4
(403) 984-5197   *SIC* 1382

ALTUS ENERGY SERVICES LTD   p 43
222 3 AVE SW SUITE 740, CALGARY, AB, T2P 0B4
SIC 1389

ALTUS GEOMATICS LIMITED PARTNERSHIP   p 66
2020 4TH ST SW UNIT 310, CALGARY, AB, T2S 1W3
(403) 508-7770   *SIC* 8713

ALTUS GEOMATICS LIMITED PARTNERSHIP   p 99
17327 106A AVE NW, EDMONTON, AB, T5S 1M7
(780) 481-3399   *SIC* 8713

ALTUS GEOMATICS LIMITED PARTNERSHIP   p 941
33 YONGE ST SUITE 500, TORONTO, ON, M5E 1G4
(416) 641-9500   *SIC* 8713

ALTUS GROUP   p 66
See ALTUS GEOMATICS LIMITED PARTNERSHIP

ALTUS GROUP   p 99
See ALTUS GEOMATICS LIMITED PARTNERSHIP

ALTUS GROUP   p 941
See ALTUS GEOMATICS LIMITED PARTNERSHIP

ALTUS GROUP LIMITED   p 311
1055 WEST GEORGIA ST SUITE 2500, VANCOUVER, BC, V6E 0B6
(604) 683-5591   *SIC* 6722

ALTUS GROUP LIMITED   p 941
33 YONGE ST SUITE 500, TORONTO, ON, M5E 1G4
(416) 641-9500   *SIC* 6722

ALTUS GROUP LIMITED   p 1201
1100 BOUL RENE-LEVESQUE O BUREAU 1600, MONTREAL, QC, H3B 4N4
(514) 392-7700   *SIC* 6531

ALUFORME LTEE   p 1083
2000 RUE DE LIERRE, COTE SAINT-LUC, QC, H7G 4Y4
(450) 669-6690   *SIC* 3271

ALUM-TEK INDUSTRIES LTD   p 179
26221 30A AVE, ALDERGROVE, BC, V4W 2W6
SIC 3448

ALUMA SYSTEMS INC   p 127
GD LCD MAIN, FORT MCMURRAY, AB, T9H 3E2
(780) 790-4852   *SIC* 1799

ALUMA SYSTEMS INC   p 494
2 MANCHESTER CRT, BOLTON, ON, L7E 2J3
(905) 669-5282   *SIC* 7353

ALUMA-FENCE   p 1022
See GRECO ALUMINUM RAILINGS LTD

ALUMABRITE ANODIZING, DIV   p 608
See KROMET INTERNATIONAL INC

ALUMET MFG., INC   p 198
2660 BARNET HWY, COQUITLAM, BC, V3B 1B7
(604) 464-5451   *SIC* 5023

ALUMI-BUNK CORPORATION   p 566
5 KEPPEL ST, DUNDALK, ON, N0C 1B0
(800) 700-2865   *SIC* 3713

ALUMICO ARCHITECTURAL INC   p 1166
4343 RUE HOCHELAGA BUREAU 100, MONTREAL, QC, H1V 1C2
(514) 255-4343   *SIC* 5031

ALUMICO METAL & OXIDATION INC   p 1166
4343 RUE HOCHELAGA BUREAU 100, MONTREAL, QC, H1V 1C2
(514) 255-4343   *SIC* 3471

ALUMICOR INTERNATIONAL INC   p 582
290 HUMBERLINE DR, ETOBICOKE, ON, M9W 5S2
(416) 745-4222   *SIC* 3479

ALUMICOR LIMITED   p 582
290 HUMBERLINE DR SUITE 1, ETOBICOKE, ON, M9W 5S2
(416) 745-4222   *SIC* 3479

ALUMIER MD   p 782
See BEAUTYNEXT GROUP INC

ALUMINART ARCHITECTURAL   p 1049
See GESTION JUSTERO INC

ALUMINART PRODUCTS LIMITED   p 501
1 SUMMERLEA RD, BRAMPTON, ON, L6T 4V2
(905) 791-7521   *SIC* 3442

ALUMINERIE ALOUETTE INC   p 1367
400 CH DE LA POINTE-NOIRE, SEPT-ILES, QC, G4R 5M9
(418) 964-7000   *SIC* 3334

ALUMINERIE DE BAIE COMEAU   p 1052
See ALCOA CANADA CIE

ALUMINERIE DE BAIE-COMEAU   p 1090
See ALCOA CANADA CIE

ALUMINERIE DE BAIE-COMEAU   p 1201
See ALCOA CANADA CIE

ALUMINERIE DE BECANCOUR INC   p 1055
5555 RUE PIERRE-THIBAULT BUREAU 217, BECANCOUR, QC, G9H 2T7
(819) 294-6101   *SIC* 3463

ALUMINIUM ANDRE GAGNON INC   p 1347
1225 RANG DE LA RIVIERE N, SAINT-LIN-LAURENTIDES, QC, J5M 1Y7
(450) 439-3324   *SIC* 1629

ALUMINIUM B. BOUCHARD INC   p 1233
125 RUE DE LA POINTE-LANGLOIS, MONTREAL, QC, H7L 3J4
(450) 622-9543   *SIC* 1761

ALUMINIUM CARUSO & FILS INC   p 1239
5528 RUE DE CASTILLE, MONTREAL-NORD, QC, H1G 3E5
(514) 326-2274   *SIC* 3442

ALUMINIUM DUCHESNE   p 1403
See DUCHESNE ET FILS LTEE

ALUMINIUM J CLEMENT INC   p 1158
1535 117 RTE, MONT-TREMBLANT, QC, J8E 2X9
(819) 425-7122   *SIC* 1629

ALUMINIUM PIPE SYSTEMS   p 83
See SKOCDOPOLE CONSTRUCTION LTD

ALUMINUM ASSOCIATES   p 651
See HOMEWAY COMPANY LIMITED

ALUMINUM CURTAINWALL SYSTEMS INC   p 216
1820 KRYCZKA PL, KAMLOOPS, BC, V1S 1S4
(250) 372-3600   *SIC* 3449

ALUMINUM MOLD & PATTERN LTD   p 782
15 VANLEY CRES, NORTH YORK, ON, M3J 2B7
(416) 749-3000   *SIC* 3544

ALUMINUM WAREHOUSE   p 584
See EXTRUDE-A-TRIM INC

ALUMITECH ARCHITECTURAL GLASS & METAL LIMITED   p 440
10 BLUEWATER RD, BEDFORD, NS, B4B 1G9
(902) 832-1200   *SIC* 1799

ALUMNAE THEATRE COMPANY   p 932
70 BERKELEY ST, TORONTO, ON, M5A 2W6
(416) 364-4170   *SIC* 7922

ALVIN BUCKWOLD CHILD DEVELOPMENT PROGRAM   p 1433
See SASKATCHEWAN HEALTH AUTHORITY

ALVOPETRO ENERGY LTD   p 43
525 8 AVE SW SUITE 1700, CALGARY, AB, T2P 1G1
(587) 794-4224   *SIC* 1311

ALWAYS A DOLLAR PLUS   p 788
496 LAWRENCE AVE W, NORTH YORK, ON, M6A 1A1
(416) 785-8500   *SIC* 5411

ALWEATHER WINDOWS & DOORS LIMITED   p 445
27 TROOP AVE, DARTMOUTH, NS, B3B 2A7
(902) 468-2605   *SIC* 5211

ALYKHAN VELJI DESIGNS INC   p 20
217 4 ST NE, CALGARY, AB, T2E 3S1
(403) 617-2406   *SIC* 7389

ALYRIN OPERATIONS LTD   p 458
10 RAGGED LAKE BLVD SUITE 8, HALIFAX, NS, B3S 1C2
(902) 450-0056   *SIC* 5461

ALYSSA FOODS, DIV OF   p 461
See PUBNICO TRAWLERS LIMITED

ALZAC HOLDINGS LTD   p 99
18011 105 AVE NW, EDMONTON, AB, T5S 2E1
(780) 447-4303   *SIC* 7389

ALZHEIMER SOCIETY OF B.C.   p 292
828 8TH AVE W SUITE 300, VANCOUVER, BC, V5Z 1E2
(604) 681-6530   *SIC* 7389

ALZHEIMER SOCIETY OF CANADA   p 923
20 EGLINTON AVE W SUITE 1200, TORONTO, ON, M4R 1K8
(416) 488-8772   *SIC* 8399

AM INSPECTION LTD   p 1405
501 RAILWAY ST N, CABRI, SK, S0N 0J0
(306) 587-2620   *SIC* 7389

AM PM SERVICE   p 180
See 406106 ALBERTA INC

AM730   p 330
See CORUS ENTERTAINMENT INC

AMA NSG INC   p 719
6699 CAMPOBELLO RD, MISSISSAUGA, ON, L5N 2L7
(905) 826-3922   *SIC* 8748

AMA TRAVEL   p 118
See ALBERTA MOTOR ASSOCIATION TRAVEL AGENCY LTD

AMADA CANADA LTD   p 1110
885 RUE GEORGES-CROS, GRANBY, QC, J2J 1E8
(450) 378-0111   *SIC* 5084

AMAKO CONSTRUCTION LTD   p 241
1000 3RD ST W SUITE 300, NORTH VANCOUVER, BC, V7P 3J6
(604) 990-6766   *SIC* 1522

AMALGAMATED DAIRIES LIMITED   p 1042
79 WATER ST SUITE 1, SUMMERSIDE, PE, C1N 1A6
(902) 888-5088   *SIC* 2026

AMALGAME   p 1372
See CUISINE IDEALE INC

AMAN ENTERPRISES 1989 LTD   p 224
20255 102 AVE, LANGLEY, BC, V1M 4B4
(604) 513-0462   *SIC* 4213

AMARANTH HEALTH AND WELLNESS   p 74
See AMARANTH WHOLE FOODS MARKET INC

AMARANTH WHOLE FOODS MARKET INC   p 74
7 ARBOUR LAKE DR NW, CALGARY, AB, T3G 5G8
(403) 547-6333   *SIC* 5499

AMARO INC   p 1298
4061 GRAND RANG SAINTE-CATHERINE, SAINT-CUTHBERT, QC, J0K 2C0
(514) 593-5144   *SIC* 5149

AMAX HEALTH INC   p 883
27 SEAPARK DR UNIT 1, ST CATHARINES, ON, L2M 6S5
(905) 682-8070   *SIC* 5047

AMAYA   p 967
See STARS GROUP INC, THE

AMAZING KOBOTIC INDUSTRIES INC   p 704
5671 KENNEDY RD, MISSISSAUGA, ON, L4Z 3E1
(905) 712-1000   *SIC* 3444

AMAZING PERSONA, THE   p 431
See PERSONA COMMUNICATIONS INC

AMAZING PERSONA, THE   p 899
See PERSONA COMMUNICATIONS INC

AMAZON CANADA FULFILLMENT SERVICES INC   p 719
6363 MILLCREEK DR, MISSISSAUGA, ON, L5N 1L8
(289) 998-0300   *SIC* 5192

AMBASSADOR BUILDING MAINTENANCE LIMITED   p 1022
628 MONMOUTH RD, WINDSOR, ON, N8Y 3L1
(519) 255-1107   *SIC* 7349

AMBASSADOR MECHANICAL L.P.   p 353
400 FORT WHYTE WAY UNIT 110, OAK BLUFF, MB, R4G 0B1
(204) 231-1094   *SIC* 1711

AMBASSADOR SALES (SOUTHERN) LTD   p 13
4110 76 AVE SE, CALGARY, AB, T2C 2J2
(403) 720-2012   *SIC* 5211

AMBASSATOURS GRAY LINE   p 454
See ATLANTIC AMBASSATOURS LIMITED

AMBASSATOURS GRAYLINE   p 454
See AMBASSATOURS LIMITED

AMBASSATOURS LIMITED   p 454
6575 BAYNE ST, HALIFAX, NS, B3K 0H1

(902) 423-6242   SIC 4725
AMBICO LIMITED p 595
1120 CUMMINGS AVE, GLOUCESTER, ON, K1J 7R8
(613) 746-4663   SIC 3442
AMBROSE p 75
See AMBROSE UNIVERSITY COLLEGE
AMBROSE UNIVERSITY COLLEGE p 75
150 AMBROSE CIR SW, CALGARY, AB, T3H 0L5
(403) 410-2000   SIC 8221
AMBULANCE CHICOUTIMI INC p 1080
784 BOUL BARRETTE, CHICOUTIMI, QC, G7J 3Z7
(418) 543-5045   SIC 4119
AMBULANCE NEW BRUNSWICK INC p 406
210 JOHN ST SUITE 101, MONCTON, NB, E1C 0B8
(506) 872-6500   SIC 4119
AMBULANCE SLN p 1080
See AMBULANCE CHICOUTIMI INC
AMBULANCES DE LA GATINEAU, LES p 1103
See COOPERATIVE DES PARAMEDICS DE L'OUTAOUAIS
AMBULANCES SAINT HYACINTHE p 1312
See DESSERCOM INC
AMBURG LIMITED p 747
13 INDUSTRIAL BLVD, NAPANEE, ON, K7R 1M7
(613) 354-4371   SIC 5399
AMBYINT INC p 20
1440 AVIATION PK NE SUITE 119, CALGARY, AB, T2E 7E2
(800) 205-1311   SIC 5084
AMC FORM TECHNOLOGIES p 351
35 HEADINGLEY ST, HEADINGLEY, MB, R4H 0A8
(204) 633-8800   SIC 5211
AMCA SALES LIMITED p 445
1000 WINDMILL RD SUITE 22, DARTMOUTH, NS, B3B 1L7
(902) 468-1501   SIC 5141
AMCAN-JUMAX INC p 1307
3300 2E RUE, SAINT-HUBERT, QC, J3Y 8Y7
(450) 445-8888   SIC 5085
AMCO FARMS INC p 644
523 WILKINSON DR, LEAMINGTON, ON, N8H 1A6
(519) 326-9095   SIC 0191
AMCO PRODUCE INC p 644
523 WILKINSON DR, LEAMINGTON, ON, N8H 3V5
(519) 326-9095   SIC 5148
AMCO WHOLESALE p 249
See NORTHERN HARDWARE & FURNITURE CO., LTD
AMCOR CANADA p 1127
See AMCOR PACKAGING CANADA, INC
AMCOR PACKAGING CANADA, INC p 508
95 BISCAYNE CRES, BRAMPTON, ON, L6W 4R2
(905) 450-5579   SIC 2657
AMCOR PACKAGING CANADA, INC p 1127
2150 RUE ONESIME-GAGNON, LACHINE, QC, H8T 3M8
SIC 2657
AMCOR RIGID PLASTICS - BRAMPTON p 508
See AMCOR RIGID PLASTICS ATLANTIC, INC
AMCOR RIGID PLASTICS ATLANTIC, INC p 508
95 BISCAYNE CRES, BRAMPTON, ON, L6W 4R2
(905) 450-5579   SIC 3089
AMD MEDICOM INC p 1248
2555 CH DE L'AVIATION, POINTE-CLAIRE, QC, H9P 2Z2
(514) 633-1111   SIC 3842
AMDIL NORTH AMERICA p 704
See AMHIL ENTERPRISES
AMDOCS CANADIAN MANAGED SER-

VICES INC p 691
1705 TECH AVE UNIT 2, MISSISSAUGA, ON, L4W 0A2
(905) 614-4000   SIC 8742
AMDOCS CANADIAN MANAGED SERVICES INC p 1332
2351 BOUL ALFRED-NOBEL BUREAU 200, SAINT-LAURENT, QC, H4S 0B2
(514) 338-3100   SIC 7371
AMEC p 944
See AMEC FOSTER WHEELER NCL LIMITED
AMEC BDR LIMITED p 43
401 9 AVE SW SUITE 1300, CALGARY, AB, T2P 3C5
(403) 283-0060   SIC 8711
AMEC BLACK & MCDONALD LIMITED p 445
11 FRAZEE AVE, DARTMOUTH, NS, B3B 1Z4
(902) 474-3700   SIC 1731
AMEC CONSTRUCTION INC p 1121
312 RUE JOSEPH-GAGNE S, LA BAIE, QC, G7B 3P6
(418) 544-8885   SIC 1542
AMEC EARTH & ENVIRONMENTAL DIV OF p 1095
See WOOD CANADA LIMITED
AMEC EARTH & ENVIRONMENTAL, DIV OF p 187
See WOOD CANADA LIMITED
AMEC EARTH & ENVIRONMENTAL, DIV OF p 799
See WOOD CANADA LIMITED
AMEC EARTH & ENVIRONMENTAL, DIV OF p 873
See WOOD CANADA LIMITED
AMEC EARTH & EVIRONMENTAL DIVISION p 301
See WOOD CANADA LIMITED
AMEC EC SERVICES p 796
See AMEC FOSTER WHEELER INC
AMEC ENGINEERING p 43
See AMEC FOSTER WHEELER INC
AMEC ENVIRONMENT & INFRASTRUCTURE, DIV OF p 111
See WOOD CANADA LIMITED
AMEC FOSTER WHEELER p 528
See WOOD CANADA LIMITED
AMEC FOSTER WHEELER INC p 43
801 6 AVE SW SUITE 900, CALGARY, AB, T2P 3W3
(403) 298-4170   SIC 6712
AMEC FOSTER WHEELER INC p 429
133 CROSBIE RD, ST. JOHN'S, NL, A1B 1H3
(709) 724-1900   SIC 7373
AMEC FOSTER WHEELER INC p 796
2020 WINSTON PARK DR SUITE 700, OAKVILLE, ON, L6H 6X7
(905) 829-5400   SIC 8711
AMEC FOSTER WHEELER INC p 796
2020 WINSTON PARK DR SUITE 700, OAKVILLE, ON, L6H 6X7
(905) 829-5400   SIC 6719
AMEC FOSTER WHEELER NCL LIMITED p 944
700 UNIVERSITY AVE SUITE 200, TORONTO, ON, M5G 1X6
(416) 592-2102   SIC 8999
AMEC USINAGE INC p 1292
110 RUE DES GRANDS-LACS, SAINT-AUGUSTIN-DE-DESMAURES, QC, G3A 2K1
(418) 878-4133   SIC 3599
AMECO SERVICES INC p 139
6909 42 ST UNIT 101, LEDUC, AB, T9E 0W1
(780) 440-6633   SIC 7353
AMELCO ELECTRIC (CALGARY) LTD p 20
2230 22 ST NE, CALGARY, AB, T2E 8B7

(403) 250-1270   SIC 1731
AMENAGEMENT GRANRIVE INC p 1193
600 BOUL DE MAISONNEUVE O BUREAU 2600, MONTREAL, QC, H3A 3J2
(514) 499-8300   SIC 6531
AMENAGEMENTS RICHARD LTEE, LES p 1108
110 RUE COURT, GRANBY, QC, J2G 4Y9
(450) 372-3019   SIC 6719
AMER SPORTS CANADA INC p 187
4250 MANOR ST, BURNABY, BC, V5G 1B2
(604) 454-9900   SIC 3949
AMER SPORTS CANADA INC p 238
2220 DOLLARTON HWY UNIT 110, NORTH VANCOUVER, BC, V7H 1A8
(604) 960-3001   SIC 5091
AMER SPORTS CANADA INC p 286
2770 BENTALL ST, VANCOUVER, BC, V5M 4H4
(604) 960-3001   SIC 3949
AMERICAN & EFIRD p 1047
See AMERICAN & EFIRD CANADA INCORPOREE
AMERESCO CANADA INC p 850
30 LEEK CRES SUITE 301, RICHMOND HILL, ON, L4B 4N4
(888) 483-7627   SIC 3825
AMERICA ONLINE CANADA INC p 406
11 OCEAN LIMITED WAY, MONCTON, NB, E1C 0H1
SIC 4899
AMERICA ONLINE CANADA INC p 978
99 SPADINA AVE SUITE 200, TORONTO, ON, M5V 3P8
(416) 263-8100   SIC 7319
AMERICAN & EFIRD CANADA INCORPOREE p 1047
8301 BOUL RAY-LAWSON, ANJOU, QC, H1J 1X9
(514) 352-4800   SIC 2284
AMERICAN BUS PRODUCTS p 568
See LEEDS TRANSIT INC
AMERICAN CUMO MINING CORPORATION p 292
638 MILLBANK RD, VANCOUVER, BC, V5Z 4B7
(604) 689-7902   SIC 1044
AMERICAN CUSTOM ROTOMOLDING p 364
See ACR CANADA CORPORATION
AMERICAN EAGLE OUTFITTERS CANADA CORPORATION p 744
450 COURTNEYPARK DR W, MISSISSAUGA, ON, L5W 1Y6
(289) 562-8000   SIC 5651
AMERICAN EXPRESS p 766
See AMEX CANADA INC
AMERICAN HOTEL INCOME PROPERTIES REIT LP p 302
925 GEORGIA ST W SUITE 800, VANCOUVER, BC, V6C 3L2
(604) 630-3134   SIC 6798
AMERICAN IRON & METAL LP p 609
75 STEEL CITY CRT, HAMILTON, ON, L8H 3Y2
(905) 547-5533   SIC 4953
AMERICAN PAPER EXPORT INC p 326
1080 HOWE ST UNIT 506, VANCOUVER, BC, V6Z 2T1
(604) 298-7092   SIC 5113
AMERICAN POULTRY SERVICES LTD p 682
63 ELORA ST, MILDMAY, ON, N0G 2J0
(800) 963-3488   SIC 0751
AMERICAN STANDARD p 732
See LIXIL CANADA INC
AMERICAN TRANSPORTATION & LOGISTICS (AT&L) CANADA INC p 1084
400 BOUL SAINT-MARTIN O BUREAU 206, COTE SAINT-LUC, QC, H7M 3Y8
(514) 316-6496   SIC 4731

AMERICAS SILVER CORPORATION p 948
145 KING ST W SUITE 2870, TORONTO, ON, M5H 1J8
(416) 848-9503   SIC 1081
AMERIGO RESOURCES LTD p 302
355 BURRARD ST SUITE 1260, VANCOUVER, BC, V6C 2G8
(604) 681-2802   SIC 1021
AMERIMARK, DIV OF p 902
See MCBRIDE METAL FABRICATING CORPORATION
AMES TILE & STONE LTD p 237
415 BOYNE ST SUITE 301, NEW WESTMINSTER, BC, V3M 5K2
(604) 515-3486   SIC 5032
AMEUBLEMENT BRANCHAUD INC p 1100
52 RTE 105, EGAN, QC, J9E 3A9
(819) 449-2610   SIC 5021
AMEUBLEMENT DE BUREAU AMBIANCE p 1240
See CIMTEL (QUEBEC) INC
AMEUBLEMENT DE BUREAU FOCUS p 1392
See GROUPE AMEUBLEMENT FOCUS INC
AMEUBLEMENT DOREL p 1402
See INDUSTRIES DOREL INC, LES
AMEUBLEMENTS ARTELITE INC p 1047
10251 BOUL RAY-LAWSON, ANJOU, QC, H1J 1L6
(514) 493-6113   SIC 5712
AMEUBLEMENTS EL RAN LTEE p 1249
2751 RTE TRANSCANADIENNE, POINTE-CLAIRE, QC, H9R 1B4
(514) 630-5656   SIC 2512
AMEUBLEMENTS GILBERT LTEE, LES p 1332
8855 BOUL HENRI-BOURASSA O, SAINT-LAURENT, QC, H4S 1P7
SIC 2542
AMEUBLEMENTS TANGUAY INC p 1078
1990 BOUL TALBOT, CHICOUTIMI, QC, G7H 7Y3
(418) 698-4411   SIC 5712
AMEUBLEMENTS TANGUAY INC p 1276
7200 RUE ARMAND-VIAU, QUEBEC, QC, G2C 2A7
(800) 826-4829   SIC 5712
AMEUBLEMENTS TANGUAY INC p 1385
2200 BOUL DES RECOLLETS, TROIS-RIVIERES, QC, G8Z 3X5
(819) 373-1111   SIC 5712
AMEUBLEMENTS THOMASVILLE p 1251
See INTERIEURS MOBILIA INC, LES
AMEX CANADA INC p 666
80 MICRO CRT SUITE 300, MARKHAM, ON, L3R 9Z5
(905) 475-2177   SIC 6153
AMEX CANADA INC p 766
2225 SHEPPARD AVE E, NORTH YORK, ON, M2J 5C2
(905) 474-8000   SIC 6099
AMEX FRASERIDGE REALTY p 290
6325 FRASER ST SUITE 200, VANCOUVER, BC, V5W 3A3
(604) 322-3272   SIC 6531
AMEX FREIGHT INC p 477
7066 SMITH INDUSTRIAL DR, AMHERSTBURG, ON, N0R 1J0
(519) 726-4444   SIC 4731
AMF AUTOMATION TECHNOLOGIES COMPANY OF CANADA p 1372
1025 RUE CABANA BUREAU 1, SHERBROOKE, QC, J1K 2M4
(819) 563-3111   SIC 3556
AMF CANADA p 1372
See AMF AUTOMATION TECHNOLOGIES COMPANY OF CANADA
AMG LONDON INC p 653
230 VICTORIA ST, LONDON, ON, N6A 2C2
(519) 667-0660   SIC 6324
AMG METALS INC p 880
21 BALES DR W, SHARON, ON, L0G 1V0

(905) 953-4111 *SIC* 3365

AMGEN BRITISH COLUMBIA INC *p* 182
7990 ENTERPRISE ST, BURNABY, BC,
V5A 1V7
(604) 415-1800 *SIC* 5122

AMGEN CANADA INC *p* 719
6775 FINANCIAL DR SUITE 100, MISSIS-
SAUGA, ON, L5N 0A4
(905) 285-3000 *SIC* 5122

AMH CANADA LTEE *p* 1284
391 RUE SAINT-JEAN-BAPTISTE E, RI-
MOUSKI, QC, G5L 1Z2
(418) 724-4105 *SIC* 3548

AMHERST CONCRETE PUMPING LIMITED
p 870
105 NANTUCKET BLVD, SCARBOROUGH,
ON, M1P 2N5
(416) 752-2431 *SIC* 1771

AMHERST CRANE RENTALS LIMITED *p*
870
105 NANTUCKET BLVD, SCARBOROUGH,
ON, M1P 2N5
(416) 752-2602 *SIC* 7359

AMHERST TOYOTA *p* 438
See *CGW AUTOMOTIVE GROUP LIMITED*

AMHERST, TOWN OF *p* 438
98 VICTORIA ST E, AMHERST, NS, B4H
1X6
(902) 667-7743 *SIC* 4953

AMHERSTVIEW FOODLAND *p* 477
See *976736 ONTARIO LIMITED*

AMHIL ENTERPRISES *p* 704
400 TRADERS BLVD E, MISSISSAUGA,
ON, L4Z 1W7
(905) 890-5261 *SIC* 3089

AMHIL ENTERPRISES LTD *p* 704
400 TRADERS BLVD E, MISSISSAUGA,
ON, L4Z 1W7
(905) 890-5261 *SIC* 3089

AMI *p* 687
See *AMI AIR MANAGEMENT INC*

AMI AIR MANAGEMENT INC *p* 687
3223 ORLANDO DR, MISSISSAUGA, ON,
L4V 1C5
(905) 694-9676 *SIC* 3822

AMI AUTO INC *p* 1076
191 BOUL SAINT-JEAN-BAPTISTE,
CHATEAUGUAY, QC, J6K 3B9
(450) 692-9600 *SIC* 5511

AMI HONDA, L' *p* 1288
See *2732-2304 QUEBEC INC*

AMI JUNIOR MAZDA, L' *p* 1078
See *AUTOMOBILES CHICOUTIMI (1986)
INC*

AMI-CO *p* 1344
See *MAISON AMI-CO (1981) INC, LA*

AMICA AT BEARBROOK *p* 594
See *AMICA MATURE LIFESTYLES INC*

AMICA AT ERIN MILLS *p* 718
See *AMICA MATURE LIFESTYLES INC*

AMICA AT SWAN LAKE *p* 665
See *AMICA MATURE LIFESTYLES INC*

AMICA AT WINDSOR *p* 1022
4909 RIVERSIDE DR E SUITE 207, WIND-
SOR, ON, N8Y 0A4
(519) 948-5500 *SIC* 6513

AMICA MATURE LIFESTYLES INC *p* 594
2645 INNES RD SUITE 342, GLOUCES-
TER, ON, K1B 3J7
(613) 837-8720 *SIC* 8361

AMICA MATURE LIFESTYLES INC *p* 665
6360 16TH AVE SUITE 336, MARKHAM,
ON, L3P 7Y6
(905) 201-6058 *SIC* 8361

AMICA MATURE LIFESTYLES INC *p* 718
4620 KIMBERMOUNT AVE, MISSIS-
SAUGA, ON, L5M 5W5
(905) 816-9163 *SIC* 8361

AMICA MATURE LIFESTYLES INC *p* 948
20 QUEEN ST W SUITE 2700, TORONTO,
ON, M5H 3R3
(416) 487-2020 *SIC* 8361

AMICA SENIOR LIFESTYLES INC *p* 948
20 QUEEN ST W SUITE 3200, TORONTO,

ON, M5H 3R3
(416) 487-2020 *SIC* 6531
See *AMICO INFRASTRUCTURES INC*

AMICO CANADA INC *p* 520
1080 CORPORATE DR, BURLINGTON,
ON, L7L 5R6
(905) 335-4474 *SIC* 3499

AMICO CLINICAL SOLUTIONS CORP *p* 850
85 FULTON WAY, RICHMOND HILL, ON,
L4B 2N4
(905) 764-0800 *SIC* 3841

AMICO CORPORATION *p* 850
85 FULTON WAY, RICHMOND HILL, ON,
L4B 2N4
(905) 764-0800 *SIC* 3569

AMICO INFRASTRUCTURES INC *p* 807
2199 BLACKACRE DR SUITE 100, OLD-
CASTLE, ON, N0R 1L0
(519) 737-1577 *SIC* 1623

AMICO PATIENT CARE CORPORATION *p*
850
85 FULTON WAY, RICHMOND HILL, ON,
L4B 2N4
(905) 764-0800 *SIC* 5047

AMICO-ISG *p* 520
See *AMICO CANADA INC*

AMIMAC (2002) LTEE *p* 1116
3499 RUE DE L'ENERGIE, JONQUIERE,
QC, G7X 0C1
(418) 542-3531 *SIC* 5084

AMIMOC *p* 1280
See *AUCLAIR & MARTINEAU INC*

AMIOT, MARIUS INC *p* 1284
350 2E RUE E, RIMOUSKI, QC, G5L 7J4
(418) 723-1155 *SIC* 5013

AMIR KITCHEN *p* 1237
See *9168-9406 QUEBEC INC*

AMIRIX SYSTEMS INC *p* 440
20 ANGUS MORTON DR, BEDFORD, NS,
B4B 0L9
(902) 450-1700 *SIC* 3674

AMITY GOODWILL INDUSTRIES *p* 613
225 KING WILLIAM ST, HAMILTON, ON,
L8R 1B1
(905) 526-8482 *SIC* 8699

AMITY-COOINDA PACKAGING SERVICES
p 241
1070 ROOSEVELT CRES, NORTH VAN-
COUVER, BC, V7P 1M3
(604) 985-7491 *SIC* 7389

AMIX GROUP *p* 237
See *AMIX MARINE PROJECTS LTD*

AMIX MARINE PROJECTS LTD *p* 237
625 AGNES ST UNIT 425, NEW WESTMIN-
STER, BC, V3M 5Y4
(604) 516-0857 *SIC* 4499

AMJ CAMPBELL INC *p* 734
7075 TOMKEN RD, MISSISSAUGA, ON,
L5S 1R7
(905) 795-3785 *SIC* 4214

**AMJ CAMPBELL INTERNATIONAL -
TORONTO** *p* 736
See *1776963 ONTARIO INC*

AMJ CAMPBELL VAN LINES *p* 208
See *112792 CANADA INC*

AMJ CAMPBELL VAN LINES *p* 678
See *1300323 ONTARIO INC*

AMJ VAN LINES *p* 734
See *AMJ CAMPBELL INC*

AMNOR INDUSTRIES INC *p* 1289
8 RUE DOYON, ROUYN-NORANDA, QC,
J9X 7B4
(819) 762-9044 *SIC* 7699

AMO *p* 948
See *ASSOCIATION OF MUNICIPALITIES
OF ONTARIO*

AMOPHARM INC *p* 1045
82 1RE AV E, AMOS, QC, J9T 4B2
(819) 727-1234 *SIC* 5912

AMOR CONSTRUCTION *p* 1001
See *176026 CANADA INC*

AMOS 3601 *p* 1280
See *RADIO-ONDE INC*

AMOS TOYOTA *p* 1045
See *9056-4725 QUEBEC INC*

AMOUR HOSIERY, L' *p* 1179
See *MANUFACTURE DE BAS CULOTTES
LAMOUR INC*

AMP SOLAR GROUP INC *p* 712
55 PORT ST E UNIT A, MISSISSAUGA, ON,
L5G 4P3
(905) 271-7800 *SIC* 4911

AMPACET CANADA COMPANY *p* 636
101 SASAGA DR, KITCHENER, ON, N2C
2G8
(519) 748-5576 *SIC* 2816

AMPAK INC *p* 1134
4225 DES LAURENTIDES (A-15) E, LAVAL-
OUEST, QC, H7L 5W5
(450) 682-4141 *SIC* 5085

AMPCO GRAFIX DIV OF *p* 199
See *AMPCO MANUFACTURERS INC*

AMPCO MANUFACTURERS INC *p* 199
9 BURBIDGE ST SUITE 101, COQUITLAM,
BC, V3K 7B2
(604) 472-3800 *SIC* 2759

AMPCO MANUFACTURERS INC *p* 199
9 BURBIDGE ST UNIT 101, COQUITLAM,
BC, V3K 7B2
SIC 2759

AMPERE LIMITED *p* 786
15 TORBARRIE RD, NORTH YORK, ON,
M3L 1G5
(416) 661-3330 *SIC* 1731

AMPHENOL CANADA CORP *p* 864
605 MILNER AVE, SCARBOROUGH, ON,
M1B 5X6
(416) 291-4401 *SIC* 5065

**AMPHENOL TECHNICAL PRODUCTS IN-
TERNATIONAL CO** *p*
383
2110 NOTRE DAME AVE, WINNIPEG, MB,
R3H 0K1
(204) 697-2222 *SIC* 3679

AMPHORA MAINTENANCE SERVICES INC
p 919
707A DANFORTH AVE, TORONTO, ON,
M4J 1L2
(416) 461-0401 *SIC* 7349

AMPLC *p* 1082
See *ARCELORMITTAL PRODUITS LONGS
CANADA S.E.N.C.*

AMPRO *p* 1313
See *PRODUITS FORESTIERS AMPRO
INC*

AMPRO ELECTRIC LTD *p* 650
406 FIRST ST, LONDON, ON, N5W 4N1
(519) 439-9748 *SIC* 5999

AMRE SUPPLY COMPANY LIMITED *p* 125
1259 91 ST SW STE 201, EDMONTON, AB,
T6X 1E9
(780) 461-2929 *SIC* 5064

AMS *p* 330
See *ADVANCED MILLWRIGHT SERVICES
LTD*

AMS *p* 630
See *ALMA MATER SOCIETY OF QUEEN'S
UNIVERSITY INCORPORATED*

AMS *p* 830
See *APOLLO MANAGEMENT SERVICES
LTD*

AMS COMPUTER GROUP *p* 188
See *CANADIAN AUTOMATED MANAGE-
MENT SYSTEMS LTD*

AMS IMAGING INC *p* 748
77 AURIGA DR UNIT 17, NEPEAN, ON,
K2E 7Z7
(613) 723-1668 *SIC* 5044

AMSCAN CANADA *p* 782
See *AMSCAN DISTRIBUTORS (CANADA)
LTD*

AMSCAN DISTRIBUTORS (CANADA) LTD *p*
782
1225 FINCH AVE W, NORTH YORK, ON,
M3J 2E8
(800) 363-6662 *SIC* 5199

AMSCO CAST PRODUCTS (CANADA) INC

p 356
35 MERCY ST, SELKIRK, MB, R1A 1N5
(204) 482-4442 *SIC* 3325

AMSTED CANADA INC *p* 362
104 REGENT AVE E, WINNIPEG, MB, R2C
0C1
(204) 222-4252 *SIC* 3462

AMSTED CANADA INC *p* 362
2500 DAY ST, WINNIPEG, MB, R2C 3A4
(204) 222-4252 *SIC* 3462

AMSTERDAM BREWING CO. LIMITED *p*
917
45 ESANDAR DR UNIT 2, TORONTO, ON,
M4G 4C5
(416) 504-1040 *SIC* 2082

AMSTERDAM PRODUCTS LTD *p* 561
2 MONTREAL RD, CORNWALL, ON, K6H
6L4
(613) 933-7393 *SIC* 7389

AMT *p* 648
See *ADJ HOLDINGS INC*

AMT ELECTROSURGERY INC *p* 637
20 STECKLE PL UNIT 16, KITCHENER,
ON, N2E 2C3
(519) 895-0452 *SIC* 5047

AMT MANAGEMENT SERVICES *p* 376
360 MAIN ST SUITE 3000, WINNIPEG, MB,
R3C 4G1
(204) 957-4868 *SIC* 8742

AMTEK ENGINEERING SERVICES LTD *p*
595
1900 CITY PARK DR SUITE 510,
GLOUCESTER, ON, K1J 1A3
(613) 749-3990 *SIC* 8711

AMTEX *p* 702
See *XENTEX TRADING INC*

AMUSEMENTS AIRBOUNCE SENC, LES *p*
1394
29 AV PASOLD, VAUDREUIL-DORION, QC,
J7V 2W9
(450) 424-0214 *SIC* 7359

AMVEX *p* 850
See *ALDACO INDUSTRIES INC*

AMVIC INC *p* 764
501 MCNICOLL AVE, NORTH YORK, ON,
M2H 2E2
(416) 410-5674 *SIC* 3271

AMWAY CANADA CORPORATION *p* 657
375 EXETER RD, LONDON, ON, N6E 2Z3
(519) 685-7700 *SIC* 5122

AMWAY GLOBAL *p* 657
See *AMWAY CANADA CORPORATION*

AMYLIOR INC *p* 1394
3190 RUE F.-X.-TESSIER, VAUDREUIL-
DORION, QC, J7V 5V5
(450) 424-0288 *SIC* 2514

AMYSYSTEMS *p* 1394
See *AMYLIOR INC*

AN OPTIMUM PARTNER *p* 1196
See *GROUPE OPTIMUM INC*

ANACHEMIA CANADA CO *p* 1125
255 RUE NORMAN, LACHINE, QC, H8R
1A3
(514) 489-5711 *SIC* 5049

ANACHEMIA SCIENCE *p* 1125
See *ANACHEMIA CANADA CO*

ANACONDA MINING INC *p* 948
150 YORK ST SUITE 410, TORONTO, ON,
M5H 3S5
(416) 304-6622 *SIC* 1041

ANAERGIA INC *p* 521
4210 SOUTH SERVICE RD, BURLINGTON,
ON, L7L 4X5
(905) 766-3333 *SIC* 2869

**ANAGO (NON) RESIDENTIAL RE-
SOURCES INC** *p*
837
252 DELAWARE ST, PARKHILL, ON, N0M
2K0
(519) 294-6238 *SIC* 8361

ANAGO RESOURCES *p* 837
See *ANAGO (NON) RESIDENTIAL RE-
SOURCES INC*

ANALOGIC CANADA CORPORATION *p*

1328
4950 RUE LEVY, SAINT-LAURENT, QC, H4R 2P1
(514) 856-6920   SIC 8731

ANALYTIQUE IPERCEPTIONS   p 1205
See IPERCEPTIONS INC

ANARCHIST MOUNTAIN FIRE DEPART-MENT   p 242
115 GRIZZLY RD, OSOYOOS, BC, V0H 1V6
SIC 7389

ANATOLIA GROUP INC   p 1029
8300 HUNTINGTON RD, WOODBRIDGE, ON, L4L 1A5
(905) 771-3800   SIC 5032

ANATOME INC   p 729
5800 AVEBURY RD UNIT 3, MISSIS-SAUGA, ON, L5R 3M3
(905) 502-7200   SIC 5044

ANB CANADA INC   p 754
25 MILLARD AVE W UNIT 1, NEWMARKET, ON, L3X 7R5
(905) 953-9777   SIC 5122

ANCAST INDUSTRIES LTD   p 380
1350 SASKATCHEWAN AVE, WINNIPEG, MB, R3E 0L2
(204) 786-7911   SIC 3322

ANCASTER HIGH SCHOOL   p 477
See HAMILTON-WENTWORTH DISTRICT SCHOOL BOARD, THE

ANCASTER OLD MILL INC   p 477
548 OLD DUNDAS RD, ANCASTER, ON, L9G 3J4
(905) 648-1828   SIC 6712

ANCASTER TOYOTA INC   p 477
30 MASON DR, ANCASTER, ON, L9G 3K9
(905) 648-9910   SIC 5511

ANCHOR CONCRETE PRODUCTS LIM-ITED   p 630
1645 SYDENHAM RD, KINGSTON, ON, K7L 4V4
(613) 546-6683   SIC 3272

ANCHOR CONSTRUCTION INDUSTRIAL PRODUCTS LTD   p 383
1810 DUBLIN AVE, WINNIPEG, MB, R3H 0H3
(204) 633-0064   SIC 5072

ANCHOR DANLY INC   p 1021
2590 OUELLETTE AVE, WINDSOR, ON, N8X 1L7
(519) 966-4431   SIC 3544

ANCHOR PACKING   p 1131
See ROBCO INC

ANCIA   p 1137
See ANCIA PERSONNEL INC

ANCIA PERSONNEL INC   p 1137
469 AV TANIATA BUREAU 400, LEVIS, QC, G6W 5M6
SIC 7361

ANCO CHEMICALS INC   p 664
85 MALMO CRT, MAPLE, ON, L6A 1R4
(905) 832-2276   SIC 5169

ANCO CONTRACTING INC   p 1029
140 REGINA RD UNIT 15, WOODBRIDGE, ON, L4L 8N1
(905) 652-2353   SIC 5032

ANCRAGES CANADIENS   p 1307
See AMCAN-JUMAX INC

ANCTIL, DIVISION ENVIRONNEMENT   p 1299
See ANCTIL, J. INC

ANCTIL, J. INC   p 1299
3110 RTE 222, SAINT-DENIS-DE-BROMPTON, QC, J0B 2P0
(819) 846-2747   SIC 5211

AND 07 CONSULTING   p 608
674 QUEENSTON RD, HAMILTON, ON, L8G 1A3
(905) 561-8960   SIC 8748

AND AGENCY INC   p 769
1220 SHEPPARD AVE E SUITE 100, NORTH YORK, ON, M2K 2S5
(416) 493-6111   SIC 8732

ANDALOS BAKERY AND PASTRY   p 1325
See BOULANGERIE ANDALOS INC

ANDE CAPITAL CORP   p 357
2976 DAY ST, SPRINGFIELD, MB, R2C 2Z2
(204) 777-5345   SIC 6712

ANDEANGOLD LTD   p 329
701 GEORGIA ST W SUITE 1500, VAN-COUVER, BC, V7Y 1K8
(604) 608-6172   SIC 1081

ANDEROL CANADA   p 568
See LANXESS CANADA CO./CIE

ANDERSON COLLEGIATE VOCATIONAL INSTITUTE   p 1014
See DURHAM DISTRICT SCHOOL BOARD

ANDERSON CONSULTING   p 744
See 2207544 ONTARIO INC

ANDERSON DDB HEALTH & LIFESTYLE   p 930
See OMNICOM CANADA CORP

ANDERSON MERCHANDISERS-CANADA, INC.   p 850
60 LEEK CRES SUITE B, RICHMOND HILL, ON, L4B 1H1
SIC 5099

ANDERSON MOTORS LTD   p 1413
3333 6TH AVE E, PRINCE ALBERT, SK, S6V 8C8
(306) 765-3000   SIC 5511

ANDERSON PUMP HOUSE LTD   p 1412
9802 THATCHER AVE, NORTH BATTLE-FORD, SK, S9A 3W2
(306) 937-7741   SIC 5074

ANDERSON RENTAL AND PAVING LTD   p 1431
3430 IDYLWYLD DR N, SASKATOON, SK, S7L 5Y7
(306) 934-2000   SIC 1611

ANDERSON VACATIONS   p 65
See MARSHALL ANDERSON TOURS LTD

ANDERSON WATTS LTD   p 183
6336 DARNLEY ST, BURNABY, BC, V5B 3B1
(604) 291-7751   SIC 5141

ANDERSON, DON HAULAGE LIMITED   p 598
36 GORDON COLLINS DR, GORMLEY, ON, L0H 1G0
(416) 798-7737   SIC 4213

ANDERSON, GORD AUTOMOTIVE GROUP INC   p 1034
1267 DUNDAS ST, WOODSTOCK, ON, N4S 7V9
(519) 537-2326   SIC 5511

ANDERSON, RHONDA MPA KPMG LLP LAWYER   p 87
10175 101 ST NW UNIT 2200, EDMON-TON, AB, T5J 0H3
(780) 429-7300   SIC 8111

ANDERSON-MCTAGUE & ASSOCIATES LTD   p 414
154 PRINCE WILLIAM ST, SAINT JOHN, NB, E2L 2B6
(506) 632-5020   SIC 6411

ANDERSON-MCTAGUE INSURANCE AGENCY   p 414
158 PRINCE WILLIAM ST, SAINT JOHN, NB, E2L 2B6
(506) 632-5000   SIC 6411

ANDERSONS CHRYSLER, DIV   p 1413
See ANDERSON MOTORS LTD

ANDOLA FIBRES LTD   p 631
740 PROGRESS AVE, KINGSTON, ON, K7M 4W9
(613) 389-1261   SIC 5131

ANDORRA BUILDING MAINTENANCE LTD   p 573
46 CHAUNCEY AVE, ETOBICOKE, ON, M8Z 2Z4
(416) 537-7772   SIC 7349

ANDRE ROY ET SYLVAIN BOISSELLE PHARMACIENS INC   p 1376
369 BOUL FISET, SOREL-TRACY, QC, J3P 3R3
(450) 746-7840   SIC 5912

ANDRE SIMON INC   p 1384
425 RUE DESSUREAULT, TROIS-RIVIERES, QC, G8T 2L8
(819) 373-1013   SIC 5531

ANDRE TARDIFF AGENCY LIMITED   p 565
140 COLONISATION AVE N, DRYDEN, ON, P8N 2Z5
(807) 223-4324   SIC 5171

ANDRE'S AUDIOTRONIC   p 220
See ANDRE'S T.V. SALES & SERVICE LTD

ANDRE'S T.V. SALES & SERVICE LTD   p 220
2153 SPRINGFIELD RD, KELOWNA, BC, V1Y 7X1
(250) 861-4101   SIC 5731

ANDRE, JEAN-GUY LTEE   p 1105
692 BOUL GREBER, GATINEAU, QC, J8V 3P8
(819) 243-6181   SIC 5531

ANDRE, T. A. & SONS (ONTARIO) LIMITED   p 629
30 RIGNEY ST, KINGSTON, ON, K7K 6Z2
(613) 549-8060   SIC 1542

ANDREW AGENCIES LTD   p 360
322 7TH AVE S, VIRDEN, MB, R0M 2C0
(204) 748-2734   SIC 6411

ANDREW PELLER LIMITED   p 599
697 SOUTH SERVICE RD, GRIMSBY, ON, L3M 4E8
(905) 643-4131   SIC 2084

ANDREW PELLER LIMITED   p 760
1249 NIAGARA STONE RD, NIAGARA ON THE LAKE, ON, L0S 1J0
(905) 468-7123   SIC 2084

ANDREWS & CO   p 811
See HARTEL FINANCIAL MANAGEMENT CORPORATION

ANDREWS & GEORGE COMPANY LIM-ITED   p 291
125 3RD AVE W, VANCOUVER, BC, V5Y 1E6
(604) 876-0466   SIC 5149

ANDREWS MAILING SERVICE LTD   p 480
226 INDUSTRIAL PKY N UNIT 7, AURORA, ON, L4G 4C3
(905) 503-1700   SIC 7331

ANDREWS REALTY LTD   p 292
650 41ST AVE W SUITE 410, VANCOU-VER, BC, V5Z 2M9
(604) 263-2823   SIC 6531

ANDREWS, DENNY FORD SALES INC   p 99
18208 STONY PLAIN RD NW, EDMONTON, AB, T5S 1A7
(780) 489-9999   SIC 5511

ANDRITZ AUTOMATION LTD   p 253
13700 INTERNATIONAL PL SUITE 100, RICHMOND, BC, V6V 2X8
(604) 214-9248   SIC 8711

ANDRITZ HYDRO CANADA INC   p 1074
7920 RUE SAMUEL-HATT BUREAU 7902, CHAMBLY, QC, J3L 6W4
(450) 658-5554   SIC 8711

ANDRITZ HYDRO CANADA INC   p 1249
6100 RTE TRANSCANADIENNE, POINTE-CLAIRE, QC, H9R 1B9
(514) 428-6700   SIC 8711

ANDRITZ LTEE   p 1127
2260 32E AV, LACHINE, QC, H8T 3H4
(514) 631-7700   SIC 5084

ANDRITZ SEPARATION   p 1127
See ANDRITZ LTEE

ANDROID - BRAMPTON, L.L.C.   p 498
14 PRECIDIO CRT, BRAMPTON, ON, L6S 6E3
(905) 458-4774   SIC 3694

ANDROID INDUSTRIES - BRAMPTON   p 498
See ANDROID - BRAMPTON, L.L.C.

ANDY LOGISTIQUE INC   p 1364
4225 BOUL HEBERT, SALABERRY-DE-VALLEYFIELD, QC, J6S 6J2
(514) 667-8494   SIC 4731

ANDY TRAINING CENTRE   p 1364
See ANDY TRANSPORT INC

ANDY TRANSPORT INC   p 1364
4225 BOUL HEBERT, SALABERRY-DE-VALLEYFIELD, QC, J6S 6J2
(514) 667-8500   SIC 4213

ANDY'S TIRE SHOP LIMITED   p 468
146 ROBIE ST, TRURO, NS, B2N 1L1
(902) 897-1669   SIC 5531

ANE STEWART LTD   p 451
730 CENTRAL AVE, GREENWOOD, NS, B0P 1N0
(902) 765-6338   SIC 5531

ANECDOTE, L'   p 1055
See STATION MONT-SAINTE-ANNE INC

ANGEL SEAFOODS LTD   p 290
8475 FRASER ST, VANCOUVER, BC, V5X 3Y1
(604) 254-2824   SIC 5146

ANGEL STAR HOLDINGS LTD   p 336
740 BURDETT AVE SUITE 1901, VICTO-RIA, BC, V8W 1B2
(250) 382-4221   SIC 7011

ANGELCARE   p 1072
See DEVELOPPEMENTS ANGELCARE INC, LES

ANGELL HASMAN & ASSOCIATES RE-ALTY LTD   p 342
1544 MARINE DR SUITE 203, WEST VAN-COUVER, BC, V7V 1H8
(604) 921-1188   SIC 6531

ANGELO'S BAKERY AND DELI   p 658
See 1279028 ONTARIO LIMITED

ANGELO'S GARDEN CENTRE LIMITED   p 548
1801 HIGHWAY 7, CONCORD, ON, L4K 1V4
(905) 669-9220   SIC 5261

ANGELS PHARMACEUTICAL SERVICES LTD   p 714
2458 DUNDAS ST W UNIT 13, MISSIS-SAUGA, ON, L5K 1R8
(905) 823-7895   SIC 5912

ANGELS THERE FOR YOU   p 266
12031 2ND AVE SUITE 100, RICHMOND, BC, V7E 3L6
(604) 271-4427   SIC 8399

ANGERS TOYOTA   p 1311
See AUTOMOBILES J. D. A. INC

ANGIE'S KITCHEN INC   p 883
1761 ERB'S RD, ST AGATHA, ON, N0B 2L0
(519) 747-1700   SIC 5812

ANGIOTECH PHARMACEUTICALS, INC   p 302
355 BURRARD ST SUITE 1100, VANCOU-VER, BC, V6C 2G8
(604) 221-7676   SIC 8731

ANGLES HAIR DESIGN   p 75
See ANGLES SALON INC

ANGLES SALON INC   p 75
555 STRATHCONA BLVD SW SUITE 420, CALGARY, AB, T3H 2Z9
(403) 242-6057   SIC 7231

ANGLICAN APPEAL   p 931
See ANGLICAN CHURCH OF CANADA

ANGLICAN CHURCH OF CANADA   p 931
80 HAYDEN ST SUITE 400, TORONTO, ON, M4Y 3G2
(416) 924-9192   SIC 8661

ANGLICAN DIOCESE OF OTTAWA   p 825
See INCORPORATION SYNOD DIOCESE OF OTTAWA

ANGLICAN DIOCESE OF TORONTO   p 939
See INCORPORATED SYNOD OF THE DIOCESE OF TORONTO, THE

ANGLO AMERICAN CEDAR PRODUCTS LTD   p 232
7160 BEATTY DR, MISSION, BC, V2V 6B4
(604) 826-7185   SIC 5031

ANGLO CANADIAN MOTORS   p 99
See ATKIN, MICHAEL HOLDINGS INC

ANGLO ORIENTAL LIMITED   p 666
255 SHIELDS CRT, MARKHAM, ON, L3R 8V2

(905) 752-0612   *SIC 5023*
ANGLOCOM INC   *p 1257*
300 RUE SAINT-PAUL BUREAU 210, QUE-
BEC, QC, G1K 7R1
(418) 529-6928   *SIC 7389*
**ANGLOPHONE SOUTH SCHOOL DIS-
TRICT (ASD-S)**   *p*
411
398 HAMPTON RD, QUISPAMSIS, NB, E2E
4V5
(506) 847-6200   *SIC 8211*
**ANGLOPHONE SOUTH SCHOOL DIS-
TRICT (ASD-S)**   *p*
413
490 WOODWARD AVE, SAINT JOHN, NB,
E2K 5N3
(506) 658-5300   *SIC 8211*
**ANGLOPHONE SOUTH SCHOOL DIS-
TRICT (ASD-S)**   *p*
418
55 LEONARD DR, SUSSEX, NB, E4E 2P8
(506) 432-2017   *SIC 8211*
ANGLOPHONE WEST SCHOOL DISTRICT
p 399
499 CLIFFE ST, FREDERICTON, NB, E3A
9P5
(506) 457-6898   *SIC 8211*
ANGLOPHONE WEST SCHOOL DISTRICT
p 400
1135 PROSPECT ST, FREDERICTON, NB,
E3B 3B9
(506) 453-5454   *SIC 8211*
ANGLOPHONE WEST SCHOOL DISTRICT
p 400
300 PRIESTMAN ST, FREDERICTON, NB,
E3B 6J8
(506) 453-5435   *SIC 8211*
**ANGUS CONSULTING MANAGEMENT LIM-
ITED**   *p*
778
1125 LESLIE ST, NORTH YORK, ON, M3C
2J6
(416) 443-8300   *SIC 7349*
ANGUS G FOODS INC   *p 442*
588 PORTLAND ST, DARTMOUTH, NS,
B2W 2M3
(902) 435-3181   *SIC 5812*
ANGUS GEOSOLUTIONS INC   *p 620*
13029 STEELES AVE, HORNBY, ON, L0P
1E0
(905) 876-0700   *SIC 8748*
ANGUS SYSTEMS GROUP LIMITED *p 778*
1125 LESLIE ST, NORTH YORK, ON, M3C
2J6
(416) 385-8550   *SIC 7372*
ANGUS, H.H. AND ASSOCIATES LIMITED*p*
778
1127 LESLIE ST, NORTH YORK, ON, M3C
2J6
(416) 443-8200   *SIC 8711*
ANGUS-MILLER LTD   *p 414*
40 WELLINGTON ROW, SAINT JOHN, NB,
E2L 3H3
(506) 633-7000   *SIC 6411*
ANI PHARMACEUTICALS CANADA INC *p*
796
400 IROQUOIS SHORE RD, OAKVILLE,
ON, L6H 1M5
(905) 337-4500   *SIC 2834*
ANI-MAT INC   *p 1375*
395 RUE RODOLPHE-RACINE, SHER-
BROOKE, QC, J1R 0S7
(819) 821-2091   *SIC 2273*
ANIKA HOLDINGS INC   *p 390*
1700 WAVERLEY ST SUITE B, WINNIPEG,
MB, R3T 5V7
(204) 269-9551   *SIC 5511*
ANIMAL HEALTH, DIV OF   *p 521*
*See BOEHRINGER INGELHEIM (CANADA)
LTD*
ANIMAL SAFETY PUBLICATIONS *p 407*
295 ENGLISH DR, MONCTON, NB, E1E
0J3
(506) 858-7807   *SIC 7311*

ANIMALERIE DYNO INC   *p 1254*
2377 BOUL LOUIS-XIV, QUEBEC, QC, G1C
1B2
(418) 661-7128   *SIC 5999*
ANIMANIA   *p 1070*
See GROUPE VETERI MEDIC INC
ANIMATION SQUEEZE STUDIO INC *p 1257*
520 BOUL CHAREST E BUREAU 340,
QUEBEC, QC, G1K 3J3
(418) 476-1786   *SIC 7336*
ANIMATIONS ARCHY   *p 1271*
See PRODUCTIONS ARCHY'S INC, LES
**ANIMIKII OZOSON CHILD AND FAMILY
SERVICES INC**   *p 373*
313 PACIFIC AVE UNIT 3, WINNIPEG, MB,
R3A 0M2
(204) 944-0040   *SIC 8399*
ANIPET ANIMAL SUPPLIES INC   *p 278*
19038 24 AVE, SURREY, BC, V3Z 3S9
(604) 536-3367   *SIC 5199*
ANISHINABEK NATION   *p 564*
See UNION OF ONTARIO INDIANS
ANIXTER CANADA INC   *p 729*
200 FOSTER CRES, MISSISSAUGA, ON,
L5R 3Y5
(905) 568-8999   *SIC 5063*
ANIXTER CANADA INC   *p 1127*
3000 RUE LOUIS-A.-AMOS, LACHINE, QC,
H8T 3P8
(514) 636-3636   *SIC 5063*
**ANIXTER POWER SOLUTIONS CANADA
INC**   *p 546*
188 PURDY RD, COLBORNE, ON, K0K 1S0
(905) 355-2474   *SIC 5085*
ANJINNOV CONSTRUCTION INC   *p 1246*
13550 BOUL HENRI-BOURASSA E,
POINTE-AUX-TREMBLES, QC, H1A 0A4
(514) 353-3000   *SIC 1542*
ANKER-HOLTH, DIV OF   *p 509*
*See MAGNUM INTEGRATED TECHNOLO-
GIES INC*
ANM INDUSTRIES (2005) INC   *p 1019*
2500 CENTRAL AVE, WINDSOR, ON, N8W
4J5
(519) 258-2550   *SIC 3471*
**ANMAR MECHANICAL AND ELECTRICAL
CONTRACTORS LTD**   *p 647*
199 MUMFORD RD, LIVELY, ON, P3Y 0A4
(705) 692-0888   *SIC 1711*
ANN DAVIS SRVC   *p 196*
See DAVIS, ANN TRANSITION SOCIETY
ANN-LOUISE JEWELLERS LTD   *p 288*
18 2ND AVE E, VANCOUVER, BC, V5T 1B1
(604) 873-6341   *SIC 5944*
ANNABEL CANADA INC   *p 1098*
1645 RUE HAGGERTY, DRUM-
MONDVILLE, QC, J2C 5P7
(819) 472-1367   *SIC 2261*
ANNABLE FOODS LTD   *p 284*
850 FARWELL ST, TRAIL, BC, V1R 3T8
(250) 368-3363   *SIC 5411*
**ANNACIS ISLAND WASTE WATER TREAT-
MENT PLANT**   *p*
206
*See GREATER VANCOUVER REGIONAL
DISTRICT*
ANNANDALE LEASING LIMITED   *p 843*
GD, PICKERING, ON, L1V 2R1
(905) 683-5722   *SIC 5511*
**ANNAPOLIS EAST ELEMENTARY
SCHOOL**   *p 441*
*See ANNAPOLIS VALLEY REGIONAL
SCHOOL BOARD*
**ANNAPOLIS VALLEY DISTRICT HEALTH
AUTHORITY**   *p 459*
150 EXHIBITION ST, KENTVILLE, NS, B4N
5E3
(902) 678-7381   *SIC 8062*
**ANNAPOLIS VALLEY REGIONAL SCHOOL
BOARD**   *p 439*
1941 HWY 1, AUBURN, NS, B0P 1A0
(902) 847-4440   *SIC 8211*
**ANNAPOLIS VALLEY REGIONAL SCHOOL
BOARD**   *p 441*

121 ORCHARD ST RR 3, BERWICK, NS,
B0P 1E0
(902) 538-4600   *SIC 8211*
**ANNAPOLIS VALLEY REGIONAL SCHOOL
BOARD**   *p 470*
225 PAYZANT DR, WINDSOR, NS, B0N 2T0
(902) 792-6740   *SIC 8211*
**ANNAPOLIS VALLEY REGIONAL SCHOOL
BOARD**   *p 471*
75 GREENWICH RD S, WOLFVILLE, NS,
B4P 2R2
(902) 542-6060   *SIC 8211*
**ANNAPOLIS VALLEY WORK ACTIVITY SO-
CIETY**   *p*
459
11 OPPORTUNITY LANE, KENTVILLE, NS,
B4N 3V7
(902) 679-2755   *SIC 6733*
**ANNE & MAX TANENBAUM COMMUNITY
HEBREW ACADEMY OF TORONTO**   *p 664*
9600 BATHURST ST, MAPLE, ON, L6A 3Z8
SIC 8211
ANNE J. MACARTHUR PS   *p 683*
See HALTON DISTRICT SCHOOL BOARD
ANNETTE'S DONUTS LIMITED   *p 997*
1965 LAWRENCE AVE W, TORONTO, ON,
M9N 1H5
(416) 656-3444   *SIC 2051*
ANNETTE'S KEEPSAKES   *p 343*
GD, WHITE ROCK, BC, V4B 5L5
(604) 538-5890   *SIC 5099*
ANNEX BUSINESS MEDIA   *p 880*
*See ANNEX PUBLISHING & PRINTING
INC*
ANNEX CONSULTING GROUP INC *p 327*
555 BURRARD ST SUITE 950, VANCOU-
VER, BC, V7X 1M8
(604) 638-8878   *SIC 8742*
ANNEX PUBLISHING & PRINTING INC *p*
880
105 DONLY DR S, SIMCOE, ON, N3Y 4N5
(519) 428-3471   *SIC 2721*
ANNEX-NEWCOM LIMITED PARTNERSHIP
p 775
80 VALLEYBROOK DR, NORTH YORK, ON,
M3B 2S9
(416) 442-5600   *SIC 2721*
ANNEXAIR INC   *p 1098*
1125 RUE BERGERON, DRUM-
MONDVILLE, QC, J2C 7V5
(819) 475-3302   *SIC 3564*
ANNISONS LTD   *p 880*
140 QUEENSWAY E, SIMCOE, ON, N3Y
4Y7
(519) 426-1513   *SIC 5014*
ANODIZING & PAINT T.N.M INC   *p 1249*
21 CH DE L'AVIATION, POINTE-CLAIRE,
QC, H9R 4Z2
(514) 335-7001   *SIC 3471*
**ANODYNE ELECTRONICS HOLDING
CORP**   *p 221*
1925 KIRSCHNER RD UNIT 15,
KELOWNA, BC, V1Y 4N7
(250) 763-1088   *SIC 5065*
**ANODYNE ELECTRONICS MANUFACTUR-
ING CORP**   *p*
221
1925 KIRSCHNER RD UNIT 15,
KELOWNA, BC, V1Y 4N7
(250) 763-1088   *SIC 5065*
ANOVA   *p 655*
*See ANOVA: A FUTURE WITHOUT VIO-
LENCE*
ANOVA: A FUTURE WITHOUT VIOLENCE*p*
655
255 HORTON ST E FL 3, LONDON, ON,
N6B 1L1
(519) 642-3003   *SIC 8699*
ANSELL CANADA INC   *p 1088*
105 RUE LAUDER, COWANSVILLE, QC,
J2K 2K8
(450) 266-1850   *SIC 5122*
ANSWER 365   *p 455*
See HMC COMMUNICATIONS INC

ANSWER GARDEN PRODUCTS LTD, THE*p*
178
27715 HUNTINGDON RD, ABBOTSFORD,
BC, V4X 1B6
(604) 856-6221   *SIC 5191*
ANSWER PLUS   *p 612*
See PASWORD GROUP INC, THE
ANSWER PRECISION TOOL INC   *p 636*
146 OTONABEE DR, KITCHENER, ON,
N2C 1L6
(519) 748-0079   *SIC 5013*
ANSWERNET   *p 578*
See TELEPARTNERS CALL CENTRE INC
**ANSWERPLUS COMMUNICATION SER-
VICES INC**   *p*
233
235 BASTION ST SUITE 205, NANAIMO,
BC, V9R 3A3
(250) 753-7587   *SIC 7389*
ANSWERPLUS COMMUNICATIONS *p 233*
*See ANSWERPLUS COMMUNICATION
SERVICES INC*
ANT & BEE CORPORATION   *p 978*
123 JOHN ST, TORONTO, ON, M5V 2E2
(416) 646-2811   *SIC 7361*
ANTEK MADISON PLASTICS CORP *p 878*
100 FINCHDENE SQ, SCARBOROUGH,
ON, M1X 1C1
(416) 321-1170   *SIC 5162*
ANTELOPE HILLS CONSTRUCTION LTD *p*
666
80 TIVERTON CRT SUITE 300, MARKHAM,
ON, L3R 0G4
(905) 477-7609   *SIC 1522*
ANTEX DESIGNS INC   *p 704*
330 BRITANNIA RD E, MISSISSAUGA, ON,
L4Z 1X9
(905) 507-8778   *SIC 2211*
ANTEX WESTERN LTD   *p 371*
1340 CHURCH AVE, WINNIPEG, MB, R2X
1G4
(204) 633-4815   *SIC 1752*
ANTHEM ACQUISITION LTD   *p 327*
SUITE 1100 BENTALL IV, 1055 DUNSMUIR
ST, VANCOUVER, BC, V7X 1K8
(604) 689-3040   *SIC 6531*
ANTHEM INDUSTRIAL, A DIV OF   *p 327*
See ANTHEM WORKS LTD
ANTHEM MEDIA GROUP INC   *p 991*
171 EAST LIBERTY ST SUITE 230,
TORONTO, ON, M6K 3P6
(416) 987-7841   *SIC 4833*
**ANTHEM MEDIA SPORTS & ENTERTAIN-
MENT**   *p*
991
See ANTHEM MEDIA GROUP INC
**ANTHEM RIVERFRONT LAND LIMITED
PARTNERSHIP**   *p 43*
104 2 ST SW, CALGARY, AB, T2P 0C7
(403) 536-8802   *SIC 6553*
ANTHEM WORKS LTD   *p 327*
1055 DUNSMUIR STREET, VANCOUVER,
BC, V7X 1K8
(604) 689-3040   *SIC 6553*
ANTHONY   *p 1178*
*See ENTREPRISES ERNEST (MTL) LTEE,
LES*
ANTHONY CLARK INSURANCE   *p 68*
See HERITAGE HILL INSURANCE LTD
ANTHONY INSURANCE INCORPORATED*p*
432
35 BLACKMARSH RD, ST. JOHN'S, NL,
A1E 1S4
(709) 758-5500   *SIC 6411*
ANTHONY SUZUKI KELOWNA   *p 219*
See ANTHONY'S AUTO SALES INC
ANTHONY'S AUTO SALES INC   *p 219*
2759 HIGHWAY 97 N, KELOWNA, BC, V1X
4J8
(250) 861-6163   *SIC 5511*
ANTHOS ENGINEERING   *p 733*
See 701466 ONTARIO LIMITED
ANTHRATECH WESTERN INC   *p 12*
4450 46 AVE SE, CALGARY, AB, T2B 3N7

(403) 255-7377   SIC 5074
ANTIPASTOS DI ROMA   p 887
See ROMAN DELI LTD
ANTIROUILLE METROPOLITAIN INC   p 1384
3175 BOUL THIBEAU, TROIS-RIVIERES, QC, G8T 1G4
(819) 378-8787   SIC 7549
ANTISTAR CLOTHING   p 1327
See VETEMENTS MAJCO INC
ANTLER EXPRESS LTD   p 104
16389 130 AVE NW, EDMONTON, AB, T5V 1K5
(780) 447-1639   SIC 7389
ANTON MANUFACTURING   p 556
See MULTIMATIC INC
ANTONACCI CLOTHES LIMITED   p 786
99 NORFINCH DR, NORTH YORK, ON, M3N 1W8
(416) 663-4093   SIC 5136
ANTONACCI FINE CUSTOM TAILORING p 786
See ANTONACCI CLOTHES LIMITED
ANTRIM TRUCK CENTER LTD   p 478
580 WHITE LAKE RD, ARNPRIOR, ON, K7S 3G9
(613) 623-9618   SIC 5012
ANTRIM WESTERN STAR   p 478
See ANTRIM TRUCK CENTER LTD
AOC RESINS AND COATINGS COMPANY p 602
38 ROYAL RD, GUELPH, ON, N1H 1G3
(519) 821-5180   SIC 2821
AOF SERVICE ALIMENTAIRE INC   p 1098
2150 RUE SIGOUIN, DRUMMONDVILLE, QC, J2C 5Z4
(819) 477-5353   SIC 5087
AOGS   p 435
See ARCTIC OIL & GAS SERVICES INC
AOL CANADA   p 406
See AMERICA ONLINE CANADA INC
AOL CANADA   p 978
See AMERICA ONLINE CANADA INC
AON BENFIELD CANADA ULC   p 978
225 KING ST W SUITE 1000, TORONTO, ON, M5V 3M2
(416) 979-3300   SIC 8748
AON CANADA INC   p 326
900 HOWE ST, VANCOUVER, BC, V6Z 2M4
(604) 688-4442   SIC 6411
AON CANADA INC   p 959
20 BAY ST SUITE 2400, TORONTO, ON, M5J 2N8
(416) 868-5500   SIC 6411
AON CANADA INC   p 1201
700 RUE DE LA GAUCHETIERE O UNITE 1800, MONTREAL, QC, H3B 0A5
(514) 842-5000   SIC 6411
AON GLOBAL PROFESSIONS PRACTICE p 1206
See MINET INC
AON HEWITT INC   p 978
225 KING ST W SUITE 1600, TORONTO, ON, M5V 3M2
(416) 542-5500   SIC 8999
AON HEWITT INC   p 1201
700 RUE DE LA GAUCHETIERE O BUREAU 1900, MONTREAL, QC, H3B 0A7
(514) 845-6231   SIC 8999
AON HEWITT INC   p 1271
2600 BOUL LAURIER BUREAU 750, QUEBEC, QC, G1V 4W2
(418) 650-1119   SIC 8999
AON INC   p 840
307 AYLMER ST N, PETERBOROUGH, ON, K9J 7M4
(705) 742-5445   SIC 6553
AON INSURANCE MANAGERS   p 326
See AON CANADA INC
AON PARIZEAU INC   p 1201
700 RUE DE LA GAUCHETIERE O BUREAU 1700, MONTREAL, QC, H3B 0A4
(514) 842-5000   SIC 6411
AON REED STENHOUSE INC   p 43

600 3 AVE SW SUITE 1800, CALGARY, AB, T2P 0G5
(403) 267-7010   SIC 6411
AON REED STENHOUSE INC   p 87
10025 102A AVE NW SUITE 900, EDMONTON, AB, T5J 0Y2
(780) 423-9801   SIC 6411
AON REED STENHOUSE INC   p 296
401 GEORGIA ST W SUITE 1200, VANCOUVER, BC, V6B 5A1
(604) 688-4442   SIC 6411
AON REED STENHOUSE INC   p 959
20 BAY ST SUITE 2400, TORONTO, ON, M5J 2N8
(416) 868-5500   SIC 6411
AON REED STENHOUSE INC   p 1201
700 DE LA GAUCHETIERE O BUREAU 1800, MONTREAL, QC, H3B 0A4
(514) 842-5000   SIC 6411
AON RISK SOLUTION   p 959
See AON CANADA INC
AOR   p 20
See ADVANCED ORTHOMOLECULAR RESEARCH INC
AOT ENERGY CANADA INC   p 43
520 3 AVE SW SUITE 3120, CALGARY, AB, T2P 0R3
(403) 770-2700   SIC 5172
AOT ENERGY CANADA NATURAL GAS INC   p 43
520 3 AVE SW UNIT 3120, CALGARY, AB, T2P 0R3
(403) 770-2700   SIC 5172
AOT TECHNOLOGIES   p 330
See APPSONTIME TECHNOLOGIES LTD
AP FOUNDERS LP   p 968
79 WELLINGTON ST W SUITE 3500, TORONTO, ON, M5K 1K7
(416) 306-9800   SIC 6282
AP INFRASTRUCTURE SOLUTIONS LP p 1
26229 TWP RD 531A, ACHESON, AB, T7X 5A4
(780) 444-1560   SIC 3272
AP INFRASTRUCTURE SOLUTIONS LP p 12
4300 50 AVE SE SUITE 217, CALGARY, AB, T2B 2T7
(403) 248-3171   SIC 3272
AP INFRASTRUCTURE SOLUTIONS LP p 13
8916 48 ST SE, CALGARY, AB, T2C 2P9
(403) 204-8500   SIC 3312
AP INFRASTRUCTURE SOLUTIONS LP p 257
7900 NELSON RD, RICHMOND, BC, V6W 1G4
(604) 278-9766   SIC 3312
AP INFRASTRUCTURE SOLUTIONS LP p 548
3300 HIGHWAY 7 SUITE 500, CONCORD, ON, L4K 4M3
(647) 795-9250   SIC 3312
AP INFRASTRUCTURE SOLUTIONS LP p 1316
800 BOUL PIERRE-TREMBLAY, SAINT-JEAN-SUR-RICHELIEU, QC, J2X 4W8
(450) 346-4481   SIC 3312
AP MARTIN PHARMACEUTICAL SUPPLIES LTD   p 253
13711 MAYFIELD PL UNIT 150, RICHMOND, BC, V6V 2G9
(604) 273-8899   SIC 5122
AP&C REVETEMENTS & POUDRES AVANCEES INC   p 1061
3765 RUE LA VERENDRYE BUREAU 110, BOISBRIAND, QC, J7H 1R8
(450) 434-1004   SIC 3479
AP&C UNE SOCIETE DE GE ADDITIVE p 1061
See AP&C REVETEMENTS & POUDRES AVANCEES INC
APACO IMAGING LAB   p 873
See 1387208 ONTARIO LTD

APAF   p 1333
See ENTREPRISES D'ALIMENTATION POUR ANIMAUX FAMILIER (A.P.A.F) INC, LES
APANS HEALTH SERVICES   p 837
See PARK LANE TERRACE LIMITED
APC FILTRATION INC   p 515
10C ABBOTT CRT UNIT 303, BRANTFORD, ON, N3S 0E7
(888) 689-1235   SIC 2674
APD AUTOMOTIVE PARTS DISTRIBUTORS p 153
See EXHAUST MASTERS INC
APEGA   p 87
See ASSOCIATION OF PROFESSIONAL ENGINEERS AND GEOSCIENTISTS OF ALBERTA, THE
APEL EXTRUSIONS LIMITED   p 13
7929 30 ST SE, CALGARY, AB, T2C 1H7
(403) 279-3321   SIC 3354
APETITO CANADA LIMITED   p 501
12 INDELL LANE, BRAMPTON, ON, L6T 3Y3
(905) 799-1022   SIC 2038
APEX   p 43
See APEX DISTRIBUTION INC
APEX ALUMINUM EXTRUSIONS LTD p 224
9767 201 ST, LANGLEY, BC, V1M 3E7
(604) 882-3542   SIC 3354
APEX BRANDED SOLUTIONS INC   p 548
21 GRANITERIDGE RD SUITE 1, CONCORD, ON, L4K 5M9
(905) 760-9946   SIC 5122
APEX COMMUNICATIONS INC   p 273
13734 104 AVE SUITE 201, SURREY, BC, V3T 1W5
(604) 583-6685   SIC 5999
APEX DISTRIBUTION INC   p 43
407 2 ST SW SUITE 550, CALGARY, AB, T2P 2Y3
(403) 268-7333   SIC 5084
APEX FOODSOURCE LTD   p 176
30530 PROGRESSIVE WAY, ABBOTSFORD, BC, V2T 6W3
(604) 854-1492   SIC 5149
APEX GARAGE STORE   p 407
See APEX INDUSTRIES INC
APEX INDUSTRIES INC   p 407
100 MILLENNIUM BLVD, MONCTON, NB, E1E 2G8
(506) 867-1600   SIC 3442
APEX INVESTIGATION & SECURITY INC p 907
391 OLIVER RD, THUNDER BAY, ON, P7B 2G2
(807) 344-8491   SIC 7381
APEX LIMITED PARTNERSHIP   p 41
1710 14 AVE NW SUITE 300, CALGARY, AB, T2N 4Y6
(403) 210-3473   SIC 1521
APEX MOTOR EXPRESS LTD   p 498
60 WARD RD, BRAMPTON, ON, L6S 4L5
(905) 789-5000   SIC 4213
APEX MOUNTAIN RESORT (1997) LTD p 243
324 STRAYHORSE RD, PENTICTON, BC, V2A 6J9
(250) 292-8222   SIC 7999
APEX OILFIELD SERVICES (2000) INC p 158
5402 BLINDMAN CRES, RED DEER COUNTY, AB, T4S 2M4
(403) 314-3385   SIC 7353
APEX REALTY EXECUTIVES   p 20
1212 31 AVE NE SUITE 105, CALGARY, AB, T2E 7S8
(403) 250-5803   SIC 6531
APEX REFORESTATION LTD   p 296
GD STN TERMINAL, VANCOUVER, BC, V6B 3P7
(604) 736-0063   SIC 8748
APEX RESULTS REALTY INC   p 526
2465 WALKER'S LINE, BURLINGTON, ON, L7M 4K4

(905) 332-4111   SIC 6531
APEX WIRELESS   p 273
See APEX COMMUNICATIONS INC
APEX-NIAGARA TOOL LTD   p 885
54 CATHERINE ST, ST CATHARINES, ON, L2R 7R5
(905) 704-1797   SIC 5251
APG DISPLAYS   p 716
See ADVANCED PRESENTATION PRODUCTS INC
APGN INC   p 1058
1270 BOUL MICHELE-BOHEC, BLAINVILLE, QC, J7C 5S4
(450) 939-0799   SIC 3564
API   p 108
See ALBERTA PETROLEUM INDUSTRIES LTD
API TECHNOLOGIES, DIV OF   p 624
See FILTRAN LIMITED
APLIN & MARTIN CONSULTANTS LTD p 275
12448 82 AVE SUITE 201, SURREY, BC, V3W 3E9
(604) 597-9189   SIC 8711
APLIN, DAVID & ASSOCIATES INC   p 27
140 10 AVE SE STE 500, CALGARY, AB, T2G 0R1
(403) 261-9000   SIC 7361
APLIN, DAVID GROUP   p 27
See APLIN, DAVID & ASSOCIATES INC
APM CONSTRUCTION SERVICES INC p 1040
16 MCCARVILLE ST, CHARLOTTETOWN, PE, C1E 2A6
(902) 569-8400   SIC 1542
APO PRODUCTS LTD   p 913
5590 FINCH AVE E UNIT 1, TORONTO, ON, M1B 1T1
(416) 321-5412   SIC 5141
APOBIOLOGIX   p 792
See APOTEX INC
APOLLO FOREST PRODUCTS LTD p 213
2555 TACHIE RD, FORT ST. JAMES, BC, V0J 1P0
(250) 996-8297   SIC 0851
APOLLO HEALTH AND BEAUTY CARE INC p 782
1 APOLLO PL, NORTH YORK, ON, M3J 0H2
(416) 758-3700   SIC 2679
APOLLO MACHINE   p 112
See APOLLO MACHINE & WELDING LTD
APOLLO MACHINE & WELDING LTD p 112
4141 93 ST NW, EDMONTON, AB, T6E 5Y3
(780) 463-3060   SIC 3533
APOLLO MANAGEMENT SERVICES LTD p 830
1200 PRINCE OF WALES DR SUITE D, OTTAWA, ON, K2C 3Y4
(613) 225-7969   SIC 6531
APOLLO MEDICAL LTD   p 413
379 SOMERSET ST, SAINT JOHN, NB, E2K 2Y5
(506) 693-3330   SIC 5047
APOLLO MICROWAVES   p 1094
See MICRO-ONDES APOLLO LTEE
APOLLO SHEET METAL LTD   p 199
2095 BRIGANTINE DR, COQUITLAM, BC, V3K 7B8
(604) 525-8299   SIC 1711
APOPHARMA INC   p 792
200 BARMAC DR, NORTH YORK, ON, M9L 2Z7
(416) 749-9300   SIC 2834
APOTEX FERMENTATION INC   p 393
50 SCURFIELD BLVD, WINNIPEG, MB, R3Y 1G4
(204) 989-6830   SIC 2834
APOTEX INC   p 582
50 STEINWAY BLVD SUITE 3, ETOBICOKE, ON, M9W 6Y3
(416) 675-0338   SIC 2834
APOTEX INC   p 792
200 BARMAC DR, NORTH YORK, ON, M9L

2Z7

(800) 268-4623   *SIC* 2834

APOTEX INC
285 GARRYRAY DR, NORTH YORK, ON, M9L 1P2
(416) 749-9300   *SIC* 2834

APOTEX INC   *p* 855
380 ELGIN MILLS RD E, RICHMOND HILL, ON, L4C 5H2
(905) 884-2050   *SIC* 2834

APOTEX INC   *p* 996
150 SIGNET DR, TORONTO, ON, M9L 1T9
(416) 401-7328   *SIC* 2834

APOTEX INTERNATIONAL INC   *p* 792
150 SIGNET DR, NORTH YORK, ON, M9L 1T9
(416) 749-9300   *SIC* 6712

APOTEX PHARMACEUTICAL HOLDINGS INC   *p* 792
150 SIGNET DR, NORTH YORK, ON, M9L 1T9
(416) 749-9300   *SIC* 8731

APOTEX PHARMACHEM INC   *p* 516
11 SPALDING DR, BRANTFORD, ON, N3T 6B7
(519) 756-8942   *SIC* 2834

APOTEX PHARMACHEM INC   *p* 516
34 SPALDING DR, BRANTFORD, ON, N3T 6B8
(519) 756-8942   *SIC* 2834

APOTRES DE L'AMOUR INFINI CANADA, LES   *p* 1159
290 7E RANG, MONT-TREMBLANT, QC, J8E 1Y4
(819) 425-7257   *SIC* 8661

APOTRES DE L'AMOUR INFINI LES EDITIONS MAGNIFICAT, LES   *p* 1159
See APOTRES DE L'AMOUR INFINI CANADA, LES

APP CANADA   *p* 511
See ASIA PULP & PAPER (CANADA) LTD

APP PARKING   *p* 131
See ALL PEACE PROTECTION LTD

APP-TRIM   *p* 873
See APPAREL TRIMMINGS INC

APPAIDE   *p* 1193
See APPDIRECTE CANADA INC

APPALACHE VALLEY   *p* 1342
See S. BOUDRIAS HORTICOLE INC

APPAREL RESOURCE GROUP INC   *p* 872
80 ROLARK DR, SCARBOROUGH, ON, M1R 4G2
SIC 5137

APPAREL TRIMMINGS INC   *p* 873
20 COMMANDER BLVD, SCARBOROUGH, ON, M1S 3L9
(416) 298-8836   *SIC* 2387

APPARTEMENTS DU SQUARE ANGUS, LES   *p* 1169
See INVESTISSEMENT IMMOBILIER CCSM LTEE

APPARTEMENTS L'EXCELSIOR, LES   *p* 1069
See SOCIETE DE GESTION COGIR INC

APPDIRECTE CANADA INC   *p* 1193
2050 RUE DE BLEURY, MONTREAL, QC, H3A 2J5
(514) 876-4449   *SIC* 7371

APPELEZ MAURICE COURRIER   *p* 1331
See 2931028 CANADA INC

APPELT'S DIAMONDS   *p* 385
See APPELT'S JEWELLERY LTD

APPELT'S JEWELLERY LTD   *p* 385
305 MADISON ST UNIT C, WINNIPEG, MB, R3J 1H9
(204) 774-2829   *SIC* 5944

APPLANIX CORPORATION   *p* 850
85 LEEK CRES, RICHMOND HILL, ON, L4B 3B3
(289) 695-6000   *SIC* 3829

APPLE AUTO GLASS   *p* 216
See CENTURY GLASS (85) LTD

APPLE CANADA INC   *p* 959

120 BREMNER BLVD SUITE 1600, TORONTO, ON, M5J 0A8
(647) 943-4400   *SIC* 5045

APPLE EXPRESS   *p* 691
See 9517154 CANADA LTD

APPLE ONE EMPLOYMENT SERVICES   *p* 578
See APPLEONE SERVICES LTD

APPLE SECURITY INC   *p* 343
15216 NORTH BLUFF RD SUITE 604, WHITE ROCK, BC, V4B 0A7
(604) 507-9577   *SIC* 7389

APPLE STORE   *p* 959
See APPLE CANADA INC

APPLE VALLEY FOODS INCORPORATED   *p* 459
14 CALKIN DR, KENTVILLE, NS, B4N 1J5
(902) 679-4701   *SIC* 2051

APPLEBEE'S   *p* 1017
See APPLESHORE RESTAURANTS INC

APPLEBEE'S NEIGHBORHOOD GRILL & BAR   *p* 759
See KERRIO CORPORATION

APPLEBEE'S NEIGHBOURHOOD GRILL & BAR   *p* 104
See HANSON RESTAURANTS INC

APPLEBY COLLEGE   *p* 802
540 LAKESHORE RD W, OAKVILLE, ON, L6K 3P1
(905) 845-4681   *SIC* 8211

APPLEONE SERVICES LTD   *p* 578
50 PAXMAN RD SUITE 6, ETOBICOKE, ON, M9C 1B7
(416) 622-0100   *SIC* 7361

APPLESHORE RESTAURANTS INC   *p* 1017
11865 COUNTY RD 42, WINDSOR, ON, N8N 2M1
(519) 979-7800   *SIC* 8741

APPLETON ELECTRIC   *p* 568
See APPLETON GROUP CANADA, LTD

APPLETON GROUP CANADA, LTD   *p* 568
99 UNION ST, ELMIRA, ON, N3B 3L7
(519) 669-9222   *SIC* 3644

APPLEWOOD AIR-CONDITIONING LIMITED   *p* 711
3525 HAWKESTONE RD, MISSISSAUGA, ON, L5C 2V1
(905) 275-4500   *SIC* 1711

APPLEWOOD CHEVROLET OLDSMOBILE CADILLAC   *p* 716
See APPLEWOOD HOLDINGS INC

APPLEWOOD HOLDINGS INC   *p* 716
3000 WOODCHESTER DR, MISSISSAUGA, ON, L5L 2R4
(905) 828-2221   *SIC* 5511

APPLEWOOD KIA   *p* 227
See APPLEWOOD MOTORS INC

APPLEWOOD MOTORS INC   *p* 227
19764 LANGLEY BYPASS, LANGLEY, BC, V3A 7B1
(604) 533-7881   *SIC* 5511

APPLEWOOD NISSAN INC   *p* 270
15257 FRASER HWY, SURREY, BC, V3R 3P3
(604) 589-1775   *SIC* 5511

APPLIANCE ADVANTAGE   *p* 540
See KEYESBURY DISTRIBUTORS LIMITED

APPLICATION SYSTEMS GROUP   *p* 595
See A.S.G. INC

APPLIED BIOLOGICAL MATERIALS INC   *p* 253
1-3671 VIKING WAY, RICHMOND, BC, V6V 2J5
(604) 247-2416   *SIC* 8731

APPLIED CONSUMER & CLINICAL EVALUATIONS INC   *p* 716
2575B DUNWIN DR, MISSISSAUGA, ON, L5L 3N9
(905) 828-0493   *SIC* 8731

APPLIED ELECTRONICS LIMITED   *p* 691
1260 KAMATO RD, MISSISSAUGA, ON,

L4W 1Y1
(905) 625-4321   *SIC* 5099

APPLIED INDUSTRIAL FLOORING CANADA   *p* 572
See PREFERRED POLYMER COATINGS LTD

APPLIED INDUSTRIAL TECHNOLOGIES   *p* 652
See SCS SUPPLY GROUP INC

APPLIED INDUSTRIAL TECHNOLOGIES, LP   *p* 1434
143 WHEELER ST, SASKATOON, SK, S7P 0A4
(306) 931-0888   *SIC* 5085

APPLIED SYSTEMS CANADA ULC   *p* 719
6865 CENTURY AVENUE SUITE 3000, MISSISSAUGA, ON, L5N 2E2
(905) 363-6500   *SIC* 4213

APPLIED WIRING (GEORGETOWN) INC.   *p* 593
2 ROSETTA ST, GEORGETOWN, ON, L7G 3P2
(905) 873-1717   *SIC* 3644

APPLIED WIRING ASSEMBLIES INC   *p* 593
2 ROSETTA ST, GEORGETOWN, ON, L7G 3P2
(905) 873-1717   *SIC* 5191

APPLUS RTD   *p* 110
See RTD QUALITY SERVICES INC

APPNOVATION TECHNOLOGIES INC   *p* 294
190 ALEXANDER ST SUITE 600, VANCOUVER, BC, V6A 1B5
(604) 568-0313   *SIC* 7374

APPRENTISSAGE EN LIGNE BRIDGE   *p* 1200
See TECHNOMEDIA FORMATION INC

APPROVISIONNEMENT DE NAVIRES CLIPPER INC   *p* 1209
770 RUE MILL, MONTREAL, QC, H3C 1Y3
(514) 937-9561   *SIC* 5088

APPS CARTAGE INC   *p* 737
6495 TOMKEN RD, MISSISSAUGA, ON, L5T 2X7
(905) 451-2720   *SIC* 4212

APPS INTERNATIONAL   *p* 737
See APPS CARTAGE INC

APPS TRANSPORT GROUP INC   *p* 737
6495 TOMKEN RD, MISSISSAUGA, ON, L5T 2X7
(905) 451-2720   *SIC* 6712

APPSONTIME TECHNOLOGIES LTD   *p* 330
320-645 FORT ST, VANCOUVER, BC, V8W 1G2
(778) 433-1268   *SIC* 8748

APR-CHU DE QUEBEC   *p* 1269
See CHU DE QUEBEC - UNIVERSITE LAVAL

APRI INSURANCE SOLUTIONS INC   *p* 850
165 EAST BEAVER CREEK RD SUITE 18, RICHMOND HILL, ON, L4B 2N2
(866) 877-3600   *SIC* 6411

APRIL CANADA INC   *p* 1071
3250 BOUL LAPINIERE BUREAU 100, BROSSARD, QC, J4Z 3T8
(855) 745-2020   *SIC* 6411

APRIL MARINE CANADA INC   *p* 1071
4405 BOUL LAPINIERE, BROSSARD, QC, J4Z 3T5
(450) 671-6147   *SIC* 6331

APRIL POINT LODGE   *p* 333
See OAK BAY MARINA LTD

APRIL SUPER FLO INC   *p* 1121
9 RUE BELAND, L'ISLE-VERTE, QC, G0L 1K0
(418) 898-5151   *SIC* 5172

APSEA   *p* 451
See ATLANTIC PROVINCES SPECIAL EDUCATION AUTHORITY

APTALIS PHARMA CANADA ULC   *p* 1158
597 BOUL SIR-WILFRID-LAURIER, MONT-SAINT-HILAIRE, QC, J3H 6C4
(450) 467-5100   *SIC* 5122

APTIM SERVICES CANADA CORP   *p* 162
15 TURBO DR UNIT 1, SHERWOOD PARK,

AB, T8H 2J6
(780) 467-2411   *SIC* 8711

APTN   *p* 374
See ABORIGINAL PEOPLE'S TELEVISION NETWORK INCORPORATED

APTOS CANADA INC   *p* 1332
9300 RTE TRANSCANADIENNE BUREAU 300, SAINT-LAURENT, QC, H4S 1K5
(514) 426-0822   *SIC* 7371

APTS   *p* 1144
See ALLIANCE DU PERSONNEL PROFESSIONNEL ET TECHNIQUE DE LA SANTE ET DES SERVICES SOCIAUX

APTS   *p* 1279
See ALLIANCE PERSONNELLE PROFESSIONELLE ET TECHNIQUE DE LA SANTE ET DES SERVICES SOCIAUX

APVE INVESTMENTS INC   *p* 1401
9 AV FORDEN, WESTMOUNT, QC, H3Y 2Y6
SIC 6211

APX HOSPITALITY MANAGEMENT INC   *p* 99
18335 105 AVE NW SUITE 101, EDMONTON, AB, T5S 2K9
(780) 484-1515   *SIC* 7011

AQC   *p* 1060
See AIREAU QUALITE CONTROLE INC

AQTR   *p* 1201
See ASSOCIATION QUEBECOISE DES TRANSPORTS

AQUA 7 REGIONAL WATER COMMISSION   *p* 169
GD, THREE HILLS, AB, T0M 2A0
(403) 443-5541   *SIC* 4941

AQUA AIR SYSTEMS LTD   *p* 108
8703 50 ST NW, EDMONTON, AB, T6B 1E7
(780) 465-8011   *SIC* 5075

AQUA BEAUCE   *p* 1353
See BEAUCE EAU INC

AQUA CAD   *p* 1245
See AQUA DATA INC

AQUA DATA INC   *p* 1245
95 5E AV, PINCOURT, QC, J7W 5K8
(514) 425-1010   *SIC* 7373

AQUA INDUSTRIAL LTD   *p* 127
9912 FRANKLIN AVE SUITE 205, FORT MCMURRAY, AB, T9H 2K5
(780) 799-7300   *SIC* 1791

AQUA INSURAQUA INSURANCE   *p* 92
13220 ST ALBERT TRAIL NW SUITE 302, EDMONTON, AB, T5L 4W1
(780) 448-0100   *SIC* 6411

AQUA LEADER   *p* 1130
See CRYSTAL WATER INVESTMENTS COMPANY

AQUA PLEASURE   *p* 1261
See 9378-7471 QUEBEC INC

AQUA Q   *p* 548
See AP INFRASTRUCTURE SOLUTIONS LP

AQUA SAND BOND   *p* 1362
See PRODUITS DESIGNER ALLIANCE INC

AQUA SOLUTIONS   *p* 1321
See RBF INTERNATIONAL LTEE

AQUA STOP   *p* 1329
See GANT PARIS DU CANADA LTEE, LE

AQUA-BRILLE   *p* 1399
See PEINTURE SYLTECK INC

AQUA-NOR DIV   *p* 545
See FORTIER BEVERAGES LIMITED

AQUA-POWER CLEANERS (1979) LTD   *p* 402
65 ROYAL PARKWAY, FREDERICTON, NB, E3G 0J9
(506) 458-1113   *SIC* 7349

AQUACLEAR FILTRATION   *p* 99
10518 180 ST NW UNIT 101, EDMONTON, AB, T5S 2P1
(780) 809-3146   *SIC* 5074

AQUACULTURE DEVELOPMENT BRANCH   *p* 336
3RD FL, VICTORIA, BC, V8W 2Z7

SIC 8748
AQUAFUCHSIA   *p 1401*
4881 RUE SHERBROOKE O, WEST-
MOUNT, QC, H3Z 1G9
(514) 489-8466   *SIC 5148*
AQUAPRAXIS   *p 1215*
See WSP CANADA INC
AQUAREHAB EAU POTABLE INC *p 1233*
2145 RUE MICHELIN, MONTREAL, QC,
H7L 5B8
(450) 687-3472   *SIC 1623*
AQUAREHAB INC   *p 1233*
2145 RUE MICHELIN, MONTREAL, QC,
H7L 5B8
(450) 687-3472   *SIC 1623*
**AQUARIUM SERVICES WAREHOUSE OUT-
LETS INC**   *p*
1029
441 CHRISLEA RD, WOODBRIDGE, ON,
L4L 8N4
(905) 851-1858   *SIC 6794*
AQUASHELL HOLDINGS INC   *p 470*
13915 ROUTE 6, WALLACE, NS, B0K 1Y0
(902) 257-2920   *SIC 2092*
**AQUATECH CANADIAN WATER SERVICES
INC.**   *p 80*
BAY 5 41070 COOK RD, COCHRANE, AB,
T4C 1A1
(403) 932-4507   *SIC 4941*
**AQUATECH SOCIETE DE GESTION DE
L'EAU INC**   *p 1141*
2099 BOUL FERNAND-LAFONTAINE,
LONGUEUIL, QC, J4G 2J4
(450) 646-5200   *SIC 4941*
**AQUATECK WATER SYSTEMS DISTRIBU-
TORS LTD**   *p*
815
2700 LANCASTER RD SUITE 116, OT-
TAWA, ON, K1B 4T7
(613) 526-4613   *SIC 5084*
AQUATERA UTILITIES INC   *p 131*
11101 104 AVE, GRANDE PRAIRIE, AB,
T8V 8H6
(780) 532-9725   *SIC 4953*
AQUATERRA CORPORATION   *p 257*
6560 MCMILLAN WAY, RICHMOND, BC,
V6W 1L2
(604) 232-7610   *SIC 5963*
AQUATERRA CORPORATION   *p 691*
1200 BRITANNIA RD E, MISSISSAUGA,
ON, L4W 4T5
(905) 795-6500   *SIC 5149*
AQUICON CONSTRUCTION CO. LTD   *p 501*
131 DELTA PARK BLVD SUITE 1, BRAMP-
TON, ON, L6T 5M8
(905) 458-1313   *SIC 1542*
AQUIFER DISTRIBUTION LTD   *p 1426*
227 VENTURE CRES, SASKATOON, SK,
S7K 6N8
(306) 242-1567   *SIC 5074*
AQUIFER INVESTMENTS LTD   *p 1426*
227A VENTURE CRES, SASKATOON, SK,
S7K 6N8
(306) 242-1567   *SIC 6719*
AQUIFER PUMP DISTRIBUTING LTD   *p*
1426
227A VENTURE CRES, SASKATOON, SK,
S7K 6N8
(306) 242-1567   *SIC 5084*
AQUIFORM DISTRIBUTORS LTD   *p 278*
19296 25 AVE, SURREY, BC, V3Z 3X1
(604) 541-0500   *SIC 5091*
AQUILA CEDAR PRODUCTS LTD   *p 242*
1282 ALBERNI HWY, PARKSVILLE, BC,
V9P 2C9
(250) 248-5922   *SIC 5031*
AQUILINI INVESTMENT GROUP INC *p 296*
800 GRIFFITHS WAY, VANCOUVER, BC,
V6B 6G1
(604) 687-8813   *SIC 6512*
AQUILINI INVESTMENT GROUP INC *p 406*
1005 MAIN ST, MONCTON, NB, E1C 1G9
(506) 854-6340   *SIC 7011*
AQUILINI PROPERTIES LIMITED PART-

NERSHIP   *p*
1187
215 RUE SAINT-JACQUES UNITE 120,
MONTREAL, QC, H2Y 1M6
(514) 847-9547   *SIC 6512*
AQUILNI GROUP PROPERTIES LP   *p 400*
659 QUEEN ST, FREDERICTON, NB, E3B
1C3
(506) 455-3371   *SIC 7011*
AQUINOX PHARMACEUTICALS INC *p 288*
887 GREAT NORTHERN WAY SUITE 450,
VANCOUVER, BC, V5T 4T5
(604) 629-9223   *SIC 5912*
AR BOYCO IMAGE OPTOMETRY   *p 198*
See A.B. IMAGE OPTICS INC
**AR-LINE SECURITY AND INVESTIGATION
LTD**   *p 568*
34 BIRCH RD, ELLIOT LAKE, ON, P5A 2E2
SIC 6211
ARAGON MARKETING GROUP   *p 1186*
See 2040830 ONTARIO INC
ARAIGNEE   *p 1183*
See TRICOTS LELA INC, LES
ARAMARK CANADA LTD.   *p 117*
125 UNIVERSITY CAMPUS NW, EDMON-
TON, AB, T6G 2H6
(780) 492-5800   *SIC 5812*
ARAMARK CANADA LTD.   *p 451*
923 ROBIE ST, HALIFAX, NS, B3H 3C3
(902) 420-5599   *SIC 5812*
ARAMARK CANADA LTD.   *p 573*
811 ISLINGTON AVE, ETOBICOKE, ON,
M8Z 5W8
(416) 255-1331   *SIC 5812*
ARAMARK CANADA LTD.   *p 842*
2151 EAST BANK DR, PETERBOROUGH,
ON, K9L 1Z8
SIC 5812
ARAMARK CANADA LTD.   *p 907*
955 OLIVER RD, THUNDER BAY, ON, P7B
5E1
(807) 343-8142   *SIC 5812*
ARAMARK CANADA LTD.   *p 974*
21 CLASSIC AVE SUITE 1008, TORONTO,
ON, M5S 2Z3
(416) 598-2424   *SIC 5812*
ARAMARK ENTERTAINMENT SERVICES *p*
296
*See ARAMARK ENTERTAINMENT SER-
VICES (CANADA) INC*
**ARAMARK ENTERTAINMENT SERVICES
(CANADA) INC**   *p 221*
1223 WATER ST, KELOWNA, BC, V1Y 9V1
(250) 979-0878   *SIC 8742*
**ARAMARK ENTERTAINMENT SERVICES
(CANADA) INC**   *p 296*
800 GRIFFITHS WAY, VANCOUVER, BC,
V6B 6G1
(604) 780-7623   *SIC 8742*
**ARAMARK ENTERTAINMENT SERVICES
(CANADA) INC**   *p 626*
1000 PALLADIUM DR SUITE 107, KANATA,
ON, K2V 1A4
(613) 599-0230   *SIC 8742*
ARAMARK MANAGED SERVICES   *p 117*
See ARAMARK CANADA LTD.
ARAMARK MANAGED SERVICES   *p 573*
See ARAMARK CANADA LTD.
ARAMARK MANAGED SERVICES   *p 907*
See ARAMARK CANADA LTD.
ARAMARK QUEBEC INC   *p 1338*
4900 RUE FISHER, SAINT-LAURENT, QC,
H4T 1J6
(514) 341-7770   *SIC 5812*
**ARAMARK REMOTE WORKPLACE SER-
VICES LTD**   *p*
112
9647 45 AVE NW, EDMONTON, AB, T6E
5Z8
(780) 437-5665   *SIC 5812*
ARANA GARDENING SUPPLIES LIMITED *p*
737
6300 KENNEDY RD UNIT 1, MISSIS-
SAUGA, ON, L5T 2X5

(905) 670-8500   *SIC 5193*
ARAUCO CANADA LIMITED   *p 418*
151 CHURCH ST, ST STEPHEN, NB, E3L
5H1
(506) 466-2370   *SIC 5039*
ARAUCO CANADA LIMITED   *p 666*
80 TIVERTON CRT SUITE 701, MARKHAM,
ON, L3R 0G4
(905) 475-9686   *SIC 2631*
ARAUCO CANADA LIMITED   *p 861*
657 BASE LINE, SAULT STE. MARIE, ON,
P6A 5K6
(705) 253-0770   *SIC 2493*
ARAUCO NORTH AMERICA   *p 418*
See ARAUCO CANADA LIMITED
ARAUCO NORTH AMERICA   *p 666*
See ARAUCO CANADA LIMITED
ARAXI RESTAURANT & BAR   *p 342*
See ALIK ENTERPRISES LTD
ARBEC, BOIS D'OEUVRE INC   *p 1124*
1053 BOUL DUCHARME, LA TUQUE, QC,
G9X 3C3
(819) 523-2765   *SIC 2421*
ARBELL DISTRIBUTION PRODUCTS *p 520*
See 1542053 ONTARIO LIMITED
**ARBELL, DIV DE ELECTRONIQUES AC-
TIVE TECH**   *p*
1091
See ELECTRONIQUES ARBELL INC
ARBITREX   *p 1273*
*See SERVICES CONSEILS ARBITREX
INC, LES*
ARBOR MEMORIAL   *p 995*
See ARBOR MEMORIAL SERVICES INC
ARBOR MEMORIAL SERVICES INC *p 995*
2 JANE ST SUITE 101, TORONTO, ON,
M6S 4W8
(416) 763-3230   *SIC 6553*
ARBORCARE TREE SERVICE LTD   *p 77*
10100 114 AVE SE, CALGARY, AB, T3S
0A5
(403) 273-6378   *SIC 0783*
ARBORG & DISTRICT HEALTH CENTER *p*
345
GD, ARBORG, MB, R0C 0A0
(204) 376-5247   *SIC 8062*
ARBORG PERSONAL CARE HOME *p 345*
*See INTERLAKE REGIONAL HEALTH AU-
THORITY INC*
ARBORICULTURE DE BEAUCE INC *p 1055*
364E RTE DU PRESIDENT-KENNEDY,
BEAUCEVILLE, QC, G5X 1N9
(418) 774-6217   *SIC 0721*
ARBORITE, DIV OF   *p 1133*
See WILSONART CANADA ULC
ARBOUR AUTOMOBILES LTEE   *p 1085*
2475 BOUL CHOMEDEY, COTE SAINT-
LUC, QC, H7T 2R2
(450) 681-8110   *SIC 5521*
ARBOUR VOLKSWAGEN   *p 1085*
See ARBOUR AUTOMOBILES LTEE
ARBRE BLEU DONNEES CELLULAIRES *p*
1331
See SPECTRIS CANADA INC
ARBRE JOYEUX INC   *p 1356*
1077 271 RTE, SAINTE-CLOTILDE-DE-
BEAUCE, QC, G0N 1C0
(418) 427-3363   *SIC 5199*
ARBUTUS BIOPHARMA CORPORATION *p*
191
8900 GLENLYON PKY SUITE 100, BURN-
ABY, BC, V5J 5J8
(604) 419-3200   *SIC 2834*
ARBUTUS CARE CENTRE   *p 322*
See REVERA INC
ARBUTUS CLUB, THE   *p 320*
2001 NANTON AVE, VANCOUVER, BC,
V6J 4A1
(604) 266-7166   *SIC 7997*
ARBUTUS COVE ENTERPRISES INC *p 336*
650 HERALD ST, VICTORIA, BC, V8W 1S7
(250) 598-1387   *SIC 5146*
ARBUTUS ROOFING & DRAINS (2006) LTD
p 259

4260 VANGUARD RD, RICHMOND, BC,
V6X 2P5
(604) 272-7277   *SIC 1761*
ARBUTUS RV & MARINE SALES LTD *p 232*
2603 SACKVILLE RD, MERVILLE, BC, V0R
2M0
(250) 337-2174   *SIC 5571*
ARBY'S   *p 41*
See SUNNY HOLDINGS LIMITED
ARC   *p 259*
*See ARTHRITIS RESEARCH CENTRE SO-
CIETY OF CANADA, THE*
ARC BUSINESS SOLUTIONS INC   *p 87*
10088 102 AVE NW SUITE 2507, EDMON-
TON, AB, T5J 2Z1
(780) 702-5022   *SIC 7379*
ARC INDUSTRIES   *p 526*
See COMMUNITY LIVING BURLINGTON
ARC INDUSTRIES   *p 532*
466 FRANKLIN BLVD, CAMBRIDGE, ON,
N1R 8G6
(519) 621-0680   *SIC 8331*
ARC INDUSTRIES   *p 533*
See COMMUNITY LIVING CAMBRIDGE
ARC INDUSTRIES   *p 602*
*See COMMUNITY LIVING GUELPH
WELLINGTON*
ARC LINE CONSTRUCTION LTD   *p 7*
GD STN MAIN, BROOKS, AB, T1R 1E4
(403) 362-4315   *SIC 1623*
ARC PROTECTION CORP   *p 208*
7351 VANTAGE WAY UNIT 3, DELTA, BC,
V4G 1C9
(604) 345-0215   *SIC 6289*
ARC RESOURCES LTD   *p 43*
308 4 AVE SW SUITE 1200, CALGARY, AB,
T2P 0H7
(403) 503-8600   *SIC 1381*
ARC'TERYX EQUIPMENT DIV.   *p 187*
See AMER SPORTS CANADA INC
ARC'TERYX EQUIPMENT DIV.   *p 238*
See AMER SPORTS CANADA INC
ARC'TERYX EQUIPMENT DIV.   *p 286*
See AMER SPORTS CANADA INC
ARC-EN-CIEL   *p 1388*
See MARGARINE THIBAULT INC
ARCA FINANCIAL GROUP INC   *p 1007*
237 LABRADOR DR, WATERLOO, ON, N2K
4M8
(519) 745-8500   *SIC 6282*
ARCADIAN PROJECTS INC   *p 483*
1439 GINGERICH RD UNIT 2, BADEN, ON,
N3A 3J7
(519) 804-9697   *SIC 5211*
ARCADIS CANADA INC   *p 691*
4005 HICKORY DR, MISSISSAUGA, ON,
L4W 1L1
(905) 614-1978   *SIC 8748*
ARCADIS CANADA INC   *p 850*
121 GRANTON DR UNIT 12, RICHMOND
HILL, ON, L4B 3N4
(905) 764-9380   *SIC 8748*
ARCAN DEVELOPMENTS LTD   *p 342*
1675 27TH ST, WEST VANCOUVER, BC,
V7V 4K9
(604) 925-1247   *SIC 8069*
ARCAN GROUP INC   *p 435*
112 TALTHEILEI DR, YELLOWKNIFE, NT,
X1A 0E9
(867) 873-2520   *SIC 1542*
ARCANE   *p 653*
See ARCANE DIGITAL INC
ARCANE DIGITAL INC   *p 653*
304 TALBOT ST, LONDON, ON, N6A 2R4
(226) 289-2445   *SIC 7311*
ARCANE HORIZON INC   *p 383*
1313 BORDER ST UNIT 62, WINNIPEG,
MB, R3H 0X4
(204) 897-5482   *SIC 8611*
ARCELORMITTAL COTEAU-DU-LAC INC *p*
1088
25 RUE DE L'ACIER, COTEAU-DU-LAC,
QC, J0P 1B0
(450) 763-0915   *SIC 3479*

ARCELORMITTAL COTEAU-DU-LAC LIMITED PARTNERSHIP   p
1088
25 RUE DE L'ACIER, COTEAU-DU-LAC, QC, J0P 1B0
(450) 763-0915   SIC 3479

ARCELORMITTAL DOFASCO G.P.   p 611
1330 BURLINGTON ST E, HAMILTON, ON, L8N 3J5
(905) 548-7200   SIC 3479

ARCELORMITTAL EXPLOITATION MINIERE CANADA S.E.N.C.   p 1144
1010 RUE DE SERIGNY, LONGUEUIL, QC, J4K 5G7
(418) 766-2000   SIC 1011

ARCELORMITTAL PRODUITS LONGS CANADA S.E.N.C.   p 1082
3900 RTE DES ACIERIES, CONTRE-COEUR, QC, J0L 1C0
(450) 587-8600   SIC 3312

ARCELORMITTAL PRODUITS LONGS CANADA S.E.N.C.   p 1082
4000 RTE DES ACIERIES, CONTRE-COEUR, QC, J0L 1C0
(450) 587-8600   SIC 3312

ARCELORMITTAL PRODUITS LONGS CANADA S.E.N.C.   p 1082
2050 RTE DES ACIERIES, CONTRE-COEUR, QC, J0L 1C0
(450) 587-2012   SIC 3312

ARCELORMITTAL PRODUITS LONGS CANADA S.E.N.C.   p 1145
2555 CH DU LAC, LONGUEUIL, QC, J4N 1C1
(450) 442-7700   SIC 3316

ARCELORMITTAL PRODUITS LONGS CANADA S.E.N.C.   p 1223
5900 RUE SAINT-PATRICK, MONTREAL, QC, H4E 1B3
(514) 762-5260   SIC 3312

ARCELORMITTAL TAILORED BLANKS AMERICAS LIMITED   p 548
55 CONFEDERATION PKY, CONCORD, ON, L4K 4Y7
(905) 761-1525   SIC 3542

ARCELORMITTAL TAILORED BLANKS MERELBEKE   p 548
See ARCELORMITTAL TAILORED BLANKS AMERICAS LIMITED

ARCELORMITTAL TUBULAR PRODUCTS CANADA G.P.   p 510
14 HOLTBY AVE, BRAMPTON, ON, L6X 2M3
(905) 451-2400   SIC 3714

ARCELORMITTAL TUBULAR PRODUCTS CANADA G.P.   p 1034
193 GIVINS ST, WOODSTOCK, ON, N4S 5Y8
(519) 537-6671   SIC 3714

ARCH CHEMICALS CANADA, INC   p 803
160 WARNER DR, OAKVILLE, ON, L6L 6E7
(905) 847-9878   SIC 5169

ARCHAMBAULT   p 1164
See GROUPE ARCHAMBAULT INC

ARCHAMBAULT, J. L. PHARMACIEN   p
1295
12 BOUL CLAIREVUE O BUREAU 39, SAINT-BRUNO, QC, J3V 1P8
(450) 653-1528   SIC 5912

ARCHANGEL FIREWORKS INC   p 387
104 PEMBINA HWY, WINNIPEG, MB, R3L 2C8
(204) 943-3332   SIC 5999

ARCHBISHOP DENIS O'CONNOR CATHOLIC HIGH SCHOOL   p 474
See DURHAM CATHOLIC DISTRICT SCHOOL BOARD

ARCHBISHOP MC O'NEILL HIGH SCHOOL   p 1420
See BOARD OF EDUCATION OF THE REGINA ROMAN CATHOLIC SEPARATE SCHOOL DIVISION NO. 81

ARCHBISHOP O'LEARY CATHOLIC HIGH SCHOOL   p 84

See EDMONTON CATHOLIC SCHOOLS

ARCHBISHOP ROMERO CATHOLIC SECONDARY SCHOOL   p
994
See TORONTO CATHOLIC DISTRICT SCHOOL BOARD

ARCHDIOCESE OF ST BONIFACE, THE   p
364
151 DE LA CATHEDRALE AVE, WINNIPEG, MB, R2H 0H6
(204) 237-9851   SIC 8661

ARCHE DAYBREAK, L'   p 856
11339 YONGE ST, RICHMOND HILL, ON, L4S 1L1
(905) 884-3454   SIC 8361

ARCHEAN ENERGY LTD   p 43
324 8 AVE SW SUITE 1000, CALGARY, AB, T2P 2Z2
(403) 237-9600   SIC 5541

ARCHEAN RESOURCES LTD   p 431
140 WATER ST SUITE 903, ST. JOHN'S, NL, A1C 6H6
(709) 758-1700   SIC 1081

ARCHER TRUCK SERVICES LIMITED   p
885
260 DUNKIRK RD, ST CATHARINES, ON, L2R 7K6
(905) 685-6532   SIC 5511

ARCHER'S POULTRY FARM LIMITED p 518
15738 COUNTY ROAD 2, BRIGHTON, ON, K0K 1H0
(613) 475-0820   SIC 5191

ARCHEVEQUE & RIVEST LTEE, L'   p 1282
96 BOUL INDUSTRIEL, REPENTIGNY, QC, J6A 4X6
(450) 581-4480   SIC 1542

ARCHEVEQUE CATHOLIQUE ROMAIN DE QUEBEC, L'   p 1270
1073 BOUL RENE-LEVESQUE O, QUEBEC, QC, G1S 4R5
(418) 688-1211   SIC 8661

ARCHIBALD, GRAY & MCKAY LTD   p 657
3514 WHITE OAK RD, LONDON, ON, N6E 2Z9
(519) 685-5300   SIC 5995

ARCHIDIOCESE DE MONCTON   p 397
452 RUE AMIRAULT, DIEPPE, NB, E1A 1G3
(506) 857-9531   SIC 8661

ARCHIE MCCOY (HAMILTON) LIMITED   p
999
1890 HIGHWAY 5 W, TROY, ON, L0R 2B0
(519) 647-3411   SIC 3321

ARCHIE'S SACKVILLE BOTTLE EXCHANGE LIMITED   p
461
446 SACKVILLE DR, LOWER SACKVILLE, NS, B4C 2R8
(902) 865-9010   SIC 7389

ARCHIES SURF SHOP   p 652
See 11292580 ONTARIO LIMITED

ARCHIPELAGO MARINE RESEARCH LTD p
339
525 HEAD ST SUITE 1, VICTORIA, BC, V9A 5S1
(250) 383-4535   SIC 8732

ARCHITECTES DE MESSAGERIE   p 1211
See NETGOVERN INC

ARCHITECTURAL DIVISION   p 641
See AECOM CANADA LTD

ARCHITECTURAL ORNAMENT INC p 548
55 BRADWICK DR, CONCORD, ON, L4K 1K5
SIC 2821

ARCHITECTURAL PRECAST STRUCTURES LTD   p
224
9844 199A ST, LANGLEY, BC, V1M 2X7
(604) 888-1968   SIC 1771

ARCHITECTURE49 INC   p 390
1600 BUFFALO PL, WINNIPEG, MB, R3T 6B8
(204) 477-1260   SIC 8712

ARCHIVE IRON MOUNTAIN   p 1241
See IRON MOUNTAIN CANADA OPERA-

TIONS ULC

ARCHIVES DU SEMINAIRE SAINT-JOSEPH DE TROIS-RIVIERES   p
1388
See SEMINAIRE DES TROIS-RIVIERES

ARCHIVES IRON MOUNTAIN   p 504
See IRON MOUNTAIN CANADA OPERATIONS ULC

ARCHIVES IRON MOUNTAIN   p 554
See IRON MOUNTAIN CANADA OPERATIONS ULC

ARCHWAY INSURANCE INC   p 438
81 VICTORIA ST E, AMHERST, NS, B4H 1X7
(902) 667-0800   SIC 6411

ARCIS SEISMIC SOLUTIONS CORP   p 43
250 5 ST SW SUITE 2100, CALGARY, AB, T2P 0R4
(403) 781-1700   SIC 1382

ARCLIN CANADA LTD   p 544
56 WILLMOTT ST, COBOURG, ON, K9A 4S3
(905) 372-1896   SIC 2821

ARCO RESOURCES CORP   p 302
570 GRANVILLE ST SUITE 1200, VANCOUVER, BC, V6C 3P1
(604) 689-8336   SIC 1081

ARCOLA CO-OPERATIVE ASSOCIATION LIMITED   p 1404
HWY 13, ARCOLA, SK, S0C 0G0
(306) 455-2393   SIC 5171

ARCON ELECTRIC LTD   p 648
1065 CLARKE RD, LONDON, ON, N5V 3B3
(519) 451-6699   SIC 1731

ARCON METAL PROCESSING INC   p 855
105 INDUSTRIAL RD, RICHMOND HILL, ON, L4C 2Y4
SIC 3469

ARCONAS   p 729
See ARCONAS INVESTMENTS LTD

ARCONAS CORPORATION   p 729
5700 KEATON CRES UNIT 1, MISSISSAUGA, ON, L5R 3H5
(905) 272-0727   SIC 2531

ARCONAS INVESTMENTS LTD   p 729
5700 KEATON CRES UNIT 1, MISSISSAUGA, ON, L5R 3H5
(905) 272-0727   SIC 2531

ARCOTEC QUEBEC   p 1263
See 9190-5730 QUEBEC INC

ARCTEC ALLOYS LIMITED   p 20
4304 10 ST NE, CALGARY, AB, T2E 6K3
(403) 250-9355   SIC 5085

ARCTIC BEVERAGES LP   p 356
107 MOUNTAIN VIEW RD UNIT 2, ROSSER, MB, R0H 1E0
(204) 633-8686   SIC 5149

ARCTIC CHILLER LTD   p 161
100 CREE RD, SHERWOOD PARK, AB, T8A 3X8
(780) 449-0459   SIC 5149

ARCTIC CO-OPERATIVES LIMITED   p 371
1645 INKSTER BLVD, WINNIPEG, MB, R2X 2W7
(204) 697-1625   SIC 5099

ARCTIC CRANE SERVICE LTD   p 134
14915 89 ST, GRANDE PRAIRIE, AB, T8X 0J2
(780) 814-6990   SIC 7389

ARCTIC DOVE LIMITED   p 435
8 TANK FARM RD, INUVIK, NT, X0E 0T0
(867) 777-3226   SIC 5171

ARCTIC GLACIER   p 373
See AGI CCAA INC

ARCTIC HOLDINGS & LEASING LTD p 435
135 KAM LAKE RD, YELLOWKNIFE, NT, X1A 0G3
(867) 920-4844   SIC 1611

ARCTIC OIL & GAS SERVICES INC   p 435
170 MACKENZIE RD, INUVIK, NT, X0E 0T0
(867) 777-8700   SIC 5812

ARCTIC PACKAGING INDUSTRIES INC   p
1010
295 FROBISHER DR, WATERLOO, ON,

N2V 2G4
(519) 885-2161   SIC 5199

ARCTIC SPAS   p 169
See BLUE FALLS MANUFACTURING LTD

ARCTURUS REALTY CORPORATION p 578
191 THE WEST MALL SUITE 400, ETOBICOKE, ON, M9C 5K8
(905) 943-4100   SIC 6531

ARCURVE INC   p 63
902 11 AVE SW SUITE 300, CALGARY, AB, T2R 0E7
(403) 242-4361   SIC 7372

ARDENE   p 1335
See PLACEMENTS ARDEN INC, LES

ARDENT MILLS ULC   p 1215
2110 RUE NOTRE-DAME O, MONTREAL, QC, H3J 1N2
(514) 939-8051   SIC 2041

ARDENT MILLS ULC   p 1426
95 33RD ST E, SASKATOON, SK, S7K 0R8
(306) 665-7200   SIC 2044

ARDENT SPORTSWEAR INCORPORATED   p 291
125 3RD AVE W, VANCOUVER, BC, V5Y 1E6
(604) 879-3268   SIC 5136

ARDENTON CAPITAL CORPORATION   p
311
1021 WEST HASTINGS ST UNIT 2400, VANCOUVER, BC, V6E 0C3
(604) 833-4899   SIC 6162

ARDENTON FINANCIAL   p 311
See ARDENTON CAPITAL CORPORATION

ARDO VLM   p 1091
See ALIMENTS VLM INC, LES

ARDROSSAN JUNIOR SENIOR HIGH   p 4
See ELK ISLAND PUBLIC SCHOOLS REGIONAL DIVISION NO. 14

ARENA BOURGET   p 1283
See COLLEGE BOURGET

ARENA CHENIER   p 1142
See SOGEP INC

ARENA DES CANADIENS INC, L'   p 1209
1275 RUE SAINT-ANTOINE O, MONTREAL, QC, H3C 5L2
(514) 932-2582   SIC 7941

ARENA DU ROCKET, L'   p 1210
See CLUB DE HOCKEY CANADIEN, INC

ARENA W.B. SCOTT   p 1375
See UNIVERSITE BISHOP'S

ARENS, MIKE BUILDING MATERIALS LTD   p 542
124 KEIL DR S SUITE 1719, CHATHAM, ON, N7M 3H1
(519) 354-0700   SIC 5211

AREO-FEU LTEE   p 1309
5205 RUE J.-A.-BOMBARDIER, SAINT-HUBERT, QC, J3Z 1G4
(450) 651-2240   SIC 5087

ARES VENTURES INC   p 1433
668 UNIVERSITY DR, SASKATOON, SK, S7N 0J2
(306) 241-1435   SIC 1521

ARGENT FISHERIES (2007) LIMITED p 450
501 MAIN ST, GLACE BAY, NS, B1A 4X5
(902) 849-1005   SIC 0912

ARGENTIA FREEZERS & TERMINALS LIMITED   p
423
GD, FRESHWATER PB, NL, A0B 1W0
(709) 227-5603   SIC 4222

ARGO   p 752
See ONTARIO DRIVE & GEAR LIMITED

ARGO CANADA HOLDING ULC   p 648
3020 GORE RD, LONDON, ON, N5V 4T7
(519) 457-3400   SIC 6712

ARGO LUMBER   p 664
See ARGO LUMBER INC

ARGO LUMBER INC   p 664
10275 KEELE ST, MAPLE, ON, L6A 3Y9
(905) 832-2251   SIC 5031

ARGO ROAD MAINTENANCE (SOUTH OKANAGAN) INC   p 243
290 WATERLOO AVE, PENTICTON, BC,

V2A 7N3

(250) 493-6969   SIC 1611
ARGO SALES INC   p 43
717 7 AVE SW SUITE 1300, CALGARY, AB,
T2P 0Z3

(403) 265-6633   SIC 3443
ARGO SALES INC   p 145
925 23 ST SW, MEDICINE HAT, AB, T1A
8R1

(403) 526-3142   SIC 3443
ARGON SOLUTION   p 816
See 9111735 CANADA INC
ARGONAUT GOLD INC   p 985
1 FIRST CANADIAN PLACE SUITE 3400,
TORONTO, ON, M5X 1A4

SIC 1081
ARGOS CARPETS LTD   p 750
1914 MERIVALE RD, NEPEAN, ON, K2G
1E8

(613) 226-6573   SIC 5023
ARGUS CARRIERS LTD   p 184
3839 MYRTLE ST, BURNABY, BC, V5C 4G1

(604) 433-2066   SIC 4212
ARGUS MACHINE CO. LTD   p 112
5820 97 ST NW, EDMONTON, AB, T6E 3J1

(780) 434-9451   SIC 3494
ARGUS MAZDA AUTO   p 1107
See 174761 CANADA INC
ARGUS TELECOM INTERNATIONAL INC p
1328
2505 RUE GUENETTE, SAINT-LAURENT,
QC, H4R 2E9

(514) 331-0840   SIC 5065
ARGYLE COBBLERS LTD   p 451
1663 ARGYLE ST, HALIFAX, NS, B3J 2B5

(902) 492-3018   SIC 5812
ARGYLE SECONDARY SCHOOL   p 239
See SCHOOL DISTRICT NO. 44 (NORTH
VANCOUVER)
ARI FINANCIAL SERVICES INC   p 711
1270 CENTRAL PKY W SUITE 500, MIS-
SISSAUGA, ON, L5C 4P4

(905) 803-8000   SIC 8741
ARI FLEET SERVICES OF CANADA INC p
859
1000 DEGURSE RD, SARNIA, ON, N7T
7H5

(519) 332-3739   SIC 4789
ARIAN PHOSPHATE   p 1078
See ARIANNE PHOSPHATE INC
ARIANA HOLDINGS INC   p 692
4544 EASTGATE PKY, MISSISSAUGA, ON,
L4W 3W6

(905) 238-6300   SIC 2033
ARIANNE PHOSPHATE INC   p 1078
393 RUE RACINE E BUREAU 200,
CHICOUTIMI, QC, G7H 1T2

(418) 549-7316   SIC 1475
ARISE TECHNOLOGIES CORP   p 535
150 WERLICH DR SUITE 5, CAMBRIDGE,
ON, N1T 1N6

SIC 5211
ARISS CONTROLS & ELECTRIC INC p 139
6800 39 ST, LEDUC, AB, T9E 0Z4

(780) 986-1147   SIC 1731
ARISS MANUFACTURING   p 478
See LINAMAR CORPORATION
ARISTOCRAT   p 1398
See WOOD WYANT CANADA INC
ARITZIA INC   p 294
611 ALEXANDER ST SUITE 118, VANCOU-
VER, BC, V6A 1E1

(604) 251-3132   SIC 5651
ARITZIA LP   p 294
611 ALEXANDER ST SUITE 118, VANCOU-
VER, BC, V6A 1E1

(604) 251-3132   SIC 5621
ARITZIA LP   p 329
701 GEORGIA ST W SUITE 53D, VANCOU-
VER, BC, V7Y 1K8

(604) 681-9301   SIC 5621
ARIVA   p 738
See DOMTAR INC
ARIVA DIV OF   p 1127

See DOMTAR INC
ARIZONA SILVER EXPLORATION INC   p
302
750 WEST PENDER ST SUITE 804, VAN-
COUVER, BC, V6C 2T7

(604) 833-4278   SIC 1041
ARJO   p 729
See ARJO CANADA INC
ARJO CANADA INC   p 729
90 MATHESON BLVD W SUITE 350, MIS-
SISSAUGA, ON, L5R 3R3

(905) 238-7880   SIC 5047
ARJOHUNTLEIGH MAGOG INC   p 1147
2001 RUE TANGUAY, MAGOG, QC, J1X
5Y5

(819) 868-0441   SIC 3841
ARKEMA CANADA INC   p 1055
655 BOUL ALPHONSE-DESHAIES, BE-
CANCOUR, QC, G9H 2Y8

(819) 294-9965   SIC 2819
ARLA FOODS INC   p 548
675 RIVERMEDE RD, CONCORD, ON, L4K
2G9

(905) 669-9393   SIC 5451
ARLANXEO CANADA INC   p 859
1265 VIDAL ST S, SARNIA, ON, N7T 7M2

(519) 337-8251   SIC 2822
ARLBERG HOLDINGS INC   p 1332
4505 RUE COUSENS, SAINT-LAURENT,
QC, H4S 1X5

SIC 6712
ARLIE'S SPORT SHOP (DOWNTOWN) LTD
p 883
17 KEEFER RD, ST CATHARINES, ON,
L2M 6K4

(905) 684-8134   SIC 5621
ARLYN ENTERPRISES LTD   p 13
6303 30 ST SE UNIT 112, CALGARY, AB,
T2C 1R4

(403) 279-2223   SIC 5172
ARM AGENCE DE RECOUVREMENT INC p
1387
985 RUE ROYALE BUREAU 201, TROIS-
RIVIERES, QC, G9A 4H7

(819) 375-3327   SIC 7322
ARM RIVER COLONY   p 1409
See ARM RIVER FARMING CO. LTD
ARM RIVER FARMING CO. LTD   p 1409
GD, LUMSDEN, SK, S0G 3C0

(306) 731-2819   SIC 0191
ARMADA COLONY   p 144
GD, LOMOND, AB, T0L 1G0

(403) 792-3388   SIC 0191
ARMADA TOOLWORKS LIMITED   p 645
6 LOF DR, LINDSAY, ON, K9V 4S5

(705) 328-9599   SIC 3089
ARMAND AUTOMOBILES LTEE   p 1074
542 BOUL PERRON, CARLETON, QC, G0C
1J0

(418) 364-3382   SIC 5511
ARMAND GENEST & FILS   p 1262
See LA-BIL INC
ARMAND GUAY   p 1280
See GUAY INC
ARMAND H. COUTURE LTD   p 619
1226 FRONT ST, HEARST, ON, P0L 1N0

(705) 362-4941   SIC 5171
ARMANEAU AUTOS INC   p 1159
140 BOUL TACHE O, MONTMAGNY, QC,
G5V 3A5

(418) 248-2323   SIC 5511
ARMATEC SURVIVABILITY CORP   p 565
1 NEWTON AVE, DORCHESTER, ON, N0L
1G4

(519) 268-2999   SIC 3795
ARMATURE DNS 2000 INC   p 1239
11001 AV JEAN-MEUNIER, MONTREAL-
NORD, QC, H1G 4S7

(514) 324-1141   SIC 3625
ARMATURE ELECTRIC LIMITED   p 191
3811 NORTH FRASER WAY, BURNABY,
BC, V5J 5J2

(604) 879-6141   SIC 1731
ARMATURES BOIS-FRANCS INC   p 1399

249 BOUL DE LA BONAVENTURE, VICTO-
RIAVILLE, QC, G6T 1V5

(819) 758-7501   SIC 3443
ARMAUR PLUMBING LTD   p 224
20085 100A AVE UNIT 1, LANGLEY, BC,
V1M 3G4

(604) 888-1255   SIC 1711
ARMBRO TRANSPORT INC   p 737
6050 DIXIE RD, MISSISSAUGA, ON, L5T
1A6

(416) 213-7299   SIC 4731
ARMO-TOOL LIMITED   p 662
9827 LONGWOODS RD, LONDON, ON,
N6P 1P2

(519) 652-3700   SIC 3544
ARMOIRES CAMBOARD   p 1154
See ARMOIRES FABRITEC LTEE
ARMOIRES CONTESSA INC   p 1394
370 RUE JOSEPH-CARRIER, VAUDREUIL-
DORION, QC, J7V 5V5

(450) 455-6682   SIC 2434
ARMOIRES CUISINES ACTION   p 1134
See 2757-5158 QUEBEC INC
ARMOIRES CUISINES ACTION   p 1316
See 2757-5158 QUEBEC INC
ARMOIRES CUISINES ACTION   p 1363
See 2757-5158 QUEBEC INC
ARMOIRES DE CUISINE BERNIER INC p
1137
1955 3E RUE BUREAU 70, LEVIS, QC,
G6W 5M6

(418) 839-8142   SIC 2434
ARMOIRES DISTINCTION INC   p 1284
180 AV LEONIDAS S, RIMOUSKI, QC, G5L
2T2

(418) 723-6857   SIC 5211
ARMOIRES FABRITEC LTEE   p 1068
80 BOUL DE L'AEROPORT, BROMONT,
QC, J2L 1S9

(450) 534-1659   SIC 2434
ARMOIRES FABRITEC LTEE   p 1154
1230 RUE INDUSTRIELLE, MONT-JOLI,
QC, G5H 3S2

(418) 775-7010   SIC 2434
ARMOIRES MIRALIS   p 1291
See MIRALIS INC
**ARMOR MACHINE & MANUFACTURING
LIMITED**   p 120
9962 29 AVE NW, EDMONTON, AB, T6N
1A2

(780) 465-6152   SIC 3599
ARMOR PERSONNEL   p 510
See PINPOINT CAREERS INC
ARMOROOF DIV OF   p 509
See IKO INDUSTRIES LTD
ARMOROOF DIV OF   p 619
See IKO INDUSTRIES LTD
ARMOROOF DIV OF   p 663
See IKO INDUSTRIES LTD
ARMOUR STEEL SUPPLY LIMITED   p 891
540 SEAMAN ST, STONEY CREEK, ON,
L8E 3X7

(905) 388-7751   SIC 5051
ARMOUR TRANSPORT   p 448
See POLE STAR TRANSPORT INCORPO-
RATED
ARMOUR TRANSPORT INC   p 408
689 EDINBURGH DR, MONCTON, NB, E1E
2L4

(506) 857-0205   SIC 4213
ARMOUR TRANSPORT INC   p 445
80 GUILDFORD AVE, DARTMOUTH, NS,
B3B 0G3

(902) 468-8855   SIC 4213
ARMOUR TRANSPORTATION SYSTEMS p
408
See ARMOUR TRANSPORT INC
ARMOUR TRANSPORTATION SYSTEMS p
445
See ARMOUR TRANSPORT INC
**ARMOUR TRANSPORTATION SYSTEMS
INC**   p 408
689 EDINBURGH DR, MONCTON, NB, E1E
2L4

(506) 857-0205   SIC 6712
ARMOUR VALVE LTD   p 873
126 MILNER AVE, SCARBOROUGH, ON,
M1S 3R2

(416) 299-0780   SIC 5085
ARMOUR-CLAD CONTRACTING INC   p 99
18035 114 AVE NW, EDMONTON, AB, T5S
1T8

SIC 1542
ARMSTRONG & QUAILE ASSOCIATES INC
p 663
5858 RIDEAU VALLEY DR N, MANOTICK,
ON, K4M 1B3

(613) 692-0751   SIC 6211
ARMSTRONG ELEMENTARY SCHOOL   p
188
See BURNABY SCHOOL BOARD DIS-
TRICT 41
ARMSTRONG FLUID TECHNOLOGY p 869
See S. A. ARMSTRONG LIMITED
ARMSTRONG MILLING CO. LTD   p 607
1021 HALDIMAND RD UNIT 20,
HAGERSVILLE, ON, N0A 1H0

(905) 779-2473   SIC 2048
**ARMSTRONG MONITORING CORPORA-
TION, THE**   p
831
215 COLONNADE RD S, OTTAWA, ON,
K2E 7K3

(613) 225-9531   SIC 3829
ARMSTRONG PARTNERSHIP LP   p 778
23 PRINCE ANDREW PL, NORTH YORK,
ON, M3C 2H2

(416) 444-3050   SIC 8743
ARMSTRONG PLAZA LTD   p 839
142 HUNTER ST E, PETERBOROUGH,
ON, K9H 1G6

(705) 743-8253   SIC 5411
ARMSTRONG REGIONAL CO-OPERATIVE
p 179
973 OTTER LAKE CROSS RD, ARM-
STRONG, BC, V0E 1B6

(250) 546-9438   SIC 5541
ARMSTRONG REGIONAL COOPERATIVEp
179
973 OTTER LAKE CROSS RD, ARM-
STRONG, BC, V0E 1B6

(250) 546-9438   SIC 5171
ARMSTRONG STORE LIMITED   p 840
760 SHERBROOKE ST, PETERBOR-
OUGH, ON, K9J 2R1

(705) 742-3321   SIC 5411
ARMSTRONG TOP PACK LTD   p 644
500 COUNTY RD 18, LEAMINGTON, ON,
N8H 3V5

(519) 326-3273   SIC 7389
ARMSTRONG'S COMMUNICATION LTD   p
397
380 SALMON RIVER MOUTH RD, COAL
CREEK, NB, E4A 2T7

(506) 339-6066   SIC 7382
ARMSTRONG, O.H. LIMITED   p 460
1478 PARK ST, KINGSTON, NS, B0P 1R0

(902) 765-3311   SIC 5147
ARMTEC   p 13
See AP INFRASTRUCTURE SOLUTIONS
LP
ARMTEC   p 370
See ARMTEC INC
ARMTEC CANADA CULVERT   p 99
See ARMTEC INC
ARMTEC HOLDINGS LIMITED   p 602
370 SPEEDVALE AVE W SUITE 101,
GUELPH, ON, N1H 7M7

(519) 822-0210   SIC 3272
ARMTEC INC   p 99
10423 178 ST NW UNIT 201, EDMONTON,
AB, T5S 1R5

(780) 487-3404   SIC 3498
ARMTEC INC   p 370
2500 FERRIER ST, WINNIPEG, MB, R2V
4P6

(204) 338-9311   SIC 3312
ARMVIEW ESTATES   p 459

See SHANNEX INCORPORATED
ARMY & NAVY p 296
See ARMY & NAVY DEPT. STORE LIMITED
ARMY & NAVY DEPT. STORE LIMITEDp 84
100 LONDONDERRY MALL UNIT A, ED-
MONTON, AB, T5C 3C8
SIC 5399
ARMY & NAVY DEPT. STORE LIMITED p
236
502 COLUMBIA ST, NEW WESTMINSTER,
BC, V3L 1B1
(604) 526-4661   SIC 5311
ARMY & NAVY DEPT. STORE LIMITED p
296
74 CORDOVA ST W, VANCOUVER, BC,
V6B 1C9
(604) 683-9660   SIC 5311
ARMY & NAVY DEPT. STORE LIMITED p
296
27 HASTINGS ST W SUITE 25, VANCOU-
VER, BC, V6B 1G5
(604) 682-6644   SIC 5311
ARMY & NAVY DEPT. STORE NO.12 p 84
See ARMY & NAVY DEPT. STORE LIMITED
ARNASON INDUSTRIES LTD p 356
9094 HWY 1, ROSSER, MB, R0H 1E0
(204) 633-2567   SIC 1623
ARNE'S TRAILER SALES p 365
See ARNE'S WELDING LTD
ARNE'S WELDING LTD p 365
835 MISSION ST, WINNIPEG, MB, R2J 0A4
(204) 233-7111   SIC 3715
ARNEG CANADA INC p 1129
18 RUE RICHELIEU, LACOLLE, QC, J0J
1J0
(450) 246-3837   SIC 3585
**ARNETT & BURGESS OIL FIELD CON-
STRUCTION LIMITED** p
160
4510 50 ST, SEDGEWICK, AB, T0B 4C0
(780) 384-4050   SIC 1623
ARNETT & BURGESS PIPELINERS LTD p
161
4510 50 ST S, SEDGEWICK, AB, T0B 4C0
(780) 384-4050   SIC 1623
ARNO ELECTRIC p 1386
See ARNO ELECTRIQUE LTEE
ARNO ELECTRIQUE LTEE p 1386
2300 BOUL DES RECOLLETS, TROIS-
RIVIERES, QC, G8Z 3X5
(819) 379-5222   SIC 1731
ARNO HOLDINGS LTD p 538
201B PRESTON PKY, CAMBRIDGE, ON,
N3H 5E8
(519) 653-3171   SIC 6712
ARNOLD BROS. TRANSPORT LTD p 365
739 LAGIMODIERE BLVD, WINNIPEG, MB,
R2J 0T8
(204) 257-6666   SIC 4213
ARNOLD WINDSHIELD DISTRIBUTORS p
111
See WINDSHIELD SURGEONS LTD
ARNON p 830
See ARNON DEVELOPMENT CORPORA-
TION LIMITED
**ARNON DEVELOPMENT CORPORATION
LIMITED** p 830
1801 WOODWARD DR, OTTAWA, ON, K2C
0R3
(613) 226-2000   SIC 6553
ARNONE TRANSPORT LIMITED p 907
300 WATER ST S, THUNDER BAY, ON, P7B
6P6
(807) 345-1478   SIC 4213
ARNOTT CONSTRUCTION LIMITED p 681
2 BERTRAM INDUSTRIAL PKY SUITE 1,
MIDHURST, ON, L0L 1X0
(705) 735-9121   SIC 1623
ARNPRIOR AEROSPACE INC p 478
107 BASKIN DR, ARNPRIOR, ON, K7S 3M1
(613) 623-4267   SIC 3728
ARNPRIOR BUILDERS SUPPLIES, DIV OF
p 479
See M. SULLIVAN & SON LIMITED

ARNPRIOR CHRYSLER LTD p 478
205 MADAWASKA BLVD, ARNPRIOR, ON,
K7S 1S6
(613) 623-4256   SIC 5511
ARNPRIOR LEGION BRANCH 174 p 479
See ROYAL CANADIAN LEGION, THE
ARNPRIOR OTTAWA AUTO PARTS LTD p
478
5445 MADAWASKA BLVD, ARNPRIOR, ON,
K7S 3H4
(613) 623-7361   SIC 5531
ARNPRIOR REGIONAL HEALTH p 478
350 JOHN ST N, ARNPRIOR, ON, K7S 2P6
(613) 623-7962   SIC 8062
**ARNSBY, M. F. PROPERTY MANAGEMENT
LTD** p 651
924 OXFORD ST E, LONDON, ON, N5Y 3J9
(519) 455-6080   SIC 6531
ARO INC p 1175
1001 RUE SHERBROOKE E BUREAU 700,
MONTREAL, QC, H2L 1L3
(514) 322-1414   SIC 7322
ARODAL SERVICES LTD p 253
2631 VIKING WAY SUITE 248, RICHMOND,
BC, V6V 3B5
(604) 274-0477   SIC 7349
AROMAFORCE p 1091
See BIOFORCE CANADA INC
AROMATHEQUE INC p 1154
26 AV DU DOCTEUR-RENE-A.-LEPAGE,
MONT-JOLI, QC, G5H 1R2
(418) 775-8841   SIC 5912
AROMATIK p 1393
See SUPPLEMENTS AROMATIK INC
ARP AUTOMATION CONTROLS INC p 135
80042 475 AVE E UNIT 200, HIGH RIVER,
AB, T1V 1M3
(403) 652-7130   SIC 3625
**ARPAC STORAGE SYSTEMS CORPORA-
TION** p
208
7663 PROGRESS WAY, DELTA, BC, V4G
1A2
(604) 940-4000   SIC 2542
ARPI'S INDUSTRIES LTD p 13
6815 40 ST SE, CALGARY, AB, T2C 2W7
(403) 236-2444   SIC 1711
ARPI'S NORTH INC p 92
14445 123 AVE NW, EDMONTON, AB, T5L
2Y1
(780) 452-2096   SIC 1711
ARRAY CANADA INC p 870
45 PROGRESS AVE, SCARBOROUGH,
ON, M1P 2Y6
(416) 299-4865   SIC 3993
ARRAY MARKETING p 870
See ARRAY CANADA INC
ARRELL YOUTH CENTRE p 614
See BANYAN COMMUNITY SERVICES
INC
ARRIMAGE DU SAINT-LAURENT, DIV DE p
1259
See QUEBEC STEVEDORING COMPANY
LTD
ARRISCRAFT CANADA INC p 538
875 SPEEDSVILLE RD, CAMBRIDGE, ON,
N3H 4R6
(519) 653-3275   SIC 3281
ARRK CANADA HOLDINGS, INC p 1004
17 ELM DR S, WALLACEBURG, ON, N8A
5E8
(519) 627-6078   SIC 5261
**ARRKANN TRAILER & SPORT CENTRE
LTD** p 121
1904 80 AVE NW, EDMONTON, AB, T6P
1N2
(780) 440-4811   SIC 5561
**ARROW AND SLOCAN LAKES COMMU-
NITY SERVICES** p
233
205 6 AVE NW, NAKUSP, BC, V0G 1R0
(250) 265-3674   SIC 8399
ARROW CAPITAL MANAGEMENT INC p
936

36 TORONTO ST SUITE 750, TORONTO,
ON, M5C 2C5
(416) 323-0477   SIC 6211
**ARROW CONSTRUCTION PRODUCTS
LIMITED** p 402
50 GERVAIS CRT, FREDERICTON, NB,
E3C 1L4
(506) 458-9610   SIC 5039
ARROW DIVERSIFIED FUND p 936
36 TORONTO ST SUITE 750, TORONTO,
ON, M5C 2C5
(416) 323-0477   SIC 6722
ARROW ECS CANADA LIMITED p 737
171 SUPERIOR BLVD UNIT 2, MISSIS-
SAUGA, ON, L5T 2L6
(905) 670-4699   SIC 7372
ARROW ELECTRONICS CANADA LTD p
737
171 SUPERIOR BLVD SUITE 2, MISSIS-
SAUGA, ON, L5T 2L6
(905) 565-4405   SIC 5065
ARROW ENGINEERING INC p 92
13167 146 ST NW SUITE 202, EDMON-
TON, AB, T5L 4S8
(780) 801-6100   SIC 8711
ARROW FASTENER CANADA p 1339
See DISTRIBUTEURS JARDEL INC, LES
ARROW FURNITURE LTD p 794
35 ARROW RD, NORTH YORK, ON, M9M
2L4
(416) 743-1530   SIC 5712
ARROW GAMES CORPORATION p 758
6199 DON MURIE ST, NIAGARA FALLS,
ON, L2G 0B1
(905) 354-7300   SIC 5092
ARROW GAMES CORPORATION p 848
9515 MONTROSE RD UNIT 2, PORT
ROBINSON, ON, L0S 1K0
(905) 354-7300   SIC 5092
ARROW PACKING COMPANY p 318
See CALKINS & BURKE LIMITED
ARROW PLUMBING INC p 862
594 SECOND LINE E, SAULT STE. MARIE,
ON, P6B 4K1
(705) 759-8316   SIC 5251
ARROW RELOAD SYSTEMS INC p 161
53309 RANGE ROAD 232 UNIT 38, SHER-
WOOD PARK, AB, T8A 4V2
(780) 464-4640   SIC 4789
ARROW SPEED CONTROLS LIMITED p
253
13851 BRIDGEPORT RD, RICHMOND, BC,
V6V 1J6
(604) 321-4033   SIC 3625
**ARROW TRANSPORTATION SYSTEMS
INC** p 216
1805 MISSION FLATS RD, KAMLOOPS,
BC, V2C 1A9
(250) 374-6715   SIC 4212
**ARROW TRANSPORTATION SYSTEMS
INC** p 302
999 HASTINGS ST W SUITE 1300, VAN-
COUVER, BC, V6C 2W2
(604) 324-1333   SIC 4213
**ARROW WELDING & INDUSTRIAL SUP-
PLIES INC** p
99
17811 107 AVE NW, EDMONTON, AB, T5S
1R8
(780) 483-2050   SIC 5084
ARROW-WEST EQUIPMENT LTD p 1
53016 HWY 60 UNIT 109, ACHESON, AB,
T7X 5A7
(780) 962-4490   SIC 5082
ARROW/BELL COMPONENTS p 737
See ARROW ELECTRONICS CANADA LTD
**ARROWHEAD DEVELOPMENT CORPO-
RATION** p
349
101 YELLOWQUILL TRAIL W, EDWIN, MB,
R0H 0G0
(204) 252-2731   SIC 5541
ARROWHEAD SPRING WATER LTD p 33
5730 BURBANK RD SE, CALGARY, AB,

T2H 1Z4
SIC 5499
ARROWQUIP p 393
See NORTHQUIP INC
ARROWSMITH LODGE p 242
See ARROWSMITH REST HOME SOCI-
ETY
ARROWSMITH POTTERS GUILD p 242
600 ALBERNI HWY, PARKSVILLE, BC, V9P
1J9
(250) 954-1872   SIC 8399
ARROWSMITH REST HOME SOCIETY p
242
266 MOILLIET ST S SUITE 1, PARKSVILLE,
BC, V9P 1M9
(250) 947-9777   SIC 8051
ARROWSMITH SEARCH & RESCUE p 252
3241 ALBERNI HWY, QUALICUM BEACH,
BC, V9K 1Y6
(250) 752-7774   SIC 8999
ARROWSMITH SERVICES p 245
See PORT ALBERNI ASSOCIATION FOR
COMMUNITY LIVING
ARSANDCO INVESTMENTS LIMITEDp 935
111 CARLTON ST, TORONTO, ON, M5B
2G3
(416) 977-8000   SIC 7011
**ARSENAL ART CONTEMPORAIN (MON-
TREAL)** p
1072
See CEDAROME CANADA INC
ARSENAL CLEANING SERVICES LTD p
876
80 NASHDENE RD UNIT 7, SCARBOR-
OUGH, ON, M1V 5E4
(416) 321-8777   SIC 7349
ARSENAULT BROS. CONSTRUCTION LTD
p 1042
5 HILLSIDE AVE, SUMMERSIDE, PE, C1N
4H3
(902) 888-2689   SIC 1522
ARSLAN AUTOMOTIVE CANADA LTEE p
1249
84 AV LEACOCK, POINTE-CLAIRE, QC,
H9R 1H1
(514) 694-1113   SIC 5511
ARSLANIAN CUTTING WORKS NWT LTDp
435
106 ARCHIBALD ST, YELLOWKNIFE, NT,
X1A 2P4
(867) 873-0138   SIC 3915
ARSYSTEMS INTERNATIONAL INC p 666
2770 14TH AVE SUITE 101, MARKHAM,
ON, L3R 0J1
(905) 968-3096   SIC 7389
ART GALLERY OF ONTARIO p 977
317 DUNDAS ST W SUITE 535, TORONTO,
ON, M5T 1G4
(416) 977-0414   SIC 8412
ART INSTITUTE OF VANCOUVER INC, THE
p 286
2665 RENFREW ST, VANCOUVER, BC,
V5M 0A7
(604) 683-9200   SIC 8221
ART INSTITUTE OF VANCOUVER, THE p
286
See ART INSTITUTE OF VANCOUVER
INC, THE
ART KNAPP PLANTLAND p 279
See MUD BAY NURSERIES LTD
ART KNAPP PLANTLAND & FLORISTS p
246
See WIMCO NURSERIES LTD
ART LINEN MANUFACTURING p 1169
See DECORS DE MAISON COMMON-
WEALTH INC
ART SHOPPE LIMITED p 923
2131 YONGE ST, TORONTO, ON, M4S 2A7
(416) 487-3211   SIC 5712
ART-IS-IN BAKERY INC p 824
250 CITY CENTRE AVE UNIT 112, OT-
TAWA, ON, K1R 6K7
(613) 695-1226   SIC 5461
ARTAFLEX INC p 850

174 WEST BEAVER CREEK RD, RICH-
MOND HILL, ON, L4B 1B4
(905) 470-0109   *SIC* 3679
ARTCRAFT   *p 1049*
See *LUSTRE ARTCRAFT DE MONTREAL
LTEE*
ARTCRAFT COMPANY INC   *p 548*
309 PENNSYLVANIA AVE, CONCORD, ON,
L4K 5R9
(905) 660-1919   *SIC* 5131
ARTCRAFT ELECTRIC LIMITED   *p 501*
8050 TORBRAM RD, BRAMPTON, ON, L6T
3T2
(905) 791-1551   *SIC* 3645
ARTE GROUP INC   *p 20*
4300 5 ST NE, CALGARY, AB, T2E 7C3
(403) 640-4559   *SIC* 1541
ARTE STRUCTURES   *p 20*
See *ARTE GROUP INC*
ARTEC CONSTRUCTION   *p 38*
See *870892 ALBERTA LTD*
ARTECH DIGITAL ENTERTAINMENT INC *p*
828
6 HAMILTON AVE N, OTTAWA, ON, K1Y
4R1
(613) 728-4880   *SIC* 7371
ARTECH STUDIOS   *p 828*
See *ARTECH DIGITAL ENTERTAINMENT
INC*
ARTEK GROUP LIMITED, THE   *p 274*
12140 103A AVE, SURREY, BC, V3V 7Y9
(604) 584-2131   *SIC* 1542
ARTEK VANCOUVER, DIV OF   *p 274*
See *ARTEK GROUP LIMITED, THE*
ARTELITE   *p 1047*
See *AMEUBLEMENTS ARTELITE INC*
ARTEMANO   *p 1142*
See *RODI DESIGN INC*
ARTERRA WINES CANADA, INC   *p 737*
441 COURTNEYPARK DR E, MISSIS-
SAUGA, ON, L5T 2V3
(905) 564-6900   *SIC* 2084
ARTERRA WINES CANADA, INC   *p 1288*
175 CH DE MARIEVILLE, ROUGEMONT,
QC, J0L 1M0
(450) 469-3104   *SIC* 5182
ARTEX SPORTSWEAR INC   *p 876*
40 TIFFIELD RD UNIT 9, SCARBOROUGH,
ON, M1V 5B6
(416) 755-3382   *SIC* 2253
ARTEX SYSTEMS INC   *p 548*
523 BOWES RD, CONCORD, ON, L4K 1J5
(905) 669-1425   *SIC* 5032
ARTHON INDUSTRIES LIMITED   *p 219*
1790 K.L.O. RD UNIT 9, KELOWNA, BC,
V1W 3P6
(250) 764-6144   *SIC* 1442
**ARTHRITIS RESEARCH CENTRE SOCIETY
OF CANADA, THE**   *p 259*
5591 NO. 3 RD, RICHMOND, BC, V6X 2C7
(604) 879-7511   *SIC* 8733
ARTHRITIS SOCIETY, THE   *p 944*
393 UNIVERSITY AVE SUITE 1700,
TORONTO, ON, M5G 1E6
(416) 979-7228   *SIC* 7389
ARTHUR A WISHART LIBRARY   *p 861*
See *ALGOMA UNIVERSITY*
**ARTHUR CHRYSLER DODGE JEEP LIM-
ITED**   *p*
479
165 CATHERINE ST W, ARTHUR, ON, N0G
1A0
(519) 848-2016   *SIC* 5511
ARTHUR ROGER & ASSOCIES INC *p 1134*
2010 BOUL DAGENAIS O, LAVAL-OUEST,
QC, H7L 5W2
(450) 963-5080   *SIC* 5141
ARTHUR VOADEN SECONDARY SCHOOL
p 890
See *THAMES VALLEY DISTRICT SCHOOL
BOARD*
ARTICLES DE CUIR J E FOURNIER *p 1183*
See *GROUPE YELLOW INC*
ARTICLES EN CUIR C.B.M. INC   *p 1227*

8370 RUE LABARRE, MONTREAL, QC,
H4P 2E7
(514) 738-5858   *SIC* 5199
ARTICLES INTERNATIONAUX   *p 1157*
See *STOKES INC*
ARTICLES MENAGERS DURA INC   *p 1361*
2105 BOUL DAGENAIS O, SAINTE-ROSE,
QC, H7L 5W9
(450) 622-3872   *SIC* 5021
ARTIFACT ACCELERATED LEARNING   *p*
1187
See *ARTIFACT LOGICIEL INC*
ARTIFACT LOGICIEL INC   *p 1187*
300 RUE DU SAINT-SACREMENT BUREAU
223, MONTREAL, QC, H2Y 1X4
(514) 286-6665   *SIC* 3999
ARTIFICIAL LIFT   *p 149*
See *SCHLUMBERGER CANADA LIMITED*
ARTIKA FOR LIVING INC   *p 1127*
1756 50E AV, LACHINE, QC, H8T 2V5
(514) 249-4557   *SIC* 3641
ARTIKA MAISON   *p 1127*
See *ARTIKA FOR LIVING INC*
**ARTIS REAL ESTATE INVESTMENT
TRUST**   *p 376*
220 PORTAGE AVE SUITE 600, WIN-
NIPEG, MB, R3C 0A5
(204) 947-1250   *SIC* 6722
ARTIS REIT   *p 376*
See *ARTIS REAL ESTATE INVESTMENT
TRUST*
ARTIS REIT   *p 376*
See *ARTIS US HOLDINGS II GP, INC*
ARTIS US HOLDINGS II GP, INC   *p 376*
360 MAIN ST SUITE 300, WINNIPEG, MB,
R3C 3Z3
(204) 947-1250   *SIC* 6519
**ARTISTIC DEVELOPMENT SUPPORT
GROUP**   *p 856*
27 NAPANEE ST, RICHMOND HILL, ON,
L4E 0X3
SIC 8062
ARTISTIC LANDSCAPE DESIGNS LIMITED
p 826
2079 ARTISTIC PL, OTTAWA, ON, K1V 8A8
(613) 733-8220   *SIC* 0781
ARTISTIC STAIRS LTD   *p 13*
3504 80 AVE SE, CALGARY, AB, T2C 1J3
(403) 279-5898   *SIC* 2431
ARTISTIC STUCCO LTD   *p 81*
GD, DE WINTON, AB, T0L 0X0
(403) 888-7412   *SIC* 1542
ARTISTS EMPORIUM   *p 383*
See *BALCO INC*
ARTIZAN   *p 1249*
See *CHANDELLES ET CREATIONS ROBIN
INC*
ARTMETCO INC   *p 1328*
2375 RUE COHEN, SAINT-LAURENT, QC,
H4R 2N5
(514) 339-2707   *SIC* 3444
ARTON BEADS CRAFT INC   *p 978*
523 QUEEN ST W, TORONTO, ON, M5V
2B4
(416) 504-1168   *SIC* 5088
ARTOPEX INC   *p 1110*
800 RUE VADNAIS, GRANBY, QC, J2J 1A7
(450) 378-0189   *SIC* 2522
ARTOPEX INC   *p 1233*
2129 RUE BERLIER, MONTREAL, QC, H7L
3M9
(450) 973-9655   *SIC* 2522
ARTRON LABORATORIES INC   *p 191*
3938 NORTH FRASER WAY, BURNABY,
BC, V5J 5H6
(604) 415-9757   *SIC* 3841
ARTS COMMONS   *p 27*
See *CALGARY CENTRE FOR PERFORM-
ING ARTS*
ARTS UMBRELLA   *p 319*
See *CHILDREN'S ARTS UMBRELLA AS-
SOCIATION*
ARTSMARKETING SERVICES INC   *p 932*
260 KING ST E SUITE 500, TORONTO, ON,

M5A 4L5
(416) 941-9000   *SIC* 7389
ARVA INDUSTRIES INC   *p 889*
43 GAYLORD RD, ST THOMAS, ON, N5P
3R9
(519) 637-1855   *SIC* 3599
ARVA LIMITED   *p 773*
4120 YONGE ST SUITE 310, NORTH
YORK, ON, M2P 2B8
(416) 222-0842   *SIC* 1623
ARXIUM INC   *p 388*
96 NATURE PARK WAY, WINNIPEG, MB,
R3P 0X8
(204) 943-0066   *SIC* 3845
ARYZTA CANADA CO   *p 515*
115 SINCLAIR BLVD SUITE 1, BRANT-
FORD, ON, N3S 7X6
(519) 720-2000   *SIC* 5145
ARZ GROUP OF COMPANIES LIMITED   *p*
766
279 YORKLAND BLVD, NORTH YORK, ON,
M2J 1S5
(416) 847-0350   *SIC* 5399
ARZON LIMITED   *p 521*
4485 MAINWAY, BURLINGTON, ON, L7L
7P3
(905) 332-5600   *SIC* 3353
**AS DU RANGEMENT RIVE-NORD/ RIVE-
SUD INC**   *p*
1074
1635 BOUL LEBEL BUREAU 302, CHAM-
BLY, QC, J3L 0R8
(514) 792-4036   *SIC* 1799
ASAHI REFINING CANADA LTD   *p 508*
130 GLIDDEN RD, BRAMPTON, ON, L6W
3M8
(905) 453-6120   *SIC* 3339
ASANKO GOLD INC   *p 311*
1066 HASTINGS ST W SUITE 680, VAN-
COUVER, BC, V6E 3X2
(604) 683-8193   *SIC* 1011
ASBEX LTD   *p 817*
2280 STEVENAGE DR UNIT 200, OTTAWA,
ON, K1G 3W3
(613) 228-1080   *SIC* 1799
ASBURY BUILDING SERVICES INC   *p 573*
323 EVANS AVE, ETOBICOKE, ON, M8Z
1K2
SIC 7349
ASBURY WILKINSON INC   *p 521*
1115 SUTTON DR, BURLINGTON, ON, L7L
5Z8
(905) 332-0862   *SIC* 5051
ASCENDANT RESOURCES INC   *p 968*
79 WELLINGTON ST W SUITE 2100,
TORONTO, ON, M5K 1H1
(647) 796-0066   *SIC* 1081
ASCENSEURS DESIGN INC   *p 1263*
1865 RUE A.-R.-DECARY, QUEBEC, QC,
G1N 3Z8
(418) 681-2023   *SIC* 5084
ASCENSEURS RE-NO   *p 723*
See *KONE INC*
**ASCENT REAL ESTATE MANAGEMENT
CORPORATION**   *p 184*
2176 WILLINGDON AVE, BURNABY, BC,
V5C 5Z9
(604) 521-7653   *SIC* 6531
ASCO   *p 425*
See *ASCO CANADA LIMITED*
ASCO AEROSPACE CANADA LTD   *p 208*
8510 RIVER RD, DELTA, BC, V4G 1B5
(604) 946-4900   *SIC* 3429
ASCO CANADA LIMITED   *p 425*
10 CORISANDE DR, MOUNT PEARL, NL,
A1N 5A4
(709) 748-7800   *SIC* 4225
ASCO CONSTRUCTION LTD   *p 619*
1125 TUPPER ST UNIT 1, HAWKESBURY,
ON, K6A 3T5
(613) 632-0121   *SIC* 1542
ASCO NUMATICS   *p 517*
See *EMERSON ELECTRIC CANADA LIM-
ITED*

ASCOT   *p 1054*
See *PEINTURE UCP INC*
ASCS CANADIAN SIGNAL CORPORATION
p 1013
606 BEECH ST W, WHITBY, ON, L1N 7T8
(905) 665-4300   *SIC* 3679
ASD SOLUTIONS LTD   *p 734*
190 STATESMAN DR, MISSISSAUGA, ON,
L5S 1X7
(519) 271-4900   *SIC* 5045
ASDR   *p 1148*
See *ASDR CANADA INC*
ASDR CANADA INC   *p 1148*
691 RUE ROYALE, MALARTIC, QC, J0Y
1Z0
(819) 757-3039   *SIC* 6712
ASDR CANADA INC   *p 1390*
1462 RUE DE LA QUEBECOISE, VAL-
D'OR, QC, J9P 5H4
(819) 757-3039   *SIC* 4953
ASDR ENVIRONNEMENT   *p 1390*
See *ASDR CANADA INC*
ASEBP   *p 118*
See *ALBERTA SCHOOL EMPLOYEE BEN-
EFIT PLAN, THE*
ASECO INTEGRATED SYSTEMS   *p 803*
See *CALLISTO INTEGRATION LTD*
**ASENESKAK CASINO LIMITED PARTNER-
SHIP**   *p*
359
GD STN MAIN, THE PAS, MB, R9A 1K2
(204) 627-2250   *SIC* 7999
**ASENIWUCHE DEVELOPMENT CORPO-
RATION**   *p*
130
10028 99 ST, GRANDE CACHE, AB, T0E
0Y0
(780) 827-5510   *SIC* 1389
ASENTUS CONSULTING GROUP LTD   *p*
296
1286 HOMER ST, SUITE 200, VANCOU-
VER, BC, V6B 2Y5
(604) 609-9993   *SIC* 8741
ASEQ   *p 1201*
See *ALLIANCE POUR LA SANTE ETUDI-
ANTE AU QUEBEC INC*
ASHBURN GOLF CLUB   *p 457*
See *HALIFAX GOLF & COUNTRY CLUB,
LIMITED*
ASHBURY COLLEGE INCORPORATED   *p*
820
362 MARIPOSA AVE, OTTAWA, ON, K1M
0T3
(613) 749-5954   *SIC* 8211
**ASHCROFT & ASSOCIATES NATURAL
STONE LTD**   *p 594*
381297 CONCESSION 17, GEORGIAN
BLUFFS, ON, N0H 2T0
(519) 534-5966   *SIC* 1411
ASHCROFT HOMES - CENTRAL PARK INC
p 748
18 ANTARES DR UNIT 102, NEPEAN, ON,
K2E 1A9
(613) 226-7266   *SIC* 1521
ASHERN GARAGE LTD   *p 345*
2 MAIN ST, ASHERN, MB, R0C 0E0
(204) 768-2835   *SIC* 5541
ASHERN SERVICE   *p 345*
See *ASHERN GARAGE LTD*
ASHKYLE LTD   *p 405*
101 LEWISVILLE RD, MONCTON, NB, E1A
2K5
(506) 859-6969   *SIC* 5712
ASHLAND CANADA CORP   *p 713*
2620 ROYAL WINDSOR DR, MISSIS-
SAUGA, ON, L5J 4E7
(800) 274-5263   *SIC* 5169
ASHLAND CONSTRUCTION   *p 548*
See *ASHLAND PAVING LTD*
ASHLAND PAVING LTD   *p 548*
340 BOWES RD, CONCORD, ON, L4K 1K1
(905) 660-3060   *SIC* 1611
ASHLEY CARPETS LTD   *p 95*
14340 111 AVE NW, EDMONTON, AB, T5M

2P4
 (780) 454-9503   *SIC* 5713
ASHLEY FINE FLOORS   *p* 95
 See ASHLEY CARPETS LTD
ASHLEY FURNITURE HOME STORE *p* 892
 See FURNITURE INVESTMENT GROUP INC
ASHMORE LIMITED   *p* 419
 3307 ROUTE 101, TRACYVILLE, NB, E5L 1N7
 (506) 459-7777   *SIC* 6712
ASHPRIOR CHARITABLE FOUNDATION *p* 781
 See DMS PROPERTY MANAGEMENT LTD
ASHTON CASSE-CROUTE INC   *p* 1261
 1100 AV GALIBOIS BUREAU 250, QUE-BEC, QC, G1M 3M7
 (418) 682-2288   *SIC* 5812
ASI   *p* 537
 See AUTOMATED SOLUTIONS INTERNA-TIONAL INC
ASI   COMPUTER   TECHNOLOGIES (CANADA) CORP   *p* 666
 3930 14TH AVE UNIT 1, MARKHAM, ON, L3R 0A8
 (905) 470-1000   *SIC* 5045
ASI GROUP LTD   *p* 891
 566 ARVIN AVE, STONEY CREEK, ON, L8E 5P1
 (905) 643-3283   *SIC* 1629
ASIA LINK COMPUTER INC   *p* 850
 45A WEST WILMOT ST UNIT 5 7, RICH-MOND HILL, ON, L4B 2P2
 (905) 731-1928   *SIC* 5045
ASIA PULP & PAPER (CANADA) LTD *p* 511
 20 HEREFORD ST SUITE 15, BRAMPTON, ON, L6Y 0M1
 (905) 450-2100   *SIC* 5113
ASIAN MINERAL RESOURCES LIMITED *p* 948
 120 ADELAIDE ST W SUITE 2500, TORONTO, ON, M5H 1T1
 (416) 360-3412   *SIC* 1061
ASIAN TELEVISION NETWORK INTERNA-TIONAL LIMITED   *p* 666
 330 COCHRANE DR, MARKHAM, ON, L3R 8E4
 (905) 948-8199   *SIC* 4833
ASIG   *p* 728
 See ASIG CANADA LTD
ASIG CANADA LTD   *p* 511
 8501 MISSISSAUGA RD SUITE 302, BRAMPTON, ON, L6Y 5G8
 (905) 497-4114   *SIC* 5172
ASIG CANADA LTD   *p* 728
 5600 SILVER DART DR, MISSISSAUGA, ON, L5P 1C4
 (905) 694-2846   *SIC* 5172
ASIG CANADA LTD   *p* 1431
 2515 AIRPORT RD SUITE 7, SASKATOON, SK, S7L 1M4
 (306) 651-6018   *SIC* 5172
ASIGRA INC   *p* 916
 79 BRISBANE ROAD, TORONTO, ON, M3J 2K3
 (416) 736-8111   *SIC* 7371
ASKAN ARTS LIMITED   *p* 782
 20 TORO RD, NORTH YORK, ON, M3J 2A7
 (416) 398-2333   *SIC* 7699
ASKEW'S ENTERPRISES LTD   *p* 267
 111 LAKESHORE DR NE, SALMON ARM, BC, V1E 4N3
 (250) 832-2668   *SIC* 6712
ASKEW'S FOOD   *p* 267
 See ASKEW'S ENTERPRISES LTD
ASKEW'S FOOD SERVICE LTD   *p* 267
 111 LAKESHORE DR NE, SALMON ARM, BC, V1E 4N3
 (250) 832-2064   *SIC* 5411
ASKEW'S FOODS   *p* 267
 See ASKEW'S FOOD SERVICE LTD
ASL AQFLOW   *p* 266
 See ASL ENVIRONMENTAL SCIENCES

INC
ASL CONSULTING   *p* 582
 See ASL ENTERPRISES INC
ASL DISTRIBUTION SERVICES LIMITED *p* 796
 2160 BUCKINGHAM RD, OAKVILLE, ON, L6H 6M7
 (905) 829-5141   *SIC* 4225
ASL ENTERPRISES INC   *p* 582
 155 REXDALE BLVD SUITE 800, ETOBI-COKE, ON, M9W 5Z8
 (416) 740-6996   *SIC* 8741
ASL ENVIRONMENTAL SCIENCES INC *p* 266
 6703 RAJPUR PL UNIT 1, SAANICHTON, BC, V8M 1Z5
 (250) 656-0177   *SIC* 8748
ASL GLOBAL LOGISTICS   *p* 498
 See 1579901 ONTARIO INC
ASL PRINT FX LTD   *p* 1029
 1 ROYAL GATE BLVD UNIT A, WOOD-BRIDGE, ON, L4L 8Z7
 (416) 798-7310   *SIC* 2759
ASLCHEM INTERNATIONAL INC   *p* 259
 4871 SHELL RD SUITE 1260, RICHMOND, BC, V6X 3Z6
 (604) 270-8824   *SIC* 5052
ASM CANADA, INC   *p* 666
 160 MCNABB ST SUITE 330, MARKHAM, ON, L3R 4E4
 (905) 475-9623   *SIC* 5141
ASMODEE CANADA INC   *p* 1283
 31 RUE DE LA COOPERATIVE, RIGAUD, QC, J0P 1P0
 (450) 424-0655   *SIC* 5092
ASPASIE INC   *p* 1387
 2106   RUE   BELLEFEUILLE,   TROIS-RIVIERES, QC, G9A 3Y9
 (819) 379-2157   *SIC* 3999
ASPECT RETAIL LOGISTICS INC   *p* 844
 1400 CHURCH ST, PICKERING, ON, L1W 4C1
 (905) 428-9947   *SIC* 4225
ASPEN CUSTOM TRAILERS   *p* 139
 3914 81 AVE, LEDUC, AB, T9E 0C3
 (780) 980-1925   *SIC* 5088
ASPEN FAMILY AND COMMUNITY NET-WORK SOCIETY   *p* 20
 2609 15 ST NE SUITE 200, CALGARY, AB, T2E 8Y4
 (403) 219-3477   *SIC* 8699
ASPEN PLANERS LTD   *p* 232
 1375 HOUSTON ST, MERRITT, BC, V1K 1B8
 (250) 378-9266   *SIC* 2421
ASPEN PLANERS LTD   *p* 274
 12745 116 AVE, SURREY, BC, V3V 7H9
 (604) 580-2781   *SIC* 2421
ASPEN PROPERTIES LTD   *p* 43
 150 9 AVE SW UNIT 1510, CALGARY, AB, T2P 3H9
 (403) 216-2660   *SIC* 6531
ASPEN REGIONAL HEALTH   *p* 138
 9503 BEAVER HILL RD, LAC LA BICHE, AB, T0A 2C0
 (780) 623-4472   *SIC* 8621
ASPEN RIDGE HOMES   *p* 548
 See ALBERO RIDGE HOMES LTD
ASPEN VIEW PUBLIC SCHOOL DIVISION NO. 78   *p* 4
 3600 48 AVE SUITE 19, ATHABASCA, AB, T9S 1M8
 (780) 675-7080   *SIC* 8211
ASPEN-DUNHILL HOLDINGS LTD   *p* 880
 HIGHWAY 2 W SUITE 6, SHANNONVILLE, ON, K0K 3A0
 (613) 966-6895   *SIC* 5541
ASPENHEIM COLONY FARMS LTD   *p* 345
 GD, BAGOT, MB, R0H 0E0
 (204) 274-2782   *SIC* 0191
ASPENHEIM COLONY OF HUTTERIAN BRETHREN - TRUST   *p* 345
 See ASPENHEIM COLONY FARMS LTD

ASPENWOOD   *p* 199
 See SCHOOL DISTRICT NO. 43 (COQUIT-LAM)
ASPHALTE DESJARDINS INC   *p* 1381
 3030 RUE ANDERSON, TERREBONNE, QC, J6Y 1W1
 (450) 430-7160   *SIC* 1611
ASPHALTE, BETON, CARRIERES RIVE-NORD INC   *p* 1153
 5605 RTE ARTHUR-SAUVE, MIRABEL, QC, J7N 2W4
 (450) 258-4242   *SIC* 1611
ASPHALTE, BETON, CARRIERES RIVE-NORD INC   *p* 1291
 134 RTE DU LONG-SAULT, SAINT-ANDRE-D'ARGENTEUIL, QC, J0V 1X0
 (450) 258-4242   *SIC* 5082
ASPIN KEMP & ASSOCIATES HOLDING CORP   *p* 1041
 23 BROOK ST, MONTAGUE, PE, C0A 1R0
 (902) 361-3135   *SIC* 6712
ASPIN KEMP & ASSOCIATES INC   *p* 1041
 23 BROOK ST, MONTAGUE, PE, C0A 1R0
 (902) 361-3135   *SIC* 8711
ASPIRATEUR EN GROS   *p* 1289
 See PRODUITS SANITAIRES NORFIL INC
ASPLUNDH CANADA ULC   *p* 179
 26050 31B AVE, ALDERGROVE, BC, V4W 2Z6
 (604) 856-2222   *SIC* 0783
ASPLUNDH CANADA ULC   *p* 450
 645 PRATT AND WHITNEY DR SUITE 1, GOFFS, NS, B2T 0H4
 (902) 468-8733   *SIC* 7299
ASPLUNDH CANADA ULC   *p* 1380
 3366 RUE JACOB-JORDAN, TERRE-BONNE, QC, J6X 4J6
 (450) 968-1888   *SIC* 0783
ASPLUNDH TREE SERVICE ULC   *p* 450
 See ASPLUNDH CANADA ULC
ASPOL FORD   *p* 204
 See ASPOL MOTORS (1982) LTD
ASPOL MOTORS (1982) LTD   *p* 204
 1125 102 AVE, DAWSON CREEK, BC, V1G 2C2
 (250) 782-5804   *SIC* 5511
ASPOTOGAN CONSOLIDATED ELEMEN-TARY SCHOOL   *p* 441
 See SOUTH SHORE REGIONAL SCHOOL BOARD
ASRJ COMMUNICATIONS INC   *p* 532
 179 MORRISON DR, CALEDONIA, ON, N3W 1A8
 SIC 4899
ASSA ABLOY DOOR GROUP INC   *p* 1029
 101 ASHBRIDGE CIR, WOODBRIDGE, ON, L4L 3R5
 (416) 749-2111   *SIC* 3442
ASSA ABLOY ENTRANCE SYSTEM CANADA INC   *p* 716
 4020A SLADEVIEW CRES SUITE 4, MIS-SISSAUGA, ON, L5L 6B1
 (905) 608-9242   *SIC* 1796
ASSA ABLOY OF CANADA LTD   *p* 548
 160 FOUR VALLEY DR, CONCORD, ON, L4K 4T9
 (905) 738-2466   *SIC* 5072
ASSANTE CAPITAL MANAGEMENT LTD *p* 936
 2 QUEEN ST E SUITE 1900, TORONTO, ON, M5C 3G7
 (416) 348-9994   *SIC* 6211
ASSANTE FINANCIAL MANAGEMENT *p* 630
 264 KING ST E, KINGSTON, ON, K7L 3A9
 (613) 549-8602   *SIC* 6282
ASSANTE FINANCIAL MANAGEMENT LTD *p* 1010
 855 BIRCHMOUNT DR, WATERLOO, ON, N2V 2R7
 (519) 886-3257   *SIC* 8741

ASSANTE WEALTH MANAGEMENT *p* 936
 See ASSANTE CAPITAL MANAGEMENT LTD
ASSANTE   WEALTH   MANAGEMENT (CANADA) LTD   *p* 971
 199 BAY ST SUITE 2700, TORONTO, ON, M5L 1E2
 (416) 348-9994   *SIC* 6712
ASSEAU-BPR   *p* 1266
 See BPR INC
ASSELS SEAFOOD INC   *p* 1376
 11 132 RTE, SHIGAWAKE, QC, G0C 3E0
 SIC 2092
ASSEMBLE-RITE, LTD   *p* 1018
 2755 LAUZON PKY, WINDSOR, ON, N8T 3H5
 (519) 945-8464   *SIC* 8741
ASSEMBLY INTERNATIONAL INC   *p* 1021
 3233 DEVON DR, WINDSOR, ON, N8X 4L5
 SIC 5013
ASSEMBLY OF FIRST NATIONS   *p* 825
 See NATIONAL INDIAN BROTHERHOOD
ASSEMBLY OF MANITOBA CHIEFS SEC-RETARIAT INC   *p* 374
 275 PORTAGE AVE SUITE 200, WIN-NIPEG, MB, R3B 2B3
 (204) 956-0610   *SIC* 8651
ASSENT COMPLIANCE INC   *p* 820
 525 COVENTRY RD, OTTAWA, ON, K1K 2C5
 (613) 369-8390   *SIC* 7371
ASSINIBOIA DOWNS   *p* 386
 See MANITOBA JOCKEY CLUB INC
ASSINIBOIA ELEMENTARY   *p* 1411
 See PRAIRIE SOUTH SCHOOL DIVISION NO 210
ASSINIBOINE CREDIT UNION LIMITED, THE   *p* 376
 200 MAIN ST 6TH FL, WINNIPEG, MB, R3C 1A8
 (204) 958-8588   *SIC* 6062
ASSINIBOINE GORDON INN ON THE PARK *p* 385
 See GORDON HOTELS & MOTOR INNS LTD
ASSINIBOINE PARK CONSERVANCY *p* 389
 See ZOOLOGICAL SOCIETY OF MANI-TOBA
ASSINIBOINE PARK CONSERVANCY INC *p* 388
 55 PAVILION CRES, WINNIPEG, MB, R3P 2N6
 (204) 927-6002   *SIC* 8699
ASSOCIATE VETERINARY CLINIC (1981) LTD   *p* 33
 7140 12 ST SE, CALGARY, AB, T2H 2Y4
 (403) 541-0815   *SIC* 0742
ASSOCIATED AUCTIONEERS INC   *p* 650
 1881 SCANLAN ST, LONDON, ON, N5W 6C3
 (519) 453-7182   *SIC* 7389
ASSOCIATED BRANDS INC   *p* 891
 944 HIGHWAY 8, STONEY CREEK, ON, L8E 5S3
 (905) 643-1211   *SIC* 2099
ASSOCIATED ENGINEERING (B.C.) LTD *p* 286
 2889 12TH AVE E SUITE 500, VANCOU-VER, BC, V5M 4T5
 (604) 293-1411   *SIC* 8711
ASSOCIATED ENGINEERING (BC)   *p* 187
 See ASSOCIATED ENGINEERING GROUP LTD
ASSOCIATED ENGINEERING (ONT.) LTD *p* 577
 304 THE EAST MALL SUITE 800, ETOBI-COKE, ON, M9B 6E2
 (416) 622-9502   *SIC* 8711
ASSOCIATED ENGINEERING (SASK) LTD *p* 1431
 2225 NORTHRIDGE DR SUITE 1, SASKA-TOON, SK, S7L 6X6
 (306) 653-4969   *SIC* 8711

ASSOCIATED ENGINEERING ALBERTA LTD *p 74*
600 CROWFOOT CRES NW SUITE 400, CALGARY, AB, T3G 0B4
(403) 262-4500   *SIC 8711*

ASSOCIATED ENGINEERING ALBERTA LTD *p 87*
9888 JASPER AVE NW SUITE 500, EDMONTON, AB, T5J 5C6
(780) 451-7666   *SIC 8711*

ASSOCIATED ENGINEERING GROUP LTD *p 87*
9888 JASPER AVE NW SUITE 500, EDMONTON, AB, T5J 5C6
(780) 451-7666   *SIC 8711*

ASSOCIATED ENGINEERING GROUP LTD *p 187*
4940 CANADA WAY SUITE 300, BURNABY, BC, V5G 4K6
(604) 293-1411   *SIC 8711*

ASSOCIATED HEALTH SYSTEMS INC *p 275*
8145 130 ST UNIT 6, SURREY, BC, V3W 7X4
(604) 591-8012   *SIC 5047*

ASSOCIATED HEBREW SCHOOLS OF TORONTO *p 775*
252 FINCH AVE W, NORTH YORK, ON, M2R 1M9
(416) 494-7666   *SIC 8211*

ASSOCIATED LABELS *p 200*
See *ELLWORTH INDUSTRIES LTD*

ASSOCIATED LABELS & PRINTING LTD *p 199*
61 CLIPPER ST, COQUITLAM, BC, V3K 6X2
(604) 525-4764   *SIC 2679*

ASSOCIATED MARITIME PHARMACIES LIMITED *p 449*
269 HIGHWAY 214 UNIT 2, ELMSDALE, NS, B2S 1K1
(902) 883-8018   *SIC 5912*

ASSOCIATED MATERIALS CANADA LIMITED *p 13*
4069 112 AVE SE SUITE 7, CALGARY, AB, T2C 0J4
(403) 640-0906   *SIC 3444*

ASSOCIATED MATERIALS CANADA LIMITED *p 521*
1001 CORPORATE DR, BURLINGTON, ON, L7L 5V5
(905) 319-5561   *SIC 3444*

ASSOCIATED MATERIALS CANADA LIMITED *p 1249*
2501 AUT TRANSCANADIENNE, POINTE-CLAIRE, QC, H9R 1B3
(514) 426-7801   *SIC 3444*

ASSOCIATED MINING CONSTRUCTION INC *p 1417*
2491 ALBERT ST N, REGINA, SK, S4P 3A2
(306) 206-5000   *SIC 1474*

ASSOCIATED PAVING & MATERIALS LTD *p 521*
5365 MUNRO CRT, BURLINGTON, ON, L7L 5M7
(905) 637-1966   *SIC 1611*

ASSOCIATED PRO-CLEANING SERVICES CORP *p 666*
3400 14TH AVE SUITE 39, MARKHAM, ON, L3R 0H7
(905) 477-6966   *SIC 7349*

ASSOCIATED TUBE CANADA, DIV OF *p 674*
See *SAMUEL, SON & CO., LIMITED*

ASSOCIATION B.C.S *p 1374*
80 CH MOULTON HILL, SHERBROOKE, QC, J1M 2K4
(819) 566-0227   *SIC 8211*

ASSOCIATION CHRETIENNE DES JEUNES FEMMES DE MONTREAL *p 1212*
1355 BOUL RENE-LEVESQUE O BUREAU 208, MONTREAL, QC, H3G 1T3
(514) 866-9941   *SIC 7032*

ASSOCIATION COOPERATIVE FORESTIERE DE ST-ELZEAR *p 1299*
215 RTE DE L'EGLISE, SAINT-ELZEAR-DE-BONAVENTURE, QC, G0C 2W0
(418) 534-2596   *SIC 2421*

ASSOCIATION D'ENTRAIDE LE CHAINON INC, L' *p 1184*
4373 AV DE L'ESPLANADE, MONTREAL, QC, H2W 1T2
(514) 845-0151   *SIC 8322*

ASSOCIATION D'HOSPITALISATION CANASSURANCE *p 1193*
550 RUE SHERBROOKE O, MONTREAL, QC, H3A 1B9
(514) 286-7658   *SIC 6321*

ASSOCIATION DE BIENFAISSANCE ET DE RETRAITE DES POLICIERS DE LA VILLE DE MONTREAL *p 1173*
480 RUE GILFORD BUREAU 200, MONTREAL, QC, H2J 1N3
(514) 527-8061   *SIC 6371*

ASSOCIATION DES CROISIERES DU SAINT-LAURENT *p 1284*
84 RUE SAINT-GERMAIN E BUREAU 206, RIMOUSKI, QC, G5L 1A6
(418) 725-0135   *SIC 6331*

ASSOCIATION DES EMPLOYEURS MARITIME, L' *p 1209*
2100 AV PIERRE-DUPUY, MONTREAL, QC, H3C 3R5
(514) 878-3721   *SIC 8631*

ASSOCIATION DES ETUDIANTS DU CEGEP ST-LAURENT INC *p 1323*
625 AV SAINTE-CROIX, SAINT-LAURENT, QC, H4L 3X7
(514) 747-4026   *SIC 8699*

ASSOCIATION DES ETUDIANTS DU COLLEGE REGIONAL CHAMPLAIN L' *p 1271*
790 AV NEREE-TREMBLAY, QUEBEC, QC, G1V 4K2
(418) 656-6921   *SIC 8211*

ASSOCIATION DES MANOEUVRES INTERPROVINCIAUX (AMI), L' *p 1176*
565 BOUL CREMAZIE E BUREAU 3800, MONTREAL, QC, H2M 2V6
(514) 381-8780   *SIC 8631*

ASSOCIATION DES PARENTS DE L'EXTERNAT SAINT-JEAN-EUDES *p 1144*
See *EXTERNAT SAINT-JEAN-EUDES*

ASSOCIATION DES POMPIERS DE MONTREAL INC *p 1168*
2655 PLACE CHASSE 2E ETAGE, MONTREAL, QC, H1Y 2C3
(514) 527-9691   *SIC 8631*

ASSOCIATION DES RESIDENTS ET RESIDENTES DU CENTRE D'ACCEUIL DE GATINEAU, L' *p 1103*
134 RUE JEAN-RENE-MONETTE, GATINEAU, QC, J8P 7C3
(819) 966-6450   *SIC 8361*

ASSOCIATION DU TRANSPORT AERIEN INTERNATIONAL (IATA) *p 1229*
800 RUE DU SQUARE-VICTORIA BUREAU 1538, MONTREAL, QC, H4Z 1A1
(514) 874-0202   *SIC 8611*

ASSOCIATION ECHEC ET MATHEMATIQUES *p 1185*
3423 RUE SAINT-DENIS BUREAU 400, MONTREAL, QC, H2X 3L2
(514) 845-8352   *SIC 5092*

ASSOCIATION ETUDIANTE DE L'UNIVERSITE MCGILL *p 1193*
3600 RUE MCTAVISH BUREAU 1200, MONTREAL, QC, H3A 0G3
(514) 398-6800   *SIC 8699*

ASSOCIATION FOR COMMUNITY LIVING-STEINBACH BRANCH INC *p 358*
395 MAIN ST, STEINBACH, MB, R5G 1Z4
(204) 326-7539   *SIC 8699*

ASSOCIATION INTERNATIONALE DES ETUDIANTS EN SCIENCES ECONOMIQUES ET COMMERCIALES *p 1185*
315 RUE SAINTE-CATHERINE E BUREAU 213, MONTREAL, QC, H2X 3X2
(514) 987-3288   *SIC 8621*

ASSOCIATION NORD-AMERICAINE DE SERVICE DE PARTAGE DE VEHICULES *p 1203*
See *COMMUNAUTO INC*

ASSOCIATION OF MUNICIPALITIES OF ONTARIO *p 948*
200 UNIVERSITY AVE SUITE 801, TORONTO, ON, M5H 3C6
(416) 971-9856   *SIC 6282*

ASSOCIATION OF NEIGHBOURHOOD HOUSES OF BRITISH COLUMBIA *p 288*
3102 MAIN ST SUITE 203, VANCOUVER, BC, V5T 3G7
(604) 875-9111   *SIC 8399*

ASSOCIATION OF PROFESSIONAL ENGINEERS AND GEOSCIENTISTS OF ALBERTA, THE *p 87*
10060 JASPER AVE NW SUITE 1500, EDMONTON, AB, T5J 4A2
(780) 426-3990   *SIC 8621*

ASSOCIATION PARITAIRE POUR LA SANTE ET LA SECURITE DU TRAVAIL DU SECTEUR AFFAIRES SOCIALES *p 1166*
5100 RUE SHERBROOKE E BUREAU 950, MONTREAL, QC, H1V 3R9
(514) 253-6871   *SIC 8631*

ASSOCIATION PROVINCIALE DES CONSTRUCTEURS D'HABITATIONS DU QUEBEC INC *p 1051*
5930 BOUL LOUIS-H.-LAFONTAINE, ANJOU, QC, H1M 1S7
(514) 353-9960   *SIC 8611*

ASSOCIATION QUEBECOISE D'ETABLISSEMENT DE SANTE & DES SERVICES SOCIAUX *p 1193*
505 BOUL DE MAISONNEUVE O BUREAU 400, MONTREAL, QC, H3A 3C2
(514) 842-4861   *SIC 8399*

ASSOCIATION QUEBECOISE DES TRANSPORTS *p 1201*
1255 RUE UNIVERSITY BUREAU 200, MONTREAL, QC, H3B 3X4
(514) 523-6444   *SIC 8621*

ASSOCIATION SOGERIVE INC *p 1142*
101 CH DE LA RIVE, LONGUEUIL, QC, J4H 4C9
(450) 442-9575   *SIC 4493*

ASSOCIATION TOURISTIQUE REGIONALE DE CHARLEVOIX INC *p 1122*
495 BOUL DE COMPORTE, LA MALBAIE, QC, G5A 3G3
(418) 665-4454   *SIC 7389*

ASSOCIATION TOURISTIQUE REGIONALE DE MONTREAL, L' *p 1207*
See *OFFICE DES CONGRES ET DU TOURISME DU GRAND MONTREAL INC. L'*

ASSOCIATION YWCA DE QUEBEC, L' *p 1270*
855 AV HOLLAND, QUEBEC, QC, G1S 3S5
(418) 683-2155   *SIC 8699*

ASSOCIES SPORTIFS DE MONTREAL, SOCIETE EN COMMANDITE, LES *p 1218*
6105 AV DU BOISE, MONTREAL, QC, H3S 2V9
(514) 737-0000   *SIC 7991*

ASSUMPTION COLLAGE SCHOOL *p 516*
See *BRANT HALDIMAND NORFOLK CATHOLIC DISTRICT SCHOOL BOARD*

ASSUMPTION COLLEGE CATHOLIC HIGH SCHOOL *p 1025*
See *WINDSOR-ESSEX CATHOLIC DISTRICT SCHOOL BOARD, THE*

ASSUMPTION COLLEGE SCHOOL *p 516*
See *BRANT HALDIMAND NORFOLK CATHOLIC DISTRICT SCHOOL BOARD*

ASSUMPTION LIFE *p 406*
See *ASSUMPTION MUTUAL LIFE INSURANCE COMPANY*

ASSUMPTION MUTUAL LIFE INSURANCE COMPANY *p 406*
770 MAIN ST, MONCTON, NB, E1C 1E7
(506) 853-6040   *SIC 6311*

ASSUMPTION PLACE LIMITED *p 406*
770 MAIN ST, MONCTON, NB, E1C 1E7
(506) 853-5420   *SIC 6512*

ASSURACTION *p 1203*
See *EGR INC*

ASSURANCE 5000 *p 1045*
See *TREMBLAY ASSURANCE LTEE*

ASSURANCE 5000 INC *p 1151*
89 RUE SAINT-ANDRE, METABETCHOUAN-LAC-A-LA-CROIX, QC, G8G 1V5
(418) 349-5000   *SIC 6411*

ASSURANCE BEAULIEU *p 1268*
See *CAPITALE ASSURANCES GENERALES INC, LA*

ASSURANCE BRIAN BROCHET *p 1376*
See *LUSSIER DALE PARIZEAU INC*

ASSURANCE BURROWES INC *p 1168*
2600 BOUL SAINT-JOSEPH E BUREAU 206, MONTREAL, QC, H1Y 2A4
(514) 522-2661   *SIC 6411*

ASSURANCE DECENNALE *p 1170*
See *RACINE & CHAMBERLAND INC*

ASSURANCE ET GESTION DE RISQUES *p 1106*
815 BOUL DE LA CARRIERE BUREAU 102, GATINEAU, QC, J8Y 6T4
SIC 6411

ASSURANCE JONES INC *p 1129*
103 AV BETHANY, LACHUTE, QC, J8H 2L2
(450) 562-8555   *SIC 6411*

ASSURANCE MARTIN & CYR *p 1076*
See *GROUPE DPJL INC*

ASSURANCE MURDOCH, CREVIER *p 1227*
See *HUB INTERNATIONAL QUEBEC LIMITEE*

ASSURANCE PROMUTUEL PORTNEUF-CHAMPLAIN *p 1294*
See *PROMUTUEL PORTNEUF-CHAMPLAIN SOCIETE, MUTUAL D'ASSURANCE GENERALE*

ASSURANCE ROY YELLE INC *p 1088*
106 RUE CHURCH, COWANSVILLE, QC, J2K 1T8
(450) 263-0110   *SIC 6411*

ASSURANCE TREMBLAY *p 1151*
See *ASSURANCE 5000 INC*

ASSURANCE VOYAGE RSA INC *p 1371*
1910 RUE KING O BUREAU 200, SHERBROOKE, QC, J1J 2E2
(819) 780-0064   *SIC 6411*

ASSURANCE VOYAGES COMPARAISON *p 1273*
See *SSQ DISTRIBUTION INC*

ASSURANCES COTE, GUIMOND, LAFOND & ASSOCIES INC *p 1045*
221 1RE AV E, AMOS, QC, J9T 1H5
(819) 732-5371   *SIC 6411*

ASSURANCES DCPA *p 1159*
See *DUBE COOKE PEDICELLI INC*

ASSURANCES DU GRANIT, LES *p 1124*
See *ASSURANCES FORTIN, GAGNON ET LEBRUN INC*

ASSURANCES ETERNA INC *p 1270*
1134 GRANDE ALLEE O BUREAU 400, QUEBEC, QC, G1S 1E5
(418) 266-1000   *SIC 6282*

ASSURANCES FONTAINE LEMAY & ASS INC, LES *p 1135*
5331 RUE SAINT-GEORGES, LEVIS, QC, G6V 4N4
(418) 835-1150   *SIC 6411*

ASSURANCES FORTIN FRECHETTE p 1137
See LEMIEUX ASSURANCES INC
ASSURANCES FORTIN FRECHETTE p 1306
See LEMIEUX ASSURANCES INC
ASSURANCES FORTIN, GAGNON ET LE-BRUN INC p 1124
4138 RUE LAVAL, LAC-MEGANTIC, QC, G6B 1B3
(819) 583-1208   SIC 6331
ASSURANCES GENERALES BANQUE NATIONAL INC p 1201
1100 BOUL ROBERT-BOURASSA UNITE 11, MONTREAL, QC, H3B 3A5
(514) 871-7507   SIC 6331
ASSURANCES GROULX p 1105
See ASSURANCES ROLAND GROULX INC, LES
ASSURANCES GROUPE CONCORDE INC p 1087
3820 BOUL LEVESQUE O BUREAU 101, COTE SAINT-LUC, QC, H7V 1E8
(450) 973-2822   SIC 6331
ASSURANCES GROUPE VEZINA p 1084
999 BOUL SAINT-MARTIN O, COTE SAINT-LUC, QC, H7S 1M5
(450) 663-6880   SIC 6411
ASSURANCES J.Y. MARCOUX & ASSOCIES INC p 1359
1017 BOUL VACHON N BUREAU 100, SAINTE-MARIE, QC, G6E 1M3
(418) 387-6604   SIC 6411
ASSURANCES JEAN-CLAUDE LECLERC INC p 1100
230 BOUL SAINT-JOSEPH O, DRUM-MONDVILLE, QC, J2E 0G3
(819) 477-3156   SIC 6411
ASSURANCES JOE ANGELONE INC p 1051
7811 BOUL LOUIS-H.-LAFONTAINE BUREAU 201, ANJOU, QC, H1K 4E4
(514) 353-1331   SIC 6411
ASSURANCES LAREAU ROUSSILLON p 1242
See LAREAU - COURTIERS D'ASSURANCES INC
ASSURANCES MICHEL BROSSEAU LTEE p 1156
5665 AV ROYALMOUNT BUREAU 200, MONT-ROYAL, QC, H4P 2P9
(514) 288-9141   SIC 6411
ASSURANCES MORIN ET ASSOCIES p 1109
See COURTIKA ASSURANCES INC
ASSURANCES PROVENCHER VERREAULT & ASSOCIES INC p 1071
7055 BOUL TASCHEREAU BUREAU 620, BROSSARD, QC, J4Z 1A7
(450) 676-7707   SIC 6411
ASSURANCES R.P.B. p 1365
See ROCHEFORT, PERRON, BILLETTE INC
ASSURANCES ROBICHAUD INSURANCE BROKERS INC p 627
37 RIVERSIDE DR, KAPUSKASING, ON, P5N 1A7
(705) 335-2371   SIC 6411
ASSURANCES ROBILLARD p 1303
See ASSURANCES ROBILLARD & ASSOCIES INC, LES
ASSURANCES ROBILLARD & ASSOCIES INC, LES p 1303
461 CH DE JOLIETTE BUREAU 100, SAINT-FELIX-DE-VALOIS, QC, J0K 2M0
(450) 889-5557   SIC 6311
ASSURANCES ROLAND GROULX INC, LES p 1105
540 BOUL DE L'HOPITAL BUREAU 200, GATINEAU, QC, J8V 3T2

(819) 243-0242   SIC 6411
ASSURANCES SAGUENAY INC p 1115
2655 BOUL DU ROYAUME BUREAU 102, JONQUIERE, QC, G7S 4S9
(418) 699-1100   SIC 6411
ASSURANCES SHINK BOURGON p 1365
See ASSURANCIA SHINK DECELLES INC
ASSURANCIA GROUPE BROSSEAU INC p 1072
1 AV LIBERTE, CANDIAC, QC, J5R 3X8
(450) 635-1155   SIC 6411
ASSURANCIA SHINK DECELLES INC p 1365
45 RUE VICTORIA E, SALABERRY-DE-VALLEYFIELD, QC, J6T 2L4
(450) 377-8585   SIC 6411
ASSURANT LIFE OF CANADA p 754
1111 DAVIS DRIVE, NEWMARKET, ON, L3Y 9E5
(888) 977-3752   SIC 6311
ASSURANT LIFE OF CANADA MARKHAM p 666
95 ROYAL CREST CRT UNIT 19, MARKHAM, ON, L3R 9X5
(905) 943-4447   SIC 6311
ASSURANT SERVICES CANADA INC p 771
5000 YONGE ST SUITE 2000, NORTH YORK, ON, M2N 7E9
(416) 733-3360   SIC 6351
ASSURANT SOLUTIONS p 771
See ASSURANT SERVICES CANADA INC
ASSURED PACKAGING DIVISION p 554
See K-G SPRAY-PAK INC
ASSUREXPERTS INC p 1277
540 RUE MICHEL-FRAGASSO, QUEBEC, QC, G2E 5N4
(418) 871-2289   SIC 6411
ASSURIS p 935
250 YONGE ST SUITE 3110, TORONTO, ON, M5B 2L7
(416) 359-2001   SIC 6411
AST TRUST COMPANY (CANADA) p 936
1 TORONTO ST SUITE 1200, TORONTO, ON, M5C 2V6
(416) 682-3800   SIC 8741
ASTA FOOD p 1291
See ALIMENTS ASTA INC
ASTALDI CANADA INC p 424
358 HAMILTON RIVER RD, HAPPY VALLEY-GOOSE BAY, NL, A0P 1C0
(709) 896-4470   SIC 1541
ASTELLAS PHARMA CANADA, INC p 666
675 COCHRANE DR SUITE 500, MARKHAM, ON, L3R 0B8
(905) 470-7990   SIC 5122
ASTENJOHNSON DRYER FABRIC p 623
See ASTENJOHNSON, INC
ASTENJOHNSON, INC p 623
48 RICHARDSON SIDE RD, KANATA, ON, K2K 1X2
(613) 592-5851   SIC 2221
ASTENJOHNSON, INC p 623
1243 TERON RD, KANATA, ON, K2K 1X2
(613) 592-5851   SIC 2299
ASTENJOHNSON, INC p 1365
213 BOUL DU HAVRE, SALABERRY-DE-VALLEYFIELD, QC, J6S 1R9
(450) 373-2425   SIC 2299
ASTLEY GILBERT LIMITED p 787
42 CARNFORTH RD, NORTH YORK, ON, M4A 2K7
(416) 288-8666   SIC 2759
ASTON HILL VIP INCOME FUND p 968
77 KING ST W SUITE 2110, TORONTO, ON, M5K 2A1
(416) 583-2300   SIC 6733
ASTOR & YORK RETAIL BC LTD p 918
1721 BAYVIEW AVE UNIT 202, TORONTO, ON, M4G 3C1
(416) 434-2900   SIC 6531
ASTOUND GROUP INC, THE p 805
1215 NORTH SERVICE RD W UNIT A, OAKVILLE, ON, L6M 2W2
(905) 465-0474   SIC 7389

ASTRA DESIGN SYSTEMS INC p 692
5155 CREEKBANK RD, MISSISSAUGA, ON, L4W 1X2
(905) 282-9000   SIC 5084
ASTRA TRADE FINISHING LIMITED p 864
390 TAPSCOTT RD SUITE 1, SCARBOROUGH, ON, M1B 2Y9
(416) 291-2272   SIC 2631
ASTRAL BROADCASTING GROUP INC p 1214
1616 BOUL RENE-LEVESQUE O BUREAU 300, MONTREAL, QC, H3H 1P8
(514) 939-3150   SIC 4833
ASTRAL MEDIA AFFICHAGE, S.E.C. p 1193
1800 AV MCGILL COLLEGE BUREAU 2700, MONTREAL, QC, H3A 3J6
(514) 939-5000   SIC 7312
ASTRAL MEDIA OUTDOOR p 978
See BELL MEDIA INC
ASTRAL MEDIA RADIO ATLANTIC INC p 400
206 ROOKWOOD AVE, FREDERICTON, NB, E3B 2M2
(506) 451-9111   SIC 4832
ASTRAL MEDIA RADIO INC p 926
2 ST CLAIR AVE W SUITE 200, TORONTO, ON, M4V 1L6
(416) 323-5200   SIC 4832
ASTRAL MEDIA RADIO INC p 1214
2100 RUE SAINTE-CATHERINE O BUREAU 1000, MONTREAL, QC, H3H 2T3
(514) 529-3200   SIC 4832
ASTRAL TELEVISION NETWORK, DIV OF p 922
See BELL MEDIA INC
ASTRAZENECA CANADA INC p 703
1004 MIDDLEGATE RD SUITE 5000, MISSISSAUGA, ON, L4Y 1M4
(905) 277-7111   SIC 2834
ASTRO INSURANCE 1000 INC p 142
542 7 ST S UNIT 100, LETHBRIDGE, AB, T1J 2H1
(403) 320-6700   SIC 6411
ASTRONICS LSI CANADA p 1095
See SYSTEMES LUMINESCENT CANADA INC
ASURION CANADA, INC p 406
11 OCEAN LIMITED WAY, MONCTON, NB, E1C 0H1
(506) 386-9200   SIC 4899
AT EAZE p 870
See 1905405 ONTARIO LIMITED
AT FILMS INC p 107
4605 101A AVE NW, EDMONTON, AB, T6A 0L3
(780) 450-7760   SIC 1742
AT LIMITED PARTNERSHIP p 398
365 CH CANADA, EDMUNDSTON, NB, E3V 1W2
(506) 737-2345   SIC 5031
AT&S (ADVANCE TANKS & SYSTEMS) p 1149
See RESERVOIRS GIL-FAB INTERNATIONAL INC, LES
AT&T ENTERPRISES CANADA CO p 903
55 COMMERCE VALLEY DR W SUITE 700, THORNHILL, ON, L3T 7V9
(905) 762-7390   SIC 4899
AT&T GLOBAL SERVICES CANADA CO p 903
55 COMMERCE VALLEY DR W SUITE 700, THORNHILL, ON, L3T 7V9
(905) 762-7390   SIC 4899
AT-TAIBAH HALAL p 119
See OSMAN GLOBAL TRADING LTD
ATA p 197
See ATCHELITZ THREHERMEN'S ASSOCIATION
ATAC RESOURCES LTD p 297
510 HASTINGS ST W SUITE 1016, VANCOUVER, BC, V6B 1L8
(604) 687-2522   SIC 1041
ATACAMA PACIFIC GOLD CORPORATION p 936

25 ADELAIDE ST E SUITE 1900, TORONTO, ON, M5C 3A1
(416) 861-8267   SIC 1041
ATB p 281
See AGGRESSIVE TUBE BENDING INC
ATB FINANCIAL p 87
10020 100 ST NW SUITE 2100, EDMONTON, AB, T5J 0N3
(780) 408-7000   SIC 6036
ATC POLYMERES FORMULES p 1099
See SCOTT BADER ATC INC
ATC-FROST MAGNETICS INC p 796
1130 EIGHTH LINE, OAKVILLE, ON, L6H 2R4
(905) 844-6681   SIC 3677
ATC-FROST MAGNETICS INC p 1008
550 PARKSIDE DR UNIT D6, WATERLOO, ON, N2L 5V4
(905) 844-6681   SIC 3677
ATCHELITZ THREHERMEN'S ASSOCIATION p 197
44146 LUCKAKUCK WAY, CHILLIWACK, BC, V2R 4A7
(604) 858-2119   SIC 7389
ATCHISON, S. W. PLUMBING & HEATING LTD p 660
4186 RANEY CRES UNIT 4, LONDON, ON, N6L 1C3
(519) 652-0673   SIC 1711
ATCO ELECTRIC p 131
See ATCO ELECTRIC LTD
ATCO ELECTRIC LTD p 87
10035 105 ST NW, EDMONTON, AB, T5J 2V6
(780) 420-7310   SIC 4911
ATCO ELECTRIC LTD p 131
9717 97 AVE, GRANDE PRAIRIE, AB, T8V 6L9
(780) 538-7032   SIC 4911
ATCO ELECTRIC LTD p 135
GD, HANNA, AB, T0J 1P0
(403) 854-5141   SIC 4911
ATCO ENERGY SOLUTIONS LTD p 63
909 11 AVE SW SUITE 800, CALGARY, AB, T2R 1L7
(403) 292-7500   SIC 4911
ATCO FRONTEC LTD p 63
909 11 AVE SW SUITE 300, CALGARY, AB, T2R 1L7
(403) 245-7757   SIC 7011
ATCO GAS p 63
See ATCO GAS AND PIPELINES LTD
ATCO GAS p 108
See ATCO GAS AND PIPELINES LTD
ATCO GAS p 291
115 3RD AVE W, VANCOUVER, BC, V5Y 1E6
SIC 4924
ATCO GAS AND PIPELINES LTD p 20
4415 12 ST NE, CALGARY, AB, T2E 4R1
(403) 245-7857   SIC 4923
ATCO GAS AND PIPELINES LTD p 63
1040 11 AVE SW, CALGARY, AB, T2R 0G3
(403) 245-7551   SIC 4923
ATCO GAS AND PIPELINES LTD p 63
909 11 AVE SW SUITE 1200, CALGARY, AB, T2R 1L7
(403) 245-7060   SIC 4923
ATCO GAS AND PIPELINES LTD p 108
5623 82 AVE NW, EDMONTON, AB, T6B 0E8
(780) 733-2552   SIC 0721
ATCO GAS, DIV OF p 63
See ATCO GAS AND PIPELINES LTD
ATCO GROUP p 73
See ATCO LTD
ATCO ITEK p 87
See CANADIAN UTILITIES LIMITED
ATCO LTD p 73
5302 FORAND ST SW, CALGARY, AB, T3E 8B4
(403) 292-7500   SIC 4911

ATCO MIDSTREAM LTD *p 43*
240 4 AVE SW SUITE 900, CALGARY, AB, T2P 4H4
(403) 513-3700 *SIC 4899*

ATCO POWER *p 135*
See *ATCO ELECTRIC LTD*

ATCO POWER (2010) LTD *p 63*
919 11 AVE SW SUITE 400, CALGARY, AB, T2R 1P3
(403) 209-6900 *SIC 4911*

ATCO POWER CANADA LTD *p 63*
919 11 AVE SW SUITE 400, CALGARY, AB, T2R 1P3
(403) 209-6900 *SIC 4911*

ATCO STRUCTURES & LOGISTICS LTD *p 73*
115 PEACEKEEPERS DR, CALGARY, AB, T3E 7X4
(403) 662-8500 *SIC 1742*

ATCO TECHNOLOGY MANAGEMENT LTD *p 87*
10035 105 ST, EDMONTON, AB, T5J 2V6
(403) 292-7500 *SIC 4911*

ATCO TWO RIVERS LODGING CONSTRUCTION LIMITED PARTNERSHIP *p 73*
4838 RICHARD RD SW SUITE 300, CALGARY, AB, T3E 6L1
(403) 662-8500 *SIC 1541*

ATCO WATER, DIV OF *p 63*
See *ATCO ENERGY SOLUTIONS LTD*

ATEDM *p 1173*
See *AUTISME ET TROUBLES ENVAHISSANTS DU DEVELOPPEMENT MONTR AL*

ATEK DEVELOPMENTS INC *p 153*
6320 50 AVE UNIT 405, RED DEER, AB, T4N 4C6
(403) 342-4885 *SIC 1542*

ATELIER ABACO INC *p 1047*
9100 RUE CLAVEAU, ANJOU, QC, H1J 1Z4
(514) 355-6182 *SIC 7389*

ATELIER D'OUTILS ELECTRIQUES SHERBROOKE *p 1048*
See *DORSON LTEE*

ATELIER D'USINAGE *p 1280*
See *MACHINERIE P.W. INC*

ATELIER DE MECANIQUE PREMONT INC *p 1266*
2495 BOUL WILFRID-HAMEL, QUEBEC, QC, G1P 2H9
(418) 683-0563 *SIC 5012*

ATELIER DE READAPTATION AU TRAVAIL DE BEAUCE INC, L' *p 1321*
1280 AV DU PALAIS, SAINT-JOSEPH-DE-BEAUCE, QC, G0S 2V0
(418) 397-4341 *SIC 7349*

ATELIER DE TRI DES MATIERES PLASTIQUES RECYCLABLES DU QUEBEC INC *p 1233*
3405 BOUL INDUSTRIEL, MONTREAL, QC, H7L 4S3
(450) 667-5347 *SIC 2821*

ATELIER DES VIEILLES FORGES INC *p 1386*
1000 PLACE BOLAND, TROIS-RIVIERES, QC, G8Z 4H2
(819) 376-1834 *SIC 4783*

ATELIER DESIGN *p 1375*
See *MOBILIER DE BUREAU LOGIFLEX INC*

ATELIER DIESEL FOURNIER *p 1353*
See *ADF DIESEL MONTREAL INC*

ATELIER DU CRAN *p 1078*
See *CENTRE D'ENTRAINEMENT A LA VIE DE CHICOUTIMI INC*

ATELIER GERARD BEAULIEU INC *p 417*
164 RUE MGR-MARTIN E, SAINT-QUENTIN, NB, E8A 1W1
(506) 235-2243 *SIC 3443*

ATELIER KOLLONTAI INC *p 1174*
2065 RUE PARTHENAIS BUREAU 389, MONTREAL, QC, H2K 3T1

(514) 223-4899 *SIC 5961*

ATELIER LA FLECHE DE FER INC, L' *p 1063*
1730 RUE EIFFEL, BOUCHERVILLE, QC, J4B 7W1
(450) 552-9150 *SIC 8322*

ATELIER LA FLECHE DE FER INC, L' *p 1307*
3800 RUE RICHELIEU, SAINT-HUBERT, QC, J3Y 7B1
(450) 656-9150 *SIC 7629*

ATELIER M.C AUTO XPERT *p 1170*
See *ENTREPOT DE MONTREAL 1470 INC*

ATELIER PEPIN INC *p 1242*
1369 BOUL LOUIS-FRECHETTE, NICOLET, QC, J3T 1M3
(819) 293-5584 *SIC 7389*

ATELIER POLY-TECK *p 1371*
See *DEFI POLYTECK*

ATELIER POLY-TECK INC *p 1373*
151 RUE LEGER, SHERBROOKE, QC, J1L 2G8
(819) 563-6636 *SIC 3081*

ATELIER TAC *p 1320*
See *GROUPE LEV-FAB INC*

ATELIER UBI, L' *p 1183*
See *UBISOFT DIVERTISSEMENTS INC*

ATELIERS ACTIBEC 2000 INC, LES *p 1112*
508 GRANDE ALLEE O, GRANDE-RIVIERE-OUEST, QC, G0C 1W0
(418) 385-1414 *SIC 4953*

ATELIERS B.G. INC, LES *p 1370*
2980 RUE KING E, SHERBROOKE, QC, J1G 5J2
(819) 346-2195 *SIC 3399*

ATELIERS BEAU-ROC INC, LES *p 1002*
300 RUE UNIVERSELLE, VARS, ON, K0A 3H0
(613) 443-0044 *SIC 3713*

ATELIERS D'ELLE, LES *p 1256*
See *FOND SRS DE L'ETABLISSEMENT DE DETENTION DE QUEBEC, LE*

ATELIERS FERROVIAIRES DE MONT-JOLI INC, LES *p 1357*
125 RUE DE L'EXPANSION, SAINTE-FLAVIE, QC, G0J 2L0
(418) 775-7174 *SIC 7389*

ATELIERS G. PAQUETTE INC *p 1282*
104 RUE LAROCHE, REPENTIGNY, QC, J6A 7M5
(450) 654-6744 *SIC 7629*

ATELIERS LEOPOLD DESROSIERS INC *p 1150*
60 RUE BRILLANT, MATANE, QC, G4W 0J9
(418) 562-2640 *SIC 7389*

ATELIERS MANUTEX INC, LES *p 1289*
230 AV MARCEL-BARIL, ROUYN-NORANDA, QC, J9X 7C1
(819) 764-4415 *SIC 5136*

ATELIERS T.A.Q. INC *p 1277*
5255 RUE RIDEAU, QUEBEC, QC, G2E 5H5
(418) 871-4912 *SIC 7389*

ATELIERS TRANSITION INC, LES *p 1311*
1255 RUE DELORME BUREAU 103, SAINT-HYACINTHE, QC, J2S 2J3
(450) 771-2747 *SIC 7389*

ATHABASCA CATERING LIMITED PARTNERSHIP *p 1433*
335 PACKHAM AVE SUITE 120, SASKATOON, SK, S7N 4S1
(306) 242-8008 *SIC 5812*

ATHABASCA OIL CORPORATION *p 43*
215 9 AVE SW SUITE 1200, CALGARY, AB, T2P 1K3
(403) 237-8227 *SIC 5172*

ATHABASCA TRIBAL COUNCIL LTD *p 127*
9206 MCCORMICK DR, FORT MCMURRAY, AB, T9H 1C7
(780) 791-6538 *SIC 8699*

ATHABASCA UNIVERSITY *p 4*
1 UNIVERSITY DR, ATHABASCA, AB, T9S 3A3

(780) 675-6100 *SIC 8221*

ATHLETE'S CARE SPORTS MEDICINE CENTRES INC *p 766*
505 CONSUMERS RD SUITE 809, NORTH YORK, ON, M2J 4V8
(416) 479-8562 *SIC 8011*

ATHLETIC KNIT *p 993*
See *BERNARD ATHLETIC KNIT & ENTERPRISES LIMITED*

ATHLETICA *p 1008*
See *ATHLETICA SPORT SYSTEMS INC*

ATHLETICA SPORT SYSTEMS INC *p 1008*
554 PARKSIDE DR, WATERLOO, ON, N2L 5Z4
(519) 747-1856 *SIC 3949*

ATHOL MURRAY COLLEGE OF NOTRE DAME *p 1438*
49 MAIN ST, WILCOX, SK, S0G 5E0
(306) 732-2080 *SIC 8211*

ATHOS *p 1259*
See *LEPINE-CLOUTIER LTEE*

ATI *p 750*
See *ALGONQUIN COLLEGE OF APPLIED ARTS AND TECHNOLOGY*

ATI TECHNOLOGIES ULC *p 678*
1 COMMERCE VALLEY DR E, MARKHAM, ON, L3T 7X6
(905) 882-2600 *SIC 3577*

ATI TELECOM INTERNATIONAL, COMPANY *p 112*
4336 97 ST NW, EDMONTON, AB, T6E 5R9
(780) 424-9100 *SIC 4899*

ATICO MINING CORPORATION *p 302*
543 GRANVILLE ST UNIT 501, VANCOUVER, BC, V6C 1X8
(604) 633-9022 *SIC 1021*

ATIKOKAN GENERAL HOSPITAL *p 479*
120 DOROTHY ST, ATIKOKAN, ON, P0T 1C1
(807) 597-4215 *SIC 8062*

ATIMI SOFTWARE INC *p 302*
800 PENDER ST W SUITE 800, VANCOUVER, BC, V6C 2V6
(778) 372-2800 *SIC 7372*

ATIRA PROPERTY MANAGEMENT INC *p 294*
405 POWELL ST, VANCOUVER, BC, V6A 1G7
(604) 439-8848 *SIC 8741*

ATIS LP *p 408*
70 RIDEOUT ST, MONCTON, NB, E1E 1E2
(506) 853-8080 *SIC 5039*

ATIS PORTES ET FENETRES CORP. *p 1381*
2175 BOUL DES ENTREPRISES, TERREBONNE, QC, J6Y 1W9
(450) 492-0404 *SIC 2431*

ATIS S.E.C. *p 1144*
1111 RUE SAINT-CHARLES O, LONGUEUIL, QC, J4K 5G4
(450) 928-0101 *SIC 2431*

ATITUDES RESTAURANT & BISTRO, L' *p 436*
See *YELLOWKNIFE INN LTD*

ATKIN, MICHAEL HOLDINGS INC *p 99*
17415 103 AVE NW, EDMONTON, AB, T5S 1J4
(780) 486-5100 *SIC 5511*

ATKINSON & TERRY INSURANCE BROKERS *p 207*
8067 120 ST SUITE 120, DELTA, BC, V4C 6P7
(604) 596-3350 *SIC 6411*

ATKINSON HOME BUILDING CENTRE *p 618*
See *BMP (1985) LIMITED*

ATKINSON, LEO G FISHERIES LIMITED *p 442*
89 DANIELS HEAD RD RR 1, CLARKS HARBOUR, NS, B0W 1P0
(902) 745-3047 *SIC 5146*

ATLANTA GOLD INC *p 985*
100 KING ST W SUITE 5600, TORONTO,

ON, M5X 1C9
(416) 777-0013 *SIC 1041*

ATLANTIA HOLDINGS INCORPORATED *p 241*
949 3RD ST W SUITE 121, NORTH VANCOUVER, BC, V7P 3P7
(604) 985-7257 *SIC 5045*

ATLANTIC ACURA *p 457*
See *FAIRVIEW COVE AUTO LIMITED*

ATLANTIC AIR-COOLED ENGINES DIV *p 409*
See *ROBERT K. BUZZELL LIMITED*

ATLANTIC ALARM & SOUND LTD *p 397*
489 AV ACADIE SUITE 200, DIEPPE, NB, E1A 1H7
(506) 853-9315 *SIC 6211*

ATLANTIC ALL-WEATHER WINDOWS LTD *p 411*
49 EAST MAIN ST, PORT ELGIN, NB, E4M 2X9
(506) 538-2361 *SIC 3089*

ATLANTIC AMBASSATOURS LIMITED *p 454*
6575 BAYNE ST, HALIFAX, NS, B3K 0H1
(902) 423-6242 *SIC 4111*

ATLANTIC BAPTIST SENIOR CITIZENS HOMES INC *p 408*
35 ATLANTIC BAPTIST AVE, MONCTON, NB, E1E 4N3
(506) 858-7870 *SIC 6712*

ATLANTIC BEEF PRODUCTS INC *p 1038*
95 TRAIN STATION RD, ALBANY, PE, C0B 1A0
(902) 437-2727 *SIC 2011*

ATLANTIC BUILDING CLEANING LIMITED *p 452*
1505 BARRINGTON ST SUITE 1310, HALIFAX, NS, B3J 3K5
(902) 420-1497 *SIC 7349*

ATLANTIC BUSINESS INTERIOR *p 448*
See *TAR INVESTMENTS LIMITED*

ATLANTIC BUSINESS INTERIORS LIMITED *p 445*
30 TROOP AVE, DARTMOUTH, NS, B3B 1Z1
(902) 468-3200 *SIC 5021*

ATLANTIC CANADA WORLD TRADE CENTRE *p 454*
See *TRADE CENTRE LIMITED*

ATLANTIC CAR STEREO LIMITED *p 443*
26 LAKECREST DR, DARTMOUTH, NS, B2X 1T8
(902) 435-0600 *SIC 5531*

ATLANTIC CARRIER TRANSICOLD, DIV OF *p 742*
See *REEFER SALES & SERVICE (TORONTO) INCORPORATED*

ATLANTIC CATCH DATA LIMITED *p 452*
1801 HOLLIS ST SUITE 1220, HALIFAX, NS, B3J 3N4
(902) 422-4745 *SIC 3823*

ATLANTIC CENTRAL *p 455*
See *CREDIT UNION CENTRAL OF NOVA SCOTIA*

ATLANTIC CENTRAL *p 455*
6074 LADY HAMMOND RD SUITE B, HALIFAX, NS, B3K 2R7
(902) 453-0680 *SIC 6351*

ATLANTIC CHICAN SEAFOOD *p 442*
See *3274876 NOVA SCOTIA LIMITED*

ATLANTIC COATED PAPERS LTD *p 1013*
1605 MCEWEN DR, WHITBY, ON, L1N 7L4
(416) 299-1675 *SIC 2672*

ATLANTIC COMPRESSED AIR LTD *p 408*
484 EDINBURGH DR, MONCTON, NB, E1E 2L1
(506) 858-9500 *SIC 5084*

ATLANTIC CONTROLS DIV OF *p 1118*
See *CONTROLES LAURENTIDE LTEE*

ATLANTIC CUSTOM BROKERS *p 431*
233 DUCKWORTH ST SUITE 301, ST. JOHN'S, NL, A1C 1G8

(709) 745-8700   *SIC* 4731
ATLANTIC DODGE   *p* 463
See 3213695 NOVA SCOTIA LIMITED
ATLANTIC EDM   *p* 1356
See INDUSTRIES ELIRA INC
ATLANTIC FABRICS LIMITED   *p* 443
114 WOODLAWN RD, DARTMOUTH, NS, B2W 2S7
(902) 434-1440   *SIC* 5949
ATLANTIC GOLD CORPORATION   *p* 327
595 BURRARD ST SUITE 3083, VANCOUVER, BC, V7X 1L3
(604) 689-5564   *SIC* 1479
ATLANTIC GROCERY DISTRIBUTORS LIMITED   *p* 421
1 HOPE AVE, BAY ROBERTS, NL, A0A 1G0
(709) 786-9720   *SIC* 5141
ATLANTIC GYM & SPORTS   *p* 1264
See GROUPE SPORTS-INTER PLUS INC, LE
ATLANTIC HIGHWAYS MANAGEMENT CORPORATION LIMITED   *p* 450
209 COBEQUID PASS, GREAT VILLAGE, NS, B0M 1L0
(902) 668-2211   *SIC* 4785
ATLANTIC HOTELS PARTNERSHIP   *p* 297
510 HASTINGS ST W, VANCOUVER, BC, V6B 1L8
(604) 687-8813   *SIC* 7011
ATLANTIC INDUSTRIAL CLEANERS, DIV OF   *p* 416
See ENVIROSYSTEMS INCORPORATED
ATLANTIC INDUSTRIAL CLEANERS, DIV OF   *p* 446
See ENVIROSYSTEMS INCORPORATED
ATLANTIC INDUSTRIES LIMITED   *p* 412
32 YORK ST, SACKVILLE, NB, E4L 4R4
(506) 364-4600   *SIC* 3499
ATLANTIC LOTTERY CORPORATION INC*p* 406
922 MAIN ST, MONCTON, NB, E1C 8W6
(506) 867-5800   *SIC* 7999
ATLANTIC LUBRICANTS   *p* 469
See INTEC INVESTMENT HOLDINGS INC
ATLANTIC MARINE PRODUCTS   *p* 421
See BARRY GROUP INC
ATLANTIC MAZDA   *p* 397
See ATLANTIC MOTORS LTD
ATLANTIC MINERALS LIMITED   *p* 422
22 COMMERCIAL ST, CORNER BROOK, NL, A2H 2V2
(709) 634-8255   *SIC* 1422
ATLANTIC MINERALS LIMITED   *p* 427
GD, PORT AU PORT, NL, A0N 1T0
(709) 644-2447   *SIC* 1011
ATLANTIC MOBILITY PRODUCTS   *p* 440
See ATLANTIC MOBILITY PRODUCTS LIMITED PARTNERSHIP
ATLANTIC MOBILITY PRODUCTS LIMITED PARTNERSHIP   *p* 440
200 BLUEWATER RD UNIT 1, BEDFORD, NS, B4B 1G9
(902) 481-6699   *SIC* 5065
ATLANTIC MOTORS LTD   *p* 397
665 BOUL FERDINAND, DIEPPE, NB, E1A 7G1
(506) 852-8225   *SIC* 5511
ATLANTIC NEWSPRINT COMPANY, DIV   *p* 1013
See ATLANTIC PACKAGING PRODUCTS LTD
ATLANTIC PACKAGING PRODUCTS LTD *p* 621
45 CHISHOLM DR, INGERSOLL, ON, N5C 2C7
(800) 268-5620   *SIC* 2653
ATLANTIC PACKAGING PRODUCTS LTD *p* 692
5711 ATLANTIC DR, MISSISSAUGA, ON, L4W 1H3
(800) 268-5620   *SIC* 2653
ATLANTIC PACKAGING PRODUCTS LTD *p* 870

111 PROGRESS AVE, SCARBOROUGH, ON, M1P 2Y9
(416) 298-5456   *SIC* 2679
ATLANTIC PACKAGING PRODUCTS LTD *p* 870
111 PROGRESS AVE, SCARBOROUGH, ON, M1P 2Y9
(416) 298-8101   *SIC* 2679
ATLANTIC PACKAGING PRODUCTS LTD *p* 876
118 TIFFIELD RD, SCARBOROUGH, ON, M1V 5N2
(800) 268-5620   *SIC* 2653
ATLANTIC PACKAGING PRODUCTS LTD *p* 876
55 MILLIKEN BLVD, SCARBOROUGH, ON, M1V 1V3
(416) 298-5508   *SIC* 2653
ATLANTIC PACKAGING PRODUCTS LTD *p* 876
45 MILLIKEN BLVD, SCARBOROUGH, ON, M1V 1V3
(416) 298-5566   *SIC* 2676
ATLANTIC PACKAGING PRODUCTS LTD *p* 1013
1900 THICKSON RD S, WHITBY, ON, L1N 9E1
(905) 686-5944   *SIC* 2621
ATLANTIC PET DISTRIBUTING, DIV OF   *p* 1013
See LEIS PET DISTRIBUTING INC
ATLANTIC PILOTAGE AUTHORITY   *p* 452
1791 BARRINGTON ST SUITE 1801, HALIFAX, NS, B3J 3K9
(902) 426-2550   *SIC* 4499
ATLANTIC POTATO DISTRIBUTORS LTD *p* 411
42 INDUSTRIAL PARK ST, PERTH-ANDOVER, NB, E7H 2J2
(506) 273-6501   *SIC* 5148
ATLANTIC POULTRY INCORPORATED   *p* 465
791 BELCHER ST SUITE 1, PORT WILLIAMS, NS, B0P 1T0
(902) 678-1335   *SIC* 0259
ATLANTIC POWER (WILLIAMS LAKE) LTD *p* 343
4455 MACKENZIE AVE N, WILLIAMS LAKE, BC, V2G 5E8
(250) 392-6394   *SIC* 4911
ATLANTIC PRIVATE PROTECTION SERVICE   *p* 445
7 MELLOR AVE UNIT 12, DARTMOUTH, NS, B3B 0E8
(902) 468-9002   *SIC* 7381
ATLANTIC PROMOTIONS INC   *p* 1141
770 BOUL GUIMOND, LONGUEUIL, QC, J4G 1V6
(514) 871-1671   *SIC* 5023
ATLANTIC PROVINCES SPECIAL EDUCATION AUTHORITY   *p* 451
5940 SOUTH ST, HALIFAX, NS, B3H 1S6
(902) 423-8469   *SIC* 8211
ATLANTIC READY MIX   *p* 422
280 HUMBER RD, CORNER BROOK, NL, A2H 7H1
(709) 634-1885   *SIC* 5032
ATLANTIC READY MIX   *p* 427
See ATLANTIC MINERALS LIMITED
ATLANTIC READY-MIX, DIV OF   *p* 422
See ATLANTIC MINERALS LIMITED
ATLANTIC RETAIL CO-OPERATIVES FEDERATION   *p* 406
123 HALIFAX ST, MONCTON, NB, E1C 9R6
(506) 858-6000   *SIC* 5141
ATLANTIC RETIREMENT CONCEPTS INC*p* 399
10 BARTON CRES SUITE 504, FREDERICTON, NB, E3A 5S3
(506) 450-7088   *SIC* 6513
ATLANTIC ROOFERS LIMITED   *p* 397

118 CH COCAGNE CROSS, COCAGNE, NB, E4R 2J2
(506) 576-6683   *SIC* 1761
ATLANTIC SHELLFISH   *p* 421
See BARRY GROUP INC
ATLANTIC SKY SERVICE   *p* 450
647 BARNES DR, GOFFS, NS, B2T 1K3
(902) 873-3575   *SIC* 4522
ATLANTIC SPEEDY PROPANE   *p* 419
668 MAIN ST, WOODSTOCK, NB, E7M 2C8
SIC 4924
ATLANTIC SPEEDY PROPANE   *p* 467
546 GEORGE ST, SYDNEY, NS, B1P 1K7
SIC 4924
ATLANTIC SPEEDY PROPANE   *p* 471
65A STARRS RD, YARMOUTH, NS, B5A 2T2
(902) 742-8305   *SIC* 4924
ATLANTIC SUPERSTORE   *p* 463
See ATLANTIC WHOLESALERS LTD
ATLANTIC SUPERSTORE   *p* 464
See ATLANTIC WHOLESALERS LTD
ATLANTIC SUPERSTORE   *p* 470
See ATLANTIC WHOLESALERS LTD
ATLANTIC SUPERSTORE, THE   *p* 412
See ATLANTIC WHOLESALERS LTD
ATLANTIC SUPERSTORE, THE   *p* 449
See ATLANTIC WHOLESALERS LTD
ATLANTIC TOURS LIMITED   *p* 455
2631 KING ST, HALIFAX, NS, B3K 4T7
(902) 423-6242   *SIC* 4725
ATLANTIC TOWING LIMITED   *p* 414
300 UNION ST SUITE 2, SAINT JOHN, NB, E2L 4Z2
(506) 648-2750   *SIC* 4492
ATLANTIC TRAILER & EQUIPMENT LTD *p* 425
8 LINTROS PL, MOUNT PEARL, NL, A1N 5K2
(709) 745-3260   *SIC* 5083
ATLANTIC WALLBOARD LIMITED PARTNERSHIP   *p* 412
30 JERVIS LANE, SAINT JOHN, NB, E2J 0A9
(506) 633-3311   *SIC* 4924
ATLANTIC WHOLESALERS   *p* 457
See LOBLAW PROPERTIES LIMITED
ATLANTIC WHOLESALERS LTD   *p* 394
700 ST. PETER AVE, BATHURST, NB, E2A 2Y7
(506) 547-3180   *SIC* 5411
ATLANTIC WHOLESALERS LTD   *p* 408
100 BAIG BLVD, MONCTON, NB, E1E 1C8
(506) 852-2000   *SIC* 5141
ATLANTIC WHOLESALERS LTD   *p* 409
89 TRINITY DR, MONCTON, NB, E1G 2J7
(506) 383-4919   *SIC* 5411
ATLANTIC WHOLESALERS LTD   *p* 410
1198 ONONDAGA ST, OROMOCTO, NB, E2V 1B8
(506) 357-5982   *SIC* 5411
ATLANTIC WHOLESALERS LTD   *p* 411
425 COVERDALE RD, RIVERVIEW, NB, E1B 3K3
(506) 387-5992   *SIC* 5411
ATLANTIC WHOLESALERS LTD   *p* 412
168 ROTHESAY AVE, SAINT JOHN, NB, E2J 2B5
(506) 648-1320   *SIC* 5411
ATLANTIC WHOLESALERS LTD   *p* 413
650 SOMERSET ST, SAINT JOHN, NB, E2K 2Y7
(506) 658-6054   *SIC* 5411
ATLANTIC WHOLESALERS LTD   *p*418
10 LOWER COVE RD, SUSSEX, NB, E4E 0B7
(506) 433-9820   *SIC* 5411
ATLANTIC WHOLESALERS LTD   *p* 419
3409 RUE PRINCIPALE SUITE 31, TRACADIE-SHEILA, NB, E1X 1C7
(506) 393-1155   *SIC* 5411
ATLANTIC WHOLESALERS LTD   *p* 419
350 CONNELL ST, WOODSTOCK, NB, E7M

5G8
(506) 328-1100   *SIC* 5411
ATLANTIC WHOLESALERS LTD   *p* 438
126 ALBION ST S, AMHERST, NS, B4H 2X3
(902) 661-0703   *SIC* 5411
ATLANTIC WHOLESALERS LTD   *p* 439
1650 BEDFORD HWY, BEDFORD, NS, B4A 4J7
(902) 832-3117   *SIC* 5411
ATLANTIC WHOLESALERS LTD   *p* 441
21 DAVISON DR, BRIDGEWATER, NS, B4V 3K8
(902) 543-1809   *SIC* 5411
ATLANTIC WHOLESALERS LTD   *p* 442
920 COLE HARBOUR RD, DARTMOUTH, NS, B2V 2J5
(902) 462-4500   *SIC* 5411
ATLANTIC WHOLESALERS LTD   *p* 449
295 HIGHWAY 214, ELMSDALE, NS, B2S 2L1
(902) 883-1180   *SIC* 5411
ATLANTIC WHOLESALERS LTD   *p* 449
470 WARWICK ST, DIGBY, NS, B0V 1A0
(902) 245-4108   *SIC* 5411
ATLANTIC WHOLESALERS LTD   *p* 450
155 RESERVE ST, GLACE BAY, NS, B1A 4W3
(902) 842-9609   *SIC* 5411
ATLANTIC WHOLESALERS LTD   *p* 451
1075 BARRINGTON ST, HALIFAX, NS, B3H 4P1
(902) 492-3240   *SIC* 5411
ATLANTIC WHOLESALERS LTD   *p* 456
3711 JOSEPH HOWE DR, HALIFAX, NS, B3L 4H8
(902) 468-8866   *SIC* 5411
ATLANTIC WHOLESALERS LTD   *p* 458
210 CHAIN LAKE DR, HALIFAX, NS, B3S 1C5
(902) 450-5317   *SIC* 5411
ATLANTIC WHOLESALERS LTD   *p* 461
745 SACKVILLE DR, LOWER SACKVILLE, NS, B4E 2R2
(902) 864-2299   *SIC* 5411
ATLANTIC WHOLESALERS LTD   *p* 463
9064 COMMERCIAL ST, NEW MINAS, NS, B4N 3E4
(902) 681-0665   *SIC* 5411
ATLANTIC WHOLESALERS LTD   *p* 464
125 KING ST SUITE 321, NORTH SYDNEY, NS, B2A 3S1
(902) 794-7111   *SIC* 5411
ATLANTIC WHOLESALERS LTD   *p* 467
1225 KINGS RD, SYDNEY, NS, B1S 1E1
(902) 539-7657   *SIC* 5411
ATLANTIC WHOLESALERS LTD   *p* 470
11 COLE DR, WINDSOR, NS, B0N 2T0
(902) 798-9537   *SIC* 5411
ATLANTIC WHOLESALERS LTD   *p* 1038
465 UNIVERSITY AVE, CHARLOTTETOWN, PE, C1A 4N9
(902) 569-2850   *SIC* 5411
ATLANTIC WHOLESALERS LTD   *p* 1041
509 MAIN ST, MONTAGUE, PE, C0A 1R0
(902) 838-5421   *SIC* 5411
ATLANTIC WHOLESALERS LTD   *p* 1042
535 GRANVILLE ST, SUMMERSIDE, PE, C1N 6N4
(902) 888-1581   *SIC* 5411
ATLANTIC WINDOWS   *p* 411
See ATLANTIC ALL-WEATHER WINDOWS LTD
ATLANTICA DIVERSIFIED TRANSPORTATION SYSTEMS   *p* 421
5 MYERS AVE, CLARENVILLE, NL, A5A 1T5
(709) 466-7052   *SIC* 4213
ATLANTICA DIVERSIFIED TRANSPORTATION SYSTEMS INC   *p* 445
10 MORRIS DR UNIT 19, DARTMOUTH, NS, B3B 1K8
SIC 4731

ATLANTICA MECHANICAL CONTRAC-TORS INCORPORATED *p* 445
9 RALSTON AVE, DARTMOUTH, NS, B3B 1H5
(902) 468-2300   *SIC 1711*

ATLANTIS *p* 1231
See *CENTRE DE CONDITIONNEMENT PHYSIQUE ATLANTIS INC.*

ATLANTIS POMPE STE-FOY INC *p* 1263
1844 BOUL WILFRID-HAMEL, QUEBEC, QC, G1N 3Z2
(418) 681-7301   *SIC 5084*

ATLANTIS TRANSPORTATION SERVICES INC *p* 728
6500 SILVER DART DR, MISSISSAUGA, ON, L5P 1C4
(905) 672-5171   *SIC 4213*

ATLAS ACCESSOIRES D'AUTOS *p* 1231
See *PIECES D'AUTOS TRANSBEC INC, LES*

ATLAS AIR CONDITIONING *p* 796
See *ATLAS SERVICE COMPANY INC*

ATLAS ARTISTES *p* 1211
See *L'ARENA DES CANADIENS INC*

ATLAS BEARINGS CORPORATION *p* 501
8043 DIXIE RD, BRAMPTON, ON, L6T 3V1
(905) 790-0283   *SIC 5085*

ATLAS CANADA *p.* 796
See *ATLAS VAN LINES (CANADA) LTD*

ATLAS CARGO *p* 687
See *ATLAS INTERNATIONAL FREIGHT FORWARDING INC*

ATLAS COPCO CANADA INC *p* 647
200 MUMFORD RD SUITE A, LIVELY, ON, P3Y 1L2
(705) 673-6711   *SIC 5082*

ATLAS COPCO CANADA INC *p* 737
1025 TRISTAR DR, MISSISSAUGA, ON, L5T 1W5
(289) 562-0100   *SIC 5082*

ATLAS COPCO COMPRESSORS CANADA, DIV OF *p* 737
See *ATLAS COPCO CANADA INC*

ATLAS COPCO CONSTRUCTION AND MINING CANADA, DIV OF *p* 647
See *ATLAS COPCO CANADA INC*

ATLAS COPCO MINING & ROCK EXCAVATION TECHNIQUE CANADA *p* 737
See *ATLAS COPCO CANADA INC*

ATLAS CORPORATION, THE *p* 549
111 ORTONA CRT, CONCORD, ON, L4K 3M3
(905) 669-6825   *SIC 1542*

ATLAS FLUID SYSTEM, DIV OF *p* 1002
See *MARTINREA AUTOMOTIVE INC*

ATLAS GRAHAM *p* 384
See *JOSEPH & COMPANY LTD*

ATLAS GRAHAM FURGALE LTD *p* 383
1725 SARGENT AVE, WINNIPEG, MB, R3H 0C5
(204) 775-4451   *SIC 3991*

ATLAS GRAPHIC SUPPLY INC *p* 666
121 WHITEHALL DR, MARKHAM, ON, L3R 9T1
(905) 948-9800   *SIC 5199*

ATLAS HOLDINGS COMPANY LIMITED *p* 501
8043 DIXIE RD, BRAMPTON, ON, L6T 3V1
(905) 791-3888   *SIC 3429*

ATLAS HYDRAULICS INC *p* 515
369 ELGIN ST, BRANTFORD, ON, N3S 7P5
(519) 756-8210   *SIC 3492*

ATLAS INTERNATIONAL FREIGHT FORWARDING INC *p* 687
6365 NORTHWEST DR SUITE 18, MISSISSAUGA, ON, L4V 1J8
(905) 673-5000   *SIC 4731*

ATLAS PAINTING & RESTORATIONS LTD *p* 253
5020 NO. 7 RD, RICHMOND, BC, V6V 1R7
(604) 244-8244   *SIC 1542*

ATLAS PAPER BAG COMPANY LIMITED *p* 876
90 DYNAMIC DR, SCARBOROUGH, ON, M1V 2V1
(416) 293-2125   *SIC 2674*

ATLAS POLAR COMPANY LIMITED *p* 916
60 NORTHLINE RD, TORONTO, ON, M4B 3E5
(416) 751-7740   *SIC 5084*

ATLAS POWER SWEEPING LTD *p* 183
2796 NORLAND AVE, BURNABY, BC, V5B 3A6
(604) 294-6333   *SIC 4959*

ATLAS SERVICE COMPANY INC *p* 796
2590 BRISTOL CIR UNIT 1, OAKVILLE, ON, L6H 6Z7
(905) 279-3440   *SIC 1711*

ATLAS TIRE WHOLESALE INC *p* 737
6200 TOMKEN RD, MISSISSAUGA, ON, L5T 1X7
(905) 670-7354   *SIC 5014*

ATLAS TRAILER COACH PRODUCTS LTD *p* 20
2530 21 ST NE, CALGARY, AB, T2E 7L3
(403) 291-1225   *SIC 5013*

ATLAS TUBE CANADA ULC *p* 618
200 CLARK ST, HARROW, ON, N0R 1G0
(519) 738-5000   *SIC 3317*

ATLAS TUBE CANADA ULC *p* 1011
160 DAIN AVE, WELLAND, ON, L3B 5Y6
(905) 735-7473   *SIC 3317*

ATLAS VAN LINES (CANADA) LTD *p* 796
485 NORTH SERVICE RD E, OAKVILLE, ON, L6H 1A5
(905) 844-0701   *SIC 4731*

ATLAS-APEX ROOFING INC *p* 582
65 DISCO RD, ETOBICOKE, ON, M9W 1M2
(416) 421-6244   *SIC 1761*

ATLATSA RESOURCES CORPORATION *p* 302
666 BURRARD ST SUITE 1700, VANCOUVER, BC, V6C 2X8
(604) 631-1300   *SIC 1081*

ATLIFIC HOTELS *p* 1187
See *ATLIFIC INC*

ATLIFIC INC *p* 138
210 VILLAGE RD, LAKE LOUISE, AB, T0L 1E0
(403) 522-3791   *SIC 7011*

ATLIFIC INC *p* 336
728 HUMBOLDT ST, VICTORIA, BC, V8W 3Z5
(250) 480-3800   *SIC 7011*

ATLIFIC INC *p* 390
1330 PEMBINA HWY, WINNIPEG, MB, R3T 2B4
(204) 452-4747   *SIC 7011*

ATLIFIC INC *p* 582
231 CARLINGVIEW DR, ETOBICOKE, ON, M9W 5E8
(416) 675-0411   *SIC 7011*

ATLIFIC INC *p* 758
4960 CLIFTON HILL, NIAGARA FALLS, ON, L2G 3N4
(905) 358-3293   *SIC 7011*

ATLIFIC INC *p* 1142
900 RUE SAINT-CHARLES E, LONGUEUIL, QC, J4H 3Y2
(450) 646-8100   *SIC 7011*

ATLIFIC INC *p* 1187
250 RUE SAINT-ANTOINE O BUREAU 400, MONTREAL, QC, H2Y 0A3
(514) 509-5500   *SIC 8741*

ATM FOODS LTD *p* 207
8037 120 ST, DELTA, BC, V4C 6P7
SIC 5411

ATMOSPHERE *p* 23
See *FGL SPORTS LTD*

ATMOSPHERE *p* 1104
1100 BOUL MALONEY O, GATINEAU, QC, J8T 6G3
(819) 243-3711   *SIC 5941*

ATMOSPHERE *p* 1271
See *9023-4436 QUEBEC INC*

ATMOSPHERE *p* 1371
See *9147-8453 QUEBEC INC*

ATMOSPHERE SPORTS - PLAIN AIR 590 *p* 1379
See *GROUPE LALIBERTE SPORTS INC*

ATMPRQ *p* 1233
See *ATELIER DE TRI DES MATIERES PLASTIQUES RECYCLABLES DU QUEBEC INC*

ATOCAS DE L'ERABLE INC, LES *p* 1245
2249 RUE GARNEAU, PLESSISVILLE, QC, G6L 2Y7
(819) 621-7166   *SIC 0171*

ATOM-JET INDUSTRIES (2002) LTD *p* 347
2110 PARK AVE, BRANDON, MB, R7B 0R9
(204) 728-8590   *SIC 3599*

ATOMIC ENERGY OF CANADA LIMITED *p* 354
GD, PINAWA, MB, R0E 1L0
(204) 753-2311   *SIC 2819*

ATOMIC ENERGY OF CANADA LIMITED *p* 541
286 PLANT RD STN 508A, CHALK RIVER, ON, K0J 1J0
(613) 584-3311   *SIC 4911*

ATOMIC ENERGY OF CANADA LIMITED *p* 913
GD, TIVERTON, ON, N0G 2T0
SIC 2819

ATOMIC FICTION CANADA, INC *p* 1193
2050 RUE DE BLEURY BUREAU 800, MONTREAL, QC, H3A 2J5
(514) 600-0399   *SIC 7819*

ATOS INC *p* 737
6375 SHAWSON DR, MISSISSAUGA, ON, L5T 1S7
(905) 819-5761   *SIC 7379*

ATPAC INC *p* 1160
10700 BOUL HENRI-BOURASSA E, MONTREAL, QC, H1C 1G9
(514) 881-8888   *SIC 5013*

ATRAHAN TRANSFORMATION INC *p* 1403
860 CH DES ACADIENS, YAMACHICHE, QC, G0X 3L0
(819) 296-3791   *SIC 2011*

ATRC ENTERPRISES *p* 165
5005 42 ST SS 2, ST PAUL, AB, T0A 3A2
(780) 645-3227   *SIC 5541*

ATRENS-COUNSEL INSURANCE BROKERS *p* 719
See *ATRENS-COUNSEL INSURANCE BROKERS INC*

ATRENS-COUNSEL INSURANCE BROKERS INC *p* 719
7111 SYNTEX DR SUITE 200, MISSISSAUGA, ON, L5N 8C3
(905) 567-6222   *SIC 6411*

ATRF *p* 97
See *ALBERTA TEACHERS' RETIREMENT FUND BOARD*

ATRIA NETWORKS LP *p* 639
301 VICTORIA ST N, KITCHENER, ON, N2H 5E1
(888) 623-0623   *SIC 4899*

ATRIPCO DELIVERY SERVICE *p* 576
See *TRAILERMASTER FREIGHT CARRIERS LTD*

ATRIUM GROUP INC, THE *p* 452
1515 DRESDEN ROW, HALIFAX, NS, B3J 4B1
(902) 425-5700   *SIC 5431*

ATRIUM INNOVATIONS INC *p* 1401
3500 BOUL DE MAISONNEUVE O BUREAU 2405, WESTMOUNT, QC, H3Z 3C1
(514) 205-6240   *SIC 2023*

ATRIUM MORTGAGE INVESTMENT CORPORATION *p* 936
20 ADELAIDE ST E SUITE 900, TORONTO, ON, M5C 2T6
(416) 867-1053   *SIC 6163*

ATRONIC *p* 1218

See *EMBIX COMPAGNIE D'IMPORTATIONS DE MONTRES LTEE*

ATS *p* 13
See *3618358 CANADA INC*

ATS ADVANCE MANUFACTURING, DIV OF *p* 538
See *ATS AUTOMATION TOOLING SYSTEMS INC*

ATS ANDLAUER TRANSPORTATION SERVICES INC *p* 99
11264 186 ST NW, EDMONTON, AB, T5S 2W2
(780) 440-4005   *SIC 4731*

ATS AUTOMATION *p* 968
100 WELLINGTON ST W, TORONTO, ON, M5K 1J2
(416) 601-1555   *SIC 5962*

ATS AUTOMATION TOOLING SYSTEMS INC *p* 538
730 FOUNTAIN ST SUITE 2B, CAMBRIDGE, ON, N3H 4R7
(519) 653-6500   *SIC 3569*

ATS SERVICES LTD *p* 748
35 AURIGA DR SUITE 213, NEPEAN, ON, K2E 8B7
(613) 288-9139   *SIC 4899*

ATS TEST INC *p* 1029
600 CHRISLEA RD, WOODBRIDGE, ON, L4L 8K9
(905) 850-8600   *SIC 3823*

ATS TRAFFIC - ALBERTA LTD *p* 121
9015 14 ST NW, EDMONTON, AB, T6P 0C9
(780) 440-4114   *SIC 3993*

ATS TRAFFIC GROUP LTD *p* 121
9015 14 ST NW, EDMONTON, AB, T6P 0C9
(780) 440-4114   *SIC 3812*

ATS TRAFFIC-BRITISH COLUMBIA LTD *p* 122
7798 16 ST NW, EDMONTON, AB, T6P 1L9
(780) 440-4114   *SIC 3669*

ATTABOTICS INC *p* 20
7944 10 ST NE, CALGARY, AB, T2E 8W1
(403) 909-8230   *SIC 8742*

ATTACHES ET SUSPENSION MONTREAL-NORD *p*
1161
8065 BOUL HENRI-BOURASSA E, MONTREAL, QC, H1E 2Z3
(514) 643-4106   *SIC 5531*

ATTACHES INDUSTRIELLES USCAN LTEE, LES *p* 1091
87A BOUL BRUNSWICK, DOLLARD-DES-ORMEAUX, QC, H9B 2J5
(514) 684-2940   *SIC 5085*

ATTACHES KINGSTON *p* 1367
See *TENAQUIP LIMITEE*

ATTACHES METRICAN *p* 1101
See *FABORY CANADA INC*

ATTAR METALS INC *p* 737
1856 ROMANI CRT, MISSISSAUGA, ON, L5T 1J1
(905) 670-1491   *SIC 5093*

ATTFIELD, ROGER INC *p* 762
GD, NOBLETON, ON, L0G 1N0
(416) 675-1231   *SIC 7948*

ATTFIELD, ROGER RACING STABLE *p* 762
See *ATTFIELD, ROGER INC*

ATTIC, THE *p* 245
4760 JOHNSTON RD, PORT ALBERNI, BC, V9Y 5M3
(250) 723-2143   *SIC 8699*

ATTITUDES IMPORT INC *p* 1101
3025 BOUL LE CORBUSIER, FABREVILLE, QC, H7L 4C3
(450) 681-4147   *SIC 5199*

ATTO & ASSOCIATES INSURANCE BROKERS INC *p* 704
5660 MCADAM RD SUITE A1, MISSISSAUGA, ON, L4Z 1T2
(905) 890-1412   *SIC 6411*

ATTRACTION IMAGES PRODUCTIONS INC *p* 1183

5455 AV DE GASPE BUREAU 804, MON-
TREAL, QC, H2T 3B3
(514) 285-7001   SIC 7922

ATTRACTION INC   p 1124
672 RUE DU PARC, LAC-DROLET, QC,
G0Y 1C0
(819) 549-2477   SIC 5136

ATTRELL AUTO HOLDINGS LIMITED p 513
110 CANAM CRES, BRAMPTON, ON, L7A
1A9
(905) 451-7235   SIC 5511

ATTRELL HYUNDAI   p 513
See ATTRELL MOTOR CORPORATION

ATTRELL MOTOR CORPORATION   p 513
100 CANAM CRES, BRAMPTON, ON, L7A
1A9
(905) 451-1699   SIC 5511

ATTRELL TOYOTA   p 513
See ATTRELL AUTO HOLDINGS LIMITED

**ATTRIDGE TRANSPORTATION INCORPO-
RATED**   p
521
5439 HARVESTER RD, BURLINGTON, ON,
L7L 5J7
(905) 333-4047   SIC 4151

**ATTRIDGE TRANSPORTATION INCORPO-
RATED**   p
1005
27 MILL ST S, WATERDOWN, ON, L0R 2H0
(905) 690-2632   SIC 4141

ATV FARMS   p 620
See 1758691 ONTARIO INC

ATX NETWORKS   p 475
See TRISCAP CANADA, INC

AU BON MARCHE   p 1168
See BLINDS TO GO INC

AU BON SOIN   p 1164
See MORIN, JEAN-GUY INC

AU CARROSSIER INC   p 1289
1355 AV LARIVIERE, ROUYN-NORANDA,
QC, J9X 6M6
(819) 762-5000   SIC 5511

AU DRAGON FORGE   p 1344
See GROUPE ADF INC

AU LIT   p 923
See AU LIT FINE LINENS INC

AU LIT FINE LINENS INC   p 923
2049 YONGE ST, TORONTO, ON, M4S 2A2
(416) 489-7992   SIC 5719

AU PAIN DORE   p 1167
See BD APD INC

AU ROYAUME CHRYSLER DODGE JEEP p
1354
700 RUE PRINCIPALE, SAINTE-AGATHE-
DES-MONTS, QC, J8C 1L3
(819) 326-4524   SIC 5511

AU VIEUX DULUTH EXPRESS (MD) p 1333
See ENTREPRISES MTY TIKI MING INC,
LES

**AUBAINERIE CONCEPT MODE GALERIES
LAVAL**   p 1236
See CORPORATION A.U.B. INC

AUBAINERIE CONCEPT MODE INC, L'   p
1390
965 RUE GERMAIN, VAL-D'OR, QC, J9P
7H7
(819) 824-4377   SIC 5651

AUBAINERIE CONCEPT MODE, L   p 1076
80 BOUL D'ANJOU, CHATEAUGUAY, QC,
J6K 1C3
(450) 699-0444   SIC 5651

AUBAINERIE CONCEPT MODE, L'   p 1130
See E.D.M. LASALLE INC

AUBAINERIE JEAN TALON   p 1225
See CROTEAU, J. A. (1989) INC

AUBAINERIE MASCOUCHE   p 1149
See CONCEPT MASCOUCHE INC

AUBAINERIE, L'   p 1062
See JOCELYN CROTEAU INC

AUBAINERIE, L'   p 1114
See CROTEAU, MARCEL INC

AUBAINERIE, L'   p 1173
See CROTEAU, PIERRE INC

AUBAINERIE, L'   p 1285

See R. CROTEAU RIMOUSKI INC

AUBAINES LEE   p 1179
See NOXS INC

AUBE KIA   p 1390
See GROUPE AUBE LTEE

AUBE, J.-P. RESTAURANT SERVICES LTD
p 912
522 ALGONQUIN BLVD E UNIT 520, TIM-
MINS, ON, P4N 1B7
(705) 264-7323   SIC 5812

AUBERGE & SPA LE NORDIK INC   p 1077
16 CH NORDIK, CHELSEA, QC, J9B 2P7
(819) 484-1112   SIC 7991

AUBERGE BROMONT   p 1068
See CHATEAU BROMONT INC

AUBERGE DE LA POINTE INC   p 1285
10 BOUL CARTIER, RIVIERE-DU-LOUP,
QC, G5R 6A1
(418) 862-3514   SIC 7011

AUBERGE DE LA RIVE INC   p 1376
165 CH SAINTE-ANNE, SOREL-TRACY,
QC, J3P 6J7
(450) 742-5691   SIC 7011

AUBERGE DU COTEAU   p 1288
See FERME C.M.J.I. ROBERT INC

AUBERGE DU LAC SACACOMIE INC   p
1291
4000 CH YVON-PLANTE, SAINT-ALEXIS-
DES-MONTS, QC, J0K 1V0
(819) 265-4444   SIC 7011

AUBERGE DU PORTAGE LTEE   p 1243
671 RTE DU FLEUVE, NOTRE-DAME-DU-
PORTAGE, QC, G0L 1Y0
(418) 862-3601   SIC 7011

AUBERGE DU TRESOR INC   p 1268
20 RUE SAINTE-ANNE, QUEBEC, QC, G1R
3X2
(418) 694-1876   SIC 7011

AUBERGE JASEUR BOREAL   p 1377
See CONSTRUCTIONS PROCO INC

AUBERGE LAC-A-L'EAU-CLAIRE   p 1291
See SIMDAR INC

**AUBERGE LE BALUCHON, GAS-
TRONOMIE.SPA.PLEIN ET CULTURE**   p
1350
See CONCEPT ECO-PLEIN AIR LE BALU-
CHON INC

AUBERGE SAINT-ANTOINE INC   p 1257
10 RUE SAINT-ANTOINE, QUEBEC, QC,
G1K 4C9
(418) 692-2211   SIC 7011

AUBERGE STONEHAM   p 1378
See DISTRIBUTIONS LMC LTEE, LES

AUBERGE SUR LA ROUTE, L'   p 1187
426 RUE SAINT-GABRIEL, MONTREAL,
QC, H2Y 2Z9
(514) 954-1041   SIC 6311

AUBIN & ST-PIERRE INC   p 1123
350 RUE RAYGO, LA PRESENTATION, QC,
J0H 1B0
(450) 796-2966   SIC 5083

**AUBURN HEIGHTS RETIREMENT RESI-
DENCE**   p
77
See ALL SENIORS CARE LIVING CEN-
TRES LTD

AUBURN RENTALS   p 93
See DENILLE INDUSTRIES LTD

AUCERNA   p 42
See 3ES INNOVATION INC

AUCLAIR & MARTINEAU INC   p 1280
2277 RUE DE LA FAUNE, QUEBEC, QC,
G3E 1S9
(418) 842-1943   SIC 3144

AUDCOMP   p 477
See AUDCOMP GROUP INC

AUDCOMP GROUP INC   p 477
611 TRADEWIND DR SUITE 100, AN-
CASTER, ON, L9G 4V5
(905) 304-1775   SIC 5734

AUDEAMUS   p 858
1546 ROLLIN RD, SAINT-PASCAL-
BAYLON, ON, K0A 3N0
SIC 8062

AUDI AUTOHAUS   p 335
1101 YATES ST, VICTORIA, BC, V8V 3N1
(250) 590-5849   SIC 5511

AUDI BARRIE   p 622
See 2311390 ONTARIO INC

AUDI CANADA INC   p 473
777 BAYLY ST W, AJAX, ON, L1S 7G7
(905) 428-4826   SIC 5511

AUDI CENTRE OAKVILLE   p 806
See OAKVILLE VOLKSWAGEN INC

AUDI DOWNTOWN TORONTO   p 934
See TRANSCONTINENTAL FINE CARS
LTD

AUDI KITCHENER-WATERLOO   p 635
See CROSBY AUDI INC

AUDI LEVIS   p 1139
See 190937 CANADA LTEE

AUDI OF RICHMOND   p 254
See COWELL MOTORS LTD

AUDI ST-BRUNO   p 1295
See 9458778 CANADA LIMITED

AUDI WINDSOR   p 1018
See 2494719 ONTARIO INC

AUDI WINNIPEG   p 389
See WAM MOTORS GP INC

**AUDICO SERVICES LIMITED PARTNER-
SHIP**   p
948
390 BAY ST SUITE 1900, TORONTO, ON,
M5H 2Y2
(416) 361-1622   SIC 8721

AUDIENCEVIEW   p 978
2ND FLOOR, TORONTO, ON, M5V 3C7
(416) 687-2100   SIC 8748

AUDIO VIDEO D.G.   p 1264
See GESTION QUEMAR INC

AUDIO VIDEO UNLIMITED   p 200
See GLASWEGIAN ENTERPRISES INC

**AUDIO VISUAL SERVICES (CANADA)
CORPORATION**   p 1029
180 TROWERS RD UNIT 28, WOOD-
BRIDGE, ON, L4L 8A6
(647) 724-0880   SIC 7359

**AUDIO VISUAL SYSTEMS INTEGRATION
INC**   p 27
3636 7 ST SE, CALGARY, AB, T2G 2Y8
(403) 255-4123   SIC 5999

AUDIO WAREHOUSE LTD   p 1420
1329 LORNE ST, REGINA, SK, S4R 2K2
(306) 525-8128   SIC 5731

AUDIO ZONE INC   p 1187
444 RUE SAINT-PAUL E, MONTREAL, QC,
H2Y 3V1
(514) 931-9466   SIC 7389

AUDITORIUM DE VERDUN   p 1397
See VILLE DE MONTREAL

AUDMET CANADA LTD   p 719
6950 CREDITVIEW RD, MISSISSAUGA,
ON, L5N 0A6
(905) 677-3231   SIC 3842

**AUDY FARLEY LALANDE LA BERGE ET
ASSOCIES**   p 1343
See CIMA+ S.E.N.C.

AUF   p 1219
See AGENCE UNIVERSITAIRE DE LA
FRANCOPHONIE

AUGUST CORPORATE PARTNERS INC   p
184
4445 LOUGHEED HWY SUITE 1001,
BURNABY, BC, V5C 0E4
(604) 731-0441   SIC 6712

AUGUST ELECTRONICS INC   p 20
1810 CENTRE AVE NE, CALGARY, AB, T2E
0A6
(403) 273-3131   SIC 3699

AULAC IRVING BIG STOP   p 394
See BENICK SERVICES INC

AULD PHILLIPS   p 197
See AULD PHILLIPS LTD

AULD PHILLIPS LTD   p 197
8040 EVANS RD, CHILLIWACK, BC, V2R
5R8
(604) 792-8518   SIC 5621

AUNTIE ANNE'S PRETZELS   p 491

See INTEGRICO INC

AUPE.   p 97
See ALBERTA UNION OF PROVINCIAL
EMPLOYEES, THE

AURA   p 389
See MACCHIA ENTERPRISES LTD

AURA MINERALS INC   p 948
155 UNIVERSITY AVE SUITE 1240,
TORONTO, ON, M5H 3B7
(416) 649-1033   SIC 1041

AURACLEAN   p 990
See AURACLEAN BUILDING MAINTE-
NANCE INC

**AURACLEAN BUILDING MAINTENANCE
INC**   p 990
104 GREENLAW AVE, TORONTO, ON,
M6H 3V5
(416) 561-6137   SIC 7349

AURAY CAPITAL CANADA INC   p 1201
600 RUE DE LA GAUCHETIERE O BU-
REAU 2740, MONTREAL, QC, H3B 4L8
(514) 499-8440   SIC 6726

AURCANA CORPORATION   p 302
789 PENDER ST W SUITE 850, VANCOU-
VER, BC, V6C 1H2
(604) 331-9333   SIC 1021

AUREOLE PHARMACEUTIQUE CANADA p
1152
See HALO PHARMACEUTICAL CANADA
INC

AUREUS ENERGY SERVICES INC   p 79
9510 78 AVE, CLAIRMONT, AB, T8X 0M2
(780) 567-3009   SIC 3567

AURIUM PHARMA INC   p 549
7941 JANE ST SUITE 105, CONCORD, ON,
L4K 4L6
(905) 669-9057   SIC 5912

AURORA BIOMED INC   p 294
1001 PENDER ST E, VANCOUVER, BC,
V6A 1W2
(604) 215-8700   SIC 8731

AURORA CANNABIS INC   p 311
1199 HASTINGS ST W SUITE 1500, VAN-
COUVER, BC, V6E 3T5
SIC 2833

AURORA CHRYSLER   p 480
See CHEVALIER CHRYSLER INC

AURORA COLLEGE   p 435
50 CONIBEAR CRES, FORT SMITH, NT,
X0E 0P0
(867) 872-7000   SIC 8221

AURORA ELEMENTARY SCHOOL   p 159
See WILD ROSE SCHOOL DIVISION NO.
66

AURORA FILTERS   p 875
See ALL-WELD COMPANY LIMITED

AURORA HELICOPTERS LTD   p 127
410 SNOW EAGLE DR, FORT MCMURRAY,
AB, T9H 0H7
(780) 743-5588   SIC 4522

**AURORA HOME HARDWARE & BUILDING
CENTRE**   p 480
See BARFITT BROS. HARDWARE (AU-
RORA) LTD

**AURORA IMPORTING & DISTRIBUTING
LIMITED**   p 734
815 GANA CRT, MISSISSAUGA, ON, L5S
1P2
(905) 670-1855   SIC 5149

AURORA INSTRUMENTS LTD   p 294
1001 PENDER ST E, VANCOUVER, BC,
V6A 1W2
(604) 215-8700   SIC 3821

AURORA TOYOTA   p 480
See AUTO GROUP AURORA INC

AURREA SIGNATURE INC   p 1063
1205 RUE AMPERE BUREAU 201,
BOUCHERVILLE, QC, J4B 7M6
(450) 650-2151   SIC 6411

AURREA SIGNATURE MD   p 1063
See AURREA SIGNATURE INC

**AURUM CERAMIC DENTAL LABORATO-
RIES LTD**   p
66

115 17 AVE SW, CALGARY, AB, T2S 0A1

(403) 228-5120   *SIC* 6712

AURYN RESOURCES INC   *p* 311

1199 HASTINGS ST W SUITE 600, VANCOUVER, BC, V6E 3T5

(778) 729-0600   *SIC* 1081

AUSENCO ENGINEERING CANADA INC *p* 43

401 9 AVE SW STE 1430, CALGARY, AB, T2P 3C5

(403) 705-4100   *SIC* 1382

AUSENCO ENGINEERING CANADA INC *p* 297

855 HOMER ST, VANCOUVER, BC, V6B 2W2

(604) 684-9311   *SIC* 8711

AUSTCO COMMUNICATION SYSTEMS *p* 577

See AUSTCO MARKETING & SERVICE (CANADA) LIMITED

AUSTCO MARKETING & SERVICE (CANADA) LIMITED   *p* 577

940 THE EAST MALL SUITE 101, ETOBICOKE, ON, M9B 6J7

(888) 670-9997   *SIC* 5065

AUSTIN METAL LIMITED PARTNERSHIP *p* 183

5414 GORING ST, BURNABY, BC, V5B 3A3

(604) 291-7381   *SIC* 5084

AUSTIN O'BRIEN CATHOLIC HIGH SCHOOL   *p* 109

See EDMONTON CATHOLIC SEPARATE SCHOOL DISTRICT NO.7

AUSTIN POWDER LTD   *p* 202

4919 ISLAND HWY N, COURTENAY, BC, V9N 5Z2

(250) 334-2624   *SIC* 5169

AUSTIN STEEL GROUP INC   *p* 498

39 PROGRESS CRT, BRAMPTON, ON, L6S 5X2

(905) 799-3324   *SIC* 3312

AUSTRALIS CAPITAL INC.   *p* 297

510 SEYMOUR ST SUITE 900, VANCOUVER, BC, V6B 3J5

SIC 5122

AUTHENTIC CONCIERGE AND SECURITY SERVICES INC   *p* 994

2333 DUNDAS ST W SUITE 206, TORONTO, ON, M6R 3A6

(416) 777-1812   *SIC* 7381

AUTHENTIC T-SHIRT COMPANY ULC, THE *p* 323

850 KENT AVE SOUTH W, VANCOUVER, BC, V6P 3G1

(778) 732-0258   *SIC* 5136

AUTHENTIC WINE AND SPIRITS MERCHANTS   *p* 191

7432 FRASER PARK DR, BURNABY, BC, V5J 5B9

(604) 708-5022   *SIC* 5182

AUTHENTIQUE POSE CAFE INC, L' *p* 1304

9555 10E AV, SAINT-GEORGES, QC, G5Y 8J8

(418) 228-3191   *SIC* 5046

AUTISME ET TROUBLES ENVAHISSANTS DU DEVELOPPEMENT MONTR AL   *p* 1173

4450 RUE SAINT-HUBERT BUREAU 320, MONTREAL, QC, H2J 2W9

(514) 524-6114   *SIC* 8611

AUTO AMBASSADEUR INC   *p* 1085

2000 BOUL CHOMEDEY, COTE SAINT-LUC, QC, H7T 2W3

(450) 686-2710   *SIC* 5511

AUTO BOULEVARD SAINT-MARTIN INC *p* 1085

2450 BOUL CHOMEDEY, COTE SAINT-LUC, QC, H7T 2X3

(450) 682-1212   *SIC* 5511

AUTO BUGATTI INC   *p* 1093

825 AV AVOCA, DORVAL, QC, H9P 1G4

(514) 636-8750   *SIC* 5511

AUTO CLASSIQUE DE LAVAL INC   *p* 1363

3131 DESSTE NORD LAVAL (A-440) O,

SAINTE-ROSE, QC, H7P 5P2

(450) 681-2500   *SIC* 5511

AUTO CLEARING (1982) LTD   *p* 1431

331 CIRCLE DR W, SASKATOON, SK, S7L 5S8

(306) 244-2186   *SIC* 7532

AUTO CONTROL MEDICAL INC   *p* 719

6695 MILLCREEK DR UNIT 6, MISSISSAUGA, ON, L5N 5R8

(905) 814-6350   *SIC* 5047

AUTO DETAILS 1995   *p* 1092

See LAVE AUTO A LA MAIN STEVE INC

AUTO ELECTRIC SERVICE LTD   *p* 1420

1360 BROAD ST, REGINA, SK, S4R 1Y5

(306) 525-2551   *SIC* 5013

AUTO FRANK & MICHEL INC   *p* 1063

5790 BOUL SAINTE-ANNE RR 1, BOISCHATEL, QC, G0A 1H0

(418) 822-2252   *SIC* 5511

AUTO FRANK ET MICHEL INC   *p* 1063

5790 BOUL SAINTE-ANNE, BOISCHATEL, QC, G0A 1H0

(418) 822-6686   *SIC* 5511

AUTO FRANK MICHEL CHARLEVOIX INC *p* 1122

2060 BOUL DE COMPORTE, LA MALBAIE, QC, G5A 3C5

(418) 665-6431   *SIC* 5511

AUTO GALLERY 1994 LTD   *p* 1420

609 WINNIPEG ST, REGINA, SK, S4R 8P2

(306) 525-6700   *SIC* 5511

AUTO GALLERY OF WINNIPEG   *p* 386

See 4695900 MANITOBA LTD

AUTO GALLERY SUZUKI SUBARU   *p* 1420

See AUTO GALLERY 1994 LTD

AUTO GROUP AURORA INC   *p* 480

669 WELLINGTON ST E, AURORA, ON, L4G 0C9

(905) 727-1948   *SIC* 5511

AUTO GROUP NEWMARKET INC   *p* 754

1171 DAVIS DR, NEWMARKET, ON, L3Y 8R1

(905) 953-2890   *SIC* 5511

AUTO HAUS FORT GARRY (1981) LTD   *p* 387

660 PEMBINA HWY, WINNIPEG, MB, R3M 2M5

(204) 284-7520   *SIC* 5511

AUTO HAUS VOLKSWAGEN   *p* 387

See AUTO HAUS FORT GARRY (1981) LTD

AUTO HOUSE HONDA   *p* 860

See HENTSCHEL, HART INC

AUTO IMPORTATION TERREBONNE INC *p* 1379

1295 CAR MASSON, TERREBONNE, QC, J6W 6J7

SIC 5511

AUTO L.P. TREMBLAY, LTEE   *p* 1078

1330 BOUL DU ROYAUME O, CHICOUTIMI, QC, G7H 5B1

(418) 549-3320   *SIC* 5511

AUTO LAC INC   *p* 405

2491 KING GEORGE HWY, MIRAMICHI, NB, E1V 6W3

(506) 773-9448   *SIC* 5399

AUTO LIST OF CANADA   *p* 362

See ALC - AUTO LIST OF CANADA INC

AUTO LOISIRS   *p* 1190

See PRESSE (2018) INC, LA

AUTO MACHINERY   *p* 402

See VAST-AUTO DISTRIBUTION ATLANTIC LTD

AUTO MACHINERY AND GENERAL SUPPLY COMPANY, LIMITED   *p* 400

50 WHITING RD, FREDERICTON, NB, E3B 5V5

(506) 453-1600   *SIC* 5013

AUTO MAXIMUM   *p* 1346

See VAST-AUTO DISTRIBUTION LTEE

AUTO METIVIER INC   *p* 1135

160 RTE DU PRESIDENT-KENNEDY, LEVIS, QC, G6V 6E1

(418) 837-4701   *SIC* 5511

AUTO MODENA INC.   *p* 1227

3980 RUE JEAN-TALON O, MONTREAL, QC, H4P 1V6

(514) 337-7274   *SIC* 5012

AUTO MONT CHEVROLET BUICK GMC LTEE   *p* 1154

1300 BOUL ALBINY-PAQUETTE, MONT-LAURIER, QC, J9L 1M7

(819) 623-1122   *SIC* 5511

AUTO MOTION LIMITED   *p* 468

568 PRINCE ST, TRURO, NS, B2N 1G3

(902) 893-2288   *SIC* 5065

AUTO MSHOP   *p* 1307

4535 AV THIBAULT BUREAU 1, SAINT-HUBERT, QC, J3Y 7N1

(579) 720-7747   *SIC* 5511

AUTO PARTS CENTRES   *p* 650

See CANUSA AUTOMOTIVE WAREHOUSING INC

AUTO PARTS NETWORK   *p* 426

See CANADIAN AUTO RECYCLING LIMITED

AUTO PARTS PLUS   *p* 118

10341 58 AVE NW, EDMONTON, AB, T6H 5E4

(780) 437-4917   *SIC* 5013

AUTO PARTS PLUS   *p* 1068

See UNI-SELECT QUEBEC INC

AUTO PARTS PLUS   *p* 1155

See PIECES D'AUTO LEON GRENIER (1987) INC, LES

AUTO PARTS PLUS   *p* 1308

See PIECES D'AUTO SUPER INC

AUTO PLUS J.F. HAMEL INC   *p* 1058

255 BOUL DE LA SEIGNEURIE O, BLAINVILLE, QC, J7C 4N3

(450) 435-4455   *SIC* 5511

AUTO PRO NIAGARA   *p* 591

See CENTRAL MOTORS (PELHAM) LTD

AUTO SENATEUR INC   *p* 1235

255 BOUL SAINT-MARTIN E, MONTREAL, QC, H7M 1Z1

(450) 663-2020   *SIC* 5511

AUTO SUTURE   *p* 1333

See COVIDIEN CANADA ULC

AUTO TRADER   *p* 580

See TRADER CORPORATION

AUTO USA   *p* 1297

See AUTOMOBILE EN DIRECT.COM INC

AUTO VALUE   *p* 1148

See PEINTURE & PIECES D.R. INC

AUTO WAREHOUSING COMPANY CANADA LIMITED   *p* 813

1150 STEVENSON RD S SUITE 1, OSHAWA, ON, L1J 0B3

(905) 725-6549   *SIC* 4789

AUTO WEST BMW   *p* 261

See M T K AUTO WEST LTD

AUTO WEST INFINITI LTD   *p* 253

13720 SMALLWOOD PL, RICHMOND, BC, V6V 1W8

SIC 5511

AUTO-KOOL   *p* 1128

See KOOLIAN ENTREPRISES INC, LES

AUTO-MATRIX CONTROLES   *p* 1357

See VENTILABEC INC

AUTO-NET AUTOMOBILE SALES LTD *p* 162

10 BROADWAY BLVD, SHERWOOD PARK, AB, T8H 2A2

(780) 449-5775   *SIC* 5511

AUTO-PAK   *p* 561

See BENSON GROUP INC

AUTOBUS AUGER INC   *p* 1137

880 RUE DE SAINT-ROMUALD, LEVIS, QC, G6W 5M6

(418) 833-2181   *SIC* 4151

AUTOBUS AUGER METROPOLITAIN INC *p* 1076

147 RUE PRINCIPALE, CHATEAUGUAY, QC, J6K 1G2

(450) 691-1654   *SIC* 4111

AUTOBUS BRUNET INC, LES   *p* 1319

986 RUE DES LACS, SAINT-JEROME, QC,

J5L 1T4

(450) 438-8363   *SIC* 4151

AUTOBUS C MONGEAU   *p* 1320

See TRANSCOBEC (1987) INC

AUTOBUS DU VILLAGE INC, LES   *p* 1102

65 RUE THIBAULT, GATINEAU, QC, J8L 3Z1

(819) 281-9235   *SIC* 4151

AUTOBUS GRANBY INC   *p* 1110

1254 RUE PRINCIPALE, GRANBY, QC, J2J 0M2

(450) 378-9951   *SIC* 4142

AUTOBUS IDEAL INC   *p* 1239

5101 BOUL INDUSTRIEL, MONTREAL-NORD, QC, H1G 3H1

(514) 323-2355   *SIC* 4151

AUTOBUS LA QUEBECOISE INC   *p* 1108

545 RUE DE VERNON, GATINEAU, QC, J9J 3K4

(819) 770-1070   *SIC* 4151

AUTOBUS LA QUEBECOISE INC   *p* 1278

607 6E AVENUE DE L'AEROPORT, QUEBEC, QC, G2G 2T4

(418) 872-5525   *SIC* 4151

AUTOBUS LACHENAIE   *p* 1282

See SABEM, SEC

AUTOBUS LASALLE INC   *p* 1369

149 RUE WEST, SHAWVILLE, QC, J0X 2Y0

(819) 647-5696   *SIC* 4142

AUTOBUS LAVAL LTEE   *p* 1254

445 RUE DES ALLEGHANYS BUREAU 201, QUEBEC, QC, G1C 4N4

(418) 667-3265   *SIC* 4151

AUTOBUS MAHEUX LTEE, LES   *p* 1123

156 393 RTE S, LA SARRE, QC, J9Z 2X2

(819) 333-2217   *SIC* 4151

AUTOBUS MAHEUX LTEE, LES   *p* 1390

855 BOUL BARRETTE, VAL-D'OR, QC, J9P 0J8

(819) 825-4767   *SIC* 4151

AUTOBUS OUTAOUAIS   *p* 1108

See AUTOBUS LA QUEBECOISE INC

AUTOBUS RIVE-NORD LTEE   *p* 1232

1325 MONTEE MASSON, MONTREAL, QC, H7E 4P2

(450) 661-7140   *SIC* 4151

AUTOBUS TERREMONT LTEE   *p* 1150

343 CH DES ANGLAIS, MASCOUCHE, QC, J7L 3P8

(450) 477-1500   *SIC* 4151

AUTOBUS TRANSCO   *p* 1161

See AUTOBUS TRANSCO (1988) INC

AUTOBUS TRANSCO (1988) INC   *p* 1130

8201 RUE ELMSLIE, LASALLE, QC, H8N 2W6

(514) 363-4315   *SIC* 4151

AUTOBUS TRANSCO (1988) INC   *p* 1161

7975 BOUL HENRI-BOURASSA E, MONTREAL, QC, H1E 1N9

(514) 648-8625   *SIC* 4151

AUTOBUS TRANSCOBEC (1987) INC, LES *p* 1319

21 RUE JOHN-F.-KENNEDY, SAINT-JEROME, QC, J7Y 4B4

(450) 432-9748   *SIC* 4151

AUTOBUS YVES SEGUIN & FILS INC *p* 1381

1730 RUE EFFINGHAM, TERREBONNE, QC, J6Y 1R7

(450) 433-6958   *SIC* 4151

AUTOCANADA INC   *p* 104

15511 123 AVE NW UNIT 200, EDMONTON, AB, T5V 0C3

(866) 938-0561   *SIC* 5511

AUTOCAR HELIE INC.   *p* 1055

3505 BOUL DE PORT-ROYAL, BECANCOUR, QC, G9H 1Y2

(819) 371-1177   *SIC* 4151

AUTOCAR METROPOLITAIN   *p* 1076

See 4345240 CANADA INC

AUTOCARS ORLEANS EXPRESS INC *p* 1210

740 RUE NOTRE-DAME O BUREAU 1000, MONTREAL, QC, H3C 3X6

▲ Public Company   ■ Public Company Family Member   **HQ** Headquarters   **BR** Branch   **SL** Single Location

(514) 395-4000   *SIC* 4131
AUTOCOM MANUFACTURING   *p* 605
See LINAMAR CORPORATION
AUTODATA SOLUTIONS COMPANY   *p* 653
100 DUNDAS ST SUITE 500, LONDON, ON, N6A 5B6
(519) 451-2323   *SIC* 7371
AUTODESK CANADA CIE   *p* 932
210 KING ST E, TORONTO, ON, M5A 1J7
(416) 362-9181   *SIC* 7371
AUTODESK CANADA CIE   *p* 1210
10 RUE DUKE, MONTREAL, QC, H3C 2L7
(514) 393-1616   *SIC* 7371
AUTODROME ST-EUSTACHE   *p* 1301
See 4397291 CANADA INC
AUTOFILL PRODUCTS   *p* 1054
See SCHOLLE IPN CANADA LTD
AUTOGAS PROPANE LTD   *p* 191
5605 BYRNE RD, BURNABY, BC, V5J 3J1
(604) 433-4900   *SIC* 5984
AUTOGENE INDUSTRIES NORTH BAY INC   *p* 762
1811 SEYMOUR ST, NORTH BAY, ON, P1A 0C7
(705) 474-0350   *SIC* 7692
AUTOLINE PRODUCTS LTD   *p* 367
675 GOLSPIE ST, WINNIPEG, MB, R2K 2V2
(204) 668-8242   *SIC* 3592
AUTOLINX EXPRESS INC   *p* 494
12673 COLERAINE DR, BOLTON, ON, L7E 3B5
(905) 951-1900   *SIC* 4212
AUTOLIV CANADA INC   *p* 666
7455 BIRCHMOUNT RD, MARKHAM, ON, L3R 5C2
(905) 475-1468   *SIC* 2394
AUTOLIV CANADA INC   *p* 911
20 AUTOLIV DR, TILBURY, ON, N0P 2L0
(519) 682-1083   *SIC* 2394
AUTOLOAN SOLUTIONS LTD   *p* 996
80 JUTLAND RD, TORONTO, ON, M8Z 2G6
(888) 300-9769   *SIC* 6141
AUTOLOANS.CA   *p* 996
See AUTOLOAN SOLUTIONS LTD
AUTOLOG   *p* 1058
See AUTOLOG, GESTION DE LA PRODUCTION INC
AUTOLOG, GESTION DE LA PRODUCTION INC   *p* 1058
1240 BOUL MICHELE-BOHEC, BLAINVILLE, QC, J7C 5S4
(450) 434-8389   *SIC* 7379
AUTOLUX LTD   *p* 844
970 BROCK RD, PICKERING, ON, L1W 2A1
(416) 266-1500   *SIC* 4111
AUTOMANN HEAVY DUTY CANADA ULC *p* 508
350 FIRST GULF BLVD, BRAMPTON, ON, L6W 4T5
(905) 654-6500   *SIC* 5013
AUTOMATED SOLUTIONS INTERNATIONAL INC   *p* 537
25 MILLING RD SUITE 204, CAMBRIDGE, ON, N3C 1C3
(519) 220-0071   *SIC* 5962
AUTOMATED STEEL DETAILING ASSOCIATES LTD   *p* 582
77 BELFIELD RD UNIT 100, ETOBICOKE, ON, M9W 1G6
(416) 241-6967   *SIC* 7389
AUTOMATES VEN INC   *p* 1098
2375 RUE POWER, DRUMMONDVILLE, QC, J2C 6Z5
(819) 477-1133   *SIC* 5962
AUTOMATIC COATING LIMITED   *p* 873
211 NUGGET AVE, SCARBOROUGH, ON, M1S 3B1
(416) 335-7500   *SIC* 3479
AUTOMATIC SYSTEMES AMERIQUE INC *p* 1069
4005 BOUL MATTE BUREAU D,

BROSSARD, QC, J4Y 2P4
(450) 659-0737   *SIC* 1731
AUTOMATIC WELDING MACHINE SUPPLY CO   *p* 639
See E. & E. SEEGMILLER LIMITED
AUTOMATION METSO CANADA   *p* 1330
See METSO FLOW CONTROL CANADA LTD
AUTOMATION ONE BUSINESS SYSTEMS INC   *p* 284
1365 BOUNDARY RD, VANCOUVER, BC, V5K 4T9
(604) 233-7702   *SIC* 5044
AUTOMATISATION JRT INC   *p* 1266
405 AV GALILEE, QUEBEC, QC, G1P 4M6
(418) 871-6016   *SIC* 3613
AUTOMATISATION MARINE ET SIMULATION POUR CENTRALES L-3   *p* 1340
See L3 MAPPS INC
AUTOMATISATION MCKESSON CANADA *p* 1098
See CORPORATION MCKESSON CANADA, LA
AUTOMATISATION ROCKWELL CANADA *p* 1071
See ROCKWELL AUTOMATION CANADA LTD
AUTOMAXX AUTOMOTIVE SALES, DIV OF *p* 40
See VARSITY PLYMOUTH CHRYSLER (1994) LTD
AUTOMEX   *p* 1340
See LANIEL (CANADA) INC
AUTOMOBILE EN DIRECT.COM INC *p* 1297
360 RTE 132, SAINT-CONSTANT, QC, J5A 1M3
(450) 638-6664   *SIC* 5511
AUTOMOBILE ET TOURING CLUB DU QUEBEC (A.T.C.Q.)   *p* 1278
444 RUE BOUVIER, QUEBEC, QC, G2J 1E3
(418) 624-2424   *SIC* 8699
AUTOMOBILE G.R. COREE LONGUEUIL LTEE   *p* 1141
1680 BOUL MARIE-VICTORIN, LONGUEUIL, QC, J4G 1A5
(450) 670-2080   *SIC* 5511
AUTOMOBILE KAMOURASKA (1992) INC *p* 1349
255 AV PATRY, SAINT-PASCAL, QC, G0L 3Y0
(418) 492-3432   *SIC* 5511
AUTOMOBILE NATIONAL (1999) INC   *p* 1304
585 90E RUE, SAINT-GEORGES, QC, G5Y 3L1
(418) 228-8838   *SIC* 5511
AUTOMOBILE PAILLE INC   *p* 1057
700 AV GILLES-VILLENEUVE, BERTHIERVILLE, QC, J0K 1A0
(450) 836-6291   *SIC* 5511
AUTOMOBILE PAQUIN LTEE   *p* 1296
17 RUE PRINCIPALE N, SAINT-BRUNO-DE-GUIGUES, QC, J0Z 2G0
(819) 728-2289   *SIC* 5511
AUTOMOBILE PIERRE METHOT INC   *p* 1397
885 RUE NOTRE-DAME E, VICTORIAVILLE, QC, G6P 4B8
(819) 758-5858   *SIC* 5511
AUTOMOBILES AUMONT (1977) INC, LES *p* 1243
357 BOUL ANTONIO-BARRETTE, NOTRE-DAME-DES-PRAIRIES, QC, J6E 1G1
(450) 759-3449   *SIC* 5511
AUTOMOBILES B. G. P. INC   *p* 1304
8800 BOUL LACROIX, SAINT-GEORGES, QC, G5Y 2B5
(418) 228-5825   *SIC* 5511
AUTOMOBILES BAURORE 2000 LTEE, LES *p* 1103
975 CH DE MASSON, GATINEAU, QC, J8M 1R4

(819) 986-6714   *SIC* 5511
AUTOMOBILES BELLEM INC, LES   *p* 1154
2050 BOUL ALBINY-PAQUETTE BUREAU 3, MONT-LAURIER, QC, J9L 3G5
(819) 623-7341   *SIC* 5511
AUTOMOBILES BERNIER & CREPEAU LTEE   *p* 1389
3100 BOUL SAINT-JEAN, TROIS-RIVIERES, QC, G9B 2M9
(819) 377-3077   *SIC* 5511
AUTOMOBILES BOUCHARD & FILS INC *p* 1154
1800 BOUL JACQUES-CARTIER, MONT-JOLI, QC, G5H 2W8
(418) 775-4378   *SIC* 5511
AUTOMOBILES BOUCHARD & FILS INC *p* 1285
401 AV LEONIDAS S, RIMOUSKI, QC, G5M 1A1
(418) 722-4388   *SIC* 5511
AUTOMOBILES BROSSARD BUICK   *p* 1069
See BROSSARD CHEVROLET BUICK GMC INC
AUTOMOBILES CANDIAC INC, LES   *p* 1089
30 132 RTE, DELSON, QC, J5B 1H3
(450) 632-2220   *SIC* 5511
AUTOMOBILES CARMER 1990 INC   *p* 1075
417 BOUL RENE-LEVESQUE O, CHANDLER, QC, G0C 1K0
(418) 689-4467   *SIC* 5511
AUTOMOBILES CHICOUTIMI (1986) INC *p* 1078
545 BOUL DU ROYAUME O, CHICOUTIMI, QC, G7H 5B1
(418) 545-6555   *SIC* 5511
AUTOMOBILES DES SEIGNEURS INC   *p* 1379
893 RUE L?ON-MARTEL, TERREBONNE, QC, J6W 2K4
(450) 471-6602   *SIC* 5511
AUTOMOBILES DONALD BRASSARD INC *p* 1380
2850 CH GASCON, TERREBONNE, QC, J6X 4H6
(450) 477-0555   *SIC* 5511
AUTOMOBILES DU BOULEVARD 2000 INC *p* 1243
3260 RTE DU PRESIDENT-KENNEDY, NOTRE-DAME-DES-PINS, QC, G0M 1K0
(418) 774-4100   *SIC* 5521
AUTOMOBILES DUCLOS LONGUEUIL   *p* 1308
See DUCLOS LONGUEUIL CHRYSLER DODGE JEEP RAM INC
AUTOMOBILES F.M. INC   *p* 1311
5705 AV TRUDEAU, SAINT-HYACINTHE, QC, J2S 1H5
(450) 773-4736   *SIC* 6712
AUTOMOBILES FAIRVIEW INC   *p* 1249
15 AV AUTO PLAZA, POINTE-CLAIRE, QC, H9R 5Z7
(514) 630-3666   *SIC* 5511
AUTOMOBILES FRANCOIS ST-JEAN INC, LES   *p* 1243
560 131 RTE, NOTRE-DAME-DES-PRAIRIES, QC, J6E 0M2
(450) 752-1212   *SIC* 5521
AUTOMOBILES HYUNDAI RUBY AUTO   *p* 1382
2272 RUE NOTRE-DAME E, THETFORD MINES, QC, G6G 2W2
(418) 338-4665   *SIC* 5521
AUTOMOBILES ILE-PERROT INC   *p* 1120
40 BOUL DON-QUICHOTTE, L'ILE-PERROT, QC, J7V 6N5
(514) 453-8416   *SIC* 5511
AUTOMOBILES J. D. A. INC   *p* 1311
3395 BOUL LAFRAMBOISE, SAINT-HYACINTHE, QC, J2S 4Z7
(450) 774-9191   *SIC* 5511
AUTOMOBILES JALBERT   *p* 1266
See ALIMENTS KRISPY KERNELS INC
AUTOMOBILES L F B INC, LES   *p* 1149
118 MONTEE MASSON, MASCOUCHE,

QC, J7K 3B5
(450) 474-2428   *SIC* 5511
AUTOMOBILES LA SEIGNEURIE (1990) INC, LES   *p* 1074
850 BOUL DE PERIGNY BUREAU 112, CHAMBLY, QC, J3L 1W3
(450) 658-6699   *SIC* 5511
AUTOMOBILES LAPORTE, REJEAN & FILS LTEE   *p* 1349
1881 RUE PRINCIPALE, SAINT-NORBERT, QC, J0K 3C0
(450) 836-3783   *SIC* 5511
AUTOMOBILES LEVEILLE INC   *p* 1379
1369 MONTEE MASSON, TERREBONNE, QC, J6W 6A6
(450) 471-4117   *SIC* 5511
AUTOMOBILES LEVIKO (1991) LTEE   *p* 1135
144 RTE DU PRESIDENT-KENNEDY, LEVIS, QC, G6V 6C9
(418) 833-7140   *SIC* 5511
AUTOMOBILES MAUGER FORD INC   *p* 1112
119 GRANDE ALLEE E, GRANDE-RIVIERE, QC, G0C 1V0
(418) 385-2118   *SIC* 5511
AUTOMOBILES MAURICE PARENT INC   *p* 1261
205 RUE ETIENNE-DUBREUIL, QUEBEC, QC, G1M 4A6
(418) 627-4601   *SIC* 5511
AUTOMOBILES MET-HAM INC   *p* 1249
575 BOUL SAINT-JEAN, POINTE-CLAIRE, QC, H9R 3K1
(514) 685-5555   *SIC* 5511
AUTOMOBILES PERRON (CHICOUTIMI) INC   *p* 1078
930 BOUL TALBOT, CHICOUTIMI, QC, G7H 4B4
(418) 549-7633   *SIC* 5511
AUTOMOBILES POPULAR INC, LES *p* 1173
5441 RUE SAINT-HUBERT, MONTREAL, QC, H2J 2Y4
(514) 274-5471   *SIC* 5511
AUTOMOBILES REGATE INC   *p* 1365
1325 BOUL MONSEIGNEUR-LANGLOIS, SALABERRY-DE-VALLEYFIELD, QC, J6S 1C1
(450) 373-4372   *SIC* 5511
AUTOMOBILES RELAIS 2000 INC   *p* 1371
2059 RUE KING O, SHERBROOKE, QC, J1J 2E9
(819) 563-6622   *SIC* 5511
AUTOMOBILES RIMAR INC   *p* 1346
5500 BOUL METROPOLITAIN E, SAINT-LEONARD, QC, H1S 1A6
(514) 253-4888   *SIC* 5511
AUTOMOBILES ROBERGE LTEE   *p* 1254
545 RUE CLEMENCEAU, QUEBEC, QC, G1C 7B6
(418) 666-2000   *SIC* 5511
AUTOMOBILES ROCHMAT INC   *p* 1191
1124 RUE DE BLEURY, MONTREAL, QC, H2Z 1N4
(514) 879-1550   *SIC* 5511
AUTOMOBILES ROYAUME LTEE   *p* 1078
533 BOUL DU ROYAUME O, CHICOUTIMI, QC, G7H 5B1
(418) 543-9393   *SIC* 5511
AUTOMOBILES SENEX LTEE   *p* 1366
851 7E AV, SENNETERRE, QC, J0Y 2M0
(819) 737-2291   *SIC* 5511
AUTOMOBILES SILVER STAR (MONTREAL) INC   *p* 1227
7800 BOUL DECARIE, MONTREAL, QC, H4P 2H4
(514) 735-5501   *SIC* 5511
AUTOMOBILES ST-EUSTACHE INC   *p* 1058
16 RUE DE BRAINE, BLAINVILLE, QC, J7B 1Z1
(514) 927-8977   *SIC* 5511
AUTOMOBILES ULSAN LTEE   *p* 1093
1625 BOUL HYMUS, DORVAL, QC, H9P

1J5
(514) 683-5702   *SIC* 5511

AUTOMOBILES VAL ESTRIE INC   *p* 1373
4141 RUE KING O, SHERBROOKE, QC,
J1L 1P5
(819) 563-4466   *SIC* 5511

AUTOMOBILES VIEILLES FORGES LTEE *p*
1389
1500 BOUL ARTHUR-ROUSSEAU, TROIS-
RIVIERES, QC, G9B 0X4
(819) 373-2355   *SIC* 5511

**AUTOMOBILES VILLENEUVE JOLIETTE
(1996) INC**   *p* 1243
570   131   RTE,   NOTRE-DAME-DES-
PRAIRIES, QC, J6E 0M2
(450) 759-8155   *SIC* 5511

**AUTOMOTIVE PROPERTIES REAL ESTATE
INVESTMENT TRUST**   *p* 936
133 KING ST E SUITE 300, TORONTO, ON,
M5C 1G6
(647) 789-2440   *SIC* 6719

AUTOMOTIVE SYSTEMS GROUP   *p* 808
*See JOHNSON CONTROLS NOVA SCOTIA
U.L.C.*

AUTOMOTIVE WAREHOUSE   *p* 760
See 465912 ONTARIO INC

AUTOMOTIVE WHOLESALE INC   *p* 870
2380 LAWRENCE AVE E, SCARBOR-
OUGH, ON, M1P 2R5
(416) 285-6363   *SIC* 5511

AUTONEUM CANADA LTD   *p* 648
1800 HURON ST, LONDON, ON, N5V 3A6
(519) 659-0560   *SIC* 2299

AUTONEUM CANADA LTD   *p* 911
1451 BELL MILL SIDEROAD, TILLSON-
BURG, ON, N4G 4H8
(519) 842-6411   *SIC* 2299

AUTOPLUS   *p* 1068
See UNI-SELECT INC

AUTOPLUS   *p* 1245
See PIECES D'AUTO PINCOURT INC, LES

AUTOPLUS RESOURCES LTD   *p* 27
4620 BLACKFOOT TRAIL SE, CALGARY,
AB, T2G 4G2
(403) 243-6200   *SIC* 5511

AUTOPNEU   *p* 1261
See PNEUS RATTE INC

AUTOPNEU AUCLAIR   *p* 1268
See SERVICE DE PNEUS AUCLAIR INC

AUTOPORT LIMITED   *p* 449
1180 MAIN RD, EASTERN PASSAGE, NS,
B3G 0B5
(902) 465-6050   *SIC* 4226

AUTOPRICE CANADA   *p* 692
*See AUTOTEK CAR SALES & SERVICE
(1996) LTD*

**AUTOPRO AUTOMATION CONSULTANTS
LTD**   *p* 10
525 28 ST SE SUITE 360, CALGARY,
T2A 6W9
(403) 569-6480   *SIC* 8711

**AUTOPRO AUTOMATION CONSULTANTS
LTD**   *p* 134
11039 78 AVE SUITE 103, GRANDE
PRAIRIE, AB, T8W 2J7
(780) 539-2450   *SIC* 8711

AUTORITE DES MARCHES FINANCIERS *p*
1229
*See GOUVERNEMENT DE LA PROVINCE
DE QUEBEC*

AUTOS ALBERTA   *p* 142
See DAVIS GMC BUICK LTD

**AUTOS ECONOMIQUES CASAVANT INC,
LES**   *p* 1311
350 RUE DANIEL-JOHNSON E, SAINT-
HYACINTHE, QC, J2S 8W5
(450) 774-1724   *SIC* 5511

AUTOS J. G. PINARD & FILS LTEE   *p* 1359
1219 125 RTE, SAINTE-JULIENNE, QC,
J0K 2T0
(450) 831-2211   *SIC* 5511

AUTOS JEAN-FRANCOIS HAMEL LTEE *p*
1300
332 RUE DUBOIS, SAINT-EUSTACHE, QC,

J7P 4W9
(450) 491-0440   *SIC* 5511

AUTOS R. CHAGNON DE GRANBY INC   *p*
1110
1711 RUE PRINCIPALE, GRANBY, QC, J2J
0M9
(450) 378-9963   *SIC* 5511

AUTOS YOMO INC, LES   *p* 1386
5225 BOUL JEAN-XXIII, TROIS-RIVIERES,
QC, G8Z 4A5
(819) 374-3330   *SIC* 5511

AUTOSENSE AUTO PARTS   *p* 487
See MODERN SALES CO-OP

**AUTOTEK CAR SALES & SERVICE (1996)
LTD**   *p* 692
1630 MATHESON BLVD SUITE 1, MISSIS-
SAUGA, ON, L4W 1Y4
(905) 625-4100   *SIC* 5511

AUTOTEK ELECTROPLATING LTD   *p* 582
20 HUDDERSFIELD RD, ETOBICOKE, ON,
M9W 5Z6
(416) 674-0063   *SIC* 3471

AUTOTEMP INC   *p* 21
3419 12 ST NE SUITE 3, CALGARY, AB,
T2E 6S6
(403) 250-7837   *SIC* 7539

AUTOTOWN SALES CORPORATION   *p* 390
1717 WAVERLEY ST SUITE 400, WIN-
NIPEG, MB, R3T 6A9
(204) 269-1600   *SIC* 5521

AUTOTUBE LIMITED   *p* 897
300 HIGH ST E, STRATHROY, ON, N7G
4C5
(519) 245-1742   *SIC* 3312

AUTOVAC   *p* 623
See ASTENJOHNSON, INC

AUTOWEST INC   *p* 370
2150 MCPHILLIPS ST, WINNIPEG, MB,
R2V 3C8
(204) 632-7135   *SIC* 5521

AUTRUCHE   *p* 1141
See AUTRUCHE VARIETES INC

AUTRUCHE VARIETES INC   *p* 1141
715 RUE DELAGE BUREAU 700,
LONGUEUIL, QC, J4G 2P8
(450) 670-2323   *SIC* 5199

AUVENTS MULTIPLES INC   *p* 1056
1505A RUE DE L'INDUSTRIE, BELOEIL,
QC, J3G 0S5
(450) 446-4182   *SIC* 3444

AUVENTS PRESTIGE   *p* 1163
See ACME AWNINGS PRESTIGE

AUX MILLE ET UNE SAISONS   *p* 560
See UNFI CANADA, INC

AUX P'TITS SOINS   *p* 1161
See METRO RICHELIEU INC

**AUXILIAIRE DE L'HOPITAL GENERAL JUIF
SIR MORTIMER B. DAVIS INC, LES**   *p* 1219
3755   CH   DE   LA   COTE-SAINTE-
CATHERINE   BUREAU A018, MONTREAL,
QC, H3T 1E2
(514) 340-8216   *SIC* 5511

**AUXILIAIRES BENEVOLES DU CEN-
TRE D'HEBERGEMENT DE BEAUCEVILLE
(CBH)**   *p* 1055
253 108 RTE, BEAUCEVILLE, QC, G5X 2Z3
(418) 774-3304   *SIC* 8093

AV & R VISION & ROBOTIQUES INC*p* 1210
269 RUE PRINCE, MONTREAL, QC, H3C
2N4
(514) 788-1420   *SIC* 8742

AV GROUP NB INC   *p* 410
103 PINDER RD, NACKAWIC, NB, E6G
1W4
(506) 575-3391   *SIC* 2611

AV TERRACE BAY INC   *p* 902
21 MILL RD, TERRACE BAY, ON, P0T 2W0
(807) 825-1075   *SIC* 2611

AV-CANADA INC   *p* 702
1655 QUEENSWAY E UNIT 2, MISSIS-
SAUGA, ON, L4X 2Z5
(905) 566-5500   *SIC* 7359

AV-TECH   *p* 1264
See LOGIC-CONTROLE INC

AV-TECH INC   *p* 1263
2300 RUE LEON-HARMEL BUREAU 101,
QUEBEC, QC, G1N 4L2
(418) 686-2300   *SIC* 1711

AVALANCHE CANADA   *p* 253
1596 ILLECILLEWAET RD, REVELSTOKE,
BC, V0E 2S1
(250) 837-2141   *SIC* 8699

AVALANT INTERNATIONAL LTD   *p* 43
315 8 AVE SW, CALGARY, AB, T2P 4K1
SIC 4925

AVALON ADVANCED MATERIALS INC   *p*
948
130   ADELAIDE   ST   W   SUITE   1901,
TORONTO, ON, M5H 3P5
(416) 364-4938   *SIC* 1021

AVALON COAL SALT & OIL LTD   *p* 422
69   COLEY'S   PT   N,   COLEYS   POINT
SOUTH, NL, A0A 1X0
(709) 753-4000   *SIC* 5169

AVALON FORD SALES   *p* 429
See AVALON FORD SALES 1996 LIMITED

AVALON FORD SALES 1996 LIMITED*p* 429
80 WYATT BLVD, ST. JOHN'S, NL, A1B 3N9
(709) 754-7500   *SIC* 5511

AVALON MUSIC   *p* 556
See MOOD MEDIA ENTERTAINMENT LTD

AVALON RETIREMENT CENTER   *p* 807
See 488491 ONTARIO INC

AVALON SALT   *p* 422
See AVALON COAL SALT & OIL LTD

AVANADE CANADA INC   *p* 692
5450 EXPLORER DR SUITE 400, MISSIS-
SAUGA, ON, L4W 5N1
(416) 641-5111   *SIC* 7371

AVANCE MERCANTILE   *p* 1204
See EVOLOCITY FINANCIAL GROUP INC

AVANCEZ ASSEMBLY CANADA, ULC   *p*
1024
599 SPRUCEWOOD AVE, WINDSOR, ON,
N9C 0B3
(226) 221-8800   *SIC* 3011

AVANT   *p* 1054
See ROLF C. HAGEN INC

**AVANT IMAGING & INTEGRATED MEDIA
INC**   *p* 480
205 INDUSTRIAL PKY N UNIT 1, AURORA,
ON, L4G 4C4
(905) 841-6444   *SIC* 2752

AVANT SLEEP   *p* 921
See 2188262 ONTARIO LTD

AVANT-GARDE FABRICS   *p* 1051
See TISSUS MASTER LTEE, LES

AVANTAGE 2 MILLIONS   *p* 1180
See PRIMMUM INSURANCE COMPANY

AVANTAGE BUREAU CHEZ SOI   *p* 1180
*See COMPAGNIE D'ASSURANCES GEN-
ERALES TD*

AVANTAGE FORD INC   *p* 1120
30   BOUL   DON-QUICHOTTE,   L'ILE-
PERROT, QC, J7V 6N5
(514) 453-5850   *SIC* 5511

AVANTAGE PLUS INC   *p* 1171
5420 RUE CHAPLEAU, MONTREAL, QC,
H2G 2E4
(514) 525-2000   *SIC* 1542

AVANTE LOGIXX INC   *p* 775
1959 LESLIE ST, NORTH YORK, ON, M3B
2M3
(416) 923-6984   *SIC* 1731

AVANTE SECURITY   *p* 777
See SECURE 724 LTD

AVANTE SECURITY INC   *p* 775
1959 LESLIE ST, NORTH YORK, ON, M3B
2M3
(416) 923-2435   *SIC* 7382

AVANTGARD INVESTMENTS INC   *p* 571
3526 LAKE SHORE BLVD W, ETOBICOKE,
ON, M8W 1N6
(416) 252-0066   *SIC* 5511

AVANTGLIDE   *p* 1350
See GROUPE DUTAILIER INC

AVANTIS COOPERATIVE   *p* 1360
See COOP AVANTIS

AVAYA CANADA CORP   *p* 666
11 ALLSTATE PKY SUITE 300, MARKHAM,
ON, L3R 9T8
(905) 474-6000   *SIC* 4899

AVC INSURANCE SERVICES INC   *p* 297
650 GEORGIA ST W SUITE 11588, VAN-
COUVER, BC, V6B 4N8
(604) 685-6431   *SIC* 8742

AVCOM SYSTEMS INC   *p* 199
1312 KETCH CRT UNIT 101, COQUITLAM,
BC, V3K 6W1
(604) 944-8650   *SIC* 3829

AVCORP INDUSTRIES INC   *p* 208
10025 RIVER WAY, DELTA, BC, V4G 1M7
(604) 582-1137   *SIC* 3728

**AVEDA TRANSPORTATION AND ENERGY
SERVICES INC**   *p* 43
435 4 AVE SW SUITE 300, CALGARY, AB,
T2P 3A8
(403) 264-4950   *SIC* 1389

AVENEX   *p* 259
*See AVENEX COATING TECHNOLOGIES
INC*

AVENEX COATING TECHNOLOGIES INC *p*
259
11938 BRIDGEPORT RD UNIT 260, RICH-
MOND, BC, V6X 1T2
(604) 716-4599   *SIC* 3089

AVENIDA CARPENTRY LTD   *p* 737
6801 COLUMBUS RD, MISSISSAUGA, ON,
L5T 2G9
(905) 565-0813   *SIC* 1751

AVENIR D'ENFANTS   *p* 1223
*See SOCIETE DE GESTION DU FONDS
POUR LE DEVELOPPEMENT DES JEUNES
ENFANTS*

AVENIR TRADING CORP   *p* 43
808 1 ST SW SUITE 300, CALGARY, AB,
T2P 1M9
(403) 237-9949   *SIC* 4924

AVENSYS SOLUTIONS INC   *p* 1338
178 RUE MERIZZI, SAINT-LAURENT, QC,
H4T 1S4
(514) 738-6766   *SIC* 5084

AVENTECH INTERNATIONAL INC   *p* 1261
850 BOUL PIERRE-BERTRAND BUREAU
185, QUEBEC, QC, G1M 3K8
(418) 843-8966   *SIC* 5051

AVENTUR ENERGY CORP   *p* 213
10493 ALDER CRES, FORT ST. JOHN, BC,
V1J 4M7
(250) 785-7093   *SIC* 1389

AVENTURIA TOURS   *p* 1244
See WINDIGO AVENTURE INC

**AVENUE INDUSTRIAL SUPPLY COMPANY
LIMITED**   *p* 850
35 STAPLES AVE SUITE 110, RICHMOND
HILL, ON, L4B 4W6
(877) 304-1270   *SIC* 5084

AVENUE MACHINERY CORP   *p* 174
1521 SUMAS WAY, ABBOTSFORD, BC,
V2S 8M9
(604) 792-4111   *SIC* 5083

AVENUE MEDICAL CENTRE   *p* 516
See BANNESTER, DR LESLIE R

AVENUE MOTOR WORKS INC   *p* 1029
681   ROWNTREE   DAIRY   RD,   WOOD-
BRIDGE, ON, L4L 5T9
(905) 850-2268   *SIC* 5013

AVENUE PONTIAC BUICK GMC INC*p* 1285
140   MONTEE   INDUSTRIELLE-ET-
COMMERCIALE,   RIMOUSKI,   QC,   G5M
1B1
(418) 725-2001   *SIC* 5511

AVERNA TECHNOLOGIES INC   *p* 1210
87 RUE PRINCE BUREAU 510, MON-
TREAL, QC, H3C 2M7
(514) 842-7577   *SIC* 3825

AVERSAN INC   *p* 729
30 EGLINTON AVE W SUITE 500, MISSIS-
SAUGA, ON, L5R 3E7
(416) 289-1554   *SIC* 8711

AVERTEX UTILITY SOLUTIONS INC *p* 863
205235 COUNTY RD 109, SCARBOR-

OUGH, ON, L9W 0T8
(519) 942-3030   *SIC* 1623
AVERY CONSTRUCTION LIMITED   *p* 863
940 SECOND LINE W SUITE B, SAULT STE. MARIE, ON, P6C 2L3
(705) 759-4800   *SIC* 1611
AVERY DENNISON CANADA CORPORA-TION   *p* 844
1840 CLEMENTS RD, PICKERING, ON, L1W 3Y2
(905) 837-4700   *SIC* 2672
AVERY WEIGH-TRONIX TM   *p* 1228
See WEIGH-TRONIX CANADA, ULC
AVERY'S FARM MARKETS LIMITED   *p* 451
619 CENTRAL AVE, GREENWOOD, NS, B0P 1R0
(902) 765-0224   *SIC* 5431
AVESORO RESOURCES INC   *p* 971
199 BAY ST SUITE 5300, TORONTO, ON, M5L 1B9
SIC 1041
AVG (OEAM) INC   *p* 876
605 MIDDLEFIELD RD UNIT 1, SCARBOR-OUGH, ON, M1V 5B9
(416) 321-2978   *SIC* 5531
AVG (OEM) INC   *p* 876
50 TIFFIELD RD UNIT 1, SCARBOROUGH, ON, M1V 5B7
(416) 321-2978   *SIC* 5013
AVH CHIPMAN   *p* 460
See NOVA SCOTIA HEALTH AUTHORITY
AVI-SPL   *p* 851
See AVI-SPL CANADA LTD
AVI-SPL CANADA LTD   *p* 851
35 EAST BEAVER CREEK RD SUITE 1, RICHMOND HILL, ON, L4B 1B3
(866) 797-5635   *SIC* 4813
AVIALL (CANADA) LTD   *p* 685
7150 TORBRAM RD SUITE 15, MISSIS-SAUGA, ON, L4T 3Z8
(905) 676-1695   *SIC* 5088
AVIANOR INC   *p* 1153
12405 RUE SERVICE A-2, MIRABEL, QC, J7N 1E4
SIC 3728
AVIATION STARLINK INC   *p* 1093
9025 AV RYAN, DORVAL, QC, H9P 1A2
(514) 631-7500   *SIC* 4522
AVICOLE   *p* 1136
See EXCELDOR COOPERATIVE
AVICOMAX INC   *p* 1098
500 RUE LABONTE, DRUMMONDVILLE, QC, J2C 6X9
(819) 471-5000   *SIC* 2015
AVID TECHNOLOGY CANADA CORP   *p* 1185
3510 BOUL SAINT-LAURENT BUREAU 300, MONTREAL, QC, H2X 2V2
(514) 845-1636   *SIC* 7371
AVIGILON CORPORATION   *p* 297
555 ROBSON ST 3RD FL, VANCOUVER, BC, V6B 3K9
(604) 629-5182   *SIC* 3651
AVINA FRESH PRODUCE LTD   *p* 178
28265 58 AVE, ABBOTSFORD, BC, V4X 2E8
(604) 856-9833   *SIC* 0182
AVINO SILVER & GOLD MINES LTD   *p* 302
570 GRANVILLE ST SUITE 900, VANCOU-VER, BC, V6C 3P1
(604) 682-3701   *SIC* 1044
AVION GOLD CORPORATION   *p* 948
65 QUEEN ST W SUITE 820, TORONTO, ON, M5H 2M5
(416) 861-9500   *SIC* 1081
AVION SERVICES CORP   *p* 383
2000 WELLINGTON AVE SUITE 503, WIN-NIPEG, MB, R3H 1C1
(204) 784-5800   *SIC* 7381
AVIS   *p* 597
See AVISCAR INC
AVIS   *p* 1092
See AVISCAR INC

AVISCAR INC   *p* 582
1 CONVAIR DR, ETOBICOKE, ON, M9W 6Z9
(416) 213-8400   *SIC* 7514
AVISCAR INC   *p* 597
180 PAUL BENOIT DR, GLOUCESTER, ON, K1V 2E5
(613) 521-7541   *SIC* 7514
AVISCAR INC   *p* 1092
975 BOUL ROMEO-VACHON N BUREAU 317, DORVAL, QC, H4Y 1H2
(514) 636-1902   *SIC* 7514
AVISCEN   *p* 1110
See STEDFAST INC
AVISINA PROPERTIES LTD   *p* 187
3787 CANADA WAY UNIT 200, BURNABY, BC, V5G 1G5
(604) 419-6000   *SIC* 8741
AVISON YOUNG (CANADA) INC   *p* 959
18 YORK ST SUITE 400, TORONTO, ON, M5J 2T8
(416) 955-0000   *SIC* 8742
AVISON YOUNG ADVISORS AND MAN-AGERS INC   *p* 948
257 ADELAIDE ST W SUITE 400, TORONTO, ON, M5H 1X9
(416) 343-0078   *SIC* 6531
AVISON YOUNG COMMERCIAL REAL ES-TATE (ONTARIO) INC   *p* 959
18 YORK ST SUITE 400, TORONTO, ON, M5J 2T8
(416) 955-0000   *SIC* 6531
AVIV INTERNATIONAL TRADE CORPORA-TION   *p* 666
31 TELSON RD SUITE 2, MARKHAM, ON, L3R 1E4
(905) 479-5047   *SIC* 5136
AVIVA   *p* 1177
See AVIVA CANADA INC
AVIVA CANADA   *p* 87
See AVIVA INSURANCE COMPANY OF CANADA
AVIVA CANADA INC   *p* 444
99 WYSE RD SUITE 1600, DARTMOUTH, NS, B3A 4S5
(902) 460-3100   *SIC* 6411
AVIVA CANADA INC   *p* 679
10 AVIVA WAY SUITE 100, MARKHAM, ON, L6G 0G1
(416) 288-1800   *SIC* 6411
AVIVA CANADA INC   *p* 1177
555 RUE CHABANEL O BUREAU 900, MONTREAL, QC, H2N 2H8
(514) 850-4100   *SIC* 6411
AVIVA CANADA INC   *p* 1201
630 BOUL RENE-LEVESQUE O BUREAU 900, MONTREAL, QC, H3B 1S6
(514) 876-5029   *SIC* 6331
AVIVA COMPAGNIE D'ASSURANCE DU CANADA   *p* 1201
See AVIVA INSURANCE COMPANY OF CANADA
AVIVA INSURANCE COMPANY OF CANADA   *p* 43
140 4 AVE SW SUITE 2400, CALGARY, AB, T2P 3W4
(403) 750-0600   *SIC* 6331
AVIVA INSURANCE COMPANY OF CANADA   *p* 87
10250 101 ST NW SUITE 1700, EDMON-TON, AB, T5J 3P4
(780) 428-1822   *SIC* 6331
AVIVA INSURANCE COMPANY OF CANADA   *p* 326
1125 HOWE ST SUITE 1100, VANCOU-VER, BC, V6Z 2Y6
(604) 669-2626   *SIC* 6331
AVIVA INSURANCE COMPANY OF CANADA   *p* 612
1 KING ST W SUITE 600, HAMILTON, ON, L8P 1A4

(289) 391-2600   *SIC* 6331
AVIVA INSURANCE COMPANY OF CANADA   *p* 653
255 QUEENS AVE SUITE 1500, LONDON, ON, N6A 5R8
(519) 672-2880   *SIC* 6331
AVIVA INSURANCE COMPANY OF CANADA   *p* 868
2206 EGLINTON AVE E SUITE 160, SCAR-BOROUGH, ON, M1L 4S8
(416) 288-1800   *SIC* 6331
AVIVA INSURANCE COMPANY OF CANADA   *p* 948
121 KING ST W SUITE 1400, TORONTO, ON, M5H 3T9
SIC 6411
AVIVA INSURANCE COMPANY OF CANADA   *p* 1201
630 BOUL RENE-LEVESQUE O BUREAU 700, MONTREAL, QC, H3B 1S6
(514) 399-1200   *SIC* 6331
AVIVA TRADERS   *p* 1201
See AVIVA CANADA INC
AVIYA AEROSPACE SYSTEMS   *p* 719
See AVIYA TECHNOLOGIES INC
AVIYA TECHNOLOGIES INC   *p* 719
2495 MEADOWPINE BLVD, MISSIS-SAUGA, ON, L5N 6C3
(905) 812-9995   *SIC* 7373
AVIZO EXPERTS-CONSEILS INC   *p* 1372
1125 RUE DE CHERBOURG, SHER-BROOKE, QC, J1K 0A8
(819) 346-4342   *SIC* 8748
AVJET   *p* 1098
See AVJET HOLDING INC
AVJET HOLDING INC   *p* 1098
1525 BOUL SAINT-JOSEPH, DRUM-MONDVILLE, QC, J2C 2E9
(819) 479-1000   *SIC* 5172
AVL MANUFACTURING INC   *p* 613
243 QUEEN ST N, HAMILTON, ON, L8R 3N6
(905) 545-7660   *SIC* 8711
AVMAX AIRCRAFT LEASING INC   *p* 21
380 MCTAVISH RD NE SUITE 3, CALGARY, AB, T2E 7G5
(403) 735-3299   *SIC* 5088
AVMAX AVIATION SERVICES INC   *p* 1394
264 RUE ADRIEN-PATENAUDE, VAUDREUIL-DORION, QC, J7V 5V5
(450) 424-9636   *SIC* 4581
AVMAX GROUP INC   *p* 21
2055 PEGASUS RD NE, CALGARY, AB, T2E 8C3
(403) 291-2464   *SIC* 4581
AVMAX GROUP INC   *p* 21
275 PALMER RD NE, CALGARY, AB, T2E 7G4
(403) 250-2644   *SIC* 7622
AVMAX GROUP INC   *p* 21
380 MCTAVISH RD NE, CALGARY, AB, T2E 7G5
(403) 735-3299   *SIC* 4581
AVMAX INTERIEURS EXECUTIFS (AIE)   *p* 1394
See AVMAX AVIATION SERVICES INC
AVMOR LTEE   *p* 1233
950 RUE MICHELIN, MONTREAL, QC, H7L 5C1
(450) 629-8074   *SIC* 2842
AVNET CANADA   *p* 719
See AVNET INTERNATIONAL (CANADA) LTD
AVNET INTERNATIONAL (CANADA) LTD   *p* 719
6950 CREDITVIEW RD UNIT 2, MISSIS-SAUGA, ON, L5N 0A6
(905) 812-4400   *SIC* 5065
AVOCETTE TECHNOLOGIES INC   *p* 236
422 SIXTH ST 2ND FLR, NEW WESTMIN-STER, BC, V3L 3B2
(604) 395-6000   *SIC* 7371
AVOGESCO INC   *p* 1201
1 PLACE VILLE-MARIE BUREAU 1300,

MONTREAL, QC, H3B 0E6
(514) 925-6300   *SIC* 8741
AVOKERIE HEALTHCARE INC   *p* 582
10 HUMBERLINE DR UNIT 301, ETOBI-COKE, ON, M9W 6J5
(416) 628-7151   *SIC* 8059
AVON CANADA   *p* 1249
See AVON CANADA INC
AVON CANADA INC   *p* 143
10 PURDUE CRT W, LETHBRIDGE, AB, T1K 4R8
SIC 2844
AVON CANADA INC   *p* 1249
5500 RTE TRANSCANADIENNE, POINTE-CLAIRE, QC, H9R 1B6
(514) 695-3371   *SIC* 5122
AVON MAITLAND DISTRICT SCHOOL BOARD   *p* 589
92 GIDLEY E, EXETER, ON, N0M 1S0
(519) 235-0880   *SIC* 8211
AVON MAITLAND DISTRICT SCHOOL BOARD   *p* 646
155 MAITLAND AVE S, LISTOWEL, ON, N4W 2M4
(519) 291-1880   *SIC* 8211
AVON MAITLAND DISTRICT SCHOOL BOARD   *p* 895
428 FORMAN AVE, STRATFORD, ON, N5A 6R7
(519) 271-9740   *SIC* 8211
AVON MAITLAND DISTRICT SCHOOL BOARD   *p* 1026
231 MADILL DR E, WINGHAM, ON, N0G 2W0
(519) 357-1800   *SIC* 8211
AVON VALLEY FLORAL   *p* 411
See ROYAL GARDENS LIMITED
AVON VALLEY FLORAL   *p* 450
See AVON VALLEY FLORAL INC
AVON VALLEY FLORAL INC   *p* 450
285 TOWN RD RR 2, FALMOUTH, NS, B0P 1L0
(902) 798-8381   *SIC* 0181
AVON VIEW HIGH SCHOOL   *p* 470
See ANNAPOLIS VALLEY REGIONAL SCHOOL BOARD
AVONDALE CONSTRUCTION LIMITED   *p* 458
49 HOBSONS LAKE DR, HALIFAX, NS, B3S 0E4
(902) 876-1818   *SIC* 1542
AVONDALE STORES LIMITED   *p* 623
4520 JORDAN RD, JORDAN STATION, ON, L0R 1S0
(905) 562-4173   *SIC* 5411
AVONLEA HOMES LTD   *p* 142
1111 3 AVE S, LETHBRIDGE, AB, T1J 0J5
(403) 320-1989   *SIC* 1521
AVONLEA MASTER BUILDER   *p* 142
See AVONLEA HOMES LTD
AVONLEA VILLAGE   *p* 1042
GD, NORTH RUSTICO, PE, C0A 1X0
(902) 963-3050   *SIC* 4725
AVOTUS CORPORATION   *p* 729
110 MATHESON BLVD W SUITE 300, MIS-SISSAUGA, ON, L5R 4G7
(905) 890-9199   *SIC* 4899
AVOTUS INC   *p* 1249
116 AV PENDENNIS, POINTE-CLAIRE, QC, H9R 1H6
SIC 7389
AVRIL SUPERMARCHE SANTE   *p* 1108
See 9020-5758 QUEBEC INC
AVRON FOODS LIMITED   *p* 549
277 BASALTIC RD, CONCORD, ON, L4K 4W8
(800) 997-9752   *SIC* 5141
AVW TELAV AUDIO VISUAL SERVICES   *p* 817
2295 ST. LAURENT BLVD, OTTAWA, ON, K1G 4H6
(613) 526-3121   *SIC* 7359
AWARD   *p* 1398
See SANI-MARC INC

AWC MANUFACTURING LP p 605
163 CURTIS DR, GUELPH, ON, N1K 1S9
(519) 822-0577   SIC 3499

AWG NORTHERN INDUSTRIES INC p 269
3424 16 HWY E RR 6, SMITHERS, BC, V0J 2N6
(250) 847-9211   SIC 8741

AWI p 12
See ANTHRATECH WESTERN INC

AWNBCO FOODS LTD p 1412
2142 100TH ST, NORTH BATTLEFORD, SK, S9A 0X6
(306) 445-9453   SIC 5963

AWP p 278
See ADVANCE WIRE PRODUCTS LTD

AXA ASSISTANCE CANADA INC p 1193
2001 BOUL ROBERT-BOURASSA BUREAU 1850, MONTREAL, QC, H3A 2L8
(514) 285-9053   SIC 6411

AXA ASSURANCES INC p 311
1090 GEORGIA ST W SUITE 1350, VANCOUVER, BC, V6E 3V7
SIC 6311

AXA ASSURANCES INC p 432
35 BLACKMARSH RD, ST. JOHN'S, NL, A1E 1S4
(709) 726-8974   SIC 6311

AXA ASSURANCES INC p 1193
2020 BOUL ROBERT-BOURASSA BUREAU 100, MONTREAL, QC, H3A 2A5
(514) 282-1914   SIC 6311

AXA ASSURANCES INC p 1271
2640 BOUL LAURIER BUREAU 900, QUEBEC, QC, G1V 5C2
SIC 6311

AXA GENERAL INSURANCE p 1193
See AXA ASSURANCES INC

AXA INSURANCE (CANADA) p 770
5700 YONGE ST SUITE 1400, NORTH YORK, ON, M2M 4K2
(416) 218-4175   SIC 6331

AXA PACIFIC INSURANCE p 311
See AXA ASSURANCES INC

AXALTA COATING SYSTEMS CANADA COMPANY p 473
408 FAIRALL ST, AJAX, ON, L1S 1R6
(905) 683-5500   SIC 5013

AXE MUSIC INC p 83
11931 WAYNE GRETZKY DRIVE NORTHBOUND NW, EDMONTON, AB, T5B 1Y4
(780) 471-2001   SIC 5736

AXEL KRAFT INTERNATIONAL LIMITED p 480
99 ENGELHARD DR, AURORA, ON, L4G 3V1
(905) 841-6840   SIC 5122

AXENS CANADA SPECIALTY ALUMINAS INC p 519
4000 DEVELOPMENT DR, BROCKVILLE, ON, K6V 5V5
(613) 342-7462   SIC 2819

AXEP PLUS p 1253
See MARCHE DOMINIC PICHE INC

AXIA FIBRENET p 63
See AXIA NETMEDIA CORPORATION

AXIA NETMEDIA CORPORATION p 63
220 12 AVE SW SUITE 110, CALGARY, AB, T2R 0E9
(403) 538-4000   SIC 4813

AXIA SECURITE p 1160
See AXIA SERVICES

AXIA SERVICES p 1160
13025 RUE JEAN-GROU, MONTREAL, QC, H1A 3N6
(514) 642-3250   SIC 7349

AXIA SUPERNET LTD p 63
220 12 AVE SW SUITE 110, CALGARY, AB, T2R 0E9
(403) 538-4000   SIC 4813

AXIM CONSTRUCTION INC p 1317
650 RUE BOUCHER BUREAU 106, SAINT-JEAN-SUR-RICHELIEU, QC, J3B 7Z8
(450) 358-3885   SIC 1542

AXIOM GROUP INC p 480

115 MARY ST, AURORA, ON, L4G 1G3
(905) 727-2878   SIC 3541

AXIOM MILLWRIGHTING & FABRICATION INC p 535
55 SAVAGE DR, CAMBRIDGE, ON, N1T 1S5
(519) 620-2000   SIC 1796

AXIOM PLASTICS INC p 480
115 MARY ST, AURORA, ON, L4G 1G3
(905) 727-2878   SIC 3089

AXIOM REAL-TIME METRICS INC p 997
1 CITY VIEW DR, TORONTO, ON, M9W 5A5
(905) 845-9779   SIC 7371

AXIOMATIC TECHNOLOGIES CORPORATION p 704
5915 WALLACE ST, MISSISSAUGA, ON, L4Z 1Z8
(905) 602-9270   SIC 3679

AXION INSURANCE SERVICES INC p 851
95 MURAL ST SUITE 205, RICHMOND HILL, ON, L4B 3G2
(905) 731-3118   SIC 6411

AXION LEE INSURANCE p 851
See AXION INSURANCE SERVICES INC

AXIS p 1130
See ECLAIRAGE AXIS INC

AXIS DATABASE MARKETING GROUP INC p 692
1331 CRESTLAWN DR UNIT A, MISSISSAUGA, ON, L4W 2P9
(416) 503-3210   SIC 8732

AXIS FAMILY RESOURCES LTD p 344
321 SECOND AVE N, WILLIAMS LAKE, BC, V2G 2A1
(250) 392-1000   SIC 8399

AXIS INSURANCE GROUP p 327
See AXIS INSURANCE MANAGERS INC

AXIS INSURANCE MANAGERS INC p 327
555 BURRARD ST. BOX 275 UNIT 400, VANCOUVER, BC, V7X 1M8
(604) 731-5328   SIC 6411

AXIS SORTING INC p 602
300 WILLOW RD UNIT 102B, GUELPH, ON, N1H 7C6
(519) 212-4990   SIC 7549

AXIUM AUTOMATION p 1051
See SYMBOTIC CANADA ULC

AXIUM SOLUTIONS ULC p 199
1963 LOUGHEED HWY, COQUITLAM, BC, V3K 3T8
(604) 468-6820   SIC 7371

AXON INTEGRATION & DEVELOPPEMENT p 1188
See GROUPE ASKIDA INC

AXOR CONSTRUCTION CANADA INC p 1193
1555 RUE PEEL BUREAU 1100, MONTREAL, QC, H3A 3L8
(514) 846-4000   SIC 1542

AXSUN INC p 1309
4900 RUE ARMAND-FRAPPIER BUREAU 450, SAINT-HUBERT, QC, J3Z 1G5
(450) 445-3003   SIC 4731

AXTON INCORPORATED p 205
441 DERWENT PL, DELTA, BC, V3M 5Y9
(604) 522-2731   SIC 3399

AXXESS INTERNATIONAL COURTIERS EN DOUANES INC p 734
1804 ALSTEP DR UNIT 1, MISSISSAUGA, ON, L5S 1W1
(905) 672-0270   SIC 4731

AXXESS INTERNATIONAL COURTIERS EN DOUANES INC p 1187
360 RUE SAINT-JACQUES BUREAU 1200, MONTREAL, QC, H2Y 1P5
(514) 849-9377   SIC 4731

AXXESS LOGISTICS, DIV OF p 1026
See 864884 ONTARIO INC

AXYS TECHNOLOGIES INC p 268
2035 MILLS RD W, SIDNEY, BC, V8L 5X2
(250) 655-5850   SIC 8748

AXYZ INTERNATIONAL INC p 521

5330 SOUTH SERVICE RD, BURLINGTON, ON, L7L 5L1
(905) 634-4940   SIC 3553

AY HOLDINGS ONTARIO INC p 948
150 YORK ST SUITE 900, TORONTO, ON, M5H 3S5
(416) 955-0000   SIC 6712

AY ROYAUME FORD p 1354
See AU ROYAUME CHRYSLER DODGE JEEP

AYA KITCHENS p 702
See AYA KITCHENS AND BATHS LTD

AYA KITCHENS AND BATHS LTD p 702
1551 CATERPILLAR RD, MISSISSAUGA, ON, L4X 2Z6
(905) 848-1999   SIC 2434

AYLMER VALU-MART p 482
See 1214288 ONTARIO LIMITED

AYLWARDS (1986) LIMITED p 425
200 ATLANTIC ST SUITE 192, MARYSTOWN, NL, A0E 2M0
(709) 279-2202   SIC 5251

AYLWARDS HOME CENTRE p 425
See AYLWARDS (1986) LIMITED

AYR FARMERS' MUTUAL INSURANCE COMPANY p 482
1400 NORTHUMBERLAND ST RR 1, AYR, ON, N0B 1E0
(519) 632-7413   SIC 6331

AYR MOTOR EXPRESS INC p 419
46 POPLAR ST, WOODSTOCK, NB, E7M 4G2
(506) 325-2205   SIC 4213

AYRE & OXFORD INC p 95
13455 114 AVE NW UNIT 203, EDMONTON, AB, T5M 2E2
(780) 448-4984   SIC 6531

AYRLINE LEASING INC p 483
2558 CEDAR CREEK RD SS 2, AYR, ON, N0B 1E0
(519) 740-8209   SIC 6712

AZ GROUP p 1035
847 BERKSHIRE DR, WOODSTOCK, ON, N4S 8R6
(519) 421-2423   SIC 8611

AZ HOME AND GIFTS p 259
See AZ TRADING CO. LTD

AZ TRADING CO. LTD p 259
7080 RIVER RD SUITE 223, RICHMOND, BC, V6X 1X5
(604) 214-3600   SIC 5947

AZARGA METALS CORP p 343
15782 MARINE DR UNIT 1, WHITE ROCK, BC, V4B 1E6
(604) 536-2711   SIC 1021

AZARGA URANIUM CORP p 343
15782 MARINE DR UNIT 1, WHITE ROCK, BC, V4B 1E6
(604) 536-2711   SIC 1081

AZELIS CANADA INC p 1063
1570 RUE AMPERE BUREAU 106, BOUCHERVILLE, QC, J4B 7L4
(450) 449-6363   SIC 5169

AZGA INSURANCE AGENCY CANADA LTD p 641
4273 KING ST E, KITCHENER, ON, N2P 2E9
(519) 742-2800   SIC 6411

AZGA SERVICE CANADA INC p 641
4273 KING ST E, KITCHENER, ON, N2P 2E9
(519) 742-2800   SIC 8322

AZIMUTH THREE COMMUNICATIONS p 501
See AZIMUTH THREE ENTERPRISES INC

AZIMUTH THREE ENTERPRISES INC p 501
127 DELTA PARK BLVD, BRAMPTON, ON, L6T 5M8
(437) 370-7160   SIC 1731

AZIZ, J. & A. LIMITED p 782
1635 FLINT RD, NORTH YORK, ON, M3J 2J6
(416) 787-0365   SIC 5131

AZROCK p 1101

See TARKETT INC

AZTEC ELECTRICAL SUPPLY INC p 549
25 NORTH RIVERMEDE RD UNIT 4-10, CONCORD, ON, L4K 5V4
(905) 761-7762   SIC 5063

AZUMA FOODS (CANADA) CO., LTD p 253
11451 TWIGG PL, RICHMOND, BC, V6V 3C9
(604) 325-1129   SIC 5146

AZURITE HOLDINGS LTD p 236
225 EDWORTHY WAY, NEW WESTMINSTER, BC, V3L 5G4
(604) 527-1120   SIC 6712

B

B & A PETROLEUM LTD p 1436
2004 SOUTH SERVICE RD W, SWIFT CURRENT, SK, S9H 5J5
(306) 773-8890   SIC 5983

B & B CONTRACTING GROUP p 278
See B & B CONTRACTING LTD

B & B CONTRACTING LTD p 278
3077 188 ST SUITE 100, SURREY, BC, V3Z 9V5
(604) 539-7200   SIC 4212

B & B DIXON AUTOMOTIVE INC p 754
395 HARRY WALKER PKY N UNIT 3, NEWMARKET, ON, L3Y 7B3
(905) 895-5184   SIC 5013

B & B ELECTRONICS LTD p 125
4316 SAVARYN DR SW, EDMONTON, AB, T6X 1Z9
(780) 439-3901   SIC 5731

B & B LINE CONSTRUCTION LTD p 427
1274 KENMOUNT RD, PARADISE, NL, A1L 1N3
(709) 722-1112   SIC 1623

B & B SALES LIMITED p 422
27 UNION ST, CORNER BROOK, NL, A2H 5P9
(709) 639-8991   SIC 5087

B & C FOOD DISTRIBUTORS LTD p 266
6711 BUTLER CRES, SAANICHTON, BC, V8M 1Z7
(250) 544-2333   SIC 5147

B & G KERR SALES LTD p 629
1040 DIVISION ST SUITE 694, KINGSTON, ON, K7K 0C3
(613) 546-1922   SIC 5531

B & G TRUCK & TRAILER REPAIRS p 563
See 884262 ONTARIO INC

B & I TRUCK PARTS INC p 486
480 DUNLOP ST W, BARRIE, ON, L4N 9W5
(705) 737-3201   SIC 5531

B & L HOMES FOR CHILDREN LTD p 374
470 NOTRE DAME AVE SUITE 200, WINNIPEG, MB, R3B 1R5
(204) 774-6089   SIC 8399

B & M HOME HARDWARE BUILDING CENTRE p 151
See 645373 ALBERTA LTD

B & R HOLDINGS INC p 916
32 CRANFIELD RD, TORONTO, ON, M4B 3H3
(416) 701-9800   SIC 2672

B & W INSURANCE AGENCIES p 275
8434 120 ST SUITE 108, SURREY, BC, V3W 7S2
(604) 591-7891   SIC 6331

B A S P BUY & SELL PRESS LTD, THE p 184
4664 LOUGHEED HWY SUITE 202, BURNABY, BC, V5C 5T5
(604) 540-4455   SIC 2711

B B FAMILY CONVENIENCE p 1006
See BRADSHAW BROS. PETROLEUM LTD.

B C FEDERATION OF LABOUR (CLC) p 288
5118 JOYCE ST SUITE 200, VANCOUVER, BC, V5R 4H1
(604) 430-1421   SIC 6371

B C FUNDRAISERS p 290
8278 MANITOBA ST, VANCOUVER, BC,

V5X 3A2
SIC 8699
B D *p* 796
See BECTON DICKINSON CANADA INC
B D L *p* 70
See BREWERS' DISTRIBUTOR LTD
B F GOODRICH *p* 965
See POLYCORP LTD
B I V PUBLICATIONS LTD *p* 288
102 4TH AVE E, VANCOUVER, BC, V5T
1G2
(604) 669-8500 *SIC* 2711
B J ELECTRIC SUPPLIES LTD *p* 112
4143 97 ST NW, EDMONTON, AB, T6E 6E9
(780) 461-2334 *SIC* 5063
B J'S TRUCK CENTRE *p* 1038
See B J'S TRUCK PARTS INC
B J'S TRUCK PARTS INC *p* 1038
502 BRACKLEY PT RD, CHARLOTTE-
TOWN, PE, C1A 8C2
(902) 566-4205 *SIC* 5531
B K A OFFICE INC *p* 782
675 PETROLIA RD, NORTH YORK, ON,
M3J 2N6
(416) 665-2466 *SIC* 5065
B L S ASPHALT INC *p* 1420
711 TORONTO ST, REGINA, SK, S4R 8G1
(306) 775-0080 *SIC* 1611
B M W ELITE AUTOMOBILES INC *p* 595
1040 OGILVIE RD, GLOUCESTER, ON, K1J
8G9
(613) 749-7700 *SIC* 5511
B S I INSURANCE BROKERS LTD *p* 351
16 3RD AVENUE EAST, LETELLIER, MB,
R0G 1C0
(204) 737-2471 *SIC* 6411
B SQUARED AIRSOFT LTD *p* 95
14574 116 AVE NW, EDMONTON, AB, T5M
3E9
(780) 884-8292 *SIC* 5099
B T Y GROUP *p* 291
See BTY CONSULTANCY GROUP INC
**B TAYLOR HOME HARDWARE BUILDING
CENTRE** *p* 565
See 2699001 CANADA LIMITED
B TOWN GROUP *p* 590
See 1759800 ONTARIO INC
B WYZE INC *p* 666
20 VALLEYWOOD DR UNIT 100,
MARKHAM, ON, L3R 6G1
(905) 780-0444 *SIC* 8742
B WYZE SOLUTIONS *p* 666
See B WYZE INC
B&J MUSIC *p* 1053
See INDUSTRIES JAM LTEE, LES
B&M EMPLOYMENT INC *p* 786
168 OAKDALE RD UNIT 8, NORTH YORK,
ON, M3N 2S5
SIC 7361
B&N MANAGEMENT *p* 972
51 TRANBY AVE, TORONTO, ON, M5R 1N4
(613) 321-7401 *SIC* 7361
B+H CHIL DESIGN *p* 320
1706 1ST AVE W SUITE 400, VANCOU-
VER, BC, V6J 0E4
(604) 688-8571 *SIC* 7389
B-LINE TIRE & AUTO SUPPLY LTD *p* 165
32 RAYBORN CRES, ST. ALBERT, AB, T8N
4B1
(780) 458-7619 *SIC* 5014
B-LINE UTILITIES LTD *p* 151
5703 48 AVE, OLDS, AB, T4H 1V1
(403) 556-8563 *SIC* 1623
B. & C. LIST (1982) LTD *p* 290
8278 MANITOBA ST, VANCOUVER, BC,
V5X 3A2
(604) 482-3100 *SIC* 2721
B. & C. NIGHTINGALE FARMS LTD *p* 643
1931 WINDHAM RD 19 RR 1, LA SALETTE,
ON, N0E 1H0
(519) 582-2461 *SIC* 0191
B. & K. INTERNATIONAL CORPORATION *p*
392
34 WATERFRONT RD, WINNIPEG, MB,

R3X 1L2
(204) 654-4785 *SIC* 5159
B. BRAUN OF CANADA, LTD *p* 720
6711 MISSISSAUGA RD SUITE 504, MIS-
SISSAUGA, ON, L5N 2W3
(905) 363-4335 *SIC* 5047
B. C. GAS INC. *p* 216
910 COLUMBIA ST W, KAMLOOPS, BC,
V2C 1L2
SIC 4924
B. C. GAS UTILITY LTD. *p* 203
110 SLATER RD NW, CRANBROOK, BC,
V1C 5C8
(250) 426-6388 *SIC* 4923
B. D. R. SERVICES LTD *p* 371
11 YARD ST, WINNIPEG, MB, R2W 5J6
(204) 586-8227 *SIC* 1711
B. GINGRAS ENTERPRISES LTD *p* 112
4505 101 ST NW, EDMONTON, AB, T6E
5C6
(780) 435-3355 *SIC* 7349
B. K. FER OUVRE INC *p* 1295
1800 RUE MARIE-VICTORIN, SAINT-
BRUNO, QC, J3V 6B9
(514) 820-7423 *SIC* 3441
B. KAMINS-CHEMIST *p* 1251
See KAMINS DERMATOLOGIQUE, INC
B. MCDOWELL EQUIPMENT LIMITED *p*
899
2018 KINGSWAY, SUDBURY, ON, P3B 4J8
(705) 566-8190 *SIC* 5084
B. TERFLOTH + CIE (CANADA) INC *p* 1401
3500 BOUL DE MAISONNEUVE O UNITE
2360, WESTMOUNT, QC, H3Z 3C1
(514) 939-2341 *SIC* 5141
B.& R. ECKEL'S TRANSPORT LTD *p* 6
5514B 50 AVE, BONNYVILLE, AB, T9N 2K8
(780) 826-3889 *SIC* 1389
B.A. BLACKTOP LTD *p* 238
111 FORESTER ST SUITE 201, NORTH
VANCOUVER, BC, V7H 0A6
(604) 985-0611 *SIC* 1611
B.B. BARGOON'S (1996) CORP *p* 549
8201 KEELE ST UNIT 1, CONCORD, ON,
L4K 1Z4
(905) 761-5065 *SIC* 5712
B.B. INVESTMENTS INC *p* 76
388 COUNTRY HILLS BLVD NE SUITE 600,
CALGARY, AB, T3K 5J6
(403) 226-7171 *SIC* 5812
**B.C. COMFORT AIR CONDITIONING LIM-
ITED** *p*
191
7405 LOWLAND DR, BURNABY, BC, V5J
5A8
(604) 439-3344 *SIC* 1711
B.C. CUSTOM CAR ASSOCIATION *p* 232
32670 DYKE RD, MISSION, BC, V2V 4J5
(604) 826-6315 *SIC* 8699
B.C. FASTENERS & TOOLS (2000) LTD *p*
275
12824 78 AVE UNIT 101, SURREY, BC,
V3W 8E7
(604) 599-5455 *SIC* 5085
B.C. FASTENERS & TOOLS LTD *p* 221
1960 WINDSOR RD SUITE 3, KELOWNA,
BC, V1Y 4R5
(250) 868-9222 *SIC* 5085
B.C. INSTRUMENTS *p* 879
See B.C. PRECISION INC
B.C. LOTTOTECH INTERNATIONAL INC *p*
216
74 SEYMOUR ST W, KAMLOOPS, BC, V2C
1E2
(250) 828-5500 *SIC* 7999
B.C. PRECISION INC *p* 879
41 PROCTOR RD, SCHOMBERG, ON, L0G
1T0
(905) 939-7323 *SIC* 3545
B.C. TREE FRUITS LIMITED *p* 221
1473 WATER ST, KELOWNA, BC, V1Y 1J6
(250) 470-4200 *SIC* 5148
B.C.A.A. HOLDINGS LTD *p* 187
4567 CANADA WAY, BURNABY, BC, V5G

4T1
(604) 268-5000 *SIC* 6411
B.C.A.A. TRAVEL, DIV OF *p* 187
See B.C.A.A. HOLDINGS LTD
B.F.L. ENERGY SERVICES LTD *p* 6
5610 54 AVE, BONNYVILLE, AB, T9N 2N3
SIC 3441
B.G.E. SERVICE & SUPPLY LTD *p* 118
5711 103A ST NW, EDMONTON, AB, T6H
2J6
(780) 436-6960 *SIC* 5085
B.I. GROUP *p* 1178
See BEAUMARCHE INC
B.L. INTIMATE APPAREL CANADA INC *p*
1178
9500 RUE MEILLEUR BUREAU 111, MON-
TREAL, QC, H2N 2B7
(514) 858-9254 *SIC* 5137
B.L.T. CONSTRUCTION SERVICES INC *p*
918
953A EGLINTON AVE E, TORONTO, ON,
M4G 4B5
(416) 755-2505 *SIC* 1541
B.M.I. CONSTRUCTION CO. LIMITED *p* 844
1058 COPPERSTONE DR SUITE 1, PICK-
ERING, ON, L1W 3V8
(905) 686-4287 *SIC* 1542
B.O.B. HEADQUARTERS INC *p* 346
658 18TH ST UNIT 2, BRANDON, MB, R7A
5B4
(204) 728-7470 *SIC* 5961
B.P.D.L. INC *p* 1044
890 RUE DES PINS O, ALMA, QC, G8B 7R3
(418) 668-6161 *SIC* 8742
B.R.T. DISTRIBUTING LTD *p* 627
1368 HIGHWAY 7, KEENE, ON, K9J 0G6
(705) 295-6832 *SIC* 5199
B.R.T. PET FOODS, DIV OF *p* 627
See B.R.T. DISTRIBUTING LTD
B.S.D. LOGISTICS INC *p* 508
350 RUTHERFORD RD S SUITE 202,
BRAMPTON, ON, L6W 3M2
(289) 801-4045 *SIC* 4213
B.T.E. ASSEMBLY LTD *p* 646
801 TREMAINE AVE S, LISTOWEL, ON,
N4W 3G9
(519) 291-5322 *SIC* 3089
**B.U.I.L.D. BUILDING URBAN INDUSTRIES
FOR LOCAL DEVELOPMENT INC** *p* 371
765 MAIN ST UNIT 200, WINNIPEG, MB,
R2W 3N5
(204) 943-5981 *SIC* 1521
B.W.S. MANUFACTURING LTD *p* 396
29 HAWKINS RD, CENTREVILLE, NB, E7K
1A4
(506) 276-4567 *SIC* 3715
B2B *p* 944
See B2B BANK
B2B BANK *p* 944
199 BAY ST SUITE 600, TORONTO, ON,
M5G 1M5
(647) 826-7979 *SIC* 6021
B2B BANK DEALER SERVICES *p* 944
See B2B BANK FINANCIAL SERVICES INC
B2B BANK FINANCIAL SERVICES INC *p*
944
199 BAY ST SUITE 610, TORONTO, ON,
M5G 1M5
(416) 926-0221 *SIC* 6282
B2GOLD CORP *p* 328
595 BURRARD ST SUITE 3100, VANCOU-
VER, BC, V7X 1L7
(604) 681-8371 *SIC* 1041
B3CG INTERCONNECT INC *p* 1301
310 BOUL INDUSTRIEL, SAINT-
EUSTACHE, QC, J7R 5R4
(450) 491-4040 *SIC* 4899
B3CG INTERCONNEXION *p* 1301
See B3CG INTERCONNECT INC
B3INTELLIGENCE LTD *p* 915
100 SHEPPARD AVE E SUITE 503,
TORONTO, ON, M2N 6N5
(416) 549-8000 *SIC* 8732
BAAGWATING COMMUNITY ASSOCIA-

TION *p*
848
22521 ISLAND RD, PORT PERRY, ON, L9L
1B6
(905) 985-3337 *SIC* 7999
BABEL *p* 1216
See SERVICES DE JEUX BABEL INC
BABESKIN BODYCARE INC *p* 341
815 MARGAREE PL, WEST VANCOUVER,
BC, V7T 2J5
(604) 922-1883 *SIC* 5122
BABINE FOREST PRODUCTS LIMITED *p*
194
19479 16 HWY E RR 3, BURNS LAKE, BC,
V0J 1E3
(250) 692-7177 *SIC* 2421
BABINEAU, D. DRUGS INC *p* 1017
11500 TECUMSEH RD E SUITE 1118,
WINDSOR, ON, N8N 1L7
(519) 735-2121 *SIC* 5912
BABLAKE LTD *p* 70
11800 40 ST SE, CALGARY, AB, T2Z 4T1
(403) 248-3559 *SIC* 6712
BABY ENROUTE *p* 829
See 8463859 CANADA INC
BABY LOVE - TRADE MARK *p* 1328
See CHAUSSURES M & M INC
BACARDI CANADA INC *p* 572
3250 BLOOR ST W SUITE 1050, ETOBI-
COKE, ON, M8X 2X9
(905) 451-6100 *SIC* 2085
BACHLY CONSTRUCTION *p* 494
See C. S. BACHLY BUILDERS LIMITED
BACINIL *p* 1059
See DUCHESNAY INC
BACK ALLEY, THE *p* 27
See 376599 ALBERTA INC
BACKCHECK DIV OF *p* 281
*See CHECKWELL SOLUTIONS CORPO-
RATION*
BACKERHAUS VEIT LTD *p* 737
6745 INVADER CRES, MISSISSAUGA, ON,
L5T 2B6
(905) 850-9229 *SIC* 2053
BACKRACK *p* 525
See THI CANADA INC
BACKWOODS CONTRACTING LTD *p* 125
1259 91 ST SW UNIT 301, EDMONTON,
AB, T6X 1E9
(587) 880-2937 *SIC* 1389
BACKWOODS ENERGY SERVICES *p* 125
See BACKWOODS CONTRACTING LTD
BACON AMERICA *p* 1311
See ALIMENTS PRINCE, S.E.C.
BAD BOY FURNITURE & APPLIANCES *p*
792
*See BAD BOY FURNITURE WAREHOUSE
LIMITED*
**BAD BOY FURNITURE WAREHOUSE LIM-
ITED** *p*
792
500 FENMAR DR, NORTH YORK, ON, M9L
2V5
(416) 667-7546 *SIC* 5712
**BADALI'S, JOE ITALIAN RESTAURANT &
BAR** *p* 959
*See BADALI'S, JOE PIAZZA ON FRONT
INC*
BADALI'S, JOE PIAZZA ON FRONT INC *p*
959
156 FRONT ST W, TORONTO, ON, M5J 2L6
(416) 977-3064 *SIC* 5812
**BADANAI CHEVROLET OLDSMOBILE
CADILLAC** *p* 907
See BADANAI MOTORS LTD
BADANAI MOTORS LTD *p* 907
399 MEMORIAL AVE, THUNDER BAY, ON,
P7B 3Y4
(807) 683-4900 *SIC* 5511
BADGER DAYLIGHTING LTD *p* 64
919 11TH AVE SW SUITE 400, CALGARY,
AB, T2R 1P3
(403) 264-8500 *SIC* 1389
BADMINTON AND RACQUET CLUB OF

TORONTO, THE p 926
25 ST CLAIR AVE W, TORONTO, ON, M4V 1K6
(416) 921-2159 *SIC 7997*

BAE NEWPLAN p 426
See SNC-LAVALIN INC

BAE-NEWPLAN GROUP LIMITED p 425
1133 TOPSAIL RD, MOUNT PEARL, NL, A1N 5G2
(709) 368-0118 *SIC 8711*

BAFFIN BUILDING SYSTEMS p 748
See 4577 NUNAVUT LIMITED

BAG TEX PACKAGING INC p 836
10 SPRUCE ST, PARIS, ON, N3L 1R6
(519) 442-0499 *SIC 5199*

BAGEL-BAGEL p 815
See EBAM ENTERPRISES LTD

BAGELCHESSE p 1292
See FROMAGERIE BERGERON INC

BAGHAI DEVELOPMENT LIMITED p 915
678 SHEPPARD AVE E UNIT H, TORONTO, ON, M2K 1B7
(416) 449-5994 *SIC 0212*

BAGOS BUN BAKERY LTD p 33
303 58 AVE SE SUITE 3, CALGARY, AB, T2H 0P3
(403) 252-3660 *SIC 2051*

BAGOS BUN BAKERY LTD p 371
232 JARVIS AVE, WINNIPEG, MB, R2W 3A1
(204) 586-8409 *SIC 5461*

BAGUETTECO p 1127
See BOULART INC

BAIE DE BEAUPORT p 1257
See CLUB NAUTIQUE DE LA BAIE DE BEAUPORT

BAIE STE-ANNE CO-OPERATIVE LTD p 394
5575 ROUTE 117, BAIE-SAINTE-ANNE, NB, E9A 1E6
(506) 228-4211 *SIC 5411*

BAIE STE-ANNE SEAFOODS (2014) INC p 399
143 CH ESCUMINAC POINT, ESCUMINAC, NB, E9A 1V6
(506) 228-4444 *SIC 2091*

BAIE, LA p 1287
See HUDSON'S BAY COMPANY

BAIG BLVD MOTORS INC p 408
1820 MAIN ST, MONCTON, NB, E1E 4S7
(506) 857-2950 *SIC 5511*

BAILEY HELICOPTERS LTD p 21
600 PALMER RD NE, CALGARY, AB, T2E 7R3
(403) 219-2770 *SIC 4522*

BAILEY METAL PROCESSING LIMITED p 521
1211 HERITAGE RD, BURLINGTON, ON, L7L 4Y1
(905) 336-5111 *SIC 7389*

BAILEY METAL PRODUCTS LIMITED p 549
1 CALDARI RD, CONCORD, ON, L4K 3Z9
(905) 738-9267 *SIC 3312*

BAILEY WEST INC p 275
7715 129A ST, SURREY, BC, V3W 6A2
(604) 590-5100 *SIC 3444*

BAILEY WEST PROCESSING INC p 549
1 CALDARI RD, CONCORD, ON, L4K 3Z9
(905) 738-9267 *SIC 5051*

BAILEY'S WELDING & CONSTRUCTION INC p 82
6205 56 AVE, DRAYTON VALLEY, AB, T7A 1S5
(780) 542-3578 *SIC 1799*

BAILEY-HUNT LIMITED p 549
1 CALDARI RD, CONCORD, ON, L4K 3Z9
(905) 738-9267 *SIC 3312*

BAILLARGEON - MSA INC p 1317
800 RUE DES CARRIERES, SAINT-JEAN-SUR-RICHELIEU, QC, J3B 2P2
(450) 346-4441 *SIC 6712*

BAILLOT, JULES & FILS LIMITEE p 1107
960 BOUL SAINT-JOSEPH, GATINEAU, QC, J8Z 1T3

(819) 777-5261 *SIC 5511*

BAIN & COMPANY CANADA, INC p 928
2 BLOOR ST E, TORONTO, ON, M4W 1A8
(416) 929-1888 *SIC 8742*

BAIN DEPOT p 1058
See BAIN DEPOT INC

BAIN DEPOT INC p 1058
1200 BOUL MICHELE-BOHEC, BLAINVILLE, QC, J7C 5S4
(450) 433-6930 *SIC 5719*

BAIN MAGIQUE p 1173
See RENOVATIONS MARTIN MARTIN INC

BAIN MAGIQUE p 1301
See 130355 CANADA INC

BAIN MAGIQUE p 1301
See DISTRIBUTION BATH FITTER INC

BAINE JOHNSTON CORPORATION p 428
410 EAST WHITE HILLS RD, ST. JOHN'S, NL, A1A 5J7
(709) 576-1780 *SIC 6712*

BAINS OCEANIA INC. p 1383
591 RUE DES ENTREPRISES, THETFORD MINES, QC, G6H 4B2
(418) 332-4224 *SIC 3272*

BAINS TRAVEL LIMITED p 290
6550 FRASER ST, VANCOUVER, BC, V5X 3T3
(604) 324-2277 *SIC 4724*

BAINS ULTRA INC p 1140
956 CH OLIVIER, LEVIS, QC, G7A 2N1
(418) 831-4344 *SIC 3089*

BAINS ULTRA INC p 1140
1200 CH INDUSTRIEL BUREAU 4, LEVIS, QC, G7A 1B1
(418) 831-7132 *SIC 5999*

BAINULTRA p 1140
See BAINS ULTRA INC

BAIRD MACGREGOR INSURANCE BRO-KERS INC p 920
825 QUEEN ST E, TORONTO, ON, M4M 1H8
(416) 778-8000 *SIC 6411*

BAJAJ DRUGS LIMITED p 580
1530 ALBION RD SUITE 925, ETOBICOKE, ON, M9V 1B4
(416) 741-7711 *SIC 5912*

BAJAR, ANTONIO GREENHOUSES LIM-ITED p 754
18545 KEELE ST, NEWMARKET, ON, L3Y 4V9
(905) 775-2773 *SIC 5193*

BAKA p 577
See BAKA COMMUNICATIONS, INC

BAKA COMMUNICATIONS, INC p 577
630 THE EAST MALL, ETOBICOKE, ON, M9B 4B1
(416) 641-2800 *SIC 5999*

BAKE INC p 21
See CANADIAN TEST CASE 192

BAKEMARK CANADA p 253
See BAKEMARK INGREDIENTS CANADA LIMITED

BAKEMARK INGREDIENTS CANADA LIM-ITED p 253
2480 VIKING WAY, RICHMOND, BC, V6V 1N2
(604) 303-1700 *SIC 5149*

BAKER ATLAS p 44
See BAKER HUGHES CANADA COMPANY

BAKER HUGHES CANADA COMPANY p 13
4839 90 AVE SE SUITE FRNT, CALGARY, AB, T2C 2S8
(403) 531-5300 *SIC 1389*

BAKER HUGHES CANADA COMPANY p 44
401 9 AVE SW SUITE 1000, CALGARY, AB, T2P 3C5
(403) 537-3400 *SIC 5084*

BAKER HUGHES CANADA COMPANY p 44
401 9 AVE SW SUITE 1300, CALGARY, AB, T2P 3C5
SIC 5169

BAKER HUGHES CANADA COMPANY p 108
9010 34 ST NW, EDMONTON, AB, T6B 2V1
(780) 465-9495 *SIC 1389*

BAKER HUGHES CANADA COMPANY p 139
3905 71 AVE, LEDUC, AB, T9E 0R8
(780) 612-3150 *SIC 1389*

BAKER HUGHES CANADA COMPANY p 139
7016 45 ST, LEDUC, AB, T9E 7E7
(780) 986-5559 *SIC 5084*

BAKER HUGHES CANADA COMPANY p 155
4089 77 ST, RED DEER, AB, T4P 2T3
(403) 357-1401 *SIC 1389*

BAKER HUGHES CANADA COMPANY p 155
7880 EDGAR INDUSTRIAL DR, RED DEER, AB, T4P 3R2
(403) 340-3015 *SIC 1389*

BAKER HUGHES CANADA COMPANY p 158
1901 BROADWAY AVE E, REDCLIFF, AB, T0J 2P0
SIC 1389

BAKER HUGHES INC p 44
401 9 AVE SW SUITE 1000, CALGARY, AB, T2P 3C5
(403) 537-3400 *SIC 3533*

BAKER OIL TOOLS p 44
See BAKER HUGHES CANADA COMPANY

BAKER STREET BAKERY INC p 578
130 THE WEST MALL, ETOBICOKE, ON, M9C 1B9
(416) 785-9666 *SIC 5149*

BAKER SUPPLY LTD p 233
33 CLIFF ST, NANAIMO, BC, V9R 5E6
(250) 754-6315 *SIC 5013*

BAKER, BERTRAND, CHASSE & GOGUEN CLAIM SERVICES LIMITED p 709
3660 HURONTARIO ST SUITE 601, MIS-SISSAUGA, ON, L5B 3C4
(905) 279-8880 *SIC 6411*

BAKER, G.R. MEMORIAL HOSPITAL p 252
See NORTHERN HEALTH AUTHORITY

BAKER, WALTER & CHANTAL SALES LTD p 477
1060 WILSON ST W, ANCASTER, ON, L9G 3K9
(905) 304-0000 *SIC 5531*

BAKERY DELUXE COMPANY p 794
50 MARMORA ST, NORTH YORK, ON, M9M 2X5
(416) 746-1010 *SIC 2051*

BAKKER, J. C. & SONS LIMITED p 885
1360 THIRD ST SUITE 3, ST CATHARINES, ON, L2R 6P9
(905) 935-4533 *SIC 5193*

BAKTERA p 1066
See LABORATOIRES SUISSE INC, LES

BALAMORE FARM LTD p 450
9036 HIGHWAY 2, GREAT VILLAGE, NS, B0M 1L0
(902) 668-2005 *SIC 0191*

BALANCED FINANCIAL SERVICES LTD p 322
2309 41ST AVE W SUITE 202, VANCOU-VER, BC, V6M 2A3
(604) 261-8509 *SIC 6282*

BALCO INC p 383
1610 ST JAMES ST, WINNIPEG, MB, R3H 0L2
(204) 772-2421 *SIC 5199*

BALI p 1178
See CREATIONS NOC NOC INC

BALISCUS p 1319
See CENTRE DE PLOMBERIE ST-JEROME INC

BALISCUS L'ESPACE EAU ET PLOMBERIE p 1170
See DESCHENES & FILS LTEE

BALIVERNES BOUTIQUE p 1265
See ROBOVER INC

BALL CONSTRUCTION (CANADA) INC p 635
5 SHIRLEY AVE, KITCHENER, ON, N2B 2E6
(519) 742-5851 *SIC 6712*

BALL CONSTRUCTION INC p 635
5 SHIRLEY AVE, KITCHENER, ON, N2B 2E6
(519) 742-5851 *SIC 1542*

BALL CONSTRUCTION LTD p 635
5 SHIRLEY AVE, KITCHENER, ON, N2B 2E6
(519) 742-5851 *SIC 1521*

BALL HARRISON HANSELL EMPLOYEE BENEFITS INSURANCE AGENCY LTD p 891
1040 SOUTH SERVICE RD, STONEY CREEK, ON, L8E 6G3
(905) 643-1017 *SIC 6321*

BALL PACKAGING PRODUCTS CANADA CORP p 1013
1506 WENTWORTH ST, WHITBY, ON, L1N 7C1
(905) 666-3600 *SIC 3411*

BALL TECHNOLOGIES AVANCEES D'ALUMINIUM CANADA S.E.C. p 1372
2205 RUE ROY, SHERBROOKE, QC, J1K 1B8
(819) 563-3589 *SIC 3341*

BALLARD POWER SYSTEMS INC p 191
9000 GLENLYON PKY, BURNABY, BC, V5J 5J8
(604) 454-0900 *SIC 3674*

BALLIN INC p 1297
2100 AV DE L'UNION, SAINT-CESAIRE, QC, J0L 1T0
(450) 469-4957 *SIC 2339*

BALLIN INC p 1332
2825 RUE BRABANT-MARINEAU, SAINT-LAURENT, QC, H4S 1R8
(514) 333-5501 *SIC 2325*

BALLYCLIFFE LODGE LIMITED p 473
70 STATION ST, AJAX, ON, L1S 1R9
(905) 683-7321 *SIC 8051*

BALMORAL HALL - SCHOOL FOR GIRLS p 376
630 WESTMINSTER AVE, WINNIPEG, MB, R3C 3S1
(204) 784-1600 *SIC 8211*

BALMORAL INVESTMENTS LTD p 267
2476 MOUNT NEWTON CROSS RD, SAANICHTON, BC, V8M 2B8
(250) 652-1146 *SIC 7011*

BALMORAL INVESTMENTS LTD p 340
101 ISLAND HWY, VICTORIA, BC, V9B 1E8
(250) 388-7807 *SIC 7011*

BALMORAL SAVE EASY p 394
647 DES PIONNIERS AVE, BALMORAL, NB, E8E 1B3
(506) 826-2545 *SIC 5411*

BALOG AUCTION SERVICES INC p 142
GD, LETHBRIDGE, AB, T1J 3Y2
(403) 320-1980 *SIC 5154*

BALTA IMPORTS LTD p 754
17600 YONGE ST SUITE 43, NEWMAR-KET, ON, L3Y 4Z1
(905) 853-5281 *SIC 5099*

BAMBERGER POLYMERS (CANADA) CORP p 720
2000 ARGENTIA RD SUITE 306, MISSIS-SAUGA, ON, L5N 1P7
(905) 821-9400 *SIC 5162*

BAMBORA INC p 334
2659 DOUGLAS ST SUITE 302, VICTORIA, BC, V8T 4M3
(250) 472-2326 *SIC 8741*

BAMFORD PRODUCE COMPANY LIMITED p 703
2501 STANFIELD RD SUITE A, MISSIS-SAUGA, ON, L4Y 1R6
(905) 615-9400 *SIC 5148*

BANANA REPUBLIC p 935
See GAP (CANADA) INC

BANBRICO LIMITED p 532
480 COLLIER MACMILLAN DR, CAM-

BRIDGE, ON, N1R 6R5
(905) 668-9174   *SIC* 5051

BANC PROPERTIES LIMITED   *p* 439
30 DAMASCUS RD SUITE 215, BEDFORD, NS, B4A 0C1
(902) 461-6450   *SIC* 6531

BANCROFT MOTORS LTD   *p* 484
29668 HWY 62 NORTH RR 2, BANCROFT, ON, K0L 1C0
(613) 332-3437   *SIC* 5511

BANCTEC (CANADA), INC   *p* 666
100 ALLSTATE PKY SUITE 400, MARKHAM, ON, L3R 6H3
(905) 475-6060   *SIC* 7371

BANDIT ENERGY SERVICES   *p* 143
500018 RR21 & HWY 16 WEST, LLOYD-MINSTER, AB, T9V 3C5
(780) 875-8764   *SIC* 4619

BANDSTRA TRANSPORTATION   *p* 251
See MANITOULIN TRANSPORTATION

BANDSTRA TRANSPORTATION SYSTEMS LTD   *p* 269
3394 HWY 16 E, SMITHERS, BC, V0J 2N0
(250) 847-2057   *SIC* 4213

BANFF CARIBOU PROPERTIES LTD   *p* 4
229 BEAR ST SUITE 300, BANFF, AB, T1L 1H8
(403) 762-2642   *SIC* 7011

BANFF LODGING COMPANY   *p* 4
See BANFF CARIBOU PROPERTIES LTD

BANFF PARK LODGE   *p* 4
See FUJI STARLIGHT EXPRESS CO., LTD

BANFF/LAKE LOUISE CENTRE RESERVATIONS   *p* 65
See SUNSHINE VILLAGE CORPORATION

BANIERE IGA EXTRA, LA   *p* 1255
See SOBEYS CAPITAL INCORPORATED

BANISTER PIPELINE CONSTRUCTION   *p* 1232
See SIMARD-BEAUDRY CONSTRUCTION INC

BANISTER RESEARCH & CONSULTING INC   *p* 91
11223 99 AVE NW, EDMONTON, AB, T5K 0G9
(780) 451-4444   *SIC* 8732

BANK OF CANADA   *p* 815
234 WELLINGTON ST, OTTAWA, ON, K1A 0G9
(613) 782-8111   *SIC* 6011

BANK OF CHINA (CANADA) LTD   *p* 903
50 MINTHORN BLVD SUITE 600, THORN-HILL, ON, L3T 7X8
(905) 771-6886   *SIC* 6021

BANK OF MONTREAL   *p* 236
610 SIXTH ST SUITE 125, NEW WESTMIN-STER, BC, V3L 3C2
(604) 665-3770   *SIC* 6021

BANK OF MONTREAL   *p* 527
865 HARRINGTON CRT, BURLINGTON, ON, L7N 3P3
SIC 6021

BANK OF MONTREAL   *p* 877
3550 PHARMACY AVE, SCARBOROUGH, ON, M1W 3Z3
(416) 490-4300   *SIC* 6021

BANK OF MONTREAL   *p* 1187
119 RUE SAINT-JACQUES, MONTREAL, QC, H2Y 1L6
(514) 877-7373   *SIC* 6021

BANK OF MONTREAL HOLDING INC *p* 985
100 KING ST W 21ST FLOOR, TORONTO, ON, M5X 1A1
(416) 359-5003   *SIC* 6211

BANK OF MONTREAL INSTITUTE FOR LEARNING   *p* 877
See BANK OF MONTREAL

BANK OF MONTREAL SECURITIES CANADA   *p* 986
See BMO NESBITT BURNS INC

BANK OF NOVA SCOTIA TRUST COMPANY, THE   *p* 937

1 QUEEN ST E SUITE 1200, TORONTO, ON, M5C 2W5
(416) 866-7829   *SIC* 6021

BANK OF NOVA SCOTIA, THE   *p* 302
409 GRANVILLE ST UNIT 700, VANCOU-VER, BC, V6C 1T2
(604) 630-4000   *SIC* 6021

BANK OF NOVA SCOTIA, THE   *p* 302
815 HASTINGS ST W SUITE 300, VAN-COUVER, BC, V6C 1B4
SIC 6021

BANK OF NOVA SCOTIA, THE   *p* 377
200 PORTAGE AVE, WINNIPEG, MB, R3C 2R7
(204) 985-3011   *SIC* 6021

BANK OF NOVA SCOTIA, THE   *p* 948
44 KING ST W SCOTIA PLAZA, TORONTO, ON, M5H 1H1
(416) 866-6161   *SIC* 6733

BANK OF NOVA SCOTIA, THE   *p* 1193
1002 RUE SHERBROOKE O BUREAU 200, MONTREAL, QC, H3A 3L6
(514) 499-5432   *SIC* 6021

BANK OF NOVA SCOTIA, THE   *p* 1193
1002 RUE SHERBROOKE O BUREAU 600, MONTREAL, QC, H3A 3L6
(514) 287-3600   *SIC* 6021

BANK OF NOVA SCOTIA, THE   *p* 1214
1922 RUE SAINTE-CATHERINE O BU-REAU 300, MONTREAL, QC, H3H 1M4
SIC 6021

BANK STREET KIA   *p* 597
See 1364279 ONTARIO INC

BANK STREET MAZDA   *p* 597
See DIRECT MOTOR COMPANY LTD

BANKERS PETROLEUM LTD   *p* 44
3700-888 3 ST SW, CALGARY, AB, T2P 5C5
(403) 513-2699   *SIC* 1382

BANKING TRANSFORMED   *p* 1213
See CGI INC

BANLIEUE FORD INC   *p* 1292
344 RUE LAURIER, SAINT-APOLLINAIRE, QC, G0S 2E0
(418) 881-2323   *SIC* 5511

BANNERMAN ENTERPRISES INC   *p* 213
9820 93 AVE, FORT ST. JOHN, BC, V1J 6J8
(250) 787-1142   *SIC* 5531

BANNERMAN, BOB CHRYSLER DODGE & JEEP   *p* 778
See BANNERMAN, BOB MOTORS LIM-ITED

BANNERMAN, BOB MOTORS LIMITED   *p* 778
888 DON MILLS RD, NORTH YORK, ON, M3C 1V6
(416) 444-0888   *SIC* 5511

BANNESTER, DR LESLIE R   *p* 516
221 BRANT AVE SUITE 1, BRANTFORD, ON, N3T 3J2
(519) 753-8666   *SIC* 8011

BANNEX PARTNERSHIP   *p* 167
6610 50 AVE, STETTLER, AB, T0C 2L2
(403) 742-4737   *SIC* 5211

BANNIERE ESSO   *p* 1233
See COUCHE-TARD INC

BANNISTER CHEVROLET BUICK GMC VERNON INC   *p* 331
4703 27 ST, VERNON, BC, V1T 4Y8
(250) 542-2647   *SIC* 5511

BANNISTER GM VERNON   *p* 331
See BANNISTER CHEVROLET BUICK GMC VERNON INC

BANQ   *p* 1175
See BIBLIOTHEQUE ET ARCHIVES NA-TIONALES DU QUEBEC

BANQ   *p* 1284
See BIBLIOTHEQUE ET ARCHIVES NA-TIONALES DU QUEBEC

BANQUE CAPITAL ONE (SUCCURSALE CANADIENNE)   *p* 1217
See CAPITAL ONE BANK (CANADA BRANCH)

BANQUE DE DEVELOPPEMENT DU CANADA   *p* 1201

5 PLACE VILLE-MARIE BUREAU 400, MONTREAL, QC, H3B 5E7
(514) 283-5904   *SIC* 6141

BANQUE LAURENTIENNE DU CANADA *p* 1213
1360 BOUL RENE-LEVESQUE O BUREAU 600, MONTREAL, QC, H3G 0E5
(514) 284-4500   *SIC* 6712

BANQUE NATIONALE ASSURANCES   *p* 1201
See BANQUE NATIONALE DU CANADA

BANQUE NATIONALE DU CANADA   *p* 44
407 8 AVE SW SUITE 1000, CALGARY, AB, T2P 1E5
(403) 294-4917   *SIC* 6021

BANQUE NATIONALE DU CANADA   *p* 44
450 1 ST SW SUITE 2800, CALGARY, AB, T2P 5H1
(403) 266-1116   *SIC* 8741

BANQUE NATIONALE DU CANADA   *p* 985
130 KING ST W SUITE 3200, TORONTO, ON, M5X 2A2
(647) 252-5380   *SIC* 6021

BANQUE NATIONALE DU CANADA *p* 1187
500 PLACE D'ARMES BUREAU 500, MON-TREAL, QC, H2Y 2W3
(514) 394-6642   *SIC* 6021

BANQUE NATIONALE DU CANADA *p* 1201
1100 BOUL ROBERT-BOURASSA BU-REAU 12E, MONTREAL, QC, H3B 3A5
(514) 866-6755   *SIC* 6531

BANQUE NATIONALE DU CANADA *p* 1201
600 RUE DE LA GAUCHETIERE O BU-REAU 4E, MONTREAL, QC, H3B 4L3
(514) 394-4385   *SIC* 6021

BANQUE NATIONALE DU CANADA *p* 1268
333 GRANDE ALLEE E BUREAU 400, QUEBEC, QC, G1R 5W3
(418) 521-6400   *SIC* 6021

BANQUE NATIONALE DU CANADA *p* 1328
1130 BOUL MARCEL-LAURIN, SAINT-LAURENT, QC, H4R 1J7
(514) 332-4220   *SIC* 6021

BANQUE SCOTIA   *p* 948
See BANK OF NOVA SCOTIA, THE

BANRO CORPORATION   *p* 985
100 KING ST W SUITE 7070, TORONTO, ON, M5X 2A1
(416) 366-2221   *SIC* 1041

BANRO INVESTMENT SOLUTIONS CORP *p* 985
100 KING ST W UNIT 5602, TORONTO, ON, M5X 2A2
(416) 948-5271   *SIC* 6282

BANTING MEMORIAL HIGH SCHOOL *p* 476
See SIMCOE COUNTY DISTRICT SCHOOL BOARD, THE

BANTREL CO.   *p* 67
600-1201 GLENMORE TRAIL SW, CAL-GARY, AB, T2V 4Y8
(403) 290-5000   *SIC* 8711

BANTREL CO.   *p* 67
1201 GLENMORE TRAIL SW SUITE 1061, CALGARY, AB, T2V 4Y8
(403) 290-5000   *SIC* 8711

BANTREL CO.   *p* 108
4999 98 AVE NW UNIT 401, EDMONTON, AB, T6B 2X3
(780) 462-5600   *SIC* 8711

BANWELL GARDENS   *p* 1017
3000 BANWELL RD, WINDSOR, ON, N8N 0B3
(519) 735-3204   *SIC* 8051

BANYAN COMMUNITY SERVICES INC   *p* 614
688 QUEENSDALE AVE E UNIT 2B, HAMIL-TON, ON, L8V 1M1
(905) 545-0133   *SIC* 8699

BAP TRUCKING   *p* 498
See 1957444 ONTARIO INC

BAPTIST HOUSING MINISTRIES SOCIETY, THE   *p* 335
1002 VANCOUVER ST SUITE 112, VICTO-RIA, BC, V8V 3V8

(250) 384-1313   *SIC* 8361

BAR BLACK JACK   *p* 1301
See CONSTRUCTIONS LOUISBOURG LTEE

BAR CAPPUCINO   *p* 1159
See STATION MONT-TREMBLANT SOCI-ETE EN COMMANDITE

BAR CHEZ BABE   *p* 1383
See INVESTISSEMENTS BABE INC

BAR DEN FOODS LTD   *p* 219
590 HIGHWAY 33 W UNIT 12, KELOWNA, BC, V1X 6A8
(250) 762-9234   *SIC* 5411

BAR HYDRAULICS INC   *p* 615
1632 UPPER OTTAWA ST, HAMILTON, ON, L8W 3P2
(905) 385-2257   *SIC* 5084

BAR L'EVASION ENR   *p* 1397
See 2166-2440 QUEBEC INC

BAR SPECTACLE LE VIEUX SHACK *p* 1321
See PRODUITS JUPITER INC, LES

BAR SUITE 701   *p* 1190
See RESTAURANT AIX INC

BAR-B-DEE FARMS LTD   *p* 496
GD, BORNHOLM, ON, N0K 1A0
(519) 347-2966   *SIC* 5153

BARBARIAN SPORTSWEAR INC   *p* 642
575 TRILLIUM DR, KITCHENER, ON, N2R 1J9
(519) 895-1932   *SIC* 2329

BARBEQUES GALORE & WOOD FIRE-PLACES, DIV OF   *p* 26
See TRADEX SUPPLY LTD

BARBER GROUP INVESTMENTS INC *p* 601
485 SOUTHGATE DR, GUELPH, ON, N1G 3W6
SIC 5039

BARBER MOTORS (1963) LTD   *p* 1437
1 GOVERNMENT RD, WEYBURN, SK, S4H 0N8
(306) 842-6531   *SIC* 5511

BARBER STEWART MCVITTIE & WAL-LACE INSURANCE BROKERS LTD   *p* 766
6 LANSING SQ SUITE 230, NORTH YORK, ON, M2J 1T5
(416) 493-0050   *SIC* 6411

BARBER-COLLINS SECURITY SERVICES LTD   *p* 1007
245 LABRADOR DR UNIT 1, WATERLOO, ON, N2K 4M8
(519) 745-1111   *SIC* 7381

BARBO, DIV DE   *p* 1280
See ALFRED CLOUTIER LIMITEE

BARBOUR LIVING HERITAGE VILLAGE *p* 427
GD, NEWTOWN, NL, A0G 3L0
(709) 536-3220   *SIC* 8699

BARBOUR'S FOOD MARKET LIMITED *p* 544
6708 35 HWY RR 1, COBOCONK, ON, K0M 1K0
(705) 454-1414   *SIC* 5411

BARCLAY SALES LTD   *p* 246
1441 KEBET WAY, PORT COQUITLAM, BC, V3C 6L3
(604) 945-1010   *SIC* 5074

BARCO MATERIALS HANDLING LIMITED *p* 848
24 KERR CRES SUITE 3, PUSLINCH, ON, N0B 2J0
(519) 763-1037   *SIC* 2426

BARCOL DOOR LTD   *p* 92
14820 YELLOWHEAD TRAIL NW, EDMON-TON, AB, T5L 3C5
(780) 452-7140   *SIC* 5211

BARCOL DOORS & WINDOWS   *p* 92
See BARCOL DOOR LTD

BARD CANADA INC   *p* 796
2715 BRISTOL CIR UNIT 1, OAKVILLE, ON, L6H 6X5
(289) 291-8000   *SIC* 3841

BARDON SUPPLIES LIMITED   *p* 490

405 COLLEGE ST E, BELLEVILLE, ON, K8N 4Z6
(613) 966-5643   *SIC* 5074
BARE SPORTS CANADA LTD   *p* 191
3711 NORTH FRASER WAY SUITE 50, BURNABY, BC, V5J 5J2
(604) 235-2630   *SIC* 3069
BARETTE BERNARD   *p* 1104
See BARETTE BERNARD - ENERFLAMME INC
BARETTE BERNARD - ENERFLAMME INC *p* 1104
37 RUE DE VALCOURT, GATINEAU, QC, J8T 8G9
(819) 243-0143   *SIC* 4961
BARETTE BERNARD - ENERFLAMME INC *p* 1104
36 RUE DE VARENNES BUREAU 1, GATINEAU, QC, J8T 0B6
(819) 243-0143   *SIC* 1711
BARFITT BROS. HARDWARE (AURORA) LTD   *p* 480
289 WELLINGTON ST E, AURORA, ON, L4G 6H6
(905) 727-4751   *SIC* 5251
BARGAIN GIANT STORES   *p* 1231
See MAGASINS HART INC
BARGAIN SHOP, THE   *p* 689
See RED APPLE STORES INC
BARIATRIX NUTRITION INC   *p* 1127
4905 RUE FAIRWAY, LACHINE, QC, H8T 1B7
(514) 633-7455   *SIC* 5499
BARIL ELECTRIQUE   *p* 1398
See OUTIL MAG INC
BARIL FORD LINCOLN INC   *p* 1311
6875 BOUL LAURIER O, SAINT-HYACINTHE, QC, J2S 9A5
(514) 454-7070   *SIC* 5511
BARIL MANUFACTURIER INC   *p* 1384
579 BOUL SAINTE-MADELEINE, TROIS-RIVIERES, QC, G8T 9J8
(819) 693-3871   *SIC* 5074
BARKERVILLE GOLD MINES LTD   *p* 948
155 UNIVERSITY AVE SUITE 1410, TORONTO, ON, M5H 3B7
(416) 775-3671   *SIC* 1041
BARKMAN CONCRETE LTD   *p* 358
152 BRANDT ST, STEINBACH, MB, R5G 0R2
(204) 326-3445   *SIC* 5032
BARLBOROUGH BUSINESS ENTERPRISES LTD   *p* 161
192 ORDZE AVE, SHERWOOD PARK, AB, T8B 1M6
(780) 449-1616   *SIC* 6712
BARLEY MILL BREW PUB & SPORTS BISTRO   *p* 243
See BARLEY MILL PUB LTD, THE
BARLEY MILL PUB LTD, THE   *p* 243
2460 SKAHA LAKE RD, PENTICTON, BC, V2A 6E9
(250) 493-8000   *SIC* 5921
BARN, THE   *p* 614
See METRO RICHELIEU INC
BARNABE & SAURETTE INSURANCE BROKERS   *p* 351
See B S I INSURANCE BROKERS LTD
BARNABE KIA   *p* 1315
See GESTION GREGOIRE INC
BARNABE MAZDA   *p* 1315
See GESTIONS J.B. GREGOIRE INC
BARNABE MAZDA DE BROSSARD   *p* 1069
See INVESTISSEMENTS J.B. GREGOIRE INC
BARNABE NISSAN DE CHATEAUGUAY INC   *p* 1076
187 BOUL SAINT-JEAN-BAPTISTE, CHATEAUGUAY, QC, J6K 3B4
(450) 691-9541   *SIC* 5511
BARNES & CASTLE   *p* 788
See BENIX & CO. INC
BARNES COMMUNICATIONS INC   *p* 941

1 YONGE ST SUITE 1504, TORONTO, ON, M5E 1E5
(416) 367-5000   *SIC* 6282
BARNES J.D., LIMITED   *p* 667
140 RENFREW DR SUITE 100, MARKHAM, ON, L3R 6B3
(905) 477-3600   *SIC* 8713
BARNES WHEATON CHEVROLET CADILLAC LTD   *p* 196
46125 OLDS DR, CHILLIWACK, BC, V2P 0B5
(604) 792-1391   *SIC* 5511
BARNES, D.F. LIMITED   *p* 432
22 SUDBURY ST, ST. JOHN'S, NL, A1E 2V1
(709) 579-5041   *SIC* 3441
BARNETT, WINNIFRED MARY KAY CONSULTANT   *p* 658
185 HUNT CLUB DR, LONDON, ON, N6H 3Y8
(519) 471-7227   *SIC* 5961
BARNEY RIVER INVESTMENTS LIMITED *p* 771
4576 YONGE ST SUITE 300, NORTH YORK, ON, M2N 6N4
(416) 620-7200   *SIC* 6513
BARNIM HOLDINGS INC   *p* 520
593771 HWY 59, BURGESSVILLE, ON, N0J 1C0
(519) 424-9865   *SIC* 5014
BARNSTON ISLAND HERB CORPORATION   *p* 281
148 BARNSTON ISLAND, SURREY, BC, V4N 4R1
(604) 581-8017   *SIC* 5159
BAROMETER CAPITAL MANAGEMENT INC   *p* 959
1 UNIVERSITY AVE SUITE 1800, TORONTO, ON, M5J 2P1
(416) 775-3080   *SIC* 6211
BARON INSURANCE AGENCIES GROUP INC   *p* 331
5301 25 AVE SUITE 119, VERNON, BC, V1T 9R1
(250) 545-6565   *SIC* 6411
BARON INSURANCE BROKER GROUP *p* 331
See BARON INSURANCE AGENCIES GROUP INC
BARON OILFIELD SUPPLY   *p* 131
9515 108 ST, GRANDE PRAIRIE, AB, T8V 5R7
(780) 532-5661   *SIC* 5084
BARON SPORTS   *p* 1133
See SAIL PLEIN AIR INC
BARONET INC   *p* 1359
234 AV BARONET, SAINTE-MARIE, QC, G6E 2R1
(418) 209-1009   *SIC* 2511
BARR-AG LTD   *p* 151
5837 IMPERIAL DR, OLDS, AB, T4H 1G6
(403) 507-8660   *SIC* 5191
BARRA HOLDINGS INC   *p* 907
285 MEMORIAL AVE, THUNDER BAY, ON, P7B 6H4
(807) 345-6564   *SIC* 6712
BARRACUDA HEATING SERVICE LTD   *p* 450
152 HOLLAND RD, FLETCHERS LAKE, NS, B2T 1A1
(902) 576-3020   *SIC* 1711
BARRCANA HOMES INC   *p* 4
59504 RANGE RD 32, BARRHEAD, AB, T7N 1A4
(780) 305-0505   *SIC* 2452
BARRDAY PROTECTIVE SOLUTIONS *p* 537
See BARRDAY, INC
BARRDAY, INC   *p* 537
260 HOLIDAY INN DR, CAMBRIDGE, ON, N3C 4E8
(519) 621-3620   *SIC* 2299
BARREAU DU HAUT CANADA   *p* 953

See LAW SOCIETY OF UPPER CANADA, THE
BARREAU DU QUEBEC, LE   *p* 1187
445 BOUL SAINT-LAURENT BUREAU 100, MONTREAL, QC, H2Y 3T8
(514) 954-3400   *SIC* 8621
BARRETT CORPORATION   *p* 419
300 LOCKHART MILL RD, WOODSTOCK, NB, E7M 6B9
(506) 328-8853   *SIC* 5091
BARRETT HIDES INC   *p* 486
75 WELHAM RD, BARRIE, ON, L4N 8Y3
(705) 734-9905   *SIC* 5159
BARRETTE REMAN   *p* 1317
See BARRETTEBOIS INC
BARRETTE-CHAPAIS LTEE   *p* 1317
583 CH DU GRAND-BERNIER N, SAINT-JEAN-SUR-RICHELIEU, QC, J3B 8K1
(450) 357-7000   *SIC* 2421
BARRETTEBOIS INC   *p* 1317
583 CH DU GRAND-BERNIER N, SAINT-JEAN-SUR-RICHELIEU, QC, J3B 8K1
(450) 357-7000   *SIC* 2511
BARRHAVEN CHRYSLER DODGE JEEP RAM   *p* 835
See MOTOR WORKS ONE HOLDINGS INC
BARRHAVEN MAZDA   *p* 835
See MOTOR WORKS TWO HOLDINGS INC
BARRHAVEN SOBEYS   *p* 751
See 1470341 ONTARIO INC
BARRHEAD COMPOSITE HIGH SCHOOL *p* 4
See PEMBINA HILLS REGIONAL DIVISION 7
BARRHEAD IGA   *p* 167
See FRESON MARKET LTD
BARRICK GOLD CORPORATION   *p* 959
161 BAY ST SUITE 3700, TORONTO, ON, M5J 2S1
(416) 861-9911   *SIC* 1041
BARRIE AUTO AUCTION LTD   *p* 486
434 TIFFIN ST, BARRIE, ON, L4N 9W8
(705) 725-8183   *SIC* 5012
BARRIE CENTRAL COLLEGIATE INSTITUTE   *p* 488
See SIMCOE COUNTY DISTRICT SCHOOL BOARD, THE
BARRIE FORD   *p* 486
55 MAPLEVIEW DR W, BARRIE, ON, L4N 9H7
(705) 737-2310   *SIC* 5511
BARRIE HARLEY-DAVIDSON   *p* 485
See 1235054 ONTARIO LIMITED
BARRIE HONDA AUTO SALES   *p* 487
See JOHNSTON, KERV MOTORS (1996) LTD
BARRIE MEMORIAL HOSPITAL FOUNDATION   *p* 1113
10 RUE KING BUREAU 200, HUNTINGDON, QC, J0S 1H0
(450) 829-3877   *SIC* 8322
BARRIE MINOR BASEBALL ASSOCIATION *p* 486
14 BROADMOOR AVE, BARRIE, ON, L4N 3M9
(705) 726-1441   *SIC* 8699
BARRIE NATIONAL PINES GOLF & COUNTRY CLUB   *p* 484
GD STN MAIN, BARRIE, ON, L4M 4S8
(705) 431-7000   *SIC* 7997
BARRIE NORTH COLLEGIATE   *p* 485
See SIMCOE COUNTY DISTRICT SCHOOL BOARD, THE
BARRIE RECREATION LTD   *p* 486
65 HART DR, BARRIE, ON, L4N 5M3
(705) 733-2280   *SIC* 5551
BARRIE WELDING & MACHINE (1974) LIMITED   *p* 486
39 ANNE ST S, BARRIE, ON, L4N 2C7

(705) 726-1444   *SIC* 3599
BARRINGTON CONSULTING GROUP INCORPORATED, THE   *p* 452
1326 BARRINGTON ST, HALIFAX, NS, B3J 1Z1
(902) 491-4462   *SIC* 8741
BARRINGTON MARKET SUPERSTORE   *p* 451
See ATLANTIC WHOLESALERS LTD
BARRON POULTRY LIMITED   *p* 477
7470 COUNTY ROAD 18, AMHERSTBURG, ON, N9V 2Y7
(519) 726-5250   *SIC* 2015
BARROW SAFETY SERVICES INC   *p* 136
889 SWITZER DR, HINTON, AB, T7V 1V1
(780) 865-7763   *SIC* 8748
BARRY CALLEBAUT CANADA INC *p* 1311
2950 RUE NELSON, SAINT-HYACINTHE, QC, J2S 1Y7
(450) 774-9131   *SIC* 2066
BARRY GROUP   *p* 394
See BARRY GROUP INC
BARRY GROUP INC   *p* 394
12 ALLEE FRIGAULT, ANSE-BLEUE, NB, E8N 2J2
  SIC 5421
BARRY GROUP INC   *p* 421
GD, CATALINA, NL, A0C 1J0
(709) 469-2849   *SIC* 5093
BARRY GROUP INC   *p* 421
1 MASONIC TERRACE, CLARENVILLE, NL, A5A 1N2
(709) 466-7186   *SIC* 2092
BARRY GROUP INC   *p* 422
415 GRIFFIN DR, CORNER BROOK, NL, A2H 3E9
(709) 785-7387   *SIC* 5146
BARRY GROUP INC   *p* 423
GD, DOVER, NL, A0G 1X0
(709) 537-5888   *SIC* 2091
BARRY PHARMACY LTD   *p* 400
1040 PROSPECT ST SUITE 172, FREDERICTON, NB, E3B 3C1
(506) 451-1567   *SIC* 5912
BARRY PHILLIPS DRUGS LIMITED   *p* 572
3010 BLOOR ST W, ETOBICOKE, ON, M8X 1C2
(416) 234-0136   *SIC* 5912
BARRY'S BAY CUSTOM WOODWORKING AND BUILDERS' SUPPLY LTD   *p* 489
306 JOHN ST, BARRYS BAY, ON, K0J 1B0
(613) 756-2794   *SIC* 5211
BARRY'S BAY DAIRY LTD   *p* 489
15 DUNN ST, BARRYS BAY, ON, K0J 1B0
(613) 756-2018   *SIC* 5143
BARRY'S BAY HOME HARDWARE BUILDING CENTRE   *p* 489
See BARRY'S BAY CUSTOM WOODWORKING AND BUILDERS' SUPPLY LTD
BARRY'S BAY METRO   *p* 489
28 BAY ST, BARRYS BAY, ON, K0J 1B0
(613) 756-7097   *SIC* 5411
BARRY, ART FORD SALES LTD   *p* 139
8012 SPARROW CRES, LEDUC, AB, T9E 7G1
(780) 986-1100   *SIC* 5511
BARRY, D F & ASSOCIATES INC   *p* 445
7 MELLOR AVE UNIT 12, DARTMOUTH, NS, B3B 0E8
(902) 468-9001   *SIC* 7389
BARRYMORE FURNITURE CO. LTD   *p* 788
1168 CALEDONIA RD, NORTH YORK, ON, M6A 2W5
(416) 532-2891   *SIC* 2512
BARTECH GROUP, THE   *p* 704
See BARTECH TECHNICAL SERVICES OF CANADA, LTD
BARTECH TECHNICAL SERVICES OF CANADA, LTD   *p* 704
160 TRADERS BLVD E SUITE 112, MISSISSAUGA, ON, L4Z 3K7
(905) 502-9914   *SIC* 7361

▲ Public Company   ■ Public Company Family Member   **HQ** Headquarters   **BR** Branch   **SL** Single Location

BARTEK INGREDIENTS INC   p 891
421 SEAMAN ST, STONEY CREEK, ON, L8E 3J4
(905) 662-1127   SIC 2869

BARTEL BULK FREIGHT INC   p 352
405 STAMPEDE DR, MORRIS, MB, R0G 1K0
(204) 746-2053   SIC 4213

BARTEL FREIGHT   p 352
See BARTEL BULK FREIGHT INC

BARTELSE HOLDINGS LIMITED   p 535
162 SAVAGE DR, CAMBRIDGE, ON, N1T 1S4
(519) 622-2500   SIC 2048

BARTERPAY INC   p 891
102-1040 SOUTH SERVICE RD, STONEY CREEK, ON, L8E 6G3
(905) 777-0660   SIC 7389

BARTEX   p 1302
See TRI-TEXCO INC

BARTHOLOMEWS BAR & GRILL   p 336
See EXECUTIVE HOUSE LTD

BARTIN PIPE & PILING SUPPLY LTD.   p 13
6835 GLENMORE TRAIL SE, CALGARY, AB, T2C 2S2
(403) 279-7473   SIC 5051

BARTLE & GIBSON CO LTD   p 83
13475 FORT RD NW, EDMONTON, AB, T5A 1C6
(780) 472-2850   SIC 5074

BARTLETT, H J ELECTRIC INC   p 425
51 DUNDEE AVE UNIT 1, MOUNT PEARL, NL, A1N 4R6
(709) 747-2204   SIC 1731

BARTON AUTO PARTS LIMITED   p 610
367 CANNON ST E UNIT 361, HAMILTON, ON, L8L 2C3
(905) 522-5124   SIC 5013

BARTON RETIREMENT INC   p 615
1430 UPPER WELLINGTON ST, HAMILTON, ON, L9A 5H3
(905) 385-2111   SIC 6513

BARTON SECONDARY SCHOOL   p 614
See HAMILTON-WENTWORTH DISTRICT SCHOOL BOARD, THE

BARTON, BLACK & ROBERTSON INSURANCE SERVICES LTD   p 216
206 SEYMOUR ST UNIT 100, KAMLOOPS, BC, V2C 6P5
(250) 314-6217   SIC 6411

BARTONAIR FABRICATIONS INC   p 610
394 SHERMAN AVE N, HAMILTON, ON, L8L 6P1
(905) 524-2234   SIC 3291

BARTSIDE FARMS   p 1037
3302 HALDIMAND ROAD 9, YORK., ON, N0A 1R0
(905) 692-2766   SIC 5154

BARZOTTI WOODWORKING LIMITED   p 606
2 WATSON RD S, GUELPH, ON, N1L 1E2
(519) 821-3670   SIC 5211

BAS A.Y.K. INC, LES   p 1345
5505 BOUL DES GRANDES-PRAIRIES, SAINT-LEONARD, QC, H1R 1B3
(514) 279-4648   SIC 2252

BASALITE CONCRETE PRODUCTS-VANCOUVER ULC   p 275
8650 130 ST, SURREY, BC, V3W 1G1
(604) 596-3844   SIC 3272

BASE LINE DRAFTING SERVICES INC   p 549
30 PENNSYLVANIA AVE UNIT 3B, CONCORD, ON, L4K 4A5
(905) 660-7017   SIC 7389

BASEBALL EASTON   p 1118
See EASTON HOCKEY CANADA, INC

BASECRETE INC   p 1030
396 CHRISLEA RD, WOODBRIDGE, ON, L4L 8A8
(905) 265-9983   SIC 1542

BASF AGRICULTURAL SPECIALTIES LTD   p 1435
3835 THATCHER AVE, SASKATOON, SK, S7R 1A3
(306) 373-3060   SIC 6331

BASF CANADA INC   p 729
100 MILVERTON DR UNIT 500, MISSISSAUGA, ON, L5R 4H1
(289) 360-1300   SIC 2821

BASF CANADA INC   p 729
100 MILVERTON DR FLOOR 5, MISSISSAUGA, ON, L5R 4H1
(289) 360-1300   SIC 2821

BASF CANADA INC   p 1023
845 WYANDOTTE ST W, WINDSOR, ON, N9A 5Y1
(519) 256-3155   SIC 2851

BASI   p 1392
See BOMBARDIER PRODUITS RECREATIFS INC

BASIC FASHION SERVICE   p 547
See 1422545 ONTARIO INC

BASIC FUN, LTD   p 692
1200 AEROWOOD DR UNIT 27-28, MISSISSAUGA, ON, L4W 2S7
(905) 629-3836   SIC 3944

BASIC PACKAGING INDUSTRIES INC   p 704
5591 MCADAM RD, MISSISSAUGA, ON, L4Z 1N4
(905) 890-0922   SIC 2842

BASIC SPIRIT INCORPORATED   p 465
73 WATER ST, PUGWASH, NS, B0K 1L0
(902) 243-3390   SIC 5199

BASICS OFFICE PRODUCTS LTD   p 538
1040 FOUNTAIN ST N SUITE 1, CAMBRIDGE, ON, N3E 1A3
(519) 653-8984   SIC 5044

BASILIQUE NOTRE-DAME DE MONTREAL   p 1188
See FABRIQUE DE LA PAROISSE NOTRE-DAME DE MONTREAL, LA

BASILIQUE SAINTE-ANNE-DE-BEAUPRE   p 1354
10018 AV ROYALE, SAINTE-ANNE-DE-BEAUPRE, QC, G0A 3C0
(418) 827-3781   SIC 8661

BASIN CONTRACTING LIMITED   p 449
100 BEDROCK LANE, ELMSDALE, NS, B2S 2B1
(902) 883-2235   SIC 1611

BASKIN FINANCIAL SERVICES INC   p 926
95 ST CLAIR AVE W SUITE 900, TORONTO, ON, M4V 1N6
(416) 969-9540   SIC 6282

BASKIN WEALTH SERVICES   p 926
See BASKIN FINANCIAL SERVICES INC

BASQ INTERNATIONAL INC   p 1156
8515 PLACE DEVONSHIRE BUREAU 214, MONT-ROYAL, QC, H4P 2K1
(514) 733-0066   SIC 7389

BASQUE, GILLES SALES LTD   p 404
878 ROUTE 113, INKERMAN, NB, E8P 1C9
(506) 336-4738   SIC 5013

BASS PRO SHOPS CANADA INC   p 549
1 BASS PRO MILLS DR, CONCORD, ON, L4K 5W4
(905) 761-4000   SIC 5941

BASSANO FARMS LTD   p 10
923 28 ST NE, CALGARY, AB, T2A 7X1
(403) 273-4557   SIC 5148

BASSANO GROWERS   p 10
See BASSANO FARMS LTD

BASSE FRERES ALIMENTATION ORIENTALE (2013) INC   p 1235
4555 NORD LAVAL (A-440) O, MONTREAL, QC, H7P 4W6
(450) 781-1255   SIC 5145

BASSE NUTS   p 1235
See BASSE FRERES ALIMENTATION ORIENTALE (2013) INC

BASSETT & WALKER INTERNATIONAL INC   p 932
2 BERKELEY ST SUITE 502, TORONTO, ON, M5A 4J5
(416) 363-7070   SIC 5142

BASSETT DIRECT   p 854
See ROSENEATH DIRECT OPERATING CORPORATION

BASSETT PETROLEUM DISTRIBUTORS LTD   p 435
43013 MACKENZIE HWY, HAY RIVER, NT, X0E 0R9
(867) 874-8500   SIC 5171

BAST TIRECRAFT   p 1006
1 BAST PL, WATERLOO, ON, N2J 4G8
(519) 664-2282   SIC 5531

BAST, PAUL & ASSOCIATES   p 636
625 WABANAKI DR UNIT 4, KITCHENER, ON, N2C 2G3
(519) 893-3500   SIC 8741

BASTILLE, J. M. INC   p 1285
396 RUE TEMISCOUATA BUREAU 744, RIVIERE-DU-LOUP, QC, G5R 2Z2
(418) 862-3346   SIC 5093

BASTILLE, MARTIN INC   p 1285
227 RTE DE L'ANSE-AU-PERSIL, RIVIERE-DU-LOUP, QC, G5R 5Z5
(418) 862-1705   SIC 5051

BAT CANADA   p 1223
See IMPERIAL TOBACCO CANADA LIMITEE

BATCO MANUFACTURING, DIV OF   p 388
See AG GROWTH INTERNATIONAL INC

BATCO-REM   p 1436
201 INDUSTRIAL DR, SWIFT CURRENT, SK, S9H 5R4
SIC 3523

BATEAUX PRINCECRAFT INC   p 1253
725 RUE SAINT-HENRI, PRINCEVILLE, QC, G6L 5C2
(819) 364-5581   SIC 3732

BATEMAN FOODS (1995) LTD   p 83
13504 VICTORIA TRAIL NW, EDMONTON, AB, T5A 5C9
(780) 432-1535   SIC 5411

BATESVILLE CANADA LTD   p 734
2390 ANSON DR, MISSISSAUGA, ON, L5S 1G2
(905) 673-7717   SIC 5087

BATESVILLE CASKET CANADA, DIV OF   p 723
See HILL-ROM CANADA LTD

BATH & BODY WORKS (CANADA) CORP   p 1093
1608 BOUL SAINT-REGIS, DORVAL, QC, H9P 1H6
(514) 684-7700   SIC 5719

BATH & BODY WORKS INC   p 718
5100 ERIN MILLS PKY, MISSISSAUGA, ON, L5M 4Z5
(905) 820-1112   SIC 5719

BATH MILL INC   p 176
2637 DEACON ST, ABBOTSFORD, BC, V2T 6L4
(604) 302-2284   SIC 5099

BATHURST CLARK RESOURCE LIBRARY   p 663
See VAUGHAN PUBLIC LIBRARIES

BATHURST FINE CARS INC   p 394
2300 ST. PETER AVE, BATHURST, NB, E2A 7K2
(506) 548-4569   SIC 5511

BATHURST HONDA   p 394
See BATHURST FINE CARS INC

BATHURST LUMBER, DIV OF   p 396
See FORNEBU LUMBER COMPANY INC

BATHURST, CITY OF   p 394
14 SEAN COUTURIER AVE, BATHURST, NB, E2A 6X2
(506) 549-3300   SIC 7999

BATIMAT   p 649
See EMCO CORPORATION

BATIMENTS CANADA   p 1142
See CANADA BETON ET DECORATIONS INC

BATIMENTS DOMEX, LES   p 1353
See INDUSTRIES HARNOIS INC, LES

BATISE INVESTMENTS LIMITED   p 785
3625 DUFFERIN ST UNIT 503, NORTH YORK, ON, M3K 1N4
(416) 635-7520   SIC 6553

BATISSE COMMERCIALE   p 1401
See 159585 CANADA INC

BATITECH LTEE   p 1378
578 RUE COMMERCIALE N, TEMISCOUATA-SUR-LE-LAC, QC, G0L 1E0
(418) 854-0854   SIC 1521

BATON ROUGE RESTAURANT   p 788
See BOZIKIS FOOD GROUP

BATON ROUGE STEAKHOUSE & BAR   p 1228
See GROUPE RESTAURANTS IMVESCOR INC

BATTERIES ELECTRIQUES QUEBEC   p 1312
See GROUPE MASKA INC

BATTERIES EXPERT LONGUEUIL   p 1144
See VITRERIE LONGUEUIL INC

BATTERY HOTEL & SUITES   p 428
See BATTERY MANAGEMENT INC

BATTERY MANAGEMENT INC   p 428
100 SIGNAL HILL RD, ST. JOHN'S, NL, A1A 1B3
SIC 7011

BATTIST, GERALD TRUCKING LIMITED   p 463
2559 GRANTON RD SUITE 3, NEW GLASGOW, NS, B2H 5C6
(902) 396-1398   SIC 4212

BATTISTELLIS'   p 647
See 1144259 ONTARIO LIMITED

BATTLE RIVER IMPLEMENTS LTD   p 78
4717 38 ST, CAMROSE, AB, T4V 3W9
(780) 672-4463   SIC 5999

BATTLE RIVER REGIONAL DIVISION 31   p 78
5402 48A AVE, CAMROSE, AB, T4V 0L3
(780) 672-6131   SIC 8211

BATTLEFIELD EQUIPMENT RENTAL, DIV OF   p 427
See TOROMONT INDUSTRIES LTD

BATTLEFIELD EQUIPMENT RENTALS   p 893
See TOROMONT INDUSTRIES LTD

BATTLEFIELD GRAPHICS INC   p 521
5355 HARVESTER RD, BURLINGTON, ON, L7L 5K4
(905) 333-4114   SIC 2752

BATTLEFIELD PRESS   p 521
See BATTLEFIELD GRAPHICS INC

BATTLEFORDS AND DISTRICT CO-OPERATIVE LTD   p 1412
9800 TERRITORIAL DR SUITE 1, NORTH BATTLEFORD, SK, S9A 3W6
(306) 445-9800   SIC 5171

BATTLEFORDS CO-OP   p 1412
See BATTLEFORDS AND DISTRICT CO-OPERATIVE LTD

BATTLEFORDS UNION HOSPITAL   p 1412
See GOVERNMENT OF SASKATCHEWAN

BAU-VAL INC   p 1063
210 BOUL DE MONTARVILLE BUREAU 2006, BOUCHERVILLE, QC, J4B 6T3
(514) 875-4270   SIC 1429

BAUER HOCKEY LTD   p 720
6925 CENTURY AVE UNIT 600, MISSISSAUGA, ON, L5N 7K2
(905) 363-3200   SIC 3949

BAUER PARTNERSHIP   p 687
6490 VISCOUNT RD, MISSISSAUGA, ON, L4V 1H3
SIC 6712

BAUMAN, T & W ENTERPRISES INC   p 1030
7835 HIGHWAY 50 UNIT 14 & 15, WOODBRIDGE, ON, L4L 1A5
(905) 264-0080   SIC 5013

BAUMEIER CORPORATION   p 538
1050 FOUNTAIN ST N, CAMBRIDGE, ON,

N3H 4R7
(519) 650-5553   *SIC* 3599
BAUSCH + LOMB   *p* 1362
See SANTE BAUSCH, CANADA INC
BAUSCH HEALTH COMPANIES INC *p* 1361
2150 BOUL SAINT-ELZEAR O, SAINTE-ROSE, QC, H7L 4A8
(514) 744-6792   *SIC* 2834
BAVARIA AUTOHAUS (1997) LTD   *p* 99
18925 STONY PLAIN RD NW, EDMONTON, AB, T5S 2Y4
(780) 484-0000   *SIC* 5511
BAVARIA BMW   *p* 99
See BAVARIA AUTOHAUS (1997) LTD
BAWATING COLLEGIATE & VOCATION SCHOOL   *p* 862
See ALGOMA DISTRICT SCHOOL BOARD
BAXTER CORPORATION   *p* 476
89 CENTRE ST S, ALLISTON, ON, L9R 1J4
(705) 435-6261   *SIC* 5122
BAXTER CORPORATION   *p* 720
7125 MISSISSAUGA RD, MISSISSAUGA, ON, L5N 0C2
(905) 369-6000   *SIC* 2834
BAXTER, BERT TRANSPORT LTD *p* 1406
301 KENSINGTON AVE, ESTEVAN, SK, S4A 2A1
(306) 634-3616   *SIC* 1389
BAXTROM INDEPENDENT GROCERY   *p* 561
31 NINTH ST E, CORNWALL, ON, K6H 6R3
(613) 938-8040   *SIC* 5411
BAY   *p* 146
See HUDSON'S BAY COMPANY
BAY CITY INSURANCE SERVICES LTD   *p* 238
1199 LYNN VALLEY RD SUITE 121, NORTH VANCOUVER, BC, V7J 3H2
(604) 986-1155   *SIC* 6411
BAY FERRIES LIMITED   *p* 1038
94 WATER ST, CHARLOTTETOWN, PE, C1A 1A6
(902) 566-3838   *SIC* 4449
BAY GROWERS INC   *p* 544
828114 GREY ROAD 40, CLARKSBURG, ON, N0H 1J0
(519) 599-7568   *SIC* 5992
BAY HAVEN NURSING HOME INC   *p* 546
499 HUME ST SUITE 18, COLLINGWOOD, ON, L9Y 4H8
(705) 445-6501   *SIC* 8051
BAY HAVEN SENIOR CARE COMMUNITY *p* 546
See BAY HAVEN NURSING HOME INC
BAY HILL CONTRACTING LTD   *p* 278
19122 21 AVE, SURREY, BC, V3Z 3M3
(604) 536-3306   *SIC* 1731
BAY OF QUINTE MUTUAL INSURANCE CO *p* 845
13379 LOYALIST PKY, PICTON, ON, K0K 2T0
(613) 476-2145   *SIC* 6331
BAY ST GEORGE RESIDENTIAL SUPPORT *p* 434
30B ATLANTIC AVE, STEPHENVILLE, NL, A2N 2E9
(709) 643-9762   *SIC* 6531
BAY TRAVEL, THE   *p* 453
See MARITIME TRAVEL INC
BAY, THE   *p* 8
See HUDSON'S BAY COMPANY
BAY, THE   *p* 35
See HUDSON'S BAY COMPANY
BAY, THE   *p* 51
See HUDSON'S BAY COMPANY
BAY, THE   *p* 84
See HUDSON'S BAY COMPANY
BAY, THE   *p* 104
See HUDSON'S BAY COMPANY
BAY, THE   *p* 119
See HUDSON'S BAY COMPANY
BAY, THE   *p* 142
See HUDSON'S BAY COMPANY
BAY, THE   *p* 157

See HUDSON'S BAY COMPANY
BAY, THE   *p* 190
See HUDSON'S BAY COMPANY
BAY, THE   *p* 216
See HUDSON'S BAY COMPANY
BAY, THE   *p* 243
See HUDSON'S BAY COMPANY
BAY, THE   *p* 249
See HUDSON'S BAY COMPANY
BAY, THE   *p* 262
See HUDSON'S BAY COMPANY
BAY, THE   *p* 293
See HUDSON'S BAY COMPANY
BAY, THE   *p* 305
See HUDSON'S BAY COMPANY
BAY, THE   *p* 341
See HUDSON'S BAY COMPANY
BAY, THE   *p* 378
See HUDSON'S BAY COMPANY
BAY, THE   *p* 382
See HUDSON'S BAY COMPANY
BAY, THE   *p* 407
See HUDSON'S BAY COMPANY
BAY, THE   *p* 457
See HUDSON'S BAY COMPANY
BAY, THE   *p* 503
See HUDSON'S BAY COMPANY
BAY, THE   *p* 530
See HUDSON'S BAY COMPANY
BAY, THE   *p* 533
See HUDSON'S BAY COMPANY
BAY, THE   *p* 585
See HUDSON'S BAY COMPANY
BAY, THE   *p* 632
See HUDSON'S BAY COMPANY
BAY, THE   *p* 657
See HUDSON'S BAY COMPANY
BAY, THE   *p* 658
See HUDSON'S BAY COMPANY
BAY, THE   *p* 671
See HUDSON'S BAY COMPANY
BAY, THE   *p* 710
See HUDSON'S BAY COMPANY
BAY, THE   *p* 718
See HUDSON'S BAY COMPANY
BAY, THE   *p* 789
See HUDSON'S BAY COMPANY
BAY, THE   *p* 797
See HUDSON'S BAY COMPANY
BAY, THE   *p* 814
See HUDSON'S BAY COMPANY
BAY, THE   *p* 821
See HUDSON'S BAY COMPANY
BAY, THE   *p* 855
See HUDSON'S BAY COMPANY
BAY, THE   *p* 868
See HUDSON'S BAY COMPANY
BAY, THE   *p* 887
See HUDSON'S BAY COMPANY
BAY, THE   *p* 1155
See HUDSON'S BAY COMPANY
BAY, THE   *p* 1250
See HUDSON'S BAY COMPANY
BAY, THE   *p* 1427
See HUDSON'S BAY COMPANY
BAY-BLOOR RADIO INC   *p* 928
55 BLOOR ST W, TORONTO, ON, M4W 1A5
(416) 967-1122   *SIC* 5731
BAYBRIDGE SENIOR LIVING   *p* 948
See AMICA SENIOR LIFESTYLES INC
BAYCADD SOLUTIONS INC   *p* 828
1296 CARLING AVE, OTTAWA, ON, K1Z 7K8
(613) 298-4918   *SIC* 4899
BAYCOAT LIMITED   *p* 607
244 LANARK ST, HAMILTON, ON, L8E 4B3
(905) 561-0965   *SIC* 3479
BAYCOMP COMPANY   *p* 521
5035 NORTH SERVICE RD, BURLINGTON, ON, L7L 5V2
(905) 332-0991   *SIC* 5162
BAYCOR INDUSTRIES LTD   *p* 44
404 6 AVE SW SUITE 300, CALGARY, AB,

T2P 0R9
(403) 294-0600   *SIC* 6211
BAYCREST CENTRE FOR GERIATRIC CARE   *p* 988
3560 BATHURST ST, TORONTO, ON, M6A 2E1
(416) 785-2500   *SIC* 8069
BAYCREST HOSPITAL   *p* 988
See BAYCREST CENTRE FOR GERIATRIC CARE
BAYER CROPSCIENCE INC   *p* 13
160 QUARRY PARK BLVD SE SUITE 200, CALGARY, AB, T2C 3G3
(403) 723-7400   *SIC* 2879
BAYER CROPSCIENCE INC   *p* 1415
295 HENDERSON DR, REGINA, SK, S4N 6C2
(306) 721-4500   *SIC* 5191
BAYER CROPSCIENCE INC   *p* 1426
5 CLUMBERS HWY 41, SASKATOON, SK, S7K 7E9
(306) 477-9400   *SIC* 5191
BAYER HEALTHCARE   *p* 859
See BAYER INC
BAYER HEALTHCARE, DIV OF   *p* 692
See BAYER INC
BAYER INC   *p* 692
2920 MATHESON BLVD E SUITE 1, MISSISSAUGA, ON, L4W 5R6
(416) 248-0771   *SIC* 5122
BAYER INC   *p* 859
1265 VIDAL ST S, SARNIA, ON, N7T 7M2
(519) 337-8251   *SIC* 2822
BAYLIN TECHNOLOGIES INC   *p* 667
60 COLUMBIA WAY SUITE 205, MARKHAM, ON, L3R 0C9
(416) 805-9127   *SIC* 3661
BAYLIS MEDICAL CANADA   *p* 692
See BAYLIS MEDICALE CIE INC
BAYLIS MEDICALE CIE INC   *p* 692
2645 MATHESON BLVD E, MISSISSAUGA, ON, L4W 5S4
(905) 602-4875   *SIC* 5047
BAYLIS MEDICALE CIE INC   *p* 1338
5959 RTE TRANSCANADIENNE, SAINT-LAURENT, QC, H4T 1A1
(514) 488-9801   *SIC* 5047
BAYMAG INC   *p* 68
10655 SOUTHPORT RD SW SUITE 800, CALGARY, AB, T2W 4Y1
(403) 271-9400   *SIC* 1459
BAYNES SOUND OYSTER LTD   *p* 284
5848 ISLAND HWY, UNION BAY, BC, V0R 3B0
(250) 335-2111   *SIC* 5146
BAYRIDGE SECONDARY SCHOOL   *p* 632
See LIMESTONE DISTRICT SCHOOL BOARD
BAYRIDGE TRANSPORT LTD   *p* 259
9900 RIVER DR, RICHMOND, BC, V6X 3S3
(604) 278-6622   *SIC* 4213
BAYSHORE BROADCASTING CORPORATION   *p* 835
270 9 ST E, OWEN SOUND, ON, N4K 5P5
(519) 376-2030   *SIC* 4832
BAYSHORE HEALTHCARE LTD   *p* 292
See BAYSHORE HEALTHCARE LTD.
BAYSHORE HEALTHCARE LTD   *p* 333
See BAYSHORE HEALTHCARE LTD.
BAYSHORE HEALTHCARE LTD   *p* 385
See BAYSHORE HEALTHCARE LTD.
BAYSHORE HEALTHCARE LTD   *p* 408
See BAYSHORE HEALTHCARE LTD.
BAYSHORE HEALTHCARE LTD   *p* 413
See BAYSHORE HEALTHCARE LTD.
BAYSHORE HEALTHCARE LTD   *p* 456
See BAYSHORE HEALTHCARE LTD.
BAYSHORE HEALTHCARE LTD   *p* 542
See BAYSHORE HEALTHCARE LTD.
BAYSHORE HEALTHCARE LTD   *p* 562
See BAYSHORE HEALTHCARE LTD.
BAYSHORE HEALTHCARE LTD   *p* 614
See BAYSHORE HEALTHCARE LTD.

BAYSHORE HEALTHCARE LTD   *p* 826
See BAYSHORE HEALTHCARE LTD.
BAYSHORE HEALTHCARE LTD   *p* 881
See BAYSHORE HEALTHCARE LTD.
BAYSHORE HEALTHCARE LTD   *p* 884
See BAYSHORE HEALTHCARE LTD.
BAYSHORE HEALTHCARE LTD   *p* 900
See BAYSHORE HEALTHCARE LTD.
BAYSHORE HEALTHCARE LTD   *p* 1022
See BAYSHORE HEALTHCARE LTD.
BAYSHORE HEALTHCARE LTD.   *p* 292
555 12TH AVE W UNIT 410, VANCOUVER, BC, V5Z 3X7
(604) 873-2545   *SIC* 8082
BAYSHORE HEALTHCARE LTD.   *p* 333
1512 FORT ST, VICTORIA, BC, V8S 5J2
(250) 370-2253   *SIC* 8082
BAYSHORE HEALTHCARE LTD.   *p* 385
1700 NESS AVE, WINNIPEG, MB, R3J 3Y1
(204) 943-7124   *SIC* 8049
BAYSHORE HEALTHCARE LTD.   *p* 408
50 DRISCOLL CRES SUITE 201, MONCTON, NB, E1E 3R8
(506) 857-9992   *SIC* 8082
BAYSHORE HEALTHCARE LTD.   *p* 413
600 MAIN ST SUITE C150, SAINT JOHN, NB, E2K 1J5
(506) 633-9588   *SIC* 8082
BAYSHORE HEALTHCARE LTD.   *p* 456
7071 BAYERS RD SUITE 237, HALIFAX, NS, B3L 2C2
(902) 425-7683   *SIC* 8059
BAYSHORE HEALTHCARE LTD.   *p* 542
857 GRAND AVE W SUITE 206, CHATHAM, ON, N7L 4T1
(519) 354-2019   *SIC* 8059
BAYSHORE HEALTHCARE LTD.   *p* 562
112 SECOND ST W, CORNWALL, ON, K6J 1G5
(613) 938-1691   *SIC* 8082
BAYSHORE HEALTHCARE LTD.   *p* 614
755 CONCESSION ST SUITE 100, HAMILTON, ON, L8V 1C4
(905) 523-5999   *SIC* 8082
BAYSHORE HEALTHCARE LTD.   *p* 714
2101 HADWEN RD, MISSISSAUGA, ON, L5K 2L3
(905) 822-8075   *SIC* 8082
BAYSHORE HEALTHCARE LTD.   *p* 826
310 HUNT CLUB RD SUITE 202, OTTAWA, ON, K1V 1C1
(613) 733-4408   *SIC* 8082
BAYSHORE HEALTHCARE LTD.   *p* 881
94 BECKWITH ST N, SMITHS FALLS, ON, K7A 2C1
(613) 283-1400   *SIC* 8082
BAYSHORE HEALTHCARE LTD.   *p* 884
282 LINWELL RD SUITE 205, ST CATHARINES, ON, L2N 6N5
(905) 688-5214   *SIC* 8322
BAYSHORE HEALTHCARE LTD.   *p* 900
2120 REGENT ST SUITE 8, SUDBURY, ON, P3E 3Z9
(705) 523-6668   *SIC* 8082
BAYSHORE HEALTHCARE LTD.   *p* 1022
1275 WALKER RD SUITE 10, WINDSOR, ON, N8Y 4X9
(519) 973-5411   *SIC* 8082
BAYSHORE SPECIALTY RX LTD   *p* 667
233 ALDEN RD, MARKHAM, ON, L3R 3W6
(905) 474-0822   *SIC* 5961
BAYSIDE CHRYSLER DODGE LTD   *p* 394
1374 ST. PETER AVE, BATHURST, NB, E2A 3A5
(506) 546-6606   *SIC* 5511
BAYSIDE MIDDLE SCHOOL   *p* 180
See SCHOOL DISTRICT 63 (SAANICH)
BAYSIDE POWER L.P.   *p* 412
509 BAYSIDE DR, SAINT JOHN, NB, E2J 1B4
(506) 694-1400   *SIC* 4911
BAYTECH PLASTICS INC   *p* 681
16403 HWY 12, MIDLAND, ON, L4R 4L6
(705) 526-7801   *SIC* 3089

BAYTECH PLASTICS INC   *p* 681
320 ELIZABETH ST, MIDLAND, ON, L4R
1Y9
(705) 526-7801   *SIC* 3089
BAYTEX ENERGY CORP   *p* 44
520 3 AVE SW SUITE 2800, CALGARY, AB,
T2P 0R3
(587) 952-3000   *SIC* 1311
BAYVIEW CHRYSLER DODGE LTD   *p* 859
255 INDIAN RD S, SARNIA, ON, N7T 3W5
(519) 336-2189   *SIC* 5511
BAYVIEW CONSTRUCTION LTD   *p* 353
4000 MCGILLIVRAY BLVD, OAK BLUFF,
MB, R4G 0B5
(204) 254-7761   *SIC* 1611
**BAYVIEW FLOWERS (JORDAN STATION)
LTD**   *p* 623
3764 JORDAN RD, JORDAN STATION, ON,
L0R 1S0
(905) 562-7321   *SIC* 5193
BAYVIEW GLEN SCHOOL   *p* 776
See MACMARMON FOUNDATION
BAYVIEW HILL ELEMENTARY SCHOOL   *p*
854
*See YORK REGION DISTRICT SCHOOL
BOARD*
BAYVIEW HOSPITALITY INC   *p* 944
108 CHESTNUT ST, TORONTO, ON, M5G
1R3
(416) 977-5000   *SIC* 7011
BAYVIEW SECONDARY SCHOOL   *p* 856
*See YORK REGION DISTRICT SCHOOL
BOARD*
BAYVIEW TRUCKS & EQUIPMENT LTD   *p*
412
315 MCALLISTER DR, SAINT JOHN, NB,
E2J 2S8
(800) 561-9911   *SIC* 5511
BAYVIEW VILLA NURSING HOME   *p* 769
See EXTENDICARE (CANADA) INC
BAYWEST MANAGEMENT CORPORATION
p 275
13468 77 AVE, SURREY, BC, V3W 6Y3
(604) 591-6060   *SIC* 6531
BAYWOOD ENTERPRISES   *p* 762
See 611421 ONTARIO INC.
BAYWOOD HOMES   *p* 785
See 2069718 ONTARIO LIMITED
BAYWOOD HOMES PARTNERSHIP   *p* 785
1140 SHEPPARD AVE W UNIT 12, NORTH
YORK, ON, M3K 2A2
(416) 633-7333   *SIC* 6552
BAZAAR & NOVELTY   *p* 758
See ARROW GAMES CORPORATION
BAZAAR MARKETING   *p* 887
See 1271591 ONTARIO INC
BB EDUCATION   *p* 1217
See BRAULT & BOUTHILLIER LTEE
BBA INC   *p* 582
10 CARLSON CRT SUITE 420, ETOBI-
COKE, ON, M9W 6L2
(416) 585-2115   *SIC* 8711
BBA INC   *p* 1158
375 BOUL SIR-WILFRID-LAURIER, MONT-
SAINT-HILAIRE, QC, J3H 6C3
(450) 464-2111   *SIC* 8711
BBA INC   *p* 1193
2020 BOUL ROBERT-BOURASSA, MON-
TREAL, QC, H3A 2A5
(514) 866-2111   *SIC* 8711
BBA-TOP CONTROL   *p* 1158
See BBA INC
BBA-TOP CONTROL   *p* 1193
See BBA INC
BBCG   *p* 709
*See BAKER, BERTRAND, CHASSE &
GOGUEN CLAIM SERVICES LIMITED*
BBDO   *p* 928
See BBDO CANADA CORP
BBDO CANADA CORP   *p* 928
2 BLOOR ST W SUITE 3200, TORONTO,
ON, M4W 3E2
(416) 972-1505   *SIC* 7311
BBDO CANADA CORP   *p* 928

2 BLOOR ST W SUITE SUITE 3200,
TORONTO, ON, M4W 3R6
(416) 972-1505   *SIC* 7311
BBE EXPEDITING LTD   *p* 134
1759 35 AVE E, GRANDE PRAIRIE, AB,
T9E 0V6
(780) 890-8611   *SIC* 4731
BBO SERVICES LIMITED PARTNERSHIP *p*
653
380 WELLINGTON ST SUITE 1600, LON-
DON, ON, N6A 5B5
(519) 679-0450   *SIC* 7389
BBS SECURITIES INC   *p* 773
4100 YONGE ST SUITE 506, NORTH
YORK, ON, M2P 2B5
(416) 235-0200   *SIC* 6211
BBT TRANSPORT LTD   *p* 419
1999 CH VAL-DOUCET, VAL-DOUCET, NB,
E8R 1Z5
(506) 764-8004   *SIC* 4731
BBW INTERNATIONAL INC   *p* 71
75 EDGEVALLEY CIR NW, CALGARY, AB,
T3A 4Y9
  SIC 7389
BC AMBULANCE SERVICE   *p* 267
*See EMERGENCY AND HEALTH SER-
VICES COMMISSION*
BC AND YUKON DIVISION, THE   *p* 293
See CANADIAN CANCER SOCIETY
BC ASSURES   *p* 1080
*See BILODEAU COUTURE ASSURANCES
INC*
BC BIOMEDICAL LABORATORIES LTD   *p*
275
7455 130 ST, SURREY, BC, V3W 1H8
(604) 507-5000   *SIC* 8071
BC CANCER AGENCY   *p* 221
See BC CANCER FOUNDATION
BC CANCER FOUNDATION   *p* 221
399 ROYAL AVE, KELOWNA, BC, V1Y 5L3
(250) 712-3900   *SIC* 8069
BC CANCER FOUNDATION   *p* 274
13750 96 AVE, SURREY, BC, V3V 1Z2
(604) 930-2098   *SIC* 8621
**BC CANCER, A PART OF THE PROVIN-
CIAL HEALTH SERVICES AUTHORITY**   *p*
293
*See PROVINCIAL HEALTH SERVICES AU-
THORITY*
**BC CANCER, PART OF THE PROVINCIAL
HEALTH SERVICES AUTHORITY**   *p* 275
*See PROVINCIAL HEALTH SERVICES AU-
THORITY*
**BC CANCER, PART OF THE PROVINCIAL
HEALTH SERVICES AUTHORITY**   *p* 293
*See PROVINCIAL HEALTH SERVICES AU-
THORITY*
**BC CANCER, PART OF THE PROVINCIAL
HEALTH SERVICES AUTHORITY**   *p* 333
*See PROVINCIAL HEALTH SERVICES AU-
THORITY*
**BC CENTRE FOR EXCELLENCE IN HIV
AIDS**   *p* 326
1081 BURRARD ST SUITE 608, VANCOU-
VER, BC, V6Z 1Y6
(604) 806-8477   *SIC* 8732
**BC CHILDREN'S HOSPITAL FOUNDATION
(BCCHF)**   *p* 292
*See BRITISH COLUMBIA'S CHILDREN'S
HOSPITAL FOUNDATION*
**BC CLINICAL AND SUPPORT SERVICES
SOCIETY**   *p* 226
See FRASER HEALTH AUTHORITY
BC CORPS OF COMMISSIONAIRES   *p* 303
*See CANADIAN CORPS OF COMMIS-
SIONAIRES NATIONAL OFFICE, THE*
BC FERRIES   *p* 336
*See BRITISH COLUMBIA FERRY SER-
VICES INC*
BC FRESH VEGETABLES INC   *p* 210
4363 KING ST, DELTA, BC, V4K 0A5
(604) 946-3139   *SIC* 5148
**BC GOVERNMENT AND SERVICE EM-
PLOYEES' UNION**   *p*

188
4925 CANADA WAY, BURNABY, BC, V5G
1M1
(604) 291-9611   *SIC* 8631
**BC GOVERNMENT AND SERVICE EM-
PLOYEES' UNION**   *p*
188
4911 CANADA WAY SUITE 101, BURNABY,
BC, V5G 3W3
(604) 291-9611   *SIC* 8631
BC HYDRO   *p* 297
*See BRITISH COLUMBIA HYDRO AND
POWER AUTHORITY*
BC MAISON D'EDITION   *p* 1397
See BUROPRO CITATION INC
BC NDP   *p* 186
See NEW DEMOCRATIC PARTY OF B.C.
BC PENSION CORPORATION   *p* 334
2995 JUTLAND RD, VICTORIA, BC, V8T
5J9
(250) 356-8548   *SIC* 6371
BC SPCA   *p* 288
*See BRITISH COLUMBIA SOCIETY FOR
THE PREVENTION OF CRUELTY TO ANI-
MALS, THE*
BC STEVENS COMPANY   *p* 208
8188 SWENSON WAY, DELTA, BC, V4G 1J6
(604) 634-3088   *SIC* 5047
BC TREE FRUITS COOPERATIVE   *p* 221
1473 WATER ST, KELOWNA, BC, V1Y 1J6
(250) 470-4200   *SIC* 5148
BC UNDERGROUND   *p* 220
See R 870 HOLDINGS LTD
BC2 GROUPE CONSEIL INC   *p* 1187
85 RUE SAINT-PAUL O BUREAU 300,
MONTREAL, QC, H2Y 3V4
(514) 507-3600   *SIC* 8748
BCA RESEARCH INC   *p* 1193
1002 RUE SHERBROOKE O BUREAU
1600, MONTREAL, QC, H3A 3L6
(514) 499-9550   *SIC* 6282
BCAA INSURANCE   *p* 188
*See BRITISH COLUMBIA AUTOMOBILE
ASSOCIATION*
BCB CORPORATE SERVICES LTD   *p* 241
1000 14TH ST W UNIT 100, NORTH VAN-
COUVER, BC, V7P 3P3
(778) 340-1060   *SIC* 8741
BCC HOLDINGS INC   *p* 67
1912 13 ST SW, CALGARY, AB, T2T 3P6
(403) 617-0806   *SIC* 6712
BCE INC   *p* 1395
1 CARREFOUR ALEXANDER-GRAHAM-
BELL BUREAU A-8-1, VERDUN, QC, H3E
3B3
(888) 932-6666   *SIC* 4899
BCF CAPITAL S.E.N.C   *p* 1201
1100 BOUL RENE-LEVESQUE O BUREAU
2500, MONTREAL, QC, H3B 5C9
(514) 397-8500   *SIC* 8111
BCF INVESTMENTS INC   *p* 208
9829 RIVER RD, DELTA, BC, V4G 1B4
(604) 583-3474   *SIC* 2091
BCG LOGISTICS (2000) INC   *p* 803
1300 SOUTH SERVICE RD W, OAKVILLE,
ON, L6L 5T7
(905) 238-3444   *SIC* 4731
BCG LOGISTICS GROUP   *p* 803
See BCG LOGISTICS (2000) INC
BCGEU   *p* 188
*See BC GOVERNMENT AND SERVICE
EMPLOYEES' UNION*
BCIMC   *p* 336
*See BRITISH COLUMBIA INVESTMENT
MANAGEMENT CORPORATION*
BCIMC REALTY CORPORATION   *p* 334
2950 JUTLAND RD UNIT 300, VICTORIA,
BC, V8T 5K2
(778) 410-7100   *SIC* 6531
BCIT   *p* 188
*See BRITISH COLUMBIA INSTITUTE OF
TECHNOLOGY, THE*
BCM INSURANCE COMPANY   *p* 1012
See BERTIE AND CLINTON MUTUAL IN-

SURANCE COMPANY
BCMEA   *p* 294
*See BRITISH COLUMBIA MARITIME EM-
PLOYERS ASSOCIATION*
BCNU   *p* 184
See BRITISH COLUMBIA NURSES UNION
BCOM COMPUTER CENTRE INC   *p* 105
15051 118 AVE NW, EDMONTON, AB, T5V
1H9
(780) 481-8855   *SIC* 5734
BCP   *p* 1184
See PUBLICIS CANADA INC
BCP CONSTRUCTION   *p* 169
See 825209 ALBERTA LTD
BCP LTEE   *p* 1185
3530 BOUL SAINT-LAURENT BUREAU
300, MONTREAL, QC, H2X 2V1
(514) 285-0077   *SIC* 7311
BCP PLUMBING SUPPLIES, DIV OF   *p* 385
See ROBINSON, B.A. CO. LTD
BCP REPUTATION   *p* 1185
See BCP LTEE
BCR   *p* 142
See BRIDGE COUNTY RACEWAY LTD
BD - CANADA   *p* 720
See BECTON DICKINSON CANADA INC
BD APD INC   *p* 1167
3075 RUE DE ROUEN, MONTREAL, QC,
H1W 3Z2
(514) 528-8877   *SIC* 5149
BD BIOSCIENCES   *p* 720
2280 ARGENTIA RD, MISSISSAUGA, ON,
L5N 6H8
  SIC 5047
BD CANADA LTD   *p* 311
1100 MELVILLE ST UNIT 210, VANCOU-
VER, BC, V6E 4A6
(604) 296-3500   *SIC* 5461
BD DIAGNOSTIC   *p* 1266
See GENEOHM SCIENCES CANADA INC
BD DIAGNOSTICS   *p* 1267
See INFECTIO DIAGNOSTIC INC
BD DIESEL PERFORMANCE   *p* 174
See BD ENGINE BRAKE INC
BD ENGINE BRAKE INC   *p* 174
33541 MACLURE RD, ABBOTSFORD, BC,
V2S 7W2
(604) 853-6096   *SIC* 3465
BDA INC   *p* 570
12 DRUMMOND ST SUITE 1, ETOBICOKE,
ON, M8V 1Y8
(416) 251-1757   *SIC* 1542
BDC   *p* 1201
*See BANQUE DE DEVELOPPEMENT DU
CANADA*
BDI CANADA INC   *p* 737
6235 TOMKEN RD, MISSISSAUGA, ON,
L5T 1K2
(905) 238-3392   *SIC* 5085
BDI DISTRIBUTION   *p* 1045
See BEN DESHAIES INC
BDL   *p* 102
See MTE LOGISTIX EDMONTON INC
BDO CANADA   *p* 667
See BDO CANADA LLP
BDO CANADA & ASSOCIATES LTD *p* 937
36 TORONTO ST SUITE 600, TORONTO,
ON, M5C 2C5
(416) 369-3100   *SIC* 8721
BDO CANADA INC   *p* 302
925 GEORGIA ST W SUITE 600, VANCOU-
VER, BC, V6C 3L2
(604) 688-5421   *SIC* 8721
BDO CANADA LIMITED   *p* 527
3115 HARVESTER RD SUITE 400,
BURLINGTON, ON, L7N 3N8
(905) 639-9500   *SIC* 8111
BDO CANADA LIMITED   *p* 959
123 FRONT ST W SUITE 1200, TORONTO,
ON, M5J 2M2
(416) 865-0210   *SIC* 8111
BDO CANADA LLP   *p* 44
903 8 AVE SW SUITE 620, CALGARY, AB,
T2P 0P7

(403) 266-5608   *SIC* 8721
BDO CANADA LLP   *p* 302
925 GEORGIA ST W SUITE 600, VANCOUVER, BC, V6C 3L2
(604) 688-5421   *SIC* 8721
BDO CANADA LLP   *p* 377
200 GRAHAM AVE SUITE 700, WINNIPEG, MB, R3C 4L5
(204) 956-7200   *SIC* 8721
BDO CANADA LLP   *p* 527
3115 HARVESTER RD SUITE 400, BURLINGTON, ON, L7N 3N8
(905) 639-9500   *SIC* 8721
BDO CANADA LLP   *p* 667
60 COLUMBIA WAY SUITE 300, MARKHAM, ON, L3R 0C9
(905) 946-1066   *SIC* 8721
BDO CANADA LLP   *p* 709
1 CITY CENTRE DR SUITE 1700, MISSISSAUGA, ON, L5B 1M2
(905) 270-7700   *SIC* 8721
BDO CANADA LLP   *p* 941
20 WELLINGTON ST E SUITE 500, TORONTO, ON, M5E 1C5
(416) 865-0111   *SIC* 8721
BDO CANADA LLP   *p* 969
66 WELLINGTON ST W SUITE 3600, TORONTO, ON, M5K 1H1
(416) 865-0200   *SIC* 8748
BDO CANADA LLP   *p* 1112
289 RUE PRINCIPALE, GRENVILLE, QC, J0V 1J0
SIC 8721
BDO CANADA LLP   *p* 1201
1000 RUE DE LA GAUCHETIERE O BUREAU 200, MONTREAL, QC, H3B 4W5
(514) 931-0841   *SIC* 8721
BDO DUNWOODY   *p* 302
See *BDO CANADA LIMITED*
BDO DUNWOODY   *p* 527
See *BDO CANADA LIMITED*
BDO DUNWOODY   *p* 959
See *BDO CANADA LIMITED*
BDP, ULC   *p* 582
10 CARLSON CRT SUITE 801, ETOBICOKE, ON, M9W 6L2
(905) 602-0200   *SIC* 4731
BDP INTERNATIONAL   *p* 582
See *BDP CANADA, ULC*
BE   *p* 501
See *BRAMPTON ENGINEERING INC*
BE PRESSURE SUPPLY INC   *p* 176
30585 PROGRESSIVE WAY, ABBOTSFORD, BC, V2T 6W3
(604) 850-6662   *SIC* 3589
BEA FISHER CENTRE INC, THE   *p* 143
3514 51 AVE, LLOYDMINSTER, AB, T9V 1C8
(780) 875-3633   *SIC* 8322
BEACH I G A   *p* 920
See *BEACH SUPERMARKETS LIMITED*
BEACH & ASSOCIATES LIMITED   *p* 959
95 WELLINGTON ST W SUITE 1120, TORONTO, ON, M5J 2N7
(416) 368-9680   *SIC* 6411
BEACH GROVE NURSING HOME   *p* 1040
See *PROVINCE OF PEI*
BEACH POINT PROCESSING COMPANY *p* 1042
75 WHARF LANE, MURRAY HARBOUR, PE, C0A 1V0
(902) 962-4340   *SIC* 2091
BEACH SUPERMARKETS LIMITED   *p* 920
2040 QUEEN ST E, TORONTO, ON, M4L 1J4
(416) 694-3011   *SIC* 5411
BEACHCOMBER HOME & LEISURE LTD *p* 331
5309 26 ST, VERNON, BC, V1T 7G4
(250) 542-3399   *SIC* 5021
BEACHCOMBER HOT TUBS GROUP *p* 275
13245 COMBER WAY, SURREY, BC, V3W 5V8
(604) 502-4733   *SIC* 3999

BEACHCOMBER HOT TUBS INC   *p* 275
13245 COMBER WAY, SURREY, BC, V3W 5V8
(604) 591-8611   *SIC* 5091
BEACON COMMUNITY SERVICES   *p* 268
9860 THIRD ST, SIDNEY, BC, V8L 4R2
(250) 658-6407   *SIC* 8699
BEACON HERALD, THE   *p* 895
See *1032451 B.C. LTD*
BEACON INTERNATIONAL DESPATCH LIMITED   *p* 687
2-6300 NORTHWEST DR, MISSISSAUGA, ON, L4V 1J7
(416) 640-0434   *SIC* 4731
BEACON INTERNATIONAL WAREHOUSING LTD   *p* 514
325 WEST ST SUITE B110, BRANTFORD, ON, N3R 3V6
SIC 4731
BEACON LITE LTD   *p* 817
4070 BELGREEN DR, OTTAWA, ON, K1G 3N2
(613) 737-7337   *SIC* 7359
BEACON ROOFING SUPPLY CANADA COMPANY   *p* 1247
13145 RUE PRINCE-ARTHUR, POINTE-AUX-TREMBLES, QC, H1A 1A9
(514) 642-8998   *SIC* 5039
BEACON UNDERWRITING LTD   *p* 329
700 GEORGIA ST W SUITE 1488, VANCOUVER, BC, V7Y 1K8
(604) 685-6533   *SIC* 6331
BEACONSFIELD HIGH SCHOOL   *p* 1054
See *LESTER B. PEARSON SCHOOL BOARD*
BEADERS CHOICE   *p* 1058
See *9106-5235 QUEBEC INC*
BEAIRSTO & ASSOCIATES ENGINEERING LTD   *p* 131
10940 92 AVE, GRANDE PRAIRIE, AB, T8V 6B5
(780) 532-4919   *SIC* 8711
BEAM CANADA INC   *p* 572
3280 BLOOR ST W UNIT 510, ETOBICOKE, ON, M8X 2X3
(416) 849-7300   *SIC* 5182
BEAR CLAW CASINO   *p* 1405
See *SASKATCHEWAN INDIAN GAMING AUTHORITY INC*
BEAR CREEK CONTRACTING LTD   *p* 283
3550 16 HWY E, THORNHILL, BC, V8G 5J3
(250) 635-4345   *SIC* 1629
BEAR SCARE LTD   *p* 5
5905 44 AVE, BEAUMONT, AB, T4X 0J1
(780) 717-0139   *SIC* 8748
BEAR TRAIL   *p* 1016
See *COUPLES RESORT INC*
BEAR, JOHN PONTIAC BUICK CADILLAC LTD   *p* 616
1200 UPPER JAMES ST, HAMILTON, ON, L9C 3B1
(905) 575-9400   *SIC* 5511
BEARD WINTER LLP   *p* 948
130 ADELAIDE ST W SUITE 701, TORONTO, ON, M5H 2K4
(416) 593-5555   *SIC* 8111
BEARDY'S & OKEMASIS WILLOW CREE FIRST NATION EDUCATION AUTHORITY *p* 1405
GD, DUCK LAKE, SK, S0K 1J0
(306) 467-4441   *SIC* 6732
BEARSKIN AIRLINES   *p* 359
See *BEARSKIN LAKE AIR SERVICE LP*
BEARSKIN AIRLINES   *p* 881
See *BEARSKIN LAKE AIR SERVICE LP*
BEARSKIN AIRLINES   *p* 910
See *BEARSKIN LAKE AIR SERVICE LP*
BEARSKIN LAKE AIR SERVICE LP   *p* 359
585 6TH AVE S, STONEWALL, MB, R0C 2Z0
SIC 8299
BEARSKIN LAKE AIR SERVICE LP   *p* 881
7 AIRPORT RD, SIOUX LOOKOUT, ON, P8T 1J6
(807) 737-3473   *SIC* 4522
BEARSKIN LAKE AIR SERVICE LP   *p* 910
1475 WALSH ST W, THUNDER BAY, ON, P7E 4X6
(807) 577-1141   *SIC* 4512
BEARSKIN LAKE AIR SERVICE LP   *p* 910
216 ROUND BLVD SUITE 2, THUNDER BAY, ON, P7E 3N9
(807) 475-0006   *SIC* 4512
BEARSPAW CONTRACTING INC   *p* 212
2200 BALMER DR SUITE 2, ELKFORD, BC, V0B 1H0
SIC 1541
BEARSTONE ENVIRONMENTAL SOLUTIONS INC   *p* 44
435 4 AVE SW SUITE 500, CALGARY, AB, T2P 3A8
(403) 984-9798   *SIC* 4959
BEARTOOTH HOLDINGS LIMITED   *p* 432
689 WATER ST, ST. JOHN'S, NL, A1E 1B5
(709) 726-6932   *SIC* 5147
BEASLEY, WILLIAM ENTERPRISES LIMITED   *p* 959
9 QUEENS QUAY W, TORONTO, ON, M5J 2H3
(416) 203-0405   *SIC* 7996
BEAT 94.5 FM   *p* 291
See *0781337 B.C. LTD*
BEAT GOES ON, THE   *p* 1006
See *1449132 ONTARIO LIMITED*
BEATTIE HOMES LTD   *p* 70
3165 114 AVE SE, CALGARY, AB, T2Z 3X2
SIC 1521
BEATTIE STATIONERY LIMITED   *p* 886
399 VANSICKLE RD SUITE 3056, ST CATHARINES, ON, L2S 3T4
(905) 688-4040   *SIC* 5943
BEATTIE'S BASICS   *p* 886
See *BEATTIE STATIONERY LIMITED*
BEATTY FLOORS LTD   *p* 285
1840 PANDORA ST, VANCOUVER, BC, V5L 1M7
(604) 254-9571   *SIC* 1752
BEATTY FOODS LTD   *p* 473
374 QUEEN ST E, ACTON, ON, L7J 2Y5
(519) 853-9128   *SIC* 5812
BEATTY FOODS LTD   *p* 508
372 MAIN ST N, BRAMPTON, ON, L6V 1P8
(905) 455-2841   *SIC* 5812
BEATTY FOODS LTD   *p* 512
160 SANDALWOOD PKY E, BRAMPTON, ON, L6Z 1Y5
(905) 840-0700   *SIC* 5812
BEAU CADEAU & PANIER PANACHE *p* 1253
See *PANIER & CADEAU INC, LE*
BEAUBOIS GROUP INC   *p* 1304
521 6E AV N, SAINT-GEORGES, QC, G5Y 0H1
(418) 228-5104   *SIC* 2431
BEAUCE AUTO (2000) INC   *p* 1055
405 BOUL RENAULT, BEAUCEVILLE, QC, G5X 1N7
(418) 774-9801   *SIC* 5511
BEAUCE CARNAVAL INC   *p* 1304
1340 BOUL DIONNE, SAINT-GEORGES, QC, G5Y 3V6
(418) 228-8008   *SIC* 7999
BEAUCE DISTRIBUTION T.V.   *p* 1212
See *VIDEOTRON LTEE*
BEAUCE EAU INC   *p* 1353
175 CH DES FONDS, SAINT-VICTOR, QC, G0M 2B0
(418) 588-3289   *SIC* 5149
BEAUCE METAL INC   *p* 1304
11855 35E AV, SAINT-GEORGES, QC, G5Y 5B9
(418) 228-5566   *SIC* 5051
BEAUCHESNE, EDOUARD (1985) INC *p* 1348
3211 RUE DE L'INDUSTRIE, SAINT-MATHIEU-DE-BELOEIL, QC, J3G 4S5
(450) 467-8776   *SIC* 5039
BEAUDEV GESTIONS INC   *p* 1063
102 CH DU TREMBLAY, BOUCHERVILLE, QC, J4B 6Z6
SIC 5947
BEAUDRY & CADRIN INC   *p* 1247
12225 BOUL METROPOLITAIN E, POINTE-AUX-TREMBLES, QC, H1B 5R3
(514) 352-5620   *SIC* 5149
BEAUDRY & LAPOINTE LTEE   *p* 1123
1 111 RTE O BUREAU 1110, LA SARRE, QC, J9Z 1R5
(819) 333-2266   *SIC* 5511
BEAUDRY EQUIPEMENTS LAITIERS   *p* 1347
See *BEAUDRY MORIN INC*
BEAUDRY MORIN INC   *p* 1347
565 RUE PRINCIPALE, SAINT-LEONARD-D'ASTON, QC, J0C 1M0
(819) 399-2403   *SIC* 5084
BEAUDRY, JEAN-PAUL LTEE   *p* 1247
12225 BOUL METROPOLITAIN E, POINTE-AUX-TREMBLES, QC, H1B 5R3
(514) 352-5620   *SIC* 5141
BEAUFIELD RESOURCES INC   *p* 1193
1801 MCGILL COLLEGE AVE BUREAU 950, MONTREAL, QC, H3A 2N4
(514) 842-3443   *SIC* 1041
BEAUGARTE (QUEBEC INC)   *p* 1271
2590 BOUL LAURIER UNITE 150, QUEBEC, QC, G1V 4M6
SIC 5812
BEAUGARTE (QUEBEC) INC   *p* 1271
2600 BOUL LAURIER, QUEBEC, QC, G1V 4W1
SIC 5812
BEAULAC TRANSPORT   *p* 1138
See *DISTRIBUTIONS BEAULAC, CARL INC, LES*
BEAULIEU & LAMOUREUX INC   *p* 1294
283 BOUL SIR-WILFRID-LAURIER, SAINT-BASILE-LE-GRAND, QC, J3N 1M2
(450) 653-1752   *SIC* 5063
BEAULIEU BAKERY LTD   *p* 810
2122 ST. JOSEPH BLVD, ORLEANS, ON, K1C 1E6
(613) 837-2525   *SIC* 5461
BEAULIEU CANADA   *p* 1044
See *COMPAGNIE BEAULIEU CANADA*
BEAULIEU DECOR   *p* 1284
See *BEAULIEU DECOR D'ASTOUS & FRERES INC*
BEAULIEU DECOR D'ASTOUS & FRERES INC   *p* 1284
385 2E RUE E, RIMOUSKI, QC, G5L 2G4
(418) 723-9487   *SIC* 5713
BEAULIEU, CLAUDE SPORT INC   *p* 1352
75 AV DE LA GARE BUREAU E1, SAINT-SAUVEUR, QC, J0R 1R6
(450) 227-8632   *SIC* 5941
BEAULNE & RHEAUME   *p* 1345
See *AGENCE ANDRE BEAULNE LTEE*
BEAUMARCHE INC   *p* 1178
9124 BOUL SAINT-LAURENT, MONTREAL, QC, H2N 1M9
(514) 382-4062   *SIC* 5137
BEAUMARK PROTECTION SERVICES *p* 76
20 COUNTRY HILLS MEWS NW, CALGARY, AB, T3K 4S4
(403) 803-1567   *SIC* 7381
BEAUMONT HUSKY   *p* 5
See *1162095 ALBERTA LTD*
BEAUMONT SOBEYS   *p* 5
See *SOBEYS CAPITAL INCORPORATED*
BEAUMONT STANLEY INC   *p* 322
2125 41ST AVE W, VANCOUVER, BC, V6M 1Z3
(604) 266-9177   *SIC* 5944
BEAUPORT HYUNDAI   *p* 1254
See *AUTOMOBILES ROBERGE LTEE*
BEAUPORT MAZDA   *p* 1254
See *9118-8706 QUEBEC INC*
BEAUPORT NISSAN   *p* 1255

See LOCATION 18E RUE INC
BEAUPRE CAPITALE CHRYSLER INC p
1261
225 RUE DU MARAIS, QUEBEC, QC, G1M
3C8
(418) 687-2604   SIC 5511

BEAUSEJOUR CONSUMERS CO-OPERATIVE LIMITED p
345
605 PARK AVE, BEAUSEJOUR, MB, R0E
0C0
(204) 268-2605   SIC 5171

BEAUSEJOUR HEALTH CENTRE p 345
See NORTH EASTMAN HEALTH ASSOCI-ATION INC

BEAUSEJOUR SHELL p 1391
See RAYMOND BEAUSEJOUR (1989) INC

BEAUSEJOUR TOWN FIRE HALL p 380
1369 ERIN ST, WINNIPEG, MB, R3E 2S7
(204) 792-8627   SIC 7389

BEAUTE STAR BEDARD INC p 1133
1700 RUE FLEETWOOD, LAVAL, QC, H7N
0C6
(450) 967-7827   SIC 5122

BEAUTIFUL PLAINS SCHOOL DIVISION p
353
213 MOUNTAIN AVE, NEEPAWA, MB, R0J
1H0
(204) 476-2387   SIC 8211

BEAUTY EXPRESS CANADA INC p 679
170 DUFFIELD DR SUITE 200, MARKHAM,
ON, L6G 1B5
(905) 258-0684   SIC 7231

BEAUTY SUPPLY WAREHOUSE p 786
See REX BEAUTY INC.

BEAUTY SYSTEMS GROUP (CANADA) INC
p 720
2345 ARGENTIA RD SUITE 102, MISSIS-SAUGA, ON, L5N 8K4
(905) 696-2600   SIC 5087

BEAUTYNEXT GROUP INC p 782
436 LIMESTONE CRES, NORTH YORK,
ON, M3J 2S4
(416) 665-6616   SIC 5122

BEAUTYROCK HOLDINGS INC p 492
3 APPLEWOOD DR SUITE 3, BELLEVILLE,
ON, K8P 4E3
(613) 932-2525   SIC 7389

BEAUVAIS & VERRET INC p 1263
2181 RUE LEON-HARMEL, QUEBEC, QC,
G1N 4N5
(418) 688-1336   SIC 1542

BEAUVAIS LTEE p 1072
264 AV LIBERTE, CANDIAC, QC, J5R 6X1
(514) 871-0226   SIC 5148

BEAUWARD SHOPPING CENTRES LTD p
1301
430 BOUL ARTHUR-SAUVE BUREAU
6010, SAINT-EUSTACHE, QC, J7R 6V7
(450) 473-6831   SIC 6512

BEAUWARD SHOPPING CENTRES LTD p
1311
3200 BOUL LAFRAMBOISE BUREAU 1009,
SAINT-HYACINTHE, QC, J2S 4Z5
(450) 773-8282   SIC 6512

BEAVER AIR SERVICES p 359
See BEAVER AIR SERVICES LIMITED
PARTNERSHIP

BEAVER AIR SERVICES LIMITED PART-NERSHIP p
359
2 GRACE LAKE RD, THE PAS, MB, R9A
1M3
(204) 623-7160   SIC 4512

BEAVER BRAE SECONDARY SCHOOL p
628
See KEEWATIN PATRICIA DISTRICT
SCHOOL BOARD

BEAVER BROOK ANTIMONY MINE INC p
423
GD, GLENWOOD, NL, A0G 2K0
(709) 679-5866   SIC 1099

BEAVER BUS LINES LIMITED p 365
339 ARCHIBALD ST, WINNIPEG, MB, R2J

0W6
(204) 989-7007   SIC 4142

BEAVER CREEK CO-OP ASSN LIMITED p
139
HWY 15 & 831, LAMONT, AB, T0B 2R0
(780) 895-2241   SIC 5171

BEAVER ELECTRICAL MACHINERY LTD p
192
7440 LOWLAND DR, BURNABY, BC, V5J
5A4
(604) 431-5000   SIC 7694

BEAVER ENTERPRISES p 435
See BEAVER ENTERPRISES LIMITED
PARTNERSHIP

BEAVER ENTERPRISES LIMITED PART-NERSHIP p
435
GD, FORT LIARD, NT, X0G 0A0
(867) 770-2203   SIC 1611

BEAVER FASHIONS LIMITED p 1169
3565 RUE JARRY E BUREAU 109, MON-TREAL, QC, H1Z 4K6
(514) 721-1180   SIC 7389

BEAVER HILL AUCTION SERVICES LTD p
169
GD, TOFIELD, AB, T0B 4J0
(780) 662-9384   SIC 5154

BEAVER LODGE p 432
See BROWNING HARVEY LIMITED

BEAVER LUMBER p 899
See CARRINGTONS BUILDING CENTRE
LTD

BEAVER MACHINE CORPORATION p 754
250 HARRY WALKER PKY N UNIT 1, NEW-MARKET, ON, L3Y 7B4
(905) 836-4700   SIC 3581

BEAVER PLASTICS LTD p 1
11581 272 ST, ACHESON, AB, T7X 6E9
(780) 962-4433   SIC 3089

BEAVER TRUCK CENTER p 370
See WINNIPEG EQUIPMENT SALES LTD

BEAVER VALLEY STONE LIMITED p 667
8081 WOODBINE AVE, MARKHAM, ON,
L3R 2P1
(416) 222-2424   SIC 5999

BEAVERLODGE MUNICIPAL HOSPITAL p 5
See GOVERNMENT OF THE PROVINCE
OF ALBERTA

BEAVERS DENTAL p 746
See SYBRON CANADA LP

BEAZLEY CANADA LIMITED p 959
55 UNIVERSITY AVE SUITE 550,
TORONTO, ON, M5J 2H7
(416) 601-2155   SIC 6411

BEBE CONFORT p 1279
See J.M. CLEMENT LTEE

BECHTEL QUEBEC LIMITEE p 1193
1500 BOUL ROBERT-BOURASSA BU-REAU 910, MONTREAL, QC, H3A 3S7
SIC 8711

**BECK, WILSON M INSURANCE SERVICES
INC** p 192
8678 GREENALL AVE SUITE 303, BURN-ABY, BC, V5J 3M6
(604) 437-6200   SIC 6411

BECKLEY FARM LODGE FOUNDATION p
335
530 SIMCOE ST, VICTORIA, BC, V8V 4W4
(250) 381-4421   SIC 8051

BECKLEY FARM LODGE SOCIETY p 335
See BECKLEY FARM LODGE FOUNDA-TION

BECKMAN COULTER CANADA INC p 720
7075 FINANCIAL DR, MISSISSAUGA, ON,
L5N 6V8
(905) 819-1234   SIC 5047

BECTON DICKINSON CANADA INC p 720
2100 DERRY RD W SUITE 100, MISSIS-SAUGA, ON, L5N 0B3
(905) 288-6000   SIC 5047

BECTON DICKINSON CANADA INC p 796
2771 BRISTOL CIR, OAKVILLE, ON, L6H
6R5
SIC 5047

BECTROL INC p 1311
4550 AV BEAUDRY, SAINT-HYACINTHE,
QC, J2S 8A5
(450) 774-1330   SIC 5063

BEDARD, DIV DE p 1111
See SHERMAG IMPORT INC

BEDARD, JACQUES EXCAVATION LIM-ITED p
748
3006 TENTH LINE RD, NAVAN, ON, K4B
1H8
(613) 824-3208   SIC 1794

BEDCO, DIVISION DE GERODON INC p
1084
2305 AV FRANCIS-HUGHES, COTE SAINT-LUC, QC, H7S 1N5
(514) 384-2820   SIC 3499

BEDCOLAB LTEE p 1084
2305 AV FRANCIS-HUGHES, COTE SAINT-LUC, QC, H7S 1N5
(514) 384-2820   SIC 5049

BEDDINGTON HEIGHTS COMMUNITY AS-SOCIATION p
76
375 BERMUDA DR NW, CALGARY, AB, T3K
2J5
(403) 295-8837   SIC 8699

BEDESSEE IMPORTS LTD p 870
2 GOLDEN GATE CRT, SCARBOROUGH,
ON, M1P 3A5
(416) 292-2400   SIC 5142

BEDFORD BIOFUELS INC p 44
510 5 ST SW SUITE 1500, CALGARY, AB,
T2P 3S2
(403) 648-6100   SIC 8748

BEDFORD LIONS CLUB p 439
36 HOLLAND AVE, BEDFORD, NS, B4A
1L9
(902) 835-0862   SIC 8699

BEDFORD, DIV OF p 690
See TIMKEN CANADA LP

BEDONDAINE p 1258
See BENJO INC

BEDWELL VAN LINES LIMITED p 844
1051 TOY AVE, PICKERING, ON, L1W 3N9
(905) 686-0002   SIC 4214

BEE BELL HEALTH BAKERY INC p 112
10416 80 AVE NW, EDMONTON, AB, T6E
5T7
SIC 5461

BEE CLEAN p 112
See B. GINGRAS ENTERPRISES LTD

BEE CLEAN CENTRAL p 368
See CORREIA ENTERPRISES LTD

BEE MAID HONEY LIMITED p 383
625 ROSEBERRY ST, WINNIPEG, MB, R3H
0T4
(204) 786-8977   SIC 5149

BEE-CLEAN p 112
See BEE-CLEAN BUILDING MAINTE-NANCE INCORPORATED

BEE-CLEAN (TORONTO) LTD p 918
2 THORNCLIFFE PARK DR UNIT 22,
TORONTO, ON, M4H 1H2
(416) 410-6181   SIC 7349

BEE-CLEAN BUILDING MAINTENANCE p
918
See BEE-CLEAN (TORONTO) LTD

BEE-CLEAN BUILDING MAINTENANCE IN-CORPORATED p
112
4505 101 ST NW, EDMONTON, AB, T6E
5C6
(780) 435-3355   SIC 7349

BEE-CLEAN BUILDING MAINTENANCE IN-CORPORATED p
1415
1555 MCDONALD ST UNIT A, REGINA, SK,
S4N 6H7
(306) 757-8020   SIC 7349

BEEBE, D LUMBER CO LTD p 747
199 JIM KIMMETT BLVD, NAPANEE, ON,
K7R 3L1
(613) 354-3315   SIC 5251

BEECHGROVE COUNTRY FOODS INC p
866
20 MINUK ACRES, SCARBOROUGH, ON,
M1E 4Y6
(416) 283-8777   SIC 2011

BEECHWOOD AGRI SERVICES INC p 837
123 KING ST, PARKHILL, ON, N0M 2K0
(519) 294-0474   SIC 5153

BEEDIE CONSTRUCTION CO LTD p 188
3030 GILMORE DIVERS, BURNABY, BC,
V5G 3B4
(604) 435-3321   SIC 8741

BEEDIE SCHOOL OF BUSINESS p 309
See SIMON FRASER UNIVERSITY

BEEFEATER MOTOR INN HOTEL p 1406
See SYMONS THE BAKER LTD

BEEFEATERS INC p 866
885 PROGRESS AVE SUITE 318, SCAR-BOROUGH, ON, M1H 3G3
(416) 289-1554   SIC 5147

**BEELAND CO-OPERATIVE ASSOCIATION
LIMITED** p 1437
1101 99 ST, TISDALE, SK, S0E 1T0
(306) 873-2688   SIC 5171

BEEMAID HONEY p 384
See MANITOBA COOPERATIVE HONEY
PRODUCERS LIMITED

BEENOX INC p 1257
305 BOUL CHAREST E BUREAU 700,
QUEBEC, QC, G1K 3H3
(418) 522-2468   SIC 7371

BEER STORE DISTRIBUTION CENTRE p
508
See BREWERS RETAIL INC

BEER STORE, THE p 661
See BREWERS RETAIL INC

BEER STORE, THE p 692
See BREWERS RETAIL INC

BEER STORE, THE p 817
See BREWERS RETAIL INC

BEER STORE, THE p 891
See BREWERS RETAIL INC

BEGHELLI CANADA INC p 667
3900 14TH AVE SUITE 1, MARKHAM, ON,
L3R 4R3
(905) 948-9500   SIC 3646

BEHAN CONSTRUCTION LIMITED p 544
GD LCD MAIN, COBOURG, ON, K9A 4K1
(905) 372-9862   SIC 1623

BEHAVIOUR INSTITUTE p 611
57 YOUNG ST, HAMILTON, ON, L8N 1V1
(905) 570-0777   SIC 8999

BEHAVIOUR INTERACTIF INC p 1182
6666 RUE SAINT-URBAIN, MONTREAL,
QC, H2S 3H1
(514) 843-4484   SIC 7371

**BEHAVIOURAL HEALTH FOUNDATION
INC, THE** p 392
35 DE LA DIGUE AVE, WINNIPEG, MB,
R3V 1M7
(204) 269-3430   SIC 8322

BEHCHO KO DEVELOPMENT CORPORA-TION p
436
25 STANTON PLAZA, YELLOWKNIFE, NT,
X1A 2P3
(867) 920-7288   SIC 5169

BEHLEN INDUSTRIES LP p 346
927 DOUGLAS ST, BRANDON, MB, R7A
7B3
(204) 728-1188   SIC 1541

BEHR CANADA p 10
See BEHR PROCESS CANADA LTD

BEHR PROCESS CANADA LTD p 10
2750 CENTRE AVE NE, CALGARY, AB, T2A
2L3
(403) 273-0226   SIC 5198

BEIERSDORF CANADA INC p 1332
2344 BOUL ALFRED-NOBEL BUREAU
100A, SAINT-LAURENT, QC, H4S 0A4
(514) 956-4330   SIC 5122

BEIGNES M.W.M. INC., LES p 1144
895 RUE SAINT-LAURENT O, LONGUEUIL,
QC, J4K 2V1

(450) 677-6363   *SIC* 5461
BEILY'S PUB & GRILL   *p* 1423
See *101055401 SASKATCHEWAN LTD*
BEISEKER COLONY   *p* 5
See *HUTTERIAN BRETHRAN CHURCH OF BEISEKER*
BEKAR & ASSOCIATES ENTERPRISES LIMITED   *p* 197
45737 LUCKAKUCK WAY, CHILLIWACK, BC, V2R 4E8
(604) 858-4199   *SIC* 5699
BEKINS MOVING AND STORAGE (CANADA) LTD   *p* 278
3779 190 ST, SURREY, BC, V3Z 0P6
(604) 270-1120   *SIC* 4214
BEL CONTRACTING   *p* 183
See *BELPACIFIC EXCAVATING & SHORING LIMITED PARTNERSHIP*
BEL VOLT SALES LIMITED   *p* 870
1350 BIRCHMOUNT RD, SCARBOROUGH, ON, M1P 2E4
(416) 757-2277   *SIC* 5063
BEL-AIR AUTOMOBILES INC   *p* 820
450 MCARTHUR AVE, OTTAWA, ON, K1K 1G4
(613) 741-3270   *SIC* 5511
BELAIR DIRECT   *p* 831
See *COMPAGNIE D'ASSURANCE BELAIR INC, LA*
BELAIR DIRECT   *p* 944
See *COMPAGNIE D'ASSURANCE BELAIR INC, LA*
BELAIR DIRECT   *p* 1051
See *COMPAGNIE D'ASSURANCE BELAIR INC, LA*
BELAIR DIRECT   *p* 1279
See *COMPAGNIE D'ASSURANCE BELAIR INC, LA*
BELAIR NETWORKS INC   *p* 623
603 MARCH RD, KANATA, ON, K2K 2M5
(613) 254-7070   *SIC* 4813
BELAND LAPOINTE   *p* 1140
See *CONSTRUCTIONS BELAND & LAPOINTE INC, LES*
BELANGER CONSTRUCTION   *p* 543
See *BELANGER, R.M. LIMITED*
BELANGER CONSTRUCTION (1981) INC *p* 543
100 RADISSON AVE, CHELMSFORD, ON, P0M 1L0
(705) 855-4555   *SIC* 1611
BELANGER FORD LINCOLN CENTRE LTD, THE   *p* 543
204 MICHAEL ST, CHELMSFORD, ON, P0M 1L0
(705) 855-4504   *SIC* 5511
BELANGER LAMINES INC   *p* 1063
1435 RUE JOLIOT-CURIE, BOUCHERVILLE, QC, J4B 7M4
(450) 449-3447   *SIC* 2541
BELANGER SAUVE S.E.N.C.R.L.   *p* 1201
5 PLACE VILLE-MARIE BUREAU 900, MONTREAL, QC, H3B 2G2
(514) 878-3081   *SIC* 8111
BELANGER, R.M. LIMITED   *p* 543
100 RADISSON AVE, CHELMSFORD, ON, P0M 1L0
(705) 855-4555   *SIC* 1542
BELANGER-VT INDUSTRIES   *p* 1063
See *BELANGER LAMINES INC*
BELCAM INC   *p* 1072
9 BOUL MONTCALM N BUREAU 400, CANDIAC, QC, J5R 3L5
(450) 619-1112   *SIC* 5122
BELCAN CANADA INC   *p* 1249
1000 BOUL SAINT-JEAN BUREAU 715, POINTE-CLAIRE, QC, H9R 5P1
(514) 697-9212   *SIC* 8711
BELCARRA   *p* 141
See *TRIPLE M HOUSING LTD*
BELCHIM CROP PROTECTION CANADA INC   *p* 600
104 COOPER DR UNIT 3, GUELPH, ON, N1C 0A4

(519) 826-7878   *SIC* 5191
BELCREST NURSING HOMES LIMITED   *p* 492
250 BRIDGE ST W SUITE 241, BELLEVILLE, ON, K8P 5N3
(613) 968-4434   *SIC* 8051
BELDEN   *p* 1332
See *BELDEN CANADA INC*
BELDEN CANADA INC   *p* 1332
2310 BOUL ALFRED-NOBEL, SAINT-LAURENT, QC, H4S 2B4
(514) 822-2345   *SIC* 3315
BELER HOLDINGS INC   *p* 716
4050A SLADEVIEW CRES SUITE 1A, MISSISSAUGA, ON, L5L 5Y5
(905) 569-1277   *SIC* 5199
BELFAST MINI MILLS LTD   *p* 1038
1820 GARFIELD RD, BELFAST, PE, C0A 1A0
(902) 659-2430   *SIC* 3552
BELFIORE'S VALUMART   *p* 639
385 FREDERICK ST, KITCHENER, ON, N2H 2P2
(519) 571-7248   *SIC* 5411
BELFOR (CANADA) INC   *p* 99
17408 116 AVE NW, EDMONTON, AB, T5S 2X2
(780) 455-5566   *SIC* 1799
BELFOR (CANADA) INC   *p* 275
7677D 132 ST, SURREY, BC, V3W 4M8
(604) 599-9980   *SIC* 1799
BELFOR (CANADA) INC   *p* 284
3300 BRIDGEWAY, VANCOUVER, BC, V5K 1H9
(604) 432-1123   *SIC* 1799
BELFOR PROPERTY & RESTORATION   *p* 275
See *BELFOR (CANADA) INC*
BELFOR RESTORATION SERVICES   *p* 99
See *BELFOR (CANADA) INC*
BELFOR RESTORATION SERVICES   *p* 284
See *BELFOR (CANADA) INC*
BELFRY ARTS CENTRE   *p* 334
See *BELFRY THEATRE SOCIETY, THE*
BELFRY THEATRE SOCIETY, THE   *p* 334
1291 GLADSTONE AVE, VICTORIA, BC, V8T 1G5
(250) 385-6815   *SIC* 7922
BELHUMEUR DOORS   *p* 1194
See *CORPORATION INTERNATIONALE MASONITE*
BELIMO AIRCONTROLS (CAN.) INC *p* 704
5845 KENNEDY RD, MISSISSAUGA, ON, L4Z 2G3
(905) 712-3118   *SIC* 5063
BELISLE   *p* 1348
See *BELISLE SOLUTION-NUTRITION INC*
BELISLE SOLUTION-NUTRITION INC   *p* 1348
196 CH DES PATRIOTES, SAINT-MATHIAS-SUR-RICHELIEU, QC, J3L 6A7
(450) 658-8733   *SIC* 2048
BELISLE, G. HOLDINGS (LONDON) LIMITED   *p* 660
4231 BLAKIE RD, LONDON, ON, N6L 1B8
(519) 652-5183   *SIC* 1711
BELL   *p* 1396
See *COMPAGNIE DE TELEPHONE BELL DU CANADA OU BELL CANADA, LA*
BELL   *p* 1396
See *BELL MOBILITE INC*
BELL & MACKENZIE CO. LTD   *p* 610
500 SHERMAN AVE N, HAMILTON, ON, L8L 8J6
(905) 527-6000   *SIC* 5032
BELL - GRASSLANDS   *p* 1422
4609 GORDON RD, REGINA, SK, S4W 0B7
(306) 779-1910   *SIC* 8748
BELL ALIANT REGIONAL COMMUNICATIONS INC   *p* 406
27 ALMA ST, MONCTON, NB, E1C 4Y2
(506) 860-8655   *SIC* 4899

BELL ALIANT REGIONAL COMMUNICATIONS INC   *p* 413
1 BRUNSWICK PL SUITE 1800, SAINT JOHN, NB, E2K 1B5
(800) 665-6000   *SIC* 4899
BELL ALIANT REGIONAL COMMUNICATIONS INC   *p* 414
GD, SAINT JOHN, NB, E2L 4K2
(506) 658-7169   *SIC* 4899
BELL ALIANT REGIONAL COMMUNICATIONS INC   *p* 425
760 TOPSAIL RD SUITE 2110, MOUNT PEARL, NL, A1N 3J5
(709) 739-2122   *SIC* 4899
BELL ALIANT REGIONAL COMMUNICATIONS INC   *p* 452
1505 BARRINGTON ST SUITE 1102, HALIFAX, NS, B3J 3K5
(902) 487-4609   *SIC* 4899
BELL ALIANT REGIONAL COMMUNICATIONS, LIMITED PARTNERSHIP   *p* 452
1505 BARRINGTON ST, HALIFAX, NS, B3J 3K5
(888) 214-7896   *SIC* 4899
BELL AND HOWELL CANADA LTD   *p* 851
30 MURAL ST UNIT 6, RICHMOND HILL, ON, L4B 1B5
(416) 747-2200   *SIC* 7629
BELL BAKER   *p* 834
See *RENSERVALL LIMITED*
BELL CANADA   *p* 413
See *BELL ALIANT REGIONAL COMMUNICATIONS INC*
BELL CANADA   *p* 721
See *COMPAGNIE DE TELEPHONE BELL DU CANADA OU BELL CANADA, LA*
BELL CANADA ENTREPRISES   *p* 1395
See *BCE INC*
BELL CITY AUTO CENTRE INC   *p* 516
100 OLD ONONDAGA RD E, BRANTFORD, ON, N3T 5L4
(800) 265-8498   *SIC* 5511
BELL CONFERENCING INC   *p* 692
5099 CREEKBANK RD SUITE B4, MISSISSAUGA, ON, L4W 5N2
(905) 602-3900   *SIC* 7389
BELL DISTRIBUTION BUREAU DE MONTREAL   *p* 1096
See *BELL MOBILITE INC*
BELL DISTRIBUTORS RGD   *p* 716
See *BELL LIFESTYLE PRODUCTS INC*
BELL EXPRESSVU INC   *p* 775
115 SCARSDALE RD, NORTH YORK, ON, M3B 2R2
(416) 383-6299   *SIC* 4899
BELL EXPRESSVU INC   *p* 778
100 WYNFORD DR SUITE 300, NORTH YORK, ON, M3C 4B4
(416) 383-6600   *SIC* 4841
BELL EXPRESSVU INC   *p* 1096
200 BOUL BOUCHARD BUREAU 72, DORVAL, QC, H9S 1A8
(514) 828-6600   *SIC* 4833
BELL FLAVORS & FRAGRANCES (CANADA) CO   *p* 1069
3800 RUE ISABELLE BUREAU H, BROSSARD, QC, J4Y 2R3
(450) 444-3819   *SIC* 2087
BELL HELICOPTER TEXTRON CANADA LIMITEE   *p* 1152
12800 RUE DE L'AVENIR, MIRABEL, QC, J7J 1R4
(450) 971-6500   *SIC* 3721
BELL HELICOPTERE TEXTRON   *p* 1152
See *BELL HELICOPTER TEXTRON CANADA LIMITEE*
BELL HIGH SCHOOL   *p* 751
See *OTTAWA-CARLETON DISTRICT SCHOOL BOARD*

BELL LIFESTYLE PRODUCTS INC   *p* 716
3164 PEPPER MILL CRT UNIT 1-8, MISSISSAUGA, ON, L5L 4X4
(905) 820-7000   *SIC* 5122
BELL MEDIA INC   *p* 75
80 PATINA RISE SW, CALGARY, AB, T3H 2W4
(403) 240-5600   *SIC* 4833
BELL MEDIA INC   *p* 99
18520 STONY PLAIN RD NW SUITE 100, EDMONTON, AB, T5S 1A8
(780) 486-2800   *SIC* 4833
BELL MEDIA INC   *p* 326
750 BURRARD ST SUITE 300, VANCOUVER, BC, V6Z 2V6
(604) 608-2868   *SIC* 4833
BELL MEDIA INC   *p* 326
969 ROBSON ST UNIT 500, VANCOUVER, BC, V6Z 1X5
(604) 871-9000   *SIC* 4832
BELL MEDIA INC   *p* 377
345 GRAHAM AVE SUITE 400, WINNIPEG, MB, R3C 5S6
(204) 788-3300   *SIC* 4833
BELL MEDIA INC   *p* 455
2885 ROBIE ST, HALIFAX, NS, B3K 5Z4
(902) 453-4000   *SIC* 4833
BELL MEDIA INC   *p* 638
864 KING ST W, KITCHENER, ON, N2G 1E8
(519) 578-1313   *SIC* 4833
BELL MEDIA INC   *p* 659
1 COMMUNICATIONS RD, LONDON, ON, N6J 4Z1
(519) 686-8810   *SIC* 4832
BELL MEDIA INC   *p* 821
87 GEORGE ST, OTTAWA, ON, K1N 9H7
(613) 224-1313   *SIC* 4833
BELL MEDIA INC   *p* 873
9 CHANNEL NINE CRT, SCARBOROUGH, ON, M1S 4B5
(416) 332-5000   *SIC* 4833
BELL MEDIA INC   *p* 922
50 EGLINTON AVE E SUITE 1, TORONTO, ON, M4P 1A6
(416) 924-6664   *SIC* 4833
BELL MEDIA INC   *p* 978
299 QUEEN ST W, TORONTO, ON, M5V 2Z5
(416) 591-5757   *SIC* 4833
BELL MEDIA INC   *p* 978
720 KING ST W SUITE 1000, TORONTO, ON, M5V 2T3
SIC 7922
BELL MEDIA INC   *p* 978
444 FRONT ST W, TORONTO, ON, M5V 2S9
(416) 585-5000   *SIC* 5192
BELL MEDIA INC   *p* 1174
1205 AV PAPINEAU, MONTREAL, QC, H2K 4R2
(514) 273-6311   *SIC* 4833
BELL MEDIA INC   *p* 1175
1717 BOUL RENE-LEVESQUE E, MONTREAL, QC, H2L 4T9
(514) 529-3200   *SIC* 4832
BELL MEDIA INC   *p* 1175
1717 BOUL RENE-LEVESQUE E BUREAU 120, MONTREAL, QC, H2L 4T9
(514) 529-3200   *SIC* 4832
BELL MEDIA INC   *p* 1426
216 1ST AVE N, SASKATOON, SK, S7K 3W3
(306) 665-8600   *SIC* 4833
BELL MEDIA RADIO S.E.N.C.   *p* 1193
1800 AV MCGILL COLLEGE UNITE 1600, MONTREAL, QC, H3A 3K9
(514) 939-5000   *SIC* 4832
BELL MOBILITE INC   *p* 286
2925 VIRTUAL WAY SUITE 400, VANCOUVER, BC, V5M 4X5
(604) 678-4160   *SIC* 4899
BELL MOBILITE INC   *p* 595

1420 BLAIR PL SUITE 700, GLOUCESTER, ON, K1J 9L8
SIC 5063

BELL MOBILITE INC   p 692
5055 SATELLITE DR UNIT 1, MISSISSAUGA, ON, L4W 5K7
SIC 5731

BELL MOBILITE INC   p 1096
200 BOUL BOUCHARD BUREAU 500, DORVAL, QC, H9S 5X5
(514) 333-3336   SIC 5999

BELL MOBILITE INC   p 1396
1 CARREFOUR ALEXANDER-GRAHAM-BELL BUREAU A-7, VERDUN, QC, H3E 3B3
(514) 870-6550   SIC 4899

BELL MOBILITY   p 286
See COMPAGNIE DE TELEPHONE BELL DU CANADA OU BELL CANADA, LA

BELL MOBILITY   p 560
See TOTALLY ONE COMMUNICATIONS INC

BELL MOBILITY CENTRES   p 790
See WIRELESS PERSONAL COMMUNICATIONS INC

BELL MOBILITY INC   p 286
See BELL MOBILITE INC

BELL MTS INC   p 346
517 18TH ST, BRANDON, MB, R7A 5Y9
(204) 727-4500   SIC 4841

BELL MTS INC   p 377
333 MAIN ST, WINNIPEG, MB, R3C 4E2
(204) 225-5687   SIC 4841

BELL SOLUTIONS TECHNIQUES   p 1307
See BELL TECHNICAL SOLUTIONS INC

BELL TECHNICAL SOLUTIONS INC   p 750
1740 WOODROFFE AVE, NEPEAN, ON, K2G 3R8
(613) 746-4465   SIC 4899

BELL TECHNICAL SOLUTIONS INC p 1063
75 RUE J.-A.-BOMBARDIER SUITE 200, BOUCHERVILLE, QC, J4B 8P1
(450) 449-1120   SIC 1731

BELL TECHNICAL SOLUTIONS INC p 1307
6396 GRANDE ALLEE, SAINT-HUBERT, QC, J3Y 8J8
(450) 678-0100   SIC 4899

BELL TRAILER SALES   p 1427
See G. J. BELL ENTERPISES LTD

BELL WORLD   p 855
See CENTURY CELLULAR (RICHMOND HILL) CORPORATION

BELL, TEMPLE   p 944
393 UNIVERSITY AVE SUITE 1300, TORONTO, ON, M5G 1E6
(416) 581-8200   SIC 8111

BELL, W S CARTAGE   p 640
See 553562 ONTARIO LIMITED

BELL-CAMP MANUFACTURING INC p 621
543925 CLARKE RD E, INGERSOLL, ON, N5C 3J8
(519) 485-3120   SIC 3499

BELL-GAZ LTEE   p 1303
5300 CH DE SAINT-GABRIEL, SAINT-FELIX-DE-VALOIS, QC, J0K 2M0
(450) 889-5944   SIC 5984

BELLA FLOR CANADA   p 657
444 NEWBOLD ST, LONDON, ON, N6E 1K3
(800) 667-1902   SIC 5112

BELLA HOSIERY MILLS INC   p 1225
1401 RUE LEGENDRE O BUREAU 200, MONTREAL, QC, H4N 2R9
(514) 274-6500   SIC 3842

BELLAI BROTHERS CONSTRUCTION LTD p 824
440 LAURIER AVE W SUITE 200, OTTAWA, ON, K1R 7X6
(613) 782-2932   SIC 1771

BELLAIR HOMES   p 771
See 7667965 CANADA INC

BELLAMERE WINERY AND EVENTS CENTRE   p 658
See 657720 ONTARIO LTD

BELLAMY AUTOTECHNIC LTD   p 1420

2640 AVONHURST DR, REGINA, SK, S4R 3J4
(306) 525-4555   SIC 5511

BELLAMY KIA   p 1420
See BELLAMY AUTOTECHNIC LTD

BELLAMY SOFTWARE   p 74
See SYLOGIST LTD

BELLARE INDUSTRIAL COATINGS INC p 21
636 36 AVE NE, CALGARY, AB, T2E 2L7
(403) 295-9676   SIC 5198

BELLATRIX EXPLORATION LTD   p 44
800 5 AVE SW UNIT 1920, CALGARY, AB, T2P 3T6
(403) 266-8670   SIC 1381

BELLATRIX EXPLORATION LTD   p 82
5516 INDUSTRIAL RD, DRAYTON VALLEY, AB, T7A 1R1
(403) 266-8670   SIC 1381

BELLE   p 1333
See CONGLOM INC

BELLE BAY PRODUCTS   p 396
See BELLE BAY PRODUCTS LTD

BELLE BAY PRODUCTS LTD   p 396
10 RUE DU QUAI, CARAQUET, NB, E1W 1B6
(506) 727-4414   SIC 2092

BELLE GUEULE & DESSIN   p 1173
See BRASSEURS GMT INC, LES

BELLE PLAINE COLONY   p 1404
See HUTTERITE BRETHREN CHURCH OF BELLE PLAINE

BELLE RIVER DISTRICT HIGH SCHOOL p 490
See GREATER ESSEX COUNTY DISTRICT SCHOOL BOARD

BELLE RIVER ENTERPRISES LTD   p 1038
GD, BELLE RIVER, PE, C0A 1B0
(902) 962-2248   SIC 2092

BELLE-PAK PACKAGING INC   p 667
7465 BIRCHMOUNT RD, MARKHAM, ON, L3R 5X9
(905) 475-5151   SIC 2673

BELLEMARE ABRASIFS & MINERAUX p 1388
See SDF ABRASIF INC

BELLEMONT POWELL LTEE   p 1064
1570 RUE AMPERE UNITE 508, BOUCHERVILLE, QC, J4B 7L4
(450) 641-2661   SIC 5141

BELLEROSE COMPOSITE HIGH SCHOOL p 166
See ST. ALBERT PUBLIC SCHOOL DISTRICT NO. 5565

BELLEVILLE CHRYSLER DODGE JEEP p 490
See 621509 ONTARIO INC

BELLEVILLE METAL SALES LIMITED p 490
222 UNIVERSITY AVE, BELLEVILLE, ON, K8N 5S5
(613) 968-2188   SIC 5051

BELLEVILLE TOYOTA   p 491
See MID-WAY MOTORS (QUINTE) LIMITED

BELLEVUE FABRICATING LTD   p 490
525 BELLEVUE DR, BELLEVILLE, ON, K8N 4Z5
(613) 968-6721   SIC 3441

BELLINA LINGERIE   p 1170
See HAMILTON LINGERIE (1978) LTD

BELLISSIMA   p 37
See SERENA FASHIONS (ALBERTA) LTD

BELLISSIMA   p 322
See SERENA FASHIONS LTD

BELLIVEAU MOTORS LIMITED   p 442
1484 HIGHWAY 1, CHURCH POINT, NS, B0W 1M0
(902) 769-0706   SIC 5511

BELLIVO TRANSFORMATION INC   p 1354
1505 RTE LUPIEN, SAINTE-ANGELE-DE-PREMONT, QC, J0K 1R0
(819) 268-5199   SIC 7299

BELLUCCI   p 1180

See DISTRIBUTIONS BELLUCCI LTEE, LES

BELLVILLE VOLKSWAGON   p 492
See NORTH FRONT MOTORS INC

BELLWOODS CENTRES FOR COMMUNITY LIVING INC   p 778
789 DON MILLS RD SUITE 701, NORTH YORK, ON, M3C 1T5
(416) 696-9663   SIC 8361

BELLWYCK PACKAGING INC   p 521
977 CENTURY DR, BURLINGTON, ON, L7L 5J8
(905) 631-4475   SIC 7389

BELLWYCK PACKAGING INC   p 835
GD, OWEN SOUND, ON, N4K 5N9
(800) 265-3708   SIC 2657

BELLWYCK PACKAGING INC   p 914
21 FINCHDENE SQ, TORONTO, ON, M1X 1A7
(416) 752-1210   SIC 2657

BELLWYCK PACKAGING SOLUTIONS p 521
See BELLWYCK PACKAGING INC

BELLWYCK PACKAGING SOLUTIONS p 835
See BELLWYCK PACKAGING INC

BELLWYCK PACKAGING SOLUTIONS p 914
See BELLWYCK PACKAGING INC

BELLY QUEBEC   p 1372
See A. & R. BELLEY INC

BELMONT   p 714
See TAKARA COMPANY, CANADA, LTD

BELMONT FINANCIAL GROUP INC, THE p 443
33 ALDERNEY DR UNIT 7TH, DARTMOUTH, NS, B2Y 2N4
(902) 465-5687   SIC 6411

BELMONT HOUSE   p 974
See TORONTO AGED MEN'S AND WOMEN'S HOMES, THE

BELMONT LONG TERM CARE FACILITY p 492
See BELCREST NURSING HOMES LIMITED

BELMONT MEAT PRODUCTS LIMITED p 792
230 SIGNET DR, NORTH YORK, ON, M9L 1V2
(416) 749-7250   SIC 2011

BELMONT PRESS LIMITED   p 680
5 BODINGTON CRT, MARKHAM, ON, L6G 1A6
(905) 940-4900   SIC 7389

BELMONT PROPERTIES   p 319
1401 BROADWAY W SUITE 302, VANCOUVER, BC, V6H 1H6
(604) 736-2841   SIC 6141

BELMONT PROPERTY MANAGEMENT p 788
See BLEEMAN HOLDINGS LIMITED

BELMONT SECONDARY SCHOOL   p 340
See SCHOOL DISTRICT NO 62 (SOOKE)

BELO SUN MINING CORP   p 949
65 QUEEN ST W SUITE 800, TORONTO, ON, M5H 2M5
(416) 309-2137   SIC 1041

BELOW THE BELT   p 112
See BELOW THE BELT STORE (VANCOUVER) LTD

BELOW THE BELT LTD   p 112
5611 86 ST NW, EDMONTON, AB, T6E 6H7
(780) 469-5301   SIC 5611

BELOW THE BELT STORE (VANCOUVER) LTD   p 112
5611 86 ST NW, EDMONTON, AB, T6E 6H7
(780) 469-5301   SIC 5611

BELPACIFIC EXCAVATING & SHORING LIMITED PARTNERSHIP   p 183
3183 NORLAND AVE, BURNABY, BC, V5B 3A9
(604) 291-1255   SIC 1623

BELROCK CONSTRUCTION GENERAL

CONTRACTOR LIMITED   p 549
185 ADESSO DR, CONCORD, ON, L4K 3C4
(905) 669-9481   SIC 1542

BELRON CANADA INCORPOREE   p 1169
8288 BOUL PIE-IX, MONTREAL, QC, H1Z 3T6
(514) 593-7000   SIC 7536

BELTERRA CORPORATION   p 205
1609 DERWENT WAY, DELTA, BC, V3M 6K8
(604) 540-0044   SIC 5084

BELTPACK   p 1340
See LAIRD CONTROLS CANADA LIMITED

BELUGA   p 1240
See CHAUSSURES DE LUCA MONTREAL INC

BELVEDERE GOLF & COUNTRY CLUB p 162
51418 HWY 21 S, SHERWOOD PARK, AB, T8H 2T2
(780) 467-2025   SIC 7997

BELVEDERE HEIGHTS   p 837
See DISTRICT OF PARRY SOUND (WEST) BELVEDERE HEIGHTS HOME FOR THE AGED

BELVIKA TRADE & PACKAGING LTD p 734
A-450 EXPORT BLVD, MISSISSAUGA, ON, L5S 2A4
(905) 502-7444   SIC 7389

BELWOOD POULTRY LIMITED   p 477
4272 4TH CONC N, AMHERSTBURG, ON, N9V 2Y9
(519) 736-2236   SIC 5144

BELYER INSURANCE LTD   p 1019
3390 WALKER RD SUITE 300, WINDSOR, ON, N8W 3S1
(519) 915-4667   SIC 6411

BELZILE   p 1079
See PETROLES R.L. INC, LES

BELZILE, BEAUMIER ET BELZILE SENC p 1111
765 6E AV, GRAND-MERE, QC, G9T 2H8
(819) 538-8606   SIC 5912

BEMA AUTOSPORT BMW   p 1424
See BEMA IMPORTS INC

BEMA IMPORTS INC   p 1424
607 BRAND CRT, SASKATOON, SK, S7J 5L3
(306) 955-0900   SIC 5511

BEMIS FLEXIBLE PACKAGING CANADA LIMITED   p 794
130 ARROW RD, NORTH YORK, ON, M9M 2M1
(416) 742-8910   SIC 2657

BEMIS FLEXIBLE PACKAGING MILPRINT, DIV OF   p 794
See BEMIS FLEXIBLE PACKAGING CANADA LIMITED

BEN CALF ROBE SOCIETY OF EDMONTON   p 83
12046 77 ST NW, EDMONTON, AB, T5B 2G7
(780) 477-6648   SIC 8322

BEN DESHAIES INC   p 1045
431 6E RUE O, AMOS, QC, J9T 2V5
(819) 732-6466   SIC 5141

BEN MACHINE PRODUCTS COMPANY INCORPORATED   p 1027
8065 HUNTINGTON RD SUITE 1, WOODBRIDGE, ON, L4H 3T9
(905) 856-7707   SIC 3499

BEN MOSS JEWELLERS   p 374
See BEN MOSS JEWELLERS WESTERN CANADA LTD

BEN MOSS JEWELLERS WESTERN CANADA LTD   p 374
201 PORTAGE AVE SUITE 300, WINNIPEG, MB, R3B 3K6
(204) 947-6682   SIC 5944

BEN-MOR   p 1313
See CABLES BEN-MOR INC, LES

BENCH   p 301
See 10SHEET SERVICES INC
BENCH   p 1157
See MARQUES DE VETEMENTS
FREEMARK TEC INC
BENCH COLONY   p 1435
See BENCH HUTTERIAN BRETHREN
CORP
BENCH HUTTERIAN BRETHREN CORP p
1435
  HWY 13 W, SHAUNAVON, SK, S0N 2M0
  (306) 297-3270   SIC 0111
BENCH PRESS LTD, THE   p 598
  2402 STOUFFVILLE RD RR 1, GORMLEY,
  ON, L0H 1G0
  (905) 887-3043   SIC 7312
BENCHMARK ATHLETIC INC   p 729
  6085 BELGRAVE RD, MISSISSAUGA, ON,
  L5R 4E6
  (905) 361-2390   SIC 5137
BENCHMARK BUILDING SYSTEMS LTD p
200
  145 SCHOOLHOUSE ST SUITE 13, CO-
  QUITLAM, BC, V3K 4X8
  (604) 524-6533   SIC 1542
BEND ALL AUTOMOTIVE ULC   p 483
  115 WANLESS CRT, AYR, ON, N0B 1E0
  (519) 623-2003   SIC 3671
BEND ALL AUTOMOTIVE ULC   p 483
  575 WAYDOM DR, AYR, ON, N0B 1E0
  (519) 623-2001   SIC 3499
BEND ALL AUTOMOTIVE ULC   p 483
  655 WAYDOM DR, AYR, ON, N0B 1E0
  (519) 623-2002   SIC 5015
BEND ALL AUTOMOTIVE ULC   p 535
  445 DOBBIE DR, CAMBRIDGE, ON, N1T
  1S9
  (519) 623-2001   SIC 3499
BEND ALL MANUFACTURING   p 483
  See BEND ALL AUTOMOTIVE ULC
BENDALE BUSINESS & TECHNICAL IN-
STITUTE   p
872
  See TORONTO DISTRICT SCHOOL
  BOARD
BENECO PACKAGING   p 736
  See SHEEN LEGEND PACKAGING CORP
BENEDICT HOLDINGS LTD   p 165
  390 ST ALBERT TRAIL, ST. ALBERT, AB,
  T8N 5J9
  (780) 459-5447   SIC 5541
BENEFIT PLAN ADMINISTRATORS LIM-
ITED   p
576
  90 BURNHAMTHORPE RD, ETOBICOKE,
  ON, M9A 1H2
  (905) 275-6466   SIC 8742
BENEFIT PLAN ADMINISTRATORS LIM-
ITED   p
709
  90 BURNHAMTHORPE RD W SUITE 300,
  MISSISSAUGA, ON, L5B 3C3
  (905) 275-6466   SIC 8742
BENEFITS BY DESIGN INC   p 245
  2755 LOUGHEED HWY SUITE 500, PORT
  COQUITLAM, BC, V3B 5Y9
  (604) 464-0313   SIC 6411
BENEVITO FOODS INC   p 577
  17 VICKERS RD, ETOBICOKE, ON, M9B
  1C1
  SIC 2051
BENEVITY, INC   p 21
  611 MEREDITH RD NE UNIT 700, CAL-
  GARY, AB, T2E 2W5
  (403) 237-7875   SIC 7371
BENEVOLES DE LA RESIDENCE YVON-
BRUNET INC, LES   p
1223
  6250 AV NEWMAN, MONTREAL, QC, H4E
  4K4
  (514) 765-8000   SIC 8361
BENGARD MANUFACTURING, DIV OF   p
697
  See LOXCREEN CANADA LTD

BENGOUGH CO-OPERATIVE LIMITED   p
1404
  140 3 ST E, BENGOUGH, SK, S0C 0K0
  (306) 268-2040   SIC 5171
BENICK SERVICES INC   p 394
  170 AULAC RD, AULAC, NB, E4L 2X2
  (506) 536-1339   SIC 5541
BENISTI IMPORTATION ET EXPORTATION
p 1226
  See   IMPORTATIONS-EXPORTATIONS
  BENISTI INC
BENISTI USA LLC   p 1225
  1650 RUE CHABANEL O, MONTREAL, QC,
  H4N 3M8
  (514) 384-0140   SIC 5136
BENIX & CO. INC   p 788
  98 ORFUS RD, NORTH YORK, ON, M6A
  1L9
  (416) 784-0732   SIC 5719
BENJO INC   p 1258
  520 BOUL CHAREST E BUREAU 233,
  QUEBEC, QC, G1K 3J3
  (418) 640-0001   SIC 5945
BENKO SEWER SERVICES   p 64
  See BADGER DAYLIGHTING LTD
BENNETT CHEVROLET CADILLAC LTD p
532
  445 HESPELER RD, CAMBRIDGE, ON,
  N1R 6J2
  (519) 621-1250   SIC 5511
BENNETT DESIGN ASSOCIATES INC   p
1001
  10 DOUGLAS RD UNIT 2, UXBRIDGE, ON,
  L9P 1S9
  (905) 852-4617   SIC 7389
BENNETT DUNLOP FORD SALES (1993)
LIMITED   p 1420
  770 BROAD ST, REGINA, SK, S4R 8H7
  (306) 522-6612   SIC 5511
BENNETT JONES LLP   p 44
  855 2 ST SW SUITE 4500, CALGARY, AB,
  T2P 4K7
  (403) 298-3100   SIC 8111
BENNETT JONES LLP   p 985
  3400 ONE FIRST CANADIAN PL,
  TORONTO, ON, M5X 1A4
  (416) 863-1200   SIC 8111
BENNETT MECHANICAL INSTALLATION
(2001) LTD   p 682
  524 6TH CONCESSION RD W, MILL-
  GROVE, ON, L0R 1V0
  (905) 689-7242   SIC 1711
BENNETT MECHANICAL INSTALLATIONS
(2001) LTD   p 682
  524 SIXTH CONC W, MILLGROVE, ON,
  L0R 1V0
  (905) 689-7242   SIC 1629
BENNETT MECHANICAL INSTALLATIONS
LTD   p 682
  524 6TH CONCESSION RD W, MILL-
  GROVE, ON, L0R 1V0
  SIC 1629
BENNETT RESTAURANT LTD   p 429
  54 KENMOUNT RD, ST. JOHN'S, NL, A1B
  1W2
  (709) 754-1254   SIC 5812
BENNETT'S BAKERY LIMITED   p 907
  899 TUNGSTEN ST, THUNDER BAY, ON,
  P7B 6H2
  (807) 344-2931   SIC 5149
BENNETT'S HOME FURNISHINGS LIM-
ITED   p
539
  13 FRONT ST S, CAMPBELLFORD, ON,
  K0L 1L0
  (705) 653-1188   SIC 5211
BENNETT'S LIMITED   p 424
  165 HAMILTON RIVER RD, HAPPY
  VALLEY-GOOSE BAY, NL, A0P 1E0
  (709) 896-5024   SIC 5541
BENNETT'S ULTRAMAR   p 424
  See BENNETT'S LIMITED
BENNETT'S VALUE MART   p 630
  See DJD DEVELOPMENT CORPORATION

BENNETT, KEN ENTERPRISES INC   p 417
  173 MAIN ST, SHEDIAC, NB, E4P 2A5
  (506) 533-9788   SIC 5531
BENNY STARK LIMITED   p 993
  200 UNION ST, TORONTO, ON, M6N 3M9
  (416) 654-3464   SIC 5093
BENOIT JOBIN INC   p 1284
  25 RUE SAINT-GERMAIN E, RIMOUSKI,
  QC, G5L 1A3
  (418) 725-0742   SIC 1542
BENOIT OILFIELD CONSTRUCTION (1997)
LTD   p 79
  302 RUPERT ST, CHAUVIN, AB, T0B 0V0
  (780) 858-3794   SIC 1623
BENOIT OILFIELD CONSTRUCTION LTD p
79
  302 RUPERT ST, CHAUVIN, AB, T0B 0V0
  (780) 858-3794   SIC 1623
BENS PHARMACY   p 540
  See COUNTRY DRUG STORES LTD
BENSIMON BYRNE INC   p 978
  225 WELLINGTON ST W, TORONTO, ON,
  M5V 3G7
  (416) 922-2211   SIC 7311
BENSON AUTO PARTS   p 1104
  See BENSON GROUP INC
BENSON B A & SON LTD   p 284
  266 1ST AVE, TRAIL, BC, V1R 4V2
  (250) 368-6428   SIC 5171
BENSON BEVERLY TIRE   p 566
  See BEVERLY GROUP INC, THE
BENSON GROUP INC   p 561
  700 EDUCATION RD, CORNWALL, ON,
  K6H 6B8
  (613) 933-1700   SIC 5013
BENSON GROUP INC   p 1104
  95 BOUL GREBER, GATINEAU, QC, J8T
  3P9
  (819) 669-6555   SIC 5013
BENSON INDUSTRIES LIMITED   p 267
  2201 KEATING CROSS RD, SAANICHTON,
  BC, V8M 2A5
  (250) 652-4417   SIC 2434
BENSON KEARLEY & ASSOCIATES IN-
SURANCE BROKERS LTD   p
754
  17705 LESLIE ST SUITE 101, NEWMAR-
  KET, ON, L3Y 3E3
  (905) 898-3815   SIC 6411
BENSON KEARLEY IFG   p 754
  See BENSON KEARLEY & ASSOCIATES
  INSURANCE BROKERS LTD
BENSON OIL   p 284
  See BENSON B A & SON LTD
BENSON, GARRY W ENTERPRISES LTD p
39
  40 HUNTERHORN DR NE, CALGARY, AB,
  T2K 6H2
  SIC 5531
BENTALL KENNEDY LP   p 959
  1 YORK ST SUITE 1100, TORONTO, ON,
  M5J 0B6
  (416) 681-3400   SIC 6282
BENTALLGREENOAK (CANADA) LIMITED
PARTNERSHIP   p 328
  1055 DUNSMUIR ST SUITE 1800, VAN-
  COUVER, BC, V7X 1B1
  (604) 661-5000   SIC 6531
BENTALLGREENOAK (CANADA) LIMITED
PARTNERSHIP   p 328
  1055 DUNSMUIR ST SUITE 1800, VAN-
  COUVER, BC, V7X 1L3
  (604) 646-2800   SIC 6531
BENTALLGREENOAK (CANADA) LIMITED
PARTNERSHIP   p 582
  10 CARLSON CRT SUITE 500, ETOBI-
  COKE, ON, M9W 6L2
  (416) 674-7707   SIC 6531
BENTALLGREENOAK (CANADA) LIMITED
PARTNERSHIP   p 959
  1 YORK ST SUITE 1100, TORONTO, ON,
  M5J 0B6
  (416) 681-3400   SIC 6531
BENTLEY MONTREAL   p 1227

See MOTEURS DECARIE INC, LES
BENTLEYS OF LONDON SLACKS LTD   p
371
  1309 MOUNTAIN AVE, WINNIPEG, MB,
  R2X 2Y1
  (204) 786-6081   SIC 2339
BENTO INC   p 667
  25 CENTURIAN DR SUITE 208,
  MARKHAM, ON, L3R 5N8
  (905) 513-0028   SIC 5812
BENTO NOUVEAU   p 815
  See 1496519 ONTARIO INC
BENTO SUSHI   p 667
  See BENTO INC
BERARDINI, FERNANDO INC   p 1325
  80 RUE STINSON, SAINT-LAURENT, QC,
  H4N 2E7
  (514) 744-9412   SIC 5143
BERCO AUTOMOTIVE SUPPLY LIMITED p
792
  163 MILVAN DR SUITE 1, NORTH YORK,
  ON, M9L 1Z8
  (416) 749-0231   SIC 5511
BERCOMAC LIMITEE   p 1044
  92 RUE FORTIN N, ADSTOCK, QC, G0N
  1S0
  (418) 422-2252   SIC 3523
BERENDSEN FLUID POWER LTD   p 878
  35 IRONSIDE CRES UNIT A, SCARBOR-
  OUGH, ON, M1X 1G5
  (416) 335-5557   SIC 5084
BERESKIN & PARR LLP   p 949
  40 KING ST W 4TH FL, TORONTO, ON,
  M5H 3Y2
  (416) 364-7311   SIC 8111
BERESKIN & PARR MANAGEMENT   p 949
  See BERESKIN & PARR LLP
BERETTA FARMS INC   p 582
  80 GALAXY BLVD UNIT 1, ETOBICOKE,
  ON, M9W 4Y8
  (416) 674-5609   SIC 0119
BERETTA PIPELINE CONSTRUCTION LTD
p 1409
  GD, LLOYDMINSTER, SK, S9V 0X5
  (780) 875-6522   SIC 1623
BERETTA PROTECTIVE SERVICES INTER-
NATIONAL INC   p
112
  9404 58 AVE NW, EDMONTON, AB, T6E
  0B6
  (780) 481-6348   SIC 7381
BERG CHILLING SYSTEMS INC   p 870
  51 NANTUCKET BLVD, SCARBOROUGH,
  ON, M1P 2N5
  (416) 755-2221   SIC 3585
BERGA RECYCLING INC   p 1133
  3055 BOUL SAINT-MARTIN O BUREAU
  T500, LAVAL, QC, H7T 0J3
  (514) 949-7244   SIC 5051
BERGER BLANC INC, LE   p 1160
  9825 BOUL HENRI-BOURASSA E, MON-
  TREAL, QC, H1C 1G5
  (514) 494-2002   SIC 8699
BERGER MIX   p 395
  See BERGER PEAT MOSS ENR
BERGER PEAT MOSS ENR   p 395
  149 BAY DU VIN RIVER RD, BAY DU VIN,
  NB, E1N 5P4
  (800) 463-5582   SIC 5261
BERGER PEATMOSS   p 394
  See TOURBIERES BERGER LTEE, LES
BERGERON   p 1067
  See SERVICES MATREC INC
BERGERON MAYBOIS, DIV OF   p 1046
  See TRANSPORT TFI 23 S.E.C.
BERICAP INC   p 521
  835 SYSCON CRT, BURLINGTON, ON, L7L
  6C5
  (905) 634-2248   SIC 5085
BERICAP NORTH AMERICA   p 521
  See BERICAP INC
BERK'S INTERTRUCK LTD   p 234
  2230 MCCULLOUGH RD, NANAIMO, BC,
  V9S 4M8

(250) 758-5217   *SIC* 5511
BERKELEY GLADSTONE RIDGE   *p* 455
See BERKELEY HOLDINGS LIMITED
BERKELEY HOLDINGS LIMITED   *p* 455
2633 GLADSTONE ST SUITE 312, HALI-
FAX, NS, B3K 4W3
(902) 492-3700   *SIC* 6513
BERKLEY CANADA INC   *p* 949
145 KING ST W SUITE 1000, TORONTO,
ON, M5H 1J8
(416) 304-1178   *SIC* 6351
BERKSHIRE GROUP   *p* 1324
See 3653340 CANADA INC
**BERKSHIRE HATHAWAY SPECIALTY IN-
SURANCE**   *p*
959
200 BAY ST, TORONTO, ON, M5J 2J2
(647) 846-7803   *SIC* 6311
BERLINES TRANSIT INC   *p* 1058
719 BOUL INDUSTRIEL BUREAU 102B,
BLAINVILLE, QC, J7C 3V3
(450) 437-3589   *SIC* 4151
BERLITZ CANADA INC   *p* 709
3660 HURONTARIO ST SUITE 302, MIS-
SISSAUGA, ON, L5B 3C4
(905) 896-0215   *SIC* 8299
BERMAN FALK INC   *p* 224
9499 198 ST, LANGLEY, BC, V1M 3B8
(604) 882-8903   *SIC* 5963
BERMEX   *p* 1150
See MEUBLES BDM + INC
BERMEX INTERNATIONAL INC   *p* 1150
215 BOUL OUEST, MASKINONGE, QC,
J0K 1N0
(819) 601-8702   *SIC* 2511
BERMINGHAM CONSTRUCTION   *p* 610
*See BERMINGHAM FOUNDATION SOLU-
TIONS LIMITED*
**BERMINGHAM FOUNDATION SOLUTIONS
LIMITED**   *p* 610
600, FERGUSON AVE N, HAMILTON, ON,
L8L 4Z9
(905) 528-7924   *SIC* 1629
**BERNARD ATHLETIC KNIT & ENTER-
PRISES LIMITED**   *p*
993
2 SCARLETT RD, TORONTO, ON, M6N 4J6
(416) 766-6151   *SIC* 5137
BERNARDI BUILDING SUPPLY LTD   *p* 792
469 GARYRAY DR, NORTH YORK, ON,
M9L 1P9
(416) 741-0941   *SIC* 5039
BERNARDO METAL PRODUCTS LIMITED*p*
737
170 CAPITAL CRT, MISSISSAUGA, ON,
L5T 2R8
(905) 362-1252   *SIC* 3499
BERNIER & CREPEAU (1988) LTEE   *p* 1098
160 BOUL SAINT-JOSEPH, DRUM-
MONDVILLE, QC, J2C 2A8
(819) 477-8503   *SIC* 5511
BERNIER, A D INC   *p* 1129
229 2E AV, LAMBTON, QC, G0M 1H0
(418) 486-7461   *SIC* 5211
**BERNT GILBERTSON ENTERPRISES LIM-
ITED**   *p*
850
3107 HURON LINE HWY 548, RICHARDS
LANDING, ON, P0R 1J0
(705) 246-2076   *SIC* 1611
BERNZOMATIC, DIV OF   *p* 801
See NEWELL BRANDS CANADA ULC
BERO INVESTMENTS LTD   *p* 283
14948 32 AVE, SURREY, BC, V4P 3R5
(604) 536-3644   *SIC* 5511
**BERRIS MANGAN CHARTERED ACCOUN-
TANTS**   *p*
320
1827 5TH AVE W, VANCOUVER, BC, V6J
1P5
SIC 8721
BERRY & SMITH TRUCKING LTD   *p* 243
301 WARREN AVE E, PENTICTON, BC,
V2A 3M1

(250) 492-4042   *SIC* 4213
BERRY FRESH FARMS   *p* 590
1760 BALFOUR ST, FENWICK, ON, L0S
1C0
(905) 892-8231   *SIC* 0171
BERRY PLASTICS CANADA INC   *p* 866
595 CORONATION DR, SCARBOROUGH,
ON, M1E 2K4
(416) 281-6000   *SIC* 3081
BERSACO, INC   *p* 1112
717 RUE DE LA MONTAGNE, GRANDES-
BERGERONNES, QC, G0T 1G0
(418) 232-1100   *SIC* 2448
BERT FRENCH & SON LIMITED   *p* 848
126 GREER RD SUITE 1, PORT SYDNEY,
ON, P0B 1L0
(705) 385-2311   *SIC* 1521
BERT'S ELECTRIC (2001) LTD   *p* 176
2258 PEARDONVILLE RD, ABBOTSFORD,
BC, V2T 6J8
(604) 850-8731   *SIC* 1731
**BERTIE AND CLINTON MUTUAL INSUR-
ANCE COMPANY**   *p*
1012
1003 NIAGARA ST, WELLAND, ON, L3C
1M5
(905) 735-1234   *SIC* 6331
BERTINI MODA   *p* 1332
See BALLIN INC
BERTOLIN, S. PHARMACY LTD   *p* 33
6455 MACLEOD TRAIL S UNIT Y003, CAL-
GARY, AB, T2H 0K4
(403) 253-2424   *SIC* 5912
BERTOZZI, ADRIANO IMPORTING INC   *p*
582
2070 CODLIN CRES UNIT 2, ETOBICOKE,
ON, M9W 7J2
(416) 213-0075   *SIC* 5141
**BERTRAM CONSTRUCTION & DESIGN
LTD**   *p* 486
25 GEORGE ST UNIT E, BARRIE, ON, L4N
2G5
(705) 726-0254   *SIC* 1541
BERTRAM DRILLING CORP   *p* 79
347 CARADOC AVE, CARBON, AB, T0M
0L0
(403) 572-3591   *SIC* 1382
**BERTRAND CONSTRUCTION L'ORIGNAL,
UNE DIVISION DE COLACEM CANADA**   *p*
1086
See COLACEM CANADA INC
**BERTRAND DISTRIBUTEUR EN ALIMEN-
TATION**   *p*
1065
See GROUPE COLABOR INC
**BERUBE CHEVROLET CADILLAC BUICK
GMC LTEE**   *p* 1286
101 BOUL CARTIER, RIVIERE-DU-LOUP,
QC, G5R 2N3
(418) 862-6324   *SIC* 5511
**BERWICK RETIREMENT COMMUNITIES
LTD**   *p* 198
1700 COMOX AVE, COMOX, BC, V9M 4H4
(250) 339-1690   *SIC* 8361
BERWIL LTEE   *p* 1169
8651 9E AV BUREAU 1, MONTREAL, QC,
H1Z 3A1
(514) 376-0121   *SIC* 1711
BESCO BEAUTE (1980) LTEE   *p* 1221
5770 CH UPPER-LACHINE, MONTREAL,
QC, H4A 2B3
(514) 481-1115   *SIC* 5122
BESNER   *p* 1139
See TRANSPORT TFI 6 S.E.C.
BESRA GOLD INC   *p* 937
10 KING ST E SUITE 500, TORONTO, ON,
M5C 1C3
(416) 572-2525   *SIC* 1081
**BESS AND MOE GREENBERG FAMILY
HILLEL LODGE, THE**   *p* 829
*See OTTAWA JEWISH HOME FOR THE
AGED*
**BESSEMER AND LAKE ERIE RAILROAD
COMPANY**   *p* 1202

935 RUE DE LA GAUCHETIERE O BU-
REAU 11, MONTREAL, QC, H3B 2M9
(514) 399-4536   *SIC* 4011
BESSETTE AUTOMOBILE INC   *p* 1088
395 RUE DE LA RIVIERE, COWANSVILLE,
QC, J2K 1N4
(450) 263-4000   *SIC* 5511
BESSETTE ET BOUDREAU INC   *p* 1392
680 RTE 143, VAL-JOLI, QC, J1S 0G6
(819) 845-7722   *SIC* 4212
BESSNER GALLAY KREISMAN   *p* 1401
4150 RUE SAINTE-CATHERINE O BU-
REAU 600, WESTMOUNT, QC, H3Z 2Y5
(514) 908-3600   *SIC* 8721
BEST ADVICE FINANCIAL SERVICES INC   *p* 766
250 CONSUMERS RD SUITE 1111,
NORTH YORK, ON, M2J 4V6
(416) 490-1474   *SIC* 8741
BEST ADVICE INSURANCE   *p* 766
*See BEST ADVICE FINANCIAL SERVICES
INC*
BEST BAKING INC   *p* 573
166 NORSEMAN ST, ETOBICOKE, ON,
M8Z 2R4
(416) 536-1330   *SIC* 5149
BEST BUY   *p* 156
See BEST BUY CANADA LTD
BEST BUY   *p* 445
See BEST BUY CANADA LTD
BEST BUY   *p* 529
See BEST BUY CANADA LTD
BEST BUY   *p* 567
See BEST BUY CANADA LTD
BEST BUY   *p* 626
See BEST BUY CANADA LTD
BEST BUY   *p* 636
See BEST BUY CANADA LTD
BEST BUY   *p* 820
See BEST BUY CANADA LTD
BEST BUY   *p* 870
See BEST BUY CANADA LTD
BEST BUY   *p* 1030
See BEST BUY CANADA LTD
BEST BUY   *p* 1069
See BEST BUY CANADA LTD
BEST BUY CANADA LTD   *p* 33
6909 MACLEOD TRAIL SW, CALGARY, AB,
T2H 0L6
SIC 5734
BEST BUY CANADA LTD   *p* 69
350 SHAWVILLE BLVD SE UNIT 110, CAL-
GARY, AB, T2Y 3S4
(403) 509-9120   *SIC* 5734
BEST BUY CANADA LTD   *p* 87
10304 109 ST NW, EDMONTON, AB, T5J
1M3
(780) 498-5505   *SIC* 5731
BEST BUY CANADA LTD   *p* 156
5001 19 ST UNIT 800, RED DEER, AB, T4R
3R1
(403) 314-5645   *SIC* 5731
BEST BUY CANADA LTD   *p* 192
8800 GLENLYON PKY, BURNABY, BC, V5J
5K3
(604) 435-8223   *SIC* 5731
BEST BUY CANADA LTD   *p* 224
19890 92A AVE, LANGLEY, BC, V1M 3A9
(604) 419-5500   *SIC* 5999
BEST BUY CANADA LTD   *p* 341
2100 PARK ROYAL S, WEST VANCOUVER,
BC, V7T 2W4
(604) 913-3336   *SIC* 5731
BEST BUY CANADA LTD   *p* 445
119 GALE TERR, DARTMOUTH, NS, B3B
0C4
(902) 468-0075   *SIC* 5731
BEST BUY CANADA LTD   *p* 498
9200 AIRPORT RD, BRAMPTON, ON, L6S
6G6
(905) 494-7000   *SIC* 5065
BEST BUY CANADA LTD   *p* 529
1200 BRANT ST UNIT 1, BURLINGTON,
ON, L7P 5C6

(905) 332-4758   *SIC* 5731
BEST BUY CANADA LTD   *p* 567
175 GREEN LANE E, EAST GWILLIM-
BURY, ON, L9N 0C9
(905) 954-1262   *SIC* 5731
BEST BUY CANADA LTD   *p* 596
1525 CITY PARK DR, GLOUCESTER, ON,
K1J 1H3
(613) 747-7636   *SIC* 5731
BEST BUY CANADA LTD   *p* 626
255 KANATA AVE UNIT D1, KANATA, ON,
K2T 1K5
SIC 5999
BEST BUY CANADA LTD   *p* 626
745 KANATA AVE SUITE GG1, KANATA,
ON, K2T 1H9
(613) 287-3912   *SIC* 5731
BEST BUY CANADA LTD   *p* 636
215 FAIRWAY RD S, KITCHENER, ON, N2C
1X2
(519) 783-0333   *SIC* 5731
BEST BUY CANADA LTD   *p* 641
50 GATEWAY PARK DR, KITCHENER, ON,
N2P 2J4
SIC 5731
BEST BUY CANADA LTD   *p* 651
1735 RICHMOND ST SUITE 111, LONDON,
ON, N5X 3Y2
(519) 640-2900   *SIC* 5731
BEST BUY CANADA LTD   *p* 729
6075 MAVIS RD UNIT 1, MISSISSAUGA,
ON, L5R 4G6
(905) 361-8251   *SIC* 5999
BEST BUY CANADA LTD   *p* 754
17890 YONGE ST, NEWMARKET, ON, L3Y
8S1
SIC 5999
BEST BUY CANADA LTD   *p* 795
2625A WESTON RD, NORTH YORK, ON,
M9N 3V8
(416) 242-6162   *SIC* 5731
BEST BUY CANADA LTD   *p* 814
1471 HARMONY RD N, OSHAWA, ON, L1K
0Z6
(905) 433-4455   *SIC* 5731
BEST BUY CANADA LTD   *p* 820
380 COVENTRY RD, OTTAWA, ON, K1K
2C6
(613) 212-0333   *SIC* 5731
BEST BUY CANADA LTD   *p* 826
2210 BANK ST UNIT B1, OTTAWA, ON, K1V
1J5
(613) 526-7450   *SIC* 5731
BEST BUY CANADA LTD   *p* 858
1380 EXMOUTH ST, SARNIA, ON, N7S 3X9
(519) 542-4388   *SIC* 5731
BEST BUY CANADA LTD   *p* 870
480 PROGRESS AVE, SCARBOROUGH,
ON, M1P 5J1
(416) 296-7020   *SIC* 5731
BEST BUY CANADA LTD   *p* 1000
8601 WARDEN AVE SUITE 1,
UNIONVILLE, ON, L3R 0B5
SIC 5731
BEST BUY CANADA LTD   *p* 1030
7850 WESTON RD SUITE 1, WOOD-
BRIDGE, ON, L4L 9N8
(905) 264-3191   *SIC* 5731
BEST BUY CANADA LTD   *p* 1064
584 CH DE TOURAINE BUREAU 101,
BOUCHERVILLE, QC, J4B 8S5
SIC 5999
BEST BUY CANADA LTD   *p* 1069
8480 BOUL LEDUC UNIT 100, BROSSARD,
QC, J4Y 0K7
(450) 766-2300   *SIC* 5731
BEST BUY CANADA LTD   *p* 1078
1401 BOUL TALBOT, CHICOUTIMI, QC,
G7H 5N6
(418) 698-6701   *SIC* 5731
BEST BUY CANADA LTD   *p* 1130
7077 BOUL NEWMAN, LASALLE, QC, H8N
1X1
(514) 368-6570   *SIC* 5731

BEST BUY CANADA LTD   p 1214
2313 RUE SAINTE-CATHERINE O BU-
REAU 108, MONTREAL, QC, H3H 1N2
    SIC 5731
BEST BUY CANADA LTD   p 1249
6321 RTE TRANSCANADIENNE UNITE
121, POINTE-CLAIRE, QC, H9R 5A5
    (514) 428-1999   *SIC* 5999
BEST BUY HOUSING INC   p 351
4250 PORTAGE AVE, HEADINGLEY, MB,
R4H 1C6
    (204) 895-2393   *SIC* 5211
BEST BUY MEDICAL SUPPLIES INC p 406
211 BROMLEY AVE SUITE 7, MONCTON,
NB, E1C 5V5
    (506) 851-1644   *SIC* 5047
BEST BUY MOBILE HOMES   p 351
    See BEST BUY HOUSING INC
**BEST CHOICE OCEAN CONTAINER TER-
MINAL INC**   p
642
11339 ALBION VAUGHAN RD, KLEIN-
BURG, ON, L0J 1C0
    SIC 4214
BEST COST FOOD LTD   p 338
3555 DOUGLAS ST, VICTORIA, BC, V8Z
3L6
    SIC 5411
BEST EXPRESS HOT SHOT TRUCKING p
217
    See HOT SHOT TRUCKING (1990) LTD
BEST MADE TOYS INTERNATIONAL INC p
782
120 SAINT REGIS CRES N, NORTH YORK,
ON, M3J 1Z3
    (416) 630-6665   *SIC* 5092
BEST MADE TOYS INTERNATIONAL, ULC
p 782
120 SAINT REGIS CRES N, NORTH YORK,
ON, M3J 1Z3
    (416) 630-6665   *SIC* 3942
BEST THERATRONICS LTD   p 623
413 MARCH RD SUITE 25, KANATA, ON,
K2K 0E4
    (613) 591-2100   *SIC* 3841
BEST WAY STONE LIMITED   p 1030
8821 WESTON RD, WOODBRIDGE, ON,
L4L 1A6
    (416) 747-0988   *SIC* 3272
BEST WEST PET FOODS INC   p 383
1150 ST JAMES ST, WINNIPEG, MB, R3H
0K7
    (204) 783-0952   *SIC* 5999
BEST WESTERN CAIRN CROFT HOTEL p
758
    See CADE HOLDING INC
**BEST WESTERN CHARTERHOUSE HO-
TELS**   p
376
    See 1379025 ONTARIO LIMITED
BEST WESTERN GLENGARRY   p 469
    *See GLENGARRY MOTEL AND RESTAU-
RANT LIMITED*
BEST WESTERN GUILDWOOD INN p 846
    See GUILDWOOD INN LIMITED, THE
BEST WESTERN HOTEL UNIVERSEL p
1098
    See GESTION J.L.T. UNIVERSELLE INC
BEST WESTERN LAMPLIGHTER INNp 656
    *See LAMPLIGHTER INNS (LONDON) LIM-
ITED*
**BEST WESTERN LAMPLIGHTER INN &
CONFERENCE CENTRE**   p 654
    *See LAMPLIGHTER INNS (LONDON) LIM-
ITED*
**BEST WESTERN NORTH BAY HOTEL AND
CONFERENCE CENTRE, THE**   p 762
    See INVEST REIT
BEST WESTERN PACIFIC INN   p 281
    See SOUTH SURREY HOTEL LTD
BEST WESTERN PARKWAY INN   p 562
    See NORBRO HOLDINGS LTD
**BEST WESTERN PLUS CHATEAU
GRANVILLE HOTEL**   p 326

    See CHATEAU GRANVILLE INC
BEST WESTERN PRIMROSE HOTEL, THE
p 935
    See ARSANDCO INVESTMENTS LIMITED
BEST WESTERN RAINBOW COUNTRY INN
p 197
    See LICKMAN TRAVEL CENTRE INC
BEST WESTERN SANDS HOTEL   p 318
1755 DAVIE ST, VANCOUVER, BC, V6G
1W5
    (604) 682-1831   *SIC* 7011
BEST WESTERN SANDS HOTEL   p 331
3914 32 ST, VERNON, BC, V1T 5P1
    (250) 545-3755   *SIC* 7011
**BEST WESTERN THE WESTERLY HOTEL,
DIV OF**   p 203
    See COURTENAY LODGE LTD
BEST WESTERN VERNON LODGE HOTEL
p 318
    See BEST WESTERN SANDS HOTEL
BEST WESTERN VILLAGE PARK INN p 41
    See ROYAL HOST INC
BEST WESTERN WAYSIDE INN   p 172
    See PEACE HILLS INVESTMENTS LTD
BEST WESTERN WAYSIDE INN & SUITE p
144
    See WAYSIDE MANAGEMENT LTD
BEST WESTERN WHEELS INN   p 542
    See BRAD-LEA MEADOWS LIMITED
BEST-BACKED   p 1362
    See MAPEI INC
BESTAR INC   p 1125
4220 RUE VILLENEUVE, LAC-MEGANTIC,
QC, G6B 2C3
    (819) 583-1017   *SIC* 2511
BESTBUY DISTRIBUTORS LIMITED p 687
3355 AMERICAN DR, MISSISSAUGA, ON,
L4V 1Y7
    (905) 673-0444   *SIC* 5013
BESTCO FOOD MART   p 580
    See 1794318 ONTARIO INC
BESTECH   p 899
    *See BOUDREAU-ESPLEY-PITRE CORPO-
RATION*
BESTILE APPAREL INC   p 866
841 PROGRESS AVE, SCARBOROUGH,
ON, M1H 2X4
    SIC 5136
BESTSELLER   p 1180
    *See BESTSELLER VENTES EN GROS
CANADA INC*
BESTSELLER FASHION   p 1181
    *See VENTE AU DETAIL BESTSELLER
CANADA INC*
**BESTSELLER   VENTES   EN   GROS
CANADA INC**   p 1180
225 RUE DE LIEGE O, MONTREAL, QC,
H2P 1H4
    (514) 381-4392   *SIC* 5136
BESTWAY CARTAGE LIMITED   p 737
6505 VIPOND DR, MISSISSAUGA, ON, L5T
1J9
    (905) 565-8877   *SIC* 4212
BETA-CALCO INC   p 782
25 KODIAK CRES, NORTH YORK, ON, M3J
3E5
    (416) 531-9942   *SIC* 3645
BETA-TECH INC   p 486
318 SAUNDERS RD, BARRIE, ON, L4N 9Y2
    (705) 797-0119   *SIC* 3544
BETAPLEX INC   p 1238
132 RUE PRINCIPALE, MONTREAL, QC,
H7X 3V2
    (450) 969-3300   *SIC* 1521
BETCO ENTERPRISES LTD   p 403
120 MCLEAN AVE, HARTLAND, NB, E7P
2K5
    (506) 375-4671   *SIC* 1542
BETEL HOME FOUNDATION   p 350
96 1ST AVE, GIMLI, MB, R0C 1B1
    (204) 642-5556   *SIC* 8051
BETH TZEDEC CONGREGATION INCp 972
1700 BATHURST ST, TORONTO, ON, M5P
3K3

    (416) 781-3511   *SIC* 8661
BETH TZEDEC MEMORIAL PARK   p 972
    See BETH TZEDEC CONGREGATION INC
**BETHANIA   MENNONITE   PERSONAL
CARE HOME INC**   p 367
1045 CONCORDIA AVE, WINNIPEG, MB,
R2K 3S7
    (204) 667-0795   *SIC* 8361
BETHANY AIRDRIE   p 3
    See BETHANY CARE SOCIETY
BETHANY CARE CENTRE CALGARY p 41
    See BETHANY CARE SOCIETY
BETHANY CARE SOCIETY   p 3
1736 1 AVE NW SUITE 725, AIRDRIE, AB,
T4B 2C4
    (403) 948-6022   *SIC* 8051
BETHANY CARE SOCIETY   p 12
2915 26 AVE SE UNIT 100, CALGARY, AB,
T2B 2W6
    (403) 210-4600   *SIC* 8322
BETHANY CARE SOCIETY   p 41
916 18A ST NW SUITE 3085, CALGARY,
AB, T2N 1C6
    (403) 284-0161   *SIC* 8051
BETHANY CARE SOCIETY   p 76
19 HARVEST GOLD MANOR NE, CAL-
GARY, AB, T3K 4Y1
    (403) 226-8200   *SIC* 8051
BETHANY CARE SOCIETY   p 80
32 QUIGLEY DR UNIT 1000, COCHRANE,
AB, T4C 1X9
    (403) 932-6422   *SIC* 8051
BETHANY CARE SOCIETY   p 156
99 COLLEGE CIR, RED DEER, AB, T4R
0M3
    (403) 357-3700   *SIC* 8322
BETHANY HARVEST HILLS   p 76
    See BETHANY CARE SOCIETY
BETHEL WINDOWS & DOORS LTD   p 80
1504 12 ST, COALDALE, AB, T1M 1M3
    (403) 345-4401   *SIC* 5211
BETHESDA COMMUNITY SERVICES INC p
906
3280 SCHMON PKY, THOROLD, ON, L2V
4Y6
    (905) 684-6918   *SIC* 8399
**BETHESDA HOME FOR THE MENTALLY
HANDICAPPED INC**   p 906
3280 SCHMON PKY, THOROLD, ON, L2V
4Y6
    (905) 684-6918   *SIC* 8399
**BETHESDA HOME FOR THE MENTALLY
HANDICAPPED INC**   p 1003
3950 FLY RD RR 1, VINELAND, ON, L0R
2C0
    (905) 562-4184   *SIC* 8399
BETHESDA HOSPITAL   p 358
    See SOUTHERN HEALTH-SANTE SUD
BETHESDA PROGRAMS   p 906
    *See BETHESDA HOME FOR THE MEN-
TALLY HANDICAPPED INC*
BETHESDA PROGRAMS   p 1003
    *See BETHESDA HOME FOR THE MEN-
TALLY HANDICAPPED INC*
BETON ALLIANCE   p 1150
    See BETON PROVINCIAL LTEE
BETON AMIX LTEE   p 1108
600B RUE DE VERNON, GATINEAU, QC,
J9J 3K5
    (819) 770-5092   *SIC* 3273
BETON BARRETTE INC   p 1390
1000 BOUL BARRETTE, VAL-D'OR, QC,
J9P 0J8
    (819) 825-8112   *SIC* 5032
BETON BELLEMARE   p 1388
    See THOMAS BELLEMARE LTEE
BETON BOLDUC INC   p 1359
1358 2E RUE DU PARC-INDUSTRIEL,
SAINTE-MARIE, QC, G6E 1G8
    (418) 387-2634   *SIC* 3272
BETON BOURGEOIS   p 1082
    See A. & J.L. BOURGEOIS LTEE
BETON CHEVALIER INC   p 1055
152 39E AV, BEAUCEVILLE, QC, G5X 3S4

    (418) 774-4747   *SIC* 5211
BETON CHEVALIER INC   p 1378
50   CH   ROURKE,   STONEHAM-ET-
TEWKESBURY, QC, G3C 0W3
    (418) 848-1966   *SIC* 5032
BETON DUNBRICK   p 1079
    See GAZON SAVARD (SAGUENAY) INC
BETON GRANBY   p 1299
    *See   CARRIERES   DE   ST-DOMINIQUE
LTEE, LES*
BETON LAGACE   p 1254
    See ENTREPRISES L.T. LTEE, LES
BETON METROPOLITAIN   p 1307
    See 9338-4337 QUEBEC INC
BETON MOBILE ST-ALPHONSE   p 1318
    See MSA INFRASTRUCTURES INC
BETON OPTIMAL   p 1351
    See GROUPE ABS INC
BETON PREFABRIQUE DU RICHELIEU INC
p 1044
890 RUE DES PINS O, ALMA, QC, G8B 7R3
    (418) 668-6161   *SIC* 3273
BETON PROVINCIAL FINANCE LTEE   p
1150
1825 AV DU PHARE O, MATANE, QC, G4W
3M6
    (418) 562-0074   *SIC* 6712
BETON PROVINCIAL LTEE   p 1150
1825 AV DU PHARE O, MATANE, QC, G4W
3M6
    (418) 562-0074   *SIC* 6712
BETON ROYAL   p 1378
    See BETON CHEVALIER INC
BETON ST-MARC   p 1348
    See GRAYMONT (PORTNEUF) INC
BETONEL MD   p 1067
    *See PPG ARCHITECTURAL COATINGS
CANADA INC*
BETONNIERES MODERNES, LES   p 1381
    See ASPHALTE DESJARDINS INC
BETONS PREFABRIQUES DU LAC INC   p
1044
890 RUE DES PINS O, ALMA, QC, G8B 7R3
    (418) 668-6161   *SIC* 3272
**BETONS   PREFABRIQUES   TRANS-
CANADA INC**   p
1044
890 RUE DES PINS O, ALMA, QC, G8B 7R3
    (418) 668-6161   *SIC* 1771
**BETTER BEEF-CARGILL MEAT SOLU-
TIONS, DIV OF**   p
600
    See CARGILL LIMITED
BETTER BUILT   p 209
    *See NORTHWESTERN SYSTEMS COR-
PORATION*
BETTER SOFTWARE COMPANY INC, THE
p 832
303 TERRY FOX DR SUITE 101, OTTAWA,
ON, K2K 3J1
    (613) 627-3506   *SIC* 7372
BETTER WELLNESS JMC LTD   p 634
1221 WEBER ST E SUITE 1086, KITCH-
ENER, ON, N2A 1C2
    (519) 748-2430   *SIC* 5912
BEURLING ACADEMY   p 1397
    *See   LESTER B.   PEARSON SCHOOL
BOARD*
BEVCO   p 281
    See BEVCO SALES INTERNATIONAL INC
BEVCO SALES INTERNATIONAL INCp 281
9354 194 ST, SURREY, BC, V4N 4E9
    (604) 888-1455   *SIC* 5084
BEVENDALE ENTERPRISES LTD   p 343
1380   ALPHA LAKE RD   SUITE   4,
WHISTLER, BC, V8E 0H9
    (604) 932-5506   *SIC* 5411
BEVERLY CREST MOTOR INN LTD   p 106
3414 118 AVE NW, EDMONTON, AB, T5W
0Z4
    (780) 474-0456   *SIC* 7011
BEVERLY GROUP INC, THE   p 566
525 6 HWY, DUNDAS, ON, L9H 7K1
    (905) 525-9240   *SIC* 5531

BEVERTEC CST INC p 692
5025 ORBITOR DR BLDG 6 UNIT 400, MISSISSAUGA, ON, L4W 4Y5
(416) 695-7525 SIC 7379

BEVO FARMS LTD p 226
7170 GLOVER RD, LANGLEY, BC, V2Y 2R1
(604) 888-0420 SIC 0161

BEWORKS INC p 990
946 QUEEN ST W, TORONTO, ON, M6J 1G8
(416) 920-1921 SIC 8742

BEXEL INC p 1225
9001 BOUL DE L'ACADIE BUREAU 200, MONTREAL, QC, H4N 3H7
(514) 858-2222 SIC 0251

BEYOND DIGITAL IMAGING INC p 667
36 APPLE CREEK BLVD, MARKHAM, ON, L3R 4Y4
(905) 415-1888 SIC 7384

BEYOND ENERGY & TRADE INC p 44
205 5 AVE SW SUITE 1870, CALGARY, AB, T2P 2V7
(403) 531-2699 SIC 4924

BEYOND ENERGY SERVICES & TECHNOLOGY CORP p 44
444 5 AVE SW, CALGARY, AB, T2P 2T8
(403) 506-1514 SIC 1381

BEYOND TECHNOLOGIES p 1212
See SOLUTIONS BEYOND TECHNOLOGIES INC

BEYOND THE RACK p 1337
See 7098961 CANADA INC

BEYOND WIRELESS INC p 898
444 BARRYDOWNE RD UNIT 3, SUDBURY, ON, P3A 3T3
(705) 525-7091 SIC 4812

BF WORKPLACE p 383
See BUSINESS FURNISHINGS (1996) LTD

BFCO INC p 1054
5 RUE PAUL-RENE-TREMBLAY, BAIE-SAINT-PAUL, QC, G3Z 3E4
(418) 435-3682 SIC 2499

BFG CANADA LTD p 593
88 TODD RD, GEORGETOWN, ON, L7G 4R7
(905) 873-8744 SIC 2099

BFG ENTERPRISE SERVICES p 678
See BURMAN & FELLOWS GROUP INC

BFI CANADA p 160
See WASTE CONNECTIONS OF CANADA INC

BFI CANADA p 497
See WASTE CONNECTIONS OF CANADA INC

BFI CANADA p 561
See WASTE CONNECTIONS OF CANADA INC

BFI CANADA p 595
See WASTE CONNECTIONS OF CANADA INC

BFI CONSTRUCTORS LTD p 112
8404 MCINTYRE RD NW, EDMONTON, AB, T6E 6V3
(780) 485-2703 SIC 1541

BFL CANADA p 1193
See BFL CANADA RISQUES ET ASSURANCES INC

BFL CANADA INSURANCE SERVICES INC p 41
1167 KENSINGTON CRES NW SUITE 200, CALGARY, AB, T2N 1X7
(403) 451-4132 SIC 6311

BFL CANADA INSURANCE SERVICES INC p 311
1177 HASTINGS ST W SUITE 200, VANCOUVER, BC, V6E 2K3
(604) 669-9600 SIC 6411

BFL CANADA RISK AND INSURANCE SERVICES INC p 949
181 UNIVERSITY AVE SUITE 1700, TORONTO, ON, M5H 3M7
(416) 599-5530 SIC 6411

BFL CANADA RISQUES ET ASSURANCES

INC p 1193
2001 AV MCGILL COLLEGE BUREAU 2200, MONTREAL, QC, H3A 1G1
(514) 843-3632 SIC 6411

BFS 2002 p 1293
See PREVERCO INC

BG DESIGN p 1195

BG DISTRIBUTION p 596
See BRUNET-GOULARD AGENCIES INC

BGI p 667
See BGI BENCHMARK GROUP INTERNATIONAL INC

BGI BENCHMARK GROUP INTERNATIONAL INC p 667
207-30 CENTURIAN DR, MARKHAM, ON, L3R 8B8
(905) 305-8900 SIC 8741

BGIS GLOBAL INTEGRATED SOLUTIONS CANADA LP p 667
4175 14TH AVE SUITE 300, MARKHAM, ON, L3R 0J2
(905) 943-4100 SIC 6531

BGIS O&M SOLUTIONS INC p 1185
87 RUE ONTARIO O BUREAU 200, MONTREAL, QC, H2X 0A7
(514) 840-8660 SIC 6531

BGK CONSULTANTS p 1401
See BESSNER GALLAY KREISMAN

BGL CONTRACTORS CORP p 1010
608 COLBY DR, WATERLOO, ON, N2V 1A2
(519) 725-5000 SIC 1542

BGL SOFT p 1166
See OBJECTIF LUNE INC

BGLA INC p 1258
50 COTE DINAN, QUEBEC, QC, G1K 8N6
(418) 694-9041 SIC 8712

BGRS LIMITED p 778
39 WYNFORD DR, NORTH YORK, ON, M3C 3K5
(416) 510-5600 SIC 7389

BHD TUBULAR LIMITED p 108
6903 72 AVE NW, EDMONTON, AB, T6B 3A5
(780) 434-6824 SIC 5051

BHI INSTALLATIONS INC p 501
278 ORENDA RD, BRAMPTON, ON, L6T 4X6
(905) 791-2850 SIC 1751

BHM MEDICAL p 1147
See ARJOHUNTLEIGH MAGOG INC

BI VIEW BUILDING SERVICES LTD p 692
5004 TIMBERLEA BLVD UNIT 26-29, MISSISSAUGA, ON, L4W 5C5
(905) 712-1831 SIC 7349

BIALIK HEBREW DAY SCHOOL p 790
2760 BATHURST ST, NORTH YORK, ON, M6B 3A1
(416) 783-3346 SIC 8211

BIALIK HIGH SCHOOL p 1083
See JEWISH PEOPLE'S SCHOOLS AND PERETZ SCHOOLS INC

BIALIK, DON & ASSOCIATES p 44
255 5 AVE SW SUITE 3100, CALGARY, AB, T2P 3G6
(403) 515-6900 SIC 7379

BIAMONTE INVESTMENTS LTD p 760
7600 LUNDY'S LANE, NIAGARA FALLS, ON, L2H 1H1
(905) 354-2211 SIC 5812

BIASUCCI DEVELOPMENTS INC p 863
544 WELLINGTON ST W, SAULT STE. MARIE, ON, P6C 3T6
(705) 946-8701 SIC 1542

BIBBY STE CROIX p 1357
See CANADA PIPE COMPANY ULC

BIBEAU p 1303
See USINES D'AUTRAY LTEE, LES

BIBLAIRIE G.G.C. LTEE p 1371
1567 RUE KING O, SHERBROOKE, QC, J1J 2C6
(819) 566-0344 SIC 5192

BIBLIOCENTRE, DIV OF p 866

See CENTENNIAL COLLEGE OF APPLIED ARTS & TECHNOLOGY, THE

BIBLIOCOMMONS INC p 978
119 SPADINA AVE SUITE 1000, TORONTO, ON, M5V 2L1
(647) 436-6381 SIC 7374

BIBLIOTHEQUE ET ARCHIVES NATIONALES DU QUEBEC p 1175
See GOUVERNEMENT DE LA PROVINCE DE QUEBEC

BIBLIOTHEQUE ET ARCHIVES NATIONALES DU QUEBEC p 1175
475 BOUL DE MAISONNEUVE E, MONTREAL, QC, H2L 5C4
(514) 873-1100 SIC 8231

BIBLIOTHEQUE ET ARCHIVES NATIONALES DU QUEBEC p 1284
337 RUE MOREAULT, RIMOUSKI, QC, G5L 1P4
(418) 727-3500 SIC 8231

BIBLIOTHEQUE GABRIELLE ROY p 1259
See INSTITUT CANADIEN DE QUEBEC, L'

BIC INC p 786
155 OAKDALE RD, NORTH YORK, ON, M3N 1W2
(416) 742-9173 SIC 5122

BIC SPORT p 786
See BIC INC

BICKNELL, PETER AUTOMOTIVE INC p 883
117 CUSHMAN RD, ST CATHARINES, ON, L2M 6S9
(905) 685-3184 SIC 5511

BICYCLES QUILICOT INC, LES p 1364
232 RUE SAINT-CHARLES LOCAL 90, SAINTE-THERESE, QC, J7E 2B4
(450) 420-2222 SIC 5941

BICYCLES QUILICOT PERFORMANCE p 1364
See BICYCLES QUILICOT INC, LES

BID GROUP TECHNOLOGIES LTD p 330
See BID GROUP TECHNOLOGIES LTD

BID GROUP TECHNOLOGIES LTD p 330
3446 MOUNTAIN VIEW RD, VANDERHOOF, BC, V0J 3A2
(250) 567-2578 SIC 3441

BID GROUP TECHNOLOGIES LTD p 1152
18095 RUE LAPOINTE, MIRABEL, QC, J7J 1E3
(450) 435-2121 SIC 3553

BID GROUP TECHNOLOGIES LTD p 1304
4000 40E RUE, SAINT-GEORGES, QC, G5Y 8G4
(418) 228-8911 SIC 3553

BIDCOR SALES AND MARKETING INC p 692
2785 SKYMARK AVE SUITE 14, MISSISSAUGA, ON, L4W 4Y3
SIC 5141

BIDELL EQUIPMENT LIMITED PARTNERSHIP p 14
6900 112 AVE SE, CALGARY, AB, T2C 4Z1
(403) 235-5877 SIC 3563

BIDELL GAS COMPRESSION p 19
See TOTAL ENERGY SERVICES INC

BIDGOOD'S SUPERMARKET p 423
See BIDGOOD'S WHOLESALE LIMITED

BIDGOOD'S WHOLESALE LIMITED p 423
355 MAIN RD, GOULDS, NL, A1S 1J9
(709) 368-3125 SIC 5411

BIENA INC p 1311
2955 RUE CARTIER, SAINT-HYACINTHE, QC, J2S 1L4
(450) 778-7505 SIC 2023

BIESSE CANADA INC p 1152
18005 RUE LAPOINTE, MIRABEL, QC, J7J 0G2
(450) 437-5534 SIC 5084

BIG 4 DODGE JEEP p 33
See BIG 4 MOTORS LTD

BIG 4 MOTORS LTD p 33
7330 MACLEOD TRAIL SE, CALGARY, AB, T2H 0L9
(403) 252-6671 SIC 5511

BIG 8 BEVERAGES LIMITED p 466
120 NORTH FOORD ST, STELLARTON, NS, B0K 0A2
(902) 755-6333 SIC 2086

BIG AL p 1134
See MANUFACTURE TRIPLE G. INC

BIG AL'S AQUARIUM SERVICES p 1029
See AQUARIUM SERVICES WAREHOUSE OUTLETS INC

BIG BILL p 1081
See CODET INC

BIG BLUE BUBBLE INC p 653
220 DUNDAS ST SUITE 900, LONDON, ON, N6A 1H3
(519) 649-0071 SIC 5734

BIG BRANDS INC p 14
5329 72 AVE SE, CALGARY, AB, T2C 4X6
(587) 470-5810 SIC 5122

BIG CARROT NATURAL FOOD MARKET p 919
See 546073 ONTARIO LIMITED

BIG COUNTRY ENERGY SERVICES LIMITED PARTNERSHIP p 172
3905 35 ST SUITE 3, WHITECOURT, AB, T7S 0A2
(780) 706-2141 SIC 1623

BIG COUNTRY HOSPITAL p 151
See ALBERTA HEALTH SERVICES

BIG D PRODUCTS LTD p 331
7861 HWY 97 SUITE 1, VERNON, BC, V1B 3R9
SIC 5023

BIG EARL RADIO p 104
See NEWCAP INC

BIG FREIGHT SYSTEMS INC p 371
10 HUTCHINGS ST, WINNIPEG, MB, R2X 2X1
(204) 772-3434 SIC 4213

BIG FREIGHT WAREHOUSING p 371
See BIG FREIGHT SYSTEMS INC

BIG G HOLDINGS LTD p 1413
GD, PENNANT STATION, SK, S0N 1X0
(306) 626-3249 SIC 0119

BIG HEARTS HOLDINGS LTD p 259
5760 MINORU BLVD SUITE 203, RICHMOND, BC, V6X 2A9
(604) 278-3318 SIC 8059

BIG I TOWING p 14
See CITY WIDE TOWING AND RECOVERY SERVICE LTD

BIG LAKES DODGE LTD p 135
5109 41 ST, HIGH PRAIRIE, AB, T0G 1E0
(780) 523-5007 SIC 5511

BIG M FORD LINCOLN LTD p 146
1312 TRANS CANADA WAY SE, MEDICINE HAT, AB, T1B 3Z9
(403) 527-4406 SIC 5511

BIG MOO ICE CREAM PARLOURS, THE p 169
4603 LAKESHORE DR, SYLVAN LAKE, AB, T4S 1C3
(403) 887-5533 SIC 5451

BIG RED DOG INC p 342
4122 VILLAGE GREEN SUITE 5, WHISTLER, BC, V0N 1B4
(604) 938-9656 SIC 4725

BIG RED MARKET p 906
See 633569 ONTARIO LIMITED

BIG RED MARKETS p 906
See 1729787 ONTARIO LIMITED

BIG RED OIL PRODUCTS INC p 844
1915 CLEMENTS RD SUITE 7, PICKERING, ON, L1W 3V1
(905) 420-0001 SIC 5172

BIG RIG COLLISION AND PAINT LTD p 174
933 COUTTS WAY, ABBOTSFORD, BC, V2S 7M2
(604) 857-4915 SIC 7532

BIG RIG COLLISION REPAIRS p 118

See 402909 ALBERTA LTD

BIG RIG HEAVY DUTY PARTS p 174
See BIG RIG COLLISION AND PAINT LTD

BIG ROCK BREWERY INC p 14
5555 76 AVE SE SUITE 1, CALGARY, AB, T2C 4L8
(403) 720-3239 *SIC 2082*

BIG SHO FOODS LTD p 998
130 QUEEN ST N, TOTTENHAM, ON, L0G 1W0
(905) 936-6157 *SIC 5812*

BIG SKY FARMS INC p 1407
10333 8TH AVE E, HUMBOLDT, SK, S0K 2A1
(306) 682-5041 *SIC 0213*

BIG TROUT LAKE BAND PERSONNEL OFFICE p 493
GD, BIG TROUT LAKE, ON, P0V 1G0
SIC 8699

BIG WHITE SKI RESORT LTD p 218
5315 BIG WHITE RD, KELOWNA, BC, V1P 1P4
(250) 765-3101 *SIC 7011*

BIGELOW FOWLER CLINIC p 142
1605 9 AVE S, LETHBRIDGE, AB, T1J 1W2
(403) 327-3121 *SIC 8011*

BIGGAR p 945
See FETHERSTONHAUGH & CO.

BIGGS AND NARCISO CONSTRUCTION SERVICES INC p 667
181 BENTLEY ST SUITE 14, MARKHAM, ON, L3R 3Y1
(905) 470-8788 *SIC 1799*

BIGNUCOLO INCORPORATED p 541
13 BEECH ST, CHAPLEAU, ON, P0M 1K0
(705) 864-0774 *SIC 5411*

BIGRIDGE BREWING CORPORATION p 271
5580 152 ST, SURREY, BC, V3S 5J9
(604) 574-2739 *SIC 2082*

BIGTECH p 677
See BIGTECH CLI INC

BIGTECH CLI INC p 677
5990 14TH AVE, MARKHAM, ON, L3S 4M4
(905) 695-0100 *SIC 7378*

BIJORKA p 1250
See DIAMANT ELINOR INC.

BIJOUTERIE CARMEN INC p 1325
700 RUE HODGE AVE SUITE 200, SAINT-LAURENT, QC, H4N 2V2
(514) 273-1718 *SIC 5094*

BIJOUTERIE EDOUARD p 1241
See 137448 CANADA INC

BIJOUTERIE JACOBUS p 1274
See GROUPE JACOBUS INC

BIJOUTERIE LATENDRESSE p 1178
See BIJOUTIERS DOUCET 1993 INC, LES

BIJOUTERIE LAVIGUEUR LTEE p 1310
3981 RUE DE MONT-ROYAL BUREAU 100, SAINT-HUBERT, QC, J4T 2H4
(450) 672-3233 *SIC 5944*

BIJOUTIERS DOUCET 1993 INC, LES p 1178
9250 RUE MEILLEUR BUREAU 201, MONTREAL, QC, H2N 2A5
(514) 385-4500 *SIC 5944*

BIK HYDRAULICS LTD p 582
41 CLAIREVILLE DR UNIT A, ETOBICOKE, ON, M9W 5Z7
(416) 679-3838 *SIC 5084*

BIKINI VILLAGE p 1166
See BOUTIQUE LA VIE EN ROSE INC

BIKY p 1345
See SOCIETE EN COMMANDITE CANADELLE

BILD p 775
See BUILDING INDUSTRY AND LAND DEVELOPMENT ASSOCIATION

BILGEN, BERK INSURANCE LTD p 112
8925 51 AVE NW SUITE 311, EDMONTON, AB, T6E 5J3
(780) 822-6042 *SIC 6411*

BILL GOSLING OUTSOURCING HOLDING CORP p 754
16635 YONGE ST SUITE 26, NEWMARKET, ON, L3X 1V6
(905) 470-8181 *SIC 6712*

BILL HOWICH CHRYSLER JEEP p 194
See BILL HOWICH CHRYSLER LTD

BILL HOWICH CHRYSLER LTD p 194
2777 ISLAND HWY, CAMPBELL RIVER, BC, V9W 2H4
(250) 287-9133 *SIC 5511*

BILL MATTHEWS' AUTOHAUS LIMITED p 429
575 KENMOUNT RD, ST. JOHN'S, NL, A1B 3P9
(709) 726-4424 *SIC 5511*

BILL MATTICK'S RESTAURANT & LOUNGE p 338
See CORDOVA BAY GOLF COURSE LTD

BILLABONG p 1334
See GSM (CANADA) PTY LTD

BILLABONG ROAD & BRIDGE MAINTENANCE INC p 283
5630 16 HWY W, TERRACE, BC, V8G 0C6
(250) 638-7918 *SIC 1611*

BILLETTE & VINCENT p 1360
See 9016-0003 QUEBEC INC

BILLY BEATS p 1340
See MEGA BRANDS INC

BILLY GRUFF MARKETING LTD p 198
2310 ALBERNI HWY, COOMBS, BC, V0R 1M0
(250) 248-6272 *SIC 5411*

BILODEAU p 1243
See NATURE 3M INC

BILODEAU AUTOS p 1354
See BILODEAU, CECIL AUTOS LTEE

BILODEAU COUTURE ASSURANCES INC p 1080
31 RUE RACINE O, CHICOUTIMI, QC, G7J 1E4
(418) 698-0999 *SIC 6331*

BILODEAU, CECIL AUTOS LTEE p 1354
9641 BOUL SAINTE-ANNE, SAINTE-ANNE-DE-BEAUPRE, QC, G0A 3C0
(418) 827-3773 *SIC 5511*

BILODEAU, L. & FILS LTEE p 1064
1405 RUE GRAHAM-BELL BUREAU 101, BOUCHERVILLE, QC, J4B 6A1
(450) 449-6542 *SIC 4724*

BILTON WELDING AND MANUFACTURING LTD p 136
5815 37 ST, INNISFAIL, AB, T4G 1S8
(403) 227-7799 *SIC 3533*

BIMCOR INC p 1202
1000 RUE DE LA GAUCHETIERE O BUREAU 1300, MONTREAL, QC, H3B 5A7
(514) 394-4750 *SIC 6282*

BIMEDA-MTC ANIMAL HEALTH INC p 537
420 BEAVERDALE RD, CAMBRIDGE, ON, N3C 2W4
(519) 654-8000 *SIC 2834*

BIMINI UNITED CHURCH CAMP p 757
3180 113 RD, NEWTON, ON, N0K 1V0
(519) 271-4129 *SIC 7032*

BINARY STREAM SOFTWARE INC p 182
4238 LOZELLS AVE UNIT 201, BURNABY, BC, V5A 0C4
(604) 522-6300 *SIC 7371*

BINDER CONSTRUCTION LIMITED p 95
11635 160 ST NW, EDMONTON, AB, T5M 3Z3
(780) 452-2740 *SIC 1542*

BINGEMANS INC p 635
425 BINGEMANS CENTRE DR, KITCHENER, ON, N2B 3X7
(519) 744-1555 *SIC 5812*

BINGHAM MEMORIAL HOSPITAL p 680
507 8TH AVE, MATHESON, ON, P0K 1N0
(705) 273-2424 *SIC 8062*

BINGO KELOWNA CHANCES GAMING ENTERTAINMENT p 221
1585 SPRINGFIELD RD, KELOWNA, BC, V1Y 5V5
(250) 860-9577 *SIC 7999*

BINGO PAPER COMPANY, THE p 20
See 800743 ALBERTA LTD

BINGO VEZINA INC p 1343
6125 BOUL METROPOLITAIN E, SAINT-LEONARD, QC, H1P 1X7
(514) 321-5555 *SIC 5092*

BINKS INSURANCE BROKERS LIMITED p 830
2625 QUEENSVIEW DR SUITE 100B, OTTAWA, ON, K2B 8K2
(613) 226-1350 *SIC 6411*

BINNIE p 188
See BINNIE, R.F. & ASSOCIATES LTD

BINNIE, R.F. & ASSOCIATES LTD p 188
300-4940 CANADA WAY, BURNABY, BC, V5G 4K6
(604) 420-1721 *SIC 8711*

BIO AGRI MIX LP p 745
11 ELLENS ST, MITCHELL, ON, N0K 1N0
(519) 348-9865 *SIC 2834*

BIO BANQUE GENIZON p 1204
See GENOME QUEBEC

BIO BASIC CANADA INC p 667
20 KONRAD CRES SUITE 1, MARKHAM, ON, L3R 8T4
(905) 474-4493 *SIC 5169*

BIO BISCUIT INC p 1311
5505 AV TRUDEAU BUREAU 15, SAINT-HYACINTHE, QC, J2S 1H5
(450) 778-1349 *SIC 2047*

BIO PED FOOT CARE CENTRE p 796
See BIO PED FRANCHISING INC

BIO PED FRANCHISING INC p 796
2150 WINSTON PARK DR UNIT 21, OAKVILLE, ON, L6H 5V1
(905) 829-0505 *SIC 6794*

BIO-RAD LABORATORIES (CANADA) LIMITED p 737
1329 MEYERSIDE DR, MISSISSAUGA, ON, L5T 1C9
(905) 364-3435 *SIC 5049*

BIOAMP p 1226
See NCH CANADA INC

BIOCARBURANTS ENERKEM ALBERTA p 124
See ENERKEM ALBERTA BIOFUELS LP

BIOFORCE CANADA INC p 1091
66 BOUL BRUNSWICK, DOLLARD-DES-ORMEAUX, QC, H9B 2L3
(514) 421-3441 *SIC 5149*

BIOFORET p 1167
See LALLEMAND INC

BIOGEOSCIENCE INSTITUTE p 41
See GOVERNORS OF THE UNIVERSITY OF CALGARY, THE

BIOMATIK CORPORATION p 538
140 MCGOVERN DR UNIT 9, CAMBRIDGE, ON, N3H 4R7
(519) 489-7195 *SIC 5122*

BIOMEDIC p 1276
See FAMILIPRIX INC

BIOMEDICAL INDUSTRY GROUP INC p 820
532 MONTREAL RD SUITE 362, OTTAWA, ON, K1K 4R4
(613) 745-4139 *SIC 5047*

BIOMERIEUX CANADA, INC p 1332
7815 BOUL HENRI-BOURASSA O, SAINT-LAURENT, QC, H4S 1P7
(514) 336-7321 *SIC 5047*

BIONEST p 1369
See TECHNOLOGIES BIONEST INC

BIONEUTRA GLOBAL CORPORATION p 120
9608 25 AVE NW, EDMONTON, AB, T6N 1J4
(780) 466-1481 *SIC 5149*

BIONX CANADA p 480
See BIONX INTERNATIONAL CORPORATION

BIONX INTERNATIONAL CORPORATION p 480
455 MAGNA DR, AURORA, ON, L4G 7A9
(905) 726-9105 *SIC 3625*

BIOPAK LIMITED p 113
7824 51 AVE NW, EDMONTON, AB, T6E 6W2
SIC 2023

BIOPHARM p 1059
See NEOPHARM LABS INC

BIOREM INC p 848
7496 WELLINGTON RD 34, PUSLINCH, ON, N0B 2J0
(519) 767-9100 *SIC 3822*

BIOREX INC p 1268
295 CH SAINTE-FOY, QUEBEC, QC, G1R 1T5
(418) 522-4945 *SIC 8748*

BIOSCRYPT INC p 667
50 ACADIA AVE UNIT 200, MARKHAM, ON, L3R 0B3
(905) 624-7700 *SIC 3663*

BIOSITE p 1393
See GSI ENVIRONNEMENT INC

BIOSPHERA p 1304
See AUTHENTIQUE POSE CAFE INC, L'

BIOSTEEL SPORTS NUTRITION INC p 790
1-87 WINGOLD AVE, NORTH YORK, ON, M6B 1P8
(416) 322-7833 *SIC 5122*

BIOSYENT INC p 582
170 ATTWELL DR SUITE 520, ETOBICOKE, ON, M9W 5Z5
(905) 206-0013 *SIC 2834*

BIOTHERM CANADA p 1197
See L'OREAL CANADA INC

BIOTRONIK CANADA INC p 578
185 THE WEST MALL SUITE 1000, ETOBICOKE, ON, M9C 5L5
(416) 620-0069 *SIC 5047*

BIOVECTRA INC p 1040
11 AVIATION AVE, CHARLOTTETOWN, PE, C1E 0A1
(902) 566-9116 *SIC 2834*

BIOVECTRA INC p 1040
29 MCCARVILLE ST, CHARLOTTETOWN, PE, C1E 2A7
(902) 566-9116 *SIC 2834*

BIOWARE CORP p 118
4445 CALGARY TRAIL NW SUITE 200, EDMONTON, AB, T6H 5R7
(780) 430-0164 *SIC 7371*

BIRCH HILL EQUITY PARTNERS II LTD p 969
100 WELLINGTON ST W SUITE 2300, TORONTO, ON, M5K 1B7
(416) 775-3800 *SIC 6211*

BIRCH HILL EQUITY PARTNERS MANAGEMENT INC p 969
100 WELLINGTON ST W SUITE 2300, TORONTO, ON, M5K 1A1
(416) 775-3800 *SIC 6726*

BIRCH STREET SEAFOODS LTD p 449
31 BIRCH ST, DIGBY, NS, B0V 1A0
(902) 245-6551 *SIC 5142*

BIRCHCLIFF ENERGY LTD p 44
600 3RD AVE SW SUITE 1000, CALGARY, AB, T2P 0G5
(403) 261-6401 *SIC 1382*

BIRCHES NURSING HOME, THE p 463
See TWIN OAKS SENIOR CITIZENS ASSOCIATION

BIRCHGROVE CAPITAL CORPORATION LTD p 445
7 MELLOR AVE UNIT 1, DARTMOUTH, NS, B3B 0E8
(902) 453-9300 *SIC 6531*

BIRCHGROW REALTY p 448
See RE/MAX NOVA REAL ESTATE

BIRCHLAND PLYWOOD - VENEER LIMITED p 903
50 GENELLE ST, THESSALON, ON, P0R 1L0

(705) 842-2430   *SIC* 2435
BIRCHWOOD CHEVROLET BUICK GMC *p*
386
See BIRCHWOOD PONTIAC BUICK LIM-
ITED
BIRCHWOOD FURNITURE CO INC   *p* 12
4770 46 AVE SE, CALGARY, AB, T2B 3T7
(403) 252-5111   *SIC* 2512
BIRCHWOOD HONDA WEST   *p* 386
3965 PORTAGE AVE SUITE 75, WIN-
NIPEG, MB, R3K 2H5
(204) 888-4542   *SIC* 5511
BIRCHWOOD PONTIAC BUICK LIMITED *p*
386
3965 PORTAGE AVE UNIT 40, WINNIPEG,
MB, R3K 2H1
(204) 837-5811   *SIC* 5511
BIRD CONSTRUCTION COMPANY   *p* 381
1055 ERIN ST, WINNIPEG, MB, R3G 2X1
(204) 775-7141   *SIC* 1542
BIRD CONSTRUCTION COMPANY LIM-
ITED   *p*
257
6900 GRAYBAR RD SUITE 2370, RICH-
MOND, BC, V6W 0A5
(604) 271-4600   *SIC* 1542
BIRD CONSTRUCTION COMPANY LIM-
ITED   *p*
692
5700 EXPLORER DR SUITE 400, MISSIS-
SAUGA, ON, L4W 0C6
(905) 602-4122   *SIC* 1542
BIRD CONSTRUCTION INC   *p* 692
5700 EXPLORER DR SUITE 400, MISSIS-
SAUGA, ON, L4W 0C6
(905) 602-4122   *SIC* 1542
BIRD ENTREPRENEURS GENERAUX
LTEE   *p* 1249
1870 BOUL DES SOURCES BUREAU 200,
POINTE-CLAIRE, QC, H9R 5N4
(514) 426-1333   *SIC* 1611
BIRD STAIRS   *p* 400
See BIRD, J.W. AND COMPANY LIMITED
BIRD, J.W. AND COMPANY LIMITED *p* 400
670 WILSEY RD, FREDERICTON, NB, E3B
7K4
(506) 453-9915   *SIC* 5039
BIRD-STAIRS LTD   *p* 400
670 WILSEY RD, FREDERICTON, NB, E3B
7K4
(506) 453-9915   *SIC* 5063
BIRLA CARBON   *p* 609
See BIRLA CARBON CANADA LTD
BIRLA CARBON CANADA LTD   *p* 609
755 PARKDALE AVE N, HAMILTON, ON,
L8H 7N5
(905) 544-3343   *SIC* 2895
BIRNAM EXCAVATING LTD   *p* 1005
7046 NAUVOO RD, WARWICK TOWNSHIP,
ON, N0N 1J4
(519) 828-3449   *SIC* 1623
BIRON   *p* 1077
See 9170-7570 QUEBEC INC
BIRON DIAGNOSTIC   *p* 1069
See BIRON LABORATOIRE MEDICAL INC
BIRON LABORATOIRE MEDICAL INC   *p*
1069
4105 BOUL MATTE, BROSSARD, QC, J4Y
2P4
(514) 866-6146   *SIC* 8071
BIRTHRIGHT   *p* 917
777 COXWELL AVE, TORONTO, ON, M4C
3C6
(416) 469-1111   *SIC* 8399
BIRTHRIGHT INTERNATIONAL   *p* 917
See BIRTHRIGHT
BIRTLEY COAL TESTING, DIV OF   *p* 185
See GWIL INDUSTRIES INC
BISCUITERIE DOMINIC INC   *p* 1114
285 RUE SAINT-CHARLES-BORROMEE N,
JOLIETTE, QC, J6E 4R8
(450) 756-2637   *SIC* 5461
BISCUITS LECLERC LTEE   *p* 1292
91 RUE DE ROTTERDAM, SAINT-

AUGUSTIN-DE-DESMAURES, QC, G3A
1T1
(418) 878-2601   *SIC* 2052
BISCUITS LECLERC LTEE   *p* 1292
70 RUE DE ROTTERDAM, SAINT-
AUGUSTIN-DE-DESMAURES, QC, G3A
1S9
(418) 878-2601   *SIC* 2052
BISHARA PHARMA INC   *p* 1185
3575 AV DU PARC BUREAU 5602, MON-
TREAL, QC, H2X 3P9
(514) 849-6176   *SIC* 5912
BISHOP & ASSOCIATES   *p* 70
See BISHOP, DONALD H. PROFESSIONAL
CORPORATION
BISHOP & MCKENZIE LLP   *p* 87
10180 101 ST SUITE 2300, EDMONTON,
AB, T5J 1V3
(780) 426-5550   *SIC* 8111
BISHOP ALLEN ACADEMY   *p* 573
See TORONTO CATHOLIC DISTRICT
SCHOOL BOARD
BISHOP CARROLL HIGH SCHOOL   *p* 73
See CALGARY ROMAN CATHOLIC SEPA-
RATE SCHOOL DISTRICT #1
BISHOP GRANDIN SENIOR HIGH SCHOOL
p 68
See CALGARY ROMAN CATHOLIC SEPA-
RATE SCHOOL DISTRICT #1
BISHOP MACDONELL CATHOLIC HIGH
SCHOOL   *p* 607
See WELLINGTON CATHOLIC DISTRICT
SCHOOL BOARD
BISHOP OF VICTORIA CORPORATION
SOLE   *p* 337
4044 NELTHORPE ST SUITE 1, VICTORIA,
BC, V8X 2A1
(250) 479-1331   *SIC* 8661
BISHOP P.F. REDING SECONDARY   *p* 683
See HALTON CATHOLIC DISTRICT
SCHOOL BOARD
BISHOP RYAN CATHOLIC SECONDARY
SCHOOL   *p* 617
See HAMILTON-WENTWORTH CATHOLIC
SCHOOL BOARD
BISHOP STRACHAN SCHOOL, THE   *p* 926
298 LONSDALE RD, TORONTO, ON, M4V
1X2
(416) 483-4325   *SIC* 8211
BISHOP'S COLLEGE SCHOOL   *p* 1374
See ASSOCIATION B.C.S
BISHOP, DONALD H. PROFESSIONAL
CORPORATION   *p* 70
11410 27 ST SE UNIT 6, CALGARY, AB,
T2Z 3R6
(403) 974-3937   *SIC* 8042
BISON FIRE PROTECTION INC   *p* 362
35 BOYS RD, WINNIPEG, MB, R2C 2Z2
(204) 237-3473   *SIC* 7389
BISON TRANSPORT INC   *p* 8
234090 WRANGLER RD, CALGARY, AB,
P1X 0K2
(403) 444-0555   *SIC* 4731
BISON TRANSPORT INC   *p* 162
80 LIBERTY RD, SHERWOOD PARK, AB,
T8H 2J6
(780) 416-7736   *SIC* 4213
BISON TRANSPORT INC   *p* 383
1001 SHERWIN RD, WINNIPEG, MB, R3H
0T8
(204) 833-0000   *SIC* 4213
BISON TRANSPORT INC   *p* 692
5850 SHAWSON DR, MISSISSAUGA, ON,
L4W 3W5
(905) 364-4401   *SIC* 4213
BISON VIEW TRAILERS   *p* 346
See STEVE'S LIVESTOCK TRANSPORTA-
TION (BLUMENORT) LTD
BISSETT FASTENERS LIMITED   *p* 200
63 FAWCETT RD, COQUITLAM, BC, V3K
6V2
(604) 540-0200   *SIC* 5085
BISSETT RESOURCE CONSULTANTS LTD
p 44

839 5 AVE SW SUITE 250, CALGARY, AB,
T2P 3C8
(403) 263-0073   *SIC* 1389
BISSON AUTO PARTS   *p* 1382
See A. BISSON ET FILS LTEE
BISSON CHEVROLET INC   *p* 1382
2257 RUE NOTRE-DAME E, THETFORD
MINES, QC, G6G 2W4
(418) 335-7571   *SIC* 5511
BISSON EXPERT   *p* 1309
See ROGER BISSON INC
BISSONNETTE YOUR INDEPENDENT
GROCER   *p* 820
See 1437716 ONTARIO LIMITED
BISTRO DU BOUCHER   *p* 1269
See GROUPE RESTOS PLAISIRS INC, LE
BISTROPLUS MARTIN   *p* 1114
See MARTIN-PRODUITS DE BUREAU INC
BITUMAR INC   *p* 1238
11155 RUE SAINTE-CATHERINE E,
MONTREAL-EST, QC, H1B 0A4
(514) 645-4561   *SIC* 2911
BITUMINEX LIMITED   *p* 365
29 TERRACON PL, WINNIPEG, MB, R2J
4B3
(204) 237-6253   *SIC* 7359
BIZERBA CANADA INC   *p* 720
2810 ARGENTIA RD UNIT 9, MISSIS-
SAUGA, ON, L5N 8L2
(905) 816-0498   *SIC* 5084
BIZOU   *p* 1359
See BIZOU INTERNATIONAL INC
BIZOU INTERNATIONAL INC   *p* 1304
8585 BOUL LACROIX, SAINT-GEORGES,
QC, G5Y 5L6
(418) 227-0424   *SIC* 5944
BIZOU INTERNATIONAL INC   *p* 1359
1490 3E AV DU PARC-INDUSTRIEL,
SAINTE-MARIE, QC, G6E 3T9
(418) 387-8481   *SIC* 5944
BJ PIPELINE INSPECTION SERVICES *p* 13
See BAKER HUGHES CANADA COMPANY
BJ SERVICES HOLDINGS CANADA ULC *p*
44
215 9 AVE SW UNIT 800, CALGARY, AB,
T2P 1K3
(587) 324-2058   *SIC* 1382
BJ TAKE INC   *p* 567
220 RAMSEY DR, DUNNVILLE, ON, N1A
0A7
(905) 774-5988   *SIC* 3646
BK INDUSTRIES   *p* 1295
See B. K. FER OUVRE INC
BKI RISK MANAGEMENT   *p* 23
See KANE, BRIAN INSURANCE AGEN-
CIES LTD
BLACK & DECKER CANADA INC   *p* 519
100 CENTRAL AVE W, BROCKVILLE, ON,
K6V 4N8
(613) 342-6641   *SIC* 5084
BLACK & MCDONALD GROUP LIMITED *p*
928
2 BLOOR ST E SUITE 2100, TORONTO,
ON, M4W 1A8
(416) 920-5100   *SIC* 1711
BLACK & MCDONALD LIMITED   *p* 380
401 WESTON ST SUITE A, WINNIPEG,
MB, R3E 3H4
(204) 774-4403   *SIC* 1711
BLACK & MCDONALD LIMITED   *p* 428
29 OTTAWA ST, ST. JOHN'S, NL, A1A 2R9
(709) 896-2639   *SIC* 1711
BLACK & MCDONALD LIMITED   *p* 445
60 CUTLER AVE, DARTMOUTH, NS, B3B
0J6
(902) 468-3101   *SIC* 1711
BLACK & MCDONALD LIMITED   *p* 819
2460 DON REID DR, OTTAWA, ON, K1H
1E1
(613) 526-1226   *SIC* 1731
BLACK & MCDONALD LIMITED   *p* 878
31 PULLMAN CRT, SCARBOROUGH, ON,
M1X 1E4
(416) 298-9977   *SIC* 1711

BLACK & MCDONALD LIMITED   *p* 878
35 PULLMAN CRT, SCARBOROUGH, ON,
M1X 1E4
(416) 298-9977   *SIC* 1711
BLACK & MCDONALD LIMITED   *p* 928
2 BLOOR ST E SUITE 2100, TORONTO,
ON, M4W 1A8
(416) 920-5100   *SIC* 1711
BLACK & MCDONALD SHEET METAL AND
CUSTOM FABRICATION   *p* 878
See BLACK & MCDONALD LIMITED
BLACK BOND BOOKS LTD   *p* 232
32555 LONDON AVE SUITE 344, MISSION,
BC, V2V 6M7
(604) 814-2650   *SIC* 5942
BLACK BOND BOOKS LTD   *p* 280
15562 24 AVE UNIT 1, SURREY, BC, V4A
2J5
(604) 536-4444   *SIC* 5942
BLACK BOX NETWORK SERVICES *p* 768
See NORSTAN CANADA LTD
BLACK CANYON   *p* 1332
See BULA CANADA INC
BLACK CAT WEAR PARTS LTD   *p* 108
5604 59 ST NW, EDMONTON, AB, T6B 3C3
(780) 465-6666   *SIC* 3531
BLACK CAT WEAR PARTS LTD   *p* 108
5720 59 ST NW, EDMONTON, AB, T6B 3L4
(780) 465-6666   *SIC* 3531
BLACK CAT WEAR PARTS LTD   *p* 356
71 RAILWAY ST, SELKIRK, MB, R1A 4L4
(204) 482-9046   *SIC* 3531
BLACK CREEK COMMUNITY HEALTH
CENTRE   *p* 786
2202 JANE ST SUITE 5, NORTH YORK,
ON, M3M 1A4
(416) 249-8000   *SIC* 8011
BLACK CREEK PIONEER VILLAGE *p* 784
See TORONTO AND REGION CONSERVA-
TION AUTHORITY
BLACK DIAMOND CAMPS   *p* 44
See BLACK DIAMOND GROUP LIMITED
BLACK DIAMOND CAMPS, DIV OF   *p* 44
See BLACK DIAMOND LIMITED PARTNER-
SHIP
BLACK DIAMOND GROUP LIMITED   *p* 44
440 2 AVE SW SUITE 1000, CALGARY, AB,
T2P 5E9
(403) 206-4747   *SIC* 7353
BLACK DIAMOND LIMITED PARTNERSHIP
p 44
440 2 AVE SW SUITE 1000, CALGARY, AB,
T2P 5E9
(403) 206-4747   *SIC* 7359
BLACK DIAMOND MANAGEMENT GROUP
CORPORATION   *p* 709
77 CITY CENTRE DR, MISSISSAUGA, ON,
L5B 1M5
(289) 201-7898   *SIC* 6211
BLACK FEATHER HOLDINGS INCORPO-
RATED   *p*
989
250 BOWIE AVE, TORONTO, ON, M6E 4Y2
(416) 780-9850   *SIC* 2339
BLACK GOLD REGIONAL DIVISION #18 *p*
5
5417 43 AVE, BEAUMONT, AB, T4X 1K1
(780) 929-6282   *SIC* 8211
BLACK GOLD REGIONAL DIVISION #18 *p*
81
105 ATHABASCA AVE, DEVON, AB, T9G
1A4
(780) 987-3709   *SIC* 8211
BLACK GOLD REGIONAL DIVISION #18 *p*
148
1101 5 ST SUITE 301, NISKU, AB, T9E 7N3
(780) 955-6025   *SIC* 8211
BLACK GOLD REGIONAL SCHOOLS *p* 148
See BLACK GOLD REGIONAL DIVISION
#18
BLACK KNIGHT INN LTD   *p* 156
2929 50 AVE, RED DEER, AB, T4R 1H1
(403) 343-6666   *SIC* 7011
BLACK PALM AVIARIES OF CANADA INC

p 866
4251 KINGSTON RD, SCARBOROUGH, ON, M1E 2M5
(416) 283-4262   *SIC 5511*
BLACK PRESS   *p 336*
See ISLAND PUBLISHERS LTD
BLACK PRESS GROUP LTD   *p 156*
2950 BREMNER AVE, RED DEER, AB, T4R 1M9
(403) 343-2400   *SIC 2711*
BLACK PRESS GROUP LTD   *p 174*
34375 GLADYS AVE, ABBOTSFORD, BC, V2S 2H5
(604) 853-1144   *SIC 2711*
BLACK PRESS GROUP LTD   *p 219*
2495 ENTERPRISE WAY, KELOWNA, BC, V1X 7K2
(250) 766-4688   *SIC 2711*
BLACK PRESS GROUP LTD   *p 333*
3175 BEACH DR, VICTORIA, BC, V8R 6L7
(250) 480-3220   *SIC 2711*
BLACK ROCK   *p 963*
See ISHARES U.S. HIGH YIELD BOND IN-DEX ETF (CAD-HEDGED)
BLACK SAXON III INC   *p 762*
201 PINEWOOD PARK DR, NORTH BAY, ON, P1B 8Z4
(705) 472-0810   *SIC 7011*
BLACK STREET PRODUCTIONS LTD *p 291*
2339 COLUMBIA ST SUITE 202, VANCOUVER, BC, V5Y 3Y3
(604) 257-4720   *SIC 7812*
BLACK SUN RISING INC   *p 113*
10548 82 AVE NW SUITE G, EDMONTON, AB, T6E 2A4
SIC 5082
BLACK TIGER FUELS LTD   *p 163*
GD, SLAVE LAKE, AB, T0G 2A0
(780) 849-3616   *SIC 5172*
BLACK TOP CABS LTD   *p 326*
777 PACIFIC ST, VANCOUVER, BC, V6Z 2R7
(604) 683-4567   *SIC 5541*
BLACK VELVET DISTILLING CO, THE   *p 140*
See CONSTELLATION BRANDS SCHENLEY ULC
BLACK, SHARON RE/MAX KELOWNA   *p 221*
1553 HARVEY AVE SUITE 100, KELOWNA, BC, V1Y 6G1
(250) 717-5040   *SIC 6531*
BLACKBERRY LIMITED   *p 1007*
2200 UNIVERSITY AVE E, WATERLOO, ON, N2K 0A7
(519) 888-7465   *SIC 7371*
BLACKBROOK CHEMICAL LTD   *p 754*
1245 MAPLE HILL CRT SUITE 1, NEWMARKET, ON, L3Y 9E8
SIC 2899
BLACKBURN & BLACKBURN INC   *p 1078*
980 BOUL DE L'UNIVERSITE E, CHICOUTIMI, QC, G7H 6H1
(418) 549-4900   *SIC 5044*
BLACKBURN + H.P.   *p 1281*
21 RUE ROLLET, REPENTIGNY, QC, J5Y 3R3
SIC 4924
BLACKBURN RADIO INC   *p 653*
700 RICHMOND ST UNIT 102, LONDON, ON, N6A 5C7
(519) 679-8680   *SIC 4832*
BLACKBURN SERVICE D'INVENTAIRE INC   *p 1078*
125 RUE DUBE, CHICOUTIMI, QC, G7H 2V3
(418) 543-4567   *SIC 7389*
BLACKCOMB SKIING ENTERPRISES LIMITED PARTNERSHIP   *p 343*
4545 BLACKCOMB WAY, WHISTLER, BC, V8E 0X9
(604) 932-3141   *SIC 7011*
BLACKFOOT INN   *p 33*

See BLACKFOOT MOTOR INN LTD
BLACKFOOT MOTOR INN LTD   *p 33*
5940 BLACKFOOT TRAIL SE, CALGARY, AB, T2H 2B5
(403) 252-2253   *SIC 7011*
BLACKFOOT MOTORCYCLE LTD   *p 27*
6 HIGHFIELD CIR SE, CALGARY, AB, T2G 5N5
(403) 243-2636   *SIC 5571*
BLACKFOOT MOTOSPORTS   *p 27*
See BLACKFOOT MOTORCYCLE LTD
BLACKIE CONSTRUCTION INC   *p 713*
2133 ROYAL WINDSOR DR UNIT 22, MISSISSAUGA, ON, L5J 1K5
SIC 1542
BLACKLINE SAFETY CORP   *p 27*
803 24 AVE SE UNIT 100, CALGARY, AB, T2G 1P5
(403) 451-0327   *SIC 3663*
BLACKMONT CAPITAL   *p 307*
See MACQUARIE CAPITAL MARKETS CANADA LTD
BLACKNED, JAMES   *p 1400*
9 RUE PONTAX, WASKAGANISH, QC, J0M 1R0
(819) 895-8694   *SIC 1611*
BLACKPEARL RESOURCES INC   *p 44*
215 9 AVE SW UNIT 900, CALGARY, AB, T2P 1K3
(403) 215-8313   *SIC 1382*
BLACKS PHOTO   *p 1182*
See PROS DE LA PHOTO (QUEBEC) INC, LES
BLACKSTOCK FORD LINCOLN SALES LTD   *p 808*
207155 9 HWY, ORANGEVILLE, ON, L9W 2Z7
(519) 941-5431   *SIC 5511*
BLACKSTONE PRODUCTIONS INC   *p 291*
112 6TH AVE W, VANCOUVER, BC, V5Y 1K6
(604) 623-3369   *SIC 7812*
BLACKSTRAP HOSPITALITY CORPORATION   *p 1424*
1125 LOUISE AVE, SASKATOON, SK, S7H 2P8
(306) 931-1030   *SIC 6712*
BLACKWOOD BUILDING CENTRE   *p 174*
See BLACKWOOD BUILDING CENTRE LTD
BLACKWOOD BUILDING CENTRE LTD   *p 174*
33050 SOUTH FRASER WAY, ABBOTSFORD, BC, V2S 2A9
(604) 853-6471   *SIC 5211*
BLACKWOOD PARTNERS CORPORATION *p 937*
110 YONGE ST SUITE 1500, TORONTO, ON, M5C 1T4
(416) 603-3900   *SIC 6282*
BLAIKIES DODGE CHRYSLER LIMITED   *p 468*
28 WADDELL ST, TRURO, NS, B2N 4A2
(902) 893-4381   *SIC 5511*
BLAINVILLE CHRYSLER DODGE INC   *p 1058*
249 BOUL DE LA SEIGNEURIE O, BLAINVILLE, QC, J7C 4N3
(450) 419-5337   *SIC 5511*
BLAINVILLE FORD INC   *p 1058*
600 BOUL DU CURE-LABELLE, BLAINVILLE, QC, J7C 2H9
(450) 430-9181   *SIC 5511*
BLAIR BUILDING MATERIALS INC   *p 664*
10445 KEELE ST, MAPLE, ON, L6A 3Y9
(416) 798-4996   *SIC 5211*
BLAIR'S FERTILIZER LTD   *p 1409*
GD, LANIGAN, SK, S0K 2M0
(306) 365-3150   *SIC 5191*
BLAIS & LANGLOIS INC   *p 1398*
345 RUE CARTIER, VICTORIAVILLE, QC, G6R 1E3
(819) 739-2905   *SIC 1542*

BLAIS RECREATIF   *p 1289*
See LOCATION BLAIS INC
BLAKE, A. E. VENTES LTEE   *p 1328*
3588 BOUL POIRIER, SAINT-LAURENT, QC, H4R 2J5
(514) 332-4214   *SIC 5169*
BLAKE, CASSELS & GRAYDON LLP   *p 44*
855 2 ST SW SUITE 3500, CALGARY, AB, T2P 4J8
(403) 260-9600   *SIC 8111*
BLAKE, CASSELS & GRAYDON LLP   *p 328*
595 BURRARD ST SUITE 2600, VANCOUVER, BC, V7X 1L3
(604) 631-3300   *SIC 8111*
BLAKE, CASSELS & GRAYDON LLP   *p 971*
199 BAY ST SUITE 4000, TORONTO, ON, M5L 1A9
(416) 863-2400   *SIC 8111*
BLAKE, CASSELS & GRAYDON LLP   *p 1202*
1 PLACE VILLE-MARIE BUREAU 3000, MONTREAL, QC, H3B 4N8
(514) 982-4000   *SIC 8111*
BLAKENY FUELS   *p 407*
See FUNDY ENERGY LIMITED
BLAKES SERVICES INC   *p 971*
199 BAY ST, TORONTO, ON, M5L 1A9
(416) 863-2603   *SIC 8741*
BLANCHARD   *p 1002*
See GFL ENVIRONMENTAL INC
BLANCHARD FOUNDRY, DIVISION OF   *p 1427*
See HARMON INTERNATIONAL INDUSTRIES INC
BLANCHARD, A. INC   *p 1056*
4350 AV ARSENEAULT, BECANCOUR, QC, G9H 1V8
(819) 233-2349   *SIC 5511*
BLANCHETT NEON LIMITED   *p 93*
12850 ST ALBERT TRAIL NW, EDMONTON, AB, T5L 4H6
(780) 453-2441   *SIC 3993*
BLANCHETTE & BLANCHETTE INC *p 1400*
520 2E AV, WEEDON, QC, J0B 3J0
(819) 877-2622   *SIC 2421*
BLANCHETTE VACHON & ASSOCIES CA SENC   *p 1359*
See 9178-8562 QUEBEC INC
BLANCHETTE VACHON ET ASSOCIES CA SENCRL   *p 1139*
8149 RUE DU MISTRAL BUREAU 202, LEVIS, QC, G6X 1G5
(418) 387-3636   *SIC 8721*
BLANCHETTE VACHON ET ASSOCIES CA SENCRL   *p 1359*
266 AV DU COLLEGE, SAINTE-MARIE, QC, G6E 3Y4
(418) 387-3636   *SIC 8721*
BLANEY MCMURTRY LLP   *p 937*
2 QUEEN ST E SUITE 1500, TORONTO, ON, M5C 3G5
(416) 593-1221   *SIC 8111*
BLAST   *p 1371*
See PRODUITS AMERICAN BILTRITE (CANADA) LTEE
BLAST RADIUS INC   *p 297*
509 RICHARDS ST, VANCOUVER, BC, V6B 2Z6
(604) 647-6500   *SIC 7374*
BLAST RADIUS INC   *p 979*
99 SPADINA AVE SUITE 200, TORONTO, ON, M5V 3P8
(416) 214-4220   *SIC 7374*
BLASTCO CORPORATION   *p 516*
57 WEST ONONDAGA RD W SS 13, BRANTFORD, ON, N3T 5M1
(519) 756-9050   *SIC 1721*
BLASTECH   *p 518*
See T.F. WARREN GROUP INC
BLAZE KING   *p 244*
See VALLEY COMFORT SYSTEMS INC
BLC CAPITAL   *p 523*
See LBC CAPITAL INC
BLEAK HOUSE SENIOR'S CENTRE   *p 370*

1637 MAIN ST, WINNIPEG, MB, R2V 1Y8
(204) 338-4723   *SIC 8699*
BLEEMAN HOLDINGS LIMITED   *p 788*
970 LAWRENCE AVE W SUITE 304, NORTH YORK, ON, M6A 3B6
(416) 256-3900   *SIC 6531*
BLENDTEK FINE INGREDIENTS INC *p 538*
32 CHERRY BLOSSOM RD, CAMBRIDGE, ON, N3H 4R7
(519) 279-4401   *SIC 5169*
BLENHEIM COMMUNITY VILLAGE RETIREMENT RESIDENCE   *p 493*
See REVERA LONG TERM CARE INC
BLENHEIM SOBEY'S   *p 493*
20210 COMMUNICATION RD, BLENHEIM, ON, N0P 1A0
(519) 676-9044   *SIC 5411*
BLESSED CARDINAL NEWMAN SECONDARY SCHOOL   *p 869*
See TORONTO CATHOLIC DISTRICT SCHOOL BOARD
BLESSED KATERI SCHOOL   *p 641*
See WATERLOO CATHOLIC DISTRICT SCHOOL BOARD
BLETSOE ENTERPRISES INC   *p 643*
1 QUEEN ST, LAKEFIELD, ON, K0L 2H0
(705) 652-3202   *SIC 5411*
BLEU TECH   *p 1342*
See BLEU TECH MONTREAL INC
BLEU TECH MONTREAL INC   *p 1342*
4150 CHOMEDEY (A-13) O, SAINT-LAURENT, QC, H7R 6E9
(450) 767-2890   *SIC 8712*
BLEUETIERES SENCO INC, LES   *p 1302*
1459 BOUL DU SACRE-COEUR, SAINT-FELICIEN, QC, G8K 1B3
(418) 679-1472   *SIC 5142*
BLEUETS FORTIN & FILS INC   *p 1090*
555 RUE DE QUEN, DOLBEAU-MISTASSINI, QC, G8L 5M3
(418) 276-8611   *SIC 5142*
BLEUETS MISTASSINI LTEE   *p 1090*
555 RUE DE QUEN, DOLBEAU-MISTASSINI, QC, G8L 5M3
(418) 276-8611   *SIC 5142*
BLEUETS SAUVAGES DU QUEBEC INC, LES   *p 1296*
698 RUE MELANCON BUREAU 160, SAINT-BRUNO-LAC-SAINT-JEAN, QC, G0W 2L0
(418) 343-2410   *SIC 5142*
BLF REIT   *p 1068*
See COGIR APARTMENTS REAL ESTATE INVESTMENT TRUST
BLG   *p 44*
See BORDEN LADNER GERVAIS LLP
BLG   *p 302*
See BORDEN LADNER GERVAIS LLP
BLG   *p 822*
See BORDEN LADNER GERVAIS LLP
BLG   *p 949*
See BORDEN LADNER GERVAIS LLP
BLG   *p 1202*
See BORDEN LADNER GERVAIS LLP
BLINDS BY VERTICAN INC   *p 145*
549 17 ST SW, MEDICINE HAT, AB, T1A 7W5
(403) 527-9084   *SIC 5719*
BLINDS TO GO INC   *p 1163*
3100 BOUL DE L'ASSOMPTION, MONTREAL, QC, H1N 3S4
(514) 259-9955   *SIC 2591*
BLINDS TO GO INC   *p 1168*
3510 BOUL SAINT-JOSEPH E, MONTREAL, QC, H1X 1W6
(514) 255-4000   *SIC 5719*
BLITZ DIRECT, DATA & PROMOTION   *p 1214*
See VISION 7 COMMUNICATIONS INC
BLIZZARD COURIER SERVICE LTD *p 775*
1937 LESLIE ST, NORTH YORK, ON, M3B 2M3

(416) 444-0596   *SIC* 7389
BLM DECK DIVISION INC   *p* 642
120 MCBRINE DR, KITCHENER, ON, N2R 1E7
(519) 894-0008   *SIC* 4731
BLM GROUP INC, THE   *p* 642
120 MCBRINE DR, KITCHENER, ON, N2R 1E7
(519) 748-9880   *SIC* 4213
BLM TRANSPORTATION GROUP   *p* 642
See BLM GROUP INC, THE
BLOMMER CHOCOLATE COMPANY OF CANADA INC   *p* 539
103 SECOND AVE, CAMPBELLFORD, ON, K0L 1L0
(705) 653-5821   *SIC* 2066
BLONDEAU TAXI LIMITEE   *p* 815
2161 BANTREE ST, OTTAWA, ON, K1B 4X3
SIC 4151
BLONDEAU TRANSPORTATION   *p* 815
See BLONDEAU TAXI LIMITEE
BLONDO CANADA   *p* 1331
See SML CANADA ACQUISITION CORP
BLOOD TRIBE DEPARTMENT OF HEALTH INC   *p* 166
MAIN ST, STAND OFF, AB, T0L 1Y0
(403) 737-3888   *SIC* 8399
BLOOD TRIBE DEPARTMENT OF HEALTH INC   *p* 167
GD, STAND OFF, AB, T0L 1Y0
(403) 737-2102   *SIC* 8099
BLOOD TRIBE EMERGENCY SERVICES   *p* 167
See BLOOD TRIBE DEPARTMENT OF HEALTH INC
BLOOMSTAR BOUQUET   *p* 691
See 3856011 CANADA INC
BLOUNT CANADA INC   *p* 602
505 EDINBURGH RD N, GUELPH, ON, N1H 6L4
(519) 822-6870   *SIC* 3568
BLOUNT HOLDINGS LTD   *p* 602
505 EDINBURGH RD N, GUELPH, ON, N1H 6L4
(519) 822-6870   *SIC* 3425
BLOW MOLD GROUP   *p* 516
See WENTWORTH MOLD LTD
BLS ASPHALT & LANDSCAPE CONSTRUCTION   *p* 1420
See B L S ASPHALT INC
BLT FOODS LTD   *p* 412
499 ROTHESAY AVE, SAINT JOHN, NB, E2J 2C6
(506) 633-1098   *SIC* 5812
BLU'S CLOTHING LTD   *p* 113
4719 101 ST NW, EDMONTON, AB, T6E 5C6
(780) 437-3991   *SIC* 5621
BLU'S WOMENS WEAR   *p* 113
See BLU'S CLOTHING LTD
BLUE BIRD CABS LTD   *p* 334
2612 QUADRA ST, VICTORIA, BC, V8T 4E4
(250) 382-2222   *SIC* 4121
BLUE BOY MOTOR HOTEL LTD   *p* 290
725 MARINE DR SE, VANCOUVER, BC, V5X 2T9
(604) 321-6611   *SIC* 7011
BLUE BUS   *p* 241
See CORPORATION OF THE DISTRICT OF WEST VANCOUVER, THE
BLUE CASTLE GAMES INC   *p* 184
4401 STILL CREEK DR UNIT 300, BURNABY, BC, V5C 6G9
(604) 299-5626   *SIC* 7372
BLUE CIRCLE INSURANCE LTD   *p* 27
3402 8 ST SE UNIT 200, CALGARY, AB, T2G 5S7
(403) 770-4949   *SIC* 6411
BLUE CREST INTERFAITH HOME   *p* 423
See EASTERN REGIONAL INTEGRATED HEALTH AUTHORITY
BLUE CROSS LIFE INSURANCE COMPANY OF CANADA   *p*

406
644 MAIN ST SUITE 500, MONCTON, NB, E1C 1E2
(506) 853-1811   *SIC* 6311
BLUE CROSS LIFE INSURANCE COMPANY OF CANADA   *p* 1417
1870 ALBERT ST SUITE 100, REGINA, SK, S4P 4B7
(306) 525-5025   *SIC* 6411
BLUE ELEPHANT REALTY INC   *p* 979
548 KING ST W SUITE 202, TORONTO, ON, M5V 1M3
(416) 504-6133   *SIC* 6531
BLUE FALLS MANUFACTURING LTD *p* 169
4549 52 ST, THORSBY, AB, T0C 2P0
(780) 789-2626   *SIC* 3999
BLUE GIANT EQUIPMENT CORPORATION   *p* 508
85 HEART LAKE RD, BRAMPTON, ON, L6W 3K2
(905) 457-3900   *SIC* 3569
BLUE GOOSE CAPITAL CORP   *p* 949
80 RICHMOND ST W SUITE 1502, TORONTO, ON, M5H 2A4
(416) 363-5151   *SIC* 0259
BLUE HERON SUPPORT SERVICES ASSOCIATION   *p* 4
GD STN MAIN, BARRHEAD, AB, T7N 1B8
(780) 674-4944   *SIC* 8361
BLUE HIVE   *p* 931
See YOUNG & RUBICAM GROUP OF COMPANIES ULC, THE
BLUE IMP PLAYGROUND EQUIPMENT   *p* 146
See SCOTT, S.F. MANUFACTURING CO. LIMITED
BLUE LINE DISTRIBUTION LIMITED *p* 683
8175 LAWSON RD, MILTON, ON, L9T 5E5
(905) 875-4630   *SIC* 4213
BLUE LINE TAXI   *p* 611
See BLUE LINE TRANSPORTATION LTD
BLUE LINE TRANSPORTATION LTD   *p* 611
160 JOHN ST S, HAMILTON, ON, L8N 2C4
(905) 525-2583   *SIC* 4121
BLUE MOOSE CLOTHING COMPANY LTD *p* 371
90 SUTHERLAND AVE UNIT 100, WINNIPEG, MB, R2W 3C7
(204) 783-2557   *SIC* 3143
BLUE MOUNTAIN CHRYSLER LTD   *p* 546
9950 26 HWY, COLLINGWOOD, ON, L9Y 3Z1
(705) 445-2740   *SIC* 5511
BLUE MOUNTAIN PLASTICS INC   *p* 880
400 SECOND LINE, SHELBURNE, ON, L0N 1S5
(519) 925-3550   *SIC* 4953
BLUE MOUNTAIN RESORT   *p* 298
See INTRAWEST ULC
BLUE MOUNTAIN RESORT   *p* 493
See INTRAWEST ULC
BLUE OCEAN CONTACT CENTERS INC   *p* 456
7051 BAYERS RD SUITE 400, HALIFAX, NS, B3L 4V2
(902) 722-3300   *SIC* 7389
BLUE PINE ENTERPRISES LTD   *p* 278
18960 34A AVE, SURREY, BC, V3Z 1A7
(604) 535-3026   *SIC* 0782
BLUE PLANET BY PAJAR   *p* 1183
See PAJAR DISTRIBUTION LTD
BLUE RIBBON INCOME FUND   *p* 959
181 BAY ST SUITE 2930, TORONTO, ON, M5J 2T3
(416) 642-6000   *SIC* 6722
BLUE RIDGE LUMBER INC   *p* 173
GD STN MAIN, WHITECOURT, AB, T7S 1S1
(780) 648-6200   *SIC* 5031
BLUE RUBY   *p* 322
See BEAUMONT STANLEY INC
BLUE SKY FINANCIAL GROUP INC   *p* 762

128 MCINTYRE ST W SUITE 100, NORTH BAY, ON, P1B 2Y6
(705) 497-3723   *SIC* 6411
BLUE SPIKE BEVERAGES   *p* 1225
See 9127-2021 QUEBEC INC
BLUE SPRINGS GOLF CLUB   *p* 473
See CLUBLINK CORPORATION ULC
BLUE STAR FORD LINCOLN SALES LTD *p* 880
121 QUEENSWAY E, SIMCOE, ON, N3Y 4M5
(519) 426-3673   *SIC* 5511
BLUE STAR NUTRACEUTICALS INC *p* 492
180 NORTH FRONT ST UNIT 6, BELLEVILLE, ON, K8P 3B9
(613) 968-2278   *SIC* 5149
BLUE STREAK ELECTRONICS INC   *p* 549
30 MOYAL CRT, CONCORD, ON, L4K 4R8
(905) 669-4812   *SIC* 3694
BLUE TREE HOTELS GP ULC   *p* 87
10135 100 ST NW, EDMONTON, AB, T5J 0N7
(780) 426-3636   *SIC* 7011
BLUE TREE HOTELS INVESTMENT (CANADA), LTD   *p* 318
1601 BAYSHORE DR, VANCOUVER, BC, V6G 2V4
(604) 682-3377   *SIC* 7011
BLUE TREE HOTELS INVESTMENT (CANADA), LTD   *p* 959
WESTIN HARBOUR CASTLE, TORONTO, ON, M5J 1A6
(416) 869-1600   *SIC* 7011
BLUE WATER AGENCIES LIMITED   *p* 445
40 TOPPLE DR, DARTMOUTH, NS, B3B 1L6
(902) 468-4900   *SIC* 5088
BLUE WATER BRIDGE AUTHORITY   *p* 846
See BLUE WATER BRIDGE CANADA
BLUE WATER BRIDGE CANADA   *p* 846
1555 VENETIAN BLVD SUITE 436, POINT EDWARD, ON, N7T 0A9
(519) 336-2720   *SIC* 4785
BLUE WATER GROUP   *p* 445
See BLUE WATER AGENCIES LIMITED
BLUE WATER IGA   *p* 563
420 LYNDOCH ST, CORUNNA, ON, N0N 1G0
(519) 862-5213   *SIC* 5411
BLUE-CON CONSTRUCTION   *p* 648
See BLUE-CON INC
BLUE-CON INC   *p* 648
1915 CRUMLIN RD, LONDON, ON, N5V 3B8
(519) 659-2400   *SIC* 1623
BLUEARTH RENEWABLES INC   *p* 64
214 11 AVE SW SUITE 400, CALGARY, AB, T2R 0K1
(403) 668-1575   *SIC* 4911
BLUEBIRD INVESTMENTS LIMITED *p* 423
12 DUGGAN ST, GRAND FALLS-WINDSOR, NL, A2A 2K6
(709) 489-5403   *SIC* 1542
BLUEBIX SOLUTIONS INCORPORATED   *p* 916
1110 FINCH AVE W SUITE 612, TORONTO, ON, M3J 2T2
(416) 319-5486   *SIC* 7361
BLUECAT NETWORKS, INC   *p* 773
4100 YONGE ST SUITE 300, NORTH YORK, ON, M2P 2B5
(416) 646-8400   *SIC* 7379
BLUECIRCLE INSURANCE BROKERS *p* 27
See BLUE CIRCLE INSURANCE LTD
BLUEDROP PERFORMANCE LEARNING INC   *p* 431
18 PRESCOTT ST, ST. JOHN'S, NL, A1C 3S4
(709) 739-9000   *SIC* 3699
BLUEDROP SIMULATION SERVICES INC *p* 458
36 SOLUTIONS DR SUITE 300, HALIFAX, NS, B3S 1N2
(800) 563-3638   *SIC* 3728
BLUEDROP TRAINING & SIMULATION INC

p 458
36 SOLUTIONS DR SUITE 300, HALIFAX, NS, B3S 1N2
(800) 563-3638   *SIC* 3728
BLUEGENESIS.COM CORP   *p* 687
5915 AIRPORT RD SUITE 800, MISSISSAUGA, ON, L4V 1T1
(905) 673-3232   *SIC* 4813
BLUELINE NEW HOLLAND   *p* 460
See VALLEY INDUSTRIES (2007) LTD
BLUERIVER TRADING LTD   *p* 782
369 RIMROCK ROAD, NORTH YORK, ON, M3J 3G2
(416) 638-8543   *SIC* 5149
BLUESHORE FINANCIAL CREDIT UNION *p* 240
1250 LONSDALE AVE, NORTH VANCOUVER, BC, V7M 2H6
(604) 983-4500   *SIC* 6062
BLUESTAR CANADA   *p* 1340
See INTELLICO - IDS INC
BLUESTONE RESOURCES INC   *p* 302
800 PENDER ST W UNIT 1020, VANCOUVER, BC, V6C 2V6
(604) 646-4534   *SIC* 1041
BLUETREE HOMES LTD   *p* 328
1055 DUNSMUIR ST SUITE 2000, VANCOUVER, BC, V7X 1L5
(604) 648-1800   *SIC* 1521
BLUEVALE COLLEGIATE INSTITUTE   *p* 1007
See WATERLOO REGION DISTRICT SCHOOL BOARD
BLUEWATER DISTRICT SCHOOL BOARD *p* 835
1550 8TH ST E, OWEN SOUND, ON, N4K 0A2
(519) 376-2010   *SIC* 8211
BLUEWATER DISTRICT SCHOOL BOARD *p* 847
780 GUSTAVUS ST SS 4, PORT ELGIN, ON, N0H 2C4
(519) 832-2091   *SIC* 8211
BLUEWATER HEALTH   *p* 842
450 BLANCHE ST, PETROLIA, ON, N0N 1R0
(519) 464-4400   *SIC* 8062
BLUEWATER HEALTH   *p* 859
89 NORMAN ST, SARNIA, ON, N7T 6S3
(519) 464-4400   *SIC* 8062
BLUEWATER OFFICE EQUIPMENT LTD   *p* 597
223 HURON RD, GODERICH, ON, N7A 2Z8
(519) 524-9863   *SIC* 5045
BLUEWATER POWER CORPORATION   *p* 859
855 CONFEDERATION ST SUITE 716, SARNIA, ON, N7T 2E4
(519) 337-8201   *SIC* 4911
BLUEWATER POWER DISTRIBUTION CORPORATION   *p* 859
855 CONFEDERATION ST, SARNIA, ON, N7T 2E4
(519) 337-8201   *SIC* 4911
BLUEWATER RECYCLING ASSOCIATION *p* 621
415 CANADA AVE, HURON PARK, ON, N0M 1Y0
(519) 228-6678   *SIC* 4953
BLUEWAVE ENERGY   *p* 435
See BASSETT PETROLEUM DISTRIBUTORS LTD
BLUEWAVE ENERGY LTD   *p* 445
30 OLAND CRT, DARTMOUTH, NS, B3B 1V2
(902) 481-0515   *SIC* 5541
BLUM CANADA LIMITED   *p* 737
7135 PACIFIC CIR, MISSISSAUGA, ON, L5T 2A8
(905) 670-7920   *SIC* 5072
BLUMENGART COLONY FARMS LTD *p* 354
GD, PLUM COULEE, MB, R0G 1R0
(204) 829-3687   *SIC* 0191
BLUMENSCHEIN HOLDINGS LTD   *p* 124

11750 30 AVE SW, EDMONTON, AB, T6W 1A8

SIC 5411

BLUMETRIC ENVIRONMENTAL INC *p* 540
3108 CARP RD, CARP, ON, K0A 1L0
(613) 839-3053   SIC 1623

BLUNDELL SEAFOODS LTD *p* 259
11351 RIVER RD, RICHMOND, BC, V6X 1Z6
(604) 270-3300   SIC 5146

BLUNDEN CONSTRUCTION (1995) LIMITED *p* 458
519 HERRING COVE RD, HALIFAX, NS, B3R 1X3
(902) 477-2531   SIC 1541

BLUSH LANE ORGANIC PRODUCE LTD *p* 75
10 ASPEN STONE BLVD SW SUITE 3000, CALGARY, AB, T3H 0K3
(403) 210-1247   SIC 5148

BLYLEVEN ENTERPRISES INC *p* 836
363 GOVERNORS RD E, PARIS, ON, N3L 3E1
(519) 752-4436   SIC 5261

BLYTH & COMPANY TRAVEL LIMITED *p* 972
13 HAZELTON AVE, TORONTO, ON, M5R 2E1
(416) 964-2569   SIC 4724

BLYTH EDUCATION *p* 972
See BLYTH EDUCATIONAL GROUP INC

BLYTH EDUCATIONAL GROUP INC *p* 972
160 AVENUE RD, TORONTO, ON, M5R 2H8
(416) 960-3552   SIC 8748

BMB GLOBAL SOURCING *p* 1231
See DISTRIBUTIONS B.M.B. (1985) S.E.C., LES

BMC SOFTWARE CANADA INC *p* 903
50 MINTHORN BLVD SUITE 200, THORNHILL, ON, L3T 7X8
(905) 707-4600   SIC 7372

BMF *p* 527
See BURLINGTON MERCHANDISING & FIXTURES INC

BMG HOLDINGS LTD *p* 404
32 SAWYER RD, JACKSONVILLE, NB, E7M 3B7
(506) 328-8853   SIC 5091

BMI CANADA INC *p* 1061
3437 BOUL DE LA GRANDE-ALLEE, BOIS-BRIAND, QC, J7H 1H5
(450) 434-1313   SIC 5074

BML MULTI TRADES GROUP LTD *p* 515
32 RYAN PL, BRANTFORD, ON, N3S 7S1
(905) 777-7879   SIC 1711

BMML HOLDINGS *p* 1417
2103 11TH AVE SUITE 700, REGINA, SK, S4P 4G1
(306) 347-8300   SIC 6712

BMO *p* 236
See BANK OF MONTREAL

BMO *p* 527
See BANK OF MONTREAL

BMO ASSET MANAGEMENT INC *p* 985
100 KING ST W 43RD FLOOR, TORONTO, ON, M5X 1A1
(416) 359-5000   SIC 6282

BMO CAPITAL MARKETS *p* 985
See BMO NESBITT BURNS INC

BMO FONDS D'INVESTISSEMENT *p* 985
See BMO INVESTMENTS INC

BMO INVESTMENTS INC *p* 985
100 KING ST W 43RD FLOOR, TORONTO, ON, M5X 1A1
(416) 359-5003   SIC 6722

BMO INVESTORLINE INC *p* 985
100 KING ST W 21ST FLOOR, TORONTO, ON, M5X 2A1
(416) 867-6300   SIC 6211

BMO LIFE ASSURANCE COMPANY *p* 941
60 YONGE ST, TORONTO, ON, M5E 1H5
(416) 596-3900   SIC 6411

BMO LIFE INSURANCE COMPANY *p* 941

60 YONGE ST 11TH FLOOR, TORONTO, ON, M5E 1H5
(416) 596-3900   SIC 6311

BMO NESBITT BURNS *p* 1187
See BANK OF MONTREAL

BMO NESBITT BURNS INC *p* 44
525 8 AVE SW SUITE 3200, CALGARY, AB, T2P 1G1
(403) 261-9550   SIC 6211

BMO NESBITT BURNS INC *p* 377
360 MAIN ST SUITE 1400, WINNIPEG, MB, R3C 3Z3
(204) 949-2183   SIC 6211

BMO NESBITT BURNS INC *p* 825
979 BANK ST 6TH FL, OTTAWA, ON, K1S 5K5
(613) 562-6400   SIC 6211

BMO NESBITT BURNS INC *p* 985
100 KING ST W FL 38, TORONTO, ON, M5X 1H3
(416) 365-6029   SIC 6211

BMO NESBITT BURNS INC *p* 985
100 KING ST W UNIT 1, TORONTO, ON, M5X 2A1
(416) 643-1778   SIC 6211

BMO NESBITT BURNS INC *p* 986
1 FIRST CANADIAN PL 21ST FL, TORONTO, ON, M5X 1H3
(416) 359-4000   SIC 6211

BMO PRIVATE INVESTMENT COUNSEL INC *p* 986
100 KING ST W, TORONTO, ON, M5X 1H3
(416) 359-5001   SIC 6211

BMP *p* 1027
See BEN MACHINE PRODUCTS COMPANY INCORPORATED

BMP (1985) LIMITED *p* 618
5276 HINCHINBROOKE RD, HARTINGTON, ON, K0H 1W0
(613) 372-2838   SIC 5211

BMP MECHANICAL LTD *p* 33
6420 6A ST SE SUITE 110, CALGARY, AB, T2H 2B7
(403) 816-4409   SIC 1711

BMP METALS INC *p* 501
18 CHELSEA LANE, BRAMPTON, ON, L6T 3Y4
(905) 799-2002   SIC 3499

BMR *p* 1065
See GROUPE BMR INC

BMR *p* 1075
See OSTIGUY ET FRERES INC

BMR *p* 1077
See BOIS DE CONSTRUCTION CHENEVILLE INC, LES

BMR *p* 1301
See RENOVAPRIX INC

BMR *p* 1365
See MATERIAUX MIRON INC

BMR *p* 1399
See J. DROLET & FILS LTEE

BMR *p* 1400
See MATERIAUX DE CONSTRUCTION LETOURNEAU INC

BMR AGRIZONE *p* 1065
See GROUPE BMR INC

BMR MATCO *p* 1063
See 7577010 CANADA INC

BMS CANADA *p* 1336
See SOCIETE BRISTOL-MYERS SQUIBB CANADA, LA

BMT CANADA LTD *p* 623
311 LEGGET DR, KANATA, ON, K2K 1Z8
(613) 592-2830   SIC 8711

BMT INSURANCE & FINANCIAL SERVICES *p* 912
See BMT INSURANCE BROKERS LIMITED

BMT INSURANCE BROKERS LIMITED *p* 912
65 MAPLE ST S, TIMMINS, ON, P4N 1Y6
(705) 268-9988   SIC 6411

BMW *p* 827
See OTTO'S SERVICE CENTRE LIMITED

BMW AUTOHAUS *p* 906
See TRANSGLOBAL FINE CARS LTD

BMW CANADA INC *p* 856
50 ULTIMATE DR, RICHMOND HILL, ON, L4S 0C8
(905) 770-1758   SIC 5012

BMW CANBEC *p* 1227
See CANBEC AUTOMOBILE INC

BMW GRAND RIVER *p* 635
See 2142242 ONTARIO INC

BMW GROUP CANADA *p* 856
See BMW CANADA INC

BMW KINGSTON *p* 631
See 2445120 ONTARIO INC

BMW LAVAL *p* 1085
See AUTO BOULEVARD SAINT-MARTIN INC

BMW LEVIS *p* 1136
See GROUPE AUTOMOTIVE HOLAND LEVIS INC

BMW MINI LAVAL *p* 53
See LMB AUTOMOBILE INC

BMW OF MISSISSAUGA *p* 695
See FERRI, R AUTOMOBILES INC

BMW PRODUCTS & SERVICES *p* 144
See WEATHERFORD ARTIFICIAL LIFT SYSTEMS CANADA LTD

BMW SARNIA *p* 860
See SARNIA FINE CARS 2019 INC

BMW STE-JULIE *p* 1358
1633 BOUL ARMAND-FRAPPIER, SAINTE-JULIE, QC, J3E 3R6
(450) 922-1633   SIC 5521

BMW STORE LTD, THE *p* 320
2040 BURRARD ST, VANCOUVER, BC, V6J 3H5
(604) 659-3200   SIC 5511

BMW TORONTO *p* 920
See 2176542 ONTARIO LTD

BMW VILLE DE QUEBEC *p* 1261
See 9258-0547 QUEBEC INC

BMW VILLE DE QUEBEC *p* 1261
See 9182-2452 QUEBEC INC

BMW WEST ISLAND *p* 1093
See BOURASSA WEST ISLAND INC

BO-BEBE *p* 1084
See 3717291 CANADA INC

BOA-FRANC INC *p* 1304
1255 98E RUE, SAINT-GEORGES, QC, G5Y 8J5
(418) 227-1181   SIC 2426

BOA-FRANC, S.E.N.C. *p* 1304
1255 98E RUE, SAINT-GEORGES, QC, G5Y 8J5
(418) 227-1181   SIC 2426

BOARD OF EDUCATION OF SASKATOON SCHOOL DIVISION NO. 13 OF SASKATCHEWAN, THE *p* 1424
1905 PRESTON AVE, SASKATOON, SK, S7J 2E7
(306) 683-7850   SIC 8211

BOARD OF EDUCATION OF SASKATOON SCHOOL DIVISION NO. 13 OF SASKATCHEWAN, THE *p* 1426
310 21ST ST E, SASKATOON, SK, S7K 1M7
(306) 683-8200   SIC 8211

BOARD OF EDUCATION OF SASKATOON SCHOOL DIVISION NO. 13 OF SASKATCHEWAN, THE *p* 1431
2220 RUSHOLME RD, SASKATOON, SK, S7L 4A4
(306) 683-7800   SIC 8211

BOARD OF EDUCATION OF SCHOOL DISTRICT #82 (COAST M *p* 223
1491 KINGFISHER AVE N, KITIMAT, BC, V8C 1E9
(250) 632-6174   SIC 8211

BOARD OF EDUCATION OF SCHOOL DISTRICT #82 (COAST M *p* 283
3430 SPARKS ST, TERRACE, BC, V8G 2V3
(250) 638-0306   SIC 8211

BOARD OF EDUCATION OF SCHOOL DISTRICT NO. 06 (ROCKY MOUNTAIN), THE *p* 216
1535 14TH ST SUITE 4, INVERMERE, BC, V0A 1K4
(250) 342-9213   SIC 8211

BOARD OF EDUCATION OF SCHOOL DISTRICT NO. 23 (CENTRAL OKANAGAN), THE *p* 219
1040 HOLLYWOOD RD S, KELOWNA, BC, V1X 4N2
(250) 860-8888   SIC 8211

BOARD OF EDUCATION OF SCHOOL DISTRICT NO. 23 (CENTRAL OKANAGAN), THE *p* 219
3130 GORDON DR, KELOWNA, BC, V1W 3M4
(250) 870-5106   SIC 8211

BOARD OF EDUCATION OF SCHOOL DISTRICT NO. 23 (CENTRAL OKANAGAN), THE *p* 219
705 RUTLAND RD N, KELOWNA, BC, V1X 3B6
(250) 870-5134   SIC 8211

BOARD OF EDUCATION OF SCHOOL DISTRICT NO. 23 (CENTRAL OKANAGAN), THE *p* 221
1079 RAYMER AVE, KELOWNA, BC, V1Y 4Z7
(250) 870-5105   SIC 8211

BOARD OF EDUCATION OF SCHOOL DISTRICT NO. 35 (LANGLEY) *p* 227
4875 222 ST, LANGLEY, BC, V3A 3Z7
(604) 534-7891   SIC 8211

BOARD OF EDUCATION OF SCHOOL DISTRICT NO. 39 (VANC *p* 322
See BOARD OF EDUCATION OF SCHOOL DISTRICT NO. 39 (VANCOUVER), THE

BOARD OF EDUCATION OF SCHOOL DISTRICT NO. 39 (VANCOUVER), THE *p* 286
2600 BROADWAY E, VANCOUVER, BC, V5M 1Y5
(604) 713-8215   SIC 8211

BOARD OF EDUCATION OF SCHOOL DISTRICT NO. 39 (VANCOUVER), THE *p* 287
1755 55TH AVE E, VANCOUVER, BC, V5P 1Z7
(604) 713-8278   SIC 8211

BOARD OF EDUCATION OF SCHOOL DISTRICT NO. 39 (VANCOUVER), THE *p* 288
6454 KILLARNEY ST, VANCOUVER, BC, V5S 2X7
(604) 713-8950   SIC 8211

BOARD OF EDUCATION OF SCHOOL DISTRICT NO. 39 (VANCOUVER), THE *p* 292
5025 WILLOW ST SUITE 39, VANCOUVER, BC, V5Z 3S1
(604) 713-8927   SIC 8211

BOARD OF EDUCATION OF SCHOOL DISTRICT NO. 39 (VANCOUVER), THE *p* 320
1580 BROADWAY W, VANCOUVER, BC, V6J 5K8
(604) 713-5000   SIC 8211

BOARD OF EDUCATION OF SCHOOL DISTRICT NO. 39 (VANCOUVER), THE *p* 322
2250 EDDINGTON DR, VANCOUVER, BC, V6L 2E7
(604) 713-8974   SIC 8211

BOARD OF EDUCATION OF SCHOOL DISTRICT NO. 39 (VANCOUVER), THE *p* 322
2706 TRAFALGAR ST, VANCOUVER, BC, V6K 2J6
(604) 713-8961   SIC 8211

BOARD OF EDUCATION OF SCHOOL DISTRICT NO. 39 (VANCOUVER), THE *p*

322
6360 MAPLE ST, VANCOUVER, BC, V6M
4M2
(604) 713-8200   *SIC* 8211
**BOARD OF EDUCATION OF SCHOOL DIS-
TRICT NO. 39 (VANCOUVER), THE**   *p*
323
7055 HEATHER ST, VANCOUVER, BC, V6P
3P7
(604) 713-8189   *SIC* 8211
**BOARD OF EDUCATION OF SCHOOL DIS-
TRICT NO. 39 (VANCOUVER), THE**   *p*
324
3939 16TH AVE W, VANCOUVER, BC, V6R
3C9
(604) 713-8171   *SIC* 8211
**BOARD OF EDUCATION OF SCHOOL DIS-
TRICT NO. 57 (PRINCE GEORGE), THE**   *p*
248
4540 HANDLEN RD, PRINCE GEORGE,
BC, V2K 2J8
(250) 962-9271   *SIC* 8211
**BOARD OF EDUCATION OF SCHOOL DIS-
TRICT NO. 57 (PRINCE GEORGE), THE**   *p*
249
2100 FERRY AVE, PRINCE GEORGE, BC,
V2L 4R5
(250) 561-6800   *SIC* 8211
**BOARD OF EDUCATION OF SCHOOL DIS-
TRICT NO. 57 (PRINCE GEORGE), THE**   *p*
249
747 WINNIPEG ST, PRINCE GEORGE, BC,
V2L 2V3
(250) 563-7124   *SIC* 8211
**BOARD OF EDUCATION OF SCHOOL DIS-
TRICT NO. 57 (PRINCE GEORGE), THE**   *p*
250
2901 GRIFFITHS AVE, PRINCE GEORGE,
BC, V2M 2S7
(250) 562-6441   *SIC* 8211
**BOARD OF EDUCATION OF SCHOOL DIS-
TRICT NO. 61 (GREATER VICTORIA)**   *p*
332
3970 GORDON HEAD RD, VICTORIA, BC,
V8N 3X3
(250) 477-6977   *SIC* 8211
**BOARD OF EDUCATION OF SCHOOL DIS-
TRICT NO. 61 (GREATER VICTORIA)**   *p*
333
3963 BORDEN ST, VICTORIA, BC, V8P
3H9
(250) 479-1696   *SIC* 8211
**BOARD OF EDUCATION OF SCHOOL DIS-
TRICT NO. 61 (GREATER VICTORIA)**   *p*
334
1260 GRANT ST, VICTORIA, BC, V8T 1C2
(250) 388-5456   *SIC* 8211
**BOARD OF EDUCATION OF SCHOOL DIS-
TRICT NO. 61 (GREATER VICTORIA)**   *p*
338
556 BOLESKINE RD, VICTORIA, BC, V8Z
1E8
(250) 475-3212   *SIC* 8211
**BOARD OF EDUCATION OF SCHOOL DIS-
TRICT NO. 61 (GREATER VICTORIA)**   *p*
338
957 BURNSIDE RD W, VICTORIA, BC, V8Z
6E9
(250) 479-8271   *SIC* 8211
**BOARD OF EDUCATION OF SCHOOL DIS-
TRICT NO. 61 (GREATER VICTORIA)**   *p*
339
847 COLVILLE RD, VICTORIA, BC, V9A
4N9
(250) 382-9226   *SIC* 8211
**BOARD OF EDUCATION OF SCHOOL DIS-
TRICT NO. 91 (NECHAKO LAKE), THE**   *p*
330
153 CONNAUGHT ST E, VANDERHOOF,
BC, V0J 3A0
(250) 567-2284   *SIC* 8211
**BOARD OF EDUCATION OF THE CHI-
NOOK SCHOOL DIVISION NO. 211 OF
SASKATCHEWAN**   *p* 1436

2100 GLADSTONE ST E, SWIFT CUR-
RENT, SK, S9H 3W7
(306) 778-9200   *SIC* 8211
**BOARD OF EDUCATION OF THE GOOD
SPIRIT SCHOOL DIVISION NO. 204 OF
SASKATCHEWAN**   *p* 1438
150 GLADSTONE AVE N, YORKTON, SK,
S3N 2A8
(306) 786-5560   *SIC* 8211
**BOARD OF EDUCATION OF THE LIV-
ING SKY SCHOOL DIVISION NO. 202
SASKATCHEWAN**   *p* 1412
1791 110TH ST, NORTH BATTLEFORD,
SK, S9A 2Y2
(306) 445-6101   *SIC* 8211
**BOARD OF EDUCATION OF THE LIV-
ING SKY SCHOOL DIVISION NO. 202
SASKATCHEWAN**   *p* 1412
509 PIONEER AVE, NORTH BATTLEFORD,
SK, S9A 4A5
(306) 937-7702   *SIC* 8211
**BOARD OF EDUCATION OF THE REGINA
ROMAN CATHOLIC SEPARATE SCHOOL
DIVISION NO. 81**   *p* 1417
1027 COLLEGE AVE, REGINA, SK, S4P
1A7
(306) 791-7230   *SIC* 8211
**BOARD OF EDUCATION OF THE REGINA
ROMAN CATHOLIC SEPARATE SCHOOL
DIVISION NO. 81**   *p* 1420
134 ARGYLE ST, REGINA, SK, S4R 4C3
(306) 791-7240   *SIC* 8211
**BOARD OF EDUCATION REGINA SCHOOL
DIVISION NO. 4 OF SASKATCHEWAN**   *p*
1422
3838 E BUCKINGHAM DR, REGINA, SK,
S4V 3A1
(306) 791-8585   *SIC* 8211
**BOARD OF EDUCATION REGINA SCHOOL
DIVISION NO. 4 OF SASKATCHEWAN**   *p*
1423
5255 ROCHDALE BLVD, REGINA, SK, S4X
4M8
(306) 523-3400   *SIC* 8211
**BOARD OF EDUCATION SCHOOL DIS-
TRICT #38 (RICHMOND)**   *p*
253
4151 JACOMBS RD, RICHMOND, BC, V6V
1N7
(604) 668-6430   *SIC* 8211
**BOARD OF EDUCATION SCHOOL DIS-
TRICT #38 (RICHMOND)**   *p*
262
7171 MINORU BLVD, RICHMOND, BC, V6Y
1Z3
(604) 668-6400   *SIC* 8211
**BOARD OF EDUCATION SCHOOL DIS-
TRICT #38 (RICHMOND)**   *p*
262
7811 GRANVILLE AVE, RICHMOND, BC,
V6Y 3E3
(604) 668-6000   *SIC* 8211
**BOARD OF EDUCATION SCHOOL DIS-
TRICT #38 (RICHMOND)**   *p*
262
9500 NO. 4 RD, RICHMOND, BC, V7A 2Y9
(604) 668-6575   *SIC* 8211
**BOARD OF EDUCATION SCHOOL DIS-
TRICT #38 (RICHMOND)**   *p*
266
4251 GARRY ST, RICHMOND, BC, V7E 2T9
(604) 718-4050   *SIC* 8211
**BOARD OF EDUCATION SCHOOL DIS-
TRICT #38 (RICHMOND)**   *p*
266
6600 WILLIAMS RD, RICHMOND, BC, V7E
1K5
(604) 668-6668   *SIC* 8211
**BOARD OF EDUCATION SCHOOL DIS-
TRICT #38 (RICHMOND)**   *p*
266
9200 NO. 1 RD, RICHMOND, BC, V7E 6L5
(604) 668-6615   *SIC* 8211
BOARD OF GOVERNERS OF BOW VALLEY

COLLEGE, THE   *p* 27
345 6 AVE SE, CALGARY, AB, T2G 4V1
(403) 410-1400   *SIC* 8221
**BOARD OF GOVERNOR'S OF RED RIVER
COLLEGE, THE**   *p* 383
2055 NOTRE DAME AVE, WINNIPEG, MB,
R3H 0J9
(204) 632-3960   *SIC* 8222
**BOARD OF GOVERNORS OF EXHIBITION
PLACE, THE**   *p* 991
100 PRINCES BLVD SUITE 1, TORONTO,
ON, M6K 3C3
(416) 263-3600   *SIC* 7999
**BOARD OF HEALTH FOR THE DISTRICT
OF ALGOMA HEALTH UNIT**   *p* 862
294 WILLOW AVE, SAULT STE. MARIE,
ON, P6B 0A9
(705) 942-4646   *SIC* 8011
**BOARD OF HEALTH FOR THE TIMISKAM-
ING HEALTH UNIT**   *p*
753
421 SHEPHERDSON RD, NEW LISKEARD,
ON, P0J 1P0
(705) 647-4305   *SIC* 8099
**BOARD OF MANAGEMENT OF THE
TORONTO ZOO**   *p* 864
361A OLD FINCH AVE, SCARBOROUGH,
ON, M1B 5K7
(416) 392-5929   *SIC* 7999
BOARD OF SCHOOL TRUSTEES   *p* 320
1580 BROADWAY W, VANCOUVER, BC,
V6J 5K8
(604) 713-5000   *SIC* 8211
**BOARD OF SCHOOL TRUSTEES OF
SCHOOL DISTRICT #40 (NEW WESTMIN-
STER), THE**   *p*
237
1001 COLUMBIA ST, NEW WESTMIN-
STER, BC, V3M 1C4
(604) 517-6240   *SIC* 8211
**BOARD OF SCHOOL TRUSTEES OF
SCHOOL DISTRICT NO. 45**   *p* 341
1250 CHARTWELL DR, WEST VANCOU-
VER, BC, V7S 2R2
(604) 981-1100   *SIC* 8211
**BOARD OF TRUSTEES OF HORIZON
SCHOOL DIVISION NO 67**   *p* 169
6302 56 ST, TABER, AB, T1G 1Z9
(403) 223-3547   *SIC* 8211
**BOARD OF TRUSTEES OF THE RED DEER
PUBLIC SCHOOL DISTRICT NO. 104, THE** *p*
153
4204 58 ST, RED DEER, AB, T4N 2L6
(403) 347-1171   *SIC* 8211
**BOARD OF TRUSTEES OF THE RED DEER
PUBLIC SCHOOL DISTRICT NO. 104, THE** *p*
156
150 LOCKWOOD AVE, RED DEER, AB,
T4R 2M4
(403) 342-6655   *SIC* 8211
**BOARDROOM SNOWBOARD SHOP, DIV
OF**   *p* 239
See HIGH OUTPUT SPORTS CANADA INC
BOARDSHOP, THE   *p* 659
See EAST LONDON SPORTS LIMITED
BOARDSUITE CORP   *p* 949
372 BAY ST SUITE 1800, TORONTO, ON,
M5H 2W9
SIC 7372
**BOARDWALK REAL ESTATE INVEST-
MENT TRUST**   *p*
64
1501 1 ST SW SUITE 200, CALGARY, AB,
T2R 0W1
(403) 531-9255   *SIC* 6531
**BOARDWALK REIT LIMITED PARTNER-
SHIP**   *p*
64
1501 1 ST SW SUITE 200, CALGARY, AB,
T2R 0W1
(403) 531-9255   *SIC* 6513
BOARDWALK RENTAL COMMUNITIES   *p*
64
See BOARDWALK REAL ESTATE INVEST-

MENT TRUST
BOARDWALK RENTAL COMMUNITIES   *p*
64
*See BOARDWALK REIT LIMITED PART-
NERSHIP*
BOART LONGYEAR CANADA   *p* 713
2442 SOUTH SHERIDAN WAY, MISSIS-
SAUGA, ON, L5J 2M7
(905) 822-7922   *SIC* 1799
BOAT ROCKER RIGHTS INC   *p* 932
595 ADELAIDE ST E, TORONTO, ON, M5A
1N8
(416) 591-0065   *SIC* 7371
BOATHOUSE   *p* 883
*See ARLIE'S SPORT SHOP (DOWNTOWN)
LTD*
BOATHOUSE RESTAURANTS OF CANADA
p 343
14935 MARINE DR, WHITE ROCK, BC,
V4B 1C3
(604) 536-7320   *SIC* 5812
BOB DALE GLOVES & IMPORTS LTD *p* 108
4504 82 AVE NW, EDMONTON, AB, T6B
2S4
(780) 469-2100   *SIC* 5136
**BOB DALE OILFIELD CONSTRUCTION
LTD**   *p* 82
5309 56TH AVE, DRAYTON VALLEY, AB,
T7A 1S7
(780) 542-4834   *SIC* 1629
**BOB MACQUARRIE RECREATION COM-
PLEX - ORLEANS**   *p*
810
See CITY OF OTTAWA
BOB MYERS CHEVROLET OLDS   *p* 474
*See MYERS, BOB CHEVROLET OLDSMO-
BILE LTD*
BOB RUMBALL CENTRE FOR THE DEAF *p*
769
*See ONTARIO MISSION FOR THE DEAF,
THE*
BOB'S NO FRILLS   *p* 529
571 BRANT ST, BURLINGTON, ON, L7R
2G6
(866) 987-6453   *SIC* 5411
BOBCAT OF REGINA LTD   *p* 1417
GD LCD MAIN, REGINA, SK, S4P 2Z4
(306) 347-7600   *SIC* 5084
BOBCAT OF SASKATOON   *p* 1435
See FGI SUPPLY LTD
BOBCAT OF TORONTO   *p* 505
See OAKEN HOLDINGS INC
BOBLEN CASES   *p* 1172
See ETUIS BOBLEN CASES INC
**BOBRICK WASHROOM EQUIPMENT COM-
PANY**   *p*
872
45 ROLARK DR, SCARBOROUGH, ON,
M1R 3B1
(416) 298-1611   *SIC* 3431
BOCA BOYS HOLDINGS INC   *p* 1401
1 CAR WESTMOUNT BUREAU 1100,
WESTMOUNT, QC, H3Z 2P9
(514) 341-5600   *SIC* 6712
BOCAN MATERIAUX   *p* 1321
*See COMPAGNIE EAGLE LUMBER LIMI-
TEE, LA*
BOCCIOLETTI, J & M SALES LTD   *p* 131
11311 99 ST, GRANDE PRAIRIE, AB, T8V
2H6
(780) 539-9292   *SIC* 5531
BOCK   *p* 538
See BOCK NORTH AMERICA LTD
BOCK NORTH AMERICA LTD   *p* 538
18 CHERRY BLOSSOM RD, CAMBRIDGE,
ON, N3H 4R7
(519) 653-3334   *SIC* 3089
BOCKSTAEL CONSTRUCTION LIMITED *p*
365
100 PAQUIN RD UNIT 200, WINNIPEG, MB,
R2J 3V4
(204) 233-7135   *SIC* 1542
BODKIN FINANCIAL CORPORATION *p* 716
2150 DUNWIN DR SUITE 1, MISSIS-

SAUGA, ON, L5L 5M8
(905) 820-4550   *SIC* 6159
BODNAR DRILLING LTD   *p* 358
23 DELAURIER DR, STE ROSE DU LAC,
MB, R0L 1S0
(204) 447-2755   *SIC* 1481
BODNAR, KEN ENTERPRISES INC *p* 532
75 DUNDAS ST, CAMBRIDGE, ON, N1R
6G5
(519) 621-8180   *SIC* 5531
BODTKER GROUP OF COMPANIES LTD *p*
14
7905 46 ST SE, CALGARY, AB, T2C 2Y6
(403) 279-2191   *SIC* 6712
BODY GLOVE   *p* 1341
See SGS SPORTS INC
BODY PLUS   *p* 183
6200 DARNLEY ST SUITE 204, BURNABY,
BC, V5B 3B1
SIC 5122
**BODY PLUS NUTRITIONAL PRODUCTS
INC**   *p* 864
130 MCLEVIN AVE UNIT 5, SCARBOR-
OUGH, ON, M1B 3R6
(416) 332-1881   *SIC* 5149
BODY SHOP CANADA LIMITED, THE *p* 788
1 YORKDALE RD SUITE 510, NORTH
YORK, ON, M6A 3A1
(416) 782-2948   *SIC* 6794
BODYLINE AUTO RECYCLERS   *p* 607
See BODYLINE INC
BODYLINE INC   *p* 607
185 BANCROFT ST, HAMILTON, ON, L8E
4L4
(905) 573-7000   *SIC* 5511
BOEHMER BOX LP   *p* 637
120 TRILLIUM DR, KITCHENER, ON, N2E
2C4
(519) 576-2480   *SIC* 2652
BOEHMER BOX LP   *p* 642
1560 BATTLER RD, KITCHENER, ON, N2R
1J6
(519) 576-2480   *SIC* 2652
**BOEHMERS CRONIN EMERY ACCENT
HEATING & COOLING**   *p* 1006
*See MIDWESTERN ONTARIO SERVICE
EXPERT*
BOEHRINGER INGELHEIM (CANADA) LTD
p 521
5180 SOUTH SERVICE RD, BURLINGTON,
ON, L7L 5H4
(905) 639-0333   *SIC* 5122
BOEHRINGER INGELHEIM (CANADA) LTD
p 1084
2100 RUE CUNARD, COTE SAINT-LUC,
QC, H7S 2G5
SIC 8731
BOEING CANADA OPERATIONS LTD *p* 385
99 MURRAY PARK RD, WINNIPEG, MB,
R3J 3M6
(204) 888-2300   *SIC* 3728
BOEING CANADA WINNIPEG, DIV OF *p*
385
See BOEING CANADA OPERATIONS LTD
BOESE FOODS INTERNATIONAL INC *p*
521
4145 NORTH SERVICE RD 2ND FL,
BURLINGTON, ON, L7L 6A3
(289) 288-5304   *SIC* 5141
BOHN PETROLEUM SERVICES LTD *p* 173
3449 33 ST, WHITECOURT, AB, T7S 1X4
(780) 778-8551   *SIC* 1389
BOHNE SPRING INDUSTRIES LIMITED *p*
573
60 CORONET RD, ETOBICOKE, ON, M8Z
2M1
(416) 231-9000   *SIC* 5085
**BOILER INSPECTION AND INSURANCE
COMPANY OF CANADA, THE**   *p* 949
390 BAY ST SUITE 2000, TORONTO, ON,
M5H 2Y2
(416) 363-5491   *SIC* 6331
BOILERMAKER'S BENEFIT & TRUST *p* 667
See BOILERMAKER'S NATIONAL BENE-

FIT PLANS
**BOILERMAKER'S NATIONAL BENEFIT
PLANS**   *p* 667
45 MCINTOSH DR, MARKHAM, ON, L3R
8C7
(905) 946-2530   *SIC* 6371
BOIRON CANADA INC   *p* 1295
1300 RUE RENE-DESCARTES, SAINT-
BRUNO, QC, J3V 0B7
(450) 723-2066   *SIC* 5122
BOIRON DOLISOS   *p* 1295
See BOIRON CANADA INC
BOIS AISE DE MONTREAL INC   *p* 1137
1190A RUE DE COURCHEVEL BUREAU
420, LEVIS, QC, G6W 0M5
(418) 832-4200   *SIC* 5031
BOIS B.S.L MATANE   *p* 1154
See BOIS BSL INC
BOIS BSL INC   *p* 1154
1081 BOUL INDUSTRIEL, MONT-JOLI, QC,
G5H 3K8
(418) 775-5360   *SIC* 5023
BOIS CINTRE MSGB   *p* 1299
See ESCALIERS GRENIER, GILLES INC
BOIS CLO-VAL   *p* 1364
*See COMPAGNIE COMMONWEALTH PLY-
WOOD LTEE, LA*
BOIS D' OEUVRE CEDRICO   *p* 1124
See GROUPE CEDRICO INC
BOIS D'INGENIERIE RESOLU-LP *p* 1130
*See BOIS D'INGENIERIE RESOLU-LP
LAROUCHE INC*
**BOIS   D'INGENIERIE   RESOLU-LP
LAROUCHE INC**   *p* 1130
900 CH DU LAC-HIPPOLYTE, LAROUCHE,
QC, G0W 1Z0
(418) 547-2828   *SIC* 2448
BOIS D'OEUVRE CEDRICO INC   *p* 1074
562 RTE 132 E, CAUSAPSCAL, QC, G0J
1J0
(418) 756-5727   *SIC* 5099
BOIS D'OEUVRE CEDRICO INC   *p* 1253
39 RUE SAINT-JEAN-BAPTISTE, PRICE,
QC, G0J 1Z0
(418) 775-7516   *SIC* 2431
BOIS DAAQUAM INC   *p* 1271
2590 BOUL LAURIER BUREAU 740, QUE-
BEC, QC, G1V 4M6
SIC 2421
BOIS DAAQUAM INC   *p* 1322
370   RTE   204,   SAINT-JUST-DE-
BRETENIERES, QC, G0R 3H0
(418) 244-3601   *SIC* 2421
**BOIS DE CONSTRUCTION CHENEVILLE
INC, LES**   *p* 1077
99 RUE ALBERT-FERLAND, CHENEVILLE,
QC, J0V 1E0
(819) 428-3903   *SIC* 5211
BOIS DE PLANCHER P.G. INC, LES *p* 1299
2424 RUE PRINCIPALE, SAINT-EDOUARD-
DE-LOTBINIERE, QC, G0S 1Y0
(418) 796-2328   *SIC* 2426
BOIS DE SCIAGE LAFONTAINE INC *p* 1361
144 RANG LAFONTAINE, SAINTE-
PERPETUE-DE-L'ISLET, QC, G0R 3Z0
(418) 359-2500   *SIC* 2421
BOIS DE STRUCTURE LEE   *p* 1362
See METALTECH-OMEGA INC
BOIS EXPANSION INC   *p* 1216
9750 BOUL SAINT-LAURENT, MONTREAL,
QC, H3L 2N3
(514) 381-5626   *SIC* 5031
BOIS FRANC MODEL   *p* 1299
See BOIS DE PLANCHER P.G. INC, LES
BOIS FRANCS D.V. INC, LES   *p* 1102
131 RUE PRINCIPALE, FASSETT, QC, J0V
1H0
(819) 423-2338   *SIC* 5031
BOIS HAMEL   *p* 1299
See CLERMOND HAMEL LTEE
BOIS INDIFOR INC, LES   *p* 1271
2590 BOUL LAURIER BUREAU 1040, QUE-
BEC, QC, G1V 4M6
(418) 877-2294   *SIC* 5031

BOIS KENNEBEC - USINE 001   *p* 1305
See BOIS KENNEBEC LTEE
BOIS KENNEBEC LTEE   *p* 1305
8475 25E AV, SAINT-GEORGES, QC, G6A
1M8
(418) 228-1414   *SIC* 2431
BOIS MARSOUI G.D.S. INC   *p* 1149
2 RTE DE LA MINE CANDEGO, MARSOUI,
QC, G0E 1S0
(418) 288-5635   *SIC* 2421
BOIS NOBLES KA'N'ENDA   *p* 1204
See FOREX INC
BOIS NOBLES KA'N'ENDA LTEE   *p* 1154
701 RUE IBERVILLE, MONT-LAURIER, QC,
J9L 3W7
(819) 623-2445   *SIC* 2421
**BOIS OUVRE DE BEAUCEVILLE (1992)
INC**   *p* 1055
201 134E RUE, BEAUCEVILLE, QC, G5X
3H9
(418) 774-3606   *SIC* 2431
BOIS OUVRES WATERVILLE INC   *p* 1400
525 RUE PRINCIPALE N, WATERVILLE,
QC, J0B 3H0
(819) 837-2476   *SIC* 5084
BOIS POULIN INC, LES   *p* 1124
658 RUE POULIN, LAC-DROLET, QC, G0Y
1C0
(819) 549-2090   *SIC* 2421
**BOIS PRECIEUX QUEBEC CANADA 1993
INC**   *p* 1082
3100 RTE 108 BUREAU 4, COOKSHIRE-
EATON, QC, J0B 1M0
(866) 624-0243   *SIC* 5099
BOIS ROCHER PERCE G.D.S.   *p* 1149
See BOIS MARSOUI G.D.S. INC
BOIS TURCOTTE LTEE   *p* 1390
1338 3E AV, VAL-D'OR, QC, J9P 1V5
(819) 824-3661   *SIC* 5039
BOIS-FRANCS   *p* 1350
See 2730-8303 QUEBEC INC
BOISACO INC   *p* 1290
648 CH DU MOULIN BUREAU 250,
SACRE-COEUR-SAGUENAY, QC, G0T 1Y0
(418) 236-4633   *SIC* 2421
BOISE ALLJOIST LTD   *p* 417
70 RUE INDUSTRIELLE, SAINT-JACQUES,
NB, E7B 1T1
(506) 735-3561   *SIC* 2499
BOISE NOTRE DAME, LES RESIDENCES *p*
1241
See 6423264 CANADA INC
BOISE ST-FRANCIS INC, LE   *p* 1056
1981 RUE BERNARD-PILON, BELOEIL,
QC, J3G 4S5
(450) 446-8221   *SIC* 6531
**BOISERIES LUSSIER, DIV DE QUINCAIL-
LERIE RICHELIEU**   *p*
1335
See QUINCAILLERIE RICHELIEU LTEE
BOISERIES MILLE ILES   *p* 1161
See BOISERIES RAYMOND INC
BOISERIES RAYMOND INC   *p* 1161
11880 56E AV, MONTREAL, QC, H1E 2L6
(514) 494-1141   *SIC* 2431
BOISJOLI, DORIA LTEE   *p* 1402
730 RUE BOISJOLI, WICKHAM, QC, J0C
1S0
(819) 398-6813   *SIC* 0251
BOISVERT AUTO   *p* 1064
See BOISVERT, P.E. AUTO LTEE
BOISVERT PONTIAC BUICK LTD   *p* 1058
470   BOUL   DU   CURE-LABELLE,
BLAINVILLE, QC, J7C 2H2
(450) 430-9400   *SIC* 5511
BOISVERT, P.E. AUTO LTEE   *p* 1064
2   BOUL   MARIE-VICTORIN,
BOUCHERVILLE, QC, J4B 1V5
(514) 527-8215   *SIC* 5511
BOITE A GRAINS INC, LA   *p* 1106
581 BOUL SAINT-JOSEPH, GATINEAU,
QC, J8Y 4A6
(819) 771-3000   *SIC* 5499
BOITE A PAIN CAFE NAPOLI   *p* 1258

*See BOULANGERIE ARTISANALE LA
BOITE A PAIN INC*
BOITEOUVERTE.CA   *p* 1330
See SERVICES J. SONIC INC
BOKIT MC   *p* 1140
See MATERIAUX BOMAT INC
BOLD EVENT CREATIVE INC   *p* 182
7570 CONRAD ST, BURNABY, BC, V5A
2H7
(604) 437-7677   *SIC* 3999
BOLDER GRAPHICS INCORPORATED *p* 14
10 SMED LANE SE UNIT 110, CALGARY,
AB, T2C 4T5
(403) 259-0054   *SIC* 7336
BOLDT POOL CONSTRUCTION LTD *p* 884
20 NIHAN DR, ST CATHARINES, ON, L2N
1L1
(905) 934-0937   *SIC* 5999
BOLDT POOLS & SPAS   *p* 884
See BOLDT POOL CONSTRUCTION LTD
**BOLDUC MANUFACTURIER DE PRO-
DUITS DE BETON**   *p*
1359
See BETON BOLDUC INC
BOLERO SHELLFISH PROCESSING INC *p*
417
1324 ROUTE 335, SAINT-SIMON, NB, E8P
2B2
(506) 727-5217   *SIC* 2091
BOLESS INC   *p* 1107
15 RUE BUTEAU BUREAU 220, GATINEAU,
QC, J8Z 1V4
(819) 770-3028   *SIC* 1542
BOLIVAR HOLDINGS LTD   *p* 273
10280 CITY PKY, SURREY, BC, V3T 4C2
(604) 589-8299   *SIC* 5941
BOLLORE LOGISTIQUES CANADA INC *p*
1332
3400   RUE   DOUGLAS-B.-FLOREANI,
SAINT-LAURENT, QC, H4S 1V2
(514) 956-7870   *SIC* 4731
BOLSHOI   *p* 1319
See ENTREPRISES ROLLAND INC, LES
BOLT   *p* 1378
See RAYONIER A.M. CANADA G.P.
BOLT AND NUT SUPPLY LIMITED *p* 532
384 FRANKLIN BLVD, CAMBRIDGE, ON,
N1R 8G5
(519) 623-0370   *SIC* 5085
BOLT OFFSITE LTD   *p* 14
7007 84 ST SE, CALGARY, AB, T2C 4T6
(403) 921-5318   *SIC* 1521
BOLT SECURITY SYSTEMS   *p* 98
See 569398 ALBERTA LTD
BOLT SUPPLY HOUSE LTD, THE   *p* 27
3909 MANCHESTER RD SE UNIT C, CAL-
GARY, AB, T2G 4A1
(403) 245-2818   *SIC* 5085
BOLTHOUSE FARMS CANADA INC *p* 1013
303 MILO RD, WHEATLEY, ON, N0P 2P0
(519) 825-3412   *SIC* 5431
BOLTON STEEL TUBE CO. LTD   *p* 494
455A PIERCEY RD, BOLTON, ON, L7E 5B8
(905) 857-6830   *SIC* 3312
BOLTON SUPERMARKETS LTD   *p* 737
6790 PACIFIC CIR, MISSISSAUGA, ON,
L5T 1N8
(905) 670-1204   *SIC* 5411
BOLTS PLUS INCORPORATED   *p* 685
7100 TORBRAM RD, MISSISSAUGA, ON,
L4T 4B5
(905) 673-5554   *SIC* 5072
BOLZANO HOLDINGS LTD   *p* 338
477 BOLESKINE RD, VICTORIA, BC, V8Z
1E7
(250) 475-1441   *SIC* 2431
BOMBARDIER   *p* 1295
*See BOMBARDIER TRANSPORTATION
CANADA HOLDING INC*
BOMBARDIER A?RONAUTIQUE   *p* 762
See BOMBARDIER INC
BOMBARDIER A?RONAUTIQUE   *p* 1093
See BOMBARDIER INC
BOMBARDIER AERONAUTIQUE   *p* 1328

See *BOMBARDIER INC*
BOMBARDIER AERONAUTIQUE   p 785
See *BOMBARDIER INC*
BOMBARDIER AERONAUTIQUE   p 1092
See *BOMBARDIER INC*
BOMBARDIER AERONAUTIQUE   p 1202
See *BOMBARDIER INC*
BOMBARDIER AERONAUTIQUE   p 1338
See *BOMBARDIER INC*
BOMBARDIER AERONAUTIQUE   p 1410
See *BOMBARDIER INC*
BOMBARDIER INC   p 631
1059 TAYLOR-KIDD BLVD, KINGSTON, ON,
K7M 6J9
(613) 384-3100   *SIC* 2754
BOMBARDIER INC   p 737
6291 ORDAN DR, MISSISSAUGA, ON, L5T
1G9
(905) 795-7869   *SIC* 4111
BOMBARDIER INC   p 762
1500 AIRPORT RD, NORTH BAY, ON, P1B
8G2
SIC 8711
BOMBARDIER INC   p 785
123 GARRATT BLVD, NORTH YORK, ON,
M3K 1Y5
(416) 633-7310   *SIC* 3721
BOMBARDIER INC   p 1092
200 CH DE LA COTE-VERTU BUREAU
1110, DORVAL, QC, H4S 2A3
(514) 420-4000   *SIC* 3721
BOMBARDIER INC   p 1093
9501 AV RYAN, DORVAL, QC, H9P 1A2
(514) 855-5000   *SIC* 8711
BOMBARDIER INC   p 1202
800 BOUL RENE-LEVESQUE O 29E
ETAGE, MONTREAL, QC, H3B 1Y8
(514) 861-9481   *SIC* 3743
BOMBARDIER INC   p 1295
1101 RUE PARENT, SAINT-BRUNO, QC,
J3V 6E6
(450) 441-2020   *SIC* 4111
BOMBARDIER INC   p 1328
1800 BOUL MARCEL-LAURIN, SAINT-
LAURENT, QC, H4R 1K2
(514) 855-5000   *SIC* 3812
BOMBARDIER INC   p 1338
8575 CH DE LA COTE-DE-LIESSE, SAINT-
LAURENT, QC, H4T 1G5
(514) 344-6620   *SIC* 8249
BOMBARDIER INC   p 1410
GD, MOOSE JAW, SK, S6H 7Z8
(306) 694-2222   *SIC* 8299
**BOMBARDIER PRODUITS RECREATIFS
INC**   p 1392
565 RUE DE LA MONTAGNE BUREAU 210,
VALCOURT, QC, J0E 2L0
(450) 532-2211   *SIC* 3799
**BOMBARDIER PRODUITS RECREATIFS
INC**   p 1392
726 RUE SAINT-JOSEPH, VALCOURT, QC,
J0E 2L0
(450) 532-2211   *SIC* 3799
BOMBARDIER TRANSPORT   p 737
See *BOMBARDIER INC*
BOMBARDIER TRANSPORT   p 1122
See *BOMBARDIER TRANSPORTATION
CANADA INC*
BOMBARDIER TRANSPORT   p 1295
See *BOMBARDIER TRANSPORTATION
CANADA INC*
BOMBARDIER TRANSPORTATION   p 1295
See *BOMBARDIER INC*
**BOMBARDIER TRANSPORTATION
CANADA HOLDING INC**   p 1295
1101 RUE PARENT, SAINT-BRUNO, QC,
J3V 6E6
(450) 441-2020   *SIC* 6712
**BOMBARDIER TRANSPORTATION
CANADA INC**   p 909
1001 MONTREAL ST, THUNDER BAY, ON,
P7C 4V6
(807) 475-2810   *SIC* 3743
BOMBARDIER TRANSPORTATION

CANADA INC   p 1122
230 RTE O BUREAU 130, LA POCATIERE,
QC, G0R 1Z0
(418) 856-1232   *SIC* 5088
**BOMBARDIER TRANSPORTATION
CANADA INC**   p 1295
1101 RUE PARENT, SAINT-BRUNO, QC,
J3V 6E6
(450) 441-3193   *SIC* 7363
BOMBARIDER TRANSPORT   p 909
See *BOMBARDIER TRANSPORTATION
CANADA INC*
BOMBAY COMPANY, THE   p 500
See *446987 ONTARIO INC*
BON REGARD   p 1222
See *BONLOOK INC*
BONANZA GARDEN CENTRE   p 737
See *BOLTON SUPERMARKETS LTD*
BONANZA LALUMIERE   p 1346
See *2941902 CANADA INC*
BONASOURCE INC   p 960
144 FRONT ST W SUITE 725, TORONTO,
ON, M5J 2L7
(416) 410-4059   *SIC* 7374
BONAVENTURE COMMUNICATION   p 1387
See *GROUPE CLR INC*
BONAVISTA BOVI HOME/MAISON INC   p 1156
8515 PLACE DEVONSHIRE BUREAU 100,
MONT-ROYAL, QC, H4P 2K1
(514) 273-6300   *SIC* 5023
BONAVISTA ENERGY CORPORATION p 44
525 8 AVE SW SUITE 1500, CALGARY, AB,
T2P 1G1
(403) 213-4300   *SIC* 1311
BONAVISTA FABRICS   p 1156
See *BONAVISTA BOVI HOME/MAISON INC*
BONBONS OINK OINK INC, LES   p 1227
4810 RUE JEAN-TALON O, MONTREAL,
QC, H4P 2N5
(514) 731-4555   *SIC* 2064
BONCHEFF GREENHOUSES INC   p 573
382 OLIVEWOOD RD, ETOBICOKE, ON,
M8Z 2Z9
(416) 233-1800   *SIC* 5148
BONCHEFF HERBS   p 573
See *BONCHEFF GREENHOUSES INC*
BONCOR CONTAINERS   p 1330
See *MITCHEL-LINCOLN PACKAGING LTD*
BOND BRAND LOYALTY INC   p 744
6900 MARITZ DR, MISSISSAUGA, ON,
L5W 1L8
(905) 696-9400   *SIC* 8741
BOND CONSTRUCTION INC   p 127
295 MACDONALD CRES, FORT MCMUR-
RAY, AB, T9H 4B7
(780) 743-3448   *SIC* 1542
BOND HEAD GOLF RESORT INC   p 490
4805 7TH LINE RR 1, BEETON, ON, L0G
1A0
(905) 778-9400   *SIC* 7992
BOND PLACE HOTEL LTD   p 935
65 DUNDAS ST E, TORONTO, ON, M5B
2G8
(416) 362-6061   *SIC* 7011
BOND-A-PLY ALBERTA   p 128
See *GENRON ENTERPRISES LTD*
BONDAR'S FINE FURNITURE LTD   p 33
6999 11 ST SE BAY SUITE 110, CALGARY,
AB, T2H 2S1
(403) 253-8200   *SIC* 5712
**BONDFIELD CONSTRUCTION COMPANY
LIMITED**   p 549
407 BASALTIC RD, CONCORD, ON, L4K
4W8
(416) 667-8422   *SIC* 1542
BONDI PRODUCE CO. LTD   p 995
188 NEW TORONTO ST, TORONTO, ON,
M8V 2E8
(416) 252-7799   *SIC* 5148
BONDUELLE AMERIQUE DE NORD p 1299
See *BONDUELLE CANADA INC*
BONDUELLE AMERIQUE DU NORD p 1297
See *BONDUELLE CANADA INC*

BONDUELLE CANADA INC   p 621
583278 HAMILTON RD, INGERSOLL, ON,
N5C 3J7
(519) 485-0282   *SIC* 5142
BONDUELLE CANADA INC   p 1217
600 RUE HENRI BOURASSA O BUREAU
630, MONTREAL, QC, H3M 3E2
(514) 384-4281   *SIC* 2037
BONDUELLE CANADA INC   p 1297
1055 RTE 112, SAINT-CESAIRE, QC, J0L
1T0
(450) 469-3159   *SIC* 5149
BONDUELLE CANADA INC   p 1299
540 CH DES PATRIOTES, SAINT-DENIS-
SUR-RICHELIEU, QC, J0H 1K0
(450) 787-3411   *SIC* 2033
BONDUELLE CANADA INC   p 1360
316 RUE SAINT-JOSEPH RR 2, SAINTE-
MARTINE, QC, J0S 1V0
(450) 427-2130   *SIC* 2033
BONE STRUCTURE MD   p 1236
See *SIMPLE CONCEPT INC*
BONHOMME   p 597
See *BYTOWN LUMBER INC*
BONI DESIGN   p 1295
See *EQUIPEMENT BONI INC*
BONICA PRECISION (CANADA) INC p 253
3830 JACOMBS RD UNIT 105, RICHMOND,
BC, V6V 1Y6
(604) 270-0812   *SIC* 5094
BONICHOIX   p 1089
See *MARCHE FRECHETTE INC*
BONLOOK INC   p 1222
4020 RUE SAINT-AMBROISE BUREAU
489, MONTREAL, QC, H4C 2C7
(855) 943-5566   *SIC* 5995
BONNE BAY HEALTH CENTRE   p 427
See *WESTERN REGIONAL INTEGRATED
HEALTH AUTHORITY, THE*
BONNECHERE MANOR   p 849
See *CORPORATION OF THE COUNTY OF
RENFREW*
BONNES GATERIES 2007 INC   p 1349
710 RTE LAGUEUX, SAINT-NICOLAS, QC,
G7A 1A7
(418) 831-4948   *SIC* 5149
BONNETERIE BELLA INC.   p 972
1191 BATHURST ST, TORONTO, ON, M5R
3H4
(416) 537-2137   *SIC* 2251
BONNETERIE BELLA INC.   p 1225
1401 RUE LEGENDRE O, MONTREAL, QC,
H4N 2R9
(514) 381-8519   *SIC* 2251
BONNETT'S ENERGY CORP   p 134
65007 HWY 43, GRANDE PRAIRIE, AB,
T8W 5E7
(403) 264-3010   *SIC* 1389
BONNETT'S ENERGY SERVICES LP p 134
65007 HWY 43, GRANDE PRAIRIE, AB,
T8W 5E7
(780) 532-5700   *SIC* 1389
BONNETT'S WIRELINE, DIV   p 134
See *BONNETT'S ENERGY SERVICES LP*
BONNEVILLE MODULAR HOMES   p 1355
See *INDUSTRIES BONNEVILLE LTEE,
LES*
BONNIE & CLYDE   p 1297
See *LUDIK DESIGNER CONFISEUR INC*
BONNIE DOON SAFEWAY   p 112
See *SOBEYS WEST INC*
BONNIE TOGS   p 744
See *GENUINE CANADIAN CORP, THE*
BONNY'S TAXI LTD   p 192
5759 SIDLEY ST, BURNABY, BC, V5J 5E6
(604) 435-8233   *SIC* 4121
BONNYMAN AUTOMOTIVE   p 463
See *BONNYMAN MITSUBISHI*
BONNYMAN MITSUBISHI   p 463
29 CRESCENT DR, NEW MINAS, NS, B4N
3G7
SIC 5511
BONNYVILLE DODGE LTD   p 6
5605 50 AVE, BONNYVILLE, AB, T9N 2L1

(780) 826-2999   *SIC* 5511
**BONNYVILLE REGIONAL FIRE AUTHOR-
ITY**   p
6
4407 50 AVE, BONNYVILLE, AB, T9N 2H3
(780) 826-4755   *SIC* 7389
BONNYVILLE WELDING LTD   p 6
PT OF NE 14-616 W 4TH, BONNYVILLE,
AB, T9N 2J3
(780) 826-3847   *SIC* 1623
BONTE FOODS LIMITED   p 397
615 RUE CHAMPLAIN, DIEPPE, NB, E1A
7Z7
(506) 857-0025   *SIC* 2011
BONTERRA ENERGY CORP   p 64
1015 4 ST SW SUITE 901, CALGARY, AB,
T2R 1J4
(403) 262-5307   *SIC* 1311
BONTERRA RESOURCES INC   p 302
200 BURRARD ST SUITE 1680, VANCOU-
VER, BC, V6C 3L6
(604) 678-5308   *SIC* 1041
BONUS METAL CANADA INC   p 1240
10171 AV PELLETIER, MONTREAL-NORD,
QC, H1H 3R2
(514) 321-4820   *SIC* 5084
BOOK CITY   p 974
See *BOOKMASTERS LTD*
BOOK DEPOT INC   p 907
67 FRONT ST N, THOROLD, ON, L2V 1X3
(905) 680-7230   *SIC* 5192
BOOK EXPRESS   p 256
See *RAINCOAST BOOK DISTRIBUTION
LTD*
BOOKMASTERS LTD   p 974
501 BLOOR ST W SUITE 30, TORONTO,
ON, M5S 1V8
(416) 961-4496   *SIC* 5942
BOOKSHELF OF GUELPH LIMITED   p 602
41 QUEBEC ST, GUELPH, ON, N1H 2T1
(519) 821-3311   *SIC* 5942
BOOM TOWN CASINO   p 128
See *GAMEHOST INC*
BOOMCO DECOR INC   p 549
255 BASS PRO MILLS DR SUITE, CON-
CORD, ON, L4K 0A2
(905) 660-0677   *SIC* 5712
BOOMCO DECOR INC   p 659
760 WHARNCLIFFE RD S, LONDON, ON,
N6J 2N4
(519) 686-1441   *SIC* 5712
BOOMTOWN CASINO   p 157
See *GAMEHOST INC*
BOOMU MARKETING DIV OF   p 927
See *ACCUMARK PARTNERS INC*
BOONE FOOD SERVICES LIMITED   p 456
6960 MUMFORD RD SUITE 300, HALIFAX,
NS, B3L 4P1
(902) 453-5330   *SIC* 5812
**BOONE PLUMBING AND HEATING SUP-
PLY INC**   p
594
1282 ALGOMA RD SUITE 613, GLOUCES-
TER, ON, K1B 3W8
(613) 746-8560   *SIC* 5074
BOOSTER JUICE   p 165
See *1529813 ALBERTA LTD*
BOOTH INDUSTRIES, A DIV OF   p 919
See *GOVERNING COUNCIL OF THE SAL-
VATION ARMY IN CANADA, THE*
BOOTLEGGER   p 257
See *BOOTLEGGER CLOTHING INC*
BOOTLEGGER CLOTHING INC   p 257
6651 FRASERWOOD PL UNIT 250, RICH-
MOND, BC, V6W 1J3
(604) 276-8400   *SIC* 5621
BORALEX ENERGY CREATOR   p 1117
See *BORALEX INC*
BORALEX INC   p 1117
36 RUE LAJEUNESSE, KINGSEY FALLS,
QC, J0A 1B0
(819) 363-6363   *SIC* 4911
BORDEN LADNER GERVAIS LLP   p 44
520 3 AVE SW SUITE 1900, CALGARY, AB,

T2P 0R3
(403) 232-9500   *SIC* 8111
BORDEN LADNER GERVAIS LLP   p 302
200 BURRARD ST SUITE 1200, VANCOUVER, BC, V6C 3L6
(604) 687-5744   *SIC* 8111
BORDEN LADNER GERVAIS LLP   p 822
100 QUEEN ST SUITE 1100, OTTAWA, ON, K1P 1J9
(613) 237-5160   *SIC* 8111
BORDEN LADNER GERVAIS LLP   p 949
22 ADELAIDE ST W SUITE 3400, TORONTO, ON, M5H 4E3
(416) 367-6000   *SIC* 8111
BORDEN LADNER GERVAIS LLP   p 1202
1000 RUE DE LA GAUCHETIERE O BUREAU 900, MONTREAL, QC, H3B 5H4
(514) 879-1212   *SIC* 8111
BORDEN METAL PRODUCTS (CANADA) LIMITED   p 490
50 DAYFOOT ST, BEETON, ON, L0G 1A0
(905) 729-2229   *SIC* 3446
BORDER CHEMICAL COMPANY LIMITEDp 385
2147 PORTAGE AVE, WINNIPEG, MB, R3J 0L4
(204) 837-1383   *SIC* 2819
BORDER CITY BUILDING CENTRE LTD   p 143
2802 50 AVE, LLOYDMINSTER, AB, T9V 2S3
(780) 875-7762   *SIC* 5251
BORDER CITY CASTINGS   p 591
See 1083211 ONTARIO LTD
BORDER CITY R.V. CENTRE LTD   p 1409
GD LCD MAIN, LLOYDMINSTER, SK, S9V 0X5
(403) 875-0345   *SIC* 5571
BORDER GLASS & ALUMINUM   p 374
See BORDER GROUP OF COMPANIES INC, THE
BORDER GROUP OF COMPANIES INC, THE   p 374
53 HIGGINS AVE, WINNIPEG, MB, R3B 0A8
(204) 957-7200   *SIC* 3442
BORDER INVESTIGATION AND SECURITY INC   p 410
303 ROUTE 170, OAK BAY, NB, E3L 3Y2
(506) 466-6303   *SIC* 6211
BORDER PAVING LTD   p 155
6711 GOLDEN WEST AVE, RED DEER, AB, T4P 1A7
(403) 343-1177   *SIC* 1611
BORDER STEEL LIMITED   p 1021
3209 DEVON DR, WINDSOR, ON, N8X 4L5
(519) 966-0760   *SIC* 5051
BORDER TRENDS INC   p 692
5496 GORVAN DR, MISSISSAUGA, ON, L4W 3E8
(905) 238-1807   *SIC* 5023
BORDERLAND CO-OPERATIVE LIMITED p 1411
704 MAIN ST, MOOSOMIN, SK, S0G 3N0
(306) 435-4655   *SIC* 5411
BORDERWARE TECHNOLOGIES INC   p 709
50 BURNHAMTHORPE RD W SUITE 502, MISSISSAUGA, ON, L5B 3C2
(905) 804-1855   *SIC* 7371
BOREA CONSTRUCTION ULC   p 1140
562 RUE OLIVIER, LEVIS, QC, G7A 2N6
(418) 626-2314   *SIC* 1541
BOREAL WELL SERVICES   p 131
13701 99 ST, GRANDE PRAIRIE, AB, T8V 7N9
(780) 513-3400   *SIC* 1381
BOREALE   p 1058
See BRASSEURS DU NORD INC, LES
BOREALIS CAPITAL CORPORATIONp 960
200 BAY ST SUITE 200, TORONTO, ON, M5J 2J2
(416) 361-1011   *SIC* 6282
BOREALIS HOLDINGS TRUST MANAGE-

MENT INC   p
960
200 BAY ST S SUITE 2100, TORONTO, ON, M5J 2J2
(416) 361-1011   *SIC* 1731
BOREALIS INFRASTRUCTURE MANAGE-MENT INC   p
960
200 BAY ST SUITE 2100, TORONTO, ON, M5J 2J2
(416) 361-1011   *SIC* 6162
BOREALIS INVESTMENTS INC   p 949
100 ADELAIDE ST W SUITE 900, TORONTO, ON, M5H 0E2
(416) 361-1011   *SIC* 6719
BOREK CONSTRUCTION LTD   p 204
9630 RD 223, DAWSON CREEK, BC, V1G 4H8
(250) 782-5561   *SIC* 1389
BORETS CANADA LTD   p 148
2305 8 ST, NISKU, AB, T9E 7Z3
(780) 955-4799   *SIC* 5084
BORETS-WEATHERFORD   p 148
See BORETS CANADA LTD
BORETTA CONSTRUCTION 2002 LTD   p
365
1383 DUGALD RD, WINNIPEG, MB, R2J 0H3
(204) 237-7375   *SIC* 1542
BORLAND CONSTRUCTION (1989) LIMITED   p
365
751 LAGIMODIERE BLVD, WINNIPEG, MB, R2J 0T8
(204) 255-6444   *SIC* 1611
BOS INNOVATIONS INC   p 565
500 HUDSON DR, DORCHESTER, ON, N0L 1G5
(519) 268-8563   *SIC* 3569
BOS. & CO.   p 526
See 602667 ONTARIO LTD
BOSA CONSTRUCTION INC   p 302
838 HASTINGS ST W UNIT 1100, VANCOUVER, BC, V6C 0A6
(604) 299-1363   *SIC* 1522
BOSA ENTERPRISE CORPORATION p 302
838 HASTINGS ST W SUITE 1100, VANCOUVER, BC, V6C 0A6
(604) 299-1363   *SIC* 6712
BOSA FOODS   p 284
See A. BOSA & CO. LTD
BOSA PROPERTIES INC   p 302
838 W HASTINGS ST, VANCOUVER, BC, V6C 2X1
(604) 412-0313   *SIC* 6531
BOSA PROPERTIES INC   p 302
838 HASTINGS ST W SUITE 1201, VANCOUVER, BC, V6C 0A6
(604) 299-1363   *SIC* 6733
BOSCH REXROTH CANADA CORP p 1011
490 PRINCE CHARLES DR S, WELLAND, ON, L3B 5X7
(905) 735-0510   *SIC* 5084
BOSCUS CANADA INC   p 1249
900 AV SELKIRK, POINTE-CLAIRE, QC, H9R 3S3
(514) 694-9805   *SIC* 5031
BOSE LIMITED   p 678
280 HILLMOUNT RD SUITE 5, MARKHAM, ON, L6C 3A1
(905) 887-5950   *SIC* 5065
BOSHART INDUSTRIES INC   p 685
25 WHALEY AVE, MILVERTON, ON, N0K 1M0
(519) 595-4444   *SIC* 5085
BOSLEY REAL ESTATE LTD   p 923
290 MERTON ST, TORONTO, ON, M4S 1A9
(416) 322-8000   *SIC* 6531
BOSS BAKERY & RESTAURANT   p 294
See BOSS BAKERY & RESTAURANT LTD, THE
BOSS BAKERY & RESTAURANT LTD, THE p 294
532 MAIN ST, VANCOUVER, BC, V6A 2T9

(604) 683-3860   *SIC* 5461
BOSS LUBRICANTS   p 13
See ARLYN ENTERPRISES LTD
BOSS STEEL LIMITED   p 855
320 NEWKIRK RD, RICHMOND HILL, ON, L4C 3G7
(888) 301-6403   *SIC* 5051
BOSTON CONSULTING GROUP OF CANADA LIMITED, THE   p 960
181 BAY ST SUITE 2400, TORONTO, ON, M5J 2T3
(416) 955-4200   *SIC* 8741
BOSTON PIZZA   p 69
See 668977 ALBERTA INC
BOSTON PIZZA   p 120
See FOREVER IN DOUGH INC
BOSTON PIZZA   p 128
See FORT MCMURRAY PIZZA LTD
BOSTON PIZZA   p 129
See 301726 ALBERTA LTD
BOSTON PIZZA   p 150
See 945575 ALBERTA LTD
BOSTON PIZZA   p 164
See SPRUCE GROVE PIZZA LTD
BOSTON PIZZA   p 356
See 3177743 MANITOBA LTD
BOSTON PIZZA   p 515
See WAY, G RESTAURANTS SERVICES LTD
BOSTON PIZZA   p 806
See TOOR & ASSOCIATES INC
BOSTON PIZZA   p 840
See BOSTON PIZZA INTERNATIONAL INC
BOSTON PIZZA   p 1013
See 476982 BRITISH COLUMBIA LTD
BOSTON PIZZA   p 1051
See BOSTON PIZZA INTERNATIONAL INC
BOSTON PIZZA   p 1394
52 BOUL DE LA CITE-DES-JEUNES, VAUDREUIL-DORION, QC, J7V 9L5
(450) 455-4464   *SIC* 2038
BOSTON PIZZA 111   p 76
See B.B. INVESTMENTS INC
BOSTON PIZZA 505   p 736
See 1327601 ONTARIO INC
BOSTON PIZZA CAPILANO   p 107
See M & V ENTERPRISES LTD
BOSTON PIZZA INTERNATIONAL INC   p 259
10760 SHELLBRIDGE WAY UNIT 100, RICHMOND, BC, V6X 3H1
(604) 270-1108   *SIC* 6794
BOSTON PIZZA INTERNATIONAL INC   p 840
821 RYE ST, PETERBOROUGH, ON, K9J 6X1
(705) 740-2775   *SIC* 5812
BOSTON PIZZA INTERNATIONAL INC   p 1051
7300 BOUL DES ROSERAIES, ANJOU, QC, H1M 2T5
(514) 788-4848   *SIC* 5812
BOSTON PIZZA INTERNATIONAL INC   p 1086
450 PROM DU CENTROPOLIS, COTE SAINT-LUC, QC, H7T 3C2
(450) 688-2229   *SIC* 5812
BOSTON PIZZA OKOTOKS 149   p 151
See TOMANICK GROUP, THE
BOSTON PIZZA ORLEANS   p 811
3884 INNES RD, ORLEANS, ON, K1W 1K9
(613) 590-0881   *SIC* 5812
BOSTON PIZZA ROYALTIES INCOME FUND   p 259
10760 SHELLBRIDGE WAY UNIT 100, RICHMOND, BC, V6X 3H1
(604) 270-1108   *SIC* 5812
BOSTON SCIENTIFIC LTD   p 737
6430 VIPOND DR, MISSISSAUGA, ON, L5T 1W8
(705) 291-6900   *SIC* 3841
BOSTON'S CHEV-OLDS-CADILLAC-GEO LTD   p 862
415 PIM ST, SAULT STE. MARIE, ON, P6B

2T9
SIC 5511
BOT CONSTRUCTION LIMITED   p 803
1224 SPEERS RD, OAKVILLE, ON, L6L 5B6
(905) 827-4167   *SIC* 1611
BOTHWELL   p 537
See SAMUEL, SON & CO., LIMITED
BOTHWELL CHEESE INC   p 353
61 MAIN ST N, NEW BOTHWELL, MB, R0A 1C0
(204) 388-4666   *SIC* 2022
BOTHWELL-ACCURATE CO. INC.   p 687
6675 REXWOOD RD, MISSISSAUGA, ON, L4V 1V1
(905) 673-0615   *SIC* 1761
BOTSFORD FISHERIES LTD   p 411
2112 ROUTE 950, PETIT-CAP, NB, E4N 2J8
(506) 577-4327   *SIC* 5146
BOTTEGA NICASTRO INC, LA   p 821
64 GEORGE ST, OTTAWA, ON, K1N 5V9
(613) 789-7575   *SIC* 5411
BOTTLE DEPOT, THE   p 337
See ADANAC RECOVERY LTD
BOUCHARD & BLANCHETTE MARINE LIMITEE   p 1367
60 RUE RETTY, SEPT-ILES, QC, G4R 3E1
(418) 968-2505   *SIC* 7389
BOUCHARD FORD   p 1285
See AUTOMOBILES BOUCHARD & FILS INC
BOUCHARD PARENT ASSOCIES INC   p 1244
1185 AV BERNARD, OUTREMONT, QC, H2V 1V5
(514) 271-4820   *SIC* 6531
BOUCHEES D'AMOUR   p 1311
See BARRY CALLEBAUT CANADA INC
BOUCHER & JONES FUELS   p 1006
See BOUCHER & JONES INC
BOUCHER & JONES INC   p 1006
155 ROGER ST SUITE 1, WATERLOO, ON, N2J 1B1
(519) 653-3501   *SIC* 5171
BOUCHER LORTIE INC   p 1278
850 RUE DES ROCAILLES BUREAU 1124, QUEBEC, QC, G2J 1A5
(418) 623-2323   *SIC* 1711
BOUCHER RONALD & FILS INC   p 1360
851 RTE PRINCIPALE, SAINTE-MELANIE, QC, J0K 3A0
(450) 889-8363   *SIC* 5411
BOUCHER, O. & FILS LIMITEE   p 1357
2045 BOUL SAINT-ELZEAR O, SAINTE-DOROTHEE, QC, H7L 3N7
(450) 682-2400   *SIC* 5147
BOUCHER, MARC PHARMACIEN   p 1261
5 RUE MARIE-DE-L'INCARNATION, QUEBEC, QC, G1M 3J4
SIC 5912
BOUCHERIE CHARCUTERIE PERRON INC p 1350
145 AV ALBERT-PERRON, SAINT-PRIME, QC, G8J 1L3
(418) 251-3131   *SIC* 5147
BOUCHERIE COTE INC   p 1320
952A RUE LABELLE, SAINT-JEROME, QC, J7Z 5M8
(450) 438-4159   *SIC* 6512
BOUCHERIE DENIS COUTURE INC p 1257
825 4E AV, QUEBEC, QC, G1J 3A6
(418) 648-2633   *SIC* 5141
BOUCHERIE LE BIFTHEQUE   p 1340
See LE BIFTHEQUE INC
BOUCHERIE LE CHAROLAIS   p 1356
See MARCHE G. CARDINAL INC
BOUCHERIE VEILLEUX INC   p 1360
1000 BOUL VACHON N, SAINTE-MARIE, QC, G6E 1M2
(418) 386-5744   *SIC* 5141
BOUCHIER CONTRACTING LTD   p 127
GD LCD MAIN, FORT MCMURRAY, AB, T9H 3E2
(780) 828-4010   *SIC* 1629
BOUCHIER GROUP   p 127

See BOUCHIER CONTRACTING LTD
BOUCLAIR HOME p 1249
See BOUCLAIR INC
BOUCLAIR INC p 1249
152 AV ALSTON, POINTE-CLAIRE, QC,
H9R 6B4
(514) 426-0115   *SIC 5719*
BOUCTOUCHE PHARMACY LTD p 395
30 IRVING BLVD SUITE 200, BOUC-
TOUCHE, NB, E4S 3L2
(506) 743-2434   *SIC 5912*
**BOUDREAU-ESPLEY-PITRE CORPORA-
TION** p
899
1040 LORNE ST UNIT 3, SUDBURY, ON,
P3C 4R9
(705) 675-7720   *SIC 8711*
BOUFFARD SANITAIRE INC p 1150
75 RUE SAVARD, MATANE, QC, G4W 0H9
(418) 562-5116   *SIC 4953*
BOUILLOIRE FALMEC INC p 1044
200 RUE DES PINS O BUREAU 109, ALMA,
QC, G8B 6P9
(418) 668-0788   *SIC 3443*
BOULANG PREMIERE MOISSON GARS p
1200
See 3169693 CANADA INC
**BOULANGERIE & PATISSERIE LAMON-
TAGNE**
1397
See 9098-8585 QUEBEC INC
BOULANGERIE ANDALOS INC p 1325
350 BOUL LEBEAU, SAINT-LAURENT, QC,
H4N 1R5
(514) 856-0983   *SIC 2051*
**BOULANGERIE ARTISANALE LA BOITE A
PAIN INC** p 1258
289 RUE SAINT-JOSEPH E, QUEBEC, QC,
G1K 3B1
(418) 647-3666   *SIC 5461*
BOULANGERIE AU PAIN DORE p 1064
See BRIDOR INC
BOULANGERIE BEAUSEJOUR p 1044
See PATISSERIE GAUDET INC
BOULANGERIE BON MARCHE CANTOR p
1169
See 2920409 CANADA INC
**BOULANGERIE CASCHER DE MONTREAL
LTEE** p 1227
7005 AV VICTORIA, MONTREAL, QC, H4P
2N9
(514) 739-3651   *SIC 5149*
**BOULANGERIE ET FROMENT ET DE SEVE
INC** p 1171
2355 RUE BEAUBIEN E, MONTREAL, QC,
H2G 1N3
(514) 722-4301   *SIC 2051*
BOULANGERIE GADOUA LTEE p 1122
170 BOUL TASCHEREAU BUREAU 220, LA
PRAIRIE, QC, J5R 5H6
(450) 245-3326   *SIC 2051*
BOULANGERIE GADOUA LTEE p 1353
561 RUE PRINCIPALE, SAINT-THOMAS,
QC, J0K 3L0
SIC 5461
BOULANGERIE GEORGES INC p 1370
2000 RUE KING E, SHERBROOKE, QC,
J1G 5G6
(819) 564-3002   *SIC 5461*
BOULANGERIE GONDOLE INC p 1325
225 RUE BENJAMIN-HUDON, SAINT-
LAURENT, QC, H4N 1J1
(514) 956-5555   *SIC 5149*
**BOULANGERIE LES MOULINS LA
FAYETTE** p 1352
*See BOULANGERIE LES MOULINS LA
FAYETTE INC*
**BOULANGERIE LES MOULINS LA
FAYETTE INC** p 1352
7 AV DE L'EGLISE, SAINT-SAUVEUR, QC,
J0R 1R0
(450) 227-2632   *SIC 2051*
BOULANGERIE MULTI-MARQUES p 1166
See MULTI-MARQUES INC

BOULANGERIE PATISSERIE DUMAS INC p
1266
2391 AV WATT, QUEBEC, QC, G1P 3X2
(418) 658-2037   *SIC 2051*
BOULANGERIE PREMIERE MOISSON p
1085
See 3761045 CANADA INC
BOULANGERIE PREMIERE MOISSON p
1145
See 3116506 CANADA INC
BOULANGERIE PREMIERE MOISSON p
1166
See 3122298 CANADA INC
BOULANGERIE PREMIERE MOISSON p
1173
See 4048873 CANADA INC
BOULANGERIE PREMIERE MOISSON p
1182
See 7979134 CANADA INC
BOULANGERIE PREMIERE MOISSON p
1222
See 9015-9492 QUEBEC INC
BOULANGERIE PREMIERE MOISSON p
1382
See 2850401 CANADA INC
BOULANGERIE PREMIERE MOISSON p
1393
See 3367771 CANADA INC
BOULANGERIE SAINT-DONAT ENR p 1299
See 2318-4211 QUEBEC INC
BOULANGERIE SAINTE MARTINE p 1360
See DARE FOODS LIMITED
BOULANGERIE ST THOMAS p 1353
See BOULANGERIE GADOUA LTEE
BOULANGERIE ST-METHODE p 1071
6000 AV AUTEUIL, BROSSARD, QC, J4Z
1N3
(450) 766-0678   *SIC 5461*
BOULANGERIE ST-METHODE INC p 1044
14 RUE PRINCIPALE E, ADSTOCK, QC,
G0N 1S0
(418) 422-2246   *SIC 5461*
BOULANGERIE VACHON INC p 1343
8770 BOUL LANGELIER BUREAU 230,
SAINT-LEONARD, QC, H1P 3C6
(514) 326-5084   *SIC 5149*
BOULANGERIE VACHON INC p 1360
380 RUE NOTRE-DAME N, SAINTE-
MARIE, QC, G6E 2K7
(418) 387-5421   *SIC 5149*
BOULANGERIES COMAS INC, LES p 1343
6325 BOUL DES GRANDES-PRAIRIES BU-
REAU 5, SAINT-LEONARD, QC, H1P 1A5
(514) 323-1880   *SIC 5142*
BOULANGERIES RENE ULC, LES p 1053
375 AV LEE, BAIE-D'URFE, QC, H9X 3S3
(514) 457-4500   *SIC 2051*
**BOULANGERIES WESTON QUEBEC LIMI-
TEE** p
1145
2700 BOUL JACQUES-CARTIER E,
LONGUEUIL, QC, J4N 1L5
(450) 448-7246   *SIC 2051*
BOULART INC p 1127
1355 32E AV, LACHINE, QC, H8T 3H2
(514) 631-4040   *SIC 2051*
BOULDER CREEK GOLF COURSE LTD p
139
333 BOULDER CREEK DR SUITE 3, LANG-
DON, AB, T0J 1X3
(403) 936-8777   *SIC 6712*
BOULET LEMELIN YACHT INC p 1258
1125 BOUL CHAMPLAIN, QUEBEC, QC,
G1K 0A2
(418) 681-5655   *SIC 5551*
BOULET, G.A. INC p 1353
501 RUE SAINT-GABRIEL, SAINT-TITE,
QC, G0X 3H0
(418) 365-5174   *SIC 3144*
BOULEVARD CHEVROLET INC p 1285
374 MONTEE INDUSTRIELLE-ET-
COMMERCIALE, RIMOUSKI, QC, G5M
1X1
(888) 844-5489   *SIC 5511*

BOULEVARD CLUB LIMITED, THE p 991
1491 LAKE SHORE BLVD W, TORONTO,
ON, M6K 3C2
(416) 532-3341   *SIC 7997*
**BOULEVARD DODGE CHRYSLER JEEP
(2000) INC** p 1325
2955 CH DE LA COTE-DE-LIESSE, SAINT-
LAURENT, QC, H4N 2N3
(514) 748-2955   *SIC 5511*
**BOULEVARD METROPOLITAIN AUTOMO-
BILE INC** p
1325
100 BOUL MONTPELLIER, SAINT-
LAURENT, QC, H4N 0H8
(514) 748-0100   *SIC 5511*
BOULEVARD TOYOTA p 1261
See 4488601 CANADA INC
BOULONS PLUS p 1151
See 2962-9060 QUEBEC INC
BOULOT VERS..., LE p 1166
4447 RUE DE ROUEN, MONTREAL, QC,
H1V 1H1
(514) 259-2312   *SIC 8699*
BOUNDARY FORD & RV SALES p 1409
See BOUNDARY FORD SALES LTD
BOUNDARY FORD SALES LTD p 143
2502 50 AVE, LLOYDMINSTER, AB, T9V
2S3
(780) 872-7755   *SIC 5511*
BOUNDARY FORD SALES LTD p 1409
2405 50 AVE, LLOYDMINSTER, SK, S9V
1Z7
(306) 825-4481   *SIC 5511*
BOUNDARY HOSPITAL p 215
7649 22ND ST, GRAND FORKS, BC, V0H
1H2
(250) 443-2100   *SIC 8062*
BOUNDLESS ADVENTURES INC p 836
7513 RIVER RD, PALMER RAPIDS, ON,
K0J 2E0
(613) 758-2702   *SIC 8699*
BOURASSA ALIMENTATION p 1354
See S. BOURASSA (STE-AGATHE) LTEE
**BOURASSA AUTOMOBILES INTERNA-
TIONAL INC** p
1363
2800 BOUL CHOMEDEY, SAINTE-ROSE,
QC, H7P 5Z9
(450) 681-0028   *SIC 5511*
BOURASSA BOYER SOLUTION INC p 1394
3323 BOUL DE LA GARE, VAUDREUIL-
DORION, QC, J7V 8W5
(450) 424-7000   *SIC 8748*
BOURASSA WEST ISLAND INC p 1093
2000 PLACE TRANSCANADIENNE, DOR-
VAL, QC, H9P 2X5
(514) 683-2000   *SIC 5511*
BOURASSA, S. (ST-SAUVEUR) LTEE p
1352
105B AV GUINDON RR 6, SAINT-
SAUVEUR, QC, J0R 1R6
(450) 227-4737   *SIC 5411*
BOURBEAU, GERARD & FILS INC p 1256
8285 1RE AV, QUEBEC, QC, G1G 4C1
(418) 623-5401   *SIC 5193*
BOURDON, EDOUARD & FILS INC p 1181
760 RUE JEAN-TALON E, MONTREAL, QC,
H2R 1V1
(514) 270-5226   *SIC 5411*
BOURGABEC INC p 1268
600 GRANDE ALLEE E, QUEBEC, QC,
G1R 2K5
(418) 522-0393   *SIC 5813*
BOURGAULT INDUSTRIES LTD p 1436
500 HWY UNIT 368 N, ST BRIEUX, SK, S0K
3V0
(306) 275-2300   *SIC 3523*
BOURGAULT INDUSTRIES LTD p 1436
501 BARBIER DR, ST BRIEUX, SK, S0K
3V0
(306) 275-2300   *SIC 1761*
BOURGEOIS MOTORS LIMITED p 681
281 CRANSTON CRES, MIDLAND, ON,
L4R 4L1

(705) 526-2278   *SIC 5511*
**BOURGEOIS-COTE-FORGET & ASSO-
CIATES INSURANCE BROKERS** p
810
2712 ST. JOSEPH BLVD, ORLEANS, ON,
K1C 1G5
(613) 824-0441   *SIC 6411*
BOURGIE URGEL p 1155
*See SERVICES COMMEMORATIFS CELE-
BRIS INC*
BOURQUE INDUSTRIAL LTD p 416
85 INDUSTRIAL DR, SAINT JOHN, NB,
E2R 1A4
(506) 633-7740   *SIC 3499*
BOURQUE SECURITY SERVICES NS p 457
176 BEDFORD HWY, HALIFAX, NS, B3M
2J8
(902) 832-2456   *SIC 6289*
BOURQUE, A ACIER ET METAUX INC p
1375
137 CH GODIN, SHERBROOKE, QC, J1R
0S6
(819) 569-6960   *SIC 5093*
**BOURSE CANADIENNE DE PRODUITS DE-
RIVES** p
1229
See BOURSE DE MONTREAL INC
BOURSE DE MONTREAL INC p 1229
800 RUE DU SQUARE-VICTORIA 4E
ETAGE, MONTREAL, QC, H4Z 1A1
(514) 871-2424   *SIC 6231*
BOUSQUET TECHNOLOGIES INC p 1358
2121 RUE NOBEL BUREAU 101, SAINTE-
JULIE, QC, J3E 1Z9
(514) 874-9050   *SIC 3433*
BOUTEILLES & EMBALLAGE UNIS p 1361
*See BOUTEILLES RECYCLEES DU QUE-
BEC (B.R.Q) INC, LES*
**BOUTEILLES RECYCLEES DU QUEBEC
(B.R.Q) INC, LES** p 1361
1400 BOUL DAGENAIS O, SAINTE-ROSE,
QC, H7L 5C7
(450) 622-1600   *SIC 7389*
BOUTETTE & BARNETT INC p 648
1950 OXFORD ST E, LONDON, ON, N5V
2Z8
(519) 679-1770   *SIC 5075*
**BOUTETTE & BARNETT TRADE DISTRI-
BUTION CENTRE** p
648
See BOUTETTE & BARNETT INC
BOUTHILLETTE PARIZEAU INC p 1216
9825 RUE VERVILLE, MONTREAL, QC,
H3L 3E1
(514) 383-3747   *SIC 8711*
BOUTIK BUZZY p 1084
See 9213-0699 QUEBEC INC
BOUTIN, V. EXPRESS INC p 1246
1397 RUE SAVOIE, PLESSISVILLE, QC,
G6L 1J8
(819) 362-7333   *SIC 4213*
BOUTIQUE AGRICOLE LE CAMPAGNARD p 1153
See MONDOU, REAL INC
BOUTIQUE ALENTOUR p 1373
*See COOPERATIVE D'ALENTOUR,
GROSSISTE EN ALIMENTATION NA-
TURELLE DES CANTONS DE L'EST*
BOUTIQUE BOUCHERVILLE p 1320
See H. CHALUT LTEE
BOUTIQUE BUZZY p 1233
See 9227-6898 QUEBEC INC
BOUTIQUE COLORI INC p 1325
2255 CH DE LA COTE-DE-LIESSE, SAINT-
LAURENT, QC, H4N 2M6
(514) 858-7494   *SIC 5621*
**BOUTIQUE COMMUNAUTAIRE FRIPE-
PRIX RENAISSANCE** p
1181
*See INDUSTRIES GOODWILL RENAIS-
SANCE MONTREAL INC*
**BOUTIQUE DE GOLF LE GRAND PORT-
NEUF** p
1253

See *GOLF DU GRAND PORTNEUF INC,*
LE
BOUTIQUE ELECTRONIQUE, LA *p* 1091
See *2758792 CANADA INC*
BOUTIQUE ET MAGASIN A RAYONS
LINEN CHEST   *p* 1134
See *BOUTIQUE LINEN CHEST (PHASE II)*
INC
BOUTIQUE FOYER PROPANE EXPRESSE
p 1109
See *GAZ PROPANE RAINVILLE INC*
BOUTIQUE LA VIE EN ROSE INC *p* 1166
4320 AV PIERRE-DE COUBERTIN, MON-
TREAL, QC, H1V 1A6
(514) 256-9446   *SIC* 5632
BOUTIQUE LE PENTAGONE INC *p* 1378
301 RUE EDWARD-ASSH, STE-
CATHERINE-DE-LA-J-CARTIE, QC, G3N
1A3
(418) 875-1839   *SIC* 5621
BOUTIQUE LINEN CHEST (PHASE II) INC*p*
1134
4455 DES LAURENTIDES (A-15) E, LAVAL-
OUEST, QC, H7L 5X8
(514) 331-5260   *SIC* 5719
BOUTIQUE LINEN CHEST (PHASE II) INC*p*
1155
2305 CH ROCKLAND BUREAU 500, MONT-
ROYAL, QC, H3P 3E9
(514) 341-7810   *SIC* 5714
BOUTIQUE M   *p* 1213
See *MUSEE DES BEAUX-ARTS DE MON-*
TREAL
BOUTIQUE MARIE CLAIRE INC *p* 1047
8501 BOUL RAY-LAWSON, ANJOU, QC,
H1J 1K6
(514) 354-0650   *SIC* 5621
BOUTIQUE NEW LOOK SIGNATURE *p*
1205
See *GROUPE VISION NEW LOOK INC*
BOUTIQUE OF LEATHERS LTD, THE *p* 70
12012 44 ST SE, CALGARY, AB, T2Z 4A2
(403) 259-2726   *SIC* 5948
BOUTIQUE OPTION INC   *p* 1060
120 CH DE LA GRANDE-COTE, BOIS-
BRIAND, QC, J7G 1B9
(450) 433-2999   *SIC* 5621
BOUTIQUE ORIGINE   *p* 1227
See *CARPETTE MULTI DESIGN C.M.D.*
INC
BOUTIQUE TRISTAN & ISEUT INC *p* 1215
20 RUE DES SEIGNEURS, MONTREAL,
QC, H3K 3K3
(514) 937-4601   *SIC* 5621
BOUTIQUE UNISEXE JOVEN INC *p* 1328
3616 BOUL POIRIER, SAINT-LAURENT,
QC, H4R 2J5
(514) 382-5940   *SIC* 5611
BOUTIQUE WAVE SANS FIL   *p* 182
See *GLENTEL INC*
BOUTIQUE WEB INSO   *p* 1184
See *SOLUTIONS INFORMATIQUES INSO*
INC
BOUTIQUES SAN FRANCISCO   *p* 1385
4125 BOUL DES FORGES, TROIS-
RIVIERES, QC, G8Y 1W1
(819) 375-8727   *SIC* 5961
BOUTRY CANADA LTEE   *p* 1169
2170 AV CHARLAND, MONTREAL, QC,
H1Z 1B1
SIC 5087
BOUVET, ANDRE LTEE   *p* 1056
1840 BOUL DE PORT-ROYAL, BECAN-
COUR, QC, G9H 0K7
(819) 233-2357   *SIC* 1794
BOUVIER INC, LE   *p* 1275
2335 BOUL BASTIEN, QUEBEC, QC, G2B
1B3
(418) 842-9160   *SIC* 5812
BOUVILLIONS-BELLERIVE INC   *p* 1135
80 RUE JACQUES-NAU BUREAU 102,
LEVIS, QC, G6V 9J4
(418) 838-9611   *SIC* 5142
BOUVRY EXPORTS CALGARY LTD *p* 33

222 58 AVE SW SUITE 312, CALGARY, AB,
T2H 2S3
(403) 253-0717   *SIC* 2011
BOUVRY EXPORTS CALGARY LTD *p* 127
GD, FORT MACLEOD, AB, T0L 0Z0
(403) 553-4431   *SIC* 2011
BOUYGUES ENERGIES AND SERVICES
CANADA LIMITED   *p* 273
9801 KING GEORGE BLVD UNIT 125,
SURREY, BC, V3T 5H5
(604) 585-3358   *SIC* 8741
BOVE DRUGS LIMITED   *p* 516
320 COLBORNE ST W SUITE 1152,
BRANTFORD, ON, N3T 1M2
(519) 759-8133   *SIC* 5912
BOW CITY   *p* 21
See *BOW CITY DELIVERY (1989) LTD*
BOW CITY DELIVERY (1989) LTD *p* 21
1423 45 AVE NE BAY CTR, CALGARY, AB,
T2E 2P3
(403) 250-5329   *SIC* 7389
BOW CYCLE & MOTOR CO LTD *p* 72
8525 BOWFORT RD NW, CALGARY, AB,
T3B 2V2
(403) 288-5421   *SIC* 5511
BOW CYCLE & SPORTS LTD   *p* 72
6501 BOWNESS RD NW, CALGARY, AB,
T3B 0E8
(403) 288-5422   *SIC* 5941
BOW GROUPE DE PLOMBERIE INC*p* 1108
15 RUE VITTIE, GRANBY, QC, J2G 6N8
(450) 372-5481   *SIC* 3089
BOW GROUPE DE PLOMBERIE INC*p* 1157
5700 CH DE LA COTE-DE-LIESSE, MONT-
ROYAL, QC, H4T 1B1
(514) 735-5551   *SIC* 3089
BOW MEL CHRYSLER LTD   *p* 211
461 TRANS CANADA HWY, DUNCAN, BC,
V9L 3R7
(250) 748-8144   *SIC* 5511
BOW METALLICS   *p* 1157
See *BOW GROUPE DE PLOMBERIE INC*
BOW RIVER ENERGY LTD   *p* 44
321 6 AVE SW SUITE 500, CALGARY, AB,
T2P 3H3
(403) 475-4100   *SIC* 1382
BOW RIVER PROPERTY MANAGEMENT &
LEASING   *p* 66
See *ENTERPRISE UNIVERSAL INC*
BOW VALLEY COLLEGE   *p* 27
See *BOARD OF GOVERNERS OF BOW*
VALLEY COLLEGE, THE
BOW VALLEY INSURANCE SERVICES
(1992) LTD   *p* 67
9805 HORTON RD SW, CALGARY, AB, T2V
2X5
(403) 297-9400   *SIC* 6411
BOW VIEW MANOR   *p* 72
See *BRENDA STRAFFORD FOUNDATION*
LTD, THE
BOWATER CANADIAN LIMITED   *p* 1210
111 BOUL ROBERT-BOURASSA UNITE
5000, MONTREAL, QC, H3C 2M1
(514) 875-2160   *SIC* 2621
BOWATER PRODUITS FORESTIERS DU
CANADA ULC   *p* 1202
1155 METCALFE RUE BUREAU 800, MON-
TREAL, QC, H3B 5H2
SIC 2621
BOWDEN PO   *p* 815
See *CANADA POST CORPORATION*
BOWEN MANUFACTURING LIMITED *p* 546
188 KING ST E RR 2, COLBORNE, ON,
K0K 1S0
(905) 355-3757   *SIC* 6712
BOWERS MEDICAL SUPPLY   *p* 210
See *RADION LABORATORIES LTD*
BOWMAN FUELS LTD   *p* 486
265 BURTON AVE, BARRIE, ON, L4N 2R9
(705) 726-6071   *SIC* 5172
BOWMANVILLE FOOD LAND   *p* 496
225 KING ST E, BOWMANVILLE, ON, L1C
1P8
(905) 697-7256   *SIC* 5411

BOWNE ENTERPRISE SOLUTIONS, DIV
OF   *p* 780
See *RR DONELLEY CANADA FINANCIAL*
COMPANY
BOWNESS BAKERY (ALBERTA) INC *p* 21
4280 23 ST NE SUITE 1, CALGARY, AB,
T2E 6X7
(403) 250-9760   *SIC* 2051
BOWNESS HIGH SCHOOL   *p* 72
See *CALGARY BOARD OF EDUCATION*
BOXBERG HOLDING LTD   *p* 520
6124 ANNA ST, BRUNNER, ON, N0K 1C0
(519) 595-8903   *SIC* 6411
BOXES NEXT DAY INC   *p* 573
54 ATOMIC AVE, ETOBICOKE, ON, M8Z
5L1
(416) 253-7350   *SIC* 2653
BOXMASTER, DIV OF   *p* 263
See *CROWN CORRUGATED COMPANY*
BOXPILOT   *p* 945
See *GRAYMATTER DIRECT (CANADA)*
INC
BOYAUX MULTIFLEX   *p* 1344
See *HEBDRAULIQUE INC*
BOYD AUTOBODY & GLASS   *p* 386
See *BOYD GROUP INC, THE*
BOYD AUTOBODY AND GLASS   *p* 220
See *ABOUGOUSH COLLISION INC*
BOYD DISTRIBUTORS   *p* 220
See *INSUL-WEST BUILDING MATERIALS*
LTD
BOYD GROUP HOLDINGS INC   *p* 386
3570 PORTAGE AVE, WINNIPEG, MB, R3K
0Z8
(204) 895-1244   *SIC* 7538
BOYD GROUP INC, THE   *p* 386
3570 PORTAGE AVE, WINNIPEG, MB, R3K
0Z8
(204) 895-1244   *SIC* 7532
BOYD GROUP INCOME FUND   *p* 383
1745 ELLICE AVE, WINNIPEG, MB, R3H
1A6
(204) 895-1244   *SIC* 7532
BOYD MOVING & STORAGE LTD   *p* 815
1255 LEEDS AVE UNIT 1, OTTAWA, ON,
K1B 3W2
(613) 244-4444   *SIC* 4214
BOYD SECONDARY SCHOOL   *p* 266
See *BOARD OF EDUCATION SCHOOL*
DISTRICT #38 (RICHMOND)
BOYER HOLDINGS LTD   *p* 907
391 OLIVER RD, THUNDER BAY, ON, P7B
2G2
(807) 344-8491   *SIC* 6712
BOYER TRUCK SALES   *p* 909
See *WESTERN STAR SALES THUNDER*
BAY LTD
BOYER, MICHAEL PONTIAC BUICK GMC
(1988) LTD   *p* 843
715 KINGSTON RD, PICKERING, ON, L1V
1A9
(905) 831-2693   *SIC* 5511
BOYLAN GROUP LTD, THE   *p* 145
540 18 ST SW, MEDICINE HAT, AB, T1A
8A7
(403) 526-7799   *SIC* 5912
BOYLAN'S PHOTOCOPY CENTRE   *p* 145
See *BOYLAN GROUP LTD, THE*
BOYNE CLARKE NS LAW   *p* 444
See *BOYNECLARKE LLP*
BOYNE LODGE PERSONAL CARE HOME*p*
348
See *BOYNE VALLEY HOSTEL CORPORA-*
TION, THE
BOYNE PUBLIC SCHOOL   *p* 682
See *HALTON DISTRICT SCHOOL BOARD*
BOYNE VALLEY HOSTEL CORPORATION,
THE   *p* 348
120 4TH AVE SW RR 3, CARMAN, MB, R0G
0J0
(204) 745-6715   *SIC* 8361
BOYNECLARKE LLP   *p* 444
99 WYSE RD SUITE 600, DARTMOUTH,
NS, B3A 4S5

(902) 469-9500   *SIC* 8111
BOYS & GIRLS CLUB OF OTTAWA *p* 830
2825 DUMAURIER AVE, OTTAWA, ON, K2B
7W3
(613) 828-0428   *SIC* 8641
BOYS & GIRLS CLUBS OF EDMONTON,
THE   *p* 85
9425 109A AVE NW, EDMONTON, AB, T5H
1G1
(780) 424-8181   *SIC* 8322
BOYS & GIRLS CLUBS OF HAMILTON *p*
609
See *HAMILTON EAST KIWANIS BOYS &*
GIRLS CLUB INCORPORATED
BOYS AND GIRLS CLUB OF NIAGARA *p*
758
6681 CULP ST, NIAGARA FALLS, ON, L2G
2C5
(905) 357-2444   *SIC* 8641
BOYS AND GIRLS CLUBS FOUNDATION
OF SOUTH COAST BC   *p* 288
2875 ST. GEORGE ST, VANCOUVER, BC,
V5T 3R8
(604) 879-6554   *SIC* 8399
BOYS AND GIRLS CLUBS OF SOUTH
COAST BC   *p* 288
See *BOYS AND GIRLS CLUBS FOUNDA-*
TION OF SOUTH COAST BC
BOYS' AND GIRLS' CLUBS OF GREATER
VANCOUVER   *p* 288
2875 ST. GEORGE ST, VANCOUVER, BC,
V5T 3R8
(604) 879-9118   *SIC* 8322
BOZIKIS FOOD GROUP   *p* 788
216 YONGE BLVD, NORTH YORK, ON,
M5M 3H8
SIC 6712
BP CANADA   *p* 860
See *PLAINS MIDSTREAM CANADA ULC*
BP CANADA   *p* 1130
See *CIE MATERIAUX DE CONSTRUCTION*
BP CANADA, LA
BP CANADA ENERGY COMPANY   *p* 44
240 4 AVE SW, CALGARY, AB, T2P 4H4
(403) 233-1313   *SIC* 1311
BP CANADA ENERGY MARKETING CORP
p 45
240 4 AVE SW, CALGARY, AB, T2P 4H4
(403) 233-1313   *SIC* 5172
BP INVESTMENTS & HOLDINGS   *p* 861
See *510127 ONTARIO LIMITED*
BPDL   *p* 1044
See *BETONS PREFABRIQUES DU LAC*
INC
BPDR   *p* 1044
See *BETON PREFABRIQUE DU RICHE-*
LIEU INC
BPO PROPERTIES LTD   *p* 960
181 BAY ST SUITE 330, TORONTO, ON,
M5J 2T3
(416) 363-9491   *SIC* 6719
BPONOVO INC   *p* 914
3660 MIDLAND AVE UNIT V3022,
TORONTO, ON, M1V 0B8
(416) 479-0416   *SIC* 4899
BPR   *p* 1167
See *TETRA TECH INDUSTRIES INC*
BPR INC   *p* 1266
4655 BOUL WILFRID-HAMEL, QUEBEC,
QC, G1P 2J7
(418) 871-8151   *SIC* 8711
BPRE SAINT LOUIS HOLDINGS, LIMITED
PARTNERSHIP   *p* 311
1075 GEORGIA ST W SUITE 2010, VAN-
COUVER, BC, V6E 3C9
(604) 806-3350   *SIC* 6712
BPSR CORPORATION   *p* 570
123 FOURTH ST, ETOBICOKE, ON, M8V
2Y6
(905) 999-9999   *SIC* 5311
BPSR NOVELTIES   *p* 570
See *BPSR CORPORATION*
BPWOOD LTD   *p* 243
186 NANAIMO AVE W UNIT 102, PENTIC-

TON, BC, V2A 1N4
(250) 493-9339   SIC 5031
BRABER EQUIPMENT LTD   p 174
34425 MCCONNELL RD SUITE 117, AB-
BOTSFORD, BC, V2S 7P1
(604) 850-7770   SIC 5083
BRABY MOTORS LTD   p 267
1250 TRANS CANADA HWY SW, SALMON
ARM, BC, V1E 1T1
(250) 832-8053   SIC 5511
BRACCO IMAGING CANADA   p 1048
See E-Z-EM CANADA INC
BRACKENRIG ENTERPRISES INC   p 678
2900 MAJOR MACKENZIE DR E,
MARKHAM, ON, L6C 0G6
(416) 907-8237   SIC 5531
BRACKNELL CORPORATION   p 996
195 THE WEST MALL STE 302, TORONTO,
ON, M9C 5K1
SIC 1711
BRAD, D FARM LTD   p 836
4939 BRADLEY LINE, PAIN COURT, ON,
N0P 1Z0
SIC 0161
BRAD-LEA MEADOWS LIMITED   p 542
615 RICHMOND ST, CHATHAM, ON, N7M
1R2
(519) 436-5506   SIC 7011
BRADEN-BURRY EXPEDITING   p 134
See BBE EXPEDITING LTD
BRADFORD & DISTRICT PRODUCE LTD p
497
355 DISSETTE ST, BRADFORD, ON, L3Z
3H1
(905) 775-9633   SIC 5148
**BRADFORD CO-OPERATIVE STORAGE
LIMITED**   p 497
61 BRIDGE ST, BRADFORD, ON, L3Z 3H3
(905) 775-3317   SIC 0723
BRADFORD DISTRICT HIGH SCHOOL   p
497
See   SIMCOE   COUNTY   DISTRICT
SCHOOL BOARD, THE
**BRADFORD GREENHOUSES GARDEN
GALLERY**   p 497
See BRADFORD GREENHOUSES LIM-
ITED
**BRADFORD GREENHOUSES GARDEN
GALLERY**   p 883
See BRADFORD GREENHOUSES LIM-
ITED
BRADFORD GREENHOUSES LIMITED   p
497
2433 12TH CONC, BRADFORD, ON, L3Z
2B2
(905) 775-4769   SIC 5191
BRADFORD GREENHOUSES LIMITED   p
883
4346 HWY 90, SPRINGWATER, ON, L9X
1T7
(705) 725-9913   SIC 5261
BRADFORD WHITE - CANADA INC   p 593
9 BRIGDEN GATE, GEORGETOWN, ON,
L7G 0A3
(905) 203-0600   SIC 5064
**BRADKEN CANADA MANUFACTURED
PRODUCTS LTD**   p 937
90   RICHMOND   ST   E   SUITE   4000,
TORONTO, ON, M5C 1P1
(416) 975-8251   SIC 3325
**BRADKEN CANADA MANUFACTURED
PRODUCTS LTD**   p 1154
105 AV DE LA FONDERIE, MONT-JOLI,
QC, G5H 1W2
(418) 775-4358   SIC 3321
BRADLEY AIR SERVICES LIMITED   p 626
20 COPE DR, KANATA, ON, K2M 2V8
(613) 254-6200   SIC 4522
BRADLEY AIR SERVICES LIMITED   p 826
100 THAD JOHNSON PVT, OTTAWA, ON,
K1V 0R1
(613) 254-6200   SIC 8322
BRADLEY AIR-CONDITIONING LIMITED p
549

150 CONNIE CRES SUITE 14, CONCORD,
ON, L4K 1L9
(905) 660-5400   SIC 1711
BRADLEY STEEL PROCESSORS INC   p
362
1201 REGENT AVE W, WINNIPEG, MB,
R2C 3B2
(204) 987-2080   SIC 3441
**BRADLEY'S COMMERCIAL INSURANCE
LIMITED**   p 890
1469   STITTSVILLE   MAIN   ST,
STITTSVILLE, ON, K2S 0C8
(613) 836-2473   SIC 6411
BRADNER B.C. ORGANIC FEED LTD p 178
28670 58 AVE, ABBOTSFORD, BC, V4X
2E8
(604) 835-3299   SIC 0254
BRADNER FARMS   p 178
See BRADNER B.C. ORGANIC FEED LTD
BRADON CONSTRUCTION LTD   p 78
250031 MOUNTAIN VIEW TRAIL, CAL-
GARY, AB, T3Z 3S3
(403) 229-4022   SIC 1521
BRADSHAW BROS. PETROLEUM LTD.   p
1006
308 MAIN ST S, WATERFORD, ON, N0E
1Y0
(519) 443-8611   SIC 5983
BRADSHAW CANADA HOLDINGS, INC   p
1027
200 ZENWAY BLVD SUITE 3, WOOD-
BRIDGE, ON, L4H 0L6
(905) 264-2246   SIC 6211
BRADVIN TRAILER SALES LTD   p 131
10920 87 AVE, GRANDE PRAIRIE, AB, T8V
8K4
(780) 539-6260   SIC 5084
BRADY OILFIELD SERVICES L.P.   p 1407
1 MERGEN ST, HALBRITE, SK, S0C 1H0
(306) 458-2344   SIC 1389
BRAEBURY   p 629
See BRAEBURY HOMES CORPORATION
BRAEBURY HOMES CORPORATION p 629
366 KING ST E SUITE 400, KINGSTON,
ON, K7K 6Y3
(613) 546-3400   SIC 1521
BRAEMAR   p 744
See   AMERICAN   EAGLE   OUTFITTERS
CANADA CORPORATION
**BRAGG COMMUNICATIONS INCORPO-
RATED**   p
455
6080 YOUNG ST SUITE 800, HALIFAX, NS,
B3K 5L2
(902) 453-2800   SIC 4841
BRAGG LUMBER COMPANY LIMITED   p
442
1536 WYVRN RD, COLLINGWOOD COR-
NER, NS, B0M 1E0
(902) 686-3254   SIC 0171
BRAGO CONSTRUCTION INC   p 1231
5535 RUE MAURICE-CULLEN, MON-
TREAL, QC, H7C 2T8
(450) 661-1121   SIC 1521
BRAHAM & ASSOCIATES INC   p 833
251 BANK ST, OTTAWA, ON, K2P 1X3
(613) 294-4589   SIC 6211
BRAIN BUSTER INC   p 667
206 TELSON RD, MARKHAM, ON, L3R 1E6
(905) 604-5055   SIC 5945
BRAIN INJURED GROUP SOCIETY   p 249
1070 4TH AVE, PRINCE GEORGE, BC, V2L
3J1
(250) 564-2447   SIC 8699
**BRAIN INJURY COMMUNITY RE-ENTRY
(NIAGARA) INC**   p 907
3340 SCHMON PKWY UNIT 2, THOROLD,
ON, L2V 4Y6
(905) 687-6788   SIC 8399
BRAIN MATTERS   p 884
314 LAKE ST SUITE 2, ST CATHARINES,
ON, L2N 4H4
SIC 8999
BRAINS II SOLUTIONS, INC   p 667

165 KONRAD CRES, MARKHAM, ON, L3R
9T9
(905) 946-8700   SIC 5045
**BRAKING & SUSPENSION PRODUCT
CENTER**   p 912
See ZF AUTOMOTIVE CANADA LIMITED
**BRAMALEA SALES PARTS DISTRIBUTION
CENTRE**   p 503
See   FORD   MOTOR   COMPANY   OF
CANADA, LIMITED
BRAMALEA TOYOTA   p 500
See POLICARO INVESTMENTS LIMITED
BRAMGATE AUTOMOTIVE INC   p 508
268 QUEEN ST E, BRAMPTON, ON, L6V
1B9
(905) 459-6040   SIC 5511
BRAMGATE LEASING INC   p 508
268 QUEEN ST E, BRAMPTON, ON, L6V
1B9
(905) 459-6040   SIC 5511
BRAMGATE VOLKSWAGEN   p 508
See BRAMGATE AUTOMOTIVE INC
BRAMPTON BRICK LIMITED   p 513
225 WANLESS DR, BRAMPTON, ON, L7A
1E9
(905) 840-1011   SIC 3251
**BRAMPTON CALEDON COMMUNITY LIV-
ING**   p
510
34 CHURCH ST W, BRAMPTON, ON, L6X
1H3
(905) 453-8841   SIC 8322
**BRAMPTON CENTENNIAL SECONDARY
SCHOOL**   p 512
See PEEL DISTRICT SCHOOL BOARD
BRAMPTON CESSNA   p 544
See BRAMPTON FLYING CLUB
BRAMPTON CHRYSLER DODGE JEEP   p
512
See 1035312 ONTARIO LIMITED
BRAMPTON CIVIC HOSPITAL   p 498
See WILLIAM OSLER HEALTH SYSTEM
BRAMPTON ENGINEERING INC   p 501
8031 DIXIE RD, BRAMPTON, ON, L6T 3V1
(905) 793-3000   SIC 3559
**BRAMPTON FIRE & EMERGENCY SER-
VICES**   p
509
See CORPORATION OF THE CITY OF
BRAMPTON, THE
BRAMPTON FLYING CLUB   p 544
13691 MCLAUGHLIN RD, CHELTENHAM,
ON, L7C 2B2
(416) 798-7928   SIC 8299
BRAMPTON GUARDIAN   p 717
See METROLAND MEDIA GROUP LTD
BRAMPTON LIBRARY   p 508
See   BRAMPTON   PUBLIC   LIBRARY
BOARD, THE
BRAMPTON MITSUBISHI   p 510
See 1512804 ONTARIO INC
BRAMPTON NORTH NISSAN   p 513
195 CANAM CRES, BRAMPTON, ON, L7A
1G1
(905) 459-1600   SIC 5511
BRAMPTON NORTH SUPERCENTRE p 508
See WAL-MART CANADA CORP
**BRAMPTON PUBLIC LIBRARY BOARD,
THE**   p 508
65 QUEEN ST E, BRAMPTON, ON, L6W
3L6
(905) 793-4636   SIC 8231
BRAMWOOD FOREST INC   p 582
38 TABER RD, ETOBICOKE, ON, M9W 3A8
(416) 747-7244   SIC 5031
BRANCH 133 LEGION VILLAGE INC p 544
111 HIBERNIA ST SUITE 220, COBOURG,
ON, K9A 4Y7
(905) 372-8705   SIC 6513
**BRANCH FINANCE CORPORATION LIM-
ITED**   p
881
5 CHAMBERS ST, SMITHS FALLS, ON,
K7A 2Y2

(613) 283-5555   SIC 6799
BRANCH VENTURE CAPITAL SERVICE   p
881
See BRANCH FINANCE CORPORATION
LIMITED
BRANCHAUD - BUCKINGHAM   p 1100
See AMEUBLEMENT BRANCHAUD INC
BRANCHERS, LES   p 1321
See LUNETTERIE BRANCHES INC., LES
BRANCY ONE HOLDINGS LTD   p 848
140 PRESCOTT CENTRE DR, PRESCOTT,
ON, K0E 1T0
(613) 925-4217   SIC 5531
**BRAND ENERGY SOLUTION (CANADA)
LTD**   p 27
601 34 AVE SE, CALGARY, AB, T2G 1V2
(403) 243-0283   SIC 3644
BRAND FELT OF CANADA LIMITED   p 702
2559 WHARTON GLEN AVE, MISSIS-
SAUGA, ON, L4X 2A8
(905) 279-6680   SIC 2231
BRANDALLIANCE ONTARIO   p 1002
See BRANDALLIANCE, INC
BRANDALLIANCE ONTARIO INC   p 1007
640 BRIDGE ST W, WATERLOO, ON, N2K
4M9
(519) 746-2055   SIC 5199
BRANDALLIANCE, INC   p 1002
10   ROYBRIDGE   GATE   SUITE   202,
VAUGHAN, ON, L4H 3M8
(905) 819-0155   SIC 5199
BRANDES INVESTMENT PARTNERS p 960
See BRANDES INVESTMENT PARTNERS
& CO.
**BRANDES INVESTMENT PARTNERS &
CO.**   p 960
20 BAY ST SUITE 400, TORONTO, ON, M5J
2N8
(416) 306-5700   SIC 6282
BRANDETTE WELL SERVICING LTD   p 82
3202 63 ST, DRAYTON VALLEY, AB, T7A
1R6
(780) 542-3404   SIC 1389
BRANDON CHRYSLER DODGE (1987) LTD
p 347
3250 VICTORIA AVE, BRANDON, MB, R7B
3Y4
(204) 728-3396   SIC 5013
**BRANDON CLINIC MEDICAL CORPORA-
TION**   p
346
620 DENNIS ST, BRANDON, MB, R7A 5E7
(204) 728-4440   SIC 8011
BRANDON COMMUNITY OPTIONS INC   p
346
136 11TH ST, BRANDON, MB, R7A 4J4
(204) 571-5770   SIC 8322
BRANDON MCC TRIFTH SHOP   p 347
See MENNONITE CENTRAL COMMITTEE
CANADA
BRANDON PETROLEUM   p 108
See BRANDON PETROLEUM SALES LTD
BRANDON PETROLEUM SALES LTD p 108
3515 76 AVE NW, EDMONTON, AB, T6B
2S8
(780) 413-1826   SIC 5171
BRANDON POLICE SERVICE   p 346
See BRANDON, CITY OF
BRANDON SCHOOL DIVISION, THE   p 346
1031 6TH ST, BRANDON, MB, R7A 4K5
(204) 729-3100   SIC 8211
BRANDON SCHOOL DIVISION, THE   p 346
1930 1ST ST, BRANDON, MB, R7A 6Y6
(204) 729-3900   SIC 8211
BRANDON SCHOOL DIVISION, THE   p 347
715 MCDIARMID DR, BRANDON, MB, R7B
2H7
(204) 729-3170   SIC 8211
BRANDON, CITY OF   p 346
1020 VICTORIA AVE, BRANDON, MB, R7A
1A9
(204) 729-2345   SIC 7381
**BRANDS INTERNATIONAL CORPORA-
TION**   p

754
594 NEWPARK BLVD, NEWMARKET, ON, L3X 2S2
(905) 830-4404   SIC 2844
BRANDT AGRICULTURAL PRODUCTS   p 1417
302 MILL ST, REGINA, SK, S4P 3E1
(306) 791-7557   SIC 3535
BRANDT ENGINEERED PRODUCTS p 1417
See BRANDT AGRICULTURAL PROD-UCTS
BRANDT GROUP OF COMPANIES,THE   p 1423
3710 EASTGATE DR SUITE 1, REGINA, SK, S4Z 1A5
(306) 347-1499   SIC 1542
BRANDT INDUSTRIES CANADA LTD   p 1417
13 AVE & PINKIE RD, REGINA, SK, S4P 3A1
(306) 791-7777   SIC 3523
BRANDT MEATS & DELICATESSEN p 702
See BRANDT, G. MEAT PACKERS LIMITED
BRANDT TRACTOR LTD   p 99
10630 176 ST NW, EDMONTON, AB, T5S 1M2
(780) 484-6613   SIC 5084
BRANDT TRACTOR LTD   p 1417
HWY 1 E, REGINA, SK, S4P 3R8
(306) 791-7777   SIC 5084
BRANDT, G. MEAT PACKERS LIMITED   p 702
1878 MATTAWA AVE, MISSISSAUGA, ON, L4X 1K1
(905) 279-4460   SIC 2013
BRANDT, PAUL TRUCKING LTD   p 352
226 STATION ST S, MORRIS, MB, R0G 1K0
(204) 746-2555   SIC 4213
BRANDVENTURE INC   p 667
335 RENFREW DR SUITE 202, MARKHAM, ON, L3R 9S9
(888) 277-9737   SIC 5141
BRANKSOME HALL   p 928
10 ELM AVE, TORONTO, ON, M4W 1N4
(416) 920-9741   SIC 8211
BRANT ALCOVE REHABILITATION SER-VICES   p 516
See ST. LEONARD'S COMMUNITY SER-VICES
BRANT COLONY   p 7
See HUTTERIAN BRETHREN OF BRANT, THE
BRANT FOOD CENTER LTD   p 516
94 GREY ST, BRANTFORD, ON, N3T 2T5
(519) 756-8002   SIC 5431
BRANT   HALDIMAND   NORFOLK CATHOLIC DISTRICT SCHOOL BOARD p 514
80 PARIS RD, BRANTFORD, ON, N3R 1H9
(519) 759-2318   SIC 8211
BRANT   HALDIMAND   NORFOLK CATHOLIC DISTRICT SCHOOL BOARD p 514
322 FAIRVIEW DR, BRANTFORD, ON, N3R 2X6
(519) 756-6369   SIC 8211
BRANT   HALDIMAND   NORFOLK CATHOLIC DISTRICT SCHOOL BOARD p 516
257 SHELLARD'S LANE, BRANTFORD, ON, N3T 5L5
(519) 751-2030   SIC 8211
BRANT   HALDIMAND   NORFOLK CATHOLIC DISTRICT SCHOOL BOARD p 880
128 EVERGREEN HILL RD, SIMCOE, ON, N3Y 4K1
(519) 429-3600   SIC 8211
BRANT INSTORE CORPORATION   p 515
254 HENRY ST, BRANTFORD, ON, N3S 7R5
(800) 265-8480   SIC 2759
BRANT INSTORE CORPORATION   p 516

555 GREENWICH ST, BRANTFORD, ON, N3T 5T3
(519) 759-4361   SIC 2759
BRANT MUTUAL INSURANCE COMPANY p 514
20 HOLIDAY DR, BRANTFORD, ON, N3R 7J4
(519) 752-0088   SIC 6311
BRANT SCREEN CRAFT   p 515
See BRANT INSTORE CORPORATION
BRANT SECURITIES LIMITED   p 960
220 BAY ST SUITE 300, TORONTO, ON, M5J 2W4
(416) 596-4599   SIC 6211
BRANT TELEPHONE INC   p 527
3190 HARVESTER RD SUITE 101, BURLINGTON, ON, L7N 3T1
(905) 632-2000   SIC 5999
BRANTCO CONSTRUCTION   p 533
See EKUM-SEKUM INCORPORATED
BRANTFORD CHRYSLER DODGE JEEP LTD   p 514
180 LYNDEN RD, BRANTFORD, ON, N3R 8A3
(519) 753-7331   SIC 5511
BRANTFORD COLLEGIATE & VOCA-TIONAL INSTITUTE   p 517
See GRAND ERIE DISTRICT SCHOOL BOARD
BRANTFORD ENGINEERING AND CON-STRUCTION LIMITED   p 515
54 EWART AVE, BRANTFORD, ON, N3S 0H4
(519) 759-1160   SIC 1623
BRANTFORD EXPOSITOR   p 517
See OSPREY MEDIA PUBLISHING INC
BRANTFORD FINE CARS LIMITED   p 517
378 KING GEORGE RD SUITE 6, BRANT-FORD, ON, N3T 5L8
(519) 753-3168   SIC 5511
BRANTFORD HOME HARDWARE   p 514
See 2030413 ONTARIO LIMITED
BRANTFORD HONDA   p 517
See BRANTFORD FINE CARS LIMITED
BRANTFORD NISSAN INC   p 514
338 KING GEORGE RD, BRANTFORD, ON, N3R 5M1
(519) 756-9240   SIC 5511
BRANTFORD TOYOTA   p 514
See HOGEWONING MOTORS LTD
BRANTHAVEN HOMES 2000 INC   p 521
720 OVAL CRT, BURLINGTON, ON, L7L 6A9
(905) 333-8364   SIC 1521
BRANTMAC MANAGEMENT LIMITED p 514
73 KING GEORGE RD, BRANTFORD, ON, N3R 5K2
(519) 756-7350   SIC 5812
BRANTTEL NETWORKS   p 527
See BRANT TELEPHONE INC
BRANTWOOD CENTRE   p 517
See BRANTWOOD RESIDENTIAL DEVEL-OPMENT CENTRE
BRANTWOOD COLONY FARMS LTD p 354
GD, OAKVILLE, MB, R0H 0Y0
(204) 267-2527   SIC 0119
BRANTWOOD RESIDENTIAL DEVELOP-MENT CENTRE   p 517
25 BELL LANE, BRANTFORD, ON, N3T 1E1
(519) 753-2658   SIC 8361
BRAR CAPITAL CORP   p 796
2320 BRISTOL CIR UNIT 3, OAKVILLE, ON, L6H 5S3
(905) 844-1291   SIC 2759
BRASS APPLE ENTERPRISES INC   p 213
9320 82A AVE, FORT ST. JOHN, BC, V1J 6S2
SIC 1521
BRASS WORKS LTD   p 371
511 JARVIS AVE, WINNIPEG, MB, R2W

3A8
(204) 582-3737   SIC 3312
BRASSARD BURO INC   p 1266
2747 AV WATT, QUEBEC, QC, G1P 3X3
(418) 657-5500   SIC 5112
BRASSARD GOULET YARGEAU   p 1268
See BRASSARD GOULET YARGEAU SER-VICES FINANCIERS INTEGRES INC
BRASSARD GOULET YARGEAU SER-VICES FINANCIERS INTEGRES INC   p 1268
686 GRANDE ALLEE E BUREAU 100, QUEBEC, QC, G1R 2K5
(418) 682-5853   SIC 8741
BRASSELER CANADA INC   p 1256
4500 BOUL HENRI-BOURASSA BUREAU 230, QUEBEC, QC, G1H 3A5
(418) 622-1195   SIC 5047
BRASSERIE FLEURIMONT   p 1370
See GESTION LOUMA INC
BRASSERIE LABATT   p 1131
See LABATT BREWING COMPANY LIM-ITED
BRASSERIE LABATT   p 1132
See LABATT BREWING COMPANY LIM-ITED
BRASSERIE MCAUSLAN INC, LA   p 1222
5080 RUE SAINT-AMBROISE, MONTREAL, QC, H4C 2G1
(514) 939-3060   SIC 2082
BRASSEUR TRANSPORT INC   p 1123
1250 RUE INDUSTRIELLE, LA PRAIRIE, QC, J5R 5G4
(450) 444-7079   SIC 4213
BRASSERS DU MONDE INC   p 1311
3755 RUE PICARD PORTE 2, SAINT-HYACINTHE, QC, J2S 1H3
(450) 250-2611   SIC 5181
BRASSEURS DU NORD INC, LES   p 1058
875 BOUL MICHELE-BOHEC BUREAU 221, BLAINVILLE, QC, J7C 5J6
(450) 979-8400   SIC 2082
BRASSEURS GMT INC, LES   p 1173
5585 RUE DE LA ROCHE, MONTREAL, QC, H2J 3K3
(514) 274-4941   SIC 2082
BRASSEURS RJ INC, LES   p 1173
5585 RUE DE LA ROCHE, MONTREAL, QC, H2J 3K3
(514) 274-4941   SIC 2082
BRASSO NISSAN LTD   p 33
195 GLENDEER CIR SE, CALGARY, AB, T2H 2S8
(403) 253-5555   SIC 5511
BRATTYS LLP   p 549
7501 KEELE ST SUITE 200, CONCORD, ON, L4K 1Y2
(905) 760-2600   SIC 8111
BRAULT & BOUTHILLIER LTEE   p 1217
700 AV BEAUMONT, MONTREAL, QC, H3N 1V5
(514) 273-9186   SIC 5049
BRAULT & MARTINEAU   p 1104
See GROUPE BMTC INC
BRAULT ET MARTINEAU   p 1238
See GROUPE BMTC INC
BRAULT, OMER INC   p 1317
865 RUE AUBRY, SAINT-JEAN-SUR-RICHELIEU, QC, J3B 7R4
(450) 347-3342   SIC 1761
BRAUN ASSOCIATES LIMITED   p 859
201 FRONT ST N SUITE 405, SARNIA, ON, N7T 7T9
(519) 336-4590   SIC 7361
BRAUN HORTICULTURE   p 747
See BRAUN NURSERY LIMITED
BRAUN NURSERY LIMITED   p 747
2004 GLANCASTER RD, MOUNT HOPE, ON, L0R 1W0
(905) 648-1911   SIC 0181
BRAUN-VALLEY ASSOCIATES   p 859
See BRAUN ASSOCIATES LIMITED
BRAVAD   p 1371
See 9114-9534 QUEBEC INC

BRAVADO DESIGNS LTD   p 775
60 SCARSDALE RD UNIT 100, NORTH YORK, ON, M3B 2R7
(416) 466-8652   SIC 5137
BRAVO PRODUCTS & EXPORTS INC p 771
170 SHEPPARD AVE E SUITE 303A, NORTH YORK, ON, M2N 3A4
(416) 590-9605   SIC 5142
BRAVO REALTY LIMITED   p 21
2116 27 AVE NE SUITE 122, CALGARY, AB, T2E 7A6
(403) 818-2020   SIC 6531
BRAWO BRASSWORKING LIMITED   p 520
500 ONTARIO ST N, BURKS FALLS, ON, P0A 1C0
(705) 382-3637   SIC 3351
BRAXCO LIMITED   p 414
130 STATION ST, SAINT JOHN, NB, E2L 3H6
(506) 633-9040   SIC 5411
BRAY'S FUELS LIMITED   p 755
19870 HWY 11, NEWMARKET, ON, L3Y 4V9
(905) 775-3120   SIC 5172
BRAYER, L. A. INDUSTRIES LTD   p 113
3811 93 ST NW, EDMONTON, AB, T6E 5K5
(780) 462-4812   SIC 1711
BRAZILIAN   CANADIAN   COFFEE AL-BERTA INC   p 33
6812 6 ST SE BAY SUITE J, CALGARY, AB, T2H 2K4
SIC 5141
BRAZILIAN CANADIAN COFFEE CO. LTD p 582
1260 MARTIN GROVE RD, ETOBICOKE, ON, M9W 4X3
(416) 749-2000   SIC 5149
BRAZILIAN COFFEE   p 582
See BRAZILIAN CANADIAN COFFEE CO. LTD
BRAZILIAN COFFEE CALGARY   p 33
See BRAZILIAN CANADIAN COFFEE AL-BERTA INC
BRAZZO CONTRACTORS (CALGARY) LTD p 14
2624 54 AVE SE UNIT 1, CALGARY, AB, T2C 1R5
(403) 279-1983   SIC 1711
BREADKO BAKERY   p 737
See BREADKO NATIONAL BAKING LTD
BREADKO NATIONAL BAKING LTD   p 737
6310 KESTREL RD, MISSISSAUGA, ON, L5T 1Z3
(905) 670-4949   SIC 5461
BREAKAWAY GAMING CENTRE   p 1023
655 CRAWFORD AVE, WINDSOR, ON, N9A 5C7
(519) 256-0001   SIC 7999
BREAKER TECHNOLOGY LTD   p 903
35 ELGIN ST, THORNBURY, ON, N0H 2P0
(519) 599-2015   SIC 3532
BREAKWATER FISHERIES LIMITED p 423
23 HILL VIEW DR, COTTLESVILLE, NL, A0G 1S0
SIC 2092
BREAKWATER FISHERIES LIMITED p 462
13311 HWY 104 AULD'S COVE, MUL-GRAVE, NS, B0E 2G0
SIC 5146
BREAKWATER RESOURCES LTD p 1134
KM 42 RTE 1000, LEBEL-SUR-QUEVILLON, QC, J0Y 1X0
(819) 755-5550   SIC 1081
BREAKWATER RESOURCES LTD p 1288
8900 RANG DES PONTS, ROUYN-NORANDA, QC, J0Z 1P0
(819) 637-2075   SIC 1081
BREATHER   p 1183
See PRODUITS BREATHER INC
BREAU, RAYMOND LTD   p 398
131 RUE DE L'EGLISE, EDMUNDSTON, NB, E3V 1J9
(506) 735-5559   SIC 5912

BREBEUF COLLEGE SECONDARY SCHOOL *p 770*
See TORONTO CATHOLIC DISTRICT SCHOOL BOARD
BRECK CONSTRUCTION *p 1426*
6 CORY LANE, SASKATOON, SK, S7K 3J7
(306) 242-5532   *SIC 1799*
BRECKLES INSURANCE BROKERS LIMITED *p*
1000
85 ENTERPRISE BLVD SUITE 401, UNIONVILLE, ON, L6G 0B5
(905) 752-4747   *SIC 6411*
BRECON FOODS INC *p 1249*
189 BOUL HYMUS BUREAU 406, POINTE-CLAIRE, QC, H9R 1E9
(514) 426-8140   *SIC 5142*
BREEN'S ENTERPRISES LIMITED *p 428*
104 CHARTER AVE, ST. JOHN'S, NL, A1A 1P2
(709) 726-9040   *SIC 5461*
BREEN'S ULTRAMAR *p 428*
See BREEN'S ENTERPRISES LIMITED
BREEZE DRIED INC *p 911*
1300 JACKSON SUITE 2, TILLSONBURG, ON, N4G 4G7
(519) 688-0224   *SIC 2426*
BREEZE WOOD FOREST PRODUCTS *p*
911
See BREEZE DRIED INC
BREITHAUPT COMMUNITY CENTRE *p 639*
See CORPORATION OF THE CITY OF KITCHENER
BRELCOR HOLDINGS LTD *p 113*
8635 63 AVE NW, EDMONTON, AB, T6E 0E8
(780) 465-1466   *SIC 5072*
BREMNER INTERNATIONAL *p 878*
See BREMNER, GORDON C. INTERNATIONAL INC
BREMNER, GORDON C. INTERNATIONAL INC *p 878*
420 FINCHDENE SQ, SCARBOROUGH, ON, M1X 1C2
(416) 321-6943   *SIC 4731*
BREMO INC *p 1292*
214 138 RTE, SAINT-AUGUSTIN-DE-DESMAURES, QC, G3A 2X9
(418) 878-4070   *SIC 3052*
BRENCO INDUSTRIES LTD *p 208*
10030 RIVER WAY, DELTA, BC, V4G 1M9
(604) 584-2700   *SIC 3441*
BRENDA STRAFFORD FOUNDATION LTD, THE *p 72*
4628 MONTGOMERY BLVD NW, CALGARY, AB, T3B 0K7
(403) 288-1780   *SIC 8051*
BRENDONN HOLDINGS LTD *p 356*
JUNCTION OF HWY SUITE 16, RUSSELL, MB, R0J 1W0
(204) 773-2268   *SIC 5171*
BRENLO LTD *p 582*
41 RACINE RD, ETOBICOKE, ON, M9W 2Z4
(416) 749-6857   *SIC 2431*
BRENNAN PAVING & CONSTRUCTION LTD *p 680*
505 MILLER AVE, MARKHAM, ON, L6G 1B2
(905) 475-1440   *SIC 1611*
BRENNAN PAVING LIMITED *p 680*
505 MILLER AVE, MARKHAM, ON, L6G 1B2
(905) 475-1440   *SIC 1611*
BRENNAN PONTIAC BUICK GMC LTD *p*
918
1860 BAYVIEW AVE, TORONTO, ON, M4G 0C3
(416) 485-0350   *SIC 5511*
BRENNEIS MARKET GARDENS INC *p 87*
GD STN MAIN, EDMONTON, AB, T5J 2G8
(780) 473-7733   *SIC 5431*
BRENNER & ASSOCIATES INC *p 1010*
630 SUPERIOR DR, WATERLOO, ON, N2V

2C6
(519) 746-0439   *SIC 6712*
BRENNER MECHANICAL INC *p 1010*
630 SUPERIOR DR, WATERLOO, ON, N2V 2C6
(519) 746-0439   *SIC 1711*
BRENNTAG CANADA INC *p 573*
43 JUTLAND RD, ETOBICOKE, ON, M8Z 2G6
(416) 259-8231   *SIC 5169*
BRENNTAG CANADA INC *p 1332*
9999 RTE TRANSCANADIENNE, SAINT-LAURENT, QC, H4S 1V1
(514) 333-7820   *SIC 5169*
BRENNTAG TORONTO *p 573*
See BRENNTAG CANADA INC
BRENTA CONSTRUCTION INC *p 183*
2810 NORLAND AVE, BURNABY, BC, V5B 3A6
(604) 430-5887   *SIC 1542*
BRENTRIDGE FORD SALES LTD *p 172*
5604 41 AVE, WETASKIWIN, AB, T9A 3M7
(780) 352-6048   *SIC 5511*
BRENTWOOD BAY LODGE LTD *p 180*
849 VERDIER AVE, BRENTWOOD BAY, BC, V8M 1C5
(250) 544-2079   *SIC 7991*
BRENTWOOD BAY RESORT & SPA *p 180*
See BRENTWOOD BAY LODGE LTD
BRENTWOOD CLASSICS LIMITED *p 549*
57 ADESSO DR, CONCORD, ON, L4K 3C7
(905) 761-0195   *SIC 2512*
BRENTWOOD CO-OP *p 40*
See CALGARY CO-OPERATIVE ASSOCIATION LIMITED
BRENTWOOD COLLEGE ASSOCIATION *p*
232
2735 MT BAKER RD, MILL BAY, BC, V0R 2P1
(250) 743-5521   *SIC 8211*
BRENTWOOD COLLEGE SCHOOL *p 232*
See BRENTWOOD COLLEGE ASSOCIATION
BRENTWOOD FOUNDATION *p 1021*
2335 DOUGALL AVE SUITE 42, WINDSOR, ON, N8X 1S9
(519) 946-3115   *SIC 8699*
BRENTWOOD SAFEWAY *p 40*
See SOBEYS WEST INC
BRENTWOOD TRUE VALUE FOOD CENTRE *p*
180
See TRUE VALUE FOOD CENTRE LTD
BRESCIA UNIVERSITY COLLEGE *p 658*
See URSULINE RELIGIOUS OF THE DIOCESE OF LONDON IN ONTARIO
BRETON & THIBAULT LTEE *p 1289*
333 BOUL RIDEAU, ROUYN-NORANDA, QC, J9X 5Y6
(819) 797-4949   *SIC 5251*
BRETON AGRI-MANAGEMENT INC *p 1294*
1312 RUE SAINT-GEORGES, SAINT-BERNARD, QC, G0S 2G0
(418) 475-6601   *SIC 8741*
BRETON TRADITION 1944 INC *p 1294*
1312 RUE SAINT-GEORGES, SAINT-BERNARD, QC, G0S 2G0
(418) 475-6601   *SIC 2011*
BRETON, DENIS CHEVROLET LTEE *p 1300*
364 RUE DUBOIS, SAINT-EUSTACHE, QC, J7P 4W9
(450) 472-3200   *SIC 5511*
BRETT CHEVROLET CADILLAC *p 412*
183 ROTHESAY AVE, SAINT JOHN, NB, E2J 2B4
(506) 634-5555   *SIC 5511*
BRETT-YOUNG SEEDS LIMITED *p 392*
HWY 330 AND HWY 100 SW CORNER, WINNIPEG, MB, R3V 1L5
(204) 261-7932   *SIC 5191*
BRETT-YOUNG SEEDS LIMITED PARTNERSHIP *p*
392
GD, WINNIPEG, MB, R3V 1L5

(204) 261-7932   *SIC 5191*
BRETTYOUNG *p 392*
See BRETT-YOUNG SEEDS LIMITED
BREUVAGES APPALACHES INC, LES *p*
1397
925 RUE NOTRE-DAME O, VICTORIAVILLE, QC, G6P 7L1
SIC 5149
BREVILLE *p 1324*
See BREVILLE CANADA S.E.C.
BREVILLE CANADA S.E.C. *p 1324*
9800 CAVENDISH BLVD STE 250, SAINT-LAURENT, QC, H4M 2V9
(514) 683-3535   *SIC 5064*
BREVITAS CONSULTING INC *p 851*
70 EAST BEAVER CREEK RD SUITE 24, RICHMOND HILL, ON, L4B 3B2
(289) 819-1339   *SIC 8742*
BREWBAKER'S *p 400*
See 053944 NB INC
BREWBAKERS *p 401*
See ROSS VENTURES LTD
BREWERS CAR PARTS PLUS *p 533*
See GRAND VALLEY DISTRIBUTORS INC
BREWERS RETAIL INC *p 508*
69 FIRST GULF BLVD, BRAMPTON, ON, L6W 4T8
(905) 450-2799   *SIC 5181*
BREWERS RETAIL INC *p 661*
280 SOVEREIGN RD, LONDON, ON, N6M 1B3
(519) 451-3699   *SIC 5921*
BREWERS RETAIL INC *p 692*
9800 EXPLORER DR, MISSISSAUGA, ON, L4W 5L2
(905) 361-1005   *SIC 5921*
BREWERS RETAIL INC *p 817*
2750 SWANSEA CRES, OTTAWA, ON, K1G 6R8
(613) 738-8615   *SIC 5921*
BREWERS RETAIL INC *p 891*
414 DEWITT RD, STONEY CREEK, ON, L8E 4B7
(905) 664-7921   *SIC 5921*
BREWERS' DISTRIBUTOR LTD *p 70*
11500 29 ST SE SUITE 101, CALGARY, AB, T2Z 3W9
(800) 661-2337   *SIC 4225*
BREWERS' DISTRIBUTOR LTD *p 246*
1711 KINGSWAY AVE, PORT COQUITLAM, BC, V3C 0B6
(604) 927-4055   *SIC 5181*
BREWIS, CHARLES LIMITED *p 605*
995 WOODLAWN RD W, GUELPH, ON, N1K 1C9
(519) 836-0645   *SIC 5511*
BREWMASTER COFFEE ENTERPRISES (M.H.) INC *p 145*
764 7 ST SE, MEDICINE HAT, AB, T1A 1K6
(403) 526-0791   *SIC 5141*
BREWS SUPPLY LTD *p 70*
12203 40 ST SE, CALGARY, AB, T2Z 4E6
(403) 243-1144   *SIC 5063*
BREWSTER INC *p 4*
100 GOPHER ST, BANFF, AB, T1L 1J3
(403) 762-6700   *SIC 4725*
BREWSTER INC *p 4*
GD STN MAIN, BANFF, AB, T1L 1H1
(403) 762-3331   *SIC 7011*
BRI-AL FISHER SERVICES INC *p 883*
1678 ERB'S RD, ST AGATHA, ON, N0B 2L0
(519) 747-1606   *SIC 5541*
BRI-CHEM CORP *p 1*
27075 ACHESON RD, ACHESON, AB, T7X 6B1
(780) 962-9490   *SIC 2899*
BRI-STEEL DISTRIBUTION *p 122*
See GLOBAL ALLOY PIPE AND SUPPLY, INC
BRIADCO TOOL & MOULD INC *p 807*
5605 ROSCON INDUSTRIAL DR, OLD-CASTLE, ON, N0R 1L0
(519) 737-1760   *SIC 3544*
BRIAN DOMELLE ENTERPRISES LIMITED

p 918
459-825 EGLINTON AVE E, TORONTO, ON, M4G 4G9
(416) 422-0303   *SIC 5251*
BRIAN JESSEL BMW *p 286*
See JESSEL, BRIAN AUTOSPORT INC
BRIAN KURTZ TRUCKING LTD *p 518*
6960 SPEEDVALE RD W RR 2, BRESLAU, ON, N0B 1M0
(519) 836-5821   *SIC 4213*
BRIANS POULTRY SERVICES LTD *p 682*
GD, MILDMAY, ON, N0G 2J0
(519) 367-2675   *SIC 0751*
BRIARLANE RENTAL PROPERTY MANAGEMENT INC *p*
667
85 SPY CRT SUITE 100, MARKHAM, ON, L3R 4Z4
(905) 944-9406   *SIC 6513*
BRIARS ESTATES LIMITED *p 623*
55 HEDGE RD RR 1, JACKSONS POINT, ON, L0E 1L0
(800) 465-2376   *SIC 7011*
BRIARS INN & COUNTRY CLUB *p 623*
See BRIARS ESTATES LIMITED
BRICK *p 95*
See BRICK WAREHOUSE LP, THE
BRICK LTD, THE *p 95*
16930 114 AVE NW, EDMONTON, AB, T5M 3S2
(780) 930-6000   *SIC 5712*
BRICK WAREHOUSE LP, THE *p 95*
16930 114 AVE NW, EDMONTON, AB, T5M 3S2
(780) 930-6000   *SIC 6712*
BRICK WAREHOUSE LP, THE *p 182*
3100 PRODUCTION WAY SUITE 103, BURNABY, BC, V5A 4R4
(604) 415-4900   *SIC 5712*
BRICK WAREHOUSE LP, THE *p 219*
948 MCCURDY RD SUITE 100, KELOWNA, BC, V1X 2P7
(250) 765-2220   *SIC 5712*
BRICK WAREHOUSE LP, THE *p 702*
1607 DUNDAS ST E, MISSISSAUGA, ON, L4X 1L5
(905) 629-2900   *SIC 5712*
BRICK WAREHOUSE LP, THE *p 737*
6765 KENNEDY RD, MISSISSAUGA, ON, L5T 0A2
(905) 696-3400   *SIC 5712*
BRICK WAREHOUSE LP, THE *p 870*
19 WILLIAM KITCHEN RD, SCARBOROUGH, ON, M1P 5B7
(416) 751-3383   *SIC 5712*
BRICK WAREHOUSE LP, THE *p 1030*
137 CHRISLEA RD, WOODBRIDGE, ON, L4L 8N6
(905) 850-5300   *SIC 5712*
BRICK, THE *p 167*
See BANNEX PARTNERSHIP
BRICK, THE *p 182*
See BRICK WAREHOUSE LP, THE
BRICK, THE *p 219*
See BRICK WAREHOUSE LP, THE
BRICKLOK SURFACING *p 340*
See VAN ISLE BRICKLOK SURFACING & LANDSCAPE SUPPLIES LTD
BRICOR MECHANICAL LTD *p 219*
1778 BARON RD, KELOWNA, BC, V1X 7G9
(250) 861-6696   *SIC 1711*
BRIDGE 8 INVESTMENTS INC *p 14*
7805 46 ST SE, CALGARY, AB, T2C 2Y5
(403) 236-0305   *SIC 6712*
BRIDGE CITY CHRYSLER DODGE JEEP LTD *p 142*
3216 1 AVE S, LETHBRIDGE, AB, T1J 4H2
(403) 328-3325   *SIC 5511*
BRIDGE COUNTY RACEWAY LTD *p 142*
GD LCD MAIN, LETHBRIDGE, AB, T1J 3Y2
SIC 7948
BRIDGE ELECTRIC CORP *p 262*
11091 HAMMERSMITH GATE, RICHMOND, BC, V7A 5E6

(604) 273-2744   *SIC* 1731
BRIDGE GAP CHATEAU INC   *p* 87
10111 BELLAMY HILL NW, EDMONTON, AB, T5J 1N7
(780) 428-6611   *SIC* 7011
BRIDGE SYSTEMS   *p* 338
See BRIDGE, P.R. SYSTEMS LTD
BRIDGE, P.R. SYSTEMS LTD   *p* 338
455 BANGA PL SUITE 108, VICTORIA, BC, V8Z 6X5
(250) 475-3766   *SIC* 1731
BRIDGEHEAD (2000) INC   *p* 824
130 ANDERSON ST, OTTAWA, ON, K1R 6T7
(613) 231-5488   *SIC* 5812
BRIDGEMARK BRANDING & DESIGN   *p* 709
33 CITY CENTRE DR SUITE 380, MISSISSAUGA, ON, L5B 2N5
(905) 281-7240   *SIC* 7389
BRIDGEMARQ REAL ESTATE SERVICES INC   *p* 779
39 WYNFORD DR, NORTH YORK, ON, M3C 3K5
(416) 510-5800   *SIC* 6719
BRIDGEPOINT LOGISTICS INC   *p* 549
20 BARNES CRT UNIT 2, CONCORD, ON, L4K 4L4
(416) 307-2100   *SIC* 4731
BRIDGER, BOB ENTERPRISES INC   *p* 211
2929 GREEN RD, DUNCAN, BC, V9L 0C1
(250) 748-5557   *SIC* 5531
BRIDGES   *p* 221
See BRIDGES TRANSITIONS INC
BRIDGES CHEVROLET   *p* 1412
See NBFG AUTO LTD
BRIDGES TRANSITIONS INC   *p* 221
1726 DOLPHIN AVE UNIT 205, KELOWNA, BC, V1Y 9R9
(250) 869-4200   *SIC* 7372
BRIDGES, DAVID INC   *p* 365
360 DAWSON RD N, WINNIPEG, MB, R2J 0S7
(204) 233-0500   *SIC* 3399
BRIDGES-OVER-BARRIERS   *p* 600
See GUELPH SERVICES FOR THE AUTISTIC
BRIDGESTONE CANADA INC   *p* 729
5770 HURONTARIO ST SUITE 400, MISSISSAUGA, ON, L5R 3G5
(877) 468-6270   *SIC* 5014
BRIDGESTONE CANADA INC   *p* 1035
1200 DUNDAS ST, WOODSTOCK, ON, N4S 7V9
(519) 537-6231   *SIC* 2296
BRIDGESTONE CANADA INC   *p* 1114
1200 BOUL FIRESTONE, JOLIETTE, QC, J6E 2W5
(450) 756-1061   *SIC* 3011
BRIDGEWATER BANK   *p* 45
926 5 AVE SW SUITE 150, CALGARY, AB, T2P 0N7
(866) 243-4301   *SIC* 6021
BRIDGEWATER HONDA   *p* 441
See STACY'S AUTO RANCH LIMITED
BRIDGEWATER MAZDA   *p* 459
15230 HIGHWAY 3, HEBBVILLE, NS, B4V 6X5
(902) 530-9666   *SIC* 5511
BRIDGEWATER PHARMACY LIMITED   *p* 441
215 DOMINION ST, BRIDGEWATER, NS, B4V 2K7
(902) 543-3418   *SIC* 5912
BRIDGEWATER PHARMASAVE   *p* 441
See BRIDGEWATER PHARMACY LIMITED
BRIDON BEKAERT LE GROUPE CABLES *p* 1251
See INDUSTRIES DE CABLES D'ACIER LTEE
BRIDOR INC   *p* 1064
1370   RUE   GRAHAM-BELL, BOUCHERVILLE, QC, J4B 6H5
(450) 641-1265   *SIC* 2053

BRIERCREST COLLEGE   *p* 1405
See BRIERCREST COLLEGE AND SEMINARY
BRIERCREST COLLEGE AND SEMINARY *p* 1405
510 COLLEGE DR, CARONPORT, SK, S0H 0S0
(306) 756-3200   *SIC* 8221
BRIERE GILBERT + ASSOCIES ARCHITECTES   *p* 1258
See BGLA INC
BRIGGS, GEORGE L. AERIE 4269 FRATERNAL ORDER OF EAGLES   *p* 1011
3 CENTRE ST, WEBBWOOD, ON, P0P 2G0
(705) 869-4269   *SIC* 8699
BRIGHOLME INC   *p* 667
4118 14TH AVE, MARKHAM, ON, L3R 0J3
(905) 475-0043   *SIC* 5021
BRIGHOLME INTERIORS GROUP   *p* 667
See BRIGHOLME INC
BRIGHT HARVEST ENTERPRISE INC *p* 259
2620 SIMPSON RD SUITE 140, RICHMOND, BC, V6X 2P9
(604) 278-6680   *SIC* 5141
BRIGHTER FUTURES   *p* 846
GD, PIKANGIKUM, ON, P0V 2L0
(807) 773-5300   *SIC* 6411
BRIGHTER MECHANICAL LIMITED   *p* 188
107-4585 CANADA WAY, BURNABY, BC, V5G 4L6
(604) 279-0901   *SIC* 1711
BRIGHTON SOBEYS   *p* 518
See 1151377 ONTARIO INC
BRIGHTON-BEST INTERNATIONAL, (CANADA) INC   *p* 501
7900 GOREWAY DR SUITE 1, BRAMPTON, ON, L6T 5W6
(905) 791-2000   *SIC* 5085
BRIGHTPATH EARLY LEARNING INC *p* 14
200 RIVERCREST DR SE SUITE 201, CALGARY, AB, T2C 2X5
(403) 705-0362   *SIC* 8299
BRIGHTSPARK   *p* 995
See EDUCATOURS LTD
BRIGIL CONSTRUCTION INC   *p* 1107
3354 BOUL DES GRIVES BUREAU 3, GATINEAU, QC, J9A 0A6
(819) 243-7392   *SIC* 1521
BRIMELL AUTOMOTIVE SERVICES LIMITED   *p* 873
5060 SHEPPARD AVE E, SCARBOROUGH, ON, M1S 4N3
(416) 292-2241   *SIC* 7532
BRIMELL GROUP, THE   *p* 873
See BRIMELL AUTOMOTIVE SERVICES LIMITED
BRIMELL MOTORS LIMITED   *p* 873
5060 SHEPPARD AVE E, SCARBOROUGH, ON, M1S 4N3
(416) 292-2241   *SIC* 5511
BRIMELL TOYOTA   *p* 873
See BRIMELL MOTORS LIMITED
BRINDLEY AUCTION SERVICE LTD   *p* 567
37110 DUNGANNON RD, DUNGANNON, ON, N0M 1R0
(519) 529-7625   *SIC* 5083
BRINK FOREST PRODUCTS LTD   *p* 249
2023 RIVER RD, PRINCE GEORGE, BC, V2L 5S8
(250) 564-0412   *SIC* 2421
BRINK'S   *p* 10
See BRINK'S CANADA LIMITED
BRINK'S   *p* 648
See BRINK'S CANADA LIMITED
BRINK'S CANADA   *p* 815
See BRINK'S CANADA LIMITED
BRINK'S CANADA LIMITED   *p* 10
640 28 ST NE UNIT 8, CALGARY, AB, T2A 6R3
(403) 272-2259   *SIC* 7381
BRINK'S CANADA LIMITED   *p* 93

14680 134 AVE NW, EDMONTON, AB, T5L 4T4
(780) 453-5057   *SIC* 7381
BRINK'S CANADA LIMITED   *p* 288
247 1ST AVE E, VANCOUVER, BC, V5T 1A7
(604) 875-6221   *SIC* 7381
BRINK'S CANADA LIMITED   *p* 445
19 ILSLEY AVE, DARTMOUTH, NS, B3B 1L5
(902) 468-7124   *SIC* 7381
BRINK'S CANADA LIMITED   *p* 571
95 BROWNS LINE, ETOBICOKE, ON, M8W 3S2
(416) 461-0261   *SIC* 7381
BRINK'S CANADA LIMITED   *p* 610
75 LANSDOWNE AVE, HAMILTON, ON, L8L 8A3
(905) 549-5997   *SIC* 7381
BRINK'S CANADA LIMITED   *p* 648
1495 SPANNER ST, LONDON, ON, N5V 1Z1
(519) 659-3457   *SIC* 7381
BRINK'S CANADA LIMITED   *p* 720
2233 ARGENTIA RD SUITE 400, MISSISSAUGA, ON, L5N 2X7
(905) 306-9600   *SIC* 7381
BRINK'S CANADA LIMITED   *p* 815
2755 LANCASTER RD, OTTAWA, ON, K1B 4V8
(613) 521-8650   *SIC* 7381
BRINK'S HAMILTON   *p* 610
See BRINK'S CANADA LIMITED
BRINKHAUS FACTORY   *p* 1196
See GROUPE BIRKS INC
BRINKS TORONTO   *p* 571
See BRINK'S CANADA LIMITED
BRIO GOLD INC   *p* 949
22 ADELAIDE ST W UNIT 2020, TORONTO, ON, M5H 4E3
(416) 860-6310   *SIC* 1081
BRIO INSURANCE   *p* 358
13 BRANDT ST SUITE 1, STEINBACH, MB, R5G 0C2
(204) 326-3870   *SIC* 6411
BRIQUE & PAVE DONAT FORTIER   *p* 1314
2036 RANG DE LA RIVIERE, SAINT-ISIDORE, QC, G0S 2S0
(418) 882-5879   *SIC* 3241
BRIQUE ET PAVE CHICOINE   *p* 1080
See GROUPE GIROUX MACONNEX INC
BRIQUE ET PIERRE MONTREAL INC *p* 1231
1070 MONTEE MASSON, MONTREAL, QC, H7C 2R2
(514) 321-8402   *SIC* 5032
BRIQUES & PIERRE NADON   *p* 1344
See GIVESCO INC
BRIS EQUITIES LTD   *p* 1426
75 24TH ST E, SASKATOON, SK, S7K 0K3
(306) 652-1660   *SIC* 6712
BRISBIN BROOK BEYNON, ARCHITECTS *p* 949
14 DUNCAN ST SUITE 400, TORONTO, ON, M5H 3G8
(416) 591-8999   *SIC* 8712
BRISBIN BROOK BEYNON,INTERIORS *p* 949
See BRISBIN BROOK BEYNON, ARCHITECTS
BRISDALE PUBLIC SCHOOL   *p* 513
See PEEL DISTRICT SCHOOL BOARD
BRISTER GROUP-MORRISBURG   *p* 746
See BRISTER INSURANCE BROKERS LTD
BRISTER INSURANCE BROKERS LTD *p* 746
83 MAIN ST, MORRISBURG, ON, K0C 1X0
(613) 543-3731   *SIC* 6411
BRISTOL AEROSPACE LIMITED   *p* 383
660 BERRY ST, WINNIPEG, MB, R3H 0S5
(204) 775-8331   *SIC* 3728
BRISTOL MACHINE WORKS LIMITED *p* 900

2100 ALGONQUIN RD, SUDBURY, ON, P3E 4Z6
(705) 522-1550   *SIC* 3599
BRISTOW, TERRY DRUGS LTD   *p* 900
2015 LONG LAKE RD, SUDBURY, ON, P3E 4M8
(705) 522-3030   *SIC* 5912
BRITA   *p* 509
See CLOROX COMPANY OF CANADA, LTD, THE
BRITA CANADA CORPORATION   *p* 508
150 BISCAYNE CRES, BRAMPTON, ON, L6W 4V3
(905) 789-2465   *SIC* 5074
BRITACAN FACILITIES MANAGEMENT GROUP INC   *p* 766
505 CONSUMERS RD SUITE 1010, NORTH YORK, ON, M2J 4V8
(416) 494-2007   *SIC* 7389
BRITCO BUILDING SYSTEMS   *p* 224
See BRITCO MANAGEMENT INC
BRITCO LP   *p* 178
1825 TOWER DR, AGASSIZ, BC, V0M 1A2
(604) 796-2257   *SIC* 2452
BRITCO MANAGEMENT INC   *p* 224
20091 91A AVE UNIT 100, LANGLEY, BC, V1M 3A2
(604) 455-8000   *SIC* 2452
BRITE BLINDS LTD   *p* 182
4275 PHILLIPS AVE SUITE C, BURNABY, BC, V5A 2X4
(604) 420-8820   *SIC* 5719
BRITE-LITE CALGARY   *p* 12
See BRITE-LITE INC
BRITE-LITE INC   *p* 12
2880 45 AVE SE UNIT 252, CALGARY, AB, T2B 3M1
(403) 720-6877   *SIC* 5063
BRITESTONE HUTTERIAN BRETHREN *p* 79
GD, CARBON, AB, T0M 0L0
(403) 572-3046   *SIC* 0119
BRITISH COLUMBIA AUTOMOBILE ASSOCIATION   *p* 188
4567 CANADA WAY, BURNABY, BC, V5G 4T1
(604) 268-5500   *SIC* 8699
BRITISH COLUMBIA CENTRE FOR ABILITY ASSOCIATION   *p* 288
2805 KINGSWAY, VANCOUVER, BC, V5R 5H9
(604) 451-5511   *SIC* 8093
BRITISH COLUMBIA CENTRE FOR DISEASE CONTROL AND PREVENTION SOCIETY BRANCH   *p* 292
655 12TH AVE W, VANCOUVER, BC, V5Z 4R4
(604) 660-0584   *SIC* 8011
BRITISH COLUMBIA COLLEGE OF NURSING PROFESSIONALS   *p* 302
200 GRANVILLE ST SUITE 900, VANCOUVER, BC, V6C 1S4
(604) 742-6200   *SIC* 8621
BRITISH COLUMBIA CONSERVATION FOUNDATION, THE   *p* 271
17564 56A AVE SUITE 206, SURREY, BC, V3S 1G3
(604) 576-1433   *SIC* 0971
BRITISH COLUMBIA CORPS OF COMMISSIONAIRES   *p* 303
595 HOWE ST UNIT 801, VANCOUVER, BC, V6C 2T5
(604) 646-3330   *SIC* 7381
BRITISH COLUMBIA FEDERATION OF RETIRED UNION MEMBERS   *p* 288
5118 JOYCE ST SUITE 200, VANCOUVER, BC, V5R 4H1
(604) 688-4565   *SIC* 6371

BRITISH COLUMBIA FERRY SERVICES INC *p 336*
1321 BLANSHARD ST SUITE 500, VICTORIA, BC, V8W 0B7
(250) 381-1401 *SIC 4482*

BRITISH COLUMBIA HYDRO AND POWER AUTHORITY *p 297*
333 DUNSMUIR ST, VANCOUVER, BC, V6B 5R3
(604) 224-9376 *SIC 4911*

BRITISH COLUMBIA INSTITUTE OF TECHNOLOGY, THE *p 188*
3700 WILLINGDON AVE, BURNABY, BC, V5G 3H2
(604) 434-5734 *SIC 8221*

BRITISH COLUMBIA INVESTMENT MANAGEMENT CORPORATION *p 336*
750 PANDORA AVE, VICTORIA, BC, V8W 0E4
(778) 410-7100 *SIC 6722*

BRITISH COLUMBIA LIFE AND CASUALTY COMPANY *p 188*
4250 CANADA WAY, BURNABY, BC, V5G 4W6
(604) 419-8000 *SIC 6311*

BRITISH COLUMBIA LOTTERY CORPORATION *p 216*
74 SEYMOUR ST W, KAMLOOPS, BC, V2C 1E2
(250) 828-5500 *SIC 7993*

BRITISH COLUMBIA MARITIME EMPLOYERS ASSOCIATION *p 294*
349 RAILWAY ST SUITE 500, VANCOUVER, BC, V6A 1A4
(604) 688-1155 *SIC 8631*

BRITISH COLUMBIA MEDICAL ASSOCIATION (CANADIAN MEDICAL ASSOCIATION - B.C. DIVISION) *p 320*
1665 BROADWAY W SUITE 115, VANCOUVER, BC, V6J 5A4
(604) 736-5551 *SIC 8621*

BRITISH COLUMBIA MENTAL HEALTH SOCIETY *p 199*
2601 LOUGHEED HWY, COQUITLAM, BC, V3C 4J2
(604) 524-7000 *SIC 8063*

BRITISH COLUMBIA NURSES UNION *p 184*
4060 REGENT ST, BURNABY, BC, V5C 6P5
(604) 433-2268 *SIC 8631*

BRITISH COLUMBIA RAPID TRANSIT COMPANY LTD *p 181*
6800 14TH AVE, BURNABY, BC, V3N 4S7
(604) 520-3641 *SIC 4111*

BRITISH COLUMBIA SOCIETY FOR THE PREVENTION OF CRUELTY TO ANIMALS, THE *p 288*
1245 7TH AVE E, VANCOUVER, BC, V5T 1R1
(604) 681-7271 *SIC 8699*

BRITISH COLUMBIA TEACHER'S FEDERATION *p 292*
550 6TH AVE W SUITE 100, VANCOUVER, BC, V5Z 4P2
(604) 871-2283 *SIC 8621*

BRITISH COLUMBIA'S CHILDREN'S HOSPITAL FOUNDATION *p 292*
938 28TH AVE W, VANCOUVER, BC, V5Z 4H4
(604) 875-2444 *SIC 8699*

BRITISH COLUMBIA'S CHILDRENS HOSPITAL *p 319*
4480 OAK ST SUITE B321, VANCOUVER, BC, V6H 3V4
(604) 875-2345 *SIC 8069*

BRITISH COLUMBIA'S WOMEN'S HOSPI-TAL AND HEALTH CENTRE FOUNDATION *p 319*
4500 OAK ST RM D310, VANCOUVER, BC, V6H 3N1
(604) 875-2270 *SIC 7389*

BRITISH CONFECTIONERY COMPANY (1982) LIMITED *p 426*
7 PANTHER PL, MOUNT PEARL, NL, A1N 5B7
(709) 747-2377 *SIC 6712*

BRITISH CONFECTIONERY COMPANY LIMITED *p 429*
187 KENMOUNT RD SUITE 2, ST. JOHN'S, NL, A1B 3P9
(709) 747-2377 *SIC 2679*

BRITISH EMPIRE FUELS INC *p 494*
41 COUNTRY RD SUITE 36, BOBCAYGEON, ON, K0M 1A0
(705) 738-2121 *SIC 5983*

BRITISH FASTENING SYSTEMS LIMITED *p 782*
155 CHAMPAGNE DR UNIT 10, NORTH YORK, ON, M3J 2C6
(416) 631-9400 *SIC 5085*

BRITISH FINE CARS LTD *p 99*
17007-111 AVE, EDMONTON, AB, T5S 0J5
(780) 484-1818 *SIC 5511*

BRITISH GROUP OF COMPANIES, THE *p 429*
See *BRITISH CONFECTIONERY COMPANY LIMITED*

BRITISH PACIFIC TRANSPORT HOLDINGS LTD *p 224*
9975 199B ST, LANGLEY, BC, V1M 3G4
(604) 882-5880 *SIC 6712*

BRITMAN PACKAGING SERVICES *p 473*
See *2179267 ONTARIO LTD*

BRITTANY INTERNATIONAL *p 1051*
See *VETEMENTS GOLDEN BRAND (CANADA) LTEE*

BRO-DART LIBRARY SUPPLIES *p 514*
See *BRODART CANADA COMPANY*

BROAD COVE FISHERIES *p 449*
1631 CULLODEN RD, DIGBY, NS, B0V 1A0
(902) 532-7301 *SIC 5146*

BROADCAST NEWS *p 937*
See *CANADIAN PRESS, THE*

BROADCOM CANADA LTD *p 253*
13711 INTERNATIONAL PL UNIT 200, RICHMOND, BC, V6V 2Z8
(604) 233-8500 *SIC 7371*

BROADGRAIN COMMODITIES INC *p 937*
18 KING ST E SUITE 900, TORONTO, ON, M5C 1C4
(416) 504-0070 *SIC 5153*

BROADMEAD CARE SOCIETY *p 337*
4579 CHATTERTON WAY, VICTORIA, BC, V8X 4Y7
(250) 656-0717 *SIC 8051*

BROADRIDGE *p 667*
See *BROADRIDGE CUSTOMER COMMUNICATIONS CANADA, ULC*

BROADRIDGE CUSTOMER COMMUNICATIONS CANADA, ULC *p 667*
2601 14TH AVE, MARKHAM, ON, L3R 0H9
(905) 470-2000 *SIC 2759*

BROADRIDGE FINANCIAL SOLUTION *p 303*
See *BROADRIDGE SOFTWARE LIMITED*

BROADRIDGE FINANCIAL SOLUTIONS (CANADA) INC *p 949*
4 KING ST W SUITE 500, TORONTO, ON, M5H 1B6
(416) 350-0099 *SIC 7374*

BROADRIDGE INVESTOR COMMUNICATIONS CORPORATION *p 730*
5970 CHEDWORTH WAY, MISSISSAUGA, ON, L5R 4G5
(905) 507-5100 *SIC 8748*

BROADRIDGE SOFTWARE LIMITED *p 303*
510 BURRARD ST SUITE 600, VANCOUVER, BC, V6C 3A8

(604) 687-2133 *SIC 7374*

BROADRIDGE SOFTWARE LIMITED *p 949*
4 KING ST W SUITE 500, TORONTO, ON, M5H 1B6
(416) 350-0999 *SIC 7371*

BROADSTREET DATA SOLUTIONS INC *p 773*
10 YORK MILLS RD SUITE 214, NORTH YORK, ON, M2P 2G4
(416) 792-2000 *SIC 4899*

BROADVIEW FOUNDATION *p 868*
3555 DANFORTH RD, SCARBOROUGH, ON, M1L 1E3
(416) 466-2173 *SIC 8361*

BROADVIEW NURSING CENTRE LIMITED *p 881*
210 BROCKVILLE ST, SMITHS FALLS, ON, K7A 3Z4
(613) 283-1845 *SIC 8051*

BROADVIEW PUBLIC SCHOOL *p 829*
See *OTTAWA-CARLETON DISTRICT SCHOOL BOARD*

BROADWAY AUTO SALES *p 497*
See *435682 ONTARIO LIMITED*

BROADWAY CONSTRUCTION, DIV OF *p 382*
See *PHOENIX ENTERPRISES LTD*

BROADWAY PAVING LTD, THE *p 1247*
3620 39E AV, POINTE-AUX-TREMBLES, QC, H1A 3V1
(514) 642-5811 *SIC 1611*

BROADWAY PENTECOSTAL CARE ASSOCIATION *p 319*
1377 LAMEY'S MILL RD, VANCOUVER, BC, V6H 3S9
(604) 733-1441 *SIC 8051*

BROADWAY PENTECOSTAL LODGE *p 319*
See *BROADWAY PENTECOSTAL CARE ASSOCIATION*

BROADWAY REFRIGERATION AND AIR CONDITIONING CO. LTD *p 183*
2433 HOLDOM AVE, BURNABY, BC, V5B 5A1
(604) 255-2461 *SIC 1711*

BROCCOLINI CONSTRUCTION (TORONTO) INC *p 692*
2680 MATHESON BLVD E SUITE 104, MISSISSAUGA, ON, L4W 0A5
(416) 242-7772 *SIC 1542*

BROCK CANADA *p 147*
See *BROCK CONSTRUCTION LTD*

BROCK CANADA FIELD SERVICES LTD *p 148*
3735 8 ST UNIT 200, NISKU, AB, T9E 8J8
(780) 465-9016 *SIC 1799*

BROCK CANADA INC *p 148*
3735 8 ST, NISKU, AB, T9E 8J8
(780) 465-9016 *SIC 1389*

BROCK CANADA INDUSTRIAL LTD *p 148*
3735 8 ST, NISKU, AB, T9E 8J8
(780) 465-9016 *SIC 1799*

BROCK CANADA MANAGEMENT CORPORATION *p 113*
8925 62 AVE NW, EDMONTON, AB, T6E 5L2
(780) 465-9016 *SIC 8741*

BROCK CANADA WEST LTD *p 200*
1650 BRIGANTINE DR SUITE 100, COQUITLAM, BC, V3K 7B5
(604) 519-6788 *SIC 1799*

BROCK CONSTRUCTION LTD *p 147*
3735 8 ST, MEDICINE HAT, AB, T9E 8J8
(403) 526-8930 *SIC 6719*

BROCK SOLUTIONS HOLDINGS INC *p 636*
88 ARDELT AVE, KITCHENER, ON, N2C 2C9
(519) 571-1522 *SIC 6712*

BROCK SOLUTIONS INC *p 636*
88 ARDELT AVE, KITCHENER, ON, N2C 2C9
(519) 571-1522 *SIC 8748*

BROCK SOLUTIONS INC *p 636*

90 ARDELT AVE, KITCHENER, ON, N2C 2C9
(519) 571-1522 *SIC 3491*

BROCK UNIVERSITY *p 886*
1812 SIR ISAAC BROCK WAY, ST CATHARINES, ON, L2S 3A1
(905) 688-5550 *SIC 8221*

BROCK UNIVERSITY WELLNESS INSTITUTE, DIV OF *p 886*
See *BROCK UNIVERSITY*

BROCK WHITE CANADA ULC *p 371*
879 KEEWATIN ST, WINNIPEG, MB, R2X 2S7
(204) 694-3600 *SIC 5039*

BROCKMANN CHOCOLATE INC *p 208*
7863 PROGRESS WAY, DELTA, BC, V4G 1A3
(604) 946-4111 *SIC 2066*

BROCKVILLE & AREA COMMUNITY LIVING ASSOCIATION *p 519*
6 GLENN WOOD PL SUITE 100, BROCKVILLE, ON, K6V 2T3
(613) 342-2953 *SIC 8322*

BROCKVILLE AREA CENTRE FOR DEVELOPMENTALLY HANDICAPPED PERSONS INC *p 519*
61 KING ST E, BROCKVILLE, ON, K6V 1B2
SIC 8322

BROCKVILLE GENERAL HOSPITAL *p 519*
42 GARDEN ST, BROCKVILLE, ON, K6V 2C3
(613) 345-5649 *SIC 8062*

BROCKVILLE GENERAL HOSPITAL *p 519*
75 CHARLES ST, BROCKVILLE, ON, K6V 1S8
(613) 345-5645 *SIC 8062*

BROCKVILLE HARDWARE ENTERPRISES INC *p 519*
584 STEWART BLVD, BROCKVILLE, ON, K6V 7H2
(613) 342-4421 *SIC 5251*

BROCKVILLE HOME HARDWARE *p 519*
See *BROCKVILLE HARDWARE ENTERPRISES INC*

BROCKVILLE MOTOR SALES LIMITED *p 519*
1240 STEWART BLVD, BROCKVILLE, ON, K6V 7H2
(613) 342-5244 *SIC 5511*

BROCKVILLE POLICE ASSOCIATION *p 519*
2269 PARKEDALE AVE W, BROCKVILLE, ON, K6V 3G9
(613) 342-0127 *SIC 8631*

BROCO AUTO GLASS & UPHOLSTERY *p 200*
See *BROTHERS COMPANY GLASS CAR CARE LTD*

BRODA ENTERPRISES INC *p 635*
560 BINGEMANS CENTRE DR, KITCHENER, ON, N2B 3X9
(519) 746-8080 *SIC 3842*

BRODA GROUP HOLDINGS LIMITED PARTNERSHIP *p 1414*
4271 5TH AVE E, PRINCE ALBERT, SK, S6W 0A5
(306) 764-5337 *SIC 1522*

BRODA GROUP OF COMPANIES *p 1414*
See *NORTH AMERICAN ROCK & DIRT INC*

BRODA SEATING *p 635*
See *BRODA ENTERPRISES INC*

BRODART CANADA COMPANY *p 514*
109 ROY BLVD, BRANTFORD, ON, N3R 7K1
SIC 2531

BRODY COMPANY LTD, THE *p 411*
199 HAMPTON RD SUITE 606, QUISPAMSIS, NB, E2E 4L9
(506) 849-4123 *SIC 5399*

BROFORT INC *p 817*
2161 THURSTON DR, OTTAWA, ON, K1G 6C9

(613) 746-8580   *SIC 1751*
BROGAN SAFETY SUPPLY LTD   *p 131*
12002 101 AVE SUITE 101, GRANDE PRAIRIE, AB, T8V 8B1
(780) 539-9004   *SIC 5099*
BROKERAGE SERVICES, DIV OF   *p 376*
See W. H. ESCOTT COMPANY LIMITED
BROKERFORCE INSURANCE INC   *p 766*
200 CONSUMERS RD SUITE 608, NORTH YORK, ON, M2J 4R4
(416) 494-2696   *SIC 6411*
BROKERHOUSE DISTRIBUTORS INC   *p 582*
108 WOODBINE DOWNS BLVD UNIT 4, ETOBICOKE, ON, M9W 5S6
(416) 798-3537   *SIC 5962*
BROKERS TRUST INSURANCE GROUP INC   *p 549*
2780 HIGHWAY 7 SUITE 201, CONCORD, ON, L4K 3R9
(416) 427-5251   *SIC 6411*
BROMLEY FOODS LTD   *p 139*
5421 50 ST, LEDUC, AB, T9E 6Z7
(780) 986-2289   *SIC 5411*
BROMLEY MECHANICAL SERVICES *p 145*
See ARGO SALES INC
BROMPTON FUNDS   *p 960*
See BROMPTON GROUP LIMITED
BROMPTON FUNDS LIMITED   *p 960*
181 BAY ST SUITE 2930, TORONTO, ON, M5J 2T3
(416) 642-9061   *SIC 6722*
BROMPTON GROUP LIMITED   *p 960*
181 BAY ST SUITE 2930, TORONTO, ON, M5J 2T3
(416) 642-6000   *SIC 6722*
BROMPTON SPLIT BANC CORP   *p 960*
181 BAY ST SUITE 2930, TORONTO, ON, M5J 2T3
(416) 642-9061   *SIC 6726*
BROMWICH & SMITH INC   *p 45*
1000 9 AVE SW SUITE 201, CALGARY, AB, T2P 2Y6
(855) 884-9243   *SIC 8111*
BRON   *p 1035*
See ROBERTS WELDING & FABRICATING LTD
BRON & SONS NURSERY CO. LTD *p 215*
3315 CARSON RD, GRAND FORKS, BC, V0H 1H4
(250) 442-2014   *SIC 5193*
BRONCO INDUSTRIES INC   *p 208*
7988 82 ST, DELTA, BC, V4G 1L8
(604) 940-8821   *SIC 3211*
BRONSKILL & CO. INC   *p 979*
662 KING ST W SUITE 101, TORONTO, ON, M5V 1M7
(416) 703-8689   *SIC 7389*
BRONZART CASTING LTD   *p 14*
4315 64 AVE SE SUITE 1, CALGARY, AB, T2C 2C8
(403) 279-6584   *SIC 5051*
BROOK CROMPTON LTD   *p 582*
264 ATTWELL DR, ETOBICOKE, ON, M9W 5B2
(416) 675-3844   *SIC 5063*
BROOK RESTORATION LTD   *p 582*
11 KELFIELD ST, ETOBICOKE, ON, M9W 5A1
(416) 663-7976   *SIC 1542*
BROOKDALE TREELAND NURSERIES LIMITED   *p 879*
6050 17TH SIDEROAD, SCHOMBERG, ON, L0G 1T0
(905) 859-4571   *SIC 0181*
BROOKE RADIOLOGY & ASSOCIATES *p 320*
See REM TEK ENTERPRISES LTD
BROOKFIELD ASSET MANAGEMENT INC *p 960*
181 BAY ST SUITE 300, TORONTO, ON, M5J 2T3
(416) 363-9491   *SIC 6512*
BROOKFIELD BRP CANADA CORP *p 1104*

480 BOUL DE LA CITE BUREAU 200, GATINEAU, QC, J8T 8R3
(819) 561-2722   *SIC 6712*
BROOKFIELD CAPITAL PARTNERS II L.P. *p 960*
181 BAY ST SUITE 300, TORONTO, ON, M5J 2T3
(416) 363-9491   *SIC 3088*
BROOKFIELD CAPITAL PARTNERS LTD *p 960*
181 BAY ST SUITE 300, TORONTO, ON, M5J 2T3
(416) 363-9491   *SIC 8741*
BROOKFIELD HIGH SCHOOL   *p 827*
See OTTAWA-CARLETON DISTRICT SCHOOL BOARD
BROOKFIELD ICE CREAM LIMITED *p 432*
314 LEMARCHANT RD, ST. JOHN'S, NL, A1E 1R2
(709) 738-4652   *SIC 2024*
BROOKFIELD INFRASTRUCTURE PARTNERS L.P. *p 960*
181 BAY ST SUITE 300, TORONTO, ON, M5J 2T3
(416) 363-9491   *SIC 8711*
BROOKFIELD PRIVATE EQUITY INC *p 960*
181 BAY ST SUITE 300, TORONTO, ON, M5J 2T3
(416) 363-9491   *SIC 6722*
BROOKFIELD PROPERTIES   *p 958*
See 8961182 CANADA INC
BROOKFIELD PROPERTIES MANAGEMENT CORPORATION   *p 960*
181 BAY ST SUITE 300, TORONTO, ON, M5J 2T3
(416) 369-2300   *SIC 6531*
BROOKFIELD PROPERTY PARTNERS L.P. *p 960*
181 BAY ST SUITE 300, TORONTO, ON, M5J 2T3
(416) 363-9491   *SIC 6798*
BROOKFIELD RENEWABLE ENERGY MARKETING LP   *p 1105*
41 RUE VICTORIA, GATINEAU, QC, J8X 2A1
(819) 561-2722   *SIC 4911*
BROOKFIELD RENEWABLE ENERGY PARTNERS L.P.   *p 1105*
41 RUE VICTORIA, GATINEAU, QC, J8X 2A1
(819) 561-2722   *SIC 8731*
BROOKFIELD RENEWABLE PARTNERS L.P.   *p 960*
181 BAY ST SUITE 300, TORONTO, ON, M5J 2T3
(416) 363-9491   *SIC 4911*
BROOKFIELD RENEWABLE TRADING AND MARKETING LP   *p 1105*
41 RUE VICTORIA, GATINEAU, QC, J8X 2A1
(819) 561-2722   *SIC 4911*
BROOKFIELD RESIDENTIAL PROPERTIES INC   *p 73*
4906 RICHARD RD SW, CALGARY, AB, T3E 6L1
(403) 231-8900   *SIC 6553*
BROOKLIN ESTATES GENERAL PARTNER INC.   *p 1030*
3700 STEELES AVE W SUITE 800, WOODBRIDGE, ON, L4L 8M9
(905) 850-8508   *SIC 6553*
BROOKLYN POWER CORPORATION *p 441*
65 BOWATER MERSEY HAULING RD, BROOKLYN, NS, B0J 1H0
(902) 354-2299   *SIC 4911*
BROOKLYN VOLUNTEER FIRE DEPARTMENT   *p 441*
995 HWY 215, BROOKLYN, NS, B0J 1H0
(902) 757-2043   *SIC 7389*
BROOKS ASPHALT AND AGGREGATE

LTD   *p 7*
PO BOX 686 STN MAIN, BROOKS, AB, T1R 1B6
(403) 362-5597   *SIC 1611*
BROOKS HEALTH CENTRE   *p 7*
See ALBERTA HEALTH SERVICES
BROOKS IGA   *p 1003*
See REID'S FOODLAND
BROOKS INDUSTRIAL METALS LTD   *p 7*
221 7TH ST E, BROOKS, AB, T1R 1B3
(403) 362-3544   *SIC 5999*
BROOKSIDE RETIREMENT RESIDENCE *p 857*
See REVERA INC
BROOKSTREET HOTEL CORPORATION *p 623*
525 LEGGET DR, KANATA, ON, K2K 2W2
(613) 271-3582   *SIC 7011*
BROOKVILLE CARRIERS VAN LIMITED PARTNERSHIP   *p 416*
65 ALLOY DR, SAINT JOHN, NB, E2M 7S9
(506) 633-7555   *SIC 4213*
BROOKVILLE CARRIERS VAN, DIV OF *p 416*
See LAIDLAW CARRIERS VAN LP
BROOKVILLE CARRIERS VAN, DIV OF *p 849*
See LAIDLAW CARRIERS VAN LP
BROOKVILLE MANUFACTURING COMPANY   *p 412*
See 059884 N.B. INC
BROPAC   *p 1239*
See BROSSARD FRERES INC
BROSE CANADA INC   *p 661*
1500 MAX BROSE DR, LONDON, ON, N6N 1P7
(519) 644-5200   *SIC 3679*
BROSSARD CHEVROLET BUICK GMC INC *p 1069*
2555 BOUL MATTE, BROSSARD, QC, J4Y 2P4
(450) 619-6666   *SIC 5511*
BROSSARD FRERES INC   *p 1239*
10848 AV MOISAN, MONTREAL-NORD, QC, H1G 4N7
(514) 321-4121   *SIC 5149*
BROSSARD MAZDA   *p 1069*
See 9096-9080 QUEBEC INC
BROTHER INTERNATIONAL   *p 1091*
See CORPORATION INTERNATIONAL BROTHER (CANADA) LTEE, LA
BROTHERS COMPANY GLASS CAR CARE LTD   *p 200*
802 BRUNETTE AVE, COQUITLAM, BC, V3K 1C4
(604) 517-0215   *SIC 1793*
BROTHERS MEAT LIMITED   *p 455*
2665 AGRICOLA ST, HALIFAX, NS, B3K 4C7
(902) 455-8774   *SIC 5147*
BROUE-ALLIANCE INC   *p 1101*
3838 BOUL LEMAN, FABREVILLE, QC, H7E 1A1
(450) 661-0281   *SIC 2082*
BROUGHTON'S   *p 766*
See BROUGHTON, B. COMPANY LIMITED
BROUGHTON, B. COMPANY LIMITED *p 766*
322 CONSUMERS RD, NORTH YORK, ON, M2J 1P8
(416) 690-4777   *SIC 5192*
BROUILLETTE & FRERE INC   *p 1096*
4500 BOUL SAINT-JOSEPH, DRUMMONDVILLE, QC, J2A 1A7
(819) 475-7114   *SIC 5211*
BROUILLETTE AUTOMOBILE   *p 1313*
See ST-HYACINTHE CHRYSLER JEEP DODGE INC
BROUILLETTE AUTOMOBILE INC   *p 1311*
2750 RUE LAFONTAINE, SAINT-HYACINTHE, QC, J2S 2N6
(450) 773-8551   *SIC 5511*
BROUWER CONSTRUCTION (1981) LTD *p*

885
1880 KING ST, ST CATHARINES, ON, L2R 6P7
(905) 984-3060   *SIC 1542*
BROUWER TURF   *p 628*
See KESMAC INC
BROWN & ASSOCIATES PLANNING GROUP LTD   *p 45*
215 9 AVE SW SUITE 600, CALGARY, AB, T2P 1K3
(403) 269-4733   *SIC 8748*
BROWN BROS MANAGEMENT LTD   *p 290*
270 MARINE DR SE, VANCOUVER, BC, V5X 2S6
(604) 321-5100   *SIC 5511*
BROWN BROS. AGENCIES LIMITED   *p 336*
1125 BLANSHARD ST, VICTORIA, BC, V8W 2H7
(250) 385-8771   *SIC 6411*
BROWN WINDOW CORPORATION   *p 549*
185 SNOW BLVD SUITE 2, CONCORD, ON, L4K 4N9
(905) 738-6045   *SIC 5211*
BROWN'S CLEANERS   *p 824*
See BROWN'S CLEANERS AND TAILORS LIMITED
BROWN'S CLEANERS AND TAILORS LIMITED   *p 824*
270 CITY CENTRE AVE, OTTAWA, ON, K1R 7R7
(613) 235-5181   *SIC 7216*
BROWN'S FINE FOOD SERVICES INC *p 630*
844 DIVISION ST, KINGSTON, ON, K7K 4C3
(613) 546-3246   *SIC 5812*
BROWN'S FINE FOODS SERVICES   *p 630*
See BROWN'S FINE FOOD SERVICES INC
BROWN'S FUEL   *p 781*
See 2124688 ONTARIO LIMITED
BROWN'S GENERAL STORE LTD   *p 150*
31 SOUTHRIDGE DR SUITE 171, OKOTOKS, AB, T1S 2N3
(403) 995-3798   *SIC 5912*
BROWN'S PAVING LTD   *p 418*
20 PLANT RD, SUSSEX CORNER, NB, E4E 2W9
(506) 433-4721   *SIC 1611*
BROWN, AL G. & ASSOCIATES   *p 788*
970 LAWRENCE AVE W SUITE 501, NORTH YORK, ON, M6A 3B6
(416) 787-6176   *SIC 6411*
BROWN, BARRIE PONTIAC BUICK GMC LTD   *p 194*
2700 ISLAND HWY, CAMPBELL RIVER, BC, V9W 2H5
SIC 5511
BROWN, BOB BUICK GMC LTD   *p 243*
1010 WESTMINSTER AVE W, PENTICTON, BC, V2A 1L6
(250) 493-7121   *SIC 5511*
BROWN, DAVID UNITED LTD   *p 441*
761 CAMBRIDGE RD, CAMBRIDGE, NS, B0P 1G0
(902) 538-8088   *SIC 4213*
BROWN, JIM & SONS TRUCKING   *p 807*
See 662117 ONTARIO INC
BROWNE & CO   *p 667*
505 APPLE CREEK BLVD UNIT 2, MARKHAM, ON, L3R 5B1
(905) 475-6104   *SIC 3262*
BROWNE'S AUTO SUPPLIES LIMITED   *p 426*
1075 TOPSAIL RD, MOUNT PEARL, NL, A1N 5G1
(709) 364-9397   *SIC 5511*
BROWNING HARVEY LIMITED   *p 432*
15 ROPEWALK LANE, ST. JOHN'S, NL, A1E 4P1
(709) 579-4116   *SIC 2086*
BROWNLEE LLP   *p 87*
10155 102 ST NW SUITE 2200, EDMONTON, AB, T5J 4G8

---

(780) 497-4800   *SIC* 8111
BROWNLEE'S METRO   *p* 839
See BROWNLEE, RONALD (1994) LTD
BROWNLEE, RONALD (1994) LTD   *p* 839
50 WILSON ST W, PERTH, ON, K7H 2N4
(613) 267-4921   *SIC* 5411
BROWNS   *p* 1328
See CHAUSSURES BROWNS INC
BROWNS' CHEVROLET LIMITED   *p* 204
12109 8 ST, DAWSON CREEK, BC, V1G
5A5
(250) 782-9155   *SIC* 5511
BROWNSBURG ELECTRONIK INC   *p* 1129
741 RUE LOWE, LACHUTE, QC, J8H 4N9
(450) 562-5211   *SIC* 3677
**BROWNSTONE INVESTMENT PLANNING
INC**   *p* 377
444 ST MARY AVE SUITE 1122, WIN-
NIPEG, MB, R3C 3T1
(204) 944-9911   *SIC* 6282
BROWNSVILLE HOLDINGS INC   *p* 482
GD LCD MAIN, AYLMER, ON, N5H 2R7
(519) 866-3446   *SIC* 6712
BRP INC   *p* 1392
726 RUE SAINT-JOSEPH, VALCOURT, QC,
J0E 2L0
(450) 532-2211   *SIC* 5012
BRR LOGISTICS LIMITED   *p* 542
24 MCGREGOR PL, CHATHAM, ON, N7M
5J4
(519) 352-4120   *SIC* 5143
BRS CANADA ACQUISITION INC   *p* 486
92 CAPLAN AVE SUITE 108, BARRIE, ON,
L4N 9J2
(705) 719-7922   *SIC* 5091
**BRUCE CHEVROLET PONTIAC BUICK
GMC LIMITED**   *p* 462
394 MAIN ST, MIDDLETON, NS, B0S 1P0
(902) 825-3494   *SIC* 5511
BRUCE GM   *p* 462
*See BRUCE CHEVROLET PONTIAC
BUICK GMC LIMITED*
BRUCE POWER L.P.   *p* 913
177 TIE RD MUNICIPAL KINCARDINE RR
2, TIVERTON, ON, N0G 2T0
(519) 361-2673   *SIC* 4911
BRUCE POWER L.P.   *p* 944
700 UNIVERSITY AVE SUITE 200,
TORONTO, ON, M5G 1X6
(519) 361-2673   *SIC* 4911
BRUCE R. SMITH LIMITED   *p* 880
51 PARK RD, SIMCOE, ON, N3Y 4J9
(519) 426-0904   *SIC* 4212
BRUCE TELECOM   *p* 913
See MUNICIPALITY OF KINCARDINE, THE
BRUCE'S COUNTRY MARKET   *p* 230
See SEA FRESH FISH LTD
BRUCE'S FOUR SEASONS (1984) LTD   *p*
360
TRANSCANADA HWY N, VIRDEN, MB,
R0M 2C0
(204) 748-1539   *SIC* 5561
**BRUCE-GREY CATHOLIC DISTRICT
SCHOOL BOARD**   *p* 617
799 16TH AVE, HANOVER, ON, N4N 3A1
(519) 364-5820   *SIC* 8211
**BRUCE-GREY CATHOLIC DISTRICT
SCHOOL BOARD**   *p* 1004
450 ROBINSON ST, WALKERTON, ON,
N0G 2V0
(519) 881-1900   *SIC* 8211
BRUCKNER SUPPLY CANADA   *p* 677
See WESCO DISTRIBUTION CANADA LP
BRUDERHEIM ENERGY TERMINAL LTD   *p*
27
500 CENTRE ST SE SUITE 2600, CAL-
GARY, AB, T2G 1A6
(403) 766-2000   *SIC* 5169
BRUHAM AUTOMOTIVE INC   *p* 1000
5201 HIGHWAY 7 E, UNIONVILLE, ON, L3R
1N3
(905) 948-8222   *SIC* 5511
BRUIN'S PLUMBING & HEATING LTD   *p* 155
7026 JOHNSTONE DR, RED DEER, AB,

T4P 3Y6
(403) 343-6060   *SIC* 1711
BRUKER LTD   *p* 683
2800 HIGHPOINT DR, MILTON, ON, L9T
6P4
(905) 876-4641   *SIC* 5049
BRULE FOODS LTD   *p* 526
4000 MAINWAY SUITE 3, BURLINGTON,
ON, L7M 4B9
(905) 319-2663   *SIC* 5461
BRULE HOLDINGS LTD   *p* 452
5686 SPRING GARDEN RD, HALIFAX, NS,
B3J 1H5
(902) 423-6766   *SIC* 6712
BRULERIE DES MONTS INC.   *p* 1352
197 RUE PRINCIPALE, SAINT-SAUVEUR,
QC, J0R 1R0
(450) 227-6157   *SIC* 5499
BRULERIE GRANDE RESERVE INC *p* 1372
930 RUE BLAIS, SHERBROOKE, QC, J1K
2B7
(819) 564-8844   *SIC* 5149
BRULERIE TATUM   *p* 1372
See CAFE FARO INC
BRUN FISHERIES LTD   *p* 411
73 CH DE L'ILE, PETIT-CAP, NB, E4N 2G6
(506) 577-1157   *SIC* 5146
BRUN-WAY HIGHWAYS OPERATIONS INC
p 403
1754 ROUTE 640, HANWELL, NB, E3C 2B2
(506) 474-7750   *SIC* 1611
BRUNEAU ELECTRIQUE INC   *p* 1114
527 BOUL DOLLARD, JOLIETTE, QC, J6E
4M5
(450) 759-6606   *SIC* 1731
BRUNELLE, GUY INC   *p* 1165
4450 RUE BELANGER, MONTREAL, QC,
H1T 1B5
(514) 729-0008   *SIC* 1721
BRUNET   *p* 1045
See AMOPHARM INC
BRUNET   *p* 1247
*See MCMAHON DISTRIBUTEUR PHAR-
MACEUTIQUE INC*
BRUNET   *p* 1275
See GESTION BBFD INC
BRUNET   *p* 1357
*See PRODUITS DE BETON CASAUBON
INC, LES*
BRUNET   *p* 1398
*See JEAN-SEBASTIEN CROTEAU IS-
ABELLE ANNE ROBITAILLE INC*
BRUNET ET CLOUTIER   *p* 1319
See AUTOBUS BRUNET INC, LES
BRUNET-GOULARD AGENCIES INC *p* 596
5370 CANOTEK RD UNIT 21, GLOUCES-
TER, ON, K1J 9E8
(613) 748-7377   *SIC* 5065
BRUNICO COMMUNICATIONS LTD *p* 979
366 ADELAIDE ST W SUITE 100,
TORONTO, ON, M5V 1R9
(416) 408-2300   *SIC* 2721
BRUNO & NICK INC   *p* 1182
6766 RUE MARCONI, MONTREAL, QC,
H2S 3J7
(514) 272-8998   *SIC* 5141
**BRUNO'S CONTRACTING (THUNDER
BAY) LIMITED**   *p* 907
665 HEWITSON ST, THUNDER BAY, ON,
P7B 5V5
(807) 623-1855   *SIC* 1611
BRUNO'S FINE FOODS   *p* 572
*See BRUNO'S FINE FOODS (ETOBICOKE)
LTD*
BRUNO'S FINE FOODS (ETOBICOKE) LTD
p 572
4242 DUNDAS ST W SUITE 15, ETOBI-
COKE, ON, M8X 1Y6
(416) 234-1106   *SIC* 5411
BRUNO'S FINE FOODS (NORTH) LTD *p* 855
9665 BAYVIEW AVE SUITE 29, RICHMOND
HILL, ON, L4C 9V4
(905) 737-4280   *SIC* 5411
BRUNSWICK ENTERPRISES LIMITED   *p*

362
125 BISMARCK ST, WINNIPEG, MB, R2C
2Z2
(204) 224-1472   *SIC* 5051
BRUNSWICK HINO INC   *p* 411
20 SMITH ST, PETITCODIAC, NB, E4Z 4W1
(506) 756-2250   *SIC* 5511
BRUNSWICK NEWS INC   *p* 406
939 MAIN ST, MONCTON, NB, E1C 8P3
(506) 859-4900   *SIC* 2711
BRUNSWICK PIPELINE   *p* 415
*See EMERA BRUNSWICK PIPELINE COM-
PANY LTD*
BRUNSWICK STEEL   *p* 362
*See BRUNSWICK ENTERPRISES LIM-
ITED*
BRUNSWICK VALLEY LUMBER INC *p* 399
367 MAIN ST SUITE 1, FREDERICTON,
NB, E3A 1E6
(506) 457-1900   *SIC* 5031
BRYAN & COMPANY LLP   *p* 87
10180 101 ST NW SUITE 2600, EDMON-
TON, AB, T5J 3Y2
(780) 423-5730   *SIC* 8111
**BRYAN'S FARM & INDUSTRIAL SUPPLY
LTD**   *p* 849
4062 HIGHWAY 6 RR 2, PUSLINCH, ON,
N0B 2J0
(519) 837-0710   *SIC* 5083
BRYAN'S FASHIONS LTD   *p* 285
1950 FRANKLIN ST, VANCOUVER, BC,
V5L 1R2
(604) 255-1890   *SIC* 5621
BRYAN'S FUEL   *p* 808
See 941-2401 HEATING LTD
BRYAN, J GASCON INVESTMENTS INC   *p*
283
5100 16 HWY W SUITE 486, TERRACE,
BC, V8G 5S5
(250) 635-7178   *SIC* 5251
BRYANT CANADA   *p* 1361
See CARRIER ENTERPRISE CANADA, L.P.
BRYDSON GROUP LTD   *p* 931
557 CHURCH ST, TORONTO, ON, M4Y 2E2
(416) 964-4525   *SIC* 7991
BRYJON ENTERPRISES LTD   *p* 381
925 MILT STEGALL DR, WINNIPEG, MB,
R3G 3H7
(204) 786-8756   *SIC* 7359
BRYMARK INSTALLATIONS GROUP INC *p*
246
1648 BROADWAY ST, PORT COQUITLAM,
BC, V3C 2M8
(604) 944-1206   *SIC* 1711
**BRYSON & ASSOCIATES INSURANCE
BROKERS LTD**   *p* 475
541 BAYLY ST E, AJAX, ON, L1Z 1W7
(905) 426-8787   *SIC* 6411
BRYSTON LTD   *p* 840
677 NEAL DR, PETERBOROUGH, ON, K9J
6X7
(705) 742-5325   *SIC* 3651
BRYTE P MANAGEMENT   *p* 521
*See ASSOCIATED PAVING & MATERIALS
LTD*
BRYTEX BUILDING SYSTEMS INC   *p* 113
5610 97 ST NW, EDMONTON, AB, T6E 3J1
(780) 437-7970   *SIC* 3448
BRYTOR INTERNATIONAL MOVING INC *p*
734
275 EXPORT BLVD, MISSISSAUGA, ON,
L5S 1Y4
(905) 564-8855   *SIC* 7389
BSA   *p* 1344
*See INGREDIENTS ALIMENTAIRES BSA
INC, LES*
BSI EQUIPEMENTIER   *p* 1044
See BOUILLOIRE FALMEC INC
BSI GROUP CANADA INC   *p* 687
6205B AIRPORT RD SUITE 108, MISSIS-
SAUGA, ON, L4V 1E3
(416) 620-9991   *SIC* 8741
BSL ENTREPRENEUR GENERAL   *p* 1292
See CONSTRUCTION BSL INC

BSL PROPERTY GROUP INC   *p* 45
335 8 AVE SW, CALGARY, AB, T2P 1C9
(403) 253-1100   *SIC* 4213
BSM SERVICES (1998) LTD   *p* 405
948 CH ROYAL, MEMRAMCOOK, NB, E4K
1Y8
(506) 862-0810   *SIC* 1711
BSM TECHNOLOGIES INC   *p* 582
75 INTERNATIONAL BLVD SUITE 100,
ETOBICOKE, ON, M9W 6L9
(866) 768-4771   *SIC* 7379
BSM TECHNOLOGIES LTD   *p* 188
4299 CANADA WAY SUITE 215, BURNABY,
BC, V5G 1H3
(604) 434-7337   *SIC* 3699
BSM TECHNOLOGIES LTD   *p* 583
75 INTERNATIONAL BLVD SUITE 100,
ETOBICOKE, ON, M9W 6L9
(416) 675-1201   *SIC* 3699
BSN MEDICAL INC   *p* 1235
4455 NORD LAVAL (A-440) O UNITE 255,
MONTREAL, QC, H7P 4W6
(450) 978-0738   *SIC* 5047
BT LAW LIMITED PARTNERSHIP   *p* 944
393 UNIVERSITY AVE SUITE 1300,
TORONTO, ON, M5G 1E6
(416) 581-8200   *SIC* 8741
BTB REIT   *p* 1213
*See FONDS DE PLACEMENT IMMOBILIER
BTB*
BTC INDIAN HEALTH SERVICE INC *p* 1412
1192 101ST ST SUITE 103, NORTH BAT-
TLEFORD, SK, S9A 0Z6
(306) 937-6700   *SIC* 8099
BTE TRANSPORT GROUP   *p* 646
See B.T.E. ASSEMBLY LTD
BTI   *p* 903
See BREAKER TECHNOLOGY LTD
BTI BLUETOOTH TECHNOLOGIES INC   *p*
800
169 ROBINSON ST, OAKVILLE, ON, L6J
5W7
SIC 5065
BTK INVESTMENTS LIMITED   *p* 409
2600 MOUNTAIN RD, MONCTON, NB, E1G
3T6
(506) 859-6000   *SIC* 5541
BTN   *p* 879
*See BROOKDALE TREELAND NURS-
ERIES LIMITED*
BTN ATLANTIC   *p* 395
See 615317 NB INC
BTNX INC   *p* 667
570 HOOD RD UNIT 23, MARKHAM, ON,
L3R 4G7
(905) 944-9565   *SIC* 2835
BTY CONSULTANCY GROUP INC   *p* 291
2288 MANITOBA ST, VANCOUVER, BC,
V5Y 4B5
(604) 734-3126   *SIC* 8742
BUANDERIE BLANCHELLE INC, LA *p* 1282
94 RUE DE NORMANDIE, REPENTIGNY,
QC, J6A 4W2
(450) 585-1218   *SIC* 7218
BUANDERIE BLANCHELLE INC, LA *p* 1316
825 AV MONTRICHARD, SAINT-JEAN-
SUR-RICHELIEU, QC, J2X 5K8
(450) 347-4390   *SIC* 7218
**BUANDERIE CENTRALE DE MONTREAL
INC**   *p* 1163
7250 RUE JOSEPH-DAOUST, MONTREAL,
QC, H1N 3N9
(514) 253-1635   *SIC* 7218
BUANDERIE VILLERAY LTEE   *p* 1166
4740 RUE DE ROUEN, MONTREAL, QC,
H1V 3T7
(514) 259-4531   *SIC* 7218
BUCHANAN LUMBER DIV OF   *p* 84
*See BUCHANAN, GORDON ENTER-
PRISES LTD*
BUCHANAN LUMBER DIV OF   *p* 135
*See BUCHANAN, GORDON ENTER-
PRISES LTD*
BUCHANAN LUMBER SALES   *p* 908

See *BUCHANAN SALES INC*

BUCHANAN SALES INC *p 908*
1120 PREMIER WAY, THUNDER BAY, ON,
P7B 0A3
　SIC 5099

**BUCHANAN, GORDON ENTERPRISES
LTD** *p 84*
34 AIRPORT RD NW, EDMONTON, AB,
T5G 0W7
　(780) 424-2202　*SIC 2421*

**BUCHANAN, GORDON ENTERPRISES
LTD** *p 135*
1 RAILWAY AVE, HIGH PRAIRIE, AB, T0G
1E0
　(780) 523-4544　*SIC 2421*

BUCHNER MANUFACTURING INC *p 837*
30004 HWY 48, PEFFERLAW, ON, L0E 1N0
　(705) 437-1734　*SIC 3444*

BUCK CONSULTANTS LIMITED *p 979*
155 WELLINGTON ST W SUITE 3000,
TORONTO, ON, M5V 3L3
　(416) 865-0060　*SIC 8748*

BUCK OR TWO *p 1031*
See *EXTREME RETAIL CANADA INC*

BUCK'S AUTO PARTS *p 375*
See *SAMETCO AUTO INC*

BUCKET SHOP INC, THE *p 913*
24 GOVERNMENT RD S, TIMMINS, ON,
P4R 1N4
　(705) 531-2658　*SIC 5085*

BUCKEYE CANADA CO. *p 208*
7979 VANTAGE WAY, DELTA, BC, V4G 1A6
　SIC 2621

BUCKHAM TRANSPORT LIMITED *p 484*
HWY 28, BAILIEBORO, ON, K0L 1B0
　(705) 939-6311　*SIC 4213*

BUCKINGHAM CHRYSLER JEEP DODGEp
1103
See *7531877 CANADA LTEE*

BUCKINGHAM REALTY (WINDSOR) LTD p
1019
4573 TECUMSEH RD E, WINDSOR, ON,
N8W 1K6
　(519) 948-8171　*SIC 6531*

BUCKINGHAM TOYOTA *p 1103*
See *11084836 CANADA INC.*

**BUCKLAND CUSTOMS BROKERS LIM-
ITED** p
889
73 GAYLORD RD, ST THOMAS, ON, N5P
3R9
　(519) 631-4944　*SIC 4731*

BUCKLAND FREIGHT SERVICES *p 889*
See *BUCKLAND CUSTOMS BROKERS
LIMITED*

BUCKLER AQUATICS LIMITED *p 764*
562 MCNICOLL AVE, NORTH YORK, ON,
M2H 2E1
　(416) 499-0151　*SIC 7999*

BUCKLEY CARTAGE LIMITED *p 692*
1905 SHAWSON DR, MISSISSAUGA, ON,
L4W 1T9
　(905) 564-3211　*SIC 4213*

BUCKLEY INSURANCE BROKERS LTD p
755
247 MAIN ST S, NEWMARKET, ON, L3Y
3Z4
　(905) 836-7283　*SIC 6411*

BUCKLEY, W. K. INVESTMENTS LIMITEDp
692
5230 ORBITOR DR, MISSISSAUGA, ON,
L4W 5G7
　SIC 6719

BUCKWOLD WESTERN *p 1426*
See *BRIS EQUITIES LTD*

BUCKWOLD WESTERN LTD *p 1426*
3239 FAITHFULL AVE UNIT 70, SASKA-
TOON, SK, S7K 8H4
　(306) 652-1660　*SIC 5023*

BUDA JUICE CANADA *p 782*
See *2469447 ONTARIO LIMITED*

BUDD'S MAZDA *p 805*
1501 NORTH SERVICE RD W, OAKVILLE,
ON, L6M 2W2

---

　(905) 827-4242　*SIC 5511*

BUDD, STUART & SONS LIMITED *p 803*
2454 SOUTH SERVICE RD W, OAKVILLE,
ON, L6L 5M9
　(905) 845-3577　*SIC 5511*

BUDDS BMW OF OAKVILLE *p 803*
See *BUDDS HAMILTON LIMITED*

BUDDS CHEVROLET CADILLAC BUICK p
802
410 SOUTH SERVICE RD W, OAKVILLE,
ON, L6K 2H4
　(888) 992-2620　*SIC 5511*

BUDDS HAMILTON LIMITED *p 803*
2454 SOUTH SERVICE RD W, OAKVILLE,
ON, L6L 5M9
　(905) 845-3577　*SIC 5511*

BUDGET CAR & TRUCK RENTAL *p 338*
See *BUDGET RENT-A-CAR OF VICTORIA
LTD*

BUDGET CAR & TRUCK RENTALS *p 283*
See *GEORDY RENTALS INC*

**BUDGET CAR & TRUCK RENTALS OF OT-
TAWA LTD** p
817
851 INDUSTRIAL AVE, OTTAWA, ON, K1G
4L3
　(613) 739-4231　*SIC 7513*

BUDGET CAR AND TRUCK RENTAL *p 234*
See *DEVON TRANSPORT LTD*

BUDGET CAR SALES *p 324*
See *MONTCALM VENTURES LTD*

BUDGET LOCATION *p 1246*
See *LOCATION HEBERT 2000 LTEE*

BUDGET LOCATION D'AUTOS *p 1320*
See *GIRALDEAU INTER-AUTO INC*

BUDGET PROPANE (1998) *p 1366*
See *ENERGIE P38 INC*

BUDGET RENT A CAR *p 910*
See *R B D MARKETING INC*

BUDGET RENT A CAR *p 1440*
See *WHITEHORSE MOTORS LIMITED*

BUDGET RENT A CAR OF BC LTD *p 259*
7080 RIVER RD UNIT 203, RICHMOND,
BC, V6X 1X5
　(604) 678-1124　*SIC 7514*

BUDGET RENT-A-CAR *p 261*
See *PHELPS LEASING LTD*

BUDGET RENT-A-CAR OF CALGARY p 31
See *PRAIRIE VIEW HOLDINGS LTD*

**BUDGET RENT-A-CAR OF EDMONTON
LTD** *p 113*
4612 95 ST NW, EDMONTON, AB, T6E 5Z6
　(780) 448-2060　*SIC 7514*

BUDGET RENT-A-CAR OF VICTORIA LTDp
338
3657 HARRIET RD, VICTORIA, BC, V8Z
3T1
　(250) 953-5300　*SIC 7514*

BUDGETAUTO INC *p 583*
1 CONVAIR DR, ETOBICOKE, ON, M9W
6Z9
　(416) 213-8400　*SIC 7514*

**BUENA VISTA TELEVISION DISTRIBU-
TION** p
984
See *WALT DISNEY COMPANY (CANADA)
LTD, THE*

BUFFALO AIR EXPRESS *p 95*
See *BUFFALO PARCEL COURIER SER-
VICE LTD*

BUFFALO AIRWAYS LTD *p 435*
25 INDUSTRIAL DR, HAY RIVER, NT, X0E
0R6
　(867) 874-3333　*SIC 4512*

**BUFFALO AND FORT ERIE PUBLIC
BRIDGE COMPANY** *p 591*
100 QUEEN ST, FORT ERIE, ON, L2A 3S6
　(905) 871-1608　*SIC 4785*

BUFFALO CANOE CLUB *p 857*
4475 ERIE RD SUITE 1, RIDGEWAY, ON,
L0S 1N0
　(905) 894-2750　*SIC 7997*

BUFFALO COAL CORP *p 949*
65 QUEEN ST W, TORONTO, ON, M5H

2M5
　(416) 309-2957　*SIC 1221*

**BUFFALO INSPECTION SERVICES (2005)
INC** *p 108*
3867 ROPER RD NW, EDMONTON, AB,
T6B 3S5
　(780) 486-7344　*SIC 8734*

BUFFALO INTERNATIONAL *p 1216*
See *BUFFALO INTERNATIONAL INC*

BUFFALO INTERNATIONAL INC *p 1216*
400 RUE SAUVE O, MONTREAL, QC, H3L
1Z8
　(514) 388-3551　*SIC 2211*

BUFFALO LODGE *p 128*
See *NORALTA LODGE LTD*

BUFFALO MOUNTAIN LODGE *p 66*
See *CANADIAN ROCKY MOUNTAIN RE-
SORTS LTD*

**BUFFALO PARCEL COURIER SERVICE
LTD** *p 95*
11310 153 ST NW, EDMONTON, AB, T5M
1X6
　(780) 455-9283　*SIC 7389*

**BUFFALO RIVER MINI MART & GAS BAR
INC** *p 1405*
GD, DILLON, SK, S0M 0S0
　(306) 282-2177　*SIC 5541*

**BUFFALO TRAIL PUBLIC SCHOOLS RE-
GIONAL DIVISION NO. 28** p
171
1041 10A ST, WAINWRIGHT, AB, T9W 2R4
　(780) 842-6144　*SIC 8211*

BUFFET LA PLAZA *p 1193*
See *9191-1404 QUEBEC INC*

BUGABOOS EYEWEAR (U.S.A) INC *p 241*
758 HARBOURSIDE DR, NORTH VAN-
COUVER, BC, V7P 3R7
　(604) 924-2393　*SIC 5099*

BUGATTI INTERNATIONAL *p 1061*
See *GROUPE BUGATTI INC, LE*

BUGDEN, E L LIMITED *p 422*
199 RIVERSIDE DR, CORNER BROOK,
NL, A2H 4A1
　(709) 634-6177　*SIC 5141*

BUHLER EZEE-ON, INC *p 170*
5110 62 ST, VEGREVILLE, AB, T9C 1N6
　(780) 632-2126　*SIC 3523*

BUHLER FURNITURE INC *p 383*
700 KING EDWARD ST, WINNIPEG, MB,
R3H 1B4
　(204) 775-7799　*SIC 2511*

BUHLER INDUSTRIES INC *p 352*
301 MOUNTAIN ST S, MORDEN, MB, R6M
1X7
　(204) 822-4467　*SIC 3523*

BUHLER INDUSTRIES INC *p 390*
1260 CLARENCE AVE, WINNIPEG, MB,
R3T 1T2
　(204) 661-8711　*SIC 3523*

BUHLER INDUSTRIES INC *p 390*
1260 CLARENCE AVE SUITE 112, WIN-
NIPEG, MB, R3T 1T2
　(204) 661-8711　*SIC 3523*

BUHLER VERSATILE INC *p 390*
1260 CLARENCE AVE, WINNIPEG, MB,
R3T 1T2
　(204) 284-6100　*SIC 3523*

BUHLER VERSATILE INDUSTRIES *p 1426*
NORTH CORMAN INDUSTRIAL PARK,
SASKATOON, SK, S7K 0A1
　(306) 931-3000　*SIC 5033*

BUILD IT *p 737*
See *BUILD IT BY DESIGN (2014) INC*

BUILD IT BY DESIGN (2014) INC *p 737*
1580 TRINITY DR UNIT 12, MISSISSAUGA,
ON, L5T 1L6
　(905) 696-0468　*SIC 1542*

BUILD-A-MOLD, DIV OF *p 1022*
See *A.P. PLASMAN INC*

BUILDDIRECT.COM TECHNOLOGIES INCp
297
401 GEORGIA ST W SUITE 2200, VAN-
COUVER, BC, V6B 5A1
　(604) 662-8100　*SIC 5039*

BUILDERS FURNITURE LTD *p 367*
695 WASHINGTON AVE, WINNIPEG, MB,
R2K 1M4
　(204) 668-0783　*SIC 2541*

BUILDERS' SUPPLIES *p 738*
See *CATLEN HOLDINGS LIMITED*

**BUILDING & MAINTENANCE INDUSTRIES
(BMI)** *p 833*
See *4089171 CANADA INC*

BUILDING AUTOMATION *p 827*
See *SIEMENS CANADA LIMITED*

BUILDING DEPARTMENT *p 381*
See *WINNIPEG SCHOOL DIVISION*

**BUILDING INDUSTRY AND LAND DEVEL-
OPMENT ASSOCIATION** p
775
20 UPJOHN RD SUITE 100, NORTH YORK,
ON, M3B 2V9
　(416) 391-3445　*SIC 8611*

BUILDING PRODUCTS CANADA *p 1132*
See *CIE MATERIAUX DE CONSTRUCTION
BP CANADA, LA*

BUILDINGS DIVISION *p 256*
See *STUART OLSON BUILDINGS LTD*

BUILDMASTER *p 1304*
See *GROUPE CANAM INC*

BUILDSCALE, INC *p 639*
8 QUEEN ST N UNIT 1, KITCHENER, ON,
N2H 2G8
　(800) 530-3878　*SIC 7372*

**BUILT BY ENGINEERS CONSTRUCTION
INC** *p 532*
520 COLLIER MACMILLAN DR SUITE 8,
CAMBRIDGE, ON, N1R 6R6
　(519) 620-8886　*SIC 8711*

BUILT TO SELL INC *p 917*
2175 QUEEN ST E UNIT 302, TORONTO,
ON, M4E 1E5
　(416) 628-9754　*SIC 5734*

BUIST MOTOR PRODUCTS LTD *p 158*
4230 50 AVE, RIMBEY, AB, T0C 2J0
　(403) 843-2244　*SIC 5511*

BUL RIVER MINERAL CORPORATIONp 27
4723 1 ST SW SUITE 350, CALGARY, AB,
T2G 4Y8
　SIC 1081

BULA CANADA INC *p 1332*
4005 RUE SARTELON, SAINT-LAURENT,
QC, H4S 2A6
　(514) 270-4222　*SIC 5136*

BULK BARN FOODS LIMITED *p 480*
320 DON HILLOCK DR, AURORA, ON, L4G
0G9
　(905) 726-5000　*SIC 5141*

BULK CARRIERS (P.E.I) LIMITED *p 1041*
779 BANNOCKBURN RD, CORNWALL, PE,
C0A 1H0
　(902) 675-2600　*SIC 4213*

**BULK PLUS LOGISTICS LIMITED PART-
NERSHIP** p
713
452 SOUTHDOWN RD, MISSISSAUGA,
ON, L5J 2Y4
　(905) 403-7854　*SIC 4731*

BULK SISTERS *p 1160*
See *IMPORTATIONS & DISTRIBUTIONS
B.H. INC*

BULK TRANSFER SYSTEMS INC *p 642*
11339 ALBION VAUGHAN RD, KLEIN-
BURG, ON, L0J 1C0
　(905) 893-2626　*SIC 4212*

BULKLEY VALLEY DISTRICT HOSPITAL p
269
See *BULKLEY VALLEY HEALTH COUNCIL*

BULKLEY VALLEY HEALTH COUNCIL p
269
3950 8 AVE, SMITHERS, BC, V0J 2N0
　(250) 847-2611　*SIC 8062*

BULL DOG *p 1065*
See *GRAYMONT (QC) INC*

BULL MOOSE TUBE LIMITED *p 529*
2170 QUEENSWAY DR, BURLINGTON,
ON, L7R 3T1
　(905) 637-8261　*SIC 3312*

BULL, HOUSSER & TUPPER LLP *p 297*
510 GEORGIA ST W SUITE 1800, VAN-COUVER, BC, V6B 0M3
(604) 687-6575   *SIC 8111*

BULLDOG BAG LTD *p 253*
13631 VULCAN WAY, RICHMOND, BC, V6V 1K4
(604) 273-8021   *SIC 2674*

BULLETIN *p 1327*
See TRICOT MONDIAL INC

BULLETPROOF SOLUTIONS INC *p 402*
25 ALISON BLVD, FREDERICTON, NB, E3C 2N5
(506) 452-8558   *SIC 6211*

BULLFROG POWER INC *p 979*
366 ADELAIDE ST W SUITE 701, TORONTO, ON, M5V 1R9
(416) 360-3464   *SIC 4911*

BULLYS SPORT & ENTERTAINMENT CEN-TRE *p*
142
See ROCKY MOUNTAIN TURF CLUB INC

BULOVA WATCH COMPANY LIMITED *p 864*
39 CASEBRIDGE CRT, SCARBOROUGH, ON, M1B 5N4
(416) 751-7151   *SIC 5094*

BULYEA COMMUNITY CO-OPERATIVE AS-SOCIATION LIMITED, THE *p*
1404
GD, BULYEA, SK, S0G 0L0
(306) 725-4911   *SIC 5171*

BUMPER TO BUMPER *p 80*
See 370071 ALBERTA LTD

BUMPER TO BUMPER *p 98*
See 970426 ALBERTA LTD

BUMPER TO BUMPER *p 435*
See TDC CONTRACTING LTD

BUNCHES FLOWER COMPANY *p 117*
7108 109 ST NW, EDMONTON, AB, T6G 1B8
(780) 447-5359   *SIC 5992*

BUNGE CANADA *p 803*
See BUNGE CANADA HOLDINGS 1 ULC

BUNGE CANADA HOLDINGS 1 ULC *p 803*
2190 SOUTH SERVICE RD W, OAKVILLE, ON, L6L 5N1
(905) 825-7900   *SIC 2079*

BUNGE CANADA HOLDINGS 1 ULC *p 803*
2190 SOUTH SERVICE RD W, OAKVILLE, ON, L6L 5N1
(905) 825-7900   *SIC 6712*

BUNGE DU CANADA LTEE *p 1258*
300 RUE DALHOUSIE, QUEBEC, QC, G1K 8M8
(418) 692-3761   *SIC 3523*

BUNGE GRAIN DU CANADA INC *p 1310*
6120 RUE DES SEIGNEURS E, SAINT-HYACINTHE, QC, J2R 1Z9
SIC 5153

BUNGE GRAIN DU CANADA INC *p 1359*
60 RUE SAINT-SIMON, SAINTE-MADELEINE, QC, J0H 1S0
SIC 5153

BUNGE OF CANADA LTD *p 610*
515 VICTORIA AVE N, HAMILTON, ON, L8L 8G7
(905) 527-9121   *SIC 2076*

BUNGE OF CANADA LTD *p 803*
2190 SOUTH SERVICE RD W, OAKVILLE, ON, L6L 5N1
(905) 825-7900   *SIC 2079*

BUNN-O-MATIC CORPORATION OF CANADA *p 480*
280 INDUSTRIAL PKY S, AURORA, ON, L4G 3T9
(905) 841-2866   *SIC 3589*

BUNNY'S FOOD SERVICE LIMITED *p 563*
1540 HIGHWAY 2, COURTICE, ON, L1E 2R6
(905) 434-2444   *SIC 5962*

BUNTAIN INSURANCE AGENCIES LTD *p*
324
3707 10TH AVE W, VANCOUVER, BC, V6R 2G5

(604) 224-2373   *SIC 6411*

BUNTY'S BUBBLE BATH *p 373*
See 2792924 MANITOBA LTD

BUNZL CANADA INC *p 527*
3150 HARVESTER RD SUITE 100, BURLINGTON, ON, L7N 3W8
(289) 289-1200   *SIC 5113*

BUNZL CANADA INC *p 537*
400 JAMIESON PKY, CAMBRIDGE, ON, N3C 4N3
(519) 651-2233   *SIC 5084*

BUNZL DISTRIBUTION *p 527*
See BUNZL CANADA INC

BUPONT MOTORS INC *p 913*
1180 RIVERSIDE DR, TIMMINS, ON, P4R 1A2
(705) 268-2226   *SIC 5511*

BUR-CYCLE *p 1300*
See GRENIER POPULAIRE DES BASSES LAURENTIDES

BURDIFILEK INC *p 977*
183 BATHURST ST SUITE 300, TORONTO, ON, M5T 2R7
(416) 703-4334   *SIC 7389*

BUREAU ADMINISTRATIF *p 1253*
See BOIS D'OEUVRE CEDRICO INC

BUREAU AIDE JURIDIQUE *p 1142*
See CENTRE COMMUNAUTAIRE JU-RIDIQUE DE LA RIVE-SUD

BUREAU D'AFFAIRE D'ANJOU *p 1048*
See ENERGIR INC

BUREAU D'EVALUATION DE QUEBEC INC *p 1261*
275 RUE METIVIER BUREAU 170, QUE-BEC, QC, G1M 3X8
(418) 871-6777   *SIC 7389*

BUREAU DE NORMALISATION DU QUE-BEC (BNQ) *p*
1266
See CENTRE DE RECHERCHE INDUS-TRIELLE DU QUEBEC

BUREAU DE POSTES DE BELOEIL *p 1056*
See CANADA POST CORPORATION

BUREAU DES INTERVIEWEURS PROFES-SIONNELS (B.I.P.) (1988) INC *p*
1193
2021 AV UNION BUREAU 1221, MON-TREAL, QC, H3A 2S9
(514) 288-1980   *SIC 8732*

BUREAU EN GROS *p 854*
See STAPLES CANADA ULC

BUREAU VERITAS - INSPECTORATE *p*
1239
See MANASTE INSPECTION QUALITY QUANTITY (CANADA) INC

BUREAU VERITAS CANADA (2019) INC *p*
21
2021 41 AVE NE, CALGARY, AB, T2E 6P2
(403) 291-3077   *SIC 8734*

BUREAU VERITAS CANADA (2019) INC *p*
108
6744 50 ST NW, EDMONTON, AB, T6B 3M9
(780) 378-8500   *SIC 8734*

BUREAU VERITAS CANADA (2019) INC *p*
188
4606 CANADA WAY, BURNABY, BC, V5G 1K5
(604) 734-7276   *SIC 8734*

BUREAU VERITAS CANADA (2019) INC *p*
440
200 BLUEWATER RD SUITE 201, BED-FORD, NS, B4B 1G9
(902) 420-0203   *SIC 8731*

BUREAU VERITAS CANADA (2019) INC *p*
720
1919 MINNESOTA CRT SUITE 500, MIS-SISSAUGA, ON, L5N 0C9
(905) 288-2150   *SIC 8734*

BUREAU VERITAS CANADA (2019) INC *p*
1338
889 MONTEE DE LIESSE, SAINT-LAURENT, QC, H4T 1P5
(514) 448-9001   *SIC 8748*

BUREAU VERITAS COMMODITIES

CANADA LTD *p 323*
9050 SHAUGHNESSY ST, VANCOUVER, BC, V6P 6E5
(604) 253-3158   *SIC 8734*

BUREAU VETERINAIRE DE LA RIVWE SUD *p 1267*
See HOPITAL VETERINAIRE DAUBIGNY

BUREAUTIQUE COTE-SUD INC *p 1159*
49 RUE SAINT-JEAN-BAPTISTE E, MONT-MAGNY, QC, G5V 1J6
(418) 248-4949   *SIC 5112*

BURGEONVEST BICK SECURITIES LIM-ITED *p*
612
21 KING ST W SUITE 1100, HAMILTON, ON, L8P 4W7
(905) 528-6505   *SIC 6211*

BURGER KING *p 509*
See MILLS GROUP INC, THE

BURGER KING *p 579*
See REDBERRY FRANCHISING CORP

BURGER KING *p 1356*
See 9070-9734 QUEBEC INC

BURGESS TRANSPORTATION SERVICES INC *p 411*
20 SMITH ST, PETITCODIAC, NB, E4Z 4W1
(506) 756-2250   *SIC 4213*

BURGESS, JOHN WILLIAM ENTERPRISES INC *p 703*
799 DUNDAS ST E, MISSISSAUGA, ON, L4Y 2B7
(905) 566-4982   *SIC 5812*

BURGUNDY ASSET MANAGEMENT LTD *p*
960
181 BAY ST SUITE 4510, TORONTO, ON, M5J 2T3
(416) 869-3222   *SIC 6211*

BURGUNDY ASSET MANAGEMENT LTD *p*
1194
1501 AV MCGILL COLLEGE BUREAU 2090, MONTREAL, QC, H3A 3M8
(514) 844-8091   *SIC 8741*

BURKE MEDIA *p 86*
See MCCALLUM PRINTING GROUP INC

BURKE'S AUTO SALES *p 463*
2757 WESTVILLE RD, NEW GLASGOW, NS, B2H 5C6
(902) 755-2522   *SIC 5511*

BURKE'S RESTORATION *p 755*
See BURKE'S RESTORATION INC

BURKE'S RESTORATION INC *p 755*
17705 LESLIE ST UNIT 7, NEWMARKET, ON, L3Y 8C6
(905) 895-2456   *SIC 1521*

BURKE'S RESTORATION INC *p 792*
98 MILVAN DR, NORTH YORK, ON, M9L 1Z6
(416) 744-2456   *SIC 1521*

BURKERT CONTROMATIC INC *p 521*
5002 SOUTH SERVICE RD, BURLINGTON, ON, L7L 5Y7
(905) 632-3033   *SIC 5085*

BURKERT FLUID CONTROL SYSTEMS *p*
521
See BURKERT CONTROMATIC INC

BURLINGTON ACCOUNTING *p 527*
See BDO CANADA LLP

BURLINGTON AUTOMATION CORPORA-TION *p*
566
63 INNOVATION DR, DUNDAS, ON, L9H 7L8
(905) 689-7771   *SIC 3541*

BURLINGTON BUISNESS FORMS *p 530*
See BURLINGTON BUSINESS FORMS INC

BURLINGTON BUSINESS FORMS INC *p*
530
2289 FAIRVIEW ST UNIT 208, BURLING-TON, ON, L7R 2E3
(905) 632-4611   *SIC 8743*

BURLINGTON CONVENTION CENTRE *p*
521
1120 BURLOAK DR, BURLINGTON, ON,

L7L 6P8
(905) 319-0319   *SIC 7389*

BURLINGTON GOLF AND COUNTRY CLUB LIMITED *p 531*
422 NORTH SHORE BLVD E, BURLING-TON, ON, L7T 1W9
(905) 634-7726   *SIC 7997*

BURLINGTON HYDRO ELECTRIC INC *p*
530
1340 BRANT ST, BURLINGTON, ON, L7R 3Z7
(905) 332-1851   *SIC 4911*

BURLINGTON HYDRO INC *p 530*
1340 BRANT ST, BURLINGTON, ON, L7R 3Z7
(905) 332-1851   *SIC 4911*

BURLINGTON HYUNDAI *p 529*
See 2853167 CANADA INC

BURLINGTON LAIDLAW *p 526*
See FIRSTCANADA ULC

BURLINGTON MAZDA *p 527*
805 WALKER'S LINE, BURLINGTON, ON, L7N 2G1
(905) 333-1790   *SIC 5511*

BURLINGTON MAZDA *p 528*
See TAGGEL AUTOMOBILE INC

BURLINGTON MERCHANDISING & FIX-TURES INC *p*
527
3100 HARVESTER RD UNIT 8, BURLING-TON, ON, L7N 3W8
(905) 332-6652   *SIC 7389*

BURLINGTON POST, THE *p 523*
See METROLAND MEDIA GROUP LTD

BURLINGTON RESOURCES *p 82*
See CONOCOPHILLIPS WESTERN CANADA PARTNERSHIP

BURLINGTON TOYOTA *p 528*
See 1028918 ONTARIO INC

BURLINGTON-FAIRVIEW NISSAN LTD *p*
521
4111 NORTH SERVICE RD, BURLINGTON, ON, L7L 4X6
(905) 681-2162   *SIC 5521*

BURLOAK TOOL & DIE LTD *p 526*
3121 MAINWAY, BURLINGTON, ON, L7M 1A4
(905) 331-6838   *SIC 8711*

BURLODGE CANADA LTD *p 716*
3400 RIDGEWAY DR UNIT 14, MISSIS-SAUGA, ON, L5L 0A2
(905) 790-1881   *SIC 5141*

BURMAC MANAGEMENT LIMITED *p 468*
710 PRINCE ST, TRURO, NS, B2N 1G6
SIC 6512

BURMAN & FELLOWS GROUP INC *p 678*
170 TRAVAIL RD, MARKHAM, ON, L3S 3J1
(905) 472-1056   *SIC 1731*

BURMAN UNIVERSITY *p 138*
6730 UNIVERSITY DR ROOM A104, LA-COMBE, AB, T4L 2E5
(403) 782-3381   *SIC 8221*

BURN BRAE FARMS *p 1354*
See FERME ST-ZOTIQUE LTEE

BURNABY HOSPITAL *p 189*
See FRASER HEALTH AUTHORITY

BURNABY LAKE GREENHOUSES LTD *p*
281
17250 80 AVE, SURREY, BC, V4N 6J6
(604) 576-2088   *SIC 0181*

BURNABY LAKE GREENHOUSES LTD *p*
281
17250 80 AVE, SURREY, BC, V4N 6J6
(604) 576-2088   *SIC 5083*

BURNABY MOUNTAIN SECONDARY SCHOOL *p 180*
See BURNABY SCHOOL BOARD DIS-TRICT 41

BURNABY NORTH SECONDARY SCHOOL *p 184*
See BURNABY SCHOOL BOARD DIS-TRICT 41

BURNABY PARKS & RECREATION *p 190*
See CITY OF BURNABY

BURNABY PUBLIC LIBRARY p 189
6100 WILLINGDON AVE, BURNABY, BC,
V5H 4N5
(604) 436-5400 SIC 8231

BURNABY SCHOOL BOARD DISTRICT 41
p 180
8800 EASTLAKE DR, BURNABY, BC, V3J
7X5
(604) 296-6870 SIC 8211

BURNABY SCHOOL BOARD DISTRICT 41
p 181
7777 18TH ST, BURNABY, BC, V3N 5E5
(604) 296-6885 SIC 8211

BURNABY SCHOOL BOARD DISTRICT 41
p 181
8580 16TH AVE, BURNABY, BC, V3N 1S6
(604) 296-6890 SIC 8211

BURNABY SCHOOL BOARD DISTRICT 41
p 184
4600 PARKER ST, BURNABY, BC, V5C 3E2
(604) 296-6865 SIC 8211

BURNABY SCHOOL BOARD DISTRICT 41
p 184
751 HAMMARSKJOLD DR RM 115, BURN-
ABY, BC, V5B 4A1
SIC 8211

BURNABY SCHOOL BOARD DISTRICT 41
p 188
5325 KINCAID ST, BURNABY, BC, V5G
1W2
(604) 296-6900 SIC 8211

BURNABY SCHOOL BOARD DISTRICT 41
p 189
4404 SARDIS ST, BURNABY, BC, V5H 1K7
SIC 8211

BURNABY SCHOOL BOARD DISTRICT 41
p 189
6060 MARLBOROUGH AVE, BURNABY,
BC, V5H 3L7
(604) 296-9021 SIC 8211

BURNABY SCHOOL BOARD DISTRICT 41
p 192
5455 RUMBLE ST, BURNABY, BC, V5J 2B7
(604) 296-6880 SIC 8211

BURNABY SOUTH SECONDARY SCHOOL
p 192
See BURNABY SCHOOL BOARD DIS-
TRICT 41

BURNAC PRODUCE p 587
See PRO PAK PACKAGING LIMITED

BURNAC PRODUCE LIMITED p 1027
80 ZENWAY BLVD, WOODBRIDGE, ON,
L4H 3H1
(905) 856-9064 SIC 5148

BURNBRAE FARMS LIMITED p 663
3356 COUNTY ROAD 27, LYN, ON, K0E
1M0
(613) 345-5651 SIC 5144

BURNCO MANUFACTURING INC p 549
40 CITRON CRT, CONCORD, ON, L4K 2P5
(905) 761-6155 SIC 3569

BURNCO ROCK PRODUCTS LTD p 34
155 GLENDEER CIR SE SUITE 200, CAL-
GARY, AB, T2H 2S8
(403) 255-2600 SIC 3273

BURNDY CANADA INC p 844
870 BROCK RD, PICKERING, ON, L1W 1Z8
(905) 752-5400 SIC 3643

BURNETT, LEO COMPANY LTD p 928
175 BLOOR ST E NORTH TOWER SUITE
1200, TORONTO, ON, M4W 3R9
(416) 925-5997 SIC 7311

BURNSIDE FLOORING DIV OF p 446
See INSTALL-A-FLOR LIMITED

BURNSTEIN, DR. & ASSOCIATES p 800
1484 CORNWALL RD, OAKVILLE, ON, L6J
7W5
(905) 844-3240 SIC 8299

BURO & CIE p 1351
See PAPETERIE ST-REMI INC

BURO DESIGN INTERNATIONAL p 1343
See BURO DESIGN INTERNATIONAL A.Q.
INC

BURO DESIGN INTERNATIONAL A.Q. INC

p 1343
5715 BOUL METROPOLITAIN E, SAINT-
LEONARD, QC, H1P 1X3
(514) 955-6644 SIC 2521

BURO DESIGN INTERNATIONAL A.Q. INC
p 1347
125 RUE QUINTAL, SAINT-LIN-
LAURENTIDES, QC, J5M 2S8
(450) 439-8554 SIC 2521

BUROPRO CITATION INC p 1397
505 BOUL JUTRAS E, VICTORIAVILLE,
QC, G6P 7H4
(819) 752-7777 SIC 5112

BURQUITLAM CARE SOCIETY p 200
560 SYDNEY AVE, COQUITLAM, BC, V3K
6A4
SIC 8051

BURQUITLAM LIONS CARE CENTRE p 200
See BURQUITLAM CARE SOCIETY

BURRARD ACURA AUTO PLAZA p 320
See BURRARD IMPORTS LTD

BURRARD IMPORTS LTD p 320
2430 BURRARD ST, VANCOUVER, BC,
V6J 5L3
(604) 736-8890 SIC 5511

BURRELL OVERHEAD DOOR CO. LIMITED
p 549
1853 HIGHWAY 7, CONCORD, ON, L4K
1V4
(905) 669-1711 SIC 6712

BURRITO BOYZ DISTRIBUTION INC p 573
21 JUTLAND RD, ETOBICOKE, ON, M8Z
2G6
(416) 251-8536 SIC 5149

BURRITT BROS. CARPET p 285
See BEATTY FLOORS LTD

**BURROWES COURTIERS
D'ASSURANCES** p 1168
2647 PLACE CHASSE, MONTREAL, QC,
H1Y 2C3
(514) 522-2661 SIC 6411

BURROWES INSURANCE BROKERS p
1068
See WILLIAM E. BURROWES INC

BURROWING OWL ESTATE WINERY p 242
See BURROWING OWL VINEYARDS LTD

BURROWING OWL VINEYARDS LTD p 242
100 BURROWING OWL PL, OLIVER, BC,
V0H 1T0
(250) 498-0620 SIC 2084

BURROWS & KEEWATIN SAFEWAY p 370
See SOBEYS WEST INC

BURSTALL NGL STORAGE L.P. p 45
222 3 AVE SW SUITE 900, CALGARY, AB,
T2P 0B4
(403) 296-0140 SIC 4922

BUS GARAGE p 217
See SCHOOL DISTRICT 73 (KAM-
LOOPS/THOMPSON)

BUSHMASTER HUNTING & FISHING p 993
See EVERLITE LUGGAGE MANUFACTUR-
ING LIMITED

BUSHTUKAH INC p 828
203 RICHMOND RD, OTTAWA, ON, K1Z
6W4
SIC 5941

BUSHWAKKER BREWING COMPANY LTD
p 1420
2206 DEWDNEY AVE, REGINA, SK, S4R
1H3
(306) 359-7276 SIC 2082

BUSINESS FURNISHINGS (1996) LTD p 383
1741 WELLINGTON AVE, WINNIPEG, MB,
R3H 0G1
(204) 489-4191 SIC 5112

BUSINESS IMPROVEMENT GROUP INC p
605
400 MICHENER RD SUITE 3, GUELPH,
ON, N1K 1E4
(519) 823-1110 SIC 8748

BUSINESS IN VANCOUVER p 288
See B I V PUBLICATIONS LTD

BUSINESS SOLUTIONS DIVISION p 928
See CANON CANADA INC

BUSINESS SYSTEMS p 736
See 2213802 ONTARIO INC

BUSINESS TRAVEL NETWORK INC p 928
1027 YONGE ST SUITE 103, TORONTO,
ON, M4W 2K9
(416) 924-6000 SIC 4724

BUSKRO INTERNATIONAL LTD p 844
1738 ORANGEBROOK CRT UNIT 1, PICK-
ERING, ON, L1W 3G8
(905) 839-6018 SIC 3577

BUSREL INC p 1325
200 RUE DESLAURIERS, SAINT-
LAURENT, QC, H4N 1V8
(514) 336-0000 SIC 7311

BUSTARD BROTHERS LIMITED p 1008
575 DAVENPORT RD, WATERLOO, ON,
N2L 5Z3
(519) 884-5888 SIC 5511

BUSTARD CHRYSLER p 1008
See BUSTARD BROTHERS LIMITED

BUSTERS TOWING 1987 LTD p 289
104 1ST AVE E, VANCOUVER, BC, V5T
1A4
(604) 685-8181 SIC 7549

**BUSY BEE EXPRESS LINES INCORPO-
RATED** p
27
4127 16 ST SE, CALGARY, AB, T2G 3R9
(403) 233-2353 SIC 4731

BUSY BEE MACHINE TOOLS LTD p 549
130 GREAT GULF DR, CONCORD, ON,
L4K 5W1
(905) 738-5115 SIC 5251

BUSY-BEE SANITARY SUPPLIES INC p
113
4004 97 ST NW UNIT 24, EDMONTON, AB,
T6E 6N1
(780) 462-0075 SIC 5087

BUTCHART GARDENS LTD, THE p 180
800 BENVENUTO AVE, BRENTWOOD
BAY, BC, V8M 1J8
(250) 652-5256 SIC 8422

BUTCHER BLOCK, THE p 204
See LAWRENCE MEAT PACKING CO. LTD

BUTCHER BOYS ENTERPRISES LTD p 331
4803 PLEASANT VALLEY RD, VERNON,
BC, V1B 3L7
(250) 542-2968 SIC 5411

BUTCHER BOYS FOOD MARKET p 331
See BUTCHER BOYS ENTERPRISES LTD

**BUTCHER ENGINEERING ENTERPRISES
LIMITED, THE** p 621
17 UNDERWOOD RD, INGERSOLL, ON,
N5C 3K1
(519) 425-0999 SIC 7538

**BUTCHER ENGINEERING ENTERPRISES
LIMITED, THE** p 1018
2755 LAUZON PKY, WINDSOR, ON, N8T
3H5
(519) 944-9200 SIC 4783

BUTCHER ENTERPRISES p 1018
See BUTCHER ENGINEERING ENTER-
PRISES LIMITED, THE

BUTCHER SHOPPE, THE p 573
See 573349 ONTARIO LIMITED

BUTLER AUTO & RV CENTRE p 216
See BUTLER AUTO SALES LTD

BUTLER AUTO SALES LTD p 216
142 TRANQUILLE RD, KAMLOOPS, BC,
V2B 3G1
(250) 554-2518 SIC 5511

BUTLER BROTHERS SUPPLIES LTD p 267
1851 KEATING CROSS RD UNIT 101,
SAANICHTON, BC, V8M 1W9
(250) 652-1680 SIC 3273

BUTLER BUILDINGS CANADA p 492
5 HARVEST CRES, BELLEVILLE, ON, K8P
4M2
SIC 1541

BUTLER BYERS INSURANCE LTD p 1426
301 4TH AVE N, SASKATOON, SK, S7K 2L8
(306) 653-2233 SIC 6411

**BUTLER CHEVROLET PONTIAC BUICK
CADILLAC LTD** p 837

1370 PEMBROKE ST W, PEMBROKE, ON,
K8A 7M3
(613) 735-3147 SIC 5511

**BUTLER RIDGE ENERGY SERVICES
(2011) LTD** p 216
8908 CLARKE AVE, HUDSON'S HOPE, BC,
V0C 1V0
(250) 783-2363 SIC 5211

BUTORAC, DON LIMITED p 532
90 PINEBUSH RD, CAMBRIDGE, ON, N1R
8J8
(519) 623-3360 SIC 5531

BUTTCON HOLDINGS LIMITED p 549
8000 JANE ST SUITE 401, CONCORD, ON,
L4K 5B8
(905) 907-4242 SIC 1541

BUTTCON LIMITED p 549
8000 JANE ST, CONCORD, ON, L4K 5B8
(905) 907-4242 SIC 1541

BUTTE COLONY p 1404
GD, BRACKEN, SK, S0N 0G0
(306) 298-4445 SIC 8741

BUTTERBALL p 617
See EXCELDOR FOODS LTD

BUTTERFLY p 1244
See LAUZON - PLANCHERS DE BOIS EX-
CLUSIFS INC

BUY & SELL PRESS p 184
See B A S P BUY & SELL PRESS LTD, THE

BUY SELL TRADE p 895
945 ERIE ST, STRATFORD, ON, N5A 6S4
(519) 271-6824 SIC 5013

BUY-LOW FOODS LTD p 14
7100 44 ST SE, CALGARY, AB, T2C 2V7
(403) 236-6300 SIC 5411

BUY-LOW FOODS LTD p 281
19580 TELEGRAPH TRAIL, SURREY, BC,
V4N 4H1
(604) 888-1121 SIC 5411

BUYATAB ONLINE INC p 297
B1 788 BEATTY ST, VANCOUVER, BC, V6B
2M1
(604) 678-3275 SIC 5961

BUYERS GROUP OF MISSISSAUGA INC p
667
205 TORBAY RD SUITE 12, MARKHAM,
ON, L3R 3W4
(905) 948-1911 SIC 5072

BUYNFLY FOOD LIMITED p 425
208 HUMBER AVE, LABRADOR CITY, NL,
A2V 1K9
(709) 944-4003 SIC 5411

BV LABS p 720
See BUREAU VERITAS CANADA (2019)
INC

BVL CONSTRUCTION SERVICES INC p
171
GD, WABASCA, AB, T0G 2K0
SIC 3533

BW TECHNOLOGIES BY HONEYWELL p
27
See BW TECHNOLOGIES PARTNERSHIP

BW TECHNOLOGIES LTD p 10
2840 2 AVE SE, CALGARY, AB, T2A 7X9
(403) 248-9226 SIC 3829

BW TECHNOLOGIES PARTNERSHIP p 27
4411 6 ST SE SUITE 110, CALGARY, AB,
T2G 4E8
(403) 248-9226 SIC 3829

BW VISTA RAILINGS p 231
See VISTA RAILING SYSTEMS INC

BWAY PACKAGING CANADA p 804
See ROPAK CANADA INC

BWI p 932
See BASSETT & WALKER INTERNA-
TIONAL INC

BWIRELESS COMMUNICATIONS INC p 297
555 ROBSON ST UNIT 1, VANCOUVER,
BC, V6B 1A6
(604) 689-8488 SIC 5999

BWM INDUSTRIAL AUTOMATION DIV p
486
See BARRIE WELDING & MACHINE (1974)
LIMITED

BWXT CANADA LTD p 532
581 CORONATION BLVD, CAMBRIDGE, ON, N1R 3E9
(519) 621-2130   SIC 3621

BWXT CANADA LTD p 532
581 CORONATION BLVD, CAMBRIDGE, ON, N1R 5V3
(519) 621-2130   SIC 3621

BWXT ISOTOPE TECHNOLOGIES p 532
See BWXT ITG CANADA, INC

BWXT ITG CANADA, INC p 532
581 CORONATION BLVD, CAMBRIDGE, ON, N1R 5V3
(613) 592-3400   SIC 2834

BWXT ITG CANADA, INC p 832
447 MARCH RD, OTTAWA, ON, K2K 1X8
(613) 592-3400   SIC 2834

BWXT NUCLEAR ENERGY CANADA INC p 840
1160 MONAGHAN RD, PETERBOROUGH, ON, K9J 0A8
(855) 696-9588   SIC 2819

BYBLOS BAKERY LTD p 21
2479 23 ST NE, CALGARY, AB, T2E 8J8
(403) 250-3711   SIC 2051

BYEXPRESS CORPORATION p 826
2471 HOLLY LN, OTTAWA, ON, K1V 7P2
(613) 739-3000   SIC 4731

BYLANDS NURSERIES LTD p 341
1600 BYLAND RD, WEST KELOWNA, BC, V1Z 1H6
(250) 769-7272   SIC 0181

BYLES, A. S. SUPPLIES LIMITED p 393
1711 KENASTON BLVD, WINNIPEG, MB, R3Y 1V5
(204) 269-9630   SIC 5311

BYNG GROUP LTD, THE p 549
511 EDGELEY BLVD UNIT 2, CONCORD, ON, L4K 4G4
(905) 660-5454   SIC 7389

BYNG PLASTERING AND TILE LIMITED p 549
511 EDGELEY BLVD UNIT 2, CONCORD, ON, L4K 4G4
(905) 660-5454   SIC 1742

BYRNE CREEK SECONDARY SCHOOL p 181
See BURNABY SCHOOL BOARD DISTRICT 41

BYTEK AUTOMOBILES INC p 817
1325 ST. LAURENT BLVD, OTTAWA, ON, K1G 0Z7
(613) 745-6885   SIC 5511

BYTOWN CATERING p 596
See STUDY BREAK LIMITED

BYTOWN INVESTMENTS p 833
See 595799 ONTARIO LTD

BYTOWN LUMBER INC p 597
1740 QUEENSDALE AVE, GLOUCESTER, ON, K1T 1J6
(613) 733-9303   SIC 5211

BYZ CONSTRUCTION INC p 147
2196 BRIER PARK PL NW, MEDICINE HAT, AB, T1C 1S6
SIC 1794

C

(C.C.A.) COMMERCIAL CREDIT ADJUSTERS LTD p 374
300-317 DONALD ST, WINNIPEG, MB, R3B 2H6
(204) 958-5850   SIC 7322

?COLE DUSHCESS PARK SECONDARE p 249
See BOARD OF EDUCATION OF SCHOOL DISTRICT NO. 57 (PRINCE GEORGE), THE

?COLE SECONDAIRE LES SEIGNEURIES p 1350
See COMMISSION SCOLAIRE DE LA RIVERAINE

C & B DISPLAY PACKAGING INC p 713
2560 SOUTH SHERIDAN WAY, MISSISSAUGA, ON, L5J 2M4

(905) 823-7770   SIC 2653

C & C INSURANCE CONSULTANTS LTD p 643
22425 JEFFERIES RD UNIT 6, KOMOKA, ON, N0L 1R0
(519) 657-1446   SIC 6411

C & C MOTOR SALES LTD p 1015
1705 DUNDAS ST W, WHITBY, ON, L1P 1Y9
(905) 430-6666   SIC 5511

C & D CLEANING & SECURITY SERVICES LIMITED p 458
106 CHAIN LAKE DR UNIT 2A, HALIFAX, NS, B3S 1A8
(902) 450-5654   SIC 7349

C & E EXPRESS INC p 512
1B CONESTOGA DR SUITE 101, BRAMPTON, ON, L6Z 4N5
(905) 495-7934   SIC 4789

C & G VILLAGE INN p 353
2193 HWY 59, NIVERVILLE, MB, R0A 1E0
(204) 388-4283   SIC 5541

C & K HAPPY FARMS LTD p 227
22950 16 AVE, LANGLEY, BC, V2Z 1K7
(604) 533-8307   SIC 0191

C & M p 1181
See C & M TEXTILES INC

C & M SEEDS p 836
See C & M SEEDS MANUFACTURING INC

C & M SEEDS MANUFACTURING INC p 836
6180 5TH LINE RR 3, PALMERSTON, N0G 2P0
(519) 343-2126   SIC 5191

C & M TEXTILES INC p 1181
7500 RUE SAINT-HUBERT, MONTREAL, QC, H2R 2N6
(514) 272-0247   SIC 5949

C & R VENTURES INC p 388
1857 GRANT AVE SUITE A, WINNIPEG, MB, R3N 1Z2
(204) 489-1086   SIC 5461

C & S AUTO PARTS LIMITED p 873
151 NUGGET AVE, SCARBOROUGH, ON, M1S 3B1
(416) 754-8500   SIC 5013

C & T RENTALS & SALES LTD p 377
116 WHEATFIELD RD, WINNIPEG, MB, R3C 2E6
(204) 594-7368   SIC 5082

C & V FARMS p 476
See ONTARIO POTATO DIST. (ALLISTON) INC. 1991

C A PIPPY PARK COMMISSION p 429
460 ALLANDALE RD, ST. JOHN'S, NL, A1B 4E8
(709) 753-7110   SIC 7992

C A R S p 153
See CENTRAL ALBERTA RESIDENCE SOCIETY

C A S COMMUNICATIONS SERVICES LIMITED p 865
503 CENTENNIAL RD N, SCARBOROUGH, ON, M1C 2A5
(416) 724-8333   SIC 7389

C AND C ENTERPRISES p 564
See 1329481 ONTARIO INC

C B ENGINEERING LTD p 27
5040 12A ST SE, CALGARY, AB, T2G 5K9
(403) 259-6220   SIC 5084

C C A C p 859
See SARNIA/LAMBTON COMMUNITY CARE ACCESS CENTRE

C D I MOBILIER DE BUREAU p 1187
See CIME DECOR INC

C DESIGN p 1178
See CABRELLI INC

C E C I p 1168
See CENTRE D'ETUDE ET DE COOPERATION INTERNATIONALE

C E P LOCAL 30 p 416
1216 SAND COVE RD UNIT 15, SAINT JOHN, NB, E2M 5V8
(506) 635-5786   SIC 8631

C F & R SERVICES INC p 844
1920 CLEMENTS RD, PICKERING, ON, L1W 3V6
(905) 426-3891   SIC 8743

C F I B p 773
See CANADIAN FEDERATION OF INDEPENDENT BUSINESS

C F L p 942
See CANADIAN FOOTBALL LEAGUE

C F V S A R p 174
See CENTRAL FRASER VALLEY SEARCH & RESCUE SOCIETY

C G U INSURANCE p 43
See AVIVA INSURANCE COMPANY OF CANADA

C H A p 1270
See HOPITAL DU ST-SACREMENT DU CENTRE HOSPITALIER AFFILIE UQ

C H R CENTRAL PRODUCTION PHARMACY p 21
1119 55 AVE NE, CALGARY, AB, T2E 6W1
SIC 2834

C H S L D SHAWVILLE p 1369
See CENTRE D'ACCEUIL PONTIAC

C H S L D VIGI SAINT AUGUSTIN p 1294
See VIGI SANTE LTEE

C H S PHARMACY LIMITED p 812
117 KING ST E, OSHAWA, ON, L1H 1B9
(905) 576-9096   SIC 5912

C H S PHARMACY LIMITED p 844
590 GRANITE CRT SUITE 4, PICKERING, ON, L1W 3X6
(905) 420-7335   SIC 5912

C I T C p 766
See CANADIAN INSTITUTE OF TRAVEL COUNSELLORS OF ONTARIO

C I V T p 326
See BELL MEDIA INC

C J A D p 1215
See STANDARD BROADCAST PRODUCTIONS LTD

C J I PROPERTIES INC p 891
237 ARVIN AVE, STONEY CREEK, ON, L8E 5S6
(905) 664-8448   SIC 6712

C L CONSULTANTS LIMITED p 21
3601 21 ST NE SUITE A, CALGARY, AB, T2E 6T5
(403) 250-3982   SIC 8999

C L S C DU VIEUX LACHINE p 1126
1900 RUE NOTRE-DAME, LACHINE, QC, H8S 2G2
(514) 639-0650   SIC 8399

C L S C HUNTINGDON p 1113
See BARRIE MEMORIAL HOSPITAL FOUNDATION

C L S C KATERI p 1072
See CENTRE LOCAL DES SERVICES COMMUNAUTAIRES KATERI INC

C L S C LA PETITE PATRIE p 1182
6520 RUE DE SAINT-VALLIER, MONTREAL, QC, H2S 2P7
(514) 273-4508   SIC 8399

C L S C LE NOROIS p 1045
See CENTRE LOCAL DES SERVICES COMMUNAUTAIRES LE NOROIS

C L S C OLIVIER-GUIMOND p 1164
5810 RUE SHERBROOKE E, MONTREAL, QC, H1N 1B2
(514) 255-2365   SIC 8082

C L S C PLATEAU MONT-ROYAL p 1172
4689 AV PAPINEAU, MONTREAL, QC, H2H 1V4
(514) 521-7663   SIC 8322

C L S C SAINT-LEONARD p 1343
5540 RUE JARRY E, SAINT-LEONARD, QC, H1P 1T9
(514) 328-3460   SIC 8093

C LA CANADIENNE p 1156
See ENTREPRISES LA CANADIENNE INC

C M M p 720
See CANADIAN MEASUREMENT-METROLOGY INC

C M M T Q p 1180
See CORPORATION DES MAITRES MECANICIENS EN TUYAUTERIE DU QUEBEC

C M P p 483
See CMP AUTOMATION INC

C MAR SERVICES (CANADA) LTD p 434
20 BEAR COVE RD, WITLESS BAY, NL, A0A 4K0
(709) 334-2033   SIC 8741

C N p 911
See COMPAGNIE DES CHEMINS DE FER NATIONAUX DU CANADA

C N RAIL p 93
See COMPAGNIE DES CHEMINS DE FER NATIONAUX DU CANADA

C N RAIL p 859
See COMPAGNIE DES CHEMINS DE FER NATIONAUX DU CANADA

C N RAIL p 1410
See COMPAGNIE DES CHEMINS DE FER NATIONAUX DU CANADA

C R E I T p 928
See CHOICE PROPERTIES REAL ESTATE INVESTMENT TRUST

C S C p 1213
See COMPUTER SCIENCES CANADA INC

C S G BRODERIE & SOIE INTERNATIONALE INC p 1157
8660 CH DARNLEY BUREAU 102, MONT-ROYAL, QC, H4T 1M4
(514) 738-3899   SIC 7389

C S N p 1370
See CONSEIL CENTRAL DES SYNDICATS NATIANAUX DE L'ESTRIE

C T M GATINEAU p 1107
73 RUE JEAN-PROULX, GATINEAU, QC, J8Z 1W2
(819) 777-0999   SIC 8748

C W A p 1417
See CANADIAN WESTERN AGRIBITION ASSOCIATION

C&C PACKING LIMITED PARTNERSHIP p 1343
6800 BOUL DES GRANDES-PRAIRIES, SAINT-LEONARD, QC, H1P 3P3
(514) 939-2273   SIC 2011

C&M ELECTRIC LTD p 540
3038 CARP RD, CARP, ON, K0A 1L0
(613) 839-3232   SIC 1731

C&O APPAREL INC p 192
3788 NORTH FRASER WAY, BURNABY, BC, V5J 5G1
(604) 451-9799   SIC 2329

C&S GROUP OPERATIONS LTD p 184
2820 INGLETON AVE, BURNABY, BC, V5G 6G7
(604) 435-4431   SIC 5032

C-COM SATELLITE SYSTEMS INC p 815
2574 SHEFFIELD RD, OTTAWA, ON, K1B 3V7
(613) 745-4110   SIC 3663

C-CORE p 429
1 MORRISSEY RD, ST. JOHN'S, NL, A1B 3X5
(709) 864-8354   SIC 8711

C-FER TECHNOLOGIES (1999) INC p 120
200 KARL CLARK RD NW, EDMONTON, AB, T6N 1H2
(780) 450-3300   SIC 8748

C-LIVING INC p 779
71 BARBER GREENE RD, NORTH YORK, ON, M3C 2A2
(416) 391-5777   SIC 7389

C-MAC MICROCIRCUITS ULC p 1373
3000 BOUL INDUSTRIEL, SHERBROOKE, QC, J1L 1V8
(819) 821-4524   SIC 5411

C-MAC MICROSYSTEMS SOLUTIONS p 1373
See C-MAC MICROCIRCUITS ULC

C-VISION LIMITED p 438
21 TANTRAMAR CRES, AMHERST, NS,

B4H 4S8
(902) 667-1228 *SIC* 3672
C-W AGENCIES INC *p* 291
2020 YUKON ST, VANCOUVER, BC, V5Y
3N8
(604) 879-9080 *SIC* 8732
C. & C. WOOD PRODUCTS LTD *p* 252
1751 QUESNEL-HIXON RD, QUESNEL,
BC, V2J 5Z5
(250) 992-7471 *SIC* 2431
C. & J. CLARK CANADA LIMITED *p* 796
2881 BRIGHTON RD, OAKVILLE, ON, L6H
6C9
(905) 829-1825 *SIC* 5139
C. B. S. CONSTRUCTION LTD *p* 127
150 MACKAY CRES, FORT MCMURRAY,
AB, T9H 4W8
(780) 743-1810 *SIC* 1629
C. CARON *p* 1150
See *9223-3196 QUEBEC INC*
C. CROTEAU INC *p* 1282
220 BOUL BRIEN, REPENTIGNY, QC, J6A
7E9
(450) 581-7373 *SIC* 5651
C. D. R. YOUNG'S AGGREGATES INC *p* 846
31 HWY 35, PONTYPOOL, ON, L0A 1K0
(705) 277-3972 *SIC* 5032
C. DECICCO AGENCIES INC *p* 692
1035 STACEY CRT, MISSISSAUGA, ON,
L4W 2X7
(905) 238-1485 *SIC* 5122
C. FRAPPIER ELECTRIQUE INC *p* 1132
9607 RUE CLEMENT, LASALLE, QC, H8R
4B4
(514) 363-1712 *SIC* 1731
C. HEAD LIMITED *p* 10
3516 8 AVE NE SUITE 326, CALGARY, AB,
T2A 6K5
(403) 248-6400 *SIC* 5251
C. KEAY INVESTMENTS LTD *p* 208
9076 RIVER RD, DELTA, BC, V4G 1B5
(604) 940-0210 *SIC* 7519
C. R. PLASTIC PRODUCTS INC *p* 895
1172 ERIE ST, STRATFORD, ON, N4Z 0A1
(519) 271-1288 *SIC* 2519
C. ROULEAU GRANIT *p* 1378
See *GRANIT C. ROULEAU INC*
C. S. BACHLY BUILDERS LIMITED *p* 494
27 NIXON RD, BOLTON, ON, L7E 1J7
(905) 951-3100 *SIC* 1521
C. VALLEY PAVING LTD *p* 642
10535 HWY 50, KLEINBURG, ON, L0J 1C0
(416) 736-4220 *SIC* 1611
C. WALKER GROUP INC *p* 341
1455 BELLEVUE AVE SUITE 300, WEST
VANCOUVER, BC, V7T 1C3
(604) 922-6563 *SIC* 8741
C.A. FISCHER LUMBER CO. LTD *p* 95
16210 114 AVE NW SUITE 200, EDMON-
TON, AB, T5M 2Z5
(780) 453-1994 *SIC* 5211
C.A. SPENCER *p* 1235
See *CASLUMBER INC*
C.A. SPENCER INC *p* 1235
2930 BOUL DAGENAIS O, MONTREAL,
QC, H7P 1T1
(450) 622-2420 *SIC* 5031
C.A.F. *p* 1254
See *CHARLES-AUGUSTE FORTIER INC*
C.A.H.Y. *p* 1108
See *7643454 CANADA INC*
C.A.S.A.R.A YUKON *p* 1440
25 PILGRIM PL UNIT 2, WHITEHORSE, YT,
Y1A 0M7
(867) 668-6431 *SIC* 4512
C.A.T. & DESSIN *p* 1088
See *C.A.T. INC*
C.A.T. INC *p* 1088
4 RUE DU TRANSPORT, COTEAU-DU-
LAC, QC, J0P 1B0
(450) 763-6363 *SIC* 4213
C.B. CONSTANTINI LTD *p* 326
910-980 HOWE ST, VANCOUVER, QC, V6Z
0C8

(604) 669-1212 *SIC* 6799
C.B. INVESTMENTS LTD *p* 158
28042 HWY 11 SUITE 207, RED DEER
COUNTY, AB, T4S 2L4
(403) 346-2948 *SIC* 2051
C.B. POWELL LIMITED *p* 692
2475 SKYMARK AVE SUITE 1, MISSIS-
SAUGA, ON, L4W 4Y6
(905) 206-7797 *SIC* 5141
C.B.R. LASER INC *p* 1246
340 RTE 116, PLESSISVILLE, QC, G6L 2Y2
(819) 362-9339 *SIC* 7389
C.B.U. PUBLICATIONS LTD *p* 833
420 O'CONNOR ST SUITE 1600, OTTAWA,
ON, K2P 1W4
(613) 230-0721 *SIC* 2721
C.C. MARINE DISTRIBUTORS INC *p* 755
460 HARRY WALKER PKY S, NEWMAR-
KET, ON, L3Y 8E3
(905) 830-0000 *SIC* 5088
C.C.O.H.T.A. *p* 825
See *CANADIAN AGENCY FOR DRUGS
AND TECHNOLOGIES IN HEALTH (CADTH)*
C.C.T. LOGISTICS SERVICES *p* 733
See *1149318 ONTARIO INC*
C.D.E *p* 1319
See *152429 CANADA INC*
C.D.M.S *p* 1194
See *CHRIS DANIELLE MICRO SOLU-
TIONS (CDMS) INC*
C.D.M.V. INC *p* 1311
2999 BOUL CHOQUETTE, SAINT-
HYACINTHE, QC, J2S 6H5
(450) 771-2368 *SIC* 5047
C.E. COPIE EXPRESS *p* 1131
See *2853477 CANADA INC*
C.E.R. *p* 1349
See *CONSTRUCTION ENERGIE RENOU-
VELABLE S.E.N.C.*
C.E.V. INC *p* 1167
3055 RUE ADAM, MONTREAL, QC, H1W
3Y7
(514) 521-8253 *SIC* 5065
C.F.F. HOLDINGS INC *p* 609
1840 BURLINGTON ST E, HAMILTON, ON,
L8H 3L4
(905) 549-2603 *SIC* 5051
C.F.F. STAINLESS STEELS INC *p* 609
1840 BURLINGTON ST E, HAMILTON, ON,
L8H 3L4
(905) 549-2603 *SIC* 5051
C.G. AIR SYSTEMES INC *p* 1378
207 RUE INDUSTRIELLE, STE-
MARGUERITE-DE-DORCHESTER, QC,
G0S 2X0
(418) 935-7075 *SIC* 3842
C.G. INDUSTRIAL SPECIALTIES LTD *p* 290
558 E KENT AVE SOUTH, VANCOUVER,
BC, V5X 4V6
(604) 263-1671 *SIC* 5085
**C.G. MAINTENANCE & SANITARY PROD-
UCTS INC** *p*
782
40 SAINT REGIS CRES, NORTH YORK,
ON, M3J 1Y5
SIC 5087
C.G.F.A *p* 1356
See *COOPERATIVE DE GESTION
FORESTIERE DES APPALACHES*
C.H. ROBINSON COMPANY (CANADA) LTD
p 549
610 APPLEWOOD CRES UNIT 601, CON-
CORD, ON, L4K 0E3
(905) 851-8865 *SIC* 4731
C.H. ROBINSON MONDIAL CANADA, LTEE
p 1210
645 RUE WELLINGTON BUREAU 400,
MONTREAL, QC, H3C 0L1
(514) 288-2161 *SIC* 4731
**C.H. ROBINSON PROJECT LOGISTICS
LTD** *p* 21
6715 8 ST NE SUITE 102, CALGARY, AB,
T2E 7H7
(403) 295-1505 *SIC* 4731

C.H.S.L.D. BAYVIEW INC *p* 1253
27 CH DU BORD-DU-LAC LAKESHORE,
POINTE-CLAIRE, QC, H9S 4H1
(514) 695-9384 *SIC* 8051
C.H.U.S. *p* 1370
See *CENTRE HOSPITALIER UNIVERSI-
TAIRE DE SHERBROOKE*
C.I.A *p* 1212
See *ALITHYA CANADA INC*
C.I.A.Q. *p* 1311
See *CENTRE D'INSEMINATION ARTIFI-
CIELLE DU QUEBEC (C.I.A.Q.) SOCIETE EN
COMMANDITE*
C.I.C IMPORTATIONS NATURELLES *p* 1066
See *LA COMPAGNIE D'IMPORTATION DE
COSMETIQUES LIMITEE*
C.I.C. *p* 1417
See *CROWN INVESTMENTS CORPORA-
TION OF SASKATCHEWAN*
C.I.F. CONSTRUCTION LTD *p* 250
6171 OTWAY RD, PRINCE GEORGE, BC,
V2M 7B4
(250) 564-8174 *SIC* 1541
C.I.F. METAL LTEE *p* 1382
1900 RUE SETLAKWE, THETFORD
MINES, QC, G6G 8B2
(418) 338-6250 *SIC* 3365
C.I.H.I. *p* 829
See *CANADIAN INSTITUTE FOR HEALTH
INFORMATION*
C.J. DIGITAL *p* 708
See *C.J. GRAPHICS INC*
C.J. GRAPHICS INC *p* 708
560 HENSALL CIR, MISSISSAUGA, ON,
L5A 1Y1
(416) 588-0808 *SIC* 2752
C.J. MARKETING LTD *p* 851
50 EAST WILMOT ST, RICHMOND HILL,
ON, L4B 3Z3
(905) 886-8885 *SIC* 5199
C.J.C. COULTER INVESTMENTS 2006 INC
p 1021
1324 WINDSOR AVE, WINDSOR, ON, N8X
3L9
(519) 253-7422 *SIC* 5712
C.J.W. PHARMACY INCORPORATED *p* 602
104 SILVERCREEK PKY N, GUELPH, ON,
N1H 7B4
(519) 821-5080 *SIC* 5912
C.L. MALACH COMPANY (1997) LTD *p* 353
3501 MCGILLIVRAY BLVD, OAK BLUFF,
MB, R4G 0B5
(204) 895-8002 *SIC* 3444
C.L.S.C. DU HAVRE *p* 1376
30 RUE FERLAND, SOREL-TRACY, QC,
J3P 3C7
(450) 746-4545 *SIC* 8093
C.L.S.C. MALAUZE *p* 1151
See *GOUVERNEMENT DE LA PROVINCE
DE QUEBEC*
C.L.S.C. MONTREAL-NORD *p* 1176
1615 AV EMILE-JOURNAULT, MONTREAL,
QC, H2M 2G3
(514) 384-2000 *SIC* 8361
C.M. BRAKE INC *p* 546
118 COUNTY ROAD 31, COLBORNE, ON,
K0K 1S0
(905) 265-0265 *SIC* 3069
C.M.A REFRIGERATION *p* 1218
See *CARMICHAEL ENGINEERING LTD*
**C.M.S. COMMERCIAL MECHANICAL SER-
VICES LTD** *p*
878
2721 MARKHAM RD UNIT 10, SCARBOR-
OUGH, ON, M1X 1L5
(416) 609-9992 *SIC* 1711
C.O.M. RESOURCES LTD *p* 34
6223 2 ST SE SUITE 165, CALGARY, AB,
T2H 1J5
(403) 299-9400 *SIC* 8711
C.P. LOEWEN ENTERPRISES LTD *p* 358
77 PTH 52 W, STEINBACH, MB, R5G 1B2
(204) 326-6446 *SIC* 3444
C.P. VEGETABLE OIL INC *p* 501

10 CARSON CRT UNIT 2, BRAMPTON,
ON, L6T 4P8
(905) 792-2309 *SIC* 5149
C.P.C. C'PAS CHER U *p* 1375
See *MAGASINS C.P.C. INC, LES*
C.P.U. DESIGN INC *p* 1263
2323 BOUL DU VERSANT-NORD BUREAU
100, QUEBEC, QC, G1N 4P4
(418) 681-6974 *SIC* 5045
C.R. COMPREF *p* 1167
See *ENTREPRISES ELECTRIQUES L.M.
INC, LES*
C.R. LAURENCE OF CANADA LIMITED *p*
549
65 TIGI CRT, CONCORD, ON, L4K 5E4
(905) 303-7966 *SIC* 3211
**C.R.A. COLLATERAL RECOVERY & AD-
MINISTRATION INC** *p*
27
1289 HIGHFIELD CRES SE UNIT 109, CAL-
GARY, AB, T2G 5M2
(403) 240-3450 *SIC* 7381
C.R.A.D.A.C.L. *p* 194
See *CAMPBELL RIVER AND DISTRICT
ASSOCIATION FOR COMMUNITY LIVING*
C.S.A GROUP *p* 583
See *CANADIAN STANDARDS ASSOCIA-
TION*
C.S.D.C.C.S. *p* 770
See *CONSEIL SCOLAIRE DE DISTRICT
CATHOLIQUE CENTRE-SUD*
C.S.T. CONSULTANTS INC *p* 766
2235 SHEPPARD AVE E UNIT 1600,
NORTH YORK, ON, M2J 5B8
(416) 445-7377 *SIC* 6732
C.T. CONSULTANTS INC *p* 1399
1696 BOUL DES LAURENTIDES, VIMONT,
QC, H7M 2P4
(514) 375-0377 *SIC* 7361
C.T. CONTROL TEMP LTD *p* 184
4340 DAWSON ST, BURNABY, BC, V5C
4B6
(604) 298-2000 *SIC* 5078
C.T.M. ADHESIF *p* 1047
See *C.T.M. ADHESIVES INC*
C.T.M. ADHESIVES INC *p* 1047
8320 RUE GRENACHE, ANJOU, QC, H1J
1C5
(514) 321-5540 *SIC* 5169
C.T.M. GATINEAU *p* 1048
See *CENTRE DE TELEPHONE MOBILE
LTEE*
C.T.M.A. TRAVERSIER LTEE *p* 1073
435 CH AVILA-ARSENEAU, CAP-AUX-
MEULES, QC, G4T 1J3
(418) 986-6600 *SIC* 4424
C.T.M.A. VACANCIER *p* 1073
See *NAVIGATION MADELEINE INC*
C.T.S. FOOD BROKERS INC *p* 1127
5025 RUE FRANCOIS-CUSSON, LA-
CHINE, QC, H8T 3K1
(514) 956-0356 *SIC* 5147
C.W. CARRY LTD *p* 113
5815 75 ST NW, EDMONTON, AB, T6E 0T3
(780) 465-0381 *SIC* 5051
**C/S CONSTRUCTION SPECIALTIES COM-
PANY** *p*
720
2240 ARGENTIA RD, MISSISSAUGA, ON,
L5N 2K7
(905) 274-3611 *SIC* 3446
C2 GROUP INC *p* 518
350 WOOLWICH ST S, BRESLAU, ON, N0B
1M0
(519) 648-3118 *SIC* 1522
C2 MEDIA *p* 253
See *C2 MEDIA CANADA ULC*
C2 MEDIA CANADA ULC *p* 253
14291 BURROWS RD, RICHMOND, BC,
V6V 1K9
(604) 270-4000 *SIC* 2759
C4MEDIA INC *p* 570
2267 LAKE SHORE BLVD W, ETOBICOKE,
ON, M8V 3X2

(647) 917-4470   *SIC* 8748
C5 GROUP INC   *p* 972
1329 BAY ST SUITE 300, TORONTO, ON, M5R 2C4
(416) 926-8200   *SIC* 6719
CAA   *p* 817
See CAA NORTH & EAST ONTARIO
CAA   *p* 828
See CANADIAN AUTOMOBILE ASSOCIATION
CAA (MANITOBA)   *p* 382
See MML CLUB SERVICES LTD
CAA ATLANTIC LIMITED   *p* 412
378 WESTMORLAND RD, SAINT JOHN, NB, E2J 2G4
(506) 634-1400   *SIC* 8699
CAA CLUB GROUP   *p* 903
60 COMMERCE VALLEY DR E, THORNHILL, ON, L3T 7P9
(905) 771-3000   *SIC* 8699
CAA INSURANCE COMPANY   *p* 903
60 COMMERCE VALLEY DR E, THORNHILL, ON, L3T 7P9
(905) 771-3000   *SIC* 6331
CAA MANITOBA   *p* 382
See MANITOBA MOTOR LEAGUE, THE
CAA NIAGARA   *p* 907
3271 SCHMON PKY, THOROLD, ON, L2V 4Y6
(905) 984-8585   *SIC* 8699
CAA NORTH & EAST ONTARIO   *p* 817
2151 THURSTON DR, OTTAWA, ON, K1G 6C9
(613) 820-1890   *SIC* 8699
CAA QUEBEC   *p* 1278
See AUTOMOBILE ET TOURING CLUB DU QUEBEC (A.T.C.Q.)
CAA SASKATCHEWAN   *p* 1421
See SASKATCHEWAN MOTOR CLUB
CAA SOUTH CENTRAL ONTARIO   *p* 903
See CAA CLUB GROUP
CAA TRAVEL (SOUTH CENTRAL ONTARIO) INC.   *p* 903
60 COMMERCE VALLEY DR E, THORNHILL, ON, L3T 7P9
(905) 771-3000   *SIC* 4724
CAA-QUEBEC   *p* 1213
See CANADIAN AUTOMOBILE ASSOCIATION
CAAT PENSION PLAN   *p* 935
See COLLEGES OF APPLIED ARTS & TECHNOLOGY PENSION PLAN
CAB-R-SON   *p* 1374
See TECHNOLOGIES DUAL-ADE INC
CABAN   *p* 974
See CLUB MONACO CORP
CABANE A SUCRE CONSTANTIN (1992) INC   *p* 1301
1054 BOUL ARTHUR-SAUVE, SAINT-EUSTACHE, QC, J7R 4K3
(450) 473-2374   *SIC* 2099
CABELA'S   *p* 21
See CABELA'S RETAIL CANADA INC
CABELA'S CANADA   *p* 365
See CABELA'S RETAIL CANADA INC
CABELA'S CANADA   *p* 388
See CABELA'S RETAIL CANADA INC
CABELA'S RETAIL CANADA INC   *p* 21
851 64 AVE NE, CALGARY, AB, T2E 3B8
(403) 910-0200   *SIC* 5941
CABELA'S RETAIL CANADA INC   *p* 365
25 DE BAETS ST, WINNIPEG, MB, R2J 4G5
(204) 788-4867   *SIC* 5941
CABELA'S RETAIL CANADA INC   *p* 388
580 STERLING LYON PKY, WINNIPEG, MB, R3P 1E9
(204) 786-8966   *SIC* 5941
CABICO   *p* 883
See ELMWOOD GROUP LIMITED, THE
CABICO BOUTIQUE   *p* 1082
See GROUPE CABICO INC
CABINET DE RELATIONS PUBLIQUES NATIONAL INC, LE   *p*

979
320 FRONT ST W SUITE 1600, TORONTO, ON, M5V 3B5
(416) 586-0180   *SIC* 8743
CABLE BRIDGE ENTERPRISES LIMITED *p* 476
6015 HIGHWAY 89, ALLISTON, ON, L9R 1A4
(705) 435-5501   *SIC* 7011
CABLE CONTROL SYSTEMS INC   *p* 796
2800 COVENTRY RD, OAKVILLE, ON, L6H 6R1
(905) 829-9910   *SIC* 1799
CABLE PUBLIC AFFAIRS CHANNEL INC *p* 822
45 O'CONNOR ST SUITE 1750, OTTAWA, ON, K1P 1A4
SIC 4841
CABLECOM DIV.   *p* 460
See EMERA UTILITY SERVICES INCORPORATED
CABLES BEN-MOR INC, LES   *p* 1313
1105 RUE LEMIRE, SAINT-HYACINTHE, QC, J2T 1L8
(450) 778-0022   *SIC* 5051
CABLESHOPPE INC, THE   *p* 870
1410 BIRCHMOUNT RD, SCARBOROUGH, ON, M1P 2E3
(416) 293-3634   *SIC* 1731
CABLEVISION HAUT ST-LAURENT *p* 1121
See DERY TELECOM INC
CABO DRILLING (ONTARIO) CORP   *p* 634
34 DUNCAN AVE N, KIRKLAND LAKE, ON, P2N 3L3
(705) 567-9311   *SIC* 1799
CABOT CANADA LTD   *p* 859
800 TASHAMOO AVE, SARNIA, ON, N7T 7N4
(519) 336-2261   *SIC* 2895
CABOT FORD LINCOLN SALES LIMITED *p* 429
177 KENMOUNT RD, ST. JOHN'S, NL, A1B 3P9
(709) 722-6600   *SIC* 5511
CABOT MANUFACTURING ULC   *p* 397
521 BOUL FERDINAND, DIEPPE, NB, E1A 7G1
(506) 386-2868   *SIC* 3275
CABRELLI DESIGN   *p* 1178
See GROUPE CABRELLI INC
CABRELLI INC   *p* 1178
9200 RUE MEILLEUR BUREAU 300, MONTREAL, QC, H2N 2A9
(514) 384-4750   *SIC* 5137
CAC ENTERPRISES GROUP INC   *p* 190
4538 KINGSWAY UNIT 619, BURNABY, BC, V5H 4T9
(604) 430-8835   *SIC* 5051
CAC RECYCLING   *p* 190
See CAC ENTERPRISES GROUP INC
CACADES GROUPE CARTON PLAT EAST ANGUS   *p* 1100
See CASCADES CANADA ULC
CACEIS (CANADA) LIMITED   *p* 705
1 ROBERT SPECK PKY SUITE 1510, MISSISSAUGA, ON, L4Z 3M3
(905) 281-4145   *SIC* 8741
CACHE EXPLORATION INC   *p* 210
4770 72ND ST, DELTA, BC, V4K 3N3
(604) 306-5285   *SIC* 1041
CACHERE CLASSIQUE   *p* 1157
See 9256-5589 QUEBEC INC
CACR DE ST BONIFACE   *p* 364
See ARCHDIOCESE OF ST BONIFACE, THE
CACTUS (ISP) INTERNET INC   *p* 1106
490 BOUL SAINT-JOSEPH BUREAU 300, GATINEAU, QC, J8Y 3Y7

(819) 778-0313   *SIC* 4813
CACTUS CAFE BARLOW LTD   *p* 292
550 BROADWAY W, VANCOUVER, BC, V5Z 0E9
(604) 714-2025   *SIC* 5812
CACTUS CLUB   *p* 259
See CACTUS RESTAURANTS LTD
CACTUS CLUB CAFE   *p* 184
See CACTUS RESTAURANTS LTD
CACTUS CLUB CAFE   *p* 219
See CACTUS RESTAURANTS LTD
CACTUS CLUB CAFE   *p* 292
See CACTUS CAFE BARLOW LTD
CACTUS CLUB CAFE   *p* 320
See CACTUS RESTAURANTS LTD
CACTUS COMMERCE   *p* 1106
See CACTUS (ISP) INTERNET INC
CACTUS RESTAURANTS LTD   *p* 184
4219B LOUGHEED HWY, BURNABY, BC, V5C 3Y6
(604) 291-6606   *SIC* 5812
CACTUS RESTAURANTS LTD   *p* 219
1575 BANKS RD SUITE 200, KELOWNA, BC, V1X 7Y8
(250) 763-6752   *SIC* 5812
CACTUS RESTAURANTS LTD   *p* 259
5500 NO. 3 RD, RICHMOND, BC, V6X 2C8
(604) 244-9969   *SIC* 5812
CACTUS RESTAURANTS LTD   *p* 292
550 BROADWAY W SUITE 201, VANCOUVER, BC, V5Z 0E9
(604) 714-2025   *SIC* 5812
CACTUS RESTAURANTS LTD   *p* 320
1530 BROADWAY W, VANCOUVER, BC, V6J 5K9
(604) 733-0434   *SIC* 5812
CAD CONSTRUCTION LTD   *p* 421
19 SAWDUST ROAD, BAY ROBERTS, NL, A0A 1G0
SIC 1542
CAD INDUSTRIES FERROVIAIRES LTEE *p* 1126
155 BOUL MONTREAL-TORONTO, LACHINE, QC, H8S 1B4
(514) 634-3131   *SIC* 4789
CAD TEK INC   *p* 583
321 HUMBERLINE DR, ETOBICOKE, ON, M9W 5T6
(416) 679-9780   *SIC* 5051
CADBURY   *p* 991
See KRAFT HEINZ CANADA ULC
CADE HOLDING INC   *p* 758
6400 LUNDY'S LANE, NIAGARA FALLS, ON, L2G 1T6
(905) 356-1161   *SIC* 7011
CADEUL   *p* 1258
See CONFEDERATION DES ASSOCIATIONS D'ETUDIANTS ET D'ETUDIANTES DE L'UNIVERSITE LAVAL (CADEU
CADEX ELECTRONICS INC   *p* 258
22000 FRASERWOOD WAY, RICHMOND, BC, V6W 1J6
(604) 231-7777   *SIC* 3825
CADEX INC   *p* 1316
755 AV MONTRICHARD, SAINT-JEAN-SUR-RICHELIEU, QC, J2X 5K8
(450) 348-6774   *SIC* 3821
CADIEUX & ASSOCIES S.E.N.C.   *p* 1129
225 RUE PRINCIPALE, LACHUTE, QC, J8H 2Z7
(450) 562-5285   *SIC* 5072
CADILLAC CHEVROLET BUICK GMC DU WEST ISLAND LTEE   *p* 1091
3650 BOUL DES SOURCES, DOLLARD-DES-ORMEAUX, QC, H9B 1Z9
(514) 683-6555   *SIC* 5511
CADILLAC FAIRVIEW CORPORATION LIMITED, THE   *p* 935
220 YONGE ST SUITE 110, TORONTO, ON, M5B 2H1
(416) 598-8700   *SIC* 6512
CADILLAC FAIRVIEW CORPORATION LIMITED, THE   *p*

949
20 QUEEN ST W SUITE 500, TORONTO, ON, M5H 3R4
(416) 598-8200   *SIC* 6512
CADILLAC HUMMER OF LONDON   *p* 658
600 OXFORD ST W, LONDON, ON, N6H 1T9
(519) 472-1199   *SIC* 5511
CADILLAC VENTURES INC   *p* 941
65 FRONT ST E SUITE 200, TORONTO, ON, M5E 1B5
(416) 203-7722   *SIC* 1041
CADOGAN HALL   *p* 8
GD, CADOGAN, AB, T0B 0T0
(780) 753-2963   *SIC* 6512
CADORATH AEROSPACE INC   *p* 369
2070 LOGAN AVE, WINNIPEG, MB, R2R 0H9
(204) 633-2707   *SIC* 3728
CADRE LOGIS + NET   *p* 1132
See CENTRE D'ACTION DE DEVELOPPEMENT ET DE RECHERCHE EN EMPLOYABILITE
CADRES COLUMBIA INC   *p* 1164
6251 RUE NOTRE-DAME E, MONTREAL, QC, H1N 2E9
(514) 253-2999   *SIC* 2499
CADRES VERBEC INC   *p* 1395
101 MONTEE CALIXA-LAVALLEE, VERCHERES, QC, J0L 2R0
(450) 583-3378   *SIC* 5031
CADROPORTE MANUFACTURIER INC   *p* 1058
700 BOUL INDUSTRIEL, BLAINVILLE, QC, J7C 3V4
(450) 434-9000   *SIC* 5211
CAE FORMATION POUR L'AVIATION MILITAIRE INC   *p* 1405
15 WING MOOSE JAW BLDG 160, BUSHELL PARK, SK, S0H 0N0
(306) 694-2719   *SIC* 8249
CAE INC   *p* 1338
8585 CH DE LA COTE-DE-LIESSE, SAINT-LAURENT, QC, H4T 1G6
(514) 341-6780   *SIC* 3699
CAE INTERNATIONAL HOLDINGS LIMITED   *p* 1338
8585 CH DE LA COTE-DE-LIESSE, SAINT-LAURENT, QC, H4T 1G6
(514) 341-6780   *SIC* 6712
CAE MILITARY AVIATION TRAINING INC *p* 1405
See CAE FORMATION POUR L'AVIATION MILITAIRE INC
CAE SANTE CANADA INC   *p* 1338
8585 CH DE LA COTE-DE-LIESSE, SAINT-LAURENT, QC, H4T 1G6
(514) 341-6780   *SIC* 3699
CAESARS WINDSOR   *p* 1024
See WINDSOR CASINO LIMITED
CAFAS FUELING, ULC   *p* 1092
780 BOUL STUART-GRAHAM S, DORVAL, QC, H4Y 1G2
(514) 636-3770   *SIC* 5172
CAFE DE MONTREAL   *p* 765
See TANGERINE BANK
CAFE DEPOT INC, LE   *p* 1171
2464 RUE JEAN-TALON E, MONTREAL, QC, H2E 1W2
(514) 281-2067   *SIC* 6794
CAFE DES ECLUSIERS   *p* 1190
See SOCIETE DU VIEUX-PORT DE MONTREAL INC
CAFE DU MONDE   *p* 1259
See GROUPE RESTOS PLAISIRS INC, LE
CAFE FARO   *p* 1372
See BRULERIE GRANDE RESERVE INC
CAFE FARO INC   *p* 1372
930 RUE BLAIS, SHERBROOKE, QC, J1K 2B7
(819) 564-8844   *SIC* 5149
CAFE HOLT TMA482, 017   *p* 929

See HOLT, RENFREW & CIE, LIMITEE
CAFE HUBERT SAINT-JEAN DISTRIBUTION *p*
1370
See CAFE VITTORIA INC
CAFE MARC ROBITAILLE INC *p 1044*
850 AV TANGUAY, ALMA, QC, G8B 5Y3
(418) 668-8022 *SIC 5149*
CAFE MORGANE *p 1387*
See CAFE MORGANE ROYALE INC
CAFE MORGANE ROYALE INC *p 1387*
4945 BOUL GENE-H.-KRUGER, TROIS-RIVIERES, QC, G9A 4N5
(819) 694-1118 *SIC 5499*
CAFE SELENA *p 1170*
See SERVICES DE CAFE VAN HOUTTE INC
CAFE VIENNE *p 1210*
See GROUPE CAFE VIENNE 1998 INC, LE
CAFE VITTORIA INC *p 1370*
1625 RUE BELVEDERE S, SHERBROOKE, QC, J1H 4E4
(819) 564-8226 *SIC 5149*
CAFE, LE *p 824*
See NATIONAL ARTS CENTRE CORPORATION
CAFES VIENNE PRESS INC, LES *p 1210*
1422 RUE NOTRE-DAME O, MONTREAL, QC, H3C 1K9
(514) 935-5553 *SIC 6712*
CAFRAMO LIMITED *p 594*
501273 GREY ROAD 1, GEORGIAN BLUFFS, ON, N0H 2T0
(519) 534-1080 *SIC 3564*
CAGE AU SPORT, LA *p 1205*
See GROUPE SPORTSCENE INC
CAGE AUX SPORTS, LA *p 1065*
See GROUPE SPORTSCENE INC
CAGE AUX SPORTS, LA *p 1077*
See 3111326 CANADA INC
CAGE AUX SPORTS, LA *p 1227*
See GROUPE SPORTSCENE INC
CAIG *p 960*
See CANADIAN AVIATION INSURANCE MANAGERS LTD
CAIN LAMARRE CASGRAIN WELLS *p*
1078
See CAIN LAMARRE CASGRAIN WELLS, S.E.N.C.R.L.
CAIN LAMARRE CASGRAIN WELLS, S.E.N.C.R.L. *p 1078*
255 RUE RACINE E BUREAU 600, CHICOUTIMI, QC, G7H 7L2
(418) 545-4580 *SIC 8111*
CAIN LAMARRE CASGRAIN WELLS, S.E.N.C.R.L. *p*
630 BOUL RENE-LEVESQUE O BUREAU 2780, MONTREAL, QC, H3B 1S6
(514) 393-4580 *SIC 8111*
CAISSE D'ECONOMIE SOLIDAIRE DESJARDINS *p*
1258
155 BOUL CHAREST E BUREAU 500, QUEBEC, QC, G1K 3G6
(418) 647-1527 *SIC 6062*
CAISSE DE BEAUPORT *p 1254*
See CAISSE DESJARDINS DE BEAUPORT
CAISSE DESJARDINS - CENTREDE SERVICE *p*
1173
1685 RUE RACHEL E, MONTREAL, QC, H2J 2K6
(514) 524-3551 *SIC 6159*
CAISSE DESJARDINS CHARLES-LEMOYNE *p*
1322
477 AV VICTORIA, SAINT-LAMBERT, QC, J4P 2J1
(450) 671-3733 *SIC 6062*
CAISSE DESJARDINS D'AMOS *p 1046*
2 RUE PRINCIPALE N, AMOS, QC, J9T 2K6
SIC 6062
CAISSE DESJARDINS DE BEAUPORT *p*

1254
799 RUE CLEMENCEAU, QUEBEC, QC, G1C 8J7
(418) 660-3119 *SIC 6062*
CAISSE DESJARDINS DE BOUCHERVILLE *p 1064*
1071 BOUL DE MONTARVILLE, BOUCHERVILLE, QC, J4B 6R2
(450) 655-9041 *SIC 6062*
CAISSE DESJARDINS DE CHICOUTIMI *p*
1078
245 RUE RACINE E, CHICOUTIMI, QC, G7H 1S4
(418) 549-3224 *SIC 6062*
CAISSE DESJARDINS DE CHOMEDEY *p 1087*
3075 BOUL CARTIER O, COTE SAINT-LUC, QC, H7V 1J4
(450) 688-0900 *SIC 6062*
CAISSE DESJARDINS DE DRUM-MONDVILLE *p*
1098
460 BOUL SAINT-JOSEPH, DRUM-MONDVILLE, QC, J2C 2A8
(819) 474-2524 *SIC 6062*
CAISSE DESJARDINS DE GRANBY-HAUTE-YAMASKA *p*
1108
450 RUE PRINCIPALE, GRANBY, QC, J2G 2X1
(450) 777-5353 *SIC 6062*
CAISSE DESJARDINS DE HULL-AYLMER *p*
1106
250 BOUL SAINT-JOSEPH, GATINEAU, QC, J8Y 3X6
(819) 776-3000 *SIC 6062*
CAISSE DESJARDINS DE HULL-AYLMER *p*
1107
219 BOUL DU PLATEAU, GATINEAU, QC, J9A 0N4
(819) 776-3000 *SIC 6062*
CAISSE DESJARDINS DE JONQUIERE *p*
1116
2358 RUE SAINT-DOMINIQUE, JONQUIERE, QC, G7X 0M7
(418) 695-1850 *SIC 6062*
CAISSE DESJARDINS DE L'ERABLE *p*
1246
1658 RUE SAINT-CALIXTE, PLESSISVILLE, QC, G6L 1P9
(819) 362-3236 *SIC 6062*
CAISSE DESJARDINS DE L'OUEST DE LA MAURICIE *p 1146*
75 AV SAINT-LAURENT BUREAU 300, LOUISEVILLE, QC, J5V 1J6
(819) 228-9422 *SIC 6062*
CAISSE DESJARDINS DE L'OUEST DE LA MONTEREGIE *p 1151*
724 BOUL SAINT-JEAN-BAPTISTE, MERCIER, QC, J6R 0B2
(450) 698-2204 *SIC 6062*
CAISSE DESJARDINS DE L'OUEST DE LAVAL *p 1363*
440 CHOMEDEY (A-13) O, SAINTE-ROSE, QC, H7X 3S9
(450) 962-1800 *SIC 6062*
CAISSE DESJARDINS DE LA CHAUDIERE *p 1137*
1190B RUE DE COURCHEVEL BUREAU 103, LEVIS, QC, G6W 0M6
(418) 839-8819 *SIC 6062*
CAISSE DESJARDINS DE LA REGION DE SAINT-HYACINTHE *p 1311*
1697 RUE GIROUARD O, SAINT-HYACINTHE, QC, J2S 2Z9
(450) 768-3030 *SIC 6062*
CAISSE DESJARDINS DE LA REGION DE THETFORD *p 1382*
300 BOUL FRONTENAC E, THETFORD MINES, QC, G6G 7M8
(418) 338-3591 *SIC 6062*
CAISSE DESJARDINS DE LA VALLEE DES PAYS-D'EN-HAUT *p 1352*
218 RUE PRINCIPALE, SAINT-SAUVEUR,

QC, J0R 1R0
(450) 227-3712 *SIC 6062*
CAISSE DESJARDINS DE LORIMIER-VILLERAY *p*
1171
2050 BOUL ROSEMONT, MONTREAL, QC, H2G 1T1
(514) 376-7676 *SIC 6062*
CAISSE DESJARDINS DE MERCIER-ROSEMONT *p*
1346
6955 RUE JEAN-TALON E, SAINT-LEONARD, QC, H1S 1N2
(514) 254-7878 *SIC 6062*
CAISSE DESJARDINS DE QUEBEC *p 1258*
135 RUE SAINT-VALLIER O, QUEBEC, QC, G1K 1J9
(418) 687-2810 *SIC 6062*
CAISSE DESJARDINS DE QUEBEC *p 1263*
150 RUE MARIE-DE-L'INCARNATION, QUEBEC, QC, G1N 4G8
(418) 687-2810 *SIC 6062*
CAISSE DESJARDINS DE RIMOUSKI *p*
1284
100 RUE JULIEN-REHEL, RIMOUSKI, QC, G5L 0G6
(418) 723-3368 *SIC 6062*
CAISSE DESJARDINS DE SAINT-ANTOINE-DES-LAURENTIDES *p*
1320
663 BOUL SAINT-ANTOINE, SAINT-JEROME, QC, J7Z 3B8
(450) 436-5331 *SIC 6062*
CAISSE DESJARDINS DE SAINT-HUBERT *p 1307*
2400 BOUL GAETAN-BOUCHER, SAINT-HUBERT, QC, J3Y 5B7
(450) 443-0047 *SIC 6062*
CAISSE DESJARDINS DE SAINTE-FOY *p*
1274
990 AV DE BOURGOGNE BUREAU 200, QUEBEC, QC, G1W 0E8
(418) 653-0515 *SIC 6062*
CAISSE DESJARDINS DE SAINTE-FOY *p*
1275
3211 CH SAINTE-FOY, QUEBEC, QC, G1X 1R3
(418) 653-0515 *SIC 6062*
CAISSE DESJARDINS DE SALABERRY-DE-VALLEYFIELD *p*
1365
120 RUE ALEXANDRE, SALABERRY-DE-VALLEYFIELD, QC, J6S 3K4
(450) 377-4177 *SIC 6062*
CAISSE DESJARDINS DE SALABERRY-DE-VALLEYFIELD *p*
1366
15 RUE SAINT-THOMAS, SALABERRY-DE-VALLEYFIELD, QC, J6T 4J1
(450) 377-4177 *SIC 6062*
CAISSE DESJARDINS DE SAULT-AU-RECOLLET-MONTREAL-NORD *p*
1240
10205 BOUL PIE-IX, MONTREAL-NORD, QC, H1H 3Z4
(514) 322-9310 *SIC 6062*
CAISSE DESJARDINS DE SILLERY–SAINT-LOUIS-DE-FRANCE *p*
1271
1444 AV MAGUIRE, QUEBEC, QC, G1T 1Z3
(418) 681-3566 *SIC 6062*
CAISSE DESJARDINS DE VIMONT-AUTEUIL *p*
1232
5350 BOUL DES LAURENTIDES, MONTREAL, QC, H7K 2J8
(450) 669-2694 *SIC 6062*
CAISSE DESJARDINS DES BOIS-FRANCS *p 1397*
300 BOUL DES BOIS-FRANCS S, VICTORIAVILLE, QC, G6P 7W7
(819) 758-9421 *SIC 6062*
CAISSE DESJARDINS DES GRANDS

BOULEVARDS DE LAVAL *p 1133*
3111 BOUL SAINT-MARTIN O, LAVAL, QC, H7T 0K2
(450) 667-9950 *SIC 6062*
CAISSE DESJARDINS DES POLICIERS ET POLICIERES *p 1173*
460 RUE GILFORD, MONTREAL, QC, H2J 1N3
(514) 847-1004 *SIC 6062*
CAISSE DESJARDINS DES RIVIERES DE QUEBEC *p 1276*
2287 AV CHAUVEAU, QUEBEC, QC, G2C 0G7
(418) 842-1214 *SIC 6062*
CAISSE DESJARDINS DES SEIGNEURIES DE BELLECHASE *p 1297*
2807 AV ROYALE, SAINT-CHARLES-DE-BELLECHASSE, QC, G0R 2T0
(418) 887-3337 *SIC 6062*
CAISSE DESJARDINS DES SEIGNEURIES DE LA FRONTIERE *p 1242*
373 RUE SAINT-JACQUES, NAPIERVILLE, QC, J0J 1L0
(450) 245-3391 *SIC 6062*
CAISSE DESJARDINS DES TROIS-RIVIERES *p*
1387
1200 RUE ROYALE, TROIS-RIVIERES, QC, G9A 4J2
(819) 376-1200 *SIC 6062*
CAISSE DESJARDINS DES VERTS-SOMMETS DE L'ESTRIE *p*
1081
155 RUE CHILD, COATICOOK, QC, J1A 2B4
(819) 849-0434 *SIC 6062*
CAISSE DESJARDINS DU CARREFOUR DES LACS *p 1090*
572 AV JACQUES-CARTIER, DISRAELI, QC, G0N 1E0
(418) 449-2652 *SIC 6062*
CAISSE DESJARDINS DU CENTRE-DE-LA-MAURICIE *p*
1368
444 5E RUE DE LA POINTE, SHAWINIGAN, QC, G9N 1E6
(819) 536-4404 *SIC 6062*
CAISSE DESJARDINS DU CENTRE-VILLE DE QUEBEC *p 1258*
See CAISSE DESJARDINS DE QUEBEC
CAISSE DESJARDINS DU COEUR DE BEL-LECHASSE *p*
1291
730 RTE BEGIN, SAINT-ANSELME, QC, G0R 2N0
(418) 885-4421 *SIC 6062*
CAISSE DESJARDINS DU COEUR-DE-L'ILE *p*
1171
2050 BOUL ROSEMONT, MONTREAL, QC, H2G 1T1
(514) 376-7676 *SIC 6062*
CAISSE DESJARDINS DU HAUT-RICHELIEU *p*
1315
175 BOUL OMER-MARCIL, SAINT-JEAN-SUR-RICHELIEU, QC, J2W 0A3
(450) 359-5933 *SIC 6062*
CAISSE DESJARDINS DU HAUT-RICHELIEU *p*
1316
730 BOUL D'IBERVILLE, SAINT-JEAN-SUR-RICHELIEU, QC, J2X 3Z9
(450) 357-5000 *SIC 6062*
CAISSE DESJARDINS DU LAC-MEMPHREMAGOG *p*
1147
230 RUE PRINCIPALE O, MAGOG, QC, J1X 2A5
SIC 6062
CAISSE DESJARDINS DU LAC-MEMPHREMAGOG *p*
1148
342 RUE PRINCIPALE, MANSONVILLE,

QC, J0E 1X0

(819) 843-3328   *SIC* 6036

CAISSE DESJARDINS DU MONT-SAINT-BRUNO   *p* 1295

1649 RUE MONTARVILLE, SAINT-BRUNO, QC, J3V 3T8

(450) 653-3646   *SIC* 6062

CAISSE DESJARDINS DU NORD DE LANAUDIERE   *p* 1114

275 RUE BEAUDRY N, JOLIETTE, QC, J6E 6A7

(450) 756-0999   *SIC* 8741

CAISSE DESJARDINS DU NORD DE LAVAL   *p* 1361

396 BOUL CURE-LABELLE, SAINTE-ROSE, QC, H7L 4T7

(450) 622-8130   *SIC* 6062

CAISSE DESJARDINS DU NORD DE SHERBROOKE   *p* 1371

1845 RUE KING O, SHERBROOKE, QC, J1J 2E4

(819) 566-0050   *SIC* 6062

CAISSE DESJARDINS DU SUD DE LA CHAUDIERE   *p* 1304

10555 BOUL LACROIX, SAINT-GEORGES, QC, G5Y 1K2

(418) 228-8824   *SIC* 6062

CAISSE DESJARDINS DU SUD DE LA CHAUDIERE   *p* 1304

1275 BOUL DIONNE, SAINT-GEORGES, QC, G5Y 0R4

(418) 227-7000   *SIC* 8741

CAISSE DESJARDINS GODEFROY *p* 1056

4265 BOUL DE PORT-ROYAL, BECAN-COUR, QC, G9H 1Z3

(819) 233-2333   *SIC* 6062

CAISSE DESJARDINS PIERRE-BOUCHER *p* 1145

2401 BOUL ROLAND-THERRIEN, LONGUEUIL, QC, J4N 1C5

(450) 468-7411   *SIC* 6062

CAISSE DESJARDINS PIERRE-LE-GARDEUR   *p* 1282

477 RUE NOTRE-DAME, REPENTIGNY, QC, J6A 2T6

(450) 585-5555   *SIC* 6062

CAISSE DESJARDINS THERESE-DE-BLAINVILLE   *p* 1364

201 BOUL DU CURE-LABELLE, SAINTE-THERESE, QC, J7E 2X6

(450) 430-6550   *SIC* 6062

CAISSE POPULAIRE   *p* 899

See CAISSE POPULAIRE DES VOYAGEURS INC

CAISSE POPULAIRE DE BOUCTOUCHE *p* 395

See CAISSE POPULAIRE KENT-SUD LTEE

CAISSE POPULAIRE DE LA PRAIRIE   *p* 1123

450 BOUL TASCHEREAU, LA PRAIRIE, QC, J5R 1V1

(450) 659-5431   *SIC* 6062

CAISSE POPULAIRE DE SAINT-BONIFACE LIMITEE, LA   *p* 364

205 PROVENCHER BLVD SUITE 100, WINNIPEG, MB, R2H 0G4

(204) 237-8874   *SIC* 8742

CAISSE POPULAIRE DES VOYAGEURS INC   *p* 899

531 NOTRE DAME AVE, SUDBURY, ON, P3C 5L1

(705) 674-4234   *SIC* 6062

CAISSE POPULAIRE DESJARDINS CANADIENNE ITALIENNE   *p* 1182

6999 BOUL SAINT-LAURENT, MONTREAL, QC, H2S 3E1

(514) 270-4124   *SIC* 6062

CAISSE POPULAIRE DESJARDINS D'ALMA   *p* 1044

600 RUE COLLARD, ALMA, QC, G8B 1N4

(418) 669-1414   *SIC* 6062

CAISSE POPULAIRE DESJARDINS DE

CHARLESBOURG   *p* 1256

155 76E RUE E, QUEBEC, QC, G1H 1G4

(418) 626-1146   *SIC* 6062

CAISSE POPULAIRE DESJARDINS DE L'ENVOLEE   *p* 1058

1070 BOUL DU CURE-LABELLE, BLAINVILLE, QC, J7C 2M7

(450) 430-4603   *SIC* 6062

CAISSE POPULAIRE DESJARDINS DE L'ENVOLEE   *p* 1152

13845 BOUL DU CURE-LABELLE, MIRABEL, QC, J7J 1A1

(450) 430-4603   *SIC* 6062

CAISSE POPULAIRE DESJARDINS DE RICHELIEU-SAINT-MATHIAS   *p* 1283

1111 3E RUE, RICHELIEU, QC, J3L 3Z2

(450) 658-0649   *SIC* 6062

CAISSE POPULAIRE DESJARDINS DE SAINT-LAURENT, LA   *p* 1323

1460 RUE DE L'EGLISE, SAINT-LAURENT, QC, H4L 2H6

(514) 748-8821   *SIC* 6062

CAISSE POPULAIRE DESJARDINS DES MILLE-ILES   *p* 1231

4433 BOUL DE LA CONCORDE E, MONTREAL, QC, H7C 1M4

(450) 661-7274   *SIC* 6062

CAISSE POPULAIRE DESJARDINS DES RAMEES   *p* 1120

1278 CH DE LA VERNIERE, L'ETANG-DU-NORD, QC, G4T 3E6

(418) 986-2319   *SIC* 6062

CAISSE POPULAIRE DESJARDINS DU BASSIN-DE-CHAMBLY   *p* 1074

455 BOUL BRASSARD, CHAMBLY, QC, J3L 4V6

(450) 658-0691   *SIC* 6062

CAISSE POPULAIRE DESJARDINS DU PIEMONT LAURENTIEN   *p* 1119

1638 RUE NOTRE-DAME, L'ANCIENNE-LORETTE, QC, G2E 3B6

(418) 872-1445   *SIC* 6062

CAISSE POPULAIRE DESJARDINS LE MANOIR   *p* 1149

820 MONTEE MASSON, MASCOUCHE, QC, J7K 3B6

(450) 474-2474   *SIC* 6062

CAISSE POPULAIRE KENT-SUD LTEE *p* 395

196 IRVING BLVD, BOUCTOUCHE, NB, E4S 3L7

(506) 576-6666   *SIC* 6062

CAISSE POPULAIRE LA PRAIRIE LTEE *p* 357

130 CENTRALE AVE, STE ANNE, MB, R5H 1J3

(204) 422-8896   *SIC* 6062

CAISSE POPULAIRE LA VALLEE LTEE *p* 403

181 BOUL BROADWAY, GRAND-SAULT/GRAND FALLS, NB, E3Z 2J8

(506) 473-3660   *SIC* 6062

CAISSE POPULAIRE LES GRANDS BOULEVARD   *p* 1085

1535 BOUL SAINT-MARTIN O, COTE SAINT-LUC, QC, H7S 1N1

(450) 668-4000   *SIC* 6411

CAISSE POPULAIRE TRILLIUM INC *p* 596

1173 CYRVILLE RD, GLOUCESTER, ON, K1J 7S6

(613) 745-2123   *SIC* 6062

CAISSE SAINT JEAN BAPTIST   *p* 1098

See CAISSE DESJARDINS DE DRUMMONDVILLE

CAISSEN WATER TECHNOLOGIES INC *p* 538

265 INDUSTRIAL RD, CAMBRIDGE, ON, N3H 4R7

(800) 265-7841   *SIC* 5963

CAISSES DESJARDINS   *p* 1076

See FEDERATION DES CAISSES DESJARDINS DU QUEBEC

CAISSES DESJARDINS DES BERGES DE ROUSSILLON   *p* 1297

296 VOIE DE LA DESSERTE, SAINT-CONSTANT, QC, J5A 2C9

(450) 632-2820   *SIC* 6062

CAISSIECO ENTERPRISES LTD   *p* 443

24 FOREST HILLS PKY, DARTMOUTH, NS, B2W 6E4

(902) 462-6100   *SIC* 5999

CAJUN'S CLOTHING STORE   *p* 471

See ACADIA STUDENTS' UNION INC

CAKES UNLIMITED   *p* 372

See ICE CREAM UNLIMITED INC

CAL-MATRIX METROLOGY   *p* 1091

See TRANSCAT CANADA INC

CALABRIA MARKET & DELI INC   *p* 393

139 SCURFIELD BLVD, WINNIPEG, MB, R3Y 1L6

(204) 487-1700   *SIC* 5411

CALADO AND LIMA HOME IMPROVEMENT INC   *p* 868

15 MANSION AVE, SCARBOROUGH, ON, M1L 1A5

(416) 782-0110   *SIC* 1521

CALAHOO MEATS LTD   *p* 168

3 54416 RGE RD 280, STURGEON COUNTY, AB, T8R 1Z5

(780) 458-2136   *SIC* 5147

CALAIS FARMS LTD   *p* 174

33418 DOWNES RD, ABBOTSFORD, BC, V2S 7T4

(604) 852-1660   *SIC* 0191

CALALTA SUPPLY LTD   *p* 21

3800 19 ST NE UNIT 8, CALGARY, AB, T2E 6V2

(403) 250-3195   *SIC* 5063

CALCON MANAGEMENT, L.P.   *p* 27

700 CENTRE ST SE, CALGARY, AB, T2G 5P6

(403) 537-4426   *SIC* 8741

CALCULATED INCENTIVES INC   *p* 906

109 ROSEDALE HEIGHTS DR, THORNHILL, ON, L4J 4V9

SIC 5199

CALDER CENTRE   *p* 1425

See SASKATCHEWAN HEALTH AUTHORITY

CALDIC CANADA INC   *p* 720

6980 CREDITVIEW RD, MISSISSAUGA, ON, L5N 8E2

(905) 812-7300   *SIC* 2043

CALDON WOODS GOLFS CLUB   *p* 494

See CLUBLINK CORPORATION ULC

CALDWELL & ROSS LIMITED   *p* 402

195 DOAK RD, FREDERICTON, NB, E3C 2E6

(506) 453-1333   *SIC* 1611

CALDWELL PARTNERS INTERNATIONAL INC, THE   *p* 972

165 AVENUE RD SUITE 600, TORONTO, ON, M5R 3S4

(416) 920-7702   *SIC* 7311

CALDWELL ROACH INSURANCE   *p* 468

See CALDWELL-ROACH AGENCIES LIMITED

CALDWELL SECURITIES LTD   *p* 949

150 KING ST W SUITE 1710, TORONTO, ON, M5H 1J9

(416) 862-7755   *SIC* 6211

CALDWELL, C. MARK ENTERPRISE LTD *p* 76

388 COUNTRY HILLS BLVD NE UNIT 200, CALGARY, AB, T3K 5J6

(403) 226-9550   *SIC* 5251

CALDWELL-ROACH AGENCIES LIMITED *p* 468

643 PRINCE ST, TRURO, NS, B2N 1G5

(902) 893-4204   *SIC* 6411

CALEA HOMECARE, DIV OF   *p* 692

See CALEA LTD

CALEA LTD   *p* 692

2785 SKYMARK AVE UNIT 2, MISSISSAUGA, ON, L4W 4Y3

(905) 238-1234   *SIC* 5122

CALEDON CREEK MECHANICAL LIMITED

p 532

18023 HORSESHOE HILL RD, CALEDON VILLAGE, ON, L7K 2B8

(519) 927-0190   *SIC* 1711

CALEDON EAST FOODLAND   *p* 531

15771 AIRPORT RD SUITE 4A, CALEDON EAST, ON, L7C 1K2

(905) 584-9677   *SIC* 5411

CALEDON PROPANE INC   *p* 494

1 BETOMAT CRT, BOLTON, ON, L7E 2V9

(905) 857-1448   *SIC* 5984

CALEDON TUBING, DIV OF   *p* 888

See 2008788 ONTARIO LIMITED

CALEDONIA PRODUCE DISTRIBUTORS *p* 739

See GREENGROCER INC, THE

CALEDONIA TRANSPORTATION CO *p* 617

See 944622 ONTARIO LIMITED

CALEGO INTERNATIONAL INC   *p* 1338

6265 CH DE LA COTE-DE-LIESSE BUREAU 200, SAINT-LAURENT, QC, H4T 1C3

(514) 334-2117   *SIC* 5099

CALENDAR CLUB OF CANADA   *p* 836

See CALENDAR CLUB OF CANADA LIMITED PARTNERSHIP

CALENDAR CLUB OF CANADA LIMITED PARTNERSHIP   *p* 836

6 ADAMS ST SUITE A, PARIS, ON, N3L 3X4

(519) 442-8355   *SIC* 5945

CALENDAR, THE   *p* 219

See BLACK PRESS GROUP LTD

CALENDRIER DREAM TEAM   *p* 1402

See RNC MEDIA INC

CALERES CANADA, INC   *p* 839

1857 ROGERS RD, PERTH, ON, K7H 1P7

(613) 267-0348   *SIC* 5139

CALEY ORTHODONTIC LABORATORY LIMITED   *p* 1008

151 PARK ST, WATERLOO, ON, N2L 1Y5

(519) 742-1467   *SIC* 3843

CALFOREX   *p* 45

See CALGARY FOREIGN EXCHANGE LTD

CALFRAC WELL SERVICES LTD   *p* 45

411 8 AVE SW, CALGARY, AB, T2P 1E3

(866) 770-3722   *SIC* 1389

CALFRAC WELL SERVICES LTD   *p* 155

7310 EDGAR INDUSTRIAL DR, RED DEER, AB, T4P 3R2

(866) 772-3722   *SIC* 1381

CALGARY AGGREGATE RECYCLING LTD *p* 14

6020 94 AVE SE, CALGARY, AB, T2C 3Z3

(403) 279-8330   *SIC* 4953

CALGARY AIRPORT AUTHORITY, THE *p* 21

2000 AIRPORT RD NE, CALGARY, AB, T2E 6W5

(403) 735-1200   *SIC* 4581

CALGARY ALTERNATIVE SUPPORT SERVICES INC   *p* 41

1240 KENSINGTON RD NW SUITE 408, CALGARY, AB, T2N 3P7

(403) 283-0611   *SIC* 8322

CALGARY BMW   *p* 33

See 504147 ALBERTA LTD

CALGARY BOARD OF EDUCATION   *p* 8

3020 52 ST NE, CALGARY, AB, T1Y 5P4

(403) 280-6565   *SIC* 8211

CALGARY BOARD OF EDUCATION   *p* 10

1304 44 ST SE, CALGARY, AB, T2A 1M8

(403) 272-6665   *SIC* 8211

CALGARY BOARD OF EDUCATION   *p* 34

47 FYFFE RD SE, CALGARY, AB, T2H 1B9

(403) 777-6420   *SIC* 8211

CALGARY BOARD OF EDUCATION   *p* 34

9019 FAIRMOUNT DR SE, CALGARY, AB, T2H 0Z4

(403) 259-5585   *SIC* 8211

CALGARY BOARD OF EDUCATION   *p* 40

5220 NORTHLAND DR NW, CALGARY, AB, T2L 2J6

(403) 289-9241   *SIC* 8211

CALGARY BOARD OF EDUCATION   *p* 40

6620 4 ST NW, CALGARY, AB, T2K 1C2
(403) 274-2240   *SIC 8211*
CALGARY BOARD OF EDUCATION   *p 41*
1019 1 ST NW, CALGARY, AB, T2M 2S2
(403) 276-5521   *SIC 8211*
CALGARY BOARD OF EDUCATION   *p 41*
3009 MORLEY TRAIL NW, CALGARY, AB,
T2M 4G9
(403) 289-2551   *SIC 8211*
CALGARY BOARD OF EDUCATION   *p 41*
512 18 ST NW, CALGARY, AB, T2N 2G5
(403) 777-6380   *SIC 8211*
CALGARY BOARD OF EDUCATION   *p 64*
1221 8 ST SW, CALGARY, AB, T2R 0L4
(403) 817-4000   *SIC 8211*
CALGARY BOARD OF EDUCATION   *p 66*
641 17 AVE SW, CALGARY, AB, T2S 0B5
(403) 228-5363   *SIC 8211*
CALGARY BOARD OF EDUCATION   *p 68*
2266 WOODPARK AVE SW, CALGARY, AB,
T2W 2Z8
(403) 251-8022   *SIC 8211*
CALGARY BOARD OF EDUCATION   *p 68*
910 75 AVE SW, CALGARY, AB, T2V 0S6
(403) 253-2261   *SIC 8211*
CALGARY BOARD OF EDUCATION   *p 72*
4627 77 ST NW, CALGARY, AB, T3B 2N6
(403) 286-5092   *SIC 8211*
CALGARY BOARD OF EDUCATION   *p 73*
2336 53 AVE SW, CALGARY, AB, T3E 1L2
(403) 243-4500   *SIC 8211*
CALGARY BOARD OF EDUCATION   *p 73*
2519 RICHMOND RD SW SUITE 168, CAL-
GARY, AB, T3E 4M2
(403) 777-7200   *SIC 8221*
CALGARY BOARD OF EDUCATION   *p 73*
5111 21 ST SW, CALGARY, AB, T3E 1R9
(403) 243-8880   *SIC 8211*
CALGARY C MOTORS LP   *p 34*
125 GLENDEER CIR SE, CALGARY, AB,
T2H 2S8
(403) 255-8111   *SIC 5511*
**CALGARY CATHOLIC IMMIGRATION SO-
CIETY**   *p 64*
1111 11 AVE SW SUITE 103, CALGARY,
AB, T2R 0G5
(403) 262-5692   *SIC 8322*
**CALGARY CATHOLIC IMMIGRATION SO-
CIETY**   *p 64*
1111 11 AVE SW UNIT 111, CALGARY, AB,
T2R 0G5
(403) 262-2006   *SIC 8322*
CALGARY CATHOLIC SCHOOL DISTRICT
p 45
*See CALGARY ROMAN CATHOLIC SEPA-
RATE SCHOOL DISTRICT #1*
**CALGARY CENTRE FOR PERFORMING
ARTS**   *p 27*
205 8 AVE SE SUITE 1205, CALGARY, AB,
T2G 0K9
(403) 294-7455   *SIC 7929*
CALGARY CHAMBER OF COMMERCE   *p 27*
237 8 AVE SE SUITE 600, CALGARY, AB,
T2G 5C3
(403) 750-0400   *SIC 8611*
CALGARY CO-OP   *p 21*
*See CALGARY CO-OPERATIVE ASSOCIA-
TION LIMITED*
CALGARY CO-OP   *p 34*
*See CALGARY CO-OPERATIVE ASSOCIA-
TION LIMITED*
CALGARY CO-OP   *p 39*
*See CALGARY CO-OPERATIVE ASSOCIA-
TION LIMITED*
CALGARY CO-OP   *p 74*
*See CALGARY CO-OPERATIVE ASSOCIA-
TION LIMITED*
CALGARY CO-OP   *p 168*
*See CALGARY CO-OPERATIVE ASSOCIA-
TION LIMITED*
CALGARY CO-OP HOME HEALTH CARE

LIMITED   *p 39*
9309 MACLEOD TRAIL SW SUITE 3, CAL-
GARY, AB, T2J 0P6
(403) 252-2266   *SIC 5137*
**CALGARY CO-OPERATIVE ASSOCIATION
LIMITED**   *p 10*
3330 17 AVE SE SUITE 5, CALGARY, AB,
T2A 0P9
(403) 299-4461   *SIC 5411*
**CALGARY CO-OPERATIVE ASSOCIATION
LIMITED**   *p 21*
540 16 AVE NE, CALGARY, AB, T2E 1K4
(403) 299-4276   *SIC 5411*
**CALGARY CO-OPERATIVE ASSOCIATION
LIMITED**   *p 34*
151 86 AVE SE UNIT 110, CALGARY, AB,
T2H 3A5
(403) 219-6025   *SIC 5411*
**CALGARY CO-OPERATIVE ASSOCIATION
LIMITED**   *p 39*
1221 CANYON MEADOWS DR SE SUITE
95, CALGARY, AB, T2J 6G2
(403) 299-4350   *SIC 5411*
**CALGARY CO-OPERATIVE ASSOCIATION
LIMITED**   *p 40*
4122 BRENTWOOD RD NW SUITE 4, CAL-
GARY, AB, T2L 1K8
(403) 299-4301   *SIC 5411*
**CALGARY CO-OPERATIVE ASSOCIATION
LIMITED**   *p 74*
35 CROWFOOT WAY NW, CALGARY, AB,
T3G 2L4
(403) 216-4500   *SIC 5411*
**CALGARY CO-OPERATIVE ASSOCIATION
LIMITED**   *p 168*
320 2ND ST, STRATHMORE, AB, T1P 1K1
(403) 934-3121   *SIC 5411*
**CALGARY CONVENTION CENTRE AU-
THORITY**   *p 27*
120 9 AVE SE, CALGARY, AB, T2G 0P3
(403) 261-8500   *SIC 7389*
CALGARY COUNSELLING CENTRE   *p 28*
105 12 AVE SE SUITE 100, CALGARY, AB,
T2G 1A1
(403) 265-4980   *SIC 8322*
**CALGARY DISTRICT PIPE TRADES
HEALTH & WELFARE AND PENSION
PLANS**   *p 8*
2635 37 AVE NE SUITE 110, CALGARY, AB,
T1Y 5Z6
(403) 250-3534   *SIC 6371*
**CALGARY DROP-IN & REHAB CENTRE
SOCIETY**   *p 28*
1 DERMOT BALDWIN WAY SE, CALGARY,
AB, T2G 0P8
(403) 266-3600   *SIC 8399*
CALGARY E M S   *p 8*
See EMERGENCY MEDICAL SERVICES
**CALGARY ELKS LODGE #4 SOCIETY OF
THE B.P.O.E. OF CANADA**   *p 21*
2502 6 ST NE, CALGARY, AB, T2E 3Z3
(403) 250-7391   *SIC 7992*
CALGARY ELKS LODGE & GOLF CLUB   *p 21*
*See CALGARY ELKS LODGE #4 SOCIETY
OF THE B.P.O.E. OF CANADA*
CALGARY ENERGY CENTRE NO. 2 INC   *p 78*
14417 68 ST NE, CALGARY, AB, T4B 2T4
(403) 567-5135   *SIC 4911*
**CALGARY EXHIBITION AND STAMPEDE
LIMITED**   *p 28*
1410 OLYMPIC WAY SE, CALGARY, AB,
T2G 2W1
(403) 261-0101   *SIC 7999*
CALGARY FASTENERS & TOOLS LTD *p 28*
1288 42 AVE SE UNIT 1, CALGARY, AB,
T2G 5P1
(403) 287-5340   *SIC 5085*
CALGARY FASTENERS AND TOOLS   *p 27*
See 700635 ALBERTA LTD
CALGARY FLAMES HOCKEY CLUB   *p 28*
See CALGARY FLAMES LIMITED PART-

NERSHIP
**CALGARY FLAMES LIMITED PARTNER-
SHIP**   *p 28*
555 SADDLEDOME RISE SE, CALGARY,
AB, T2G 2W1
(403) 777-2177   *SIC 7941*
CALGARY FOREIGN EXCHANGE LTD *p 45*
255 5 AVE SUITE 480, CALGARY, AB, T2P
3G6
(403) 290-0400   *SIC 6099*
**CALGARY FRENCH & INTERNATIONAL
SCHOOL SOCIETY, THE**   *p 75*
700 77 ST SW, CALGARY, AB, T3H 5R1
(403) 240-1500   *SIC 8299*
CALGARY FUEL STOP   *p 12*
See CANADIAN TRUCKSTOPS LTD
CALGARY GYMNASTICS CENTRE   *p 72*
179 CANADA OLYMPIC RD SW, CALGARY,
AB, T3B 5R5
(403) 242-1171   *SIC 7999*
CALGARY H MOTORS LP   *p 21*
1920 23 ST NE, CALGARY, AB, T2E 8N3
(403) 250-9990   *SIC 5511*
CALGARY HANDI-BUS ASSOCIATION *p 21*
231 37 AVE NE, CALGARY, AB, T2E 8J2
(403) 276-8028   *SIC 8322*
CALGARY HARLEY-DAVIDSON   *p 23*
*See HARLEY-DAVIDSON OF SOUTHERN
ALBERTA INC*
CALGARY HERALD, THE   *p 25*
See POSTMEDIA NETWORK INC
CALGARY HOMELESS FOUNDATION *p 28*
615 MACLEOD TRAIL SE SUITE 1500,
CALGARY, AB, T2G 4T8
(403) 237-6456   *SIC 8699*
CALGARY HONDA   *p 38*
See 504148 ALBERTA INC
CALGARY HOUSING COMPANY   *p 72*
See CALHOME PROPERTIES LTD
**CALGARY HUMANE SOCIETY FOR PRE-
VENTION OF CRUELTY TO ANIMALS**   *p 14*
4455 110 AVE SE, CALGARY, AB, T2C 2T7
(403) 205-4455   *SIC 8699*
CALGARY HYUNDAI   *p 21*
See CALGARY H MOTORS LP
**CALGARY IMMIGRANT WOMEN'S ASSO-
CIATION**   *p 28*
138 4 AVE SE SUITE 200, CALGARY, AB,
T2G 4Z6
(403) 517-8830   *SIC 8399*
CALGARY IMPOUND   *p 28*
See CALGARY PARKING AUTHORITY
CALGARY INTERNATIONAL AIRPORT *p 21*
*See CALGARY AIRPORT AUTHORITY,
THE*
CALGARY ITALIAN BAKERY LTD   *p 34*
5310 5 ST SE, CALGARY, AB, T2H 1L2
(403) 255-3515   *SIC 2051*
CALGARY M VEHICLES GP INC   *p 34*
168 GLENDEER CIRCLE SE, CALGARY,
AB, T2H 2V4
(403) 253-6800   *SIC 5511*
CALGARY METAL RECYCLING INC   *p 28*
3415 OGDEN RD SE, CALGARY, AB, T2G
4N4
(403) 262-4542   *SIC 5093*
**CALGARY OLYMPIC DEVELOPMENT AS-
SOCIATION**   *p 72*
88 CANADA OLYMPIC RD SW, CALGARY,
AB, T3B 5R5
(403) 247-5452   *SIC 7999*
CALGARY PARKING AUTHORITY   *p 28*
400 39 AVE SE, CALGARY, AB, T2G 5P8
(403) 537-7100   *SIC 7521*
CALGARY PETERBILT LTD   *p 70*
11550 44 ST SE, CALGARY, AB, T2Z 4A2
(403) 235-2550   *SIC 5012*
CALGARY PETROLEUM CLUB   *p 45*
319 5 AVE SW, CALGARY, AB, T2P 0L5
(403) 269-7981   *SIC 8641*

CALGARY PLAZA HOTEL LTD   *p 10*
1316 33 ST NE, CALGARY, AB, T2A 6B6
(403) 248-8888   *SIC 7011*
CALGARY PUBLIC LIBRARY   *p 28*
800 3 ST SE, CALGARY, AB, T2G 2E7
(403) 260-2712   *SIC 8231*
CALGARY R&D CENTRE   *p 71*
See TRICAN WELL SERVICE LTD
**CALGARY RAMADA DOWNTOWN LIMITED
PARTNERSHIP**   *p 45*
708 8 AVE SW, CALGARY, AB, T2P 1H2
(403) 263-7600   *SIC 7011*
**CALGARY REAL ESTATE BOARD CO-
OPERATIVE LIMITED**   *p 21*
300 MANNING RD NE, CALGARY, AB, T2E
8K4
(403) 263-4940   *SIC 8611*
**CALGARY ROMAN CATHOLIC SEPARATE
SCHOOL DISTRICT #1**   *p 40*
877 NORTHMOUNT DR NW, CALGARY,
AB, T2L 0A3
(403) 500-2026   *SIC 8211*
**CALGARY ROMAN CATHOLIC SEPARATE
SCHOOL DISTRICT #1**   *p 45*
1000 5 AVE SW SUITE 1, CALGARY, AB,
T2P 4T9
(403) 500-2000   *SIC 8211*
**CALGARY ROMAN CATHOLIC SEPARATE
SCHOOL DISTRICT #1**   *p 66*
111 18 AVE SW SUITE 1, CALGARY, AB,
T2S 0B8
(403) 500-2024   *SIC 8211*
**CALGARY ROMAN CATHOLIC SEPARATE
SCHOOL DISTRICT #1**   *p 68*
111 HADDON RD SW, CALGARY, AB, T2V
2Y2
(403) 500-2047   *SIC 8211*
**CALGARY ROMAN CATHOLIC SEPARATE
SCHOOL DISTRICT #1**   *p 73*
4624 RICHARD RD SW, CALGARY, AB,
T3E 6L1
(403) 500-2056   *SIC 8211*
CALGARY SCIENCE CENTRE SOCIETY   *p 21*
220 ST GEORGES DR NE, CALGARY, AB,
T2E 5T2
(403) 817-6800   *SIC 8412*
CALGARY SCIENTIFIC INC   *p 28*
1210 20 AVE SE SUITE 208, CALGARY, AB,
T2G 1M8
(403) 270-7159   *SIC 7374*
CALGARY SCOPE SOCIETY   *p 21*
219 18 ST SE, CALGARY, AB, T2E 6J5
(403) 509-0200   *SIC 8322*
CALGARY SILVER LININGS FOUNDATION   *p 67*
2009 33 AVE SW SUITE 2, CALGARY, AB,
T2T 1Z5
(403) 536-4025   *SIC 8062*
CALGARY STAMPEDE   *p 28*
*See CALGARY EXHIBITION AND STAM-
PEDE LIMITED*
CALGARY STOCKYARDS LTD   *p 34*
5925 12 ST SE RM 200, CALGARY, AB, T2H
2M3
(403) 234-7429   *SIC 5154*
CALGARY SUN, THE   *p 20*
See 1032451 B.C. LTD
CALGARY TELECOM   *p 76*
See FRIENDLY TELECOM INC
CALGARY TELUS CONVENTION CENTRE
p 27
*See CALGARY CONVENTION CENTRE
AUTHORITY*
CALGARY TOWER FACILITIES LTD   *p 45*
101 9 AVE SW, CALGARY, AB, T2P 1J9
(403) 266-7171   *SIC 5812*
CALGARY URBAN PROJECT SOCIETY   *p 64*
1001 10 AVE SW, CALGARY, AB, T2R 0B7
(403) 221-8780   *SIC 8093*
CALGARY V MOTORS LP   *p 40*
4849 NORTHLAND DR NW, CALGARY, AB,

T2L 2K3
(403) 286-4849 *SIC* 5511
CALGARY VALVE & FITTING INC *p* 10
3202 12 AVE NE, CALGARY, AB, T2A 6N8
(403) 243-5646 *SIC* 5085
CALGARY YOUNG MEN'S CHRISTIAN AS-SOCIATION *p*
68
11 HADDON RD SW, CALGARY, AB, T2V 2X8
SIC 8399
CALGARY YOUNG MEN'S CHRISTIAN AS-SOCIATION *p*
69
See *CALGARY YOUNG MEN'S CHRISTIAN ASSOCIATION, THE*
CALGARY YOUNG MEN'S CHRISTIAN AS-SOCIATION *p*
74
See *CALGARY YOUNG MEN'S CHRISTIAN ASSOCIATION, THE*
CALGARY YOUNG MEN'S CHRISTIAN AS-SOCIATION *p*
126
GD, EXSHAW, AB, T0L 2C0
(403) 673-3858 *SIC* 8621
CALGARY YOUNG MEN'S CHRISTIAN AS-SOCIATION, THE *p*
45
101 3 ST SW, CALGARY, AB, T2P 4G6
(403) 269-6701 *SIC* 8399
CALGARY YOUNG MEN'S CHRISTIAN AS-SOCIATION, THE *p*
69
333 SHAWVILLE BLVD SE SUITE 400, CALGARY, AB, T2Y 4H3
(403) 256-5533 *SIC* 8322
CALGARY YOUNG MEN'S CHRISTIAN AS-SOCIATION, THE *p*
74
8100 JOHN LAURIE BLVD NW, CALGARY, AB, T3G 3S3
(403) 547-6576 *SIC* 8399
CALGARY YOUNG WOMEN'S CHRISTIAN ASSOCIATION *p* 28
1715 17 AVE SE, CALGARY, AB, T2G 5J1
(403) 262-0498 *SIC* 8399
CALGARY YOUNG WOMEN'S CHRISTIAN ASSOCIATION, THE *p* 28
320 5 AVE SE, CALGARY, AB, T2G 0E5
(403) 263-1550 *SIC* 8322
CALGARY ZOO *p* 21
See *CALGARY ZOOLOGICAL SOCIETY, THE*
CALGARY ZOOLOGICAL SOCIETY, THE *p* 21
1300 ZOO RD NE, CALGARY, AB, T2E 7V6
(403) 232-9300 *SIC* 7999
CALHEX INDUSTRIES LTD *p* 14
9515 48 ST SE, CALGARY, AB, T2C 2R1
(403) 225-4395 *SIC* 3443
CALHOME PROPERTIES LTD *p* 72
820 PINE PL SW, CALGARY, AB, T3C 3N1
(403) 217-7933 *SIC* 6514
CALHOUN FOODS LAND *p* 682
6 CENTURY BLVD, MILLBROOK, ON, L0A 1G0
(705) 932-2139 *SIC* 5411
CALIAN GROUP LTD *p* 835
770 PALLADIUM DR, OTTAWA, ON, K2V 1C8
(613) 599-8600 *SIC* 8711
CALIAN LTD *p* 835
4-770 PALLADIUM DR, OTTAWA, ON, K2V 1C8
(613) 599-8600 *SIC* 4899
CALIAN LTD *p* 1202
700 RUE DE LA GAUCHETIERE O BU-REAU 26E, MONTREAL, QC, H3B 5M2
SIC 7361
CALIAN LTD *p* 1433
18 INNOVATION BLVD, SASKATOON, SK, S7N 3R1
(306) 931-3425 *SIC* 4899

CALIBRE BEAUTE *p* 853
See *QUADRANT COSMETICS CORP*
CALIBRE SALES INC *p* 549
8162 KEELE ST, CONCORD, ON, L4K 2A5
(905) 660-3603 *SIC* 5113
CALIFORNIA CLEANING *p* 505
See *QUIET HARMONY INC*
CALIFORNIA INNOVATIONS INC *p* 788
36 DUFFLAW RD, NORTH YORK, ON, M6A 2W1
(416) 590-7700 *SIC* 5078
CALIFORNIA L.I.N.E. INC *p* 1297
701 RANG SAINT-PIERRE N UNIT? 1, SAINT-CONSTANT, QC, J5A 0R2
(450) 632-9000 *SIC* 4212
CALKINS & BURKE HOLDINGS LTD *p* 318
1500 GEORGIA ST W SUITE 800, VAN-COUVER, BC, V6G 2Z6
(604) 669-3741 *SIC* 2092
CALKINS & BURKE LIMITED *p* 318
1500 GEORGIA ST W SUITE 800, VAN-COUVER, BC, V6G 2Z6
(604) 669-3741 *SIC* 5146
CALL CENTRE INC, THE *p* 429
5 PIPPY PL SUITE 7, ST. JOHN'S, NL, A1B 3X2
(709) 722-3730 *SIC* 7389
CALL ROACH'S YELLOW TAXI *p* 907
See *ROACH'S TAXI (1988) LTD*
CALL-US INFO LTD *p* 455
6009 QUINPOOL RD, HALIFAX, NS, B3K 5J7
SIC 7389
CALL2RECYCLE CANADA, INC *p* 995
5140 YONGE ST UNIT 1570, TORONTO, ON, M7A 2K2
(888) 224-9764 *SIC* 3356
CALLBECKS HOME HARDWARE *p* 1042
See *CALLBECKS LTD*
CALLBECKS LTD *p* 1042
613 WATER ST E, SUMMERSIDE, PE, C1N 4H8
(902) 436-1100 *SIC* 5211
CALLIDUS CAPITAL CORPORATION *p* 960
181 BAY ST UNIT 4620, TORONTO, ON, M5J 2T3
(416) 945-3016 *SIC* 8741
CALLISTO INTEGRATION LTD *p* 803
635 FOURTH LINE UNIT 16, OAKVILLE, ON, L6L 5W4
(905) 339-0059 *SIC* 7373
CALLNOVO *p* 914
See *BPONOVO INC*
CALLOWAY REIT (CARLETON) INC *p* 549
700 APPLEWOOD CRES SUITE 200, CON-CORD, ON, L4K 5X3
(905) 326-6400 *SIC* 6798
CALLOWAY REIT (SOUTH KEYS) INC *p* 549
700 APPLEWOOD CRES SUITE 20, CON-CORD, ON, L4K 5X3
(905) 326-6400 *SIC* 6798
CALM AIR INTERNATIONAL LP *p* 383
930 FERRY RD, WINNIPEG, MB, R3H 0Y8
(204) 778-6471 *SIC* 4512
CALMONT LEASING LTD *p* 93
14610 YELLOWHEAD TRAIL NW, EDMON-TON, AB, T5L 3C5
(780) 454-0491 *SIC* 7513
CALMONT TRUCK CENTRE LTD *p* 99
11403 174 ST NW, EDMONTON, AB, T5S 2P4
(780) 451-2680 *SIC* 5511
CALMONT TRUCK RENTAL & LEASING *p* 93
See *CALMONT LEASING LTD*
CALNASH TRUCKING LTD *p* 138
1 PARKER RD, LAC LA BICHE, AB, T0A 2C0
SIC 4213
CALROC INDUSTRIES INC *p* 143
6847 66 ST, LLOYDMINSTER, AB, T9V 3R7
(780) 875-8802 *SIC* 5082
CALSCO SOLVENTS LIMITED *p* 876
4120 MIDLAND AVE, SCARBOROUGH,

ON, M1V 4S8
(416) 293-0123 *SIC* 5169
CALSPER DEVELOPMENTS INC *p* 549
7501 KEELE ST SUITE 100, CONCORD, ON, L4K 1Y2
(905) 761-8200 *SIC* 1521
CALTECH GROUP LTD *p* 64
1011 1 ST SW SUITE 520, CALGARY, AB, T2R 1J2
(403) 263-8055 *SIC* 8713
CALTEST ENERGY SERVICES LTD *p* 64
602 12 AVE SW SUITE 610, CALGARY, AB, T2R 1J3
SIC 4925
CALTEX TRANSPORT *p* 1127
See *COURTIER DOUANES INTERNA-TIONAL SKYWAY LTEE*
CALTRAX INC *p* 28
1805 30 AVE SE, CALGARY, AB, T2G 4X8
(403) 234-0585 *SIC* 4789
CALVARY PLACE PERSONAL CARE HOME *p* 380
See *3885136 MANITOBA ASSOCIATION INC*
CALVIN KLEIN *p* 983
See *PVH CANADA, INC*
CALVIN KLEVIN *p* 1341
See *PVH CANADA, INC*
CAM CHAIN CO. LTD *p* 276
8355 128 ST, SURREY, BC, V3W 4G1
(604) 599-1522 *SIC* 3462
CAM CLARK FORD LINCOLN LTD *p* 241
833 AUTOMALL DR, NORTH VANCOU-VER, BC, V7P 3R8
(604) 980-3673 *SIC* 7532
CAM CLARK FORD RICHMOND LTD *p* 253
13580 SMALLWOOD PL, RICHMOND, BC, V6V 2C1
(604) 273-7331 *SIC* 5531
CAM CLARK FORD SALES LTD *p* 2
925 VETERANS BLVD NW BAY 1, AIR-DRIE, AB, T4A 2G6
(403) 948-6660 *SIC* 5511
CAM DISTRIBUTORS LTD *p* 14
7095 64 ST SE UNIT 20, CALGARY, AB, T2C 5C3
(403) 720-0076 *SIC* 5085
CAM INDUSTRIAL *p* 14
See *CAM DISTRIBUTORS LTD*
CAM TRAN CO. LTD *p* 546
203 PURDY RD, COLBORNE, ON, K0K 1S0
(905) 355-3224 *SIC* 3612
CAM-RAIL *p* 1310
See *BUNGE GRAIN DU CANADA INC*
CAM-RON INSURANCE BROKERS LIM-ITED *p*
806
4579 OIL SPRINGS LINE, OIL SPRINGS, ON, N0N 1P0
(519) 834-2833 *SIC* 6411
CAM-SCOTT TRANSPORT LTD *p* 1013
1900 BOUNDARY RD, WHITBY, ON, L1N 8P8
(905) 438-9555 *SIC* 4212
CAM-SLIDE *p* 754
See *MAGNA SEATING INC*
CAM-TAG INDUSTRIES INC *p* 597
2783 FENTON RD, GLOUCESTER, ON, K1T 3T8
(613) 822-1921 *SIC* 3365
CAM-TRAC BERNIERES INC *p* 1140
830 CH OLIVIER, LEVIS, QC, G7A 2N1
(418) 831-2324 *SIC* 5999
CAM-TRAC RIMOUSKI *p* 1140
See *CAM-TRAC BERNIERES INC*
CAMA WOODLANDS NURSING HOME *p* 529
159 PANIN RD, BURLINGTON, ON, L7P 5A6
(905) 681-6441 *SIC* 8051
CAMACC SYSTEMS INC *p* 267
2261 KEATING CROSS RD UNIT 200B, SAANICHTON, BC, V8M 2A5
(250) 652-3406 *SIC* 5065

CAMAD *p* 870
See *CAMERON ADVERTISING DISPLAYS LIMITED*
CAMALOR MFG. INC *p* 519
100 CENTRAL AVE W, BROCKVILLE, ON, K6V 4N8
(613) 342-2259 *SIC* 3499
CAMBIE COMMUNITY CENTRE *p* 256
See *RICHMOND, CITY OF*
CAMBIE ROOFING & DRAINAGE CON-TRACTORS *p*
290
See *CAMBIE ROOFING CONTRACTORS LTD*
CAMBIE ROOFING CONTRACTORS LTD *p* 290
1367 E KENT AVE NORTH, VANCOUVER, BC, V5X 4T6
(604) 261-1111 *SIC* 1761
CAMBIUM INC *p* 839
52 HUNTER ST E, PETERBOROUGH, ON, K9H 1G5
(705) 742-7900 *SIC* 8748
CAMBLI INTERNATIONAL *p* 1318
See *GROUPE CAMBLI INC*
CAMBODIA SUPPORT GROUP SOCIETY *p* 223
135 THOMPSON ST, KIMBERLEY, BC, V1A 1T9
(250) 427-2159 *SIC* 8699
CAMBRIA DESIGN BUILD *p* 754
See *1148044 ONTARIO LTD*
CAMBRIA FABSHOP-TORONTO INC *p* 494
41 SIMPSON RD, BOLTON, ON, L7E 2R6
(905) 951-1011 *SIC* 2541
CAMBRIAN COLLEGE OF APPLIED ARTS & TECHNOLOGY, THE *p* 898
1400 BARRYDOWNE RD, SUDBURY, ON, P3A 3V8
(705) 566-8101 *SIC* 8222
CAMBRIAN CREDIT UNION LIMITED *p* 377
225 BROADWAY, WINNIPEG, MB, R3C 5R4
(204) 925-2600 *SIC* 6062
CAMBRIAN FLOWER DISTRIBUTION *p* 833
See *CAMBRIAN TRADING HOUSE LTD*
CAMBRIAN FORD SALES INC *p* 898
1615 KINGSWAY ST, SUDBURY, ON, P3A 4S9
(705) 560-3673 *SIC* 5511
CAMBRIAN INSURANCE BROKERS LIM-ITED *p*
900
130 PARIS ST SUITE 1, SUDBURY, ON, P3E 3E1
(705) 673-5000 *SIC* 6411
CAMBRIAN SOLUTIONS INC *p* 800
627 LYONS LANE SUITE 300, OAKVILLE, ON, L6J 5Z7
(905) 338-3172 *SIC* 5169
CAMBRIAN TRADING HOUSE LTD *p* 833
153 GILMOUR ST, OTTAWA, ON, K2P 0N8
(613) 233-3111 *SIC* 5193
CAMBRIDGE AND NORTH DUMFRIES EN-ERGY PLUS INC *p*
532
1500 BISHOP ST N, CAMBRIDGE, ON, N1R 7N6
(519) 621-3530 *SIC* 4911
CAMBRIDGE BRASS, INC *p* 535
140 ORION PL, CAMBRIDGE, ON, N1T 1R9
(519) 621-5520 *SIC* 3432
CAMBRIDGE CENTRE HONDA *p* 532
See *405 AUTO SALES INC*
CAMBRIDGE CLUB *p* 949
See *CAMBRIDGE GROUP OF CLUB*
CAMBRIDGE COUNTRY MANOR *p* 538
See *CARESSANT-CARE NURSING AND RETIREMENT HOMES LIMITED*
CAMBRIDGE FIRE DEPARTMENT *p* 533
See *CORPORATION OF THE CITY OF CAMBRIDGE, THE*
CAMBRIDGE GLOBAL PAYMENTS *p* 949
See *CAMBRIDGE MERCANTILE CORP*

CAMBRIDGE GROUP OF CLUB   p 949
100 RICHMOND ST W SUITE 444, TORONTO, ON, M5H 3K6
(416) 862-1077   SIC 7991

CAMBRIDGE MACK   p 533
See CENTRAL AUTOMOTIVE SERVICES LIMITED

CAMBRIDGE MEMORIAL HOSPITAL p 532
700 CORONATION BLVD, CAMBRIDGE, ON, N1R 3G2
(519) 621-2330   SIC 8062

CAMBRIDGE MERCANTILE CORP   p 949
212 KING ST W SUITE 400, TORONTO, ON, M5H 1K5
(416) 646-6401   SIC 6099

CAMBRIDGE PRO FAB INC   p 517
84 SHAVER RD, BRANTFORD, ON, N3T 5M1
(519) 751-4351   SIC 3621

CAMBRIDGE PUBLIC LIBRARY BOARD, THE   p 535
1 NORTH SQUARE, CAMBRIDGE, ON, N1S 2K6
(519) 621-0460   SIC 8231

CAMBRIDGE SUITES HOTEL   p 452
See CENTENNIAL HOTELS LIMITED

CAMBRIDGE SUITES HOTEL SYDNEY   p 467
See TREIT HOLDINGS 21 INC

CAMBRIDGE SUITES LIMITED, THE   p 452
1601 LOWER WATER ST SUITE 700, HALIFAX, NS, B3J 3P6
(902) 421-1601   SIC 7011

CAMBRIDGE TOYOTA   p 539
See EAGLE NORTH HOLDINGS INC

CAMBRIDGE VOLKSWAGEN INC   p 532
275 HESPELER RD, CAMBRIDGE, ON, N1R 3H8
(519) 621-8989   SIC 5511

CAMBRIDGE WOODEN TOY CO   p 532
See ARC INDUSTRIES

CAMBRIDGE, LE   p 1252
See PLACEMENTS CAMBRIDGE INC

CAMCARB CO2 LTD   p 792
155 SIGNET DR, NORTH YORK, ON, M9L 1V1
(416) 745-1304   SIC 5169

CAMCO ACURA   p 828
See CAMCO AUTOMOBILES INC

CAMCO AUTOMOBILES INC   p 828
1475 CARLING AVE, OTTAWA, ON, K1Z 7L9
(613) 728-8888   SIC 5511

CAMCOURT HOLDINGS LTD   p 203
660 ENGLAND AVE, COURTENAY, BC, V9N 2N4
(250) 338-1383   SIC 5411

CAMDON CONSTRUCTION LTD   p 155
6780 76 ST, RED DEER, AB, T4P 4G6
(403) 343-1233   SIC 1542

CAMECO CORPORATION   p 1432
2121 11TH ST W, SASKATOON, SK, S7M 1J3
(306) 956-6200   SIC 1094

CAMECO FUEL MANUFACTURING INC   p 544
2C ST NORTHAM INDUSTRIAL PK, COBOURG, ON, K9A 4K5
(905) 372-0147   SIC 3545

CAMEO CRAFTS   p 1127
See CORPORATION MULTI-COLOR MONTREAL CANADA

CAMEO KNITTING   p 1192
See 4207602 CANADA INC

CAMERON & ASSOCIATES INSURANCE CONSULTANTS LTD   p 960
55 YORK ST SUITE 400, TORONTO, ON, M5J 1R7
(416) 350-5822   SIC 6411

CAMERON ADVERTISING DISPLAYS LIMITED   p 870
12 NANTUCKET BLVD, SCARBOROUGH, ON, M1P 2N4

(416) 752-7220   SIC 7319

CAMERON FLOW SYSTEMS LTD   p 21
7944 10 ST NE, CALGARY, AB, T2E 8W1
(403) 291-4814   SIC 3825

CAMERON HEIGHTS COLLEGIATE INSTITUTE   p 639
See WATERLOO REGION DISTRICT SCHOOL BOARD

CAMERON INDUSTRIES INC   p 600
309 ELIZABETH ST, GUELPH, ON, N1E 2X8
(519) 824-3561   SIC 2672

CAMERON LIBRARY   p 117
See GOVERNORS OF THE UNIVERSITY OF ALBERTA, THE

CAMERON STEEL INC   p 645
52 WALSH RD SUITE 3, LINDSAY, ON, K9V 4R3
(705) 878-0544   SIC 3599

CAMEX   p 148
See CAMEX EQUIPMENT SALES & RENTALS INC

CAMEX EQUIPMENT SALES & RENTALS INC   p 148
1806 2 ST, NISKU, AB, T9E 0W8
(780) 955-2770   SIC 7353

CAMFIL CANADA INC   p 550
2700 STEELES AVE W, CONCORD, ON, L4K 3C8
(905) 660-0688   SIC 3569

CAMFIL CANADA INC   p 1233
2785 AV FRANCIS-HUGHES, MONTREAL, QC, H7L 3J6
(450) 629-3030   SIC 5085

CAMFIL FARR FILTERS   p 550
See CAMFIL CANADA INC

CAMH   p 990
See CENTRE FOR ADDICTION AND MENTAL HEALTH

CAMI ASSEMBLY   p 621
See GENERAL MOTORS OF CANADA COMPANY

CAMILION SOLUTIONS, INC   p 904
123 COMMERCE VALLEY DR E SUITE 800, THORNHILL, ON, L3T 7W8
SIC 7371

CAMILLE FINANCIAL   p 49
See ENERVEST MANAGEMENT LTD

CAMION FREIGHTLINER MONT-LAURIER INC   p 1124
325 CH DU GOLF, LAC-DES-ECORCES, QC, J0W 1H0
(819) 623-7177   SIC 5511

CAMION VOLVO MONTREAL   p 1093
See 9093451 CANADA INC

CAMIONNAGE TOWTAL   p 1158
See TRANSPORT A. LABERGE ET FILS INC

CAMIONS A & R DUBOIS INC   p 1314
2745 RUE PRINCIPALE, SAINT-JEAN-BAPTISTE, QC, J0L 2B0
(450) 464-4631   SIC 5531

CAMIONS FREIGHTLINER M.B. TROIS-RIVIERES LTEE   p 1389
300 RUE QUENNEVILLE, TROIS-RIVIERES, QC, G9B 1X6
(819) 377-9997   SIC 5511

CAMIONS FREIGHTLINER QUEBEC DIVISION LEVIS INC   p 1135
865 RUE ARCHIMEDE, LEVIS, QC, G6V 7M5
(418) 837-3661   SIC 5511

CAMIONS FREIGHTLINER QUEBEC INC p 1266
2380 AV DALTON, QUEBEC, QC, G1P 3X1
(418) 657-2425   SIC 5511

CAMIONS FREIGHTLINER RIVIERE-DU-LOUP INC   p 1286
100 BOUL INDUSTRIEL, RIVIERE-DU-LOUP, QC, G5R 0K5

(418) 862-3192   SIC 5012

CAMIONS FREIGHTLINER STERLING DRUMMONDVILLE INC   p 1096
5770 PLACE KUBOTA BUREAU 4, DRUMMONDVILLE, QC, J2B 6V4
(819) 474-2264   SIC 5541

CAMIONS INTER-ANJOU INC   p 1047
8300 RUE EDISON, ANJOU, QC, H1J 1S8
(514) 353-9720   SIC 5012

CAMIONS INTER-ESTRIE (1991) INC, LES   p 1373
250 RUE LEGER, SHERBROOKE, QC, J1L 1M1
(819) 564-6677   SIC 5511

CAMIONS INTERNATIONAL ELITE LTEE   p 1261
265 RUE ETIENNE-DUBREUIL, QUEBEC, QC, G1M 4A6
(418) 687-9510   SIC 5511

CAMIONS INTERNATIONAL WEST ISLAND INC   p 1333
6100 CH SAINT-FRANCOIS, SAINT-LAURENT, QC, H4S 1B7
(514) 333-4412   SIC 5521

CAMIONS LAGUE INC   p 1064
205 CH DU TREMBLAY, BOUCHERVILLE, QC, J4B 6L6
(450) 655-6940   SIC 7538

CAMIONS LUSSIER-LUSSICAM INC p 1358
1341 RUE PRINCIPALE, SAINTE-JULIE, QC, J3E 0C4
(450) 649-1265   SIC 5012

CAMIONS MASKA INC   p 1348
690 MONT?E MONETTE, SAINT-MATHIEU-DE-LAPRAIRIE, QC, J0L 2H0
(450) 444-5600   SIC 5012

CAMIONS RAY-LAWSON   p 1113
See CENTRE DU CAMION GAMACHE INC

CAMOPLAST SOLIDEAL - CENTRE TECHNIQUE   p 1147
See CAMSO INC

CAMOSUN COLLEGE   p 333
3100 FOUL BAY RD, VICTORIA, BC, V8P 5J2
(250) 370-3550   SIC 8221

CAMP AGUDAH   p 788
129 MCGILLIVRAY AVE, NORTH YORK, ON, M5M 2Y7
(416) 781-7101   SIC 7032

CAMP B B-RIBACK   p 68
1607 90 AVE SW, CALGARY, AB, T2V 4V7
SIC 7032

CAMP DE JOUR DU CENTRE DE LOISIRS IMMACULEE-CONCEPTION   p 1172
See CENTRE PERE SABLON

CAMP FORMING LTD   p 794
105 RIVALDA RD, NORTH YORK, ON, M9M 2M6
(416) 745-8680   SIC 1771

CAMP KINTAIL   p 597
85153 BLUEWATER HWY, GODERICH, ON, N7A 3X9
(519) 529-7317   SIC 8699

CAMP KINTAIL SUMMER OFFICE   p 597
See CAMP KINTAIL

CAMP KODIAK   p 716
See 1234121 ONTARIO LIMITED

CAMP MOTIVACTION   p 1084
See RECREGESTION LE GROUPE INC

CAMP PAPILLON   p 1291
See SOCIETE POUR LES ENFANTS HANDICAPES DU QUEBEC

CAMP TAMARACK   p 1432
See TAMARACK FOUNDATION

CAMP USA-MONDE   p 1184
See MAKWA AVENTURES INC, LES

CAMP WAHANOWIN LIMITED   p 923
227 EGLINTON AVE W, TORONTO, ON, M4R 1A9
(416) 482-2600   SIC 7032

CAMP WINNEBAGOE INC   p 972
4 SILVERWOOD AVE, TORONTO, ON, M5P 1W4

(416) 486-1110   SIC 7032

CAMP WINSTON FOUNDATION   p 922
55 EGLINTON AVE E SUITE 312, TORONTO, ON, M4P 1G8
(416) 487-6229   SIC 8699

CAMPAGNE MAJEURE 2014-2019   p 1270
See ARCHEVEQUE CATHOLIQUE ROMAIN DE QUEBEC, L'

CAMPANA SYSTEMS INC   p 1010
103 RANDALL DR UNIT 2, WATERLOO, ON, N2V 1C5
(226) 336-8085   SIC 7371

CAMPARI CANADA   p 599
See FORTY CREEK DISTILLERY LTD

CAMPBELL & CAMERON INC   p 1130
1855 AV DOLLARD, LASALLE, QC, H8N 1T9
(514) 762-9777   SIC 5511

CAMPBELL AND KENNEDY ELECTRIC (1996) LIMITED   p 550
242 APPLEWOOD CRES SUITE 11, CONCORD, ON, L4K 4E5
(905) 761-8550   SIC 1731

CAMPBELL BROS. MOVERS LIMITED   p 661
55 MIDPARK CRES, LONDON, ON, N6N 1A9
(519) 681-5710   SIC 4214

CAMPBELL COMPANY OF CANADA p 570
60 BIRMINGHAM ST, ETOBICOKE, ON, M8V 2B8
(416) 251-1131   SIC 2032

CAMPBELL COMPANY OF CANADA p 646
1400 MITCHELL RD S, LISTOWEL, ON, N4W 3G7
SIC 5142

CAMPBELL CONSTRUCTION LTD   p 338
559 KELVIN RD, VICTORIA, BC, V8Z 1C4
(250) 475-1300   SIC 1542

CAMPBELL FORD SALES LTD   p 828
1500 CARLING AVE, OTTAWA, ON, K1Z 0A3
(613) 725-3611   SIC 5511

CAMPBELL HELICOPTERS LTD   p 176
30740 THRESHOLD DR, ABBOTSFORD, BC, V2T 6H5
(604) 852-1122   SIC 4522

CAMPBELL MONUMENT COMPANY LIMITED   p 490
712 DUNDAS ST W, BELLEVILLE, ON, K8N 4Z2
(613) 966-5154   SIC 5999

CAMPBELL RIVER AND DISTRICT ASSOCIATION FOR COMMUNITY LIVING   p 194
1153 GREENWOOD ST, CAMPBELL RIVER, BC, V9W 3C5
(250) 287-9731   SIC 8399

CAMPBELL RIVER FISHING CO LTD p 194
1330 HOMEWOOD RD, CAMPBELL RIVER, BC, V9W 6Y5
(250) 286-0887   SIC 5142

CAMPBELL SCIENTIFIC (CANADA) CORP   p 93
14532 131 AVE NW, EDMONTON, AB, T5L 4X4
(780) 454-2505   SIC 7629

CAMPBELL TOYOTA   p 542
See CAMPBELL, BOB MOTORS LTD

CAMPBELL TRAVEL LTD   p 297
181 KEEFER PL SUITE 201, VANCOUVER, BC, V6B 6C1
(604) 688-2913   SIC 4724

CAMPBELL'S AUTOMATED RECORDS MANAGEMENT   p 661
See CAMPBELL BROS. MOVERS LIMITED

CAMPBELL'S CONCRETE   p 1040
See CAMPBELL'S CONCRETE LTD

CAMPBELL'S CONCRETE LTD   p 1040
420 MOUNT EDWARD RD, CHARLOTTETOWN, PE, C1E 2A1
(902) 368-3442   SIC 5032

CAMPBELL, BOB MOTORS LTD   p 542

296 RICHMOND ST, CHATHAM, ON, N7M 1P6

(519) 352-4740   SIC 5511

CAMPBELL, JAMES INC   p 645
333 KENT ST W, LINDSAY, ON, K9V 2Z7

(705) 324-6668   SIC 5812

CAMPBELL, JAMES INC   p 840
978 LANSDOWNE ST W, PETERBOROUGH, ON, K9J 1Z9

(705) 743-6731   SIC 5812

CAMPBELL, RON G SALES LTD   p 140
1240 2A AVE N SUITE 2, LETHBRIDGE, AB, T1H 0E4

(403) 320-6191   SIC 5531

CAMPBELL, SCOTT DODGE LTD   p 1412
3042 99TH ST HWY SUITE 4, NORTH BATTLEFORD, SK, S9A 3W8

(306) 445-6640   SIC 5511

CAMPBELLFORD DISTRICT HIGH SCHOOL   p 539
See KAWARTHA PINE RIDGE DISTRICT SCHOOL BOARD

CAMPBELLFORD MEMORIAL HOSPITAL p 539
146 OLIVER RD, CAMPBELLFORD, ON, K0L 1L0

(705) 653-1140   SIC 8062

CAMPBELLFORD WHOLESALE COMPANY LTD   p 539
11 INDUSTRIAL DR SUITE 1, CAMPBELLFORD, ON, K0L 1L0

(705) 653-3640   SIC 5194

CAMPBELLTON NURSING HOME INC   p 396
101 DOVER ST, CAMPBELLTON, NB, E3N 3K6

(506) 789-7350   SIC 8051

CAMPBELLTON REGIONAL HOSPITAL   p 396
See RESTIGOUCHE HEALTH AUTHORITY

CAMPING MART   p 1348
See VR ST-CYR INC

CAMPING VILLAGE HISTORIQUE DE VAL-JALBERT   p 1075
See CORPORATION DU PARC REGIONAL DE VAL-JALBERT

CAMPIO FURNITURE LIMITED   p 1030
5770 HIGHWAY 7 UNIT 1, WOODBRIDGE, ON, L4L 1T8

(905) 850-6636   SIC 2512

CAMPIO GROUP   p 1030
See CAMPIO FURNITURE LIMITED

CAMPION MARINE INC   p 219
200 CAMPION ST, KELOWNA, BC, V1X 7S8

(250) 765-7795   SIC 3732

CAMPOR ENVIRONNEMENT INC   p 1286
98 RUE DES EQUIPEMENTS, RIVIERE-DU-LOUP, QC, G5R 5W9

(418) 867-8577   SIC 4953

CAMPS BRUCHESI   p 1307
See PLEIN AIR BRUCHESI INC

CAMPTECH II CIRCUITS INC   p 667
81 BENTLEY ST, MARKHAM, ON, L3R 3L1

(905) 477-8790   SIC 3672

CAMPUS   p 1175
1111 RUE SAINTE-CATHERINE E, MONTREAL, QC, H2L 2G6

(514) 526-9867   SIC 5813

CAMPUS DE LEVIS   p 1137
See UNIVERSITE DU QUEBEC

CAMPUS DU FORT SAINT-JEAN   p 1317
See CORPORATION DU FORT ST-JEAN

CAMPUS ENERGY PARTNERS LP   p 45
355 4 AVE SW SUITE 1700, CALGARY, AB, T2P 0J1

(403) 691-7575   SIC 4922

CAMPUS LIVING CENTRES INC   p 578
5405 EGLINTON AVE W SUITE 214, ETOBICOKE, ON, M9C 5K6

(416) 620-0635   SIC 1531

CAMPUS LONGUEUIL   p 1145

See UNIVERSITE DE SHERBROOKE

CAMPUS NOTRE-DAME-DE-FOY   p 1292
5000 RUE CLEMENT-LOCKQUELL, SAINT-AUGUSTIN-DE-DESMAURES, QC, G3A 1B3

(418) 872-8041   SIC 8221

CAMPUS TOWER SUITE HOTEL   p 117
11145 87 AVE NW, EDMONTON, AB, T6G 0Y1

(780) 439-6060   SIC 7389

CAMROSE ASSOCIATION FOR COMMUNITY LIVING   p 78
4604 57 ST, CAMROSE, AB, T4V 2E7

(780) 672-0257   SIC 8361

CAMROSE CHRYSLER LTD   p 78
3511 48 AVE, CAMROSE, AB, T4V 0K9

(780) 672-2476   SIC 5511

CAMROSE REGIONAL EXHIBITION AND AGRICULTURAL SOCIETY   p 78
4250 EXHIBITION DR, CAMROSE, AB, T4V 4Z8

(780) 672-3640   SIC 7389

CAMROSE SOBEYS CORP   p 78
4820 66 ST, CAMROSE, AB, T4V 4P6

(780) 672-5969   SIC 5411

CAMROVA RESOURCES INC   p 303
890 W PENDER SUITE 600, VANCOUVER, BC, V6C 1J9

(604) 685-2323   SIC 1481

CAMSO DISTRIBUTION CANADA INC   p 692
5485 TOMKEN RD, MISSISSAUGA, ON, L4W 3Y3

(416) 674-5441   SIC 5014

CAMSO INC   p 1147
2675 RUE MACPHERSON, MAGOG, QC, J1X 0E6

(819) 868-1500   SIC 8731

CAMSO INC   p 1147
2633 RUE MACPHERSON, MAGOG, QC, J1X 0E6

(819) 868-1500   SIC 3011

CAMTAC MANUFACTURING   p 605
See LINAMAR CORPORATION

CAMTX CORPORATION   p 972
106 AVENUE RD, TORONTO, ON, M5R 2H3

(416) 920-0500   SIC 2211

CAN ALTA BINDERY CORP   p 113
8445 DAVIES RD NW, EDMONTON, AB, T6E 4N3

(780) 466-9973   SIC 5943

CAN ART ALUMINUM EXTRUSION INC   p 501
85 PARKSHORE DR, BRAMPTON, ON, L6T 5M1

(905) 791-1464   SIC 3354

CAN MAR CONTRACTING LIMITED   p 583
169 CITY VIEW DR, ETOBICOKE, ON, M9W 5B1

(416) 674-8791   SIC 1542

CAN WEST PROJECTS INC   p 75
85 FREEPORT BLVD NE SUITE 202, CALGARY, AB, T3J 4X8
SIC 1623

CAN-60 INCOME ETF   p 960
95 WELLINGTON ST W SUITE 1400, TORONTO, ON, M5J 2N7

(416) 642-1289   SIC 6722

CAN-AM   p 737
See CANADIAN AMERICAN BOXED MEAT CORP

CAN-AM AUTO GLASS & SUPPLIES   p 118
See CRYSTAL GLASS CANADA LTD

CAN-AM CASTERS & WHEELS, DIV OF   p 533
See COLSON GROUP CANADA, INC

CAN-AM CHAINS   p 276
See CAM CHAIN CO. LTD

CAN-AM CHRYSLER   p 405
See CAN-AM MOTORS LTD

CAN-AM GEOMATICS CORP   p 64
340 12 AVE SW SUITE 900, CALGARY, AB, T2R 1L5

(403) 269-8887   SIC 8713

CAN-AM MOTORS LTD   p 405
40 MORTON AVE, MONCTON, NB, E1A 3H9

(506) 852-8210   SIC 5511

CAN-AM PEPPER COMPANY LTD   p 482
52999 JOHN WISE LINE, AYLMER, ON, N5H 2R5

(519) 773-3250   SIC 0161

CAN-AM PRODUCE & TRADING LTD p 294
886 MALKIN AVE, VANCOUVER, BC, V6A 2K7

(604) 253-8834   SIC 5148

CAN-AM RV CENTRE   p 662
See CAN-AM TRAILERS LIMITED

CAN-AM TRAILERS LIMITED   p 662
6068 COLONEL TALBOT RD, LONDON, ON, N6P 1J1

(519) 652-3284   SIC 5561

CAN-AM TRAVEL STOPS INC   p 1438
1203 HWY 1, WHITEWOOD, SK, S0G 5C0

(306) 735-2565   SIC 5541

CAN-AM WEST CARRIERS INC   p 174
400 RIVERSIDE RD, ABBOTSFORD, BC, V2S 7M4

(604) 857-1375   SIC 4213

CAN-AQUA INTERNATIONAL LTEE   p 1233
2250 BOUL DAGENAIS O, MONTREAL, QC, H7L 5Y2

(450) 625-3088   SIC 5074

CAN-AR COACH, DIV OF   p 559
See TOKMAKJIAN INC

CAN-BEC IMMOBILIER INC   p 1350
1260 RUE PRINCIPALE E, SAINT-PAUL-D'ABBOTSFORD, QC, J0E 1A0

(450) 379-2088   SIC 1541

CAN-BOW MOTORS LTD   p 78
707 RAILWAY AVE, CANMORE, AB, T1W 1P2

(403) 678-4222   SIC 5511

CAN-CARE HEALTH SERVICES INC p 771
45 SHEPPARD AVE E SUITE 204, NORTH YORK, ON, M2N 5W9

(647) 725-1048   SIC 8082

CAN-CELL INDUSTRIES INC   p 93
14735 124 AVE NW, EDMONTON, AB, T5L 3B2

(780) 447-1255   SIC 2621

CAN-DER CONSTRUCTION LTD   p 113
5410 97 ST NW, EDMONTON, AB, T6E 5C1

(780) 436-2980   SIC 1522

CAN-ENG FURNACES INTERNATIONAL LTD   p 757
6800 MONTROSE RD, NIAGARA FALLS, ON, L2E 6V5

(905) 356-1327   SIC 3567

CAN-ENG PARTNERS LTD   p 757
6800 MONTROSE RD, NIAGARA FALLS, ON, L2E 6V5

(905) 356-1327   SIC 3567

CAN-FIT-PRO, DIV OF   p 878
See CANADIAN FITNESS PROFESSIONALS INC

CAN-MED HEALTHCARE   p 457
See I.M.P. GROUP LIMITED

CAN-OP   p 910
See 1796640 ONTARIO LIMITED

CAN-PET DISTRIBUTORS INC   p 550
84 DONEY CRES SUITE C, CONCORD, ON, L4K 3A8

(905) 738-3663   SIC 5199

CAN-RAD BEAUTY LIMITED   p 786
125 NORFINCH DR SUITE 100, NORTH YORK, ON, M3N 1W8

(416) 663-7373   SIC 5087

CAN-SAVE SUPPLY AND DISTRIBUTION p 486
411 BAYVIEW DR, BARRIE, ON, L4N 8Y2

(705) 722-7283   SIC 5039

CAN-SCAN IMPORTS   p 125
See NORDIC HOLDINGS LTD

CAN-SURE UNDERWRITING   p 329
See BEACON UNDERWRITING LTD

CAN-SURE UNDERWRITING LTD   p 329
700 GEORGIA ST W SUITE 1488, VAN-

COUVER, BC, V7Y 1A1

(604) 685-6533   SIC 6351

CANA CONSTRUCTION CO. LTD   p 34
5720 4 ST SE SUITE 100, CALGARY, AB, T2H 1K7

(403) 255-5521   SIC 1542

CANA HIGH VOLTAGE LTD   p 34
5720 4 ST SE UNIT 100, CALGARY, AB, T2H 1K7

(403) 247-3121   SIC 8711

CANA IMPORT EXPORT LTD   p 573
1589 THE QUEENSWAY UNIT 1, ETOBICOKE, ON, M8Z 5W9

(416) 252-8652   SIC 5199

CANA LIMITED   p 34
5720 4 ST SE SUITE 100, CALGARY, AB, T2H 1K7

(403) 255-5521   SIC 2421

CANA PROJECT MANAGEMENT LTD p 34
5720 4 ST SE UNIT 100, CALGARY, AB, T2H 1K7

(403) 255-5521   SIC 8741

CANA SERVICES LTD   p 34
5720 4 ST SE SUITE 100, CALGARY, AB, T2H 1K7

(403) 255-5521   SIC 8741

CANA UTILITIES LTD   p 34
5720 4 ST SE UNIT 100, CALGARY, AB, T2H 1K7

(403) 255-5521   SIC 1623

CANA-DATUM MOULDS LTD   p 573
55 GOLDTHORNE AVE, ETOBICOKE, ON, M8Z 5S7

(416) 252-1212   SIC 3544

CANABO   p 548
See ALEAFIA HEALTH INC

CANAC   p 1278
See CANAC-MARQUIS GRENIER LTEE

CANAC IMMOBILIER INC   p 1119
6235 BOUL WILFRID-HAMEL, L'ANCIENNE-LORETTE, QC, G2E 5W2

(418) 872-2874   SIC 5211

CANAC IMMOBILIER INC   p 1255
947 AV ROYALE, QUEBEC, QC, G1E 1Z9

(418) 667-1729   SIC 5039

CANAC IMMOBILIER INC   p 1278
5355 BOUL DES GRADINS, QUEBEC, QC, G2J 1C8

(418) 667-1313   SIC 5039

CANAC IMMOBILIER INC   p 1285
228 RUE DES NEGOCIANTS, RIMOUSKI, QC, G5M 1B6

(418) 723-0007   SIC 5211

CANAC-MARQUIS GRENIER LTEE p 1278
5355 BOUL DES GRADINS, QUEBEC, QC, G2J 1C8

(418) 667-1313   SIC 6719

CANACCORD GENUITY CORP   p 45
450 1 ST SW SUITE 2200, CALGARY, AB, T2P 5H1

(403) 508-3800   SIC 6211

CANACCORD GENUITY CORP   p 330
609 GRANVILLE ST SUITE 2200, VANCOUVER, BC, V7Y 1H2

(604) 643-7300   SIC 6211

CANACCORD GENUITY CORP   p 1202
1250 BOUL RENE-LEVESQUE O BUREAU 2000, MONTREAL, QC, H3B 4W8
SIC 6211

CANACCORD GENUITY GROUP INC p 330
609 GRANVILLE ST VAN UNIT 2200, VANCOUVER, BC, V7Y 1H2

(604) 643-7300   SIC 6211

CANACOL ENERGY LTD   p 45
585 8 AVE SW SUITE 2650, CALGARY, AB, T2P 1G1

(403) 561-1648   SIC 1311

CANAD CORPORATION LTD   p 354
2401 SASKATCHEWAN AVE W, PORTAGE LA PRAIRIE, MB, R1N 4A6

(204) 857-9745   SIC 7011

CANAD CORPORATION LTD   p 369
930 JEFFERSON AVE SUITE 3, WINNIPEG, MB, R2P 1W1

(204) 697-1495   *SIC 4724*
CANAD CORPORATION OF CANADA INC*p* 370
2100 MCPHILLIPS ST, WINNIPEG, MB, R2V 3T9
(204) 633-0024   *SIC 7011*
CANAD CORPORATION OF MANITOBA LTD   *p* 362
826 REGENT AVE W, WINNIPEG, MB, R2C 3A8
(204) 224-1681   *SIC 7011*
CANAD CORPORATION OF MANITOBA LTD   *p* 365
1034 ELIZABETH RD, WINNIPEG, MB, R2J 1B3
(204) 253-2641   *SIC 7011*
CANAD CORPORATION OF MANITOBA LTD   *p* 369
930 JEFFERSON AVE SUITE 3, WINNIPEG, MB, R2P 1W1
(204) 697-1495   *SIC 7011*
CANAD CORPORATION OF MANITOBA LTD   *p* 390
1792 PEMBINA HWY, WINNIPEG, MB, R3T 2G2
(204) 269-6955   *SIC 7011*
CANAD INNS EXPRESS FORT GARRY (CELEBRATIONS, ALLEY CATZ, THE BEACH NIGHT CLUB)   *p* 369
See CANAD CORPORATION OF MANITOBA LTD
CANAD INNS GARDEN CITY   *p* 370
See CANAD CORPORATION OF CANADA INC
CANAD TRANSCONA INN   *p* 362
See CANAD CORPORATION OF MANITOBA LTD
CANADA ADMINISTRATION   *p* 1258
271 RUE DE L'ESTUAIRE, QUEBEC, QC, G1K 8S8
(418) 648-3645   *SIC 4731*
CANADA AGRIGROW   *p* 1021
1243 ELM AVE, WINDSOR, ON, N8X 2B6
(519) 915-8882   *SIC 5191*
CANADA AUTO REMARKETING SUPERSTORE   *p* 118
See 392268 ALBERTA LTD
CANADA AVIATION AND SPACE MUSEUM *p* 817
See CANADA SCIENCE AND TECHNOLOGY MUSEUMS CORPORATION
CANADA BETON ET DECORATIONS INC *p* 1142
777 RUE D'AUVERGNE, LONGUEUIL, QC, J4H 3T9
(450) 463-7084   *SIC 1611*
CANADA BREAD COMPANY, LIMITED *p* 14
4320 80 AVE SE, CALGARY, AB, T2C 4N6
(403) 203-1675   *SIC 2051*
CANADA BREAD COMPANY, LIMITED   *p* 105
12151 160 ST NW, EDMONTON, AB, T5V 1M4
(780) 451-4663   *SIC 2051*
CANADA BREAD COMPANY, LIMITED   *p* 226
6350 203 ST, LANGLEY, BC, V2Y 1L9
(604) 532-8200   *SIC 2051*
CANADA BREAD COMPANY, LIMITED   *p* 406
235 BOTSFORD ST, MONCTON, NB, E1C 4X9
(506) 857-9158   *SIC 2051*
CANADA BREAD COMPANY, LIMITED   *p* 550
711 RIVERMEDE RD, CONCORD, ON, L4K 2G9
(905) 660-3034   *SIC 2051*
CANADA BREAD COMPANY, LIMITED   *p* 577
10 FOUR SEASONS PL SUITE 1200, ETOBICOKE, ON, M9B 6H7
(416) 622-2040   *SIC 2051*

CANADA BREAD COMPANY, LIMITED   *p* 578
35 RAKELY CRT SUITE 1, ETOBICOKE, ON, M9C 5A5
(416) 622-2040   *SIC 2051*
CANADA BREAD COMPANY, LIMITED   *p* 615
155 NEBO RD SUITE 1, HAMILTON, ON, L8W 2E1
(905) 387-3935   *SIC 5149*
CANADA BREAD COMPANY, LIMITED   *p* 993
130 CAWTHRA AVE, TORONTO, ON, M6N 3C2
(416) 626-4382   *SIC 2051*
CANADA BREAD COMPANY, LIMITED   *p* 1361
3455 AV FRANCIS-HUGHES, SAINTE-ROSE, QC, H7L 5A5
(450) 669-2222   *SIC 5461*
CANADA BREAD DOUGH DELIGHT *p* 1002
See DOUGH DELIGHT LTD
CANADA BREAD FROZEN BAKERY   *p* 14
See CANADA BREAD COMPANY, LIMITED
CANADA BRICK, THE REAL MC COY*p* 530
See MERIDIAN BRICK CANADA LTD
CANADA BROKERLINK (ONTARIO) INC *p* 68
1201 GLENMORE TRAIL SW SUITE 100, CALGARY, AB, T2V 4Y8
(403) 209-6300   *SIC 6411*
CANADA BROKERLINK INC   *p* 64
1400 1 ST SW SUITE 200, CALGARY, AB, T2R 0V8
(403) 290-1541   *SIC 6411*
CANADA BUILDS COMPANY LTD   *p* 645
423 COUNTY RD 36 UNIT 2, LINDSAY, ON, K9V 4R3
(705) 324-8777   *SIC 1521*
CANADA CARTAGE   *p* 14
See CANADA CARTAGE SYSTEM LIMITED PARTNERSHIP
CANADA CARTAGE DIVERSIFIED ULC   *p* 734
1115 CARDIFF BLVD, MISSISSAUGA, ON, L5S 1L8
(905) 564-2115   *SIC 4212*
CANADA CARTAGE SYSTEM LIMITED PARTNERSHIP   *p* 14
4700 102 AVE SE, CALGARY, AB, T2C 2X8
(403) 296-0290   *SIC 4213*
CANADA CARTAGE SYSTEM LIMITED PARTNERSHIP   *p* 734
1115 CARDIFF BLVD, MISSISSAUGA, ON, L5S 1L8
(905) 564-2115   *SIC 4731*
CANADA CLEAN FUELS INC   *p* 782
4425 CHESSWOOD DR, NORTH YORK, ON, M3J 2C2
(416) 521-9533   *SIC 4212*
CANADA COLORS AND CHEMICALS (EASTERN) LIMITED   *p* 928
175 BLOOR ST E SUITE 1300, TORONTO, ON, M4W 3R8
(416) 443-5500   *SIC 5169*
CANADA COLORS AND CHEMICALS LIMITED   *p* 928
175 BLOOR ST E SUITE 1300, TORONTO, ON, M4W 3R8
(416) 443-5500   *SIC 5162*
CANADA COMPOUND CORPORATION   *p* 1030
391 ROWNTREE DAIRY RD, WOODBRIDGE, ON, L4L 8H1
(905) 856-5005   *SIC 5149*
CANADA COUNCIL FOR THE ARTS   *p* 822
150 ELGIN ST, OTTAWA, ON, K1P 5V8
(613) 566-4414   *SIC 6732*
CANADA DEPOSIT INSURANCE CORPORATION   *p* 822
50 O'CONNOR ST 17TH FL, OTTAWA, ON, K1P 6L2

(613) 996-2081   *SIC 6399*
CANADA DEVELOPMENT INVESTMENT CORPORATION   *p* 972
1240 BAY ST SUITE 302, TORONTO, ON, M5R 2A7
(416) 966-2221   *SIC 6719*
CANADA DIAGNOSTICS CENTRES   *p* 36
See MR IMAGING CORP
CANADA DIRECT   *p* 1094
See GESTION CANADADIRECT INC
CANADA DOUGH DELIGHT   *p* 550
See CANADA BREAD COMPANY, LIMITED
CANADA DRAYAGE INC   *p* 1127
4415 RUE FAIRWAY, LACHINE, QC, H8T 1B5
(514) 639-7878   *SIC 4212*
CANADA DRIVES LTD   *p* 328
555 BURRARD ST SUITE 600, VANCOUVER, BC, V7X 1M8
(888) 865-6402   *SIC 6141*
CANADA DRUGS CUSTOMER CARE *p* 364
See 5177007 MANITOBA LTD
CANADA DRUGS LTD   *p* 365
16 TERRACON PL, WINNIPEG, MB, R2J 4G7
SIC 5912
CANADA DRY MOTT'S INC   *p* 730
30 EGLINTON AVE W SUITE 600, MISSISSAUGA, ON, L5R 3E7
(905) 712-4121   *SIC 2086*
CANADA EMPLOYMENT & IMMIGRATION UNION   *p* 822
275 SLATER ST UNIT 1204, OTTAWA, ON, K1P 5H9
(613) 236-9634   *SIC 8631*
CANADA ENTERPRISES STEVEDORING AND TERMINALS   *p* 1189
See LOGISTEC ARRIMAGE INC
CANADA FENG TAI INTERNATIONAL INC*p* 764
1100 GORDON BAKER RD, NORTH YORK, ON, M2H 3B3
(416) 497-6666   *SIC 5141*
CANADA FIBERS LTD   *p* 782
35 VANLEY CRES SUITE 500, NORTH YORK, ON, M3J 2B7
SIC 4953
CANADA FIBERS LTD   *p* 997
130 ARROW RD, TORONTO, ON, M9M 2M1
(416) 253-0400   *SIC 5093*
CANADA FOOD EQUIPMENT LTD   *p* 573
45 VANSCO RD, ETOBICOKE, ON, M8Z 5Z8
(416) 253-5100   *SIC 5084*
CANADA FORGINGS INC   *p* 1011
130 HAGAR WELLAND, WELLAND, ON, L3B 5P8
(905) 735-1220   *SIC 3462*
CANADA GAMES AQUATIC CENTRE *p* 217
See KAMLOOPS, THE CORPORATION OF THE CITY OF
CANADA GAMES AQUATIC CENTRE *p* 415
See SAINT JOHN AQUATIC CENTRE COMMISSION
CANADA GAMES POOL   *p* 236
See CORPORATION OF THE CITY OF NEW WESTMINSTER
CANADA GARDENWORKS LTD   *p* 184
6250 LOUGHEED HWY, BURNABY, BC, V5B 2Z9
(604) 299-0621   *SIC 5261*
CANADA GARLIC IMPORTING INC   *p* 705
315 TRADERS BLVD E UNIT 2, MISSISSAUGA, ON, L4Z 3E4
(905) 501-8868   *SIC 5148*
CANADA GOLDEN FORTUNE POTASH CORP   *p* 1426
402 21ST ST E UNIT 200, SASKATOON, SK, S7K 0C3
(306) 668-6877   *SIC 1474*
CANADA GOOSE   *p* 989
See BLACK FEATHER HOLDINGS INCORPORATED
CANADA GOOSE HOLDINGS INC   *p* 989

250 BOWIE AVE, TORONTO, ON, M6E 4Y2
(416) 780-9850   *SIC 2331*
CANADA GOOSE INC   *p* 989
250 BOWIE AVE, TORONTO, ON, M6E 4Y2
(416) 780-9850   *SIC 5611*
CANADA GREEN BUILDING COUNCIL   *p* 821
47 CLARENCE ST SUITE 202, OTTAWA, ON, K1N 9K1
(613) 288-8097   *SIC 8611*
CANADA GUARANTY MORTGAGE INSURANCE COMPANY   *p* 937
1 TORONTO ST SUITE 400, TORONTO, ON, M5C 2V6
(416) 640-8924   *SIC 6351*
CANADA HEALTH INFOWAY   *p* 949
150 KING ST W SUITE 1300, TORONTO, ON, M5H 1J9
(416) 979-4606   *SIC 8748*
CANADA HEALTH INFOWAY   *p* 953
See INFOROUTE SANTE DU CANADA INC
CANADA ICI CAPITAL CORPORATION*p* 87
10180 101 ST NW SUITE 3540, EDMONTON, AB, T5J 3S4
(780) 990-1144   *SIC 6163*
CANADA IMPERIAL OIL LIMITED   *p* 45
237 4 AVE SW SUITE 2480, CALGARY, AB, T2P 0H6
(800) 567-3776   *SIC 5172*
CANADA IMPERIAL OIL LIMITED   *p* 859
602 CHRISTINA ST S, SARNIA, ON, N7T 7M5
(519) 339-2000   *SIC 5172*
CANADA INN EXPRESS FORT GARY*p* 390
See CANAD CORPORATION OF MANITOBA LTD
CANADA INNS WINDSORS PARK   *p* 365
See CANAD CORPORATION OF MANITOBA LTD
CANADA INTERNATIONAL TRAVEL SERVICE INC   *p* 1009
794 PARIS BLVD, WATERLOO, ON, N2T 2Z2
(519) 746-0579   *SIC 4724*
CANADA LANDS COMPANY CLC LIMITED *p* 960
1 UNIVERSITY AVE SUITE 1700, TORONTO, ON, M5J 2P1
(416) 214-1250   *SIC 6531*
CANADA LANDS COMPANY CLC LIMITED *p* 979
301 FRONT ST W, TORONTO, ON, M5V 2T6
(416) 868-6937   *SIC 6531*
CANADA LIFE   *p* 977
See GREAT-WEST LIFE ASSURANCE COMPANY, THE
CANADA LIFE ASSURANCE COMPANY, THE   *p* 944
330 UNIVERSITY AVE SUITE 2, TORONTO, ON, M5G 1R8
(416) 597-1440   *SIC 6311*
CANADA LIFE ASSURANCE COMPANY, THE   *p* 1417
1901 SCARTH ST SUITE 414, REGINA, SK, S4P 4L4
(306) 751-6000   *SIC 6311*
CANADA LIFE FINANCIAL CORPORATION *p* 944
330 UNIVERSITY AVE, TORONTO, ON, M5G 1R7
(416) 597-1440   *SIC 6351*
CANADA LIFE MORTGAGE SERVICES LTD *p* 944
330 UNIVERSITY AVE, TORONTO, ON, M5G 1R8
(416) 597-6981   *SIC 6163*
CANADA LIVESTOCK ADVANCE ASSOCIATION   *p* 385
See CANADIAN CANOLA GROWERS ASSOCIATION

CANADA LOYAL FINANCIAL p 796
See CANADA LOYAL INSURANCE AGENCY LIMITED

CANADA LOYAL FINANCIAL LIMITED p 796
2866 PORTLAND DR, OAKVILLE, ON, L6H 5W8
(905) 829-5514   SIC 6311

CANADA LOYAL INSURANCE AGENCY LIMITED p 796
2866 PORTLAND DR, OAKVILLE, ON, L6H 5W8
(905) 829-5514   SIC 6411

CANADA MALTING CO. LIMITED p 28
3316 BONNYBROOK RD SE, CALGARY, AB, T2G 4M9
(403) 571-7000   SIC 2083

CANADA MANITOBA BUSINESS SERVICE CENTRE p 377
240 GRAHAM AVE SUITE 250, WINNIPEG, MB, R3C 0J7
(204) 984-2272   SIC 8999

CANADA MILLENNIUM SCHOLARSHIP FOUNDATION p 1194
1000 RUE SHERBROOKE O UNITE 800, MONTREAL, QC, H3A 3G4
SIC 8699

CANADA NATIONAL OWN COMPANY (CNOC) p 919
71 THORNCLIFFE PARK DR SUITE 403, TORONTO, ON, M4H 1L3
(647) 520-9004   SIC 6799

CANADA NEWSWIRE p 961
See CNW GROUP LTD

CANADA PALLET CORP p 544
755 DIVISION ST, COBOURG, ON, K9A 3T1
(905) 373-0761   SIC 2448

CANADA PENSION PLAN INVESTMENT BOARD p 937
1 QUEEN ST E, TORONTO, ON, M5C 2W5
(416) 868-4075   SIC 6719

CANADA PIPE COMPANY ULC p 1349
106 MONTEE BASSE, SAINT-OURS, QC, J0G 1P0
(450) 785-2205   SIC 3322

CANADA PIPE COMPANY ULC p 1357
6200 RUE PRINCIPALE, SAINTE-CROIX, QC, G0S 2H0
(418) 926-3262   SIC 3312

CANADA PLACE p 303
See CANADA PLACE CORPORATION

CANADA PLACE CORPORATION p 303
999 CANADA PL SUITE 100, VANCOUVER, BC, V6C 3E1
(604) 775-7200   SIC 6512

CANADA POST CORPORATION p 236
24 OVENS AVE, NEW WESTMINSTER, BC, V3L 1Z2
(604) 516-7802   SIC 4311

CANADA POST CORPORATION p 637
70 TRILLIUM DR, KITCHENER, ON, N2E 0E2
(519) 748-3056   SIC 4311

CANADA POST CORPORATION p 815
2701 RIVERSIDE DR, OTTAWA, ON, K1A 1M2
(613) 734-8440   SIC 4311

CANADA POST CORPORATION p 815
2701 RIVERSIDE DR, OTTAWA, ON, K1A 1L5
(613) 734-8440   SIC 4311

CANADA POST CORPORATION p 815
2701 RIVERSIDE DR, OTTAWA, ON, K1A 0B1
(613) 734-8440   SIC 4311

CANADA POST CORPORATION p 870
280 PROGRESS AVE, SCARBOROUGH, ON, M1P 5H8
(416) 299-4577   SIC 4311

CANADA POST CORPORATION p 884
163 SCOTT ST, ST CATHARINES, ON, L2N 1H3
(905) 934-9792   SIC 4311

CANADA POST CORPORATION p 1030
21 HAIST AVE SUITE 1, WOODBRIDGE, ON, L4L 5V5
(905) 851-1237   SIC 4311

CANADA POST CORPORATION p 1056
595 BOUL SIR-WILFRID-LAURIER, BELOEIL, QC, J3G 4J1
SIC 4311

CANADA POST CORPORATION p 1061
4570 RUE AMBROISE-LAFORTUNE, BOISBRIAND, QC, J7H 0E5
(450) 435-4527   SIC 4311

CANADA POST CORPORATION p 1078
1939 RUE DES SAPINS UNITE 1, CHICOUTIMI, QC, G7H 0H7
(418) 690-0350   SIC 4311

CANADA POST CORPORATION p 1164
6700 RUE SHERBROOKE E, MONTREAL, QC, H1N 1C9
(514) 259-3233   SIC 4311

CANADA POST CORPORATION p 1263
660 RUE GRAHAM-BELL, QUEBEC, QC, G1N 0B2
(418) 847-2160   SIC 4311

CANADA POST CORPORATION p 1278
6700 BOUL PIERRE-BERTRAND BUREAU 200, QUEBEC, QC, G2J 0B6
SIC 4311

CANADA POST CORPORATION p 1338
555 RUE MCARTHUR BUREAU 1506, SAINT-LAURENT, QC, H4T 1T4
(514) 345-4571   SIC 4311

CANADA POST CORPORATION p 1384
1285 RUE NOTRE-DAME E, TROIS-RIVIERES, QC, G8T 4J9
(819) 691-4215   SIC 4311

CANADA POWERTRAIN, DIV OF p 100
See CRANE CARRIER (CANADA) LIMITED

CANADA PROTECTION PLAN p 779
See CANADA PROTECTION PLAN INC

CANADA PROTECTION PLAN INC p 779
250 FERRAND DR SUITE 1100, NORTH YORK, ON, M3C 3G8
(416) 447-6060   SIC 6411

CANADA PUMP AND POWER (CPP) CORPORATION p 4
53113 RANGE ROAD 211, ARDROSSAN, AB, T8G 2C5
(780) 922-1178   SIC 5084

CANADA PURE SPRING WATER, DIV OF p 784
See TEL-E CONNECT SYSTEMS LTD

CANADA REVENUE AGENCY p 414
126 PRINCE WILLIAM ST, SAINT JOHN, NB, E2L 2B6
(506) 636-4623   SIC 8721

CANADA REVENUE AGENCY SAINT JOHN PSO p 414
See CANADA REVENUE AGENCY

CANADA ROAD CARRIER LTD p 207
11440 73 AVE, DELTA, BC, V4C 1B7
(604) 502-0240   SIC 7389

CANADA SAFEWAY p 65
See SOBEYS WEST INC

CANADA SAFEWAY p 322
See SOBEYS WEST INC

CANADA SAFEWAY # 165 p 179
See SOBEYS WEST INC

CANADA SAFEWAY #838 p 97
See SOBEYS WEST INC

CANADA SAFEWAY 263 p 25
See SOBEYS WEST INC

CANADA SAFEWAY 76 p 202
See SOBEYS WEST INC

CANADA SAFEWAY NO. 171 p 268
See SOBEYS WEST INC

CANADA SCAFFOLD SUPPLY CO. LTD p 253
11331 TWIGG PL, RICHMOND, BC, V6V 3C9
(604) 324-7691   SIC 3446

CANADA SCIENCE AND TECHNOLOGY MUSEUMS CORPORATION p 817

2421 LANCASTER RD, OTTAWA, ON, K1G 5A3
(613) 991-3044   SIC 8412

CANADA SECURITY SERVICES LTD p 200
91 GOLDEN DR SUITE 27, COQUITLAM, BC, V3K 6R2
SIC 7381

CANADA SPORTSWEAR CORP p 792
230 BARMAC DR, NORTH YORK, ON, M9L 2Z3
(416) 740-8020   SIC 5136

CANADA STAMP p 659
See STERLING MARKING PRODUCTS INC

CANADA STAMPINGS LTD p 1036
1299 COMMERCE WAY, WOODSTOCK, ON, N4V 0A2
(519) 537-6245   SIC 3469

CANADA STEAMSHIP LINES p 1188
See GROUPE CSL INC

CANADA STEEL SERVICE CENTRE INC p 648
25 CUDDY BLVD, LONDON, ON, N5V 3Y3
(519) 453-5600   SIC 5051

CANADA TAXES p 870
200 TOWN CENTRE CRT SUITE 475, SCARBOROUGH, ON, M1P 4Y3
(800) 267-6999   SIC 7389

CANADA TORONTO EAST MISSION p 867
30 SEMINOLE AVE, SCARBOROUGH, ON, M1J 1N1
SIC 8661

CANADA TORONTO EAST MISSION p 989
851 OSSINGTON AVE, TORONTO, ON, M6G 3V2
(416) 531-0535   SIC 8661

CANADA TOUR SYSTEM INC p 297
510 HASTINGS ST W SUITE 1308, VANCOUVER, BC, V6B 1L8
(604) 681-9747   SIC 4724

CANADA TUBEFORM INC p 661
2879 INNOVATION DR, LONDON, ON, N6M 0B6
(519) 451-9995   SIC 3465

CANADA UKRAINE FOUNDATION p 573
145 EVANS AVE UNIT 300, ETOBICOKE, ON, M8Z 5X8
(416) 966-9700   SIC 8699

CANADA WATERWORKS INC p 583
35 SHAFT RD, ETOBICOKE, ON, M9W 4M3
(416) 244-4848   SIC 5039

CANADA WEST BOOT FACTORY OUTLET p 371
See CANADA WEST SHOE MANUFACTURING INC

CANADA WEST HARVEST CENTRE INC p 1406
8 INDUSTRIAL DR, EMERALD PARK, SK, S4L 1B6
(306) 525-2300   SIC 5083

CANADA WEST SHOE MANUFACTURING INC p 371
1250 FIFE ST, WINNIPEG, MB, R2X 2N6
(204) 632-4110   SIC 5661

CANADA WEST TRUCK CENTRE p 1431
3750 IDYLWYLD DR N SUITE 107, SASKATOON, SK, S7L 6G3
(306) 934-1110   SIC 5012

CANADA WEST VETERINARY SPECIALISTS AND CRITICAL CARE HOSPITAL p 286
See 534422 B.C. LTD

CANADA WIDE MEDIA LIMITED p 184
4180 LOUGHEED HWY SUITE 102, BURNABY, BC, V5C 6A7
(604) 299-7311   SIC 2721

CANADA WINDOWS & DOORS p 1013
See 921983 ONTARIO INC

CANADA WINNIPEG AREA CONTROL p 386
See NAV CANADA

CANADA WORLD YOUTH INC p 1215
2330 RUE NOTRE-DAME O BUREAU 300, MONTREAL, QC, H3J 1N4

(514) 931-3526   SIC 8641

CANADA WORLDWIDE SERVICES INC p 501
9 VAN DER GRAAF CRT, BRAMPTON, ON, L6T 5E5
(905) 671-1771   SIC 7389

CANADA YOUTH ORANGE NETWORK INC p 285
1638 PANDORA ST, VANCOUVER, BC, V5L 1L6
(604) 254-7733   SIC 2086

CANADA'S NATIONAL BALLET SCHOOL p 931
400 JARVIS ST, TORONTO, ON, M4Y 2G6
(416) 964-3780   SIC 7911

CANADA'S NATIONAL LABORATORY FOR PARTICLE AND NUCLEAR PHYSICS p 325
See TRIUMF

CANADA'S WONDERLAND COMPANY p 1003
9580 JANE ST, VAUGHAN, ON, L6A 1S6
(905) 832-7000   SIC 7996

CANADA-ISRAEL SECURITIES LIMITED p 782
801-1120 FINCH AVE W, NORTH YORK, ON, M3J 3H7
(416) 789-3351   SIC 6211

CANADADRUGS.COM p 365
See CANADA DRUGS LTD

CANADAWIDE FRUIT WHOLESALERS INC p 1225
1370 RUE DE BEAUHARNOIS O BUREAU 200, MONTREAL, QC, H4N 1J5
(514) 382-3232   SIC 5148

CANADAWIDE SCIENTIFIC LIMITED p 817
2300 WALKLEY RD SUITE 4, OTTAWA, ON, K1G 6B1
(613) 736-8811   SIC 5049

CANADAY'S APPAREL LTD p 1410
115 CORONATION DR, MOOSE JAW, SK, S6H 4P3
(306) 692-6406   SIC 2325

CANADEL FURNITURE p 1146
See CANADEL INC

CANADEL INC p 1146
700 RUE CANADEL, LOUISEVILLE, QC, J5V 3A4
(819) 228-8471   SIC 2511

CANADIAN ADDICTION TREATMENT PHARMACY LP p 678
175 COMMERCE VALLEY DR W, MARKHAM, ON, L3T 7P6
(905) 773-3884   SIC 5122

CANADIAN AGENCY FOR DRUGS AND TECHNOLOGIES IN HEALTH (CADTH) p 825
865 CARLING AVE SUITE 600, OTTAWA, ON, K1S 5S8
(613) 226-2553   SIC 8731

CANADIAN AIR-CRANE LTD p 208
7293 WILSON AVE, DELTA, BC, V4G 1E5
(604) 940-1715   SIC 2411

CANADIAN ALCOHOL CO p 876
See CALSCO SOLVENTS LIMITED

CANADIAN ALPINE CENTRE p 138
203 VILLAGE RD, LAKE LOUISE, AB, T0L 1E0
(403) 522-2200   SIC 7389

CANADIAN ALPINE SKI TEAM, DIV OF p 72
See ALPINE CANADA ALPIN

CANADIAN AMERICAN BOXED MEAT CORP p 737
6905 KENDERRY GATE SUITE 2, MISSISSAUGA, ON, L5T 2Y8
(905) 949-8882   SIC 5147

CANADIAN ANALYTICAL LABORATORIES INC p 720
6733 KITIMAT RD, MISSISSAUGA, ON, L5N 1W3
(416) 286-3332   SIC 8734

CANADIAN APARTMENT PROPERTIES REAL ESTATE INVESTMENT TRUST p 941
11 CHURCH ST SUITE 401, TORONTO,

ON, M5E 1W1
　(416) 861-9404　SIC 6722
CANADIAN ART PRINTS INC　p 265
　6311 WESTMINSTER HWY UNIT 110, RICHMOND, BC, V7C 4V4
　(604) 207-0165　SIC 5199
CANADIAN ARTISTS' REPRESENTATION (MANITOBA) INC　p 374
　100 ARTHUR ST SUITE 407, WINNIPEG, MB, R3B 1H3
　(204) 943-7211　SIC 8699
CANADIAN ASSOCIATES OF THE BEN-GURION UNIVERSITY OF NEGEV INC, THE　p 782
　1000 FINCH AVE W SUITE 506, NORTH YORK, ON, M3J 2V5
　(416) 665-8054　SIC 8399
CANADIAN ASSOCIATION FOR CO-OPERATIVE EDUCATION　p
974
　720 SPADINA AVE SUITE 202, TORONTO, ON, M5S 2T9
　(416) 483-3311　SIC 8621
CANADIAN ASSOCIATION FOR COMMU-NITY LIVING　p
813
　850 KING ST W UNIT 20, OSHAWA, ON, L1J 8N5
　(905) 436-2500　SIC 8399
CANADIAN ASSOCIATION OF CLERGY　p
614
　114 ARKELL ST, HAMILTON, ON, L8S 1N7
　(905) 522-3775　SIC 8621
CANADIAN ASSOCIATION OF PETROLEUM PRODUCERS　p 45
　350 7 AVE SW SUITE 2100, CALGARY, AB, T2P 3N9
　(403) 267-1100　SIC 8611
CANADIAN ASSOCIATION OF PROFES-SIONAL EMPLOYEES　p
822
　100 QUEEN ST SUITE 400, OTTAWA, ON, K1P 1J9
　(613) 236-9181　SIC 8631
CANADIAN ASSOCIATION OF TOKEN COLLECTORS　p 473
　273 MILL ST E, ACTON, ON, L7J 1J7
　(519) 853-3812　SIC 7699
CANADIAN AUSTIN GROUP HOLDINGS ULC　p 1396
　4 PLACE DU COMMERCE, VERDUN, QC, H3E 1J4
　(514) 281-4040　SIC 6719
CANADIAN AUTO RECYCLING LIMITED　p
426
　6 COREY KING DR, MOUNT PEARL, NL, A1N 0A2
　(709) 747-2000　SIC 5531
CANADIAN AUTO WORKERS　p 637
　See UNIFOR
CANADIAN AUTOMATED BANK MA-CHINES INC　p
278
　17637 1 AVE SUITE 101, SURREY, BC, V3Z 9S1
　(866) 538-2982　SIC 5044
CANADIAN AUTOMATED MANAGEMENT SYSTEMS LTD　p 188
　3707 WAYBURNE DR, BURNABY, BC, V5G 3L1
　(604) 430-5677　SIC 5962
CANADIAN AUTOMATION & TOOL INTER-NATIONAL INC　p
738
　6811 EDWARDS BLVD, MISSISSAUGA, ON, L5T 2S2
　(905) 795-1232　SIC 5962
CANADIAN AUTOMOBILE ASSOCIATIONp
828
　1545 CARLING AVE SUITE 500, OTTAWA, ON, K1Z 8P9
　(613) 247-0117　SIC 8699
CANADIAN AUTOMOBILE ASSOCIATIONp
1213

　1180 RUE DRUMMOND BUREAU 610, MONTREAL, QC, H3G 2S1
　(855) 861-5750　SIC 1541
CANADIAN AUTOMOTIVE INSTITUTE, THE　p 622
　3722 FAIRWAY RD, INNISFIL, ON, L9S 1A5
　　SIC 7299
CANADIAN AUTOPARTS TOYOTA INC　p
208
　7233 PROGRESS WAY, DELTA, BC, V4G 1E7
　(604) 946-5636　SIC 3714
CANADIAN AVIATION INSURANCE MAN-AGERS LTD　p
960
　200 BAY ST SUITE 2310, TORONTO, ON, M5J 2J1
　(416) 865-0252　SIC 6411
CANADIAN BABBITT BEARINGS LTD　p
513
　64 DALKEITH DR, BRANTFORD, ON, N3P 1N6
　(519) 752-5471　SIC 5085
CANADIAN BANC CORP　p 979
　200 FRONT ST W SUITE 2510, TORONTO, ON, M5V 3K2
　(416) 304-4440　SIC 6722
CANADIAN BANK NOTE COMPANY, LIM-ITED　p
748
　18 AURIGA DR, NEPEAN, ON, K2E 7T9
　(613) 722-3421　SIC 2796
CANADIAN BANK NOTE COMPANY, LIM-ITED　p
828
　975 GLADSTONE AVE, OTTAWA, ON, K1Y 4W5
　(613) 722-3421　SIC 2759
CANADIAN BANK NOTE COMPANY, LIM-ITED　p
828
　145 RICHMOND RD, OTTAWA, ON, K1Z 1A1
　(613) 722-3421　SIC 2759
CANADIAN BANKERS ASSOCIATION, THE　p 971
　199 BAY ST 30TH FL, TORONTO, ON, M5L 1G2
　(416) 362-6092　SIC 8611
CANADIAN BAR ASSOCIATION, THEp 822
　66 SLATER ST SUITE 1200, OTTAWA, ON, K1P 5H1
　(613) 237-2925　SIC 8621
CANADIAN BASE OPERATORS INC　p 546
　101 PRETTY RIVER PKY S SUITE 6, COLLINGWOOD, ON, L9Y 4M8
　(705) 446-9019　SIC 7538
CANADIAN BEARINGS LTD　p 734
　1600 DREW RD, MISSISSAUGA, ON, L5S 1S5
　(905) 670-7422　SIC 5085
CANADIAN BENEFITS CONSULTING GROUP INC　p 922
　2300 YONGE ST SUITE 3000, TORONTO, ON, M4P 1E4
　(416) 483-5896　SIC 6321
CANADIAN BIBLE COLLEGE　p 1422
　4400 4TH AVE, REGINA, SK, S4T 0H8
　(306) 545-0210　SIC 8221
CANADIAN BIOENERGY CORPORATIONp
240
　221 ESPLANADE W SUITE 310, NORTH VANCOUVER, BC, V7M 3J3
　(604) 947-0040　SIC 5172
CANADIAN BLOOD SERVICES　p 45
　200 BARCLAY PARADE SW UNIT 10, CAL-GARY, AB, T2P 4R5
　　SIC 8099
CANADIAN BLOOD SERVICES　p 817
　1800 ALTA VISTA DR, OTTAWA, ON, K1G 4J5
　(613) 739-2300　SIC 8099
CANADIAN BLOOD SERVICES　p 928
　2 BLOOR ST W, TORONTO, ON, M4W 3E2

　(613) 739-2300　SIC 8099
CANADIAN BRASS & COPPER CO　p 550
　225 DONEY CRES SUITE 1, CONCORD, ON, L4K 1P6
　(416) 736-0797　SIC 5051
CANADIAN BROADCASTING CORPORA-TION　p
41
　1724 WESTMOUNT BLVD NW, CALGARY, AB, T2N 3G7
　(403) 521-6000　SIC 4832
CANADIAN BROADCASTING CORPORA-TION　p
87
　123 EDMONTON CITY CENTRE NW, ED-MONTON, AB, T5J 2Y8
　(780) 468-7777　SIC 4833
CANADIAN BROADCASTING CORPORA-TION　p
297
　700 HAMILTON ST, VANCOUVER, BC, V6B 2R5
　(604) 662-6000　SIC 4832
CANADIAN BROADCASTING CORPORA-TION　p
406
　250 ARCHIBALD ST, MONCTON, NB, E1C 8N8
　　SIC 4832
CANADIAN BROADCASTING CORPORA-TION　p
429
　95 UNIVERSITY AVE, ST. JOHN'S, NL, A1B 1Z4
　(709) 576-5000　SIC 4833
CANADIAN BROADCASTING CORPORA-TION　p
452
　5600 SACKVILLE ST, HALIFAX, NS, B3J 1L2
　(902) 420-4483　SIC 4832
CANADIAN BROADCASTING CORPORA-TION　p
822
　181 QUEEN ST, OTTAWA, ON, K1P 1K9
　(613) 288-6000　SIC 4833
CANADIAN BROADCASTING CORPORA-TION　p
979
　250 FRONT ST W, TORONTO, ON, M5V 3G5
　(416) 205-3311　SIC 4832
CANADIAN BROADCASTING CORPORA-TION　p
979
　205 WELLINGTON ST W RM 4E301 B, TORONTO, ON, M5V 3G7
　(416) 205-5807　SIC 4833
CANADIAN BROADCASTING CORPORA-TION　p
979
　205 WELLINGTON ST W UNIT 9A211, TORONTO, ON, M5V 3G7
　(416) 205-3072　SIC 4833
CANADIAN BROADCASTING CORPORA-TION　p
1175
　1400 BOUL RENE-LEVESQUE E, MON-TREAL, QC, H2L 2M2
　(514) 597-6000　SIC 4833
CANADIAN BROADCASTING CORPORA-TION　p
1268
　888 RUE SAINT-JEAN UNITE 224, QUE-BEC, QC, G1R 5H6
　(418) 656-8206　SIC 4832
CANADIAN BROADCASTING CORPORA-TION　p
1417
　2440 BROAD ST, REGINA, SK, S4P 0A5
　(306) 347-9540　SIC 4832
CANADIAN BUSINESS MACHINES LIM-ITED　p
683

　8750 HOLGATE CRES, MILTON, ON, L9T 0K3
　(905) 878-0648　SIC 3499
CANADIAN CANCER SOCIETY　p 252
　172 2 AVE W, QUALICUM BEACH, BC, V9K 1T7
　　SIC 8399
CANADIAN CANCER SOCIETY　p 293
　565 10TH AVE W SUITE 44, VANCOUVER, BC, V5Z 4J4
　(604) 879-9131　SIC 7389
CANADIAN CANCER SOCIETY　p 926
　55 ST CLAIR AVE W SUITE 300, TORONTO, ON, M4V 2Y7
　(416) 961-7223　SIC 8399
CANADIAN CANCER SOCIETY　p 926
　55 ST CLAIR AVE W SUITE 500, TORONTO, ON, M4V 2Y7
　(416) 961-7223　SIC 8399
CANADIAN CANCER SOCIETY　p 1165
　5151 BOUL DE L'ASSOMPTION, MON-TREAL, QC, H1T 4A9
　(514) 255-5151　SIC 8399
CANADIAN CANNABIS CLINICS　p 885
　80 KING STREET, ST CATHARINES, ON, L2R 7G1
　(289) 273-3851　SIC 8011
CANADIAN CANOLA GROWERS ASSOCI-ATION　p
385
　1661 PORTAGE AVE SUITE 400, WIN-NIPEG, MB, R3J 3T7
　(204) 788-0090　SIC 8611
CANADIAN CAPITAL CORPORATIONp 990
　1022 BLOOR ST W SUITE 300, TORONTO, ON, M6H 1M2
　(416) 495-0909　SIC 6712
CANADIAN CAPSULE EQUIPMENT LIM-ITED　p
1021
　2510 OUELLETTE AVE SUITE 102, WIND-SOR, ON, N8X 1L4
　(519) 966-1122　SIC 3559
CANADIAN CARD SYSTEMS　p 667
　See CANCARD INC
CANADIAN CART SALES, DIV OF　p 757
　See TURF CARE PRODUCTS CANADA LIMITED
CANADIAN CENTER FOR CHILD PROTEC-TION INC　p
388
　615 ACADEMY RD, WINNIPEG, MB, R3N 0E7
　(204) 945-5735　SIC 8699
CANADIAN CENTRAL　p 937
　See CREDIT UNION CENTRAL OF CANADA
CANADIAN CENTRAL GUAGE LABORA-TORY, THE DIV OF　p
502
　See COX, FRANK J SALES LIMITED
CANADIAN CENTRE ON SUBSTANCE ABUSE　p 822
　75 ALBERT ST SUITE 500, OTTAWA, ON, K1P 5E7
　(613) 235-4048　SIC 8732
CANADIAN CHAMBER OF COMMERCE, THE　p 822
　275 SLATER ST SUITE 1700, OTTAWA, ON, K1P 5H9
　(613) 238-4000　SIC 8699
CANADIAN CLAIMS SERVICES INC　p 99
　17958 106 AVE, EDMONTON, AB, T5S 1V4
　(780) 443-1185　SIC 6411
CANADIAN CLAIMS SERVICES-VANCOUVER
99
　See CCS ADJUSTERS INC
CANADIAN CLOTHING INTERNATIONAL INC　p 864
　541 CONLINS RD, SCARBOROUGH, ON, M1B 5S1
　(416) 335-1300　SIC 5137
CANADIAN CO CO TOURS, INC　p 4

220 BEAR ST SUITE 306, BANFF, AB, T1L 1A2
(403) 762-5600   SIC 4725
CANADIAN COASTAL RESOURCES LTD p 45
202 6 AVE SW SUITE 900, CALGARY, AB, T2P 2R9
SIC 1311
CANADIAN COIN & CURRENCY CORP p 855
10355 YONGE ST, RICHMOND HILL, ON, L4C 3C1
(905) 883-5300   SIC 5094
CANADIAN COLLEGE OF NATUROPATHIC MEDICINE p 769
See INSTITUTE OF NATUROPATHIC EDUCATION AND RESEARCH
CANADIAN CONDOMINIUM MANAGEMENT CORP p 108
9440 49 ST NW SUITE 230, EDMONTON, AB, T6B 2M9
(780) 485-0505   SIC 1531
CANADIAN CONSTRUCTION MATERIALS ENGINEERING & TESTING INC p 192
6991 CURRAGH AVE, BURNABY, BC, V5J 4V6
(604) 436-9111   SIC 8734
CANADIAN CONTRACT CLEANING SPECIALISTS, INC p 21
1420 40 AVE NE SUITE 3, CALGARY, AB, T2E 6L1
(403) 259-5560   SIC 7349
CANADIAN CONTRACT CLEANING SPECIALISTS, INC p 135
603 10 AVE SE, HIGH RIVER, AB, T1V 1K2
SIC 7349
CANADIAN CONTRACT CLEANING SPECIALISTS, INC p 155
7550 40 AVE, RED DEER, AB, T4P 2H8
(403) 348-8440   SIC 7349
CANADIAN CONTRACT CLEANING SPECIALISTS, INC p 851
10 EAST WILMOT ST UNIT 25, RICHMOND HILL, ON, L4B 1G9
(905) 707-0410   SIC 7349
CANADIAN COPYRIGHT LICENSING AGENCY p 942
1 YONGE ST SUITE 800, TORONTO, ON, M5E 1E5
(416) 868-1620   SIC 6794
CANADIAN CORPS OF COMMISSIONAIRES 153
See CANADIAN CORPS OF COMMISSIONAIRES NATIONAL OFFICE, THE
CANADIAN CORPS OF COMMISSIONAIRES (MANITOBA AND NORTHWESTERN ONTARIO DIVISION) p 381
290 BURNELL ST, WINNIPEG, MB, R3G 2A7
(204) 942-5993   SIC 7381
CANADIAN CORPS OF COMMISSIONAIRES (NEWFOUNDLAND) p 429
207A KENMOUNT RD, ST. JOHN'S, NL, A1B 3P9
(709) 754-0757   SIC 7381
CANADIAN CORPS OF COMMISSIONAIRES (NORTHERN ALBERTA) p 97
10633 124 ST NW SUITE 101, EDMONTON, AB, T5N 1S5
(780) 451-1974   SIC 7381
CANADIAN CORPS OF COMMISSIONAIRES (OTTAWA DIVISION) p 748
24 COLONNADE RD N, NEPEAN, ON, K2E 7J6
(613) 228-0715   SIC 7381

CANADIAN CORPS OF COMMISSIONAIRES (SOUTHERN ALBERTA) p 21
1107 53 AVE NE, CALGARY, AB, T2E 6X9
(403) 244-4664   SIC 7381
CANADIAN CORPS OF COMMISSIONAIRES BELLEVILLE DETACHMENT QUINTE AREA p 490
See CANADIAN CORPS OF COMMISSIONAIRES NATIONAL OFFICE, THE
CANADIAN CORPS OF COMMISSIONAIRES MID ISLAND OPERATIONS 234
See CANADIAN CORPS OF COMMISSIONAIRES NATIONAL OFFICE, THE
CANADIAN CORPS OF COMMISSIONAIRES NATIONAL OFFICE, THE p 142
1222 3 AVE S, LETHBRIDGE, AB, T1J 0J9
(403) 327-1222   SIC 8621
CANADIAN CORPS OF COMMISSIONAIRES NATIONAL OFFICE, THE p 153
4807 50 AVE SUITE 107, RED DEER, AB, T4N 4A5
(403) 314-4142   SIC 7381
CANADIAN CORPS OF COMMISSIONAIRES NATIONAL OFFICE, THE p 234
711 NORTHUMBERLAND AVE, NANAIMO, BC, V9S 5C5
(250) 754-1042   SIC 7381
CANADIAN CORPS OF COMMISSIONAIRES NATIONAL OFFICE, THE p 303
595 HOWE ST SUITE 801, VANCOUVER, BC, V6C 2T5
(604) 646-3330   SIC 7381
CANADIAN CORPS OF COMMISSIONAIRES NATIONAL OFFICE, THE p 337
928 CLOVERDALE AVE, VICTORIA, BC, V8X 2T3
(250) 727-7755   SIC 7381
CANADIAN CORPS OF COMMISSIONAIRES NATIONAL OFFICE, THE p 409
41 MECCA DR, MONCTON, NB, E1G 1B7
(506) 384-2020   SIC 7381
CANADIAN CORPS OF COMMISSIONAIRES NATIONAL OFFICE, THE p 490
314 PINNACLE ST UNIT 2, BELLEVILLE, ON, K8N 3B4
(613) 962-6500   SIC 6289
CANADIAN CORPS OF COMMISSIONAIRES NATIONAL OFFICE, THE p 561
14 THIRD ST E, CORNWALL, ON, K6H 2C7
(613) 932-2594   SIC 7381
CANADIAN CORPS OF COMMISSIONAIRES NATIONAL OFFICE, THE p 748
24 COLONNADE RD N, NEPEAN, ON, K2E 7J6
SIC 7381
CANADIAN CORPS OF COMMISSIONAIRES NATIONAL OFFICE, THE p 1038
15 ST. PETERS RD, CHARLOTTETOWN, PE, C1A 5N1
(902) 894-7026   SIC 8621
CANADIAN CORPS OF COMMISSIONAIRES NATIONAL OFFICE, THE p 1420
122 ALBERT ST, REGINA, SK, S4R 2N2
(306) 757-0998   SIC 7381
CANADIAN CORPS OF COMMISSIONAIRES NATIONAL OFFICE, THE p 1426
493 2ND AVE N, SASKATOON, SK, S7K 2C1
(306) 244-6588   SIC 7381
CANADIAN CORPS OF COMMISSION-

AIRES NORTH SASKACHEWAN, DIV OF p 1426
See CANADIAN CORPS OF COMMISSIONAIRES NATIONAL OFFICE, THE
CANADIAN CORRECTIONAL MANAGEMENT INC 405
4 AIRPORT DR, MIRAMICHI, NB, E1N 3W4
(506) 624-2160   SIC 7381
CANADIAN COUNCIL ON REHABILITATION AND WORK, THE p 923
477 MOUNT PLEASANT RD SUITE 105, TORONTO, ON, M4S 2L9
(416) 260-3060   SIC 8748
CANADIAN COURIER LTD p 423
20 AV ROE, GANDER, NL, A1V 0H5
(709) 256-3528   SIC 4731
CANADIAN CURTIS REFRIGERATION INC p 891
881 ARVIN AVE, STONEY CREEK, ON, L8E 5N8
(905) 643-1977   SIC 3585
CANADIAN CUSTOM PACKAGING p 785
See TRAFALGAR INDUSTRIES OF CANADA LIMITED
CANADIAN DEAFBLIND ASSOCIATION ONTARIO CHAPTER p 517
54 BRANT AVE FL 3, BRANTFORD, ON, N3T 3G8
SIC 8399
CANADIAN DENTAL RELIEF INTERNATIONAL p 994
203 PARKSIDE DR, TORONTO, ON, M6R 2Z2
SIC 8062
CANADIAN DEPOSITORY FOR SECURITIES LIMITED, THE p 949
85 RICHMOND ST W, TORONTO, ON, M5H 2C9
(416) 365-8400   SIC 6289
CANADIAN DEVELOPMENT CONSULTANTS INTERNATIONAL INC p 303
541 HOWE ST UNIT 200, VANCOUVER, BC, V6C 2C2
(604) 633-1849   SIC 8732
CANADIAN DEWATERING (2006) LTD p 122
8350 1 ST NW, EDMONTON, AB, T6P 1X2
(780) 400-2260   SIC 5084
CANADIAN DEWATERING L.P. p 122
8350 1 ST NW, EDMONTON, AB, T6P 1X2
(780) 400-2260   SIC 5084
CANADIAN DINERS (1995) L.P. LTD p 820
1130 ST. LAURENT BLVD, OTTAWA, ON, K1K 3B6
(613) 747-9190   SIC 5812
CANADIAN DOORMAT AND MOP SERVICES p 85
See CANADIAN LINEN AND UNIFORM SERVICE CO
CANADIAN DRAPERY HARDWARE LTD p 782
150 STEEPROCK DR, NORTH YORK, ON, M3J 2T4
(416) 630-6900   SIC 5023
CANADIAN EGG MARKETING AGENCY p 833
21 FLORENCE ST, OTTAWA, ON, K2P 0W6
(613) 238-2514   SIC 5144
CANADIAN ELECTROCOATING LTD p 1024
945 PRINCE RD, WINDSOR, ON, N9C 2Z4
(519) 977-7523   SIC 3479
CANADIAN EMPLOYMENT CONTRACTORS INC p 702
2077 DUNDAS ST E UNIT 101, MISSISSAUGA, ON, L4X 1M2
(905) 282-9578   SIC 7361
CANADIAN ENERGY SERVICES INC p 45

700 4 AVE SW SUITE 1400, CALGARY, AB, T2P 3J4
(403) 269-2800   SIC 1381
CANADIAN ENGINEERED PRODUCTS AND SALES LTD p 208
7449 HUME AVE SUITE 6, DELTA, BC, V4G 1C3
(604) 940-8188   SIC 5075
CANADIAN ENGINEERED WOOD PRODUCTS LTD p 169
1 ERICKSON DR, SYLVAN LAKE, AB, T4S 1P5
(403) 887-6677   SIC 5031
CANADIAN ENGINEERING AND TOOL COMPANY LIMITED, THE p 1024
2265 SOUTH CAMERON BLVD, WINDSOR, ON, N9B 3P6
(519) 969-1618   SIC 3544
CANADIAN EXECUTIVE SERVICE ORGANIZATION p 944
700 BAY ST SUITE 800, TORONTO, ON, M5G 1Z6
(416) 961-2376   SIC 8699
CANADIAN FEDERATION OF INDEPENDENT BUSINESS 773
4141 YONGE ST SUITE 401, NORTH YORK, ON, M2P 2A8
(416) 222-8022   SIC 8611
CANADIAN FEDERATION OF UNIVERSITY WOMEN p 268
GD, SALT SPRING ISLAND, BC, V8K 2W1
SIC 8399
CANADIAN FERTILIZERS LIMITED p 145
1250 52 ST NW, MEDICINE HAT, AB, T1A 7R9
(403) 527-8887   SIC 2873
CANADIAN FINE MOTORS INC p 872
1882 LAWRENCE AVE E, SCARBOROUGH, ON, M1R 2Y5
(416) 588-8899   SIC 5521
CANADIAN FISH GUYS p 355
390 REGGIE LEACH DR, RIVERTON, MB, R0C 2R0
(204) 378-5510   SIC 0273
CANADIAN FISHING COMPANY LIMITED, THE p 294
301 WATERFRONT RD E, VANCOUVER, BC, V6A 0B3
(604) 681-0211   SIC 5146
CANADIAN FITNESS PROFESSIONALS INC p 878
225 SELECT AVE SUITE 110, SCARBOROUGH, ON, M1X 0B5
(416) 493-3515   SIC 7999
CANADIAN FLOORING & RENOVATIONS p 322
See ZAD HOLDINGS LTD
CANADIAN FLUORESCENT INDUSTRIES p 562
See SIGNIFY CANADA LTD
CANADIAN FOOTBALL LEAGUE p 942
50 WELLINGTON ST E 3RD FL, TORONTO, ON, M5E 1C8
(416) 322-9650   SIC 8699
CANADIAN FOOTWEAR (1982) LTD p 373
128 ADELAIDE ST, WINNIPEG, MB, R3A 0W5
(204) 944-7463   SIC 5661
CANADIAN FOREST PRODUCTS LTD p 180
36654 HART HWY, BEAR LAKE, BC, V0J 3G0
(250) 972-4700   SIC 2421
CANADIAN FOREST PRODUCTS LTD p 213
9312 259 RD LCD MAIN, FORT ST. JOHN, BC, V1J 4M6
(250) 787-3600   SIC 5031
CANADIAN FOREST PRODUCTS LTD p 215
1397 MORICE RIVER FOREST SERVICE

RD RR 1, HOUSTON, BC, V0J 1Z1
(250) 845-5200   *SIC 2421*
CANADIAN FOREST PRODUCTS LTD *p*
230
MILL RD, MACKENZIE, BC, V0J 2C0
(250) 997-3271   *SIC 2421*
CANADIAN FOREST PRODUCTS LTD *p*
236
430 CANFOR AVE, NEW WESTMINSTER,
BC, V3L 5G2
SIC 2421
CANADIAN FOREST PRODUCTS LTD *p*
249
5162 NORTHWOOD PULP MILL RD,
PRINCE GEORGE, BC, V2L 4W2
(250) 962-3500   *SIC 2421*
CANADIAN FOREST PRODUCTS LTD *p*
250
2789 PULP MILL RD, PRINCE GEORGE,
BC, V2N 2K3
(250) 563-0161   *SIC 2421*
CANADIAN FOREST PRODUCTS LTD *p*
250
2533 PRINCE GEORGE PULPMILL RD,
PRINCE GEORGE, BC, V2N 2K3
(250) 563-0161   *SIC 2421*
CANADIAN FOREST PRODUCTS LTD *p*
283
8300 CHERRY AVE E, TAYLOR, BC, V0C
2K0
(250) 789-9300   *SIC 2421*
CANADIAN FOREST PRODUCTS LTD *p*
323
1700 75TH AVE W UNIT 100, VANCOU-
VER, BC, V6P 6G2
(604) 661-5241   *SIC 2421*
CANADIAN FOREST PRODUCTS LTD *p*
330
1399 BEARHEAD RD, VANDERHOOF, BC,
V0J 3A2
(250) 567-4725   *SIC 2421*
CANADIAN FOREST PRODUCTS LTD *p*
344
GD, WOSS, BC, V0N 3P0
(250) 281-2300   *SIC 2421*
**CANADIAN FOUNDATION FOR HEALTH-
CARE IMPROVEMENT (CFHI)** *p*
822
150 KENT ST SUITE 200, OTTAWA, ON,
K1P 0E4
(613) 728-2238   *SIC 8621*
**CANADIAN FOUNDATION FOR THE
AMERICAS** *p 821*
1 NICHOLAS ST SUITE 720, OTTAWA, ON,
K1N 7B7
(613) 562-0005   *SIC 8699*
CANADIAN FREIGHTWAYS *p 94*
See TRANSPORT TFI 7 S.E.C
CANADIAN FREIGHTWAYS *p 183*
See TRANSPORT TFI 7 S.E.C
CANADIAN FREIGHTWAYS *p 1337*
See TRANSPORT TFI 7 S.E.C
**CANADIAN FRUIT & PRODUCE COMPANY
INC** *p 572*
165 THE QUEENSWAY SUITE 306, ETOBI-
COKE, ON, M8Y 1H8
(416) 259-5007   *SIC 5148*
**CANADIAN FUR SHOP OF SAITOH LIM-
ITED** *p*
960
65 HARBOUR SQ SUITE 1204, TORONTO,
ON, M5J 2L4
(416) 364-5885   *SIC 5948*
CANADIAN GAS & ELECTRIC INC *p 67*
1324 17 AVE SW SUITE 500, CALGARY,
AB, T2T 5S8
(403) 269-9379   *SIC 4911*
CANADIAN GATEWAY *p 906*
See YYZ TRAVEL SERVICES (INT'L) INC
**CANADIAN GENERAL INVESTMENTS LIM-
ITED** *p*
937
10 TORONTO ST, TORONTO, ON, M5C 2B7
(416) 366-2931   *SIC 6726*

CANADIAN GENERAL-TOWER LIMITED *p*
533
52 MIDDLETON ST, CAMBRIDGE, ON,
N1R 5T6
(519) 623-1633   *SIC 3081*
**CANADIAN GOODWILL INDUSTRIES
CORP** *p 374*
70 PRINCESS ST, WINNIPEG, MB, R3B
1K2
(204) 943-6435   *SIC 8699*
CANADIAN GRAND HOLIDAY *p 260*
*See GRAND PACIFIC TRAVEL & TRADE
(CANADA) CORP*
CANADIAN GRAPHICS WEST INC *p 290*
8285 MAIN ST, VANCOUVER, BC, V5X 3L7
(604) 324-1246   *SIC 5136*
CANADIAN GROUP, THE *p 792*
430 SIGNET DR SUITE A, NORTH YORK,
ON, M9L 2T6
(416) 746-3388   *SIC 5092*
CANADIAN GUIDE RAIL CORPORATION *p*
349
2840 WENZEL ST, EAST ST PAUL, MB,
R2E 1E7
(204) 222-2142   *SIC 3441*
CANADIAN HEARING SOCIETY *p 972*
271 SPADINA RD, TORONTO, ON, M5R
2V3
(416) 928-2502   *SIC 5999*
CANADIAN HEART RESEARCH CENTRE *p*
766
259 YORKLAND RD SUITE 200, NORTH
YORK, ON, M2J 0B5
(416) 977-8010   *SIC 8731*
CANADIAN HEATING PRODUCTS INC *p*
229
27342 GLOUCESTER WAY, LANGLEY, BC,
V4W 4A1
(604) 607-6422   *SIC 3429*
CANADIAN HELICOPTERS LIMITED *p 134*
1000 AIRPORT RD SUITE 4500, GRANDE
PRAIRIE, AB, T9E 0V3
(780) 429-6900   *SIC 4522*
CANADIAN HERITAGE DESIGN *p 241*
See COUNTRY FURNITURE LTD
CANADIAN HOBBYCRAFT LIMITED *p 550*
445 EDGELEY BLVD UNIT 1, CONCORD,
ON, L4K 4G1
(905) 738-6556   *SIC 5092*
**CANADIAN HOME BUILDERS' ASSOCIA-
TION OF BRITISH COLUMBIA** *p*
188
3700 WILLINGDON AVE, BURNABY, BC,
V5G 3H2
(604) 432-7112   *SIC 8621*
CANADIAN HOME SECURITY *p 715*
See EPIC DEALS INC
**CANADIAN HOSPITAL SPECIALTIES LIM-
ITED** *p*
796
2810 COVENTRY RD, OAKVILLE, ON, L6H
6R1
(905) 825-9300   *SIC 5047*
CANADIAN HYDRO DEVELOPERS, INC *p*
64
110 12 AVE SW, CALGARY, AB, T2R 0G7
(403) 267-7110   *SIC 4911*
**CANADIAN IMPERIAL BANK OF COM-
MERCE** *p*
971
199 BAY ST COMMERCE CRT W,
TORONTO, ON, M5L 1A2
(416) 980-3096   *SIC 6021*
CANADIAN INDUSTRIAL PARAMEDICS *p*
122
8917 13 ST NW, EDMONTON, AB, T6P 0C7
(780) 467-4262   *SIC 8322*
**CANADIAN INSTITUTE FOR HEALTH IN-
FORMATION** *p*
829
495 RICHMOND RD SUITE 600, OTTAWA,
ON, K2A 4B2
(613) 241-7860   *SIC 8011*
CANADIAN INSTITUTE FOR HEALTH IN-

FORMATION   *p*
922
90 EGLINTON AVE E SUITE 300,
TORONTO, ON, M4P 2Y3
(416) 481-2002   *SIC 8361*
**CANADIAN INSTITUTE OF TRAVEL COUN-
SELLORS OF ONTARIO** *p*
766
505 CONSUMERS RD SUITE 406, NORTH
YORK, ON, M2J 4V8
(416) 484-4450   *SIC 8621*
CANADIAN INSURANCE BROKERS INC *p*
922
1 EGLINTON AVE E SUITE 415,
TORONTO, ON, M4P 3A1
(416) 486-0951   *SIC 6411*
CANADIAN INTERMODAL SERVICES LTD
p 14
5402 44 ST SE, CALGARY, AB, T2C 4M8
(403) 920-0577   *SIC 5085*
**CANADIAN INTERNATIONAL FREIGHT
FORWARDERS ASSOCIATION INC** *p 583*
170 ATTWELL DR UNIT 480, ETOBICOKE,
ON, M9W 5Z5
(416) 234-5100   *SIC 4731*
**CANADIAN INTERNATIONAL GRAINS IN-
STITUTE** *p*
377
303 MAIN ST SUITE 1000, WINNIPEG, MB,
R3C 3G7
(204) 983-5344   *SIC 8743*
**CANADIAN INTERNATIONAL MILITARY
GAMES CORPORATION** *p 949*
357 BAY ST SUITE 300, TORONTO, ON,
M5H 2T7
(416) 364-0001   *SIC 8699*
CANADIAN IPG *p 889*
See CANADIAN IPG CORPORATION
CANADIAN IPG CORPORATION *p 889*
130 WOODWORTH AVE, ST THOMAS, ON,
N5P 3K1
(519) 637-1945   *SIC 5084*
CANADIAN JOURNAL OF SURGERY *p 817*
See CANADIAN MEDICAL ASSOCIATION
CANADIAN KAWASAKI MOTORS INC *p 868*
101 THERMOS RD, SCARBOROUGH, ON,
M1L 4W8
(416) 445-7775   *SIC 5012*
CANADIAN KENNEL CLUB, THE *p 583*
200 RONSON DR SUITE 400, ETOBICOKE,
ON, M9W 5Z9
(416) 675-5511   *SIC 8621*
CANADIAN KENWORTH COMPANY *p 725*
See PACCAR OF CANADA LTD
**CANADIAN KRAFT PAPER INDUSTRIES
LIMITED** *p 359*
HWY 10 N, THE PAS, MB, R9A 1L4
(204) 623-7411   *SIC 2621*
CANADIAN KROWN DEALERS INC *p 879*
35 MAGNUM DR, SCHOMBERG, ON, L0G
1T0
(905) 939-8750   *SIC 5169*
CANADIAN LABOUR CONGRESS *p 826*
2841 RIVERSIDE DR, OTTAWA, ON, K1V
8X7
(613) 521-3400   *SIC 8631*
CANADIAN LAWYER MAGAZINE INC *p 480*
240 EDWARD ST, AURORA, ON, L4G 3S9
(905) 841-6480   *SIC 5192*
**CANADIAN LIFE AND HEALTH INSUR-
ANCE ASSOCIATION INC** *p*
969
79 WELLINGTON ST W SUITE 2300,
TORONTO, ON, M5K 1G8
(416) 777-2221   *SIC 8611*
**CANADIAN LIFE AND HEALTH INSUR-
ANCE OMBUDSERVICE** *p*
937
20 TORONTO ST SUITE 710, TORONTO,
ON, M5C 2B8
(416) 777-9002   *SIC 6311*
CANADIAN LIGHT SOURCE INC *p 1433*
44 INNOVATION BLVD, SASKATOON, SK,
S7N 2V3

(306) 657-3500   *SIC 8733*
**CANADIAN LINEN AND UNIFORM SER-
VICE CO** *p*
28
4525 MANILLA RD SE, CALGARY, AB, T2G
4B6
(403) 243-8080   *SIC 7213*
**CANADIAN LINEN AND UNIFORM SER-
VICE CO** *p*
85
8631 STADIUM RD NW, EDMONTON, AB,
T5H 3W9
(780) 665-3905   *SIC 7213*
**CANADIAN LINEN AND UNIFORM SER-
VICE CO** *p*
184
2750 GILMORE AVE, BURNABY, BC, V5C
4T9
(778) 331-6200   *SIC 7213*
**CANADIAN LINEN AND UNIFORM SER-
VICE CO** *p*
369
1860 KING EDWARD ST, WINNIPEG, MB,
R2R 0N2
(204) 633-7261   *SIC 7213*
**CANADIAN LINEN AND UNIFORM SER-
VICE CO** *p*
445
41 THORNHILL DR SUITE 136, DART-
MOUTH, NS, B3B 1R9
(902) 468-2155   *SIC 7213*
**CANADIAN LINEN AND UNIFORM SER-
VICE CO** *p*
486
116 VICTORIA ST, BARRIE, ON, L4N 2J1
(705) 739-0573   *SIC 7213*
**CANADIAN LINEN AND UNIFORM SER-
VICE CO** *p*
573
20 ATOMIC AVE, ETOBICOKE, ON, M8Z
5L1
(416) 354-3100   *SIC 7213*
**CANADIAN LINEN AND UNIFORM SER-
VICE CO** *p*
652
155 ADELAIDE ST S, LONDON, ON, N5Z
3K8
(519) 686-5000   *SIC 7213*
**CANADIAN LINEN AND UNIFORM SER-
VICE CO** *p*
786
75 NORFINCH DR SUITE 1, NORTH YORK,
ON, M3N 1W8
(416) 849-5100   *SIC 7218*
**CANADIAN LINEN AND UNIFORM SER-
VICE CO** *p*
817
1695 RUSSELL RD, OTTAWA, ON, K1G
0N1
(613) 736-9975   *SIC 7213*
**CANADIAN LINEN AND UNIFORM SER-
VICE CO** *p*
1415
180 N LEONARD ST, REGINA, SK, S4N
5V7
(306) 721-4848   *SIC 7213*
**CANADIAN LIQUIDS PROCESSORS LIM-
ITED** *p*
610
15 BIGGAR AVE, HAMILTON, ON, L8L 3Z3
(888) 312-1000   *SIC 4953*
CANADIAN LOCATORS INC *p 10*
525 28 ST SE SUITE 201, CALGARY, AB,
T2A 6W9
(403) 263-6310   *SIC 8742*
CANADIAN LOCATORS INC *p 99*
18215 114 AVE NW UNIT 101, EDMON-
TON, AB, T5S 2P6
(780) 487-7553   *SIC 1623*
**CANADIAN LOGISTICS SYSTEMS LIM-
ITED** *p*
324
3433 BROADWAY W SUITE 201, VANCOU-
VER, BC, V6R 2B4

(604) 731-8001 *SIC 4785*
CANADIAN LUMBER LTD *p 361*
139 NORTH RAILWAY AVE, WINKLER, MB, R6W 1J4
(204) 325-5319 *SIC 5211*
CANADIAN LYNDEN TRANSPORT LTD *p 1*
27340 ACHESON RD, ACHESON, AB, T7X 6B1
(780) 960-9444 *SIC 4213*
CANADIAN MALARTIC GP *p 1148*
100 CH DU LAC MOURIER, MALARTIC, QC, J0Y 1Z0
(819) 757-2225 *SIC 1041*
CANADIAN MARITIME ENGINEERING LIMITED *p*
445
90 THORNHILL DR, DARTMOUTH, NS, B3B 1S3
(902) 468-1888 *SIC 3599*
CANADIAN MARKETING ASSOCIATION *p*
960
55 UNIVERSITY AVE SUITE 603, TORONTO, ON, M5J 2H7
(416) 391-2362 *SIC 8611*
CANADIAN MARKETING TEST CASE 200 LIMITED *p 730*
5770 HURONTARIO ST, MISSISSAUGA, ON, L5R 3G5
(800) 986-5569 *SIC 3949*
CANADIAN MARKETING TEST CASE 201 LIMITED *p 730*
5770 HURONTARIO ST, MISSISSAUGA, ON, L5R 3G5
SIC 5087
CANADIAN MARKETING TEST CASE 204 LIMITED *p 730*
5770 HURONTARIO ST, MISSISSAUGA, ON, L5R 3G5
SIC 5091
CANADIAN MARKETING TEST CASE 206 LIMITED *p 730*
5770 HURONTARIO ST, MISSISSAUGA, ON, L5R 3G5
(905) 555-5555 *SIC 2732*
CANADIAN MARKETING TEST CASE 217*p*
730
5770 HURONTARIO ST, MISSISSAUGA, ON, L5R 3G5
SIC 6719
CANADIAN MDF PRODUCTS COMPANY *p*
93
14810 131 AVE NW SUITE 2, EDMONTON, AB, T5L 4Y3
(780) 452-5406 *SIC 5211*
CANADIAN MEASUREMENT-METROLOGY INC *p 720*
2433 MEADOWVALE BLVD, MISSISSAUGA, ON, L5N 5S2
(905) 819-7878 *SIC 5085*
CANADIAN MEDIA FUND *p 942*
50 WELLINGTON ST E, TORONTO, ON, M5E 1C8
(416) 214-4400 *SIC 8399*
CANADIAN MEDICAL ASSOCIATION *p 817*
1867 ALTA VISTA DR, OTTAWA, ON, K1G 5W8
(613) 731-9331 *SIC 8621*
CANADIAN MEDICAL PROTECTIVE ASSOCIATION, THE *p*
825
875 CARLING AVE SUITE 928, OTTAWA, ON, K1S 5P1
(613) 725-2000 *SIC 8621*
CANADIAN MEMORIAL CHIROPRACTIC COLLEGE *p 764*
6100 LESLIE ST, NORTH YORK, ON, M2H 3J1
(416) 482-2340 *SIC 8221*
CANADIAN MENNONITE UNIVERSITY *p*
388
500 SHAFTESBURY BLVD, WINNIPEG, MB, R3P 2N2
(204) 487-3300 *SIC 8221*
CANADIAN MENTAL HEALTH ASSOCIA-

TION TORONTO BRANCH, THE *p*
788
700 LAWRENCE AVE W SUITE 480, NORTH YORK, ON, M6A 3B4
(416) 789-7957 *SIC 8011*
CANADIAN MENTAL HEALTH ASSOCIATION TORONTO BRANCH, THE *p*
811
60 BOND ST W, OSHAWA, ON, L1G 1A5
(905) 436-8760 *SIC 8011*
CANADIAN MENTAL HEALTH ASSOCIATION, MIDDLESEX *p*
655
534 QUEENS AVE, LONDON, ON, N6B 1Y6
(519) 668-0624 *SIC 8621*
CANADIAN MENTAL HEALTH ASSOCIATION, NIAGARA BRANCH *p*
885
15 WELLINGTON ST, ST CATHARINES, ON, L2R 5P7
(905) 641-5222 *SIC 8011*
CANADIAN MENTAL HEALTH ASSOCIATION, PETERBOROUGH BRANCH *p*
839
466 GEORGE ST N, PETERBOROUGH, ON, K9H 3R7
(705) 748-6711 *SIC 8011*
CANADIAN MENTAL HEALTH ASSOCIATION, SIMCOE COUNTY BRANCH *p*
486
15 BRADFORD ST, BARRIE, ON, L4N 1W2
(705) 726-5033 *SIC 8011*
CANADIAN MENTAL HEALTH ASSOCIATION, THUNDER BAY BRANCH *p*
907
200 VAN NORMAN ST, THUNDER BAY, ON, P7A 4B8
(807) 345-5564 *SIC 8621*
CANADIAN MENTAL HEALTH ASSOCIATION, WINDSOR-ESSEX COUNTY BRANCH *p 1021*
1400 WINDSOR AVE, WINDSOR, ON, N8X 3L9
(519) 255-7440 *SIC 8011*
CANADIAN MENTAL HEALTH ASSOCIATION-COCHRANE-TIMISKAMING BRANCH *p 912*
330 SECOND AVE SUITE 201, TIMMINS, ON, P4N 8A4
(705) 267-8100 *SIC 8011*
CANADIAN MENTAL HEALTH ASSOCIATION/PEEL BRANCH *p*
511
7700 HURONTARIO ST SUITE 314, BRAMPTON, ON, L6Y 4M3
(905) 451-1718 *SIC 8011*
CANADIAN MENTAL HEALTH ASSOCIATION/PEEL BRANCH *p*
511
7700 HURONTARIO ST SUITE 601, BRAMPTON, ON, L6Y 4M3
(905) 451-2123 *SIC 8621*
CANADIAN METAL AND FIBRE LTD *p 343*
1392 JOHNSTON RD, WHITE ROCK, BC, V4B 3Z2
(604) 535-2793 *SIC 5541*
CANADIAN MILK MANUFACTURING INC *p*
519
198 PEARL ST E, BROCKVILLE, ON, K6V 1R4
(613) 970-5566 *SIC 2023*
CANADIAN MINI-WAREHOUSE PROPERTIES COMPANY *p*
720
1740 ARGENTIA RD, MISSISSAUGA, ON, L5N 3K3
(905) 677-0363 *SIC 4225*
CANADIAN MIST DISTILLERS LIMITED *p*
546
202 MACDONALD RD, COLLINGWOOD, ON, L9Y 4J2
(705) 445-4690 *SIC 2085*
CANADIAN MOUNTAIN HOLIDAYS LIMITED PARTNERSHIP *p*

4
217 BEAR ST, BANFF, AB, T1L 1J6
(403) 762-7100 *SIC 7011*
CANADIAN MUSEUM OF NATURE *p 833*
240 MCLEOD ST, OTTAWA, ON, K2P 2R1
(613) 566-4700 *SIC 8412*
CANADIAN MUSICAL REPRODUCTION RIGHTS AGENCY LIMITED, THE *p 974*
56 WELLESLEY ST W SUITE 320, TORONTO, ON, M5S 2S3
(416) 926-1966 *SIC 6794*
CANADIAN N D E TECHNOLOGY LTD *p*
583
124 SKYWAY AVE, ETOBICOKE, ON, M9W 4Y9
(416) 213-8000 *SIC 5084*
CANADIAN NATIONAL EXHIBITION ASSOCIATION *p*
991
210 PRINCES BLVD, TORONTO, ON, M6K 3C3
(416) 263-3600 *SIC 7996*
CANADIAN NATIONAL INSTITUTE FOR THE BLIND, THE *p 918*
1929 BAYVIEW AVE, TORONTO, ON, M4G 3E8
(416) 486-2500 *SIC 8331*
CANADIAN NATIONAL RAILWAY *p 84*
See COMPAGNIE DES CHEMINS DE FER NATIONAUX DU CANADA
CANADIAN NATIONAL RAILWAY *p 1203*
See COMPAGNIE DES CHEMINS DE FER NATIONAUX DU CANADA
CANADIAN NATIONAL RAILWAYS PENSION TRUST FUND *p*
1202
5 PLACE VILLE-MARIE BUREAU 1100, MONTREAL, QC, H3B 2G2
(514) 399-5963 *SIC 6726*
CANADIAN NATIONAL SPORTSMEN'S SHOWS (1989) LIMITED *p 705*
30 VILLAGE CENTRE PL, MISSISSAUGA, ON, L4Z 1V9
(905) 361-2677 *SIC 7389*
CANADIAN NATIONAL STEEL CORPORATION *p*
78
5302 39 ST, CAMROSE, AB, T4V 2N8
(780) 672-3116 *SIC 3312*
CANADIAN NATURAL RESOURCES LIMITED *p*
6
GD STN MAIN, BONNYVILLE, AB, T9N 2J6
(780) 826-8110 *SIC 1311*
CANADIAN NATURAL RESOURCES LIMITED *p*
45
324 8 AVE SW SUITE 1800, CALGARY, AB, T2P 2Z2
(403) 517-6700 *SIC 1311*
CANADIAN NATURAL RESOURCES LIMITED *p*
45
855 2 ST SW SUITE 2100, CALGARY, AB, T2P 4J8
(403) 517-6700 *SIC 1311*
CANADIAN NATURAL RESOURCES LIMITED *p*
131
9705 97 ST, GRANDE PRAIRIE, AB, T8V 8B9
(780) 831-7475 *SIC 1311*
CANADIAN NETWORK INSTALLATIONS LTD *p 667*
1351 RODICK RD UNIT 6, MARKHAM, ON, L3R 5K4
(905) 946-2188 *SIC 4899*
CANADIAN NIAGARA HOTELS INC *p 757*
5685 FALLS AVE 3RD-5TH FL, NIAGARA FALLS, ON, L2E 6W7
(905) 374-4444 *SIC 7011*
CANADIAN NIAGARA HOTELS INC *p 758*
5875 FALLS AVE, NIAGARA FALLS, ON, L2G 3K7

(905) 374-4444 *SIC 7011*
CANADIAN NIAGARA POWER INC *p 591*
1130 BERTIE ST, FORT ERIE, ON, L2A 5Y2
(905) 871-0330 *SIC 4911*
CANADIAN NORTH INC *p 21*
150 PALMER RD NE, CALGARY, AB, T2E 7R3
(780) 890-8600 *SIC 4729*
CANADIAN NORTH INC *p 21*
580 PALMER RD NE SUITE 200, CALGARY, AB, T2E 7R3
(403) 503-2310 *SIC 4512*
CANADIAN NORTHERN SHIELD INSURANCE COMPANY *p*
297
555 HASTINGS ST W UNIT 1900, VANCOUVER, BC, V6B 4N6
(604) 662-2900 *SIC 6411*
CANADIAN NUCLEAR LABORATORIES LTD *p 541*
286 PLANT RD, CHALK RIVER, ON, K0J 1J0
(613) 584-3311 *SIC 2819*
CANADIAN NUCLEAR SOCIETY *p 944*
655 BAY ST, TORONTO, ON, M5G 2K4
(416) 977-7620 *SIC 8999*
CANADIAN NURSES ASSOCIATION *p 833*
50 DRIVEWAY, OTTAWA, ON, K2P 1E2
(613) 232-6424 *SIC 8748*
CANADIAN OATS MILLING LTD *p 168*
55021 RGE RD 234A, STURGEON COUNTY, AB, T8T 2A9
(780) 973-9102 *SIC 5153*
CANADIAN OLYMPIC COMMITTEE *p 925*
21 ST CLAIR AVE E SUITE 900, TORONTO, ON, M4T 1L9
(416) 962-0262 *SIC 8699*
CANADIAN OPERA COMPANY *p 932*
227 FRONT ST E, TORONTO, ON, M5A 1E8
(416) 363-6671 *SIC 7922*
CANADIAN OVERSEAS MARKETING CORPORATION *p 291*
2020 YUKON ST, VANCOUVER, BC, V5Y 3N8
SIC 7331
CANADIAN PACIFIC RAILWAY COMPANY*p*
253
420 VICTORIA RD, REVELSTOKE, BC, V0E 2S0
(250) 837-8229 *SIC 4011*
CANADIAN PACIFIC RAILWAY COMPANY*p*
1083
5901 AV WESTMINSTER, COTE SAINT-LUC, QC, H4W 2J9
(514) 483-7102 *SIC 4011*
CANADIAN PACIFIC RAILWAY COMPANY*p*
1210
1100 RUE DE LA GAUCHETIERE, MONTREAL, QC, H3C 3E4
(514) 395-5151 *SIC 4111*
CANADIAN PACIFIC RAILWAY COMPANY*p*
1410
3 MANITOBA ST W, MOOSE JAW, SK, S6H 1P8
(306) 693-5421 *SIC 4011*
CANADIAN PACIFIC RAILWAY LIMITED *p*
14
7550 OGDEN DALE RD SE, CALGARY, AB, T2C 4X9
(888) 333-6370 *SIC 4011*
CANADIAN PAPER CONNECTION INC *p*
550
200 VICEROY RD UNIT 1, CONCORD, ON, L4K 3N8
(905) 669-2222 *SIC 5113*
CANADIAN PARALYMPIC COMMITTEE *p*
833
225 METCALFE ST SUITE 310, OTTAWA, ON, K2P 1P9
(613) 569-4333 *SIC 8699*
CANADIAN PARAMEDICAL SERVICES INC *p 34*
7053 FARRELL RD SE SUITE 5, CALGARY,

AB, T2H 0T3
(403) 259-8399   *SIC* 8049

CANADIAN PARKS & WILDERNESS SOCIETY *p* 824
250 CITY CENTRE AVE SUITE 506, OTTAWA, ON, K1R 6K7
(613) 569-7226   *SIC* 8999

CANADIAN PARTNERSHIP AGAINST CANCER CORPORATION *p* 949
145 KING ST W STE 900, TORONTO, ON, M5H 1J8
(416) 915-9222   *SIC* 8733

CANADIAN PAYMENTS ASSOCIATION *p* 824
350 ALBERT ST UNIT 800, OTTAWA, ON, K1R 1A4
(613) 238-4173   *SIC* 8741

CANADIAN PAYROLL ASSOCIATION, THE *p* 928
250 BLOOR ST E SUITE 1600, TORONTO, ON, M4W 1E6
(416) 487-3380   *SIC* 8611

CANADIAN PHOENIX STEEL PRODUCTS, DIV OF *p* 573
See 1045761 ONTARIO LIMITED

CANADIAN POSTMASTERS AND ASSISTANTS ASSOCIATION *p* 820
281 QUEEN MARY ST, OTTAWA, ON, K1K 1X1
(613) 745-2095   *SIC* 8621

CANADIAN PREMIER AUTOMOTIVE LTD *p* 660
1065 WHARNCLIFFE RD S, LONDON, ON, N6L 1J9
(519) 680-1800   *SIC* 7515

CANADIAN PREMIER LIFE INSURANCE COMPANY *p* 771
25 SHEPPARD AVE W, NORTH YORK, ON, M2N 6S6
(416) 883-6300   *SIC* 6311

CANADIAN PRESS, THE *p* 937
36 KING ST E SUITE 301, TORONTO, ON, M5C 2L9
(416) 364-0321   *SIC* 7383

CANADIAN PRESS, THE *p* 1187
215 RUE SAINT-JACQUES UNITE 100, MONTREAL, QC, H2Y 1M6
(514) 849-3212   *SIC* 7383

CANADIAN PRINCESS RESORT *p* 284
See OAK BAY MARINA LTD

CANADIAN PROTECTION PROVIDERS INC *p* 766
251 CONSUMERS RD SUITE 1200, NORTH YORK, ON, M2J 4R3
(647) 330-0313   *SIC* 6211

CANADIAN PUBLIC ACCOUNTABILITY BOARD *p* 949
150 YORK ST SUITE 900, TORONTO, ON, M5H 3S5
(416) 913-8260   *SIC* 8721

CANADIAN PUBLIC HEALTH ASSOCIATION *p* 828
1565 CARLING AVE SUITE 300, OTTAWA, ON, K1Z 8R1
(613) 725-3769   *SIC* 8621

CANADIAN REAL ESTATE ASSOCIATION, THE *p* 833
200 CATHERINE ST 6H FL, OTTAWA, ON, K2P 2K9
(613) 237-7111   *SIC* 8611

CANADIAN RED CROSS *p* 1396
See CANADIAN RED CROSS SOCIETY, THE

CANADIAN RED CROSS SOCIETY, THE *p* 445
133 TROOP AVE, DARTMOUTH, NS, B3B 2A7
(902) 496-0103   *SIC* 8059

CANADIAN RED CROSS SOCIETY, THE *p* 561

165 MONTREAL RD, CORNWALL, ON, K6H 1B2
SIC 8059

CANADIAN RED CROSS SOCIETY, THE *p* 833
400 COOPER ST SUITE 8000, OTTAWA, ON, K2P 2H8
(613) 740-1900   *SIC* 8322

CANADIAN RED CROSS SOCIETY, THE *p* 1396
6 PLACE DU COMMERCE, VERDUN, QC, H3E 1P4
(514) 362-2930   *SIC* 8322

CANADIAN REFORMED SOCIETY FOR A HOME FOR THE AGED INC *p* 529
4486 GUELPH LINE, BURLINGTON, ON, L7P 0N2
(905) 335-3636   *SIC* 8051

CANADIAN REFRIGERATION SUPPLY *p* 851
See EASTERN REFRIGERATION SUPPLY CO. LIMITED

CANADIAN REGIONAL ENGINEERING CENTRE *p* 812
See GENERAL MOTORS OF CANADA COMPANY

CANADIAN RENEWABLE ENERGY ACADEMY *p* 1002
445 EDGELEY BOULEVARD, VAUGHAN, ON, L4K 4G1
(647) 832-0553   *SIC* 4924

CANADIAN RENEWABLE ENERGY CORPORATION *p* 1026
4 LINE RD SUITE 209, WOLFE ISLAND, ON, K0H 2Y0
(613) 385-2045   *SIC* 4911

CANADIAN RESEARCH DATA CENTER NETWORK *p* 614
1280 MAIN ST W, HAMILTON, ON, L8S 4M1
(905) 525-9140   *SIC* 8732

CANADIAN ROAD BUILDERS INC *p* 1
26120 ACHESON RD, ACHESON, AB, T7X 6B3
(780) 962-7800   *SIC* 1611

CANADIAN ROCKIE MATSUTAKE LTD *p* 259
8740 BECKWITH RD SUITE 110, RICHMOND, BC, V6X 1V5
SIC 5141

CANADIAN ROCKY MOUNTAIN RESORTS LTD *p* 66
332 17 AVE SW, CALGARY, AB, T2S 0A8
(403) 233-8066   *SIC* 7011

CANADIAN ROYALTIES INC *p* 1202
800 BOUL RENE-LEVESQUE O BUREAU 410, MONTREAL, QC, H3B 1X9
(514) 879-1688   *SIC* 1081

CANADIAN SALT COMPANY *p* 126
See K+S SEL WINDSOR LTEE

CANADIAN SCHOLARSHIP TRUST FOUNDATION *p* 766
2225 SHEPPARD AVE E SUITE 600, NORTH YORK, ON, M2J 5C2
(416) 445-7377   *SIC* 6732

CANADIAN SCIENCE AND TECHNOLOGY GROWTH FUND INC *p* 986
130 KING ST W SUITE 2200, TORONTO, ON, M5X 2A2
SIC 6722

CANADIAN SCIENCE CENTRE FOR HUMAN AND ANIMAL HEALTH *p* 380
1015 ARLINGTON ST SUITE A1010, WINNIPEG, MB, R3E 3P6
(204) 789-6001   *SIC* 8733

CANADIAN SECURITIES EXCHANGE *p* 986
See CNSX MARKETS INC

CANADIAN SHAREOWNER INVESTMENT *p* 949
See CANADIAN SHAREOWNERS ASSOCIATION

CANADIAN SHAREOWNERS ASSOCIATION *p* 949

170 UNIVERSITY AVE SUITE 704, TORONTO, ON, M5H 3B3
(416) 595-9600   *SIC* 6282

CANADIAN SOCCER ASSOCIATION INCORPORATED, THE *p* 833
237 METCALFE ST, OTTAWA, ON, K2P 1R2
(613) 237-7678   *SIC* 8699

CANADIAN SOCIETY OF IMMIGRATION CONSULTANTS *p* 949
390 BAY ST SUITE 1600, TORONTO, ON, M5H 2Y2
(416) 572-2800   *SIC* 7389

CANADIAN SOLAR INC *p* 605
545 SPEEDVALE AVE W, GUELPH, ON, N1K 1E6
(519) 837-1881   *SIC* 3312

CANADIAN SPECIAL OLYMPICS INC *p* 925
60 ST CLAIR AVE E SUITE 700, TORONTO, ON, M4T 1N5
(416) 927-9050   *SIC* 8699

CANADIAN SPECIALTY METALS ULC *p* 583
81 STEINWAY BLVD, ETOBICOKE, ON, M9W 6H6
(416) 213-0000   *SIC* 5051

CANADIAN SPRINGS *p* 691
See AQUATERRA CORPORATION

CANADIAN SPRINGS WATER COMPANY *p* 257
See AQUATERRA CORPORATION

CANADIAN STANDARD HOME SERVICES *p* 932
See 2456317 ONTARIO LTD

CANADIAN STANDARDS ASSOCIATION *p* 254
13799 COMMERCE PKY, RICHMOND, BC, V6V 2N9
(604) 273-4581   *SIC* 8734

CANADIAN STANDARDS ASSOCIATION *p* 583
178 REXDALE BLVD, ETOBICOKE, ON, M9W 1R3
(416) 747-4000   *SIC* 8734

CANADIAN STARTER DRIVES INC *p* 792
176 MILVAN DR, NORTH YORK, ON, M9L 1Z9
(416) 748-1458   *SIC* 7538

CANADIAN STEEL NETWORK INC *p* 738
6445 KENNEDY RD UNIT A, MISSISSAUGA, ON, L5T 2W4
(905) 670-2900   *SIC* 5051

CANADIAN STORES *p* 570
See A B C COMPANY LIMITED

CANADIAN STRUCTURAL & MECHANICAL LTD *p* 858
1399 LOUGAR AVE, SARNIA, ON, N7S 5N5
(519) 383-6525   *SIC* 1711

CANADIAN TAMIL ACADEMY *p* 873
8 MILNER AVE, SCARBOROUGH, ON, M1S 3P8
(416) 757-2006   *SIC* 8211

CANADIAN TECHNICAL CENTRE *p* 670
See GENERAL MOTORS OF CANADA COMPANY

CANADIAN TENNIS ASSOCIATION *p* 786
1 SHOREHAM DR SUITE 200, NORTH YORK, ON, M3N 3A7
(416) 665-9777   *SIC* 8699

CANADIAN TEST CASE 101 LTD *p* 730
5770 HURONTARIO ST, MISSISSAUGA, ON, L5R 3G5
SIC 2899

CANADIAN TEST CASE 11 *p* 730
5770 HURONTARIO ST, MISSISSAUGA, ON, L5R 3G5
SIC 7389

CANADIAN TEST CASE 110 *p* 730
5770 HURONTARIO ST, MISSISSAUGA, ON, L5R 3G5
SIC 3949

CANADIAN TEST CASE 111 *p* 730
5770 HURONTARIO ST, MISSISSAUGA, ON, L5R 3G5
SIC 3949

CANADIAN TEST CASE 117 *p* 730
5770 HURONTARIO ST, MISSISSAUGA, ON, L5R 3G5
SIC 5137

CANADIAN TEST CASE 120-TEST *p* 720
6750 CENTURY AVE SUITE 305, MISSISSAUGA, ON, L5N 0B7
(905) 812-5920   *SIC* 5083

CANADIAN TEST CASE 145 *p* 730
5770 HURONTARIO ST, MISSISSAUGA, ON, L5R 3G5
SIC 2834

CANADIAN TEST CASE 158 *p* 1194
505 BOUL DE MAISONNEUVE O BUREAU 906, MONTREAL, QC, H3A 3C2
(514) 904-1496   *SIC* 5499

CANADIAN TEST CASE 16 *p* 720
6750 CENTURY AVE SUITE 305, MISSISSAUGA, ON, L5N 2V8
(905) 812-5920   *SIC* 7389

CANADIAN TEST CASE 165 *p* 730
5770 HURONTARIO ST, MISSISSAUGA, ON, L5R 3G5
SIC 2421

CANADIAN TEST CASE 167 *p* 730
5770 HURONTARIO ST, MISSISSAUGA, ON, L5R 3G5
SIC 7389

CANADIAN TEST CASE 168 INC. *p* 730
5770 HURONTARIO ST, MISSISSAUGA, ON, L5R 3G5
SIC 3714

CANADIAN TEST CASE 168 INC. *p* 1085
1450 RUE CUNARD, COTE SAINT-LUC, QC, H7S 2B7
SIC 3714

CANADIAN TEST CASE 169 DIV *p* 730
See CANADIAN TEST CASE 168 INC.

CANADIAN TEST CASE 172 *p* 720
6750 CENTURY AVE SUITE 305, MISSISSAUGA, ON, L5N 0B7
SIC 5311

CANADIAN TEST CASE 173 *p* 720
6750 CENTURY AVE, SUITE 305, MISSISSAUGA, ON, L5N 0B7
(905) 812-5920   *SIC* 3732

CANADIAN TEST CASE 174 *p* 570
123 FOURTH ST, ETOBICOKE, ON, M8V 2Y6
(905) 812-5920   *SIC* 7389

CANADIAN TEST CASE 174 *p* 730
5770 HURONTARIO ST, MISSISSAUGA, ON, L5R 3G5
SIC 6021

CANADIAN TEST CASE 176 *p* 720
6750 CENTURY AVE SUITE 305, MISSISSAUGA, ON, L5N 2V8
(905) 812-5920   *SIC* 5812

CANADIAN TEST CASE 177 CORP *p* 720
6750 CENTURY AVE SUITE 305, MISSISSAUGA, ON, L5N 2V8
(905) 812-5920   *SIC* 5812

CANADIAN TEST CASE 185 *p* 720
6750 CENTURY AVE SUITE 300, MISSISSAUGA, ON, L5N 0B7
(905) 812-5920   *SIC* 3714

CANADIAN TEST CASE 187 *p* 720
6750 CENTURY AVE SUITE 305, MISSISSAUGA, ON, L5N 2V8
(905) 812-5920   *SIC* 5812

CANADIAN TEST CASE 192 *p* 21
1110 CENTRE ST NE SUITE 204, CALGARY, AB, T2E 2R2
(403) 276-5546   *SIC* 3714

CANADIAN TEST CASE 20 *p* 720
6750 CENTURY AVE SUITE 305, MISSISSAUGA, ON, L5N 0B7
(905) 812-5920   *SIC* 8741

CANADIAN TEST CASE 21 *p* 720
6750 CENTURY AVE SUITE 305, MISSIS-

SAUGA, ON, L5N 2V8
(905) 812-5920   *SIC* 1044
CANADIAN TEST CASE 22   *p* 730
5770 HURONTARIO ST, MISSISSAUGA,
ON, L5R 3G5
SIC 7389
CANADIAN TEST CASE 27 LTD   *p* 730
5770 HURONTARIO ST, MISSISSAUGA,
ON, L5R 3G5
SIC 2992
CANADIAN TEST CASE 29-B   *p* 720
6750 CENTURY AVE SUITE 305, MISSIS-
SAUGA, ON, L5N 2V8
(905) 812-5922   *SIC* 6324
CANADIAN TEST CASE 30, DIVISION*p* 730
See *CANADIAN TEST CASE 74*
CANADIAN TEST CASE 31 LTD   *p* 720
6750 CENTURY AVE SUITE 305, MISSIS-
SAUGA, ON, L5N 2V8
(905) 812-5920   *SIC* 5199
CANADIAN TEST CASE 36 LIMITED *p* 720
6750 CENTURY AVE SUITE 305, MISSIS-
SAUGA, ON, L5N 2V8
SIC 5331
CANADIAN TEST CASE 44   *p* 730
5770 HURONTARIO ST, MISSISSAUGA,
ON, L5R 3G5
SIC 7389
CANADIAN TEST CASE 49 LTD   *p* 720
6750 CENTURY AVE SUITE 305, MISSIS-
SAUGA, ON, L5N 2V8
(905) 812-5920   *SIC* 6311
CANADIAN TEST CASE 52   *p* 730
5770 HURONTARIO ST, MISSISSAUGA,
ON, L5R 3G5
SIC 3949
CANADIAN TEST CASE 56   *p* 708
5770 HURONTARIO ST, MISSISSAUGA,
ON, L5A 4G4
SIC 2421
CANADIAN TEST CASE 62   *p* 720
6750 CENTURY AVE SUITE 305, MISSIS-
SAUGA, ON, L5N 2V8
(437) 999-9999   *SIC* 8748
CANADIAN TEST CASE 65   *p* 720
6750 CENTURY AVE SUITE 305, MISSIS-
SAUGA, ON, L5N 2V8
(905) 812-5920   *SIC* 1011
CANADIAN TEST CASE 74   *p* 730
5770 HURONTARIO ST, MISSISSAUGA,
ON, L5R 3G5
SIC 7389
CANADIAN TEST CASE 87   *p* 720
6750 CENTURY AVE SUITE 305, MISSIS-
SAUGA, ON, L5N 2V8
(905) 812-5920   *SIC* 5932
CANADIAN TEST CASE 95 INC   *p* 730
5770 HURONTARIO ST, MISSISSAUGA,
ON, L5R 3G5
SIC 8711
CANADIAN TEXTILE RECYCLING LIMITED
p 521
5385 MUNRO CRT, BURLINGTON, ON, L7L
5M7
(905) 632-1464   *SIC* 5093
CANADIAN THEOLOGICAL SEMINARY *p*
1422
See *CANADIAN BIBLE COLLEGE*
CANADIAN THERMO WINDOWS INC   *p*
1030
75 ROWNTREE DAIRY RD, WOOD-
BRIDGE, ON, L4L 6C8
(905) 856-8805   *SIC* 3442
CANADIAN THREADALL   *p* 535
See *CANADIAN THREADALL LIMITED*
CANADIAN THREADALL LIMITED   *p* 535
130 TURNBULL CRT, CAMBRIDGE, ON,
N1T 1J2
(519) 576-3360   *SIC* 5085
CANADIAN TIRE   *p* 3
See *MILLER FAMILY SALES AND SERVICE
LTD*
CANADIAN TIRE   *p* 4
See *LESAGE, L.T. HOLDINGS LTD*

CANADIAN TIRE   *p* 39
See *BENSON, GARRY W ENTERPRISES
LTD*
CANADIAN TIRE   *p* 69
250 SHAWVILLE WAY SE, CALGARY, AB,
T2Y 3J1
(403) 201-2002   *SIC* 5014
CANADIAN TIRE   *p* 70
See *GREG SAARI MERCHANDISING LTD*
CANADIAN TIRE   *p* 71
See *DAVENPORT SALES & AUTO SER-
VICE LTD*
CANADIAN TIRE   *p* 73
See *GRIFA, BLAISE LTD*
CANADIAN TIRE   *p* 76
See *CALDWELL, C. MARK ENTERPRISE
LTD*
CANADIAN TIRE   *p* 77
See *LINCIA CORPORATION*
CANADIAN TIRE   *p* 79
1110 GATEWAY AVE, CANMORE, AB, T1W
0J1
(403) 678-3295   *SIC* 5014
CANADIAN TIRE   *p* 104
See *FEIST ENTERPRISES LTD*
CANADIAN TIRE   *p* 107
See *MACKINTOSH, K.J. SALES LTD*
CANADIAN TIRE   *p* 119
See *M. & P. VARLEY ENTERPRISES LTD*
CANADIAN TIRE   *p* 135
1 GATEWAY BLVD SS 1 SUITE 908, HIGH
LEVEL, AB, T0H 1Z0
(780) 926-1908   *SIC* 5531
CANADIAN TIRE   *p* 139
See *LAURION, S. & J. LIMITED*
CANADIAN TIRE   *p* 140
See *CAMPBELL, RON G SALES LTD*
CANADIAN TIRE   *p* 144
See *KAVANAGH INVESTMENTS LTD*
CANADIAN TIRE   *p* 154
See *MURRAY, DON A. HOLDINGS LTD*
CANADIAN TIRE   *p* 157
See *MACLEAN, K. T. (KEN) LIMITED*
CANADIAN TIRE   *p* 159
See *CML BOSWELL HOLDINGS LTD*
CANADIAN TIRE   *p* 167
See *WARDELL, A & M SALES LTD*
CANADIAN TIRE   *p* 168
900 PINE RD SUITE 109, STRATHMORE,
AB, T1P 0A2
(403) 934-9733   *SIC* 5531
CANADIAN TIRE   *p* 169
62 THEVENAZ IND. TRAIL UNIT 200, SYL-
VAN LAKE, AB, T4S 0B6
(403) 887-0581   *SIC* 5531
CANADIAN TIRE   *p* 170
See *MALGO, JA SALES LTD*
CANADIAN TIRE   *p* 172
See *DEWLING, S & C SALES LTD*
CANADIAN TIRE   *p* 176
32513 SOUTH FRASER WAY SUITE 434,
ABBOTSFORD, BC, V2T 4N5
(604) 870-4134   *SIC* 5531
CANADIAN TIRE   *p* 195
See *RON DITTBERNER LTD*
CANADIAN TIRE   *p* 197
See *NADEAU, MARCEL MANAGEMENT
INC*
CANADIAN TIRE   *p* 203
See *HEERINGA, J.L. ENTERPRISES LTD*
CANADIAN TIRE   *p* 204
See *M.R. BAULDIC ENTERPRISES INC*
CANADIAN TIRE   *p* 211
See *BRIDGER, BOB ENTERPRISES INC*
CANADIAN TIRE   *p* 218
See *JUUSOLA, JACK SALES LTD*
CANADIAN TIRE   *p* 220
See *GOSTLIN, K E ENTERPRISES LTD*
CANADIAN TIRE   *p* 234
4585 UPLANDS DR, NANAIMO, BC, V9T
6M8
(250) 585-5485   *SIC* 5014
CANADIAN TIRE   *p* 239
See *T MACRAE FAMILY SALES LTD*

CANADIAN TIRE   *p* 242
34017 97TH ST, OLIVER, BC, V0H 1T0
(250) 498-8473   *SIC* 5014
CANADIAN TIRE   *p* 243
See *MACMILLAN, DOUG ENTERPRISES
LTD*
CANADIAN TIRE   *p* 245
See *HOPE DISTRIBUTION & SALES INC*
CANADIAN TIRE   *p* 252
See *DESUTTER INVESTMENTS INC*
CANADIAN TIRE   *p* 259
3511 NO. 3 RD, RICHMOND, BC, V6X 2B8
(604) 273-2939   *SIC* 5251
CANADIAN TIRE   *p* 268
See *ENDRESS SALES AND DISTRIBU-
TION LTD*
CANADIAN TIRE   *p* 274
See *WILLIAMS, DAVE & PAT SALES LTD*
CANADIAN TIRE   *p* 278
See *WALDIE, D.S. HOLDINGS INCORPO-
RATED*
CANADIAN TIRE   *p* 283
See *TYSACH HIGGINS LTD*
CANADIAN TIRE   *p* 284
See *T & L GREGORINI ENTERPRISES INC*
CANADIAN TIRE   *p* 287
See *GREATER VANCOUVER ASSOCIATE
STORES LTD*
CANADIAN TIRE   *p* 333
See *WEAVER, J & D HOLDINGS LTD*
CANADIAN TIRE   *p* 339
See *K A R INDUSTRIES LIMITED*
CANADIAN TIRE   *p* 340
See *TIM CURRY SALES LIMITED*
CANADIAN TIRE   *p* 346
See *J. GRANT WALLACE HOLDINGS LTD*
CANADIAN TIRE   *p* 358
See *NURKKALA, HJ INVESTMENTS*
CANADIAN TIRE   *p* 382
See *ENGLAND, PAUL SALES LTD*
CANADIAN TIRE   *p* 393
See *BYLES, A. S. SUPPLIES LIMITED*
CANADIAN TIRE   *p* 394
See *GESTION ROGER THERIAULT*
CANADIAN TIRE   *p* 394
See *GAUDREAU, MARC INC*
CANADIAN TIRE   *p* 394
See *GESTION GILLES CHARTRAND INC*
CANADIAN TIRE   *p* 400
See *SEMEGEN, MICHEL HOLDINGS LTD*
CANADIAN TIRE   *p* 401
See *GUITARD, CHARLES MERCHANDIS-
ING LTD*
CANADIAN TIRE   *p* 403
See *GESTION GIACOMO D'AMICO INC*
CANADIAN TIRE   *p* 405
See *CEDM TOWER LTD*
CANADIAN TIRE   *p* 407
See *GESTION REMI GAUTHIER INC*
CANADIAN TIRE   *p* 410
See *FITCHCO ENTERPRISES INC*
CANADIAN TIRE   *p* 417
See *BENNETT, KEN ENTERPRISES INC*
CANADIAN TIRE   *p* 418
See *GEORGE, JS ENTERPRISES LTD*
CANADIAN TIRE   *p* 419
See *LEMAY, G & S HOLDINGS INC*
CANADIAN TIRE   *p* 420
See *LANDRY, CLAUDE INVESTMENTS
INC*
CANADIAN TIRE   *p* 420
See *K & J PECK SALES LTD*
CANADIAN TIRE   *p* 422
See *SEARS, WC HOLDINGS INC*
CANADIAN TIRE   *p* 423
See *DUNGEY, D.B. HOLDINGS INC*
CANADIAN TIRE   *p* 425
500 VANIER AVE, LABRADOR CITY, NL,
A2V 2W7
(709) 944-7740   *SIC* 5014
CANADIAN TIRE   *p* 430
See *L & L MCCAW HOLDINGS LTD*
CANADIAN TIRE   *p* 436
See *W.J. PARISEAU SALES LTD*

CANADIAN TIRE   *p* 438
See *SOEHNER SALES LIMITED*
CANADIAN TIRE   *p* 438
See *SHIRLEY, STEWART A ENTER-
PRISES LIMITED*
CANADIAN TIRE   *p* 439
150 DAMASCUS RD, BEDFORD, NS, B4A
0E5
(902) 835-1060   *SIC* 5531
CANADIAN TIRE   *p* 444
See *ACHESON, ALAN J. LIMITED*
CANADIAN TIRE   *p* 444
See *ACHESON, A.J. SALES LIMITED*
CANADIAN TIRE   *p* 449
269 HIGHWAY 214, ELMSDALE, NS, B2S
1K1
(902) 883-1771   *SIC* 5014
CANADIAN TIRE   *p* 450
See *A & E WARDELL LTD*
CANADIAN TIRE   *p* 451
See *ANE STEWART LTD*
CANADIAN TIRE   *p* 458
16 DENTITH RD, HALIFAX, NS, B3R 2H9
(902) 477-5608   *SIC* 5251
CANADIAN TIRE   *p* 463
See *DEREK HUTCHISON SALES LIMITED*
CANADIAN TIRE   *p* 468
See *2891379 CANADA INC*
CANADIAN TIRE   *p* 470
See *D & L GUITARD SALES INC*
CANADIAN TIRE   *p* 476
See *TALLON, DENNIS M. & ASSOCIATES
INC*
CANADIAN TIRE   *p* 477
See *BAKER, WALTER & CHANTAL SALES
LTD*
CANADIAN TIRE   *p* 481
See *M. & A. WRIGHT CO. LIMITED*
CANADIAN TIRE   *p* 482
See *MARTIN, LOUIS MERCHANDISING
LTD*
CANADIAN TIRE   *p* 484
See *HODGKINSON A & G SALES LTD*
CANADIAN TIRE   *p* 494
99 MCEWAN DR E SUITE 2, BOLTON, ON,
L7E 2Z7
(905) 857-5425   *SIC* 5251
CANADIAN TIRE   *p* 496
See *DOTY, RONALD T. LIMITED*
CANADIAN TIRE   *p* 497
See *TEN BUSS LIMITED*
CANADIAN TIRE   *p* 498
See *I & D MCEWEN LTD*
CANADIAN TIRE   *p* 514
30 LYNDEN RD, BRANTFORD, ON, N3R
8A4
(519) 751-2878   *SIC* 5531
CANADIAN TIRE   *p* 519
2360 PARKEDALE AVE, BROCKVILLE, ON,
K6V 7J5
(613) 342-5841   *SIC* 5531
CANADIAN TIRE   *p* 532
See *BUTORAC, DON LIMITED*
CANADIAN TIRE   *p* 532
See *BODNAR, KEN ENTERPRISES INC*
CANADIAN TIRE   *p* 541
See *GESTION FSTG INC*
CANADIAN TIRE   *p* 542
See *PILON, RAYMOND J. ENTERPRISES
LTD*
CANADIAN TIRE   *p* 544
See *MAGASIN RENE VEILLEUX INC*
CANADIAN TIRE   *p* 545
See *MOULTON, RALPH HOLDINGS LTD*
CANADIAN TIRE   *p* 546
See *DANIEL S. WEBSTER HOLDINGS LIM-
ITED*
CANADIAN TIRE   *p* 560
See *VELANOFF, JACK HOLDINGS LIM-
ITED*
CANADIAN TIRE   *p* 564
See *H.S. PIKE HOLDINGS INC*
CANADIAN TIRE   *p* 565
See *VANDERVAART SALES & SERVICE*

LTD

CANADIAN TIRE p 566
See LOMBARDI, ALDO SALES INC

CANADIAN TIRE p 567
See RYAN, D.C. SALES INC

CANADIAN TIRE p 568
See PORTENGEN, R. HOME AND AUTO INC

CANADIAN TIRE p 569
See MCMASTER, PAT & MARLEEN ENTERPRISES LTD

CANADIAN TIRE p 570
See MAL WHITLOCK ENTERPRISES LTD

CANADIAN TIRE p 576
See TALKA ENTERPRISES LTD

CANADIAN TIRE p 578
See WAKEHAM TAYLOR HOLDINGS INC

CANADIAN TIRE p 587
See ORFORD SALES LTD

CANADIAN TIRE p 590
See K & J FAMILY HOLDINGS LTD

CANADIAN TIRE p 591
See MILLS-ROY ENTERPRISES LIMITED

CANADIAN TIRE p 596
See TREVOR J LOWE INC

CANADIAN TIRE p 597
4792 BANK ST, GLOUCESTER, ON, K1T 3W7
(613) 822-2163   SIC 5014

CANADIAN TIRE p 597
See RUBIN, MARILYN D. SALES & SERVICE INC

CANADIAN TIRE p 604
See PMD RETAIL SALES INC

CANADIAN TIRE p 617
896 10TH ST, HANOVER, ON, N4N 3P2
(519) 364-2870   SIC 5531

CANADIAN TIRE p 619
See CRONIER, J.P. ENTERPRISES INC

CANADIAN TIRE p 619
See LEGER, D L SALES INC

CANADIAN TIRE p 620
See MOSER, K.G. LIMITED

CANADIAN TIRE p 626
See UNITED MALWOOD MERCHANTS INC

CANADIAN TIRE p 627
See GESTION DOMINIC PAQUETTE INC

CANADIAN TIRE p 628
See 1146490 ONTARIO INC

CANADIAN TIRE p 629
See CANADIANTIRE

CANADIAN TIRE p 629
See B & G KERR SALES LTD

CANADIAN TIRE p 633
640 CATARAQUI WOODS DR, KINGSTON, ON, K7P 2Y5
(613) 384-1766   SIC 5531

CANADIAN TIRE p 634
See MEDEIROS, PAUL ENTERPRISES LIMITED

CANADIAN TIRE p 635
See CARKAE ENGLISH SALES LTD

CANADIAN TIRE p 637
See POLLOCK, PAUL S. ENTERPRISES LTD

CANADIAN TIRE p 645
See RICHARD, MARIAN ENTERPRISES LTD

CANADIAN TIRE p 646
See FOX, DOMINIC LIMITED

CANADIAN TIRE p 656
See LATTANVILLE HOLDINGS CORPORATION

CANADIAN TIRE p 660
See DODSON, JIM SALES LTD

CANADIAN TIRE p 678
See BRACKENRIG ENTERPRISES INC

CANADIAN TIRE p 678
7650 MARKHAM RD, MARKHAM, ON, L3S 4S1
(905) 472-1638   SIC 5541

CANADIAN TIRE p 681
See H.G. CAMPBELL ENTERPRISES LTD

CANADIAN TIRE p 683
See GRANT, JAMIE & BARB SALES LTD

CANADIAN TIRE p 711
See ELIK, MIKE LIMITED

CANADIAN TIRE p 714
See TREMBLAY, C.J. INVESTMENTS INC

CANADIAN TIRE p 746
See TELFER, S & T MERCHANDISING LTD

CANADIAN TIRE p 746
See PROULX, MICHEL STORE INC

CANADIAN TIRE p 748
See ZYWOT, T. HOLDINGS LIMITED

CANADIAN TIRE p 751
See R.J. BONNEVILLE ENTERPRISES INC

CANADIAN TIRE p 753
See WHITE, BART SALES LTD

CANADIAN TIRE p 758
See EXCEL RETAIL LIMITED

CANADIAN TIRE p 763
See LAMONT, PAUL AUTOMOTIVE LTD

CANADIAN TIRE p 769
See SELLORS, ERIC R. HOLDINGS LIMITED

CANADIAN TIRE p 781
See LEVY, JEFF INVESTMENTS LTD

CANADIAN TIRE p 805
See COLLIN & DIANA PARKER SALES LTD

CANADIAN TIRE p 806
1550 SIMMONS, ODESSA, ON, K0H 2H0
(613) 386-3457   SIC 5541

CANADIAN TIRE p 811
See CLAUDE L'HEUREUX HOLDINGS INC

CANADIAN TIRE p 830
See VALIFF SALES INC

CANADIAN TIRE p 836
See CIERE, PIETER ENTERPRISES INC

CANADIAN TIRE p 838
See DENANCO SALES LTD

CANADIAN TIRE p 839
1050 CHEMONG RD, PETERBOROUGH, ON, K9H 7S2
(705) 745-1388   SIC 5014

CANADIAN TIRE p 839
See P & R HOFSTATTER SALES LTD

CANADIAN TIRE p 842
See SALKELD, C. & S. ENTERPRISES LTD

CANADIAN TIRE p 846
See GARON, LAWRENCE M ENTERPRISES LTD

CANADIAN TIRE p 848
See BRANCY ONE HOLDINGS LTD

CANADIAN TIRE p 851
250 SILVER LINDEN DR SUITE 87, RICHMOND HILL, ON, L4B 4W7
(905) 731-3100   SIC 5531

CANADIAN TIRE p 856
11720 YONGE ST, RICHMOND HILL, ON, L4E 0K4
(905) 884-9009   SIC 5531

CANADIAN TIRE p 857
See JEMARICA INC

CANADIAN TIRE p 863
See LAWLESS, M.J. HOLDINGS LTD

CANADIAN TIRE p 867
See FOX, JOHN A LTD

CANADIAN TIRE p 869
See LEROUX, K. D. SALES LTD

CANADIAN TIRE p 874
See GRANDVIEW SALES & DISTRIBUTION LTD

CANADIAN TIRE p 880
See ANNISONS LTD

CANADIAN TIRE p 882
See PARISIEN, J.W. ENTERPRISES LTD

CANADIAN TIRE p 886
See DRAVES, BRIAN H MERCHANDISING LTD

CANADIAN TIRE p 889
See SCHMIDT, JACK SUPPLIES LIMITED

CANADIAN TIRE p 897
See CROPLEY, PAUL J & D SALES LTD

CANADIAN TIRE p 898
See MARCHAND, PIERRE STORE INC

CANADIAN TIRE p 900

See DEMERS, MICHEL STORE INC

CANADIAN TIRE p 911
See STONE, BRUCE ENTERPRISES LTD

CANADIAN TIRE p 917
2681 DANFORTH AVE SUITE 273, TORONTO, ON, M4C 1L4
(416) 690-6069   SIC 5531

CANADIAN TIRE p 988
See MCCARTHY ELLIS MERCANTILE LTD

CANADIAN TIRE p 988
See 1557483 ONTARIO INC

CANADIAN TIRE p 1004
74 MCNAUGHTON AVE SUITE 135, WALLACEBURG, ON, N8A 1R9
(519) 627-4251   SIC 5531

CANADIAN TIRE p 1005
See FILES, JIM & DEANNA SALES & SERVICES LIMITED

CANADIAN TIRE p 1009
See YOUNG, J. & S. MERCHANTS LTD

CANADIAN TIRE p 1011
158 PRIMEWAY DRIVE, WELLAND, ON, L3B 0A1
(905) 732-1371   SIC 5014

CANADIAN TIRE p 1015
See ROSS DREY LIMITED

CANADIAN TIRE p 1019
See SKELLY, ROBERT E. LIMITED

CANADIAN TIRE p 1024
See MORRISON, DAVID W. ENTERPRISES LTD

CANADIAN TIRE p 1026
See WRANK ENTERPRISES LTD

CANADIAN TIRE p 1040
See MACEACHERN, K & A HOLDINGS LTD

CANADIAN TIRE p 1064
See DUBREUIL, GILLES LTEE

CANADIAN TIRE p 1070
See ENTREPRISES FRANCOIS BRIEN LTEE, LES

CANADIAN TIRE p 1074
3400 BOUL FRECHETTE, CHAMBLY, QC, J3L 6Z6
(450) 447-8393   SIC 5014

CANADIAN TIRE p 1078
See 9032-8402 QUEBEC INC

CANADIAN TIRE p 1081
85 RUE WELLINGTON, COATICOOK, QC, J1A 2H6
SIC 5014

CANADIAN TIRE p 1089
See ENTREPRISES PAUL WOODSTOCK LTEE

CANADIAN TIRE p 1090
See ENTREPRISES PIERRE LAUZON LTEE

CANADIAN TIRE p 1091
3079 BOUL DES SOURCES, DOLLARD-DES-ORMEAUX, QC, H9B 1Z6
(514) 684-9750   SIC 5531

CANADIAN TIRE p 1092
See ENTREPRISES MICHEL HAMELIN INC, LES

CANADIAN TIRE p 1099
See MAGASIN ST-JEAN, ALAIN INC

CANADIAN TIRE p 1104
See ENTREPRISES JACQUES CARIGNAN LTEE, LES

CANADIAN TIRE p 1115
See ENTREPRISES J.P. LAROCHELLE INC, LES

CANADIAN TIRE p 1117
See CANADIAN TIRE ASSOCIATE STORES & AUTO CENTRES

CANADIAN TIRE p 1122
See GESTION MARIO ROY INC

CANADIAN TIRE p 1123
See GESTION MARC-ANDRE LORD INC

CANADIAN TIRE p 1125
See GESTION STEFANO ROVER INC

CANADIAN TIRE p 1130
See GESTIONS JEAN-MARC GAGNE LTEE

CANADIAN TIRE p 1135

100 RTE DU PRESIDENT-KENNEDY, LEVIS, QC, G6V 6C9
(418) 833-5525   SIC 5531

CANADIAN TIRE p 1138
See GESTION REJEAN LEGER INC

CANADIAN TIRE p 1147
See INVESTISSEMENTS JEAN C. LAPIERRE LTEE

CANADIAN TIRE p 1150
145 RUE PIUZE, MATANE, QC, G4W 0H7
(418) 562-5144   SIC 5014

CANADIAN TIRE p 1159
See INVESTISSEMENTS MICHEL DESLAURIERS INC, LES

CANADIAN TIRE p 1159
See 9050-4283 QUEBEC INC

CANADIAN TIRE p 1160
See GESTION ANDRE R. VAILLANCOURT LTEE

CANADIAN TIRE p 1162
See ENTREPRISES ROLAND DOYON

CANADIAN TIRE p 1167
See ENTREPRISES HENRI RAVARY LTEE, LES

CANADIAN TIRE p 1170
See GESTION RENE J. BEAUDOIN INC

CANADIAN TIRE p 1220
See LEROUX, SYLVAIN M. ENTREPRISES LTD

CANADIAN TIRE p 1232
See GESTIONS REJEAN SAVARD LTEE

CANADIAN TIRE p 1262
See GESTION J. M. LEROUX LTEE

CANADIAN TIRE p 1282
See FRENETTE, GEFFREY LTEE

CANADIAN TIRE p 1296
See INVESTISSEMENT PIERRE MARCOTTE LIMITEE, LES

CANADIAN TIRE p 1302
See J.M. DUBRIS LTEE

CANADIAN TIRE p 1310
See ENTREPRISES PIERRE L BOULOS INC, LES

CANADIAN TIRE p 1317
See ENTREPRISES RAYMOND LEWIS INC, LES

CANADIAN TIRE p 1346
See LEGARE, DUPERRE INC

CANADIAN TIRE p 1346
6565 RUE JEAN-TALON E, SAINT-LEONARD, QC, H1S 1N2
(514) 257-9350   SIC 5531

CANADIAN TIRE p 1354
See ENTREPRISES DE VENTE LEWIS, R. INC, LES

CANADIAN TIRE p 1367
See ENTREPRISES MARIO LAROCHELLE INC, LES

CANADIAN TIRE p 1379
See GESTION FAMILLE BUCCI INC

CANADIAN TIRE p 1382
4785 BOUL LAURIER, TERREBONNE, QC, J7M 1C3
(450) 477-4013   SIC 5531

CANADIAN TIRE p 1385
See MAGASIN MARC-ANDRE ST-JACQUES INC

CANADIAN TIRE p 1390
See DUMAIS, ALBERT INC

CANADIAN TIRE p 1394
See GESTIONS REJEAN POITRAS INC, LES

CANADIAN TIRE p 1397
See ENTREPRISES JOEL GIRARD INC, LES

CANADIAN TIRE p 1410
See K.M. TURNBULL SALES INC

CANADIAN TIRE p 1410
See PENNER, P & A SALES INC

CANADIAN TIRE p 1411
See PUGLIA, P. M. SALES LTD

CANADIAN TIRE p 1422
See ROSSDREY LTD

CANADIAN TIRE p 1436

▲ Public Company   ■ Public Company Family Member   **HQ** Headquarters   **BR** Branch   **SL** Single Location

See DEGUIRE, MICHEL HOLDINGS INC
CANADIAN TIRE p 1437
See CAYEN, J.C. HOLDINGS LTD
CANADIAN TIRE p 1438
277 BROADWAY ST E SUITE 287, YORK-
TON, SK, S3N 3G7
(306) 783-9744 SIC 5541
CANADIAN TIRE p 1438
See HARVEY, R & J ADVENTURES LTD
CANADIAN TIRE p 1440
18 CHILKOOT WAY, WHITEHORSE, YT,
Y1A 6T5
(867) 668-3652 SIC 5531
CANADIAN TIRE #075 p 814
See HAYHURST, GEORGE LIMITED
CANADIAN TIRE #089 p 1289
See GESTION GILLES ST-MICHEL INC
CANADIAN TIRE #115 p 1365
See ENTREPRISES MICHEL CHOINIERE
INC, LES
CANADIAN TIRE #131 p 1368
See GESTION MARCEL G GAGNE INC
CANADIAN TIRE #300 p 1235
See CANTIN, DENIS R LTEE
CANADIAN TIRE #305 p 500
See R. B. BELL (SUPPLIES) LIMITED
CANADIAN TIRE #320 p 1284
See ENTREPRISES GHISLAIN G FORTIN
LTEE
CANADIAN TIRE #405 p 1278
See GESTION GERALD SAVARD INC
CANADIAN TIRE #493 p 80
See HATCH, ROBERT RETAIL INC
CANADIAN TIRE 005 p 484
See SUNSTRUM, GARRY W. SALES LIM-
ITED
CANADIAN TIRE 138 p 1111
See MICHEL THIBAUDEAU INC
CANADIAN TIRE 169 p 723
See INGLIS, D.W. LIMITED
CANADIAN TIRE 182 p 994
See TALLON, TIMOTHY J SALES INC
CANADIAN TIRE 184 p 1255
See GESTION JEAN PAQUETTE INC
**CANADIAN TIRE 229 GLACE BAY NOVA
SCOTIA** p 450
See CANADIAN TIRE ASSOCIATES
STORE
CANADIAN TIRE 272 p 751
See TEX-DON LTD
CANADIAN TIRE 294 p 580
See G. C. LOH MERCHANDISING LTD
CANADIAN TIRE 342 p 1276
See GUILLEMETTE, JEAN-PAUL INC
CANADIAN TIRE 395 p 204
See RICHARD REINDERS SALES LTD
CANADIAN TIRE 428 p 162
See K RICE RETAILING INC
CANADIAN TIRE 486 p 283
See BRYAN, J GASCON INVESTMENTS
INC
CANADIAN TIRE 57 p 646
See CASSIE CO ENTERPRISES LTD
CANADIAN TIRE 690 p 1101
See GESTION GUY L'HEUREUX INC
CANADIAN TIRE 71 p 760
See RATTRAY, WILLIAM HOLDINGS LTD
CANADIAN TIRE ASSOC STORE p 428
See MARSHALL, JAMES B ENTERPRISES
LTD
CANADIAN TIRE ASSOC STORE #78 p 837
See D & F CLOUTIER GROUP ENTER-
PRISES INC
CANADIAN TIRE ASSOC STORE 465 p 457
See WEICKERT, C & R ENTERPRISES LTD
CANADIAN TIRE ASSOCIATE STORE p 10
See C. HEAD LIMITED
CANADIAN TIRE ASSOCIATE STORE p 84
See DAVENPORT SALES & AUTO SER-
VICE LTD
CANADIAN TIRE ASSOCIATE STORE p
127
1 HOSPITAL ST, FORT MCMURRAY, AB,
T9H 5C1

(780) 791-6400 SIC 5531
CANADIAN TIRE ASSOCIATE STORE p
136
868 CARMICHAEL LANE, HINTON, AB,
T7V 1Y6
(780) 865-6198 SIC 5531
CANADIAN TIRE ASSOCIATE STORE p
157
See DANDCO ENTERPRISES LTD
CANADIAN TIRE ASSOCIATE STORE p
177
See JBE HOME & AUTO LIMITED
CANADIAN TIRE ASSOCIATE STORE p
192
7200 MARKET CROSS, BURNABY, BC,
V5J 0A2
(604) 451-5888 SIC 5531
CANADIAN TIRE ASSOCIATE STORE p
203
1100 VICTORIA AVE N, CRANBROOK, BC,
V1C 6G7
(250) 489-5563 SIC 5531
CANADIAN TIRE ASSOCIATE STORE p
226
See G.A. VALLANCE HOLDINGS LIMITED
CANADIAN TIRE ASSOCIATE STORE p
276
7599 KING GEORGE BLVD, SURREY, BC,
V3W 5A8
(604) 572-3739 SIC 5531
CANADIAN TIRE ASSOCIATE STORE p
362
See HUTCHISON, W A LTD
CANADIAN TIRE ASSOCIATE STORE p
365
See GIRTON MANAGEMENT LTD
CANADIAN TIRE ASSOCIATE STORE p
418
250 KING ST, ST STEPHEN, NB, E3L 2E5
(506) 466-4110 SIC 5531
CANADIAN TIRE ASSOCIATE STORE p
422
See ROBERT G. AYLWARD SALES LTD
CANADIAN TIRE ASSOCIATE STORE p
456
6203 QUINPOOL RD SUITE 44, HALIFAX,
NS, B3L 4P6
(902) 422-4598 SIC 5251
CANADIAN TIRE ASSOCIATE STORE p
463
See TOM MARA ENTERPRISE LIMITED
CANADIAN TIRE ASSOCIATE STORE p
565
409 GOVERNMENT ST, DRYDEN, ON, P8N
2P4
(807) 223-6644 SIC 5531
CANADIAN TIRE ASSOCIATE STORE p
633
See DERBYSHIRE E.D. & SONS LIMITED
CANADIAN TIRE ASSOCIATE STORE p
657
See SANDY MCTYRE RETAIL LTD
CANADIAN TIRE ASSOCIATE STORE p
660
See DONALD F. JOHNSTON HOLDINGS
LTD
CANADIAN TIRE ASSOCIATE STORE p
795
See 2931621 CANADA INC
CANADIAN TIRE ASSOCIATE STORE p
798
See KAVCO SALES LTD
CANADIAN TIRE ASSOCIATE STORE p
814
1333 WILSON RD N SUITE 336, OSHAWA,
ON, L1K 2B8
(905) 433-5575 SIC 5541
CANADIAN TIRE ASSOCIATE STORE p
887
See MARTIN HOME & AUTO LTD
CANADIAN TIRE ASSOCIATE STORE p
896
See FINCH, BARRY ENTERPRISES LTD
CANADIAN TIRE ASSOCIATE STORE p

898
See MCNAMARA, MERVIN J. INC
CANADIAN TIRE ASSOCIATE STORE p
918
See BRIAN DOMELLE ENTERPRISES LIM-
ITED
CANADIAN TIRE ASSOCIATE STORE p
1006
See MCDONALD, PHIL ENTERPRISES
LTD
CANADIAN TIRE ASSOCIATE STORE p
1406
See L & M MERCIER ENTERPRISES INC
CANADIAN TIRE ASSOCIATE STORE p
1433
See DAVE DEPLAEDT RETAIL SALES LTD
CANADIAN TIRE ASSOCIATE STORE #094
p 858
See PETER CHARLES ANSLEY HOLD-
INGS LIMITED
CANADIAN TIRE ASSOCIATE STORE #444
p 486
See DERBYSHIRE, D MERCHANDISING
LTD
CANADIAN TIRE ASSOCIATE STORE LTD
p 267
2090 10 AVE SW, SALMON ARM, BC, V1E
0E1
(250) 832-5474 SIC 5531
**CANADIAN TIRE ASSOCIATE STORE, DIV
OF** p 562
See MISTEREL INC
CANADIAN TIRE ASSOCIATE STORES p
356
See ROB WILLITTS SALES LTD
**CANADIAN TIRE ASSOCIATE STORES &
AUTO CENTRES** p 1117
16821 RTE TRANSCANADIENNE UNITE
149, KIRKLAND, QC, H9H 5J1
(514) 697-4761 SIC 5531
CANADIAN TIRE ASSOCIATES STORE p
450
130 RESERVE ST, GLACE BAY, NS, B1A
4W5
(902) 842-0700 SIC 5251
CANADIAN TIRE ASSOCIATES STORE 254
p 412
See ADRA SALES INC
**CANADIAN TIRE ASSOCIATES STORES
ALL DEPARTMENTS** p 1420
655 ALBERT ST, REGINA, SK, S4R 2P4
(306) 525-9027 SIC 5531
CANADIAN TIRE AUTOMOTIVE PARTS p
807
See 4137566 CANADA LTD
CANADIAN TIRE BAIE COMEAU p 1053
See GESTION BENOIT GUILLEMETTE
INC
CANADIAN TIRE BLAINVILLE p 1059
See GESTION M.L.B. CARDINAL LTEE
CANADIAN TIRE CORPORATION, LIMITED
p 924
2180 YONGE ST, TORONTO, ON, M4S 2B9
(416) 480-3000 SIC 5531
CANADIAN TIRE EXPRESS p 920
See OLIVER, PETER M SALES LTD
CANADIAN TIRE GAS BAR p 502
See DIAMO ENTERPRISES INC
CANADIAN TIRE GAS BAR p 908
943 FORT WILLIAM RD, THUNDER BAY,
ON, P7B 3A6
(807) 346-8070 SIC 5541
CANADIAN TIRE GRANDE PRAIRIE p 131
See BOCCIOLETTI, J & M SALES LTD
CANADIAN TIRE INTER CITY p 908
See NEARING, ROBERT C. HOLDINGS
INC
CANADIAN TIRE KINCARDINE p 629
811 DURHAM ST, KINCARDINE, ON, N2Z
3B8
(519) 395-2886 SIC 5531
CANADIAN TIRE MAGASIN ASSOCIATES p
1368
1555 RUE TRUDEL, SHAWINIGAN, QC,

G9N 8K8
(819) 537-3888 SIC 5013
**CANADIAN TIRE MAGASINS ASSOCIES
#318 ET #099** p 1328
See 4178963 CANADA INC
CANADIAN TIRE MIRAMICHI p 405
See AUTO LAC INC
CANADIAN TIRE NO 361 p 332
See TURNER, GRANT C. T. ENTER-
PRISES INC
CANADIAN TIRE NO 482 p 267
See D & K CROSS SALES LTD.
CANADIAN TIRE OWEN SOUND p 835
See ERSSER, A. J. HOLDINGS LTD
CANADIAN TIRE REAL ESTATE LIMITED p
924
2180 YONGE ST, TORONTO, ON, M4S 2B9
(416) 480-3000 SIC 6531
CANADIAN TIRE REAL ESTATE LIMITED p
1146
2211 BOUL ROLAND-THERRIEN BUREAU
256, LONGUEUIL, QC, J4N 1P2
(450) 448-1177 SIC 6531
CANADIAN TIRE ROSEMERE p 1287
See MARTINEAU, REAL INC
CANADIAN TIRE SERVICE p 1414
See JENKINS, MALCOLM J. (HOLDINGS)
LTD
CANADIAN TIRE SERVICES LIMITED p
1011
1000 EAST MAIN ST, WELLAND, ON, L3B
3Z3
(905) 735-3131 SIC 6153
CANADIAN TIRE SHAWNESSY p 69
See HLADY, RONALD H. AUTO SALES LTD
CANADIAN TIRE SOUTHPARK p 119
See STEVEN K. LEE AND CO. LTD
CANADIAN TIRE STORE p 83
See CROZIER, DONNA & JOHN LIMITED
CANADIAN TIRE STORE p 143
See LACHANCE, B.D. SALES LTD
CANADIAN TIRE STORE p 213
See BANNERMAN ENTERPRISES INC
CANADIAN TIRE STORE p 235
See GWENAL HOLDINGS LTD
CANADIAN TIRE STORE p 492
See MCCULLOUGH, D.E. ENTERPRISES
LTD
CANADIAN TIRE STORE p 755
See FORD, WAYNE SALES LIMITED
CANADIAN TIRE STORE p 1414
See JENKINS, MALCOLM J. MERCHAN-
DISING LTD
CANADIAN TIRE STORE #127 p 1001
See HIGGINS, PATRICK J ENTERPRISES
LTD
CANADIAN TIRE STORE 313 p 39
See DAND AUTO PARTS LIMITED
CANADIAN TIRE STORE 321 p 906
See GOODLAD, JOHN P. SALES INC
CANADIAN TIRE STORE 40 p 599
See R J J HOLDINGS LTD
CANADIAN TIRE, DIV OF p 443
See CAISSIECO ENTERPRISES LTD
**CANADIAN TOLLING COMPANY INTER-
NATIONAL INC** p
1027
6300 STEELES AVE W, WOODBRIDGE,
ON, L4H 1J1
(905) 265-4070 SIC 4785
CANADIAN TOOL & DIE LTD p 390
1331 CHEVRIER BLVD, WINNIPEG, MB,
R3T 1Y4
(204) 453-6833 SIC 3469
**CANADIAN TOURISM HUMAN RESOURCE
COUNCIL** p 822
151 SLATER ST SUITE 608, OTTAWA, ON,
K1P 5H3
(613) 231-6949 SIC 8699
CANADIAN TRADE INTERNATIONAL, INC
p 1431
2241 HANSELMAN AVE SUITE 8, SASKA-
TOON, SK, S7L 6A7
(306) 931-4111 SIC 5039

▲ Public Company   ■ Public Company Family Member   **HQ** Headquarters   **BR** Branch   **SL** Single Location

CANADIAN TRAVEL TEAM   p 241
935 MARINE DR SUITE 304, NORTH VAN-COUVER, BC, V7P 1S3
(604) 990-7370   SIC 4725
CANADIAN TRUCKSTOPS LTD   p 12
2515 50 AVE SE, CALGARY, AB, T2B 3R8
(403) 236-2515   SIC 5541
CANADIAN TUBULARS (1997) LTD   p 45
825 8 AVE SW SUITE 4100, CALGARY, AB, T2P 2T4
(403) 266-2218   SIC 5051
CANADIAN TURNER CONSTRUCTION COMPANY LTD   p 942
48 YONGE ST, TORONTO, ON, M5E 1G6
(416) 607-8300   SIC 1542
CANADIAN ULTRAMAR COMPANY   p 429
39 PIPPY PL, ST. JOHN'S, NL, A1B 3X2
(709) 754-1880   SIC 5983
CANADIAN UNICEF COMMITTEE   p 924
2200 YONGE ST SUITE 1100, TORONTO, ON, M4S 2C6
(416) 482-4444   SIC 8399
CANADIAN UNION OF BREWERY AND GENERAL WORKERS LOCAL 325   p 583
1 CARLINGVIEW DR, ETOBICOKE, ON, M9W 5E5
(416) 675-2648   SIC 8631
CANADIAN UNION OF POSTAL WORKERS
p 833
377 BANK ST, OTTAWA, ON, K2P 1Y3
(613) 236-7238   SIC 8631
CANADIAN UNION OF PUBLIC EMPLOY-EES   p
188
4940 CANADA WAY SUITE 500, BURNABY, BC, V5G 4T3
(604) 291-1940   SIC 8631
CANADIAN UNION OF PUBLIC EMPLOY-EES   p
377
275 BROADWAY SUITE 403B, WINNIPEG, MB, R3C 4M6
(204) 942-6524   SIC 8631
CANADIAN UNION OF PUBLIC EMPLOY-EES   p
817
1375 ST. LAURENT BLVD, OTTAWA, ON, K1G 0Z7
(613) 237-1590   SIC 8631
CANADIAN UNIVERSITIES RECIPROCAL INSURANCE EXCHANGE   p 521
5500 NORTH SERVICE RD SUITE 901, BURLINGTON, ON, L7L 6W6
(905) 336-3366   SIC 6321
CANADIAN URBAN LIMITED   p 85
10572-105 ST NW, EDMONTON, AB, T5H 2W7
(780) 424-7722   SIC 8742
CANADIAN UTILITIES LIMITED   p 73
5302 FORAND ST, CALGARY, AB, T3E 8B4
(403) 292-7500   SIC 4924
CANADIAN UTILITIES LIMITED   p 87
10035 105 ST NW, EDMONTON, AB, T5J 1C8
(780) 420-7209   SIC 4911
CANADIAN UTILITY CONSTRUCTION CORP   p 182
7950 VENTURE ST, BURNABY, BC, V5A 1V3
SIC 1623
CANADIAN UTILITY CONSTRUCTION CORP   p 184
4333 STILL CREEK DR SUITE 300, BURN-ABY, BC, V5C 6S6
(604) 574-6640   SIC 1623
CANADIAN UTILITY CONSTRUCTION CORP   p 271
6739 176 ST UNIT 1, SURREY, BC, V3S 4G6
(604) 576-9358   SIC 1623
CANADIAN VIEWPOINT INC   p 855
9350 YONGE ST SUITE 206, RICHMOND HILL, ON, L4C 5G2
(905) 770-1770   SIC 8732

CANADIAN VINYLTEK WINDOWS CORPO-RATION   p
205
587 EBURY PL, DELTA, BC, V3M 6M8
(604) 540-0029   SIC 5211
CANADIAN WARPLANE HERITAGE INC   p
747
9280 AIRPORT RD, MOUNT HOPE, ON, L0R 1W0
(905) 679-4183   SIC 8699
CANADIAN WARPLANE HERITAGE MU-SEUM   p
747
See CANADIAN WARPLANE HERITAGE INC
CANADIAN WASTE   p 1146
See WM QUEBEC INC
CANADIAN WESTERN AGGREGATE   p 131
See D & J ISLEY & SONS CONTRACTING LTD
CANADIAN WESTERN AGRIBITION ASSO-CIATION   p
1417
GD LCD MAIN, REGINA, SK, S4P 2Z4
(306) 565-0565   SIC 7999
CANADIAN WESTERN BANK   p 87
10303 JASPER AVE NW SUITE 3000, ED-MONTON, AB, T5J 3N6
(780) 423-8888   SIC 6021
CANADIAN WESTERN BANK   p 303
666 BURRARD ST 22ND FL, VANCOUVER, BC, V6C 2X8
(604) 669-0081   SIC 6021
CANADIAN WESTERN TRUST COMPANY p
297
750 CAMBIE ST SUITE 300, VANCOUVER, BC, V6B 0A2
(604) 685-2081   SIC 6091
CANADIAN WILDERNESS ADVENTURES LTD   p 342
4545 BLACKCOMB WAY, WHISTLER, BC, V0N 1B4
(604) 938-1554   SIC 5571
CANADIAN WILDLIFE FEDERATION   p 626
350 MICHAEL COWPLAND DR, KANATA, ON, K2M 2W1
(613) 599-9594   SIC 8999
CANADIAN WIRELESS   p 480
See CANADIAN WIRELESS COMMUNICA-TIONS INC
CANADIAN WIRELESS COMMUNICA-TIONS INC   p
480
10-91 FIRST COMMERCE DR, AURORA, ON, L4G 0G2
(905) 726-2652   SIC 5999
CANADIAN-BRITISH CONSULTING GROUP LIMITED   p 452
1489 HOLLIS ST, HALIFAX, NS, B3J 3M5
(902) 421-7241   SIC 6712
CANADIANTIRE   p 629
811 DURHAM ST, KINCARDINE, ON, N2Z 3B8
(519) 395-2886   SIC 5531
CANADIEN NATIONAL   p 1139
See COMPAGNIE DES CHEMINS DE FER NATIONAUX DU CANADA
CANADIENNE DE CROISSANCE   p 1168
3795 RUE MASSON BUREAU 108, MON-TREAL, QC, H1X 1S7
SIC 8741
CANADO/NACAN EQUIPEMENT INC   p
1328
5782 BOUL THIMENS, SAINT-LAURENT, QC, H4R 2K9
(514) 333-0077   SIC 5084
CANADOIL FORGE LTEE   p 1056
805 BOUL ALPHONSE-DESHAIES, BE-CANCOUR, QC, G9H 2Y8
(819) 294-6600   SIC 3462
CANADORE COLLEGE OF APPLIED ARTS AND TECHNOLOGY   p 762
100 COLLEGE DR, NORTH BAY, ON, P1B 8K9

(705) 474-7600   SIC 8222
CANADREAM CAMPERS   p 160
See CANADREAM INC
CANADREAM CORPORATION   p 160
292154 CROSSPOINTE DR, ROCKY VIEW COUNTY, AB, T4A 0V2
(403) 291-1000   SIC 7519
CANADREAM INC   p 160
292154 CROSSPOINTE DR, ROCKY VIEW COUNTY, AB, T4A 0V2
SIC 7519
CANADREAM RV RENTALS & SALES   p
160
See CANADREAM CORPORATION
CANAF   p 311
See CANAF INVESTMENTS INC
CANAF INVESTMENTS INC   p 311
1111 MELVILLE ST BUREAU 1100, VAN-COUVER, BC, V6E 3V6
(604) 283-6110   SIC 1221
CANAFRIC INC   p 883
15 SEAPARK DR, ST CATHARINES, ON, L2M 6S5
(905) 688-9588   SIC 5142
CANAGRO EXPORTS INC   p 361
24084 HWY 3 E, WINKLER, MB, R6W 4B1
(204) 325-5090   SIC 5083
CANALISATIONS KARIC, LES   p 1133
See SERVICES INFRASPEC INC
CANALTA CONTROLS LTD   p 155
6759 65 AVE, RED DEER, AB, T4P 1X5
(403) 342-4494   SIC 5084
CANALTA HOTELS   p 82
See SMH MANAGEMENT INC
CANAM   p 1303
See GROUPE CANAM INC
CANAM   p 1304
See CANAM BATIMENTS ET STRUC-TURES INC
CANAM BATIMENTS ET STRUCTURES INC   p 734
See CANAM BATIMENTS ET STRUC-TURES INC
CANAM BATIMENTS ET STRUCTURES INC   p 734
1739 DREW RD, MISSISSAUGA, ON, L5S 1J5
(905) 671-3460   SIC 3441
CANAM BATIMENTS ET STRUCTURES INC   p 1304
11505 1RE AV BUREAU 500, SAINT-GEORGES, QC, G5Y 7X3
(418) 582-3331   SIC 3441
CANAM BRIDGES   p 1264
See GROUPE CANAM INC
CANAM BUILDING ENVELOPE SPECIAL-ISTS INC   p
919
50 BETH NEALSON DR, TORONTO, ON, M4H 1M6
(416) 467-3485   SIC 5033
CANAM PLASTICS 2000 INC   p 494
30 HOLLAND DR, BOLTON, ON, L7E 1G6
(905) 951-6166   SIC 2821
CANAM PONTS CANADA INC   p 1263
1445 RUE DU GRAND-TRONC, QUEBEC, QC, G1N 4G1
(418) 683-2561   SIC 1622
CANAM-BRIDGES   p 1263
See CANAM PONTS CANADA INC
CANAMARAUNITED, DIV OF   p 114
See DIVERSITY TECHNOLOGIES COR-PORATION
CANAMEX-CARBRA TRANSPORTATION SERVICES INC   p 685
7415 TORBRAM RD, MISSISSAUGA, ON, L4T 1G8
(905) 458-5363   SIC 4213
CANAPAN MEATS   p 1085
See DELI-PORC INC
CANAPEN GROUP F COMPANIES, THE   p
87
See CANAPEN INVESTMENTS LTD
CANAPEN INVESTMENTS LTD   p 87

10020 101A AVE NW SUITE 800, EDMON-TON, AB, T5J 3G2
(780) 428-0511   SIC 6512
CANARAIL   p 1209
See SYSTRA CANADA INC
CANARCTIC   p 1204
See FEDNAV LIMITEE
CANARD IMPERIAL DE BROME LTEE   p
1306
243 RTE 249, SAINT-GEORGES-DE-WINDSOR, QC, J0A 1J0
(819) 828-2219   SIC 0259
CANARD LIBERE - ESPACE GOURMAAD, LE   p 1306
See CANARD IMPERIAL DE BROME LTEE
CANARD LIBERE - ESPACE GOURMAND, LE   p 1118
See CANARDS DU LAC BROME LTEE
CANARDS DU LAC BROME LTEE   p 1118
40 CH DU CENTRE, KNOWLTON, QC, J0E 1V0
(450) 242-3825   SIC 2015
CANARINO NISSAN   p 762
See 1121121 ONTARIO INC
CANARM LTD   p 519
2157 PARKEDALE AVE, BROCKVILLE, ON, K6V 0B4
(613) 342-5424   SIC 5063
CANAROPA (1954) INC   p 1127
1725 50E AV, LACHINE, QC, H8T 3C8
(514) 636-6466   SIC 5072
CANARX SERVICES INC   p 1021
235 EUGENIE ST W SUITE 105D, WIND-SOR, ON, N8X 2X7
(519) 973-1735   SIC 5122
CANASSISTANCE INC   p 1194
550 RUE SHERBROOKE O, MONTREAL, QC, H3A 3S3
(800) 264-1852   SIC 8741
CANASSURANCE COMPAGNIE D'ASSURANCE INC   p 1194
550 RUE SHERBROOKE O BUREAU B9, MONTREAL, QC, H3A 3S3
(514) 286-8400   SIC 6321
CANATOM NPM   p 715
See SNC-LAVALIN NUCLEAR INC
CANAVISION   p 1101
See INCOSPEC COMMUNICATIONS INC
CANAWAY HOLDINGS LTD   p 333
3651 SHELBOURNE ST SUITE 4, VICTO-RIA, BC, V8P 4H1
(250) 477-2218   SIC 5411
CANBEC AUTOMOBILE INC   p 1227
4070 RUE JEAN-TALON O, MONTREAL, QC, H4P 1V5
(514) 289-6464   SIC 5511
CANCABLE INC   p 612
100 KING ST W UNIT 700, HAMILTON, ON, L8P 1A2
(905) 769-9705   SIC 1731
CANCADE COMPANY LIMITED   p 346
1651 12TH ST, BRANDON, MB, R7A 7L1
(204) 728-4450   SIC 3523
CANCARB LIMITED   p 147
1702 BRIER PARK CRES NW, MEDICINE HAT, AB, T1C 1T9
(403) 527-1121   SIC 2895
CANCARD INC   p 667
177 IDEMA RD SUITE 8, MARKHAM, ON, L3R 1A9
(416) 449-8111   SIC 5084
CANCER CARE ONTARIO   p 630
25 KING ST W, KINGSTON, ON, K7L 5P9
(613) 544-2630   SIC 8069
CANCER CARE ONTARIO   p 908
980 OLIVER RD, THUNDER BAY, ON, P7B 6V4
(807) 343-1610   SIC 8731
CANCER CARE ONTARIO   p 944
620 UNIVERSITY AVE SUITE 1500, TORONTO, ON, M5G 2L7
(416) 971-9800   SIC 8733
CANCERCARE MANITOBA   p 380
675 MCDERMOT AVE UNIT 4025, WIN-

NIPEG, MB, R3E 0V9

(204) 787-2197   *SIC* 8069

CANCERCARE MANITOBA FOUNDATION INC *p* 380

675 MCDERMOT AVE SUITE 1160, WIN-NIPEG, MB, R3E 0V9

(204) 787-4143   *SIC* 8069

CANCOIL THERMAL CORPORATION*p* 630

991 JOHN F. SCOTT RD, KINGSTON, ON, K7L 4V3

(613) 541-1235   *SIC* 3585

CANCOM BROADCAST SOLUTIONS *p* 715

See SHAW SATELLITE SERVICES INC

CANCOM SECURITY INC *p* 782

1183 FINCH AVE W UNIT 205, NORTH YORK, ON, M3J 2G2

(416) 763-0000   *SIC* 7381

CANCORD DRILLING, DIV OF *p* 158

See HARDROCK BITS & OILFIELD SUP-PLIES LTD

CANDA SIX FORTUNE ENTERPRISE CO. LTD *p* 192

8138 NORTH FRASER WAY, BURNABY, BC, V5J 0E7

(604) 432-9000   *SIC* 5149

CANDAN ENTERPRISES LTD *p* 227

20257 LANGLEY BYPASS, LANGLEY, BC, V3A 6K9

(604) 530-3645   *SIC* 5571

CANDAN R.V. CENTER *p* 228

See TRAVELAND R.V. RENTALS LTD

CANDAN RV CENTER *p* 227

See CANDAN ENTERPRISES LTD

CANDEAL.CA INC *p* 932

152 KING ST E SUITE 400, TORONTO, ON, M5A 1J3

(416) 814-7800   *SIC* 6231

CANDET *p* 583

See CANADIAN N D E TECHNOLOGY LTD

CANDIAC TOYOTA *p* 1072

See 9123-2165 QUEBEC INC

CANDO RAIL SERVICES LTD *p* 346

740 ROSSER AVE SUITE 400, BRANDON, MB, R7A 0K9

(204) 725-2627   *SIC* 1629

CANDO TIE DEPOT *p* 346

See CANDO RAIL SERVICES LTD

CANDUCT INDUSTRIES LIMITED *p* 660

4575 BLAKIE RD, LONDON, ON, N6L 1P8

(519) 652-9014   *SIC* 2655

CANDYM ENTERPRISES LTD *p* 680

95 CLEGG RD, MARKHAM, ON, L6G 1B9

(905) 474-1555   *SIC* 5199

CANEAST FOODS LIMITED *p* 851

70 EAST BEAVER CREEK RD UNIT 204, RICHMOND HILL, ON, L4B 3B2

(905) 771-6051   *SIC* 5141

CANEDA TRANSPORT LTD *p* 12

4330 46 AVE SE, CALGARY, AB, T2B 3N7

(403) 236-7900   *SIC* 4213

CANEM SYSTEMS LTD *p* 95

11320 151 ST NW, EDMONTON, AB, T5M 4A9

(780) 454-0381   *SIC* 1731

CANEM SYSTEMS LTD *p* 254

13351 COMMERCE PKY SUITE 1358, RICHMOND, BC, V6V 2X7

(604) 214-8650   *SIC* 1731

CANEM SYSTEMS LTD *p* 254

1600 VALMONT WAY SUITE 100, RICH-MOND, BC, V6V 1Y4

(604) 273-1131   *SIC* 1731

CANERECTOR INC *p* 764

1 SPARKS AVE, NORTH YORK, ON, M2H 2W1

(416) 225-6240   *SIC* 3443

CANERECTOR INC *p* 885

23 SMITH ST, ST CATHARINES, ON, L2R 6Y6

(905) 684-2022   *SIC* 3441

CANEX BUILDING SUPPLIES LTD *p* 197

46070 KNIGHT RD, CHILLIWACK, BC, V2R 1B7

(604) 858-8188   *SIC* 5039

CANEXUS CHEMICALS CANADA LTD *p* 45

144 4 AVE SW UNIT 2100, CALGARY, AB, T2P 3N4

(403) 571-7300   *SIC* 5169

CANFARM PULSE INC *p* 390

1427 SOMERVILLE AVE, WINNIPEG, MB, R3T 1C3

(204) 298-3595   *SIC* 5153

CANFIN CAPITAL GROUP INC *p* 800

2829 SHERWOOD HEIGHTS DR SUITE 102, OAKVILLE, ON, L6J 7R7

(905) 829-0020   *SIC* 8741

CANFOR *p* 213

See CANADIAN FOREST PRODUCTS LTD

CANFOR *p* 215

See CANADIAN FOREST PRODUCTS LTD

CANFOR - PLATEAU *p* 330

See CANADIAN FOREST PRODUCTS LTD

CANFOR - TAYLOR *p* 283

See CANADIAN FOREST PRODUCTS LTD

CANFOR ADMINISTRATION CENTRE*p* 249

See CANADIAN FOREST PRODUCTS LTD

CANFOR CORPORATION *p* 323

1700 75TH AVE W SUITE 100, VANCOU-VER, BC, V6P 6G2

(604) 661-5241   *SIC* 2421

CANFOR MACKENZIE DIVISION *p* 230

See CANADIAN FOREST PRODUCTS LTD

CANFOR PULP *p* 250

See CANADIAN FOREST PRODUCTS LTD

CANFOR PULP LTD *p* 250

5353 NORTHWOOD PULP MILL RD, PRINCE GEORGE, BC, V2N 2K3

(250) 962-3666   *SIC* 2611

CANFOR PULP PRODUCTS INC *p* 323

1700 75TH AVE W UNIT 230, VANCOU-VER, BC, V6P 6G2

(604) 661-5241   *SIC* 2621

CANFOR RESEARCH & DEVELOPMENT CENTRE *p* 323

See CANADIAN FOREST PRODUCTS LTD

CANFORGE *p* 1011

See CANADA FORGINGS INC

CANGAS SOLUTIONS INC *p* 45

555 4 AVE SW SUITE 1250, CALGARY, AB, T2P 3E7

(403) 930-0123   *SIC* 4924

CANICKEL MINING LIMITED *p* 360

GD, WABOWDEN, MB, R0B 1S0

(204) 689-2972   *SIC* 1081

CANIMEX INC *p* 1098

285 RUE SAINT-GEORGES, DRUM-MONDVILLE, QC, J2C 4H3

(819) 477-1335   *SIC* 3429

CANKOSH INC *p* 667

7030 WOODBINE AVE SUITE 500, MARKHAM, ON, L3R 6G2

(905) 943-7990   *SIC* 5963

CANLAK INC *p* 1089

674 RUE PRINCIPALE BUREAU 309, DAV-ELUYVILLE, QC, G0Z 1C0

(819) 367-3264   *SIC* 2851

CANLAN ICE SPORTS CORP *p* 184

6501 SPROTT ST, BURNABY, BC, V5B 3B8

(604) 291-0626   *SIC* 7999

CANLAN ICE SPORTS CORP *p* 1068

5880 BOUL TASCHEREAU, BROSSARD, QC, J4W 1M6

(450) 462-2113   *SIC* 7999

CANLAN ICE SPORTS ET DESSIN *p* 1069

See QUATRE GLACES (1994) INC, LES

CANLIGHT MANAGEMENT INC *p* 692

5160 EXPLORER DR SUITE 17, MISSIS-SAUGA, ON, L4W 4T7

(905) 625-1522   *SIC* 6719

CANLOG (LA MAISON DE BOIS CANADI-ENNE) *p* 1074

See FABRICATION SCANDINAVE INC

CANLYTE, DIV OF *p* 1129

See SIGNIFY CANADA LTD

CANMEC INDUSTRIEL INC *p* 1080

1750 RUE LA GRANDE, CHICOUTIMI, QC, G7K 1H7

(418) 543-9151   *SIC* 3569

CANMEC LA BAIE INC *p* 1121

3453 CH DES CHUTES, LA BAIE, QC, G7B 3N8

(418) 544-3391   *SIC* 5085

CANMEC LAJOIE SOMEC *p* 1080

See CANMEC INDUSTRIEL INC

CANMET MATERIALS *p* 613

See NATURAL RESOURCES CANADA

CANMORE GENERAL HOSPITAL *p* 78

See ALBERTA HEALTH SERVICES

CANN-AMM EXPORTS INC *p* 230

23638 RIVER RD UNIT 1, MAPLE RIDGE, BC, V2W 1B7

(604) 466-9121   *SIC* 5093

CANNEBERGES ATOKA INC *p* 1148

3025 RTE 218, MANSEAU, QC, G0X 1V0

(819) 356-2001   *SIC* 0171

CANNEBERGES BECANCOUR MANAGE-MENT INC *p* 1347

94 RANG SAINT-FRANCOIS, SAINT-LOUIS-DE-BLANDFORD, QC, G0Z 1B0

(819) 364-3853   *SIC* 5148

CANNEPP *p* 208

See CANADIAN ENGINEERED PROD-UCTS AND SALES LTD

CANNERY SEAFOOD RESTAURANT *p* 285

See SILVERBIRCH NO. 41 OPERATIONS LIMITED PARTNERSHIP

CANNIMED LTD *p* 1426

RR 5 LCD MAIN, SASKATOON, SK, S7K 3J8

(306) 975-1207   *SIC* 2834

CANNING CONTRACTING LIMITED *p* 738

525 ABILENE DR, MISSISSAUGA, ON, L5T 2H7

SIC 1542

CANNON AUTOMOTIVE SOLUTIONS *p* 1024

See ELECTROMAC GROUP INC, THE

CANNON DESIGN ARCHITECTURE INC *p* 318

1500 GEORGIA ST W SUITE 710, VAN-COUVER, BC, V6G 2Z6

(250) 388-0115   *SIC* 8712

CANNON SECURITY AND PATROL SER-VICES *p* 812

23 SIMCOE ST S FL 2, OSHAWA, ON, L1H 4G1

(416) 742-9994   *SIC* 7381

CANNOR NURSERIES (1989) LTD *p* 174

34261 MARSHALL RD, ABBOTSFORD, BC, V2S 1L8

SIC 5261

CANNTRUST HOLDINGS INC *p* 1027

9200 WESTON RD, WOODBRIDGE, ON, L4H 2P8

(647) 872-2300   *SIC* 5993

CANOE EIT INCOME FUND *p* 45

421 7 AVE SW SUITE 2750, CALGARY, AB, T2P 4K9

(403) 571-5554   *SIC* 6726

CANOE INC *p* 932

333 KING ST E SUITE 1, TORONTO, ON, M5A 0E1

(416) 947-2154   *SIC* 4813

CANOLA COUNCIL OF CANADA *p* 374

167 LOMBARD AVE UNIT 400, WINNIPEG, MB, R3B 0T6

(204) 982-2100   *SIC* 7389

CANON CANADA INC *p* 511

8000 MISSISSAUGA RD, BRAMPTON, ON, L6Y 5Z7

(905) 863-8000   *SIC* 5044

CANON CANADA INC *p* 928

175 BLOOR ST E SUITE 1200, TORONTO, ON, M4W 3R8

(416) 491-9330   *SIC* 5999

CANON MEDICAL SYSTEMS *p* 667

See CANON MEDICAL SYSTEMS CANADA LIMITED

CANON MEDICAL SYSTEMS CANADA LIMITED *p* 667

75 TIVERTON CT, MARKHAM, ON, L3R 4M8

(800) 668-9729   *SIC* 3845

CANOPTEC *p* 1325

See ESSILOR GROUPE CANADA INC

CANOPY GROWTH CORPORATION *p* 881

1 HERSHEY DR, SMITHS FALLS, ON, K7A 0A8

(855) 558-9333   *SIC* 6712

CANORO RESOURCES LTD *p* 45

717 7 AVE SW SUITE 700, CALGARY, AB, T2P 0Z3

(403) 543-5747   *SIC* 1311

CANPAR CARRIER *p* 22

See CANPAR TRANSPORT L.P.

CANPAR COURIER *p* 501

See CANPAR TRANSPORT L.P.

CANPAR TRANSPORT L.P. *p* 22

707 BARLOW TRAIL SE UNIT D, CAL-GARY, AB, T2E 8C2

(800) 387-9335   *SIC* 7389

CANPAR TRANSPORT L.P. *p* 182

8399 EASTLAKE DR, BURNABY, BC, V5A 4W2

(604) 421-3452   *SIC* 4731

CANPAR TRANSPORT L.P. *p* 501

201 WESTCREEK BLVD SUITE 102, BRAMPTON, ON, L6T 0G8

(905) 499-2690   *SIC* 7389

CANPAR TRANSPORT L.P. *p* 570

205 NEW TORONTO ST, ETOBICOKE, ON, M8V 0A1

(416) 869-1332   *SIC* 4213

CANPAR TRANSPORT L.P. *p* 1004

18 INDUSTRIAL RD, WALKERTON, ON, N0G 2V0

(519) 881-2770   *SIC* 4731

CANPEPTIDE INC *p* 1249

265 BOUL HYMUS BUREAU 1500, POINTE-CLAIRE, QC, H9R 1G6

(514) 697-2168   *SIC* 2834

CANPLAS INDUSTRIES LTD *p* 486

500 VETERANS DR, BARRIE, ON, L4N 9J5

(705) 726-3361   *SIC* 3088

CANPLEX PROFILES INC *p* 848

1 EASY ST, PORT PERRY, ON, L9L 1B2

(905) 985-2759   *SIC* 2821

CANPOTEX LIMITED *p* 1426

111 2ND AVE S SUITE 400, SASKATOON, SK, S7K 3R7

(306) 931-2200   *SIC* 5191

CANPRO CONSTRUCTION LTD *p* 338

555 DUPPLIN RD, VICTORIA, BC, V8Z 1C2

(250) 475-0975   *SIC* 1542

CANPRO KING-REED LP. *p* 764

155 GORDON BAKER RD SUITE 101, NORTH YORK, ON, M2H 3N5

(416) 449-8677   *SIC* 6719

CANRAM *p* 1329

See EXPERTS EN MEMOIRE INTERNA-TIONALE INC, LES

CANRIG DRILLING TECHNOLOGY LTD *p* 14

5250 94 AVE SE, CALGARY, AB, T2C 3Z3

(403) 279-3466   *SIC* 1389

CANRIM PACKAGING LTD *p* 221

1125 RICHTER ST, KELOWNA, BC, V1Y 2K6

(250) 762-3332   *SIC* 2085

CANROOF CORPORATION INC *p* 920

560 COMMISSIONERS ST, TORONTO, ON, M4M 1A7

(416) 461-8122   *SIC* 5211

CANROS GRP INC *p* 856

30 VIA RENZO DR SUITE 255, RICHMOND HILL, ON, L4S 0B8

(905) 918-0640   *SIC* 3532

CANSEL *p* 192

See CANSEL SURVEY EQUIPMENT INC

CANSEL SURVEY EQUIPMENT INC *p* 192

3900 NORTH FRASER WAY, BURNABY, BC, V5J 5H6

(604) 299-5766   *SIC* 5049

CANSEW INC p 1178
111 RUE CHABANEL O BUREAU 101, MONTREAL, QC, H2N 1C9
(514) 382-2807 *SIC* 2284

CANSHIP UGLAND LTD p 429
1315 TOPSAIL RD, ST. JOHN'S, NL, A1B 3N4
(709) 782-3333 *SIC* 4424

CANSIT p 1223
See IMAFLEX INC

CANSO CREDIT INCOME FUND p 851
100 YORK BLVD SUITE 501, RICHMOND HILL, ON, L4B 1J8
(416) 640-4275 *SIC* 6726

CANSO FORD SALES (2005) LIMITED p 464
9 MACINTOSH RD, PORT HAWKESBURY, NS, B9A 3K4
(902) 625-1338 *SIC* 5541

CANSTAR CONSTRUCTION LTD p 200
78 FAWCETT RD, COQUITLAM, BC, V3K 6V5
(604) 549-0099 *SIC* 1799

CANSTAR RESTORATIONS p 200
See CANSTAR CONSTRUCTION LTD

CANSTEM LEASING SERVICES p 906
See ROY FOSS MOTORS LTD

CANTAK CORPORATION p 45
355 4 AVE SW SUITE 1050, CALGARY, AB, T2P 0J1
(403) 269-5536 *SIC* 5051

CANTAX p 1372
See WOLTERS KLUWER CANADA LIMITED

CANTEC SECURITY SERVICES INC p 885
140 WELLAND AVE UNIT 5, ST CATHARINES, ON, L2R 2N6
(905) 687-9500 *SIC* 7381

CANTECH p 563
See COMPAGNIE CANADIAN TECHNICAL TAPE LTEE

CANTECH TUBULAR SERVICES LTD p 155
7983 EDGAR INDUSTRIAL DR SUITE A, RED DEER, AB, T4P 3R2
SIC 5051

CANTEGA TECHNOLOGIES INC p 95
11603 165 ST NW, EDMONTON, AB, T5M 3Z1
(780) 448-9700 *SIC* 3699

CANTELON ENTERPRISES INC p 73
2529 17 AVE SW, CALGARY, AB, T3E 0A2
(403) 246-1176 *SIC* 6712

CANTERBURY COFFEE p 108
See CANTERBURY FOOD SERVICE (ALTA) LTD

CANTERBURY COFFEE p 192
See CANTERBURY FOOD SERVICE LTD

CANTERBURY COFFEE CORPORATION p 192
8080 NORTH FRASER WAY UNIT 1, BURNABY, BC, V5J 0E6
(604) 431-4400 *SIC* 5149

CANTERBURY FOOD SERVICE (ALTA) LTD p 108
4803 93 AVE NW, EDMONTON, AB, T6B 3A2
(780) 468-6363 *SIC* 5149

CANTERBURY FOOD SERVICE LTD p 192
8080 NORTH FRASER WAY UNIT 1, BURNABY, BC, V5J 0E6
(604) 431-4400 *SIC* 5499

CANTERBURY FOUNDATION p 98
8403 142 ST NW SUITE 125, EDMONTON, AB, T5R 4L3
(780) 483-5361 *SIC* 8361

CANTERBURY HIGH SCHOOL p 818
See OTTAWA-CARLETON DISTRICT SCHOOL BOARD

CANTERBURY HOUSE BOOKSTORE p 826
See SAINT PAUL UNIVERSITY

CANTERBURY ROOFING LTD p 28
3810 16 ST SE, CALGARY, AB, T2G 3R7
(403) 234-8582 *SIC* 1761

CANTERRA SEEDS (2002) LTD p 390

1475 CHEVRIER BLVD UNIT 201, WINNIPEG, MB, R3T 1Y7
(204) 988-9750 *SIC* 5191

CANTERRA SEEDS HOLDINGS LTD p 390
1475 CHEVRIER BLVD UNIT 201, WINNIPEG, MB, R3T 1Y7
(204) 988-9750 *SIC* 5191

CANTEX CANADA LIMITED p 872
2 ROLARK DR, SCARBOROUGH, ON, M1R 4G2
(416) 751-4567 *SIC* 5131

CANTIN BEAUTE LTEE p 1266
2495 AV DALTON, QUEBEC, QC, G1P 3S5
(418) 654-0444 *SIC* 5087

CANTIN GAGNON ASSURANCES INC p 1116
2463 RUE SAINT-DOMINIQUE, JONQUIERE, QC, G7X 6K4
(418) 542-7575 *SIC* 6411

CANTIN, DENIS R LTEE p 1235
1450 BOUL LE CORBUSIER, MONTREAL, QC, H7N 6J5
(450) 682-9922 *SIC* 5311

CANTINE LUCIE INC p 1311
5825 AV DESJARDINS, SAINT-HYACINTHE, QC, J2S 1A4
(450) 774-8585 *SIC* 5963

CANTOL CORP p 667
199 STEELCASE RD W, MARKHAM, ON, L3R 2M4
(905) 475-6141 *SIC* 2842

CANTON POULTRY MEATS INC p 1010
670 SUPERIOR DR, WATERLOO, ON, N2V 2C6
(519) 746-1390 *SIC* 5144

CANTOR'S GROCERY LTD p 380
1445 LOGAN AVE, WINNIPEG, MB, R3E 1S1
(204) 774-1679 *SIC* 5411

CANTRAV SERVICES INC p 291
22 2ND AVE W, VANCOUVER, BC, V5Y 1B3
(604) 708-2500 *SIC* 8741

CANTU BATHROOMS & HARDWARE LTD p 290
8351 ONTARIO ST, VANCOUVER, BC, V5X 3E8
(604) 688-1252 *SIC* 5074

CANTWELL CULLEN & COMPANY INC p 803
1131 SOUTH SERVICE RD W, OAKVILLE, ON, L6L 6K4
(905) 825-3255 *SIC* 3679

CANUCK AMUSEMENTS AND MERCHANDISING LTD p 73
3911 37 ST SW, CALGARY, AB, T3E 6L6
(403) 249-6641 *SIC* 5092

CANUCK COMPOUNDERS INC p 533
180 SHELDON DR UNIT 12, CAMBRIDGE, ON, N1R 6V1
(519) 621-6521 *SIC* 2821

CANUCK INDUSTRIES p 610
See FIBRE LAMINATIONS LTD

CANUCKS CENTRE FOR BC HOCKEY, THE p 297
800 GRIFFITHS WAY SUITE 4, VANCOUVER, BC, V6B 6G1
(604) 899-7770 *SIC* 7997

CANUCKS SPORTS & ENTERTAINMENT CORPORATION p 297
800 GRIFFITHS WAY, VANCOUVER, BC, V6B 6G1
(604) 899-7400 *SIC* 7941

CANUS CONSTRUCTION INC p 93
13030 146 ST NW, EDMONTON, AB, T5L 2H7
SIC 1542

CANUSA AUTOMOTIVE WAREHOUSING INC p 650
2290 SCANLAN ST, LONDON, ON, N5W 6G7
(519) 268-7070 *SIC* 5511

CANWEL BUILDING MATERIALS GROUP LTD p 311

1055 GEORGIA ST W SUITE 1100, VANCOUVER, BC, V6E 0B6
(604) 432-1400 *SIC* 5039

CANWEL BUILDING MATERIALS LTD p 311
1055 WEST GEORGIA ST SUITE 1100, VANCOUVER, BC, V6E 3P3
(604) 432-1400 *SIC* 5039

CANWELL INSURANCE AND FINANCIAL SERVICES INC p 665
121 ROBINSON ST, MARKHAM, ON, L3P 1P2
SIC 6411

CANWEST DHI p 606
See ONTARIO DAIRY HERD IMPROVEMENT CORPORATION

CANWEST INNOVATIONS p 178
See 0962358 B.C. LTD

CANWEST PROPANE PARTNERSHIP p 46
440 2 AVE SW SUITE 1700, CALGARY, AB, T2P 5E9
(403) 206-4000 *SIC* 5084

CANWEST WIRE ROPE INC p 281
9323 194 ST SUITE 200, SURREY, BC, V4N 4G1
SIC 5051

CANWORLD FOODS LTD p 996
320 NORTH QUEEN ST SUITE 100, TORONTO, ON, M9C 5K4
(416) 233-1900 *SIC* 5147

CANXPRESS p 379
See TRANSX LTD

CANXPRESS LTD p 70
11400 27 ST SE, CALGARY, AB, T2Z 3R6
(403) 236-9088 *SIC* 4213

CANYON CREEK SOUP COMPANY LTD p 74
60 CROWFOOT CRES NW SUITE 204, CALGARY, AB, T3G 3J9
SIC 2032

CANYON CREEK STEAK & CHOPHOUSE p 711
See SIR CORP

CANYON CREEK TOYOTA INC p 39
370 CANYON MEADOWS DR SE, CALGARY, AB, T2J 7C6
(403) 278-6066 *SIC* 5511

CANYON PLUMBING & HEATING LTD p 70
3185 114 AVE SE, CALGARY, AB, T2Z 3X2
(403) 258-1505 *SIC* 1711

CANYON SERVICES GROUP INC p 46
645 7 AVE SW SUITE 2900, CALGARY, AB, T2P 4G8
(403) 266-0202 *SIC* 1389

CANYON TECHNICAL SERVICES LTD p 46
255 5 AVE SW SUITE 2900, CALGARY, AB, T2P 3G6
(403) 355-2300 *SIC* 1389

CANYON TECHNICAL SERVICES LTD p 79
9102 102 ST SUITE 55, CLAIRMONT, AB, T8X 5G8
(780) 357-2250 *SIC* 1389

CANYON TECHNICAL SERVICES LTD p 153
28042 HWY 11 UNIT 322, RED DEER, AB, T4N 5H3
SIC 1389

CANYON TECHNICAL SERVICES LTD p 1406
548 BOURQUIN RD, ESTEVAN, SK, S4A 2A7
(306) 637-3360 *SIC* 1389

CAON SERVICES INC p 28
1143 42 AVE SE, CALGARY, AB, T2G 1Z3
(403) 279-6641 *SIC* 1711

CAOUTCHOUC ET PLASTIQUES FALPACO INC p 1110
825 RUE J.-A.-BOMBARDIER, GRANBY, QC, J2J 1E9
(450) 378-3348 *SIC* 5085

CAP GEMINI p 946
See NEW HORIZON SYSTEM SOLUTIONS INC

CAPABLE BUILDING CLEANING LTD p 399
158 CLARK ST, FREDERICTON, NB, E3A 2W7
(506) 458-9343 *SIC* 7349

CAPCO p 986
100 KING ST W SUITE 5010, TORONTO, ON, M5X 1C7
(416) 923-4570 *SIC* 8742

CAPE p 822
See CANADIAN ASSOCIATION OF PROFESSIONAL EMPLOYEES

CAPE BALD PACKERS, LIMITED p 396
2618 CH ACADIE, CAP-PELE, NB, E4N 1E3
(506) 577-4316 *SIC* 5146

CAPE BREEZE SEAFOODS LIMITED p 465
3203 MAIN RD, PORT LA TOUR, NS, B0W 2T0
(902) 768-2550 *SIC* 2092

CAPE BRETON BEVERAGES LIMITED p 449
65 HARBOUR DR, EDWARDSVILLE, NS, B2A 4T7
(902) 564-4536 *SIC* 2086

CAPE BRETON COUNTY HOMEMAKERS AGENCY p 466
5 DETHERIDGE DR SUITE 1, SYDNEY, NS, B1L 1B8
(902) 562-5003 *SIC* 8059

CAPE BRETON DISTRICT HEALTH AUTHORITY p 467
1482 GEORGE ST, SYDNEY, NS, B1P 1P3
(902) 567-8000 *SIC* 8062

CAPE BRETON ISLAND HOUSING AUTHORITY p 467
18 DOLBIN ST, SYDNEY, NS, B1P 1S5
(902) 539-8520 *SIC* 8399

CAPE BRETON REGIONAL HOSPITAL p 467
See CAPE BRETON DISTRICT HEALTH AUTHORITY

CAPE BRETON UNIVERSITY p 466
1250 GRAND LAKE RD, SYDNEY, NS, B1M 1A2
(902) 539-5300 *SIC* 8221

CAPE BRETON-VICTORIA REGIONAL SCHOOL BOARD p 465
999 GABARUS HWY, PRIME BROOK, NS, B1L 1E5
(902) 562-4595 *SIC* 8211

CAPE BRETON-VICTORIA REGIONAL SCHOOL BOARD p 467
275 GEORGE ST, SYDNEY, NS, B1P 1J7
(902) 564-8293 *SIC* 8211

CAPE BROYLE SEA PRODUCTS LIMITED p 421
GD, CAPE BROYLE, NL, A0A 1P0
(709) 432-2400 *SIC* 2092

CAPE CARE SERVICES (1996) LTD p 466
4 DRYDEN AVE, SYDNEY, NS, B1N 3K4
(902) 562-2444 *SIC* 8399

CAPE COD WOOD SIDINGS DIV OF p 459
See MARWOOD LTD

CAPE-MAN HOLDINGS LTD p 165
11 ESTATE CRES, ST. ALBERT, AB, T8N 5X2
(780) 459-0510 *SIC* 3442

CAPEL ELECTRIQUE p 1157
See FRANKLIN EMPIRE INC

CAPELLA TELECOMMUNICATIONS INC p 1101
2065 RUE MICHELIN, FABREVILLE, QC, H7L 5B7
(450) 686-0033 *SIC* 4899

CAPESPAN AMERIQUE DU NORD p 1338
See CAPESPAN NORTH AMERICA INC

CAPESPAN NORTH AMERICA INC p 1338
6700 CH DE LA COTE-DE-LIESSE BUREAU 301, SAINT-LAURENT, QC, H4T 2B5
(514) 739-9181 *SIC* 5148

CAPEZIO p 973
See MARKIO DESIGNS INC

CAPGEMINI CANADA INC p 949

200 UNIVERSITY AVE SUITE 1100, TORONTO, ON, M5H 3C6
(416) 365-4400   SIC 8742

CAPILANO HIGHWAY SERVICES COMPANY p 341
118 BRIDGE RD, WEST VANCOUVER, BC, V7P 3R2
(604) 983-2411   SIC 1611

CAPILANO SUSPENSION BRIDGE LTD p 242
3735 CAPILANO RD SUITE 1889, NORTH VANCOUVER, BC, V7R 4J1
(604) 985-7474   SIC 4724

CAPILANO UNIVERSITY p 239
2055 PURCELL WAY SUITE 284, NORTH VANCOUVER, BC, V7J 3H5
(604) 986-1911   SIC 8221

CAPILANO VOLKSWAGEN INC p 241
1151 MARINE DR, NORTH VANCOUVER, BC, V7P 1T1
(604) 985-0694   SIC 5511

CAPILANO, DIV OF p 230
See ROPAK CANADA INC

CAPILEX-BEAUTE LTEE p 1266
2670 AV DALTON, QUEBEC, QC, G1P 3S4
(418) 653-2500   SIC 5087

CAPILEX-BEAUTE MONTREAL p 1266
See CAPILEX-BEAUTE LTEE

CAPITAL BUILDING SUPPLIES LTD p 250
4150 COWART RD, PRINCE GEORGE, BC, V2N 6H9
(250) 562-1125   SIC 5039

CAPITAL CARE p 84
See KIPNESS CENTRE FOR VETERANS INC

CAPITAL CARE GROUP INC p 91
9925 109 ST NW SUITE 500, EDMONTON, AB, T5K 2J8
(780) 448-2400   SIC 8051

CAPITAL CARE GROUP INC p 98
8740 165 ST NW SUITE 438, EDMONTON, AB, T5R 2R8
(780) 341-2300   SIC 8059

CAPITAL CARE LYNNWOOD p 98
See CAPITAL CARE GROUP INC

CAPITAL CHRYSLER JEEP DODGE RAM p 125
See CAPITAL MOTORS LP

CAPITAL CITY PAVING LTD p 267
6588 BRYN RD, SAANICHTON, BC, V8M 1X6
(250) 652-3626   SIC 1611

CAPITAL CRANE LIMITED p 426
20 SAGONA AVE, MOUNT PEARL, NL, A1N 4R2
(709) 748-8888   SIC 7353

CAPITAL D'AMERIQUE CDPQ INC p 1191
1000 PLACE JEAN-PAUL-RIOPELLE BUREAU 12E, MONTREAL, QC, H2Z 2B3
(514) 842-3261   SIC 6371

CAPITAL DESJARDINS INC p 1135
100 AV DES COMMENDEURS, LEVIS, QC, G6V 7N5
(418) 835-8444   SIC 6722

CAPITAL DESSAU INC p 1236
1200 BOUL SAINT-MARTIN O BUREAU 300, MONTREAL, QC, H7S 2E4
(514) 281-1010   SIC 8742

CAPITAL DODGE CHRYSLER JEEP LIMITED p 626
2500 PALLADIUM DR SUITE 1200, KANATA, ON, K2V 1E2
(613) 271-7114   SIC 5511

CAPITAL DRYWALL SYSTEMS LTD p 501
396 DEERHURST DR, BRAMPTON, ON, L6T 5H9
(905) 458-1112   SIC 1742

CAPITAL ENGINEERING p 99
17187 114 AVE NW SUITE 101, EDMONTON, AB, T5S 2N5
(780) 488-2504   SIC 8711

CAPITAL F p 1230

See GESTION DESJARDINS CAPITAL INC

CAPITAL FOOD SERVICE p 410
See ROLLY'S WHOLESALE LTD

CAPITAL FORD LINCOLN INC p 1423
1201 N PASQUA ST, REGINA, SK, S4X 4P7
(306) 543-5410   SIC 5511

CAPITAL GROUP p 960
See CAPITAL INTERNATIONAL ASSET MANAGEMENT (CANADA), INC.

CAPITAL HONDA p 1040
See JOLOWAY LTD

CAPITAL HYUNDAI p 429
See CAPITAL MOTORS LIMITED

CAPITAL INDUSTRIAL SALES & SERVICE LTD p 122
851 77 AVE NW, EDMONTON, AB, T6P 1S9
(780) 440-4467   SIC 5084

CAPITAL INSURANCE BROKER p 105
See JIMSAR BUSINESS SERVICES INC

CAPITAL INTERNATIONAL ASSET MANAGEMENT (CANADA), INC. p 960
181 BAY ST SUITE 3730, TORONTO, ON, M5J 2T3
(416) 815-2134   SIC 6722

CAPITAL IRON (1997) LTD p 334
1900 STORE ST, VICTORIA, BC, V8T 4R4
(250) 385-9703   SIC 5251

CAPITAL MANAGEMENT LTD p 91
9747 104 ST NW SUITE 1604, EDMONTON, AB, T5K 0Y6
(780) 428-6511   SIC 1531

CAPITAL MORTGAGES p 748
18 DEAKIN ST SUITE 106, NEPEAN, ON, K2E 8B7
(613) 228-3888   SIC 6162

CAPITAL MOTORS p 204
See CAPITAL MOTORS (1985) LTD

CAPITAL MOTORS (1985) LTD p 204
1609 ALASKA AVE, DAWSON CREEK, BC, V1G 1Z9
(250) 782-8589   SIC 5511

CAPITAL MOTORS LIMITED p 429
479 KENMOUNT RD, ST. JOHN'S, NL, A1B 3P9
(709) 726-0288   SIC 5511

CAPITAL MOTORS LP p 125
1311 101 ST SW, EDMONTON, AB, T6X 1A1
(780) 435-4711   SIC 5511

CAPITAL OFFICE INTERIORS LIMITED p 749
16 ANTARES DR, NEPEAN, ON, K2E 7Y7
(613) 723-2000   SIC 5021

CAPITAL ONE BANK (CANADA BRANCH) p 1217
950 AV BEAUMONT, MONTREAL, QC, H3N 1V5
(800) 481-3239   SIC 6153

CAPITAL ONE SERVICES (CANADA) INC p 771
5140 YONGE ST SUITE 1900, NORTH YORK, ON, M2N 6L7
(416) 549-2500   SIC 6153

CAPITAL PACKERS HOLDINGS INC p 83
12907 57 ST NW, EDMONTON, AB, T5A 0E7
(780) 476-1391   SIC 6719

CAPITAL PACKERS INC p 83
12907 57 ST NW, EDMONTON, AB, T5A 0E7
(780) 476-1391   SIC 2011

CAPITAL PAPER PRODUCTS LIMITED p 459
27 CALKIN DR, KENTVILLE, NS, B4N 3V7
(902) 678-6767   SIC 5113

CAPITAL PAPER RECYCLING LTD p 14
10595 50 ST SE, CALGARY, AB, T2C 3E3
(403) 543-3322   SIC 5044

CAPITAL PARKING INC p 824
400 SLATER ST SUITE 2102, OTTAWA, ON, K1R 7S7
(613) 593-8820   SIC 7521

CAPITAL PAVING INC p 849

4459 CONCESSION 7, PUSLINCH, ON, N0B 2J0
(519) 822-4511   SIC 1611

CAPITAL PONTIAC BUICK CADILLAC GMC LTD p 1423
4020 ROCHDALE BLVD, REGINA, SK, S4X 4P7
(306) 525-5211   SIC 5511

CAPITAL POWER (K3) LIMITED PARTNERSHIP p 87
10065 JASPER AVE NW, EDMONTON, AB, T5J 3B1
(780) 392-5305   SIC 5063

CAPITAL POWER CORPORATION p 85
10423 101 ST NW SUITE 1200, EDMONTON, AB, T5H 0E9
(780) 392-5100   SIC 4911

CAPITAL PRINTING & FORMS INC p 93
14133 128A AVE NW, EDMONTON, AB, T5L 4P5
(780) 453-5039   SIC 5112

CAPITAL PRINTING & FORMS INK p 93
See CAPITAL PRINTING & FORMS INC

CAPITAL READY MIX LIMITED p 429
TRANS CANADA HWY, ST. JOHN'S, NL, A1B 3N4
(709) 364-5008   SIC 3273

CAPITAL REGION HOUSING CORPORATION p 91
10232 112 ST NW, EDMONTON, AB, T5K 1M4
(780) 408-3301   SIC 6531

CAPITAL REGIONAL p 1230
See CAPITAL REGIONAL ET COOPERATIF DESJARDINS

CAPITAL REGIONAL ET COOPERATIF DESJARDINS p 1230
2 COMPLEXE DESJARDINS O BUREAU 1717, MONTREAL, QC, H5B 1B8
(514) 281-2322   SIC 6719

CAPITAL S AUTO SALES p 346
See CAPITAL S ENTERPRISES LTD

CAPITAL S ENTERPRISES LTD p 346
GD, BRANDON, MB, R7A 5Y1
(204) 730-0097   SIC 5521

CAPITAL SAFETY GROUP CANADA ULC p 734
260 EXPORT BLVD, MISSISSAUGA, ON, L5S 1Y9
(905) 795-9333   SIC 3842

CAPITAL SECURITY & INVESTIGATIONS p 562
504 PITT ST, CORNWALL, ON, K6J 3R5
(613) 937-4111   SIC 7381

CAPITAL SEWER SERVICES INC p 1027
401 VAUGHAN VALLEY BLVD, WOODBRIDGE, ON, L4H 3B5
(905) 522-0522   SIC 1799

CAPITAL STIKLY INC p 1178
225 RUE CHABANEL O BUREAU 200, MONTREAL, QC, H2N 2C9
(514) 381-5393   SIC 5136

CAPITAL STONEWORKS, DIV OF p 792
See YORK MARBLE TILE & TERRAZZO INC

CAPITAL SUBARU p 430
See HOWARD MOTORS INC

CAPITAL TOOL & DESIGN LTD. p 550
270 SPINNAKER WAY SUITE 13, CONCORD, ON, L4K 4W1
(905) 760-8088   SIC 3312

CAPITAL TRAITEUR p 1191
See CAPITAL TRAITEUR MONTREAL INC

CAPITAL TRAITEUR MONTREAL INC p 1191
159 RUE SAINT-ANTOINE O BUREAU 400, MONTREAL, QC, H2Z 2A7
(514) 875-1897   SIC 5812

CAPITAL TRAITEUR MONTREAL INC p 1191
201 AV VIGER O, MONTREAL, QC, H2Z 1X7

(514) 871-3111   SIC 5812

CAPITAL TRANSIT INC p 1263
2035 RUE DU HAUT-BORD BUREAU 300, QUEBEC, QC, G1N 4R7
(418) 914-0777   SIC 6159

CAPITAL WEST INSURANCE SERVICES p 231
22785 DEWDNEY TRUNK RD, MAPLE RIDGE, BC, V2X 3K4
(604) 476-1227   SIC 6411

CAPITALE ASSURANCES GENERALES INC, LA p 1268
625 RUE JACQUES-PARIZEAU, QUEBEC, QC, G1R 2G5
(418) 781-1618   SIC 6321

CAPITALE ASSUREUR DE L'ADMINISTRATION PUBLIQUE INC, LA p 1268
625 RUE JACQUES-PARIZEAU, QUEBEC, QC, G1R 2G5
(418) 644-4106   SIC 6311

CAPITALE CARD p 1268
See CAPITALE ASSUREUR DE L'ADMINISTRATION PUBLIQUE INC, LA

CAPITALE GESTION FINANCIERE INC, LA p 1271
650-2875 BOUL LAURIER, QUEBEC, QC, G1V 5B1
(418) 644-0038   SIC 6411

CAPITALE GROUPE FINANCIER INC, LA p 1268
625 RUE JACQUES-PARIZEAU, QUEBEC, QC, G1R 2G5
(418) 644-4229   SIC 6712

CAPITALE IMMOBILIERE MFQ INC, LA p 1268
625 RUE JACQUES-PARIZEAU, QUEBEC, QC, G1R 2G5
(418) 644-4267   SIC 6531

CAPITALE MUTUELLE DE L'ADMINISTRATION PUBLIQUE, LA p 1268
625 RUE JACQUES-PARIZEAU, QUEBEC, QC, G1R 2G5
(418) 644-4229   SIC 6311

CAPITALE NISSAN p 1262
See SOVEA AUTOS LTEE

CAPITALE QUEBEC CHAMPLAIN, LA p 1261
See 9049-8049 QUEBEC INC

CAPITALE, LA p 1271
See CAPITALE GESTION FINANCIERE INC, LA

CAPITOL HILL COMMUNITY ASSOCIATION p 41
1531 21 AVE NW, CALGARY, AB, T2M 1L9
(403) 289-0859   SIC 8399

CAPITOL STEEL CORPORATION p 380
1355 SASKATCHEWAN AVE, WINNIPEG, MB, R3E 3K4
(204) 889-9980   SIC 3441

CAPLAN INDUSTRIES INC p 208
6800 DENNETT PL, DELTA, BC, V4G 1N4
(604) 946-3100   SIC 5072

CAPMATIC LTEE p 1239
12180 BOUL ALBERT-HUDON, MONTREAL-NORD, QC, H1G 3K7
(514) 322-0062   SIC 3565

CAPO INDUSTRIES LIMITED p 521
1200 CORPORATE DR, BURLINGTON, ON, L7L 5R6
(905) 332-6626   SIC 2899

CAPOL INC p 1309
5132 RUE J.-A.-BOMBARDIER, SAINT-HUBERT, QC, J3Z 1H1
(450) 766-8707   SIC 5141

CAPP p 45
See CANADIAN ASSOCIATION OF PETROLEUM PRODUCERS

CAPPRODUCTS, LTD p 544
25 WINNIPEG RD RR 5, CLINTON, ON, N0M 1L0
(519) 482-5000   SIC 3499

CAPREIT p 941

See *CANADIAN APARTMENT PROPER-*
TIES REAL ESTATE INVESTMENT TRUST
CAPRI BAGELS & BUNS   *p* 787
See *ONTARIO BAKERY SUPPLIES LIM-*
ITED
CAPRICMW INSURANCE SERVICES LTD *p*
221
    1500 HARDY ST SUITE 100, KELOWNA,
BC, V1Y 8H2
    (250) 860-2426   *SIC* 6411
CAPRION BIOSCIENCES INC   *p* 1185
    201 AV DU PRESIDENT-KENNEDY BU-
REAU 3900, MONTREAL, QC, H2X 3Y7
    (514) 360-3600   *SIC* 2834
CAPRION PROTEOME   *p* 1185
    See *CAPRION BIOSCIENCES INC*
CAPS 'N PLUGS   *p* 499
    See *JAY CEE ENTERPRISES LIMITED*
CAPSERVCO   *p* 222
    See *GRANT THORNTON LLP*
CAPSERVCO   *p* 298
    See *GRANT THORNTON LLP*
CAPSERVCO   *p* 670
    See *GRANT THORNTON LLP*
CAPSERVCO LIMITED PARTNERSHIP *p*
452
    2000 BARRINGTON ST SUITE 1100, HALI-
FAX, NS, B3J 3K1
    (902) 421-1734   *SIC* 8721
CAPSERVCO LIMITED PARTNERSHIP *p*
960
    50 BAY ST SUITE 1200, TORONTO, ON,
M5J 3A5
    (416) 366-4240   *SIC* 8721
CAPSTAN HAULING LTD   *p* 134
    10903 78 AVE, GRANDE PRAIRIE, AB,
T8W 2L2
    (780) 402-3110   *SIC* 1389
**CAPSTONE BLOWOUT RECOVERY, CAP-
STONE ABANDONMENTS**   *p*
2
    32 EAST LAKE CIR NE, AIRDRIE, AB, T4A
2K1
    (403) 437-8587   *SIC* 1389
**CAPSTONE INFRASTRUCTURE CORPO-
RATION**   *p*
979
    155 WELLINGTON ST W SUITE 2930,
TORONTO, ON, M5V 3H1
    (416) 649-1300   *SIC* 4911
CAPSTONE MINING CORP   *p* 297
    510 GEORGIA ST W SUITE 2100, VAN-
COUVER, BC, V6B 0M3
    (604) 684-8894   *SIC* 1081
**CAPSULES AMCOR FLEXIBLES CANADA
INC**   *p* 1297
    2301 RTE 112, SAINT-CESAIRE, QC, J0L
1T0
    (450) 469-0777   *SIC* 3466
CAPT-AIR INC   *p* 1183
    5860 BOUL SAINT-LAURENT, MONTREAL,
QC, H2T 1T3
    (514) 273-4331   *SIC* 5087
CAPTAIN DAN'S INC   *p* 397
    463 CHAMPLAIN ST, DIEPPE, NB, E1A 1P2
    (506) 872-7621   *SIC* 2092
CAPTEL INC   *p* 1387
    9395 BOUL PARENT BUREAU 2, TROIS-
RIVIERES, QC, G9A 5E1
    (819) 373-1454   *SIC* 1623
CAPWORK LABORATORY INC   *p* 254
    13982 CAMBIE RD SUITE 113, RICH-
MOND, BC, V6V 2K2
    (604) 233-7060   *SIC* 5149
CAR LOT ETC INC, THE   *p* 898
    2231 LASALLE BLVD, SUDBURY, ON, P3A
2A9
    (705) 560-3999   *SIC* 5521
**CAR PARK MANAGEMENT SERVICES LIM-
ITED**   *p*
931
    40 ISABELLA ST, TORONTO, ON, M4Y 1N1
    (416) 920-3382   *SIC* 7521
CAR-BER TESTING SERVICES   *p* 846

See *CAR-BER TESTING SERVICES INC*
CAR-BER TESTING SERVICES INC *p* 846
    911 MICHIGAN AVE, POINT EDWARD, ON,
N7V 1H2
    (519) 336-7775   *SIC* 8734
CARA FOODS   *p* 368
    1221 ST MARY'S RD, WINNIPEG, MB, R2M
5L5
    (204) 254-2128   *SIC* 5812
CARA FOODS INTERNATIONAL LTD *p* 856
    1620 ELGIN MILLS RD E, RICHMOND
HILL, ON, L4S 0B2
    (905) 508-4139   *SIC* 5812
CARA HOLDINGS LIMITED   *p* 972
    21 BEDFORD RD SUITE 200, TORONTO,
ON, M5R 2J9
    (905) 760-2244   *SIC* 5812
CARA OPERATIONS LIMITED   *p* 994
    See *RECIPE UNLIMITED CORPORATION*
CARA OPERATIONS LIMITED   *p* 1092
    See *RECIPE UNLIMITED CORPORATION*
CARA OPERATIONS QUEBEC LTD   *p* 550
    199 FOUR VALLEY DR, CONCORD, ON,
L4K 0B8
    (905) 760-2244   *SIC* 5812
CARA OPERATIONS QUEBEC LTD   *p* 573
    1001 THE QUEENSWAY, ETOBICOKE, ON,
M8Z 6C7
    (416) 255-0464   *SIC* 5812
CARAT CANADA INC   *p* 979
    276 KING ST W SUITE 400, TORONTO,
ON, M5V 1J2
    (416) 504-3965   *SIC* 7311
CARAT CANADA INC   *p* 1184
    4446 BOUL SAINT-LAURENT BUREAU
500, MONTREAL, QC, H2W 1Z5
    (514) 287-2555   *SIC* 7311
CARAT COMMANDITE   *p* 1194
    See *CARAT STRATEGEM INC*
CARAT STRATEGEM INC   *p* 1194
    400 BOUL DE MAISONNEUVE O BUREAU
250, MONTREAL, QC, H3A 1L4
    (514) 284-4446   *SIC* 7311
CARAVAN AVIATION   *p* 1077
    See *CHANTIERS DE CHIBOUGAMAU
LTEE, LES*
CARAVAN LOGISTICS INC   *p* 803
    2284 WYECROFT RD, OAKVILLE, ON, L6L
6M1
    (905) 338-5885   *SIC* 4213
CARBERRY INTERNATIONAL   *p* 383
    See *CARBERRY INTERNATIONAL
SPORTS INC*
**CARBERRY INTERNATIONAL SPORTS
INC**   *p* 383
    820 BRADFORD ST, WINNIPEG, MB, R3H
0N5
    (204) 632-4222   *SIC* 5091
CARBON CONSTRUCTORS INC   *p* 28
    3915 8 ST SE, CALGARY, AB, T2G 3A5
    (403) 203-4900   *SIC* 1542
CARBON ENGINEERING LTD   *p* 269
    37321 GALBRAITH RD, SQUAMISH, BC,
V8B 0A2
    (778) 386-1457   *SIC* 2813
CARBON STEEL PROFILES LIMITED *p* 498
    2190 WILLIAMS PKY, BRAMPTON, ON,
L6S 5X7
    (905) 799-2427   *SIC* 7389
CARBONMASTERS   *p* 200
    See *CARBONMASTERS INNOVATION LTD*
CARBONMASTERS INNOVATION LTD *p*
200
    35 LEEDER ST, COQUITLAM, BC, V3K 3V5
    (778) 684-2096   *SIC* 5075
CARBOTECH INTERNATIONAL   *p* 1245
    See *4170083 CANADA INC*
CARCANADA CORPORATION   *p* 663
    5791 REGIONAL ROAD 73, MANOTICK,
ON, K4M 1A5
    (613) 489-1212   *SIC* 5511
CARCONE'S AUTO RECYCLING LIMITED *p*
480
    1030 BLOOMINGTON RD SUITE 2, AU-

RORA, ON, L4G 0L7
    (905) 773-5778   *SIC* 5013
CARDEAGER AUTO BODY   *p* 355
    See *CARDEAGER FORD SALES SERVICE
& AUTO BODY LTD*
**CARDEAGER FORD SALES SERVICE &
AUTO BODY LTD**   *p* 355
    GD, ROBLIN, MB, R0L 1P0
    (204) 937-8386   *SIC* 5511
CARDEL CONSTRUCTION LTD   *p* 14
    180 QUARRY PARK BLVD SE, CALGARY,
AB, T2C 3G3
    (403) 258-1511   *SIC* 6712
CARDEL HOMES LIMITED PARTNERSHIP
p 14
    180 QUARRY PARK BLVD SE SUITE 200,
CALGARY, AB, T2C 3G3
    (403) 258-1511   *SIC* 1521
CARDERO'S RESTAURANT   *p* 318
    See *SEQUOIA COMPANY OF RESTAU-
RANTS INC*
**CARDIGAN LOBSTER SUPPERS & JOCKS
LOUNGE**   *p* 1038
    See *MACDONALD, J A COMPANY*
CARDINAL   *p* 633
    See *CARDINAL MOVERS KINGSTON INC*
CARDINAL CAPITAL MANAGEMENT INC *p*
383
    1780 WELLINGTON AVE SUITE 506, WIN-
NIPEG, MB, R3H 1B3
    (204) 783-0716   *SIC* 6282
CARDINAL CARETAKERS CO LIMITED   *p*
876
    80 DYNAMIC DR, SCARBOROUGH, ON,
M1V 2V1
    SIC 7349
**CARDINAL CARTER CATHOLIC HIGH
SCHOOL**   *p* 482
    See *YORK CATHOLIC DISTRICT SCHOOL
BOARD*
CARDINAL COURIERS LTD   *p* 687
    6600 GOREWAY DR UNIT D, MISSIS-
SAUGA, ON, L4V 1S6
    (905) 507-4111   *SIC* 7389
CARDINAL ENERGY LTD   *p* 46
    400 3 AVE SW SUITE 600, CALGARY, AB,
T2P 4H2
    (403) 234-8681   *SIC* 1311
CARDINAL FASTENERS   *p* 865
    See *TALBOT SALES LIMITED*
**CARDINAL FINE CABINETRY CORPORA-
TION**   *p*
660
    165 EXETER RD, LONDON, ON, N6L 1A4
    (519) 652-3295   *SIC* 5712
CARDINAL HEALTH CANADA INC   *p* 550
    1000 TESMA WAY, CONCORD, ON, L4K
5R8
    (905) 417-2900   *SIC* 5047
CARDINAL HEALTH CANADA INC   *p* 738
    1330 MEYERSIDE DR, MISSISSAUGA,
ON, L5T 1C2
    (905) 761-0068   *SIC* 5047
CARDINAL MEAT SPECIALISTS LIMITED *p*
501
    155 HEDGEDALE RD, BRAMPTON, ON,
L6T 5P3
    (905) 459-4436   *SIC* 2013
CARDINAL MOVERS KINGSTON INC *p* 633
    921 WOODBINE RD, KINGSTON, ON, K7P
2X4
    (289) 395-0003   *SIC* 4212
**CARDINAL NEWMAN SECONDARY
SCHOOL**   *p* 894
    See *HAMILTON-WENTWORTH CATHOLIC
SCHOOL BOARD*
CARDINAL RIVER COALS LTD   *p* 136
    GD, HINTON, AB, T7V 1V5
    (780) 692-5100   *SIC* 1221
CARDINAL RIVER OPERATIONS   *p* 136
    See *TECK COAL LIMITED*
CARDIOLOGY PLUS   *p* 22
    See *CARDIOLOGY PLUS (CALGARY) INC*
CARDIOLOGY PLUS (CALGARY) INC *p* 22

803 1 AVE NE SUITE 306, CALGARY, AB,
T2E 7C5
    (403) 571-8600   *SIC* 8734
CARDIOMED SUPPLIES INC   *p* 645
    199 ST DAVID ST, LINDSAY, ON, K9V 5K7
    (705) 328-2518   *SIC* 5047
CARDONE INDUSTRIES ULC   *p* 99
    17803 111 AVE NW, EDMONTON, AB, T5S
2X3
    (780) 444-5033   *SIC* 5013
CARDSTON ELEMENTARY SCHOOL   *p* 79
    See *WESTWIND SCHOOL DIVISION #74*
CARDTRONICS CANADA HOLDINGS INC *p*
10
    1420 28 ST NE SUITE 6, CALGARY, AB,
T2A 7W6
    (403) 207-1500   *SIC* 6099
CARDTRONICS CANADA HOLDINGS INC *p*
687
    3269 AMERICAN DR SUITE 1, MISSIS-
SAUGA, ON, L4V 1V4
    (905) 678-7373   *SIC* 6099
**CARDTRONICS CANADA OPERATIONS
INC**   *p* 10
    1420 28 ST NE SUITE 6, CALGARY, AB,
T2A 7W6
    (403) 207-1500   *SIC* 8741
CARE COUNTS HEALTH SERVICES *p* 259
    See *BIG HEARTS HOLDINGS LTD*
**CAREER PARTNERS INTERNATIONAL/
HAZELL & ASSOCIATES**   *p* 925
    See *MIMERI INVESTMENTS LTD*
**CAREFIRST SENIORS AND COMMUNITY
SERVICES ASSOCIATION**   *p* 876
    300 SILVER STAR BLVD, SCARBOROUGH,
ON, M1V 0G2
    (416) 502-2323   *SIC* 8322
**CAREFOR HEALTH & COMMUNITY SER-
VICES**   *p*
817
    760 BELFAST RD, OTTAWA, ON, K1G 6M8
    (613) 749-7557   *SIC* 8621
**CAREFOR HEALTH & COMMUNITY SER-
VICES**   *p*
838
    425 CECELIA ST, PEMBROKE, ON, K8A
1S7
    (613) 732-9993   *SIC* 8082
CAREFREE COACH & RV LTD   *p* 108
    4510 51 AVE NW, EDMONTON, AB, T6B
2W2
    (780) 438-2008   *SIC* 5561
CAREFREE RV LTD   *p* 108
    4510 51 AVE NW, EDMONTON, AB, T6B
2W2
    (780) 438-2008   *SIC* 5521
CAREMED SERVICES INC   *p* 866
    1200 MARKHAM RD SUITE 220, SCAR-
BOROUGH, ON, M1H 3C3
    (416) 438-4577   *SIC* 8082
CAREMED SERVICES INC   *p* 1013
    1450 HOPKINS ST SUITE 205, WHITBY,
ON, L1N 2C3
    (905) 666-6656   *SIC* 8059
CAREPARTNERS   *p* 642
    See *8262900 CANADA INC*
CAREPARTNERS INC   *p* 642
    139 WASHBURN DR, KITCHENER, ON,
N2R 1S1
    (519) 748-5002   *SIC* 8011
CARESSANT CARE LINDSAY   *p* 645
    See *CARESSANT-CARE NURSING AND
RETIREMENT HOMES LIMITED*
CARESSANT CARE MARMORA   *p* 680
    See *CARESSANT-CARE NURSING AND
RETIREMENT HOMES LIMITED*
**CARESSANT CARE NURSING HOME
COBDEN**   *p* 544
    12 WREN DR, COBDEN, ON, K0J 1K0
    (613) 646-2109   *SIC* 8051
**CARESSANT-CARE NURSING AND RE-
TIREMENT HOMES LIMITED**   *p*
538
    3680 SPEEDSVILLE RD SUITE 3, CAM-

BRIDGE, ON, N3H 4R6
(519) 650-0100   SIC 8051
CARESSANT-CARE NURSING AND RE-TIREMENT HOMES LIMITED   p
618
24 LOUISE ST, HARRISTON, ON, N0G 1Z0
(519) 338-3700   SIC 8051
CARESSANT-CARE NURSING AND RE-TIREMENT HOMES LIMITED   p
645
114 MCLAUGHLIN RD, LINDSAY, ON, K9V 6L1
(705) 324-0300   SIC 8051
CARESSANT-CARE NURSING AND RE-TIREMENT HOMES LIMITED   p
645
240 MARY ST W, LINDSAY, ON, K9V 5K5
(705) 324-1913   SIC 8051
CARESSANT-CARE NURSING AND RE-TIREMENT HOMES LIMITED   p
680
58 BURSTHALL ST, MARMORA, ON, K0K 2M0
(613) 472-3130   SIC 8051
CARESSANT-CARE NURSING AND RE-TIREMENT HOMES LIMITED   p
890
15 BONNIE PL, ST THOMAS, ON, N5R 5T8
(519) 633-6493   SIC 8051
CARESSANT-CARE NURSING AND RE-TIREMENT HOMES LIMITED   p
902
94 WILLIAM ST S SUITE 202, TAVISTOCK, ON, N0B 2R0
(519) 655-2344   SIC 8051
CARESSANT-CARE NURSING AND RE-TIREMENT HOMES LIMITED   p
1035
264 NORWICH AVE, WOODSTOCK, ON, N4S 3V9
(519) 539-0408   SIC 8051
CARESSANT-CARE NURSING AND RE-TIREMENT HOMES LIMITED   p
1035
81 FYFE AVE, WOODSTOCK, ON, N4S 8Y2
(519) 539-6461   SIC 8051
CARESTREAM HEALTH CANADA COM-PANY   p
550
8800 DUFFERIN ST SUITE 201, CON-CORD, ON, L4K 0C5
(905) 532-0877   SIC 3843
CARETEK INTEGRATED BUSINESS SO-LUTIONS INC   p
501
1900 CLARK BLVD UNIT 8, BRAMPTON, ON, L6T 0E9
(416) 630-9555   SIC 5734
CARETEK IT SOLUTIONS   p 501
See CARETEK INTEGRATED BUSINESS SOLUTIONS INC
CAREWEST   p 68
10301 SOUTHPORT LANE SW, CALGARY, AB, T2W 1S7
(403) 943-8140   SIC 8059
CAREWEST   p 75
6363 SIMCOE RD SW, CALGARY, AB, T3H 4M3
(403) 240-7950   SIC 8051
CAREWEST ROYAL PARK   p 68
See CAREWEST
CAREY INDUSTRIAL SERVICES LTD p 129
9918A 102 ST, FORT SASKATCHEWAN, AB, T8L 2C3
(780) 998-1919   SIC 7361
CAREY MANAGEMENT INC   p 40
5445 8 ST NE, CALGARY, AB, T2K 5R9
(403) 275-7360   SIC 6712
CARFAIR COMPOSITES INC   p 365
692 MISSION ST, WINNIPEG, MB, R2J 0A3
(204) 233-0671   SIC 3299
CARFINCO INCOME FUND   p 113
4245 97 ST NW SUITE 300, EDMONTON,

AB, T6E 5Y7
(780) 413-7549   SIC 6722
CARGAIR   p 1308
See MAX AVIATION INC
CARGAIR LTEE   p 1307
6100 RTE DE L'AEROPORT, SAINT-HUBERT, QC, J3Y 8Y9
(450) 656-4783   SIC 4522
CARGESCO (2002) INC   p 1297
2325 BOUL INDUSTRIEL, SAINT-CESAIRE, QC, J0L 1T0
(450) 469-3168   SIC 5084
CARGILL   p 1377
See PROVIMI CANADA ULC
CARGILL ANIMAL NUTRITION DIV p 1307
See CARGILL LIMITED
CARGILL FOODS   p 135
See CARGILL LIMITED
CARGILL FOODS   p 583
See CARGILL LIMITED
CARGILL FOODS   p 1074
See CARGILL LIMITED
CARGILL LIMITED   p 135
472 AVENUE & HWY SUITE 2A, HIGH RIVER, AB, T1V 1P4
(403) 652-4688   SIC 2011
CARGILL LIMITED   p 377
240 GRAHAM AVE SUITE 300, WINNIPEG, MB, R3C 0J7
(204) 947-0141   SIC 5153
CARGILL LIMITED   p 583
71 REXDALE BLVD, ETOBICOKE, ON, M9W 1P1
SIC 2011
CARGILL LIMITED   p 600
781 YORK RD, GUELPH, ON, N1E 6N1
(519) 823-5200   SIC 2011
CARGILL LIMITED   p 648
10 CUDDY BLVD, LONDON, ON, N5V 5E3
(519) 453-4996   SIC 2015
CARGILL LIMITED   p 1035
404 MAIN ST, WOODSTOCK, ON, N4S 7X5
(519) 539-8561   SIC 2048
CARGILL LIMITED   p 1074
7901 RUE SAMUEL-HATT, CHAMBLY, QC, J3L 6V7
(450) 447-4600   SIC 5153
CARGILL LIMITED   p 1307
5928 BOUL COUSINEAU BUREAU 300, SAINT-HUBERT, QC, J3Y 7R9
(450) 676-8607   SIC 5191
CARGILL NUTRENA FEEDS   p 377
See CARGILL LIMITED
CARGILL VALUE ADDED MEATS   p 648
See CARGILL LIMITED
CARGO COVER   p 1221
See OCEANWIDE CANADA INC
CARGOJET   p 714
See CARGOJET HOLDINGS LTD
CARGOJET   p 747
See CARGOJET INC
CARGOJET AIRWAYS LTD   p 714
2281 NORTH SHERIDAN WAY, MISSIS-SAUGA, ON, L5K 2S3
(905) 501-7373   SIC 4512
CARGOJET HOLDINGS LIMITED PART-NERSHIP   p
714
2281 NORTH SHERIDAN WAY, MISSIS-SAUGA, ON, L5K 2S3
(905) 501-7373   SIC 6712
CARGOJET HOLDINGS LTD   p 714
2281 NORTH SHERIDAN WAY, MISSIS-SAUGA, ON, L5K 2S3
(905) 501-7373   SIC 4581
CARGOJET INC   p 714
2281 NORTH SHERIDAN WAY, MISSIS-SAUGA, ON, L5K 2S3
(905) 501-7373   SIC 4512
CARGOJET INC   p 747
9300 AIRPORT RD SUITE 320, MOUNT HOPE, ON, L0R 1W0
(905) 679-9127   SIC 4512
CARGOJET PARTNERSHIP   p 705

350 BRITANNIA RD E UNIT 5 6, MISSIS-SAUGA, ON, L4Z 1X9
(905) 501-7373   SIC 4512
CARGOLUTION INC   p 1092
800 BOUL STUART-GRAHAM S BUREAU 360, DORVAL, QC, H4Y 1J6
(514) 636-2576   SIC 4731
CARIBBEAN ICE CREAM COMPANY LTD p
787
130 BERMONDSEY RD, NORTH YORK, ON, M4A 1X5
(416) 759-3277   SIC 5141
CARIBBEAN INTERNATIONAL SUPPLY LIMITED   p 550
160 APPLEWOOD CRES SUITE 21, CON-CORD, ON, L4K 4H2
SIC 5046
CARIBOO CENTRAL RAILROAD CON-TRACTING LTD   p
219
307 BANKS RD UNIT 209, KELOWNA, BC, V1X 6A1
(778) 478-1745   SIC 1629
CARIBOO CHEVROLET BUICK GMC LTD p
344
370 MACKENZIE AVE S, WILLIAMS LAKE, BC, V2G 1C7
(250) 392-7185   SIC 5511
CARIBOO CHEVROLET OLDSMOBILE PONTIAC BUICK GMC LTD   p 344
370 MACKENZIE AVE S, WILLIAMS LAKE, BC, V2G 1C7
(250) 392-7185   SIC 5511
CARIBOO FOREST CONSULTANTS LTD p
252
335 VAUGHAN ST, QUESNEL, BC, V2J 2T1
SIC 8741
CARIBOO GM   p 344
See CARIBOO CHEVROLET BUICK GMC LTD
CARIBOO HELICOPTER SKIING (88) LTD p
180
1 HARRWOOD DR, BLUE RIVER, BC, V0E 1J0
(250) 673-8381   SIC 7011
CARIBOO HILL SECONDARY SCHOOL   p
181
See BURNABY SCHOOL BOARD DIS-TRICT 41
CARIBOO KEEPSAKES   p 252
See QUESNEL CRAFTERS SOCIETY
CARIBOO MEMORIAL HOSPITAL   p 344
517 SIXTH AVE N SUITE 401, WILLIAMS LAKE, BC, V2G 2G8
(250) 392-4411   SIC 8062
CARIBOO PRESS   p 333
See BLACK PRESS GROUP LTD
CARIBOO PRESS PRINTING & PUBLISH-ING LTD   p
219
2495 ENTERPRISE WAY, KELOWNA, BC, V1X 7K2
(250) 763-3212   SIC 8748
CARIBOO PULP & PAPER COMPANY p 252
50 NORTH STAR RD, QUESNEL, BC, V2J 3J6
(250) 992-0200   SIC 2611
CARIBOO STEEL CENTRE   p 344
See TASCO SUPPLIES LTD
CARIBOU ROAD SERVICES LTD   p 248
5201 52ND AVE, POUCE COUPE, BC, V0C 2C0
(250) 786-5440   SIC 5082
CARILLION CANADA INC   p 550
7077 KEELE ST, CONCORD, ON, L4K 0B6
(905) 532-5200   SIC 1611
CARILLION CANADA INC   p 828
1145 CARLING AVE SUITE 1317, OTTAWA, ON, K1Z 7K4
(613) 722-6521   SIC 8741
CARILLION CONSTRUCTION   p 550
See CARILLION CANADA INC
CARILLION CONSTRUCTION INC   p 550
7077 KEELE ST, CONCORD, ON, L4K 0B6

(905) 532-5200   SIC 8741
CARILLION SERVICE ROH   p 828
See CARILLION CANADA INC
CARIS   p 401
See UNIVERSAL SYSTEMS LTD
CARISTRAP INTERNATIONAL INC p 1085
1760 BOUL FORTIN, COTE SAINT-LUC, QC, H7S 1N8
(450) 667-4700   SIC 3199
CARKAE ENGLISH SALES LTD   p 635
1080 VICTORIA ST N SUITE 139, KITCH-ENER, ON, N2B 3C4
(519) 744-1153   SIC 5531
CARL SQUARED PRODUCTIONS INC   p
979
901 KING ST W SUITE 301, TORONTO, ON, M5V 3H5
(416) 483-9773   SIC 7922
CARL ZEISS CANADA LIMITED   p 776
45 VALLEYBROOK DR, NORTH YORK, ON, M3B 2S6
(416) 449-4660   SIC 5995
CARLE FORD INC   p 1102
901 RUE DOLLARD, GATINEAU, QC, J8L 3T4
(819) 986-3000   SIC 5511
CARLETON CO-OPERATIVE LIMITED   p
399
8818 MAIN ST, FLORENCEVILLE-BRISTOL, NB, E7L 3G2
(506) 392-5587   SIC 5411
CARLETON KIRK LODGE NURSING HOME p 416
2 CARLETON KIRK PL, SAINT JOHN, NB, E2M 5B8
(506) 643-7040   SIC 8051
CARLETON MUSHROOM FARMS LIMITED p 811
6280 DALMENY RD, OSGOODE, ON, K0A 2W0
(613) 826-2868   SIC 0182
CARLETON PLACE & DISTRICT MEMO-RIAL HOSPITAL   p
540
211 LAKE AVE E, CARLETON PLACE, ON, K7C 1J4
(613) 257-2200   SIC 8069
CARLETON PLACE DRUG MART INC p 540
47 LANSDOWNE AVE, CARLETON PLACE, ON, K7C 3S9
(613) 257-1414   SIC 5912
CARLETON PLACE IDA DRUG MART p 540
See CARLETON PLACE DRUG MART INC
CARLETON UNIVERSITY   p 825
1125 COLONEL BY DR, OTTAWA, ON, K1S 5B6
(613) 520-2600   SIC 8221
CARLING FRUIT INC   p 829
1855 CARLING AVE, OTTAWA, ON, K2A 1E4
(613) 722-6106   SIC 5431
CARLING MOTORS CO LTD   p 829
1840 CARLING AVE, OTTAWA, ON, K2A 1C5
(613) 706-8082   SIC 5511
CARLING PROPANE INC   p 620
19752 HOLLAND LANDING RD UNIT 201, HOLLAND LANDING, ON, L9N 0A1
(905) 952-0146   SIC 5541
CARLINGVIEW MANOR   p 830
See REVERA LONG TERM CARE INC
CARLISLE DEVELOPMENTS INC   p 8
2891 SUNRIDGE WAY NE UNIT 230, CAL-GARY, AB, T1Y 7K7
(403) 571-8400   SIC 1521
CARLISLE GROUP   p 8
2891 SUNRIDGE WAY NE UNIT 230, CAL-GARY, AB, T1Y 7K7
(403) 571-8400   SIC 8741
CARLOU MARKETING INC   p 1431
820 45TH ST W, SASKATOON, SK, S7L 6A5
(306) 664-1188   SIC 5047
CARLS GROCERY (DIV OF)   p 469

See POTTIER'S GENERAL STORES LIMITED

CARLSON BODY SHOP SUPPLY LTD *p* 113
5308 97 ST NW, EDMONTON, AB, T6E 5W5
(780) 438-0808   *SIC* 5013

CARLSON MARKETING *p* 1190
See ONE10 CANADA HOLDINGS ULC

CARLSON WAGONLIT *p* 428
See CARLSON WAGONLIT CANADA

CARLSON WAGONLIT CANADA *p* 428
92 ELIZABETH AVE, ST. JOHN'S, NL, A1A
1W7
(709) 726-2900   *SIC* 4724

CARLSON WAGONLIT CANADA *p* 692
2425 MATHESON BLVD E SUITE 600, MIS-
SISSAUGA, ON, L4W 5K4
(905) 740-3500   *SIC* 4724

CARLSON WAGONLIT CANADA *p* 830
885 MEADOWLANDS DR SUITE 401, OT-
TAWA, ON, K2C 3N2
(613) 274-6969   *SIC* 4724

CARLSON WAGONLIT TRAVEL *p* 589
See ELLISON TRAVEL & TOURS LTD

CARLSON WAGONLIT TRAVEL *p* 690
See 1437782 ONTARIO INC

CARLSON WAGONLIT TRAVEL *p* 692
See CARLSON WAGONLIT CANADA

CARLSON WAGONLIT TRAVEL *p* 830
See CARLSON WAGONLIT CANADA

CARLSON, G. W. CONSTRUCTION LTD *p* 233
78 ESPLANADE, NANAIMO, BC, V9R 4Y8
SIC 1542

CARLSTAR GROUP ULC, THE *p* 1010
645 MCMURRAY RD, WATERLOO, ON,
N2V 2B7
(519) 885-0630   *SIC* 5085

CARLSUN ENERGY SOLUTIONS INC *p* 847
1606 BRUCE-SAUGEEN TLINE, PORT EL-
GIN, ON, N0H 2C5
(519) 832-4075   *SIC* 8741

CARLTON CARDS LIMITED *p* 692
1820 MATHESON BLVD UNIT B1, MISSIS-
SAUGA, ON, L4W 0B3
(905) 219-6410   *SIC* 5112

**CARLTON COMPREHENSIVE HIGH
SCHOOL** *p* 1414
*See SASKATCHEWAN RIVER SCHOOL DI-
VISION #119*

CARLTON ONE ENGAGEMENT ULC *p* 851
38 LEEK CRES 4TH FL, RICHMOND HILL,
ON, L4B 4N8
(905) 477-3971   *SIC* 8742

CARLYLE KING BRANCH LIBRARY *p* 1430
See SASKATOON PUBLIC LIBRARY

CARLYLE MOTOR PRODUCTS LTD *p* 1405
GD, CARLYLE, SK, S0C 0R0
(306) 453-6741   *SIC* 5511

CARMACKS ENTERPRISES LTD *p* 127
GD LCD MAIN, FORT MCMURRAY, AB,
T9H 3E2
(780) 598-1376   *SIC* 1611

CARMACKS ENTERPRISES LTD *p* 148
701 25 AVE, NISKU, AB, T9E 0C1
(780) 955-5545   *SIC* 1611

CARMACKS INDUSTRIES *p* 127
See CARMACKS ENTERPRISES LTD

CARMAN'S FOTO SOURCE *p* 895
See 402424 ONTARIO LIMITED

CARMANA PLAZA *p* 314
See KBK NO 51 VENTURES LTD

**CARMANAH TECHNOLOGIES CORPORA-
TION** *p* 339
203 HARBOUR RD SUITE 4, VICTORIA,
BC, V9A 3S2
(250) 380-0052   *SIC* 5074

**CARMANAH TECHNOLOGIES CORPORA-
TION** *p* 339
250 BAY ST, VICTORIA, BC, V9A 3K5
(250) 380-0052   *SIC* 3648

CARMAX *p* 430
See IMPORT AUTO PLAZA INC

CARMEN & FRANKS GARAGE LTD *p* 867
2584 EGLINTON AVE E, SCARBOROUGH,
ON, M1K 2R5
(416) 261-7219   *SIC* 5511

**CARMEN WATCHES DIV OF CARMEN
JEWELLERY** *p* 1325
See BIJOUTERIE CARMEN INC

CARMEUSE LIME (CANADA) LIMITED *p* 621
374681 COUNTY RD 6, INGERSOLL, ON,
N5C 3K5
(519) 423-6283   *SIC* 3274

CARMEUSE NATURAL CHEMICALS *p* 621
See CARMEUSE LIME (CANADA) LIMITED

CARMICHAEL ENGINEERING LTD *p* 1218
3822 AV DE COURTRAI, MONTREAL, QC,
H3S 1C1
(514) 735-4361   *SIC* 8711

**CARNAGHAN THORNE INSURANCE
GROUP INC.** *p* 415
10 CROWN ST, SAINT JOHN, NB, E2L 2X5
(506) 634-1177   *SIC* 6311

CARNAVAL DE QUEBEC INC *p* 1260
205 BOUL DES CEDRES, QUEBEC, QC,
G1L 1N8
(418) 626-3716   *SIC* 7999

CARNBRO LTD *p* 598
HWY 540 B, GORE BAY, ON, P0P 1H0
(705) 282-2723   *SIC* 4731

CARNEIL GROUP INC, THE *p* 365
1035 MISSION ST, WINNIPEG, MB, R2J
0A4
(204) 233-0671   *SIC* 1721

CARO ANALYTICAL SERVICES LTD *p* 254
4011 VIKING WAY UNIT 110, RICHMOND,
BC, V6V 2K9
(604) 279-1499   *SIC* 8734

CAROL AUTOMOBILE LIMITED *p* 425
55 AVALON DR, LABRADOR CITY, NL, A2V
1K3
(709) 944-2000   *SIC* 5511

**CAROL WABUSH CO-OP SOCIETY LIM-
ITED** *p* 425
500 VANIER AVE, LABRADOR CITY, NL,
A2V 2W7
SIC 5411

CAROLINA HOMES INC *p* 69
230 EVERSYDE BLVD SW SUITE 2101,
CALGARY, AB, T2Y 0J4
(403) 256-5544   *SIC* 1521

CARON *p* 1102
*See MAISON DE LA POMME DE FRE-
LIGHSBURG INC*

CARON & GUAY INC *p* 1055
95 RUE INDUSTRIELLE, BEAUPRE, QC,
G0A 1E0
(418) 827-2459   *SIC* 3089

CARON & GUAY INC *p* 1261
615 BOUL PIERRE-BERTRAND, QUEBEC,
QC, G1M 3J3
(418) 683-7534   *SIC* 5211

CARON AUTOMOBILES INC *p* 1159
75 BOUL TACHE E, MONTMAGNY, QC,
G5V 1B6
(418) 248-7877   *SIC* 5511

CARON CONTRUCTION *p* 1295
See CONSTRUCTIONS BRI INC, LES

CARON ET GUAY, PORTES & FENETRES *p* 1055
See CARON & GUAY INC

CARON TRANSLATION CENTRE LTD *p* 822
130 SLATER ST SUITE 700, OTTAWA, ON,
K1P 6E2
(613) 230-4611   *SIC* 7389

CARON, CAMILLE INC *p* 1150
9 RUE NOTTAWAY, MATAGAMI, QC, J0Y
2A0
SIC 5211

CAROPAC INC *p* 1357
736 3E RANG, SAINTE-CLOTILDE-DE-
CHATEAUGUAY, QC, J0L 1W0
(450) 826-3145   *SIC* 5148

CAROPHIL INC *p* 1219

CARPE DIEM *p* 499
*See CARPE DIEM RESIDENTIAL TREAT-
MENT HOMES FOR CHILDREN INC*

**CARPE DIEM RESIDENTIAL TREATMENT
HOMES FOR CHILDREN INC** *p* 499
9355 DIXIE RD, BRAMPTON, ON, L6S 1J7
(905) 799-2947   *SIC* 8361

CARPEDIA GROUP INTERNATIONAL INC *p* 800
75 NAVY ST, OAKVILLE, ON, L6J 2Z1
(905) 337-3407   *SIC* 8742

CARPENTER CANADA CO *p* 14
5800 36 ST SE, CALGARY, AB, T2C 2A9
(403) 279-2466   *SIC* 3089

CARPENTER CANADA CO *p* 1030
500 HANLAN RD, WOODBRIDGE, ON, L4L
3P6
(416) 743-5689   *SIC* 1751

**CARPENTERS DISTRICT COUNCIL OF
ONTARIO TRAINING TRUST FUND, THE** *p* 1030
222 ROWNTREE DAIRY RD, WOOD-
BRIDGE, ON, L4L 9T2
SIC 8699

**CARPENTERS LOCAL UNION 27 JOINT
APPRENTICESHIP AND TRAINING TRUST
FUND INC** *p* 1030
222 ROWNTREE DAIRY RD, WOOD-
BRIDGE, ON, L4L 9T2
(905) 652-5507   *SIC* 8331

CARPET CARE SYSTEMS *p* 580
34 ASHMOUNT CRES, ETOBICOKE, ON,
M9R 1C7
(416) 247-7311   *SIC* 5087

CARPETTE MULTI DESIGN C.M.D. INC *p* 1227
8134 BOUL DECARIE BUREAU A, MON-
TREAL, QC, H4P 2S8
(514) 344-8877   *SIC* 5023

CARPETTES LANART INC *p* 1317
300 RUE SAINT-LOUIS, SAINT-JEAN-SUR-
RICHELIEU, QC, J3B 1Y4
(450) 348-4843   *SIC* 5023

CARPROOF *p* 653
See CARPROOF CORPORATION

CARPROOF CORPORATION *p* 653
130 DUFFERIN AVE SUITE 1101, LON-
DON, ON, N6A 5R2
(866) 835-8612   *SIC* 6411

CARPROOF.COM *p* 653
See 3823202 CANADA INC

CARQUEST CANADA LTD *p* 583
35 WORCESTER RD SUITE 1, ETOBI-
COKE, ON, M9W 1K9
(416) 679-3045   *SIC* 4225

CARQUEST CANADA LTD *p* 1064
1670 RUE EIFFEL BUREAU 100,
BOUCHERVILLE, QC, J4B 7W1
(450) 641-5757   *SIC* 4225

CARQUEST DISTRIBUTION CENTER *p* 1064
See CARQUEST CANADA LTD

**CARR & COMPANY INSURANCE BRO-
KERS LTD** *p* 819
1980 OGILVIE RD, OTTAWA, ON, K1J 9L3
(613) 706-1806   *SIC* 6411

CARREFOUR 440 CHEVROLET *p* 1086
*See GROUPE AUTOMOBILES LAURUS
LTEE*

CARREFOUR CHAREST *p* 1272
*See FONDS DE PLACEMENT IMMOBILIER
COMINAR*

**CARREFOUR DE LA SANTE ET DES SER-
VICES SOCIAUX DU VAL-SAINT-FRANCOIS** *p* 1403
79 RUE ALLEN BUREAU 501, WINDSOR,
QC, J1S 2P8
(819) 542-2777   *SIC* 8361

**CARREFOUR DE LA SSS DU VAL SAINT-
FRANCOIS** *p* 1403

*See CARREFOUR DE LA SANTE ET
DES SERVICES SOCIAUX DU VAL-SAINT-
FRANCOIS*

**CARREFOUR DE LA VOITURE IMPORTEE
INC** *p* 1311
200 RUE DANIEL-JOHNSON E, SAINT-
HYACINTHE, QC, J2S 8W5
(514) 856-7878   *SIC* 5511

CARREFOUR DU CAMION R.D.L. *p* 1286
*See CAMIONS FREIGHTLINER RIVIERE-
DU-LOUP INC*

CARREFOUR FINANCIER SOLIDAIRE *p* 1174
*See FONDACTION, LE FONDS DE DEVEL-
OPPEMENT DE LA CSN POUR LA COOP-
ERATION ET L'EMPLOI*

CARREFOUR FORMATION MAURICIE *p* 1368
*See COMMISSION SCOLAIRE DE
L'ENERGIE*

CARREFOUR FRONTENAC *p* 1382
See 9130-1093 QUEBEC INC

**CARREFOUR JEUNESSE-EMPLOI TROIS-
RIVIERES/MRC DES CHENAUX** *p* 1384
580 RUE BARKOFF BUREAU 300, TROIS-
RIVIERES, QC, G8T 9T7
(819) 376-0179   *SIC* 8699

CARREFOUR NISSAN *p* 1107
See 174762 CANADA INC

CARREFOUR RICHELIEU *p* 1197
*See IMMEUBLES CARREFOUR RICHE-
LIEU LTEE, LES*

CARREFOUR SAINT-GEORGES *p* 1271
See 9130-1093 QUEBEC INC

**CARREFOUR SUZUKI-SUBARU AUTOMO-
BILES** *p* 1361
See 9020-7697 QUEBEC INC

**CARRIAGE HILLS RESORT CORPORA-
TION** *p* 484
1101 HORSESHOE VALLEY RD W, BAR-
RIE, ON, L4M 4Y8
(705) 835-0087   *SIC* 7011

**CARRIAGE HILLS VACATION OWNERS
ASSOCIATION** *p* 880
90 HIGHLAND DR, SHANTY BAY, ON, L0L
2L0
(705) 835-5858   *SIC* 7011

CARRIAGE HOUSE INN *p* 34
See CARRIAGE HOUSE MOTOR INN LTD

CARRIAGE HOUSE MOTOR INN LTD *p* 34
9030 MACLEOD TRAIL SE, CALGARY, AB,
T2H 0M4
(403) 253-1101   *SIC* 7011

CARRIER CENTERS INC *p* 1035
645 ATHLONE AVE, WOODSTOCK, ON,
N4S 7V8
(519) 539-0971   *SIC* 5511

CARRIER EMERGENCY *p* 514
See CARRIER TRUCK CENTER INC

CARRIER EMERGENCY *p* 1035
See CARRIER TRUCK CENTER INC

CARRIER ENTERPRISE CANADA, L.P. *p* 734
195 STATESMAN DR, MISSISSAUGA, ON,
L5S 1X4
(905) 672-0606   *SIC* 5075

CARRIER ENTERPRISE CANADA, L.P. *p* 1361
2025 BOUL DAGENAIS O, SAINTE-ROSE,
QC, H7L 5V1
(514) 324-5050   *SIC* 5075

CARRIER FOREST PRODUCTS LTD *p* 250
4722 CONTINENTAL WAY, PRINCE
GEORGE, BC, V2N 5S5
(250) 963-9664   *SIC* 3599

CARRIER LUMBER LTD *p* 250
4722 CONTINENTAL WAY, PRINCE
GEORGE, BC, V2N 5S5
(250) 563-9271   *SIC* 2421

CARRIER SEKANI FAMILY SERVICES SO-

CIETY *p*
249
987 4TH AVE, PRINCE GEORGE, BC, V2L
3H7
(250) 562-3591 *SIC* 8399
CARRIER TRUCK CENTER INC *p* 514
6 EDMONDSON ST, BRANTFORD, ON,
N3R 7J3
(519) 752-5431 *SIC* 5511
CARRIER TRUCK CENTER INC *p* 1035
645 ATHLONE AVE, WOODSTOCK, ON,
N4S 7V8
(519) 539-9837 *SIC* 5531
CARRIERE BERNIER LTEE *p* 1316
25 CH DU PETIT-BERNIER, SAINT-JEAN-
SUR-RICHELIEU, QC, J2Y 1B8
(514) 875-2841 *SIC* 1422
CARRIERE D'ACTON VALE LTEE *p* 1044
525 116 RTE, ACTON VALE, QC, J0H 1A0
(450) 546-3201 *SIC* 3273
CARRIERE INDUSTRIAL SUPPLY LIMITED
p 647
190 MAGILL ST, LIVELY, ON, P3Y 1K7
(705) 692-4784 *SIC* 5082
**CARRIERE MONT-BRUNO DIVISION DE
CONSTRUCTION DJL** *p* 1064
See *CONSTRUCTION DJL INC*
CARRIERE ST-EUSTACHE LTEE *p* 1300
555 AV MATHERS, SAINT-EUSTACHE, QC,
J7P 4C1
(450) 430-9090 *SIC* 1422
**CARRIERES DE ST-DOMINIQUE LTEE,
LES** *p* 1299
700 RUE PRINCIPALE, SAINT-
DOMINIQUE, QC, J0H 1L0
(450) 774-2591 *SIC* 3273
CARRIERES DUCHARME INC, LES *p* 1113
564 CH DE COVEY HILL, HAVELOCK, QC,
J0S 2C0
(450) 247-2787 *SIC* 3281
CARRINGTON-O'BRIEN FOODS LTD *p* 158
GD, ROCKY MOUNTAIN HOUSE, AB, T4T
1T1
(403) 845-2110 *SIC* 5411
CARRINGTONS BUILDING CENTRE LTD *p*
899
82 LORNE ST, SUDBURY, ON, P3C 4N8
(705) 673-9511 *SIC* 5211
CARROLL SOUTH SHORE MOTORS INC *p*
441
GD LCD MAIN, BRIDGEWATER, NS, B4V
2V8
(902) 543-2493 *SIC* 5511
CARROLL SOUTH SORE GM *p* 441
See *CARROLL SOUTH SHORE MOTORS
INC*
CARROSSIER PROCOLOR PIE IX *p* 1170
See *PIE IX DODGE CHRYSLER 2000 INC*
**CARROSSIER PROCOLOR SHERBROOKE
OUEST** *p* 1373
See *AUTOMOBILES VAL ESTRIE INC*
CARROSSIER PROCOLOR WEEDON *p*
1401
See *WEEDON AUTOMOBILE (1977) INC*
**CARROT RIVER CO-OPERATIVE LIMITED,
THE** *p* 1405
1002 MAIN ST, CARROT RIVER, SK, S0E
0L0
(306) 768-2622 *SIC* 8699
CARRUS INVESTMENTS LTD *p* 808
GD STN A, ORANGEVILLE, ON, L9W 2Z4
(519) 941-6221 *SIC* 5511
CARRUTHERS NICOL INSURANCE INC *p*
835
1230 2ND AVE E, OWEN SOUND, ON, N4K
2J3
(519) 376-5350 *SIC* 6411
CARS R US LTD *p* 461
183 SACKVILLE DR, LOWER SACKVILLE,
NS, B4C 2R5
(902) 864-1109 *SIC* 5521
CARSON & WEEKS INSURANCE BROKERS LIMITED *p*
665

59 MAIN ST N, MARKHAM, ON, L3P 1X7
(905) 294-0722 *SIC* 6411
CARSON AIR LTD *p* 218
00-6197 AIRPORT WAY, KELOWNA, BC,
V1V 2S2
(250) 765-7776 *SIC* 4522
CARSON CUSTOM BROKERS LIMITED *p*
278
17735 1 AVE SUITE 260, SURREY, BC, V3Z
9S1
(604) 538-4966 *SIC* 4731
CARSON FEED & SUPPLY, DIV OF *p* 646
See *DAVID CARSON FARMS & AUCTION
SERVICES LTD*
CARSON FREIGHT SYSTEMS *p* 278
See *CARSON CUSTOM BROKERS LIMITED*
CARSON WELDING *p* 1438
See *AECOM CANADA LTD*
CARSON'S *p* 839
See *883481 ONTARIO INC*
CARSTAR AUTOMOTIVE CANADA *p* 615
See *1716871 ONTARIO INC*
CARTE INTERNATIONAL INC *p* 369
1995 LOGAN AVE, WINNIPEG, MB, R2R
0H8
(204) 633-7220 *SIC* 3612
CARTE INTERNATIONAL INC *p* 1074
2032 AV BOURGOGNE BUREAU 107,
CHAMBLY, QC, J3L 1Z6
(450) 447-5815 *SIC* 5065
CARTEL PACKAGING *p* 1252
See *PENTAGON GRAPHICS LTD*
CARTER *p* 511
72 LINKS LANE, BRAMPTON, ON, L6Y 5H1
(416) 574-3770 *SIC* 4724
CARTER BROTHERS LTD *p* 404
1797 ROUTE 134, LAKEVILLE-
WESTMORLAND, NB, E1H 1A1
(506) 383-9150 *SIC* 1623
**CARTER CHEVROLET CADILLAC BUICK
GMC BURNABY LTD** *p* 185
4550 LOUGHEED HWY, BURNABY, BC,
V5C 3Z5
(604) 291-6474 *SIC* 5511
**CARTER CHEVROLET CADILLAC BUICK
GMC NORTHSHORE LTD** *p* 241
800 AUTOMALL DR, NORTH VANCOUVER, BC, V7P 3R8
(604) 987-5231 *SIC* 5511
CARTER DODGE CHRYSLER LTD *p* 185
4650 LOUGHEED HWY, BURNABY, BC,
V5C 4A6
(604) 299-2681 *SIC* 5511
CARTER GM *p* 241
See *CARTER CHEVROLET CADILLAC
BUICK GMC NORTHSHORE LTD*
CARTER HONDA *p* 320
See *CARTER MOTOR CARS LTD*
CARTER MOTOR CARS LTD *p* 320
2390 BURRARD ST, VANCOUVER, BC,
V6J 3J1
(604) 736-2821 *SIC* 5511
CARTER, DWAYNE ENTERPRISES LTD *p*
386
3401 PORTAGE AVE, WINNIPEG, MB, R3K
0W9
(204) 949-6022 *SIC* 5812
CARTER, HOWARD LEASE LTD *p* 185
4550 LOUGHEED HWY, BURNABY, BC,
V5C 3Z5
(604) 291-8899 *SIC* 7515
CARTER, JACK CHEVROLET CADILLAC *p*
70
See *GLENMAC CORPORATION LTD*
CARTES CARLTON *p* 1131
See *SFP CANADA LTD*
**CARTES, TIMBRES & MONNAIES STE-
FOY** *p*
1271
See *CARTES, TIMBRES ET MONNAIE
STE-FOY INC*
**CARTES, TIMBRES ET MONNAIE STE-FOY
INC** *p* 1271

2740 BOUL LAURIER, QUEBEC, QC, G1V
4P7
(418) 658-5639 *SIC* 7389
CARTHO SERVICES *p* 825
See *OSLER, HOSKIN & HARCOURT LLP*
CARTHOS SERVICES LP *p* 986
1 1ST CANADIAN PL, TORONTO, ON, M5X
1B8
(416) 362-2111 *SIC* 8741
CARTHOS SERVICES LP *p* 1202
1000 RUE DE LA GAUCHETIERE O BUREAU 2100, MONTREAL, QC, H3B 4W5
(514) 904-8100 *SIC* 8111
CARTIER *p* 1297
See *EMBALLAGES JEAN CARTIER INC*
CARTIER CHEVROLET BUICK GMC LTEE
p 1281
1475 BOUL PIE-XI S, QUEBEC, QC, G3K
1H1
(418) 847-6000 *SIC* 5511
CARTIER ENERGIE EOLIENNE INC *p* 1144
1111 RUE SAINT-CHARLES O BUREAU
1155E, LONGUEUIL, QC, J4K 5G4
(450) 928-0426 *SIC* 4911
CARTIER HOUSE CARE CENTRE LTD *p*
200
1419 CARTIER AVE, COQUITLAM, BC,
V3K 2C6
(604) 939-4654 *SIC* 8361
CARTIER KITCHENS INC *p* 501
8 CHELSEA LANE, BRAMPTON, ON, L6T
3Y4
(905) 793-0063 *SIC* 2434
CARTIER PLACE SUITE HOTEL AND RESIDENCE *p*
834
See *FIDELITAS HOLDING COMPANY LIMITED*
CARTOUCHES CERTIFIEES INC *p* 1183
160 RUE SAINT-VIATEUR E BUREAU 411,
MONTREAL, QC, H2T 1A8
(888) 573-6787 *SIC* 5085
CARUSO CLUB *p* 900
See *SOCIETY CARUSO CLUB OF SUDBURY*
CARVEST PROPERTIES LIMITED *p* 662
3800 COLONEL TALBOT RD, LONDON,
ON, N6P 1H5
(519) 653-4124 *SIC* 6531
CARVETH CARE CENTRE *p* 592
See *CARVETH NURSING HOME LIMITED*
CARVETH NURSING HOME LIMITED *p* 592
375 JAMES ST, GANANOQUE, ON, K7G
2Z1
(613) 382-4752 *SIC* 8051
CAS OF ALGOMA *p* 862
See *CHILDREN'S AID SOCIETY OF ALGOMA*
CASA BELLA WINDOWS INC *p* 685
7630 AIRPORT RD, MISSISSAUGA, ON,
L4T 4G6
(416) 650-1033 *SIC* 3089
CASA BELLA WINDOWS INC *p* 786
124 NORFINCH DR, NORTH YORK, ON,
M3N 1X1
(416) 650-1033 *SIC* 2431
CASA CUBANA *p* 1327
See *SPIKE MARKS INC*
CASA ITALIA *p* 507
See *ZADI FOODS LIMITED*
CASA VERDE HEALTH CENTRE *p* 784
See *PARAGON HEALTH CARE INC*
CASANA FURNITURE COMPANY LTD *p*
363
90 LEXINGTON PK, WINNIPEG, MB, R2G
4H2
(204) 988-3189 *SIC* 5021
CASATI NATURAL GAS *p* 498
7 ADRIATIC CRES, BRAMPTON, ON, L6P
1W7
(905) 460-4023 *SIC* 4924
CASAVANT FRERES S.E.C *p* 1311
900 RUE GIROUARD E, SAINT-
HYACINTHE, QC, J2S 2Y2

(450) 773-5001 *SIC* 3931
CASCADE (CANADA) LTD *p* 692
5570 TIMBERLEA BLVD, MISSISSAUGA,
ON, L4W 4M6
(905) 629-7777 *SIC* 3537
CASCADE (CANADA) LTD *p* 849
4 NICHOLAS BEAVER RD, PUSLINCH, ON,
N0B 2J0
(519) 763-3675 *SIC* 3537
CASCADE AEROSPACE INC *p* 176
1337 TOWNLINE RD, ABBOTSFORD, BC,
V2T 6E1
(604) 850-7372 *SIC* 4581
CASCADE AQUA-TECH LTD *p* 184
3215 NORLAND AVE SUITE 100, BURNABY, BC, V5B 3A9
(604) 291-6101 *SIC* 5169
CASCADE BOXBOARD GROUP, THE *p* 734
See *CASCADES CANADA ULC*
**CASCADE INSURANCE AGENCIES
(BURNABY) INC** *p* 190
4683 KINGSWAY, BURNABY, BC, V5H 2B3
SIC 6411
CASCADE PROCESS CONTROLS LTD *p* 7
420 AQUADUCT DR, BROOKS. AB, T1R
1C8
(403) 362-4722 *SIC* 1731
CASCADE SERVICES LTD *p* 213
9619 81 AVE, FORT ST. JOHN, BC, V1J 6P6
(250) 785-0236 *SIC* 1389
CASCADE SONOCO DIV KINGSEY FALLS
p 1117
See *CASCADES SONOCO INC*
CASCADES *p* 1117
See *CASCADES CANADA ULC*
**CASCADES BOXBOARD GROUP
TORONTO** *p* 920
See *CASCADES CANADA ULC*
CASCADES BOXBOARD GROUP, DIV OF *p*
367
See *CASCADES CANADA ULC*
CASCADES CANADA ULC *p* 34
416 58 AVE SE, CALGARY, AB, T2H 0P4
(403) 531-3800 *SIC* 2653
CASCADES CANADA ULC *p* 235
800 MAUGHAN RD, NANAIMO, BC, V9X
1J2
(250) 722-3396 *SIC* 4953
CASCADES CANADA ULC *p* 254
3300 VIKING WAY, RICHMOND, BC, V6V
1N6
(604) 273-7321 *SIC* 2653
CASCADES CANADA ULC *p* 367
531 GOLSPIE ST, WINNIPEG, MB, R2K
2T9
(204) 667-6600 *SIC* 2657
CASCADES CANADA ULC *p* 382
680 WALL ST, WINNIPEG, MB, R3G 2T8
(204) 786-5761 *SIC* 2653
CASCADES CANADA ULC *p* 408
232 BAIG BLVD, MONCTON, NB, E1E 1C8
(506) 869-2200 *SIC* 2653
CASCADES CANADA ULC *p* 486
35 FRASER CRT, BARRIE, ON, L4N 5J5
(705) 737-0470 *SIC* 5999
CASCADES CANADA ULC *p* 515
434 HENRY ST, BRANTFORD, ON, N3S
7W1
(519) 756-5264 *SIC* 4953
CASCADES CANADA ULC *p* 550
655 CREDITSTONE RD SUITE 41, CONCORD, ON, L4K 5P9
(905) 760-3900 *SIC* 2653
CASCADES CANADA ULC *p* 571
450 EVANS AVE, ETOBICOKE, ON, M8W
2T5
(416) 255-8541 *SIC* 2657
CASCADES CANADA ULC *p* 574
66 SHORNCLIFFE RD, ETOBICOKE, ON,
M8Z 5K1
(416) 231-2525 *SIC* 2611
CASCADES CANADA ULC *p* 734
7447 BRAMALEA RD, MISSISSAUGA, ON,
L5S 1C4

(905) 671-2940 *SIC 2631*
CASCADES CANADA ULC *p 734*
7830 TRANMERE DR SUITE UNIT, MISSISSAUGA, ON, L5S 1L9
(905) 678-8211 *SIC 7389*
CASCADES CANADA ULC *p 864*
5910 FINCH AVE E, SCARBOROUGH, ON, M1B 5P8
(416) 412-3500 *SIC 2679*
CASCADES CANADA ULC *p 888*
304 JAMES ST S, ST MARYS, ON, N4X 1B7
(519) 284-1840 *SIC 2653*
CASCADES CANADA ULC *p 920*
495 COMMISSIONERS ST, TORONTO, ON, M4M 1A5
(416) 461-8261 *SIC 2631*
CASCADES CANADA ULC *p 998*
300 MARMORA ST, TRENTON, ON, K8V 5R8
SIC 2679
CASCADES CANADA ULC *p 1072*
75 BOUL MARIE-VICTORIN, CANDIAC, QC, J5R 1C2
(450) 444-6500 *SIC 2621*
CASCADES CANADA ULC *p 1072*
77 BOUL MARIE-VICTORIN, CANDIAC, QC, J5R 1C2
(450) 444-6400 *SIC 2676*
CASCADES CANADA ULC *p 1096*
500 RUE LAUZON, DRUMMONDVILLE, QC, J2B 2Z3
(819) 472-5757 *SIC 3089*
CASCADES CANADA ULC *p 1100*
248 RUE WARNER, EAST ANGUS, QC, J0B 1R0
(819) 832-5300 *SIC 2631*
CASCADES CANADA ULC *p 1116*
4010 CH SAINT-ANDRE, JONQUIERE, QC, G7Z 0A5
SIC 2631
CASCADES CANADA ULC *p 1117*
467 BOUL MARIE-VICTORIN, KINGSEY FALLS, QC, J0A 1B0
(819) 363-5600 *SIC 2676*
CASCADES CANADA ULC *p 1117*
404 BOUL MARIE-VICTORIN, KINGSEY FALLS, QC, J0A 1B0
(819) 363-5100 *SIC 6712*
CASCADES CANADA ULC *p 1126*
63 BOUL SAINT-JOSEPH, LACHINE, QC, H8S 2K9
(514) 595-2870 *SIC 4953*
CASCADES CANADA ULC *p 1129*
115 RUE DE LA PRINCESSE, LACHUTE, QC, J8H 4M3
(450) 562-8585 *SIC 2676*
CASCADES CANADA ULC *p 1166*
2755 RUE VIAU, MONTREAL, QC, H1V 3J4
(514) 251-3800 *SIC 2652*
CASCADES CANADA ULC *p 1166*
2755 RUE VIAU, MONTREAL, QC, H1V 3J4
(514) 251-3800 *SIC 2631*
CASCADES CANADA ULC *p 1236*
2345 DES LAURENTIDES (A-15) E, MONTREAL, QC, H7S 1Z7
(450) 688-1152 *SIC 2676*
CASCADES CANADA ULC *p 1295*
1061 RUE PARENT, SAINT-BRUNO, QC, J3V 6R7
(450) 461-8600 *SIC 2631*
CASCADES CANADA ULC *p 1378*
520 RUE COMMERCIALE N, TEMISCOUATA-SUR-LE-LAC, QC, G0L 1E0
(418) 854-2803 *SIC 2631*
CASCADES CANADA ULC *p 1394*
400 RUE FORBES, VAUDREUIL-DORION, QC, J7V 6N8
(450) 455-5731 *SIC 2631*
CASCADES CANADA ULC *p 1399*
400 BOUL DE LA BONAVENTURE, VICTORIAVILLE, QC, G6T 1V8
(819) 758-3177 *SIC 2653*
CASCADES CENTRE DE TRANSFORMA-

TION *p*
1319
See ENTREPRISES ROLLAND INC, LES
CASCADES CIP, UNE DIV DE CASCADES CANADA ULC *p 1117*
See CASCADES CS+ INC
CASCADES CONTAINER BOARD PACKAGING *p*
998
See CASCADES CANADA ULC
CASCADES CONTAINERBOARD PACKAGING - ART & DIE *p*
571
See CASCADES CANADA ULC
CASCADES CONTAINERBOARD PACKAGING - JELLCO *p*
486
See CASCADES CANADA ULC
CASCADES CONTAINERBOARD PACKAGING - MISSISSAUGA *p*
734
See CASCADES CANADA ULC
CASCADES CS+ INC *p 1069*
9500 AV ILLINOIS, BROSSARD, QC, J4Y 3B7
(450) 923-3300 *SIC 8711*
CASCADES CS+ INC *p 1117*
15 RUE LAMONTAGNE, KINGSEY FALLS, QC, J0A 1B0
(819) 363-5971 *SIC 8711*
CASCADES CS+ INC *p 1117*
471 BOUL MARIE-VICTORIN, KINGSEY FALLS, QC, J0A 1B0
(819) 363-5700 *SIC 8711*
CASCADES CS+ INC *p 1117*
465 BOUL MARIE-VICTORIN, KINGSEY FALLS, QC, J0A 1B0
(819) 363-5920 *SIC 2631*
CASCADES EMBALLAGE CARTONCAISSE *p*
1166
See CASCADES CANADA ULC
CASCADES EMBALLAGE CARTONCAISSE, UNE DIVISION DE CASCADES CANADA ULC *p 1295*
See CASCADES CANADA ULC
CASCADES GIE *p 1117*
See CASCADES CS+ INC
CASCADES GROUPE PAPIERS FINS INC *p*
720
7280 WEST CREDIT AVE, MISSISSAUGA, ON, L5N 5N1
(905) 813-9400 *SIC 2621*
CASCADES GROUPE TISSU *p 1117*
See CASCADES CANADA ULC
CASCADES GROUPE TISSU LACHUTE *p*
1129
See CASCADES CANADA ULC
CASCADES GROUPE TISSU-CANDIAC *p*
1072
See CASCADES CANADA ULC
CASCADES GROUPE TISSUS LAVAL *p*
1236
See CASCADES CANADA ULC
CASCADES INC *p 1117*
455 BOUL MARIE-VICTORIN, KINGSEY FALLS, QC, J0A 1B0
(819) 363-5300 *SIC 3081*
CASCADES INC *p 1117*
404 BOUL MARIE-VICTORIN, KINGSEY FALLS, QC, J0A 1B0
(819) 363-5100 *SIC 2621*
CASCADES INOPAK *p 1096*
See CASCADES CANADA ULC
CASCADES PLASTIQUES DIV DE *p 1117*
See CASCADES INC
CASCADES RECOVERY+ *p 235*
See CASCADES CANADA ULC
CASCADES RECOVERY+ *p 515*
See CASCADES CANADA ULC
CASCADES RECOVERY+ - TORONTO *p*
574
See CASCADES CANADA ULC
CASCADES RECUPERATION + *p 1126*

See CASCADES CANADA ULC
CASCADES SONOCO INC *p 1117*
457 BOUL MARIE-VICTORIN, KINGSEY FALLS, QC, J0A 1B0
(819) 363-5400 *SIC 2679*
CASCADES TISSUE GROUP - CANDIAC *p*
1072
See CASCADES CANADA ULC
CASCADES TRANSIT *p 1117*
See CASCADES TRANSPORT INC
CASCADES TRANSPORT INC *p 1117*
2 RUE PARENTEAU, KINGSEY FALLS, QC, J0A 1B0
(819) 363-5800 *SIC 4213*
CASCADIA METALS LTD *p 208*
7630 BERG RD, DELTA, BC, V4G 1G4
(604) 946-3890 *SIC 5051*
CASCADIA MOTIVATION INC *p 153*
4646 RIVERSIDE DR SUITE 14A, RED DEER, AB, T4N 6Y5
(403) 340-8687 *SIC 4724*
CASE 'N DRUM OIL INC *p 657*
3462 WHITE OAK RD, LONDON, ON, N6E 2Z9
(519) 681-3772 *SIC 5172*
CASE MANOR *p 494*
28 BOYD ST, BOBCAYGEON, ON, K0M 1A0
(705) 738-2374 *SIC 8051*
CASE NEW HOLLAND *p 1434*
See CNH INDUSTRIAL CANADA, LTD
CASERA CREDIT UNION LIMITED *p 362*
1300 PLESSIS RD, WINNIPEG, MB, R2C 2Y6
(204) 958-6300 *SIC 6062*
CASEY CONCRETE LIMITED *p 438*
96 PARK ST, AMHERST, NS, B4H 2R7
(902) 667-3395 *SIC 3273*
CASEY CONCRETE LIMITED *p 468*
69 GLENWOOD DR, TRURO, NS, B2N 1E9
(902) 895-1618 *SIC 3273*
CASEY HOUSE HOSPICE INC *p 931*
119 ISABELLA ST, TORONTO, ON, M4Y 1P2
(416) 962-7600 *SIC 8051*
CASEY TRANSPORTATION COMPANY LIMITED *p 629*
1312 WELLINGTON ST W SUITE 1, KING CITY, ON, L7B 1K5
SIC 4151
CASH & CARRY *p 182*
See H.Y. LOUIE CO. LIMITED
CASH & CARRY CARPETS *p 145*
See JOUJAN BROTHERS FLOORING INC
CASH & CARRY LUMBER MART LTD *p*
1412
11301 6TH AVE, NORTH BATTLEFORD, SK, S9A 2N5
(306) 445-3350 *SIC 5211*
CASH 4 YOU CORP *p 533*
250 DUNDAS ST S UNIT 10, CAMBRIDGE, ON, N1R 8A8
(519) 620-1900 *SIC 6099*
CASH BACK *p 50*
See H & R BLOCK CANADA, INC
CASH CANADA FINANCIAL CENTERS LTD *p 108*
8170 50 ST NW SUITE 325, EDMONTON, AB, T6B 1E6
(780) 424-1080 *SIC 6163*
CASH NOW *p 667*
See CASH NOWPLUS INC
CASH NOWPLUS INC *p 667*
3100 STEELES AVE E SUITE 906, MARKHAM, ON, L3R 8T3
(905) 470-0084 *SIC 6099*
CASH STORE FINANCIAL SERVICES INC, THE *p 105*
15511 123 AVE NW, EDMONTON, AB, T5V 0C3
(780) 408-5110 *SIC 6141*
CASH STORE INC, THE *p 99*
17631 103 AVE NW, EDMONTON, AB, T5S 1N8
(780) 408-5110 *SIC 6141*

CASHN *p 998*
See CHILDREN'S AID SOCIETY OF HALDIMAND AND NORFOLK, THE
CASHTECH CURRENCY PRODUCTS *p 736*
See QWINSTAR CANADA INC
CASINO ABS *p 112*
See PURE CANADIAN GAMING CORP
CASINO BY VANSHAW *p 147*
See VANSHAW ENTERPRISES LTD
CASINO DE CHARLEVOIX, LE *p 1122*
See SOCIETE DES CASINOS DU QUEBEC INC, LA
CASINO DE MONTREAL *p 1199*
See SOCIETE DES CASINOS DU QUEBEC INC, LA
CASINO DE MONTREAL *p 1212*
See SOCIETE DES CASINOS DU QUEBEC INC, LA
CASINO GATINEAU ACURA *p 1106*
See 6358101 CANADA INC
CASINO LETHBRIDGE *p 142*
See PURE CANADIAN GAMING CORP
CASINO NANAIMO *p 233*
See GREAT CANADIAN CASINOS INC
CASINO NEW NOUVEAU-BRUNSWICK *p*
409
See SONCO GAMING NEW BRUNSWICK LIMITED PARTNERSHIP
CASINO NIAGARA LIMITED *p 758*
5705 FALLS AVE, NIAGARA FALLS, ON, L2G 3K6
(905) 374-3598 *SIC 7999*
CASINO NIAGARA LIMITED *p 758*
5705 FALLS AVE, NIAGARA FALLS, ON, L2G 7M9
(905) 374-6928 *SIC 7999*
CASINO RAMA INC *p 849*
5899 RAMA RD, RAMA, ON, L3V 6H6
(705) 329-3325 *SIC 7999*
CASINO REGINA *p 1418*
See SASKATCHEWAN GAMING CORPORATION
CASINO TROPICAL PLANTS LTD. *p 271*
4148 184TH ST, SURREY, BC, V3S 0R5
(604) 576-1156 *SIC 0179*
CASINOYELLOWHEAD *p 106*
See PURE CANADIAN GAMING CORP
CASIO CANADA LTD *p 667*
141 MCPHERSON ST, MARKHAM, ON, L3R 3L3
(905) 248-4400 *SIC 5099*
CASLUMBER INC *p 1235*
2885 BOUL DAGENAIS O, MONTREAL, QC, H7P 1T2
(450) 622-2420 *SIC 6712*
CASMAN BUILDING SOLUTIONS INC *p*
127
330 MACKENZIE BLVD, FORT MCMURRAY, AB, T9H 4C4
(780) 791-9283 *SIC 1542*
CASMAN GROUP OF COMPANIES *p 127*
See CASMAN INC
CASMAN INC *p 127*
330 MACKENZIE BLVD, FORT MCMURRAY, AB, T9H 4C4
(780) 791-9283 *SIC 1611*
CASMAN INDUSTRIAL CONSTRUCTION INC *p 127*
330 MACKENZIE BLVD, FORT MCMURRAY, AB, T9H 4C4
(780) 791-9283 *SIC 1629*
CASPEN DRUGS LTD *p 124*
3945 34 ST NW SUITE 371, EDMONTON, AB, T6T 1L5
(780) 461-6768 *SIC 5912*
CASSELLHOLME HOME FOR THE AGED *p 762*
400 OLIVE ST, NORTH BAY, ON, P1B 6J4
(705) 474-4250 *SIC 8361*
CASSELS BROCK & BLACKWELL LLP *p 950*
40 KING ST W SUITE 2100, TORONTO, ON, M5H 3C2
(416) 869-5300 *SIC 8111*

▲ Public Company   ■ Public Company Family Member   **HQ** Headquarters   **BR** Branch   **SL** Single Location

CASSENS TRANSPORT LTD   p 661
1237 GREEN VALLEY RD, LONDON, ON, N6N 1E4
(519) 690-2603   SIC 4212
CASSIDY'S TRANSFER & STORAGE LIMITED   p 838
1001 MCKAY ST, PEMBROKE, ON, K8A 6X7
(613) 735-6881   SIC 4213
CASSIE CO ENTERPRISES LTD   p 646
500 MITCHELL RD S, LISTOWEL, ON, N4W 3G7
(519) 291-1960   SIC 5251
CAST METAL SERVICES   p 937
See BRADKEN CANADA MANUFACTURED PRODUCTS LTD
CAST-STONE PRECAST INC   p 494
487 PIERCEY RD, BOLTON, ON, L7E 5B8
(905) 857-6111   SIC 3272
CASTEL ROC   p 1216
See REVE ALCHIMIQUE INC
CASTFORGE   p 1302
See POWERCAST INC
CASTLE BUILDING CENTRES GROUP LTD   p 730
100 MILVERTON DR SUITE 400, MISSISSAUGA, ON, L5R 4H1
(905) 564-3307   SIC 7389
CASTLE FUELS (2008) INC   p 216
1639 TRANS CANADA HWY E, KAMLOOPS, BC, V2C 3Z5
(250) 372-5035   SIC 5172
CASTLE METALS   p 719
See A. M. CASTLE & CO. (CANADA) INC
CASTLE MOUNTAIN RESORT INC   p 152
GD, PINCHER CREEK, AB, T0K 1W0
(403) 627-5101   SIC 7011
CASTLE RESOURCES INC   p 969
79 WELLINGTON ST W SUITE 2100, TORONTO, ON, M5K 1H1
(416) 593-8300   SIC 1081
CASTLE ROCK CONTRACTING LTD   p 167
967 BOULDER BLVD SUITE 101, STONY PLAIN, AB, T7Z 0E7
(780) 968-6828   SIC 1542
CASTLE ROCK RESEARCH CORPORATION   p 87
10180 101 ST NW SUITE 2410, EDMONTON, AB, T5J 3S4
(780) 448-9619   SIC 2731
CASTLE ROYALE   p 1083
See CSH CASTEL ROYAL INC
CASTONGUAY G.P.   p 593
640 GARSON CONISTON RD, GARSON, ON, P3L 1R3
(705) 693-3887   SIC 1629
CASTOOL TOOLING SYSTEMS   p 1001
See EXCO TECHNOLOGIES LIMITED
CASTOR COLONY   p 79
See HUTTERIAN BRETHREN CHURCH OF CASTOR
CAT AND FIDDLE SPORTS BAR   p 247
See MILLERS LANDING PUB LTD
CAT RENTAL STORE, THE   p 102
See RAYDON RENTALS LTD
CATALENT ONTARIO LIMITED   p 1024
2125 AMBASSADOR DR, WINDSOR, ON, N9C 3R5
(519) 969-5404   SIC 2899
CATALENT WINDSOR OPERATIONS   p 1024
See CATALENT ONTARIO LIMITED
CATALOG SALES, DIV OF   p 724
See MAPLEHURST BAKERIES INC
CATALYST CAPITAL GROUP INC, THE   p 961
181 BAY ST SUITE 4700, TORONTO, ON, M5J 2T3
(416) 945-3003   SIC 6726
CATALYST LLP   p 14
200 QUARRY PARK BLVD SE SUITE 250, CALGARY, AB, T2C 5E3

(403) 296-0082   SIC 8721
CATALYST PAPER CORPORATION   p 204
8541 HAY ROAD N, CROFTON, BC, V0R 1R0
(250) 246-6100   SIC 2621
CATALYST PAPER CORPORATION   p 245
4000 STAMP AVE, PORT ALBERNI, BC, V9Y 5J7
(250) 723-2161   SIC 2621
CATALYST PAPER CORPORATION   p 248
5775 ASH AVE, POWELL RIVER, BC, V8A 4R3
(604) 483-3722   SIC 2621
CATALYST PAPER CORPORATION   p 264
3600 LYSANDER LANE SUITE 200 FL 2, RICHMOND, BC, V7B 1C3
(604) 247-4400   SIC 2621
CATALYST PAPER CORPORATION   p 274
10555 TIMBERLAND RD, SURREY, BC, V3V 3T3
(604) 953-0373   SIC 2621
CATALYST PULP AND PAPER SALES INC   p 264
3600 LYSANDER LANE 2ND FL, RICHMOND, BC, V7B 1C3
(604) 247-4400   SIC 5099
CATANIA WORLDWIDE   p 708
See CATANIA, M. L. COMPANY LIMITED
CATANIA, M. L. COMPANY LIMITED   p 708
575 ORWELL ST SUITE 3, MISSISSAUGA, ON, L5A 2W4
(416) 236-9394   SIC 5148
CATECH SYSTEMS LTD   p 667
201 WHITEHALL DR UNIT 4, MARKHAM, ON, L3R 9Y3
(905) 477-0160   SIC 1731
CATELECTRIC INC   p 873
125 COMMANDER BLVD, SCARBOROUGH, ON, M1S 3M7
(416) 299-4864   SIC 3479
CATELLI   p 578
See CATELLI FOODS CORPORATION
CATELLI FOODS CORPORATION   p 205
1631 DERWENT WAY, DELTA, BC, V3M 6K8
(604) 525-2278   SIC 2099
CATELLI FOODS CORPORATION   p 578
401 THE WEST MALL SUITE 11, ETOBICOKE, ON, M9C 5J5
(416) 626-3500   SIC 2099
CATELLI FOODS CORPORATION   p 607
80 BROCKLEY DR, HAMILTON, ON, L8E 3C5
(905) 560-6200   SIC 2098
CATELLI FOODS CORPORATION   p 1164
6890 RUE NOTRE-DAME E, MONTREAL, QC, H1N 2E5
(514) 256-1601   SIC 2098
CATERERS (YORK) LIMITED   p 781
37 SOUTHBOURNE AVE, NORTH YORK, ON, M3H 1A4
SIC 5812
CATERPILLAR   p 370
See TOROMONT INDUSTRIES LTD
CATERPILLAR OF CANADA CORPORATION   p 1030
3700 STEELES AVE W SUITE 902, WOODBRIDGE, ON, L4L 8K8
(905) 265-5802   SIC 5082
CATHAY FOREST PRODUCTS CORP   p 851
30 WERTHEIM CRT SUITE 14, RICHMOND HILL, ON, L4B 1B9
SIC 0851
CATHAY IMPORTERS 2000 LIMITED   p 254
12631 VULCAN WAY, RICHMOND, BC, V6V 1J7
(604) 233-0050   SIC 5099
CATHEDRAL ENERGY SERVICES LTD   p 34
6030 3 ST SE, CALGARY, AB, T2H 1K2
(403) 265-2560   SIC 1381
CATHEDRALE (BASILIQUE) MARIE-REINE-DU- MONDE ET SAINT-JACQUES   p 1215

See CORPORATION ARCHIEPISCOPALE CATHOLIQUE ROMAINE DE MONTREAL, LA
CATHELLE INC   p 1355
19925 CH SAINTE-MARIE, SAINTE-ANNE-DE-BELLEVUE, QC, H9X 3Y3
(514) 428-8888   SIC 5063
CATHERWOOD TOWING LTD   p 232
32885 MISSION WAY SUITE 101, MISSION, BC, V2V 6E4
(604) 826-9221   SIC 4492
CATHOLIC CEMETERIES OF THE DIOCESE OF HAMILTON   p 531
600 SPRING GARDENS RD, BURLINGTON, ON, L7T 1J1
(905) 522-7727   SIC 6531
CATHOLIC CEMETERIES-ARCHDIOCESE OF TORONTO   p 771
4950 YONGE ST SUITE 206, NORTH YORK, ON, M2N 6K1
(416) 733-8544   SIC 7261
CATHOLIC CENTRAL SECONDARY SCHOOL   p 1022
See WINDSOR-ESSEX CATHOLIC DISTRICT SCHOOL BOARD, THE
CATHOLIC CHARITIES   p 113
See CATHOLIC SOCIAL SERVICES
CATHOLIC CHILDREN'S AID SOCIETY OF HAMILTON-WENTWORTH   p 611
735 KING ST E, HAMILTON, ON, L8M 1A1
(905) 525-2012   SIC 8322
CATHOLIC CHILDREN'S AID SOCIETY OF TORONTO, THE   p 931
26 MAITLAND ST, TORONTO, ON, M4Y 1C6
(416) 395-1500   SIC 8322
CATHOLIC CHILDREN'S AID SOCIETY OF TORONTO, THE   p 990
900 DUFFERIN ST SUITE 219, TORONTO, ON, M6H 4A9
(416) 395-1500   SIC 8322
CATHOLIC DISTRICT SCHOOL BOARD OF EASTERN ONTARIO   p 519
40 CENTRAL AVE W, BROCKVILLE, ON, K6V 4N5
(613) 342-4911   SIC 8211
CATHOLIC DISTRICT SCHOOL BOARD OF EASTERN ONTARIO   p 562
1500A CUMBERLAND ST, CORNWALL, ON, K6J 5V9
(613) 932-0349   SIC 8211
CATHOLIC EDUCATION CENTER   p 640
See WATERLOO CATHOLIC DISTRICT SCHOOL BOARD
CATHOLIC EDUCATION CENTRE   p 132
See GRANDE PRAIRIE CATHOLIC SCHOOL DISTRICT 28
CATHOLIC FAMILY SERVICE OF CALGARY, THE   p 64
707 10 AVE SW SUITE 250, CALGARY, AB, T2R 0B3
(403) 233-2360   SIC 8322
CATHOLIC FAMILY SERVICES OF HAMILTON   p 614
2B-688 QUEENSDALE AVE E, HAMILTON, ON, L8V 1M1
(905) 527-3823   SIC 8399
CATHOLIC FAMILY SERVICES OF PEEL-DUFFERIN   p 501
60 WEST DR SUITE 201, BRAMPTON, ON, L6T 3T6
(905) 450-1608   SIC 8699
CATHOLIC IMMIGRATION CENTRE OTTAWA   p 833
219 ARGYLE AVE SUITE 500, OTTAWA, ON, K2P 2H4
(613) 232-9634   SIC 8331
CATHOLIC INDEPENDENT SCHOOLS OF NELSON DIOCESE, THE   p 219

3665 BENVOULIN RD, KELOWNA, BC, V1W 4M7
(250) 762-2905   SIC 8211
CATHOLIC INDEPENDENT SCHOOLS OF VANCOUVER ARCHDIOCESE, THE   p 293
4885 SAINT JOHN PAUL II WAY, VANCOUVER, BC, V5Z 0G3
(604) 683-9331   SIC 8661
CATHOLIC INDEPENDENT SCHOOLS, DIOCESE OF VICTORIA   p 337
4044 NELTHORPE ST SUITE 1, VICTORIA, BC, V8X 2A1
(250) 727-6893   SIC 8211
CATHOLIC PASTORAL CENTRE   p 67
See IONA HOLDINGS CORPORATION
CATHOLIC PASTORAL CENTRE   p 926
See ROMAN CATHOLIC EPISCOPAL CORPORATION FOR THE DIOCESE OF TORONTO, IN CANADA
CATHOLIC SCHOOL BOARD   p 293
See CATHOLIC INDEPENDENT SCHOOLS OF VANCOUVER ARCHDIOCESE, THE
CATHOLIC SOCIAL SERVICES   p 85
10709 105 ST NW, EDMONTON, AB, T5H 2X3
(780) 424-3545   SIC 8399
CATHOLIC SOCIAL SERVICES   p 113
8815 99 ST NW, EDMONTON, AB, T6E 3V3
(780) 432-1137   SIC 8361
CATHOLIC SOCIAL SERVICES   p 153
5104 48 AVE, RED DEER, AB, T4N 3T8
(403) 347-8844   SIC 8361
CATHOLIC SOCIAL SERVICES   p 172
5206 51 AVE, WETASKIWIN, AB, T9A 0V4
(780) 352-5535   SIC 8361
CATLEN HOLDINGS LIMITED   p 738
7361 PACIFIC CIR, MISSISSAUGA, ON, L5T 2A4
(905) 362-1161   SIC 5039
CATLIE SUITES HOTEL, LE   p 1197
See INVESTISSEMENTS RAMAN 'S.E.N.C.', LES
CATLIN CANADA INC   p 937
100 YONGE ST SUITE 1200, TORONTO, ON, M5C 2W1
(416) 928-5586   SIC 6211
CATONS LTD   p 138
3806 53 AVE, LACOMBE, AB, T4L 0A9
(403) 786-9999   SIC 5083
CATP   p 678
See CANADIAN ADDICTION TREATMENT PHARMACY LP
CATTLEX LTD   p 351
GD, HAMIOTA, MB, R0M 0T0
(204) 764-2471   SIC 5154
CAULFEILD APPAREL GROUP LTD   p 782
1400 WHITEHORSE RD, NORTH YORK, ON, M3J 3A7
(416) 636-5900   SIC 5136
CAUSEWAY RESTAURANTS LTD   p 336
812 WHARF ST, VICTORIA, BC, V8W 1T3
(250) 381-2244   SIC 5812
CAVALCADE COLOUR LAB INC   p 620
34 KING WILLIAM ST, HUNTSVILLE, ON, P1H 1G5
(705) 789-9603   SIC 7384
CAVALCADE FORD LTD   p 496
420 ECCLESTONE DR, BRACEBRIDGE, ON, P1L 1R1
(705) 645-8731   SIC 5511
CAVALIER CANDIES LTD   p 374
185 BANNATYNE AVE, WINNIPEG, MB, R3B 0R4
(204) 957-8777   SIC 2064
CAVALIER ENTERPRISES LTD   p 8
2620 32 AVE NE, CALGARY, AB, T1Y 6B8
(403) 291-0107   SIC 7011
CAVALIER ENTERPRISES LTD   p 1426
620 SPADINA CRES E, SASKATOON, SK, S7K 3T5
(306) 652-6770   SIC 7011
CAVALIER ET DESSIN   p 1064
See EMBALLAGES CARROUSEL INC, LES
CAVALIER LAND LTD   p 22

1223 31 AVE NE SUITE 100, CALGARY, AB, T2E 7W1
(403) 264-5188   *SIC 6712*

CAVALIER TOOL & MANUFACTURING LTD *p 1019*
3450 WHEELTON DR, WINDSOR, ON, N8W 5A7
(519) 944-2144   *SIC 3544*

CAVALIER TRANSPORTATION SERVICES INC *p 494*
14091 HUMBER STATION RD, BOLTON, ON, L7E 0Z9
(905) 857-6981   *SIC 4731*

CAVAN CONTRACTORS LTD *p 113*
3722 91 ST NW, EDMONTON, AB, T6E 5M3
(780) 462-5311   *SIC 1542*

CAVANAGH'S FOOD MARKET LIMITED *p 468*
86 MAIN ST, TRURO, NS, B2N 4G6
SIC 5411

CAVCO FOOD SERVICES LTD *p 637*
715 OTTAWA ST S, KITCHENER, ON, N2E 3H5
(519) 569-7224   *SIC 5812*

CAVCO FOOD SERVICES LTD *p 641*
431 HIGHLAND RD W, KITCHENER, ON, N2M 3C6
(519) 578-8630   *SIC 5812*

CAVE SPRING CELLARS LTD *p 623*
3836 MAIN ST RR 1, JORDAN STATION, ON, L0R 1S0
(905) 562-3581   *SIC 5182*

CAVE SPRING VINEYARDS *p 623*
See *CAVE SPRING CELLARS LTD*

CAVELL, EDITH CARE CENTRE *p 142*
See *CHANTELLE MANAGEMENT LTD*

CAVENDISH AGRI SERVICES LIMITED *p 397*
100 MIDLAND DR, DIEPPE, NB, E1A 6X4
(506) 858-7777   *SIC 5261*

CAVENDISH FARMS CORPORATION *p 397*
100 MIDLAND DR, DIEPPE, NB, E1A 6X4
(506) 858-7777   *SIC 5142*

CAVENDISH PRODUCE, DIV OF *p 397*
See *CAVENDISH FARMS CORPORATION*

CAW CANADA *p 477*
See *UNIFOR*

CAW COMMUNITY CHILD CARE AND DEVELOPMENT SERVICES INC *p 1019*
3450 YPRES AVE SUITE 100, WINDSOR, ON, N8W 5K9
SIC 8611

CAW LOCAL 105 *p 565*
See *UNIFOR*

CAW LOCAL 1839 *p 492*
See *UNIFOR*

CAW LOCAL 31 *p 632*
See *UNIFOR*

CAW LOCAL 4401 *p 887*
See *UNIFOR*

CAW LOCAL 542 *p 486*
26 LORENA ST, BARRIE, ON, L4N 4P4
(705) 739-3532   *SIC 8611*

CAW LOCAL 973 *p 507*
See *UNIFOR*

CAWTHORN INVESTMENTS LTD *p 22*
6700 9 ST NE, CALGARY, AB, T2E 8K6
(403) 295-5855   *SIC 6712*

CAWTHRA GARDENS LONGTERM CARE *p 708*
See *CHARTWELL RETIREMENT RESIDENCES*

CAWTHRA PARK SECONDARY SCHOOL *p 713*
See *PEEL DISTRICT SCHOOL BOARD*

CAXTON MARK INC *p 644*
10 IROQUOIS RD, LEAMINGTON, ON, N8H 3V7
(519) 322-1002   *SIC 5044*

CAYEN, J.C. HOLDINGS LTD *p 1437*
1240 SIMS AVE, WEYBURN, SK, S4H 3N9
(306) 842-4600   *SIC 5531*

CAYER, JEAN-CLAUDE ENTERPRISES LTD *p 645*
708 LIMOGES RD, LIMOGES, ON, K0A 2M0
(613) 443-2293   *SIC 5072*

CAYUGA DISPLAYS INC *p 541*
88 TALBOT ST E, CAYUGA, ON, N0A 1E0
(905) 772-5214   *SIC 2541*

CAYUGA MATERIALS & CONSTRUCTION CO. LIMITED *p 541*
4219 HIGHWAY 3 RR 4, CAYUGA, ON, N0A 1E0
(905) 772-3331   *SIC 1422*

CAYUGA MUTUAL INSURANCE COMPANY *p 541*
23 KING ST, CAYUGA, ON, N0A 1E0
(905) 772-5498   *SIC 6411*

CAZZA PETITE *p 1179*
See *MODES CAZZA INC*

CB INDUSTRIAL PART NETWORK *p 526*
2100 CLIPPER CRES, BURLINGTON, ON, L7M 2P5
(905) 639-1907   *SIC 5084*

CB PARTNERS CORPORATION *p 108*
4703 52 AVE NW, EDMONTON, AB, T6B 3R6
(780) 395-3300   *SIC 1542*

CB RICHARD ELLIS GLOBAL CORPORATE SERVICES LTD *p 937*
18 KING ST E UNIT 1100, TORONTO, ON, M5C 1C4
(416) 775-3975   *SIC 6512*

CB SUPPLIES LTD *p 278*
3325 190 ST, SURREY, BC, V3Z 1A7
(604) 535-5088   *SIC 5074*

CBA EXPERTS-CONSEILS *p 1216*
See *BOUTHILLETTE PARIZEAU INC*

CBB *p 513*
See *CANADIAN BABBITT BEARINGS LTD*

CBC *p 297*
See *CANADIAN BROADCASTING CORPORATION*

CBC *p 452*
See *CANADIAN BROADCASTING CORPORATION*

CBC *p 822*
See *CANADIAN BROADCASTING CORPORATION*

CBC *p 979*
See *CANADIAN BROADCASTING CORPORATION*

CBC *p 1175*
See *CANADIAN BROADCASTING CORPORATION*

CBC PENSION BOARD OF TRUSTEES *p 822*
99 BANK ST SUITE 191, OTTAWA, ON, K1P 6B9
(613) 688-3900   *SIC 6371*

CBC RADIO CANADA *p 1417*
See *CANADIAN BROADCASTING CORPORATION*

CBC SPECIALTY METALS *p 550*
See *CANADIAN BRASS & COPPER CO*

CBC TV *p 429*
See *CANADIAN BROADCASTING CORPORATION*

CBC/CBRT/CBR *p 41*
See *CANADIAN BROADCASTING CORPORATION*

CBCI TELECOM *p 1127*
See *CBCI TELECOM CANADA INC*

CBCI TELECOM CANADA INC *p 1127*
2260 46E AV, LACHINE, QC, H8T 2P3
(514) 422-9333   *SIC 4899*

CBCL *p 452*
See *CANADIAN-BRITISH CONSULTING GROUP LIMITED*

CBCL LIMITED *p 452*
1489 HOLLIS ST, HALIFAX, NS, B3J 3M5
(902) 421-7241   *SIC 8711*

CBI HEALTH *p 572*
See *CBI LIMITED*

CBI HEALTH CENTRE *p 64*

See *CBI LIMITED*

CBI HOME HEALTH *p 608*
See *CBI LIMITED*

CBI LIMITED *p 64*
1400 1 ST SW SUITE 500, CALGARY, AB, T2R 0V8
(403) 232-8770   *SIC 8049*

CBI LIMITED *p 492*
11 BAY BRIDGE RD, BELLEVILLE, ON, K8P 3P6
(613) 962-3426   *SIC 8741*

CBI LIMITED *p 572*
3300 BLOOR ST W SUITE 900, ETOBICOKE, ON, M8X 2X2
(800) 463-2225   *SIC 8049*

CBI LIMITED *p 608*
45 GODERICH RD, HAMILTON, ON, L8E 4W8
(905) 777-1255   *SIC 8741*

CBI MANUFACTURING LTD *p 143*
702 1 AVE NW, LINDEN, AB, T0M 1J0
(403) 546-3851   *SIC 3713*

CBL *p 668*
See *CBL DATA RECOVERY TECHNOLOGIES INC*

CBL DATA RECOVERY TECHNOLOGIES INC *p 668*
590 ALDEN RD SUITE 105, MARKHAM, ON, L3R 8N2
(905) 479-9938   *SIC 7375*

CBM CANADA BUILDING MATERIALS *p 496*
See *ST. MARYS CEMENT INC. (CANADA)*

CBM CANADA BUILDING MATERIALS *p 889*
See *ST. MARYS CEMENT INC. (CANADA)*

CBM METAL *p 683*
See *CANADIAN BUSINESS MACHINES LIMITED*

CBM-CANADA BUILDING MAT CO *p 918*
See *ST. MARYS CEMENT INC. (CANADA)*

CBN COMMERCIAL SOLUTIONS *p 828*
See *CANADIAN BANK NOTE COMPANY, LIMITED*

CBRE CALEDON CAPITAL MANAGEMENT INC *p 950*
141 ADELAIDE ST W SUITE 1500, TORONTO, ON, M5H 3L5
(416) 861-0700   *SIC 6722*

CBRE LIMITED *p 46*
See *CBRE LIMITEE*

CBRE LIMITED *p 311*
See *CBRE LIMITEE*

CBRE LIMITED *p 766*
See *CBRE LIMITEE*

CBRE LIMITED *p 950*
See *CBRE LIMITEE*

CBRE LIMITEE *p 46*
530 8 AVE SW SUITE 500, CALGARY, AB, T2P 3S8
(403) 536-1290   *SIC 6531*

CBRE LIMITEE *p 311*
1021 HASTINGS ST W SUITE 2500, VANCOUVER, BC, V6E 0C3
(604) 319-1374   *SIC 6531*

CBRE LIMITEE *p 766*
2001 SHEPPARD AVE E SUITE 300, NORTH YORK, ON, M2J 4Z8
(416) 494-0600   *SIC 6531*

CBRE LIMITEE *p 950*
145 KING ST W SUITE 1100, TORONTO, ON, M5H 1J8
(416) 362-2244   *SIC 8748*

CBRE LIMITEE *p 950*
40 KING ST W SUITE 4100, TORONTO, ON, M5H 3Y2
(416) 947-7661   *SIC 6531*

CBS *p 127*
See *C. B. S. CONSTRUCTION LTD*

CBS CANADA HOLDINGS CO *p 710*
See *OUTFRONT MEDIA CANADA LP*

CBS OUTDOOR CANADA *p 571*
See *OUTFRONT MEDIA CANADA LP*

CBS PARTS LTD *p 281*

9505 189 ST SUITE 9505, SURREY, BC, V4N 5L8
(604) 888-1944   *SIC 5013*

CBV COLLECTION SERVICES LTD *p 185*
4664 LOUGHEED HWY UNIT 20, BURNABY, BC, V5C 5T5
(604) 687-4559   *SIC 7322*

CBV COLLECTIONS *p 185*
See *CBV COLLECTION SERVICES LTD*

CCA *p 864*
See *COMMON COLLECTION AGENCY INC*

CCAC *p 509*
See *CENTRAL WEST COMMUNITY CARE ACCESS CENTRE*

CCAC *p 900*
See *NORTH EAST COMMUNITY CARE ACCESS CENTRE*

CCAC OXFORD *p 1035*
See *COMMUNITY CARE ACCESS CENTRE - OXFORD*

CCAS HAMILTON *p 611*
See *CATHOLIC CHILDREN'S AID SOCIETY OF HAMILTON-WENTWORTH*

CCC PLASTICS *p 928*
See *CANADA COLORS AND CHEMICALS LIMITED*

CCCSI *p 851*
See *CANADIAN CONTRACT CLEANING SPECIALISTS, INC*

CCD LIMITED PARTNERSHIP *p 734*
1115 CARDIFF BLVD, MISSISSAUGA, ON, L5S 1L8
(905) 564-2115   *SIC 6712*

CCFC *p 668*
See *CHRISTIAN CHILDREN'S FUND OF CANADA*

CCFC *p 925*
See *CROHN'S AND COLITIS CANADA*

CCFGLM ONTARIO LIMITED *p 574*
1255 THE QUEENSWAY, ETOBICOKE, ON, M8Z 1S1
(416) 252-5000   *SIC 5812*

CCG *p 551*
See *CONCORD CONCRETE GROUP INC*

CCI ENTERTAINMENT LTD *p 926*
210 ST CLAIR AVE W 4 FL, TORONTO, ON, M4V 1R2
(416) 964-8750   *SIC 6712*

CCI INC *p 99*
17816 118 AVE NW, EDMONTON, AB, T5S 2W3
(780) 784-1990   *SIC 7373*

CCI RESEARCH *p 808*
See *CCI RESEARCH INC*

CCI RESEARCH INC *p 808*
71 BROADWAY, ORANGEVILLE, ON, L9W 1K1
(519) 938-9552   *SIC 8732*

CCI WIRELESS *p 22*
See *CORRIDOR COMMUNICATIONS, INC*

CCIS *p 64*
See *CALGARY CATHOLIC IMMIGRATION SOCIETY*

CCL INDUSTRIES INC *p 914*
111 GORDON BAKER RD SUITE 801, TORONTO, ON, M2H 3R1
(416) 756-8500   *SIC 2672*

CCL INDUSTRIES INC *p 1295*
1315 RUE RENE-DESCARTES, SAINT-BRUNO, QC, J3V 0B7
(450) 653-3071   *SIC 2679*

CCL INTERNATIONAL INC *p 764*
105 GORDON BAKER RD SUITE 800, NORTH YORK, ON, M2H 3P8
(416) 756-8500   *SIC 2679*

CCL PROPERTIES LTD *p 297*
475 GEORGIA ST W SUITE 800, VANCOUVER, BC, V6B 4M9
(604) 684-7117   *SIC 6531*

CCM HOCKEY *p 1331*
See *SPORT MASKA INC*

CCMET GROUP *p 192*
See *CANADIAN CONSTRUCTION MATE-*

RIALS ENGINEERING & TESTING INC
CCNQ p 1269
See COMMISSION DE LA CAPITALE NA-
TIONALE DU QUEBEC
CCPEDQ p 1164
See FEDERATION DES CAISSES DES-
JARDINS DU QUEBEC
CCQ p 1176
See COMMISSION DE LA CONSTRUC-
TION DU QUEBEC
CCR p 625
See 1737868 ONTARIO INC.
CCREST LABORATORIES p 1344
See EURO-PHARM INTERNATIONAL
CANADA INC
CCRW p 923
See CANADIAN COUNCIL ON REHABILI-
TATION AND WORK, THE
CCS ADJUSTERS INC p 99
10120 175 ST NW, EDMONTON, AB, T5S
1L1
(780) 443-1185   SIC 6411
CCS CONTRACTING LTD p 100
18039 114 AVE NW, EDMONTON, AB, T5S
1T8
(780) 481-1776   SIC 1761
CCS INDUSTRIALS p 813
See LAKESHORE MILL SUPPLIES LTD
CCSL p 473
See CORPORATE CONTRACTING SER-
VICES LTD
CCSSSBJ p 1081
See CONSEIL CRI DE LA SANTE ET DES
SERVICES SOCIAUX DE LA BAIE JAMES
CCT CANADA INC p 734
6900 TRANMERE DR, MISSISSAUGA, ON,
L5S 1L9
(905) 362-9198   SIC 4731
CCT GLOBAL SOURCING INC p 550
40 BRADWICK DR UNIT 5, CONCORD, ON,
L4K 1K9
(905) 326-8452   SIC 5099
CCTF p 648
See CCTF CORPORATION
CCTF CORPORATION p 521
4151 NORTH SERVICE RD UNIT 2,
BURLINGTON, ON, L7L 4X6
(905) 335-5320   SIC 8721
CCTF CORPORATION p 648
2124 OXFORD ST E, LONDON, ON, N5V
0B7
(519) 453-3488   SIC 5084
**CCV INSURANCE & FINANCIAL SERVICES
INC** p 510
32 QUEEN ST W, BRAMPTON, ON, L6X
1A1
(905) 459-6066   SIC 6411
CCWI-CANADA p 687
See CONGO CORPORATE WOODS IN-
CORPORATED
CD PLUS GROUP OF STORES p 502
See ENTERTAINMENT ONE GP LIMITED
CDA INDUSTRIES INC p 844
1055 SQUIRES BEACH RD, PICKERING,
ON, L1W 4A6
(905) 686-7000   SIC 2541
CDA NEILSON MARKETING p 844
See CDA INDUSTRIES INC
CDA-TEQ QUEBEC INC p 1215
1201 RUE DE CONDE, MONTREAL, QC,
H3K 2E4
(514) 789-0529   SIC 5142
CDB CONSTRUCTION p 1319
See CONSTRUCTION DEMATHIEU &
BARD (CDB) INC
CDC p 207
See WALLACE & CAREY INC
CDC p 1030
See CARPENTERS DISTRICT COUNCIL
OF ONTARIO TRAINING TRUST FUND, THE
CDC CONSTRUCTION LTD p 291
16 4TH AVE W SUITE 300, VANCOUVER,
BC, V5Y 1G3
(604) 873-6656   SIC 1542

CDC FOODS p 850
See 1272227 ONTARIO INC
CDC FOODS INC p 851
21 EAST WILMOT ST UNIT 2, RICHMOND
HILL, ON, L4B 1A3
(905) 763-2929   SIC 5141
CDCI p 303
See CANADIAN DEVELOPMENT CON-
SULTANTS INTERNATIONAL INC
CDE ELECTRIQUE p 1319
See CENTRE DE DISTRIBUTION ELEC-
TRIQUE LIMITEE
CDI COLLEGE p 310
See VANCOUVER CAREER COLLEGE
(BURNABY) INC
CDI COMPUTER DEALERS INC p 680
130 SOUTH TOWN CENTRE BLVD,
MARKHAM, ON, L6G 1B8
(905) 946-1119   SIC 5045
**CDI EDUCATION (ALBERTA) LIMITED
PARTNERSHIP** p 273
13401 108 AVE SUITE 360, SURREY, BC,
V3T 5T3
(604) 915-7288   SIC 8211
CDI SPACES p 111
See SPACES INC
CDIC p 972
See CANADA DEVELOPMENT INVEST-
MENT CORPORATION
CDM CANADA p 894
See CHRISTIAN BLIND MISSION INTER-
NATIONAL
CDN CERTIFIED IMPORTERS, DIV OF p 93
See DONG-PHUONG ORIENTAL MARKET
LTD
CDN CONTROLS LTD p 131
10306 118 ST, GRANDE PRAIRIE, AB, T8V
3X9
(780) 532-8151   SIC 1731
CDN ENERGY AND POWER CORP p 14
10550 42 ST SE SUITE 107, CALGARY, AB,
T2C 5C7
(403) 236-0333   SIC 5063
**CDN POWER PAC ELECTRICAL MECHAN-
ICAL, DIV OF** p
1
See KINSEY ENTERPRISES INC
CDN TECHNOLOGY p 1013
901 BURNS ST E, WHITBY, ON, L1N 0E6
(905) 430-7295   SIC 3699
CDP CAPITAL - AMERIQUE p 1191
See CAPITAL D'AMERIQUE CDPQ INC
CDP CAPITAL-CI p 1191
See CDP CAPITAL-CONSEIL IMMOBILIER
INC
CDP CAPITAL-CONSEIL IMMOBILIER INC
p 1191
1000 PLACE JEAN-PAUL-RIOPELLE BU-
REAU A 300, MONTREAL, QC, H2Z 2B3
(514) 875-3360   SIC 6722
CDS p 668
See COMPUTER DATA SOURCE CANADA
CORP
CDS p 949
See CANADIAN DEPOSITORY FOR SECU-
RITIES LIMITED, THE
**CDS CLEARING AND DEPOSITORY SER-
VICES INC** p
950
85 RICHMOND ST W, TORONTO, ON, M5H
2C9
(416) 365-8400   SIC 6211
CDS DOORS, DIV OF p 668
See COMMERCIAL DRYWALL SUPPLY
(ONTARIO) INC
CDS SYSTEMS p 1129
See SYSTEMES DE LIGNES
D'EXTRUSION FABE INC
CDSL CANADA LIMITED p 720
2480 MEADOWVALE BLVD SUITE 100,
MISSISSAUGA, ON, L5N 8M6
(905) 858-7100   SIC 7379
CDSL CANADA LIMITED p 1417
1900 ALBERT ST UNIT 700, REGINA, SK,

S4P 4K8
(306) 761-4000   SIC 7379
CDSPI p 776
155 LESMILL RD, NORTH YORK, ON, M3B
2T8
(416) 296-9401   SIC 6411
CDW CANADA CORP p 687
5925 AIRPORT RD UNIT 800, MISSIS-
SAUGA, ON, L4V 1W1
(647) 259-1034   SIC 5045
CDW CANADA CORP p 996
185 THE WEST MALL SUITE 1700,
TORONTO, ON, M9C 1B8
(647) 288-5700   SIC 5045
CE DE CANDY COMPANY LIMITED p 755
150 HARRY WALKER PKY N, NEWMAR-
KET, ON, L3Y 7B2
(905) 853-7171   SIC 2064
**CEA CENTRE REGIONAL INTEGRE DE
FORMATION** p 1109
See COMMISSION SCOLAIRE DU VAL-
DES-CERFS
CEA LAURE CONON p 1078
See COMMISSION SCOLAIRE DES
RIVES-DU-SAGUENAY
CEB CANADA INC p 1258
400 BOULEVARD JEAN-LESAGE UNITE
500, QUEBEC, QC, G1K 8W1
(418) 523-6663   SIC 5734
CEB INVESTMENTS INC p 28
250 42 AVE SE, CALGARY, AB, T2G 1Y4
(403) 265-4155   SIC 1731
CEC p 693
See COMPUTER ENHANCEMENT COR-
PORATION
CEC p 1187
See COMMISSION FOR ENVIRONMEN-
TAL COOPERATION
CEC PERSONNEL SOLUTIONS p 702
See CANADIAN EMPLOYMENT CON-
TRACTORS INC
CEC SERVICES LIMITED (AURORA) p 629
16188 BATHURST ST, KING CITY, ON, L7B
1K5
(905) 713-3711   SIC 1731
CECCE p 596
See CONSEIL DES ECOLES
CATHOLIQUES DE LANGUE FRANCAISE
DU CENTRE-EST
CECCONI SIMONE INC p 990
1335 DUNDAS ST W, TORONTO, ON, M6J
1Y3
(416) 588-5900   SIC 7389
CEDA p 108
See CEDA FIELD SERVICES LP
CEDA FIELD SERVICES LP p 108
6005 72A AVE NW, EDMONTON, AB, T6B
2J1
(780) 377-4306   SIC 7699
CEDA INTERNATIONAL CORPORATION p
39
11012 MACLEOD TRAIL SE SUITE 625,
CALGARY, AB, T2J 6A5
(403) 253-3233   SIC 2819
CEDAR DRIVE JUNIOR PUBLIC SCHOOL p
867
See TORONTO DISTRICT SCHOOL
BOARD
**CEDAR GROVE BUILDING PRODUCTS
LTD** p 276
8073 132 ST, SURREY, BC, V3W 4N5
(604) 590-3106   SIC 5211
CEDAR GROVE ROOFING SUPPLY p 276
See CEDAR GROVE BUILDING PROD-
UCTS LTD
CEDAR JUICE p 972
See COLD PRESS CORP, THE
CEDAR SPRING BOTTLED WATER p 554
See HAYHOE EQUIPMENT AND SUPPLY
LTD
**CEDAR SPRINGS HEALTH RACQUET &
SPORTS CLUB** p 527
See CEDAR SPRINGS TENNIS LIMITED
CEDAR SPRINGS TENNIS LIMITED p 527

960 CUMBERLAND AVE, BURLINGTON,
ON, L7N 3J6
(905) 632-9758   SIC 7997
CEDARBRAE COLLEGIATE INSTITUTE p
867
See TORONTO DISTRICT SCHOOL
BOARD
CEDARGLEN GROUP INC, THE p 34
550 71 AVE SE SUITE 140, CALGARY, AB,
T2H 0S6
(403) 255-2000   SIC 1521
CEDARGLEN HOMES p 34
See CEDARGLEN GROUP INC, THE
CEDARLANE CORPORATION p 521
4410 PALETTA CRT, BURLINGTON, ON,
L7L 5R2
(289) 288-0001   SIC 2836
CEDARLANE LABORATORIES p 521
See CEDARLANE CORPORATION
CEDAROME CANADA INC p 1072
21 RUE PAUL-GAUGUIN, CANDIAC, QC,
J5R 3X8
(450) 659-8000   SIC 5149
CEDARS AT COBBLE HILL p 198
See CEDARS DISCOVERY CENTRE LTD
CEDARS DISCOVERY CENTRE LTD p 198
3741 HOLLAND AVE, COBBLE HILL, BC,
V0R 1L0
(250) 733-2006   SIC 8093
CEDARSTONE ENHANCED CARE p 469
See SHANNEX INCORPORATED
CEDARVALE LODGE p 628
See SPECIALTY CARE INC
**CEDARVALE LODGE/SWEETBRIAR
LODGE** p 558
See SPECIALTY CARE INC
CEDARWAY FLORAL INC p 489
4665 BARTLETT RD, BEAMSVILLE, ON,
L0R 1B1
(905) 563-4338   SIC 5193
CEDARWOOD VILLAGE p 881
See MAPLEWOOD NURSING HOME LIM-
ITED
CEDM TOWER LTD p 405
2491 KING GEORGE HWY, MIRAMICHI,
NB, E1V 6W3
(506) 773-9446   SIC 5531
CEDROM-SNI INC p 1244
825 AV QUERBES BUREAU 200, OUT-
REMONT, QC, H2V 3X1
(514) 278-6060   SIC 4899
CEGEP CHAMPLAIN ST LAWRENCE p
1271
See ASSOCIATION DES ETUDIANTS DU
COLLEGE REGIONAL CHAMPLAIN L'
CEGEP D'AHUNTSIC p 1176
See COLLEGE AHUNTSIC
CEGEP DE BAIE-COMEAU p 1053
537 BOUL BLANCHE, BAIE-COMEAU, QC,
G5C 2B2
(418) 589-5707   SIC 8221
CEGEP DE GASPE p 1102
See COLLEGE D'ENSEIGNEMENT GEN-
ERALE & PROFESSIONNEL DE LA GASPE-
SIE & DES ILES
CEGEP DE GRANBY p 1109
See CEGEP DE GRANBY HAUTE-
YAMASKA
CEGEP DE GRANBY HAUTE-YAMASKA p
1109
235 RUE SAINT-JACQUES, GRANBY, QC,
J2G 3N1
(450) 372-6614   SIC 8221
CEGEP DE LA POCATIERE p 1122
See COLLEGE D'ENSEIGNEMENT
GENERAL & PROFESSIONEL DE LA
POCATIERE
CEGEP DE MATANE p 1150
See COLLEGE D'ENSEIGNEMENT GEN-
ERAL & PROFESSIONNEL DE MATANE
CEGEP DE RIVIERE-DU-LOUP p 1286
See COLLEGE D'ENSEIGNEMENT GEN-
ERAL ET PROFESSIONNEL DE RIVIERE-
DU-LOUP

CEGEP DE SAINT-HYACINTHE p 1312
See COLLEGE D'ENSEIGNEMENT GEN-
ERAL ET PROFESSIONEL DE SAINT-
HYACINTHE

CEGEP DE SEPT-ILES p 1367
See COOPERATIVE ETUDIANTE DU
CEGEP DE SEPT-ILES

CEGEP DE SOREL-TRACY p 1377
See COLLEGE D'ENSEIGNEMENT GEN-
ERAL ET PROFESSIONNEL SOREL-TRACY

CEGEP DE THETFORD p 1382
671 BOUL FRONTENAC O, THETFORD
MINES, QC, G6G 1N1
(418) 338-8591 SIC 8221

CEGEP DE TROIS-RIVIERES p 1386
3500 RUE DE COURVAL, TROIS-
RIVIERES, QC, G8Z 1T2
(819) 376-1721 SIC 8222

CEGEP DE VICTORIAVILLE p 1397
See COLLEGE D'ENSEIGNEMENT GEN-
ERAL ET PROFESSIONNEL DE VICTORIAV-
ILLE

CEGEP DU VIEUX MONTREAL p 1185
See FONDATION DU CEGEP DU VIEUX
MONTREAL, LA

CEGEP FRANCOIS-XAVIER-GARNEAU p
1270
See COLLEGE D'ENSEIGNEMENT GEN-
ERAL ET PROFESSIONEL FRANCOIS-
XAVIER-GARNEAU

CEGEP GERALD-GODIN p 1358
See COLLEGE D'ENSEIGNEMENT GEN-
ERAL ET PROFESSIONNEL GERALD-
GODIN

CEGEP HERITAGE COLLEGE p 1106
325 BOUL DE LA CITE-DES-JEUNES,
GATINEAU, QC, J8Y 6T3
(819) 778-2270 SIC 8221

CEGEP LIMOILOU p 1257
See REGIE DES CLUBS D'EXCELLENCE
COLLEGE D'ENSEIGNEMENT GENERAL
ET PROFESSIONNEL DE LIMOILOU

CEGEP MARIE-VICTORIN p 1163
See COLLEGE D'ENSEIGNEMENT
GENERAL ET PROFESSIONNEL MARIE-
VICTORIN

**CEGEP REGIONAL DE LANAUDIERE A
TERREBONNE** p 1380
See FONDATION DU CEGEP REGIONAL
DE LANAUDIERE

CEGEP VANIER COLLEGE p 1323
See VANIER COLLEGE OF GENERAL AND
VOCATIONAL EDUCATION

CEGERCO INC p 1078
255 RUE RACINE E BUREAU 595,
CHICOUTIMI, QC, G7H 7L2
(418) 690-3432 SIC 1522

CEGERCO INC p 1080
1180 RUE BERSIMIS, CHICOUTIMI, QC,
G7K 1A5
(418) 543-6159 SIC 1611

CEGERTEC INC p 1071
4805 BOUL LAPINIERE BUREAU 4300,
BROSSARD, QC, J4Z 0G2
(450) 656-3356 SIC 8621

CEH p 1135
See CONSTRUCTIONS E. HUOT INC

**CEI - ARCHITECTURE PLANNING INTERI-
ORS** p
318
1500 GEORGIA ST W SUITE 500, VAN-
COUVER, BC, V6G 2Z6
(604) 687-1898 SIC 8712

CEILI'S IRISH PUB & RESTAURANT p 42
See 817936 ALBERTA LTD

CEL p 1426
See COMMUNITY ELECTRIC LTD

CELADON p 527
See CELADON IMPORTS INC

CELADON IMPORTS INC p 527
3345 NORTH SERVICE RD UNIT 107,
BURLINGTON, ON, L7N 3G2
(905) 335-6444 SIC 5023

CELANESE CANADA ULC p 87

4405 101 AVE, EDMONTON, AB, T5J 2K1
(780) 468-0800 SIC 2821

CELANESE CANADA ULC p 1064
50 BOUL MARIE-VICTORIN BUREAU 100,
BOUCHERVILLE, QC, J4B 1V5
(450) 655-0396 SIC 2819

CELCO CONTROLS LTD p 371
78 HUTCHINGS ST, WINNIPEG, MB, R2X
3B1
(204) 788-1677 SIC 3613

CELERITY BUILDERS LTD p 361
GD, WINKLER, MB, R6W 4B3
(204) 362-4003 SIC 1522

CELERO SOLUTIONS INC p 34
8500 MACLEOD TRAIL SE SUITE 350N,
CALGARY, AB, T2H 2N1
(403) 258-5900 SIC 8742

CELESTICA INC p 916
844 DON MILLS RD, TORONTO, ON, M3C
1V7
(416) 448-5800 SIC 3589

CELESTICA INTERNATIONAL INC p 779
844 DON MILLS RD, NORTH YORK, ON,
M3C 1V7
(416) 448-5800 SIC 3679

CELESTICA INTERNATIONAL LP p 716
3333 UNITY DR SUITE A, MISSISSAUGA,
ON, L5L 3S6
(416) 448-2559 SIC 3812

CELESTICA INTERNATIONAL LP p 755
213 HARRY WALKER PKY S, NEWMAR-
KET, ON, L3Y 8T3
(416) 448-2559 SIC 3672

CELESTICA INTERNATIONAL LP p 916
844 DON MILLS RD, TORONTO, ON, M3C
1V7
(416) 448-2559 SIC 3672

CELGENE CANADA INC p 721
6755 MISSISSAUGA RD SUITE 600, MIS-
SISSAUGA, ON, L5N 7Y2
(289) 291-0200 SIC 5122

CELIA HARBOUR HOLDINGS LTD p 1440
29 LEWES BLVD, WHITEHORSE, YT, Y1A
4S5
(867) 667-7860 SIC 5411

CELLAY CANADA INC p 668
30 ROYAL CREST CRT SUITE 8,
MARKHAM, ON, L3R 9W8
SIC 5193

CELLCOM WIRELESS INC p 271
17650 66A AVE, SURREY, BC, V3S 4S4
(604) 575-1700 SIC 4899

CELLMART COMMUNICATIONS INC p 259
5300 NO. 3 RD SUITE 432, RICHMOND,
BC, V6X 2X9
(604) 247-2355 SIC 4812

CELLO PRODUCTS INC p 533
210 AVENUE RD, CAMBRIDGE, ON, N1R
8H5
(519) 621-9150 SIC 3432

CELLPAGE p 1222
See PROTEC INVESTIGATION AND SE-
CURITY INC

**CELLULAR BABY CELL PHONE ACCES-
SORIES SPECIALIST LTD** p
190
4710 KINGSWAY UNIT 1028, BURNABY,
BC, V5H 4M2
(604) 437-9977 SIC 5999

**CELLULAR CONCEPTS OF NOVA SCOTIA
LIMITED** p 455
3232 BARRINGTON ST, HALIFAX, NS, B3K
2X7
(902) 423-0167 SIC 5999

CELLULAR POINT p 1029
See 1359238 ONTARIO INC.

CELLULAR SOLUTION p 1337
See 3294269 CANADA INC

CELSIAIR p 1121
See OUELLET CANADA INC

CELTIC EXPLORATION ULC p 46
505 3 ST SW SUITE 500, CALGARY, AB,
T2P 3E6
(403) 201-5340 SIC 1382

CELTRADE CANADA INC p 685
7566 BATH RD, MISSISSAUGA, ON, L4T
1L2
(905) 678-1322 SIC 2035

CEMATRIX CORPORATION p 14
5440 53 ST SE, CALGARY, AB, T2C 4B6
(403) 219-0484 SIC 3272

CEMENTATION CANADA INC p 762
590 GRAHAM DR, NORTH BAY, ON, P1B
7S1
(705) 472-3381 SIC 1241

CEMTOL MANUFACTURING p 605
See LINAMAR CORPORATION

CENDREX-ARCO METAL p 1162
See INDUSTRIES CENDREX INC, LES

CENGEA SOLUTIONS INC p 311
1188 GEORGIA ST W SUITE 560, VAN-
COUVER, BC, V6E 4A2
(604) 697-6400 SIC 7372

CENOVUS ENERGY p 28
See CENOVUS FCCL LTD

CENOVUS ENERGY INC p 46
500 CENTRE ST SE, CALGARY, AB, T2P
0M5
(403) 766-2000 SIC 1382

CENOVUS FCCL LTD p 28
500 CENTRE ST SE SUITE 766, CALGARY,
AB, T2G 1A6
(403) 766-2000 SIC 1311

CENTAUR IMPORT MOTORS (1977) LTD p
28
3819 MACLEOD TRAIL SW, CALGARY, AB,
T2G 2R3
(403) 287-2544 SIC 5511

CENTAUR PRODUCTS INC p 182
3145 THUNDERBIRD CRES, BURNABY,
BC, V5A 3G1
(604) 357-3510 SIC 1752

CENTAUR SUBARU p 28
See CENTAUR IMPORT MOTORS (1977)
LTD

CENTCOM CONSTRUCTION LTD p 34
7220 FISHER ST SE SUITE 310, CAL-
GARY, AB, T2H 2H8
(403) 252-5571 SIC 1542

CENTENNIAL 89 CORP p 28
4412 MANILLA RD SE SUITE 1, CALGARY,
AB, T2G 4B7
(403) 214-0044 SIC 2011

**CENTENNIAL CENTRE OF SCIENCE AND
TECHNOLOGY** p 779
770 DON MILLS RD, NORTH YORK, ON,
M3C 1T3
(416) 429-4100 SIC 8412

**CENTENNIAL COLLEGE OF APPLIED
ARTS & TECHNOLOGY, THE** p 866
941 PROGRESS AVE, SCARBOROUGH,
ON, M1G 3T8
(416) 289-5000 SIC 8222

CENTENNIAL FOODSERVICE p 28
4412 MANILLA RD SE SUITE 1, CALGARY,
AB, T2G 4B7
(403) 214-0044 SIC 5142

CENTENNIAL FOODSERVICE p 254
12759 VULCAN WAY UNIT 108, RICH-
MOND, BC, V6V 3C8
(604) 273-5261 SIC 2011

CENTENNIAL HOTELS LIMITED p 452
1515 SOUTH PARK ST, HALIFAX, NS, B3J
2L2
(902) 423-6331 SIC 7011

CENTENNIAL HOTELS LIMITED p 452
1583 BRUNSWICK ST, HALIFAX, NS, B3J
3P5
(902) 420-0555 SIC 7011

CENTENNIAL OPTICAL LIMITED p 786
158 NORFINCH DR, NORTH YORK, ON,
M3N 1X6
(416) 739-8539 SIC 5049

CENTENNIAL PLACE p 682
2 CENTENNIAL LANE RR 3, MILLBROOK,
ON, L0A 1G0
(705) 932-4464 SIC 8051

CENTENNIAL PONTIAC BUICK GMC LTD p

413
160 ROTHESAY AVE, SAINT JOHN, NB,
E2J 2B5
(506) 634-2020 SIC 5511

CENTENNIAL REGIONAL HIGH SCHOOL p
1112
See RIVERSIDE SCHOOL BOARD

CENTENNIAL SECONDARY SCHOOL p
199
See SCHOOL DISTRICT NO. 43 (COQUIT-
LAM)

CENTENNIAL SECONDARY SCHOOL p
492
See HASTINGS AND PRINCE EDWARD
DISTRICT SCHOOL BOARD

CENTENNIAL SPECIAL CARE HOME p
1406
See SASKATCHEWAN HEALTH AUTHOR-
ITY

CENTENNIAL SUPPLY LTD p 361
526 CENTENNIAL ST, WINKLER, MB, R6W
1J4
(204) 325-8261 SIC 5171

CENTENNIAL WINDOWS KITCHENER p
648
See CENTENNIAL WINDOWS LTD

CENTENNIAL WINDOWS LTD p 648
687 SOVEREIGN RD, LONDON, ON, N5V
4K8
(519) 451-0508 SIC 1751

CENTENOKA PARK MALL p 268
See R.P. JOHNSON CONSTRUCTION LTD

**CENTER FOR ARTS & TECHNOLOGY
OKANAGAN** p 223
See TEC THE EDUCATION COMPANY INC

CENTERFIRE CONTRACTING LTD p 3
236 STONY MOUNTAIN RD SUITE 106,
ANZAC, AB, T0P 1J0
(780) 334-2277 SIC 1389

CENTERLINE (WINDSOR) LIMITED p 643
595 MORTON DR, LASALLE, ON, N9J 3T8
(519) 734-6886 SIC 3548

CENTERLINE (WINDSOR) LIMITED p 643
655 MORTON DR, LASALLE, ON, N9J 3T9
(519) 734-8330 SIC 3548

CENTERLINE (WINDSOR) LIMITED p 1026
415 MORTON DR, WINDSOR, ON, N9J 3T8
(519) 734-8464 SIC 3599

CENTERLINE GEOMATICS LTD p 127
GD LCD MAIN, FORT MCMURRAY, AB,
T9H 3E2
(780) 881-4696 SIC 8713

CENTERRA GOLD INC p 961
1 UNIVERSITY AVE SUITE 1500,
TORONTO, ON, M5J 2P1
(416) 204-1953 SIC 1081

CENTIMARK LTD p 692
5597 TIMBERLEA BLVD, MISSISSAUGA,
ON, L4W 2S4
(905) 206-0255 SIC 1761

CENTINEL SECURITY p 8
3132 26 ST NE UNIT 335, CALGARY, AB,
T1Y 6Z1
(403) 237-8485 SIC 7381

CENTOCO PLASTICS LIMITED p 1019
2450 CENTRAL AVE, WINDSOR, ON, N8W
4J3
(519) 948-2300 SIC 2499

CENTR REG INTEGRE DE FORMATION p
1109
See COMMISSION SCOLAIRE DU VAL-
DES-CERFS

CENTRA CONSTRUCTION GROUP LTD p
224
20178 98 AVE, LANGLEY, BC, V1M 3G1
(604) 882-5010 SIC 1751

CENTRA GAS MANITOBA INC. p 358
175 NORTH FRONT DR, STEINBACH, MB,
R5G 1X3
(204) 326-9805 SIC 4924

CENTRA INDUSTRIES INC p 538
24 CHERRY BLOSSOM RD, CAMBRIDGE,
ON, N3H 4R7
(519) 650-2828 SIC 3369

CENTRACARE p 416
414 BAY ST, SAINT JOHN, NB, E2M 7L4
(506) 649-2550   SIC 8063

CENTRAIDE DU GRAND MONTREAL p
1194
493 RUE SHERBROOKE O, MONTREAL,
QC, H3A 1B6
(514) 288-1261   SIC 8399

CENTRAIDE LAURENTIDES p 1058
880 BOUL MICHELE-BOHEC BUREAU
107, BLAINVILLE, QC, J7C 5E2
(450) 436-1584   SIC 7389

CENTRAIDE MONTREAL p 1194
See CENTRAIDE DU GRAND MONTREAL

CENTRAL AGENCIES INC p 78
4870 51 ST, CAMROSE, AB, T4V 1S1
(780) 679-2170   SIC 6411

CENTRAL AIR EQUIPMENT LTD p 28
1322 HASTINGS CRES SE, CALGARY, AB,
T2G 4C9
(403) 243-8003   SIC 5084

CENTRAL ALBERTA CO-OP LTD p 153
6201 46 AVE, RED DEER, AB, T4N 6Z1
(403) 309-8913   SIC 5411

CENTRAL ALBERTA GREENHOUSES LTD
p 5
GD, BLACKFALDS, AB, T0M 0J0
(403) 885-4606   SIC 5193

**CENTRAL ALBERTA RESIDENCE SOCI-
ETY** p
153
5000 50 AVE SUITE 300, RED DEER, AB,
T4N 6C2
(403) 342-4550   SIC 8699

**CENTRAL AUTO PARTS DISTRIBUTORS
LTD** p 28
34 HIGHFIELD CIR SE, CALGARY, AB, T2G
5N5
(403) 259-8655   SIC 5013

**CENTRAL AUTOMOTIVE SERVICES LIM-
ITED** p
533
1220 FRANKLIN BLVD, CAMBRIDGE, ON,
N1R 8B7
(519) 653-7161   SIC 5511

CENTRAL BAKERY DEMPSTER p 993
See CANADA BREAD COMPANY, LIMITED

CENTRAL BEAUTY SUPPLY LIMITED p 650
300 ASHLAND AVE, LONDON, ON, N5W
4E4
(519) 453-4590   SIC 5087

**CENTRAL BUILDERS' SUPPLY P.G. LIM-
ITED** p
250
1501 CENTRAL ST W, PRINCE GEORGE,
BC, V2N 1P6
(250) 563-1538   SIC 1541

CENTRAL BUILDING SUPPLIES p 415
See MARITIME HOME IMPROVEMENT
LIMITED

**CENTRAL CANADA FUELS & LUBRI-
CANTS INC** p
910
910 COMMERCE ST, THUNDER BAY, ON,
P7E 6E9
(807) 475-4259   SIC 5172

CENTRAL CANADIAN GLASS LTD p 550
60 SNOW BLVD UNIT 1, CONCORD, ON,
L4K 4B3
(905) 660-1676   SIC 5039

CENTRAL CARRIERS (EDMONTON) LTD p
105
13008 163 ST NW, EDMONTON, AB, T5V
1L6
(780) 447-1610   SIC 4231

CENTRAL CCAC p 771
See CENTRAL COMMUNITY CARE AC-
CESS CENTRE

CENTRAL CITY ASPHALT LTD p 5
39327 RANGE RD, BLACKFALDS, AB, T0M
0J0
(403) 346-5050   SIC 1611

**CENTRAL CITY BREWERS & DISTILLERS
LTD** p 270

11411 BRIDGEVIEW DR, SURREY, BC,
V3R 0C2
(604) 588-2337   SIC 5921

**CENTRAL COMMUNITY CARE ACCESS
CENTRE** p 771
45 SHEPPARD AVE E SUITE 700, NORTH
YORK, ON, M2N 5W9
(416) 222-2241   SIC 8011

CENTRAL DISTRIBUTION CENTRE p 642
See WEBER SUPPLY COMPANY INC

CENTRAL DRUG STORES LTD, THE p 233
495 DUNSMUIR ST, NANAIMO, BC, V9R
6B9
(250) 753-6401   SIC 5912

**CENTRAL EAST LOCAL HEALTH INTE-
GRATION NETWORK** p
1014
See GOVERNMENT OF ONTARIO

CENTRAL FAIRBANK LUMBER p 550
See CENTRAL LUMBER LIMITED

CENTRAL FOODS CO. LTD p 263
12160 HORSESHOE WAY, RICHMOND,
BC, V7A 4V5
(604) 271-9797   SIC 5431

**CENTRAL FRASER VALLEY SEARCH &
RESCUE SOCIETY** p 174
1594 RIVERSIDE RD, ABBOTSFORD, BC,
V2S 8J2
(604) 852-7271   SIC 8999

CENTRAL FRESH MARKET p 638
See CENTRAL MEAT MARKET (KITCH-
ENER) LIMITED

CENTRAL GARAGE LTD p 394
76 RUE NOTRE DAME, ATHOLVILLE, NB,
E3N 3Z2
(506) 753-7731   SIC 5511

**CENTRAL GRAPHICS AND CONTAINER
GROUP LTD** p 692
5526 TIMBERLEA BLVD, MISSISSAUGA,
ON, L4W 2T7
(905) 238-8400   SIC 2653

CENTRAL GROUP, THE p 692
See CENTRAL GRAPHICS AND CON-
TAINER GROUP LTD

CENTRAL HARDWARE LTD p 212
701 BASS AVE, ENDERBY, BC, V0E 1V2
(250) 838-6474   SIC 5211

CENTRAL HAVEN SPECIAL CARE HOME p
1431
1020 AVENUE I N, SASKATOON, SK, S7L
2H7
(306) 844-4040   SIC 8051

**CENTRAL HOME IMPROVEMENT WARE-
HOUSE** p
438
35 MARKET ST, ANTIGONISH, NS, B2G
3B5
(902) 863-6882   SIC 1521

**CENTRAL HOME IMPROVEMENT WARE-
HOUSE** p
463
610 RIVER RD E, NEW GLASGOW, NS,
B2H 3S1
(902) 755-2555   SIC 1521

CENTRAL HOME IMPROVEMENT, DIV OF p
467
See NOVA CAPITAL INCORPORATED

**CENTRAL IRRIGATION SUPPLY OF
CANADA INC** p 550
272 BRADWICK DR, CONCORD, ON, L4K
1K8
(905) 532-0977   SIC 5083

CENTRAL LAUNDRY & LINEN SERVICES p
443
See CROTHALL SERVICES CANADA INC

CENTRAL LUMBER LIMITED p 550
1900 STEELES AVE W, CONCORD, ON,
L4K 1A1
(416) 736-6263   SIC 5031

CENTRAL MACHINE & MARINE INC p 859
649 MCGREGOR SIDE RD, SARNIA, ON,
N7T 7H5
(519) 337-3722   SIC 3599

CENTRAL MACHINERY & METALS p 686

See MARX METALS LIMITED

**CENTRAL MEAT MARKET (KITCHENER)
LIMITED** p 638
760 KING ST W, KITCHENER, ON, N2G
1E6
(519) 576-9400   SIC 5411

CENTRAL MEMORIAL HIGH SCHOOL p 73
See CALGARY BOARD OF EDUCATION

CENTRAL MONTESSORI SCHOOL p 771
See CENTRAL MONTESSORI SCHOOLS
INC

CENTRAL MONTESSORI SCHOOLS INC p
771
200 SHEPPARD AVE E, NORTH YORK,
ON, M2N 3A9
(416) 222-5940   SIC 8211

CENTRAL MOTORS (PELHAM) LTD p 591
227 HWY 20, FONTHILL, ON, L0S 1E6
(905) 892-2653   SIC 5511

CENTRAL MOUNTAIN AIR LTD p 264
4180 AGAR DR, RICHMOND, BC, V7B 1A3
(604) 207-0130   SIC 4512

CENTRAL MOUNTAIN AIR LTD p 269
6431 AIRPORT RD, SMITHERS, BC, V0J
2N2
(250) 877-5000   SIC 4512

**CENTRAL NOVA SCOTIA CIVIC CENTER
SOCIETY** p 468
625 ABENAKI RD, TRURO, NS, B2N 0G6
(902) 893-2224   SIC 8611

**CENTRAL OKANAGAN BOYS & GIRLS
CLUB** p 221
1434 GRAHAM ST, KELOWNA, BC, V1Y
3A8
(250) 762-3914   SIC 8699

**CENTRAL OKANAGAN CHILD DEVELOP-
MENT ASSOCIATION** p
221
1546 BERNARD AVE, KELOWNA, BC, V1Y
6R9
(250) 763-5100   SIC 8699

**CENTRAL ONTARIO DAIRY DISTRIBUTING
INC** p 705
5820 KENNEDY RD, MISSISSAUGA, ON,
L4Z 2C3
(905) 501-9168   SIC 5143

CENTRAL ONTARIO DAIRY DISTRIBUTION
p 705
260 BRUNEL RD SUITE B, MISSISSAUGA,
ON, L4Z 1T5
(905) 507-0084   SIC 5141

**CENTRAL ONTARIO HEALTHCARE PRO-
CUREMENT ALLIANCE** p
851
95 MURAL ST SUITE 300, RICHMOND
HILL, ON, L4B 3G2
(905) 886-5319   SIC 6712

CENTRAL ONTARIO WEB p 485
See 1637136 ONTARIO INC

CENTRAL PARK LODGES p 98
See REVERA INC

CENTRAL PEACE HEALTH COMPLEX p
164
5010 45TH AVE, SPIRIT RIVER, AB, T0H
3G0
(780) 864-3993   SIC 8062

CENTRAL PEEL SECONDARY SCHOOL p
508
See PEEL DISTRICT SCHOOL BOARD

CENTRAL PLAINS CO-OPERATIVE LTD p
1407
203 MAIN ST, ESTON, SK, S0L 1A0
(306) 882-2601   SIC 5399

CENTRAL PLAINS CO-OPERATIVE LTD p
1423
117 1ST AVE E, ROSETOWN, SK, S0L 2V0
(306) 882-2601   SIC 5171

CENTRAL PRECAST INC p 749
25 BONGARD AVE, NEPEAN, ON, K2E 6V2
(613) 225-9510   SIC 3272

**CENTRAL REGIONAL HEALTH AUTHOR-
ITY** p
421
25 PLEASANTVIEW RD, BOTWOOD, NL,

A0H 1E0
(709) 257-2874   SIC 8051

**CENTRAL REGIONAL HEALTH AUTHOR-
ITY** p
423
50 UNION ST, GRAND FALLS-WINDSOR,
NL, A2A 2E1
(709) 292-2500   SIC 8062

CENTRAL ROAST INC p 738
6880 COLUMBUS RD, MISSISSAUGA, ON,
L5T 2G1
(416) 661-7366   SIC 5145

CENTRAL SERVICE STATION LIMITED p
428
160   FLATBAY   JUNCTION   RD,   ST
GEORGES, NL, A0N 1Z0
(709) 647-3500   SIC 1611

CENTRAL STAMPINGS LIMITED p 1019
2525 CENTRAL AVE, WINDSOR, ON, N8W
4J6
(519) 945-1111   SIC 3469

CENTRAL SUN MINING INC p 328
595 BURRARD ST SUITE 3100, VANCOU-
VER, BC, V7X 1L7
(604) 681-8371   SIC 1081

CENTRAL TECHNICAL SCHOOL p 976
See   TORONTO   DISTRICT   SCHOOL
BOARD

CENTRAL TECHNOLOGY SERVICES p 800
See CENTRAL TECHNOLOGY SERVICES
CORPORATION

**CENTRAL TECHNOLOGY SERVICES COR-
PORATION** p
800
1400 CORNWALL RD UNIT 5, OAKVILLE,
ON, L6J 7W5
(905) 829-9480   SIC 7377

CENTRAL TORONTO ACADEMY p 990
See   TORONTO   DISTRICT   SCHOOL
BOARD

**CENTRAL   TORONTO   COMMUNITY
HEALTH CENTRES** p 979
168   BATHURST   ST   SUITE   3199,
TORONTO, ON, M5V 2R4
(416) 703-8480   SIC 8621

**CENTRAL TRANSPORT REFRIGERATION
(MAN.) LTD** p 382
986 WALL ST SUITE 480, WINNIPEG, MB,
R3G 2V3
(204) 772-2481   SIC 5078

CENTRAL TRUCK EQUIPMENT INC p 142
3521 1 AVE S, LETHBRIDGE, AB, T1J 4H1
(403) 328-4189   SIC 5511

CENTRAL VICTORIA SECURITY LTD p 334
612 GARBALLY RD, VICTORIA, BC, V8T
2K2
   SIC 7381

CENTRAL WELDING & IRON WORKS p
762
See 1510610 ONTARIO INC

**CENTRAL WEST COMMUNITY CARE AC-
CESS CENTRE** p
509
199 COUNTY COURT BLVD, BRAMPTON,
ON, L6W 4P3
(905) 796-0040   SIC 8049

**CENTRAL WEST SPECIALIZED DEVELOP-
MENTAL SERVICES** p
526
3782 STAR LANE, BURLINGTON, ON, L7M
5A0
(905) 336-4248   SIC 8322

**CENTRAL WEST SPECIALIZED DEVELOP-
MENTAL SERVICES** p
802
53 BOND ST, OAKVILLE, ON, L6K 1L8
(905) 844-7864   SIC 8322

CENTRAL WIRE INDUSTRIES LTD p 839
1 NORTH ST, PERTH, ON, K7H 2S2
(613) 267-3752   SIC 3312

CENTRALE - HAMEL-CRT, DIV OF p 1299
See HAMEL-CRT S.E.N.C.

CENTRALE ASHTON INC p 1364
104B RUE TURGEON, SAINTE-THERESE,

QC, J7E 3H9

(450) 435-6468   *SIC* 7381

CENTRALE DES SYNDICATS DEMOCRA-TIQUES *p*
1274

990 AV DE BOURGOGNE BUREAU 600, QUEBEC, QC, G1W 0E8

(418) 529-2956   *SIC* 8631

CENTRALE DES SYNDICATS DU QUEBEC (CSQ), LA *p 1163*

9405 RUE SHERBROOKE E, MONTREAL, QC, H1L 6P3

(514) 356-8888   *SIC* 8631

CENTRALE DES SYNDICATS DU QUEBEC (CSQ), LA *p 1258*

320 RUE SAINT-JOSEPH E BUREAU 100, QUEBEC, QC, G1K 9E7

(514) 356-8888   *SIC* 8631

CENTRAP INC *p 1154*

1111 RUE INDUSTRIELLE, MONT-JOLI, QC, G5H 3T9

(418) 775-7202   *SIC* 2431

CENTRE DISTRIBUTION FRUITS ET LEGUMES *p 1067*

See PROVIGO DISTRIBUTION INC

CENTRE ACCEUIL HENRIETTE CERE *p*
1307

6435 CH DE CHAMBLY, SAINT-HUBERT, QC, J3Y 3R6

(450) 678-3291   *SIC* 8361

CENTRE ADMINISTRATIF *p 1054*

See COMMISSION SCOLAIRE DE CHARLEVOIX, LA

CENTRE ADMINISTRATIF DE STE ANNE DES MONTS *p 1355*

See COMMISSION SCOLAIRE DES CHIC-CHOCS

CENTRE ADMINISTRATION KAMOURASKA-CHAUDIERE-APPALACHES *p*
1382

See CAISSE DESJARDINS DE LA REGION DE THETFORD

CENTRE AGRICOLE COATICOOK INC *p*
1081

525 RUE MAIN O, COATICOOK, QC, J1A 1R2

(819) 849-2663   *SIC* 5083

CENTRE AGRICOLE J.L.D. INC *p 1232*

3900 SUD LAVAL (A-440) E, MONTREAL, QC, H7E 5N2

(514) 373-4999   *SIC* 5083

CENTRE AGRICOLE NICOLET-YAMASKA INC *p 1242*

2025 BOUL LOUIS-FRECHETTE, NICO-LET, QC, J3T 1M4

(819) 293-4441   *SIC* 5083

CENTRE AUTO COLLISION LIMITED *p 933*

354 RICHMOND ST E, TORONTO, ON, M5A 1P7

(416) 364-1116   *SIC* 7532

CENTRE BAY YACHT STATION LTD *p 239*

1103 HERITAGE BLVD, NORTH VANCOU-VER, BC, V7J 3G8

(604) 986-0010   *SIC* 6719

CENTRE BOURGET *p 1247*

See CENTRE D'HEBERGEMENT ET DE SOINS DE LONGUE DUREE BOURGET INC

CENTRE CANADIEN D'ARCHITECURE *p*
1214

1920 RUE BAILE, MONTREAL, QC, H3H 2S6

(514) 939-7028   *SIC* 8412

CENTRE CDP CAPITAL *p 1191*

See FONDS SOCIAL DES EMPLOYES DE LA CAISSE DE DEPOT ET PLACEMENT DU QUEBEC

CENTRE CITY CAPITAL LIMITED *p 712*

15 STAVEBANK RD S SUITE 804, MISSIS-SAUGA, ON, L5G 2T2

(905) 891-7770   *SIC* 7011

CENTRE CITY CAPITAL LIMITED *p 712*

1 PORT ST E SUITE 301, MISSISSAUGA, ON, L5G 4N1

(905) 274-5212   *SIC* 6553

CENTRE CITY REAL ESTATE INC *p 249*

1679 15TH AVE, PRINCE GEORGE, BC, V2L 3X2

(250) 552-2757   *SIC* 6531

CENTRE COMMERCIAL D'ASBESTOS
1052

See COOP ALIMENTAIRE DE LA REGION D'ASBESTOS

CENTRE COMMERCIAL PROMENADES ST-NOEL *p 1382*

100 1RE RUE BUREAU 12, THETFORD MINES, QC, G6G 4Y2

(418) 338-6066   *SIC* 6512

CENTRE COMMUNAUTAIRE DE LOISIR DE LA COTE-DES-NEIGES *p 1219*

5347 CH DE LA COTE-DES-NEIGES, MON-TREAL, QC, H3T 1Y4

(514) 733-1478   *SIC* 8322

CENTRE COMMUNAUTAIRE FRANCO-PHONE WINDSOR-ESSEX-KENT INC *p*
1018

7515 FOREST GLADE DR, WINDSOR, ON, N8T 3P5

(519) 948-5545   *SIC* 7299

CENTRE COMMUNAUTAIRE JURIDIQUE DE LA RIVE-SUD *p 1142*

101 BOUL ROLAND-THERRIEN BUREAU 301, LONGUEUIL, QC, J4H 4B9

(450) 928-7655   *SIC* 8111

CENTRE COMMUNAUTAIRE JURIDIQUE DE MONTREAL *p 1194*

425 BOUL DE MAISONNEUVE O BUREAU 600, MONTREAL, QC, H3A 3K5

(514) 864-2111   *SIC* 8111

CENTRE COMMUNAUTAIRE LEONARDO DA VINCI *p 1345*

8370 BOUL LACORDAIRE, SAINT-LEONARD, QC, H1R 3Y6

(514) 955-8350   *SIC* 8322

CENTRE COPL *p 1274*

See UNIVERSITE LAVAL

CENTRE CULTUREL & SPORTIF REGINA ASSUMPTA *p 1171*

See COLLEGE REGINA ASSUMPTA (1995)

CENTRE D HEBERGEMENT SAINTE-ANNE *p*
1154

See CENTRE HOSPITALIER ET CENTRE DE READAPTATION ANTOINE-LABELLE

CENTRE D' HEBERGEMENT ET DE SOINS DE LONGUE DUREE HEATHER INC *p 1281*

3931 RUE LAKESHORE DRIVE, RAWDON, QC, J0K 1S0

(450) 834-3070   *SIC* 8361

CENTRE D' HEBERGEMENT ST MARC DES CARRIERES *p 1347*

See CENTRE DE SANTE ET DE SER-VICES SOCIAUX DE PORTNEUF

CENTRE D'HEBERGEMENT ST-ANTOINE-DE-PADOUE *p*
1347

See GOUVERNEMENT DE LA PROVINCE DE QUEBEC

CENTRE D'ACCEUIL DANTE *p 1165*

See HOPITAL SANTA CABRINI

CENTRE D'ACCEUIL JEANNE CREVIER *p*
1064

151 RUE DE MUY, BOUCHERVILLE, QC, J4B 4W7

SIC 8361

CENTRE D'ACCEUIL PONTIAC *p 1369*

290 RUE MARION, SHAWVILLE, QC, J0X 2Y0

(819) 647-5755   *SIC* 8361

CENTRE D'ACCUEIL DU HAUT-ST LAU-RENT (CHSLD) *p*
1244

65 RUE HECTOR, ORMSTOWN, QC, J0S 1K0

(450) 829-2346   *SIC* 8361

CENTRE D'ACCUEIL FATHER DOWD *p*
1218

6565 CH HUDSON BUREAU 217, MON-

TREAL, QC, H3S 2T7

SIC 8361

CENTRE D'ACCUEIL MARCELLE FERRON *p 1069*

8600 BOUL MARIE-VICTORIN, BROSSARD, QC, J4X 1A1

(450) 923-1430   *SIC* 8361

CENTRE D'ACCUEIL ROGER SEGUIN *p*
544

435 LEMAY ST RR 1, CLARENCE CREEK, ON, K0A 1N0

(613) 488-2053   *SIC* 8361

CENTRE D'ACCUEIL SAINT-JOSEPH DE LEVIS INC *p 1135*

107 RUE SAINT-LOUIS, LEVIS, QC, G6V 4G9

(418) 833-3414   *SIC* 8051

CENTRE D'ACTION DE DEVELOPPEMENT ET DE RECHERCHE EN EMPLOYABILITE *p*
1132

1005 RUE D'UPTON, LASALLE, QC, H8R 2V2

(514) 367-3576   *SIC* 8399

CENTRE D'APPELS TIGERTEL *p 1200*

See TIGERTEL COMMUNICATIONS INC

CENTRE D'EBERGEMENT ANDREE PER-RAULT *p*
1312

See CSSS RICHELIEU-YAMASKA CH DE LA MRC D'ACTON

CENTRE D'EBERGEMENT GAMELIN LAVERGNE *p 1174*

See CENTRE DE SANTE ET DE SER-VICES SOCIAUX JEANNE-MANCE

CENTRE D'EDUCATION DES ADULTES DU CHEMIN-DU-ROY *p 1385*

See COMMISSION SCOLAIRE DU CHEMIN-DU-ROY

CENTRE D'ENTRAINEMENT A LA VIE DE CHICOUTIMI INC *p 1078*

766 RUE DU CENACLE, CHICOUTIMI, QC, G7H 2J2

(418) 549-4003   *SIC* 8361

CENTRE D'ESTIMATION LA CAPITALE QUEBEC *p 1261*

See BUREAU D'EVALUATION DE QUEBEC INC

CENTRE D'ETUDE ET DE COOPERATION INTERNATIONALE *p 1168*

3000 RUE OMER-LAVALLEE, MONTREAL, QC, H1Y 3R8

(514) 875-9911   *SIC* 8322

CENTRE D'ETUDES INTERAMERICAINES *p 1274*

See UNIVERSITE LAVAL

CENTRE D'EVALUATION & READAPTION PHYSIQUE C.E.R.P. INC *p 1235*

3095 NORD LAVAL (A-440) O, MONTREAL, QC, H7P 4W5

(450) 688-0445   *SIC* 8049

CENTRE D'HEBERGEMENT CHAMPLAIN *p*
1069

See CENTRE DE SANTE ET DE SER-VICES SOCIAUX CHAMPLAIN

CENTRE D'HEBERGEMENT CHAMPLAIN-DES-MONTAGNES *p*
1280

See GROUPE CHAMPLAIN INC

CENTRE D'HEBERGEMENT CHAMPLAIN-JEAN-LOUIS-LAPIERRE *p*
1298

See GROUPE CHAMPLAIN INC

CENTRE D'HEBERGEMENT DE CHATEAU-GUAY *p*
1076

See CENTRE INTEGRE DE SANTE ET DE SERVICES SOCIAUX DE LA MONTEREGIE-OUEST

CENTRE D'HEBERGEMENT DE CONTRE-COEUR *p*
1082

See CENTRE DE SANTE ET DE SER-VICES SOCIAUX PIERRE-BOUCHER

CENTRE D'HEBERGEMENT DE LA

PINIERE *p 1231*

See CENTRE DE SANTE ET DE SER-VICES SOCIAUX DE LAVAL

CENTRE D'HEBERGEMENT DE LA RIVE, LE *p 1399*

See PRODIMAX INC

CENTRE D'HEBERGEMENT DE LACHINE *p*
1126

See CENTRE DE SANTE ET DE SER-VICES SOCIAUX DE DORVAL-LACHINE-LASALLE

CENTRE D'HEBERGEMENT DE NAZAIRE PICHE *p 1126*

150 15E AV BUREAU 319, LACHINE, QC, H8S 3L9

(514) 637-2326   *SIC* 8361

CENTRE D'HEBERGEMENT DE SAINT-BENOIT, LE *p*
1153

See CENTRE INTEGRE DE SANTE ET DE SERVICES SOCIAUX DES LAURENTIDES

CENTRE D'HEBERGEMENT DRAPEAU-DESCHAMBAULT *p*
1364

See CENTRE DE SANTE ET DE SER-VICES SOCIAUX DE THERESE-DE-BLAINVILLE

CENTRE D'HEBERGEMENT DU BOISE LTEE *p 1274*

3690 BOUL NEILSON, QUEBEC, QC, G1W 0A9

(418) 781-0471   *SIC* 8361

CENTRE D'HEBERGEMENT DU FARGY *p*
1255

See CENTRE INTEGRE UNIVERSITAIRE DE SANTE ET DE SERVICES SOCIAUX DE LA CAPITALE-NATIONALE, LE

CENTRE D'HEBERGEMENT ET DE SOINS DE LONGUE DUREE BOURGET INC *p 1247*

11570 RUE NOTRE-DAME E, POINTE-AUX-TREMBLES, QC, H1B 2X4

(514) 645-1673   *SIC* 8051

CENTRE D'HEBERGEMENT ET DE SOINS DE LONGUE DUREE LOUISE-FAUBERT INC *p 1319*

300 RUE DU DOCTEUR-CHARLES-LEONARD, SAINT-JEROME, QC, J7Y 0N2

(450) 710-1770   *SIC* 8059

CENTRE D'HEBERGEMENT ET DE SOINS DE LONGUE DUREE MONT-ROYAL *p 1155*

See VIGI SANTE LTEE

CENTRE D'HEBERGEMENT ET DE SOINS DE LONGUE DUREE PIERREFONDS *p 1245*

See VIGI SANTE LTEE

CENTRE D'HEBERGEMENT ET DE SOINS DE LONGUE DUREE PROVIDENCE SAINT-JOSEPH INC *p*
1165

5605 RUE BEAUBIEN E BUREAU 114, MONTREAL, QC, H1T 1X4

(514) 254-4991   *SIC* 8661

CENTRE D'HEBERGEMENT FERNAND LAROCQUE *p 1357*

See GOUVERNEMENT DE LA PROVINCE DE QUEBEC

CENTRE D'HEBERGEMENT HUBERT MAI-SON NEUVE *p*
1287

See CLSC-CHSLD THERESE DE BLAINVILLE

CENTRE D'HEBERGEMENT LA PIETA *p*
1105

See CENTRE DE SANTE ET DE SER-VICES SOCIAUX DE GATINEAU

CENTRE D'HEBERGEMENT NOTRE DAME DE LOURDES & SAINT CHARLES *p 1259*

See GOUVERNEMENT DE LA PROVINCE DE QUEBEC

CENTRE D'HEBERGEMENT SAINTE-DOROTHEE *p*
1238

See CENTRE DE SANTE ET DE SER-VICES SOCIAUX DE LAVAL

CENTRE D'HEBERGEMENT SOIN

LONGUE DUREE MRC DE MASKINONGE, LE   *p* 1146
181 6E AV, LOUISEVILLE, QC, J5V 1V2
(819) 228-2706   *SIC* 8361

CENTRE D'HEBERGEMENT ST-JEAN-EUDES INC   *p*
1256
6000 3E AV O, QUEBEC, QC, G1H 7J5
(418) 627-1124   *SIC* 8051

CENTRE D'HEBERGEMENT ST-VINCENT DE MARIE INC   *p* 1323
1175 BOUL DE LA COTE-VERTU, SAINT-LAURENT, QC, H4L 5J1
(514) 744-1175   *SIC* 8051

CENTRE D'HEBERGEMENT YVONNE-SYLVAIN   *p*
1255
See CENTRE DE SANTE ET DE SERVICES SOCIAUX DE QUEBEC-NORD

CENTRE D'HERBEGREMNT DE DORVAL *p*
1096
See CHSLD LACHINE, NAZAIRE PICHE ET FOYER DORVAL, LES

CENTRE D'INFORMATION RX LTEE *p* 1392
245 RUE JEAN-COUTU, VARENNES, QC, J3X 0E1
(450) 646-9760   *SIC* 7376

CENTRE D'INITIATIVE TECHNOLOGIQUE DE MONTREAL (CITEC)   *p* 1336
See TECHNOPARC MONTREAL

CENTRE D'INSEMINATION ARTIFICIELLE DU QUEBEC (C.I.A.Q.) SOCIETE EN COMMANDITE   *p*
1311
3450 RUE SICOTTE, SAINT-HYACINTHE, QC, J2S 2M2
(450) 774-1141   *SIC* 8093

CENTRE DE BENEVOLAT DE LA TUQUE INC   *p* 1124
497 RUE SAINT-ANTOINE, LA TUQUE, QC, G9X 2Y3
   SIC 8322

CENTRE DE CARROSSERIE SAUVAGEAU *p* 1351
See LOCATION SAUVAGEAU INC

CENTRE DE CONDITIONNEMENT PHYSIQUE ATLANTIS INC   *p* 1399
1201 BOUL DES LAURENTIDES, VIMONT, QC, H7M 2X9
(450) 629-1500   *SIC* 3949

CENTRE DE CONDITIONNEMENT PHYSIQUE INC.   *p* 1231
4745 AV DES INDUSTRIES, MONTREAL, QC, H7C 1A1
(450) 664-2285   *SIC* 3949

CENTRE DE CONDITIONNEMENT PHYSIQUE L'OPTION SANTE   *p* 1177
See SPORTS MONTREAL INC

CENTRE DE CONFORMITE ICC INC *p* 1093
88 AV LINDSAY, DORVAL, QC, H9P 2T8
(514) 636-8146   *SIC* 5199

CENTRE DE CONGRES DE SAINT-HYACINTHE   *p*
1311
See 9343-0114 QUEBEC INC

CENTRE DE COULEE SHAWINIGAN A/S CLD DE SHAWINIGAN   *p* 1081
See SOTREM (1993) INC

CENTRE DE COUPE PREMOULE DE QUEBEC   *p*
1267
See PREMOULE INC

CENTRE DE DISTRIBUTION COUCHE-TARD   *p*
1234
See DISTRIBUTION COUCHE-TARD INC

CENTRE DE DISTRIBUTION ELECTRIQUE LIMITEE   *p* 1319
298 RUE DE MARTIGNY O, SAINT-JEROME, QC, J7Y 4C9
(450) 438-1263   *SIC* 5063

CENTRE DE DISTRIBUTION GROUPE ALDO   *p* 1329
See GROUPE ALDO INC, LE

CENTRE DE DISTRIBUTION ROBERT   *p*
1065
See GROUPE ROBERT INC

CENTRE DE DISTRIBUTION VITESSE   *p*
1127
See CORPORATION TRANSPORT VITESSE

CENTRE DE FORMATION ECONOLER   *p*
1258
See ECONOLER INC

CENTRE DE FORMATION PROFESSIONNEL DE LEVIS   *p*
1136
See COMMISSION SCOLAIRE DES NAVIGATEURS

CENTRE DE FORMATION PROFESSIONNEL QUALITECH   *p*
1384
See COMMISSION SCOLAIRE DU CHEMIN-DU-ROY

CENTRE DE FORMATION PROFESSIONNELLE   *p*
1390
See COMMISSION SCOLAIRE DE L'OR-ET-DES-BOIS

CENTRE DE FORMATION PROFESSIONNELLE BEL-AVENIR   *p*
1385
See COMMISSION SCOLAIRE DU CHEMIN-DU-ROY

CENTRE DE FORMATION PROFESSIONNELLE DE BLACK LAKE   *p*
1383
See COMMISSION SCOLAIRE DES APPALACHES

CENTRE DE FORMATION PROFESSIONNELLE MARIE ROLLET   *p*
1271
See COMMISSION SCOLAIRE DES DECOUVREURS

CENTRE DE FORMATION PROFESSIONNELLE PAVILLON BEGIN   *p*
1045
See COMMISSION SCOLAIRE DU LAC-ST-JEAN

CENTRE DE FORMATION PROFESSIONNELLE PIERRE DUPUY   *p*
1146
1150 CH DU TREMBLAY, LONGUEUIL, QC, J4N 1A2
(450) 468-4000   *SIC* 8211

CENTRE DE GOLF, LE VERSANT INC   *p*
1381
2075 COTE DE TERREBONNE, TERREBONNE, QC, J6Y 1H6
(450) 964-2291   *SIC* 7992

CENTRE DE GRAINS   *p* 1398
See VIVACO, GROUPE COOPERATIF

CENTRE DE L'AUTO BLAIN, MARIO INC, LE   *p* 1151
545 BOUL LAURIER, MCMASTERVILLE, QC, J3G 6P2
(450) 464-4551   *SIC* 5511

CENTRE DE L'ESCALIER INC   *p* 1380
3535 BOUL DES ENTREPRISES, TERREBONNE, QC, J6X 4J9
(514) 592-0241   *SIC* 2431

CENTRE DE LA NATURE DU MONT-SAINT-HILAIRE   *p*
1158
422 CH DES MOULINS, MONT-SAINT-HILAIRE, QC, J3G 4S6
(450) 467-1755   *SIC* 8999

CENTRE DE LA PETITE ENFANCE LA GIBOULEE   *p*
1238
531 RUE HUBERDEAU, MONTREAL, QC, H7X 1P6
(450) 689-6442   *SIC* 8351

CENTRE DE LA PETITE ENFANCE PARC-EN-CIEL   *p*
1090
888 RUE SAINT-ANTOINE, DISRAELI, QC, G0N 1E0

(418) 449-3004   *SIC* 8351

CENTRE DE LA SANTE ET DU SERVICES SOCIAUX DE LA BASSE COTE-NORD   *p*
1147
1070 BOUL DOCTEUR-CAMILLE-MARCOUX, LOURDES-DE-BLANC-SABLON, QC, G0G 1W0
(418) 461-2144   *SIC* 8062

CENTRE DE LA SARRE   *p* 1123
See UNIVERSITE DU QUEBEC

CENTRE DE LANGUES INTERNATIONALES CHARPENTIER   *p*
1371
20 RUE BRYANT, SHERBROOKE, QC, J1J 3E4
(819) 822-2542   *SIC* 8299

CENTRE DE LOCATION G.M. INC   *p* 1152
12075 RUE ARTHUR-SICARD BUREAU 101, MIRABEL, QC, J7J 0E9
(450) 434-0505   *SIC* 7359

CENTRE DE MAINTENANCE ANDY INC, LE *p* 1365
4225 BOUL HEBERT, SALABERRY-DE-VALLEYFIELD, QC, J6S 6J2
(514) 667-8500   *SIC* 4731

CENTRE DE MATERIAUX COMPOSITES *p*
1321
170 RUE DU PARC, SAINT-JOSEPH-DE-BEAUCE, QC, G0S 2V0
(418) 397-6514   *SIC* 8631

CENTRE DE MECANIQUE DU GOLFE INC *p*
1367
336 AV NOEL, SEPT-ILES, QC, G4R 1L7
(418) 962-4057   *SIC* 5084

CENTRE DE MEDECINE SPORTIVE DE LAVAL ET PHYSIO PLUS   *p* 1235
See CENTRE D'EVALUATION & READAPTION PHYSIQUE C.E.R.P. INC

CENTRE DE MELANGE D'ENGRAIS *p* 1306
See AGRILAIT, COOPERATIVE AGRICOLE

CENTRE DE MOTOS INC   *p*
8705 BOUL TASCHEREAU, BROSSARD, QC, J4Y 1A4
(450) 443-4488   *SIC* 5571

CENTRE DE PIECES ET SERVICES EXPERT INC   *p*
1169
8260 BOUL PIE-IX, MONTREAL, QC, H1Z 3T6
(514) 943-5755   *SIC* 5064

CENTRE DE PLOMBERIE ST-JEROME INC *p* 1173
1075 BOUL DU GRAND-HERON, SAINT-JEROME, QC, J5L 1G2
(450) 436-2318   *SIC* 1711

CENTRE DE PORTES ET FENETRES NOUVELLE   *p*
1244
See CONSTRUCTION MICHEL MALTAIS INC

CENTRE DE PREVENTION DU SUICIDE: ACCALMIE   *p* 1387
1905 RUE ROYALE, TROIS-RIVIERES, QC, G9A 4K8
(819) 378-8585   *SIC* 8999

CENTRE DE PROTECTION ET DE READAPTATION DE LA COTE-NORD   *p*
1053
835 BOUL JOLLIET, BAIE-COMEAU, QC, G5C 1P5
(418) 589-9927   *SIC* 8361

CENTRE DE PSYCHOLOGIE GOUIN INC *p*
1216
39 BOUL GOUIN O, MONTREAL, QC, H3L 1H9
(514) 331-5530   *SIC* 8049

CENTRE DE READAPTATION CONSTANCE LETHBRIDGE   *p*
1222
See GOUVERNEMENT DE LA PROVINCE DE QUEBEC

CENTRE DE READAPTATION CONSTANCE LETHBRIDGE, LE   *p*
1221

7005 BOUL DE MAISONNEUVE O, MONTREAL, QC, H4B 1T3
(514) 487-1770   *SIC* 8093

CENTRE DE READAPTATION EN DEFICIENCE INTELLECTUELLE ET TED   *p*
1135
55 RUE DU MONT-MARIE, LEVIS, QC, G6V 0B8
(418) 833-3218   *SIC* 8361

CENTRE DE READAPTATION EN DEFICIENCE INTELLECTUELLE ET TED   *p*
1159
20 AV COTE, MONTMAGNY, QC, G5V 1Z9
(418) 248-4970   *SIC* 8361

CENTRE DE READAPTATION EN DEFICIENCE PHYSIQUE LE BOUCLIER   *p*
1114
1075 BOUL FIRESTONE BUREAU 1000, JOLIETTE, QC, J6E 6X6
(450) 755-2741   *SIC* 8011

CENTRE DE READAPTATION EN DEFICIENCE PHYSIQUE LE BOUCLIER   *p*
1320
225 RUE DU PALAIS, SAINT-JEROME, QC, J7Z 1X7
(450) 560-9898   *SIC* 8011

CENTRE DE READAPTATION INTERNATIONAL   *p*
1386
3450 RUE SAINTE-MARGUERITE, TROIS-RIVIERES, QC, G8Z 1X3
(819) 691-7536   *SIC* 5047

CENTRE DE READAPTATION LA MAISON *p* 1289
7 9E RUE, ROUYN-NORANDA, QC, J9X 2A9
(819) 762-6592   *SIC* 8011

CENTRE DE READAPTATION LA MYRIADE, LE   *p*
1149
1280 CH SAINT-HENRI, MASCOUCHE, QC, J7K 2N1
(450) 474-4175   *SIC* 8361

CENTRE DE READAPTATION LE BOUCLIER   *p* 1320
See CENTRE DE READAPTATION EN DEFICIENCE PHYSIQUE LE BOUCLIER

CENTRE DE READAPTATION LE GOUVERNAIL   *p*
1255
See FONDATION DU CENTRE JEUNESSE DE QUEBEC

CENTRE DE READAPTATION LUCIE-BRUNEAU   *p*
1172
See CENTRE INTEGRE UNIVERSITAIRE SANTE ET SERVICES SOCIAUX DU CENTRE-SUD-DE-L'ILE-DE-MONTREAL

CENTRE DE READAPTATION MAB-MACKAY   *p*
1222
7000 RUE SHERBROOKE O, MONTREAL, QC, H4B 1R3
(514) 489-8201   *SIC* 8093

CENTRE DE READAPTATION MARIE ENFANT   *p*
1219
See CENTRE HOSPITALIER UNIVERSITAIRE SAINTE-JUSTINE

CENTRE DE READAPTATION MARIE ENFANT DU CHU SAINTE-JUSTINE   *p* 1165
See CENTRE HOSPITALIER UNIVERSITAIRE SAINTE-JUSTINE

CENTRE DE READAPTATION POUR LES JEUNES EN DIFFICULTE D'ADAPTATION DE JOLIETTE   *p* 1114
See CENTRES JEUNESSE DE LANAUDIERE, LES

CENTRE DE READAPTATION SPECIALISE EN SURDITE ET EN COMMUNICATION   *p*
1175
See INSTITUT RAYMOND-DEWAR

CENTRE DE RECEPTION LE MADISON

INC p 1345
8750 BOUL PROVENCHER, SAINT-LEONARD, QC, H1R 3N7
(514) 374-7428 *SIC* 7299

CENTRE DE RECHERCHE DE L'INSTITUT DE CARDIOLOGIE DE MONTREAL p 1165
See INSTITUT DE CARDIOLOGIE DE MONTREAL

CENTRE DE RECHERCHE EN INFECTIOLOGIE (CRI) p 1271
2705 BOUL LAURIER BUREAU RC 709, QUEBEC, QC, G1V 4G2
(418) 654-2705 *SIC* 8748

CENTRE DE RECHERCHE FERNAD SEGUIN p 1164
See FONDATION DE L'INSTITUT UNIVERSITAIRE EN SANTE MENTALE DE MONTREAL

CENTRE DE RECHERCHE INDUSTRIELLE DU QUEBEC p 1266
333 RUE FRANQUET, QUEBEC, QC, G1P 4C7
(418) 659-1550 *SIC* 8731

CENTRE DE RECHERCHE INFORMATIQUE DE MONTREAL INC p 1217
405 AV OGILVY BUREAU 101, MONTREAL, QC, H3N 1M3
(514) 840-1234 *SIC* 8731

CENTRE DE REFERENCE EN AGRICULTURE ET AGROALIMENTAIRE DU QUEBEC p 1271
2875 BOUL LAURIER UNITE 900, QUEBEC, QC, G1V 5B1
(418) 523-5411 *SIC* 8699

CENTRE DE RENOVATION ANDRE LESPERANCE INC p 1364
227 BOUL RENE-A.-ROBERT, SAINTE-THERESE, QC, J7E 4L1
(450) 430-6220 *SIC* 5211

CENTRE DE RENOVATION F D S INC p 1116
3460 BOUL SAINT-FRANCOIS UNITE B001, JONQUIERE, QC, G7X 8L3
(418) 548-4676 *SIC* 5211

CENTRE DE RENOVATION G. HARVEY p 1348
See MATERIAUX AUDET INC

CENTRE DE RENOVATION RAYMOND BOIES INC p 1055
215 RUE LACHANCE, BEAUPRE, QC, G0A 1E0
(418) 827-4531 *SIC* 5211

CENTRE DE RENOVATION RAYMOND BOIES INC p 1075
8540 BOUL SAINTE-ANNE, CHATEAU-RICHER, QC, G0A 1N0
(418) 824-4533 *SIC* 5211

CENTRE DE RENOVATION TERREBONNE INC p 1380
1505 CH GASCON, TERREBONNE, QC, J6X 2Z6
(450) 471-6631 *SIC* 5251

CENTRE DE RESSOURCES EDUCATIVES ET COMMUNAUTAIRES POUR ADULTES p 1171
10770 RUE CHAMBORD, MONTREAL, QC, H2C 2R8
(514) 596-7629 *SIC* 7389

CENTRE DE SANTE & DE SERVICES SOCIAUX DE MATANE p 1150
349 AV SAINT-JEROME, MATANE, QC, G4W 3A8
(418) 562-5741 *SIC* 8611

CENTRE DE SANTE D'EASTMAN INC p 1100
895 CH DES DILIGENCES, EASTMAN, QC, J0E 1P0
(450) 297-3009 *SIC* 7991

CENTRE DE SANTE DE LA HAUT ST CHARLES p 1275

1105
273 RUE LAURIER, GATINEAU, QC, J8X 3W8
(819) 966-6420 *SIC* 8062

CENTRE DE SANTE ET DE SERVICES SOCIAUX DE L'OUEST-DE-L'ILE p 1249
160 AV STILLVIEW, POINTE-CLAIRE, QC, H9R 2Y2
(514) 630-2225 *SIC* 8062

CENTRE DE SANTE ET DE SERVICES SOCIAUX DE LA HAUTE-GASPESIE p 1355
50 RUE DU BELVEDERE, SAINTE-ANNE-DES-MONTS, QC, G4V 1X4
(418) 797-2744 *SIC* 8621

CENTRE DE SANTE ET DE SERVICES SOCIAUX DE LA MAINGANIE p 1113
1035 PROM DES ANCIENS, HAVRE-SAINT-PIERRE, QC, G0G 1P0
(418) 538-2212 *SIC* 8093

CENTRE DE SANTE ET DE SERVICES SOCIAUX DE LA MRC DE COATICOOK p 1081
138 RUE JEANNE-MANCE, COATICOOK, QC, J1A 1W3
(819) 849-4876 *SIC* 8062

CENTRE DE SANTE ET DE SERVICES SOCIAUX DE LA POINTE-DE-L'ILE p 1163
4900 BOUL LAPOINTE, MONTREAL, QC, H1K 4W9
(514) 353-1227 *SIC* 8361

CENTRE DE SANTE ET DE SERVICES SOCIAUX DE LA POMMERAIE, LE p 1378
50 RUE WESTERN, SUTTON, QC, J0E 2K0
(450) 538-3332 *SIC* 8361

CENTRE DE SANTE ET DE SERVICES SOCIAUX DE LA VALLEE-DE-L'OR p 1148
1141 RUE ROYALE, MALARTIC, QC, J0Y 1Z0
(819) 825-5858 *SIC* 8062

CENTRE DE SANTE ET DE SERVICES SOCIAUX DE LA VALLEE-DE-L'OR p 1390
1265 BOUL FOREST, VAL-D'OR, QC, J9P 5H3
(819) 825-5858 *SIC* 8011

CENTRE DE SANTE ET DE SERVICES SOCIAUX DE LA VALLEE-DE-LA-BATISCAN p 1355
60 RUE DE LA FABRIQUE BUREAU 217, SAINTE-ANNE-DE-LA-PERADE, QC, G0X 2J0
(418) 325-2313 *SIC* 8051

CENTRE DE SANTE ET DE SERVICES SOCIAUX DE LA VALLEE-DE-LA-BATISCAN p 1358
90 RANG RIVIERE VEILLETTE, SAINTE-GENEVIEVE-DE-BATISCAN, QC, G0X 2R0
(418) 362-2727 *SIC* 8399

CENTRE DE SANTE ET DE SERVICES SOCIAUX DE LA VALLEE-DE-LA-GATINEAU p 1148
See FONDATION SANTE VALLEE-DE-LA-GATINEAU

CENTRE DE SANTE ET DE SERVICES SOCIAUX DE LA VIEILLE-CAPITALE p 1258
50 RUE SAINT-JOSEPH E, QUEBEC, QC, G1K 3A5
(418) 529-2572 *SIC* 8322

CENTRE DE SANTE ET DE SERVICES SOCIAUX DE LA VIEILLE-CAPITALE p 1261
1451 BOUL PERE-LELIEVRE BUREAU 363, QUEBEC, QC, G1M 1N8
(418) 683-2516 *SIC* 8361

CENTRE DE SANTE ET DE SERVICES SOCIAUX DE LA VIEILLE-CAPITALE p 1268

55 CH SAINTE-FOY, QUEBEC, QC, G1R 1S9
(418) 641-2572 *SIC* 8011

CENTRE DE SANTE ET DE SERVICES SOCIAUX DE LAVAL p 1084
1755 BOUL RENE-LAENNEC, COTE SAINT-LUC, QC, H7M 3L9
(450) 668-1010 *SIC* 8099

CENTRE DE SANTE ET DE SERVICES SOCIAUX DE LAVAL p 1092
1515 BOUL CHOMEDEY, DORVAL, QC, H7V 3Y7
(450) 978-8300 *SIC* 8062

CENTRE DE SANTE ET DE SERVICES SOCIAUX DE LAVAL p 1231
4895 RUE SAINT-JOSEPH, MONTREAL, QC, H7C 1H6
(450) 661-3305 *SIC* 8361

CENTRE DE SANTE ET DE SERVICES SOCIAUX DE LAVAL p 1238
350 BOUL SAMSON O, MONTREAL, QC, H7X 1J4
(450) 689-0933 *SIC* 8361

CENTRE DE SANTE ET DE SERVICES SOCIAUX DE LAVAL p 1241
800 BOUL CHOMEDEY BUREAU 200, MONTREAL-OUEST, QC, H7V 3Y4
(450) 682-2952 *SIC* 8399

CENTRE DE SANTE ET DE SERVICES SOCIAUX DE MEMPHREMAGOG p 1147
See GOUVERNEMENT DE LA PROVINCE DE QUEBEC

CENTRE DE SANTE ET DE SERVICES SOCIAUX DE PORTNEUF p 1092
250 BOUL GAUDREAU BUREAU 370, DONNACONA, QC, G3M 1L7
(418) 285-3025 *SIC* 8361

CENTRE DE SANTE ET DE SERVICES SOCIAUX DE PORTNEUF p 1347
444 RUE BEAUCHAMP, SAINT-MARC-DES-CARRIERES, QC, G0A 4B0
(418) 268-3511 *SIC* 8361

CENTRE DE SANTE ET DE SERVICES SOCIAUX DE PORTNEUF p 1348
1045 BOUL BONA-DUSSAULT, SAINT-MARC-DES-CARRIERES, QC, G0A 4B0
(418) 268-3571 *SIC* 7991

CENTRE DE SANTE ET DE SERVICES SOCIAUX DE PORTNEUF p 1351
700 RUE SAINT-CYRILLE BUREAU 850, SAINT-RAYMOND, QC, G3L 1W1
(418) 337-4611 *SIC* 8062

CENTRE DE SANTE ET DE SERVICES SOCIAUX DE QUEBEC-NORD p 1055
11000 RUE DES MONTAGNARDS, BEAUPRE, QC, G0A 1E0
(418) 827-3726 *SIC* 8062

CENTRE DE SANTE ET DE SERVICES SOCIAUX DE QUEBEC-NORD p 1254
4E ETAGE 2915, AV DU BOURG-ROYAL, QUEBEC, QC, G1C 3S2
(418) 661-5666 *SIC* 8011

CENTRE DE SANTE ET DE SERVICES SOCIAUX DE QUEBEC-NORD p 1255
3365 RUE GUIMONT, QUEBEC, QC, G1E 2H1
(418) 663-8171 *SIC* 8361

CENTRE DE SANTE ET DE SERVICES SOCIAUX DE QUEBEC-NORD p 1256
190 76E RUE E, QUEBEC, QC, G1H 7K4

See CENTRE DE SANTE ET DE SERVICES SOCIAUX DE QUEBEC-NORD

CENTRE DE SANTE DE LA HAUT ST CHARLES p 1281
See CENTRE DE SANTE ET DE SERVICES SOCIAUX DE QUEBEC-NORD-CLSC DE LA JACQUES-CARTIER -VAL-BELA

CENTRE DE SANTE DE TEMISCAMING INC p 1378
180 RUE ANVIK, TEMISCAMING, QC, J0Z 3R0
SIC 8062

CENTRE DE SANTE ET DE SERVICE SOCIAUX DE LA REGION DE THETFORD 1382
1717 RUE NOTRE-DAME E, THETFORD MINES, QC, G6G 2V4
(418) 338-7777 *SIC* 8399

CENTRE DE SANTE ET DE SERVICE SOCIAUX DU HAUT SAINT-FRANCOIS, LE 1400
245 RUE SAINT-JANVIER, WEEDON, QC, J0B 3J0
SIC 7041

CENTRE DE SANTE ET DE SERVICE SOCIAUX LES ESKERS DE L'ABITIBI p 1046
632 1RE RUE O, AMOS, QC, J9T 2N2
(819) 732-3271 *SIC* 8062

CENTRE DE SANTE ET DE SERVICES SOCIAUX - INSTITUT UNIVERSITAIRE DE GERIATRIE DE SHERBROOKE p 1371
375 RUE ARGYLL, SHERBROOKE, QC, J1J 3H5
(819) 780-2222 *SIC* 8099

CENTRE DE SANTE ET DE SERVICES SOCIAUX CHAMPLAIN p 1069
5050 PLACE NOGENT, BROSSARD, QC, J4Y 2K3
(450) 672-3328 *SIC* 8322

CENTRE DE SANTE ET DE SERVICES SOCIAUX DE BEAUCE p 1304
12523 25E AV, SAINT-GEORGES, QC, G5Y 5N6
(418) 228-2244 *SIC* 8399

CENTRE DE SANTE ET DE SERVICES SOCIAUX DE CHICOUTIMI p 1078
1236 RUE D'ANGOULEME, CHICOUTIMI, QC, G7H 6P9
(418) 698-3907 *SIC* 8361

CENTRE DE SANTE ET DE SERVICES SOCIAUX DE CHICOUTIMI p 1078
305 RUE SAINT-VALLIER, CHICOUTIMI, QC, G7H 5H6
(418) 541-1046 *SIC* 8011

CENTRE DE SANTE ET DE SERVICES SOCIAUX DE DORVAL-LACHINE-LASALLE p 1126
650 PLACE D'ACCUEIL, LACHINE, QC, H8S 3Z5
(514) 634-7161 *SIC* 8361

CENTRE DE SANTE ET DE SERVICES SOCIAUX DE DORVAL-LACHINE-LASALLE p 1126
1900 RUE NOTRE-DAME BUREAU 262, LACHINE, QC, H8S 2G2
(514) 639-0650 *SIC* 7991

CENTRE DE SANTE ET DE SERVICES SOCIAUX DE DORVAL-LACHINE-LASALLE p 1131
650 16E AV, LASALLE, QC, H8P 2S3
(514) 637-2351 *SIC* 8062

CENTRE DE SANTE ET DE SERVICES SOCIAUX DE GATINEAU p 1104
85 RUE BELLEHUMEUR BUREAU 301, GATINEAU, QC, J8T 8B7
(819) 966-6016 *SIC* 8062

CENTRE DE SANTE ET DE SERVICES SOCIAUX DE GATINEAU p

(418) 628-6808   *SIC* 8011
CENTRE DE SANTE ET DE SERVICES SO-CIAUX DE QUEBEC-NORD   *p*
1275
11999 RUE DE L'HOPITAL BUREAU 217, QUEBEC, QC, G2A 2T7
(418) 843-2572   *SIC* 8399
CENTRE DE SANTE ET DE SERVICES SOCIAUX DE QUEBEC-NORD-CLSC DE LA JACQUES-CARTIER -VAL-BELA   *p* 1281
1465 RUE DE L'ETNA, QUEBEC, QC, G3K 2S2
(418) 843-2572   *SIC* 8699
CENTRE DE SANTE ET DE SERVICES SO-CIAUX DE RIVIERE-DU-LOUP   *p*
1286
28 RUE JOLY, RIVIERE-DU-LOUP, QC, G5R 3H2
(418) 862-6385   *SIC* 8059
CENTRE DE SANTE ET DE SERVICES SO-CIAUX DE THERESE-DE-BLAINVILLE   *p*
1364
125 RUE DUQUET, SAINTE-THERESE, QC, J7E 0A5
(450) 430-4553   *SIC* 8322
CENTRE DE SANTE ET DE SERVICES SO-CIAUX DU COEUR-DE-L'ILE   *p*
1182
See SYNDICAT DES PROFESSION-NELLES EN SOINS DU CENTRE DE SANTE ET SERVICES SOCIAUX DU COEUR DE
CENTRE DE SANTE ET DE SERVICES SO-CIAUX DU PONTIAC   *p*
1254
2135 RUE DE LA TERRASSE-CADIEUX, QUEBEC, QC, G1C 1Z2
(418) 667-3910   *SIC* 8051
CENTRE DE SANTE ET DE SERVICES SO-CIAUX DU SUD-OUEST-VERDUN   *p*
1223
6161 RUE LAURENDEAU, MONTREAL, QC, H4E 3X6
(514) 762-2777   *SIC* 8062
CENTRE DE SANTE ET DE SERVICES SO-CIAUX DU SUD-OUEST-VERDUN   *p*
1396
4000 BOUL LASALLE, VERDUN, QC, H4G 2A3
(514) 362-1000   *SIC* 8062
CENTRE DE SANTE ET DE SERVICES SO-CIAUX JEANNE-MANCE   *p*
1174
1440 RUE DUFRESNE, MONTREAL, QC, H2K 3J3
(514) 527-8921   *SIC* 8361
CENTRE DE SANTE ET DE SERVICES SO-CIAUX LA POMMERAIE   *p*
1056
34 RUE SAINT-JOSEPH, BEDFORD, QC, J0J 1A0
(450) 248-4304   *SIC* 8621
CENTRE DE SANTE ET DE SERVICES SO-CIAUX LA POMMERAIE   *p*
1101
800 RUE SAINT-PAUL, FARNHAM, QC, J2N 2K6
(450) 293-3167   *SIC* 8361
CENTRE DE SANTE ET DE SERVICES SO-CIAUX LUCILLE-TEASDALE   *p*
1164
7445 RUE HOCHELAGA, MONTREAL, QC, H1N 3V2
(514) 251-6000   *SIC* 8322
CENTRE DE SANTE ET DE SERVICES SO-CIAUX LUCILLE-TEASDALE   *p*
1164
5810 RUE SHERBROOKE E, MONTREAL, QC, H1N 1B2
(514) 255-2365   *SIC* 8322
CENTRE DE SANTE ET DE SERVICES SO-CIAUX LUCILLE-TEASDALE   *p*
1167
3095 RUE SHERBROOKE E, MONTREAL, QC, H1W 1B2

(514) 523-0991   *SIC* 6513
CENTRE DE SANTE ET DE SERVICES SO-CIAUX PIERRE-BOUCHER   *p*
1082
4700 RTE MARIE-VICTORIN, CONTRE-COEUR, QC, J0L 1C0
(450) 468-8410   *SIC* 8361
CENTRE DE SANTE ET DE SERVICES SO-CIAUX PIERRE-BOUCHER   *p*
1145
1333 BOUL JACQUES-CARTIER E, LONGUEUIL, QC, J4M 2A5
(450) 468-8410   *SIC* 8062
CENTRE DE SANTE ET DE SERVICES SO-CIAUX PIERRE-DE S   *p*
1376
See CSSS PIERRE-DE SAUREL
CENTRE DE SANTE ET DE SERVICES SO-CIAUX QUEBECNORD   *p*
1055
See GOUVERNEMENT DE LA PROVINCE DE QUEBEC
CENTRE DE SANTE ET DES SERVICES SOCIAUX DE LA HAUTE-COTE-NORD   *p*
1378
162 RUE DES JESUITES, TADOUSSAC, QC, G0T 2A0
(418) 235-4588   *SIC* 8062
CENTRE DE SANTE ET SERVICES SOCI-AUX DE MONTMAGNY - L'ISLET   *p*
1159
22 AV COTE, MONTMAGNY, QC, G5V 1Z9
(418) 248-0639   *SIC* 8062
CENTRE DE SANTE ET SERVICES SOCI-AUX DE MONTMAGNY - L'ISLET   *p*
1302
10 RUE ALPHONSE, SAINT-FABIEN-DE-PANET, QC, G0R 2J0
(418) 249-2572   *SIC* 8062
CENTRE DE SANTE ET SERVICES SOCI-AUX DE PAPINEAU   *p*
1291
14 RUE SAINT-ANDRE, SAINT-ANDRE-AVELLIN, QC, J0V 1W0
(819) 983-7341   *SIC* 8361
CENTRE DE SANTE ET SERVICES SOCI-AUX DU PONTIAC   *p*
1369
200 RUE ARGUE, SHAWVILLE, QC, J0X 2Y0
(819) 647-2211   *SIC* 8099
CENTRE DE SANTE INUULITSIVIK   *p* 1254
GD, PUVIRNITUQ, QC, J0M 1P0
(819) 988-2957   *SIC* 8062
CENTRE DE SANTE PAUL GILBERT *p* 1139
9330 BOUL DU CENTRE-HOSPITALIER, LEVIS, QC, G6X 1L6
(418) 380-8993   *SIC* 8069
CENTRE DE SANTE TULATTAVIK DE L'UNGAVA   *p* 1118
GD, KUUJJUAQ, QC, J0M 1C0
(819) 964-2905   *SIC* 8051
CENTRE DE SERVICE   *p* 1148
See CAISSE DESJARDINS DU LAC-MEMPHREMAGOG
CENTRE DE SERVICE AUTEUIL   *p* 1232
See CAISSE DESJARDINS DE VIMONT-AUTEUIL
CENTRE DE SERVICE BEAUBIEN *p* 1346
See CAISSE DESJARDINS DE MERCIER-ROSEMONT
CENTRE DE SERVICE BERNARD-RACICOT   *p*
1307
See CAISSE DESJARDINS DE SAINT-HUBERT
CENTRE DE SERVICE BLAINVILLE *p* 1152
See CAISSE POPULAIRE DESJARDINS DE L'ENVOLEE
CENTRE DE SERVICE BROMONT   *p* 1108
See CAISSE DESJARDINS DE GRANBY-HAUTE-YAMASKA
CENTRE DE SERVICE CANDIAC   *p* 1297
See CAISSES DESJARDINS DES BERGES

DE ROUSSILLON
CENTRE DE SERVICE CHARLEMAGNE   *p*
1282
See CAISSE DESJARDINS PIERRE-LE GARDEUR
CENTRE DE SERVICE CHRIST-ROI *p* 1046
See CAISSE DESJARDINS D'AMOS
CENTRE DE SERVICE COMPTON   *p* 1081
See CAISSE DESJARDINS DES VERTS-SOMMETS DE L'ESTRIE
CENTRE DE SERVICE D'EASTMAN *p* 1147
See CAISSE DESJARDINS DU LAC-MEMPHREMAGOG
CENTRE DE SERVICE DAGENAIS *p* 1363
See CAISSE DESJARDINS DE L'OUEST DE LAVAL
CENTRE DE SERVICE DE BOIS-DES-FILIONS—LORRAINE   *p*
1364
See CAISSE DESJARDINS THERESE-DE BLAINVILLE
CENTRE DE SERVICE DE CAP-AUX-MEULES   *p*
1120
See CAISSE POPULAIRE DESJARDINS DES RAMEES
CENTRE DE SERVICE DE LA COLLINE   *p*
1275
See CAISSE DESJARDINS DE SAINTE-FOY
CENTRE DE SERVICE DE LA MONTAGNE
p 1387
See CAISSE DESJARDINS DES TROIS-RIVIERES
CENTRE DE SERVICE DE LOURDES   *p*
1246
See CAISSE DESJARDINS DE L'ERABLE
CENTRE DE SERVICE DE SAINT-LAMBERT-DE-LAUZON   *p*
1137
See CAISSE DESJARDINS DE LA CHAUDIERE
CENTRE DE SERVICE DES POLICIERS ET POLICIERES MUNICIPAUX DU QUEBEC   *p*
1173
See CAISSE DESJARDINS DES POLICIERS ET POLICIERES
CENTRE DE SERVICE DUVERNAY *p* 1231
See CAISSE POPULAIRE DESJARDINS DES MILLE-ILES
CENTRE DE SERVICE EN SANTE SECU-RITE DU QUEBEC   *p*
1385
See SHOPPING WEB PLUS INC
CENTRE DE SERVICE FINANCIER AUX ENTREPRISES CAISSES DESJARDINS DES HAUTES-MAREES   *p* 1271
See CAISSE DESJARDINS DE SILLERY–SAINT-LOUIS-DE-FRANCE
CENTRE DE SERVICE FLEURY   *p* 1182
See CAISSE POPULAIRE DESJARDINS CANADIENNE ITALIENNE
CENTRE DE SERVICE LAC-MASSON   *p* 1352
See CAISSE DESJARDINS DE LA VALLEE DES PAYS-D'EN-HAUT
CENTRE DE SERVICE LAROUCHE *p* 1116
See CAISSE DESJARDINS DE JON-QUIERE
CENTRE DE SERVICE LOISIRS QUEBEC *p* 1171
See CAISSE DESJARDINS DE LORIMIER-VILLERAY
CENTRE DE SERVICE MONTPELLIER   *p*
1323
See CAISSE POPULAIRE DESJARDINS DE SAINT-LAURENT, LA
CENTRE DE SERVICE SAINT-BASILE-LE-GRAND   *p*
1295
See CAISSE DESJARDINS DU MONT-SAINT-BRUNO
CENTRE DE SERVICE SAINT-THOMAS   *p*
1365

See CAISSE DESJARDINS DE SALABERRY-DE-VALLEYFIELD
CENTRE DE SERVICE UNIPNEU   *p* 1067
See PNEUS UNIMAX LTEE
CENTRE DE SERVICES ANGUS   *p* 1171
See CAISSE DESJARDINS DU COEUR-DE-L'ILE
CENTRE DE SERVICES BEAUCEVILLE   *p*
1304
See CAISSE DESJARDINS DU SUD DE LA CHAUDIERE
CENTRE DE SERVICES BEAULAC-GARTHBY   *p*
1090
See CAISSE DESJARDINS DU CAR-REFOUR DES LACS
CENTRE DE SERVICES BEAUMONT   *p*
1297
See CAISSE DESJARDINS DES SEIGNEURIES DE BELLECHASE
CENTRE DE SERVICES BECANCOUR   *p*
1056
See CAISSE DESJARDINS GODEFROY
CENTRE DE SERVICES BOULEVARD   *p*
1098
See CAISSE DESJARDINS DE DRUM-MONDVILLE
CENTRE DE SERVICES DE LAC-SAINT-CHARLES   *p*
1256
See CAISSE POPULAIRE DESJARDINS DE CHARLESBOURG
CENTRE DE SERVICES DE PAIE CGI INC *p*
1176
1611 BOUL CREMAZIE E 7TH FLOOR, MONTREAL, QC, H2M 2P2
(514) 850-6300   *SIC* 8721
CENTRE DE SERVICES DU CARREFOUR DE L'ESTRIE   *p* 1371
See CAISSE DESJARDINS DU NORD DE SHERBROOKE
CENTRE DE SERVICES DU PLATEAU   *p*
1107
See CAISSE DESJARDINS DE HULL-AYLMER
CENTRE DE SERVICES FABREVILLE   *p*
1361
See CAISSE DESJARDINS DU NORD DE LAVAL
CENTRE DE SERVICES FLEURY   *p* 1240
See CAISSE DESJARDINS DE SAULT-AU-RECOLLET-MONTREAL-NORD
CENTRE DE SERVICES FORT ST-LOUIS *p*
1064
See CAISSE DESJARDINS DE BOUCHERVILLE
CENTRE DE SERVICES LA MAURICIENNE
p 1368
See CAISSE DESJARDINS DU CENTRE-DE-LA-MAURICIE
CENTRE DE SERVICES LA PLAINE *p* 1149
See CAISSE POPULAIRE DESJARDINS LE MANOIR
CENTRE DE SERVICES LA PRESENTA-TION   *p*
1311
See CAISSE DESJARDINS DE LA REGION DE SAINT-HYACINTHE
CENTRE DE SERVICES LABRECQUE   *p*
1044
See CAISSE POPULAIRE DESJARDINS D'ALMA
CENTRE DE SERVICES LACOLLE *p* 1242
See CAISSE DESJARDINS DES SEIGNEURIES DE LA FRONTIERE
CENTRE DE SERVICES MONTREAL *p* 1258
See CAISSE D'ECONOMIE SOLIDAIRE DESJARDINS
CENTRE DE SERVICES PARTAGES-MATERIEL ROULANT ET ATELIERS, LE *p*
1167
See VILLE DE MONTREAL
CENTRE DE SERVICES SAINT-BARNABE *p*
1146

See CAISSE DESJARDINS DE L'OUEST DE LA MAURICIE
CENTRE DE SERVICES SAINT-EMILE p 1276
See CAISSE DESJARDINS DES RIVIERES DE QUEBEC
CENTRE DE SERVICES SAINTE-CLAIRE p 1291
See CAISSE DESJARDINS DU COEUR DE BELLECHASSE
CENTRE DE SERVICES SAINTE-MARTINE p 1151
See CAISSE DESJARDINS DE L'OUEST DE LA MONTEREGIE
CENTRE DE SERVICES SAMSON p 1087
See CAISSE DESJARDINS DE CHOMEDEY
CENTRE DE SERVICES VAL-BELAIR p 1119
See CAISSE POPULAIRE DESJARDINS DU PIEMONT LAURENTIEN
CENTRE DE SKI BROMONT p 1068
See SKI BROMONT.COM, SOCIETE EN COMMANDITE
CENTRE DE SKI MONT LA RESERVE p 1299
See COMPAGNIE IMMOBILIERE GUEYMARD & ASSOCIES LTEE
CENTRE DE SKI MONT-RIGAUD p 1283
See 2735-3861 QUEBEC INC
CENTRE DE SOINS DE LONGUE DUREE MONTFORT p 820
705 MONTREAL RD, OTTAWA, ON, K1K 0M9
(613) 746-8602   *SIC* 8741
CENTRE DE SPIRITUALITE DES URSULINES p 1275
See PROVINCE DU QUEBEC DE L'UNION CANADIENNE DES MONIALES DE L'ORDRE DE SAINTE-URSULE
CENTRE DE TECHNOLOGIES INFORMATIQUES GROUPE ACCESS p 1226
See 3096-3227 QUEBEC INC
CENTRE DE TELEPHONE MOBILE LTEE p 1048
9680 BOUL DU GOLF BUREAU 1, ANJOU, QC, H1J 2Y7
(514) 645-9271   *SIC* 5999
CENTRE DE TESTS ELECTRONIQUES p 1252
See TECHNOLOGIES MPB INC, LES
CENTRE DE TOXICOLOGIE DU QUEBEC p 1272
See INSTITUT NATIONALE DE SANTE PUBLIQUE DU QUEBEC
CENTRE DE TRANSPORT LASALLE p 1131
See SOCIETE DE TRANSPORT DE MONTREAL
CENTRE DE VISION DELSON p 1089
See CENTRE DE VISION DELSON INC
CENTRE DE VISION DELSON INC p 1089
70 132 RTE BUREAU 104, DELSON, QC, J5B 0A1
(450) 638-5212   *SIC* 8042
CENTRE DENTAIDE p 1199
See SOCIETE DE SERVICES DENTAIRES (A.C.D.Q.) INC
CENTRE DES CONGRES DE BOUCHERVILLE p 1063
See 9138-4438 QUEBEC INC
CENTRE DES CONGRES DE QUEBEC p 1270
See SOCIETE DU CENTRE DES CONGRES DE QUEBEC
CENTRE DES RECOLLETS-FOUCHER SOCIETE EN COMMANDITE p 1194
1555 RUE PEEL BUREAU 700, MONTREAL, QC, H3A 3L8
(514) 940-1555   *SIC* 6719

CENTRE DIOCESAN p 397
See ARCHIDIOCESE DE MONCTON
CENTRE DISTRIBUTION p 285
See CENTRE SKATEBOARD DISTRIBUTION LTD
CENTRE DOLLARD CORMIER p 1177
See GOUVERNEMENT DE LA PROVINCE DE QUEBEC
CENTRE DU BRICOLEUR LACHINE LTEE p 1126
650 RUE NOTRE-DAME BUREAU 1849, LACHINE, QC, H8S 2B3
(514) 637-3767   *SIC* 5039
CENTRE DU CAMION (AMIANTE) p 1383
See 3358097 CANADA INC
CENTRE DU CAMION (AMIANTE) INC p 1383
4680 BOUL FRONTENAC E, THETFORD MINES, QC, G6H 4G5
(418) 338-8588   *SIC* 5511
CENTRE DU CAMION (BEAUCE) INC, LE p 1305
8900 25E AV, SAINT-GEORGES, QC, G6A 1K5
(418) 228-8005   *SIC* 5012
CENTRE DU CAMION BEAUDOIN INC p 1096
5360 RUE SAINT-ROCH S, DRUMMONDVILLE, QC, J2B 6V4
(819) 478-8186   *SIC* 5511
CENTRE DU CAMION D'AMOS INC p 1046
145 RTE 111 E, AMOS, QC, J9T 3A2
(819) 732-6471   *SIC* 5531
CENTRE DU CAMION GAMACHE INC p 1113
609 RUE PRINCIPALE, ILE-AUX-NOIX, QC, J0J 1G0
(450) 246-3881   *SIC* 5521
CENTRE DU CAMION MONT-LAURIER INC, LE p 1154
3763 CH DE LA LIEVRE N, MONT-LAURIER, QC, J9L 3G4
(819) 623-3433   *SIC* 5531
CENTRE DU CAMION STE-MARIE INC, LE p 1310
5400 RUE MARTINEAU, SAINT-HYACINTHE, QC, J2R 1T8
(450) 796-4004   *SIC* 5511
CENTRE DU CAMION THIBAULT p 1290
See THIBAULT CHEVROLET CADILLAC BUICK GMC DE ROUYN-NORANDA LTEE
CENTRE DU GOLF U.F.O. INC p 1152
9500 RANG SAINTE-HENRIETTE, MIRABEL, QC, J7J 2A1
(514) 990-8392   *SIC* 7997
CENTRE DU PIN LIMITEE, LE p 1184
225 RUE JOSEPH-TISON, MONTREAL, QC, H2V 4S5
(514) 278-5551   *SIC* 5193
CENTRE DU PNEUS VILLEMAIRE p 1300
See GARAGE VILLEMAIRE & FILS INC
CENTRE DU POSEUR PROFESSIONNEL p 1327
See PROSOL INC
CENTRE DU SABLON p 1237
See CORPORATION DU CENTRE DU SABLON INC
CENTRE DU SPORT ALARY INC p 1321
1324 BOUL SAINT-ANTOINE, SAINT-JEROME, QC, J7Z 7M2
(450) 436-2242   *SIC* 5571
CENTRE DU SPORT LAC-ST-JEAN INC p 1075
1454 RUE PRINCIPALE, CHAMBORD, QC, G0W 1G0
(418) 342-6202   *SIC* 5561
CENTRE DU TRAVAIL p 1089
See COTE-RECO INC
CENTRE DUFFERIN DISTRICT HIGH SCHOOL p 880
See UPPER GRAND DISTRICT SCHOOL BOARD, THE
CENTRE ENGRAIS MINERAUX p 1352
390 263 RTE, SAINT-SEBASTIEN-DE-

FRONTENAC, QC, G0Y 1M0
(819) 652-2266   *SIC* 2874
CENTRE ETUDIANTS HILLEL p 1219
See FEDERATION CJA
CENTRE FINANCIER AUX ENTREPRISES - QUEBEC-CAPITALE p 1254
3333 RUE DU CARREFOUR BUREAU 280, QUEBEC, QC, G1C 5R9
(418) 660-2229   *SIC* 8741
CENTRE FINANCIER AUX ENTREPRISES DE LA CAPITALE p 1255
See FEDERATION DES CAISSES DESJARDINS DU QUEBEC
CENTRE FINANCIER AUX ENTREPRISES DES CAISSES DESJARDINS CHAUDIERE-SUD p 1304
See CAISSE DESJARDINS DU SUD DE LA CHAUDIERE
CENTRE FINANCIER AUX ENTREPRISES DESJARDINS LEVIS LOTBINIERE p 1135
1610 BOUL ALPHONSE-DESJARDINS BUREAU 600, LEVIS, QC, G6V 0H1
(418) 834-4343   *SIC* 8741
CENTRE FINANCIER AUX ENTREPRISES DESJARDINS TROIS-RIVIERES p 1386
2000 BOUL DES RECOLLETS, TROIS-RIVIERES, QC, G8Z 3X4
(819) 376-4000   *SIC* 8741
CENTRE FINANCIER AUX ENTREPRISES DESJARDINS VALLEE DU RICHELIEU-YAMASKA p 1074
See CAISSE POPULAIRE DESJARDINS DU BASSIN-DE-CHAMBLY
CENTRE FINANCIER AUX ENTREPRISES JOLIETTE-DE-LANAUDIERE p 1114
See CAISSE DESJARDINS DU NORD DE LANAUDIERE
CENTRE FINANCIER S.F.L. DU LITTORAL INC p 1286
290 BOUL DE L'HOTEL-DE-VILLE BUREAU 200, RIVIERE-DU-LOUP, QC, G5R 5C6
(418) 862-4980   *SIC* 6311
CENTRE FOR ADDICTION AND MENTAL HEALTH p 918
175 BRENTCLIFFE RD, TORONTO, ON, M4G 0C5
(416) 425-3930   *SIC* 8093
CENTRE FOR ADDICTION AND MENTAL HEALTH p 974
33 RUSSELL ST, TORONTO, ON, M5S 2S1
(416) 535-8501   *SIC* 8093
CENTRE FOR ADDICTION AND MENTAL HEALTH p 990
1001 QUEEN ST W SUITE 301, TORONTO, ON, M6J 1H4
(416) 535-8501   *SIC* 8093
CENTRE FOR ADDICTION AND MENTAL HEALTH FOUNDATION p 990
100 STOKES ST FL 5, TORONTO, ON, M6J 1H4
(416) 979-6909   *SIC* 8699
CENTRE FOR ADDICTION MENTAL HEALTH p 918
See DONWOOD INSTITUTE, THE
CENTRE FOR AFFORDABLE WATER AND SANITATION TECHNOLOGY (CAWST) p 34
6020 2 ST SE UNIT B12, CALGARY, AB, T2H 2L8
(403) 243-3285   *SIC* 8399
CENTRE FOR AUTISM SERVICES ALBERTA p 113
4752 99 ST NW, EDMONTON, AB, T6E 5H5
(780) 488-6600   *SIC* 8699
CENTRE FOR CHILD DEVELOPMENT OF THE LOWER MAINLAND, THE p 274
9460 140 ST, SURREY, BC, V3V 5Z4
(604) 584-1361   *SIC* 8322
CENTRE FOR CHILD DEVELOPMENT, THE p 274
See CENTRE FOR CHILD DEVELOPMENT OF THE LOWER MAINLAND, THE

CENTRE FOR COMMUNICATIONS AND INFORMATION TECHNOLOGY, DIV OF p 982
See ONTARIO CENTRES OF EXCELLENCE INC
CENTRE FOR CONTINUING EDUCATION p 1214
See UNIVERSITE CONCORDIA
CENTRE FOR EDUCATION AND TRAINING p 710
See QUALITY CONTINUOUS IMPROVEMENT CENTRE FOR COMMUNITY EDUCATION AND TRAINING
CENTRE FOR GLOBAL STUDIES, THE p 333
3800 FINNERTY RD SUITE 3800, VICTORIA, BC, V8P 5C2
(250) 472-4990   *SIC* 8699
CENTRE FOR HIP HEALTH AND MOBILITY p 294
See VANCOUVER COASTAL HEALTH AUTHORITY
CENTRE FOR MARINE CNG INC p 433
130 SOUTHSIDE RD, ST. JOHN'S, NL, A1E 0A2
SIC 4924
CENTRE FOR MOLECULAR MEDICINE AND THERAPEUTIC p 293
950 28TH AVE W SUITE 3109, VANCOUVER, BC, V5Z 4H4
(604) 875-3535   *SIC* 8732
CENTRE FOR PHENOGENOMICS INC, THE p 977
25 ORDE ST, TORONTO, ON, M5T 3H7
(647) 837-5811   *SIC* 8733
CENTRE FOR RESEARCH IN EARTH AND SPACE TECHNOLOGY p 782
4850 KEELE ST, NORTH YORK, ON, M3J 3K1
(416) 736-5247   *SIC* 8733
CENTRE FOR SKILLS DEVELOPMENT & TRAINING, THE p 521
5151 NEW ST, BURLINGTON, ON, L7L 1V3
(905) 637-3393   *SIC* 8299
CENTRE FORMATION DU TRANSPORT ROUTIER p 1152
See COMMISSION SCOLAIRE DE LA RIVIERE-DU-NORD
CENTRE FORMATION PROFESSIONNELLE DE NEUFCHATEL p 1276
See COMMISSION SCOLAIRE DE LA CAPITALE, LA
CENTRE GERIATRIQUE DE BEL AGE p 1342
See SANTE COURVILLE INC
CENTRE GESTION DES AVOIRS p 1315
See CAISSE DESJARDINS DU HAUT-RICHELIEU
CENTRE HEBERGEMENT JEANNE-LEBER p 1164
See CENTRE DE SANTE ET DE SERVICES SOCIAUX LUCILLE-TEASDALE
CENTRE HERBERGEMENT DE DONNACONA p 1092
See CENTRE DE SANTE ET DE SERVICES SOCIAUX DE PORTNEUF
CENTRE HI-FI p 1346
See 149667 CANADA INC
CENTRE HONDA p 933
See CENTRE AUTO COLLISION LIMITED
CENTRE HOSPITALIER AMBULATOIRE REGIONAL DE LAVAL p 1092
1515 BOUL CHOMEDEY BUREAU 160, DORVAL, QC, H7V 3Y7
(450) 978-8300   *SIC* 8062
CENTRE HOSPITALIER DE BEDFORD p 1056
34 RUE SAINT-JOSEPH, BEDFORD, QC, J0J 1A0
(450) 248-4304   *SIC* 8069
CENTRE HOSPITALIER DE L'UNIVERSITE

DE MONTREAL p 1175
1560 RUE SHERBROOKE E, MONTREAL, QC, H2L 4M1
(800) 224-7737 SIC 8062
CENTRE HOSPITALIER DE L'UNIVERSITE DE MONTREAL p 1175
See CENTRE HOSPITALIER DE L'UNIVERSITE DE MONTREAL
CENTRE HOSPITALIER DE L'UNIVERSITE DE MONTREAL p 1185
1058 RUE SAINT-DENIS, MONTREAL, QC, H2X 3J4
(514) 890-8000 SIC 8062
CENTRE HOSPITALIER DE L'UNIVERSITE DE MONTREAL p 1185
See CENTRE HOSPITALIER DE L'UNIVERSITE DE MONTREAL
CENTRE HOSPITALIER DE L'UNIVERSITE DE MONTREAL p 1185
850 RUE SAINT-DENIS, MONTREAL, QC, H2X 0A9
(514) 890-8000 SIC 8062
CENTRE HOSPITALIER DE LACHINE DU CUSM p 1131
See CENTRE DE SANTE ET DE SERVICES SOCIAUX DE DORVAL-LACHINE-LASALLE
CENTRE HOSPITALIER DE ST. MARY'S p 1219
3830 AV LACOMBE, MONTREAL, QC, H3T 1M5
(514) 345-3511 SIC 8062
CENTRE HOSPITALIER DE TRACADIE p 419
See REGIONAL HEALTH AUTHORITY A
CENTRE HOSPITALIER DE TROIS-PISTOLES p 1384
550 RUE NOTRE-DAME E, TROIS-PISTOLES, QC, G0L 4K0
(418) 851-1111 SIC 8069
CENTRE HOSPITALIER DU CENTRE LA MAURICIE p 1368
1265 RUE TRUDEL BUREAU 6, SHAWINIGAN, QC, G9N 8T3
(819) 539-8371 SIC 7363
CENTRE HOSPITALIER DU CENTRE LA MAURICIE p 1368
243 1RE RUE DE LA POINTE, SHAWINIGAN, QC, G9N 1K2
SIC 8361
CENTRE HOSPITALIER ET CENTRE DE READAPTATION ANTOINE-LABELLE p 1154
411 RUE DE LA MADONE, MONT-LAURIER, QC, J9L 1S1
(819) 623-5940 SIC 8361
CENTRE HOSPITALIER ET CENTRE DE READAPTATION ANTOINE-LABELLE p 1287
See CENTRE HOSPITALIER ET CENTRE DE READAPTATION ANTOINE-LABELLE
CENTRE HOSPITALIER ET CENTRE DE READAPTATION ANTOINE-LABELLE p 1287
1525 RUE L'ANNONCIATION N, RIVIERE-ROUGE, QC, J0T 1T0
(819) 275-2411 SIC 8062
CENTRE HOSPITALIER MONT-SINAI-MONTREAL p 1083
5690 BOUL CAVENDISH, COTE SAINT-LUC, QC, H4W 1S7
(514) 369-2222 SIC 8062
CENTRE HOSPITALIER REGIONAL DE TROIS-RIVIERES p 1386
1991 BOUL DU CARMEL, TROIS-RIVIERES, QC, G8Z 3R9
(819) 697-3333 SIC 8069
CENTRE HOSPITALIER UNIVERSITAIRE DE QUEBEC p 1260
10 RUE DE L'ESPINAY BUREAU 520, QUEBEC, QC, G1L 3L5
(418) 525-4444 SIC 8062

CENTRE HOSPITALIER UNIVERSITAIRE DE QUEBEC p 1268
11 COTE DU PALAIS, QUEBEC, QC, G1R 2J6
(418) 525-4444 SIC 8062
CENTRE HOSPITALIER UNIVERSITAIRE DE QUEBEC p 1268
11 COTE DU PALAIS BUREAU 3431, QUEBEC, QC, G1R 2J6
(418) 525-4444 SIC 8062
CENTRE HOSPITALIER UNIVERSITAIRE DE QUEBEC p 1269
9 RUE MCMAHON, QUEBEC, QC, G1R 3S3
(418) 691-5281 SIC 8732
CENTRE HOSPITALIER UNIVERSITAIRE DE QUEBEC p 1271
See CENTRE HOSPITALIER UNIVERSITAIRE DE QUEBEC
CENTRE HOSPITALIER UNIVERSITAIRE DE QUEBEC p 1271
2705 BOUL LAURIER BUREAU 2211, QUEBEC, QC, G1V 4G2
(418) 525-4444 SIC 8062
CENTRE HOSPITALIER UNIVERSITAIRE DE QUEBEC p 1280
775 RUE SAINT-VIATEUR UNITE 130A, QUEBEC, QC, G2L 2Z3
SIC 8062
CENTRE HOSPITALIER UNIVERSITAIRE DE SHERBROOKE p 1370
3001 12E AV N, SHERBROOKE, QC, J1H 5N4
(819) 346-1110 SIC 8621
CENTRE HOSPITALIER UNIVERSITAIRE SAINTE-JUSTINE p 1165
5200 RUE BELANGER, MONTREAL, QC, H1T 1C9
(514) 374-1710 SIC 8093
CENTRE HOSPITALIER UNIVERSITAIRE SAINTE-JUSTINE p 1219
3175 CH DE LA COTE-SAINTE-CATHERINE, MONTREAL, QC, H3T 1C5
(514) 345-4931 SIC 8069
CENTRE HOSTIPALIER DE L'UNIVERSITE DE MONTREAL (CHUM) p 1186
See UNITE DE SANTE INTERNATIONALE
CENTRE INFORMATIQUE DNB LIMITEE p 1229
800 PLACE VICTORIA BUREAU 2700, MONTREAL, QC, H4Z 1B7
SIC 5045
CENTRE INRS-INSTITUT ARMAND-FRAPPIER p 1087
See INSTITUTE NATIONAL DE LA RECHERCHE SCIENTIFIQUE
CENTRE INTEGRE DE MECANIQUE INDUSTRIELLE DE LA CHAUDIERE CIMIC p 1304
See COMMISSION SCOLAIRE DE LA BEAUCE-ETCHEMIN
CENTRE INTEGRE DE MECANIQUE, DE METALLURGIE ET D'ELECTRICITE CIMME p 1323
See COMMISSION SCOLAIRE MARGUERITE-BOURGEOYS
CENTRE INTEGRE DE SANTE ET DE SERVICES SOCIAUX DE LA MONTEREGIE-OUEST p 1076
95 CH DE LA HAUTE-RIVIERE, CHATEAUGUAY, QC, J6K 3P1
(450) 692-8231 SIC 8322
CENTRE INTEGRE DE SANTE ET DE SERVICES SOCIAUX DE LA MONTEREGIE-OUEST p 1123
500 AV DE BALMORAL, LA PRAIRIE, QC, J5R 4N5
(450) 659-9148 SIC 8361
CENTRE INTEGRE DE SANTE ET DE SERVICES SOCIAUX DE LA MONTEREGIE-OUEST p 1317

315 RUE MACDONALD BUREAU 105, SAINT-JEAN-SUR-RICHELIEU, QC, J3B 8J3
(450) 348-6121 SIC 8361
CENTRE INTEGRE DE SANTE ET DE SERVICES SOCIAUX DE LANAUDIERE p 1114
See GOUVERNEMENT DE LA PROVINCE DE QUEBEC
CENTRE INTEGRE DE SANTE ET DE SERVICES SOCIAUX DE LANAUDIERE p 1321
11 RUE BOYER, SAINT-JEROME, QC, J7Z 2K5
(450) 432-7588 SIC 8049
CENTRE INTEGRE DE SANTE ET DE SERVICES SOCIAUX DE LANAUDIERE p 1379
1317 BOUL DES SEIGNEURS, TERREBONNE, QC, J6W 5B1
(450) 471-2881 SIC 8011
CENTRE INTEGRE DE SANTE ET DE SERVICES SOCIAUX DES ILES p 1073
430 CH PRINCIPAL, CAP-AUX-MEULES, QC, G4T 1R9
(418) 986-2121 SIC 8062
CENTRE INTEGRE DE SANTE ET DE SERVICES SOCIAUX DES LAURENTIDES p 1153
9100 RUE DUMOUCHEL, MIRABEL, QC, J7N 5A1
(450) 258-2481 SIC 7041
CENTRE INTEGRE DE SANTE ET DE SERVICES SOCIAUX DES LAURENTIDES p 1301
29 CH D'OKA, SAINT-EUSTACHE, QC, J7R 1K6
(450) 491-1233 SIC 8062
CENTRE INTEGRE DE SANTE ET DE SERVICES SOCIAUX DES LAURENTIDES p 1321
500 BOUL DES LAURENTIDES BUREAU 1010, SAINT-JEROME, QC, J7Z 4M2
(450) 436-8622 SIC 8011
CENTRE INTEGRE DE SANTE ET DE SERVICES SOCIAUX DES LAURENTIDES p 1321
290 RUE DE MONTIGNY, SAINT-JEROME, QC, J7Z 5T3
(450) 432-2777 SIC 8011
CENTRE INTEGRE DE SANTE ET DE SERVICES SOCIAUX DES LAURENTIDES p 1354
125 CH DU TOUR-DU-LAC, SAINTE-AGATHE-DES-MONTS, QC, J8C 1B4
(819) 326-6221 SIC 8361
CENTRE INTEGRE DE SANTE ET DE SERVICES SOCIAUX DU BAS-SAINT-LAURENT p 1284
355 BOUL SAINT-GERMAIN, RIMOUSKI, QC, G5L 3N2
(418) 724-3000 SIC 8399
CENTRE INTEGRE UNIVERSITAIRE DE SANTE ET DE SERVICES SOCIAUX DE L'ESTRIE p 1371
375 RUE ARGYLL, SHERBROOKE, QC, J1J 3H5
(819) 780-2222 SIC 8621
CENTRE INTEGRE UNIVERSITAIRE DE SANTE ET DE SERVICES SOCIAUX DE LA CAPITALE-NATIONALE, LE p 1255
700 BOUL DES CHUTES, QUEBEC, QC, G1E 2B7
(418) 663-9934 SIC 8361
CENTRE INTEGRE UNIVERSITAIRE SANTE ET SERVICES SOCIAUX DU CENTRE-SUD-DE-L'ILE-DE-MONTREAL p 1163
8147 RUE SHERBROOKE E, MONTREAL, QC, H1L 1A7
(514) 356-4500 SIC 8322
CENTRE INTEGRE UNIVERSITAIRE SANTE ET SERVICES SOCIAUX DU CENTRE-SUD-DE-L'ILE-DE-MONTREAL

p 1165
4675 RUE BELANGER, MONTREAL, QC, H1T 1C2
(514) 593-3979 SIC 8011
CENTRE INTEGRE UNIVERSITAIRE SANTE ET SERVICES SOCIAUX DU CENTRE-SUD-DE-L'ILE-DE-MONTREAL p 1172
2222 AV LAURIER E, MONTREAL, QC, H2H 1C4
(514) 527-4527 SIC 8011
CENTRE INTEGRE UNIVERSITAIRE SANTE ET SERVICES SOCIAUX DU CENTRE-SUD-DE-L'ILE-DE-MONTREAL p 1172
2275 AV LAURIER E, MONTREAL, QC, H2H 2N8
(514) 527-4527 SIC 8011
CENTRE INTEGRE UNIVERSITAIRE SANTE ET SERVICES SOCIAUX DU CENTRE-SUD-DE-L'ILE-DE-MONTREAL p 1183
155 BOUL SAINT-JOSEPH E, MONTREAL, QC, H2T 1H4
(514) 593-2044 SIC 8011
CENTRE INTEGRE UNIVERSITAIRE SANTE ET SERVICES SOCIAUX DU CENTRE-SUD-DE-L'ILE-DE-MONTREAL p 1185
3430 RUE JEANNE-MANCE, MONTREAL, QC, H2X 2J9
(514) 842-1147 SIC 8011
CENTRE INTERNATIONAL DE COURSE AUTOMOBILE (ICAR) INC p 1153
12800 BOUL HENRI-FABRE, MIRABEL, QC, J7N 0A6
(514) 955-4227 SIC 8699
CENTRE INTERNATIONAL DE RECHERCHE EN ALIMENTATION ANIMALE DE ST-HYACINTHE p 1310
See JEFO NUTRITION INC
CENTRE IOS p 1227
See 9186-5758 QUEBEC INC
CENTRE ISLAND FOOD SERVICES LTD p 574
84 ADVANCE RD, ETOBICOKE, ON, M8Z 2T7
(416) 234-2345 SIC 5812
CENTRE JARDIN BOURBEAU p 1256
See BOURBEAU, GERARD & FILS INC
CENTRE JEUNESSE COTE NORD p 1053
See CENTRE DE PROTECTION ET DE READAPTATION DE LA COTE-NORD
CENTRE JEUNESSE DE L'ESTRIE p 1370
340 RUE DUFFERIN, SHERBROOKE, QC, J1H 4M7
(819) 822-2727 SIC 8322
CENTRE JEUNESSE DE L'ESTRIE p 1375
8475 CH BLANCHETTE, SHERBROOKE, QC, J1N 3A3
(819) 864-4221 SIC 8361
CENTRE JEUNESSE DE LA MAURICIE ET DU CENTRE-DU-QUE p 1096
See CENTRE JEUNESSE DE LA MAURICIE ET DU CENTRE-DU-QUEBEC, LE
CENTRE JEUNESSE DE LA MAURICIE ET DU CENTRE-DU-QUEBEC, LE p 1096
3100 BOUL LEMIRE, DRUMMONDVILLE, QC, J2B 7R2
(819) 477-5115 SIC 8361
CENTRE JEUNESSE DE LA MAURICIE ET DU CENTRE-DU-QUEBEC, LE p 1386
1455 BOUL DU CARMEL, TROIS-RIVIERES, QC, G8Z 3R7
(819) 378-5481 SIC 8322
CENTRE JEUNESSE DE LA MAURICIE ET DU CENTRE-DU-QUEBEC, LE p 1386
2735 RUE PAPINEAU, TROIS-RIVIERES, QC, G8Z 1N8
(819) 378-8635 SIC 8322
CENTRE JEUNESSE DE LAVAL p 1084
See GOUVERNEMENT DE LA PROVINCE

DE QUEBEC

CENTRE JEUNESSE DE MONTREAL MONT ST-ANTOINE *p* 1163
See CENTRE INTEGRE UNIVERSITAIRE SANTE ET SERVICES SOCIAUX DU CENTRE-SUD-DE-L'ILE-DE-MONTREAL

CENTRE JEUNESSE DE QUEBEC SERVICE D'URGENCE SOCIALE *p* 1256
See GOUVERNEMENT DE LA PROVINCE DE QUEBEC

CENTRE JEUNESSE DES LAURENTIDES*p* 1319
358 RUE LAVIOLETTE, SAINT-JEROME, QC, J7Y 2T1
(450) 432-9753 *SIC* 8322

CENTRE JEUNESSE DES LAURENTIDES*p* 1354
See CENTRE INTEGRE DE SANTE ET DE SERVICES SOCIAUX DES LAURENTIDES

CENTRE JEUNESSE VAL DU LAC *p* 1375
See CENTRE JEUNESSE DE L'ESTRIE

CENTRE LA TRAVERSEE *p* 1171
1460 BOUL CREMAZIE E, MONTREAL, QC, H2E 1A2
(514) 321-4984 *SIC* 8361

CENTRE LAFLECHE GRAND-MERE*p* 1368
555 AV DE LA STATION, SHAWINIGAN, QC, G9N 1V9
(819) 536-0071 *SIC* 8361

CENTRE LE CARDINAL INC *p* 1247
12900 RUE NOTRE-DAME E, POINTE-AUX-TREMBLES, QC, H1A 1R9
(514) 645-0095 *SIC* 8069

CENTRE LE ROYER *p* 1051
See GROUPE ROY SANTE INC

CENTRE LEASEHOLD IMPROVEMENTS LIMITED *p* 843
1315 PICKERING PKY UNIT 205, PICKERING, ON, L1V 7G5
(905) 492-6131 *SIC* 1542

CENTRE LOCAL DE SANTE COMMUNAUTAIRE DE JOLIETTE *p* 1114
See GOUVERNEMENT DE LA PROVINCE DE QUEBEC

CENTRE LOCAL DES SERVICES COMMUNAUTAIRES KATERI INC *p* 1072
90 BOUL MARIE-VICTORIN, CANDIAC, QC, J5R 1C1
(450) 659-7661 *SIC* 8399

CENTRE LOCAL DES SERVICES COMMUNAUTAIRES LE NOROIS *p* 1045
100 RUE SAINT-JOSEPH, ALMA, QC, G8B 7A6
(418) 668-4563 *SIC* 8399

CENTRE LOUIS-JOLLIET *p* 1260
See COMMISSION SCOLAIRE DE LA CAPITALE, LA

CENTRE MARAICHER EUGENE GUINOIS JR INC *p* 1357
555 4E RANG, SAINTE-CLOTILDE-DE-CHATEAUGUAY, QC, J0L 1W0
(450) 826-3207 *SIC* 0161

CENTRE MASSICOTTE INC *p* 1261
687 BOUL PIERRE-BERTRAND, QUEBEC, QC, G1M 2E4
(418) 687-4340 *SIC* 5712

CENTRE MEDICAL PHYSIMED *p* 1339
See GROUPE SANTE PHYSIMED INC

CENTRE MGR VICTOR TREMBLAY *p* 1078
See CENTRE DE SANTE ET DE SERVICES SOCIAUX DE CHICOUTIMI

CENTRE MONTEREGIEN DE READAPTATION *p* 1307
5300 CH DE CHAMBLY, SAINT-HUBERT, QC, J3Y 3N7
(450) 676-7447 *SIC* 7991

CENTRE NUMERIQUE DE LA CAPITALE *p* 1258
See COPIES DE LA CAPITALE INC, LES

CENTRE OASIS SURF INC *p* 1069
9520 BOUL LEDUC BUREAU 1, BROSSARD, QC, J4Y 0B3
(450) 486-7873 *SIC* 5411

CENTRE OPTOMETRIQUE DE GRANBY INC *p* 1110
220 RUE SAINT-JUDE N, GRANBY, QC, J2J 0C2
(450) 372-1031 *SIC* 5047

CENTRE ORTHOPEDIQUE CDD *p* 1097
See 9060-1899 QUEBEC INC

CENTRE PERE SABLON *p* 1172
4265 AV PAPINEAU, MONTREAL, QC, H2H 1T3
(514) 527-1256 *SIC* 7997

CENTRE RAIL-CONTROL *p* 1095
See SYSTEMES RAILTERM INC, LES

CENTRE READAPTATION DE GASPESIE *p* 1102
150 RUE MGR-ROSS BUREAU 550, GASPE, QC, G4X 2R8
(418) 368-2306 *SIC* 8093

CENTRE READAPTATION LA RESSOURSE *p* 1106
See GOUVERNEMENT DE LA PROVINCE DE QUEBEC

CENTRE RECREATIF EDOUARD RIVET *p* 1238
See SODEM INC

CENTRE RECREOTOURISTIQUE DE SHIP-SHAW *p* 1079
See SOCIETE DE GESTION DE LA ZONE PORTUAIRE DE CHICOUTIMI INC

CENTRE RECREOTOURISTIQUE MONTJOYE *p* 1073
See SODEM INC

CENTRE REGIONAL DE SANTE ET DE SERVICES SOCIAUX DE LA BAIE-JAMES *p* 1077
51 3E RUE, CHIBOUGAMAU, QC, G8P 1N1
(418) 748-2676 *SIC* 8062

CENTRE REGIONAL DE TRANSBORDEMENT ET TRAINS ROUTIERS DU SAGUENAY-LAC-ST-JEAN *p* 1116
See SERVICES NOLITREX INC

CENTRE SAINT-MICHEL FORMATION POUR ADULTS *p* 1370
See COMMISSION SCOLAIRE DE LA REGION-DE-SHERBROOKE

CENTRE SCOLAIRE COMMUNAUTAIRE LA FONTAINE *p* 410
700 RUE PRINCIPALE, NEGUAC, NB, E9G 1N4
(506) 776-3808 *SIC* 8211

CENTRE SCOLAIRE ETOILE DE L'ACADIE *p* 462
See CONSEIL SCOLAIRE ACADIEN PROVINCIAL

CENTRE SEGAL DES ARTS DE LA SCENE *p* 1219
5170 CH DE LA COTE-SAINTE-CATHERINE, MONTREAL, QC, H3W 1M7
(514) 739-7944 *SIC* 7922

CENTRE SERVICES CLIENTS ET INNOVATION *p* 1139
See TEKNION ROY & BRETON INC

CENTRE SHERATON LIMITED PARTNERSHIP, LE *p* 1202
1201 BOUL RENE-LEVESQUE O BUREAU 217, MONTREAL, QC, H3B 2L7
(514) 878-2000 *SIC* 7011

CENTRE SKATEBOARD DISTRIBUTION LTD *p* 285
1486 E PENDER ST, VANCOUVER, BC, V5L 1V8
(604) 629-0000 *SIC* 5091

CENTRE SOCIAL DES COLS BLANCS DE L'ILE DE MONTREAL *p* 1178
See CENTRE SOCIAL DES FONCTIONNAIRES MUNICIPAUX DE MONTREAL

CENTRE SOCIAL DES FONCTIONNAIRES MUNICIPAUX DE MONTREAL *p* 1178
8790 AV DU PARC, MONTREAL, QC, H2N 1Y6
(514) 842-9463 *SIC* 8641

CENTRE SPORTIF PALADIUM INC *p* 1142
475 BOUL ROLAND-THERRIEN, LONGUEUIL, QC, J4H 4A6
(450) 646-9995 *SIC* 7999

CENTRE ST-AUGUSTIN *p* 1254
See CENTRE DE SANTE ET DE SERVICES SOCIAUX DU PONTIAC

CENTRE STREET CHURCH *p* 22
3900 2 ST NE, CALGARY, AB, T2E 9C1
(403) 293-3900 *SIC* 8661

CENTRE TECHNO-PNEU INC *p* 1285
445 RUE DE L'EXPANSION, RIMOUSKI, QC, G5M 1B4
(418) 724-4104 *SIC* 5531

CENTRE UBANISATION CULTURE ET SOCIETE *p* 1260
See UNIVERSITE DU QUEBEC

CENTRE UNIVERSITAIRE DE SANTE MCGILL *p* 1221
1001 BOUL DECARIE, MONTREAL, QC, H4A 3J1
(514) 934-1934 *SIC* 8062

CENTRE VETERINAIRE D.M.V. *p* 1128
See GROUPE DIMENSION MULTI VETERINAIRE INC, LE

CENTRE WELLINGTON *p* 1397
See INSTITUT UNIVERSITAIRE EN SANTE MENTALE DOUGLAS

CENTRE Y DU PARC, LE *p* 1184
See YMCA DU QUEBEC, LES

CENTRECORP MANAGEMENT SERVICES LIMITED *p* 668
2851 JOHN ST SUITE 1, MARKHAM, ON, L3R 5R7
(905) 477-9200 *SIC* 6512

CENTRES D'EVALUATION DE LA TECHNOLOGIE INC *p* 1210
740 RUE SAINT-MAURICE, MONTREAL, QC, H3C 1L5
(514) 954-3665 *SIC* 8631

CENTRES DE DONNEES ESTRUXTURE INC *p* 1229
800 RUE DU SQUARE-VICTORIA BUREAU 1, MONTREAL, QC, H4Z 1B7
(514) 369-2209 *SIC* 8999

CENTRES DE LA JEUNESSE ET DE LA FAMILLE BATSHAW, L *p* 1253
3065 BOUL DU CURE-LABELLE, PREVOST, QC, J0R 1T0
(450) 224-8234 *SIC* 8322

CENTRES DE LA JEUNESSE ET DE LA FAMILLE BATSHAW, L *p* 1401
5 RUE WEREDALE PARK, WESTMOUNT, QC, H3Z 1Y5
(514) 989-1885 *SIC* 8322

CENTRES DENTAIRES LAPOINTE INC *p* 1142
116 RUE GUILBAULT, LONGUEUIL, QC, J4H 2T2
(450) 679-2300 *SIC* 8021

CENTRES JEUNESSE CHAUDIERE-APPALACHES, LES *p* 1135
100 RTE MONSEIGNEUR-BOURGET BUREAU 300, LEVIS, QC, G6V 2Y9
(418) 837-9331 *SIC* 8322

CENTRES JEUNESSE DE L'OUTAOUAIS, LES *p* 1105
105 BOUL SACRE-COEUR BUREAU 1, GATINEAU, QC, J8X 1C5
(819) 771-6631 *SIC* 8322

CENTRES JEUNESSE DE LANAUDIERE, LES *p* 1114
1170 RUE LADOUCEUR, JOLIETTE, QC, J6E 3W7
(450) 759-0755 *SIC* 8641

CENTRETOWN CITIZENS OTTAWA CORPORATION *p* 833
415 GILMOUR ST UNIT 200, OTTAWA, ON, K2P 2M8
(613) 234-4065 *SIC* 8699

CENTRETOWN COMMUNITY HEALTH CENTRE *p* 833
420 COOPER ST, OTTAWA, ON, K2P 2N6
(613) 233-4443 *SIC* 8093

CENTREVILLE AMUSEMENT PARK *p* 959
See BEASLEY, WILLIAM ENTERPRISES LIMITED

CENTRIA COMMERCE INC *p* 1086
3131 BOUL SAINT-MARTIN O BUREAU 500, COTE SAINT-LUC, QC, H7T 2Z5
(514) 874-0122 *SIC* 8742

CENTRIC GROUP, THE *p* 668
161 ALDEN RD UNIT 9, MARKHAM, ON, L3R 3W7
(905) 415-9577 *SIC* 8743

CENTRIC HEALTH CORPORATION *p* 923
20 EGLINTON AVE W SUITE 2100, TORONTO, ON, M4R 1K8
(416) 927-8400 *SIC* 8742

CENTRILIFT *p* 139
See BAKER HUGHES CANADA COMPANY

CENTRILIFT A BAKER HUGHES COMPANY *p* 46
401 9 AVE SW SUITE 1000, CALGARY, AB, T2P 3C5
(403) 537-3400 *SIC* 5013

CENTRILIFT, A DIVISION OF *p* 46
See CENTRILIFT A BAKER HUGHES COMPANY

CENTRIS *p* 1396
See CIGM

CENTRIX ENVIRONNEMENT INC *p* 1139
5314 AV DES BELLES-AMOURS BUREAU 104, LEVIS, QC, G6X 1P2
(418) 988-3888 *SIC* 6712

CENTRON CONSTRUCTION LIMITED *p* 39
8826 BLACKFOOT TRAIL SE UNIT 104, CALGARY, AB, T2J 3J1
(403) 252-1120 *SIC* 1542

CENTRON EAGLE RIDGE *p* 39
See CENTRON GROUP OF COMPANIES INC

CENTRON GROUP OF COMPANIES INC *p* 39
8826 BLACKFOOT TRAIL SE SUITE 104, CALGARY, AB, T2J 3J1
(403) 252-1120 *SIC* 1542

CENTURA (HAMILTON) LIMITED *p* 615
140 NEBO RD, HAMILTON, ON, L8W 2E4
(905) 383-5100 *SIC* 5023

CENTURA (OTTAWA) LIMITED *p* 988
950 LAWRENCE AVE W, TORONTO, ON, M6A 1C4
(416) 785-5151 *SIC* 5023

CENTURA (TORONTO) LIMITED *p* 788
950 LAWRENCE AVE W, NORTH YORK, ON, M6A 1C4
(416) 785-5165 *SIC* 5032

CENTURA (VANCOUVER) LIMITED *p* 188
4616 CANADA WAY, BURNABY, BC, V5G 1K5
(604) 298-8453 *SIC* 5032

CENTURA BRANDS *p* 700
See ROBINSON FORGIONE GROUP INC

CENTURA BRANDS INC *p* 693
1200 AEROWOOD DR UNIT 50, MISSISSAUGA, ON, L4W 2S7
(905) 602-1965 *SIC* 5122

CENTURA FLOOR & WALL FASHIONS *p* 188
See CENTURA (VANCOUVER) LIMITED

CENTURA FLOOR & WALL FASHIONS *p* 448
See TANGRAM SURFACES INC

CENTURA FLOOR & WALL TILE *p* 615
See CENTURA (HAMILTON) LIMITED

CENTURA FLOOR AND WALL FASHIONS*p* 788

See CENTURA (TORONTO) LIMITED
CENTURA LIMITED   *p 788*
950 LAWRENCE AVE W, NORTH YORK, ON, M6A 1C4
(416) 785-5165   *SIC 5023*
CENTURA LONDON   *p 657*
See RAM DISTRIBUTORS LIMITED
CENTURA OTTAWA   *p 988*
See CENTURA (OTTAWA) LIMITED
CENTURA QUEBEC LTEE   *p 1338*
5885 CH DE LA COTE-DE-LIESSE, SAINT-LAURENT, QC, H4T 1C3
(514) 336-4311   *SIC 5032*
CENTURA TILE   *p 788*
See CENTURA LIMITED
CENTURION ASSET MANAGEMENT INC *p 771*
25 SHEPPARD AVE W SUITE 710, NORTH YORK, ON, M2N 6S6
(416) 733-5600   *SIC 6531*
CENTURION MECHANICAL LTD   *p 73*
2509 DIEPPE AVE SW UNIT 301, CALGARY, AB, T3E 7J9
(403) 452-6761   *SIC 1711*
CENTURY 21   *p 484*
See CENTURY 21 B J ROTH REALTY LTD
CENTURY 21   *p 668*
See CENTURY 21 KING'S QUAY REAL ESTATE INC
CENTURY 21 ASSOCIATES INC   *p 705*
5659 MCADAM RD UNIT C1, MISSISSAUGA, ON, L4Z 1N9
(905) 279-8888   *SIC 6531*
CENTURY 21 ASSURANCE REALTY LTD *p 221*
251 HARVEY AVE, KELOWNA, BC, V1Y 6C2
(250) 869-0101   *SIC 6531*
CENTURY 21 ATRIA REALTY INC   *p 851*
1550 16TH AVE UNIT C SUITE 200 SOUTH, RICHMOND HILL, ON, L4B 3K9
(905) 883-1988   *SIC 6531*
CENTURY 21 B J ROTH REALTY LTD *p 484*
355 BAYFIELD ST SUITE 5, BARRIE, ON, L4M 3C3
(705) 721-9111   *SIC 6531*
CENTURY 21 BAMBER REALTY LTD   *p 67*
1612 17 AVE SW, CALGARY, AB, T2T 0E3
(403) 875-4653   *SIC 6531*
CENTURY 21 BEST SELLERS LTD   *p 705*
4 ROBERT SPECK PKY SUITE 150, MISSISSAUGA, ON, L4Z 1S1
(905) 273-4211   *SIC 6531*
CENTURY 21 CAMDEC REAL ESTATE LTD *p 873*
4544 SHEPPARD AVE E SUITE 100, SCARBOROUGH, ON, M1S 1V2
(416) 298-2800   *SIC 6531*
CENTURY 21 CARRIE REALTY LTD   *p 368*
1046 ST MARY'S RD, WINNIPEG, MB, R2M 5S6
(204) 987-2100   *SIC 6531*
CENTURY 21 CARRIE.COM   *p 368*
See CENTURY 21 CARRIE REALTY LTD
CENTURY 21 COASTAL REALTY LTD *p 276*
12837 76 AVE SUITE 217, SURREY, BC, V3W 2V3
(604) 599-4888   *SIC 6531*
CENTURY 21 COLONIAL REALTY INC *p 1038*
111 ST. PETERS RD, CHARLOTTETOWN, PE, C1A 5P1
(902) 566-2121   *SIC 6531*
CENTURY 21 FIRST CANADIAN CORP *p 655*
420 YORK ST SUITE 21, LONDON, ON, N6B 1R1
(519) 673-3390   *SIC 6531*
CENTURY 21 HERITAGE HOUSE LTD *p 1035*
871 DUNDAS ST, WOODSTOCK, ON, N4S 1G8
(519) 539-5646   *SIC 6531*
CENTURY 21 IN TOWN REALTY   *p 326*

See NECHAKO REAL ESTATE LTD
CENTURY 21 KING'S QUAY REAL ESTATE INC   *p 668*
7300 WARDEN AVE SUITE 401, MARKHAM, ON, L3R 9Z6
(905) 940-3428   *SIC 6531*
CENTURY 21 LANTHORN REAL ESTATE LTD   *p 491*
266 FRONT ST UNIT 202, BELLEVILLE, ON, K8N 2Z2
(613) 967-2100   *SIC 6531*
CENTURY 21 MAX-IMMO   *p 1236*
See 2945-9609 QUEBEC INC
CENTURY 21 MILLENNIUM INC   *p 509*
350 RUTHERFORD RD S SUITE 10, BRAMPTON, ON, L6W 4N6
(905) 450-8300   *SIC 6531*
CENTURY 21 NEW AGE REALTY INC *p 718*
5618 TENTH LINE W UNIT 9, MISSISSAUGA, ON, L5M 7L9
(905) 567-1411   *SIC 6531*
CENTURY 21 NEW CONCEPT LTD   *p 776*
1993 LESLIE ST, NORTH YORK, ON, M3B 2M3
(416) 449-7600   *SIC 6531*
CENTURY 21 PEOPLE'S CHOICE REALTY INC   *p 997*
1780 ALBION RD SUITE 2, TORONTO, ON, M9V 1C1
(416) 742-8000   *SIC 6531*
CENTURY 21 PERCY FULTON LTD   *p 876*
2911 KENNEDY RD, SCARBOROUGH, ON, M1V 1S8
(416) 298-0465   *SIC 6531*
CENTURY 21 PLATINUM REALTY   *p 118*
See 921325 ALBERTA LTD
CENTURY 21 PROFESSIONAL GROUP INC *p 514*
32 CHARING CROSS ST, BRANTFORD, ON, N3R 2H2
(519) 756-3900   *SIC 6531*
CENTURY 21 QUEENSWOOD REALTY LTD *p 332*
2558 SINCLAIR RD, VICTORIA, BC, V8N 1B8
(250) 477-1100   *SIC 6531*
CENTURY 21 REGAL REALTY INC   *p 873*
4030 SHEPPARD AVE E SUITE 2, SCARBOROUGH, ON, M1S 1S6
(416) 291-0929   *SIC 6531*
CENTURY 21 SKYLARK REAL ESTATE LTD   *p 734*
1510 DREW RD UNIT 6, MISSISSAUGA, ON, L5S 1W7
(905) 673-3100   *SIC 6531*
CENTURY 21 TODAY REALTY LTD   *p 591*
225 GARRISON RD, FORT ERIE, ON, L2A 1M8
(905) 871-2121   *SIC 6531*
CENTURY 21 UNITED REALTY INC BROKAGE   *p 840*
387 GEORGE ST S, PETERBOROUGH, ON, K9J 3E1
(705) 743-4444   *SIC 6531*
CENTURY 21 VISION LTD   *p 1221*
5517 AV DE MONKLAND, MONTREAL, QC, H4A 1C8
(514) 481-2126   *SIC 6531*
CENTURY 21 WESTMAN REALTY LTD.   *p 347*
2915 VICTORIA AVE, BRANDON, MB, R7B 2N6
(204) 725-0555   *SIC 6531*
CENTURY 21 YOUR NUMBER ONE REALTY INC BROKERAGE   *p 770*
6400 YONGE ST SUITE 200, NORTH YORK, ON, M2M 3X4
SIC 6531
CENTURY 21-JOHN DEVRIES LTD   *p 625*
444 HAZELDEAN RD, KANATA, ON, K2L 1V2
(613) 836-2570   *SIC 6531*

CENTURY AGRO LTD   *p 1420*
845 BROAD ST UNIT 207, REGINA, SK, S4R 8G9
(306) 949-7182   *SIC 5153*
CENTURY CELLULAR (RICHMOND HILL) CORPORATION   *p 855*
10520 YONGE ST SUITE 26, RICHMOND HILL, ON, L4C 3C7
(905) 884-0000   *SIC 5065*
CENTURY GARDENS RECREATION CENTRE   *p 508*
See CORPORATION OF THE CITY OF BRAMPTON, THE
CENTURY GLASS (85) LTD   *p 216*
1110 VICTORIA ST, KAMLOOPS, BC, V2C 2C5
(250) 374-1274   *SIC 5211*
CENTURY GROUP LANDS CORPORATION *p 237*
11 EIGHTH ST 10TH FL, ANVIL CENTRE, NEW WESTMINSTER, BC, V3M 3N7
(604) 943-2203   *SIC 6531*
CENTURY HOLDINGS LTD   *p 237*
11 EIGHTH ST, NEW WESTMINSTER, BC, V3M 3N7
(604) 943-2203   *SIC 6512*
CENTURY HONDA   *p 468*
See 3278724 NOVA SCOTIA LIMITED
CENTURY INTERNATIONAL ARMS LTD *p 1338*
353 RUE ISABEY, SAINT-LAURENT, QC, H4T 1Y2
(514) 731-8883   *SIC 5091*
CENTURY LANE KITCHENS INC.   *p 219*
800 MCCURDY RD, KELOWNA, BC, V1X 2P7
(250) 765-2366   *SIC 5031*
CENTURY PACIFIC FOUNDRY   *p 275*
See 302084 B.C. LTD
CENTURY PACIFIC FOUNDRY LTD   *p 276*
8239 128 ST, SURREY, BC, V3W 4G1
(604) 596-7451   *SIC 3325*
CENTURY PLAZA HOTEL   *p 326*
See CENTURY PLAZA LTD
CENTURY PLAZA LTD   *p 326*
1015 BURRARD ST, VANCOUVER, BC, V6Z 1Y5
(604) 687-0575   *SIC 7011*
CENTURY PRODUCTS   *p 1324*
See 2946-4617 QUEBEC INC
CENTURY SECONDARY SCHOOL   *p 1024*
See GREATER ESSEX COUNTY DISTRICT SCHOOL BOARD
CENTURYAMADEUS   *p 1156*
See INDUSTRIES CENTURY INC, LES
CEP LOCAL 1119   *p 215*
See UNIFOR
CEPEO   *p 817*
See CONSEIL DES ECOLES PUBLIQUES DE L'EST DE L'ONTARIO
CEPSA CHIMIE BECANCOUR INC   *p 1056*
5250 BOUL BECANCOUR, BECANCOUR, QC, G9H 3X3
(819) 294-1414   *SIC 2819*
CEQUENCE ENERGY LTD   *p 46*
215-9TH AVE SW SUITE 1400, CALGARY, AB, T2P 1K3
(403) 229-3050   *SIC 1382*
CERA-PRO ECOLOGICAL   *p 1047*
See ADHESIFS PROMA INC
CERAGRES LES-BAINS   *p 1326*
See GROUPE CARREAUX CERAGRES INC
CERAGRES TILE GROUP   *p 790*
170 TYCOS DR, NORTH YORK, ON, M6B 1W8
(416) 286-3553   *SIC 5032*
CERAMIQUE DECORS M.S.F. INC   *p 1266*
2750 AV DALTON, QUEBEC, QC, G1P 3S4
(418) 781-0955   *SIC 5713*
CERAMIQUE ITAL-NORD LTEE   *p 1245*
569 BOUL DES LAURENTIDES BUREAU 117, PIEDMONT, QC, J0R 1K0

(450) 227-8866   *SIC 5032*
CERAMIQUES B.G.   *p 1152*
See 9173-1307 QUEBEC INC
CERAMIQUES ROYAL LTEE, LES   *p 1343*
8845 RUE PASCAL-GAGNON, SAINT-LEONARD, QC, H1P 1Z4
(514) 324-0002   *SIC 5032*
CERATEC INC   *p 1263*
414 AV SAINT-SACREMENT, QUEBEC, QC, G1N 3Y3
(418) 681-0101   *SIC 5032*
CERATEC INC   *p 1325*
1620 BOUL JULES-POITRAS, SAINT-LAURENT, QC, H4N 1Z3
(514) 956-0341   *SIC 5032*
CERATEC VAUDREUIL   *p 1325*
See CERATEC INC
CERCUEILS ALLIANCE CASKETS INC *p 398*
355 DU POUVOIR CH, EDMUNDSTON, NB, E3V 4K1
(506) 739-6226   *SIC 3995*
CEREALEX INC   *p 1352*
666 RANG DU RUISSEAU-DES-ANGES S, SAINT-ROCH-DE-L'ACHIGAN, QC, J0K 3H0
(450) 588-3132   *SIC 5153*
CEREBRAL PALSY PARENT COUNCIL OF TORONTO   *p 678*
379 CHURCH ST SUITE 402, MARKHAM, ON, L6B 0T1
(905) 513-2756   *SIC 8399*
CERES GLOBAL AG CORP   *p 846*
2 SHERWOOD FOREST LN, PORT COLBORNE, ON, L3K 5V8
(905) 834-5924   *SIC 6211*
CERESCO   *p 1353*
See SG CERESCO INC
CERICOLA FARMS   *p 497*
See SURE FRESH FOODS INC
CERIDIAN CANADA LTD   *p 8*
2618 HOPEWELL PL NE SUITE 310, CALGARY, AB, T1Y 7J7
(403) 262-6035   *SIC 8721*
CERIDIAN CANADA LTD   *p 323*
1200 73RD AVE W SUITE 1400, VANCOUVER, BC, V6P 6G5
(604) 267-6200   *SIC 8721*
CERIDIAN CANADA LTD   *p 377*
125 GARRY ST, WINNIPEG, MB, R3C 3P2
(204) 947-9400   *SIC 7361*
CERIDIAN CANADA LTD   *p 668*
675 COCHRANE DR SUITE 515N, MARKHAM, ON, L3R 0B8
(905) 947-7000   *SIC 8721*
CERIDIAN CANADA LTD   *p 693*
5600 EXPLORER DR SUITE 400, MISSISSAUGA, ON, L4W 4Y2
(905) 282-8100   *SIC 8721*
CERIDIAN CANADA LTD   *p 1333*
8777 RTE TRANSCANADIENNE, SAINT-LAURENT, QC, H4S 1Z6
(514) 908-3000   *SIC 8721*
CERIDIAN LIFEWORKS SERVICES   *p 668*
See CERIDIAN CANADA LTD
CERIKO ASSELIN LOMBARDI INC   *p 1333*
3005 RUE HALPERN, SAINT-LAURENT, QC, H4S 1P5
(514) 956-5511   *SIC 1542*
CERMAQ CANADA LTD   *p 194*
919 ISLAND HWY UNIT 203, CAMPBELL RIVER, BC, V9W 2C2
(250) 286-0022   *SIC 0273*
CERMAQ CANADA LTD   *p 283*
61 4TH ST, TOFINO, BC, V0R 2Z0
(250) 725-1255   *SIC 2048*
CERMEX CANADA   *p 1238*
See SIDEL CANADA INC
CERTAINTEED CANADA, INC   *p 1027*
61 ROYAL GROUP CRES, WOODBRIDGE, ON, L4H 1X9
(905) 652-5200   *SIC 3296*
CERTAINTEED GYPSUM CANADA, INC *p 205*
1070 DERWENT WAY, DELTA, BC, V3M

5R1
(604) 527-1405   *SIC* 3275
CERTAINTEED GYPSUM CANADA, INC *p*
1356
700 1RE AV, SAINTE-CATHERINE, QC, J5C
1C5
(450) 632-5440   *SIC* 3275
**CERTAS DIRECT COMPAGNIE
D'ASSURANCE** *p* 705
3 ROBERT SPECK PKY, MISSISSAUGA,
ON, L4Z 2G5
(905) 306-3900   *SIC* 6331
**CERTAS HOME AND AUTO INSURANCE
COMPANY** *p* 1136
6300 BOUL GUILLAUME-COUTURE,
LEVIS, QC, G6V 6P9
(418) 835-4900   *SIC* 6411
CERTEK HEAT MACHINES INC *p* 171
11101 ST WEMBLEY ST, WEMBLEY, AB,
T0H 3S0
(780) 832-3962   *SIC* 1389
CERTEX SOLUTIONS *p* 948
See 1576640 ONTARIO LTD
CERTEX-20-ANS *p* 1307
*See CERTEX-CENTRE DE RECUPERA-
TION ET DE RECYCLAGE DU TEXTILE INC*
**CERTEX-CENTRE DE RECUPERATION ET
DE RECYCLAGE DU TEXTILE INC** *p* 1307
7500 GRANDE ALLEE, SAINT-HUBERT,
QC, J3Y 0V7
(450) 926-1733   *SIC* 4953
CERTICOM CORP *p* 693
4701 TAHOE BLVD, MISSISSAUGA, ON,
L4W 0B5
(905) 507-4220   *SIC* 7372
**CERTIFIED GENERAL ACCOUNTANTS
ASSOCIATION OF BRITISH COLUMBIA** *p*
297
555 HASTINGS ST W SUITE 800, VAN-
COUVER, BC, V6B 4N6
(604) 872-7222   *SIC* 8621
**CERTIFIED GENERAL ACCOUNTANTS
ASSOCIATION OF CANADA** *p* 192
4200 NORTH FRASER WAY SUITE 100,
BURNABY, BC, V5J 5K7
(604) 408-6660   *SIC* 8621
CERTIFIED RADIO SOUTH, DIV OF *p* 125
See B & B ELECTRONICS LTD
CERUM DENTAL SUPPLIES LTD *p* 66
115 17 AVE SW, CALGARY, AB, T2S 0A1
(403) 228-5199   *SIC* 5047
CERVELO CYCLES INC *p* 788
15 LESWYN RD UNIT 1, NORTH YORK,
ON, M6A 1J8
(416) 782-6789   *SIC* 3751
CERVO-POLYGAZ INC *p* 1080
1371 RUE DE LA MANIC, CHICOUTIMI,
QC, G7K 1G7
(418) 696-1212   *SIC* 5169
CERVOL SERVICE GROUP INC *p* 716
2295 DUNWIN DR UNIT 4, MISSISSAUGA,
ON, L5L 3S4
(905) 569-0557   *SIC* 1711
CERVUS AG EQUIPMENT LP *p* 76
333 96 AVE NE SUITE 5201, CALGARY, AB,
T3K 0S3
(403) 567-0339   *SIC* 0851
**CERVUS CONTRACTORS EQUIPMENT
LTD** *p* 76
333 96 AVE NE SUITE 5201, CALGARY, AB,
T3K 0S3
(877) 567-0339   *SIC* 5082
CERVUS CORPORATION *p* 76
120 COUNTRY HILLS LANDNG NW SUITE
205, CALGARY, AB, T3K 5P3
(403) 567-0339   *SIC* 6712
CERVUS EQUIPMENT CORP *p* 76
333 96 AVE NE UNIT 5201, CALGARY, AB,
T3K 0S3
(403) 567-0339   *SIC* 5082
CERVUS EQUIPMENT CORPORATION *p* 76
333 96 AVE NE SUITE 5201, CALGARY, AB,
T3K 0S3
(403) 567-0339   *SIC* 5084

CERVUS LP *p* 76
333 96 AVE NE SUITE 5201, CALGARY, AB,
T3K 0S3
(403) 275-2215   *SIC* 5999
CES ENERGY SOLUTIONS CORP *p* 46
332 6 AVE SW SUITE 1400, CALGARY, AB,
T2P 0B2
(403) 269-2800   *SIC* 1382
CES ENERGY SOLUTIONS CORP *p* 1405
HIGHWAY 9 S, CARLYLE, SK, S0C 0R0
(306) 453-4470   *SIC* 1382
CESIDIO ALTERNATE ENERGY *p* 855
298 DEMAINE CRES, RICHMOND HILL,
ON, L4C 2W5
(416) 822-6750   *SIC* 4924
CESIUM *p* 1156
See CESIUM TELECOM INCORPORATED
CESIUM TELECOM INCORPORATED *p*
1156
5798 RUE FERRIER, MONT-ROYAL, QC,
H4P 1M7
(514) 798-8686   *SIC* 5065
CESL ENGINEERING *p* 323
See CESL LIMITED
CESL LIMITED *p* 323
8898 HEATHER ST UNIT 107, VANCOU-
VER, BC, V6P 3S8
SIC 8731
CESO *p* 944
*See CANADIAN EXECUTIVE SERVICE
ORGANIZATION*
**CESSCO FABRICATION & ENGINEERING
LIMITED** *p* 113
7310 99 ST NW, EDMONTON, AB, T6E 3R8
(780) 433-9531   *SIC* 3499
CETAL *p* 1133
179 BOUL LAURIER, LAURIER-STATION,
QC, G0S 1N0
(418) 728-3119   *SIC* 2448
CEV *p* 1167
See C.E.V. INC
CEVA FREIGHT CANADA CORP *p* 693
1880 MATHESON BLVD E, MISSISSAUGA,
ON, L4W 5N4
(905) 672-3456   *SIC* 4731
CEVA LOGISTICS *p* 499
See CEVA LOGISTICS CANADA, ULC
CEVA LOGISTICS CANADA, ULC *p* 499
2600 NORTH PARK DR, BRAMPTON, ON,
L6S 6E2
(905) 789-2904   *SIC* 4212
CEVA LOGISTICS CANADA, ULC *p* 648
15745 ROBIN'S HILL RD, LONDON, ON,
N5V 0A5
(519) 659-2382   *SIC* 4731
CEWP *p* 169
*See CANADIAN ENGINEERED WOOD
PRODUCTS LTD*
CEZINC *p* 1366
*See ZINC ELECTROLYTIQUE DU CANADA
LIMITEE*
CF INDUSTRIES *p* 145
See CANADIAN FERTILIZERS LIMITED
**CFB ESQUIMALT MILITARY FAMILY RE-
SOURCE CENTRE** *p*
339
1505 ESQUIMALT RD, VICTORIA, BC, V9A
7N2
(250) 363-8628   *SIC* 8399
CFE LEVIS LOTBINIERE BELLE CHASSE *p*
1135
*See CENTRE FINANCIER AUX EN-
TREPRISES DESJARDINS LEVIS LOT-
BINIERE*
CFG *p* 333
*See CENTRE FOR GLOBAL STUDIES,
THE*
CFGE *p* 1389
See COGECO MEDIA INC
CFGO *p* 821
87 GEORGE ST, OTTAWA, ON, K1N 9H7
(613) 789-2486   *SIC* 7313
CFI *p* 1146
See CYRILLE FRIGON (1996) INC

CFIS LANGUAGE SCHOOLS *p* 75
*See CALGARY FRENCH & INTERNA-
TIONAL SCHOOL SOCIETY, THE*
CFMI-FM *p* 330
See CORUS ENTERTAINMENT INC
CFN PRECISION LTD *p* 550
1000 CREDITSTONE RD, CONCORD, ON,
L4K 4P8
(905) 669-8191   *SIC* 3812
CFO RENTALS INC *p* 1437
GD LCD MAIN, WEYBURN, SK, S4H 2J7
(306) 842-3454   *SIC* 5082
CFOS RADIO *p* 835
*See BAYSHORE BROADCASTING COR-
PORATION*
CFR CHEMICALS INC *p* 46
525 8 AVE SW SUITE 1920, CALGARY, AB,
T2P 1G1
(587) 320-1097   *SIC* 5169
CFRN TV *p* 99
See BELL MEDIA INC
CFS *p* 614
*See CATHOLIC FAMILY SERVICES OF
HAMILTON*
CG CANADIAN GLOVE CORP *p* 972
67 KIMBARK BLVD, TORONTO, ON, M5N
2X9
(416) 939-5066   *SIC* 3069
CG MAINTENANCE *p* 782
*See C.G. MAINTENANCE & SANITARY
PRODUCTS INC*
CGA CANADA *p* 192
*See CERTIFIED GENERAL ACCOUN-
TANTS ASSOCIATION OF CANADA*
CGA-BC *p* 297
*See CERTIFIED GENERAL ACCOUN-
TANTS ASSOCIATION OF BRITISH
COLUMBIA*
CGC GYPSUM *p* 155
7550 40 AVE, RED DEER, AB, T4P 2H8
(403) 277-0586   *SIC* 3699
CGC INC *p* 470
GD, WINDSOR, NS, B0N 2T0
(902) 798-4676   *SIC* 1499
CGC INC *p* 607
55 THIRD LINE RD, HAGERSVILLE, ON,
N0A 1H0
(905) 768-3331   *SIC* 3275
CGC INC *p* 709
350 BURNHAMTHORPE RD W SUITE 500,
MISSISSAUGA, ON, L5B 3J1
(905) 803-5600   *SIC* 3275
CGC INC *p* 803
735 FOURTH LINE, OAKVILLE, ON, L6L
5B7
(905) 337-5100   *SIC* 1761
CGC INC *p* 1164
7200 RUE NOTRE-DAME E, MONTREAL,
QC, H1N 3L6
(514) 255-4061   *SIC* 3275
CGFPC *p* 1426
*See CANADA GOLDEN FORTUNE
POTASH CORP*
CGG SERVICES (CANADA) INC *p* 75
3675 63 AVE NE, CALGARY, AB, T3J 5K1
(403) 291-1434   *SIC* 7371
CGI *p* 88
*See CONSEILLERS EN GESTION ET IN-
FORMATIQUE CGI INC*
CGI *p* 596
*See CONSEILLERS EN GESTION ET IN-
FORMATIQUE CGI INC*
CGI *p* 720
See CDSL CANADA LIMITED
CGI *p* 935
*See CONSEILLERS EN GESTION ET IN-
FORMATIQUE CGI INC*
CGI *p* 937
*See CANADIAN GENERAL INVESTMENTS
LIMITED*
CGI *p* 1078
*See CONSEILLERS EN GESTION ET IN-
FORMATIQUE CGI INC*
CGI *p* 1176

CGI *p* 1213
*See CONSEILLERS EN GESTION ET IN-
FORMATIQUE CGI INC*
CGI *p* 1258
*See CONSEILLERS EN GESTION ET IN-
FORMATIQUE CGI INC*
CGI *p* 1417
See CDSL CANADA LIMITED
CGI DEVELOPMENT INC *p* 426
20 SAGONA AVE, MOUNT PEARL, NL,
A1N 4R2
(709) 748-8888   *SIC* 1521
CGI INC *p* 1213
1350 BOUL RENE-LEVESQUE O SUITE
25E, MONTREAL, QC, H3G 1T4
(514) 841-3200   *SIC* 7371
CGI POSTES CANADA *p* 1263
1940 RUE LEON-HARMEL, QUEBEC, QC,
G1N 4K3
(418) 682-8663   *SIC* 4311
CGIS *p* 290
See C.G. INDUSTRIAL SPECIALTIES LTD
CGL MANUFACTURING INC *p* 605
151 ARROW RD, GUELPH, ON, N1K 1S8
(519) 836-0322   *SIC* 3599
**CGL-GRS SWISS CANADIAN GEM LAB
INC** *p* 303
409 GRANVILLE ST SUITE 510, VANCOU-
VER, BC, V6C 1T2
(604) 687-0091   *SIC* 8734
CGRIFF21 HOLDINGS INC *p* 680
25 BODRINGTON CRT, MARKHAM, ON,
L6G 1B6
(905) 940-9334   *SIC* 7699
CGSDS/SHDVGS *p* 899
*See SUDBURY DEVELOPMENTAL SER-
VICES*
CGT *p* 533
*See CANADIAN GENERAL-TOWER LIM-
ITED*
CGTA GIFT SHOW *p* 583
42 VOYAGER CRT S, ETOBICOKE, ON,
M9W 5M7
(416) 679-0170   *SIC* 7389
CGTV GAMES LTD *p* 311
1199 PENDER ST W SUITE 800, VANCOU-
VER, BC, V6E 2R1
SIC 7371
CGV BUILDERS INC *p* 545
56 CONNAUGHT AVE, COCHRANE, ON,
P0L 1C0
(705) 272-5404   *SIC* 1542
CGW AUTOMOTIVE GROUP LIMITED *p* 438
34 LORD AMHERST DR, AMHERST, NS,
B4H 4W6
(902) 667-8348   *SIC* 5511
CGX ENERGY INC *p* 950
333 BAY ST SUITE 1100, TORONTO, ON,
M5H 2R2
(416) 364-5569   *SIC* 1389
CH 2015 *p* 1086
See CONCEPTION HABITAT 2015 INC
CH TELEVISION *p* 335
See POSTMEDIA NETWORK INC
CH2M HILL CANADA LIMITED *p* 190
4720 KINGSWAY SUITE 2100, BURNABY,
BC, V5H 4N2
(604) 684-3282   *SIC* 8711
CH2M HILL CANADA LIMITED *p* 766
245 CONSUMERS RD SUITE 400, NORTH
YORK, ON, M2J 1R3
(416) 499-9000   *SIC* 8711
**CH2M HILL CONSTRUCTION CANADA,
LTD** *p* 28
1100 1 ST SE SUITE 1400, CALGARY, AB,
T2G 1B1
(403) 232-9800   *SIC* 1541
CH2M HILL ENERGY CANADA LTD *p* 14
205 QUARRY PARK BLVD SE, CALGARY,
AB, T2C 3E7
(403) 407-6000   *SIC* 8748
CHABERTON ESTATE WINERY *p* 227

See DOMAINE DE CHABERTON ESTATES LTD

CHABOT CARROSSERIE INC p 1159
264 CH DES POIRIER, MONTMAGNY, QC, G5V 4S5
(418) 234-1525   *SIC 7532*

CHADO p 1156
See GROUPE DYNAMITE INC

CHADWICK FOOD SERVICE MANAGEMENT INCORPORATED p 439
200 WATERFRONT DR SUITE 225, BEDFORD, NS, B4A 4J4
SIC 5812

CHAFFEY-BURKE ELEMENTARY SCHOOL p 189
See BURNABY SCHOOL BOARD DISTRICT 41

CHAGNON HONDA p 1110
See AUTOS R. CHAGNON DE GRANBY INC

CHAGNON, J. M. p 1081
See CENTRE AGRICOLE COATICOOK INC

CHAI POULTRY INC p 920
115 SAULTER ST S, TORONTO, ON, M4M 3K8
SIC 5144

CHAINES DE TRACTION QUEBEC LTEE p 1048
9401 BOUL PARKWAY, ANJOU, QC, H1J 1N4
(514) 353-9210   *SIC 5072*

CHAINES TELE ASTRAL p 1214
See ASTRAL BROADCASTING GROUP INC

CHAINON, LE p 1184
See ASSOCIATION D'ENTRAIDE LE CHAINON INC, L'

CHAIRMAN'S BRAND CORPORATION p 870
77 PROGRESS AVE, SCARBOROUGH, ON, M1P 2Y7
(416) 288-8515   *SIC 6794*

CHAITON & CHAITON p 771
See CHAITON MANAGEMENT LTD

CHAITON MANAGEMENT LTD p 771
185 SHEPPARD AVE W, NORTH YORK, ON, M2N 1M9
(416) 222-8888   *SIC 8111*

CHALAIR ELECTRIK p 1296
See STELPRO DESIGN INC

CHALET CHEVROLET OLDSMOBILE LTD p 223
1142 304TH ST, KIMBERLEY, BC, V1A 3H6
(250) 427-4895   *SIC 5511*

CHALET GM p 223
See CHALET CHEVROLET OLDSMOBILE LTD

CHALEUR REGIONAL HOSPITAL p 394
See REGIONAL HEALTH AUTHORITY A

CHALLAND PIPELINE LTD p 159
HWY 11 S, ROCKY MOUNTAIN HOUSE, AB, T4T 1B4
(403) 845-2469   *SIC 1623*

CHALLENGER BUILDING SUPPLIES LTD p 140
3304 8 AVE N, LETHBRIDGE, AB, T1H 5C9
(403) 327-8501   *SIC 5039*

CHALLENGER ENGINEERING p 107
See CHALLENGER GEOMATICS LTD

CHALLENGER GEOMATICS LTD p 107
9945 50 ST NW SUITE 200, EDMONTON, AB, T6A 0L4
(780) 424-5511   *SIC 8713*

CHALLENGER INVESTMENTS INC p 538
300 MAPLE GROVE RD, CAMBRIDGE, ON, N3E 1B7
(519) 653-6226   *SIC 4213*

CHALLENGER LOGISTICS INC p 538
300 MAPLE GROVE RD, CAMBRIDGE, ON, N3E 1B7
(519) 653-6226   *SIC 4731*

CHALLENGER MOTOR FREIGHT INC p 538
300 MAPLE GROVE RD, CAMBRIDGE, ON,

N3E 1B7
(519) 653-6226   *SIC 4213*

CHALLENGER MOTOR FREIGHT INC p 1093
2770 AV ANDRE, DORVAL, QC, H9P 1K6
(514) 684-2025   *SIC 4213*

CHALMERS FUELS INC p 836
6630 HWY 23, PALMERSTON, ON, N0G 2P0
(519) 343-3023   *SIC 5983*

CHALMERS INVESTMENT CORP LTD p 28
727 42 AVE SE, CALGARY, AB, T2G 1Y8
(403) 243-6642   *SIC 5812*

CHALMERS SUSPENSION INTERNATIONAL INC p 687
6400 NORTHAM DR, MISSISSAUGA, ON, L4V 1J1
(905) 362-6400   *SIC 3715*

CHALUT, A . AUTO LTEE p 1243
250 BOUL ANTONIO-BARRETTE, NOTRE-DAME-DES-PRAIRIES, QC, J6E 6J5
(450) 756-1638   *SIC 5511*

CHAMARD, JACQUES & FILS INC p 1282
619 BOUL IBERVILLE, REPENTIGNY, QC, J6A 2C5
(450) 581-0101   *SIC 5411*

CHAMBERS ELECTRICAL CORP p 200
204 CAYER ST UNIT 101, COQUITLAM, BC, V3K 5B1
(604) 526-5688   *SIC 1731*

CHAMBLY HONDA p 1074
See AUTOMOBILES LA SEIGNEURIE (1990) INC, LES

CHAMBLY KIA p 1074
See 4486404 CANADA INC.

CHAMBLY MAZDA p 1074
See 4427814 CANADA INC

CHAMBORD SPORT YAMAHA p 1075
See CENTRE DU SPORT LAC-ST-JEAN INC

CHAMBRE DE COMMERCE DU MONTREAL METROPOLITAIN p 1187
380 RUE SAINT-ANTOINE O BUREAU 6000, MONTREAL, QC, H2Y 3X7
(514) 871-4000   *SIC 8611*

CHAMBRE DE LA SECURITE FINANCIERE p 1185
300 RUE LEO-PARISEAU BUREAU 2600, MONTREAL, QC, H2X 4B8
(514) 282-5777   *SIC 6351*

CHAMBRE IMMOBILIERE DU GRAND MONTREAL p 1396
600 CH DU GOLF, VERDUN, QC, H3E 1A8
(514) 762-2440   *SIC 8611*

CHAMCO INDUSTRIES LTD p 2
553 KINGSVIEW WAY SE SUITE 110, AIRDRIE, AB, T4A 0C9
(403) 945-8134   *SIC 5084*

CHAMCO INDUSTRIES LTD p 77
8900 VENTURE AVE SE, CALGARY, AB, T3S 0A2
(403) 777-1200   *SIC 5084*

CHAMOIS CAR WASH CORP, THE p 362
85 REENDERS DR, WINNIPEG, MB, R2C 5E8
(204) 669-9700   *SIC 7542*

CHAMOIS, THE p 363
See REENDERS CAR WASH LTD

CHAMP INDUSTRIES p 365
See BRIDGES, DAVID INC

CHAMP'S MUSHROOM'S GROUP p 179
See CHAMP'S MUSHROOMS INC

CHAMP'S MUSHROOMS INC p 179
3151 260 ST, ALDERGROVE, BC, V4W 2Z6
(604) 607-0789   *SIC 0182*

CHAMPAG INC p 1395
1156 RTE MARIE-VICTORIN, VERCHERES, QC, J0L 2R0
(450) 583-3350   *SIC 0182*

CHAMPAGNE EDITION INC p 140
57425 RGE RD 253, LEGAL, AB, T0G 1L0
(780) 961-3229   *SIC 3069*

CHAMPAGNE, GERARD LTEE p 1396
5144 RUE BANNANTYNE, VERDUN, QC, H4G 1G5
(514) 766-3536   *SIC 5411*

CHAMPION CHEVROLET BUICK GMC LTD p 284
2880 HIGHWAY DR, TRAIL, BC, V1R 2T3
(250) 368-9134   *SIC 5511*

CHAMPION IRON MINES LIMITED p 937
20 ADELAIDE ST E SUITE 200, TORONTO, ON, M5C 2T6
(416) 866-2200   *SIC 1081*

CHAMPION MOYER DIEBEL p 623
See MOYER DIEBEL LIMITED

CHAMPION PRODUCTS CORP p 1022
2601 WYANDOTTE ST E, WINDSOR, ON, N8Y 0A5
(519) 252-5414   *SIC 5113*

CHAMPIONCASES.COM p 1335
See NEXT SUCCESS INC

CHAMPLAIN DODGE CHRYSLER LTEE p 1396
3350 RUE WELLINGTON, VERDUN, QC, H4G 1T5
(514) 761-4801   *SIC 5511*

CHAMPLAIN LHIN p 596
1900 CITY PARK DR SUITE 204, GLOUCESTER, ON, K1J 1A3
(613) 747-6784   *SIC 6324*

CHAMPLAIN MOTORS LIMITED p 408
1810 MAIN ST, MONCTON, NB, E1E 4S7
(506) 857-1800   *SIC 5511*

CHAMPLAIN NISSAN p 408
See CHAMPLAIN MOTORS LIMITED

CHANCELLOR PARK INC p 429
270 PORTUGAL COVE RD SUITE 219, ST. JOHN'S, NL, A1B 4N6
(709) 754-1165   *SIC 8051*

CHANCES KELOWNA p 221
See BINGO KELOWNA CHANCES GAMING ENTERTAINMENT

CHANDELLES ET CREATIONS ROBIN INC p 1249
151 AV ALSTON, POINTE-CLAIRE, QC, H9R 5V9
(514) 426-5999   *SIC 5137*

CHANDLER SALES p 413
See IRVING, J. D. LIMITED

CHANDLER, DEAN ROOFING LIMITED p 868
275 COMSTOCK RD, SCARBOROUGH, ON, M1L 2H2
(416) 751-7840   *SIC 1761*

CHANDOS CONSTRUCTION LTD p 120
9604 20 AVE NW, EDMONTON, AB, T6N 1G1
(780) 436-8617   *SIC 1542*

CHANEL CANADA ULC p 1072
55 BOUL MARIE-VICTORIN, CANDIAC, QC, J5R 1B6
(450) 659-1981   *SIC 5122*

CHANGE HEALTHCARE CANADA COMPANY p 259
10711 CAMBIE RD SUITE 130, RICHMOND, BC, V6X 3G5
(604) 279-5422   *SIC 7371*

CHANGEPOINT CANADA ULC p 851
30 LEEK CRES SUITE 300, RICHMOND HILL, ON, L4B 4N4
(905) 886-7000   *SIC 7371*

CHANGFENG ENERGY INC p 668
32 SOUTH UNIONVILLE AVE SUITE 2036-2038, MARKHAM, ON, L3R 9S6
(647) 313-0066   *SIC 4923*

CHANGFENG ENERGY INC p 668
32 SOUTH UNIONVILLE AVENUE, MARKHAM, ON, L3R 9S6
(647) 313-0066   *SIC 4923*

CHANGFENG ENERGY INC. p 961
55 UNIVERSITY AVE, TORONTO, ON, M5J 2H7
SIC 4923

CHANMPENOISE, LA p 1270

CHANNEL CONTROL MERCHANTS CORPORATION p 515
225 HENRY ST UNIT 5B, BRANTFORD, ON, N3S 7R4
(519) 770-3403   *SIC 5199*

CHANNEL GATE TECHNOLOGIES INC p 185
4170 STILL CREEK DR SUITE 310, BURNABY, BC, V5C 6C6
(604) 683-0313   *SIC 5961*

CHANNEL ZERO p 994
See OUAT MEDIA INC

CHANTALE'S BED & BREAKFAST INC p 406
1234 MAIN ST, MONCTON, NB, E1C 1H7
SIC 6712

CHANTELLE MANAGEMENT LTD p 142
1255 5 AVE S, LETHBRIDGE, AB, T1J 0V6
(403) 328-6631   *SIC 8051*

CHANTIER DAVIE CANADA INC p 1136
22 RUE GEORGE-D.-DAVIE, LEVIS, QC, G6V 0K4
(418) 837-5841   *SIC 4493*

CHANTIERS DE CHIBOUGAMAU LTEE, LES p 1077
521 CH MERRILL, CHIBOUGAMAU, QC, G8P 2K7
(418) 748-6481   *SIC 2439*

CHANTLER TRANSPORT INC p 622
3235 CLIFFORD CRT, INNISFIL, ON, L9S 3V8
(705) 431-4022   *SIC 4213*

CHAOS FESTIVAL p 1185
See FESTIVAL JUSTE POUR RIRE

CHAPAIS ENERGIE, SOCIETE EN COMMANDITE p 942
67 YONGE ST SUITE 810, TORONTO, ON, M5E 1J8
SIC 4911

CHAPDELAINE ASSURANCE ET SERVICES FINANCIERS INC p 1056
220 RUE BREBEUF, BELOEIL, QC, J3G 5P3
(450) 464-2112   *SIC 6411*

CHAPELLERIE JEAN MYRIAM INC, LA p 1178
555 RUE CHABANEL O UNITE 303, MONTREAL, QC, H2N 2H8
(514) 383-0549   *SIC 5137*

CHAPELLERIE, LA p 1178
See CHAPELLERIE JEAN MYRIAM INC, LA

CHAPITEAUX CLASSIC INC, LES p 1247
12301 BOUL METROPOLITAIN E, POINTE-AUX-TREMBLES, QC, H1B 5R3
(514) 645-4555   *SIC 5999*

CHAPMAN FIRE PROTECTION A DIVISION OF p 331
See CHAPMAN MECHANICAL LTD

CHAPMAN MECHANICAL LTD p 331
901 WADDINGTON DR, VERNON, BC, V1T 9E2
(250) 545-9040   *SIC 1711*

CHAPMAN'S ICE CREAM p 664
See CHAPMAN'S, DAVID ICE CREAM LIMITED

CHAPMAN'S, DAVID ICE CREAM LIMITED p 664
100 CHAPMAN'S CRES, MARKDALE, ON, N0C 1H0
(519) 986-3131   *SIC 2024*

CHAPPLE FUELS LIMITED p 542
175 BOTHWELL ST, CHATHAM, ON, N7M 5J5
(519) 351-7194   *SIC 4212*

CHAPTERS p 9
See INDIGO BOOKS & MUSIC INC

CHAPTERS p 981
See INDIGO BOOKS & MUSIC INC

CHAPTERS p 1205

See INDIGO BOOKS & MUSIC INC
CHAPTERS DISTRIBUTION   *p 504*
See INDIGO BOOKS & MUSIC INC
CHARBONNEAU MESSAGER RAPIDE   *p 1110*
See MESSAGER RAPIDE INC
CHARCOAL STEAK HOUSE INC   *p 634*
2980 KING ST E, KITCHENER, ON, N2A 1A9
(519) 893-6570   *SIC 5812*
CHARCUTERIE DE BRETAGE   *p 1058*
See CHARCUTERIE LA TOUR EIFFEL INC
CHARCUTERIE L. FORTIN LIMITEE   *p 1045*
5371 AV DU PONT N, ALMA, QC, G8E 1T9
(418) 347-3365   *SIC 2013*
CHARCUTERIE LA TOUR EIFFEL INC   *p 1058*
1020 BOUL MICHELE-BOHEC, BLAINVILLE, QC, J7C 5E2
(450) 979-0001   *SIC 2011*
CHARCUTERIE LA TOUR EIFFEL INC   *p 1261*
485 RUE DES ENTREPRENEURS, QUE-BEC, QC, G1M 2V2
(418) 687-2840   *SIC 5147*
CHARCUTERIE PARISIENNE   *p 1130*
See ALIMENTS LEVITTS (CANADA) INC, LES
CHAREST AUTOMOBILE LTEE   *p 1399*
275 BOUL PIERRE-ROUX E BUREAU 443, VICTORIAVILLE, QC, G6T 1S9
(819) 758-8271   *SIC 5511*
CHAREST INTERNATIONAL   *p 1399*
See CHAREST AUTOMOBILE LTEE
CHAREST, F. LTEE   *p 1305*
1085 42E RUE N, SAINT-GEORGES, QC, G5Z 0T9
(418) 228-9747   *SIC 5194*
CHAREX INC   *p 1153*
14940 RUE LOUIS-M.-TAILLON, MIRABEL, QC, J7N 2K4
(450) 475-1135   *SIC 1522*
CHARGER LOGISTICS INC   *p 501*
25 PRODUCTION RD, BRAMPTON, ON, L6T 4N8
(905) 793-3525   *SIC 4212*
CHARIOT CARRIERS INC   *p 34*
5760 9 ST SE UNIT 105, CALGARY, AB, T2H 1Z9
(403) 640-0822   *SIC 5091*
CHARITAS HEALTH GROUP   *p 91*
See ALBERTA HEALTH SERVICES
CHARL   *p 1092*
See CENTRE HOSPITALIER AMBULA-TOIRE REGIONAL DE LAVAL
CHARL-POL INC   *p 1121*
4653 CH SAINT-ANICET, LA BAIE, QC, G7B 0J4
(418) 544-7355   *SIC 3569*
CHARL-POL INC   *p 1121*
805 RUE DE L'INNOVATION, LA BAIE, QC, G7B 3N8
(418) 677-1518   *SIC 3569*
CHARL-POL INC   *p 1253*
440 RUE LUCIEN-THIBODEAU, PORT-NEUF, QC, G0A 2Y0
(418) 286-4881   *SIC 3569*
CHARLAMARA HOLDINGS INC   *p 540*
2962 CARP RD, CARP, ON, K0A 1L0
(613) 831-9039   *SIC 1522*
CHARLAND CHEVROLET CADILLAC BUICK GMC LTEE   *p 1109*
595 RUE BOIVIN, GRANBY, QC, J2G 2M1
(450) 372-4242   *SIC 5511*
CHARLEBOIS, MAURICE ALIMENTATION LTEE   *p 1245*
267 RUE MARIE-CLAUDE, PLAISANCE, QC, J0V 1S0
SIC 5142
CHARLEBOIS-TREPANIER ET ASSOCIES 2009 INC   *p 1106*
815 BOUL DE LA CARRIERE BUREAU 102, GATINEAU, QC, J8Y 6T4
(819) 777-5246   *SIC 6411*

CHARLES BELANGER & FILS   *p 1049*
See GASTIER M.P. INC
CHARLES IGA   *p 1400*
See ENTREPRISES EMILE CHARLES & FILS LTEE
CHARLES LAKE PROVINCIAL PK   *p 643*
See FRIENDS OF CHARLESTON LAKE PARK, THE
CHARLES LAPIERRE INC   *p 1333*
5600 RUE KIERAN, SAINT-LAURENT, QC, H4S 2B5
(514) 337-6990   *SIC 5084*
CHARLES P ALLEN HIGH SCHOOL   *p 440*
See HALIFAX REGIONAL SCHOOL BOARD
CHARLES RIVER LABORATOIRIES PRE-CLINICAL SERVICES MONTREAL   *p 1366*
See LABORATOIRES CHARLES RIVER MONTREAL ULC
CHARLES RIVER LABORATORIES MON-TREAL ULC   *p 1370*
See LABORATOIRES CHARLES RIVER MONTREAL ULC
CHARLES TAYLOR ADJUSTING   *p 46*
See CHARLES TAYLOR CONSULTING SERVICES (CANADA) INC
CHARLES TAYLOR CONSULTING SER-VICES (CANADA) INC   *p 46*
321 6 AVE SW SUITE 910, CALGARY, AB, T2P 3H3
(403) 266-3336   *SIC 6411*
CHARLES TENNANT & COMPANY   *p 794*
See CHARLES TENNANT & COMPANY (CANADA) LIMITED
CHARLES TENNANT & COMPANY (CANADA) LIMITED   *p 794*
34 CLAYSON RD, NORTH YORK, ON, M9M 2G8
(416) 741-9264   *SIC 2869*
CHARLES-AUGUSTE FORTIER INC   *p 1254*
424 BOUL RAYMOND, QUEBEC, QC, G1C 8K9
(418) 661-0043   *SIC 1794*
CHARLESBOIS TREPANIER   *p 1106*
See ASSURANCE ET GESTION DE RISQUES
CHARLESBOURG AUTOMOBILES LTEE   *p 1256*
16070 BOUL HENRI-BOURASSA, QUE-BEC, QC, G1G 3Z8
(418) 623-9843   *SIC 5511*
CHARLESBOURG TOYOTA   *p 1256*
See CHARLESBOURG AUTOMOBILES LTEE
CHARLESGLEN LTD   *p 77*
7687 110 AVE NW SUITE 7687, CALGARY, AB, T3R 1R8
(403) 241-0888   *SIC 5511*
CHARLESGLEN TOYOTA   *p 77*
See CHARLESGLEN LTD
CHARLESWOOD SAFEWAY   *p 389*
See SOBEYS WEST INC
CHARLIE'S HOT SHOT   *p 1406*
See BAXTER, BERT TRANSPORT LTD
CHARLIE'S MEAT & SEAFOOD SUPPLY LTD   *p 869*
61 SKAGWAY AVE, SCARBOROUGH, ON, M1M 3T9
(416) 261-1312   *SIC 5147*
CHARLOTTE COUNTY CHEVROLET BUICK GMC LTD   *p 398*
137 ROUTE 170, DUFFERIN CHARLOTTE CO, NB, E3L 3X5
(506) 466-0640   *SIC 5511*
CHARLOTTE COUNTY HUMANE RE-SOURCES INC   *p 418*
15 MARKS ST, ST STEPHEN, NB, E3L 2A9
(506) 466-5081   *SIC 8741*
CHARLOTTE ELEANOR ENGLEHART HOSPITAL   *p 842*
450 BLANCHE ST, PETROLIA, ON, N0N

1R0
(519) 882-4325   *SIC 8062*
CHARLOTTE PRODUCTS LTD   *p 840*
2060 FISHER DR, PETERBOROUGH, ON, K9J 6X6
(705) 740-2880   *SIC 2842*
CHARLOTTETOWN SUPER STORE   *p 1038*
See ATLANTIC WHOLESALERS LTD
CHARLTOM RESTAURANTS LIMITED   *p 455*
3630 KEMPT RD, HALIFAX, NS, B3K 4X8
(902) 832-2103   *SIC 5812*
CHARLTON & HILL LIMITED   *p 140*
2620 5 AVE N, LETHBRIDGE, AB, T1H 6J6
(403) 328-2665   *SIC 1711*
CHARM DIAMOND CENTRES   *p 443*
See CHARM JEWELRY LIMITED
CHARM JEWELRY LIMITED   *p 443*
140 PORTLAND ST, DARTMOUTH, NS, B2Y 1J1
(902) 463-7177   *SIC 5944*
CHARRON EDITEUR   *p 1175*
See GROUPE SOGIDES INC
CHARRON TRANSPORT LIMITED   *p 542*
123 BYNG AVE, CHATHAM, ON, N7M 6C6
(519) 352-8970   *SIC 4212*
CHARTER BUILDING CO DIV OF   *p 887*
See LADSON PROPERTIES LIMITED
CHARTER BUS LINES OF BC   *p 210*
See VANCOUVER TOURS AND TRANSIT LTD
CHARTERED PROFESSIONAL ACCOUN-TANTS OF ALBERTA   *p 46*
444 7 AVE SW SUITE 800, CALGARY, AB, T2P 0X8
(403) 299-1300   *SIC 8621*
CHARTERED PROFESSIONAL ACCOUN-TANTS OF ALBERTA   *p 89*
See INSTITUTE OF CHARTERED AC-COUNTANTS OF ALBERTA
CHARTERED PROFESSIONAL ACCOUN-TANTS OF BRITISH COLUMBIA   *p 297*
555 HASTINGS ST W UNIT 800, VANCOU-VER, BC, V6B 4N5
(604) 872-7222   *SIC 8621*
CHARTERED PROFESSIONAL ACCOUN-TANTS OF CANADA   *p 979*
277 WELLINGTON ST W SUITE 600, TORONTO, ON, M5V 3H2
(416) 977-3222   *SIC 8621*
CHARTERED PROFESSIONAL ACCOUN-TANTS OF ONTARIO   *p 928*
69 BLOOR ST E, TORONTO, ON, M4W 1B3
(416) 962-1841   *SIC 8621*
CHARTIS   *p 1193*
See AIG INSURANCE COMPANY OF CANADA
CHARTON-HOBBS INC   *p 1396*
3000 BOUL RENE-LEVESQUE BUREAU 400, VERDUN, QC, H3E 1T9
(514) 353-8955   *SIC 5169*
CHARTRAND FORD (VENTES) INC   *p 1083*
1610 BOUL SAINT-MARTIN E, COTE SAINT-LUC, QC, H7G 4W6
(450) 669-6110   *SIC 5511*
CHARTRAND INDEPENDENT GROCER   *p 753*
See CHARTRAND, R. J. HOLDINGS LIM-ITED
CHARTRAND'S INDEPENDENT INC   *p 544*
4764 REGIONAL ROAD 15 RR 4, CHELMS-FORD, ON, P0M 1L0
(705) 855-4588   *SIC 5411*
CHARTRAND, R. J. HOLDINGS LIMITED   *p 753*
55 SCOTT ST, NEW LISKEARD, ON, P0J 1P0
(705) 647-8844   *SIC 5411*
CHARTRIGHT AIR GROUP   *p 734*
See CHARTRIGHT AIR INC

CHARTRIGHT AIR INC   *p 734*
2450 DERRY RD E, MISSISSAUGA, ON, L5S 1B2
(905) 671-4674   *SIC 8742*
CHARTWELL   *p 744*
See COMPASS GROUP CANADA LTD
CHARTWELL CLASSIC OAKVILLE   *p 796*
180 OAK PARK BLVD SUITE 221, OAKVILLE, ON, L6H 0A6
(905) 257-0095   *SIC 6513*
CHARTWELL COUNTRY COTTAGE RE-TIREMENT RESIDENCE   *p 162*
75 CRANFORD WAY, SHERWOOD PARK, AB, T8H 2B9
(780) 417-0757   *SIC 6513*
CHARTWELL MASTER CARE LP   *p 714*
2065 LEANNE BLVD, MISSISSAUGA, ON, L5K 2L6
(905) 822-4663   *SIC 8052*
CHARTWELL MASTER CARE LP   *p 730*
100 MILVERTON DR SUITE 700, MISSIS-SAUGA, ON, L5R 4H1
(905) 501-9219   *SIC 8322*
CHARTWELL MASTER CARE LP   *p 805*
2140 BARONWOOD DR, OAKVILLE, ON, L6M 4V6
(905) 827-2405   *SIC 8052*
CHARTWELL OASIS ST-JEAN, RESI-DENCE POUR RETRAITES   *p 1316*
See CSH L'OASIS ST. JEAN INC
CHARTWELL PARK PLACE RETIREMENT RESIDENCE   *p 480*
See CSH PARK PLACE MANOR INC
CHARTWELL QUEBEC (MEL) HOLDINGS INC   *p 1232*
3245 BOUL SAINT-MARTIN E, MONTREAL, QC, H7E 4T6
(450) 661-0911   *SIC 8361*
CHARTWELL RETIREMENT RESIDENCES   *p 480*
32 MILL ST, AURORA, ON, L4G 2R9
(905) 727-1939   *SIC 8051*
CHARTWELL RETIREMENT RESIDENCES   *p 578*
495 THE WEST MALL, ETOBICOKE, ON, M9C 5S3
(416) 622-7094   *SIC 8059*
CHARTWELL RETIREMENT RESIDENCES   *p 678*
380 CHURCH ST SUITE 421, MARKHAM, ON, L6B 1E1
(905) 472-3320   *SIC 8059*
CHARTWELL RETIREMENT RESIDENCES   *p 708*
590 LOLITA GDNS SUITE 355, MISSIS-SAUGA, ON, L5A 4N8
(905) 306-9984   *SIC 8051*
CHARTWELL RETIREMENT RESIDENCES   *p 730*
100 MILVERTON DR SUITE 700, MISSIS-SAUGA, ON, L5R 4H1
(905) 501-9219   *SIC 6719*
CHARTWELL RETIREMENT RESIDENCES   *p 730*
See CHARTWELL MASTER CARE LP
CHARTWELL RETIREMENT RESIDENCES   *p 760*
120 WELLNGTON ST, NIAGARA ON THE LAKE, ON, L0S 1J0
(905) 468-2111   *SIC 8051*
CHARTWELL RETIREMENT RESIDENCES   *p 805*
2140 BARONWOOD DR SUITE 225, OAKVILLE, ON, L6M 4V6
(905) 827-2405   *SIC 8059*
CHARTWELL SENIOR HOUSING   *p 921*
See CSH FOUR TEDDINGTON PARK INC
CHARTWELL SENIORS HOUSING REAL ESTATE INVESTMENT TRUST   *p 730*
See CHARTWELL RETIREMENT RESI-DENCES
CHARTWELL STUDENT DINING SER-

VICES   p
542
See COMPASS GROUP CANADA LTD
CHARTWELL WATERFORD   p 805
See CHARTWELL MASTER CARE LP
CHARTWELL WENLEIGH LONG TERM
CARE RESIDENCE   p 714
See CHARTWELL MASTER CARE LP
CHARTWELLS   p 445
See COMPASS GROUP CANADA LTD
CHASE AND CHASE FISH & OYSTER, THE
p 957
See TEMPERENCECO INC
CHASE PAYMENTECH SOLUTIONS p 866
100 CONSILIUM PL SUITE 1400, SCAR-
BOROUGH, ON, M1H 3E3
(416) 940-6300   SIC 7389
CHASE RIVER COUNTRY GROCER p 233
See H & W FOOD COUNTRY
CHASM SAWMILLS   p 174
See WEST FRASER MILLS LTD
CHASSE TOYOTA   p 1173
See GROUPE CHASSE INC
CHAT RADIO 94.5 FM   p 158
See PATTISON, JIM BROADCAST GROUP
LTD
CHATEAU BONNE ENTENTE INC   p 1275
3400 CH SAINTE-FOY, QUEBEC, QC, G1X
1S6
(418) 650-4550   SIC 7011
CHATEAU BROMONT INC   p 1068
90 RUE DE STANSTEAD, BROMONT, QC,
J2L 1K6
(450) 534-3433   SIC 7011
CHATEAU CHAMPLAIN   p 1202
See CHATEAU CHAMPLAIN LIMITED
PARTNERSHIP
CHATEAU CHAMPLAIN LIMITED PART-
NERSHIP   1202
1050 RUE DE LA GAUCHETIERE O, MON-
TREAL, QC, H3B 4C9
(514) 878-9000   SIC 7011
CHATEAU DE CHAMPLAIN   p 414
300 BOARS HEAD RD SUITE 119, SAINT
JOHN, NB, E2K 5C2
(506) 633-1195   SIC 6411
CHATEAU DES CHARMES WINES LTD p
888
1025 YORK RD, ST DAVIDS, ON, L0S 1P0
(905) 262-4219   SIC 5921
CHATEAU GARDENS NIAGARA   p 760
See CHARTWELL RETIREMENT RESI-
DENCES
CHATEAU GRANVILLE INC   p 326
1100 GRANVILLE ST, VANCOUVER, BC,
V6Z 2B6
(604) 669-7070   SIC 7011
CHATEAU INC, LE   p 1325
105 BOUL MARCEL-LAURIN, SAINT-
LAURENT, QC, H4N 2M3
(514) 738-7000   SIC 5621
CHATEAU JASPER   p 137
See JAS DAY INVESTMENTS LTD
CHATEAU LACOMBE HOTEL   p 87
See BRIDGE GAP CHATEAU INC
CHATEAU LACOMBE HOTEL LTD   p 88
10111 BELLAMY HILL NW, EDMONTON,
AB, T5J 1N7
(780) 428-6611   SIC 7011
CHATEAU LAURIER HOTEL GP INC p 821
1 RIDEAU ST, OTTAWA, ON, K1N 8S7
(613) 241-1414   SIC 7011
CHATEAU LOUIS   p 84
See CHATEAU LOUIS HOTEL & CONFER-
ENCE CENTRE LTD
CHATEAU LOUIS HOTEL & CONFERENCE
CENTRE LTD   p 84
11727 KINGSWAY NW, EDMONTON, AB,
T5G 3A1
(780) 452-7770   SIC 7011
CHATEAU M.T. INC   p 1159
3045 CH DE LA CHAPELLE, MONT-
TREMBLANT, QC, J8E 1E1

(819) 681-7000   SIC 7011
CHATEAU OTTAWA HOTEL INC   p 822
150 ALBERT ST, OTTAWA, ON, K1P 5G2
(613) 238-1500   SIC 7011
CHATEAU RICHER MILL   p 1075
See PF RESOLU CANADA INC
CHATEAU VICTORIA HOTEL & SUITES p
336
See ANGEL STAR HOLDINGS LTD
CHATEAU WESTMOUNT INC   p 1401
1860 BOUL DE MAISONNEUVE O, WEST-
MOUNT, QC, H3Z 3G2
(514) 369-3000   SIC 7041
CHATEAUGUAY NISSAN   p 1076
See BARNABE NISSAN DE CHATEAU-
GUAY INC
CHATEAUGUAY PACKAGING   p 1183
See EMBALLAGE CADEAU NOBLE INC
CHATEAUWORKS & DESIGN   p 1325
See CHATEAU INC, LE
CHATHAM KENT FAMILY YMCA   p 542
See CHATHAM KENT FAMILY YOUNG
MEN'S CHRISTIAN ASSOCIATION, THE
CHATHAM KENT FAMILY YOUNG MEN'S
CHRISTIAN ASSOCIATION, THE p 542
101 COURTHOUSE LANE, CHATHAM, ON,
N7L 0B5
SIC 8641
CHATHAM KENT HOME HARDWARE
BUILDING CENTRE   p 542
See ARENS, MIKE BUILDING MATERIALS
LTD
CHATHAM, W. T ASSOCIATES LTD p 880
83 MAPLE ST, SIMCOE, ON, N3Y 2G1
(519) 426-0379   SIC 4925
CHATHAM-KENT CHILDREN'S SERVICES
p 542
495 GRAND AVE W, CHATHAM, ON, N7L
1C5
(519) 352-0440   SIC 8322
CHATHAM-KENT HEALTH ALLIANCE p
542
See PUBLIC GENERAL HOSPITAL SOCI-
ETY OF CHATHAM, THE
CHATHAM-KENT PUC   p 543
See PUBLIC UTILITIES COMMISSION
FOR THE MUNICIPALITY OF CHATHAM-
KENT
CHATHAM-KENT SECONDARY SCHOOL p
542
See LAMBTON KENT DISTRICT SCHOOL
BOARD
CHATR MOBILE   p 930
See ROGERS COMMUNICATIONS
CANADA INC
CHATTERS LIMITED PARTNERSHIP p 158
271 BURNT PARK DR, RED DEER
COUNTY, AB, T4S 0K7
(403) 342-5055   SIC 7231
CHAUFFAGE RDL PG INC   p 1286
160 RUE LOUIS-PHILIPPE-LEBRUN,
RIVIERE-DU-LOUP, QC, G5R 5W8
(418) 862-5351   SIC 5172
CHAUFFEUR EXPRESS LOCATION INC. p
1387
3346 RUE BELLEFEUILLE, TROIS-
RIVIERES, QC, G9A 3Z3
(819) 697-3555   SIC 7361
CHAUHAN PHARMACY SERVICES LTD p
509
160 MAIN ST S SUITE 2, BRAMPTON, ON,
L6W 2E1
(905) 451-0111   SIC 5912
CHAUSSURES BO-PIEDS INC   p 1144
2626 RUE PAPINEAU, LONGUEUIL, QC,
J4K 3M4
(450) 651-9222   SIC 5661
CHAUSSURES BROWNS INC   p 1328
2255 RUE COHEN, SAINT-LAURENT, QC,
H4R 2N7
(514) 334-5000   SIC 5661
CHAUSSURES DE LUCA MONTREAL INC
p 1240
9999 BOUL SAINT-MICHEL, MONTREAL-

NORD, QC, H1H 5G7
(514) 279-4541   SIC 3144
CHAUSSURES GILBERT   p 1276
See JEAN-PAUL FORTIN (1997) INC
CHAUSSURES L'INTERVALLE INC p 1228
4345 BOUL POIRIER, MONTREAL, QC,
H4R 2A4
(438) 386-4555   SIC 5139
CHAUSSURES M & M INC   p 1328
4350 BOUL THIMENS, SAINT-LAURENT,
QC, H4R 2P2
(514) 738-8210   SIC 5139
CHAUSSURES PANDA   p 1059
See GROUPE PANDA DETAIL INC
CHAUSSURES RALLYE INC   p 1048
10001 BOUL RAY-LAWSON, ANJOU, QC,
H1J 1L6
(514) 353-5888   SIC 3021
CHAUSSURES REGENCE INC   p 1280
655 RUE DE L'ARGON, QUEBEC, QC, G2N
2G7
(418) 849-7997   SIC 3144
CHAUSSURES RUBINO INC, LES p 1343
9300 RUE DU PRADO, SAINT-LEONARD,
QC, H1P 3B4
(514) 326-0566   SIC 5661
CHAUSSURES S T C INC, LES   p 1048
10100 RUE COLBERT, ANJOU, QC, H1J
2J8
(514) 351-0675   SIC 5139
CHAUSSURES TENDANCE   p 1144
See CHAUSSURES BO-PIEDS INC
CHAVES ESSO   p 533
See CHAVES GAS BARS LIMITED
CHAVES GAS BARS LIMITED   p 533
31 DUNDAS ST S, CAMBRIDGE, ON, N1R
8N9
(519) 622-1301   SIC 5541
CHBABC   p 188
See CANADIAN HOME BUILDERS' ASSO-
CIATION OF BRITISH COLUMBIA
CHC HELICOPTER HOLDING S.A.R.L. p
264
4740 AGAR DR, RICHMOND, BC, V7B 1A3
(604) 276-7500   SIC 4522
CHC HELICOPTERS CANADA INC p 264
4740 AGAR DR, RICHMOND, BC, V7B 1A3
(604) 276-7500   SIC 4522
CHCH HAMILTON   p 612
See CHCH TV
CHCH TV   p 612
163 JACKSON ST W, HAMILTON, ON, L8P
0A8
(905) 522-1101   SIC 4833
CHD MAINTENANCE LIMITED   p 790
274 VIEWMOUNT AVE, NORTH YORK, ON,
M6B 1V2
(416) 782-5071   SIC 7349
CHEBOGUE FISHERIES LIMITED p 471
98 CLIFF ST, YARMOUTH, NS, B5A 3J9
(902) 742-9157   SIC 4213
CHEBUCTO VENTURES CORP   p 213
8911 117 AVE, FORT ST. JOHN, BC, V1J
6B8
(250) 787-7501   SIC 5812
CHECKER CABS LTD   p 10
316 MERIDIAN RD SE, CALGARY, AB, T2A
1X2
(403) 299-9999   SIC 4212
CHECKER COURIER   p 10
See CHECKER CABS LTD
CHECKER INDUSTRIAL LTD   p 1022
3345 WYANDOTTE ST E, WINDSOR, ON,
N8Y 1E9
(519) 258-2022   SIC 5085
CHECKERS, DIV OF   p 531
See COUGAR SHOES INC
CHECKPOINT CHRYSLER LTD   p 885
357 ONTARIO ST, ST CATHARINES, ON,
L2R 5L3
(905) 688-2802   SIC 5511
CHECKPOINT GMC PONTIAC BUICK LTD p
405
349 KING GEORGE HWY, MIRAMICHI, NB,

E1V 1L2
(506) 622-7091   SIC 5511
CHECKWELL SOLUTIONS CORPORATION
p 281
19433 96 AVE SUITE 200, SURREY, BC,
V4N 4C4
(604) 506-4663   SIC 8748
CHEDER CHABAD   p 782
900 ALNESS ST UNIT 203, NORTH YORK,
ON, M3J 2H6
(416) 663-1972   SIC 8699
CHEEMA CLEANING SERVICES LTD p 531
12366 AIRPORT RD, CALEDON, ON, L7C
2W1
(905) 951-7156   SIC 7349
CHEEMO   p 93
See HERITAGE FROZEN FOODS LTD
CHEEP INSURANCE   p 443
GD, DARTMOUTH, NS, B2Y 3Y3
(902) 463-1675   SIC 6411
CHEER SPORT SHARKS LIMITED p 538
600 BOXWOOD DR, CAMBRIDGE, ON,
N3E 1A5
(519) 653-1221   SIC 8699
CHEESECAKE CAFE, THE   p 9
See PINEHILL MANAGEMENT CORP
CHEF BOMBAY   p 108
See ALIYA'S FOODS LIMITED
CHEF DE FILE EN LOCATION DESSIN p
1049
See GROUPE LOU-TEC INC
CHEF REDI MEATS   p 1431
See CHEF-REDI MEATS INC
CHEF-REDI MEATS INC   p 1431
501 45TH ST W SUITE 11, SASKATOON,
SK, S7L 5Z9
(306) 665-3266   SIC 5147
CHEFS WITHOUT LIMITS   p 571
See PRO IT PLUS INC.
CHEK   p 334
See 0859291 B.C. LTD
CHELL GROUP CORPORATION   p 583
14 METEOR DR, ETOBICOKE, ON, M9W
1A4
(416) 675-3536   SIC 7371
CHELSEY PARK RETIREMENT COMMU-
NITY   p
658
312 OXFORD ST W, LONDON, ON, N6H
4N7
(519) 434-3164   SIC 6513
CHELSEY PARK RETIREMENT COMMU-
NITY   p
658
See DIVERSICARE CANADA MANAGE-
MENT SERVICES CO., INC
CHELTENHAM NURSING HOME   p 775
See DIVERSICARE CANADA MANAGE-
MENT SERVICES CO., INC
CHELTON TECHNOLOGIES CANADA LIM-
ITED   p
221
1925 KIRSCHNER RD SUITE 14,
KELOWNA, BC, V1Y 4N7
(250) 763-2232   SIC 3663
CHEMAINUS HEALTH CARE CENTRE p
196
9909 ESPLANADE ST, CHEMAINUS, BC,
V0R 1K1
(250) 737-2040   SIC 8069
CHEMAINUS SAWMILL   p 196
See WESTERN FOREST PRODUCTS INC
CHEMARKETING INDUSTRIES INC p 716
2155 DUNWIN DR UNIT 15, MISSIS-
SAUGA, ON, L5L 4M1
(905) 607-6800   SIC 5169
CHEMCO ELECTRICAL CONTRACTORS
LTD   p 127
210 MACALPINE CRES SUITE 6, FORT
MCMURRAY, AB, T9H 4A6
(780) 714-6206   SIC 1731
CHEMCO ELECTRICAL CONTRACTORS
LTD   p 148
3135 4 ST, NISKU, AB, T9E 8L1

(780) 436-9570 *SIC 1731*
CHEMETALL CANADA, LIMITED *p 501*
1 KENVIEW BLVD SUITE 110, BRAMP-
TON, ON, L6T 5E6
(905) 791-1628 *SIC 5169*
CHEMETICS INC *p 286*
2930 VIRTUAL WAY SUITE 200, VANCOU-
VER, BC, V5M 0A5
(604) 734-1200 *SIC 8711*
CHEMFAB INDUSTRIES INC *p 563*
466 POLYMOORE DR, CORUNNA, ON,
N0N 1G0
(519) 862-1433 *SIC 1711*
**CHEMICAL LIME COMPANY OF CANADA
INC** *p 224*
102 B AVENUE SUITE 20303, LANGLEY,
BC, V1M 4B4
(604) 888-2575 *SIC 2899*
CHEMICALS MARKETING DIVISION *p 60*
See SUNCOR ENERGY MARKETING INC
CHEMIN DE FER QNS&L *p 1367*
*See COMPAGNIE DE CHEMIN DE FER
DU LITTORAL NORD DE QUEBEC ET DU
LABRADOR INC*
CHEMINEE LINING E. *p 895*
*See CLEAVER-BROOKS OF CANADA LIM-
ITED*
**CHEMINEES SECURITE INTERNATIONAL
LTEE** *p 1233*
2125 RUE MONTEREY, MONTREAL, QC,
H7L 3T6
(450) 973-9999 *SIC 3317*
**CHEMINS DE FER QUEBEC-GATINEAU
INC** *p 1225*
9001 BOUL DE L'ACADIE BUREAU 600,
MONTREAL, QC, H4N 3H5
(514) 948-6999 *SIC 4111*
CHEMISE EMPIRE LTEE *p 1146*
451 AV SAINT-LAURENT, LOUISEVILLE,
QC, J5V 1K4
(819) 228-2821 *SIC 2321*
CHEMISES L. L. LESSARD INC *p 1321*
1195 AV DU PALAIS, SAINT-JOSEPH-DE-
BEAUCE, QC, G0S 2V0
(418) 397-5665 *SIC 7389*
CHEMLINE PLASTICS LIMITED *p 904*
55 GUARDSMAN RD, THORNHILL, ON,
L3T 6L2
(905) 889-7890 *SIC 5085*
**CHEMNORTH SYSTEMS AND SERVICES
COMPANY LTD** *p 568*
30 TIMBER RD SUITE 2, ELLIOT LAKE,
ON, P5A 2T1
(705) 461-9821 *SIC 5087*
**CHEMONG HOME HARDWARE BUILDING
CENTRE** *p 840*
See 1853865 ONTARIO INC
CHEMOURS CANADA COMPANY, THE *p 721*
2233 ARGENTIA RD UNIT 402, MISSIS-
SAUGA, ON, L5N 2X7
(905) 816-2310 *SIC 2816*
CHEMQUE *p 587*
*See ROYAL ADHESIVES & SEALANTS
CANADA LTD*
CHEMROY CANADA *p 501*
See CHEMROY CHEMICALS LIMITED
CHEMROY CANADA INC *p 501*
106 SUMMERLEA RD, BRAMPTON, ON,
L6T 4X3
(905) 789-0701 *SIC 5169*
CHEMROY CHEMICALS LIMITED *p 501*
106 SUMMERLEA RD, BRAMPTON, ON,
L6T 4X3
(905) 789-0701 *SIC 5169*
CHEMSYNERGY INC *p 521*
1100 BURLOAK DR SUITE 101, BURLING-
TON, ON, L7L 6B2
(905) 827-4900 *SIC 5169*
CHEMTECH INTERNATIONAL *p 256*
*See RGM CHEMTECH INTERNATIONAL
INC*
CHEMTRADE ELECTROCHEM INC *p 46*
144 4 AVE SW SUITE 2100, CALGARY, AB,

T2P 3N4
SIC 2812
CHEMTRADE ELECTROCHEM INC *p 238*
100 AMHERST AVE, NORTH VANCOU-
VER, BC, V7H 1S4
(604) 929-1107 *SIC 2812*
CHEMTRADE ELECTROCHEM INC *p 238*
100 AMHERST AVE, NORTH VANCOU-
VER, BC, V7H 1S4
(604) 929-1107 *SIC 2899*
CHEMTRADE LOGISTICS (US) INC *p 764*
155 GORDON BAKER RD SUITE 300,
NORTH YORK, ON, M2H 3N5
(416) 496-5856 *SIC 5169*
CHEMTRADE LOGISTICS INC *p 764*
155 GORDON BAKER RD UNIT 300,
NORTH YORK, ON, M2H 3N5
(416) 496-5856 *SIC 2819*
CHEMTRADE LOGISTICS INCOME FUND *p 765*
155 GORDON BAKER RD SUITE 300,
NORTH YORK, ON, M2H 3N5
(416) 496-5856 *SIC 2819*
**CHEMTRADE PERFORMANCE CHEMI-
CALS CANADA INC** *p 765*
155 GORDON BAKER RD SUITE 300,
NORTH YORK, ON, M2H 3N5
(416) 496-5856 *SIC 5169*
**CHEMTRADE PERFORMANCE CHEMI-
CALS US, LLC** *p 765*
155 GORDON BAKER RD SUITE 300,
NORTH YORK, ON, M2H 3N5
(416) 496-5856 *SIC 5169*
**CHEMTRADE WEST LIMITED PARTNER-
SHIP** *p 765*
155 GORDON BAKER RD SUITE 300,
NORTH YORK, ON, M2H 3N5
(416) 496-5856 *SIC 5169*
CHENAIL FRUITS ET LEGUMES INC *p 1180*
340 RUE BELLARMIN, MONTREAL, QC,
H2P 1G5
(514) 858-7540 *SIC 5148*
CHENAIL IMPORT-EXPORT *p 1180*
See CHENAIL FRUITS ET LEGUMES INC
CHENG SHIN RUBBER CANADA, INC *p 499*
400 CHRYSLER DR UNIT C, BRAMPTON,
ON, L6S 5Z5
(905) 789-0882 *SIC 5085*
CHENIER MOTORS LTD *p 913*
1276 RIVERSIDE DR, TIMMINS, ON, P4R
1A4
(705) 264-9528 *SIC 5541*
**CHENOY'S DELICATESSEN & STEAK
HOUSE INC** *p 1091*
3616 BOUL SAINT-JEAN, DOLLARD-DES-
ORMEAUX, QC, H9G 1X1
(514) 620-2584 *SIC 5812*
CHEO *p 819*
*See CHILDRENS HOSPITAL OF EASTERN
ONTARIO*
**CHEO-AUTISM PROGRAM EASTERN ON-
TARIO** *p 819*
401 SMYTH RD, OTTAWA, ON, K1H 8L1
(613) 745-5963 *SIC 8699*
CHEP CANADA INC *p 721*
7400 EAST DANBRO CRES, MISSIS-
SAUGA, ON, L5N 8C6
(905) 790-2437 *SIC 7359*
CHERBOURG *p 1370*
*See EQUIPEMENT SANITAIRE CHER-
BOURG (1977) INC*
CHERISON ENTERPRISES INC *p 550*
53 COURTLAND AVE SUITE 1, CONCORD,
ON, L4K 3T2
(905) 882-6168 *SIC 5199*
CHEROVAN HOLDINGS LTD *p 337*
4400 CHATTERTON WAY SUITE 301, VIC-
TORIA, BC, V8X 5J2

(250) 881-7878 *SIC 6712*
CHERRY FOREST PRODUCTS *p 848*
*See BARCO MATERIALS HANDLING LIM-
ITED*
CHERRY HILL CLUB, LIMITED *p 857*
912 CHERRY HILL BLVD, RIDGEWAY, ON,
L0S 1N0
(905) 894-1122 *SIC 7997*
CHERRY INSURANCE LTD *p 1426*
350 3RD AVE S, SASKATOON, SK, S7K
1M5
(306) 653-2313 *SIC 6411*
CHERRYFIELD CONTRACTING LTD *p 409*
1050 MCLAUGHLIN DR, MONCTON, NB,
E1G 3R2
SIC 1623
CHERUBINI METAL WORKS LIMITED *p 445*
570 AV WILKINSON, DARTMOUTH, NS,
B3B 0J4
(902) 468-5630 *SIC 1622*
CHERVIN INC *p 1010*
20 BENJAMIN RD, WATERLOO, ON, N2V
2J9
(519) 885-3542 *SIC 2511*
CHES SPECIAL RISK INC *p 986*
130 KING ST W 19TH FL, TORONTO, ON,
M5X 1C9
(647) 480-1515 *SIC 6411*
CHESSWOOD GROUP LIMITED *p 776*
156 DUNCAN MILL RD SUITE 15, NORTH
YORK, ON, M3B 3N2
(416) 386-3099 *SIC 8741*
CHESTER CARTAGE *p 864*
See CHESTER CARTAGE & MOVERS LTD
CHESTER CARTAGE & MOVERS LTD *p 864*
1995 MARKHAM RD, SCARBOROUGH,
ON, M1B 2W3
(416) 754-7716 *SIC 4212*
CHESTER PHARMACY LTD *p 441*
3785 HWY 3, CHESTER, NS, B0J 1J0
(902) 275-3518 *SIC 5912*
CHESTER PHARMASAVE *p 441*
See CHESTER PHARMACY LTD
CHESTER VILLAGE *p 868*
See BROADVIEW FOUNDATION
**CHESTER VOLUNTEER FIRE DEPART-
MENT** *p 441*
149 CENTRAL ST, CHESTER, NS, B0J 1J0
(902) 275-5113 *SIC 7389*
CHESTERMERE SAFEWAY *p 79*
See SOBEYS WEST INC
CHESTWOOD STATIONERY LIMITED *p 668*
100 STEELCASE RD E SUITE 105,
MARKHAM, ON, L3R 1E8
(905) 475-5542 *SIC 5112*
CHESTWOOD-NEZEY DISTRIBUTION *p 668*
See CHESTWOOD STATIONERY LIMITED
CHET CONSTRUCTION LTD *p 174*
33759 MOREY AVE SUITE 1, ABBOTS-
FORD, BC, V2S 2W5
(604) 859-1441 *SIC 1623*
CHETICAMP COOP LTD. *p 442*
15081 CABOT TRAIL RD, CHETICAMP, NS,
B0E 1H0
(902) 224-2066 *SIC 5039*
CHETWYND FOREST INDUSTRIES *p 196*
See WEST FRASER MILLS LTD
CHEUNG, ARTHUR PHARMACY LIMITED *p 796*
240 LEIGHLAND AVE, OAKVILLE, ON, L6H
3H6
(905) 842-3730 *SIC 5912*
CHEUNG, HARRY PHARMACIES LTD *p 920*
970 QUEEN ST E SUITE 823, TORONTO,
ON, M4M 1J8
(416) 462-0062 *SIC 5912*
CHEVALIER AUTOMOBILES INC *p 866*
4334 KINGSTON RD, SCARBOROUGH,
ON, M1E 2M8
(416) 281-1234 *SIC 5511*
CHEVALIER CHRYSLER INC *p 480*
14535 YONGE ST, AURORA, ON, L4G 6L1

(905) 841-1233 *SIC 5511*
**CHEVALIERS DE COLOMB THETFORD-
MINES, LES** *p 1382*
95 9E RUE N, THETFORD MINES, QC,
G6G 5J1
(418) 335-6444 *SIC 8699*
CHEVRETTE REPARATION *p 1115*
See TECHNODIESEL INC
CHEVRIER LAPORTE & ASSOCIES INC *p 1290*
319 RUE NOTRE-DAME, ROXTON FALLS,
QC, J0H 1E0
SIC 6311
CHEVROLET BUICK GMC *p 166*
*See RON HODGSON CHEVROLET BUICK
GMC LTD*
CHEVROLET TRUCKS LTD *p 113*
10727 82 AVE NW, EDMONTON, AB, T6E
2B1
(780) 439-0071 *SIC 5511*
CHEVRON *p 262*
See 22 ENTERPRISES LTD
CHEVRON *p 271*
See D.W.P. DISTRIBUTORS LTD
CHEVRON CANADA LIMITED *p 185*
355 WILLINGDON AVE N, BURNABY, BC,
V5C 1X4
(604) 257-4040 *SIC 2911*
CHEVRON CANADA LIMITED *p 311*
1050 PENDER ST W SUITE 1200, VAN-
COUVER, BC, V6E 3T4
(604) 668-5300 *SIC 2911*
CHEVRON CANADA RESOURCES *p 311*
See CHEVRON CANADA LIMITED
**CHEVRON CONSTRUCTION SERVICES
LTD** *p 559*
4475 COUNTY 15 RD, BROCKVILLE, ON,
K6V 5T2
(613) 926-0690 *SIC 1541*
CHEVRON CORP. *p 312*
1050 PENDER ST W SUITE 1200, VAN-
COUVER, BC, V6E 3T4
(604) 668-5671 *SIC 4923*
CHEVRON RESOURCES LTD *p 46*
500 5 AVE SW SUITE 700, CALGARY, AB,
T2P 0L7
(403) 234-5000 *SIC 1311*
CHEVY FARM *p 104*
See WESTGATE CHEVROLET LTD
CHEW EXCAVATING LTD *p 334*
575 GORGE RD E, VICTORIA, BC, V8T
2W5
(250) 386-7586 *SIC 1794*
CHEWTERS CHOCOLATES (1992) INC *p 205*
1648 DERWENT WAY, DELTA, BC, V3M
6R9
(888) 515-7117 *SIC 2066*
CHEYENNE HOLDINGS INC *p 185*
3855 HENNING DR SUITE 109, BURNABY,
BC, V5C 6N3
(604) 291-9000 *SIC 1542*
CHEZ ASHTON *p 1261*
See ASHTON CASSE-CROUTE INC
CHEZ CORA *p 1364*
See FRANCHISES CORA INC
CHEZ DAGOBERT *p 1268*
See BOURGABEC INC
CHEZ HENRI MAJEAU ET FILS INC *p 1297*
30 RUE DE LA VISITATION, SAINT-
CHARLES-BORROMEE, QC, J6E 4M8
(450) 759-1113 *SIC 5812*
CHEZ PIGGY RESTAURANT LIMITED *p 630*
44 PRINCESS ST, KINGSTON, ON, K7L
1A4
(613) 544-7790 *SIC 5461*
CHEZ PIGGY RESTAURANT LIMITED *p 630*
68R PRINCESS ST, KINGSTON, ON, K7L
1A5
(613) 549-7673 *SIC 2051*
CHFD CHANNEL 4 *p 907*
*See THUNDER BAY ELECTRONICS LIM-
ITED*

CHG BLOOR HOLDINGS INC p 972
1221 BAY ST, TORONTO, ON, M5R 3P5
(647) 348-7000 *SIC 5812*
CHIBOUGAMAU AUTOMOBILE INC p 1077
859 3E RUE, CHIBOUGAMAU, QC, G8P 1R1
(418) 748-2634 *SIC 5511*
CHIBOUGAMAU DIAMOND DRILLING p 1077
See FORAGES CHIBOUGAMAU LTEE
CHIC RESTO-POP INC, LE p 1167
1500 AV D'ORLEANS, MONTREAL, QC, H1W 3R1
(514) 521-4089 *SIC 5812*
CHICAGO 58 p 1030
See CHICAGO 58 FOOD PRODUCTS LIMITED
CHICAGO 58 FOOD PRODUCTS LIMITED p 1030
135 HAIST AVE, WOODBRIDGE, ON, L4L 5V6
(905) 265-1044 *SIC 5147*
CHICAGO, CENTRAL & PACIFIC RAILROAD COMPANY p 1202
935 RUE DE LA GAUCHETIERE O, MONTREAL, QC, H3B 2M9
(514) 399-4536 *SIC 4011*
CHICO'S FAS CANADA, CO. p 452
1959 UPPER WATER ST SUITE 900, HALIFAX, NS, B3J 3N2
(888) 855-4986 *SIC 6512*
CHICOUTIMI CHRYSLER p 1078
See CHICOUTIMI CHRYSLER DODGE JEEP INC
CHICOUTIMI CHRYSLER DODGE JEEP INC p 1078
829 BOUL TALBOT, CHICOUTIMI, QC, G7H 4B5
(418) 549-2873 *SIC 5511*
CHIEF HAULING CONTRACTORS INC p 14
5654 55 ST SE, CALGARY, AB, T2C 3G9
(403) 215-4312 *SIC 4212*
CHIEF ISAAC INCORPORATED p 1440
1371 2 AVE, DAWSON, YT, Y0B 1G0
(867) 993-5384 *SIC 6799*
CHIEF MEDICAL SUPPLIES LTD p 22
411 19 ST SE, CALGARY, AB, T2E 6J7
(403) 207-6034 *SIC 2834*
CHIEFTAIN AUTO PARTS (1987) INC p 249
555 3RD AVE, PRINCE GEORGE, BC, V2L 3C2
(250) 562-1258 *SIC 5013*
CHIEFTAIN WAREHOUSING p 249
See CHIEFTAIN AUTO PARTS (1987) INC
CHIGNECTO CENTRAL REGIONAL SCHOOL BOARD p 468
60 LORNE ST, TRURO, NS, B2N 3K3
(902) 897-8900 *SIC 8211*
CHIGNECTO CENTRAL REGIONAL SCHOOL BOARD p 468
34 LORNE ST, TRURO, NS, B2N 3K3
(902) 896-5700 *SIC 8211*
CHIL-CON PRODUCTS, DIV OF p 514
See HT INDUSTRIAL LTD
CHILD & FAMILY SERVICES OF WESTERN MANITOBA p 346
800 MCTAVISH AVE, BRANDON, MB, R7A 7L4
(204) 726-6030 *SIC 8322*
CHILD AND FAMILY BENEFITS SERVICES p 798
See KINARK CHILD AND FAMILY SERVICES
CHILD FIND MANITOBA p 388
See CANADIAN CENTER FOR CHILD PROTECTION INC
CHILD WELFARE p 896
See HURON-PERTH CHILDREN'S AID SOCIETY
CHILDREN AND FAMILY SERVICES FOR YORK REGION p 755
16915 LESLIE ST, NEWMARKET, ON, L3Y 9A1

(905) 895-2318 *SIC 8322*
CHILDREN'S & WOMEN'S HEALTH CENTRE OF BRITISH COLUMBIA BRANCH p 319
4500 OAK ST, VANCOUVER, BC, V6H 3N1
(604) 875-2424 *SIC 8069*
CHILDREN'S & WOMEN'S HEALTH CENTRE OF BRITISH COLUMBIA BRANCH p 320
1770 7TH AVE W SUITE 260, VANCOUVER, BC, V6J 4Y6
(604) 733-6721 *SIC 8721*
CHILDREN'S AID SOCIETY p 839
See CHILDREN'S AID SOCIETY OF THE COUNTY OF LANARK AND THE TOWN OF SMITHS FALLS, THE
CHILDREN'S AID SOCIETY p 861
See WINDSOR-ESSEX CHILDREN'S AID SOCIETY
CHILDREN'S AID SOCIETY OF ALGOMA p 862
191 NORTHERN AVE E, SAULT STE. MARIE, ON, P6B 4H8
(705) 949-0162 *SIC 8322*
CHILDREN'S AID SOCIETY OF HALDIMAND AND NORFOLK, THE p 998
70 TOWN CENTRE DR, TOWNSEND, ON, N0A 1S0
(519) 587-5437 *SIC 8322*
CHILDREN'S AID SOCIETY OF HAMILTON, THE p 608
26 ARROWSMITH RD, HAMILTON, ON, L8E 4H8
(905) 522-1121 *SIC 8322*
CHILDREN'S AID SOCIETY OF OXFORD COUNTY p 1035
712 PEEL ST, WOODSTOCK, ON, N4S 0B4
(519) 539-6176 *SIC 8322*
CHILDREN'S AID SOCIETY OF THE CITY OF SARNIA AND THE COUNTY OF LAMBTON p 861
161 KENDALL ST, SARNIA, ON, N7V 4G6
(519) 336-0623 *SIC 8322*
CHILDREN'S AID SOCIETY OF THE COUNTY OF LANARK AND THE TOWN OF SMITHS FALLS, THE p 839
8 HERRIOTT ST, PERTH, ON, K7H 1S9
(613) 264-9991 *SIC 8399*
CHILDREN'S AID SOCIETY OF THE COUNTY OF RENFREW p 838
77 MARY ST SUITE 100, PEMBROKE, ON, K8A 5V4
(613) 735-6866 *SIC 8322*
CHILDREN'S AID SOCIETY OF THE DISTRICT OF NIPISSING & PARRY SOUND, THE p 763
433 MCINTYRE ST W, NORTH BAY, ON, P1B 2Z3
(705) 472-0910 *SIC 8322*
CHILDREN'S AID SOCIETY OF THE DISTRICTS OF SUDBURY AND MANITOULIN, THE p 898
319 LASALLE BLVD UNIT 3, SUDBURY, ON, P3A 1W7
(705) 566-3113 *SIC 8322*
CHILDREN'S AID SOCIETY OF THE NIAGARA REGION, THE p 887
82 HANNOVER DR, ST CATHARINES, ON, L2W 1A4
(905) 937-7731 *SIC 8322*
CHILDREN'S AID SOCIETY OF THE REGION OF PEEL, THE p 709
101 QUEENSWAY W SUITE 500, MISSISSAUGA, ON, L5B 2P7
SIC 8399
CHILDREN'S AID SOCIETY OF THE REGION OF PEEL, THE p 721
6860 CENTURY AVE, MISSISSAUGA, ON, L5N 2W5
(905) 363-6131 *SIC 8322*
CHILDREN'S AID SOCIETY OF THE RE-

GIONAL MUNICIPALITY OF HALTON p 521
1445 NORJOHN CRT, BURLINGTON, ON, L7L 0E6
(905) 333-4441 *SIC 8322*
CHILDREN'S AID SOCIETY OF THE REGIONAL MUNICIPALITY OF WATERLOO, THE p 636
200 ARDELT AVE, KITCHENER, ON, N2C 2L9
(519) 576-0540 *SIC 8322*
CHILDREN'S AID SOCIETY OF TORONTO p 782
20 DE BOERS DR SUITE 250, NORTH YORK, ON, M3J 0H1
(416) 924-4646 *SIC 8322*
CHILDREN'S AID SOCIETY OF TORONTO p 931
30 ISABELLA ST, TORONTO, ON, M4Y 1N1
(416) 924-4646 *SIC 8322*
CHILDREN'S ARTS UMBRELLA ASSOCIATION p 319
1286 CARTWRIGHT ST, VANCOUVER, BC, V6H 3R8
(604) 681-5268 *SIC 8299*
CHILDREN'S CENTRE FOR ABILITY p 288
See BRITISH COLUMBIA CENTRE FOR ABILITY ASSOCIATION
CHILDREN'S EDUCATION FUNDS p 738
See CHILDREN'S EDUCATIONAL FOUNDATION OF CANADA, THE
CHILDREN'S EDUCATIONAL FOUNDATION OF CANADA, THE p 738
6705 TOMKEN RD UNIT 236, MISSISSAUGA, ON, L5T 2J6
SIC 6733
CHILDREN'S FOUNDATION, THE p 286
2750 18TH AVE E, VANCOUVER, BC, V5M 4W8
(604) 434-9101 *SIC 8399*
CHILDREN'S HOSPITAL FOUNDATION OF MANITOBA INC, TH p 380
715 MCDERMOT AVE SUITE 513, WINNIPEG, MB, R3E 3P4
(204) 789-3968 *SIC 8733*
CHILDREN'S HOUSE MONTESSORI, THE p 1025
2611 LABELLE ST, WINDSOR, ON, N9E 4G4
(519) 969-5278 *SIC 8351*
CHILDREN'S PLACE (CANADA), LP, THE p 730
6040 CANTAY RD, MISSISSAUGA, ON, L5R 4J2
(905) 502-0353 *SIC 5641*
CHILDREN'S WISH FOUNDATION OF CANADA, THE p 843
1101 KINGSTON RD SUITE 350, PICKERING, ON, L1V 1B5
(905) 839-8882 *SIC 7389*
CHILDREN'S WORLD ACADEMY (CWA) p 1131
See LESTER B. PEARSON SCHOOL BOARD
CHILDRENS AID SOCIETY UNITED COUNTIES STORMONT, DUNDAS & GLENGARRY p 562
150 BOUNDARY RD, CORNWALL, ON, K6H 6J5
(613) 933-2292 *SIC 8322*
CHILDRENS HOSPITAL OF EASTERN ONTARIO p 819
401 SMYTH RD, OTTAWA, ON, K1H 8L1
(613) 737-7600 *SIC 8069*
CHILI'S TEXAS GRILL p 123
See SPEEDY CREEK (2011) LTD
CHILIS TEXAS GRILL p 119
See SPEEDY CREEK (2011) LTD
CHILL FRESH PRODUCE INC p 533
1170 FRANKLIN BLVD UNIT B, CAMBRIDGE, ON, N1R 7J2

(519) 896-0124 *SIC 5148*
CHILLIWACK GENERAL HOSPITAL p 196
45600 MENHOLM RD, CHILLIWACK, BC, V2P 1P7
(604) 795-4141 *SIC 8062*
CHILLIWACK HEALTH UNIT p 196
See FRASER HEALTH AUTHORITY
CHILLIWACK SECONDARY SCHOOL p 197
See SCHOOL DISTRICT NO 33 CHILLIWACK
CHILLIWACK TAXI LTD p 196
45877 HOCKING AVE, CHILLIWACK, BC, V2P 1B5
(604) 795-9111 *SIC 4121*
CHIMIE PARACHEM p 1238
See CHIMIE PARACHEM S.E.C.
CHIMIE PARACHEM INC p 1238
3500 AV BROADWAY, MONTREAL-EST, QC, H1B 5B4
(514) 640-2200 *SIC 1311*
CHIMIE PARACHEM S.E.C. p 1238
3500 AV BROADWAY, MONTREAL-EST, QC, H1B 5B4
(514) 640-2200 *SIC 1311*
CHIMO CONSTRUCTION (2014) LIMITED p 429
136 CROSBIE RD SUITE 409, ST. JOHN'S, NL, A1B 3K3
(709) 739-5900 *SIC 1542*
CHIMO YOUTH RETREAT CENTRE p 85
10585 111 ST NW SUITE 103, EDMONTON, AB, T5H 3E8
(780) 420-0324 *SIC 8322*
CHIN RADIO/TV INTERNATIONAL p 990
See RADIO 1540 LIMITED
CHINA EDUCATION RESOURCES INC p 297
515 PENDER ST W SUITE 300, VANCOUVER, BC, V6B 6H5
(604) 331-2388 *SIC 5999*
CHINA GOLD INTERNATIONAL RESOURCES CORP LTD p 328
505 BURRARD ST SUITE 660, VANCOUVER, BC, V7X 1M4
(604) 609-0598 *SIC 1081*
CHINA KELI ELECTRIC COMPANY LTD p 328
555 BURRARD ST SUITE 900, VANCOUVER, BC, V7X 1M8
SIC 3679
CHINA'S TIME-HONORED BRAND p 677
See WING ON NEW GROUP CANADA INC
CHINESE ACADEMY FOUNDATION, THE p 40
6600 4 ST NW, CALGARY, AB, T2K 1C2
(403) 777-7663 *SIC 8299*
CHINGUACOUSY SECONDARY SCHOOL p 499
See PEEL DISTRICT SCHOOL BOARD
CHINOOK CREDIT UNION LTD p 7
99 2 ST W, BROOKS, AB, T1R 1B9
(403) 362-4233 *SIC 6062*
CHINOOK ENERGY INC p 46
222 3RD AV SW SUITE 1610, CALGARY, AB, T2P 0B4
(403) 261-6883 *SIC 1382*
CHINOOK FUELS LTD p 127
160 MACKAY CRES, FORT MCMURRAY, AB, T9H 4W8
(780) 743-2381 *SIC 5171*
CHINOOK GAS CO-OP LTD p 147
125 8 AVE NW, MILK RIVER, AB, T0K 1M0
(403) 647-3588 *SIC 4923*
CHINOOK INFRASTRUCTURE p 70
3131 114 AVE SE SUITE 100, CALGARY, AB, T2Z 3X2
(403) 355-1655 *SIC 1611*
CHINOOK LEARNING SERVICES p 73
See CALGARY BOARD OF EDUCATION
CHINOOK REGIONAL HOSPITAL p 142
See ALBERTA HEALTH SERVICES
CHINOOK VILLAGE p 145
See CHINOOK VILLAGE HOUSING SOCI-

ETY

CHINOOK VILLAGE HOUSING SOCIETY *p* 145
2801 13 AVE SE, MEDICINE HAT, AB, T1A 3R1
(403) 526-6951   *SIC* 6514

CHINOOKS EDGE SCHOOL DIVISION NO. 73 *p* 136
4904 50 ST, INNISFAIL, AB, T4G 1W4
(403) 227-7070   *SIC* 8211

CHINTZ & COMPANY *p* 336
See *CHINTZ & COMPANY DECORATIVE FURNISHINGS INC*

CHINTZ & COMPANY DECORATIVE FURNISHINGS INC *p* 336
1720 STORE ST, VICTORIA, BC, V8W 1V5
(250) 381-2404   *SIC* 5719

CHIOVITTI BANANA COMPANY LIMITED *p* 574
26 MAGNIFICENT RD, ETOBICOKE, ON, M8Z 4T3
(416) 251-3774   *SIC* 5148

CHIP REIT NO 16 OPERATIONS LIMITED PARTNERSHIP *p* 84
11830 KINGSWAY NW SUITE 906, EDMONTON, AB, T5G 0X5
(780) 454-9521   *SIC* 7011

CHIP REIT NO 18 OPERATIONS LIMITED PARTNERSHIP *p* 142
320 SCENIC DR S, LETHBRIDGE, AB, T1J 4B4
(403) 328-1123   *SIC* 7011

CHIP REIT NO 23 OPERATIONS LIMITED PARTNERSHIP *p* 693
5050 ORBITOR DR, MISSISSAUGA, ON, L4W 4X2
(905) 238-9600   *SIC* 7011

CHIPMAN OUTREACH INC *p* 396
12 CIVIC CRT, CHIPMAN, NB, E4A 2H9
(506) 339-5639   *SIC* 8621

CHIPPAWA VOLUNTEER FIREFIGHTER ASSOCIATION *p* 758
8696 BANTING AVE, NIAGARA FALLS, ON, L2G 6Z8
(905) 295-4398   *SIC* 7389

CHIRO FOODS LIMITED *p* 104
17118 90 AVE NW, EDMONTON, AB, T5T 4C8
(780) 438-8848   *SIC* 5812

CHIRO FOODS LIMITED *p* 118
5041 GATEWAY BLVD NW UNIT 100, EDMONTON, AB, T6H 4R7
(780) 438-8848   *SIC* 5812

CHISHOLM CENTRE *p* 800
See *BURNSTEIN, DR. & ASSOCIATES*

CHISHOLM, R. FOOD SERVICES INC *p* 762
140 LAKESHORE DR, NORTH BAY, ON, P1A 2A8
(705) 474-9770   *SIC* 5812

CHISHOLM, RONALD A. LIMITED *p* 928
2 BLOOR ST W SUITE 3300, TORONTO, ON, M4W 3K3
(416) 967-6000   *SIC* 5141

CHIU, WALLY DRUGS LTD *p* 769
2528 BAYVIEW AVE, NORTH YORK, ON, M2L 1A9
(416) 816-1823   *SIC* 5912

CHIVA AUTO GOUP INC *p* 721
2290 BATTLEFORD RD, MISSISSAUGA, ON, L5N 3K6
(905) 812-8882   *SIC* 5511

CHMP *p* 1202
See *COGECO MEDIA ACQUISITIONS INC*

CHOCOLAT JEAN-TALON *p* 1328
See *CONFISERIES REGAL INC*

CHOCOLAT LAMONTAGNE INC *p* 1373
4045 RUE DE LA GARLOCK, SHERBROOKE, QC, J1L 1W9
(819) 564-1014   *SIC* 2066

CHOCOLAT PERFECTION INC *p* 1142
570 BOUL ROLAND-THERRIEN BUREAU 217, LONGUEUIL, QC, J4H 3V9
(450) 674-4546   *SIC* 5149

CHOCOLATERIE BERBARD CALLEBAUT *p* 22
See *COCOCO CHOCOLATIERS INC*

CHOCOLATERIE LA CABOSSE D'OR INC *p* 1244
973 CH OZIAS-LEDUC, OTTERBURN PARK, QC, J3G 4S6
(450) 464-6937   *SIC* 2064

CHOCOLATS COLOMBE *p* 1047
128 235 RTE, ANGE-GARDIEN, QC, J0E 1E0
(450) 293-0129   *SIC* 5149

CHOCOLATS FAVORIS *p* 1276
See *CHOCOLATS FAVORIS INC, LES*

CHOCOLATS FAVORIS INC, LES *p* 1276
4355 RUE JEAN-MARCHAND BUREAU 101, QUEBEC, QC, G2C 0N2
(418) 915-9311   *SIC* 2026

CHOEUR DU CEGEP DE SHERBROOKE *p* 1370
475 RUE DU CEGEP, SHERBROOKE, QC, J1E 4K1
(819) 564-6350   *SIC* 8221

CHOHAN CARRIERS LTD *p* 281
15760 110 AVE, SURREY, BC, V4N 4Z1
(604) 888-1855   *SIC* 4213

CHOICE CANNING COMPANY INC *p* 1002
3100 STEELES AVE W SUITE 603, VAUGHAN, ON, L4K 3R1
(905) 918-3866   *SIC* 5146

CHOICE HOTELS CANADA INC *p* 693
5015 SPECTRUM WAY SUITE 400, MISSISSAUGA, ON, L4W 0E4
(905) 602-2222   *SIC* 6794

CHOICE OFFICE PERSONNEL LTD *p* 88
10025 102A AVE NW SUITE 1102, EDMONTON, AB, T5J 2Z2
(780) 424-6816   *SIC* 7363

CHOICE PROPERTIES REAL ESTATE INVESTMENT TRUST *p* 928
175 BLOOR ST E SUITE 1400N, TORONTO, ON, M4W 3R8
(416) 324-7840   *SIC* 6798

CHOICES MARKET *p* 210
See *WALLSA HOLDINGS LTD*

CHOICES MARKET SOUTH SURREY *p* 283
See *3248 KING GEORGE HWY HOLDINGS LTD*

CHOKO AUTHENTIC APPAREL *p* 1001
See *CHOKO MOTORSPORTS INC*

CHOKO MOTORSPORTS INC *p* 1001
19 ANDERSON BLVD, UXBRIDGE, ON, L9P 0C7
(905) 642-1010   *SIC* 5136

CHOM 97.7 *p* 1193
See *BELL MEDIA RADIO S.E.N.C.*

CHOMEDEY HYUNDAI *p* 1085
See *2552-4018 QUEBEC INC*

CHOMEDEY KIA *p* 1241
See *4335325 CANADA INC*

CHOMEDEY NISSAN INC *p* 1086
2465 BOUL CURE-LABELLE, COTE SAINT-LUC, QC, H7T 1R3
(450) 682-4400   *SIC* 5511

CHOMEDEY/DESLAURIERS FORD LINCOLN INC *p* 1235
2705 BOUL CHOMEDEY, MONTREAL, QC, H7P 0C2
(450) 666-3673   *SIC* 5511

CHONG LEE SEA FOOD *p* 285
See *347942 B. C. LTD*

CHOO KIN ENTERPRISES LTD *p* 195
984 SHOPPERS ROW, CAMPBELL RIVER, BC, V9W 2C5
SIC 5912

CHORUS AVIATION INC *p* 445
3 SPECTACLE LAKE DR, DARTMOUTH, NS, B3B 1W8
(902) 873-5000   *SIC* 4512

CHOTV CFGSTV *p* 1107
See *RNC MEDIA INC*

CHOUINARD, A. & FILS INC *p* 1354

10505 BOUL SAINTE-ANNE, SAINTE-ANNE-DE-BEAUPRE, QC, G0A 3C0
(418) 827-5569   *SIC* 5421

CHOWN ELECTRICAL CONTRACTORS LTD *p* 105
12230 163 ST NW, EDMONTON, AB, T5V 1S2
(780) 447-4525   *SIC* 1731

CHOYS HOLDINGS INCORPORATED *p* 259
4751 SHELL RD SUITE 2, RICHMOND, BC, V6X 3H4
(604) 270-6882   *SIC* 5147

CHRIMA IRON WORK LIMITED *p* 895
559 DOURO ST, STRATFORD, ON, N5A 0E3
(519) 271-5399   *SIC* 3499

CHRIMA METAL FABRICATION *p* 895
See *CHRIMA IRON WORK LIMITED*

CHRIS & STACEY'S NO FRILLS *p* 712
1250 SOUTH SERVICE RD, MISSISSAUGA, ON, L5E 1V4
(905) 891-1021   *SIC* 5411

CHRIS AND BETH NO FRILLS LTD *p* 811
1050 SIMCOE ST N SUITE 754, OSHAWA, ON, L1G 4W5
(905) 728-3100   *SIC* 5411

CHRIS DANIELLE MICRO SOLUTIONS (CDMS) INC *p* 1194
550 RUE SHERBROOKE O BUREAU 250, MONTREAL, QC, H3A 1B9
(514) 286-2367   *SIC* 7379

CHRIS' NO FRILLS *p* 578
See *1057362 ONTARIO LTD*

CHRIST THE KING SECONDARY *p* 593
See *HALTON CATHOLIC DISTRICT SCHOOL BOARD*

CHRIST THE TEACHER CATHOLIC SCHOOLS DIVISION 212 *p* 138
45A PALLISER WAY, YORKTON, SK, S3N 4C5
(306) 783-8787   *SIC* 8211

CHRISTIAN & MISSIONARY ALLIANCE - CANADIAN PACIFIC DISTRICT *p* 276
7565 132 ST SUITE 107, SURREY, BC, V3W 1K5
SIC 8661

CHRISTIAN AND MISSIONARY ALLIANCE IN CANADA, THE *p* 685
7560 AIRPORT RD UNIT 1, MISSISSAUGA, ON, L4T 4H4
(416) 674-7878   *SIC* 8661

CHRISTIAN BLIND MISSION INTERNATIONAL *p* 894
GD, STOUFFVILLE, ON, L4A 7Z9
(905) 640-6464   *SIC* 8661

CHRISTIAN CHILDREN'S FUND OF CANADA *p* 668
1200 DENISON ST, MARKHAM, ON, L3R 8G6
(905) 754-1001   *SIC* 8699

CHRISTIAN HORIZONS *p* 641
4278 KING ST E, KITCHENER, ON, N2P 2G5
(519) 650-0966   *SIC* 8361

CHRISTIAN LABOUR ASSOCIATION OF CANADA *p* 105
14920 118 AVE NW, EDMONTON, AB, T5V 1B8
(780) 454-6181   *SIC* 8611

CHRISTIAN LABOUR ASSOCIATION OF CANADA *p* 721
2335 ARGENTIA RD, MISSISSAUGA, ON, L5N 0A3
(905) 812-2855   *SIC* 8631

CHRISTIANSON PIPE INC *p* 135
GD STN MAIN, HIGH RIVER, AB, T1V 1M2
(403) 652-4336   *SIC* 5051

CHRISTIE *p* 638
See *CHRISTIE DIGITAL SYSTEMS CANADA INC*

CHRISTIE BROWN & CO BAKERY *p* 1166
See *KRAFT HEINZ CANADA ULC*

CHRISTIE DIGITAL SYSTEMS CANADA

INC *p* 638
809 WELLINGTON ST N, KITCHENER, ON, N2G 4Y7
(519) 744-8005   *SIC* 3861

CHRISTIE GARDENS APARTMENTS AND CARE INC *p* 989
600 MELITA CRES, TORONTO, ON, M6G 3Z4
(416) 530-1330   *SIC* 8051

CHRISTIE INNOMED INC *p* 1301
516 RUE DUFOUR, SAINT-EUSTACHE, QC, J7R 0C3
(450) 472-9120   *SIC* 5047

CHRISTIE LAKE KIDS *p* 820
400 COVENTRY RD, OTTAWA, ON, K1K 2C7
(613) 742-6922   *SIC* 7033

CHRISTIE LITES *p* 571
See *966850 ONTARIO INC*

CHRISTIE LITES TORONTO LTD *p* 571
100 CARSON ST UNIT A, ETOBICOKE, ON, M8W 3R9
(416) 644-1010   *SIC* 5049

CHRISTIE SCHOOL SUPPLY MANITOBA *p* 346
705 PACIFIC AVE, BRANDON, MB, R7A 0H8
(204) 727-1423   *SIC* 5943

CHRISTIE'S DAIRY LIMITED *p* 489
4819 UNION RD, BEAMSVILLE, ON, L0R 1B4
(905) 563-8841   *SIC* 5143

CHRISTIE'S OFFICE PLUS *p* 346
See *CHRISTIE SCHOOL SUPPLY MANITOBA*

CHRISTIE, B. L. INVESTMENTS INC *p* 908
581 RED RIVER RD, THUNDER BAY, ON, P7B 1H4
(807) 344-6666   *SIC* 5943

CHRISTINA RIVER ENTERPRISES LIMITED PARTNERSHIP *p* 127
GD LCD MAIN, FORT MCMURRAY, AB, T9H 3E2
(780) 334-2446   *SIC* 2448

CHRISTINE'S HOLDINGS INC *p* 1424
3310 8TH ST E UNIT 440, SASKATOON, SK, S7H 5M3
(306) 373-5556   *SIC* 5912

CHRISTMAS FOREVER *p* 185
See *HOLLAND IMPORTS INC*

CHRISTOFFERSEN, READ JONES LTD *p* 319
1285 BROADWAY W UNIT 300, VANCOUVER, BC, V6H 3X8
(604) 738-0048   *SIC* 8711

CHRISTOPHER YEE DRUGS LTD *p* 668
5000 HIGHWAY 7 E, MARKHAM, ON, L3R 4M9
(905) 477-6320   *SIC* 5912

CHRISTOPHER'S WELDING LTD *p* 82
GD, DIDSBURY, AB, T0M 0W0
SIC 1389

CHROMATOGRAPHIC SPECIALTIES INC *p* 519
300 LAURIER BLVD, BROCKVILLE, ON, K6V 5W1
(613) 342-4678   *SIC* 5049

CHROME DATA SOLUTIONS, LP *p* 650
345 SASKATOON ST, LONDON, ON, N5W 4R4
(519) 451-2323   *SIC* 7371

CHROME SOLUTIONS *p* 653
See *AUTODATA SOLUTIONS COMPANY*

CHRONICLE JOURNAL, THE *p* 908
75 CUMBERLAND ST S, THUNDER BAY, ON, P7B 1A3
(807) 343-6200   *SIC* 2711

CHRONO AVIATION INC *p* 1278
706A 7E AV DE L'AEROPORT, QUEBEC, QC, G2J 2T6
(418) 529-4444   *SIC* 4522

CHRYSALIS *p* 93
See *CHRYSALIS: AN ALBERTA SOCIETY*

FOR CITIZENS WITH DISABILITIES
CHRYSALIS: AN ALBERTA SOCIETY FOR CITIZENS WITH DISABILITIES *p 93*
13325 ST ALBERT TRAIL NW, EDMONTON, AB, T5L 4R3
(780) 454-9656   *SIC 8331*
CHRYSLER CANADA *p 1019*
See *FCA CANADA INC*
CHRYSLER CANADA *p 1023*
See *FCA CANADA INC*
CHRYSLER CANADA *p 1250*
See *FCA CANADA INC*
CHRYSLER DODGE *p 1098*
See *BERNIER & CREPEAU (1988) LTEE*
CHRYSLER DODGE JEEP *p 528*
See *UNIQUE CHRYSLER DODGE JEEP LTD*
CHRYSLER DODGE JEEP *p 1389*
See *AUTOMOBILES BERNIER & CREPEAU LTEE*
CHRYSLER FINANCIAL SERVICES CANADA INC *p 1023*
1 RIVERSIDE DR W, WINDSOR, ON, N9A 5K3
(519) 973-2000   *SIC 6153*
CHRYSLER JEEP *p 394*
See *CENTRAL GARAGE LTD*
CHRYSLER WINDSOR *p 1023*
See *FCA CANADA INC*
CHSLD *p 1281*
See *CENTRE D' HEBERGEMENT ET DE SOINS DE LONGUE DUREE HEATHER INC*
CHSLD CENTRE D'HEBERGEMENT ROBERT CLICHE *p 1168*
See *GOUVERNEMENT DE LA PROVINCE DE QUEBEC*
CHSLD DE GATINEAU - MAISON BON SEJOUR *p 1103*
See *ASSOCIATION DES RESIDENTS ET RESIDENTES DU CENTRE D'ACCEUIL DE GATINEAU, L'*
CHSLD L'ORCHIDEE BLANCHE *p 1232*
See *ORCHIDEE BLANCHE CENTRE D'HEBERGEMENT SOINS LONGUE DUREE INC, L*
CHSLD LACHINE, NAZAIRE PICHE ET FOYER DORVAL, LES *p 1096*
225 AV DE LA PRESENTATION, DORVAL, QC, H9S 3L7
(514) 631-9094   *SIC 8361*
CHSLD LE CHATEAU *p 1057*
See *GROUPE CHAMPLAIN INC*
CHSLD LOUISE-FAUBERT *p 1319*
See *CENTRE D'HEBERGEMENT ET DE SOINS DE LONGUE DUREE LOUISE-FAUBERT INC*
CHSLD MARIE-CLARET INC *p 1240*
3345 BOUL HENRI-BOURASSA E, MONTREAL-NORD, QC, H1H 1H6
(514) 322-4380   *SIC 8361*
CHSLD PROVIDENCE NOTRE-DAME DE LOURDES INC *p 1166*
1870 BOUL PIE-IX, MONTREAL, QC, H1V 2C6
(514) 527-4595   *SIC 8051*
CHSLD TREFLE D'OR, LES CENTRE D'HEBERGEMENT DE ST REMI *p 1351*
See *GOUVERNEMENT DE LA PROVINCE DE QUEBEC*
CHSLD VIGI BROSSARD *p 1071*
See *VIGI SANTE LTEE*
CHSLD VIGI ET BLAIS *p 1150*
See *VIGI SANTE LTEE*
CHSLD VIGI ET LES CHUTES *p 1369*
See *VIGI SANTE LTEE*
CHSLD VIGI MONTEREGIE *p 1310*
See *VIGI SANTE LTEE*
CHSLD VIGI REINE ELIZABETH *p 1221*
See *VIGI SANTE LTEE*
CHSLD VIGI SHERMONT *p 1371*
See *VIGI SANTE LTEE*
CHSM & C MANAGEMENT *p 977*
474 BATHURST ST SUITE 300, TORONTO,

ON, M5T 2S6
(416) 964-1115   *SIC 8111*
CHU DE QUEBEC - UNIVERSITE LAVAL *p 1269*
11 COTE DU PALAIS, QUEBEC, QC, G1R 2J6
(418) 525-4444   *SIC 8733*
CHUANG'S COMPANY LTD *p 668*
110 DENISON ST UNIT 8, MARKHAM, ON, L3R 1B6
(905) 415-2812   *SIC 5149*
CHUBB DU CANADA COMPANY D'ASSURANCE *p 1202*
See *CHUBB INSURANCE COMPANY OF CANADA*
CHUBB EDWARDS *p 1184*
See *CSG SECURITY CORPORATION*
CHUBB EDWARDS SECURITY *p 701*
See *UTC FIRE & SECURITY CANADA INC*
CHUBB INSURANCE COMPANY OF CANADA *p 971*
199 BAY ST SUITE 2500, TORONTO, ON, M5L 1E2
(416) 863-0550   *SIC 6331*
CHUBB INSURANCE COMPANY OF CANADA *p 1202*
1250 BOUL RENE-LEVESQUE O BUREAU 2700, MONTREAL, QC, H3B 4W8
(514) 938-4000   *SIC 6331*
CHUBB SECURITY SYSTEMS *p 693*
See *CSG SECURITY CORPORATION*
CHUBB SECURITY SYSTEMS, DIV OF *p 693*
See *CSG SECURITY CORPORATION*
CHUCK'S AUTO SUPPLY LTD *p 344*
861 MACKENZIE AVE S, WILLIAMS LAKE, BC, V2G 3X8
(250) 398-7012   *SIC 5013*
CHUDD'S CHRYSLER LTD *p 350*
231 GD, GIMLI, MB, R0C 1B0
(204) 642-8555   *SIC 5511*
CHUDLEIGH'S APPLE FARM LTD *p 683*
624 MCGEACHIE DR, MILTON, ON, L9T 3Y5
(905) 878-2725   *SIC 0175*
CHUDLEIGH'S LTD *p 683*
8501 CHUDLEIGH WAY, MILTON, ON, L9T 0L9
(905) 878-8781   *SIC 5461*
CHUM SATELLITE SERVICES *p 678*
See *CHUM SATELLITE SERVICES LIMITED*
CHUM SATELLITE SERVICES LIMITED *p 678*
280 HILLMOUNT RD UNIT 6, MARKHAM, ON, L6C 3A1
(905) 475-1661   *SIC 7313*
CHUM, LE *p 1185*
See *CENTRE HOSPITALIER DE L'UNIVERSITE DE MONTREAL*
CHUNG DAHM IMMERSION SCHOOL *p 238*
See *CHUNG DAHM IMMERSION SCHOOL, VANCOUVER INC*
CHUNG DAHM IMMERSION SCHOOL, VANCOUVER INC *p 238*
2420 DOLLARTON HWY, NORTH VANCOUVER, BC, V7H 2Y1
SIC 8299
CHUNG HING CO. LTD *p 290*
8595 FRASER ST, VANCOUVER, BC, V5X 3Y1
(604) 324-7411   *SIC 5141*
CHUNG, A. T. PHARMACY LIMITED *p 995*
2290 BLOOR ST W SUITE 989, TORONTO, ON, M6S 1N9
(416) 769-1105   *SIC 5912*
CHUQ *p 1268*
See *CENTRE HOSPITALIER UNIVERSITAIRE DE QUEBEC*
CHUQ PAVILLON HOTEL DIEU DE QUEBEC *p 1269*
See *CENTRE HOSPITALIER UNIVERSITAIRE DE QUEBEC*

CHURCH & DWIGHT CANADA CORP *p 734*
635 SECRETARIAT CRT, MISSISSAUGA, ON, L5S 0A5
(905) 696-6570   *SIC 2834*
CHURCH BREWING COMPANY LTD, THE *p 471*
329 MAIN ST, WOLFVILLE, NS, B4P 1C8
(902) 818-8277   *SIC 2082*
CHURCH OF JESUS CHRIST OF LATTER DAY SAINTS, THE *p 989*
See *CANADA TORONTO EAST MISSION*
CHURCH OF ST. JOHN & ST. STEPHEN HOME INC, THE *p 414*
130 UNIVERSITY AVE, SAINT JOHN, NB, E2K 4K3
(506) 643-6001   *SIC 8051*
CHURCHILL FALL LABRADOR CORPORATION *p 421*
GD, CHURCHILL FALLS, NL, A0R 1A0
(709) 925-8298   *SIC 4911*
CHURCHILL FALLS (LABRADOR) CORPORATION LIMITED *p 430*
500 COLUMBUS DR, ST. JOHN'S, NL, A1B 4K7
(709) 737-1450   *SIC 4911*
CHURCHILL FALLS PO *p 815*
See *CANADA POST CORPORATION*
CHURCHILL HIGH SCHOOL *p 387*
See *WINNIPEG SCHOOL DIVISION*
CHURCHILL REGIONAL HEALTH AUTHORITY INC *p 348*
162 LAVERENDRYE AVE, CHURCHILL, MB, R0B 0E0
(204) 675-8881   *SIC 8062*
CHURCHILL RETIREMENT COMMUNITY, THE *p 90*
See *REVERA INC*
CHURCHILL RHA *p 348*
See *CHURCHILL REGIONAL HEALTH AUTHORITY INC*
CHURGIN, ARNOLD SHOES LIMITED *p 46*
227 8 AVE SW, CALGARY, AB, T2P 1B7
(403) 262-3366   *SIC 5661*
CI FINANCIAL CORP *p 937*
2 QUEEN ST E, TORONTO, ON, M5C 3G7
(416) 364-1145   *SIC 6282*
CI FOODS *p 574*
See *CENTRE ISLAND FOOD SERVICES LTD*
CI INVESTMENTS INC *p 937*
1 QUEEN ST E SUITE 2000, TORONTO, ON, M5C 3W5
(416) 364-1145   *SIC 6282*
CIBA VISION CANADA DIV *p 725*
See *NOVARTIS PHARMA CANADA INC*
CIBA VISION CANADA INC *p 721*
2 RIMINI MEWS, MISSISSAUGA, ON, L5N 4K1
SIC 5048
CIBA VISION DIV. *p 721*
See *CIBA VISION CANADA INC*
CIBC ASSET MANAGEMENT HOLDINGS INC *p 971*
COMMERCE CRT W, TORONTO, ON, M5L 1A2
(416) 980-2211   *SIC 6282*
CIBC ASSET MANAGEMENT INC *p 961*
18 YORK ST SUITE 140, TORONTO, ON, M5J 2T8
(416) 364-5620   *SIC 6282*
CIBC ASSET MANAGEMENT INC *p 1194*
1500 BOUL ROBERT-BOURASSA BUREAU 800, MONTREAL, QC, H3A 3S6
(514) 875-7040   *SIC 6282*
CIBC INVESTOR SERVICES INC *p 971*
199 BAY ST, TORONTO, ON, M5L 1A2
(416) 980-3343   *SIC 6282*
CIBC INVESTOR SERVICES INC *p 1202*
1155 BOUL RENE-LEVESQUE O BUREAU 1501, MONTREAL, QC, H3B 2J6
(514) 876-3343   *SIC 6282*

CIBC INVESTORS EDGE *p 971*
See *CIBC INVESTOR SERVICES INC*
CIBC INVESTORS EDGE *p 1202*
See *CIBC INVESTOR SERVICES INC*
CIBC MELLON GLOBAL SECURITIES SERVICES COMPANY *p 653*
150 DUFFERIN AVE 5TH FL, LONDON, ON, N6A 5N6
(519) 873-2218   *SIC 6091*
CIBC MELLON GLOBAL SECURITIES SERVICES COMPANY *p 961*
1 YORK ST SUITE 500, TORONTO, ON, M5J 0B6
(416) 643-5000   *SIC 6091*
CIBC MELLON TRUST COMPANY *p 961*
1 YORK ST SUITE 900, TORONTO, ON, M5J 0B6
(416) 643-5000   *SIC 6211*
CIBC MORTGAGES INC *p 942*
33 YONGE ST SUITE 700, TORONTO, ON, M5E 1G4
(416) 865-1999   *SIC 6163*
CIBC SECURITIES INC *p 950*
200 KING ST W SUITE 700, TORONTO, ON, M5H 4A8
(416) 980-2211   *SIC 6722*
CIBC WOOD GUNDY *p 88*
See *CIBC WORLD MARKETS INC*
CIBC WOOD GUNDY *p 374*
See *CIBC WORLD MARKETS INC*
CIBC WOOD GUNDY *p 833*
See *CIBC WORLD MARKETS INC*
CIBC WOOD GUNDY *p 904*
See *CIBC WORLD MARKETS INC*
CIBC WOOD GUNDY *p 961*
See *CIBC WORLD MARKETS INC*
CIBC WOOD GUNDY *p 1194*
See *CIBC WORLD MARKETS INC*
CIBC WOOD GUNDY *p 1202*
See *CIBC WORLD MARKETS INC*
CIBC WORLD MARKETS INC *p 88*
10180 101 ST NW SUITE 1800, EDMONTON, AB, T5J 3S4
(780) 429-8900   *SIC 6211*
CIBC WORLD MARKETS INC *p 374*
1 LOMBARD PL SUITE 1000, WINNIPEG, MB, R3B 3N9
(204) 942-0311   *SIC 6211*
CIBC WORLD MARKETS INC *p 833*
150 ELGIN ST, OTTAWA, ON, K2P 1L4
(613) 237-5775   *SIC 6211*
CIBC WORLD MARKETS INC *p 904*
123 COMMERCE VALLEY DR E SUITE 100, THORNHILL, ON, L3T 7W8
(905) 762-2300   *SIC 6211*
CIBC WORLD MARKETS INC *p 961*
161 BAY ST, TORONTO, ON, M5J 2S1
(416) 594-7000   *SIC 6211*
CIBC WORLD MARKETS INC *p 961*
181 BAY ST SUITE 600, TORONTO, ON, M5J 2T3
SIC 6211
CIBC WORLD MARKETS INC *p 1194*
600 BOUL DE MAISONNEUVE O BUREAU 3050, MONTREAL, QC, H3A 3J2
(514) 847-6300   *SIC 6211*
CIBC WORLD MARKETS INC *p 1202*
1 PLACE VILLE-MARIE BUREAU 4125, MONTREAL, QC, H3B 3P9
(514) 392-7600   *SIC 6211*
CIBELYE IMPORT-EXPORT *p 1138*
See *GLOBCO INTERNATIONAL INC*
CIBS CONSTRUCTION *p 619*
See *MAYLAN CONSTRUCTION SERVICES INC*
CIBT EDUCATION GROUP INC *p 293*
777 BROADWAY W UNIT 1200, VANCOUVER, BC, V5Z 4J7
(604) 871-9909   *SIC 6282*
CICAME ENERGIE INC *p 1309*
5400 RUE J.-A.-BOMBARDIER, SAINT-HUBERT, QC, J3Z 1G8
(450) 679-7778   *SIC 3643*
CICCARELLI GROUP *p 477*

See CICCARELLI, OTTAVIO & SON CONTRACTING LTD

CICCARELLI, OTTAVIO & SON CONTRACTING LTD *p* 477
807 GARNER RD E SUITE 1, ANCASTER, ON, L9G 3K9
(905) 648-5178   *SIC* 4959

CICHLID WHOLESALE LTD *p* 14
7503 35 ST SE UNIT 25, CALGARY, AB, T2C 1V3
(403) 720-8355   *SIC* 5199

CID BISSETT FASTENERS LIMITED *p* 499
175 SUN PAC BLVD UNIT 2A, BRAMPTON, ON, L6S 5Z6
(905) 595-0411   *SIC* 5072

CIDRERIE MILTON *p* 1356
See CIDRERIE MILTON INC

CIDRERIE MILTON INC *p* 1356
5 137 RTE N, SAINTE-CECILE-DE-MILTON, QC, J0E 2C0
(450) 777-2442   *SIC* 0175

CIE CANADA TIRE INC, LA *p* 1053
21500 AUT TRANSCANADIENNE, BAIE-D'URFE, QC, H9X 4B7
(514) 457-0155   *SIC* 5014

CIE CANADIENNE DE PAPIER & D'EMBALLAGE LTEE *p* 1333
3001 RUE BRABANT-MARINEAU, SAINT-LAURENT, QC, H4S 1V5
(514) 333-4040   *SIC* 5113

CIE CANADIENNE DE PRODUITS OPTIQUES LTEE, LA *p* 1227
8360 RUE MAYRAND, MONTREAL, QC, H4P 2C9
(514) 737-6777   *SIC* 5049

CIE D'ECLAIRAGE UNION LTEE, LA *p* 1227
8150 BOUL DECARIE, MONTREAL, QC, H4P 2S8
(514) 340-5000   *SIC* 5063

CIE D'ENSEIGNES MONTREAL NEON *p* 1086
See ENSEIGNES MONTREAL NEON INC

CIE D'ENSIGNES MONTREAL NEON *p* 1233
See 3093-6975 QUEBEC INC

CIE D'HABILLEMENT SE CE LTEE, LA *p* 1338
6445 CH DE LA COTE-DE-LIESSE, SAINT-LAURENT, QC, H4T 1S9
(514) 341-4400   *SIC* 5137

CIE D'IMPORTATION DE NOUVEAUTES STEIN INC, LA *p* 1325
865 RUE DESLAURIERS, SAINT-LAURENT, QC, H4N 1X3
(514) 334-3366   *SIC* 5137

CIE DANAWARES *p* 1127
1860 32E AV, LACHINE, QC, H8T 3J7
(514) 342-5555   *SIC* 5092

CIE ELECTRIQUE BRITTON LTEE, LA *p* 1156
8555 CH DEVONSHIRE BUREAU 213, MONT-ROYAL, QC, H4P 2L3
(514) 342-5520   *SIC* 1731

CIE MATERIAUX DE CONSTRUCTION BP CANADA, LA *p* 1114
See CIE MATERIAUX DE CONSTRUCTION BP CANADA, LA

CIE MATERIAUX DE CONSTRUCTION BP CANADA, LA *p* 1114
351 RUE ALICE, JOLIETTE, QC, J6E 8P2
(450) 682-4428   *SIC* 2429

CIE MATERIAUX DE CONSTRUCTION BP CANADA, LA *p* 1130
2850 AV DOLLARD, LASALLE, QC, H8N 2V2
(514) 364-0161   *SIC* 5199

CIE MATERIAUX DE CONSTRUCTION BP CANADA, LA *p* 1132
9500 RUE SAINT-PATRICK, LASALLE, QC, H8R 1R8
(514) 364-0161   *SIC* 2429

CIE MATERIAUX DE CONSTRUCTION BP CANADA, LA *p* 1132
9510 RUE SAINT-PATRICK, LASALLE, QC, H8R 1R9
(514) 364-0161   *SIC* 2493

CIE MCCORMICK CANADA CO., LA *p* 648
600 CLARKE RD, LONDON, ON, N5V 3K5
(519) 432-7311   *SIC* 2099

CIE SAFRAN CABINE CANADA *p* 1118
See SAFRAN CABIN CANADA CO.

CIE. MYLES INTERNATIONAL *p* 1177
See 9076-5223 QUEBEC INC

CIELO PRINT INC *p* 824
250 CITY CENTRE AVE SUITE 138, OTTAWA, ON, K1R 6K7
(613) 232-1112   *SIC* 7389

CIENA CANADA, INC *p* 832
385 TERRY FOX DR, OTTAWA, ON, K2K 0L1
(613) 670-2000   *SIC* 3571

CIERE, PIETER ENTERPRISES INC *p* 836
31 MECHANIC ST, PARIS, ON, N3L 1K1
(519) 442-2312   *SIC* 5531

CIF LAB CASEWORK SOLUTIONS INC *p* 550
56 EDILCAN DR, CONCORD, ON, L4K 3S6
(905) 738-5821   *SIC* 3821

CIF LAB SOLUTIONS LP *p* 550
53 COURTLAND AVE SUITE 1, CONCORD, ON, L4K 3T2
(905) 738-5821   *SIC* 3821

CIFFA *p* 583
See CANADIAN INTERNATIONAL FREIGHT FORWARDERS ASSOCIATION INC

CIGM *p* 1396
600 CH DU GOLF, VERDUN, QC, H3E 1A8
(514) 762-5264   *SIC* 6531

CIGNA LIFE INSURANCE COMPANY OF CANADA *p* 866
100 CONSILIUM PL SUITE 301, SCARBOROUGH, ON, M1H 3E3
(416) 290-6666   *SIC* 6321

CIHI *p* 922
See CANADIAN INSTITUTE FOR HEALTH INFORMATION

CIK TELECOM INC *p* 766
282 CONSUMERS RD, NORTH YORK, ON, M2J 1P8
(416) 800-4111   *SIC* 4899

CIM-CONSEIL EN IMMOBILISATION ET MANAGEMENT INC *p* 1191
440 BOUL RENE-LEVESQUE O BUREAU 1700, MONTREAL, QC, H2Z 1V7
(514) 393-4563   *SIC* 8741

CIMA + *p* 1343
See CIMA CANADA INC

CIMA CANADA INC *p* 1343
3400 BOUL DU SOUVENIR SUITE 600, SAINT-LAURENT, QC, H7V 3Z2
(514) 337-2462   *SIC* 8741

CIMA+ S.E.N.C. *p* 1103
420 BOUL MALONEY E BUREAU 201, GATINEAU, QC, J8P 7N8
(819) 663-9294   *SIC* 8711

CIMA+ S.E.N.C. *p* 1210
740 RUE NOTRE-DAME O UNITE 900, MONTREAL, QC, H3C 3X6
(514) 337-2462   *SIC* 8711

CIMA+ S.E.N.C. *p* 1279
1145 BOUL LEBOURGNEUF BUREAU 300, QUEBEC, QC, G2K 2K8
(418) 623-3373   *SIC* 8711

CIMA+ S.E.N.C. *p* 1343
3400 BOUL DU SOUVENIR BUREAU 600, SAINT-LAURENT, QC, H7V 3Z2
(514) 337-2462   *SIC* 8711

CIMA+ S.E.N.C. *p* 1373
3385 RUE KING O, SHERBROOKE, QC, J1L 1P8
(819) 565-3385   *SIC* 8711

CIMARRON PROJECTS LTD *p* 34
6025 11 ST SE SUITE 300, CALGARY, AB, T2H 2Z2
(403) 252-3436   *SIC* 8711

CIMAX LA BELLECHASSOISE *p* 1048
See EXCAVATIONS PAYETTE LTEE, LES

CIMCO REFRIGERATION *p* 934
See TOROMONT INDUSTRIES LTD

CIMCOOL METAL WORKING FLUIDS *p* 523
See MILACRON CANADA CORP

CIMCORP AUTOMATION LTD *p* 599
635 SOUTH SERVICE RD, GRIMSBY, ON, L3M 4E8
(905) 643-9700   *SIC* 3569

CIME DECOR INC *p* 1187
420 RUE MCGILL BUREAU 100, MONTREAL, QC, H2Y 2G1
(514) 842-2463   *SIC* 5021

CIMENT MCINNIS INC *p* 1213
832 BOUL RENE-LEVESQUE O BUREAU 205, MONTREAL, QC, H3G 2W2
(438) 382-3331   *SIC* 2891

CIMENT QUEBEC INC *p* 1123
1250 CH SAINT-JOSE, LA PRAIRIE, QC, J5R 6A9
(450) 444-7942   *SIC* 3273

CIMENT QUEBEC INC *p* 1294
145 BOUL DU CENTENAIRE, SAINT-BASILE, QC, G0A 3G0
(418) 329-2100   *SIC* 3241

CIMENT ST-LAURENT *p* 1114
See CRH CANADA GROUP INC

CIMENTERIE PORT-DANIEL *p* 1174
See SOCIETE DE GESTION REJEAN & SERGE AUCOIN INTERNATIONAL INC

CIMS LIMITED PARTNERSHIP *p* 246
1610 INDUSTRIAL AVE, PORT COQUITLAM, BC, V3C 6N3
(604) 472-4300   *SIC* 1541

CIMTEK INC *p* 521
5328 JOHN LUCAS DR, BURLINGTON, ON, L7L 6A6
(905) 331-6338   *SIC* 7373

CIMTEL (QUEBEC) INC *p* 1240
71 AV WESTMINSTER N, MONTREAL-OUEST, QC, H4X 1Y8
(514) 481-4344   *SIC* 5065

CINCOM SYSTEMS OF CANADA LTD *p* 708
2085 HURONTARIO ST SUITE 500, MISSISSAUGA, ON, L5A 4G1
(905) 279-4220   *SIC* 5045

CINDERCRETE PRODUCTS LIMITED *p* 1417
HWY 1 E, REGINA, SK, S4P 3A1
(306) 789-2636   *SIC* 3271

CINE-PARC ST-EUSTACHE INC *p* 1300
555 AV MATHERS, SAINT-EUSTACHE, QC, J7P 4C1
(514) 879-1707   *SIC* 7833

CINEFLIX MEDIA INC *p* 979
110 SPADINA AVE SUITE 400, TORONTO, ON, M5V 2K4
(416) 531-2500   *SIC* 7929

CINEGROUPE INTERACTIF INC *p* 1175
1010 RUE SAINTE-CATHERINE E, MONTREAL, QC, H2L 2G3
(514) 524-7567   *SIC* 7372

CINEMA BANQUE SCOTIA MONTREAL *p* 1202
See CINEPLEX ODEON CORPORATION

CINEMA CINEPLEX BROSSARD & VIP *p* 1070
See CINEPLEX ODEON CORPORATION

CINEMA CINEPLEX LAVAL *p* 1086
See CINEPLEX ODEON CORPORATION

CINEMAS GUZZO INC *p* 1379
1055 CH DU COTEAU, TERREBONNE, QC, J6W 5Y8
(450) 961-2945   *SIC* 7832

CINEMATRONIX *p* 276
See EAGLE CINEMATRONICS INC

CINEPLEX CINEMAS MISSISSAUGA *p* 709
See CINEPLEX ODEON CORPORATION

CINEPLEX CINEMAS SOUTH EDMONTON *p* 120
See CINEPLEX ODEON CORPORATION

CINEPLEX CINEMAS WESTMOUNT & VIP *p* 660

See CINEPLEX ODEON CORPORATION

CINEPLEX ENTERTAINMENT *p* 925
See CINEPLEX ENTERTAINMENT LIMITED PARTNERSHIP

CINEPLEX ENTERTAINMENT *p* 925
See CINEPLEX INC

CINEPLEX ENTERTAINMENT LIMITED PARTNERSHIP *p* 120
1725 99 ST NW, EDMONTON, AB, T6N 1K5
(587) 585-3760   *SIC* 7999

CINEPLEX ENTERTAINMENT LIMITED PARTNERSHIP *p* 925
1303 YONGE ST, TORONTO, ON, M4T 2Y9
(416) 323-6600   *SIC* 7832

CINEPLEX INC *p* 925
1303 YONGE ST SUITE 300, TORONTO, ON, M4T 2Y9
(416) 323-6600   *SIC* 7822

CINEPLEX ODEON CORPORATION *p* 104
8882 170 ST NW SUITE 3030, EDMONTON, AB, T5T 4M2
(780) 444-2400   *SIC* 7832

CINEPLEX ODEON CORPORATION *p* 120
1525 99 ST NW, EDMONTON, AB, T6N 1K5
(780) 436-3675   *SIC* 7832

CINEPLEX ODEON CORPORATION *p* 326
900 BURRARD ST, VANCOUVER, BC, V6Z 3G5
(604) 630-1407   *SIC* 7832

CINEPLEX ODEON CORPORATION *p* 382
817 ST JAMES ST, WINNIPEG, MB, R3G 3L9
(204) 774-1001   *SIC* 7832

CINEPLEX ODEON CORPORATION *p* 596
2385 CITY PARK DR, GLOUCESTER, ON, K1J 1G1
(613) 749-5861   *SIC* 7832

CINEPLEX ODEON CORPORATION *p* 660
755 WONDERLAND RD S, LONDON, ON, N6K 1M6
(519) 474-2152   *SIC* 7832

CINEPLEX ODEON CORPORATION *p* 709
309 RATHBURN RD W, MISSISSAUGA, ON, L5B 4C1
(905) 275-4969   *SIC* 7832

CINEPLEX ODEON CORPORATION *p* 925
1303 YONGE ST, TORONTO, ON, M4T 2Y9
(416) 323-6600   *SIC* 7832

CINEPLEX ODEON CORPORATION *p* 979
259 RICHMOND ST W, TORONTO, ON, M5V 3M6
(416) 368-5600   *SIC* 7832

CINEPLEX ODEON CORPORATION *p* 1070
9350 BOUL LEDUC, BROSSARD, QC, J4Y 0B3
(450) 678-5542   *SIC* 7832

CINEPLEX ODEON CORPORATION *p* 1086
2800 AV DU COSMODOME, COTE SAINT-LUC, QC, H7T 2X1
(450) 978-0212   *SIC* 7832

CINEPLEX ODEON CORPORATION *p* 1202
977 RUE SAINTE-CATHERINE O, MONTREAL, QC, H3B 4W3
(514) 842-0549   *SIC* 7832

CINNABON *p* 533
See CINNAGARD INC

CINNAGARD INC *p* 533
120 MAIN ST UNIT 3, CAMBRIDGE, ON, N1R 1V7
(519) 622-3188   *SIC* 2051

CINNAROLL BAKERIES LIMITED *p* 22
2140 PEGASUS RD NE, CALGARY, AB, T2E 8G8
(403) 255-4556   *SIC* 5461

CINNZEO BAKERIES *p* 158
See C.B. INVESTMENTS LTD

CINNZEO DIV *p* 22
See CINNAROLL BAKERIES LIMITED

CINRAM CANADA OPERATIONS ULC *p* 864
2255 MARKHAM RD, SCARBOROUGH, ON, M1B 2W3
(416) 298-8190   *SIC* 5045

CINRAM CANADA OPERATIONS ULC *p*

873
400 NUGGET AVE, SCARBOROUGH, ON, M1S 4A4
(416) 332-9000   *SIC* 3652

CINRAM GROUP   *p* 864
See *CINRAM CANADA OPERATIONS ULC*

CINRAM INTERNATIONAL INCOME FUND   *p* 864
2255 MARKHAM RD, SCARBOROUGH, ON, M1B 2W3
(416) 298-8190   *SIC* 6722

CINTAS CANADA LIMITED   *p* 28
1235 23 AVE SE, CALGARY, AB, T2G 5S5
SIC 7218

CINTAS CANADA LIMITED   *p* 229
5293 272 ST, LANGLEY, BC, V4W 1P1
(604) 857-2281   *SIC* 7218

CINTAS CANADA LIMITED   *p* 650
30 CHARTERHOUSE CRES, LONDON, ON, N5W 5V5
(519) 453-5010   *SIC* 7218

CINTAS CANADA LIMITED   *p* 716
4170 SLADEVIEW CRES UNIT 2, MISSISSAUGA, ON, L5L 0A1
(416) 763-4400   *SIC* 7218

CINTAS CANADA LIMITED   *p* 755
255 HARRY WALKER PKY S SUITE 1, NEWMARKET, ON, L3Y 8Z5
(905) 853-4409   *SIC* 7213

CINTAS CANADA LIMITED   *p* 786
149 EDDYSTONE AVE, NORTH YORK, ON, M3N 1H5
(416) 743-5070   *SIC* 7218

CINTAS CANADA LIMITED   *p* 1064
1470 RUE NOBEL, BOUCHERVILLE, QC, J4B 5H3
(450) 449-4747   *SIC* 7218

CINTEX INTERNATIONAL (CANADA) LIMITED   *p* 693
5195 MAINGATE DR, MISSISSAUGA, ON, L4W 1G4
(905) 795-8052   *SIC* 5091

CINTUBE LTEE   *p* 1074
1577 RUE WATTS, CHAMBLY, QC, J3L 2Z3
(450) 658-5140   *SIC* 3498

CINTUBE LTEE   *p* 1126
333 BOUL SAINT-JOSEPH BUREAU 105, LACHINE, QC, H8S 2K9
(514) 634-3592   *SIC* 3498

CIOC   *p* 51
See *HAMMERHEAD RESOURCES INC*

CIOCIARO CLUB OF WINDSOR INC   *p* 807
3745 NORTH TALBOT RD, OLDCASTLE, ON, N0R 1L0
(519) 737-6153   *SIC* 8641

CIOT CANADA   *p* 1178
See *CIOT INC*

CIOT INC   *p* 1178
9151 BOUL SAINT-LAURENT, MONTREAL, QC, H2N 1N2
(514) 382-5180   *SIC* 5032

CIP   *p* 122
See *CANADIAN INDUSTRIAL PARAMEDICS*

CIPA LUMBER CO. LTD   *p* 205
797 CARLISLE RD, DELTA, BC, V3M 5P4
(604) 523-2250   *SIC* 2436

CIPHER PHARMACEUTICALS INC   *p* 796
209 OAK PARK BLVD SUITE 501, OAKVILLE, ON, L6H 0M2
(905) 602-5840   *SIC* 2834

CIR COMMERCIAL REALTY INC   *p* 1417
2505 11TH AVE SUITE 200, REGINA, SK, S4P 0K6
(306) 789-8300   *SIC* 6531

CIRBA INC   *p* 680
179 ENTERPRISE BLVD UNIT 400, MARKHAM, ON, L6G 0E7
(905) 731-0090   *SIC* 7371

CIRCA ENTERPRISES INC   *p* 68
10333 SOUTHPORT RD SW SUITE 535, CALGARY, AB, T2W 3X6
(403) 258-2011   *SIC* 3643

CIRCA TELECOM, DIV OF   *p* 68
See *CIRCA ENTERPRISES INC*

CIRCLE DRIVE SPECIAL CARE HOME INC   *p* 1435
3055 PRESTON AVE, SASKATOON, SK, S7T 1C3
(306) 955-4800   *SIC* 8051

CIRCLE K   *p* 1233
See *ALIMENTATION COUCHE-TARD INC*

CIRCLE OF CARE   *p* 773
See *CIRCLE OF HOME CARE SERVICES (TORONTO)*

CIRCLE OF HOME CARE SERVICES (TORONTO)   *p* 773
4211 YONGE ST SUITE 401, NORTH YORK, ON, M2P 2A9
(416) 635-2860   *SIC* 8059

CIRCUIT ACURA   *p* 1279
See *9220-3785 QUEBEC INC*

CIRCUIT CENTER INC   *p* 870
175 MIDWEST RD, SCARBOROUGH, ON, M1P 3A6
(416) 285-5550   *SIC* 3672

CIRCUIT ICAR   *p* 1153
See *CENTRE INTERNATIONAL DE COURSE AUTOMOBILE (ICAR) INC*

CIRCUIT TECH INC   *p* 668
399 DENISON ST, MARKHAM, ON, L3R 1B7
(905) 474-9227   *SIC* 3672

CIRCUL-AIRE INC   *p* 1328
3999 BOUL DE LA COTE-VERTU, SAINT-LAURENT, QC, H4R 1R2
(514) 337-3331   *SIC* 3564

CIRCUS WORLD DISPLAYS LIMITED   *p* 760
4080 MONTROSE RD, NIAGARA FALLS, ON, L2H 1J9
(905) 353-0732   *SIC* 3651

CIRION BIOPHARMA RECHERCHE INC   *p* 1233
3150 RUE DELAUNAY, MONTREAL, QC, H7L 5E1
(450) 688-6445   *SIC* 6712

CIRQUE DU SOLEIL CANADA INC   *p* 1169
8400 2E AV, MONTREAL, QC, H1Z 4M6
(514) 722-2324   *SIC* 7999

CIRQUE DU SOLEIL INC   *p* 1169
CIRQUE DU SOLEIL, MONTREAL, QC, H1Z 4M6
(514) 722-2324   *SIC* 7999

CIS   *p* 219
See *CATHOLIC INDEPENDENT SCHOOLS OF NELSON DIOCESE, THE*

CIS   *p* 650
See *CORPORATE INVESTIGATIVE SERVICES LTD*

CIS INSURANCE BROKERS (CANADA) LTD   *p* 904
505 HIGHWAY 7 E SUITE 328, THORNHILL, ON, L3T 7T1
(905) 889-2268   *SIC* 6411

CIS NAVIGATION   *p* 1189
See *NAVIGATION DES ETATS INDEPENDANTS DU COMMONWEALTH INC*

CISCO SYSTEMS CANADA CO   *p* 961
88 QUEENS QUAY W SUITE 2700, TORONTO, ON, M5J 0B8
(416) 306-7000   *SIC* 5065

CISCO SYSTEMS CANADA CO   *p* 1194
1800 AV MCGILL COLLEGE BUREAU 700, MONTREAL, QC, H3A 3J6
(514) 847-6800   *SIC* 5999

CISCO SYSTEMS CO.   *p* 873
100 MIDDLEFIELD RD UNIT 1, SCARBOROUGH, ON, M1S 4M6
(416) 299-6888   *SIC* 5065

CISOLIFT DISTRIBUTION INC   *p* 1306
192 RUE SYLVESTRE, SAINT-GERMAIN-DE-GRANTHAM, QC, J0C 1K0
(819) 395-3838   *SIC* 5084

CISSS DE LANAUDIERE - LE BOUCLIER   *p* 1321
See *CENTRE INTEGRE DE SANTE ET DE SERVICES SOCIAUX DE LANAUDIERE*

CISSS DE LAURENTIDES, LE   *p* 1321
See *CENTRE INTEGRE DE SANTE ET DE SERVICES SOCIAUX DES LAURENTIDES*

CISSS DES ILES   *p* 1073
See *CENTRE INTEGRE DE SANTE ET DE SERVICES SOCIAUX DES ILES*

CISSS DU BAS-SAINT-LAURENT   *p* 1284
See *CENTRE INTEGRE DE SANTE ET DE SERVICES SOCIAUX DU BAS-SAINT-LAURENT*

CISTEK SOLUTIONS INC.   *p* 46
SUITE 1000 605 5 AVE SW, CALGARY, AB, T2P 3H5
(403) 264-0018   *SIC* 4922

CITADEL COMMERCE CORP   *p* 192
8610 GLENLYON PKY UNIT 130, BURNABY, BC, V5J 0B6
(604) 299-6924   *SIC* 7372

CITADEL HIGH   *p* 451
See *HALIFAX REGIONAL SCHOOL BOARD*

CITADEL INCOME FUND   *p* 925
1300 YONGE ST SUITE 300, TORONTO, ON, M4T 1X3
(416) 361-9673   *SIC* 6726

CITADELLE CHEVROLET CADILLAC BUICK GMC LTEE   *p* 1136
89 RTE DU PRESIDENT-KENNEDY, LEVIS, QC, G6V 6C8
(418) 835-1171   *SIC* 5511

CITADELLE COOPERATIVE DE PRODUCTEURS DE SIROP D'ERABLE   *p* 1246
2100 AV SAINT-LAURENT, PLESSISVILLE, QC, G6L 2R3
(819) 362-3241   *SIC* 2099

CITAIR, INC   *p* 620
73 MILL RD, HENSALL, ON, N0M 1X0
(519) 262-2600   *SIC* 3792

CITCO (CANADA) INC   *p* 452
5151 GEORGE ST SUITE 700, HALIFAX, NS, B3J 1M5
(902) 442-4242   *SIC* 8741

CITCO (CANADA) INC   *p* 928
2 BLOOR ST E SUITE 2700, TORONTO, ON, M4W 1A8
(416) 966-9200   *SIC* 8742

CITE CHRYSLER PLYMOUTH   *p* 1107
See *3041000 CANADA INC*

CITE COLLEGIALE, LA   *p* 820
801 AVIATION PKY, OTTAWA, ON, K1K 4R3
(613) 742-2483   *SIC* 8222

CITE DES JEUNES A.-M. SORMANY D'EDMUNDSTON   *p* 398
See *DISTRICT SCOLAIRE 3*

CITE NISSAN   *p* 1218
See *105262 CANADA INC*

CITE VIVA   *p* 1380
See *GROUPE EDIFIO INC*

CITE-JARDIN   *p* 1104
See *9095-1302 QUEBEC INC*

CITERNES BEDARD INC   *p* 1222
5785 PLACE TURCOT, MONTREAL, QC, H4C 1V9
(514) 937-1670   *SIC* 3443

CITERNES EXPERTS INC   *p* 1231
4545 AV DES INDUSTRIES, MONTREAL, QC, H7C 1A1
(514) 323-5510   *SIC* 5085

CITI CARDS CANADA INC   *p* 730
5900 HURONTARIO ST, MISSISSAUGA, ON, L5R 0B8
(905) 285-7500   *SIC* 6153

CITIBANK CANADA   *p* 937
1 TORONTO ST SUITE 1200, TORONTO, ON, M5C 2V6
(416) 369-6399   *SIC* 6153

CITIBANK CANADA   *p* 961
123 FRONT ST W SUITE 1900, TORONTO, ON, M5J 2M3
(416) 947-5500   *SIC* 6021

CITIBANK VISA   *p* 937
See *CITIBANK CANADA*

CITICAPITAL   *p* 961

See *CITICORP VENDOR FINANCE, LTD*

CITICORP VENDOR FINANCE, LTD   *p* 961
123 FRONT ST W SUITE 1500, TORONTO, ON, M5J 2M3
(800) 991-4046   *SIC* 6159

CITIGROUP GLOBAL MARKETS CANADA INC   *p* 693
2920 MATHESON BLVD E, MISSISSAUGA, ON, L4W 5R6
(905) 624-9889   *SIC* 6722

CITIGROUP GLOBAL MARKETS CANADA INC   *p* 961
161 BAY ST SUITE 4600, TORONTO, ON, M5J 2S1
(416) 866-2300   *SIC* 6211

CITIGUARD SECURITY SERVICES INC   *p* 870
1560 BRIMLEY RD SUITE 201, SCARBOROUGH, ON, M1P 3G9
(416) 431-6888   *SIC* 7381

CITILOGISTICS INC   *p* 583
22 HUDDERSFIELD RD, ETOBICOKE, ON, M9W 5Z6
(416) 251-5545   *SIC* 7389

CITITEL INC   *p* 84
11830 111 AVE NW SUITE 202, EDMONTON, AB, T5G 0E1
(780) 489-1212   *SIC* 7389

CITIWELL INTERNATIONAL INC   *p* 782
401 MAGNETIC DR UNIT 9, NORTH YORK, ON, M3J 3G9
SIC 5092

CITIZEN RELATIONS   *p* 1258
See *CITOYEN OPTIMUM S.E.C.*

CITOXLAB AMERIQUE DU NORD INC   *p* 1241
445 BOUL ARMAND-FRAPPIER, MONTREAL-OUEST, QC, H7V 4B3
(450) 973-2240   *SIC* 8731

CITOYEN OPTIMUM S.E.C.   *p* 1258
300 RUE SAINT-PAUL BUREAU 300, QUEBEC, QC, G1K 7R1
(418) 647-2727   *SIC* 4899

CITOYEN RELATIONS INC   *p* 1258
300 RUE SAINT-PAUL BUREAU 300, QUEBEC, QC, G1K 7R1
(418) 521-3744   *SIC* 4899

CITY CHRYSLER JEEP   *p* 145
See *CITY PLYMOUTH CHRYSLER (MEDICINE HAT) LTD*

CITY ADULT LEARNING CENTRE   *p* 920
See *TORONTO DISTRICT SCHOOL BOARD*

CITY AUTO SERVICE LTD   *p* 235
803 BAKER ST, NELSON, BC, V1L 4J8
(250) 352-5346   *SIC* 5511

CITY BREAD CO. LTD, THE   *p* 371
232 JARVIS AVE, WINNIPEG, MB, R2W 3A1
(204) 586-8409   *SIC* 2051

CITY BREAD CO. LTD, THE   *p* 371
238 DUFFERIN AVE, WINNIPEG, MB, R2W 2X6
(204) 586-8409   *SIC* 2051

CITY BUICK CHEVROLET CADILLAC GMC LTD   *p* 764
1900 VICTORIA PARK AVE, NORTH YORK, ON, M1R 1T6
(416) 751-5920   *SIC* 5511

CITY CAB (BRANTFORD-DARLING STREET) LIMITED   *p* 517
40 DALHOUSIE ST, BRANTFORD, ON, N3T 2H8
(519) 759-7800   *SIC* 4121

CITY CAB INC   *p* 1038
168 PRINCE ST, CHARLOTTETOWN, PE, C1A 4R6
(902) 892-6567   *SIC* 4121

CITY CENTRE CAMPUS   *p* 301
See *VANCOUVER COMMUNITY COLLEGE*

CITY CENTRE CARE SOCIETY   *p* 297
415 PENDER ST W, VANCOUVER, BC, V6B 1V2

(604) 681-9111   *SIC* 8051
CITY CHEVROLET GEO OLDSMOBILE LTD
p 610
155 CANNON ST E, HAMILTON, ON, L8L
2A6

SIC 5511
CITY CHRYSLER   *p* 422
*See CITY MOTORS A LIMITED PARTNER-
SHIP*
CITY COIN VENDING SERVICES LTD *p* 68
9212 HORTON RD SW UNIT J, CALGARY,
AB, T2V 2X4
(403) 253-0324   *SIC* 5962
CITY ELECTRIC SUPPLY CORPORATIONp
531
10 PERDUE CRT UNIT 6, CALEDON, ON,
L7C 3M6
(905) 495-0535   *SIC* 5063
CITY FISH   *p* 8
See 1294711 ALBERTA LTD
CITY FORD SALES LTD   *p* 124
14750 MARK MESSIER TRAIL NW, ED-
MONTON, AB, T6V 1H5
(780) 454-2000   *SIC* 5511
CITY HONDA   *p* 430
See KENMOUNT MOTORS INC
CITY HOTELS LIMITED   *p* 431
251 EMPIRE AVE SUITE 103, ST. JOHN'S,
NL, A1C 3H9
(709) 738-3989   *SIC* 7011
CITY LUMBER & MILLWORK   *p* 105
See CITY LUMBER CORPORATION
CITY LUMBER CORPORATION   *p* 105
15711 128 AVE NW, EDMONTON, AB, T5V
1K4
(780) 447-1344   *SIC* 5039
CITY MAZDA   *p* 454
See 2187878 NOVA SCOTIA LIMITED
CITY MOTORS A LIMITED PARTNERSHIPp
422
119 O'CONNELL DR, CORNER BROOK,
NL, A2H 5M6
(709) 637-1000   *SIC* 5511
CITY NATIONAL LEASING DIV   *p* 764
*See CITY BUICK CHEVROLET CADILLAC
GMC LTD*
CITY OF ABBOTSFORD   *p* 176
3106 CLEARBROOK RD, ABBOTSFORD,
BC, V2T 4N6
(604) 855-0500   *SIC* 7999
CITY OF ABBOTSFORD   *p* 176
32270 GEORGE FERGUSON WAY, AB-
BOTSFORD, BC, V2T 2L1
(604) 853-3566   *SIC* 7389
**CITY OF BURLINGTON ROAD & PARK
MAINTENANCE**   *p* 527
*See CORPORATION OF THE CITY OF
BURLINGTON*
CITY OF BURNABY   *p* 185
240 WILLINGDON AVE, BURNABY, BC,
V5C 5E9
(604) 298-7946   *SIC* 7999
CITY OF BURNABY   *p* 190
6533 NELSON AVE, BURNABY, BC, V5H
0C2

SIC 8322
CITY OF CALGARY, THE   *p* 28
315 10 AVE SE SUITE 101, CALGARY, AB,
T2G 0W2
(403) 268-5153   *SIC* 8399
CITY OF DELTA   *p* 207
7815 112 ST, DELTA, BC, V4C 4V9
(604) 952-3075   *SIC* 7999
CITY OF GREATER SUDBURY, THE *p* 898
960 NOTRE DAME AVE SUITE D, SUD-
BURY, ON, P3A 2T4
(705) 566-4270   *SIC* 8059
CITY OF GREATER SUDBURY, THE *p* 900
1700 KINGSWAY RD, SUDBURY, ON, P3E
3L7
(705) 675-3333   *SIC* 4111
**CITY OF KAWARTHA LAKES FIRE RES-
CUE SERVICE**   *p*
645

*See CORPORATION OF THE CITY OF
KAWARTHA LAKES, THE*
CITY OF OTTAWA   *p* 810
1490 YOUVILLE DR, ORLEANS, ON, K1C
2X8
(613) 580-9600   *SIC* 7999
CITY OF OTTAWA   *p* 817
1500 ST. LAURENT BLVD, OTTAWA, ON,
K1G 0Z8
(613) 741-6440   *SIC* 4111
CITY OF REGINA, THE   *p* 1420
333 WINNIPEG ST, REGINA, SK, S4R 8P2
(306) 777-7726   *SIC* 4111
CITY OF REGINA, THE   *p* 1420
333 WINNIPEG ST, REGINA, SK, S4R 8P2
(306) 777-7780   *SIC* 4131
CITY OF SURREY, THE   *p* 271
6651 148 ST FL 3, SURREY, BC, V3S 3C7
(604) 591-4152   *SIC* 8711
CITY OF WATERLOO SERVICE CENTER *p*
1007
*See CORPORATION OF THE CITY OF WA-
TERLOO, THE*
CITY OFFICE REIT, INC   *p* 312
1075 GEORGIA ST W SUITE 2010, VAN-
COUVER, BC, V6E 3C9
(604) 806-3366   *SIC* 6798
**CITY PLYMOUTH CHRYSLER (MEDICINE
HAT) LTD**   *p* 145
982 REDCLIFF DR SW, MEDICINE HAT,
AB, T1A 5E4
(403) 526-6944   *SIC* 5511
CITY PROJECTS LTD   *p* 185
4483 JUNEAU ST, BURNABY, BC, V5C 4C4
(604) 874-5566   *SIC* 1542
CITY RENTALS   *p* 900
*See DELLELCE CONSTRUCTION &
EQUIPMENT LTD*
CITY TAXI   *p* 517
*See CITY CAB (BRANTFORD-DARLING
STREET) LIMITED*
CITY TIRE & AUTO CENTRE LIMITEDp 426
1123 TOPSAIL RD, MOUNT PEARL, NL,
A1N 5G2
(709) 364-6808   *SIC* 7538
CITY TIRE CENTRE   *p* 1432
See MARKET TIRE (1976) LTD
CITY WEST   *p* 251
*See CITY WEST CABLE & TELEPHONE
CORP*
CITY WEST CABLE & TELEPHONE CORP
p 251
248 3RD AVE W, PRINCE RUPERT, BC,
V8J 1L1
(250) 624-2111   *SIC* 4899
CITY WIDE CATERING   *p* 691
See 888930 ONTARIO INC
**CITY WIDE TOWING AND RECOVERY SER-
VICE LTD**   *p*
14
10885 84 ST SE, CALGARY, AB, T2C 5A6
(403) 798-0876   *SIC* 7549
CITY WIRELESS   *p* 8
2150 29 ST NE SUITE 10, CALGARY, AB,
T1Y 7G4

SIC 3651
CITY-CORE MESSENGER SERVICES LTDp
294
1185 GRANT ST, VANCOUVER, BC, V6A
2J7
(604) 254-9218   *SIC* 7389
CITYHOUSING FIRST PLACE HAMILTON *p*
611
350 KING ST E SUITE 300, HAMILTON, ON,
L8N 3Y3
(905) 525-9800   *SIC* 6531
CITYWIDE DOOR & HARDWARE INC   *p*
1030
80 VINYL CRT, WOODBRIDGE, ON, L4L
4A3
(905) 265-2444   *SIC* 5072
CIUSSS DE L'ESTRIE - CHUS   *p* 1371
*See CENTRE DE SANTE ET DE SER-
VICES SOCIAUX - INSTITUT UNIVERSI-*

TAIRE DE GERIATRIE DE SHERBROOKE
CIUSSS DE L'ESTRIE - CHUS   *p* 1371
*See CENTRE INTEGRE UNIVERSITAIRE
DE SANTE ET DE SERVICES SOCIAUX DE
L'ESTRIE*
**CIUSSS DE LA MAURICIE-ET-DU-CENTRE-
DU-QUEBEC**   *p*
1389
11931 RUE NOTRE-DAME O, TROIS-
RIVIERES, QC, G9B 6W9
(819) 377-2441   *SIC* 8069
**CIUSSS DU CENTRE-SUD-DE-L'ILE-DE-
MONTREAL**   *p*
1183
*See CENTRE INTEGRE UNIVERSI-
TAIRE SANTE ET SERVICES SOCIAUX
DU CENTRE-SUD-DE-L'ILE-DE-MONTREAL*
CIVEO CANADA LIMITED PARTNERSHIP *p*
113
3790 98 ST NW, EDMONTON, AB, T6E 6B4
(780) 463-8872   *SIC* 7389
CIVEO CORPORATION   *p* 113
3790 98 ST NW, EDMONTON, AB, T6E 6B4
(780) 463-8872   *SIC* 7021
CIVEO STRUCTURES INC   *p* 100
21216 113 AVE NW, EDMONTON, AB, T5S
1Y6
(780) 447-2333   *SIC* 1521
CIVIC HONDA D.D.O.   *p* 1091
See GARAGE CIVIC LIMITEE
CIVIC MOTORS LTD   *p* 820
1171 ST. LAURENT BLVD, OTTAWA, ON,
K1K 3B7
(613) 741-6676   *SIC* 5511
CIVIC POWER SPORTS   *p* 171
10111 107 ST, WESTLOCK, AB, T7P 1W9
(780) 349-5277   *SIC* 3949
CIVIC TIRE & BATTERY (WESTLOCK) LTD
p 172
10111 107 ST, WESTLOCK, AB, T7P 1W9
(780) 349-3351   *SIC* 5531
**CIVIL SERVICE SUPERANNUATION
BOARD**   *p* 377
444 ST MARY AVE SUITE 1200, WIN-
NIPEG, MB, R3C 3T1
(204) 946-3200   *SIC* 6371
CIWA   *p* 28
*See CALGARY IMMIGRANT WOMEN'S
ASSOCIATION*
CJ OILFIELD CONSTRUCTION LTD *p* 167
4607 42 ST, STETTLER, AB, T0C 2L0
(403) 742-1102   *SIC* 1541
CJBQ RADIO   *p* 491
*See QUINTE BROADCASTING COMPANY
LIMITED*
CJCB   *p* 458
*See MARITIME BROADCASTING SYSTEM
LIMITED*
CJMCQ   *p* 1386
*See CENTRE JEUNESSE DE LA
MAURICIE ET DU CENTRE-DU-QUEBEC,
LE*
CKB CONSTRUCTION (2004) LTD   *p* 100
10828 209 ST NW, EDMONTON, AB, T5S
1Z9
(780) 453-6611   *SIC* 1794
CKBL - FM   *p* 1425
See 629112 SASKATCHEWAN LTD
CKF INC   *p* 227
19878 57A AVE, LANGLEY, BC, V3A 6G6
(604) 530-9121   *SIC* 2821
CKF INC   *p* 459
48 PRINCE ST, HANTSPORT, NS, B0P 1P0
(902) 684-3231   *SIC* 3086
CKF INC   *p* 583
218 BELFIELD RD, ETOBICOKE, ON, M9W
1H3
(416) 249-4612   *SIC* 3086
CKF INC   *p* 583
30 IRON ST, ETOBICOKE, ON, M9W 5E1
(416) 249-2207   *SIC* 2679
CKMS-FM 100.3   *p* 1008
200 UNIVERSITY AVE W, WATERLOO, ON,
N2L 3G1

SIC 4832
CKNX AM   *p* 653
See BLACKBURN RADIO INC
CKNY-FM   *p* 330
See CORUS ENTERTAINMENT INC
CKR GLOBAL   *p* 766
*See XPERA RISK MITIGATION & INVESTI-
GATION LP*
CKRM NEWS   *p* 1417
1900 ROSE ST, REGINA, SK, S4P 0A9
(306) 546-6200   *SIC* 6794
CKRN (RADIO)   *p* 1289
See RNC MEDIA INC
CKST AM   *p* 326
See BELL MEDIA INC
CKWX NEWS   *p* 293
2440 ASH ST SUITE 1130, VANCOUVER,
BC, V5Z 4J6
(604) 873-2599   *SIC* 7383
CLAC   *p* 721
*See CHRISTIAN LABOUR ASSOCIATION
OF CANADA*
CLACE HOLDINGS LTD   *p* 335
903 YATES ST, VICTORIA, BC, V8V 3M4
(250) 381-6000   *SIC* 5411
CLAIMS MANAGEMENT SERVICES *p* 689
See SEDGWICK CMS CANADA INC
CLAIMSECURE INC   *p* 709
1 CITY CENTRE DR SUITE 620, MISSIS-
SAUGA, ON, L5B 1M2
(705) 673-2541   *SIC* 6324
CLAIMSECURE INC   *p* 899
40 ELM ST SUITE 225, SUDBURY, ON, P3C
0A2
(705) 673-2541   *SIC* 6324
CLAIMSPRO   *p* 125
See SCM INSURANCE SERVICES INC
CLAIMSPRO LP   *p* 693
1550 ENTERPRISE RD SUITE 310, MIS-
SISSAUGA, ON, L4W 4P4
(905) 671-0185   *SIC* 6411
CLAIR DE LUNE   *p* 1340
See PRODUITS CLAIR DE LUNE INC
CLAIR FOYER INC   *p* 1046
841 3E RUE O, AMOS, QC, J9T 2T4
(819) 732-6511   *SIC* 8361
**CLAIR INDUSTRIAL DEVELOPMENT COR-
PORATION LTD**   *p*
397
14 AV 2 IEME INDUSTRIEL, CLAIR, NB,
E7A 2B1
(506) 992-2152   *SIC* 2429
CLAIRE'S STORES CANADA CORP *p* 986
100 KING ST W SUITE 6600, TORONTO,
ON, M5X 2A1
(800) 252-4737   *SIC* 5632
CLAIRO PRECISION   *p* 1232
See RTI-CLARO INC
CLAIRVEST GROUP INC   *p* 925
22 ST CLAIR AVE E SUITE 1700,
TORONTO, ON, M4T 2S3
(416) 925-9270   *SIC* 6726
CLAN PANNETON (1993) INC, LE   *p* 1216
2660 RUE MULLINS, MONTREAL, QC, H3K
1P4
(514) 937-0707   *SIC* 4214
CLARA INDUSTRIAL SERVICES LIMITEDp
910
1130 COMMERCE ST, THUNDER BAY, ON,
P7E 6E9
(807) 475-4608   *SIC* 1721
CLARE'S CYCLE & SPORTS LTD   *p* 590
799 HWY 20, FENWICK, ON, L0S 1C0
(905) 892-2664   *SIC* 5571
CLAREMONT SECONDARY SCHOOLp 338
See SCHOOL DISTRICT 63 (SAANICH)
CLARENCE ENTERPRISES LIMITED *p* 465
10029 HIGHWAY 1, SAULNIERVILLE, NS,
B0W 2Z0
(902) 769-3458   *SIC* 5411
CLARENCE FARM SERVICES LIMITED *p*
468
70 INDUSTRIAL AVE, TRURO, NS, B2N
6V2

(902) 895-5434 *SIC* 2048
CLARENCE FULTON SECONDARY SCHOOL *p* 331
See SCHOOL DISTRICT NO 22 (VERNON)
CLARENCE SHOPPING MART *p* 465
See CLARENCE ENTERPRISES LIMITED
CLARENDON FOUNDATION (CHESHIRE HOMES) INC *p* 933
25 HENRY LANE TERR SUITE 442, TORONTO, ON, M5A 4B6
SIC 8699
CLARENVILLE AREA CONSUMERS CO-OPERATIVE SOCIETY LTD *p* 421
238 MEMORIAL DR, CLARENVILLE, NL, A5A 1N9
(709) 466-2622 *SIC* 5411
CLARIANT (CANADA) INC *p* 1333
4600 RUE COUSENS, SAINT-LAURENT, QC, H4S 1X3
(514) 334-1117 *SIC* 5169
CLARIANT PLASTICS & COATINGS CANADA INC *p*
2 LONE OAK CRT, ETOBICOKE, ON, M9C 5R9
(416) 847-7000 *SIC* 5169
CLARICA LIFE INSURANCE COMPANY *p* 1019
3200 DEZIEL DR SUITE 508, WINDSOR, ON, N8W 5K8
(519) 974-3200 *SIC* 6311
CLARIDGE HOMES CORPORATION *p* 833
210 GLADSTONE AVE SUITE 2001, OTTAWA, ON, K2P 0Y6
(613) 233-6030 *SIC* 6553
CLARINGTON CENTRAL SECONDARY SCHOOL *p* 496
See KAWARTHA PINE RIDGE SCHOOL BOARD
CLARINGTON HONDA AUTO POWERHOUSE *p* 496
See CLAYTON AUTOMOTIVE GROUP INC
CLARINS CANADA INC *p* 1363
815 CHOMEDEY (A-13) E, SAINTE-ROSE, QC, H7W 5N4
(450) 688-0144 *SIC* 5122
CLARINS SKIN SPA *p* 1363
See CLARINS CANADA INC
CLARION CANADA INC *p* 796
2239 WINSTON PARK DR, OAKVILLE, ON, L6H 5R1
(905) 829-4600 *SIC* 5064
CLARION HOTEL QUEBEC *p* 1274
See 9187-7571 QUEBEC INC
CLARION MEDICAL TECHNOLOGIES INC *p* 535
125 FLEMING DR, CAMBRIDGE, ON, N1T 2B8
(519) 620-3900 *SIC* 5047
CLARION NURSING HOMES LIMITED *p* 893
337 HIGHWAY 8, STONEY CREEK, ON, L8G 1E7
(905) 664-2281 *SIC* 8051
CLARION RESORT *p* 762
See BLACK SAXON III INC
CLARIUS MOBILE HEALTH CORP *p* 188
3605 GILMORE WAY SUITE 350, BURNABY, BC, V5G 4X5
(778) 800-9975 *SIC* 3829
CLARK *p* 1047
See ALIMENTS OUIMET-CORDON BLEU INC
CLARK AG SYSTEMS LTD *p* 532
186 GREENS RD, CALEDONIA, ON, N3W 1X2
(905) 765-4401 *SIC* 5083
CLARK BUILDERS *p* 108
See CB PARTNERS CORPORATION
CLARK COMPANIES *p* 532
See CLARK AG SYSTEMS LTD
CLARK CONSTRUCTION *p* 3
See 330558 ALBERTA LTD

CLARK CONSTRUCTION *p* 136
GD STN MAIN, HINTON, AB, T7V 1T9
(780) 865-5822 *SIC* 1389
CLARK OIL CO. LTD *p* 419
GD STN MAIN, WOODSTOCK, NB, E7M 6B9
(506) 328-3243 *SIC* 5172
CLARK TOYOTA *p* 400
See CLARK, JIM MOTORS LTD
CLARK'S AUTO CENTRE LTD *p* 1042
110 WALKER AVE, SUMMERSIDE, PE, C1N 6V9
(902) 436-5800 *SIC* 5511
CLARK'S CHEVROLET CADILLAC *p* 400
See CLARK, J & SON LIMITED
CLARK'S SUPPLY AND SERVICE LTD *p* 1410
1650 STADACONA ST W, MOOSE JAW, SK, S6H 4P8
(306) 693-4334 *SIC* 5084
CLARK'S TOYOTA *p* 1042
See CLARK'S AUTO CENTRE LTD
CLARK, DROUIN, LEFEBVRE INC *p* 1064
1301 RUE GAY-LUSSAC, BOUCHERVILLE, QC, J4B 7K1
(450) 449-4171 *SIC* 5141
CLARK, H. PHARMACY INC *p* 880
454 NORFOLK ST S, SIMCOE, ON, N3Y 2X3
(519) 426-6580 *SIC* 5912
CLARK, J & SON LIMITED *p* 400
820 PROSPECT ST, FREDERICTON, NB, E3B 4Z2
(506) 452-1010 *SIC* 5511
CLARK, JIM MOTORS LTD *p* 400
35 ALISON BLVD, FREDERICTON, NB, E3B 4Z9
(506) 452-2200 *SIC* 5511
CLARK, KENNEDY COMPANY, LIMITED *p* 580
15 LEADING RD, ETOBICOKE, ON, M9V 4B7
(416) 743-5911 *SIC* 5084
CLARK, RON AND ASSOCIATES (2006) INC *p* 280
2195 KING GEORGE BLVD, SURREY, BC, V4A 5A3
SIC 1542
CLARKDALE MOTORS LTD *p* 290
4575 MAIN ST, VANCOUVER, BC, V5V 3R4
(604) 872-5431 *SIC* 5511
CLARKDALE VOLKSWAGEN *p* 290
See CLARKDALE MOTORS LTD
CLARKE ROLLER & RUBBER LIMITED *p* 601
485 SOUTHGATE DR, GUELPH, ON, N1G 3W6
(519) 763-7655 *SIC* 5169
CLARKE ROLLER & RUBBER LIMITED *p* 738
6225 KENNEDY RD, MISSISSAUGA, ON, L5T 2S8
(905) 564-3215 *SIC* 3069
CLARKE TRANSPORT *p* 550
See CLARKE TRANSPORT INC
CLARKE TRANSPORT INC *p* 501
201 WESTCREEK BLVD SUITE 200, BRAMPTON, ON, L6T 5S6
(905) 291-3000 *SIC* 4731
CLARKE TRANSPORT INC *p* 550
751 BOWES RD SUITE 2, CONCORD, ON, L4K 5C9
(416) 665-5585 *SIC* 4213
CLARKE, DOUGLAS K INSURANCE BROKERS LIMITED *p* 668
151 ESNA PARK DR SUITE 26, MARKHAM, ON, L3R 3B1
SIC 6311
CLARKSDALE PUBLIC SCHOOL *p* 529
See HALTON DISTRICT SCHOOL BOARD
CLARKSON CONSTRUCTION COMPANY LIMITED *p* 803
1224 SPEERS RD, OAKVILLE, ON, L6L 5B6

(905) 827-4167 *SIC* 8721
CLARKSON DIV *p* 714
See PPG CANADA INC
CLARKSON SECONDARY SCHOOL *p* 714
See PEEL DISTRICT SCHOOL BOARD
CLAROCITY CORPORATION *p* 34
6940 FISHER RD SE SUITE 200, CALGARY, AB, T2H 0W3
(403) 984-9246 *SIC* 7374
CLASS 1 *p* 538
See CLASS 1 INCORPORATED
CLASS 1 INCORPORATED *p* 538
565 BOXWOOD DR, CAMBRIDGE, ON, N3E 1A5
(519) 650-2355 *SIC* 3841
CLASSE AUDIO INC *p* 1127
5070 RUE FRANCOIS-CUSSON, LACHINE, QC, H8T 1B3
(514) 636-6384 *SIC* 3699
CLASSIC CARE PHARMACY CORPORATION *p* 521
1320 HEINE CRT, BURLINGTON, ON, L7L 6L9
(905) 631 9027 *SIC* 5999
CLASSIC COMMUNITIES *p* 145
See CLASSIC CONSTRUCTION LTD
CLASSIC CONSTRUCTION LTD *p* 145
671 INDUSTRIAL AVE SE, MEDICINE HAT, AB, T1A 3L5
(403) 528-2793 *SIC* 1522
CLASSIC DENTAL LABORATORIES LTD *p* 66
115 17 AVE SW, CALGARY, AB, T2S 0A1
(403) 228-5120 *SIC* 8072
CLASSIC DODGE CHRYSLER INC *p* 486
145 BRADFORD ST, BARRIE, ON, L4N 3B2
(705) 795-1431 *SIC* 5511
CLASSIC FIRE PROTECTION INC *p* 792
645 GARYRAY DR, NORTH YORK, ON, M9L 1P9
(416) 740-3000 *SIC* 7389
CLASSIC FIREPLACE DISTRIBUTORS & CENTRAL AIR HEATING & AIR CONDITIONING *p* 71
See LENNOX INDUSTRIES (CANADA) LTD
CLASSIC FREIGHT *p* 445
See CLASSIC FREIGHT SYSTEMS (2011) LIMITED
CLASSIC FREIGHT SYSTEMS (2011) LIMITED *p* 445
50 JOSEPH ZATZMAN DR, DARTMOUTH, NS, B3B 1N8
(902) 481-3701 *SIC* 4213
CLASSIC HONDA *p* 512
See 985178 ONTARIO INC
CLASSIC KITCHENS & CABINETS LIMITED *p* 22
1122 40 AVE NE, CALGARY, AB, T2E 5T8
(403) 250-9470 *SIC* 2434
CLASSIC PACKAGING CORPORATION *p* 200
1580 BRIGANTINE DR SUITE 100, COQUITLAM, BC, V3K 7C1
(604) 523-6700 *SIC* 7389
CLASSIC TILE CONTRACTORS LIMITED *p* 521
1175 APPLEBY LINE UNIT B2, BURLINGTON, ON, L7L 5H9
(905) 335-1700 *SIC* 1752
CLASSICO GOURMET *p* 776
See KRAFT HEINZ CANADA ULC
CLAUDE AUTO (1984) INC *p* 1154
330 BOUL ALBINY-PAQUETTE, MONT-LAURIER, QC, J9L 1J9
(819) 623-3511 *SIC* 5511
CLAUDE CROTEAU ET FILLES INC *p* 1384
500 RUE BARKOFF, TROIS-RIVIERES, QC, G8T 9P5
(819) 379-4566 *SIC* 5651
CLAUDE L'HEUREUX HOLDINGS INC *p*

811
3910 INNES RD SUITE 422, ORLEANS, ON, K1W 1K9
(613) 830-7000 *SIC* 5531
CLAUDE NEON LIMITEE *p* 1249
1868 BOUL DES SOURCES BUREAU 200, POINTE-CLAIRE, QC, H9R 5R2
(514) 693-9436 *SIC* 3993
CLAUDE RESOURCES INC *p* 1408
1112 FINLAYSON ST, LA RONGE, SK, S0J 1L0
(306) 635-2015 *SIC* 1041
CLAUDE RESOURCES INC *p* 1408
GD, LA RONGE, SK, S0J 1L0
(306) 635-2015 *SIC* 1041
CLAUDE RESOURCES INC *p* 1431
2100 AIRPORT DR SUITE 202, SASKATOON, SK, S7L 6M6
(306) 668-7505 *SIC* 1041
CLAVIERS MEMTRONIK, LES *p* 1170
See MEMTRONIK INNOVATIONS INC
CLAYBAR CONTRACTING INC *p* 566
424 MACNAB ST, DUNDAS, ON, L9H 2L3
(905) 627-8000 *SIC* 1799
CLAYBURN INDUSTRIES LTD *p* 174
33765 PINE ST, ABBOTSFORD, BC, V2S 5C1
(604) 859-5288 *SIC* 3255
CLAYBURN REFRACTORIES *p* 174
See CLAYBURN INDUSTRIES LTD
CLAYTON AUTOMOTIVE GROUP INC *p* 496
29 SPICER SQ, BOWMANVILLE, ON, L1C 5M2
(905) 697-2333 *SIC* 5511
CLAYTON'S HERITAGE MARKET *p* 268
See TRAIL BAY DEVELOPMENTS LTD
CLB MEDIA INC *p* 480
240 EDWARD ST SUITE 1, AURORA, ON, L4G 3S9
SIC 2721
CLC *p* 826
See CANADIAN LABOUR CONGRESS
CLDH MEADOWVALE INC *p* 721
6750 MISSISSAUGA RD, MISSISSAUGA, ON, L5N 2L3
(905) 826-0940 *SIC* 7011
CLE CAPITAL INC *p* 1386
2200 RUE DE LA SIDBEC S, TROIS-RIVIERES, QC, G8Z 4H1
(819) 373-8000 *SIC* 6159
CLEAN ENERGY COMPRESSION *p* 197
See IMW INDUSTRIES INC
CLEAN HARBORS CANADA INC *p* 563
4090 TELFER RD, CORUNNA, ON, N0N 1G0
(519) 864-1021 *SIC* 4953
CLEAN HARBORS ENERGY AND INDUSTRIAL SERVICES CORP *p* 127
26 AIRPORT RD, FORT MCMURRAY, AB, T9H 5B4
(780) 743-0222 *SIC* 7349
CLEAN HARBORS ENERGY AND INDUSTRIAL SERVICES CORP *p* 139
3902 77 AVE, LEDUC, AB, T9E 0B6
(780) 980-1868 *SIC* 7349
CLEAN HARBORS ENERGY AND INDUSTRIAL SERVICES CORP *p* 159
235133 RYAN RD, ROCKY VIEW COUNTY, AB, T1X 0K1
(403) 236-9891 *SIC* 7349
CLEAN HARBORS SURFACE RENTALS PARTNERSHIP *p* 46
222 3 AVE SW SUITE 900, CALGARY, AB, T2P 0B4
(403) 543-7325 *SIC* 1389
CLEAN HARBORS SURFACE RENTALS PARTNERSHIP *p* 139
3902 77 AVE, LEDUC, AB, T9E 0B6
(780) 980-1868 *SIC* 1389
CLEAN PROPREMENT FAIT *p* 1140
See SERVICE D'ENTRETIEN CLEAN IN-

TERNATIONAL INC

CLEAN WATER WORKS INC   *p 815*
1800 BANTREE ST, OTTAWA, ON, K1B 5L6
(613) 745-2444   *SIC 1623*
CLEAN-BRITE SERVICES OF REGINA LTD
p 1420
1201 OSLER ST, REGINA, SK, S4R 1W4
(306) 352-9953   *SIC 7349*
CLEANMARK GROUP INC   *p 950*
141 ADELAIDE ST W SUITE 1000, TORONTO, ON, M5H 3L5
(416) 364-0677   *SIC 7349*
CLEANRIVER RECYCLING SOLUTIONS INC   *p 480*
189 EARL STEWART DR UNIT 1, AURORA, ON, L4G 6V5
(905) 717-4984   *SIC 4953*
CLEANTEK INDUSTRIES INC   *p 160*
261106 WAGON WHEEL CRES SUITE 1, ROCKY VIEW COUNTY, AB, T4A 0E2
(403) 567-8700   *SIC 1389*
CLEAR PACIFIC TRADING LTD   *p 263*
12160 HORSESHOE WAY SUITE 120, RICHMOND, BC, V7A 4V5
   SIC 5146
CLEAR VIEW HOME FURNISHINGS LTD *p 413*
428 ROTHESAY AVE, SAINT JOHN, NB, E2J 2C4
(506) 634-1966   *SIC 5712*
CLEARBROOK GRAIN & MILLING COMPANY LIMITED   *p 176*
2425 TOWNLINE RD, ABBOTSFORD, BC, V2T 6L6
(604) 850-1108   *SIC 2048*
CLEARBROOK PLAZA   *p 176*
See IMAGE PLUS
CLEARDALE COLONY   *p 80*
See HUTTERIAN BRETHREN CHURCH OF CLEARDALE
CLEARESULT CANADA INC   *p 944*
393 UNIVERSITY AVE SUITE 1622, TORONTO, ON, M5G 1E6
(416) 504-3400   *SIC 8711*
CLEARPATH ROBOTICS INC   *p 642*
1425 STRASBURG RD UNIT 2A, KITCHENER, ON, N2R 1H2
(519) 513-2416   *SIC 8742*
CLEARSTREAM ENERGY SERVICES INC *p 46*
311 6 AVE SW SUITE 415, CALGARY, AB, T2P 3H2
(587) 318-0997   *SIC 8741*
CLEARSTREAM ENERGY SERVICES LIMITED PARTNERSHIP   *p 80*
141 2 AVE E, COCHRANE, AB, T4C 2B9
(403) 932-9565   *SIC 1389*
CLEARSTREAM TRANSPORTATION SERVICES LP   *p 108*
7809 34 ST NW, EDMONTON, AB, T6B 2V5
(780) 410-1960   *SIC 1389*
CLEARTECH HOLDINGS LTD   *p 1426*
1500 QUEBEC AVE, SASKATOON, SK, S7K 1V7
(306) 664-2522   *SIC 6712*
CLEARTECH INDUSTRIES INC   *p 105*
12720 INLAND WAY NW, EDMONTON, AB, T5V 1K2
(800) 387-7503   *SIC 2819*
CLEARTECH INDUSTRIES INC   *p 1426*
1500 QUEBEC AVE, SASKATOON, SK, S7K 1V7
(306) 664-2522   *SIC 2819*
CLEARTECH INDUSTRIES LIMITED PARTNERSHIP   *p 1426*
1500 QUEBEC AVE, SASKATOON, SK, S7K 1V7
(306) 664-2522   *SIC 5169*
CLEARVIEW COLONY LTD   *p 349*
GD, ELM CREEK, MB, R0G 0N0

(204) 436-2187   *SIC 5211*
CLEARVIEW CONSUMER CO-OP LTD *p 358*
365 PTH 12 N, STEINBACH, MB, R5G 1V1
(204) 346-2667   *SIC 5411*
CLEARVIEW HORTICULTURAL PRODUCTS INC   *p 229*
5343A 264 ST SUITE 1, LANGLEY, BC, V4W 1J7
(604) 856-6131   *SIC 5992*
CLEARVIEW INDUSTRIES LTD   *p 792*
45 FENMAR DR, NORTH YORK, ON, M9L 1M1
(416) 745-6666   *SIC 3442*
CLEARVIEW PATIO DOORS   *p 792*
See CLEARVIEW INDUSTRIES LTD
CLEARWATER ARCTIC SURF CLAM COMPANY, DIV OF   *p 439*
See CLEARWATER SEAFOODS LIMITED PARTNERSHIP
CLEARWATER DEEP SEA TRAWLERS *p 462*
See THORNVALE HOLDINGS LIMITED
CLEARWATER ENERGY SERVICES LP *p 127*
355 MACKENZIE BLVD, FORT MCMURRAY, AB, T9H 5E2
(780) 743-2171   *SIC 1541*
CLEARWATER FABRICATION   *p 122*
See CLEARWATER FABRICATION GP INC
CLEARWATER FABRICATION GP INC *p 122*
5710 17 ST NW, EDMONTON, AB, T6P 1S4
(780) 464-4230   *SIC 1791*
CLEARWATER FINE FOODS   *p 440*
See THORNVALE HOLDINGS LIMITED
CLEARWATER SEAFOOD   *p 423*
See CLEARWATER SEAFOODS LIMITED PARTNERSHIP
CLEARWATER SEAFOODS   *p 439*
See CLEARWATER SEAFOODS HOLDINGS INC
CLEARWATER SEAFOODS HOLDINGS INC   *p 439*
757 BEDFORD HWY, BEDFORD, NS, B4A 3Z7
(902) 443-0550   *SIC 2092*
CLEARWATER SEAFOODS LIMITED PARTNERSHIP   *p 423*
1 PLANT RD, GRAND BANK, NL, A0E 1W0
(709) 832-1550   *SIC 5146*
CLEARWATER SEAFOODS LIMITED PARTNERSHIP   *p 439*
757 BEDFORD HWY, BEDFORD, NS, B4A 3Z7
(902) 443-0550   *SIC 2092*
CLEARWAY CONSTRUCTION INC   *p 550*
379 BOWES RD, CONCORD, ON, L4K 1J1
(905) 761-6955   *SIC 1623*
CLEARWAY GROUP   *p 559*
See TESTON PIPELINES LIMITED
CLEARWEST SOLUTIONS INC   *p 226*
8700 200 ST SUITE 310, LANGLEY, BC, V2Y 0G4
(604) 888-5050   *SIC 5999*
CLEAVER-BROOKS OF CANADA LIMITED   *p 895*
161 LORNE AVE W, STRATFORD, ON, N5A 6S4
(519) 271-9220   *SIC 3443*
CLEF DE SOL INC, LA   *p 1277*
445 AV SAINT-JEAN-BAPTISTE BUREAU 220, QUEBEC, QC, G2E 5N7
(418) 627-0840   *SIC 5999*
CLEF DES CHAMPS, LA   *p 1391*
See HERBORISTERIE LA CLEF DES CHAMPS INC
CLEMENT FOODS LTD   *p 385*
1881 PORTAGE AVE, WINNIPEG, MB, R3J 0H3

(204) 988-4810   *SIC 5411*
CLEMENT GAGNON ET JACINTHE DESJARDINS, PHARMACIENS (S.E.N.C.) *p 1242*
145 CH CYR, NEW RICHMOND, QC, G0C 2B0
(418) 392-4451   *SIC 5912*
CLEMENT, CHRYSLER DODGE LTEE *p 1146*
77 RUE DE L'EGLISE N, LORRAINVILLE, QC, J0Z 2R0
(819) 625-2187   *SIC 5511*
CLERMOND HAMEL LTEE   *p 1299*
25 7E RANG S, SAINT-EPHREM-DE-BEAUCE, QC, G0M 1R0
(418) 484-2888   *SIC 2421*
CLERMONT   *p 1075*
See 141517 CANADA LTEE
CLERMONT, MARIETTE INC   *p 1236*
2300 BOUL LE CORBUSIER, MONTREAL, QC, H7S 2C9
(450) 934-7502   *SIC 5712*
CLEVE'S SPORTING GOODS LIMITED *p 445*
30 THORNHILL DR, DARTMOUTH, NS, B3B 1S1
(902) 468-1885   *SIC 5941*
CLEVE'S SPORTING GOODS LIMITED *p 471*
76 STARRS RD, YARMOUTH, NS, B5A 2T5
(902) 742-8135   *SIC 5941*
CLEVELAND RANGE LTD   *p 550*
8251 KEELE ST, CONCORD, ON, L4K 1Z1
(905) 660-4747   *SIC 3589*
CLEVEST SOLUTIONS INC   *p 254*
13700 INTERNATIONAL PL SUITE 200, RICHMOND, BC, V6V 2X8
(604) 214-9700   *SIC 7371*
CLHIA   *p 969*
See CANADIAN LIFE AND HEALTH INSURANCE ASSOCIATION INC
CLHIO   *p 937*
See CANADIAN LIFE AND HEALTH INSURANCE OMBUDSERVICE
CLI GROUP   *p 843*
See CENTRE LEASEHOLD IMPROVEMENTS LIMITED
CLIANTHA RESEARCH   *p 696*
See INFLAMAX RESEARCH LIMITED
CLIC   *p 1371*
See CENTRE DE LANGUES INTERNATIONALES CHARPENTIER
CLICKFREE AUTOMATIC BACK UP *p 854*
See STORAGE APPLIANCE CORPORATION
CLIENTLOGIC   *p 409*
See SITEL CANADA CORPORATION
CLIFF TOWING   *p 95*
See CTS EQUIPMENT TRANSPORT LTD
CLIFFORD MASONRY (ONTARIO) LIMITED *p 870*
1190 BIRCHMOUNT RD, SCARBOROUGH, ON, M1P 2B8
(416) 691-2341   *SIC 1542*
CLIFFORD RESTORATION LIMITED *p 871*
1190 BIRCHMOUNT RD, SCARBOROUGH, ON, M1P 2B8
(416) 691-2341   *SIC 1542*
CLIFFS RESSOURCES NATURELLES *p 1367*
See MINES WABUSH
CLIFTON ASSOCIATES LTD   *p 1415*
340 MAXWELL CRES, REGINA, SK, S4N 5Y5
(306) 721-7611   *SIC 8711*
CLIMAT-CONTROL PL   *p 1141*
See CLIMAT-CONTROL SB INC
CLIMAT-CONTROL SB INC   *p 1141*
800 RUE JEAN-NEVEU, LONGUEUIL, QC, J4G 2M1
(514) 789-0456   *SIC 1711*
CLIMATE CHANGE EMISSIONS MANAGEMENT (CCEMC) CORPORATION *p 162*

300 PALISADES WAY, SHERWOOD PARK, AB, T8H 2T9
(780) 417-1920   *SIC 7389*
CLIMATISATION BEAUBIEN   *p 1169*
See QUINCAILLERIE BEAUBIEN INC
CLIMATISATION VALLEE & FILS INC *p 1282*
83 RUE LAROCHE, REPENTIGNY, QC, J6A 7M3
(450) 581-4360   *SIC 1711*
CLINIC PHARMACY   *p 812*
See C H S PHARMACY LIMITED
CLINICAL RESEARCH DENTAL SUPPLIES & SERVICES INC   *p 653*
167 CENTRAL AVE SUITE 200, LONDON, ON, N6A 1M6
(519) 641-3066   *SIC 5047*
CLINIQUE COMMUNAUTAIRE POINTE-ST-CHARLES   *p 1216*
500 AV ASH, MONTREAL, QC, H3K 2R4
(514) 937-9251   *SIC 8011*
CLINIQUE D'OPTOMETRIE IRIS   *p 1289*
See 9085-7160 QUEBEC INC
CLINIQUE D'OPTOMETRIE MIOSIS *p 1106*
See GROUPE MIOSIS, S.E.N.C.R.L.
CLINIQUE DE PHYSIOTHERAPIE LAVALTRIE ENR.   *p 1134*
See 9006-5855 QUEBEC INC
CLINIQUE DE PREVENTION EN SEXUALITE   *p 1368*
See CENTRE HOSPITALIER DU CENTRE LA MAURICIE
CLINIQUE DE RECHERCHE DES TRAITEMENTS HORMONAUX   *p 1272*
See ENDOCEUTICS INC
CLINIQUE DU PIED EQUILIBRE   *p 1237*
See LABORATOIRE VICTHOM INC
CLINIQUE MEDICALE FUSEY   *p 1385*
See JEAN-FRANCOIS GAUTHIER ET ALEXANDRE RIVARD, PHARMACIENS S.E.N.C
CLINIQUE OPTOMETRIE DE SHERBROOKE   *p 1371*
See OPTAGEX INC
CLINIQUE SANTE VOYAGE SAINT-LUC *p 1175*
1560 RUE SHERBROOKE E, MONTREAL, QC, H2L 4M1
(514) 890-8332   *SIC 4724*
CLINTON PUBLIC HOSPITAL, THE *p 544*
See HURON PERTH HEALTHCARE ALLIANCE
CLINTON PUBLIC HOSPITAL, THE *p 896*
See HURON PERTH HEALTHCARE ALLIANCE
CLIO   *p 189*
See THEMIS SOLUTIONS INC
CLIO/OZ   *p 789*
See MAINLINE FASHIONS INC
CLIPPER CONSTRUCTION LIMITED *p 501*
16 MELANIE DR SUITE 200, BRAMPTON, ON, L6T 4K9
(905) 790-2333   *SIC 1794*
CLIVENCO INC   *p 1263*
1185 RUE PHILIPPE-PARADIS BUREAU 200, QUEBEC, QC, G1N 4E2
(418) 682-6373   *SIC 1711*
CLKL   *p 634*
See COMMUNITY LIVING KIRKLAND LAKE
CLOC   *p 812*
See COMMUNITY LIVING OSHAWA/CLARINGTON
CLOROX COMPANY OF CANADA, LTD, THE   *p 509*
150 BISCAYNE CRES, BRAMPTON, ON, L6W 4V3
(905) 595-8200   *SIC 5169*
CLOROX COMPANY OF CANADA, LTD,

THE *p 808*
101 JOHN ST, ORANGEVILLE, ON, L9W 2R1
(519) 941-0720 *SIC 2673*

CLOSE TO HOME *p 73*
3507 17 AVE SW SUITE A, CALGARY, AB, T3E 0B6
(403) 543-0550 *SIC 8699*

CLOSER TO HOME COMMUNITY SERVICE *p 73*
See CLOSE TO HOME

CLOSING THE GAP HEALTHCARE GROUP INC *p 693*
2810 MATHESON BLVD E SUITE 100, MISSISSAUGA, ON, L4W 4X7
(905) 306-0202 *SIC 8059*

CLOTHES OUT TRADING *p 789*
See DACURY AGENCIES CORPORATION

CLOTURE SPEC-II INC *p 1064*
65 RUE DE MONTGOLFIER, BOUCHERVILLE, QC, J4B 8C4
(450) 449-7732 *SIC 5039*

CLOTURES ARBOIT INC, LES *p 1120*
230 RUE ARBOIT, L'ASSOMPTION, QC, J5W 4P5
(450) 589-8484 *SIC 3273*

CLOTURES JERMAR INC. *p 1394*
877 RTE HARWOOD, VAUDREUIL-DORION, QC, J7V 8P2
(450) 732-1121 *SIC 5039*

CLOUD-RIDER DESIGNS LTD *p 1420*
1260 8TH AVE, REGINA, SK, S4R 1C9
(306) 761-2119 *SIC 3429*

CLOUMATIC *p 1319*
See 2969-9477 QUEBEC INC

CLOUTHIER, BILL & SONS LTD *p 838*
17 BRANDON AVE, PEMBROKE, ON, K8A 6W5
(613) 735-4194 *SIC 5511*

CLOUTIER, EUGENE INC *p 1281*
1659 RUE DES ROSELINS, QUEBEC, QC, G3E 1G2
(418) 842-2087 *SIC 3131*

CLOUTIER, N. V. INC *p 1371*
2550 RUE KING O, SHERBROOKE, QC, J1J 2H1
(819) 346-3911 *SIC 5511*

CLOVER INSURANCE GROUP *p 1030*
3800 STEELES AVE W SUITE 201, WOODBRIDGE, ON, L4L 4G9
(905) 851-7774 *SIC 6411*

CLOVER LEAF CHEESE *p 22*
See CLOVER LEAF CHEESE LTD

CLOVER LEAF CHEESE LTD *p 22*
1201 45 AVE NE, CALGARY, AB, T2E 2P2
(403) 250-3780 *SIC 5143*

CLOVER TOOL MANUFACTURING LTD *p 550*
8271 KEELE ST SUITE 3, CONCORD, ON, L4K 1Z1
(905) 669-1999 *SIC 3469*

CLOVERDALE INVESTMENTS LTD *p 279*
2630 CROYDON DR STE 400, SURREY, BC, V3Z 6T3
(604) 594-6211 *SIC 6712*

CLOVERDALE PAINT INC *p 279*
2630 CROYDON DR UNIT 400, SURREY, BC, V3Z 6T3
(604) 596-6261 *SIC 2851*

CLOVERLEAF GROCERY *p 569*
See CLOVERLEAF GROCERY (EMO) LIMITED

CLOVERLEAF GROCERY (EMO) LIMITED *p 569*
5970 HWY 11, EMO, ON, P0W 1E0
(807) 482-2793 *SIC 5411*

CLOVIS ISABELLE ET FILS INC. *p 1348*
2420 RUE PRINCIPALE, SAINT-MICHEL, QC, J0L 2J0
(450) 454-7200 *SIC 0161*

CLOW CANADA INC *p 609*
1757 BURLINGTON ST E, HAMILTON, ON, L8H 3L5
(905) 548-9604 *SIC 5085*

CLS CATERING *p 728*
See CLS CATERING SERVICES LTD

CLS CATERING SERVICES LTD *p 264*
3560 JERICHO RD, RICHMOND, BC, V7B 1C2
(604) 273-4438 *SIC 5812*

CLS CATERING SERVICES LTD *p 728*
2950 CONVAIR DR, MISSISSAUGA, ON, L5P 1A2
(905) 676-3218 *SIC 5812*

CLSC BASSE-VILLE LIMOILOU VANIER *p 1258*
See CENTRE DE SANTE ET DE SERVICES SOCIAUX DE LA VIEILLE-CAPITALE

CLSC DE BELLECHASSE SOCIAL *p 1343*
100A RUE MONSEIGNEUR-BILODEAU, SAINT-LAZARE-DE-BELLECHASSE, QC, G0R 3J0
(418) 883-2227 *SIC 8399*

CLSC DE DORVAL-LACHINE *p 1126*
See CENTRE DE SANTE ET DE SERVICES SOCIAUX DE DORVAL-LACHINE-LASALLE

CLSC DE SAINT JEROME *p 1321*
See GOUVERNEMENT DE LA PROVINCE DE QUEBEC

CLSC DE SAINT-FABIEN-DE-PANET *p 1302*
See CENTRE DE SANTE ET SERVICES SOCIAUX DE MONTMAGNY - L'ISLET

CLSC DE SAINT-MICHEL *p 1169*
3355 RUE JARRY E, MONTREAL, QC, H1Z 2E5
(514) 374-8223 *SIC 8399*

CLSC ET CENTRE D'HEBERGEMENT PETITE-NATION *p 1291*
See CENTRE DE SANTE ET SERVICES SOCIAUX DE PAPINEAU

CLSC JEAN-OLIVIER-CHENIER *p 1301*
See CENTRE INTEGRE DE SANTE ET DE SERVICES SOCIAUX DES LAURENTIDES

CLSC LA SOURCE *p 1256*
See CENTRE DE SANTE ET DE SERVICES SOCIAUX DE QUEBEC-NORD

CLSC LAMATER DE TERREBONNE *p 1379*
See CENTRE INTEGRE DE SANTE ET DE SERVICES SOCIAUX DE LANAUDIERE

CLSC LES ESKERS *p 1046*
See CENTRE DE SANTE ET DE SERVICE SOCIAUX LES ESKERS DE L'ABITIBI

CLSC ORLEANS *p 1055*
See CENTRE DE SANTE ET DE SERVICES SOCIAUX DE QUEBEC-NORD

CLSC SIMONNE-MONET-CHARTRAND *p 1145*
1303 BOUL JACQUES-CARTIER E, LONGUEUIL, QC, J4M 2Y8
(450) 463-2850 *SIC 8399*

CLSC-CHSLD D'AUTRAY *p 1357*
2410 RUE PRINCIPALE, SAINTE-ELISABETH, QC, J0K 2J0
(450) 759-8355 *SIC 7389*

CLSC-CHSLD DU RUISSEAU-PAPINEAU *p 1241*
See CENTRE DE SANTE ET DE SERVICES SOCIAUX DE LAVAL

CLSC-CHSLD THERESE DE BLAINVILLE *p 1287*
365 CH DE LA GRANDE-COTE, ROSEMERE, QC, J7A 1K4
(450) 621-3760 *SIC 8361*

CLT INTERNATIONAL *p 864*
See CLT LOGISTICS, INC

CLT LOGISTICS, INC *p 864*
5900 FINCH AVE E, SCARBOROUGH, ON, M1B 5P8
(416) 686-4199 *SIC 5122*

CLUB AT BOND HEAD, THE *p 490*
See BOND HEAD GOLF RESORT INC

CLUB AUTO ROADSIDE SERVICES LTD *p 904*
60 COMMERCE VALLEY DR E, THORNHILL, ON, L3T 7P9
(905) 771-4001 *SIC 7549*

CLUB COFFEE L.P. *p 583*
55 CARRIER DR SUITE 1, ETOBICOKE, ON, M9W 5V9
(416) 675-1300 *SIC 5149*

CLUB COOP D'AMOS *p 1046*
See CLUB COOPERATIF DE CONSOMMATION D'AMOS

CLUB COOPERATIF DE CONSOMMATION D'AMOS *p 1046*
421 12E AV E, AMOS, QC, J9T 3H1
(819) 732-5281 *SIC 5411*

CLUB DE GOLF ACTON VALE INC *p 1044*
1000 RTE 116, ACTON VALE, QC, J0H 1A0
(450) 549-5885 *SIC 7992*

CLUB DE GOLF CHATEAUGUAY *p 1135*
See CLUB DE GOLF DE BELLE VUE (1984) INC

CLUB DE GOLF DE BELLE VUE (1984) INC *p 1135*
880 BOUL DE LERY, LERY, QC, J6N 1B7
(450) 692-6793 *SIC 7997*

CLUB DE GOLF DE LA VALLEE DU RICHELIEU INC, LE *p 1358*
100 CH DU GOLF, SAINTE-JULIE, QC, J3E 1Y1
(450) 649-1511 *SIC 7997*

CLUB DE GOLF DE LACHUTE (CANADA) *p 1129*
See 9175-2527 QUEBEC INC

CLUB DE GOLF DE ROSEMERE *p 1287*
282 BOUL LABELLE, ROSEMERE, QC, J7A 2H6
(450) 437-7555 *SIC 7997*

CLUB DE GOLF FONTAINEBLEAU *p 1058*
See CLUBLINK CORPORATION ULC

CLUB DE GOLF GLENDALE *p 1152*
See CENTRE DU GOLF U.F.O. INC

CLUB DE GOLF ISLESMERE *p 1248*
See CLUBLINK CORPORATION ULC

CLUB DE GOLF LE BLAINVILLIER INC *p 1058*
200 RUE DU BLAINVILLIER, BLAINVILLE, QC, J7C 4X6
(450) 433-1444 *SIC 7997*

CLUB DE GOLF SUMMERLEA INC *p 1394*
1000 RTE DE LOTBINIERE, VAUDREUIL-DORION, QC, J7V 0H5
(450) 455-0921 *SIC 7997*

CLUB DE GOLF TERREBONNE INC *p 1380*
3555 CH MARTIN, TERREBONNE, QC, J6X 0B2
(450) 477-1817 *SIC 6712*

CLUB DE GOLF WHITLOCK *p 1113*
128 COTE SAINT-CHARLES, HUDSON, QC, J0P 1H0
(450) 458-5305 *SIC 7997*

CLUB DE HOCKEY CANADIEN, INC *p 1210*
1275 RUE SAINT-ANTOINE O, MONTREAL, QC, H3C 5L2
(514) 932-2582 *SIC 7941*

CLUB DE HOCKEY LES VOLTIGEURS *p 1098*
300 RUE COCKBURN, DRUMMONDVILLE, QC, J2C 4L6
(819) 477-9400 *SIC 7941*

CLUB DE SOCCER LA PLAINE INC. *p 1382*
6900 RUE GUERIN, TERREBONNE, QC, J7M 1L9
(450) 477-0372 *SIC 7941*

CLUB ITALIA LODGE NO 5 *p 760*
See CLUB ITALIA,NIAGARA, ORDER SONS OF ITALY OF CANADA

CLUB ITALIA,NIAGARA, ORDER SONS OF ITALY OF CANADA *p 760*
2525 MONTROSE RD, NIAGARA FALLS, ON, L2H 0T9
(905) 374-7388 *SIC 7299*

CLUB LA CITE *p 1185*
See 6038263 CANADA INC

CLUB LAVAL-SUR-LE-LAC, LE *p 1236*
150 RUE LES PEUPLIERS, MONTREAL, QC, H7R 1J0
(450) 627-2643 *SIC 7992*

CLUB MAA INC *p 1194*

2070 RUE PEEL, MONTREAL, QC, H3A 1W6
(514) 845-2233 *SIC 7997*

CLUB MED VENTES CANADA INC *p 1401*
3500 BOUL DE MAISONNEUVE O BUREAU 1500, WESTMOUNT, QC, H3Z 3C1
(514) 937-1428 *SIC 4725*

CLUB MEUBLES AVANTAGES *p 1101*
See MEUBLES DENIS RIEL INC

CLUB MONACO CORP *p 974*
157 BLOOR ST W, TORONTO, ON, M5S 1P7
(416) 591-8837 *SIC 5621*

CLUB NAUTIQUE DE LA BAIE DE BEAUPORT *p*
1 BOUL HENRI-BOURASSA, QUEBEC, QC, G1J 1W8
(418) 266-0722 *SIC 8621*

CLUB NUAGE *p 1326*
See MODE CAPITAL INC, LA

CLUB PAPETIER, LE *p 1284*
See 9144-1923 QUEBEC INC

CLUB PISCINE *p 1245*
See CLUB PISCINE PLUS C.P.P.Q. (WEST ISLAND) INC, LE

CLUB PISCINE *p 1261*
See CENTRE MASSICOTTE INC

CLUB PISCINE *p 1388*
See PISCINES LAUNIER INC

CLUB PISCINE PLUS C.P.P.Q. (LONGUEUIL) INC, LE *p 1141*
620 RUE JEAN-NEVEU, LONGUEUIL, QC, J4G 1P1
(450) 463-3112 *SIC 5999*

CLUB PISCINE PLUS C.P.P.Q. (WEST ISLAND) INC, LE *p 1245*
14920 BOUL DE PIERREFONDS, PIERREFONDS, QC, H9H 4G2
(514) 696-2582 *SIC 5999*

CLUB PISCINE PLUS QUEBEC C.P.P.Q. INC, LE *p 1060*
888 BOUL INDUSTRIEL, BOIS-DES-FILION, QC, J6Z 4V1
(450) 965-9249 *SIC 6794*

CLUB PLEIN AIR LA CORDEE *p 1174*
See CORDEE PLEIN AIR INC, LA

CLUB PRO *p 550*
See CLUB PRO ADULT ENTERTAINMENT INC

CLUB PRO ADULT ENTERTAINMENT INC *p 550*
170 DOUGHTON RD, CONCORD, ON, L4K 1R4
(905) 669-6422 *SIC 5813*

CLUB SNOB *p 1179*
See SOCIETE DE COMMERCE ACADEX INC

CLUB TREMBLANT INC *p 1159*
121 RUE CUTTLE, MONT-TREMBLANT, QC, J8E 1B9
SIC 7011

CLUB VIDEO ECLAIR INC *p 1281*
1889 BOUL PIE-XI N, QUEBEC, QC, G3J 1P4
(418) 845-1212 *SIC 7841*

CLUB VIDEO SUTTON INC *p 1070*
9160 BOUL LEDUC BUREAU 410, BROSSARD, QC, J4Y 0E3
(514) 251-8118 *SIC 7371*

CLUB VOYAGE DUMOULIN *p 1061*
See DESTINATIONS ESCAPA INC

CLUB VOYAGE MALAVOY *p 1168*
See VOYAGES MALAVOY INC

CLUB VOYAGES LA FORFAITERIE *p 1378*
See FORFAITERIE INC, LA

CLUB VOYAGES SOLERAMA *p 1300*
See 9064-6795 QUEBEC INC

CLUB VOYAGES SOLERAMA *p 1300*
See 9368-7952 QUEBEC INC

CLUBLINK CORPORATION ULC *p 473*
13448 DUBLIN LINE SUITE 1, ACTON, ON, L7J 2L7

▲ Public Company ■ Public Company Family Member **HQ** Headquarters **BR** Branch **SL** Single Location

(519) 853-0904   *SIC 7992*
CLUBLINK CORPORATION ULC   *p 494*
15608 REGIONAL ROAD 50, BOLTON, ON, L7E 3E5
(905) 880-1400   *SIC 7992*
CLUBLINK CORPORATION ULC   *p 567*
109 ROYAL TROON LANE, DUNROBIN, ON, K0A 1T0
(613) 832-3804   *SIC 7992*
CLUBLINK CORPORATION ULC   *p 593*
11742 TENTH LINE SUITE 4, GEORGE-TOWN, ON, L7G 4S7
(905) 877-8468   *SIC 7992*
CLUBLINK CORPORATION ULC   *p 598*
12657 WOODBINE AVE S, GORMLEY, ON, L0H 1G0
(905) 888-1219   *SIC 7992*
CLUBLINK CORPORATION ULC   *p 622*
8165 10 SIDEROAD SUITE 11, INNISFIL, ON, L9S 4T3
(705) 431-7000   *SIC 7992*
CLUBLINK CORPORATION ULC   *p 629*
14700 BATHURST ST, KING CITY, ON, L7B 1K5
(905) 713-6875   *SIC 7992*
CLUBLINK CORPORATION ULC   *p 629*
15675 DUFFERIN ST, KING CITY, ON, L7B 1K5
(905) 841-3730   *SIC 7992*
CLUBLINK CORPORATION ULC   *p 748*
4999 BOUNDARY RD, NAVAN, ON, K4B 1P5
(613) 822-1454   *SIC 7992*
CLUBLINK CORPORATION ULC   *p 894*
14001 WARDEN AVE, STOUFFVILLE, ON, L4A 3T4
(905) 888-1100   *SIC 7992*
CLUBLINK CORPORATION ULC   *p 1058*
1 BOUL DE FONTAINEBLEAU, BLAINVILLE, QC, J7B 1L4
(450) 434-7569   *SIC 7992*
CLUBLINK CORPORATION ULC   *p 1248*
1199 CH DU BORD-DE-L'EAU, POINTE-CLAIRE, QC, H7Y 1A9
(450) 689-4130   *SIC 7992*
CLUBLINK ONE MEMBERSHIP MORE GOLF   *p 629*
See TWC ENTERPRISES LIMITED
CLUETT HOLDINGS INC   *p 445*
629 WINDMILL RD, DARTMOUTH, NS, B3B 1B6
(902) 466-5328   *SIC 6712*
CLUTE, BOB GM   *p 491*
See CLUTE, BOB PONTIAC BUICK GMC LTD
CLUTE, BOB PONTIAC BUICK GMC LTD *p 491*
6692 HWY 62, BELLEVILLE, ON, K8N 4Z5
(613) 962-4584   *SIC 5511*
CLUTE, BOB SATURN   *p 490*
See 1607408 ONTARIO INC
CLV GROUP INC   *p 833*
485 BANK ST SUITE 200, OTTAWA, ON, K2P 1Z2
(613) 728-2000   *SIC 6531*
CLYDE UNION CANADA LIMITED   *p 521*
4151 NORTH SERVICE RD UNIT 1, BURLINGTON, ON, L7L 4X6
(905) 315-3800   *SIC 3561*
CLYVANOR LTEE   *p 1304*
2125 95E RUE BUREAU 1, SAINT-GEORGES, QC, G5Y 8J1
(418) 228-7690   *SIC 2439*
CMA   *p 960*
See CANADIAN MARKETING ASSOCIATION
CMA CGM (CANADA) INC   *p 1210*
740 RUE NOTRE-DAME O BUREAU 1330, MONTREAL, QC, H3C 3X6
(514) 908-7001   *SIC 4412*
CMB INSURANCE BROKERS   *p 125*
See MCDONALD & BYCHKOWSKI LTD
CMBC   *p 185*
See COAST MOUNTAIN BUS COMPANY

CMBC   *p 236*
See COAST MOUNTAIN BUS COMPANY LTD
CMBC   *p 263*
See COAST MOUNTAIN BUS COMPANY LTD
CMC   *p 1333*
See CONSTRUCTIONS DE MAUSOLEES CARRIER INC, LES
CMC ELECTRONIQUE INC   *p 832*
415 LEGGET DR, OTTAWA, ON, K2K 2B2
(613) 592-6500   *SIC 8711*
CMC ELECTRONIQUE INC   *p 1324*
600 BOUL DR.-FREDERIK-PHILIPS, SAINT-LAURENT, QC, H4M 2S9
(514) 748-3148   *SIC 8711*
CMC PAPER CONVERERS   *p 782*
See CANADA FIBERS LTD
CMC PAPER CONVERTERS   *p 997*
See CANADA FIBERS LTD
CMCC   *p 764*
See CANADIAN MEMORIAL CHIROPRACTIC COLLEGE
CME   *p 729*
See ALLIANCES DES MANUFACTURIERS ET DES EXPORTATEURS DU CANADA
CMG   *p 40*
See COMPUTER MODELLING GROUP LTD
CMH HELI-SKIING & HIKING   *p 4*
See CANADIAN MOUNTAIN HOLIDAYS LIMITED PARTNERSHIP
CMHA   *p 486*
See CANADIAN MENTAL HEALTH ASSOCIATION, SIMCOE COUNTY BRANCH
CMHA   *p 655*
See CANADIAN MENTAL HEALTH ASSOCIATION, MIDDLESEX
CMHA   *p 788*
See CANADIAN MENTAL HEALTH ASSOCIATION TORONTO BRANCH, THE
CMHA   *p 811*
See CANADIAN MENTAL HEALTH ASSOCIATION TORONTO BRANCH, THE
CMHA   *p 839*
See CANADIAN MENTAL HEALTH ASSOCIATION, PETERBOROUGH BRANCH
CMHA   *p 885*
See CANADIAN MENTAL HEALTH ASSOCIATION, NIAGARA BRANCH
CMHA   *p 907*
See CANADIAN MENTAL HEALTH ASSOCIATION, THUNDER BAY BRANCH
CMHA   *p 912*
See CANADIAN MENTAL HEALTH ASSOCIATION-COCHRANE-TIMISKAMING BRANCH
CMHA   *p 1021*
See CANADIAN MENTAL HEALTH ASSOCIATION, WINDSOR-ESSEX COUNTY BRANCH
CMHA PEEL DUFFERIN   *p 511*
See CANADIAN MENTAL HEALTH ASSOCIATION/PEEL BRANCH
CMHA RESSOURCE CENTRE   *p 511*
See CANADIAN MENTAL HEALTH ASSOCIATION/PEEL BRANCH
CMI COSMETIC MANUFACTURERS INC *p 550*
90 MOYAL CRT, CONCORD, ON, L4K 4R8
(905) 879-1999   *SIC 5122*
CMI INTERLANGUES INC   *p 833*
412 MACLAREN ST, OTTAWA, ON, K2P 0M8
(613) 236-3763   *SIC 8299*
CMIC SUCCESS LTD   *p 916*
4850 KEELE ST, TORONTO, ON, M3J 3K1
(416) 736-0123   *SIC 5942*
CML ATC   *p 1107*
See SOLACOM TECHNOLOGIES INC
CML BOSWELL HOLDINGS LTD   *p 159*
5440 46 ST, ROCKY MOUNTAIN HOUSE, AB, T4T 1B3

(403) 846-0077   *SIC 5531*
CML CANADIAN MORTGAGE LENDER *p 26*
See VERICO CML CANADIAN MORTGAGE LENDER INC
CML HEALTHCARE INC   *p 744*
60 COURTNEYPARK DR W UNIT 1, MISSISSAUGA, ON, L5W 0B3
(905) 565-0043   *SIC 8071*
CMM   *p 519*
See CANADIAN MILK MANUFACTURING INC
CMN CALGARY INC   *p 46*
335 8 AVE SW SUITE 1000, CALGARY, AB, T2P 1C9
(403) 266-5544   *SIC 6531*
CMN GLOBAL INC   *p 904*
150 COMMERCE VALLEY DR W SUITE 900, THORNHILL, ON, L3T 7Z3
(905) 669-4333   *SIC 8011*
CMP - CLASSIC AUTOMOTIVE LTD   *p 10*
1313 36 ST NE, CALGARY, AB, T2A 6P9
(403) 207-1002   *SIC 7538*
CMP AUTOMATION INC   *p 483*
229 BOIDA AVE SUITE 1, AYR, ON, N0B 1E0
(519) 740-6035   *SIC 3599*
CMP AUTOMOTIVE INC   *p 10*
1313 36 ST NE, CALGARY, AB, T2A 6P9
(403) 207-1000   *SIC 7538*
CMP GROUP LTD   *p 208*
7733 PROGRESS WAY, DELTA, BC, V4G 1A3
(604) 940-2010   *SIC 5051*
CMP SOLUTIONS MECANIQUES AVANCEES LTEE   *p 1075*
1241 RUE DES CASCADES, CHATEAU-GUAY, QC, J6J 4Z2
(450) 691-5510   *SIC 3499*
CMRRA   *p 974*
See CANADIAN MUSICAL REPRODUCTION RIGHTS AGENCY LIMITED, THE
CMS CREATIVE MANAGEMENT SERVICES LIMITED   *p 377*
330 ST MARY AVE SUITE 750, WINNIPEG, MB, R3C 3Z5
(204) 944-0789   *SIC 8741*
CMW INSURANCE SERVICES LTD *p 185*
1901 ROSSER AVE UNIT 700, BURNABY, BC, V5C 6R6
(604) 294-3301   *SIC 6411*
CN ATLANTIC ZONE   *p 408*
See COMPAGNIE DES CHEMINS DE FER NATIONAUX DU CANADA
CN EQUIPMENT   *p 362*
See COMPAGNIE DES CHEMINS DE FER NATIONAUX DU CANADA
CN INTERMODAL   *p 1338*
See COMPAGNIE DES CHEMINS DE FER NATIONAUX DU CANADA
CN INVESTMENT, DIV   *p 1203*
See COMPAGNIE DES CHEMINS DE FER NATIONAUX DU CANADA
CN INVESTMENT, DIV OF   *p 1202*
See CANADIAN NATIONAL RAILWAYS PENSION TRUST FUND
CN NORTH AMERICA   *p 551*
See COMPAGNIE DES CHEMINS DE FER NATIONAUX DU CANADA
CN RAIL   *p 550*
See COMPAGNIE DES CHEMINS DE FER NATIONAUX DU CANADA
CN RAILS   *p 979*
See COMPAGNIE DES CHEMINS DE FER NATIONAUX DU CANADA
CN RAILWAY   *p 250*
See COMPAGNIE DES CHEMINS DE FER NATIONAUX DU CANADA
CN TOWER   *p 960*
See CANADA LANDS COMPANY CLC LIMITED
CN TOWER   *p 979*
See CANADA LANDS COMPANY CLC LIMITED

CN WORLDWIDE   *p 761*
See CN WORLDWIDE DISTRIBUTION SERVICES (CANADA) INC
CN WORLDWIDE DISTRIBUTION SERVICES (CANADA) INC   *p 761*
303 TOWNLINE RD SUITE 200, NIAGARA ON THE LAKE, ON, L0S 1J0
(905) 641-3139   *SIC 4225*
CNA   *p 434*
See COLLEGE OF THE NORTH ATLANTIC
CNA CANADA   *p 969*
See CONTINENTAL CASUALTY COMPANY
CNA CANADA, INC   *p 969*
66 WELLINGTON ST W SUITE 3700, TORONTO, ON, M5K 1J5
(416) 542-7300   *SIC 6411*
CNB COMPUTERS INC   *p 687*
6400 NORTHWEST DR, MISSISSAUGA, ON, L4V 1K1
(905) 501-0099   *SIC 5045*
CNC   *p 250*
See COLLEGE OF NEW CALEDONIA, THE
CNC AUTOMATION   *p 1354*
See 2778751 CANADA INC
CNC PRECISION PROFILES PLUS   *p 1436*
See BOURGAULT INDUSTRIES LTD
CNEA   *p 991*
See CANADIAN NATIONAL EXHIBITION ASSOCIATION
CNESST   *p 1258*
See COMMISSION DES NORMES, DE L'EQUITE, DE LA SANTE ET DE LA SECURITE DU TRAVAIL, LA
CNH INDUSTRIAL CANADA, LTD   *p 1434*
1000 71ST ST E, SASKATOON, SK, S7P 0B5
(306) 934-3500   *SIC 3523*
CNI   *p 667*
See CANADIAN NETWORK INSTALLATIONS LTD
CNIB   *p 918*
See CANADIAN NATIONAL INSTITUTE FOR THE BLIND, THE
CNIM CANADA INC   *p 1210*
1499 RUE WILLIAM, MONTREAL, QC, H3C 1R4
(514) 932-1220   *SIC 3534*
CNL   *p 541*
See CANADIAN NUCLEAR LABORATORIES LTD
CNOOC MARKETING CANADA   *p 46*
801 7 AVE SW SUITE 1700, CALGARY, AB, T2P 3P7
(403) 699-4000   *SIC 4911*
CNOOC PETROLEUM NORTH AMERICA ULC   *p 28*
500 CENTRE ST SE SUITE 2300, CALGARY, AB, T2G 1A6
(403) 699-4000   *SIC 1382*
CNR (ECHO) RESOURCES INC   *p 46*
855 2 ST SW SUITE 2500, CALGARY, AB, T2P 4J8
SIC 1311
CNRL   *p 131*
See CANADIAN NATURAL RESOURCES LIMITED
CNS   *p 297*
See CANADIAN NORTHERN SHIELD INSURANCE COMPANY
CNSX MARKETS INC   *p 986*
100 KING ST W SUITE 7210, TORONTO, ON, M5X 1E1
(416) 572-2000   *SIC 6231*
CNW GROUP LTD   *p 961*
88 QUEENS QUAY W SUITE 3000, TORONTO, ON, M5J 0B8
(416) 863-9350   *SIC 4899*
CO DARA VENTURES LTD   *p 243*
5500 CLEMENTS CRES SUITE 80, PEACHLAND, BC, V0H 1X5
(250) 767-9054   *SIC 5541*
CO-FO CONCRETE FORMING CON-

STRUCTION LIMITED p
653
72 ANN ST, LONDON, ON, N6A 1P9
(519) 432-2391 *SIC 3273*

CO-OP p 139
See *BEAVER CREEK CO-OP ASSN LIMITED*

CO-OP p 1424
See *SOBEYS WEST INC*

CO-OP ATLANTIC p 406
See *ATLANTIC RETAIL CO-OPERATIVES FEDERATION*

CO-OP DES DEUX RIVES p 1243
1455 AV DU ROCHER BUREAU 102, NOR-MANDIN, QC, G8M 3X5
(418) 274-2910 *SIC 5211*

CO-OP GAS BAR p 366
See *RED RIVER COOPERATIVE LTD*

CO-OP REFINERY COMPLEX p 1415
See *CONSUMERS' CO-OPERATIVE REFINERIES LIMITED*

CO-OP SASKATOON STONEBRID p 1435
106 STONEBRIDGE BLVD, SASKATOON, SK, S7T 0J1
(306) 933-0306 *SIC 5411*

CO-OP, REGINA GAS BAR p 1422
4705 GORDON RD, REGINA, SK, S4W 0B7
(306) 791-9388 *SIC 5541*

CO-OPERATIVE DE BOUCTOUCHE LTD , (LA) p 395
191 IRVING BLVD, BOUCTOUCHE, NB, E4S 3K3
(506) 743-1960 *SIC 5411*

CO-OPERATIVE DE SAINT-QUENTIN LTEE p 417
145 RUE CANADA, SAINT-QUENTIN, NB, E8A 1J4
(506) 235-2083 *SIC 5411*

CO-OPERATIVE DEVELOPMENT FOUNDATION OF CANADA p
833
275 BANK ST SUITE 400, OTTAWA, ON, K2P 2L6
(613) 238-6711 *SIC 8699*

CO-OPERATIVE REGIONALE DE NIPISSING-SUDBURY LIMITED p 1003
4 RUE PRINCIPALE, VERNER, ON, P0H 2M0
(705) 594-2354 *SIC 5191*

CO-OPERATIVE SUPERANNUATION SOCIETY p
1426
333 3RD AVE N SUITE 501, SASKATOON, SK, S7K 2M2
(306) 244-1539 *SIC 6371*

CO-OPERATORS GENERAL INSURANCE COMPANY p 406
10 RECORD ST, MONCTON, NB, E1C 0B2
(506) 853-1215 *SIC 6311*

CO-OPERATORS GENERAL INSURANCE COMPANY p 602
130 MACDONELL ST, GUELPH, ON, N1H 2Z6
(519) 824-4400 *SIC 6411*

CO-OPERATORS GENERAL INSURANCE COMPANY p 711
1270 CENTRAL PKY W SUITE 600, MISSISSAUGA, ON, L5C 4P4
SIC 6411

CO-OPERATORS GROUP LIMITED, THE p
602
130 MACDONELL ST, GUELPH, ON, N1H 2Z6
(519) 824-4400 *SIC 6331*

CO-OPERATORS GROUP LIMITED, THE p
668
7300 WARDEN AVE SUITE 110, MARKHAM, ON, L3R 9Z6
(905) 470-7300 *SIC 6411*

CO-OPERATORS GROUP LIMITED, THE p
1417
1920 COLLEGE AVE, REGINA, SK, S4P 1C4
(306) 347-6200 *SIC 6411*

CO-OPERATORS, THE p 602
See *CO-OPERATORS GROUP LIMITED, THE*

CO-OPERATORS, THE p 668
See *CO-OPERATORS GROUP LIMITED, THE*

CO-PAK PACKAGING CORP p 583
1231 MARTIN GROVE RD, ETOBICOKE, ON, M9W 4X2
(905) 799-0092 *SIC 7389*

CO-PAR ELECTRIC LTD p 124
1132 156 ST SW, EDMONTON, AB, T6W 1A4
(780) 453-1414 *SIC 1731*

COACH p 452
See *COACH STORES CANADA CORPORATION*

COACH CANADA p 492
See *TRENTWAY-WAGAR INC*

COACH CANADA p 690
See *TRENTWAY-WAGAR INC*

COACH CANADA p 842
See *TRENTWAY-WAGAR INC*

COACH STORES CANADA CORPORATION p 452
1959 UPPER WATER ST SUITE 900, HALIFAX, NS, B3J 3N2
(866) 995-9956 *SIC 5632*

COACHMAN INSURANCE COMPANY p 577
10 FOUR SEASONS PL SUITE 200, ETOBICOKE, ON, M9B 6H7
(416) 255-3417 *SIC 6331*

COADY INTERNATIONAL INSTITUTE p 438
See *ST. FRANCIS XAVIER UNIVERSITY*

COAL ISLAND LTD p 259
10991 SHELLBRIDGE WAY SUITE 310, RICHMOND, BC, V6X 3C6
(604) 873-4312 *SIC 2436*

COAL MOUNTAIN OPERATIONS p 269
See *TECK COAL LIMITED*

COAL VALLEY MOTOR PRODUCTS LTD p 212
16 MANITOU RD, FERNIE, BC, V0B 1M5
(250) 423-9288 *SIC 5511*

COALISION INC p 1187
700 RUE SAINT-ANTOINE E BUREAU 110, MONTREAL, QC, H2Y 1A6
(514) 798-3534 *SIC 2339*

COAST 2000 TERMINALS LTD p 258
16080 PORTSIDE RD SUITE 100, RICHMOND, BC, V6W 1M1
(604) 270-3625 *SIC 4231*

COAST BASTION INN p 233
See *COAST HOTELS LIMITED*

COAST BUILDING SUPPLIES LTD p 276
8484 128 ST UNIT 100, SURREY, BC, V3W 4G3
(604) 590-0055 *SIC 5032*

COAST CAPITAL p 273
See *COAST CAPITAL SAVINGS FEDERAL CREDIT UNION*

COAST CAPITAL INSURANCE SERVICES LTD p 339
1499 ADMIRALS RD, VICTORIA, BC, V9A 2P8
(250) 483-7000 *SIC 6411*

COAST CAPITAL REAL ESTATE LTD p 337
4460 CHATTERTON WAY SUITE 110, VICTORIA, BC, V8X 5J2
(250) 477-5353 *SIC 6531*

COAST CAPITAL SAVINGS FEDERAL CREDIT UNION p 273
9900 KING GEORGE BLVD SUITE 800, SURREY, BC, V3T 0K7
(604) 517-7400 *SIC 6062*

COAST CAPITAL SAVINGS FEDERAL CREDIT UNION p 274
9900 KING GEORGE BLVD 4TH FL, SURREY, BC, V3T 0K7
(778) 945-3225 *SIC 6159*

COAST CLAIM SERVICE LTD p 334
2727 QUADRA ST SUITE 6, VICTORIA, BC, V8T 4E5
(250) 386-3111 *SIC 6411*

COAST COUNTRY FINANCIAL p 203
See *COAST COUNTRY INSURANCE SERVICES LTD*

COAST COUNTRY INSURANCE SERVICES LTD p 203
426 8TH ST, COURTENAY, BC, V9N 1N5
(250) 334-3443 *SIC 6411*

COAST DISCOVERY INN & MARINA p 195
See *COAST HOTELS LIMITED*

COAST DISTRIBUTION SYSTEM, THE p 1296
See *NTP/STAG CANADA INC*

COAST EDMONTON PLAZA HOTEL p 88
See *COAST HOTELS LIMITED*

COAST ENERGY CANADA INC p 46
530 8 AVE SW SUITE 920, CALGARY, AB, T2P 3S8
(403) 508-6700 *SIC 4924*

COAST FRASER ENTERPRISES LTD p 312
1177 WEST HASTINGS ST SUITE 2101, VANCOUVER, BC, V6E 2K3
(604) 498-1110 *SIC 5031*

COAST HOTELS AND RESORTS p 249
See *COAST HOTELS LIMITED*

COAST HOTELS AND RESORTS p 312
See *COAST HOTELS LIMITED*

COAST HOTELS LIMITED p 88
10155 105 ST NW, EDMONTON, AB, T5J 1E2
(780) 423-4811 *SIC 7011*

COAST HOTELS LIMITED p 195
975 SHOPPERS ROW, CAMPBELL RIVER, BC, V9W 2C4
(250) 287-9225 *SIC 7011*

COAST HOTELS LIMITED p 233
11 BASTION ST, NANAIMO, BC, V9R 6E4
(250) 753-6601 *SIC 7011*

COAST HOTELS LIMITED p 249
770 BRUNSWICK ST, PRINCE GEORGE, BC, V2L 2C2
(250) 563-0121 *SIC 7011*

COAST HOTELS LIMITED p 312
1090 GEORGIA ST W SUITE 900, VANCOUVER, BC, V6E 3V7
(604) 682-7982 *SIC 7011*

COAST HOTELS LIMITED p 318
1763 COMOX ST, VANCOUVER, BC, V6G 1P6
(604) 688-7711 *SIC 7011*

COAST INDUSTRIAL CONSTRUCTION LTD p 251
110 1ST AVE W SUITE 260, PRINCE RUPERT, BC, V8J 1A8
(250) 624-4327 *SIC 1542*

COAST MOUNTAIN BUS COMPANY LTD p 185
3855 KITCHENER ST SUITE 420, BURNABY, BC, V5C 3L8
(604) 205-6111 *SIC 4111*

COAST MOUNTAIN BUS COMPANY LTD p 236
287 NELSON'S CRT SUITE 700, NEW WESTMINSTER, BC, V3L 0E7
(778) 375-6400 *SIC 4111*

COAST MOUNTAIN BUS COMPANY LTD p 263
11133 COPPERSMITH WAY, RICHMOND, BC, V7A 5E8
(604) 277-7787 *SIC 4142*

COAST MOUNTAIN CHEVROLET PONTIAC BUICK GMC LTD p 269
4038 16 HWY E RR 6, SMITHERS, BC, V0J 2N6
(250) 847-2214 *SIC 5511*

COAST MOUNTAIN COLLEGE p 283
5331 MCCONNELL AVE, TERRACE, BC, V8G 4X2
(250) 635-6511 *SIC 8221*

COAST MOUNTAIN GEOLOGICAL LTD p 303
625 HOWE ST SUITE 488, VANCOUVER, BC, V6C 2T6
(604) 681-0209 *SIC 8999*

COAST MOUNTAIN GM p 269
See *COAST MOUNTAIN CHEVROLET PONTIAC BUICK GMC LTD*

COAST PLAZA AT STANLEY PARK p 318
See *COAST HOTELS LIMITED*

COAST PLAZA HOTEL p 10
See *CALGARY PLAZA HOTEL LTD*

COAST POWERTRAIN LTD p 236
420 CANFOR AVE, NEW WESTMINSTER, BC, V3L 5G2
(604) 520-6125 *SIC 5531*

COAST RANGE CONCRETE LTD p 230
1011 HWY 99 N, LILLOOET, BC, V0K 1V0
(250) 256-7803 *SIC 5032*

COAST REALTY GROUP (QUALICUM) LTD p 252
689 MEMORIAL AVE, QUALICUM BEACH, BC, V9K 1S8
(250) 752-3375 *SIC 6531*

COAST SPAS p 226
See *COAST SPAS MANUFACTURING INC*

COAST SPAS MANUFACTURING INC p 226
6315 202 ST, LANGLEY, BC, V2Y 1N1
(604) 514-8111 *SIC 3999*

COAST STORAGE & CONTAINERS LTD p 268
5674 TEREDO ST SUITE 102, SECHELT, BC, V0N 3A0
(604) 883-2444 *SIC 7359*

COAST TIRE & AUTO SERVICE LTD p 414
130 SOMERSET ST SUITE 150, SAINT JOHN, NB, E2K 2X4
(506) 674-9620 *SIC 5531*

COAST TO COAST DEALER SERVICES INC p 610
1945 KING ST E SUITE 100, HAMILTON, ON, L8K 1W2
(905) 578-7477 *SIC 6399*

COAST TO COAST HELICOPTERS INC p 5
27312 TOWNSHIP RD 394 UNIT 237, BLACKFALDS, AB, T0M 0J0
(403) 885-5220 *SIC 4522*

COAST TO COAST NEWSSTAND SERVICES LTD p
873
5230 FINCH AVE E SUITE 1, SCARBOROUGH, ON, M1S 4Z9
(416) 754-3900 *SIC 5192*

COAST TO COAST VIDEO SALES LTD p
237
1109 ROYAL AVE, NEW WESTMINSTER, BC, V3M 1K4
(604) 525-9355 *SIC 5099*

COAST TO COAST WARRANTY p 610
See *COAST TO COAST DEALER SERVICES INC*

COAST UNDERWRITERS LTD p 297
650 GEORGIA ST W UNIT 2690, VANCOUVER, BC, V6B 4N7
(604) 683-5631 *SIC 6331*

COAST WHOLESALE APPLIANCES INC p 290
8488 MAIN ST, VANCOUVER, BC, V5X 4W8
(604) 321-6644 *SIC 5722*

COASTAL BLENDING & PACKAGING p 415
See *HIGHLANDS BLENDING & PACKAGING G.P.*

COASTAL COMMUNITY CREDIT UNION p 233
59 WHARF ST SUITE 220, NANAIMO, BC, V9R 2X3
(250) 741-3200 *SIC 6062*

COASTAL COMMUNITY CREDIT UNION p 233
59 WHARF ST UNIT 220, NANAIMO, BC, V9R 2X3
(250) 716-2331 *SIC 6062*

COASTAL COMMUNITY INSURANCE AGENCIES LTD p 233
50 TENTH ST SUITE 111, NANAIMO, BC, V9R 6L1
SIC 6411

COASTAL COMMUNITY INSURANCE SERVICES 2007 LTD p

233
59 WHARF ST SUITE 220, NANAIMO, BC,
V9R 2X3
(888) 741-1010   SIC 6311

COASTAL CULTURE   p 1038
See COASTAL CULTURE INC

COASTAL CULTURE INC   p 1038
156 QUEEN ST, CHARLOTTETOWN, PE,
C1A 4B5
(902) 894-3146   SIC 5947

COASTAL DOOR & FRAME INC   p 445
40 RADDALL AVE, DARTMOUTH, NS, B3B
1T2
(902) 468-2333   SIC 5039

COASTAL ENTERPRISES LTD   p 398
48 DIPPER HARBOUR RD, DIPPER HAR-
BOUR, NB, E5J 1X2
(506) 659-2781   SIC 5146

COASTAL INSURANCE SERVICES LTD   p
185
4350 STILL CREEK DR SUITE 400, BURN-
ABY, BC, V5C 0G5
(604) 269-1000   SIC 6411

COASTAL MARINE LIMITED   p 426
1256 TOPSAIL RD, MOUNT PEARL, NL,
A1N 5E8
(709) 747-0159   SIC 5551

COASTAL MOUNTAIN FUELS   p 195
See CR 92 HOLDINGS LTD

COASTAL OUTDOORS   p 426
See COASTAL MARINE LIMITED

COASTAL PACIFIC XPRESS INC   p 271
5355 152 ST SUITE 105, SURREY, BC, V3S
5A5
(604) 575-4200   SIC 4213

COASTAL RANGE SYSTEMS INC   p 188
6400 ROBERTS ST SUITE 200, BURNABY,
BC, V5G 4C9
(604) 473-2100   SIC 5045

**COASTAL RESTORATIONS & MASONRY
LIMITED**   p 450
8 MILLS DR, GOODWOOD, NS, B3T 1P3
(902) 876-8333   SIC 1771

COASTAL SHIPPING LIMITED   p 425
128 MAIN ST, LEWISPORTE, NL, A0G 3A0
(709) 535-6944   SIC 4424

COASTAL TRANSPORT LIMITED   p 415
22 GERMAIN ST SUITE 104, SAINT JOHN,
NB, E2L 2E5
(506) 642-0520   SIC 4482

**COASTAL ZONE RESEARCH INSTITUTE
INC**   p 417
232B AV DE L'EGLISE, SHIPPAGAN, NB,
E8S 1J2
(506) 336-6600   SIC 8733

COASTLAND WOOD INDUSTRIES LTD   p
233
84 ROBARTS ST SUITE 2, NANAIMO, BC,
V9R 2S5
(250) 754-1962   SIC 2436

COATINGS & RELATED PRODUCTS   p 557
See PPG CANADA INC

COATINGS 85 LTD   p 738
6995 DAVAND DR, MISSISSAUGA, ON,
L5T 1L5
(905) 564-1711   SIC 3471

COATS BELL   p 1027
See COATS CANADA INC

COATS CANADA INC   p 1027
10 ROYBRIDGE GATE SUITE 200, WOOD-
BRIDGE, ON, L4H 3M8
(905) 850-9200   SIC 5092

COBALT 27 CAPITAL CORP   p 950
4 KING ST W SUITE 401, TORONTO, ON,
M5H 1B6
(647) 846-7765   SIC 1061

COBB'S AG FOODS LTD   p 169
5015 50 ST SUITE 2, SYLVAN LAKE, AB,
T4S 1P9
SIC 5411

COBDEN AGRICULTURAL SOCIETY   p 544
43 ASTROLABE RD, COBDEN, ON, K0J
1K0
(613) 646-2426   SIC 6519

COBEQUID EDUCATIONAL CENTRE   p 468
See CHIGNECTO CENTRAL REGIONAL
SCHOOL BOARD

COBER   p 642
See COBER PRINTING LIMITED

COBER PRINTING LIMITED   p 642
1351 STRASBURG RD, KITCHENER, ON,
N2R 1H2
(519) 745-7136   SIC 2752

COBOCONK IGA   p 544
See BARBOUR'S FOOD MARKET LIMITED

**COBOURG DISTRICT COLLEGIATE INSTI-
TUTE EAST**   p
545
See KAWARTHA PINE RIDGE DISTRICT
SCHOOL BOARD

COBOURG NISSAN LTD   p 545
831 DIVISION ST, COBOURG, ON, K9A
5R9
(905) 372-3963   SIC 5511

COBRA ELECTRIC LTD   p 281
9688 190 ST, SURREY, BC, V4N 3M9
(604) 594-1633   SIC 1731

COBRA FIXATIONS CIE LTEE   p 1048
8051 BOUL METROPOLITAIN E, ANJOU,
QC, H1J 1J8
(514) 354-2240   SIC 3965

COBRA INTEGRATED SYSTEMS LTDp 185
4427 DAWSON ST, BURNABY, BC, V5C
4B8
(604) 664-7671   SIC 5065

**COBRA INTERNATIONAL SYSTEMES DE
FIXATIONS CIE LTEE**   p 1048
8051 BOUL METROPOLITAIN E, ANJOU,
QC, H1J 1J8
(514) 354-2240   SIC 6712

COBS BREAD   p 311
See BD CANADA LTD

COBURN REALTY LTD   p 750
1415 WOODROFFE AVE, NEPEAN, ON,
K2G 1V9
(613) 226-8790   SIC 6531

COCA-COLA BOTTLING   p 460
See COCA-COLA LTD

COCA-COLA BOTTLING   p 933
See COCA-COLA REFRESHMENTS
CANADA COMPANY

COCA-COLA BOTTLING COMPANY   p 22
See COCA-COLA CANADA BOTTLING
LIMITED

**COCA-COLA CANADA BOTTLING LIM-
ITED**   p
22
3851 23 ST NE, CALGARY, AB, T2E 6T2
(403) 291-3111   SIC 2086

**COCA-COLA CANADA BOTTLING LIM-
ITED**   p
120
9621 27 AVE NW, EDMONTON, AB, T6N
1E7
(780) 450-2653   SIC 2086

**COCA-COLA CANADA BOTTLING LIM-
ITED**   p
372
1331 INKSTER BLVD, WINNIPEG, MB, R2X
1P6
(204) 633-2590   SIC 2086

**COCA-COLA CANADA BOTTLING LIM-
ITED**   p
460
20 LAKESIDE PARK DR, LAKESIDE, NS,
B3T 1L8
(902) 876-8661   SIC 2086

**COCA-COLA CANADA BOTTLING LIM-
ITED**   p
501
15 WESTCREEK BLVD, BRAMPTON, ON,
L6T 5T4
(905) 874-7202   SIC 2086

**COCA-COLA CANADA BOTTLING LIM-
ITED**   p
661
950 GREEN VALLEY RD, LONDON, ON,
N6N 1E3

(800) 241-2653   SIC 2086

**COCA-COLA CANADA BOTTLING LIM-
ITED**   p
792
24 FENMAR DR, NORTH YORK, ON, M9L
1L8
(416) 741-0440   SIC 2086

**COCA-COLA CANADA BOTTLING LIM-
ITED**   p
933
335 KING ST E, TORONTO, ON, M5A 1L1
(416) 424-6000   SIC 2086

**COCA-COLA CANADA BOTTLING LIM-
ITED**   p
1415
355 HENDERSON DR, REGINA, SK, S4N
6B9
(800) 218-2653   SIC 5149

COCA-COLA LTD   p 460
20 LAKESIDE PARK DR, LAKESIDE, NS,
B3T 1L8
(902) 876-8661   SIC 5149

COCA-COLA LTD   p 765
3389 STEELES AVE E SUITE 500, NORTH
YORK, ON, M2H 3S8
SIC 5149

COCA-COLA LTD   p 1387
8500 BOUL INDUSTRIEL, TROIS-
RIVIERES, QC, G9A 5E1
(819) 694-4000   SIC 2086

**COCA-COLA REFRESHMENTS CANADA
COMPANY**   p 219
406 OLD VERNON RD SUITE 100,
KELOWNA, BC, V1X 4R2
(250) 491-3414   SIC 2086

**COCA-COLA REFRESHMENTS CANADA
COMPANY**   p 258
7200 NELSON RD, RICHMOND, BC, V6W
1G4
(416) 424-6000   SIC 4225

**COCA-COLA REFRESHMENTS CANADA
COMPANY**   p 609
1575 BARTON ST E, HAMILTON, ON, L8H
7K6
(905) 548-3206   SIC 2086

**COCA-COLA REFRESHMENTS CANADA
COMPANY**   p 933
335 KING ST E, TORONTO, ON, M5A 1L1
(416) 424-6000   SIC 2086

**COCA-COLA REFRESHMENTS CANADA
COMPANY**   p 1164
2750 BOUL DE L'ASSOMPTION, MON-
TREAL, QC, H1N 2G9
(514) 254-9411   SIC 2086

**COCA-COLA REFRESHMENTS CANADA
COMPANY**   p 1261
990 AV GODIN, QUEBEC, QC, G1M 2X9
(418) 686-4884   SIC 5149

COCCOLI   p 1225
See CREATIONS ROBO INC

COCHON DINGUE, LE   p 1259
See GROUPE RESTOS PLAISIRS INC, LE

**COCHRANE DISTRICT SOCIAL SERVICES
ADMINISTRATION BOARD**   p 912
500 ALGONQUIN BLVD E, TIMMINS, ON,
P4N 1B7
(705) 268-7722   SIC 8399

COCHRANE DODGE   p 80
See COCHRANE MOTOR PRODUCTS LTD

COCHRANE DODGE CHRYSLER JEEP   p
80
See 641100 ALBERTA LTD

COCHRANE DSSAB   p 912
See COCHRANE DISTRICT SOCIAL SER-
VICES ADMINISTRATION BOARD

COCHRANE GROUP INC   p 66
320 23 AVE SW SUITE 104, CALGARY, AB,
T2S 0J2
(403) 262-3638   SIC 8711

COCHRANE MOTOR PRODUCTS LTD   p 80
6 RIVER HEIGHTS DR, COCHRANE, AB,
T4C 0N8
(403) 932-4072   SIC 5511

COCHRANE TEMISKAMING RESOURCE

CENTRE   p 912
600 TOKE ST, TIMMINS, ON, P4N 6W1
(705) 267-8181   SIC 8052

COCHRANE'S PHARMASAVE   p 471
See COCHRANE, D. ROSS PHARMACY
LIMITED

**COCHRANE, D. ROSS PHARMACY LIM-
ITED**   p
471
442 MAIN ST, WOLFVILLE, NS, B4P 1E2
(902) 542-3624   SIC 5912

COCHRANE/EMPRESS V PARTNERSHIP   p
80
262145 RANGE ROAD 43, COCHRANE,
AB, T4C 2J8
(403) 932-8555   SIC 4619

COCO ASHPHALT ENGINEERING, DIV OF
p 785
See COCO PAVING INC

COCO PAVING INC   p 491
6520 HWY 62, BELLEVILLE, ON, K8N 4Z5
(613) 962-3461   SIC 1611

COCO PAVING INC   p 496
3075 MAPLE GROVE RD, BOWMANVILLE,
ON, L1C 6N2
(905) 697-0400   SIC 1611

COCO PAVING INC   p 599
4139 HWY 34, GREEN VALLEY, ON, K0C
1L0
(613) 525-1750   SIC 1611

COCO PAVING INC   p 785
949 WILSON AVE, NORTH YORK, ON, M3K
1G2
(416) 633-9670   SIC 1611

COCOCO CHOCOLATIERS INC   p 22
2320 2 AVE SE, CALGARY, AB, T2E 6J9
(403) 265-5777   SIC 2066

COCONUT GROVE INTIMATES   p 668
See COCONUT GROVE PADS INC

COCONUT GROVE PADS INC   p 668
525 DENISON ST UNIT 1, MARKHAM, ON,
L3R 1B8
(905) 752-0566   SIC 2342

CODAN RADIO COMMUNICATIONS   p 335
See DANIELS ELECTRONICS LTD

CODET   p 1081
See 9099-9012 QUEBEC INC

CODET INC   p 1081
49 RUE MAPLE, COATICOOK, QC, J1A
1C3
(819) 849-4819   SIC 2326

CODIAC TRANSIT   p 408
See MONCTON, CITY OF

COENTREPRISE LVM - INSPEC-SOL   p
1266
See ENGLOBE CORP

**COENTREPRISE MANUTENTION QUEBEC
ET GAUTHIER INTERLIFT**   p 1251
See MANUTENTION QUEBEC INC

COENTREPRISE TRANSELEC-ARNO   p
1085
2075 BOUL FORTIN, COTE SAINT-LUC,
QC, H7S 1P4
(514) 382-1550   SIC 4911

COFACE CANADA   p 766
See COFACE SERVICES CANADA COM-
PANY

COFACE SERVICES CANADA COMPANY p
766
251 CONSUMERS RD SUITE 910, NORTH
YORK, ON, M2J 4R3
(647) 426-4730   SIC 8741

COFFEE CONNECTION LTD, THE   p 10
401 33 ST NE UNIT 3, CALGARY, AB, T2A
7R3
(403) 269-5977   SIC 7389

COFFEE COOP, THE   p 895
693 ERIE ST, STRATFORD, ON, N4Z 1A1
(519) 271-6127   SIC 5461

COFFEE TIME   p 870
See CHAIRMAN'S BRAND CORPORA-
TION

COFFEE TIME   p 871
See COFFEE TIME DONUTS INCORPO-

RATED
COFFEE TIME DONUTS INCORPORATEDp
871
77 PROGRESS AVE, SCARBOROUGH,
ON, M1P 2Y7
(416) 288-8515   *SIC 6794*
COFFRAGE ALLIANCE LTEE   p 1083
2000 RUE DE LIERRE, COTE SAINT-LUC,
QC, H7G 4Y4
(514) 326-5200   *SIC 1542*
COFFRAGE CCC   p 1279
See *COFFRAGES DOMINIC LTEE, LES*
COFFRAGE MAGMA (10 ANS) INC p 1231
1500 RUE MARCEL-BENOIT, MONTREAL,
QC, H7C 0A9
(450) 664-4989   *SIC 1799*
COFFRAGE MEGAFORME INC   p 1232
2500 MONTEE SAINT-FRANCOIS, MON-
TREAL, QC, H7E 4P2
SIC 1799
COFFRAGES ATLANTIQUE INC   p 1058
41   RUE   GASTON-DUMOULIN,
BLAINVILLE, QC, J7C 6B4
(450) 437-5353   *SIC 1799*
COFFRAGES DOMINIC LTEE, LES p 1279
6921 BOUL PIERRE-BERTRAND, QUE-
BEC, QC, G2K 1M1
(418) 626-3271   *SIC 1799*
COFFRAGES L.D. INC   p 1139
2621 AV DE LA ROTONDE, LEVIS, QC,
G6X 2M2
(418) 832-7070   *SIC 1799*
COFFRAGES SYNERGY   p 1134
See *9090-5092 QUEBEC INC*
COFLEX PACKAGING DIV OF DLP   p 1238
See *DE LUXE PRODUITS DE PAPIER INC*
COFOMO INC   p 1202
1000 RUE DE LA GAUCHETIERE O UNITE
1500, MONTREAL, QC, H3B 4X5
(514) 866-0039   *SIC 7379*
COFORCE INC   p 1048
11301 RUE MIRABEAU, ANJOU, QC, H1J
2S2
(514) 354-3430   *SIC 8361*
COG-VEYOR SYSTEMS INC   p 1030
371 HANLAN RD, WOODBRIDGE, ON, L4L
3T1
(416) 798-7333   *SIC 5084*
COGAN   p 1380
See *PRODUITS DE FIL ET DE METAL CO-
GAN LTEE*
COGECO & DESSIN   p 1202
See *COGECO INC*
COGECO COMMUNICATIONS INC   p 1202
5 PLACE VILLE-MARIE BUREAU 1700,
MONTREAL, QC, H3B 0B3
(514) 874-2600   *SIC 4841*
COGECO CONNEXION INC   p 1202
5 PLACE VILLE-MARIE BUREAU 1700,
MONTREAL, QC, H3B 0B3
(514) 764-4700   *SIC 4841*
COGECO INC   p 1202
5 PLACE VILLE-MARIE BUREAU 1700,
MONTREAL, QC, H3B 0B3
(514) 764-4700   *SIC 4832*
COGECO MEDIA ACQUISITIONS INC   p
1202
5 PLACE VILLE-MARIE BUREAU 1700,
MONTREAL, QC, H3B 0B3
(514) 764-4700   *SIC 6712*
COGECO MEDIA INC   p 1389
4141   BOUL   SAINT-JEAN,   TROIS-
RIVIERES, QC, G9B 2M8
(819) 691-1001   *SIC 7922*
COGENT POWER INC   p 527
845 LAURENTIAN DR, BURLINGTON, ON,
L7N 3W7
(905) 637-3033   *SIC 4911*
COGHLAN'S LTD   p 390
121 IRENE ST, WINNIPEG, MB, R3T 4C7
(204) 284-9550   *SIC 5091*
**COGIR APARTMENTS REAL ESTATE IN-
VESTMENT TRUST**   p
1068

7250 BOUL TASCHEREAU BUREAU 200,
BROSSARD, QC, J4W 1M9
(450) 672-5090   *SIC 6531*
COGIR GENERAL PARTNERSHIP   p 1069
See *SOCIETE DE GESTION COGIR
S.E.N.C.*
COGIRES INC   p 1269
1220 PLACE GEORGE-V O, QUEBEC, QC,
G1R 5B8
(418) 522-3848   *SIC 7011*
COGNERA   p 46
530 8 AVE SW SUITE 920, CALGARY, AB,
T2P 3S8
(403) 218-2010   *SIC 8741*
COGNITIVE SCIENCE PROGRAM   p 785
See *YORK UNIVERSITY*
**COGNIZANT TECHNOLOGY SOLUTIONS
CANADA, INC**   p 977
241 SPADINA AVE SUITE 500, TORONTO,
ON, M5T 2E2
(647) 827-0412   *SIC 7379*
COGSDALE CORPORATION   p 1040
3 LOWER MALPEQUE RD, CHARLOTTE-
TOWN, PE, C1E 1R4
(902) 892-3101   *SIC 7371*
COH   p 1061
See *REEL COH INC*
COH PROJETS ET SERVICES INC   p 1060
801 BOUL DU CURE-BOIVIN, BOIS-
BRIAND, QC, J7G 2J2
(450) 430-6500   *SIC 3531*
COHEN & COHEN   p 748
See *1770918 ONTARIO INC*
COHEN'S HOME FURNISHINGS LIMITED p
426
24 GLENCOE DR, MOUNT PEARL, NL,
A1N 4P6
(709) 739-6631   *SIC 5712*
COHEN, JERRY FORWARDERS LTD   p
1127
5203 RUE FAIRWAY, LACHINE, QC, H8T
3K8
(514) 635-1033   *SIC 4213*
COHENDAV INC   p 1338
153 RUE GRAVELINE, SAINT-LAURENT,
QC, H4T 1R4
(514) 342-6700   *SIC 6712*
COHERENT CANADA INC   p 713
1222 APRIL DR, MISSISSAUGA, ON, L5J
3J7
(905) 823-5808   *SIC 3699*
COHPA   p 851
See *CENTRAL ONTARIO HEALTHCARE
PROCUREMENT ALLIANCE*
COI   p 29
See *CONTEMPORARY OFFICE INTERI-
ORS LTD*
COIFFURE BEL-AGE QUEBEC   p 1224
See *UNITES MOBILES DE COIFFURE DE
MONTREAL INC, LES*
COILED TUBING DISTRICT, DIV OF   p 155
See *BAKER HUGHES CANADA COMPANY*
COILPLUS   p 621
See *COILPLUS CANADA INC*
COILPLUS CANADA INC   p 621
18 UNDERWOOD RD, INGERSOLL, ON,
N5C 3V6
(519) 485-6393   *SIC 5051*
COINAMATIC CANADA INC   p 730
301 MATHESON BLVD W, MISSISSAUGA,
ON, L5R 3G3
(905) 755-1946   *SIC 7215*
COIT SERVICES   p 189
See *GENTLE CARE DRAPERY & CARPET
CLEANERS LTD*
COJALY INC   p 1394
601 AV SAINT-CHARLES, VAUDREUIL-
DORION, QC, J7V 8G4
(450) 455-0409   *SIC 5812*
COL-FAX   p 1236
See *GRAND MARCHE COL-FAX INC*
COLABOR LIMITED PARTNERSHIP   p 648
580 INDUSTRIAL RD, LONDON, ON, N5V
1V1

(800) 265-9267   *SIC 5141*
COLABOR LIMITED PARTNERSHIP   p 648
580 INDUSTRIAL RD, LONDON, ON, N5V
1V1
(519) 453-3410   *SIC 5141*
COLABOR LIMITED PARTNERSHIP   p 738
6270 KENWAY DR, MISSISSAUGA, ON,
L5T 2N3
(905) 795-2400   *SIC 5142*
COLABOR LIMITED PARTNERSHIP   p 817
100 LEGACY RD, OTTAWA, ON, K1G 5T8
(613) 737-7000   *SIC 5141*
COLABOR SKOR DISTRIBUTION   p 558
See *SKOR FOOD SERVICE LTD*
COLACEM CANADA INC   p 1086
2540 BOUL DANIEL-JOHNSON BUREAU
808 8E ETAGE, COTE SAINT-LUC, QC, H7T
2S3
(450) 686-1221   *SIC 1422*
COLAROME   p 1309
See *CAPOL INC*
COLAS CANADA INC   p 915
4950 YONGE ST SUITE 2400, TORONTO,
ON, M2N 6K1
(416) 293-5443   *SIC 1611*
COLASANTI FARMS LIMITED   p 858
1550 ROAD 3 E, RUTHVEN, ON, N0P 2G0
(519) 326-3287   *SIC 5812*
COLAUTTI CONSTRUCTION LTD   p 597
2562 DEL ZOTTO AVE, GLOUCESTER,
ON, K1T 3V7
(613) 822-1440   *SIC 1623*
COLAUTTI GROUP   p 597
See *COLAUTTI CONSTRUCTION LTD*
COLCHESTER CO-OP   p 468
See *COLCHESTER CO-OPERATIVE SER-
VICES LIMITED*
**COLCHESTER CO-OPERATIVE SERVICES
LIMITED**   p 468
339 WILLOW ST SUITE A, TRURO, NS,
B2N 5A6
(902) 893-9470   *SIC 5411*
**COLCHESTER RESIDENTIAL SERVICES
SOCIETY**   p 468
35 COMMERCIAL ST SUITE 201, TRURO,
NS, B2N 3H9
(902) 893-4273   *SIC 8322*
COLD LAKE FOODS   p 81
See *SOBEYS CAPITAL INCORPORATED*
COLD NORTH SEAFOODS LIMITED   p 425
2 WATER ST, LA SCIE, NL, A0K 3M0
SIC 2092
COLD NORTH SEAFOODS LIMITED   p 426
157 GLENCOE DR SUITE 200, MOUNT
PEARL, NL, A1N 4S7
(709) 368-9955   *SIC 5146*
COLD PRESS CORP, THE   p 972
176 ST GEORGE ST, TORONTO, ON, M5R
2M7
(416) 934-5034   *SIC 5149*
COLD SPRINGS FARM   p 634
See *THAMES VALLEY PROCESSORS LTD*
COLD STORAGE   p 700
See *S.D.R. DISTRIBUTION SERVICES*
COLDSTAR SOLUTIONS INC   p 340
937 DUNFORD AVE UNIT 1, VICTORIA,
BC, V9B 2S4
(250) 391-7425   *SIC 4212*
COLDSTREAM CONCRETE LIMITED p 621
402 QUAKER LANE, ILDERTON, ON, N0M
2A0
(519) 666-0604   *SIC 3272*
COLDWATER FOODLAND   p 546
77 COLDWATER RD, COLDWATER, ON,
L0K 1E0
(705) 686-7700   *SIC 5411*
COLDWELL BANKER   p 190
See *N R S WESTBURN REALTY LTD*
COLDWELL BANKER   p 813
See *R.M.R REAL ESTATE LIMITED*
COLDWELL BANKER   p 1040
See *PARKER REALTY LTD*
**COLDWELL BANKER 1ST LONDON REAL
ESTATE**   p 657

See *1ST LONDON REAL ESTATE SER-
VICES INC*
COLDWELL BANKER COBURN REALTY p
750
See *COBURN REALTY LTD*
**COLDWELL BANKER FIRST OTTAWA RE-
ALTY**   p
890
See *FIRST OTTAWA REALTY INC*
**COLDWELL BANKER FIRST OTTAWA RE-
ALTY LTD**   p
828
1419 CARLING AVE SUITE 219, OTTAWA,
ON, K1Z 7L6
(613) 728-2664   *SIC 6531*
**COLDWELL BANKER HOME & FAMILY RE-
ALTY LTD**   p
803
1515 REBECCA ST SUITE 25, OAKVILLE,
ON, L6L 5G8
(905) 825-3305   *SIC 6531*
**COLDWELL BANKER HOMEFRONT RE-
ALTY**   p
514
See *HOMEFRONT REALTY INC*
COLDWELL BANKER HORIZON REALTY p
221
See *COLDWELL BANKER HORIZON RE-
ALTY LTD*
**COLDWELL BANKER HORIZON REALTY
LTD**   p 221
1470 HARVEY AVE SUITE 14, KELOWNA,
BC, V1Y 9K8
(250) 860-7500   *SIC 6531*
**COLDWELL BANKER MOMENTUM RE-
ALTY**   p
884
See *MOMENTUM REALTY INC*
**COLDWELL BANKER NATIONAL PRE-
FERRED PROPERTIES**   p
388
1530 TAYLOR AVE SUITE 6, WINNIPEG,
MB, R3N 1Y1
(204) 985-4300   *SIC 6531*
**COLDWELL BANKER NEUMANN REAL
ESTATE**   p 601
See *COLDWELL BANKER NEUMANN
HERB REAL ESTATE LTD*
**COLDWELL BANKER NEUMANN HERB
REAL ESTATE LTD**   p 601
824 GORDON ST SUITE 201, GUELPH,
ON, N1G 1Y7
(519) 821-3600   *SIC 6531*
**COLDWELL BANKER NEUMANN REAL
ESTATE**   p 601
824 GORDON ST UNIT 201, GUELPH, ON,
N1G 1Y7
(519) 821-3600   *SIC 6531*
**COLDWELL BANKER PETER BENNIGER
REALTY**   p 640
See *PETER BENNINGER REALTY LTD*
COLDWELL BANKER PREMIER REALTY p
323
See *STERN REALTY (1994) LTD*
**COLDWELL BANKER PROPERTIES UN-
LIMITED REALTY LTD**   p
918
874 EGLINTON AVE E, TORONTO, ON,
M4G 2L1
(416) 424-1300   *SIC 6531*
**COLDWELL BANKER RHODES & COM-
PANY**   p
833
See *COLDWELL BANKER RHODES &
COMPANY LTD*
**COLDWELL BANKER RHODES & COM-
PANY LTD**   p
833
100 ARGYLE AVE, OTTAWA, ON, K2P 1B6
(613) 236-9551   *SIC 6531*
COLDWELL BANKER SARAZEN REALTYp
826
See *SARAZEN REALTY LTD*
COLDWELL CASE REALTY   p 919

836 DANFORTH AVE, TORONTO, ON, M4J
1L6
(416) 690-7771 *SIC* 6531
COLE CARRIERS CORP *p* 609
89 GLOW AVE, HAMILTON, ON, L8H 3V7
(905) 548-0979 *SIC* 4212
COLE ENGINEERING GROUP LTD *p* 668
70 VALLEYWOOD DR, MARKHAM, ON,
L3R 4T5
(905) 940-6161 *SIC* 8711
COLE HARBOUR PLACE *p* 443
See COMMUNITY BUILDERS INC
COLE INTERNATIONAL INC *p* 22
1111 49 AVE NE, CALGARY, AB, T2E 8V2
(403) 262-2771 *SIC* 4731
COLEMAN CARE CENTRE *p* 485
See 477281 ONTARIO LTD
COLEMAN CONTAINERS LIMITED *p* 574
54 ATOMIC AVE, ETOBICOKE, ON, M8Z
5L1
(416) 253-7441 *SIC* 2653
COLEMAN'S FOOD CENTRE STORES *p*
434
See FOCENCO LIMITED
COLEMAN, DOUG TRUCKING LTD *p* 648
540 FIRST ST, LONDON, ON, N5V 1Z3
(519) 451-4349 *SIC* 4212
**COLES RETIREMENT PLANNING CON-
SULTANTS** *p*
452
2000 BARRINGTON ST, HALIFAX, NS, B3J
3K1
(902) 423-0350 *SIC* 6411
COLET PACKAGING *p* 738
See COLET SHIPPING SUPPLIES INC
COLET SHIPPING SUPPLIES INC *p* 738
165 ANNAGEM BLVD, MISSISSAUGA, ON,
L5T 2V1
(905) 670-4919 *SIC* 5113
COLGATE-PALMOLIVE CANADA INC *p* 687
6400 NORTHWEST DR, MISSISSAUGA,
ON, L4V 1K1
SIC 2844
COLGATE-PALMOLIVE CANADA INC *p* 779
895 DON MILLS RD, NORTH YORK, ON,
M3C 1W3
(416) 421-6000 *SIC* 2844
**COLIN PLOTKIN & SONS CONSULTING
INC** *p* 258
12011 RIVERSIDE WAY SUITE 210, RICH-
MOND, BC, V6W 1K6
(604) 241-9639 *SIC* 6321
COLIO ESTATE WINES INC *p* 693
5900 AMBLER DR SUITE 7, MISSIS-
SAUGA, ON, L4W 2N3
(905) 949-4246 *SIC* 5921
COLISPRO INC *p* 1307
3505 BOUL LOSCH, SAINT-HUBERT, QC,
J3Y 5T7
(450) 445-7171 *SIC* 7389
COLITREX *p* 1211
See INTELCOM COURRIER CANADA INC
COLL?GE QUEEN OF ANGEL *p* 1096
See QUEEN OF ANGELS ACADEMY INC
COLLABERA CANADA INC *p* 705
1 ROBERT SPECK PKY UNIT 900, MISSIS-
SAUGA, ON, L4Z 3M3
(416) 639-6250 *SIC* 7361
COLLABORATIVE STRUCTURES LIMITED
p 537
6683 ELLIS RD, CAMBRIDGE, ON, N3C
2V4
(519) 658-2750 *SIC* 1542
COLLECTCENTS INC *p* 738
1450 MEYERSIDE DR UNIT 200, MISSIS-
SAUGA, ON, L5T 2N5
(905) 670-7575 *SIC* 7322
COLLECTES CODERR *p* 1045
See PAPIERS SOLIDERR INC, LES
COLLECTION ARIANNE INC *p* 1225
1655 RUE DE LOUVAIN O, MONTREAL,
QC, H4N 1G6
(514) 385-9393 *SIC* 2341
COLLECTION CONRAD C INC *p* 1178

9320 BOUL SAINT-LAURENT BUREAU
200, MONTREAL, QC, H2N 1N7
(514) 385-9599 *SIC* 2337
COLLECTION IME *p* 1061
See JENO NEUMAN ET FILS INC
COLLECTION SONDER *p* 1184
See SONDER CANADA INC
**COLLECTIONS DE STYLE R.D. INTERNA-
TIONALES LTEE, LES** *p*
1227
5275 RUE FERRIER BUREAU 200, MON-
TREAL, QC, H4P 1L7
(514) 342-1222 *SIC* 5137
COLLECTIONS PIACENTE *p* 1231
See COLLECTIONS UNIMAGE INC
COLLECTIONS SHAN INC, LES *p* 1400
4390 SUD LAVAL (A-440) O, VIMONT, QC,
H7T 2P7
(450) 687-7101 *SIC* 2339
COLLECTIONS UNIMAGE INC *p* 1231
5620 RUE ERNEST-CORMIER, MON-
TREAL, QC, H7C 2T5
(450) 661-6444 *SIC* 5699
COLLECTOR CARS *p* 493
See RM CLASSIC CARS INC
COLLEGA INTERNATIONAL INC *p* 776
210 LESMILL RD, NORTH YORK, ON, M3B
2T5
(416) 754-1444 *SIC* 5122
COLLEGE AHUNTSIC *p* 1176
9155 RUE SAINT HUBERT, MONTREAL,
QC, H2M 1Y8
(514) 389-5921 *SIC* 8221
**COLLEGE AND ASSOCIATION OF REGIS-
TERED NURSES OF ALBERTA** *p*
95
11620 168 ST NW, EDMONTON, AB, T5M
4A6
(780) 451-0043 *SIC* 8621
COLLEGE ANTOINE-GIROUARD *p* 1312
700 RUE GIROUARD E, SAINT-
HYACINTHE, QC, J2S 2Y2
SIC 8221
**COLLEGE AVENUE SECONDARY
SCHOOL** *p* 1035
*See THAMES VALLEY DISTRICT SCHOOL
BOARD*
COLLEGE BEAUBOIS *p* 1245
4901 RUE DU COLLEGE-BEAUBOIS,
PIERREFONDS, QC, H8Y 3T4
(514) 684-7642 *SIC* 8211
COLLEGE BOURGET *p* 1283
65 RUE SAINT-PIERRE, RIGAUD, QC, J0P
1P0
(450) 451-0815 *SIC* 8221
COLLEGE CATHOLIC SAMUEL-GENEST *p*
820
*See CONSEIL DES ECOLES
CATHOLIQUES DE LANGUE FRANCAISE
DU CENTRE-EST*
COLLEGE CHARLEMAGNE *p* 1245
See COLLEGE CHARLEMAGNE INC
COLLEGE CHARLEMAGNE INC *p* 1245
5000 RUE PILON, PIERREFONDS, QC,
H9K 1G4
(514) 626-7060 *SIC* 8221
**COLLEGE CHARLES-LEMOYNE DE
LONGUEUIL INC** *p* 1144
1430 RUE PATENAUDE, LONGUEUIL, QC,
J4K 5H4
(450) 463-1592 *SIC* 8211
**COLLEGE CHARLES-LEMOYNE DE
LONGUEUIL INC** *p* 1146
901 CH TIFFIN, LONGUEUIL, QC, J4P 3G6
(514) 875-0505 *SIC* 8211
COLLEGE D'AFFAIRES ELLIS (1974) INC *p*
1098
235 RUE MOISAN, DRUMMONDVILLE, QC,
J2C 1W9
(819) 477-3113 *SIC* 8221
**COLLEGE D'ENSEIGNEMENT GENERAL
& PROFESSIONEL DE LA POCATIERE** *p*
1122
140 4E AV, LA POCATIERE, QC, G0R 1Z0

(418) 856-1525 *SIC* 8221
**COLLEGE D'ENSEIGNEMENT GENERAL
& PROFESSIONNEL DE MATANE** *p* 1150
616 AV SAINT-REDEMPTEUR, MATANE,
QC, G4W 1L1
(418) 562-1240 *SIC* 8221
**COLLEGE D'ENSEIGNEMENT GENERAL
ET PROFESSIONEL DE SAINT-HYACINTHE**
p 1312
3000 AV BOULLE, SAINT-HYACINTHE, QC,
J2S 1H9
(450) 773-6800 *SIC* 8222
**COLLEGE D'ENSEIGNEMENT GENERAL
ET PROFESSIONEL FRANCOIS-XAVIER-
GARNEAU** *p*
1270
1640 BOUL DE L'ENTENTE, QUEBEC, QC,
G1S 4S7
(418) 688-8310 *SIC* 8222
**COLLEGE D'ENSEIGNEMENT GENERAL
ET PROFESSIONEL MARIE-VICTORIN** *p*
1163
7000 RUE MARIE-VICTORIN, MONTREAL,
QC, H1G 2J6
(514) 325-0150 *SIC* 8221
**COLLEGE D'ENSEIGNEMENT GENERAL
ET PROFESSIONNEL DE RIVIERE-DU-
LOUP** *p*
1286
80 RUE FRONTENAC, RIVIERE-DU-LOUP,
QC, G5R 1R1
(418) 862-6903 *SIC* 8221
**COLLEGE D'ENSEIGNEMENT GENERAL
ET PROFESSIONNEL DE SAINTE-FOY** *p*
1272
See COOPSCO SAINTE-FOY
**COLLEGE D'ENSEIGNEMENT GENERAL
ET PROFESSIONNEL DE VICTORIAVILLE** *p*
1397
475 RUE NOTRE-DAME E, VICTORIAV-
ILLE, QC, G6P 4B3
(819) 758-6401 *SIC* 8221
**COLLEGE D'ENSEIGNEMENT GEN-
ERAL ET PROFESSIONNEL EDOUARD-
MONTPETIT** *p*
1143
945 CH DE CHAMBLY, LONGUEUIL, QC,
J4H 3M6
(450) 679-2631 *SIC* 8222
**COLLEGE D'ENSEIGNEMENT GENERAL
ET PROFESSIONNEL GERALD-GODIN** *p*
1358
15615 BOUL GOUIN O, SAINTE-
GENEVIEVE, QC, H9H 5K8
(514) 626-2666 *SIC* 8221
**COLLEGE D'ENSEIGNEMENT GENERAL
ET PROFESSIONNEL JOHN ABBOTT** *p*
1355
21275 RUE LAKESHORE, SAINTE-ANNE-
DE-BELLEVUE, QC, H9X 3L9
(514) 457-6610 *SIC* 8221
**COLLEGE D'ENSEIGNEMENT GENERAL
ET PROFESSIONNEL SOREL-TRACY** *p*
1377
3000 BOUL DE TRACY, SOREL-TRACY,
QC, J3R 5B9
(450) 742-6651 *SIC* 8221
**COLLEGE D'ENSEIGNEMENT GENERALE
& PROFESSIONNEL DE LA GASPESIE &
DES ILES** *p* 1102
96 RUE JACQUES-CARTIER, GASPE, QC,
G4X 2S8
(418) 368-2201 *SIC* 8221
COLLEGE DAWSON *p* 1220
3040 RUE SHERBROOKE O, MONTREAL,
QC, H3Z 1A4
(514) 931-8731 *SIC* 8222
COLLEGE DE L'ASSOMPTION *p* 1120
*See CORPORATION DU COLLEGE DE
L'ASSOMPTION, LA*
COLLEGE DE LEVIS *p* 1136
9 RUE MONSEIGNEUR-GOSSELIN BU-
REAU 109, LEVIS, QC, G6V 5K1
(418) 833-1249 *SIC* 8221

COLLEGE DE MONT-ROYAL *p* 1163
2165 RUE BALDWIN, MONTREAL, QC,
H1L 5A7
(514) 351-7851 *SIC* 8221
COLLEGE DE MONTREAL *p* 1214
1931 RUE SHERBROOKE O, MONTREAL,
QC, H3H 1E3
(514) 933-7397 *SIC* 8221
COLLEGE DE ROSEMONT *p* 1168
6400 16E AV, MONTREAL, QC, H1X 2S9
(514) 376-1620 *SIC* 8222
COLLEGE DE SAINT-BONIFACE *p* 364
200 DE LA CATHEDRALE AVE, WINNIPEG,
MB, R2H 0H7
(204) 233-0210 *SIC* 8221
COLLEGE DES MEDECINS DU QUEBEC *p*
1202
1250 BOUL RENE-LEVESQUE O BUREAU
3500, MONTREAL, QC, H3B 0G2
(514) 933-4441 *SIC* 8621
COLLEGE EDOUARD-MONTPETIT *p* 1143
*See COLLEGE D'ENSEIGNEMENT GEN-
ERAL ET PROFESSIONNEL EDOUARD-
MONTPETIT*
**COLLEGE ELLIS CAMPUS DE DRUM-
MONDVILLE** *p*
1098
*See COLLEGE D'AFFAIRES ELLIS (1974)
INC*
COLLEGE ESTHER-BLONDIN *p* 1314
101 RUE SAINTE-ANNE, SAINT-JACQUES,
QC, J0K 2R0
(450) 839-7652 *SIC* 8211
COLLEGE FORD LINCOLN LTD *p* 142
3975 1 AVE S, LETHBRIDGE, AB, T1J 4P8
(403) 329-0333 *SIC* 5511
COLLEGE FRANCAIS (1965) INC *p* 1144
1391 RUE BEAUREGARD, LONGUEUIL,
QC, J4K 2M3
(450) 670-7391 *SIC* 8211
**COLLEGE FRANCAIS ANNEXE RIVE SUD
PRIMAIRE** *p* 1144
See COLLEGE FRANCAIS (1965) INC
COLLEGE FRANCOIS-DE-LAVAL *p* 1269
6 RUE DE LA VIEILLE-UNIVERSITE BU-
REAU 70, QUEBEC, QC, G1R 5X8
(418) 694-1020 *SIC* 8211
COLLEGE HEIGHTS S.S. *p* 600
*See UPPER GRAND DISTRICT SCHOOL
BOARD, THE*
**COLLEGE INTERNATIONAL DES MAR-
CELLINES** *p*
1401
See VILLA SAINTE MARCELLINE
**COLLEGE INTERNATIONAL MARIE DE
FRANCE** *p* 1219
4635 CH QUEEN-MARY, MONTREAL, QC,
H3W 1W3
(514) 737-1177 *SIC* 8211
COLLEGE JEAN DE LA MENNAIS *p* 1123
870 CH DE SAINT-JEAN, LA PRAIRIE, QC,
J5R 2L5
(450) 659-7657 *SIC* 8211
COLLEGE JEAN-EUDES INC *p* 1168
3535 BOUL ROSEMONT, MONTREAL, QC,
H1X 1K7
(514) 376-5740 *SIC* 8211
COLLEGE JESUS MARIE DE SILLERY *p*
1271
2047 CH SAINT-LOUIS, QUEBEC, QC, G1T
1P3
(418) 687-9250 *SIC* 8211
COLLEGE LAFLECHE *p* 1386
1687 BOUL DU CARMEL, TROIS-
RIVIERES, QC, G8Z 3R8
(819) 375-7346 *SIC* 8221
COLLEGE LASALLE *p* 1214
2120 RUE SAINTE-CATHERINE O, MON-
TREAL, QC, H3H 1M7
(514) 939-2006 *SIC* 8249
COLLEGE LASALLE INDUSTRIE *p* 1214
See 131427 CANADA INC
COLLEGE LAVAL *p* 1231
1275 AV DU COLLEGE, MONTREAL, QC.

H7C 1W8
(450) 661-7714   *SIC* 8211
COLLEGE LETENDRE   *p 1235*
1000 BOUL DE L'AVENIR, MONTREAL, QC, H7N 6J6
(450) 688-9933   *SIC* 8221
COLLEGE LOUIS RIEL   *p 364*
See *DIVISION SCOLAIRE FRANCO-MANITOBAINE*
COLLEGE LOWER CANADA, LE   *p 1221*
See *LOWER CANADA COLLEGE*
COLLEGE MARIE-DE-L'INCARNATION *p 1387*
725 RUE HART, TROIS-RIVIERES, QC, G9A 4R9
(819) 379-3223   *SIC* 8211
COLLEGE MERICI   *p 1270*
755 GRANDE ALLEE O BUREAU 683, QUEBEC, QC, G1S 1C1
(418) 683-1591   *SIC* 8221
COLLEGE MONT SACRE-COEUR   *p 1110*
210 RUE DENISON E, GRANBY, QC, J2H 2R6
(450) 372-6882   *SIC* 8222
COLLEGE MONT-ROYAL   *p 1163*
See *COLLEGE DE MONT-ROYAL*
COLLEGE MONT-SAINT-LOUIS   *p 1171*
1700 BOUL HENRI-BOURASSA E, MONTREAL, QC, H2C 1J3
(514) 382-1560   *SIC* 8211
COLLEGE NOTRE-DAME   *p 899*
See *CONSEIL SCOLAIRE DE DISTRICT CATHOLIQUE DU NOUVEL-ONTARIO, LE*
COLLEGE NOTRE-DAME-DE-LOURDES *p 1146*
845 CH TIFFIN, LONGUEUIL, QC, J4P 3G5
(450) 670-4740   *SIC* 8211
COLLEGE O'SULLIVAN DE MONTREAL INC   *p 1213*
1191 RUE DE LA MONTAGNE, MONTREAL, QC, H3G 1Z2
(514) 866-4622   *SIC* 8244
COLLEGE OF EDUCATION   *p 1434*
See *UNIVERSITY OF SASKATCHEWAN*
COLLEGE OF ENGINEERING   *p 1434*
See *UNIVERSITY OF SASKATCHEWAN*
COLLEGE OF NEW CALEDONIA, THE   *p 250*
3330 22ND AVE, PRINCE GEORGE, BC, V2N 1P8
(250) 562-2131   *SIC* 8221
COLLEGE OF NEW CALEDONIA, THE   *p 252*
100 CAMPUS WAY, QUESNEL, BC, V2J 7K1
(250) 991-7500   *SIC* 8222
COLLEGE OF NURSES OF ONTARIO *p 972*
101 DAVENPORT RD, TORONTO, ON, M5R 3P1
(416) 928-0900   *SIC* 8621
COLLEGE OF NURSING   *p 1434*
See *UNIVERSITY OF SASKATCHEWAN*
COLLEGE OF PHYSICIANS & SURGEONS OF ALBERTA   *p 88*
10020 100 ST NW SUITE 2700, EDMONTON, AB, T5J 0N3
(780) 423-4764   *SIC* 8011
COLLEGE OF PHYSICIANS AND SURGEONS OF ONTARIO   *p 944*
80 COLLEGE ST, TORONTO, ON, M5G 2E2
(416) 967-2600   *SIC* 8621
COLLEGE OF REGISTERED NURSES OF BC   *p 320*
2855 ARBUTUS ST, VANCOUVER, BC, V6J 3Y8
(604) 736-7331   *SIC* 8621
COLLEGE OF THE NORTH ATLANTIC *p 434*
432 MASSACHUSETTS DR, STEPHENVILLE, NL, A2N 3C1
(709) 643-7868   *SIC* 8211
COLLEGE OF THE ROCKIES   *p 203*
2700 COLLEGE WAY, CRANBROOK, BC,

V1C 5L7
(250) 489-2751   *SIC* 8222
COLLEGE PARK MOTOR PRODUCTS LTD *p 170*
4512 RAILWAY AVE, VERMILION, AB, T9X 1E9
(780) 853-4646   *SIC* 5511
COLLEGE PRINTERS   *p 261*
See *POSTMEDIA NETWORK INC*
COLLEGE REGINA ASSUMPTA (1995)   *p 1171*
1750 RUE SAURIOL E, MONTREAL, QC, H2C 1X4
(514) 382-9998   *SIC* 8211
COLLEGE SAINT-ALEXANDRE DE LA GATINEAU   *p 1105*
2425 RUE SAINT-LOUIS, GATINEAU, QC, J8V 1E7
(819) 561-3812   *SIC* 8221
COLLEGE SAINT-BERNARD   *p 1096*
25 AV DES FRERES-DE-LA-CHARITE, DRUMMONDVILLE, QC, J2B 6A2
(819) 478-3330   *SIC* 8211
COLLEGE SAINT-CHARLES-GARNIER, LE *p 1270*
1150 BOUL RENE-LEVESQUE O, QUEBEC, QC, G1S 1V7
(418) 681-0107   *SIC* 8221
COLLEGE SAINT-MAURICE   *p 1312*
630 RUE GIROUARD O, SAINT-HYACINTHE, QC, J2S 2Y3
(450) 773-7478   *SIC* 8221
COLLEGE SAINT-SACREMENT   *p 1379*
901 RUE SAINT-LOUIS, TERREBONNE, QC, J6W 1K1
(450) 471-6615   *SIC* 8211
COLLEGE SAINTE MARCELLAINE *p 1224*
9155 BOUL GOUIN O, MONTREAL, QC, H4K 1C3
(514) 334-9651   *SIC* 8211
COLLEGE SAINTE-ANNE   *p 1126*
1250 BOUL SAINT-JOSEPH, LACHINE, QC, H8S 2M8
(514) 637-3571   *SIC* 8221
COLLEGE SCOLAIRE CATHOLIQUE FRANCO OUEST   *p 832*
See *CONSEIL DES ECOLES CATHOLIQUES DE LANGUE FRANCAISE DU CENTRE-EST*
COLLEGE SHAWINIGAN   *p 1368*
2263 AV DU COLLEGE, SHAWINIGAN, QC, G9N 6V8
(819) 539-6401   *SIC* 8221
COLLEGE STANISLAS INCORPORE   *p 1244*
780 BOUL DOLLARD, OUTREMONT, QC, H2V 3G5
(514) 273-9521   *SIC* 8211
COLLEGE STE-ANNE-DE-LA POCATIERE *p 1122*
100 4E AV, LA POCATIERE, QC, G0R 1Z0
(418) 856-3012   *SIC* 8221
COLLEGES OF APPLIED ARTS & TECHNOLOGY PENSION PLAN   *p 935*
250 YONGE ST UNIT 2900, TORONTO, ON, M5B 2L7
(416) 673-9000   *SIC* 6371
COLLEY, BORLAND & VALE INSURANCE BROKERS LIMITED   *p 1000*
4591 HIGHWAY 7 E SUITE 200, UNIONVILLE, ON, L3R 1M6
(905) 477-2720   *SIC* 6411
COLLICUTT ENERGY SERVICES CORP *p 155*
8133 EDGAR INDUSTRIAL CLOSE, RED DEER, AB, T4P 3R4
(403) 309-9250   *SIC* 5063
COLLIERS INTERNATIONAL   *p 379*
See *PRATT MCGARRY INC*
COLLIERS INTERNATIONAL   *p 961*
See *COLLIERS MACAULAY NICOLLS INC*
COLLIERS INTERNATIONAL   *p 1194*
See *COLLIERS INTERNATIONAL (QUE-*

BEC) INC
COLLIERS INTERNATIONAL   *p 1417*
See *CIR COMMERCIAL REALTY INC*
COLLIERS INTERNATIONAL (QUEBEC) INC   *p 1194*
1800 AV MCGILL COLLEGE BUREAU 400, MONTREAL, QC, H3A 3J6
(514) 866-1900   *SIC* 6531
COLLIERS INTERNATIONAL CANADA   *p 303*
See *COLLIERS MACAULAY NICOLLS INC*
COLLIERS INTERNATIONAL GROUP INC *p 961*
181 BAY ST SUITE 1400, TORONTO, ON, M5J 2V1
(416) 777-2200   *SIC* 6531
COLLIERS INTERNATIONAL GROUP INC *p 974*
1140 BAY ST SUITE 4000, TORONTO, ON, M5S 2B4
(416) 960-9500   *SIC* 6531
COLLIERS MACAULAY NICOLLS INC   *p 47*
335 8 AVE SW 900 ROYAL BANK BLDG, CALGARY, AB, T2P 1C9
(403) 265-9180   *SIC* 6531
COLLIERS MACAULAY NICOLLS INC *p 303*
200 GRANVILLE ST UNIT 19, VANCOUVER, BC, V6C 1S4
(604) 681-4111   *SIC* 6531
COLLIERS MACAULAY NICOLLS INC *p 961*
181 BAY ST UNIT 1400, TORONTO, ON, M5J 2V1
(416) 777-2200   *SIC* 8611
COLLIERS MCCLOCKLIN REAL ESTATE CORP   *p 1426*
728 SPADINA CRES E SUITE 101, SASKATOON, SK, S7K 3H2
(306) 653-4410   *SIC* 6531
COLLIERS PROJECT LEADERS INC *p 831*
2720 IRIS ST, OTTAWA, ON, K2C 1E6
(613) 820-6610   *SIC* 8741
COLLIN & DIANA PARKER SALES LTD   *p 805*
1100 KERR ST, OAKVILLE, ON, L6M 0L4
(905) 844-0202   *SIC* 5531
COLLINGWOOD CARS INC   *p 546*
10230 26 HWY, COLLINGWOOD, ON, L9Y 0A5
(705) 444-1414   *SIC* 5511
COLLINGWOOD COLLEGIATE INSTITUTE *p 547*
See *SIMCOE COUNTY DISTRICT SCHOOL BOARD, THE*
COLLINGWOOD GENERAL AND MARINE HOSPITAL, THE   *p 546*
459 HUME ST, COLLINGWOOD, ON, L9Y 1W9
(705) 445-2550   *SIC* 8062
COLLINGWOOD NEIGHBOURHOOD HOUSE   *p 288*
See *COLLINGWOOD NEIGHBOURHOOD HOUSE SOCIETY*
COLLINGWOOD NEIGHBOURHOOD HOUSE SOCIETY   *p 288*
5288 JOYCE ST, VANCOUVER, BC, V5R 6C9
(604) 435-0323   *SIC* 8399
COLLINGWOOD SCHOOL   *p 341*
See *COLLINGWOOD SCHOOL SOCIETY*
COLLINGWOOD SCHOOL SOCIETY *p 341*
2605 WENTWORTH AVE, WEST VANCOUVER, BC, V7S 3H4
(604) 925-8375   *SIC* 8211
COLLINGWOOD SCHOOL SOCIETY *p 341*
70 MORVEN DR, WEST VANCOUVER, BC, V7S 1B2
(604) 925-3331   *SIC* 8211
COLLINGWOOD SCHOOL WENTWORTH *p 341*
See *COLLINGWOOD SCHOOL SOCIETY*
COLLINGWOOD TOYOTA   *p 546*
See *COLLINGWOOD CARS INC*
COLLINS AEROSPACE   *p 803*
See *GOODRICH AEROSPACE CANADA*

LTD
COLLINS AUTO PARTS   *p 873*
See *C & S AUTO PARTS LIMITED*
COLLINS BARRELL CHARTER ACCOUNTANTS   *p 86*
See *1067863 ALBERTA LTD*
COLLINS BARROW KAWARTHAS LLP   *p 840*
272 CHARLOTTE ST, PETERBOROUGH, ON, K9J 2V4
(705) 742-3418   *SIC* 8721
COLLINS BARROW MONTREAL   *p 1203*
625 BOUL RENE-LEVESQUE O BUREAU 1100, MONTREAL, QC, H3B 1R2
(514) 866-8533   *SIC* 8721
COLLINS BARROW OTTAWA LLP   *p 751*
301 MOODIE DR SUITE 400, NEPEAN, ON, K2H 9C4
(613) 820-8010   *SIC* 8721
COLLINS BARROW TORONTO LLP   *p 950*
11 KING ST W SUITE 700, TORONTO, ON, M5H 4C7
(416) 480-0160   *SIC* 8721
COLLINS BARROW VICTORIA LTD   *p 336*
645 FORT ST SUITE 540, VICTORIA, BC, V8W 1G2
(250) 386-0500   *SIC* 8721
COLLINS BARROW, SUDBURY - NIPISSING LLP   *p 898*
1174 ST. JEROME ST, SUDBURY, ON, P3A 2V9
(705) 560-5592   *SIC* 8721
COLLINS BUREAU   *p 543*
See *ERIE & MAIN CONSULTING INC*
COLLINS CONCESSIONS LIMITED   *p 758*
8621 EARL THOMAS AVE, NIAGARA FALLS, ON, L2G 0B5
SIC 2064
COLLINS FAMILY CARS INC   *p 660*
1035 WHARNCLIFFE RD S, LONDON, ON, N6L 1J9
(519) 690-1600   *SIC* 5511
COLLINS INDUSTRIES   *p 107*
See *401919 ALBERTA LTD*
COLLINS INDUSTRIES LTD   *p 108*
3740 73 AVE NW, EDMONTON, AB, T6B 2Z2
(780) 440-1796   *SIC* 3441
COLLINS MANUFACTURING CO. LTD *p 224*
9835 199A ST SUITE 5, LANGLEY, BC, V1M 2X7
(604) 888-2812   *SIC* 3713
COLLINS RANKIN INSURANCE BROKERS *p 637*
645 WESTMOUNT RD E, KITCHENER, ON, N2E 3S3
SIC 6411
COLLUS POWERSTREAM CORP   *p 546*
43 STEWART RD, COLLINGWOOD, ON, L9Y 4M7
(705) 445-1800   *SIC* 4911
COLOMER CANADA, LTD   *p 738*
1055 COURTNEYPARK DR E SUITE A, MISSISSAUGA, ON, L5T 1M7
(905) 565-7047   *SIC* 5131
COLONIAL   *p 1019*
See *COLONIAL TOOL GROUP INC*
COLONIAL CHEVROLET LTD   *p 755*
18100 YONGE ST, NEWMARKET, ON, L3Y 8V1
(905) 895-1171   *SIC* 5511
COLONIAL COLLISION CENTRE/ COLONIAL HONDA   *p 455*
See *DONPAT INVESTMENTS LIMITED*
COLONIAL FARMS LTD   *p 179*
3830 OKANAGAN ST, ARMSTRONG, BC, V0E 1B0
(250) 546-3008   *SIC* 2015
COLONIAL GARAGE & DISTRIBUTORS LIMITED   *p 433*
355 HAMILTON AVE, ST. JOHN'S, NL, A1E

1K1
(709) 579-4011   *SIC* 5013
COLONIAL TOOL GROUP INC   *p* 1019
1691 WALKER RD, WINDSOR, ON, N8W
3P1
(519) 253-2461   *SIC* 3541
COLONY FORD LINCOLN SALES INC   *p*
508
300 QUEEN ST E, BRAMPTON, ON, L6V
1C2
(905) 451-4094   *SIC* 5511
COLONY MOTOR PRODUCTS   *p* 1407
See COLONY PONTIAC BUICK LTD
COLONY PONTIAC BUICK LTD   *p* 1407
331 MAIN ST, HUMBOLDT, SK, S0K 2A1
(306) 682-2661   *SIC* 5511
COLOPLAST CANADA CORPORATION   *p*
796
2401   BRISTOL   CIR   SUITE   205A,
OAKVILLE, ON, L6H 6P1
(877) 820-7008   *SIC* 5047
COLOR AD PACKAGING LTD   *p* 365
200 BEGHIN AVE, WINNIPEG, MB, R2J
3W2
(204) 777-7770   *SIC* 3086
COLOR COMPASS CORPORATION   *p* 113
5308 97 ST NW, EDMONTON, AB, T6E 5W5
(780) 438-0808   *SIC* 6712
COLOR STEELS INC   *p* 906
251 RACCO PKY, THORNHILL, ON, L4J
8X9
(905) 879-0300   *SIC* 5051
COLORFAST CORPORATION   *p* 118
6115 GATEWAY BLVD NW, EDMONTON,
AB, T6H 2H3
SIC 7384
COLORI   *p* 1325
See BOUTIQUE COLORI INC
COLORIDE INC   *p* 1146
80 AV SAINT-MARTIN, LOUISEVILLE, QC,
J5V 1B4
(819) 228-5553   *SIC* 3999
COLORTECH INC   *p* 502
8027 DIXIE RD, BRAMPTON, ON, L6T 3V1
(888) 557-8324   *SIC* 2865
COLOSSUS MINERALS INC   *p* 986
100 KING ST W SUITE 5600, TORONTO,
ON, M5X 1C9
SIC 1041
COLOURFAST PRINTING   *p* 693
*See COLOURFAST SECURE CARD TECH-
NOLOGY INC*
**COLOURFAST SECURE CARD TECHNOL-
OGY INC**   *p*
693
5380 TIMBERLEA BLVD, MISSISSAUGA,
ON, L4W 2S6
(905) 206-9477   *SIC* 3089
COLOURS ART   *p* 86
*See K.R.S. TECHNICAL SERVICES LIM-
ITED*
COLSON GROUP CANADA, INC   *p* 533
1600 BISHOP ST N SUITE 300, CAM-
BRIDGE, ON, N1R 7N6
(519) 623-9420   *SIC* 3499
COLT CANADA CORPORATION   *p* 636
1036 WILSON AVE, KITCHENER, ON, N2C
1J3
(519) 893-6840   *SIC* 3484
COLT CHEMICAL, DIV OF   *p* 622
See COMET CHEMICAL COMPANY LTD
COLT RESOURCES INC   *p* 1187
500   PLACE   D'ARMES   BUREAU   1800,
MONTREAL, QC, H2Y 2W2
(438) 259-3315   *SIC* 1081
COLTA HOLDINGS   *p* 552
*See EMPIRE CONTINENTAL MANAGE-
MENT INC*
COLTS AND OLD PORT CIGAR COMPANY
p 1144
*See   GROUPE   TABAC   SCANDINAVE
CANADA INC*
COLUMBIA ALUMINUM PRODUCTS   *p* 209
See PHOENIX GLASS INC

**COLUMBIA BUILDING MAINTENANCE CO
LTD**   *p* 782
65 MARTIN ROSS AVE UNIT 1, NORTH
YORK, ON, M3J 2L6
(416) 663-5020   *SIC* 7349
COLUMBIA COLLEGE   *p* 22
See COLUMBIA COLLEGE CORP
COLUMBIA COLLEGE   *p* 297
555 SEYMOUR ST SUITE 500, VANCOU-
VER, BC, V6B 3H6
(604) 683-8360   *SIC* 8221
COLUMBIA COLLEGE CORP   *p* 22
802 MANNING RD NE, CALGARY, AB, T2E
7N8
(403) 235-9300   *SIC* 8299
COLUMBIA CONTAINERS LTD   *p* 285
2319 COMMISSIONER ST, VANCOUVER,
BC, V5L 1A4
(604) 254-9461   *SIC* 5084
COLUMBIA ENERGY INC   *p* 334
2659 DOUGLAS ST SUITE 200, VICTORIA,
BC, V8T 4M3
(250) 474-3533   *SIC* 4924
COLUMBIA FOREST PRODUCTS LTD   *p*
858
HWY 17 E, RUTHERGLEN, ON, P0H 2E0
(705) 776-7622   *SIC* 5031
COLUMBIA FOREST PRODUCTS, DIV   *p*
619
See LEVESQUE PLYWOOD LIMITED
COLUMBIA FUELS, DIV OF   *p* 154
*See PARKLAND INDUSTRIES LIMITED
PARTNERSHIP*
COLUMBIA INDUSTRIES LTD   *p* 14
7150 112 AVE SE, CALGARY, AB, T2C 4Z1
(403) 236-3420   *SIC* 3728
COLUMBIA INTERNATIONAL COLLEGE   *p*
614
*See   COLUMBIA   PRIVATE   SECONDARY
SCHOOL INC*
COLUMBIA KITCHEN CABINETS LTD   *p*
176
2221 TOWNLINE RD, ABBOTSFORD, BC,
V2T 6H1
(604) 850-3538   *SIC* 2434
COLUMBIA MANUFACTURING CO. LTD   *p*
192
4575 TILLICUM ST, BURNABY, BC, V5J
5K9
(604) 437-3377   *SIC* 5031
COLUMBIA PLASTICS LTD   *p* 271
19320 60 AVE, SURREY, BC, V3S 3M2
(604) 530-9990   *SIC* 3089
**COLUMBIA   PRIVATE   SECONDARY
SCHOOL INC**   *p* 614
1003 MAIN ST W SUITE 163, HAMILTON,
ON, L8S 4P3
(905) 572-7883   *SIC* 8211
COLUMBIA REMTEC MANUFACTURING   *p*
1075
See REMTEC INC
**COLUMBIA SPORTSWEAR CANADA LIM-
ITED**   *p*
661
1425 MAX BROSE DR SUITE 1, LONDON,
ON, N6N 0A2
(519) 644-5000   *SIC* 5136
COLUMBIA SPORTSWEAR CANADA LP   *p*
661
1425 MAX BROSE DR SUITE 1, LONDON,
ON, N6N 0A2
(519) 644-5000   *SIC* 5136
COLUMBUS CENTRE OF TORONTO   *p* 788
901 LAWRENCE AVE W SUITE 306,
NORTH YORK, ON, M6A 1C3
(416) 789-7011   *SIC* 8322
COLUMBUS CLUB   *p* 490
See KNIGHTS OF COLUMBUS
COLUMBUS GOLD CORP   *p* 297
1090 HAMILTON ST, VANCOUVER, BC,
V6B 2R9
(604) 634-0970   *SIC* 1041
COLUMBUS LINE CANADA INC   *p* 303
900 HASTINGS ST W SUITE 600, VAN-

COUVER, BC, V6C 1E5
SIC 5411
COLUMBUS LONG TERM CARE SOCIETY
p 323
704 69TH AVE W, VANCOUVER, BC, V6P
2W3
(604) 321-4405   *SIC* 8361
COLUMBUS RESIDENCE   *p* 323
*See COLUMBUS LONG TERM CARE SO-
CIETY*
COLVILLE MANOR   *p* 1042
See PROVINCE OF PEI
COLWIN ELECTRIC GROUP   *p* 248
2829 MURRAY ST, PORT MOODY, BC, V3H
1X3
(604) 461-2181   *SIC* 1731
COM DEV INTERNATIONAL LTD   *p* 533
155 SHELDON DR, CAMBRIDGE, ON, N1R
7H6
(519) 622-2300   *SIC* 3669
COM DEV LTD   *p* 533
155 SHELDON DR, CAMBRIDGE, ON, N1R
7H6
(519) 622-2300   *SIC* 3669
COM DEV SPACE   *p* 533
See COM DEV LTD
**COM-NET (COMMUNICATION CABLING
AND NETWORK SOLUTIONS) INC**   *p* 817
2191 THURSTON DR, OTTAWA, ON, K1G
6C9
(613) 247-7778   *SIC* 1731
COM-TEL MARKETING INC   *p* 550
163 BUTTERMILL AVE SUITE 1, CON-
CORD, ON, L4K 3X8
(905) 738-1494   *SIC* 5963
COMAINTEL INC   *p* 1369
121 AV CHAHOON BUREAU 100, SHAW-
INIGAN, QC, G9T 7G1
(819) 538-6583   *SIC* 3567
COMARK HOLDINGS INC   *p* 298
650 GEORGIA ST W SUITE 2900, VAN-
COUVER, BC, V6B 4N9
(604) 646-3790   *SIC* 6712
COMAX, COOPERATIVE AGRICOLE   *p* 1310
4880 RUE DES SEIGNEURS E, SAINT-
HYACINTHE, QC, J2R 1Z5
(450) 799-3211   *SIC* 2048
COMBAT   *p* 819
5390 CANOTEK RD UNIT 20, OTTAWA,
ON, K1J 1H8
SIC 3949
COMBAT DES CLIPS (MC)   *p* 1206
See MUSIQUEPLUS INC
COMBATBALL   *p* 387
See VBALLS TARGET SYSTEMS INC
COMBINED METAL INDUSTRIES INC   *p* 792
505 GARYRAY DR, NORTH YORK, ON,
M9L 1P9
(416) 743-7730   *SIC* 5093
COMBO PETITES   *p* 1234
See MAGASIN LAURA (P.V.) INC
COMBOPLATE   *p* 1305
See MANAC INC
COMCARE (CANADA) LIMITED   *p* 400
168 BRUNSWICK ST, FREDERICTON, NB,
E3B 1G6
SIC 8059
COMCARE (CANADA) LIMITED   *p* 406
30 GORDON ST SUITE 105, MONCTON,
NB, E1C 1L8
(506) 853-9112   *SIC* 7363
COMCARE (CANADA) LIMITED   *p* 456
7071 BAYERS RD SUITE 1151, HALIFAX,
NS, B3L 2C2
(902) 453-0838   *SIC* 8051
COMCARE (CANADA) LIMITED   *p* 656
339 WELLINGTON RD SUITE 200, LON-
DON, ON, N6C 5Z9
(800) 663-5775   *SIC* 8049
COMCARE (CANADA) LIMITED   *p* 880
8 QUEENSWAY E SUITE 4, SIMCOE, ON,
N3Y 4M3
(519) 426-5122   *SIC* 8059
COMCARE (CANADA) LIMITED   *p* 881

52 ABBOTT ST N UNIT 3, SMITHS FALLS,
ON, K7A 1W3
SIC 7363
COMCARE HEALTH SERVICES   *p* 406
See COMCARE (CANADA) LIMITED
COMCARE HEALTH SERVICES   *p* 456
See COMCARE (CANADA) LIMITED
COMCARE HEALTH SERVICES   *p* 656
See COMCARE (CANADA) LIMITED
COMCARE HEALTH SERVICES   *p* 880
See COMCARE (CANADA) LIMITED
COMCARE HEALTH SERVICES   *p* 881
See COMCARE (CANADA) LIMITED
COMDA THE CALENDAR PEOPLE   *p* 791
See 1120423 ONTARIO LIMITED
COMEAU'S SEA FOODS LIMITED   *p* 465
60 SAULNIERVILLE RD, SAULNIERVILLE,
NS, B0W 2Z0
(902) 769-2101   *SIC* 2092
COMEAU'S SEA FOODS LIMITED   *p* 465
GD, PUBNICO, NS, B0W 2W0
(902) 762-3333   *SIC* 2092
COMEAU, C. L. CO, LTD   *p* 396
117 BOUL ST-PIERRE O, CARAQUET, NB,
E1W 1B6
(506) 727-3411   *SIC* 5141
**COMEAUVILLE SEAFOOD PRODUCTS
LIMITED**   *p* 465
GD, SAULNIERVILLE, NS, B0W 2Z0
(902) 769-2266   *SIC* 5146
COMENCO   *p* 1051
*See   COMENCO   SERVICES   AUX   IM-
MEUBLES INC*
**COMENCO SERVICES AUX IMMEUBLES
INC**   *p* 1051
8150 BOUL METROPOLITAIN E BUREAU
310, ANJOU, QC, H1K 1A1
(514) 389-7233   *SIC* 6531
COMET CHEMICAL COMPANY LTD   *p* 622
3463 THOMAS ST, INNISFIL, ON, L9S 3W4
(705) 436-5580   *SIC* 5169
**COMET STRIP ENTERPRISES (CANADA)
LTD**   *p* 254
5375 PARKWOOD PL SUITE 1, RICH-
MOND, BC, V6V 2N1
(604) 278-4005   *SIC* 5092
COMETAL INC   *p* 1137
2965   BOUL   GUILLAUME-COUTURE,
LEVIS, QC, G6W 6N6
(418) 839-8831   *SIC* 5075
COMEX FOOD PRODUCTION INC   *p* 303
586 HORNBY ST, VANCOUVER, BC, V6C
2E7
(604) 971-4745   *SIC* 5812
COMFORT FURNITURE GALLERIES   *p* 100
17109 109 AVE NW, EDMONTON, AB, T5S
2H8
(780) 481-7800   *SIC* 5712
COMFORT INN & SUITES   *p* 340
See BALMORAL INVESTMENTS LTD
COMFORT INN CLIFTON HILL   *p* 759
See HOCO LIMITED
COMFORT INN NIAGARA FALLS   *p* 758
See ATLIFIC INC
COMFORT SHOP, THE   *p* 39
*See CALGARY CO-OP HOME HEALTH
CARE LIMITED*
COMFORT SYSTEM SOLUTIONS INC   *p* 705
150 BRITANNIA RD E UNIT 1, MISSIS-
SAUGA, ON, L4Z 2A4
(905) 568-1661   *SIC* 5075
COMFORTING CARE LTD   *p* 199
657 GATENSBURY ST, COQUITLAM, BC,
V3J 5G9
SIC 8049
COMFREE   *p* 1139
See DP IMMOBILIER QUEBEC INC
COMINAR CONSTRUCTION S.E.C.   *p* 1271
2820 BOUL LAURIER BUREAU 850, QUE-
BEC, QC, G1V 0C1
(418) 681-8151   *SIC* 1542
**COMISSION DE LA SANTE ET DE LA SE-
CURITE**   *p*
1106

See GOUVERNEMENT DE LA PROVINCE DE QUEBEC

COMISSION SCOLAIRE DE LANGUE FRANCAISE, LA *p* 1043
1596 124 RTE, WELLINGTON STATION, PE, C0B 2E0
(902) 854-2975   *SIC* 8211

COMITE CONJOINT ACPQ FPPQ SEPQ *p* 1143
See ELEVEURS DE PORCS DU QUEBEC LES

COMITE PARITAIRE DE L'INDUSTRIE DES SERVICES AUTOMOBILES DE LA REGION DE MONTREAL *p* 1182
509 RUE BELANGER BUREAU 165, MONTREAL, QC, H2S 1G5
(514) 288-3003   *SIC* 8621

COMITE PARITAIRE DES AGENTS DE SECURITE *p* 1051
7450 BOUL DES GALERIES D'ANJOU UNITE 490, ANJOU, QC, H1M 3M3
(514) 493-9105   *SIC* 8631

COMMAND FISHING AND PIPE RECOVERY LTD *p* 140
24521 TOWNSHIP ROAD 510, LEDUC COUNTY, AB, T4X 0T4
(780) 979-2220   *SIC* 1389

COMMANDER HOLDINGS INC *p* 1038
3 MOUNT EDWARD RD, CHARLOTTETOWN, PE, C1A 5R7
(902) 566-2295   *SIC* 5983

COMMANDER WAREHOUSE EQUIPMENT LTD *p* 241
930 1ST ST W SUITE 119, NORTH VANCOUVER, BC, V7P 3N4
(604) 980-8511   *SIC* 5084

COMMANDITE FPI PRO INC *p* 1194
2000 RUE MANSFIELD BUREAU 920, MONTREAL, QC, H3A 2Z6
(514) 933-9552   *SIC* 6153

COMMANDITE KRUGER BROMPTON INC *p* 1218
3285 CH DE BEDFORD, MONTREAL, QC, H3S 1G5
(514) 737-1131   *SIC* 2621

COMMDOOR ALUMINUM *p* 1030
471 CHRISLEA RD SUITE 1, WOODBRIDGE, ON, L4L 8N6
(416) 743-3667   *SIC* 3365

COMMERCE AUTOMOBILE S.G.C. CORPORATION *p* 1047
7010 BOUL HENRI-BOURASSA E, ANJOU, QC, H1E 7K7
(514) 324-7777   *SIC* 5511

COMMERCE GLOBAL DU PAPIER *p* 1393
See 3427277 CANADA INC

COMMERCE INTERNATIONAL MANHATTAN INC *p* 1338
6150 RTE TRANSCANADIENNE, SAINT-LAURENT, QC, H4T 1X5
(514) 388-5588   *SIC* 5136

COMMERCE JARDINO FRESH INC *p* 1161
8145 AV MARCO-POLO, MONTREAL, QC, H1E 5Y8
(514) 664-5566   *SIC* 5148

COMMERCE KOLTECH LTEE *p* 1338
943 RUE REVERCHON, SAINT-LAURENT, QC, H4T 4L2
(514) 739-4111   *SIC* 5169

COMMERCIAL ALCOHOL *p* 503
See GREENFIELD GLOBAL QUEBEC INC

COMMERCIAL ALCOHOL DIV OF *p* 939
See GREENFIELD GLOBAL, INC

COMMERCIAL AQUATIC SUPPLIES *p* 238
See DB PERKS & ASSOCIATES LTD

COMMERCIAL BAKERIES CORP *p* 786
45 TORBARRIE RD, NORTH YORK, ON, M3L 1G5
(416) 247-5478   *SIC* 2052

COMMERCIAL BEARING SERVICE *p* 113

See COMMERCIAL SOLUTIONS INC

COMMERCIAL BEARING SERVICE (1966) LTD. *p* 113
4203 95 ST NW SUITE 1966, EDMONTON, AB, T6E 5R6
(780) 432-1611   *SIC* 5085

COMMERCIAL BUILDING SERVICE LTD *p* 1415
819 ARCOLA AVE, REGINA, SK, S4N 0S9
(306) 757-5332   *SIC* 7349

COMMERCIAL CLEANING SERVICES LIMITED *p* 443
166 BRAEMAR DR, DARTMOUTH, NS, B2X 2T3
(902) 435-9500   *SIC* 7349

COMMERCIAL DRYWALL SUPPLY (ONTARIO) INC *p* 668
235 DON PARK RD, MARKHAM, ON, L3R 1C2
(905) 415-7777   *SIC* 5211

COMMERCIAL EQUIPMENT CORP *p* 205
591 CHESTER RD, DELTA, BC, V3M 6G7
(604) 526-6126   *SIC* 5082

COMMERCIAL LIGHTING PRODUCTS LTD *p* 205
1535 CLIVEDEN AVE, DELTA, BC, V3M 6P7
(604) 540-4999   *SIC* 5063

COMMERCIAL LINES & CLAIMS *p* 715
See ROYAL & SUN ALLIANCE INSURANCE COMPANY OF CANADA

COMMERCIAL LOGISTICS INC *p* 258
16133 BLUNDELL RD, RICHMOND, BC, V6W 0A3
(604) 276-1300   *SIC* 4731

COMMERCIAL MARKETING *p* 665
See 788265 ONTARIO LIMITED

COMMERCIAL MECHANICAL SERVICES *p* 878
See C.M.S. COMMERCIAL MECHANICAL SERVICES LTD

COMMERCIAL ROLL FORMED PRODUCTS LIMITED *p* 502
225 PARKHURST SQ, BRAMPTON, ON, L6T 5H5
(905) 790-5665   *SIC* 3316

COMMERCIAL SOLUTIONS INC *p* 113
4203 95 ST NW, EDMONTON, AB, T6E 5R6
(780) 432-1611   *SIC* 5085

COMMERCIAL SPRING AND TOOL COMPANY LIMITED *p* 705
160 WATLINE AVE, MISSISSAUGA, ON, L4Z 1R1
(905) 568-3899   *SIC* 3495

COMMERCIAL SWITCHGEAR LIMITED *p* 906
175 RACCO PKWY, THORNHILL, ON, L4J 8X9
(905) 669-9270   *SIC* 3613

COMMERCIAL TIRE AUTO SERVICE *p* 826
See 1562067 ONTARIO INC

COMMERCIAL TRANSPORT (NORTHERN) LIMITED *p* 647
70 MAGILL ST, LIVELY, ON, P3Y 1K7
(705) 692-4727   *SIC* 4213

COMMERCIAL TRUCK EQUIPMENT *p* 205
See COMMERCIAL EQUIPMENT CORP

COMMERCIAL WELDING LTD *p* 361
130 CANADA ST, WINKLER, MB, R6W 0J3
(204) 325-4195   *SIC* 6531

COMMERICAL CLEANING SERVICE *p* 883
See 1434378 ONTARIO INC

COMMISSION DE LA CAPITALE NATIONALE DU QUEBEC *p* 1269
525 BOUL RENE-LEVESQUE E BUREAU RC, QUEBEC, QC, G1R 5S9
(418) 528-0773   *SIC* 8743

COMMISSION DE LA CONSTRUCTION DU QUEBEC *p* 1176
1201 BOUL CREMAZIE E, MONTREAL, QC, H2M 0A6
(514) 593-3121   *SIC* 8611

COMMISSION DE LA CONSTRUCTION DU QUEBEC *p* 1176
8485 AV CHRISTOPHE-COLOMB, MONTREAL, QC, H2M 0A7
(514) 341-7740   *SIC* 8611

COMMISSION DE LA SANTE ET DES SERVICES SOCIAUX PREMIERE NATION DU QUEBEC ET DU LABRADOR *p* 1401
250 RUE CHEF-MICHEL-LAVEAU, WENDAKE, QC, G0A 4V0
(418) 842-1540   *SIC* 8399

COMMISSION DES NORMES, DE L'EQUITE, DE LA SANTE ET DE LA SECURITE DU TRAVAIL, LA *p* 1258
524 RUE BOURDAGES BUREAU 370, QUEBEC, QC, G1K 7E2
(877) 639-0744   *SIC* 6331

COMMISSION DES SERVICES ELECTRIQUES DE LA VILLE DE MONTREAL *p* 1172
See COMMISSION DES SERVICES ELECTRIQUES DE MONTREAL

COMMISSION DES SERVICES ELECTRIQUES DE MONTREAL *p* 1172
4305 RUE HOGAN, MONTREAL, QC, H2H 2N2
(514) 868-3111   *SIC* 1799

COMMISSION FOR ENVIRONMENTAL COOPERATION *p* 1187
393 RUE SAINT-JACQUES BUREAU 200, MONTREAL, QC, H2Y 1N9
(514) 350-4300   *SIC* 8748

COMMISSION SCOLAIRE ABITIBI *p* 1123
24 5E AV E, LA SARRE, QC, J9Z 1K8
(819) 333-5591   *SIC* 8211

COMMISSION SCOLAIRE AU COEUR DES VALLEES *p* 1102
582 RUE MACLAREN E, GATINEAU, QC, J8L 2W2
(819) 986-8511   *SIC* 8211

COMMISSION SCOLAIRE CRIE (LA) *p* 1081
11 MAAMUU, CHISASIBI, QC, J0M 1E0
(819) 855-2833   *SIC* 8211

COMMISSION SCOLAIRE CRIE (LA) *p* 1154
203 MAIN ST, MISTISSINI, QC, G0W 1C0
(418) 923-2764   *SIC* 8211

COMMISSION SCOLAIRE DE CHARLEVOIX, LA *p* 1054
200 RUE SAINT-AUBIN, BAIE-SAINT-PAUL, QC, G3Z 2R2
(418) 435-2824   *SIC* 8211

COMMISSION SCOLAIRE DE CHARLEVOIX, LA *p* 1054
200 RUE SAINT-AUBIN UNITE 102, BAIE-SAINT-PAUL, QC, G3Z 2R2
(418) 435-2824   *SIC* 8211

COMMISSION SCOLAIRE DE CHARLEVOIX, LA *p* 1122
88 RUE DES CIMES, LA MALBAIE, QC, G5A 1T3
(418) 665-3791   *SIC* 8211

COMMISSION SCOLAIRE DE KAMOURASKA RIVIERE-DU-LOUP *p* 1286
320 RUE SAINT-PIERRE, RIVIERE-DU-LOUP, QC, G5R 3V3
(418) 862-8203   *SIC* 8211

COMMISSION SCOLAIRE DE KAMOURASKA RIVIERE-DU-LOUP *p* 1349
525 AV DE L'EGLISE, SAINT-PASCAL, QC, G0L 3Y0
(418) 856-7030   *SIC* 8211

COMMISSION SCOLAIRE DE L'ENERGIE *p* 1353
405 BOUL SAINT-JOSEPH RR 1, SAINT-TITE, QC, G0X 3H0
(418) 365-5191   *SIC* 8211

COMMISSION SCOLAIRE DE L'ENERGIE *p* 1368
5105 AV ALBERT-TESSIER BUREAU 840, SHAWINIGAN, QC, G9N 7A3
(819) 539-2265   *SIC* 8211

COMMISSION SCOLAIRE DE L'ENERGIE *p* 1368
5285 AV ALBERT TESSIER, SHAWINIGAN, QC, G9N 6T9
(819) 539-2285   *SIC* 8211

COMMISSION SCOLAIRE DE L'ENERGIE *p* 1369
1200 RUE DE VAL-MAURICIE, SHAWINIGAN, QC, G9P 2L9
(819) 536-5675   *SIC* 8211

COMMISSION SCOLAIRE DE L'ESTUAIRE *p* 1053
620 RUE JALBERT, BAIE-COMEAU, QC, G5C 0B8
(418) 589-0806   *SIC* 8211

COMMISSION SCOLAIRE DE L'OR-ET-DES-BOIS *p* 1390
125 RUE SELF, VAL-D'OR, QC, J9P 3N2
(819) 825-6366   *SIC* 8211

COMMISSION SCOLAIRE DE L'OR-ET-DES-BOIS *p* 1390
799 BOUL FOREST, VAL-D'OR, QC, J9P 2L4
(819) 825-4220   *SIC* 8211

COMMISSION SCOLAIRE DE L'OR-ET-DES-BOIS *p* 1390
125 RUE SELF, VAL-D'OR, QC, J9P 3N2
(819) 825-4670   *SIC* 8211

COMMISSION SCOLAIRE DE LA BAIE JAMES *p* 1077
596 4E RUE, CHIBOUGAMAU, QC, G8P 1S3
(418) 748-7621   *SIC* 8211

COMMISSION SCOLAIRE DE LA BEAUCE-ETCHEMIN *p* 1304
11700 25E AV, SAINT-GEORGES, QC, G5Y 8B8
(418) 228-1993   *SIC* 8211

COMMISSION SCOLAIRE DE LA BEAUCE-ETCHEMIN *p* 1304
1925 118E RUE, SAINT-GEORGES, QC, G5Y 7R7
(418) 228-5541   *SIC* 8211

COMMISSION SCOLAIRE DE LA BEAUCE-ETCHEMIN *p* 1304
2121 119E RUE, SAINT-GEORGES, QC, G5Y 5S1
(418) 228-8964   *SIC* 8211

COMMISSION SCOLAIRE DE LA BEAUCE-ETCHEMIN *p* 1321
695 AV ROBERT-CLICHE, SAINT-JOSEPH-DE-BEAUCE, QC, G0S 2V0
(418) 397-6841   *SIC* 8211

COMMISSION SCOLAIRE DE LA BEAUCE-ETCHEMIN *p* 1348
30A CH DE LA POLYVALENTE BUREAU 3033, SAINT-MARTIN, QC, G0M 1B0
(418) 228-5541   *SIC* 8211

COMMISSION SCOLAIRE DE LA BEAUCE-ETCHEMIN *p* 1350
2105 25E AV, SAINT-PROSPER-DE-DORCHESTER, QC, G0M 1Y0
(418) 594-8231   *SIC* 8211

COMMISSION SCOLAIRE DE LA CAPITALE, LA *p* 1257
1640 8E AV, QUEBEC, QC, G1J 3N5
(418) 686-4040   *SIC* 8211

COMMISSION SCOLAIRE DE LA CAPITALE, LA *p* 1258
See COMMISSION SCOLAIRE DE LA CAPITALE, LA

COMMISSION SCOLAIRE DE LA CAPI-
TALE, LA   p
1258
  50 RUE DU CARDINAL-MAURICE-ROY,
QUEBEC, QC, G1K 8S9
  (418) 686-4040   SIC 8211
COMMISSION SCOLAIRE DE LA CAPI-
TALE, LA   p
1258
  125 RUE DES COMMISSAIRES O BUREAU
210, QUEBEC, QC, G1K 1M7
  (418) 686-4040   SIC 5049
COMMISSION SCOLAIRE DE LA CAPI-
TALE, LA   p
1260
  1201 RUE DE LA POINTE-AUX-LIEVRES,
QUEBEC, QC, G1L 4M1
  (418) 686-4040   SIC 8211
COMMISSION SCOLAIRE DE LA CAPI-
TALE, LA   p
1260
  1625 BOUL BENOIT-XV, QUEBEC, QC, G1L
2Z3
  (418) 686-4040   SIC 8211
COMMISSION SCOLAIRE DE LA CAPI-
TALE, LA   p
1263
  1060 RUE BORNE, QUEBEC, QC, G1N 1L9
  (418) 686-4040   SIC 8331
COMMISSION SCOLAIRE DE LA CAPI-
TALE, LA   p
1270
  555 CH SAINTE-FOY, QUEBEC, QC, G1S
2J9
  (418) 686-4040   SIC 8211
COMMISSION SCOLAIRE DE LA CAPI-
TALE, LA   p
1275
  158 BOUL DES ETUDIANTS, QUEBEC,
QC, G2A 1N8
  (418) 686-4040   SIC 8211
COMMISSION SCOLAIRE DE LA CAPI-
TALE, LA   p
1276
  3400 AV CHAUVEAU, QUEBEC, QC, G2C
1A1
  (418) 686-4040   SIC 8331
COMMISSION SCOLAIRE DE LA CAPI-
TALE, LA   p
1276
  3600 AV CHAUVEAU, QUEBEC, QC, G2C
1A1
  (418) 686-4040   SIC 8211
COMMISSION SCOLAIRE DE LA COTE-
DU-SUD, LA   p
1159
  141 BOUL TACHE E, MONTMAGNY, QC,
G5V 1B9
  (418) 248-2370   SIC 8211
COMMISSION SCOLAIRE DE LA COTE-
DU-SUD, LA   p
1291
  825 RTE BEGIN, SAINT-ANSELME, QC,
G0R 2N0
  (418) 885-4431   SIC 8211
COMMISSION SCOLAIRE DE LA COTE-
DU-SUD, LA   p
1299
  70 RTE SAINT-GERARD, SAINT-DAMIEN-
DE-BUCKLAND, QC, G0R 2Y0
  (418) 789-1001   SIC 8211
COMMISSION SCOLAIRE DE LA JON-
QUIERE   p
1115
  3450 BOUL DU ROYAUME, JONQUIERE,
QC, G7S 5T2
  (418) 547-5781   SIC 8211
COMMISSION SCOLAIRE DE LA JON-
QUIERE   p
1115
  2215 BOUL MELLON BUREAU 101, JON-
QUIERE, QC, G7S 3G4
  (418) 548-3113   SIC 8211
COMMISSION SCOLAIRE DE LA JON-

QUIERE   p
1116
  1954 RUE DES ETUDIANTS, JONQUIERE,
QC, G7X 4B1
  (418) 542-3571   SIC 8211
COMMISSION SCOLAIRE DE LA
MOYENNE-COTE-NORD   p 1113
  See GOUVERNEMENT DE LA PROVINCE
DE QUEBEC
COMMISSION SCOLAIRE DE LA
MOYENNE-COTE-NORD, LA   p 1113
  1235 RUE DE LA DIGUE, HAVRE-SAINT-
PIERRE, QC, G0G 1P0
  (418) 538-3044   SIC 8211
COMMISSION SCOLAIRE DE LA POINTE-
DE-L'ILE   p
1163
  8205 RUE FONTENEAU, MONTREAL, QC,
H1K 4E1
  (514) 353-9970   SIC 8211
COMMISSION SCOLAIRE DE LA POINTE-
DE-L'ILE   p
1239
  6051 BOUL MAURICE-DUPLESSIS,
MONTREAL-NORD, QC, H1G 1Y6
  (514) 328-3200   SIC 8211
COMMISSION SCOLAIRE DE LA POINTE-
DE-L'ILE   p
1239
  11480 BOUL ROLLAND, MONTREAL-
NORD, QC, H1G 3T9
  (514) 328-3570   SIC 8211
COMMISSION SCOLAIRE DE LA POINTE-
DE-L'ILE   p
1240
  11411 AV PELLETIER, MONTREAL-NORD,
QC, H1H 3S3
  (514) 328-3250   SIC 8211
COMMISSION SCOLAIRE DE LA POINTE-
DE-L'ILE   p
1240
  10748 BOUL SAINT-VITAL, MONTREAL-
NORD, QC, H1H 4T3
  (514) 328-3272   SIC 8211
COMMISSION SCOLAIRE DE LA POINTE-
DE-L'ILE   p
1247
  550 53E AV, POINTE-AUX-TREMBLES, QC,
H1A 2T7
  (514) 642-9520   SIC 8211
COMMISSION SCOLAIRE DE LA POINTE-
DE-L'ILE   p
1343
  5950 RUE HONORE-MERCIER, SAINT-
LEONARD, QC, H1P 3E4
  (514) 321-8475   SIC 8211
COMMISSION SCOLAIRE DE LA REGION-
DE-SHERBROOKE   p
1370
  135 RUE KING O, SHERBROOKE, QC, J1H
1P4
  (819) 822-5520   SIC 8211
COMMISSION SCOLAIRE DE LA REGION-
DE-SHERBROOKE   p
1370
  405 RUE SARA, SHERBROOKE, QC, J1H
5S6
  (819) 822-5455   SIC 8211
COMMISSION SCOLAIRE DE LA REGION-
DE-SHERBROOKE   p
1370
  825 RUE BOWEN S, SHERBROOKE, QC,
J1G 2G2
  (819) 822-5444   SIC 8211
COMMISSION SCOLAIRE DE LA REGION-
DE-SHERBROOKE   p
1370
  955 RUE DE CAMBRIDGE, SHER-
BROOKE, QC, J1H 1E2
  (819) 822-5400   SIC 8211
COMMISSION SCOLAIRE DE LA REGION-
DE-SHERBROOKE   p
1372
  2955 BOUL DE L'UNIVERSITE BUREAU

822, SHERBROOKE, QC, J1K 2Y3
  (819) 822-5540   SIC 8211
COMMISSION SCOLAIRE DE LA REGION-
DE-SHERBROOKE   p
1372
  2965 BOUL DE L'UNIVERSITE, SHER-
BROOKE, QC, J1K 2X6
  (819) 822-5540   SIC 8211
COMMISSION SCOLAIRE DE LA REGION-
DE-SHERBROOKE   p
1375
  4076 BOUL DE L'UNIVERSITE, SHER-
BROOKE, QC, J1N 2Y1
  (819) 822-5577   SIC 8211
COMMISSION SCOLAIRE DE LA
RIVERAINE   p 1242
  375 RUE DE MONSEIGNEUR-BRUNAULT,
NICOLET, QC, J3T 1Y6
  (819) 293-5821   SIC 8211
COMMISSION SCOLAIRE DE LA
RIVERAINE   p 1347
  401 RUE GERMAIN, SAINT-LEONARD-
D'ASTON, QC, J0C 1M0
  (819) 399-2122   SIC 8211
COMMISSION SCOLAIRE DE LA
RIVERAINE   p 1350
  165 218 RTE, SAINT-PIERRE-LES-
BECQUETS, QC, G0X 2Z0
  (819) 263-2323   SIC 8211
COMMISSION SCOLAIRE DE LA RIVIERE-
DU-NORD   p
1129
  452 AV D'ARGENTEUIL BUREAU 103,
LACHUTE, QC, J8H 1W9
  (450) 562-8841   SIC 8211
COMMISSION SCOLAIRE DE LA RIVIERE-
DU-NORD   p
1152
  17000 RUE AUBIN, MIRABEL, QC, J7J 1B1
  (450) 435-0167   SIC 8299
COMMISSION SCOLAIRE DE LA RIVIERE-
DU-NORD   p
1321
  1155 AV DU PARC, SAINT-JEROME, QC,
J7Z 6X6
  (450) 438-1296   SIC 8211
COMMISSION SCOLAIRE DE LA RIVIERE-
DU-NORD   p
1321
  535 RUE FILION, SAINT-JEROME, QC, J7Z
1J6
  (450) 436-1560   SIC 8211
COMMISSION SCOLAIRE DE LA RIVIERE-
DU-NORD   p
1321
  600 36E AV, SAINT-JEROME, QC, J7Z 5W2
  (450) 436-1858   SIC 8211
COMMISSION SCOLAIRE DE LA
SEIGNEURIE-DES-MILLE-ILE   p 1061
  See COMMISSION SCOLAIRE DE LA
SEIGNEURIE-DES-MILLE-ILES
COMMISSION SCOLAIRE DE LA
SEIGNEURIE-DES-MILLE-ILES   p 1061
  2700 RUE JEAN-CHARLES-BONENFANT,
BOISBRIAND, QC, J7H 1P1
  (450) 433-5455   SIC 8211
COMMISSION SCOLAIRE DE LA
SEIGNEURIE-DES-MILLE-ILES   p 1301
  430 BOUL ARTHUR-SAUVE BUREAU
3050, SAINT-EUSTACHE, QC, J7R 6V7
  (450) 974-7000   SIC 8211
COMMISSION SCOLAIRE DE LA
SEIGNEURIE-DES-MILLE-ILES   p 1364
  8 RUE TASSE, SAINTE-THERESE, QC,
J7E 1V3
  (450) 433-5445   SIC 8211
COMMISSION SCOLAIRE DE LA
SEIGNEURIE-DES-MILLE-ILES   p 1364
  401 BOUL DU DOMAINE, SAINTE-
THERESE, QC, J7E 4S4
  (450) 433-5400   SIC 8211
COMMISSION SCOLAIRE DE LA VALLEE-
DES-TISSERANDS, LA   p
1055

  250 RUE GAGNON, BEAUHARNOIS, QC,
J6N 2W8
  (450) 225-2260   SIC 8211
COMMISSION SCOLAIRE DE LA VALLEE-
DES-TISSERANDS, LA   p
1366
  70 RUE LOUIS VI-MAJOR, SALABERRY-
DE-VALLEYFIELD, QC, J6T 3G2
  (450) 371-2004   SIC 8211
COMMISSION SCOLAIRE DE LAVAL   p
1085
  955 BOUL SAINT-MARTIN O BUREAU 144,
COTE SAINT-LUC, QC, H7S 1M5
  (450) 662-7000   SIC 8211
COMMISSION SCOLAIRE DE LAVAL   p
1232
  1740 MONTEE MASSON, MONTREAL,
QC, H7E 4P2
  (450) 662-7000   SIC 8331
COMMISSION SCOLAIRE DE MONTREAL
p 1163
  5850 AV DE CARIGNAN, MONTREAL, QC,
H1M 2V4
  (514) 596-4134   SIC 8211
COMMISSION SCOLAIRE DE MONTREAL
p 1163
  2800 BOUL LAPOINTE, MONTREAL, QC,
H1L 5M1
  (514) 596-5035   SIC 8211
COMMISSION SCOLAIRE DE MONTREAL
p 1164
  6200 AV PIERRE-DE COUBERTIN, MON-
TREAL, QC, H1N 1S4
  (514) 596-4140   SIC 8211
COMMISSION SCOLAIRE DE MONTREAL
p 1164
  5555 RUE SHERBROOKE E, MONTREAL,
QC, H1N 1A2
  (514) 596-5100   SIC 8211
COMMISSION SCOLAIRE DE MONTREAL
p 1166
  1860 AV MORGAN, MONTREAL, QC, H1V
2R2
  (514) 596-4844   SIC 8211
COMMISSION SCOLAIRE DE MONTREAL
p 1166
  2455 AV LETOURNEUX, MONTREAL, QC,
H1V 2N9
  (514) 596-4949   SIC 8211
COMMISSION SCOLAIRE DE MONTREAL
p 1168
  3737 RUE SHERBROOKE E, MONTREAL,
QC, H1X 3B3
  (514) 596-6000   SIC 8211
COMMISSION SCOLAIRE DE MONTREAL
p 1168
  6855 16E AV, MONTREAL, QC, H1X 2T5
  (514) 596-4166   SIC 8211
COMMISSION SCOLAIRE DE MONTREAL
p 1169
  2901 RUE DE LOUVAIN E, MONTREAL,
QC, H1Z 1J7
  (514) 596-5353   SIC 8211
COMMISSION SCOLAIRE DE MONTREAL
p 1171
  8200 RUE ROUSSELOT, MONTREAL, QC,
H2E 1Z6
  (514) 596-4350   SIC 8211
COMMISSION SCOLAIRE DE MONTREAL
p 1171
  1350 BOUL CREMAZIE E, MONTREAL,
QC, H2E 1A1
  (514) 596-4300   SIC 8211
COMMISSION SCOLAIRE DE MONTREAL
p 1172
  2110 BOUL SAINT-JOSEPH E, MON-
TREAL, QC, H2H 1E7
  (514) 596-5700   SIC 8211
COMMISSION SCOLAIRE DE MONTREAL
p 1180
  8200 BOUL SAINT-LAURENT, MONTREAL,
QC, H2P 2L8
  (514) 596-5400   SIC 8211
COMMISSION SCOLAIRE DE MONTREAL

p 1180
1205 RUE JARRY E, MONTREAL, QC, H2P 1W9
(514) 596-4160   *SIC* 8211
COMMISSION SCOLAIRE DE MONTREAL p 1182
6555 RUE DE NORMANVILLE, MONTREAL, QC, H2S 2B8
(514) 596-4940   *SIC* 8211
COMMISSION SCOLAIRE DE MONTREAL p 1183
6080 AV DE L'ESPLANADE, MONTREAL, QC, H2T 3A3
(514) 596-4800   *SIC* 8211
COMMISSION SCOLAIRE DE MONTREAL p 1217
11845 BOUL DE L'ACADIE BUREAU 281, MONTREAL, QC, H3M 2T4
(514) 596-5280   *SIC* 8211
COMMISSION SCOLAIRE DE MONTREAL p 1220
6300 CH DE LA COTE-SAINT-LUC, MONTREAL, QC, H3X 2H4
(514) 596-5920   *SIC* 8211
COMMISSION SCOLAIRE DE MONTREAL p 1222
717 RUE SAINT-FERDINAND, MONTREAL, QC, H4C 2T3
(514) 596-5960   *SIC* 8211
COMMISSION SCOLAIRE DE MONTREAL p 1224
12055 RUE DEPATIE, MONTREAL, QC, H4J 1W9
(514) 596-5565   *SIC* 8211
COMMISSION SCOLAIRE DE PORTNEUF p 1351
400 BOUL CLOUTIER, SAINT-RAYMOND, QC, G3L 3M8
(418) 337-6721   *SIC* 8211
COMMISSION SCOLAIRE DE ROUYN-NORANDA p 1289
70 RUE DES OBLATS E, ROUYN-NORANDA, QC, J9X 3N6
(819) 762-8161   *SIC* 8211
COMMISSION SCOLAIRE DE SAINT-HYACINTHE, LA p 1044
1450 3E AV, ACTON VALE, QC, J0H 1A0
(450) 546-5575   *SIC* 8211
COMMISSION SCOLAIRE DE SAINT-HYACINTHE, LA p 1312
2255 AV SAINTE-ANNE, SAINT-HYACINTHE, QC, J2S 5H7
(450) 773-8401   *SIC* 8211
COMMISSION SCOLAIRE DE SAINT-HYACINTHE, LA p 1312
2700 AV T.-D.-BOUCHARD, SAINT-HYACINTHE, QC, J2S 7G2
(450) 773-8408   *SIC* 8211
COMMISSION SCOLAIRE DE SOREL-TRACY 1376
265 RUE DE RAMEZAY, SOREL-TRACY, QC, J3P 4A5
(450) 742-5901   *SIC* 8211
COMMISSION SCOLAIRE DE SOREL-TRACY p 1377
2800 BOUL DES ERABLES, SOREL-TRACY, QC, J3R 2W4
(450) 746-3510   *SIC* 8211
COMMISSION SCOLAIRE DES AFFLU-ENTS p 1281
250 BOUL LOUIS-PHILIPPE-PICARD, REPENTIGNY, QC, J5Y 3W9
(450) 492-3578   *SIC* 8211
COMMISSION SCOLAIRE DES AFFLU-ENTS p 1379
400 MONTEE DUMAIS, TERREBONNE, QC, J6W 5W9
(450) 492-3613   *SIC* 8211
COMMISSION SCOLAIRE DES AFFLU-ENTS p 1380
1659 BOUL DES SEIGNEURS, TERRE-BONNE, QC, J6X 3E3
(450) 492-3622   *SIC* 8211
COMMISSION SCOLAIRE DES AP-PALACHES 1382
561 RUE SAINT-PATRICK, THETFORD MINES, QC, G6G 5W1
(418) 338-7831   *SIC* 8211
COMMISSION SCOLAIRE DES AP-PALACHES 1382
650 RUE LAPIERRE, THETFORD MINES, QC, G6G 7P1
(418) 338-7800   *SIC* 8211
COMMISSION SCOLAIRE DES AP-PALACHES 1383
499 RUE SAINT-DESIRE, THETFORD MINES, QC, G6H 1L7
(418) 423-4291   *SIC* 8211
COMMISSION SCOLAIRE DES BOIS-FRANCS p 1246
1159 RUE SAINT-JEAN, PLESSISVILLE, QC, G6L 1E1
(819) 362-3226   *SIC* 8211
COMMISSION SCOLAIRE DES BOIS-FRANCS p 1397
40 BOUL DES BOIS-FRANCS N, VICTORI-AVILLE, QC, G6P 1E5
(819) 758-6453   *SIC* 8211
COMMISSION SCOLAIRE DES BOIS-FRANCS p 1397
20 RUE DE L'ERMITAGE, VICTORIAVILLE, QC, G6P 1J5
(819) 752-4591   *SIC* 8211
COMMISSION SCOLAIRE DES CHENES p 1096
457 RUE DES ECOLES BUREAU 846, DRUMMONDVILLE, QC, J2B 1J3
(819) 478-6700   *SIC* 8211
COMMISSION SCOLAIRE DES CHENES p 1098
265 RUE SAINT-FELIX, DRUMMONDVILLE, QC, J2C 5M1
(819) 478-6600   *SIC* 8211
COMMISSION SCOLAIRE DES CHENES p 1098
175 RUE PELLETIER, DRUMMONDVILLE, QC, J2C 2W1
(819) 474-0750   *SIC* 8211
COMMISSION SCOLAIRE DES CHIC-CHOCS p 1355
170 BOUL SAINTE-ANNE O, SAINTE-ANNE-DES-MONTS, QC, G4V 1R8
(418) 763-2206   *SIC* 8211
COMMISSION SCOLAIRE DES DECOU-VREURS p 1270
1255 AV DU CHANOINE-MOREL, QUE-BEC, QC, G1S 4B1
(418) 684-0064   *SIC* 8211
COMMISSION SCOLAIRE DES DECOU-VREURS p 1271
3000 BOUL HOCHELAGA, QUEBEC, QC, G1V 3Y4
(418) 652-2159   *SIC* 8211
COMMISSION SCOLAIRE DES DECOU-VREURS p 1271
945 AV WOLFE BUREAU 100, QUEBEC, QC, G1V 4E2
(418) 652-2121   *SIC* 8211
COMMISSION SCOLAIRE DES DECOU-VREURS p 1275
1505 RUE DES GRANDES-MAREES, QUE-BEC, QC, G1Y 2T3
(418) 652-2196   *SIC* 8211
COMMISSION SCOLAIRE DES DECOU-VREURS p 1275
3643 AV DES COMPAGNONS, QUEBEC, QC, G1X 3Z6
(418) 652-2170   *SIC* 8211
COMMISSION SCOLAIRE DES DRAVEURS p 1103
360 BOUL LA VERENDRYE E, GATINEAU, QC, J8P 6K7
(819) 663-9241   *SIC* 8211
COMMISSION SCOLAIRE DES DRAVEURS p 1104
9 RUE SAINTE-YVONNE BUREAU 253, GATINEAU, QC, J8T 1X6
(819) 568-0233   *SIC* 8211
COMMISSION SCOLAIRE DES GRANDES-SEIGNEURIES p 1072
4 AV DE CHAMPAGNE, CANDIAC, QC, J5R 4W3
(514) 380-8899   *SIC* 8211
COMMISSION SCOLAIRE DES GRANDES-SEIGNEURIES p 1089
35 RUE BOARDMAN, DELSON, QC, J5B 2C3
(514) 380-8899   *SIC* 8211
COMMISSION SCOLAIRE DES GRANDES-SEIGNEURIES p 1123
50 BOUL TASCHEREAU BUREAU 310, LA PRAIRIE, QC, J5R 4V3
(514) 380-8899   *SIC* 8211
COMMISSION SCOLAIRE DES GRANDES-SEIGNEURIES p 1123
1100 BOUL TASCHEREAU, LA PRAIRIE, QC, J5R 1W8
(514) 380-8899   *SIC* 8211
COMMISSION SCOLAIRE DES HAUTES-RIVIERES p 1149
677 RUE DESJARDINS, MARIEVILLE, QC, J3M 1R1
(450) 460-4491   *SIC* 8211
COMMISSION SCOLAIRE DES HAUTES-RIVIERES p 1297
1881 AV SAINT-PAUL, SAINT-CESAIRE, QC, J0L 1T0
(450) 469-3187   *SIC* 8211
COMMISSION SCOLAIRE DES HAUTES-RIVIERES p 1316
365 AV LANDRY, SAINT-JEAN-SUR-RICHELIEU, QC, J2X 2P6
(450) 347-1225   *SIC* 8211
COMMISSION SCOLAIRE DES HAUTES-RIVIERES p 1316
940 BOUL DE NORMANDIE, SAINT-JEAN-SUR-RICHELIEU, QC, J3A 1A7
(450) 348-0413   *SIC* 8211
COMMISSION SCOLAIRE DES HAUTES-RIVIERES p 1316
511 RUE PIERRE-CAISSE, SAINT-JEAN-SUR-RICHELIEU, QC, J3A 1N5
(450) 348-0958   *SIC* 8211
COMMISSION SCOLAIRE DES HAUTES-RIVIERES p 1317
151 RUE NOTRE-DAME, SAINT-JEAN-SUR-RICHELIEU, QC, J3B 6M9
(450) 348-4747   *SIC* 8211
COMMISSION SCOLAIRE DES HAUTES-RIVIERES p 1317
210 RUE NOTRE-DAME, SAINT-JEAN-SUR-RICHELIEU, QC, J3B 6N3
(450) 359-6411   *SIC* 8211
COMMISSION SCOLAIRE DES HAUTS-CANTONS 1081
311 RUE SAINT-PAUL E, COATICOOK, QC, J1A 1G1
(819) 849-4825   *SIC* 8211
COMMISSION SCOLAIRE DES HAUTS-CANTONS p 1100
308 RUE PALMER, EAST ANGUS, QC, J0B 1R0
(819) 832-4953   *SIC* 8211
COMMISSION SCOLAIRE DES HAUTS-CANTONS 1125
3409 RUE LAVAL, LAC-MEGANTIC, QC, G6B 1A5
(819) 583-3023   *SIC* 8211
COMMISSION SCOLAIRE DES ILES p 1120
1419 CH DE L'ETANG-DU-NORD, L'ETANG-DU-NORD, QC, G4T 3B9
(418) 986-5511   *SIC* 8211
COMMISSION SCOLAIRE DES LAUREN-TIDES p 1159
700 BOUL DU DOCTEUR-GERVAIS, MONT-TREMBLANT, QC, J8E 2T3
(819) 425-3743   *SIC* 8211
COMMISSION SCOLAIRE DES LAUREN-TIDES p 1354
13 RUE SAINT-ANTOINE, SAINTE-AGATHE-DES-MONTS, QC, J8C 2C3
(819) 324-8670   *SIC* 8211
COMMISSION SCOLAIRE DES LAUREN-TIDES p 1354
258 BOUL DE SAINTE-ADELE, SAINTE-ADELE, QC, J8B 0K6
(450) 240-6220   *SIC* 8211
COMMISSION SCOLAIRE DES MONTS-ET-MAREES p 1046
See COMMISSION SCOLAIRE DES MONTS-ET-MAREES
COMMISSION SCOLAIRE DES MONTS-ET-MAREES p 1046
93 AV DU PARC BUREAU 3, AMQUI, QC, G5J 2L8
(418) 629-6200   *SIC* 8211
COMMISSION SCOLAIRE DES MONTS-ET-MAREES p 1046
95 AV DU PARC, AMQUI, QC, G5J 2L8
(418) 629-6200   *SIC* 8211
COMMISSION SCOLAIRE DES NAVIGA-TEURS p 1136
30 RUE VINCENT-CHAGNON, LEVIS, QC, G6V 4V6
(418) 838-8400   *SIC* 8221
COMMISSION SCOLAIRE DES NAVIGA-TEURS p 1136
55 RUE DES COMMANDEURS, LEVIS, QC, G6V 6P5
(418) 838-8402   *SIC* 8211
COMMISSION SCOLAIRE DES NAVIGA-TEURS p 1136
6045 RUE SAINT-GEORGES, LEVIS, QC, G6V 4K6
(418) 838-8548   *SIC* 8211
COMMISSION SCOLAIRE DES NAVIGA-TEURS p 1137
1860 1RE RUE BUREAU 90, LEVIS, QC, G6W 5M6
(418) 839-0500   *SIC* 8211
COMMISSION SCOLAIRE DES NAVIGA-

TEURS   *p*
1139
3724 AV DES EGLISES, LEVIS, QC, G6X
1X4
(418) 839-0500   *SIC* 8211
COMMISSION SCOLAIRE DES NAVIGA-
TEURS   *p*
1291
1134 RUE DU CENTENAIRE, SAINT-
AGAPIT, QC, G0S 1Z0
(418) 888-3961   *SIC* 8211
COMMISSION SCOLAIRE DES NAVIGA-
TEURS   *p*
1349
368 RTE DU PONT, SAINT-NICOLAS, QC,
G7A 2V3
(418) 834-2461   *SIC* 8211
COMMISSION SCOLAIRE DES NAVIGA-
TEURS   *p*
1357
6380 RUE GARNEAU, SAINTE-CROIX, QC,
G0S 2H0
(418) 796-0503   *SIC* 8211
COMMISSION SCOLAIRE DES PATRIOTES
p 1056
225 RUE HUBERT, BELOEIL, QC, J3G 2S8
(450) 467-9309   *SIC* 8211
COMMISSION SCOLAIRE DES PATRIOTES
p 1056
725 RUE DE LEVIS, BELOEIL, QC, J3G
2M1
(450) 467-0262   *SIC* 8211
COMMISSION SCOLAIRE DES PATRIOTES
p 1074
535 BOUL BRASSARD, CHAMBLY, QC, J3L
6H3
(450) 461-5908   *SIC* 8211
COMMISSION SCOLAIRE DES PATRIOTES
p 1158
525 RUE JOLLIET, MONT-SAINT-HILAIRE,
QC, J3H 3N2
(450) 467-0261   *SIC* 8211
COMMISSION SCOLAIRE DES PATRIOTES
p 1295
1740 RUE ROBERVAL, SAINT-BRUNO, QC,
J3V 3R3
(450) 441-2919   *SIC* 8211
COMMISSION SCOLAIRE DES PATRIOTES
p 1295
221 BOUL CLAIREVUE E, SAINT-BRUNO,
QC, J3V 5J3
(450) 653-1541   *SIC* 8211
COMMISSION SCOLAIRE DES PHARES *p*
1284
250 BOUL ARTHUR-BUIES O, RIMOUSKI,
QC, G5L 7A7
(418) 724-3439   *SIC* 8211
COMMISSION   SCOLAIRE   DES
PREMIERES-SEIGNEURIES   *p* 1055
See *COMMISSION SCOLAIRE DES*
PREMIERES-SEIGNEURIES
COMMISSION   SCOLAIRE   DES
PREMIERES-SEIGNEURIES   *p* 1055
10975 BOUL SAINTE-ANNE, BEAUPRE,
QC, G0A 1E0
(418) 821-8053   *SIC* 8211
COMMISSION   SCOLAIRE   DES
PREMIERES-SEIGNEURIES   *p* 1254
See *COMMISSION SCOLAIRE DES*
PREMIERES-SEIGNEURIES
COMMISSION   SCOLAIRE   DES
PREMIERES-SEIGNEURIES   *p* 1254
2233 AV ROYALE, QUEBEC, QC, G1C 1P3
(418) 821-8988   *SIC* 8211
COMMISSION   SCOLAIRE   DES
PREMIERES-SEIGNEURIES   *p* 1254
2265 AV LARUE, QUEBEC, QC, G1C 1J9
(418) 821-4220   *SIC* 8211
COMMISSION   SCOLAIRE   DES
PREMIERES-SEIGNEURIES   *p* 1255
2740 AV SAINT-DAVID, QUEBEC, QC, G1E
4K7
(418) 666-4500   *SIC* 8211
COMMISSION   SCOLAIRE   DES

PREMIERES-SEIGNEURIES   *p* 1255
See *COMMISSION SCOLAIRE DES*
PREMIERES-SEIGNEURIES
COMMISSION   SCOLAIRE   DES
PREMIERES-SEIGNEURIES   *p* 1255
645 AV DU CENACLE, QUEBEC, QC, G1E
1B3
(418) 666-4666   *SIC* 8211
COMMISSION   SCOLAIRE   DES
PREMIERES-SEIGNEURIES   *p* 1255
643 AV DU CENACLE, QUEBEC, QC, G1E
1B3
(418) 666-4666   *SIC* 8211
COMMISSION   SCOLAIRE   DES
PREMIERES-SEIGNEURIES   *p* 1256
800 RUE DE LA SORBONNE, QUEBEC,
QC, G1H 1H1
(418) 622-7821   *SIC* 8331
COMMISSION   SCOLAIRE   DES
PREMIERES-SEIGNEURIES   *p* 1256
See *COMMISSION SCOLAIRE DES*
PREMIERES-SEIGNEURIES
COMMISSION   SCOLAIRE   DES
PREMIERES-SEIGNEURIES   *p* 1280
700 RUE DE L'ARGON, QUEBEC, QC, G2N
2G5
(418) 634-5580   *SIC* 8299
COMMISSION   SCOLAIRE   DES
PREMIERES-SEIGNEURIES   *p* 1280
See *COMMISSION SCOLAIRE DES*
PREMIERES-SEIGNEURIES
COMMISSION SCOLAIRE DES RIVES-DU-
SAGUENAY   *p*
1077
350 RUE SAINT-GERARD, CHICOUTIMI,
QC, G7G 1J2
(418) 541-4343   *SIC* 8211
COMMISSION SCOLAIRE DES RIVES-DU-
SAGUENAY   *p*
1078
847   RUE   GEORGES-VANIER,
CHICOUTIMI, QC, G7H 4M1
(418) 698-5170   *SIC* 8211
COMMISSION SCOLAIRE DES RIVES-DU-
SAGUENAY   *p*
1078
985 RUE BEGIN, CHICOUTIMI, QC, G7H
4P1
(418) 698-5185   *SIC* 8211
COMMISSION SCOLAIRE DES RIVES-DU-
SAGUENAY   *p*
1078
36   RUE   JACQUES-CARTIER   E,
CHICOUTIMI, QC, G7H 1W2
(418) 698-5000   *SIC* 8211
COMMISSION SCOLAIRE DES RIVES-DU-
SAGUENAY   *p*
1121
1802 AV JOHN-KANE, LA BAIE, QC, G7B
1K2
(418) 544-2843   *SIC* 8211
COMMISSION SCOLAIRE DES SAMARES
p 1057
881   RUE   PIERRE-DE-LESTAGE,
BERTHIERVILLE, QC, J0K 1A0
(450) 758-3599   *SIC* 8211
COMMISSION SCOLAIRE DES SAMARES
p 1281
3144 18E AV BUREAU 760, RAWDON, QC,
J0K 1S0
(450) 758-3749   *SIC* 8211
COMMISSION SCOLAIRE DES SAMARES
p 1303
4671 RUE PRINCIPALE BUREAU 190,
SAINT-FELIX-DE-VALOIS, QC, J0K 2M0
(450) 439-6046   *SIC* 8211
COMMISSION SCOLAIRE DES SAMARES
p 1352
60 MONTEE REMI-HENRI, SAINT-ROCH-
DE-L'ACHIGAN, QC, J0K 3H0
(450) 588-7410   *SIC* 8211
COMMISSION SCOLAIRE DES SOMMETS
p 1052
430 5E AV, ASBESTOS, QC, J1T 1X2

(819) 879-5413   *SIC* 8211
COMMISSION SCOLAIRE DES SOMMETS
p 1403
250 RUE SAINT-GEORGES, WINDSOR,
QC, J1S 1K4
(819) 845-2728   *SIC* 8211
COMMISSION SCOLAIRE DU CHEMIN-DU-
ROY   *p*
1384
500   RUE   DES   ERABLES,   TROIS-
RIVIERES, QC, G8T 9S4
(819) 373-1422   *SIC* 8211
COMMISSION SCOLAIRE DU CHEMIN-DU-
ROY   *p*
1384
501   RUE   DES   ERABLES,   TROIS-
RIVIERES, QC, G8T 5J2
(819) 375-8931   *SIC* 8211
COMMISSION SCOLAIRE DU CHEMIN-DU-
ROY   *p*
1385
3750   RUE   JEAN-BOURDON,   TROIS-
RIVIERES, QC, G8Y 2A5
(819) 379-8714   *SIC* 8211
COMMISSION SCOLAIRE DU CHEMIN-DU-
ROY   *p*
1385
3750   RUE   JEAN-BOURDON,   TROIS-
RIVIERES, QC, G8Y 2A5
(819) 691-3366   *SIC* 8211
COMMISSION SCOLAIRE DU CHEMIN-DU-
ROY   *p*
1386
1725   BOUL   DU   CARMEL,   TROIS-
RIVIERES, QC, G8Z 3R8
(819) 379-5822   *SIC* 8211
COMMISSION SCOLAIRE DU CHEMIN-DU-
ROY   *p*
1389
365 RUE CHAVIGNY, TROIS-RIVIERES,
QC, G9B 1A7
(819) 377-4391   *SIC* 8211
COMMISSION SCOLAIRE DU FER *p* 1367
110 RUE COMEAU, SEPT-ILES, QC, G4R
1J4
(418) 964-2811   *SIC* 8211
COMMISSION SCOLAIRE DU FLEUVE ET
DES LACS   *p* 1378
14   RUE   DU   VIEUX-CHEMIN,
TEMISCOUATA-SUR-LE-LAC,   QC,   G0L
1E0
(418) 854-2370   *SIC* 8211
COMMISSION SCOLAIRE DU FLEUVE ET
DES LACS   *p* 1384
455 RUE JENKIN, TROIS-PISTOLES, QC,
G0L 4K0
SIC 8211
COMMISSION SCOLAIRE DU LAC-ST-
JEAN   *p*
1045
850 AV B?GIN, ALMA, QC, G8B 2X6
(418) 669-6063   *SIC* 8211
COMMISSION SCOLAIRE DU LITTORAL *p*
1367
789 RUE BEAULIEU, SEPT-ILES, QC, G4R
1P8
(418) 962-5558   *SIC* 8211
COMMISSION SCOLAIRE DU PAYS-DES-
BLEUETS   *p*
1090
300   AV   JEAN-DOLBEAU,   DOLBEAU-
MISTASSINI, QC, G8L 2T7
(418) 276-0984   *SIC* 8211
COMMISSION SCOLAIRE DU PAYS-DES-
BLEUETS   *p*
1287
171 BOUL DE LA JEUNESSE, ROBERVAL,
QC, G8H 2N9
(418) 275-3110   *SIC* 8211
COMMISSION SCOLAIRE DU VAL-DES-
CERFS   *p*
1088
222 RUE MERCIER, COWANSVILLE, QC,
J2K 3R9

(450) 263-6660   *SIC* 8211
COMMISSION SCOLAIRE DU VAL-DES-
CERFS   *p*
1109
55 RUE COURT, GRANBY, QC, J2G 9N6
(450) 372-0221   *SIC* 8211
COMMISSION SCOLAIRE DU VAL-DES-
CERFS   *p*
1109
700 RUE DENISON O, GRANBY, QC, J2G
4G3
(450) 378-8544   *SIC* 8249
COMMISSION SCOLAIRE DU VAL-DES-
CERFS   *p*
1109
1111 RUE SIMONDS S, GRANBY, QC, J2G
9H7
(450) 378-9981   *SIC* 8211
COMMISSION SCOLAIRE DU VAL-DES-
CERFS   *p*
1110
549 RUE FOURNIER, GRANBY, QC, J2J
2K5
(450) 777-7536   *SIC* 8211
COMMISSION   SCOLAIRE   EASTERN
TOWNSHIPS   *p* 1088
224 RUE MERCIER, COWANSVILLE, QC,
J2K 5C3
(450) 263-3772   *SIC* 8211
COMMISSION   SCOLAIRE   EASTERN
TOWNSHIPS   *p* 1147
340 RUE SAINT-JEAN-BOSCO, MAGOG,
QC, J1X 1K9
(819) 868-3100   *SIC* 8211
COMMISSION   SCOLAIRE   ENGLISH-
MONTREAL   *p*
1239
See *FONDATION EDUCATIVE DE LA COM-*
MISSION SCOLAIRE ENGLISH-MONTREAL,
LA
COMMISSION   SCOLAIRE   ENGLISH-
MONTREAL   *p*
1329
See *FONDATION EDUCATIVE DE LA COM-*
MISSION SCOLAIRE ENGLISH-MONTREAL,
LA
COMMISSION   SCOLAIRE   ENGLISH-
MONTREAL   *p*
1346
See *FONDATION EDUCATIVE DE LA COM-*
MISSION SCOLAIRE ENGLISH-MONTREAL,
LA
COMMISSION SCOLAIRE HARRICANA *p*
1046
850 1RE RUE E, AMOS, QC, J9T 2H8
(819) 732-3221   *SIC* 8211
COMMISSION SCOLAIRE HARRICANA *p*
1046
800 1RE RUE E, AMOS, QC, J9T 2H8
(819) 732-3221   *SIC* 8211
COMMISSION SCOLAIRE KATIVIK *p* 1113
PR, INUKJUAK, QC, J0M 1M0
(819) 254-8211   *SIC* 8211
COMMISSION SCOLAIRE KATIVIK *p* 1254
GD, PUVIRNITUQ, QC, J0M 1P0
(819) 988-2960   *SIC* 8211
COMMISSION SCOLAIRE KATIVIK *p* 1324
9800 BOUL CAVENDISH BUREAU 400,
SAINT-LAURENT, QC, H4M 2V9
(514) 482-8220   *SIC* 8211
COMMISSION SCOLAIRE MARGUERITE-
BOURGEOYS   *p*
1127
50 34E AV, LACHINE, QC, H8T 1Z2
(514) 748-4662   *SIC* 8211
COMMISSION SCOLAIRE MARGUERITE-
BOURGEOYS   *p*
1131
8585 RUE GEORGE, LASALLE, QC, H8P
1G5
(514) 595-2052   *SIC* 8211
COMMISSION SCOLAIRE MARGUERITE-
BOURGEOYS   *p*
1132

9199 RUE CENTRALE, LASALLE, QC, H8R
2J9
(514) 595-2044   SIC 8211
**COMMISSION SCOLAIRE MARGUERITE-
BOURGEOYS**   p
1155
50 AV MONTGOMERY, MONT-ROYAL, QC,
H3R 2B3
(514) 731-2761   SIC 8211
**COMMISSION SCOLAIRE MARGUERITE-
BOURGEOYS**   p
1155
1101 CH ROCKLAND, MONT-ROYAL, QC,
H3P 2X8
(514) 739-6311   SIC 8211
**COMMISSION SCOLAIRE MARGUERITE-
BOURGEOYS**   p
1249
311 AV INGLEWOOD, POINTE-CLAIRE,
QC, H9R 2Z8
(514) 855-4225   SIC 8211
**COMMISSION SCOLAIRE MARGUERITE-
BOURGEOYS**   p
1253
3 AV SAINTE-ANNE, POINTE-CLAIRE, QC,
H9S 4P6
(514) 855-4236   SIC 8211
**COMMISSION SCOLAIRE MARGUERITE-
BOURGEOYS**   p
1323
1100 BOUL DE LA COTE-VERTU, SAINT-
LAURENT, QC, H4L 4V1
(514) 855-4500   SIC 8211
**COMMISSION SCOLAIRE MARGUERITE-
BOURGEOYS**   p
1325
235 RUE BLEIGNIER, SAINT-LAURENT,
QC, H4N 1B1
(514) 332-0742   SIC 8211
**COMMISSION SCOLAIRE MARGUERITE-
BOURGEOYS**   p
1328
2395 BOUL THIMENS, SAINT-LAURENT,
QC, H4R 1T4
(514) 332-3190   SIC 8211
**COMMISSION SCOLAIRE MARIE-
VICTORIN**   p
1069
8350 BOUL PELLETIER, BROSSARD, QC,
J4X 1M8
(450) 465-6290   SIC 8211
**COMMISSION SCOLAIRE MARIE-
VICTORIN**   p
1070
3055 BOUL DE ROME, BROSSARD, QC,
J4Y 1S9
(450) 443-0010   SIC 8211
**COMMISSION SCOLAIRE MARIE-
VICTORIN**   p
1143
13 RUE SAINT-LAURENT E, LONGUEUIL,
QC, J4H 4B7
(450) 670-0730   SIC 8211
**COMMISSION SCOLAIRE MARIE-
VICTORIN**   p
1143
444 RUE DE GENTILLY E, LONGUEUIL,
QC, J4H 3X7
(450) 651-6800   SIC 8211
**COMMISSION SCOLAIRE MARIE-
VICTORIN**   p
1146
1250 CH DU TREMBLAY, LONGUEUIL, QC,
J4N 1A2
(450) 468-0833   SIC 8211
**COMMISSION SCOLAIRE MARIE-
VICTORIN**   p
1308
5095 RUE AURELE, SAINT-HUBERT, QC,
J3Y 2E6
(450) 678-0145   SIC 8211
**COMMISSION SCOLAIRE MARIE-
VICTORIN**   p
1308

7450 BOUL COUSINEAU, SAINT-HUBERT,
QC, J3Y 3L4
(450) 678-2080   SIC 8211
**COMMISSION SCOLAIRE MARIE-
VICTORIN**   p
1309
1600 RUE DE MONACO, SAINT-HUBERT,
QC, J3Z 1B7
(450) 462-3844   SIC 8211
**COMMISSION SCOLAIRE MARIE-
VICTORIN**   p
1310
3855 GRANDE ALLEE, SAINT-HUBERT,
QC, J4T 2V8
(450) 678-2781   SIC 8211
**COMMISSION SCOLAIRE MARIE-
VICTORIN**   p
1310
3875 GRANDE ALLEE, SAINT-HUBERT,
QC, J4T 2V8
(450) 676-0261   SIC 8211
COMMISSION SCOLAIRE NEW FRONTIER
p 1076
210 RUE MCLEOD, CHATEAUGUAY, QC,
J6J 2H4
(450) 691-3230   SIC 8211
COMMISSION SCOLAIRE NEW FRONTIER
p 1076
214 RUE MCLEOD, CHATEAUGUAY, QC,
J6J 2H4
(450) 691-1440   SIC 8211
**COMMISSION SCOLAIRE PIERRE-NEVEU,
LA**   p 1154
525 RUE DE LA MADONE, MONT-
LAURIER, QC, J9L 1S4
(819) 623-4310   SIC 8211
COMMISSIONAIRES   p 337
See CANADIAN CORPS OF COMMIS-
SIONAIRES NATIONAL OFFICE, THE
COMMISSIONAIRES (GREAT LAKES)   p
657
1112 DEARNESS DR UNIT 14, LONDON,
ON, N6E 1N9
(519) 433-6763   SIC 7381
COMMISSIONAIRES (GREAT LAKES)   p
796
2947 PORTLAND DR, OAKVILLE, ON, L6H
5S4
(416) 364-4496   SIC 7381
COMMISSIONAIRES BC   p 303
See BRITISH COLUMBIA CORPS OF
COMMISSIONAIRES
COMMISSIONAIRES GREAT LAKES p 657
See COMMISSIONAIRES (GREAT LAKES)
COMMISSIONAIRES, THE   p 561
See CANADIAN CORPS OF COMMIS-
SIONAIRES NATIONAL OFFICE, THE
**COMMISSO BROS. & RACCO ITALIAN
BAKERY INC**   p 992
8 KINCORT ST, TORONTO, ON, M6M 3E1
(416) 651-7671   SIC 2051
COMMISSO'S FRESH FOODS   p 760
See 1788741 ONTARIO INC
COMMODITY IMPORT INC   p 1342
845 AV MUNCK, SAINT-LAURENT, QC,
H7S 1A9
(514) 384-4690   SIC 6719
COMMON COLLECTION AGENCY INC   p
864
5900 FINCH AVE E SUITE 200A, SCAR-
BOROUGH, ON, M1B 5P8
(416) 297-7077   SIC 7322
COMMONWEALTH HOSPITALITY LTD   p
451
1980 ROBIE ST, HALIFAX, NS, B3H 3G5
(902) 423-1161   SIC 7011
COMMONWEALTH HOSPITALITY LTD   p
527
3063 SOUTH SERVICE RD, BURLINGTON,
ON, L7N 3E9
(905) 639-4443   SIC 7011
COMMONWEALTH HOSPITALITY LTD   p
693
5090 EXPLORER DR SUITE 700, MISSIS-

SAUGA, ON, L4W 4T9
(905) 602-6224   SIC 7011
COMMONWEALTH LEGAL INC   p 961
145 WELLINGTON ST W SUITE 901,
TORONTO, ON, M5J 1H8
(416) 703-3755   SIC 8111
**COMMONWELL MUTUAL INSURANCE
GROUP, THE**   p 645
336 ANGELINE ST S, LINDSAY, ON, K9V
0J8
(705) 324-2146   SIC 6331
COMMUNAUTO INC   p 1203
1117 RUE SAINTE-CATHERINE O BU-
REAU 806, MONTREAL, QC, H3B 1H9
(514) 842-4545   SIC 7515
COMMUNICATION DEMO INC   p 1187
407 RUE MCGILL BUREAU 311, MON-
TREAL, QC, H2Y 2G3
(514) 985-2523   SIC 7389
COMMUNICATION DEMO INC   p 1266
925 AV NEWTON BUREAU 220, QUEBEC,
QC, G1P 4M2
(418) 877-0704   SIC 7389
COMMUNICATION MARKETING PALM   p
1207
See PALM COMMUNICATION MARKETING
INC
COMMUNICATION PL   p 1254
See 9084-2733 QUEBEC INC
COMMUNICATION SERVICES   p 865
See C A S COMMUNICATIONS SERVICES
LIMITED
COMMUNICATIONA ID EST   p 1190
See OGILVY MONTREAL INC
**COMMUNICATIONS & POWER INDUS-
TRIES CANADA INC**   p
593
45 RIVER DR UPPER LEVEL, GEORGE-
TOWN, ON, L7G 2J4
(905) 877-0161   SIC 3663
**COMMUNICATIONS & POWER INDUS-
TRIES CANADA INC**   p
593
LOWER LEVEL 45 RIVER DR, GEORGE-
TOWN, ON, L7G 2J4
(905) 877-0161   SIC 3663
COMMUNICATIONS AIRBUS DS   p 1107
See VESTA SOLUTIONS COMMUNICA-
TIONS CORP
COMMUNICATIONS COMPROD   p 1064
See COMPROD INC
COMMUNICATIONS FORMEDIC INC p 668
20 TORBAY RD, MARKHAM, ON, L3R 1G6
(905) 415-1940   SIC 4899
**COMMUNICATIONS GROUP RED DEER
LTD**   p 155
7434 50 AVE, RED DEER, AB, T4P 1X7
(403) 347-0777   SIC 4899
COMMUNICATIONS INTERVOX INC, LES p
1375
6420 CH DE SAINT-ELIE, SHERBROOKE,
QC, J1R 0P6
(819) 563-3222   SIC 5065
COMMUNICATIONS LMT INC   p 1194
1500 AV MCGILL COLLEGE, MONTREAL,
QC, H3A 3J5
(514) 285-9263   SIC 5065
COMMUNICATIONS MEDIA GO DESIGN p
1223
See COMMUNICATIONS MEDPLAN INC
COMMUNICATIONS MEDPLAN INC p 1223
2077 RUE CABOT, MONTREAL, QC, H4E
1E2
(514) 767-6166   SIC 8748
**COMMUNICATIONS METRO-MONTREAL
INC**   p 1218
3901 RUE JEAN-TALON O BUREAU 200,
MONTREAL, QC, H3R 2G4
(514) 736-6767   SIC 7389
COMMUNICATIONS POMERLEAU INC p
1046
111 BOUL MERCIER, AMOS, QC, J9T 2P2
(819) 732-5377   SIC 4899
COMMUNICATIONS TMP WORLDWIDE p

1198
See MONSTER WORLDWIDE CANADA
INC
COMMUNICATIONS TRANSCRIPT INC p
1194
625 AV DU PRESIDENT-KENNEDY BU-
REAU 800, MONTREAL, QC, H3A 1K2
(514) 874-9134   SIC 7389
COMMUNICATIONS TRISPEC INC, LES p
1344
8500 RUE PASCAL-GAGNON, SAINT-
LEONARD, QC, H1P 1Y4
(514) 328-2025   SIC 5065
COMMUNITECH CORPORATION   p 638
151 CHARLES ST W SUITE 100, KITCH-
ENER, ON, N2G 1H6
(519) 888-9944   SIC 8611
**COMMUNITY & NEIGHBOURHOOD SER-
VICES**   p
28
See CITY OF CALGARY, THE
**COMMUNITY & PRIMARY HEALTH CARE-
LANARK, LEEDS & GRENVILLE**   p 519
2235 PARKEDALE AVE, BROCKVILLE, ON,
K6V 6B2
(613) 342-1747   SIC 8399
COMMUNITY BUILDERS INC   p 443
51 FOREST HILLS PKY SUITE 1, DART-
MOUTH, NS, B2W 6C6
(902) 464-5100   SIC 7997
COMMUNITY CARE ACCESS CENTRE   p
620
See MUSKOKA ALGONQUIN HEALTH-
CARE
**COMMUNITY CARE ACCESS CENTRE -
OXFORD**   p 1035
1147 DUNDAS ST, WOODSTOCK, ON, N4S
8W3
(519) 539-1284   SIC 8082
**COMMUNITY CARE ACCESS CENTRE NI-
AGARA**   p
884
149 HARTZEL RD, ST CATHARINES, ON,
L2P 1N6
(905) 684-9441   SIC 8082
COMMUNITY CARE SERVICES   p 705
See COMMUNITY HOMEMAKERS LTD
COMMUNITY CLUB   p 882
219 5TH ST, SMOOTH ROCK FALLS, ON,
P0L 2B0
(705) 338-2336   SIC 8641
**COMMUNITY CONNECTIONS SOCIETY OF
SOUTHEAST BC**   p 203
209 16TH AVE N, CRANBROOK, BC, V1C
5S8
(250) 426-2976   SIC 7361
COMMUNITY CONSUMERS COOP p 425
See CAROL WABUSH CO-OP SOCIETY
LIMITED
**COMMUNITY EDUCATION NETWORK FOR
SOUTH WESTERN NEWFOUNDLAND** p 434
See COMMUNITY EDUCATION NETWORK
INC
COMMUNITY EDUCATION NETWORK INC
p 434
31 GALLANT ST, STEPHENVILLE, NL, A2N
2B5
(709) 643-4891   SIC 8399
COMMUNITY ELECTRIC LTD   p 1426
811 58TH ST E, SASKATOON, SK, S7K 6X5
(306) 477-8822   SIC 1731
COMMUNITY FARM STORE LTD, THE p 211
330 DUNCAN ST SUITE 101, DUNCAN,
BC, V9L 3W4
(250) 748-6223   SIC 5149
COMMUNITY FIRST DEVELOPMENTS INC
p 788
2171 AVENUE RD SUITE 303, NORTH
YORK, ON, M5M 4B4
(416) 932-9249   SIC 8742
**COMMUNITY HEALTH SERVICES (SASKA-
TOON) ASSOCIATION LIMITED**   p
1426
455 2ND AVE N, SASKATOON, SK, S7K

2C2
(306) 652-0300   SIC 8011
COMMUNITY HOMEMAKERS LTD   p 705
160 TRADERS BLVD E SUITE 103, MISSIS-SAUGA, ON, L4Z 3K7
(905) 275-0544   SIC 8082
COMMUNITY LIFECARE INC   p 656
81 GRAND AVE, LONDON, ON, N6C 1M2
(519) 432-1162   SIC 6513
COMMUNITY LIVING - FORT ERIE   p 591
615 INDUSTRIAL DR, FORT ERIE, ON, L2A 5M4
(905) 871-6770   SIC 8322
COMMUNITY LIVING ACCESS   p 880
See COMMUNITY LIVING ACCESS SUP-PORT SERVICES
COMMUNITY LIVING ACCESS SUPPORT SERVICES   p 880
89 CULVER ST, SIMCOE, ON, N3Y 2V5
(519) 426-0007   SIC 8399
COMMUNITY LIVING ALGOMA   p 862
99 NORTHERN AVE E, SAULT STE. MARIE, ON, P6B 4H5
(705) 253-1700   SIC 8322
COMMUNITY LIVING BELLEVILLE AND AREA   p 491
91 MILLENNIUM PKY, BELLEVILLE, ON, K8N 4Z5
(613) 969-7407   SIC 8059
COMMUNITY LIVING BRANT   p 515
366 DALHOUSIE ST, BRANTFORD, ON, N3S 3W2
(519) 756-2662   SIC 8322
COMMUNITY LIVING BURLINGTON   p 526
3057 MAINWAY, BURLINGTON, ON, L7M 1A1
(905) 335-6711   SIC 8322
COMMUNITY LIVING CAMBRIDGE   p 533
466 FRANKLIN BLVD, CAMBRIDGE, ON, N1R 8G6
(519) 621-0680   SIC 8331
COMMUNITY LIVING CAMBRIDGE   p 538
1124 VALENTINE DR, CAMBRIDGE, ON, N3H 2N8
(519) 650-5091   SIC 8361
COMMUNITY LIVING DURHAM NORTH   p 848
60 VANEDWARD DR UNIT 2, PORT PERRY, ON, L9L 1G3
(905) 985-8511   SIC 8361
COMMUNITY LIVING ELGIN   p 889
400 TALBOT ST, ST THOMAS, ON, N5P 1B8
(519) 631-9222   SIC 8361
COMMUNITY LIVING ESSEX COUNTY   p 1017
13158 TECUMSEH RD E, WINDSOR, ON, N8N 3T6
(519) 979-0057   SIC 8322
COMMUNITY LIVING GEORGINA   p 902
See CORPORATION OF THE TOWN OF GEORGINA, THE
COMMUNITY LIVING GUELPH WELLINGTON   p 602
8 ROYAL RD, GUELPH, ON, N1H 1G3
(519) 824-2480   SIC 8299
COMMUNITY LIVING GUELPH WELLINGTON   p 602
8 ROYAL RD, GUELPH, ON, N1H 1G3
(519) 824-2480   SIC 8322
COMMUNITY LIVING GUELPH WELLINGTON   p 746
135 FERGUS ST S, MOUNT FOREST, ON, N0G 2L2
(519) 323-4050   SIC 8322
COMMUNITY LIVING HALDIMAND   p 541
2256 RIVER RD E, CAYUGA, ON, N0A 1E0
(905) 772-3344   SIC 8322
COMMUNITY LIVING KINGSTON AND DISTRICT   p 631

541 DAYS RD UNIT 6, KINGSTON, ON, K7M 3R8
(613) 546-6613   SIC 8322
COMMUNITY LIVING KIRKLAND LAKE   p 634
51 GOVERNMENT RD W, KIRKLAND LAKE, ON, P2N 2E5
(705) 567-9331   SIC 8399
COMMUNITY LIVING LONDON INC   p 652
180 ADELAIDE ST S SUITE 4, LONDON, ON, N5Z 3L1
(519) 686-3000   SIC 8322
COMMUNITY LIVING LONDON INC   p 652
190 ADELAIDE ST S, LONDON, ON, N5Z 3L1
(519) 686-3000   SIC 8322
COMMUNITY LIVING NEWMAR-KET/AURORA DISTRICT   p 755
195 HARRY WALKER PKY N, NEWMAR-KET, ON, L3Y 7B3
(905) 773-6346   SIC 8399
COMMUNITY LIVING NORTH BAY   p 763
161 MAIN ST E, NORTH BAY, ON, P1B 1A9
(705) 476-3288   SIC 8322
COMMUNITY LIVING NORTH HALTON   p 683
500 VALLEYVIEW CRES, MILTON, ON, L9T 3L2
(905) 693-0528   SIC 8322
COMMUNITY LIVING NORTH HALTON   p 683
917 NIPISSING RD, MILTON, ON, L9T 5E3
(905) 878-2337   SIC 8322
COMMUNITY LIVING OAKVILLE   p 802
301 WYECROFT RD, OAKVILLE, ON, L6K 2H2
(905) 844-0146   SIC 8399
COMMUNITY LIVING ONTARIO   p 776
240 DUNCAN MILL RD SUITE 403, NORTH YORK, ON, M3B 3S6
(416) 447-4348   SIC 8322
COMMUNITY LIVING OS-HAWA/CLARINGTON   p 812
39 WELLINGTON AVE E, OSHAWA, ON, L1H 3Y1
(905) 576-3011   SIC 8361
COMMUNITY LIVING OWEN SOUND AND DISTRICT   p 835
769 4TH AVE E, OWEN SOUND, ON, N4K 2N5
(519) 371-9251   SIC 8399
COMMUNITY LIVING PARRY SOUND   p 837
38 JOSEPH ST, PARRY SOUND, ON, P2A 2G5
(705) 746-9330   SIC 8399
COMMUNITY LIVING PRINCE EDWARD   p 845
67 KING ST UNIT 1, PICTON, ON, K0K 2T0
(613) 476-6038   SIC 8699
COMMUNITY LIVING RENFREW COUNTY SOUTH   p 849
326 RAGLAN ST S, RENFREW, ON, K7V 1R5
(613) 432-6763   SIC 8399
COMMUNITY LIVING TIMMINS INTERGRA-TION COMMUNAUTAIRE   p 912
166 BROUSSEAU AVE, TIMMINS, ON, P4N 5Y4
(705) 268-8811   SIC 8322
COMMUNITY LIVING TORONTO   p 574
288 JUDSON ST UNIT 17, ETOBICOKE, ON, M8Z 5T6
(416) 252-1171   SIC 7389
COMMUNITY LIVING TORONTO   p 782
1122 FINCH AVE W UNIT 18, NORTH YORK, ON, M3J 3J5
(416) 225-7166   SIC 8322
COMMUNITY LIVING TORONTO   p 972
20 SPADINA RD, TORONTO, ON, M5R 2S7
(416) 968-0650   SIC 8322
COMMUNITY LIVING TORONTO   p 972

20 SPADINA RD SUITE 257, TORONTO, ON, M5R 2S7
(416) 968-0650   SIC 8742
COMMUNITY LIVING WALKERTON AND DISTRICT   p 1004
19 DURHAM ST E, WALKERTON, ON, N0G 2V0
(519) 881-0233   SIC 7361
COMMUNITY LIVING WALLACEBURG   p 1004
1100 DUFFERIN AVE, WALLACEBURG, ON, N8A 2W1
(519) 627-0776   SIC 8699
COMMUNITY LIVING WEST NIPISSING   p 898
120 NIPISSING ST, STURGEON FALLS, ON, P2B 1J6
(705) 753-3143   SIC 8059
COMMUNITY LIVING WINDSOR   p 1019
2840 TEMPLE DR, WINDSOR, ON, N8W 5J5
(519) 944-2464   SIC 8322
COMMUNITY LIVING YORK SOUTH   p 855
101 EDWARD AVE, RICHMOND HILL, ON, L4C 5E5
(905) 884-9110   SIC 8361
COMMUNITY LIVING-GRIMSBY, LINCOLN AND WEST LINCOLN   p 489
5041 KING ST, BEAMSVILLE, ON, L0R 1B0
(905) 563-4115   SIC 8322
COMMUNITY LIVING-STORMONT COUNTY   p 563
280 NINTH ST W, CORNWALL, ON, K6J 3A6
(613) 938-9550   SIC 8059
COMMUNITY LODGE INCORPORATED   p 467
320 ALEXANDRA ST, SYDNEY, NS, B1S 2G1
(902) 539-5267   SIC 8361
COMMUNITY NATURAL FOODS LTD   p 34
202 61 AVE SW, CALGARY, AB, T2H 0B4
(403) 930-6363   SIC 5411
COMMUNITY NATURAL FOODS LTD   p 34
6120 1A ST SW, CALGARY, AB, T2H 0G3
(403) 252-0011   SIC 5499
COMMUNITY NATURAL FOODS LTD   p 72
1304 10 AVE SW, CALGARY, AB, T3C 0J2
(403) 930-6363   SIC 5499
COMMUNITY RESPITE SERVICE   p 380
1155 NOTRE DAME AVE, WINNIPEG, MB, R3E 3G1
(204) 953-2400   SIC 8399
COMMUNITY SAVINGS CREDIT UNION   p 274
13450 102 AVE SUITE 1600, SURREY, BC, V3T 5X3
(604) 654-2000   SIC 6062
COMMUNITY SERVICES   p 603
See GUELPH, CITY OF
COMMUNITY SUPPORT CONNECTIONS-MEALS ON WHEELS AND MORE   p 1008
420 WEBER ST N UNIT L, WATERLOO, ON, N2L 4E7
(519) 772-8787   SIC 5963
COMMUNITY THERAPY SERVICES INC   p 383
1555 ST JAMES ST UNIT 201, WINNIPEG, MB, R3H 1B5
(204) 949-0533   SIC 8699
COMMUNITY, THE   p 991
See PULP & FIBER INC
COMO   p 1325
See COMO DIFFUSION INC
COMO DIFFUSION INC   p 1325
103 BOUL MARCEL-LAURIN, SAINT-LAURENT, QC, H4N 2M3
(514) 286-2666   SIC 5137
COMOR SPORTS CENTRE LTD   p 320
1793 4TH AVE W, VANCOUVER, BC, V6J 1M2
(604) 734-0212   SIC 5941
COMOR-GO PLAY OUTSIDE   p 320

See COMOR SPORTS CENTRE LTD
COMOX VALLEY DISTRIBUTION LTD   p 233
140 TENTH ST, NANAIMO, BC, V9R 6Z5
(250) 754-7773   SIC 4213
COMOX VALLEY DODGE CHRYSLER JEEP LTD   p 203
4847 ISLAND HWY N, COURTENAY, BC, V9N 5Y8
(250) 338-5451   SIC 5511
COMOX VALLEY HYUNDAI   p 203
See CVH AUTO INC
COMOX VALLEY REGIONAL DISTRICT   p 195
225 DOGWOOD ST S, CAMPBELL RIVER, BC, V9W 8C8
(250) 287-9234   SIC 7999
COMOX VALLEY SENIORS VILLAGE   p 203
See PR SENIORS HOUSING MANAGE-MENT LTD
COMOX VALLEY SPORTS & AQUATIC CENTRES   p 203
See TOWN OF COMOX, THE
COMOX VALLEY TRANSITION SOCIETY   p 203
625 ENGLAND AVE, COURTENAY, BC, V9N 2N5
(250) 897-0511   SIC 8699
COMP-TECH MFG. INC   p 776
58 SCARSDALE RD, NORTH YORK, ON, M3B 2R7
(416) 510-1035   SIC 3469
COMPACT MOULD LIMITED   p 1030
120 HAIST AVE, WOODBRIDGE, ON, L4L 5V4
(905) 851-7724   SIC 3544
COMPAGNIE 2 AMERIKS INC, LA   p 1233
2300 RUE MICHELIN, MONTREAL, QC, H7L 5C3
(438) 380-3330   SIC 5149
COMPAGNIE ABITIBIBOWATER DU CANADA   p 1209
See ABITIBIBOWATER CANADA INC
COMPAGNIE AMERICAINE DE FER & METAUX INC, LA   p 1238
9100 BOUL HENRI-BOURASSA E, MONTREAL-EST, QC, H1E 2S4
(514) 494-2000   SIC 3341
COMPAGNIE AMERICAINE DE FER & METAUX INC, LA   p 1257
999 BOUL MONTMORENCY, QUEBEC, QC, G1J 3W1
(418) 649-1000   SIC 3341
COMPAGNIE ARCHER-DANIELS-MIDLAND DU CANADA   p 1072
See ADM AGRI-INDUSTRIES COMPANY
COMPAGNIE BEAULIEU CANADA   p 1044
335 RUE DE ROXTON, ACTON VALE, QC, J0H 1A0
(450) 546-5000   SIC 2273
COMPAGNIE BEAULIEU CANADA   p 1101
1144 BOUL MAGENTA E, FARNHAM, QC, J2N 1C1
SIC 2273
COMPAGNIE BEAULIEU CANADA   p 1402
1003 RUE PRINCIPALE RR 21, WICKHAM, QC, J0C 1S0
SIC 2282
COMPAGNIE BROADSIGN CANADA   p 1203
1100 BOUL ROBERT-BOURASSA 12E ETAGE, MONTREAL, QC, H3B 3A5
(514) 399-1184   SIC 7371
COMPAGNIE CANADIAN TECHNICAL TAPE LTEE   p 563
1400 ROSEMOUNT AVE, CORNWALL, ON, K6J 3E6
(613) 932-3105   SIC 2672
COMPAGNIE CANADIAN TECHNICAL TAPE LTEE   p 1325
455 BOUL DE LA COTE-VERTU, SAINT-LAURENT, QC, H4N 1E8
(514) 334-1510   SIC 2672
COMPAGNIE COMMERCIALE EMEGO LTEE, LA   p 1130

7373 RUE CORDNER, LASALLE, QC, H8N 2R5

(514) 365-0202   SIC 5139

COMPAGNIE COMMONWEALTH PLY-WOOD LTEE, LA p 1364

15 BOUL DU CURE-LABELLE, SAINTE-THERESE, QC, J7E 2X1

(450) 435-6541   SIC 2435

COMPAGNIE COMMONWEALTH PLY-WOOD LTEE, LA p 1368

1155 AV DE LA FONDERIE, SHAWINIGAN, QC, G9N 1W9

(819) 537-6621   SIC 2435

COMPAGNIE D'ACIER ARCHIDROME DU CANADA LTEE, LA p 1308

3100 BOUL LOSCH, SAINT-HUBERT, QC, J3Y 3V8

(450) 678-4444   SIC 5051

COMPAGNIE D'APPAREILS ELEC-TRIQUES PEERLESS LTEE p 1132

9145 RUE BOIVIN, LASALLE, QC, H8R 2E5

(514) 595-1671   SIC 1731

COMPAGNIE D'ARRIMAGE EMPIRE LTEE p 1187

500 PLACE D'ARMES BUREAU 2800, MONTREAL, QC, H2Y 2W2

(514) 288-2221   SIC 4731

COMPAGNIE D'ASSURANCE BELAIR INC, LA p 831

1111 PRINCE OF WALES DR SUITE 200, OTTAWA, ON, K2C 3T2

(613) 744-3279   SIC 6411

COMPAGNIE D'ASSURANCE BELAIR INC, LA p 944

700 UNIVERSITY AVE SUITE 1100, TORONTO, ON, M5G 0A2

(416) 250-6363   SIC 6331

COMPAGNIE D'ASSURANCE BELAIR INC, LA p 1051

7101 RUE JEAN-TALON E BUREAU 300, ANJOU, QC, H1M 3T6

(514) 270-1700   SIC 6331

COMPAGNIE D'ASSURANCE BELAIR INC, LA p 1279

5400 BOUL DES GALERIES BUREAU 500, QUEBEC, QC, G2K 2B4

(418) 877-1199   SIC 6331

COMPAGNIE D'ASSURANCE DU QUEBEC p 1194

1001 BOUL DE MAISONNEUVE O BU-REAU 1400, MONTREAL, QC, H3A 3C8

(514) 844-1116   SIC 6331

COMPAGNIE D'ASSURANCE HABITATION ET AUTO TD p 668

675 COCHRANE DR SUITE 100, MARKHAM, ON, L3R 0B8

(905) 415-8400   SIC 6411

COMPAGNIE D'ASSURANCE MISSISQUOI, LA p 1203

5 PLACE VILLE-MARIE UNITE 1400, MON-TREAL, QC, H3B 2G2

(514) 875-5790   SIC 6331

COMPAGNIE D'ASSURANCE MISSISQUOI, LA p 1203

See ECONOMICAL MUTUAL INSURANCE COMPANY

COMPAGNIE D'ASSURANCE SONNET 1203

5 PLACE VILLE-MARIE BUREAU 1400, MONTREAL, QC, H3B 0A8

(514) 875-5790   SIC 6331

COMPAGNIE D'ASSURANCE WAWANESA p 1157

See WAWANESA MUTUAL INSURANCE COMPANY, THE

COMPAGNIE D'ASSURANCES GEN-ERALES TD 1180

50 BOUL CREMAZIE O BUREAU 1200, MONTREAL, QC, H2P 1B6

(514) 382-6060   SIC 6311

COMPAGNIE D'ECHANTILLONS NA-TIONAL LIMITEE p 1161

11500 BOUL ARMAND-BOMBARDIER, MONTREAL, QC, H1E 2W9

(514) 648-4000   SIC 2782

COMPAGNIE D'EDITION ANDRE PAQUE-TTE INC, LA p 619

1100 ABERDEEN ST, HAWKESBURY, ON, K6A 1K7

(613) 632-4155   SIC 2711

COMPAGNIE D'ENTRETIEN BRITE-LITE LTEE p 1361

940 RUE BERGAR, SAINTE-ROSE, QC, H7L 4Z8

(450) 669-3803   SIC 5083

COMPAGNIE DE CHEMIN DE FER DU LITTORAL NORD DE QUEBEC ET DU LABRADOR INC p 1367

1 RUE RETTY, SEPT-ILES, QC, G4R 3C7

(418) 968-7400   SIC 4011

COMPAGNIE DE CHEMIN DE FER ROBERVAL-SAGUENAY INC, LA p 1115

1955 BOUL MELLON EDIFICE 1001, JON-QUIERE, QC, G7S 4L2

(418) 699-2714   SIC 4011

COMPAGNIE DE COMMERCE A.S. & F. LTEE p 1216

9850 RUE MEILLEUR, MONTREAL, QC, H3L 3J4

(514) 385-5568   SIC 5136

COMPAGNIE DE CONSTRUCTION ET DE DEVELOPPEMENT CRIE LTEE, LA p 1232

3983 BOUL LITE, MONTREAL, QC, H7E 1A3

(450) 661-1102   SIC 1522

COMPAGNIE DE CUIVRE HIGHLAND p 1144

See HIGHLAND COPPER COMPANY INC

COMPAGNIE DE DYNAMIQUE AVANCEE LTEE, LA p 1295

1700 RUE MARIE-VICTORIN, SAINT-BRUNO, QC, J3V 6B9

(450) 653-7220   SIC 3535

COMPAGNIE DE GESTION ALCOA-LAURALCO p 1090

1 BOUL DES SOURCES, DESCHAM-BAULT, QC, G0A 1S0

(418) 286-5287   SIC 3354

COMPAGNIE DE LOCATION D'EQUIPEMENT CLE p 1386

See CLE CAPITAL INC

COMPAGNIE DE PAPIERS WHITE BIRCH CANADA p 1257

10 BOUL DES CAPUCINS, QUEBEC, QC, G1J 0G9

(418) 525-2500   SIC 2621

COMPAGNIE DE POISSONS DE MON-TREAL LTEE, LA p 1216

1647 RUE SAINT-PATRICK, MONTREAL, QC, H3K 3G9

(514) 486-9537   SIC 5146

COMPAGNIE DE PRODUITS FAVORITE, LA p 1237

See OIL-DRI CANADA ULC

COMPAGNIE DE RECYCLAGE DE PA-PIERS MD INC, LA p 1076

235 BOUL INDUSTRIEL, CHATEAUGUAY, QC, J6J 4Z2

(450) 699-3425   SIC 4953

COMPAGNIE DE TELEPHONE BELL DU CANADA OU BELL CANADA, LA p 88

10104 103 AVE NW SUITE 2800, EDMON-TON, AB, T5J 0H8

(780) 409-6800   SIC 4899

COMPAGNIE DE TELEPHONE BELL DU CANADA OU BELL CANADA, LA p 286

2980 VIRTUAL WAY, VANCOUVER, BC, V5M 4X3

SIC 5963

COMPAGNIE DE TELEPHONE BELL DU CANADA OU BELL CANADA, LA p 312

1066 HASTINGS ST W SUITE 1500, VAN-COUVER, BC, V6E 3X2

(604) 484-1010   SIC 4899

COMPAGNIE DE TELEPHONE BELL DU CANADA OU BELL CANADA, LA p 721

7111 SYNTEX DR, MISSISSAUGA, ON, L5N 8C3

SIC 4899

COMPAGNIE DE TELEPHONE BELL DU CANADA OU BELL CANADA, LA p 851

9133 LESLIE ST, RICHMOND HILL, ON, L4B 4N1

(905) 762-9137   SIC 7379

COMPAGNIE DE TELEPHONE BELL DU CANADA OU BELL CANADA, LA p 969

100 WELLINGTON ST W, TORONTO, ON, M5K 1J3

(416) 365-7200   SIC 4813

COMPAGNIE DE TELEPHONE BELL DU CANADA OU BELL CANADA, LA p 979

21 CANNIFF ST, TORONTO, ON, M5V 3G1

(647) 393-3039   SIC 4813

COMPAGNIE DE TELEPHONE BELL DU CANADA OU BELL CANADA, LA p 1272

2715 BOUL DU VERSANT-NORD, QUE-BEC, QC, G1V 1A3

(418) 691-1080   SIC 4899

COMPAGNIE DE TELEPHONE BELL DU CANADA OU BELL CANADA, LA p 1396

1 CARREF ALEXANDER-GRAHAM-BELL, VERDUN, QC, H3E 3B3

SIC 4899

COMPAGNIE DE TELEPHONE BELL DU CANADA OU BELL CANADA, LA p 1396

1 CARREF ALEXANDER-GRAHAM-BELL TOWER A-7-1, VERDUN, QC, H3E 3B3

(514) 786-8424   SIC 4899

COMPAGNIE DE VETEMENTS C-IN2 INC p 1338

8750 CH DE LA COTE-DE-LIESSE BU-REAU 100, SAINT-LAURENT, QC, H4T 1H2

(514) 344-9660   SIC 5136

COMPAGNIE DE VILLEGIATURE ET DE DEVELOPEMENT GRAND LODGE INC, LA p 1159

2396 RUE LABELLE, MONT-TREMBLANT, QC, J8E 1T8

(819) 425-2734   SIC 7011

COMPAGNIE DE VILLEGIATURE LGL 1159

See LGL RESORTS COMPANY

COMPAGNIE DE VOLAILLES MAXI, LA p 1347

See MAXI CANADA INC

COMPAGNIE DES CHEMINS DE FER NA-TIONAUX DU CANADA p 84

10229 127 AVE NW, EDMONTON, AB, T5E 0B9

(780) 472-3452   SIC 4011

COMPAGNIE DES CHEMINS DE FER NA-TIONAUX DU CANADA p 84

11703 127 AVE NW, EDMONTON, AB, T5E 0C9

(780) 472-3486   SIC 4011

COMPAGNIE DES CHEMINS DE FER NA-TIONAUX DU CANADA p 93

12103 127 AVE NW, EDMONTON, AB, T5L 4X7

(780) 472-3261   SIC 4011

COMPAGNIE DES CHEMINS DE FER NA-TIONAUX DU CANADA p 93

12646 124 ST NW, EDMONTON, AB, T5L 0N9

(780) 472-3078   SIC 4111

COMPAGNIE DES CHEMINS DE FER NA-TIONAUX DU CANADA p 218

309 CN RD, KAMLOOPS, BC, V2H 1K3

(250) 828-6331   SIC 4111

COMPAGNIE DES CHEMINS DE FER NA-TIONAUX DU CANADA p 250

1108 INDUSTRIAL WAY, PRINCE GEORGE, BC, V2N 5S1

(250) 561-4190   SIC 4111

COMPAGNIE DES CHEMINS DE FER NA-TIONAUX DU CANADA p 270

13477 116 AVE, SURREY, BC, V3R 6W4

(604) 589-6552   SIC 4111

COMPAGNIE DES CHEMINS DE FER NA-TIONAUX DU CANADA p 362

150 PANDORA AVE W, WINNIPEG, MB, R2C 4H5

(204) 235-2626   SIC 4789

COMPAGNIE DES CHEMINS DE FER NA-TIONAUX DU CANADA p 398

194 RUE ST-FRANCOIS, EDMUNDSTON, NB, E3V 1E9

(506) 735-1201   SIC 4011

COMPAGNIE DES CHEMINS DE FER NA-TIONAUX DU CANADA p 408

255 HUMP YARD RD, MONCTON, NB, E1E 4S3

(506) 853-2866   SIC 4231

COMPAGNIE DES CHEMINS DE FER NA-TIONAUX DU CANADA p 491

257 AIRPORT PKY, BELLEVILLE, ON, K8N 4Z6

(613) 969-2247   SIC 4011

COMPAGNIE DES CHEMINS DE FER NA-TIONAUX DU CANADA p 550

73 DIESEL DR UNIT 1B, CONCORD, ON, L4K 1B9

SIC 4011

COMPAGNIE DES CHEMINS DE FER NA-TIONAUX DU CANADA p 551

GD, CONCORD, ON, L4K 1B9

(905) 669-3302   SIC 4011

COMPAGNIE DES CHEMINS DE FER NA-TIONAUX DU CANADA p 551

GD, CONCORD, ON, L4K 1B9

(905) 669-3009   SIC 4789

COMPAGNIE DES CHEMINS DE FER NA-TIONAUX DU CANADA p 574

123 JUDSON ST, ETOBICOKE, ON, M8Z 1A4

(416) 253-6395   SIC 4011

COMPAGNIE DES CHEMINS DE FER NA-TIONAUX DU CANADA p 650

363 EGERTON ST, LONDON, ON, N5W 6B1

SIC 7699

COMPAGNIE DES CHEMINS DE FER NA-TIONAUX DU CANADA p 859

699 MACGREGOR RD, SARNIA, ON, N7T 7H8

(519) 339-1253   SIC 4011

COMPAGNIE DES CHEMINS DE FER NA-TIONAUX DU CANADA p 911

1825 BROADWAY AVE, THUNDER BAY, ON, P7K 1M8

SIC 4011

COMPAGNIE DES CHEMINS DE FER NA-TIONAUX DU CANADA p 979

277 FRONT ST W, TORONTO, ON, M5V 2X4

(888) 888-5909   SIC 4111

COMPAGNIE DES CHEMINS DE FER NA-TIONAUX DU CANADA p

1002
1 ADMINISTRATION RD, VAUGHAN, ON,
L4K 1B9
(905) 669-3128   *SIC* 4011
**COMPAGNIE DES CHEMINS DE FER NA-
TIONAUX DU CANADA**   *p*
1139
2600 AV DE LA ROTONDE, LEVIS, QC,
G6X 2M1
SIC 4011
**COMPAGNIE DES CHEMINS DE FER NA-
TIONAUX DU CANADA**   *p*
1203
935 RUE DE LA GAUCHETIERE 16E
ETAGE O, MONTREAL, QC, H3B 2M9
(514) 399-5430   *SIC* 4011
**COMPAGNIE DES CHEMINS DE FER NA-
TIONAUX DU CANADA**   *p*
1203
5 PLACE VILLE-MARIE BUREAU 1100,
MONTREAL, QC, H3B 2G2
(514) 399-4811   *SIC* 4011
**COMPAGNIE DES CHEMINS DE FER NA-
TIONAUX DU CANADA**   *p*
1338
4500 RUE HICKMORE, SAINT-LAURENT,
QC, H4T 1K2
(514) 734-2288   *SIC* 4013
**COMPAGNIE DES CHEMINS DE FER NA-
TIONAUX DU CANADA**   *p*
1366
171 4E RUE O, SENNETERRE, QC, J0Y
2M0
(819) 737-8121   *SIC* 4111
**COMPAGNIE DES CHEMINS DE FER NA-
TIONAUX DU CANADA**   *p*
1410
GD, MELVILLE, SK, S0A 2P0
SIC 4111
COMPAGNIE DIVERSIFIEE DE L'EST LTEE
p 1249
131 BOUL HYMUS, POINTE-CLAIRE, QC,
H9R 1E7
(514) 694-5353   *SIC* 3497
**COMPAGNIE DIVERSIFIEE EDELSTEIN
LTEE, LA**   *p* 1241
9001 CH AVON BUREAU 100, MONTREAL-
OUEST, QC, H4X 2G8
(514) 489-8689   *SIC* 5113
COMPAGNIE DU BOIS FRANC DZD INC, LA
p 1319
450 BOUL ROLAND-GODARD, SAINT-
JEROME, QC, J7Y 4G8
(450) 431-1643   *SIC* 5031
**COMPAGNIE EAGLE LUMBER LIMITEE,
LA**   *p* 1321
435 BOUL JEAN-BAPTISTE-ROLLAND E,
SAINT-JEROME, QC, J7Z 4J4
(450) 432-4004   *SIC* 5211
COMPAGNIE FILTERFAB   *p* 883
See FILTERFAB COMPANY
COMPAGNIE FRANCE FILM INC   *p* 1175
505 RUE SHERBROOKE E BUREAU 2401,
MONTREAL, QC, H2L 4N3
(514) 844-0680   *SIC* 6512
COMPAGNIE GE AVIATION CANADA, LA *p*
1068
2 BOUL DE L'AEROPORT, BROMONT, QC,
J2L 1S6
(450) 534-0917   *SIC* 8711
COMPAGNIE GESTIMET INC, LA   *p* 1384
3175 BOUL THIBEAU, TROIS-RIVIERES,
QC, G8T 1G4
(819) 371-8456   *SIC* 6712
COMPAGNIE HOWMET CANADA   *p* 1234
See HOWMET CANADA COMPANY
**COMPAGNIE IMMOBILIERE GUEYMARD &
ASSOCIES LTEE**   *p* 1299
251   CH FUSEY, SAINT-DONAT-DE-
MONTCALM, QC, J0T 2C0
(819) 424-1373   *SIC* 6719
**COMPAGNIE INTERNATIONALE DE PRO-
DUITS ALIMENTAIRES ET COMMERCE DE
DETAIL INC**   *p* 1185

1615 RUE SAINT-DENIS, MONTREAL, QC,
H2X 3K3
(514) 287-3555   *SIC* 5149
COMPAGNIE KATOEN NATIE CANADA   *p*
100
18210 109 AVE NW, EDMONTON, AB, T5S
2K2
(780) 489-9040   *SIC* 4225
**COMPAGNIE MARITIME MEDITERRA-
NEENNE (CANADA)**   *p*
1189
*See MEDITERRANEAN SHIPPING COM-
PANY (CANADA) INC*
COMPAGNIE MEXX CANADA   *p* 1325
905 RUE HODGE, SAINT-LAURENT, QC,
H4N 2B3
(514) 383-5555   *SIC* 5137
COMPAGNIE MINIERE IOC INC   *p* 425
2 AVALON DR, LABRADOR CITY, NL, A2V
2Y6
(709) 944-8400   *SIC* 1011
COMPAGNIE MINIERE IOC INC   *p* 1203
1190   AV   DES   CANADIENS-DE-
MONTREAL BUREAU 400, MONTREAL,
QC, H3B 0E3
(418) 968-7400   *SIC* 1011
COMPAGNIE MINIERE IOC INC   *p* 1367
1 RUE RETTY, SEPT-ILES, QC, G4R 3C7
(418) 968-7400   *SIC* 1011
COMPAGNIE MOTOPARTS INC   *p* 1246
1124   RUE   SAINT-CALIXTE,
PLESSISVILLE, QC, G6L 1N8
(819) 362-7373   *SIC* 5085
COMPAGNIE NALCO CANADA   *p* 530
See NALCO CANADA CO.
COMPAGNIE NORMAND LTEE, LA *p* 1349
340 RUE TACHE, SAINT-PASCAL, QC, G0L
3Y0
(418) 492-2712   *SIC* 3524
COMPAGNIE OTTO JANGL LTEE   *p* 1376
294 RANG SAINT-PAUL, SHERRINGTON,
QC, J0L 2N0
(450) 247-2758   *SIC* 5091
COMPAGNIE REGITAN LTEE, LA   *p* 1093
1420 RTE TRANSCANADIENNE, DORVAL,
QC, H9P 1H7
(514) 685-8282   *SIC* 5194
COMPAGNIE TOP TUBES   *p* 1060
870 BOUL INDUSTRIEL, BOIS-DES-
FILION, QC, J6Z 4V7
(450) 621-9600   *SIC* 3999
COMPAGNIE U.S. COTON (CANADA), LA *p*
1127
2100 52E AV BUREAU 100, LACHINE, QC,
H8T 2Y5
SIC 3842
COMPAGNIE U.S. SAMPLE   *p* 1161
*See COMPAGNIE D'ECHANTILLONS NA-
TIONAL LIMITEE*
**COMPAGNIE WW HOTELS (POINTE-
CLAIRE)**   *p*
1249
6700 RTE TRANSCANADIENNE, POINTE-
CLAIRE, QC, H9R 1C2
(514) 697-7110   *SIC* 7011
COMPAIR CANADA INC   *p* 803
2390 SOUTH SERVICE RD W, OAKVILLE,
ON, L6L 5M9
(905) 847-0688   *SIC* 5084
**COMPANY'S COMING PUBLISHING LIM-
ITED**   *p*
120
2311 96 ST NW, EDMONTON, AB, T6N 1G3
(780) 450-6223   *SIC* 2731
COMPAQ   *p* 624
*See ESIT CANADA ENTERPRISE SER-
VICES CO*
COMPASS   *p* 159
See COMPASS ENERGY SYSTEMS LTD
**COMPASS CONSTRUCTION RESOURCES
LTD**   *p* 988
2700 DUFFERIN ST UNIT 77, TORONTO,
ON, M6B 4J3
(416) 789-9819   *SIC* 1542

COMPASS ENERGY SYSTEMS LTD   *p* 159
285028 FRONTIER RD, ROCKY VIEW
COUNTY, AB, T1X 0V9
(403) 262-2487   *SIC* 3491
COMPASS FINANCIAL   *p* 377
428 PORTAGE AVE SUITE 204, WIN-
NIPEG, MB, R3C 0E2
(204) 940-3950   *SIC* 6722
**COMPASS FOOD SALES COMPANY LIM-
ITED**   *p*
480
260 INDUSTRIAL PKY N, AURORA, ON,
L4G 4C3
(905) 713-0167   *SIC* 5141
COMPASS GROUP CANADA LTD   *p* 238
1640 ELECTRA BLVD SUITE 123, NORTH
SAANICH, BC, V8L 5V4
(250) 655-3718   *SIC* 5812
COMPASS GROUP CANADA LTD   *p* 445
10 MORRIS DR SUITE 35, DARTMOUTH,
NS, B3B 1K8
(902) 466-0150   *SIC* 5963
COMPASS GROUP CANADA LTD   *p* 452
1800 ARGYLE ST SUITE 401, HALIFAX,
NS, B3J 3N8
SIC 5812
COMPASS GROUP CANADA LTD   *p* 542
285 MCNAUGHTON AVE E, CHATHAM,
ON, N7L 2G7
(519) 358-7111   *SIC* 5812
COMPASS GROUP CANADA LTD   *p* 744
1 PROLOGIS BLVD SUITE 400, MISSIS-
SAUGA, ON, L5W 0G2
(905) 795-5100   *SIC* 5812
COMPASS GROUP CANADA LTD   *p* 1426
35 22ND ST E, SASKATOON, SK, S7K 0C8
(306) 975-7790   *SIC* 5812
COMPASS MINERAL   *p* 597
*See COMPASS MINERALS CANADA
CORP*
COMPASS MINERALS CANADA CORP   *p*
597
245 REGENT ST, GODERICH, ON, N7A
3Y5
(519) 524-8351   *SIC* 2899
COMPASS MINERALS CANADA CORP   *p*
597
300 NORTH HARBOUR RD W, GODERICH,
ON, N7A 3Y9
(519) 524-8351   *SIC* 1481
COMPASS MINERALS CANADA CORP   *p*
721
6700 CENTURY AVE SUITE 202, MISSIS-
SAUGA, ON, L5N 6A4
(905) 567-0231   *SIC* 1479
COMPASSION HOME CARE INC   *p* 421
GD, BAY ROBERTS, NL, A0A 1G0
(709) 786-8677   *SIC* 8322
COMPASSION HOME HEALTH SERVICES *p*
421
See COMPASSION HOME CARE INC
**COMPASSIONATE RESOURCE WARE-
HOUSE**   *p*
339
831 DEVONSHIRE RD SUITE 2, VICTORIA,
BC, V9A 4T5
(250) 381-4483   *SIC* 8699
COMPES INTERNATIONAL LIMITED *p* 502
25 DEVON RD, BRAMPTON, ON, L6T 5B6
(905) 458-5994   *SIC* 3544
COMPETITION CHEVROLET LTD   *p* 167
40 BOULDER BLVD, STONY PLAIN, AB,
T7Z 1V7
(780) 963-6121   *SIC* 5511
COMPETITION COMPOSITES INC   *p* 479
251 FIFTH AVE, ARNPRIOR, ON, K7S 3M3
(613) 599-6951   *SIC* 2655
COMPETITION TOYOTA LTD   *p* 651
1515 ROB PANZER RD, LONDON, ON, N5X
0M7
(519) 451-3880   *SIC* 5511
COMPLETE AVIATION SERVICES LTD *p*
840
SS 5 STN DELIVERY CENTRE, PETER-

BOROUGH, ON, K9J 6X6
(705) 745-8626   *SIC* 5172
COMPLETE CARE INC   *p* 370
1801 MAIN ST, WINNIPEG, MB, R2V 2A2
(204) 949-5090   *SIC* 8051
**COMPLETE COMMUNICATION SYSTEMS
INC**   *p* 893
905 QUEENSTON RD, STONEY CREEK,
ON, L8G 1B6
(905) 664-1158   *SIC* 5999
COMPLETE INNOVATIONS HOLDINGS INC
p 961
88 QUEENS QUAY W SUITE 200,
TORONTO, ON, M5J 0B8
(905) 944-0863   *SIC* 7371
COMPLETE SPRING & TRAILER SERVICE
p 486
See B & I TRUCK PARTS INC
COMPLEX SUPPLY INC   *p* 757
PO BOX 300 STN MAIN, NIAGARA FALLS,
ON, L2E 6T3
(905) 374-6928   *SIC* 7999
COMPLEXE AUTO 440 DE LAVAL INC   *p*
1086
3670 SUD LAVAL (A-440) O, COTE SAINT-
LUC, QC, H7T 2H6
(450) 682-3670   *SIC* 5511
**COMPLEXE DE L'AUTO PARK AVENUE
INC**   *p* 1345
4505 BOUL METROPOLITAIN E BUREAU
201, SAINT-LEONARD, QC, H1R 1Z4
(514) 899-9000   *SIC* 5511
COMPLEXE OASIS ST-JEAN   *p* 1316
See 2550-7856 QUEBEC INC
COMPLEXE SOUTHWEST ONE   *p* 774
*See DORCHESTER OAKS CORPORA-
TION*
COMPLYWORKS LTD   *p* 73
4838 RICHARD RD SW SUITE 600, CAL-
GARY, AB, T3E 6L1
(403) 219-4792   *SIC* 8742
COMPO RECYCLE   *p* 1077
See SERVICES SANITAIRES MAJ INC
COMPOSANTES LIPPERT   *p* 1111
See GROUPE LCI CANADA, INC
COMPOSANTES THERMOVISION   *p* 1318
See PRODUITS THERMOVISION INC
COMPOSITES VCI INC   *p* 1347
830 12E AV BUREAU 915, SAINT-LIN-
LAURENTIDES, QC, J5M 2V9
(450) 302-4646   *SIC* 3699
COMPOUNDS FELIX INC, LES   *p* 1308
3455 RUE RICHELIEU, SAINT-HUBERT,
QC, J3Y 7P9
(450) 443-6888   *SIC* 2672
**COMPREHENSIVE CARE INTERNA-
TIONAL INC**   *p*
991
173 DUFFERIN ST SUITE 200, TORONTO,
ON, M6K 3H7
(416) 531-5950   *SIC* 8742
COMPRESSCO CANADA INC   *p* 15
5050 76 AVE SE, CALGARY, AB, T2C 2X2
(403) 279-5866   *SIC* 5084
COMPRESSEURS QUEBEC   *p* 1327
See 10079952 CANADA INC
COMPRESSEURS QUEBEC A K ENR   *p*
1328
2431 RUE GUENETTE, SAINT-LAURENT,
QC, H4R 2E9
(514) 337-0566   *SIC* 5084
COMPRESSION TECHNOLOGY INC *p* 213
10911 89 AVE, FORT ST. JOHN, BC, V1J
6V2
(250) 787-8655   *SIC* 3563
COMPRESSOR ESSENTIALS DIV.   *p* 803
See COMPAIR CANADA INC
**COMPRESSOR PRODUCTS INTERNA-
TIONAL CANADA INC**   *p*
113
6308 DAVIES RD NW, EDMONTON, AB,
T6E 4M9
(780) 468-5145   *SIC* 7699
COMPROD INC   *p* 1064

---

88 BOUL INDUSTRIEL, BOUCHERVILLE, QC, J4B 2X2
(450) 641-1454 *SIC 4899*

COMPTANT.COM *p 1172*
See GROUPE COMPTANT QUEBEC INC

COMPTEC S. G. INC *p 1381*
1115 RUE ARMAND-BOMBARDIER, TERREBONNE, QC, J6Y 1S9
(450) 965-8166 *SIC 7389*

COMPTOIR AGRICOLE DE ST-HYACINTHE *p 1313*
4420 RUE SAINT-PIERRE O, SAINT-HYACINTHE, QC, J2T 5G8
SIC 5083

COMPTOIR D'ENTRAIDE DE LACHUTE *p 1058*
See CENTRAIDE LAURENTIDES

COMPTOIRS MOULES RIVE-NORD INC, LES *p 1254*
414 BOUL RAYMOND, QUEBEC, QC, G1C 0L6
(418) 667-8814 *SIC 5039*

COMPTON, CLARKE FINANCIAL INC *p 172*
5402 56 ST, WETASKIWIN, AB, T9A 2B3
(780) 352-3311 *SIC 5511*

COMPUCOM CANADA CO. *p 693*
1830 MATHESON BLVD UNIT 1, MISSISSAUGA, ON, L4W 0B3
(289) 261-3000 *SIC 5045*

COMPUCOM SYSTEMS *p 693*
See COMPUCOM CANADA CO.

COMPUGEN INC *p 856*
100 VIA RENZO DR, RICHMOND HILL, ON, L4S 0B8
(905) 707-2000 *SIC 7373*

COMPUGEN SYSTEMS LTD *p 10*
1440 28 ST NE SUITE 3, CALGARY, AB, T2A 7W6
(403) 571-4400 *SIC 7373*

COMPUGEN SYSTEMS LTD *p 856*
100 VIA RENZO DR, RICHMOND HILL, ON, L4S 0B8
(905) 707-2000 *SIC 6712*

COMPUMEDIA DESIGN *p 1070*
See ENSEIGNES CMD INC

COMPUSTAT CONSULTANTS INC *p 808*
67 FIRST ST, ORANGEVILLE, ON, L9W 2E6
(519) 938-9552 *SIC 8732*

COMPUSULT *p 426*
See COMPUSULT LIMITED

COMPUSULT LIMITED *p 426*
40 BANNISTER ST, MOUNT PEARL, NL, A1N 1W1
(709) 745-7914 *SIC 7371*

COMPUTER BOULEVARD INC *p 383*
1250 ST JAMES ST UNIT B, WINNIPEG, MB, R3H 0L1
(204) 775-3202 *SIC 5045*

COMPUTER DATA SOURCE CANADA CORP *p 668*
3780 14TH AVE UNIT 106, MARKHAM, ON, L3R 9Y5
(905) 474-2100 *SIC 5734*

COMPUTER ENHANCEMENT CORPORATION *p 693*
5112 TIMBERLEA BLVD SUITE 2, MISSISSAUGA, ON, L4W 2S5
(905) 625-9100 *SIC 5045*

COMPUTER MEDIA GROUP, THE *p 817*
See COMPUTER MEDIA PRODUCTS LTD

COMPUTER MEDIA PRODUCTS LTD *p 817*
250 TREMBLAY RD SUITE 520, OTTAWA, ON, K1G 3J8
(613) 226-7071 *SIC 5045*

COMPUTER METHODS INTERNATIONAL CORP *p 782*
4850 KEELE ST, NORTH YORK, ON, M3J 3K1
(416) 736-0123 *SIC 7371*

COMPUTER MODELLING GROUP LTD *p 40*
3710 33 ST NW, CALGARY, AB, T2L 2M1
(403) 531-1300 *SIC 7371*

COMPUTER PARTS 2000 *p 551*
See COMSALE COMPUTER INC

COMPUTER RESEARCH INSTITUTE OF MONTREAL *p 1217*
See CENTRE DE RECHERCHE INFORMATIQUE DE MONTREAL INC

COMPUTER ROOM SERVICES CORPORATION *p 475*
75 CHAMBERS DR UNIT 6, AJAX, ON, L1Z 1E1
(905) 686-4000 *SIC 1731*

COMPUTER SCIENCES CANADA INC *p 624*
555 LEGGET DR, KANATA, ON, K2K 2X3
(613) 591-1810 *SIC 7373*

COMPUTER SCIENCES CANADA INC *p 1213*
1360 BOUL RENE-LEVESQUE O BUREAU 300, MONTREAL, QC, H3G 2W7
SIC 7379

COMPUTER TALK TECHNOLOGY INC *p 904*
150 COMMERCE VALLEY DR W UNIT 800, THORNHILL, ON, L3T 7Z3
(905) 882-5000 *SIC 7371*

COMPUTER TRENDS CANADA *p 34*
5738 BURBANK CRES SE, CALGARY, AB, T2H 1Z6
SIC 5311

COMPUTER UPGRADING SPECIALISTS LTD *p 77*
232 MAHOGANY TERR SE, CALGARY, AB, T3M 0T5
(403) 271-3800 *SIC 7373*

COMPUTERSHARE *p 1194*
See COMPUTERSHARE TRUST COMPANY OF CANADA

COMPUTERSHARE CANADA INC *p 961*
100 UNIVERSITY AVE SUITE 800, TORONTO, ON, M5J 2Y1
(416) 263-9200 *SIC 6712*

COMPUTERSHARE TRUST COMPANY OF CANADA *p 961*
100 UNIVERSITY AVE SUITE 800, TORONTO, ON, M5J 2Y1
(416) 263-9200 *SIC 6733*

COMPUTERSHARE TRUST COMPANY OF CANADA *p 1194*
1500 BOUL ROBERT-BOURASSA BUREAU 700, MONTREAL, QC, H3A 3S8
(514) 982-7888 *SIC 6733*

COMPUTRONIX CORPORATION *p 97*
10216 124 ST NW SUITE 200, EDMONTON, AB, T5N 4A3
(780) 454-3700 *SIC 7371*

COMPUVISION SYSTEMS INC *p 105*
15511 123 AVE NW SUITE 101, EDMONTON, AB, T5V 0C3
(587) 525-7600 *SIC 7379*

COMSALE COMPUTER INC *p 551*
111 SNIDERCROFT RD, CONCORD, ON, L4K 2J8
(905) 761-6466 *SIC 5045*

COMSALE COMPUTER INC *p 664*
158 WALLENBERG DR, MAPLE, ON, L6A 4M2
(647) 648-2323 *SIC 5045*

COMSATEC INC *p 532*
61 HIGH ST N, CALLANDER, ON, P0H 1H0
(705) 752-4342 *SIC 4924*

COMSTOCK CANADA LTD *p 652*
1200 TRAFALGAR ST, LONDON, ON, N5Z 1H5
SIC 1711

COMTECH MANUFACTURING *p 603*
See LINAMAR CORPORATION

COMTEK ADVANCED STRUCTURES LTD *p 521*
1360 ARTISANS CRT, BURLINGTON, ON, L7L 5Y2
(905) 331-8121 *SIC 5088*

COMTRONIC COMPUTER INC *p 851*
30 KINNEAR CRT UNIT 1, RICHMOND HILL, ON, L4B 1K8
(905) 881-3606 *SIC 5045*

COMWAVE *p 781*
See COMWAVE TELECOM INC

COMWAVE NETWORKS INC *p 782*
61 WILDCAT RD, NORTH YORK, ON, M3J 2P5
(866) 288-5779 *SIC 4899*

COMWAVE TELECOM INC *p 781*
4884 DUFFERIN ST UNIT 1, NORTH YORK, ON, M3H 5S8
(416) 663-9700 *SIC 8732*

CON-CAST PIPE INC *p 849*
299 BROCK RD S, PUSLINCH, ON, N0B 2J0
(519) 763-8655 *SIC 3272*

CON-DRAIN COMPANY (1983) LIMITED *p 551*
30 FLORAL PKY SUITE 100, CONCORD, ON, L4K 4R1
(905) 669-5400 *SIC 1623*

CON-DRAIN COMPANY LIMITED *p 551*
30 FLORAL PKY SUITE 100, CONCORD, ON, L4K 4R1
(416) 798-7153 *SIC 1623*

CON-ELCO LTD *p 551*
200 BRADWICK DR, CONCORD, ON, L4K 1K8
(905) 669-4942 *SIC 1623*

CON-PRO INDUSTRIES CANADA LTD *p 365*
765 MARION ST, WINNIPEG, MB, R2J 0K6
(204) 233-3717 *SIC 1542*

CON-STRADA CONSTRUCTION INC *p 551*
30 FLORAL PKY, CONCORD, ON, L4K 4R1
(905) 660-6000 *SIC 1611*

CON-TACT MASONRY LTD *p 807*
2504 BINDER CRES SUITE 1, OLDCASTLE, ON, N0R 1L0
(519) 737-1852 *SIC 1741*

CON-WALL CNCRETE INC *p 657*
525 EXETER RD, LONDON, ON, N6E 2Z3
(519) 681-6910 *SIC 1771*

CON-WEST CONTRACTING LTD *p 284*
1311 KOOTENAY ST SUITE 250, VANCOUVER, BC, V5K 4Y3
(604) 294-5067 *SIC 1629*

CONA RESOURCES LTD *p 47*
421 7 AVE SW SUITE 1900, CALGARY, AB, T2P 4K9
(403) 930-3000 *SIC 2911*

CONAGRA FOODS CANADA INC *p 565*
759 WELLINGTON ST, DRESDEN, ON, N0P 1M0
(519) 683-4422 *SIC 2032*

CONAGRA FOODS CANADA INC *p 693*
5055 SATELLITE DR UNIT 1-2, MISSISSAUGA, ON, L4W 5K7
(416) 679-4200 *SIC 2032*

CONAGRA LAMB WESTON *p 169*
See LAMB WESTON CANADA ULC

CONAIR CONSUMER PRODUCTS ULC *p 1027*
100 CONAIR PKY, WOODBRIDGE, ON, L4H 0L2
(905) 851-5162 *SIC 5064*

CONAIR GROUP INC *p 176*
1510 TOWER ST, ABBOTSFORD, BC, V2T 6H5
(604) 855-1171 *SIC 0851*

CONALJAN INC *p 1174*
4045 RUE PARTHENAIS, MONTREAL, QC, H2K 3T8
(514) 522-2121 *SIC 6719*

CONBORA FORMING INC *p 551*
109 EDILCAN DR, CONCORD, ON, L4K 3S6
(905) 738-7979 *SIC 1771*

CONCASSAGE T.C.G. INC *p 1078*
111 RUE DES ROUTIERS, CHICOUTIMI, QC, G7H 5B1
(418) 698-4949 *SIC 1422*

CONCASSES DE LA RIVE-SUD INC *p 1135*
333 CH DES SABLES, LEVIS, QC, G6C 1B5

(418) 838-7444 *SIC 1429*

CONCENTRA BANK *p 1426*
333 3RD AVE N, SASKATOON, SK, S7K 2M2
(306) 956-5100 *SIC 6021*

CONCENTRIX *p 812*
See CONCENTRIX TECHNOLOGIES SERVICES (CANADA) LIMITED

CONCENTRIX TECHNOLOGIES SERVICES (CANADA) LIMITED *p 411*
720 COVERDALE RD, RIVERVIEW, NB, E1B 3L8
(506) 860-5900 *SIC 4899*

CONCENTRIX TECHNOLOGIES SERVICES (CANADA) LIMITED *p 443*
375 PLEASANT ST SUITE 103, DARTMOUTH, NS, B2Y 4N4
(902) 428-9999 *SIC 4899*

CONCENTRIX TECHNOLOGIES SERVICES (CANADA) LIMITED *p 687*
6725 AIRPORT RD 6TH FL, MISSISSAUGA, ON, L4V 1V2
(416) 380-3800 *SIC 8721*

CONCENTRIX TECHNOLOGIES SERVICES (CANADA) LIMITED *p 812*
1189 COLONEL SAM DR, OSHAWA, ON, L1H 8W8
(416) 380-3800 *SIC 4899*

CONCEPT 2000 REAL ESTATE (1989) INCORPORATED *p 270*
15127 100 AVE SUITE 103, SURREY, BC, V3R 0N9
(604) 583-2000 *SIC 6531*

CONCEPT ALIMENTAIRE L'EPICIER *p 1161*
See ALIMENTATION L'EPICIER INC

CONCEPT ECO-PLEIN AIR LE BALUCHON INC *p 1350*
3550 CH DES TREMBLES RR 3, SAINT-PAULIN, QC, J0K 3G0
(819) 268-2695 *SIC 5812*

CONCEPT ELECTRIC LTD *p 29*
1260 HIGHFIELD CRES SE, CALGARY, AB, T2G 5M3
(403) 287-8777 *SIC 1731*

CONCEPT GOURMET DU VILLAGE *p 1242*
See CONCEPT GOURMET DU VILLAGE ULC

CONCEPT GOURMET DU VILLAGE ULC *p 1242*
539 CH DU VILLAGE, MORIN-HEIGHTS, QC, J0R 1H0
(800) 668-2314 *SIC 5149*

CONCEPT GROUP *p 29*
See CONCEPT ELECTRIC LTD

CONCEPT JP INC *p 1101*
2089 RUE MICHELIN, FABREVILLE, QC, H7L 5B7
(800) 795-2595 *SIC 5087*

CONCEPT MASCOUCHE INC *p 1149*
161 MONTEE MASSON BUREAU 44, MASCOUCHE, QC, J7K 3B4
(450) 474-3315 *SIC 5651*

CONCEPT MAT INC *p 1150*
41 RUE BRILLANT, MATANE, QC, G4W 0J7
(418) 562-6680 *SIC 5031*

CONCEPT MODE STE-FOY INC *p 1274*
999 AV DE BOURGOGNE BUREAU A1, QUEBEC, QC, G1W 4S6
(418) 653-3214 *SIC 5621*

CONCEPT PLASTICS LIMITED *p 517*
27 CATHARINE AVE, BRANTFORD, ON, N3T 1X5
(519) 759-1900 *SIC 3089*

CONCEPT S21 *p 1212*
See TINK PROFITABILITE NUMERIQUE INC

CONCEPT SAINT-BRUNO INC *p 1112*
3844 BOUL TASCHEREAU, GREENFIELD PARK, QC, J4V 2H9
(450) 466-0422 *SIC 5137*

CONCEPTION GENIK INC *p 1321*
715 RUE NOBEL BUREAU 108, SAINT-JEROME, QC, J7Z 7A3

(450) 436-7706　　*SIC 5084*
CONCEPTION HABITAT 2015 INC　*p 1086*
2400 BOUL DANIEL-JOHNSON, COTE SAINT-LUC, QC, H7T 3A4
(450) 902-2007　　*SIC 1522*
CONCEPTROMEC 2001　　　　*p 1147*
See CONCEPTROMEC INC
CONCEPTROMEC EXPORTATION INC　*p 1147*
1780 BOUL INDUSTRIEL, MAGOG, QC, J1X 4V9
(819) 847-3627　　*SIC 8711*
CONCEPTROMEC INC　　　　*p 1147*
1782 BOUL INDUSTRIEL, MAGOG, QC, J1X 4V9
(819) 847-3627　　*SIC 3559*
CONCEPTS MANHATTAN INTERNA-TIONAL　　　　　　　　　　*p 1340*
See MANHATTAN INTERNATIONAL CON-CEPTS INC
CONCEPTS ON WHEELS INC　*p 668*
2600 JOHN ST UNIT 224, MARKHAM, ON, L3R 3W3
(905) 513-1595　　*SIC 5085*
CONCEPTS ZONE INC, LES　*p 1173*
4246 RUE SAINT-DENIS, MONTREAL, QC, H2J 2K8
(514) 845-3530　　*SIC 5719*
CONCEPTWAVE SOFTWARE INC　*p 687*
5935 AIRPORT RD SUITE 1105, MISSIS-SAUGA, ON, L4V 1W5
　　SIC 7371
CONCERT INFRASTRUCTURE LTD　*p 326*
1190 HORNBY ST, VANCOUVER, BC, V6Z 2K5
(604) 688-9460　　*SIC 6211*
CONCERT PROPERTIES LTD　*p 326*
1190 HORNBY ST, VANCOUVER, BC, V6Z 2K5
(604) 688-9460　　*SIC 6531*
CONCERT REAL ESTATE CORPORATION　*p 326*
1190 HORNBY ST, VANCOUVER, BC, V6Z 2K5
(604) 688-9460　　*SIC 6553*
CONCESSIONNAIRE DCK CANADA　*p 1179*
See RAND ACCESSORIES INC
CONCESSIONNAIRE HONDA DE　*p 1316*
400 RUE LABERGE, SAINT-JEAN-SUR-RICHELIEU, QC, J3A 1G5
(450) 347-7567　　*SIC 5511*
CONCHE SEAFOODS LTD　　*p 422*
2 HAMBOUR DR, CONCHE, NL, A0K 1Y0
(709) 622-4111　　*SIC 5146*
CONCIERGERIE SPEICO INC　*p 1130*
7651 RUE CORDNER, LASALLE, QC, H8N 2X2
(514) 364-0777　　*SIC 7349*
CONCORD ADEX DEVELOPMENTS CORP　*p 769*
1001 SHEPPARD AVE E, NORTH YORK, ON, M2K 1C2
(416) 813-0999　　*SIC 6553*
CONCORD ADEX INC　　　*p 979*
23 SPADINA AVE, TORONTO, ON, M5V 3M5
(416) 813-0333　　*SIC 1542*
CONCORD CONCRETE & DRAIN LTD　*p 551*
109 EDILCAN DR, CONCORD, ON, L4K 3S6
(416) 736-0277　　*SIC 1771*
CONCORD CONCRETE GROUP INC *p 551*
125 EDILCAN DR, CONCORD, ON, L4K 3S6
(905) 738-7979　　*SIC 4213*
CONCORD CONFECTIONS　　*p 559*
See TOOTSIE ROLL OF CANADA ULC
CONCORD COORDINATES INC　*p 871*
2220 MIDLAND AVE UNIT 21 23, SCAR-BOROUGH, ON, M1P 3E6
　　SIC 5136
CONCORD ENERGY WELL SERVICES *p 51*

See HIGH ARCTIC ENERGY SERVICES INC
CONCORD FOOD CENTRE INC　*p 906*
1438 CENTRE ST, THORNHILL, ON, L4J 3N1
(905) 886-2180　　*SIC 5411*
CONCORD IDEA CORP　　　*p 668*
3993 14TH AVE, MARKHAM, ON, L3R 4Z6
(905) 513-7686　　*SIC 4899*
CONCORD MACHINE TOOL, DIV OF *p 1017*
See CONCORDE PRECISION MACHINING INC
CONCORD METAL MANUFACTURING INC　*p 551*
121 SPINNAKER WAY, CONCORD, ON, L4K 2T2
(905) 738-2127　　*SIC 2542*
CONCORD NATIONAL　　　*p 447*
See MITCHELL AGENCIES LIMITED
CONCORD NATIONAL (PRAIRIE DIVISION) *p 23*
See GARROD FOOD BROKERS LTD
CONCORD NATIONAL PACIFIC, DIV OF *p 240*
See CONCORD SALES LTD
CONCORD PREMIUM MEATS LTD　*p 551*
125 EDILCAN DR, CONCORD, ON, L4K 3S6
(905) 738-7979　　*SIC 5147*
CONCORD PREMIUM MEATS LTD　*p 1301*
160 RUE WILLIAMS, SAINT-EUSTACHE, QC, J7R 0A4
(450) 623-7676　　*SIC 5147*
CONCORD PROJECTS LTD　　*p 363*
1277 HENDERSON HWY SUITE 200, WIN-NIPEG, MB, R2G 1M3
(204) 339-1651　　*SIC 1541*
CONCORD SALES LTD　　　*p 240*
1124 LONSDALE AVE SUITE 400, NORTH VANCOUVER, BC, V7M 2H1
(604) 986-7341　　*SIC 5141*
CONCORD SCREEN INC　　*p 755*
1311 KERRISDALE BLVD, NEWMARKET, ON, L3Y 8Z8
(905) 953-8100　　*SIC 5085*
CONCORD SECURITY CORPORATION　*p 190*
4710 KINGSWAY SUITE 925, BURNABY, BC, V5H 4M2
(604) 689-4005　　*SIC 7381*
CONCORD STEEL CENTRE LIMITED　*p 1030*
147 ASHBRIDGE CIR, WOODBRIDGE, ON, L4L 3R5
(905) 856-1717　　*SIC 5051*
CONCORD TRANSPORTATION INC　*p 583*
96 DISCO RD, ETOBICOKE, ON, M9W 0A3
(416) 679-7400　　*SIC 4213*
CONCORDE AIRPORT SERVICES　*p 22*
See CONCORDE BAGGAGE SERVICES INC
CONCORDE AUTOMOBILE (1990) LTEE *p 1312*
3003 RUE PICARD, SAINT-HYACINTHE, QC, J2S 1H2
(450) 774-5336　　*SIC 5511*
CONCORDE BAGGAGE SERVICES INC　*p 22*
2000 AIRPORT RD NE, CALGARY, AB, T2E 6W5
(403) 735-5317　　*SIC 7349*
CONCORDE FOOD SERVICES (1996) LTD *p 1424*
1171 8TH ST E, SASKATOON, SK, S7H 0S3
(306) 668-3000　　*SIC 5812*
CONCORDE PRECISION MACHINING INC　*p 1017*
469 SILVER CREEK INDUSTRIAL DR, WINDSOR, ON, N8N 4W2
(519) 727-3287　　*SIC 3544*
CONCORDIA FURNITURE LTD　*p 1048*
11001 RUE SECANT, ANJOU, QC, H1J 1S6
(514) 355-5100　　*SIC 5712*
CONCORDIA HOSPITAL　　*p 367*

1095 CONCORDIA AVE, WINNIPEG, MB, R2K 3S8
(204) 667-1560　　*SIC 8062*
CONCORDIA UNIVERSITY COLLEGE OF ALBERTA　　　　　　　　*p 83*
7128 ADA BLVD NW, EDMONTON, AB, T5B 4E4
(780) 479-8481　　*SIC 8221*
CONCORDIA UNIVERSITY OF EDMONTON *p 83*
See CONCORDIA UNIVERSITY COLLEGE OF ALBERTA
CONCOURS MOLD INC　　*p 1017*
465 JUTRAS DR S, WINDSOR, ON, N8N 5C4
(519) 727-9949　　*SIC 3544*
CONCRETE PRODUCTS LIMITED　*p 428*
260 EAST WHITE HILLS RD, ST. JOHN'S, NL, A1A 5J7
(709) 368-3171　　*SIC 3273*
CONCRETE SOLUTIONS, DIV OF　*p 411*
See WARREN READY-MIX LTD
CONDAIR HUMIDITY LTD　　*p 597*
2740 FENTON RD, GLOUCESTER, ON, K1T 3T7
(613) 822-0335　　*SIC 3585*
CONDILLO FOODS, DIV OF　　*p 3*
See OLD DUTCH FOODS LTD
CONDOMINIUM FIRST MANAGEMENT SERVICES LTD　　　　　　*p 47*
840 7 AVE SW SUITE 600, CALGARY, AB, T2P 3G2
(403) 299-1810　　*SIC 6531*
CONDOR CHIMIQUES INC　*p 1298*
2645 BOUL TERRA-JET BUREAU B, SAINT-CYRILLE-DE-WENDOVER, QC, J1Z 1B3
(819) 474-6661　　*SIC 2911*
CONDOR PETROLEUM INC　　*p 47*
2400 144 4 AVE SW, CALGARY, AB, T2P 3N4
(403) 201-9694　　*SIC 1382*
CONDOR PROPERTIES　　　*p 551*
See CONDOR PROPERTIES LTD
CONDOR PROPERTIES LTD　*p 551*
1500 HIGHWAY 7, CONCORD, ON, L4K 5Y4
(905) 907-1500　　*SIC 6531*
CONDOR SECURITY　　　*p 781*
4610 DUFFERIN ST UNIT 1B, NORTH YORK, ON, M3H 5S4
(416) 410-4035　　*SIC 7381*
CONDRAIN GROUP　　　*p 551*
See CON-DRAIN COMPANY LIMITED
CONECO EQUIPMENT　　　*p 97*
See SMS EQUIPMENT INC
CONECO EQUIPMENT　　　*p 129*
See SMS EQUIPMENT INC
CONESTOGA COLD STORAGE (QUEBEC) LIMITED　　　　　　　*p 1093*
10000 AV RYAN, DORVAL, QC, H9P 3A1
(514) 631-5040　　*SIC 4225*
CONESTOGA COLD STORAGE LIMITED *p 637*
299 TRILLIUM DR, KITCHENER, ON, N2E 1W9
(519) 748-5415　　*SIC 4222*
CONESTOGA COLLEGE COMMUNICA-TIONS CORPORATION　　　*p 638*
299 DOON VALLEY DR, KITCHENER, ON, N2G 4M4
(519) 748-5220　　*SIC 8222*
CONESTOGA COLLEGE INSTITUTE OF TECHNOLOGY AND ADVANCED LEARN-ING　　　　　　　　　*p 638*
299 DOON VALLEY DR, KITCHENER, ON, N2G 4M4
(519) 748-5220　　*SIC 8222*
CONESTOGA MEAT PACKERS LTD　*p 518*
313 MENNO ST, BRESLAU, ON, N0B 1M0
(519) 648-2506　　*SIC 5147*
CONESTOGA MEATS　　　*p 518*

See CONESTOGA MEAT PACKERS LTD
CONESTOGA PIPE & SUPPLY CANADA CORPORATION　　　　　　*p 47*
736 8 AVE SW SUITE 430, CALGARY, AB, T2P 1H4
(403) 444-5554　　*SIC 5051*
CONESTOGA PIPER AND SUPPLY CANADA CORP　　　　　　*p 6*
1010 1ST AVE E, BOW ISLAND, AB, T0K 0G0
(403) 545-2935　　*SIC 1389*
CONESTOGA STUDENTS INCORPO-RATED　　　　　　　　　*p 638*
299 DOON VALLEY DR, KITCHENER, ON, N2G 4M4
(519) 748-5131　　*SIC 8641*
CONESTOGO AGRI SYSTEMS INC　*p 476*
7506 WELLINGTON ROAD 11, ALMA, ON, N0B 1A0
(519) 638-3022　　*SIC 5083*
CONESTOGO MECHANICAL INC　*p 640*
50 DUMART PL, KITCHENER, ON, N2K 3C7
(519) 579-6740　　*SIC 1711*
CONETEC INVESTIGATIONS LTD　*p 254*
12140 VULCAN WAY, RICHMOND, BC, V6V 1J8
(604) 273-4311　　*SIC 0711*
CONEXUS CREDIT UNION　*p 1417*
See CONEXUS CREDIT UNION 2006
CONEXUS CREDIT UNION 2006　*p 1413*
2800 2ND AVE W, PRINCE ALBERT, SK, S6V 5Z4
(306) 953-6100　　*SIC 6062*
CONEXUS CREDIT UNION 2006　*p 1417*
1960 ALBERT ST SUITE 205, REGINA, SK, S4P 2T1
(800) 667-7477　　*SIC 6062*
CONFECTION 4E DIMENSION LTEE　*p 417*
11 RUE INDUSTRIELLE, SAINT-LEONARD, NB, E7E 2A9
(506) 423-7660　　*SIC 2337*
CONFECTION B L INC　　*p 397*
681 RUE PRINCIPALE, CLAIR, NB, E7A 2H3
(506) 992-3602　　*SIC 2335*
CONFECTION D. N. G.　　*p 1375*
See ADMINISTRATION BEAULIEU INC
CONFECTION PAGAR INC　*p 1109*
451 RUE EDOUARD, GRANBY, QC, J2G 3Z4
(450) 375-5398　　*SIC 7389*
CONFECTION ST METHODE INC　*p 1044*
228 RUE NOTRE-DAME N, ADSTOCK, QC, G0N 1S0
(418) 422-2206　　*SIC 2325*
CONFECTIONS STROMA INC., LES *p 1169*
3565 RUE JARRY E BUREAU 501, MON-TREAL, QC, H1Z 4K6
(514) 381-8422　　*SIC 7389*
CONFEDERATION BRIDGE　*p 1038*
See STRAIT CROSSING BRIDGE LIMITED
CONFEDERATION CENTRE BOX OFFICE *p 1039*
145 RICHMOND ST, CHARLOTTETOWN, PE, C1A 1J1
(902) 628-1864　　*SIC 6512*
CONFEDERATION CENTRE OF THE ARTS *p 1039*
See FATHERS OF CONFEDERATION BUILDINGS TRUST
CONFEDERATION COLLEGE　*p 909*
See CONFEDERATION COLLEGE OF AP-PLIED ARTS AND TECHNOLOGY, THE
CONFEDERATION COLLEGE OF APPLIED ARTS AND TECHNOLOGY, THE　*p 909*
1450 NAKINA DR, THUNDER BAY, ON, P7C 4W1
(807) 475-6110　　*SIC 8222*
CONFEDERATION DES ASSOCIATIONS D'ETUDIANTS ET D'ETUDIANTES DE L'UNIVERSITE LAVAL (CADEU　*p 1258*
PAVILLON MAURICE-POLLACK BUREAU

2265, QUEBEC, QC, G1K 7P4
(418) 656-7931   *SIC* 8641
CONFEDERATION DES SYNDICATS NA-
TIONAUX (C.S.N.)   *p*
1174
1601 AV DE LORIMIER, MONTREAL, QC,
H2K 4M5
(514) 529-4993   *SIC* 8631
CONFEDERATION FREEZERS   *p* 506
See STERLING PACKERS LIMITED
CONFEDERATION SAFEWAY   *p* 1432
See SOBEYS WEST INC
CONFERENCE BOARD OF CANADA, THE
p 819
See AERIC INC
CONFERENCE WORLD TOURS   *p* 769
1200 SHEPPARD AVE E SUITE 201,
NORTH YORK, ON, M2K 2S5
(416) 221-6411   *SIC* 4724
CONFI-DENT INC   *p* 668
90 NOLAN CRT UNIT 14, MARKHAM, ON,
L3R 4L9
(905) 474-4444   *SIC* 5047
CONFIDENCE MANAGEMENT LTD   *p* 388
275 COMMERCE DR, WINNIPEG, MB, R3P
1B3
(204) 487-2500   *SIC* 8741
CONFISERIE MONDOUX INC   *p* 1083
1610 PLACE DE LIERRE, COTE SAINT-
LUC, QC, H7G 4X7
(450) 669-1311   *SIC* 5145
CONFISERIE SWEET FACTORY, LA *p* 1236
See INDULBEC INC
CONFISERIES REGAL INC   *p* 1233
1625 BOUL DAGENAIS O, MONTREAL,
QC, H7L 5A3
(450) 628-6700   *SIC* 5145
CONFISERIES REGAL INC   *p* 1328
4620 BOUL THIMENS, SAINT-LAURENT,
QC, H4R 2B2
(514) 333-8540   *SIC* 5145
CONFORM WORKS INC   *p* 47
GD LCD 1, CALGARY, AB, T2P 2G8
(403) 243-2250   *SIC* 1541
CONFORT EXPERT INC   *p* 1048
9771 BOUL METROPOLITAIN E, ANJOU,
QC, H1J 0A4
(514) 640-7711   *SIC* 1711
CONFORTCHEM INC   *p* 1249
76 BOUL HYMUS, POINTE-CLAIRE, QC,
H9R 1E3
(514) 332-1140   *SIC* 5169
CONFORTEC   *p* 1398
See MEUBLES CATHEDRA INC
CONGEBEC CAPITAL LTEE   *p* 1063
5780 BOUL SAINTE-ANNE, BOISCHATEL,
QC, G0A 1H0
(418) 822-4077   *SIC* 6719
CONGEBEC INC   *p* 1261
810 AV GODIN, QUEBEC, QC, G1M 2X9
(418) 683-3491   *SIC* 4222
CONGEBEC LOGISTIQUE INC   *p* 390
1555 CHEVRIER BLVD UNIT A, WIN-
NIPEG, MB, R3T 1Y7
(204) 475-5570   *SIC* 4222
CONGEBEC LOGISTIQUE INC   *p* 1261
810 AV GODIN, QUEBEC, QC, G1M 2X9
(418) 683-3491   *SIC* 6712
CONGELATEUR DE L'ERABLE   *p* 1245
See ATOCAS DE L'ERABLE INC, LES
CONGLOM   *p* 685
See CONGLOM FUTURCHEM INC
CONGLOM FUTURCHEM INC   *p* 685
7385 BREN RD SUITE 3, MISSISSAUGA,
ON, L4T 1H3
SIC 3648
CONGLOM INC   *p* 254
11488 EBURNE WAY UNIT 130, RICH-
MOND, BC, V6V 3E1
(604) 629-1338   *SIC* 5141
CONGLOM INC   *p* 1328
4600 BOUL POIRIER, SAINT-LAURENT,
QC, H4R 2C5
(514) 333-6666   *SIC* 5122

CONGLOM INC   *p* 1333
2600 AV MARIE-CURIE, SAINT-LAURENT,
QC, H4S 2C3
(514) 333-6666   *SIC* 5063
CONGO CORPORATE WOODS INCORPO-
RATED   *p*
687
5935 AIRPORT RD, MISSISSAUGA, ON,
L4V 1W5
(647) 388-6615   *SIC* 2499
CONGREGATION DES SOEURS DE
NOTRE-DAME DU PERPETUEL SECOURS
p 1299
159 RUE COMMERCIALE, SAINT-DAMIEN-
DE-BUCKLAND, QC, G0R 2Y0
(418) 789-2112   *SIC* 8661
CONIFEX INC   *p* 213
300 TAKLA RD, FORT ST. JAMES, BC, V0J
1P0
(250) 996-8241   *SIC* 2421
CONIFEX TIMBER INC   *p* 330
700 WEST GEORGIA ST SUITE 980, VAN-
COUVER, BC, V7Y 1B6
(604) 216-2949   *SIC* 2421
CONKRISDA HOLDINGS LIMITED   *p* 657
1150 WELLINGTON RD, LONDON, ON,
N6E 1M3
(519) 681-0600   *SIC* 7011
CONMAR JANITORIAL CO. LTD   *p* 161
50 RIDGEVIEW CRT, SHERWOOD PARK,
AB, T8A 6B4
(780) 441-5459   *SIC* 7349
CONMED   *p* 591
See CRESCENT PARK LODGE
CONMED DEVELOPMENTS INC   *p* 591
4 HAGEY AVE, FORT ERIE, ON, L2A 1W3
(905) 871-8330   *SIC* 8051
CONMED LINVATEC   *p* 724
See LINVATEC CANADA ULC
CONNACHER OIL AND GAS LIMITED *p* 47
640 5 AVE SW SUITE 1040, CALGARY, AB,
T2P 3G4
(403) 538-6201   *SIC* 1382
CONNAISSEURS DE BOIS   *p* 1170
See LANGEVIN & FOREST LTEE
CONNECT   *p* 262
See GROUP CONNECT LTD, THE
CONNECT CONVEYOR BELTING INC*p* 683
405 INDUSTRIAL DR UNIT 128, MILTON,
ON, L9T 5B1
(905) 878-5552   *SIC* 5085
CONNECT INSURE   *p* 831
1111 PRINCE OF WALES DR, OTTAWA,
ON, K2C 3T2
(613) 723-0670   *SIC* 6289
CONNECT LOGISTICS SERVICES INC   *p*
165
50 CORRIVEAU AVE, ST. ALBERT, AB, T8N
3T5
(780) 458-4492   *SIC* 4226
CONNECT NORTH AMERICA CORPORA-
TION   *p*
394
275 MAIN ST SUITE 600, BATHURST, NB,
E2A 1A9
(506) 545-9450   *SIC* 7389
CONNECT SOCIETY   *p* 118
6240 113 ST NW, EDMONTON, AB, T6H
3L2
(780) 454-9581   *SIC* 8699
CONNECTEURS ELECTRIQUES WECO
INC   *p* 1118
18050 RTE TRANSCANADIENNE, KIRK-
LAND, QC, H9J 4A1
(514) 694-9136   *SIC* 3613
CONNECTIVIA   *p* 1145
See TECHNOLOGY EVALUATION CEN-
TERS INC
CONNECTIVIA   *p* 1210
See CENTRES D'EVALUATION DE LA
TECHNOLOGIE INC
CONNECTRA TECHNOLOGIES INC *p* 125
1803 91 ST SUITE 102, EDMONTON, AB,
T6X 0W8

(888) 731-5210   *SIC* 8742
CONNEX ONTARIO   *p* 851
See CONNEX TELECOMMUNICATIONS
INC
CONNEX TELECOMMUNICATIONS COR-
PORATION   *p*
851
44 EAST BEAVER CREEK RD SUITE 16,
RICHMOND HILL, ON, L4B 1G8
(905) 944-6500   *SIC* 6712
CONNEX TELECOMMUNICATIONS INC *p*
851
44 EAST BEAVER CREEK RD UNIT 16,
RICHMOND HILL, ON, L4B 1G8
(905) 944-6500   *SIC* 4899
CONNEXION TECHNIC INC   *p* 1254
989 AV NORDIQUE BUREAU 100, QUE-
BEC, QC, G1C 0C7
(418) 660-6276   *SIC* 1799
CONNEXION TRUCK CENTRE LTD   *p* 369
440 OAK POINT HWY, WINNIPEG, MB,
R2R 1V3
(204) 633-3333   *SIC* 5511
CONNON NURSERIES   *p* 566
See NEIL VANDER KRUK HOLDINGS INC
CONNON NURSERIES   *p* 857
See A.V.K. NURSERY HOLDINGS INC
CONNOR BROS., DIV OF   *p* 395
See CONNORS BROS. CLOVER LEAF
SEAFOODS COMPANY
CONNOR CLARK & LUNN PRIVATE CAPI-
TAL LTD   *p*
986
130 KING ST W UNIT 1400, TORONTO,
ON, M5X 2A2
(416) 214-6325   *SIC* 6722
CONNOR, CLARK & LUNN FINANCIAL
GROUP   *p* 312
1111 GEORGIA ST W SUITE 2200, VAN-
COUVER, BC, V6E 4M3
(604) 685-4465   *SIC* 8732
CONNOR, CLARK & LUNN INVESTMENT
MANAGEMENT LTD   *p* 312
1111 GEORGIA ST W UNIT 2300, VAN-
COUVER, BC, V6E 4M3
(604) 685-2020   *SIC* 6282
CONNOR, CLARK & LUNN WHOLESALE
FINANCE INC   *p* 986
130 KING STREET W SUITE 1400,
TORONTO, ON, M5X 1C8
(416) 862-2020   *SIC* 6211
CONNORS BROS. CLOVER LEAF
SEAFOODS COMPANY   *p* 395
180 BRUNSWICK ST, BLACKS HARBOUR,
NB, E5H 1G6
(506) 456-3391   *SIC* 5146
CONNORS BROS. CLOVER LEAF
SEAFOODS COMPANY   *p* 668
80 TIVERTON CRT SUITE 600, MARKHAM,
ON, L3R 0G4
(905) 474-0608   *SIC* 5146
CONNORS TRANSFER LIMITED   *p* 466
39 CONNORS LN, STELLARTON, NS, B0K
0A2
(902) 752-1142   *SIC* 4213
CONOCOPHILLIPS   *p* 47
See CONOCOPHILLIPS CANADA RE-
SOURCES CORP
CONOCOPHILLIPS CANADA   *p* 47
See CONOCOPHILLIPS WESTERN
CANADA PARTNERSHIP
CONOCOPHILLIPS CANADA RESOURCES
p 47
See CONOCOPHILLIPS WESTERN
CANADA PARTNERSHIP
CONOCOPHILLIPS CANADA RESOURCES
CORP   *p* 47
401 9 AVE SW SUITE 1600, CALGARY, AB,
T2P 3C5
(403) 233-4000   *SIC* 1311
CONOCOPHILLIPS WESTERN CANADA
PARTNERSHIP   *p* 47
401 9 AVE SW SUITE 1600, CALGARY, AB,
T2P 3C5

(403) 233-4000   *SIC* 1382
CONOCOPHILLIPS WESTERN CANADA
PARTNERSHIP   *p* 47
401 9TH AVE SW, CALGARY, AB, T2P 2H7
(403) 233-4000   *SIC* 1311
CONOCOPHILLIPS WESTERN CANADA
PARTNERSHIP   *p* 82
GD STN MAIN, DRAYTON VALLEY, AB,
T7A 1T1
SIC 1311
CONOLIFT   *p* 879
See KROPF INDUSTRIAL INC
CONPHARM LTD   *p* 1420
303 N ALBERT ST, REGINA, SK, S4R 3C3
(306) 777-8010   *SIC* 5912
CONRAD BROTHERS LIMITED   *p* 443
31 CONO DR, DARTMOUTH, NS, B2W 3Y2
(902) 435-3233   *SIC* 3281
CONREZ GROUP LTD, THE   *p* 919
366 DANFORTH AVE SUITE A, TORONTO,
ON, M4K 1N8
(416) 449-7444   *SIC* 6794
CONROS CORPORATION   *p* 776
41 LESMILL RD, NORTH YORK, ON, M3B
2T3
(416) 751-4343   *SIC* 2499
CONSBEC INC   *p* 1001
2736 BELISLE DR, VAL CARON, ON, P3N
1B3
(705) 897-4971   *SIC* 1799
CONSCORP INC   *p* 1344
6800 BOUL DES GRANDES-PRAIRIES,
SAINT-LEONARD, QC, H1P 3P3
(514) 939-2273   *SIC* 2011
CONSEIL CENTRAL DES SYNDICATS NA-
TIANAUX DE L'ESTRIE   *p*
1370
180 COTE DE L'ACADIE, SHERBROOKE,
QC, J1H 2T3
(819) 563-6515   *SIC* 8631
CONSEIL CRI DE LA SANTE ET DES SER-
VICES SOCIAUX DE LA BAIE JAMES   *p*
1081
GD, CHISASIBI, QC, J0M 1E0
(819) 855-9001   *SIC* 8062
CONSEIL DE RECHERCHES EN SCI-
ENCES HUMAINES   *p*
825
See SOCIAL SCIENCES AND HUMANI-
TIES RESEARCH COUNCIL OF CANADA
CONSEIL DES ECOLES CATHOLIQUES DE
LANGUE FRANCAISE DU CENTRE-EST   *p*
596
4000 LABELLE ST, GLOUCESTER, ON,
K1J 1A1
(613) 744-2555   *SIC* 8211
CONSEIL DES ECOLES CATHOLIQUES DE
LANGUE FRANCAISE DU CENTRE-EST   *p*
820
704 CARSON'S RD, OTTAWA, ON, K1K
2H3
(613) 744-8344   *SIC* 8211
CONSEIL DES ECOLES CATHOLIQUES DE
LANGUE FRANCAISE DU CENTRE-EST   *p*
832
2675 DRAPER AVE, OTTAWA, ON, K2H
7A1
SIC 8211
CONSEIL DES ECOLES PUBLIQUES DE
L'EST DE L'ONTARIO   *p* 811
500 MILLENNIUM BLVD, ORLEANS, ON,
K4A 4X3
(613) 833-0018   *SIC* 8211
CONSEIL DES ECOLES PUBLIQUES DE
L'EST DE L'ONTARIO   *p* 817
2445 ST. LAURENT BLVD, OTTAWA, ON,
K1G 6C3
(613) 742-8960   *SIC* 8211
CONSEIL INTERNATIONAL DES AERO-
PORTS   *p*
1229
800 RUE SQ VICTORIA BUREAU 1810,
MONTREAL, QC, H4Z 1G8
(514) 373-1224   *SIC* 4581

CONSEIL REGIONAL MAURICIE ET CEN-TRE DU QUEBEC (FTQ) *p*
1387
7080 RUE MARION BUREAU 101, TROIS-RIVIERES, QC, G9A 6G4
(819) 378-4049 *SIC 8631*
CONSEIL SANTA MARIA 2267 *p 1134*
173 RUE RENE-PHILIPPE, LEMOYNE, QC, J4R 2J9
(450) 671-1580 *SIC 8699*
CONSEIL SCOLAIRE ACADIEN PROVINCIAL *p*
462
9248 ROUTE 1, METEGHAN RIVER, NS, B0W 2L0
(902) 769-5458 *SIC 8211*
CONSEIL SCOLAIRE ACADIEN PROVINCIAL *p*
464
3435 RTE 206, PETIT DE GRAT, NS, B0E 2L0
(902) 226-5232 *SIC 8211*
CONSEIL SCOLAIRE CATHOLIQUE DE DISTRICT DES GRANDES RIVIERES, LE *p*
627
75 QUEEN ST, KAPUSKASING, ON, P5N 1H5
(705) 335-6091 *SIC 8211*
CONSEIL SCOLAIRE CATHOLIQUE DE DISTRICT DES GRANDES RIVIERES, LE *p*
912
896 RIVERSIDE DR, TIMMINS, ON, P4N 3W2
(705) 267-1421 *SIC 8211*
CONSEIL SCOLAIRE CATHOLIQUE MON-AVENIR *p*
770
110 DREWRY AVE, NORTH YORK, ON, M2M 1C8
(416) 397-6564 *SIC 8211*
CONSEIL SCOLAIRE CATHOLIQUE PROVIDENCE *p*
1018
7515 FOREST GLADE DR, WINDSOR, ON, N8T 3P5
(519) 948-9227 *SIC 8211*
CONSEIL SCOLAIRE CENTRE-NORD *p 111*
8627 91 ST NW SUITE 322, EDMONTON, AB, T6C 3N1
(780) 468-5250 *SIC 8211*
CONSEIL SCOLAIRE DE DISTRICT CATHOLIQUE CENTRE-SUD *p 770*
110 DREWRY AVE, NORTH YORK, ON, M2M 1C8
(416) 250-1754 *SIC 8211*
CONSEIL SCOLAIRE DE DISTRICT CATHOLIQUE DE L'EST ONTARIEN *p 562*
510 MCCONNELL AVE, CORNWALL, ON, K6H 4M1
(613) 933-0172 *SIC 8211*
CONSEIL SCOLAIRE DE DISTRICT CATHOLIQUE DE L'EST ONTARIEN *p 619*
572 KITCHENER ST SUITE 8E, HAWKESBURY, ON, K6A 2P3
(613) 632-7055 *SIC 8211*
CONSEIL SCOLAIRE DE DISTRICT CATHOLIQUE DE L'EST ONTARIEN *p 643*
875 COUNTY ROAD 17, L'ORIGNAL, ON, K0B 1K0
(613) 675-4691 *SIC 8211*
CONSEIL SCOLAIRE DE DISTRICT CATHOLIQUE DE L'EST ONTARIEN *p 857*
1535 DU PARC AVE, ROCKLAND, ON, K4K 1C3
(613) 446-5169 *SIC 8211*
CONSEIL SCOLAIRE DE DISTRICT CATHOLIQUE DU NOUVEL-ONTARIO, LE *p 899*
201 JOGUES ST, SUDBURY, ON, P3C 5L7
(705) 673-5626 *SIC 8211*
CONSEIL SCOLAIRE DE DISTRICT CATHOLIQUE DU NOUVEL-ONTARIO, LE *p 899*
100 LEVIS ST, SUDBURY, ON, P3C 2H1

(705) 674-7484 *SIC 8211*
CONSEIL SCOLAIRE DE DISTRICT DU GRAND NORD DE L'ONTARIO *p 899*
296 VAN HORNE ST, SUDBURY, ON, P3B 1H9
(705) 671-1533 *SIC 8211*
CONSEIL SCOLAIRE DISTRICT NO 5 *p 394*
915 ST. ANNE ST, BATHURST, NB, E2A 6X1
(506) 547-2785 *SIC 8211*
CONSEIL SCOLAIRE DISTRICT NO 5 *p 396*
45A RUE DU VILLAGE, CAMPBELLTON, NB, E3N 3G4
(506) 789-2250 *SIC 8211*
CONSEIL SCOLAIRE DU DISTRICT DU NORD-EST DE L'ONTARIO *p 763*
2345 CONNAUGHT AVE, NORTH BAY, ON, P1B 0A3
(705) 497-8700 *SIC 8211*
CONSEIL SCOLAIRE FRANCOPHONE DE LA COLOMBIE-BRITANNIQUE *p 254*
13511 COMMERCE PKY UNIT 100, RICHMOND, BC, V6V 2J8
(604) 214-2600 *SIC 8211*
CONSEIL SCOLAIRE VIAMONDE *p 791*
116 CORNELIUS PKY, NORTH YORK, ON, M6L 2K5
(416) 614-0844 *SIC 8211*
CONSEILLERS EN GESTION COWATER-SOGEMA INTERNATIONAL *p*
822
See COWATERSOGEMA INTERNATIONAL INC
CONSEILLERS EN GESTION ET INFOR-MATIQUE CGI INC *p*
88
10303 JASPER AVE NW SUITE 800, EDMONTON, AB, T5J 3N6
(780) 409-2200 *SIC 7379*
CONSEILLERS EN GESTION ET INFOR-MATIQUE CGI INC *p*
596
1410 BLAIR PL, GLOUCESTER, ON, K1J 9B9
(613) 740-5900 *SIC 7379*
CONSEILLERS EN GESTION ET INFOR-MATIQUE CGI INC *p*
935
250 YONGE ST SUITE 2000, TORONTO, ON, M5B 2L7
(416) 363-7827 *SIC 8741*
CONSEILLERS EN GESTION ET INFOR-MATIQUE CGI INC *p*
1078
930 RUE JACQUES-CARTIER E 3RD FLOOR, CHICOUTIMI, QC, G7H 7K9
(418) 696-6789 *SIC 7379*
CONSEILLERS EN GESTION ET INFOR-MATIQUE CGI INC *p*
1176
9555 AV CHRISTOPHE-COLOMB, MONTREAL, QC, H2M 2E3
(514) 374-7777 *SIC 4899*
CONSEILLERS EN GESTION ET INFOR-MATIQUE CGI INC *p*
1213
1350 BOUL RENE-LEVESQUE O 15E ETAGE, MONTREAL, QC, H3G 1T4
(514) 841-3200 *SIC 6712*
CONSEILLERS EN GESTION ET INFOR-MATIQUE CGI INC *p*
1258
410 BOUL CHAREST E BUREAU 700, QUEBEC, QC, G1K 8G3
(418) 623-0101 *SIC 7379*
CONSEILLERS EN PLACEMENTS GOOD-MAN & COMPANY *p*
939
See GOODMAN & COMPANY, INVESTMENT COUNSEL LTD
CONSEILLERS LOGISIL INC, LES *p 1213*
1440 RUE SAINTE-CATHERINE O BU-REAU 400, MONTREAL, QC, H3G 1R8
SIC 7379

CONSEILLERS, FISCALITE AMERICAINE *p*
1199
See RICHTER S.E.N.C.R.L.
CONSEILS PPI *p 1396*
See PPI QUEBEC ADVISORY INC
CONSEJO DE PROMOCION TURISTICA DE MEXICO S.A. DE C.A. *p 303*
999 HASTINGS ST W SUITE 1110, VANCOUVER, BC, V6C 2W2
SIC 7389
CONSENSO CREATIONS INC *p 1225*
1565 RUE CHABANEL O, MONTREAL, QC, H4N 2W3
SIC 5136
CONSERVATORY GROUP *p 676*
See VIEWMARK HOMES LTD
CONSERVATORY GROUP, THE *p 666*
See ANTELOPE HILLS CONSTRUCTION LTD
CONSERVING CANADA'S WETLANDS *p*
359
See DUCKS UNLIMITED CANADA
CONSITE CONSTRUCTION LTD *p 29*
1802 17 AVE SE, CALGARY, AB, T2G 1K4
(403) 265-0700 *SIC 1771*
CONSOLIDATED AVIATION FUELING OF TORONTO, ULC *p 728*
5600 SILVER DART DR, MISSISSAUGA, ON, L5P 1A2
(905) 694-2846 *SIC 5172*
CONSOLIDATED BOTTLE CORPORATION *p 993*
77 UNION ST, TORONTO, ON, M6N 3N2
(800) 561-1354 *SIC 5199*
CONSOLIDATED DEALERS CO-OPERATIVE INC *p*
1030
441 HANLAN RD, WOODBRIDGE, ON, L4L 3T1
(905) 264-7022 *SIC 5013*
CONSOLIDATED FASTFRATE INC *p 15*
11440 54 ST SE, CALGARY, AB, T2C 4Y6
(403) 264-1687 *SIC 4731*
CONSOLIDATED FASTFRATE INC *p 88*
7725 101 ST, EDMONTON, AB, T5J 2M1
(780) 439-0061 *SIC 4731*
CONSOLIDATED FASTFRATE INC *p 1027*
9701 HIGHWAY 50, WOODBRIDGE, ON, L4H 2G4
(905) 893-2600 *SIC 4213*
CONSOLIDATED FASTFRATE INC *p 1127*
4415 RUE FAIRWAY, LACHINE, QC, H8T 1B5
(514) 639-7747 *SIC 4731*
CONSOLIDATED GYPSUM SUPPLY LTD *p*
100
11660 170 ST NW, EDMONTON, AB, T5S 1J7
(780) 452-7786 *SIC 5039*
CONSOLIDATED MONITORING LTD *p 91*
9707 110 ST NW SUITE 404, EDMONTON, AB, T5K 2L9
(780) 488-3777 *SIC 7381*
CONSOLIDATED RESTAURANTS LIMITED *p 443*
620 PORTLAND ST, DARTMOUTH, NS, B2W 2M3
(902) 434-8814 *SIC 5812*
CONSOLIDATED TURF EQUIPMENT (1965) LTD *p 383*
986 POWELL AVE, WINNIPEG, MB, R3H 0H6
(204) 633-7276 *SIC 5083*
CONSOLIDATION TCG *p 1079*
See DYNAMITAGE T.C.G. (1993) INC
CONSOLTEX INC *p 1088*
400 RUE WILLARD, COWANSVILLE, QC, J2K 3A2
(514) 333-8800 *SIC 2299*
CONSOLTEX INC *p 1216*
560 BOUL HENRI-BOURASSA O BUREAU 302, MONTREAL, QC, H3L 1P4
(514) 333-8800 *SIC 2299*
CONSORTIUM DES MARQUES PRIVEES

PBC INC, LES *p 1396*
3000 BOUL RENE-LEVESQUE BUREAU 330, VERDUN, QC, H3E 1T9
(514) 768-4122 *SIC 5149*
CONSORTIUM M.R. CANADA LTEE *p 1152*
14243 BOUL DU CURE-LABELLE, MIRABEL, QC, J7J 1M2
(514) 328-6060 *SIC 1541*
CONSORTIUM PL *p 1396*
See CONSORTIUM DES MARQUES PRIVEES PBC INC, LES
CONSORTIUM POMERLEAU VERREAULT ACCIONA *p 1237*
See VERREAULT INC
CONSORTIUM PONT MOHAWK CPM *p*
1116
GD, KAHNAWAKE, QC, J0L 1B0
(450) 635-6063 *SIC 1622*
CONSTANT AIR-FLO *p 1288*
See MATERIEL INDUSTRIEL LTEE, LE
CONSTANT FIRE PROTECTION SYSTEMS LTD *p 15*
5442 56 AVE SE, CALGARY, AB, T2C 4M6
(403) 279-7973 *SIC 7389*
CONSTELLATION BRANDS SCHENLEY ULC *p 140*
2925 9 AVE N, LETHBRIDGE, AB, T1H 5E3
(403) 317-2100 *SIC 2085*
CONSTELLATION SOFTWARE INC *p 937*
20 ADELAIDE ST E SUITE 1200, TORONTO, ON, M5C 2T6
(416) 861-2279 *SIC 7371*
CONSTRUCTION *p 266*
See EMIL ANDERSON MAINTENANCE CO. LTD
CONSTRUCTION & GENERAL WORKERS UNION LOCAL NO. 92 *p 85*
10319 106 AVE NW SUITE 104, EDMONTON, AB, T5H 0P4
(780) 426-6630 *SIC 8631*
CONSTRUCTION ALBERT JEAN LTEE *p*
1174
4045 RUE PARTHENAIS, MONTREAL, QC, H2K 3T8
(514) 522-2121 *SIC 1542*
CONSTRUCTION ARNO INC *p 1386*
2300 BOUL DES RECOLLETS, TROIS-RIVIERES, QC, G8Z 3X5
(819) 379-5222 *SIC 1623*
CONSTRUCTION AUBIN, LAVAL LTEE *p*
1379
1470 RUE NATIONALE, TERREBONNE, QC, J6W 6M1
(514) 640-0622 *SIC 1542*
CONSTRUCTION AUDET & KNIGHT *p 1290*
See 9015-6472 QUEBEC INC
CONSTRUCTION B M L, DIV.DE SINTRA *p*
1140
See SINTRA INC
CONSTRUCTION BAO INC *p 1161*
7875 AV MARCO-POLO, MONTREAL, QC, H1E 1N8
(514) 648-2272 *SIC 1771*
CONSTRUCTION BAU-VAL INC *p 1058*
87 RUE EMILIEN-MARCOUX BUREAU 101, BLAINVILLE, QC, J7C 0B4
(514) 788-4660 *SIC 1611*
CONSTRUCTION BERNARD BORDELEAU INC. *p 1297*
100 RUE ROMEO-GAUDREAULT, SAINT-CHARLES-BORROMEE, QC, J6E 0A1
(450) 752-2660 *SIC 1522*
CONSTRUCTION BERTRAND DIONNE INC *p 1098*
1555 RUE JANELLE, DRUMMONDVILLE, QC, J2C 5S5
(819) 472-2559 *SIC 1542*
CONSTRUCTION BLACKNED ENR *p 1400*
See BLACKNED, JAMES
CONSTRUCTION BML *p 1287*
See SINTRA INC
CONSTRUCTION BOREA *p 1140*
See BOREA CONSTRUCTION ULC
CONSTRUCTION BROCCOLINI INC *p 1117*

16766 RTE TRANSCANADIENNE UNITE 500, KIRKLAND, QC, H9H 4M7
(514) 737-0076   *SIC* 1542
CONSTRUCTION BSL INC   *p* 1292
315 RUE DE ROTTERDAM, SAINT-AUGUSTIN-DE-DESMAURES, QC, G3A 2E5
(418) 878-4448   *SIC* 1542
CONSTRUCTION C.A.L.   *p* 1333
See CERIKO ASSELIN LOMBARDI INC
CONSTRUCTION CITADELLE INC   *p* 1254
419 RUE DES MONTEREGIENNES, QUEBEC, QC, G1C 7J7
(418) 661-9351   *SIC* 1542
CONSTRUCTION COUTURE & TANGUAY *p* 1140
See 9124-4905 QUEBEC INC
CONSTRUCTION CYBCO INC   *p* 1338
7089 RTE TRANSCANADIENNE, SAINT-LAURENT, QC, H4T 1A2
(514) 284-2228   *SIC* 1542
CONSTRUCTION DEMATHIEU & BARD (CDB) INC   *p* 1319
170 BOUL ROLAND-GODARD, SAINT-JEROME, QC, J7Y 4P7
(450) 569-8043   *SIC* 1622
CONSTRUCTION DERIC INC   *p* 1277
5145 RUE RIDEAU, QUEBEC, QC, G2E 5H5
(418) 781-2228   *SIC* 1541
CONSTRUCTION DIMCO INC.   *p* 1161
8601 BOUL HENRI-BOURASSA E BUREAU 100, MONTREAL, QC, H1E 1P4
(514) 494-1001   *SIC* 1611
CONSTRUCTION DINAMO INC   *p* 1119
6023 BOUL WILFRID-HAMEL, L'ANCIENNE-LORETTE, QC, G2E 2H3
(418) 871-6226   *SIC* 1541
CONSTRUCTION DISTRIBUTION & SUPPLY COMPANY INC   *p* 1002
300 CONFEDERATION PKWY UNIT 3, VAUGHAN, ON, L4K 4T8
(416) 665-8006   *SIC* 5211
CONSTRUCTION DJL INC   *p* 1064
1550 RUE AMPERE BUREAU 200, BOUCHERVILLE, QC, J4B 7L4
(450) 641-8000   *SIC* 1611
CONSTRUCTION DJL INC   *p* 1106
20 RUE EMILE-BOND, GATINEAU, QC, J8Y 3M7
(819) 770-2300   *SIC* 1611
CONSTRUCTION DJL INC   *p* 1223
6200 RUE SAINT-PATRICK, MONTREAL, QC, H4E 1B3
(514) 766-8256   *SIC* 1611
CONSTRUCTION DJL INC   *p* 1295
580 RANG DES VINGT-CINQ E, SAINT-BRUNO, QC, J3V 0G6
(450) 653-2423   *SIC* 1422
CONSTRUCTION DJL INC   *p* 1368
3200 BOUL HUBERT-BIERMANS, SHAWINIGAN, QC, G9N 0A4
(819) 539-2271   *SIC* 1611
CONSTRUCTION DROLET, MARC INC *p* 1277
5475 RUE RIDEAU, QUEBEC, QC, G2E 5V9
(418) 871-7574   *SIC* 1521
CONSTRUCTION ENERGIE RENOUVELABLE S.E.N.C.   *p* 1349
178 132 RTE E, SAINT-OMER, QC, G0C 2Z0
(418) 364-6027   *SIC* 3621
CONSTRUCTION ET PAVAGE BOISVERT INC   *p* 1300
180 BOUL DE LA GABELLE, SAINT-ETIENNE-DES-GRES, QC, G0X 2P0
(819) 374-7297   *SIC* 1794
CONSTRUCTION ET PAVAGE PORTNEUF INC   *p* 1348
599 BOUL BONA-DUSSAULT, SAINT-MARC-DES-CARRIERES, QC, G0A 4B0
(418) 268-3558   *SIC* 1611

CONSTRUCTION FASTENERS & TOOLS LTD   *p* 1426
504 45TH A ST E, SASKATOON, SK, S7K 0W7
(306) 668-8880   *SIC* 5085
CONSTRUCTION G-NESIS INC   *p* 1236
4915 RUE LOUIS-B.-MAYER, MONTREAL, QC, H7P 0E5
(514) 370-8303   *SIC* 1623
CONSTRUCTION G. THERRIEN 2010 INC *p* 1242
3885 BOUL LOUIS-FRECHETTE, NICOLET, QC, J3T 1T7
(819) 293-6921   *SIC* 1542
CONSTRUCTION GARBARINO INC   *p* 1402
4795 RUE SAINTE-CATHERINE O BUREAU 302, WESTMOUNT, QC, H3Z 1S8
(514) 731-5654   *SIC* 1521
CONSTRUCTION GARNIER LTEE   *p* 1101
3980 BOUL LEMAN, FABREVILLE, QC, H7E 1A1
(450) 661-6470   *SIC* 1623
CONSTRUCTION GELY INC   *p* 1119
1781 RTE DE L'AEROPORT, L'ANCIENNE-LORETTE, QC, G2G 2P5
(418) 871-3368   *SIC* 1611
CONSTRUCTION GERATEK LTEE   *p* 1373
535 RUE PEPIN, SHERBROOKE, QC, J1L 1X3
(819) 564-2933   *SIC* 1542
CONSTRUCTION GILLES LANTHIER INC *p* 1144
2119 RUE SAINTE-HELENE, LONGUEUIL, QC, J4K 3T5
(450) 670-8238   *SIC* 1542
CONSTRUCTION GOLDER   *p* 1226
See GOLDER CONSTRUCTION INC
CONSTRUCTION IB MAURITANIE   *p* 1289
See INDUSTRIES BLAIS INC, LES
CONSTRUCTION IDEAL DE GRANBY INC *p* 1110
65 RUE SAINT-JUDE S, GRANBY, QC, J2J 2N2
(450) 378-2301   *SIC* 1542
CONSTRUCTION IRENEE PAQUET & FILS INC   *p* 1172
1300 RUE SAINT-ZOTIQUE E, MONTREAL, QC, H2G 1G5
(514) 273-3910   *SIC* 1542
CONSTRUCTION J. & R. SAVARD LTEE *p* 1307
1201 BOUL MARTEL, SAINT-HONORE-DE-CHICOUTIMI, QC, G0V 1L0
(418) 543-5933   *SIC* 1794
CONSTRUCTION J.C. LEPAGE LTEE *p* 1244
254 132 RTE, PABOS MILLS, QC, G0C 2J0
(418) 689-0568   *SIC* 6531
CONSTRUCTION J.C. LEPAGE LTEE *p* 1284
569 RUE DE LAUSANNE, RIMOUSKI, QC, G5L 4A7
(418) 724-4239   *SIC* 1542
CONSTRUCTION J.P.L.   *p* 1106
See JPL APRES SINISTRE INC
CONSTRUCTION JOBIN, BENOIT   *p* 1284
See BENOIT JOBIN INC
CONSTRUCTION JULIEN DALPE INC *p* 1360
350 CH DES PRES, SAINTE-MARIE-SALOME, QC, J0K 2Z0
(450) 754-2059   *SIC* 1542
CONSTRUCTION KIEWIT CIE   *p* 1133
3055 BOUL SAINT-MARTIN O BUREAU 200, LAVAL, QC, H7T 0J3
(450) 435-5756   *SIC* 8711
CONSTRUCTION L.F.G. INC   *p* 1349
178 RTE 132 E, SAINT-OMER, QC, G0C 2Z0
(418) 364-7082   *SIC* 1541
CONSTRUCTION LA-RAY DIVISION ROUYN-NORANDA   *p* 1289
950 RUE SAGUENAY, ROUYN-NORANDA, QC, J9X 7B6

(819) 762-9345   *SIC* 1521
CONSTRUCTION LANOUE, PASCAL INC *p* 1163
8400 RUE SHERBROOKE E, MONTREAL, QC, H1L 1B2
(514) 544-8999   *SIC* 1522
CONSTRUCTION LARIVIERE LTEE *p* 1108
640 RUE AUGUSTE-MONDOUX, GATINEAU, QC, J9J 3K3
(819) 770-2280   *SIC* 1794
CONSTRUCTION LECLERC & PELLETIER INC   *p* 1367
475 AV PERREAULT, SEPT-ILES, QC, G4R 1K6
(418) 962-2499   *SIC* 1542
CONSTRUCTION LONGER INC   *p* 1373
175 RUE LEGER, SHERBROOKE, QC, J1L 1M2
(819) 564-0115   *SIC* 1542
CONSTRUCTION M.G.P. INC   *p* 1299
140 RTE 271 S, SAINT-EPHREM-DE-BEAUCE, QC, G0M 1R0
(418) 484-5740   *SIC* 1522
CONSTRUCTION MANCHAOW INC *p* 1081
2 CLUSTER F7, CHISASIBI, QC, J0M 1E0
(819) 855-2046   *SIC* 1522
CONSTRUCTION MARATHON   *p* 1337
See 7190891 CANADA INC
CONSTRUCTION MARIEVILLE INC *p* 1149
2010 RUE DU PONT, MARIEVILLE, QC, J3M 1J9
(450) 460-7955   *SIC* 1542
CONSTRUCTION MAURICE BILODEAU INC   *p* 1135
401 RUE DU GRAND-TRONC, LEVIS, QC, G6K 1K8
(418) 831-4024   *SIC* 1521
CONSTRUCTION MICHEL GAGNON LTEE *p* 1263
2250 RUE LEON-HARMEL BUREAU 200, QUEBEC, QC, G1N 4L2
(418) 687-3824   *SIC* 1742
CONSTRUCTION MICHEL MALTAIS INC *p* 1244
775 RTE 132 E, NOUVELLE, QC, G0C 2E0
(418) 794-2605   *SIC* 1521
CONSTRUCTION NCL   *p* 1171
See 2313-3606 QUEBEC INC
CONSTRUCTION PAROX INC   *p* 1056
1655 RUE DE L'INDUSTRIE, BELOEIL, QC, J3G 0S5
(450) 813-9655   *SIC* 1522
CONSTRUCTION PASCAL   *p* 1051
8020 BOUL METROPOLITAIN E, ANJOU, QC, H1K 1A1
(514) 493-1054   *SIC* 1542
CONSTRUCTION PG4   *p* 1247
See PG4 CONSTRUCTION CORP.
CONSTRUCTION POLARIS INC   *p* 1278
500 -797 BOUL LEBOURGNEUF, QUEBEC, QC, G2J 0B5
(418) 861-9877   *SIC* 1794
CONSTRUCTION PROMEC   *p* 1288
See 2242974 CANADA INC
CONSTRUCTION RAOUL PELLETIER (1997) INC   *p* 1137
3650 BOUL GUILLAUME-COUTURE, LEVIS, QC, G6W 7L3
(418) 837-9833   *SIC* 1794
CONSTRUCTION RAYMOND ET FILS INC, LES   *p* 1152
14243 BOUL DU CURE-LABELLE, MIRABEL, QC, J7J 1M2
(450) 979-4847   *SIC* 1521
CONSTRUCTION RENO-GAUTHIER ENTREPRENEUR GENERAL INC   *p* 1073
1266 RUE DE VIMY, CANTON TREMBLAY, QC, G7G 5H8
(418) 543-8602   *SIC* 1542
CONSTRUCTION SAFETY ASSOCIATION OF ONTARIO   *p* 583
21 VOYAGER CRT S, ETOBICOKE, ON, M9W 5M7

SIC 8611
CONSTRUCTION SANTE MONTREAL *p* 1186
See SANTE MONTREAL COLLECTIF CJV, S.E.C.
CONSTRUCTION SOCAM LTEE   *p* 1233
3300 AV FRANCIS-HUGHES, MONTREAL, QC, H7L 5A7
(450) 662-9000   *SIC* 1542
CONSTRUCTION SOLIMEC   *p* 1156
See ENTREPRISES DE CONSTRUCTION DAWCO INC
CONSTRUCTION SOTER INC   *p* 1232
4085 RANG SAINT-ELZEAR E, MONTREAL, QC, H7E 4P2
(450) 664-2818   *SIC* 1611
CONSTRUCTION SOTER INC   *p* 1236
4915 RUE LOUIS-B.-MAYER, MONTREAL, QC, H7P 0E5
(450) 664-2818   *SIC* 1521
CONSTRUCTION TALBON INC   *p* 1289
203 BOUL INDUSTRIEL, ROUYN-NORANDA, QC, J9X 6P2
(819) 797-0122   *SIC* 1541
CONSTRUCTION TAWICH INC   *p* 1401
16 RTE BEAVER, WEMINDJI, QC, J0M 1L0
(819) 978-0264   *SIC* 1611
CONSTRUCTION TECHNIPRO BSL *p* 1284
See 168287 CANADA INC
CONSTRUCTION TECHNIPRO BSL *p* 1284
See 9275-0181 QUEBEC INC
CONSTRUCTION TEMBEC   *p* 1207
See RAYONIER A.M. COMPAGNIE DE CONSTRUCTION INC
CONSTRUCTION VERGO   *p* 1361
See CONSTRUCTION VERGO 2011 INC
CONSTRUCTION VERGO 2011 INC *p* 1361
1463 RUE BERLIER, SAINTE-ROSE, QC, H7L 3Z1
(450) 967-2220   *SIC* 1542
CONSTRUCTION VP INC   *p* 1302
1450 RTE 117, SAINT-FAUSTIN-LAC-CARRE, QC, J0T 1J2
SIC 1521
CONSTRUCTION YVAN BOISVERT INC *p* 1300
180 BOUL DE LA GABELLE, SAINT-ETIENNE-DES-GRES, QC, G0X 2P0
(819) 374-7277   *SIC* 1794
CONSTRUCTIONN FASTECH   *p* 1124
See ACIER FASTECH INC
CONSTRUCTIONS 3P INC   *p* 1070
3955 RUE ISABELLE, BROSSARD, QC, J4Y 2R2
(450) 659-6000   *SIC* 1711
CONSTRUCTIONS BE-CON INC, LES *p* 1279
1054 BOUL BASTIEN BUREAU 418, QUEBEC, QC, G2K 1E6
(418) 626-3583   *SIC* 1542
CONSTRUCTIONS BEAUCE-ATLAS INC, LES   *p* 1360
600 1RE AV DU PARC-INDUSTRIEL, SAINTE-MARIE, QC, G6E 1B5
(418) 387-4872   *SIC* 5051
CONSTRUCTIONS BELAND & LAPOINTE INC, LES   *p* 1140
723 CH INDUSTRIEL, LEVIS, QC, G7A 1B5
(418) 831-8638   *SIC* 1542
CONSTRUCTIONS BINET INC, LES *p* 1294
227 RTE 271, SAINT-BENOIT-LABRE, QC, G0M 1P0
(418) 228-1578   *SIC* 1542
CONSTRUCTIONS BOB-SON INC *p* 1052
2264 AV DU LABRADOR, BAIE-COMEAU, QC, G4Z 3C4
(418) 296-0064   *SIC* 1611
CONSTRUCTIONS BRI INC, LES   *p* 1295
585 RUE SAGARD, SAINT-BRUNO, QC, J3V 6C1
(450) 461-3310   *SIC* 1794
CONSTRUCTIONS CJRB INC, LES *p* 1381
3000 RUE ANDERSON, TERREBONNE, QC, J6Y 1W1

▲ Public Company   ■ Public Company Family Member   **HQ** Headquarters   **BR** Branch   **SL** Single Location

(450) 965-1110   *SIC* 1623
CONSTRUCTIONS CONCREATE LTEE *p* 1333
5840 RUE DONAHUE, SAINT-LAURENT, QC, H4S 1C1
(514) 335-0412   *SIC* 1622
CONSTRUCTIONS DANIEL LOISELLE INC, LES *p* 1312
1350 AV ST-JACQUES, SAINT-HYACINTHE, QC, J2S 6M6
SIC 1542
CONSTRUCTIONS DE CASTEL INC, LES *p* 1076
265 BOUL INDUSTRIEL, CHATEAUGUAY, QC, J6J 4Z2
(450) 699-2036   *SIC* 1542
CONSTRUCTIONS DE MAUSOLEES CARRIER INC, LES *p* 1333
7575 BOUL THIMENS, SAINT-LAURENT, QC, H4S 2A2
(514) 832-3733   *SIC* 1542
CONSTRUCTIONS E. HUOT INC *p* 1135
15 RUE DE L'ARENA BUREAU 400, LEVIS, QC, G6J 0B1
(418) 836-7310   *SIC* 1542
CONSTRUCTIONS E.D.B. INC *p* 1392
545 RTE 249, VAL-JOLI, QC, J1S 0E6
(819) 845-5436   *SIC* 3554
CONSTRUCTIONS EDGUY INC, LES *p* 1360
500 1RE AV DU PARC-INDUSTRIEL, SAINTE-MARIE, QC, G6E 1B5
(418) 387-6270   *SIC* 1794
CONSTRUCTIONS EMBEC *p* 1217
See ESTIMATIONS DE CONSTRUCTION DU QUEBEC INC
CONSTRUCTIONS EXCEL S.M. INC, LES *p* 1360
1083 BOUL VACHON N BUREAU 300, SAINTE-MARIE, QC, G6E 1M8
(418) 386-1442   *SIC* 1541
CONSTRUCTIONS FABMEC INC *p* 1078
1590 BOUL DU ROYAUME O BUREAU 4, CHICOUTIMI, QC, G7H 5B1
(418) 549-3636   *SIC* 1522
CONSTRUCTIONS FGP INC, LES *p* 1294
33 MONTEE ROBERT, SAINT-BASILE-LE-GRAND, QC, J3N 1L7
(450) 441-2727   *SIC* 1542
CONSTRUCTIONS JEL BERGERON *p* 1397
91 RUE MONFETTE, VICTORIAVILLE, QC, G6P 0B7
(819) 795-3030   *SIC* 1521
CONSTRUCTIONS LEO BAROLET INC, LES *p* 1401
250 2E AV, WEEDON, QC, J0B 3J0
(819) 877-2378   *SIC* 1521
CONSTRUCTIONS LOUISBOURG LTEE *p* 1301
699 BOUL INDUSTRIEL, SAINT-EUSTACHE, QC, J7R 6C3
(450) 623-7100   *SIC* 8711
CONSTRUCTIONS MAXERA INC, LES *p* 1346
7675 RUE LESPINAY, SAINT-LEONARD, QC, H1S 3C6
(514) 254-9002   *SIC* 8361
CONSTRUCTIONS METHODEX INC, LES *p* 1080
676 RUE DES ACTIONNAIRES, CHICOUTIMI, QC, G7J 5A8
(418) 545-2280   *SIC* 1542
CONSTRUCTIONS NOMADE *p* 1355
See 9131-1050 QUEBEC INC
CONSTRUCTIONS PEPIN ET FORTIN INC, LES *p* 1398
371 AV PIE-X, VICTORIAVILLE, QC, G6R 0L6
(819) 357-9274   *SIC* 1542
CONSTRUCTIONS PLACO INC, LES *p* 1078
2700 BOUL TALBOT BUREAU 41, CHICOUTIMI, QC, G7H 5B1
(418) 545-3362   *SIC* 1542

CONSTRUCTIONS PROCO INC *p* 1377
516 172 RTE O, ST-NAZAIRE-DU-LAC-ST-JEAN, QC, G0W 2V0
(418) 668-3371   *SIC* 1541
CONSTRUCTIONS QUORUM INC *p* 1224
5200 RUE SAINT-PATRICK BUREAU 200, MONTREAL, QC, H4E 4N9
(514) 822-2882   *SIC* 1522
CONSTRUCTIONS RELIANCE INC, LES *p* 1127
3285 BOUL JEAN-BAPTISTE-DESCHAMPS, LACHINE, QC, H8T 3E4
(514) 631-7999   *SIC* 1522
CONSTRUCTIONS RICOR INC *p* 1113
1214 RUE DE L'ESCALE, HAVRE-SAINT-PIERRE, QC, G0G 1P0
(418) 538-3201   *SIC* 1542
CONSULAIR GASTON BOULANGER *p* 1263
See CONSULAIR INC
CONSULAIR INC *p* 1263
2022 RUE LAVOISIER BUREAU 125, QUEBEC, QC, G1N 4L5
(418) 650-5960   *SIC* 7389
CONSULATE GENERAL OF THE REPUBLIC OF KOREA COMMERCIAL SECTION *p* 950
65 QUEEN ST W SUITE 600, TORONTO, ON, M5H 2M5
(416) 368-3399   *SIC* 6799
CONSULTANT AUTO 360 *p* 1212
See SOLUTIONS MEDIAS 360 INC
CONSULTANTS A.G.I.R. *p* 1235
See 9273743 CANADA INC
CONSULTANTS AECOM INC *p* 1084
1 PLACE LAVAL BUREAU 200, COTE SAINT-LUC, QC, H7N 1A1
(450) 967-1260   *SIC* 8711
CONSULTANTS AECOM INC *p* 1185
85 RUE SAINTE-CATHERINE O, MONTREAL, QC, H2X 3P4
(514) 287-8500   *SIC* 8711
CONSULTANTS AECOM INC *p* 1266
4700 BOUL WILFRID-HAMEL, QUEBEC, QC, G1P 2J9
(418) 871-2444   *SIC* 8711
CONSULTANTS ATHENA *p* 1309
See AREO-FEU LTEE
CONSULTANTS CAPGEMINI *p* 949
See CAPGEMINI CANADA INC
CONSULTANTS COMMERCIAUX DELMAR *p* 1127
See DELMAR INTERNATIONAL INC
CONSULTANTS DE L'ARCTIQUE INC, LES *p* 1048
10200 RUE MIRABEAU, ANJOU, QC, H1J 1T6
(514) 353-3552   *SIC* 7389
CONSULTANTS F. DRAPEAU INC *p* 1348
2005 CH DE L'INDUSTRIE, SAINT-MATHIEU-DE-BELOEIL, QC, J3G 0S4
(450) 467-2642   *SIC* 7699
CONSULTANTS LUPIEN ROULEAU INC *p* 1064
1550 RUE AMPERE BUREAU 301, BOUCHERVILLE, QC, J4B 7L4
(450) 449-7333   *SIC* 7389
CONSULTANTS MESAR INC *p* 1389
4500 RUE CHARLES-MALHIOT, TROIS-RIVIERES, QC, G9B 0V4
(819) 537-5771   *SIC* 8711
CONSULTANTS RELLIM *p* 1209
See W.B.C. CORPORATION
CONSULTANTS S.P.I. INC *p* 1300
136C RUE SAINT-LAURENT, SAINT-EUSTACHE, QC, J7P 5G1
(514) 288-8868   *SIC* 7381
CONSULTANTS VFP INC *p* 1387
1455 RUE CHAMPLAIN, TROIS-RIVIERES, QC, G9A 5X4
(819) 378-6159   *SIC* 8711
CONSULTATION EN TECHNOLOGIE DE L'INFORMATION ET DES COMUNICATIONS DACSYS INC *p* 1145

612 RUE DU CAPRICORNE, LONGUEUIL, QC, J4L 4X2
(514) 260-1616   *SIC* 8741
CONSULTEC LTD *p* 993
139 MULOCK AVE, TORONTO, ON, M6N 1G9
(416) 236-2426   *SIC* 8711
CONSUMER DIVISION *p* 684
See RECOCHEM INC
CONSUMER/SURVIVOR BUSINESS COUNCIL OF ONTARIO *p* 994
1499 QUEEN ST W SUITE 203, TORONTO, ON, M6R 1A3
(416) 504-1693   *SIC* 8399
CONSUMERS COMMUNITY CO-OP *p* 416
3300 WESTFIELD RD, SAINT JOHN, NB, E2M 7A4
SIC 5411
CONSUMERS' CO-OPERATIVE REFINERIES LIMITED *p* 1415
550E E 9TH AVE N, REGINA, SK, S4N 7B3
(306) 721-5353   *SIC* 2911
CONSUMERS' CO-OPERATIVE REFINERIES LIMITED *p* 1415
580 PARK ST, REGINA, SK, S4N 5A9
(306) 719-4353   *SIC* 2911
CONSUN CONTRACTING LTD *p* 127
195 MACDONALD CRES, FORT MCMURRAY, AB, T9H 4B3
(780) 743-3163   *SIC* 1629
CONTACT NORTH/CONTACT NORD *p* 908
1139 ALLOY DR SUITE 104, THUNDER BAY, ON, P7B 6M8
(807) 344-1616   *SIC* 8742
CONTACT RESOURCE SERVICES INC *p* 715
2225 ERIN MILLS PKWY, MISSISSAUGA, ON, L5K 2P0
(905) 855-8106   *SIC* 7322
CONTACT SERVICES INC *p* 298
128 PENDER ST W FLR 6-7, VANCOUVER, BC, V6B 1R8
(604) 688-5523   *SIC* 8748
CONTAINER CORPORATION OF CANADA *p* 851
See CONTAINER CORPORATION OF CANADA LTD
CONTAINER CORPORATION OF CANADA LTD *p* 851
68 LEEK CRES, RICHMOND HILL, ON, L4B 1H1
(905) 764-3777   *SIC* 3085
CONTAINER WEST *p* 14
See CANADIAN INTERMODAL SERVICES LTD
CONTAINERWEST *p* 254
See CONTAINERWEST MANUFACTURING LTD
CONTAINERWEST MANUFACTURING LTD *p* 254
11660 MITCHELL RD, RICHMOND, BC, V6V 1T7
(604) 322-0533   *SIC* 5085
CONTAINERWORLD FORWARDING SERVICES INC *p* 258
16133 BLUNDELL RD, RICHMOND, BC, V6W 0A3
(604) 276-1300   *SIC* 4731
CONTANT *p* 1230
See GROUPE CONTANT INC
CONTAX INC *p* 928
893 YONGE ST, TORONTO, ON, M4W 2H2
(416) 927-1913   *SIC* 8741
CONTEMPORARY OFFICE INTERIORS LTD *p* 29
2206 PORTLAND ST SE, CALGARY, AB, T2G 4M6
(403) 265-1133   *SIC* 5021
CONTENANTS DURABAC INC, LES *p* 1110
22 CH MILTON, GRANBY, QC, J2J 0P2

(450) 378-1723   *SIC* 3443
CONTENANTS I.M.L. D'AMERIQUE DU NORD INC, LES *p* 1350
2625 344 RTE, SAINT-PLACIDE, QC, J0V 2B0
(450) 258-3130   *SIC* 3089
CONTENANTS IML CANADA *p* 1350
See CONTENANTS I.M.L. D'AMERIQUE DU NORD INC, LES
CONTENT MANAGEMENT CORPORATION *p* 904
50 MINTHORN BLVD SUITE 800, THORNHILL, ON, L3T 7X8
(905) 889-6555   *SIC* 7376
CONTI ELECTRIC COMPANY OF CANADA *p* 1019
2861 TEMPLE DR, WINDSOR, ON, N8W 5E5
(519) 250-8212   *SIC* 1731
CONTINENTAL ALLOYS & SERVICES INC *p* 47
1440-530 8 AVE SW, CALGARY, AB, T2P 3S8
(403) 216-5150   *SIC* 5084
CONTINENTAL AUTOMOTIVE CANADA *p* 542
See CONTINENTAL TIRE CANADA, INC
CONTINENTAL BUILDING PRODUCTS CANADA INC *p* 1074
8802 BOUL INDUSTRIEL, CHAMBLY, QC, J3L 4X3
(450) 447-3206   *SIC* 1499
CONTINENTAL CABINET COMPANY INCORPORATED *p* 648
547 CLARKE RD, LONDON, ON, N5V 2E1
(519) 455-3830   *SIC* 2431
CONTINENTAL CAPITAL *p* 1338
See CONTINENTAL INVESTISSEMENTS CAPITAL INC
CONTINENTAL CARGO SYSTEMS INC *p* 734
7175 TRANMERE DR UNIT 1B, MISSISSAUGA, ON, L5S 1N4
(905) 405-0096   *SIC* 4731
CONTINENTAL CARTAGE *p* 1
See 689803 ALBERTA LTD
CONTINENTAL CARTAGE INC *p* 1
26215 TWP RD 531A UNIT 412, ACHESON, AB, T7X 5A4
(780) 452-9414   *SIC* 4213
CONTINENTAL CASUALTY COMPANY *p* 969
66 WELLINGTON ST W SUITE 3700, TORONTO, ON, M5K 1E9
(416) 542-7300   *SIC* 6331
CONTINENTAL CHAIN & RIGGING LTD *p* 108
7011 GIRARD RD NW, EDMONTON, AB, T6B 2C4
(780) 437-2701   *SIC* 3462
CONTINENTAL CONVEYOR (ONTARIO) LIMITED *p* 747
100 RICHMOND BLVD, NAPANEE, ON, K7R 4A4
(613) 354-3318   *SIC* 5084
CONTINENTAL COSMETICS LTD *p* 551
390 MILLWAY AVE, CONCORD, ON, L4K 3V8
(905) 660-0622   *SIC* 5122
CONTINENTAL CURRENCY EXCHANGE *p* 813
See 1022481 ONTARIO INC
CONTINENTAL DECON *p* 504
See JORDAHL CANADA INC
CONTINENTAL DIV DE *p* 1368
See CONSTRUCTION DJL INC
CONTINENTAL ELECTRICAL MOTOR SERVICES (NORTHERN) LTD *p* 122
8909 15 ST NW, EDMONTON, AB, T6P 0B8
(780) 410-8800   *SIC* 7694
CONTINENTAL ELECTRICAL MOTOR SERVICES LTD *p* 29
4015 8 ST SE SUITE 201, CALGARY, AB.

T2G 3A5

(403) 236-9428 *SIC* 7694

CONTINENTAL GOLD INC *p* 979
155 WELLINGTON ST W SUITE 2920, TORONTO, ON, M5V 3H1
(416) 583-5610 *SIC* 1041

CONTINENTAL GROUP *p* 29
See CONTINENTAL ELECTRICAL MOTOR SERVICES LTD

CONTINENTAL GROUP *p* 122
See CONTINENTAL ELECTRICAL MOTOR SERVICES (NORTHERN) LTD

CONTINENTAL IMAGING PRODUCTS *p* 63
See 702856 ALBERTA LTD

CONTINENTAL INN *p* 98
See WESTVIEW INN LTD

CONTINENTAL INVESTISSEMENTS CAPITAL INC *p* 1338
7575 RTE TRANSCANADIENNE STE 100, SAINT-LAURENT, QC, H4T 1V6
(514) 875-6661 *SIC* 7389

CONTINENTAL LABORATORIES (1985) LTD *p* 22
3601 21 ST NE UNIT A, CALGARY, AB, T2E 6T5
(403) 250-3982 *SIC* 1389

CONTINENTAL MINERALS CORPORATION *p* 303
800 PENDER ST W SUITE 1020, VANCOUVER, BC, V6C 2V6
(604) 684-6365 *SIC* 1081

CONTINENTAL MUSHROOM CORPORATION (1989) LTD *p* 681
2545 NINTH LINE RD, METCALFE, ON, K0A 2P0
SIC 0182

CONTINENTAL NEWSPAPERS (CANADA) LTD *p* 221
550 DOYLE AVE, KELOWNA, BC, V1Y 7V1
(250) 763-4000 *SIC* 2711

CONTINENTAL ROOFING *p* 255
See ORIGINAL ROOF MAINTAINER INC

CONTINENTAL SAUSAGE CO. LTD *p* 290
3585 MAIN ST, VANCOUVER, BC, V5V 3N4
(604) 874-0332 *SIC* 5147

CONTINENTAL TIRE CANADA, INC *p* 542
700 PARK AVENUE E, CHATHAM, ON, N7M 5M7
(519) 352-6700 *SIC* 5014

CONTINENTAL TRAVEL BUREAU LTD *p* 377
222 OSBORNE ST N, WINNIPEG, MB, R3C 1V4
(204) 989-8575 *SIC* 4724

CONTINU-GRAPH INC *p* 1325
409 BOUL LEBEAU, SAINT-LAURENT, QC, H4N 1S2
(514) 331-0741 *SIC* 2752

CONTINUING LEGAL EDUC, THE *p* 298
845 CAMBIE ST SUITE 500, VANCOUVER, BC, V6B 4Z9
(604) 669-3544 *SIC* 8621

CONTINUING STUDIES *p* 222
See OKANAGAN COLLEGE

CONTINUOUS COLOUR COAT LIMITED *p* 583
1430 MARTIN GROVE RD, ETOBICOKE, ON, M9W 4Y1
(416) 743-7980 *SIC* 3479

CONTITECH CANADA, INC *p* 721
6711 MISSISSAUGA RD SUITE 01, MISSISSAUGA, ON, L5N 2W3
(905) 366-2010 *SIC* 3069

CONTITECH CANADA, INC *p* 745
79 ARTHUR ST, MITCHELL, ON, N0K 1N0
SIC 3559

CONTITECH CANADA, INC *p* 835
3225 3RD AVE E, OWEN SOUND, ON, N4K 5N3
SIC 3714

CONTITECH CANADA, INC *p* 1291

127 RANG PARENT, SAINT-ALPHONSE-DE-GRANBY, QC, J0E 2A0
(450) 375-5050 *SIC* 3069

CONTOUR EARTHMOVING LTD *p* 159
285019 WRANGLER WAY, ROCKY VIEW COUNTY, AB, T1X 0K3
(403) 275-0154 *SIC* 1629

CONTRACT PHARMACEUTICALS LIMITED CANADA *p* 721
2145 MEADOWPINE BLVD 1ST FL, MISSISSAUGA, ON, L5N 6R8
(905) 821-7600 *SIC* 2834

CONTRACT PHARMACEUTICALS LIMITED CANADA *p* 721
7600 EAST DANBRO CRES, MISSISSAUGA, ON, L5N 6L6
(905) 821-7600 *SIC* 2834

CONTRACTEURS ARMSERV INC *p* 1333
6400 RUE VANDEN-ABEELE, SAINT-LAURENT, QC, H4S 1R9
(514) 333-5340 *SIC* 5074

CONTRANS CORP *p* 1036
1179 RIDGEWAY RD, WOODSTOCK, ON, N4V 1E3
(519) 421-4600 *SIC* 6712

CONTRANS FLATBED GROUP GP INC *p* 607
80 THIRD LINE RD, HAGERSVILLE, ON, N0A 1H0
(905) 768-3375 *SIC* 4213

CONTRANS GROUP INC *p* 683
100 MARKET DR, MILTON, ON, L9T 3H5
(905) 693-8088 *SIC* 4449

CONTRANS GROUP INC *p* 839
42 LANARK RD, PERTH, ON, K7H 3K5
(613) 267-2007 *SIC* 4482

CONTRANS HOLDING II LP *p* 1036
1179 RIDGEWAY RD, WOODSTOCK, ON, N4V 1E3
(519) 421-4600 *SIC* 6712

CONTRE-PLAQUE ST-CASIMIR INC *p* 1296
420 RTE GUILBAULT, SAINT-CASIMIR, QC, G0A 3L0
(418) 339-2313 *SIC* 2435

CONTREPLAQUE & PLACAGE CANADA INC *p* 1364
15 BOUL DU CURE-LABELLE, SAINTE-THERESE, QC, J7E 2X1
(450) 435-6541 *SIC* 5031

CONTRLE TECHNIQUE APPLIQUE *p* 1128
See INTERTEK TESTING SERVICES NA LTD

CONTROL INNOVATIONS INC *p* 15
11222 42 ST SE, CALGARY, AB, T2C 0J9
(403) 720-0277 *SIC* 1389

CONTROL TECH 2011 LTD *p* 134
11001 78 AVE, GRANDE PRAIRIE, AB, T8W 2J7
(780) 539-7114 *SIC* 8748

CONTROL TECHNOLOGY INC *p* 5
4305 SOUTH ST, BLACKFALDS, AB, T0C 0B0
(403) 885-2677 *SIC* 1389

CONTROLE ROUTIER QUEBEC *p* 1336
See SOCIETE D'ASSURANCES AUTOMOBILES DE QUEBEC

CONTROLE TOTAL LOGISTIQUE INC *p* 1394
200 AV L'OYOLA-SCHMIDT, VAUDREUIL-DORION, QC, J7V 8P2
(450) 424-1700 *SIC* 4731

CONTROLES A.C. INC, LES *p* 1137
2185 5E RUE, LEVIS, QC, G6W 5M6
(418) 834-2777 *SIC* 5075

CONTROLES AC *p* 1137
See CONTROLES A.C. INC, LES

CONTROLES I.S.I. INC, LES *p* 1333
4030 CH DU BOIS-FRANC, SAINT-LAURENT, QC, H4S 1A7
(514) 338-1562 *SIC* 8748

CONTROLES LAURENTIDE LTEE *p* 1118
18000 RTE TRANSCANADIENNE, KIRKLAND, QC, H9J 4A1
(514) 697-9230 *SIC* 5085

CONTROLES PROVAN ASSOCIES INC, LES *p* 1333
2315 RUE HALPERN, SAINT-LAURENT, QC, H4S 1S3
(514) 332-3230 *SIC* 5084

CONTROLLED ENVIRONMENTS LIMITED *p* 384
590 BERRY ST, WINNIPEG, MB, R3H 0R9
(204) 786-6451 *SIC* 3821

CONTROLS & EQUIPMENT LTD *p* 408
185 MILLENNIUM BLVD, MONCTON, NB, E1E 2G7
(506) 857-8836 *SIC* 1731

CONVALESCENT HOME OF WINNIPEG, THE *p* 387
276 HUGO ST N, WINNIPEG, MB, R3M 2N6
(204) 453-4663 *SIC* 8051

CONVATEC CANADA LTEE *p* 1093
1425 RTE TRANSCANADIENNE BUREAU 250, DORVAL, QC, H9P 2W9
(514) 822-5985 *SIC* 5047

CONVECTAIR-NMT INC *p* 1364
30 CAR SICARD, SAINTE-THERESE, QC, J7E 3X6
(450) 951-4367 *SIC* 5063

CONVENIENCE GROUP INC *p* 571
10 BUTTERICK RD, ETOBICOKE, ON, M8W 3Z8
(416) 233-6900 *SIC* 5031

CONVENTION CENTRE CORPORATION, THE *p* 377
375 YORK AVE SUITE 243, WINNIPEG, MB, R3C 3J3
(204) 956-1720 *SIC* 7389

CONVENTRY MOTORS LIMITED *p* 390
1717 WAVERLEY ST UNIT 520, WINNIPEG, MB, R3T 6A9
(204) 475-3982 *SIC* 5511

CONVERGE CONSTRUCTION LTD *p* 233
31413 GILL AVE UNIT 108, MISSION, BC, V4S 0C4
(604) 814-3401 *SIC* 1521

CONVERGE TECHNOLOGY PARTNERS INC *p* 961
161 BAY ST SUITE 4420, TORONTO, ON, M5J 2S1
SIC 7372

CONVERGE TECHNOLOGY SOLUTIONS CORP. *p* 961
161 BAY ST SUITE 2325, TORONTO, ON, M5J 2S1
(416) 360-3995 *SIC* 7371

CONVERGINT TECHNOLOGIES LTD *p* 34
6020 11 ST SE SUITE 2, CALGARY, AB, T2H 2L7
(403) 291-3241 *SIC* 8711

CONVERSANT INTELLECTUAL PROPERTY MANAGEMENT INC *p* 832
515 LEGGET DR SUITE 704, OTTAWA, ON, K2K 3G4
(613) 576-3000 *SIC* 3825

CONVERTER CORE INC *p* 509
155 ORENDA RD UNIT 1, BRAMPTON, ON, L6W 1W3
(905) 459-6566 *SIC* 5113

CONVERTISSEUR DE PAPIERS ARTEAU, DIVISION DE PAPIERS ET EMBALLAGES ARTEAU *p* 1162
See PAPIERS ET EMBALLAGES ARTEAU INC

CONVEY-ALL INDUSTRIES INC *p* 361
130 CANADA ST, WINKLER, MB, R6W 0J3
(204) 325-4195 *SIC* 3523

CONVIRON *p* 384
See CONTROLLED ENVIRONMENTS LIMITED

CONVOY SUPPLY LTD *p* 276
8183 130 ST, SURREY, BC, V3W 7X4
(604) 591-5381 *SIC* 5039

CONVOYEUR CONTINENTAL & USINAGE LTEE *p* 1382
470 RUE SAINT-ALPHONSE S, THETFORD MINES, QC, G6G 3V8

(418) 338-4682 *SIC* 3599

CONWAY JACQUES COURTIERS *p* 1203
1250 BOUL RENE-LEVESQUE O, MONTREAL, QC, H3B 4W8
(514) 935-4242 *SIC* 6311

CONXCORP LTD *p* 738
6350 NETHERHART RD UNIT 2, MISSISSAUGA, ON, L5T 1K3
(866) 815-2669 *SIC* 3648

COOK & COOKE INSURANCE BROKERS *p* 359
See SWAN VALLEY AGENCIES LTD

COOK (CANADA) INC *p* 894
165 MOSTAR ST, STOUFFVILLE, ON, L4A 0Y2
(905) 640-7110 *SIC* 5047

COOKE AQUACULTURE INC *p* 395
874 MAIN ST, BLACKS HARBOUR, NB, E5H 1E6
(506) 456-6600 *SIC* 0912

COOKE INC *p* 395
669 MAIN ST, BLACKS HARBOUR, NB, E5H 1K1
(506) 456-6600 *SIC* 0912

COOKE, CHARLIE INSURANCE AGENCY LTD *p* 1039
125 POWNAL ST SUITE 1, CHARLOTTETOWN, PE, C1A 3W4
(902) 566-5666 *SIC* 6411

COOKIES BY GEORGE *p* 86
See 683060 ALBERTA LTD

COOKIES GRILL *p* 197
44335 YALE RD SUITE 3A, CHILLIWACK, BC, V2R 4H2
(604) 792-0444 *SIC* 5461

COOKS ISI INSURANCE *p* 1418
See HARVARD WESTERN VENTURES INC

COOKSON MOTORS LTD *p* 221
1150 GORDON DR, KELOWNA, BC, V1Y 3E4
(250) 763-2327 *SIC* 5511

COOKSTOWN AUTO CENTRE LTD *p* 561
5046 5TH, COOKSTOWN, ON, L0L 1L0
(416) 364-0743 *SIC* 5093

COOKSVILLE CHRYSLER DODGE JEEP *p* 708
See COOKSVILLE DODGE CHRYSLER INC

COOKSVILLE DODGE CHRYSLER INC *p* 708
290 DUNDAS ST E, MISSISSAUGA, ON, L5A 1W9
(905) 279-3031 *SIC* 5511

COOKSVILLE STEEL LIMITED *p* 708
510 HENSALL CIR, MISSISSAUGA, ON, L5A 1Y1
(905) 277-9538 *SIC* 3441

COOL *p* 1292
See ENTREPOTS E.F.C. INC, LES

COOL BEER BREWING CO. INCORPORATED *p* 574
164 EVANS AVE, ETOBICOKE, ON, M8Z 1J4
(416) 255-7100 *SIC* 5181

COOL CREEK ENERGY LTD *p* 218
455 DENE DR, KAMLOOPS, BC, V2H 1J1
(250) 374-0614 *SIC* 5983

COOLEY, DEAN GM *p* 348
See COOLEY, DEAN MOTORS LTD

COOLEY, DEAN MOTORS LTD *p* 348
1600 MAIN ST S, DAUPHIN, MB, R7N 3B3
(204) 638-4026 *SIC* 7538

COOLTECH AIR SYSTEMS LTD *p* 494
37 NIXON RD, BOLTON, ON, L7E 1K1
(905) 951-0885 *SIC* 1711

COONEY BULK SALES LIMITED *p* 491
77 BELLEVUE DR, BELLEVILLE, ON, K8N 4Z5
(613) 962-6666 *SIC* 4212

COONEY GROUP INC *p* 491
77 BELLEVUE DR, BELLEVILLE, ON, K8N 4Z5

(613) 962-6666   *SIC* 6712
COONEY TRANSPORT LTD   *p* 491
77 BELLEVUE DR, BELLEVILLE, ON, K8N
4Z5
(613) 962-6666   *SIC* 4213
COOP AGRODOR, LA   *p* 1384
*See COOPERATIVE AGRO-ALIMENTAIRE
DES VALLEES, OUTAOUAIS-LAURENTIDES*
**COOP ALIMENTAIRE DE LA REGION
D'ASBESTOS**   *p* 1052
511 1RE AV, ASBESTOS, QC, J1T 3P6
(819) 879-5427   *SIC* 5411
COOP AVANTIS   *p* 1360
500 RTE CAMERON BUREAU 100,
SAINTE-MARIE, QC, G6E 0L9
(418) 386-2667   *SIC* 5191
COOP CHAMBORD   *p* 1075
*See   COOPERATIVE
D'APPROVISIONNEMENT DE CHAMBORD*
COOP COMAX, LA   *p* 1310
See COMAX, COOPERATIVE AGRICOLE
COOP D'ELECTRICITE   *p* 1315
*See   COOPERATIVE   REGIONALE
D'ELECTRICITE DE ST-JEAN-BAPTISTE-
DE-ROUVILLE*
**COOP DE LA POLYVALENTE DE
THETFORD-MINES**   *p* 1382
561 RUE SAINT-PATRICK, THETFORD
MINES, QC, G6G 5W1
(418) 338-7832   *SIC* 5943
COOP DE LA RIVIERE DU SUD   *p* 1377
*See SOCIETE COOPERATIVE AGRICOLE
DE LA RIVIERE-DU-SUD*
COOP DE STE-PERPETUE, LA   *p* 1361
*See   MAGASIN   CO-OP   DE   STE-
PERPETUE, CTE L'ISLET*
**COOP DE TRAVAIL EN AMENAGEMENT
FORESTIER DE GRANDE-VALLEE** *p* 1112
39C RUE SAINT-FRANCOIS-XAVIER E,
GRANDE-VALLEE, QC, G0E 1K0
(418) 393-3339   *SIC* 0851
**COOP DES CANTONS COOPERATIVE
AGRICOLE**   *p* 1081
96 RUE MAIN E, COATICOOK, QC, J1A
1N2
(819) 849-9833   *SIC* 5153
COOP DES MONTEREGIENNES, LA *p* 1109
61 RUE SAINTE-THERESE, GRANBY, QC,
J2G 7K2
(450) 378-2667   *SIC* 5191
COOP DU CEGEP DE LIMOILOU   *p* 1272
*See COOPERATIVE DE L'UNIVERSITE
LAVAL*
COOP FEDEREE, LA   *p* 1064
1580 RUE EIFFEL, BOUCHERVILLE, QC,
J4B 5Y1
(450) 449-6344   *SIC* 5191
COOP FEDEREE, LA   *p* 1225
9001 BOUL DE L'ACADIE, MONTREAL,
QC, H4N 3H7
(514) 384-6450   *SIC* 6519
COOP FEDEREE, LA   *p* 1225
9001 BOUL DE L'ACADIE BUREAU 200,
MONTREAL, QC, H4N 3H7
(514) 858-2222   *SIC* 5191
COOP FEDEREE, LA   *p* 1298
249 RUE PRINCIPALE, SAINT-DAMASE,
QC, J0H 1J0
(450) 797-2691   *SIC* 5191
COOP FEDEREE, LA   *p* 1310
3250 BOUL LAURIER E, SAINT-
HYACINTHE, QC, J2R 2B6
(450) 773-6661   *SIC* 5144
COOP FEDEREE, LA   *p* 1314
3380 RUE PRINCIPALE BUREAU 430,
SAINT-JEAN-BAPTISTE, QC, J0L 2B0
(450) 467-2875   *SIC* 2015
COOP FEDEREE, LA   *p* 1386
4225 RUE SAINT-JOSEPH BUREAU 379,
TROIS-RIVIERES, QC, G8Z 4G3
(819) 379-8551   *SIC* 5072
COOP FORESTIERE DE STE-ROSE *p* 1363
184 RUE DU QUAI, SAINTE-ROSE-DU-
NORD, QC, G0V 1T0

SIC 0851
COOP HEC MONTREAL   *p* 1219
*See COOPERATIVE DE L'ECOLE DES
HAUTES ETUDES COMMERCIALES*
COOP IGA CARREFOUR   *p* 1045
*See COOPERATIVE DES CONSOMMA-
TEURS D'ALMA*
COOP MATAPEDIENNE, LA   *p* 1046
*See   MATAPEDIENNE   COOPERATIVE
AGRICOLE, LA*
COOP NOVAGO, LA   *p* 1114
839 RUE PAPINEAU, JOLIETTE, QC, J6E
2L6
(418) 873-2535   *SIC* 8699
COOP PURDEL, LA   *p* 1284
155 RUE SAINT-JEAN-BAPTISTE E, RI-
MOUSKI, QC, G5L 1Y7
(418) 736-4363   *SIC* 5083
COOP UNICOOP, LA   *p* 1360
See UNICOOP, COOPERATIVE AGRICOLE
**COOP UNIFRONTIERES - SECTEUR
AGRICOLE/CENTRE DE MELANGE -
NAPIERVILLE, LA**
See COOP UNIFRONTIERES, LA   *p* 1298
COOP UNIFRONTIERES, LA   *p* 1298
4 RANG SAINT-ANDRE, SAINT-CYPRIEN-
DE-NAPIERVILLE, QC, J0J 1L0
(450) 245-3308   *SIC* 5153
COOP VAL-NORD, LA   *p* 1114
*See   COOPERATIVE   AGRICOLE
PROFID'OR*
COOPER BARGING SERVICE LTD   *p* 212
GD, FORT NELSON, BC, V0C 1R0
(250) 774-3359   *SIC* 4449
COOPER CONSTRUCTION LIMITED *p* 796
2381 BRISTOL CIR SUITE C-200,
OAKVILLE, ON, L6H 5S9
(905) 829-0444   *SIC* 1542
COOPER CROUSE-HINDS   *p* 730
*See COOPER INDUSTRIES (ELECTRI-
CAL) INC*
COOPER EQUIPMENT RENTALS LIMITED
p 738
6335 EDWARDS BLVD, MISSISSAUGA,
ON, L5T 2W7
(877) 329-6531   *SIC* 7353
COOPER INDUSTRIES (CANADA) INC
p 730
5925 MCLAUGHLIN RD, MISSISSAUGA,
ON, L5R 1B8
(905) 501-3000   *SIC* 6712
COOPER INDUSTRIES (ELECTRICAL) INC
p 730
5925 MCLAUGHLIN RD, MISSISSAUGA,
ON, L5R 1B8
(905) 501-3000   *SIC* 5211
COOPER INDUSTRIES (ELECTRICAL) INC
p 730
5925 MCLAUGHLIN RD, MISSISSAUGA,
ON, L5R 1B8
(905) 507-4000   *SIC* 4911
COOPER LIGHTING, DIV OF   *p* 730
*See COOPER INDUSTRIES (ELECTRI-
CAL) INC*
COOPER MARKET LTD   *p* 216
804 LAVAL CRES, KAMLOOPS, BC, V2C
5P3
SIC 5411
COOPER'S FOODS   *p* 216
See COOPER MARKET LTD
COOPER'S IRON & METAL INC   *p* 933
130 COMMISSIONERS ST, TORONTO, ON,
M5A 1A8
(416) 461-0733   *SIC* 5093
COOPER, R J CONSTRUCTION LTD *p* 250
1937 OGILVIE ST S, PRINCE GEORGE,
BC, V2N 1X2
(250) 563-4649   *SIC* 1542
**COOPER-STANDARD   AUTOMOTIVE
CANADA LIMITED**   *p* 593
346 GUELPH ST, GEORGETOWN, ON,
L7G 4B5
(905) 873-6921   *SIC* 2891
COOPER-STANDARD   AUTOMOTIVE

CANADA LIMITED   *p* 594
268 APPIN RD RR 4, GLENCOE, ON, N0L
1M0
(519) 287-2450   *SIC* 3714
**COOPER-STANDARD   AUTOMOTIVE
CANADA LIMITED**   *p* 895
703 DOURO ST, STRATFORD, ON, N5A
3T1
(519) 271-3360   *SIC* 2891
**COOPER-STANDARD   AUTOMOTIVE
CANADA LIMITED**   *p* 895
703 DOURO ST, STRATFORD, ON, N5A
3T1
(519) 271-3360   *SIC* 3069
**COOPER-STANDARD   AUTOMOTIVE
CANADA LIMITED**   *p* 1373
3995 BOUL INDUSTRIEL, SHERBROOKE,
QC, J1L 2S7
(819) 562-4440   *SIC* 3465
**COOPER-STANDARD   AUTOMOTIVE
CANADA LIMITED**   *p* 1373
4045 RUE BRODEUR, SHERBROOKE, QC,
J1L 1K4
(819) 562-4440   *SIC* 3465
**COOPER-STANDARD   AUTOMOTIVE
CANADA LIMITED**   *p* 1375
4870 RUE ROBERT BOYD, SHER-
BROOKE, QC, J1R 0W8
(819) 562-4440   *SIC* 3465
COOPERATION ECHANGE CANADA INC *p*
1229
975 BOUL ROMEO-VACHON-AEROPORT
N, MONTREAL, QC, H4V 1H1
(514) 828-0068   *SIC* 6231
**COOPERATIVE AGRICOLE D'EMBRUN
LIMITED, LA**   *p* 569
926 NOTRE DAME ST, EMBRUN, ON, K0A
1W0
(613) 443-2892   *SIC* 5191
**COOPERATIVE AGRICOLE D'EMBRUN
LIMITED, LA**   *p* 569
GD, EMBRUN, ON, K0A 1W0
(613) 443-2892   *SIC* 5411
**COOPERATIVE AGRICOLE DES AP-
PALACHES**   *p*
1133
303 CH DE LA GROSSE-?LE, LAURI-
ERVILLE, QC, G0S 1P0
(819) 385-4272   *SIC* 2048
COOPERATIVE AGRICOLE DU PRE-VERT
p 1384
1316 RUE SAINTE-MARIE, TINGWICK,
QC, J0A 1L0
(819) 359-2255   *SIC* 5251
COOPERATIVE AGRICOLE PROFID'OR *p*
1114
839 RUE PAPINEAU, JOLIETTE, QC, J6E
2L6
(450) 759-4041   *SIC* 5191
COOPERATIVE AGRICOLE-APPALACHE *p*
1147
120 RUE SAINT-PIERRE, LYSTER, QC,
G0S 1V0
(819) 389-5553   *SIC* 8699
**COOPERATIVE AGRO-ALIMENTAIRE DES
VALLEES, OUTAOUAIS-LAURENTIDES** *p*
1384
340 RUE LYON, THURSO, QC, J0X 3B0
(819) 985-4839   *SIC* 5191
COOPERATIVE   D'ALBANEL *p* 1044
287 RUE DE L'EGLISE, ALBANEL, QC,
G8M 3J9
(418) 279-3183   *SIC* 5411
**COOPERATIVE   D'ALENTOUR,
GROSSISTE EN ALIMENTATION NA-
TURELLE DES CANTONS DE L'EST**   *p*
1373
4740 BOUL INDUSTRIEL, SHERBROOKE,
QC, J1L 3A3
(819) 562-3443   *SIC* 5149

**COOPERATIVE D'APPROVISIONNEMENT
DE CHAMBORD**   *p* 1075
1945 RTE 169, CHAMBORD, QC, G0W 1G0
(418) 342-6495   *SIC* 5411
**COOPERATIVE D'APPROVISIONNEMENTS
DE STE-JULIE**   *p* 1358
1590 RUE PRINCIPALE, SAINTE-JULIE,
QC, J3E 1W6
(450) 922-5555   *SIC* 5072
**COOPERATIVE D'HABITATION LE TRAIT
D'UNION DE GATINEAU**   *p* 1104
29 RUE D'ORLEANS BUREAU 101,
GATINEAU, QC, J8T 5T9
(819) 561-9702   *SIC* 6514
**COOPERATIVE DE CARAQUET LIMITEE,
LA**   *p* 396
121 BOUL ST-PIERRE O, CARAQUET, NB,
E1W 1B6
(506) 727-1930   *SIC* 5411
**COOPERATIVE   DE   GESTION
FORESTIERE DES APPALACHES**   *p* 1356
519   RTE   PRINCIPALE,   SAINTE-
APOLLINE-DE-PATTON, QC, G0R 2P0
(418) 469-3033   *SIC* 2411
**COOPERATIVE DE L'ECOLE DES HAUTES
ETUDES COMMERCIALES**   *p* 1219
5255 AV DECELLES BUREAU 2340, MON-
TREAL, QC, H3T 2B1
(514) 340-6396   *SIC* 5942
**COOPERATIVE DE L'UNIVERSITE DE
SHERBROOKE**   *p* 1372
2500 BOUL DE L'UNIVERSITE BUREAU B5
014, SHERBROOKE, QC, J1K 2R1
(819) 821-3599   *SIC* 5411
COOPERATIVE DE L'UNIVERSITE LAVAL *p*
1272
2305 RUE DE L'UNIVERSITE BUREAU
1100, QUEBEC, QC, G1V 0B4
(418) 656-2600   *SIC* 6712
**COOPERATIVE DE ROGERSVILLE LIMI-
TEE, LA**   *p*
412
28 BOUCHER ST, ROGERSVILLE, NB, E4Y
1X5
(506) 775-6131   *SIC* 5411
**COOPERATIVE DE SERVICES A DOMICILE
BEAUCE-NORD**   *p* 1321
700 AV ROBERT-CLICHE, SAINT-JOSEPH-
DE-BEAUCE, QC, G0S 2V0
(418) 397-8283   *SIC* 8399
COOPERATIVE DE SHEDIAC LIMITEE, LA
p 417
335 MAIN ST, SAINT-LEOLIN, NB, E4P 2B1
(506) 532-4441   *SIC* 5411
**COOPERATIVE DE TRANSPORT MAR-
ITIME AERIEN ASSOCIATION COOPERA-
TIVE**   *p*
1073
435 CH AVILA-ARSENEAU, CAP-AUX-
MEULES, QC, G4T 1J3
(418) 986-6600   *SIC* 4213
**COOPERATIVE DE TRAVAILLEURS
FORESTIERS EAUBOIS**   *p* 1355
48 3E AV O, SAINTE-ANNE-DES-MONTS,
QC, G4V 1J5
(418) 763-2255   *SIC* 0851
**COOPERATIVE DES CONSOMATEURS DE
CHARLESBOURG**   *p* 1280
1233 BOUL LOUIS-XIV, QUEBEC, QC, G2L
1L9
(418) 628-2525   *SIC* 5411
**COOPERATIVE DES CONSOMMATEURS
D'ALMA**   *p* 1045
705 AV DU PONT N, ALMA, QC, G8B 6T5
(418) 662-7405   *SIC* 5411
**COOPERATIVE DES CONSOMMATEURS
DE FERMONT**   *p* 1102
299 LE CARREFOUR, FERMONT, QC, G0G
1J0
SIC 5411
**COOPERATIVE DES CONSOMMATEURS
DE LORETTEVILLE**   *p* 1275
250 RUE LOUIS-IX, QUEBEC, QC, G2B 1L4
(418) 842-2341   *SIC* 5411

COOPERATIVE DES CONSOMMATEURS DE STE-FOY p 1274
999 AV DE BOURGOGNE, QUEBEC, QC, G1W 4S6
(418) 658-6472   SIC 5411

COOPERATIVE DES ENCANS D'ANIMAUX DU BAS-SAINT-LAURENT p 1284
3229 132 RTE O, RIMOUSKI, QC, G0L 1B0
(418) 736-5788   SIC 5154

COOPERATIVE DES PARAMEDICS DE L'OUTAOUAIS p 1103
505 BOUL DES AFFAIRES, GATINEAU, QC, J8R 0B2
(819) 643-5005   SIC 4119

COOPERATIVE DES PARAMEDICS DU TEMISCOUATA p 1378
148 RUE DE L'EGLISE, TEMISCOUATA-SUR-LE-LAC, QC, G0L 1X0
(418) 899-2047   SIC 5047

COOPERATIVE DES PECHEURS DE CAP DAUPHIN p 1112
51 CH SHORE, GROSSE-ILE, QC, G4T 6A4
(418) 985-2321   SIC 5421

COOPERATIVE DES TRAVAILLEURS ET TRAVAILLEUSES PREMIER DEFI LAVAL 1342
1111 BOUL DES LAURENTIDES, SAINT-LAURENT, QC, H7N 5B5
(450) 668-7085   SIC 5812

COOPERATIVE DES TRAVAILLEUSES ET TRAVAILLEURS EN RESTAURATION LA DEMOCRATE p 1167
2901 RUE SHERBROOKE E, MONTREAL, QC, H1W 1B2
SIC 5812

COOPERATIVE ETUDIANTE DU CEGEP DE SEPT-ILES p 1367
175 RUE DE LA VERENDRYE, SEPT-ILES, QC, G4R 5B7
(418) 962-9848   SIC 8221

COOPERATIVE FORESTIERE DE FERLAND-BOILLEAU p 1102
445 381 RTE, FERLAND-ET-BOILLEAU, QC, G0V 1H0
(418) 676-2626   SIC 2411

COOPERATIVE FORESTIERE DE PETIT-PARIS p 1347
576 RUE GAUDREAULT, SAINT-LUDGER-DE-MILOT, QC, G0W 2B0
(418) 373-2575   SIC 2411

COOPERATIVE FORESTIERE DU BAS ST-MAURICE p 1294
1410 BOUL TRUDEL E, SAINT-BONIFACE-DE-SHAWINIGAN, QC, G0X 2L0
(819) 535-6262   SIC 8699

COOPERATIVE FORESTIERE DU HAUT ST-MAURICE p 1124
50 RUE BOSTONNAIS, LA TUQUE, QC, G9X 2E8
(819) 523-2737   SIC 2411

COOPERATIVE FORESTIERE HAUT PLAN VERT LAC-DES-AIGLES p 1124
109 RUE PRINCIPALE, LAC-DES-AIGLES, QC, G0K 1V0
(418) 779-2612   SIC 2411

COOPERATIVE FORESTIERE ST-DOMINIQUE p 1299
289 RUE PRINCIPALE, SAINT-DOMINIQUE-DU-ROSAIRE, QC, J0Y 2K0
(819) 732-5723   SIC 0851

COOPERATIVE NOTRE-DAME LIMITEE , LA p 419
2616 CH VAL-DOUCET, VAL-DOUCET, NB, E8R 1Z2
(506) 764-3394   SIC 5411

COOPERATIVE REGIONALE D'ELECTRICITE DE ST-JEAN-BAPTISTE-DE-ROUVILLE p 1315
3113 RUE PRINCIPALE, SAINT-JEAN-BAPTISTE, QC, J0L 2B0

(450) 467-5583   SIC 4911

COOPERATIVE REGIONALE DE LA BAIE LTEE, LA p 419
3430 RUE PRINCIPALE, TRACADIE-SHEILA, NB, E1X 1C8
(506) 395-1700   SIC 5411

COOPSCO SAINT-HYACINTHE p 1312
3000 AV BOULLE, SAINT-HYACINTHE, QC, J2S 1H9
(450) 774-2727   SIC 5734

COOPSCO SAINT-HYACINTHE p 1312
3230 RUE SICOTTE, SAINT-HYACINTHE, QC, J2S 2M2
(450) 778-6504   SIC 8222

COOPSCO SAINTE-FOY p 1272
2410 CH SAINTE-FOY, QUEBEC, QC, G1V 1T3
(418) 659-6600   SIC 5942

COOPTEL COOP DE TELECOMMUNICATION p 1392
5521 CH DE L'AEROPORT, VALCOURT, QC, J0E 2L0
(450) 532-2667   SIC 4813

COORDINATE INDUSTRIES LTD p 797
2251 WINSTON PARK DR, OAKVILLE, ON, L6H 5R1
(905) 829-0099   SIC 3728

COORDINATED MANAGEMENT SERVICES p 379
See PITBLADO LLP

COORSTEK ADVANCED MATERIALS HAMILTON ULC p 836
45 CURTIS AVE N, PARIS, ON, N3L 3W1
(519) 442-6395   SIC 3255

COORSTEK ENGINEERED METALS p 648
See ADJ INDUSTRIES INC

COPAP COMMERCE INC p 1249
755 BOUL SAINT-JEAN BUREAU 305, POINTE-CLAIRE, QC, H9R 5M9
(514) 693-9150   SIC 5111

COPAP INC p 1249
755 BOUL SAINT-JEAN BUREAU 305, POINTE-CLAIRE, QC, H9R 5M9
(514) 693-9150   SIC 2295

COPCAN CIVIL p 235
See COPCAN CONTRACTING LTD

COPCAN CONTRACTING LTD p 235
1920 BALSAM RD, NANAIMO, BC, V9X 1T5
(250) 754-7260   SIC 1794

COPENHAGEN DANISH p 1343
See BOULANGERIES COMAS INC, LES

COPERNIC INC p 1258
400 BOUL JEAN-LESAGE BUREAU 345, QUEBEC, QC, G1K 8W1
(418) 524-4661   SIC 7371

COPERNICUS STUDIOS INC p 452
1226 HOLLIS ST SUITE 100, HALIFAX, NS, B3J 1T6
(902) 474-5194   SIC 8999

COPICOM INC p 1317
50 RUE SAINT-JACQUES, SAINT-JEAN-SUR-RICHELIEU, QC, J3B 2J9
(450) 347-8252   SIC 5044

COPIES DE LA CAPITALE INC, LES p 1258
235 BOUL CHAREST E, QUEBEC, QC, G1K 3G8
(418) 648-1911   SIC 2752

COPIEXPRESS p 1265
See 24184863 QUEBEC INC

COPISCOPE INC p 1325
460 BOUL MONTPELLIER BUREAU 267, SAINT-LAURENT, QC, H4N 2G7
(514) 744-3610   SIC 5065

COPOL INTERNATIONAL LTD.-PACKAGING FILMS p 464
69 HARTIGAN DR, NORTH SYDNEY, NS, B0A 1H0
(902) 794-9685   SIC 3081

COPP BUILDING MATERIALS LIMITED p 653
45 YORK ST, LONDON, ON, N6A 1A4
(519) 679-9000   SIC 5039

COPP'S BUILDALL p 653
See COPP BUILDING MATERIALS LIMITED

COPPA'S FRESH MARKET p 780
See 2360083 ONTARIO LIMITED

COPPER BAY HOLDINGS INC p 520
9 BENNETT ST, BRUCE MINES, ON, P0R 1C0
(705) 785-3506   SIC 5541

COPPER BAY SHELL/ NUGGET FOOD STORE p 520
See COPPER BAY HOLDINGS INC

COPPER CORE LIMITED p 583
275 CARRIER DR, ETOBICOKE, ON, M9W 5Y8
(416) 675-1177   SIC 3433

COPPER CREEK GOLF CLUB p 642
See COPPER CREEK LIMITED PARTNERSHIP

COPPER CREEK LIMITED PARTNERSHIP p 642
11191 HWY 27, KLEINBURG, ON, L0J 1C0
(905) 893-3370   SIC 7992

COPPER MOUNTAIN MINING CORPORATION p 303
700 PENDER ST W SUITE 1700, VANCOUVER, BC, V6C 1G8
(604) 682-2992   SIC 1021

COPPER TERRACE LIMITED p 542
91 TECUMSEH RD, CHATHAM, ON, N7M 1B3
(519) 354-5442   SIC 8051

COPPER TERRACE LONG TERM CARE p 542
See COPPER TERRACE LIMITED

COPPERLEAF TECHNOLOGIES INC p 286
2920 VIRTUAL WAY SUITE 140, VANCOUVER, BC, V5M 0C4
(604) 639-9700   SIC 7371

COPPERLINE EXCAVATING LTD p 164
375 SASKATCHEWAN AVE, SPRUCE GROVE, AB, T7X 3A1
(780) 968-3805   SIC 1796

COPPLEY LTD p 613
56 YORK BLVD, HAMILTON, ON, L8R 0A2
(905) 529-1112   SIC 5136

COPYRIGHTER p 1208
See ROBIC, S.E.N.C.R.L.

COQUITLAM CHRYSLER p 199
See COQUITLAM CHRYSLER DODGE JEEP LTD

COQUITLAM CHRYSLER DODGE JEEP LTD p 199
2960 CHRISTMAS WAY, COQUITLAM, BC, V3C 4E6
(604) 464-6611   SIC 5511

COQUITLAM CRUISESHIPCENTERS p 200
1021 AUSTIN AVE, COQUITLAM, BC, V3K 3N9
(604) 937-7125   SIC 4724

COQUITLAM SUPERMARKETS LTD p 198
1163 PINETREE WAY SUITE 1056, COQUITLAM, BC, V3B 8A9
(604) 552-6108   SIC 5411

COQUITLAM, CITY OF p 200
1120 BRUNETTE AVE, COQUITLAM, BC, V3K 1G2
(604) 664-1636   SIC 8299

CORA FRANCHISE GROUP INC, THE p 685
2798 THAMESGATE DR UNIT 1, MISSISSAUGA, ON, L4T 4E8
(905) 673-2672   SIC 6794

CORAL BEACH FARMS LTD p 224
16351 CARRS LANDING RD, LAKE COUNTRY, BC, V4V 1A9
(250) 766-5393   SIC 2035

CORAL CANADA WIDE LTD p 8
2150 29 ST NE UNIT 30, CALGARY, AB, T1Y 7G4
(403) 571-9200   SIC 1711

CORAL ENERGY p 665
30 AVONDALE CRES, MARKHAM, ON, L3P 2K1

SIC 4925

CORAL GOLD RESOURCES LTD p 303
570 GRANVILLE ST SUITE 900, VANCOUVER, BC, V6C 3P1
(604) 682-3701   SIC 1081

CORAL OILFIELD SERVICES INC p 134
15303 94 ST SUITE 15303, GRANDE PRAIRIE, AB, T8X 0L2
(780) 402-9800   SIC 1389

CORAM CONSTRUCTION p 112
See 511670 ALBERTA LTD

CORAM CONSTRUCTION p 1419
See 511670 ALBERTA LTD

CORBEC INC p 1126
1 RUE PROVOST BUREAU 201, LACHINE, QC, H8S 4H2
(514) 364-4000   SIC 3399

CORBEILLE - BORDEAUX - CARTIERVILLE, LA p 1224
5080 RUE DUDEMAINE, MONTREAL, QC, H4J 1N6
(514) 856-0838   SIC 8999

CORBETT CREEK W C P C P p 1013
See CORBETT CREEK WATER POLLUTION CONTROL PLANT

CORBETT CREEK WATER POLLUTION CONTROL PLANT p 1013
2400 FORBES ST, WHITBY, ON, L1N 8M3
(905) 576-9844   SIC 5084

CORBETT OFFICE EQUIPMENT LTD p 331
3306 30 AVE, VERNON, BC, V1T 2C8
(250) 549-2236   SIC 5044

CORBETT'S SKIS & SNOWBOARDS INC p 803
2278 SPEERS RD, OAKVILLE, ON, L6L 2X8
(905) 338-7713   SIC 5941

CORBY SPIRIT AND WINE LIMITED p 979
225 KING ST W SUITE 1100, TORONTO, ON, M5V 3M2
(416) 479-2400   SIC 2085

CORDEE PLEIN AIR INC, LA p 1086
2777 BOUL SAINT-MARTIN O, COTE SAINT-LUC, QC, H7T 2Y7
(514) 524-1326   SIC 5941

CORDEE PLEIN AIR INC, LA p 1174
2159 RUE SAINTE-CATHERINE E, MONTREAL, QC, H2K 2H9
(514) 524-1326   SIC 5941

CORDOVA BAY GOLF COURSE LTD p 338
5333 CORDOVA BAY RD, VICTORIA, BC, V8Y 2L3
(250) 658-4445   SIC 7992

CORDY OILFIELD SERVICES INC p 15
5366 55 ST SE, CALGARY, AB, T2C 3G9
(403) 262-7667   SIC 1382

CORE ARCHITECTS INC p 933
130 QUEENS QUAY E SUITE 700, TORONTO, ON, M5A 0P6
(416) 343-0400   SIC 8712

CORE ENERGY RECOVERY SOLUTIONS INC p 285
1455 GEORGIA ST E, VANCOUVER, BC, V5L 2A9
(604) 488-1132   SIC 8731

CORE GEOLOGY BUILDING p 20
See AGAT LABORATORIES LTD

CORE GOLD INC p 312
1166 ALBERNI ST SUITE 1201, VANCOUVER, BC, V6E 3Z3
(604) 345-4822   SIC 1041

CORE INSURANCE CLAIMS CONTRACTING INC p 792
94 KENHAR DR UNIT 10, NORTH YORK, ON, M9L 1N2
(416) 740-9400   SIC 6411

CORE LABORATORIES CANADA LTD p 22
2810 12 ST NE, CALGARY, AB, T2E 7P7
(403) 250-4000   SIC 8734

CORE LABORATORIES CANADA LTD p 158
39139 HIGHWAY 2A UNIT 5409, RED DEER COUNTY, AB, T4S 2A8
(403) 340-1017   SIC 1389

CORE LOGISTICS p 687
See AIRLINE EXPRESS SERVICES INC
CORE LOGISTICS INTERNATIONAL INC p 687
3133 ORLANDO DR, MISSISSAUGA, ON, L4V 1C5
(905) 670-2000 *SIC 4581*
CORE SECURITY p 274
See CORE SECURITY GROUP INC
CORE SECURITY GROUP INC p 274
13456 108 AVE, SURREY, BC, V3T 2K1
(604) 583-2673 *SIC 7381*
CORE(CLIENT ONGOING REHABILITATION AND EQUALITY) ASSOCIATION p 145
412 3 ST SE, MEDICINE HAT, AB, T1A 0H1
(403) 527-3302 *SIC 8322*
COREIO INC p 1030
55 DIRECTOR CRT, WOODBRIDGE, ON, L4L 4S5
(905) 264-8520 *SIC 5045*
COREL COMPUTER p 828
See COREL CORPORATION
COREL CORPORATION p 828
1600 CARLING AVE SUITE 100, OTTAWA, ON, K1Z 8R7
(613) 728-8200 *SIC 7371*
COREM p 1263
1180 RUE DE LA MINERALOGIE, QUEBEC, QC, G1N 1X7
(418) 527-8211 *SIC 8732*
CORES WORLDWIDE INCORPORATED p 440
674 HIGHWAY 214, BELNAN, NS, B2S 2N2
(902) 883-1611 *SIC 5084*
CORESLAB INTERNATIONAL INC p 891
332 JONES RD SUITE 8, STONEY CREEK, ON, L8E 5N2
(905) 643-0220 *SIC 6712*
CORESLAB STRUCTURES (ONT) INC p 566
205 CORESLAB DR, DUNDAS, ON, L9H 0B3
(905) 689-3993 *SIC 3272*
COREWORX INC p 639
22 FREDERICK ST SUITE 800, KITCHENER, ON, N2H 6M6
(519) 772-3181 *SIC 5045*
COREY CRAIG LTD p 406
713 MAIN ST, MONCTON, NB, E1C 1E3
(506) 856-8050 *SIC 5812*
COREY FEED MILLS p 402
See COREY NUTRITION COMPANY INC
COREY FORD LTD p 420
336 CONNELL ST, WOODSTOCK, NB, E7M 5E2
(506) 328-8828 *SIC 5511*
COREY NUTRITION COMPANY INC p 402
136 HODGSON RD, FREDERICTON, NB, E3C 2G4
(506) 444-7744 *SIC 2048*
COREYDALE CONTRACTING CO p 501
See CLIPPER CONSTRUCTION LIMITED
CORIL HOLDINGS LTD p 29
1100 1 ST SE SUITE 600, CALGARY, AB, T2G 1B1
(403) 231-7700 *SIC 6719*
CORINEX COMMUNICATION p 312
See CORINEX COMMUNICATIONS CORP
CORINEX COMMUNICATIONS CORP p 312
1090 PENDER ST W SUITE 1000, VANCOUVER, BC, V6E 2N7
(604) 692-0520 *SIC 3669*
CORINTHIAN DISTRIBUTORS LTD p 192
8118 NORTH FRASER WAY UNIT 1, BURNABY, BC, V5J 0E5
(604) 431-5058 *SIC 5141*
CORITY p 928
See CORITY SOFTWARE INC
CORITY SOFTWARE INC p 928
250 BLOOR ST E 1ST FL, TORONTO, ON, M4W 1E6
(416) 863-6800 *SIC 7371*
CORIX CONTROL SOLUTIONS LIMITED

PARTNERSHIP p 113
8803 58 AVE NW, EDMONTON, AB, T6E 5X1
(780) 468-6950 *SIC 1389*
CORIX GROUP OF COMPANIES p 312
See CORIX INFRASTRUCTURE INC
CORIX INFRASTRUCTURE INC p 312
1188 GEORGIA ST W SUITE 1160, VANCOUVER, BC, V6E 4A2
(604) 697-6700 *SIC 6712*
CORIX UTILITIES INC p 312
1188 GEORGIA ST W SUITE 1160, VANCOUVER, BC, V6E 4A2
(604) 697-6700 *SIC 1623*
CORIX WATER SYSTEMS INC p 254
1128 BURDETTE ST, RICHMOND, BC, V6V 2Z3
(604) 273-4987 *SIC 3589*
CORLIVING DISTRIBUTION LTD p 279
2252 190 ST, SURREY, BC, V3Z 3W7
(604) 542-7650 *SIC 5021*
CORMA INC p 551
10 MCCLEARY CRT, CONCORD, ON, L4K 2Z3
(905) 669-9397 *SIC 3559*
CORMARK SECURITIES (USA) LIMITED p 961
220 BAY ST SUITE 2800, TORONTO, ON, M5J 2W4
(416) 362-7485 *SIC 6211*
CORMARK SECURITIES INC p 961
200 BAY ST S SUITE 2800, TORONTO, ON, M5J 2J2
(416) 362-7485 *SIC 6211*
CORMER AEROSPACE p 372
See CORMER GROUP INDUSTRIES INC
CORMER GROUP INDUSTRIES INC p 372
33 BENTALL ST, WINNIPEG, MB, R2X 2Z7
(204) 987-6400 *SIC 3728*
CORMODE & DICKSON CONSTRUCTION (1983) LTD p 95
11450 160 ST NW UNIT 200, EDMONTON, AB, T5M 3Y7
(780) 701-9300 *SIC 1541*
CORNEAU CANTIN LEBOURGNEUF p 1078
See 9142-5454 QUEBEC INC
CORNELIUS p 1153
See TREVI FABRICATION INC
CORNELL CONSTRUCTION LIMITED p 517
410 HARDY RD, BRANTFORD, ON, N3T 5L8
(519) 753-3125 *SIC 1611*
CORNELL INSURANCE BROKERS LTD p 668
275 RENFREW DR SUITE 208, MARKHAM, ON, L3R 0C8
(905) 471-3868 *SIC 6411*
CORNER BROOK PULP AND PAPER LIMITED p 422
1 MILLS RD, CORNER BROOK, NL, A2H 6B9
(709) 637-3104 *SIC 2621*
CORNERSTONE BUILDERS LTD p 491
195 BELLEVUE DR, BELLEVILLE, ON, K8N 4Z5
(613) 968-3501 *SIC 1542*
CORNERSTONE CO-OPERATIVE p 165
5017 42 ST SUITE 3, ST PAUL, AB, T0A 3A2
(780) 645-3351 *SIC 5411*
CORNERSTONE COURIER INC p 637
219 SHOEMAKER ST, KITCHENER, ON, N2E 3B3
(519) 741-0446 *SIC 7389*
CORNERSTONE GROUP OF COMPANIES LIMITED p 923
20 EGLINTON AVE W 4TH FLOOR, TORONTO, ON, M4R 1K8
(416) 932-9555 *SIC 8742*
CORNERSTONE INSURANCE BROKERS LTD p 1030
8001 WESTON RD SUITE 300, WOODBRIDGE, ON, L4L 9C8

(905) 856-1981 *SIC 6411*
CORNERSTONE LOGISTICS LP p 797
2180 BUCKINGHAM RD SUITE 204, OAKVILLE, ON, L6H 6H1
(905) 339-1456 *SIC 4731*
CORNERSTONE SOBEYS p 146
See 783814 ALBERTA LTD
CORNERSTONE STRUCTRUAL RESTORATION INC p 639
85 EDWIN ST, KITCHENER, ON, N2H 4N7
(519) 745-8121 *SIC 1542*
CORNIES FARMS LTD p 633
1545 KRATZ RD, KINGSVILLE, ON, N9Y 3K4
(519) 733-5416 *SIC 0191*
CORNWALL COMMUNITY HOSPITAL p 562
840 MCCONNELL AVE, CORNWALL, ON, K6H 5S5
(613) 938-4240 *SIC 8062*
CORNWALL ELECTRIC p 562
See CORNWALL STREET RAILWAY LIGHT AND POWER COMPANY LIMITED
CORNWALL FRUIT p 562
See CORNWALL FRUIT SUPPLY LIMITED
CORNWALL FRUIT SUPPLY LIMITED p 562
1424 LASCELLE AVE, CORNWALL, ON, K6H 3L2
SIC 5141
CORNWALL GRAVEL COMPANY LTD p 563
390 ELEVENTH ST W, CORNWALL, ON, K6J 3B2
(613) 932-6571 *SIC 1611*
CORNWALL IRVING 24 & MAINWAY CENTRE p 563
3250 BROOKDALE AVE, CORNWALL, ON, K6K 1W3
(613) 933-5668 *SIC 5983*
CORNWALL NISSAN p 562
See 1497665 ONTARIO INC
CORNWALL STREET RAILWAY LIGHT AND POWER COMPANY LIMITED p 562
1001 SYDNEY ST, CORNWALL, ON, K6H 3K1
(613) 932-0123 *SIC 4911*
CORNWALLIS CHEVROLET BUICK GMC LIMITED p 463
9184 COMMERCIAL ST, NEW MINAS, NS, B4N 3E5
(902) 681-8300 *SIC 5511*
CORO MINING CORP p 303
625 HOWE ST SUITE 1280, VANCOUVER, BC, V6C 2T6
(604) 682-5546 *SIC 1021*
CORONA COMPANY p 995
See CORONA JEWELLERY COMPANY LTD
CORONA JEWELLERY COMPANY LTD p 995
16 RIPLEY AVE, TORONTO, ON, M6S 3P1
(416) 762-2222 *SIC 3911*
CORONACH CO-OPERATIVE ASSOCIATION LIMITED, THE p 1405
112 CENTRE ST, CORONACH, SK, S0H 0Z0
(306) 267-2010 *SIC 5171*
CORONADO CONTRACTING CORP p 88
TH PO BOX 17 STN MAIN, EDMONTON, AB, T5J 2G9
(780) 449-1654 *SIC 1611*
CORONET WALLPAPERS (ONTARIO) LIMITED p 583
88 RONSON DR, ETOBICOKE, ON, M9W 1B9
(416) 245-2900 *SIC 5198*
COROPLAST DIV p 305
See GREAT PACIFIC ENTERPRISES INC
COROPLAST DIV p 1111
See GREAT PACIFIC ENTERPRISES INC
CORPA HOLDINGS INC p 521
2000 APPLEBY LINE SUITE G3, BURLINGTON, ON, L7L 7H7

(905) 331-1333 *SIC 8741*
CORPORATE ASSETS INC p 996
373 MUNSTER AVE, TORONTO, ON, M8Z 3C8
(416) 962-9600 *SIC 7389*
CORPORATE CLASSICS CATERERS p 241
See TEJAZZ MANAGEMENT SERVICES INC
CORPORATE CLEANING SERVICES LTD p 231
20285 STEWART CRES SUITE 402, MAPLE RIDGE, BC, V2X 8G1
(604) 465-4699 *SIC 7217*
CORPORATE CONTRACTING SERVICES LTD p 473
575 WESTNEY RD S, AJAX, ON, L1S 4N7
(416) 291-8644 *SIC 1542*
CORPCRATE COURIERS LOGISTICS ULC p 290
8350 PRINCE EDWARD ST, VANCOUVER, BC, V5X 3R9
SIC 7389
CORPORATE ELECTRIC LIMITED p 289
2233 QUEBEC ST, VANCOUVER, BC, V5T 3A1
(604) 879-0551 *SIC 1731*
CORPORATE IMAGES p 279
See CORLIVING DISTRIBUTION LTD
CORPORATE INVESTIGATIVE SERVICES LTD p 650
544 EGERTON ST, LONDON, ON, N5W 3Z8
(519) 652-2163 *SIC 7381*
CORPORATE MANAGEMENT p 138
See GOVERNMENT OF THE PROVINCE OF ALBERTA
CORPORATE SECURITY SUPPLY LTD p 384
891 CENTURY ST SUITE A, WINNIPEG, MB, R3H 0M3
(204) 989-1000 *SIC 5099*
CORPORATE TRAVEL MANAGEMENT SOLUTIONS INC p 781
5000 DUFFERIN ST SUITE 219B, NORTH YORK, ON, M3H 5T5
(416) 665-2867 *SIC 4724*
CORPORATIF RENAUD INC p 1314
3445 BOUL LAFRAMBOISE, SAINT-HYACINTHE, QC, J4T 2G1
(450) 462-9991 *SIC 5521*
CORPORATION A.U.B. INC p 1236
1605 BOUL LE CORBUSIER, MONTREAL, QC, H7S 1Z3
(450) 681-3317 *SIC 5651*
CORPORATION ABBVIE p 1333
8401 RTE TRANSCANADIENNE, SAINT-LAURENT, QC, H4S 1Z1
(514) 906-9700 *SIC 2834*
CORPORATION ADFAST p 1333
2685 RUE DIAB, SAINT-LAURENT, QC, H4S 1E7
(514) 337-7307 *SIC 6712*
CORPORATION ALLIANCE DYNAMIQUE p 1086
3065 BOUL LE CARREFOUR, COTE SAINT-LUC, QC, H7T 1C7
(450) 688-0688 *SIC 5251*
CORPORATION ANRAD p 1328
See ANALOGIC CANADA CORPORATION
CORPORATION ARCHIEPISCOPALE CATHOLIQUE ROMAINE DE MONTREAL, LA p 1215
2000 RUE SHERBROOKE O, MONTREAL, QC, H3H 1G4
(514) 931-7311 *SIC 8661*
CORPORATION ASICS CANADA p 1370
101 RUE DES ABENAQUIS BUREAU 201, SHERBROOKE, QC, J1H 1H1
(819) 566-8866 *SIC 5139*
CORPORATION AURIFERE MONARQUES p 1352
68 AV DE LA GARE UNITE 205, SAINT-SAUVEUR, QC, J0R 1R0

(819) 736-4581   SIC 1081

CORPORATION BIONETIX INTERNA-TIONAL p
1355

21040 RUE DAOUST, SAINTE-ANNE-DE-BELLEVUE, QC, H9X 4C7

(514) 457-2914   SIC 5122

CORPORATION BNP PARIBAS CANADA p
1194

1981 AV MCGILL COLLEGE BUREAU 515, MONTREAL, QC, H3A 2W8

(514) 285-6000   SIC 6021

CORPORATION CHAMPION PIPE LINE LIMITEE p 1174

1717 RUE DU HAVRE, MONTREAL, QC, H2K 2X3

(514) 598-3444   SIC 4922

CORPORATION COMMERCIALE CRES-CENT p
1156

5430 AV ROYALMOUNT, MONT-ROYAL, QC, H4P 1H7

(514) 739-3355   SIC 7389

CORPORATION COMPAGNONS DE MON-TREAL p
1168

2602 BEAUBIEN E, MONTREAL, QC, H1Y 1G5

(514) 727-4444   SIC 8399

CORPORATION COMPUWARE DU CANADA p 1187

500 PLACE D'ARMES BUREAU 1800, MONTREAL, QC, H2Y 2W2

(438) 259-3300   SIC 5045

CORPORATION CONS p 1344

See CONSCORP INC

CORPORATION COPNICK, LA p 1222

6198 RUE NOTRE-DAME O, MONTREAL, QC, H4C 1V4

(514) 937-9306   SIC 5093

CORPORATION CULTURELLE DE SHAW-INIGAN p
1368

2100 BOUL DES HETRES, SHAWINIGAN, QC, G9N 8R8

(819) 539-1888   SIC 8699

CORPORATION D'ACIER ALLIANCE, LA p
1083

1060 BOUL DES LAURENTIDES, COTE SAINT-LUC, QC, H7G 2W1

(514) 382-5780   SIC 5051

CORPORATION D'ACQUISITION ROLL p
1322

See ROCTEST LTEE

CORPORATION D'ECLAIRAGE GREEN-LITE, LA p
1249

115 BOUL BRUNSWICK BUREAU 102, POINTE-CLAIRE, QC, H9R 5N2

(514) 695-9090   SIC 5063

CORPORATION D'HABITATION JEANNE-MANCE, LA p
1185

150 RUE ONTARIO E BUREAU 1, MON-TREAL, QC, H2X 1H1

(514) 872-1221   SIC 7389

CORPORATION D'OR INTEGRA p 314

See INTEGRA GOLD CORP

CORPORATION DE CEGEP ANDRE-LAURENDEAU p
1130

1111 RUE LAPIERRE BUREAU 300, LASALLE, QC, H8N 2J4

(514) 364-3320   SIC 8221

CORPORATION DE DEVELOPPEMENT CULTUREL DE TROIS-RIVIERES p
1387

1425 PLACE DE L'HOTEL-DE-VILLE, TROIS-RIVIERES, QC, G9A 4S7

(819) 372-4614   SIC 6531

CORPORATION DE DEVELOPPEMENT CUIRS BENTLEY INC, LA p 1143

375 BOUL ROLAND-THERRIEN BUREAU 210, LONGUEUIL, QC, J4H 4A6

(450) 651-5000   SIC 6712

CORPORATION DE FESTIVAL DE MONTGOLFIERES DE SAINT-JEAN-SUR-RICHELIEU INC p
1317

5 CH DE L'AEROPORT, SAINT-JEAN-SUR-RICHELIEU, QC, J3B 7B5

(450) 346-6000   SIC 7999

CORPORATION DE GESTION E.A. MI-CHOT, LA p
1221

5038 RUE SHERBROOKE O, MONTREAL, QC, H4A 1S7

(514) 484-3531   SIC 5912

CORPORATION DE GESTION POSITRON CANADA p 1227

5101 RUE BUCHAN SUITE 220, MON-TREAL, QC, H4P 2R9

(514) 345-2220   SIC 6712

CORPORATION DE L'ECOLE DES HAUTES ETUDES COMMERCIALES DE MONTREAL p 1219

3000 CH DE LA COTE-SAINTE-CATHERINE, MONTREAL, QC, H3T 2A7

(514) 340-6000   SIC 8221

CORPORATION DE L'ECOLE POLYTECH-NIQUE DE MONTREAL p
1219

2900 BOUL EDOUARD-MONTPETIT, MON-TREAL, QC, H3T 1J4

(514) 340-4711   SIC 8221

CORPORATION DE LA SALLE ALBERT-ROUSSEAU, LA p
1272

2410 CH SAINTE-FOY, QUEBEC, QC, G1V 1T3

(418) 659-6629   SIC 6512

CORPORATION DE SECURITE GARDA CANADA p 88

10250 101 ST NW SUITE 1010, EDMON-TON, AB, T5J 3P4

(780) 425-5000   SIC 7381

CORPORATION DE SECURITE GARDA CANADA p 128

8600 FRANKLIN AVE SUITE 606, FORT MCMURRAY, AB, T9H 4G8

(780) 791-7087   SIC 6289

CORPORATION DE SECURITE GARDA CANADA p 703

2345 STANFIELD RD UNIT 400, MISSIS-SAUGA, ON, L4Y 3Y3

(416) 915-9500   SIC 7349

CORPORATION DE SECURITE GARDA WORLD p 1210

1390 RUE BARRE, MONTREAL, QC, H3C 5X9

(514) 281-2811   SIC 7381

CORPORATION DE SECURITE GARDA WORLD p 1426

316 2ND AVE N, SASKATOON, SK, S7K 2B9

(306) 242-3330   SIC 7381

CORPORATION DE SERVICE DE LA CHAMBRE DES NOTAIRES DU QUEBEC, LA p 1194

1801 AV MCGILL COLLEGE BUREAU 600, MONTREAL, QC, H3A 0A7

(514) 879-1793   SIC 8621

CORPORATION DE SERVICE DES NO-TAIRES DU QUEBEC p
1194

See CORPORATION DE SERVICE DE LA CHAMBRE DES NOTAIRES DU QUEBEC, LA

CORPORATION DE SOINS DE LA SANTE HOSPIRA p
1118

17300 RTE TRANSCANADIENNE, KIRK-LAND, QC, H9J 2M5

(514) 695-0500   SIC 6712

CORPORATION DE VALVES TRUELINE, LA p 1355

20675 BOUL INDUSTRIEL, SAINTE-ANNE-DE-BELLEVUE, QC, H9X 4B2

(514) 457-5777   SIC 5085

CORPORATION DES ALIMENTS I-D p 1237

1800 SUD LAVAL (A-440) O, MONTREAL, QC, H7S 2E7

(450) 687-2680   SIC 5141

CORPORATION DES HOTELS INTER-CONTINENTAL (MONTREAL), LA p
1187

360 RUE SAINT-ANTOINE O, MONTREAL, QC, H2Y 3X4

(514) 987-9900   SIC 7011

CORPORATION DES MAITRES MECANI-CIENS EN TUYAUTERIE DU QUEBEC p
1180

8175 BOUL SAINT-LAURENT, MONTREAL, QC, H2P 2M1

(514) 382-2668   SIC 8621

CORPORATION DES PILOTES DU BAS SAINT-LAURENT INC p 1258

240 RUE DALHOUSIE, QUEBEC, QC, G1K 8M8

(418) 692-0444   SIC 4499

CORPORATION DES PILOTES DU SAINT-LAURENT CENTRAL INC p
1387

1350 RUE ROYALE BUREAU 800, TROIS-RIVIERES, QC, G9A 4J4

(819) 379-8882   SIC 4499

CORPORATION DU CENTRE DU SABLON INC p 1237

755 CH DU SABLON, MONTREAL, QC, H7W 4H5

(450) 688-8961   SIC 8322

CORPORATION DU COLLEGE DE L'ASSOMPTION, LA p 1120

270 BOUL DE L'ANGE-GARDIEN, L'ASSOMPTION, QC, J5W 1R7

(450) 589-5621   SIC 8221

CORPORATION DU FORT ST-JEAN p 1317

15 RUE JACQUES-CARTIER N, SAINT-JEAN-SUR-RICHELIEU, QC, J3B 8R8

(450) 358-6900   SIC 6531

CORPORATION DU PARC REGIONAL DE VAL-JALBERT p 1075

95 RUE SAINT-GEORGES, CHAMBORD, QC, G0W 1G0

(418) 275-3132   SIC 8412

CORPORATION DU THEATRE L'ETOILE p
1070

6000 BOUL DE ROME BUREAU 240, BROSSARD, QC, J4Y 0B6

(450) 676-1030   SIC 6512

CORPORATION EFUNDRAISING.COM INC p 1210

33 RUE PRINCE BUREAU 200, MON-TREAL, QC, H3C 2M7

SIC 7389

CORPORATION EPIDERMA INC p 1272

2590 BOUL LAURIER BUREAU 330, QUE-BEC, QC, G1V 4M6

(418) 651-8678   SIC 7231

CORPORATION FINANCIERE BROME INC p 1194

550 RUE SHERBROOKE O BUREAU 700, MONTREAL, QC, H3A 1B9

(514) 842-2975   SIC 6351

CORPORATION FINANCIERE J. DE-SCHAMPS INC p
1255

755 BOUL DES CHUTES, QUEBEC, QC, G1E 2C2

(418) 667-3322   SIC 6712

CORPORATION FINANCIERE QUEBE-COISE INC p
1055

500 BOUL DU BEAU-PRE, BEAUPRE, QC, G0A 1E0

(418) 827-5211   SIC 6712

CORPORATION FINANCIERE THINKING CAPITAL p
1220

4200 BOUL DORCHESTER O BUREAU 300, MONTREAL, QC, H3Z 1V2

(866) 889-9412   SIC 6211

CORPORATION GARDAWORLD SER-VICES TRANSPORT DE VALEURS CANADA p 1248

1390 RUE BARRE, POINTE-AUX-TREMBLES, QC, H3C 5X9

(514) 281-2811   SIC 6211

CORPORATION GROUPE PHARMESSOR p
1346

5000 BOUL METROPOLITAIN E, SAINT-LEONARD, QC, H1S 3G7

(514) 725-1212   SIC 5122

CORPORATION HAGGAR CANADA p 783

See HAGGAR CANADA CO.

CORPORATION INTERACTIVE EIDOS p
1194

400 BOUL DE MAISONNEUVE O 6E ETAGE, MONTREAL, QC, H3A 1L4

(514) 670-6300   SIC 7371

CORPORATION INTERNATIONAL BROTHER (CANADA) LTEE, LA p 1091

1 RUE HOTEL-DE-VILLE, DOLLARD-DES-ORMEAUX, QC, H9B 3H6

(514) 685-0600   SIC 5084

CORPORATION INTERNATIONALE MA-SONITE p
1194

1501 AV MCGILL COLLEGE SUITE 26E, MONTREAL, QC, H3A 3N9

(514) 841-6400   SIC 2431

CORPORATION LEEDS GRENVILLE & LA-NARK DISTRICT HEALTH UNIT, THE p
519

458 LAURIER BLVD SUITE 200, BROCKVILLE, ON, K6V 7K5

(613) 345-5685   SIC 8399

CORPORATION MAGIL CONSTRUCTION p
1225

1655 RUE DE BEAUHARNOIS O BUREAU 16, MONTREAL, QC, H4N 1J6

(514) 341-9899   SIC 8741

CORPORATION MAURICE-RATTE p 1397

905 BOUL DES BOIS-FRANCS S, VICTO-RIAVILLE, QC, G6P 5W1

(819) 357-8217   SIC 8661

CORPORATION MCKESSON CANADA, LA p 100

10931 177 ST NW, EDMONTON, AB, T5S 1P6

(780) 486-8700   SIC 5122

CORPORATION MCKESSON CANADA, LA p 200

71 GLACIER ST, COQUITLAM, BC, V3K 5Z1

(604) 942-7111   SIC 5122

CORPORATION MCKESSON CANADA, LA p 687

6355 VISCOUNT RD, MISSISSAUGA, ON, L4V 1W2

(905) 671-4586   SIC 5122

CORPORATION MCKESSON CANADA, LA p 1098

650 RUE BERGERON, DRUMMONDVILLE, QC, J2C 0E2

(819) 850-5400   SIC 5122

CORPORATION MCKESSON CANADA, LA p 1169

8290 BOUL PIE-IX BUREAU 1, MON-TREAL, QC, H1Z 4E8

(514) 593-4531   SIC 5122

CORPORATION MCKESSON CANADA, LA p 1276

2655 RUE DE CELLES, QUEBEC, QC, G2C 1K7

(418) 845-3061   SIC 5122

CORPORATION MCKESSON CANADA, LA p 1328

4705 RUE DOBRIN, SAINT-LAURENT, QC, H4R 2P7

(514) 745-2100   SIC 5122

CORPORATION MICRO BIRD INC p 1100

3000 RUE GIRARDIN, DRUMMONDVILLE, QC, J2E 0A1

(819) 477-8222   SIC 3713

CORPORATION MODASUITE p 1183

See MODASUITE INC

CORPORATION MORGUARD p 709

55 CITY CENTRE DR SUITE 800, MISSIS-

SAUGA, ON, L5B 1M3
(905) 281-3800   *SIC* 6531

CORPORATION MORGUARD   *p* 824
350 SPARKS ST SUITE 402, OTTAWA, ON,
K1R 7S8
(613) 237-6373   *SIC* 6519

CORPORATION MULTI-COLOR MON-
TREAL CANADA   *p*
1127
1925 32E AV, LACHINE, QC, H8T 3J1
(514) 341-4850   *SIC* 2752

CORPORATION NOTRE-DAME DE BON-
SECOURS, LA   *p*
1270
990 RUE GERARD-MORISSET, QUEBEC,
QC, G1S 1X6
(418) 681-4637   *SIC* 8361

CORPORATION OF COUNCIL OF MINIS-
TERS OF EDUCATION CANADA, THE   *p*
926
95 ST CLAIR AVE W SUITE 1106,
TORONTO, ON, M4V 1N6
(416) 962-8100   *SIC* 8621

CORPORATION OF DELTA, THE   *p* 207
See CITY OF DELTA

CORPORATION OF HALDIMAND COUNTY,
THE   *p* 567
657 LOCK ST W SUITE A, DUNNVILLE,
ON, N1A 1V9
(800) 265-2818   *SIC* 8361

CORPORATION OF MASSEY HALL AND
ROY THOMSON HALL, THE   *p* 961
60 SIMCOE ST, TORONTO, ON, M5J 2H5
(416) 593-4822   *SIC* 6512

CORPORATION OF NORFOLK COUNTY   *p*
880
44 ROB BLAKE WAY, SIMCOE, ON, N3Y
0E3
(519) 426-0902   *SIC* 8051

CORPORATION OF THE CITY OF BRAMP-
TON, THE   *p*
508
340 VODDEN ST E, BRAMPTON, ON, L6V
2N2
(905) 874-2814   *SIC* 7999

CORPORATION OF THE CITY OF BRAMP-
TON, THE   *p*
509
8 RUTHERFORD RD S, BRAMPTON, ON,
L6W 3J1
(905) 874-2700   *SIC* 7389

CORPORATION OF THE CITY OF
BURLINGTON   *p* 527
3330 HARVESTER RD, BURLINGTON, ON,
L7N 3M8
(905) 333-6166   *SIC* 7349

CORPORATION OF THE CITY OF CAM-
BRIDGE, THE   *p*
533
1625 BISHOP ST N, CAMBRIDGE, ON,
N1R 7J4
(519) 621-6001   *SIC* 7389

CORPORATION OF THE CITY OF COURTE-
NAY, THE   *p*
203
489 OLD ISLAND HWY, COURTENAY, BC,
V9N 3P5
(250) 338-5371   *SIC* 7999

CORPORATION OF THE CITY OF FREDER-
ICTON   *p*
400
520 YORK ST, FREDERICTON, NB, E3B
3R2
(506) 460-2020   *SIC* 1389

CORPORATION OF THE CITY OF
KAWARTHA LAKES, THE   *p* 645
220 ANGELINE ST S, LINDSAY, ON, K9V
0J8
(705) 324-3558   *SIC* 8361

CORPORATION OF THE CITY OF
KAWARTHA LAKES, THE   *p* 645
9 CAMBRIDGE ST N, LINDSAY, ON, K9V
4C4
(705) 324-5731   *SIC* 7389

CORPORATION OF THE CITY OF
KINGSTON, THE   *p* 630
175 RIDEAU ST SUITE 416, KINGSTON,
ON, K7K 3H6
(613) 530-2818   *SIC* 8361

CORPORATION OF THE CITY OF
KINGSTON, THE   *p* 632
1114 LEN BIRCHALL WAY, KINGSTON,
ON, K7M 9A1
(613) 389-6404   *SIC* 4581

CORPORATION OF THE CITY OF KITCH-
ENER   *p*
638
200 KING ST W, KITCHENER, ON, N2G
4V6
(519) 741-2345   *SIC* 1611

CORPORATION OF THE CITY OF KITCH-
ENER   *p*
639
350 MARGARET AVE, KITCHENER, ON,
N2H 4J8
(519) 741-2502   *SIC* 8322

CORPORATION OF THE CITY OF NEW
WESTMINSTER   *p* 236
1 SIXTH AVE E, NEW WESTMINSTER, BC,
V3L 4G6
(604) 519-1000   *SIC* 7389

CORPORATION OF THE CITY OF NEW
WESTMINSTER   *p* 236
65 SIXTH AVE E, NEW WESTMINSTER,
BC, V3L 4G6
(604) 526-4281   *SIC* 7999

CORPORATION OF THE CITY OF NORTH
BAY, THE   *p* 763
119 PRINCESS ST W, NORTH BAY, ON,
P1B 6C2
(705) 474-5662   *SIC* 7389

CORPORATION OF THE CITY OF OSHAWA
p 813
199 ADELAIDE AVE W, OSHAWA, ON, L1J
7B1
(905) 433-1239   *SIC* 7389

CORPORATION OF THE CITY OF PETER-
BOROUGH, THE   *p*
840
151 LANSDOWNE ST W, PETERBOR-
OUGH, ON, K9J 1Y4
(705) 743-3561   *SIC* 8322

CORPORATION OF THE CITY OF SAULT
STE MARIE, THE   *p* 861
269 QUEEN ST E, SAULT STE. MARIE, ON,
P6A 1Y9
(705) 759-5251   *SIC* 7389

CORPORATION OF THE CITY OF THUN-
DER BAY, THE   *p*
907
523 ALGOMA ST N, THUNDER BAY, ON,
P7A 5C2
SIC 8361

CORPORATION OF THE CITY OF THUN-
DER BAY, THE   *p*
908
1046 LITHIUM DR, THUNDER BAY, ON,
P7B 6G3
(807) 623-4400   *SIC* 4899

CORPORATION OF THE CITY OF
TORONTO   *p* 578
400 THE WEST MALL, ETOBICOKE, ON,
M9C 5S1
(416) 394-3600   *SIC* 8051

CORPORATION OF THE CITY OF
VAUGHAN, THE   *p* 1030
9201 ISLINGTON AVE, WOODBRIDGE,
ON, L4L 1A6
(905) 832-8564   *SIC* 8322

CORPORATION OF THE CITY OF WATER-
LOO, THE   *p*
1007
265 LEXINGTON CRT, WATERLOO, ON,
N2K 1W9
(519) 886-2310   *SIC* 7389

CORPORATION OF THE CITY OF WATER-
LOO, THE   *p*
1008

101 FATHER DAVID BAUER DR, WATER-
LOO, ON, N2L 0B4
(519) 886-1177   *SIC* 7299

CORPORATION OF THE CITY OF WIND-
SOR   *p*
1019
3540 NORTH SERVICE RD E, WINDSOR,
ON, N8W 5X2
(519) 974-2277   *SIC* 4959

CORPORATION OF THE CITY OF WIND-
SOR   *p*
1023
815 GOYEAU ST, WINDSOR, ON, N9A 1H7
(519) 253-6573   *SIC* 7389

CORPORATION OF THE CITY OF WIND-
SOR   *p*
1025
1881 CABANA RD W, WINDSOR, ON, N9G
1C7
(519) 253-6060   *SIC* 8361

CORPORATION OF THE COUNTY OF
BRUCE, THE   *p* 1016
671 FRANK ST, WIARTON, ON, N0H 2T0
(519) 534-1113   *SIC* 8051

CORPORATION OF THE COUNTY OF DUF-
FERIN, THE   *p*
880
151 CENTRE ST, SHELBURNE, ON, L9V
3R7
(519) 925-2140   *SIC* 8322

CORPORATION OF THE COUNTY OF EL-
GIN   *p*
482
475 TALBOT ST E, AYLMER, ON, N5H 3A5
(519) 773-9205   *SIC* 8361

CORPORATION OF THE COUNTY OF EL-
GIN   *p*
889
39232 FINGAL LINE, ST THOMAS, ON,
N5P 3S5
(519) 631-0620   *SIC* 8361

CORPORATION OF THE COUNTY OF ES-
SEX, THE   *p*
644
175 TALBOT ST E, LEAMINGTON, ON, N8H
1L9
(519) 326-5731   *SIC* 8361

CORPORATION OF THE COUNTY OF
GREY   *p* 567
575 SADDLER ST, DURHAM, ON, N0G 1R0
(519) 369-6035   *SIC* 8051

CORPORATION OF THE COUNTY OF
LAMBTON   *p* 591
39 MORRIS ST, FOREST, ON, N0N 1J0
(519) 786-2151   *SIC* 8059

CORPORATION OF THE COUNTY OF
LAMBTON   *p* 842
3958 PETROLIA LINE RR 4, PETROLIA,
ON, N0N 1R0
(519) 882-3797   *SIC* 4119

CORPORATION OF THE COUNTY OF
LAMBTON   *p* 859
749 DEVINE ST, SARNIA, ON, N7T 1X3
(519) 336-3720   *SIC* 8361

CORPORATION OF THE COUNTY OF
LAMBTON   *p* 859
6362 TELFER RD, SARNIA, ON, N7T 7H4
(519) 882-2442   *SIC* 4119

CORPORATION OF THE COUNTY OF
LAMBTON   *p* 1037
789 BROADWAY ST, WYOMING, ON, N0N
1T0
(519) 845-0801   *SIC* 8741

CORPORATION OF THE COUNTY OF MID-
DLESEX   *p*
897
599 ALBERT ST, STRATHROY, ON, N7G
1X1
(519) 245-2520   *SIC* 8361

CORPORATION OF THE COUNTY OF
NORTHUMBERLAND   *p* 545
983 BURNHAM ST SUITE 1321,
COBOURG, ON, K9A 5J6
(905) 372-8759   *SIC* 8361

CORPORATION OF THE COUNTY OF REN-
FREW   *p*
849
470 ALBERT ST, RENFREW, ON, K7V 4L5
(613) 432-4873   *SIC* 8361

CORPORATION OF THE COUNTY OF SIM-
COE   *p*
809
12 GRACE AVE, ORILLIA, ON, L3V 2K2
(705) 325-1504   *SIC* 8361

CORPORATION OF THE DISTRICT OF
SAANICH, THE   *p* 337
760 VERNON AVE, VICTORIA, BC, V8X
2W6
(250) 475-5500   *SIC* 7389

CORPORATION OF THE DISTRICT OF
WEST VANCOUVER, THE   *p* 241
221 LLOYD AVE, NORTH VANCOUVER,
BC, V7P 3M2
(604) 985-7777   *SIC* 4111

CORPORATION OF THE REGIONAL MU-
NICIPALITY OF DURHAM, THE   *p*
811
600 OSHAWA BLVD N SUITE 208, OS-
HAWA, ON, L1G 5T9
(905) 579-3313   *SIC* 8741

CORPORATION OF THE REGIONAL MU-
NICIPALITY OF DURHAM, THE   *p*
1013
105 CONSUMERS DR, WHITBY, ON, L1N
6A3
(905) 668-7721   *SIC* 4941

CORPORATION OF THE REGIONAL MU-
NICIPALITY OF DURHAM, THE   *p*
1014
632 DUNDAS ST W, WHITBY, ON, L1N 5S3
(905) 668-5851   *SIC* 8361

CORPORATION OF THE REGIONAL MU-
NICIPALITY OF DURHAM, THE   *p*
1016
825 CONLIN RD, WHITBY, ON, L1R 3K3
(905) 655-3344   *SIC* 1611

CORPORATION OF THE TOWN OF AJAX,
THE   *p* 473
435 MONARCH AVE, AJAX, ON, L1S 2G7
(905) 683-3050   *SIC* 7389

CORPORATION OF THE TOWN OF
GEORGINA, THE   *p* 902
26943 48 HWY RR 2, SUTTON WEST, ON,
L0E 1R0
(905) 722-8947   *SIC* 8361

CORPORATION OF THE TOWN OF
WHITBY, THE   *p* 1014
500 VICTORIA ST W, WHITBY, ON, L1N
9G4
(905) 668-7765   *SIC* 7999

CORPORATION OF TRINITY COLLEGE
SCHOOL, THE   *p* 847
55 DEBLAQUIRE ST N, PORT HOPE, ON,
L1A 4K7
(905) 885-4565   *SIC* 8211

CORPORATION OPTIMUM   *p* 1195
425 BOUL DE MAISONNEUVE O BUREAU
1700, MONTREAL, QC, H3A 3G5
(514) 288-2010   *SIC* 6712

CORPORATION PRESSE COMMERCE   *p*
1338
3339 RUE GRIFFITH BUREAU 4, SAINT-
LAURENT, QC, H4T 1W5
(514) 333-5041   *SIC* 5994

CORPORATION REBOX   *p* 1341
See REBOX CORP

CORPORATION REGIONALE DE DEVEL-
OPPEMENT DE LA RECUPERATION ET DU
RECYCLAGE REGION 02   *p* 1045
1000 BOUL SAINT-JUDE, ALMA, QC, G8B
3L1
(418) 668-8502   *SIC* 5932

CORPORATION SAVARIA   *p* 1342
4350 DESSTE CHOMEDEY (A-13) O,
SAINT-LAURENT, QC, H7R 6E9
(450) 681-5655   *SIC* 3999

CORPORATION SCIENTIFIQUE CLAISSE,
LA   *p* 1268

See SPECTRIS CANADA INC

CORPORATION SENZA, LA *p* 551
8960 JANE ST, CONCORD, ON, L4K 2M9
SIC 5632

CORPORATION SENZA, LA *p* 1093
1608 BOUL SAINT-REGIS, DORVAL, QC,
H9P 1H6
(514) 684-7700 *SIC* 5632

CORPORATION SERVICES MONERIS
687
3190 ORLANDO DR, MISSISSAUGA, ON,
L4V 1R5
SIC 7378

CORPORATION SERVICES MONERIS *p*
1338
7350 RTE TRANSCANADIENNE, SAINT-
LAURENT, QC, H4T 1A3
(514) 733-0443 *SIC* 7389

CORPORATION SIGVARIS *p* 1158
See SIGVARIS CORPORATION

CORPORATION STARLINK INC *p* 1093
9025 AV RYAN, DORVAL, QC, H9P 1A2
(514) 631-7500 *SIC* 6712

CORPORATION STELLAR CANADA INC *p*
1176
255 BOUL CREMAZIE E BUREAU 400,
MONTREAL, QC, H2M 1L5
(514) 850-6900 *SIC* 4813

CORPORATION STERIS CANADA *p* 1255
See STERIS CANADA ULC

CORPORATION TRANSPORT VITESSE *p*
1127
1111 46E AV, LACHINE, QC, H8T 3C5
(514) 631-2777 *SIC* 4213

CORPORATION TRIBOSPEC, LA *p* 1132
220 AV LAFLEUR, LASALLE, QC, H8R 4C9
(514) 595-7579 *SIC* 6712

CORPORATION WEAVEXX *p* 460
See XERIUM CANADA INC

CORPORATION XPRIMA.COM *p* 1241
420 BOUL ARMAND-FRAPPIER BUREAU
200, MONTREAL-OUEST, QC, H7V 4B4
(450) 681-5868 *SIC* 7374

**CORPORATION ZEDBED INTERNATIONAL
INC** *p* 1368
5352 RUE BURRILL, SHAWINIGAN, QC,
G9N 0C3
(819) 539-1112 *SIC* 5021

**CORRADO CARPENTER CONTRACTOR
LIMITED** *p* 551
445 EDGELEY BLVD SUITE 20, CON-
CORD, ON, L4K 4G1
(905) 660-4411 *SIC* 1751

CORREIA ENTERPRISES LTD *p* 368
375 NAIRN AVE, WINNIPEG, MB, R2L 0W8
(204) 668-4420 *SIC* 7349

CORRELIEU SECONDARY SCHOOL *p* 252
See SCHOOL DISTRICT #28

CORREVIO PHARMA CORP *p* 320
1441 CREEKSIDE DR 6 FL, VANCOUVER,
BC, V6J 4S7
(604) 677-6905 *SIC* 8731

CORRIDOR COMMUNICATIONS, INC *p* 22
465 AVIATION RD NE SUITE 137, CAL-
GARY, AB, T2E 7H8
(888) 240-2224 *SIC* 4813

CORRIDOR RESOURCES INC *p* 452
5475 SPRING GARDEN RD SUITE 301,
HALIFAX, NS, B3J 3T2
(902) 429-4511 *SIC* 1321

CORRPAR INDUSTRIES LTD *p* 755
17775 LESLIE ST, NEWMARKET, ON, L3Y
3E3
(905) 836-4599 *SIC* 2653

CORRPRO CANADA, INC *p* 100
10848 214 ST NW, EDMONTON, AB, T5S
2A7
(780) 447-4565 *SIC* 8711

CORRPRO CANADA, INC *p* 213
8607 101 ST, FORT ST. JOHN, BC, V1J 5K4
(250) 787-9100 *SIC* 8711

CORSA COAL CORP *p* 937
110 YONGE ST SUITE 601, TORONTO,
ON, M5C 1T4

SIC 1081

CORSIM CONSTRUCTION INC *p* 1172
2003 RUE GILFORD, MONTREAL, QC,
H2H 1H2
(514) 345-9320 *SIC* 1522

CORSINI INTERNATIONAL *p* 1343
See 4507525 CANADA INC

CORSTEEL HYDRAULICS *p* 547
See 1923921 ONTARIO INC

CORTAGE SOURCE, THE *p* 565
See WINCHESTER AUBURN MILLS INC

CORTEX DISTRIBUTION LTD *p* 1058
40 RUE EMILIEN-MARCOUX BUREAU 10,
BLAINVILLE, QC, J7C 0B5
(450) 686-9999 *SIC* 5087

CORTINA KITCHENS INC *p* 1030
70 REGINA RD, WOODBRIDGE, ON, L4L
8L6
(905) 264-6464 *SIC* 2434

**CORUS AUDIO & ADVERTISING SER-
VICES LTD** *p*
47
630 3 AVE SW SUITE 501, CALGARY, AB,
T2P 4L4
(403) 716-6500 *SIC* 4832

CORUS ENTERTAINMENT *p* 47
*See CORUS AUDIO & ADVERTISING SER-
VICES LTD*

CORUS ENTERTAINMENT INC *p* 330
700 GEORGIA ST W SUITE 2000, VAN-
COUVER, BC, V7Y 1K8
(604) 687-5177 *SIC* 4832

CORUS ENTERTAINMENT INC *p* 933
25 DOCKSIDE DR, TORONTO, ON, M5A
0B5
(416) 479-7000 *SIC* 4832

CORUS ENTERTAINMENT INC *p* 1230
800 RUE DE LA GAUCHETIERE O BU-
REAU 1100, MONTREAL, QC, H5A 1M1
(514) 767-9250 *SIC* 7922

CORUS ENTERTAINMENT, DIV OF *p* 1184
See TOON BOOM ANIMATION INC

CORUS MEDIA HOLDINGS INC *p* 22
222 23 ST NE, CALGARY, AB, T2E 7N2
(403) 235-7777 *SIC* 4833

CORUS MEDIA HOLDINGS INC *p* 118
5325 ALLARD WAY NW, EDMONTON, AB,
T6H 5B8
(780) 436-1250 *SIC* 7822

CORUS MEDIA HOLDINGS INC *p* 445
14 AKERLEY BLVD, DARTMOUTH, NS,
B3B 1J3
(902) 481-7400 *SIC* 4833

CORUS MEDIA HOLDINGS INC *p* 779
81 BARBER GREENE RD, NORTH YORK,
ON, M3C 2A2
(416) 446-5311 *SIC* 4833

CORUS MEDIA HOLDINGS INC *p* 933
25 DOCKSIDE DR, TORONTO, ON, M5A
0B5
(416) 479-7000 *SIC* 4833

CORVET CONSTRUCTION (1977) LTD *p*
157
37565 HIGHWAY 2 SUITE 107, RED DEER
COUNTY, AB, T4E 1B4
(403) 340-3535 *SIC* 1623

CORVETTE PARTS WORLD WIDE *p* 274
*See CORVETTE SPECIALTIES AUTO
GROUP LTD*

**CORVETTE SPECIALTIES AUTO GROUP
LTD** *p* 274
11180 SCOTT RD, SURREY, BC, V3V 8B8
(604) 580-8388 *SIC* 5511

CORVEX MANUFACTURING *p* 605
See LINAMAR CORPORATION

CORY MINE, DIV OF *p* 1429
*See POTASH CORPORATION OF
SASKATCHEWAN INC*

COS *p* 1227
*See CIE CANADIENNE DE PRODUITS OP-
TIQUES LTEE, LA*

COSBEC INC *p* 1338
699 RUE GOUGEON, SAINT-LAURENT,
QC, H4T 2B4

(514) 336-2411 *SIC* 5087

COSCO *p* 328
*See COSCO SHIPPING LINES (CANADA)
INC*

COSCO SHIPPING LINES (CANADA) INC *p*
328
1055 DUNSMUIR ST SUITE 2288, VAN-
COUVER, BC, V7X 1K8
(604) 689-8989 *SIC* 4491

COSECO INSURANCE COMPANY *p* 730
See COSECO INSURANCE INC.

COSECO INSURANCE INC. *p* 730
5600 CANCROSS CRT, MISSISSAUGA,
ON, L5R 3E9
(905) 507-6156 *SIC* 6331

COSELLA-DORKEN *p* 489
See DORKEN SYSTEMS INC

COSIMO MINNELLA INVESTMENTS INC *p*
384
1680 NOTRE DAME AVE UNIT 7, WIN-
NIPEG, MB, R3H 1H6
(204) 786-0001 *SIC* 5087

COSMA INTERNATIONAL (CANADA) INC *p*
502
2550 STEELES AVE, BRAMPTON, ON, L6T
5R3
SIC 3714

COSMACEUTICAL RESEARCH LAB INC *p*
276
12920 84 AVE, SURREY, BC, V3W 1K7
(604) 590-1373 *SIC* 2844

COSMETICA LABORATORIES INC *p* 868
1960 EGLINTON AVE E, SCARBOROUGH,
ON, M1L 2M5
(416) 615-2400 *SIC* 2844

COSMETIQUES LISE WATIER *p* 1128
See GROUPE MARCELLE INC

COSMO COMMUNICATIONS CANADA INC
p 678
55 TRAVAIL RD UNIT 2, MARKHAM, ON,
L3S 3J1
(905) 209-0488 *SIC* 5065

COSMO GOLF CANADA *p* 1426
*See COSMOPOLITAN INDUSTRIES GOLF
CANADA LTD*

COSMO MOTORS LTD *p* 259
3511 NO. 3 RD, RICHMOND, BC, V6X 2B8
(604) 273-0333 *SIC* 5511

COSMO MUSIC *p* 856
See COSMO MUSIC COMPANY LTD

COSMO MUSIC COMPANY LTD *p* 856
10 VIA RENZO DR, RICHMOND HILL, ON,
L4S 0B6
(905) 770-5222 *SIC* 5736

**COSMOPOLITAN INDUSTRIES GOLF
CANADA LTD** *p* 1426
1302B ALBERTA AVE, SASKATOON, SK,
S7K 1R5
(306) 477-4653 *SIC* 5091

COSMOPOLITAN INDUSTRIES LTD *p* 1427
28 34TH ST E, SASKATOON, SK, S7K 3Y2
(306) 664-3158 *SIC* 2611

COSMOS FURNITURE LTD *p* 502
1055 CLARK BLVD, BRAMPTON, ON, L6T
3W4
(905) 790-2676 *SIC* 5021

COSMOS I BOTTLE DEPOT *p* 155
7428 49 AVE SUITE 1, RED DEER, AB, T4P
1M2
(403) 342-2034 *SIC* 7389

COSOLTEC INC *p* 1086
3080 BOUL LE CARREFOUR, COTE
SAINT-LUC, QC, H7T 2R5
(450) 682-0000 *SIC* 1542

COSSETTE *p* 992
See VISION 7 COMMUNICATIONS INC

COSSETTE *p* 1212
See 7660715 CANADA INC

COSSETTE COMMUNICATION *p* 1214
See VISION 7 COMMUNICATIONS INC

COSSETTE COMMUNICATION INC *p* 991
32 ATLANTIC AVE, TORONTO, ON, M6K
1X8
(416) 922-2727 *SIC* 4899

COSSETTE DIGITAL INC *p* 1258
300 RUE SAINT-PAUL BUREAU 300, QUE-
BEC, QC, G1K 7R1
(418) 647-2727 *SIC* 4899

COST LESS EXPRESS LTD *p* 200
11 BURBIDGE ST SUITE 204, COQUIT-
LAM, BC, V3K 7B2
(604) 444-4467 *SIC* 5044

COSTCO *p* 8
See COSTCO WHOLESALE CANADA LTD

COSTCO *p* 34
See COSTCO WHOLESALE CANADA LTD

COSTCO *p* 105
See COSTCO WHOLESALE CANADA LTD

COSTCO *p* 131
See COSTCO WHOLESALE CANADA LTD

COSTCO *p* 143
See COSTCO WHOLESALE CANADA LTD

COSTCO *p* 147
See COSTCO WHOLESALE CANADA LTD

COSTCO *p* 157
See COSTCO WHOLESALE CANADA LTD

COSTCO *p* 216
See COSTCO WHOLESALE CANADA LTD

COSTCO *p* 219
See COSTCO WHOLESALE CANADA LTD

COSTCO *p* 245
See COSTCO WHOLESALE CANADA LTD

COSTCO *p* 276
See COSTCO WHOLESALE CANADA LTD

COSTCO *p* 298
See COSTCO WHOLESALE CANADA LTD

COSTCO *p* 362
See COSTCO WHOLESALE CANADA LTD

COSTCO *p* 393
See COSTCO WHOLESALE CANADA LTD

COSTCO *p* 475
See COSTCO WHOLESALE CANADA LTD

COSTCO *p* 486
See COSTCO WHOLESALE CANADA LTD

COSTCO *p* 509
See COSTCO WHOLESALE CANADA LTD

COSTCO *p* 574
See COSTCO WHOLESALE CANADA LTD

COSTCO *p* 594
See COSTCO WHOLESALE CANADA LTD

COSTCO *p* 633
See COSTCO WHOLESALE CANADA LTD

COSTCO *p* 641
See COSTCO WHOLESALE CANADA LTD

COSTCO *p* 657
See COSTCO WHOLESALE CANADA LTD

COSTCO *p* 658
See COSTCO WHOLESALE CANADA LTD

COSTCO *p* 678
See COSTCO WHOLESALE CANADA LTD

COSTCO *p* 716
See COSTCO WHOLESALE CANADA LTD

COSTCO *p* 840
See COSTCO WHOLESALE CANADA LTD

COSTCO *p* 856
See COSTCO WHOLESALE CANADA LTD

COSTCO *p* 884
See COSTCO WHOLESALE CANADA LTD

COSTCO *p* 899
See COSTCO WHOLESALE CANADA LTD

COSTCO *p* 1019
See COSTCO WHOLESALE CANADA LTD

COSTCO *p* 1030
See COSTCO WHOLESALE CANADA LTD

COSTCO *p* 1061
See COSTCO WHOLESALE CANADA LTD

COSTCO *p* 1072
See COSTCO WHOLESALE CANADA LTD

COSTCO *p* 1225
See COSTCO WHOLESALE CANADA LTD

COSTCO *p* 1249
See COSTCO WHOLESALE CANADA LTD

COSTCO *p* 1275
See COSTCO WHOLESALE CANADA LTD

COSTCO *p* 1278
See COSTCO WHOLESALE CANADA LTD

COSTCO *p* 1308
See COSTCO WHOLESALE CANADA LTD

COSTCO *p 1373*
See COSTCO WHOLESALE CANADA LTD

COSTCO *p 1387*
See COSTCO WHOLESALE CANADA LTD

COSTCO *p 1435*
See COSTCO WHOLESALE CANADA LTD

COSTCO CANADA HOLDINGS INC *p 749*
415 WEST HUNT CLUB RD, NEPEAN, ON, K2E 1C5
(613) 221-2000 *SIC 6712*

COSTCO MONTREAL *p 1216*
See COSTCO WHOLESALE CANADA LTD

COSTCO STORE#1076 *p 160*
See COSTCO WHOLESALE CANADA LTD

COSTCO WHOLESALE *p 226*
See COSTCO WHOLESALE CANADA LTD

COSTCO WHOLESALE *p 1064*
See COSTCO WHOLESALE CANADA LTD

COSTCO WHOLESALE *p 1104*
See COSTCO WHOLESALE CANADA LTD

COSTCO WHOLESALE CANADA *p 1422*
See COSTCO WHOLESALE CANADA LTD

COSTCO WHOLESALE CANADA LTD *p 2*
1003 HAMILTON BLVD NE, AIRDRIE, AB, T4A 0G2
(403) 945-4267 *SIC 4731*

COSTCO WHOLESALE CANADA LTD *p 8*
2853 32 ST NE, CALGARY, AB, T1Y 6T7
(403) 299-1610 *SIC 5099*

COSTCO WHOLESALE CANADA LTD *p 34*
99 HERITAGE GATE SE, CALGARY, AB, T2H 3A7
(403) 313-7650 *SIC 5099*

COSTCO WHOLESALE CANADA LTD *p 77*
11588 SARCEE TRAIL NW SUITE 543, CALGARY, AB, T3R 0A1
(403) 516-3700 *SIC 5099*

COSTCO WHOLESALE CANADA LTD *p 105*
12450 149 ST NW SUITE 154, EDMONTON, AB, T5V 1G9
(780) 453-8470 *SIC 5099*

COSTCO WHOLESALE CANADA LTD *p 131*
9901 116 ST UNIT 102, GRANDE PRAIRIE, AB, T8V 6H6
(780) 538-2911 *SIC 5099*

COSTCO WHOLESALE CANADA LTD *p 143*
3200 MAYOR MAGRATH DR S, LETHBRIDGE, AB, T1K 6Y6
(403) 320-8917 *SIC 5099*

COSTCO WHOLESALE CANADA LTD *p 147*
2350 BOX SPRINGS BLVD NW BOX SUITE 593, MEDICINE HAT, AB, T1C 0C8
(403) 581-5700 *SIC 5099*

COSTCO WHOLESALE CANADA LTD *p 157*
37400 HIGHWAY 2 UNIT 162, RED DEER COUNTY, AB, T4E 1B9
(403) 340-3736 *SIC 5099*

COSTCO WHOLESALE CANADA LTD *p 160*
293020 CROSSIRON COMMON SUITE 300, ROCKY VIEW COUNTY, AB, T4A 0J6
(403) 516-5050 *SIC 5099*

COSTCO WHOLESALE CANADA LTD *p 162*
2201 BROADMOOR BLVD, SHERWOOD PARK, AB, T8H 0A1
(780) 410-2520 *SIC 5099*

COSTCO WHOLESALE CANADA LTD *p 174*
1127 SUMAS WAY, ABBOTSFORD, BC, V2S 8H2
(604) 850-3458 *SIC 5099*

COSTCO WHOLESALE CANADA LTD *p 182*
3550 BRIGHTON AVE SUITE 51, BURNABY, BC, V5A 4W3
(604) 420-2668 *SIC 5099*

COSTCO WHOLESALE CANADA LTD *p 216*

1675 VERSATILE DR, KAMLOOPS, BC, V1S 1W7
(250) 374-5336 *SIC 5099*

COSTCO WHOLESALE CANADA LTD *p 219*
2479 HIGHWAY 97 N, KELOWNA, BC, V1X 4J2
(250) 868-9515 *SIC 5099*

COSTCO WHOLESALE CANADA LTD *p 226*
20499 64 AVE, LANGLEY, BC, V2Y 1N5
(604) 539-8901 *SIC 5099*

COSTCO WHOLESALE CANADA LTD *p 245*
2370 OTTAWA ST, PORT COQUITLAM, BC, V3B 7Z1
(604) 552-2228 *SIC 5099*

COSTCO WHOLESALE CANADA LTD *p 250*
2555 RANGE RD SUITE 158, PRINCE GEORGE, BC, V2N 4G8
(250) 561-0784 *SIC 5099*

COSTCO WHOLESALE CANADA LTD *p 259*
9151 BRIDGEPORT RD SUITE 54, RICHMOND, BC, V6X 3L9
(604) 270-3647 *SIC 5099*

COSTCO WHOLESALE CANADA LTD *p 276*
7423 KING GEORGE BLVD SUITE 55, SURREY, BC, V3W 5A8
(604) 596-7435 *SIC 5099*

COSTCO WHOLESALE CANADA LTD *p 298*
605 EXPO BLVD, VANCOUVER, BC, V6B 1V4
(604) 622-5050 *SIC 5099*

COSTCO WHOLESALE CANADA LTD *p 340*
799 MCCALLUM RD, VICTORIA, BC, V9B 6A2
(250) 391-1151 *SIC 5099*

COSTCO WHOLESALE CANADA LTD *p 362*
1499 REGENT AVE W, WINNIPEG, MB, R2C 4M4
(204) 654-4214 *SIC 5099*

COSTCO WHOLESALE CANADA LTD *p 384*
1315 ST JAMES ST SUITE 57, WINNIPEG, MB, R3H 0K9
(204) 788-4415 *SIC 5099*

COSTCO WHOLESALE CANADA LTD *p 393*
2365 MCGILLIVRAY BLVD SUITE 1, WINNIPEG, MB, R3Y 0A1
(204) 487-5100 *SIC 5399*

COSTCO WHOLESALE CANADA LTD *p 409*
25 TRINITY DR SUITE 217, MONCTON, NB, E1G 2J7
(506) 858-7959 *SIC 5399*

COSTCO WHOLESALE CANADA LTD *p 428*
28 STAVANGER DR, ST. JOHN'S, NL, A1A 5E8
(709) 738-8610 *SIC 5141*

COSTCO WHOLESALE CANADA LTD *p 458*
230 CHAIN LAKE DR, HALIFAX, NS, B3S 1C5
(902) 450-1078 *SIC 5099*

COSTCO WHOLESALE CANADA LTD *p 475*
150 KINGSTON RD E, AJAX, ON, L1Z 1E5
(905) 619-6677 *SIC 5099*

COSTCO WHOLESALE CANADA LTD *p 478*
100 LEGEND CRT SUITE 1105, ANCASTER, ON, L9K 1J3
(905) 304-0344 *SIC 5099*

COSTCO WHOLESALE CANADA LTD *p 486*
41 MAPLEVIEW DR E, BARRIE, ON, L4N

9A9
(705) 728-2350 *SIC 5099*

COSTCO WHOLESALE CANADA LTD *p 509*
100 BISCAYNE CRES, BRAMPTON, ON, L6W 4S1
(905) 450-2092 *SIC 5099*

COSTCO WHOLESALE CANADA LTD *p 529*
1225 BRANT ST, BURLINGTON, ON, L7P 1X7
(905) 336-6714 *SIC 5099*

COSTCO WHOLESALE CANADA LTD *p 567*
18182 YONGE ST, EAST GWILLIMBURY, ON, L9N 0J3
(905) 954-4733 *SIC 5311*

COSTCO WHOLESALE CANADA LTD *p 574*
50 QUEEN ELIZABETH BLVD SUITE 524, ETOBICOKE, ON, M8Z 1M1
(416) 251-2832 *SIC 5399*

COSTCO WHOLESALE CANADA LTD *p 594*
1900 CYRVILLE RD, GLOUCESTER, ON, K1B 1A5
(613) 748-9966 *SIC 5199*

COSTCO WHOLESALE CANADA LTD *p 633*
1015 CENTENNIAL DR, KINGSTON, ON, K7P 3B7
(613) 549-2527 *SIC 5141*

COSTCO WHOLESALE CANADA LTD *p 641*
4438 KING ST E SUITE 512, KITCHENER, ON, N2P 2G4
(519) 650-3662 *SIC 5399*

COSTCO WHOLESALE CANADA LTD *p 657*
4313 WELLINGTON RD S, LONDON, ON, N6E 2Z8
(519) 680-1027 *SIC 5141*

COSTCO WHOLESALE CANADA LTD *p 658*
693 WONDERLAND RD N SUITE 530, LONDON, ON, N6H 4L1
(519) 474-5301 *SIC 5099*

COSTCO WHOLESALE CANADA LTD *p 678*
65 KIRKHAM DR SUITE 545, MARKHAM, ON, L3S 0A9
(905) 201-3502 *SIC 5099*

COSTCO WHOLESALE CANADA LTD *p 680*
1 YORKTECH DR SUITE 151, MARKHAM, ON, L6G 1A6
(905) 477-5718 *SIC 5099*

COSTCO WHOLESALE CANADA LTD *p 716*
3180 LAIRD RD, MISSISSAUGA, ON, L5L 6A5
(905) 828-3340 *SIC 5099*

COSTCO WHOLESALE CANADA LTD *p 730*
5900 RODEO DR SUITE 526, MISSISSAUGA, ON, L5R 3S9
(905) 568-4828 *SIC 5099*

COSTCO WHOLESALE CANADA LTD *p 749*
415 WEST HUNT CLUB RD, NEPEAN, ON, K2E 1C5
(613) 221-2010 *SIC 5099*

COSTCO WHOLESALE CANADA LTD *p 750*
1849 MERIVALE RD SUITE 540, NEPEAN, ON, K2G 1E3
(613) 727-4786 *SIC 5141*

COSTCO WHOLESALE CANADA LTD *p 840*
485 THE PARKWAY, PETERBOROUGH, ON, K9J 0B3
(705) 750-2600 *SIC 5199*

COSTCO WHOLESALE CANADA LTD *p 856*

35 JOHN BIRCHALL RD SUITE 592, RICHMOND HILL, ON, L4S 0B2
(905) 780-2100 *SIC 5099*

COSTCO WHOLESALE CANADA LTD *p 872*
1411 WARDEN AVE SUITE 537, SCARBOROUGH, ON, M1R 2S3
(416) 288-0033 *SIC 5099*

COSTCO WHOLESALE CANADA LTD *p 884*
3 NORTH SERVICE RD, ST CATHARINES, ON, L2N 7R1
(905) 646-2008 *SIC 5141*

COSTCO WHOLESALE CANADA LTD *p 899*
1465 KINGSWAY, SUDBURY, ON, P3B 0A5
(705) 524-8255 *SIC 5141*

COSTCO WHOLESALE CANADA LTD *p 1019*
4411 WALKER RD, SUITE 534, WINDSOR, ON, N8W 3T6
(519) 972-1899 *SIC 5399*

COSTCO WHOLESALE CANADA LTD *p 1030*
71 COLOSSUS DR SUITE 547, WOODBRIDGE, ON, L4L 9J8
(905) 264-8337 *SIC 5199*

COSTCO WHOLESALE CANADA LTD *p 1048*
7373 RUE BOMBARDIER, ANJOU, QC, H1J 2V2
(514) 493-4814 *SIC 5099*

COSTCO WHOLESALE CANADA LTD *p 1061*
3600 AV DES GRANDES TOURELLES, BOISBRIAND, QC, J7H 0A1
(450) 420-4500 *SIC 5099*

COSTCO WHOLESALE CANADA LTD *p 1064*
635 CH DE TOURAINE, BOUCHERVILLE, QC, J4B 5E4
(450) 645-2631 *SIC 5099*

COSTCO WHOLESALE CANADA LTD *p 1072*
60 RUE STRASBOURG, CANDIAC, QC, J5R 0B4
(450) 444-3453 *SIC 5099*

COSTCO WHOLESALE CANADA LTD *p 1078*
2500 BOUL TALBOT, CHICOUTIMI, QC, G7H 5B1
(418) 696-1112 *SIC 5199*

COSTCO WHOLESALE CANADA LTD *p 1104*
1100 BOUL MALONEY O BUREAU 542, GATINEAU, QC, J8T 6G3
(819) 246-4005 *SIC 5099*

COSTCO WHOLESALE CANADA LTD *p 1216*
300 RUE BRIDGE, MONTREAL, QC, H3K 2C3
(514) 938-5170 *SIC 5399*

COSTCO WHOLESALE CANADA LTD *p 1225*
1015 RUE DU MARCHE-CENTRAL, MONTREAL, QC, H4N 3J8
(514) 381-1251 *SIC 5399*

COSTCO WHOLESALE CANADA LTD *p 1236*
2999 NORD LAVAL A-440 O, MONTREAL, QC, H7P 5P4
(450) 686-7420 *SIC 5099*

COSTCO WHOLESALE CANADA LTD *p 1249*
5701 RTE TRANSCANADIENNE, POINTE-CLAIRE, QC, H9R 1B7
(514) 426-5052 *SIC 5099*

COSTCO WHOLESALE CANADA LTD *p 1275*
3233 AV WATT, QUEBEC, QC, G1X 4W2
(418) 656-0666 *SIC 5099*

COSTCO WHOLESALE CANADA LTD *p 1278*
440 RUE BOUVIER, QUEBEC, QC, G2J

1E3
(418) 627-5100   SIC 5099
COSTCO WHOLESALE CANADA LTD   p 1308
5025 BOUL COUSINEAU, SAINT-HUBERT, QC, J3Y 3K7
(450) 443-3618   SIC 5099
COSTCO WHOLESALE CANADA LTD   p 1373
3400 RUE KING O, SHERBROOKE, QC, J1L 1C9
(819) 822-2121   SIC 5199
COSTCO WHOLESALE CANADA LTD   p 1387
3000 BOUL DES RECOLLETS, TROIS-RIVIERES, QC, G9A 6J2
(819) 693-5758   SIC 5399
COSTCO WHOLESALE CANADA LTD   p 1422
665 UNIVERSITY PARK DR SUITE 520, REGINA, SK, S4V 2V8
(306) 789-8838   SIC 5099
COSTCO WHOLESALE CANADA LTD   p 1435
115 MARQUIS DR W, SASKATOON, SK, S7R 1C7
(306) 933-4262   SIC 5099
COSTCO WHOLESALE STORE # 519 p 458
See COSTCO WHOLESALE CANADA LTD
COSTI IMMIGRANT SERVICES   p 989
1710 DUFFERIN ST, TORONTO, ON, M6E 3P2
(416) 658-1600   SIC 8322
COSTINIUK, D PHARMACY LTD   p 884
600 ONTARIO ST, ST CATHARINES, ON, L2N 7H8
(905) 937-3532   SIC 5912
COSYN TECHNOLOGY   p 111
See WORLEYPARSONSCORD LP
COTA HEALTH   p 933
550 QUEEN ST E SUITE 201, TORONTO, ON, M5A 1V2
(888) 785-2779   SIC 8049
COTE OUELLET THIVIERGE NOTAIRES INC   p 1286
646 RUE LAFONTAINE BUREAU 100, RIVIERE-DU-LOUP, QC, G5R 3C8
(418) 863-5050   SIC 7389
COTE TASCHEREAU SAMSON DEMERS S.E.N.C.R.L   p 1270
871 GRANDE ALLEE O BUREAU 100, QUEBEC, QC, G1S 2L1
(418) 688-9375   SIC 7389
COTE, CLAUDE ASSURANCES ENR   p 1088
106 RUE CHURCH, COWANSVILLE, QC, J2K 1T8
(450) 263-0597   SIC 6411
COTE, REGIS ET ASSOCIES ARCHITECTES   p 1086
2990 AV PIERRE-PELADEAU BUREAU 200, COTE SAINT-LUC, QC, H7T 0B1
SIC 8712
COTE-RECO INC   p 1089
100 12E AV, DESCHAILLONS-SUR-SAINT-LAURENT, QC, G0S 1G0
(819) 292-2323   SIC 5139
COTNAM, DAN DRUGS LTD   p 911
200 BROADWAY ST, TILLSONBURG, ON, N4G 5A7
(519) 842-3521   SIC 5912
COTON EN FLEUR   p 1179
See MODES CORWIK INC
COTRAC FORD LINCOLN SALES INC   p 567
204 CURRIE RD, DUTTON, ON, N0L 1J0
(519) 762-3506   SIC 5511
COTT BEVERAGES CANADA   p 687
See COTT CORPORATION
COTT CORPORATION   p 687
6525 VISCOUNT RD, MISSISSAUGA, ON, L4V 1H6
(905) 672-1900   SIC 2086

COTTON CANDY INC   p 721
2600 ARGENTIA RD, MISSISSAUGA, ON, L5N 5V4
(905) 858-2600   SIC 5199
COTTON INC   p 757
2125 FRUITBELT DR, NIAGARA FALLS, ON, L2E 6S4
(905) 262-2000   SIC 1794
COTTON READY MIX   p 757
See COTTON INC
COTTONWOOD GOLF & COUNTRY CLUB   p 127
88008 226 AVE E, FOOTHILLS, AB, T1S 4A6
(403) 938-7216   SIC 7997
COTTONWOODS CARE CENTRE   p 222
See INTERIOR HEALTH AUTHORITY
COTY CANADA INC   p 1093
1255 RTE TRANSCANADIENNE BUREAU 200, DORVAL, QC, H9P 2V4
(514) 421-5050   SIC 5122
COU HOLDING ASSOCIATION INC   p 944
180 DUNDAS ST W SUITE 1100, TORONTO, ON, M5G 1Z8
(416) 979-2165   SIC 8621
COUCHE-TARD INC   p 1233
4204 BOUL INDUSTRIEL, MONTREAL, QC, H7L 0E3
(450) 662-6632   SIC 5541
COUGAR DRILLING SOLUTIONS INC p 122
7319 17 ST NW, EDMONTON, AB, T6P 1P1
(780) 440-2400   SIC 7353
COUGAR FUELS LTD   p 6
5602 54 AVE, BONNYVILLE, AB, T9N 2N3
(780) 826-3043   SIC 5983
COUGAR GLOBAL INVESTMENTS LIMITED PARTNERSHIP   p 950
357 BAY ST SUITE 1001, TORONTO, ON, M5H 2T7
(416) 368-5255   SIC 6211
COUGAR HELICOPTERS INC   p 428
10 AV JETSTREAM, ST. JOHN'S, NL, A1A 0R7
(709) 758-4800   SIC 4522
COUGAR SHOES INC   p 531
2 MASONRY CRT, BURLINGTON, ON, L7T 4A8
(905) 639-0100   SIC 5139
COUGAR TOOL   p 122
See COUGAR DRILLING SOLUTIONS INC
COUGHLIN & ASSOCIATES LTD   p 817
466 TREMBLAY RD, OTTAWA, ON, K1G 3R1
(613) 231-2266   SIC 6411
COUGHLIN INSURANCE BROKERS   p 387
See COUGHLIN, GUY INSURANCE AGENCY LTD
COUGHLIN, GUY INSURANCE AGENCY LTD   p 387
1170 TAYLOR AVE UNIT 4, WINNIPEG, MB, R3M 3Z4
(204) 953-4600   SIC 6411
COUILLARD CONSTRUCTION LIMITEE   p 1081
228 RUE MAIN E, COATICOOK, QC, J1A 1N2
(819) 849-9181   SIC 1611
COULOMBE QUEBEC LIMITEE   p 1263
2300 RUE CYRILLE-DUQUET, QUEBEC, QC, G1N 2G5
(418) 687-2700   SIC 2086
COULSON AIRCRANE LTD   p 245
4890 CHERRY CREEK RD, PORT ALBERNI, BC, V9Y 8E9
(250) 723-8118   SIC 4522
COULSON FOREST PRODUCTS LIMITED p 245
4890 CHERRY CREEK RD, PORT ALBERNI, BC, V9Y 8E9
(250) 723-8118   SIC 2411
COULTER WATER METER SERVICE p 621
See ERTH (HOLDINGS) INC
COULTER'S FURNITURE   p 1021

See C.J.C. COULTER INVESTMENTS 2006 INC
COULTER'S PHARMACY (LONDON) LTD p 660
1051 WONDERLAND RD S, LONDON, ON, N6K 3X4
(519) 472-2222   SIC 5912
COUMELIE INC   p 1264
2300 RUE CYRILLE-DUQUET, QUEBEC, QC, G1N 2G5
(418) 687-2700   SIC 6712
COUNCIL OF MINISTERS OF EDUCATION CANADA   p 926
See CORPORATION OF COUNCIL OF MINISTERS OF EDUCATION CANADA, THE
COUNSEL GROUP FUNDS   p 693
2680 SKYMARK AVE SUITE 700, MISSISSAUGA, ON, L4W 5L6
(905) 625-9885   SIC 6211
COUNSEL PORTFOLIO SERVICES INC   p 693
2680 SKYMARK AVE SUITE 700, MISSISSAUGA, ON, L4W 5L6
(905) 625-9885   SIC 6722
COUNSEL SELECT SMALL CAP   p 693
2680 SKYMARK AVE UNIT 700, MISSISSAUGA, ON, L4W 5L6
(905) 625-9885   SIC 6722
COUNTERFORCE CORPORATION   p 408
1077 ST GEORGE BLVD, MONCTON, NB, E1E 4C9
(506) 862-5500   SIC 7382
COUNTERFORCE CORPORATION   p 693
2740 MATHESON BLVD E UNIT 2A, MISSISSAUGA, ON, L4W 4X3
(905) 282-6200   SIC 7382
COUNTERPATH CORPORATION   p 328
505 BURRARD ST SUITE 300, VANCOUVER, BC, V7X 1M3
(604) 320-3344   SIC 7379
COUNTRY 95.5 FM   p 217
See PATTISON, JIM BROADCAST GROUP LTD
COUNTRY CHRYSLER   p 136
See COUNTRY ENTERPRISES LTD
COUNTRY CLUB DE MONTREAL, LE   p 1323
5 RUE RIVERSIDE, SAINT-LAMBERT, QC, J4S 1B7
(450) 671-6181   SIC 7997
COUNTRY CLUB TOWERS   p 789
See JOSTEN DEVELOPMENTS LIMITED
COUNTRY CROSS ROADS SERVICE   p 1437
GD, WAKAW, SK, S0K 4P0
(306) 233-5553   SIC 5541
COUNTRY DAY SCHOOL, THE   p 629
13415 DUFFERIN ST, KING CITY, ON, L7B 1K5
(905) 833-5366   SIC 8211
COUNTRY DRUG STORES LTD   p 540
6 CAMERON ST E, CANNINGTON, ON, L0E 1E0
(705) 432-2644   SIC 5912
COUNTRY ENTERPRISES LTD   p 136
1103 14 ST SE, HIGH RIVER, AB, T1V 1L5
SIC 5511
COUNTRY FURNITURE LTD   p 241
1365 PEMBERTON AVE, NORTH VANCOUVER, BC, V7P 2R6
(604) 985-9700   SIC 5021
COUNTRY GROCER   p 196
See ISLAND INDEPENDENT BUYING GROUP LTD
COUNTRY GROCER SALTSPRING   p 268
See 123 ENTERPRISES LTD
COUNTRY HILLS TOYOTA   p 75
See 1009931 ALBERTA LTD
COUNTRY JUNCTION DIV OF   p 172
See WETASKIWIN CO-OPERATIVE ASSOCIATION LIMITED
COUNTRY LUMBER LTD   p 227
22538 FRASER HWY, LANGLEY, BC, V2Z 2T8

(604) 533-4447   SIC 5211
COUNTRY MEADOWS RETIREMENT RESIDENCE   p 520
See BOXBERG HOLDING LTD
COUNTRY POULTRY   p 1005
7705 4TH LINE SUITE 2, WALLENSTEIN, ON, N0B 2S0
(519) 698-9930   SIC 0212
COUNTRY PRIME MEATS LTD   p 224
3171 97 HWY, LAC LA HACHE, BC, V0K 1T1
(250) 396-4111   SIC 2011
COUNTRY PRODUCE (ORILLIA) LTD p 809
301 WESTMOUNT DR N, ORILLIA, ON, L3V 6Y4
(705) 325-9902   SIC 5431
COUNTRY R.V.   p 220
See FRASERWAY RV GP LTD
COUNTRY SIGNS   p 998
See 1339022 ONTARIO LTD
COUNTRY TERRACE   p 643
See OMNI HEALTH COUNTRY TERRACE NURSING HOME
COUNTRY VILLAGE HEALTH CARE CENTRE   p 882
440 COUNTY RD 8 SUITE 8, SOUTH WOODSLEE, ON, N0R 1V0
(519) 839-4812   SIC 8051
COUNTRYSIDE CHRYSLER DODGE LIMITED   p 569
458 TALBOT ST N, ESSEX, ON, N8M 2W6
(519) 776-5287   SIC 5511
COUNTRYSIDE FARMS   p 359
See WIELER ENTERPRISES LTD
COUNTRYWIDE HOMES LTD   p 551
1500 HIGHWAY 7, CONCORD, ON, L4K 5Y4
(905) 907-1500   SIC 1522
COUNTY LINE FARMS LTD   p 158
GD, RIMBEY, AB, T0C 2J0
(403) 843-6275   SIC 0191
COUNTY OF FORTY MILE NO 8   p 126
GD, ETZIKOM, AB, T0K 0W0
(403) 666-2082   SIC 1611
COUNTY OF LENNOX & ADDINGTON p 747
309 BRIDGE ST W SUITE 113, NAPANEE, ON, K7R 2G4
SIC 8059
COUNTY OF TWO HILLS NATURAL GAS p 170
5606 51 ST, TWO HILLS, AB, T0B 4K0
(780) 657-2800   SIC 4924
COUNTY STETTLER HOUSING AUTHORITY, THE   p 167
611 50TH AVE, STETTLER, AB, T0C 2L1
(403) 742-9220   SIC 6513
COUNTY STETTLER HOUSING AUTHORITY, THE   p 167
620 47TH AVE SUITE 111, STETTLER, AB, T0C 2L1
(403) 742-2953   SIC 6513
COUPAL & FILS INC   p 1159
349 117 RTE, MONT-TREMBLANT, QC, J8E 2X4
(819) 425-8771   SIC 5211
COUPE LASER ULTRA INC   p 1250
205 BOUL BRUNSWICK BUREAU 400, POINTE-CLAIRE, QC, H9R 1A5
(514) 333-8156   SIC 7389
COUPLES RESORT INC   p 1016
139 GALEAIRY LAKE RD, WHITNEY, ON, K0J 2M0
(613) 637-1179   SIC 7011
COURANT MECANICA   p 1336
See SOLUTIONS MECANICA INC, LES
COURCHESNE, LAROSE, LIMITEE p 1048
9761 BOUL DES SCIENCES, ANJOU, QC, H1J 0A6
(514) 525-6381   SIC 5148

COUREY, GEORGE INC   p 1231
6620 RUE ERNEST-CORMIER, MON-TREAL, QC, H7C 2T5
(450) 661-6620   SIC 5023
COURIER COMPANY LTD, THE   p 989
1219 ST CLAIR AVE W, TORONTO, ON, M6E 1B5
(416) 504-7373   SIC 7389
COURONNES PLUS.COM INC, LES p 1102
9 RUE DES CERISIERS, GASPE, QC, G4X 2M1
(418) 368-3670   SIC 3999
COURRIER DE ST-HYACINTHE   p 1312
See DBC COMMUNICATIONS INC
COURRIER PUROLATOR   p 1330
See PUROLATOR INC
COURRIER PUROLATOR   p 1362
See PUROLATOR INC
COURRIER RAPIDE SERVICE   p 1126
640 RUE NOTRE-DAME, LACHINE, QC, H8S 2B3
(514) 866-8727   SIC 7389
COURT GROUP OF COMPANIES LTD, THE   p 530
490 ELIZABETH ST, BURLINGTON, ON, L7R 2M2
(905) 333-5002   SIC 6712
COURT HOLDINGS LIMITED   p 489
5071 KING ST, BEAMSVILLE, ON, L0R 1B0
(905) 563-0782   SIC 3694
COURTAGE BGL LTEE   p 1187
300 RUE DU SAINT-SACREMENT BUREAU 123, MONTREAL, QC, H2Y 1X4
(514) 288-8111   SIC 4731
COURTAGE EN LIGNE DISNAT   p 1209
See VALEURS MOBILIERES DESJARDINS INC
COURTAGE ESCOMPTE BANQUE LAU-RENTIENNE   p 1214
See VALEURS MOBILIERES BANQUE LAURENTIENNE INC
COURTENAY LODGE LTD   p 203
1590 CLIFFE AVE, COURTENAY, BC, V9N 2K4
(250) 338-7741   SIC 7011
COURTENAY RECREATION CENTRE p 203
See CORPORATION OF THE CITY OF COURTENAY, THE
COURTENAY TOYOTA   p 203
See RICE AUTOMOTIVE INVESTMENTS LTD
COURTESY AIR   p 1404
See 947786 ALBERTA LTD
COURTESY CHEVROLET LTD.   p 574
1635 THE QUEENSWAY, ETOBICOKE, ON, M8Z 1T8
SIC 5511
COURTESY CHRYSLER DODGE (1987) LTD   p 34
125 GLENDEER CIR SE, CALGARY, AB, T2H 2S8
(403) 255-8111   SIC 5511
COURTESY CHRYSLER DODGE JEEP p 35
125 GLENDEER CIR SE, CALGARY, AB, T2H 2S8
(403) 255-9100   SIC 5511
COURTESY CHRYSLER DODGE JEEP RAM   p 34
See CALGARY C MOTORS LP
COURTESY FORD LINCOLN SALES LIM-ITED   p 659
684 WHARNCLIFFE RD S, LONDON, ON, N6J 2N4
(519) 680-1200   SIC 5511
COURTESY FREIGHT SYSTEMS LTD p 909
340 SIMPSON ST, THUNDER BAY, ON, P7C 3H7
(807) 623-3278   SIC 4231
COURTESY MITSUBISHI   p 34
See CALGARY M VEHICLES GP INC
COURTEX   p 1231
See COUREY, GEORGE INC

COURTICE HEALTH CENTRE   p 813
See OSHAWA CLINIC
COURTIER DOUANES INTERNATIONAL SKYWAY LTEE   p 1127
9230 CH DE LA COTE-DE-LIESSE, LA-CHINE, QC, H8T 1A1
(514) 636-0250   SIC 4731
COURTIER MULTI PLUS INC   p 1172
5650 RUE D'IBERVILLE BUREAU 630, MONTREAL, QC, H2G 2B3
(514) 376-0313   SIC 6411
COURTIERS EN DOUANES GENERAL INC, LES   p 1187
112 RUE MCGILL BUREAU 200, MON-TREAL, QC, H2Y 2E5
(514) 876-1704   SIC 4731
COURTIERS EN TRANSPORT G.M.R. INC, LES   p 1138
2111 4E RUE BUREAU 100, LEVIS, QC, G6W 5M6
(418) 839-5768   SIC 4731
COURTIERS INTER-QUEBEC INC, LES p 1254
900 BOUL RAYMOND, QUEBEC, QC, G1B 3G3
SIC 6531
COURTIERS INTER-QUEBEC INC, LES p 1256
805 RUE DE NEMOURS, QUEBEC, QC, G1H 6Z5
(418) 622-7537   SIC 6531
COURTIKA ASSURANCES INC   p 1109
800 RUE PRINCIPALE SUITE 206, GRANBY, QC, J2G 2Y8
(450) 372-5801   SIC 6411
COURTNEY WHOLESALE CONFEC-TIONERY LIMITED   p 648
600 THIRD ST, LONDON, ON, N5V 2C2
(519) 451-7440   SIC 5145
COURTNEY'S DISTRIBUTING INC   p 847
1941 CONCESSION RD 5, PORT HOPE, ON, L1A 3V5
(905) 786-1106   SIC 5141
COURTYARD BY MARRIOTT - TORONTO-AIRPORT   p 582
See ATLIFIC INC
COURTYARD BY MARRIOTT CALGARY AIRPORT   p 76
See MITCHELL GROUP ALBERTA INC
COURTYARD BY MARRIOTT OTTAWA p 821
See MARKET SQUARE LIMITED PART-NERSHIP
COURTYARD BY MARRIOTT, THE   p 932
See YONGE STREET HOTEL LTD
COURVILLE, DAN CHEVROLET LTD p 900
2601 REGENT ST, SUDBURY, ON, P3E 6K6
(705) 523-2438   SIC 5511
COUSINEAU FARMS   p 1298
See JARDINS PAUL COUSINEAU & FILS INC, LES
COUSINS CURRIE DIVISION OF SILGAN PLASTICS CANADA   p 1033
See SILGAN PLASTICS CANADA INC
COUTTS COURIER COMPANY LTD   p 1415
606 HENDERSON DR, REGINA, SK, S4N 5X3
(306) 569-9300   SIC 7389
COUTTS, WILLIAM E. COMPANY, LIMITED p 480
100 VANDORF SIDEROAD, AURORA, ON, L4G 3G9
SIC 5947
COUTTS, WILLIAM E. COMPANY, LIMITED p 668
3762 14TH AVE UNIT 100, MARKHAM, ON, L3R 0G7
(416) 492-1300   SIC 2771
COUTURE C G H INC   p 1298
12 RUE BELANGER, SAINT-DAMASE-DES-AULNAIES, QC, G0R 2X0
(418) 598-3208   SIC 2339

COUTURE PARFUMS & COSMETICS LTD p 574
997 THE QUEENSWAY, ETOBICOKE, ON, M8Z 1P3
(416) 597-3232   SIC 5999
COUTURE VOIE EXPRESS   p 1294
See 9048-9493 QUEBEC INC
COUTURE, ALFRED LIMITEE   p 1291
420 RUE PRINCIPALE, SAINT-ANSELME, QC, G0R 2N0
(418) 885-4425   SIC 0723
COUTURE, ARMAND & FILS INC   p 1079
1080 BOUL TALBOT, CHICOUTIMI, QC, G7H 4B6
(418) 543-1521   SIC 7011
COUVENT MONT SAINT JOSEPH   p 820
See SISTERS OF CHARITY OF OTTAWA, THE
COUVERTURE MONTREAL-NORD LTEE p 1344
8200 RUE LAFRENAIE, SAINT-LEONARD, QC, H1P 2A9
(514) 324-8300   SIC 1761
COUVERTURES ST-LEONARD INC, LES p 1162
11365 55E AV, MONTREAL, QC, H1E 2R2
(514) 648-1118   SIC 1761
COUVOIR BOIRE & FRERES INC   p 1402
532 9E RANG, WICKHAM, QC, J0C 1S0
(819) 398-6807   SIC 0251
COUVOIR RAMSAY   p 1303
See POIRIER-BERARD LTEE
COUVOIR SCOTT LTEE   p 1366
1798 RTE DU PRESIDENT-KENNEDY, SCOTT, QC, G0S 3G0
(418) 387-2323   SIC 0254
COUVOIR UNIK INC   p 1158
222 104 RTE, MONT-SAINT-GREGOIRE, QC, J0J 1K0
(450) 347-0126   SIC 0254
COUVRE PLANCHERS MAURICE PEL-LETIER   p 1138
See COUVRE-PLANCHERS PELLETIER INC
COUVRE-PLANCHER HAUTE VILLE INC p 1124
14 CH DU BOISE, LAC-BEAUPORT, QC, G3B 2A2
(418) 841-0440   SIC 5023
COUVRE-PLANCHERS PELLETIER INC p 1138
4600 BOUL GUILLAUME-COUTURE, LEVIS, QC, G6W 5N6
(418) 837-3681   SIC 5713
COVALON TECHNOLOGIES LTD   p 693
1660 TECH AVE UNIT 5, MISSISSAUGA, ON, L4W 5S7
(905) 568-8400   SIC 8731
COVANA   p 1098
See CANIMEX INC
COVANTA BURNABY RENEWABLE EN-ERGY, INC / ENERGIE RENOUVELABLE COVANTA BURNABY, INC   p 181
5150 RIVERBEND DR, BURNABY, BC, V3N 4V3
(604) 521-1025   SIC 4961
COVANTA SOLUTIONS ENVIRONNEMEN-TALES INC   p 1074
7860 RUE SAMUEL-HATT, CHAMBLY, QC, J3L 6W4
(450) 447-1212   SIC 4953
COVE GUEST HOME, THE   p 467
See COMMUNITY LODGE INCORPO-RATED
COVE PROPERTIES LTD   p 123
316-14127 23 AVE NW, EDMONTON, AB, T6R 0G4
(780) 469-2683   SIC 1522
COVE VIEW PHARMACY INC   p 413
407 WESTMORLAND RD SUITE 194, SAINT JOHN, NB, E2J 3S9
(506) 636-7777   SIC 5912

COVENANT HEALTH   p 119
3033 66 ST NW, EDMONTON, AB, T6K 4B2
(780) 735-9000   SIC 8062
COVENANT HOUSE TORONTO   p 935
20 GERRARD ST E, TORONTO, ON, M5B 2P3
(416) 598-4898   SIC 8322
COVENANT HOUSE VANCOUVER   p 298
326 PENDER ST W, VANCOUVER, BC, V6B 1T1
(604) 647-4480   SIC 8399
COVENTREE INC   p 961
161 BAY ST 27TH FL, TORONTO, ON, M5J 2S1
(416) 815-0700   SIC 6211
COVENTRY HOMES INC   p 100
17615 111 AVE NW, EDMONTON, AB, T5S 0A1
(780) 453-5100   SIC 1521
COVENTRY NORTH JAGUAR LAND ROVER   p 1030
123 AUTO PARK CIR, WOODBRIDGE, ON, L4L 9S5
(647) 990-3433   SIC 5511
COVEO SOLUTIONS INC   p 1274
3175 CH DES QUATRE-BOURGEOIS BU-REAU 200, QUEBEC, QC, G1W 2K7
(418) 263-1111   SIC 7371
COVER ALL NORTH INC   p 131
GD LCD MAIN, GRANDE PRAIRIE, AB, T8V 2Z7
(780) 532-0366   SIC 1541
COVER FX SKIN CARE INC   p 782
1681 FLINT RD, NORTH YORK, ON, M3J 2W8
(866) 424-3332   SIC 5122
COVER-ALL COMPUTER SERVICES CORP p 871
1170 BIRCHMOUNT RD, SCARBOROUGH, ON, M1P 5E3
(416) 752-8100   SIC 7372
COVERDELL CANADA CORPORATION p 1195
1801 AV MCGILL COLLEGE BUREAU 800, MONTREAL, QC, H3A 2N4
(514) 847-7800   SIC 7389
COVERED BRIDGE POTATO CHIP COM-PANY INC   p 418
149 ST THOMAS RD, ST THOMAS, NB, E7P 2X6
(506) 375-2447   SIC 4225
COVERTECH FABRICATING INC   p 583
279 HUMBERLINE DR SUITE 1, ETOBI-COKE, ON, M9W 5T6
(416) 798-1340   SIC 3089
COVERTECH FLEXIBLE PACKAGING p 583
See COVERTECH FABRICATING INC
COVEY BASICS   p 402
See COVEY OFFICE GROUP INC
COVEY OFFICE GROUP INC   p 402
250 ALISON BLVD, FREDERICTON, NB, E3C 0A9
(506) 458-8333   SIC 5112
COVIA CANADA LTD   p 577
10 FOUR SEASONS PL SUITE 600, ETO-BICOKE, ON, M9B 6H7
(416) 626-1500   SIC 1459
COVIA CANADA LTEE   p 1153
11974 RTE SIR-WILFRID-LAURIER, MIRABEL, QC, J7N 1P5
(450) 438-1238   SIC 1481
COVIDIEN CANADA ULC   p 1333
8455 RTE TRANSCANADIENNE, SAINT-LAURENT, QC, H4S 1Z1
(514) 332-1220   SIC 2834
COVIDIEN CANADA ULC   p 1333
8455 RTE TRANSCANADIENNE, SAINT-LAURENT, QC, H4S 1Z1
(877) 664-8926   SIC 5047
COVIDIEN MANUFACTURING   p 1333
See COVIDIEN CANADA ULC
COVILAC COOPERATIVE AGRICOLE p 1054

40 RUE DE L'EGLISE, BAIE-DU-FEBVRE, QC, J0G 1A0
(450) 783-6491 *SIC* 7389
COVINGTON CAPITAL CORPORATION *p* 942
87 FRONT ST E SUITE 400, TORONTO, ON, M5E 1B8
(416) 504-5419 *SIC* 6722
COWAN BUICK GMC LTD *p* 496
166 KING ST E, BOWMANVILLE, ON, L1C 1N8
(905) 623-3396 *SIC* 5511
COWAN GRAPHICS INC *p* 109
4864 93 AVE NW, EDMONTON, AB, T6B 2P8
(780) 577-5700 *SIC* 2759
COWAN IMAGING GROUP *p* 109
See COWAN GRAPHICS INC
COWAN INSURANCE GROUP LTD *p* 538
705 FOUNTAIN ST N, CAMBRIDGE, ON, N3H 4R7
(519) 650-6360 *SIC* 6411
COWAN, FRANK COMPANY LIMITED *p* 848
75 MAIN ST N, PRINCETON, ON, N0J 1V0
(519) 458-4331 *SIC* 6411
COWANSVILLE TOYOTA *p* 1088
See 9122-8171 QUEBEC INC
COWATERSOGEMA INTERNATIONAL INC *p* 822
275 SLATER ST SUITE 1600, OTTAWA, ON, K1P 5H9
(613) 722-6434 *SIC* 8741
COWBOYS COUNTRY SALOON LTD *p* 100
10102 180 ST NW, EDMONTON, AB, T5S 1N4
SIC 5813
COWDEN-WOODS DESIGN BUILDERS LTD *p* 486
249 SAUNDERS RD UNIT 1, BARRIE, ON, L4N 9A3
(705) 721-8422 *SIC* 1542
COWELL IMPORTS INC *p* 254
5680 PARKWOOD CRES, RICHMOND, BC, V6V 0B5
(604) 273-6068 *SIC* 5511
COWELL MOTORS LTD *p* 254
5600 PARKWOOD CRES, RICHMOND, BC, V6V 0B5
(604) 279-9663 *SIC* 5511
COWI NORTH AMERICA LTD *p* 239
400-138 13TH ST E, NORTH VANCOUVER, BC, V7L 0E5
(604) 986-1222 *SIC* 8712
COWICHAN DISTRICT HOSPITAL *p* 212
See VANCOUVER ISLAND HEALTH AUTHORITY
COWICHAN INDEPENDENT LIVING *p* 211
See COWICHAN VALLEY INDEPENDENT LIVING RESOURCES CENTRE SOCIETY
COWICHAN VALLEY INDEPENDENT LIVING RESOURCES CENTRE SOCIETY *p* 211
121 FIRST ST UNIT 103, DUNCAN, BC, V9L 1R1
(250) 746-3930 *SIC* 8699
COWIE *p* 1225
See 9356-1405 QUEBEC INC.
COWIE INC *p* 1110
660 RUE BERNARD, GRANBY, QC, J2J 0H6
(450) 375-7500 *SIC* 5146
COWPER INC *p* 1126
677 7E AV, LACHINE, QC, H8S 3A1
(514) 637-6746 *SIC* 5084
COWS *p* 1040
See COWS PRINCE EDWARD ISLAND INC
COWS PRINCE EDWARD ISLAND INC *p* 1040
397 CAPITAL DR, CHARLOTTETOWN, PE, C1E 2E2
(902) 566-5558 *SIC* 6712
COX & PALMER *p* 452
1959 UPPER WATER ST SUITE 1100, HALIFAX, NS, B3J 3N2

(902) 491-4118 *SIC* 8111
COX BROS. POULTRY FARM LIMITED *p* 462
7520 215 HWY, MAITLAND, NS, B0N 1T0
(902) 261-2823 *SIC* 0259
COX CONSTRUCTION LIMITED *p* 602
965 YORK RD, GUELPH, ON, N1H 6K5
(519) 824-6570 *SIC* 1611
COX MECHANICAL LTD *p* 165
65 CORRIVEAU AVE, ST. ALBERT, AB, T8N 5A3
(780) 459-2530 *SIC* 1711
COX, FRANK J SALES LIMITED *p* 502
40 WEST DR, BRAMPTON, ON, L6T 3T6
(905) 457-9190 *SIC* 5049
COX, G W CONSTRUCTION LTD *p* 140
1210 31 ST N, LETHBRIDGE, AB, T1H 5J8
(403) 328-1346 *SIC* 1794
CP DISTRIBUTORS LTD *p* 1434
3719 KOCHAR AVE, SASKATOON, SK, S7P 0B8
(306) 242-3315 *SIC* 5039
CP ENERGY MARKETING INC *p* 47
505 2 ST SW SUITE 84, CALGARY, AB, T2P 1N8
(403) 717-4600 *SIC* 8711
CP ENERGY MARKETING L.P. *p* 85
2000-10423 101 ST NW, EDMONTON, AB, T5H 0E8
(403) 717-4600 *SIC* 4911
CP TECH *p* 1328
See CP TECH CORPORATION
CP TECH CORPORATION *p* 1328
2300 RUE COHEN, SAINT-LAURENT, QC, H4R 2N8
(514) 333-0030 *SIC* 3479
CPA ALBERTA *p* 46
See CHARTERED PROFESSIONAL ACCOUNTANTS OF ALBERTA
CPA CANADA *p* 979
See CHARTERED PROFESSIONAL ACCOUNTANTS OF CANADA
CPA MONTREAL *p* 1182
See COMITE PARITAIRE DE L'INDUSTRIE DES SERVICES AUTOMOBILES A LA REGION DE MONTREAL
CPA ONTARIO *p* 928
See CHARTERED PROFESSIONAL ACCOUNTANTS OF ONTARIO
CPAB *p* 949
See CANADIAN PUBLIC ACCOUNTABILITY BOARD
CPABC *p* 297
See CHARTERED PROFESSIONAL ACCOUNTANTS OF BRITISH COLUMBIA
CPAC *p* 822
See CABLE PUBLIC AFFAIRS CHANNEL INC
CPAS SYSTEMS INC *p* 779
250 FERRAND DR 7TH FLOOR, NORTH YORK, ON, M3C 3G8
(416) 422-0563 *SIC* 7371
CPC PUMPS INTERNATIONAL INC *p* 522
5200 MAINWAY, BURLINGTON, ON, L7L 5Z1
(289) 288-4753 *SIC* 3561
CPHC *p* 519
See COMMUNITY & PRIMARY HEALTH CARE- LANARK, LEEDS & GRENVILLE
CPI CANADA *p* 593
See COMMUNICATIONS & POWER INDUSTRIES CANADA INC
CPI CARD GROUP-CANADA INC *p* 551
460 APPLEWOOD CRES, CONCORD, ON, L4K 4Z3
(905) 761-8222 *SIC* 2675
CPI CORROSION *p* 1237
See LVM INC
CPI SERVICE *p* 113
See COMPRESSOR PRODUCTS INTERNATIONAL CANADA INC
CPK INTERIOR PRODUCTS INC *p* 847
128 PETER ST, PORT HOPE, ON, L1A 1C4
(905) 885-7231 *SIC* 3714

CPL *p* 721
See CONTRACT PHARMACEUTICALS LIMITED CANADA
CPM FOODS LTD *p* 344
1324 BROADWAY AVE S, WILLIAMS LAKE, BC, V2G 4N2
(250) 392-4919 *SIC* 6712
CPP *p* 1333
See CIE CANADIENNE DE PAPIER & D'EMBALLAGE LTEE
CPP INVESTMENT BOARD *p* 937
See CANADA PENSION PLAN INVESTMENT BOARD
CPP INVESTMENT BOARD *p* 937
See CPPIB EQUITY INVESTMENTS INC
CPP INVESTMENT BOARD REAL ESTATE HOLDINGS INC *p* 937
1 QUEEN ST E SUITE 2500, TORONTO, ON, M5C 2W5
(416) 868-4075 *SIC* 6719
CPPIB EQUITY INVESTMENTS INC *p* 937
1 QUEEN ST E SUITE 2500, TORONTO, ON, M5C 2W5
(416) 868-4075 *SIC* 6211
CPR *p* 1083
See CANADIAN PACIFIC RAILWAY COMPANY
CPR *p* 1210
See CANADIAN PACIFIC RAILWAY COMPANY
CPR *p* 1410
See CANADIAN PACIFIC RAILWAY COMPANY
CPS *p* 1422
See NUTRIEN AG SOLUTIONS (CANADA) INC
CPS WOOD PRODUCTS *p* 544
See CANADA PALLET CORP
CPT CANADA POWER TECHNOLOGY LIMITED *p* 705
161 WATLINE AVE, MISSISSAUGA, ON, L4Z 1P2
(905) 890-6900 *SIC* 5084
CPT GLOBAL CONSULTING CORPORATION *p* 986
100 KING ST W SUITE 5600, TORONTO, ON, M5X 1C9
(416) 642-2886 *SIC* 8742
CPU *p* 1264
See CPU SERVICE D'ORDINATEUR INC
CPU SERVICE D'ORDINATEUR INC *p* 1264
2323 BOUL DU VERSANT-NORD BUREAU 100, QUEBEC, QC, G1N 4P4
(418) 681-1234 *SIC* 7378
CR 92 HOLDINGS LTD *p* 195
1720 MAPLE ST, CAMPBELL RIVER, BC, V9W 3G2
(250) 287-4214 *SIC* 5172
CRAAQ *p* 1271
See CENTRE DE REFERENCE EN AGRICULTURE ET AGROALIMENTAIRE DU QUEBEC
CRABBE LUMBER *p* 399
See H. J. CRABBE & SONS, LTD
CRABBY JOES BAR *p* 725
See OBSIDIAN GROUP INC
CRABIERS DU NORD INC, LES *p* 1253
428 RUE PRINCIPALE, PORTNEUF-SUR-MER, QC, G0T 1P0
(418) 238-2132 *SIC* 2091
CRAIG EVAN CORPORATION, THE *p* 648
2480 HURON ST UNIT 3, LONDON, ON, N5V 0B1
(519) 455-6760 *SIC* 4899
CRAIG HOLME NURSING HOME *p* 473
See CRAIGWIEL GARDENS
CRAIG KIELBURGER SECONDARY SCHOOL *p* 683
See HALTON DISTRICT SCHOOL BOARD
CRAIG MANUFACTURING LTD *p* 403
96 MCLEAN AVE, HARTLAND, NB, E7P 2K5

(506) 375-4493 *SIC* 3441
CRAIG MCDONALD REDDON INSURANCE BROKERS LTD *p* 617
467 10TH ST SUITE 200, HANOVER, ON, N4N 1R3
(519) 364-3540 *SIC* 6311
CRAIG PACKAGING LIMITED *p* 623
5911 CARMEN RD S, IROQUOIS, ON, K0E 1K0
(613) 652-4856 *SIC* 2653
CRAIG STREET BREWING COMPANY *p* 211
25 CRAIG ST, DUNCAN, BC, V9L 1V7
(250) 737-2337 *SIC* 2082
CRAIG, JAN DRUG STORE LTD *p* 1026
6020 MALDEN RD, WINDSOR, ON, N9H 1S8
(519) 969-9971 *SIC* 5912
CRAIG, MCDONALD, REDDON INSURANCE BROKERS LTD *p* 1004
12 COLBORNE ST S, WALKERTON, ON, N0G 2V0
(519) 881-2701 *SIC* 6411
CRAIGWIEL GARDENS *p* 473
221 AILSA CRAIG MAIN ST, AILSA CRAIG, ON, N0M 1A0
(519) 293-3215 *SIC* 6513
CRAIGWOOD YOUTH SERVICES *p* 473
26996 NEW ONTARIO RD, AILSA CRAIG, ON, N0M 1A0
(519) 232-4301 *SIC* 8322
CRAIK CO-OPERATIVE ASSOCIATION LIMITED, THE *p* 1405
309 3RD ST, CRAIK, SK, S0G 0V0
(306) 734-2612 *SIC* 5171
CRAILIN LOGISTICS SERVICES INC *p* 622
14722 HEART LAKE RD, INGLEWOOD, ON, L7C 2J7
(905) 838-3215 *SIC* 4731
CRAIN'S CONSTRUCTION *p* 663
See 1059895 ONTARIO INC
CRAINS' CONSTRUCTION LIMITED *p* 663
1800 MAYBERLY 2 ELPHIN RD, MABERLY, ON, K0H 2B0
(613) 268-2308 *SIC* 1794
CRAKMEDIA NETWORK *p* 1257
See 4355768 CANADA INC
CRANBERRY GOLF RESORT *p* 546
See LAW CRANBERRY RESORT LIMITED
CRANBROOK DODGE *p* 203
1725 CRANBROOK ST N, CRANBROOK, BC, V1C 3S9
(888) 697-0855 *SIC* 5521
CRANBROOK GLEN ENTERPRISES LIMITED *p* 937
119 CHURCH ST, TORONTO, ON, M5C 2G5
(416) 868-0872 *SIC* 5946
CRANBROOK GLEN ENTERPRISES LIMITED *p* 1182
6229 RUE SAINT-HUBERT, MONTREAL, QC, H2S 2L9
(514) 274-6577 *SIC* 5946
CRANBROOK SOCIETY FOR COMMUNITY LIVING *p* 203
1629 BAKER ST SUITE 100, CRANBROOK, BC, V1C 1B4
(250) 426-7588 *SIC* 8322
CRANE CANADA CO. *p* 1027
141 ROYAL GROUP CRES, WOODBRIDGE, ON, L4H 1X9
(416) 244-5351 *SIC* 5085
CRANE CARRIER (CANADA) LIMITED *p* 100
11523 186 ST NW, EDMONTON, AB, T5S 2W6
(780) 443-2493 *SIC* 5013
CRANE PLUMBING CANADA CORP *p* 895
15 CRANE AVE, STRATFORD, ON, N5A 6S4
SIC 3431

CRANE SERVICE SYSTEMS INC p 891
419 MILLEN RD, STONEY CREEK, ON,
L8E 2P6
(905) 664-9900   *SIC* 7389
CRANE, JOHN CANADA INC p 891
423 GREEN RD, STONEY CREEK, ON, L8E
3A1
(905) 662-6191   *SIC* 3061
CRANE, JOHN CANADA INC p 891
423 GREEN RD, STONEY CREEK, ON, L8E
3A1
(905) 662-6191   *SIC* 3499
CRANESMART SYSTEMS INC p 113
4908 97 ST NW, EDMONTON, AB, T6E 5S1
(780) 437-2986   *SIC* 5084
CRANFIELD GENERAL CONTRACTING p
916
See EVAGELOU ENTERPRISES INC
CRATE AND BARREL CANADA INC p 39
100 ANDERSON RD SE SUITE 273, CAL-
GARY, AB, T2J 3V1
(403) 278-7020   *SIC* 5712
CRATEX INDUSTRIES (CALGARY) LTD p
15
3347 57 AVE SE, CALGARY, AB, T2C 0B2
(403) 203-0880   *SIC* 4783
CRATEX INDUSTRIES LTD p 109
4735 82 AVE NW, EDMONTON, AB, T6B
0E5
(780) 468-4769   *SIC* 4783
CRAVO EQUIPMENT LTD p 517
30 WHITE SWAN RD, BRANTFORD, ON,
N3T 5L4
(519) 759-8226   *SIC* 3448
CRAWFORD & COMPANY (CANADA) INC p
640
539 RIVERBEND DR, KITCHENER, ON,
N2K 3S3
(519) 578-5540   *SIC* 6411
CRAWFORD & COMPANY (CANADA) INC p
1006
180 KING ST S UNIT 610, WATERLOO, ON,
N2J 1P8
(519) 578-9800   *SIC* 6411
CRAWFORD CHRYSLER JEEP DODGE p
543
*See RIVERVIEW SERVICE CENTRE LIM-
ITED*
CRAWFORD CLASS ACTION SERVICES p
1006
*See CRAWFORD & COMPANY (CANADA)
INC*
**CRAWFORD GENERAL CONTRACTING
INC** p 1017
507 BIRKDALE CRT, WINDSOR, ON, N8N
4B3
(519) 567-8411   *SIC* 1542
CRAWFORD MARINE SERVICES p 286
2985 VIRTUAL WAY SUITE 280, VANCOU-
VER, BC, V5M 4X7
(604) 436-2277   *SIC* 5541
CRAWFORD METAL CORPORATION p 771
132 SHEPPARD AVE W SUITE 200,
NORTH YORK, ON, M2N 1M5
(416) 224-1515   *SIC* 5051
CRAWFORD PACKAGING EQUIPMENT p
648
See CRAWFORD PACKAGING INC
CRAWFORD PACKAGING INC p 502
115 WALKER DR UNIT A, BRAMPTON, ON,
L6T 5P5
(800) 265-4993   *SIC* 5084
CRAWFORD PACKAGING INC p 648
3036 PAGE ST, LONDON, ON, N5V 4P2
(519) 659-0507   *SIC* 5199
CRAWFORD PROVINCIAL p 502
See CRAWFORD PACKAGING INC
**CRAWFORD SMITH & SWALLOW CHAR-
TERED ACCOUNTANTS LLP** p
757
4741 QUEEN ST, NIAGARA FALLS, ON,
L2E 2M2
(905) 356-4200   *SIC* 8721
CRAWFORD, ALLAN ASSOCIATES LIM-

ITED p
705
5805 KENNEDY RD, MISSISSAUGA, ON,
L4Z 2G3
(905) 890-2010   *SIC* 5065
CRAZY JOE'S DRAPERY STORE p 781
See 1079746 ONTARIO LIMITED
CRC SOGEMA INC p 1144
1111 RUE SAINT-CHARLES O BUREAU
454, LONGUEUIL, QC, J4K 5G4
(450) 651-2800   *SIC* 8742
CRDI CHAUDIERE-APPALACHES p 1159
*See CENTRE DE READAPTATION EN DE-
FICIENCE INTELLECTUELLE ET TED*
CRDI DE QUEBEC p 1256
*See GOUVERNEMENT DE LA PROVINCE
DE QUEBEC*
CRDITED DE CHAUDIERE-APPALACHES p
1135
*See CENTRE DE READAPTATION EN DE-
FICIENCE INTELLECTUELLE ET TED*
CRE TRANSPORT p 1381
See 9138-7472 QUEBEC INC
CREA p 833
*See CANADIAN REAL ESTATE ASSOCIA-
TION, THE*
CREAFORM INC p 1138
4700 RUE DE LA PASCALINE, LEVIS, QC,
G6W 0L9
(418) 833-4446   *SIC* 7373
CREAM SODA p 1341
See TRIO-SELECTION INC
CREATE-A-TREAT p 584
*See GIVE AND GO PREPARED FOODS
CORP*
CREATECH GROUP, THE p 1395
See 6362222 CANADA INC
CREATION STRATEGIQUE ABSOLUE INC
p 1397
1097 RUE NOTRE-DAME O BUREAU 100,
VICTORIAVILLE, QC, G6P 7L1
(819) 752-8888   *SIC* 8748
CREATION TECHNOLOGIES INC p 192
8999 FRASERTON CRT, BURNABY, BC,
V5J 5H8
(604) 430-4336   *SIC* 3679
CREATION TECHNOLOGIES LP p 192
8997 FRASERTON CRT SUITE 102, BURN-
ABY, BC, V5J 5H8
(604) 430-4336   *SIC* 3679
CREATION TECHNOLOGIES LP p 192
8999 FRASERTON CRT, BURNABY, BC,
V5J 5H8
(604) 430-4336   *SIC* 3679
CREATION TECHNOLOGIES LP p 680
110 CLEGG RD, MARKHAM, ON, L6G 1E1
(866) 754-5004   *SIC* 3679
CREATION TECHNOLOGIES LP p 721
6820 CREDITVIEW RD, MISSISSAUGA,
ON, L5N 0A9
(877) 812-4212   *SIC* 3679
CREATIONS BRONZE p 1094
See JOSEPH RIBKOFF INC
CREATIONS CLAIRE BELL INC p 1178
8955 BOUL SAINT-LAURENT BUREAU
301, MONTREAL, QC, H2N 1M5
(514) 270-1477   *SIC* 5137
CREATIONS G.S.L. INC p 1178
9494 BOUL SAINT-LAURENT BUREAU
800, MONTREAL, QC, H2N 1P4
(514) 273-0422   *SIC* 5137
CREATIONS JADE p 1052
See 135456 CANADA INC
CREATIONS MALO INC p 1241
750 BOUL CURE-LABELLE BUREAU 200,
MONTREAL-OUEST, QC, H7V 2T9
(450) 682-6561   *SIC* 3911
CREATIONS MORIN INC, LES p 1096
2575 BOUL SAINT-JOSEPH, DRUM-
MONDVILLE, QC, J2B 7V4
(819) 474-4664   *SIC* 2399
CREATIONS NATHALIE BARBARA p 1178
See CREATIONS G.S.L. INC
CREATIONS NOC NOC INC p 1178

9600 RUE MEILLEUR BUREAU 750, MON-
TREAL, QC, H2N 2E3
(514) 381-2554   *SIC* 5137
CREATIONS ROBO INC p 1225
1205 RUE DE LOUVAIN O, MONTREAL,
QC, H4N 1G6
(514) 382-6501   *SIC* 5137
CREATIONS SERGIO CANUTO INC p 1169
3637 BOUL CREMAZIE E, MONTREAL,
QC, H1Z 2J4
(514) 729-1116   *SIC* 7389
CREATIONS VERNOVA, LES p 1359
See NOVATECH CANADA INC
CREATIVE AVENUES INC p 64
211 10 AVE SW, CALGARY, AB, T2R 0A4
(403) 292-0360   *SIC* 7389
CREATIVE BAG CO. LTD, THE p 783
1100 LODESTAR RD UNIT 1, NORTH
YORK, ON, M3J 2Z4
(416) 631-6444   *SIC* 5113
CREATIVE CONCEPTS D.V.R. INC p 113
4404 94 ST NW, EDMONTON, AB, T6E 6T7
(780) 438-3044   *SIC* 5199
CREATIVE DOOR SERVICES LTD p 105
14904 135 AVE NW, EDMONTON, AB, T5V
1R9
(780) 483-1789   *SIC* 1751
CREATIVE OUTDOOR ADVERTISING p 598
See BENCH PRESS LTD, THE
CREATIVE SALMON COMPANY LTD p 283
612 CAMPBELL ST, TOFINO, BC, V0R 2Z0
(250) 725-2884   *SIC* 0273
CREATIVE TRAVEL SOLUTIONS INC p 923
118 EGLINTON AVE W SUITE 500,
TORONTO, ON, M4R 2G4
(416) 485-6387   *SIC* 4724
CRECA p 1171
*See CENTRE DE RESSOURCES ED-
UCATIVES ET COMMUNAUTAIRES POUR
ADULTES*
CREDENTIAL p 312
*See CREDENTIAL FINANCIAL STRATE-
GIES INC*
CREDENTIAL FINANCIAL INC p 312
1111 GEORGIA ST W SUITE 800, VAN-
COUVER, BC, V6E 4T6
(604) 714-3800   *SIC* 8741
**CREDENTIAL FINANCIAL STRATEGIES
INC** p 312
1111 GEORGIA ST W SUITE 800, VAN-
COUVER, BC, V6E 4T6
(604) 742-8259   *SIC* 8742
CREDENTIAL SECURITIES INC p 312
1111 GEORGIA ST W SUITE 800, VAN-
COUVER, BC, V6E 4T6
(604) 714-3900   *SIC* 6211
**CREDIT BUREAU OF CANADA COLLEC-
TIONS** p
738
See COLLECTCENTS INC
**CREDIT BUREAU OF STRATFORD (1970)
LTD** p 895
61 LORNE AVE E SUITE 96, STRATFORD,
ON, N5A 6S4
(519) 271-6211   *SIC* 7323
CREDIT COMMERCIALE C.C.F.M. p 1194
*See CORPORATION FINANCIERE BROME
INC*
CREDIT RISK MANAGEMENT CANADA p
895
*See CREDIT BUREAU OF STRATFORD
(1970) LTD*
**CREDIT SUISSE SECURITIES (CANADA)
INC** p 986
1 FIRST CANADIAN PL SUITE 2900,
TORONTO, ON, M5X 1C9
(416) 352-4500   *SIC* 6211
**CREDIT UNION CENTRAL ALBERTA LIM-
ITED** p
35
8500 MACLEOD TRAIL SE SUITE 350N,
CALGARY, AB, T2H 2N1
(403) 258-5900   *SIC* 6062
CREDIT UNION CENTRAL NOVA SCOTIA p

455
*See CREDIT UNION CENTRAL OF
CANADA*
CREDIT UNION CENTRAL OF CANADA p
179
2941 272 ST, ALDERGROVE, BC, V4W 3R3
(604) 856-7724   *SIC* 6062
CREDIT UNION CENTRAL OF CANADA p
455
6074 LADY HAMMOND RD, HALIFAX, NS,
B3K 2R7
(902) 453-0680   *SIC* 6062
CREDIT UNION CENTRAL OF CANADA p
937
151 YONGE ST SUITE 1000, TORONTO,
ON, M5C 2W7
(416) 232-1262   *SIC* 6111
**CREDIT UNION CENTRAL OF MANITOBA
LIMITED** p 374
317 DONALD ST SUITE 400, WINNIPEG,
MB, R3B 2H6
(204) 985-4700   *SIC* 8611
**CREDIT UNION CENTRAL OF NOVA SCO-
TIA** p
455
6074 LADY HAMMOND RD, HALIFAX, NS,
B3K 2R7
(902) 453-0680   *SIC* 6289
**CREDIT UNION DEPOSIT GUARANTEE
CORPORATION** p 88
10104 103 AVE NW SUITE 2000, EDMON-
TON, AB, T5J 0H8
(780) 428-6680   *SIC* 6399
**CREDIT UNION DEPOSIT GUARANTEE
CORPORATION** p 377
200 GRAHAM AVE SUITE 390, WINNIPEG,
MB, R3C 4L5
(204) 942-8480   *SIC* 6399
**CREDIT VALLEY ANIMAL CENTRE LIM-
ITED** p
893
111 HIGHWAY 8, STONEY CREEK, ON,
L8G 1C1
(905) 662-6719   *SIC* 0742
CREDIT VW CANADA, INC p 1328
4865 RUE MARC-BLAIN BUREAU 300,
SAINT-LAURENT, QC, H4R 3B2
(514) 332-4333   *SIC* 6159
CREE CANADA CORP p 687
6889 REXWOOD RD UNIT 3, MISSIS-
SAUGA, ON, L4V 1R2
(905) 671-1991   *SIC* 5063
CREE SCHOOL BOARD p 1081
See COMMISSION SCOLAIRE CRIE (LA)
CREE WAY GAS WEST LTD p 1432
2511 22ND ST W, SASKATOON, SK, S7M
0V9
(306) 975-0125   *SIC* 5541
CREE-ASKI SERVICES LTD FIELD OFFICE
p 746
196 FERGUSON RD, MOOSONEE, ON,
P0L 1Y0
(705) 336-2828   *SIC* 1521
CREE-WAY GAS LTD p 1433
343 PACKHAM AVE, SASKATOON, SK,
S7N 4S1
(306) 955-8823   *SIC* 5541
CREEKBANK TRANSPORT, DIV OF p 701
See TRIANGLE FREIGHT SERVICES LTD
CREEKSIDE MARKET INC p 343
2071 LAKE PLACID RD SUITE 305,
WHISTLER, BC, V8E 0B6
(604) 938-9301   *SIC* 5411
CREEMORE SPRINGS BREWERY LIMITED
p 564
139 MILL ST SUITE 369, CREEMORE, ON,
L0M 1G0
(705) 466-2240   *SIC* 2082
**CREIGHTON & COMPANY INSURANCE
BROKERS LTD** p 705
315 MATHESON BLVD E, MISSISSAUGA,
ON, L4Z 1X8
(905) 890-0090   *SIC* 6411
CREIGHTON ROCK DRILL LIMITED p 734

2222 DREW RD, MISSISSAUGA, ON, L5S 1B1
(905) 673-8200   *SIC* 5082
CREIT MANAGEMENT L.P.   p 928
175 BLOOR ST E SUITE 500N, TORONTO, ON, M4W 3R8
(416) 628-7771   *SIC* 6531
CREMES GLACEES LEBEL, LES   p 1129
See AGROPUR COOPERATIVE
CRESCENT HEIGHTS HIGH SCHOOL p 41
See CALGARY BOARD OF EDUCATION
CRESCENT HEIGHTS HIGH SCHOOLp 146
See MEDICINE HAT SCHOOL DISTRICT NO. 76
CRESCENT PARK LODGE   p 591
See CONMED DEVELOPMENTS INC
CRESCENT PARK LODGE   p 591
4 HAGEY AVE, FORT ERIE, ON, L2A 1W3
(905) 871-8330   *SIC* 8051
CRESCENT POINT ENERGY CORP   p 47
585 8 AVE SW SUITE 2000, CALGARY, AB, T2P 1G1
(403) 693-0020   *SIC* 1311
CRESCENT POINT ENERGY CORP p 1405
801 RAILWAY AVE, CARLYLE, SK, S0C 0R0
(306) 453-3236   *SIC* 1311
CRESCITA THERAPEUTICS INC   p 721
6733 MISSISSAUGA RD SUITE 610, MISSISSAUGA, ON, L5N 6J5
(905) 673-4295   *SIC* 8731
CRESSEY DEVELOPMENT CORPORATION   p
293
555 8TH AVE W SUITE 200, VANCOUVER, BC, V5Z 1C6
(604) 683-1256   *SIC* 1522
CREST CIRCUIT   p 665
See 656706 ONTARIO INC
CREST HOTEL LTD   p 251
222 1ST AVE W, PRINCE RUPERT, BC, V8J 1A8
(250) 624-6771   *SIC* 7011
CREST MOLD TECHNOLOGY INC   p 807
2055 BLACKACRE DR RR 1, OLDCASTLE, ON, N0R 1L0
(519) 737-1546   *SIC* 3089
CREST REALTY LTD   p 240
2609 WESTVIEW DR SUITE 101, NORTH VANCOUVER, BC, V7N 4M2
(604) 985-1321   *SIC* 6531
CRESTLINE COACH LTD   p 1434
126 WHEELER ST, SASKATOON, SK, S7P 0A9
(306) 934-8844   *SIC* 3711
CRESTON PET ADOPTION & WELFARE SOCIETY   p 204
2805 LOWER WYNNDEL RD, CRESTON, BC, V0B 1G8
(250) 428-7297   *SIC* 8699
CRESTON VALLEY GLEANERS SOCIETYp 204
807 CANYON ST, CRESTON, BC, V0B 1G3
(250) 428-4106   *SIC* 8399
CRESTVIEW CHRYSLER DODGE JEEP   p 1420
601 ALBERT ST, REGINA, SK, S4R 2P4
(306) 992-2443   *SIC* 5511
CRESTVIEW STRATEGY INC   p 823
222 QUEEN ST SUITE 1201, OTTAWA, ON, K1P 5V9
(613) 232-3192   *SIC* 8748
CRESTWOOD ENGINEERING COMPANY LTD   p 226
6217 205 ST, LANGLEY, BC, V2Y 1N7
(604) 533-8675   *SIC* 5013
CRESTWOOD SCHOOL   p 779
See FOREST HILL LEARNING CENTRE LIMITED
CREW ENERGY INC   p 47
250 5 ST SW SUITE 800, CALGARY, AB, T2P 0R4
(403) 266-2088   *SIC* 1311
CRFA
See RESTAURANTS CANADA

CRH CANADA GROUP INC   p 551
2300 STEELES AVE W SUITE 400, CONCORD, ON, L4K 5X6
(905) 532-3000   *SIC* 3531
CRH CANADA GROUP INC   p 668
7655 WOODBINE AVE, MARKHAM, ON, L3R 2N4
(905) 475-6631   *SIC* 3273
CRH CANADA GROUP INC   p 683
9410 DUBLIN LINE, MILTON, ON, L9T 2X7
(905) 878-6051   *SIC* 1481
CRH CANADA GROUP INC   p 713
2391 LAKESHORE RD W, MISSISSAUGA, ON, L5J 1K1
(905) 822-1653   *SIC* 3241
CRH CANADA GROUP INC   p 802
690 DORVAL DR SUITE 200, OAKVILLE, ON, L6K 3W7
(905) 842-2741   *SIC* 8711
CRH CANADA GROUP INC   p 803
585 MICHIGAN DR SUITE 1, OAKVILLE, ON, L6L 0G1
(905) 842-2741   *SIC* 1521
CRH CANADA GROUP INC   p 1114
966 CH DES PRAIRIES, JOLIETTE, QC, J6E 0L4
(450) 756-1076   *SIC* 3241
CRH CANADA GROUP INC   p 1141
435 RUE JEAN-NEVEU, LONGUEUIL, QC, J4G 2P9
(450) 651-1117   *SIC* 3241
CRH CANADA GROUP INC   p 1141
435 RUE JEAN-NEVEU, LONGUEUIL, QC, J4G 2P9
(450) 651-1117   *SIC* 3273
CRH MEDICAL CORPORATION   p 303
999 CANADA PL SUITE 578, VANCOUVER, BC, V6C 3E1
(604) 633-1440   *SIC* 3841
CRI CANADA   p 185
See CRI CREDIT GROUP SERVICES INC
CRI CANADA INC   p 111
8925 82 AVE NW SUITE 207, EDMONTON, AB, T6C 0Z2
(780) 469-3808   *SIC* 6712
CRI CREDIT GROUP SERVICES INC p 185
4185 STILL CREEK DR UNIT 350A, BURNABY, BC, V5C 6G9
(604) 438-7785   *SIC* 6411
CRIBIT SEEDS   p 1013
See WINTERMAR FARMS (1989) LTD
CRIBTEC INC   p 1277
5145 RUE RIDEAU, QUEBEC, QC, G2E 5H5
(418) 622-5992   *SIC* 1731
CRICH HOLDINGS AND BUILDINGS LIMITED   p
653
560 WELLINGTON ST, LONDON, ON, N6A 3R4
(519) 434-1808   *SIC* 6719
CRIDGE CENTRE FOR THE FAMILY, THE p
334
1307 HILLSIDE AVE SUITE 414, VICTORIA, BC, V8T 0A2
(250) 384-8058   *SIC* 8322
CRIMP CIRCUITS INC   p 783
675 PETROLIA RD, NORTH YORK, ON, M3J 2N6
(416) 665-2466   *SIC* 3672
CRIMSON TIDE FISHERIES   p 423
See BARRY GROUP INC
CRISIS CENTRE NORTH BAY   p 763
198 SECOND AVE W, NORTH BAY, ON, P1B 3K9
SIC 8399
CRISTINI AMERIQUE DU NORD INCp 1129
700 BOUL CRISTINI, LACHUTE, QC, J8H 4N3
(450) 562-5511   *SIC* 2679
CRISTOMEL INC   p 1324
100 BOUL ALEXIS-NIHON BUREAU 105, SAINT-LAURENT, QC, H4M 2N6
(514) 747-1575   *SIC* 5045

CRITERION CATALYSTS & TECHNOLOGIES CANADA, INC   p
118
5241 CALGARY TRAIL NW UNIT 810, EDMONTON, AB, T6H 5G8
(780) 438-4188   *SIC* 2819
CRITES & RIDDELL INC   p 1130
2695 AV DOLLARD, LASALLE, QC, H8N 2J8
(514) 368-8641   *SIC* 5112
CRITES & RIDDELL PROMO   p 1130
See CRITES & RIDDELL INC
CRITICAL CONTROL ENERGY SERVICES CORP   p 29
140 10 AVE SE SUITE 800, CALGARY, AB, T2G 0R1
(403) 705-7500   *SIC* 7371
CRITICAL CONTROL ENERGY SERVICES CORP   p 88
10130 103 ST NW SUITE 1500, EDMONTON, AB, T5J 3N9
(780) 423-3100   *SIC* 7371
CRITICAL CONTROL ENERGY SERVICES CORP   p 91
10045 111 ST NW, EDMONTON, AB, T5K 2M5
(780) 423-3100   *SIC* 8742
CRITICAL MASS INC   p 979
425 ADELAIDE ST W, TORONTO, ON, M5V 3C1
(416) 673-5275   *SIC* 7374
CRITICAL PATH COURIERS LTD   p 693
1257 KAMATO RD, MISSISSAUGA, ON, L4W 2M2
(905) 212-8333   *SIC* 7389
CRITTERS & CROPS LTD   p 160
GD, ROSEMARY, AB, T0J 2W0
(403) 378-4934   *SIC* 0291
CRIUS ENERGY TRUST   p 986
100 KING ST W SUITE 3400, TORONTO, ON, M5X 1A4
(416) 644-1753   *SIC* 4924
CRL SYNERGY   p 66
See 1391130 ALBERTA LTD
CRNBC   p 320
See COLLEGE OF REGISTERED NURSES OF BC
CROATION CLUB KARLOVAC   p 683
1880 THOMPSON RD S, MILTON, ON, L9T 2X5
(905) 878-6185   *SIC* 8651
CROCS CANADA INC   p 851
1455 16TH AVE UNIT 7, RICHMOND HILL, ON, L4B 4W5
(905) 747-3366   *SIC* 3021
CROCUS PLAINS REGIONAL SECONDARY SCHOOL   p
346
See BRANDON SCHOOL DIVISION, THE
CRODA CANADA LIMITED   p 906
221 RACCO PKY UNIT A, THORNHILL, ON, L4J 8X9
(905) 886-1383   *SIC* 5169
CROESUS FINANSOFT INC   p 1241
600 BOUL ARMAND-FRAPPIER BUREAU 200, MONTREAL-OUEST, QC, H7V 4B4
(450) 662-6101   *SIC* 7371
CROFAM MANAGEMENT INC   p 915
501 CONSUMERS RD, TORONTO, ON, M2J 5E2
(416) 391-0400   *SIC* 7359
CROFT, MICHAEL SAND & GRAVEL INC p
590
400421 GREY RD SUITE 4, FLESHERTON, ON, N0C 1E0
(519) 924-2429   *SIC* 1611
CROFTERS FOOD LTD   p 837
7 GREAT NORTH RD, PARRY SOUND, ON, P2A 2X8
(705) 746-6301   *SIC* 2033
CROFTERS ORGANIC   p 837
See CROFTERS FOOD LTD
CROFTON MANOR   p 323
See REVERA INC

CROFTON MILL   p 204
See CATALYST PAPER CORPORATION
CROFTON, DIV OF   p 264
See CATALYST PAPER CORPORATION
CROHN'S AND COLITIS CANADA   p 925
60 ST CLAIR AVE E SUITE 600, TORONTO, ON, M4T 1N5
(416) 920-5035   *SIC* 8399
CROISIERES AML INC   p 1258
124 RUE SAINT-PIERRE, QUEBEC, QC, G1K 4A7
(866) 856-6668   *SIC* 4424
CROISIERES DU PORT DE MONTREAL   p 1258
See CROISIERES AML INC
CROISSANTERIE BLANVILLE   p 1059
See PETITE BRETONNE INC, LA
CROISSANTS D' OLIVIER LTD, LES   p 200
12 KING EDWARD ST UNIT 101, COQUITLAM, BC, V3K 0E7
(778) 285-8662   *SIC* 2051
CROISSANTS DE BERCY   p 1266
See BOULANGERIE PATISSERIE DUMAS INC
CROIX BLEUE DU QUEBEC (LA)   p 1193
See ASSOCIATION D'HOSPITALISATION CANASSURANCE
CROIX BLEUE MEDAVIE   p 1198
See MEDAVIE INC
CROMBIE DEVELOPMENTS LIMITEDp 452
2000 BARRINGTON ST SUITE 1210, HALIFAX, NS, B3J 3K1
SIC 6512
CROMBIE DEVELOPMENTS LIMITEDp 466
115 KING ST, STELLARTON, NS, B0K 1S0
(902) 755-4440   *SIC* 6512
CROMBIE REAL ESTATE INVESTMENT TRUST   p 463
610 EAST RIVER RD SUITE 200, NEW GLASGOW, NS, B2H 3S2
(902) 755-8100   *SIC* 6798
CROMBIE REIT   p 453
See HALIFAX DEVELOPMENTS
CRONE GEOPHYSICS & EXPLORATION LTD   p 721
2135 MEADOWPINE BLVD, MISSISSAUGA, ON, L5N 6L5
(905) 814-0100   *SIC* 3829
CRONIER, J.P. ENTERPRISES INC   p 619
1330 FRONT ST, HEARST, ON, P0L 1N0
(705) 362-5822   *SIC* 5531
CRONKITE, DIV OF   p 528
See WOLSELEY CANADA INC
CROOKS, J R HEALTH CARE SERVICES INC   p 908
285 MEMORIAL AVE, THUNDER BAY, ON, P7B 6H4
(807) 345-6564   *SIC* 5999
CROP INC   p 1195
550 RUE SHERBROOKE O BUREAU 900, MONTREAL, QC, H3A 1B9
(514) 807-9431   *SIC* 8732
CROP MANAGEMENT NETWORK INC p 78
4232 41 ST SUITE 110, CAMROSE, AB, T4V 4E5
(587) 322-2767   *SIC* 5191
CROP PRODUCTION SERVICES (CPS)p 39
See AGRIUM INC
CROPLEY, PAUL J & D SALES LTD   p 897
24614 ADELAIDE RD, STRATHROY, ON, N7G 2P8
(519) 245-2704   *SIC* 5531
CROPPER MOTORS   p 1412
See CROPPER, A.G. ENTERPRISES LTD
CROPPER, A.G. ENTERPRISES LTDp 1412
501 5TH AVE N, NAICAM, SK, S0K 2Z0
(306) 874-2011   *SIC* 5511
CROQUE-MOI   p 1062
See PLAISIRS GASTRONOMIQUES INC
CROSBIE JOB INSURANCE LIMITEDp 430
1 CROSBIE PL SUITE 201, ST. JOHN'S, NL, A1B 3Y8
(709) 726-5414   *SIC* 6411
CROSBIE SALAMIS LIMITED   p 428

80 HEBRON WAY, ST. JOHN'S, NL, A1A 0L9

(709) 722-5377   SIC 1799

CROSBY AUDI INC   p 635
2350 SHIRLEY DR, KITCHENER, ON, N2B 3X5

(519) 514-0100   SIC 5511

CROSBY MOLASSES COMPANY LIMITED p 413
327 ROTHESAY AVE, SAINT JOHN, NB, E2J 2C3

(506) 634-7515   SIC 5149

CROSBY PROPERTY MANAGEMENT LTD p 326
777 HORNBY ST SUITE 600, VANCOUVER, BC, V6Z 1S4

(604) 683-8900   SIC 6513

CROSS & NORMAN (1986) LTD   p 227
20027 FRASER HWY, LANGLEY, BC, V3A 4E4

(604) 534-7927   SIC 5511

CROSS BORDERS CONSULTING LTD   p 1413
PO BOX 509, PILOT BUTTE, SK, S0G 3Z0

(306) 781-4484   SIC 1381

CROSS BORDERS DRILLING   p 1413
See CROSS BORDERS CONSULTING LTD

CROSS COUNTRY MANUFACTURING   p 352
See 5274398 MANITOBA LTD

CROSS LAKE EDUCATION AUTHORITY p 348
GD, CROSS LAKE, MB, R0B 0J0

(204) 676-3030   SIC 8211

CROSS PACIFIC INVESTMENT GROUP INC p 200
62 FAWCETT RD SUITE 13, COQUITLAM, BC, V3K 6V5

(604) 522-8144   SIC 5141

CROSS, DR G B MEMORIAL HOSPITAL p 421
67 MANITOBA DR, CLARENVILLE, NL, A5A 1K3

(709) 466-3411   SIC 8062

CROSSALTA GAS STORAGE & SERVICES LTD   p 47
700 2 ST SW SUITE 1600, CALGARY, AB, T2P 2W1

(403) 298-3575   SIC 4922

CROSSBY DEWAR INC   p 813
1143 WENTWORTH ST W SUITE 201, OSHAWA, ON, L1J 8P7

(905) 683-5102   SIC 1751

CROSSEY ENGINEERING LTD   p 766
2255 SHEPPARD AVE E, NORTH YORK, ON, M2J 4Y1

(416) 497-3111   SIC 8711

CROSSFIELD ENVIRONMENTAL CONSULTANTS OF CANADA LIMITED   p 629
242 BURNS BLVD, KING CITY, ON, L7B 1E1

(905) 833-2108   SIC 7389

CROSSFIELD PLANT INTERIOR   p 629
See CROSSFIELD ENVIRONMENTAL CONSULTANTS OF CANADA LIMITED

CROSSING COMPANY INCORPORATED, THE   p 148
1807 8 ST, NISKU, AB, T9E 7S8

(780) 955-5051   SIC 1623

CROSSLINX TRANSIT SOLUTIONS CONSTRUCTORS GP   p 771
4711 YONGE ST UNIT 1500, NORTH YORK, ON, M2N 6K8

(416) 679-6116   SIC 8742

CROSSMARK CANADA INC   p 693
5580 EXPLORER DR SUITE 300, MISSISSAUGA, ON, L4W 4Y1

SIC 8743

CROSSROADS C & I DISTRIBUTORS p 98
See 518162 ALBERTA INC

CROSSROADS CHRISTIAN COMMUNICATIONS INCORPORATED   p 530

1295 NORTH SERVICE RD, BURLINGTON, ON, L7R 4M2

(905) 845-5100   SIC 4833

CROSSROADS ESSO   p 639
593 VICTORIA ST N, KITCHENER, ON, N2H 5E9

(519) 741-0424   SIC 5541

CROSSROADS FAMILY OF MINISTRIES   p 530
See CROSSROADS CHRISTIAN COMMUNICATIONS INCORPORATED

CROSSROADS GAS CO-OP LTD   p 137
36060 RANGE ROAD 282, INNISFAIL, AB, T4G 1T5

(403) 227-4861   SIC 4924

CROSSROADS PONTIAC BUICK LIMITED p 423
295 AIRPORT BLVD, GANDER, NL, A1V 1Y9

(709) 651-3500   SIC 5511

CROSSROADS REGIONAL HEALTH AUTHORITY   p 82
4550 MADSEN AVE, DRAYTON VALLEY, AB, T7A 1N8

(780) 542-5321   SIC 8062

CROSSTOWN CHRYSLER DODGE JEEP RAM   p 106
See XTOWN MOTORS LP

CROSSTOWN METAL INDUSTRIES LTD   p 270
13133 115 AVE SUITE 100, SURREY, BC, V3R 2V8

(604) 589-3133   SIC 3444

CROSSTOWN OLDSMOBILE CHEVROLET LTD   p 898
280 FALCONBRIDGE RD, SUDBURY, ON, P3A 5K3

(705) 566-4804   SIC 5511

CROSSWINDS INTERNET COMMUNICATIONS INC   p 942
1 YONGE ST, TORONTO, ON, M5E 1E5

(416) 364-2202   SIC 4813

CROTEAU, J. A. (1989) INC   p 1225
1001 RUE DU MARCHE-CENTRAL LOCAL A11, MONTREAL, QC, H4N 1J8

(514) 382-3403   SIC 5651

CROTEAU, MARCEL INC   p 1114
990 RUE PAPINEAU BUREAU 5, JOLIETTE, QC, J6E 2L7

(450) 756-1221   SIC 5651

CROTEAU, PIERRE INC   p 1173
1490 AV DU MONT-ROYAL E BUREAU 3, MONTREAL, QC, H2J 1Y9

(514) 521-0059   SIC 5621

CROTHALL SERVICES CANADA INC p 443
300 PLEASANT ST SUITE 10, DARTMOUTH, NS, B2Y 3S3

(902) 464-3115   SIC 7219

CROUSTILLES YUM YUM, DIV DE   p 1400
See ALIMENTS KRISPY KERNELS INC

CROUTE DOREE, LA   p 1345
See DELICOUKI INC

CROVEN CRYSTALS   p 1015
See WENZEL INTERNATIONAL INC

CROWDCARE CORPORATION   p 851
120 EAST BEAVER CREEK RD SUITE 202, RICHMOND HILL, ON, L4B 4V1

(647) 559-9190   SIC 7371

CROWE FOUNDRY LIMITED   p 537
95 SHEFFIELD ST, CAMBRIDGE, ON, N3C 1C4

SIC 3321

CROWE SOBERMAN LLP   p 925
2 ST CLAIR AVE E SUITE 1100, TORONTO, ON, M4T 2T5

(416) 964-7633   SIC 8721

CROWELLS PHARMACY LTD   p 458
205 HERRING COVE RD SUITE 505, HALIFAX, NS, B3P 1L1

(902) 477-4650   SIC 5912

CROWFLIGHT MINERALS   p 360

See CANICKEL MINING LIMITED

CROWFOOT DODGE   p 74
See CROWFOOT DODGE CHRYSLER INC

CROWFOOT DODGE CHRYSLER INC p 74
20 CROWFOOT RISE NW, CALGARY, AB, T3G 3S7

(403) 241-0300   SIC 5511

CROWFOOT FORD   p 75
See DUFFIN FAMILY HOLDINGS LTD

CROWFOOT H MOTORS LP   p 75
710 CROWFOOT CRESCENT NW, CALGARY, AB, T3G 4S3

(403) 252-8833   SIC 5511

CROWFOOT HYUNDAI   p 75
See CROWFOOT H MOTORS LP

CROWFOOT IMAGE AUTO BODY LTD p 75
141 CROWFOOT WAY NW UNIT 25, CALGARY, AB, T3G 4B7

(403) 547-4932   SIC 5511

CROWFOOT LIQUOR STORE   p 74
See 586307 ALBERTA LTD

CROWN 44   p 226
See WESTLAM INDUSTRIES LTD

CROWN ACURA   p 390
See ANIKA HOLDINGS INC

CROWN BUILDING SUPPLIES LTD   p 276
7550 132 ST UNIT 10, SURREY, BC, V3W 4M7

(604) 591-5555   SIC 5039

CROWN CAP (1987) LTD   p 380
1130 WALL ST, WINNIPEG, MB, R3E 2R9

(204) 775-7740   SIC 2353

CROWN CAPITAL ENTERPRISES INC   p 1415
1801 E TURVEY RD UNIT 7, REGINA, SK, S4N 3A4

(306) 546-8030   SIC 6712

CROWN CAPITAL PARTNERS INC   p 47
888 3 ST SW FL 10, CALGARY, AB, T2P 5C5

(403) 775-2554   SIC 8741

CROWN CORRUGATED COMPANY   p 263
13911 GARDEN CITY RD, RICHMOND, BC, V7A 2S5

(604) 277-7111   SIC 2653

CROWN FOOD SERVICE EQUIPMENT LTD p 786
70 OAKDALE RD, NORTH YORK, ON, M3N 1V9

(416) 746-2358   SIC 3589

CROWN INVESTMENTS CORPORATION OF SASKATCHEWAN   p 1417
2400 COLLEGE AVE SUITE 400, REGINA, SK, S4P 1C8

(306) 787-6851   SIC 4911

CROWN ISLE RESORT & GOLF COMMUNITY   p 203
See SILVERADO LAND CORP

CROWN LIFT TRUCKS   p 742
See RYDER MATERIAL HANDLING ULC

CROWN METAL PACKAGING CANADA LP p 15
4455 75 AVE SE, CALGARY, AB, T2C 2K8

(403) 236-0241   SIC 3411

CROWN METAL PACKAGING CANADA LP p 997
21 FENMAR DR, TORONTO, ON, M9L 2Y9

(416) 741-6002   SIC 3411

CROWN METAL PACKAGING CANADA LP p 1333
5789 RUE CYPIHOT, SAINT-LAURENT, QC, H4S 1R3

(514) 956-8900   SIC 3411

CROWN NISSAN   p 390
1717 WAVERLEY ST SUITE 700, WINNIPEG, MB, R3T 6A9

(204) 269-4685   SIC 5511

CROWN PLASTICS EXTUSSION CO p 1028
See ROYAL GROUP, INC

CROWN PLAZA FREDERICTON LORD BEAVER BROOK HOTEL, DIV OF   p 400
See AQUILNI GROUP PROPERTIES LP

CROWN PLAZA HOTEL   p 825

See DELTA HOTELS NO. 12 LIMITED PARTNERSHIP

CROWN POINT ENERGY INC   p 47
GD, CALGARY, AB, T2P 0T8

(403) 232-1150   SIC 1382

CROWN PROPERTY MANAGEMENT INC p 944
400 UNIVERSITY AVE SUITE 1900, TORONTO, ON, M5G 1S5

(416) 927-1851   SIC 6531

CROWN RELOCATIONS   p 522
See CROWN WORLDWIDE LTD

CROWN RIDGE HEALTH CARE SERVICES INC   p 492
37 WILKIE ST, BELLEVILLE, ON, K8P 4E4

(613) 966-1323   SIC 8051

CROWN RIDGE HEALTH CARE SERVICES INC   p 998
106 CROWN ST, TRENTON, ON, K8V 6R3

(613) 392-1289   SIC 8051

CROWN RIDGE PLACE   p 998
See CROWN RIDGE HEALTH CARE SERVICES INC

CROWN SHRED & RECYCLING INC p 1415
225 E 6TH AVE, REGINA, SK, S4N 6A6

(306) 545-5454   SIC 4953

CROWN STAR FOODS-EDMONTON   p 108
See 620126 ALBERTA LTD

CROWN WALLPAPER + FABRICS   p 583
See CORONET WALLPAPERS (ONTARIO) LIMITED

CROWN WORLDWIDE LTD   p 522
1375 ARTISANS CRT, BURLINGTON, ON, L7L 5Y2

(905) 827-4899   SIC 4783

CROWNE PLAZA CHATEAU LACOMBE p 88
See CHATEAU LACOMBE HOTEL LTD

CROWNE PLAZA MONCTON DOWNTOWN p 406
See AQUILINI INVESTMENT GROUP INC

CROWNE PLAZA MONCTON DOWNTOWN HOTEL   p 406
1005 MAIN ST, MONCTON, NB, E1C 1G9

(506) 854-6340   SIC 7011

CROWNHILL PACKAGING LTD   p 502
8905 GOREWAY DR, BRAMPTON, ON, L6T 0B7

(905) 494-1191   SIC 5199

CROWSNEST PASS HEALTH CENTRE p 6
See ALBERTA HEALTH SERVICES

CROZIER, DONNA & JOHN LIMITED p 83
13211 FORT RD NW, EDMONTON, AB, T5A 1C3

(780) 473-2394   SIC 5531

CRP PRODUCTS   p 895
See C. R. PLASTIC PRODUCTS INC

CRS   p 248
See CARIBOU ROAD SERVICES LTD

CRS   p 380
See COMMUNITY RESPITE SERVICE

CRS   p 715
See CONTACT RESOURCE SERVICES INC

CRS CRANESYSTEMS INC   p 162
333 STRATHMOOR WAY, SHERWOOD PARK, AB, T8H 2K2

(780) 416-8800   SIC 3531

CRSS   p 468
See COLCHESTER RESIDENTIAL SERVICES SOCIETY

CRT - EBC, S.E.N.C.   p 1064
95 RUE J.-A.-BOMBARDIER BUREAU 4, BOUCHERVILLE, QC, J4B 8P1

SIC 7363

CRT - EBC, S.E.N.C.   p 1136
870 RUE ARCHIMEDE, LEVIS, QC, G6V 7M5

(418) 833-8073   SIC 7363

CRT CONSTRUCTION INC   p 1136
870 RUE ARCHIMEDE, LEVIS, QC, G6V 7M5

(418) 833-8073   SIC 1622

CRT-HAMEL   p 1136

870 RUE ARCHIMEDE, LEVIS, QC, G6V 7M5
(418) 833-8073 *SIC* 1542
CRUICKSHANK FORD *p* 795
2062 WESTON RD, NORTH YORK, ON, M9N 1X5
(416) 244-6461 *SIC* 5511
CRUICKSHANK-GLENGARRY DIVISION *p* 599
See COCO PAVING INC
CRUISE CANADA INC *p* 8
2980 26 ST NE, CALGARY, AB, T1Y 6R7
(403) 291-4963 *SIC* 7519
CRUISE CONCEPT *p* 290
See BAINS TRAVEL LIMITED
CRUISEPLUS MANAGEMENT LTD *p* 230
7143 CAILLET RD, LANTZVILLE, BC, V0R 2H0
(250) 390-0220 *SIC* 4724
CRUISESHIPCENTERS INTERNATIONAL INC *p* 312
1055 HASTINGS ST W SUITE 400, VANCOUVER, BC, V6E 2E9
(604) 685-1221 *SIC* 6794
CRUPI GROUP, THE *p* 876
See D. CRUPI & SONS LIMITED
CRUST CRAFT INC *p* 93
13211 146 ST NW, EDMONTON, AB, T5L 4S8
(780) 466-1333 *SIC* 5461
CRUSTACES DES MONTS INC, LES *p* 1355
1 RUE DU PARC-INDUSTRIEL, SAINTE-ANNE-DES-MONTS, QC, G4V 2V9
(418) 763-5561 *SIC* 2092
CRYOCATH TECHNOLOGY *p* 1251
See MEDTRONIC CRYOCATH LP
CRYOPAK INDUSTRIES (2007) ULC *p* 205
1081 CLIVEDEN AVE SUITE 110, DELTA, BC, V3M 5V1
(604) 515-7977 *SIC* 3822
CRYOVAC *p* 717
See SEALED AIR (CANADA) CO./CIE
CRYSTAL CLAIRE COSMETICS INC *p* 873
165 MILNER AVE, SCARBOROUGH, ON, M1S 4G7
(416) 421-1882 *SIC* 2844
CRYSTAL CONSULTING INC *p* 279
2677 192 ST UNIT 108, SURREY, BC, V3Z 3X1
(778) 294-4425 *SIC* 1751
CRYSTAL FOUNTAINS HOLDINGS INC *p* 551
60 SNOW BLVD SUITE 3, CONCORD, ON, L4K 4B3
(905) 660-6674 *SIC* 3499
CRYSTAL GLASS CANADA LTD *p* 118
6424 GATEWAY BLVD NW, EDMONTON, AB, T6H 2H9
(780) 652-2512 *SIC* 7536
CRYSTAL GROUP HOLDINGS INC. *p* 873
165 MILNER AVE, SCARBOROUGH, ON, M1S 4G7
(416) 421-9299 *SIC* 6712
CRYSTAL INFOSOFT *p* 933
186 FREDERICK ST, TORONTO, ON, M5A 4L4
SIC 7371
CRYSTAL INTERNATIONAL *p* 873
See CRYSTAL INTERNATIONAL (GROUP) INC.
CRYSTAL INTERNATIONAL (GROUP) INC. *p* 873
165 MILNER AVE, SCARBOROUGH, ON, M1S 4G7
(416) 421-9299 *SIC* 2844
CRYSTAL MOUNTAIN RESORTS LTD *p* 219
GD RPO BANKS CENTRE, KELOWNA, BC, V1X 4K3
SIC 7011
CRYSTAL PARK SCHOOL *p* 132
See GRANDE PRAIRIE PUBLIC SCHOOL DISTRICT #2357
CRYSTAL WATER INVESTMENTS COMPANY *p*

1130
7050 RUE SAINT-PATRICK, LASALLE, QC, H8N 1V2
(514) 363-3232 *SIC* 3949
CS AUTOMOTIVE TUBING INC *p* 661
2400 INNOVATION DR, LONDON, ON, N6M 0C5
(519) 453-0123 *SIC* 3317
CS DESIGN *p* 1178
See CANSEW INC
CS WIND CANADA INC *p* 1017
9355 ANCHOR DR, WINDSOR, ON, N8N 5A8
(519) 735-0973 *SIC* 3523
CSA *p* 1214
See UNION DES ARTISTES
CSA GROUP *p* 583
See CANADIAN STANDARDS ASSOCIATION.
CSA INTERNATIONAL *p* 254
See CANADIAN STANDARDS ASSOCIATION
CSA TRANSPORTATION *p* 571
See 669779 ONTARIO LTD
CSC *p* 624
See COMPUTER SCIENCES CANADA INC
CSC LA FONTAINE *p* 410
See DISTRICT SCOLAIRE FRANCOPHONE NORD-EST
CSC VIC ROYAL *p* 1399
See VICTORIAVILLE & CO INC
CSCL *p* 203
See CRANBROOK SOCIETY FOR COMMUNITY LIVING
CSCL DU HAUT ST FRANCOIS *p* 1400
See CENTRE DE SANTE ET DE SERVICE SOCIAUX DU HAUT SAINT-FRANCOIS, LE
CSD *p* 1274
See CENTRALE DES SYNDICATS DEMOCRATIQUES
CSD, A DIV OF *p* 792
See CANADIAN STARTER DRIVES INC
CSDCEO *p* 643
See CONSEIL SCOLAIRE DE DISTRICT CATHOLIQUE DE L'EST ONTARIEN
CSDM *p* 1168
See COMMISSION SCOLAIRE DE MONTREAL
CSF INTERNATIONAL *p* 1282
See EQUIPEMENTS DE SUPERMARCHES CONCEPT INTERNATIONAL INC
CSG INDUSTRIES *p* 86
See 8056323 CANADA INC
CSG SECURITY CORPORATION *p* 693
5201 EXPLORER DR, MISSISSAUGA, ON, L4W 4H1
(905) 629-1446 *SIC* 3699
CSG SECURITY CORPORATION *p* 693
2740 MATHESON BLVD E UNIT 1, MISSISSAUGA, ON, L4W 4X3
(905) 629-2600 *SIC* 5065
CSG SECURITY CORPORATION *p* 1184
6680 AV DU PARC, MONTREAL, QC, H2V 4H9
(514) 272-7700 *SIC* 1731
CSH CASTEL ROYAL INC *p* 1083
5740 BOUL CAVENDISH BUREAU 2006, COTE SAINT-LUC, QC, H4W 2T8
SIC 8361
CSH DEVONSHIRE SENIORS INC *p* 1023
901 RIVERSIDE DR W, WINDSOR, ON, N9A 7J6
(519) 252-2273 *SIC* 6513
CSH DOMAINE CASCADE *p* 1368
695 7E RUE DE LA POINTE, SHAWINIGAN, QC, G9N 8K2
(819) 536-4463 *SIC* 6513
CSH FOUR TEDDINGTON PARK INC *p* 921
4 TEDDINGTON PARK AVE, TORONTO, ON, M4N 2C3
(416) 481-2986 *SIC* 6513
CSH L'OASIS ST. JEAN INC *p* 1316
1050 RUE STEFONI, SAINT-JEAN-SUR-RICHELIEU, QC, J3A 1T5

(450) 349-5861 *SIC* 8361
CSH PARK PLACE MANOR INC *p* 480
15055 YONGE ST, AURORA, ON, L4G 6T4
(905) 727-2952 *SIC* 6513
CSH ROYAL OAK LTC INC *p* 633
1750 DIVISION RD N SUITE 415, KINGSVILLE, ON, N9Y 4G7
(519) 733-9303 *SIC* 8059
CSH WOODHAVEN LTC INC *p* 678
380 CHURCH ST, MARKHAM, ON, L6B 1E1
(905) 472-3320 *SIC* 8361
CSI *p* 312
See CREDENTIAL SECURITIES INC
CSI *p* 638
See CONESTOGA STUDENTS INCORPORATED
CSI *p* 870
See CABLESHOPPE INC, THE
CSI *p* 979
See CSI GLOBAL EDUCATION INC
CSI CHEMICAL COMPANY LTD *p* 259
2560 SHELL RD SUITE 3013, RICHMOND, BC, V6X 0B8
(604) 278-1071 *SIC* 5169
CSI GLOBAL EDUCATION INC *p* 979
200 WELLINGTON ST W SUITE 1200, TORONTO, ON, M5V 3G2
(416) 364-9130 *SIC* 8299
CSI LOGISTICS *p* 622
See CRAILIN LOGISTICS SERVICES INC
CSL COMMERCIAL SWITCHGEAR LIMITED *p* 906
See COMMERCIAL SWITCHGEAR LIMITED
CSM COMPRESSOR INC *p* 120
9330 27 AVE NW, EDMONTON, AB, T6N 1B2
(780) 435-5722 *SIC* 7699
CSPGNO *p* 899
See CONSEIL SCOLAIRE DE DISTRICT DU GRAND NORD DE L'ONTARIO
CSPQ *p* 1269
See GOUVERNEMENT DE LA PROVINCE DE QUEBEC
CSQ *p* 1258
See CENTRALE DES SYNDICATS DU QUEBEC (CSQ), LA
CSR COSMETIC SOLUTIONS INC *p* 486
149 VICTORIA ST, BARRIE, ON, L4N 2J6
(705) 728-5917 *SIC* 2844
CSSS *p* 1159
See CENTRE DE SANTE ET SERVICES SOCIAUX DE MONTMAGNY - L'ISLET
CSSS DE BEDFORD *p* 1056
See CENTRE DE SANTE ET DE SERVICES SOCIAUX LA POMMERAIE
CSSS DE L'HEMATITE *p* 1102
1 RUE ALEXANDRE, FERMONT, QC, G0G 1J0
(418) 287-5461 *SIC* 8011
CSSS DE LA BASE COTE-NORD *p* 1147
See CENTRE DE LA SANTE ET DU SERVICES SOCIAUX DE LA BASSE COTE-NORD
CSSS DE LA VALLEE-DE-LA-GATINEAU , LE *p* 1148
See FONDATION SANTE VALLEE-DE-LA-GATINEAU
CSSS DE PORTNEUF *p* 1348
See CENTRE DE SANTE ET DE SERVICES SOCIAUX DE PORTNEUF
CSSS DU PONTIAC *p* 1369
See CENTRE DE SANTE ET SERVICES SOCIAUX DU PONTIAC
CSSS JARDIN ROUSSILLON *p* 1123
See CENTRE INTEGRE DE SANTE ET DE SERVICES SOCIAUX DE LA MONTEREGIE-OUEST
CSSS PAPINEAU *p* 1102
See SYNDICAT DES PROFESSIONNELLES DE LA SANTE DU RESEAU PAPINEAU, SPSRP-FIQ
CSSS PIERRE-DE-SAUREL *p* 1376

400 AV DE L'HOTEL-DIEU, SOREL-TRACY, QC, J3P 1N5
(450) 746-6000 *SIC* 8062
CSSS RESIDENCE DOCTEUR JOSEPH GARCEAU *p* 1368
See CENTRE HOSPITALIER DU CENTRE LA MAURICIE
CSSS RICHELIEU-YAMASKA CH DE LA MRC D'ACTON *p* 1312
1955 AV PRATTE, SAINT-HYACINTHE, QC, J2S 7W5
(450) 771-4536 *SIC* 7021
CSSSC *p* 1078
See CENTRE DE SANTE ET DE SERVICES SOCIAUX DE CHICOUTIMI
CSSSG *p* 1106
See GOUVERNEMENT DE LA PROVINCE DE QUEBEC
CSSSPNQL *p* 1401
See COMMISSION DE LA SANTE ET DES SERVICES SOCIAUX PREMIERE NATION DU QUEBEC ET DU LABRADOR
CST *p* 705
See COMMERCIAL SPRING AND TOOL COMPANY LIMITED
CST INVESTOR SERVICES INC *p* 950
320 BAY ST SUITE 1000, TORONTO, ON, M5H 4A6
(888) 402-1644 *SIC* 6231
CSV MIDSTREAM SOLUTIONS CORP *p* 47
355 4 AVE SW SUITE 700, CALGARY, AB, T2P 0J1
(587) 316-6900 *SIC* 4923
CT CONSTRUCTION LTD *p* 571
55 BROWNS LINE, ETOBICOKE, ON, M8W 3S2
(416) 588-8707 *SIC* 1622
CT REAL ESTATE INVESTMENT TRUST *p* 922
2180 YONGE ST, TORONTO, ON, M4P 2V8
(416) 480-2029 *SIC* 6798
CT REIT *p* 922
See CT REAL ESTATE INVESTMENT TRUST
CTC *p* 1399
See C.T. CONSULTANTS INC
CTD *p* 390
See CANADIAN TOOL & DIE LTD
CTFS *p* 1011
See CANADIAN TIRE SERVICES LIMITED
CTG BRANDS INC *p* 551
123 GREAT GULF DR, CONCORD, ON, L4K 5V1
(905) 761-3330 *SIC* 5092
CTI INDUSTRIES INC *p* 864
5621 FINCH AVE E UNIT 3, SCARBOROUGH, ON, M1B 2T9
(416) 297-8738 *SIC* 3679
CTL CORP *p* 797
1660 NORTH SERVICE RD E SUITE 102, OAKVILLE, ON, L6H 7G3
(905) 815-9510 *SIC* 6159
CTL-WDW LTD *p* 851
9130 LESLIE ST UNIT 204, RICHMOND HILL, ON, L4B 0B9
(416) 781-3635 *SIC* 7322
CTM INTERNATIONAL GIFTWARE INC *p* 1239
11420 BOUL ALBERT-HUDON, MONTREAL-NORD, QC, H1G 3J6
(514) 324-4200 *SIC* 5199
CTMA *p* 1073
See COOPERATIVE DE TRANSPORT MARITIME AERIEN ASSOCIATION COOPERATIVE
CTMS *p* 781
See CORPORATE TRAVEL MANAGEMENT SOLUTIONS INC
CTP DISTRIBUTORS CUSTOM TRUCK PARTS INC *p* 131
13313 100 ST, GRANDE PRAIRIE, AB, T8V 4H4
(780) 538-2211 *SIC* 5013
CTR AUTO/INDUSTRIAL SUPPLY *p* 382

See CENTRAL TRANSPORT REFRIGERATION (MAN.) LTD

CTR REFRIGERATION AND FOOD STORE EQUIPMENT LTD p 12
4840 52 ST SE, CALGARY, AB, T2B 3R2
(403) 444-2877 *SIC 1711*

CTS EQUIPMENT TRANSPORT LTD p 95
11480 156 ST NW, EDMONTON, AB, T5M 3N2
(780) 451-3900 *SIC 7549*

CTS OF CANADA CO p 718
80 THOMAS ST, MISSISSAUGA, ON, L5M 1Y9
(905) 826-1141 *SIC 3679*

CTSD p 1270
See COTE TASCHEREAU SAMSON DEMERS S.E.N.C.R.L

CTU ELITE p 326
See ELITE INSURANCE COMPANY

CTV p 1174
See BELL MEDIA INC

CTV ATLANTIC p 455
See BELL MEDIA INC

CTV OTTAWA p 821
See BELL MEDIA INC

CTV SASKATOON p 1426
See BELL MEDIA INC

CTV SPECIALTY TELEVISION INC p 638
864 KING ST W, KITCHENER, ON, N2G 1E8
SIC 4833

CTV SPECIALTY TELEVISION INC p 899
699 FROOD RD, SUDBURY, ON, P3C 5A3
(705) 674-8301 *SIC 4833*

CTV TELEVISION p 75
See BELL MEDIA INC

CTV WINNIPEG p 377
See BELL MEDIA INC

CU INC p 73
5302 FORAND ST SW 4TH FL, CALGARY, AB, T3E 8B4
(403) 292-7500 *SIC 4931*

CUBE PACKAGING SOLUTIONS INC p 480
200 INDUSTRIAL PKY N, AURORA, ON, L4G 4C3
(905) 750-2823 *SIC 3089*

CUBEX LIMITED p 369
42 ST PAUL BLVD, WINNIPEG, MB, R2P 2W5
(204) 336-0008 *SIC 5082*

CUCO RESOURCES LTD p 950
155 UNIVERSITY AVE SUITE 1230, TORONTO, ON, M5H 3B7
(647) 247-1381 *SIC 1021*

CUDDY FARMS p 652
See CUDDY INTERNATIONAL CORPORATION

CUDDY FARMS p 897
See CUDDY GROUP LIMITED

CUDDY FARMS LIMITED 2008 p 897
28429 CENTRE RD, STRATHROY, ON, N7G 3H6
(519) 245-1592 *SIC 0253*

CUDDY GROUP LIMITED p 897
28429 CENTRE RD, STRATHROY, ON, N7G 3H6
(519) 245-1592 *SIC 0253*

CUDDY INTERNATIONAL CORPORATION p 652
1226 TRAFALGAR ST, LONDON, ON, N5Z 1H5
(800) 265-1061 *SIC 2015*

CUETS FINANCIAL LTD p 1417
2055 ALBERT ST, REGINA, SK, S4P 2T8
(306) 566-1269 *SIC 7389*

CUF p 573
See CANADA UKRAINE FOUNDATION

CUI-CANADA, INC p 783
39 KODIAK CRES, NORTH YORK, ON, M3J 3E5
(416) 630-8108 *SIC 5999*

CUIRS BENTLEY INC p 1338
6125 CH DE LA COTE-DE-LIESSE, SAINT-LAURENT, QC, H4T 1C8

(514) 341-9333 *SIC 5948*

CUISINE ADVENTURES p 1091
See PLATS DU CHEF ULC, LES

CUISINE CROTONE INC p 1161
9800 BOUL MAURICE-DUPLESSIS, MONTREAL, QC, H1C 1G1
(514) 648-3553 *SIC 2434*

CUISINE IDEALE INC p 1372
980 RUE PANNETON, SHERBROOKE, QC, J1K 2B2
(819) 566-2401 *SIC 2434*

CUISINE KARO p 1381
See ALIMENTS MARTEL INC

CUISINE ROYAL p 1343
See CERAMIQUES ROYAL LTEE, LES

CUISINE SOLEIL p 1390
See 9192-4548 QUEBEC INC

CUISINES BEAUREGARD INC p 1110
655 RUE SIMONDS S, GRANBY, QC, J2J 1C2
(450) 375-0707 *SIC 5211*

CUISINES CUSTOM DIAMOND INTERNATIONAL p 1342
See CUSTOM DIAMOND INTERNATIONAL INC

CUISINES GASPESIENNES p 1150
See CUISINES GASPESIENNES MATANE LTEE, LES

CUISINES GASPESIENNES MATANE LTEE, LES p 1150
85 RUE DU PORT BUREAU 1, MATANE, QC, G4W 3M6
(418) 562-5757 *SIC 2013*

CUISINES LAURIER INC p 1133
266 RUE DE LA STATION, LAURIER-STATION, QC, G0S 1N0
(418) 728-3630 *SIC 2434*

CUISINES NUTRI-DELI INC, LES p 1321
535 RUE FILION, SAINT-JEROME, QC, J7Z 1J6
(450) 438-5278 *SIC 5812*

CUISINES VALENCIA p 1294
See R.C.M. MODULAIRE INC

CUISITEC LTEE p 1321
175 RUE MICHENER, SAINT-JOSEPH-DE-BEAUCE, QC, G0S 2V0
(418) 397-5432 *SIC 5211*

CUISIVIANDES p 1294
See BRETON TRADITION 1944 INC

CULASSES DU FUTUR L. R. INC, LES p 1149
1390 AV DE LA GARE, MASCOUCHE, QC, J7K 2Z2
(514) 966-3450 *SIC 3714*

CULBERSON, RALPH B & SONS LTD p 404
682 ROUTE 560, JACKSONVILLE, NB, E7M 3J8
(506) 328-4366 *SIC 0134*

CULINARY CAPERS CATERING INC p 320
1545 3RD AVE W, VANCOUVER, BC, V6J 1J8
(604) 875-0123 *SIC 5812*

CULINARY PAPERS INC p 1014
125 CONSUMERS DR, WHITBY, ON, L1N 1C4
(905) 668-7533 *SIC 2671*

CULLEN DIESEL POWER LTD p 281
9300 192 ST, SURREY, BC, V4N 3R8
(604) 888-1211 *SIC 5084*

CULLEN WESTERN STAR TRUCK INC p 174
380 RIVERSIDE RD SUITE 3, ABBOTSFORD, BC, V2S 7M4
(604) 504-5904 *SIC 5511*

CULLEN, BARRY CHEVROLET CADILLAC LTD p 605
905 WOODLAWN RD W, GUELPH, ON, N1K 1B7
(519) 824-0210 *SIC 5511*

CULLEN, BRIAN MOTORS LIMITED p 885
386 ONTARIO ST, ST CATHARINES, ON, L2R 5L8
(905) 684-8745 *SIC 5511*

CULLEN, RAY CHEVROLET LTD p 659
730 WHARNCLIFFE RD S, LONDON, ON, N6J 2N4
(519) 686-2875 *SIC 5511*

CULLIGAN p 1438
See CULLIGAN OF CANADA ULC

CULLIGAN DU SUD-OUEST QUEBEC p 519
See EASTERN ONTARIO WATER TECHNOLOGY LTD

CULLIGAN OF BELLEVILLE p 492
See GOOD WATER COMPANY LTD, THE

CULLIGAN OF CANADA ULC p 1438
76 SEVENTH AVE S SUITE 1, YORKTON, SK, S3N 3V2
(306) 782-2648 *SIC 5999*

CULLIGAN WATER p 538
See CAISSEN WATER TECHNOLOGIES INC

CULLIGAN WATER CONDITIONING p 1434
See WESTERN WATER INDUSTRIES

CULLIGAN WATER CONDITIONING (BARRIE) LIMITED p 486
15 MORROW RD, BARRIE, ON, L4N 3V7
(705) 728-4782 *SIC 5074*

CULLIGAN WEST TORONTO p 502
8985 AIRPORT RD, BRAMPTON, ON, L6T 5T2
(416) 798-7670 *SIC 5963*

CULLITON INC p 895
473 DOURO ST, STRATFORD, ON, N5A 3S9
(519) 271-1981 *SIC 1711*

CULP, J. E. TRANSPORT LTD p 489
4815 MERRITT RD, BEAMSVILLE, ON, L0R 1B1
(905) 563-5055 *SIC 4212*

CULTURE SHAWINIGAN p 1368
See CORPORATION CULTURELLE DE SHAWINIGAN

CULTURES DE CHEZ NOUS INC, LES p 1356
1120 9E RANG, SAINTE-BRIGITTE-DES-SAULTS, QC, J0C 1E0
(819) 336-4846 *SIC 0161*

CUMAF DU LAC p 1045
5791 AV DU PONT N, ALMA, QC, G8E 1X1
SIC 7389

CUMBERLAND HEALTH CENTRE p 204
See VANCOUVER ISLAND HEALTH AUTHORITY

CUMBERLAND PAVING AND CONTRACTING p 445
8 MOORE RD, DARTMOUTH, NS, B3B 1J2
(902) 832-9062 *SIC 1611*

CUMBERLAND SENIOR CARE CORPORATION p 465
262 CHURCH ST, PUGWASH, NS, B0K 1L0
(902) 243-2504 *SIC 8361*

CUMIS GENERAL INSURANCE COMPANY p 530
151 NORTH SERVICE RD, BURLINGTON, ON, L7R 4C2
(905) 632-1221 *SIC 6331*

CUMIS GROUP LIMITED, THE p 530
151 NORTH SERVICE RD, BURLINGTON, ON, L7R 4C2
(800) 263-9120 *SIC 6311*

CUMIS LIFE INSURANCE COMPANY p 530
151 NORTH SERVICE RD, BURLINGTON, ON, L7R 4C2
(905) 632-1221 *SIC 6311*

CUMMING & DOBBIE (1986) LTD p 346
3000 VICTORIA AVE E, BRANDON, MB, R7A 7L2
(204) 726-0790 *SIC 1794*

CUMMINGS PHARMACY LTD p 420
370 CONNELL ST, WOODSTOCK, NB, E7M 5G9
(506) 328-8801 *SIC 5912*

CUMMINS EST DU CANADA SEC p 738

7175 PACIFIC CIR, MISSISSAUGA, ON, L5T 2A8
(905) 795-0050 *SIC 5084*

CUMMINS EST DU CANADA SEC p 1250
7200 RTE TRANSCANADIENNE, POINTE-CLAIRE, QC, H9R 1C2
(514) 695-8410 *SIC 5084*

CUMMINS EST DU CANADA SEC p 1378
3614 RTE TEWKESBURY, STONEHAM-ET-TEWKESBURY, QC, G3C 2L8
(418) 848-6464 *SIC 5063*

CUMMINS WESTERN CANADA LIMITED PARTNERSHIP p 12
4887 35 ST SE, CALGARY, AB, T2B 3H6
(403) 569-1122 *SIC 5084*

CUMMINS WESTERN CANADA LIMITED PARTNERSHIP p 100
11751 181 ST NW, EDMONTON, AB, T5S 2K5
(780) 455-2151 *SIC 5084*

CUMMINS WESTERN CANADA LIMITED PARTNERSHIP p 281
18452 96 AVE, SURREY, BC, V4N 3P8
(604) 882-5000 *SIC 5084*

CUNARD COURT HIGHRISE p 455
2065 BRUNSWICK ST SUITE 1706, HALIFAX, NS, B3K 5T8
(902) 407-8845 *SIC 1522*

CUNDARI p 979
See CUNDARI GROUP LTD

CUNDARI GROUP LTD p 979
26 DUNCAN ST, TORONTO, ON, M5V 2B9
(416) 510-1771 *SIC 7311*

CUNNINGHAM LINDSEY CANADA CLAIMS SERVICES LTD p 709
50 BURNHAMTHORPE RD W SUITE 1102, MISSISSAUGA, ON, L5B 3C2
(905) 896-8181 *SIC 8748*

CUNNINGHAM LINDSEY CANADA LIMITED p 611
46 JACKSON ST E, HAMILTON, ON, L8N 1L1
(905) 528-1481 *SIC 6411*

CUNNINGHAM LINDSEY CANADA LIMITED p 612
25 MAIN ST W SUITE 1810, HAMILTON, ON, L8P 1H1
(905) 528-1481 *SIC 6411*

CUNNINGHAM LINDSEY CANADA LIMITED p 1317
523 BOUL DU SEMINAIRE N BUREAU 103, SAINT-JEAN-SUR-RICHELIEU, QC, J3B 5L8
SIC 6411

CUPE p 817
See CANADIAN UNION OF PUBLIC EMPLOYEES

CUPE BRITISH COLUMBIA REGIONAL OFFICE p 188
See CANADIAN UNION OF PUBLIC EMPLOYEES

CUPE LOCAL 2153 p 377
See CANADIAN UNION OF PUBLIC EMPLOYEES

CUPS p 64
See CALGARY URBAN PROJECT SOCIETY

CUPW p 833
See CANADIAN UNION OF POSTAL WORKERS

CURALEAF HOLDINGS, INC p 303
666 BURRARD ST SUITE 1700, VANCOUVER, BC, V6C 2X8
(604) 218-4766 *SIC 1081*

CURIE p 521
See CANADIAN UNIVERSITIES RECIPROCAL INSURANCE EXCHANGE

CURLCO INDUSTRIES INC p 566
85 LITTLE JOHN RD SUITE 1585, DUNDAS, ON, L9H 4H1
(905) 628-4287 *SIC 7231*

CURRAN & BRIGGS LIMITED p 1042
40 ALL WEATHER HWY, SUMMERSIDE, PE, C1N 4J8
(902) 436-2163   *SIC* 1611

CURRAN & HERRIDGE CONSTRUCTION CO., LIMITED p 859
283 CONFEDERATION ST, SARNIA, ON, N7T 2A3
(519) 332-3610   *SIC* 1541

CURRAN CONTRACTORS LTD p 859
283 CONFEDERATION ST, SARNIA, ON, N7T 2A3
(519) 332-3610   *SIC* 1541

CURRIE TRUCK CENTRE p 681
See CURRIE, DONALD TRUCKS INC

CURRIE, DONALD TRUCKS INC p 681
2 CURRIE DR, MIDHURST, ON, L9X 0N3
(705) 734-1953   *SIC* 7538

CURRY MOTORS LIMITED p 607
5065 COUNTY RD 21 RR 3, HALIBURTON, ON, K0M 1S0
(705) 457-2765   *SIC* 5511

CURTICE SECONDARY SCHOOL p 563
See KAWARTHA PINE RIDGE DISTRICT SCHOOL BOARD

CURTIS CARPETS LTD p 390
1280 PEMBINA HWY, WINNIPEG, MB, R3T 2B2
(204) 452-8100   *SIC* 5713

CURTIS CONSTRUCTION LTD p 1417
2930 PASQUA ST N, REGINA, SK, S4P 3H1
(306) 543-3944   *SIC* 4212

CURTIS GORDON MOTOR HOTEL p 367
See GORDON HOTELS & MOTOR INNS LTD

CURTIS INSURANCE LIMITED p 776
1500 DON MILLS RD SUITE 501, NORTH YORK, ON, M3B 3K4
(416) 447-4499   *SIC* 6411

CURTIS INTERNATIONAL LTD p 734
7045 BECKETT DR UNIT 15, MISSISSAUGA, ON, L5S 2A3
(416) 674-2123   *SIC* 5065

CURTISS WRIGHT CONTROLS EMBEDDED COMPUTING p 626
See DY 4 SYSTEMS INC

CURTISS-WRIGHT CONTROLS EM TECHNOLOGIES p 895
See NOVATRONICS INC

CURTISS-WRIGHT DEFENSE SOLUTIONS p 711
See INDAL TECHNOLOGIES INC

CURTISS-WRIGHT FLOW CONTROL COMPANY CANADA p 517
15 SHAVER RD, BRANTFORD, ON, N3T 5M1
(519) 756-4800   *SIC* 3494

CURTISS-WRIGHT NUCLEAR CANADA p 517
See CURTISS-WRIGHT FLOW CONTROL COMPANY CANADA

CUSCO FABRICATORS LLC p 855
305 ENFORD RD, RICHMOND HILL, ON, L4C 3E9
(905) 883-1214   *SIC* 3569

CUSHMAN & WAKEFIELD p 88
See CW EDMONTON INC

CUSHMAN & WAKEFIELD ASSET SERVICES ULC p 937
1 QUEEN ST E SUITE 300, TORONTO, ON, M5C 2W5
(416) 955-0595   *SIC* 6531

CUSHMAN & WAKEFIELD LTD p 330
See CUSHMAN & WAKEFIELD ULC

CUSHMAN & WAKEFIELD LTD p 731
See CUSHMAN & WAKEFIELD ULC

CUSHMAN & WAKEFIELD LTEE p 1195
999 BOUL DE MAISONNEUVE O BUREAU 1500, MONTREAL, QC, H3A 3L4
(514) 841-5011   *SIC* 6531

CUSHMAN & WAKEFIELD ULC p 330
700 GEORGIA ST W, VANCOUVER, BC, V7Y 1K8
(604) 683-3111   *SIC* 6531

CUSHMAN & WAKEFIELD ULC p 731
5770 HURONTARIO ST SUITE 200, MISSISSAUGA, ON, L5R 3G5
(905) 568-9500   *SIC* 6531

CUSHMAN & WAKEFIELD ULC p 961
161 BAY ST SUITE 1500, TORONTO, ON, M5J 2S1
(416) 862-0611   *SIC* 6531

CUSM p 1221
See CENTRE UNIVERSITAIRE DE SANTE MCGILL

CUSTOM AIR CONDITIONING LTD p 246
1835 BROADWAY ST, PORT COQUITLAM, BC, V3C 4Z1
(604) 945-7728   *SIC* 1711

CUSTOM ALUMINUM, INC p 551
40 ROMINA DR UNIT 2, CONCORD, ON, L4K 4Z7
(905) 669-8459   *SIC* 7389

CUSTOM CASTINGS LIMITED p 365
2015 DUGALD RD, WINNIPEG, MB, R2J 0H3
(204) 663-9142   *SIC* 3365

CUSTOM COLOUR IMAGING p 792
See CUSTOM COLOUR LABS INC

CUSTOM COLOUR LABS INC p 792
5703 STEELES AVE W, NORTH YORK, ON, M9L 1S7
(416) 630-2020   *SIC* 7384

CUSTOM CONCRETE NORTHERN, DIV OF p 488
See SARJEANT COMPANY LIMITED, THE

CUSTOM COUNTERTOPS p 1431
See FLOFORM INDUSTRIES LTD

CUSTOM COURIER CO. LTD p 1431
501 PAKWA PL SUITE 2, SASKATOON, SK, S7L 6A3
(306) 653-8500   *SIC* 7389

CUSTOM DIAMOND INTERNATIONAL INC p 1342
895 AV MUNCK, SAINT-LAURENT, QC, H7S 1A9
(450) 668-0330   *SIC* 3469

CUSTOM ELECTRIC LTD p 22
1725 27 AVE NE, CALGARY, AB, T2E 7E1
(403) 736-0205   *SIC* 1731

CUSTOM ENERGIZED AIR LTD p 113
9555 62 AVE NW, EDMONTON, AB, T6E 0E1
(780) 465-2247   *SIC* 5082

CUSTOM FABRICATORS & MACHINISTS LIMITED p 416
45 GIFFORD RD, SAINT JOHN, NB, E2M 5K7
(506) 648-2226   *SIC* 3599

CUSTOM FOAM SYSTEMS LTD p 637
360 TRILLIUM DR, KITCHENER, ON, N2E 2K6
(519) 748-1700   *SIC* 3086

CUSTOM HELICOPTERS LTD p 357
706 SOUTH GATE RD, ST ANDREWS, MB, R1A 3P8
(204) 338-7953   *SIC* 4522

CUSTOM HOUSE ULC p 279
409-2626 CROYDON DR, SURREY, BC, V3Z 0S8
(604) 560-8060   *SIC* 6099

CUSTOM LEATHER CANADA LIMITED p 635
460 BINGEMANS CENTRE DR, KITCHENER, ON, N2B 3X9
(519) 741-2070   *SIC* 2387

CUSTOM MARBLE p 349
See CLEARVIEW COLONY LTD

CUSTOM MARINE DESIGN & SUPPLY LIMITED p 468
29 GREENS POINT RD, TRENTON, NS, B0K 1X0
(902) 752-2827   *SIC* 5551

CUSTOM PLASTICS INTERNATIONAL LIMITED p 545
887 D'ARCY ST, COBOURG, ON, K9A 4B4
(905) 372-2281   *SIC* 3089

CUSTOM TRAVEL SOLUTIONS INC p 66
2424 4 ST SW SUITE 800, CALGARY, AB, T2S 2T4
(403) 272-1000   *SIC* 4724

CUSTOM TRUCK PARTS p 131
See CTP DISTRIBUTORS CUSTOM TRUCK PARTS INC

CUSTOM TRUCK SALES INC p 1415
520 PARK ST, REGINA, SK, S4N 0T6
(306) 569-9021   *SIC* 5511

CUSTOM VACUUM SERVICES LTD p 148
904 29 AVE, NISKU, AB, T9E 1B7
(780) 955-9344   *SIC* 5722

CUSTOM WOOD p 581
See 875578 ONTARIO LIMITED

CUSTOM WOOD FABRICATING COMPANY p 586
See MILTEX CONSTRUCTION LIMITED

CUSTOMER EXPRESSIONS CORP p 830
2255 CARLING AVE SUITE 500, OTTAWA, ON, K2B 7Z5
(613) 244-5111   *SIC* 4813

CUSTOMIZED DELIVERY SERVICE INC p 668
3075 14TH AVE SUITE 209, MARKHAM, ON, L3R 0G9
(905) 475-5908   *SIC* 7389

CUSTOMPLAN FINANCIAL ADVISORS INC p 318
1500 GEORGIA ST W SUITE 1900, VANCOUVER, BC, V6G 2Z6
(604) 687-7773   *SIC* 8741

CUT KNIFE HEALTH COMPLEX PRAIRIE NORTH HEALTH DISTRICT p 1405
102 DION AVE, CUT KNIFE, SK, S0M 0N0
(306) 398-4977   *SIC* 6324

CUT TECHNOLOGIES p 1138
460 3E AV BUREAU 100, LEVIS, QC, G6W 5M6
(418) 834-7772   *SIC* 5084

CUTLER FOREST PRODUCTS INC p 1027
81 ROYAL GROUP CRES UNIT A, WOODBRIDGE, ON, L4H 1X9
(905) 212-1414   *SIC* 5031

CUTLER GROUP p 1027
See CUTLER FOREST PRODUCTS INC

CUTTERS CHOICE p 649
See LASER SALES INC

CVC SLING SHOT TRANSPORTATION INC p 205
1345 DERWENT WAY, DELTA, BC, V3M 5V9
(604) 515-9462   *SIC* 4731

CVH AUTO INC p 203
GOLD ISLAND HWY, COURTENAY, BC, V9N 3P1
(250) 334-2441   *SIC* 5511

CVS CONTROLS LTD p 113
3900 101 ST NW, EDMONTON, AB, T6E 0A5
(780) 437-3055   *SIC* 3491

CVS CRUISE VICTORIA LTD p 335
185 DALLAS RD, VICTORIA, BC, V8V 1A1
(250) 386-8652   *SIC* 4725

CVS PRODUCTIONS p 1070
See CLUB VIDEO SUTTON INC

CVS SIGHT SEEING p 335
See CVS CRUISE VICTORIA LTD

CVTECH INC p 1098
300 RUE LABONTE, DRUMMONDVILLE, QC, J2C 6X9
(819) 477-3232   *SIC* 3566

CVTECH R ET D p 1098
See CVTECH INC

CW EDMONTON INC p 88
10088 102 AVE NW UNIT 2700, EDMONTON, AB, T5J 2Z1
(780) 420-1177   *SIC* 6531

CW PROFESSIONAL SERVICES (CANADA) ULC p 1187
500 RUE SAINT-JACQUES, MONTREAL, QC, H2Y 1S1
(514) 281-1888   *SIC* 7379

CWA MECANIQUE DE PROCEDE p 1306
See ALLEN ENTREPRENEUR GENERAL INC

CWB GROUP - INDUSTRY SERVICES CORP p 683
8260 PARKHILL DR, MILTON, ON, L9T 5V7
(905) 542-1312   *SIC* 8621

CWB MAXIUM FINANCIAL INC p 851
30 VOGELL RD SUITE 1, RICHMOND HILL, ON, L4B 3K6
(905) 780-6150   *SIC* 6159

CWB NATIONAL LEASING INC p 390
1525 BUFFALO PL, WINNIPEG, MB, R3T 1L9
(204) 954-9000   *SIC* 6159

CWC p 47
See CWC ENERGY SERVICES CORP

CWC ENERGY SERVICES CORP p 47
205 5 AVE SW SUITE 610, CALGARY, AB, T2P 2V7
(403) 264-2177   *SIC* 1382

CWH DISTRIBUTION SERVICES INC p 583
1245 MARTIN GROVE RD, ETOBICOKE, ON, M9W 4X2
(416) 674-5826   *SIC* 4212

CWI CLIMATEWORX INTERNATIONAL INC p 502
18 CHELSEA LANE, BRAMPTON, ON, L6T 3Y4
(905) 405-0800   *SIC* 5075

CWL p 82
See CHRISTOPHER'S WELDING LTD

CWP CONSTRUCTORS LTD p 113
8702 48 AVE NW SUITE 210, EDMONTON, AB, T6E 5L1
(780) 757-5834   *SIC* 1521

CWP INDUSTRIEL INC p 1187
407 RUE MCGILL BUREAU 315, MONTREAL, QC, H2Y 2G3
(514) 871-2120   *SIC* 5031

CWS INDUSTRIES (MFG) CORP p 122
7622 18 ST NW, EDMONTON, AB, T6P 1Y6
(780) 469-9185   *SIC* 3545

CWS INDUSTRIES (MFG) CORP p 281
19490 92 AVE, SURREY, BC, V4N 4G7
(604) 888-9008   *SIC* 3531

CWS LOGISTICS LTD p 390
1664 SEEL AVE, WINNIPEG, MB, R3T 4X5
(204) 474-2278   *SIC* 4225

CWS VENTURES INC p 281
19490 92 AVE, SURREY, BC, V4N 4G7
(604) 888-9008   *SIC* 3531

CWSDS PASSPORT p 683
917 NIPISSING RD UNIT 1A, MILTON, ON, L9T 5E3
(905) 693-8885   *SIC* 6371

CWT CONCIERGE p 1054
53 MAPLE CRES, BEACONSFIELD, QC, H9W 4T3
(514) 695-7215   *SIC* 4724

CXD MAINTENANCE SERVICE LTD p 113
6276 92 ST NW, EDMONTON, AB, T6E 3A7
(780) 391-1565   *SIC* 7539

CY RHEAULT CONSTRUCTION LTD p 912
273 THIRD AVE SUITE 404, TIMMINS, ON, P4N 1E2
(705) 268-3445   *SIC* 1542

CYBA STEVENS MANAGEMENT GROUP INC p 22
5735 7 ST NE SUITE 100, CALGARY, AB, T2E 8V3
(403) 291-3288   *SIC* 5141

CYBERLINK PACIFIC TELECOMMUNICATIONS LIMITED p 303
888 DUNSMUIR ST SUITE 868, VANCOUVER, BC, V6C 3K4
(604) 708-9688   *SIC* 4899

CYCLE DEVINCI INC p 1080
1555 RUE DE LA MANIC, CHICOUTIMI,

QC, G7K 1G8
(418) 549-6218   *SIC* 3751
CYCLE WORKS MOTORSPORTS LTD *p*
113
5688 75 ST NW, EDMONTON, AB, T6E 5X6
(780) 440-3200   *SIC* 5599
CYCLES LAMBERT INC   *p* 1139
1000 RUE DES RIVEURS, LEVIS, QC, G6Y
9G3
(418) 835-1685   *SIC* 6712
CYCLO VAC   *p* 1059
See INDUSTRIES TROVAC LIMITEE, LES
CYCLONE MANUFACTURING INCORPO-RATED   *p*
721
7300 RAPISTAN CRT, MISSISSAUGA, ON,
L5N 5S1
(905) 567-5601   *SIC* 3728
CYGNUS MARKETING INC   *p* 1188
507 PLACE D'ARMES BUREAU 1519,
MONTREAL, QC, H2Y 2W8
(514) 284-5569   *SIC* 8742
CYMAX CANADA   *p* 185
*See CHANNEL GATE TECHNOLOGIES
INC*
CYMBRIA CORPORATION   *p* 974
150 BLOOR ST W SUITE 500, TORONTO,
ON, M5S 2X9
(416) 963-9353   *SIC* 6726
CYME INTERNATIONAL T & D INC   *p* 1295
1485 RUE ROBERVAL BUREAU 104,
SAINT-BRUNO, QC, J3V 3P8
(450) 461-3655   *SIC* 7371
CYNTECH CONSTRUCTION LTD   *p* 159
235061 WRANGLER LINK, ROCKY VIEW
COUNTY, AB, T1X 0K3
(403) 228-1767   *SIC* 5085
CYONI   *p* 285
See CANADA YOUTH ORANGE NET-WORK INC
CYPHER SYSTEMS GROUP INC   *p* 1019
3600 RHODES DR, WINDSOR, ON, N8W
5A4
(519) 945-4943   *SIC* 7371
CYPRESS COLONY FARMS LTD   *p* 348
GD, CYPRESS RIVER, MB, R0K 0P0
(204) 743-2185   *SIC* 0291
CYPRESS HEALTH REGION   *p* 1436
440 CENTRAL AVE S, SWIFT CURRENT,
SK, S9H 3G6
    SIC 8361
CYPRESS MANAGEMENT LTD   *p* 221
537 LEON AVE SUITE 200, KELOWNA, BC,
V1Y 2A9
(250) 763-4323   *SIC* 6712
CYPRESS MOTORS (SC)   *p* 1436
2234 SOUTH SERVICE RD W, SWIFT
CURRENT, SK, S9H 5J7
(306) 778-3673   *SIC* 5511
CYPRESS REGIONAL HOSPITAL   *p* 1436
See SASKATCHEWAN HEALTH AUTHOR-ITY
CYPRESS SECURITY (2013) INC   *p* 276
7028 120 ST SUITE 203, SURREY, BC,
V3W 3M8
(778) 564-4088   *SIC* 7381
CYRILLE FRIGON (1996) INC   *p* 1146
1351 BOUL SAINT-LAURENT O, LOUI-SEVILLE, QC, J5V 2L4
(819) 228-9491   *SIC* 5153
CYRO CANADA INC   *p* 758
6515 BARKER ST, NIAGARA FALLS, ON,
L2G 1Y6
(905) 677-1388   *SIC* 2821
CYRS LTEE   *p* 1235
1789 BOUL DES LAURENTIDES, MON-TREAL, QC, H7M 2P7
    SIC 5621
CYRVILLE CHRYSLER DODGE JEEP LTD *p*
820
900 ST. LAURENT BLVD, OTTAWA, ON,
K1K 3B3
(613) 745-7051   *SIC* 5511
CYTEC CANADA INC   *p* 760

9061 GARNER RD, NIAGARA FALLS, ON,
L2H 0Y2
(905) 356-9000   *SIC* 2819
**CYTRONICS HOLDING CORPORATION
LTD**   *p* 1155
3333 BOUL GRAHAM BUREAU 101,
MONT-ROYAL, QC, H3R 3L5
(514) 382-0820   *SIC* 6719
**CYV CHEVROLET PONTIAC BUICK GMC
LTD**   *p* 420
324 CONNELL ST, WOODSTOCK, NB, E7M
5E2
(506) 799-0110   *SIC* 5511
CYZOTRIM ENR   *p* 1370
See 3101-2883 QUEBEC INC

D

D & A COLLECTION CORPORATION *p* 705
75 WATLINE AVE SUITE 142, MISSIS-SAUGA, ON, L4Z 3E5
(905) 507-1147   *SIC* 7322
D & A GROUP SERVICES   *p* 705
See D & A COLLECTION CORPORATION
D & B COMPANIES OF CANADA LTD, THE *p* 406
*See D&B COMPANIES OF CANADA ULC,
THE*
D & D ASSOCIATES LEASING   *p* 904
See D & D ASSOCIATES LTD
D & D ASSOCIATES LTD   *p* 904
8199 YONGE ST SUITE 401, THORNHILL,
ON, L3T 2C6
(905) 881-5575   *SIC* 6733
D & D ENERGY SERVICES LTD   *p* 134
9201 163 AVE, GRANDE PRAIRIE, AB, T8X
0B6
(780) 402-0383   *SIC* 4213
D & D WELL SERVICES   *p* 134
See D & D ENERGY SERVICES LTD
**D & F CLOUTIER GROUP ENTERPRISES
INC**   *p* 837
30 PINE DR, PARRY SOUND, ON, P2A 3B8
(705) 746-4033   *SIC* 5251
D & H CANADA ULC   *p* 511
7975 HERITAGE RD SUITE 20, BRAMP-TON, ON, L6Y 5X5
(905) 796-0030   *SIC* 5065
D & H GROUP CHARTERED ACCOUN-TANTS   *p*
319
1333 BROADWAY W, VANCOUVER, BC,
V6H 4C1
(604) 731-5881   *SIC* 8721
D & J ISLEY & SONS CONTRACTING LTD *p*
131
11517 89 AVE, GRANDE PRAIRIE, AB, T8V
5Z2
(780) 539-7580   *SIC* 2411
D & K CROSS SALES LTD.   *p* 267
1151 10 AVE SW SUITE 300, SALMON
ARM, BC, V1E 1T3
(250) 832-9600   *SIC* 5251
D & L CRANSTON HOLDINGS LTD   *p* 145
1601 DUNMORE RD SE SUITE 107,
MEDICINE HAT, AB, T1A 1Z8
(800) 665-5122   *SIC* 6794
D & L GUITARD SALES INC   *p* 470
5130 ST MARGARETS BAY RD, UPPER
TANTALLON, NS, B3Z 1E2
(902) 826-2800   *SIC* 5251
D & L SALES LIMITED   *p* 873
150 MIDDLEFIELD RD, SCARBOROUGH,
ON, M1S 4L6
(416) 423-1133   *SIC* 5199
D & M CANADA   *p* 672
See MARANTZ CANADA INC
D & M LOCATING LTD   *p* 1437
4 2ND STREET W, TROSSACHS, SK, S0C
2N0
(306) 354-7907   *SIC* 7389
D & R CUSTOM STEEL FABRICATION   *p*
844
See 242408 STEEL FABRICATION LIM-ITED

D & S FURNITURE GALLERIES LTD   *p* 382
1425 ELLICE AVE, WINNIPEG, MB, R3G
0G3
(204) 783-8500   *SIC* 5712
D & S MEAT PRODUCTS LTD   *p* 473
220 CLEMENTS RD W UNIT 1, AJAX, ON,
L1S 3K5
(905) 427-9229   *SIC* 5147
D & V ELECTRONICS LTD   *p* 1027
130 ZENWAY BLVD, WOODBRIDGE, ON,
L4H 2Y7
(905) 264-7646   *SIC* 3694
D & W FORWARDERS INC   *p* 509
81 ORENDA RD, BRAMPTON, ON, L6W
1V7
(905) 459-3560   *SIC* 4213
D & W GROUP INC   *p* 623
2173 HIGHWAY 3, JARVIS, ON, N0A 1J0
(519) 587-2273   *SIC* 5999
D B D AUTO INC   *p* 1235
1215 BOUL DES LAURENTIDES, MON-TREAL, QC, H7M 2Y1
(450) 668-6393   *SIC* 5511
D C SECURITY INC   *p* 583
22 GOODMARK PL UNIT 20, ETOBICOKE,
ON, M9W 6R2
(416) 213-1995   *SIC* 6211
D DENISON CONSULTANTS   *p* 921
1535 MOUNT PLEASANT RD, TORONTO,
ON, M4N 2V1
(416) 484-1893   *SIC* 8748
D F X DISTRIBUTION   *p* 716
See BELER HOLDINGS INC
D G DUNBAR INSURANCE BROKER LIM-ITED   *p*
653
255 QUEENS AVE SUITE 1050, LONDON,
ON, N6A 5R8
(519) 642-0858   *SIC* 6411
D K FORD SALES LTD   *p* 139
6559 SPARROW DR, LEDUC, AB, T9E 7L1
(780) 986-2929   *SIC* 5511
D W I SERVICE LIMITED   *p* 423
738 MAIN RD, GOULDS, NL, A1S 1J2
(709) 745-7054   *SIC* 4789
D W POPPY SECONDARY SCHOOL   *p* 227
See SCHOOL DISTRICT NO. 35 (LANG-LEY)
D&B COMPANIES OF CANADA ULC, THE *p*
406
1234 MAIN ST SUITE 2001, MONCTON,
NB, E1C 1H7
(506) 867-2000   *SIC* 7323
D&B COMPANIES OF CANADA ULC, THE *p*
721
6750 CENTURY AVE SUITE 305, MISSIS-SAUGA, ON, L5N 2V8
    SIC 7323
D&D CABLE VISION   *p* 62
See VIDEON CABLESYSTEMS INC
D&D SECURITIES INC   *p* 950
150 YORK ST SUITE 1714, TORONTO, ON,
M5H 3S5
(416) 363-0201   *SIC* 6211
D&G LANDSCAPING INC   *p* 599
1341 COKER ST, GREELY, ON, K4P 1A1
(613) 821-4444   *SIC* 1611
D'ALESIO'S FOOD MARKET   *p* 610
See 1389773 ONTARIO INC
D'ALESSANDRO INVESTMENTS LIMITED
p 571
3526 LAKE SHORE BLVD W, ETOBICOKE,
ON, M8W 1N6
(416) 252-2277   *SIC* 5511
D'ANGELO BRANDS   *p* 691
See 2156775 ONTARIO INC
D'ANGELO BRANDS   *p* 692
See ARIANA HOLDINGS INC
D'ARTAGNAN   *p* 1338
See CORPORATION PRESSE COM-MERCE
D'AVERSA, NINO BAKERY LIMITED   *p* 783
1 TORO RD, NORTH YORK, ON, M3J 2A4
(416) 638-3271   *SIC* 5461

D'ENTREMONT, PAUL MARINE LTD   *p* 470
2616 HWY 3, WEST PUBNICO, NS, B0W
3S0
(902) 762-3301   *SIC* 5541
D'SA, MEL M. INC   *p* 184
6508 HASTINGS ST SUITE 214, BURN-ABY, BC, V5B 1S2
(604) 291-0638   *SIC* 5912
D+H   *p* 669
See DH CORPORATION
D+H LIMITED PARTNERSHIP   *p* 962
120 BREMNER BLVD 30TH FL, TORONTO,
ON, M5J 0A8
(416) 696-7700   *SIC* 6211
D-BOX   *p* 1141
See D-BOX TECHNOLOGIES INC
D-BOX TECHNOLOGIES INC   *p* 1141
2172 RUE DE LA PROVINCE, LONGUEUIL,
QC, J4G 1R7
(450) 442-3003   *SIC* 3625
D-THIND DEVELOPMENT LTD   *p* 190
700-4211 KINGSWAY, BURNABY, BC, V5H
1Z6
(604) 451-7780   *SIC* 1522
D-WAVE SYSTEMS INC   *p* 188
3033 BETA AVE, BURNABY, BC, V5G 4M9
(604) 630-1428   *SIC* 5734
D. & A.'S PET FOOD 'N MORE LTD   *p* 279
19347 24 AVE UNIT 105, SURREY, BC, V3Z
3S9
(604) 591-5990   *SIC* 5999
D. & R. ELECTRONICS CO. LTD   *p* 494
8820 GEORGE BOLTON PKY, BOLTON,
ON, L7E 2Y4
(905) 951-9997   *SIC* 3669
D. A. TOWNLEY & ASSOCIATES LTD *p* 188
4400 DOMINION ST SUITE 160, BURN-ABY, BC, V5G 4G3
(604) 299-7482   *SIC* 6411
D. CRUPI & SONS LIMITED   *p* 876
85 PASSMORE AVE, SCARBOROUGH,
ON, M1V 4K9
(416) 291-1986   *SIC* 1611
D. G. BEVAN INSURANCE BROKERS LTD
p 486
166 SAUNDERS RD UNIT 6, BARRIE, ON,
L4N 9A4
(705) 726-3381   *SIC* 6411
D. GRANT CONSTRUCTION LIMITED *p* 662
9887 LONGWOODS RD, LONDON, ON,
N6P 1P2
(519) 652-2949   *SIC* 1542
**D. KRAHN INSURANCE & FINANCIAL
SERVICES INC**   *p* 1427
75 LENORE DR SUITE 1, SASKATOON,
SK, S7K 7Y1
(306) 384-7216   *SIC* 6321
D. L. PAGANI LIMITED   *p* 601
716 GORDON ST, GUELPH, ON, N1G 1Y6
(519) 836-1240   *SIC* 7011
D. PECK PLUMBING   *p* 857
15 MYRTLE ST, RIDGETOWN, ON, N0P
2C0
(519) 360-5913   *SIC* 1711
D. R. BRENTON LIMITED   *p* 460
2 LAKESIDE PARK DR UNIT 5, LAKESIDE,
NS, B3T 1L7
(902) 876-7879   *SIC* 5099
D. R. PERRY PHARMACY LTD   *p* 143
2045 MAYOR MAGRATH DR S UNIT 102,
LETHBRIDGE, AB, T1K 2S2
(403) 328-5509   *SIC* 5912
D.A. BUILDING SYSTEMS LTD   *p* 140
2808 2 AVE N, LETHBRIDGE, AB, T1H 0C2
(403) 328-4427   *SIC* 1541
D.A.R.E. (DRUG ABUSE RESISTANCE ED-UCATION) ONTARIO   *p*
490
See GOVERNMENT OF ONTARIO
D.A.R.T.S.   *p* 82
See DRUMHELLER AND REGION TRAN-SITION SOCIETY
D.B. KENNEY FISHERIES LIMITED   *p* 470
301 WATER ST, WESTPORT, NS, B0V 1H0

(902) 839-2023   *SIC* 5146

D.C. DRUGS LIMITED   *p* 933
467 PARLIAMENT ST, TORONTO, ON, M5A 3A3
(416) 925-4121   *SIC* 5912

D.C.M. MECHANICAL LTD   *p* 35
6335 10 ST SE SUITE 6, CALGARY, AB, T2H 2Z9
(403) 255-9161   *SIC* 1711

D.D. DISTRIBUTION LUBRIFIANTS INC   *p* 1351
69 BOUL SAINT-REMI, SAINT-REMI, QC, J0L 2L0
(450) 454-3978   *SIC* 5172

D.F. BARNES SERVICES LIMITED   *p* 433
22 SUDBURY ST, ST. JOHN'S, NL, A1E 2V1
(709) 579-5041   *SIC* 3312

D.G.B. FRUITERIE   *p* 1174
See HECTOR LARIVEE INC

D.G.C. CONTRACTING INC   *p* 164
40 DIAMOND AVE, SPRUCE GROVE, AB, T7X 3A8
SIC 1623

D.G.S. CONSTRUCTION COMPANY LTD *p* 270
13761 116 AVE UNIT A101, SURREY, BC, V3R 0T2
(604) 584-2214   *SIC* 1542

D.H. RAPELJE LODGE   *p* 1012
See REGIONAL MUNICIPALITY OF NIAGARA, THE

D.J. DRILLING (2004) LTD   *p* 279
19286 21 AVE UNIT 104, SURREY, BC, V3Z 3M3
(604) 541-1362   *SIC* 1081

D.J. INDUSTRIAL SALES AND MANUFACTURING INC   *p* 551
25 NORTH RIVERMEDE RD UNIT 1, CONCORD, ON, L4K 5V4
(416) 798-7575   *SIC* 5084

D.J. KNOLL TRANSPORT LTD   *p* 1406
4 GREAT PLAINS INDUSTRIAL DR, EMERALD PARK, SK, S4L 1B6
(306) 789-4824   *SIC* 4213

D.L.G.L. IMMOBILIERE LTEE   *p* 1058
850 BOUL MICHELE-BOHEC, BLAINVILLE, QC, J7C 5E2
(450) 979-4646   *SIC* 7371

D.L.G.L. LTEE   *p* 1058
850 BOUL MICHELE-BOHEC, BLAINVILLE, QC, J7C 5E2
(450) 979-4646   *SIC* 7371

D.M. EXPRESS   *p* 95
11616 145 ST NW, EDMONTON, AB, T5M 1V8
(780) 454-1188   *SIC* 7389

D.M. SERVANT PHARMACY LIMITED *p* 444
21 MICMAC BLVD SUITE 129, DARTMOUTH, NS, B3A 4K6
(902) 463-3321   *SIC* 5912

D.M.C. SOUDURE INC   *p* 1147
1816 RTE 111 E, MACAMIC, QC, J0Z 2S0
(819) 782-2514   *SIC* 1799

D.M.S. MECHANICAL LTD   *p* 187
7449 CONWAY AVE UNIT 104, BURNABY, BC, V5E 2P7
(604) 437-8996   *SIC* 1711

D.M.S. PLUMBING HEATING AND AIR CONDITIONING   *p* 187
See D.M.S. MECHANICAL LTD

D.O.T FURNITURE LIMITED   *p* 703
3105 DIXIE RD, MISSISSAUGA, ON, L4Y 4E3
(416) 252-2228   *SIC* 5712

D.O.T. FURNITURE PATIO EXPERTS *p* 703
See D.O.T FURNITURE LIMITED

D.S.L. DIAGNOSTIC PRODUCTS INCORPORATED   *p*
668
50   VALLEYWOOD   DR   SUITE   1, MARKHAM, ON, L3R 6E9
(905) 470-0431   *SIC* 5047

D.W.P. DISTRIBUTORS LTD   *p* 271

5504 176 ST, SURREY, BC, V3S 4C3
(604) 576-2961   *SIC* 5172

D.W.S. ROOFING AND WATERPROOFING SERVICES INC   *p* 597
2562 DEL ZOTTO AVE, GLOUCESTER, ON, K1T 3V7
(613) 260-7700   *SIC* 1761

D2 TECHNOLOGIE INC   *p* 1328
2119 BOUL MARCEL-LAURIN, SAINT-LAURENT, QC, H4R 1K4
(514) 904-5888   *SIC* 5999

D2L CORPORATION   *p* 638
151 CHARLES ST W SUITE 400, KITCHENER, ON, N2G 1H6
(519) 772-0325   *SIC* 7373

DAAM GALVANIZING - EDMONTON *p* 109
See DAAM GALVANIZING CO. LTD

DAAM GALVANIZING CO. LTD   *p* 109
9390 48 ST NW, EDMONTON, AB, T6B 2R3
(780) 468-6868   *SIC* 3479

DAC AVIATION INTERNATIONAL LTEE *p* 1132
9371 RUE WANKLYN, LASALLE, QC, H8R 1Z2
(514) 876-0135   *SIC* 4581

DAC GROUP   *p* 769
See DAC GROUP (HOLDINGS) LIMITED

DAC GROUP (HOLDINGS) LIMITED *p* 769
1210 SHEPPARD AVE E SUITE 500, NORTH YORK, ON, M2K 1E3
(416) 492-4322   *SIC* 7311

DAC GROUP/CANADA LTD   *p* 769
1210 SHEPPARD AVE E SUITE 500, NORTH YORK, ON, M2K 1E3
(416) 492-4322   *SIC* 7311

DACKIR DISTRIBUTIONS   *p* 211
5305 12 AVE, DELTA, BC, V4M 2B1
(604) 318-1235   *SIC* 5192

DACOTA FREIGHT SERVICE LTD   *p* 203
1474 THEATRE RD, CRANBROOK, BC, V1C 7G1
(250) 426-3808   *SIC* 4731

DACRO INDUSTRIES INC   *p* 113
9325 51 AVE NW, EDMONTON, AB, T6E 4W8
(780) 434-8900   *SIC* 3443

DACSYS   *p* 1145
See CONSULTATION EN TECHNOLOGIE DE L'INFORMATION ET DES COMUNICATIONS DACSYS INC

DACURY AGENCIES CORPORATION *p* 789
59 SAMOR RD, NORTH YORK, ON, M6A 1J2
(416) 781-2171   *SIC* 5137

DAD'S COOKIES   *p* 871
See KRAFT HEINZ CANADA ULC

DAFCO FILTRATION GROUP CORPORATION   *p*
693
5390 AMBLER DR, MISSISSAUGA, ON, L4W 1G9
(905) 624-9165   *SIC* 3569

DAGMAR RESORT LIMITED   *p* 479
1220 LAKERIDGE RD RR 1, ASHBURN, ON, L0B 1A0
(905) 649-2002   *SIC* 7011

DAGMAR SKI RESORT   *p* 479
See DAGMAR RESORT LIMITED

DAHL BROTHERS (CANADA) LIMITED *p* 713
2600 SOUTH SHERIDAN WAY, MISSISSAUGA, ON, L5J 2M4
(905) 822-2330   *SIC* 6712

DAHL VALVE LIMITED   *p* 713
2600 SOUTH SHERIDAN WAY, MISSISSAUGA, ON, L5J 2M4
(905) 822-2330   *SIC* 3494

DAHNAY LOGISTICS CANADA LTD *p* 703
2501 STANFIELD RD, MISSISSAUGA, ON, L4Y 1R6
(289) 803-1982   *SIC* 4731

DAI TOKU HOLDINGS COMPANY LTD *p* 294
1575 VERNON DR, VANCOUVER, BC, V6A

3P8
(604) 253-5111   *SIC* 6712

DAIGNEAULT & FRERE (1966) INC *p* 1316
400 RUE LABERGE, SAINT-JEAN-SUR-RICHELIEU, QC, J3A 1G5
(450) 347-7567   *SIC* 5511

DAIGNEAULT FERLAND ASSURANCES INC   *p* 1060
181 RUE HENRY-BESSEMER BUREAU 103, BOIS-DES-FILION, QC, J6Z 4S9
(450) 621-3666   *SIC* 6311

DAIGNEAULT PROVOST JOLY LEBRUN INC   *p* 1076
185 BOUL SAINT-JEAN-BAPTISTE BUREAU 100, CHATEAUGUAY, QC, J6K 3B4
(450) 691-9913   *SIC* 6411

DAIKIN (MC)   *p* 1141
See DAIKIN APPLIED CANADA INC

DAIKIN APPLIED CANADA INC   *p* 1141
603 RUE BERIAULT, LONGUEUIL, QC, J4G 1Z1
(450) 674-2442   *SIC* 5075

DAILY GLEANER   *p* 402
See   UNIVERSITY   PRESS   OF   NEW BRUNSWICK

DAILY HERALD TRIBUNE, THE   *p* 131
See 1032451 B.C. LTD

DAILY SEAFOOD INC   *p* 919
135 BLAKE ST, TORONTO, ON, M4J 3E2
(416) 461-9449   *SIC* 5146

DAIMLER CHRYSLER   *p* 1088
See BESSETTE AUTOMOBILE INC

DAIMLER TRUCK FINANCIAL   *p* 697
See MERCEDES-BENZ FINANCIAL SERVICES CANADA CORPORATION

DAINOLITE LIMITED   *p* 738
1401 COURTNEYPARK DR E UNIT 2, MISSISSAUGA, ON, L5T 2E4
(905) 564-1262   *SIC* 5063

DAINTY FOODS   *p* 1401
See ALIMENTS DAINTY FOODS INC, LES

DAIRY FARMERS OF CANADA   *p* 833
21 FLORENCE ST, OTTAWA, ON, K2P 0W6
(613) 236-9997   *SIC* 8611

DAIRY FARMERS OF NEW BRUNSWICK *p* 412
29 MILK BOARD RD, ROACHVILLE, NB, E4G 2G7
(506) 432-4330   *SIC* 5143

DAIRY FARMERS OF ONTARIO   *p* 721
6780 CAMPOBELLO RD, MISSISSAUGA, ON, L5N 2L8
(905) 821-8970   *SIC* 8611

DAIRY PRODUCTS IN MOTION INC *p* 738
6045 EDWARDS BLVD, MISSISSAUGA, ON, L5T 2W7
(905) 565-5210   *SIC* 5143

DAIRY QUEEN   *p* 124
See E.B.C. HOLDINGS LTD

DAIRY QUEEN   *p* 143
See PETERS DAIRY BAR LTD

DAIRY QUEEN   *p* 153
See HDQ INVESTMENTS LTD

DAIRY QUEEN   *p* 161
See BARLBOROUGH BUSINESS ENTERPRISES LTD

DAIRY QUEEN BRAZIER   *p* 412
See BLT FOODS LTD

DAIRY QUEEN BRAZIER STORE   *p* 1039
See MITTON, V CO LTD

DAIRY QUEEN CANADA INC   *p* 530
1111 INTERNATIONAL BLVD, BURLINGTON, ON, L7R 3Y3
(905) 639-1492   *SIC* 8742

DAIRY QUEEN RESTAURANT   *p* 224
See HABENDUM HOLDING LTD

DAIRY TREATS   *p* 788
See 593631 ONTARIO LIMITED

DAIRYLAND AGRO SUPPLY LTD   *p* 1435
4030 THATCHER AVE, SASKATOON, SK, S7R 1A2
(306) 242-5850   *SIC* 5083

DAIRYTOWN PROCESSING LTD   *p* 412
49 MILK BOARD RD, ROACHVILLE, NB,

E4G 2G7
(506) 432-1950   *SIC* 2026

DAIRYWORLD FOODS   *p* 20
See AGRIFOODS INTERNATIONAL CO-OPERATIVE LTD

DAISY INTELLIGENCE CORPORATION *p* 551
2300 STEELES AVE W STE 250, CONCORD, ON, L4K 5X6
(905) 642-2629   *SIC* 7372

DAIWA DISTRIBUTION (ONTARIO) INC *p* 668
361 ALDEN RD, MARKHAM, ON, L3R 3L4
(905) 940-2889   *SIC* 5045

DAJCOR ALUMINUM LTD   *p* 542
155 IRWIN ST, CHATHAM, ON, N7M 0N5
(519) 351-2424   *SIC* 3354

DAJO HOLDINGS LTD   *p* 408
1810 MAIN ST, MONCTON, NB, E1E 4S7
(506) 852-8210   *SIC* 5511

DAKERYN INDUSTRIES LTD   *p* 240
233 1ST ST W SUITE 210, NORTH VANCOUVER, BC, V7M 1B3
(604) 986-0323   *SIC* 5031

DAKIN NEWS SYSTEMS INC   *p* 718
238 QUEEN ST S SUITE 2, MISSISSAUGA, ON, L5M 1L5
(905) 826-0862   *SIC* 6794

DAKON CONSTRUCTION LTD   *p* 1010
275 FROBISHER DR UNIT 1, WATERLOO, ON, N2V 2G4
(519) 746-0920   *SIC* 1542

DAKOTA COLLEGIATE INSTITUTE *p* 368
See LOUIS RIEL SCHOOL DIVISION

DAL-TILE OF CANADA ULC   *p* 551
40 GRANITERIDGE RD UNIT 1, CONCORD, ON, L4K 5M8
(905) 738-2099   *SIC* 5032

DALCON CONSTRUCTION   *p* 1272
See DALCON INC

DALCON INC   *p* 1272
2820 BOUL LAURIER BUREAU 1050, QUEBEC, QC, G1V 0C1
(418) 781-6300   *SIC* 1542

DALE   MATHESON   CARR-HILTON LABONTE LLP   *p* 312
1140 PENDER ST W SUITE 1500, VANCOUVER, BC, V6E 4G1
(604) 687-4747   *SIC* 8721

DALE PARIZEAU MORRIS MACKENZIE *p* 1269
See LUSSIER DALE PARIZEAU INC

DALEX CANADA INC   *p* 551
157 ADESSO DR, CONCORD, ON, L4K 3C3
(905) 738-2070   *SIC* 5087

DALFEN'S LIMITED   *p* 1402
4444 RUE SAINTE-CATHERINE O BUREAU 100, WESTMOUNT, QC, H3Z 1R2
(514) 938-1050   *SIC* 6512

DALHOUSIE NURSING HOME INC   *p* 397
296 VICTORIA ST UNIT 1, DALHOUSIE, NB, E8C 2R8
(506) 684-7800   *SIC* 8051

DALHOUSIE UNIVERSITY   *p* 451
1276 SOUTH PARK ST RM 225, HALIFAX, NS, B3H 2Y9
(902) 473-7736   *SIC* 8221

DALHOUSIE UNIVERSITY   *p* 451
5850 COLLEGE ST UNIT 13B, HALIFAX, NS, B3H 1X5
(902) 494-6850   *SIC* 8221

DALHOUSIE UNIVERSITY   *p* 451
6135 UNIVERSITY AVE RM 3030, HALIFAX, NS, B3H 4P9
(902) 494-1440   *SIC* 8221

DALHOUSIE UNIVERSITY   *p* 451
6299 SOUTH ST, HALIFAX, NS, B3H 4J1
(902) 494-2211   *SIC* 8221

DALHOUSIE UNIVERSITY   *p* 468
62 CUMMING DR, TRURO, NS, B2N 5E3
(902) 893-6600   *SIC* 8221

DALIMONTE, M. PHARMACY LTD   *p* 664
2943 MAJOR MACKENZIE DR SUITE 1,

MAPLE, ON, L6A 3N9
(905) 832-9954   SIC 5912
DALISA   p 1317
See MULTI-PORTIONS INC
DALKOTECH INC   p 1375
9330 BOUL BOURQUE, SHERBROOKE, QC, J1N 0G2
(819) 868-1997   SIC 7692
DALL CONTRACTING LTD   p 212
GD, FORT NELSON, BC, V0C 1R0
(250) 774-7251   SIC 5171
DALLAIRE FOREST KIROUAC, COMPTABLES PROFESSIONNELS AGRES, S.E.N.C.R.L.   p 1272
1175 AV LAVIGERIE BUREAU 580, QUEBEC, QC, G1V 4P1
(418) 650-2266   SIC 8721
DALLOV HOLDINGS LIMITED   p 530
441 MAPLE AVE, BURLINGTON, ON, L7S 1L8
(905) 639-2264   SIC 8051
DALMAC ENERGY INC   p 113
4934 89 ST NW, EDMONTON, AB, T6E 5K1
(780) 988-8510   SIC 1382
DALMAC OILFIELD SERVICES INC   p 114
4934 89 ST NW, EDMONTON, AB, T6E 5K1
(780) 988-8510   SIC 1389
DALMACIJA FORMING LTD   p 749
11 GIFFORD ST SUITE 201, NEPEAN, ON, K2E 7S3
(613) 727-1371   SIC 1771
DALMAR MOTORS LIMITED   p 659
475 WHARNCLIFFE RD S, LONDON, ON, N6J 2N1
(519) 433-3181   SIC 5511
DALMAR VOLKSWAGEN AUDI   p 659
See DALMAR MOTORS LIMITED
DALREN LIMITED   p 545
8781 DALE RD, COBOURG, ON, K9A 4J9
(905) 377-1080   SIC 1542
DALRON CONSTRUCTION LIMITED   p 899
130 ELM ST, SUDBURY, ON, P3C 1T6
(705) 560-9770   SIC 1521
DALTCO ELECTRIC & SUPPLY (1979) LTD   p 630
26 LAPPANS LANE, KINGSTON, ON, K7K 6Z4
(613) 546-3677   SIC 5065
DALTON CHEMICAL LABORATORIES INC   p 916
349 WILDCAT RD, TORONTO, ON, M3J 2S3
(416) 661-2102   SIC 2834
DALTON COMPANY LTD, THE   p 988
1140 CASTLEFIELD AVE, TORONTO, ON, M6B 1E9
(416) 789-4195   SIC 1541
DALTON PHARMA SERVICES   p 916
See DALTON CHEMICAL LABORATORIES INC
DALTON TIMMIS INSURANCE GROUP INC   p 478
35 STONE CHURCH RD, ANCASTER, ON, L9K 1S5
(905) 648-3922   SIC 6331
DALTON WHITE FARMS & SUPPLIES LIMITED   p 564
802 JAMES ST, DELHI, ON, N4B 2E1
(519) 582-2864   SIC 0132
DALZIEL ENTERPRISES LTD   p 81
3439 HWY 580, CREMONA, AB, T0M 0R0
(403) 337-3264   SIC 5191
DAMA CONSTRUCTION   p 1093
See 9028-7939 QUEBEC INC
DAMAFRUIT   p 1298
See DEVELOPPEMENT BONNET INC
DAMAR ESSO   p 1410
See DAMAR HOLDINGS LTD
DAMAR HOLDINGS LTD   p 1410
1920 HWY 6 S, MELFORT, SK, S0E 1A0
(306) 752-9066   SIC 5541
DAMAR SECURITY SYSTEMS   p 860
See LAMBTON COMMUNICATIONS LIM-

ITED
DAMCO CANADA INC   p 693
5700 EXPLORER DR UNIT 101, MISSISSAUGA, ON, L4W 0C6
(866) 361-3073   SIC 4731
DAMCO DISTRIBUTION CANADA INC   p 208
8400 RIVER RD, DELTA, BC, V4G 1B5
(604) 940-1357   SIC 4731
DAMS FORD LINCOLN SALES LTD   p 271
19330 LANGLEY BYPASS, SURREY, BC, V3S 7R2
(604) 532-9921   SIC 5511
DAMSAR INC   p 1171
8115 AV PAPINEAU, MONTREAL, QC, H2E 2H7
(514) 374-0177   SIC 5499
DAN AGENCY INC   p 979
276 KING ST W SUITE 100, TORONTO, ON, M5V 1J2
(416) 929-9700   SIC 7311
DAN AGENCY INC   p 1222
3970 RUE SAINT-AMBROISE, MONTREAL, QC, H4C 2C7
(514) 848-0010   SIC 7311
DAN NEL COACH LINES COMPANY LIMITED   p 883
12 KEEFER RD SUITE 10, ST CATHARINES, ON, L2M 7N9
(905) 934-1124   SIC 4151
DAN'S PRODUCE LIMITED   p 760
7201 BEECHWOOD RD, NIAGARA FALLS, ON, L2H 0W8
(905) 356-1560   SIC 5148
DAN-D FOODS (TORONTO) LTD   p 551
45 BASALTIC RD UNIT 5, CONCORD, ON, L4K 1G5
(905) 889-7807   SIC 5141
DAN-D FOODS LTD   p 263
11760 MACHRINA WAY, RICHMOND, BC, V7A 4V1
(604) 274-3263   SIC 5141
DAN-JEN MECHANICAL LTD   p 260
11786 RIVER RD SUITE 146, RICHMOND, BC, V6X 3Z3
(604) 232-4545   SIC 1711
DANA CANADA CORPORATION   p 486
120 WELHAM RD, BARRIE, ON, L4N 8Y4
(705) 737-2300   SIC 3714
DANA CANADA CORPORATION   p 489
5095 SOUTH SERVICE RD, BEAMSVILLE, ON, L0R 1B0
SIC 5013
DANA CANADA CORPORATION   p 533
401 FRANKLIN BLVD, CAMBRIDGE, ON, N1R 8G8
(519) 621-1303   SIC 3714
DANA CANADA CORPORATION   p 542
1010 RICHMOND ST, CHATHAM, ON, N7M 5J5
(519) 351-1221   SIC 2298
DANA CANADA CORPORATION   p 746
205 INDUSTRIAL DR, MOUNT FOREST, ON, N0G 2L1
(519) 323-9494   SIC 3443
DANA CANADA CORPORATION   p 802
656 KERR ST, OAKVILLE, ON, L6K 3E4
(905) 849-1200   SIC 3714
DANA CANADA CORPORATION   p 803
1400 ADVANCE RD, OAKVILLE, ON, L6L 6L6
(905) 825-8856   SIC 3443
DANA CANADA CORPORATION   p 888
500 JAMES ST S, ST MARYS, ON, N4X 1B4
SIC 3714
DANA HOSPITALITY LIMITED PARTNERSHIP   p 800
2898 SOUTH SHERIDAN WAY SUITE 200, OAKVILLE, ON, L6J 7L5
(905) 829-0292   SIC 5812
DANA LOGIC INC   p 1203
1155 BOUL RENE-LEVESQUE O BUREAU

2500, MONTREAL, QC, H3B 2K4
(514) 845-5326   SIC 7372
DANACA TRANSPORT MONTREAL LTEE   p 1141
2555 RUE JEAN-DESY, LONGUEUIL, QC, J4G 1G6
(450) 463-0020   SIC 4212
DANBY   p 602
See DANBY PRODUCTS LIMITED
DANBY PRODUCTS LIMITED   p 602
5070 WHITELAW RD, GUELPH, ON, N1H 6Z9
(519) 837-0920   SIC 5064
DAND AUTO PARTS LIMITED   p 39
9940 MACLEOD TRAIL SE SUITE 3, CALGARY, AB, T2J 3K9
(403) 278-4040   SIC 5311
DANDCO ENTERPRISES LTD   p 157
2510 50 AVE, RED DEER, AB, T4R 1M3
(403) 342-2223   SIC 5531
DANDY OIL PRODUCTS LTD   p 105
15630 118 AVE NW, EDMONTON, AB, T5V 1C4
(780) 452-1104   SIC 5172
DANESCO INC   p 1118
18111 RTE TRANSCANADIENNE, KIRKLAND, QC, H9J 3K1
(514) 694-9111   SIC 5023
DANFREIGHT SYSTEMS INC   p 1114
1400 CH LASALLE, JOLIETTE, QC, J6E 0L8
(450) 755-6190   SIC 4213
DANGO INC   p 397
725 ROUTE 945 SUITE A, CORMIER-VILLAGE, NB, E4P 5Y4
(506) 533-6272   SIC 7389
DANIA HOME SOCIETY   p 188
4279 NORLAND AVE, BURNABY, BC, V5G 3Z6
(604) 299-1370   SIC 8361
DANIADOWN HOME   p 290
See DANIADOWN QUILTS LTD
DANIADOWN QUILTS LTD   p 290
1270 MARINE DR SE, VANCOUVER, BC, V5X 2V9
(604) 324-8766   SIC 5719
DANICA IMPORTS LTD   p 291
348 7TH AVE W, VANCOUVER, BC, V5Y 1M4
(604) 255-6150   SIC 5023
DANIEL ET DANIEL CATERING INC   p 933
248 CARLTON ST, TORONTO, ON, M5A 2L1
(416) 968-9275   SIC 5812
DANIEL LAVOIE PHARMACIEN INC   p 1304
11400 1RE AVE, SAINT-GEORGES, QC, G5Y 5S4
(418) 227-1515   SIC 5912
DANIEL MCINTYRE COLLEGIATE INSTITUTE   p 381
See WINNIPEG SCHOOL DIVISION
DANIEL S. WEBSTER HOLDINGS LIMITED   p 546
89 BALSAM ST, COLLINGWOOD, ON, L9Y 3Y6
(705) 445-4169   SIC 5531
DANIELS CORPORATION, THE   p 933
130 QUEENS QUAY E 8 FL, TORONTO, ON, M5A 0P6
(416) 598-2129   SIC 6799
DANIELS ELECTRONICS LTD   p 335
43 ERIE ST, VICTORIA, BC, V8V 1P8
(250) 382-8268   SIC 3669
DANIELS GROUP INC, THE   p 933
130 QUEENS QUAY E 8 FL, TORONTO, ON, M5A 0P6
(416) 598-2129   SIC 6531
DANIELS HR CORPORATION   p 933
130 QUEENS QUAY E 8 FL, TORONTO, ON, M5A 0P6
(416) 598-2129   SIC 1522
DANIELS KIMBER PHYSIOTHERAPY CLINIC P.C. LTD   p 1424

3907 8TH ST E SUITE 304, SASKATOON, SK, S7H 5M7
(306) 652-5151   SIC 8049
DANIELS LR CORPORATION   p 933
130 QUEENS QUAY E 8 FL, TORONTO, ON, M5A 0P6
(416) 598-2129   SIC 8712
DANIELS MIDTOWN CORPORATION   p 933
130 QUEENS QUAY E 8 FL, TORONTO, ON, M5A 0P6
(416) 598-2129   SIC 1522
DANIELS SERVICE CENTRE LTD   p 857
21180 VICTORIA RD, RIDGETOWN, ON, N0P 2C0
(519) 674-5493   SIC 7538
DANIELS SHARPSMART CANADA LIMITED   p 509
52 BRAMSTEELE RD SUITE 8, BRAMPTON, ON, L6W 3M5
(905) 793-2966   SIC 5047
DANIELS, ETLIN   p 794
1850 WILSON AVE, NORTH YORK, ON, M9M 1A1
(416) 741-7336   SIC 5063
DANIS CONSTRUCTION INC   p 1377
13000 RTE MARIE-VICTORIN, SOREL-TRACY, QC, J3R 0J9
SIC 3273
DANKA MDS   p 1328
5924 BOUL HENRI-BOURASSA O, SAINT-LAURENT, QC, H4R 1V9
(514) 339-5000   SIC 5044
DANNY PROFESSIONAL SERVICES   p 1027
See CONAIR CONSUMER PRODUCTS ULC
DANNY'S NO FRILLS   p 611
See 717940 ONTARIO LIMITED
DANONE CANADA   p 1064
See DANONE INC
DANONE INC   p 1064
100 RUE DE LAUZON, BOUCHERVILLE, QC, J4B 1E6
(450) 655-7331   SIC 2026
DANS UN JARDIN CANADA INC   p 1064
240 BOUL INDUSTRIEL, BOUCHERVILLE, QC, J4B 2X4
(450) 449-2121   SIC 5999
DANS UN JARDIN INC   p 1064
240 BOUL INDUSTRIEL, BOUCHERVILLE, QC, J4B 2X4
(450) 449-2121   SIC 6712
DANSON DECOR INC   p 1333
3425 RUE DOUGLAS-B.-FLOREANI, SAINT-LAURENT, QC, H4S 1Y6
(514) 335-2435   SIC 5199
DANZER CANADA INC   p 567
402725 HWY 4, DURHAM, ON, N0G 1R0
(519) 369-3310   SIC 3861
DAOUST, JACQUES COATINGS MANAGEMENT INC   p 533
32 MCKENZIE ST, CAMBRIDGE, ON, N1R 4E1
(519) 624-1515   SIC 3471
DAOUST, PAUL CONSTRUCTION GROUP INC   p 596
5424 CANOTEK RD, GLOUCESTER, ON, K1J 1E9
(613) 590-1694   SIC 1542
DAPASOFT INC   p 914
111 GORDON BAKER SUITE 600, TORONTO, ON, M2H 3R1
(416) 847-4080   SIC 7371
DAPC   p 891
See DYNAMIC & PROTO CIRCUITS INC
DAPHNE FLOWER IMPORTS   p 736
See 421229 ONTARIO LIMITED
DAPP POWER L.P.   p 172
RR 1, WESTLOCK, AB, T7P 2N9
(780) 954-2089   SIC 4911
DAQUIN SALES   p 831
See 119155 CANADA LIMITED
DARCOR CASTERS   p 571

See DARCOR LIMITED

DARCOR LIMITED p 571
7 STAFFORDSHIRE PL, ETOBICOKE, ON,
M8W 1T1
(416) 255-8563 SIC 3562

DARDEN RESTAURANTS INC , DIV OF p
688
See GENERAL MILLS RESTAURANTS INC

DARE FOODS LIMITED p 265
6751 ELMBRIDGE WAY, RICHMOND, BC,
V7C 4N1
(604) 233-1117 SIC 2051

DARE FOODS LIMITED p 538
25 CHERRY BLOSSOM RD, CAMBRIDGE,
ON, N3H 4R7
(519) 893-5500 SIC 2051

DARE FOODS LIMITED p 683
725 STEELES AVE E, MILTON, ON, L9T
5H1
(905) 875-1223 SIC 2064

DARE FOODS LIMITED p 1322
845 AV SAINT-CHARLES, SAINT-
LAMBERT, QC, J4P 2A2
(450) 671-6121 SIC 2051

DARE FOODS LIMITED p 1360
15 RANG DUBUC, SAINTE-MARTINE, QC,
J0S 1V0
(450) 427-8410 SIC 2051

DARGAL INTERLINE p 221
See DARGAL INTERLINE CRUISE &
TOURS LTD

**DARGAL INTERLINE CRUISE & TOURS
LTD** p 221
1632 DICKSON AVE SUITE 200,
KELOWNA, BC, V1Y 7T2
(250) 861-3223 SIC 4725

DARLING INTERNATIONAL CANADA INCp
468
169 LOWER TRURO RD, TRURO, NS, B2N
5C1
(902) 895-2801 SIC 4953

DARLING INTERNATIONAL CANADA INCp
535
485 PINEBUSH RD, CAMBRIDGE, ON, N1T
0A6
(519) 780-3342 SIC 4953

DARLING INTERNATIONAL CANADA INCp
566
880 5 HWY W, DUNDAS, ON, L9H 5E2
(905) 628-2258 SIC 4953

DARLING INTERNATIONAL CANADA INCp
745
8406 WELLINGTON COUNTY RR,
MOOREFIELD, ON, N0G 2K0
(519) 638-3081 SIC 4953

DARLING INTERNATIONAL CANADA INCp
1356
605 1RE AV, SAINTE-CATHERINE, QC, J5C
1C5
(450) 632-3250 SIC 4953

DARONA p 1298
See MOULAGE SOUS PRESSION A.M.T.
INC

DARPEX p 1167
See SOLOTECH INC

DART AEROSPACE LTD p 619
1270 ABERDEEN ST, HAWKESBURY, ON,
K6A 1K7
(613) 632-5200 SIC 5088

DART CANADA INC p 864
2121 MARKHAM RD, SCARBOROUGH,
ON, M1B 2W3
(416) 293-2877 SIC 2656

DART MESSENGER & COURIER SERVICE
p 364
See 2851262 MANITOBA LTD

**DARTMOUTH CHRYSLER DODGE JEEP
RAM** p 443
See DARTMOUTH MOTORS LP

DARTMOUTH CROSSING LIMITED p 445
34 LOGIEALMOND CLOSE, DARTMOUTH,
NS, B3B 0C8
(902) 445-8883 SIC 7389

DARTMOUTH HIGH SCHOOL p 444

See HALIFAX REGIONAL SCHOOL
BOARD

DARTMOUTH MOTORS LP p 443
61 ATHORPE DR, DARTMOUTH, NS, B2W
1K9
(902) 469-9050 SIC 7532

DARTMOUTH SENIOR CARE SOCIETY p
443
10 MOUNT HOPE AVE, DARTMOUTH, NS,
B2Y 4K1
(902) 469-3702 SIC 8051

DARTMOUTH SPORTSPLEX p 444
See DARTMOUTH SPORTSPLEX COM-
MUNITY ASSOCIATION

**DARTMOUTH SPORTSPLEX COMMUNITY
ASSOCIATION** p 444
110 WYSE RD, DARTMOUTH, NS, B3A
1M2
(902) 464-2600 SIC 7997

DARVIC ENTERPRISES LTD p 340
2435 MILLSTREAM RD, VICTORIA, BC,
V9B 3R5
(250) 391-6082 SIC 5541

DARVONDA NURSERIES LTD p 226
6690 216 ST, LANGLEY, BC, V2Y 2N9
(604) 530-6889 SIC 0181

DARWIN CONSTRUCTION (CANADA) LTD
p 238
197 FORESTER ST SUITE 404, NORTH
VANCOUVER, BC, V7H 0A6
(604) 929-7944 SIC 1542

DARYL-EVANS MECHANICAL LTD p 200
211 SCHOOLHOUSE ST UNIT 1, COQUIT-
LAM, BC, V3K 4X9
(604) 525-3523 SIC 1711

DAS p 48
See DOW AGROSCIENCES CANADA INC.

**DAS LEGAL PROTECTION INSURANCE
COMPANY LIMITED** p 950
390 BAY ST SUITE 1610, TORONTO, ON,
M5H 2Y2
(416) 342-5400 SIC 6331

DASCO STORAGE SOLUTIONS LTD p 502
346 ORENDA RD, BRAMPTON, ON, L6T
1G1
(905) 792-7080 SIC 5044

DASH HUDSON INC p 452
1668 BARRINGTON ST UNIT 600, HALI-
FAX, NS, B3J 2A2
(902) 298-2795 SIC 7372

DASHWOOD INDUSTRIES INC p 541
69323 RICHMOND ST, CENTRALIA, ON,
N0M 1K0
(519) 228-6624 SIC 5211

DASKO HOLDINGS LTD p 220
1830 UNDERHILL ST, KELOWNA, BC, V1X
5P8
(250) 862-5242 SIC 5541

DASONG ZAO CAMPAIGN, THE p 914
3469 SHEPPARD AVE E, TORONTO, ON,
M1T 3K5
(647) 641-7292 SIC 8651

DASSAULT SYSTEMES CANADA INC p
1188
393 RUE SAINT-JACQUES BUREAU 300,
MONTREAL, QC, H2Y 1N9
(514) 940-2949 SIC 7373

**DASSAULT SYSTEMES CANADA INNOVA-
TION TECHNOLOGIES** p
1188
See DASSAULT SYSTEMES CANADA INC

**DASSAULT SYSTEMES CANADA SOFT-
WARE INC** p
312
1066 HASTINGS ST W SUITE 1100, VAN-
COUVER, BC, V6E 3X1
(604) 684-6550 SIC 7371

**DATA & AUDIO-VISUAL ENTERPRISES
HOLDINGS INC** p 962
161 BAY ST SUITE 2300, TORONTO, ON,
M5J 2S1
(416) 361-1959 SIC 6712

DATA ACCESS SOLUTIONS INC p 851
15 WERTHEIM CRT UNIT 107, RICHMOND

HILL, ON, L4B 3H7
(905) 370-9960 SIC 4813

DATA CABLE COMPANY INC, THE p 808
31 ROBB BLVD, ORANGEVILLE, ON, L9W
3L1
(519) 941-7020 SIC 3679

DATA CIRCUITS p 674
See QTA CIRCUITS LTD

**DATA COMMUNICATIONS MANAGEMENT
CORP** p 72
1311 9 AVE SW SUITE 300, CALGARY, AB,
T3C 0H9
(403) 272-7440 SIC 2759

**DATA COMMUNICATIONS MANAGEMENT
CORP** p 125
9503 12 AVE SW, EDMONTON, AB, T6X
0C3
(780) 462-9700 SIC 5112

**DATA COMMUNICATIONS MANAGEMENT
CORP** p 499
9195 TORBRAM RD, BRAMPTON, ON, L6S
6H2
(905) 791-3151 SIC 2761

**DATA COMMUNICATIONS MANAGEMENT
CORP** p 738
80 AMBASSADOR DR, MISSISSAUGA,
ON, L5T 2Y9
(905) 696-8884 SIC 2759

**DATA COMMUNICATIONS MANAGEMENT
CORP** p 1098
1750 RUE JEAN-BERCHMANS-MICHAUD,
DRUMMONDVILLE, QC, J2C 7S2
(819) 472-1111 SIC 2761

**DATA COMMUNICATIONS MANAGEMENT
CORP** p 1110
855 BOUL INDUSTRIEL, GRANBY, QC, J2J
1A6
SIC 2761

DATA DIRECT GROUP INC p 734
2001 DREW RD UNIT 1, MISSISSAUGA,
ON, L5S 1S4
(905) 564-0150 SIC 7331

DATA GATHERING SERVICE INC p 161
320 SIOUX RD SUITE 110, SHERWOOD
PARK, AB, T8A 3X6
(780) 467-9575 SIC 6331

DATA GROUP OF COMPANIES p 125
See DATA COMMUNICATIONS MANAGE-
MENT CORP

DATA GROUP OF COMPANIES p 1110
See DATA COMMUNICATIONS MANAGE-
MENT CORP

DATA GROUP OF COMPANIES, THE p 499
See DATA COMMUNICATIONS MANAGE-
MENT CORP

DATA INTEGRITY INC p 856
30 VIA RENZO DR UNIT 3, RICHMOND
HILL, ON, L4S 0B8
(416) 638-0111 SIC 5045

DATA PARCEL EXPRESS INCORPORATED
p 738
6500 VAN DEEMTER CRT, MISSISSAUGA,
ON, L5T 1S1
(905) 564-5555 SIC 4731

DATA PROBE INC p 364
297 ST MARY'S RD, WINNIPEG, MB, R2H
1J5
SIC 8732

DATA WEST SOLUTIONS p 802
See OPEN SOLUTIONS CANADA INC

DATA WIRING SOLUTIONS INC p 426
1170 TOPSAIL RD SUITE 3, MOUNT
PEARL, NL, A1N 5E8
(709) 747-2150 SIC 1623

DATALOG TECHNOLOGY INC p 15
10707 50 ST SE, CALGARY, AB, T2C 3E5
(403) 243-2024 SIC 1389

DATAVISUAL p 819
See DATAVISUAL MARKETING INC

DATAVISUAL MARKETING INC p 819
1101 POLYTEK ST SUITE 500, OTTAWA,
ON, K1J 0B3
(613) 741-9898 SIC 5099

DATAWAVE SYSTEMS INC p 254

13575 COMMERCE PKY SUITE 110, RICH-
MOND, BC, V6V 2L1
(604) 295-1800 SIC 4813

DATAWIND INC p 734
7895 TRANMERE DR SUITE 207, MISSIS-
SAUGA, ON, L5S 1V9
(905) 671-0202 SIC 4813

DATCOM p 873
1361 HUNTINGWOOD DR UNIT 13, SCAR-
BOROUGH, ON, M1S 3J1
(416) 293-2866 SIC 5051

DATEK INDUSTRIAL TECHNOLOGIES LTD
p 199
3268 CHARTWELL GREEN, COQUITLAM,
BC, V3E 3M9
(604) 468-8615 SIC 5084

DATRAN BAS ST-LAURENT INC p 1285
290 AV DE L'INDUSTRIE, RIMOUSKI, QC,
G5M 1W4
SIC 5198

DATUM GROUP p 573
See CANA-DATUM MOULDS LTD

DAUBOIS INC p 1344
6155 BOUL DES GRANDES-PRAIRIES,
SAINT-LEONARD, QC, H1P 1A5
(514) 328-1253 SIC 5032

DAUDET CREEK CONTRACTING LTD p
224
495 QUATSINO BLVD, KITIMAT, BC, V8C
2G7
(250) 632-4831 SIC 1522

DAUPHIN CO-OP p 348
See DAUPHIN CONSUMERS COOPERA-
TIVE LTD

**DAUPHIN CONSUMERS COOPERATIVE
LTD** p 348
18 3RD AVE NE, DAUPHIN, MB, R7N 0Y6
(204) 638-6003 SIC 5411

**DAUPHIN GENERAL HOSPITAL FOUNDA-
TION, THE** p
348
625 3RD ST SW, DAUPHIN, MB, R7N 1R7
(204) 638-3010 SIC 8641

DAUPHIN PERSONAL CARE HOME INC p
348
625 3RD ST SW, DAUPHIN, MB, R7N 1R7
(204) 638-3010 SIC 8059

**DAUPHIN REGIONAL COMPREHENSIVE
SECONDARY SCHOOL** p 349
See MOUNTAIN VIEW SCHOOL DIVISION

DAUPHIN REGIONAL HEALTH CENTRE p
348
625 3RD ST SW, DAUPHIN, MB, R7N 1R7
(204) 638-3010 SIC 8062

**DAV-BAR-DAL INSURANCE SERVICES
LTD** p 142
300 10 ST S, LETHBRIDGE, AB, T1J 2M6
(403) 320-1010 SIC 6411

DAVCO WELDING & CRANES p 171
See DAVCO WELDING LTD

DAVCO WELDING LTD p 171
GD STN MAIN, WAINWRIGHT, AB, T9W
1M3
(780) 842-5559 SIC 1799

DAVE & BUSTERS OF CANADA p 548
See 6131646 CANADA INC

DAVE DEPLAEDT RETAIL SALES LTD p
1433
1731 PRESTON AVE N SUITE 133, SASKA-
TOON, SK, S7N 4V2
(306) 373-3666 SIC 5251

DAVE MOORE FUELS LTD p 589
315 MAIN ST N SUITE 3, EXETER, ON,
N0M 1S3
(519) 235-0853 SIC 5172

DAVE WOOD MAZDA p 754
See 967961 ONTARIO LIMITED

DAVE'S COMMERCIAL CLEANING p 463
See SHANNON, BRENDA CONTRACTS
LIMITED

DAVE'S CRUISES p 235
6490 PTARMIGAN WAY, NANAIMO, BC,
V9V 1V7
(250) 390-1115 SIC 4724

DAVENHILL SENIOR LIVING p 931
See YONGE-ROSEDALE CHARITABLE FOUNDATION

DAVENPORT REALTY BROKERAGE p 1010
See 2615267 ONTARIO INC

DAVENPORT SALES & AUTO SERVICE LTD p 71
5404 DALTON DR NW SUITE 299, CALGARY, AB, T3A 2C3
(403) 288-1100 SIC 5531

DAVENPORT SALES & AUTO SERVICE LTD p 84
11839 KINGSWAY NW, EDMONTON, AB, T5G 3J7
(780) 413-8473 SIC 5531

DAVENPORT SUBARU OF ORILLIA p 809
See 1176356 ONTARIO INC

DAVEY TREE EXPERT CO. OF CANADA, LIMITED p 118
5622 103A ST NW, EDMONTON, AB, T6H 2J5
(780) 428-8733 SIC 0783

DAVEY TREE EXPERT CO. OF CANADA, LIMITED p 233
13 VICTORIA CRES SUITE 20, NANAIMO, BC, V9R 5B9
(250) 755-1288 SIC 5261

DAVEY TREE EXPERT CO. OF CANADA, LIMITED p 477
611 TRADEWIND DR SUITE 500, ANCASTER, ON, L9G 4V5
(905) 333-1034 SIC 7999

DAVEY TREE SERVICES p 233
See DAVEY TREE EXPERT CO. OF CANADA, LIMITED

DAVEY TREE SERVICES DIV p 477
See DAVEY TREE EXPERT CO. OF CANADA, LIMITED

DAVIAN CONSTRUCTION LTD p 380
740 LOGAN AVE, WINNIPEG, MB, R3E 1M9
(204) 783-7251 SIC 1542

DAVID & CLAUDE HOLDINGS CANADA INC p 533
30 COWANSVIEW RD, CAMBRIDGE, ON, N1R 7N3
(519) 622-2320 SIC 5085

DAVID & MARY THOMSON COLLEGIATE INSTITUTE p 872
See TORONTO DISTRICT SCHOOL BOARD

DAVID BROWN SYSTEM (CANADA) INC p 1053
20375 AV CLARK-GRAHAM, BAIE-D'URFE, QC, H9X 3T5
(514) 457-7700 SIC 3566

DAVID CARSON FARMS & AUCTION SERVICES LTD p 646
5531 PERTH LINE 86, LISTOWEL, ON, N4W 3G8
(519) 291-2049 SIC 5154

DAVID CORDINGLEY TRANSPORT CORP p 515
148 MOHAWK ST, BRANTFORD, ON, N3S 7G5
(519) 752-7810 SIC 4212

DAVID OPPENHEIMER & ASSOCIATES GENERAL PARTNERSHIP p 200
11 BURBIDGE ST SUITE 101, COQUITLAM, BC, V3K 7B2
(604) 461-6779 SIC 0181

DAVID SHAW SILVERWARE NORTH AMERICA LTD p 783
85 MARTIN ROSS AVE, NORTH YORK, ON, M3J 2L5
(416) 736-0492 SIC 5094

DAVID SHAW TABLEWARE p 783
See DAVID SHAW SILVERWARE NORTH AMERICA LTD

DAVID SULLIVAN GROUP OF COMPANIES LTD, THE p 298
489 ROBSON ST, VANCOUVER, BC, V6B 6L9
(604) 684-5714 SIC 5411

DAVID SUZUKI FOUNDATION, THE p 322
2211 4TH AVE W UNIT 219, VANCOUVER, BC, V6K 4S2
(604) 732-4228 SIC 8699

DAVID THOMPSON HEALTH REGION p 68
See ALBERTA HEALTH SERVICES

DAVID THOMPSON SECONDARY SCHOOL p 216
See BOARD OF EDUCATION OF SCHOOL DISTRICT NO. 06 (ROCKY MOUNTAIN), THE

DAVID THOMPSON SECONDARY SCHOOL p 287
See BOARD OF EDUCATION OF SCHOOL DISTRICT NO. 39 (VANCOUVER), THE

DAVID YOUNGSON & ASSOCIATES LIMITED p 916
12 CRANFIELD RD UNIT 200, TORONTO, ON, M4B 3G8
(416) 441-9696 SIC 5199

DAVID'S VACATION CLUB RENTALS p 657
4-1106 DEARNESS DR, LONDON, ON, N6E 1N9
(519) 686-7694 SIC 4724

DAVIDSON & COMPANY CHARTERED ACCOUNTANTS LLP p 330
609 GRANDVILLE ST SUITE 1200, VANCOUVER, BC, V7Y 1G6
(604) 687-0947 SIC 8721

DAVIDSON & SONS CUSTOMS BROKERS LTD p 312
1188 GEORGIA ST W SUITE 1220, VANCOUVER, BC, V6E 4A2
(604) 681-5132 SIC 4731

DAVIDSON DELAPLANTE INSURANCE BROKERS LTD p 912
100 THIRD AVE, TIMMINS, ON, P4N 1C3
(705) 268-1011 SIC 6411

DAVIDSON ENMAN LUMBER LIMITED p 15
9515 44 ST SE, CALGARY, AB, T2C 2P7
(403) 279-5525 SIC 2439

DAVIDSON ENMAN LUMBER LIMITED p 29
452 42 AVE SE, CALGARY, AB, T2G 1Y5
(403) 243-2566 SIC 5211

DAVIDSON ENMAN LUMBER TRUSS, DIV OF p 29
See DAVIDSON ENMAN LUMBER LIMITED

DAVIDSON SHELL p 1405
See 6132511 CANADA LTD

DAVIDSTEA INC p 1156
5430 RUE FERRIER, MONT-ROYAL, QC, H4P 1M2
(514) 739-0006 SIC 5499

DAVIE STREET MANAGEMENT SERVICES LTD p 298
322 DAVIE ST, VANCOUVER, BC, V6B 5Z6
(604) 642-6787 SIC 7011

DAVIES p 1195
See DAVIES WARD PHILLIPS & VINEBERG LLP

DAVIES AUTO ELECTRIC LIMITED p 702
2571 WHARTON GLEN AVE, MISSISSAUGA, ON, L4X 2A8
(905) 279-6300 SIC 5511

DAVIES WARD PHILLIPS & VINEBERG LLP p 979
155 WELLINGTON ST W, TORONTO, ON, M5V 3J7
(416) 863-0900 SIC 8111

DAVIES WARD PHILLIPS & VINEBERG LLP p 1195
1501 AV MCGILL COLLEGE BUREAU 2600, MONTREAL, QC, H3A 3N9
(514) 841-6400 SIC 8111

DAVIS & MCCAULEY FUELS LTD p 648
660 CLARKE RD, LONDON, ON, N5V 3A9
(519) 453-6900 SIC 5172

DAVIS & WILLMOT INC p 917
2060 QUEEN ST E SUITE 51504, TORONTO, ON, M4E 1C9

SIC 5094

DAVIS AGENCY OF OTTAWA LIMITED p 751
3161 GREENBANK RD UNIT A7, NEPEAN, ON, K2J 4H9
(613) 825-0755 SIC 5947

DAVIS AND COMPANY p 303
See DAVIS MANAGEMENT LTD

DAVIS CAMPUS p 512
See SHERIDAN COLLEGE INSTITUTE OF TECHNOLOGY AND ADVANCED LEARNING

DAVIS CONTROLS LIMITED p 797
2200 BRISTOL CIR, OAKVILLE, ON, L6H 5R3
(905) 829-2000 SIC 5084

DAVIS FUEL COMPANY LIMITED p 520
22 KING ST, BURFORD, ON, N0E 1A0
(519) 449-2417 SIC 5172

DAVIS GMC BUICK LTD p 142
115 WT HILL BLVD S, LETHBRIDGE, AB, T1J 4T6
(403) 329-4444 SIC 5511

DAVIS GMC BUICK LTD p 146
1450 TRANS CANADA WAY SE, MEDICINE HAT, AB, T1B 4M2
(403) 527-1115 SIC 7532

DAVIS GROUP OF COMPANIES CORP p 669
25 RIVIERA DR SUITE 7, MARKHAM, ON, L3R 8N4
(905) 477-7440 SIC 2782

DAVIS HENDERSON INTERCHEQUES p 962
See D+H LIMITED PARTNERSHIP

DAVIS HENDERSON INTERCHEQUES p 1141
See DH CORPORATION

DAVIS INDUSTRIES p 663
4855 520 HWY, MAGNETAWAN, ON, P0A 1P0
SIC 1522

DAVIS LLP p 47
250 2 ST SW SUITE 1000, CALGARY, AB, T2P 0C1
(403) 296-4470 SIC 8111

DAVIS LLP p 303
666 BURRARD ST SUITE 2800, VANCOUVER, BC, V6C 2Z7
(604) 687-9444 SIC 8111

DAVIS MANAGEMENT LTD p 303
666 BURRARD ST SUITE 2800, VANCOUVER, BC, V6C 2Z7
(604) 687-9444 SIC 8741

DAVIS MANAGEMENT LTD p 986
100 KING ST W UNIT 60, TORONTO, ON, M5X 2A1
(416) 365-3500 SIC 8111

DAVIS MARTINDALE PROFESSIONAL CORPORATION p 659
373 COMMISSIONERS RD W, LONDON, ON, N6J 1Y4
(519) 673-3141 SIC 8748

DAVIS STRAIT FISHERIES LIMITED p 458
71 MCQUADE LAKE CRES, HALIFAX, NS, B3S 1C4
(902) 450-5115 SIC 5146

DAVIS VALU-MART p 847
See DAVIS, GARY FOOD STORES LIMITED

DAVIS YOUR INDEPENDENT GROCER p 847
20 JOCELYN ST, PORT HOPE, ON, L1A 3V5
(905) 885-1867 SIC 5411

DAVIS, ANN TRANSITION SOCIETY p 196
9046 YOUNG RD, CHILLIWACK, BC, V2P 4R6
(604) 792-2760 SIC 8999

DAVIS, GARY FOOD STORES LIMITED p 847
177 TORONTO RD, PORT HOPE, ON, L1A 3V5
SIC 5411

DAVIS, PERCY H. LIMITED p 1413
4 ABBOTT AVE, NORTH PORTAL, SK, S0C 1W0
(306) 927-2165 SIC 4731

DAVIS, W.R. ENGINEERING LIMITED p 815
1260 OLD INNES RD SUITE 606, OTTAWA, ON, K1B 3V3
(613) 748-5500 SIC 3674

DAVISON CATALYST p 1365
See GCP CANADA INC

DAVPART INC p 771
4576 YONGE ST UNIT 700, NORTH YORK, ON, M2N 6N4
(416) 222-3010 SIC 6531

DAVROC TESTING LABORATORIES INC p 499
2051 WILLIAMS PKY UNIT 21, BRAMPTON, ON, L6S 5T3
(905) 792-7792 SIC 8734

DAWE, STAN LTD p 422
191 RIVERSIDE DR, CORNER BROOK, NL, A2H 2N2
(709) 639-9131 SIC 5211

DAWN FOOD PRODUCTS (CANADA), LTD p 502
275 STEELWELL RD, BRAMPTON, ON, L6T 0C8
(289) 505-4640 SIC 5149

DAWNAL QUICK SERVE LTD p 216
1465 TRANS CANADA HWY W, KAMLOOPS, BC, V1S 1A1
(250) 374-1922 SIC 5812

DAWNAL QUICK SERVE LTD p 216
661 FORTUNE DR, KAMLOOPS, BC, V2B 2K7
(250) 376-0222 SIC 5812

DAWNAL QUICK SERVE LTD p 217
500 NOTRE DAME DR UNIT 800, KAMLOOPS, BC, V2C 6T6
(250) 314-3686 SIC 5812

DAWSCO COFFEE SERVICE LTD p 29
4325 1 ST SE, CALGARY, AB, T2G 2L2
(403) 250-7494 SIC 7389

DAWSON & KEENAN INSURANCE & FINANCIAL SERVICES p 861
See DAWSON & KEENAN INSURANCE LTD

DAWSON & KEENAN INSURANCE LTD p 861
121 BROCK ST, SAULT STE. MARIE, ON, P6A 3B6
(705) 949-3740 SIC 6411

DAWSON CO-OP p 204
See DAWSON CO-OPERATIVE UNION

DAWSON CO-OPERATIVE UNION p 204
10200 8 ST SUITE 3, DAWSON CREEK, BC, V1G 3P8
(250) 782-2217 SIC 5171

DAWSON CONSTRUCTION LIMITED p 217
1212 MCGILL RD, KAMLOOPS, BC, V2C 6N6
(250) 374-3657 SIC 1611

DAWSON COURT HOME FOR THE AGED p 907
See CORPORATION OF THE CITY OF THUNDER BAY, THE

DAWSON WALLACE CONSTRUCTION LTD p 109
4611 ELENIAK RD NW, EDMONTON, AB, T6B 2N1
(780) 466-8700 SIC 1542

DAWSON'S OFFICE COFFEE SERVICES p 29
See DAWSCO COFFEE SERVICE LTD

DAY & NIGHT CARRIERS LTD p 693
1270 AEROWOOD DR, MISSISSAUGA, ON, L4W 1B7
SIC 4213

DAY & ROSS DEDICATED LOGISTICS p 721
6711 MISSISSAUGA RD SUITE 410, MISSISSAUGA, ON, L5N 2W3
(905) 285-2355 SIC 4212

DAY & ROSS INC p 403
398 MAIN ST, HARTLAND, NB, E7P 1C6
(506) 375-4401 *SIC* 4213

DAY & ROSS INC p 409
623 MAPLETON RD, MONCTON, NB, E1G
2K5
(866) 329-7677 *SIC* 4213

DAY & ROSS INC p 513
170 VAN KIRK DR, BRAMPTON, ON, L7A
1K9
(905) 846-6300 *SIC* 4213

DAY & ROSS TRANSPORTATION GROUP p
403
See DAY & ROSS INC

DAY TRANSPORT p 483
See DAY, WILLIAM CONSTRUCTION LIM-
ITED

DAY, GUY R. & SON LIMITED p 418
78 MILLTOWN BLVD, ST STEPHEN, NB,
E3L 1G6
(506) 466-3330 *SIC* 6411

DAY, WILLIAM CONSTRUCTION LIMITED p
483
2500 ELM ST, AZILDA, ON, P0M 1B0
(705) 682-1555 *SIC* 7359

DAYBAR INDUSTRIES LIMITED p 502
50 WEST DR, BRAMPTON, ON, L6T 2J4
(905) 625-8000 *SIC* 3442

DAYS INN p 884
See 1264316 ONTARIO INC

DAYS INN p 913
See SENATOR HOTELS LIMITED

DAYS INN & SUITES WEST EDMONTON p
100
10010 179A ST NW, EDMONTON, AB, T5S
2T1
(780) 444-4440 *SIC* 7011

DAYS INN REGINA p 1424
See DIMENSION 3 HOSPITALITY CORPO-
RATION

DAYS INN-LUNDY'S LANE p 759
See NIAGARA HOSPITALITY HOTELS INC

DAYSLAND HEALTH CENTRE p 81
See ALBERTA HEALTH SERVICES

DAYTON SUPERIOR CANADA LTD p 738
6650 PACIFIC CIR, MISSISSAUGA, ON,
L5T 1V6
(416) 798-2000 *SIC* 3444

DAYTONA CAPITAL CORPORATION p 100
11504 170 ST NW SUITE 101, EDMON-
TON, AB, T5S 1J7
(780) 452-2288 *SIC* 1522

DAYTONA FREIGHT SYSTEMS INC p 494
124 COMMERCIAL RD, BOLTON, ON, L7E
1K4
(416) 744-2020 *SIC* 4213

DAYTONA HOMES p 100
See DAYTONA CAPITAL CORPORATION

DB PERKS & ASSOCIATES LTD p 238
2411 DOLLARTON HWY SUITE 102,
NORTH VANCOUVER, BC, V7H 0A3
(604) 980-2805 *SIC* 5091

DB-AECON PONT ST-JACQUES S.E.P p
1319
170 BOUL ROLAND-GODARD, SAINT-
JEROME, QC, J7Y 4P7
(450) 569-8043 *SIC* 1622

DBC COMMUNICATIONS INC p 1312
655 AV SAINTE-ANNE, SAINT-
HYACINTHE, QC, J2S 5G4
(450) 773-3190 *SIC* 4899

DBC MARINE SAFETY SYSTEMS LTD p
205
1689 CLIVEDEN AVE, DELTA, BC, V3M 6V5
(604) 278-3221 *SIC* 3732

DBC S.E.P. p 1319
170 BOUL ROLAND-GODARD, SAINT-
JEROME, QC, J7Y 4P7
(450) 569-8043 *SIC* 1629

DBG p 738
See DBG CANADA LIMITED

DBG CANADA LIMITED p 738
110 AMBASSADOR DR, MISSISSAUGA,
ON, L5T 2X8

(905) 362-2311 *SIC* 3499

DBG CANADA LIMITED p 1036
980 JULIANA DR, WOODSTOCK, ON, N4V
1B9

SIC 3469

DBG GROUP LTD p 738
110 AMBASSADOR DR, MISSISSAUGA,
ON, L5T 2X8
(905) 670-1555 *SIC* 3499

DBM OPTIX INC p 1361
1630 BLVD DAGENAIS O, SAINTE-ROSE,
QC, H7L 5C7
(450) 622-3100 *SIC* 3827

DBPC GROUP OF COMPANIES LTD p 767
250 CONSUMERS RD SUITE 605, NORTH
YORK, ON, M2J 4V6
(416) 755-9198 *SIC* 7361

DBR TECHNOLOGY CENTER DIVISION p
121
See SCHLUMBERGER CANADA LIMITED

DBRAND INC p 980
500 KING ST W 3RD FL, TORONTO, ON,
M5V 1L9
(647) 282-3711 *SIC* 5999

DBRS LIMITED p 950
181 UNIVERSITY AVE SUITE 700,
TORONTO, ON, M5H 3M7
(416) 593-5577 *SIC* 6289

DBS p 690
See 1503647 ONTARIO LIMITED

DC FOODS & SUNRISE FARMS p 1011
See SUNWEST FOODS PROCESSORS
LTD

DC PAYMENTS PHYSICAL p 10
See CARDTRONICS CANADA HOLDINGS
INC

DCB BUSINESS SYSTEMS GROUP INC p
491
175 LAHR DR, BELLEVILLE, ON, K8N 5S2
(613) 966-6315 *SIC* 5999

DCC p 767
See DOMINION COLOUR CORPORATION

DCH MOTORS LTD p 260
4211 NO. 3 RD, RICHMOND, BC, V6X 2C3
(604) 278-8999 *SIC* 5511

DCL INTERNATIONAL INC p 551
241 BRADWICK DR, CONCORD, ON, L4K
1K5
(905) 660-6450 *SIC* 3714

DCM p 162
See DCM INTEGRATED SOLUTIONS INC

DCM INTEGRATED SOLUTIONS INC p 162
56 LIBERTY RD, SHERWOOD PARK, AB,
T8H 2J6
(780) 464-6733 *SIC* 1629

DCR EXPRESS p 1288
See ROBERT TRANSPORT SPECIALIZED
INC

DCR LOGISTICS INC p 1289
150 AV MARCEL-BARIL, ROUYN-
NORANDA, QC, J9X 7C1
(819) 764-4944 *SIC* 4731

DCR STRATEGIES INC p 693
2680 SKYMARK AVE SUITE 420, MISSIS-
SAUGA, ON, L4W 5L6
(905) 212-9100 *SIC* 7389

DCS p 128
See DEMERS CONTRACTING SERVICES
LTD

DCSR INVESTMENT CORP p 486
455 WELHAM RD, BARRIE, ON, L4N 8Z6
(705) 726-5841 *SIC* 3569

DCT CHAMBERS TRUCKING LTD p 269
4631 FARSTAD WAY RR 1, SKOOKUM-
CHUCK, BC, V0B 2E0
(250) 422-3535 *SIC* 4212

DCT CHAMBERS TRUCKING LTD p 331
600 WADDINGTON DR, VERNON, BC, V1T
8T6
(250) 549-2157 *SIC* 4212

DDB CANADA p 326
See OMNICOM CANADA CORP

DDJLR ONTARIO LTD p 716
2477 MOTORWAY BLVD, MISSISSAUGA,

ON, L5L 3R2
(905) 828-8488 *SIC* 5511

DDL p 774
See DOCUMENT DIRECTION LIMITED

DDS WIRELESS INTERNATIONAL INC p
263
11920 FORGE PL, RICHMOND, BC, V7A
4V9
(604) 241-1441 *SIC* 3663

DE BEERS CANADA INC p 22
1601 AIRPORT RD NE SUITE 300, CAL-
GARY, AB, T2E 6Z8
(403) 930-0991 *SIC* 1499

DE CHAMPLAIN DESIGN INC p 1350
812 BOUL DE L'INDUSTRIE, SAINT-PAUL,
QC, J0K 3E0
(450) 760-2098 *SIC* 5136

**DE DUTCH PANNEKOEK HOUSE RESTAU-
RANTS INC** p
281
8484 162 ST SUITE 108, SURREY, BC, V4N
1B4
(604) 543-3101 *SIC* 6794

DE GRANDPRE CHAIT S.E.N.C.R.L. p 1203
1000 RUE DE LA GAUCHETIERE O BU-
REAU 2900, MONTREAL, QC, H3B 4W5
(514) 878-4311 *SIC* 8111

**DE HAVILLAND AIRCRAFT OF CANADA
LIMITED** p 916
123 GARRATT BLVD, TORONTO, ON, M3K
1Y5
(416) 633-7310 *SIC* 3721

DE JONG ENTERPRISES p 796
See DE JONG, WM ENTERPRISES INC

DE JONG, WM ENTERPRISES INC p 796
773451 59 HWY RR 3, NORWICH, ON, N0J
1P0
(519) 424-9007 *SIC* 4213

DE LA FONTAINE p 1373
See DELAFONTAINE INC

DE LA FONTAINE & ASSOCIES INC p 1070
7503 BOUL TASCHEREAU BUREAU B,
BROSSARD, QC, J4Y 1A2
(450) 676-8335 *SIC* 5072

DE LA FONTAINE & ASSOCIES INC p 1380
3700 RUE PASCAL-GAGNON, TERRE-
BONNE, QC, J6X 4J2
(450) 471-2982 *SIC* 5031

**DE LAGE LANDEN FINANCIAL SERVICES
CANADA INC** p 803
3450 SUPERIOR CRT UNIT 1, OAKVILLE,
ON, L6L 0C4
(905) 465-3160 *SIC* 6159

DE LUXE PRODUITS DE PAPIER INC p
1238
200 AV MARIEN, MONTREAL-EST, QC,
H1B 4V2
(514) 645-4571 *SIC* 2671

DE RIGUEUR INC p 622
2521 BOWMAN ST, INNISFIL, ON, L9S 0E9
(705) 733-7700 *SIC* 5082

**DE THOMAS WEALTH MANAGEMENT
CORP** p 851
9033 LESLIE ST UNIT 1, RICHMOND HILL,
ON, L4B 4K3
(905) 731-9800 *SIC* 6282

DE'LONGHI CANADA INC p 731
6150 MCLAUGHLIN RD SUITE 2, MISSIS-
SAUGA, ON, L5R 4E1
(905) 362-2340 *SIC* 5064

DEACRO INDUSTRIES LTD p 738
135 CAPITAL CRT, MISSISSAUGA, ON,
L5T 2R8
(905) 564-6556 *SIC* 3554

**DEAFBLIND SERVICES SOCIETY OF
BRITISH COLUMBIA** p 290
3369 FRASER ST SUITE 212, VANCOU-
VER, BC, V5V 4C2
SIC 8699

DEALER SERVICES GROUP p 1063
See ADP CANADA CO

DEALERSHIP INVESTMENTS LIMITED p 84
13145 97 ST NW, EDMONTON, AB, T5E
4C4

(780) 476-6221 *SIC* 5511

DEALERTRACK CANADA INC p 693
2700 MATHESON BLVD E SUITE 702, MIS-
SISSAUGA, ON, L4W 4V9
(905) 281-6200 *SIC* 7372

DEALNET CAPITAL CORP p 950
4 KING ST W SUITE 1700, TORONTO, ON,
M5H 1B6
(905) 695-8557 *SIC* 6159

DEALS 4 U p 405
See MORRIS WHOLESALE LTD

DEAN AND BARB NO FRILLS p 542
See DEAN MILLS NO FRILLS

**DEAN CONSTRUCTION COMPANY LIM-
ITED** p
1026
2720 FRONT RD, WINDSOR, ON, N9J 2N5
(519) 734-8999 *SIC* 1629

DEAN INDUSTRIES, INC p 153
4915 54 ST 3RD FLR, RED DEER, AB, T4N
2G7

SIC 5051

DEAN MILLS NO FRILLS p 542
100 WILLIAM ST S, CHATHAM, ON, N7M
4S4
(519) 351-0355 *SIC* 5411

DEAN MYERS CHRYSLER DODGE p 1007
See WATERLOO DODGE CHRYSLER LTD

DEAN MYERS LEASING (1995) p 788
See 1125278 ONTARIO LTD

DEAN SEELY BOBDALE p 82
See BOB DALE OILFIELD CONSTRUC-
TION LTD

DEAN'S FOOD BASICS p 862
701 PINE ST, SAULT STE. MARIE, ON, P6B
3G2
(705) 949-8929 *SIC* 5411

**DEANS KNIGHT CAPITAL MANAGEMENT
LTD** p 303
999 HASTINGS ST W SUITE 730, VAN-
COUVER, BC, V6C 2W2
(604) 669-0212 *SIC* 6722

DEARBORN MOTORS LTD p 217
2555 TRANS CANADA HWY E, KAM-
LOOPS, BC, V2C 4B1
(250) 372-7101 *SIC* 5511

DEB CANADIAN HYGIENE p 518
See SC JOHNSON PROFESSIONAL CA
INC

DEBEERS CANADA EXPLORATION p 919
65 OVERLEA BLVD SUITE 300, TORONTO,
ON, M4H 1P1
(416) 645-1710 *SIC* 1382

DEBLY ENTERPRISES LIMITED p 415
170 ASHBURN RD, SAINT JOHN, NB, E2L
3T5
(506) 696-2936 *SIC* 1611

DEBRADEE ENTERPRISES LTD p 1432
123 AUDITORIUM AVE, SASKATOON, SK,
S7M 5S8
(306) 525-8600 *SIC* 5137

DEBRADEE WEDDINGS p 1432
See DEBRADEE ENTERPRISES LTD

DEBRO INC. p 499
11 AUTOMATIC RD, BRAMPTON, ON, L6S
4K6
(905) 799-8200 *SIC* 5169

DECA CABLES INC p 998
150 NORTH MURRAY ST, TRENTON, ON,
K8V 6R8
(613) 392-3585 *SIC* 3496

DECACER p 1140
See 9020-2292 QUEBEC INC

DECALCOMANIE CREATIF GRAHAM p
1128
See GRAHAM CREATIVE DECAL INC

DECAREL INC p 1402
4434 RUE SAINTE-CATHERINE O, WEST-
MOUNT, QC, H3Z 1R2
(514) 935-6462 *SIC* 1542

DECAREL INTERNATIONAL p 1402
See DECAREL INC

DECARIE SATURN SAAB p 1220
See 405-4547 CANADA INC

DECAST LTD p 1000
8807 COUNTY ROAD 56, UTOPIA, ON, L0M 1T0
(800) 461-5632   *SIC* 3272

DECATHLON CANADA INC p 1068
2151 BOUL LAPINIERE, BROSSARD, QC, J4W 2T5
(514) 962-7545   *SIC* 5941

DECHANT CONSTRUCTION (WESTERN) LTD p 213
4801 44 AVE, FORT NELSON, BC, V0C 1R0
(250) 775-6064   *SIC* 1389

DECHANT CONSTRUCTION LTD p 135
11004 97 ST, HIGH LEVEL, AB, T0H 1Z0
(780) 926-4411   *SIC* 1611

DECIEM DISTRIBUTION INC p 933
517 RICHMOND ST E, TORONTO, ON, M5A 1R4
(416) 203-3992   *SIC* 5999

DECIEM INC p 933
517 RICHMOND ST E, TORONTO, ON, M5A 1R4
(416) 203-3992   *SIC* 5999

DECIMA INC p 922
2345 YONGE ST SUITE 704, TORONTO, ON, M4P 2E5
(416) 962-9109   *SIC* 8732

DECISION RESOURCES GROUP (DRG) p 930
See MILLENNIUM RESEARCH GROUP INC

DECISIONONE CORPORATION p 851
44 EAST BEAVER CREEK RD UNIT 19, RICHMOND HILL, ON, L4B 1G8
(905) 882-1555   *SIC* 7378

DECISIONONE CORPORATION p 1329
2505 RUE COHEN, SAINT-LAURENT, QC, H4R 2N5
(514) 338-1927   *SIC* 7378

DECISIVE DIVIDEND CORPORATION p 221
1674 BERTRAM ST UNIT 201, KELOWNA, BC, V1Y 9G4
(250) 870-9146   *SIC* 6719

DECK STORE INC, THE p 997
789 ARROW RD SUITE 10, TORONTO, ON, M9M 2L4
(416) 749-3963   *SIC* 5211

DECKER AUTO RECREATION MARINE p 422
See DECKER MOTORS LIMITED

DECKER COLONY FARMS LTD p 349
GD, DECKER, MB, R0M 0K0
(204) 764-2481   *SIC* 0191

DECKER COLONY OF HUTTERIAN BRETHREN TRUST p 349
See DECKER COLONY FARMS LTD

DECKER LAKE FOREST PRODUCTS LTD p 194
GD, BURNS LAKE, BC, V0J 1E0
(250) 698-7304   *SIC* 2421

DECKER MOTORS LIMITED p 422
245 MEMORIAL DR, CLARENVILLE, NL, A5A 1R4
(709) 466-2394   *SIC* 5511

DECO ADHESIVE PRODUCTS (1985) LIMITED p 583
28 GREENSBORO DR, ETOBICOKE, ON, M9W 1E1
(416) 247-7878   *SIC* 7336

DECO LABELS & FLEXIBLE PACKAGING p 583
See DECO ADHESIVE PRODUCTS (1985) LIMITED

DECO SIGNALISATION INC p 1048
9225 RUE DU PARCOURS, ANJOU, QC, H1J 3A8
(514) 494-1004   *SIC* 3993

DECO WINDSHIELD REPAIR INC p 72
1602 42 ST SW, CALGARY, AB, T3C 1Z5
(403) 829-6289   *SIC* 7536

DECOLIN INC p 1178
9150 AV DU PARC, MONTREAL, QC, H2N 1Z2
(514) 384-2910   *SIC* 5023

DECOMA INTERNATIONAL, DIV OF p 481
See MAGNA INTERNATIONAL INC

DECOR & MORE INC p 797
1171 INVICTA DR, OAKVILLE, ON, L6H 4M1
(905) 844-1300   *SIC* 7389

DECOR CABINET COMPANY p 352
See DECOR CABINETS LTD

DECOR CABINETS LTD p 352
200 ROUTE 100, MORDEN, MB, R6M 1Y4
(204) 822-6151   *SIC* 2434

DECOR EXPERT EXPO p 1141
See 3022528 CANADA INC

DECOR GRATES INCORPORATED p 473
4 CHISHOLM CRT, AJAX, ON, L1S 4N8
(647) 777-3544   *SIC* 3446

DECOR STRUCTURES CORP p 866
735 PROGRESS AVE, SCARBOROUGH, ON, M1H 2W7
(416) 498-9379   *SIC* 5191

DECOR-REST FURNITURE LTD p 1030
511 CHRISLEA RD SUITE 8, WOODBRIDGE, ON, L4L 8N6
(905) 856-5956   *SIC* 2512

DECORATIVE FOUNTAIN CO, DIV OF p 551
See CRYSTAL FOUNTAINS HOLDINGS INC

DECORIUM p 783
See FURNCO FURNITURE INTERNATIONAL DISTRIBUTORS LTD

DECORS DE MAISON COMMONWEALTH INC p 1169
8800 BOUL PIE-IX, MONTREAL, QC, H1Z 3V1
(514) 384-8290   *SIC* 5131

DECOUPAGE M.P.S. INC p 1339
123 MONTEE DE LIESSE, SAINT-LAURENT, QC, H4T 1S6
(514) 744-8291   *SIC* 5084

DECOUSTICS p 1027
See CERTAINTEED CANADA, INC

DECTRO INTERNATIONAL p 1266
See DECTRONIQUE (1984) INC

DECTRON INC p 1329
3999 BOUL DE LA COTE-VERTU, SAINT-LAURENT, QC, H4R 1R2
(514) 336-3330   *SIC* 3585

DECTRON INTERNATIONALE INC p 1329
3999 BOUL DE LA COTE-VERTU, SAINT-LAURENT, QC, H4R 1R2
(514) 336-3330   *SIC* 3585

DECTRONIQUE (1984) INC p 1266
1000 BOUL DU PARC-TECHNOLOGIQUE, QUEBEC, QC, G1P 4S3
(418) 650-0303   *SIC* 3999

DEDICATED FREIGHT CARRIERS INC p 419
634 ROUTE 590, WATERVILLE CARLETON CO, NB, E7P 1B7
(506) 375-1010   *SIC* 4731

DEE ENTERPRISES LTD p 200
455 NORTH RD, COQUITLAM, BC, V3K 3V9
(604) 937-1205   *SIC* 5411

DEE, ROSE E. (INTERNATIONAL) LIMITED p 992
1450 CASTLEFIELD AVE, TORONTO, ON, M6M 1Y6
(416) 658-2222   *SIC* 5131

DEELEY HARLEY DAVIDSON p 551
See DEELEY, FRED IMPORTS LTD.

DEELEY, FRED IMPORTS LTD. p 551
830 EDGELEY BLVD, CONCORD, ON, L4K 4X1
(905) 660-3500   *SIC* 5012

DEELEY, TREV MOTORCYCLES (1991) LTD p 286
1875 BOUNDARY RD, VANCOUVER, BC, V5M 3Y7
(604) 291-1875   *SIC* 5571

DEEM MANAGEMENT SERVICES LIMITED p 848

990 EDWARD ST, PRESCOTT, ON, K0E 1T0
(613) 925-2834   *SIC* 8051

DEEM MANAGEMENT SERVICES LIMITED p 1007
229 LEXINGTON RD, WATERLOO, ON, N2K 2E1
(519) 772-1026   *SIC* 8051

DEEP CLEAN AUTOMATIC CLEANING & RESTORATION INC p 608
26 BURFORD RD UNIT 200, HAMILTON, ON, L8E 3C7
(905) 578-3445   *SIC* 1521

DEEP RIVER AND DISTRICT HOSPITAL CORPORATION p 564
117 BANTING DR, DEEP RIVER, ON, K0J 1P0
(613) 584-2484   *SIC* 8062

DEEPAK INTERNATIONAL LTD p 986
1 FIRST CANADIAN PL UNIT 6000, TORONTO, ON, M5X 1B5
SIC 3915

DEER COUNTRY EQUIPMENT p 358
See REIMER FARM SUPPLIES LTD

DEER LAKE POWER COMPANY DIV OF p 422
See CORNER BROOK PULP AND PAPER LIMITED

DEER LAKE SALES & SERVICE LTD p 192
5965 KINGSWAY, BURNABY, BC, V5J 1H1
(604) 434-2488   *SIC* 5511

DEER LODGE HOTELS LTD p 1431
106 CIRCLE DR W, SASKATOON, SK, S7L 4L6
(306) 242-8881   *SIC* 7011

DEER PARK HOLDINGS LTD p 153
7150 50 AVE, RED DEER, AB, T4N 6A5
(403) 343-8800   *SIC* 7011

DEER POINT SOBEYS p 39
See LLAP HOLDINGS LTD

DEERBOINE COLONY FARMS LTD p 345
GD, ALEXANDER, MB, R0K 0A0
(204) 728-7383   *SIC* 0119

DEERBOINE COLONY OF HUTTERIAN BRETHREN TRUST p 345
See DEERBOINE COLONY FARMS LTD

DEERBROOK REALTY INC p 1021
59 EUGENIE ST E, WINDSOR, ON, N8X 2X9
(519) 972-1000   *SIC* 6531

DEERFIELD COLONY p 145
See DEERFIELD HUTTERIAN BRETHERN

DEERFIELD HUTTERIAN BRETHERN p 145
GD, MAGRATH, AB, T0K 1J0
(403) 758-6461   *SIC* 0762

DEERFOOT INN & CASINO INC p 70
11500 35 ST SE SUITE 1000, CALGARY, AB, T2Z 3W4
(403) 236-7529   *SIC* 7011

DEERHURST RESORT p 621
See SKYLINE DEERHURST RESORT INC

DEERLAND FARM EQUIPMENT (1985) LTD p 130
8599 112 ST, FORT SASKATCHEWAN, AB, T8L 3V3
(780) 998-3249   *SIC* 5083

DEERMART EQUIPMENT SALES LTD p 155
6705 GOLDEN WEST AVE, RED DEER, AB, T4P 1A7
(403) 343-2238   *SIC* 5999

DEETAG LTD p 648
649 THIRD ST, LONDON, ON, N5V 2C1
(519) 659-4673   *SIC* 5085

DEFAVERI GROUP CONTRACTING INC p 891
1259 ARVIN AVE, STONEY CREEK, ON, L8E 0H7
(905) 560-2555   *SIC* 1541

DEFEHR FURNITURE p 363
See DEFEHR FURNITURE (2009) LTD

DEFEHR FURNITURE (2009) LTD p 363
125 FURNITURE PARK, WINNIPEG, MB, R2G 1B9

(204) 988-5630   *SIC* 2511

DEFENCE CONSTRUCTION (1951) LIMITED p 824
350 ALBERT ST SUITE 1900, OTTAWA, ON, K1R 1A4
(613) 998-9548   *SIC* 8741

DEFENCE CONSTRUCTION CANADA p 824
See DEFENCE CONSTRUCTION (1951) LIMITED

DEFENCE UNLIMITED p 823
See DEFENCE UNLIMITED INTERNATIONAL CORP

DEFENCE UNLIMITED INTERNATIONAL CORP p 823
251 LAURIER AVE W SUITE 900, OTTAWA, ON, K1P 5J6
(613) 366-3677   *SIC* 7389

DEFFOSSES ET VALLEE S.E.N.C p 1281
1065 BOUL PIE-XI N BUREAU 263, QUEBEC, QC, G3K 2S5
(418) 840-0337   *SIC* 5912

DEFI IRIS p 1086
See IRIS, GROUPE VISUEL (1990) INC, LE

DEFI POLYTECK p 1371
1255 BOUL QUEEN-VICTORIA, SHERBROOKE, QC, J1J 4N6
(819) 348-1209   *SIC* 7699

DEFI RECUP-AIR p 1082
See SUNRISE TRADEX CORP

DEFLECTEUR AIRFLOW p 1222
See 2956-1198 QUEBEC INC

DEFLECTO CANADA LTD p 883
221 BUNTING RD, ST CATHARINES, ON, L2M 3Y2
(905) 641-8872   *SIC* 3444

DEGELDER CONSTRUCTION CO. (2010) LTD p 318
1455 GEORGIA ST W SUITE 100, VANCOUVER, BC, V6G 2T3
(604) 688-1515   *SIC* 1542

DEGELMAN INDUSTRIES LTD p 1417
272 INDUSTRIAL DR, REGINA, SK, S4P 3B1
(306) 543-4447   *SIC* 3523

DEGOEYS NURSERY AND FLOWERS p 1013
1501 RD 6, WHEATLEY, ON, N0P 2P0
(519) 326-8813   *SIC* 5191

DEGROOT'S NURSERIES p 859
1840 LONDON LINE, SARNIA, ON, N7T 7H2
(519) 542-3436   *SIC* 0181

DEGROOT-HILL CHEVROLET BUICK GMC LTD p 911
HWY 3, TILLSONBURG, ON, N4G 4H3
(519) 842-9026   *SIC* 5511

DEGUIRE, MICHEL HOLDINGS INC p 1436
1811 22ND AVE NE, SWIFT CURRENT, SK, S9H 5B7
(306) 773-0654   *SIC* 5531

DEHL HOLDINGS LTD p 221
1465 ELLIS ST SUITE 100, KELOWNA, BC, V1Y 2A3
(250) 762-5434   *SIC* 6712

DEI, CHARLES CONSTRUCTION LTD p 136
GD, HINES CREEK, AB, T0H 2A0
(780) 494-3838   *SIC* 1389

DEL EQUIPMENT p 755
See DIESEL EQUIPMENT LIMITED

DEL INDUSTRIAL METALS INC p 502
7653 BRAMALEA RD, BRAMPTON, ON, L6T 5V3
(905) 595-1222   *SIC* 5051

DEL MANAGEMENT SOLUTIONS INC p 781
4810 DUFFERIN ST SUITE E, NORTH YORK, ON, M3H 5S8
(416) 661-3070   *SIC* 6512

DEL METALS p 502
See DEL INDUSTRIAL METALS INC

DEL MONTE CANADA INC p 565
GD, DRESDEN, ON, N0P 1M0

(519) 683-4422 *SIC* 2032
DEL PROPERTY MANAGEMENT INC *p* 781
109-4800 DUFFERIN ST, NORTH YORK, ON, M3H 5S9
(416) 661-3151 *SIC* 6531
DEL SOL GREENHOUSES INC *p* 633
1665 GRAHAM, KINGSVILLE, ON, N9Y 2E4
(519) 733-8373 *SIC* 5148
DEL WINDOWS & DOORS INC *p* 891
241 ARVIN AVE, STONEY CREEK, ON, L8E 2L9
(905) 561-4335 *SIC* 3089
DEL'S PASTRY LIMITED *p* 574
344 BERING AVE, ETOBICOKE, ON, M8Z 3A7
(416) 231-4383 *SIC* 2051
DELAFONTAINE INC *p* 1373
4115 RUE BRODEUR, SHERBROOKE, QC, J1L 1K4
(819) 348-1219 *SIC* 3442
DELAGAR DIVISION *p* 1072
See BELCAM INC
DELANEY HOLDINGS INC *p* 361
200 PACIFIC ST, WINKLER, MB, R6W 0K2
(204) 325-7376 *SIC* 3321
DELAWANA INN & RESORT *p* 620
See 1212360 ONTARIO LIMITED
DELBIGIO, KEN PHARMACY LTD *p* 387
43 OSBORNE ST, WINNIPEG, MB, R3L 1Y2
(204) 958-7000 *SIC* 5912
DELCAN INTERNATIONAL CORPORATION *p*
669
625 COCHRANE DR SUITE 500, MARKHAM, ON, L3R 9R9
(905) 943-0500 *SIC* 8711
DELCO AUTOMATION INC *p* 1435
3735 THATCHER AVE, SASKATOON, SK, S7R 1B8
(306) 244-6449 *SIC* 3625
DELCO FIREPLACES LTD *p* 227
20679 LANGLEY BYPASS, LANGLEY, BC, V3A 5E8
(604) 530-2166 *SIC* 5023
DELCOM BUSINESS SOLUTIONS *p* 1325
See COPISCOPE INC
DELCOSECURITY *p* 1435
See DELCO AUTOMATION INC
DELFT BLUE *p* 536
See GROBER INC
DELFT BLUE VEAL INC *p* 535
162 SAVAGE DR, CAMBRIDGE, ON, N1T 1S4
(519) 622-2500 *SIC* 2011
DELFT BLUE, DIV OF *p* 536
See GROBER INC
DELGADO FOODS INTERNATIONAL LIMITED *p*
263
12031 NO. 5 RD, RICHMOND, BC, V7A 4E9
(604) 241-8175 *SIC* 6712
DELGANT (CIVILS) *p* 494
See DELGANT CONSTRUCTION LIMITED
DELGANT CONSTRUCTION LIMITED *p* 494
7 MARCONI CRT, BOLTON, ON, L7E 1H3
(905) 857-7858 *SIC* 1542
DELHI IGA *p* 564
227 MAIN STREET OF DELHI, DELHI, ON, N4B 2M4
(519) 582-0990 *SIC* 5411
DELHI INDUSTRIES INC *p* 519
2157 PARKEDALE AVE, BROCKVILLE, ON, K6V 0B4
(613) 342-5424 *SIC* 3564
DELHI LONG TERM CARE CENTER *p* 564
See DELHI NURSING HOME LIMITED
DELHI NURSING HOME LIMITED *p* 564
750 GIBRALTER ST, DELHI, ON, N4B 3B3
(519) 582-3400 *SIC* 8051
DELI-PORC INC *p* 1085
1805 BOUL INDUSTRIEL, COTE SAINT-LUC, QC, H7S 1P5
(450) 629-0294 *SIC* 2011

DELICANA NORD-OUEST INC *p* 1289
680 AV CHAUSSE, ROUYN-NORANDA, QC, J9X 4B9
(819) 762-3555 *SIC* 5147
DELICES DE DAWN, LES *p* 1339
See G.D. NIRVANA INC
DELICES DE LA FORET - VALLI *p* 1307
See 3523462 CANADA INC
DELICOUKI INC *p* 1345
5695 BOUL DES GRANDES-PRAIRIES BUREAU 118, SAINT-LEONARD, QC, H1R 1B3
(514) 731-2705 *SIC* 5149
DELISLE AUTO LTEE *p* 1174
2815 RUE SHERBROOKE E, MONTREAL, QC, H2K 1H2
(514) 523-1122 *SIC* 5511
DELISLE CLUB *p* 925
1521 YONGE ST SUITE 303, TORONTO, ON, M4T 1Z2
SIC 7991
DELL FINANCIAL SERVICES CANADA LIMITED *p* 765
155 GORDON BAKER RD SUITE 501, NORTH YORK, ON, M2H 3N5
(800) 864-8156 *SIC* 6159
DELLA SIEGA ENTERPRISES LTD *p* 151
6700 46 ST SUITE 300, OLDS, AB, T4H 0A2
(403) 556-7384 *SIC* 5411
DELLCOM AEROSPACE *p* 547
See 2119485 ALBERTA LTD
DELLELCE CONSTRUCTION & EQUIPMENT LTD *p*
900
1375 REGENT ST SUITE 2, SUDBURY, ON, P3E 6K4
SIC 4212
DELMAR CHEMICALS INC *p* 1132
9321 RUE AIRLIE, LASALLE, QC, H8R 2B2
(514) 366-7950 *SIC* 2833
DELMAR CONSTRUCTION LIMITED *p* 471
77 PARADE ST SUITE 1, YARMOUTH, NS, B5A 3B3
(902) 742-4672 *SIC* 1542
DELMAR INTERNATIONAL INC *p* 1127
10636 CH DE LA COTE-DE-LIESSE, LACHINE, QC, H8T 1A5
(514) 636-8800 *SIC* 4731
DELMAS *p* 1210
See CMA CGM (CANADA) INC
DELMAS CO-OPERATIVE ASSOCIATION *p*
231
1562 MAIN ST, MASSET, BC, V0T 1M0
(250) 626-3933 *SIC* 5411
DELN CONSTRUCTION INC *p* 1008
550 CONESTOGO RD, WATERLOO, ON, N2L 4E3
(519) 880-9863 *SIC* 1521
DELNOR CONSTRUCTION LTD *p* 109
3609 74 AVE NW, EDMONTON, AB, T6B 2T7
(780) 469-1304 *SIC* 1542
DELOITTE *p* 669
See DELOITTE LLP
DELOITTE *p* 950
See DELOITTE MANAGEMENT SERVICES LP
DELOITTE *p* 1270
See DELOITTE RESTRUCTURING INC
DELOITTE & TOUCHE MANAGEMENT CONSULTANTS *p* 452
1969 UPPER WATER ST SUITE 1500, HALIFAX, NS, B3J 3R7
(902) 422-8541 *SIC* 8741
DELOITTE & TOUCHE MANAGEMENT CONSULTANTS *p* 779
1 CONCORDE GATE SUITE 200, NORTH YORK, ON, M3C 3N6
(416) 601-6150 *SIC* 8111
DELOITTE & TOUCHE MANAGEMENT CONSULTANTS *p* 823
See DELOITTE LLP
DELOITTE & TOUCHE MANAGEMENT CONSULTANTS *p* 962
181 BAY ST SUITE 1400, TORONTO, ON,

M5J 2V1
(416) 601-6150 *SIC* 8741
DELOITTE E.R.S. *p* 1210
See DELOITTE ERS INC
DELOITTE ERS INC *p* 1210
1190 AV DES CANADIENS-DE-MONTREAL BUREAU 500, MONTREAL, QC, H3C 0M7
(514) 393-7115 *SIC* 8721
DELOITTE LLP *p* 47
850 2 ST SW SUITE 700, CALGARY, AB, T2P 0R8
(403) 267-1700 *SIC* 8721
DELOITTE LLP *p* 88
10180 101 ST NW SUITE 2000, EDMONTON, AB, T5J 4E4
(780) 421-3611 *SIC* 8721
DELOITTE LLP *p* 328
1055 DUNSMUIR ST SUITE 2800, VANCOUVER, BC, V7X 1P4
(604) 669-4466 *SIC* 8721
DELOITTE LLP *p* 452
1969 UPPER WATER ST SUITE 1500, HALIFAX, NS, B3J 3R7
(902) 422-8541 *SIC* 8721
DELOITTE LLP *p* 529
1005 SKYVIEW DR SUITE 202, BURLINGTON, ON, L7P 5B1
(905) 315-6770 *SIC* 8721
DELOITTE LLP *p* 638
195 JOSEPH ST, KITCHENER, ON, N2G 1J6
(519) 650-7600 *SIC* 8721
DELOITTE LLP *p* 669
15 ALLSTATE PKY SUITE 400, MARKHAM, ON, L3R 5B4
SIC 8742
DELOITTE LLP *p* 771
5140 YONGE ST SUITE 1700, NORTH YORK, ON, M2N 6L7
(416) 601-6150 *SIC* 8721
DELOITTE LLP *p* 823
100 QUEEN ST SUITE 1600, OTTAWA, ON, K1P 5T8
(613) 236-2442 *SIC* 8721
DELOITTE LLP *p* 823
100 QUEEN ST SUITE 800, OTTAWA, ON, K1P 5T8
(613) 236-2442 *SIC* 8741
DELOITTE LLP *p* 950
22 ADELAIDE ST W SUITE 200, TORONTO, ON, M5H 0A9
(416) 601-6150 *SIC* 8721
DELOITTE LLP *p* 950
8 ADELAIDE ST W SUITE 200, TORONTO, ON, M5H 0A9
(416) 601-6150 *SIC* 8721
DELOITTE LLP *p* 1079
901 BOUL TALBOT BUREAU 400, CHICOUTIMI, QC, G7H 0A1
(418) 549-6650 *SIC* 6733
DELOITTE LLP *p* 1371
1802 RUE KING O BUREAU 300, SHERBROOKE, QC, J1J 0A2
(819) 823-1616 *SIC* 8111
DELOITTE LLP *p* 1427
122 1ST AVE S SUITE 400, SASKATOON, SK, S7K 7E5
(306) 343-4400 *SIC* 8721
DELOITTE MANAGEMENT SERVICES *p*
328
See DELOITTE LLP
DELOITTE MANAGEMENT SERVICES *p*
950
See DELOITTE LLP
DELOITTE MANAGEMENT SERVICES LP *p*
950
121 KING ST W SUITE 300, TORONTO, ON, M5H 3T9
(416) 775-2364 *SIC* 8721
DELOITTE RESTRUCTURING INC *p* 1086
2540 BOUL DANIEL-JOHNSON BUREAU 210, COTE SAINT-LUC, QC, H7T 2S3
(450) 978-3500 *SIC* 8721

DELOITTE RESTRUCTURING INC *p* 1270
925 GRANDE ALLEE O BUREAU 400, QUEBEC, QC, G1S 4Z4
(418) 624-3333 *SIC* 8721
DELOITTE RESTRUCTURING INC *p* 1387
1500 RUE ROYALE BUREAU 250, TROIS-RIVIERES, QC, G9A 6E6
(819) 691-1212 *SIC* 8721
DELOM SERVICES INC *p* 1160
13065 RUE JEAN-GROU, MONTREAL, QC, H1A 3N6
(514) 642-8220 *SIC* 7694
DELOM SOLUTIONS *p* 1160
See DELOM SERVICES INC
DELOUPE INC *p* 1302
102 RUE DU PARC-INDUSTRIEL, SAINT-EVARISTE-DE-FORSYTH, QC, G0M 1S0
(418) 459-6443 *SIC* 3715
DELPHI ENERGY CORP *p* 47
333 7 AVE SW SUITE 2300, CALGARY, AB, T2P 2Z1
(403) 265-6171 *SIC* 1382
DELPHI SOLUTIONS CORP *p* 669
7550 BIRCHMOUNT RD, MARKHAM, ON, L3R 6C6
SIC 7622
DELSAER-GESTIONNAIRES DE PROJETS *p* 1372
See SERVICES EXP INC., LES
DELSTAR ENERGIE INC *p* 1160
12885 RUE JEAN-GROU, MONTREAL, QC, H1A 3N6
(514) 642-8222 *SIC* 7699
DELTA AGGREGATES LTD *p* 208
7469 HUME AVE, DELTA, BC, V4G 1C3
(604) 940-1300 *SIC* 5032
DELTA BEAUSEJOUR *p* 407
See INNVEST REAL ESTATE INVESTMENT TRUST
DELTA BEVERAGES INC *p* 1030
21 MARYCROFT AVE, WOODBRIDGE, ON, L4L 5Y6
(905) 850-8077 *SIC* 2086
DELTA BINGO *p* 885
See 301061 ONTARIO LIMITED
DELTA BOW VALLEY HOTEL *p* 29
See DELTA HOTELS LIMITED
DELTA CALGARY AIRPORT HOTEL *p* 22
See DELTA HOTELS LIMITED
DELTA CALGARY SOUTH *p* 39
See HOSPITALITY INNS LTD
DELTA CEDAR PRODUCTS LTD *p* 207
10104 RIVER RD, DELTA, BC, V4C 2R3
(604) 583-4159 *SIC* 2421
DELTA CEDAR SPECIALTIES LTD *p* 207
10104 RIVER RD, DELTA, BC, V4C 2R3
(604) 589-9006 *SIC* 2499
DELTA CO-OPERATIVE ASSOCIATION LTD, THE *p* 1437
130 SECOND AVE W, UNITY, SK, S0K 4L0
(306) 228-2662 *SIC* 5411
DELTA CONTROLS INC *p* 271
17850 56 AVE, SURREY, BC, V3S 1C7
(604) 574-9444 *SIC* 3613
DELTA COUNTRY FARMS (BC) LTD *p* 210
3752 ARTHUR DR, DELTA, BC, V4K 3N2
(604) 940-1881 *SIC* 5149
DELTA EDMONTON CENTRE SUITE HOTEL *p*
88
See DELTA HOTELS LIMITED
DELTA EDMONTON SOUTH *p* 118
See DELTA HOTELS NO. 2 LIMITED PARTNERSHIP
DELTA EDMONTON SOUTH HOTEL AND CONFERENCE CENTER *p* 118
See DELTA HOTELS LIMITED
DELTA ELEVATOR COMPANY LIMITED *p*
638
509 MILL ST, KITCHENER, ON, N2G 2Y5
(519) 745-5789 *SIC* 7699
DELTA FAUCET CANADA *p* 889
See MASCO CANADA LIMITED
DELTA FREDERICTON *p* 400

See DELTA HOTELS NO. 32 LIMITED PART-NERSHIP
DELTA GRANDVIEW RESORT (MUSKOKA) p 620
See DELTA HOTELS LIMITED
DELTA HELICOPTERS LTD p 168
26004 TWP RD 544 UNIT 13, STURGEON COUNTY, AB, T8T 0B6
(780) 458-3564   *SIC 4522*
DELTA HOSPITAL p 210
See GOVERNMENT OF THE PROVINCE OF BRITISH COLUMBIA
DELTA HOTELS BY MARRIOTT BARRING-TON p 453
See LEADON (BARRINGTON) OPERA-TIONS LP
DELTA HOTELS LIMITED p 22
2001 AIRPORT RD NE, CALGARY, AB, T2E 6Z8
(403) 291-2600   *SIC 8741*
DELTA HOTELS LIMITED p 29
209 4 AVE SE, CALGARY, AB, T2G 0C6
(403) 266-1980   *SIC 8741*
DELTA HOTELS LIMITED p 88
10222 102 ST NW, EDMONTON, AB, T5J 4C5
(780) 429-3900   *SIC 8741*
DELTA HOTELS LIMITED p 118
4404 GATEWAY BLVD NW, EDMONTON, AB, T6H 5C2
(780) 434-6415   *SIC 7011*
DELTA HOTELS LIMITED p 264
3500 CESSNA DR, RICHMOND, BC, V7B 1C7
(604) 278-1241   *SIC 8741*
DELTA HOTELS LIMITED p 298
550 HASTINGS ST W, VANCOUVER, BC, V6B 1L6
(604) 689-8188   *SIC 7011*
DELTA HOTELS LIMITED p 339
45 SONGHEES RD, VICTORIA, BC, V9A 6T3
(250) 360-2999   *SIC 7011*
DELTA HOTELS LIMITED p 377
350 ST MARY AVE, WINNIPEG, MB, R3C 3J2
(204) 944-7278   *SIC 7011*
DELTA HOTELS LIMITED p 400
1133 REGENT ST, FREDERICTON, NB, E3B 3Z2
SIC 8741
DELTA HOTELS LIMITED p 415
39 KING ST, SAINT JOHN, NB, E2L 4W3
(506) 648-1981   *SIC 8741*
DELTA HOTELS LIMITED p 467
300 ESPLANADE ST, SYDNEY, NS, B1P 1A7
(902) 562-7500   *SIC 8741*
DELTA HOTELS LIMITED p 620
939 60 HWY, HUNTSVILLE, ON, P1H 1B2
(705) 789-4417   *SIC 8741*
DELTA HOTELS LIMITED p 638
105 KING ST E, KITCHENER, ON, N2G 2K8
(519) 569-4588   *SIC 8741*
DELTA HOTELS LIMITED p 655
325 DUNDAS ST, LONDON, ON, N6B 1T9
(519) 679-6111   *SIC 8741*
DELTA HOTELS LIMITED p 694
5444 DIXIE RD SUITE 47, MISSISSAUGA, ON, L4W 2L2
(905) 624-1144   *SIC 8741*
DELTA HOTELS LIMITED p 721
6750 MISSISSAUGA RD, MISSISSAUGA, ON, L5N 2L3
(905) 821-1981   *SIC 8741*
DELTA HOTELS LIMITED p 824
361 QUEEN ST, OTTAWA, ON, K1R 0C7
SIC 8741
DELTA HOTELS LIMITED p 969
77 KING ST W SUITE 2300, TORONTO, ON, M5K 2A1
SIC 8741
DELTA HOTELS LIMITED p 1039

18 QUEEN ST, CHARLOTTETOWN, PE, C1A 4A1
(902) 566-2222   *SIC 8741*
DELTA HOTELS LIMITED p 1373
2685 RUE KING O, SHERBROOKE, QC, J1L 1C1
(819) 822-1989   *SIC 8741*
DELTA HOTELS LIMITED p 1417
1919 SASKATCHEWAN DR SUITE 100, REGINA, SK, S4P 4H2
(306) 525-5255   *SIC 8741*
DELTA HOTELS NO. 12 LIMITED PART-NERSHIP p 825
101 LYON ST N, OTTAWA, ON, K1R 5T9
(613) 237-1508   *SIC 7011*
DELTA HOTELS NO. 12 LIMITED PART-NERSHIP p 1312
1200 RUE JOHNSON O, SAINT-HYACINTHE, QC, J2S 7K7
SIC 7011
DELTA HOTELS NO. 2 LIMITED PARTNER-SHIP p 118
4404 GATEWAY BLVD NW, EDMONTON, AB, T6H 5C2
(780) 434-6415   *SIC 7011*
DELTA HOTELS NO. 32 LIMITED PART-NERSHIP p 400
225 WOODSTOCK RD, FREDERICTON, NB, E3B 2H8
(506) 451-7929   *SIC 7011*
DELTA LONDON ARMOURIES HOTEL p 656
See INNVEST HOTELS (LONDON) LTD
DELTA MEADOWVALE RESORT & CON-FERENCE CENTRE p 721
See CLDH MEADOWVALE INC
DELTA NATIONAL p 1280
See GESTION GAEVAN INC
DELTA OTTAWA HOTEL AND SUITES p 824
See DELTA HOTELS LIMITED
DELTA PACIFIC SEAFOODS LTD p 210
6001 60 AVE, DELTA, BC, V4K 0B2
(604) 946-5160   *SIC 2092*
DELTA PANEL, DIV OF p 205
See CIPA LUMBER CO. LTD
DELTA PHARMA INC p 1093
1655 RTE TRANSCANADIENNE, DORVAL, QC, H9P 1J1
(514) 685-7311   *SIC 5912*
DELTA POWER EQUIPMENT p 589
See 1476399 ONTARIO LIMITED
DELTA POWER EQUIPMENT LTD p 589
71301 LONDON RD, EXETER, ON, N0M 1S3
(519) 235-2121   *SIC 5999*
DELTA PRINCE EDWARD HOTEL p 1039
See DELTA HOTELS LIMITED
DELTA ROCK & SAND LTD p 1436
1910 SOUTH RAILWAY ST E, SWIFT CUR-RENT, SK, S9H 4G6
(306) 773-9808   *SIC 4212*
DELTA SCHOOL DISTRICT NO.37 p 207
11447 82 AVE, DELTA, BC, V4C 5J6
(604) 596-7471   *SIC 8211*
DELTA SCHOOL DISTRICT NO.37 p 207
9115 116 ST, DELTA, BC, V4C 5W8
(604) 594-6100   *SIC 8211*
DELTA SCHOOL DISTRICT NO.37 p 208
11584 LYON RD, DELTA, BC, V4E 2K4
(604) 946-4101   *SIC 8211*
DELTA SCHOOL DISTRICT NO.37 p 210
4615 51 ST, DELTA, BC, V4K 2V8
(604) 946-4194   *SIC 8211*
DELTA SCHOOL DISTRICT NO.37 p 211
750 53 ST, DELTA, BC, V4M 3B7
(604) 943-7407   *SIC 8211*
DELTA SECONDARY SCHOOL p 210
See DELTA SCHOOL DISTRICT NO.37
DELTA SHERBROOKE p 1373

2685 RUE KING O, SHERBROOKE, QC, J1L 1C1
(819) 822-1989   *SIC 7011*
DELTA STAR p 1316
See TRANSFORMATEURS DELTA STAR INC
DELTA SUNSHINE TAXI (1972) LTD p 276
12837 76 AVE UNIT 203, SURREY, BC, V3W 2V3
(604) 594-5444   *SIC 4121*
DELTA TEXTILES INC p 200
61 GLACIER ST, COQUITLAM, BC, V3K 5Z1
(604) 942-2214   *SIC 5131*
DELTA TORONTO AIRPORT HOTEL p 585
See KSD ENTERPRISES LTD
DELTA TORONTO AIRPORT WEST p 694
See DELTA HOTELS LIMITED
DELTA TOUR AND TRAVEL SERVICES (CANADA) INC p 260
5611 COONEY RD SUITE 160, RICH-MOND, BC, V6X 3J6
(604) 233-0081   *SIC 4724*
DELTA TOUR VANCOUVER p 260
See DELTA TOUR AND TRAVEL SER-VICES (CANADA) INC
DELTA TROIS-RIVIERES p 1387
See 2343-7393 QUEBEC INC
DELTA VANCOUVER AIRPORT HOTEL p 264
See DELTA HOTELS LIMITED
DELTA VANCOUVER SUITE HOTEL p 298
See DELTA HOTELS LIMITED
DELTA VIEW FARMS LTD p 210
3330 41B ST, DELTA, BC, V4K 3N2
(604) 946-1776   *SIC 0182*
DELTA VIEW HABILITATION CENTRE LTD p 210
9341 BURNS DR, DELTA, BC, V4K 3N3
(604) 501-6700   *SIC 7389*
DELTA VIEW LIFE ENRICHMENT CEN-TRES LTD p 210
9341 BURNS DR, DELTA, BC, V4K 3N3
(604) 501-6700   *SIC 8052*
DELTA WAREHOUSES, DIV OF p 150
See UNION TRACTOR LTD
DELTA WINNIPEG p 377
See DELTA HOTELS LIMITED
DELTA WIRE & MFG p 618
29 DELTA DR, HARROW, ON, N0R 1G0
(519) 738-3514   *SIC 3535*
DELTA-Q TECHNOLOGIES CORP p 188
3755 WILLINGDON AVE, BURNABY, BC, V5G 3H3
(604) 327-8244   *SIC 3629*
DELTAWARE SYSTEMS INC p 1039
176 GREAT GEORGE ST SUITE 300, CHARLOTTETOWN, PE, C1A 4K9
(902) 368-8122   *SIC 7371*
DELTON CABINET MFG LTD p 93
14135 128 AVE NW, EDMONTON, AB, T5L 3H3
(780) 413-2260   *SIC 5211*
DELTRO ELECTRIC LTD p 702
1706 MATTAWA AVE, MISSISSAUGA, ON, L4X 1K1
(905) 566-9816   *SIC 1731*
DELUXE ALARMS INC p 551
9000 KEELE ST UNIT 12, CONCORD, ON, L4K 0B3
(416) 410-3020   *SIC 3699*
DELUXE FRENCH FRIES p 414
See MAC'S FOODS LTD
DELUXE LABORATORIES p 980
See DELUXE TORONTO LTD
DELUXE TORONTO LTD p 980
901 KING ST W SUITE 700, TORONTO, ON, M5V 3H5
(416) 364-4321   *SIC 7819*
DELUXE VANCOUVER LTD p 291
50 2ND AVE W, VANCOUVER, BC, V5Y 1B3
(604) 872-7000   *SIC 7812*
DELVED LTD p 851

88A E BEAVER CREEK RD UNIT A, RICH-MOND HILL, ON, L4B 4A8
(289) 597-5140   *SIC 5013*
DELVIEW ADULT LEARNING CENTRE p 207
See DELTA SCHOOL DISTRICT NO.37
DELVIRO ENERGY p 997
See DELVIRO INC
DELVIRO INC p 997
94 BROCKPORT DR, TORONTO, ON, M9W 7J8
(416) 502-3434   *SIC 3646*
DEMAC MEDIA INC p 935
211 YONGE ST SUITE 600, TORONTO, ON, M5B 1M4
(416) 670-1322   *SIC 7372*
DEMAN CONSTRUCTION CORP p 703
776 DUNDAS ST E SUITE 201, MISSIS-SAUGA, ON, L4Y 2B6
(905) 277-0363   *SIC 1542*
DEMATIC LIMITED p 721
6750 CENTURY AVE SUITE 302, MISSIS-SAUGA, ON, L5N 2V8
(877) 567-7300   *SIC 5084*
DEMENAGEMENT KING'S TRANSFER IN-TERNATIONAL INC p 1210
287 RUE ELEANOR, MONTREAL, QC, H3C 2C1
(514) 932-2957   *SIC 4213*
DEMENAGEMENT LE CLAN PANNETON p 1216
See CLAN PANNETON (1993) INC, LE
DEMENAGEMENT MONT-BRUNO/LAKESHORE INC p 1295
1900 RUE MARIE-VICTORIN, SAINT-BRUNO, QC, J3V 6B9
(450) 653-7891   *SIC 4213*
DEMENAGEMENT OUTAOUAIS INC p 1107
150 RUE JEAN-PROULX, GATINEAU, QC, J8Z 1V3
(819) 771-1634   *SIC 4214*
DEMENAGEURS MELDRUM, LES p 1222
See MELDRUM THE MOVER INC
DEMERS p 1140
See PRODUCTIONS HORTICOLES DE-MERS INC, LES
DEMERS BEAULNE S.E.N.C.R.L. p 1195
1800 AV MCGILL COLLEGE BUREAU 600, MONTREAL, QC, H3A 3J6
(514) 878-9631   *SIC 8721*
DEMERS BRAUN MANUFACTURIER D'AMBULANCES INC p 1057
28 RUE RICHELIEU, BELOEIL, QC, J3G 4N5
(450) 467-4683   *SIC 3713*
DEMERS CONTRACTING SERVICES LTD p 128
240 MACLENNAN CRES, FORT MCMUR-RAY, AB, T9H 4G1
(780) 799-3222   *SIC 1611*
DEMERS, AMBULANCE MANUFACTURER INC p 1057
28 RUE RICHELIEU, BELOEIL, QC, J3G 4N5
(450) 467-4683   *SIC 3713*
DEMERS, MICHEL STORE INC p 900
2259 REGENT ST, SUDBURY, ON, P3E 5M9
(705) 523-5800   *SIC 5531*
DEMERS, ROBERT & GILLES INC p 1381
3055 RUE DES BATISSEURS, TERRE-BONNE, QC, J6Y 0A2
(450) 477-2727   *SIC 5032*
DEMEX p 1080
See DEMOLITION ET EXCAVATION DE-MEX INC
DEMEYERE CHRYSLER LIMITED p 880
144 QUEENSWAY E, SIMCOE, ON, N3Y 4K8
(519) 426-3010   *SIC 5511*
DEMILEC INC p 1060
870 BOUL DU CURE-BOIVIN, BOIS-

BRIAND, QC, J7G 2A7
(866) 345-3916   *SIC* 2899
DEMIX BETON   *p* 1141
See *CRH CANADA GROUP INC*
DEMIX CONSTRUCTION   *p* 1141
See *CRH CANADA GROUP INC*
DEMO SPECIALISTE   *p* 1161
See *DEMOSPEC DECONSTRUCTION INC*
DEMOLITION ET EXCAVATION DEMEX INC
p 1080
2253 CH DE LA RESERVE, CHICOUTIMI,
QC, G7J 0C9
(418) 698-2222   *SIC* 1795
DEMOLITION ST-PIERRE   *p* 1369
See *EXCAVATION RENE ST-PIERRE INC*
DEMON OILFIELD SERVICES INC   *p* 81
812 LAUT AVE, CROSSFIELD, AB, T0M
0S0
(403) 946-4800   *SIC* 1389
DEMOSPEC DECONSTRUCTION INC   *p*
1161
10000 BOUL HENRI-BOURASSA E, MON-
TREAL, QC, H1C 1T1
(514) 648-6366   *SIC* 1795
DEMOTEC   *p* 1078
See *CEGERCO INC*
DEMOTEC   *p* 1080
See *CEGERCO INC*
DEMPSEY CORPORATION   *p* 920
47 DAVIES AVE, TORONTO, ON, M4M 2A9
(416) 461-0844   *SIC* 5169
DEMPSTER BREAD, DIV OF   *p* 226
See *CANADA BREAD COMPANY, LIMITED*
DEMPSTER BREAD, DIV OF   *p* 577
See *CANADA BREAD COMPANY, LIMITED*
DEMPSTER BREAD, DIV OF   *p* 615
See *CANADA BREAD COMPANY, LIMITED*
DEMRELL   *p* 499
See *MCDONALD'S RESTAURANTS OF
CANADA LIMITED*
DEMTEC INC   *p* 1253
50 BOUL INDUSTRIEL, PRINCEVILLE, QC,
G6L 4P2
(819) 364-2043   *SIC* 1522
DEMUTH STEEL PRODUCTS INC   *p* 1008
419 ALBERT ST, WATERLOO, ON, N2L 3V2
(519) 884-2980   *SIC* 5083
DEMYSH GROUP INC   *p* 713
2568 ROYAL WINDSOR DR, MISSIS-
SAUGA, ON, L5J 1K7
SIC 3612
DEMYSH METAL   *p* 713
See *DEMYSH GROUP INC*
DEN AT NICKLAUS NORTH   *p* 343
See *GOLFBC HOLDINGS INC*
DEN-O-TECH INTERNATIONAL   *p* 1197
See *LOGICIELS DTI INC*
DENANCO SALES LTD   *p* 838
1104 PEMBROKE ST E, PEMBROKE, ON,
K8A 8S2
(613) 735-0000   *SIC* 5531
DENAULT, BERGERON & ASSOCIES INC *p*
1203
1100 BOUL RENE-LEVESQUE O BUREAU
1520, MONTREAL, QC, H3B 4N4
SIC 7363
DENCAN RESTAURANTS INC   *p* 320
1755 BROADWAY W SUITE 310, VANCOU-
VER, BC, V6J 4S5
(604) 730-6620   *SIC* 5812
DENCAN RESTAURANTS INC   *p* 331
4201 32 ST SUITE 6501, VERNON, BC,
V1T 5P3
(250) 542-0079   *SIC* 5812
DENDROTIK INC   *p* 1274
3083 CH DES QUATRE-BOURGEOIS BU-
REAU 100, QUEBEC, QC, G1W 2K6
(418) 653-7066   *SIC* 5082
DENE SKY SITE SERVICES LTD   *p* 79
351 RICHARD ST, CHARD, AB, T0P 1G0
(780) 559-2202   *SIC* 1629
DENFIELD LIVESTOCK SALES LTD *p* 564
12952 SIXTEEN MILE RD, DENFIELD, ON,
N0M 1P0

(519) 666-1140   *SIC* 5154
DENHAM FORD SALES LTD   *p* 172
5601 45 AVE, WETASKIWIN, AB, T9A 2G2
(780) 352-6043   *SIC* 5511
DENHAM HOLDINGS LTD   *p* 137
4412 50 ST, INNISFAIL, AB, T4G 1P7
(403) 227-3311   *SIC* 6712
DENHAM INN & SUITES   *p* 139
See *PEACE HILLS INVESTMENTS LTD*
DENI'S FOOD BASICS   *p* 993
See *1416018 ONTARIO LIMITED*
DENILLE INDUSTRIES LTD   *p* 93
14440 YELLOWHEAD TRAIL NW, EDMON-
TON, AB, T5L 3C5
(780) 413-0900   *SIC* 7519
DENIS CROTEAU INC   *p* 1106
9 BOUL MONTCLAIR BUREAU 19,
GATINEAU, QC, J8Y 2E2
(819) 770-6886   *SIC* 5651
DENIS MORRIS CATHOLIC HIGH SCHOOL
p 887
See *NIAGARA CATHOLIC DISTRICT
SCHOOL BOARD*
DENIS OFFICE SUPPLIES   *p* 406
123 LUTZ ST, MONCTON, NB, E1C 5E8
(506) 853-8920   *SIC* 5112
DENIS OFFICE SUPPLIES   *p* 1134
See *FOURNITURES DE BUREAU DENIS
INC*
DENIS, MAURICE ET FILS INC   *p* 1233
1745 RUE GUILLET, MONTREAL, QC, H7L
5B1
(450) 687-3840   *SIC* 1711
DENISON MINES CORP   *p* 962
1100 40 UNIVERSITY AVE, TORONTO, ON,
M5J 1T1
(416) 979-1991   *SIC* 1094
DENMAR INC   *p* 1266
2365 AV WATT, QUEBEC, QC, G1P 3X2
(418) 654-2888   *SIC* 6712
DENNINGER'S FOODS OF THE WORLD *p*
611
See *DENNINGER, R. LIMITED*
DENNINGER, R. LIMITED   *p* 611
284 KING ST E, HAMILTON, ON, L8N 1B7
(905) 528-8468   *SIC* 2013
**DENNIS CHEVROLET PONTIAC BUICK
GMC LTD**   *p* 422
24 CONFEDERATION DR, CORNER
BROOK, NL, A2H 6G7
(709) 634-8248   *SIC* 5511
DENNIS JACKSON SEED SERVICE LTD *p*
565
1315 JACKSON ST, DRESDEN, ON, N0P
1M0
(519) 683-4413   *SIC* 5153
DENNIS LOU AUTOMOTIVE & MARINE *p*
620
See *MUSKOKA AUTO PARTS LIMITED*
DENNISON AUTO LTD   *p* 241
828 AUTOMALL DR, NORTH VANCOU-
VER, BC, V7P 3R8
(604) 929-6736   *SIC* 5511
DENNY BUS LINES LTD   *p* 473
5414 ERIN FOURTH LINE, ACTON, ON,
L7J 2L8
(519) 833-9117   *SIC* 4151
DENNY'S RESTAURANT   *p* 320
See *DENCAN RESTAURANTS INC*
DENNY'S RESTAURANT   *p* 331
See *DENCAN RESTAURANTS INC*
DENNY'S RESTAURANT   *p* 1013
See *1413249 ONTARIO INC*
DENRAY TIRE LTD   *p* 369
344 OAK POINT HWY, WINNIPEG, MB,
R2R 1V1
(204) 632-7339   *SIC* 3011
DENSI CORPORATION   *p* 1295
1100 RUE PARENT, SAINT-BRUNO, QC,
J3V 6L8
(450) 441-1300   *SIC* 3955
DENSIFY   *p* 680
See *CIRBA INC*
DENSIGRAPHIX KOPI   *p* 1295

See *DENSI CORPORATION*
DENSO MANUFACTURING CANADA, INC *p*
606
900 SOUTHGATE DR, GUELPH, ON, N1L
1K1
(519) 837-6600   *SIC* 5013
DENSO SALES CANADA, INC   *p* 705
195 BRUNEL RD, MISSISSAUGA, ON, L4Z
1X3
(905) 890-0890   *SIC* 5013
DENTAL BRANDS FOR LESS INC   *p* 669
61 AMBER ST, MARKHAM, ON, L3R 3J7
(905) 669-9329   *SIC* 5047
DENTAL WINGS INC   *p* 1166
2251 AV LETOURNEUX, MONTREAL, QC,
H1V 2N9
(514) 807-8485   *SIC* 7371
DENTALCORP HEALTH SERVICES ULC *p*
962
181 BAY ST STE 2600, TORONTO, ON,
M5J 2T3
(416) 558-8338   *SIC* 8621
DENTONS CANADA LLP   *p* 47
850 2 ST SW SUITE 1500, CALGARY, AB,
T2P 0R8
(403) 268-7000   *SIC* 8111
DENTONS CANADA LLP   *p* 88
10180 101 ST NW SUITE 2900, EDMON-
TON, AB, T5J 3V5
(780) 423-7100   *SIC* 8111
DENTONS CANADA LLP   *p* 303
250 HOWE ST SUITE 2000, VANCOUVER,
BC, V6C 3R8
(604) 687-4460   *SIC* 8111
DENTONS CANADA LLP   *p* 823
99 BANK ST SUITE 1420, OTTAWA, ON,
K1P 1H4
(613) 783-9600   *SIC* 8111
DENTONS CANADA LLP   *p* 969
77 KING ST W SUITE 400, TORONTO, ON,
M5K 2A1
(416) 863-4511   *SIC* 8111
DENTONS CANADA LLP   *p* 1203
1 PLACE VILLE-MARIE BUREAU 3900,
MONTREAL, QC, H3B 4M7
(514) 878-8800   *SIC* 8111
DENTSPLY CANADA LTD   *p* 1030
161 VINYL CRT, WOODBRIDGE, ON, L4L
4A3
(905) 851-6060   *SIC* 5047
DENTSU AEGIS NETWORK CANADA INC *p*
1195
400 BOUL DE MAISONNEUVE O BUREAU
250, MONTREAL, QC, H3A 1L4
(514) 284-4446   *SIC* 6712
**DENTSU AEGIS NETWORK ENTERPRISE
SOLUTIONS INC**   *p* 962
1 UNIVERSITY AVE 10FL, TORONTO, ON,
M5J 2P1
(416) 473-6287   *SIC* 7311
DENTSU AGENT NETWORK   *p* 962
See *DENTSU AEGIS NETWORK ENTER-
PRISE SOLUTIONS INC*
DENTSUBOS INC   *p* 1222
See *DAN AGENCY INC*
DENURE TOURS LTD   *p* 645
71 MOUNT HOPE ST, LINDSAY, ON, K9V
5N5
(705) 324-9161   *SIC* 4725
DEODATO, TONY & SONS LIMITED   *p* 632
100 BINNINGTON CRT, KINGSTON, ON,
K7M 8N1
(613) 548-3073   *SIC* 5148
**DEPANAGO VENTES INSTITUTION-
NELLES, DIV DE**   *p*
1265
See *SAVARD ORTHO CONFORT INC*
DEPANNEUR BELANGER XI   *p* 1248
See *4501403 CANADA INC*
DEPANNEUR BELANGER XL   *p* 1246
See *4501403 CANADA INC*
DEPANNEUR CADEKO   *p* 1366
43 BOUL JOUBERT E, SAYABEC, QC, G0J
3K0

(418) 536-5495   *SIC* 5411
DEPANNEUR DES ORMEAUX   *p* 1384
See *ENTREPRISES MARC DONTIGNY
INC*
DEPANNEUR LA ROCHELIERE   *p* 1323
See *RESTAURANT-BAR LA ROCHELIERE
INC*
DEPANNEUR LE FRIGO   *p* 1305
See *PLACEMENTS M DROUIN INC, LES*
DEPANNEUR LUCAR NAPIERVILLE *p* 1316
See *PETROLES C.L. INC, LES*
DEPANNEUR NEWVIQ'VI INC   *p* 1118
1285 RUE GORDON, KUUJJUAQ, QC, J0M
1C0
(819) 964-2228   *SIC* 5411
DEPANNEUR PETRO-CANADA   *p* 1262
See *PETROLES CADEKO INC*
DEPANNEUR VAL MAHER INC   *p* 1109
1000 CH DENISON E, GRANBY, QC, J2G
8C7
(450) 375-2041   *SIC* 5411
DEPANNEURS MAC'S, LES   *p* 914
See *MAC'S CONVENIENCE STORES INC*
DEPARTEMENT DE GENIE MECANIQUE *p*
1274
See *UNIVERSITE LAVAL*
DEPARTEMENT DES COMMUNICATIONS *p*
1338
See *CANADA POST CORPORATION*
DEPARTMENT OF ANATOMY   *p* 451
See *DALHOUSIE UNIVERSITY*
DEPARTMENT OF ASIAN STUDIES   *p* 325
See *UNIVERSITY OF BRITISH COLUMBIA,
THE*
DEPARTMENT OF BOTANY   *p* 325
See *UNIVERSITY OF BRITISH COLUMBIA,
THE*
**DEPARTMENT OF CHEMICAL ENGINEER-
ING & APPLIED CHEMISTRY**   *p*
975
See *GOVERNING COUNCIL OF THE UNI-
VERSITY OF TORONTO, THE*
DEPARTMENT OF CHEMISTRY   *p* 975
See *GOVERNING COUNCIL OF THE UNI-
VERSITY OF TORONTO, THE*
**DEPARTMENT OF COMMUNITY SERVICES
CHILD WELFARE**   *p* 463
161 TERRA COTTA DR, NEW GLASGOW,
NS, B2H 6B6
(902) 755-5950   *SIC* 7389
**DEPARTMENT OF COMPUTER SYSTEMS
& NETWORKS RESEARCH GROUP**   *p* 975
See *GOVERNING COUNCIL OF THE UNI-
VERSITY OF TORONTO, THE*
**DEPARTMENT OF ECOLOGY AND EVOLU-
TIONARY**   *p*
975
See *GOVERNING COUNCIL OF THE UNI-
VERSITY OF TORONTO, THE*
**DEPARTMENT OF ELECTRICAL COM-
PUTER & ENGINEERING**   *p*
975
See *GOVERNING COUNCIL OF THE UNI-
VERSITY OF TORONTO, THE*
**DEPARTMENT OF ELECTRICAL ENGI-
NEERS**   *p*
974
See *GOVERNING COUNCIL OF THE UNI-
VERSITY OF TORONTO, THE*
DEPARTMENT OF ENGLISH   *p* 972
See *GOVERNING COUNCIL OF THE UNI-
VERSITY OF TORONTO, THE*
**DEPARTMENT OF FAMILY AND COMMU-
NITY MEDICINE**   *p*
977
See *GOVERNING COUNCIL OF THE UNI-
VERSITY OF TORONTO, THE*
**DEPARTMENT OF GEOGRAPHY & PLAN-
NING**   *p*
975
See *GOVERNING COUNCIL OF THE UNI-
VERSITY OF TORONTO, THE*
DEPARTMENT OF IMMUNOLOGY   *p* 975
See *GOVERNING COUNCIL OF THE UNI-*

VERSITY OF TORONTO, THE
DEPARTMENT OF LABORATORY MEDICINE & PATHOBIOLOGY   *p* 945
See GOVERNING COUNCIL OF THE UNIVERSITY OF TORONTO, THE
DEPARTMENT OF MATHEMATICAL & STATISTICAL SCIENCES   *p* 117
See GOVERNORS OF THE UNIVERSITY OF ALBERTA, THE
DEPARTMENT OF MATHEMATICS   *p* 325
See UNIVERSITY OF BRITISH COLUMBIA, THE
DEPARTMENT OF MATHEMATICS   *p* 975
See GOVERNING COUNCIL OF THE UNIVERSITY OF TORONTO, THE
DEPARTMENT OF MEDICAL IMAGING   *p* 977
See GOVERNING COUNCIL OF THE UNIVERSITY OF TORONTO, THE
DEPARTMENT OF MEDICINE   *p* 945
See GOVERNING COUNCIL OF THE UNIVERSITY OF TORONTO, THE
DEPARTMENT OF MOLECULAR GENETICS   *p* 975
See GOVERNING COUNCIL OF THE UNIVERSITY OF TORONTO, THE
DEPARTMENT OF NATIONAL DEFENCE AND THE CANADIAN ARMED FORCES   *p* 1132
9401 RUE WANKLYN, LASALLE, QC, H8R 1Z2
(514) 366-4310   *SIC* 7389
DEPARTMENT OF OBSTETRICS AND GYNAECOLOGY   *p* 945
See GOVERNING COUNCIL OF THE UNIVERSITY OF TORONTO, THE
DEPARTMENT OF OPHTHALMOLOGY   *p* 819
See OTTAWA HOSPITAL, THE
DEPARTMENT OF ORTHOPAEDICS   *p* 294
See UNIVERSITY OF BRITISH COLUMBIA, THE
DEPARTMENT OF PAEDIATRICS   *p* 945
See GOVERNING COUNCIL OF THE UNIVERSITY OF TORONTO, THE
DEPARTMENT OF PHARMACOLOGY AND TOXICOLOGY   *p* 975
See GOVERNING COUNCIL OF THE UNIVERSITY OF TORONTO, THE
DEPARTMENT OF PHILOSOPHY   *p* 972
See GOVERNING COUNCIL OF THE UNIVERSITY OF TORONTO, THE
DEPARTMENT OF PHYSIOLOGY   *p* 975
See GOVERNING COUNCIL OF THE UNIVERSITY OF TORONTO, THE
DEPARTMENT OF PSYCHIATRY   *p* 977
See GOVERNING COUNCIL OF THE UNIVERSITY OF TORONTO, THE
DEPARTMENT OF RADIOLOGY   *p* 289
See UNIVERSITY OF BRITISH COLUMBIA, THE
DEPARTMENT OF SOCIOLOGY   *p* 975
See GOVERNING COUNCIL OF THE UNIVERSITY OF TORONTO, THE
DEPARTMENT OF SOIL SCIENCE   *p* 1434
See UNIVERSITY OF SASKATCHEWAN
DEPATIE FINANCIAL SERVICES   *p* 138
See SUN LIFE FINANCIAL AND DEPATIE FINANCIAL SERVICES INC
DEPENDABLE ANODIZING LIMITED   *p* 669
268 DON PARK RD SUITE 1, MARKHAM, ON, L3R 1C3
(905) 475-1229   *SIC* 3471
DEPENDABLE HOMETECH   *p* 612
See CANCABLE INC
DEPENDABLE TRUCK AND TANK LIMITED   *p* 509
275 CLARENCE ST, BRAMPTON, ON, L6W 3R3
(905) 453-6724   *SIC* 3443
DEPENDABLEHOMETECH   *p* 530

See OCP COMMUNICATIONS INC
DEPMAR FLIGHT HOLDINGS INC   *p* 1431
HANGAR 10 JOHN G. DIEFENBAKER AIRPORT, SASKATOON, SK, S7L 6S1
(306) 931-8552   *SIC* 5172
DEPOSIT INSURANCE CORPORATION OF ONTARIO   *p* 771
4711 YONGE ST SUITE 700, NORTH YORK, ON, M2N 6K8
(416) 325-9444   *SIC* 6399
DEPOT ENTREPOT   *p* 1127
See DOVERCO INC
DEPOT K   *p* 1164
See CANADA POST CORPORATION
DEPT OF COMPUTER SCIENCE   *p* 325
See UNIVERSITY OF BRITISH COLUMBIA, THE
DEPT OF MEDICINE   *p* 1434
See UNIVERSITY OF SASKATCHEWAN
DEPT OF SURGERY   *p* 1434
See UNIVERSITY OF SASKATCHEWAN
DEQ SYSTEMS CORP   *p* 1138
1840 1RE RUE BUREAU 103A, LEVIS, QC, G6W 5M6
(418) 839-3012   *SIC* 6799
DERAGON AUTO-CITE INC   *p* 1088
797 BOUL JEAN-JACQUES-BERTRAND, COWANSVILLE, QC, J2K 0H9
(450) 266-0101   *SIC* 5511
DERAGON FORD   *p* 1088
See DERAGON AUTO-CITE INC
DERBYSHIRE E.D. & SONS LIMITED   *p* 633
2560 PRINCESS ST SUITE 417, KINGSTON, ON, K7P 2S8
(613) 384-4414   *SIC* 5531
DERBYSHIRE, D MERCHANDISING LTD   *p* 486
75 MAPLEVIEW DR W, BARRIE, ON, L4N 9H7
(705) 792-0920   *SIC* 5531
DEREK HUTCHISON SALES LIMITED   *p* 463
9212 COMMERCIAL ST, NEW MINAS, NS, B4N 5J5
(902) 681-4576   *SIC* 5251
DEREK K. HO PHARMACY LTD   *p* 1000
8601 WARDEN AVE, UNIONVILLE, ON, L3R 0B5
(905) 479-0772   *SIC* 5912
DERKO'S SERVICE LTD   *p* 134
5008 50 AVE, GRASSLAND, AB, T0A 1V0
(780) 525-3931   *SIC* 5171
DERMA SCIENCES CANADA INC   *p* 873
104 SHORTING RD, SCARBOROUGH, ON, M1S 3S4
(416) 299-4003   *SIC* 2834
DERMALOGICA (CANADA) LTD   *p* 980
720 KING ST W SUITE 300, TORONTO, ON, M5V 2T3
(416) 368-2286   *SIC* 5122
DERMOLAB PHARMA LTEE   *p* 1358
1421 RUE NOBEL, SAINTE-JULIE, QC, J3E 1Z4
(450) 649-8886   *SIC* 2834
DEROS   *p* 639
See CROSSROADS ESSO
DEROS ESSO   *p* 640
See VICTORIA ST GAS BAR LTD
DEROUARD MOTOR PRODUCTS LTD   *p* 628
1405 RAILWAY ST, KENORA, ON, P9N 0B3
(807) 467-4450   *SIC* 5511
DERRICK DODGE (1980) LTD   *p* 118
6211 104 ST NW, EDMONTON, AB, T6H 2K8
(780) 435-9500   *SIC* 5511
DERRICK GOLF AND WINTER CLUB   *p* 119
3500 119 ST NW, EDMONTON, AB, T6J 5P5
(780) 437-1833   *SIC* 7997
DERY AUTOMOBILE LTEE   *p* 1316
1055 BOUL DU SEMINAIRE N, SAINT-JEAN-SUR-RICHELIEU, QC, J3A 1R7
(450) 359-9000   *SIC* 5511

DERY TELECOM INC   *p* 1121
1013 RUE BAGOT, LA BAIE, QC, G7B 2N6
(418) 544-3358   *SIC* 4841
DERY TOYOTA LTEE   *p* 1315
250 RUE MOREAU, SAINT-JEAN-SUR-RICHELIEU, QC, J2W 0E9
(450) 359-9000   *SIC* 5511
DES LAURENTIDES FORD   *p* 1321
See VOIE RAPIDE DES LAURENTIDES
DES SEIGNEURS FORD   *p* 1379
See AUTOMOBILES DES SEIGNEURS INC
DES SOURCES DODGE CHRYSLER JEEP   *p* 1091
See DES SOURCES DODGE CHRYSLER LTEE
DES SOURCES DODGE CHRYSLER LTEE   *p* 1091
3400 BOUL DES SOURCES, DOLLARD-DES-ORMEAUX, QC, H9B 1Z9
(514) 685-3310   *SIC* 5511
DESA GLASS   *p* 159
See DESA HOLDINGS LTD
DESA HOLDINGS LTD   *p* 159
285079 BLUEGRASS DR, ROCKY VIEW COUNTY, AB, T1X 0P5
(403) 230-5011   *SIC* 2431
DESALABERRY DISTRICT HEALTH CENTRE   *p* 357
See SOUTHERN HEALTH-SANTE SUD
DESCAIR INC   *p* 1170
8335 BOUL SAINT-MICHEL, MONTREAL, QC, H1Z 3E6
(514) 744-6751   *SIC* 5078
DESCARTES SYSTEMS GROUP INC, THE   *p* 1010
120 RANDALL DR, WATERLOO, ON, N2V 1C6
(519) 746-8110   *SIC* 7371
DESCH CANADA LTD   *p* 535
240 SHEARSON CRES, CAMBRIDGE, ON, N1T 1J6
(519) 621-4560   *SIC* 5084
DESCHAMPS CHEVROLET BUICK CADILLAC GMC LTEE   *p* 1358
333 BOUL ARMAND-FRAPPIER, SAINTE-JULIE, QC, J3E 0C7
(450) 649-9333   *SIC* 5511
DESCHAMPS IMPRESSION INC   *p* 1255
755 BOUL DES CHUTES, QUEBEC, QC, G1E 2C2
(418) 667-3322   *SIC* 2759
DESCHENES & FILS LTEE   *p* 1170
3901 RUE JARRY E BUREAU 100, MONTREAL, QC, H1Z 2G1
(514) 374-3110   *SIC* 5074
DESCHENES & FILS LTEE   *p* 1279
1105 RUE DES ROCAILLES, QUEBEC, QC, G2K 2K6
(418) 627-4711   *SIC* 5074
DESCO PLUMBING AND HEATING SUPPLY INC   *p* 734
7550 TRANMERE DR, MISSISSAUGA, ON, L5S 1S6
(416) 293-8219   *SIC* 5074
DESCOR INDUSTRIES INC   *p* 669
15 RIVIERA DR, MARKHAM, ON, L3R 8N4
(905) 470-0010   *SIC* 2521
DESERRES OMER   *p* 1176
See OMER DESERRES INC
DESERT CARDLOCK FUEL SERVICES LIMITED   *p* 216
1885 VERSATILE DR, KAMLOOPS, BC, V1S 1C5
(250) 374-8144   *SIC* 5172
DESGAGNES MARINE CARGO INC   *p* 1258
21 RUE DU MARCHE-CHAMPLAIN BUREAU 100, QUEBEC, QC, G1K 8Z8
(418) 692-1000   *SIC* 4412
DESGAGNES MARINE PETRO INC   *p* 1258
21 RUE DU MARCHE-CHAMPLAIN BUREAU 100, QUEBEC, QC, G1K 8Z8

(418) 692-1000   *SIC* 4412
DESHAIES & RAYMOND INC   *p* 1098
650 RUE HAGGERTY, DRUMMONDVILLE, QC, J2C 3G6
(819) 472-5486   *SIC* 1541
DESHAIES, JEAN-PAUL INC   *p* 1056
14875 BOUL BECANCOUR, BECANCOUR, QC, G9H 2L7
(819) 222-5623   *SIC* 5172
DESHARNAIS PNEUS & MECANIQUE   *p* 1265
See SERVICES DE PNEUS DESHARNAIS INC
DESHARNAIS PNEUS ET MECANIQUE   *p* 1279
See GARAGE DESHARNAIS & FILS LTEE
DESIGN BUILDING LANDSCAPE CONTRACTORS   *p* 518
See GROBE NURSERY LIMITED
DESIGN BUILT MECHANICAL INC   *p* 396
168 CRAIG RD, CHARLO, NB, E8E 2J6
(506) 684-2765   *SIC* 3441
DESIGN ELECTRONICS   *p* 757
See 828324 ONTARIO LIMITED
DESIGN FRANC ART INC   *p* 1348
29 7E RUE O, SAINT-MARTIN, QC, G0M 1B0
(418) 382-3122   *SIC* 3993
DESIGN FRANK LYMAN INC   *p* 1250
2500 BOUL DES SOURCES, POINTE-CLAIRE, QC, H9R 0B3
(514) 695-1719   *SIC* 2335
DESIGN GROUP STAFFING   *p* 86
See 416818 ALBERTA LTD
DESIGN GROUP STAFFING   *p* 88
See DESIGN GROUP STAFFING INC
DESIGN GROUP STAFFING INC   *p* 88
10012 JASPER AVE NW, EDMONTON, AB, T5J 1R2
(780) 448-5850   *SIC* 7361
DESIGN LABEL SYSTEMS INC   *p* 738
150 CAPITAL CRT, MISSISSAUGA, ON, L5T 2R8
(905) 405-1121   *SIC* 2672
DESIGN ROOFING & SHEET METAL LTD   *p* 246
1385 KINGSWAY AVE, PORT COQUITLAM, BC, V3C 1S2
(604) 944-2977   *SIC* 1761
DESIGN SOURCE INTERNATIONAL   *p* 552
See DSI UPHOLSTERY INC
DESIGN STIL   *p* 1250
See FOURNITURES DE MEUBLES ET DE LITERIE SINCA INC
DESIGNAGENCY   *p* 990
See 2161457 ONTARIO INC
DESIGNER FABRIC OUTLET LTD   *p* 991
1360 QUEEN ST W, TORONTO, ON, M6K 1L7
(416) 531-2810   *SIC* 5131
DESIGNER FABRICS   *p* 991
See DESIGNER FABRIC OUTLET LTD
DESJARDINS   *p* 1135
See CAPITAL DESJARDINS INC
DESJARDINS   *p* 1230
See DESJARDINS SOCIETE DE PLACEMENT INC
DESJARDINS   *p* 1230
See FIDUCIE DESJARDINS INC
DESJARDINS   *p* 1254
See CENTRE FINANCIER AUX ENTREPRISES - QUEBEC-CAPITALE
DESJARDINS ASSET MANAGEMENT   *p* 1230
See DESJARDINS GESTION INTERNATIONALE D'ACTIFS INC
DESJARDINS ASSURANCES   *p* 1136
See DESJARDINS ASSURANCES GENERALES INC
DESJARDINS ASSURANCES   *p* 1136
See CERTAS HOME AND AUTO INSURANCE COMPANY
DESJARDINS   ASSURANCES   GEN-

ERALES INC p
1136
6300 BOUL DE LA RIVE-SUD, LEVIS, QC,
G6V 6P9
(418) 835-4850 *SIC* 6331

DESJARDINS AUTO COLLECTION p 1262
*See JL DESJARDINS AUTO COLLECTION
INC*

DESJARDINS ENTREPRISES p 1106
*See CAISSE DESJARDINS DE HULL-
AYLMER*

DESJARDINS ENTREPRISES- RIVE-SUD p
1123
See CAISSE POPULAIRE DE LA PRAIRIE

**DESJARDINS ENTREPRISES–QUEBEC-
PORTNEUF** p
1274
*See CAISSE DESJARDINS DE SAINTE-
FOY*

**DESJARDINS ENTREPRISES-CENTRE-
DU-QUEBEC BUREAU DE VICTORIAVILLE**
p 1397
*See CAISSE DESJARDINS DES BOIS-
FRANCS*

**DESJARDINS ENTREPRISES-
LAURENTIDES** p
1320
*See CAISSE DESJARDINS DE SAINT-
ANTOINE-DES-LAURENTIDES*

DESJARDINS ENTREPRISES-SAGUENAY
p 1078
*See CAISSE DESJARDINS DE
CHICOUTIMI*

**DESJARDINS ENTREPRISESBAS-SAINT-
LAURENT** p
1284
See CAISSE DESJARDINS DE RIMOUSKI

DESJARDINS ENTREPRISESRIVE-SUD p
1145
*See CAISSE DESJARDINS PIERRE-
BOUCHER*

DESJARDINS ENTREPRISESRIVE-SUD p
1322
*See CAISSE DESJARDINS CHARLES-
LEMOYNE*

**DESJARDINS ENTREPRISESVALLEE DU
RICHELIEU-YAMASKA** p 1283
*See CAISSE POPULAIRE DESJARDINS
DE RICHELIEU-SAINT-MATHIAS*

**DESJARDINS FINANCIAL SECURITIES,
LIFE INSURANCE COMPANY** p 1230
*See DESJARDINS SECURITE FI-
NANCIERE, COMPAGNIE D'ASSURANCE
VIE*

DESJARDINS FINANCIAL SECURITY p 926
*See DESJARDINS SECURITE FI-
NANCIERE, COMPAGNIE D'ASSURANCE
VIE*

**DESJARDINS FINANCIAL SECURITY IN-
VESTMENTS** p
1269
*See DESJARDINS SECURITE FI-
NANCIERE INVESTISSEMENTS INC*

DESJARDINS FONDS DE SECURITE p
1136
See FONDS DE SECURITE DESJARDINS

DESJARDINS FORD LTEE p 1329
1150 BOUL MARCEL-LAURIN, SAINT-
LAURENT, QC, H4R 1J7
(514) 332-3850 *SIC* 5511

**DESJARDINS GESTION INTERNA-
TIONALE D'ACTIFS INC** p
1230
1 COMPLEXE DESJARDINS, MONTREAL,
QC, H5B 1B3
(514) 281-2859 *SIC* 8741

**DESJARDINS GROUPE D'ASSURANCES
GENERALES INC** p 694
5070 DIXIE RD, MISSISSAUGA, ON, L4W
1C9
(905) 366-4430 *SIC* 6411

**DESJARDINS GROUPE D'ASSURANCES
GENERALES INC** p 1136
6300 BOUL GUILLAUME-COUTURE,

LEVIS, QC, G6V 6P9
(418) 835-4850 *SIC* 6411

**DESJARDINS GROUPE D'ASSURANCES
GENERALES INC** p 1230
1 COMPLEXE DESJARDINS BUREAU 1,
MONTREAL, QC, H5B 1B1
(514) 350-8300 *SIC* 6411

**DESJARDINS GROUPE D'ASSURANCES
GENERALES INC** p 1304
15590 8E AV, SAINT-GEORGES, QC, G5Y
7X6

SIC 6411

DESJARDINS HOLDING FINANCIER INC p
1230
1 RUE COMPLEXE DESJARDINS S 40E
ETAGE, MONTREAL, QC, H5B 1J1
(418) 838-7870 *SIC* 6411

DESJARDINS INSURANCE p 705
*See CERTAS DIRECT COMPAGNIE
D'ASSURANCE*

DESJARDINS INSURANCE p 1136
*See DESJARDINS SECURITE FI-
NANCIERE, COMPAGNIE D'ASSURANCE
VIE*

**DESJARDINS SECURITE FINANCIERE IN-
VESTISSEMENTS INC** p
1269
1150 RUE DE CLAIRE-FONTAINE, QUE-
BEC, QC, G1R 5G4
(877) 647-5435 *SIC* 6282

**DESJARDINS SECURITE FINANCIERE,
COMPAGNIE D'ASSURANCE VIE** p 926
95 ST CLAIR AVE W SUITE 100,
TORONTO, ON, M4V 1N7
(416) 926-2700 *SIC* 6311

**DESJARDINS SECURITE FINANCIERE,
COMPAGNIE D'ASSURANCE VIE** p 1136
200 RUE DES COMMANDEURS, LEVIS,
QC, G6V 6R2
(418) 838-7800 *SIC* 6311

**DESJARDINS SECURITE FINANCIERE,
COMPAGNIE D'ASSURANCE VIE** p 1230
1 COMPLEXE DESJARDINS, MONTREAL,
QC, H5B 1E2
(514) 285-3000 *SIC* 6311

**DESJARDINS SECURITE FINANCIERE,
COMPAGNIE D'ASSURANCE VIE** p 1230
2 COMPLEXE DESJARDINS TOUR E,
MONTREAL, QC, H5B 1E2
(514) 350-8700 *SIC* 6311

DESJARDINS SECURITIES p 1230
*See VALEURS MOBILIERES DESJARDINS
INC*

**DESJARDINS SOCIETE DE PLACEMENT
INC** p 1230
2 COMPLEXE DESJARDINS, MONTREAL,
QC, H5B 1H5
(866) 666-1280 *SIC* 6211

DESJARDINS SOCIETE FINANCIERE INC p
1230
1 COMPLEXE DESJARDINS, MONTREAL,
QC, H5B 1J1
(418) 838-7870 *SIC* 6712

DESLAURIER CUSTOM CABINETS INC p
849
550 HALL AVE E, RENFREW, ON, K7V 2S9
(613) 432-5431 *SIC* 2541

DESLAURIERS & ASSOCIES INC p 1064
210 BOUL DE MONTARVILLE BUREAU
3015, BOUCHERVILLE, QC, J4B 6T3
(450) 641-1911 *SIC* 6411

DESMEULES AUTOMOBILES INC p 1135
182 138 RTE, LES ESCOUMINS, QC, G0T
1K0
(418) 233-2490 *SIC* 5511

DESMEULES HUYNDAI p 1235
See D B D AUTO INC

DESPRES H LTEE p 1378
44 RUE PRINCIPALE N, SUTTON, QC, J0E
2K0
(450) 538-2211 *SIC* 5411

DESPRES, LAPORTE INC p 1373
185 RUE DE LA BURLINGTON, SHER-
BROOKE, QC, J1L 1G9

(819) 566-2620 *SIC* 5046

**DESPRES-PACEY INSURANCE BROKERS
LIMITED** p 753
26 ARMSTRONG ST, NEW LISKEARD, ON,
P0J 1P0
(705) 647-6713 *SIC* 6411

DESROSIERS DISTRIBUTEURS p 594
*See BOONE PLUMBING AND HEATING
SUPPLY INC*

DESROSIERS TOYOTA p 1284
See 2846-3826 QUEBEC INC

DESSAU INC p 1237
1200 BOUL SAINT-MARTIN O BUREAU
300, MONTREAL, QC, H7S 2E4
(514) 281-1010 *SIC* 8742

DESSAU INC p 1279
1260 BOUL LEBOURGNEUF BUREAU 250,
QUEBEC, QC, G2K 2G2
(418) 626-1688 *SIC* 8711

DESSERCOM INC p 1312
592 AV SAINTE-MARIE, SAINT-
HYACINTHE, QC, J2S 4R5
(450) 773-5223 *SIC* 4119

**DESSERT CITY INVESTIGATIONS AND SE-
CURITY INC** p
217
6968 FURRER RD, KAMLOOPS, BC, V2C
4V9
(250) 828-8778 *SIC* 6211

DESSIN SHELLY p 1337
See 10033618 CANADA INC

**DESSINS DE STRUCTURE STELTEC INC,
LES** p 1364
22 BOUL DESJARDINS E BUREAU 200,
SAINTE-THERESE, QC, J7E 1C1
(450) 971-5995 *SIC* 7389

DESSINS DRUMMOND INC, LES p 1098
455 BOUL SAINT-JOSEPH BUREAU 201,
DRUMMONDVILLE, QC, J2C 7B5
(819) 477-3315 *SIC* 7389

**DESSUREAULT LEBLANC LEFEBVRE
C.A.** p 1387
950 RUE ROYALE BUREAU 104, TROIS-
RIVIERES, QC, G9A 4H8
(819) 379-0133 *SIC* 8721

**DESSUREAULT, JEAN-CLAUDE PHARMA-
CIEN** p
1297
113 RUE SAINT-PIERRE UNITE 101,
SAINT-CONSTANT, QC, J5A 0M3
(450) 632-2730 *SIC* 5912

DESTIGO (TM) p 1199
See SKYLINK VOYAGES INC

DESTINATION AUTO ENTERPRISES INC p
185
4278 LOUGHEED HWY, BURNABY, BC,
V5C 3Y5
(604) 294-2111 *SIC* 5511

DESTINATION AUTO SALES INC p 289
368 KINGSWAY, VANCOUVER, BC, V5T
3J6
(604) 873-3676 *SIC* 5511

DESTINATION AUTO VENTURES INC p 185
4278 LOUGHEED HWY, BURNABY, BC,
V5C 3Y5
(604) 294-2111 *SIC* 5511

DESTINATION CANADA 2000 p 1257
See 9277-8091 QUEBEC INC

**DESTINATION CHRYSLER JEEP DODGE
NORTHSHORE** p 185
See DESTINATION AUTO VENTURES INC

DESTINATION CHRYSLER LTD p 241
1600 MARINE DR, NORTH VANCOUVER,
BC, V7P 1T9
(888) 461-4188 *SIC* 5511

DESTINATION TOYOTA p 185
*See DESTINATION AUTO ENTERPRISES
INC*

DESTINATION TRAVEL HEALTH PLAN p
767
211 CONSUMERS RD SUITE 200, NORTH
YORK, ON, M2J 4G8
(416) 499-6616 *SIC* 6321

DESTINATION WINNIPEG INC p 374

259 PORTAGE AVE SUITE 300, WIN-
NIPEG, MB, R3B 2A9
(204) 943-1970 *SIC* 7389

DESTINATIONS ESCAPA INC p 1061
362 CH DE LA GRANDE-COTE, BOIS-
BRIAND, QC, J7G 1B1
(514) 338-1160 *SIC* 4724

DESTINATIONS ETC INC p 1195
1470 RUE PEEL BUREAU 110, MON-
TREAL, QC, H3A 1T1
(514) 849-0707 *SIC* 4724

DESTINY SOLUTIONS INC p 924
40 HOLLY ST SUITE 800, TORONTO, ON,
M4S 3C3
(416) 480-0500 *SIC* 7371

DESUTTER INVESTMENTS INC p 252
570 NEWMAN RD, QUESNEL, BC, V2J 6Z8
(250) 747-5275 *SIC* 5531

DET NORSKE VERITAS p 8
See DET NORSKE VERITAS CANADA LTD

DET NORSKE VERITAS CANADA LTD p 8
2618 HOPEWELL PL NE SUITE 150, CAL-
GARY, AB, T1Y 7J7
(403) 250-9041 *SIC* 8742

DETAIL K2 INC p 522
1080 CLAY AVE UNIT 2, BURLINGTON,
ON, L7L 0A1
(905) 335-2152 *SIC* 5199

DETECTEX SECURITY SERVICES CORP p
181
8557 GOVERNMENT ST SUITE 102,
BURNABY, BC, V3N 4S9
SIC 7381

DETON'CHO / NUNA JOINT VENTURE p
120
9839 31 AVE NW, EDMONTON, AB, T6N
1C5
(780) 434-9114 *SIC* 1629

DETOUR GOLD CORPORATION p 971
199 BAY ST SUITE 4100, TORONTO, ON,
M5L 1E2
(416) 304-0800 *SIC* 1041

DETOX ENVIRONMENTAL LTD p 496
322 BENNETT RD, BOWMANVILLE, ON,
L1C 3Z2
(905) 623-1367 *SIC* 4953

DETROIT & CANADA TUNNEL p 1023
555 GOYEAU ST, WINDSOR, ON, N9A 1H1
(519) 258-7424 *SIC* 4111

DEUCE DISPOSAL LTD p 163
240 BALSOM RD NE, SLAVE LAKE, AB,
T0G 2A0
(780) 849-3334 *SIC* 4953

DEUTSCHE BANK AG- CANADA BRANCH
p 971
199 BAY ST SUITE 4700, TORONTO, ON,
M5L 1E9
(416) 682-8000 *SIC* 6021

DEUX PAR DEUX p 1178
See GROUPE MINIMOME INC

**DEVEAU, BOURGEOIS, GAGNE, HEBERT
ET ASSOCIES S.E.N.C.R.L** p 1120
1210 CH DE LA VERNIERE BUREAU 2,
L'ETANG-DU-NORD, QC, G4T 3E6
(418) 986-4782 *SIC* 8111

DEVELOPEMENT CYREX INC p 1073
455 CH PRINCIPAL, CAP-AUX-MEULES,
QC, G4T 1E4
(418) 986-2871 *SIC* 8741

**DEVELOPMENTAL DISABILITIES ASSOCI-
ATION OF VANCOUVER-RICHMOND** p
260
3851 SHELL RD SUITE 100, RICHMOND,
BC, V6X 2W2
(604) 273-9778 *SIC* 8322

**DEVELOPMENTAL SERVICES OF LEEDS
AND GRENVILLE** p 519
*See BROCKVILLE AREA CENTRE FOR
DEVELOPMENTALLY HANDICAPPED PER-
SONS INC*

DEVELOPPEMENT BONNET INC p 1298
54 RUE PRINCIPALE, SAINT-DAMASE, QC,
J0H 1J0
(450) 797-3301 *SIC* 5143

DEVELOPPEMENT EDF EN CANADA p 1203
See DEVELOPPEMENT EDF RENOUVE-LABLES INC

DEVELOPPEMENT EDF RENOUVE-LABLES INC p 1203
1134 RUE SAINTE-CATHERINE O BUREAU 910, MONTREAL, QC, H3B 1H4
(514) 397-9997   *SIC* 1711

DEVELOPPEMENT ET PAIX p 1214
See ORGANISATION CATHOLIQUE CANADIENNE POUR LE DEVELOPPEMENT ET LA PAIX

DEVELOPPEMENT INTERNATIONAL DESJARDINS INC p 1136
150 RUE DES COMMANDEURS, LEVIS, QC, G6V 6P8
(418) 835-2400   *SIC* 8741

DEVELOPPEMENT OLYMBEC INC p 1325
333 BOUL DECARIE BUREAU 500, SAINT-LAURENT, QC, H4N 3M9
(514) 344-3334   *SIC* 6512

DEVELOPPEMENT PIEKUAKAMI ILNU-ATSH p 1150
1425 RUE OUIATCHOUAN, MASH-TEUIATSH, QC, G0W 2H0
(418) 275-8181   *SIC* 8741

DEVELOPPEMENTS ANGELCARE INC, LES p 1072
201 BOUL DE L'INDUSTRIE BUREAU 104, CANDIAC, QC, J5R 6A6
(514) 761-0511   *SIC* 3443

DEVELOPPEMENTS GERARD BROUSSEAU INC p 1256
7609 AV GRIGNON, QUEBEC, QC, G1H 6V7
(418) 626-6712   *SIC* 6512

DEVELOPPEMENTS REKERN INC, LES p 1325
333 BOUL DECARIE 5E ETAGE, SAINT-LAURENT, QC, H4N 3M9
(514) 344-3334   *SIC* 6719

DEVELUS SYSTEMS INC p 335
1112 FORT ST SUITE 600, VICTORIA, BC, V8V 3K8
(250) 388-0880   *SIC* 7371

DEVENCORE - NKF p 1203
See DEVENCORE INVESTMENTS INC

DEVENCORE INVESTMENTS INC p 1203
800 BOUL RENE-LEVESQUE O BUREAU 900, MONTREAL, QC, H3B 1X9
(514) 392-1330   *SIC* 6531

DEVENCORE LTEE p 1203
800 BOUL RENE-LEVESQUE O BUREAU 900, MONTREAL, QC, H3B 1X9
(514) 392-1330   *SIC* 6531

DEVIMCO IMMOBILIER INC p 1071
3400 RUE DE L'ECLIPSE BUREAU 310, BROSSARD, QC, J4Z 0P3
(450) 645-2525   *SIC* 6553

DEVIMCO INC p 1070
6000 BOUL DE ROME BUREAU 410, BROSSARD, QC, J4Y 0B6
(450) 645-2525   *SIC* 8741

DEVITT & FORAND CONTRACTORS INC p 35
5716 BURBANK CRES SE, CALGARY, AB, T2H 1Z6
(403) 255-8565   *SIC* 1542

DEVJO INDUSTRIES INC p 669
375 STEELCASE RD E, MARKHAM, ON, L3R 1G3
(905) 477-7689   *SIC* 6712

DEVOIR INC, LE p 1195
2050 RUE DE BLEURY, MONTREAL, QC, H3A 2J5
(514) 985-3333   *SIC* 2711

DEVON CANADA p 213
See DEVON CANADA CORPORATION

DEVON CANADA CORPORATION p 47
400 3 AVE SW SUITE 100, CALGARY, AB,
T2P 4H2
(403) 232-7100   *SIC* 1311

DEVON CANADA CORPORATION p 126
10924 92ND AVE, FAIRVIEW, AB, T0H 1L0
SIC 1382

DEVON CANADA CORPORATION p 131
9601 116 ST UNIT 101, GRANDE PRAIRIE, AB, T8V 5W3
(403) 517-6700   *SIC* 1382

DEVON CANADA CORPORATION p 168
GD, SWAN HILLS, AB, T0G 2C0
(780) 333-7800   *SIC* 5172

DEVON CANADA CORPORATION p 213
10514 87 AVE, FORT ST. JOHN, BC, V1J 5K7
SIC 1382

DEVON CHRYSLER DODGE JEEP RAM LTD p 81
7 SASKATCHEWAN AVE W, DEVON, AB, T9G 1B2
(888) 342-9117   *SIC* 5511

DEVON LUMBER p 399
See DEVON LUMBER CO. LTD

DEVON LUMBER CO. LTD p 399
200 GIBSON ST, FREDERICTON, NB, E3A 4E3
(506) 457-7123   *SIC* 5031

DEVON PROPERTIES LTD p 333
2067 CADBORO BAY RD SUITE 201, VICTORIA, BC, V8R 5G4
(250) 595-7000   *SIC* 6513

DEVON TRANSPORT LTD p 234
2501 KENWORTH RD, NANAIMO, BC, V9T 3M4
(250) 729-2400   *SIC* 7514

DEVONIAN MOTOR CORPORATION p 118
5220 GATEWAY BLVD, EDMONTON, AB, T6H 4J7
(780) 462-8846   *SIC* 5511

DEVONIAN MOTOR INCORPORATION p 100
17708 111 AVE NW, EDMONTON, AB, T5S 0A2
(780) 484-7733   *SIC* 7538

DEVONSHIRE CARE CENTRE p 124
See SUMMIT CARE CORPORATION (EDMONTON) LTD

DEVRY CUSTOM WORK LTD p 196
49259 CASTLEMAN RD, CHILLIWACK, BC, V2P 6H4
(604) 794-3874   *SIC* 6712

DEVRY GREENHOUSES (1989) LTD p 196
49259 CASTLEMAN RD, CHILLIWACK, BC, V2P 6H4
(604) 794-3874   *SIC* 5261

DEVRY GROUP OF COMPANIES p 196
See DEVRY GREENHOUSES (1989) LTD

DEVTEK AEROSPACE INC p 641
1665 HIGHLAND RD W, KITCHENER, ON, N2N 3K5
(519) 576-8910   *SIC* 3728

DEVTEK AEROSPACE INC p 1233
3675 BOUL INDUSTRIEL, MONTREAL, QC, H7L 4S3
(450) 629-3454   *SIC* 3599

DEVTEK AEROSPACE INC. p 641
See DEVTEK AEROSPACE INC

DEVTEK AEROSPACE INC. p 1233
See DEVTEK AEROSPACE INC

DEW ENGINEERING AND DEVELOPMENT ULC p 405
99 GENERAL MANSON WAY, MIRAMICHI, NB, E1N 6K6
(506) 778-8000   *SIC* 3795

DEW ENGINEERING AND DEVELOPMENT ULC p 817
3429 HAWTHORNE RD, OTTAWA, ON, K1G 4G2
(613) 736-5100   *SIC* 3795

DEWILDT CAR SALES LIMITED p 610
1600 MAIN ST E, HAMILTON, ON, L8K 1E7
(905) 312-0404   *SIC* 5511

DEWILDT CHRYSLER DODGE JEEP p 610
See DEWILDT CAR SALES LIMITED

DEWLING, S & C SALES LTD p 172
3851 56 ST, WETASKIWIN, AB, T9A 2B1
(780) 352-7175   *SIC* 5531

DEWPOINT BOTTLING COMPANY LTD p 372
326 KEEWATIN ST, WINNIPEG, MB, R2X 2R9
(204) 774-7770   *SIC* 5963

DEX p 1325
See DEX BROS. CIE DE VETEMENTS LTEE

DEX BROS. CIE DE VETEMENTS LTEE p 1325
390 RUE DESLAURIERS, SAINT-LAURENT, QC, H4N 1V8
(514) 383-2474   *SIC* 5137

DEXTER CONSTRUCTION COMPANY p 470
See MUNICIPAL CONTRACTING LIMITED

DEXTER CONSTRUCTION COMPANY LIMITED p 439
927 ROCKY LAKE DR, BEDFORD, NS, B4A 2T7
(902) 835-3381   *SIC* 1611

DEXTER CONSTRUCTION COMPANY LIMITED p 468
44 MEADOW DR, TRURO, NS, B2N 5V4
(902) 895-6952   *SIC* 1611

DEXTER MINING INC p 425
1001 LUCE ST, LABRADOR CITY, NL, A2V 2K7
(709) 944-2995   *SIC* 1794

DEXTERRA p 686
See 10647802 CANADA LIMITED

DEXTRAIL p 1151
See ENTREPRISE ROBERT THIBERT INC

DEZINECORP INC p 705
369 BRITANNIA RD E, MISSISSAUGA, ON, L4Z 2H5
SIC 5199

DFA p 1060
See DAIGNEAULT FERLAND ASSURANCES INC

DFC AUTO LTD p 220
2350 HIGHWAY 97 N, KELOWNA, BC, V1X 4H8
(250) 860-6000   *SIC* 5511

DFH REAL ESTATE LTD p 333
3914 SHELBOURNE ST, VICTORIA, BC, V8P 4J1
(250) 477-7291   *SIC* 6531

DFI p 122
See DFI CORPORATION

DFI CORPORATION p 122
2404 51 AVE NW, EDMONTON, AB, T6P 0E4
(780) 466-5237   *SIC* 3312

DGA FULFILLMENT SERVICES INC p 678
80 TRAVAIL RD UNIT 1, MARKHAM, ON, L3S 3H9
SIC 7389

DGAM p 938
See DIVERSIFIED GLOBAL ASSET MANAGEMENT CORP

DGF p 738
See DHL GLOBAL FORWARDING (CANADA) INC

DGI SUPPLY p 797
See DOALL CANADA INC

DGN MARKETING SERVICES LTD p 738
1633 MEYERSIDE DR, MISSISSAUGA, ON, L5T 1B9
(905) 670-4070   *SIC* 4225

DGS ASTRO PAVING p 213
See INTEROUTE CONSTRUCTION LTD

DH CORPORATION p 669
81 WHITEHALL DR, MARKHAM, ON, L3R 9T1
(905) 944-1231   *SIC* 6211

DH CORPORATION p 962
120 BREMNER BLVD 30 FLOOR, TORONTO, ON, M5J 0A8

(416) 696-7700   *SIC* 7371

DH CORPORATION p 1141
830 RUE DELAGE, LONGUEUIL, QC, J4G 2V4
(450) 463-6372   *SIC* 6211

DH MANUFACTURING INC p 215
1250 HOLS RD, HOUSTON, BC, V0J 1Z1
(250) 845-3390   *SIC* 2499

DHAMI, TEJI DRUGS LTD p 658
1680 RICHMOND ST SUITE 764, LONDON, ON, N6G 3Y9
(519) 663-9370   *SIC* 5912

DHILLON FOOD SERVICES LTD p 249
820 VICTORIA ST, PRINCE GEORGE, BC, V2L 5P1
(250) 563-2331   *SIC* 5812

DHL EXPRESS (CANADA) LTD p 100
10918 184 ST NW, EDMONTON, AB, T5S 2N9
(855) 345-7447   *SIC* 7389

DHL EXPRESS (CANADA) LTD p 380
130 MIDLAND ST UNIT 2, WINNIPEG, MB, R3E 3R3
(855) 345-7447   *SIC* 7389

DHL EXPRESS (CANADA) LTD p 502
18 PARKSHORE DR, BRAMPTON, ON, L6T 0G7
(905) 861-3400   *SIC* 4212

DHL GLOBAL FORWARDING (CANADA) INC p 734
1825 ALSTEP DR, MISSISSAUGA, ON, L5S 1Y5
SIC 4731

DHL GLOBAL FORWARDING (CANADA) INC p 738
6200 EDWARDS BLVD SUITE 100, MISSISSAUGA, ON, L5T 2V7
(289) 562-6500   *SIC* 4731

DHL GLOBAL FORWARDING (CANADA) INC p 1339
555 MONTEE DE LIESSE, SAINT-LAURENT, QC, H4T 1P5
(514) 344-3447   *SIC* 4731

DHL SUPPLY CHAIN (CANADA) p 731
See EXEL CANADA LTD

DHS (OSHAWA) LTD p 811
88 CENTRE ST N SUITE 1, OSHAWA, ON, L1G 4B6
(905) 571-1511   *SIC* 8621

DHS HEALTH CARE SERVICE p 811
See DHS (OSHAWA) LTD

DHX MEDIA (TORONTO PROD) LTD p 962
207 QUEENS QUAY W SUITE 550, TORONTO, ON, M5J 1A7
(416) 363-8034   *SIC* 7812

DHX MEDIA LTD p 452
1478 QUEEN ST, HALIFAX, NS, B3J 2H7
(902) 423-0260   *SIC* 7812

DI CIOCCO FARMS EASTSIDE p 644
See DI CIOCCO FARMS INCORPORATED

DI CIOCCO FARMS INCORPORATED p 644
308 TALBOT RD E, LEAMINGTON, ON, N8H 3V6
(519) 326-2339   *SIC* 0161

DI-TECH INC p 1222
2125 RUE LILY-SIMON, MONTREAL, QC, H4B 3A1
SIC 2269

DIABETES ASSOCIATION (BROOKS & DISTRICT) p 7
215 3 ST W, BROOKS, AB, T1R 0S3
SIC 8699

DIABETES CANADA p 944
522 UNIVERSITY AVE SUITE 1400, TORONTO, ON, M5G 2R5
(416) 363-3373   *SIC* 8699

DIABSOLUT INC p 1250
181 BOUL HYMUS BUREAU 100, POINTE-CLAIRE, QC, H9R 5P4
(514) 461-3314   *SIC* 8748

DIACO INTERNATIONAL INC p 29
3620 BLACKBURN RD SE, CALGARY, AB, T2G 4A5
(403) 287-4494   *SIC* 5039

DIAGEO CANADA INC *p 477*
110 ST. ARNAUD ST, AMHERSTBURG, ON, N9V 2N8
(519) 736-2161   *SIC* 2085

DIAGEO CANADA INC *p 996*
401 THE WEST MALL SUITE 800, TORONTO, ON, M9C 5P8
(416) 626-2000   *SIC* 2085

DIAGEO CANADA INC *p 1366*
1 RUE SALABERRY, SALABERRY-DE-VALLEYFIELD, QC, J6T 2G9
(450) 373-3230   *SIC* 5182

DIAGNOSTIC SERVICES OF MANITOBA INC *p 377*
155 CARLTON ST SUITE 1502, WINNIPEG, MB, R3C 3H8
(204) 926-8005   *SIC* 8741

DIAL OILFIELD SERVICES 2006 LTD *p 82*
5136 54 ST, DRAYTON VALLEY, AB, T7A 1S2
(780) 542-5879   *SIC* 1389

DIAL ONE WOLFEDALE ELECTRIC *p 557*
See OZZ ELECTRIC

DIALOG *p 29*
134 11 AVE SE SUITE 300, CALGARY, AB, T2G 0X5
(403) 541-5501   *SIC* 8712

DIALOG *p 88*
10237 104 ST NW SUITE 100, EDMONTON, AB, T5J 1B1
(780) 429-1580   *SIC* 8712

DIALOG *p 928*
2 BLOOR ST E SUITE 1000, TORONTO, ON, M4W 1A8
(416) 966-0220   *SIC* 7361

DIALOG DESIGN *p 928*
See DIALOG

DIALOGIC *p 1324*
See DIALOGIC CORPORATION

DIALOGIC CORPORATION *p 1324*
9800 CAVENDISH 5E ETAGE, SAINT-LAURENT, QC, H4M 2V9
(514) 745-5500   *SIC* 7371

DIAMANT ELINOR INC. *p 1250*
987 BOUL SAINT-JEAN, POINTE-CLAIRE, QC, H9R 5M3
(450) 688-6288   *SIC* 5944

DIAMANTS BASAL INC *p 1203*
1255 BOUL ROBERT-BOURASSA BUREAU 460, MONTREAL, QC, H3B 3B6
(514) 861-6675   *SIC* 5094

DIAMO ENTERPRISES INC *p 502*
1795 STEELES AVE E, BRAMPTON, ON, L6T 4L5
(905) 792-7108   *SIC* 5541

DIAMOND & DIAMOND CERTIFIED MG *p 780*
See TROJAN CONSOLIDATED INVESTMENTS LIMITED

DIAMOND AIRCRAFT INDUSTRIES INC *p 649*
1560 CRUMLIN, LONDON, ON, N5V 1S2
(519) 457-4000   *SIC* 3721

DIAMOND AND SCHMITT ARCHITECTS INCORPORATED *p 980*
384 ADELAIDE ST W SUITE 300, TORONTO, ON, M5V 1R7
(416) 862-8800   *SIC* 8712

DIAMOND ATHLETIC MEDICAL SUPPLIES INC *p 387*
75 POSEIDON BAY UNIT 185, WINNIPEG, MB, R3M 3E4
(204) 488-7820   *SIC* 5047

DIAMOND CO-OPERATIVE ASSOCIATION LTD *p 1408*
223 1ST AVE NE, ITUNA, SK, S0A 1N0
(306) 795-2441   *SIC* 5171

DIAMOND CONSTRUCTION *p 358*
See DIAMOND READY MIX CONCRETE LTD

DIAMOND DELIVERY SERVICES *p 277*
See R. DIAMOND GROUP OF COMPANIES LTD, THE

DIAMOND DIVERSIFIED INDUSTRIES LTD *p 442*
55 BREN ST, CORNWALLIS, NS, B0S 1H0
(902) 638-8616   *SIC* 3993

DIAMOND DRILLING TOOLS & PRECISION MACHINING *p 385*
See DIMATEC INC

DIAMOND ENERGY SERVICES INC *p 1436*
1521 NORTH SERVICE RD W, SWIFT CURRENT, SK, S9H 3S9
(306) 778-6682   *SIC* 1389

DIAMOND ESTATES WINES & SPIRITS INC *p 805*
435 NORTH SERVICE RD W UNIT 100, OAKVILLE, ON, L6M 4X8
(905) 641-1042   *SIC* 5182

DIAMOND ESTATES WINES & SPIRITS LTD *p 761*
1067 NIAGARA STONE RD, NIAGARA ON THE LAKE, ON, L0S 1J0
(905) 685-5673   *SIC* 5182

DIAMOND FIREPLACE DISTRIBUTORS LTD *p 75*
10221 15 ST NE SUITE 4, CALGARY, AB, T3J 0T1
(403) 273-0000   *SIC* 5023

DIAMOND INTERNATIONAL TRUCKS LTD *p 100*
17020 118 AVE NW, EDMONTON, AB, T5S 1S4
(780) 454-1541   *SIC* 5511

DIAMOND LODGE CO LTD *p 1404*
402 2ND AVE W, BIGGAR, SK, S0K 0M0
SIC 8361

DIAMOND PARK BUILDERS (2004) INC *p 128*
425 GREGOIRE DR SUITE 600, FORT MCMURRAY, AB, T9H 4K7
SIC 1542

DIAMOND PARKING LTD *p 318*
817 DENMAN ST, VANCOUVER, BC, V6G 2L7
(604) 681-8797   *SIC* 7521

DIAMOND PARKING SERVICES *p 318*
See DIAMOND PARKING LTD

DIAMOND PLUS *p 544*
56 ALLAN ST W, CLIFFORD, ON, N0G 1M0
(519) 327-4567   *SIC* 7389

DIAMOND PLUS SPECIALIZED *p 544*
See DIAMOND PLUS

DIAMOND READY MIX CONCRETE LTD *p 358*
399 PTH 12 N, STEINBACH, MB, R5G 1V1
(204) 326-3456   *SIC* 5032

DIAMOND SECURITY *p 660*
377 GRAND VIEW AVE, LONDON, ON, N6K 2T1
(519) 471-8095   *SIC* 7381

DIAMOND YARNS OF CANADA LTD *p 783*
155 MARTIN ROSS AVE SUITE 3, NORTH YORK, ON, M3J 2L9
(416) 736-6111   *SIC* 5199

DIAMOND-KOTE *p 342*
See WGI MANUFACTURING INC

DIAMONDGEAR *p 1*
See DIAMONDGEAR INDUSTRIAL MANUFACTURING LTD

DIAMONDGEAR INDUSTRIAL MANUFACTURING LTD *p 1*
26229 TWP RD 531A SUITE 206, ACHESON, AB, T7X 5A4
(780) 451-3912   *SIC* 5063

DIANA DOLLS FASHIONS INC *p 891*
555 BARTON ST, STONEY CREEK, ON, L8E 5S1
(905) 643-9118   *SIC* 5137

DIANNE WATTS CAMPAIGN, THE *p 276*
7327 137 ST UNIT 307, SURREY, BC, V3W 1A4
SIC 8651

DIASER MANAGEMENT (2006) LTD *p 373*
268 ELLEN ST, WINNIPEG, MB, R3A 1A7
(204) 943-8855   *SIC* 1542

DIAVIK DIAMOND MINES (2012) INC *p 436*
5201 50 AVE SUITE 300, YELLOWKNIFE, NT, X1A 3S9
(867) 669-6500   *SIC* 1499

DIBCO UNDERGROUND LIMITED *p 494*
135 COMMERCIAL RD, BOLTON, ON, L7E 1R6
(905) 857-0458   *SIC* 1622

DIBRINA & ASSOCIATES *p 900*
7 CEDAR ST SUITE 202, SUDBURY, ON, P3E 1A2
(705) 688-9011   *SIC* 6411

DIBRINA SURE BENEFITS CONSULTING INC *p 900*
62 FROOD RD SUITE 302, SUDBURY, ON, P3C 4Z3
(705) 688-9393   *SIC* 6411

DIBRINA SURE FINANCIAL GROUP INC *p 900*
62 FROOD RD SUITE 302, SUDBURY, ON, P3C 4Z3
(705) 688-9011   *SIC* 6282

DIBRINA SURE GROUP *p 900*
See DIBRINA SURE BENEFITS CONSULTING INC

DICA ELECTRONICS LTD *p 540*
160 INDUSTRIAL AVE, CARLETON PLACE, ON, K7C 3T2
(613) 257-5379   *SIC* 3672

DICK'S GARAGE LIMITED *p 861*
967 TRUNK RD, SAULT STE. MARIE, ON, P6A 5K9
(705) 759-1133   *SIC* 5511

DICK, JAMES CONSTRUCTION LIMITED *p 494*
14442 REGIONAL ROAD 50, BOLTON, ON, L7E 3E2
(905) 857-3500   *SIC* 5032

DICK, JAMES HOLDINGS LIMITED *p 494*
14442 REGIONAL RD 50, BOLTON, ON, L7E 3E2
(905) 857-3500   *SIC* 6712

DICKIE MOORE RENTAL *p 1333*
See EQUIPEMENT MOORE LTEE

DICKIE-DEE ICE CREAM VENDING BIKES & TRUCKS *p 371*
530 DUFFERIN AVE, WINNIPEG, MB, R2W 2Y6
(204) 586-5218   *SIC* 5451

DICKINSON MARINE (1997) LTD *p 200*
204 CAYER ST UNIT 407, COQUITLAM, BC, V3K 5B1
(604) 525-4444   *SIC* 5074

DICKINSON WRIGHT LLP *p 969*
222 BAY ST 18TH FL, TORONTO, ON, M5K 1H1
(416) 777-0101   *SIC* 8111

DICKNER INC *p 1284*
559 RUE DE LAUSANNE, RIMOUSKI, QC, G5L 4A7
(418) 723-7936   *SIC* 5084

DICKS AND COMPANY LIMITED *p 433*
385 EMPIRE AVE, ST. JOHN'S, NL, A1E 1W6
(709) 579-5111   *SIC* 5712

DICOCCO CONTRACTORS 2015 INC *p 859*
550 MCGREGOR SIDE RD, SARNIA, ON, N7T 7H5
(519) 344-8446   *SIC* 1521

DICOM TRANSPORTATION GROUP CANADA *p 1094*
See GLS LOGISTICS SYSTEMS CANADA LTD

DICOM TRANSPORTATION GROUP CANADA PARENT, INC *p 1093*
10500 AV RYAN, DORVAL, QC, H9P 2T7
(514) 636-8033   *SIC* 6712

DICOM TRANSPORTATION GROUP CANADA, INC *p 1094*
See GLS LOGISTICS SYSTEMS CANADA LTD

DICRETE CONSTRUCTION LTD *p 551*
71 CREDITSTONE RD, CONCORD, ON, L4K 1N3

(905) 669-9595   *SIC* 1611

DIDI *p 1326*
See NASRI INTERNATIONAL INC

DIDSBURY DISTRICT HEALTH SERVICES *p 82*
See ALBERTA HEALTH SERVICES

DIE-MAX TOOL AND DIE LTD *p 473*
23 BARR RD, AJAX, ON, L1S 3Y1
(905) 619-6554   *SIC* 3544

DIE-MOLD TOOL LIMITED *p 593*
82 TODD RD, GEORGETOWN, ON, L7G 4R7
(905) 877-3071   *SIC* 2821

DIEBOLD COMPANY OF CANADA LIMITED, THE *p 721*
6630 CAMPOBELLO RD, MISSISSAUGA, ON, L5N 2L8
(905) 817-7600   *SIC* 1731

DIEFFENBACHER NORTH AMERICA INC *p 1017*
9495 TWIN OAKS DR, WINDSOR, ON, N8N 5B8
(519) 979-6937   *SIC* 3542

DIELCO INDUSTRIAL CONTRACTORS LTD *p 661*
80 ENTERPRISE DR S, LONDON, ON, N6N 1C2
(519) 685-2224   *SIC* 1796

DIEMAX MANUFACTURING LTD *p 473*
729 FINLEY AVE, AJAX, ON, L1S 3T1
(905) 619-9380   *SIC* 3325

DIEMO MACHINE WORKS INC *p 345*
HWY 326 N, ARBORG, MB, R0C 0A0
(204) 364-2404   *SIC* 3523

DIEPPE AUTO LTEE/LTD *p 397*
600 RUE CHAMPLAIN, DIEPPE, NB, E1A 1P4
(506) 857-0444   *SIC* 5511

DIESEL ELECTRIC SERVICE *p 898*
See 510172 ONTARIO LTD

DIESEL EQUIPMENT LIMITED *p 755*
210 HARRY WALKER PKY N, NEWMARKET, ON, L3Y 7B4
(416) 421-5851   *SIC* 3713

DIESEL MARKETING *p 1212*
See SID LEE INC

DIETER'S METAL FABRICATING LIMITED *p 538*
275 INDUSTRIAL RD, CAMBRIDGE, ON, N3H 4R7
(519) 884-8555   *SIC* 3499

DIETRON TOOL & DIE INC *p 864*
64 MELFORD DR, SCARBOROUGH, ON, M1B 6B7
(416) 297-5858   *SIC* 3544

DIF INFRA IV CANADA LTD *p 980*
100 WELLINGTON ST W, TORONTO, ON, M5V 1E3
(647) 748-2088   *SIC* 6722

DIFCO *p 1195*
See DIFCO, TISSUS DE PERFORMANCE INC

DIFCO, TISSUS DE PERFORMANCE INC *p 1147*
160 RUE PRINCIPALE E, MAGOG, QC, J1X 4X5
SIC 2299

DIFCO, TISSUS DE PERFORMANCE INC *p 1195*
1411 RUE PEEL BUREAU 505, MONTREAL, QC, H3A 1S5
(819) 434-2159   *SIC* 2299

DIFFUSION ARTEQ INC *p 1159*
10 ST-JEAN-BAPTISTE E, MONTMAGNY, QC, G5V 1J7
(418) 248-3332   *SIC* 5199

DIFFUSION DIMEDIA INC *p 1325*
539 BOUL LEBEAU, SAINT-LAURENT, QC, H4N 1S2
(514) 336-3941   *SIC* 5192

DIGBY GENERAL HOSPITAL *p 449*
See NOVA SCOTIA HEALTH AUTHORITY

DIGBY TOWN AND MUNICIPAL HOUSING

CORPORATION, THE *p 449*
74 PLEASANT ST, DIGBY, NS, B0V 1A0
(902) 245-4718   *SIC 8741*

DIGI CANADA INCORPORATED *p 551*
87 MOYAL CRT, CONCORD, ON, L4K 4R8
(905) 879-0833   *SIC 5046*

DIGI117 LTD *p 240*
145 CHADWICK CRT SUITE 220, NORTH VANCOUVER, BC, V7M 3K1
(778) 772-4770   *SIC 7372*

DIGICO FABRICATION ELECTRONIQUE INC *p 1101*
950 RUE BERGAR, FABREVILLE, QC, H7L 5A1
(450) 967-7100   *SIC 8711*

DIGICO RESEAU GLOBAL INC *p 1101*
950 RUE BERGAR, FABREVILLE, QC, H7L 5A1
(450) 967-7100   *SIC 3679*

DIGICON BUILDING CONTROL SOLUTIONS LIMITED *p 446*
201 BROWNLOW AVE UNIT 11, DARTMOUTH, NS, B3B 1W2
(902) 468-2633   *SIC 5084*

DIGIFACTS SYNDICATE *p 190*
4720 KINGSWAY SUITE 900, BURNABY, BC, V5H 4N2
(604) 435-4317   *SIC 8721*

DIGIFLEX *p 1096*
See S.F. MARKETING INC

DIGITAL ATTRACTIONS INC *p 757*
6650 NIAGARA RIVER, NIAGARA FALLS, ON, L2E 6T2
(905) 371-2003   *SIC 7221*

DIGITAL CONCEPT INC *p 942*
1 YONGE ST SUITE 1801, TORONTO, ON, M5E 1W7
SIC 5065

DIGITAL PAYMENT TECHNOLOGIES CORP *p 185*
4260 STILL CREEK DR SUITE 330, BURNABY, BC, V5C 6C6
(604) 317-4055   *SIC 3824*

DIGITAL SECURITY CONTROLS *p 560*
See TYCO SAFETY PRODUCTS CANADA LTD

DIGITAL SPECIALTY CHEMICALS LIMITED *p 866*
470 CORONATION DR, SCARBOROUGH, ON, M1E 4Y4
(416) 231-2991   *SIC 2819*

DIGITCOM CANADA *p 783*
See DIGITCOM TELECOMMUNICATIONS CANADA INC

DIGITCOM TELECOMMUNICATIONS CANADA INC *p 783*
250 RIMROCK RD, NORTH YORK, ON, M3J 3A6
(416) 783-7890   *SIC 5999*

DIGITEL SYSTEMS INC *p 260*
10851 SHELLBRIDGE WAY SUITE 110, RICHMOND, BC, V6X 2W8
(604) 231-0101   *SIC 5999*

DIGITEX CANADA INC *p 157*
130 LEVA AVE, RED DEER COUNTY, AB, T4E 1B9
(403) 309-3341   *SIC 5044*

DIGNITY TRANSPORTATION INC *p 669*
50 MCINTOSH DR SUITE 110, MARKHAM, ON, L3R 9T3
(905) 470-2399   *SIC 4111*

DILAWRI AUTOMOTIVE GROUP *p 830*
See 765620 ONTARIO INC

DILAWRI CHEVROLET BUICK GMC INC *p 1104*
868 BOUL MALONEY O, GATINEAU, QC, J8T 3R6
(819) 568-5811   *SIC 5511*

DILAWRI HOLDINGS INC *p 390*
1700 WAVERLEY ST SUITE C, WINNIPEG, MB, R3T 5V7
(204) 269-1572   *SIC 5511*

DILAWRI JEEP DODGE CHRYSLER *p 748*

See 709226 ONTARIO LIMITED

DILFO MECHANICAL LIMITED *p 595*
1481 CYRVILLE RD, GLOUCESTER, ON, K1B 3L7
(613) 741-7731   *SIC 1711*

DILICO ANISHINABEK FAMILY CARE *p 592*
200 ANEMKI PL SUITE 1, FORT WILLIAM FIRST NATION, ON, P7J 1L6
(807) 623-8511   *SIC 8399*

DILL, W.C. & COMPANY INC *p 896*
PERTH LINE SUITE 26, STRATFORD, ON, N5A 6S3
SIC 7389

DILLABOUGH, D M HOLDINGS LIMITED *p 346*
1655 18TH ST, BRANDON, MB, R7A 5C6
SIC 5399

DILLON CONSULTING LIMITED *p 390*
1558 WILLSON PL, WINNIPEG, MB, R3T 0Y4
(204) 453-2301   *SIC 8711*

DILLON CONSULTING LIMITED *p 653*
130 DUFFERIN AVE SUITE 1400, LONDON, ON, N6A 5R2
(519) 438-6192   *SIC 8711*

DILLON CONSULTING LIMITED *p 767*
235 YORKLAND BLVD SUITE 800, NORTH YORK, ON, M2J 4Y8
(416) 229-4646   *SIC 8711*

DILLON CONSULTING MANAGEMENT *p 653*
See DILLON CONSULTING LIMITED

DIMA IMPORT-EXPORT INC *p 1239*
12020 BOUL ALBERT-HUDON, MONTREAL-NORD, QC, H1G 3K7
(514) 955-7295   *SIC 5149*

DIMATEC INC *p 385*
180 CREE CRES, WINNIPEG, MB, R3J 3W1
(204) 832-2828   *SIC 5084*

DIMCO DL INC *p 1162*
8601 BOUL HENRI-BOURASSA E, MONTREAL, QC, H1E 1P4
(514) 494-1001   *SIC 1611*

DIMENSION 3 HOSPITALITY CORPORATION *p 1424*
1139 8TH ST E, SASKATOON, SK, S7H 0S3
(306) 249-2882   *SIC 7011*

DIMENSION COMPOSITE INC *p 1305*
2530 95E RUE, SAINT-GEORGES, QC, G6A 1E3
(418) 228-0212   *SIC 3296*

DIMENSION DOORS *p 1061*
See DIMENSIONS PORTES ET FENETRES INC

DIMENSION HUMAINE *p 1242*
See SOGETEL INC

DIMENSIONS PORTES ET FENETRES INC *p 1061*
4065 RUE ALFRED-LALIBERTE, BOISBRIAND, QC, J7H 1P7
(450) 430-4486   *SIC 5031*

DIMERCO EXPRESS (CANADA) CORPORATION *p 694*
5100 ORBITOR DR SUITE 201, MISSISSAUGA, ON, L4W 4Z4
(905) 282-8118   *SIC 4731*

DIMPFLMEIER BAKERY LIMITED *p 574*
26 ADVANCE RD, ETOBICOKE, ON, M8Z 2T4
(416) 236-2701   *SIC 2051*

DIMPLEX NORTH AMERICA HOLDINGS LIMITED *p 538*
1367 INDUSTRIAL RD, CAMBRIDGE, ON, N3H 4W3
(519) 650-3630   *SIC 6712*

DINAMIX ALLIANCE INC *p 891*
35 SUNNYHURST AVE SUITE 2, STONEY CREEK, ON, L8E 5M9
(905) 643-9979   *SIC 5142*

DINEEN CONSTRUCTION CORPORATION *p 583*

70 DISCO RD SUITE 300, ETOBICOKE, ON, M9W 1L9
(416) 675-7676   *SIC 1541*

DINERS CLUB-EN ROUTE *p 961*
See CITIBANK CANADA

DINESEN NURSERIES LTD *p 179*
2110 272 ST, ALDERGROVE, BC, V4W 2R1
(604) 856-2290   *SIC 0181*

DINGWALL FORD SALES LTD *p 628*
927 HIGHWAY 17 E, KENORA, ON, P9N 1L9
(807) 468-6443   *SIC 5511*

DINGWELL'S MACHINERY AND SUPPLY LIMITED *p 908*
963 ALLOY DR, THUNDER BAY, ON, P7B 5Z8
(807) 623-4477   *SIC 3499*

DINO'S NOFRILLS *p 788*
See 1692038 ONTARIO LTD

DINOFF, S. DRUGS LIMITED *p 988*
523 ST CLAIR AVE W, TORONTO, ON, M6C 1A1
(416) 538-1155   *SIC 5912*

DINSDALE PERSONAL CARE HOME *p 346*
See GOVERNING COUNCIL OF THE SALVATION ARMY IN CANADA, THE

DIOCESE OF LONDON *p 655*
See ROMAN CATHOLIC EPISCOPAL CORPORATION OF THE DIOCESE OF LONDON IN ONTARIO, THE

DION MOTO INC *p 1351*
840 COTE JOYEUSE, SAINT-RAYMOND, QC, G3L 4B3
(418) 337-2776   *SIC 5571*

DION SERVICES FINANCIERS *p 1289*
1380 AV LARIVIERE, ROUYN-NORANDA, QC, J9X 4L1
(819) 797-4400   *SIC 6351*

DION, DURRELL & ASSOCIATES INC *p 935*
250 YONGE ST SUITE 2, TORONTO, ON, M5B 2L7
(416) 408-2626   *SIC 8999*

DIONDE INC *p 1101*
1660 BOUL INDUSTRIEL, FARNHAM, QC, J2N 2X8
(450) 293-3909   *SIC 6719*

DIPIETRO *p 533*
See DIPIETRO FRESH MEAT & DELICATESSEN LTD

DIPIETRO FRESH MEAT & DELICATESSEN LTD *p 533*
30 GLAMIS RD, CAMBRIDGE, ON, N1R 7H5
(519) 622-3222   *SIC 5411*

DIPLOMAT RESTAURANT, THE *p 401*
See KIL INVESTMENTS LTD

DIRCAM ELECTRIC LIMITED *p 583*
42 STEINWAY BLVD SUITE 10, ETOBICOKE, ON, M9W 6Y6
(416) 798-1115   *SIC 1731*

DIRECT ACTION IN SUPPORT OF COMMUNITY HOMES INCORPORATED *p 388*
117 VICTOR LEWIS DR UNIT 1, WINNIPEG, MB, R3P 1J6
(204) 987-1550   *SIC 8361*

DIRECT ALERT *p 1341*
See REVISION SECURITY INC

DIRECT BUY *p 667*
See BUYERS GROUP OF MISSISSAUGA INC

DIRECT CASH (LNET) *p 10*
1420 28 ST NE SUITE 6, CALGARY, AB, T2A 7W6
(403) 207-1500   *SIC 6099*

DIRECT DIAL.COM *p 655*
See THINQ TECHNOLOGIES LTD

DIRECT ENERGY *p 575*
See MARTIN AIR HEATING & AIR CONDITIONING SERVICES LIMITED

DIRECT ENERGY *p 1034*
See UNITED THERMO GROUP LTD

DIRECT ENERGY ESSENTIAL HOME SERVICES, DIV OF *p 47*

See DIRECT ENERGY MARKETING LIMITED

DIRECT ENERGY HOME SERVICES *p 814*
See PERRY MECHANICAL INC

DIRECT ENERGY MARKETING LIMITED *p 47*
525 8 AVE SW UNIT 1200, CALGARY, AB, T2P 1G1
(403) 776-2000   *SIC 1311*

DIRECT ENERGY MARKETING LIMITED *p 48*
111 5 AVE SW SUITE 1000, CALGARY, AB, T2P 3Y6
(403) 266-6393   *SIC 1311*

DIRECT ENERGY PARTNERSHIP *p 48*
525 8 AVE SW SUITE 501, CALGARY, AB, T2P 1G1
(403) 261-9810   *SIC 1731*

DIRECT EQUIPMENT LTD *p 800*
1363 CORNWALL RD, OAKVILLE, ON, L6J 7T5
(905) 844-7831   *SIC 5082*

DIRECT FIRE PROTECTION SYSTEMS *p 581*
See 6232698 CANADA INC

DIRECT FOCUS *p 373*
See DIRECT FOCUS MARKETING COMMUNICATIONS INC

DIRECT FOCUS MARKETING COMMUNICATIONS INC *p 373*
315 PACIFIC AVE, WINNIPEG, MB, R3A 0M2
(204) 947-6912   *SIC 8743*

DIRECT HORIZONTAL DRILLING INC *p 1*
26308 TWP RD 531A SUITE 3, ACHESON, AB, T7X 5A3
(780) 960-6037   *SIC 1381*

DIRECT LIMITED PARTNERSHIP *p 15*
5555 69 AVE SE SUITE 121, CALGARY, AB, T2C 4Y7
(403) 296-0291   *SIC 4212*

DIRECT LIMITED PARTNERSHIP *p 734*
1115 CARDIFF BLVD, MISSISSAUGA, ON, L5S 1L8
(905) 564-2115   *SIC 4212*

DIRECT LIQUIDATION *p 182*
See J.L. & SONS TRADING COMPANY LTD

DIRECT MOTOR COMPANY LTD *p 597*
2575 BANK ST, GLOUCESTER, ON, K1T 1M8
(613) 739-3088   *SIC 5511*

DIRECT MULTI-PAK MAILING LTD *p 669*
20 TORBAY RD, MARKHAM, ON, L3R 1G6
(905) 415-1940   *SIC 7331*

DIRECT NISSAN *p 721*
See CHIVA AUTO GOUP INC

DIRECT PLASTICS LTD *p 808*
20 STEWART CRT, ORANGEVILLE, ON, L9W 3Z9
(519) 942-8511   *SIC 2673*

DIRECT POULTRY *p 573*
See ADP DIRECT POULTRY LTD

DIRECT SALES, DIV OF *p 166*
See NILSSON BROS. INC

DIRECT SOURCE INC *p 1130*
2695 AV DOLLARD, LASALLE, QC, H8N 2J8
(514) 363-8882   *SIC 7389*

DIRECT SUPPORT CARE INC *p 755*
236 PARKVIEW CRES, NEWMARKET, ON, L3Y 2C8
(905) 895-5800   *SIC 8049*

DIRECT TIMBER INC *p 813*
1181 THORNTON RD S SUITE 1, OSHAWA, ON, L1J 8P4
(905) 571-4341   *SIC 5031*

DIRECT TRAFFIC CONTROL INC *p 467*
180 CHARLOTTE ST, SYDNEY, NS, B1P 1C5
(902) 564-8402   *SIC 7389*

DIRECT TRAFFIC MANAGEMENT INC *p 612*

70 FRID ST SUITE 8, HAMILTON, ON, L8P 4M4
(905) 529-7000   *SIC* 7389
DIRECT TRANSPORT   *p* 15
See *DIRECT LIMITED PARTNERSHIP*
DIRECT WEST CORPORATION   *p* 1415
355 LONGMAN CRES, REGINA, SK, S4N 6G3
(306) 777-0333   *SIC* 7319
DIRECTCASH PAYMENTS ULC   *p* 687
See *CARDTRONICS CANADA HOLDINGS INC*
DIRECTEUR DE POURSUITES CRIM-INELLES ET PENALES   *p* 1188
See *GOUVERNEMENT DE LA PROVINCE DE QUEBEC*
DIRECTION DE LA MAINTENANCE DES AERONEFS DU SERVICE AERIEN   *p* 1257
See *GOUVERNEMENT DE LA PROVINCE DE QUEBEC*
DIRECTION DES LABORATOIRES D'EXPERTISES ET D'ANALYSES ALI-MENTAIRES   *p* 1267
See *GOUVERNEMENT DE LA PROVINCE DE QUEBEC*
DIRECTION DES RESSOURCES HU-MAINES   *p* 1177
See *VILLE DE MONTREAL*
DIRECTION REGIONAL EMPLOI QUEBEC   *p* 1188
See *GOUVERNEMENT DE LA PROVINCE DE QUEBEC*
DIRECTIONS EAST TRADING LIMITED   *p* 783
995 FINCH AVE W, NORTH YORK, ON, M3J 2C7
(416) 661-7188   *SIC* 5632
DIRECTOR'S CHOICE   *p* 414
See *NIGHT SHIFT ANSWERING SERVICE LTD, THE*
DIRHAM CONSTRUCTION LTD   *p* 131
10127 121 AVE UNIT 201, GRANDE PRAIRIE, AB, T8V 7V3
(780) 539-4776   *SIC* 1521
DIRHAM HOMES, DIV OF   *p* 131
See *DIRHAM CONSTRUCTION LTD*
DIRK ENTERPRISES LTD   *p* 88
10235 101 ST NW SUITE 800, EDMON-TON, AB, T5J 3G1
(780) 944-9994   *SIC* 6712
DIRTT ENVIRONMENTAL SOLUTIONS LTD   *p* 15
7303 30 ST SE, CALGARY, AB, T2C 1N6
(403) 723-5000   *SIC* 2522
DISABILITY CONCEPTS INC   *p* 48
736 6 AVE SW SUITE 1500, CALGARY, AB, T2P 3T7
(403) 262-2080   *SIC* 6411
DISBROWE PONTIAC BUICK CADILLAC LTD   *p* 889
116 EDWARD ST, ST THOMAS, ON, N5P 4E6
(519) 631-2224   *SIC* 5511
DISCOUNT CAR & TRUCK RENTAL   *p* 795
See *NEW HORIZONS CAR & TRUCK RENTALS LTD*
DISCOUNT CAR & TRUCK RENTALS *p* 409
See *MONDART HOLDINGS LIMITED*
DISCOUNTERS WAREHOUSE DIV.   *p* 1002
See *CONSTRUCTION DISTRIBUTION & SUPPLY COMPANY INC*
DISCOVER BATTERY   *p* 254
See *DISCOVER ENERGY CORP*
DISCOVER ENERGY CORP   *p* 254
13511 CRESTWOOD PL UNIT 4, RICH-MOND, BC, V6V 2E9
(778) 776-3288   *SIC* 5013
DISCOVERY AIR DEFENCE SERVICES INC   *p* 1091
See *TOP ACES INC*
DISCOVERY AIR INC   *p* 436

126 CRYSTAL AVE, YELLOWKNIFE, NT, X1A 2P3
(867) 873-5350   *SIC* 4522
DISCOVERY CANADA MERCHANDISERS LTD   *p* 385
311 SAULTEAUX CRES, WINNIPEG, MB, R3J 3C7
(204) 885-7792   *SIC* 5084
DISCOVERY FOODS LTD   *p* 194
2207 GLENMORE RD UNIT 1, CAMPBELL RIVER, BC, V9H 1E1
(250) 923-7733   *SIC* 5411
DISCOVERY FORD SALES BURLINGTON LIMITED   *p* 530
850 BRANT ST, BURLINGTON, ON, L7R 2J5
(905) 632-8696   *SIC* 5511
DISCOVERY HONDA   *p* 211
See *DISCOVERY MOTORS LTD*
DISCOVERY ISLANDS ORGANICS LTD   *p* 294
880 MALKIN AVE, VANCOUVER, BC, V6A 2K6
(604) 299-1684   *SIC* 5149
DISCOVERY MOTORS LTD   *p* 211
6466 BELL MCKINNON RD, DUNCAN, BC, V9L 6C1
(250) 748-5814   *SIC* 5511
DISCOVERY ORGANICS   *p* 294
See *DISCOVERY ISLANDS ORGANICS LTD*
DISHON LIMITED   *p* 551
40 CITATION DR, CONCORD, ON, L4K 2W9
(416) 638-8900   *SIC* 3545
DISMED   *p* 550
See *CARDINAL HEALTH CANADA INC*
DISNEY CANADA INC   *p* 221
1628 DICKSON AVE SUITE 500, KELOWNA, BC, V1Y 9X1
(250) 868-8622   *SIC* 7374
DISNEY INTERACTIVE WORLD   *p* 221
See *DISNEY CANADA INC*
DISPENSARIES WHOLESALE (1991) LIM-ITED   *p* 92
10326 112 ST NW, EDMONTON, AB, T5K 1N2
(780) 426-1664   *SIC* 5122
DISPLAY-CORR   *p* 1050
See *PROMAG DISPLAYCORR CANADA INC*
DISPLAY-VU CORP   *p* 735
7045 BECKETT DR UNIT 15, MISSIS-SAUGA, ON, L5S 2A3
(416) 674-2123   *SIC* 5065
DISPRO INC   *p* 1048
10280 BOUL RAY-LAWSON, ANJOU, QC, H1J 1L8
(514) 354-5251   *SIC* 5033
DISTAMAX INC   *p* 1384
522 RUE DES ERABLES, TROIS-RIVIERES, QC, G8T 7Z6
(819) 375-2147   *SIC* 5148
DISTECH CONTROLES INC   *p* 1070
4205 PLACE JAVA, BROSSARD, QC, J4Y 0C4
(450) 444-9898   *SIC* 3822
DISTICOR DIRECT RETAILER SERVICES INC   *p* 473
695 WESTNEY RD S UNIT 14, AJAX, ON, L1S 6M9
(905) 619-6565   *SIC* 5192
DISTICOR MAGAZINE DISTRIBUTION SERVICES   *p* 814
See *MICROVITE INVESTMENTS LIMITED*
DISTIL INTERACTIVE LTD   *p* 751
16 FITZGERALD RD SUITE 200, NEPEAN, ON, K2H 8R6
SIC 5092
DISTILLERIES SAZERAC DU CANADA INC, LES   *p* 1210
950 CH DES MOULINS, MONTREAL, QC, H3C 3W5
(514) 395-3200   *SIC* 5182

DISTINCT INFRASTRUCTURE GROUP INC   *p* 583
77 BELFIELD RD UNIT 102, ETOBICOKE, ON, M9W 1G6
(416) 675-6485   *SIC* 1623
DISTINCTION BY SODEXO   *p* 1108
See *SODEXO QUEBEC LIMITEE*
DISTINCTION, LA   *p* 1114
See *9064-4048 QUEBEC INC*
DISTINCTIVE APPLIANCES INC   *p* 1237
2025 RUE CUNARD, MONTREAL, QC, H7S 2N1
(450) 687-6311   *SIC* 5064
DISTINCTIVE AUTOBODY & COLLISON CENTER LTD   *p* 413
1265 LOCH LOMOND RD, SAINT JOHN, NB, E2J 3V4
(506) 634-1765   *SIC* 5511
DISTINCTIVE HOMES   *p* 661
See *1376302 ONTARIO INC*
DISTRI-CARR LTEE   *p* 1264
214 AV SAINT-SACREMENT BUREAU 130, QUEBEC, QC, G1N 3X6
SIC 6712
DISTRIBU-PNEUS   *p* 1064
See *DISTRIBUTION STOX INC*
DISTRIBUTEL COMMUNICATIONS LIM-ITED   *p* 833
177 NEPEAN ST UNIT 300, OTTAWA, ON, K2P 0B4
(613) 237-7055   *SIC* 4899
DISTRIBUTEL COMMUNICATIONS LIM-ITED   *p* 995
3300 BLOOR ST W SUITE 800, TORONTO, ON, M8X 2X2
(416) 324-2861   *SIC* 4899
DISTRIBUTEUR DE PARE-BRISE ATLAN-TIQUE   *p* 1361
See *P.H. VITRES D'AUTOS INC*
DISTRIBUTEUR H. MIRON   *p* 1225
See *DISTRIBUTION MFG INC*
DISTRIBUTEURS D'ALIMENTS DEFEDIS INC   *p* 1363
755 CHOMEDEY (A-13) E, SAINTE-ROSE, QC, H7W 5N4
(450) 681-9500   *SIC* 5141
DISTRIBUTEURS ESSEX CONTINENTALE INC, LES   *p* 1225
985 RUE DU MARCHE-CENTRAL, MON-TREAL, QC, H4N 1K2
(514) 745-1222   *SIC* 5148
DISTRIBUTEURS JARDEL INC, LES *p* 1339
7575 RTE TRANSCANADIENNE BUREAU 405, SAINT-LAURENT, QC, H4T 1V6
(514) 321-3983   *SIC* 5112
DISTRIBUTEURS PAPINEAU   *p* 1289
See *MARCEL BARIL LTEE*
DISTRIBUTEURS TOWN LTEE   *p* 1156
5473 RUE PARE, MONT-ROYAL, QC, H4P 1P7
(514) 735-4555   *SIC* 5122
DISTRIBUTION AD WATERS (CAN) INC   *p* 1217
9805 RUE CLARK, MONTREAL, QC, H3L 2R5
(514) 381-4141   *SIC* 5074
DISTRIBUTION AVICO   *p* 1264
See *EMBALLAGE AVICO INC*
DISTRIBUTION B2U   *p* 1128
See *GROUPE CDREM INC*
DISTRIBUTION BATH FITTER INC   *p* 1301
225 RUE ROY, SAINT-EUSTACHE, QC, J7R 5R5
(450) 472-0024   *SIC* 5211
DISTRIBUTION BEN-MAR '90'   *p* 1162
See *EMBALLAGE D'ALIMENTS LATINA INC*
DISTRIBUTION CLUB TISSUS (1994) INC *p* 1308
1651 BOUL DES PROMENADES BUREAU 676, SAINT-HUBERT, QC, J3Y 5K2

(450) 462-1717   *SIC* 5949
DISTRIBUTION COTE-NORD INC   *p* 1052
12 AV ROMEO-VEZINA, BAIE-COMEAU, QC, G4Z 2W2
(418) 296-3300   *SIC* 5142
DISTRIBUTION COUCHE-TARD INC *p* 1234
4204 BOUL INDUSTRIEL, MONTREAL, QC, H7L 0E3
(450) 662-6663   *SIC* 5199
DISTRIBUTION D.M.C.   *p* 1115
See *GROUPE LD INC*
DISTRIBUTION DENIS JALBERT INC   *p* 1266
2620 AV WATT, QUEBEC, QC, G1P 3T5
(418) 658-4640   *SIC* 6712
DISTRIBUTION DIRECTE   *p* 1337
See *9248-5523 QUEBEC INC*
DISTRIBUTION DU PHARE   *p* 1049
See *KARLO CORPORATION SUPPLY & SERVICES*
DISTRIBUTION EPICERIE C.T.S. INC   *p* 1127
5025 RUE FRANCOIS-CUSSON, LA-CHINE, QC, H8T 3K1
(514) 335-3586   *SIC* 5141
DISTRIBUTION EURO STYLE   *p* 1337
See *VETEMENTS EFG INC*
DISTRIBUTION FANA SPORTS   *p* 1344
See *FANA SPORTS INC*
DISTRIBUTION FARINEX   *p* 1061
See *113712 CANADA INC*
DISTRIBUTION FISHER CAPESPAN CANADA   *p* 1339
6700 CH DE LA COTE-DE-LIESSE BU-REAU 301, SAINT-LAURENT, QC, H4T 2B5
(514) 739-9181   *SIC* 5148
DISTRIBUTION FLORALE SIERRA   *p* 1337
See *1801794 ONTARIO INC*
DISTRIBUTION FROMAGERIE BOIVIN   *p* 1121
See *2737-2895 QUEBEC INC*
DISTRIBUTION GROUP INCORPORATED *p* 433
99 BLACKMARSH RD, ST. JOHN'S, NL, A1E 1S6
(709) 579-2151   *SIC* 5046
DISTRIBUTION HARTCO   *p* 1048
See *DISTRIBUTION HARTCO SOCIETE EN COMMANDITE*
DISTRIBUTION HARTCO SOCIETE EN COMMANDITE   *p* 1048
9393 RUE LOUIS-H.-LAFONTAINE, AN-JOU, QC, H1J 1Z1
(514) 354-3810   *SIC* 5045
DISTRIBUTION HARTCO SOCIETE EN COMMANDITE   *p* 1048
9393 BOUL METROPOLITAIN E, ANJOU, QC, H1J 3C7
(514) 354-0580   *SIC* 5734
DISTRIBUTION HMH INC   *p* 1174
1815 AV DE LORIMIER, MONTREAL, QC, H2K 3W6
(514) 523-1523   *SIC* 5192
DISTRIBUTION HORIZON NATURE   *p* 1345
See *9141-1967 QUEBEC INC*
DISTRIBUTION IRIS   *p* 1379
See *LABORATOIRES LALCO INC*
DISTRIBUTION JEAN BLANCHARD INC   *p* 1375
1686 CH LALIBERTE, SHERBROOKE, QC, J1R 0C5
(819) 820-9777   *SIC* 5083
DISTRIBUTION JO-AL   *p* 1161
See *JO-AL DISTRIBUTING LTD*
DISTRIBUTION JOCA   *p* 1152
See *METAUX M.P.I. INC*
DISTRIBUTION LAURENT LEBLANC INC *p* 1317
370 RUE SAINT-LOUIS, SAINT-JEAN-SUR-RICHELIEU, QC, J3B 1Y4
(450) 346-7044   *SIC* 5088
DISTRIBUTION LE PERCO INC   *p* 1314
16535 AV PETIT, SAINT-HYACINTHE, QC, J2T 3J5

▲ Public Company   ■ Public Company Family Member   **HQ** Headquarters   **BR** Branch   **SL** Single Location

(450) 773-7146   *SIC 5962*

DISTRIBUTION LPB 2012   *p 1055*
See PNEUS BEAUCERONS INC, LES

DISTRIBUTION MFG INC   *p 1225*
387 RUE DESLAURIERS, MONTREAL, QC, H4N 1W2
(514) 344-5558   *SIC 5143*

DISTRIBUTION MIRAGE PHARMA   *p 1067*
See PROMOTIONS C.D. INC

DISTRIBUTION MMO   *p 1147*
See 4361806 CANADA INC

DISTRIBUTION NOW   *p 48*
See DNOW CANADA ULC

DISTRIBUTION OF HOLTON RECYCLING *p* 381
See HALTON RECYCLING LTD

DISTRIBUTION P.D.G.   *p 1066*
See ISN CANADA GROUP HOLDINGS INC

DISTRIBUTION PARAL   *p 1057*
See PARENT, ALAIN INC

DISTRIBUTION PHARMAPLUS INC *p 1276*
2905 RUE DE CELLES BUREAU 102, QUEBEC, QC, G2C 1W7
(418) 667-5499   *SIC 5122*

DISTRIBUTION PRAXAIR   *p 710*
See PRAXAIR CANADA INC

DISTRIBUTION PRO-PLAST   *p 1364*
See CONTREPLAQUE & PLACAGE CANADA INC

DISTRIBUTION PROPUR   *p 1291*
See LEGUPRO INC

DISTRIBUTION SINOMEX   *p 1248*
See 9156-0763 QUEBEC INC

DISTRIBUTION SOGITEX INC   *p 1390*
1201 RUE DES MANUFACTURIERS, VAL-D'OR, QC, J9P 6Y7
(819) 825-2331   *SIC 5169*

DISTRIBUTION SOMAK   *p 1235*
See SILHOUET-TONE CORPORATION

DISTRIBUTION ST-DAVID   *p 1053*
See CIE CANADA TIRE INC, LA

DISTRIBUTION STE-FOY (1982) LTEE *p* 1266
685 AV NEWTON, QUEBEC, QC, G1P 4C4
(418) 871-8133   *SIC 5039*

DISTRIBUTION STOX INC   *p 1064*
235   RUE   J.-A.-BOMBARDIER, BOUCHERVILLE, QC, J4B 8P1
(450) 449-0362   *SIC 5014*

DISTRIBUTION TOITURE MAURICIENNE *p* 1385
See STRUCTURES BARRETTE INC

DISTRIBUTION TTI   *p 1138*
See MTI CANADA INC

DISTRIBUTION VENDING PRODUCT DU CANADA   *p 589*
See VENDING PRODUCTS OF CANADA LIMITED

DISTRIBUTION VIANDES DECARIE *p 1047*
See 9395-8098 QUEBEC INC

DISTRIBUTION VTL   *p 1337*
See 9052-9025 QUEBEC INC

DISTRIBUTION WESTCO INC   *p 416*
9 RUE WESTCO, SAINT-FRANCOIS-DE-MADAWASKA, NB, E7A 1A5
(506) 992-3112   *SIC 5191*

DISTRIBUTIONNOW   *p 122*
See DNOW CANADA ULC

DISTRIBUTIONS AGRI-SOL INC   *p 1225*
1509 RUE ANTONIO-BARBEAU, MONTREAL, QC, H4N 2R5
(514) 381-4804   *SIC 5148*

DISTRIBUTIONS ALIMENTAIRES B.L.P. *p* 1233
See 149942 CANADA INC

DISTRIBUTIONS ALIMENTAIRES LE MARQUIS INC   *p* 1064
1250 RUE NOBEL BUREAU 190, BOUCHERVILLE, QC, J4B 5H1
(450) 655-4764   *SIC 5141*

DISTRIBUTIONS ALIMENTAIRES LE MARQUIS INC   *p* 1064

1630 RUE EIFFEL BUREAU 1, BOUCHERVILLE, QC, J4B 7W1
(450) 645-1999   *SIC 7389*

DISTRIBUTIONS ALIMENTAIRES MANSION INC, LES   *p* 1072
255 AV LIBERTE, CANDIAC, QC, J5R 3X8
(450) 632-5088   *SIC 5142*

DISTRIBUTIONS B.M.B. (1985) S.E.C. , LES *p* 1231
4500 RUE BERNARD-LEFEBVRE, MONTREAL, QC, H7C 0A5
(514) 382-6520   *SIC 5039*

DISTRIBUTIONS BEAULAC, CARL INC, LES   *p 1138*
15 RUE DES EMERAUDES, LEVIS, QC, G6W 6Y7
(418) 835-1414   *SIC 4213*

DISTRIBUTIONS BELLUCCI LTEE, LES *p* 1180
8145 BOUL SAINT-LAURENT, MONTREAL, QC, H2P 2M1
(514) 388-1555   *SIC 5046*

DISTRIBUTIONS CHRISTIAN DUGAS *p* 1235
See 2747-8353 QUEBEC INC

DISTRIBUTIONS CHRISTIAN PELLERIN INC   *p 1058*
719 BOUL INDUSTRIEL BUREAU 101, BLAINVILLE, QC, J7C 3V3
(450) 434-4641   *SIC 5149*

DISTRIBUTIONS D'ACIER ANICA INC, LES *p 1053*
540 AV FIRING, BAIE-D'URFE, QC, H9X 3T2
(514) 457-3071   *SIC 5051*

DISTRIBUTIONS FRANCO   *p 1263*
See 9217-5041 QUEBEC INC

DISTRIBUTIONS GYPCO (1988) INC *p* 1048
9550 BOUL RAY-LAWSON, ANJOU, QC, H1J 1L3
(514) 352-0150   *SIC 5072*

DISTRIBUTIONS J.R.V. INC   *p 1367*
818 BOUL LAURE BUREAU 101, SEPT-ILES, QC, G4R 1Y8
(418) 962-9457   *SIC 5085*

DISTRIBUTIONS JOSEE PERRAULT INC *p* 1281
3285 1E AV BUREAU 100, RAWDON, QC, J0K 1S0
(450) 834-2582   *SIC 5912*

DISTRIBUTIONS LMC LTEE, LES   *p 1378*
600 CH DU HIBOU, STONEHAM-ET-TEWKESBURY, QC, G3C 1T3
(418) 848-2415   *SIC 5941*

DISTRIBUTIONS MAROLINE INC   *p 1216*
751 RUE RICHARDSON BUREAU 4600, MONTREAL, QC, H3K 1G6
(514) 343-0448   *SIC 5064*

DISTRIBUTIONS MISSUM INC   *p 1101*
3838 BOUL LEMAN, FABREVILLE, QC, H7E 1A1
(450) 661-0281   *SIC 5141*

DISTRIBUTIONS MONDOUX, LES   *p 1083*
See CONFISERIE MONDOUX INC

DISTRIBUTIONS MONTREX INC, LES *p* 1157
5934 CH DE LA COTE-DE-LIESSE, MONT-ROYAL, QC, H4T 2A5
(514) 737-8929   *SIC 5961*

DISTRIBUTIONS MULTI-PRO INC   *p 1344*
8480 RUE CHAMP D'EAU, SAINT-LEONARD, QC, H1P 1Y3
(514) 955-1128   *SIC 5169*

DISTRIBUTIONS N.G.A   *p 1098*
See ENTREPRISES N.G.A. INC, LES

DISTRIBUTIONS NORYVE INC   *p 1046*
76 1RE AV O BUREAU 108, AMOS, QC, J9T 1T8
(819) 732-3306   *SIC 5912*

DISTRIBUTIONS PAUL-EMILE DUBE LTEE *p 1384*
489 RUE NOTRE-DAME E RR 1, TROIS-PISTOLES, QC, G0L 4K0

(418) 851-1862   *SIC 5147*

DISTRIBUTIONS YVAN NADEAU INC, LES *p 1377*
11 RANG SAINT-LEON N, STANDON, QC, G0R 4L0
(418) 642-5035   *SIC 5145*

DISTRIBUTRICES AUTOMATIQUES BEN, LES   *p 1140*
See 128388 CANADA INC

DISTRICT M INC   *p 1183*
5455 AV DE GASPE BUREAU 730, MONTREAL, QC, H2T 3B3
(888) 881-6930   *SIC 7311*

DISTRICT MUNICIPALITY OF MUSKOKA, THE   *p 496*
98 PINE ST SUITE 610, BRACEBRIDGE, ON, P1L 1N5
(705) 645-4488   *SIC 8051*

DISTRICT OF NIPPISSING SOCIAL SERVICES ADMINISTRATION BOARD   *p* 763
200 MCINTYRE ST E, NORTH BAY, ON, P1B 8V6
(705) 474-2151   *SIC 8399*

DISTRICT OF NORTH VANCOUVER MUNICIPAL PU   *p* 239
165 13TH ST E, NORTH VANCOUVER, BC, V7L 2L3
(604) 980-5021   *SIC 7389*

DISTRICT OF PARRY SOUND (WEST) BELVEDERE HEIGHTS HOME FOR THE AGED   *p 837*
21 BELVEDERE AVE, PARRY SOUND, ON, P2A 2A2
(705) 746-5871   *SIC 8361*

DISTRICT OF TIMISKAMING SOCIAL SERVICES ADMINISTRATION BOARD   *p* 634
29 DUNCAN AVE S, KIRKLAND LAKE, ON, P2N 1X5
(705) 567-9366   *SIC 8611*

DISTRICT OF WEST KELOWNA   *p 342*
3651 OLD OKANAGAN HWY, WESTBANK, BC, V4T 1P6
(250) 769-1640   *SIC 7389*

DISTRICT OF WEST KELOWNA FIRE DEPARTMENT   *p* 342
See DISTRICT OF WEST KELOWNA

DISTRICT REALTY CORPORATION   *p 828*
50 BAYSWATER AVE, OTTAWA, ON, K1Y 2E9
(613) 759-8383   *SIC 6531*

DISTRICT SCHOOL BOARD OF NIAGARA *p 591*
350 HWY 20 W, FONTHILL, ON, L0S 1E0
(905) 892-2635   *SIC 8211*

DISTRICT SCHOOL BOARD OF NIAGARA *p 599*
5 BOULTON AVE, GRIMSBY, ON, L3M 1H6
(905) 945-5416   *SIC 8211*

DISTRICT SCHOOL BOARD OF NIAGARA *p 760*
5960 PITTON RD, NIAGARA FALLS, ON, L2H 1T5
(905) 356-2401   *SIC 8211*

DISTRICT SCHOOL BOARD OF NIAGARA *p 846*
255 OMER AVE, PORT COLBORNE, ON, L3K 3Z1
(905) 834-9732   *SIC 8211*

DISTRICT SCHOOL BOARD OF NIAGARA *p 885*
34 CATHERINE ST, ST CATHARINES, ON, L2R 5E7
(905) 687-7301   *SIC 8211*

DISTRICT SCHOOL BOARD OF NIAGARA *p 885*
91 BUNTING RD, ST CATHARINES, ON, L2P 3G8
(905) 684-9461   *SIC 8211*

DISTRICT SCHOOL BOARD ONTARIO NORTH EAST   *p 634*

GD, KIRKLAND LAKE, ON, P2N 3P4
(705) 567-4981   *SIC 8211*

DISTRICT SCHOOL BOARD ONTARIO NORTH EAST   *p 753*
90 NIVEN ST, NEW LISKEARD, ON, P0J 1P0
(705) 647-7336   *SIC 8211*

DISTRICT SCHOOL BOARD ONTARIO NORTH EAST   *p 879*
153 CROATIA AVE, SCHUMACHER, ON, P0N 1G0
(705) 360-1151   *SIC 8211*

DISTRICT SCOLAIRE 11   *p 395*
37 AV RICHARD, BOUCTOUCHE, NB, E4S 3T5
(506) 743-7200   *SIC 8211*

DISTRICT SCOLAIRE 3   *p 398*
298 RUE MARTIN SUITE 3, EDMUNDSTON, NB, E3V 5E5
(506) 737-4567   *SIC 8211*

DISTRICT SCOLAIRE 3   *p 398*
300 RUE MARTIN, EDMUNDSTON, NB, E3V 0G9
(506) 735-2008   *SIC 8211*

DISTRICT SCOLAIRE FRANCOPHONE NORD-EST   *p 410*
700 RUE PRINCIPALE, NEGUAC, NB, E9G 1N4
(506) 776-3808   *SIC 8299*

DISTRICT SCOLAIRE FRANCOPHONE NORD-EST   *p 419*
3376 RUE PRINCIPALE, TRACADIE-SHEILA, NB, E1X 1A4
(506) 394-3400   *SIC 8211*

DISTRICT SCOLAIRE FRANCOPHONE NORD-EST   *p 419*
585 CHURCH ST, TRACADIE-SHEILA, NB, E1X 1G5
(506) 394-3500   *SIC 8211*

DISTRICT SCOLAIRE FRANCOPHONE NORD-EST   *p 419*
585 RUE DE L'EGLISE, TRACADIE-SHEILA, NB, E1X 1B1
(506) 394-3508   *SIC 8211*

DISTRICT SCOLAIRE FRANCOPHONE SUD   *p 395*
See DISTRICT SCOLAIRE 11

DISTRICT SCOLAIRE FRANCOPHONE SUD   *p 397*
425 RUE CHAMPLAIN, DIEPPE, NB, E1A 1P2
(506) 856-3333   *SIC 8211*

DISTROBEL INC   *p 1394*
436 RUE VALOIS, VAUDREUIL-DORION, QC, J7V 1T4
SIC 5148

DITECH PAINT CO. LTD   *p 397*
561 BOUL FERDINAND, DIEPPE, NB, E1A 7G1
(506) 384-8197   *SIC 7699*

DITECH TESTING   *p 397*
See DITECH PAINT CO. LTD

DIV DE BOW PLASTIQUES   *p 1108*
See BOW GROUPE DE PLOMBERIE INC

DIV HOWMET LAVAL CASTING   *p 1233*
See ALCOA CANADA CIE

DIVA DELIGHTS INC   *p 384*
548 KING EDWARD ST, WINNIPEG, MB, R3H 1H8
(204) 885-4376   *SIC 5461*

DIVA INTERNATIONAL INC   *p 642*
222 MCINTYRE DR, KITCHENER, ON, N2R 1E8
(519) 896-9103   *SIC 5122*

DIVACCO LIMITED   *p 694*
5191 CREEKBANK RD, MISSISSAUGA, ON, L4W 1R3
(905) 564-1711   *SIC 3479*

DIVAL DEVELOPMENTS LTD   *p 615*
90 TRINITY CHURCH RD, HAMILTON, ON, L8W 3S2
(905) 387-8214   *SIC 1794*

DIVCO LIMITEE   *p 1170*
8300 BOUL PIE-IX, MONTREAL, QC, H1Z

4E8
(514) 593-8888 *SIC 1541*
DIVERSCO SUPPLY INC *p 533*
495 CONESTOGA BLVD, CAMBRIDGE, ON, N1R 7P4
(519) 740-1210 *SIC 5085*
DIVERSE HOLDINGS LTD *p 134*
9610 62 AVE, GRANDE PRAIRIE, AB, T8W 2C3
(780) 539-6104 *SIC 6712*
DIVERSECITY COMMUNITY RESOURCES SOCIETY *p 276*
13455 76 AVE, SURREY, BC, V3W 2W3
(604) 597-0205 *SIC 8399*
DIVERSEY CANADA, INC *p 716*
3755 LAIRD RD UNIT 10, MISSISSAUGA, ON, L5L 0B3
(905) 829-1200 *SIC 2842*
DIVERSICARE CANADA MANAGEMENT SERVICES CO. INC *p 517*
612 MOUNT PLEASANT RD, BRANTFORD, ON, N3T 5L5
(519) 484-2431 *SIC 8059*
DIVERSICARE CANADA MANAGEMENT SERVICES CO., INC *p 221*
867 K.L.O. RD, KELOWNA, BC, V1Y 9G5
(250) 861-6636 *SIC 8361*
DIVERSICARE CANADA MANAGEMENT SERVICES CO., INC *p 509*
133 KENNEDY RD S, BRAMPTON, ON, L6W 3G3
(905) 459-2324 *SIC 8051*
DIVERSICARE CANADA MANAGEMENT SERVICES CO., INC *p 517*
612 MOUNT PLEASANT RD, BRANTFORD, ON, N3T 5L5
(519) 484-2431 *SIC 8051*
DIVERSICARE CANADA MANAGEMENT SERVICES CO., INC *p 517*
612 MOUNT PLEASANT RD, BRANTFORD, ON, N3T 5L5
(519) 484-2500 *SIC 8051*
DIVERSICARE CANADA MANAGEMENT SERVICES CO., INC *p 621*
263 WONHAM ST S, INGERSOLL, ON, N5C 3P6
(519) 485-3920 *SIC 8051*
DIVERSICARE CANADA MANAGEMENT SERVICES CO., INC *p 658*
312 OXFORD ST W, LONDON, ON, N6H 4N7
(519) 432-1855 *SIC 8051*
DIVERSICARE CANADA MANAGEMENT SERVICES CO., INC *p 721*
2121 ARGENTIA RD SUITE 301, MISSISSAUGA, ON, L5N 2X4
(905) 821-1161 *SIC 8051*
DIVERSICARE CANADA MANAGEMENT SERVICES CO., INC *p 775*
5935 BATHURST ST, NORTH YORK, ON, M2R 1Y8
(416) 223-4050 *SIC 8051*
DIVERSICARE CANADA MANAGEMENT SERVICES CO., INC *p 911*
16 FORT ST, TILBURY, ON, N0P 2L0
(519) 682-0243 *SIC 8059*
DIVERSICARE REALTY INVESTMENTS LIMITED *p 221*
867 K.L.O. RD, KELOWNA, BC, V1Y 9G5
(250) 861-6636 *SIC 8361*
DIVERSIFIED BRANDS DIV OF *p 905*
See *SHERWIN-WILLIAMS CANADA INC*
DIVERSIFIED GLOBAL ASSET MANAGEMENT CORP *p 938*
77 KING ST E SUITE 4310, TORONTO, ON, M5C 1G3
(416) 644-7587 *SIC 6211*
DIVERSIFIED METAL ENGINEERING *p 1040*
See *PT ENTERPRISES INC*
DIVERSIFIED PAYROLL SOLUTIONS *p 56*
See *PEO CANADA LTD*
DIVERSIFIED ROYALTY CORP *p 303*

510 BURRARD ST SUITE 902, VANCOUVER, BC, V6C 3A8
(604) 235-3146 *SIC 4953*
DIVERSIFIED TECHNOLOGY SYSTEMS INC *p 920*
1043 GERRARD ST E, TORONTO, ON, M4M 1Z7
(416) 486-6587 *SIC 8748*
DIVERSIFIED TRANSPORTATION LTD *p 88*
10014 104 ST NW UNIT 20, EDMONTON, AB, T5J 0Z1
(780) 425-0820 *SIC 4142*
DIVERSIFIED TRANSPORTATION LTD *p 114*
8351 MCINTYRE RD NW, EDMONTON, AB, T6E 5J7
(780) 468-6771 *SIC 4142*
DIVERSIFIED TRANSPORTATION LTD *p 128*
120 MACLENNAN CRES, FORT MCMURRAY, AB, T9H 4E8
(780) 743-2244 *SIC 4142*
DIVERSIFIED TRANSPORTATION LTD *p 128*
8030 GOLOSKY AVE, FORT MCMURRAY, AB, T9H 1V5
(780) 790-3960 *SIC 4111*
DIVERSIFIED TRANSPORTATION LTD *p 248*
391 NORTH NECHAKO RD, PRINCE GEORGE, BC, V2K 4K8
(250) 563-5431 *SIC 4142*
DIVERSIFIED ULBRICH - TORONTO *p 1028*
See *ULBRICH OF CANADA INC*
DIVERSIFIED ULBRICH OF CANADA *p 1027*
150 NEW HUNTINGTON RD UNIT 1, WOODBRIDGE, ON, L4H 4N4
(416) 663-7130 *SIC 5051*
DIVERSION P.L. SPORTS INC *p 1155*
2305 CH ROCKLAND BUREAU 320, MONTROYAL, QC, H3P 3E9
(514) 735-4751 *SIC 5941*
DIVERSITECH *p 1127*
See *DIVERSITECH EQUIPMENT AND SALES 1984 LTD*
DIVERSITECH EQUIPMENT AND SALES 1984 LTD *p 1127*
1200 55E AV, LACHINE, QC, H8T 3J8
(514) 631-7300 *SIC 3564*
DIVERSITY TECHNOLOGIES CORPORATION *p 114*
8750 53 AVE NW, EDMONTON, AB, T6E 5G2
(780) 440-4923 *SIC 5169*
DIVERTISSEMENT SONOMA S.E.C. *p 1402*
1 CAR WESTMOUNT BUREAU 1100, WESTMOUNT, QC, H3Z 2P9
(514) 341-5600 *SIC 5099*
DIVERTISSEMENTS GAMELOFT INC *p 1181*
7250 RUE MARCONI, MONTREAL, QC, H2R 2Z5
(514) 798-1700 *SIC 7371*
DIVESTCO INC *p 22*
1223 31 AVE NE, CALGARY, AB, T2E 7W1
(403) 237-9170 *SIC 7371*
DIVESTCO INC, DIV OF *p 22*
See *CAVALIER LAND LTD*
DIVIDEND 15 SPLIT CORP *p 980*
200 FRONT ST W SUITE 2510, TORONTO, ON, M5V 3K2
(416) 304-4443 *SIC 6722*
DIVIDEND SELECT 15 CORP *p 980*
200 FRONT ST W SUITE 2510, TORONTO, ON, M5V 3K2
(416) 304-4443 *SIC 6722*
DIVINE HARDWOOD FLOORING LTD *p 159*
235075 RYAN RD, ROCKY VIEW COUNTY, AB, T1X 0K3
(403) 285-2188 *SIC 5023*
DIVISION 2 *p 620*
See *HENSALL DISTRICT CO-OPERATIVE,*

INCORPORATED
DIVISION 2 CONTRACTING LTD *p 274*
10553 120 ST, SURREY, BC, V3V 4G4
(604) 589-4663 *SIC 4953*
DIVISION CLIENTS PROFESSIONNELS *p 1189*
See *JITNEYTRADE INC*
DIVISION DE RICHMOND *p 1371*
See *EXO-S INC*
DIVISION DES INVESTISSEMENTS DU CN *p 1203*
5 PLACE VILLE-MARIE BUREAU 101, MONTREAL, QC, H3B 2G2
(514) 399-4811 *SIC 6726*
DIVISION ECOLOBRISS *p 1385*
See *GROUPE SOUCY INC*
DIVISION GEA HOULE *p 1096*
See *GEA FARM TECHNOLOGIES CANADA INC*
DIVISION INFORMATIQUE *p 1083*
See *METRO RICHELIEU INC*
DIVISION JEANS W. GREEN *p 1328*
See *4453166 CANADA INC*
DIVISION MONDIALE DE RECHERCHE ET DEVELOPPEMENT DE PFIZER *p 1118*
See *PFIZER CANADA SRI*
DIVISION OF CONTINUING STUDIES *p 333*
See *UNIVERSITY OF VICTORIA*
DIVISION OF HAMILTON AND PARTNERS *p 48*
See *DISABILITY CONCEPTS INC*
DIVISION OF HOUSING AND ANCILLARY SERVICES *p 655*
See *UNIVERSITY OF WESTERN ONTARIO, THE*
DIVISION RADIO TRANSMETTEURS *p 1267*
See *LOAD SYSTEMS INTERNATIONAL INC*
DIVISION SCOLAIRE FRANCO-MANITOBAINE *p 351*
1263 DAWSON RD, LORETTE, MB, R0A 0Y0
(204) 878-9399 *SIC 8211*
DIVISION SCOLAIRE FRANCO-MANITOBAINE *p 364*
585 RUE ST JEAN BAPTISTE, WINNIPEG, MB, R2H 2Y2
(204) 237-8927 *SIC 8221*
DIX PERFORMANCE NORTH LTD *p 100*
11670 170 ST NW, EDMONTON, AB, T5S 1J7
(780) 465-9266 *SIC 5013*
DIXIE ELECTRIC LTD *p 552*
517 BASALTIC RD, CONCORD, ON, L4K 4W8
(905) 879-0533 *SIC 7539*
DIXIE FORD SALES LIMITED *p 694*
5495 DIXIE RD, MISSISSAUGA, ON, L4W 1E6
(905) 629-1300 *SIC 5511*
DIXIE MOTORS LP *p 694*
5515 AMBLER DR, MISSISSAUGA, ON, L4W 3Z1
(905) 238-8080 *SIC 5511*
DIXIE PLYMOUTH CHRYSLER LTD *p 502*
8050 DIXIE RD, BRAMPTON, ON, L6T 4W6
(905) 452-1000 *SIC 5511*
DIXIE SALES CANADA *p 419*
See *BARRETT CORPORATION*
DIXIE TOYOTA *p 691*
See *4247728 CANADA INC*
DIXON COMMERCIAL INVESTIGATORS (1982) INC *p 885*
91 GENEVA ST, ST CATHARINES, ON, L2R 4M9
(905) 688-0447 *SIC 7322*
DIXON GROUP CANADA LIMITED *p 369*
2200 LOGAN AVE, WINNIPEG, MB, R2R 0J2
(204) 633-5650 *SIC 5084*
DIXON HALL *p 933*

58 SUMACH ST, TORONTO, ON, M5A 3J7
(416) 863-0499 *SIC 8322*
DIXON HEATING & SHEET METAL LTD *p 271*
17741 65A AVE UNIT 101, SURREY, BC, V3S 1Z8
(604) 576-0585 *SIC 1711*
DIXON TICONDEROGA INC *p 755*
210 PONY DR UNIT 1, NEWMARKET, ON, L3Y 7B6
(905) 895-5122 *SIC 5112*
DIXON, M.J. CONSTRUCTION LIMITED *p 708*
2600 EDENHURST DR SUITE 200, MISSISSAUGA, ON, L5A 3Z8
(905) 270-7770 *SIC 1542*
DJ GALVANIZING CORPORATION *p 1024*
300 SPRUCEWOOD AVE, WINDSOR, ON, N9C 0B7
(519) 250-2120 *SIC 3479*
DJ WILL HOLDINGS LIMITED *p 153*
7150 50 AVE, RED DEER, AB, T4N 6A5
(403) 343-8800 *SIC 7011*
DJAB *p 1269*
See *MAISON SIMONS INC, LA*
DJAVAD MOWAFAGHIAN CENTRE FOR BRAIN HEALTH *p 325*
See *UNIVERSITY OF BRITISH COLUMBIA, THE*
DJB *p 886*
See *DURWARD JONES BARKWELL & COMPANY LLP*
DJB GROUPE *p 1375*
See *DISTRIBUTION JEAN BLANCHARD INC*
DJD DEVELOPMENT CORPORATION *p 630*
235 GORE RD SUITE 1, KINGSTON, ON, K7L 0C3
(613) 542-3406 *SIC 5411*
DK2 *p 522*
See *DETAIL K2 INC*
DKC GROUP *p 668*
See *CLARKE, DOUGLAS K INSURANCE BROKERS LIMITED*
DLA PIPER *p 47*
See *DAVIS LLP*
DLF PICKSEED CANADA INC *p 645*
1 GREENFIELD RD, LINDSAY, ON, K9V 4S3
(705) 878-9240 *SIC 5191*
DLK INSURANCE BROKERS LTD *p 519*
35 KING ST W, BROCKVILLE, ON, K6V 3P7
(613) 342-8663 *SIC 6411*
DLL *p 1317*
See *DISTRIBUTION LAURENT LEBLANC INC*
DLS, DIV OF *p 627*
See *SPIRENT COMMUNICATIONS OF OTTAWA LTD*
DM INFOTECH *p 1226*
See *9156-4302 QUEBEC INC*
DMB DISTRIBUTION *p 1293*
See *PLACEMENTS BOIVAIN INC*
DMC MINING SERVICES LTD *p 1030*
191 CREDITVIEW RD SUITE 400, WOODBRIDGE, ON, L4L 9T1
(905) 780-1980 *SIC 1081*
DMC SOUDURE *p 1147*
See *D.M.C. SOUDURE INC*
DMCL CHARTTERED PROFENSSIONAL ACCOUNTANT *p 312*
See *DALE MATHESON CARR-HILTON LABONTE LLP*
DMI *p 307*
See *MERCER PEACE RIVER PULP LTD*
DMI CANADA INC *p 890*
2677 WINGER RD, STEVENSVILLE, ON, L0S 1S0
(905) 382-5793 *SIC 3523*
DMR *p 1217*
See *FUJITSU CONSEIL (CANADA) INC*
DMR *p 1272*
See *FUJITSU CONSEIL (CANADA) INC*

DMS GROUP p 781
See DEL MANAGEMENT SOLUTIONS INC
DMS PROPERTY MANAGEMENT LTD p 781
4810 DUFFERIN ST SUITE E, NORTH YORK, ON, M3H 5S8
(416) 661-3070   SIC 6513
DMT DEVELOPMENT SYSTEMS GROUP INC p 390
1 RESEARCH RD UNIT 500, WINNIPEG, MB, R3T 6E3
(204) 927-1800   SIC 7371
DMW & ASSOCIATES p 692
See AXIS DATABASE MARKETING GROUP INC
DMW ELECTRICAL INSTRUMENTATION INC p 859
227 CONFEDERATION ST, SARNIA, ON, N7T 1Z9
(519) 336-3003   SIC 1731
DMX MUSIC p 35
See DMX MUSIC CANADA INC
DMX MUSIC CANADA INC p 35
7260 12 ST SE SUITE 120, CALGARY, AB, T2H 2S5
(403) 640-8525   SIC 7389
DN PHARMACY INC p 1009
658 ERB ST W, WATERLOO, ON, N2T 2Z7
(519) 886-3530   SIC 5912
DNA DATA NETWORKING AND ASSEMBLIES LTD p 192
8057 NORTH FRASER WAY, BURNABY, BC, V5J 5M8
(604) 439-1099   SIC 3678
DNA GENOTEK INC p 835
500 PALLADIUM DR UNIT 3000, OTTAWA, ON, K2V 1C2
(613) 723-5757   SIC 3829
DND HMCS HURON p 336
GD STN CSC, VICTORIA, BC, V8W 2L9
(250) 363-5482   SIC 4499
DNOW CANADA ULC p 10
1616 MERIDIAN RD NE, CALGARY, AB, T2A 2P1
(403) 569-2222   SIC 3533
DNOW CANADA ULC p 48
401 9 AVE SW SUITE 845, CALGARY, AB, T2P 3C5
(403) 531-5600   SIC 5084
DNOW CANADA ULC p 109
7127 56 AVE NW, EDMONTON, AB, T6B 3L2
(780) 465-0999   SIC 3533
DNOW CANADA ULC p 114
3550 93 ST NW, EDMONTON, AB, T6E 5N3
(780) 465-9500   SIC 3533
DNOW CANADA ULC p 114
6415 75 ST NW, EDMONTON, AB, T6E 0T3
SIC 3533
DNOW CANADA ULC p 122
2603 76 AVE NW, EDMONTON, AB, T6P 1P6
(780) 944-1000   SIC 5084
DNOW CANADA ULC p 139
6621 45 ST, LEDUC, AB, T9E 7E3
(780) 980-1490   SIC 5084
DNOW CANADA ULC p 144
6452 66 ST, LLOYDMINSTER, AB, T9V 3T6
(780) 875-5504   SIC 5084
DNOW CANADA ULC p 144
GD RPO 10, LLOYDMINSTER, AB, T9V 2H2
SIC 5084
DNR PRESSURE WELDING LTD p 167
39123 RANGE RD 19-3, STETTLER, AB, T0C 2L0
(403) 742-2859   SIC 1799
DNSSAB p 763
See DISTRICT OF NIPPISSING SOCIAL SERVICES ADMINISTRATION BOARD
DO2 INDUSTRIEL p 1090
See DOLBEAU OXYGENE INC
DOAK'S BULK FIELD p 359

See 74829 MANITOBA LTD
DOAK'S PETROLEUM LTD p 359
945 GORDON AVE, THE PAS, MB, R9A 1L6
(204) 623-2581   SIC 5171
DOALL CANADA INC p 797
2715 BRISTOL CIR, OAKVILLE, ON, L6H 6X5
(800) 923-6255   SIC 5085
DOBBIN SALES LIMITED p 1030
51 TERECAR DR UNIT 2, WOODBRIDGE, ON, L4L 0B5
(905) 264-5465   SIC 5074
DOBSON CHRYSLER DODGE JEEP p 412
See 045502 N. B. LTD
DOCK PRODUCTS CANADA INC p 649
639 SOVEREIGN RD, LONDON, ON, N5V 4K8
(519) 457-7155   SIC 1799
DOCKTOR OILFIELD TRANSPORT CORP p 82
6225 54 AVE, DRAYTON VALLEY, AB, T7A 1S8
SIC 1389
DOCTOR'S OFFICE, THE p 789
See MCI MEDICAL CLINICS INC
DOCTORS OF BC p 320
See BRITISH COLUMBIA MEDICAL ASSOCIATION (CANADIAN MEDICAL ASSOCIATION - B.C. DIVISION)
DOCU PLUS p 1210
980 RUE SAINT-ANTOINE O BUREAU 615, MONTREAL, QC, H3C 1A8
(514) 875-1616   SIC 7334
DOCUMENS p 1181
See DOCUMENS TRADUCTION INC
DOCUMENS TRADUCTION INC p 1181
7245 RUE ALEXANDRA BUREAU 301, MONTREAL, QC, H2R 2Y9
(514) 868-9899   SIC 7389
DOCUMENT COMPANY, THE p 392
See XEROX CANADA LTD
DOCUMENT COMPANY, THE p 449
See XEROX CANADA LTD
DOCUMENT DIRECTION p 774
See RICOH CANADA INC
DOCUMENT DIRECTION LIMITED p 774
4100 YONGE ST SUITE 600, NORTH YORK, ON, M2P 2B5
(416) 218-4360   SIC 5044
DOCUSYSTEMS INTEGRATIONS INC p 188
3920 NORLAND AVE SUITE 101, BURNABY, BC, V5G 4K7
SIC 5044
DODD DRIVER PERSONNEL INC p 570
2977E LAKE SHORE BLVD W SUITE L, ETOBICOKE, ON, M8V 1J8
SIC 7363
DODD'S FURNITURE LTD p 334
715 FINLAYSON ST, VICTORIA, BC, V8T 2T4
(250) 388-6663   SIC 5712
DODGE CHRYSLER DE SAINT-BASILE p 1294
See GARAGE DODGE CHRYSLER DE SAINT-BASILE INC
DODGE CHRYSLER JEEP p 1150
See TROIS DIAMANTS AUTOS (1987) LTEE
DODGE CITY p 426
See ROYAL GARAGE LIMITED, THE
DODGE CITY p 1424
See SASKATOON C AUTO LP
DODSON, JIM SALES LTD p 660
3100 WONDERLAND RD S, LONDON, ON, N6L 1A6
(519) 680-2277   SIC 5531
DOELLKEN-WOODTAPE p 506
See SURTECO CANADA LTD
DOEPKER INDUSTRIES LTD p 267
5301 40 AVE SE, SALMON ARM, BC, V1E 1X1
SIC 3715
DOEPKER INDUSTRIES LTD p 1404
300 DOEPKER AVE, ANNAHEIM, SK, S0K

0G0
(306) 598-2171   SIC 3715
DOEPKER INDUSTRIES LTD p 1411
1955 CARIBOU ST, MOOSE JAW, SK, S6H 4P2
(306) 693-2525   SIC 3715
DOHENY SECURITIES LIMITED p 385
1661 PORTAGE AVE SUITE 702, WINNIPEG, MB, R3J 3T7
(204) 925-1250   SIC 6282
DOHERTY & ASSOCIATES LTD p 823
56 SPARKS ST SUITE 700, OTTAWA, ON, K1P 5A9
(613) 238-6727   SIC 6282
DOHERTY ET ASSOCIES p 823
See DOHERTY & ASSOCIATES LTD
DOIDGE BUILDING CENTRES LTD p 629
1768 HIGHWAY 21, KINCARDINE, ON, N2Z 2Y6
(705) 645-8284   SIC 5211
DOIRON, RENEE p 411
8 RUE CENTENNIAL, RICHIBUCTO, NB, E4W 3X2
(506) 523-9403   SIC 6411
DOKA CANADA LTD./LTEE p 15
5404 36 ST SE, CALGARY, AB, T2C 1P1
(403) 243-6629   SIC 5039
DOLAN'S CONCRETE LTD p 245
4779 ROGER ST, PORT ALBERNI, BC, V9Y 3Z3
(250) 723-6442   SIC 5032
DOLARIAN, STEPHAN p 1219
5510 CH DE LA COTE-DES-NEIGES BUREAU 215, MONTREAL, QC, H3T 1Y9
(514) 344-8338   SIC 5912
DOLBEAU AUTOMOBILES LTEE p 1090
1770 BOUL WALLBERG, DOLBEAU-MISTASSINI, QC, G8L 1H8
(418) 276-0580   SIC 5511
DOLBEAU OXYGENE INC p 1090
303 8E AV BUREAU 11, DOLBEAU-MISTASSINI, QC, G8L 1Z6
(418) 276-0555   SIC 5051
DOLBEC Y. LOGISTIQUE/LOGISTICS INTERNATIONAL INC. p 1261
361 RUE DES ENTREPRENEURS, QUEBEC, QC, G1M 1B4
(418) 688-9115   SIC 4731
DOLCE INTERNATIONAL (ONTARIO) CO. p 986
130 KING ST W, TORONTO, ON, M5X 2A2
(416) 861-9600   SIC 8299
DOLEMO DEVELOPMENT CORPORATION p 29
128 2 AVE SE UNIT 200, CALGARY, AB, T2G 5J5
(403) 699-8830   SIC 6719
DOLENTE CONCRETE & DRAIN CO. p 792
52 HIGH MEADOW PL, NORTH YORK, ON, M9L 2Z5
(416) 653-6504   SIC 1623
DOLLAR FOOD MFG INC p 285
1410 ODLUM DR, VANCOUVER, BC, V5L 4X7
(604) 253-1422   SIC 5411
DOLLAR THRIFTY AUTOMOTIVE GROUP CANADA INC p 709
3660 HURONTARIO ST, MISSISSAUGA, ON, L5B 3C4
(905) 612-1881   SIC 7515
DOLLAR TREE STORES CANADA, INC p 188
3185 WILLINGDON GREEN SUITE 206, BURNABY, BC, V5G 4P3
(604) 321-2550   SIC 5999
DOLLAR'S YOUR INDEPENDANT GROCERY p 762
See 974479 ONTARIO LIMITED
DOLLARAMA p 1157
See S. ROSSY INC
DOLLARAMA INC p 1156
5805 AV ROYALMOUNT, MONT-ROYAL,

QC, H4P 0A1
(514) 737-1006   SIC 5999
DOLLARAMA L.P. p 1156
5805 AV ROYALMOUNT, MONT-ROYAL, QC, H4P 0A1
(514) 737-1006   SIC 5331
DOLLKEN WOODTAPE p 502
230 ORENDA RD, BRAMPTON, ON, L6T 1E9
(905) 673-5156   SIC 3089
DOLLO BROS. FOOD MARKET LIMITED p 685
123 25 HWY SUITE 35, MINDEN, ON, K0M 2K0
(705) 286-1121   SIC 5411
DOLLO'S I G A p 685
See DOLLO BROS. FOOD MARKET LIMITED
DOLO INVESTIGATIONS LTD p 270
10090 152 ST SUITE 408, SURREY, BC, V3R 8X8
(604) 951-1600   SIC 7389
DOLPHIN DELIVERY LTD p 182
4201 LOZELLS AVE, BURNABY, BC, V5A 2Z4
(604) 421-1115   SIC 4212
DOLPHIN TRANSPORT p 182
See DOLPHIN DELIVERY LTD
DOM INTERNATIONAL LIMITED p 871
10 GOLDEN GATE CRT, SCARBOROUGH, ON, M1P 3A5
(416) 265-3993   SIC 5146
DOM LIPA NURSING HOME p 580
See SLOVENIAN LINDEN FOUNDATION
DOM'S AUTO PARTS CO LIMITED p 563
1604 BASELINE RD, COURTICE, ON, L1E 2S5
(905) 434-4566   SIC 5531
DOM-MERIDIAN CONSTRUCTION LTD p 738
1021 MEYERSIDE DR UNIT 10, MISSISSAUGA, ON, L5T 1J6
(905) 564-5594   SIC 1623
DOMAINE CASCADE p 1368
See CSH DOMAINE CASCADE
DOMAINE DE CHABERTON ESTATES LTD p 227
1064 216 ST, LANGLEY, BC, V2Z 1R3
(604) 530-1736   SIC 2084
DOMAINE DU SKI MONT BRUNO INC p 1295
550 RANG DES VINGT-CINQ E, SAINT-BRUNO, QC, J3V 0G6
(450) 653-3441   SIC 7011
DOMAINE HONDA POINTE-AUX-TREMBLES p 1247
See 9039-8082 QUEBEC INC
DOMAINE L'HYPOTHEQUE p 1051
See FEDERATION DES CAISSES DESJARDINS DU QUEBEC
DOMAINE LAFOREST p 1245
485 170 RTE, PETIT-SAGUENAY, QC, G0V 1N0
(418) 638-5408   SIC 6159
DOMCLEAN LIMITED p 514
29 CRAIG ST, BRANTFORD, ON, N3R 7H8
(519) 752-3725   SIC 7349
DOMCO CONSTRUCTION INC p 1415
860 PARK ST, REGINA, SK, S4N 4Y3
(306) 721-8500   SIC 1542
DOME INSURANCE CORP LTD p 377
240 GRAHAM AVE SUITE 800, WINNIPEG, MB, R3C 0J7
(204) 947-2835   SIC 6331
DOME PRODUCTIONS INC p 980
1 BLUE JAYS WAY SUITE 3400, TORONTO, ON, M5V 1J3
(416) 341-2001   SIC 8741
DOMFOAM INC p 1344
6675 RUE BOMBARDIER, SAINT-LEONARD, QC, H1P 2W2
(514) 852-3959   SIC 3086
DOMFOAM INC p 1344

8785 BOUL LANGELIER, SAINT-LEONARD, QC, H1P 2C9
(514) 325-8120   *SIC 3083*

DOMFOAM INTERNATIONAL   *p 1344*
See DOMFOAM INC

DOMFOAM INTERNATIONAL INC   *p 1344*
8785 BOUL LANGELIER, SAINT-LEONARD, QC, H1P 2C9
(514) 325-8120   *SIC 3086*

DOMGEN INVESTMENTS INC   *p 1333*
9500 BOUL HENRI-BOURASSA O, SAINT-LAURENT, QC, H4S 1N8
SIC 6799

DOMINET CORPORATION   *p 874*
10 COMPASS CRT, SCARBOROUGH, ON, M1S 5R3
(416) 646-5232   *SIC 3944*

DOMINION   *p 511*
See LOBLAW COMPANIES LIMITED

DOMINION   *p 769*
See METRO ONTARIO INC

DOMINION   *p 917*
See METRO ONTARIO INC

DOMINION   *p 922*
See METRO ONTARIO INC

DOMINION & GRIMM INC   *p 1048*
8250 RUE MARCONI, ANJOU, QC, H1J 1B2
(514) 351-3000   *SIC 5099*

DOMINION 925   *p 434*
See LOBLAW FINANCIAL HOLDINGS INC

DOMINION BIOLOGICALS LIMITED   *p 446*
5 ISNOR DR, DARTMOUTH, NS, B3B 1M1
(902) 468-3992   *SIC 2836*

DOMINION BLUEPRINT & REPROGRAPHICS LTD   *p 291*
99 6TH AVE W, VANCOUVER, BC, V5Y 1K2
(604) 681-7501   *SIC 7334*

DOMINION BOND RATING SERVICES   *p 950*
See DBRS LIMITED

DOMINION CITRUS LIMITED   *p 996*
165 THE QUEENSWAY SUITE 302, TORONTO, ON, M8Y 1H8
(416) 242-8341   *SIC 5148*

DOMINION COLOUR CORPORATION *p 474*
445 FINLEY AVE, AJAX, ON, L1S 2E2
(905) 683-0231   *SIC 2816*

DOMINION COLOUR CORPORATION *p 570*
199 NEW TORONTO ST, ETOBICOKE, ON, M8V 3X4
(416) 253-4260   *SIC 2816*

DOMINION COLOUR CORPORATION *p 767*
515 CONSUMERS RD UNIT 700, NORTH YORK, ON, M2J 4Z2
(416) 791-4200   *SIC 2816*

DOMINION CORNER BROOK   *p 422*
See LOBLAWS INC

DOMINION CROWN MOULDING INC *p 174*
34450 VYE RD, ABBOTSFORD, BC, V2S 7P6
(604) 852-4224   *SIC 5031*

DOMINION DIAMOND CORPORATION   *p 436*
4920 52 ST UNIT 900, YELLOWKNIFE, NT, X1A 3T1
(867) 669-6100   *SIC 5094*

DOMINION DIAMOND EKATI ULC   *p 436*
4920 52 ST SUITE 900, YELLOWKNIFE, NT, X1A 3A3
(867) 669-9292   *SIC 1499*

DOMINION DIAMOND MINES   *p 436*
See DOMINION DIAMOND EKATI ULC

DOMINION DIVING LIMITED   *p 443*
7 CANAL ST, DARTMOUTH, NS, B2Y 2W1
(902) 434-5120   *SIC 7389*

DOMINION EQUIPMENT & CHEMICAL, DIV OF   *p 514*
See DOMCLEAN LIMITED

DOMINION FARM PRODUCE, DIV OF *p 996*
See DOMINION CITRUS LIMITED

DOMINION HAWKS CLUB   *p 449*
28 LOWER MITCHELL AVE, DOMINION, NS, B1G 1L2

(902) 849-0414   *SIC 8699*

DOMINION LENDING CENTRES INC *p 245*
2215 COQUITLAM AVE SUITE 16, PORT COQUITLAM, BC, V3B 1J6
(604) 696-1221   *SIC 6162*

DOMINION MOTORS (THUNDER BAY-1984) LTD   *p 908*
882 COPPER CRES, THUNDER BAY, ON, P7B 6C9
(807) 343-2277   *SIC 5511*

DOMINION NEON INC   *p 1048*
9225 RUE DU PARCOURS, ANJOU, QC, H1J 3A8
(514) 354-6366   *SIC 5046*

DOMINION NICKEL INVESTMENTS LTD *p 522*
834 APPLEBY LINE SUITE 1, BURLINGTON, ON, L7L 2Y7
(905) 639-9939   *SIC 5093*

DOMINION OF CANADA GENERAL INSURANCE COMPANY, THE   *p 48*
777 8 AVE SW SUITE 1700, CALGARY, AB, T2P 3R5
(403) 231-6600   *SIC 6411*

DOMINION OF CANADA GENERAL INSURANCE COMPANY, THE   *p 805*
1275 NORTH SERVICE RD W SUITE 103, OAKVILLE, ON, L6M 3G4
(905) 825-6400   *SIC 6411*

DOMINION OF CANADA GENERAL INSURANCE COMPANY, THE   *p 950*
165 UNIVERSITY AVE SUITE 101, TORONTO, ON, M5H 3B9
(416) 362-7231   *SIC 6331*

DOMINION OF CANADA GENERAL INSURANCE COMPANY, THE   *p 950*
165 UNIVERSITY AVE., TORONTO, ON, M5H 3B9
(416) 362-7231   *SIC 6411*

DOMINION PIPE & PILING LTD   *p 208*
6845 TILBURY RD, DELTA, BC, V4G 0A3
(604) 946-2655   *SIC 5051*

DOMINION PROTECTION SERVICES LTD *p 22*
1935 32 AVE NE SUITE 124, CALGARY, AB, T2E 3R1
(403) 717-1732   *SIC 5065*

DOMINION REGALIA LIMITED   *p 919*
4 OVERLEA BLVD, TORONTO, ON, M4H 1A4
(416) 752-9987   *SIC 2353*

DOMINION SAV-A-CENTRE   *p 704*
See METRO ONTARIO INC

DOMINION SAVER CENTER   *p 989*
See METRO ONTARIO INC

DOMINION SHEET METAL & ROOFING WORKS   *p 789*
113 CARTWRIGHT AVE SUITE 1, NORTH YORK, ON, M6A 1V4
(416) 789-0601   *SIC 1761*

DOMINION SIGNS   *p 1048*
See DOMINION NEON INC

DOMINION STORES   *p 724*
See METRO ONTARIO INC

DOMINION STORES #906   *p 421*
See LOBLAW COMPANIES LIMITED

DOMINION SURE SEAL LIMITED   *p 738*
6175 DANVILLE RD, MISSISSAUGA, ON, L5T 2H7
(905) 670-5411   *SIC 2891*

DOMINION VOTING SYSTEMS CORPORATION   *p 977*
215 SPADINA AVE SUITE 200, TORONTO, ON, M5T 2C7
(416) 762-8683   *SIC 5087*

DOMINO MACHINE INC   *p 114*
4040 98 ST NW, EDMONTON, AB, T6E 3L3
(780) 809-1787   *SIC 3499*

DOMINO'S PIZZA   *p 535*
See DOMINO'S PIZZA NS CO

DOMINO'S PIZZA NS CO   *p 535*
490 PINEBUSH RD UNIT 2, CAMBRIDGE, ON, N1T 0A5
(519) 748-1330   *SIC 5149*

DOMM CONSTRUCTION LTD   *p 483*
563 LOUISA ST, AYTON, ON, N0G 1C0
(519) 665-7848   *SIC 1542*

DOMO GASOLINE CORPORATION LTD *p 377*
270 FORT ST, WINNIPEG, MB, R3C 1E5
(204) 943-5920   *SIC 5541*

DOMON LTEE   *p 1126*
1950 RUE REMEMBRANCE, LACHINE, QC, H8S 1W9
(514) 637-5835   *SIC 5712*

DOMTAR CORPORATION   *p 1195*
395 BOUL DE MAISONNEUVE O BUREAU 200, MONTREAL, QC, H3A 1L6
(514) 848-5555   *SIC 2611*

DOMTAR INC   *p 217*
2005 MISSION FLATS RD, KAMLOOPS, BC, V2C 5M7
(250) 434-6000   *SIC 2421*

DOMTAR INC   *p 565*
1 DUKE ST, DRYDEN, ON, P8N 2Z7
(807) 223-2323   *SIC 2421*

DOMTAR INC   *p 569*
1 STATION RD, ESPANOLA, ON, P5E 1R6
(705) 869-2020   *SIC 2611*

DOMTAR INC   *p 738*
1330 COURTNEYPARK DR E, MISSISSAUGA, ON, L5T 1K5
(905) 670-1330   *SIC 5111*

DOMTAR INC   *p 1127*
2125 23E AV, LACHINE, QC, H8T 1X5
(514) 636-5006   *SIC 5111*

DOMTAR INC   *p 1195*
395 BOUL DE MAISONNEUVE O BUREAU 200, MONTREAL, QC, H3A 1L6
(514) 848-5555   *SIC 2611*

DOMTAR INC   *p 1392*
609 12E RANG, VAL-JOLI, QC, J1S 0H1
(819) 845-2771   *SIC 2621*

DOMTAR INC   *p 1403*
609 RANG 12, WINDSOR, QC, J1S 2L9
(800) 263-8366   *SIC 2611*

DOMTECH INC   *p 998*
40 DAVIS ST E, TRENTON, ON, K8V 6S4
(613) 394-4884   *SIC 3357*

DOMTEK INC   *p 351*
GD STN LOCKPORT, LOCKPORT, MB, R1A 3R9
(204) 981-1266   *SIC 5039*

DOMUS BUILDING CLEANING COMPANY LIMITED   *p 815*
1366 TRIOLE ST SUITE 200, OTTAWA, ON, K1B 3M4
(613) 741-7722   *SIC 7349*

DON BRENTON'S FIRE PROTECTION *p 460*
See D. R. BRENTON LIMITED

DON DOCKSTEADER MOTORS LTD *p 323*
8530 CAMBIE ST, VANCOUVER, BC, V6P 6N6
(604) 323-2200   *SIC 5511*

DON MCPHAIL MOTORS LTD   *p 618*
6332 WELLINGTON RD, HARRISTON, ON, N0G 1Z0
(519) 338-3422   *SIC 5561*

DON MICHAEL HOLDINGS INC   *p 790*
75 TYCOS DR, NORTH YORK, ON, M6B 1W3
(416) 781-7540   *SIC 5651*

DON MICHAEL HOLDINGS INC   *p 988*
1400 CASTLEFIELD AVE SUITE 2, TORONTO, ON, M6B 4N4
(416) 781-3574   *SIC 3143*

DON VALLEY HOTEL   *p 778*
See ALLIED DON VALLEY HOTEL INC

DON VALLEY NORTH TOYOTA LIMITED *p 665*
5362 HIGHWAY 7 E, MARKHAM, ON, L3P

1B9
(905) 294-8100   *SIC 5521*

DON VALLEY VOLKSWAGEN LIMITED *p 787*
1695 EGLINTON AVE E, NORTH YORK, ON, M4A 1J6
(647) 956-0498   *SIC 5511*

DON'S PHOTO SHOP LTD   *p 370*
1839 MAIN ST, WINNIPEG, MB, R2V 2A4
(204) 942-7887   *SIC 5946*

DON'S PRODUCE INC   *p 842*
1535 SNYDER'S RD E, PETERSBURG, ON, N0B 2H0
(519) 634-1077   *SIC 5148*

DONALCO INC   *p 864*
20 MELFORD DR UNIT 10, SCARBOROUGH, ON, M1B 2X6
(416) 292-7118   *SIC 1799*

DONALCO WESTERN INC   *p 114*
8218 MCINTYRE RD NW, EDMONTON, AB, T6E 5C4
(780) 448-1660   *SIC 1799*

DONALD A WILSON SECONDARY SCHOOL   *p 1015*
See DURHAM DISTRICT SCHOOL BOARD

DONALD CHOI CANADA LIMITED   *p 1010*
147 BATHURST DR, WATERLOO, ON, N2V 1Z4
(519) 886-5010   *SIC 5072*

DONALD CONSTRUCTION LIMITED *p 584*
333 HUMBERLINE DR, ETOBICOKE, ON, M9W 5X3
(416) 675-4134   *SIC 1771*

DONALD E. CHARLTON LTD   *p 176*
2035 QUEEN ST, ABBOTSFORD, BC, V2T 6J3
(604) 854-6499   *SIC 5093*

DONALD F. JOHNSTON HOLDINGS LTD *p 660*
1020 WONDERLAND RD S, LONDON, ON, N6K 3S4
(519) 680-1770   *SIC 5531*

DONALD L. DAVIDSON FUELS LTD *p 1011*
54 PINEWOOD DR, WAWA, ON, P0S 1K0
(705) 856-2166   *SIC 5171*

DONALD'S MARKET LTD   *p 285*
2342 HASTINGS ST E, VANCOUVER, BC, V5L 1V5
(604) 254-3014   *SIC 5411*

DONALDA CLUB   *p 775*
12 BUSHBURY DR, NORTH YORK, ON, M3A 2Z7
(416) 447-5575   *SIC 7997*

DONALDSON FAMILY - BRADNER FARMS *p 178*
28670 58 AVE, ABBOTSFORD, BC, V4X 2E8
(604) 857-1206   *SIC 0212*

DONATO ACADEMY OF HAIRSTYLING AND AESTHETICS   *p 709*
100 CITY CENTRE DR, MISSISSAUGA, ON, L5B 2C9
(416) 252-8999   *SIC 7231*

DONATO FRUITS ET LEGUMES INC *p 1225*
1605 RUE DE BEAUHARNOIS O, MONTREAL, QC, H4N 1J6
(514) 388-1622   *SIC 5148*

DONATO GROUP INC, THE   *p 802*
700 KERR ST SUITE 100, OAKVILLE, ON, L6K 3W5
(905) 337-7777   *SIC 5812*

DONCAR CONSTRUCTION INC   *p 1232*
4085 RANG SAINT-ELZEAR E, MONTREAL, QC, H7E 4P2
SIC 1623

DONG-PHUONG ORIENTAL MARKET LTD *p 93*
14810 131 AVE NW, EDMONTON, AB, T5L 4Y3
(780) 447-2883   *SIC 5411*

DONMAR CAR SALES LTD   *p 100*
17990 102 AVE NW, EDMONTON, AB, T5S 1M9
(780) 454-0422   *SIC 5511*

DONNACONA CHRYSLER   p 1355
See 9229-3786 QUEBEC INC
DONNELLY FARMS LTD   p 404
40 STOCKFORD RD, LANSDOWNE, NB,
E7L 4K4
(506) 375-4564   SIC 4213
DONNELLY FORD LINCOLN   p 827
See OTTAWA MOTOR SALES (1987) LIM-
ITED
DONNELLY MITSUBISHI   p 826
See HUNT CLUB AUTOMOTIVE LTD
DONNELLY PONTIAC BUICK GMC LTD p
826
2496 BANK ST, OTTAWA, ON, K1V 8S2
(613) 737-5000   SIC 5511
DONOHUE MALBAIE INC   p 1210
111 BOUL ROBERT-BOURASSA UNITE
5000, MONTREAL, QC, H3C 2M1
(514) 875-2160   SIC 2621
DONOVAN INSURANCE BROKERS INC p
1006
72 REGINA ST N, WATERLOO, ON, N2J
3A5
(519) 886-3150   SIC 6411
DONOVANS IRVING   p 426
See KARISS ENTERPRISES LIMITED
DONPAT INVESTMENTS LIMITED p 455
2657 ROBIE ST, HALIFAX, NS, B3K 4N9
(902) 453-1940   SIC 5511
DONUT DINER   p 623
See AVONDALE STORES LIMITED
DONUT TIME   p 548
See 838116 ONTARIO INC
DONWAY FORD SALES LIMITED   p 868
1975 EGLINTON AVE E, SCARBOROUGH,
ON, M1L 2N1
(416) 751-2200   SIC 5511
DONWAY LEASING   p 868
See DONWAY FORD SALES LIMITED
DONWAY PLACE   p 780
See REVERA INC
DONWOOD INSTITUTE, THE   p 918
175 BRENTCLIFFE RD, TORONTO, ON,
M4G 0C5
(416) 425-3930   SIC 8069
**DONWOOD MANOR PERSONAL CARE
HOME INC**   p 363
171 DONWOOD DR, WINNIPEG, MB, R2G
0V9
(204) 668-4410   SIC 8051
DOOLEY'S TRUCKING   p 423
See CANADIAN COURIER LTD
DOOLYS   p 1073
See DEVELOPEMENT CYREX INC
**DOORNEKAMP, H. R. CONSTRUCTION
LTD**   p 806
588 SCOTLAND RD, ODESSA, ON, K0H
2H0
(613) 386-3033   SIC 1542
**DOORTECH MFG. AND DISTRIBUTION
LTD**   p 372
530 SHEPPARD ST, WINNIPEG, MB, R2X
2P8
(204) 633-7133   SIC 5031
DOORTECH, DIV OF   p 445
See COASTAL DOOR & FRAME INC
DOPHES   p 782
See AZIZ, J. & A. LIMITED
DOPKO FOOD SERVICES LTD   p 172
5517 37A AVE, WETASKIWIN, AB, T9A 3A5
(780) 986-5322   SIC 5812
DOPPELMAYR CANADA LTD   p 220
567 ADAMS RD, KELOWNA, BC, V1X 7R9
(250) 765-3000   SIC 3799
DOPPELMAYR CANADA LTEE   p 1319
800 MONTEE SAINT-NICOLAS, SAINT-
JEROME, QC, J7Y 4C8
(450) 432-1128   SIC 3799
DOPPELMAYR CTEC   p 1319
See DOPPELMAYR CANADA LTEE
DORA CONSTRUCTION LIMITED   p 446
60 DOREY AVE SUITE 101, DARTMOUTH,
NS, B3B 0B1
(902) 468-2941   SIC 1542

DORAL HOLDINGS LIMITED   p 1012
800 NIAGARA ST, WELLAND, ON, L3C 5Z4
(905) 734-9900   SIC 6512
**DORAN STEWART OILFIELD SERVICES
(1990) LTD**   p 159
391043 752 HWY, ROCKY MOUNTAIN
HOUSE, AB, T4T 1B3
(403) 845-4044   SIC 1623
DORCHESTER CORPORATION, THE p 915
4120 YONGE ST SUITE 215, TORONTO,
ON, M2P 2C6
(416) 628-6238   SIC 6799
DORCHESTER OAKS CORPORATION p
774
120 YONGE ST SUITE 215, NORTH YORK,
ON, M2P 2B8
(416) 628-6238   SIC 6799
DOREL INDUSTRIES INC   p 562
See INDUSTRIES DOREL INC, LES
DOREL INDUSTRIES INC   p 1239
See INDUSTRIES DOREL INC, LES
DORFIN INC   p 1329
5757 BOUL THIMENS, SAINT-LAURENT,
QC, H4R 2H6
(514) 335-0333   SIC 5113
DORIGO SYSTEMS LTD   p 185
3885 HENNING DR, BURNABY, BC, V5C
6N5
(604) 294-4600   SIC 3679
DORING ENTERPRISES INC   p 350
94 7TH AVE, GIMLI, MB, R0C 1B1
(204) 642-5995   SIC 5411
DORKEN SYSTEMS INC   p 489
4655 DELTA WAY, BEAMSVILLE, ON, L0R
1B4
(905) 563-3255   SIC 5039
DORMAKABA CANADA INC   p 1227
7301 BOUL DECARIE, MONTREAL, QC,
H4P 2G7
(514) 735-5410   SIC 3699
DORMER   p 727
See SANDVIK CANADA, INC
DOROTHEA KNITTING MILLS LIMITED p
919
51 BETH NEALSON DR, TORONTO, ON,
M4H 0A4
(416) 421-3773   SIC 2253
DORPLEX INDUSTRIES LIMITED p 792
50 IRONDALE DR, NORTH YORK, ON, M9L
1R8
(416) 739-7794   SIC 3442
DORSET REALTY GROUP   p 260
See DORSET REALTY GROUP CANADA
LTD
DORSET REALTY GROUP CANADA LTD p
260
10451 SHELLBRIDGE WAY SUITE 215,
RICHMOND, BC, V6X 2W8
(604) 270-1711   SIC 6531
**DORSEY GROUP INSURANCE PLANNERS
INC, THE**   p 514
330 WEST ST UNIT 7, BRANTFORD, ON,
N3R 7V5
(519) 759-0033   SIC 6411
DORSON LTEE   p 1048
8551 BOUL PARKWAY, ANJOU, QC, H1J
1N1
(514) 351-0160   SIC 5082
DORTMANS BROS. BARN EQUIP. INC p
897
2234   EGREMONT   DR   SUITE   5,
STRATHROY, ON, N7G 3H6
(519) 247-3435   SIC 5083
DOT BENEFITS CORP   p 781
555 WILSON AVE, NORTH YORK, ON,
M3H 0C5
(416) 636-4411   SIC 6311
DOT FOODS CANADA, INC   p 502
12 BARTON CRT, BRAMPTON, ON, L6T
5H6
SIC 5141
DOT-LINE DESIGN LTD   p 851
19 EAST WILMOT ST, RICHMOND HILL,
ON, L4B 1A3

(905) 760-1133   SIC 5137
DOTS   p 85
See 595028 ALBERTA LTD
DOTY, RONALD T. LIMITED   p 496
HWY 118 W, BRACEBRIDGE, ON, P1L 1V4
(705) 645-5261   SIC 5311
DOUBLE ARROW VENTURES LTD   p 40
3630 BRENTWOOD RD NW SUITE 500,
CALGARY, AB, T2L 1K8
(403) 284-4404   SIC 5812
DOUBLE C. DISTRIBUTORS LTD p 126
6330 4 AVE, EDSON, AB, T7E 1M1
(780) 723-3141   SIC 5172
DOUBLE DIAMOND ACRES LIMITED p 633
2024 SPINKS DR, KINGSVILLE, ON, N9Y
2E5
(519) 326-1000   SIC 0182
DOUBLE DIAMOND SALES   p 633
See 1068409 ONTARIO LIMITED
DOUBLE DOUBLE FOOD GROUP   p 584
See DOUBLE DOUBLE PIZZA CHICKEN
LTD
DOUBLE DOUBLE PIZZA CHICKEN LTD p
584
1 GREENSBORO DR SUITE 28, ETOBI-
COKE, ON, M9W 1C8
(416) 241-0088   SIC 6794
DOUBLE G GAS SERVICES   p 844
962 ALLIANCE RD, PICKERING, ON, L1W
3M9
SIC 4925
DOUBLE G MECHANICAL LTD   p 109
8170 50 ST NW UNIT 430, EDMONTON,
AB, T6B 1E6
SIC 1711
DOUBLE O MARKETS LTD   p 242
GD, OLIVER, BC, V0H 1T0
SIC 5411
DOUBLE R BUILDING PRODUCTS LTD p
15
8209 30 ST SE, CALGARY, AB, T2C 1H7
(403) 236-8322   SIC 5039
DOUBLE R TRUSS AND FLOOR   p 15
See DOUBLE R BUILDING PRODUCTS
LTD
**DOUBLE RAINBOW CANADA CHINA
HOLDINGS GROUP INC**   p 856
127 FRANK ENDEAN RD, RICHMOND
HILL, ON, L4S 1V2
SIC 6211
DOUBLE STAR DRILLING (1998) LTD p 1
25180 117 AVE, ACHESON, AB, T7X 6C2
(780) 484-4276   SIC 1771
DOUBLE V CONSTRUCTION LTD   p 276
13303 78 AVE SUITE 406, SURREY, BC,
V3W 5B9
(604) 590-3131   SIC 1542
DOUBLETEX   p 980
352 ADELAIDE ST W, TORONTO, ON, M5V
1R8
(416) 593-0320   SIC 2211
DOUBLETEX   p 1217
9785 RUE JEANNE-MANCE, MONTREAL,
QC, H3L 3B6
(514) 382-1770   SIC 2211
**DOUBLETREE   BY   HILTON   HOTEL
GATINEAU-OTTAWA**   p 1108
See KENPIER INVESTISSEMENTS LIMI-
TEE
**DOUBLETREE BY HILTON TORONTO
DOWNTOWN**   p 944
See BAYVIEW HOSPITALITY INC
DOUCET MACHINERIES INC   p 1089
340 6E RUE, DAVELUYVILLE, QC, G0Z
1C0
(819) 367-2633   SIC 3553
DOUG MARSHALL MOTOR CITY LTD p 131
11044 100 ST, GRANDE PRAIRIE, AB, T8V
2N1
(780) 532-9333   SIC 5511
DOUGH DELIGHT LTD   p 1002
144 VICEROY RD, VAUGHAN, ON, L4K 2L8
SIC 2051
DOUGHTY & WILLIAMSON, DIV OF p 623

See D & W GROUP INC
DOUGLAS BARWICK INC   p 1061
599 BOUL DU CURE-BOIVIN, BOIS-
BRIAND, QC, J7G 2A8
(450) 435-3643   SIC 3498
DOUGLAS CAMPBELL LODGE   p 354
150 9TH ST SE, PORTAGE LA PRAIRIE,
MB, R1N 3T6
(204) 239-6006   SIC 6513
DOUGLAS COLLEGE   p 237
700 ROYAL AVE UNIT 2814, NEW WEST-
MINSTER, BC, V3M 5Z5
(604) 527-5400   SIC 8222
DOUGLAS FORD LINCOLN SALES LTD p
484
379 BAYFIELD ST, BARRIE, ON, L4M 3C5
(705) 728-5558   SIC 5511
DOUGLAS LAKE CATTLE COMPANY p 211
GD, DOUGLAS LAKE, BC, V0E 1S0
(250) 350-3344   SIC 0212
DOUGLAS LAKE EQUIPMENT   p 271
See DOUGLAS LAKE EQUIPMENT LIM-
ITED PARTNERSHIP
**DOUGLAS LAKE EQUIPMENT LIMITED
PARTNERSHIP**   p 211
111 DOUGLAS LAKE RD, DOUGLAS
LAKE, BC, V0E 1S0
(250) 851-2044   SIC 5083
**DOUGLAS LAKE EQUIPMENT LIMITED
PARTNERSHIP**   p 271
17924 56 AVE, SURREY, BC, V3S 1C7
(604) 576-7506   SIC 7353
DOUGLAS LAKE RANCH   p 211
See DOUGLAS LAKE CATTLE COMPANY
DOUGLAS LIGHTING CONTROLS INC p
188
3605 GILMORE WAY SUITE 280, BURN-
ABY, BC, V5G 4X5
(604) 873-2797   SIC 3625
DOVE CENTRE   p 6
6201 52 AVE, BONNYVILLE, AB, T9N 2L7
(780) 826-2552   SIC 7389
DOVE CENTRE SOCIETY   p 6
See DOVE CENTRE
DOVER BAY SECONDARY SCHOOL p 235
See   SCHOOL   DISTRICT   NO.   68
(NANAIMO-LADYSMITH)
DOVER CLIFFS   p 847
See REVERA LONG TERM CARE INC
DOVER WOODS CABINETRY (DIV OF) p
398
See TRIANGLE KITCHEN LTD
DOVERCO INC   p 1127
2111 32E AV, LACHINE, QC, H8T 3J1
(514) 420-6000   SIC 5113
DOVERCOURT BAPTIST FOUNDATION p
990
1140 BLOOR ST W, TORONTO, ON, M6H
4E6
(416) 536-6111   SIC 8361
DOW ADVANCED MATERIALS   p 866
See ROHM AND HAAS CANADA LP
DOW AGROSCIENCES CANADA INC p
1433
See DOW AGROSCIENCES CANADA INC.
DOW AGROSCIENCES CANADA INC. p 48
215 2 ST SW SUITE 2400, CALGARY, AB,
T2P 1M4
(403) 735-8800   SIC 2879
DOW AGROSCIENCES CANADA INC. p
1433
421 DOWNEY RD SUITE 101, SASKA-
TOON, SK, S7N 4L8
(800) 352-6776   SIC 2879
DOW CANADA HOLDING LP   p 48
450 1 ST SW SUITE 2100, CALGARY, AB,
T2P 5H1
(403) 267-3500   SIC 6712
DOW CHEMICAL CANADA ULC   p 48
215 2 ST SW SUITE 2400, CALGARY, AB,
T2P 1M4
(403) 267-3500   SIC 2899
DOW CHEMICAL CANADA ULC   p 130
HIGHWAY 15, FORT SASKATCHEWAN,

AB, T8L 2P4
(780) 998-8000   SIC 2899
DOW CHEMICAL CANADA ULC   p 153
GD, RED DEER, AB, T4N 6N1
(403) 885-7000   SIC 2899
DOW CHEMICAL CANADA ULC   p 794
122 ARROW RD, NORTH YORK, ON, M9M
2M1
SIC 3081
DOW CHEMICAL CANADA ULC   p 859
GD LCD MAIN, SARNIA, ON, N7T 7H7
SIC 2819
DOW HONDA   p 825
See DOW MOTORS (OTTAWA) LIMITED
DOW MOTORS (OTTAWA) LIMITED   p 825
845 CARLING AVE, OTTAWA, ON, K1S 2E7
(613) 237-2777   SIC 5511
DOWBICO SUPPLIES LIMITED   p 574
50 TITAN RD, ETOBICOKE, ON, M8Z 2J8
(416) 252-7137   SIC 5169
DOWCO CONSULTANTS LTD   p 184
2433 HOLDOM AVE, BURNABY, BC, V5B
5A1
(604) 606-5800   SIC 1791
DOWLER-KARN LIMITED   p 889
43841 TALBOT LINE, ST THOMAS, ON,
N5P 3S7
(519) 631-3810   SIC 5172
DOWLING INSURANCE BROKERS INC   p
384
1045 ST JAMES ST UNIT A, WINNIPEG,
MB, R3H 1B1
(204) 949-2600   SIC 6411
**DOWN EAST HOSPITALITY INCORPO-
RATED**   p
443
335 PRINCE ALBERT RD SUITE 1, DART-
MOUTH, NS, B2Y 1N7
(902) 434-7500   SIC 5812
DOWNEY BUILDING SUPPLIES LTD   p 411
1106 CLEVELAND AVE, RIVERVIEW, NB,
E1B 5V8
(506) 388-2400   SIC 5211
DOWNEY FORD SALES LTD   p 413
35 CONSUMERS DR, SAINT JOHN, NB,
E2J 4Z7
(506) 632-6519   SIC 5511
DOWNEY HOME HARDWARE   p 411
See DOWNEY BUILDING SUPPLIES LTD
DOWNEY'S SALES & SERVICE DIV OF   p
413
See DOWNEY FORD SALES LTD
DOWNHAM NURSERIES (1993) INC   p 897
390 YORK ST, STRATHROY, ON, N7G 2E5
SIC 5193
DOWNHILL SKIER   p 730
See CANADIAN MARKETING TEST CASE
204 LIMITED
DOWNHOLE TOOLS   p 114
See DNOW CANADA ULC
DOWNHOME SHOPPE AND GALLERY   p
431
303 WATER ST, ST. JOHN'S, NL, A1C 1B9
(709) 722-2970   SIC 6531
DOWNIE LAKE COLONY   p 1409
See HUTTERIAN BRETHREN CHURCH
OF DOWNIE LAKE INC
DOWNIE TIMBER LTD   p 253
1621 MILL ST, REVELSTOKE, BC, V0E 2S0
(250) 837-2222   SIC 2421
DOWNIE, DALE NISSAN INC   p 651
1111 OXFORD ST E, LONDON, ON, N5Y
3L7
(519) 451-4560   SIC 5511
**DOWNING STREET PROPERTY MANAGE-
MENT INC**   p
552
668 MILLWAY AVE UNIT 7, CONCORD, ON,
L4K 3V2
(905) 851-1717   SIC 6512
DOWNS CONSTRUCTION LTD   p 339
870 DEVONSHIRE RD, VICTORIA, BC, V9A
4T6
(250) 384-1390   SIC 1542

**DOWNSVIEW CHRYSLER PLYMOUTH
(1964) LTD**   p 783
199 RIMROCK RD, NORTH YORK, ON, M3J
3C6
(416) 635-1660   SIC 5511
DOWNSVIEW DRYWALL CONTRACTING   p
552
160 BASS PRO MILLS DR SUITE 200,
CONCORD, ON, L4K 0A7
(905) 660-0048   SIC 1742
**DOWNSVIEW HEATING & AIR CONDITION-
ING LTD**   p
502
4299 QUEEN ST E, BRAMPTON, ON, L6T
5V4
(905) 794-1489   SIC 1711
DOWNSVIEW KITCHENS   p 685
See DOWNSVIEW WOODWORKING LIM-
ITED
DOWNSVIEW LONG TERM CARE CENTRE
p 783
3595 KEELE ST, NORTH YORK, ON, M3J
1M7
(416) 633-3431   SIC 8051
DOWNSVIEW PLUMBING LIMITED   p 502
4299 QUEEN ST E UNIT 1, BRAMPTON,
ON, L6T 5V4
(416) 675-6215   SIC 1711
DOWNSVIEW SECONDARY SCHOOLp 786
See TORONTO DISTRICT SCHOOL
BOARD
DOWNSVIEW WOODWORKING LIMITED   p
685
2635 RENA RD, MISSISSAUGA, ON, L4T
1G6
(905) 677-9354   SIC 2434
DOWNTOWN ACURA   p 934
See TRANSASIAN FINE CARS LTD
DOWNTOWN AUTOMOTIVE INC   p 933
259 LAKE SHORE BLVD E, TORONTO, ON,
M5A 3T7
SIC 5511
**DOWNTOWN COMMUNITY HEALTH
CLINIC**   p 296
See VANCOUVER COASTAL HEALTH AU-
THORITY
DOWNTOWN EATERY (1993) LTD   p 980
563 KING ST W, TORONTO, ON, M5V 1M1
(416) 585-9200   SIC 5995
DOWNTOWN FINE CARS INC   p 933
68 PARLIAMENT ST, TORONTO, ON, M5A
0B2
(416) 603-9988   SIC 5511
**DOWNTOWN LUMBER & BUILDING SUP-
PLIES CO**   p
990
See GATHER INVESTMENTS LIMITED
DOWNTOWN MAZDA   p 933
See DOWNTOWN AUTOMOTIVE INC
DOWNTOWN PORCHE   p 933
See DOWNTOWN FINE CARS INC
DOWNTOWN REALTY LTD   p 331
4007 32 ST, VERNON, BC, V1T 5P2
(250) 260-0453   SIC 6531
DOWNTOWN TOYOTA   p 920
See 498326 ONTARIO LIMITED
DOWNTOWN WATCH   p 377
426 PORTAGE AVE SUITE 101, WIN-
NIPEG, MB, R3C 0C9
(204) 958-4620   SIC 8611
DOWNTOWN WINNIPEG BIZ   p 377
See DOWNTOWN WATCH
DOXIM SOLUTIONS INC   p 669
1380 RODICK RD SUITE 102, MARKHAM,
ON, L3R 4G5
(647) 484-0467   SIC 7371
DOYON DESPRES   p 1373
See DESPRES, LAPORTE INC
DOYON, G. T. V. (SHERBROOKE) INC   p
1373
525 RUE NORTHROP-FRYE, SHER-
BROOKE, QC, J1L 2Y3
(819) 565-3177   SIC 5731
DP ENVIRONMENTAL SERVICE INC   p 512

39 SHADYWOOD RD, BRAMPTON, ON,
L6Z 4M1
(905) 840-4480   SIC 4959
DP IMMOBILIER QUEBEC INC   p 1139
8389 AV SOUS-LE-VENT BUREAU 300,
LEVIS, QC, G6X 1K7
(418) 832-2222   SIC 6513
DP WORLD (CANADA) INC   p 294
777 CENTENNIAL RD, VANCOUVER, BC,
V6A 1A3
(604) 255-5151   SIC 4491
DP WORLD VANCOUVER   p 294
See DP WORLD (CANADA) INC
DPA ASSURANCES   p 1312
See GROUPE DESMARAIS PINSON-
NEAULT & AVARD INC
DPM INSURANCE GROUP   p 911
31 QUEEN ST N, TILBURY, ON, N0P 2L0
(519) 682-0202   SIC 6411
**DR CHARLES BEST SECONDARY
SCHOOL**   p 199
See SCHOOL DISTRICT NO. 43 (COQUIT-
LAM)
DR K A CLARK ELEMENTARY SCHOOL   p
128
See FORT MCMURRAY PUBLIC SCHOOL
DISTRICT #2833
**DR STANLEY K BERNSTEIN'S HEALTH &
DIET CLINICS**   p 777
See POST ROAD HEALTH & DIET CLINIC
DR TAX SOFTWARE   p 1155
See THOMSON REUTERS DT IMPOT ET
COMPTABILITE INC
DR. BATTERY   p 256
See RICHMOND INTERNATIONAL TECH-
NOLOGY CORP
DR. DONUT INC   p 617
2200 RYMAL RD E, HANNON, ON, L0R 1P0
(905) 692-3556   SIC 5461
**DR. GEORGES-L.-DUMONT UNIVERSITY
HOSPITAL CENTRE (DGLDUHC)**   p 407
See VITALITE HEALTH NETWORK
DR. HAUSCHKA CANADA   p 1214
See OASIS ESTHETIQUE DISTRIBUTION
INC
**DR. JOHN M. DENISON SECONDARY
SCHOOL**   p 757
See YORK REGION DISTRICT SCHOOL
BOARD
DR. OETKER CANADA LTD   p 735
2229 DREW RD, MISSISSAUGA, ON, L5S
1E5
(905) 678-1311   SIC 2038
**DR. REDDY'S LABORATORIES CANADA
INC**   p 694
2425 MATHESON BLVD E 7TH FL, MISSIS-
SAUGA, ON, L4W 5K4
(289) 201-2299   SIC 5122
DRA AMERICAS INC   p 938
44 VICTORIA ST SUITE 300, TORONTO,
ON, M5C 1Y2
(416) 800-8797   SIC 8742
**DRADER MANUFACTURING INDUSTRIES
LTD**   p 109
5750 50 ST NW, EDMONTON, AB, T6B 2Z8
(780) 440-2231   SIC 3089
DRAEGER MEDICAL CANADA INC   p 694
2425 SKYMARK AVE UNIT 1, MISSIS-
SAUGA, ON, L4W 4Y6
(905) 212-6600   SIC 5047
DRAEGER SAFETY CANADA LIMITED   p
694
2425 SKYMARK AVE UNIT 1, MISSIS-
SAUGA, ON, L4W 4Y6
(905) 212-6600   SIC 5049
DRAFTING CLINIC CANADA LIMITED, THE
p 738
1500 TRINITY DR SUITE 16, MISSIS-
SAUGA, ON, L5T 1L6
(905) 564-1300   SIC 5049
DRAGADOS CANADA INC   p 950
150 KING ST W SUITE 2103, TORONTO,
ON, M5H 1J9
(647) 260-5001   SIC 1629

DRAGAGE OCEAN DM INC   p 1258
105 RUE ABRAHAM-MARTIN UNITE 500,
QUEBEC, QC, G1K 8N1
(418) 694-1414   SIC 1629
DRAGON CITY DEVELOPMENTS INCp 977
131 BALDWIN ST, TORONTO, ON, M5T 1L7
(416) 596-8885   SIC 6512
DRAIN-ALL LTD   p 815
1611 LIVERPOOL CRT, OTTAWA, ON, K1B
4L1
(613) 739-1070   SIC 4953
DRAINAMAR   p 1248
See VEOLIA ES CANADA SERVICES IN-
DUSTRIELS INC
**DRAKA ELEVATOR PRODUCTS INCOR-
PORATED**   p
514
17 WOODYATT DR UNIT 13, BRANTFORD,
ON, N3R 7K3
(519) 758-0605   SIC 5051
DRAKE HOTEL PROPERTIES (DHP) INC   p
990
1150 QUEEN ST W, TORONTO, ON, M6J
1J3
(416) 531-5042   SIC 7011
DRAKE INTERNATIONAL INC   p 950
320 BAY ST SUITE 1400, TORONTO, ON,
M5H 4A6
(416) 216-1000   SIC 7361
DRAKE MEDOX HEALTH SERVICES   p 312
See DRAKE MEDOX HEALTH SERVICES
(VANCOUVER) INC
**DRAKE MEDOX HEALTH SERVICES (VAN-
COUVER) INC**   p
312
1166 ALBERNI ST SUITE 802, VANCOU-
VER, BC, V6E 3Z3
(604) 682-2801   SIC 8621
DRAKE PERSONNEL   p 950
See DRAKE INTERNATIONAL INC
DRAKE TOWING LTD   p 285
1553 POWELL ST, VANCOUVER, BC, V5L
5C3
(604) 251-3344   SIC 7549
DRAKKAR & ASSOCIES INC   p 1222
780 AV BREWSTER BUREAU 200, MON-
TREAL, QC, H4C 2K1
(514) 733-6655   SIC 8741
DRAKKAR RESSOURCES HUMAINES   p
1222
See DRAKKAR & ASSOCIES INC
DRANCO CONSTRUCTION LIMITED   p 584
1919 ALBION RD, ETOBICOKE, ON, M9W
5S8
(416) 675-2682   SIC 1771
DRANE, STEVE MOTERCYCLES LTDp 340
2940 ED NIXON TERR, VICTORIA, BC,
V9B 0B2
(250) 475-1345   SIC 5571
DRAPEAU   p 1348
See CONSULTANTS F. DRAPEAU INC
DRAPER WHITMAN   p 665
See 7251246 CANADA INC
DRAVES, BRIAN H MERCHANDISING LTD
p 886
431 LOUTH ST SUITE 90, ST
CATHARINES, ON, L2S 4A2
(905) 682-9275   SIC 5251
DRAYCOR CONSTRUCTION LTD   p 336
GD STN CSC, VICTORIA, BC, V8W 2L9
(250) 391-9899   SIC 1521
DRAYDEN INSURANCE LTD   p 97
10310 124 ST NW SUITE 100, EDMON-
TON, AB, T5N 1R2
(780) 482-6300   SIC 6411
DRAYTON ENTERTAINMENT INC   p 535
46 GRAND AVE S, CAMBRIDGE, ON, N1S
2L8
(519) 621-8000   SIC 7832
DRAYTON VALLEY FORD SALES LTD p 82
5214 POWER CENTRE BLVD, DRAYTON
VALLEY, AB, T7A 0A5
(780) 542-4438   SIC 5511
DRAYTON VALLEY HOME HARDWARE   p

82
See KELLY, JIM BUILDING MATERIALS LTD

DRAYTON VALLEY HOSPTIAL HEALTH CENTRE *p 82*
See CROSSROADS REGIONAL HEALTH AUTHORITY

DREAM ALTERNATIVES *p 938*
See DREAM ASSET MANAGEMENT CORPORATION

DREAM ASSET MANAGEMENT CORPORATION *p 938*
30 ADELAIDE ST E SUITE 301, TORONTO, ON, M5C 3H1
(416) 365-3535   *SIC 6531*

DREAM GLOBAL REAL ESTATE INVESTMENT TRUST *p 938*
30 ADELAIDE ST E SUITE 301, TORONTO, ON, M5C 3H1
(416) 365-3535   *SIC 6722*

DREAM GLOBAL REIT *p 938*
See DREAM GLOBAL REAL ESTATE INVESTMENT TRUST

DREAM HARD ASSET ALTERNATIVES TRUST *p 938*
30 ADELAIDE ST E SUITE 301, TORONTO, ON, M5C 3H1
(416) 365-3535   *SIC 6722*

DREAM INDUSTRIAL LP *p 938*
30 ADELAIDE ST E SUITE 301, TORONTO, ON, M5C 3H1
(416) 365-3535   *SIC 6531*

DREAM INDUSTRIAL REAL ESTATE INVESTMENT TRUST *p 938*
30 ADELAIDE STREET E SUITE 301, TORONTO, ON, M5C 3H1
(416) 365-3535   *SIC 6798*

DREAM INDUSTRIAL REIT *p 938*
See DREAM INDUSTRIAL REAL ESTATE INVESTMENT TRUST

DREAM OFFICE LP *p 938*
30 ADELAIDE ST E SUITE 301, TORONTO, ON, M5C 3H1
(416) 365-3535   *SIC 6531*

DREAM OFFICE MANAGEMENT CORP *p 938*
30 ADELAIDE ST E SUITE 301, TORONTO, ON, M5C 3H1
(416) 365-3535   *SIC 6531*

DREAM OFFICE REAL ESTATE INVESTMENT TRUST *p 938*
30 ADELAIDE ST E SUITE 301, TORONTO, ON, M5C 3H1
(416) 365-3535   *SIC 6798*

DREAM OFFICE REIT *p 938*
See DREAM OFFICE REAL ESTATE INVESTMENT TRUST

DREAM REIT INDUSTRIAL *p 938*
See DREAM UNLIMITED CORP

DREAM RIDGE HOMES CORP *p 68*
232 WOODPARK BAY SW, CALGARY, AB, T2W 6H2
(403) 616-3542   *SIC 1521*

DREAM UNLIMITED CORP *p 938*
30 ADELAIDE ST E SUITE 301, TORONTO, ON, M5C 3H1
(416) 365-3535   *SIC 6553*

DRECO *p 114*
See DRECO INTERNATIONAL HOLDINGS ULC

DRECO ENERGY SERVICES ULC *p 15*
6771 84 ST SE, CALGARY, AB, T2C 4T6
(403) 319-2333   *SIC 3533*

DRECO ENERGY SERVICES ULC *p 148*
1704 5 ST, NISKU, AB, T9E 8P8
(780) 944-3800   *SIC 3533*

DRECO ENERGY SERVICES ULC *p 148*
506 17 AVE, NISKU, AB, T9E 7T1
(780) 955-5451   *SIC 3533*

DRECO INTERNATIONAL HOLDINGS ULC *p 114*
6415 75 ST NW, EDMONTON, AB, T6E 0T3
(780) 944-3800   *SIC 3533*

DRECO RIG TECHNOLOGY & CONSTRUCTION *p 148*
See DRECO ENERGY SERVICES ULC

DRESDEN AGRICULTURAL SOCIETY *p 565*
255 PARK ST RR 5, DRESDEN, ON, N0P 1M0
(519) 683-1116   *SIC 7948*

DRESDEN INDUSTRIAL *p 857*
See KSR INTERNATIONAL INC

DRESDEN RACEWAY *p 565*
See DRESDEN AGRICULTURAL SOCIETY

DRESSER-RAND CANADA, ULC *p 114*
9330 45 AVE NW, EDMONTON, AB, T6E 6S1
(780) 436-0604   *SIC 5085*

DREVER, S. PHARMACY LIMITED *p 590*
710 TOWER ST S, FERGUS, ON, N1M 2R3
(519) 843-3160   *SIC 5912*

DREW BRADY COMPANY INC *p 805*
1155 NORTH SERVICE RD W UNIT 6, OAKVILLE, ON, L6M 3E3
(905) 815-1534   *SIC 5136*

DREW NURSING HOME *p 412*
See UNITED CHURCH HOME FOR SENIOR CITIZENS INC, THE

DREW-SMITH COMPANY LIMITED, THE *p 533*
42 AINSLIE ST N, CAMBRIDGE, ON, N1R 3J5
(519) 621-6988   *SIC 6719*

DREXEL INDUSTRIES *p 651*
See SALMON CAPITAL CORPORATION

DREXLER CONSTRUCTION LIMITED *p 857*
5274 COUNTY RD 27, ROCKWOOD, ON, N0B 2K0
(519) 856-9526   *SIC 1623*

DRIFTWOOD TICKET CENTRE *p 216*
See BRITISH COLUMBIA LOTTERY CORPORATION

DRILLING FLUIDS TREATMENT SYSTEMS INC *p 15*
7530 114 AVE SE, CALGARY, AB, T2C 4T3
(403) 279-0123   *SIC 5085*

DRILLING SERVICES DIVISION *p 59*
See SECURE ENERGY SERVICES INC

DRILLTEL SYSTEMS *p 21*
See C L CONSULTANTS LIMITED

DRISCOLL, J. F. INVESTMENT CORP *p 997*
130 KING ST, TORONTO, ON, M9N 1L5
(416) 365-7532   *SIC 6282*

DRIVE COURIER XPRESS LLC. CORPORATION *p 694*
2680 MATHESON BLVD E, MISSISSAUGA, ON, L4W 0A5
(905) 291-0888   *SIC 7389*

DRIVE PRODUCTS INC *p 1*
26230 TWP RD 531A UNIT 111, ACHESON, AB, T7X 5A4
(780) 960-6826   *SIC 5084*

DRIVE PRODUCTS INC *p 694*
1665 SHAWSON DR, MISSISSAUGA, ON, L4W 1T7
(905) 564-5800   *SIC 5084*

DRIVE STAR SHUTTLE SYSTEMS LTD *p 615*
1625 STONE CHURCH RD E, HAMILTON, ON, L8W 3Y5
(866) 378-7827   *SIC 4213*

DRIVEWYZE *p 119*
See INTELLIGENT IMAGING SYSTEMS, INC

DRIVING FORCE *p 100*
See DRIVING FORCE INC, THE

DRIVING FORCE DECKS INT'L LTD *p 176*
30691 SIMPSON RD, ABBOTSFORD, BC, V2T 6C7
(604) 514-1191   *SIC 4213*

DRIVING FORCE INC, THE *p 100*

17631 103 AVE NW, EDMONTON, AB, T5S 1N8
(780) 483-9559   *SIC 5511*

DROLET ENTREPENEUR GENERAL *p 1277*
See CONSTRUCTION DROLET, MARC INC

DRS PIVOTAL POWER *p 440*
See PIVOTAL POWER INC

DRS TECHNOLOGIES CANADA LTD *p 626*
700 PALLADIUM DR, KANATA, ON, K2V 1C6
(613) 591-6000   *SIC 3674*

DRS TECHNOLOGIES CANADA LTD *p 626*
500 PALLADIUM DR SUITE 1100, KANATA, ON, K2V 1C2
(613) 591-5800   *SIC 3674*

DRUGSTORE PHARMACY *p 512*
See WADLAND PHARMACY LIMITED

DRUGSTORE PHARMACY *p 1420*
See LOBLAWS INC

DRUGSTORE PHARMACY, THE *p 457*
See SENTINEL DRUGS LIMITED

DRUGSTORE PHARMACY, THE *p 1421*
See LOBLAWS INC

DRUMHELLER AND REGION TRANSITION SOCIETY *p 82*
105 3RD AVE E, DRUMHELLER, AB, T0J 0Y0
(403) 823-6690   *SIC 8322*

DRUMHELLER CO-OP LTD *p 82*
555 HWY 10 E, DRUMHELLER, AB, T0J 0Y0
(403) 823-5555   *SIC 5411*

DRUMMOND DESIGNS.COM *p 1098*
See DESSINS DRUMMOND INC, LES

DRUMMOND EXPORT *p 1097*
See ALIMENTS TRANS GRAS INC, LES

DRUMMOND FUELS (OTTAWA) LTD *p 749*
30 RIDEAU HEIGHTS DR, NEPEAN, ON, K2E 7A6
(613) 226-4444   *SIC 5541*

DRUMMOND HONDA *p 1097*
See 9067-7246 QUEBEC INC

DRUMMOND INFORMATIQUE LTEE *p 1096*
412 RUE HERIOT BUREAU 101, DRUMMONDVILLE, QC, J2B 1B5
(819) 477-8886   *SIC 5734*

DRUMMOND'S GAS *p 749*
See DRUMMOND FUELS (OTTAWA) LTD

DRUMMOND, GEORGE W. LIMITED *p 749*
30 RIDEAU HEIGHTS DR, NEPEAN, ON, K2E 7A6
(613) 226-4440   *SIC 1629*

DRUMMOND, SCOTT MOTORS LTD *p 539*
501 GRAND RD RR 1, CAMPBELLFORD, ON, K0L 1L0
(705) 653-2020   *SIC 5511*

DRUMMONDVILLE FORD *p 1099*
See TRADITION FORD (VENTES) LTEE

DRUMONDVILLE NISSAN *p 1097*
See 9045-4604 QUEBEC INC

DRURY'S TRANSFER REG'D *p 418*
160 STEWART AVE, SUSSEX, NB, E4E 2G2
SIC 4212

DRUXY'S FAMOUS DELI SANDWICHES *p 894*
See DRUXY'S INC

DRUXY'S INC *p 894*
52 ABBOTSFORD RD, STOUFFVILLE, ON, L4A 2C1
(416) 385-9500   *SIC 5812*

DRW CANADA CO *p 1213*
1360 BOUL RENE-LEVESQUE O BUREAU 1700, MONTREAL, QC, H3G 2W4
(514) 940-4040   *SIC 8742*

DRY ICE & GASES CO DIV *p 574*
See DOWBICO SUPPLIES LIMITED

DRYCO BUILDING SUPPLIES INC *p 227*
5955 205A ST, LANGLEY, BC, V3A 8C4
(604) 533-2313   *SIC 5039*

DRYCO DRYWALL SUPPLIES LTD *p 182*
7027 WINSTON ST, BURNABY, BC, V5A

2G7
(604) 253-4121   *SIC 5032*

DRYDEN AIR SERVICES *p 511*
See 765865 ONTARIO INC

DRYDEN BOARD OF EDUCATION *p 565*
79 CASIMIR AVE, DRYDEN, ON, P8N 2H4
(807) 223-2316   *SIC 8211*

DRYDEN CHEVROLET BUICK GMC LTD *p 565*
489 GOVERNMENT ST, DRYDEN, ON, P8N 2P6
(807) 223-7123   *SIC 5511*

DRYDEN HEIGHTS *p 812*
See DURHAM REGION NON PROFIT HOUSING CORPORATION

DRYDEN HIGH SCHOOL *p 565*
See DRYDEN BOARD OF EDUCATION

DRYDEN REGIONAL HEALTH CENTRE *p 565*
58 GOODALL ST, DRYDEN, ON, P8N 1V8
(807) 223-8200   *SIC 8062*

DRYDEN TRUCK STOP INC *p 565*
GD LCD MAIN, DRYDEN, ON, P8N 2Y6
(807) 223-2085   *SIC 5541*

DRYTAC CANADA INC *p 502*
105 NUGGETT CRT, BRAMPTON, ON, L6T 5A9
(905) 660-1748   *SIC 5169*

DRYWALL ACOUSTIC LATHING & INSULATION *p 1034*
See UNITED BROTHERHOOD OF CARPENTERS JOINERS AMERICA LOCAL 83

DS GROUP, THE *p 229*
See A.K. DRAFT SEAL LTD

DSC *p 790*
See TYCO SAFETY PRODUCTS CANADA LTD

DSD INTERNATIONAL INC *p 1382*
2515 CH DE L'AEROPORT, THETFORD MINES, QC, G6G 5R7
(418) 338-3507   *SIC 5191*

DSF *p 1266*
See DISTRIBUTION STE-FOY (1982) LTEE

DSI CANADA CIVIL, LTD *p 281*
19433 96 AVE SUITE 103, SURREY, BC, V4N 4C4
(604) 888-8818   *SIC 5039*

DSI DISPENSING SYSTEMS INTERNATIONAL INC *p 1333*
5800 BOUL THIMENS, SAINT-LAURENT, QC, H4S 1S5
(514) 433-4562   *SIC 3585*

DSI RECYCLING SYSTEMS INC *p 1006*
1595 LOBSINGER LINE SUITE 1, WATERLOO, ON, N2J 4G8
(519) 664-3586   *SIC 5074*

DSI UNDERGROUND *p 1434*
See DSI UNDERGROUND CANADA LTD

DSI UNDERGROUND CANADA LTD *p 898*
15 TOULOUSE CRES, STURGEON FALLS, ON, P2B 0A5
(705) 753-4872   *SIC 3532*

DSI UNDERGROUND CANADA LTD *p 1434*
3919 MILLAR AVE, SASKATOON, SK, S7P 0C1
(306) 244-6244   *SIC 3532*

DSI UPHOLSTERY INC *p 552*
452 MILLWAY AVE, CONCORD, ON, L4K 3V7
(905) 669-1357   *SIC 2521*

DSK *p 1220*
See LEVY PILOTTE S.E.N.C.R.L.

DSL LOGIC *p 1260*
75 RUE DES EPINETTES, QUEBEC, QC, G1L 1N6
SIC 5065

DSL LTD *p 93*
14520 128 AVE NW, EDMONTON, AB, T5L 3H6
(780) 452-7580   *SIC 5078*

DSL TRAVELLERS TOURS *p 665*
See 679475 ONTARIO INC

DSM   p 75
See DYNAMIC SOURCE MANUFACTUR-ING INC

DSM INVESTMENTS INC   p 194
959 TRANS CANADA HWY S, CACHE CREEK, BC, V0K 1H0
(250) 457-9312   *SIC* 5541

DSM NUTRITIONAL PRODUCTS CANADA INC   p 463
39 ENGLAND DR, MULGRAVE, NS, B0E 2G0
(902) 747-3500   *SIC* 2077

DSM NUTRITIONAL PRODUCTS CANADA INC   p 483
395 WAYDOM DR SUITE 2, AYR, ON, N0B 1E0
(519) 622-2200   *SIC* 5122

DSME TRENTON LTD   p 468
34 POWERPLANT RD, TRENTON, NS, B0K 1X0
(902) 753-7777   *SIC* 3441

DSS AVIATION INC   p 446
71 WRIGHT AVE, DARTMOUTH, NS, B3B 1H4
(902) 444-3788   *SIC* 5099

DST CONSULTING ENGINEERS INC p 908
605 HEWITSON ST, THUNDER BAY, ON, P7B 5V5
(807) 623-2929   *SIC* 8711

DST TRANSPORTATION   p 736
See 3580768 CANADA INC

DSTN   p 468
See DSME TRENTON LTD

DSV AIR & SEA INC   p 502
70 DRIVER RD UNIT 4, BRAMPTON, ON, L6T 5V2
(905) 629-0055   *SIC* 4731

DSV SOLUTIONS INC   p 502
8590 AIRPORT RD, BRAMPTON, ON, L6T 0C3
(905) 789-6211   *SIC* 6712

DTS COMM INC   p 486
324 SAUNDERS RD UNIT 6, BARRIE, ON, L4N 9Y2
(647) 428-8838   *SIC* 4841

DTS PHARMA INC   p 1143
1049 BOUL ROLAND-THERRIEN BUREAU 236, LONGUEUIL, QC, J4J 4L3
(450) 928-0030   *SIC* 5912

DTSSAB   p 634
See DISTRICT OF TIMISKAMING SOCIAL SERVICES ADMINISTRATION BOARD

DTZ BARNICKEY   p 296
See 540806 BC LTD

DU MAURIER LTEE   p 1222
3711 RUE SAINT-ANTOINE O, MONTREAL, QC, H4C 3P6
(514) 932-6161   *SIC* 2111

DU+ CONSEILS   p 1177
See 2854-5150 QUEBEC INC

DU-RITE MOTORS LIMITED   p 346
237 MILL RD, BOISSEVAIN, MB, R0K 0E0
(204) 534-2929   *SIC* 5083

DU-SO / JAC-SIL INC   p 1260
377 RUE DUPUY, QUEBEC, QC, G1L 1P2
(418) 626-5276   *SIC* 5013

DU-SO PIECES D'AUTO   p 1260
See DU-SO / JAC-SIL INC

DUBE & LOISELLE INC   p 1110
583 RUE DUFFERIN, GRANBY, QC, J2H 0Y5
(450) 378-9996   *SIC* 5149

DUBE AUTO SALES LIMITED   p 398
454 RUE VICTORIA, EDMUNDSTON, NB, E3V 2K5
SIC 5511

DUBE COOKE PEDICELLI INC   p 1159
370 RUE DE SAINT-JOVITE BUREAU 202, MONT-TREMBLANT, QC, J8E 2Z9
(450) 537-3646   *SIC* 6411

DUBE, R. LTEE   p 1045
370 AV BEGIN, ALMA, QC, G8B 2W8
(418) 662-3611   *SIC* 5411

DUBO DEPOT   p 1164

See DUBO ELECTRIQUE LTEE

DUBO ELECTRIQUE LTEE   p 1164
5780 RUE ONTARIO E, MONTREAL, QC, H1N 0A2
(514) 255-7711   *SIC* 5063

DUBOIS & FRERES LIMITEE   p 1246
637 AV SAINT-LOUIS, PLESSISVILLE, QC, G6L 2L9
(819) 362-7377   *SIC* 5511

DUBOIS AGRINOVATION INC   p 1351
478 RANG NOTRE-DAME, SAINT-REMI, QC, J0L 2L0
(450) 454-4641   *SIC* 5162

DUBOIS, CAMIONS ALAIN REGIS p 1314
See CAMIONS A & R DUBOIS INC

DUBOIS, ROGER INC   p 1098
285 RUE SAINT-GEORGES, DRUMMONDVILLE, QC, J2C 4H3
(819) 477-1335   *SIC* 6712

DUBORD & RAINVILLE INC   p 1329
4045 BOUL POIRIER, SAINT-LAURENT, QC, H4R 2G9
(514) 735-6111   *SIC* 5099

DUBREUIL, GILLES LTEE   p 1064
1055 BOUL DE MONTARVILLE BUREAU 332, BOUCHERVILLE, QC, J4B 6P5
(450) 655-6950   *SIC* 5014

DUBWEAR CLOTHING COMPANY   p 735
See DUBWEAR INC

DUBWEAR INC   p 735
7880 TRANMERE DR, MISSISSAUGA, ON, L5S 1L9
(905) 362-1334   *SIC* 5136

DUCA FINANCIAL SERVICES CREDIT UNION LTD   p 771
5290 YONGE ST, NORTH YORK, ON, M2N 5P9
(416) 223-8502   *SIC* 6062

DUCARTOR HOLDINGS LTD   p 950
130 ADELAIDE ST W SUITE 701, TORONTO, ON, M5H 2K4
(416) 593-5555   *SIC* 8741

DUCHARME MOTORS LTD   p 6
5714 50 AVE, BONNYVILLE, AB, T9N 2K8
(780) 826-3278   *SIC* 5511

DUCHARME SEATING   p 1343
See 4372727 CANADA INC

DUCHESNAY INC   p 1059
950 BOUL MICHELE-BOHEC, BLAINVILLE, QC, J7C 5E2
(450) 433-7734   *SIC* 2834

DUCHESNE AUTO LTEE   p 1045
450 BOUL DE QUEN, ALMA, QC, G8B 5P5
(418) 662-3431   *SIC* 5511

DUCHESNE CHEVROLET OLDSMOBILE p 1045
See DUCHESNE AUTO LTEE

DUCHESNE ET FILS LTEE   p 1403
871 BOUL DUCHESNE, YAMACHICHE, QC, G0X 3L0
(819) 296-3737   *SIC* 3315

DUCHESS ATELIER   p 95
See DUCHESS BAKE SHOP LTD

DUCHESS BAKE SHOP LTD   p 95
10718 124 ST, EDMONTON, AB, T5M 0H1
(780) 488-4999   *SIC* 5461

DUCK POND OPERATIONS   p 425
See TECK RESOURCES LIMITED

DUCK SUCKERS   p 894
See WINNERS HOME CENTRAL INC

DUCKERING'S TRANSPORT LTD   p 155
7794 47 AVENUE CLOSE, RED DEER, AB, T4P 2J9
(403) 346-8855   *SIC* 4213

DUCKS UNLIMITED CANADA   p 250
7813 RENISON PL, PRINCE GEORGE, BC, V2N 3J2
(250) 964-3825   *SIC* 8999

DUCKS UNLIMITED CANADA   p 359
1 MALLARD BAY HWY SUITE 220, STONEWALL, MB, R0C 2Z0
(204) 467-3000   *SIC* 8999

DUCLOS CHRYSLER MERCIER   p 1151
See 9264-1711 QUEBEC INC

DUCLOS LONGUEUIL CHRYSLER DODGE JEEP RAM INC   p 1308
5055 BOUL COUSINEAU, SAINT-HUBERT, QC, J3Y 3K7
(450) 656-4110   *SIC* 5511

DUECK AUTO GROUP TIRE STORE p 290
See DUECK CHEVROLET BUICK CADILLAC GMC LIMITED

DUECK CHEVROLET BUICK CADILLAC GMC LIMITED   p 290
400 MARINE DR SE, VANCOUVER, BC, V5X 4X2
(604) 324-7222   *SIC* 5012

DUECK CHEVROLET BUICK CADILLAC GMC LIMITED   p 290
400 MARINE DR SE, VANCOUVER, BC, V5X 4X2
(604) 324-7222   *SIC* 5511

DUECK GM   p 290
See DUECK CHEVROLET BUICK CADILLAC GMC LIMITED

DUECK PONTIAC BUICK GMC LIMITED p 294
888 TERMINAL AVE, VANCOUVER, BC, V6A 0A9
(604) 675-7900   *SIC* 5511

DUEDATE LOGISTICS   p 1331
See 1092072 ONTARIO INC

DUFFERIN AGGREGATES, DIV. OF p 683
See CRH CANADA GROUP INC

DUFFERIN CONCRETE   p 551
See CRH CANADA GROUP INC

DUFFERIN CONSTRUCTION COMPANY, DIV OF   p 802
See CRH CANADA GROUP INC

DUFFERIN CONSTRUCTION DIV OF p 803
See CRH CANADA GROUP INC

DUFFERIN CUSTOM CONCRETE   p 668
See CRH CANADA GROUP INC

DUFFERIN OAKS HOME FOR SENIOR CITIZENS   p 880
See CORPORATION OF THE COUNTY OF DUFFERIN, THE

DUFFERIN TRAVEL INC   p 942
35 THE ESPLANADE SUITE 200, TORONTO, ON, M5E 1Z4
(416) 369-1750   *SIC* 4725

DUFFERIN-PEEL CATHOLIC DISTRICT SCHOOL BOARD   p 499
25 CORPORATION DR, BRAMPTON, ON, L6S 6A2
(905) 791-1195   *SIC* 8211

DUFFERIN-PEEL CATHOLIC DISTRICT SCHOOL BOARD   p 499
950 NORTH PARK DR, BRAMPTON, ON, L6S 3L5
(905) 792-2282   *SIC* 8211

DUFFERIN-PEEL CATHOLIC DISTRICT SCHOOL BOARD   p 512
2 NOTRE DAME AVE, BRAMPTON, ON, L6Z 4L5
(905) 840-2802   *SIC* 8211

DUFFERIN-PEEL CATHOLIC DISTRICT SCHOOL BOARD   p 532
6500 OLD CHURCH RD, CALEDON EAST, ON, L7C 0H3
(905) 584-1670   *SIC* 8211

DUFFERIN-PEEL CATHOLIC DISTRICT SCHOOL BOARD   p 694
4235 GOLDEN ORCHARD DR, MISSISSAUGA, ON, L4W 3G1
(905) 624-4529   *SIC* 8211

DUFFERIN-PEEL CATHOLIC DISTRICT SCHOOL BOARD   p 694
635 WILLOWBANK TRAIL, MISSISSAUGA, ON, L4W 3L6
(905) 279-1554   *SIC* 8211

DUFFERIN-PEEL CATHOLIC DISTRICT SCHOOL BOARD   p 709
330 CENTRAL PKY W, MISSISSAUGA, ON, L5B 3K6
(905) 277-0326   *SIC* 8211

DUFFERIN-PEEL CATHOLIC DISTRICT

SCHOOL BOARD   p 718
2800 ERIN CENTRE BLVD, MISSISSAUGA, ON, L5M 6R5
(905) 820-3900   *SIC* 8211

DUFFERIN-PEEL CATHOLIC DISTRICT SCHOOL BOARD   p 718
3801 THOMAS ST, MISSISSAUGA, ON, L5M 7G2
(905) 285-0050   *SIC* 8211

DUFFERIN-PEEL CATHOLIC DISTRICT SCHOOL BOARD   p 731
40 MATHESON BLVD W, MISSISSAUGA, ON, L5R 1C5
(905) 890-1221   *SIC* 8211

DUFFERIN-PEEL CATHOLIC DISTRICT SCHOOL BOARD   p 744
5555 CREDITVIEW RD, MISSISSAUGA, ON, L5V 2B9
(905) 812-1376   *SIC* 8211

DUFFIN FAMILY HOLDINGS LTD   p 75
9 CROWFOOT CIR NW, CALGARY, AB, T3G 3J8
(403) 239-1115   *SIC* 6712

DUFFLET PASTRIES, A DIV OF   p 573
See BEST BAKING INC

DUFFY'S TAXI (1996) LTD   p 380
1100 NOTRE DAME AVE, WINNIPEG, MB, R3E 0N8
(204) 925-0101   *SIC* 4121

DUFORT ET LAVIGNE LTEE   p 1238
8581 PLACE MARIEN, MONTREAL-EST, QC, H1B 5W6
(514) 527-9381   *SIC* 5047

DUFORT INDUSTRIES LTD   p 384
999 KING EDWARD ST UNIT 6, WINNIPEG, MB, R3H 0R1
(204) 633-3381   *SIC* 5551

DUFOUR PONTIAC CHEVROLET INC p 1122
2040 BOUL DE COMPORTE, LA MALBAIE, QC, G5A 3C4
(418) 665-7511   *SIC* 5511

DUFRESNE FURNITURE & APPLIANCES p 389
See TDG FURNITURE INC

DUFRESNE GROUP INC, THE   p 388
116 NATURE PARK WAY, WINNIPEG, MB, R3P 0X8
(204) 989-9898   *SIC* 5021

DUFRESNE PILING COMPANY (1967) LIMITED   p 832
100 CITIGATE DR, OTTAWA, ON, K2J 6K7
(613) 739-5355   *SIC* 1794

DUFRESNE, ANDRE INSURANCE   p 1167
4061 RUE HOCHELAGA, MONTREAL, QC, H1W 1K4
(514) 256-3626   *SIC* 6411

DUFRESNE, FERNAND INC   p 1261
455 RUE DES ENTREPRENEURS BUREAU 513, QUEBEC, QC, G1M 2V2
(418) 688-1820   *SIC* 5983

DUFRESNE, L. & FILS LTEE   p 1391
2500 RUE DE L'EGLISE, VAL-DAVID, QC, J0T 2N0
(819) 322-2030   *SIC* 5411

DUFRESNE, MARC (1978) INC   p 1386
5345 RUE SAINT-JOSEPH, TROIS-RIVIERES, QC, G8Z 4M5
(819) 374-1433   *SIC* 5983

DUGGAN, PAT REAL ESTATE SERVICES LTD   p 75
156 CITADEL CLOSE NW, CALGARY, AB, T3G 4A6
(403) 547-8401   *SIC* 6531

DUHA COLOR SERVICES LIMITED   p 384
750 BRADFORD ST, WINNIPEG, MB, R3H 0N3
(204) 786-8961   *SIC* 2752

DUHA GROUP   p 384
See DUHA COLOR SERVICES LIMITED

DUKE ELECTRIC (1977) LIMITED   p 610
986 BARTON ST E, HAMILTON, ON, L8L 3C7

(905) 547-9171   *SIC 5063*
DUKE MARINE TECHNICAL SERVICES CANADA INC   *p 527*
3425 HARVESTER RD SUITE 213, BURLINGTON, ON, L7N 3N1
(800) 252-6027   *SIC 7361*
DUKE POINT SAWMILL   *p 234*
See *WESTERN FOREST PRODUCTS INC*
DULIBAN INSURANCE BROKERS LIMITED
p 591
165 HWY 20 SUITE 7, FONTHILL, ON, L0S 1E5
(905) 892-5723   *SIC 6411*
DULUTH, MISSABE AND IRON RANGE RAILWAY COMPANY   *p 1203*
935 RUE DE LA GAUCHETIERE O BUREAU 4E, MONTREAL, QC, H3B 2M9
(514) 399-4536   *SIC 4011*
DUMAIS, ALBERT INC   *p 1390*
1806 3E AV, VAL-D'OR, QC, J9P 7A9
(819) 825-9999   *SIC 5014*
DUMAS CONTRACTING LTD   *p 962*
200 BAY ST SUITE 2301, TORONTO, M5J 2J1
(416) 594-2525   *SIC 1081*
DUMAS MINING   *p 962*
See *DUMAS CONTRACTING LTD*
DUMAS YOUR INDEPENDENT GROCERS *p 900*
82 LORNE ST, SUDBURY, ON, P3C 4N8
(705) 671-3051   *SIC 5411*
DUMOULIN ELECTRONIQUE   *p 1373*
See *DOYON, G. T. V. (SHERBROOKE) INC*
DUMUR INDUSTRIES   *p 1438*
See *1343080 ALBERTA LTD*
DUN & BRADSTREET   *p 721*
See *D&B COMPANIES OF CANADA ULC, THE*
DUNBAR LUMBER SUPPLY   *p 210*
4989 BRIDGE ST, DELTA, BC, V4K 2K3
(604) 946-7322   *SIC 5031*
DUNBARTON HIGH SCHOOL   *p 843*
See *DURHAM DISTRICT SCHOOL BOARD*
DUNCAN AUTO PARTS   *p 211*
See *DUNCAN AUTO PARTS (1983) LTD*
DUNCAN AUTO PARTS (1983) LTD   *p 211*
5829 DUNCAN ST, DUNCAN, BC, V9L 3W7
(250) 746-5431   *SIC 5531*
DUNCAN CRAIG LLP   *p 88*
10060 JASPER AVE NW SUITE 2800, EDMONTON, AB, T5J 3V9
(780) 428-6036   *SIC 8111*
DUNCAN CRAIG LLP   *p 172*
4725 56 ST SUITE 103, WETASKIWIN, AB, T9A 3M2
(780) 352-1662   *SIC 8111*
DUNCAN GARAGE CAFE & BAKERY *p 211*
See *COMMUNITY FARM STORE LTD, THE*
DUNCAN WHITE SPOT   *p 211*
See *458890 B.C. LTD*
DUNCOR ENTERPRISES INC   *p 486*
101 BIG BAY POINT RD, BARRIE, ON, L4N 8M5
(705) 730-1999   *SIC 1611*
DUNDAS JAFINE INC   *p 502*
80 WEST DR, BRAMPTON, ON, L6T 3T6
(905) 450-7200   *SIC 3433*
DUNDAS MANOR LTD   *p 1016*
533 CLARENCE ST SUITE 970, WINCHESTER, ON, K0C 2K0
(613) 774-2293   *SIC 8051*
DUNDEE CORPORATION   *p 938*
1 ADELAIDE ST E SUITE 2000, TORONTO, ON, M5C 2V9
(416) 350-3388   *SIC 6211*
DUNDEE FEEDS   *p 1347*
See *MAHEU, GERARD INC*
DUNDEE PRECIOUS METALS INC   *p 938*
1 ADELAIDE ST E SUITE 500, TORONTO, ON, M5C 2V9
(416) 365-5191   *SIC 1041*
DUNDEE SECURITY   *p 875*
See *HOLLISWEALTH INC*
DUNGEY, D.B. HOLDINGS INC   *p 423*

8 CROMER AVE, GRAND FALLS-WINDSOR, NL, A2A 1X2
(709) 489-9270   *SIC 5531*
DUNKIN DONUT   *p 1376*
See *PEFOND INC*
DUNLOP STERLING TRUCK CENTRE LTD
p 140
4110 9 AVE N, LETHBRIDGE, AB, T1H 6L9
(403) 317-2450   *SIC 4212*
DUNLOP STERLING WESTERN STAR   *p 140*
See *DUNLOP STERLING TRUCK CENTRE LTD*
DUNMAC GENERAL CONTRACTORS LTD   *p 1427*
3038 FAITHFULL AVE, SASKATOON, SK, S7K 0B1
(306) 934-3044   *SIC 1542*
DUNN ENTERPRISES   *p 515*
See *COMMUNITY LIVING BRANT*
DUNN HOLDINGS INC   *p 598*
1035 MARINA RD, GRAVENHURST, ON, P1P 1R2
(705) 687-7793   *SIC 5551*
DUNN PAVING LIMITED   *p 902*
485 LITTLE BASELINE RD, TECUMSEH, ON, N8N 2L9
(519) 727-3838   *SIC 1611*
DUNN, CRAIG MOTOR CITY   *p 354*
See *DUNN, CRAIG PONTIAC BUICK GMC LTD*
DUNN, CRAIG PONTIAC BUICK GMC LTD *p 354*
2345 SISSONS DR, PORTAGE LA PRAIRIE, MB, R1N 3P1
(204) 239-5770   *SIC 5511*
DUNN-RITE FOOD PRODUCTS LTD   *p 390*
199 HAMELIN ST, WINNIPEG, MB, R3T 0P2
(204) 452-8379   *SIC 5144*
DUNNE, WILLIAM M & ASSOCIATES LIMITED   *p 1031*
10 DIRECTOR CRT SUITE 300, WOODBRIDGE, ON, L4L 7E8
(905) 856-5240   *SIC 5141*
DUNNINGTON HOLDINGS LTD   *p 1436*
1 COMMODITY DR, SUCCESS, SK, S0N 2R0
(306) 773-9748   *SIC 5153*
DUNRITE EXPRESS & HOTSHOT INC *p 109*
9435 47 ST NW, EDMONTON, AB, T6B 2R7
(780) 463-8880   *SIC 7389*
DUNSMUIR MIDDLE SCHOOL   *p 340*
See *SCHOOL DISTRICT NO 62 (SOOKE)*
DUNTON RAINVILLE SENC   *p 1229*
800 RUE DU SQUARE-VICTORIA BUREAU 43, MONTREAL, QC, H4Z 1A1
(514) 866-6743   *SIC 8111*
DUNVEGAN NORTH OILFIELD SERVICES ULC   *p 126*
GD, FAIRVIEW, AB, T0H 1L0
(780) 835-3511   *SIC 1623*
DUO COMMUNICATIONS OF CANADA LTD *p 1224*
10000 BOUL CAVENDISH, MONTREAL, QC, H4M 2V1
SIC 5099
DUOCOM CANADA   *p 1224*
See *DUO COMMUNICATIONS OF CANADA LTD*
DUOPAC PACKAGING   *p 1252*
See *PRETIUM CANADA COMPANY*
DUOPHARM INC   *p 1090*
4894 BOUL DES SOURCES BUREAU 66, DOLLARD-DES-ORMEAUX, QC, H8Y 3C7
(514) 684-6131   *SIC 5912*
DUPLIUM CORP   *p 904*
35 MINTHORN BLVD, THORNHILL, ON, L3T 7N5
(905) 709-9930   *SIC 7334*
DUPONT & DUPONT FORD   *p 1107*
See *DUPORTAGE FORD LTEE*
DUPONT & DUPONT HONDA   *p 1103*

See *7618280 CANADA INC*
DUPONT FORD LTEE   *p 1315*
190 RUE MOREAU, SAINT-JEAN-SUR-RICHELIEU, QC, J2W 2M4
(450) 359-3673   *SIC 5511*
DUPONT PIONEER   *p 721*
1919 MINNESOTA CRT, MISSISSAUGA, ON, L5N 0C9
(519) 352-6350   *SIC 5191*
DUPORTAGE FORD LTEE   *p 1107*
949 BOUL SAINT-JOSEPH, GATINEAU, QC, J8Z 1S8
(819) 778-2751   *SIC 5511*
DUPRE, CHEVROLET-CADILLAC   *p 1358*
See *DESCHAMPS CHEVROLET BUICK CADILLAC GMC LTEE*
DUPUIS MAGNA COSMETIQUES INTERNATIONAL INC   *p 1303*
191 RUE LEVEILLE, SAINT-FRANCOIS-DU-LAC, QC, J0G 1M0
(450) 568-3517   *SIC 5122*
DUPUIS, FORD LINCOLN INC   *p 541*
603 RUE ST ISIDORE, CASSELMAN, ON, K0A 1M0
(613) 764-2994   *SIC 5511*
DUPUIS, PIERRE ET CAMILLE INC *p 1163*
2150 BOUL PIERRE-BERNARD, MONTREAL, QC, H1L 4P4
(514) 351-9950   *SIC 5172*
DURA BAMBOO   *p 255*
See *IMAC ENTERPRISES CORP*
DURA CONSTRUCTION LTD   *p 1415*
555 MCDONALD ST, REGINA, SK, S4N 4X1
(306) 721-6866   *SIC 1542*
DURA KIT   *p 1361*
See *ARTICLES MENAGERS DURA INC*
DURA-LITE HEAT TRANSFER PRODUCTS LTD   *p 70*
12012 44 ST SE, CALGARY, AB, T2Z 4A2
(403) 259-2691   *SIC 3714*
DURABLE RELEASE COATERS LIMITED *p 502*
4 FINLEY RD, BRAMPTON, ON, L6T 1A9
(905) 457-2000   *SIC 3479*
DURABOND PRODUCTS LIMITED   *p 872*
55 UNDERWRITERS RD, SCARBOROUGH, ON, M1R 3B4
(416) 759-4133   *SIC 2891*
DURABOX   *p 1250*
See *EMBALLAGES SXP INC*
DURABUILT WINDOWS & DOORS INC   *p 100*
10920 178 ST NW, EDMONTON, AB, T5S 1R7
(780) 455-0440   *SIC 3442*
DURACOAT POWDER MANUFACTURING DIV   *p 600*
See *SHERWIN-WILLIAMS CANADA INC*
DURADEK   *p 276*
See *DURADEK CANADA LIMITED*
DURADEK CANADA LIMITED   *p 276*
8288 129 ST, SURREY, BC, V3W 0A6
(604) 591-5594   *SIC 5039*
DURAGUARD WHOLESALE FENCE LTD *p 100*
10624 214 ST NW, EDMONTON, AB, T5S 2A5
(780) 447-5465   *SIC 5031*
DURAL, DIV OF   *p 1094*
See *MULTIBOND INC*
DURAND & PRATT   *p 1199*
See *SERVICES DE PLACEMENT DE PERSONNEL DURAND & PRATT INC, LES*
DURAND NEIGHBOURHOOD INVESTMENTS INC   *p 612*
15 BOLD ST, HAMILTON, ON, L8P 1T3
SIC 6733
DURAPAINT INDUSTRIES LIMITED   *p 878*
247 FINCHDENE SQ SUITE 1, SCARBOROUGH, ON, M1X 1B9
(416) 754-3664   *SIC 3471*

DURAY   *p 1254*
See *TRICOTS DUVAL & RAYMOND LTEE, LES*
DURE FOODS LIMITED   *p 514*
120 ROY BLVD, BRANTFORD, ON, N3R 7K2
(519) 753-5504   *SIC 7389*
DUREZ CANADA COMPANY LTD   *p 591*
100 DUNLOP ST, FORT ERIE, ON, L2A 5M6
(905) 346-8700   *SIC 2821*
DURHAM CATHOLIC DISTRICT SCHOOL BOARD   *p 474*
80 MANDRAKE ST, AJAX, ON, L1S 5H4
(905) 427-6667   *SIC 8211*
DURHAM CATHOLIC DISTRICT SCHOOL BOARD   *p 475*
1375 HARWOOD AVE N, AJAX, ON, L1T 4G8
(905) 686-4300   *SIC 8211*
DURHAM CATHOLIC DISTRICT SCHOOL BOARD   *p 813*
650 ROSSLAND RD W, OSHAWA, ON, L1J 7C4
(905) 576-6150   *SIC 8211*
DURHAM CATHOLIC DISTRICT SCHOOL BOARD   *p 1015*
3001 COUNTRY LANE, WHITBY, ON, L1P 1M1
(905) 666-7753   *SIC 8211*
DURHAM CATHOLIC DISTRICT SCHOOL BOARD   *p 1016*
1020 DRYDEN BLVD, WHITBY, ON, L1R 2A2
(905) 666-2010   *SIC 8211*
DURHAM COLLEGE OF APPLIED ARTS AND TECHNOLOGY, THE   *p 812*
2000 SIMCOE ST N, OSHAWA, ON, L1H 7K4
(905) 721-2000   *SIC 8222*
DURHAM CUSTOM MILLWORK INC *p 811*
19 TAMBLYN RD, ORONO, ON, L0B 1M0
(905) 683-8444   *SIC 2599*
DURHAM DISTRICT SCHOOL BOARD   *p 474*
105 BAYLY ST E, AJAX, ON, L1S 1P2
(905) 683-1610   *SIC 8211*
DURHAM DISTRICT SCHOOL BOARD   *p 811*
265 HARMONY RD N, OSHAWA, ON, L1G 6L4
(905) 723-8157   *SIC 8211*
DURHAM DISTRICT SCHOOL BOARD   *p 811*
301 SIMCOE ST N, OSHAWA, ON, L1G 4T2
(905) 728-7531   *SIC 8211*
DURHAM DISTRICT SCHOOL BOARD   *p 812*
1356 SIMCOE ST S, OSHAWA, ON, L1H 4M4
(905) 725-7042   *SIC 8211*
DURHAM DISTRICT SCHOOL BOARD   *p 813*
155 GIBB ST, OSHAWA, ON, L1J 1Y4
SIC 8211
DURHAM DISTRICT SCHOOL BOARD   *p 813*
570 STEVENSON RD N, OSHAWA, ON, L1J 5P1
(905) 728-9407   *SIC 8211*
DURHAM DISTRICT SCHOOL BOARD   *p 843*
655 SHEPPARD AVE, PICKERING, ON, L1V 1G2
(905) 839-1125   *SIC 8211*
DURHAM DISTRICT SCHOOL BOARD   *p 845*
2155 LIVERPOOL RD, PICKERING, ON, L1X 1V4
(905) 420-1885   *SIC 8211*
DURHAM DISTRICT SCHOOL BOARD   *p 848*
160 ROSA ST, PORT PERRY, ON, L9L 1L7
(905) 985-7337   *SIC 8211*

DURHAM DISTRICT SCHOOL BOARD *p 1014*
400 ANDERSON ST, WHITBY, ON, L1N 3V6
(905) 668-5809 *SIC 8211*

DURHAM DISTRICT SCHOOL BOARD *p 1014*
600 HENRY ST, WHITBY, ON, L1N 5C7
(905) 666-5500 *SIC 8211*

DURHAM DISTRICT SCHOOL BOARD *p 1015*
681 ROSSLAND RD W, WHITBY, ON, L1P 1Y1
(905) 665-5057 *SIC 8211*

DURHAM DISTRICT SCHOOL BOARD *p 1016*
400 TAUNTON RD E, WHITBY, ON, L1R 2K6
(905) 686-2711 *SIC 8211*

DURHAM DODGE CHRYSLER *p 813*
See *FOREST PARK MOTORS INC*

DURHAM FURNITURE INC *p 567*
450 LAMBTON ST W, DURHAM, ON, N0G 1R0
(519) 369-2345 *SIC 2511*

DURHAM KIA *p 815*
See *JAMES CAMPBELL SERVICES LTD*

DURHAM MENTAL HEALTH SERVICES *p 1014*
519 BROCK ST S, WHITBY, ON, L1N 4K8
(905) 666-0831 *SIC 8399*

DURHAM REGION NON PROFIT HOUSING CORPORATION *p 812*
28 ALBERT ST, OSHAWA, ON, L1H 8S5
(905) 436-6610 *SIC 6531*

DURHAM REGION PLANNING *p 1014*
1615 DUNDAS ST E SUITE 4, WHITBY, ON, L1N 2L1
(905) 723-1365 *SIC 8742*

DURHAM TRUCK & EQUIPMENT SALES & SERVICE *p 474*
See *MACK SALES & SERVICE OF DURHAM INC*

DURHAMWAY BUS LINES, DIV OF *p 812*
See *473980 ONTARIO LTD*

DURISOL MATERIALS LIMITED *p 1*
67 FRID ST, HAMILTON, ON, L8P 4M3
(905) 521-0999 *SIC 6712*

DURO-COTE COMPANY LIMITED *p 502*
29 MELANIE DR, BRAMPTON, ON, L6T 4K8
SIC 3479

DUROCHER INTERNATIONAL *p 1303*
See *TRANSPORT TFI 19, S.E.C.*

DURON ONTARIO LTD *p 694*
1860 SHAWSON DR, MISSISSAUGA, ON, L4W 1R7
(905) 670-1998 *SIC 1771*

DURON PLASTICS LIMITED *p 636*
965 WILSON AVE, KITCHENER, ON, N2C 1J1
(519) 884-8011 *SIC 3089*

DUROSE MANUFACTURING LIMITED *p 600*
460 ELIZABETH ST, GUELPH, ON, N1E 6C1
(519) 822-5251 *SIC 3446*

DUROX FLOOR ACCESSORIES LIMITED *p 783*
255 STEEPROCK DR, NORTH YORK, ON, M3J 2Z5
(416) 630-4883 *SIC 5087*

DURWARD JONES BARKWELL & COMPANY LLP *p 886*
20 CORPORATE PARK DR SUITE 300, ST CATHARINES, ON, L2S 3W2
(905) 684-9221 *SIC 8721*

DURWEST CONSTRUCTION SYSTEMS (ALBERTA) LTD *p 15*
10665 46 ST SE, CALGARY, AB, T2C 5C2
(403) 253-7385 *SIC 5211*

DURWEST HOLDINGS LTD *p 337*
4400 CHATTERTON WAY SUITE 301, VICTORIA, BC, V8X 5J2

(250) 881-7878 *SIC 8741*

DUSTBANE HOLDINGS INC *p 817*
25 PICKERING PL, OTTAWA, ON, K1G 5P4
(613) 745-6861 *SIC 6712*

DUSTBANE PRODUCTS LIMITED *p 817*
25 PICKERING PL, OTTAWA, ON, K1G 5P4
(800) 387-8226 *SIC 2842*

DUSYK & BARLOW INSURANCE BROKERS LTD *p 1422*
302 UNIVERSITY PARK DR, REGINA, SK, S4V 0Y8
(306) 791-3474 *SIC 6411*

DUTCH INDUSTRIES LTD *p 1413*
500 PORTICO DRIVE, PILOT BUTTE, SK, S0G 3Z0
(306) 781-4820 *SIC 3523*

DUTCH MARKET LIMITED, THE *p 542*
80 WILLIAM ST S, CHATHAM, ON, N7M 4S3
(519) 352-2831 *SIC 5141*

DUTCHMASTER NURSERIES LIMITED *p 520*
3735 SIDELINE 16, BROUGHAM, ON, L0H 1A0
(905) 683-8211 *SIC 5193*

DUTCHMEN EQUIPMENT LTD *p 78*
4613 41 ST, CAMROSE, AB, T4V 2Y8
(780) 672-7946 *SIC 7699*

DUVAL VOLKSWAGEN INC *p 1064*
1301 RUE AMPERE, BOUCHERVILLE, QC, J4B 5Z5
(450) 679-0890 *SIC 5511*

DUVALTEX (CANADA) INC *p 1305*
2805 90E RUE, SAINT-GEORGES, QC, G6A 1K1
(418) 227-9897 *SIC 2221*

DUVALTEX INC *p 1305*
2805 90E RUE, SAINT-GEORGES, QC, G6A 1K1
(418) 227-9897 *SIC 6712*

DUVET COMFORT INC *p 874*
130 COMMANDER BLVD, SCARBOROUGH, ON, M1S 3H7
(416) 754-1455 *SIC 2329*

DUZ CHO CONSTRUCTION LIMITED PARTNERSHIP *p 196*
4821 ACCESS RD S, CHETWYND, BC, V0C 1J0
(250) 788-3120 *SIC 4619*

DV SYSTEMS INC *p 486*
490 WELHAM RD, BARRIE, ON, L4N 8Z4
(705) 728-5657 *SIC 3563*

DVA SECURITY GROUP *p 334*
See *FIRST ISLAND ARMOURED TRANSPORT (1998) LTD*

DVI LIGHTING INC *p 552*
120 GREAT GULF DR, CONCORD, ON, L4K 5W1
(905) 660-2381 *SIC 5063*

DVT GROUP, THE *p 704*
See *2142064 ONTARIO INC*

DW MANAGEMENT COMPANY *p 969*
See *DICKINSON WRIGHT LLP*

DWB CONSULTING SERVICES LTD *p 224*
3361 HELENA LAKE RD, LAC LA HACHE, BC, V0K 1T1
(250) 396-7208 *SIC 8748*

DWIGHT CRANE LTD *p 474*
131 DOWTY RD, AJAX, ON, L1S 2G3
(905) 686-3333 *SIC 7353*

DWS DATA WIRING SOLUTIONS INC *p 458*
127 CHAIN LAKE DR UNIT 1, HALIFAX, NS, B3S 1B3
(902) 445-9473 *SIC 3651*

DY 4 SYSTEMS INC *p 626*
333 PALLADIUM DR, KANATA, ON, K2V 1A6
(613) 599-9199 *SIC 3672*

DYACO CANADA INC *p 758*
5955 DON MURIE ST, NIAGARA FALLS, ON, L2G 0A9
(905) 353-8955 *SIC 5091*

DYADEM INTERNATIONAL LTD *p 765*
155 GORDON BAKER RD SUITE 401, NORTH YORK, ON, M2H 3N5
(416) 649-9200 *SIC 5045*

DYANAMEX COURIER *p 1430*
See *TFORCE FINAL MILE CANADA INC*

DYAND MECHANICAL SYSTEMS INC *p 95*
14840 115 AVE NW, EDMONTON, AB, T5M 3C1
(780) 452-5800 *SIC 5999*

DYCK INSURANCE *p 67*
See *DYCK INSURANCE SERVICE LTD*

DYCK INSURANCE AGENCY (WETASKIWIN) LTD. *p 172*
5105 47 AVE, WETASKIWIN, AB, T9A 0K4
(780) 352-9222 *SIC 6411*

DYCK INSURANCE SERVICE LTD *p 67*
24 ST SW, CALGARY, AB, T2T 5H9
(403) 246-4600 *SIC 6411*

DYER ROAD LEASING LTD *p 562*
850 EDUCATION RD, CORNWALL, ON, K6H 6B8
(613) 932-8038 *SIC 4212*

DYFOTECH INC *p 1089*
120 RUE GOODFELLOW, DELSON, QC, J5B 1V4
(450) 635-8870 *SIC 1629*

DYKELAND LODGE *p 470*
See *HANTS COUNTY RESIDENCE FOR SENIOR CITIZENS*

DYLAN RYAN TELESERVICES *p 312*
1177 HASTINGS ST W SUITE 411, VANCOUVER, BC, V6E 2K3
SIC 7389

DYMAXION COMPUTER SALES *p 452*
See *DYMAXION RESEARCH LIMITED*

DYMAXION RESEARCH LIMITED *p 452*
5515 COGSWELL ST, HALIFAX, NS, B3J 1R2
(902) 422-1973 *SIC 5734*

DYMON STORAGE CORPORATION *p 819*
1830 WALKLEY RD UNIT 1, OTTAWA, ON, K1H 8K3
(613) 247-9908 *SIC 4225*

DYMON TECHNOLOGIES INC *p 819*
1830 WALKLEY RD SUITE 2, OTTAWA, ON, K1H 8K3
(613) 247-0888 *SIC 6531*

DYN *p 783*
See *DYN EXPORTERS CANADA INC*

DYN EXPORTERS CANADA INC *p 783*
387 LIMESTONE CRES, NORTH YORK, ON, M3J 2R1
(905) 761-9559 *SIC 5932*

DYNA-FLO CONTROL VALVE SERVICES LTD *p 122*
1911 66 AVE NW, EDMONTON, AB, T6P 1M5
(780) 469-4000 *SIC 5085*

DYNABLAST INC *p 721*
2625 MEADOWPINE BLVD, MISSISSAUGA, ON, L5N 7K5
(888) 881-6667 *SIC 3589*

DYNACARE WORKPLACE *p 502*
See *DYNACARE-GAMMA LABORATORY PARTNERSHIP*

DYNACARE-GAMMA LABORATORY PARTNERSHIP *p 502*
115 MIDAIR CRT, BRAMPTON, ON, L6T 5M3
(905) 790-3515 *SIC 8071*

DYNACARE-GAMMA LABORATORY PARTNERSHIP *p 817*
750 PETER MORAND CRES, OTTAWA, ON, K1G 6S4
(613) 729-0200 *SIC 8071*

DYNACAST LTD *p 840*
710 NEAL DR, PETERBOROUGH, ON, K9J 6X7
(705) 748-9522 *SIC 3369*

DYNAENERGETICS CANADA HOLDINGS INC *p 109*
5911 56 AVE NW, EDMONTON, AB, T6B 3E2
(780) 490-0939 *SIC 1389*

DYNAENERGETICS CANADA INC *p 109*
5911 56 AVE NW, EDMONTON, AB, T6B 3E2
(780) 490-0939 *SIC 1389*

DYNAINDUSTRIAL INC *p 1427*
3326 FAITHFULL AVE, SASKATOON, SK, S7K 8H1
(306) 933-4303 *SIC 3532*

DYNALIFEDX *p 88*
10150 102 ST NW SUITE 200, EDMONTON, AB, T5J 5E2
(780) 451-3702 *SIC 8071*

DYNALIFEDX DIAGNOSTIC LABORATORY SERVICE *p 88*
See *DYNALIFEDX*

DYNALINE INDUSTRIES INC *p 100*
18070 109 AVE NW, EDMONTON, AB, T5S 2K2
(780) 453-3964 *SIC 5085*

DYNAMEX INDUSTRIAL SUPPLY LTD *p 120*
6558 28 AVE NW UNIT 295, EDMONTON, AB, T6L 6N3
(780) 904-3451 *SIC 5085*

DYNAMIC & PROTO CIRCUITS INC *p 891*
869 BARTON ST, STONEY CREEK, ON, L8E 5G6
SIC 3672

DYNAMIC AIR SHELTERS LTD *p 15*
200 RIVERCREST DR SE SUITE 170, CALGARY, AB, T2C 3K3
(403) 203-9311 *SIC 3448*

DYNAMIC ATTRACTIONS LTD *p 167*
4102 44 AVE, STETTLER, AB, T0C 2L0
SIC 3713

DYNAMIC ATTRACTIONS LTD *p 246*
1515 KINGSWAY AVE, PORT COQUITLAM, BC, V3C 1S2
(604) 639-8200 *SIC 1791*

DYNAMIC CONCRETE PUMPING INC *p 15*
10720 48 ST SE, CALGARY, AB, T2C 3E1
(403) 236-9511 *SIC 1771*

DYNAMIC DIRECT COURIER *p 855*
57 NEWKIRK RD, RICHMOND HILL, ON, L4C 3G4
SIC 7389

DYNAMIC EQUIPEMENT *p 1116*
See *6654100 CANADA INC*

DYNAMIC FOREST PRODUCTS, DIV OF *p 191*
See *TAIGA BUILDING PRODUCTS LTD*

DYNAMIC FURNITURE CORP *p 15*
5300 61 AVE SE, CALGARY, AB, T2C 4N1
(403) 236-3220 *SIC 2511*

DYNAMIC INSTALLATIONS INC *p 246*
1556 KEBET WAY, PORT COQUITLAM, BC, V3C 5M5
(604) 464-7695 *SIC 3462*

DYNAMIC MACHINE CORPORATION *p 365*
1407 DUGALD RD, WINNIPEG, MB, R2J 0H3
(204) 982-4900 *SIC 3599*

DYNAMIC PAINT PRODUCTS INC *p 721*
7040 FINANCIAL DR, MISSISSAUGA, ON, L5N 7H5
(905) 812-9319 *SIC 5198*

DYNAMIC RESCUE SYSTEMS INC *p 200*
63A CLIPPER ST, COQUITLAM, BC, V3K 6X2
(604) 522-0228 *SIC 8999*

DYNAMIC SECURITY AGENCY *p 1126*
2366 RUE VICTORIA, LACHINE, QC, H8S 1Z3
(514) 898-3598 *SIC 7381*

DYNAMIC SHELTERS INC *p 68*
10333 SOUTHPORT RD SW SUITE 523, CALGARY, AB, T2W 3X6
(403) 203-9311 *SIC 3448*

DYNAMIC SOURCE MANUFACTURING INC *p 75*
2765 48 AVE NE UNIT 117, CALGARY, AB,

T3J 5M9
(403) 516-1888   *SIC* 3679
DYNAMIC STRUCTURES LTD   *p* 246
1515 KINGSWAY AVE, PORT COQUITLAM, BC, V3C 1S2
(604) 941-9481   *SIC* 1791
DYNAMIC SUSPENSIONS, DIV OF   *p* 567
See MULTIMATIC INC
DYNAMIC TEAM SPORTS   *p* 872
See TDI-DYNAMIC CANADA ULC
DYNAMIC TECHNOLOGIES   *p* 1091
See 3081354 CANADA INC
DYNAMIC TIRE INC   *p* 1027
211 HUNTER'S VALLEY RD, WOODBRIDGE, ON, L4H 3V9
(905) 595-5558   *SIC* 5014
DYNAMITAGE CASTONGUAY LTEE   *p* 1375
5939 RUE JOYAL, SHERBROOKE, QC, J1N 1H1
(819) 864-4201   *SIC* 1389
DYNAMITAGE DU QUEBEC   *p* 1278
See CONSTRUCTION POLARIS INC
DYNAMITAGE T.C.G. (1993) INC   *p* 1079
111 RUE DES ROUTIERS, CHICOUTIMI, QC, G7H 5B1
(418) 698-5858   *SIC* 1629
DYNAMIX PROFESSIONAL VIDEO SYSTEMS INC   *p* 851
100 LEEK CRES SUITE 1, RICHMOND HILL, ON, L4B 3E6
(905) 882-4000   *SIC* 5049
DYNASTREAM INNOVATIONS   *p* 80
See GARMIN CANADA INC
DYNASTY FURNITURE MANUFACTURING INC   *p* 15
3344 54 AVE SE, CALGARY, AB, T2C 0A8
(403) 279-2958   *SIC* 2512
DYNASTY MACHINERY   *p* 1339
See FERRO TECHNIQUE LTEE
DYNASTY POWER INC   *p* 48
638 6 AVE SW UNIT 200, CALGARY, AB, T2P 0S4
(403) 613-6882   *SIC* 4911
DYNAVENTURE CORP   *p* 1431
2100 AIRPORT DR SUITE 202, SASKATOON, SK, S7L 6M6
SIC 8741
DYNE-A-PAK INC   *p* 1362
3375 AV FRANCIS-HUGHES, SAINTE-ROSE, QC, H7L 5A5
(450) 667-3626   *SIC* 3089
DYNEVOR EXPRESS LTD   *p* 584
24 BETHRIDGE RD, ETOBICOKE, ON, M9W 1N1
(416) 749-2010   *SIC* 4213
DYNEX POWER INC   *p* 624
515 LEGGET DR SUITE 800, KANATA, ON, K2K 3G4
(613) 822-2500   *SIC* 5065
DYNO NOBEL CANADA INC   *p* 15
48 QUARRY PARK BLVD SE SUITE 210, CALGARY, AB, T2C 5P2
(403) 726-7500   *SIC* 2892
DYSON & ARMSTRONG INC   *p* 1283
555 RUE CRAIG, RICHMOND, QC, J0B 2H0
(819) 826-3306   *SIC* 5511
DYSON CANADA LIMITED   *p* 980
312 ADELAIDE ST W, TORONTO, ON, M5V 1R2
(416) 849-5821   *SIC* 5087
DYTERRA CORPORATION   *p* 351
7501 WILKES AVE, HEADINGLEY, MB, R4H 1B8
(204) 885-8260   *SIC* 5083
DZOMBETA DRUG LTD   *p* 190
4827 KINGSWAY SUITE 2283, BURNABY, BC, V5H 4T6
(604) 433-2721   *SIC* 5912

E

E & L DRUGS LTD   *p* 399
269 MAIN ST, FREDERICTON, NB, E3A 1E1

(506) 451-1550   *SIC* 5912
E & T FOODS LTD   *p* 170
5203 50 AVE, VALLEYVIEW, AB, T0H 3N0
(780) 524-4424   *SIC* 5411
E B FOODS   *p* 654
See LEO'S DISTRIBUTING COMPANY CANADA LIMITED
E B M LASER INC   *p* 1292
109 RUE DES GRANDS-LACS, SAINT-AUGUSTIN-DE-DESMAURES, QC, G3A 1V9
(418) 878-3616   *SIC* 7389
E CARE CONTACT CENTERS LTD   *p* 270
15225 104 AVE SUITE 400, SURREY, BC, V3R 6Y8
(604) 587-6200   *SIC* 7389
E CONSTRUCTION LTD   *p* 122
10130 21 ST NW, EDMONTON, AB, T6P 1W7
(780) 467-7701   *SIC* 1611
E F EDUCATION FIRST   *p* 1188
See E F VOYAGES CULTURELS
E F VOYAGES CULTURELS   *p* 1188
407 RUE MCGILL BUREAU 400, MONTREAL, QC, H2Y 2G3
(800) 387-7708   *SIC* 4724
E J C   *p* 524
See SANDVIK CANADA, INC
E L CROSSLEY SECONDARY SCHOOL   *p* 591
See DISTRICT SCHOOL BOARD OF NIAGARA
E M I MUSIC CANADA   *p* 688
3109 AMERICAN DR, MISSISSAUGA, ON, L4V 0A2
SIC 5099
E MADILL OFFICE CO   *p* 233
1400 ROCKY CREEK WAY, NANAIMO, BC, V9R 5C8
(250) 754-1611   *SIC* 5044
E+COLE POLYVALENTE ARVIDA   *p* 1115
See COMMISSION SCOLAIRE DE LA JONQUIERE
E-COMM   *p* 284
See E-COMM EMERGENCY COMMUNICATIONS FOR SOUTHWEST BRITISH COLUMBIA INCORPORATED
E-COMM EMERGENCY COMMUNICATIONS FOR SOUTHWEST BRITISH COLUMBIA INCORPORATED   *p* 284
3301 PENDER ST E, VANCOUVER, BC, V5K 5J3
(604) 215-5000   *SIC* 4899
E-CYCLE SOLUTIONS INC   *p* 685
7510 BREN RD, MISSISSAUGA, ON, L4T 4H1
(905) 671-2900   *SIC* 4953
E-DJUSTER INC   *p* 749
28 CONCOURSE GATE UNIT 203, NEPEAN, ON, K2E 7T7
(866) 779-5950   *SIC* 6411
E-L FINANCIAL CORPORATION LIMITED   *p* 950
165 UNIVERSITY AVE 10TH FL, TORONTO, ON, M5H 3B8
(416) 947-2578   *SIC* 6282
E-M AIR SYSTEMS INC   *p* 552
69 ROMINA DR, CONCORD, ON, L4K 4Z9
(905) 738-0450   *SIC* 1711
E-ONE MOLI ENERGY (CANADA) LIMITED   *p* 231
20000 STEWART CRES, MAPLE RIDGE, BC, V2X 9E7
(604) 466-6654   *SIC* 3691
E-REWARDS   *p* 921
See RESEARCH NOW INC
E-TECH ELECTRICAL SERVICES INC   *p* 552
30 PENNSYLVANIA AVE, CONCORD, ON, L4K 4A5
(905) 669-4062   *SIC* 1731
E-Z-EM CANADA INC   *p* 1048
11065 BOUL LOUIS-H.-LAFONTAINE, ANJOU, QC, H1J 2Z4
(514) 353-5820   *SIC* 3295

E. & E. SEEGMILLER LIMITED   *p* 639
305 ARNOLD ST, KITCHENER, ON, N2H 6G1
(519) 579-6460   *SIC* 1611
E. & J. GALLO WINERY CANADA, LTD   *p* 722
6711 MISSISSAUGA RD SUITE 202, MISSISSAUGA, ON, L5N 2W3
(905) 819-9600   *SIC* 4731
E. BOURASSA & SONS PARTNERSHIP   *p* 1415
HWY 28 S, RADVILLE, SK, S0C 2G0
(306) 869-2277   *SIC* 5083
E. E. C. INDUSTRIES LIMITED   *p* 241
1237 WELCH ST, NORTH VANCOUVER, BC, V7P 1B3
(604) 986-5633   *SIC* 3993
E. F. MOON CONSTRUCTION LTD   *p* 354
1200 LORNE AVE E, PORTAGE LA PRAIRIE, MB, R1N 4A2
(204) 857-7871   *SIC* 1622
E. GAGNON ET FILS LTEE   *p* 1364
405 RTE 132, SAINTE-THERESE-DE-GASPE, QC, G0C 3B0
(418) 385-3011   *SIC* 2091
E. I. DUPONT CANADA - THETFORD INC   *p* 1382
1045 RUE MONFETTE E, THETFORD MINES, QC, G6G 7K7
(418) 338-8567   *SIC* 3299
E. M. PRECISE TOOL LTD   *p* 891
216 ARVIN AVE UNIT A, STONEY CREEK, ON, L8E 2L8
(905) 664-2644   *SIC* 5084
E. ROKO DISTRIBUTORS LTD   *p* 338
646 ALPHA ST, VICTORIA, BC, V8Z 1B2
(250) 381-2552   *SIC* 5072
E.B. HORSMAN & SON LTD   *p* 279
19295 25 AVE, SURREY, BC, V3Z 3X1
(778) 545-9916   *SIC* 5063
E.B.C. HOLDINGS LTD   *p* 124
12708 140 AVE NW, EDMONTON, AB, T6V 1K4
(780) 454-5258   *SIC* 6712
E.B.M LASER   *p* 1292
See 9099-7768 QUEBEC INC
E.C.E. ELECTRIQUE INC   *p* 1373
4345 RUE OUIMET, SHERBROOKE, QC, J1L 1X5
(819) 821-2222   *SIC* 1731
E.C.S. ELECTRICAL CABLE SUPPLY LTD   *p* 258
6900 GRAYBAR RD UNIT 3135, RICHMOND, BC, V6W 0A5
(604) 207-1500   *SIC* 5063
E.C.S. ENGINEERING & CONSTRUCTION LIMITED   *p* 552
51 RITIN LANE UNIT 1, CONCORD, ON, L4K 4E1
(905) 761-7009   *SIC* 1623
E.D. FEEHAN HIGH SCHOOL   *p* 1432
See ST. PAUL'S ROMAN CATHOLIC SEPARATE SCHOOL DIVISION NO 20
E.D. PRODUCTS LTD   *p* 1011
90 ATLAS AVE, WELLAND, ON, L3B 6H5
(905) 732-9473   *SIC* 3679
E.D. SMITH & SONS, LP   *p* 879
151 MAIN ST S, SEAFORTH, ON, N0K 1W0
(800) 263-9246   *SIC* 2035
E.D. SMITH FOODS, LTD   *p* 892
944 HIGHWAY 8, STONEY CREEK, ON, L8E 5S3
(905) 643-1211   *SIC* 2033
E.D.M. LASALLE INC   *p* 1130
7427 BOUL NEWMAN BUREAU 36, LASALLE, QC, H8N 1X3
(514) 365-6633   *SIC* 5311
E.E. ENGRAVER'S EXPRESS INC   *p* 227
20381 62 AVE SUITE 705, LANGLEY, BC, V3A 5E6
(604) 533-3467   *SIC* 5087
E.G. PENNER BUILDING CENTRES LTD   *p* 358
200 PARK RD W, STEINBACH, MB, R5G

1A1
(204) 326-1325   *SIC* 5211
E.H. PRICE DIVISION   *p* 367
See PRICE INDUSTRIES LIMITED
E.K. CONSTRUCTION 2000 LTD   *p* 371
11 YARD ST, WINNIPEG, MB, R2W 5J6
(204) 589-8387   *SIC* 1542
E.L.K. ENERGY INC   *p* 569
172 FOREST AVE, ESSEX, ON, N8M 3E4
(519) 776-5291   *SIC* 4911
E.M.U./RYDER   *p* 1276
See EQUIPEMENTS E.M.U. LTEE
E.O.E. GROUP INC   *p* 694
5484 TOMKEN RD UNIT 4, MISSISSAUGA, ON, L4W 2Z6
(905) 602-6400   *SIC* 5044
E.O.S. PIPELINE & FACILITIES INCORPORATED   *p* 48
736 6 AVE SW SUITE 1205, CALGARY, AB, T2P 3T7
(403) 232-8446   *SIC* 1623
E.R. PROBYN LTD   *p* 236
601 SIXTH ST UNIT 350, NEW WESTMINSTER, BC, V3L 3C1
(604) 526-8545   *SIC* 7389
E.S. FOX LIMITED   *p* 757
9127 MONTROSE RD, NIAGARA FALLS, ON, L2E 7J9
(905) 354-3700   *SIC* 1711
E.S. FOX LIMITED   *p* 900
1349 KELLY LAKE RD SUITE 1, SUDBURY, ON, P3E 5P5
(705) 522-3357   *SIC* 1541
E.S. WILLIAMS & ASSOCIATES INC   *p* 134
10514 67 AVE SUITE 306, GRANDE PRAIRIE, AB, T8W 0K8
(780) 539-4544   *SIC* 7379
E3 (EDUCATE, ENABLE, EMPOWER) COMMUNITY SERVICES INC   *p* 546
100 PRETTY RIVER PKY N, COLLINGWOOD, ON, L9Y 4X2
(705) 445-6351   *SIC* 8351
E3 COMMUNITY SERVICES   *p* 546
See E3 (EDUCATE, ENABLE, EMPOWER) COMMUNITY SERVICES INC
E88TLC90 HOLDINGS LTD   *p* 340
772 GOLDSTREAM AVE, VICTORIA, BC, V9B 2X3
(250) 478-8306   *SIC* 5411
EA SPORTS   *p* 188
See ELECTRONIC ARTS (CANADA) INC
EA SPORTS   *p* 1203
See ELECTRONIC ARTS (CANADA) INC
EAB TOOL COMPANY INC   *p* 205
584 EBURY PL, DELTA, BC, V3M 6M8
(604) 526-4595   *SIC* 5084
EABAMETOONG EDUCATION AUTHORITY   *p* 567
GD, EABAMET LAKE, ON, P0T 1L0
(807) 242-1305   *SIC* 8621
EACOM TIMBER CORPORATION   *p* 747
100 OLD NAIRN RD, NAIRN CENTRE, ON, P0M 2L0
(705) 869-4020   *SIC* 2421
EACOM TIMBER CORPORATION   *p* 1203
1100 BOUL RENE-LEVESQUE O BUREAU 2110, MONTREAL, QC, H3B 4N4
(514) 848-6815   *SIC* 2426
EAGLE AIRFIELD   *p* 540
See TEAM EAGLE LTD
EAGLE BUTTE CROSSING (TEMPO)   *p* 83
7 3RD AVE E, DUNMORE, AB, T0J 1A1
(403) 526-6552   *SIC* 5541
EAGLE CANADA, INC   *p* 35
6806 RAILWAY ST SE, CALGARY, AB, T2H 3A8
(403) 781-1192   *SIC* 1382
EAGLE CINEMATRONICS INC   *p* 276
8299 129 ST UNIT 104, SURREY, BC, V3W 0A6
(604) 592-5511   *SIC* 5099
EAGLE COPTERS LTD   *p* 22

823 MCTAVISH RD NE, CALGARY, AB, T2E 7G9
(403) 250-7370   SIC 6159
EAGLE COPTERS MAINTENANCE LTD p 22
823 MCTAVISH RD NE, CALGARY, AB, T2E 7G9
(403) 250-7370   SIC 4581
EAGLE CREEK COLONY p 1404
See HUTTERIAN BRETHREN CHURCH OF EAGLE CREEK INC
EAGLE CREEK GOLF CLUB p 567
See CLUBLINK CORPORATION ULC
EAGLE CREEK MOTOR PRODUCTS LTD p 1409
809 9TH ST W SUITE 2, MEADOW LAKE, SK, S9X 1Y2
(306) 236-4482   SIC 5511
EAGLE DRILLING SERVICES LTD p 1405
GD, CARLYLE, SK, S0C 0R0
(306) 453-2506   SIC 1781
EAGLE ENERGY INC p 48
500 4 AVE SW SUITE 2710, CALGARY, AB, T2P 2V6
(403) 531-1575   SIC 6726
EAGLE ENERGY TRUST p 48
See EAGLE ENERGY INC
EAGLE FREIGHT SYSTEM p 508
See 2326236 ONTARIO INC
EAGLE INVESTIGATIONS p 657
See EAGLE SURVEILLANCE GROUP LTD
EAGLE LAKE PROFESSIONAL LANDSCAPE SUPPLY p 168
See EAGLE LAKE TURF FARMS LTD
EAGLE LAKE TURF FARMS LTD p 168
GD STN MAIN, STRATHMORE, AB, T1P 1J5
(403) 934-6808   SIC 0181
EAGLE NORTH HOLDINGS INC p 539
2400 EAGLE ST N, CAMBRIDGE, ON, N3H 4R7
(519) 653-7030   SIC 5511
EAGLE PARK HEALTH CARE FACILITY p 252
See VANCOUVER ISLAND HEALTH AUTHORITY
EAGLE PROFESSIONAL RESOURCES INC p 823
170 LAURIER AVE W SUITE 902, OTTAWA, ON, K1P 5V5
SIC 7361
EAGLE PROFESSIONAL RESOURCES INC p 942
67 YONGE ST SUITE 200, TORONTO, ON, M5E 1J8
(416) 861-1492   SIC 7361
EAGLE QUEST GOLF CENTERS INC p 200
1001 UNITED BLVD, COQUITLAM, BC, V3K 4S8
(604) 523-6400   SIC 7999
EAGLE RIDGE CHEVROLET BUICK GMC LTD p 199
2595 BARNET HWY, COQUITLAM, BC, V3E 1K9
(604) 464-3941   SIC 5511
EAGLE RIDGE GOLF CLUB p 593
See CLUBLINK CORPORATION ULC
EAGLE RIDGE MECHANICAL CONTRACTING LTD p 246
1515 BROADWAY ST SUITE 116, PORT COQUITLAM, BC, V3C 6M2
(604) 941-1071   SIC 1711
EAGLE RIVER CHRYSLER LTD p 173
3315 CAXTON ST, WHITECOURT, AB, T7S 1P4
(780) 778-2844   SIC 5511
EAGLE SURVEILLANCE GROUP LTD p 657
1069 WELLINGTON RD SUITE 229, LONDON, ON, N6E 2H6
(519) 680-3269   SIC 7381
EAGLE TRANSPORTATION SYSTEMS, A DIV OF p 412

See R & G TRANSPORT LTD
EAGLE TRAVEL PLAZA p 911
See 908593 ONTARIO LIMITED
EAGLE WORLDWIDE FLEET MANAGEMENT p 22
See EAGLE COPTERS LTD
EAGLE'S NEST COFFEE AND BAKED GOODS INC p 484
234 HASTINGS ST N, BANCROFT, ON, K0L 1C0
(613) 332-0299   SIC 5812
EAGLE, JAMES R. HOLDINGS LIMITED p 646
172 MAIN ST W, LISTOWEL, ON, N4W 1A1
(519) 291-1011   SIC 5199
EAGLEBURGMANN CANADA INC p 683
8699 ESCARPMENT WAY SUITE 9, MILTON, ON, L9T 0J5
(905) 693-8782   SIC 5085
EAGLEPICHER ENERGY PRODUCTS ULC p 276
13136 82A AVE, SURREY, BC, V3W 9Y6
(604) 543-4350   SIC 2819
EAGLEPICHER MEDICAL POWER p 276
See EAGLEPICHER ENERGY PRODUCTS ULC
EAGLES NEST GOLF CLUB INC p 664
10000 DUFFERIN ST, MAPLE, ON, L6A 1S3
(905) 417-2300   SIC 1629
EAGLESON CONSTRUCTION p 682
See 1356594 ONTARIO LTD
EARL HAIG SECONDARY SCHOOL p 773
See TORONTO DISTRICT SCHOOL BOARD
EARL OF MARCH SECONDARY SCHOOL p 625
See OTTAWA-CARLETON DISTRICT SCHOOL BOARD
EARL PADDOCK TRANSPORTATION INC p 892
199 ARVIN AVE, STONEY CREEK, ON, L8E 2L9
(905) 667-8755   SIC 4213
EARL WILLOW PARK p 39
See EARL'S RESTAURANTS LTD
EARL'1 p 217
See EARL'S RESTAURANTS LTD
EARL'S p 22
See EARL'S RESTAURANTS CARRELL LTD
EARL'S p 41
See EARL'S RESTAURANTS LTD
EARL'S p 117
See EARL'S RESTAURANTS LTD
EARL'S p 320
See EARL'S RESTAURANTS LTD
EARL'S p 377
See EARL'S RESTAURANTS LTD
EARL'S p 1427
See EARL'S RESTAURANTS LTD
EARL'S BRIDGE PARK p 185
See EARL'S RESTAURANTS LTD
EARL'S ON TOP RESTAURANT LTD p 221
211 BERNARD AVE, KELOWNA, BC, V1Y 6N2
(250) 763-2777   SIC 5812
EARL'S PORT COQUITLAM p 246
See EARL'S RESTAURANTS LTD
EARL'S RESTAURANT p 131
See EARLS MARKET SQUARE LTD
EARL'S RESTAURANT (CLAREVIEW) LTD p 83
13330 50 ST NW, EDMONTON, AB, T5A 4Z8
(780) 473-9008   SIC 5812
EARL'S RESTAURANT (SHERWOOD PARK) LTD p 162
194 ORDZE AVE, SHERWOOD PARK, AB, T8B 1M6
(780) 449-2575   SIC 5812
EARL'S RESTAURANT (WHITE ROCK) LTD p 280

1767 152 ST SUITE 7, SURREY, BC, V4A 4N3
SIC 5812
EARL'S RESTAURANTS p 298
See EARL'S RESTAURANTS CARRELL LTD
EARL'S RESTAURANTS p 326
See EARL'S RESTAURANTS CARRELL LTD
EARL'S RESTAURANTS p 336
See EARL'S RESTAURANTS LTD
EARL'S RESTAURANTS p 1421
See EARL'S RESTAURANTS LTD
EARL'S RESTAURANTS CARRELL LTD p 22
3030 23 ST NE, CALGARY, AB, T2E 8R7
(403) 291-6700   SIC 5812
EARL'S RESTAURANTS CARRELL LTD p 298
425 CARRALL ST UNIT 200, VANCOUVER, BC, V6B 6E3
(604) 646-4880   SIC 8741
EARL'S RESTAURANTS CARRELL LTD p 326
905 HORNBY ST, VANCOUVER, BC, V6Z 1V3
(604) 682-6700   SIC 5812
EARL'S RESTAURANTS LTD p 39
10640 MACLEOD TRAIL SE, CALGARY, AB, T2J 0P8
(403) 278-7860   SIC 5812
EARL'S RESTAURANTS LTD p 41
1110 16 AVE NW, CALGARY, AB, T2M 0K8
(403) 289-2566   SIC 5812
EARL'S RESTAURANTS LTD p 66
2401 4 ST SW, CALGARY, AB, T2S 1X5
(403) 228-4141   SIC 5812
EARL'S RESTAURANTS LTD p 71
5005 DALHOUSIE DR NW SUITE 605, CALGARY, AB, T3A 5R8
(403) 247-1143   SIC 5812
EARL'S RESTAURANTS LTD p 92
11830 JASPER AVE NW, EDMONTON, AB, T5K 0N7
(780) 488-6582   SIC 5812
EARL'S RESTAURANTS LTD p 117
8629 112 ST NW, EDMONTON, AB, T6G 1K8
(780) 439-4848   SIC 5812
EARL'S RESTAURANTS LTD p 174
32900 SOUTH FRASER WAY SUITE 1, ABBOTSFORD, BC, V2S 5A1
SIC 5812
EARL'S RESTAURANTS LTD p 185
3850 LOUGHEED HWY, BURNABY, BC, V5C 6N4
(604) 291-1019   SIC 5812
EARL'S RESTAURANTS LTD p 217
1210 SUMMIT DR SUITE 800, KAMLOOPS, BC, V2C 6M1
(250) 372-3275   SIC 5812
EARL'S RESTAURANTS LTD p 246
2850 SHAUGHNESSY ST SUITE 5100, PORT COQUITLAM, BC, V3C 6K5
(604) 941-1733   SIC 5812
EARL'S RESTAURANTS LTD p 276
7236 120 ST, SURREY, BC, V3W 3M9
SIC 5812
EARL'S RESTAURANTS LTD p 320
1601 BROADWAY W, VANCOUVER, BC, V6J 1W9
(604) 736-5663   SIC 5812
EARL'S RESTAURANTS LTD p 336
1703 BLANSHARD ST, VICTORIA, BC, V8W 2J8
SIC 5812
EARL'S RESTAURANTS LTD p 341
303 MARINE DR, WEST VANCOUVER, BC, V7P 3J8
SIC 5812
EARL'S RESTAURANTS LTD p 377
191 MAIN ST, WINNIPEG, MB, R3C 1A7
(204) 989-0103   SIC 5812
EARL'S RESTAURANTS LTD p 390

2005 PEMBINA HWY, WINNIPEG, MB, R3T 5W7
SIC 5812
EARL'S RESTAURANTS LTD p 1421
2606 28TH AVE, REGINA, SK, S4S 6P3
(306) 584-7733   SIC 5812
EARL'S RESTAURANTS LTD p 1427
610 2ND AVE N, SASKATOON, SK, S7K 2C8
(306) 664-4060   SIC 5812
EARL'S STRAWBERRY HILL p 276
See EARL'S RESTAURANTS LTD
EARL'S TIN PALACE p 341
See EARL'S RESTAURANTS LTD
EARL'S TIN PALACE RESTAURANT p 92
See EARL'S RESTAURANTS LTD
EARLE M. JORGENSEN (CANADA), DIV OF p 123
See RELIANCE METALS CANADA LIMITED
EARLS INDUSTRIES LTD p 246
1616 KEBET WAY, PORT COQUITLAM, BC, V3C 5W9
(604) 941-8388   SIC 5085
EARLS MARKET SQUARE LTD p 131
9825 100 ST, GRANDE PRAIRIE, AB, T8V 6X3
(780) 538-3275   SIC 5812
EARLS PLACE p 157
See EARLS RESTAURANT (RED DEER) LTD
EARLS RESTAURANT (RED DEER) LTD p 157
2111 50 AVE, RED DEER, AB, T4R 1Z4
(403) 342-4055   SIC 5812
EARLSCOURT METAL INDUSTRIES LTD p 738
6660 ORDAN DR, MISSISSAUGA, ON, L5T 1J7
(905) 564-9000   SIC 5084
EARLY BIRD COMMUNICATORS INC p 639
111 WATER ST N, KITCHENER, ON, N2H 5B1
SIC 7334
EARLY'S FARM & GARDEN CENTRE p 1424
2615 LORNE AVE, SASKATOON, SK, S7J 0S5
(306) 931-1982   SIC 5149
EARTH & ATMOSPHERIC SCIENCES p 118
See GOVERNORS OF THE UNIVERSITY OF ALBERTA, THE
EARTH BORING CO. LIMITED p 713
1576 IFIELD RD, MISSISSAUGA, ON, L5H 3W1
(905) 277-9632   SIC 1622
EARTH POWER TRACTORS AND EQUIPMENT INC p 681
206005 HWY 26 W, MEAFORD, ON, N4L 1A5
(519) 538-1660   SIC 5083
EARTH RATED p 1225
See 9199-4467 QUEBEC INC
EARTH TECH REID CROWTHER p 69
See REID CROWTHER & PARTNERS LIMITED
EARTHCO SOIL MIXTURES INC p 552
401 BOWES RD SUITE 1, CONCORD, ON, L4K 1J4
(905) 761-6599   SIC 5191
EARTHFRESH p 522
See EARTHFRESH FARMS INC
EARTHFRESH FARMS INC p 522
1095 CLAY AVE, BURLINGTON, ON, L7L 0A1
(416) 251-2271   SIC 5148
EARTHFRESH FOODS CORP p 522
1095 CLAY AVE, BURLINGTON, ON, L7L 0A1
(416) 251-2271   SIC 5148
EARTHTECH ENGINEERING p 447
See LVM / MARITIME TESTING LIMITED
EARTHWISE CONSTRUCTION LTD p 100

20104 107 AVE NW, EDMONTON, AB, T5S 1W9

(780) 413-4235   *SIC* 1611

EARTHWISE CONTRACTING LTD   p 100
20104 107 AVE NW, EDMONTON, AB, T5S 1W9

(780) 413-4235   *SIC* 1611

EASSONS TRANSPORT LIMITED   p 442
1505 HARRINGTON RD, COLDBROOK, NS, B4N 3V7

(902) 679-1153   *SIC* 4213

EAST & WEST ALUM CRAFT LTD   p 187
7465 CONWAY AVE, BURNABY, BC, V5E 2P7

(604) 438-6261   *SIC* 3446

EAST CARDSTON COLONY   p 79
See HUTTERIAN BRETHREN CHURCH OF EAST CARDSTON (1977)

EAST CENTRAL ALBERTA CATHOLIC SEPERATE SCHOOLS REGIONAL DIVISION NO 16   p 171
1018 1 AVE, WAINWRIGHT, AB, T9W 1G9

(780) 842-3992   *SIC* 8211

EAST CENTRAL CO-OPERATIVE LIMITED   p 1408
211 1ST AVE, KELVINGTON, SK, S0A 1W0

(306) 327-4745   *SIC* 5411

EAST CENTRAL HEALTH AND PUBLIC HEATH HOMECARE AND REHABILITATION   p 170
4701 52 ST SUITE 11, VERMILION, AB, T9X 1J9

(780) 853-5270   *SIC* 8621

EAST COAST CATERING LIMITED   p 431
30 QUEEN'S RD, ST. JOHN'S, NL, A1C 2A5

(709) 576-1741   *SIC* 7389

EAST COAST CREDIT UNION LIMITED   p 438
257 MAIN ST, ANTIGONISH, NS, B2G 2C1

SIC 6062

EAST COAST INTERNATIONAL TRUCKS INC   p 410
100 URQUHART AVE, MONCTON, NB, E1H 2R5

(506) 857-2857   *SIC* 5012

EAST COAST METAL FABRICATION (2015) INC   p 449
10 MARINE DR, EDWARDSVILLE, NS, B2A 4S6

(902) 564-5600   *SIC* 3312

EAST COAST MOVING & STORAGE   p 412
See 500323 (N.B.) LTD

EAST COAST OUTFITTERS   p 461
2017 LOWER PROSPECT RD, LOWER PROSPECT, NS, B3T 1Y8

(902) 624-0334   *SIC* 4725

EAST COAST POWER SYSTEMS   p 469
See SANSOM EQUIPMENT LIMITED

EAST CUMBERLAND LODGE   p 465
See CUMBERLAND SENIOR CARE CORPORATION

EAST ELGIN CONCRETE FORMING LIMITED   p 911
10 ELM ST, TILLSONBURG, ON, N4G 0A7

(519) 842-6667   *SIC* 1771

EAST ELGIN SECONDARY SCHOOL   p 482
See THAMES VALLEY DISTRICT SCHOOL BOARD

EAST FRASER FIBER CO LTD   p 230
1000 SHEPPARD RD, MACKENZIE, BC, V0J 2C0

(250) 997-6360   *SIC* 2421

EAST HAMILTON RADIO LIMITED   p 609
1325 BARTON ST E, HAMILTON, ON, L8H 2W2

(905) 549-3581   *SIC* 5999

EAST HURON POULTRY, DIV OF   p 905
See SOFINA FOODS INC

EAST ISLE SHIPYARD   p 1041
See IRVING SHIPBUILDING INC

EAST LAKE HUSKY MARKET TRUCK STOP   p 15

5225 106 AVE SE, CALGARY, AB, T2C 5N2

(403) 236-5225   *SIC* 5541

EAST LONDON SPORTS LIMITED   p 659
406 WHARNCLIFFE RD S, LONDON, ON, N6J 2M4

(519) 673-3810   *SIC* 5941

EAST METRO AUTO LEASING, DIV OF   p 864
See FREEWAY FORD SALES LIMITED

EAST NORTHUMBERLAND SECONDARY SCHOOL   p 518
See KAWARTHA PINE RIDGE DISTRICT SCHOOL BOARD

EAST PENN CANADA   p 475
See POWER BATTERY SALES LTD

EAST SIDE MARIO'S   p 492
See 959009 ONTARIO INC

EAST SIDE MARIO'S   p 601
See PRIME RESTAURANTS

EAST SIDE MARIO'S   p 616
See PRIME RESTAURANTS INC

EAST SIDE MARIO'S   p 625
See 1172413 ONTARIO INC

EAST SIDE MARIO'S   p 648
See 1498882 ONTARIO INC

EAST SIDE MARIO'S   p 656
See 570230 ONTARIO INC

EAST SIDE MARIO'S   p 732
See PRIME RESTAURANTS INC

EAST SIDE MARIO'S   p 869
See PRIME RESTAURANTS INC

EAST SIDE MARIO'S   p 1006
450 KING ST N SUITE SIDE, WATERLOO, ON, N2J 2Z6

(226) 647-2587   *SIC* 5812

EAST SIDE MARIO'S #640   p 814
See T.T.O.C.S. LIMITED

EAST SIDE VENTILATION   p 365
See EAST SIDE VENTILATION LTD

EAST SIDE VENTILATION LTD   p 365
11 DURAND RD, WINNIPEG, MB, R2J 3T1

(204) 667-8700   *SIC* 1711

EAST YORK COLLEGIATE INSTITUTE   p 917
See TORONTO DISTRICT SCHOOL BOARD

EAST YORK HEARING CENTER   p 919
See 1185985 ONTARIO INC

EAST-COURT FORD LINCOLN SALES LIMITED   p 874
4700 SHEPPARD AVE E, SCARBOROUGH, ON, M1S 3V6

(416) 292-1171   *SIC* 5511

EASTDALE COLLEGIATE & VOCATIONAL INSTITUTE   p 811
See DURHAM DISTRICT SCHOOL BOARD

EASTERN AUTOMOTIVE WAREHOUSING, DIV OF   p 400
See AUTO MACHINERY AND GENERAL SUPPLY COMPANY, LIMITED

EASTERN CANADA RESPONSE CORPORATION LTD   p 823
275 SLATER ST SUITE 1201, OTTAWA, ON, K1P 5H9

(613) 230-7369   *SIC* 4959

EASTERN CHRYSLER DODGE JEEP   p 370
See WINNIPEG C MOTORS LP

EASTERN CONSTRUCTION COMPANY LIMITED   p 875
2075 KENNEDY RD SUITE 1200, SCARBOROUGH, ON, M1T 3V3

(416) 497-7110   *SIC* 1542

EASTERN DOOR LOGISTICS INC   p 422
3 CHURCH ST, CORNER BROOK, NL, A2H 2Z4

(709) 639-2479   *SIC* 8742

EASTERN EXPRESS LTD   p 427
21 ST. ANNE'S CRES, PARADISE, NL, A1L 3W1

(709) 754-8855   *SIC* 7389

EASTERN FABRICATORS INC   p 1041
341 GEORGETOWN RD, GEORGETOWN,

PE, C0A 1L0

(902) 283-3229   *SIC* 3441

EASTERN FENCE LIMITED   p 408
80 HENRI DUNANT ST, MONCTON, NB, E1E 1E6

(506) 857-8141   *SIC* 1799

EASTERN FOOD SERVICE   p 460
See SCOTIA FOODSERVICE LTD

EASTERN FOUNDRY LIMITED   p 422
3 WHARF RD SUITE 147, CLARENVILLE, NL, A5A 2B2

(709) 466-3814   *SIC* 5051

EASTERN HEALTH   p 426
See EASTERN REGIONAL INTEGRATED HEALTH AUTHORITY

EASTERN INDEPENDENT TELECOMMUNICATIONS LTD   p 519
100 STROWGER BLVD SUITE 112, BROCKVILLE, ON, K6V 5J9

(613) 342-9652   *SIC* 5065

EASTERN IRRIGATION DISTRICT   p 7
550 INDUSTRIAL RD W, BROOKS, AB, T0J 2A0

(403) 362-1400   *SIC* 4971

EASTERN MEAT SOLUTIONS INC   p 996
302 THE EAST MALL SUITE 500, TORONTO, ON, M9B 6C7

(416) 252-2791   *SIC* 5147

EASTERN ONTARIO HEALTH UNIT   p 563
1000 PITT ST, CORNWALL, ON, K6J 5T1

(613) 933-1375   *SIC* 8621

EASTERN ONTARIO TACCX SERVICES LLP   p 832
301 MOODY DR SUITE 400, OTTAWA, ON, K2H 9C4

(613) 820-8010   *SIC* 8721

EASTERN ONTARIO WATER TECHNOLOGY LTD   p 519
240 WALTHAM RD, BROCKVILLE, ON, K6V 7K3

(613) 498-2830   *SIC* 5999

EASTERN PLATINUM LIMITED   p 312
1188 GEORGIA ST W SUITE 1080, VANCOUVER, BC, V6E 4A2

(604) 800-8200   *SIC* 1081

EASTERN POWER DEVELOPERS   p 664
7 EAGLET CRT, MAPLE, ON, L6A 4E2

SIC 4911

EASTERN POWER LIMITED   p 570
2275 LAKE SHORE BLVD W SUITE 401, ETOBICOKE, ON, M8V 3Y3

(416) 234-1301   *SIC* 4911

EASTERN QUEBEC SEAFOODS (1998) LTD   p 1150
1600 RUE DE MATANE-SUR-MER, MATANE, QC, G4W 3M6

(418) 562-1273   *SIC* 2092

EASTERN RAILWAY SERVICES   p 396
205 ROSEBERRY ST, CAMPBELLTON, NB, E3N 2H4

(506) 753-0462   *SIC* 4789

EASTERN REFRIGERATION SUPPLY CO. LIMITED   p 851
30 VOGELL RD UNIT 5, RICHMOND HILL, ON, L4B 3K6

(905) 787-8383   *SIC* 5075

EASTERN REGIONAL INTEGRATED HEALTH AUTHORITY   p 423
1 SENIORS PL, GRAND BANK, NL, A0E 1W0

(709) 832-1660   *SIC* 8051

EASTERN REGIONAL INTEGRATED HEALTH AUTHORITY   p 426
760 TOPSAIL RD, MOUNT PEARL, NL, A1N 3J5

(709) 752-4534   *SIC* 8062

EASTERN REGIONAL INTEGRATED HEALTH AUTHORITY   p 427
1 CORRIGAN PL, PLACENTIA, NL, A0B 2Y0

(709) 227-2061   *SIC* 8051

EASTERN REGIONAL INTEGRATED

HEALTH AUTHORITY   p 431
154 LEMARCHANT RD, ST. JOHN'S, NL, A1C 5B8

(709) 777-6300   *SIC* 8062

EASTERN SCHOOL DISTRICT   p 1041
274 VALLEYFIELD RD, MONTAGUE, PE, C0A 1R0

(902) 838-0835   *SIC* 8211

EASTERN SCHOOL DISTRICT   p 1042
234 SHAKESPEARE DR, STRATFORD, PE, C1B 2V8

(902) 368-6990   *SIC* 8211

EASTERN SHORES SCHOOL BOARD   p 1242
40 RUE MOUNT-SORREL, NEW CARLISLE, QC, G0C 1Z0

(418) 752-2247   *SIC* 8211

EASTERN SIGN-PRINT LIMITED   p 466
125 NORTH FOORD ST, STELLARTON, NS, B0K 0A2

(902) 752-2722   *SIC* 2752

EASTERN TOWNSHIPS SCHOOL BOARD   p 1147
See COMMISSION SCOLAIRE EASTERN TOWNSHIPS

EASTFIELD RESOURCES LTD   p 303
325 HOWE ST SUITE 110, VANCOUVER, BC, V6C 1Z7

(604) 681-7913   *SIC* 1081

EASTGATE FORD SALES & SERVICE (82) COMPANY INC   p 609
350 PARKDALE AVE N, HAMILTON, ON, L8H 5Y3

(905) 547-2521   *SIC* 5511

EASTHOLME HOME FOR THE AGED   p 848
62 BIG BEND AVE, POWASSAN, ON, P0H 1Z0

(705) 724-2005   *SIC* 8361

EASTLINK   p 455
See BRAGG COMMUNICATIONS INCORPORATED

EASTLINK   p 455
See K-RIGHT COMMUNICATIONS LIMITED

EASTON HOCKEY CANADA, INC   p 1118
17550 RTE TRANSCANADIENNE, KIRKLAND, QC, H9J 3A3

(514) 630-9669   *SIC* 5091

EASTON'S 28 RESTAURANTS LTD   p 847
HWY 28 & 401, PORT HOPE, ON, L1A 3V6

(905) 885-1400   *SIC* 5812

EASTON'S 28 SERVICE CENTRE LTD   p 669
3100 STEELES AVE E SUITE 401, MARKHAM, ON, L3R 8T3

(905) 940-9409   *SIC* 5541

EASTON'S GROUP OF HOTELS INC   p 669
3100 STEELES AVE E SUITE 601, MARKHAM, ON, L3R 8T3

(905) 940-9409   *SIC* 7011

EASTON'S TORONTO AIRPORT HOTEL (COROGA) LP   p 669
3100 STEELES AVE E, MARKHAM, ON, L3R 8T3

(905) 940-9409   *SIC* 7011

EASTPLATS   p 312
See EASTERN PLATINUM LIMITED

EASTSIDE CHEVROLET BUICK GMC LTD   p 669
8435 WOODBINE AVE SUITE 7, MARKHAM, ON, L3R 2P4

(905) 475-7373   *SIC* 5511

EASTSIDE DODGE CHRYSLER LTD   p 11
815 36 ST NE, CALGARY, AB, T2A 4W3

(403) 273-4313   *SIC* 5511

EASTSIDE FAMILY CENTRE   p 11
495 36 ST NE SUITE 255, CALGARY, AB, T2A 6K3

(403) 299-9696   *SIC* 8699

EASTSIDE GAMES INC   p 293
555 12TH AVE W SUITE 550, VANCOUVER, BC, V5Z 3X7

(604) 568-5051   *SIC* 5734

EASTSIDE INDUSTRIAL COATINGS   p 357
See 3728111 MANITOBA LTD

EASTSIDE KIA p 20
See 967210 ALBERTA LTD

EASTSIDE PET VET HOSPITAL p 893
See CREDIT VALLEY ANIMAL CENTRE LIMITED

EASTVIEW CHEVROLET BUICK GMC LTD p 627
222 GOVERNMENT RD, KAPUSKASING, ON, P5N 2X2
(705) 335-6187   SIC 5511

EASTVIEW SECONDARY SCHOOL p 485
See SIMCOE COUNTY DISTRICT SCHOOL BOARD, THE

EASTWAY p 838
See 1555314 ONTARIO INC

EASTWAY CHRYSLER DODGE JEEP LTD p 867
2851 EGLINTON AVE E, SCARBOROUGH, ON, M1J 2E2
(416) 264-2501   SIC 5511

EASTWAY SALES & LEASING INC p 1018
9375 TECUMSEH RD E, WINDSOR, ON, N8R 1A1
(519) 979-1900   SIC 5511

EASTWAY TOYOTA & LEXUS OF WINDSOR p 1018
See EASTWAY SALES & LEASING INC

EASTWEST GOLD CORPORATION p 962
25 YORK ST 17 FL, TORONTO, ON, M5J 2V5
(416) 365-5123   SIC 1041

EASTWOOD COLLEGIATE INSTITUTE p 640
See WATERLOO REGION DISTRICT SCHOOL BOARD

EASTWOOD FOREST PRODUCTS INC p 428
112 TRANS CANADA HWY, ST JUDES, NL, A8A 3A1
(709) 635-7280   SIC 5031

EASTWOOD WOOD SPECIALTIES LTD p 883
6 PEACOCK BAY, ST CATHARINES, ON, L2M 7N8
(905) 937-3030   SIC 2426

EASY PARK p 308
See PARKING CORPORATION OF VANCOUVER, THE

EASY PLASTIC CONTAINERS CORPORATION p 552
101 JARDIN DR UNIT 10, CONCORD, ON, L4K 1X6
(905) 669-4466   SIC 3089

EASYFINANCIAL SERVICES INC p 709
33 CITY CENTRE DR SUITE 510, MISSISSAUGA, ON, L5B 2N5
(905) 272-2788   SIC 6141

EASYINSURE p 1019
See BELYER INSURANCE LTD

EAT & RUN, DIV p 114
See EDMONTON RUNNING ROOM LTD

EAT LOVE FRESH p 1340
See MISSFRESH INC

EATING NEW CREATIONS p 683
See FRESH START FOODS CANADA LTD

EATON p 3
See EATON INDUSTRIES (CANADA) COMPANY

EATON ELECTRICAL p 683
See EATON INDUSTRIES (CANADA) COMPANY

EATON ELECTRICAL, CANADIAN OPERATIONS DIV OF p 522
See EATON INDUSTRIES (CANADA) COMPANY

EATON INDUSTRIES (CANADA) COMPANY p 3
403 EAST LAKE BLVD NE, AIRDRIE, AB, T4A 2G1
(403) 948-7955   SIC 3679

EATON INDUSTRIES (CANADA) COMPANY p 522

5050 MAINWAY, BURLINGTON, ON, L7L 5Z1
(905) 333-6442   SIC 5065

EATON INDUSTRIES (CANADA) COMPANY p 584
380 CARLINGVIEW DR, ETOBICOKE, ON, M9W 5X9
(416) 798-0112   SIC 3679

EATON INDUSTRIES (CANADA) COMPANY p 683
610 INDUSTRIAL DR, MILTON, ON, L9T 5C3
(905) 875-4379   SIC 3625

EAUX NAYA INC, LES p 1166
2030 BOUL PIE-IX BUREAU 214.4, MONTREAL, QC, H1V 2C8
(514) 525-6292   SIC 5149

EAZY EXPRESS INC p 861
GD LCD MAIN, SAULT STE. MARIE, ON, P6A 5L1
(705) 253-2222   SIC 7389

EB GAMES p 502
See ELECTRONICS BOUTIQUE CANADA INC

EBAM ENTERPRISES LTD p 815
1616 MICHAEL ST, OTTAWA, ON, K1B 3T7
(613) 745-8998   SIC 5149

EBB AND FLOW FIRST NATION EDUCATION AUTHORITY p 349
GD, EBB AND FLOW, MB, R0L 0R0
(204) 448-2012   SIC 8211

EBB AND FLOW FIRST NATION EDUCATION AUTHORITY p 349
PO BOX 160, EBB AND FLOW, MB, R0L 0R0
(204) 448-2438   SIC 8211

EBB AND FLOW SCHOOL p 349
See EBB AND FLOW FIRST NATION EDUCATION AUTHORITY

EBC INC p 1119
1095 RUE VALETS, L'ANCIENNE-LORETTE, QC, G2E 4M7
(418) 872-0600   SIC 1541

EBC-NEILSON (R3-06-01) p 1119
See EBC-NEILSON, ROMAINE 3 EXCAVATIONS DERIVATION (R3-06-01) S.E.N.C.

EBC-NEILSON, ROMAINE 3 EXCAVATIONS DERIVATION (R3-06-01) S.E.N.C. p 1119
1095 RUE VALETS, L'ANCIENNE-LORETTE, QC, G2E 4M7
(418) 872-0600   SIC 1522

EBC-POMERLEAU, PJCC 62000 S.E.N.C. p 1119
1095 RUE VALETS, L'ANCIENNE-LORETTE, QC, G2E 4M7
(418) 872-0600   SIC 1522

EBC-SM (GRISE FIORD), S.E.N.C. p 1119
See EBC-SM (NUNAVUT), S.E.N.C.

EBC-SM (NUNAVUT), S.E.N.C. p 1119
1095 RUE VALETS, L'ANCIENNE-LORETTE, QC, G2E 4M7
(418) 872-0600   SIC 1542

EBCO INDUSTRIES LTD p 260
7851 ALDERBRIDGE WAY, RICHMOND, BC, V6X 2A4
(604) 278-5578   SIC 3599

EBCO METAL FINISHING LIMITED PARTNERSHIP p 254
15200 KNOX WAY, RICHMOND, BC, V6V 3A6
(604) 244-1500   SIC 3479

EBD ENTERPRISES INC p 377
29 ROY ROCHE DR, WINNIPEG, MB, R3C 2E6
(204) 633-1657   SIC 4213

EBENISTERIE A. BEAUCAGE INC p 1120
188 CH DES COMMISSAIRES, L'ASSOMPTION, QC, J5W 2T7
(450) 589-6412   SIC 2434

EBENISTERIE NORCLAIR INC p 1064
155 RUE JULES-LEGER, BOUCHERVILLE,

QC, J4B 7K8
(450) 641-1737   SIC 5712

EBENISTERIE ST-PATRICK p 1084
See 135770 CANADA LTEE

EBENISTERIE ST-URBAIN LTEE p 1347
226 RUE PRINCIPALE, SAINT-LOUIS-DE-GONZAGUE, QC, J0S 1T0
(450) 427-2687   SIC 2431

EBENISTERIES SAMSON SAMUEL INC, LES p 1074
7900 BOUL INDUSTRIEL, CHAMBLY, QC, J3L 4X3
(450) 447-7503   SIC 5712

EBERHARDT FOODS LTD p 105
12165 154 ST NW, EDMONTON, AB, T5V 1J3
(780) 454-8331   SIC 5141

EBERSPAECHER CLIMATE CONTROL SYSTEMS CANADA INC p 738
6099A VIPOND DR, MISSISSAUGA, ON, L5T 2B2
(905) 670-0960   SIC 5013

EBERSPAECHER VECTURE INC. p 552
8900 KEELE STREET UNIT 3, CONCORD, ON, L4K 2N2
(905) 761-0331   SIC 3691

EBI p 1304
See EBI ELECTRIC INC

EBI ELECTRIC INC p 1304
2250 90E RUE, SAINT-GEORGES, QC, G5Y 7J7
(418) 228-5505   SIC 1731

EBI ENERGIE INC p 1057
670 RUE DE MONTCALM, BERTHIERVILLE, QC, J0K 1A0
(450) 836-8111   SIC 1794

EBI ENVIRONNEMENT INC p 1057
670 RUE DE MONTCALM, BERTHIERVILLE, QC, J0K 1A0
(450) 836-8111   SIC 4953

EBI ENVIRONNEMENT/CDT p 1057
See EBI ENVIRONNEMENT INC

EBS CONTRACTING INC p 165
14 RAYBORN CRES SUITE 200, ST. ALBERT, AB, T8N 4B1
(780) 459-7110   SIC 6712

EBSCO CANADA LTD p 678
110 COPPER CREEK DR SUITE 305, MARKHAM, ON, L6B 0P9
(416) 297-8282   SIC 7389

EBSS p 1074
See EBENISTERIES SAMSON SAMUEL INC, LES

EBSU p 1347
See EBENISTERIE ST-URBAIN LTEE

ECCO HEATING PRODUCTS LTD p 95
14310 111 AVE NW SUITE 300, EDMONTON, AB, T5M 3Z7
(780) 452-7350   SIC 3433

ECCO HEATING PRODUCTS LTD p 228
19860 FRASER HWY, LANGLEY, BC, V3A 4C9
(604) 530-4151   SIC 3567

ECCO INVESTISSEMENT INC p 1286
54 RUE AMYOT, RIVIERE-DU-LOUP, QC, G5R 3E9
(418) 867-1695   SIC 6712

ECCO MANUFACTURING p 228
See ECCO HEATING PRODUCTS LTD

ECCO SHOES CANADA INC p 669
10 WHITEHALL DR, MARKHAM, ON, L3R 5Z7
(905) 947-8148   SIC 5139

ECCO SUPPLY p 95
See ECCO HEATING PRODUCTS LTD

ECCO TRANSPORT SERVICES LTD p 93
12841 141 ST NW, EDMONTON, AB, T5L 4N1
(780) 454-4495   SIC 4731

ECHAFAUDAGE IMPACT p 1172
See 8782601 CANADA INC

ECHAFAUDAGE PLUS (QUEBEC) INC p 1292
148 RUE D'AMSTERDAM, SAINT-

AUGUSTIN-DE-DESMAURES, QC, G3A 2R1
(418) 878-3885   SIC 1799

ECHAFAUDS PLUS (LAVAL) INC p 1362
2897 AV FRANCIS-HUGHES, SAINTE-ROSE, QC, H7L 4G8
(450) 663-1926   SIC 1799

ECHEC & MATH p 1185
See ASSOCIATION ECHEC ET MATHEMATIQUES

ECHELON FINANCIAL CORP p 118
6328 104 ST NW 2ND FLR, EDMONTON, AB, T6H 2K9
(780) 989-2777   SIC 6722

ECHELON FINANCIAL HOLDINGS INC p 694
2680 MATHESON BLVD E SUITE 300, MISSISSAUGA, ON, L4W 0A5
(905) 214-7880   SIC 6411

ECHELON GENERAL INSURANCE COMPANY p 694
2680 MATHESON BLVD E SUITE 300, MISSISSAUGA, ON, L4W 0A5
(905) 214-7880   SIC 6411

ECHELON HOME PRODUCTS LTD p 263
11120 HORSESHOE WAY UNIT 120, RICHMOND, BC, V7A 5H7
(604) 275-2210   SIC 5064

ECHELON INSURANCE p 694
See ECHELON FINANCIAL HOLDINGS INC

ECHO BRAND MANAGEMENT LTD p 276
8065 130 ST, SURREY, BC, V3W 7X4
(604) 590-4020   SIC 5099

ECHO CYCLE LTD p 104
21220 100 AVE NW, EDMONTON, AB, T5T 5X8
(780) 447-3246   SIC 5571

ECHO NDE INC p 155
53 BURNT PARK DR, RED DEER, AB, T4P 0J7
(403) 347-7042   SIC 1389

ECHO POWER GENERATION INC p 944
777 BAY ST SUITE 1910, TORONTO, ON, M5G 2C8
(416) 364-6513   SIC 4911

ECHO SEISMIC LTD p 22
4500 8A ST NE, CALGARY, AB, T2E 4J7
(403) 216-0999   SIC 1382

ECHO VILLAGE FOUNDATION p 245
4200 10TH AVE, PORT ALBERNI, BC, V9Y 4X3
(250) 724-1090   SIC 8361

ECHOTAPE p 1241
See COMPAGNIE DIVERSIFIEE EDELSTEIN LTEE, LA

ECI TECHNOLOGY GROUP INC p 876
815 MIDDLEFIELD RD UNIT 1-2, SCARBOROUGH, ON, M1V 2P9
(416) 291-2220   SIC 3679

ECKEL INDUSTRIES OF CANADA LIMITED p 746
35 ALLISON AVE, MORRISBURG, ON, K0C 1X0
(613) 543-2967   SIC 3625

ECKLER LTD p 915
5140 YONGE ST SUITE 1700, TORONTO, ON, M2N 6L7
(416) 429-3330   SIC 8999

ECKO MARINE LTD p 3
4200 47 ST, ALBERTA BEACH, AB, T0E 0A1
(780) 924-3250   SIC 5599

ECL-CDG SERVICES p 1264
See FIVES SERVICES INC

ECLAIRAGE AXIS INC p 1130
2505 RUE SENKUS, LASALLE, QC, H8N 2X8
(514) 948-6272   SIC 3648

ECLAIRAGE CONTRASTE M.L. INC p 1139
1009 RUE DU PARC-INDUSTRIEL, LEVIS, QC, G6Z 1C5
(418) 839-4624   SIC 5063

ECLAIRAGE DIMENSION PLUS *p 1182*
See ECLAIRAGE DIMENSION PLUS INC
ECLAIRAGE DIMENSION PLUS INC *p 1182*
6666 RUE SAINT-URBAIN BUREAU 320, MONTREAL, QC, H2S 3H1
(514) 332-9966 *SIC 5063*
ECLAIRAGE MIRALUX M.L. *p 1139*
See ECLAIRAGE CONTRASTE M.L. INC
ECLAIRAGE UNILIGHT LIMITEE *p 1339*
4400 RUE HICKMORE, SAINT-LAURENT, QC, H4T 1K2
(514) 769-1533 *SIC 3645*
ECLIPSE *p 431*
See ECLIPSE STORES INC
ECLIPSE AUTOMATION INC *p 535*
130 THOMPSON DR, CAMBRIDGE, ON, N1T 2E5
(519) 620-1906 *SIC 3599*
ECLIPSE PPM *p 777*
See SOLUTION Q INC
ECLIPSE STORES INC *p 431*
354 WATER ST SUITE 401, ST. JOHN'S, NL, A1C 1C4
(709) 722-0311 *SIC 5621*
ECLIPSE TRANSPORT LTD *p 179*
3120 CEMETERY RD, AGASSIZ, BC, V0M 1A1
(604) 796-8972 *SIC 4213*
ECM *p 694*
See ENGINEERED CASE MANUFACTURERS INC
ECMI LP *p 552*
125 VILLARBOIT CRES, CONCORD, ON, L4K 4K2
(905) 307-8102 *SIC 1521*
ECN CAPITAL CORP *p 962*
200 BAY ST NORTH TOWER SUITE 1625, TORONTO, ON, M5J 2J1
(416) 646-4710 *SIC 6159*
ECO ENVIRONMENT PRODUCTS (1989) LTD *p 100*
18303 107 AVE NW SUITE 1989, EDMONTON, AB, T5S 1K4
(780) 483-6232 *SIC 5047*
ECO II MANUFACTURING INC *p 876*
3391 MCNICOLL AVE UNIT 6, SCARBOROUGH, ON, M1V 2V4
(416) 292-0220 *SIC 2673*
ECO MEDICAL EQUIPMENT, DIV OF *p 100*
See ECO ENVIRONMENT PRODUCTS (1989) LTD
ECO TABS CANADA INC *p 797*
2429 LAMOKA CRT, OAKVILLE, ON, L6H 5Z7
(888) 732-6822 *SIC 5084*
ECO-FLEX *p 140*
See CHAMPAGNE EDITION INC
ECO-LOGIXX - GROSSISTE ALIMENTAIRE ET PRODUITS D'EMBALLAGES INC *p 1344*
9209 BOUL LANGELIER, SAINT-LEONARD, QC, H1P 3K9
(514) 351-3031 *SIC 5074*
ECO-PAK *p 1392*
See 2948-4292 QUEBEC INC
ECO-TEC INC *p 844*
1145 SQUIRES BEACH RD, PICKERING, ON, L1W 3T9
(905) 427-0077 *SIC 3559*
ECO-TEC LIMITED *p 844*
1145 SQUIRES BEACH RD, PICKERING, ON, L1W 3T9
(905) 427-0077 *SIC 6712*
ECOBEE INC *p 962*
207 QUEENS QUAY W SUITE 600, TORONTO, ON, M5J 1A7
(877) 932-6233 *SIC 5075*
ECOBUS, L' *p 1254*
See AUTOBUS LAVAL LTEE
ECODYNE LIMITED *p 522*
4475 CORPORATE DR, BURLINGTON, ON, L7L 5T9
(905) 332-1404 *SIC 3589*
ECOFISH RESEARCH LTD *p 203*
450 8TH ST SUITE F, COURTENAY, BC,

V9N 1N5
(250) 334-3042 *SIC 8748*
ECOFOR CONSULTING LTD *p 213*
9940 104 AVE, FORT ST. JOHN, BC, V1J 2K3
(250) 787-6009 *SIC 8748*
ECOHOME TECHNOLOGIES *p 639*
See HOGG FUEL & SUPPLY LIMITED
ECOLAB *p 694*
See ECOLAB CO.
ECOLAB CO. *p 694*
5105 TOMKEN RD SUITE 1, MISSISSAUGA, ON, L4W 2X5
(905) 238-0171 *SIC 2842*
ECOLE IGUARSIVIK *p 1254*
See COMMISSION SCOLAIRE KATIVIK
ECOLE ALTERNATIVE DES CHEMINOTS *p 1089*
See COMMISSION SCOLAIRE DES GRANDES-SEIGNEURIES
ECOLE ANNE HEBERT *p 1270*
See COMMISSION SCOLAIRE DE LA CAPITALE, LA
ECOLE ARMENIENNE SOURP HAGOP, L' *p 1224*
3400 RUE NADON, MONTREAL, QC, H4J 1P5
(514) 332-1373 *SIC 8211*
ECOLE BAIE SAINT FRANCOIS *p 1366*
See COMMISSION SCOLAIRE DE LA VALLEE-DES-TISSERANDS, LA
ECOLE BALLENAS SECONDARY SCHOOL *p 243*
See SCHOOL DISTRICT NO 69 (QUALICUM)
ECOLE BEL ESSOR *p 1146*
See COMMISSION SCOLAIRE MARIE-VICTORIN
ECOLE BETH JACOB DE RAV HIRSCHPRUNG *p 1244*
1750 AV GLENDALE, OUTREMONT, QC, H2V 1B3
(514) 731-6607 *SIC 8211*
ECOLE BROXTON PARK SCHOOL *p 164*
See PARKLAND SCHOOL DIVISION NO. 70
ECOLE CENTRE AMOS *p 1240*
See COMMISSION SCOLAIRE DE LA POINTE-DE-L'ILE
ECOLE CHOMEDEY-DE MAISONNEUVE *p 1166*
See COMMISSION SCOLAIRE DE MONTREAL
ECOLE CITE ETUDIANTE *p 1287*
See COMMISSION SCOLAIRE DU PAYS-DES-BLEUETS
ECOLE D'IBERVILLE *p 1308*
See COMMISSION SCOLAIRE MARIE-VICTORIN
ECOLE DE CONDUITE TECNIC *p 1261*
See EXCELLENTE GESTION INC
ECOLE DE CONDUITE TECNIC RIVE SUD INC *p 1308*
3285 MONTEE SAINT-HUBERT, SAINT-HUBERT, QC, J3Y 4J4
(450) 443-4104 *SIC 8299*
ECOLE DE L' ENVOL *p 1123*
See COMMISSION SCOLAIRE ABITIBI
ECOLE DE L'ETINCELLE *p 1183*
See COMMISSION SCOLAIRE DE MONTREAL
ECOLE DE L'HORIZON SOLEIL *p 1321*
See COMMISSION SCOLAIRE DE LA RIVIERE-DU-NORD
ECOLE DE LA MAGDELEINE *p 1123*
See COMMISSION SCOLAIRE DES GRANDES-SEIGNEURIES
ECOLE DE LANGUES DE LA CITE, L' *p 823*
280 ALBERT ST SUITE 500, OTTAWA, ON, K1P 5G8
(613) 569-6260 *SIC 8299*
ECOLE DE PILOTAGE DE MONT-GOLFIERES DU QUEBEC *p*

1317
See CORPORATION DE FESTIVAL DE MONTGOLFIERES DE SAINT-JEAN-SUR-RICHELIEU INC
ECOLE DE TECHNOLOGIE GAZIERE *p 1174*
See ENERGIR INC
ECOLE DE TECHNOLOGIE GAZIERE *p 1174*
See ENERGIR, S.E.C.
ECOLE DES METIERS DU SUD OUEST DE MONTREAL *p 1222*
See COMMISSION SCOLAIRE DE MONTREAL
ECOLE DES METIERS ET OCCUPATIONS DE L'INDUSTRIE DE LA CONSTRUCTION DE QUEBEC *p 1263*
See COMMISSION SCOLAIRE DE LA CAPITALE, LA
ECOLE DES MILLE-FLEURES *p 1309*
See COMMISSION SCOLAIRE MARIE-VICTORIN
ECOLE DU BAC *p 1137*
See COMMISSION SCOLAIRE DES NAVIGATEURS
ECOLE DU NOUVEAU MONDE *p 1104*
See COMMISSION SCOLAIRE DES DRAVEURS
ECOLE DU ROUTIER FUTUR-CAM *p 1096*
See PERSONNEL UNIQUE CANADA INC
ECOLE DU TOURET *p 1375*
See COMMISSION SCOLAIRE DE LA REGION-DE-SHERBROOKE
ECOLE DU TOURNESOL *p 1403*
See COMMISSION SCOLAIRE DES SOMMETS
ECOLE ELEMENTAIRE ST-JOSEPH *p 791*
See CONSEIL SCOLAIRE VIAMONDE
ECOLE EVANGELINE *p 1217*
See COMMISSION SCOLAIRE DE MONTREAL
ECOLE FELIX LECLERC *p 1249*
See COMMISSION SCOLAIRE MARGUERITE-BOURGEOYS
ECOLE GRON MORGAN PUBLIC SCHOOL *p 908*
See LAKEHEAD DISTRICT SCHOOL BOARD
ECOLE HENRI BEAULIEU *p 1325*
See COMMISSION SCOLAIRE MARGUERITE-BOURGEOYS
ECOLE HORIZON JEUNESSE *p 1241*
155 BOUL SAINTE-ROSE E, MONTREAL-OUEST, QC, H7H 1P2
(450) 662-6720 *SIC 8211*
ECOLE HOWARD S BELINGS *p 1076*
See COMMISSION SCOLAIRE NEW FRONTIER
ECOLE INTERMEDIAIRE CATHOLIQUE-PAVILLON ROCKLAND *p 857*
See CONSEIL SCOLAIRE DE DISTRICT CATHOLIQUE DE L'EST ONTARIEN
ECOLE INTERNATIONALE DU PHARE *p 1370*
See COMMISSION SCOLAIRE DE LA REGION-DE-SHERBROOKE
ECOLE JEAN DU NORD *p 1367*
See COMMISSION SCOLAIRE DU FER
ECOLE JEAN LEMAN *p 1072*
See COMMISSION SCOLAIRE DES GRANDES-SEIGNEURIES
ECOLE JOSEPH AMEDEE BELANGER *p 1317*
See COMMISSION SCOLAIRE DES HAUTES-RIVIERES
ECOLE JOSEPH-HERMAS-LECLERC *p 1109*
See COMMISSION SCOLAIRE DU VAL-DES-CERFS
ECOLE L'ODYSEE DOMINIQUE RACINE *p 1078*
See COMMISSION SCOLAIRE DES RIVES-DU-SAGUENAY
ECOLE LE CARIGNAN *p 1239*

See COMMISSION SCOLAIRE DE LA POINTE-DE-L'ILE
ECOLE LE TANDEM *p 1397*
See COMMISSION SCOLAIRE DES BOIS-FRANCS
ECOLE MARGUERITE BOURGEOYS *p 1253*
See COMMISSION SCOLAIRE MARGUERITE-BOURGEOYS
ECOLE MARGUERITE DE LAJEMMERAIS *p 1164*
See COMMISSION SCOLAIRE DE MONTREAL
ECOLE MARIE RIVIER *p 1316*
See COMMISSION SCOLAIRE DES HAUTES-RIVIERES
ECOLE MARLBOROUGH ELEMENTARY SCHOOL *p 189*
See BURNABY SCHOOL BOARD DISTRICT 41
ECOLE MGR EUCLIDE THEBERGE *p 1149*
See COMMISSION SCOLAIRE DES HAUTES-RIVIERES
ECOLE MONSEIGNEUR PARENT *p 1310*
See COMMISSION SCOLAIRE MARIE-VICTORIN
ECOLE MONTCALM *p 1372*
See FONDATION ECOLE MONTCALM INC
ECOLE NATIONALE DE CIRQUE *p 1170*
8181 2E AV, MONTREAL, QC, H1Z 4N9
(514) 982-0859 *SIC 8211*
ECOLE NOTRE DAME *p 1136*
See COMMISSION SCOLAIRE DES NAVIGATEURS
ECOLE NOTRE DAME DES RAPIDES *p 1131*
See COMMISSION SCOLAIRE MARGUERITE-BOURGEOYS
ECOLE PAUL-HUBERT *p 1284*
See COMMISSION SCOLAIRE DES PHARES
ECOLE PIERRE-DE-LESTAGE *p 1057*
See COMMISSION SCOLAIRE DES SAMARES
ECOLE POINTE LEVIS *p 1136*
See COMMISSION SCOLAIRE DES NAVIGATEURS
ECOLE POLYTECHNIQUE DE MONTREAL *p 1219*
See CORPORATION DE L'ECOLE POLYTECHNIQUE DE MONTREAL
ECOLE POLYVALENTE *p 419*
See DISTRICT SCOLAIRE FRANCOPHONE NORD-EST
ECOLE POLYVALENTE CURE MERCURE *p 1159*
See COMMISSION SCOLAIRE DES LAURENTIDES
ECOLE POLYVALENTE DE ST GEORGES *p 1304*
See COMMISSION SCOLAIRE DE LA BEAUCE-ETCHEMIN
ECOLE POLYVALENTE DES ABENAQUIS *p 1350*
See COMMISSION SCOLAIRE DE LA BEAUCE-ETCHEMIN
ECOLE POLYVALENTE JONQUIERE *p 1115*
See COMMISSION SCOLAIRE DE LA JONQUIERE
ECOLE POLYVALENTE LA SAMARE *p 1246*
See COMMISSION SCOLAIRE DES BOIS-FRANCS
ECOLE POLYVALENTE LAVIGNE *p 1129*
See COMMISSION SCOLAIRE DE LA RIVIERE-DU-NORD
ECOLE POLYVALENTE LOUIS JOSEPH PAPINEAU *p 1169*
See COMMISSION SCOLAIRE DE MONTREAL
ECOLE POLYVALENTE MARIE RIVIER *p 1098*
See COMMISSION SCOLAIRE DES CH-

ENES

ECOLE POLYVALENTE ST JEROMEp 1321
See COMMISSION SCOLAIRE DE LA RIVIERE-DU-NORD

ECOLE POLYVANTE LE CARREFOUR   p
1390
See COMMISSION SCOLAIRE DE L'OR-ET-DES-BOIS

ECOLE PRIMAIRE SECONDAIRE DES GRANDES MAREES   p 1275
See COMMISSION SCOLAIRE DES DE-COUVREURS

ECOLE PRIMAIRE DE LA SABLIERE   p
1380
See COMMISSION SCOLAIRE DES AF-FLUENTS

ECOLE PRIMAIRE GABRIELLE ROYp 1343
See COMMISSION SCOLAIRE DE LA POINTE-DE-L'ILE

ECOLE PRIMAIRE PERE-VIMONT p 1085
See COMMISSION SCOLAIRE DE LAVAL

ECOLE PUBLIQUE HERITAGE   p 763
See CONSEIL SCOLAIRE DU DISTRICT DU NORD-EST DE L'ONTARIO

ECOLE SAINT MATHIEU   p 1056
See COMMISSION SCOLAIRE DES PATRI-OTES

ECOLE SAINT MICHEL SECTEUR AUTISME   p 1270
See COMMISSION SCOLAIRE DES DE-COUVREURS

ECOLE SAINT PIERRE CLAVER   p 1172
See COMMISSION SCOLAIRE DE MON-TREAL

ECOLE SAINT-LUC   p 1220
See COMMISSION SCOLAIRE DE MON-TREAL

ECOLE   SAINTE-BERNADETTE-SOUBIROUS   p
1168
See COMMISSION SCOLAIRE DE MON-TREAL

ECOLE SAINTE-THERESE   p 1364
See COMMISSION SCOLAIRE DE LA SEIGNEURIE-DES-MILLE-ILES

ECOLE SECONDAIRE ANDRE LAUREN-DEAU   p
1308
See COMMISSION SCOLAIRE MARIE-VICTORIN

ECOLE SECONDAIRE ANJOU   p 1163
See COMMISSION SCOLAIRE DE LA POINTE-DE-L'ILE

ECOLE   SECONDAIRE   ANTOINE BROSSARD   p 1070
See COMMISSION SCOLAIRE MARIE-VICTORIN

ECOLE SECONDAIRE AUGUSTIN NOR-BET MORIN   p
1354
See COMMISSION SCOLAIRE DES LAU-RENTIDES

ECOLE SECONDAIRE BEAUMONT HIGH SCHOOL   p 5
See BLACK GOLD REGIONAL DIVISION #18

ECOLE SECONDAIRE BEAURIVAGE   p
1291
See COMMISSION SCOLAIRE DES NAVI-GATEURS

ECOLE   SECONDAIRE   BERNARD GARIEPY   p 1377
See COMMISSION SCOLAIRE DE SOREL-TRACY

ECOLE SECONDAIRE BIALIK   p 1083
See JEWISH PEOPLE'S SCHOOLS AND PERETZ SCHOOLS INC

ECOLE SECONDAIRE CALIXA LAVALEE p
1240
See COMMISSION SCOLAIRE DE LA POINTE-DE-L'ILE

ECOLE SECONDAIRE CAP JEUNESSE p
1321
See COMMISSION SCOLAIRE DE LA

RIVIERE-DU-NORD

ECOLE SECONDAIRE CARDINAL ROY   p
1258
See COMMISSION SCOLAIRE DE LA CAP-ITALE, LA

ECOLE SECONDAIRE CATHOLIQUE LA CITADELLE   p 562
See CONSEIL SCOLAIRE DE DISTRICT CATHOLIQUE DE L'EST ONTARIEN

ECOLE SECONDAIRE CAVELIER DE LASALLE   p 1132
See   COMMISSION   SCOLAIRE MARGUERITE-BOURGEOYS

ECOLE   SECONDAIRE   CHANOINE BEAUDET   p 1349
See COMMISSION SCOLAIRE DE KAMOURASKA RIVIERE-DU-LOUP

ECOLE SECONDAIRE CHARLES GRAVEL
p 1077
See COMMISSION SCOLAIRE DES RIVES-DU-SAGUENAY

ECOLE SECONDAIRE CHAVIGNY p 1389
See COMMISSION SCOLAIRE DU CHEMIN-DU-ROY

ECOLE SECONDAIRE DE CHAMBLY   p
1074
See COMMISSION SCOLAIRE DES PATRI-OTES

ECOLE SECONDAIRE DE L'ENVOL p 1349
See COMMISSION SCOLAIRE DES NAVI-GATEURS

ECOLE SECONDAIRE DE L'ESCALE   p
1052
See COMMISSION SCOLAIRE DES SOM-METS

ECOLE SECONDAIRE DE L'ILE   p 1105
See FONDATION DE LA COMMIS-SION SCOLAIRE DES PORTAGES-DE-L'OUTAOUAIS

ECOLE SECONDAIRE DE LA MONTEE   p
1370
See COMMISSION SCOLAIRE DE LA REGION-DE-SHERBROOKE

ECOLE SECONDAIRE DE NEUFCHATEL p
1276
See COMMISSION SCOLAIRE DE LA CAP-ITALE, LA

ECOLE   SECONDAIRE   DE   SAINT ANSELME   p 1291
See COMMISSION SCOLAIRE DE LA COTE-DU-SUD, LA

ECOLE SECONDAIRE DE SAINT-DAMIENp
1299
See COMMISSION SCOLAIRE DE LA COTE-DU-SUD, LA

ECOLE SECONDAIRE DES CHUTES   p
1281
See COMMISSION SCOLAIRE DES SAMARES

ECOLE SECONDAIRE DES CHUTES   p
1368
See COMMISSION SCOLAIRE DE L'ENERGIE

ECOLE SECONDAIRE DES GRANDES-MAREES   p
1121
See COMMISSION SCOLAIRE DES RIVES-DU-SAGUENAY

ECOLE SECONDAIRE DES PIONNIERS p
1386
See COMMISSION SCOLAIRE DU CHEMIN-DU-ROY

ECOLE SECONDAIRE DES RIVES p 1379
See COMMISSION SCOLAIRE DES AF-FLUENTS

ECOLE SECONDAIRE DU MONT-BRUNO p
1295
See COMMISSION SCOLAIRE DES PATRI-OTES

ECOLE SECONDAIRE DU PLATEAUp 1122
See   COMMISSION   SCOLAIRE   DE CHARLEVOIX, LA

ECOLE SECONDAIRE DU TRIOLET p 1372
See COMMISSION SCOLAIRE DE LA

REGION-DE-SHERBROOKE

ECOLE SECONDAIRE ECOLE EDOUARD-MONTPETIT   p
1164
See COMMISSION SCOLAIRE DE MON-TREAL

ECOLE   SECONDAIRE   EULALIE DUROCHER   p 1166
See COMMISSION SCOLAIRE DE MON-TREAL

ECOLE SECONDAIRE FELIX LECLERC p
1281
See COMMISSION SCOLAIRE DES AF-FLUENTS

ECOLE SECONDAIRE FERNAND LEFEB-VRE   p
1376
See COMMISSION SCOLAIRE DE SOREL-TRACY

ECOLE SECONDAIRE GEORGES VANIER
p 1180
See COMMISSION SCOLAIRE DE MON-TREAL

ECOLE SECONDAIRE HENRI BOURASSA
p 1239
See COMMISSION SCOLAIRE DE LA POINTE-DE-L'ILE

ECOLE   SECONDAIRE   JACQUES ROUSSEAU   p 1143
See COMMISSION SCOLAIRE MARIE-VICTORIN

ECOLE SECONDAIRE JEAN DE BREBEUF
p 1257
See COMMISSION SCOLAIRE DE LA CAP-ITALE, LA

ECOLE SECONDAIRE JEAN RAIMBAULTp
1098
See COMMISSION SCOLAIRE DES CH-ENES

ECOLE SECONDAIRE JOSEPH CHAR-BONNEAU   p
1171
See COMMISSION SCOLAIRE DE MON-TREAL

ECOLE SECONDAIRE JOSEPH FECTEAU
p 1382
See COMMISSION SCOLAIRE DES AP-PALACHES

ECOLE SECONDAIRE KENOGAMI p 1116
See COMMISSION SCOLAIRE DE LA JON-QUIERE

ECOLE SECONDAIRE L'ARC-EN-CIEL p
1384
See   COMMISSION   SCOLAIRE   DU FLEUVE ET DES LACS

ECOLE SECONDAIRE L'ENVOLEE p 1110
See COMMISSION SCOLAIRE DU VAL-DES-CERFS

ECOLE SECONDAIRE LA CALYPSOp 1046
See COMMISSION SCOLAIRE HARRI-CANA

ECOLE SECONDAIRE LA DECOUVERTE p
1347
See COMMISSION SCOLAIRE DE LA RIVERAINE

ECOLE SECONDAIRE LA FRONTALIERE p
1081
See   COMMISSION   SCOLAIRE   DES HAUTS-CANTONS

ECOLE SECONDAIRE LES COMPAGNONS DE QUARTIER   p 1275
See COMMISSION SCOLAIRE DES DE-COUVREURS

ECOLE SECONDAIRE LES ETCHEMINS p
1139
See COMMISSION SCOLAIRE DES NAVI-GATEURS

ECOLE SECONDAIRE LOUIS JOBINp 1351
See COMMISSION SCOLAIRE DE PORT-NEUF

ECOLE SECONDAIRE LOUIS-JACQUES-CASAULT   p
1159
See   COMMISSION   SCOLAIRE   DE LA

COTE-DU-SUD, LA

ECOLE SECONDAIRE LOUIS-RIEL p 1163
See COMMISSION SCOLAIRE DE MON-TREAL

ECOLE SECONDAIRE LOUISE TRICHET p
1163
See COMMISSION SCOLAIRE DE MON-TREAL

ECOLE SECONDAIRE LOYOLA   p 1222
7272 RUE SHERBROOKE O, MONTREAL, QC, H4B 1R2
(514) 486-1101   *SIC 8211*

ECOLE SECONDAIRE LUCIEN PAGE   p
1180
See COMMISSION SCOLAIRE DE MON-TREAL

ECOLE   SECONDAIRE   MACDONALD-CARTIER, L'   p
1308
See RIVERSIDE SCHOOL BOARD

ECOLE   SECONDAIRE   MARCELLIN-CHAMPAGNAT   p
1316
14 CH DES PATRIOTES E, SAINT-JEAN-SUR-RICHELIEU, QC, J2X 5P9
(450) 347-5343   *SIC 8211*

ECOLE SECONDAIRE MASSEY VANIER p
1088
See COMMISSION SCOLAIRE DU VAL-DES-CERFS

ECOLE SECONDAIRE MONT-ROYAL   p
1155
See   COMMISSION   SCOLAIRE MARGUERITE-BOURGEOYS

ECOLE SECONDAIRE NEPISIGUIT p 394
See CONSEIL SCOLAIRE DISTRICT NO 5

ECOLE SECONDAIRE NOTRE DAME DE ROC AMADOUR   p 1260
See COMMISSION SCOLAIRE DE LA CAP-ITALE, LA

ECOLE SECONDAIRE PANTHILE LE MAYp
1357
See COMMISSION SCOLAIRE DES NAVI-GATEURS

ECOLE SECONDAIRE PASDERMAJIAN   p
1224
See   ECOLE   ARMENIENNE   SOURP HAGOP, L'

ECOLE SECONDAIRE PAUL GERMAIN OS-TIGUY   p
1297
See   COMMISSION   SCOLAIRE   DES HAUTES-RIVIERES

ECOLE SECONDAIRE PAUL LE JEUNE p
1353
See   COMMISSION   SCOLAIRE   DE L'ENERGIE

ECOLE SECONDAIRE PIERRE BROSSEAU
p 1069
See COMMISSION SCOLAIRE MARIE-VICTORIN

ECOLE SECONDAIRE PIERRE LAPORTEp
1155
See   COMMISSION   SCOLAIRE MARGUERITE-BOURGEOYS

ECOLE SECONDAIRE POLYBEL   p 1056
See COMMISSION SCOLAIRE DES PATRI-OTES

ECOLE SECONDAIRE PUBLIQUE GISELE-LALONDE   p
811
See CONSEIL DES ECOLES PUBLIQUES DE L'EST DE L'ONTARIO

ECOLE SECONDAIRE REGIONAL DE HAWKESBURY   p 619
See CONSEIL SCOLAIRE DE DISTRICT CATHOLIQUE DE L'EST ONTARIEN

ECOLE SECONDAIRE RIVIERE DU LOUPp
1286
See   COMMISSION   SCOLAIRE   DE KAMOURASKA RIVIERE-DU-LOUP

ECOLE SECONDAIRE ROGER COMTOIS p
1275
See COMMISSION SCOLAIRE DE LA CAP-

ITALE, LA
ECOLE SECONDAIRE SAINT LAURENT *p*
1328
See COMMISSION SCOLAIRE
MARGUERITE-BOURGEOYS
ECOLE SECONDAIRE SAINT-JOSEPH DE
ST-HYACINTHE *p 1312*
2875 AV BOURDAGES N, SAINT-
HYACINTHE, QC, J2S 5S3
(450) 774-7087   *SIC 8211*
ECOLE SECONDAIRE VAL MAURICIE *p*
1369
See COMMISSION SCOLAIRE DE
L'ENERGIE
ECOLE SECONDAIRE VEILLEUX *p 1321*
See COMMISSION SCOLAIRE DE LA
BEAUCE-ETCHEMIN
ECOLE SECONDAIRES REGROUPEMENT
SUD COLLEGE SAINT LOUIS *p 1127*
See COMMISSION SCOLAIRE
MARGUERITE-BOURGEOYS
ECOLE ST GABRIEL *p 1364*
See COMMISSION SCOLAIRE DE LA
SEIGNEURIE-DES-MILLE-ILES
ECOLE ST JOSEPH *p 1310*
See COMMISSION SCOLAIRE MARIE-
VICTORIN
ECOLE ST-AMBROISE *p 1182*
See COMMISSION SCOLAIRE DE MON-
TREAL
ECOLE STE ANNE *p 401*
See SCHOOL BOARD DISTRICT 01
ECOLE STE-ODILE *p 1224*
See COMMISSION SCOLAIRE DE MON-
TREAL
ECOLE VICTOR DORE *p 1171*
See COMMISSION SCOLAIRE DE MON-
TREAL
ECOLES ET CENTRES EDUCATIF SAINT
AUBIN *p 1054*
See COMMISSION SCOLAIRE DE
CHARLEVOIX, LA
ECOLES SECONDAIRES - MONT-SAINT-
HILAIRE - OZIAS-LEDUC *p*
1158
See COMMISSION SCOLAIRE DES PATRI-
OTES
ECOLES SECONDAIRES ACHIGAN *p 1352*
See COMMISSION SCOLAIRE DES
SAMARES
ECOLES SECONDAIRES PATRIOTES DE
BEAUHARNOIS *p 1055*
See COMMISSION SCOLAIRE DE LA
VALLEE-DES-TISSERANDS, LA
ECOLIGHTING SOLUTIONS *p 1217*
See ENTRETIEN P.E.A.C.E. PLUS INC
ECOLOPHARM INC *p 1074*
8100 RUE SAMUEL-HATT, CHAMBLY, QC,
J3L 6W4
(450) 447-6307   *SIC 5122*
ECON-O-PAC LIMITED *p 871*
490 MIDWEST RD, SCARBOROUGH, ON,
M1P 3A9
(416) 750-7200   *SIC 7389*
ECONAUTO (1985) LTEE *p 1371*
2615 RUE KING O, SHERBROOKE, QC,
J1J 2H3
(819) 566-5322   *SIC 5521*
ECONO *p 1339*
See GROUPE BBH INC
ECONO-CHEM *p 72*
See 425579 ALBERTA LTD
ECONO-FAB *p 1057*
See INDUSTRIES BONNEVILLE LTEE,
LES
ECONO-RACK GROUP (2015) INC, THE *p*
515
132 ADAMS BLVD, BRANTFORD, ON, N3S
7V2
(519) 753-2227   *SIC 2542*
ECONOFAR (1988) INC *p 1068*
7400 BOUL TASCHEREAU BUREAU 71,
BROSSARD, QC, J4W 1M9
SIC 5912

ECONOFAST SHIPPING SYSTEMS INC *p*
114
9742 54 AVE NW, EDMONTON, AB, T6E
0A9
(780) 461-0578   *SIC 4731*
ECONOGLOBE *p 1199*
See SECURIGLOBE INC
ECONOLER INC *p 1258*
160 RUE SAINT-PAUL BUREAU 200, QUE-
BEC, QC, G1K 3W1
(418) 692-2592   *SIC 8748*
ECONOMICAL INSURANCE *p 612*
See ECONOMICAL MUTUAL INSURANCE
COMPANY
ECONOMICAL INSURANCE GROUP *p 48*
See ECONOMICAL MUTUAL INSURANCE
COMPANY
ECONOMICAL INSURANCE GROUP *p 770*
See ECONOMICAL MUTUAL INSURANCE
COMPANY
ECONOMICAL INSURANCE GROUP *p 825*
See ECONOMICAL MUTUAL INSURANCE
COMPANY
ECONOMICAL MUTUAL INSURANCE
COMPANY *p 48*
801 6 AVE SW SUITE 2700, CALGARY, AB,
T2P 3W2
(403) 265-8590   *SIC 6331*
ECONOMICAL MUTUAL INSURANCE
COMPANY *p 312*
1055 GEORGIA ST W SUITE 1900, VAN-
COUVER, BC, V6E 0B6
(800) 951-6665   *SIC 6331*
ECONOMICAL MUTUAL INSURANCE
COMPANY *p 446*
238A BROWNLOW AVE SUITE 310, DART-
MOUTH, NS, B3B 2B4
(902) 835-6214   *SIC 6331*
ECONOMICAL MUTUAL INSURANCE
COMPANY *p 612*
120 KING ST W SUITE 750, HAMILTON,
ON, L8P 4V2
(519) 570-8200   *SIC 6331*
ECONOMICAL MUTUAL INSURANCE
COMPANY *p 640*
590 RIVERBEND DR, KITCHENER, ON,
N2K 3S2
(519) 570-8335   *SIC 6331*
ECONOMICAL MUTUAL INSURANCE
COMPANY *p 653*
148 FULLARTON ST SUITE 1200, LON-
DON, ON, N6A 5P3
(800) 265-4441   *SIC 6331*
ECONOMICAL MUTUAL INSURANCE
COMPANY *p 770*
5700 YONGE ST SUITE 1600, NORTH
YORK, ON, M2M 4K2
(800) 268-8801   *SIC 6331*
ECONOMICAL MUTUAL INSURANCE
COMPANY *p 825*
343 PRESTON ST SUITE 500, OTTAWA,
ON, K1S 1N4
(613) 567-7060   *SIC 6331*
ECONOMICAL MUTUAL INSURANCE
COMPANY *p 1008*
111 WESTMOUNT RD S, WATERLOO, ON,
N2L 2L6
(519) 570-8200   *SIC 6331*
ECONOMICAL MUTUAL INSURANCE
COMPANY *p 1203*
5 PLACE VILLE-MARIE UNITE 1400, MON-
TREAL, QC, H3B 2G2
(514) 875-5790   *SIC 6331*
ECONOMY DRUGS LTD *p 390*
2211 PEMBINA HWY, WINNIPEG, MB, R3T
2H1
(204) 269-8113   *SIC 5912*
ECONOMY SHOE SHOP *p 451*
See ARGYLE COBBLERS LTD
ECONOMY WHEELS LTD *p 645*
129 ANGELINE ST N, LINDSAY, ON, K9V
4M9
(705) 324-5566   *SIC 5511*
ECONOSPAN STRUCTURES CORP *p 195*

472 AYLMER RD, CHASE, BC, V0E 1M1
(250) 679-3400   *SIC 3448*
ECOPURE *p 1233*
See AVMOR LTEE
ECOSYNTHETIX INC *p 526*
3365 MAINWAY SUITE 1, BURLINGTON,
ON, L7M 1A6
(905) 335-5669   *SIC 2822*
ECOSYSTEM *p 1273*
See SERVICES ENERGETIQUES
ECOSYSTEM INC, LES
ECOTEMP MANUFACTURING INC *p 1017*
8400 TWIN OAKS DR, WINDSOR, ON, N8N
5C2
SIC 3679
ECP L.P. *p 468*
50 ABBEY AVE, TRURO, NS, B2N 6W4
(902) 895-1686   *SIC 2671*
ECR INTERNATIONAL LTD *p 1004*
6800 BASE LINE, WALLACEBURG, ON,
N8A 2K6
(519) 627-0791   *SIC 3585*
ECRC *p 823*
See EASTERN CANADA RESPONSE
CORPORATION LTD
ECS COFFEE INC *p 527*
3100 HARVESTER RD UNIT 6, BURLING-
TON, ON, L7N 3W8
(905) 631-1524   *SIC 5499*
ECS VENDING *p 527*
See ECS COFFEE INC
ECSU *p 716*
See ERINDALE COLLEGE STUDENT
UNION
ECU LINE CANADA INC *p 735*
1804 ALSTEP DR SUITE 2, MISSISSAUGA,
ON, L5S 1W1
(905) 677-8334   *SIC 4731*
ECUHOME CORPORATION *p 962*
73 SIMCOE ST SUITE 308, TORONTO, ON,
M5J 1W9
(416) 593-9313   *SIC 8699*
ECYCLE SOLUTIONS *p 685*
See E-CYCLE SOLUTIONS INC
ED LEARN FORD LINCOLN LTD *p 885*
375 ONTARIO ST, ST CATHARINES, ON,
L2R 5L3
(905) 684-8791   *SIC 7515*
ED'S OK TIRE *p 352*
See ED'S TIRE SERVICE (1993) LTD
ED'S TIRE SERVICE (1993) LTD *p 352*
80 THORNHILL ST, MORDEN, MB, R6M
1C7
SIC 5531
ED. BRUNET ET ASSOCIES CANADA INC
p 1060
9 RUE DUMAS, GATINEAU, QC, J8Y 2M4
(819) 777-3877   *SIC 6712*
EDA *p 1031*
See ELECTRICITY DISTRIBUTORS ASSO-
CIATION
EDC *p 815*
See EXPORT DEVELOPMENT CANADA
EDCO DU CANADA *p 1249*
See COMPAGNIE DIVERSIFIEE DE L'EST
LTEE
EDDI'S WHOLESALE GARDEN SUPPLIES
LTD *p 229*
5744 268 ST, LANGLEY, BC, V4W 0B2
(604) 607-4447   *SIC 5261*
EDDIE BAUER OF CANADA INC *p 1031*
201 AVIVA PARK DR, WOODBRIDGE, ON,
L4L 9C1
(800) 426-8020   *SIC 5699*
EDDIE BAUER SPORTSWEAR *p 1031*
See EDDIE BAUER OF CANADA INC
EDDIE'S FAMILY FOODS *p 350*
See 600038 SASKATCHEWAN LTD
EDDIE'S HANG-UP DISPLAY LTD *p 291*
60 3RD AVE W, VANCOUVER, BC, V5Y 1E4
(604) 708-3100   *SIC 5199*
EDDY GROUP LIMITED *p 394*
660 ST. ANNE ST, BATHURST, NB, E2A
2N6

(506) 546-6631   *SIC 5074*
EDDY WHOLESALE *p 394*
See EDDY GROUP LIMITED
EDDY'S RESTAURANT SERVICES LTD *p*
427
GD, SOUTH BROOK GB, NL, A0J 1S0
(709) 657-2590   *SIC 5541*
EDDYFI NDT INC *p 1266*
3425 RUE PIERRE-ARDOUIN, QUEBEC,
QC, G1P 0B3
(418) 780-1565   *SIC 5084*
EDDYTRON *p 1054*
See NDT TECHNOLOGIES INC
EDELMAN PUBLIC RELATIONS WORLD-
WIDE CANADA INC *p*
974
150 BLOOR ST W SUITE 300, TORONTO,
ON, M5S 2X9
(416) 979-1120   *SIC 8743*
EDEM STEEL DIV OF *p 209*
See OPTIMIL MACHINERY INC
EDEN HOUSE CARE FACILITY INC *p 602*
5016 WELLINGTON ROAD 29, GUELPH,
ON, N1H 6H8
(519) 856-4622   *SIC 8051*
EDEN TEXTILES *p 86*
See SUM IT CORPORATION
EDENVALE RESTORATION SPECIALISTS
p 276
See EDENVALE RESTORATION SPECIAL-
ISTS LTD
EDENVALE RESTORATION SPECIALISTS
LTD *p 196*
8465 HARVARD PL SUITE 5, CHILLIWACK,
BC, V2P 7Z5
(604) 795-4884   *SIC 1542*
EDENVALE RESTORATION SPECIALISTS
LTD *p 276*
13260 78 AVE UNIT 24, SURREY, BC, V3W
0H6
(604) 590-1440   *SIC 1521*
EDGEMONT RETIREMENT RESIDENCE *p*
71
See REAL ESTATE INVESTMENT TRUST
EDGEN MURRAY CANADA INC *p 125*
1253 91 ST SW SUITE 302E, EDMONTON,
AB, T6X 1E9
(780) 440-1475   *SIC 5051*
EDGEPOINT *p 974*
See EDGEPOINT WEALTH MANAGEMENT
INC
EDGEPOINT CANADIAN PORTFOLIO *p*
974
150 BLOOR ST W SUITE 200, TORONTO,
ON, M5S 2X9
(416) 963-9353   *SIC 6722*
EDGEPOINT WEALTH MANAGEMENT INC
p 974
150 BLOOR ST W SUITE 500, TORONTO,
ON, M5S 2X9
(416) 963-9353   *SIC 6722*
EDGESTONE CAPITAL EQUITY PART-
NERS INC *p*
986
130 KING ST W SUITE 600, TORONTO,
ON, M5X 2A2
(416) 860-3740   *SIC 6722*
EDGEWATER CASINO *p 298*
See EDGEWATER MANAGEMENT INC
EDGEWATER GARDENS LONG-TERM
CARE CENTRE *p 567*
428 BROAD ST W, DUNNVILLE, ON, N1A
1T3
(905) 774-2503   *SIC 8051*
EDGEWATER HOLDINGS LTD *p 250*
8545 WILLOW CALE RD, PRINCE
GEORGE, BC, V2N 6Z9
(250) 561-7061   *SIC 7389*
EDGEWATER MANAGEMENT INC *p 298*
750 PACIFIC BLVD SUITE 311, VANCOU-
VER, BC, V6B 5E7
(604) 687-3343   *SIC 7011*
EDGEWELL (TM) *p 722*
See EDGEWELL PERSONAL CARE

CANADA ULC
EDGEWELL PERSONAL CARE CANADA ULC   *p* 722
6733 MISSISSAUGA RD SUITE 700, MISSISSAUGA, ON, L5N 6J5
(905) 363-2720   *SIC* 8052
EDGEWOOD CHEMICAL DEPENDENCY TREATMENT CENTRE   *p* 234
2121 BOXWOOD RD, NANAIMO, BC, V9S 4L2
(250) 751-0111   *SIC* 8093
EDGEWOOD MATTING LTD   *p* 100
18120 109 AVE NW, EDMONTON, AB, T5S 2K2
(780) 466-2084   *SIC* 5023
EDI   *p* 817
See ENCLOSURES DIRECT INC
EDICIBLE LTEE   *p* 1333
2825 RUE BRABANT-MARINEAU, SAINT-LAURENT, QC, H4S 1R8
(514) 336-0710   *SIC* 2789
EDIFICE 612 ST-JACQUES   *p* 1211
See QUEBECOR INC
EDIFICE DES ROUTIERS LOCAL 1999 CANADA INC.   *p* 1048
9393 RUE EDISON BUREAU 100, ANJOU, QC, H1J 1T4
(514) 355-1110   *SIC* 8631
EDILIVRE INC   *p* 1156
5740 RUE FERRIER, MONT-ROYAL, QC, H4P 1M7
(514) 738-0202   *SIC* 5192
EDIMEDIA   *p* 1257
See 3834310 CANADA INC
EDITEUR GUERIN LTEE   *p* 1183
4501 RUE DROLET, MONTREAL, QC, H2T 2G2
(514) 842-3481   *SIC* 2731
EDITH BOUCHARD DESIGNER   *p* 1231
See BRAGO CONSTRUCTION INC
EDITION JEUX INFINIS INC   *p* 1213
2110 RUE DRUMMOND BUREAU 200, MONTREAL, QC, H3G 1W9
SIC 5092
EDITION LE TELEPHONE ROUGE INC   *p* 1266
2555 AV WATT BUREAU 6, QUEBEC, QC, G1P 3T2
(418) 658-8122   *SIC* 7331
EDITIONS   BLAINVILLE-DEUX-MONTAGNES INC, LES   *p* 1301
53 RUE SAINT-EUSTACHE, SAINT-EUSTACHE, QC, J7R 2L2
(450) 473-1700   *SIC* 2711
EDITIONS BLAIS, YVON INC, LES   *p* 1210
75 RUE QUEEN BUREAU 4700, MONTREAL, QC, H3C 2N6
(514) 842-3937   *SIC* 8999
EDITIONS DE L'ACADIE NOUVELLE (1984) LTEE, LES   *p* 396
476 BOUL ST-PIERRE O, CARAQUET, NB, E1W 1A3
(800) 561-2255   *SIC* 2711
EDITIONS DES PARTENAIRES   *p* 1244
See FONDATION JULES & PAUL-EMILE LEGER
EDITIONS DROIT ET ENTREPRISE, LES   *p* 1210
See EDITIONS BLAIS, YVON INC, LES
EDITIONS   DU   RENOUVEAU   PEDAGOGIQUE INC   *p* 1176
1611 BOUL CREMAZIE E ETAGE 10, MONTREAL, QC, H2M 2P2
(514) 334-2690   *SIC* 2731
EDITIONS GRAND DUC, DIV   *p* 1234
See GROUPE EDUCALIVRES INC
EDITIONS GROMMELOT   *p* 1169
See CIRQUE DU SOLEIL CANADA INC
EDITIONS HURTUBISE INC   *p* 1174
1815 AV DE LORIMIER, MONTREAL, QC, H2K 3W6
(514) 523-1523   *SIC* 5192

EDITIONS NOVALIS INC, LES   *p* 1172
4475 RUE FRONTENAC, MONTREAL, QC, H2H 2S2
SIC 2721
EDITIONS PRATICO-PRATIQUES INC   *p* 1280
1685 BOUL TALBOT, QUEBEC, QC, G2N 0C6
(418) 877-0259   *SIC* 2721
EDITIONS QUEBEC-AMERIQUE INC, LES   *p* 1181
7240 RUE SAINT-HUBERT, MONTREAL, QC, H2R 2N1
(514) 499-3000   *SIC* 2741
EDITIONS ROZON CANADA   *p* 1185
See GESTION JUSTE POUR RIRE INC
EDITIONS VAUDREUIL INC   *p* 1394
480   BOUL   HARWOOD,   VAUDREUIL-DORION, QC, J7V 7H4
(450) 455-7974   *SIC* 5112
EDITIS   *p* 1175
See INTERFORUM CANADA INC
EDITO   *p* 1185
See GALLIMARD LTEE
EDJAR FOOD GROUP INC   *p* 669
7650 BIRCHMOUNT RD, MARKHAM, ON, L3R 6B9
(905) 474-0710   *SIC* 6712
EDMONDS CHEVROLET PONTIAC BUICK GMC LTD   *p* 620
138 HANES RD, HUNTSVILLE, ON, P1H 1M4
(705) 789-5507   *SIC* 5511
EDMONDS CONSTRUCTION SERVICES   *p* 455
See EDMONDS LANDSCAPE & CONSTRUCTION SERVICES LIMITED
EDMONDS GALLAGHER MCLAUGHLIN INSURANCE BROKERS LIMITED   *p* 838
270 LAKE ST, PEMBROKE, ON, K8A 7Y9
(613) 735-0621   *SIC* 6411
EDMONDS LANDSCAPE & CONSTRUCTION SERVICES LIMITED   *p* 455
2675 CLIFTON ST, HALIFAX, NS, B3K 4V4
(902) 453-5500   *SIC* 4959
EDMONTON BMW MINI EDMONTON   *p* 111
See ZP HOLDINGS INC
EDMONTON CATHOLIC SCHOOLS   *p* 84
8760 132 AVE NW, EDMONTON, AB, T5E 0X8
(780) 476-6251   *SIC* 8211
EDMONTON CATHOLIC SCHOOLS   *p* 92
See EDMONTON CATHOLIC SEPARATE SCHOOL DISTRICT NO.7
EDMONTON   CATHOLIC   SEPARATE SCHOOL DISTRICT NO.7   *p* 85
10830 109 ST NW, EDMONTON, AB, T5H 3C1
(780) 426-2010   *SIC* 8211
EDMONTON   CATHOLIC   SEPARATE SCHOOL DISTRICT NO.7   *p* 92
106 ST NW SUITE SUITE 9807, EDMONTON, AB, T5K 1C2
(780) 441-6000   *SIC* 8211
EDMONTON   CATHOLIC   SEPARATE SCHOOL DISTRICT NO.7   *p* 98
9250 163 ST NW, EDMONTON, AB, T5R 0A7
(780) 489-2571   *SIC* 8211
EDMONTON   CATHOLIC   SEPARATE SCHOOL DISTRICT NO.7   *p* 109
6110 95 AVE NW, EDMONTON, AB, T6B 1A5
(780) 466-3161   *SIC* 8211
EDMONTON   CATHOLIC   SEPARATE SCHOOL DISTRICT NO.7   *p* 119
11230 43 AVE NW, EDMONTON, AB, T6J 0X8
(780) 435-3964   *SIC* 8211
EDMONTON CITY CENTRE   *p* 88
10025 102A AVE NW SUITE 1700, EDMONTON, AB, T5J 2Z2

(780) 426-8444   *SIC* 6512
EDMONTON CITY CENTRE CHURCH CORPORATION   *p* 85
9321 JASPER AVE NW, EDMONTON, AB, T5H 3T7
(780) 424-1201   *SIC* 5812
EDMONTON COIN VENDING (1970) LTD   *p* 95
11690 147 ST NW, EDMONTON, AB, T5M 1W2
(780) 452-2727   *SIC* 5962
EDMONTON CONCERT HALL FOUNDATION   *p* 88
9720 102 AVE NW, EDMONTON, AB, T5J 4B2
(780) 429-1992   *SIC* 8399
EDMONTON DENTAL SUPPLIES LTD   *p* 85
10578 109 ST NW, EDMONTON, AB, T5H 3B2
(780) 429-2567   *SIC* 5047
EDMONTON ECONOMIC DEVELOPMENT CORPORATION   *p* 88
9797 JASPER AVE NW, EDMONTON, AB, T5J 1N9
(780) 421-9797   *SIC* 7389
EDMONTON ECONOMIC DEVELOPMENT CORPORATION   *p* 88
9990 JASPER AVE NW 3RD FL, EDMONTON, AB, T5J 1P7
(780) 424-9191   *SIC* 7389
EDMONTON EXCHANGER GROUP OF COMPANIES   *p* 114
See EDMONTON EXCHANGER & MANUFACTURING LTD
EDMONTON EXCHANGER & MANUFACTURING LTD   *p* 114
5545 89 ST NW, EDMONTON, AB, T6E 5W9
(780) 468-6722   *SIC* 3312
EDMONTON EXCHANGER & REFINERY SERVICES LTD   *p* 114
5545 89 ST NW, EDMONTON, AB, T6E 5W9
(780) 468-6722   *SIC* 7699
EDMONTON FASTENERS & TOOLS LTD   *p* 95
16409 111 AVE NW, EDMONTON, AB, T5M 2S2
(780) 484-3113   *SIC* 5085
EDMONTON GEAR CENTRE LTD   *p* 95
14811 116 AVE NW, EDMONTON, AB, T5M 3E8
(780) 452-6933   *SIC* 5013
EDMONTON HORTICULTURAL SOCIETY   *p* 100
10746 178 ST NW, EDMONTON, AB, T5S 1J3
(780) 456-3324   *SIC* 0781
EDMONTON HOUSE REALTY LTD   *p* 88
10205 100 AVE NW SUITE 3400, EDMONTON, AB, T5J 4B5
(780) 420-4040   *SIC* 6798
EDMONTON HUMANE SOCIETY FOR THE PREVENTION OF CRUELTY TO ANIMALS   *p* 105
13620 163 ST NW, EDMONTON, AB, T5V 0B2
(780) 471-1774   *SIC* 8699
EDMONTON ICE CREAM   *p* 92
See AGROPUR COOPERATIVE
EDMONTON INTERNATIONAL AIRPORT   *p* 134
See EDMONTON REGIONAL AIRPORTS AUTHORITY
EDMONTON INVESTORS GROUP LTD   *p* 84
11230 110 ST NW, EDMONTON, AB, T5G 3H7
(780) 414-4000   *SIC* 7941
EDMONTON JOURNAL, THE   *p* 90
See POSTMEDIA NETWORK INC
EDMONTON KENWORTH LTD   *p* 100
17335 118 AVE NW, EDMONTON, AB, T5S 2P5

(780) 453-3431   *SIC* 5511
EDMONTON KENWORTH PACLEASE, DIV OF   *p* 100
See EDMONTON KENWORTH LTD
EDMONTON KUBOTA LTD   *p* 105
15550 128 AVE NW, EDMONTON, AB, T5V 1S7
(780) 443-3800   *SIC* 5083
EDMONTON MENTAL HEALTH CLINIC   *p* 91
See ALBERTA HEALTH SERVICES
EDMONTON MOTORS LIMITED   *p* 92
11445 JASPER AVE NW, EDMONTON, AB, T5K 0M6
(780) 482-7809   *SIC* 5511
EDMONTON NORTHLANDS   *p* 83
7410 BORDEN PARK RD NW, EDMONTON, AB, T5B 0H8
(780) 471-8174   *SIC* 7999
EDMONTON NORTHLANDS   *p* 83
7424 118 AVE NW, EDMONTON, AB, T5B 4M9
(780) 471-7210   *SIC* 7922
EDMONTON NORTHLANDS   *p* 162
2693 BROADMOOR BLVD SUITE 132, SHERWOOD PARK, AB, T8H 0G1
(780) 471-7210   *SIC* 7999
EDMONTON NORTHSTARS ATHLETIC CLUB   *p* 83
7308 112 AVE NW, EDMONTON, AB, T5B 0E3
(780) 471-0010   *SIC* 8699
EDMONTON NUT & BOLT   *p* 113
See BRELCOR HOLDINGS LTD
EDMONTON OILERS OFFICES   *p* 84
See EDMONTON INVESTORS GROUP LTD
EDMONTON PETROLEUM CLUB   *p* 85
11110 108 ST NW SUITE 1, EDMONTON, AB, T5G 2T2
(780) 474-3411   *SIC* 8621
EDMONTON POTATO GROWERS COOPERATIVE INC   *p* 105
12220 170 ST NW, EDMONTON, AB, T5V 1L7
(780) 447-1860   *SIC* 5148
EDMONTON PUBLIC LIBRARY   *p* 88
7 SIR WINSTON CHURCHILL SQ NW, EDMONTON, AB, T5J 2V4
(780) 496-7000   *SIC* 8231
EDMONTON PUBLIC LIBRARY   *p* 88
7 SIR WINSTON CHURCHILL SQ NW SUITE 5, EDMONTON, AB, T5J 2V4
(780) 496-7050   *SIC* 8231
EDMONTON PUBLIC SCHOOL BOARD   *p* 86
See EDMONTON SCHOOL DISTRICT NO.7
EDMONTON REAL ESTATE BOARD CO-OPERATIVE LISTING BUREAU LIMITED   *p* 95
14220 112 AVE NW, EDMONTON, AB, T5M 2T8
(780) 451-6666   *SIC* 8611
EDMONTON REFINERY   *p* 91
See SUNCOR ENERGY INC
EDMONTON REGIONAL AIRPORTS AUTHORITY   *p* 134
1000 AIRPORT RD TERMINAL 1, GRANDE PRAIRIE, AB, T9E 0V3
(780) 890-8900   *SIC* 4581
EDMONTON RESEARCH CENTRE   *p* 121
See SYNCRUDE CANADA LTD
EDMONTON RUNNING ROOM LTD   *p* 114
9750 47 AVE NW, EDMONTON, AB, T6E 5P3
(780) 439-3099   *SIC* 5661
EDMONTON SCHOOL DISTRICT NO. 7   *p* 84
6804 144 AVE NW, EDMONTON, AB, T5C 3C7
(780) 408-9800   *SIC* 8211
EDMONTON SCHOOL DISTRICT NO. 7   *p* 86
1 KINGSWAY NW, EDMONTON, AB, T5H

4G9
(780) 429-8000   *SIC* 8211
EDMONTON SCHOOL DISTRICT NO. 7   *p* 111
7835 76 AVE NW, EDMONTON, AB, T6C 2N1
(780) 428-1111   *SIC* 8211
EDMONTON SCHOOL DISTRICT NO. 7   *p* 114
10450 72 AVE NW, EDMONTON, AB, T6E 0Z6
(780) 439-3957   *SIC* 8211
EDMONTON SCOTTISH SOCIETY   *p* 125
3105 101 ST SW, EDMONTON, AB, T6X 1A1
(780) 988-5357   *SIC* 7999
EDMONTON SPACE & SCIENCE FOUNDATION   *p* 95
11211 142 ST NW, EDMONTON, AB, T5M 4A1
(780) 452-9100   *SIC* 8412
EDMONTON STEEL PLATE LTD   *p* 114
5545 89 ST NW, EDMONTON, AB, T6E 5W9
(780) 468-6722   *SIC* 5051
EDMONTON SUN   *p* 107
See *1032451 B.C. LTD*
EDMONTON SUN, THE   *p* 107
See *1032451 B.C. LTD*
EDMONTON TRANSFER LTD   *p* 83
8830 126 AVE NW, EDMONTON, AB, T5B 1G9
(780) 477-1111   *SIC* 4213
EDMONTON VALVE & FITTING INC   *p* 114
4503 93 ST NW, EDMONTON, AB, T6E 5S9
(780) 437-0640   *SIC* 5085
EDMUNDSTON AUTO LTD. - EDMUNDSTON AUTO LTEE   *p* 398
121 CH CANADA, EDMUNDSTON, NB, E3V 1V7
(506) 735-4741   *SIC* 5511
EDMUNDSTON HONDA   *p* 398
See *050537 N.B. LTEE*
EDMUNDSTON REGIONAL HOSPITAL   *p* 395
See *VITALITE HEALTH NETWORK*
EDMUNDSTON TOYOTA   *p* 398
See *EDMUNDSTON AUTO LTD. - EDMUNDSTON AUTO LTEE*
EDO INTERNATIONAL FOOD INC   *p* 12
4838 32 ST SE, CALGARY, AB, T2B 2S6
(403) 215-8800   *SIC* 6794
EDO JAPAN   *p* 12
See *EDO INTERNATIONAL FOOD INC*
EDOKO FOOD IMPORTERS LTD   *p* 246
1335 KEBET WAY, PORT COQUITLAM, BC, V3C 6G1
(604) 944-7332   *SIC* 5141
EDON MANAGEMENT   *p* 29
See *EDON PROPERTIES INC*
EDON MANAGEMENT   *p* 37
See *SHAWN & ASSOCIATES MANAGEMENT LTD*
EDON MANAGEMENT   *p* 88
10030 107 ST NW, EDMONTON, AB, T5J 3E4
(780) 428-1742   *SIC* 6512
EDON PROPERTIES INC   *p* 29
1441 HASTINGS CRES SE, CALGARY, AB, T2G 4C8
(403) 245-1941   *SIC* 8741
EDPRO ENERGY GROUP INC   *p* 649
5 CUDDY BLVD, LONDON, ON, N5V 3Y3
(519) 690-0000   *SIC* 5984
EDSON CHRYSLER DODGE JEEP LTD   *p* 126
7440 4TH AVE, EDSON, AB, T7E 1V8
(780) 723-9500   *SIC* 5511
EDSON PACKAGING MACHINERY LIMITED   *p* 615
215 HEMPSTEAD DR, HAMILTON, ON, L8W 2E6

(905) 385-3201   *SIC* 3565
EDT GCV CIVIL S.E.P.   *p* 1119
1095 RUE VALETS, L'ANCIENNE-LORETTE, QC, G2E 4M7
(418) 872-0600   *SIC* 8742
EDU KIDS (DIV OF)   *p* 232
See *BLACK BOND BOOKS LTD*
EDUCATIONAL SERVICES   *p* 632
See *LIMESTONE DISTRICT SCHOOL BOARD*
EDUCATIONAL, DIV   *p* 874
See *LOUISE KOOL & GALT LIMITED*
EDUCATOR SUPPLIES LIMITED   *p* 651
2323 TRAFALGAR ST, LONDON, ON, N5Y 5S7
(519) 453-7470   *SIC* 5049
EDUCATOR'S FINANCIAL GROUP   *p* 767
2225 SHEPPARD AVE E SUITE 1105, NORTH YORK, ON, M2J 5C2
(416) 752-9410   *SIC* 6722
EDUCATOURS   *p* 1223
See *TOURS JUMPSTREET TOURS INC, LES*
EDUCATOURS LTD   *p* 995
3280 BLOOR ST W SUITE 901, TORONTO, ON, M8X 2X3
(416) 251-3390   *SIC* 4725
EDWARD COLLINS CONTRACTING LIMITED   *p* 424
2 GUY ST, JERSEYSIDE, NL, A0B 2G0
(709) 227-5509   *SIC* 1542
EDWARD CONSUMERS COOPERATIVE LTD   *p* 354
13 BROADWAY ST, PIERSON, MB, R0M 1S0
(204) 634-2418   *SIC* 5171
EDWARD D. JONES & CO. CANADA HOLDING CO., INC   *p* 709
90 BURNHAMTHORPE RD W SUITE 902, MISSISSAUGA, ON, L5B 3C3
(905) 306-8600   *SIC* 6211
EDWARD FUELS   *p* 544
See *SCRUTON-EDWARD CORP*
EDWARD FUELS LIMITED   *p* 597
263 HURON RD, GODERICH, ON, N7A 2Z8
(519) 524-8386   *SIC* 5172
EDWARD JONES   *p* 709
See *EDWARD D. JONES & CO. CANADA HOLDING CO., INC*
EDWARD SCHREYER SCHOOL   *p* 345
See *SUNRISE SCHOOL DIVISION*
EDWARDS DOORS SYSTEMS LIMITED   *p* 846
124 KENDALL ST, POINT EDWARD, ON, N7V 4G5
(519) 336-4990   *SIC* 5031
EDWARDS GARAGE LIMITED   *p* 159
4403 42ND AVE, ROCKY MOUNTAIN HOUSE, AB, T4T 1A6
(403) 845-3328   *SIC* 5511
EDWARDS GROUP   *p* 150
See *AG GROWTH INTERNATIONAL INC*
EDWARDS KENNY & BRAY LLP   *p* 317
See *YCO CORPORATE INVESTMENTS LTD*
EDWARDS LIFESCIENCES (CANADA) INC   *p* 711
1290 CENTRAL PKY W SUITE 300, MISSISSAUGA, ON, L5C 4R3
(905) 273-7138   *SIC* 5047
EECOL ELECTRIC CORP   *p* 15
11004 48 ST SE, CALGARY, AB, T2C 3E1
(403) 243-5594   *SIC* 5063
EECOL ELECTRIC CORP   *p* 69
63 SUNPARK DR SE, CALGARY, AB, T2X 3V4
(403) 253-1952   *SIC* 5063
EECOL ELECTRIC ULC   *p* 69
63 SUNPARK DR SE, CALGARY, AB, T2X 3V4
SIC 5063
EECOL HOLDINGS LTD   *p* 69

63 SUNPARK DR SE, CALGARY, AB, T2X 3V4
(403) 571-8400   *SIC* 5063
EEJAY TEXTILES   *p* 1178
See *FLAMCAN TEXTILES INC*
EENCHOKAY BIRCHSTICK SCHOOL   *p* 846
See *PIKANGIKUM EDUCATION AUTHORITY*
EF EDUCATION   *p* 1188
407 RUE MCGILL BUREAU 400, MONTREAL, QC, H2Y 2G3
(514) 904-0180   *SIC* 4724
EF INTERNATIONAL LANGUAGE SCHOOLS (CANADA) LIMITED   *p* 980
127 PORTLAND ST, TORONTO, ON, M5V 2N4
(800) 387-1463   *SIC* 7299
EFCO   *p* 593
See *EFCO CANADA CO*
EFCO CANADA CO   *p* 593
30 TODD RD, GEORGETOWN, ON, L7G 4R7
(905) 877-6957   *SIC* 3444
EFFICIENCY E1 SERVICES   *p* 446
See *EFFICIENCY NOVA SCOTIA CORP*
EFFICIENCY NOVA SCOTIA CORP   *p* 446
230 BROWNLOW AVE SUITE 300, DARTMOUTH, NS, B3B 0G5
(902) 470-3500   *SIC* 8748
EFFIGIS GEO SOLUTIONS INC   *p* 1169
4101 RUE MOLSON BUREAU 400, MONTREAL, QC, H1Y 3L1
(514) 495-6500   *SIC* 7371
EFFORT CORPORATION   *p* 611
242 MAIN ST E SUITE 240, HAMILTON, ON, L8N 1H5
(905) 528-8956   *SIC* 6719
EFFORT TRUST COMPANY, THE   *p* 611
240 MAIN ST E, HAMILTON, ON, L8N 1H5
(905) 528-8956   *SIC* 6021
EFI CONCEPTS   *p* 584
315 HUMBERLINE DR SUITE A, ETOBICOKE, ON, M9W 5T6
(416) 674-6744   *SIC* 5075
EFP DESIGNS INC   *p* 552
50 VICEROY RD SUITE 23, CONCORD, ON, L4K 3A7
(905) 669-0368   *SIC* 5211
EFW RADIOLOGY   *p* 8
2851 SUNRIDGE BLVD NE SUITE 130, CALGARY, AB, T1Y 0B7
(403) 541-1200   *SIC* 8071
EFW RADIOLOGY   *p* 77
3883 FRONT ST SE SUITE 312, CALGARY, AB, T3M 2J6
(403) 541-1200   *SIC* 8011
EG INDUSTRIES CANADA, ULC   *p* 896
291 GRIFFITH RD UNIT 2, STRATFORD, ON, N5A 6S4
(519) 273-3733   *SIC* 3089
EG TRANSPIRE   *p* 896
See *EG INDUSTRIES CANADA, ULC*
EGALE CANADA HUMAN RIGHTS TRUST   *p* 933
185 CARLTON ST, TORONTO, ON, M5A 2K7
(888) 204-7777   *SIC* 8699
EGAN TEAMBOARD INC   *p* 1031
300 HANLAN RD, WOODBRIDGE, ON, L4L 3P6
(905) 851-2826   *SIC* 2521
EGAN VISUAL INC   *p* 1031
300 HANLAN RD, WOODBRIDGE, ON, L4L 3P6
(905) 851-2826   *SIC* 2599
EGAR TOOL AND DIE LTD   *p* 535
336 PINEBUSH RD, CAMBRIDGE, ON, N1T 1Z6
(519) 623-3023   *SIC* 3469
EGG FARMERS OF CANADA   *p* 833
See *CANADIAN EGG MARKETING AGENCY*
EGGSOLUTIONS - VANDERPOLS INC   *p* 176

3911 MT LEHMAN RD, ABBOTSFORD, BC, V2T 5W5
(604) 856-4127   *SIC* 5144
EGI FINANCIAL HOLDINGS INC   *p* 694
2680 MATHESON BLVD E SUITE 300, MISSISSAUGA, ON, L4W 0A5
(905) 214-7880   *SIC* 6411
EGM   *p* 838
See *EDMONDS GALLAGHER MCLAUGHLIN INSURANCE BROKERS LIMITED*
EGR INC   *p* 1203
1100 BOUL ROBERT-BOURASSA 6E ETAGE, MONTREAL, QC, H3B 3A5
(514) 370-4800   *SIC* 6411
EGZATEK INC   *p* 1369
135 RUE OLIVA-TURGEON, SHERBROOKE, QC, J1C 0R3
(819) 846-6863   *SIC* 7699
EHATARE RETIREMENT AND NURSING HOME   *p* 866
See *ESTONIAN RELIEF COMMITTEE IN CANADA*
EHC CANADA, INC   *p* 813
1287 BOUNDARY RD, OSHAWA, ON, L1J 6Z7
(905) 432-3200   *SIC* 3534
EHC GLOBAL   *p* 813
See *EHC CANADA, INC*
EHC GLOBAL INC   *p* 813
1287 BOUNDARY RD, OSHAWA, ON, L1J 6Z7
(905) 432-3200   *SIC* 6712
EHEALTH SASKATCHEWAN   *p* 1417
2130 11TH AVE, REGINA, SK, S4P 0J5
(855) 347-5465   *SIC* 8399
EHR   *p* 609
See *EAST HAMILTON RADIO LIMITED*
EHS CANADA INC   *p* 882
2964 SOUTH GRIMSBY RD 18 RR 1, SMITHVILLE, ON, L0R 2A0
(905) 643-3343   *SIC* 8748
EI BRAND MANAGEMENT INC   *p* 1333
2520 AV MARIE-CURIE, SAINT-LAURENT, QC, H4S 1N1
(514) 344-3533   *SIC* 5137
EICHENBERG MOTORS (1971) LIMITED   *p* 911
39 BROADWAY ST, TILLSONBURG, ON, N4G 3P2
(519) 842-5953   *SIC* 5511
EIDOS-MONTREAL   *p* 1194
See *CORPORATION INTERACTIVE EIDOS*
EIGEN DEVELOPMENT LTD   *p* 320
1807 10TH AVE W SUITE 300, VANCOUVER, BC, V6J 2A9
(604) 484-0211   *SIC* 6289
EII LIMITED   *p* 526
1124 NORTHSIDE RD, BURLINGTON, ON, L7M 1H4
(905) 635-3111   *SIC* 5051
EILEEN DAILLY LEISURE POOL AND FITNESS CENTRE   *p* 185
See *CITY OF BURNABY*
EISENHAUER INSURANCE INCORPORATED   *p* 458
362 LACEWOOD DR SUITE 205, HALIFAX, NS, B3S 1M7
(902) 454-5888   *SIC* 6411
EITZ CHAIM DAY SCHOOL   *p* 790
1 VIEWMOUNT AVE, NORTH YORK, ON, M6B 1T2
(416) 789-4366   *SIC* 8211
EJ ENTERPRISE   *p* 228
20179 56 AVE, LANGLEY, BC, V3A 3Y6
(604) 514-2224   *SIC* 5084
EK'ATI SERVICES LTD   *p* 436
4910 50 AVE, YELLOWKNIFE, NT, X1A 3S5
(867) 873-8873   *SIC* 5812
EKI RENTAL   *p* 1305
See *POMERLEAU INC*
EKO   *p* 1261
See *DUFRESNE, FERNAND INC*

EKUM-SEKUM INCORPORATED   p 533
1555 BISHOP ST N UNIT 1, CAMBRIDGE, ON, N1R 7J4
(519) 622-1600   *SIC* 1771

EKUMEN   p 1172
6616 AV DES ERABLES, MONTREAL, QC, H2G 2N1
(438) 764-7433   *SIC* 7922

EL BASIL GROUP INC   p 84
13026 97 ST NW SUITE 203, EDMONTON, AB, T5E 4C6
(780) 406-7272   *SIC* 7991

EL CON   p 803
861 REDWOOD SQ SUITE 1900, OAKVILLE, ON, L6L 6R6
(905) 825-9400   *SIC* 4911

EL DIVINO PECADO   p 1281
See PRODUITS DE PATISSERIE MICHAUD INC

EL DORADO VEGETABLE FARMS LTD   p 158
860 BROADWAY AVE W, REDCLIFF, AB, T0J 2P0
(403) 548-6671   *SIC* 5148

EL-BRIS LIMITED   p 1023
933 GOYEAU ST, WINDSOR, ON, N9A 1H7
SIC 1521

EL-EN PACKAGING COMPANY LIMITED p 552
200 GREAT GULF DR, CONCORD, ON, L4K 5W1
(905) 761-5975   *SIC* 5113

EL-MET-PARTS INC   p 566
47 HEAD ST, DUNDAS, ON, L9H 3H6
(905) 628-6366   *SIC* 3469

EL-RANCHO FOOD SERVICES LIMITED p 1433
218 103RD ST E, SASKATOON, SK, S7N 1Y7
(306) 668-2600   *SIC* 5812

ELAD BUSINESS SERVICES   p 703
See 2144205 ONTARIO INC

ELAINE MAH PHARMACY LTD   p 165
140 ST ALBERT TRAIL SUITE 570, ST. ALBERT, AB, T8N 7C8
(780) 460-9222   *SIC* 5912

ELAN CONSTRUCTION LIMITED   p 8
3639 27 ST NE SUITE 100, CALGARY, AB, T1Y 5E4
(403) 291-1165   *SIC* 1542

ELAN DATAMAKERS, DIV OF   p 298
See HORTON TRADING LTD

ELASTIC PATH SOFTWARE INC   p 312
745 THURLOW ST UNIT 1400, VANCOUVER, BC, V6E 0C5
(604) 408-8078   *SIC* 7371

ELASTO PROXY INC   p 1061
4035 RUE LAVOISIER, BOISBRIAND, QC, J7H 1N1
(450) 434-2744   *SIC* 5199

ELBOW RIVER MARKETING LTD   p 48
335 8 AVE SW SUITE 810, CALGARY, AB, T2P 1C9
(403) 232-6868   *SIC* 5172

ELCAN OPTICAL TECHNOLOGIES, DIV OF p 825
See RAYTHEON CANADA LIMITED

ELCO FINANCE   p 1071
See APRIL CANADA INC

ELCO FINE FOODS INC   p 669
233 ALDEN RD, MARKHAM, ON, L3R 3W6
(604) 651-1551   *SIC* 5141

ELCO FINE FOODS LTD   p 254
13100 MITCHELL RD SUITE 120, RICHMOND, BC, V6V 1M8
(604) 324-1551   *SIC* 5141

ELCO SYSTEMS INC   p 669
215 SHIELDS CRT UNIT 4-6, MARKHAM, ON, L3R 8V2
(905) 470-0082   *SIC* 5045

ELCORA ADVANCED MATERIALS CORP p 439
275 ROCKY LAKE DR SUITE 10, BEDFORD, NS, B4A 2T3

(902) 802-8847   *SIC* 1499

ELD   p 303
See ELDORADO GOLD CORPORATION

ELDORADO GOLD CORPORATION   p 303
550 BURRARD ST 1188 BENTALL 5, VANCOUVER, BC, V6C 2B5
(604) 687-4018   *SIC* 1041

ELDORADO R V SALES LTD   p 140
711 2A AVE N, LETHBRIDGE, AB, T1H 0E1
(403) 329-3933   *SIC* 5561

ELECSO   p 1377
See 4318200 CANADA INC

ELECTRIC FOODS INC   p 11
3663 12 AVE NE, CALGARY, AB, T2A 7T1
(403) 248-7640   *SIC* 5812

ELECTRIC MOTOR SERVICE LIMITED p 114
8835 60 AVE NW, EDMONTON, AB, T6E 6L9
(780) 496-9300   *SIC* 7694

ELECTRIC POWER EQUIPMENT LIMITED p 298
1285 HOMER ST, VANCOUVER, BC, V6B 2Z2
(604) 682-4221   *SIC* 3625

ELECTRICAL COMPONENTS CANADA, INC p 911
91 LINCOLN ST, TILLSONBURG, ON, N4G 2P9
(519) 842-9063   *SIC* 3679

ELECTRICAL CONTACTS LIMITED   p 617
519 22ND AVE, HANOVER, ON, N4N 3T6
(519) 364-1878   *SIC* 3643

ELECTRICAL WHOLESALERS (CALGARY) LTD   p 22
1323 36 AVE NE, CALGARY, AB, T2E 6T6
(403) 250-7060   *SIC* 5063

ELECTRICITE GRIMARD INC   p 1080
1235 RUE BERSIMIS, CHICOUTIMI, QC, G7K 1A4
(418) 549-6352   *SIC* 1731

ELECTRICITE TRI-TECH INC   p 1096
480 BOUL STRATHMORE, DORVAL, QC, H9S 2J4
(450) 420-0111   *SIC* 1731

ELECTRICITY DISTRIBUTORS ASSOCIATION p 1031
3700 STEELES AVE W SUITE 1100, WOODBRIDGE, ON, L4L 8K8
(905) 265-5300   *SIC* 8611

ELECTRIMAT LTEE   p 1068
2180 BOUL LAPINIERE, BROSSARD, QC, J4W 1M2
(450) 462-2116   *SIC* 5063

ELECTRIQUE BRITTON   p 1156
See CIE ELECTRIQUE BRITTON LTEE, LA

ELECTRIQUE PERFECTION INC   p 1344
8685 RUE PASCAL-GAGNON, SAINT-LEONARD, QC, H1P 1Y5
(514) 376-0100   *SIC* 1731

ELECTRO AIR CANADA   p 552
See FIVE SEASONS COMFORT LIMITED

ELECTRO CABLES INC   p 998
9 RIVERSIDE DR, TRENTON, ON, K8V 5P8
(613) 394-4896   *SIC* 3357

ELECTRO CANADA LIMITED   p 988
30 TYCOS DR, TORONTO, ON, M6B 1V9
SIC 3714

ELECTRO COMPOSITES (2008) ULC p 1321
325 RUE SCOTT, SAINT-JEROME, QC, J7Z 1H3
(450) 431-2777   *SIC* 3644

ELECTRO EXPERTS   p 1169
See CENTRE DE PIECES ET SERVICES EXPERT INC

ELECTRO MECANIK PLAYFORD   p 1262
See FRANKLIN EMPIRE INC

ELECTRO SAGUENAY LTEE   p 1045
245 RUE DES HUARTS, ALMA, QC, G8E 2G1
(418) 347-3371   *SIC* 1623

ELECTRO SAGUENAY LTEE   p 1237
1555 BOUL DE L'AVENIR BUREAU 306, MONTREAL, QC, H7S 2N5
SIC 4899

ELECTRO SONIC GROUP INC   p 669
60 RENFREW DR SUITE 110, MARKHAM, ON, L3R 0E1
(905) 470-3015   *SIC* 5065

ELECTRO-5 INC   p 1373
4135 BOUL INDUSTRIEL, SHERBROOKE, QC, J1L 2S7
(819) 823-5355   *SIC* 5065

ELECTRO-MENAGERS DISTINCTIVE 1237
See DISTINCTIVE APPLIANCES INC

ELECTRO-SOLDE   p 1310
See GERMAIN LARIVIERE (1970) LTEE

ELECTRO-WIND EIFCO   p 606
See ELECTRO-WIND SUPPLY INC

ELECTRO-WIND SUPPLY INC   p 606
2 TAGGART ST, GUELPH, ON, N1L 1M5
(519) 836-2280   *SIC* 5051

ELECTROGAS MONITORS LTD   p 155
7961 49 AVE SUITE 1, RED DEER, AB, T4P 2V5
(403) 341-6167   *SIC* 5099

ELECTROGROUPE PIONEER CANADA INC p 1110
612 CH BERNARD, GRANBY, QC, J2J 0H6
(450) 378-9018   *SIC* 3612

ELECTROLAB LIMITED   p 491
631 COLLEGE ST E, BELLEVILLE, ON, K8N 0A3
(613) 962-9577   *SIC* 8748

ELECTROLAB TRAINING SYSTEMS p 491
See ELECTROLAB LIMITED

ELECTROLUX CANADA CORP   p 744
5855 TERRY FOX WAY, MISSISSAUGA, ON, L5V 3E4
(905) 813-7700   *SIC* 5064

ELECTROLUX CANADA CORP   p 1120
802 BOUL DE L'ANGE-GARDIEN, L'ASSOMPTION, QC, J5W 1T6
(450) 589-5701   *SIC* 3634

ELECTROLUX HOME PRODUCTS p 1120
See ELECTROLUX CANADA CORP

ELECTROLUX MAJOR APPLIANCES p 744
See ELECTROLUX CANADA CORP

ELECTROMAC GROUP INC, THE p 1024
1965 AMBASSADOR DR, WINDSOR, ON, N9C 3R5
(519) 969-4632   *SIC* 3469

ELECTROMAC GROUP INC, THE p 1024
600 SPRUCEWOOD AVE, WINDSOR, ON, N9C 0B2
(519) 969-4632   *SIC* 3544

ELECTROMART (ONTARIO) INC   p 609
1701 BRAMPTON ST, HAMILTON, ON, L8H 3S2
(905) 524-1555   *SIC* 5051

ELECTROMART LIGHTING & ELECTRICAL SUPPLY p 609
See ELECTROMART (ONTARIO) INC

ELECTROMEC INC   p 8
4300 26 ST NE SUITE 125, CALGARY, AB, T1Y 7H7
SIC 3679

ELECTROMEGA LIMITEE   p 1072
105 AV LIBERTE, CANDIAC, QC, J5R 3X8
(450) 635-1020   *SIC* 5084

ELECTROMIKE INC   p 1264
1375 RUE FRANK-CARREL BUREAU 2, QUEBEC, QC, G1N 2E7
(418) 681-4138   *SIC* 5065

ELECTRONIC ARTS (CANADA) INC p 188
4330 SANDERSON WAY, BURNABY, BC, V5G 4X1
(604) 456-3600   *SIC* 7371

ELECTRONIC ARTS (CANADA) INC p 1203
3 PLACE VILLE-MARIE BUREAU 12350, MONTREAL, QC, H3B 0E7
(514) 448-8800   *SIC* 7371

ELECTRONIC CONTROLS, DIV OF p 391

See PARKER HANNIFIN CANADA

ELECTRONIC IMAGING SYSTEMS CORP p 874
1361 HUNTINGWOOD DR UNIT 8, SCARBOROUGH, ON, M1S 3J1
(416) 292-0900   *SIC* 7374

ELECTRONIC METALFORM INDUSTRIES LIMITED p 669
435 STEELCASE RD E, MARKHAM, ON, L3R 2M2
(905) 475-1217   *SIC* 3499

ELECTRONIC RECYCLING ASSOCIATION OF ALBERTA, THE p 29
1301 34 AVE SE, CALGARY, AB, T2G 1V8
(403) 262-4488   *SIC* 4953

ELECTRONIC WARFARE ASSOCIATES - CANADA, LTD p 596
1223 MICHAEL ST N SUITE 200, GLOUCESTER, ON, K1J 7T2
(613) 230-6067   *SIC* 8734

ELECTRONICS BOUTIQUE CANADA INC p 502
8995 AIRPORT RD SUITE 512, BRAMPTON, ON, L6T 5T2
(905) 790-9262   *SIC* 5734

ELECTRONIQUE ABRA CORPORATION p 1327
5465 CH DE LA COTE-DE-LIESSE, SAINT-LAURENT, QC, H4P 1A1
(514) 731-0117   *SIC* 5065

ELECTRONIQUE ADDISON   p 1169
See 9117-4227 QUEBEC INC

ELECTRONIQUE DNB   p 1229
See CENTRE INFORMATIQUE DNB LIMITEE

ELECTRONIQUE S.E.M.   p 1122
See LTG RAIL CANADA LTEE

ELECTRONIQUES ARBELL INC   p 1091
3633 BOUL DES SOURCES BUREAU 208, DOLLARD-DES-ORMEAUX, QC, H9B 2K4
(514) 685-5603   *SIC* 4899

ELECTRONIQUES PROMARK INC p 1250
215 RUE VOYAGEUR, POINTE-CLAIRE, QC, H9R 6B2
(514) 426-4104   *SIC* 3679

ELECTROTEMP TECHNOLOGIES INC p 705
406 WATLINE AVE, MISSISSAUGA, ON, L4Z 1X2
(905) 488-9263   *SIC* 5999

ELECTROZAD SUPPLY CO. (SARNIA) LIMITED p 860
625 SCOTT RD, SARNIA, ON, N7T 8G3
(519) 336-8550   *SIC* 5063

ELECTROZAD SUPPLY COMPANY LIMITED p 1018
2900 JEFFERSON BLVD, WINDSOR, ON, N8T 3J2
(519) 944-2900   *SIC* 5063

ELEGANCE   p 1157
See SAFDIE & CO. INC

ELEGANCE COLONIAL INC   p 1160
3800 BOUL DU TRICENTENAIRE, MONTREAL, QC, H1B 5T8
(514) 640-1212   *SIC* 2431

ELEKTA LTEE   p 1195
2050 RUE DE BLEURY BUREAU 200, MONTREAL, QC, H3A 2J5
(514) 840-9600   *SIC* 5047

ELEMENT AI INC   p 1182
6650 RUE SAINT-URBAIN BUREAU 500, MONTREAL, QC, H2S 3G9
(514) 379-3568   *SIC* 7371

ELEMENT FLEET MANAGEMENT CORP p 962
161 BAY ST SUITE 3600, TORONTO, ON, M5J 2S1
(416) 386-1067   *SIC* 8742

ELEMENT FLEET MANAGEMENT INC p 705
4 ROBERT SPECK PKY SUITE 900, MISSISSAUGA, ON, L4Z 1S1

(905) 366-8900   *SIC* 7515
ELEMENT MATERIALS TECHNOLOGY CANADA INC   *p* 715
2395 SPEAKMAN DR SUITE 583, MISSISSAUGA, ON, L5K 1B3
(905) 822-4111   *SIC* 8734
ELEMENT TECHNICAL SERVICES INC *p* 48
810-530 8 AVE SW, CALGARY, AB, T2P 3S8
(403) 930-0246   *SIC* 1389
ELEMENTAL DATA COLLECTION INC   *p* 823
170 LAURIER AVE W SUITE 400, OTTAWA, ON, K1P 5V5
(613) 667-9352   *SIC* 8732
ELEMENTARY TEACHERS FEDERATION OF ONTARIO   *p* 931
136 ISABELLA ST, TORONTO, ON, M4Y 0B5
(416) 962-3836   *SIC* 8631
ELEMENTARY TEACHERS FEDERATION OF ONTARIO   *p* 932
136 ISABELLA ST, TORONTO, ON, M4Y 0B5
(416) 962-3836   *SIC* 8631
ELEMENTS CASINO GRAND RIVER *p* 569
See ONTARIO LOTTERY AND GAMING CORPORATION
ELEMENTS CHAUFFANTS TEMPORA   *p* 1130
See ELEMENTS CHAUFFANTS TEMPORA INC., LES
ELEMENTS CHAUFFANTS TEMPORA INC., LES   *p* 1130
2501 AV DOLLARD, LASALLE, QC, H8N 1S2
(514) 933-1649   *SIC* 3567
ELEVATE ME   *p* 244
See PROSNACK NATURAL FOODS INC
ELEVATEUR RIVE-SUD INC   *p* 1082
4065 RUE INDUSTRIELLE, CONTRECOEUR, QC, J0L 1C0
(450) 587-2500   *SIC* 5153
ELEVENTH FLOOR APPAREL LTD   *p* 584
100 RONSON DR, ETOBICOKE, ON, M9W 1B6
(416) 696-2818   *SIC* 5137
ELEVEURS DE PORCS DU QUEBEC LES *p* 1143
555 BOUL ROLAND-THERRIEN BUREAU 120, LONGUEUIL, QC, J4H 4E9
(450) 679-0540   *SIC* 2879
ELEVEURS DE PORCS DU QUEBEC, LES   *p* 1143
555 BOUL ROLAND-THERRIEN BUREAU 120, LONGUEUIL, QC, J4H 4E9
(450) 679-0540   *SIC* 8621
ELFA INSURANCE SERVICES INC   *p* 669
3950 14TH AVE UNIT 105, MARKHAM, ON, L3R 0A9
(905) 470-1038   *SIC* 6411
ELFE JUVENILE PRODUCTS   *p* 1327
See 1092072 ONTARIO INC
ELGIE BUS LINES LIMITED   *p* 661
400 SOVEREIGN RD, LONDON, ON, N6M 1A5
(519) 451-4440   *SIC* 4111
ELGIN A.C.L.   *p* 889
See COMMUNITY LIVING ELGIN
ELGIN CHRYSLER LTD   *p* 890
275 WELLINGTON ST, ST THOMAS, ON, N5R 2S6
(519) 633-2200   *SIC* 5511
ELGIN CONSTRUCTION   *p* 889
See 969774 ONTARIO LIMITED
ELGIN MALL   *p* 890
417 WELLINGTON ST SUITE 53, ST THOMAS, ON, N5R 5J5
(519) 633-4060   *SIC* 6512
ELGIN MANOR HOME FOR SENIORS *p* 889
See CORPORATION OF THE COUNTY OF ELGIN
ELGIN MANOR HOME FOR SR CITIZENS *p* 889
39262 FINGAL LINE, ST THOMAS, ON,

N5P 3S5
(519) 631-0620   *SIC* 8361
ELGIN MOTOR FREIGHT INC   *p* 661
1497 WILTON GROVE RD, LONDON, ON, N6N 1M3
(519) 644-9090   *SIC* 4213
ELGIN ST. THOMAS HEALTH UNIT   *p* 889
1230 TALBOT ST, ST THOMAS, ON, N5P 1G9
(519) 631-9900   *SIC* 8621
ELGIN ST. THOMAS PUBLIC HEALTH   *p* 889
See ELGIN ST. THOMAS HEALTH UNIT
ELGINWOOD LONG TERM CARE   *p* 857
See REVERA LONG TERM CARE INC
ELI LILLY CANADA INC   *p* 870
3650 DANFORTH AVE, SCARBOROUGH, ON, M1N 2E8
(416) 694-3221   *SIC* 2834
ELIAS WOODWORKING AND MANUFACTURING LTD   *p* 361
275 BADGER RD, WINKLER, MB, R6W 0K5
(204) 325-9962   *SIC* 2431
ELIE, JOSEPH LTEE   *p* 1052
7400 BOUL DES GALERIES D'ANJOU UNITE 300, ANJOU, QC, H1M 3M2
(514) 493-2930   *SIC* 5983
ELIK, MIKE LIMITED   *p* 711
3050 MAVIS RD SUITE 346, MISSISSAUGA, ON, L5C 1T8
(905) 270-9200   *SIC* 5251
ELIMETAL   *p* 1334
See HOLDECOM INC
ELIMETAL INC   *p* 1333
1515 BOUL PITFIELD, SAINT-LAURENT, QC, H4S 1G3
(514) 956-7400   *SIC* 3324
ELISSA GROUP CO   *p* 626
4 MARICONA WAY, KANATA, ON, K2T 1H1
(613) 799-6473   *SIC* 5148
ELITE AUTO CENTRE, DIV OF.   *p* 220
See TOTAL LEASE & TRUCK SALES LTD
ELITE CAMP SERVICES INC   *p* 164
340 ACHESON RD, SPRUCE GROVE, AB, T7X 5A7
SIC 5812
ELITE CHRYSLER JEEP INC   *p* 1376
6138 CH DE SAINT-ELIE, SHERBROOKE, QC, J1R 0L1
(819) 571-5540   *SIC* 5511
ELITE COMMUNICATIONS INC   *p* 384
585 CENTURY ST, WINNIPEG, MB, R3H 0W1
(204) 989-2995   *SIC* 4899
ELITE COMPOSITE INC   *p* 1357
1036 RUE PRINCIPALE, SAINTE-CLOTILDE-DE-BEAUCE, QC, G0N 1C0
(418) 427-2622   *SIC* 3714
ELITE CONCEPTS INC   *p* 867
1079 MIDLAND AVE, SCARBOROUGH, ON, M1K 4G7
(416) 827-3007   *SIC* 5046
ELITE CONSTRUCTION INC   *p* 552
35 ROMINA DR SUITE 100, CONCORD, ON, L4K 4Z9
(905) 660-1663   *SIC* 8741
ELITE FLEET COURIER LTD   *p* 29
3615 MANCHESTER RD SE, CALGARY, AB, T2G 3Z7
(403) 263-1247   *SIC* 7389
ELITE FORMWORK INC   *p* 77
9935 ENTERPRISE WAY SE, CALGARY, AB, T3S 0A1
(403) 236-7751   *SIC* 5211
ELITE GROUP INC   *p* 1203
1175 PLACE DU FRERE-ANDRE, MONTREAL, QC, H3B 3X9
(514) 383-4720   *SIC* 5064
ELITE GROUP TEMPORARY STAFFING, THE   *p* 708
See 2059010 ONTARIO INC
ELITE HOLDINGS INC   *p* 172
See 875647 ALBERTA LTD

ELITE INSURANCE COMPANY   *p* 326
1125 HOWE ST SUITE 1100, VANCOUVER, BC, V6Z 2Y6
(604) 669-2626   *SIC* 6411
ELITE INTERNATIONAL FOODS INC   *p* 77
10725 25 ST NE BAY 124 BLDG B, CALGARY, AB, T3N 0A4
(403) 291-0660   *SIC* 5149
ELITE PACIFIC REALTY INC   *p* 194
3010 BOUNDARY RD, BURNABY, BC, V5M 4A1
(604) 671-5259   *SIC* 6531
ELITE REALTY T. W. INC   *p* 694
5090 EXPLORER DR UNIT 7, MISSISSAUGA, ON, L4W 4X6
(905) 629-1515   *SIC* 6531
ELITE SPORTSWEAR & AWARDS LTD *p* 93
14703 118 AVE NW, EDMONTON, AB, T5L 2M7
(780) 454-9775   *SIC* 5999
ELITE SWEETS   *p* 499
See ELITE SWEETS BRANDS INC
ELITE SWEETS BRANDS INC   *p* 499
9 EDVAC DR, BRAMPTON, ON, L6S 5X8
(905) 790-9428   *SIC* 2052
ELITE WEALTH MANAGEMENT INC *p* 260
7080 RIVER RD SUITE 241, RICHMOND, BC, V6X 1X5
(604) 276-8081   *SIC* 6411
ELITREX PLUMBING LTD   *p* 1031
120 SHARER RD, WOODBRIDGE, ON, L4L 8P4
(905) 264-7418   *SIC* 1711
ELIZABETH ARDEN (CANADA) LIMITED *p* 694
1590 SOUTH GATEWAY RD, MISSISSAUGA, ON, L4W 0A8
(905) 276-4500   *SIC* 5122
ELIZABETH BRUYERE HEALTH CENTRE *p* 822
See SOEURS DE LA CHARITE D'OTTAWA, LES
ELIZABETH FRY SOC. OF HAMILTON *p* 611
85 HOLTON AVE S, HAMILTON, ON, L8M 2L4
(905) 527-3097   *SIC* 8699
ELIZABETH FRY SOCIETY OF PEEL - HALTON *p* 508
24 QUEEN ST E SUITE LO1, BRAMPTON, ON, L6V 1A3
SIC 8399
ELIZABETH GRANT INTERNATIONAL INC *p* 868
381 KENNEDY RD, SCARBOROUGH, ON, M1K 2A1
(877) 751-1999   *SIC* 5122
ELIZABETHAN CATERING SERVICES LTD *p* 164
55 ALBERTA AVE, SPRUCE GROVE, AB, T7X 4B9
(780) 962-3663   *SIC* 5812
ELIZABETHS BAKERY LTD   *p* 75
79 CROWFOOT WAY NW, CALGARY, AB, T3G 2R2
(403) 239-2583   *SIC* 5812
ELJAY IRRIGATION LTD   *p* 15
3700 78 AVE SE SUITE 3, CALGARY, AB, T2C 2L8
(403) 279-2425   *SIC* 5083
ELK ISLAND PUBLIC SCHOOLS REGIONAL DIVISION NO. 14   *p* 4
53129 RANGE ROAD 222, ARDROSSAN, AB, T8E 2M8
(780) 922-2228   *SIC* 8211
ELK ISLAND PUBLIC SCHOOLS REGIONAL DIVISION NO. 14   *p* 161
20 FESTIVAL WAY, SHERWOOD PARK, AB, T8A 4Y1
(780) 467-8816   *SIC* 8211
ELK ISLAND PUBLIC SCHOOLS RE-

GIONAL DIVISION NO. 14   *p* 162
683 WYE RD, SHERWOOD PARK, AB, T8B 1N2
(780) 464-3477   *SIC* 8211
ELK TRADING CO. LTD   *p* 185
4664 LOUGHEED HWY SUITE 174, BURNABY, BC, V5C 5T5
(604) 684-6688   *SIC* 5031
ELK VALLEY HOSPITAL   *p* 212
See INTERIOR HEALTH AUTHORITY
ELKEM METAL CANADA INC   *p* 1080
2020 CH DE LA RESERVE, CHICOUTIMI, QC, G7J 0E1
(418) 549-4171   *SIC* 3313
ELKHORN RANCH & RESORT LTD   *p* 354
3 MOOSWA DR E, ONANOLE, MB, R0J 1N0
(204) 848-2802   *SIC* 7011
ELKHORN RESORT SPA & CONFERENCE CENTRE   *p* 354
See ELKHORN RANCH & RESORT LTD
ELKVIEW OPERATIONS   *p* 269
See TECK COAL LIMITED
ELL-ROD HOLDINGS INC   *p* 811
19 TAMBLYN RD RR 1, ORONO, ON, L0B 1M0
(905) 983-5456   *SIC* 2431
ELLABEE INTERNATIONAL   *p* 1180
See IRWIN TOGS INC
ELLARD ENTERPRISES LIMITED   *p* 839
115 DRUMMOND ST W, PERTH, ON, K7H 2K8
(613) 267-4501   *SIC* 5251
ELLAS BANQUET HALL AND CONFERENCE CENTRE LTD   *p* 868
33 DANFORTH RD, SCARBOROUGH, ON, M1L 3W5
SIC 7299
ELLEMENT CONSULTING GROUP   *p* 384
503-1780 WELLINGTON AVE, WINNIPEG, MB, R3H 1B3
(204) 954-7300   *SIC* 6371
ELLERSLIE ROAD BAPTIST CHURCH SOCIETY   *p* 124
10603 ELLERSLIE RD SW, EDMONTON, AB, T6W 1A1
(780) 437-5433   *SIC* 8699
ELLETT INDUSTRIES LTD   *p* 246
1575 KINGSWAY AVE, PORT COQUITLAM, BC, V3C 1S2
(604) 941-8211   *SIC* 3443
ELLIOT LAKE FIRE DEPARTMENT   *p* 568
55 HILLSIDE DR N, ELLIOT LAKE, ON, P5A 1X5
(705) 848-3232   *SIC* 7389
ELLIOT LAKE FOODLAND   *p* 568
See 749416 ONTARIO INC
ELLIOTT COACH LINES (FERGUS) LTD *p* 590
680 GLEN GARRY CRES, FERGUS, ON, N1M 2W8
SIC 4151
ELLIOTT TURBOMACHINERY CANADA INC   *p* 530
955 MAPLE AVE, BURLINGTON, ON, L7S 2J4
(905) 333-4101   *SIC* 7699
ELLIOTT, FRED COACH LINES LIMITED *p* 606
760 VICTORIA RD S, GUELPH, ON, N1L 1C6
(519) 822-5225   *SIC* 4151
ELLIOTT-MATSUURA CANADA INC *p* 797
2120 BUCKINGHAM RD, OAKVILLE, ON, L6H 5X2
(905) 829-2211   *SIC* 5084
ELLIS GENERAL CONTRACTOR   *p* 1023
See EL-BRIS LIMITED
ELLIS PACKAGING LIMITED   *p* 844
1830 SANDSTONE MANOR, PICKERING, ON, L1W 3Y1

(905) 831-5777   *SIC 2657*

ELLIS PACKAGING WEST INC   *p* 600
136 VICTORIA RD S, GUELPH, ON, N1E
5P6
(519) 822-7060   *SIC 2657*

ELLIS PAPER BOX INC   *p* 694
2345 MATHESON BLVD E, MISSISSAUGA,
ON, L4W 5B3
(905) 212-9177   *SIC 2657*

ELLIS, THOMAS G. CENTRE   *p* 277
See SCHOOL DISTRICT NO. 36 (SURREY)

ELLIS-DON CONSTRUCTION LTD   *p* 703
1004 MIDDLEGATE RD SUITE 1000, MIS-
SISSAUGA, ON, L4Y 1M4
(877) 980-4821   *SIC 1542*

ELLISDON CONSTRUCTION LTD   *p* 649
2045 OXFORD ST E, LONDON, ON, N5V
2Z7
(519) 455-6770   *SIC 1541*

**ELLISDON CONSTRUCTION SERVICES
INC**   *p* 649
2045 OXFORD ST E, LONDON, ON, N5V
2Z7
(519) 455-6770   *SIC 1542*

ELLISDON CORPORATION   *p* 649
2045 OXFORD ST E, LONDON, ON, N5V
2Z7
(519) 455-6770   *SIC 1542*

ELLISDON FORMING LTD   *p* 649
2045 OXFORD ST E, LONDON, ON, N5V
2Z7
(519) 455-6770   *SIC 1542*

ELLISDON HOLDINGS INC   *p* 649
2045 OXFORD ST E, LONDON, ON, N5V
2Z7
(519) 455-6770   *SIC 1542*

ELLISDON INDUSTRIAL SERVICES INC *p*
125
1430 91 ST SW UNIT 101, EDMONTON,
AB, T6X 1M5
(780) 669-8530   *SIC 1629*

ELLISDON RESIDENTIAL INC   *p* 649
2045 OXFORD ST E, LONDON, ON, N5V
2Z7
(519) 455-6770   *SIC 1522*

ELLISON TRAVEL & TOURS LTD   *p* 589
311 MAIN ST N, EXETER, ON, N0M 1S3
(519) 235-2000   *SIC 4725*

**ELLWOOD SPECIALTY METALS COM-
PANY**   *p*
1019
3282 ST ETIENNE BLVD, WINDSOR, ON,
N8W 5E1
(519) 944-4411   *SIC 5051*

ELLWORTH INDUSTRIES   *p* 199
*See ASSOCIATED LABELS & PRINTING
LTD*

ELLWORTH INDUSTRIES LTD   *p* 200
61 CLIPPER ST SUITE 61, COQUITLAM,
BC, V3K 6X2
(604) 525-4764   *SIC 2672*

**ELM CREEK CO-OPERATIVE OIL & SUP-
PLIES LTD**   *p*
349
43 CHURCH AVE, ELM CREEK, MB, R0G
0N0
(204) 436-2493   *SIC 5171*

ELM GROVE LIVING CENTRE INC   *p* 991
35 ELM GROVE AVE SUITE 209,
TORONTO, ON, M6K 2J2
(416) 537-2465   *SIC 8051*

ELM HURST INN   *p* 621
415 HARRIS ST, INGERSOLL, ON, N5C
3J8
(519) 485-5321   *SIC 7011*

ELMA STEEL & EQUIPMENT LTD   *p* 646
515 TREMAINE AVE S, LISTOWEL, ON,
N4W 3G9
(519) 291-1388   *SIC 5051*

ELMARA CONSTRUCTION CO. LIMITED *p*
807
5365 WALKER RD RR 1, OLDCASTLE, ON,
N0R 1L0
(519) 737-1253   *SIC 1541*

ELMHURST LATHING AND DRYWALL LTD
p 389
3160 WILKES AVE, WINNIPEG, MB, R3S
1A7
(204) 889-8238   *SIC 1742*

ELMIRA BUS LINES, A DIV OF   *p* 606
*See ELLIOTT, FRED COACH LINES LIM-
ITED*

ELMIRA COUNTRY FAIR, THE   *p* 569
*See WOOLWICH AGRICULTURAL SOCI-
ETY*

ELMIRA DISTRICT SECONDARY SCHOOL
p 568
*See WATERLOO REGION DISTRICT
SCHOOL BOARD*

ELMIRA PET PRODUCTS LTD   *p* 568
35 MARTIN'S LANE, ELMIRA, ON, N3B 2Z5
(519) 669-3330   *SIC 2048*

ELMSDALE LANDSCAPING LIMITED *p* 449
113 ELMSDALE RD, ELMSDALE, NS, B2S
1K7
(902) 883-2291   *SIC 0782*

ELMSDALE SOD FARMS LIMITED   *p* 449
113 ELMSDALE RD, ELMSDALE, NS, B2S
1K7
(902) 883-2291   *SIC 0181*

ELMWOOD GROUP LIMITED, THE   *p* 883
570 WELLAND AVE, ST CATHARINES, ON,
L2M 5V6
(905) 688-5205   *SIC 2434*

ELMWOOD GROUP LIMITED, THE   *p* 883
570 WELLAND AVE, ST CATHARINES, ON,
L2M 5V6
(905) 688-5205   *SIC 3429*

ELMWOOD HARDWARE LTD   *p* 405
257 ELMWOOD DR, MONCTON, NB, E1A
1X4
(506) 858-8100   *SIC 5211*

ELMWOOD KITCHEN   *p* 883
See ELMWOOD GROUP LIMITED, THE

ELMWOOD PLACE   *p* 659
See REVERA LONG TERM CARE INC

ELMWOOD SCHOOL   *p* 857
*See ELMWOOD SCHOOL INCORPO-
RATED*

ELMWOOD SCHOOL INCORPORATED *p*
857
261 BUENA VISTA RD, ROCKCLIFFE, ON,
K1M 0V9
(613) 749-6761   *SIC 8211*

ELMWOOD SPA, THE   *p* 931
See BRYDSON GROUP LTD

ELOPAK CANADA INC   *p* 1061
3720 AV DES GRANDES TOURELLES,
BOISBRIAND, QC, J7H 0A1
(450) 970-2846   *SIC 2754*

ELOQUA CORPORATION   *p* 980
553 RICHMOND ST W SUITE 214,
TORONTO, ON, M5V 1Y6
(416) 864-0440   *SIC 7372*

ELRINGKLINGER CANADA, INC   *p* 644
1 SENECA RD, LEAMINGTON, ON, N8H
5P2
(519) 326-6113   *SIC 3053*

ELRINGKLINGER CANADA, INC   *p* 644
1 SENECA RD SUITE 4, LEAMINGTON,
ON, N8H 5P2
(519) 326-6113   *SIC 3714*

ELRUS AGGREGATE SYSTEMS   *p* 15
See ELRUS INC

ELRUS INC   *p* 15
4409 GLENMORE TRAIL SE, CALGARY,
AB, T2C 2R8
(403) 279-7741   *SIC 1411*

ELS MARKETING LIMITED PARTNERSHIP
p 688
3133 ORLANDO DR, MISSISSAUGA, ON,
L4V 1C5
(905) 612-1259   *SIC 4512*

ELSWOOD INVESTMENT CORPORATION *p*
328
1055 DUNSMUIR ST SUITE 3500, VAN-
COUVER, BC, V7X 1H3
(604) 691-9100   *SIC 6712*

ELTE CARPETS LIMITED   *p* 989
80 RONALD AVE, TORONTO, ON, M6E 5A2
(416) 785-7885   *SIC 5713*

ELTEX ENTERPRISES 2002 LTD   *p* 271
18927 62B AVE, SURREY, BC, V3S 8S3
(604) 599-5088   *SIC 1742*

ELTHERM CANADA INC   *p* 530
1440 GRAHAMS LN UNIT 5, BURLING-
TON, ON, L7R 2J2
(289) 812-6631   *SIC 3567*

ELTON MANUFACTURING   *p* 684
See ONTARIO DOOR SALES LTD

ELVES CHILD DEVELOPMENT CENTER *p*
97
See ELVES SPECIAL NEEDS SOCIETY

ELVES SPECIAL NEEDS SOCIETY   *p* 97
10825 142 ST NW, EDMONTON, AB, T5N
3Y7
(780) 454-5310   *SIC 8211*

ELYOD INVESTMENTS LIMITED   *p* 860
775 EXMOUTH ST, SARNIA, ON, N7T 5P7
(519) 332-6741   *SIC 5461*

ELZEN HOLDINGS LTD   *p* 95
11450 160 ST NW SUITE 200, EDMON-
TON, AB, T5M 3Y7
(780) 453-6944   *SIC 1541*

EM DYNAMICS INC   *p* 874
160 COMMANDER BLVD, SCARBOR-
OUGH, ON, M1S 3C8
(416) 293-8385   *SIC 3499*

**EM PLASTIC & ELECTRIC PRODUCTS
LIMITED**   *p* 502
14 BREWSTER RD, BRAMPTON, ON, L6T
5B7
(905) 913-3000   *SIC 5063*

EMARD BROS. LUMBER CO. LTD   *p* 562
840 TENTH ST E, CORNWALL, ON, K6H
7S2
(613) 932-5660   *SIC 5211*

EMBALLAGE AVICO INC   *p* 1264
1460 RUE PROVINCIALE, QUEBEC, QC,
G1N 4A2
(418) 682-5024   *SIC 2015*

EMBALLAGE CADEAU NOBLE INC *p* 1183
5623 AV CASGRAIN, MONTREAL, QC, H2T
1Y1
(514) 278-8500   *SIC 5199*

EMBALLAGE CANFAB INC   *p* 1216
2740 RUE SAINT-PATRICK, MONTREAL,
QC, H3K 1B8
(514) 935-5265   *SIC 2655*

EMBALLAGE CODERRE PACKAGING INC
p 1306
413 RTE 122, SAINT-GERMAIN-DE-
GRANTHAM, QC, J0C 1K0
(819) 395-4223   *SIC 2674*

EMBALLAGE D'ALIMENTS LATINA INC *p*
1162
9200 RUE ROBERT-ARMOUR BUREAU 1,
MONTREAL, QC, H1E 2H1
(514) 643-0784   *SIC 5099*

**EMBALLAGE GRAPHIC INTERNATIONAL
CANADA**   *p* 1100
*See GRAPHIC PACKAGING INTERNA-
TIONAL CANADA, ULC*

EMBALLAGE INTERPLAST   *p* 1381
See INTERPLAST PACKAGING INC

EMBALLAGE PERFORMANT INC   *p* 1088
301 BOUL GRAND N, COWANSVILLE, QC,
J2K 1A8
(450) 263-6363   *SIC 3081*

EMBALLAGE ST-JEAN LTEE   *p* 1315
80 RUE MOREAU, SAINT-JEAN-SUR-
RICHELIEU, QC, J2W 2M4
(450) 349-5871   *SIC 2673*

EMBALLAGE WORKMAN INC   *p* 1339
345 MONTEE DE LIESSE, SAINT-
LAURENT, QC, H4T 1P5
(514) 344-7227   *SIC 2671*

EMBALLAGES ALCAN LACHINE   *p* 508
See AMCOR PACKAGING CANADA, INC

**EMBALLAGES BOUDREAULT CANADA
LTEE, LES**   *p* 1106
45 RUE ADRIEN-ROBERT, GATINEAU, QC,

J8Y 3S3
(819) 777-1603   *SIC 5113*

EMBALLAGES C&C   *p* 1343
*See C&C PACKING LIMITED PARTNER-
SHIP*

EMBALLAGES CARROUSEL INC, LES   *p*
1064
1401 RUE AMPERE, BOUCHERVILLE, QC,
J4B 6C5
(450) 655-2025   *SIC 5113*

EMBALLAGES CRE-O-PACK CANADA INC
p 1157
8420 CH DARNLEY, MONT-ROYAL, QC,
H4T 1M4
(514) 343-9666   *SIC 3565*

EMBALLAGES DELTAPAC INC   *p* 1048
7575 BOUL METROPOLITAIN E, ANJOU,
QC, H1J 1J8
(514) 352-5546   *SIC 5113*

EMBALLAGES FESTIVAL INC   *p* 1339
8286 CH DE LA COTE-DE-LIESSE, SAINT-
LAURENT, QC, H4T 1G7
(514) 731-3713   *SIC 5199*

EMBALLAGES GAB - INDUSPAC   *p* 1072
See EMBALLAGES GAB LTEE, LES

EMBALLAGES GAB LTEE, LES   *p* 1072
140 BOUL DE L'INDUSTRIE, CANDIAC,
QC, J5R 1J2
(450) 444-4884   *SIC 2657*

EMBALLAGES JEAN CARTIER INC *p* 1297
2325 BOUL INDUSTRIEL, SAINT-
CESAIRE, QC, J0L 1T0
(450) 469-3168   *SIC 5084*

EMBALLAGES KRUGER S.E.C.   *p* 1218
3285 CH DE BEDFORD, MONTREAL, QC,
H3S 1G5
(514) 737-1131   *SIC 2671*

**EMBALLAGES KUSH-PACK, DIVISION DE
DORFIN**   *p* 1329
See DORFIN INC

EMBALLAGES L. BOUCHER INC, LES   *p*
1266
1360 AV GALILEE, QUEBEC, QC, G1P 4E3
(418) 681-2320   *SIC 5113*

EMBALLAGES L.P. AUBUT INC   *p* 1264
1135 RUE TAILLON, QUEBEC, QC, G1N
4G7
(418) 523-2956   *SIC 5199*

EMBALLAGES MASKA INC   *p* 1310
7450 AV PION, SAINT-HYACINTHE, QC,
J2R 1R9
(450) 796-2040   *SIC 5113*

EMBALLAGES MITCHEL-LINCOLN LTEE *p*
1099
See MITCHEL-LINCOLN PACKAGING LTD

EMBALLAGES MONTCORR LTEE, LES   *p*
1088
40 RUE INDUSTRIELLE, COTEAU-DU-
LAC, QC, J0P 1B0
(450) 763-0920   *SIC 2653*

EMBALLAGES POLIPLASTIC INC   *p* 1109
415 RUE SAINT-VALLIER, GRANBY, QC,
J2G 7Y3
(450) 378-8417   *SIC 2673*

EMBALLAGES POLYSTAR INC   *p* 1162
7975 AV MARCO-POLO, MONTREAL, QC,
H1E 1N8
(514) 648-8171   *SIC 3081*

EMBALLAGES SALERNO CANADA INC *p*
1076
2275 BOUL FORD, CHATEAUGUAY, QC,
J6J 4Z2
(450) 692-8642   *SIC 2673*

EMBALLAGES STUART INC   *p* 1156
5454 CH DE LA COTE-DE-LIESSE, MONT-
ROYAL, QC, H4P 1A5
(514) 344-5000   *SIC 2657*

EMBALLAGES SXP INC   *p* 1250
269 BOUL SAINT JEAN STE 211B,
POINTE-CLAIRE, QC, H9R 3J1
(514) 364-3269   *SIC 2631*

**EMBALLAGES TRANSCONTINENTAL
FLEXIPAK INC**   *p* 1329
5020 BOUL THIMENS, SAINT-LAURENT,

QC, H4R 2B2
(514) 335-0001   *SIC* 2673
EMBALLAGES WINPAK HEAT SEAL INC,
LES   *p* 1394
21919 CH DUMBERRY, VAUDREUIL-
DORION, QC, J7V 8P7
(450) 424-0191   *SIC* 3497
EMBARC WHISTLER   *p* 343
See INTRAWEST RESORT CLUB GROUP
EMBASSY DEVELOPMENT CORPORA-
TION   *p*
185
2025 WILLINGDON AVE SUITE 1300,
BURNABY, BC, V5C 0J3
(604) 294-0666   *SIC* 6553
EMBASSY HOTEL & SUITES   *p* 834
See GREENBERG NAIMER GROUP
EMBASSY INGREDIENTS LTD   *p* 502
5 INTERMODAL DR UNIT 1, BRAMPTON,
ON, L6T 5V9
(905) 789-3200   *SIC* 2087
EMBASSY SUITES HOTEL   *p* 758
See 2095527 ONTARIO LIMITED
EMBASSY WEST HOTEL   *p* 829
1400 CARLING AVE SUITE 517, OTTAWA,
ON, K1Z 7L8
(613) 729-4321   *SIC* 7011
EMBASSY WEST HOTEL CONFERENCE
CENTRE   *p* 829
See EMBASSY WEST HOTEL
EMBER RESOURCES INC   *p* 48
400 3 AVE SW SUITE 800, CALGARY, AB,
T2P 4H2
(403) 270-0803   *SIC* 1382
EMBERS SERVICES LIMITED   *p* 653
80 DUFFERIN AVE, LONDON, ON, N6A
1K4
(519) 672-4510   *SIC* 6512
EMBIX COMPAGNIE D'IMPORTATIONS DE
MONTRES LTEE   *p* 1218
2550 CH BATES BUREAU 301, MON-
TREAL, QC, H3S 1A7
(514) 731-3978   *SIC* 5094
EMBOUTEILLAGE COCA COLA   *p* 1261
See COCA-COLA REFRESHMENTS
CANADA COMPANY
EMBRUN ELEVATORS, DIV OF   *p* 569
See COOPERATIVE AGRICOLE
D'EMBRUN LIMITED, LA
EMBRUN FORD SALES LTD   *p* 569
608 NOTRE DAME ST, EMBRUN, ON, K0A
1W0
(613) 443-2985   *SIC* 5511
EMC   *p* 49
See EXXONMOBIL CANADA LTD
EMC   *p* 446
See EMC EMERGENCY MEDICAL CARE
INCORPORATED
EMC CORPORATION OF CANADA   *p* 951
120 ADELAIDE ST W SUITE 1400,
TORONTO, ON, M5H 1T1
(416) 628-5973   *SIC* 3577
EMC EMERGENCY MEDICAL CARE IN-
CORPORATED   *p*
446
239 BROWNLOW AVE SUITE 300, DART-
MOUTH, NS, B3B 2B2
(902) 832-8320   *SIC* 4119
EMC POWER CANADA LTD   *p* 629
2091 HIGHWAY 21, KINCARDINE, ON, N2Z
2X4
(844) 644-3627   *SIC* 1731
EMCO   *p* 521
See CCTF CORPORATION
EMCO CORPORATION   *p* 122
3011 101 AVE NW, EDMONTON, AB, T6P
1X7
(780) 440-7333   *SIC* 5074
EMCO CORPORATION   *p* 446
111 WRIGHT AVE, DARTMOUTH, NS, B3B
1K6
(902) 555-7744   *SIC* 5074
EMCO CORPORATION   *p* 649
2124 OXFORD ST E, LONDON, ON, N5V

0B7
(519) 453-9600   *SIC* 5074
EMCON SERVICES INC   *p* 232
1121 MCFARLANE WAY UNIT 105, MER-
RITT, BC, V1K 1B9
(250) 378-4176   *SIC* 1611
EMD INC   *p* 715
2695 NORTH SHERIDAN WAY SUITE 200,
MISSISSAUGA, ON, L5K 2N6
(905) 919-0200   *SIC* 5122
EMD SERONO, DIV OF   *p* 715
See EMD INC
EMD TECHNOLOGIES INCORPORATED *p*
1301
400 RUE DU PARC, SAINT-EUSTACHE,
QC, J7R 0A1
(450) 491-2100   *SIC* 3844
EMEC MACHINE TOOLS INC   *p* 739
205 ADMIRAL BLVD, MISSISSAUGA, ON,
L5T 2T3
(905) 565-3570   *SIC* 5084
EMERA BRUNSWICK PIPELINE COMPANY
LTD   *p* 415
1 GERMAIN ST SUITE 1102, SAINT JOHN,
NB, E2L 4V1
(506) 693-4214   *SIC* 4922
EMERA ENERGY INCORPORATED   *p* 452
1223 LOWER WATER ST, HALIFAX, NS,
B3J 3S8
(902) 474-7800   *SIC* 4911
EMERA INCORPORATED   *p* 453
1223 LOWER WATER ST, HALIFAX, NS,
B3J 3S8
(902) 450-0507   *SIC* 4911
EMERA UTILITY SERVICES INCORPO-
RATED   *p*
460
31 DOMINION CRES, LAKESIDE, NS, B3T
1M3
(902) 832-7999   *SIC* 1731
EMERALD HILLS GOLF & COUNTRY CLUB
p 894
See CLUBLINK CORPORATION ULC
EMERALD HILLS GOLF AND COUNTRY
CLUB   *p* 629
See CLUBLINK CORPORATION ULC
EMERALD MANAGEMENT & REALTY LTD
p 64
1036 10 AVE SW, CALGARY, AB, T2R 1M4
(403) 237-8600   *SIC* 6514
EMERAUD CANADA LIMITED   *p* 578
145 THE WEST MALL, ETOBICOKE, ON,
M9C 5P5
(416) 767-4200   *SIC* 5122
EMERGENCY AND HEALTH SERVICES
COMMISSION   *p* 224
9440 202 ST, LANGLEY, BC, V1M 4A6
(604) 215-8103   *SIC* 8099
EMERGENCY AND HEALTH SERVICES
COMMISSION   *p* 267
2261 KEATING CROSS RD, SAANICHTON,
BC, V8M 2A5
(250) 953-3298   *SIC* 4119
EMERGENCY MEDICAL SERVICES   *p* 8
3705 35 ST NE SUITE 100, CALGARY, AB,
T1Y 6C2
(403) 955-9550   *SIC* 4119
EMERGENCY MEDICAL SERVICES   *p* 842
See CORPORATION OF THE COUNTY OF
LAMBTON
EMERGENT BIOSOLUTIONS CANADA INC
p 390
155 INNOVATION DR, WINNIPEG, MB, R3T
5Y3
(204) 275-4200   *SIC* 5122
EMERGENT BIOSOLUTIONS CANADA INC
p 393
26 HENLOW BAY, WINNIPEG, MB, R3Y
1G4
(204) 275-4200   *SIC* 8731
EMERGIS INC   *p* 1158
505 BOUL SIR-WILFRID-LAURIER, MONT-
SAINT-HILAIRE, QC, J3H 4X7
(800) 363-9398   *SIC* 7371

EMERGY ENERGY SERVICES   *p* 452
See EMERA ENERGY INCORPORATED
EMERSON ELECTRIC CANADA LIMITED *p*
15
110 QUARRY PARK BLVD SE SUITE 200,
CALGARY, AB, T2C 3G3
(403) 258-6200   *SIC* 5063
EMERSON ELECTRIC CANADA LIMITED *p*
15
110 QUARRY PARK BLVD SE SUITE 200,
CALGARY, AB, T2C 3G3
(403) 258-6200   *SIC* 8711
EMERSON ELECTRIC CANADA LIMITED *p*
114
4112 91A ST NW, EDMONTON, AB, T6E
5V2
(780) 450-3600   *SIC* 3533
EMERSON ELECTRIC CANADA LIMITED *p*
517
17 AIRPORT RD, BRANTFORD, ON, N3T
5M8
(519) 758-2700   *SIC* 3492
EMERSON ELECTRIC CANADA LIMITED *p*
852
66 LEEK CRES 2ND FL, RICHMOND HILL,
ON, L4B 1H1
(905) 762-1010   *SIC* 5063
EMERSON POWER TRANSMISSION, DIV
OF   *p* 852
See EMERSON ELECTRIC CANADA LIM-
ITED
EMERSON PROCESS MANAGEMENT *p* 15
See EMERSON ELECTRIC CANADA LIM-
ITED
EMERSON PROCESS MANAGEMENT   *p*
114
See EMERSON ELECTRIC CANADA LIM-
ITED
EMERSON PROCESS MANAGEMENT, DIV
OF   *p* 15
See EMERSON ELECTRIC CANADA LIM-
ITED
EMF NUTRITION   *p* 366
See RIDLEY MF INC
EMIL ANDERSON CONSTRUCTION (EAC)
INC   *p* 221
907 ETHEL ST, KELOWNA, BC, V1Y 2W1
(250) 762-9999   *SIC* 1611
EMIL ANDERSON MAINTENANCE CO. LTD
p 266
51160 SACHE ST, ROSEDALE, BC, V0X
1X0
(604) 794-7414   *SIC* 1611
EMILY CARR SECONDARY SCHOOL   *p*
1029
See YORK REGION DISTRICT SCHOOL
BOARD
EMILY CARR UNIVERSITY OF ART & DE-
SIGN   *p*
289
520 1ST AVE E, VANCOUVER, BC, V5T
0H2
(604) 844-3800   *SIC* 8299
EMJ DATA SYSTEMS DIV OF   *p* 604
See SYNNEX CANADA LIMITED
EMJ DATA SYSTEMS, DIV OF   *p* 588
See SYNNEX CANADA LIMITED
EMMA'S BACKPORCH   *p* 529
See 975445 ONTARIO INC
EMMERSON LUMBER   *p* 607
See EMMERSON LUMBER LIMITED
EMMERSON LUMBER LIMITED   *p* 607
63 MAPLE AVE, HALIBURTON, ON, K0M
1S0
(705) 457-1550   *SIC* 5211
EMMI CANADA   *p* 1063
See 9314-8591 QUEBEC INC
EMMI'S ESSO   *p* 5
See ESSO SERVICE STATION
EMMONS GREENHOUSES INC   *p* 1000
1453 DEEBANK RD, UTTERSON, ON, P0B
1M0
(705) 769-3238   *SIC* 0181
EMONDAGE ST-GERMAIN ET FRERES

LTEE   *p* 1174
4032 AV DE LORIMIER, MONTREAL, QC,
H2K 3X7
(514) 525-7485   *SIC* 0721
EMPAQUETAGES MESSIER INC   *p* 1245
1050 RTE 133, PHILIPSBURG, QC, J0J
1N0
(450) 248-3921   *SIC* 5113
EMPAQUETEURS UNIS DE FRUITS DE
MER LTEE, LES   *p* 1344
6575 BOUL DES GRANDES-PRAIRIES,
SAINT-LEONARD, QC, H1P 3G8
(514) 322-5888   *SIC* 5146
EMPERIAL MOTEL   *p* 903
See TERRACE BAY ENTERPRISES LIM-
ITED
EMPIRE (THE CONTINENTAL) LIMITED
PARTNERSHIP   *p* 552
125 VILLARBOIT CRES, CONCORD, ON,
L4K 4K2
(905) 307-8102   *SIC* 1521
EMPIRE AUCTIONS INC   *p* 790
165 TYCOS DR, NORTH YORK, ON, M6B
1W6
(416) 784-4261   *SIC* 7389
EMPIRE CANADA   *p* 1327
See 150157 CANADA INC
EMPIRE CHEESE & BUTTER CO-
OPERATIVE   *p*
539
1120 COUNTY RD 8, CAMPBELLFORD,
ON, K0L 1L0
(705) 653-3187   *SIC* 5143
EMPIRE COMMUNITIES   *p* 552
See ECMI LP
EMPIRE COMPANY LIMITED   *p* 466
115 KING ST, STELLARTON, NS, B0K 1S0
(902) 752-8371   *SIC* 5149
EMPIRE CONTINENTAL MANAGEMENT
INC   *p* 552
125 VILLARBOIT CRES, CONCORD, ON,
L4K 4K2
(905) 307-8102   *SIC* 1521
EMPIRE FOODS LIMITED   *p* 669
205 TORBAY RD UNIT 7, MARKHAM, ON,
L3R 3W4
(905) 475-9988   *SIC* 5141
EMPIRE INDUSTRIES LTD   *p* 371
717 JARVIS AVE, WINNIPEG, MB, R2W
3B4
(204) 589-9300   *SIC* 3441
EMPIRE INVESTIGATIONS AND PROTEC-
TION SERVICES INC   *p*
844
940 BROCK RD UNIT 4, PICKERING, ON,
L1W 2A1
(905) 426-3909   *SIC* 7381
EMPIRE IPS   *p* 844
See EMPIRE INVESTIGATIONS AND PRO-
TECTION SERVICES INC
EMPIRE IRON WORKS   *p* 246
See DYNAMIC ATTRACTIONS LTD
EMPIRE KITCHEN & BATH LTD   *p* 35
5539 1 ST SE, CALGARY, AB, T2H 1H9
(403) 252-2458   *SIC* 5211
EMPIRE LANDMARK HOTEL   *p* 318
See GLOBAL GATEWAY CORP
EMPIRE LIFE   *p* 630
See EMPIRE LIFE INSURANCE COM-
PANY, THE
EMPIRE LIFE INSURANCE COMPANY, THE
p 630
259 KING ST E, KINGSTON, ON, K7L 3A8
(613) 548-1881   *SIC* 6311
EMPIRE LIFE INVESTMENTS INC   *p* 630
259 KING ST E, KINGSTON, ON, K7L 3A8
(613) 548-1881   *SIC* 6722
EMPIRE LIVING CENTRE   *p* 658
See RETIREMENT LIVING CENTRES INC
EMPIRE LIVING CENTRE INC   *p* 763
425 FRASER ST SUITE 505, NORTH BAY,
ON, P1B 3X1
(705) 474-9555   *SIC* 6513
EMPIRE ROOFING CORPORATION *p* 1023

4810 WALKER RD, WINDSOR, ON, N9A 6J3
(519) 969-7101   *SIC* 1761

EMPIRE SANDY INC   *p* 933
151 QUEENS QUAY E, TORONTO, ON, M5A 1B6
(416) 364-3244   *SIC* 4725

EMPIRE SPORT   *p* 1145
See *9119-6188 QUEBEC INC*

EMPIRE SPORTS INC   *p* 1064
1155C PLACE NOBEL, BOUCHERVILLE, QC, J4B 7L3
(450) 645-9998   *SIC* 5941

EMPIRE SPORTS INC   *p* 1146
2786 CH DU LAC BUREAU 1, LONGUEUIL, QC, J4N 1B8
(450) 646-2888   *SIC* 5941

EMPIRE SUPERMARKET (2010) LTD *p* 260
4600 NO. 3 RD UNIT 111, RICHMOND, BC, V6X 2C2
SIC 5411

EMPIRE TERRACE SUITES   *p* 763
See *EMPIRE LIVING CENTRE INC*

EMPIRE TRANSPORTATION LTD   *p* 599
263 SOUTH SERVICE RD, GRIMSBY, ON, L3M 1Y6
(905) 945-9654   *SIC* 1799

EMPLOYEE BENEFIT FUNDS ADMINISTRATION LTD   *p* 114
4224 93 ST NW SUITE 200, EDMONTON, AB, T6E 5P5
(780) 465-2882   *SIC* 6371

EMPRESS TOWERS LTD   *p* 326
1015 BURRARD ST SUITE 403, VANCOUVER, BC, V6Z 1Y5
(604) 682-4246   *SIC* 6712

EMRICK PLASTICS, DIV OF   *p* 1022
See *WINDSOR MOLD INC*

EMS AVIATION   *p* 626
See *EMS TECHNOLOGIES CANADA, LTD*

EMS CANADA, INC   *p* 40
5010 4 ST NE SUITE 207, CALGARY, AB, T2K 5X8
(403) 508-2111   *SIC* 1389

EMS TECHNOLOGIES CANADA, LTD *p* 626
400 MAPLE GROVE RD, KANATA, ON, K2V 1B8
(613) 591-6040   *SIC* 3812

EMS-TECH INC   *p* 491
699 DUNDAS ST W, BELLEVILLE, ON, K8N 4Z2
(613) 966-6611   *SIC* 8711

EMSPEC INC   *p* 1060
904 RUE JACQUES PASCHINI, BOIS-DES-FILION, QC, J6Z 4W4
(450) 430-5522   *SIC* 5063

EMTERRA ENVIRONMENTAL   *p* 526
See *HALTON RECYCLING LTD*

EMTERRA ENVIRONMENTAL   *p* 694
1611 BRITANNIA ROAD E, MISSISSAUGA, ON, L4W 1S5
(289) 562-0091   *SIC* 4953

EMULSIONS & BITUMES S.T.E.B.   *p* 1228
See *SINTRA INC*

EMW   *p* 1423
See *EMW INDUSTRIAL LTD*

EMW INDUSTRIAL LTD   *p* 1423
206 COMMERCIAL ST, SALTCOATS, SK, S0A 3R0
(306) 744-1523   *SIC* 1541

EMX ENTERPRISES LIMITED   *p* 852
250 GRANTON DR, RICHMOND HILL, ON, L4B 1H7
(905) 764-0040   *SIC* 5065

EMX ROYALTY CORPORATION   *p* 304
543 GRANVILLE ST SUITE 501, VANCOUVER, BC, V6C 1X8
(604) 688-6390   *SIC* 1481

EN-PLAS INC   *p* 864
1395 MORNINGSIDE AVE, SCARBOROUGH, ON, M1B 3J1
(416) 286-3030   *SIC* 5084

ENABIL SOLUTIONS LTD   *p* 29

---

438 11 AVE SE SUITE 500, CALGARY, AB, T2G 0Y4
(403) 398-1600   *SIC* 8721

ENBRIDGE   *p* 62
See *WESTCOAST ENERGY INC*

ENBRIDGE   *p* 1105
See *GAZIFERE INC*

ENBRIDGE COMMERCIAL SERVICES INC *p* 767
500 CONSUMERS RD, NORTH YORK, ON, M2J 1P8
(416) 492-5000   *SIC* 8741

ENBRIDGE ENERGY DISTRIBUTION INC *p* 767
500 CONSUMERS RD, NORTH YORK, ON, M2J 1P8
(416) 492-5000   *SIC* 4924

ENBRIDGE GAS NEW BRUNSWICK INC *p* 400
440 WILSEY RD SUITE 101, FREDERICTON, NB, E3B 7G5
(506) 444-7773   *SIC* 4924

ENBRIDGE GAS NEW BRUNSWICK LIMITED PARTNERSHIP   *p* 400
440 WILSEY RD SUITE 101, FREDERICTON, NB, E3B 7G5
(506) 444-7773   *SIC* 4922

ENBRIDGE INC   *p* 48
425 1 ST SW SUITE 200, CALGARY, AB, T2P 3L8
(403) 231-3900   *SIC* 4612

ENBRIDGE INCOME FUND   *p* 48
425 1 ST SW SUITE 3000, CALGARY, AB, T2P 3L8
(403) 767-3642   *SIC* 4922

ENBRIDGE OPERATIONAL SERVICES INC *p* 88
10201 JASPER AVE NW, EDMONTON, AB, T5J 3N7
(780) 420-8850   *SIC* 4923

ENBRIDGE PIPELINES (ATHABASCA) INC *p* 48
425 1 ST SW SUITE 3000, CALGARY, AB, T2P 3L8
(780) 392-4179   *SIC* 4922

ENBRIDGE PIPELINES (NW) INC   *p* 48
425 1 ST SW SUITE 3000, CALGARY, AB, T2P 3L8
SIC 4612

ENBRIDGE PIPELINES (WOODLAND) INC *p* 48
425 1 ST SW SUITE 3000, CALGARY, AB, T2P 3L8
(780) 392-4179   *SIC* 4922

ENBRIDGE PIPELINES INC   *p* 48
425 1 ST SW SUITE 200, CALGARY, AB, T2P 3L8
(403) 231-3900   *SIC* 4612

ENCAN ESP   *p* 1126
See *ENCHERES D'AUTOMOBILES ST-PIERRE (ESP) LTEE, LES*

ENCAN OUTAOUAIS LAURENTIDES *p* 1103
655 CH INDUSTRIEL, GATINEAU, QC, J8R 3M1
(819) 669-5775   *SIC* 5154

ENCAN SAWYERVILLE AUCTION   *p* 1082
See *ENCAN SAWYERVILLE INC*

ENCAN SAWYERVILLE INC   *p* 1082
512 RUE MAIN O, COATICOOK, QC, J1A 1P9
(819) 875-3577   *SIC* 5154

ENCANA CORPORATION   *p* 6
GD STN MAIN, BONNYVILLE, AB, T9N 2J6
SIC 1381

ENCANA CORPORATION   *p* 7
2249 COLLEGE DR E, BROOKS, AB, T1R 1G5
(403) 793-4400   *SIC* 1311

ENCANA CORPORATION   *p* 29
500 CENTRE ST SE, CALGARY, AB, T2G 1A6
(403) 645-2000   *SIC* 1382

ENCANA CORPORATION   *p* 134

11040 78 AVE, GRANDE PRAIRIE, AB, T8W 2M2
(780) 539-4422   *SIC* 5541

ENCANS D'ANIMAUX DU LAC ST-JEAN INC, LES   *p* 1243
1360 RANG NORD, NORMANDIN, QC, G8M 4P5
(418) 274-2233   *SIC* 5154

ENCHANTED MEADOW ESSENTIALS INC *p* 205
1480 CLIVEDEN AVE, DELTA, BC, V3M 6L9
(604) 540-2999   *SIC* 5199

ENCHERES D'AUTOMOBILES ST-PIERRE (ESP) LTEE, LES   *p* 1126
1600 RUE NORMAN, LACHINE, QC, H8S 1A9
(514) 489-3131   *SIC* 5012

ENCLOSURES DIRECT INC   *p* 817
2120 THURSTON DR, OTTAWA, ON, K1G 6E1
(613) 723-4477   *SIC* 3469

ENCON GROUP INC   *p* 596
1400 BLAIR PL SUITE 50, GLOUCESTER, ON, K1J 9B8
(613) 786-2000   *SIC* 6411

ENCORE AUTOMOBILE LTEE   *p* 1076
266 BOUL SAINT-JEAN-BAPTISTE, CHATEAUGUAY, QC, J6K 3C2
(450) 698-1060   *SIC* 5511

ENCORE CORING & DRILLING INC   *p* 29
1345 HIGHFIELD CRES SE, CALGARY, AB, T2G 5N2
(403) 287-0123   *SIC* 1381

ENCORE HONDA   *p* 1076
See *ENCORE AUTOMOBILE LTEE*

ENCORE INDUSTRIES   *p* 1240
See *2900319 CANADA INC*

ENCORE REPAIR SERVICES CANADA, ULC   *p* 552
40 NORTH RIVERMEDE RD UNIT 10, CONCORD, ON, L4K 2H3
(905) 597-5972   *SIC* 7629

ENCOREFX INC   *p* 336
517 FORT ST FL 2, VICTORIA, BC, V8W 1E7
(250) 412-5253   *SIC* 6099

ENCORP PACIFIC (CANADA)   *p* 188
4259 CANADA WAY SUITE 100, BURNABY, BC, V5G 4Y2
(604) 473-2400   *SIC* 4953

ENCRES INTERNATIONALE INX CORP *p* 1379
1247 RUE NATIONALE, TERREBONNE, QC, J6W 6H8
(450) 477-8606   *SIC* 2899

ENDEAVOUR FINANCIAL LTD   *p* 328
595 BURRARD ST SUITE 3123, VANCOUVER, BC, V7X 1J1
(604) 685-4554   *SIC* 6211

ENDEAVOUR SILVER CORP   *p* 330
609 GRANVILLE ST SUITE 1130, VANCOUVER, BC, V7Y 1G5
(604) 685-9775   *SIC* 1041

ENDEVOR CORPORATION   *p* 776
48 LESMILL RD, NORTH YORK, ON, M3B 2T5
(416) 445-5850   *SIC* 6712

ENDOCEUTICS INC   *p* 1272
2795 BOUL LAURIER BUREAU 500, QUEBEC, QC, G1V 4M7
(418) 653-0033   *SIC* 8731

ENDRAS BMW DURHAM   *p* 475
See *2176069 ONTARIO LIMITED*

ENDRESS + HAUSER CANADA LTD *p* 522
1075 SUTTON DR, BURLINGTON, ON, L7L 5Z8
(905) 681-9292   *SIC* 5084

ENDRESS SALES AND DISTRIBUTION LTD   *p* 268
4380 SUNSHINE COAST HWY RR 1, SECHELT, BC, V0N 3A1
(604) 885-6611   *SIC* 5531

ENDRIES INTERNATIONAL CANADA INC *p* 536

---

255 PINEBUSH RD UNIT A, CAMBRIDGE, ON, N1T 1B9
(519) 740-3523   *SIC* 5085

ENDUITS STEF INC   *p* 1373
4365 RUE ROBITAILLE, SHERBROOKE, QC, J1L 2K2
(819) 820-1188   *SIC* 5198

ENDURA MANUFACTURING COMPANY LIMITED   *p* 93
12425 149 ST NW, EDMONTON, AB, T5L 2J6
(780) 451-4242   *SIC* 2851

ENDURAPAK INC   *p* 372
55 PLYMOUTH ST, WINNIPEG, MB, R2X 2V5
(204) 947-1383   *SIC* 2673

ENDURON INC   *p* 385
150 CREE CRES, WINNIPEG, MB, R3J 3W1
(204) 885-2580   *SIC* 3499

ENEL GREEN POWER CANADA INC   *p* 1302
1250 RUE DE L'ENERGIE, SAINT-FELICIEN, QC, G8K 3J2
(418) 630-3800   *SIC* 4911

ENER-RIG SUPPLY INC   *p* 148
2104 7 ST SUITE 2, NISKU, AB, T9E 7Y2
(780) 955-2067   *SIC* 5063

ENERCARE CONNECTIONS INC   *p* 765
4000 VICTORIA PARK AVE, NORTH YORK, ON, M2H 3P4
(416) 649-1900   *SIC* 8611

ENERCARE INC   *p* 669
7400 BIRCHMOUNT RD, MARKHAM, ON, L3R 5V4
(416) 649-1900   *SIC* 6712

ENERCON CANADA INC   *p* 1204
700 RUE DE LA GAUCHETIERE O BUREAU 1200, MONTREAL, QC, H3B 5M2
(514) 363-7266   *SIC* 8748

ENERCON PRODUCTS LTD   *p* 114
9610 54 AVE NW, EDMONTON, AB, T6E 5V1
(780) 437-7003   *SIC* 5033

ENERCON WATER TREATMENT LTD *p* 140
3606 6 AVE N, LETHBRIDGE, AB, T1H 5C4
(403) 328-9730   *SIC* 5169

ENERCORP SAND SOLUTIONS INC   *p* 48
815 8 AVE SW SUITE 510, CALGARY, AB, T2P 3P2
(403) 217-1332   *SIC* 1389

ENERCORP SAND SOLUTIONS PARTNERSHIP   *p* 48
520 3 AVE SW UNIT 530, CALGARY, AB, T2P 0R3
(403) 217-1332   *SIC* 1382

ENERFLEX   *p* 1358
See *GAS DRIVE GLOBAL LP*

ENERFLEX INC   *p* 29
1331 MACLEOD TRL SE SUITE 904, CALGARY, AB, T2G 0K3
(403) 387-6377   *SIC* 3563

ENERFLEX SERVICE   *p* 29
See *ENERFLEX LTD*

ENERGERE INC   *p* 1204
1200 AV MCGILL COLLEGE BUREAU 700, MONTREAL, QC, H3B 4G7
(514) 848-9199   *SIC* 6712

ENERGETIC SERVICES INC   *p* 195
13366 TOMPKINS FRONTAGE RD, CHARLIE LAKE, BC, V0C 1H0
(250) 785-4761   *SIC* 1389

ENERGEX TUBE   *p* 1011
See *ATLAS TUBE CANADA ULC*

ENERGI FENESTRATION SOLUTIONS, LTD   *p* 1027
30 ROYAL GROUP CRES, WOODBRIDGE, ON, L4H 1X9
(905) 851-6637   *SIC* 3442

ENERGIE   *p* 1214
See *ASTRAL MEDIA RADIO INC*

ENERGIE 94.3 FM   *p* 1175
See *BELL MEDIA INC*

▲ Public Company   ■ Public Company Family Member   **HQ** Headquarters   **BR** Branch   **SL** Single Location

ENERGIE CONVEX ENERGY INC p 831
1771 WOODWARD DR, OTTAWA, ON, K2C
0P9
(613) 723-3141 *SIC* 5075

ENERGIE ELECTRIQUE, DIV OF p 1115
See *RIO TINTO ALCAN INC*

**ENERGIE EOLIENNE DU MONT COPPER
INC** p 1242
1500 198 RTE, MURDOCHVILLE, QC, G0E
1W0
(418) 784-2800 *SIC* 4911

ENERGIE P38 INC p 1366
683 CH LAROCQUE, SALABERRY-DE-
VALLEYFIELD, QC, J6T 4E1
(450) 373-4333 *SIC* 5984

ENERGIE VALERO INC p 1136
165 CH DES ILES, LEVIS, QC, G6V 7M5
(418) 837-3641 *SIC* 2911

ENERGIE VALERO INC p 1195
1801 AV MCGILL COLLEGE BUREAU
1300, MONTREAL, QC, H3A 2N4
(514) 982-8200 *SIC* 5172

ENERGIE VALERO INC p 1195
2200 AV MCGILL COLLEGE UNITE 400,
MONTREAL, QC, H3A 3P8
(514) 493-5201 *SIC* 5983

ENERGIE/POWER, DIV OF p 1192
See *SNC-LAVALIN INC*

ENERGIR INC p 1048
11401 AV L.-J.-FORGET, ANJOU, QC, H1J
2Z8
(514) 356-8777 *SIC* 4924

ENERGIR INC p 1130
2200 RUE DE CANNES-BRULEES,
LASALLE, QC, H8N 2Z2
(514) 367-2525 *SIC* 4924

ENERGIR INC p 1174
1717 RUE DU HAVRE, MONTREAL, QC,
H2K 2X3
(514) 598-3444 *SIC* 4924

ENERGIR, S.E.C. p 1174
1717 RUE DU HAVRE, MONTREAL, QC,
H2K 2X3
(514) 598-3444 *SIC* 4924

ENERGIZER CANADA INC p 722
6733 MISSISSAUGA RD SUITE 800, MIS-
SISSAUGA, ON, L5N 6J5
(800) 383-7323 *SIC* 3691

ENERGIZING CHEMISTRY p 859
See *ARLANXEO CANADA INC*

ENERGOLD DRILLING CORP p 304
543 GRANVILLE ST SUITE 1100, VAN-
COUVER, BC, V6C 1X8
(604) 681-9501 *SIC* 1081

ENERGY ADVANTAGE INC p 522
5515 NORTH SERVICE RD UNIT 303,
BURLINGTON, ON, L7L 6G4
(905) 319-1717 *SIC* 8748

ENERGY DODGE LTD p 1408
801 11TH AVE E, KINDERSLEY, SK, S0L
1S0
(306) 463-4131 *SIC* 5511

ENERGY FUELS INC p 938
82 RICHMOND ST E SUITE 308,
TORONTO, ON, M5C 1P1
(416) 214-2810 *SIC* 1031

**ENERGY FUNDAMENTALS GROUP LIM-
ITED PARTNERSHIP** p
662
2324 MAIN ST, LONDON, ON, N6P 1A9
(519) 652-3196 *SIC* 4922

**ENERGY HEALING VANCOUVER - KIM U-
MING** p
293
900 8TH AVE W, VANCOUVER, BC, V5Z
1E5
(604) 790-6400 *SIC* 4924

ENERGY LOGISTICS INC p 1130
2555 AV DOLLARD EDIFICE 8, LASALLE,
QC, H8N 3A9
(514) 363-9555 *SIC* 4731

ENERGY MASTER p 1178
9150 RUE MEILLEUR, MONTREAL, QC,
H2N 2A5

(514) 433-6487 *SIC* 4924

ENERGY NETWORK SERVICES INC p 852
125 WEST BEAVER CREEK RD, RICH-
MOND HILL, ON, L4B 1C6
(905) 763-2946 *SIC* 1731

ENERGY POULTRY p 1363
See *VOLAILLES REGAL INC*

ENERGY SAFETY CANADA p 22
5055 11 ST NE, CALGARY, AB, T2E 8N4
(403) 516-8000 *SIC* 8748

ENERGY SOURCE CANADA INC p 605
415 MICHENER RD, GUELPH, ON, N1K
1E8
(519) 826-0777 *SIC* 4924

ENERGY SOURCE NATURAL GAS p 605
See *ENERGY SOURCE CANADA INC*

ENERGY SOURCE NATURAL GAS INC p
605
415 MICHENER RD UNIT 1, GUELPH, ON,
N1K 1E8
(519) 826-0777 *SIC* 4924

ENERGY TRANSPORTATION GROUP p
1130
See *ENERGY LOGISTICS INC*

**ENERGY WORKS CREATIVE HEALING
ARTS** p 231
23085 118 AVENUE, MAPLE RIDGE, BC,
V2X 3J7
(604) 817-9956 *SIC* 4924

ENERKEM ALBERTA BIOFUELS LP p 124
250 AURUM RD NE SUITE 460, EDMON-
TON, AB, T6S 1G9
(780) 473-2896 *SIC* 2869

ENERKEM INC p 1195
1130 RUE SHERBROOKE O BUREAU
1500, MONTREAL, QC, H3A 2M8
(514) 875-0284 *SIC* 2869

ENERPLUS CORPORATION p 48
333 7 AVE SW SUITE 3000, CALGARY, AB,
T2P 2Z1
(403) 298-2200 *SIC* 1311

**ENERPLUS GLOBAL ENERGY MANAGE-
MENT CO** p
48
333 7 AVE SW SUITE 3000, CALGARY, AB,
T2P 2Z1
(403) 298-2200 *SIC* 8741

ENERPOWER UTILITIES INC p 552
585 APPLEWOOD CRES, CONCORD, ON,
L4K 5V7
SIC 1623

ENERSHARE TECHNOLOGY CORP p 783
87 BAKERSFIELD ST, NORTH YORK, ON,
M3J 1Z4
SIC 4923

ENERSOURCE CORPORATION p 722
2185 DERRY RD W, MISSISSAUGA, ON,
L5N 7A6
(905) 273-9050 *SIC* 4911

ENERSUL p 35
See *ENERSUL LIMITED PARTNERSHIP*

ENERSUL INC p 35
7210 BLACKFOOT TRAIL SE, CALGARY,
AB, T2H 1M5
(403) 253-5969 *SIC* 2819

ENERSUL LIMITED PARTNERSHIP p 35
7210 BLACKFOOT TRAIL SE, CALGARY,
AB, T2H 1M5
(403) 253-5969 *SIC* 1389

ENERSYS CANADA INC p 494
61 PARR BLVD UNIT 3, BOLTON, ON, L7E
4E3
(905) 951-2228 *SIC* 5063

ENERTEC RAIL EQUIPEMENT p 1058
See *9088-3570 QUEBEC INC*

ENERTRAK INC p 1363
2875 RUE JULES-BRILLANT, SAINTE-
ROSE, QC, H7P 6B2
(450) 973-2000 *SIC* 5075

**ENERVEST DIVERSIFIED MANAGEMENT
INC** p 48
700 9 AVE SW SUITE 2800, CALGARY, AB,
T2P 3V4
(403) 571-5550 *SIC* 6719

ENERVEST MANAGEMENT LTD p 49
350 7 AVE SW SUITE 3900, CALGARY, AB,
T2P 3N9
(403) 571-5550 *SIC* 6722

ENESCO CANADA CORPORATION p 739
989 DERRY RD E SUITE 303, MISSIS-
SAUGA, ON, L5T 2J8
(905) 673-9200 *SIC* 5023

ENGAGE PEOPLE INC p 669
1380 RODICK RD SUITE 300, MARKHAM,
ON, L3R 4G5
(416) 775-9180 *SIC* 7379

ENGEL'S BAKERIES LTD p 22
4709 14 ST NE UNIT 6, CALGARY, AB, T2E
6S4
(403) 250-9560 *SIC* 2051

ENGENIUM CHEMICALS CORP p 12
4333 46 AVE SE, CALGARY, AB, T2B 3N5
(403) 279-8545 *SIC* 2911

ENGHOUSE SYSTEMS LIMITED p 669
80 TIVERTON CRT SUITE 800, MARKHAM,
ON, L3R 0G4
(905) 946-3200 *SIC* 7371

ENGIE MULTITECH LTD p 722
2025 MEADOWVALE BLVD UNIT 2, MIS-
SISSAUGA, ON, L5N 5N1
(905) 812-7900 *SIC* 1711

ENGIE SERVICES INC p 1195
1001 BOUL DE MAISONNEUVE O BU-
REAU 1000, MONTREAL, QC, H3A 3C8
(514) 876-8748 *SIC* 8742

ENGINEERED AIR p 754
See *AIRTEX MANUFACTURING PART-
NERSHIP*

ENGINEERED AIR, DIV p 27
See *AIRTEX MANUFACTURING PART-
NERSHIP*

ENGINEERED ASSEMBLIES INC p 722
6535 MILLCREEK DR UNIT 75, MISSIS-
SAUGA, ON, L5N 2M2
(905) 816-2218 *SIC* 5039

**ENGINEERED CASE MANUFACTURERS
INC** p 694
5191 CREEKBANK RD, MISSISSAUGA,
ON, L4W 1R3
(905) 366-2273 *SIC* 3161

ENGINEERED COATED PRODUCTS p 469
See *INTERTAPE POLYMER INC*

ENGINEERED COATED PRODUCTS p 1324
See *GROUPE INTERTAPE POLYMER INC,
LE*

**ENGINEERED ELECTRIC CONTROLS LIM-
ITED** p
536
230 SHELDON DR, CAMBRIDGE, ON, N1T
1A8
(519) 621-5370 *SIC* 3613

**ENGINEERED FOAM PRODUCTS
CANADA, DIV** p 785
See *VPC GROUP INC*

ENGINEERED POWER GP LTD p 11
3103 14 AVE NE SUITE 20, CALGARY, AB,
T2A 7N6
(403) 235-2584 *SIC* 3692

**ENGINEERED POWER LIMITED PARTNER-
SHIP** p
11
3103 14 AVE NE UNIT 20, CALGARY, AB,
T2A 7N6
(403) 235-2584 *SIC* 3692

**ENGINEERING SEISMOLOGY GROUP
CANADA INC** p 630
20 HYPERION CRT, KINGSTON, ON, K7K
7K2
(613) 548-8287 *SIC* 1382

ENGINNERING OPERATIONS p 271
See *CITY OF SURREY, THE*

ENGLAND, PAUL SALES LTD p 382
750 ST JAMES ST, WINNIPEG, MB, R3G
3J7
(204) 943-0311 *SIC* 5399

ENGLEWOOD LOGGING, DIV OF p 344
See *CANADIAN FOREST PRODUCTS LTD*

ENGLISH BAY BATTER (TORONTO) INC p

739
6925 INVADER CRES, MISSISSAUGA, ON,
L5T 2B7
(905) 670-1110 *SIC* 2052

ENGLISH BAY BATTER L.P. p 205
904 CLIVEDEN AVE, DELTA, BC, V3M 5R5
(604) 540-0622 *SIC* 2045

ENGLISH BAY ENTERPRISES INC p 205
904 CLIVEDEN AVE, DELTA, BC, V3M 5R5
(604) 540-0622 *SIC* 6712

ENGLISH LANGUAGE INSTITUTE p 325
See *UNIVERSITY OF BRITISH COLUMBIA,
THE*

ENGLISH RIVER ENTERPRISES INC p
1405
2553 GRASSWOOD RD E, CORMAN
PARK, SK, S7T 1C8
(306) 374-9181 *SIC* 5541

ENGLOBE CORP p 1266
505 BOUL DU PARC-TECHNOLOGIQUE
SUITE 200, QUEBEC, QC, G1P 4S9
(418) 781-0191 *SIC* 0711

ENGRAIS FERTICO, LES p 1310
See *SYNAGRI S.E.C.*

ENGRAIS LAPRAIRIE p 1352
See *HOUDE, WILLIAM LTEE*

ENGRENAGE PROVINCIAL INC p 1080
1001 RUE DE LA RUPERT, CHICOUTIMI,
QC, G7K 0A2
(418) 693-8132 *SIC* 5085

ENGRENAGE PROVINCIAL INC p 1260
165 BOUL DES CEDRES, QUEBEC, QC,
G1L 1M8
(418) 683-2745 *SIC* 5085

ENGRENAGES POWER-LINK2 INC, LES p
1309
5405 RUE J.-A.-BOMBARDIER, SAINT-
HUBERT, QC, J3Z 1K3
(450) 678-0588 *SIC* 5085

ENGRENAGES SPECIALISES INC p 1283
620 RUE DESMARAIS, RICHMOND, QC,
J0B 2H0
(819) 826-3379 *SIC* 5085

ENHANCED DRILL SYSTEMS, DIV OF p 49
See *ENHANCED PETROLEUM SERVICES
PARTNERSHIP*

**ENHANCED PETROLEUM SERVICES
PARTNERSHIP** p 49
400 5 AVE SW UNIT 900, CALGARY, AB,
T2P 0L6
(403) 262-1361 *SIC* 1381

ENIRGI GROUP p 939
See *LEADFX INC*

ENJOY TREE p 1356
See *ARBRE JOYEUX INC*

ENMAX CORPORATION p 15
8820 52 ST SE SUITE 1940, CALGARY, AB,
T2C 4E7
(403) 514-3700 *SIC* 4911

ENMAX CORPORATION p 29
141 50 AVE SE SUITE 2708, CALGARY, AB,
T2G 4S7
(403) 514-3000 *SIC* 4911

ENMAX ENERGY CORPORATION p 29
141 50 AVE SE SUITE 2708, CALGARY, AB,
T2G 4S7
(403) 514-3000 *SIC* 4911

ENMAX ENERGY MARKETING INC p 29
141 50 AVE SE, CALGARY, AB, T2G 4S7
(403) 514-3000 *SIC* 4911

ENMAX POWER SERVICES CORP p 23
239 MAYLAND PL NE, CALGARY, AB, T2E
7Z8
(403) 514-3000 *SIC* 4911

ENNIS PAINT CANADA ULC p 844
850 MCKAY RD, PICKERING, ON, L1W 2Y4
(905) 686-2770 *SIC* 2851

ENNIS, J. FABRICS LTD p 114
6111 91 ST NW, EDMONTON, AB, T6E 6V6
(780) 474-5414 *SIC* 5131

ENNISKILLEN PEPPER CO. LTD p 842
4376 LASALLE LINE RR 3, PETROLIA, ON,
N0N 1R0
(519) 882-3423 *SIC* 0182

ENNISMORE FOODLAND   p 569
See SESHA ONTARIO INC
ENNOVA FACADES INC   p 1025
620 SPRUCEWOOD AVE, WINDSOR, ON, N9C 0B2
(519) 969-1740   SIC 3449
ENNS BROTHERS LTD   p 353
400 FORT WHYTE WAY UNIT 310, OAK BLUFF, MB, R4G 0B1
(204) 895-0212   SIC 5083
ENNS BROTHERS LTD   p 388
55 ROTHWELL RD, WINNIPEG, MB, R3P 2M5
(204) 475-3667   SIC 5083
ENNS PLANT FARM   p 643
See 1266093 ONTARIO LIMITED
ENRACK-SYSTEMS DIV OF   p 515
See ECONO-RACK GROUP (2015) INC, THE
ENS   p 852
See ENERGY NETWORK SERVICES INC
ENS COLLISION CENTRE   p 1427
See ENS MOTORS LTD
ENS MOTORS LTD   p 1427
285 VENTURE CRES, SASKATOON, SK, S7K 6N8
(306) 653-5611   SIC 5511
ENS, PHILIPP R LTD   p 361
301 ROBLIN BLVD, WINKLER, MB, R6W 4C4
(204) 325-4361   SIC 6712
ENSEICOM INC   p 1125
225 RUE NORMAN, LACHINE, QC, H8R 1A3
(514) 486-2626   SIC 3448
ENSEICOM SIGNS   p 1125
See ENSEICOM INC
ENSEIGNES BELANGER   p 1285
See GAGNON IMAGE INC
ENSEIGNES CMD INC   p 1070
3615B RUE ISABELLE, BROSSARD, QC, J4Y 2R2
(450) 465-1100   SIC 5099
ENSEIGNES INNOVA INC, LES   p 1048
9900 BOUL DU GOLF, ANJOU, QC, H1J 2Y7
(514) 323-6767   SIC 7389
ENSEIGNES MONTREAL NEON INCp 1086
4130 SUD LAVAL (A-440) O, COTE SAINT-LUC, QC, H7T 0H3
(450) 668-4888   SIC 3993
ENSEIGNES TRANS-CANADA   p 1048
See ENSEIGNES TRANSWORLD CIE
ENSEIGNES TRANSWORLD CIE   p 1048
9310 BOUL PARKWAY, ANJOU, QC, H1J 1N7
(514) 352-8030   SIC 3993
ENSEIGNES VISION DEK-OR INC   p 1048
9225 RUE DU PARCOURS, ANJOU, QC, H1J 3A8
(514) 354-8383   SIC 3993
ENSIGN CHRYSLER DODGE JEEP LTD   p 335
1061 YATES ST, VICTORIA, BC, V8V 3M5
(250) 386-2981   SIC 5511
ENSIGN DRILLING INC   p 49
400 5 AVE SW SUITE 1000, CALGARY, AB, T2P 0L6
(403) 262-1361   SIC 1381
ENSIGN ENERGY SERVICES INC   p 49
400 5 AVE SW SUITE 1000, CALGARY, AB, T2P 0L6
(403) 262-1361   SIC 1381
ENSIGN ROCKWELL SERVICING   p 4
See ROCKWELL SERVICING INC
ENSIGN ROCKWELL SERVICING   p 149
See ROCKWELL SERVICING INC
ENSIGN SERVICING PARTNERSHIP   p 49
400 5 AVE SW SUITE 900, CALGARY, AB, T2P 0L6
(403) 262-1361   SIC 1381
ENTABLATURE FRIEZE & PILLARS INC   p 552
50 VICEROY RD UNIT 23, CONCORD, ON,

L4K 3A7
(905) 669-0368   SIC 5211
ENTEGRA CONTROLS & ENERGY SERVICES   p 146
See 988690 ALBERTA INC
ENTEGRUS INC   p 542
320 QUEEN ST, CHATHAM, ON, N7M 2H6
(519) 352-6300   SIC 8711
ENTERA UTILITY CONTACTORS CO., LIMITED   p 785
1011 WILSON AVE, NORTH YORK, ON, M3K 1G1
(416) 746-9914   SIC 1629
ENTERO CORPORATION   p 49
1040 7 AVE SW SUITE 500, CALGARY, AB, T2P 3G9
(403) 261-1820   SIC 7371
ENTERO VISION   p 49
See ENTERO CORPORATION
ENTERPHASE CHILD AND FAMILY SERVICES INC   p 812
250 HARMONY RD S, OSHAWA, ON, L1H 6T9
SIC 8299
ENTERPRISE GROUP, INC   p 165
64 RIEL DR SUITE 2, ST. ALBERT, AB, T8N 4A4
(780) 418-4400   SIC 1629
ENTERPRISE LOCATION D'AUTOS CANADA LIMITEE   p 1092
600 RUE ARTHUR-FECTEAU, DORVAL, QC, H4Y 1K5
SIC 5511
ENTERPRISE PAPER CO. LTD   p 200
95 BRIGANTINE DR, COQUITLAM, BC, V3K 6Y9
(604) 522-6295   SIC 5113
ENTERPRISE PARIS INC   p 857
2875 RUE LAPORTE, ROCKLAND, ON, K4K 1R3
(613) 446-9948   SIC 5812
ENTERPRISE PROPERTY GROUP (MAN) INC   p 377
330 PORTAGE AVE UNIT 1000, WINNIPEG, MB, R3C 0C4
(204) 947-2242   SIC 6531
ENTERPRISE RENT-A-CAR CANADA COMPANY   p 23
2335 78 AVE NE, CALGARY, AB, T2E 7L2
(403) 250-1395   SIC 7514
ENTERPRISE RENT-A-CAR CANADA COMPANY   p 29
114 5 AVE SE, CALGARY, AB, T2G 0E2
(403) 264-0424   SIC 7514
ENTERPRISE RENT-A-CAR CANADA COMPANY   p 669
200-7390 WOODBINE AVE, MARKHAM, ON, L3R 1A5
(905) 477-1688   SIC 7514
ENTERPRISE RENT-A-CAR CANADA COMPANY   p 1092
600 RUE ARTHUR-FECTEAU, DORVAL, QC, H4Y 1K5
(514) 422-1100   SIC 7514
ENTERPRISE SQUARE   p 88
See EDMONTON PUBLIC LIBRARY
ENTERPRISE SUPPLY CHAIN GROUP   p 1221
See TECSYS INC
ENTERPRISE UNIVERSAL INC   p 66
2210 2 ST SW UNIT B250, CALGARY, AB, T2S 3C3
(403) 228-4431   SIC 6519
ENTERPRISE UNIVERSAL INC   p 72
4411 16 AVE NW, CALGARY, AB, T3B 0M3
(403) 209-4780   SIC 6512
ENTERPRISES FAWCETT, DIV OF   p 412
See 3135772 CANADA INC
ENTERPRISES MICHEL MARCHAND INC, LES   p 1379
1400 BOUL MOODY, TERREBONNE, QC,

J6W 3K9
(450) 471-9022   SIC 5812
ENTERRA HOLDINGS LTD   p 722
6925 CENTURY AVE SUITE 100, MISSISSAUGA, ON, L5N 7K2
(905) 567-4444   SIC 7363
ENTERTAINMENT LIQUIDATORS OF CANADA INC   p 702
1550 CATERPILLAR RD, MISSISSAUGA, ON, L4X 1E7
(905) 629-7283   SIC 5045
ENTERTAINMENT ONE GP LIMITED   p 502
70 DRIVER RD UNIT 1, BRAMPTON, ON, L6T 5V2
(905) 624-7337   SIC 5099
ENTERTAINMENT ONE LTD   p 980
134 PETER ST SUITE 700, TORONTO, ON, M5V 2H2
(416) 646-2400   SIC 7812
ENTOUR AUTOMOBILES INC   p 1297
270 RTE 132, SAINT-CONSTANT, QC, J5A 2C9
(450) 632-7155   SIC 5511
ENTRAIDE AGAPE   p 1255
3148 CH ROYAL, QUEBEC, QC, G1E 1V2
(418) 661-7485   SIC 8699
ENTRE-TIENS DE LA HAUTE-GASPESIE CORPORATION D'AIDE A DOMICILEp 1355
378 BOUL SAINTE-ANNE O, SAINTE-ANNE-DES-MONTS, QC, G4V 1S8
(418) 763-7163   SIC 7349
ENTREC CORPORATION   p 1
28712 114 AVE, ACHESON, AB, T7X 6E6
(780) 962-1600   SIC 7389
ENTREC CORPORATION   p 6
4902 66 ST, BONNYVILLE, AB, T9N 2R5
(780) 826-4565   SIC 4213
ENTREC CORPORATION   p 6
6708 50 AVE, BONNYVILLE, AB, T9N 0B7
(780) 826-4565   SIC 4213
ENTREE GOLD INC   p 312
1066 HASTINGS ST W SUITE 1650, VANCOUVER, BC, V6E 3X1
(604) 687-4777   SIC 1081
ENTREPOSAGE MASKA DIVISION DE GROUPE GOYETTE   p 1313
See IMMEUBLES GOYETTE INC, LES
ENTREPOSAGE MASKA LTEE   p 1312
2825 BOUL CASAVANT O, SAINT-HYACINTHE, QC, J2S 7Y4
(450) 773-9615   SIC 4225
ENTREPOSAGE SUPERVISION   p 1288
See SPECIALITES LASSONDE INC
ENTREPOSEURS DE FIBRES R & F LTEEp 1162
7975 AV MARCO-POLO, MONTREAL, QC, H1E 1N8
(514) 648-8171   SIC 3081
ENTREPOT   p 1154
See PERREAULT, YVAN & FILS INC
ENTREPOT CROISIERE   p 1226
See VOYAGES VISION DT QUEBEC-EST INC
ENTREPOT DE MONTREAL 1470 INC   p 1170
3455 RUE JARRY E, MONTREAL, QC, H1Z 2G1
(514) 374-9880   SIC 5013
ENTREPOTS E.F.C. INC, LES   p 1292
50 RUE DES GRANDS-LACS, SAINT-AUGUSTIN-DE-DESMAURES, QC, G3A 2E6
(418) 878-5660   SIC 1541
ENTREPOTS LAFRANCE INC   p 1164
7055 RUE NOTRE-DAME E, MONTREAL, QC, H1N 3R8
(514) 254-6688   SIC 4225
ENTREPOTS P C G INC, LES   p 1089
121 RUE PRINCIPALE N, DELSON, QC, J5B 1Z2
(450) 635-8053   SIC 4225
ENTREPOTS SIMARD INC, LES   p 1127
2737 RUE LOUIS-A.-AMOS, LACHINE, QC, H8T 1C3
(514) 636-9411   SIC 4225

ENTREPRENEURS BLANCHET INC, LES   p 1046
722 AV DE L'INDUSTRIE, AMOS, QC, J9T 4L9
(819) 732-5520   SIC 1611
ENTREPRENEURS ELECTRICIENS SIMPKIN LTEE   p 1221
5800 RUE SAINT-JACQUES, MONTREAL, QC, H4A 2E9
(514) 481-0125   SIC 1799
ENTREPRISE ADAPTEE D'ECONOMIE SOCIALE ET ORGANISME A BUT NON LUCRATIF   p 1103
See INTEGRATION RE SOURCE
ENTREPRISE AGRI-MONDO   p 1163
See IMPORTATIONS KROPS INC
ENTREPRISE ALLSTREAM   p 666
See ALLSTREAM BUSINESS INC
ENTREPRISE BROOKFIELD BRP CANADA   p 1104
See BROOKFIELD BRP CANADA CORP
ENTREPRISE CAMFIL FARR POWER SYSTEMS N A   p 1233
See CAMFIL CANADA INC
ENTREPRISE CLAUDE CHAGNON INC   p 1308
3500 BOUL SIR-WILFRID-LAURIER, SAINT-HUBERT, QC, J3Y 6T1
(450) 321-2446   SIC 1794
ENTREPRISE COMMERCIALE SHAH LIMITEE, L'   p 1333
3401 RUE DOUGLAS-B.-FLOREANI, SAINT-LAURENT, QC, H4S 1Y6
(514) 336-2462   SIC 2068
ENTREPRISE DE COMMUNICATIONS TANK INC   p 1210
55 RUE PRINCE, MONTREAL, QC, H3C 2M7
(514) 373-3333   SIC 7311
ENTREPRISE DE CONSTRUCTION GASTON MORIN LTEE   p 1090
310 RUE DE QUEN, DOLBEAU-MISTASSINI, QC, G8L 5N1
(418) 276-4166   SIC 6512
ENTREPRISE DE CONSTRUCTION T.E.Q. INC   p 1223
780 AV BREWSTER BUREAU 3-300, MONTREAL, QC, H4C 2K1
(514) 933-3838   SIC 1541
ENTREPRISE DE PAVAGE DION   p 1060
See PAVAGE DION INC
ENTREPRISE DE SOUDURE AEROSPATIALE, DIV DE   p 1059
See GROUPE DCM INC
ENTREPRISE FLOWCRETE   p 1310
See ADJUVANTS EUCLID CANADA INC
ENTREPRISE IEC HOLDEN   p 1339
See IEC HOLDEN INC
ENTREPRISE INDORAMA PTA MONTREAL S.E.C   p 1238
10200 RUE SHERBROOKE E, MONTREAL-EST, QC, H1B 1B4
(514) 645-7887   SIC 2821
ENTREPRISE J.M. VIDAL ET ASSOCIES   p 1223
See H.C. VIDAL LTEE
ENTREPRISE JPMA GLOBAL   p 1162
See JPMA GLOBAL INC
ENTREPRISE MINDGEEK CANADA   p 1227
See 9219-1568 QUEBEC INC
ENTREPRISE MONDOFIX   p 1059
See MONDOFIX INC
ENTREPRISE PLUS   p 1329
See DESJARDINS FORD LTEE
ENTREPRISE ROBERT THIBERT INC   p 1151
200 BOUL SAINT-JEAN-BAPTISTE BU-

REAU 212, MERCIER, QC, J6R 2L2
(450) 699-0560   *SIC* 5013
ENTREPRISE SANITAIRE F.A. LTEE *p* 1231
4799 RUE BERNARD-LEFEBVRE, MON-TREAL, QC, H7C 0A5
(450) 661-5080   *SIC* 4212
ENTREPRISE SKIRON   *p* 1260
See SKIRON INC
ENTREPRISE T.R.A. (2011) INC   *p* 1301
145 RUE DAOUST BUREAU 101, SAINT-EUSTACHE, QC, J7R 6P4
(450) 491-2940   *SIC* 5099
ENTREPRISE TELLUS, DE   *p* 1158
See EMERGIS INC
ENTREPRISE UNIGEAR   *p* 1053
See DAVID BROWN SYSTEM (CANADA) INC
ENTREPRISES A & R BROCHU CON-STRUCTION INC , LES   *p*
1295
1505 RUE MARIE-VICTORIN, SAINT-BRUNO, QC, J3V 6B7
(450) 441-7444   *SIC* 7699
ENTREPRISES A & R SAVOIE ET FILS LTEE, LES   *p* 419
2650 RUE PRINCIPALE, TRACADIE-SHEILA, NB, E1X 1A1
(506) 395-6997   *SIC* 5211
ENTREPRISES A & W ROY, LES   *p* 1046
See 2956-2584 QUEBEC INC
ENTREPRISES ACQUISIO WEB.COM *p*
1071
See ACQUISIO WEB.COM, ULC
ENTREPRISES   AGRICOLES   & FORESTIERES DE PERCE INC, LES *p* 1073
884 RUE PRINCIPALE, CAP-D'ESPOIR, QC, G0C 1G0
(418) 782-2621   *SIC* 2411
ENTREPRISES ALFRED BOIVIN INC, LES
p 1079
2205 RUE DE LA FONDERIE, CHICOUTIMI, QC, G7H 8B9
(418) 549-2457   *SIC* 1611
ENTREPRISES AMIRA INC, LES   *p* 1329
5375 BOUL HENRI-BOURASSA O, SAINT-LAURENT, QC, H4R 1C1
(514) 382-9823   *SIC* 5149
ENTREPRISES ANTONIO BARRETTE INC, LES   *p* 1254
437 RUE DES MONTEREGIENNES, QUE-BEC, QC, G1C 7J7
(418) 686-6455   *SIC* 4959
ENTREPRISES ANTONIO LAPORTE & FILS INC, LES   *p* 1243
501 RTE 131, NOTRE-DAME-DES-PRAIRIES, QC, J6E 0M1
(450) 756-1779   *SIC* 5083
ENTREPRISES B J T BOULIANNE INC, LES   *p* 1378
335 CH DU HIBOU, STONEHAM-ET-TEWKESBURY, QC, G3C 1R9
(418) 848-2637   *SIC* 5411
ENTREPRISES B. DURAND INC, LES *p*
1241
48 AV WOLSELEY N, MONTREAL-OUEST, QC, H4X 1V5
(514) 481-0368   *SIC* 6719
ENTREPRISES BARRETTE LTEE, LES *p*
1317
583 CH DU GRAND-BERNIER N, SAINT-JEAN-SUR-RICHELIEU, QC, J3B 8K1
(450) 357-7000   *SIC* 3496
ENTREPRISES BERNARD SORNIN INC, LES   *p* 1288
325 LA GRANDE-CAROLINE, ROUGE-MONT, QC, J0L 1M0
(450) 469-4934   *SIC* 3444
ENTREPRISES BOULOS,PIERRE L INC, LES   *p* 1254
705 RUE CLEMENCEAU, QUEBEC, QC, G1C 7T9
(418) 663-4334   *SIC* 5531
ENTREPRISES C. & R. MENARD INC *p*
1144

2711 RUE PAPINEAU, LONGUEUIL, QC, J4K 3M6
(450) 679-3131   *SIC* 1629
ENTREPRISES CAFECTION INC   *p* 1266
2355 AV DALTON, QUEBEC, QC, G1P 3S3
(418) 650-6162   *SIC* 3589
ENTREPRISES CANBEC CONSTRUCTION INC, LES   *p* 1125
145 RUE RICHER, LACHINE, QC, H8R 1R4
(514) 481-1226   *SIC* 1794
ENTREPRISES CANDEREL INC   *p* 1195
2000 RUE PEEL BUREAU 900, MON-TREAL, QC, H3A 2W5
(514) 842-8636   *SIC* 6712
ENTREPRISES CD VARIN INC, LES *p* 1281
285 RUE VALMONT, REPENTIGNY, QC, J5Y 3H6
(450) 654-9253   *SIC* 5411
ENTREPRISES CHRISTIAN CHADI INC, LES   *p* 1364
95 BOUL DU CURE-LABELLE BUREAU 15, SAINTE-THERESE, QC, J7E 2X6
(450) 437-5555   *SIC* 5912
ENTREPRISES CLAUDE CHAGNON INC, LES   *p* 1308
3500 BOUL SIR-WILFRID-LAURIER, SAINT-HUBERT, QC, J3Y 6T1
(450) 321-2446   *SIC* 1629
ENTREPRISES CLEMENT LAVOIE INC *p*
1082
92 RUE SAINT-JACQUES S, COATICOOK, QC, J1A 2N8
(819) 849-6374   *SIC* 5541
ENTREPRISES CLEMENT RUEL (2000) INC *p* 1096
4565 BOUL SAINT-JOSEPH, DRUM-MONDVILLE, QC, J2A 1B4
(819) 472-1107   *SIC* 5411
ENTREPRISES CLOUTIER, ALBERT LTEE, LES   *p* 1351
149 RUE ALBERT-EDOUARD, SAINT-RAYMOND, QC, G3L 2C5
(418) 337-2766   *SIC* 3842
ENTREPRISES COPAP   *p* 1249
See COPAP INC
ENTREPRISES D'ALIMENTATION POUR ANIMAUX FAMILIER (A.P.A.F) INC, LES *p*
1333
4850 CH DU BOIS-FRANC BUREAU 200, SAINT-LAURENT, QC, H4S 1A7
(514) 745-1262   *SIC* 5191
ENTREPRISES D'ELECTRICITE E.G. LTEE *p* 1323
1753 RUE GRENET, SAINT-LAURENT, QC, H4L 2R6
(514) 748-0505   *SIC* 1731
ENTREPRISES D'ELECTRICITE J.M.N. INC *p* 1150
19 RUE DURETTE, MATANE, QC, G4W 0J5
(418) 562-4009   *SIC* 1731
ENTREPRISES D'EMONDAGE L.D.L. INC, LES   *p* 1386
2300 BOUL DES RECOLLETS, TROIS-RIVIERES, QC, G8Z 3X5
(819) 694-0395   *SIC* 0783
ENTREPRISES D. GAUVREAU ENR *p* 1108
930 CH VANIER, GATINEAU, QC, J9J 3J3
(819) 682-1735   *SIC* 1629
ENTREPRISES DAVID LAUZON, LES *p*
1349
1680 RUE PRINCIPALE RR 5, SAINT-NORBERT, QC, J0K 3C0
(819) 427-5144   *SIC* 2426
ENTREPRISES DBM REFLEX INC, LES *p*
1362
1620 BOUL DAGENAIS O, SAINTE-ROSE, QC, H7L 5C7
(450) 622-3100   *SIC* 3544
ENTREPRISES DE CONSTRUCTION BON-NEAU, GUY LTEE, LES   *p*
1090
100   RUE   BOULIANNE,   DOLBEAU-MISTASSINI, QC, G8L 5L4
(418) 276-2301   *SIC* 1542

ENTREPRISES   DE   CONSTRUCTION DAWCO INC   *p* 1156
8315 CH DEVONSHIRE, MONT-ROYAL, QC, H4P 2L1
(514) 738-3033   *SIC* 1731
ENTREPRISES DE CONSTRUCTION GAS-TON MORIN (1979) LTEE   *p*
1090
310   RUE   DE   QUEN,   DOLBEAU-MISTASSINI, QC, G8L 5N1
(418) 276-4166   *SIC* 1611
ENTREPRISES DE CONSTRUCTION GI-GARI INC, LES   *p*
1079
766 RUE D'ALMA, CHICOUTIMI, QC, G7H 4E6
(418) 696-1817   *SIC* 1521
ENTREPRISES DE CONSTRUCTION RE-FRABEC INC, LES   *p*
1392
925 BOUL LIONEL-BOULET, VARENNES, QC, J3X 1P7
(450) 652-5391   *SIC* 1796
ENTREPRISES DE NETTOYAGE M.P. INC *p*
1385
1621 RUE DE LERY, TROIS-RIVIERES, QC, G8Y 7B3
SIC 7349
ENTREPRISES DE NETTOYAGE MARCEL LABBE INC   *p* 1264
340 RUE JACKSON, QUEBEC, QC, G1N 4C5
(418) 523-9411   *SIC* 7349
ENTREPRISES DE REFRIGERATION L.S. INC, LES   *p* 1234
1610 RUE GUILLET, MONTREAL, QC, H7L 5B2
(450) 682-8105   *SIC* 1711
ENTREPRISES DE VENTE LEWIS, R. INC, LES   *p* 1354
50 BOUL NORBERT-MORIN, SAINTE-AGATHE-DES-MONTS, QC, J8C 2V6
(819) 326-8900   *SIC* 5014
ENTREPRISES DERO INC   *p* 1240
9960 AV PLAZA, MONTREAL-NORD, QC, H1H 4L6
(514) 327-1108   *SIC* 3089
ENTREPRISES DOMINION BLUELINE INC, LES   *p* 1317
230 RUE FOCH BUREAU 450, SAINT-JEAN-SUR-RICHELIEU, QC, J3B 2B2
(450) 346-6827   *SIC* 5112
ENTREPRISES DONTIGNY ET TREMBLAY INC, LES   *p* 1384
15 RUE FUSEY, TROIS-RIVIERES, QC, G8T 2T3
(819) 378-2828   *SIC* 5912
ENTREPRISES DORO J.C.S. INC, LES *p*
1344
6050 BOUL DES GRANDES-PRAIRIES BU-REAU 204, SAINT-LEONARD, QC, H1P 1A2
(514) 722-3676   *SIC* 5812
ENTREPRISES DUPONT 1972 INC, LES *p*
1295
601 RUE SAGARD, SAINT-BRUNO, QC, J3V 6C1
(450) 653-9362   *SIC* 4212
ENTREPRISES ELAINE ROY INC, LES *p*
1260
2600 RUE DE LA CONCORDE, QUEBEC, QC, G1L 6A5
(418) 621-9802   *SIC* 5541
ENTREPRISES ELECTRIQUES A. & R. LTEE, LES   *p* 1310
5655   RUE   LAMOUREUX,   SAINT-HYACINTHE, QC, J2R 1S3
(450) 253-8690   *SIC* 1623
ENTREPRISES ELECTRIQUES L.M. INC, LES   *p* 1167
3006 RUE SAINTE-CATHERINE E, MON-TREAL, QC, H1W 2B8
(514) 523-2831   *SIC* 1731
ENTREPRISES   ELECTRIQUES   NADCO INC   *p* 1157

8550 CH DELMEADE, MONT-ROYAL, QC, H4T 1L7
(514) 342-2748   *SIC* 5085
ENTREPRISES EMILE CHARLES & FILS LTEE   *p* 1400
1716 RTE 105, WAKEFIELD, QC, J0X 3G0
(819) 459-2326   *SIC* 5411
ENTREPRISES EMILE CREVIER INC *p*
1329
2025 RUE LUCIEN-THIMENS, SAINT-LAURENT, QC, H4R 1K8
(514) 331-2951   *SIC* 5172
ENTREPRISES EN PLOMBERIE PIERRE POULIN, LES   *p* 1070
See CONSTRUCTIONS 3P INC
ENTREPRISES ERNEST (MTL) LTEE, LES *p* 1178
9200 RUE MEILLEUR BUREAU 101, MON-TREAL, QC, H2N 2A9
(514) 858-5258   *SIC* 5611
ENTREPRISES FRANCOIS BRIEN LTEE, LES   *p* 1070
9900   BOUL   LEDUC   BUREAU   643, BROSSARD, QC, J4Y 0B4
(450) 443-0005   *SIC* 5311
ENTREPRISES G.A. LEBLANC INC, LES *p*
1077
45 RUE ALBERT-FERLAND, CHENEVILLE, QC, J0V 1E0
(819) 428-3966   *SIC* 5411
ENTREPRISES G.N.P. INC   *p* 1399
750 BOUL PIERRE-ROUX E, VICTORIAV-ILLE, QC, G6T 1S6
(819) 752-7140   *SIC* 1623
ENTREPRISES GHISLAIN G FORTIN LTEE *p* 1284
419 BOUL JESSOP BUREAU 320, RI-MOUSKI, QC, G5L 7Y5
(418) 722-8426   *SIC* 5531
ENTREPRISES H.M. METAL INC, LES *p*
1363
583   RANG   SAINT-OVIDE,   SAINTE-SOPHIE-DE-LEVRARD, QC, G0X 3C0
(819) 288-5287   *SIC* 7692
ENTREPRISES HAMELIN   *p* 1213
See GROUPE HAMELIN INC
ENTREPRISES HENRI RAVARY LTEE, LES *p* 1167
3025 RUE SHERBROOKE E BUREAU 400, MONTREAL, QC, H1W 1B2
(514) 521-8888   *SIC* 5399
ENTREPRISES IMPORTFAB INC   *p* 1250
50 BOUL HYMUS, POINTE-CLAIRE, QC, H9R 1C9
(514) 694-0721   *SIC* 2834
ENTREPRISES ISABELLE DESJARDINS INC, LES   *p* 1319
900 BOUL GRIGNON BUREAU 116, SAINT-JEROME, QC, J7Y 3S7
(450) 438-1293   *SIC* 5912
ENTREPRISES J.C. LEVESQUE INC, LES *p*
1304
500 107E RUE, SAINT-GEORGES, QC, G5Y 8K1
(418) 228-8843   *SIC* 5014
ENTREPRISES J.G GUIMOND INC, LES *p*
1235
143 RUE DE LA STATION, MONTREAL, QC, H7M 3W1
(450) 663-7155   *SIC* 1542
ENTREPRISES J.M. CHAMPEAU, LES *p*
1347
See J.M. CHAMPEAU INC
ENTREPRISES J.P. LAROCHELLE INC, LES   *p* 1115
2290 BOUL RENE-LEVESQUE, JON-QUIERE, QC, G7S 5Y5
(418) 542-3909   *SIC* 5531
ENTREPRISES JACQUES CARIGNAN LTEE, LES   *p* 1104
700 BOUL MALONEY O, GATINEAU, QC, J8T 8K7
(819) 246-1234   *SIC* 5311
ENTREPRISES JACQUES DUFOUR & FILS

INC, LES   p 1054
106 RUE SAINTE-ANNE, BAIE-SAINT-
PAUL, QC, G3Z 1P5
(418) 435-2445   SIC 1611
ENTREPRISES JEAN-MAURICE PAP-
INEAU LTEE, LES   p
1102
14 309 RTE N BUREAU 100, FERME-
NEUVE, QC, J0W 1C0
(819) 587-3360   SIC 0851
ENTREPRISES JMC (1973) LTEE, LES   p
1072
101 CH SAINT-FRANCOIS-XAVIER, CAN-
DIAC, QC, J5R 4V4
(450) 632-4723   SIC 5812
ENTREPRISES JOEL GIRARD INC, LES   p
1397
3180 RUE WELLINGTON, VERDUN, QC,
H4G 1T3
(514) 766-8561   SIC 5531
ENTREPRISES JULIE LESSARD INC, LES
p 1382
5333 BOUL LAURIER BUREAU 180, TER-
REBONNE, QC, J7M 1W1
(450) 477-4401   SIC 5912
ENTREPRISES JULIEN BERNIER INC, LES
p 1253
46 CH DE LA SCIERIE RR 1, POINTE-
LEBEL, QC, G0H 1N0
SIC 4212
ENTREPRISES KIM LUU INC, LES   p 1240
10551 BOUL PIE-IX, MONTREAL-NORD,
QC, H1H 4A3
(514) 321-1230   SIC 5912
ENTREPRISES L.T. LTEE, LES   p 1254
1209 RUE WILBROD-ROBERT, QUEBEC,
QC, G1C 0L1
(418) 663-0555   SIC 4959
ENTREPRISES LA CANADIENNE INC   p
1156
5745 RUE PARE, MONT-ROYAL, QC, H4P
1S1
(514) 731-2112   SIC 3143
ENTREPRISES LA CHARCUTIERE LAVAL
INC   p 1232
3315 BOUL DE LA CONCORDE E, MON-
TREAL, QC, H7E 2C3
SIC 5411
ENTREPRISES LAMCOIL INC, LES   p 1236
2748 BOUL DANIEL-JOHNSON, MON-
TREAL, QC, H7P 5Z7
(450) 682-4444   SIC 7389
ENTREPRISES LARRY INC   p 1224
4200 RUE SAINT-PATRICK, MONTREAL,
QC, H4E 1A5
(514) 767-5363   SIC 5084
ENTREPRISES LAURENTIEN ELEC-
TRIQUE INC, LES   p
1217
890 BOUL CREMAZIE O, MONTREAL, QC,
H3N 1A4
(514) 276-8551   SIC 1731
ENTREPRISES LEVISIENNES INC, LES   p
1135
3104 RTE DES RIVIERES, LEVIS, QC, G6J
0B9
(418) 831-4111   SIC 1611
ENTREPRISES LEZNOFF LTEE, LES   p
1184
6525 RUE WAVERLY, MONTREAL, QC,
H2V 4M2
(514) 273-7207   SIC 5023
ENTREPRISES LIONBRIDGE (CANADA) p
1069
See LIONBRIDGE (CANADA) INC
ENTREPRISES LISE LAVOIE INC, LES   p
1149
1407 AV DE LA GARE, MASCOUCHE, QC,
J7K 3G6
(450) 474-0404   SIC 5039
ENTREPRISES LITEL INC, LES   p 1261
465 RUE METIVIER, QUEBEC, QC, G1M
2X2
(418) 527-5643   SIC 1623

ENTREPRISES LOGIX ITS   p 1132
See LOGIX ITS INC
ENTREPRISES MACBAIE INC, LES   p 1079
1401 BOUL TALBOT BUREAU 1,
CHICOUTIMI, QC, G7H 5N6
(418) 545-3593   SIC 5812
ENTREPRISES MACBAIE INC, LES   p 1079
999 BOUL TALBOT, CHICOUTIMI, QC, G7H
4B5
(418) 545-3593   SIC 5812
ENTREPRISES MACBAIE INC, LES   p 1121
1082 RUE AIME-GRAVEL, LA BAIE, QC,
G7B 2M5
(418) 545-3593   SIC 5812
ENTREPRISES MARC DONTIGNY INC   p
1384
701 BOUL THIBEAU, TROIS-RIVIERES,
QC, G8T 7A2
(819) 378-4549   SIC 5122
ENTREPRISES MARIO LAROCHELLE INC,
LES   p 1367
402 BOUL LAURE, SEPT-ILES, QC, G4R
1X5
(418) 968-1415   SIC 5531
ENTREPRISES MARSOLAIS INC, LES   p
1166
5045 RUE ONTARIO, MONTREAL, QC,
H1V 1M7
(514) 254-7171   SIC 5193
ENTREPRISES MAX FRIED INC, LES   p
1071
9125 GRANDE-ALLEE BUREAU 1,
BROSSARD, QC, J4Z 3H8
(514) 365-5154
ENTREPRISES MEADE RAY INTERNA-
TIONAL   p
1227
See MEADE RAY INTERNATIONAL INC
ENTREPRISES MICHAUDVILLE INC, LES p
1158
270 RUE BRUNET, MONT-SAINT-HILAIRE,
QC, J3H 0M6
(450) 446-9933   SIC 8711
ENTREPRISES MICHEL CAPLETTE INC   p
1130
1819 AV DOLLARD, LASALLE, QC, H8N
1T9
(514) 364-1644   SIC 5912
ENTREPRISES MICHEL CHOINIERE INC,
LES   p 1365
1770 BOUL MONSEIGNEUR-LANGLOIS,
SALABERRY-DE-VALLEYFIELD, QC, J6S
5R1
(450) 373-0123   SIC 5531
ENTREPRISES MICHEL HAMELIN INC,
LES   p 1092
223 138 RTE, DONNACONA, QC, G3M 1C1
(418) 285-1331   SIC 5531
ENTREPRISES MICHEL MARCHAND INC,
LES   p 1130
8300 BOUL NEWMAN, LASALLE, QC, H8N
1X9
(514) 365-1223   SIC 5812
ENTREPRISES MICROTEC INC, LES   p
1048
8125 BOUL DU GOLF, ANJOU, QC, H1J
0B2
(514) 388-8177   SIC 5063
ENTREPRISES MICROTEC INC, LES   p
1293
4780 RUE SAINT-FELIX, SAINT-
AUGUSTIN-DE-DESMAURES, QC, G3A
2J9
(418) 864-7924   SIC 5063
ENTREPRISES MIRCA INC, LES   p 1170
3901 RUE JARRY E BUREAU 250, MON-
TREAL, QC, H1Z 2G1
(514) 253-3110   SIC 6712
ENTREPRISES MTY TIKI MING INC, LES p
1333
8210 RTE TRANSCANADIENNE, SAINT-
LAURENT, QC, H4S 1M5
(514) 336-8885   SIC 6794
ENTREPRISES N.G.A. INC, LES   p 1098

350 RUE ROCHELEAU, DRUM-
MONDVILLE, QC, J2C 7S7
(819) 477-6891   SIC 1542
ENTREPRISES NUMESH   p 1362
See NUMESH INC
ENTREPRISES P. BONHOMME LTEE, LES
p 1107
921 BOUL SAINT-JOSEPH, GATINEAU,
QC, J8Z 1S8
(819) 561-5577   SIC 5211
ENTREPRISES P.E.B. LTEE, LES   p 1281
1190 AV DU LAC-SAINT-CHARLES, QUE-
BEC, QC, G3G 2S9
(418) 849-2841   SIC 1623
ENTREPRISES P.P. HALLE LTEE   p 1266
2610 BOUL WILFRID-HAMEL, QUEBEC,
QC, G1P 2J1
(418) 687-4740   SIC 5142
ENTREPRISES PANTHERE VERTE INC   p
1183
160 RUE SAINT-VIATEUR E BUREAU 101,
MONTREAL, QC, H2T 1A8
(514) 507-2620   SIC 5812
ENTREPRISES PAUL F. DELANEY INC   p
1073
165 CH PRINCIPAL, CAP-AUX-MEULES,
QC, G4T 1C4
(418) 986-2135   SIC 5172
ENTREPRISES PAUL WOODSTOCK LTEEp
1089
65 132 RTE, DELSON, QC, J5B 1H1
(450) 632-1700   SIC 5251
ENTREPRISES PECB, LES   p 1346
See PECB GROUP INC
ENTREPRISES PEP (2000) INC, LESp 1231
3000 RUE BERNARD-LEFEBVRE, MON-
TREAL, QC, H7C 0A5
(450) 661-5050   SIC 1794
ENTREPRISES PIERRE L BOULOS INC,
LES   p 1310
5930 RUE MARTINEAU, SAINT-
HYACINTHE, QC, J2R 2H6
(450) 796-4226   SIC 5014
ENTREPRISES PIERRE LAUZON LTEE   p
1090
1751 BOUL VEZINA BUREAU 284,
DOLBEAU-MISTASSINI, QC, G8L 3S4
(418) 276-2385   SIC 5531
ENTREPRISES PIERRE PICARD INC, LES
p 1271
1350 AV MAGUIRE BUREAU 103, QUE-
BEC, QC, G1T 1Z3
(418) 683-4492   SIC 7349
ENTREPRISES PNH INC, LES   p 1093
1985 BOUL HYMUS, DORVAL, QC, H9P
1J8
(514) 683-3279   SIC 5199
ENTREPRISES PO BO HA ENR, LES   p
1299
See HAMEL CONSTRUCTION INC
ENTREPRISES POL R INC   p 1277
5085 RUE RIDEAU, QUEBEC, QC, G2E
5H5
(418) 872-0000   SIC 5033
ENTREPRISES QMD INC, LES   p 1210
990 RUE NOTRE-DAME O BUREAU 200,
MONTREAL, QC, H3C 1K1
(514) 875-4356   SIC 1521
ENTREPRISES R & G ST-LAURENT INC   p
1052
2081 AV DU LABRADOR, BAIE-COMEAU,
QC, G4Z 3B9
(418) 589-5453   SIC 1794
ENTREPRISES R.E.R. INC   p 1077
1530 BOUL SAINTE-GENEVIEVE,
CHICOUTIMI, QC, G7G 2H1
SIC 5013
ENTREPRISES RAYMOND LEWIS INC,
LES   p 1317
855 BOUL DU SEMINAIRE N BUREAU 153,
SAINT-JEAN-SUR-RICHELIEU, QC, J3A 1J2
(450) 348-3851   SIC 5544
ENTREPRISES RECOCHEM, LES   p 1341
See RECOCHEM INC

ENTREPRISES RITE, LES   p 1050
See RITE CORPORATION
ENTREPRISES ROBERT CHARETTE INC,
LES   p 1303
1003 3E RANG, SAINT-GABRIEL-DE-
BRANDON, QC, J0K 2N0
(450) 835-7988   SIC 5144
ENTREPRISES ROLAND DOYON   p 1162
7555 BOUL MAURICE-DUPLESSIS BU-
REAU 454, MONTREAL, QC, H1E 7N2
(514) 643-2232   SIC 5251
ENTREPRISES ROLLAND INC, LES p 1319
256 BOUL JEAN-BAPTISTE-ROLLAND O,
SAINT-JEROME, QC, J7Y 0L6
(450) 569-3951   SIC 2621
ENTREPRISES ROLLAND INC, LES p 1319
980 RUE DE L'INDUSTRIE, SAINT-
JEROME, QC, J7Y 4B8
(450) 569-0040   SIC 5111
ENTREPRISES S.J.M. INC, LES   p 1048
8501 RUE JARRY, ANJOU, QC, H1J 1H7
(514) 321-2160   SIC 6712
ENTREPRISES S.M.T.R. INC   p 1288
500 RTE 112, ROUGEMONT, QC, J0L 1M0
(450) 469-3153   SIC 7538
ENTREPRISES SATELLITE, LES, DIV DE p
1355
See CATHELLE INC
ENTREPRISES SMART&FINAL, LES   p
1049
See MAYRAND LIMITEE
ENTREPRISES SOLID XPERTS   p 1336
See SOLID XPERTS INC
ENTREPRISES STERINOVA, LES   p 1313
See STERINOVA INC
ENTREPRISES SYLVIE DROLET INC   p
1368
1555 RUE TRUDEL BUREAU 131, SHAW-
INIGAN, QC, G9N 8K8
(819) 537-3888   SIC 5014
ENTREPRISES TAG, LES   p 729
See 6929818 CANADA INC
ENTREPRISES TEMBEC, LES   p 1207
See RAYONIER A.M. CANADA ENTER-
PRISES INC
ENTREPRISES TZANET INC, LES   p 1225
1375 RUE DE LOUVAIN O BUREAU 71,
MONTREAL, QC, H4N 1G6
(514) 383-0030   SIC 5046
ENTREPRISES VAGABOND INC, LES   p
1285
451 RUE DE L'EXPANSION, RIMOUSKI,
QC, G5M 1B4
(418) 724-2243   SIC 5621
ENTREPRISES VIZIMAX, LES   p 1142
See VIZIMAX INC
ENTREPRISES Z-TECH INC., LES   p 1061
4230 RUE MARCEL-LACASSE, BOIS-
BRIAND, QC, J7H 1N3
SIC 5072
ENTRETIEN 4M INC   p 1184
6300 AV DU PARC BUREAU 202, MON-
TREAL, QC, H2V 4H8
(514) 274-9933   SIC 7349
ENTRETIEN AVANGARDISTE   p 1093
See 9119-5867 QUEBEC INC
ENTRETIEN DE PISCINES SOUCY   p 1267
See PISCINES SOUCY INC
ENTRETIEN MECANIQUE BT   p 1058
See BERLINES TRANSIT INC
ENTRETIEN MENAGER LYNA   p 1358
See 188669 CANADA INC
ENTRETIEN P.E.A.C.E. PLUS INC   p 1217
950 AV OGILVY BUREAU 200, MONTREAL,
QC, H3N 1P4
(514) 273-9764   SIC 7349
ENTRETIEN PARAMEX INC   p 1389
3535 BOUL L.-P.-NORMAND, TROIS-
RIVIERES, QC, G9B 0G8
(819) 377-5533   SIC 7699
ENTRIPY CUSTOM CLOTHING   p 796
See BRAR CAPITAL CORP
ENTRO COMMUNICATIONS INC   p 962
33 HARBOUR SQ SUITE 202, TORONTO,

ON, M5J 2G2
(416) 368-1095   SIC 3993
ENTROPEX p 858
See 629728 ONTARIO LIMITED
ENTROPEX p 859
See UNITEC INC
ENTRUST DATACARD LIMITED p 624
1000 INNOVATION DR, KANATA, ON, K2K 3E7
(613) 270-3400   SIC 7371
ENTUITIVE CORPORATION p 49
150 9 AVE SW SUITE 1610, CALGARY, AB, T2P 3H9
(403) 879-1270   SIC 8711
ENTUITIVE CORPORATION p 951
200 UNIVERSITY AVE 7TH FL, TORONTO, ON, M5H 3C6
(416) 477-5832   SIC 8711
ENVELOPPE MONTREAL p 1327
See SUPREMEX INC
ENVELOPPE PREMIER p 1131
See SUPREMEX INC
ENVIREM ORGANICS INC p 404
274 ROUTE 148, KILLARNEY ROAD, NB, E3G 9E2
(506) 459-3464   SIC 2875
ENVIRO 5 INC p 1290
1101 139 RTE, ROXTON POND, QC, J0E 1Z0
(450) 777-2551   SIC 1711
ENVIRO CLEAN (NFLD.) LIMITED p 427
155 MCNAMARA DR, PARADISE, NL, A1L 0A7
(709) 781-3264   SIC 7349
ENVIRO CONNEXIONS p 1062
See WASTE CONNECTIONS OF CANADA INC
ENVIRO CONNEXIONS p 1231
See ENTREPRISE SANITAIRE F.A. LTEE
ENVIRO MUSHROOM FARM INC p 526
5200 BRITANNIA RD, BURLINGTON, ON, L7M 0S3
(905) 331-8030   SIC 0182
ENVIRO-COATINGS CANADA LTD p 713
2359 ROYAL WINDSOR DR UNIT 10, MISSISSAUGA, ON, L5J 4S9
SIC 2851
ENVIRO-TECH SURVEYS LTD p 64
1020 14 AVE SW, CALGARY, AB, T2R 0P1
(403) 345-2901   SIC 1382
ENVIRO-VAC p 282
See PARAGON REMEDIATION GROUP LTD
ENVIROBATE INC p 458
93 SUSIE LAKE CRES, HALIFAX, NS, B3S 1C3
(902) 832-0820   SIC 4959
ENVIROCLEAN BUILDING MAINTENANCE LTD p 100
17233 109 AVE NW SUITE 101, EDMONTON, AB, T5S 1H7
(780) 489-0500   SIC 7349
ENVIROMECH INDUSTRIES INC p 221
2092 ENTERPRISE WAY SUITE 100, KELOWNA, BC, V1Y 6H7
(250) 765-1777   SIC 3714
ENVIROMETAL SOLUTIONS p 611
See CUNNINGHAM LINDSEY CANADA LIMITED
ENVIRONICS ANALYTICS p 928
See ENVIRONICS ANALYTICS GROUP LTD
ENVIRONICS ANALYTICS GROUP LTD p 928
33 BLOOR ST E SUITE 400, TORONTO, ON, M4W 3H1
(416) 969-2733   SIC 8732
ENVIRONMENTAL CONTROL p 785
See YORKLAND CONTROLS LIMITED
ENVIRONMENTAL DYNAMICS LTD p 105
11810 152 ST NW, EDMONTON, AB, T5V 1E3
(780) 421-0686   SIC 1711
ENVIRONMENTAL SERVICES DIVISION OF

PUBLIC WORKS DEPARTMENT p 1019
See CORPORATION OF THE CITY OF WINDSOR
ENVIRONMENTAL SOLUTIONS REMEDIATION SERVICES p 709
See CUNNINGHAM LINDSEY CANADA CLAIMS SERVICES LTD
ENVIRONNEMENT E.S.A. p 1372
See AVIZO EXPERTS-CONSEILS INC
ENVIRONNEMENT KEMIRA QUEBEC, L' p 1393
See KEMIRA WATER SOLUTIONS CANADA INC
ENVIRONNEMENT ROUTIER NRJ INC p 1125
23 AV MILTON, LACHINE, QC, H8R 1K6
(514) 481-0451   SIC 1611
ENVIROPLAST INC p 1048
11060 BOUL PARKWAY, ANJOU, QC, H1J 1R6
(514) 352-6060   SIC 4953
ENVIROQUIP p 1140
See GROUPE ENVIRONNEMENTAL LABRIE INC
ENVIROSHAKE p 542
See 2595385 ONTARIO INC
ENVIROSOL p 1348
See FERTI TECHNOLOGIES INC
ENVIROSYSTEMS INCORPORATED p 416
55 STINSON DR, SAINT JOHN, NB, E2M 7E3
(506) 652-9178   SIC 7349
ENVIROSYSTEMS INCORPORATED p 446
11 BROWN AVE, DARTMOUTH, NS, B3B 1Z7
(902) 481-8008   SIC 2992
ENVIROTEC SERVICES INCORPORATED p 1427
100 CORY RD, SASKATOON, SK, S7K 8B7
(306) 244-9500   SIC 5211
ENVISION FINANCIAL p 196
See FIRST WEST CREDIT UNION
ENVIZION VENTURE CAPITAL CORP p 669
3601 HIGHWAY 7 E, MARKHAM, ON, L3R 0M3
(289) 301-4485   SIC 7389
ENWAVE CORPORATION p 205
1668 DERWENT WAY UNIT 1, DELTA, BC, V3M 6R9
(604) 806-6110   SIC 3569
ENWAVE ENERGY CORPORATION p 951
333 BAY ST SUITE 710, TORONTO, ON, M5H 2R2
(416) 392-6838   SIC 4961
ENWIN p 1024
See WINDSOR CANADA UTILITIES LTD
ENWIN UTILITIES LTD p 1023
787 OUELLETTE AVE SUITE 517, WINDSOR, ON, N9A 4J4
(519) 255-2727   SIC 4911
ENX INC p 1
53016 HWY 60 UNIT 703, ACHESON, AB, T7X 5A7
(780) 962-7993   SIC 5169
ENZYME TESTING LABS INC p 1319
2031 BOUL DU CURE-LABELLE, SAINT-JEROME, QC, J7Y 1S5
(450) 995-2000   SIC 7371
EODC p 815
See EODC ENGINEERING, DEVELOPING AND LICENSING, INC
EODC ENGINEERING, DEVELOPING AND LICENSING, INC p 815
1377 TRIOLE ST, OTTAWA, ON, K1B 4T4
(613) 748-5549   SIC 3462
EON BUILDING SYSTEMS INC p 266
GD, ROBERTS CREEK, BC, V0N 2W0
SIC 1521
EOS CANADA INC p 864
325 MILNER AVE SUITE 1111, SCARBOROUGH, ON, M1B 5N1
(647) 436-2605   SIC 7322
EOS NCN p 864

See EOS CANADA INC
EP SAGUENAY p 1080
See ENGRENAGE PROVINCIAL INC
EPAK INC p 372
55 PLYMOUTH ST, WINNIPEG, MB, R2X 2V5
(204) 947-1383   SIC 3081
EPALS CLASSROOM EXCHANGE INC p 834
331 COOPER ST SUITE 500, OTTAWA, ON, K2P 0G5
(613) 562-9847   SIC 4813
EPALS.COM p 834
See EPALS CLASSROOM EXCHANGE INC
EPARGNE PLACEMENTS QUEBEC BANQUE NATIONAL p 1268
See BANQUE NATIONALE DU CANADA
EPC CANADA EXPLOSIVES LTD p 634
22 GOVERNMENT RD E, KIRKLAND LAKE, ON, P2N 1A3
(705) 642-3265   SIC 2892
EPC INDUSTRIES LIMITED p 438
12 TUPPER BLVD, AMHERST, NS, B4H 4S7
(902) 667-7241   SIC 2759
EPC NORDEX p 634
See EPC CANADA EXPLOSIVES LTD
EPCOR CANADA p 85
See CP ENERGY MARKETING L.P.
EPCOR DISTRIBUTION & TRANSMISSION INC p 86
10423 101 ST NW SUITE 2000, EDMONTON, AB, T5H 0E8
(780) 412-3414   SIC 4911
EPCOR POWER DEVELOPMENT CORPORATION p 89
10065 JASPER AVE NW, EDMONTON, AB, T5J 3B1
(780) 412-3191   SIC 5063
EPCOR TECHNOLOGIES INC p 93
13410 ST ALBERT TRAIL NW, EDMONTON, AB, T5L 4P2
(780) 412-3414   SIC 8742
EPCOR UTILITIES INC p 86
10423 101 ST NW SUITE 2000, EDMONTON, AB, T5H 0E8
(780) 412-3414   SIC 4941
EPCOR WATER SERVICES INC p 86
10423 101 ST NW SUITE 2000, EDMONTON, AB, T5H 0E8
(780) 412-3850   SIC 4971
EPCOR WATER SERVICES INC p 107
10977 50 ST NW, EDMONTON, AB, T6A 2E9
(780) 969-8496   SIC 1629
EPERNAY TASTING & PROMOTIONAL COMPANY LTD, THE p 746
4 CLEVERDON BLVD, MOUNT ALBERT, ON, L0G 1M0
(905) 473-5905   SIC 8743
EPFC CORP p 64
999 8 ST SW SUITE 555, CALGARY, AB, T2R 1J5
(403) 541-9400   SIC 3498
EPI ENVIRONMENTAL PRODUCTS INC p 320
1788 BROADWAY W SUITE 801, VANCOUVER, BC, V6J 1Y1
(604) 738-6281   SIC 5169
EPIC DEALS INC p 715
2400 DUNDAS ST W SUITE 211, MISSISSAUGA, ON, L5K 2R8
(647) 478-9002   SIC 7311
EPIC FOOD SERVICES INC p 231
22987 DEWDNEY TRUNK RD, MAPLE RIDGE, BC, V2X 3K8
(604) 466-0671   SIC 5461
EPIC FOODS INC p 702
3258 WHARTON WAY, MISSISSAUGA, ON, L4X 2C1
SIC 5144
EPIC INFORMATION SOLUTIONS INC p 393

1730 MCGILLIVRAY BLVD, WINNIPEG, MB, R3Y 1A1
(204) 453-2300   SIC 5045
EPIC INVESTMENT SERVICES LIMITED PARTNERSHIP p 951
141 ADELAIDE ST W SUITE 1201, TORONTO, ON, M5H 3L5
(416) 497-9332   SIC 6531
EPIC OPPORTUNITIES INC p 384
1644 DUBLIN AVE, WINNIPEG, MB, R3H 0X5
(204) 982-4673   SIC 8322
EPIC REALTY PARTNERS INC p 767
2225 SHEPPARD AVE E SUITE 900, NORTH YORK, ON, M2J 5C2
(416) 497-9332   SIC 8742
EPICERIE CENTRE-MATIC INC p 1323
1233 RUE DES ERABLES, SAINT-LAMBERT-DE-LAUZON, QC, G0S 2W0
(418) 889-9723   SIC 5411
EPICERIE I G A p 1057
See MARCHE CROISETIERE BERTHIER INC
EPICERIE IGA COOKSHIRE p 1082
See GESTION GILLES-GENEST INC
EPICERIE QUEBEC p 1267
See METRO RICHELIEU INC
EPICERIE QUINTAL & FRERES 1978 INC p 1342
4805 BOUL ARTHUR-SAUVE, SAINT-LAURENT, QC, H7R 3X2
(450) 627-3123   SIC 5411
EPICERIE R. BUTEAU INC p 1350
2650 25E AV, SAINT-PROSPER-DE-DORCHESTER, QC, G0M 1Y0
(418) 594-8244   SIC 5411
EPICERIE R. CADIEUX & FILS INC p 1284
461 CH DE LA GRANDE-LIGNE, RIGAUD, QC, J0P 1P0
(450) 451-5318   SIC 5411
EPICERIE SALTARELLI ET FILS INC p 1224
11847 BOUL LAURENTIEN, MONTREAL, QC, H4J 2M1
(514) 331-5879   SIC 5411
EPICES ROSE VALLEY SPICES p 1332
See ALIMENTS ROSEHILL INC, LES
EPICIERS HOGUE ET FRERES INC, LES p 1355
7 BOUL SAINTE-ANNE, SAINTE-ANNE-DES-PLAINES, QC, J0N 1H0
(450) 478-1765   SIC 5411
EPICURE SELECTIONS p 268
See VICTORIAN EPICURE INC
EPIDERMA p 1272
See CORPORATION EPIDERMA INC
EPIDERMA QUEBEC INC p 1272
2590 BOUL LAURIER BUREAU 330, QUEBEC, QC, G1V 4M6
(418) 266-2027   SIC 7231
EPIROC CANADA INC p 739
1025 TRISTAR DR, MISSISSAUGA, ON, L5T 1W5
(289) 562-0100   SIC 5082
EPIROC CUSTOMER CENTRE, DIV OF p 739
See EPIROC CANADA INC
EPITRON INC p 912
841 PINE ST S, TIMMINS, ON, P4N 8S3
(705) 267-7382   SIC 5063
EPM GLOBAL SERVICES INC p 669
195 ROYAL CREST CRT, MARKHAM, ON, L3R 9X6
(905) 479-6203   SIC 3679
EPM MECANIC p 1233
See 2982897 CANADA INC
EPOCAL INC p 817
2060 WALKLEY RD, OTTAWA, ON, K1G 3P5
(613) 738-6192   SIC 8731
EPOCH TIMES p 1191
See GRANDE EPOQUE INC, LA
EPP'S PHARMACY LTD p 358
382 MAIN ST, STEINBACH, MB, R5G 1Z3
(204) 326-3747   SIC 5912

EPPENDORF CANADA LTD   p 722
2810 ARGENTIA RD UNIT 2, MISSISSAUGA, ON, L5N 8L2
(905) 826-5525   SIC 5049

EPROM INC   p 669
100 SHIELDS CRT, MARKHAM, ON, L3R 9T5
(905) 944-9000   SIC 5045

EPS LANTRIC INC   p 1339
7750 RTE TRANSCANADIENNE, SAINT-LAURENT, QC, H4T 1A5
(514) 735-4561   SIC 5051

EPSCAN INDUSTRIES LTD   p 204
600 113 AVE, DAWSON CREEK, BC, V1G 2Y6
(250) 782-9656   SIC 1731

EPSCAN INDUSTRIES LTD   p 213
10012 94 AVE, FORT ST. JOHN, BC, V1J 5J6
(250) 787-9659   SIC 5084

EPSILON ENERGY LTD   p 69
14505 BANNISTER RD SE SUITE 300, CALGARY, AB, T2X 3J3
SIC 1311

EPSILON INDUSTRIES INC   p 632
751 DALTON AVE, KINGSTON, ON, K7M 8N6
(613) 544-1133   SIC 3585

EPSILON TARGETING, DIV OF   p 914
See ICOM INFORMATION & COMMUNICATIONS L.P.

EPSON CANADA LIMITED EPSON CANADA LIMITEE   p 669
185 RENFREW DR, MARKHAM, ON, L3R 6G3
(416) 498-4574   SIC 5045

EPSTEIN COLE LLP   p 944
393 UNIVERSITY AVE SUITE 2200, TORONTO, ON, M5G 1E6
(416) 862-9888   SIC 8111

EPSYLON CONCEPT INC   p 1255
1010 AV NORDIQUE, QUEBEC, QC, G1C 0H9
(418) 661-6262   SIC 3449

EQ3   p 822
See WIELER HUNT INVESTMENTS INC

EQ3 LTD   p 363
170 FURNITURE PARK, WINNIPEG, MB, R2G 1B9
(204) 957-8018   SIC 5712

EQUAL DOOR INDUSTRIES   p 13
See AMBASSADOR SALES (SOUTHERN) LTD

EQUBE GAMING LIMITED   p 100
10493 184 ST NW SUITE 100, EDMONTON, AB, T5S 2L1
(780) 414-8890   SIC 7371

EQUICAPITA INCOME TRUST   p 75
8561 8A AVE SW SUITE 2210, CALGARY, AB, T3H 0V5
(587) 887-1538   SIC 6211

EQUIFAX CANADA CO.   p 770
5700 YONGE ST SUITE 1700, NORTH YORK, ON, M2M 4K2
(800) 278-0278   SIC 7323

EQUINOR CANADA LTD   p 49
308 4 AVE SW SUITE 3600, CALGARY, AB, T2P 0H7
(403) 234-0123   SIC 1381

EQUINOX ENGINEERING LTD   p 49
940 6 AVE SW UNIT 400, CALGARY, AB, T2P 3T1
(587) 390-1000   SIC 8711

EQUINOX GOLD CORP   p 304
700 WEST PENDER ST SUITE 1501, VANCOUVER, BC, V6C 1G8
(604) 558-0560   SIC 1021

EQUINOX INDUSTRIES INC   p 362
401 CHRISLIND ST, WINNIPEG, MB, R2C 5G4
(204) 633-7564   SIC 3299

EQUINOXE, LIFE CARE SOLUTIONS INC p 1402
4060 RUE SAINTE-CATHERINE O BU-REAU 201, WESTMOUNT, QC, H3Z 2Z3
(514) 935-2600   SIC 8059

EQUIPE D'INVENTAIRE F.M.   p 1381
See COMPTEC S. G. INC

EQUIPE DE COURSE FORESCO   p 1130
See FORESCO HOLDING INC

EQUIPE H.B. HELLER INC, L'   p 1377
175 RUE PASSENGER RR 4, STANSTEAD, QC, J0B 3E2
(819) 876-2709   SIC 5137

EQUIPE JUNIOR DE SKI DU MONT ORIG-NAL INC   p 1124
158 RANG DU MONT-ORIGNAL, LAC-ETCHEMIN, QC, G0R 1S0
(418) 625-1551   SIC 7011

EQUIPE PCJ INC   p 1144
822 RUE SAINT-LAURENT O, LONGUEUIL, QC, J4K 1C3
(450) 651-1154   SIC 5812

EQUIPE SPECTRA INC, L'   p 1195
400 BOUL DE MAISONNEUVE O 9EME ETAGE, MONTREAL, QC, H3A 1L4
(514) 525-7732   SIC 7922

EQUIPEMENT BONI INC   p 1295
1299 RUE MARIE-VICTORIN, SAINT-BRUNO, QC, J3V 6B7
(450) 653-1299   SIC 2542

EQUIPEMENT CLEMENT   p 1146
See CLEMENT, CHRYSLER DODGE LTEE

EQUIPEMENT COMAIRCO LTEE   p 1231
5535 RUE ERNEST-CORMIER, MONTREAL, QC, H7C 2S9
(450) 665-8780   SIC 5084

EQUIPEMENT D'ESSAI AEROSPATIAL C.E.L. LTEE   p 1141
715 RUE DELAGE BUREAU 400, LONGUEUIL, QC, J4G 2P8
(450) 442-9994   SIC 5088

EQUIPEMENT D'INCENDIE GLOBE INC p 1126
590 19E AV, LACHINE, QC, H8S 3S5
(514) 637-2534   SIC 5087

EQUIPEMENT D'INCENDIE PRIORITE INC p 1339
7528 CH DE LA COTE-DE-LIESSE, SAINT-LAURENT, QC, H4T 1E7
(514) 636-2431   SIC 5099

EQUIPEMENT DE BUREAU ROBERT LEGARE LTEE   p 1319
411 RUE JOHN-F.-KENNEDY, SAINT-JEROME, QC, J7Y 4B5
(450) 438-3894   SIC 5044

EQUIPEMENT DE COMBUSTION IDEAL p 1374
See PRODUITS IDEALTFC INC

EQUIPEMENT MAX-ATLAS INTERNA-TIONAL INC   p 1317
371 CH DU GRAND-BERNIER N, SAINT-JEAN-SUR-RICHELIEU, QC, J3B 4S2
(450) 346-8848   SIC 4212

EQUIPEMENT MOORE LTEE   p 1333
4955 CH SAINT-FRANCOIS, SAINT-LAURENT, QC, H4S 1P3
(514) 333-1212   SIC 5084

EQUIPEMENT QUADCO   p 1302
See QUADCO INC

EQUIPEMENT SANITAIRE CHERBOURG (1977) INC   p 1370
1051 RUE GALT E, SHERBROOKE, QC, J1G 1Y7
(819) 566-2266   SIC 5169

EQUIPEMENT ST-GERMAIN INC   p 1358
1151 RUE NOBEL, SAINTE-JULIE, QC, J3E 1Z4
(450) 443-3290   SIC 7353

EQUIPEMENT VICTORIA   p 1309
See SYSTEMS VIC INC

EQUIPEMENT WAJAX   p 1086
See INTEGRATED DISTRIBUTION SYSTEMS LIMITED PARTNERSHIP

EQUIPEMENTS A. PROVENCHER & FILS INC, LES   p 1246
2175 RUE SAINT-JEAN, PLESSISVILLE, QC, G6L 2Y4
(819) 225-0225   SIC 5083

EQUIPEMENTS ADAPTES PHYSIPRO INC, LES   p 1370
370 10E AV S, SHERBROOKE, QC, J1G 2R7
(819) 823-2252   SIC 3842

EQUIPEMENTS ADRIEN PHANEUF (LES) p 1122
23 RUE OLIVIER-MOREL, LA DURANTAYE, QC, G0R 1W0
(418) 884-2841   SIC 3131

EQUIPEMENTS ADRIEN PHANEUF INC, LES   p 1389
292 RUE PRINCIPALE, UPTON, QC, J0H 2E0
(450) 549-5811   SIC 5083

EQUIPEMENTS ARES DORVAL LTEE, LES p 1093
2000 BOUL HYMUS BUREAU 201, DORVAL, QC, H9P 1J7
(514) 683-4337   SIC 5719

EQUIPEMENTS BLANCHET   p 1377
See R.P.M. TECH INC

EQUIPEMENTS COMACT UNE DIVISION DE BID GROUP TECHNOLOGIES p 1152
See BID GROUP TECHNOLOGIES LTD

EQUIPEMENTS CONTRO VALVE INC, LES p 1070
9610 RUE IGNACE UNIT B, BROSSARD, QC, J4Y 2R4
(450) 444-5858   SIC 5084

EQUIPEMENTS D'ERABLIERE C.D.L. INC, LES   p 1343
257 RTE 279, SAINT-LAZARE-DE-BELLECHASSE, QC, G0R 3J0
(418) 883-5158   SIC 5099

EQUIPEMENTS DE FERME JAMESWAY INC   p 1377
12 RTE 249, ST-FRANCOIS-XAVIER-DE-BROMPTON, QC, J0B 2V0
(819) 845-7824   SIC 3523

EQUIPEMENTS DE SUPERMARCHES CONCEPT INTERNATIONAL INC   p 1282
429 RUE DES INDUSTRIES, REPENTIGNY, QC, J5Z 4Y8
(450) 582-3017   SIC 5078

EQUIPEMENTS E.M.U. LTEE   p 1276
3975 RUE JEAN-MARCHAND, QUEBEC, QC, G2C 2J2
(418) 767-2277   SIC 5084

EQUIPEMENTS FRONTMATEC INC p 1291
51 RTE MORISSETTE, SAINT-ANSELME, QC, G0R 2N0
(418) 885-4493   SIC 3569

EQUIPEMENTS GAETAN INC, LES p 1124
320 CH DU LAC-HURON, LAC-AUX-SABLES, QC, G0X 1M0
(418) 336-2634   SIC 1794

EQUIPEMENT INDUSTRIELS JOLIETTE INC   p 1114
1295 RUE DE LANAUDIERE, JOLIETTE, QC, J6E 3N9
(450) 756-0564   SIC 5072

EQUIPEMENTS L & L, LES   p 1244
See EQUIPEMENTS LAPLANTE & LEVESQUE LTEE, LES

EQUIPEMENTS LAGUE & MARTIN INC p 1392
555 BOUL LIONEL-BOULET, VARENNES, QC, J3X 1P7
(450) 929-2382   SIC 5083

EQUIPEMENTS LAPIERRE INC, LES p 1347
99 RUE DE L'ESCALE, SAINT-LUDGER, QC, G0M 1W0
(819) 548-5454   SIC 3569

EQUIPEMENTS LAPLANTE & LEVESQUE LTEE, LES   p 1244
780 RTE 201, ORMSTOWN, QC, J0S 1K0
(450) 829-3516   SIC 5084

EQUIPEMENTS MARQUIS INC   p 1375
1155 CH SAINT-ROCH N, SHERBROOKE, QC, J1N 0H2
(819) 822-3382   SIC 5051

EQUIPEMENTS NORDIQUES   p 1367
See 3887952 CANADA INC

EQUIPEMENTS PIERRE CHAMPIGNY LTEE   p 1044
280 RUE BONIN RR 4, ACTON VALE, QC, J0H 1A0
(450) 546-0999   SIC 5599

EQUIPEMENTS PLANNORD LTEE   p 1293
70 RUE D'ANVERS, SAINT-AUGUSTIN-DE-DESMAURES, QC, G3A 1S4
(418) 878-4007   SIC 5084

EQUIPEMENTS POWER SURVEY INTER-NATIONAL, LES   p 1339
See EQUIPEMENTS POWER SURVEY LTEE, LES

EQUIPEMENTS POWER SURVEY LTEE, LES   p 1339
7880 RTE TRANSCANADIENNE, SAINT-LAURENT, QC, H4T 1A5
(514) 333-8392   SIC 3625

EQUIPEMENTS QUE-MONT INC, LES   p 1061
3685 AV DES GRANDES TOURELLES, BOISBRIAND, QC, J7H 0E2
(514) 331-0302   SIC 5014

EQUIPEMENTS RAPCO INC, LES   p 1333
5510 RUE VANDEN-ABEELE, SAINT-LAURENT, QC, H4S 1P9
(514) 332-6562   SIC 5072

EQUIPEMENTS SIMEX   p 1252
See SIMEX DEFENCE INC

EQUIPEMENTS SOTER   p 1236
See CONSTRUCTION SOTER INC

EQUIPEMENTS SPM INC   p 1149
1290 AV DE LA GARE, MASCOUCHE, QC, J7K 2Z2
(450) 966-6616   SIC 1771

EQUIPEMENTS TENCO INC   p 1377
See TENCO INC

EQUIPEMENTS TWIN INC   p 1048
10401 BOUL PARKWAY, ANJOU, QC, H1J 1R4
(514) 353-1190   SIC 5013

EQUIPEMENTS VILLENEUVE INC   p 1077
1178 BOUL SAINTE-GENEVIEVE, CHICOUTIMI, QC, G7G 2G6
(418) 543-3600   SIC 5599

EQUIPMENT CORPS INC   p 892
1256 ARVIN AVE, STONEY CREEK, ON, L8E 0H7
(905) 545-1234   SIC 5082

EQUIPMENT D'EMBALLAGE M.M.C. LTEE p 1134
2030 BOUL DAGENAIS O, LAVAL-OUEST, QC, H7L 5W2
(450) 625-4662   SIC 5084

EQUIPMENT EXPRESS INC   p 483
60 WANLESS CRT, AYR, ON, N0B 1E0
(519) 740-8008   SIC 4213

EQUIPMENT FINANCE DEPARTMENT   p 274
See COAST CAPITAL SAVINGS FEDERAL CREDIT UNION

EQUIPMENT LAURENTIEN   p 1124
See SERVICES FORESTIERS DE MONT-LAURIER LTEE

EQUIPMENT LEASING COMPANY LTD, THE   p 480
106 BROOKEVIEW DR, AURORA, ON, L4G 6R5
(905) 629-3210   SIC 5085

EQUIPMENT SALES & SERVICE LIMITED p 584
1030 MARTIN GROVE RD, ETOBICOKE, ON, M9W 4W3
(416) 249-8141   SIC 5082

EQUIPMENT WORLD INC   p 908
988 ALLOY DR, THUNDER BAY, ON, P7B 6A5
(807) 623-9561   SIC 5084

EQUIPMENTS INDUSTRIELS I.B.S. VAL

D'OR INC, LES *p 1390*
85 RUE DES DISTRIBUTEURS, VAL-D'OR, QC, J9P 6Y1
(819) 825-3179   *SIC 5085*

EQUIREX LEASING CORP *p 802*
700 DORVAL DR UNIT 302, OAKVILLE, ON, L6K 3V3
(905) 844-4424   *SIC 6159*

EQUISOFT INC *p 1204*
1250 BOUL RENE-LEVESQUE O 33E ETAGE, MONTREAL, QC, H3B 4W8
(514) 989-3141   *SIC 7379*

EQUITABLE BANK *p 926*
30 ST CLAIR AVE W SUITE 700, TORONTO, ON, M4V 3A1
(416) 515-7000   *SIC 6021*

EQUITABLE GROUP INC *p 926*
30 ST CLAIR AVE W SUITE 700, TORONTO, ON, M4V 3A1
(416) 515-7000   *SIC 6163*

EQUITABLE LIFE INSURANCE COMPANY OF CANADA, THE *p 1006*
1 WESTMOUNT RD N, WATERLOO, ON, N2J 4C7
(519) 886-5210   *SIC 6311*

EQUITY FINANCIAL TRUST COMPANY *p 951*
200 UNIVERSITY AVE SUITE 400, TORONTO, ON, M5H 3C6
(416) 504-5050   *SIC 6289*

EQUS *p 137*
See EQUS REA LTD

EQUS REA LTD *p 137*
5803 42 ST, INNISFAIL, AB, T4G 1S8
(403) 227-4011   *SIC 4911*

ERA BANNER NEWSPAPER, THE *p 481*
See METROLAND MEDIA GROUP LTD

ERB AND ERB INSURANCE BROKERS LTD *p 635*
818 VICTORIA ST N, KITCHENER, ON, N2B 3C1
(519) 579-4270   *SIC 6331*

ERB ENTERPRISES INC *p 752*
290 HAMILTON RD, NEW HAMBURG, ON, N3A 1A2
(519) 662-2710   *SIC 6712*

ERB GROUP OF COMPANIES, THE *p 752*
290 HAMILTON RD, NEW HAMBURG, ON, N3A 1A2
(519) 662-2710   *SIC 4213*

ERB INTERNATIONAL INC *p 752*
290 HAMILTON RD, NEW HAMBURG, ON, N3A 1A2
(519) 662-2710   *SIC 7389*

ERB TRANSPORT INC *p 1394*
3001 RUE HENRY-FORD, VAUDREUIL-DORION, QC, J7V 8K2
(450) 510-2538   *SIC 4213*

ERB TRANSPORT LIMITED *p 694*
1889 BRITANNIA RD E, MISSISSAUGA, ON, L4W 1S6
(905) 670-8490   *SIC 4213*

ERB TRANSPORT LIMITED *p 752*
290 HAMILTON RD, NEW HAMBURG, ON, N3A 1A2
(519) 662-2710   *SIC 4212*

ERB TRANSPORT LIMITED *p 998*
4 RIVERSIDE DR, TRENTON, ON, K8V 5P8
(613) 965-6633   *SIC 4212*

ERCO MONDIAL *p 1102*
See SUPERIOR PLUS LP

ERCO WORLDWIDE *p 578*
See SUPERIOR PLUS LP

ERCO WORLDWIDE *p 1430*
See SUPERIOR PLUS LP

ERDENE RESOURCE DEVELOPMENT CORPORATION *p 444*
99 WYSE RD SUITE 1480, DARTMOUTH, NS, B3A 4S5
(902) 423-6419   *SIC 1081*

ERFA CANADA 2012 INC *p 1227*
8250 BOUL DECARIE BUREAU 110, MONTREAL, QC, H4P 2P5
(514) 931-3133   *SIC 5122*

ERGOCENTRIC INC *p 739*
275 SUPERIOR BLVD UNIT 2, MISSISSAUGA, ON, L5T 2L6
(905) 696-6800   *SIC 2522*

ERGOCENTRIC SEATING SYSTEMS *p 739*
See ERGOCENTRIC INC

ERGORECHERCHE LTEE *p 1237*
2101 BOUL LE CARREFOUR BUREAU 200, MONTREAL, QC, H7S 2J7
(450) 973-6700   *SIC 3842*

ERIC AUGER & SONS CONTRACTING LTD *p 171*
61 MAXIM RD, WABASCA, AB, T0G 2K0
(780) 891-3751   *SIC 1611*

ERIC HAMBER SECONDARY SCHOOL *p 292*
See BOARD OF EDUCATION OF SCHOOL DISTRICT NO. 39 (VANCOUVER), THE

ERICKSEN M-B LTD *p 124*
2120 103A ST SW, EDMONTON, AB, T6W 2P6
(780) 431-5100   *SIC 5511*

ERICKSON CONSTRUCTION (1975) LTD *p 355*
GD, RIVERTON, MB, R0C 2R0
SIC 1611

ERICKSON, DARYL HOLDINGS INC *p 1250*
263 AV LABROSSE, POINTE-CLAIRE, QC, H9R 1A3
(514) 630-7484   *SIC 6712*

ERICSSON *p 623*
See BELAIR NETWORKS INC

ERICSSON CANADA INC *p 694*
5255 SATELLITE DR, MISSISSAUGA, ON, L4W 5E3
(905) 629-6700   *SIC 4899*

ERICSSON CANADA INC *p 1156*
8400 BOUL DECARIE, MONT-ROYAL, QC, H4P 2N2
(514) 345-7900   *SIC 5065*

ERICSSON CANADA INC *p 1333*
8275 RTE TRANSCANADIENNE, SAINT-LAURENT, QC, H4S 0B6
(514) 738-8300   *SIC 5065*

ERIE & MAIN CONSULTING INC *p 543*
62 KEIL DR S, CHATHAM, ON, N7M 3G8
(519) 351-2024   *SIC 6712*

ERIE ARCHITECTURAL PRODUCTS INC *p 1017*
477 JUTRAS DR S, WINDSOR, ON, N8N 5C4
(519) 727-0372   *SIC 3442*

ERIE BEACH HOTEL LIMITED *p 847*
19 WALKER ST, PORT DOVER, ON, N0A 1N0
(519) 583-1391   *SIC 7011*

ERIE FLOORING & WOOD PRODUCTS LIMITED *p 1013*
1191 JANE ST, WEST LORNE, ON, N0L 2P0
(519) 768-1200   *SIC 2426*

ERIE GREENHOUSE STRUCTURES INC *p 911*
500 HWY 3 UNIT 2, TILLSONBURG, ON, N4G 4G8
(519) 688-6809   *SIC 1542*

ERIE MEAT PRODUCTS LIMITED *p 646*
1400 MITCHELL RD S, LISTOWEL, ON, N4W 3G7
(519) 291-6593   *SIC 2011*

ERIE MEAT PRODUCTS LIMITED *p 702*
3240 WHARTON WAY, MISSISSAUGA, ON, L4X 2C1
(905) 624-3811   *SIC 2011*

ERIE SHORES HEALTHCARE *p 644*
See LEAMINGTON DISTRICT MEMORIAL HOSPITAL

ERIE ST. CLAIR COMMUNITY CARE ACCESS CENTRE *p 543*
712 RICHMOND ST, CHATHAM, ON, N7M 5J5
(519) 436-2222   *SIC 8742*

ERIE STRUCTURES *p 911*

See ERIE GREENHOUSE STRUCTURES INC

ERIE-JAMES LIMITED *p 644*
102 QUEENS AVE, LEAMINGTON, ON, N8H 3H4
(519) 326-4417   *SIC 5148*

ERIEVIEW ACRES INC *p 633*
1930 SEACLIFF DR, KINGSVILLE, ON, N9Y 2N1
(519) 326-3013   *SIC 5159*

ERIKS INDUSTRIAL SERVICES LP *p 125*
9748 12 AVE SW, EDMONTON, AB, T6X 0J5
(780) 437-1260   *SIC 5085*

ERIN DODGE CHRYSLER LTD *p 716*
2365 MOTORWAY BLVD, MISSISSAUGA, ON, L5L 2M4
(905) 828-2004   *SIC 5511*

ERIN MILLS ACURA *p 716*
See ERIN MILLS IMPORT INC

ERIN MILLS IMPORT INC *p 716*
3025 WOODCHESTER DR, MISSISSAUGA, ON, L5L 3V3
(905) 828-5800   *SIC 5511*

ERIN MILLS LODGE *p 715*
See SIFTON PROPERTIES LIMITED

ERIN MILLS MAZDA (1994) *p 715*
See 1083153 ONTARIO LTD

ERIN MILLS MITSUBISHI *p 716*
See 2177761 ONTARIO INC

ERIN MILLS MITSUBISHI *p 716*
See DDJLR ONTARIO LTD

ERIN PARK AUTOMOTIVE PARTNERSHIP *p 716*
2411 MOTORWAY BLVD, MISSISSAUGA, ON, L5L 3R2
(905) 828-7711   *SIC 5511*

ERIN PARK TOYOTA *p 716*
See ERIN PARK AUTOMOTIVE PARTNERSHIP

ERINDALE COLLEGE STUDENT UNION *p 716*
3359 MISSISSAUGA RD, MISSISSAUGA, ON, L5L 1C6
(905) 828-5249   *SIC 8651*

ERINDALE SECONDARY SCHOOL *p 715*
See PEEL DISTRICT SCHOOL BOARD

ERINMOTORWAY INVESTMENTS LIMITED *p 716*
2380 MOTORWAY BLVD, MISSISSAUGA, ON, L5L 1X3
(905) 828-1650   *SIC 5511*

ERINOAK *p 716*
See ERINOAKKIDS CENTRE FOR TREATMENT AND DEVELOPMENT

ERINOAK KIDS CENTRE FOR TREATMENT *p 715*
2655 NORTH SHERIDAN WAY SUITE N, MISSISSAUGA, ON, L5K 2P8
(905) 855-2690   *SIC 8699*

ERINOAKKIDS CENTRE FOR TREATMENT AND DEVELOPMENT *p 716*
2277 SOUTH MILLWAY, MISSISSAUGA, ON, L5L 2M5
(905) 855-2690   *SIC 8093*

ERINWOOD FORD SALES LIMITED *p 716*
2395 MOTORWAY BLVD, MISSISSAUGA, ON, L5L 1V4
(905) 828-1600   *SIC 5511*

ERIS INFORMATION *p 776*
See ERIS INFORMATION LIMITED PARTNERSHIP

ERIS INFORMATION LIMITED PARTNERSHIP *p 776*
38 LESMILL RD SUITE 2, NORTH YORK, ON, M3B 2T5
(416) 510-5204   *SIC 7375*

ERMINESKIN JUNIOR SENIOR HIGH COMMUNITY SCHOOL *p 136*
See MIYO WAHKOHTOWIN COMMUNITY EDUCATION AUTHORITY

ERNEWEIN, JOHN LIMITED *p 1004*
18 INDUSTRIAL RD, WALKERTON, ON, N0G 2V0
(519) 881-0187   *SIC 5039*

ERNIE DEAN CHEVROLET BUICK GMC LTD *p 476*
4906 CONCESSION RD 7, ALLISTON, ON, L9R 1V3
(705) 435-4318   *SIC 5511*

ERNIE'S FITNESS EXPERTS *p 131*
11500 100 ST SUITE 1, GRANDE PRAIRIE, AB, T8V 4C2
(780) 539-9505   *SIC 5941*

ERNIE'S SPORT CENTRE (1983) LTD *p 131*
11500 100 ST UNIT 1, GRANDE PRAIRIE, AB, T8V 4C2
(780) 539-6262   *SIC 5941*

ERNIE'S SPORTS (S3) INC *p 131*
11500 100 ST UNIT 1, GRANDE PRAIRIE, AB, T8V 4C2
(780) 539-6262   *SIC 5941*

ERNIE'S SPORTS EXPERT *p 131*
See ERNIE'S SPORT CENTRE (1983) LTD

ERNST & YOUNG INC *p 377*
360 MAIN ST SUITE 2700, WINNIPEG, MB, R3C 4G9
(204) 947-6519   *SIC 8721*

ERNST & YOUNG INC *p 453*
1871 HOLLIS ST UNIT 500, HALIFAX, NS, B3J 0C3
(902) 420-1080   *SIC 8721*

ERNST & YOUNG INC *p 640*
515 RIVERBEND DR, KITCHENER, ON, N2K 3S3
(519) 744-1171   *SIC 8721*

ERNST & YOUNG INC *p 653*
255 QUEENS AVE SUITE 1800, LONDON, ON, N6A 5R8
(519) 672-6100   *SIC 8721*

ERNST & YOUNG INC *p 969*
222 BAY ST, TORONTO, ON, M5K 1J7
(416) 864-1234   *SIC 6733*

ERNST & YOUNG INC *p 1195*
900 BOUL DE MAISONNEUVE O, MONTREAL, QC, H3A 0A8
(514) 875-6060   *SIC 8721*

ERNST & YOUNG LLP *p 49*
215 2 ST SW SUITE 2200, CALGARY, AB, T2P 1M4
(403) 290-4100   *SIC 8721*

ERNST & YOUNG LLP *p 330*
700 GEORGIA ST W SUITE 2200, VANCOUVER, BC, V7Y 1K8
(604) 891-8200   *SIC 8721*

ERNST & YOUNG LLP *p 653*
1800-255 QUEENS AVE, LONDON, ON, N6A 5S8
(519) 744-1171   *SIC 8721*

ERNST & YOUNG LLP *p 823*
99 BANK ST SUITE 1600, OTTAWA, ON, K1P 6B9
(613) 232-1511   *SIC 8721*

ERNST & YOUNG LLP *p 904*
175 COMMERCE VALLEY DR W SUITE 600, THORNHILL, ON, L3T 7P6
SIC 8721

ERNST & YOUNG LLP *p 951*
100 ADELAIDE ST W SUITE 3100, TORONTO, ON, M5H 0B3
(416) 864-1234   *SIC 8721*

ERNST & YOUNG LLP *p 969*
222 BAY ST 16TH FLR, TORONTO, ON, M5K 1J7
(416) 943-2040   *SIC 8721*

ERNST & YOUNG LLP *p 1204*
1 PLACE VILLE-MARIE BUREAU 1900, MONTREAL, QC, H3B 1X9
(514) 875-6060   *SIC 8721*

ERNST & YOUNG LLP *p 1269*
90 RUE DE MAISONNEUVE, QUEBEC, QC, G1R 2C3
(514) 875-6060   *SIC 8721*

ERNST & YOUNG LLP *p 1272*
2875 BOUL LAURIER UNITE 410, QUE-

BEC, QC, G1V 0C7
(418) 524-5151   *SIC* 8721
ERNST HANSCH CONSTRUCTION LTD *p*
365
3 TERRACON PL, WINNIPEG, MB, R2J
4B3
(204) 233-7881   *SIC* 1542
ERO COPPER CORP   *p* 304
625 HOWE ST SUITE 1050, VANCOUVER,
BC, V6C 2T6
(604) 449-9244   *SIC* 1021
EROSIONCONTROLBLANKET.COM INC *p*
355
1 BROADWAY AVE, RIVERTON, MB, R0C
2R0
(204) 378-5610   *SIC* 5039
ERPI   *p* 1176
See EDITIONS DU RENOUVEAU PEDA-
GOGIQUE INC
ERRION GROUP INC   *p* 593
42 ARMSTRONG AVE, GEORGETOWN,
ON, L7G 4R9
(905) 877-7300   *SIC* 2426
ERSKINE GREEN LIMITED   *p* 776
1 VALLEYBROOK DR SUITE 201, NORTH
YORK, ON, M3B 2S7
(416) 487-3883   *SIC* 6519
ERSSER, A. J. HOLDINGS LTD   *p* 835
1605 16TH ST E, OWEN SOUND, ON, N4K
5N3
(519) 376-5220   *SIC* 5531
ERTH (HOLDINGS) INC   *p* 621
180 WHITING ST, INGERSOLL, ON, N5C
3B5
(519) 485-6038   *SIC* 7629
ESAB GROUP CANADA INC   *p* 731
6200 CANTAY RD UNIT 20, MISSISSAUGA,
ON, L5R 3Y9
(905) 670-0220   *SIC* 5084
ESAB WELDING & CUTTING PRODUCTS*p*
731
See ESAB GROUP CANADA INC
ESAM CONSTRUCTION LIMITED   *p* 658
301 OXFORD ST W, LONDON, ON, N6H
1S6
(519) 433-7291   *SIC* 6513
ESAM GROUP   *p* 658
See ESAM CONSTRUCTION LIMITED
ESBE SCIENTIFIC INDUSTRIES INC *p* 670
80 MCPHERSON ST, MARKHAM, ON, L3R
3V6
(905) 475-8232   *SIC* 5049
ESC AUTOMATION INC   *p* 271
5265 185A ST SUITE 100, SURREY, BC,
V3S 7A4
(604) 574-7790   *SIC* 5084
ESC CORPORATE SERVICES LTD   *p* 980
445 KING ST W SUITE 400, TORONTO,
ON, M5V 1K4
(416) 595-7177   *SIC* 6541
ESCALIERS GRENIER, GILLES INC *p* 1299
586 AV TEXEL, SAINT-ELZEAR, QC, G0S
2J2
(418) 387-6317   *SIC* 2431
ESCAPE FIRE PROTECTION LTD   *p* 176
30465 PROGRESSIVE WAY UNIT 8, AB-
BOTSFORD, BC, V2T 6W3
(604) 864-0376   *SIC* 7389
ESCAPE PROOF INC   *p* 800
1496 DURHAM ST, OAKVILLE, ON, L6J
2P3
(289) 837-0813   *SIC* 7549
ESCAPE PROOF QUALITY INSPECTION
SERVICES   *p* 800
See ESCAPE PROOF INC
ESCAPES RICARDO   *p* 1323
See RICARDO MEDIA INC
ESCAPES.CA   *p* 292
See SKYLAND TRAVEL INC
ESCARBILLE, L'   *p* 1386
See COLLEGE LAFLECHE
ESCENTS AROMA THERAPY   *p* 200
See ESCENTS BODY PRODUCTS INC
ESCENTS BODY PRODUCTS INC   *p* 200

18 FAWCETT RD, COQUITLAM, BC, V3K
6X9
(604) 298-9298   *SIC* 2841
ESCO LIMITED   *p* 246
1855 KINGSWAY AVE, PORT COQUITLAM,
BC, V3C 1T1
(604) 942-7261   *SIC* 3325
ESCO LIMITED   *p* 434
21 SECOND AVE, WABUSH, NL, A0R 1B0
(709) 282-3660   *SIC* 3325
ESCO LIMITED   *p* 847
185 HOPE ST S, PORT HOPE, ON, L1A
4C2
(905) 885-6301   *SIC* 3325
ESCOMPTE CHEZ LAFORTUNE INC   *p*
1071
5635 GRANDE-ALLEE BUREAU 100,
BROSSARD, QC, J4Z 3G3
(450) 462-2120   *SIC* 5912
ESCOMPTES C.F.M. INC   *p* 1358
800 MONTEE SAINTE-JULIE BUREAU 100,
SAINTE-JULIE, QC, J3E 2C4
(450) 922-6000   *SIC* 5912
ESCOMPTES FERNAND LACHANCE INC.*p*
1317
947 BOUL DU SEMINAIRE N, SAINT-JEAN-
SUR-RICHELIEU, QC, J3A 1K1
(450) 348-9251   *SIC* 5912
ESCOPHAR INC   *p* 1308
5245 BOUL COUSINEAU BUREAU 149,
SAINT-HUBERT, QC, J3Y 6J8
(450) 462-2200   *SIC* 5912
ESENTIRE, INC   *p* 536
278 PINEBUSH RD SUITE 101, CAM-
BRIDGE, ON, N1T 1Z6
(519) 651-2200   *SIC* 7372
ESG SOLUTIONS   *p* 630
See   ENGINEERING   SEISMOLOGY
GROUP CANADA INC
ESHIPPER   *p* 501
See CANADA WORLDWIDE SERVICES
INC
ESI ENERGY SERVICES INC   *p* 49
727 7 AVE SW SUITE 500, CALGARY, AB,
T2P 0Z5
(403) 262-9344   *SIC* 4911
ESI TECHNOLOGIES DE L'INFORMATION
INC   *p* 1195
1550 RUE METCALFE BUREAU 1100,
MONTREAL, QC, H3A 1X6
(514) 745-3311   *SIC* 7379
ESIGNLIVE   *p* 1228
See ONESPAN CANADA INC
ESIM   SOLUTIONS DE CHAUFFAGE
ECOLOGIQUES   *p* 1362
See ESYS ENERGIE SYSTEME INC
ESIT ADVANCED SOLUTIONS INC *p* 338
4464 MARKHAM ST SUITE 2200, VICTO-
RIA, BC, V8Z 7X8
(250) 405-4500   *SIC* 8748
ESIT CANADA ENTERPRISE SERVICES
CO   *p* 49
See ESIT CANADA ENTERPRISE SER-
VICES CO
ESIT CANADA ENTERPRISE SERVICES
CO   *p* 49
240 4 AVE SW SUITE 500, CALGARY, AB,
T2P 4H4
(403) 508-4500   *SIC* 7379
ESIT CANADA ENTERPRISE SERVICES
CO   *p* 453
1969 UPPER WATER ST, HALIFAX, NS,
B3J 3R7
(902) 000-0000   *SIC* 5734
ESIT CANADA ENTERPRISE SERVICES
CO   *p* 624
100 HERZBERG RD, KANATA, ON, K2K
3B7
(613) 592-5111   *SIC* 5045
ESIT CANADA ENTERPRISE SERVICES
CO   *p* 823
50 O'CONNOR ST SUITE 500, OTTAWA,
ON, K1P 6L2
(613) 266-9442   *SIC* 7376

ESKA INC   *p* 938
25 ADELAIDE ST E SUITE 1000,
TORONTO, ON, M5C 3A1
(416) 504-2222   *SIC* 3221
ESKA WATER   *p* 938
See ESKA INC
ESKASONI ELEMENTARY & MIDDLE
SCHOOL   *p* 450
See ESKASONI SCHOOL BOARD
ESKASONI SCHOOL BOARD   *p* 450
4645 SHORE RD, ESKASONI, NS, B1W
1K3
(902) 379-2507   *SIC* 8211
ESKASONI SCHOOL BOARD   *p* 450
4645 SHORE RD, ESKASONI, NS, B1W
1K3
(902) 379-2825   *SIC* 8211
ESKIMO EXPRESS INC   *p* 1277
5055 RUE RIDEAU BUREAU 500, QUE-
BEC, QC, G2E 5H5
(418) 681-1212   *SIC* 4213
ESKIMO   POINT   LUMBER   SUP-
PLY/AIRPORT SERVICES LTD   *p*
472
GD, ARVIAT, NU, X0C 0E0
(867) 857-2752   *SIC* 5411
ESKIMO REFRIGERATION LTD   *p* 15
4705 61 AVE SE, CALGARY, AB, T2C 4W1
(403) 279-8091   *SIC* 5078
ESKIMO STEEL LTD   *p* 162
526 STREAMBANK AVE, SHERWOOD
PARK, AB, T8H 1N1
(780) 417-9200   *SIC* 3441
ESM   *p* 1019
See ELLWOOD SPECIALTY METALS COM-
PANY
ESPACE HOUBLON EPICERIE FINE*p* 1300
See ESPACE HOUBLON INC
ESPACE HOUBLON INC   *p* 1300
180 25E AV, SAINT-EUSTACHE, QC, J7P
2V2
(450) 983-7122   *SIC* 5141
ESPACE SANTE   *p* 1216
See TRIUM MOBILIER DE BUREAU INC
ESPACE SANTE BEAUTE JOHANNE VER-
DON   *p*
1181
See GROUPE JOHANNE VERDON INC
ESPANOLA GENERAL HOSPITAL   *p* 569
825 MCKINNON DR SUITE 705, ES-
PANOLA, ON, P5E 1R4
(705) 869-1420   *SIC* 8062
ESPANOLA HOME HARDWARE   *p* 569
See MCKECHNIE, ANDY BUILDING MATE-
RIALS LTD
ESPANOLA REGIONAL HYDRO   *p* 569
598 SECOND AVE, ESPANOLA, ON, P5E
1C4
(705) 869-2771   *SIC* 4911
ESPIAL GROUP INC   *p* 834
200 ELGIN ST SUITE 1000, OTTAWA, ON,
K2P 1L5
(613) 230-4770   *SIC* 7371
ESPLANADE   (TORONTO)   SPAGHETTI
CORP   *p* 942
54 THE ESPLANADE, TORONTO, ON, M5E
1A6
(416) 864-9761   *SIC* 5812
ESPO BROTHERS MANAGEMENT I LTD *p*
174
33780 KING RD, ABBOTSFORD, BC, V2S
7P2
(604) 859-2220   *SIC* 7361
ESPUMA   *p* 1300
See LOUKIL, SAID
ESQUIMALT HIGH SCHOOL   *p* 339
See BOARD OF EDUCATION OF SCHOOL
DISTRICT NO. 61 (GREATER VICTORIA)
ESQUIMALT MFRC   *p* 339
See CFB ESQUIMALT MILITARY FAMILY
RESOURCE CENTRE
ESQUIRE PROMOTIONS, DIV OF   *p* 548
See ARTCRAFT COMPANY INC
ESRI CANADA LIMITED   *p* 779

12 CONCORDE PL SUITE 900, NORTH
YORK, ON, M3C 3R8
(416) 441-6035   *SIC* 7372
ESSAG CANADA INC   *p* 502
30 PEEL CENTRE DR, BRAMPTON, ON,
L6T 4G3
SIC 7011
ESSAR STEEL ALGOMA INC   *p* 862
See OLD STEELCO INC
ESSENCES & FRAGRANCES BELL *p* 1069
See BELL FLAVORS & FRAGRANCES
(CANADA) CO
ESSENCES ET FRAGRANCES BELL
CANADA INC   *p* 1070
3800 RUE ISABELLE, BROSSARD, QC,
J4Y 2R3
(450) 444-3819   *SIC* 5149
ESSENDANT CANADA, INC   *p* 739
6400 ORDAN DR, MISSISSAUGA, ON, L5T
2H6
(905) 670-1223   *SIC* 5099
ESSENTIAL ENERGY SERVICES LTD *p* 49
250 2 ST SW UNIT 1100, CALGARY, AB,
T2P 0C1
(403) 263-6778   *SIC* 1389
ESSENTIAL WELL SERVICE   *p* 49
See ESSENTIAL ENERGY SERVICES LTD
ESSENTIELS DE VIE WANT, LES   *p* 1180
See AGENCES WANT INC, LES
ESSEX ALUMINUM PLANT   *p* 1018
See FORD MOTOR COMPANY OF
CANADA, LIMITED
ESSEX ALUMINUM PLANT   *p* 1025
See NEMAK OF CANADA CORPORATION
ESSEX COUNTY ASSOCIATION FOR COM-
MUNITY LIVING   *p*
1017
See   COMMUNITY   LIVING   ESSEX
COUNTY
ESSEX GROUP CANADA INC   *p* 880
20 GILBERTSON DR SUITE 20, SIMCOE,
ON, N3Y 4L5
(519) 428-3900   *SIC* 3351
ESSEX HOME HARDWARE   *p* 570
See FYNBO, IB HARDWARE LTD
ESSEX POWER CORPORATION   *p* 570
360 FAIRVIEW AVE W SUITE 218, ESSEX,
ON, N8M 3G4
(519) 946-2002   *SIC* 4911
ESSEX POWER CORPORATION   *p* 807
2199 BLACKACRE DR SUITE 2, OLDCAS-
TLE, ON, N0R 1L0
(519) 946-2002   *SIC* 4911
ESSEX POWERLINES CORPORATION   *p*
570
360 FAIRVIEW AVE W SUITE 218, ESSEX,
ON, N8M 3G4
SIC 4911
ESSEX   TERMINAL   RAILWAY COMPANY,
THE   *p* 1022
1601 LINCOLN RD, WINDSOR, ON, N8Y
2J3
(519) 973-8222   *SIC* 4013
ESSEX TOPCROP SALES LIMITED   *p* 570
904 COUNTY RD 8, ESSEX, ON, N8M 2Y1
(519) 776-6411   *SIC* 2048
ESSEX WELD SOLUTIONS   *p* 570
See EWS INC
ESSEX WELD SOLUTIONS LTD   *p* 570
340 ALLEN AVE, ESSEX, ON, N8M 3G6
(519) 776-9153   *SIC* 3499
ESSEX   WINDSOR   SOLID   WASTE AU-
THORITY   *p*
570
360 FAIRVIEW AVE W SUITE 211, ESSEX,
ON, N8M 3G4
(519) 776-6441   *SIC* 4953
ESSILOR   *p* 574
See ESSILOR GROUPE CANADA INC
ESSILOR GROUPE CANADA INC   *p* 187
7541 CONWAY AVE SUITE 5, BURNABY,
BC, V5E 2P7
(604) 437-5300   *SIC* 3851
ESSILOR GROUPE CANADA INC   *p* 187

7541 CONWAY AVE SUITE 5, BURNABY, BC, V5E 2P7
(604) 437-5333   SIC 5049
ESSILOR GROUPE CANADA INC   p 574
347 EVANS AVE, ETOBICOKE, ON, M8Z 1K2
(416) 252-5458   SIC 5049
ESSILOR GROUPE CANADA INC   p 1325
371 RUE DESLAURIERS, SAINT-LAURENT, QC, H4N 1W2
(514) 337-2211   SIC 5049
ESSILOR NETWORK IN CANADA INC   p 187
See ESSILOR GROUPE CANADA INC
ESSITY CANADA INC   p 805
1275 NORTH SERVICE RD W SUITE 800, OAKVILLE, ON, L6M 3G4
(905) 339-3539   SIC 5047
ESSITY CANADA INC   p 1098
999 RUE FARRELL, DRUMMONDVILLE, QC, J2C 5P6
(819) 475-4500   SIC 5047
ESSLINGER FOODS LTD   p 522
5035 NORTH SERVICE RD, BURLINGTON, ON, L7L 5V2
(905) 332-3777   SIC 5141
ESSO   p 1134
See HALTE DU BOIS INC
ESSO (IMPERIAL OIL)   p 264
See ESSO AVITAT INTERDEL AVIATION SERVICES INC
ESSO - COOL CREEK   p 218
See COOL CREEK ENERGY LTD
ESSO AGENT   p 1011
See DONALD L. DAVIDSON FUELS LTD
ESSO AVITAT INTERDEL AVIATION SERVICES INC   p 264
5360 AIRPORT RD S, RICHMOND, BC, V7B 1B4
(604) 270-2222   SIC 5172
ESSO BULK AGENT   p 150
See MILLER SUPPLY LTD.
ESSO BULK AGENT   p 251
See YOUNG, GARY AGENCIES LTD
ESSO BULK AGENT   p 435
See ARCTIC DOVE LIMITED
ESSO SERVICE STATION   p 5
THE TRANSCANADA HWY 1 SERVICE RD, BASSANO, AB, T0J 0B0
(403) 641-3916   SIC 5541
ESSOR ASSURANCES   p 1204
See ESSOR ASSURANCES PLACEMENTS CONSEILS INC
ESSOR ASSURANCES PLACEMENTS CONSEILS INC   p 1204
1100 BOUL ROBERT-BOURASSA, MONTREAL, QC, H3B 3A5
(514) 878-9373   SIC 6411
ESSOR ASSURANCES PLACEMENTS CONSEILS INC   p 1279
5600 BOUL DES GALERIES BUREAU 600, QUEBEC, QC, G2K 2H6
(418) 692-0660   SIC 6411
ESTAMPRO INC   p 1302
104 RUE DU PARC-INDUSTRIEL, SAINT-EVARISTE-DE-FORSYTH, QC, G0M 1S0
(418) 459-3423   SIC 3599
ESTATE MORGAGE CENTER   p 406
See ESTATE MORTGAGE INC
ESTATE MORTGAGE INC   p 406
19 KATHERINE AVE, MONCTON, NB, E1C 7M7
(506) 855-5626   SIC 6211
ESTATE REALTY LTD   p 917
1052 KINGSTON RD, TORONTO, ON, M4E 1T4
(416) 690-5100   SIC 6531
ESTATE SETTLER   p 630
See GORDON'S STATE SERVICES LTD., BROKERAGE
ESTEE LAUDER COSMETICS LTD   p 874
161 COMMANDER BLVD, SCARBOROUGH, ON, M1S 3K9

(416) 292-1111   SIC 2844
ESTEE LAUDER COSMETICS LTD   p 874
161 COMMANDER BLVD, SCARBOROUGH, ON, M1S 3K9
(416) 292-1111   SIC 5122
ESTHER'S INN LTD   p 250
1151 COMMERCIAL CRES, PRINCE GEORGE, BC, V2M 6W6
(250) 562-4131   SIC 7011
ESTIMATEURS PROFESSIONELS LEROUX, BEAUDRY, PICARD & ASSOCIES INC, LES   p 1176
255 BOUL CREMAZIE E BUREAU 9E, MONTREAL, QC, H2M 1L5
(514) 384-4220   SIC 6531
ESTIMATIONS DE CONSTRUCTION DU QUEBEC INC   p 1217
78 RUE DE PORT-ROYAL E, MONTREAL, QC, H3L 1H7
SIC 1542
ESTIMATIONS GUY JALBERT 1997 INC, LES   p 1373
4520 BOUL INDUSTRIEL, SHERBROOKE, QC, J1L 2S8
(819) 566-7222   SIC 6411
ESTON HEALTH CENTRE   p 1407
822 MAIN ST, ESTON, SK, S0L 1A0
(306) 962-3667   SIC 6324
ESTON MANUFACTURING   p 603
See LINAMAR CORPORATION
ESTON MANUFACTURING, DIV OF   p 603
See LINAMAR CORPORATION
ESTONIAN RELIEF COMMITTEE IN CANADA   p 866
40 OLD KINGSTON RD, SCARBOROUGH, ON, M1E 3J5
(416) 724-6144   SIC 8699
ESTPHARM   p 1102
See PHARMACIEN MARTIN GAGNON INC
ESTRIE AUTO CENTRE   p 1375
See 2527-9829 QUEBEC INC
ESTRIE TOYOTA   p 1111
See MONTESTRIE AUTORAMA INC
ESTRIE, DIV DE   p 1073
See SINTRA INC
ESTUARY COLONY FARM   p 1409
See HUTTERIAN BRETHREN OF ESTUARY CORP
ESWIT   p 134
See WILLIAMS, E. S. & ASSOCIATES INC
ESYS ENERGIE SYSTEME INC   p 1362
3404 BOUL INDUSTRIEL, SAINTE-ROSE, QC, H7L 4R9
(450) 641-1344   SIC 3567
ETALEX INC   p 1048
8501 RUE JARRY, ANJOU, QC, H1J 1H7
(514) 351-2000   SIC 2542
ETALONNAGE TECHNIQUE   p 1094
See MCCANN EQUIPMENT LTD
ETBO TOOL & DIE   p 482
7288 RICHMOND RD, AYLMER, ON, N5H 2R5
(519) 773-5117   SIC 3541
ETD BUILDING MAINTENANCE LTD   p 323
9001 SHAUGHNESSY ST, VANCOUVER, BC, V6P 6R9
(604) 327-2555   SIC 7349
ETELLIGENT SOLUTIONS INC   p 93
11820 121 ST NW, EDMONTON, AB, T5L 5H5
(780) 452-3033   SIC 5112
ETFO   p 931
See ELEMENTARY TEACHERS FEDERATION OF ONTARIO
ETFS   p 1374
See INVESTISSEMENTS ALT2 INC
ETG COMMODITIES INC   p 739
6220 SHAWSON DR, MISSISSAUGA, ON, L5T 1J8
(416) 900-4148   SIC 6799
ETHAN ALLEN (CANADA) INC   p 1027
205 TRADE VALLEY DR SUITE B, WOODBRIDGE, ON, L4H 3N6
(905) 264-7686   SIC 5712

ETHAN ALLEN HOME INTERIORS   p 1027
See ETHAN ALLEN (CANADA) INC
ETHEREAL NAIL & BEAUTY   p 280
1688 152 ST UNIT 107, SURREY, BC, V4A 4N2
(604) 531-6889   SIC 5051
ETHOCA TECHNOLOGIES INC   p 771
100 SHEPPARD AVE E SUITE 605, NORTH YORK, ON, M2N 6N5
(416) 849-6091   SIC 5065
ETHYL CANADA INC   p 522
5045 SOUTH SERVICE RD SUITE 101, BURLINGTON, ON, L7L 5Y7
(905) 631-5470   SIC 2819
ETIQUETTES CCL MONTREAL   p 914
See CCL INDUSTRIES INC
ETIQUETTES CCL MONTREAL   p 1295
See CCL INDUSTRIES INC
ETIQUETTES FLEXO   p 1050
See PRODUITS LABELINK INC, LES
ETIQUETTES PROFECTA INC   p 1309
5050 RUE ARMAND-FRAPPIER, SAINT-HUBERT, QC, J3Z 1G5
(450) 676-0000   SIC 2672
ETL LOGISTICS, DIV OF   p 442
See EASSONS TRANSPORT LIMITED
ETOBICOKE CAMERA CLUB   p 576
76 ANGLESEY BLVD, ETOBICOKE, ON, M9A 3C1
(416) 234-2014   SIC 8699
ETOBICOKE CASTING PLANT   p 995
See FCA CANADA INC
ETOBICOKE COLLEGIATE INSTITUTE   p 577
See TORONTO DISTRICT SCHOOL BOARD
ETOBICOKE GENERAL HOSPITAL   p 581
See WILLIAM OSLER HEALTH SYSTEM
ETOBICOKE HOSPITAL VOLUNTEER ASSOCIATION GIFT SHOP   p 580
101 HUMBER COLLEGE BLVD, ETOBICOKE, ON, M9V 1R8
(416) 747-3400   SIC 5947
ETOBICOKE HUMANE SOCIETY   p 574
67 SIX POINT RD, ETOBICOKE, ON, M8Z 2X3
(416) 249-6100   SIC 8699
ETOBICOKE IRONWORKS LIMITED   p 794
141 RIVALDA RD, NORTH YORK, ON, M9M 2M6
(416) 742-7111   SIC 3446
ETOBICOKE MEDICAL CENTRE FAMILY HEALTH TEAM   p 574
85 THE EAST MALL, ETOBICOKE, ON, M8Z 5W4
(416) 621-2220   SIC 8011
ETOBICOKE SCHOOL OF THE ARTS   p 573
See TORONTO DISTRICT SCHOOL BOARD
ETOILE DODGE CHRYSLER INC, L'   p 1116
3311 BOUL DU ROYAUME, JONQUIERE, QC, G7X 0C4
(418) 542-9518   SIC 5511
ETOILE, L'   p 1070
See CORPORATION DU THEATRE L'ETOILE
ETRATECH ENTERPRISES INC   p 531
1047 COOKE BLVD, BURLINGTON, ON, L7T 4A8
(905) 681-7544   SIC 3625
ETRO CONSTRUCTION LIMITED   p 185
4727 HASTINGS ST, BURNABY, BC, V5C 2K8
(604) 492-0920   SIC 1521
ETSM TECHNICAL SERVICES LTD   p 602
407 SILVERCREEK PKY N, GUELPH, ON, N1H 8G8
(519) 827-1500   SIC 3599
ETUIS BOBLEN CASES INC   p 1172
4455 RUE FRONTENAC, MONTREAL, QC, H2H 2S2
(514) 523-8163   SIC 3161
EUCLID'S HOLDINGS LTD   p 878

275 FINCHDENE SQ UNIT 1, SCARBOROUGH, ON, M1X 1B9
(416) 321-8002   SIC 5141
EUGENE ALLARD   p 1116
See EUGENE ALLARD PRODUITS D'EMBALLAGE ET D'ENTRETIEN INC
EUGENE ALLARD PRODUITS D'EMBALLAGE ET D'ENTRETIEN INC   p 1116
2244 RUE CHAPAIS, JONQUIERE, QC, G7X 4B4
(418) 547-6654   SIC 5113
EUGENE TEXTILES (2003) INC   p 1333
1391 RUE SAINT-AMOUR, SAINT-LAURENT, QC, H4S 1T4
(514) 382-2400   SIC 5131
EURAMAX CANADA, INC   p 486
26 LORENA ST, BARRIE, ON, L4N 4P4
(705) 728-7141   SIC 2821
EUREKA   p 1180
See GROUPE LUMINAIRES INC, LE
EUREKA LIGHTING   p 1179
See 4453760 CANADA INC
EUREST-TERASEN GAS-633   p 281
16705 FRASER HWY, SURREY, BC, V4N 0E7
SIC 4923
EURO CERAMIC TILE DISTRIBUTORS LTD   p 188
4288 MANOR ST, BURNABY, BC, V5G 1B2
(604) 437-3876   SIC 5032
EURO RSCG HEALTHCARE (CANADA) INC   p 980
473 ADELAIDE ST W SUITE 300, TORONTO, ON, M5V 1T1
(416) 925-9005   SIC 7311
EURO RSCG LIFE INTERACTION, DIV OF   p 980
See EURO RSCG HEALTHCARE (CANADA) INC
EURO SUN MINING INC   p 951
65 QUEEN ST W SUITE 800, TORONTO, ON, M5H 2M5
(416) 368-7744   SIC 1041
EURO TILE & STONE INC   p 817
3103 HAWTHORNE RD, OTTAWA, ON, K1G 3V8
(613) 244-4315   SIC 5032
EURO VERVE CO. LTD   p 670
951 DENISON ST UNIT 16, MARKHAM, ON, L3R 3W9
(905) 513-8283   SIC 5137
EURO-EXCELLENCE   p 1233
See CONFISERIES REGAL INC
EURO-PHARM INTERNATIONAL CANADA INC   p 1344
9400 BOUL LANGELIER, SAINT-LEONARD, QC, H1P 3H8
(514) 324-1073   SIC 5122
EURO-RITE CABINETS LTD   p 244
19100 AIRPORT WAY SUITE 212, PITT MEADOWS, BC, V3Y 0E2
(604) 464-5060   SIC 2541
EURO-TECH CONSTRUCTION INC   p 75
855 ARBOUR LAKE RD NW, CALGARY, AB, T3G 5J2
(403) 547-1277   SIC 1542
EUROCAN PULP & PAPER, DIV OF   p 252
See WEST FRASER MILLS LTD
EUROFASE INC   p 852
33 WEST BEAVER CREEK RD, RICHMOND HILL, ON, L4B 1L8
(905) 695-2055   SIC 5063
EUROFINS BIOPHARMA PRODUCT TESTING TORONTO, INC   p 783
1111 FLINT RD UNIT 36, NORTH YORK, ON, M3J 3C7
(416) 665-2134   SIC 8734
EUROFINS ENVIRONMENT TESTING CANADA, INC   p 783
1111 FLINT RD UNIT 36, NORTH YORK, ON, M3J 3C7
(416) 665-2134   SIC 8734

EUROFINS ENVIRONMENT TESTING CANADA, INC p 1295
1390 RUE HOCQUART, SAINT-BRUNO, QC, J3V 6E1
(450) 441-5880   SIC 8734

EUROFINS ESSAIS ENVIRONNEMENTAUX p 1295
See EUROFINS ENVIRONMENT TESTING CANADA, INC

EUROFRET CANADA INC p 1059
1140 BOUL MICHELE-BOHEC, BLAINVILLE, QC, J7C 5N5
(450) 430-1313   SIC 4731

EUROHOUSE CONSTRUCTION INC p 327
2474 MARINE DR W, VANCOUVER, BC, V7V 1L1
(604) 354-6325   SIC 1521

EUROLINE WINDOWS INC p 208
7620 MACDONALD RD, DELTA, BC, V4G 1N2
(604) 940-8485   SIC 3089

EUROLINE WINDOWS INC p 338
3352 TENNYSON AVE, VICTORIA, BC, V8Z 3P6
(250) 383-8465   SIC 5031

EUROMARCHE LATINA (1980) p 1224
See EPICERIE SALTARELLI ET FILS INC

EUROMAX RESOURCES LTD p 304
595 HOWE ST 10 FL, VANCOUVER, BC, V6C 2T5
(604) 669-5999   SIC 1081

EUROPEAN BOUTIQUE p 788
See 1170760 ONTARIO LTD

EUROPEAN CREATIONS LTD p 263
12240 HORSESHOE WAY UNIT 14, RICHMOND, BC, V7A 4X9
(604) 275-0440   SIC 5137

EUROPEAN FINE FOODS CO. INC p 694
1191 CRESTLAWN DR, MISSISSAUGA, ON, L4W 1A7
(905) 206-0964   SIC 5141

EUROPUMP SYSTEMS INC p 144
6204 44 ST, LLOYDMINSTER, AB, T9V 1V9
(780) 872-7084   SIC 1389

EUROSA FARMS LTD p 180
1304 GREIG AVE, BRENTWOOD BAY, BC, V8M 1J6
(250) 652-5812   SIC 0181

EUROSPEC p 756
See NORTH AMERICAN METALS OF CANADA LTD

EUROTRADE IMPORT-EXPORT INC p 694
5484 TIMBERLEA BLVD, MISSISSAUGA, ON, L4W 2T7
(905) 624-2064   SIC 5149

EUROVIA QC CONSTRUCTION p 1065
See EUROVIA QUEBEC CONSTRUCTION INC

EUROVIA QC GP p 1065
See EUROVIA QUEBEC GRANDS PROJETS INC

EUROVIA QUEBEC CONSTRUCTION INC p 1065
1550 RUE AMPERE BUREAU 200, BOUCHERVILLE, QC, J4B 7L4
(450) 641-8000   SIC 1611

EUROVIA QUEBEC CONSTRUCTION INC p 1224
6200 RUE SAINT-PATRICK, MONTREAL, QC, H4E 1B3
(514) 766-8256   SIC 1611

EUROVIA QUEBEC CONSTRUCTION INC p 1351
104 BOUL SAINT-REMI, SAINT-REMI, QC, J0L 2L0
(450) 454-0000   SIC 1611

EUROVIA QUEBEC GRANDS PROJETS INC p 1065
1550 RUE AMPERE BUREAU 200, BOUCHERVILLE, QC, J4B 7L4
(450) 641-8000   SIC 1611

EUTECTIC CANADA INC p 1394
428 RUE AIME-VINCENT, VAUDREUIL-DORION, QC, J7V 5V5

(514) 695-7500   SIC 5085

EV LOGISTICS p 229
5111 272 ST, LANGLEY, BC, V4W 3Z2
(604) 857-6750   SIC 4213

EV LOGISTICS p 229
5111 272 ST, LANGLEY, BC, V4W 3Z2
(604) 857-6750   SIC 4225

EV LOGISTICS PERISHABLES p 229
See EV LOGISTICS

EVA'S ORIGINAL CHIMNEY p 871
See ORIGINAL CHIMNEYS INC

EVAGELOU ENTERPRISES INC p 916
39 CRANFIELD RD, TORONTO, ON, M4B 3H6
(416) 285-4774   SIC 7299

EVALUATIONS BIGRAS INC, LES p 1061
1919 BOUL LIONEL-BERTRAND BUREAU 103, BOISBRIAND, QC, J7H 1N8
(450) 420-6555   SIC 6311

EVANGELICAL LUTHERAN CHURCH IN CANADA p 293
585 41ST AVE W, VANCOUVER, BC, V5Z 2M7
(604) 261-2442   SIC 8661

EVANGELINE SECURITIES LIMITED p 470
1051 KING ST, WINDSOR, NS, B0N 2T0
(902) 792-1035   SIC 6211

EVANOV RADIO GROUP INC p 577
5312 DUNDAS ST W, ETOBICOKE, ON, M9B 1B3
(416) 213-1035   SIC 6712

EVANS CONSOLES CORPORATION p 23
1616 27 AVE NE, CALGARY, AB, T2E 8W4
(403) 291-4444   SIC 2521

EVANS ENGINE SHOP LTD p 174
33406 SOUTH FRASER WAY, ABBOTSFORD, BC, V2S 2B5
SIC 7694

EVANS HOME BUILDING CENTRE p 900
See EVANS LUMBER AND BUILDERS SUPPLY LIMITED

EVANS LUMBER AND BUILDERS SUPPLY LIMITED p 900
172 PINE ST, SUDBURY, ON, P3C 1X3
(705) 674-1921   SIC 5211

EVANS, KEN FORD SALES LTD p 211
439 TRANS CANADA HWY, DUNCAN, BC, V9L 3R7
(250) 748-5555   SIC 5511

EVASION STREET ENERGY LTD p 12
3412 33A AVE SE, CALGARY, AB, T2B 0K4
SIC 4925

EVAULT CANADA INC p 797
2315 BRISTOL CIR UNIT 200, OAKVILLE, ON, L6H 6P8
(905) 287-2600   SIC 7371

EVELYN RICHARDSON MEMORIAL ELEMENTARY SCHOOL p 471
See TRI-COUNTY REGIONAL SCHOOL BOARD

EVENKO p 1209
See ARENA DES CANADIENS INC, L'

EVENT RENTAL GROUP GP INC p 918
210 WICKSTEED AVE, TORONTO, ON, M4G 2C3
(416) 759-2611   SIC 7389

EVENT SCAPE INC p 571
4 BESTOBELL RD, ETOBICOKE, ON, M8W 4H3
(416) 231-8855   SIC 7389

EVENTIDE HOME p 757
See GOVERNING COUNCIL OF THE SALVATION ARMY IN CANADA, THE

EVENTS EAST GROUP p 453
1800 ARGYLE ST P.O. BOX 955, HALIFAX, NS, B3J 3N8
(902) 421-8686   SIC 6512

EVER GREEN ECOLOGICAL SERVICES INC p 100
20204 113 AVE NW, EDMONTON, AB, T5S 0G3
(780) 239-9419   SIC 4953

EVER GREEN ECOLOGICAL SERVICES

INC p 109
6105 76 AVE NW, EDMONTON, AB, T6B 0A7
(780) 417-2282   SIC 4953

EVEREST p 1052
See EVEREST EQUIPMENT CO

EVEREST AUTOMATION INC p 1250
227D BOUL BRUNSWICK, POINTE-CLAIRE, QC, H9R 4X5
(514) 630-9290   SIC 5084

EVEREST CLINICAL RESEARCH CORPORATION p 670
675 COCHRANE DR SUITE 408, MARKHAM, ON, L3R 0B8
(905) 752-5222   SIC 8732

EVEREST ENTERPRISES INTERNATIONAL p 10
See COFFEE CONNECTION LTD, THE

EVEREST EQUIPMENT CO p 1052
1077 RUE WESTMOUNT, AYER'S CLIFF, QC, J0B 1C0
(819) 838-4257   SIC 3713

EVEREST HOME HEALTH CARE p 711
See EVEREST NURSING & COMMUINITY CARE AGENCY INC

EVEREST INSURANCE COMPANY OF CANADA p 986
130 KING ST W SUITE 2520, TORONTO, ON, M5X 2A2
(416) 487-3900   SIC 6411

EVEREST NURSING & COMMUINITY CARE AGENCY INC p 711
2341 NIKANNA RD, MISSISSAUGA, ON, L5C 2W8
(905) 270-4426   SIC 8399

EVEREST STEEL LTD p 739
6445 KENNEDY RD UNIT C, MISSISSAUGA, ON, L5T 2W4
(905) 670-7373   SIC 5051

EVERGREEN p 928
See EVERGREEN ENVIROMENTAL FOUNDATION

EVERGREEN BAPTIST HOME p 343
1550 OXFORD ST, WHITE ROCK, BC, V4B 3R5
(604) 536-3344   SIC 8051

EVERGREEN CATHOLIC SEPARATE REGIONAL DIVISION 2 p 164
381 GROVE DR UNIT 110, SPRUCE GROVE, AB, T7X 2Y9
(780) 962-5627   SIC 8211

EVERGREEN CENTRE FOR STREET YOUTH p 978
See YONGE STREET MISSION, THE

EVERGREEN COLONY LTD p 357
GD, SOMERSET, MB, R0G 2L0
(204) 744-2596   SIC 0212

EVERGREEN COMMUNITY HEALTH CENTRE p 288
See VANCOUVER COASTAL HEALTH AUTHORITY

EVERGREEN ENERGY LTD p 79
9416 69 AVE, CLAIRMONT, AB, T8X 5B3
(780) 538-3680   SIC 1623

EVERGREEN ENVIROMENTAL FOUNDATION p 928
550 BAYVIEW AVE SUITE 300, TORONTO, ON, M4W 3X8
(416) 596-1495   SIC 8748

EVERGREEN HERBS LTD p 279
3727 184 ST, SURREY, BC, V3Z 1B8
(604) 576-2567   SIC 5148

EVERGREEN INDUSTRIES LTD p 340
1045 DUNFORD AVE, VICTORIA, BC, V9B 2S4
(250) 474-5145   SIC 4953

EVERGREEN INTERNATIONAL FOODSTUFFS LTD p 285

1944 FRANKLIN ST, VANCOUVER, BC, V5L 1R2
(604) 253-8835   SIC 5146

EVERGREEN SCHOOL DIVISION p 350
140 CENTRE AVE W, GIMLI, MB, R0C 1B1
(204) 642-6260   SIC 8211

EVERGREEN WEST REALTY p 198
2963 GLEN DR SUITE 206, COQUITLAM, BC, V3B 2P7
(604) 782-7327   SIC 6531

EVERGREENS FOUNDATION p 136
102 GOVERNMENT RD, HINTON, AB, T7V 2A6
(780) 865-5444   SIC 6513

EVERGREENS HOMES FOR SPECIAL CARE p 460
See PALMETER'S COUNTRY HOME (1986) LTD

EVERGRO CANADA INC p 208
7430 HOPCOTT RD SUITE 1, DELTA, BC, V4G 1B6
(604) 940-0290   SIC 5193

EVERLAST GROUP LTD p 510
40 HOLTBY AVE SUITE 1, BRAMPTON, ON, L6X 2M1
(905) 846-9944   SIC 4731

EVERLINK PAYMENT SERVICES INC p 904
125 COMMERCE VALLEY DR W UNIT 100, THORNHILL, ON, L3T 7W4
(905) 946-5898   SIC 6099

EVERLITE LUGGAGE MANUFACTURING LIMITED p 993
451 ALLIANCE AVE, TORONTO, ON, M6N 2J1
(416) 763-4040   SIC 5099

EVERTRUST DEVELOPMENT GROUP CANADA INC p 670
3100 STEELES AVE E SUITE 302, MARKHAM, ON, L3R 8T3
(647) 501-2345   SIC 1542

EVERTZ MICROSYSTEMS LTD p 522
5292 JOHN LUCAS DR, BURLINGTON, ON, L7L 5Z9
(905) 335-3700   SIC 3663

EVERTZ TECHNOLOGIES LIMITED p 522
5292 JOHN LUCAS DR, BURLINGTON, ON, L7L 5Z9
(905) 335-3700   SIC 3669

EVERWORKS INC p 1005
64 SPRING CREEK DR, WATERDOWN, ON, L8B 0X4
(905) 208-1668   SIC 8742

EVERYDAY STYLE LTD p 1018
7675 TRANBY AVE, WINDSOR, ON, N8S 2B7
(519) 258-7905   SIC 5963

EVIMBEC LTEE p 1138
1175 BOUL GUILLAUME-COUTURE BUREAU 200, LEVIS, QC, G6W 0S2
(418) 834-7000   SIC 8742

EVO CANADA p 1195
See EVO MERCHANT SERVICES CORP. CANADA

EVO MC p 1139
See CYCLES LAMBERT INC

EVO MERCHANT SERVICES CORP. CANADA p 1195
505 BOUL DE MAISONNEUVE O BUREAU 150, MONTREAL, QC, H3A 3C2
SIC 5046

EVOLOCITY FINANCIAL GROUP INC p 1204
1100 BOUL RENE-LEVESQUE O BUREAU 1825, MONTREAL, QC, H3B 4N4
(877) 781-0148   SIC 8742

EVOLUTION MOBILE p 1258
305 BOUL CHAREST E, QUEBEC, QC, G1K 3H3
(418) 524-3436   SIC 5065

EVOLVED ENERGY SERVICES INC p 164
PO BOX 3946 STN MAIN, SPRUCE GROVE, AB, T7X 3B2
(780) 960-2790   SIC 1389

EVONIK p 527

See EVONIK CANADA INC
EVONIK CANADA INC p 527
3380 SOUTH SERVICE RD SUITE 5,
BURLINGTON, ON, L7N 3J5
(905) 336-3423 *SIC 5169*
EVONIK OIL ADDITIVES CANADA INC p
746
12695 COUNTY ROAD 28, MORRISBURG,
ON, K0C 1X0
(613) 543-2983 *SIC 5169*
EVOQUA WATER TECHNOLOGIES LTD p
735
2045 DREW RD, MISSISSAUGA, ON, L5S
1S4
(905) 890-2803 *SIC 3589*
EVRAZ INC. NA CANADA p 15
7201 OGDEN DALE RD SE, CALGARY, AB,
T2C 2A4
(403) 279-3351 *SIC 3312*
EVRAZ INC. NA CANADA p 1417
100 ARMOUR RD. REGINA, SK, S4P 3C7
(306) 924-7700 *SIC 3312*
EVRAZ NORTH AMERICA p 15
See EVRAZ INC. NA CANADA
EVRAZ REGINA STEEL p 1417
See EVRAZ INC. NA CANADA
EVRIPOS JANITORIAL SERVICES LTD p
825
136 FLORA ST SUITE 1, OTTAWA, ON,
K1R 5R5
(613) 232-9069 *SIC 7349*
EWA-CANADA p 596
See ELECTRONIC WARFARE ASSO-
CIATES - CANADA, LTD
EWASIUK RICK W QC p 89
10180 101 ST NW SUITE 3200, EDMON-
TON, AB, T5J 3W8
(780) 497-3384 *SIC 8111*
EWING INTERNATIONAL INC p 1014
1445 HOPKINS ST, WHITBY, ON, L1N 2C2
(416) 291-1675 *SIC 3463*
EWOS p 276
See EWOS CANADA LTD
EWOS CANADA LTD p 276
7721 132 ST, SURREY, BC, V3W 4M8
(604) 591-6368 *SIC 2048*
EWS INC p 570
340 ALLEN AVE, ESSEX, ON, N8M 3G6
(519) 776-9153 *SIC 3499*
EWS LEAMINGTON p 643
See 1544982 ONTARIO INC
EXACT OILFIELD DEVELOPING LTD p 163
1412 TAMARACK RD NE, SLAVE LAKE,
AB, T0G 2A0
(780) 849-2211 *SIC 1389*
EXACTA TOOL 2010 ULC p 513
120 VAN KIRK DR, BRAMPTON, ON, L7A
1B1
(905) 840-2240 *SIC 5084*
EXACTEARTH LTD p 537
260 HOLIDAY INN DR UNIT 30, CAM-
BRIDGE, ON, N3C 4E8
(519) 622-4445 *SIC 4899*
EXAGON MARKETING INC p 552
300 CONFEDERATION PKY UNIT 4, CON-
CORD, ON, L4K 4T8
(905) 669-9627 *SIC 5199*
EXAN GROUP p 199
See AXIUM SOLUTIONS ULC
EXC HOLDINGS LTD. p 221
1631 DICKSON AVE 10TH FL, KELOWNA,
BC, V1Y 0B5
(250) 448-0030 *SIC 4214*
EXCALIBUR DRILLING LTD p 7
490 CANAL ST, BROOKS, AB, T1R 1C8
(403) 793-2092 *SIC 1381*
EXCALIBUR LEARNING RESOURCE CEN-
TRE, CANADA CORP p
630
25 MARKLAND ST, KINGSTON, ON, K7K
1S2
SIC 8249
EXCALIBUR MOTORCYCLE WORKS LIM-
ITED p

910
1425 WALSH ST W, THUNDER BAY, ON,
P7E 4X6
(807) 622-0007 *SIC 5571*
EXCALIBUR PLASTICS LTD p 633
1397 ROAD 3 E, KINGSVILLE, ON, N9Y
2E5
(519) 326-6000 *SIC 5162*
EXCAVATION DE CHICOUTIMI INC p 1080
1201 BOUL SAINT-PAUL, CHICOUTIMI,
QC, G7J 3Y2
(418) 549-8343 *SIC 1794*
EXCAVATION GERVAIS DUCLOS 2008 p
1277
See JES CONSTRUCTION INC
EXCAVATION LOISELLE ET FRERES, DIV
OF p 1365
See LOISELLE INC
EXCAVATION LOISELLE INC p 1103
See LOISELLE INC
EXCAVATION MICHEL PARADIS INC p
1302
See EXCAVATION PARADIS, MICHEL INC
EXCAVATION NORMAND MAJEAU INC p
1282
337 RUE CHARLES-MARCHAND, RE-
PENTIGNY, QC, J5Z 4N8
(450) 581-8248 *SIC 1794*
EXCAVATION PARADIS, MICHEL INC p
1302
1270 RUE NELLIGAN, SAINT-FELICIEN,
QC, G8K 1N1
(418) 679-4533 *SIC 1611*
EXCAVATION PARADIS, MICHEL INC p
1302
780 BOUL HAMEL, SAINT-FELICIEN, QC,
G8K 1X9
(418) 679-4533 *SIC 1794*
EXCAVATION R.B. GAUTHIER INC p 1159
246 RTE 117, MONT-TREMBLANT, QC, J8E
2X1
(819) 425-2074 *SIC 1794*
EXCAVATION RENE ST-PIERRE p 1369
800 RUE DE L'ARDOISE, SHERBROOKE,
QC, J1C 0J6
(819) 565-1494 *SIC 1794*
EXCAVATION RENE ST-PIERRE INC p 1369
800 RUE DE L'ARDOISE, SHERBROOKE,
QC, J1C 0J6
(819) 565-1494 *SIC 1795*
EXCAVATION ST-PIERRE ET TREMBLAY
INC p 1088
126 RUE DEAN, COWANSVILLE, QC, J2K
3Y3
(450) 266-2100 *SIC 1794*
EXCAVATIONS GILLES ST-ONGE INC, LES
p 1307
1075 CROIS DES HAUTEURS, SAINT-
HIPPOLYTE, QC, J8A 0A5
(450) 224-0555 *SIC 1794*
EXCAVATIONS LAFONTAINE INC, LES p
1136
872 RUE ARCHIMEDE BUREAU 92, LEVIS,
QC, G6V 7M5
(418) 838-2121 *SIC 1623*
EXCAVATIONS PAYETTE LTEE, LES p 1048
7900 RUE BOMBARDIER, ANJOU, QC, H1J
1A4
(514) 322-4800 *SIC 1794*
EXCAVATIONS V. ST-GERMAIN p 1358
See EQUIPEMENT ST-GERMAIN INC
EXCAVATIONS VESPO INC, LES p 1126
17 BOUL SAINT-JOSEPH, LACHINE, QC,
H8S 2K9
(514) 933-5057 *SIC 1794*
EXCEL p 10
See WALMART CANADA LOGISTICS ULC
EXCEL AUTOMOBILES MONTREAL LTEE p
1156
5400 RUE PARE, MONT-ROYAL, QC, H4P
1R3
(514) 342-6360 *SIC 5511*
EXCEL CLIMATISATION INC p 1308
4915 BOUL SIR-WILFRID-LAURIER BU-

REAU 1, SAINT-HUBERT, QC, J3Y 3X5
(450) 676-1944 *SIC 1711*
EXCEL HONDA p 1156
See EXCEL AUTOMOBILES MONTREAL
LTEE
EXCEL INSURANCE AGENCY INC p 670
80 ACADIA AVE SUITE 205, MARKHAM,
ON, L3R 9V1
(905) 470-8222 *SIC 6411*
EXCEL INSURANCE BROKERS (METRO
VANCOUVER) INC p 190
4720 KINGSWAY UNIT 2600, BURNABY,
BC, V5H 4N2
(604) 282-7719 *SIC 6411*
EXCEL LATIN AMERICA BOND FUND p
694
2810 MATHESON BLVD E SUITE 800, MIS-
SISSAUGA, ON, L4W 4X7
SIC 6722
EXCEL PLAYGREEN GROUP INC p 353
18 3 AVE S, NIVERVILLE, MB, R0A 1E0
(204) 388-9250 *SIC 0213*
EXCEL PRIX GROSSISTE EN ALIMENTA-
TION INC p
1234
1225 RUE BERGAR, MONTREAL, QC, H7L
4Z7
(450) 967-0076 *SIC 5411*
EXCEL RESOURCES SOCIETY p 86
10814 106 AVE NW SUITE 300, EDMON-
TON, AB, T5H 4E1
(780) 455-2601 *SIC 8399*
EXCEL RETAIL LIMITED p 758
6840 MCLEOD RD, NIAGARA FALLS, ON,
L2G 3G6
(905) 358-0161 *SIC 5531*
EXCEL TIRE CENTRES INC p 289
615 KINGSWAY, VANCOUVER, BC, V5T
3K5
(604) 876-1225 *SIC 5531*
EXCEL TRANSPORTATION ALBERTA INC
p 248
333 ONGMAN RD, PRINCE GEORGE, BC,
V2K 4K9
(250) 563-7356 *SIC 4212*
EXCEL TRANSPORTATION INC p 248
333 ONGMAN RD, PRINCE GEORGE, BC,
V2K 4K9
(250) 563-7356 *SIC 4212*
EXCEL-TECH LTD p 797
2568 BRISTOL CIR, OAKVILLE, ON, L6H
5S1
(905) 829-5300 *SIC 3841*
EXCELDOR COOPERATIVE p 1136
5700 RUE J.-B.-MICHAUD BUREAU 500,
LEVIS, QC, G6V 0B1
(418) 830-5600 *SIC 2015*
EXCELDOR COOPERATIVE p 1136
5700 RUE J.-B.-MICHAUD SUITE 500,
LEVIS, QC, G6V 0B1
(418) 830-5600 *SIC 2015*
EXCELDOR COOPERATIVE p 1292
1000 RTE BEGIN, SAINT-ANSELME, QC,
G0R 2N0
(418) 885-4451 *SIC 2015*
EXCELDOR COOPERATIVE p 1298
125 RUE SAINTE-ANNE GD, SAINT-
DAMASE, QC, J0H 1J0
(450) 797-3331 *SIC 2011*
EXCELDOR FOODS LTD p 617
478 14TH ST, HANOVER, ON, N4N 1Z9
(519) 364-1770 *SIC 2015*
EXCELERATOR MEDIA, DIV OF p 930
See MINDSHARE CANADA
EXCELITAS CANADA INC p 1394
22001 CH DUMBERRY, VAUDREUIL-
DORION, QC, J7V 8P7
(450) 424-3300 *SIC 3679*
EXCELL BATTERY COMPANY p 271
18525 53 AVE SUITE 133, SURREY, BC,
V3S 7A4
(604) 575-5011 *SIC 5063*
EXCELL COMMUNICATIONS p 473
See 1001943 ONTARIO LIMITED

EXCELLENCE DODGE CHRYSLER INC p
1300
250 RUE DUBOIS, SAINT-EUSTACHE, QC,
J7P 4W9
(450) 491-5555 *SIC 5511*
EXCELLENCE DODGE CHRYSLER JEEP p
1393
See 2960-7082 QUEBEC INC
EXCELLENCE FIAT p 1300
See EXCELLENCE DODGE CHRYSLER
INC
EXCELLENCE LIFE INSURANCE COM-
PANY, THE p
1176
1611 BOUL CREMAZIE E BUREAU 900,
MONTREAL, QC, H2M 2P2
(514) 327-0020 *SIC 6311*
EXCELLENTE GESTION INC p 1261
550 BOUL PERE-LELIEVRE BUREAU 100,
QUEBEC, QC, G1M 3R2
(418) 529-3868 *SIC 8299*
EXCELSIOR MINING CORP p 312
1140 PENDER ST W SUITE 1240, VAN-
COUVER, BC, V6E 4G1
(604) 681-8030 *SIC 1021*
EXCELTELECOM p 1068
See 9349-6446 QUEBEC INC
EXCENTROTECH PRECISION INC p 1031
55 WESTCREEK DR, WOODBRIDGE, ON,
L4L 9N6
(905) 856-1801 *SIC 3728*
EXCHANGE CORPORATION CANADA INC
p 264
4831 MILLER RD SUITE 206, RICHMOND,
BC, V7B 1K7
(604) 656-1700 *SIC 6099*
EXCHANGE INCOME CORPORATION p
384
1067 SHERWIN RD, WINNIPEG, MB, R3H
0T8
(204) 982-1857 *SIC 8249*
EXCHANGE SOLUTIONS INC p 938
36 TORONTO ST SUITE 1200, TORONTO,
ON, M5C 2C5
(416) 646-7000 *SIC 8741*
EXCHANGER INDUSTRIES LIMITED p 15
5811 46 ST SE SUITE 200, CALGARY, AB,
T2C 4Y5
(403) 236-0166 *SIC 3443*
EXCLUSIVE BRANDS p 739
See EXCLUSIVE CANDY AND NOVELTY
DISTRIBUTING LIMITED
EXCLUSIVE CANDY AND NOVELTY DIS-
TRIBUTING LIMITED p
739
1832 BONHILL RD, MISSISSAUGA, ON,
L5T 1C4
(905) 795-8781 *SIC 5145*
EXCLUSIVE CARE SERVICES p 570
See 671061 ONTARIO LIMITED
EXCO ENGINEERING p 670
See EXCO TECHNOLOGIES LIMITED
EXCO ENGINEERING p 755
See EXCO TECHNOLOGIES LIMITED
EXCO EXTRUSION DIES p 670
See EXCO TECHNOLOGIES LIMITED
EXCO TECHNOLOGIES LIMITED p 446
35 AKERLEY BLVD, DARTMOUTH, NS,
B3B 1J7
(902) 468-6663 *SIC 3089*
EXCO TECHNOLOGIES LIMITED p 670
130 SPY CRT, MARKHAM, ON, L3R 5H6
(905) 477-3065 *SIC 3465*
EXCO TECHNOLOGIES LIMITED p 670
130 SPY CRT UNIT 1, MARKHAM, ON, L3R
5H6
(905) 477-3065 *SIC 3544*
EXCO TECHNOLOGIES LIMITED p 755
1314 RINGWELL DR, NEWMARKET, ON.
L3Y 9C6
(905) 853-8568 *SIC 3544*
EXCO TECHNOLOGIES LIMITED p 1001
2 PARRATT RD, UXBRIDGE, ON, L9P 1R1
(905) 852-0121 *SIC 3545*

EXECAIRE p 1094
See I.M.P. GROUP LIMITED
EXECULINK TELECOM INC p 1036
1127 RIDGEWAY RD, WOODSTOCK, ON,
N4V 1E3
(877) 393-2854   SIC 4813
EXECUTIVE AIRPORT PLAZA p 260
See EXECUTIVE HOTELS GENERAL
PARTNERSHIP
EXECUTIVE CHEF p 321
See STOWE, LESLEY FINE FOODS LTD
EXECUTIVE FLIGHT CENTRE p 23
See EXECUTIVE FLIGHT CENTRE FUEL
SERVICES LTD
**EXECUTIVE FLIGHT CENTRE FUEL SER-
VICES LTD** p
23
680 PALMER RD NE SUITE 200, CAL-
GARY, AB, T2E 7R3
(403) 291-2825   SIC 5172
EXECUTIVE HOTELS & RESORTS p 185
See EXECUTIVE HOTELS GENERAL
PARTNERSHIP
EXECUTIVE HOTELS & RESORTS p 200
See EXECUTIVE HOTELS GENERAL
PARTNERSHIP
**EXECUTIVE HOTELS GENERAL PART-
NERSHIP** p
185
4201 LOUGHEED HWY, BURNABY, BC,
V5C 3Y6
(604) 298-2010   SIC 7011
**EXECUTIVE HOTELS GENERAL PART-
NERSHIP** p
200
405 NORTH RD, COQUITLAM, BC, V3K
3V9
(604) 936-9399   SIC 7011
**EXECUTIVE HOTELS GENERAL PART-
NERSHIP** p
260
7311 WESTMINSTER HWY, RICHMOND,
BC, V6X 1A3
(604) 278-5555   SIC 7011
EXECUTIVE HOUSE LTD p 336
777 DOUGLAS ST, VICTORIA, BC, V8W
2B5
(250) 388-5111   SIC 7011
EXECUTIVE MAINTENANCE SERVICES p
677
See WEREK ENTERPRISES INC
EXECUTIVE PLAZA p 202
See SAYANI INVESTMENTS LTD
**EXECUTIVE PLAZA VANCOUVER DOWN
TOWN** p 186
See SANOOR INVESTMENT LTD
EXECUTIVE ROYAL INN p 24
See P.R. DEVELOPMENTS LTD
EXECUTIVE WAITER RESOURCES INC p
321
1975 16TH AVE W, VANCOUVER, BC, V6J
2M5
(604) 689-0640   SIC 7361
EXECUTIVE WOODWORK LTD p 552
330 SPINNAKER WAY, CONCORD, ON,
L4K 4W1
(905) 669-6429   SIC 7389
EXECWAY CONSTRUCTION LTD p 864
10157 SHEPPARD AVE E, SCARBOR-
OUGH, ON, M1B 1G1
(416) 286-2019   SIC 1541
EXEL CANADA LTD p 513
100 SANDALWOOD PKY W, BRAMPTON,
ON, L7A 1A8
(905) 840-7540   SIC 4225
EXEL CANADA LTD p 731
90 MATHESON BLVD W SUITE 111, MIS-
SISSAUGA, ON, L5R 3R3
(905) 366-7700   SIC 4225
EXEL CONTRACTING INC p 540
135 WALGREEN RD, CARP, ON, K0A 1L0
(613) 831-3935   SIC 0781
EXEL LOGISTICS CANADA INC p 688
6700 NORTHWEST DR, MISSISSAUGA,

ON, L4V 1L5
SIC 5141
EXELTA GYMNASTIC p 157
See RED DEER GYMNASTIC ASSOCIA-
TION
EXELTOR INC p 1056
110 RUE DE LA RIVIERE, BEDFORD, QC,
J0J 1A0
(450) 248-4343   SIC 3965
**EXETER PRODUCE AND STORAGE COM-
PANY, LIMITED** p
590
215 THAMES RD W SS 3, EXETER, ON,
N0M 1S3
(519) 235-0141   SIC 5148
EXFO 2 PRODUCTION p 1262
See EXFO INC
EXFO INC p 1262
436 RUE NOLIN, QUEBEC, QC, G1M 1E7
(418) 683-0211   SIC 3827
EXFO INC p 1262
400 AV GODIN, QUEBEC, QC, G1M 2K2
(418) 683-0211   SIC 3827
EXHAUST MASTERS INC p 153
GD STN POSTAL BOX CTR BOX, RED
DEER, AB, T4N 5E6
(403) 885-5800   SIC 5013
**EXIDE TECHNOLOGIES CANADA CORPO-
RATION** p
722
6950 CREDITVIEW RD SUITE 3, MISSIS-
SAUGA, ON, L5N 0A6
(905) 817-1773   SIC 5063
EXIMCAN CANADA p 944
See EXPORT-IMPORT TRADE CENTRE
OF CANADA AND U.S.A. LIMITED
EXIT CERTIFIED CORPORATION p 823
220 LAURIER AVE W SUITE 1000, OT-
TAWA, ON, K1P 5Z9
(613) 232-3948   SIC 8741
EXIT REALTY ASSOCIATES p 397
260 RUE CHAMPLAIN, DIEPPE, NB, E1A
1P3
(506) 382-3948   SIC 6531
EXIT REALTY CHARLOTTE COUNTY p 418
See DAY, GUY R. & SON LIMITED
EXIT REALTY CORP. INTERNATIONAL p
722
2345 ARGENTIA RD SUITE 200, MISSIS-
SAUGA, ON, L5N 8K4
(905) 363-4050   SIC 6531
EXIT REALTY GROUP BROKERAGE p 491
5503 62 HWY, BELLEVILLE, ON, K8N 4Z7
(613) 966-9400   SIC 6531
EXIT REALTY HARE PEEL p 508
134 QUEEN ST E SUITE 100, BRAMPTON,
ON, L6V 1B2
(905) 451-2390   SIC 6531
EXIT REALTY METRO p 444
See 3100477 NOVA SCOTIA LIMITED
EXIT REALTY OPTIMUM p 446
1 GLOSTER CRT, DARTMOUTH, NS, B3B
1X9
(902) 444-3948   SIC 6531
EXKOR MANUFACTURING p 1017
See LINAMAR CORPORATION
EXO-FRUITS p 1218
See 2739-9708 QUEBEC INC
EXO-S INC p 1283
425 10E AV, RICHMOND, QC, J0B 2H0
(819) 826-5911   SIC 3089
EXO-S INC p 1371
2100 RUE KING O BUREAU 240, SHER-
BROOKE, QC, J1J 2E8
(819) 346-3967   SIC 2821
EXOCOR LTD p 886
271 RIDLEY RD W SUITE 2, ST
CATHARINES, ON, L2S 0B3
(905) 704-0603   SIC 5085
EXOPEP p 1200
See THERATECHNOLOGIES INC
EXOVA p 1250
121 BOUL HYMUS, POINTE-CLAIRE, QC,
H9R 1E6

(514) 697-3400   SIC 8734
EXP GLOBAL p 1195
See EXP SERVICES INC
EXP GLOBAL INC p 508
56 QUEEN ST E SUITE 301, BRAMPTON,
ON, L6V 4M8
(855) 225-5397   SIC 8711
EXP REALTY OF CANADA, INC p 771
4711 YONGE ST 10 FL, NORTH YORK, ON,
M2N 6K8
(866) 530-7737   SIC 6531
EXP SERVICES INC p 188
3001 WAYBURNE DR SUITE 275, BURN-
ABY, BC, V5G 4W3
(604) 874-1245   SIC 8711
EXP SERVICES INC p 401
1133 REGENT ST SUITE 300, FREDERIC-
TON, NB, E3B 3Z2
(506) 452-9000   SIC 8711
EXP SERVICES INC p 502
1595 CLARK BLVD, BRAMPTON, ON, L6T
4V1
(905) 793-9800   SIC 8711
EXP SERVICES INC p 508
56 QUEEN ST E SUITE 301, BRAMPTON,
ON, L6V 4M8
(905) 796-3200   SIC 8711
EXP SERVICES INC p 749
154 COLONNADE RD S, NEPEAN, ON,
K2E 7J5
(613) 225-9940   SIC 8711
EXP SERVICES INC p 1195
1001 BOUL DE MAISONNEUVE O BU-
REAU 800B, MONTREAL, QC, H3A 3C8
(514) 788-6158   SIC 8711
**EXP-AIR   CLIMATISATION-
REFRIGERATION** p
1142
See NAVADA LTEE
EXPEDIA CANADA CORP p 1188
63 RUE DE BRESOLES BUREAU 100,
MONTREAL, QC, H2Y 1V7
(514) 286-8180   SIC 3823
**EXPEDIA CRUISE SHIP CENTERS
KELOWNA** p 221
See EXPEDIA CRUISESHIPCENTERS
EXPEDIA CRUISE SHIP CENTRE p 725
See MISSISSAUGA CRUISE SHIP CEN-
TRE
**EXPEDIA CRUISE SHIP CENTRE FISH
CREEK** p 68
See JEMCO VENTURES INC
**EXPEDIA CRUISE SHIP CENTRE MONC-
TON** p
409
1633 MOUNTAIN RD SUITE 13, MONC-
TON, NB, E1G 1A5
(506) 386-7447   SIC 4724
**EXPEDIA CRUISE SHIP CENTRES, TER-
WILLEGAR** p
123
14256 23 AVE NW, EDMONTON, AB, T6R
3B9
(780) 822-9283   SIC 4724
EXPEDIA CRUISESHIPCENTERS p 221
1980 COOPER RD UNIT 106, KELOWNA,
BC, V1Y 8K5
(250) 763-2900   SIC 4724
**EXPEDIA CRUISESHIPCENTRES WIL-
LOWDALE** p
770
See 1529295 ONTARIO INC
**EXPEDITION HELICOPTER INTERNA-
TIONAL** p
545
See EXPEDITION HELICOPTERS INC
EXPEDITION HELICOPTERS INC p 545
190 HWY 11 W, COCHRANE, ON, P0L 1C0
(705) 272-5755   SIC 4522
EXPEDITORS CANADA INC p 731
55 STANDISH CRT SUITE 1100, MISSIS-
SAUGA, ON, L5R 4A1
(905) 290-6000   SIC 4731
EXPERIENTIAL   MARKETING   LIMITED

PARTNERSHIP p 980
49 BATHURST ST SUITE 101, TORONTO,
ON, M5V 2P2
(416) 703-3589   SIC 7922
EXPERT CHEVROLET BUICK GMC LTD p
619
500 HWY 11 E, HEARST, ON, P0L 1N0
(705) 362-8001   SIC 5511
EXPERT CUSTOMS BROKERS p 377
2595 INKSTER BLVD, WINNIPEG, MB, R3C
2E6
(204) 633-1200   SIC 4731
EXPERT GARAGE LIMITED p 619
420 HWY 11 E, HEARST, ON, P0L 1N0
(705) 362-4301   SIC 5511
EXPERT MANUFACTURING INC p 552
180 VICEROY RD, CONCORD, ON, L4K
2L8
(905) 738-7575   SIC 2522
EXPERT MOBILE COMMUNICATIONS LTD
p 131
8701 112 ST, GRANDE PRAIRIE, AB, T8V
6A4
(780) 539-3962   SIC 5065
EXPERTECH p 1164
See EXPERTECH BATISSEUR DE RE-
SEAUX INC
**EXPERTECH BATISSEUR DE RESEAUX
INC** p 1164
2555 BOUL DE L'ASSOMPTION, MON-
TREAL, QC, H1N 2G8
(866) 616-8459   SIC 1731
**EXPERTECH NETWORK INSTALLATION
INC** p 584
240 ATTWELL DR, ETOBICOKE, ON, M9W
5B2
(866) 553-5539   SIC 1623
EXPERTISES SCM LES p 1103
510 BOUL MALONEY E BUREAU 104,
GATINEAU, QC, J8P 1E7
(819) 663-6068   SIC 6411
**EXPERTS DE LA COSMETIQUE VEGE-
TALE, LES** p
1142
See YVES ROCHER AMERIQUE DU
NORD INC
**EXPERTS   EN   MEMOIRE INTERNA-
TIONALE INC, LES** p
1329
2321 RUE COHEN, SAINT-LAURENT, QC,
H4R 2N7
(514) 333-5010   SIC 5044
**EXPLOITS WELDING & MACHINE SHOP
LTD** p 424
2   QUEENSWAY,   GRAND   FALLS-
WINDSOR, NL, A2B 1J3
(709) 489-5618   SIC 3599
EXPLORANCE BLUE p 1195
See EXPLORANCE INC
EXPLORANCE INC p 1195
1470 RUE PEEL BUREAU 500, MON-
TREAL, QC, H3A 1T1
(514) 938-2111   SIC 7372
EXPLORATION BOWMORE p 1207
See OSISKO METALS INCORPORATED
EXPLORATION DATA SYSTEMS INC p 72
2410 10 AVE SW, CALGARY, AB, T3C 0K6
(403) 249-8931   SIC 1389
EXPLORATION DRILLING p 269
See MORE CORE DIAMOND DRILLING
SERVICES LTD
EXPLORER HOTEL, THE p 436
See NUNASTAR PROPERTIES INC
EXPLOS-NATURE p 1112
302 RUE DE LA RIVIERE, GRANDES-
BERGERONNES, QC, G0T 1G0
(418) 232-6249   SIC 8699
EXPO SECURITE INVESTIGATIONS INC p
1174
1600 AV DE LORIMIER BUREAU 140,
MONTREAL, QC, H2K 3W5
SIC 7389
EXPOCRETE p 2
See OLDCASTLE BUILDING PRODUCTS

CANADA, INC
EXPORT DEVELOPMENT CANADA *p* 815
150 SLATER ST, OTTAWA, ON, K1A 1K3
(613) 598-2500 *SIC* 6111
EXPORT PACKERS COMPANY INCORPO-RATED *p*
502
107 WALKER DR, BRAMPTON, ON, L6T 5K5
(905) 792-9700 *SIC* 5142
EXPORT PACKERS COMPANY LIMITED *p*
503
107 WALKER DR, BRAMPTON, ON, L6T 5K5
(905) 792-9700 *SIC* 5142
EXPORT-IMPORT TRADE CENTRE OF CANADA AND U.S.A. LIMITED *p* 944
481 UNIVERSITY AVE UNIT 301, TORONTO, ON, M5G 2E9
(416) 979-7967 *SIC* 5141
EXPOSERVICE STANDARD INC *p* 1130
2345 RUE LAPIERRE, LASALLE, QC, H8N 1B7
(514) 367-4848 *SIC* 7359
EXPOSYSTEMS CANADA *p* 878
See MCNICOL STEVENSON LIMITED
EXPOZONE *p* 1107
See 8959528 CANADA INC
EXPRESCO *p* 1332
See ALIMENTS EXPRESCO INC
EXPRESS CUSTOM *p* 243
See EXPRESS CUSTOM TRAILERS MFG. INC
EXPRESS CUSTOM TRAILERS MFG. INC *p*
243
1365 ALBERNI HWY, PARKSVILLE, BC, V9P 2B9
SIC 3537
EXPRESS DU MIDI INC, L' *p* 1356
1425 1RE AV, SAINTE-CATHERINE, QC, J5C 1C5
(450) 638-0654 *SIC* 4213
EXPRESS MAGAZINE *p* 1049
See HACHETTE DISTRIBUTION SER-VICES (CANADA) INC
EXPRESS MONDOR *p* 1129
See 2635-8762 QUEBEC INC
EXPRESS MONT-TREMBLANT *p* 1095
See SERVICES INTERNATIONALS SKY-PORT INC
EXPRESS S.R.S. *p* 1389
See TRANSPORT BELLEMARE INTERNA-TIONAL INC
EXPRESS-IT DELIVERY SERVICES (2002) INC *p* 276
13350 COMBER WAY, SURREY, BC, V3W 5V9
(604) 543-7800 *SIC* 7389
EXPRESSWAY FORD LINCOLN *p* 752
See EXPRESSWAY MOTORS LTD
EXPRESSWAY MOTORS LTD *p* 752
1554 HAYSVILLE RD, NEW HAMBURG, ON, N3A 1A3
(519) 662-3900 *SIC* 5511
EXPRESSWAY TRUCKS WATERLOO *p* 483
See VIKING TRUCK SALES INC
EXPRESSWAY TRUCKS WINDSOR *p* 663
See 905364 ONTARIO LIMITED
EXPRO GROUP CANADA INC *p* 155
8130 49 AVE CLOSE, RED DEER, AB, T4P 2V5
(877) 340-0911 *SIC* 1389
EXSPACE *p* 1067
See SYSTEMES NORBEC INC
EXTEND COMMUNICATIONS INC *p* 517
49 CHARLOTTE ST, BRANTFORD, ON, N3T 2W4
(416) 534-0477 *SIC* 7389
EXTENDICARE (CANADA) INC *p* 8
2611 37 AVE NE UNIT 7, CALGARY, AB, T1Y 5V7
(403) 228-3877 *SIC* 8051
EXTENDICARE (CANADA) INC *p* 41
1512 8 AVE NW, CALGARY, AB, T2N 1C1

(403) 289-0236 *SIC* 8051
EXTENDICARE (CANADA) INC *p* 112
8008 95 AVE NW, EDMONTON, AB, T6C 2T1
(780) 469-1307 *SIC* 8051
EXTENDICARE (CANADA) INC *p* 127
654 29TH ST, FORT MACLEOD, AB, T0L 0Z0
(403) 553-3955 *SIC* 8051
EXTENDICARE (CANADA) INC *p* 139
4309 50 ST, LEDUC, AB, T9E 6K6
(780) 986-2245 *SIC* 8051
EXTENDICARE (CANADA) INC *p* 388
2060 CORYDON AVE, WINNIPEG, MB, R3P 0N3
(204) 889-2650 *SIC* 8051
EXTENDICARE (CANADA) INC *p* 514
325 WEST ST UNIT 201, BRANTFORD, ON, N3R 3V6
(519) 756-4606 *SIC* 7363
EXTENDICARE (CANADA) INC *p* 563
812 PITT ST SUITE 16, CORNWALL, ON, K6J 5R1
(613) 932-4661 *SIC* 8051
EXTENDICARE (CANADA) INC *p* 565
40 GOODALL ST, DRYDEN, ON, P8N 1V8
(807) 223-5337 *SIC* 8049
EXTENDICARE (CANADA) INC *p* 572
56 ABERFOYLE CRES, ETOBICOKE, ON, M8X 2W4
(416) 236-1061 *SIC* 8051
EXTENDICARE (CANADA) INC *p* 615
883 UPPER WENTWORTH ST SUITE 301, HAMILTON, ON, L9A 4Y6
(905) 318-8522 *SIC* 8051
EXTENDICARE (CANADA) INC *p* 616
90 CHEDMAC DR SUITE 2317, HAMILTON, ON, L9C 7W1
(905) 318-4472 *SIC* 8051
EXTENDICARE (CANADA) INC *p* 632
309 QUEEN MARY RD, KINGSTON, ON, K7M 6P4
(613) 549-5010 *SIC* 8051
EXTENDICARE (CANADA) INC *p* 633
786 BLACKBURN MEWS, KINGSTON, ON, K7P 2N7
(613) 549-0112 *SIC* 8051
EXTENDICARE (CANADA) INC *p* 646
108 ANGELINE ST S SUITE 1, LINDSAY, ON, K9V 3L5
(705) 328-2280 *SIC* 8051
EXTENDICARE (CANADA) INC *p* 670
3000 STEELES AVE E SUITE 700, MARKHAM, ON, L3R 9W2
(905) 470-1400 *SIC* 8051
EXTENDICARE (CANADA) INC *p* 755
320 HARRY WALKER PKY N SUITE 11, NEWMARKET, ON, L3Y 7B4
SIC 8051
EXTENDICARE (CANADA) INC *p* 761
509 GLENDALE AVE SUITE 200, NIAGARA ON THE LAKE, ON, L0S 1J0
(905) 682-6555 *SIC* 8051
EXTENDICARE (CANADA) INC *p* 763
222 MCINTYRE ST W SUITE 202, NORTH BAY, ON, P1B 2Y8
(705) 495-4391 *SIC* 8051
EXTENDICARE (CANADA) INC *p* 769
550 CUMMER AVE, NORTH YORK, ON, M2K 2M2
(416) 226-1331 *SIC* 8051
EXTENDICARE (CANADA) INC *p* 796
124 LLOYD ST RR 1, NORTHBROOK, ON, K0H 2G0
(613) 336-9120 *SIC* 8051
EXTENDICARE (CANADA) INC *p* 802
700 DORVAL DR SUITE 111, OAKVILLE, ON, L6K 3V3
(905) 847-1025 *SIC* 8051
EXTENDICARE (CANADA) INC *p* 838
595 PEMBROKE ST E, PEMBROKE, ON, K8A 3L7
SIC 8059
EXTENDICARE (CANADA) INC *p* 840

80 ALEXANDER AVE, PETERBOROUGH, ON, K9J 6B4
(705) 743-7552 *SIC* 8051
EXTENDICARE (CANADA) INC *p* 866
3830 LAWRENCE AVE E SUITE 103, SCARBOROUGH, ON, M1G 1R6
(416) 439-1243 *SIC* 8051
EXTENDICARE (CANADA) INC *p* 879
15 HOLLINGER LANE, SCHUMACHER, ON, P0N 1G0
SIC 8059
EXTENDICARE (CANADA) INC *p* 907
3550 SCHMON PKY SUITE 4, THOROLD, ON, L2V 4Y6
(905) 685-6501 *SIC* 8049
EXTENDICARE (CANADA) INC *p* 1021
880 NORTH SERVICE RD E SUITE 301, WINDSOR, ON, N8X 3J5
(519) 966-5200 *SIC* 8059
EXTENDICARE (CANADA) INC *p* 1425
2225 PRESTON AVE, SASKATOON, SK, S7J 2E7
(306) 374-2242 *SIC* 8051
EXTENDICARE BAYVIEW *p* 769
See EXTENDICARE INC
EXTENDICARE CEDARS VILLA *p* 72
See EXTENDICARE INC
EXTENDICARE COBOURG *p* 545
See EXTENDICARE INC
EXTENDICARE ELMVIEW *p* 1421
See EXTENDICARE INC
EXTENDICARE FAIRMONT *p* 143
See EXTENDICARE INC
EXTENDICARE FALCONBRIDGE *p* 898
See EXTENDICARE INC
EXTENDICARE FORT MACLEOD *p* 127
See EXTENDICARE (CANADA) INC
EXTENDICARE GUILDWOOD *p* 866
See EXTENDICARE INC
EXTENDICARE HAMILTON *p* 616
See EXTENDICARE (CANADA) INC
EXTENDICARE HILLCREST *p* 41
See EXTENDICARE (CANADA) INC
EXTENDICARE HOLYROOD *p* 112
See EXTENDICARE (CANADA) INC
EXTENDICARE INC *p* 72
3330 8 AVE SW, CALGARY, AB, T3C 0E7
(403) 249-8915 *SIC* 8051
EXTENDICARE INC *p* 143
115 FAIRMONT BLVD S, LETHBRIDGE, AB, T1K 5V2
(403) 320-0120 *SIC* 8051
EXTENDICARE INC *p* 145
4706 54 ST, MAYERTHORPE, AB, T0E 1N0
(780) 786-2211 *SIC* 8051
EXTENDICARE INC *p* 155
12 MICHENER BLVD SUITE 3609, RED DEER, AB, T4P 0M1
(403) 348-0340 *SIC* 8051
EXTENDICARE INC *p* 165
4614 47 AVE, ST PAUL, AB, T0A 3A3
(780) 645-3375 *SIC* 8051
EXTENDICARE INC *p* 171
5020 57TH AVE, VIKING, AB, T0B 4N0
(780) 336-4790 *SIC* 8051
EXTENDICARE INC *p* 385
2395 NESS AVE, WINNIPEG, MB, R3J 1A5
(204) 888-3005 *SIC* 8051
EXTENDICARE INC *p* 496
264 KING ST E SUITE 306, BOW-MANVILLE, ON, L1C 1P9
(905) 623-2553 *SIC* 8051
EXTENDICARE INC *p* 496
98 PINE ST SUITE 610, BRACEBRIDGE, ON, P1L 1N5
(705) 645-4488 *SIC* 8051
EXTENDICARE INC *p* 545
130 NEW DENSMORE RD, COBOURG, ON, K9A 5W2
(905) 372-0377 *SIC* 8051
EXTENDICARE INC *p* 577
420 THE EAST MALL, ETOBICOKE, ON, M9B 3Z9
(416) 621-8000 *SIC* 8051

EXTENDICARE INC *p* 578
140 SHERWAY DR, ETOBICOKE, ON, M9C 1A4
(416) 259-2573 *SIC* 8051
EXTENDICARE INC *p* 596
1715 MONTREAL RD, GLOUCESTER, ON, K1J 6N4
(613) 741-5122 *SIC* 8051
EXTENDICARE INC *p* 632
309 QUEEN MARY RD, KINGSTON, ON, K7M 6P4
(613) 549-5010 *SIC* 8051
EXTENDICARE INC *p* 643
19 FRASER ST, LAKEFIELD, ON, K0L 2H0
(705) 652-7112 *SIC* 8051
EXTENDICARE INC *p* 646
125 COLBORNE ST E, LINDSAY, ON, K9V 6J2
(705) 878-5392 *SIC* 8051
EXTENDICARE INC *p* 653
860 WATERLOO ST, LONDON, ON, N6A 3W6
(519) 433-6658 *SIC* 8051
EXTENDICARE INC *p* 670
3000 STEELES AVE E SUITE 103, MARKHAM, ON, L3R 4T9
(905) 470-4000 *SIC* 8051
EXTENDICARE INC *p* 769
550 CUMMER AVE, NORTH YORK, ON, M2K 2M2
(416) 226-1331 *SIC* 8051
EXTENDICARE INC *p* 800
291 REYNOLDS ST SUITE 128, OAKVILLE, ON, L6J 3L5
(905) 849-7766 *SIC* 8051
EXTENDICARE INC *p* 831
2179 ELMIRA DR, OTTAWA, ON, K2C 3S1
(613) 829-3501 *SIC* 8051
EXTENDICARE INC *p* 847
360 CROFT ST SUITE 1124, PORT HOPE, ON, L1A 4K8
(905) 885-1266 *SIC* 8051
EXTENDICARE INC *p* 862
39 VAN DAELE ST, SAULT STE. MARIE, ON, P6B 4V3
(705) 949-7934 *SIC* 8051
EXTENDICARE INC *p* 866
60 GUILDWOOD PKY SUITE 327, SCAR-BOROUGH, ON, M1E 1N9
(416) 266-7711 *SIC* 8051
EXTENDICARE INC *p* 877
1020 MCNICOLL AVE SUITE 547, SCAR-BOROUGH, ON, M1W 2J6
(416) 499-2020 *SIC* 8051
EXTENDICARE INC *p* 887
283 PELHAM RD, ST CATHARINES, ON, L2S 1X7
(905) 688-3311 *SIC* 8051
EXTENDICARE INC *p* 892
199 GLOVER RD, STONEY CREEK, ON, L8E 5J2
(905) 643-1795 *SIC* 8051
EXTENDICARE INC *p* 898
281 FALCONBRIDGE RD, SUDBURY, ON, P3A 5K4
(705) 566-7980 *SIC* 8051
EXTENDICARE INC *p* 900
333 YORK ST, SUDBURY, ON, P3E 5J3
(705) 674-4221 *SIC* 8051
EXTENDICARE INC *p* 902
2475 ST. ALPHONSE ST SUITE 1238, TECUMSEH, ON, N8N 2X2
(519) 739-2998 *SIC* 8051
EXTENDICARE INC *p* 1025
1255 NORTH TALBOT RD, WINDSOR, ON, N9G 3A4
(519) 945-7249 *SIC* 8051
EXTENDICARE INC *p* 1411
1151 COTEAU ST W, MOOSE JAW, SK, S6H 5G5
(306) 693-5191 *SIC* 8051
EXTENDICARE INC *p* 1421
260 SUNSET DR, REGINA, SK, S4S 2S3
(306) 586-3355 *SIC* 8051

EXTENDICARE INC   p 1421
4125 RAE ST, REGINA, SK, S4S 3A5
(306) 586-1787   SIC 8051

EXTENDICARE INC   p 1421
4540 RAE ST, REGINA, SK, S4S 3B4
(306) 586-0220   SIC 8051

EXTENDICARE KAWARTHA LAKES   p 646
See EXTENDICARE INC

EXTENDICARE KINGSTON   p 632
See EXTENDICARE (CANADA) INC

EXTENDICARE KINGSTON   p 632
See EXTENDICARE INC

EXTENDICARE LAKEFIELD   p 643
See EXTENDICARE INC

EXTENDICARE LAURIER MANOR   p 596
See EXTENDICARE INC

EXTENDICARE LEDUC   p 139
See EXTENDICARE (CANADA) INC

EXTENDICARE LONDON   p 653
See EXTENDICARE INC

EXTENDICARE MAYERTHORPE   p 145
See EXTENDICARE INC

EXTENDICARE MICHENER HILL   p 155
See EXTENDICARE INC

EXTENDICARE MOOSE JAW   p 1411
See EXTENDICARE INC

EXTENDICARE OAKVIEW PLACE   p 385
See EXTENDICARE INC

EXTENDICARE PARKSIDE   p 1421
See EXTENDICARE INC

EXTENDICARE PETERBOROUGH   p 840
See EXTENDICARE (CANADA) INC

EXTENDICARE PORT HOPE   p 847
See EXTENDICARE INC

EXTENDICARE PRESTON   p 1425
See EXTENDICARE (CANADA) INC

EXTENDICARE SCARBOROUGH   p 866
See EXTENDICARE (CANADA) INC

EXTENDICARE SOUTHWOOD LAKES   p 1025
See EXTENDICARE INC

EXTENDICARE ST. CATHERINES   p 887
See EXTENDICARE INC

EXTENDICARE ST. PAUL   p 165
See EXTENDICARE INC

EXTENDICARE SUNSET   p 1421
See EXTENDICARE INC

EXTENDICARE TECUMSEH   p 902
See EXTENDICARE INC

EXTENDICARE TIMMINS   p 879
See EXTENDICARE (CANADA) INC

EXTENDICARE TUXEDO VILLA   p 388
See EXTENDICARE (CANADA) INC

EXTENDICARE VAN DAELE   p 862
See EXTENDICARE INC

EXTENDICARE VIKING   p 171
See EXTENDICARE INC

EXTENDICARE WEST END VILLA   p 831
See EXTENDICARE INC

EXTENDICARE YORK   p 900
See EXTENDICARE INC

EXTERIORS BY LEROY & DARCY LTD   p 140
3404 12 AVE N, LETHBRIDGE, AB, T1H 5V1
(403) 327-9113   SIC 1761

EXTERNAT SACRE-COEUR   p 1287
535 RUE LEFRANCOIS, ROSEMERE, QC, J7A 4R5
(450) 621-6720   SIC 8211

EXTERNAT SAINT-JEAN-EUDES   p 1144
2151 RUE SAINT-GEORGES, LONGUEUIL, QC, J4K 4A7
(450) 677-2184   SIC 7389

EXTRA FOODS   p 179
See LOBLAWS INC

EXTRA FOODS   p 195
See 526293 BC LTD

EXTRA FOODS   p 200
See DEE ENTERPRISES LTD

EXTRA FOODS   p 214
See 563769 B.C. LTD

EXTRA FOODS   p 252
See LOBLAWS INC

EXTRA FOODS   p 288
See FIRST GROCERY LTD

EXTRA FOODS   p 358
See LOBLAWS INC

EXTRA FOODS   p 628
See LOBLAWS INC

EXTRA FOODS   p 1410
See LOBLAWS INC

EXTRA FOODS   p 1435
See LOBLAWS INC

EXTRA FOODS & DRUGS LTD   p 286
3189 GRANDVIEW HWY, VANCOUVER, BC, V5M 2E9
(604) 439-5402   SIC 5141

EXTRA FOODS 9009   p 3

EXTRA FOODS NO. 8561   p 207
See ATM FOODS LTD

EXTRA FOODS NO. 9061   p 1428
See LOBLAWS INC

EXTRA MULTI-RESSOURCES   p 1063
See 162069 CANADA INC

EXTREME FITNESS   p 925
See DELISLE CLUB

EXTREME FITNESS GROUP INC   p 904
8281 YONGE ST, THORNHILL, ON, L3T 2C7
(905) 709-1248   SIC 7991

EXTREME RETAIL CANADA INC   p 1031
11 DIRECTOR CRT SUITE 554, WOODBRIDGE, ON, L4L 4S5
(905) 265-3160   SIC 6794

EXTREME WINDOW AND ENTRANCE SYSTEMS INC   p 408
80 LOFTUS ST, MONCTON, NB, E1E 2N2
(506) 384-3667   SIC 3089

EXTREMELY CANADIAN ADVENTURES & PROMOTIONS   p 342
See BIG RED DOG INC

EXTRUDE-A-TRIM INC   p 584
360 CARLINGVIEW DR, ETOBICOKE, ON, M9W 5X9
(416) 798-1277   SIC 5051

EXTRUDEX ALUMINUM LIMITED   p 1031
411 CHRISLEA RD, WOODBRIDGE, ON, L4L 8N4
(416) 745-4444   SIC 3354

EXTRUSIONS LAPIERRE   p 1347
See EQUIPEMENTS LAPIERRE INC, LES

EXUS PHARMACEUTICALS LTD   p 637
700 STRASBURG RD, KITCHENER, ON, N2E 2M2
(519) 576-8340   SIC 5912

EXXONMOBIL   p 459
GD, ISAACS HARBOUR, NS, B0H 1S0
(902) 387-3000   SIC 4924

EXXONMOBIL CANADA ENERGY   p 49
237 4 AVE SW, CALGARY, AB, T2P 0H6
(403) 260-7910   SIC 1382

EXXONMOBIL CANADA LTD   p 49
237 4 AVE SW SUITE 3000, CALGARY, AB, T2P 4X7
(403) 232-5300   SIC 1311

EXXONMOBIL CANADA PROPERTIES   p 49
237 4 AVE SW SUITE 4063, CALGARY, AB, T2P 0H6
(403) 260-7910   SIC 1382

EY   p 823
See ERNST & YOUNG LLP

EY   p 951
See ERNST & YOUNG LLP

EYERETURN MARKETING INC   p 922
110 EGLINTON AVE E SUITE 701, TORONTO, ON, M4P 2Y1
(416) 929-4834   SIC 7319

EYES N. OPTICS   p 998
73 DUNDAS ST W SUITE A, TRENTON, ON, K8V 3P4
(613) 392-3040   SIC 5093

EYESTAR OPTICAL (RICHMOND CENTRE)   p 254
See EYESTAR OPTICAL LTD

EYESTAR OPTICAL LTD   p 254
2639 VIKING WAY UNIT 150, RICHMOND,

BC, V6V 3B7
(604) 303-9760   SIC 5995

EYEWEAR PLACE LTD, THE   p 119
2065 111 ST NW, EDMONTON, AB, T6J 4V9
(780) 433-4888   SIC 5995

EZ-2-LOAD   p 396
See B.W.S. MANUFACTURING LTD

EZEE LEASING   p 994
See OLD MILL PONTIAC BUICK CADILLAC LIMITED

EZEFLOW INC   p 1110
985 RUE ANDRE-LINE, GRANBY, QC, J2J 1J6
(450) 375-3575   SIC 3498

EZMWD   p 12
See ZONE DIRECT MWD SERVICES LTD

F

F & D SCENE CHANGES LTD   p 29
803 24 AVE SE SUITE 2B, CALGARY, AB, T2G 1P5
(403) 233-7633   SIC 3999

F C C REPAIRS   p 155
7493 49 AVE CRES SUITE 5, RED DEER, AB, T4P 1X6
(403) 343-0092   SIC 5541

F D D C H DE JONQUIERE   p 1287
989 RUE COLLARD, ROBERVAL, QC, G8H 1X9
(418) 765-3444   SIC 6321

F D PHARMACY INC   p 788
1500 AVENUE RD, NORTH YORK, ON, M5M 3X2
(416) 781-6146   SIC 5912

F D TWO REAR OF LEEDS & LANSDOWNE   p 663
See TOWNSHIP OF LEEDS AND THE THOUSAND ISLANDS

F I OILFIELD SERVICES CANADA ULC   p 122
2880 64 AVE NW, EDMONTON, AB, T6P 1W6
(780) 463-3333   SIC 1389

F M C   p 969
See DENTONS CANADA LLP

F T Q   p 1176
See FEDERATION DES TRAVAILLEURS ET TRAVAILLEUSES DU QUEBEC (FTQ)

F&P MFG INC   p 896
275 WRIGHT BLVD, STRATFORD, ON, N5A 7Y1

SIC 3714

F&P MFG INC   p 998
1 NOLAN RD, TOTTENHAM, ON, L0G 1W0
(905) 936-3435   SIC 3714

F&P MFG., INC   p 896
See F&P MFG INC

F. D. L. COMPAGNIE LTEE   p 1218
3600 AV BARCLAY BUREAU 200, MONTREAL, QC, H3S 1K5
(514) 737-2268   SIC 6513

F. DAUDELIN ET FILS   p 1154
See 9168-1924 QUEBEC INC

F. DUFRESNE INC   p 1262
455 RUE DES ENTREPRENEURS, QUEBEC, QC, G1M 2V2
(418) 688-1820   SIC 1311

F. K. MACHINERY LIMITED   p 486
475 WELHAM RD, BARRIE, ON, L4N 8Z6
(705) 721-4200   SIC 5085

F. MENARD INC   p 1047
251 RTE 235, ANGE-GARDIEN, QC, J0E 1E0
(450) 293-3694   SIC 0213

F. P. RIDEAUVIEW INC   p 831
1430 PRINCE OF WALES DR, OTTAWA, ON, K2C 1N6
(613) 225-1240   SIC 5411

F. PAQUETTE & FILS   p 1101
See GROUPE PAQUETTE MECANIQUE DU BATIMENT INC

F.& K. MFG., CO., LIMITED   p 793
155 TURBINE DR, NORTH YORK, ON, M9L

2S7
(416) 749-3980   SIC 3542

F.A.B. RAMPES ECS. PRESTIGE   p 1162
See FABRICATION RAMPES ET ESCALIERS PRESTIGE INC

F.A.S. SEAFOOD PRODUCERS LTD   p 335
27 ERIE ST, VICTORIA, BC, V8V 1P8
(250) 383-7764   SIC 0912

F.A.S.T. FIRST AID & SURVIVAL TECHNOLOGIES LIMITED   p 209
8850 RIVER RD, DELTA, BC, V4G 1B5
(604) 940-3222   SIC 3842

F.B.B.L.   p 1180
See FAUTEUX, BRUNO, BUSSIERE, LEEWARDEN, CPA, S.E.N.C.R.L.

F.F SOUCY   p 1287
See SOCIETE EN COMMANDITE FF SOUCY WB

F.G. BRADLEY'S   p 845
See PLAYIT INCORPORATED

F.G. LISTER & CO., LIMITED   p 571
475 HORNER AVE, ETOBICOKE, ON, M8W 4X7
(416) 259-7621   SIC 5148

F.I.D. FUTUR INTERNATIONAL DIVERSIFIE INC   p 1060
926 RUE JACQUES PASCHINI, BOIS-DESFILION, QC, J6Z 4W4
(450) 621-4230   SIC 6799

F.I.T.T. TM   p 1394
See IMMUNOTEC INC

F.P. BOURGAULT TILLAGE TOOLS LTD   p 1436
200 5 AVE S, ST BRIEUX, SK, S0K 3V0
(306) 275-4500   SIC 3523

F.P.D. EAST INC   p 1127
2300 23E AV, LACHINE, QC, H8T 0A3
(514) 428-0331   SIC 5148

F.P.P.M.   p 1173
See FRATERNITE DES POLICIERS ET POLICIERES DE MONTREAL INC

F.S.S.V.S.   p 1113
See FONDATION DE LA MAISON DE SOINS PALLIATIFS DE VAUDREUIL-SOULANGES (FMSPVS)

F.W. WARD & SONS INC   p 1326
515 DESLAURIERS ST, SAINT-LAURENT, QC, H4N 1W2
(514) 858-9331   SIC 5148

F.X. LANGE INC   p 1248
10550 RUE HENRI-BOURASSA E, POINTE-AUX-TREMBLES, QC, H1C 1G6
(514) 648-7445   SIC 5051

F3 DISTRIBUTION   p 1310
See MOMENTUM DISTRIBUTION INC

FA CAPITAL MANAGEMENT INC   p 962
95 WELLINGTON ST W SUITE 1400, TORONTO, ON, M5J 2N7
(416) 642-1289   SIC 6722

FAB 3R INC   p 1387
227 BOUL DU SAINT-MAURICE, TROISRIVIERES, QC, G9A 3N8
(819) 371-8227   SIC 3469

FABCO PLASTICS WHOLESALE   p 1003
See FABCO PLASTICS WHOLESALE (ONTARIO) LIMITED

FABCO PLASTICS WHOLESALE (ONTARIO) LIMITED   p 1003
2175 TESTON RD, VAUGHAN, ON, L6A 1T3
(905) 832-0600   SIC 5162

FABCO PLASTIQUES INC   p 664
2175 TESTON RD PO BOX 2175 STN MAIN, MAPLE, ON, L6A 1T3
(905) 832-0600   SIC 5162

FABCOR 2001 INC   p 79
10202 74 AVE, CLAIRMONT, AB, T8X 5A7
(780) 532-3350   SIC 1623

FABELTA 3   p 1380
See FABELTA ALUMINIUM INC

FABELTA ALUMINIUM INC   p 1380
3840 RUE GEORGES-CORBEIL, TERRE-

BONNE, QC, J6X 4J4
(450) 477-7611　SIC 5031

FABKO FOOD LTD　p 83
8715 126 AVE NW, EDMONTON, AB, T5B 1G8
　SIC 5421

FABORY CANADA INC　p 1101
1220 RUE MICHELIN, FABREVILLE, QC, H7L 4R3
(450) 629-6900　SIC 5072

FABRENE　p 763
See FABRENE INC

FABRENE INC　p 763
240 DUPONT RD, NORTH BAY, ON, P1B 9B4
(705) 476-7057　SIC 2221

FABRI METAL　p 1246
See C.B.R. LASER INC

FABRICANA IMPORTS LTD　p 260
4591 GARDEN CITY RD, RICHMOND, BC, V6X 2K4
(604) 273-5316　SIC 5211

FABRICANT DE POELES INTERNATIONAL INC　p 1293
250 RUE DE COPENHAGUE BUREAU 1, SAINT-AUGUSTIN-DE-DESMAURES, QC, G3A 2H3
(418) 878-3040　SIC 3433

FABRICATED PLASTICS LIMITED　p 664
2175 TESTON RD, MAPLE, ON, L6A 1R3
(905) 832-8161　SIC 3299

FABRICATION BEAUCE-ATLAS INC p 1360
600 1RE AV DU PARC-INDUSTRIEL, SAINTE-MARIE, QC, G6E 1B5
(418) 387-4872　SIC 1542

FABRICATION DE MEUBLE HEMSLEY　p 1162
See GROUPE ARTITALIA INC

FABRICATION DELTA INC　p 1242
154 CH SAINT-EDGAR, NEW RICHMOND, QC, G0C 2B0
(418) 392-2624　SIC 3621

FABRICATION FRANSI INC　p 1052
32 AV BABIN, BAIE-COMEAU, QC, G4Z 3A6
(418) 296-6021　SIC 7692

FABRICATION METELEC LTEE　p 1318
300 RUE CARREAU, SAINT-JEAN-SUR-RICHELIEU, QC, J3B 2G4
(450) 346-6363　SIC 1761

FABRICATION PERFIX　p 1061
See PERFIX INC

FABRICATION RAMPES ET ESCALIERS PRESTIGE INC　p 1162
11750 AV J.-J.-JOUBERT, MONTREAL, QC, H1E 7E7
(514) 324-2107　SIC 3446

FABRICATION SCANDINAVE INC p 1074
452 BOUL PERRON, CARLETON, QC, G0C 1J0
(418) 364-6701　SIC 5099

FABRICATION STRAIN TEC　p 1249
See ARSLAN AUTOMOTIVE CANADA LTEE

FABRICATIONS DOR-VAL LTEE, LES　p 1323
11800 BOUL LAURENTIEN, SAINT-LAURENT, QC, H4K 2E1
(514) 336-7780　SIC 2531

FABRICLAND　p 11
See FABRICLAND PACIFIC LIMITED

FABRICLAND　p 217
See FABRICLAND PACIFIC LIMITED

FABRICLAND　p 992
See FABRICLAND DISTRIBUTORS (WESTERN) CORP

FABRICLAND DISTRIBUTORS (WESTERN) CORP　p 992
1450 CASTLEFIELD AVE, TORONTO, ON, M6M 1Y6
(416) 658-2200　SIC 5949

FABRICLAND DISTRIBUTORS INC p 992
1450 CASTLEFIELD AVE, TORONTO, ON, M6M 1Y6

(416) 658-2200　SIC 5949

FABRICLAND PACIFIC LIMITED　p 11
495 36 ST NE SUITE 104, CALGARY, AB, T2A 6K3
(855) 554-4840　SIC 5949

FABRICLAND PACIFIC LIMITED　p 217
2121 TRANS CANADA HWY E, KAMLOOPS, BC, V2C 4A6
(250) 374-3360　SIC 5949

FABRICMASTER INC　p 989
76 MIRANDA AVE SUITE 2, TORONTO, ON, M6E 5A1
(416) 658-2205　SIC 5131

FABRICVILLE CO. INC　p 1225
9195 RUE CHARLES-DE LA TOUR, MONTREAL, QC, H4N 1M3
(514) 383-3942　SIC 5949

FABRIMET INC　p 1096
4375 BOUL SAINT-JOSEPH, DRUMMONDVILLE, QC, J2B 1T8
(819) 472-1164　SIC 3441

FABRIQUE ARHOMA INC, LA　p 1175
1700 RUE ONTARIO E, MONTREAL, QC, H2L 1S7
(514) 598-1700　SIC 5149

FABRIQUE DE LA PAROISSE NOTRE-DAME DE MONTREAL, LA　p 1188
424 RUE SAINT-SULPICE, MONTREAL, QC, H2Y 2V5
(514) 842-2925　SIC 8661

FABRIQUE DU CARNAVAL, LA　p 1260
See CARNAVAL DE QUEBEC INC

FABRIQUE JML　p 1303
See 113514 CANADA INC

FABRIS INC.　p 892
1216 SOUTH SERVICE RD, STONEY CREEK, ON, L8E 5C4
(905) 643-4111　SIC 3599

FABRIS-MILANO GROUP LTD, THE　p 382
1035 ERIN ST, WINNIPEG, MB, R3G 2X1
(204) 783-7179　SIC 1752

FABSPEC INC　p 1376
160 RUE DU ROI, SOREL-TRACY, QC, J3P 4N5
(450) 742-0451　SIC 3443

FABTRENDS INTERNATIONAL INC p 1178
9350 AV DE L'ESPLANADE, MONTREAL, QC, H2N 1V6
(514) 382-2210　SIC 5131

FABUTAN CORPORATION　p 35
5925 3 ST SE, CALGARY, AB, T2H 1K3
(403) 640-2100　SIC 6794

FACCA INCORPORATED　p 858
2097 COUNTY RD 31 SUITE 1, RUSCOM STATION, ON, N0R 1R0
(519) 975-0377　SIC 1622

FACES　p 997
See FACES COSMETICS INC

FACES COSMETICS INC　p 997
520 GARYRAY DR, TORONTO, ON, M9L 1R1
(416) 746-7575　SIC 5999

FACILITE INFORMATIQUE　p 1204
See FACILITE INFORMATIQUE CANADA INC

FACILITE INFORMATIQUE CANADA INC p 1204
5 PLACE VILLE-MARIE BUREAU 1045, MONTREAL, QC, H3B 2G2
(514) 284-5636　SIC 7379

FACILITY ASSOCIATION　p 944
777 BAY ST SUITE 2400, TORONTO, ON, M5G 2C8
(416) 863-1750　SIC 6331

FACILITY SERVICES DEPARTMENT p 652
See THAMES VALLEY DISTRICT SCHOOL BOARD

FACTOR FORMS NIAGARA　p 758
See 2619473 ONTARIO INC

FACTOR FORMS WEST LTD　p 114
8411 MCINTYRE RD NW, EDMONTON, AB, T6E 6G3
(780) 468-1111　SIC 5112

FACTOR GAS LIQUIDS INC　p 64
611 10 AVE SW SUITE 180, CALGARY, AB, T2R 0B2
(403) 266-8778　SIC 4925

FACTORS GROUP OF NUTRITIONAL COMPANIES INC　p 200
1550 UNITED BLVD, COQUITLAM, BC, V3K 6Y2
(604) 777-1757　SIC 2833

FACTORY DIRECT COMPUTERS　p 558
See RLOGISTICS LIMITED PARTNERSHIP

FACTORY OUTLET TRAILERS INC　p 136
80010 475 AVE, HIGH RIVER, AB, T1V 1M3
(403) 603-3311　SIC 5599

FACTORY SHOE　p 639
See FACTORY SHOE (KITCHENER) LTD

FACTORY SHOE (KITCHENER) LTD p 639
686 VICTORIA ST N, KITCHENER, ON, N2H 5G1
(519) 743-2021　SIC 5661

FACULTE D'ADMINISTRATION　p 1372
See UNIVERSITE DE SHERBROOKE

FACULTY CLUB OF THE UNIVERSITY OF ALBERTA EDMONTON, THE　p 117
11435 SASKATCHEWAN DR NW, EDMONTON, AB, T6G 2G9
(780) 492-4231　SIC 5812

FACULTY MEDICINE　p 325
See UNIVERSITY OF BRITISH COLUMBIA, THE

FACULTY OF AGRICULTURE　p 468
See DALHOUSIE UNIVERSITY

FACULTY OF ARTS　p 117
See GOVERNORS OF THE UNIVERSITY OF ALBERTA, THE

FACULTY OF ARTS AND SCIENCE　p 975
See GOVERNING COUNCIL OF THE UNIVERSITY OF TORONTO, THE

FACULTY OF ARTS AND SOCIAL SCIENCES　p 451
See DALHOUSIE UNIVERSITY

FACULTY OF BIOLOGICAL & BIOMEDICAL ENGINEERING　p 1199
See ROYAL INSTITUTE FOR ADVANCEMENT OF LEARNING MCGILL

FACULTY OF DENTISTRY　p 945
See GOVERNING COUNCIL OF THE UNIVERSITY OF TORONTO, THE

FACULTY OF DENTISTRY, THE　p 325
See UNIVERSITY OF BRITISH COLUMBIA, THE

FACULTY OF EDUCATION　p 658
See UNIVERSITY OF WESTERN ONTARIO, THE

FACULTY OF ENGINEERING DIV SITE 822
See UNIVERSITY OF OTTAWA

FACULTY OF KINESIOLOGY AND PHYSICAL EDUCATION　p 975
See GOVERNING COUNCIL OF THE UNIVERSITY OF TORONTO, THE

FACULTY OF LAW　p 117
See GOVERNORS OF THE UNIVERSITY OF ALBERTA, THE

FACULTY OF LAW　p 570
See GOVERNING COUNCIL OF THE UNIVERSITY OF TORONTO, THE

FACULTY OF MEDECINE　p 41
See GOVERNORS OF THE UNIVERSITY OF CALGARY, THE

FACULTY OF MEDICINE　p 451
See DALHOUSIE UNIVERSITY

FACULTY OF MEDICINE　p 819
See UNIVERSITY OF OTTAWA

FACULTY OF MEDICINE　p 975
See GOVERNING COUNCIL OF THE UNIVERSITY OF TORONTO, THE

FACULTY OF MUSIC　p 570
See GOVERNING COUNCIL OF THE UNIVERSITY OF TORONTO, THE

FACULTY OF SOCIAL SCIENCES　p 822

See UNIVERSITY OF OTTAWA

FADY AUTO INC　p 1092
4648 BOUL SAINT-JEAN, DOLLARD-DES-ORMEAUX, QC, H9H 2A6
(514) 696-7777　SIC 5511

FAEMA　p 989
See 1100833 ONTARIO LIMITED

FAG AEROSPACE INC　p 895
See SCHAEFFLER AEROSPACE CANADA INC

FAGA GROUP INC　p 904
137 LANGSTAFF RD E, THORNHILL, ON, L3T 3M6
(905) 881-2552　SIC 1794

FAGEN & FILS　p 1204
625 RUE BELMONT, MONTREAL, QC, H3B 2M1
　SIC 5093

FAGEN INTERNATIONAL FREIGHT SERVICES　p 1322
See J. FAGEN & FILS INC

FAHRAMET, DIV OF　p 809
See KUBOTA MATERIALS CANADA CORPORATION

FAHRHALL MECHANICAL CONTRACTORS LIMITED　p 1025
3822 SANDWICH ST, WINDSOR, ON, N9C 1C1
(519) 969-7822　SIC 1711

FAHRHALL MECHANICAL HOME COMFORT　p 1025
See FAHRHALL MECHANICAL CONTRACTORS LIMITED

FAIR HAVEN UNITED CHURCH HOMES, THE　p 288
2720 48TH AVE E, VANCOUVER, BC, V5S 1G7
(604) 433-2939　SIC 8361

FAIR ISLE FORD SALES LTD　p 1039
GD STN CENTRAL, CHARLOTTETOWN, PE, C1A 7K1
(902) 368-3673　SIC 5511

FAIR, MIKE CHEVROLET BUICK GMC CADILLAC LTD　p 881
199 LOMBARD ST, SMITHS FALLS, ON, K7A 5B8
(613) 283-3882　SIC 5511

FAIRCHILD TELEVISION LTD　p 852
35 EAST BEAVER CREEK RD UNIT 8, RICHMOND HILL, ON, L4B 1B3
(905) 889-8090　SIC 4841

FAIRCREST FARMS LIMITED　p 1035
455017 45TH LINE, WOODSTOCK, ON, N4S 7V7
(519) 537-8713　SIC 5153

FAIRDEAL IMPORT & EXPORT LTD p 185
3855 HENNING DR UNIT 116, BURNABY, BC, V5C 6N3
(604) 257-2939　SIC 5199

FAIRFAX FINANCIAL HOLDINGS LIMITED p 962
95 WELLINGTON ST W SUITE 800, TORONTO, ON, M5J 2N7
(416) 367-4941　SIC 6282

FAIRFAX INDIA HOLDINGS CORPORATION　p 962
95 WELLINGTON ST W SUITE 800, TORONTO, ON, M5J 2N7
(416) 367-4755　SIC 6719

FAIRFIELD INN & SUITESSM BY MARRIOTT TORONTO AIRPORT　p 669
See EASTON'S GROUP OF HOTELS INC

FAIRFIELD PARK　p 1005
See LAPOINTE-FISHER NURSING HOME, LIMITED

FAIRFIELD PROPAGATORS LTD　p 196
10718 BELL RD, CHILLIWACK, BC, V2P 6H5
(604) 792-9988　SIC 0181

▲ Public Company　■ Public Company Family Member　**HQ** Headquarters　**BR** Branch　**SL** Single Location

FAIRHAVEN HOME p 839
881 DUTTON RD, PETERBOROUGH, ON, K9H 7S4
(705) 743-4265 *SIC 8051*

FAIRHAVEN LONG TERM CARE p 839
881 DUTTON RD, PETERBOROUGH, ON, K9H 7S4
(705) 743-0881 *SIC 8051*

FAIRHOLME COLONY FARMS LTD p 354
E 27-9-8 S, PORTAGE LA PRAIRIE, MB, R1N 3B9
(204) 252-2225 *SIC 0762*

FAIRHOLME COLONY OF HUTTERIAN BRETHREN-TRUST p 354
See FAIRHOLME COLONY FARMS LTD

FAIRLEY & STEVENS FORD LINCOLN p 446
See FAIRLEY & STEVENS LIMITED

FAIRLEY & STEVENS LIMITED p 446
580 WINDMILL RD, DARTMOUTH, NS, B3B 1B5
(902) 468-6271 *SIC 5511*

FAIRMALL LEASEHOLDS INC p 767
1800 SHEPPARD AVE E SUITE 330, NORTH YORK, ON, M2J 5A7
(416) 491-0151 *SIC 6512*

FAIRMONT BANFF SPRINGS, THE p 4
See FAIRMONT HOTELS & RESORTS INC

FAIRMONT CHATEAU LAKE LOUISE, THE p 138
See FAIRMONT HOTELS & RESORTS INC

FAIRMONT CHATEAU LAURIER p 821
See FAIRMONT HOTELS & RESORTS INC

FAIRMONT EMPRESS, THE p 336
See FAIRMONT HOTELS & RESORTS INC

FAIRMONT HOT SPRINGS RESORT LTD p 212
5225 FAIRMONT RESORT RD RR 1, FAIRMONT HOT SPRINGS, BC, V0B 1L1
(250) 345-6070 *SIC 7011*

FAIRMONT HOTEL LE REINE ELIZABETH p 1204
See FAIRMONT HOTELS & RESORTS INC

FAIRMONT HOTEL MACDONALD, THE p 89
See FAIRMONT HOTELS & RESORTS INC

FAIRMONT HOTEL VANCOUVER, THE p 304
See FAIRMONT HOTELS & RESORTS INC

FAIRMONT HOTELS & RESORTS INC p 4
405 SPRAY AVE, BANFF, AB, T1L 1J4
(403) 762-6860 *SIC 7011*

FAIRMONT HOTELS & RESORTS INC p 49
133 9 AVE SW, CALGARY, AB, T2P 2M3
(403) 262-1234 *SIC 7011*

FAIRMONT HOTELS & RESORTS INC p 49
255 BARCLAY PARADE SW, CALGARY, AB, T2P 5C2
(403) 266-7200 *SIC 7011*

FAIRMONT HOTELS & RESORTS INC p 89
10065 100 ST NW, EDMONTON, AB, T5J 0N6
(780) 424-5181 *SIC 7011*

FAIRMONT HOTELS & RESORTS INC p 137
1 LODGE RD, JASPER, AB, T0E 1E0
(780) 852-3301 *SIC 7011*

FAIRMONT HOTELS & RESORTS INC p 138
111 LAKE LOUISE DR, LAKE LOUISE, AB, T0L 1E0
(403) 522-3511 *SIC 7011*

FAIRMONT HOTELS & RESORTS INC p 264
3111 GRANT MCCONACHIE WAY, RICHMOND, BC, V7B 0A6
(604) 207-5200 *SIC 7011*

FAIRMONT HOTELS & RESORTS INC p 304
900 CANADA PL, VANCOUVER, BC, V6C 3L5
(604) 691-1991 *SIC 7011*

FAIRMONT HOTELS & RESORTS INC p 304
900 GEORGIA ST W, VANCOUVER, BC, V6C 2W6
(604) 684-3131 *SIC 7011*

FAIRMONT HOTELS & RESORTS INC p 336
721 GOVERNMENT ST, VICTORIA, BC, V8W 1W5

(250) 384-8111 *SIC 7011*

FAIRMONT HOTELS & RESORTS INC p 343
4599 CHATEAU BLVD, WHISTLER, BC, V8E 0Z5
(604) 938-8000 *SIC 7011*

FAIRMONT HOTELS & RESORTS INC p 374
2 LOMBARD PL, WINNIPEG, MB, R3B 0Y3
(204) 957-1350 *SIC 7011*

FAIRMONT HOTELS & RESORTS INC p 408
2081 MAIN ST, MONCTON, NB, E1E 1J2
(506) 877-3025 *SIC 7389*

FAIRMONT HOTELS & RESORTS INC p 418
184 ADOLPHUS ST, ST ANDREWS, NB, E5B 1T7
(506) 529-3004 *SIC 7231*

FAIRMONT HOTELS & RESORTS INC p 418
184 ADOLPHUS ST, ST ANDREWS, NB, E5B 1T7
(506) 529-8823 *SIC 7011*

FAIRMONT HOTELS & RESORTS INC p 821
1 RIDEAU ST, OTTAWA, ON, K1N 8S7
(613) 241-1414 *SIC 7011*

FAIRMONT HOTELS & RESORTS INC p 980
155 WELLINGTON ST W SUITE 3300, TORONTO, ON, M5V 0C3
(416) 874-2600 *SIC 7011*

FAIRMONT HOTELS & RESORTS INC p 1122
181 RUE RICHELIEU BUREAU 200, LA MALBAIE, QC, G5A 1X7
(418) 665-3703 *SIC 7011*

FAIRMONT HOTELS & RESORTS INC p 1159
392 RUE NOTRE-DAME, MONTEBELLO, QC, J0V 1L0
(819) 423-6341 *SIC 7011*

FAIRMONT HOTELS & RESORTS INC p 1204
900 BOUL RENE-LEVESQUE O, MONTREAL, QC, H3B 4A5
(514) 861-3511 *SIC 7011*

FAIRMONT HOTELS INC p 1201
See ACCOR MANAGEMENT CANADA INC

FAIRMONT JASPER PARK LODGE p 137
See FAIRMONT HOTELS & RESORTS INC

FAIRMONT LE CHATEAU FRONTENAC p 1269
See FRONTENAC HOTEL GP INC

FAIRMONT LE CHATEAU MONTEBELLO p 1159
See FAIRMONT HOTELS & RESORTS INC

FAIRMONT LE MANOIR RICHELIEU p 1122
See FAIRMONT HOTELS & RESORTS INC

FAIRMONT NEWFOUNDLAND, THE p 432
See HOTEL NEWFOUNDLAND (1982)

FAIRMONT PACIFIC RIM p 301
See 299 BURRARD HOTEL LIMITED PARTNERSHIP

FAIRMONT PALLISER, THE p 49
See FAIRMONT HOTELS & RESORTS INC

FAIRMONT ROYAL YORK p 966
See ROYAL YORK OPERATIONS LP

FAIRMONT SHIPPING (CANADA) LIMITED p 313
1112 PENDER ST W SUITE 300, VANCOUVER, BC, V6E 2S1
(604) 685-3318 *SIC 4731*

FAIRMONT TREMBLANT p 1159
See CHATEAU M.T. INC

FAIRMONT VANCOUVER AIRPORT HOTEL p 264
See FAIRMONT HOTELS & RESORTS INC

FAIRMONT VILLA MANAGEMENT p 212
5247 FAIRMONT CREEK RD RR 1, FAIRMONT HOT SPRINGS, BC, V0B 1L1
(250) 345-6341 *SIC 8741*

FAIRMONT WINNIPEG p 374
See FAIRMONT HOTELS & RESORTS INC

FAIRMOUNT HOME FOR THE AGED p 594
2069 BATTERSEA RD, GLENBURNIE, ON, K0H 1S0
(613) 548-9400 *SIC 8361*

FAIRMOUNT MANOIR RICHELIEU p 1122
See SOCIETE EN COMMANDITE MANOIR RICHELIEU

FAIRSTONE FINANCIAL INC p 552
See FAIRSTONE FINANCIERE INC

FAIRSTONE FINANCIERE INC p 552
1750 STEELES AVE W, CONCORD, ON, L4K 2L7
(905) 761-4538 *SIC 8742*

FAIRSTONE FINANCIERE INC p 1204
630 BOUL RENE-LEVESQUE O BUREAU 1400, MONTREAL, QC, H3B 1S6
(800) 995-2274 *SIC 6141*

FAIRSTONE SALES SOLUTIONS p 1204
See FAIRSTONE FINANCIERE INC

FAIRVERN NURSING HOME p 620
See HUNTSVILLE DISTRICT NURSING HOME INC

FAIRVIEW CHRYSLER JEEP p 402
See FAIRVIEW PLYMOUTH CHRYSLER LTD

FAIRVIEW COLONY p 81
GD, CROSSFIELD, AB, T0M 0S0
(403) 946-4524 *SIC 0119*

FAIRVIEW COVE AUTO LIMITED p 457
30 BEDFORD HWY, HALIFAX, NS, B3M 2J2
(902) 457-1555 *SIC 5511*

FAIRVIEW FITTINGS & MANUFACTURING LIMITED p 797
1170 INVICTA DR UNIT C, OAKVILLE, ON, L6H 6G1
(905) 338-0800 *SIC 5074*

FAIRVIEW HEALTH COMPLEX p 126
See ALBERTA HEALTH SERVICES

FAIRVIEW IMPORT MOTORS INC p 635
2385 SHIRLEY DR, KITCHENER, ON, N2B 3X4
(519) 893-9000 *SIC 5511*

FAIRVIEW LODGE HOME FOR AGED p 1014
See CORPORATION OF THE REGIONAL MUNICIPALITY OF DURHAM, THE

FAIRVIEW LTD p 797
1170 INVICTA DR UNIT C, OAKVILLE, ON, L6H 6G1
(905) 338-0800 *SIC 5074*

FAIRVIEW LTD p 797
1170 INVICTA DR UNIT C, OAKVILLE, ON, L6H 6G1
(905) 338-0800 *SIC 5085*

FAIRVIEW MALL p 767
See FAIRMALL LEASEHOLDS INC

FAIRVIEW MAZDA p 1249
See AUTOMOBILES MET-HAM INC

FAIRVIEW MENNONITE HOMES p 539
515 LANGS DR SUITE D, CAMBRIDGE, ON, N3H 5E4
(519) 653-2222 *SIC 8361*

FAIRVIEW NISSAN LIMITEE p 1250
345 BOUL BRUNSWICK, POINTE-CLAIRE, QC, H9R 4S1
(514) 697-5222 *SIC 5511*

FAIRVIEW PLYMOUTH CHRYSLER LTD p 402
1065 HANWELL RD, FREDERICTON, NB, E3C 1A5
(506) 458-8955 *SIC 5511*

FAIRVILLE COLONY p 5
See FAIRVILLE FARMING CO LTD

FAIRVILLE CONSTRUCTION LTD p 416
12 LINTON RD, SAINT JOHN, NB, E2M 5V4
(506) 635-1573 *SIC 1611*

FAIRVILLE FARMING CO LTD p 5
GD, BASSANO, AB, T0J 0B0
(403) 641-2404 *SIC 0191*

FAIRWAY COACHLINES INC p 365
339 ARCHIBALD ST, WINNIPEG, MB, R2J 0W6
(204) 989-7007 *SIC 4131*

FAIRWAY FORD SALES LTD p 358
236 MAIN ST, STEINBACH, MB, R5G 1Y6
(204) 326-3412 *SIC 5511*

FAIRWAY GOLF p 1236
See SUGI CANADA LTEE

FAIRWAY HOLDINGS (1994) LTD p 339
272 GORGE RD W, VICTORIA, BC, V9A 1M7
(250) 385-4814 *SIC 5411*

FAIRWAY HONDA p 423
See WINDJAMMER INVESTMENTS INC

FAIRWAY INSURANCE SERVICES INCORPORATED p 449
104 MONTAGUE ROW, DIGBY, NS, B0V 1A0
(902) 245-4741 *SIC 6411*

FAIRWAY MANAGEMENT CORPORATION LTD p 1402
4430 RUE SAINTE-CATHERINE O BUREAU 505, WESTMOUNT, QC, H3Z 3E4
(514) 935-1212 *SIC 8361*

FAIRWAY MARKET p 338
See BEST COST FOOD LTD

FAIRWAY MARKET #1 p 339
See FAIRWAY HOLDINGS (1994) LTD

FAIRWAY MARKET #4 p 333
See CANAWAY HOLDINGS LTD

FAIRWAY MARKET 3 p 340
See TRIPLE CROWN FOODS LTD

FAIRWAY MARKET GROCERY p 234
See MIDISLAND HOLDINGS LTD

FAIRWAY MARKET NO.6 p 333
See MAYFAIR VILLAGE FOODS

FAIRWAY PRODUCTS INC p 254
13611 MAYCREST WAY, RICHMOND, BC, V6V 2J4
(604) 278-1919 *SIC 5072*

FAIRWAY REALTIES p 1218
See IMMEUBLES FAIRWAY INC, LES

FAIRWAY SPECIALTY VEHICLES p 358
See FAIRWAY FORD SALES LTD

FAIRWEATHER LTD p 789
1185 CALEDONIA RD, NORTH YORK, ON, M6A 2X1
(416) 785-1771 *SIC 5621*

FAITHLIFE FINANCIAL p 1008
470 WEBER ST N, WATERLOO, ON, N2L 6J2
(519) 886-4610 *SIC 6311*

FALCK SAFETY SERVICES CANADA INCORPORATED p 443
20 ORION CRT SUITE 1, DARTMOUTH, NS, B2Y 4W6
(902) 466-7878 *SIC 8748*

FALCO ELECTRICAL SYSTEMS LTD p 29
3606 MANCHESTER RD SE, CALGARY, AB, T2G 3Z5
(403) 287-7632 *SIC 1731*

FALCO TECHNOLOGIES INC p 1123
1245 RUE INDUSTRIELLE, LA PRAIRIE, QC, J5R 2E4
(450) 444-0566 *SIC 3589*

FALCON BAKERY p 349
21 PARK BLVD, FALCON BEACH, MB, R0E 0N0
(204) 349-8993 *SIC 5149*

FALCON CAPITAL CORPORATION p 384
590 BERRY ST, WINNIPEG, MB, R3H 0R9
(204) 786-6451 *SIC 6719*

FALCON FASTENERS LIMITED p 871
251 NANTUCKET BLVD, SCARBOROUGH, ON, M1P 2P2
(416) 751-8284 *SIC 6719*

FALCON HOMES LTD p 169
17 BEJU INDUSTRIAL DR, SYLVAN LAKE, AB, T4S 2J4
(403) 887-7333 *SIC 1521*

FALCON MOTOR XPRESS LTD p 498
8 WALLABY WAY BLDG 8, BRAMPTON, ON, L6R 3C7
(866) 383-9100 *SIC 4212*

FALHER AND DISTRICT COOPERATIVE ASSOCIATION LTD, THE p 126
108 MAIN ST, FALHER, AB, T0H 1M0
(780) 837-2261 *SIC 5411*

FALLS CHEVROLET CADILLAC LTD p 760
5888 THOROLD STONE RD, NIAGARA FALLS, ON, L2J 1A2
(905) 353-9123 *SIC 5511*

FALLSVIEW NIAGARA LODGING COMPANY p 758
6733 FALLSVIEW BLVD, NIAGARA FALLS, ON, L2G 3W7
(905) 356-1944   *SIC* 7011
FALLSVIEW PLAZA HOTEL p 758
See 1712093 ONTARIO LIMITED
FALOM INC p 542
600 GRAND AVE W SUITE 10012, CHATHAM, ON, N7L 4E3
(519) 354-5842   *SIC* 6513
FALSE CREEK SURGICAL CENTRE INC p 293
555 8TH AVE W SUITE 600, VANCOUVER, BC, V5Z 1C6
(604) 739-9695   *SIC* 8011
FAMA INDUSTRIES CORPORATION p 209
7480 MACDONALD RD, DELTA, BC, V4G 1N2
(604) 952-0880   *SIC* 5031
FAMAR MONTREAL INC p 1250
3535 RTE TRANSCANADIENNE, POINTE-CLAIRE, QC, H9R 1B4
(514) 428-7488   *SIC* 2834
FAMIC TECHNOLOGIES INC p 1324
9999 BOUL CAVENDISH BUREAU 350, SAINT-LAURENT, QC, H4M 2X5
(514) 748-8050   *SIC* 5045
FAMILI-PRIX p 1115
See MEDI-PARE LTEE
FAMILIPRIX INC p 1276
6000 RUE ARMAND-VIAU BUREAU 418, QUEBEC, QC, G2C 2C5
(418) 847-3311   *SIC* 5122
FAMILIPRIX-ROY ET LEBLOND INC p 1304
899 17E RUE, SAINT-GEORGES, QC, G5Y 4W1
(418) 228-1017   *SIC* 5912
FAMILLE CHARLES IGA p 1104
See ALIMENTATIONS BECHAR INC
FAMILY & CHILDREN'S SERVICES p 838
See CHILDREN'S AID SOCIETY OF THE COUNTY OF RENFREW
FAMILY & CHILDREN'S SERVICES NIAGARA p 887
See CHILDREN'S AID SOCIETY OF THE NIAGARA REGION, THE
FAMILY AND CHILDREN'S SERVICES OF THE REGIONAL MUNICIPALITY OF WATERLOO p 636
See CHILDREN'S AID SOCIETY OF THE REGIONAL MUNICIPALITY OF WATERLOO, THE
FAMILY CENTRED PRACTICES GROUP INC p 321
1820 FIR ST UNIT 210, VANCOUVER, BC, V6J 3B1
(604) 736-0094   *SIC* 8748
FAMILY DYNAMICS p 374
393 PORTAGE AVE SUITE 401, WINNIPEG, MB, R3B 3H6
(204) 947-1401   *SIC* 8322
FAMILY FOODS p 24
See MRT ENTERPRISES INC
FAMILY FOODS PORTAGE AVENUE p 385
1881 PORTAGE AVE, WINNIPEG, MB, R3J 0H3
(204) 988-4810   *SIC* 5411
FAMILY INSURANCE SOLUTIONS INC p 313
1177 HASTINGS ST W SUITE 1400, VANCOUVER, BC, V6E 2K3
(604) 687-2655   *SIC* 6411
FAMILY LEISURE CENTRE p 39
See FAMILY LEISURE CENTRE ASSOCIATION OF SOUTHEAST CALGARY, THE
FAMILY LEISURE CENTRE ASSOCIATION OF SOUTHEAST CALGARY, THE p 39
11150 BONAVENTURE DR SE, CALGARY, AB, T2J 6R9
(403) 278-7542   *SIC* 7999

FAMILY SERVICE TORONTO p 994
202-128A STERLING RD, TORONTO, ON, M6R 2B7
(416) 595-9230   *SIC* 8322
FAMILY SIDE PURPLE SHIELD p 666
See ASSURANT LIFE OF CANADA MARKHAM
FAMILY VISION CARE LTD p 89
10088 102 AVE NW SUITE 1805, EDMONTON, AB, T5J 2Z1
(780) 423-2128   *SIC* 5995
FAMILY WEALTH ADVISORS LTD p 839
22 FOSTER ST, PERTH, ON, K7H 1R6
(613) 264-8267   *SIC* 6311
FAMILY YMCA OF REGINA p 1419
See YOUNG MENS CHRISTIAN ASSOCIATION OF REGINA
FAMME & CO. PROFESSIONAL CORPORATION p 896
125 ONTARIO ST, STRATFORD, ON, N5A 3H1
(519) 271-7581   *SIC* 8721
FAMOUS COFFEE SHOP, THE p 759
6380 FALLSVIEW BLVD UNIT R 1, NIAGARA FALLS, ON, L2G 7Y6
(905) 354-7775   *SIC* 5812
FAMOUS FOODS p 287
See FAMOUS FOODS MARKETS LTD
FAMOUS FOODS MARKETS LTD p 287
1595 KINGSWAY UNIT 101, VANCOUVER, BC, V5N 2R8
(604) 872-3019   *SIC* 5411
FAMOUS PEOPLE PLAYERS p 575
See PEOPLE PLAYERS INC
FANA SPORTS INC p 1344
6140 RUE MARIVAUX, SAINT-LEONARD, QC, H1P 3K3
(514) 648-8888   *SIC* 5136
FANCHEM LTD p 592
1012 GORE RD, FREELTON, ON, L8B 0Z5
(905) 659-3351   *SIC* 5169
FANCY POKKET CORPORATION p 408
1220 ST GEORGE BLVD, MONCTON, NB, E1E 4K7
(506) 853-7299   *SIC* 5461
FANNY BAY OYSTERS p 212
See TAYLOR SHELLFISH CANADA ULC
FANOTECH ENVIRO INC p 620
220 OLD NORTH RD, HUNTSVILLE, ON, P1H 2J4
(705) 788-3046   *SIC* 3713
FANSHAWE COLLEGE p 652
See FANSHAWE COLLEGE OF APPLIED ARTS AND TECHNOLOGY, T
FANSHAWE COLLEGE OF APPLIED ARTS AND TECHNOLOGY, T p 652
1001 BOUL FANSHAWE COLLEGE, LONDON, ON, N5Y 5R6
(519) 452-4277   *SIC* 8222
FANTAISIE D'ETAIN INC p 1402
21 AV GLADSTONE BUREAU 2, WESTMOUNT, QC, H3Z 1Z3
(514) 735-4141   *SIC* 5099
FANTASTIC CLEANING p 1419
See SIERRA VENTURES CORP
FANTASTIC-T KNITTERS INC p 285
1374 VENABLES ST, VANCOUVER, BC, V5L 2G4
(604) 255-8883   *SIC* 5136
FANUC CANADA, LTD p 722
6774 FINANCIAL DR, MISSISSAUGA, ON, L5N 7J6
(905) 812-2300   *SIC* 5084
FAR EAST FOOD PRODUCTS LIMITED p 855
273 ENFORD RD, RICHMOND HILL, ON, L4C 3E9
(905) 883-8717   *SIC* 2052
FAR EAST WATCHCASES LTD p 855
120 NEWKIRK RD UNIT 5&6, RICHMOND HILL, ON, L4C 9S7
(905) 787-9919   *SIC* 7631
FARES CONSTRUCTION LTD p 456

3480 JOSEPH HOWE DR SUITE 500, HALIFAX, NS, B3L 0B5
(902) 457-6676   *SIC* 1522
FARGEY'S DECORATING CENTRE p 153
See FARGEYS PAINT & WALL COVERINGS LTD
FARGEYS PAINT & WALL COVERINGS LTD p 153
3433 50 AVE, RED DEER, AB, T4N 3Y3
(403) 343-3133   *SIC* 5198
FARIS TEAM CORP, THE p 486
431 BAYVIEW DR UNIT 14, BARRIE, ON, L4N 8Y2
(705) 797-8485   *SIC* 6531
FARLEY MANUFACTURING INC p 849
6 KERR CRES, PUSLINCH, ON, N0B 2J0
(519) 821-5422   *SIC* 3069
FARLEYCO HEALTHCARE p 852
See FARLEYCO MARKETING INC
FARLEYCO MARKETING INC p 852
30 EAST WILMOT ST, RICHMOND HILL, ON, L4B 1A4
(905) 709-2650   *SIC* 5122
FARM BOY COMPANY INC p 562
814 SYDNEY ST, CORNWALL, ON, K6H 3J8
(613) 938-8566   *SIC* 5431
FARM BOY FRESH MARKETS p 562
See FARM BOY COMPANY INC
FARM BOY SUPERMARKET p 830
1495 RICHMOND RD, OTTAWA, ON, K2B 6R9
(613) 688-2882   *SIC* 5411
FARM BUSINESS CONSULTANTS INC p 649
2109 OXFORD ST E, LONDON, ON, N5V 2Z9
(519) 453-5040   *SIC* 7291
FARM BUSINESS CONSULTANTS LTD p 11
3015 5 AVE NE SUITE 150, CALGARY, AB, T2A 6T8
(403) 735-6105   *SIC* 8741
FARM CREDIT CANADA p 1417
1800 HAMILTON ST, REGINA, SK, S4P 4L3
(306) 780-8100   *SIC* 6159
FARM FED, DIV OF p 177
See K & R POULTRY LTD
FARM MEATS CANADA DIV p 136
See ROLLOVER PREMIUM PET FOOD LTD
FARM MUTUAL REINSURANCE PLAN INC p 536
350 PINEBUSH RD, CAMBRIDGE, ON, N1T 1Z6
(519) 740-6415   *SIC* 6331
FARM SUPPLY, DIV OF p 442
See SCOTIAN GOLD CO-OPERATIVE LIMITED
FARM-FLEET INC p 888
23703 WELLBURN RD RR 3, ST MARYS, ON, N4X 1C6
(519) 461-1499   *SIC* 5083
FARMBOY MARKETS LIMITED p 840
754 LANSDOWNE ST W, PETERBOROUGH, ON, K9J 1Z3
(705) 745-2811   *SIC* 5411
FARMBRO ALL-TRAC LTD p 716
4200 SLADEVIEW CRES, MISSISSAUGA, ON, L5L 5Z2
(905) 569-0592   *SIC* 7549
FARMER CONSTRUCTION LTD p 339
360 HARBOUR RD, VICTORIA, BC, V9A 3S1
(250) 388-5121   *SIC* 1542
FARMER INDUSTRIES GROUP INC p 339
360A HARBOUR RD, VICTORIA, BC, V9A 3S1
(250) 360-1511   *SIC* 6712
FARMER'S EDGE WEST INC p 138
3413 53 AVE, LACOMBE, AB, T4L 0C6
(403) 782-2204   *SIC* 0139
FARMER'S PICK MARKET p 831
See F. P. RIDEAUVIEW INC
FARMERS CO-OPERATIVE DAIRY LIMITED

p 455
GD, HALIFAX, NS, B3K 5Y6
SIC 5143
FARMERS DAIRY p 455
See FARMERS CO-OPERATIVE DAIRY LIMITED
FARMERS EDGE INC p 388
25 ROTHWELL RD, WINNIPEG, MB, R3P 2M5
(204) 452-3131   *SIC* 8748
FARMERS OF NORTH AMERICA p 1427
See FARMS AND FAMILIES OF NORTH AMERICA INCORPORATED
FARMERS' FRESH MUSHROOMS INC p 178
3555 ROSS RD, ABBOTSFORD, BC, V4X 1M6
(604) 857-5610   *SIC* 0182
FARMLINK MARKETING SOLUTIONS p 374
93 LOMBARD AVE SUITE 110, WINNIPEG, MB, R3B 3B1
(877) 376-5465   *SIC* 8748
FARMS AND FAMILIES OF NORTH AMERICA INCORPORATED p 1427
320 22ND ST E, SASKATOON, SK, S7K 0H1
(306) 665-2294   *SIC* 8621
FARNELL PACKAGING LIMITED p 446
30 ILSLEY AVE, DARTMOUTH, NS, B3B 1L3
(902) 468-9378   *SIC* 2673
FAROEX COMPOSITE TECHNOLOGIES p 350
See FAROEX LTD
FAROEX LTD p 350
123 ANSON ST, GIMLI, MB, R0C 1B1
(204) 642-6400   *SIC* 3299
FARONICS p 330
See FARONICS CORPORATION
FARONICS CORPORATION p 330
609 GRANVILLE ST SUITE 1400, VANCOUVER, BC, V7Y 1G5
(604) 637-3333   *SIC* 7371
FARPCNQ p 1204
See FOND D'ASSURANCE RESPONSABILITE PROFESSIONNELLE DE LA CHAMBRE DES NOTAIRES DU QUEBEC
FARPOPQ p 1196
See FONDS D'ASSURANCE RESPONSABILITE PROFESSIONNELLE DE L'ORDRE DES PHARMACIENS DU QUEBEC
FARQUHAR MASSEY WHOLESALE p 680
See MASSEY WHOLESALE LTD
FARR INSTALLATIONS LTD p 248
4912 HART HWY, PRINCE GEORGE, BC, V2K 3A1
(250) 962-0333   *SIC* 1791
FARRELLS EXCAVATING LTD p 434
2700 TRANS-CANADA HWY, ST. JOHN'S, NL, A1N 3C8
(709) 745-5904   *SIC* 1794
FARRIS, VAUGHAN, WILLS & MURPHY LLP p 330
700 GEORGIA ST W SUITE 25, VANCOUVER, BC, V7Y 1K8
(604) 684-9151   *SIC* 8111
FARROW GROUP INC p 1025
2001 HURON CHURCH RD, WINDSOR, ON, N9C 2L6
(519) 252-4415   *SIC* 6712
FARROW INTERNATIONAL p 1025
See FARROW, RUSSELL A. LIMITED
FARROW, RUSSELL A. LIMITED p 483
106 EARL THOMPSON RD, AYR, ON, N0B 1E0
(519) 740-9866   *SIC* 4731
FARROW, RUSSELL A. LIMITED p 1025
2001 HURON CHURCH RD, WINDSOR, ON, N9C 2L6
(519) 966-3003   *SIC* 4731
FAS BENEFIT ADMINISTRATORS LTD p 89
10154 108 ST NW, EDMONTON, AB, T5J

1L3

(780) 452-5161   SIC 6726

FASBEC   p 1276
See P.R. DISTRIBUTIONS INC

FASHION DISTRIBUTORS, THE   p 1126
See 115161 CANADA INC

FASKEN MARTINEAU   p 951
See FASKEN MARTINEAU DUMOULIN
LLP

FASKEN MARTINEAU DUMOULIN LLP p
304
550 BURRARD ST SUITE 2900, VANCOU-
VER, BC, V6C 0A3
(604) 631-3131   SIC 8111

FASKEN MARTINEAU DUMOULIN LLP p
951
333 BAY ST SUITE 2400, TORONTO, ON,
M5H 2T6
(416) 366-8381   SIC 8111

FASKEN MARTINEAU DUMOULIN LLP p
1229
800 RUE DU SQUARE-VICTORIA BUREAU
3700, MONTREAL, QC, H4Z 1A1
(514) 397-7400   SIC 8111

FASKEN MARTINEAU DUMOULIN LLP p
1269
140 GRANDE ALLEE E BUREAU 800,
QUEBEC, QC, G1R 5M8
(418) 640-2000   SIC 8111

FASSOM, DIV OF   p 844
See AVERY DENNISON CANADA CORPO-
RATION

FAST   p 209
See F.A.S.T. FIRST AID & SURVIVAL TECH-
NOLOGIES LIMITED

**FAST AIR EXECUTIVE AVIATION SER-
VICES**   p
385
See FAST AIR LTD

FAST AIR LTD   p 385
80 HANGAR LINE RD, WINNIPEG, MB, R3J
3Y7
(204) 982-7240   SIC 4512

FAST AS FLIGHT   p 702
See YRC FREIGHT CANADA COMPANY

FAST AS FLITE   p 187
See YRC FREIGHT CANADA COMPANY

FAST CONSULTANTS   p 1433
See FAST, DOUG & ASSOCIATES LTD

FAST LANE   p 138
See LACOMBE FORD SALES LTD

FAST TRUCKING SERVICE LTD   p 1405
1 FAST LANE, CARNDUFF, SK, S0C 0S0
(306) 482-3244   SIC 4212

FAST, DOUG & ASSOCIATES LTD p 1433
112 RESEARCH DR SUITE 112, SASKA-
TOON, SK, S7N 3R3
(306) 956-3070   SIC 8732

FASTCO CANADA   p 1393
See 168406 CANADA INC

FASTEEL INDUSTRIES LTD   p 279
19176 21 AVE, SURREY, BC, V3Z 3M3
(604) 542-8881   SIC 5051

FASTENAL CANADA LTD   p 636
900 WABANAKI DR, KITCHENER, ON, N2C
0B7
(519) 748-6566   SIC 5085

FASTENAL CANADA, LTEE   p 636
900 WABANAKI DR, KITCHENER, ON, N2C
0B7
(519) 748-6566   SIC 5085

FASTENER WAREHOUSE LTD   p 1427
820 46TH ST E, SASKATOON, SK, S7K 3V7
(306) 374-1199   SIC 5085

FASTENERS & FITTINGS INC   p 683
901 STEELES AVE E, MILTON, ON, L9T
5H3
(905) 670-2503   SIC 5085

FASTENING HOUSE INC   p 552
160 BASS PRO MILLS DR, CONCORD, ON,
L4K 0A7
(905) 669-7448   SIC 5085

FASTER LINEN SERVICE LIMITED p 574
89 TORLAKE CRES, ETOBICOKE, ON,

M8Z 1B4
(416) 252-2030   SIC 7213

FASTFRATE   p 15
See CONSOLIDATED FASTFRATE INC

FASTFRATE   p 1027
See CONSOLIDATED FASTFRATE INC

FASTFRATE   p 1127
See CONSOLIDATED FASTFRATE INC

FASTIK LABEL & SUPPLY INC   p 224
9703 199A ST, LANGLEY, BC, V1M 2X7
(604) 882-6853   SIC 7389

FASTLANE TECHNOLOGIES   p 934
See QUEST SOFTWARE CANADA INC

**FATHER BRESSANI CATHOLIC HIGH
SCHOOL**   p 1034
See YORK CATHOLIC DISTRICT SCHOOL
BOARD

FATHER LEO J AUSTIN   p 1016
See DURHAM CATHOLIC DISTRICT
SCHOOL BOARD

**FATHER MICHAEL GOETZ SECONDARY
SCHOOL**   p 709
See DUFFERIN-PEEL CATHOLIC DIS-
TRICT SCHOOL BOARD

**FATHERS OF CONFEDERATION BUILD-
INGS TRUST**   p
1039
145 RICHMOND ST, CHARLOTTETOWN,
PE, C1A 1J1
(902) 629-1166   SIC 6512

FATHOM FISH & SEAFOOD INC   p 458
339 HERRING COVE SUITE 215, HALIFAX,
NS, B3R 1V5
(902) 407-0700   SIC 5146

FATIMA AIT ADDI   p 1180
370 RUE JARRY E, MONTREAL, QC, H2P
1T9
(514) 382-4730   SIC 5912

FAUCHER INDUSTRIES   p 1344
See INDUSTRIES RAD INC

**FAURECIA EMISSIONS CONTROL TECH-
NOLOGIES CANADA, LTD**   p
503
40 SUMMERLEA RD, BRAMPTON, ON,
L6T 4X3
(905) 595-5668   SIC 3714

**FAUTEUX, BRUNO, BUSSIERE, LEEWAR-
DEN, CPA, S.E.N.C.R.L.**   p
1180
1100 BOUL CREMAZIE E BUREAU 805,
MONTREAL, QC, H2P 2X2
(514) 729-3221   SIC 8721

FAVA INVESTMENTS INC   p 552
25 INTERCHANGE WAY, CONCORD, ON,
L4K 5W3
(905) 660-4111   SIC 5063

**FAVREAU, GENDRON ASSURANCE ET
SERVICES FINANCIERS INC**   p 1055
505   RUE   DES   E?RABLES,
BEAUHARNOIS, QC, J6N 1T3
(450) 429-3755   SIC 6311

FAWCETT LUMBER   p 411
See FAWCETT, H. A. & SON LIMITED

FAWCETT TRACTOR SUPPLY LTD p 888
2126 ROAD 120, ST MARYS, ON, N4X 1C5
(519) 284-2379   SIC 5083

FAWCETT, H. A. & SON LIMITED   p 411
2 KING ST SUITE 2, PETITCODIAC, NB,
E4Z 4L2
(506) 756-3366   SIC 2421

FAYOLLE CANADA INC   p 1225
1655 RUE DE BEAUHARNOIS O, MON-
TREAL, QC, H4N 1J6
(514) 381-6970   SIC 6712

FBC   p 649
See FARM BUSINESS CONSULTANTS INC

FBI ENERGY   p 1057
See EBI ENERGIE INC

FBM CANADA GSD, INC   p 12
5155 48 AVE SE, CALGARY, AB, T2B 3S8
(403) 255-8157   SIC 5039

FBO-MONTREAL (YUL)   p 1278
See TRANS-SOL AVIATION SERVICE INC

FBT INC   p 885

413 LAKESHORE RD, ST CATHARINES,
ON, L2R 7K6
(905) 937-3333   SIC 3541

FC GEOSYNTHETIQUES INC   p 1360
1300 2E RUE DU PARC-INDUSTRIEL,
SAINTE-MARIE, QC, G6E 1G8
(418) 658-0200   SIC 5169

FCA CANADA INC   p 499
2000 WILLIAMS PKY, BRAMPTON, ON,
L6S 6B3
(905) 458-2800   SIC 1541

FCA CANADA INC   p 995
15 BROWNS LINE, TORONTO, ON, M8W
3S3
(416) 253-2300   SIC 3365

FCA CANADA INC   p 1019
2410 WALKER RD, WINDSOR, ON, N8W
3P6
(519) 973-2000   SIC 4212

FCA CANADA INC   p 1023
2199 CHRYSLER CTR, WINDSOR, ON,
N9A 4H6
(519) 973-2000   SIC 3711

FCA CANADA INC   p 1023
1 RIVERSIDE DR W, WINDSOR, ON, N9A
5K3
(519) 973-2000   SIC 3711

FCA CANADA INC   p 1250
3000 RTE TRANSCANADIENNE, POINTE-
CLAIRE, QC, H9R 1B1
(514) 630-2500   SIC 5012

FCB CANADA   p 986
See INTERPUBLIC GROUP OF COMPA-
NIES CANADA, INC, THE

FCC   p 1417
See FARM CREDIT CANADA

FCI   p 817
See FLEMING COMMUNICATIONS INC

FCL CO-OP WAREHOUSE SASKATOON p
1427
See FEDERATED CO-OPERATIVES LIM-
ITED

FCM   p 821
See FEDERATION OF CANADIAN MUNIC-
IPALITIES

FCM RECYCLING INC   p 1134
91 CH BOISJOLY, LAVALTRIE, QC, J5T 3L7
(450) 586-5185   SIC 4953

FCNQ   p 1053
See FEDERATION DES COOPERATIVES
DU NOUVEAU-QUEBEC

FCNQ CONSTRUCTION INC   p 1053
19400 AV CLARK-GRAHAM, BAIE-
D'URFE, QC, H9X 3R8
(514) 457-9375   SIC 1542

FCT   p 800
See FIRST CANADIAN TITLE COMPANY
LIMITED

FD ALPHA CANADA ACQUISITION INC p
644
128 OAK ST W, LEAMINGTON, ON, N8H
2B6
(519) 326-3173   SIC 2759

FD ALPHA CANADA ACQUISITION INC p
1085
2277 DESSTE DES LAURENTIDES (A-15)
E, COTE SAINT-LUC, QC, H7S 1Z6
(450) 680-5000   SIC 2679

FDJ FRENCH DRESSING INC   p 1178
225 RUE CHABANEL O BUREAU 200,
MONTREAL, QC, H2N 2C9
(514) 333-7171   SIC 5137

FDR   p 852
See FINANCIAL DEBT RECOVERY LIM-
ITED

FDS PRIME ENERGY SERVICES LTD p 130
11870 88 AVE UNIT 148, FORT
SASKATCHEWAN, AB, T8L 0K1
SIC 1541

FEATHERLITE INDUSTRIES LIMITED p 480
100 ENGELHARD DR, AURORA, ON, L4G
3V2
(905) 727-0031   SIC 3499

FEATURE FOODS INTERNATIONAL INC p

503
30 FINLEY RD, BRAMPTON, ON, L6T 1A9
(905) 452-7741   SIC 2035

FEATURE MILLWORK INC   p 200
204 CAYER ST UNIT 301, COQUITLAM,
BC, V3K 5B1
(604) 522-7951   SIC 5211

FEATURE WALTERS INC   p 615
1318 RYMAL RD E, HAMILTON, ON, L8W
3N1
(905) 388-7111   SIC 8712

**FEDERACION MUNDIAL DE LA
HEMOFILIA**   p 1213
See FEDERATION MONDIALE DE
L'HEMOPHILIE

**FEDERAL ATLANTIC LAKES LINE (FALL
LINE)**   p 1204
See FEDNAV INTERNATIONAL LTEE

**FEDERAL EXPRESS CANADA CORPORA-
TION**   p
23
24 AERO DR NE, CALGARY, AB, T2E 8Z9
(800) 463-3339   SIC 7389

**FEDERAL EXPRESS CANADA CORPORA-
TION**   p
185
4270 DAWSON ST, BURNABY, BC, V5C
4B1
(800) 463-3339   SIC 7389

**FEDERAL EXPRESS CANADA CORPORA-
TION**   p
264
3151 AYLMER RD, RICHMOND, BC, V7B
1L5
(800) 463-3339   SIC 7389

**FEDERAL EXPRESS CANADA CORPORA-
TION**   p
694
5985 EXPLORER DR, MISSISSAUGA, ON,
L4W 5K6
(800) 463-3339   SIC 4512

**FEDERAL EXPRESS CANADA CORPORA-
TION**   p
702
1450 CATERPILLAR RD, MISSISSAUGA,
ON, L4X 2Y1
(800) 463-3339   SIC 7389

**FEDERAL EXPRESS CANADA CORPORA-
TION**   p
735
6895 BRAMALEA RD SUITE 1, MISSIS-
SAUGA, ON, L5S 1Z7
(800) 463-3339   SIC 4215

**FEDERAL EXPRESS CANADA CORPORA-
TION**   p
1309
5005 RUE J.-A.-BOMBARDIER BUREAU A,
SAINT-HUBERT, QC, J3Z 1G4
(800) 463-3339   SIC 7389

**FEDERAL EXPRESS CANADA CORPORA-
TION**   p
1339
4041 RUE SERE, SAINT-LAURENT, QC,
H4T 2A3
(800) 463-3339   SIC 7389

**FEDERAL LIBERAL AGENCY OF
CANADA, THE**   p 823
350 ALBERT ST SUITE 920, OTTAWA, ON,
K1P 6M8
(613) 237-0740   SIC 8741

FEDERAL SCREEN PRODUCTS INC p 685
7524 BATH RD, MISSISSAUGA, ON, L4T
1L2
(905) 677-4171   SIC 3496

FEDERAL WHITE CEMENT LTD   p 569
355151 35TH LINE, EMBRO, ON, N0J 1J0
(519) 485-5410   SIC 3241

FEDERAL-MOGUL CANADA LIMITED p
722
6860 CENTURY AVE, MISSISSAUGA, ON,
L5N 2W5
(905) 761-5400   SIC 3714

FEDERAL-MOGUL WINDSOR, DIV OF p
722

See FEDERAL-MOGUL CANADA LIMITED
FEDERATED BUILDING SERVICES LIMITED *p 453 .*
1505 BARRINGTON ST SUITE 1310, HALIFAX, NS, B3J 3K5
SIC 7349

FEDERATED CO-OPERATIVES LIMITED *p 11*
2626 10 AVE NE, CALGARY, AB, T2A 2M3
(403) 531-6665 *SIC 5141*

FEDERATED CO-OPERATIVES LIMITED *p 12*
3333 52 ST SE, CALGARY, AB, T2B 1N3
(403) 531-6600 *SIC 5141*

FEDERATED CO-OPERATIVES LIMITED *p 105*
13232 170 ST NW, EDMONTON, AB, T5V 1M7
(780) 447-5700 *SIC 5141*

FEDERATED CO-OPERATIVES LIMITED *p 267*
8160 TRANS CAN HWY NE, SALMON ARM, BC, V1E 2S6
(250) 833-1200 *SIC 2436*

FEDERATED CO-OPERATIVES LIMITED *p 384*
1615 KING EDWARD ST, WINNIPEG, MB, R3H 0R7
(204) 633-8950 *SIC 5141*

FEDERATED CO-OPERATIVES LIMITED *p 1427*
604 45TH ST E, SASKATOON, SK, S7K 3T3
(306) 242-1505 *SIC 4225*

FEDERATED CO-OPERATIVES LIMITED *p 1427*
607 46TH ST E, SASKATOON, SK, S7K 0X1
SIC 5141

FEDERATED CO-OPERATIVES LIMITED *p 1427*
401 22ND ST E, SASKATOON, SK, S7K 0H2
(306) 244-3311 *SIC 4225*

FEDERATED INSURANCE COMPANY OF CANADA *p 377*
255 COMMERCE DRIVE, WINNIPEG, MB, R3C 3C9
(204) 786-6431 *SIC 6331*

FEDERATION AUTONOME DE L'ENSEIGNEMENT *p 1170*
400-8550 BOUL PIE-IX, MONTREAL, QC, H1Z 4G2
(514) 666-7763 *SIC 8631*

FEDERATION CJA *p 1219*
5151 CH DE LA COTE-SAINTE-CATHERINE, MONTREAL, QC, H3W 1M6
(514) 345-2645 *SIC 8322*

FEDERATION CJA *p 1219*
5151 CH DE LA COTE-SAINTE-CATHERINE, MONTREAL, QC, H3W 1M6
(514) 735-3541 *SIC 8322*

FEDERATION CONSTRUCTION SERVICES INC *p 80*
43220 TOWNSHIP RD 634, COLD LAKE, AB, T9M 1N1
(780) 639-0073 *SIC 1541*

FEDERATION DE L'UPA DE LA CAPITALE-NATIONALE-COTE-NORD *1277*
5185 RUE RIDEAU, QUEBEC, QC, G2E 5S2
(418) 872-0770 *SIC 0181*

FEDERATION DE L'UPA DU BAS-SAINT-LAURENT *p 1284*
284 RUE POTVIN, RIMOUSKI, QC, G5L 7P5
(418) 723-2424 *SIC 8631*

FEDERATION DE LA CSN-CONSTRUCTION *p 1312*
2000 RUE GIROUARD O BUREAU 201, SAINT-HYACINTHE, QC, J2S 3A6
(450) 261-8053 *SIC 8631*

FEDERATION DES CAISSES DESJARDINS DU QUEBEC *p 1051*
7755 BOUL LOUIS-H.-LAFONTAINE BUREAU 30711, ANJOU, QC, H1K 4M6
(514) 376-4420 *SIC 6162*

FEDERATION DES CAISSES DESJARDINS DU QUEBEC *p 1076*
235 CH DE LA HAUTE-RIVIERE, CHATEAUGUAY, QC, J6K 5B1
(450) 692-1000 *SIC 6062*

FEDERATION DES CAISSES DESJARDINS DU QUEBEC *p 1136*
100 RUE DES COMMANDEURS, LEVIS, QC, G6V 7N5
(418) 835-8444 *SIC 6062*

FEDERATION DES CAISSES DESJARDINS DU QUEBEC *p 1164*
3155 BOUL DE L'ASSOMPTION, MONTREAL, QC, H1N 3S8
(514) 253-7300 *SIC 4899*

FEDERATION DES CAISSES DESJARDINS DU QUEBEC *p 1176*
1611 BOUL CREMAZIE E BUREAU 300, MONTREAL, QC, H2M 2P2
(514) 356-5000 *SIC 8721*

FEDERATION DES CAISSES DESJARDINS DU QUEBEC *p 1191*
425 AV VIGER O BUREAU 900, MONTREAL, QC, H2Z 1W5
(514) 397-4789 *SIC 6062*

FEDERATION DES CAISSES DESJARDINS DU QUEBEC *p 1230*
1 COMPLEX DESJARDINS, MONTREAL, QC, H5B 1B2
(514) 281-7000 *SIC 6062*

FEDERATION DES CAISSES DESJARDINS DU QUEBEC *p 1255*
3333 RUE DU CARREFOUR BUREAU 280, QUEBEC, QC, G1C 5R9
(418) 660-2229 *SIC 6159*

FEDERATION DES CAISSES POPULAIRE ACADIENNES INC, LA *p 396*
295 BOUL ST-PIERRE O, CARAQUET, NB, E1W 1A4
(506) 726-4000 *SIC 6062*

FEDERATION DES COOPERATIVES DU NOUVEAU-QUEBEC *p 1053*
19950 AV CLARK-GRAHAM, BAIE-D'URFE, QC, H9X 3R8
(514) 457-9371 *SIC 5172*

FEDERATION DES EMPLOYES ET EMPLOYEES DE SERVICES PUBLICS (CSN) INC *p 1174*
1601 AV DE LORIMIER BUREAU 150, MONTREAL, QC, H2K 4M5
(514) 598-2360 *SIC 8631*

FEDERATION DES MEDECINS OMNIPRACTICIENS DU QUEBEC, LA *p 1402*
3500 BOUL DE MAISONNEUVE O BUREAU 2000, WESTMOUNT, QC, H3Z 3C1
(514) 878-1911 *SIC 8621*

FEDERATION DES MEDECINS SPECIALISTES DU QUEBEC *p 1230*
2 COMPLEXE DESJARDINS BUREAU 3000, MONTREAL, QC, H5B 1G8
(514) 350-5000 *SIC 8621*

FEDERATION DES PRODUCTEURS DE CULTURES COMMERCIALES DU QUEBEC *p 1143*
555 BOUL ROLAND-THERRIEN BUREAU 505, LONGUEUIL, QC, J4H 4G4
(450) 679-0530 *SIC 6111*

FEDERATION DES SERVICES COMMUNAUTAIRES *p 1219*
See FEDERATION CJA

FEDERATION DES TRAVAILLEURS ET TRAVAILLEUSES DU QUEBEC (FTQ) *p 1176*
565 BOUL CREMAZIE E BUREAU 12100, MONTREAL, QC, H2M 2W3
(514) 383-8000 *SIC 8631*

FEDERATION INTERPROFESSIONNELLE DE LA SANTE DU QUEBEC-FIQ *p 1195*
2050 RUE DE BLEURY, MONTREAL, QC, H3A 2J5
(514) 987-1141 *SIC 8631*

FEDERATION MONDIALE DE L'HEMOPHILIE *p 1213*
1425 BOUL RENE-LEVESQUE O BUREAU 1010, MONTREAL, QC, H3G 1T7
(514) 875-7944 *SIC 8631*

FEDERATION OF CANADIAN MUNICIPALITIES *p 821*
24 CLARENCE ST SUITE 2, OTTAWA, ON, K1N 5P3
(613) 482-8004 *SIC 8611*

FEDERATION OF ONTARIO NATURALISTS *p 951*
214 KING ST W SUITE 612, TORONTO, ON, M5H 3S6
(416) 444-8419 *SIC 8699*

FEDERATION OF SASKATCHEWAN INDIAN NATIONS *p 1433*
See FEDERATION OF SASKATCHEWAN INDIANS, INC

FEDERATION OF SASKATCHEWAN INDIANS, INC *p 1433*
103A PACKHAM AVE SUITE 100, SASKATOON, SK, S7N 4K4
(306) 665-1215 *SIC 8651*

FEDERATION QUEBECOISE DES COOPERATIVES EN MILIEU SCOLAIRE *p 1275*
3188 CH SAINTE-FOY BUREAU 200, QUEBEC, QC, G1X 1R4
(418) 650-3333 *SIC 8621*

FEDERATION-ALBERTA GAS COOPS *p 107*
9945 50 ST NW SUITE 400, EDMONTON, AB, T6A 0L4
(780) 469-3200 *SIC 4924*

FEDEX *p 694*
See FEDERAL EXPRESS CANADA CORPORATION

FEDEX FREIGHT CANADA, CORP *p 785*
1011 WILSON AVE, NORTH YORK, ON, M3K 1G1
(800) 463-3339 *SIC 4212*

FEDEX SHIP CENTRE *p 23*
See FEDERAL EXPRESS CANADA CORPORATION

FEDEX SHIP CENTRE *p 185*
See FEDERAL EXPRESS CANADA CORPORATION

FEDEX SHIP CENTRE *p 264*
See FEDERAL EXPRESS CANADA CORPORATION

FEDEX SHIP CENTRE *p 702*
See FEDERAL EXPRESS CANADA CORPORATION

FEDEX SHIP CENTRE *p 735*
See FEDERAL EXPRESS CANADA CORPORATION

FEDEX SHIP CENTRE *p 1309*
See FEDERAL EXPRESS CANADA CORPORATION

FEDEX SHIP CENTRE *p 1339*
See FEDERAL EXPRESS CANADA CORPORATION

FEDEX SUPPLY CHAIN DISTRIBUTION SYSTEM OF CANADA, INC *p 15*
6336 114 AVE SE, CALGARY, AB, T2C 4T9
(800) 463-3339 *SIC 4731*

FEDEX SUPPLY CHAIN DISTRIBUTION SYSTEM OF CANADA, INC *p 1088*
50 BOUL DUPONT, COTEAU-DU-LAC, QC, J0P 1B0
(450) 763-6400 *SIC 4731*

FEDEX TRADE NETWORKS *p 739*
See FEDEX TRADE NETWORKS TRANSPORT & BROKERAGE (CANADA), INC

FEDEX TRADE NETWORKS *p 1324*
See FEDEX TRADE NETWORKS TRANSPORT & BROKERAGE (CANADA), INC

FEDEX TRADE NETWORKS TRANSPORT & BROKERAGE (CANADA), INC *p 739*
7075 ORDAN DR, MISSISSAUGA, ON, L5T 1K6
(905) 677-7371 *SIC 4231*

FEDEX TRADE NETWORKS TRANSPORT & BROKERAGE (CANADA), INC *p 739*
7075 ORDAN DR, MISSISSAUGA, ON, L5T 1K6
(905) 677-7371 *SIC 4731*

FEDEX TRADE NETWORKS TRANSPORT & BROKERAGE (CANADA), INC *p 1324*
9800 CAVENDISH BLVD 3RD FL, SAINT-LAURENT, QC, H4M 2V9
(514) 845-3171 *SIC 4731*

FEDNAV INTERNATIONAL LTEE *p 1204*
1000 RUE DE LA GAUCHETIERE O BUREAU 3500, MONTREAL, QC, H3B 4W5
(514) 878-6500 *SIC 4412*

FEDNAV LIMITEE *p 1204*
1000 RUE DE LA GAUCHETIERE O BUREAU 3500, MONTREAL, QC, H3B 4W5
(514) 878-6500 *SIC 4412*

FEEL LIKE TALKING CONNECTIONS LTD *p 120*
9848 33 AVE NW, EDMONTON, AB, T6N 1C6
(780) 465-6055 *SIC 4899*

FEENEY R.A. LOGGING & TRUCKING LTD *p 418*
9 NEW MARKET BYE RD, SMITHFIELD, NB, E6K 2T9
SIC 7389

FEESP *p 1174*
See FEDERATION DES EMPLOYES ET EMPLOYEES DE SERVICES PUBLICS (CSN) INC

FEIST ENTERPRISES LTD *p 104*
9909 178 ST NW SUITE 288, EDMONTON, AB, T5T 6H6
(780) 444-1816 *SIC 5014*

FELBER INC *p 1346*
7275 BOUL LANGELIER, SAINT-LEONARD, QC, H1S 1V6
(514) 259-4614 *SIC 5912*

FELCO *p 1302*
See EXCAVATION PARADIS, MICHEL INC

FELCOR CANADA CO *p 584*
970 DIXON RD, ETOBICOKE, ON, M9W 1J9
(416) 675-7611 *SIC 7011*

FELDCAMP EQUIPMENT LIMITED *p 763*
701 GRAHAM DR, NORTH BAY, ON, P1B 9E6
(705) 472-5885 *SIC 5084*

FELDCAMP FLUIDPOWER *p 763*
See FELDCAMP EQUIPMENT LIMITED

FELDMAN AGENCY INC, THE *p 319*
1505 2ND AVE W SUITE 200, VANCOUVER, BC, V6H 3Y4
(604) 734-5945 *SIC 7922*

FELIX GLOBAL CORP *p 951*
80 RICHMOND ST W SUITE 1000, TORONTO, ON, M5H 2A4
(416) 512-7244 *SIC 8742*

FELLFAB *p 608*
See FELLFAB LIMITED

FELLFAB LIMITED *p 608*
2343 BARTON ST E, HAMILTON, ON, L8E 5V8
(905) 560-9230 *SIC 2399*

FELLOWES CANADA LTD *p 914*
1261 TAPSCOTT RD, TORONTO, ON, M1X 1S9
(905) 475-6320 *SIC 5113*

FELLOWES HIGH SCHOOL *p 838*
See RENFREW COUNTY DISTRICT SCHOOL BOARD

FELXIA CORPORATION *p 224*
19680 94A AVE, LANGLEY, BC, V1M 3B7
(604) 513-1266 *SIC 2621*

FEMO CONSTRUCTION LTD *p 192*
8555 GREENALL AVE SUITE 1, BURNABY,

BC, V5J 3M8
(604) 254-3999   *SIC* 1771
FEMPRO   p 1098
See FEMPRO CONSUMER PRODUCTS ULC
FEMPRO CONSUMER PRODUCTS ULC p 1098
1330 RUE JEAN-BERCHMANS-MICHAUD, DRUMMONDVILLE, QC, J2C 2Z5
(819) 475-8900   *SIC* 2676
FEN-ESCOMPTE VL   p 1137
See VITRERIE LEVIS INC
FENA INSURANCE SOLUTIONS INC p 757
4056 DORCHESTER RD UNIT 2, NIAGARA FALLS, ON, L2E 6M9
(905) 356-3362   *SIC* 6411
FENCE GUYS, THE   p 219
See MODU-LOC FENCE RENTALS LTD
FENE-TECH INC   p 1046
264 BOUL SAINT-BENOIT E, AMQUI, QC, G5J 2C5
(418) 629-4675   *SIC* 3089
FENELON COURT LONG TERM CARE CENTRE   p 590
44 WYCHWOOD CRES, FENELON FALLS, ON, K0M 1N0
(705) 887-2100   *SIC* 8051
FENELON FALLS SECONDARY SCHOOL p 590
See TRILLIUM LAKELANDS DISTRICT SCHOOL BOARD
FENERGIC INC   p 1400
17 RUE SAINTE-JEANNE-D'ARC, WARWICK, QC, J0A 1M0
(819) 358-3400   *SIC* 5211
FENESTRATION PRO-TECH   p 1381
See ATIS PORTES ET FENETRES CORP.
FENETRES ELITE INC, LES   p 1306
264 RUE DEMERS, SAINT-GILLES, QC, G0S 2P0
(418) 888-4342   *SIC* 5211
FENETRES MAGISTRAL WINDOWS INC p 1059
705 BOUL INDUSTRIEL, BLAINVILLE, QC, J7C 3V3
(450) 433-8733   *SIC* 3089
FENETRES METEO   p 1323
See METEO FENETRES ET PORTES INC
FENETRES PRISMA   p 1129
See PORTES A R D INC, LES
FENETY MARKETING SERVICES (ATLANTIC) LTD   p 408
295 ENGLISH DR, MONCTON, NB, E1E 0J3
(800) 561-4422   *SIC* 7389
FENGATE CAPITAL MANAGEMENT LTD p 969
77 KING ST W UNIT 4230, TORONTO, ON, M5K 2A1
(416) 488-4184   *SIC* 6211
FENGATE CORPORATION   p 797
2275 UPPER MIDDLE ROAD EAST SUITE 700, OAKVILLE, ON, L6H 0C3
(289) 288-3822   *SIC* 6712
FENGATE PROPERTY MANAGEMENT LTD p 527
3425 HARVESTER RD UNIT 105, BURLINGTON, ON, L7N 3N1
(289) 288-3822   *SIC* 6512
FENNER DUNLOP (BRACEBRIDGE), INC p 496
700 ECCLESTONE DR, BRACEBRIDGE, ON, P1L 1W1
(705) 645-4431   *SIC* 5085
FENPLAST INC   p 1072
160 BOUL DE L'INDUSTRIE, CANDIAC, QC, J5R 1J3
(514) 990-0012   *SIC* 3442
FENWICK, GLEN MOTORS LIMITED p 860
836 ONTARIO ST, SARNIA, ON, N7T 1N2
(519) 344-7473   *SIC* 5511
FER-PAL CONSTRUCTION LTD   p 793
171 FENMAR DR, NORTH YORK, ON, M9L

1M7
(416) 742-3713   *SIC* 1623
FERANO HOLDINGS LTD   p 817
409 INDUSTRIAL AVE, OTTAWA, ON, K1G 0Z1
(613) 523-7731   *SIC* 6712
FERBLANTERIE EDGAR ROY   p 1081
See 3099-3562 QUEBEC INC
FERCAN DEVELOPMENTS INC   p 933
193 KING ST E SUITE 200, TORONTO, ON, M5A 1J5
(416) 867-9899   *SIC* 6553
FERCO FERRURES DE BATIMENTS INC p 1362
2000 RUE BERLIER, SAINTE-ROSE, QC, H7L 4S4
(450) 973-1437   *SIC* 5072
FERGUSLEA PROPERTIES LIMITED p 830
98 WOODRIDGE CRES, OTTAWA, ON, K2B 7S9
(613) 366-5020   *SIC* 6513
FERGUSON BROS. OF ST. THOMAS LIMITED   p 889
43850 FERGUSON LINE SUITE 6, ST THOMAS, ON, N5P 3T1
(519) 631-3463   *SIC* 5153
FERGUSON CHEMICAL INNOVATION, DIV OF   p 505
See R.M. FERGUSON & COMPANY INC
FERGUSON, N. DRUGS LTD   p 759
6565 LUNDY'S LANE SUITE 799, NIAGARA FALLS, ON, L2G 1V1
(905) 354-3845   *SIC* 5912
FERGUSON-NEUDORF GLASS INC p 489
4275 NORTH SERVICE RD, BEAMSVILLE, ON, L0R 1B1
(905) 563-1394   *SIC* 1793
FERIC EASTERN, DIV OF   p 1250
See FPINNOVATIONS
FERICAR INC   p 1075
112 RTE 155, CHAMBORD, QC, G0W 1G0
(418) 342-6221   *SIC* 3715
FERIQUE GESTION DE FONDS   p 1204
See GESTION FERIQUE
FERLAC INC   p 1303
1039 RUE DE CARILLON, SAINT-FELICIEN, QC, G8K 2A2
(418) 679-1676   *SIC* 5251
FERMA IMPORT & EXPORT   p 576
See UNIBEL COMPANY LTD
FERMAR ASPHALT LIMITED   p 584
1921 ALBION RD, ETOBICOKE, ON, M9W 5S8
(416) 675-3550   *SIC* 2951
FERMAR PAVING LIMITED   p 584
1921 ALBION RD, ETOBICOKE, ON, M9W 5S8
(416) 675-3550   *SIC* 1611
FERME BETHANIE   p 1047
See AGROMEX INC
FERME BETHANIE   p 1047
See F. MENARD INC
FERME BSL   p 1294
See ALIMENTS BRETON INC
FERME C.M.J.I. ROBERT INC   p 1288
1105 LA PETITE-CAROLINE, ROUGEMONT, QC, J0L 1M0
(450) 469-3090   *SIC* 0172
FERME DES RASADES INC   p 1384
118 132 RTE E BUREAU 3095, TROIS-PISTOLES, QC, G0L 4K0
(418) 851-2366   *SIC* 5193
FERME DES VOLTIGEURS   p 1100
See VOLAILLES MARTEL INC, LES
FERME DES VOLTIGEURS INC   p 1100
2350 BOUL FOUCAULT, DRUMMONDVILLE, QC, J2E 0E8
(819) 478-7495   *SIC* 2015
FERME E NOTARO ET FILS INC, LES p 1376
307 RANG SAINT-FRANCOIS, SHERRINGTON, QC, J0L 2N0
(450) 454-3567   *SIC* 0161

FERME GENEST, LA   p 1140
See 2637-5808 QUEBEC INC
FERME H. DAIGNEAULT & FILS INC p 1357
1582 1ER RANG, SAINTE-CLOTILDE-DE-CHATEAUGUAY, QC, J0L 1W0
(450) 826-0555   *SIC* 5148
FERME LA ROSE DES VENTS   p 1154
See 9181-2958 QUEBEC INC
FERME MARAICHERE A. GUINOIS & FILS INC   p 1314
50 RANG SAINT-PHILIPPE N, SAINT-JACQUES-LE-MINEUR, QC, J0J 1Z0
(450) 515-5212   *SIC* 0161
FERME MAURICE ET PHILIPPE VAILLANCOURT INC   p 1343
6678 CH ROYAL, SAINT-LAURENT-ILE-D'ORLEANS, QC, G0A 3Z0
(418) 828-9374   *SIC* 0171
FERME ONESIME POULIOT INC   p 1315
5354 CH ROYAL, SAINT-JEAN-D'ORLEANS, QC, G0A 3W0
(418) 829-2801   *SIC* 0171
FERME ST-OURS INC   p 1349
8 RUE BOURGEOIS, SAINT-OURS, QC, J0G 1P0
(450) 785-2148   *SIC* 5144
FERME ST-ZOTIQUE LTEE   p 1354
200 69E AV, SAINT-ZOTIQUE, QC, J0P 1Z0
(450) 267-3521   *SIC* 5144
FERME VERNIER, BENOIT INC   p 1354
800 RUE PRINCIPALE, SAINT-ZOTIQUE, QC, J0P 1Z0
SIC 0161
FERMES DU SOLEIL INC, LES   p 1357
800 2E RANG UNITE 2, SAINTE-CLOTILDE-DE-CHATEAUGUAY, QC, J0L 1W0
(450) 826-3401   *SIC* 0161
FERMES HOTTE ET VAN WINDEN INC, LES   p 1298
316 RANG SAINT-ANDRE, SAINT-CYPRIEN-DE-NAPIERVILLE, QC, J0J 1L0
(450) 245-3433   *SIC* 0161
FERMES J.-F. & C. GAGNON INC., LES p 1352
804 RANG DU RUISSEAU-DES-ANGES S, SAINT-ROCH-DE-L'ACHIGAN, QC, J0K 3H0
(450) 588-2226   *SIC* 0161
FERMES LUFA INC, LES   p 1225
1400 RUE ANTONIO-BARBEAU BUREAU 201, MONTREAL, QC, H4N 1H5
(514) 669-3559   *SIC* 5148
FERMES PIGEON, ROLAND & FILS INC, LES   p 1351
1495 RANG NOTRE-DAME, SAINT-REMI, QC, J0L 2L0
(450) 454-3433   *SIC* 0161
FERMES PROLIX INC   p 1315
705 BOUL SAINT-LUC, SAINT-JEAN-SUR-RICHELIEU, QC, J2W 2G6
(450) 348-9436   *SIC* 5153
FERMES SERBI INC, LES   p 1301
841 25E AV, SAINT-EUSTACHE, QC, J7R 4K3
(450) 623-2369   *SIC* 0161
FERMES V. FORINO & FILS INC, LES p 1376
298 RANG SAINTE-MELANIE, SHERRINGTON, QC, J0L 2N0
(450) 454-6307   *SIC* 5148
FERN AND FEATHER   p 112
See BELOW THE BELT LTD
FERN BROOK SPRINGS BOTTLED WATER COMPANY LIMITED   p 593
10 BRIGDEN GATE, GEORGETOWN, ON, L7G 0A3
SIC 5149
FERNAND GILBERT LTEE   p 1079
1700 BOUL TALBOT BUREAU 400, CHICOUTIMI, QC, G7H 7Y1
(418) 549-7705   *SIC* 1794
FERNANDES GROUP, THE   p 705
260 BRUNEL RD, MISSISSAUGA, ON, L4Z

1T5
SIC 6311
FERNANDIERE INC, LA   p 1389
12500 BOUL LOUIS-LORANGER, TROIS-RIVIERES, QC, G9B 0L9
(819) 374-6977   *SIC* 2011
FERNANDO'S RESTAURANT LTD   p 326
1277 HOWE ST, VANCOUVER, BC, V6Z 1R3
SIC 6712
FERNBROOK HOMES   p 552
See FERNBROOK HOMES (WILSON) LTD
FERNBROOK HOMES   p 557
See OXVILLE HOMES LTD
FERNBROOK HOMES (LAKE OF DREAMS) LIMITED   p 552
2220 HIGHWAY 7 UNIT 5, CONCORD, ON, L4K 1W7
(416) 667-0447   *SIC* 1522
FERNBROOK HOMES (WILSON) LTD p 552
2220 HIGHWAY 7 UNIT 5, CONCORD, ON, L4K 1W7
(416) 667-0447   *SIC* 1522
FERNBROOK HOMES LIMITED   p 552
2220 HIGHWAY 7 UNIT 5, CONCORD, ON, L4K 1W7
(416) 667-0447   *SIC* 1522
FERNFOREST PUBLIC SCHOOL   p 498
See PEEL DISTRICT SCHOOL BOARD
FERNLEA FLOWERS LIMITED   p 564
1211 HIGHWAY 3, DELHI, ON, N4B 2W6
(519) 582-3060   *SIC* 0181
FERNVIEW CONSTRUCTION LIMITED p 498
10605 COLERAINE DR, BRAMPTON, ON, L6P 0V6
(905) 794-0132   *SIC* 1623
FERO WASTE & RECYCLING INC   p 408
203 DESBRISAY AVE, MONCTON, NB, E1E 0G7
(506) 855-3376   *SIC* 4953
FERONIA INC   p 962
181 BAY ST SUITE 1800, TORONTO, ON, M5J 2T9
(647) 987-7663   *SIC* 2076
FERRARI DU QUEBEC   p 1227
See AUTO MODENA INC.
FERRARI OF ONTARIO   p 1032
See MARANELLO SPORTS INC
FERRARO FOODS   p 284
See ANNABLE FOODS LTD
FERRELL BUILDERS SUPPLY LIMITED p 615
1549 RYMAL RD E, HAMILTON, ON, L8W 3N2
(905) 387-1948   *SIC* 5211
FERRELL CONTRACT - HARDWARE, DIV OF   p 615
See FERRELL BUILDERS SUPPLY LIMITED
FERRERO CANADA LIMITED   p 771
100 SHEPPARD AVE E SUITE 900, NORTH YORK, ON, M2N 6N5
(416) 590-0775   *SIC* 2064
FERRI, R AUTOMOBILES INC   p 695
4505 DIXIE RD, MISSISSAUGA, ON, L4W 5K3
(905) 625-7533   *SIC* 5511
FERRING INC   p 767
200 YORKLAND BLVD SUITE 500, NORTH YORK, ON, M2J 5C1
(416) 490-0121   *SIC* 5122
FERRING PHARMACEUTICALS   p 767
See FERRING INC
FERRO AUTOMOBILES INC   p 1367
690 AV BROCHU, SEPT-ILES, QC, G4R 2X5
(418) 962-3301   *SIC* 5511
FERRO TECHNIQUE LTEE   p 1339
819 RUE MCCAFFREY, SAINT-LAURENT, QC, H4T 1N3
(514) 341-3450   *SIC* 5084
FERROTECH MENARD INC   p 1082
665 RUE AKHURST, COATICOOK, QC, K1A

0B4
(819) 849-9474 *SIC* 7389
FERROUS PROCESSING & TRADING *p* 1022
See *ZALEV BROTHERS CO*
FERRYBANK COLONY *p* 152
See *HUTTERIAN BRETHREN CHURCH OF FERRYBANK*
FERSTEN WORLDWIDE INC *p* 1329
4600 BOUL POIRIER, SAINT-LAURENT, QC, H4R 2C5
(514) 739-1644 *SIC* 2353
FERTI TECHNOLOGIES INC *p* 1348
560 CH RHEAUME, SAINT-MICHEL, QC, J0L 2J0
(450) 454-5367 *SIC* 2874
FERUS INC *p* 49
401 9 AVE SW SUITE 1220, CALGARY, AB, T2P 3C5
(403) 517-8777 *SIC* 4925
FERUS NATURAL GAS FUELS INC *p* 49
401 9 AVE SW SUITE 1220, CALGARY, AB, T2P 3C5
(403) 517-8777 *SIC* 4925
FESTA JUICE COMPANY LTD *p* 1031
271 CHRISLEA RD, WOODBRIDGE, ON, L4L 8N6
(905) 850-5557 *SIC* 5149
FESTIVAL DE FILMS JUSTE POUR RIRE *p* 1344
See *FESTIVAL JUSTE POUR RIRE*
FESTIVAL FORD SALES (1983) LTD *p* 157
37400 HIGHWAY 2 SUITE 421, RED DEER COUNTY, AB, T4E 1B9
(403) 343-3673 *SIC* 5511
FESTIVAL JUSTE POUR RIRE *p* 1185
2101 BOUL SAINT-LAURENT, MONTREAL, QC, H2X 2T5
(514) 845-3155 *SIC* 7999
FESTIVAL JUSTE POUR RIRE *p* 1344
8375 RUE PASCAL-GAGNON, SAINT-LEONARD, QC, H1P 1Y5
SIC 8999
FESTIVAL MONDIAL DE FOLKLORE (DRUMMOND) *p* 1096
226 RUE SAINT-MARCEL, DRUMMONDVILLE, QC, J2B 2E4
(819) 472-1184 *SIC* 7999
FESTIVAL RV *p* 157
See *FESTIVAL FORD SALES (1983) LTD*
FESTO DIDACTIQUE LTEE *p* 1280
675 RUE DU CARBONE, QUEBEC, QC, G2N 2K7
(418) 849-1000 *SIC* 3999
FESTO INC *p* 695
5300 EXPLORER DR, MISSISSAUGA, ON, L4W 5G4
(905) 624-9000 *SIC* 5085
FESUK, ROBERT S. PHARMACY LTD *p* 652
759 ADELAIDE ST N, LONDON, ON, N5Y 2L7
(519) 679-4567 *SIC* 5912
FETHERSTONHAUGH *p* 823
See *FETHERSTONHAUGH & CO.*
FETHERSTONHAUGH & CO. *p* 823
55 METCALFE ST SUITE 900, OTTAWA, ON, K1P 6L5
(613) 235-4373 *SIC* 8111
FETHERSTONHAUGH & CO. *p* 945
438 UNIVERSITY AVE SUITE 1500, TORONTO, ON, M5G 2K8
(416) 598-4209 *SIC* 8111
FF SOUCY *p* 1257
See *COMPAGNIE DE PAPIERS WHITE BIRCH CANADA*
FFAW/CAW *p* 433
See *FISH FOOD & ALLIED WORKERS*
FFCA CHARTER SCHOOL SOCIETY *p* 35
7000 RAILWAY ST SE, CALGARY, AB, T2H 3A8
(403) 520-3206 *SIC* 8211
FG DELI GROUP LTD *p* 229
27101 56 AVE, LANGLEY, BC, V4W 3Y4
(604) 607-7426 *SIC* 2011

FGF BRANDS INC *p* 793
1295 ORMONT DR, NORTH YORK, ON, M9L 2W6
(416) 742-7434 *SIC* 5149
FGF BRANDS INC *p* 997
1295 ORMONT DR, TORONTO, ON, M9L 2W6
(905) 761-3333 *SIC* 2051
FGG INSPECTIONS INC *p* 162
140 PORTAGE CLOSE, SHERWOOD PARK, AB, T8H 2W2
(780) 464-3444 *SIC* 7389
FGI *p* 369
See *FORT GARRY INDUSTRIES LTD*
FGI SUPPLY LTD *p* 1435
3914 THATCHER AVE SUITE LBBY, SASKATOON, SK, S7R 1A4
(306) 931-7880 *SIC* 5082
FGL SPORTS LTD *p* 23
824 41 AVE NE, CALGARY, AB, T2E 3R3
(403) 717-1400 *SIC* 5941
FGL SPORTS LTD *p* 1021
3100 HOWARD AVE, WINDSOR, ON, N8X 3Y8
(519) 972-8379 *SIC* 5941
FGL SPORTS LTD *p* 1236
4855 RUE LOUIS-B.-MAYER, MONTREAL, QC, H7P 6C8
(450) 687-5200 *SIC* 5941
FHC ENTERPRISES LTD *p* 205
766 CLIVEDEN PL SUITE 150, DELTA, BC, V3M 6C7
(604) 549-9280 *SIC* 5399
FHE GROUP INC, THE *p* 552
260 SPINNAKER WAY UNITS 2-5, CONCORD, ON, L4K 4P9
(416) 749-1505 *SIC* 5023
FHP *p* 1084
See *PRODUITS MENAGERS FREUDENBERG INC*
FIAT CHRYSLER BRAMPTON ASSEMBLY PLANT *p* 499
See *FCA CANADA INC*
FIAT PRODUCTS, A DIV OF *p* 895
See *CRANE PLUMBING CANADA CORP*
FIBER CON *p* 551
See *CON-ELCO LTD*
FIBER CONNECTIONS INC *p* 998
80 QUEEN ST S, TOTTENHAM, ON, L0G 1W0
(800) 353-1127 *SIC* 3679
FIBERNETICS CORPORATION *p* 538
605 BOXWOOD DR SUITE 2972, CAMBRIDGE, ON, N3E 1A5
(519) 489-6700 *SIC* 4899
FIBRE DECOR *p* 122
See *FIBREWALL CANADA LTD*
FIBRE LAMINATIONS LTD *p* 610
651 BURLINGTON ST E, HAMILTON, ON, L8L 4J5
(905) 312-9152 *SIC* 3299
FIBRE NOIRE INTERNET *p* 1217
See *FIBRENOIRE INC*
FIBRECLEAN SUPPLIES LTD *p* 23
3750 19 ST NE SUITE 101, CALGARY, AB, T2E 6V2
(403) 291-3991 *SIC* 5087
FIBRECO EXPORT INC *p* 241
1209 MCKEEN AVE, NORTH VANCOUVER, BC, V7P 3H9
(604) 980-6543 *SIC* 5099
FIBRECOM *p* 427
See *B & B LINE CONSTRUCTION LTD*
FIBREK S.E.N.C. *p* 1303
4000 CH SAINT EUSEBE, SAINT-FELICIEN, QC, G8K 2R6
(418) 679-8585 *SIC* 2611
FIBRENOIRE INC *p* 1217
550 AV BEAUMONT BUREAU 320, MONTREAL, QC, H3N 1V1
(514) 907-3002 *SIC* 4813
FIBRES DE VERRE RIOUX INC, LES *p* 1358
10 RANG COTE BIC, SAINTE-FRANCOISE, QC, G0L 3B0

(418) 851-1240 *SIC* 5085
FIBRES J. C. INC, LES *p* 1074
3718 CH DE LA GRANDE-LIGNE, CHAMBLY, QC, J3L 4A7
(450) 359-4545 *SIC* 5093
FIBREWALL CANADA LTD *p* 122
1309 77 AVE NW, EDMONTON, AB, T6P 1M8
(780) 945-0561 *SIC* 5198
FIBROBEC, DIV OF *p* 1057
See *FIBROCAP INC*
FIBROCAP INC *p* 1057
201 RUE SAINT-GEORGES, BELOEIL, QC, J3G 4N4
(450) 467-8611 *SIC* 3713
FICHAULT KIA *p* 1075
See *9211-6409 QUEBEC INC*
FICODIS INC *p* 1188
465 RUE SAINT-JEAN BUREAU 708, MONTREAL, QC, H2Y 2R6
(514) 360-4007 *SIC* 5084
FIDDICK'S NURSING HOME LIMITED *p* 843
437 1ST AVE, PETROLIA, ON, N0N 1R0
(519) 882-0370 *SIC* 8051
FIDDLEHEAD AUTO SALES LIMITED *p* 467
70 DODD ST, SYDNEY, NS, B1P 1T6
(902) 539-0771 *SIC* 5511
FIDELITAS HOLDING COMPANY LIMITED *p* 834
180 COOPER ST, OTTAWA, ON, K2P 2L5
(613) 236-5000 *SIC* 7011
FIDELITY CLEARING CANADA ULC *p* 945
483 BAY ST, TORONTO, ON, M5G 2N7
(416) 216-6357 *SIC* 6211
FIDELITY CLEARING CANADA ULC *p* 945
483 BAY ST SUITE 300, TORONTO, ON, M5G 2N7
(416) 307-5200 *SIC* 6722
FIDELITY INVESTMENTS CANADA ULC *p* 935
250 YONGE ST SUITE 700, TORONTO, ON, M5B 2L7
SIC 6722
FIDELITY INVESTMENTS CANADA ULC *p* 945
483 BAY ST SUITE 200, TORONTO, ON, M5G 2N7
(416) 307-5200 *SIC* 6722
FIDELITY INVESTMENTS CANADA ULC *p* 945
See *FIDELITY RSP GLOBAL OPPORTUNITES FUND*
FIDELITY RSP GLOBAL OPPORTUNITES FUND *p* 945
483 BAY ST SUITE 300, TORONTO, ON, M5G 2N7
(416) 307-5200 *SIC* 6722
FIDO *p* 1230
See *FIDO SOLUTIONS INC*
FIDO SOLUTIONS INC *p* 1230
800 RUE DE LA GAUCHETIERE O BUREAU 4000, MONTREAL, QC, H5A 1K3
(514) 937-2121 *SIC* 4899
FIDUCIE DESJARDINS INC *p* 1230
1 COMPLEXE DESJARDINS TOUR S, MONTREAL, QC, H5B 1E4
(514) 286-9441 *SIC* 6733
FIDUCIE TECHNOLOGIES DE FIBRES AIKAWA *p* 1374
72 RUE QUEEN, SHERBROOKE, QC, J1M 2C3
(819) 562-4754 *SIC* 5111
FIDUS SYSTEMS INC *p* 832
375 TERRY FOX DR, OTTAWA, ON, K2K 0J8
(613) 595-0507 *SIC* 8711
FIELD AVIATION COMPANY INC *p* 8
4300 26 ST NE UNIT 125, CALGARY, AB, T1Y 7H7
(403) 516-8200 *SIC* 1799
FIELD AVIATION COMPANY INC *p* 735
2450 DERRY RD E, MISSISSAUGA, ON, L5S 1B2
(905) 676-1540 *SIC* 4581

FIELD AVIATION WEST LTD *p* 8
4300 26 ST NE UNIT 125, CALGARY, AB, T1Y 7H7
(403) 516-8200 *SIC* 3728
FIELD GATE ORGANICS INC *p* 621
194338 19TH LINE, INGERSOLL, ON, N5C 3J6
(519) 425-8799 *SIC* 5149
FIELD LAW *p* 89
See *FIELD LLP*
FIELD LLP *p* 49
444 7 AVE SW SUITE 400, CALGARY, AB, T2P 0X8
(403) 260-8500 *SIC* 8111
FIELD LLP *p* 89
10175 101 ST NW SUITE 2500, EDMONTON, AB, T5J 0H3
(780) 423-3003 *SIC* 8111
FIELD OF DREAMS RV LTD *p* 3
45 KINGSVIEW RD SE, AIRDRIE, AB, T4A 0A8
(403) 249-2123 *SIC* 5561
FIELD OF RV DREAMS *p* 3
See *FIELD OF DREAMS RV LTD*
FIELDGATE DEVELOPMENT AND CONSTRUCTION LTD *p* 771
5400 YONGE ST SUITE 2, NORTH YORK, ON, M2N 5R5
(416) 227-2220 *SIC* 6553
FIELDGATE HOMES *p* 771
See *FIELDGATE DEVELOPMENT AND CONSTRUCTION LTD*
FIELDING CHEMICAL TECHNOLOGIES INC *p* 711
3575 MAVIS RD, MISSISSAUGA, ON, L5C 1T7
(905) 279-5122 *SIC* 7389
FIELDPOINT SERVICE APPLICATIONS INC *p* 800
2660 SHERWOOD HEIGHTS DR SUITE 103, OAKVILLE, ON, L6J 7Y8
(905) 855-2111 *SIC* 5045
FIELDS STORES *p* 205
See *FHC ENTERPRISES LTD*
FIERA CAPITAL CORPORATION *p* 1195
1981 MCGILL COLLEGE AVE SUITE 1500, MONTREAL, QC, H3A 0H5
(514) 954-3300 *SIC* 6282
FIERA CAPITAL GESTION PRIVEE *p* 1195
See *FIERA CAPITAL CORPORATION*
FIERA FOODS COMPANY *p* 794
50 MARMORA ST, NORTH YORK, ON, M9M 2X5
(416) 746-1010 *SIC* 2053
FIESTA FARMS INC *p* 989
200 CHRISTIE ST, TORONTO, ON, M6G 3B6
(416) 537-1235 *SIC* 5411
FIFE N'DEKEL *p* 112
See *483696 ALBERTA LTD*
FIFTH AVENUE AUTO HAUS LTD *p* 11
1120 MERIDIAN RD NE, CALGARY, AB, T2A 2N9
(403) 273-2500 *SIC* 5511
FIFTH AVENUE COLLECTION LTD *p* 1411
30 STADACONA ST W, MOOSE JAW, SK, S6H 1Z1
(306) 694-8188 *SIC* 5094
FIGURE 3 *p* 951
200 UNIVERSITY AVE SUITE 200, TORONTO, ON, M5H 3C6
(416) 363-6993 *SIC* 7389
FIIX SOFTWARE *p* 995
See *MAINTENANCE ASSISTANT INC*
FILAMAT COMPOSITES INC *p* 712
880 RANGEVIEW RD, MISSISSAUGA, ON, L5E 1G9
(905) 891-3993 *SIC* 3299
FILATURE EXPERT *p* 1064
See *CONSULTANTS LUPIEN ROULEAU INC*
FILATURE LEMIEUX INC *p* 1299
125 108 RTE E, SAINT-EPHREM-DE-

BEAUCE, QC, G0M 1R0
(418) 484-2169   SIC 2281
FILBITRON MARKETING   p 670
See FILBITRON SYSTEMS GROUP INC
FILBITRON SYSTEMS GROUP INC   p 670
178 TORBAY RD, MARKHAM, ON, L3R 1G6
(905) 477-0450   SIC 5045
FILEK, STEVE DRUGS LIMITED   p 862
44 GREAT NORTHERN RD SUITE 669, SAULT STE. MARIE, ON, P6B 4Y5
(705) 949-2143   SIC 5912
FILES, JIM & DEANNA SALES & SERVICES LIMITED   p 1005
11 CLAPPISON AVE SUITE 220, WATERDOWN, ON, L8B 0Y2
(905) 690-3486   SIC 5531
FILION WAKELY THORUP ANGELETTI   p 958
See VIKING LIMITED PARTNERSHIP
FILL-MORE SEEDS INC   p 1407
1 RAILWAY AVE, FILLMORE, SK, S0G 1N0
(306) 722-3353   SIC 5153
FILLES DE JESUS, (RIMOUKI)   p 1284
949 BOUL SAINT-GERMAIN, RIMOUSKI, QC, G5L 8Y9
(418) 723-4346   SIC 8661
FILLES DE LA CHARITE DU SACRE-COEUR DE JESUS, LES   p 1370
575 RUE ALLEN, SHERBROOKE, QC, J1G 1Z1
(819) 569-9617   SIC 8661
FILLION, LOUIS ELECTRONIQUE INC   p 1164
5690 RUE SHERBROOKE E, MONTREAL, QC, H1N 1A1
(514) 254-6041   SIC 5731
FILLMORE CONSTRUCTION MANAGEMENT INC   p 114
9114 34A AVE NW, EDMONTON, AB, T6E 5P4
(780) 430-0005   SIC 1542
FILLMORE RILEY LLP   p 376
See 1700 MANAGEMENT CORPORATION
FILLMORE RILEY LLP   p 377
360 MAIN ST SUITE 1700, WINNIPEG, MB, R3C 3Z3
(204) 956-2970   SIC 8111
FILM CIRCUIT, DIV OF   p 984
See TORONTO INTERNATIONAL FILM FESTIVAL INC
FILMS SPECIALISES SIGMA CANADA, LES   p 1088
See EMBALLAGE PERFORMANT INC
FILOCHROME INC   p 1114
1355 RUE LEPINE, JOLIETTE, QC, J6E 4B7
(450) 759-1826   SIC 3496
FILS PROMPTEX   p 1094
See FILS PROMPTEX YARNS INC
FILS PROMPTEX YARNS INC   p 1094
30 AV JENKINS, DORVAL, QC, H9P 2R1
(514) 636-9928   SIC 5199
FILSINGER, W. & SONS LIMITED   p 602
55 DAWSON RD SUITE 1, GUELPH, ON, N1H 1B1
(519) 821-5744   SIC 5211
FILSPEC INC   p 1373
85 RUE DE LA BURLINGTON, SHERBROOKE, QC, J1L 1G9
(819) 573-8700   SIC 2281
FILTER SHOP, THE   p 118
See B.G.E. SERVICE & SUPPLY LTD
FILTERFAB COMPANY   p 883
16 SEAPARK DR, ST CATHARINES, ON, L2M 6S6
(905) 684-8363   SIC 3569
FILTEX VACUUMS OF CANADA   p 23
3103 CENTRE ST NW, CALGARY, AB, T2E 2X3
(403) 277-5511   SIC 5087
FILTRAN LIMITED   p 624

360 TERRY FOX DR SUITE 100, KANATA, ON, K2K 2P5
(613) 270-9009   SIC 3677
FILTRATION GROUP CANADA CORPORATION   p 739
6190 KESTREL RD, MISSISSAUGA, ON, L5T 1Z1
(905) 795-9559   SIC 3569
FILTRATION L.A.B. INC   p 1347
193 RANG DE L'EGLISE, SAINT-LIGUORI, QC, J0K 2X0
(450) 754-4222   SIC 3564
FILTRUM CONSTRUCTION   p 1262
See FILTRUM INC
FILTRUM INC   p 1262
430 RUE DES ENTREPRENEURS, QUEBEC, QC, G1M 1B3
(418) 687-0628   SIC 1629
FIN'S SEAFOOD DISTRIBUTORS   p 161
See 310104 ALBERTA LTD
FINANCE SAL   p 1270
See INDUSTRIELLE ALLIANCE, ASSURANCE ET SERVICES FINANCIERS INC
FINANCES & INDEMNISATIONS INC   p 1277
540 RUE MICHEL-FRAGASSO, QUEBEC, QC, G2E 5N4
(418) 861-9506   SIC 8741
FINANCIAL 15 SPLIT CORP   p 980
200 FRONT ST W SUITE 2510, TORONTO, ON, M5V 3K2
(416) 304-4443   SIC 6722
FINANCIAL ADVISORS ASSOCIATION OF CANADA, THE   p 980
10 LOWER SPADINA AVE SUITE 600, TORONTO, ON, M5V 2Z2
(416) 444-5251   SIC 8611
FINANCIAL DEBT RECOVERY LIMITED   p 852
40 WEST WILMOT ST UNIT 10, RICHMOND HILL, ON, L4B 1H8
(905) 771-6000   SIC 7322
FINANCIAL HORIZONS INCORPORATED   p 639
22 FREDERICK ST SUITE 112, KITCHENER, ON, N2H 6M6
(519) 742-4474   SIC 6311
FINANCIAL SOLUTION, DIV OF   p 1010
See NCR CANADA CORP
FINANCIERE AGRICOLE DU QUEBEC   p 1138
See GOUVERNEMENT DE LA PROVINCE DE QUEBEC
FINANCIERE BANQUE NATIONALE INC   p 304
666 BURRARD ST SUITE 100, VANCOUVER, BC, V6C 2X8
(604) 623-6777   SIC 6211
FINANCIERE BANQUE NATIONALE INC   p 374
200 WATERFRONT DR SUITE 400, WINNIPEG, MB, R3B 3P1
(204) 925-2250   SIC 6021
FINANCIERE BANQUE NATIONALE INC   p 1204
5E ETAGE 1155, RUE METCALFE, MONTREAL, QC, H3B 2V6
(514) 879-2222   SIC 6021
FINANCIERE BONNET INC   p 1298
54 RUE PRINCIPALE, SAINT-DAMASE, QC, J0H 1J0
(450) 797-3301   SIC 2022
FINANCIERE DES PROFESSIONNELS INC   p 1230
2 COMPLEXE DESJARDINS E BUREAU 31, MONTREAL, QC, H5B 1C2
(514) 350-5054   SIC 6722
FINANCIERE MANUVIE   p 1198
See MANUFACTURERS LIFE INSURANCE COMPANY, THE
FINANCIERE MSA, LA   p 1328
See AGENCE D'ASSURANCE VIE MANUEL SMITH LTEE
FINANCIERE SUN LIFE   p 1208

See SUN LIFE DU CANADA, COMPAGNIE D'ASSURANCE-VIE
FINASTRA   p 962
See DH CORPORATION
FINCH CHEVROLET CADILLAC BUICK GMC LTD   p 658
640 WONDERLAND RD N, LONDON, ON, N6H 3E5
(519) 657-9411   SIC 5511
FINCH HYUNDAI   p 656
300 SOUTHDALE RD E, LONDON, ON, N6C 5Y7
(519) 649-7779   SIC 7515
FINCH, BARRY ENTERPRISES LTD   p 896
1093 ONTARIO ST, STRATFORD, ON, N5A 6W6
(519) 273-2080   SIC 5531
FINCHAM AUTOMOTIVE SUPPLIES LIMITED   p 574
70 ADVANCE RD SUITE 2484, ETOBICOKE, ON, M8Z 2T7
(416) 233-5896   SIC 5511
FIND-A-CAR AUTO SALES & BROKERING INC   p 850
6104 PERTH ST, RICHMOND, ON, K0A 2Z0
SIC 5521
FINDLAY FOODS (KINGSTON) LTD   p 632
675 PROGRESS AVE, KINGSTON, ON, K7M 0C7
(613) 384-5331   SIC 5141
FINDLAY'S DRUG STORE (NEW LISKEARD) LIMITED   p 753
237 WHITEWOOD AVE UNIT 25, NEW LISKEARD, ON, P0J 1P0
(705) 647-8186   SIC 5912
FINE ANALYSIS LABORATORIES LTD   p 615
236 PRITCHARD RD, HAMILTON, ON, L8W 3P7
SIC 8734
FINE CHOICE FOODS LTD   p 254
23111 FRASERWOOD WAY, RICHMOND, BC, V6V 3B3
(604) 522-3110   SIC 2099
FINE LINE COMMUNICATIONS LTD   p 378
290 GARRY ST, WINNIPEG, MB, R3C 1H3
(204) 947-9520   SIC 8742
FINELINE SOLUTIONS   p 378
See FINE LINE COMMUNICATIONS LTD
FINES FORD LINCOLN SALES & SERVICE LTD   p 494
12435 50 HWY, BOLTON, ON, L7E 1M3
(905) 857-1252   SIC 5511
FINES FORD LINCOLN SALES&SERVICE LTD   p 494
10 SIMONA DR, BOLTON, ON, L7E 4C7
(905) 857-1252   SIC 5511
FINES HERBES AROMATIQUES FRAICHES   p 1348
See FINES HERBES DE CHEZ NOUS INC, LES
FINES HERBES DE CHEZ NOUS INC, LES   p 1348
116 CH TRUDEAU, SAINT-MATHIEU-DE-BELOEIL, QC, J3G 0E3
(450) 464-2969   SIC 5431
FINES HOME HARDWARE & BUILDING CENTRE   p 622
9 THOROLD LN, INGLESIDE, ON, K0C 1M0
(613) 537-2233   SIC 5251
FINESSE FURNITURE   p 119
See FINESSE HOME LIVING INC
FINESSE HOME LIVING INC   p 119
4210 GATEWAY BLVD NW, EDMONTON, AB, T6J 7K1
(780) 444-7100   SIC 5712
FINESSES BERGERON, LES   p 1140
See MAISON D'AFFINAGE BERGERON INC, LA
FINEST AT SEA OCEAN PRODUCTS LIMITED   p 335

27 ERIE ST, VICTORIA, BC, V8V 1P8
(250) 383-7760   SIC 2092
FINGER FOOD STUDIOS INC   p 245
2755 LOUGHEED HWY SUITE 420, PORT COQUITLAM, BC, V3B 5Y9
(604) 475-0350   SIC 7371
FINICA FOOD SPECIALTIES LIMITED   p 739
65 SUPERIOR BLVD UNIT 1, MISSISSAUGA, ON, L5T 2X9
(905) 696-2770   SIC 5143
FINISHING, DIV OF   p 673
See NORDSON CANADA, LIMITED
FINISHMASTER   p 1068
See UNI-SELECT EASTERN INC
FINKL STEEL - SOREL   p 1322
See FORGES DE SOREL CIE, LES
FINMAC LUMBER LIMITED   p 380
945 ELGIN AVE, WINNIPEG, MB, R3E 1B3
(204) 786-7694   SIC 5031
FINN WAY GENERAL CONTRACTOR INC   p 910
1301 WALSH ST W, THUNDER BAY, ON, P7E 4X6
(807) 767-2426   SIC 1542
FINNIE DISTRIBUTING (1997) INC   p 888
4188 PERTH LINE SUITE 9, ST MARYS, ON, N4X 1C5
(519) 284-2080   SIC 5191
FINNIGAN GREENHOUSE PRODUCE LTD   p 412
11021 RUE PRINCIPALE, ROGERSVILLE, NB, E4Y 2L7
(506) 775-6042   SIC 5148
FINNING CANADA   p 79
See FINNING INTERNATIONAL INC
FINNING INTERNATIONAL INC   p 79
7601 99 ST, CLAIRMONT, AB, T8X 5B1
(780) 831-2600   SIC 5082
FINNING INTERNATIONAL INC   p 289
565 GREAT NORTHERN WAY SUITE 300, VANCOUVER, BC, V5T 0H8
(604) 331-4816   SIC 5084
FIO AUTOMOTIVE CANADA CORPORATION   p 895
220 DUNN RD, STRATFORD, ON, N4Z 0A7
(519) 275-6070   SIC 3465
FIORE GOLD LTD   p 951
120 ADELAIDE ST W SUITE 1410, TORONTO, ON, M5H 1T1
(416) 639-1426   SIC 1041
FIRAN TECHNOLOGY GROUP CORPORATION   p 878
250 FINCHDENE SQ, SCARBOROUGH, ON, M1X 1A5
(416) 299-4000   SIC 3672
FIRE DEPARTMENT   p 400
See CORPORATION OF THE CITY OF FREDERICTON
FIRE DEPARTMENT   p 758
See CHIPPAWA VOLUNTEER FIRE-FIGHTER ASSOCIATION
FIRE EMERGENCY SERVICE   p 1004
510 NAPIER ST E, WALKERTON, ON, N0G 2V0
(519) 881-0642   SIC 7389
FIRE FIGHTERS ASSOCIATION LOCAL 510   p 1413
76 15TH ST E, PRINCE ALBERT, SK, S6V 1E8
SIC 8699
FIRE MONITORING OF CANADA INC   p 887
235 MARTINDALE RD UNIT 19, ST CATHARINES, ON, L2W 5X5
(905) 688-0600   SIC 7389
FIRE PROTECTION INC   p 109
6748 59 ST NW, EDMONTON, AB, T6B 3N6
(780) 469-1454   SIC 7389
FIRE SAFETY DIVISION   p 25
See SIEMENS CANADA LIMITED
FIRE TECH   p 162
See FIRE TECH FIRE PROTECTION INC
FIRE TECH FIRE PROTECTION INC   p 162

2210 PREMIER WAY UNIT 170, SHER-WOOD PARK, AB, T8H 2L2

(780) 400-3473   *SIC* 7389

FIRE-PRO   p 192

See FIRE-PRO FIRE PROTECTION LTD

FIRE-PRO FIRE PROTECTION LTD   p 192

3871 NORTH FRASER WAY SUITE 15, BURNABY, BC, V5J 5G6

(604) 299-1030   *SIC* 7389

FIREBALL EQUIPMENT LTD   p 100

17509 109A AVE NW, EDMONTON, AB, T5S 2W4

(780) 944-4818   *SIC* 5084

FIREFLY ENERGY   p 602

See AG ENERGY CO-OPERATIVE LTD

FIRELOG, DIV OF   p 776

See CONROS CORPORATION

FIREMASTER OILFIELD SERVICES INC p 49

441 5 AVE SW SUITE 570, CALGARY, AB, T2P 2V1

(403) 266-1811   *SIC* 1389

FIREMASTER OILFIELD SERVICES INC p 155

4728 78A ST CLOSE, RED DEER, AB, T4P 2J2

(403) 342-7500   *SIC* 8748

FIRENZA PLUMBING & HEATING LTD p 786

1 TORBARRIE RD, NORTH YORK, ON, M3L 1G5

(416) 247-7100   *SIC* 1711

FIREPLACE CENTER & PATIO SHOP, THE p 829

See ADVANCED PREFABS LIMITED

FIREPLACE CENTRE, THE   p 829

811 BOYD AVE, OTTAWA, ON, K2A 2C8

(613) 728-1775   *SIC* 5719

FIREPLACE PRODUCTS U.S., INC p 209

6988 VENTURE ST, DELTA, BC, V4G 1H4

(604) 946-5155   *SIC* 5719

FIRESTONE TEXTILES   p 1035

See BRIDGESTONE CANADA INC

FIRM CAPITAL   p 988

See FIRM CAPITAL PROPERTY TRUST

FIRM CAPITAL MORTGAGE INVESTMENT CORPORATION p 789

163 CARTWRIGHT AVE, NORTH YORK, ON, M6A 1V5

(416) 635-0221   *SIC* 6726

FIRM CAPITAL PROPERTY TRUST p 988

163 CARTWRIGHT AVE, TORONTO, ON, M6A 1V5

(416) 635-0221   *SIC* 6021

FIRMA FOREIGN EXCHANGE CORPORATION p 89

10205 101 ST NW SUITE 400, EDMONTON, AB, T5J 2P4

(780) 426-4946   *SIC* 6099

FIRMA FX   p 89

See FIRMA FOREIGN EXCHANGE CORPORATION

FIRST AID CENTRAL   p 1233

See 6669409 CANADA INC

FIRST AIR   p 626

See BRADLEY AIR SERVICES LIMITED

FIRST AIR   p 826

See BRADLEY AIR SERVICES LIMITED

FIRST ALERT LOCATING LTD   p 131

72022B RD 713, GRANDE PRAIRIE, AB, T8V 3A1

(780) 538-9936   *SIC* 1382

FIRST ASSET   p 938

See FIRSTASSET CANADIAN COVERTIBLE DEBENTURE FUND

FIRST ASSET CAN FINANCIALS COVERED CALL ETF p 962

95 WELLINGTON ST W SUITE 1400, TORONTO, ON, M5J 2N7

(416) 642-1289   *SIC* 6722

FIRST ASSET INVESTMENT GRADE BOND ETF p 938

2 QUEEN ST E SUITE 1200, TORONTO, ON, M5C 3G7

(416) 642-1289   *SIC* 6722

FIRST ASSET OPPORTUNITY FUND p 962

95 WELLINGTON ST W SUITE 1400, TORONTO, ON, M5J 2N7

(416) 642-1289   *SIC* 6211

FIRST AVENUE CLEARING CORPORATION p 574

47 JUTLAND RD, ETOBICOKE, ON, M8Z 2G6

(416) 259-3600   *SIC* 8732

FIRST AVENUE MEDIA ONE   p 574

See FIRST AVENUE CLEARING CORPORATION

FIRST BAUXITE CORPORATION p 304

595 HOWE ST SUITE 206, VANCOUVER, BC, V6C 2T5

SIC 1081

FIRST CANADIAN INSURANCE CORPORATION p 161

320 SIOUX RD SUITE 110, SHERWOOD PARK, AB, T8A 3X6

(780) 410-9182   *SIC* 6411

FIRST CANADIAN MANAGEMENT CORP p 190

5945 KATHLEEN AVE SUITE 220, BURNABY, BC, V5H 4J7

(604) 689-2467   *SIC* 7011

FIRST CANADIAN MESSENGER SERVICE INC p 276

13350 COMBER WAY, SURREY, BC, V3W 5V9

(604) 590-3301   *SIC* 7389

FIRST CANADIAN TITLE   p 800

See FIRST CANADIAN TITLE COMPANY LIMITED

FIRST CANADIAN TITLE   p 1326

See FIRST CANADIAN TITLE COMPANY LIMITED

FIRST CANADIAN TITLE COMPANY LIMITED p 406

1234 MAIN ST SUITE 2001, MONCTON, NB, E1C 1H7

(506) 383-6326   *SIC* 6411

FIRST CANADIAN TITLE COMPANY LIMITED p 800

2235 SHERIDAN GARDEN DR SUITE 745, OAKVILLE, ON, L6J 7Y5

(800) 307-0370   *SIC* 6361

FIRST CANADIAN TITLE COMPANY LIMITED p 800

2235 SHERIDAN GARDEN DR SUITE 745, OAKVILLE, ON, L6J 7Y5

(905) 287-1000   *SIC* 6361

FIRST CANADIAN TITLE COMPANY LIMITED p 1326

333 BOUL DECARIE BUREAU 200, SAINT-LAURENT, QC, H4N 3M9

(514) 744-1210   *SIC* 6361

FIRST CAPITAL ASSET MANAGEMENT LP p 991

85 HANNA AVE SUITE 400, TORONTO, ON, M6K 3S3

(416) 504-4114   *SIC* 6531

FIRST CAPITAL REALTY CORP p 819

1980 OGILVIE RD SUITE 149, OTTAWA, ON, K1J 9L3

SIC 8741

FIRST CAPITAL REALTY INC   p 991

85 HANNA AVE SUITE 400, TORONTO, ON, M6K 3S3

(416) 504-4114   *SIC* 6512

FIRST CHATHAM CORPORATION LTD p 543

615 RICHMOND ST, CHATHAM, ON, N7M 1R2

(519) 436-5506   *SIC* 6712

FIRST CHOICE BEVERAGE INC p 739

265 COURTNEYPARK DR E, MISSISSAUGA, ON, L5T 2T6

(905) 565-7288   *SIC* 2037

FIRST CHOICE CABINET   p 1120

See EBENISTERIE A. BEAUCAGE INC

FIRST CHOICE COURIER & MESSENGER LTD p 367

704 WATT ST, WINNIPEG, MB, R2K 2S7

(204) 661-3668   *SIC* 7389

FIRST CHOICE FOODS INC   p 192

8125 NORTH FRASER WAY, BURNABY, BC, V5J 5M8

(604) 515-8885   *SIC* 5149

FIRST CHOICE HAIR CUTTERS p 20

See ALTAVERO HAIRCARE LTD

FIRST CHOICE HAIRCUTTERS LTD p 722

6400 MILLCREEK DR, MISSISSAUGA, ON, L5N 3E7

(905) 858-8100   *SIC* 6794

FIRST CHOICE HUSKY   p 173

See FIRST CHOICE TRUCK & CAR WASH INC

FIRST CHOICE TRUCK & CAR WASH INC p 173

3530 KEPLER ST, WHITECOURT, AB, T7S 0B5

(780) 778-3377   *SIC* 5541

FIRST COBALT CORP   p 938

140 YONGE ST SUITE 201, TORONTO, ON, M5C 1X6

(416) 900-3891   *SIC* 1081

FIRST CONTACT REALTY LTD   p 487

299 LAKESHORE DR SUITE 100, BARRIE, ON, L4N 7Y9

(705) 728-4067   *SIC* 6531

FIRST DATA CANADA LIMITED p 695

2630 SKYMARK AVE SUITE 400, MISSISSAUGA, ON, L4W 5A4

(905) 602-3509   *SIC* 6099

FIRST DATA LOAN COMPANY   p 695

See FIRST DATA CANADA LIMITED

FIRST FINANCIAL UNDERWRITING SERVICES INC p 867

111 GRANGEWAY AVE SUITE 300, SCARBOROUGH, ON, M1H 3E9

(416) 750-7388   *SIC* 6211

FIRST GENERAL ENTERPRISES (ONTARIO) LTD p 986

130 KING ST SUITE 1800, TORONTO, ON, M5X 1E3

(416) 665-6680   *SIC* 1799

FIRST GENERAL SERVICES (EDMONTON) INC p 109

7311 77 AVE NW, EDMONTON, AB, T6B 0B7

(780) 463-4040   *SIC* 6321

FIRST GENERAL SERVICES (PA) LTD p 1413

32 NORTH INDUSTRIAL, PRINCE ALBERT, SK, S6V 5P7

(306) 764-7000   *SIC* 6411

FIRST GENERAL SERVICES (WINNIPEG) LTD p 390

125 FENNOLL ST UNIT 1, WINNIPEG, MB, R3T 0M2

(204) 477-0560   *SIC* 6411

FIRST GROCERY LTD   p 288

7190 KERR ST, VANCOUVER, BC, V5S 4W2

(604) 433-0434   *SIC* 5411

FIRST GULF DEVELOPMENT CORPORATION p 933

351 KING ST E 13TH FL, TORONTO, ON, M5A 0L6

(416) 773-7070   *SIC* 6552

FIRST GULF GROUP INC   p 722

6860 CENTURY AVE SUITE 1000, MISSISSAUGA, ON, L5N 2W5

(905) 812-8030   *SIC* 8741

FIRST IMPRESSIONS SPORTSWEAR &

CRESTING INC   p 35

6130 4 ST SE UNIT 7, CALGARY, AB, T2H 2B6

(403) 258-3212   *SIC* 7389

FIRST INSURANCE FUNDING OF CANADA INC p 938

20 TORONTO ST SUITE 700, TORONTO, ON, M5C 2B8

(888) 232-2238   *SIC* 6159

FIRST INTERNATIONAL COURIER SYSTEMS INC p 584

33 INTERNATIONAL BLVD, ETOBICOKE, ON, M9W 6H3

(416) 968-2000   *SIC* 7389

FIRST ISLAND ARMOURED TRANSPORT (1998) LTD p 334

612 GARBALLY RD, VICTORIA, BC, V8T 2K2

(250) 920-7114   *SIC* 7381

FIRST LADY COIFFURES   p 690

See 1459243 ONTARIO INC

FIRST LINK LOGISTICS LTD   p 722

7467 NINTH LINE, MISSISSAUGA, ON, L5N 7C3

(905) 565-1459   *SIC* 7361

FIRST LION HOLDINGS INC   p 1196

2001 AV MCGILL COLLEGE BUREAU 2200, MONTREAL, QC, H3A 1G1

(514) 843-3632   *SIC* 6411

FIRST MAJESTIC SILVER CORP p 304

925 GEORGIA ST W SUITE 1800, VANCOUVER, BC, V6C 3L2

(604) 688-3033   *SIC* 1044

FIRST MEDIA GROUP INC   p 574

536 KIPLING AVE, ETOBICOKE, ON, M8Z 5E3

(416) 252-2424   *SIC* 8999

FIRST NATIONAL FINANCIAL CORPORATION p 962

100 UNIVERSITY AVE SUITE 700, TORONTO, ON, M5J 1V6

(416) 593-1100   *SIC* 6798

FIRST NATIONAL FINANCIAL LP p 962

100 UNIVERSITY AVE SUITE 1200, TORONTO, ON, M5J 1V6

(416) 593-1100   *SIC* 6162

FIRST NATIONAL FOOD BROKERAGE p 584

26 CLAIREVILLE DR, ETOBICOKE, ON, M9W 5T9

(416) 679-0833   *SIC* 5141

FIRST NATIONS BANK OF CANADA p 1427

224 4TH AVE S SUITE 406, SASKATOON, SK, S7K 5M5

(306) 955-6739   *SIC* 6021

FIRST NATIONS FINANCIAL MANAGEMENT BOARD p 341

100 PARK ROYAL S SUITE 905, WEST VANCOUVER, BC, V7T 1A2

(604) 925-6665   *SIC* 8742

FIRST NATIONS HEALTH AUTHORITY p 341

100 PARK ROYAL S SUITE 501, WEST VANCOUVER, BC, V7T 1A2

(604) 693-6500   *SIC* 8011

FIRST NATIONS TECHNICAL INSTITUTE p 564

3 OLD YORK RD, DESERONTO, ON, K0K 1X0

(613) 396-2122   *SIC* 8244

FIRST NATIONS UNIVERSITY OF CANADA p 1421

1 FIRST NATIONS WAY, REGINA, SK, S4S 7K2

(306) 790-5950   *SIC* 8221

FIRST NICKEL INC   p 933

120 FRONT ST E SUITE 206, TORONTO, ON, M5A 4L9

(416) 362-7050   *SIC* 1061

FIRST OTTAWA REALTY INC   p 890

2 HOBIN ST, STITTSVILLE, ON, K2S 1C3

(613) 831-9628   *SIC 6531*
FIRST PIPE   *p 1053*
See INDUSTRIES REHAU INC
FIRST PLACE REALTY   *p 75*
See DUGGAN, PAT REAL ESTATE SERVICES LTD
FIRST QUANTUM MINERALS LTD   *p 304*
543 GRANVILLE ST 14TH FL, VANCOUVER, BC, V6C 1X8
(604) 688-6577   *SIC 1021*
FIRST REAL PROPERTIES LIMITED *p 612*
100 KING ST W SUITE 200, HAMILTON, ON, L8P 1A2
(905) 522-3501   *SIC 6512*
FIRST RESOLUTION MANAGEMENT CORPORATION   *p 188*
4585 CANADA WAY SUITE 320, BURNABY, BC, V5G 4L6
SIC 7322
FIRST STREET FOODS LTD   *p 171*
221 2 S, VULCAN, AB, T0L 2B0
(403) 485-6955   *SIC 5411*
FIRST STRIKE SECURITY & INVESTIGATION LTD   *p 466*
2145 KINGS RD, SYDNEY, NS, B1L 1C2
(902) 539-9991   *SIC 7381*
FIRST STUDENT   *p 169*
See FIRSTCANADA ULC
FIRST STUDENT   *p 274*
See FIRSTCANADA ULC
FIRST STUDENT   *p 477*
See FIRSTCANADA ULC
FIRST STUDENT   *p 608*
See FIRSTCANADA ULC
FIRST STUDENT CANADA   *p 522*
See FIRSTCANADA ULC
FIRST STUDENT CANADA   *p 543*
See FIRSTCANADA ULC
FIRST STUDENT CANADA   *p 752*
See FIRSTCANADA ULC
FIRST STUDENT CANADA   *p 809*
See FIRSTCANADA ULC
FIRST STUDENT CANADA   *p 835*
See FIRSTCANADA ULC
FIRST STUDENT CANADA   *p 836*
See FIRSTCANADA ULC
FIRST STUDENT CANADA   *p 896*
See FIRSTCANADA ULC
FIRST STUDENT CANADA   *p 1130*
See AUTOBUS TRANSCO (1988) INC
FIRST STUDENT CANADA   *p 1415*
See FIRSTCANADA ULC
FIRST TEAM TRANSPORT INC   *p 739*
6141 VIPOND DR, MISSISSAUGA, ON, L5T 2B2
(416) 500-8541   *SIC 4212*
FIRST TRUCK CENTRE INC   *p 95*
11313 170 ST NW, EDMONTON, AB, T5M 3P5
(780) 413-8800   *SIC 5511*
FIRST TRUCK CENTRE INC   *p 281*
18688 96 AVE, SURREY, BC, V4N 3P9
(604) 888-1424   *SIC 5012*
FIRST TRUCK CENTRE VANCOUVER   *p 281*
See FIRST TRUCK CENTRE INC
FIRST URANIUM CORPORATION   *p 969*
77 KING ST W SUITE 400, TORONTO, ON, M5K 0A1
(416) 306-3072   *SIC 1094*
FIRST WEST CREDIT UNION   *p 196*
9240 YOUNG RD, CHILLIWACK, BC, V2P 4R2
(604) 539-7300   *SIC 6062*
FIRSTASSET CANADIAN COVERTIBLE DEBENTURE FUND   *p 938*
2 QUEEN ST E SUITE 1200, TORONTO, ON, M5C 3G7
(416) 642-1289   *SIC 6722*
FIRSTBROOK CASSIE & ANDERSON LIMITED   *p 924*

1867 YONGE ST SUITE 300, TORONTO, ON, M4S 1Y5
(416) 486-1421   *SIC 6411*
FIRSTCANADA ULC   *p 169*
6304B 52 ST, TABER, AB, T1G 1J7
(403) 223-5670   *SIC 4151*
FIRSTCANADA ULC   *p 274*
12079 103A AVE, SURREY, BC, V3V 3G7
(604) 583-7060   *SIC 4151*
FIRSTCANADA ULC   *p 477*
1185 SMITH RD, ANCASTER, ON, L9G 3L1
(905) 648-1386   *SIC 4151*
FIRSTCANADA ULC   *p 497*
23 GRAY RD, BRACEBRIDGE, ON, P1L 1P8
SIC 4151
FIRSTCANADA ULC   *p 522*
1111 INTERNATIONAL BLVD, BURLINGTON, ON, L7L 6W1
(289) 288-4359   *SIC 4151*
FIRSTCANADA ULC   *p 526*
5401 DUNDAS ST, BURLINGTON, ON, L7M 0Y8
(905) 335-7010   *SIC 4151*
FIRSTCANADA ULC   *p 543*
100 CURRIE ST, CHATHAM, ON, N7M 6L9
(519) 352-1920   *SIC 4151*
FIRSTCANADA ULC   *p 608*
50 COVINGTON ST, HAMILTON, ON, L8E 2Y5
(905) 522-3232   *SIC 4151*
FIRSTCANADA ULC   *p 642*
40 MCBRINE DR, KITCHENER, ON, N2R 1E7
(519) 748-4777   *SIC 4151*
FIRSTCANADA ULC   *p 711*
3599 WOLFEDALE RD, MISSISSAUGA, ON, L5C 1V8
(905) 270-0561   *SIC 4151*
FIRSTCANADA ULC   *p 752*
1027 MOODIE DR, NEPEAN, ON, K2R 1H4
SIC 4151
FIRSTCANADA ULC   *p 761*
349 AIRPORT RD, NIAGARA ON THE LAKE, ON, L0S 1J0
(905) 688-9600   *SIC 4151*
FIRSTCANADA ULC   *p 775*
103 RAILSIDE RD, NORTH YORK, ON, M3A 1B2
(905) 294-5104   *SIC 4151*
FIRSTCANADA ULC   *p 809*
445 LACLIE ST, ORILLIA, ON, L3V 4P7
(705) 326-7376   *SIC 4151*
FIRSTCANADA ULC   *p 835*
2180 20TH ST E, OWEN SOUND, ON, N4K 5P7
(519) 376-5712   *SIC 4151*
FIRSTCANADA ULC   *p 836*
829 REST ACRES RD, PARIS, ON, N3L 3E3
SIC 4142
FIRSTCANADA ULC   *p 862*
70 INDUSTRIAL COURT A, SAULT STE. MARIE, ON, P6B 5W6
(705) 759-2192   *SIC 4151*
FIRSTCANADA ULC   *p 883*
4598 SIXTEEN RD, ST ANNS, ON, L0R 1Y0
SIC 4151
FIRSTCANADA ULC   *p 896*
4321 LINE 34, STRATFORD, ON, N5A 6S7
(519) 393-6727   *SIC 4151*
FIRSTCANADA ULC   *p 904*
120 DONCASTER AVE, THORNHILL, ON, L3T 1L3
(905) 764-6662   *SIC 4151*
FIRSTCANADA ULC   *p 1012*
1049 NIAGARA ST, WELLAND, ON, L3C 1M5
(905) 735-5944   *SIC 4151*
FIRSTCANADA ULC   *p 1415*
140 E 4TH AVE, REGINA, SK, S4N 4Z4
(306) 721-4499   *SIC 4131*
FIRSTENERGY CAPITAL CORP   *p 49*
311 6 AVE SW SUITE 1100, CALGARY, AB, T2P 3H2

(403) 262-0600   *SIC 6211*
FIRSTGROUP AMERICA   *p 72*
See GREYHOUND CANADA TRANSPORTATION ULC
FIRSTLINE MORTGAGES   *p 942*
See CIBC MORTGAGES INC
FIRSTONSITE CANADIAN HOLDINGS, INC.   *p 739*
60 ADMIRAL BLVD, MISSISSAUGA, ON, L5T 2W1
(905) 696-2900   *SIC 6712*
FIRSTONSITE RESTORATION   *p 739*
See FIRSTONSITE RESTORATION LIMITED
FIRSTONSITE RESTORATION LIMITED   *p 739*
60 ADMIRAL BLVD, MISSISSAUGA, ON, L5T 2W1
(905) 696-2900   *SIC 1799*
FIRSTONTARIO CREDIT UNION LIMITED *p 609*
1299 BARTON ST E, HAMILTON, ON, L8H 2V4
(800) 616-8878   *SIC 6062*
FIRSTONTARIO CREDIT UNION LIMITED *p 885*
3969 MONTROSE, ST CATHARINES, ON, L2R 6Z4
(905) 685-5555   *SIC 6062*
FIRSTONTARIO CREDIT UNION LIMITED *p 892*
970 SOUTH SERVICE RD SUITE 301, STONEY CREEK, ON, L8E 6A2
(905) 387-0700   *SIC 6062*
FIRSTSERVICE CORPORATION   *p 974*
1140 BAY ST SUITE 4000, TORONTO, ON, M5S 2B4
(905) 960-9500   *SIC 6519*
FIRSTSERVICE RESIDENTIAL ALBERTA LTD   *p 49*
840 7 AVE SW SUITE 1100, CALGARY, AB, T2P 3G2
(403) 299-1810   *SIC 6519*
FISCHER CANADA STAINLESS STEEL TUBING INC   *p 1010*
190 FROBISHER DR SUITE 2, WATERLOO, ON, N2V 2A2
(519) 746-0088   *SIC 3498*
FISCHER, C.A. LIMBER, CO. LTD   *p 132*
11105 100 AVE, GRANDE PRAIRIE, AB, T8V 3J9
(780) 538-1340   *SIC 5211*
FISH BASKET, THE   *p 449*
See H & H FISHERIES LIMITED
FISH CREEK EXCAVATING LTD   *p 15*
7515 84 ST SE, CALGARY, AB, T2C 4Y1
(403) 248-8222   *SIC 1794*
FISH CREEK NISSAN   *p 69*
See 969642 ALBERTA LIMITED
FISH FOOD & ALLIED WORKERS   *p 433*
368 HAMILTON AVE, ST. JOHN'S, NL, A1E 1K2
(709) 576-7276   *SIC 8631*
FISH HOUSE IN STANLEY PARK, THE   *p 317*
See 0319637 B.C. LTD
FISHER & LUDLOW, DIV OF   *p 522*
See HARRIS STEEL ULC
FISHER & LUDLOW, DIV OF   *p 892*
See HARRIS STEEL ULC
FISHER AND LUDLOW   *p 1247*
12450 BOUL INDUSTRIEL, POINTE-AUX-TREMBLES, QC, H1B 5M5
SIC 5084
FISHER BRANCH CO-OP GAS B   *p 350*
22 CACHE, FISHER BRANCH, MB, R0C 0Z0
(204) 372-6202   *SIC 5141*
FISHER POWERLINE CONSTRUCTION LTD   *p 129*
230 TAIGANOVA CRES SUITE 2B, FORT MCMURRAY, AB, T9K 0T4
(780) 713-3474   *SIC 1623*
FISHER SCIENTIFIC COMPANY   *p 749*

112 COLONNADE RD S, NEPEAN, ON, K2E 7L6
(613) 226-8874   *SIC 5049*
FISHER SCIENTIFIC COMPANY   *p 1014*
111 SCOTIA CRT, WHITBY, ON, L1N 6J6
(905) 725-7341   *SIC 5049*
FISHER WAVY   *p 900*
See ALEXANDER CENTRE INDUSTRIES LIMITED
FISHER WAVY INC   *p 910*
1344 OLIVER RD, THUNDER BAY, ON, P7G 1K4
(807) 345-5925   *SIC 3273*
FISHER'S ESSO SERVICE   *p 883*
See BRI-AL FISHER SERVICES INC
FISHER'S NO FRILLS   *p 539*
15 CANROBERT ST, CAMPBELLFORD, ON, K0L 1L0
(866) 987-6453   *SIC 5411*
FISHER, DEBBIE & LOCHHEAD, DAN *p 331*
5603 27 ST, VERNON, BC, V1T 8Z5
(250) 549-4161   *SIC 6531*
FISHERCAST   *p 839*
See FISHERCAST GLOBAL CORPORATION
FISHERCAST   *p 840*
See DYNACAST LTD
FISHERCAST GLOBAL CORPORATION   *p 839*
194 SOPHIA ST, PETERBOROUGH, ON, K9H 1E5
SIC 6712
FISHERIES AND MARINE INSTITUTE *p 432*
See MEMORIAL UNIVERSITY OF NEWFOUNDLAND
FISHERMAN'S MARKET INTERNATIONAL INCORPORATED   *p 457*
607 BEDFORD HWY, HALIFAX, NS, B3M 2L6
(902) 443-3474   *SIC 5146*
FISHIN' HOLE   *p 105*
See FISHIN' HOLE (1982) LTD, THE
FISHIN' HOLE (1982) LTD, THE   *p 105*
11829 154 ST NW, EDMONTON, AB, T5V 1G6
(780) 469-6630   *SIC 5941*
FISKARS BRAND   *p 670*
See FISKARS CANADA, INC
FISKARS CANADA, INC   *p 670*
675 COCHRANE DR, MARKHAM, ON, L3R 0B8
(905) 940-8460   *SIC 5099*
FISO TECHNOLOGIES INC   *p 1277*
500 AV SAINT-JEAN-BAPTISTE BUREAU 195, QUEBEC, QC, G2E 5R9
(418) 688-8065   *SIC 3827*
FIT FOODS LTD   *p 246*
1589 KEBET WAY, PORT COQUITLAM, BC, V3C 6L5
(604) 464-3524   *SIC 2087*
FITCH SECURITY INTEGRATION INC *p 584*
14 METEOR DR, ETOBICOKE, ON, M9W 1A4
(416) 235-1818   *SIC 5999*
FITCHCO ENTERPRISES INC   *p 410*
345 MIRAMICHI RD, OROMOCTO, NB, E2V 4T4
(506) 357-3304   *SIC 5531*
FITNESS DEPOT INC   *p 563*
700 WALLRICH AVE, CORNWALL, ON, K6J 5X4
(613) 938-8196   *SIC 5091*
FITNESS INSTITUTE LIMITED, THE   *p 969*
79 WELIINGTON ST. W 36TH FL, TORONTO, ON, M5K 1J5
(416) 865-0900   *SIC 7991*
FITNESS INSTITUTE, THE   *p 766*
See 802912 ONTARIO LIMITED
FITNESS KICKBOXING CANADA INC *p 808*
10 SECOND ST, ORANGEVILLE, ON, L9W 2B5
(519) 942-1625   *SIC 7941*
FITZGERALD & SNOW (2010) LTD   *p 1042*
190 GREENWOOD DR, SUMMERSIDE,

PE, C1N 4K2
(902) 436-9256   *SIC 1542*
FITZHENRY & WHITESIDE LIMITED   *p 670*
195 ALLSTATE PKY, MARKHAM, ON, L3R 4T8
(905) 477-9700   *SIC 5192*
FIVE BROTHERS HOSPITALITY PARTNERSHIP   *p 884*
2 NORTH SERVICE RD, ST CATHARINES, ON, L2N 4G9
(905) 934-8000   *SIC 7011*
FIVE SEASONS COMFORT LIMITED *p 552*
351 NORTH RIVERMEDE RD, CONCORD, ON, L4K 3N2
(905) 669-5620   *SIC 3564*
FIVE STAR RAGS INC   *p 735*
7500 KIMBEL ST, MISSISSAUGA, ON, L5S 1A2
(905) 405-8365   *SIC 5932*
FIVES GLOBAL SERVICES   *p 537*
See *FIVES MACHINING SYSTEMS CANADA INC*
FIVES LINE MACHINES INC   *p 1110*
1000 RUE ANDRE-LINE, GRANBY, QC, J2J 1E2
(450) 372-6480   *SIC 3541*
FIVES MACHINING SYSTEMS CANADA INC   *p 537*
70 COOPER ST, CAMBRIDGE, ON, N3C 2N4
(905) 673-7007   *SIC 5084*
FIVES SERVICES INC   *p 1264*
1580 RUE PROVINCIALE, QUEBEC, QC, G1N 4A2
(418) 656-9140   *SIC 7699*
FIVES SOLIOS ENVIRONNEMENT   *p 1196*
See *FIVES SOLIOS INC*
FIVES SOLIOS INC   *p 1196*
625 AV DU PRESIDENT-KENNEDY, MONTREAL, QC, H3A 1K2
(514) 284-0341   *SIC 5084*
FIX AUTO CANADA INC   *p 1059*
99 RUE EMILIEN-MARCOUX BUREAU 101, BLAINVILLE, QC, J7C 0B4
(450) 433-1414   *SIC 7532*
FIX AUTO ORLEANS   *p 810*
See *KEAY, JIM FORD LINCOLN SALES LTD*
FIX AUTO SAINTE-FOY   *p 1265*
See *9056-6696 QUEBEC INC*
FIXT WIRELESS INC   *p 776*
1875 LESLIE ST UNIT 4, NORTH YORK, ON, M3B 2M5
(416) 441-3498   *SIC 7629*
FIXT WIRELESS REPAIR   *p 776*
See *FIXT WIRELESS INC*
FJORD PACIFIC MARINE INDUSTRIES LTD.   *p 260*
2400 SIMPSON RD, RICHMOND, BC, V6X 2P9
(604) 270-3393   *SIC 2091*
FJORD-TECH INDUSTRIE INC   *p 1121*
2760 BOUL DE LA GRANDE-BAIE N, LA BAIE, QC, G7B 3N8
(418) 544-7091   *SIC 3625*
FJORD-TECH ROUYN-NORANDA   *p 1121*
See *FJORD-TECH INDUSTRIE INC*
FJORDS PROCESSING CANADA INC   *p 15*
115 QUARRY PARK RD SE SUITE 110, CALGARY, AB, T2C 5G9
(403) 640-4230   *SIC 3823*
FJORDS PROCESSING CANADA INC   *p 49*
237 4 AVE SW UNIT 2200, CALGARY, AB, T2P 4K3
(403) 640-4230   *SIC 1389*
FKK WHOLESALE CASH & CARRY INC   *p 790*
920 CALEDONIA RD SUITE 2, NORTH YORK, ON, M6B 3Y1
(416) 783-1197   *SIC 5145*
FLAG CHEVROLET-CHEVROLET TRUCK LTD   *p 270*
15250 104 AVE, SURREY, BC, V3R 6N8

(604) 584-7411   *SIC 5511*
FLAG NATIONAL LEASING   *p 830*
See *715137 ONTARIO LTD*
FLAG WORKS INC   *p 35*
5622 BURLEIGH CRES SE UNIT 1-4, CALGARY, AB, T2H 1Z8
(403) 265-5595   *SIC 5131*
FLAGEC INC   *p 1279*
1220 BOUL LEBOURGNEUF BUREAU 200, QUEBEC, QC, G2K 2G4
(418) 523-7015   *SIC 5912*
FLAGWORKSGROUP   *p 35*
See *FLAG WORKS INC*
FLAIR AIRLINES LTD   *p 218*
5795 AIRPORT WAY, KELOWNA, BC, V1V 1S1
(250) 491-5513   *SIC 4522*
FLAIR ENTERPRISES INC   *p 16*
3916 72 AVE SE, CALGARY, AB, T2C 2E2
(403) 219-1006   *SIC 5021*
FLAIR FLEXIBLE PACKAGING (CANADA) CORPORATION   *p 16*
4100 72 AVE SE, CALGARY, AB, T2C 2C1
(403) 207-3226   *SIC 5199* ·
FLAMAN SALES LTD   *p 1436*
GD, SOUTHEY, SK, S0G 4P0
(306) 726-4403   *SIC 5131*
FLAMBORO DOWNS HOLDINGS LIMITED   *p 566*
967 5 HWY W, DUNDAS, ON, L9H 5E2
(905) 627-3561   *SIC 7948*
FLAMBORO DOWNS RACEWAY   *p 566*
See *FLAMBORO DOWNS HOLDINGS LIMITED*
FLAMCAN TEXTILES INC   *p 1178*
9600 RUE MEILLEUR BUREAU 101, MONTREAL, QC, H2N 2E3
   SIC 5131
FLAME-TAMER FIRE & SAFETY LTD *p 503*
8058 TORBRAM RD, BRAMPTON, ON, L6T 3T2
(905) 791-3102   *SIC 5099*
FLAMINGO   *p 1050*
See *OLYMEL S.E.C.*
FLAMINGO   *p 1225*
See *COOP FEDEREE, LA*
FLAMINGO   *p 1254*
See *OLYMEL S.E.C.*
FLAMINGO   *p 1300*
See *OLYMEL S.E.C.*
FLAMINGO   *p 1313*
See *OLYMEL S.E.C.*
FLAMINGO   *p 1318*
See *OLYMEL S.E.C.*
FLAMINGO   *p 1392*
See *OLYMEL S.E.C.*
FLANAGAN FOODSERVICE INC   *p 636*
145 OTONABEE DR, KITCHENER, ON, N2C 1L7
(519) 748-6878   *SIC 5141*
FLASH COURIER SERVICES INC   *p 294*
1213 FRANCES ST, VANCOUVER, BC, V6A 1Z4
(604) 689-3278   *SIC 7389*
FLAT FEE REALTY INC   *p 487*
21 PATTERSON RD UNIT 28, BARRIE, ON, L4N 7W6
   SIC 6531
FLAT IRON   *p 574*
See *FLATIRON BUILDING GROUP INC*
FLATIRON AECON JOINT VENTURE   *p 254*
See *FLATIRON CONSTRUCTORS CANADA LIMITED*
FLATIRON BUILDING GROUP INC   *p 574*
37 ADVANCE RD UNIT 101, ETOBICOKE, ON, M8Z 2S6
(416) 749-3957   *SIC 1542*
FLATIRON CONSTRUCTORS CANADA LIMITED   *p 254*
4020 VIKING WAY SUITE 210, RICHMOND, BC, V6V 2L4
(604) 244-7343   *SIC 1611*
FLAVELLE SAWMILL COMPANY LTD *p 248*
2400 MURRAY ST, PORT MOODY, BC, V3H

4H6
(604) 939-1141   *SIC 2421*
FLB SOLUTIONS   *p 1255*
See *FRUITS ET LEGUMES BEAUPORT INC*
FLECHE AUTO (1987) LTEE, LA   *p 1053*
707 BOUL LAFLECHE, BAIE-COMEAU, QC, G5C 1C6
(418) 589-3714   *SIC 5511*
FLEET BRAKE PARTS & SERVICE LTD *p 16*
7707 54 ST SE, CALGARY, AB, T2C 4R7
(403) 476-9011   *SIC 7538*
FLEET CANADA INC   *p 591*
1011 GILMORE RD, FORT ERIE, ON, L2A 5M4
(905) 871-2100   *SIC 3728*
FLEET COMPLETE   *p 961*
See *COMPLETE INNOVATIONS HOLDINGS INC*
FLEET HEBERGEMENT   *p 1057*
See *FLEET INFORMATIQUE INC*
FLEET INFORMATIQUE INC   *p 1057*
750 RUE NOTRE-DAME BUREAU D, BERTHIERVILLE, QC, J0K 1A0
(450) 836-4877   *SIC 5045*
FLEETMIND SEON SOLUTIONS INC *p 200*
3B BURBIDGE ST SUITE 111, COQUITLAM, BC, V3K 7B2
(604) 941-0880   *SIC 3699*
FLEETWAY FACILITIES SERVICES   *p 458*
See *FLEETWAY INC*
FLEETWAY INC   *p 416*
45 GIFFORD RD, SAINT JOHN, NB, E2M 5K7
(506) 635-7733   *SIC 7363*
FLEETWAY INC   *p 458*
84 CHAIN LAKE DR SUITE 200, HALIFAX, NS, B3S 1A2
(902) 494-5700   *SIC 8711*
FLEETWAY INC   *p 823*
141 LAURIER AVE W SUITE 800, OTTAWA, ON, K1P 5J3
(613) 236-6048   *SIC 8711*
FLEETWAY TRANSPORT INC   *p 517*
31 GARNET RD, BRANTFORD, ON, N3T 5M1
(519) 753-5223   *SIC 4213*
FLEETWOOD METAL INDUSTRIES INC *p 807*
1885 BLACKACRE DR, OLDCASTLE, ON, N0R 1L0
(519) 737-1919   *SIC 3469*
FLEETWOOD METAL INDUSTRIES INC *p 835*
71 DOVER ST, OTTERVILLE, ON, N0J 1R0
(519) 879-6577   *SIC 3469*
FLEETWOOD METAL INDUSTRIES INC *p 911*
21 CLEARVIEW DR, TILLSONBURG, ON, N4G 4G8
(519) 737-1919   *SIC 3469*
FLEETWOOD PLACE HOLDINGS LTD *p 281*
16011 83 AVE, SURREY, BC, V4N 0N2
(604) 590-6860   *SIC 6712*
FLEMING CHICKS LIMITED   *p 489*
4412 ONTARIO ST, BEAMSVILLE, ON, L0R 1B0
(905) 563-4914   *SIC 0254*
FLEMING COLLEGE   *p 842*
See *SIR SANDFORD FLEMING COLLEGE OF APPLIED ARTS AND TECHNOLOGY*
FLEMING COMMUNICATIONS INC   *p 817*
920 BELFAST RD SUITE 101, OTTAWA, ON, K1G 0Z6
(613) 244-6770   *SIC 5045*
FLEMING DOOR PRODUCTS LTD.   *p 1031*
101 ASHBRIDGE CIR, WOODBRIDGE, ON, L4L 3R5
(800) 263-7515   *SIC 5211*
FLEMING FEED MILL LIMITED   *p 544*
60 IRWIN ST, CLINTON, ON, N0M 1L0
(519) 482-3438   *SIC 5191*

FLESHCON   *p 590*
See *FLESHERTON CONCRETE PRODUCTS INC*
FLESHERTON CONCRETE PRODUCTS INC   *p 590*
GD, FLESHERTON, ON, N0C 1E0
(519) 924-2429   *SIC 3273*
FLETCHER'S FINE FOODS DIV OF   *p 291*
See *SOFINA FOODS INC*
FLETCHER'S MEADOW SECONDARY SCHOOL   *p 513*
See *PEEL DISTRICT SCHOOL BOARD*
FLEURIGROS 1995 INC   *p 1266*
2365 AV WATT BUREAU 1, QUEBEC, QC, G1P 3X2
(418) 654-2888   *SIC 5193*
FLEURY MICHON   *p 1284*
See *SERVICES ALIMENTAIRES DELTA DAILYFOOD (CANADA) INC, LES*
FLEURY'S VALU MART   *p 564*
See *779173 ONTARIO LIMITED*
FLEX EXPORT   *p 1086*
2525 BOUL DANIEL-JOHNSON BUREAU 290, COTE SAINT-LUC, QC, H7T 1S9
(450) 687-3030   *SIC 7389*
FLEX GROUP   *p 1086*
See *FLEX EXPORT*
FLEX PRESSION (ONTARIO)   *p 733*
See *4166621 CANADA INC*
FLEX-N-GATE BRADFORD   *p 498*
See *VENTRA GROUP CO*
FLEX-N-GATE CANADA COMPANY   *p 840*
775 TECHNOLOGY DR, PETERBOROUGH, ON, K9J 6X7
(705) 742-3534   *SIC 3714*
FLEX-N-GATE CANADA COMPANY   *p 902*
538 BLANCHARD PK, TECUMSEH, ON, N8N 2L9
(519) 727-3931   *SIC 3465*
FLEX-O-MARK INC   *p 685*
2633 DREW RD, MISSISSAUGA, ON, L4T 1G1
(905) 678-7997   *SIC 5084*
FLEXGRAPH   *p 1315*
See *EMBALLAGE ST-JEAN LTEE*
FLEXIBLE PACKAGING, DIV OF   *p 870*
See *ATLANTIC PACKAGING PRODUCTS LTD*
FLEXIBLE SOLUTIONS INTERNATIONAL INC   *p 169*
6001 54 AVE, TABER, AB, T1G 1X4
(403) 223-2995   *SIC 3949*
FLEXIFORCE   *p 176*
See *FLEXIFORCE CANADA INC*
FLEXIFORCE CANADA INC   *p 176*
30840 PEARDONVILLE RD, ABBOTSFORD, BC, V2T 6K2
(604) 854-3660   *SIC 3429*
FLEXITALLIC CANADA LTD   *p 109*
4340 78 AVE NW, EDMONTON, AB, T6B 3J5
(780) 466-5050   *SIC 3053*
FLEXITI FINANCIAL   *p 986*
See *FLEXITI FINANCIAL INC*
FLEXITI FINANCIAL INC   *p 986*
130 KING ST W SUITE 1740, TORONTO, ON, M5X 1E1
(416) 583-1860   *SIC 6163*
FLEXLIGHT   *p 257*
See *WIDE LOYAL DEVELOPMENT LTD*
FLEXMASTER CANADA LIMITED   *p 852*
20 EAST PEARCE ST SUITE 1, RICHMOND HILL, ON, L4B 1B7
(905) 731-9411   *SIC 3599*
FLEXO PRODUCTS LIMITED   *p 760*
4777 KENT AVE, NIAGARA FALLS, ON, L2H 1J5
(905) 354-2723   *SIC 5087*
FLEXO-EXPRESS   *p 1362*
See *GROUPE LELYS INC*
FLEXOPACK   *p 1156*
See *INDUSTRIES DE PLASTIQUE TRANSCO LTEE, LES*
FLEXSTAR   *p 448*

See STELLAR INDUSTRIAL SALES LIMITED
FLEXSTAR PACKAGING p 257
See TRANSCONTINENTAL FLEXSTAR INC
FLEXTILE LTD p 571
121 THIRTIETH ST, ETOBICOKE, ON, M8W 3C1
(416) 255-1111 *SIC* 3253
FLEXTOUR p 1365
See VOYAGES BERNARD GENDRON INC
FLEXTRACK INC p 924
2200 YONGE ST SUITE 801, TORONTO, ON, M4S 2C6
(416) 545-5288 *SIC* 8741
FLEXTRONICS (CANADA) INC p 527
3430 SOUTH SERVICE RD SUITE 101, BURLINGTON, ON, L7N 3T9
(905) 592-1443 *SIC* 7371
FLEXTRONICS AUTOMOTIVE INC p 670
450 HOOD RD, MARKHAM, ON, L3R 9Z3
(800) 668-5649 *SIC* 7389
FLEXTRONICS CANADA DESIGN SERVICES INC p 624
1280 TERON RD, KANATA, ON, K2K 2C1
(613) 895-2050 *SIC* 8711
FLEXTRONICS EMS CANADA INC p 832
1280 TERON RD, OTTAWA, ON, K2K 2C1
(613) 895-2056 *SIC* 8711
FLICKA GYM CLUB p 239
123 23RD ST E, NORTH VANCOUVER, BC, V7L 3E2
(604) 985-7918 *SIC* 5961
FLIGHT CENTRE CANADA p 326
See FLIGHT CENTRE TRAVEL GROUP (CANADA) INC
FLIGHT CENTRE TRAVEL GROUP (CANADA) INC p 326
980 HOWE ST SUITE 700, VANCOUVER, BC, V6Z 0C8
(604) 682-5202 *SIC* 4724
FLIGHT NETWORK LTD p 951
145 KING ST W SUITE 1401, TORONTO, ON, M5H 1J8
(905) 829-8699 *SIC* 4724
FLIGHTEXEC p 648
See CRAIG EVAN CORPORATION, THE
FLIGHTNETWORK.COM p 951
See FLIGHT NETWORK LTD
FLIGHTSAFETY CANADA LTD p 785
95 GARRATT BLVD, NORTH YORK, ON, M3K 2A5
(416) 638-9313 *SIC* 8299
FLIGHTSAFETY CANADA LTD p 1094
9555 AV RYAN, DORVAL, QC, H9P 1A2
(514) 631-2084 *SIC* 8299
FLIGHTSAFETY INTERNATIONAL p 1094
See FLIGHTSAFETY CANADA LTD
FLIGHTSAFETY INTERNATIONAL CANADA p 785
See FLIGHTSAFETY CANADA LTD
FLINT ENERGY SERVICES p 13
See AECOM PRODUCTION SERVICES LTD
FLINT FABRICATION AND MODULARIZATION LTD p 162
180 STRATHMOOR DR, SHERWOOD PARK, AB, T8H 2B7
(780) 416-3501 *SIC* 3443
FLINT FLUID HAUL SERVICES LTD p 7
10 INDUSTRIAL RD, BROOKS, AB, T1R 1B5
(403) 793-8384 *SIC* 4212
FLINT PACKAGING PRODUCTS LTD p 552
311 CALDARI RD, CONCORD, ON, L4K 4S9
(905) 738-7205 *SIC* 2653
FLINT TUBULAR MANAGEMENT SERVICES LTD p 148
950 30 AVE, NISKU, AB, T9E 0S2
(780) 955-3380 *SIC* 1389

FLINTSHIRE FARMS INC p 591
79 PHEASANT FARM RD, FLINTON, ON, K0H 1P0
(613) 336-8552 *SIC* 5144
FLIPP CORPORATION p 572
3250 BLOOR ST W SUITE 1200, ETOBICOKE, ON, M8X 2X9
(416) 626-7092 *SIC* 7371
FLIR INTEGRATED IMAGING SOLUTIONS, INC p 258
12051 RIVERSIDE WAY, RICHMOND, BC, V6W 1K7
(604) 242-9937 *SIC* 3559
FLITE p 705
See FLITE HOCKEY INC
FLITE HOCKEY INC p 705
705 MATHESON BLVD E, MISSISSAUGA, ON, L4Z 3X9
(905) 828-6030 *SIC* 3949
FLITE LINE SERVICES (KITCHENER) INC p 518
4881 FOUNTAIN ST N SUITE 4, BRESLAU, ON, N0B 1M0
(519) 648-3404 *SIC* 5172
FLO-DRAULIC CONTROLS LTD p 593
45 SINCLAIR AVE, GEORGETOWN, ON, L7G 4X4
(905) 702-9456 *SIC* 5084
FLO-SKID MANUFACTURING INC p 16
6725 86 AVE SE, CALGARY, AB, T2C 2S4
(403) 279-6602 *SIC* 5084
FLOCHEM LTD p 603
6986 WELLINGTON ROAD 124, GUELPH, ON, N1H 6J4
(519) 763-5441 *SIC* 5169
FLOCOR INC p 892
470 SEAMAN ST, STONEY CREEK, ON, L8E 2V9
(905) 664-9230 *SIC* 5074
FLOFORM COUNTERTOPS p 390
See FLOFORM INDUSTRIES LTD
FLOFORM INDUSTRIES LTD p 390
125 HAMELIN ST, WINNIPEG, MB, R3T 3Z1
(204) 474-2334 *SIC* 2541
FLOFORM INDUSTRIES LTD p 1431
2209 SPEERS AVE, SASKATOON, SK, S7L 5X6
(306) 665-7733 *SIC* 2541
FLOGEN p 1155
See FLOGEN TECHNOLOGIES INC
FLOGEN TECHNOLOGIES INC p 1155
1255 BOUL LAIRD BUREAU 388, MONTROYAL, QC, H3P 2T1
(514) 344-8786 *SIC* 7371
FLOOD, JOHN & SONS (1961) LIMITED p 413
32 FREDERICK ST, SAINT JOHN, NB, E2J 2A9
(506) 634-1112 *SIC* 1542
FLOORRIGHT INTERIORS LTD p 143
3021 32 ST S, LETHBRIDGE, AB, T1K 7B1
(587) 800-0848 *SIC* 5211
FLORA MANUFACTURING AND DISTRIBUTING LTD p 192
7400 FRASER PARK DR, BURNABY, BC, V5J 5B9
(604) 436-6000 *SIC* 2032
FLORA-DEI p 682
632 SAFARI RD, MILLGROVE, ON, L8B 1S8
(905) 659-3354 *SIC* 5193
FLORADALE FEED MILL LIMITED p 591
2131 FLORADALE RD, FLORADALE, ON, N0B 1V0
(519) 669-5478 *SIC* 4213
FLORISTS SUPPLY LTD p 384
35 AIRPORT RD, WINNIPEG, MB, R3H 0V5
(800) 665-7378 *SIC* 5193
FLOW WATER INC p 821
110 CLARENCE ST SUITE 202, OTTAWA, ON, K1N 5P6
(613) 680-3569 *SIC* 2899
FLOWER FACTORY, THE p 383
See 7169311 MANITOBA LTD

FLOWER GROUP OPERATING LP p 623
2350 4TH AVE, JORDAN STATION, ON, L0R 1S0
(905) 562-4118 *SIC* 0181
FLOWERBUYER.COM p 802
See ACCESS FLOWER TRADING INC
FLOWR CORPORATION, THE p 670
100 ALLSTATE PKY SUITE 201, MARKHAM, ON, L3R 6H3
(905) 940-3993 *SIC* 2833
FLOWRIDER SURF LTD p 258
6700 MCMILLAN WAY, RICHMOND, BC, V6W 1J7
(604) 273-1068 *SIC* 4412
FLOWSERVE CANADA CORP p 603
225 SPEEDVALE AVE W, GUELPH, ON, N1H 1C5
(519) 824-4600 *SIC* 3561
FLOWSERVE PUMP, DIV OF p 603
See FLOWSERVE CANADA CORP
FLS INTERMEDIATE 2 ULC p 1326
400 AV SAINTE-CROIX, SAINT-LAURENT, QC, H4N 3L4
(514) 739-0939 *SIC* 6719
FLS KNELSON p 809
See FLSMIDTH LTD
FLS TRANSPORTATION SERVICES LIMITED p 1326
400 AV SAINTE-CROIX, SAINT-LAURENT, QC, H4N 3L4
(514) 739-0939 *SIC* 4731
FLSMIDTH LTD p 809
174 WEST ST S, ORILLIA, ON, L3V 6L4
(705) 325-6181 *SIC* 3532
FLUEVOG, JOHN BOOTS & SHOES LTD p 326
837 GRANVILLE ST, VANCOUVER, BC, V6Z 1K7
(604) 688-5245 *SIC* 5661
FLUEVOG, JOHN VANCOUVER LTD p 326
837 GRANVILLE ST, VANCOUVER, BC, V6Z 1K7
(604) 688-2828 *SIC* 6712
FLUID CONNECTORS DIV. p 490
See PARKER HANNIFIN CANADA
FLUID HANDLING SYSTEMS DIV p 594
See COOPER-STANDARD AUTOMOTIVE CANADA LIMITED
FLUID HOSE & COUPLING INC p 739
6150 DIXIE RD UNIT 1, MISSISSAUGA, ON, L5T 2E2
(905) 670-0955 *SIC* 5084
FLUIDSEAL INC p 254
13680 BRIDGEPORT RD SUITE 5, RICHMOND, BC, V6V 1V3
(604) 278-6808 *SIC* 5085
FLUKE ELECTRONICS CANADA INC. p 705
400 BRITANNIA RD E UNIT 1, MISSISSAUGA, ON, L4Z 1X9
(800) 363-5853 *SIC* 5063
FLUKE ELECTRONICS CANADA LP p 705
400 BRITANNIA RD E UNIT 1, MISSISSAUGA, ON, L4Z 1X9
(905) 890-7601 *SIC* 5084
FLUKE TRANSPORT LIMITED p 610
450 SHERMAN AVE N 2ND FL, HAMILTON, ON, L8L 8J6
(905) 578-0677 *SIC* 4214
FLUKE TRANSPORTATION GROUP p 610
See FLUKE TRANSPORT LIMITED
FLUOR CANADA LTD p 69
55 SUNPARK PLAZA SE, CALGARY, AB, T2X 3R4
(403) 537-4000 *SIC* 8711
FLUOR CANADA LTD p 313
1075 GEORGIA ST W SUITE 700, VANCOUVER, BC, V6E 4M7
(604) 488-2000 *SIC* 8711
FLUOR CONSTRUCTORS CANADA LTD p 69
60 SUNPARK PLAZA SE, CALGARY, AB, T2X 3Y2

(403) 537-4600 *SIC* 1541
FLUOR DANIEL p 313
See FLUOR CANADA LTD
FLUX LOGISTICS p 850
See 11198173 CANADA INC
FLUXWERX p 281
See FLUXWERX ILLUMINATION INC
FLUXWERX ILLUMINATION INC p 281
9255 194 ST, SURREY, BC, V4N 4G1
(604) 549-9379 *SIC* 3648
FLY GLOBESPAN p 293
See GLOBESPAN TRAVEL LTD
FLYHT AEROSPACE SOLUTIONS LTD p 23
1144 29 AVE NE SUITE 300E, CALGARY, AB, T2E 7P1
(403) 250-9956 *SIC* 3812
FLYING COLOURS CORP p 840
901 AIRPORT RD SUITE 120, PETERBOROUGH, ON, K9J 0E7
(705) 742-4688 *SIC* 1721
FLYING DOG, THE p 1006
See 793337 ONTARIO INC
FLYING FRESH p 264
See 420877 B.C. LTD
FLYING J CANADA INC p 747
628 COUNTY RD 41, NAPANEE, ON, K7R 3L1
(613) 354-7044 *SIC* 5541
FLYING J TRAVEL PLAZA p 747
See FLYING J CANADA INC
FLYING M TRUCK STOP p 520
See DAVIS FUEL COMPANY LIMITED
FLYNN BROS p 147
See FLYNN BROS. PROJECTS INC
FLYNN BROS. PROJECTS INC p 147
8902 95 ST, MORINVILLE, AB, T8R 1K7
(780) 939-3000 *SIC* 1541
FLYNN CANADA LTD p 159
285221 KLEYSEN WAY, ROCKY VIEW COUNTY, AB, T1X 0K1
(403) 720-8155 *SIC* 1761
FLYNN CANADA LTD p 595
5661 POWER RD, GLOUCESTER, ON, K1G 3N4
SIC 1761
FLYNN CANADA LTD p 688
6435 NORTHWEST DR, MISSISSAUGA, ON, L4V 1K2
(905) 671-3971 *SIC* 1761
FLYNN CANADA LTD p 816
2780 SHEFFIELD RD, OTTAWA, ON, K1B 3V9
(613) 696-0086 *SIC* 1761
FLYNN CANADA LTD p 892
890 ARVIN AVE, STONEY CREEK, ON, L8E 5Y8
(905) 643-9515 *SIC* 1761
FLYNN CANADA LTD p 1027
141 ROYAL GROUP CRES, WOODBRIDGE, ON, L4H 1X9
(905) 671-3971 *SIC* 1761
FLYNN PROJECTS p 147
See 1019728 ALBERTA LTD
FM GROUP OF COMPANIES p 31
See PPI SOLUTIONS INC
FMAV p 708
See FRISCHKORN AUDIO-VISUAL CORP
FMC TECHNOLOGIES COMPANY p 109
6703 68 AVE NW, EDMONTON, AB, T6B 3E3
(780) 468-9231 *SIC* 5084
FMI p 807
See FLEETWOOD METAL INDUSTRIES INC
FMI GROUP p 420
See FRANCHISE MANAGEMENT INC
FMI LOGISTICS INC p 16
7151 44 ST SE UNIT 111, CALGARY, AB, T2C 4E8
(866) 723-6660 *SIC* 4731
FMOQ p 1402
See FEDERATION DES MEDECINS OMNIPRACTICIENS DU QUEBEC, LA
FMR MECHANICAL ELECTRICAL INC p

128
330 MACKENZIE BLVD, FORT MCMUR-RAY, AB, T9H 4C4
(780) 791-9283   SIC 7623

FNF CANADA COMPANY   p 722
2700 ARGENTIA RD, MISSISSAUGA, ON, L5N 5V4
(905) 813-7174   SIC 6361

FOAM WORX   p 442
See DIAMOND DIVERSIFIED INDUSTRIES LTD

FOAMCO INDUSTRIES CORPORATION   p 552
8400 KEELE ST UNIT 2, CONCORD, ON, L4K 2A6
(416) 784-9777   SIC 3086

FOAMEX CANADA INC   p 995
415 EVANS AVE, TORONTO, ON, M8W 2T2
SIC 2821

FOCAL   p 821
See CANADIAN FOUNDATION FOR THE AMERICAS

FOCAL TECHNOLOGIES CORPORATIONp 446
77 FRAZEE AVE, DARTMOUTH, NS, B3B 1Z4
(902) 468-2263   SIC 3621

FOCENCO LIMITED   p 434
127 MAIN ST SUITE 125, STEPHENVILLE, NL, A2N 1J5
(709) 643-2885   SIC 5411

FOCENCO LIMITED   p 434
383 CONNECTICUT DR, STEPHENVILLE, NL, A2N 2Y6
(709) 637-6600   SIC 5411

FOCUS ASSESSMENTS INC   p 634
1601 RIVER RD E UNIT 10, KITCHENER, ON, N2A 3Y4
(519) 893-5972   SIC 6321

FOCUS AUTO DESIGN INC   p 16
6159 40 ST SE, CALGARY, AB, T2C 2B1
(403) 255-4711   SIC 5511

FOCUS HYUNDAI   p 368
See FOCUS MOTORS LIMITED

FOCUS MOTORS LIMITED   p 368
1066 NAIRN AVE, WINNIPEG, MB, R2L 0Y4
(204) 663-3814   SIC 5511

FOCUS PORTES & FENETRES   p 1144
See GROUPE ATIS INC

FOCUS SURVEYS   p 214
See WSP CANADA INC

FOGLER, RUBINOFF LLP   p 969
77 KING ST W SUITE 3000, TORONTO, ON, M5K 2A1
(416) 864-9700   SIC 8111

FOGO ISLAND CO-OPERATIVE SOCIETY LIMITED   p 423
22-24 GARRISON RD, FOGO, NL, A0G 2B0
(709) 266-2448   SIC 2092

FOGOLAR FURLAN CLUB   p 1019
See FOGOLAR FURLAN WINDSOR

FOGOLAR FURLAN WINDSOR   p 1019
1800 NORTH SERVICE RD E, WINDSOR, ON, N8W 1Y3
(519) 966-2230   SIC 8641

FOIRE DU LIVRE   p 1164
See LIBRAIRIE RENAUD-BRAY INC

FOLIA 2000   p 1095
See PLANTERRA LTEE

FOLIERA INC   p 489
4655 BARTLETT RD, BEAMSVILLE, ON, L0R 1B1
(905) 563-1066   SIC 5193

FOLK, DON CHEVROLET INC   p 220
2350 HIGHWAY 97 N, KELOWNA, BC, V1X 4H8
(250) 860-6000   SIC 5511

FOLLETT OF CANADA, INC   p 834
381 KENT ST SUITE 327, OTTAWA, ON, K2P 2A8
(613) 230-6148   SIC 5942

FON-TILE CORPORATION LIMITED   p 294
270 TERMINAL AVE, VANCOUVER, BC, V6A 2L6

(604) 683-9358   SIC 5032

FOND D'ASSURANCE RESPONSABILITE PROFESSIONNELLE DE LA CHAMBRE DES NOTAIRES DU QUEBEC   p 1204
1200 AV MCGILL COLLEGE BUREAU 1500, MONTREAL, QC, H3B 4G7
(514) 871-4999   SIC 6351

FOND SRS DE L'ETABLISSEMENT DE DE-TENTION DE QUEBEC, LE   p 1256
500 RUE DE LA FAUNE, QUEBEC, QC, G1G 0G9
(418) 622-7100   SIC 2752

FONDACTION, LE FONDS DE DEVEL-OPPEMENT DE LA CSN POUR LA COOP-ERATION ET L'EMPLOI   p 1174
2175 BOUL DE MAISONNEUVE E BU-REAU 103, MONTREAL, QC, H2K 4S3
(514) 525-5505   SIC 6799

FONDATION ALLO PROF   p 1173
See ALLO PROF

FONDATION CANADIENNE DU REIN, LAp 1220
5160 BOUL DECARIE BUREAU 310, MON-TREAL, QC, H3X 2H9
(514) 369-4806   SIC 8399

FONDATION CENTRAIDE DU GRAND MONTREAL   p 1196
493 RUE SHERBROOKE O, MONTREAL, QC, H3A 1B6
(514) 288-1261   SIC 8699

FONDATION CENTRE HOSPITALIER RE-GIONAL DE TROIS-RIVIERES (RSTR)   p 1387
731 RUE SAINTE-JULIE, TROIS-RIVIERES, QC, G9A 1Y1
(819) 697-3333   SIC 8062

FONDATION CHAMPLAIN ET MANOIR-DE-VERDUN   p 1397
1325 RUE CRAWFORD, VERDUN, QC, H4H 2N6
(514) 766-8513   SIC 8699

FONDATION D'AMENAGEMENT ST-PATRICK   p 1082
6767 CH DE LA COTE-SAINT-LUC BU-REAU 616, COTE SAINT-LUC, QC, H4V 2Z6
(514) 481-9609   SIC 6513

FONDATION D'ENTRAIDE BOUDDHISTE TZU CHI DU CANADA   p 1397
3988 RUE WELLINGTON BUREAU 1, VER-DUN, QC, H4G 1V3
(514) 844-2074   SIC 8699

FONDATION D'ENTRAIDE EN SANTE DES BENEVOLES DE STE-ANNE   p 1355
43 RUE SAINTE-ANNE BUREAU 3, SAINTE-ANNE-DE-BELLEVUE, QC, H9X 1L4
(514) 457-1642   SIC 8322

FONDATION D'INSTITUT CANADIEN-POLONAIS DU BIEN-ETRE INC   p 1165
5655 RUE BELANGER, MONTREAL, QC, H1T 1G2
(514) 259-2551   SIC 8052

FONDATION DE L'HOPITAL DE MON-TREAL POUR ENFANTS, LA   p 1220
3400 BOUL DE MAISONNEUVE O BU-REAU 1420, MONTREAL, QC, H3Z 3B8
(514) 934-4846   SIC 7389

FONDATION DE L'HOPITAL GENERAL JUIF SIR MORTIMER B. DAVIS   p 1219
3755 CH DE LA COTE-SAINTE-CATHERINE BUREAU A104, MONTREAL, QC, H3T 1E2
(514) 340-8251   SIC 8399

FONDATION DE L'HOPITAL SAINTE-ANNE-DE-BEAUPRE INC   p 1055
11000 RUE DES MONTAGNARDS, BEAUPRE, QC, G0A 1E0

(418) 827-3726   SIC 7389

FONDATION DE L'INSTITUT UNIVERSI-TAIRE EN SANTE MENTALE DE MON-TREAL   p 1164
7401 RUE HOCHELAGA, MONTREAL, QC, H1N 3M5
(514) 251-4000   SIC 8063

FONDATION DE L'UNIVERSITE DU QUE-BEC A MONTREAL   p 1175
405 BOUL DE MAISONNEUVE E BUREAU 2300, MONTREAL, QC, H2L 4J5
(514) 987-3030   SIC 7389

FONDATION DE L'UNIVERSITE DU QUE-BEC EN OUTAOUAIS   p 1105
283 BOUL ALEXANDRE-TACHE BUREAU F-0239, GATINEAU, QC, J8X 3X7
(819) 595-3900   SIC 8221

FONDATION DE LA COMMISSION SCO-LAIRE DES PORTAGES-DE-L'OUTAOUAISp 1105
255 RUE SAINT-REDEMPTEUR, GATINEAU, QC, J8X 2T4
(819) 771-4548   SIC 8211

FONDATION DE LA MAISON DE SOINS PALLIATIFS DE VAUDREUIL-SOULANGES (FMSPVS)   p 1113
90 RUE COMO-GARDENS, HUDSON, QC, J0P 1H0
(450) 202-2202   SIC 8399

FONDATION DE LA MAISON DU PERE   p 1175
545 RUE DE LA GAUCHETIERE E BU-REAU 296, MONTREAL, QC, H2L 5E1
(514) 843-3739   SIC 8361

FONDATION DES SOURDS DU QUEBEC (F.S.Q.) INC, LA   p 1255
3348 BOUL MONSEIGNEUR-GAUTHIER, QUEBEC, QC, G1E 2W2
(418) 660-6800   SIC 8399

FONDATION DU CARREFOUR DE LA SANTE ET DES SERVICES SOCIAUX DE MATAWINIE (CLSC - CHSLD)   p 1077
485 RUE DUPUIS, CHERTSEY, QC, J0K 3K0
(450) 882-2488   SIC 8399

FONDATION DU CEGEP DU VIEUX MON-TREAL, LA   p 1185
255 RUE ONTARIO E, MONTREAL, QC, H2X 1X6
(514) 982-3437   SIC 8221

FONDATION DU CEGEP REGIONAL DE LANAUDIERE   p 1282
781 RUE NOTRE-DAME, REPENTIGNY, QC, J5Y 1B4
(450) 470-0911   SIC 8221

FONDATION DU CEGEP REGIONAL DE LANAUDIERE   p 1380
2505 BOUL DES ENTREPRISES, TERRE-BONNE, QC, J6X 5S5
(450) 470-0933   SIC 8221

FONDATION DU CENTRE DE SANTE ET DE SERVICES SOCIAUX DE MANICOUA-GAN   p 1053
635 BOUL JOLLIET, BAIE-COMEAU, QC, G5C 1P1
(418) 589-3701   SIC 8062

FONDATION DU CENTRE DE SANTE ET DE SERVICES SOCIAUX DE TROIS-RIVIERES   p 1387
731 RUE SAINTE-JULIE, TROIS-RIVIERES, QC, G9A 1Y1
(819) 370-2100   SIC 8322

FONDATION DU CENTRE HOSPITALIER REGIONAL DE RIMOUSKI   p 1284
See FONDATION DU CENTRE RE-GIONALE DE SANTE ET DE SERVICES SOCIAUX RIMOUSKI INC

FONDATION DU CENTRE JEUNESSE DE

LA MONTEREGIE   p 1141
575 RUE ADONCOUR, LONGUEUIL, QC, J4G 2M6
(450) 679-0140   SIC 8322

FONDATION DU CENTRE JEUNESSE DE LA MONTEREGIE   p 1318
145 BOUL SAINT-JOSEPH BUREAU 200, SAINT-JEAN-SUR-RICHELIEU, QC, J3B 1W5
(450) 359-7525   SIC 8322

FONDATION DU CENTRE JEUNESSE DE LA MONTEREGIE   p 1318
See FONDATION DU CENTRE JEUNESSE DE LA MONTEREGIE

FONDATION DU CENTRE JEUNESSE DE QUEBEC   p 1255
3510 RUE CAMBRONNE, QUEBEC, QC, G1E 7H2
(418) 661-3700   SIC 8322

FONDATION DU CENTRE JEUNESSE DE QUEBEC   p 1258
540 BOUL CHAREST E, QUEBEC, QC, G1K 8L1
(418) 529-7351   SIC 8322

FONDATION DU CENTRE REGIONALE DE SANTE ET DE SERVICES SOCIAUX RI-MOUSKI INC   p 1284
150 AV ROULEAU, RIMOUSKI, QC, G5L 5T1
(418) 724-8580   SIC 8062

FONDATION DU CSSS DE VAUDREUIL-SOULANGES   p 1394
3031 BOUL DE LA GARE, VAUDREUIL-DORION, QC, J7V 9R2
(450) 455-6171   SIC 8399

FONDATION DU MOUVEMENT DU GRAAL-CANADA INC   p 1077
470 CH DES HAUTEURS, CHENEVILLE, QC, J0V 1E0
(819) 428-7001   SIC 8699

FONDATION ECOLE MONTCALM INC   p 1372
2050 BOUL DE PORTLAND, SHER-BROOKE, QC, J1J 1T9
(819) 822-5633   SIC 8211

FONDATION EDUCATIVE DE LA COMMIS-SION SCOLAIRE ENGLISH-MONTREAL, LA   p 1220
6000 AV FIELDING, MONTREAL, QC, H3X 1T4
(514) 483-7200   SIC 8211

FONDATION EDUCATIVE DE LA COMMIS-SION SCOLAIRE ENGLISH-MONTREAL, LA   p 1239
11575 AV P.-M.-FAVIER, MONTREAL-NORD, QC, H1G 6E5
(514) 328-4442   SIC 8211

FONDATION EDUCATIVE DE LA COMMIS-SION SCOLAIRE ENGLISH-MONTREAL, LA   p 1329
2505 BOUL DE LA COTE-VERTU, SAINT-LAURENT, QC, H4R 1P3
(514) 331-8781   SIC 8211

FONDATION EDUCATIVE DE LA COMMIS-SION SCOLAIRE ENGLISH-MONTREAL, LA   p 1346
7355 BOUL VIAU, SAINT-LEONARD, QC, H1S 3C2
(514) 374-6000   SIC 8211

FONDATION INTEGRATION DU QUEBEC
p 1232
See FONDATION LE PILIER

FONDATION JULES & PAUL-EMILE LEGER
p 1244
130 AV DE L'EPEE, OUTREMONT, QC, H2V 3T2
(514) 495-2409   SIC 8699

FONDATION LE PILIER   p 1224
23 AV DU RUISSEAU, MONTREAL, QC, H4K 2C8
(450) 624-9922   SIC 8361

FONDATION LE PILIER   p 1232

5273 RUE THIBAULT, MONTREAL, QC, H7K 3R5

(450) 963-3751   *SIC* 8399

FONDATION LUCIE & ANDRE CHAGNON *p* 1196

2001 AV MCGILL COLLEGE BUREAU 1000, MONTREAL, QC, H3A 1G1

(514) 380-2001   *SIC* 8699

FONDATION SANTE VALLEE-DE-LA-GATINEAU *p* 1148

309 BOUL DESJARDINS, MANIWAKI, QC, J9E 2E7

(819) 449-4690   *SIC* 8062

FONDATION SANTE VALLEE-DE-LA-GATINEAU *p* 1148

177 RUE DES OBLATS, MANIWAKI, QC, J9E 1G5

(819) 449-2513   *SIC* 8361

FONDATION SOURCE BLEU *p* 1065

1130 RUE DE MONTBRUN, BOUCHERVILLE, QC, J4B 8W6

(450) 641-3165   *SIC* 8699

FONDATION UNIVERSITAS DU CANADA *p* 1274

1035 AV WILFRID-PELLETIER BUREAU 500, QUEBEC, QC, G1W 0C5

(877) 410-7333   *SIC* 6732

FONDATION UNIVERSITE DU QUEBEC *p* 1175

405 RUE SAINTE-CATHERINE E, MONTREAL, QC, H2L 2C4

SIC 8221

FONDATION UNIVERSITE DU QUEBEC *p* 1386

See *UNIVERSITE DU QUEBEC*

FONDATION UQAM *p* 1175

See *FONDATION DE L'UNIVERSITE DU QUEBEC A MONTREAL*

FONDATIONS ROY-LAROUCHE INC *p* 1403

1695 RUE SKIROULE RR 21, WICKHAM, QC, J0C 1S0

(819) 398-7333   *SIC* 3444

FONDERIE LAPERLE, DIV DE *p* 1349

See *CANADA PIPE COMPANY ULC*

FONDERIE LEMOLTECH INC *p* 1253

30 RUE SAINT-PIERRE, PRINCEVILLE, QC, G6L 5A9

(819) 364-7616   *SIC* 3365

FONDERIE NORCAST *p* 1154

See *BRADKEN CANADA MANUFACTURED PRODUCTS LTD*

FONDERIE POITRAS LTEE *p* 1121

168 BOUL NILUS-LECLERC, L'ISLET, QC, G0R 2C0

(418) 247-5041   *SIC* 3321

FONDERIES SHELLCAST INC *p* 1239

10645 AV LAMOUREUX, MONTREAL-NORD, QC, H1G 5L4

(514) 322-3760   *SIC* 3365

FONDREC INC *p* 1152

14078 RUE DE LA CHAPELLE, MIRABEL, QC, J7J 2C8

(450) 432-2688   *SIC* 3365

FONDREMY INC *p* 1074

1465 BOUL INDUSTRIEL BUREAU 100, CHAMBLY, QC, J3L 4C4

(450) 658-7111   *SIC* 3365

FONDS AGF, LES *p* 968

See *AGF MANAGEMENT LIMITED*

FONDS D'ASSURANCE RESPONSABILITE PROFESSIONNELLE DE L'ORDRE DES PHARMACIENS DU QUEBEC *p* 1196

2020 BOUL ROBERT-BOURASSA BUREAU 2160, MONTREAL, QC, H3A 2A5

(514) 281-0300   *SIC* 6411

FONDS D'ASSURANCE RESPONSABILITE PROFESSIONNELLE DU BARREAU DU QUEBEC *p* 1188

445 BOUL SAINT-LAURENT BUREAU 300, MONTREAL, QC, H2Y 3T8

(514) 954-3452   *SIC* 6351

FONDS D'ASSURANCE-

RESPONSABILITE PROFESSIONNELLE DE L'ORDRE DES DENTISTES DU QUEBEC *p* 1198

See *ORDRE DES DENTISTES DU QUEBEC*

FONDS D'ASSURANCE-RESPONSABILITE PROFESSIONNELLE DE L'ORDRE DES DENTISTES DU QUEBEC(F.A.R. *p* 1207

See *ORDRE DES DENTISTES DU QUEBEC*

FONDS DE PLACEMENT IMMOBILIER BTB *p* 1213

1411 RUE CRESCENT BUREAU 300, MONTREAL, QC, H3G 2B3

(514) 286-0188   *SIC* 6798

FONDS DE PLACEMENT IMMOBILIER COMINAR *p* 1272

2820 BOUL LAURIER BUREAU 850, QUEBEC, QC, G1V 0C1

(418) 681-8151   *SIC* 6799

FONDS DE SECURITE DESJARDINS *p* 1136

100 AV DES COMMANDEURS, LEVIS, QC, G6V 7N5

SIC 6351

FONDS DE SOLIDARITE DES TRAVAILLEURS DU QUEBEC (F.T.Q.) *p* 1176

545 BOUL CREMAZIE E BUREAU 200, MONTREAL, QC, H2M 2W4

(514) 383-8383   *SIC* 6722

FONDS DE SOLIDARITE DES TRAVAILLEURS DU QUEBEC (F.T.Q.) *p* 1176

8717 RUE BERRI, MONTREAL, QC, H2M 2T9

(514) 383-3663   *SIC* 6722

FONDS DE SOLIDARITE FTQ *p* 1176

See *FONDS DE SOLIDARITE DES TRAVAILLEURS DU QUEBEC (F.T.Q.)*

FONDS JEAN-PIERRE-PETIT *p* 1387

See *FONDATION CENTRE HOSPITALIER REGIONAL DE TROIS-RIVIERES (RSTR)*

FONDS SOCIAL DES EMPLOYES DE LA CAISSE DE DEPOT ET PLACEMENT DU QUEBEC *p* 1191

1000 PLACE JEAN-PAUL-RIOPELLE BUREAU A12, MONTREAL, QC, H2Z 2B3

(514) 842-3261   *SIC* 6399

FONDS UNIVERSITAS, LES *p* 1274

See *FONDATION UNIVERSITAS DU CANADA*

FONG TAI INTERNATIONAL FOOD LIMITED *p* 765

1100 GORDON BAKER RD, NORTH YORK, ON, M2H 3B3

(416) 497-6666   *SIC* 5141

FONTAINE SANTE *p* 1325

See *ALIMENTS FONTAINE SANTE INC*

FONTILE KITCHEN & BATH *p* 294

See *FON-TILE CORPORATION LIMITED*

FOOD ALLERGY CANADA *p* 767

2005 SHEPPARD AVE E SUITE 800, NORTH YORK, ON, M2J 5B4

(416) 785-5666   *SIC* 7389

FOOD BANK *p* 170

4615 60 ST, VEGREVILLE, AB, T9C 1N4

(780) 632-6002   *SIC* 8699

FOOD BANKS CANADA *p* 695

5090 EXPLORER DR SUITE 203, MISSISSAUGA, ON, L4W 4T9

(905) 602-5234   *SIC* 8699

FOOD BASIC *p* 523

See *METRO ONTARIO INC*

FOOD BASIC *p* 600

See *METRO ONTARIO INC*

FOOD BASIC *p* 610

See *1290685 ONTARIO INC*

FOOD BASIC *p* 752

See *METRO ONTARIO INC*

FOOD BASIC *p* 860

See *METRO ONTARIO INC*

FOOD BASICS *p* 474

See *METRO ONTARIO INC*

FOOD BASICS *p* 508

See *METRO ONTARIO INC*

FOOD BASICS *p* 534

See *METRO ONTARIO INC*

FOOD BASICS *p* 537

See *METRO ONTARIO INC*

FOOD BASICS *p* 577

See *1690651 ONTARIO INC*

FOOD BASICS *p* 608

See *METRO ONTARIO INC*

FOOD BASICS *p* 615

See *METRO ONTARIO INC*

FOOD BASICS *p* 632

See *METRO ONTARIO INC*

FOOD BASICS *p* 636

See *METRO ONTARIO INC*

FOOD BASICS *p* 641

See *METRO ONTARIO INC*

FOOD BASICS *p* 652

See *METRO ONTARIO INC*

FOOD BASICS *p* 659

See *METRO ONTARIO INC*

FOOD BASICS *p* 679

See *METRO ONTARIO INC*

FOOD BASICS *p* 697

See *METRO ONTARIO INC*

FOOD BASICS *p* 708

See *METRO ONTARIO INC*

FOOD BASICS *p* 717

See *METRO ONTARIO INC*

FOOD BASICS *p* 768

See *METRO ONTARIO INC*

FOOD BASICS *p* 775

See *METRO ONTARIO INC*

FOOD BASICS *p* 778

See *1184038 ONTARIO LIMITED*

FOOD BASICS *p* 838

See *METRO ONTARIO INC*

FOOD BASICS *p* 862

See *METRO ONTARIO INC*

FOOD BASICS *p* 866

See *METRO ONTARIO INC*

FOOD BASICS *p* 881

See *METRO ONTARIO INC*

FOOD BASICS *p* 900

See *METRO ONTARIO INC*

FOOD BASICS *p* 904

See *METRO ONTARIO INC*

FOOD BASICS *p* 919

See *METRO ONTARIO INC*

FOOD BASICS *p* 1018

See *METRO ONTARIO INC*

FOOD BASICS *p* 1023

See *METRO ONTARIO INC*

FOOD BASICS *p* 1035

See *METRO ONTARIO INC*

FOOD DIRECTIONS INC *p* 864

120 MELFORD DR UNIT 8, SCARBOROUGH, ON, M1B 2X5

(416) 609-0016   *SIC* 2098

FOOD EQUIPMENT PARTS & SERVICE *p* 919

See *R.G. HENDERSON & SON LIMITED*

FOOD FAIR *p* 383

See *ZEIDCO INC*

FOOD FOR CHANGE *p* 1430

See *SPECIALTY DISTRIBUTING LTD*

FOOD ROLL SALES (NIAGARA) LTD *p* 759

8464 EARL THOMAS AVE, NIAGARA FALLS, ON, L2G 0B6

(905) 358-5747   *SIC* 2038

FOOD SERVICE SOLUTIONS INC *p* 722

6599 KITIMAT RD UNIT 2, MISSISSAUGA, ON, L5N 4J4

(905) 363-0309   *SIC* 5046

FOOD SUPPLIES COMPANY *p* 552

See *FOOD SUPPLIES DISTRIBUTING COMPANY INC*

FOOD SUPPLIES DISTRIBUTING COMPANY INC *p* 552

355 RAYETTE RD UNIT 10, CONCORD, ON, L4K 2G2

SIC 5149

FOOD WAREHOUSE *p* 12

See *FEDERATED CO-OPERATIVES LIMITED*

FOODELICIOUS *p* 1165

See *ALIMENTS ALASKO INC*

FOODFEST INTERNATIONAL 2000 INC *p* 552

361 CONNIE CRES, CONCORD, ON, L4K 5R2

(905) 709-4775   *SIC* 5149

FOODLAND *p* 395

See *TRA MARITIMES*

FOODLAND *p* 563

420 LYNDOCH ST, CORUNNA, ON, N0N 1G0

(519) 862-5213   *SIC* 5411

FOODLAND *p* 592

See *PARLIAMENT, ART FOODS LIMITED*

FOODLAND *p* 682

See *CALHOUN FOODS LAND*

FOODLAND *p* 746

See *2032244 ONTARIO LIMITED*

FOODLAND *p* 809

See *ABERNETHY FOODS (ORILLIA) INC*

FOODLAND STORE 6301 *p* 1036

See *WOODSTOCK INDEPENDENT GROCER ASSOCIATE, INC.*

FOODMART *p* 682

See *1031647 ONTARIO LTD*

FOODRAM MC *p* 1309

See *GROUPE FOODAROM INC*

FOOT LOCKER CANADA CO *p* 793

230 BARMAC DR, NORTH YORK, ON, M9L 2Z3

(416) 748-4210   *SIC* 5661

FOOTHILLS COMPOSITE HIGH SCHOOL AND ALBERTA HIGH SCHOOL OF FINE ARTS *p* 150

See *FOOTHILLS SCHOOL DIVISION NO. 38*

FOOTHILLS COWBOYS ASSOCIATION, THE *p* 136

609 CENTRE ST SW UNIT 7, HIGH RIVER, AB, T1V 2C2

(403) 652-1405   *SIC* 8699

FOOTHILLS CREAMERY LTD *p* 29

2825 BONNYBROOK RD SE, CALGARY, AB, T2G 4N1

(403) 263-7725   *SIC* 2021

FOOTHILLS FORD SALES *p* 136

See *HIGH RIVER FORD SALES*

FOOTHILLS FOREST PRODUCTS INC *p* 130

HIGHWAY 40 S, GRANDE CACHE, AB, T0E 0Y0

(780) 827-2225   *SIC* 2426

FOOTHILLS INDUSTRIAL PRODUCTS *p* 35

15-6143 4 ST SE, CALGARY, AB, T2H 2H9

(403) 255-3250   *SIC* 4925

FOOTHILLS LIVESTOCK AUCTION LTD *p* 167

GD, STAVELY, AB, T0L 1Z0

(403) 549-2120   *SIC* 5154

FOOTHILLS PIPE LINES (SOUTH B.C.) LTD *p* 49

112 4 AVE SW SUITE 300, CALGARY, AB, T2P 0H3

(403) 920-2000   *SIC* 4922

FOOTHILLS PIPE LINES LTD *p* 49

450 1 ST SW, CALGARY, AB, T2P 5H1

(403) 920-2000   *SIC* 4922

FOOTHILLS SCHOOL DIVISION NO. 38 *p* 136

120 5 AVE SE SUITE 38, HIGH RIVER, AB, T1V 1G2

(403) 652-3001   *SIC* 8211

FOOTHILLS SCHOOL DIVISION NO. 38 *p* 150

229 WOODHAVEN DR, OKOTOKS, AB, T1S 2A7

(403) 938-6116   *SIC* 8211
FOOTNER FOREST PRODUCTS LTD *p* 135
GD, HIGH LEVEL, AB, T0H 1Z0
(780) 841-0008   *SIC* 2493
FOOTPRINTS SECURITY GROUP, ISLAND LOSS PREVENTION *p* 243
See *FOOTPRINTS SECURITY PATROL INC*
FOOTPRINTS SECURITY PATROL INC *p* 243
GD, PARKSVILLE, BC, V9P 2G2
(250) 248-9117   *SIC* 7389
FOR *p* 1188
See *FOR. PAR SODEPLAN INC*
FOR YOUR EYES ONLY *p* 980
See *DOWNTOWN EATERY (1993) LTD*
FOR-NET INC *p* 1260
1875 AV DE LA NORMANDIE, QUEBEC, QC, G1L 3Y8
(418) 529-6103   *SIC* 7349
FOR. PAR SODEPLAN INC *p* 1188
388 RUE SAINT-JACQUES BUREAU 900, MONTREAL, QC, H2Y 1S1
(514) 871-8833   *SIC* 7389
FORACO CANADA LTD *p* 762
1839 SEYMOUR ST, NORTH BAY, ON, P1A 0C7
(705) 495-6363   *SIC* 1799
FORACTION INC *p* 1158
270 RUE BRUNET, MONT-SAINT-HILAIRE, QC, J3H 0M6
(450) 446-8144   *SIC* 1629
FORAGE ALXTREME *p* 1390
See *MACHINES ROGER INTERNATIONAL INC*
FORAGE ANDRE ROY INC *p* 1314
186 RUE BOYER, SAINT-ISIDORE-DE-LAPRAIRIE, QC, J0L 2A0
(450) 454-1244   *SIC* 1611
FORAGE CHIBOUGAMAU LTEE *p* 1289
180 BOUL INDUSTRIEL, ROUYN-NORANDA, QC, J9X 6T3
(819) 797-9144   *SIC* 1481
FORAGE LONG TROU CMAC INC *p* 1390
185 RUE DES DISTRIBUTEURS, VAL-D'OR, QC, J9P 6Y1
(819) 874-8303   *SIC* 1081
FORAGE ORBIT GARANT INC *p* 1390
3200 BOUL JEAN-JACQUES-COSSETTE, VAL-D'OR, QC, J9P 6Y6
(819) 824-2707   *SIC* 1041
FORAGE SAGUENAY INC *p* 1116
2370 RUE DE LA METALLURGIE, JONQUIERE, QC, G7X 9H2
(418) 542-5059   *SIC* 1629
FORAGES C.C.L. (1993) INC, LES *p* 1089
237 CH SAINT-FRANCOIS-XAVIER, DELSON, QC, J5B 1X8
(450) 632-3995   *SIC* 1381
FORAGES CHIBOUGAMAU LTEE *p* 1077
527 RTE 167, CHIBOUGAMAU, QC, G8P 2K5
(418) 748-3977   *SIC* 1799
FORAN MINING CORPORATION *p* 304
409 GRANVILLE ST SUITE 904, VANCOUVER, BC, V6C 1T2
(604) 488-0008   *SIC* 1081
FORBES BROS. INC *p* 514
21 LYNDEN RD SUITE 19, BRANTFORD, ON, N3R 8B8
(519) 759-8220   *SIC* 5511
FORBES BROS. LTD *p* 125
1290 91 ST SW SUITE 200, EDMONTON, AB, T6X 0P2
(780) 960-1950   *SIC* 4911
FORBES CHEVROLET *p* 442
See *2207412 NOVA SCOTIA LTD*
FORBES HEWLETT TRANSPORT INC *p* 509
156 GLIDDEN RD, BRAMPTON, ON, L6W 3L2
(905) 455-2211   *SIC* 4213
FORBES MOTORS INC *p* 640
165 WEBER ST S, KITCHENER, ON, N2J

4A6
(519) 742-4463   *SIC* 5511
FORBES WATERLOO TOYOTA *p* 1007
See *RAF ENTERPRISES INC*
FORBO FLOORING SYSTEMS *p* 580
111 WESTMORE DR, ETOBICOKE, ON, M9V 3Y6
(416) 745-4200   *SIC* 5023
FORCE COPPS PILING INC *p* 5
27312 - 213 TWP 394, BLACKFALDS, AB, T0M 0J0
(403) 341-0030   *SIC* 1629
FORCE FINANCIERE EXCEL *p* 639
See *FINANCIAL HORIZONS INCORPORATED*
FORCE INSPECTION SERVICES INC *p* 139
7500A 43 ST, LEDUC, AB, T9E 7E8
(780) 955-2370   *SIC* 7389
FORD *p* 1046
See *SOMA AUTO INC*
FORD *p* 1135
See *DESMEULES AUTOMOBILES INC*
FORD *p* 1154
See *AUTOMOBILES BOUCHARD & FILS INC*
FORD CREDIT CANADA LIMITED *p* 100
10335 172 ST NW SUITE 300, EDMONTON, AB, T5S 1K9
   SIC 8742
FORD CREDIT CANADA LIMITED *p* 800
THE CANADIAN RD, OAKVILLE, ON, L6J 5C7
(905) 845-2511   *SIC* 6141
FORD GABRIEL *p* 1222
See *FORD LINCOLN GABRIEL, S.E.C.*
FORD LINCOLN *p* 1006
455 KING ST N, WATERLOO, ON, N2J 2Z5
(877) 339-6067   *SIC* 5511
FORD LINCOLN *p* 1221
See *188461 CANADA INC*
FORD LINCOLN GABRIEL, S.E.C. *p* 1222
7100 RUE SAINT-JACQUES, MONTREAL, QC, H4B 1V2
(514) 487-7777   *SIC* 5511
FORD MOTOR COMPANY OF CANADA, LIMITED *p* 100
11604 181 ST NW, EDMONTON, AB, T5S 1M6
(780) 454-9621   *SIC* 5013
FORD MOTOR COMPANY OF CANADA, LIMITED *p* 503
8000 DIXIE RD, BRAMPTON, ON, L6T 2J7
(905) 459-2210   *SIC* 5013
FORD MOTOR COMPANY OF CANADA, LIMITED *p* 800
1 CANADIAN RD, OAKVILLE, ON, L6J 5E4
(905) 845-2511   *SIC* 3711
FORD MOTOR COMPANY OF CANADA, LIMITED *p* 1018
7654 TECUMSEH RD E, WINDSOR, ON, N8T 1E9
(519) 944-8564   *SIC* 3714
FORD MOTOR COMPANY OF CANADA, LIMITED *p* 1018
6500 CANTELON DR, WINDSOR, ON, N8T 0A6
(519) 251-4401   *SIC* 3711
FORD MOTOR COMPANY OF CANADA, LIMITED *p* 1023
2900 TRENTON ST, WINDSOR, ON, N9A 7B2
(519) 257-2000   *SIC* 3322
FORD MOTOR COMPANY OF CANADA, LIMITED *p* 1023
3223 LAUZON PKY, WINDSOR, ON, N9A 6X3
(519) 944-8784   *SIC* 5521
FORD MOTOR COMPANY OF CANADA, LIMITED *p* 1023
1000 HENRY FORD CENTRE DR, WINDSOR, ON, N9A 7E8
(519) 257-2020   *SIC* 3519
FORD MOTOR COMPANY OF CANADA, LIMITED *p* 1339

6505 RTE TRANSCANADIENNE BUREAU 200, SAINT-LAURENT, QC, H4T 1S3
(514) 744-1800   *SIC* 5012
FORD PARTS DISTRIBUTION CENTER *p* 100
See *FORD MOTOR COMPANY OF CANADA, LIMITED*
FORD WINDSOR ENGINE PLANT *p* 1023
See *FORD MOTOR COMPANY OF CANADA, LIMITED*
FORD'S, SCOTT PHARMACY LTD *p* 633
775 STRAND BLVD SUITE 11, KINGSTON, ON, K7P 2S7
(613) 384-7477   *SIC* 5912
FORD, WAYNE SALES LIMITED *p* 755
17750 YONGE ST, NEWMARKET, ON, L3Y 8P4
(905) 895-4565   *SIC* 5531
FORDING RIVER OPERATIONS *p* 212
See *TECK COAL LIMITED*
FOREIGNEXCHANGE TRANSLATIONS CANADA, INC *p* 446
10 MORRIS DR UNIT 40, DARTMOUTH, NS, B3B 1K8
(902) 468-5553   *SIC* 7389
FOREMOST INDUSTRIES LP *p* 23
1225 64 AVE NE, CALGARY, AB, T2E 8P9
(403) 295-5800   *SIC* 3531
FOREMOST INTERNATIONAL LTD *p* 731
5970 CHEDWORTH WAY SUITE B, MISSISSAUGA, ON, L5R 4G5
(905) 507-2005   *SIC* 5074
FOREMOST LLOYDMINSTER *p* 144
See *UNIVERSAL INDUSTRIES (FOREMOST) CORP*
FOREMOST UNDERWRITERS *p* 412
See *MITCHELL MCCONNELL INSURANCE LIMITED*
FORENSIC PSYCHIATRIC SERVICES COMMISSION *p* 199
70 COLONY FARM RD, COQUITLAM, BC, V3C 5X9
(604) 524-7700   *SIC* 8063
FORESCO HOLDING INC *p* 1130
498 BOUL DU ROYAUME, LAROUCHE, QC, G0W 1Z0
(418) 542-8243   *SIC* 5211
FOREST CITY CASTINGS INC *p* 889
10 HIGHBURY AVE, ST THOMAS, ON, N5P 4C7
(519) 633-2999   *SIC* 3365
FOREST CITY CONCRETE FINISHING, DIV OF *p* 911
See *EAST ELGIN CONCRETE FORMING LIMITED*
FOREST CITY FIRE PROTECTION & SECURITY *p* 652
See *FOREST CITY FIRE PROTECTION LTD*
FOREST CITY FIRE PROTECTION LTD *p* 652
160 ADELAIDE ST S UNIT A, LONDON, ON, N5Z 3L1
(519) 668-0010   *SIC* 1711
FOREST CITY GRAPHICS LIMITED *p* 661
982 HUBREY RD, LONDON, ON, N6N 1B5
(519) 668-2191   *SIC* 2771
FOREST CITY SURPLUS (1986) LIMITED *p* 650
1712 DUNDAS ST, LONDON, ON, N5W 3C9
(519) 451-0246   *SIC* 5961
FOREST CITY SURPLUS CANADA *p* 650
See *FOREST CITY SURPLUS (1986) LIMITED*
FOREST ENGINEERING RESEARCH INSTITUTE *p* 324
2601 EAST MALL, VANCOUVER, BC, V6T 1Z4
(604) 228-1555   *SIC* 8733
FOREST HEIGHTS COLLEGIATE INSTITUTE *p* 641

See *WATERLOO REGION DISTRICT SCHOOL BOARD*
FOREST HEIGHTS LONG TERM CARE CENTER *p* 641
See *REVERA LONG TERM CARE INC*
FOREST HILL *p* 625
See *OMNI HEALTH CARE LTD*
FOREST HILL LEARNING CENTRE LIMITED *p* 779
411 LAWRENCE AVE E, NORTH YORK, ON, M3C 1N9
(416) 444-5858   *SIC* 8211
FOREST HILL PLACE *p* 972
See *REVERA INC*
FOREST HILL REAL ESTATE INC *p* 771
500 SHEPPARD AVE E SUITE 201, NORTH YORK, ON, M2N 6H7
(416) 226-1987   *SIC* 6531
FOREST HILL REAL ESTATE INC *p* 972
441 SPADINA RD, TORONTO, ON, M5P 2W3
(416) 488-2875   *SIC* 6531
FOREST IGA *p* 11
See *FOREST LAWN SOBEYS*
FOREST LABORATORIES CANADA INC *p* 552
610 APPLEWOOD CRES UNIT 302, CONCORD, ON, L4K 0E3
(289) 695-4700   *SIC* 5122
FOREST LAWN CALGARY CO-OP, DIV *p* 10
See *CALGARY CO-OPERATIVE ASSOCIATION LIMITED*
FOREST LAWN HIGH SCHOOL *p* 10
See *CALGARY BOARD OF EDUCATION*
FOREST LAWN SOBEYS *p* 11
5115 17 AVE SE, CALGARY, AB, T2A 0V4
(403) 273-9339   *SIC* 5411
FOREST PARK MOTORS INC *p* 813
799 BLOOR ST W, OSHAWA, ON, L1J 5Y6
(905) 404-0525   *SIC* 5511
FORESTERIE A S L INC, LA *p* 1366
803 14E AV, SENNETERRE, QC, J0Y 2M0
(819) 737-8851   *SIC* 0851
FORESTERIE C. H. B. LTEE *p* 1368
3563 RUE TRUDEL, SHAWINIGAN, QC, G9N 6R4
(819) 731-0477   *SIC* 0851
FORESTERIE G.D.S. *p* 1089
See *PROMOBOIS G.D.S. INC*
FORESTERS ASSET MANAGEMENT INC *p* 938
20 ADELAIDE ST E SUITE 1500, TORONTO, ON, M5C 2T6
(800) 828-1540   *SIC* 6371
FORESTERS FINANCIAL INVESTMENT MANAGEMENT COMPANY OF CANADA INC *p* 771
5000 YONGE ST 8TH FLOOR, NORTH YORK, ON, M2N 7J8
(416) 883-5800   *SIC* 6722
FORESTERS LIFE INSURANCE COMPANY *p* 731
100 MILVERTON DR SUITE 400, MISSISSAUGA, ON, L5R 4H1
(905) 219-8000   *SIC* 6311
FOREVER IN DOUGH INC *p* 120
9804 22 AVE NW, EDMONTON, AB, T6N 1L1
(780) 463-9086   *SIC* 5812
FOREVER XXI ULC *p* 767
1800 SHEPPARD AVE E, NORTH YORK, ON, M2J 5A7
(416) 494-6363   *SIC* 5651
FOREWEST HOLDINGS INC *p* 228
5769 201A ST UNIT 169, LANGLEY, BC, V3A 8H9
(604) 514-8303   *SIC* 5912
FOREX INC *p* 1204
1250 BOUL RENE-LEVESQUE O BUREAU 3930, MONTREAL, QC, H3B 4W8
(514) 935-0702   *SIC* 0851
FORFAITERIE INC, LA *p* 1378
107 1RE AV, STONEHAM-ET-

TEWKESBURY, QC, G3C 0L3
(418) 848-1518 *SIC 4724*
FORGES DE SOREL CIE, LES *p 1322*
100 RUE MCCARTHY, SAINT-JOSEPH-DE-
SOREL, QC, J3R 3M8
(450) 746-4030 *SIC 3291*
FORGES DE SOREL CIE, LES *p 1322*
100 RUE MCCARTHY, SAINT-JOSEPH-DE-
SOREL, QC, J3R 3M8
(450) 746-4030 *SIC 3312*
**FORGET & SAUVE, AUDIOPROTHESISTES
S.E.N.C.**
5255 BOUL HENRI-BOURASSA O BU-
REAU 410, SAINT-LAURENT, QC, H4R 2M6
(514) 353-0001 *SIC 5999*
FORGET, JACQUES LTEE *p 1380*
2215 CH COMTOIS, TERREBONNE, QC,
J6X 4H4
(450) 477-1002 *SIC 2011*
FORINTEK, DIV OF *p 324*
See *FPINNOVATIONS*
FORKLIFT DEPOT *p 816*
See *OTTAWA EQUIPMENT & HYDRAULIC
INC*
FORM & BUILD SUPPLY INC *p 651*
1175 FRANCES ST, LONDON, ON, N5W
2L9
(519) 453-4300 *SIC 5039*
FORM SOLUTIONS *p 847*
See *2121361 ONTARIO INC*
FORMA-CON CONSTRUCTION *p 547*
See *1428508 ONTARIO LIMITED*
FORMAN FORD SALES LIMITED *p 348*
36 2ND AVE NW, DAUPHIN, MB, R7N 1H2
(204) 622-3673 *SIC 5511*
FORMAN HONDA *p 348*
See *SOUTHWEST AUTO CENTRE LTD*
FORMASHAPE *p 223*
See *WHITEWATER COMPOSITES LTD*
FORMATION PROFESSIONNELLE *p 1131*
See *LESTER B. PEARSON SCHOOL
BOARD*
FORMATIONS INC *p 93*
12220 142 ST NW, EDMONTON, AB, T5L
2G9
(780) 451-6400 *SIC 5039*
FORMCRETE (1994) LTD *p 739*
7060 PACIFIC CIR, MISSISSAUGA, ON,
L5T 2A7
(905) 669-8017 *SIC 1521*
FORMEDICA LTEE *p 1082*
4859 RUE DES ORMES, CONTRECOEUR,
QC, J0L 1C0
(450) 587-2821 *SIC 3842*
FORMET INDUSTRIES *p 889*
See *MAGNA INTERNATIONAL INC*
FORMGLAS HOLDINGS INC *p 1031*
181 REGINA RD, WOODBRIDGE, ON, L4L
8M3
(416) 635-8030 *SIC 6712*
FORMGLAS PRODUCTS LTD *p 1003*
181 REGINA RD, VAUGHAN, ON, L4L 8M3
(416) 635-8030 *SIC 3299*
FORMICA *p 1318*
See *FORMICA CANADA INC*
FORMICA CANADA INC *p 1318*
25 RUE MERCIER, SAINT-JEAN-SUR-
RICHELIEU, QC, J3B 6E9
(450) 347-7541 *SIC 3089*
**FORMING TECHNOLOGIES INCORPO-
RATED** *p*
527
3370 SOUTH SERVICE RD SUITE 203,
BURLINGTON, ON, L7N 3M6
(905) 340-3370 *SIC 7372*
FORMINTEK *p 1307*
See *9136-3283 QUEBEC INC*
FORMNET INC *p 584*
326 HUMBER COLLEGE BLVD, ETOBI-
COKE, ON, M9W 5P4
(416) 675-3404 *SIC 3444*
FORMO MOTORS LTD *p 359*
1550 MAIN ST, SWAN RIVER, MB, R0L 1Z0
(204) 734-4577 *SIC 5511*

FORMOSA SPRINGS BREWERY *p 636*
See *WATERLOO BREWING LTD*
FORMULA DISTRIBUTORS LTD *p 209*
7205 BROWN ST, DELTA, BC, V4G 1G5
(604) 946-0146 *SIC 5014*
FORMULA FORD SALES LIMITED *p 843*
940 KINGSTON RD, PICKERING, ON, L1V
1B3
(905) 420-1449 *SIC 5511*
FORMULA GROWTH LIMITED *p 1196*
1010 RUE SHERBROOKE O BUREAU
2300, MONTREAL, QC, H3A 2R7
(514) 288-5136 *SIC 6282*
FORMULA HONDA *p 865*
See *PAULDONLAM INVESTMENTS INC*
FORMULE FORD LINCOLN INC *p 1111*
1144 RUE PRINCIPALE, GRANBY, QC, J2J
0M2
(450) 777-1777 *SIC 5511*
FORMULE MAZDA *p 1285*
See *9003-4406 QUEBEC INC*
FORMULES D'AFFAIRES SUPRATECH INC
p 1111
960 RUE ANDRE-LINE, GRANBY, QC, J2J
1E2
(450) 777-1041 *SIC 2752*
FORNEBU LUMBER COMPANY INC *p 396*
5060 ROUTE 430, BRUNSWICK MINES,
NB, E2A 6W6
(506) 547-8690 *SIC 2421*
FORPAN *p 1232*
See *UNIBOARD CANADA INC*
FORREC DESIGN *p 991*
See *FORREC LTD*
FORREC LTD *p 991*
219 DUFFERIN ST SUITE 100C,
TORONTO, ON, M6K 3J1
(416) 696-8686 *SIC 1542*
**FORREST GREEN CONSULTING CORPO-
RATION** *p*
855
10520 YONGE ST UNIT 35B, RICHMOND
HILL, ON, L4C 3C7
(905) 884-3103 *SIC 8741*
**FORREST GREEN GROUP OF COMPA-
NIES** *p*
855
See *FORREST GREEN CONSULTING
CORPORATION*
FORRESTALL GROUP INC, THE *p 670*
201 WHITEHALL DR UNIT 4, MARKHAM,
ON, L3R 9Y3
SIC 7379
FORT ALBANY WING *p 591*
See *JAMES BAY GENERAL HOSPITAL*
FORT ASSURANCE *p 1220*
See *GROUPE FINANCIER FORT INC*
**FORT CALGARY PRESERVATION SOCI-
ETY** *p*
29
750 9 AVE SE, CALGARY, AB, T2G 5E1
(403) 290-1875 *SIC 8699*
FORT CITY CHRYSLER *p 213*
See *FORT CITY CHRYSLER SALES LTD*
FORT CITY CHRYSLER SALES LTD *p 213*
8424 ALASKA RD, FORT ST. JOHN, BC,
V1J 5L6
(250) 787-5220 *SIC 5511*
FORT DEARBORN *p 1085*
See *FD ALPHA CANADA ACQUISITION
INC*
FORT DISTRIBUTORS LTD *p 357*
938 MCPHILLIPS RD, ST ANDREWS, MB,
R1A 4E7
(204) 785-2180 *SIC 5169*
**FORT ERIE NATIVE CULTURAL CENTRE
INC** *p 591*
796 BUFFALO RD, FORT ERIE, ON, L2A
5H2
(905) 871-6592 *SIC 8322*
FORT ERIE NATIVE FRIENDSHIP CENTRE
p 591
See *FORT ERIE NATIVE CULTURAL CEN-
TRE INC*

**FORT ERIE TRUCK STOP & SERVICE CEN-
TRE** *p*
591
See *2097738 ONTARIO INC*
FORT GARRY FIRE TRUCKS LTD *p 378*
53 BERGEN CUTOFF RD, WINNIPEG, MB,
R3C 2E6
(204) 594-3473 *SIC 3711*
FORT GARRY INDUSTRIES LTD *p 369*
2525 INKSTER BLVD UNIT 2, WINNIPEG,
MB, R2R 2Y4
(204) 632-8261 *SIC 5013*
FORT LA BOSSE SCHOOL DIVISION *p 360*
523 9TH AVE, VIRDEN, MB, R0M 2C0
(204) 748-2692 *SIC 8211*
FORT MCKAY GROUP OF COMPANIES *p*
128
See *FORT MCKAY SERVICES LIMITED
PARTNERSHIP*
FORT MCKAY METIS GROUP LTD *p 128*
GD LCD MAIN, FORT MCMURRAY, AB,
T9H 3E2
(780) 828-4581 *SIC 1542*
**FORT MCKAY SERVICES LIMITED PART-
NERSHIP** *p*
128
GD LCD MAIN, FORT MCMURRAY, AB,
T9H 3E2
(780) 828-2400 *SIC 4225*
FORT MCMURRAY IGA *p 124*
See *BLUMENSCHEIN HOLDINGS LTD*
FORT MCMURRAY PIZZA LTD *p 128*
10202 MACDONALD AVE, FORT MCMUR-
RAY, AB, T9H 1T4
(780) 743-5056 *SIC 5812*
**FORT MCMURRAY PUBLIC SCHOOL DIS-
TRICT #2833** *p*
128
231 HARDIN ST SUITE 2833, FORT MC-
MURRAY, AB, T9H 2G2
(780) 799-7900 *SIC 8211*
**FORT MCMURRAY PUBLIC SCHOOL DIS-
TRICT #2833** *p*
128
8453 FRANKLIN AVE, FORT MCMURRAY,
AB, T9H 2J2
(780) 743-2444 *SIC 8211*
**FORT MCMURRAY PUBLIC SCHOOL DIS-
TRICT #2833** *p*
129
107 BRETT DR, FORT MCMURRAY, AB,
T9K 1V1
(780) 743-1079 *SIC 8211*
FORT MOTORS LTD *p 213*
11104 ALASKA RD, FORT ST. JOHN, BC,
V1J 5T5
(250) 785-6661 *SIC 5511*
FORT NELSON IGA *p 212*
See *399837 BC LTD*
FORT PITT FARMS INC *p 1409*
GD, LLOYDMINSTER, SK, S9V 0X5
(306) 344-4849 *SIC 0191*
FORT ROUGE AUTO SALES *p 387*
680 PEMBINA HWY, WINNIPEG, MB, R3M
2M5
(877) 792-9521 *SIC 5521*
**FORT SASKATCHEWAN COMMUNITY
HOSPITAL** *p 129*
See *ALBERTA HEALTH SERVICES*
**FORT ST JOHN CO-OPERATIVE ASSOCI-
ATION** *p*
213
10808 91 AVE, FORT ST. JOHN, BC, V1J
5R1
(250) 785-4471 *SIC 5171*
**FORT ST. JOHN HOME HARDWARE
BUILDING CENTRE** *p 213*
See *HOME HARDWARE BUILDING CEN-
TRE*
**FORT VERMILION SCHOOL DIVISON NO.
52** *p 130*
5213 RIVER RD, FORT VERMILION, AB,
T0H 1N0
(780) 927-3766 *SIC 8211*

FORT YORK C MOTORS LP *p 933*
321 FRONT ST E, TORONTO, ON, M5A
1G3
(416) 368-7000 *SIC 5511*
FORTERRA CONDUITE SOUS PRESSION *p*
1301
See *FORTERRA PRESSURE PIPE, ULC*
FORTERRA PIPE & PRECAST BC, ULC *p*
1149
1331 AV DE LA GARE, MASCOUCHE, QC,
J7K 3G6
SIC 3272
FORTERRA PIPE & PRECAST, LTD *p 533*
2099 ROSEVILLE RD SUITE 2, CAM-
BRIDGE, ON, N1R 5S3
(519) 622-7574 *SIC 3272*
FORTERRA PRESSURE PIPE, ULC *p 1000*
102 PROUSE RD, UXBRIDGE, ON, L4A
7X4
(905) 642-4383 *SIC 3272*
FORTERRA PRESSURE PIPE, ULC *p 1301*
699 BOUL INDUSTRIEL, SAINT-
EUSTACHE, QC, J7R 6C3
(450) 623-2200 *SIC 3272*
**FORTERRA TUYAUX ET PREFABRIQUES
C-B** *p 1149*
See *FORTERRA PIPE & PRECAST BC,
ULC*
**FORTES, JOE SEAFOOD & CHOP HOUSE
LTD** *p 313*
777 THURLOW ST, VANCOUVER, BC, V6E
3V5
(604) 669-1940 *SIC 5812*
FORTIER *p 1306*
146 RUE COMMERCIALE, SAINT-HENRI-
DE-LEVIS, QC, G0R 3E0
(418) 882-2205 *SIC 3273*
FORTIER AUTO (MONTREAL) LTEE *p 1052*
7000 BOUL LOUIS-H.-LAFONTAINE, AN-
JOU, QC, H1M 2X3
(514) 353-9821 *SIC 5511*
FORTIER BEVERAGES LIMITED *p 545*
158 SECOND AVE, COCHRANE, ON, P0L
1C0
(705) 272-4305 *SIC 5149*
FORTIFIED NUTRITION LIMITED *p 140*
3613 9 AVE N, LETHBRIDGE, AB, T1H 6G8
(403) 320-0401 *SIC 5191*
FORTIGATE *p 185*
See *FORTINET TECHNOLOGIES
(CANADA) ULC*
FORTIGO FREIGHT INC *p 584*
50 BELFIELD RD SUITE 5, ETOBICOKE,
ON, M9W 1G1
(416) 367-8446 *SIC 4731*
FORTIGO FREIGHT SERVICES INC *p 584*
50 BELFIELD RD SUITE 4, ETOBICOKE,
ON, M9W 1G1
(416) 367-8446 *SIC 4731*
FORTIN'S SUPPLY LTD *p 196*
45750 AIRPORT RD, CHILLIWACK, BC,
V2P 1A2
(604) 795-9739 *SIC 5013*
FORTIN, J E INC *p 1294*
116 BOUL FORTIN, SAINT-BERNARD-DE-
LACOLLE, QC, J0J 1V0
(450) 246-3867 *SIC 4213*
FORTIN, JEAN & ASSOCIES SYNDICS INC
p 1141
2360 BOUL MARIE-VICTORIN,
LONGUEUIL, QC, J4G 1B5
(450) 442-3260 *SIC 8111*
**FORTINET TECHNOLOGIES (CANADA)
ULC** *p 185*
4190 STILL CREEK DR UNIT 400, BURN-
ABY, BC, V5C 6C6
(604) 430-1297 *SIC 7379*
FORTINO'S *p 616*
See *UPPER JAMES 2004 LTD*
FORTINO'S #00081 *p 1005*
See *2156110 ONTARIO LIMITED*
FORTINO'S (HIGHWAY 7 & ANSLEY) LTD *p*
1031
3940 HIGHWAY 7, WOODBRIDGE, ON, L4L

9C3
(905) 851-5642   SIC 5411
FORTINO'S (LAWRENCE & ALLEN) LTD p
789
700 LAWRENCE AVE W, NORTH YORK,
ON, M6A 3B4
(416) 785-9843   SIC 5411
FORTINO'S (NEW STREET) LTD   p 522
5111 NEW ST SUITE 50, BURLINGTON,
ON, L7L 1V2
(905) 631-7227   SIC 5411
FORTINO'S SUPERMARKET   p 614
See FORTINOS (MALL 1994) LTD
FORTINOS   p 612
See FORTINOS (DUNDURN) LTD
FORTINOS   p 664
See LOBLAWS INC
FORTINOS (DUNDURN) LTD   p 612
50 DUNDURN ST S, HAMILTON, ON, L8P
4W3
(905) 529-4290   SIC 5411
FORTINOS (MALL 1994) LTD   p 614
65 MALL RD, HAMILTON, ON, L8V 5B8
(905) 387-7673   SIC 5411
FORTINOS (OAKVILLE) LTD   p 802
173 LAKESHORE RD W, OAKVILLE, ON,
L6K 1E7
(905) 845-3654   SIC 5411
FORTINOS 99   p 802
See FORTINOS (OAKVILLE) LTD
FORTINOS FIESTA MALL LTD   p 894
102 HIGHWAY 8, STONEY CREEK, ON,
L8G 4H3
(905) 662-3772   SIC 5411
FORTINOS SUPERMARKET LTD   p 508
60 QUARRY EDGE DR, BRAMPTON, ON,
L6V 4K2
(905) 453-3600   SIC 5411
FORTINOS SUPERMARKET LTD   p 615
1275 RYMAL RD E SUITE 2, HAMILTON,
ON, L8W 3N1
(905) 318-4532   SIC 5141
FORTINOS SUPERMARKET LTD   p 894
102 HIGHWAY 8, STONEY CREEK, ON,
L8G 4H3
(905) 664-2886   SIC 5141
FORTIS CONSTRUCTION GROUP INC p
1018
3070 JEFFERSON BLVD, WINDSOR, ON,
N8T 3G9
(519) 419-7828   SIC 1541
**FORTIS ENGINEERING & MANUFACTUR-
ING INC**   p
1427
802 57TH ST E, SASKATOON, SK, S7K 5Z2
(306) 242-4427   SIC 5051
FORTIS GROUP INC   p 1018
3070 JEFFERSON BLVD, WINDSOR, ON,
N8T 3G9
(519) 419-7828   SIC 6712
FORTIS HOSPITALITY SVC DIV OF p 433
See FORTIS PROPERTIES CORPORA-
TION
FORTIS INC   p 433
5 SPRINGDALE ST SUITE 1100, ST.
JOHN'S, NL, A1E 0E4
(709) 737-2800   SIC 4911
FORTIS PROPERTIES CORPORATION p
433
5 SPRINGDALE ST SUITE 1100, ST.
JOHN'S, NL, A1E 0E4
(709) 737-2800   SIC 6512
FORTISALBERTA INC   p 66
320 17 AVE SW, CALGARY, AB, T2S 2V1
(403) 514-4000   SIC 4911
FORTISBC ENERGY INC   p 281
16705 FRASER HWY, SURREY, BC, V4N
0E8
(604) 576-7000   SIC 4923
FORTISBC HOLDINGS INC   p 313
1111 GEORGIA ST W SUITE 1000, VAN-
COUVER, BC, V6E 4M3
(604) 443-6525   SIC 4923
FORTISBC INC   p 221

1975 SPRINGFIELD RD SUITE 100,
KELOWNA, BC, V1Y 7V7
(604) 576-7000   SIC 4911
FORTISBC PACIFIC HOLDINGS INC p 222
1975 SPRINGFIELD RD SUITE 100,
KELOWNA, BC, V1Y 7V7
(250) 469-8000   SIC 4911
FORTISONTARIO INC   p 591
1130 BERTIE ST, FORT ERIE, ON, L2A 5Y2
(905) 871-0330   SIC 4911
FORTRAN TRAFFIC SYSTEMS LIMITED p
871
470 MIDWEST RD, SCARBOROUGH, ON,
M1P 4Y5
(416) 288-1320   SIC 3669
FORTRESS CELLULOSE SPECIALISEE p
1384
See FORTRESS SPECIALTY CELLULOSE
INC
FORTRESS GLOBAL ENTERPRISES INC p
240
157 CHADWICK CRT FL 2, NORTH VAN-
COUVER, BC, V7M 3K2
(888) 820-3888   SIC 2611
FORTRESS GROUP INC   p 1010
85 BAFFIN PL, WATERLOO, ON, N2V 2C1
(519) 747-4604   SIC 5075
**FORTRESS OF LOUISBOURG ASSOCIA-
TION**   p
450
259 PARK SERVICE RD, FORTRESS OF
LOUISBOURG, NS, B1C 2L2
(902) 733-2280   SIC 5947
FORTRESS SPECIALTY CELLULOSE INCp
1384
451 RUE VICTORIA, THURSO, QC, J0X
3B0
(819) 985-2233   SIC 2611
FORTRESS TECHNOLOGY INC   p 864
51 GRAND MARSHALL DR, SCARBOR-
OUGH, ON, M1B 5N6
(416) 754-2898   SIC 3812
FORTUNA SILVER MINES INC   p 304
200 BURRARD ST SUITE 650, VANCOU-
VER, BC, V6C 3L6
(604) 484-4085   SIC 1044
FORTUNE BAY CORP   p 453
1969 UPPER WATER ST SUITE 2001, HAL-
IFAX, NS, B3J 3R7
(902) 442-1421   SIC 1041
FORTY CREEK DISTILLERY LTD   p 599
297 SOUTH SERVICE RD, GRIMSBY, ON,
L3M 1Y6
(905) 945-9225   SIC 2085
FORTY CREEK DISTILLERY LTD   p 991
1 PARDEE AVE SUITE 102, TORONTO,
ON, M6K 3H1
(905) 945-9225   SIC 2085
FORUM CANADA ULC   p 125
9503 12 AVE SW, EDMONTON, AB, T6X
0C3
(825) 410-1200   SIC 1389
FORUM NATIONAL INVESTMENTS LTD p
266
13040 NO. 2 RD SUITE 180A, RICHMOND,
BC, V7E 2G1
(604) 275-2170   SIC 8699
FORUM RESEARCH   p 974
See ACCESS RESEARCH INC
**FORWARD 600 PRECISION TOOLS & MA-
CHINERY**   p
698
See NUCLEUS DISTRIBUTION INC
FORWARD SIGNS INC   p 874
60 EMBLEM CRT, SCARBOROUGH, ON,
M1S 1B1
(416) 291-4477   SIC 3993
FORWARD VISION GROUP INC.   p 658
1828 BLUE HERON DR SUITE 37, LON-
DON, ON, N6H 0B7
(519) 471-6665   SIC 5995
FOSS FLEET MANAGEMENT   p 904
See FOSS NATIONAL LEASING LTD.
FOSS NATIONAL LEASING LTD.   p 904

125 COMMERCE VALLEY DR W SUITE
801, THORNHILL, ON, L3T 7W4
(905) 886-2522   SIC 7515
FOSSIL EPC LTD   p 148
1805 8 ST, NISKU, AB, T9E 7S8
(780) 449-0773   SIC 8741
FOSTER KIA   p 875
See FOSTER PONTIAC BUICK INC
FOSTER PARK BROKERS INC   p 101
17704 103 AVE NW SUITE 200, EDMON-
TON, AB, T5S 1J9
(780) 489-4961   SIC 6411
FOSTER PONTIAC BUICK INC   p 875
3445 SHEPPARD AVE E, SCARBOR-
OUGH, ON, M1T 3K5
(416) 291-9745   SIC 5511
FOSTER'S SEED AND FEED LTD   p 5
1120 8TH AVE W, BEAVERLODGE, AB,
T0H 0C0
(780) 354-2107   SIC 5191
**FOSTER, TOWNSEND, GRAHAM & ASSO-
CIATES LLP**   p
653
150 DUFFERIN AVE SUITE 900, LONDON,
ON, N6A 5N6
(519) 672-5272   SIC 8111
FOTIOU FRAMES LIMITED   p 1027
135 RAINBOW CREEK DR, WOOD-
BRIDGE, ON, L4H 0A4
(800) 668-8420   SIC 5023
FOTO SOURCE PHOTO SERVICE   p 1190
See PHOTO SERVICE LTEE
FOUNDATION DISTRIBUTING INC p 811
9 COBBLEDICK ST, ORONO, ON, L0B 1M0
(905) 983-1188   SIC 5049
FOUNDERS ADVANTAGE CAPITAL CORP
p 66
2207 4TH ST SW SUITE 400, CALGARY,
AB, T2S 1X1
(403) 455-9660   SIC 6211
FOUNDERS INSURANCE GROUP INC p
471
260 MAIN ST, WOLFVILLE, NS, B4P 1C4
SIC 6411
FOUNDERS INSURANCE GROUP INC. p
446
250 BROWNLOW AVE SUITE 18, DART-
MOUTH, NS, B3B 1W9
(902) 468-3529   SIC 6411
FOUNDRY, THE   p 808
See HONEYCOMB HILL HOLDINGS OF
MULMUR INC
FOUNTAIN TIRE   p 132
See FOUNTAIN TIRE (G.P.) LTD
FOUNTAIN TIRE (EDSON) LTD   p 126
4619 2 AVE, EDSON, AB, T7E 1C1
(780) 723-7666   SIC 5531
FOUNTAIN TIRE (G.P.) LTD   p 132
13003 100 ST, GRANDE PRAIRIE, AB, T8V
4H3
(780) 539-1710   SIC 5531
FOUNTAIN TIRE (SAULT STE. MARIE) LTD
p 862
55 BLACK RD, SAULT STE. MARIE, ON,
P6B 0A3
(705) 254-6664   SIC 5531
FOUNTAIN TIRE F406   p 862
See FOUNTAIN TIRE (SAULT STE. MARIE)
LTD
FOUNTAIN TIRE LTD   p 124
1006 103A ST SW SUITE 103, EDMON-
TON, AB, T6W 2P6
(780) 464-3700   SIC 5531
**FOUR COUNTIES HEALTH SERVICES
CORPORATION, THE**   p 753
1824 CONCESSION DR, NEWBURY, ON,
N0L 1Z0
(519) 693-4441   SIC 8062
FOUR POINTS BY SHERATON   p 657
See CONKRISDA HOLDINGS LIMITED
FOUR POINTS BY SHERATON   p 1256
See HOTEL & GOLF MARIGOT INC
**FOUR POINTS BY SHERATON EDMON-
TON GATEWAY**   p

125
10010 12 AVE SW, EDMONTON, AB, T6X
0P9
(780) 801-4000   SIC 7011
**FOUR POINTS BY SHERATON HOTEL ET
CENTRE DE CONFERENCES GATINEAU-
OTTAWA**   p
1105
See 35 LAURIER LIMITED PARTNERSHIP
**FOUR POINTS BY SHERATON KINGSTON
, THE**   p 631
See MELO, J.S. INC
**FOUR POINTS BY SHERATON MISSIS-
SAUGA MEDOWVALE**   p
727
See SILVER HOTEL (AMBLER) INC
FOUR POINTS EXPRESS   p 665
See 1686416 ONTARIO INC
**FOUR POINTS HOTEL SHERATON WIN-
NIPEG INTERNATIONAL AIRPORT**   p
384
1999 WELLINGTON AVE, WINNIPEG, MB,
R3H 1H5
(204) 775-5222   SIC 7011
FOUR POINTS HOTEL SUITES   p 72
See INN AT THE PARK INC
**FOUR POINTS SHERATON INTERNA-
TIONAL**   p
378
See LAKEVIEW MANAGEMENT INC
FOUR POINTS TORONTO AIRPORT p 686
See 6257 AIRPORT TORONTO HOSPITAL-
ITY INC
FOUR RIVERS CO-OPERATIVE   p 331
188 EAST STEWART ST, VANDERHOOF,
BC, V0J 3A0
(250) 567-4414   SIC 5171
**FOUR SEASONS DRYWALL SYSTEMS &
ACOUSTICS LIMITED**   p 670
200 KONRAD CRES, MARKHAM, ON, L3R
8T9
(905) 474-9960   SIC 1742
FOUR SEASONS HOLDINGS INC   p 779
1165 LESLIE ST, NORTH YORK, ON, M3C
2K8
(416) 449-1750   SIC 7011
FOUR SEASONS HOTEL MONTREAL p
1212
See 10643645 CANADA INC
FOUR SEASONS HOTEL TORONTO p 902
See PARAMITA ENTERPRISES LIMITED
**FOUR SEASONS HOTEL VANCOUVER,
THE**   p 304
See FOUR SEASONS HOTELS LIMITED
FOUR SEASONS HOTELS LIMITED p 304
791 GEORGIA ST W, VANCOUVER, BC,
V6C 2T4
(604) 689-9333   SIC 7011
FOUR SEASONS HOTELS LIMITED p 779
1165 LESLIE ST, NORTH YORK, ON, M3C
2K8
(416) 449-1750   SIC 7011
FOUR SEASONS HOTELS LIMITED p 928
60 YORKVILLE AVE, TORONTO, ON, M4W
0A4
(416) 964-0411   SIC 7011
FOUR SEASONS PALACE CATERERS LTD
p 1416
909 E ARCOLA AVE, REGINA, SK, S4N
0S2
(306) 525-8338   SIC 5921
FOUR SEASONS RESIDENCES   p 343
See FS WHISTLER HOLDINGS LIMITED
**FOUR SEASONS RESORT AND RESI-
DENCES WHISTLER**   p
343
See FS WHISTLER HOLDINGS LIMITED
FOUR SEASONS SALES   p 360
See BRUCE'S FOUR SEASONS (1984)
LTD
**FOUR SEASONS SITE DEVELOPMENT
LTD**   p 503
42 WENTWORTH CRT UNIT 1, BRAMP-
TON, ON, L6T 5K6

(905) 670-7655   *SIC* 1611
FOUR STAR DAIRY LIMITED   *p* 688
3400 AMERICAN DR, MISSISSAUGA, ON, L4V 1C1
(905) 671-8100   *SIC* 0241
FOUR STAR PLATING INDUSTRIES LIMITED   *p*
793
1162 BARMAC DR, NORTH YORK, ON, M9L 1X5
(416) 745-1742   *SIC* 3471
FOUR VALLEYS EXCAVATING & GRADING LIMITED   *p* 553
137 BOWES RD, CONCORD, ON, L4K 1H3
(905) 669-1588   *SIC* 1794
FOUR WINDS HOTELS MANAGEMENT CORP   *p* 135
10302 97 ST, HIGH LEVEL, AB, T0H 1Z0
(780) 220-1840   *SIC* 5921
FOURGONS TRANSIT INC, LES   *p* 1362
3600 BOUL INDUSTRIEL, SAINTE-ROSE, QC, H7L 4R9
(514) 382-0104   *SIC* 3713
FOURLANE FORD   *p* 137
See DENHAM HOLDINGS LTD
FOURLANE FORD SALES LTD   *p* 137
4412 50 ST, INNISFAIL, AB, T4G 1P7
(403) 227-3311   *SIC* 5511
FOURMARK MANUFACTURING INC *p* 797
2690 PLYMOUTH DR, OAKVILLE, ON, L6H 6W3
(905) 855-8777   *SIC* 3089
FOURNIER BETON   *p* 1390
See L. FOURNIER ET FILS INC
FOURNIER CHEVROLET OLDSMOBILE INC   *p* 1262
305 RUE DU MARAIS, QUEBEC, QC, G1M 3C8
(418) 687-5200   *SIC* 5511
FOURNIER CONSTRUCTION INDUSTRIELLE INC   *p*
1383
3787 BOUL FRONTENAC O, THETFORD MINES, QC, G6H 2B5
(819) 375-2888   *SIC* 1541
FOURNIER MAINTENANCE INDUSTRIELLE INC   *p*
1383
3787 BOUL FRONTENAC O, THETFORD MINES, QC, G6H 2B5
(418) 423-4241   *SIC* 7363
FOURNIER VAN & STORAGE, LIMITED   *p*
844
1051 TOY AVE, PICKERING, ON, L1W 3N9
(905) 686-0002   *SIC* 4225
FOURNITURE DE PLANCHERS INNOVATIFS INC   *p*
1065
1280 RUE GRAHAM-BELL BUREAU 1, BOUCHERVILLE, QC, J4B 6H5
(450) 641-4566   *SIC* 1752
FOURNITURES DE BUREAU DENIS INC *p*
1134
2725 RUE MICHELIN, LAVAL-OUEST, QC, H7L 5X6
(450) 681-5300   *SIC* 5712
FOURNITURES DE BUREAU DENIS INC *p*
1234
2990 BOUL LE CORBUSIER, MONTREAL, QC, H7L 3M2
(450) 687-8682   *SIC* 5112
FOURNITURES DE MEUBLES ET DE LITERIE SINCA INC   *p*
1250
870 AV ELLINGHAM, POINTE-CLAIRE, QC, H9R 3S4
(514) 697-0101   *SIC* 5072
FOURNITURES DE PLOMBERIE ET CHAUFFAGE SUTTON LTEE   *p* 1221
2174 AV DE CLIFTON, MONTREAL, QC, H4A 2N6
(514) 488-2581   *SIC* 5074
FOURNITURES INDUSTRIELLES DU QUEBEC   *p*

1265
See OUTILLAGE INDUSTRIEL QUEBEC LTEE
FOURNITURES INDUSTRIELLES DU-RAMILL   *p*
1251
See KAR INDUSTRIEL INC
FOURNITURES INDUSTRIELLES PASCO INC, LES   *p* 1246
1124 RUE SAINT-CALIXTE, PLESSISVILLE, QC, G6L 1N8
(819) 362-7345   *SIC* 6712
FOURNITURES MARITIMES R.C.I.   *p* 1080
See 9165-8021 QUEBEC INC
FOURQUEST ENERGY INC   *p* 114
7040 39 AVE NW, EDMONTON, AB, T6E 5T9
(780) 485-0690   *SIC* 1389
FOURTH-RITE CONSTRUCTION (1994) LTD   *p* 176
2609 PROGRESSIVE WAY SUITE B, ABBOTSFORD, BC, V2T 6H8
(604) 850-7684   *SIC* 1522
FOUZIA AKHTAR DRUGS LTD   *p* 580
415 THE WESTWAY SUITE 1, ETOBICOKE, ON, M9R 1H5
(416) 249-8344   *SIC* 5912
FOWLER CONSTRUCTION COMPANY LIMITED   *p*
497
1218 ROSEWARNE DR, BRACEBRIDGE, ON, P1L 0A1
(705) 645-2214   *SIC* 1611
FOX 40 INTERNATIONAL INC   *p* 608
340 GRAYS RD, HAMILTON, ON, L8E 2Z2
(905) 561-4040   *SIC* 3949
FOX CONSTRUCTORS   *p* 757
See E.S. FOX LIMITED
FOX HARB'R DEVELOPMENT LIMITED   *p* 470
1337 FOX HARBOUR RD, WALLACE, NS, B0K 1Y0
(902) 257-1801   *SIC* 7011
FOX HARB'R RESORT   *p* 470
See FOX HARB'R DEVELOPMENT LIMITED
FOX LAKE CREE NATION   *p* 350
103 FOX LAKE DR, GILLAM, MB, R0B 0L0
(204) 953-2760   *SIC* 8399
FOX RUN CANADA CORP   *p* 553
460 APPLEWOOD CRES SUITE 2, CONCORD, ON, L4K 4Z3
(905) 669-4145   *SIC* 5023
FOX RUN CRAFTSMEN   *p* 553
See FOX RUN CANADA CORP
FOX, DOMINIC LIMITED   *p* 646
377 KENT ST W, LINDSAY, ON, K9V 2Z7
(705) 324-8301   *SIC* 5531
FOX, JOHN A LTD   *p* 867
3553 LAWRENCE AVE E, SCARBOROUGH, ON, M1H 1B2
(416) 431-3888   *SIC* 5531
FOXRIDGE HOMES (MANITOBA) LTD*p* 365
30 SPEERS RD, WINNIPEG, MB, R2J 1L9
(204) 488-7578   *SIC* 1522
FOXTON FUELS LIMITED   *p* 1026
50 NORTH ST W, WINGHAM, ON, N0G 2W0
(519) 357-2664   *SIC* 5171
FOYER DE CHARLESBOURG INC   *p* 1256
7150 BOUL CLOUTIER, QUEBEC, QC, G1H 5V5
(418) 628-0456   *SIC* 8361
FOYER FARNHAM   *p* 1101
See CENTRE DE SANTE ET DE SERVICES SOCIAUX LA POMMERAIE
FOYER LA PERADE   *p* 1355
See CENTRE DE SANTE ET DE SERVICES SOCIAUX DE LA VALLEE-DE-LA-BATISCAN
FOYER NOTRE-DAME DE LOURDES INC, LE   *p* 394
2055 VALLEE LOURDES DR, BATHURST, NB, E2A 4P8

(506) 549-5085   *SIC* 8361
FOYER NOTRE-DAME DE SAINT-LEONARD INC   *p*
417
604 RUE PRINCIPALE, SAINT-LEONARD, NB, E7E 2H5
SIC 8361
FOYER PERE FISET   *p* 442
See INVERNESS MUNICIPAL HOUSING CORPORATION
FOYER RICHELIEU WELLAND   *p* 1011
655 TANGUAY AVE, WELLAND, ON, L3B 6A1
(905) 734-1400   *SIC* 8361
FOYER SAINT-ANTOINE   *p* 416
See SOCIETE D'HABITATION DE ST-ANTOINE INC
FOYER ST-FRANCOIS INC   *p* 1079
912 RUE JACQUES-CARTIER E, CHICOUTIMI, QC, G7H 2A9
(418) 549-3727   *SIC* 8361
FOYER SUTTON   *p* 1378
See CENTRE DE SANTE ET DE SERVICES SOCIAUX DE LA POMMERAIE, LE
FOYSTON, GORDON & PAYNE INC *p* 938
1 ADELAIDE ST E SUITE 2600, TORONTO, ON, M5C 2V9
(416) 362-4725   *SIC* 6722
FP CANADIAN NEWSPAPERS LIMITED PARTNERSHIP   *p* 372
1355 MOUNTAIN AVE, WINNIPEG, MB, R2X 3B6
(204) 697-7000   *SIC* 2711
FP MAILING SOLUTIONS   *p* 553
See FRANCOTYP-POSTALIA CANADA INC
FPC FLEXIBLE PACKAGING CORPORATION   *p*
868
1891 EGLINTON AVE E, SCARBOROUGH, ON, M1L 2L7
(416) 288-3060   *SIC* 2671
FPCCQ   *p* 1143
See FEDERATION DES PRODUCTEURS DE CULTURES COMMERCIALES DU QUEBEC
FPH GROUP INC   *p* 649
570 INDUSTRIAL RD, LONDON, ON, N5V 1V1
(519) 686-9965   *SIC* 5084
FPI FIREPLACE PRODUCTS INTERNATIONAL LTD   *p*
209
6988 VENTURE ST, DELTA, BC, V4G 1H4
(604) 946-5155   *SIC* 3433
FPI PRO   *p* 1194
See COMMANDITE FPI PRO INC
FPINNOVATIONS   *p* 324
2665 EAST MALL, VANCOUVER, BC, V6T 1Z4
(604) 224-3221   *SIC* 8731
FPINNOVATIONS   *p* 1250
570 BOUL SAINT-JEAN, POINTE-CLAIRE, QC, H9R 3J9
(514) 630-4100   *SIC* 8731
FPINNOVATIONS   *p* 1250
570 BOUL SAINT-JEAN, POINTE-CLAIRE, QC, H9R 3J9
(514) 630-4100   *SIC* 8733
FPINNOVATIONS   *p* 1264
300 RUE DE DIEPPE, QUEBEC, QC, G1N 3M8
(418) 659-2647   *SIC* 8731
FPM PEAT MOSS   *p* 403
See SUN GRO HORTICULTURE CANADA LTD
FPS FOOD PROCESS SOLUTIONS CORPORATION   *p*
258
7431 NELSON RD UNIT 130, RICHMOND, BC, V6W 1G3
(604) 232-2145   *SIC* 3822
FPX NICKEL CORP   *p* 313
1155 W PENDER ST SUITE 725, VANCOU-

VER, BC, V6E 2P4
(604) 681-8600   *SIC* 1061
FR RENTALS LTD   *p* 203
2495 THEATRE RD, CRANBROOK, BC, V1C 7B8
(778) 517-8388   *SIC* 7359
FR. MICHAEL MCGIVNEY CATHOLIC ACADEMY   *p* 678
See YORK CATHOLIC DISTRICT SCHOOL BOARD
FRABELS INC   *p* 1156
5580 RUE PARE, MONT-ROYAL, QC, H4P 2M1
(514) 842-8561   *SIC* 5094
FRAC SHACK INC   *p* 1
25901 114 AVE UNIT 136, ACHESON, AB, T7X 6E2
(780) 948-9898   *SIC* 1389
FRAC SHACK INTERNATIONAL INC   *p* 1
25901 114 AVE UNIT 136, ACHESON, AB, T7X 6E2
(780) 948-9898   *SIC* 1389
FRACAN STRUCTURAL STEEL   *p* 999
See FRAZIER INDUSTRIAL CO., LTD
FRACO   *p* 1348
See PRODUITS FRACO LTEE, LES
FRACTION ENERGY SERVICES LTD *p* 49
255 5 AVE SW UNIT 2900, CALGARY, AB, T2P 3G6
(403) 385-4300   *SIC* 1389
FRAM BUILDING GROUP LTD   *p* 712
141 LAKESHORE RD E, MISSISSAUGA, ON, L5G 1E8
SIC 6719
FRAMATOME CANADA LTD   *p* 844
925 BROCK RD SUITE B, PICKERING, ON, L1W 2X9
(905) 421-2600   *SIC* 1629
FRAMERS CHOICE   *p* 321
1695 2ND AVE W, VANCOUVER, BC, V6J 1H3
(604) 732-8477   *SIC* 5023
FRAMESTORE   *p* 1183
See STUDIOS FRAMESTORE INC
FRAMEWORTH CUSTOM FRAMING INC *p*
789
1198 CALEDONIA RD UNIT B, NORTH YORK, ON, M6A 2W5
(416) 781-1115   *SIC* 7699
FRAMOS TECHNOLOGIES INC   *p* 816
2733 LANCASTER DR SUITE 210, OTTAWA, ON, K1B 0A9
(613) 208-1082   *SIC* 5043
FRANCE DELICES INC   *p* 1166
5065 RUE ONTARIO E, MONTREAL, QC, H1V 3V2
(514) 259-2291   *SIC* 2051
FRANCES-KELSEY SECONDARY SCHOOL   *p* 232
See SCHOOL DISTRICT NO. 79 (COWICHAN VALLEY)
FRANCHISE MANAGEMENT INC   *p* 420
417 CONNELL ST SUITE 7, WOODSTOCK, NB, E7M 5G5
(506) 328-4631   *SIC* 5812
FRANCHISES CORA INC   *p* 1364
16 RUE SICARD BUREAU 50, SAINTE-THERESE, QC, J7E 3W7
(450) 435-2426   *SIC* 6794
FRANCIS CANADA PRODUCTS   *p* 748
See ALDUS CAPITAL CORP
FRANCIS FOODSTORE LTD   *p* 461
143 VICTORIA RD, LUNENBURG, NS, B0J 2C0
(902) 634-3751   *SIC* 5411
FRANCIS FUELS   *p* 749
See FRANCIS FUELS LTD
FRANCIS FUELS LTD   *p* 749
28 CONCOURSE GATE SUITE 105, NEPEAN, ON, K2E 7T7
(613) 723-4567   *SIC* 5983
FRANCIS INTERNATIONAL TRADING (CANADA) INC   *p* 1225
1605 RUE CHABANEL O BUREAU 300,

MONTREAL, QC, H4N 2T7
(514) 858-1088 *SIC* 2389
FRANCIS POWELL & CO. LIMITED *p 894*
180 RAM FOREST RD, STOUFFVILLE, ON, L4A 2G8
(905) 727-2518 *SIC* 1611
FRANCO FOLIES DE MONTREAL *p 1196*
400 BOUL DE MAISONNEUVE O, MONTREAL, QC, H3A 1L4
(514) 288-1040 *SIC* 8742
FRANCO-NEVADA CORPORATION *p 971*
199 BAY ST SUITE 2000, TORONTO, ON, M5L 1G9
(416) 306-6300 *SIC* 1041
FRANCOTYP-POSTALIA CANADA INC *p 553*
82 CORSTATE AVE SUITE 2000, CONCORD, ON, L4K 4X2
(905) 761-6554 *SIC* 5044
FRANK DEFEHR HOLDINGS LTD *p 363*
125 FURNITURE PARK, WINNIPEG, MB, R2G 1B9
(204) 988-5630 *SIC* 2599
FRANK FAIR INDUSTRIES LTD *p 365*
400 ARCHIBALD ST, WINNIPEG, MB, R2J 0W9
(204) 237-7987 *SIC* 3713
FRANK FLAMAN SALES LTD *p 148*
2310 SPARROW DR, NISKU, AB, T9E 8A2
(780) 955-3400 *SIC* 5999
FRANK HENRY EQUIPMENT (1987) LTD *p 114*
9810 60 AVE NW, EDMONTON, AB, T6E 0C5
(780) 434-8778 *SIC* 5084
FRANK LOGAN *p 1392*
485 249 RTE, VAL-JOLI, QC, J1S 0E8
(819) 845-4901 *SIC* 5171
FRANK'S NO FRILLS *p 866*
See 1594414 ONTARIO LIMITED
FRANKE KINDRED CANADA LIMITED *p 681*
1000 KINDRED RD, MIDLAND, ON, L4R 4K9
(705) 526-5427 *SIC* 3499
FRANKE VOLVO *p 1354*
See GARAGE FRANKE INC
FRANKIE TOMATTOS *p 665*
See 1095141 ONTARIO LIMITED
FRANKLAND CANNING CO, DIV OF *p 465*
See COMEAU'S SEA FOODS LIMITED
FRANKLIN EMPIRE INC *p 1157*
8421 CH DARNLEY, MONT-ROYAL, QC, H4T 2B2
(514) 341-3720 *SIC* 5063
FRANKLIN EMPIRE INC *p 1262*
215 RUE FORTIN, QUEBEC, QC, G1M 3M2
(418) 683-1724 *SIC* 1531
FRANKLIN TEMPLETON INVESTMENTS *p 915*
See TEMPLETON INTERNATIONAL STOCK FUND
FRANKLIN TEMPLETON INVESTMENTS CORP *p 771*
5000 YONGE ST SUITE 900, NORTH YORK, ON, M2N 0A7
(416) 957-6000 *SIC* 6282
FRANMED CONSULTANTS (1993) INC *p 951*
150 YORK ST SUITE 1500, TORONTO, ON, M5H 3S5
(416) 350-7706 *SIC* 8741
FRANSYL *p 1381*
See PRODUITS POUR TOITURES FRANSYL LTEE
FRANTIC FILMS CORPORATION *p 378*
220 PORTAGE AVE SUITE 1300, WINNIPEG, MB, R3C 0A5
(204) 949-0070 *SIC* 7819
FRARE & GALLANT LTEE *p 1100*
5530 RUE MAURICE-CULLEN, FABREVILLE, QC, H7C 2T3
(450) 664-4590 *SIC* 1541
FRASER CANYON HOSPITAL *p 215*

See FRASER HEALTH AUTHORITY
FRASER CEDAR PRODUCTS *p 230*
See STEADFAST CEDAR PRODUCTS LTD
FRASER CEDAR PRODUCTS LTD *p 230*
27400 LOUGHEED HWY, MAPLE RIDGE, BC, V2W 1L1
(604) 462-7335 *SIC* 2429
FRASER CITY MOTORS LTD *p 271*
19418 LANGLEY BYPASS, SURREY, BC, V3S 7R2
(604) 534-5355 *SIC* 5511
FRASER DIRECT DISTRIBUTION SERVICES LTD *p 683*
8300 LAWSON RD, MILTON, ON, L9T 0A4
(905) 877-4411 *SIC* 4731
FRASER FORD SALES LIMITED *p 813*
815 KING ST W, OSHAWA, ON, L1J 2L4
(905) 576-1800 *SIC* 5511
FRASER GLENBURNIE *p 999*
See TRENTON COLD STORAGE INC
FRASER HEALTH AUTHORITY *p 189*
3935 KINCAID ST, BURNABY, BC, V5G 2X6
(604) 434-3992 *SIC* 8062
FRASER HEALTH AUTHORITY *p 196*
45470 MENHOLM RD, CHILLIWACK, BC, V2P 1M2
(604) 702-4900 *SIC* 8011
FRASER HEALTH AUTHORITY *p 207*
11245 84 AVE SUITE 101, DELTA, BC, V4C 2L9
(604) 507-5400 *SIC* 8062
FRASER HEALTH AUTHORITY *p 215*
1275 7TH AVE, HOPE, BC, V0X 1L4
(604) 869-5656 *SIC* 8011
FRASER HEALTH AUTHORITY *p 226*
8521 198A ST, LANGLEY, BC, V2Y 0A1
(604) 455-1300 *SIC* 8742
FRASER HEALTH AUTHORITY *p 231*
11666 LAITY ST, MAPLE RIDGE, BC, V2X 5A3
(604) 463-4111 *SIC* 8062
FRASER HEALTH AUTHORITY *p 248*
220 BREW ST SUITE 700, PORT MOODY, BC, V3H 0H6
(604) 777-7300 *SIC* 8742
FRASER HEALTH AUTHORITY *p 274*
13401 108TH AVE SUITE 1500, SURREY, BC, V3T 5T3
(604) 953-4950 *SIC* 8059
FRASER HEALTH AUTHORITY *p 274*
13450 102 AVE SUITE 400, SURREY, BC, V3T 0H1
(604) 587-4600 *SIC* 8062
FRASER LAKE SAWMILLS *p 214*
See WEST FRASER MILLS LTD
FRASER MARINE & INDUSTRIAL, DIV. OF *p 846*
See ALGOMA CENTRAL CORPORATION
FRASER RIVER CHEVROLET BUICK GMC LTD *p 252*
340 CARSON AVE, QUESNEL, BC, V2J 2B3
(250) 992-5515 *SIC* 5511
FRASER RIVER GM *p 252*
See FRASER RIVER CHEVROLET BUICK GMC LTD
FRASER RIVER MARINE TRANSPORTATION LTD *p 230*
23888 RIVER RD, MAPLE RIDGE, BC, V2W 1B7
(604) 463-3044 *SIC* 4449
FRASER RIVER PILE & DREDGE (GP) INC *p 237*
1830 RIVER DR, NEW WESTMINSTER, BC, V3M 2A8
(604) 522-7971 *SIC* 1629
FRASER SUPPLIES (1980) LIMITED *p 441*
4147 MAIN HWY, BERWICK, NS, B0P 1E0
(902) 538-3183 *SIC* 5211
FRASER VALLEY AUCTIONS (1983) LTD *p 226*
21801 56 AVE, LANGLEY, BC, V2Y 2M9

(604) 534-3241 *SIC* 5154
FRASER VALLEY BUILDING SUPPLIES INC *p 232*
7072 WREN ST, MISSION, BC, V2V 2V9
(604) 820-1134 *SIC* 5039
FRASER VALLEY DUCK & GOOSE LTD *p 197*
4540 SIMMONS RD, CHILLIWACK, BC, V2R 4R7
(604) 823-4435 *SIC* 2015
FRASER VALLEY MEAT SUPPLIES LTD *p 196*
45735 ALEXANDER AVE, CHILLIWACK, BC, V2P 1L6
(604) 792-4723 *SIC* 5421
FRASER VALLEY PACKERS HOLDINGS LTD *p 174*
260 SHORT RD, ABBOTSFORD, BC, V2S 8A7
(604) 852-3525 *SIC* 6712
FRASER VALLEY PACKERS INC *p 174*
260 SHORT RD, ABBOTSFORD, BC, V2S 8A7
(604) 852-3525 *SIC* 0723
FRASER VALLEY REFRIGERATION LTD *p 179*
26121 FRASER HWY, ALDERGROVE, BC, V4W 2W8
(604) 856-8644 *SIC* 1711
FRASER VALLEY REGIONAL LIBRARY *p 174*
See FRASER VALLEY REGIONAL LIBRARY DISTRICT
FRASER VALLEY REGIONAL LIBRARY DISTRICT *p 174*
34589 DELAIR RD, ABBOTSFORD, BC, V2S 5Y1
(604) 859-7141 *SIC* 8231
FRASER VALLEY ROOFING LTD *p 197*
44687 CHALMER PL, CHILLIWACK, BC, V2R 0H8
(604) 795-6620 *SIC* 1761
FRASER VALLEY STEEL & WIRE LTD *p 178*
3174 MT LEHMAN RD, ABBOTSFORD, BC, V4X 2M9
(604) 856-3391 *SIC* 5051
FRASER WHARVES LTD *p 258*
13800 STEVESTON HWY, RICHMOND, BC, V6W 1A8
(604) 277-1141 *SIC* 4226
FRASERS PRO HOME CENTRE *p 441*
See FRASER SUPPLIES (1980) LIMITED
FRASERVIEW CEDAR PRODUCTS LTD *p 276*
6630 144 ST, SURREY, BC, V3W 5R5
(604) 590-3355 *SIC* 2499
FRASERWAY RV GP LTD *p 220*
3732 HIGHWAY 97 N, KELOWNA, BC, V1X 5C2
(250) 807-2898 *SIC* 5561
FRASERWAY RV LIMITED PARTNERSHIP *p 176*
30440 SOUTH FRASER WAY, ABBOTSFORD, BC, V2T 6L4
(604) 850-1976 *SIC* 5561
FRASERWAY RV RENTALS *p 176*
See FRASERWAY RV LIMITED PARTNERSHIP
FRASTELL PROPERTY MANAGEMENT INC *p 925*
22 ST CLAIR AVE E SUITE 1500, TORONTO, ON, M4T 2S3
(416) 499-3333 *SIC* 6512
FRATELLI GOUP INC *p 829*
309 RICHMOND RD, OTTAWA, ON, K1Z 6X3
(613) 722-6772 *SIC* 5812
FRATELLI RESTAURANTS *p 829*
See FRATELLI GOUP INC
FRATELLO ANALOG CAFE *p 29*
See FRATELLO GROUP INC
FRATELLO GROUP INC *p 29*
4021 9 ST SE, CALGARY, AB, T2G 3C7

(403) 265-2112 *SIC* 2095
FRATERNITE DES POLICIERS DE LA REGIE INTERMUNICIPALE ROUSSILLON INC *p 1072*
90 CH SAINT-FRANCOIS-XAVIER, CANDIAC, QC, J5R 6M6
(450) 635-9911 *SIC* 8641
FRATERNITE DES POLICIERS ET POLICIERES DE MONTREAL INC *p 1173*
480 RUE GILFORD BUREAU 300, MONTREAL, QC, H2J 1N3
(514) 527-4161 *SIC* 8631
FRATERNITE NATIONALE DES CHARPENTIERS-MENUISIERS (SECTION LOCALE 9) *p 1051*
9100 BOUL METROPOLITAIN E, ANJOU, QC, H1K 4L2
(514) 374-5871 *SIC* 8631
FRATUM PHARMA INC *p 1344*
9380 BOUL LANGELIER, SAINT-LEONARD, QC, H1P 3H8
(514) 322-6111 *SIC* 5912
FRAZIER INDUSTRIAL CO., LTD *p 999*
163 NORTH MURRAY ST, TRENTON, ON, K8V 6R7
(613) 394-6621 *SIC* 3441
FRECHETTE, JOSEE PHARMACIE *p 1052*
525 1RE AV, ASBESTOS, QC, J1T 4R1
(819) 879-6969 *SIC* 5122
FRECON CONSTRUCTION LIMITED *p 858*
1235 RUSSELL RD S, RUSSELL, ON, K4R 1E1
(613) 445-2944 *SIC* 1541
FRED C RYALL INSURANCE INC *p 705*
53 VILLAGE CENTRE PL, MISSISSAUGA, ON, L4Z 1V9
(416) 419-0240 *SIC* 6411
FRED GUY MOVING & STORAGE LTD *p 816*
1199 NEWMARKET ST, OTTAWA, ON, K1B 3V1
(613) 744-8632 *SIC* 4214
FRED VICTOR CENTRE *p 938*
59 ADELAIDE ST E SUITE 600, TORONTO, ON, M5C 1K6
(416) 364-8228 *SIC* 6513
FREDAL SOLUTIONS *p 1107*
See SPECIALISTE DU BUREAU FREDAL INC, LE
FREDERICTON DIRECT CHARGE CO-OPERATIVE LIMITED *p 402*
170 DOAK RD, FREDERICTON, NB, E3C 2G2
(506) 453-1300 *SIC* 5411
FREDERICTON HIGH SCHOOL *p 400*
See ANGLOPHONE WEST SCHOOL DISTRICT
FREDERICTON HYUNDAI *p 402*
See 609173 N.B. LTD
FREDERICTON INN *p 402*
See FREDERICTON MOTOR INN LTD
FREDERICTON INTERNATIONAL AIRPORT AUTHORITY INC *p 404*
2570 ROUTE 102 UNIT 22, LINCOLN, NB, E3B 9G1
(506) 460-0920 *SIC* 4581
FREDERICTON KIA *p 402*
See MONTEITH VENTURES INC
FREDERICTON MOTOR INN LTD *p 402*
1315 REGENT ST, FREDERICTON, NB, E3C 1A1
(506) 455-1430 *SIC* 7011
FREDERICTON NISSAN *p 401*
See HILLSIDE NISSAN LTD
FREDERICTON REGION SOLID WASTE COMMISSION *p 401*
1775 WILSEY RD, FREDERICTON, NB, E3B 7K4
(506) 453-9930 *SIC* 4953
FREDERICTON SOUTH NURSING HOME INC *p 401*
521 WOODSTOCK RD, FREDERICTON,

NB, E3B 2J2
 (506) 444-3400   *SIC* 8051
FREDERICTON VOLKSWAGEN   *p 402*
See UNITED AUTO SALES & SERVICE LTD
FREE FLOW PETROLIUM   *p 880*
See ASPEN-DUNHILL HOLDINGS LTD
FREE SPIRIT MARKET LTD   *p 1407*
615 MAIN STREET, HUMBOLDT, SK, S0K
2A0
 (306) 682-2223   *SIC* 5182
FREEBORN MOTORS LTD   *p 197*
44954 YALE RD W, CHILLIWACK, BC, V2R
4H1
 (604) 792-2724   *SIC* 5511
FREED & FREED INTERNATIONAL LTD   *p
372*
1309 MOUNTAIN AVE, WINNIPEG, MB,
R2X 2Y1
 (204) 786-6081   *SIC* 2311
FREED STORAGE LIMITED   *p 1021*
1526 OTTAWA ST, WINDSOR, ON, N8X
2G5
 (519) 258-6532   *SIC* 5611
FREED'S OF WINDSOR   *p 1021*
See FREED STORAGE LIMITED
**FREEDOM FINANCIAL SERVICES INCOR-
PORATED**   *p
442*
115 COLDBROOK VILLAGE PARK DR,
COLDBROOK, NS, B4R 1B9
 (902) 681-1100   *SIC* 8742
FREEDOM FORD SALES LIMITED   *p 112*
7505 75 ST NW, EDMONTON, AB, T6C 4H8
 (780) 465-9411   *SIC* 5511
**FREEDOM HARLEY-DAVIDSON OF OT-
TAWA**   *p
750*
See 1496201 ONTARIO INC
**FREEDOM INTERNATIONAL BROKERAGE
COMPANY**   *p 951*
181 UNIVERSITY AVE SUITE 1500,
TORONTO, ON, M5H 3M7
 (416) 367-2588   *SIC* 6211
FREEDOM PET SUPPLIES INC   *p 536*
480 THOMPSON DR, CAMBRIDGE, ON,
N1T 2K8
 (519) 624-8069   *SIC* 5149
FREEGOLD VENTURES LIMITED   *p 330*
700 GEORGIA ST W SUITE 888, VANCOU-
VER, BC, V7Y 1K8
 (604) 662-7307   *SIC* 1081
FREEHOLD ROYALTIES LTD   *p 49*
144 4 AVE SW SUITE 400, CALGARY, AB,
T2P 3N4
 (403) 221-0802   *SIC* 6792
FREEHOLD ROYALTIES PARTNERSHIP   *p
49*
144 4 AVE SW SUITE 400, CALGARY, AB,
T2P 3N4
 (403) 221-0802   *SIC* 2911
FREEMAN   *p 995*
See FREEMAN EXPOSITIONS, LTD
FREEMAN AUDIO VISUAL   *p 691*
See 3627730 CANADA INC
FREEMAN AUDIO VISUAL   *p 816*
See 3627730 CANADA INC
FREEMAN AUDIO VISUAL   *p 1126*
See 3627730 CANADA INC
FREEMAN EXPOSITIONS, LTD   *p 995*
61 BROWNS LINE, TORONTO, ON, M8W
3S2
 (416) 252-3361   *SIC* 7389
FREEMAN FORMALWEAR LIMITED   *p 787*
111 BERMONDSEY RD, NORTH YORK,
ON, M4A 2T7
 (416) 288-1222   *SIC* 7299
FREEMAN LUMBER   *p 450*
*See FREEMAN, HARRY AND SON LIM-
ITED*
FREEMAN, HARRY AND SON LIMITED   *p
450*
4804 MEEDWAY RIVER RD, GREENFIELD,
NS, B0T 1E0
 (902) 685-2792   *SIC* 5031

**FREEMARK APPAREL BRANDS RETAIL
BE INC**   *p 1156*
5640 RUE PARE, MONT-ROYAL, QC, H4P
2M1
 (514) 341-7333   *SIC* 5651
FREETEK CONSTRUCTION LTD   *p 164*
130 YELLOWHEAD RD, SPRUCE GROVE,
AB, T7X 3B5
 (780) 960-4848   *SIC* 1521
FREEWAY FORD SALES LIMITED   *p 864*
958 MILNER AVE, SCARBOROUGH, ON,
M1B 5V7
 (416) 293-3077   *SIC* 5511
FREEWAY IMPORTS LTD   *p 270*
15420 104 AVE, SURREY, BC, V3R 1N8
 (604) 583-7121   *SIC* 5511
FREEWAY MAZDA   *p 270*
See FREEWAY IMPORTS LTD
FREEWAY TRANSPORTATION INC   *p 503*
15 STRATHEARN AVE, BRAMPTON, ON,
L6T 4P1
 (905) 790-0446   *SIC* 4731
FREEWHEELING ADVENTURES   *p 459*
*See FREEWHEELING ADVENTURES IN-
CORPORATED*
**FREEWHEELING ADVENTURES INCOR-
PORATED**   *p
459*
2070 HIGHWAY 329, HUBBARDS, NS, B0J
1T0
 (902) 857-3600   *SIC* 4724
FREGEAU, B. & FILS INC   *p 1291*
402 RUE SAINT-DENIS, SAINT-
ALEXANDRE-D'IBERVILLE, QC, J0J 1S0
 (450) 346-3487   *SIC* 4212
FREIGHTCOM INC   *p 494*
77 PILLSWORTH RD UNIT 1, BOLTON, ON,
L7E 4G4
 (877) 335-8740   *SIC* 4213
FREIGHTLINER   *p 1389*
*See CAMIONS FREIGHTLINER M.B.
TROIS-RIVIERES LTEE*
FREIGHTLINER MANITOBA LTD   *p 369*
2058 LOGAN AVE, WINNIPEG, MB, R2R
0H9
 (204) 694-3000   *SIC* 5511
FREIGHTLINER OF RED DEER INC   *p 155*
8046 EDGAR INDUSTRIAL CRES, RED
DEER, AB, T4P 3R3
 (403) 309-8225   *SIC* 5511
FREIGHTLINER PRINCE GEORGE   *p 251*
See PREMIUM TRUCK & TRAILER INC
FREIGHTWORKS   *p 499*
*See MARITIME-ONTARIO FREIGHT LINES
LIMITED*
**FRENCH CONNECTION (CANADA) LIM-
ITED**   *p
980*
111 PETER ST SUITE 406, TORONTO, ON,
M5V 2H1
 (416) 640-6160   *SIC* 5651
FRENCH LANGUAGE SCHOOL BOARD   *p
1043*
*See COMISSION SCOLAIRE DE LANGUE
FRANCAISE, LA*
FRENCH'S FINE HOMES   *p 848*
See BERT FRENCH & SON LIMITED
FRENCH'S FOOD COMPANY INC, THE   *p
695*
1680 TECH AVE UNIT 2, MISSISSAUGA,
ON, L4W 5S9
 (905) 283-7000   *SIC* 5149
FRENDEL KITCHENS LIMITED   *p 695*
1350 SHAWSON DR, MISSISSAUGA, ON,
L4W 1C5
 (905) 670-7898   *SIC* 5021
FRENECO LTEE   *p 1253*
261 RUE SAINT-CHARLES, PORTNEUF,
QC, G0A 2Y0
 (418) 286-3341   *SIC* 2439
FRENETTE, GEFFREY LTEE   *p 1282*
115 BOUL BRIEN, REPENTIGNY, QC, J6A
8J3
 (450) 585-9840   *SIC* 5311

FRENO   *p 1162*
*See SERVICE DE FREINS MONTREAL
LTEE*
FRERES DU SACRE-COEUR   *p 1397*
See CORPORATION MAURICE-RATTE
FRERES MARISTES, LES   *p 1075*
7141 AV ROYALE, CHATEAU-RICHER, QC,
G0A 1N0
 (418) 824-4215   *SIC* 8661
FRESCHO   *p 534*
See SOBEYS CAPITAL INCORPORATED
FRESENIUS KABI CANADA LTD   *p 997*
165 GALAXY BLVD SUITE 100, TORONTO,
ON, M9W 0C8
 (905) 770-3711   *SIC* 5122
FRESENIUS MEDICAL CARE CANADA INC
p 852
45 STAPLES AVE SUITE 110, RICHMOND
HILL, ON, L4B 4W6
 (905) 770-0855   *SIC* 5047
FRESH - A FARE   *p 487*
See FRESH MIX LIMITED
FRESH 1 MARKETING   *p 549*
*See C.H. ROBINSON COMPANY
(CANADA) LTD*
FRESH ADVANCEMENTS INC   *p 572*
165 THE QUEENSWAY SUITE 333, ETOBI-
COKE, ON, M8Y 1H8
 (416) 259-5400   *SIC* 5148
FRESH AND WILD FOOD MARKET   *p 978*
See 576794 ONTARIO LTD
FRESH CHOICE   *p 403*
See 056729 N.B. LTD
**FRESH CHOICE FOOD DISTRIBUTION &
SERVICES**   *p 259*
See CHOYS HOLDINGS INCORPORATED
FRESH DIRECT FOODS LTD   *p 70*
11505 35 ST SE UNIT 103, CALGARY, AB,
T2Z 4B1
 (403) 508-6868   *SIC* 2099
FRESH DIRECT PRODUCE LTD   *p 294*
890 MALKIN AVE, VANCOUVER, BC, V6A
2K6
 (604) 255-1330   *SIC* 5148
FRESH HEMP FOODS LTD   *p 369*
69 EAGLE DR, WINNIPEG, MB, R2R 1V4
 (204) 953-0233   *SIC* 2032
FRESH MIX LIMITED   *p 487*
530 WELHAM RD, BARRIE, ON, L4N 8Z7
 (705) 734-1580   *SIC* 2099
FRESH SELECTIONS   *p 547*
See 2319793 ONTARIO INC
FRESH START FOODS CANADA LTD *p 683*
2705 DURANTE WAY, MILTON, ON, L9T
5J1
 (905) 878-9000   *SIC* 5148
FRESH TASTE PRODUCE LIMITED   *p 572*
165 THE QUEENSWAY SUITE 343, ETOBI-
COKE, ON, M8Y 1H8
 (416) 255-0157   *SIC* 5148
FRESHBOOKS   *p 994*
See 1924345 ONTARIO INC
FRESHCO   *p 476*
See SOBEYS CAPITAL INCORPORATED
FRESHCO   *p 512*
See SOBEYS CAPITAL INCORPORATED
FRESHCO   *p 609*
See SOBEYS CAPITAL INCORPORATED
FRESHCO   *p 615*
See SOBEYS CAPITAL INCORPORATED
FRESHCO   *p 686*
See SOBEYS CAPITAL INCORPORATED
FRESHCO   *p 764*
See SOBEYS CAPITAL INCORPORATED
FRESHCO   *p 813*
See SOBEYS CAPITAL INCORPORATED
FRESHII INC   *p 928*
1055 YONGE ST, TORONTO, ON, M4W 2L2
 (647) 350-2001   *SIC* 5812
FRESHLINE FOODS LTD   *p 703*
2501 STANFIELD RD SUITE A, MISSIS-
SAUGA, ON, L4Y 1R6
 (416) 253-6040   *SIC* 5148
FRESHOUSE FOODS LTD   *p 497*

65 REAGEN'S INDUSTRIAL PKY, BRAD-
FORD, ON, L3Z 0Z9
 (905) 775-8880   *SIC* 5149
FRESHOUSE FOODS LTD   *p 593*
71 TODD RD, GEORGETOWN, ON, L7G
4R8
 (905) 671-0220   *SIC* 5147
FRESHOUSE SALES LTD   *p 688*
6480 VISCOUNT RD UNIT 2, MISSIS-
SAUGA, ON, L4V 1H3
 (905) 671-0220   *SIC* 2011
FRESHPOINT   *p 294*
See FRESHPOINT VANCOUVER LTD
FRESHPOINT VANCOUVER LTD   *p 294*
1020 MALKIN AVE, VANCOUVER, BC, V6A
3S9
 (604) 253-1551   *SIC* 5148
FRESHPOINT VANCOUVER LTD   *p 1002*
1400 CREDITSTONE RD UNIT A,
VAUGHAN, ON, L4K 0E2
 SIC 5148
FRESHPOINT VANCOUVER, LTD   *p 1002*
See FRESHPOINT VANCOUVER LTD
FRESHSTONE BRANDS INC   *p 635*
1326 VICTORIA ST N, KITCHENER, ON,
N2B 3E2
 (519) 578-2940   *SIC* 5411
**FRESHWATER FISH MARKETING CORPO-
RATION**   *p
362*
1199 PLESSIS RD, WINNIPEG, MB, R2C
3L4
 (204) 983-6600   *SIC* 2092
FRESON MARKET LTD   *p 4*
5020 49 AVE, BARRHEAD, AB, T7N 1G4
 (780) 674-3784   *SIC* 5912
FRESON MARKET LTD   *p 7*
330 FAIRVIEW AVE W, BROOKS, AB, T1R
1K7
 SIC 5411
FRESON MARKET LTD   *p 132*
11417 99 ST, GRANDE PRAIRIE, AB, T8V
2H6
 (780) 532-2920   *SIC* 5411
FRESON MARKET LTD   *p 135*
5032 53RD AVE, HIGH PRAIRIE, AB, T0G
1E0
 (780) 523-3253   *SIC* 5411
FRESON MARKET LTD   *p 167*
4401 48 ST UNIT 130, STONY PLAIN, AB,
T7Z 1N3
 (780) 968-6924   *SIC* 5411
FREUD CANADA, INC   *p 739*
7450 PACIFIC CIR, MISSISSAUGA, ON,
L5T 2A3
 (905) 670-1025   *SIC* 5084
**FREUDENBERG-NOK SEALING TECH-
NOLOGIES**   *p
911*
See FREUDENBERG-NOK, INC
FREUDENBERG-NOK, INC   *p 911*
65 SPRUCE ST, TILLSONBURG, ON, N4G
5C4
 (519) 842-6451   *SIC* 3053
FREW ENERGY LIMITED   *p 531*
1380 GRAHAMS LANE, BURLINGTON,
ON, L7S 1W3
 (905) 637-0033   *SIC* 4925
FREW ENERGY LIMITED   *p 883*
180 CUSHMAN RD, ST CATHARINES, ON,
L2M 6T6
 (905) 685-7334   *SIC* 5172
FREW PETROLEUM   *p 812*
See FREW PETROLEUM CORPORATION
FREW PETROLEUM CORPORATION *p 812*
190 WENTWORTH ST E, OSHAWA, ON,
L1H 3V5
 (905) 723-3742   *SIC* 5172
FREY BROTHERS LIMITED   *p 619*
3435 BROADWAY ST, HAWKESVILLE, ON,
N0B 1X0
 (519) 699-4641   *SIC* 1542
FREY BUILDING CONTRACTORS   *p 619*
See FREY BROTHERS LIMITED

▲ Public Company   ■ Public Company Family Member   **HQ** Headquarters   **BR** Branch   **SL** Single Location

FREYBE GOURMET CHEF LTD   p 282
19405 94 AVE, SURREY, BC, V4N 4E6
(604) 856-5221   SIC 2038

FRIEDBERG DIRECT   p 962
See FRIEDBERG MERCANTILE GROUP LTD

FRIEDBERG MERCANTILE GROUP LTD   p 962
181 BAY ST SUITE 250, TORONTO, ON, M5J 2T3
(416) 364-1171   SIC 6221

FRIENDEFI INC   p 1184
6750 AV DE L'ESPLANADE BUREAU 320, MONTREAL, QC, H2V 4M1
(514) 397-0415   SIC 8711

FRIENDLY FAMILY FARMS LTD   p 365
500 DAWSON RD N, WINNIPEG, MB, R2J 0T1
(204) 231-5151   SIC 0191

FRIENDLY OCEAN PARK SAFEWAY   p 281
See SOBEYS WEST INC

FRIENDLY TELECOM INC   p 76
44 BERKSHIRE CRT NW, CALGARY, AB, T3K 1Z5
(403) 243-6688   SIC 4899

FRIENDS OF CHARLESTON LAKE PARK, THE   p 643
148 WOODVALE RD, LANSDOWNE, ON, K0E 1L0
(613) 659-2065   SIC 6311

FRIENDSHIP DEVELOPMENTS LTD   p 335
330 QUEBEC ST, VICTORIA, BC, V8V 1W3
(250) 381-3456   SIC 7011

FRIES TALLMAN LUMBER (1976) LTD   p 1420
1737 DEWDNEY AVE, REGINA, SK, S4R 1G5
(306) 525-2791   SIC 5211

FRIESEN EQUIPMENT LTD   p 175
339 SUMAS WAY, ABBOTSFORD, BC, V2S 8E5
(604) 864-9844   SIC 5083

FRIESEN PRINTERS   p 345
See FRIESENS CORPORATION

FRIESENS CORPORATION   p 345
1 PRINTERS WAY, ALTONA, MB, R0G 0B0
(204) 324-6401   SIC 2732

FRIGO   p 1164
See FRIGOVIANDE INC

FRIGO NATIONAL   p 683
See GORDON FOOD SERVICE CANADA LTD

FRIGOVIANDE INC   p 1164
6065 RUE HOCHELAGA, MONTREAL, QC, H1N 1X7
(514) 256-0400   SIC 5421

FRIMA STUDIO INC   p 1259
395 RUE VICTOR-REVILLON, QUEBEC, QC, G1K 3M8
(418) 529-9697   SIC 7336

FRIPES EXPORT LTD   p 871
310 MIDWEST RD, SCARBOROUGH, ON, M1P 3A9
(416) 752-5046   SIC 5932

FRISBY TIRE CO. (1974) LIMITED   p 750
1377 CLYDE AVE, NEPEAN, ON, K2G 3H7
(613) 224-2200   SIC 5531

FRISCHKORN AUDIO-VISUAL CORP   p 708
2360 TEDLO ST, MISSISSAUGA, ON, L5A 3V3
(905) 281-9000   SIC 7359

FRITO LAY CANADA   p 13
See PEPSICO CANADA ULC

FRITO LAY CANADA   p 275
See PEPSICO CANADA ULC

FRITO LAY CANADA   p 460
See PEPSICO CANADA ULC

FRITO LAY CANADA   p 539
See PEPSICO CANADA ULC

FRITO LAY CANADA   p 662
See PEPSICO CANADA ULC

FRITO LAY CANADA   p 699
See PEPSICO CANADA ULC

FRITO LAY CANADA   p 865
See PEPSICO CANADA ULC

FRITO LAY CANADA   p 1111
See PEPSICO CANADA ULC

FRITO-LAY CANADA   p 510
See PEPSICO CANADA ULC

FRITO-LAY CANADA   p 1137
See PEPSICO CANADA ULC

FRITO-LAY CANADA   p 1231
See PEPSICO CANADA ULC

FROBISHER INN   p 85
See 902776 N.W.T. LIMITED

FROBISHER INTERNATIONAL ENTERPRISE LTD   p 205
787 CLIVEDEN PL UNIT 600, DELTA, BC, V3M 6C7
(604) 523-8108   SIC 5146

FROMA-DAR   p 1165
See SAPUTO PRODUITS LAITIERS CANADA S.E.N.C.

FROMAGE LA CHAUDIERE INC   p 1125
3226 RUE LAVAL, LAC-MEGANTIC, QC, G6B 1A4
(819) 583-4664   SIC 5143

FROMAGERIE BERGERON INC   p 1292
3837 RTE MARIE-VICTORIN, SAINT-ANTOINE-DE-TILLY, QC, G0S 2C0
(418) 886-2234   SIC 2022

FROMAGERIE BOIVIN   p 1121
See 9113-0476 QUEBEC INC

FROMAGERIE DE GRANDBY   p 1110
See AGROPUR COOPERATIVE

FROMAGERIE DES BASQUES ENR   p 1384
69 132 RTE O, TROIS-PISTOLES, QC, G0L 4K0
(418) 851-2189   SIC 5143

FROMAGERIE DES NATIONS INC   p 1236
3535 NORD LAVAL (A-440) O UNITE 440, MONTREAL, QC, H7P 5G9
(450) 682-3862   SIC 5143

FROMAGERIE DU PRESBYTERE   p 1357
See 9140-5621 QUEBEC INC

FROMAGERIE HAMEL   p 1181
See FROMAGERIES PIMAR INC, LES

FROMAGERIE L'ANCETRE INC   p 1056
1615 BOUL DE PORT-ROYAL, BECANCOUR, QC, G9H 1X7
(819) 233-9157   SIC 2022

FROMAGERIE PERRON   p 1350
See ALBERT PERRON INC

FROMAGERIE POLYETHNIQUE INC, LA   p 1352
235 CH DE SAINT-ROBERT, SAINT-ROBERT, QC, J0G 1S0
(450) 782-2111   SIC 5451

FROMAGERIE VICTORIA INC, LA   p 1397
101 RUE DE L'AQUEDUC, VICTORIAVILLE, QC, G6P 1M2
(819) 752-6821   SIC 2022

FROMAGERIES PIMAR INC, LES   p 1181
220 RUE JEAN-TALON E, MONTREAL, QC, H2R 1S7
(514) 272-1161   SIC 5451

FROMAGES CDA INC   p 1049
8895 3E CROISSANT, ANJOU, QC, H1J 1B6
(514) 648-7997   SIC 5143

FROMAGES RIVIERA, LES   p 1393
See LAITERIE CHALIFOUX INC

FRONT CONSTRUCTION   p 1026
See FRONT CONSTRUCTION INDUSTRIES INC

FRONT CONSTRUCTION INDUSTRIES INC   p 1026
740 MORTON DR UNIT 1, WINDSOR, ON, N9J 3V2
(519) 250-8229   SIC 1542

FRONT HOUSE SEATING   p 759
See ADVANTAGE RESTAURANT SUPPLY INC

FRONT STREET CAPITAL   p 942
See FRONT STREET DIVERSIFIED INCOME FUND

FRONT STREET CAPITAL 2004   p 942

33 YONGE ST SUITE 600, TORONTO, ON, M5E 1G4
(416) 597-9595   SIC 6722

FRONT STREET DIVERSIFIED INCOME FUND   p 942
33 YONGE ST SUITE 600, TORONTO, ON, M5E 1G4
(416) 597-9595   SIC 6722

FRONT STREET SPECIAL OPPORTUNITIES CANADIAN FUND   p 942
33 YONGE ST SUITE 600, TORONTO, ON, M5E 1G4
(416) 597-9595   SIC 6722

FRONTENAC HOTEL GP INC   p 1269
1 RUE DES CARRIERES, QUEBEC, QC, G1R 5J5
(418) 692-3861   SIC 7011

FRONTENAK SECONDARY SCHOOL   p 632
See LIMESTONE DISTRICT SCHOOL BOARD

FRONTERA ENERGY CORPORATION   p 951
333 BAY ST SUITE 1100, TORONTO, ON, M5H 2R2
(416) 362-7735   SIC 1381

FRONTIER AUTOMOTIVE INC   p 362
1486 REGENT AVE W, WINNIPEG, MB, R2C 3A8
(204) 944-6600   SIC 5511

FRONTIER DISCOUNT HOBBIES LTD   p 491
277 FRONT ST, BELLEVILLE, ON, K8N 2Z6
(613) 967-2845   SIC 6211

FRONTIER DISTRIBUTING   p 591
See 531442 ONTARIO INC

FRONTIER LEASE & RENTAL   p 1427
See FRONTIER PETERBILT SALES LTD

FRONTIER PETERBILT SALES LTD   p 1427
303 50TH ST E, SASKATOON, SK, S7K 6C1
(306) 242-3411   SIC 5511

FRONTIER PLUMBING & HEATING SUPPLY, DIV OF   p 30
See JBW PIPE & SUPPLY LTD

FRONTIER POWER PRODUCTS LTD   p 209
7983 PROGRESS WAY, DELTA, BC, V4G 1A3
(604) 946-5531   SIC 3621

FRONTIER RESTAURANT   p 759
See HOSPITALITY MOTELS LIMITED

FRONTIER SCHOOL DIVISION   p 353
1 ROSSVILLE RD, NORWAY HOUSE, MB, R0B 1B0
(204) 359-4100   SIC 8211

FRONTIER SCHOOL DIVISION   p 365
30 SPEERS RD, WINNIPEG, MB, R2J 1L9
(204) 775-9741   SIC 8211

FRONTIER SECURITY SERVICES   p 491
See FRONTIER DISCOUNT HOBBIES LTD

FRONTIER SUPPLY CHAIN SOLUTIONS INC   p 391
555 HERVO ST STE 10, WINNIPEG, MB, R3T 3L6
(204) 784-4800   SIC 4731

FRONTIER TECHNOLOGIES   p 444
See 3043177 NOVA SCOTIA LIMITED

FRONTIER TOYOTA   p 362
See FRONTIER AUTOMOTIVE INC

FRONTIER-KEMPER CONSTRUCTORS ULC   p 239
4400 LILLOOET RD, NORTH VANCOUVER, BC, V7J 2H9
(604) 988-1665   SIC 1241

FRONTLINE CIVIL MANAGEMENT   p 162
See A & B RAIL SERVICES LTD

FRONTLINE MACHINERY LTD   p 197
43779 PROGRESS WAY, CHILLIWACK, BC, V2R 0E6
(604) 625-2009   SIC 5082

FRONTLINE SYSTEMS INC   p 592
210 JAMES A. BRENNAN RD, GANANOQUE, ON, K7G 1N7
(613) 463-9575   SIC 5084

FROST CHEVROLET   p 513

See FROST CHEVROLET BUICK GMC CADILLAC LTD

FROST CHEVROLET BUICK GMC CADILLAC LTD   p 513
150 BOVAIRD DR W, BRAMPTON, ON, L7A 0H3
(905) 459-0126   SIC 5511

FROST FIGHTER INC   p 380
1500 NOTRE DAME AVE UNIT 100, WINNIPEG, MB, R3E 0P9
(204) 775-8252   SIC 5075

FROST MANOR   p 646
See OMNI HEALTH CARE LTD

FRP CONSULTING GROUP   p 1272
See GESTION FRP INC

FRPD INVESTMENTS LIMITED PARTNERSHIP   p 237
1830 RIVER DR, NEW WESTMINSTER, BC, V3M 2A8
(604) 522-7971   SIC 1629

FRUIT D'OR INC   p 1399
306 RTE 265, VILLEROY, QC, G0S 3K0
(819) 385-1126   SIC 5149

FRUIT DOME INC   p 1157
5975 AV ANDOVER, MONT-ROYAL, QC, H4T 1H8
(514) 664-4470   SIC 5149

FRUIT OF THE LAND INC   p 906
1 PROMENADE CIR, THORNHILL, ON, L4J 4P8
(905) 761-9611   SIC 5141

FRUITERIE VAL-MONT   p 1359
See JARDINS VAL-MONT INC., LES

FRUITERIE VAL-MONT INC, LA   p 1172
2147 AV DU MONT-ROYAL E, MONTREAL, QC, H2H 1J9
(514) 523-8212   SIC 5431

FRUITERIE WAKIM   p 1106
See ORIGINAL BAKED QUALITY PITA DIPS INC, L'

FRUITICANA PRODUCE LTD   p 276
7676 129A ST, SURREY, BC, V3W 4H7
(604) 502-0005   SIC 5148

FRUITION FRUITS & FILLS   p 803
See FRUITION MANUFACTURING LIMITED

FRUITION MANUFACTURING LIMITED   p 803
2379 SPEERS RD, OAKVILLE, ON, L6L 2X9
(905) 337-6400   SIC 5142

FRUITS & LEGUMES ERIC FRECHETTE INC, LES   p 1139
750 RUE JEAN-MARCHAND, LEVIS, QC, G6Y 9G6
(418) 835-6997   SIC 5148

FRUITS & LEGUMES GAETAN BONO INC   p 1225
995 RUE DU MARCHE-CENTRAL, MONTREAL, QC, H4N 1K2
(514) 381-1387   SIC 5148

FRUITS & PASSION   p 1070
See FRUITS & PASSION BOUTIQUES INC

FRUITS & PASSION BOUTIQUES INC   p 1070
9180 BOUL LEDUC BUREAU 280, BROSSARD, QC, J4Y 0N7
(450) 678-9620   SIC 5122

FRUITS BLEUS INC, LES   p 1296
698 RUE MELANCON, SAINT-BRUNO-LAC-SAINT-JEAN, QC, G0W 2L0
(418) 343-2206   SIC 0171

FRUITS DE MER BLUEWATER INC   p 1127
1640 CROIS BRANDON BUREAU 201, LACHINE, QC, H8T 2N1
(514) 637-1171   SIC 2092

FRUITS DE MER LAGOON INC   p 1127
1301 32E AV, LACHINE, QC, H8T 3H2
(514) 383-1383   SIC 5146

FRUITS DE MER LIBERIO INC   p 1162
7337 AV JEAN-VALETS, MONTREAL, QC, H1E 3H4
(514) 750-4022   SIC 5142

FRUITS DE MER MADELEINE INC, LES p 1120
546 CH FOUGERE, L'ETANG-DU-NORD, QC, G4T 3B3
(418) 986-6016 SIC 5146

FRUITS DE MER STARBOARD INC p 1094
560 AV LEPINE, DORVAL, QC, H9P 1G2
(514) 780-1818 SIC 5146

FRUITS DORES INC p 1068
1650 RUE PANAMA BUREAU 510, BROSSARD, QC, J4W 2W4
(450) 923-5856 SIC 5148

FRUITS ET LEGUMES BEAUPORT INC p 1255
275 AV DU SEMOIR, QUEBEC, QC, G1C 7V5
(418) 661-6938 SIC 5148

FRUITS ET LEGUMES BOTSIS INC, LES p 1326
140 RUE STINSON, SAINT-LAURENT, QC, H4N 2E7
(514) 389-7676 SIC 5148

FRUITS ET LEGUMES GRANDE-ALLEE INC p 1071
4635 GRANDE-ALLEE, BROSSARD, QC, J4Z 3E9
(450) 678-3167 SIC 5431

FRUITS ET LEGUMES TARDIF INC p 1123
559 CH DE SAINT-JEAN, LA PRAIRIE, QC, J5R 2L2
(450) 659-6449 SIC 5431

FRULACT CANADA INC p 633
1295 CENTENNIAL DR, KINGSTON, ON, K7P 0R6
(613) 507-7500 SIC 5143

FRY, BENTON FORD SALES LTD p 492
321 NORTH FRONT ST, BELLEVILLE, ON, K8P 3C6
(613) 962-9141 SIC 5511

FS REALTY CENTRE CORPORATION p 709
2150 HURONTARIO ST UNIT 202E, MISSISSAUGA, ON, L5B 1M8
(416) 253-0066 SIC 6411

FS WHISTLER HOLDINGS LIMITED p 343
4591 BLACKCOMB WAY, WHISTLER, BC, V8E 0Y4
(604) 935-3400 SIC 7011

FSJ OILFIELD SERVICES p 213
8140 ALASKA RD, FORT ST. JOHN, BC, V1J 0P3
(250) 785-8935 SIC 1389

FSTQ p 1176
See FONDS DE SOLIDARITE DES TRAVAILLEURS DU QUEBEC (F.T.Q.)

FT NELSON BULK SALES LTD p 213
MILE 293 ALASKA HWY, FORT NELSON, BC, V0C 1R0
(250) 774-7340 SIC 5172

FT SERVICES p 33
See AECOM MAINTENANCE SERVICES LTD

FTG AEROSPACE - TORONTO p 878
See FIRAN TECHNOLOGY GROUP CORPORATION

FTI p 527
See FORMING TECHNOLOGIES INCORPORATED

FTI CONSULTING CANADA ULC p 969
79 WELLINGTON ST W SUITE 2010, TORONTO, ON, M5K 1B1
(416) 649-8100 SIC 8748

FTS p 340
See FTS FOREST TECHNOLOGY SYSTEMS LTD

FTS FOREST TECHNOLOGY SYSTEMS LTD p 340
1065 HENRY ENG PL, VICTORIA, BC, V9B 6B2
(250) 478-5561 SIC 3669

FUCHS LUBRICANTS CANADA LTD p 536
405 DOBBIE DR, CAMBRIDGE, ON, N1T 1S8
(519) 622-2040 SIC 5172

FUEL TRADE p 951

See FUEL TRADE INTERNATIONAL INC
FUEL TRADE INTERNATIONAL INC p 951
180 UNIVERSITY AVE UNIT 5204, TORONTO, ON, M5H 0A2
(416) 313-2912 SIC 5172

FUELS INC p 613
136 CANNON ST W, HAMILTON, ON, L8R 2B9
(905) 528-0241 . SIC 5172

FUGRO CANADA CORP p 722
2505 MEADOWVALE BLVD, MISSISSAUGA, ON, L5N 5S2
(905) 567-2870 SIC 8742

FUGRO ROADWARE, A DIVISION OF p 722
See FUGRO CANADA CORP

FUJI OPTICAL CO LTD p 852
550 HIGHWAY 7 E, RICHMOND HILL, ON, L4B 3Z4
(905) 882-5665 SIC 5995

FUJI STARLIGHT EXPRESS CO., LTD p 4
222 LYNX ST, BANFF, AB, T1L 1K5
(403) 762-4433 SIC 7011

FUJIFILM CANADA INC p 731
600 SUFFOLK CRT, MISSISSAUGA, ON, L5R 4G4
(800) 461-0416 SIC 5043

FUJIFILM VISUALSONICS INC p 921
3080 YONGE ST SUITE 6100, TORONTO, ON, M4N 3N1
(416) 484-5000 SIC 3829

FUJITEC CANADA, INC p 852
15 EAST WILMOT ST, RICHMOND HILL, ON, L4B 1A3
(905) 731-8681 SIC 5084

FUJITSU CANADA, INC p 951
155 UNIVERSITY AVE SUITE 1600, TORONTO, ON, M5H 3B7
(905) 286-9666 SIC 5045

FUJITSU CONSEIL p 823
See FUJITSU CONSEIL (CANADA) INC

FUJITSU CONSEIL (CANADA) INC p 50
606 4 ST SW SUITE 1500, CALGARY, AB, T2P 1T1
(403) 265-6001 SIC 7379

FUJITSU CONSEIL (CANADA) INC p 89
10020 101A AVE NW SUITE 1500, EDMONTON, AB, T5J 3G2
(780) 423-2070 SIC 7376

FUJITSU CONSEIL (CANADA) INC p 823
55 METCALFE ST SUITE 530, OTTAWA, ON, K1P 6L5
(613) 238-2697 SIC 8741

FUJITSU CONSEIL (CANADA) INC p 980
200 FRONT ST W SUITE 2300, TORONTO, ON, M5V 3K2
(416) 363-8661 SIC 7379

FUJITSU CONSEIL (CANADA) INC p 1217
7101 AV DU PARC BUREAU 102, MONTREAL, QC, H3N 1X9
(514) 877-3301 SIC 7379

FUJITSU CONSEIL (CANADA) INC p 1272
2960 BOUL LAURIER BUREAU 400, QUEBEC, QC, G1V 4S1
SIC 7379

FUJITSU CONSULTING p 50
See FUJITSU CONSEIL (CANADA) INC

FUJITSU CONSULTING p 89
See FUJITSU CONSEIL (CANADA) INC

FUJITSU CONSULTING p 980
See FUJITSU CONSEIL (CANADA) INC

FUJITSU FRONTECH CANADA INC p 951
155 UNIVERSITY AVE SUITE 1600, TORONTO, ON, M5H 3B7
(800) 668-8325 SIC 7699

FUJIYA FISH MARKET p 296
See SHIGS ENTERPRISES LTD

FULCRUM CAPITAL PARTNERS INC p 304
885 GEORGIA ST W SUITE 1020, VANCOUVER, BC, V6C 3E8
(604) 631-8088 SIC 6159

FULFORD SUPPLY p 1032
See NEXT PLUMBING & HYDRONICS SUPPLY INC

FULL CIRCLE ENERGY HEALING p 338

994 ABBEY RD, VICTORIA, BC, V8Y 1L2
(778) 350-3260 SIC 4924

FULL LINE AG SALES LTD p 1427
2 YELLOWHEAD INDUSTRIAL PARK LOT 2 RR 4 LCD MAIN, SASKATOON, SK, S7K 3J7
(306) 934-1546 SIC 5999

FULLER AUSTIN INC p 101
11604 186 ST NW, EDMONTON, AB, T5S 0C4
(780) 452-1701 SIC 1799

FULLER LANDAU LLP p 974
151 BLOOR ST W, TORONTO, ON, M5S 1S4
(416) 645-6500 SIC 8721

FULLER LANDAU SENCRL p 1204
1010 RUE DE LA GAUCHETIERE O BUREAU 200, MONTREAL, QC, H3B 2S1
(514) 875-2865 SIC 8721

FULLER, THOMAS CONSTRUCTION CO. LIMITED p 830
2700 QUEENSVIEW DR, OTTAWA, ON, K2B 8H6
(613) 820-6000 SIC 1542

FULLINE FARM & GARDEN EQUIPMENT LTD p 594
21911 SIMPSON RD, GLENCOE, ON, N0L 1M0
(519) 287-2840 SIC 5083

FULMER DEVELOPMENT CORPORATION, THE p 318
1500 GEORGIA ST W SUITE 1290, VANCOUVER, BC, V6G 2Z6
(604) 558-5492 SIC 5812

FUM MEDIA CORP p 313
1151 GEORGIA ST W SUITE 3205, VANCOUVER, BC, V6E 0B3
(778) 859-5882 SIC 7311

FUMOIR GRIZZLY INC p 1293
159 RUE D'AMSTERDAM, SAINT-AUGUSTIN-DE-DESMAURES, QC, G3A 2V5
(418) 878-8941 SIC 2091

FUMOIRS GASPE CURED INC, LES p 1074
65 RUE DE LA STATION, CAP-D'ESPOIR, QC, G0C 1G0
(418) 782-5920 SIC 2091

FUN FEED, DIV OF p 285
See RELAXUS PRODUCTS LTD

FUN PLANET VACATIONS p 189
See ODENZA MARKETING GROUP INC

FUN TALKING SOFTWARE LTD p 237
713 COLUMBIA ST SUITE 202, NEW WESTMINSTER, BC, V3M 1B2
(778) 999-1658 SIC 7371

FUNCTIONABILITY REHABILITATION SERVICES LP p 553
9135 KEELE ST UNIT B5, CONCORD, ON, L4K 0J4
(905) 764-2340 SIC 8049

FUNDATA CANADA INC p 776
26 LESMILL RD SUITE 1B, NORTH YORK, ON, M3B 2T5
(416) 445-5443 SIC 6289

FUNDEX INVESTMENTS INC p 553
400 APPLEWOOD CRES, CONCORD, ON, L4K 0C3
(905) 305-1651 SIC 6211

FUNDRAISING.COM p 1210
See CORPORATION EFUNDRAISING.COM INC

FUNDS FLOW CANADA INC p 803
2201 SPEERS RD, OAKVILLE, ON, L6L 2X9
SIC 7389

FUNDSERV INC p 997
130 KING ST UNIT 1700, TORONTO, ON, M9N 1L5
(416) 362-2400 SIC 8741

FUNDY BAY ENTERPRISES LTD p 398
65 DIPPER HARBOUR RD, DIPPER HARBOUR, NB, E5J 1X3
(506) 659-2890 SIC 5146

FUNDY BAY SEAFOOD p 398
See FUNDY BAY ENTERPRISES LTD

FUNDY CONSTRUCTION p 397
See FUNDY DRYWALL LTD

FUNDY DRYWALL LTD p 397
91 RUE ENGLEHART, DIEPPE, NB, E1A 8K2
(506) 383-6466 SIC 1742

FUNDY ENERGY LIMITED p 407
132 BEAVERBROOK ST, MONCTON, NB, E1C 9S8
(506) 857-3283 SIC 5074

FUNDY GRINDING & MACHINING LIMITED p 468
9 FARNHAM RD, TRURO, NS, B2N 2X6
(902) 893-4274 SIC 5084

FUNDY GRINDING MACHINE TOOL SALES p 468
See FUNDY GRINDING & MACHINING LIMITED

FUNDY GYPSUM COMPANY, A DIV OF p 470
See USG CANADIAN MINING LTD

FUNDY GYPSUM COMPANY, DIV OF p 470
See CGC INC

FUNDY HONDA p 413
See FUNDY MOTORS (1995) LTD

FUNDY MOTORS (1995) LTD p 413
160 ROTHESAY AVE, SAINT JOHN, NB, E2J 2B5
(506) 633-1333 SIC 5511

FUNDY MUTUAL INSURANCE LTD p 418
1022 MAIN ST, SUSSEX, NB, E4E 2M3
(506) 432-1535 SIC 6331

FUNDY STEVEDORING INC p 395
140 CHAMPLAIN PROM, BAYSIDE, NB, E5B 2Y2
(506) 529-8821 SIC 4491

FUNDY TEXTILE & DESIGN LIMITED p 468
189 INDUSTRIAL AVE, TRURO, NS, B2N 6V3
(902) 897-0010 SIC 2326

FUNIO p 1396
See TECHNOLOGIES IWEB INC

FUNK MOTORS p 358
See FUNK'S TOYOTA LTD

FUNK'S TOYOTA LTD p 358
57 PTH 12 N, STEINBACH, MB, R5G 1T3
(204) 326-9808 SIC 5511

FUNKS FOODS LTD p 176
2580 CLEARBROOK RD, ABBOTSFORD, BC, V2T 2Y5
SIC 5411

FUNKTIONAL LIFE SOLUTIONS p 173
See FUNKTIONAL SLEEP SOLUTIONS LTD

FUNKTIONAL SLEEP SOLUTIONS LTD p 173
4920 51ST AVE, WHITECOURT, AB, T7S 1W2
(780) 778-6461 SIC 8999

FURA p 951
See FURA GEMS INC

FURA GEMS INC p 951
65 QUEEN ST W SUITE 800, TORONTO, ON, M5H 2M5
(416) 861-2269 SIC 1499

FURLANI'S FOOD CORPORATION p 695
1730 AIMCO BLVD, MISSISSAUGA, ON, L4W 1V1
(905) 602-6102 SIC 2051

FURLONG BROTHERS LIMITED p 427
GD, PLATE COVE WEST, NL, A0C 2E0
(709) 545-2251 SIC 2092

FURNACE BELT COMPANY LIMITED, THE p 735
1874 DREW RD UNIT 7, MISSISSAUGA, ON, L5S 1J6
(905) 677-5068 SIC 5084

FURNCO FURNITURE INTERNATIONAL DISTRIBUTORS LTD p 783
363 SUPERTEST RD, NORTH YORK, ON, M3J 2M4
(416) 736-6120 SIC 5712

FURNITURE BANK p 574
25 CONNELL CRT UNIT 1, ETOBICOKE,

ON, M8Z 1E8
(416) 934-1229   *SIC* 8699
FURNITURE INVESTMENT GROUP INC *p* 892
563 BARTON ST, STONEY CREEK, ON, L8E 5S1
SIC 5712
FURRY CREEK GOLF & COUNTRY CLUB INC *p* 230
150 COUNTRY CLUB RD, LIONS BAY, BC, V0N 2E0
(604) 896-2216   *SIC* 7992
FURST-MCMIRACLE FEEDS *p* 621
See *FURST-MCNESS COMPANY OF CANADA LIMITED*
FURST-MCNESS COMPANY OF CANADA LIMITED *p* 621
30 WILSON ST, INGERSOLL, ON, N5C 4E8
(519) 485-5600   *SIC* 5191
FUSEPOINT INC *p* 722
6800 MILLCREEK DR, MISSISSAUGA, ON, L5N 4J9
(905) 363-3737   *SIC* 8741
FUSION BEAUTY *p* 926
See *FUSION BRANDS INC*
FUSION BPO SERVICES LIMITED *p* 1188
507 PLACE D'ARMES BUREAU 1000, MONTREAL, QC, H2Y 2W8
(514) 227-3126   *SIC* 7389
FUSION BRANDS INC *p* 926
40 ST CLAIR AVE W SUITE 200, TORONTO, ON, M4V 1M2
(800) 261-9110   *SIC* 5122
FUSION CINE *p* 285
See *FUSION CINE SALES & RENTALS INC*
FUSION CINE SALES & RENTALS INC *p* 285
1469 VENABLES ST, VANCOUVER, BC, V5L 2G1
(604) 879-0003   *SIC* 5065
FUSION GLASS WORKS *p* 792
See *DORPLEX INDUSTRIES LIMITED*
FUSION HOMES *p* 600
See *1266304 ONTARIO INC*
FUSION PROJECT MANAGEMENT LTD *p* 304
850 HASTINGS ST W SUITE 800, VANCOUVER, BC, V6C 1E1
(604) 629-0469   *SIC* 1521
FUSION SOLUTION INC *p* 1111
700 RUE BERNARD, GRANBY, QC, J2J 0H6
(450) 372-4994   *SIC* 7389
FUTECH HITECH INC *p* 1339
352 RUE MCARTHUR, SAINT-LAURENT, QC, H4T 1X8
(514) 351-1495   *SIC* 5063
FUTUE SHOP *p* 626
See *BEST BUY CANADA LTD*
FUTURA *p* 1216
See *CONSOLTEX INC*
FUTURA MANUFACTURIER DE PORTES ET FENETRES INC *p* 1264
1451 RUE FRANK-CARREL, QUEBEC, QC, G1N 4N7
(418) 681-7272   *SIC* 3089
FUTURA PORTES ET FENETRES *p* 1264
See *FUTURA MANUFACTURIER DE PORTES ET FENETRES INC*
FUTURE AG INC *p* 157
69 BELICH CRES, RED DEER, AB, T4S 2K5
(403) 343-6101   *SIC* 5083
FUTURE AUTO & MARINE *p* 1038
See *FUTURE SEAFOODS INC*
FUTURE BAKERY LIMITED *p* 574
106 NORTH QUEEN ST, ETOBICOKE, ON, M8Z 2E2
(416) 231-1491   *SIC* 2051
FUTURE DOORS LTD *p* 410
4009 ROUTE 115, NOTRE-DAME, NB, E4V 2G2
(506) 576-9769   *SIC* 1751
FUTURE ELECTRONICS (CDA) LTD *p* 1250

237 BOUL HYMUS, POINTE-CLAIRE, QC, H9R 5C7
(514) 694-7710   *SIC* 5065
FUTURE ELECTRONIQUE INC *p* 1250
237 BOUL HYMUS, POINTE-CLAIRE, QC, H9R 5C7
(514) 694-7710   *SIC* 5065
FUTURE HYDRAULIK INC *p* 1085
1597 RUE CUNARD, COTE SAINT-LUC, QC, H7S 2B4
(450) 687-0187   *SIC* 5084
FUTURE SALES CORPORATION *p* 670
1405 DENISON ST, MARKHAM, ON, L3R 5V2
(905) 477-1894   *SIC* 3441
FUTURE SEAFOODS INC *p* 1038
358 NEW RD, BEDEQUE, PE, C0B 1C0
(902) 887-3012   *SIC* 5146
FUTURE SHOP *p* 33
See *BEST BUY CANADA LTD*
FUTURE SHOP *p* 69
See *BEST BUY CANADA LTD*
FUTURE SHOP *p* 87
See *BEST BUY CANADA LTD*
FUTURE SHOP *p* 192
See *BEST BUY CANADA LTD*
FUTURE SHOP *p* 341
See *BEST BUY CANADA LTD*
FUTURE SHOP *p* 596
See *BEST BUY CANADA LTD*
FUTURE SHOP *p* 641
See *BEST BUY CANADA LTD*
FUTURE SHOP *p* 651
See *BEST BUY CANADA LTD*
FUTURE SHOP *p* 754
See *BEST BUY CANADA LTD*
FUTURE SHOP *p* 814
See *BEST BUY CANADA LTD*
FUTURE SHOP *p* 826
See *BEST BUY CANADA LTD*
FUTURE SHOP *p* 858
See *BEST BUY CANADA LTD*
FUTURE SHOP *p* 1000
See *BEST BUY CANADA LTD*
FUTURE SHOP *p* 1064
See *BEST BUY CANADA LTD*
FUTURE SHOP *p* 1078
See *BEST BUY CANADA LTD*
FUTURE SHOP *p* 1214
See *BEST BUY CANADA LTD*
FUTURE STEEL BUILDINGS *p* 670
See *FUTURE SALES CORPORATION*
FUTURE STEEL BUILDINGS INTL. CORP *p* 499
220 CHRYSLER DR, BRAMPTON, ON, L6S 6B6
(905) 790-8500   *SIC* 3448
FUTUREVAULT INC *p* 980
441 KING ST W UNIT 200, TORONTO, ON, M5V 1K4
(416) 560-7808   *SIC* 7389
FUTUROTO INC *p* 1351
279 AV SAINT-JACQUES, SAINT-RAYMOND, QC, G3L 4A2
(418) 337-6745   *SIC* 5511
FV FOODS *p* 868
See *8956642 CANADA CORP*
FW *p* 1329
See *FERSTEN WORLDWIDE INC*
FW GREEN HOME, THE *p* 203
1700 4TH ST S, CRANBROOK, BC, V1C 6E1
(250) 426-8016   *SIC* 8059
FWS COMMERCIAL PROJECTS LTD *p* 393
475 DOVERCOURT DR, WINNIPEG, MB, R3Y 1G4
(204) 487-2500   *SIC* 1542
FWS CONSTRUCTION LTD *p* 388
275 COMMERCE DR, WINNIPEG, MB, R3P 1B3
(204) 487-2500   *SIC* 1541
FWS HOLDINGS LTD *p* 388
275 COMMERCE DR, WINNIPEG, MB, R3P 1B3

(204) 487-2500   *SIC* 1542
FWS PHARMACY SERVICES LTD *p* 222
2271 HARVEY AVE SUITE 1360, KELOWNA, BC, V1Y 6H2
(250) 860-3764   *SIC* 5912
FX INNOVATION *p* 1143
See *GROUPE CONSEIL FXINNOVATION INC*
FX INNOVATION *p* 1196
See *GROUPE CONSEIL FXINNOVATION INC*
FXR FACTORY RACING INC *p* 353
155 OAKLAND RD, OAK BLUFF, MB, R4G 0A4
(204) 736-4406   *SIC* 5136
FYBON INDUSTRIES LIMITED *p* 503
5 TILBURY CRT, BRAMPTON, ON, L6T 3T4
(905) 291-1090   *SIC* 2297
FYI DOCTORS *p* 67
See *FYI EYE CARE SERVICES AND PRODUCTS INC*
FYI EYE CARE SERVICES AND PRODUCTS INC *p* 67
2424 4 ST SW SUITE 300, CALGARY, AB, T2S 2T4
(403) 234-2020   *SIC* 3229
FYI SERVICES ET PRODUITS QUEBEC INC *p* 1262
1100 AV GALIBOIS BUREAU A200, QUEBEC, QC, G1M 3M7
(418) 527-6682   *SIC* 5995
FYNBO, IB HARDWARE LTD *p* 570
47 WILSON AVE, ESSEX, ON, N8M 2L9
(519) 776-4646   *SIC* 5251

G

G & B BUILDING CENTRE *p* 837
See *G & B MCNABB LUMBER COMPANY LIMITED*
G & B MCNABB LUMBER COMPANY LIMITED *p* 837
22 SEGUIN ST, PARRY SOUND, ON, P2A 1B1
(705) 746-5825   *SIC* 5211
G & B SMITH FISHERIES LIMITED *p* 471
50 ROUTE 304, YARMOUTH, NS, B5A 4J8
(902) 742-5478   *SIC* 5199
G & G GENERAL SUPPLY LTD *p* 553
511 MILLWAY AVE, CONCORD, ON, L4K 3V4
(905) 669-9556   *SIC* 5074
G & H MARKETING ENTERPRISE *p* 281
See *BUY-LOW FOODS LTD*
G & L GROUP LTD *p* 553
401 BOWES RD, CONCORD, ON, L4K 1J4
(416) 798-7050   *SIC* 6712
G & L SLOTCO OILFIELD SERVICES LTD *p* 50
700 4 AVE SW SUITE 1110, CALGARY, AB, T2P 3J4
(403) 261-1717   *SIC* 3443
G & L WILCOX LIMITED *p* 567
698 SNO-DRIFTERS RD, EGANVILLE, ON, K0J 1T0
(613) 628-2424   *SIC* 5551
G & M CHEVROLET-CADILLAC LTD *p* 399
605 RUE VICTORIA, EDMUNDSTON, NB, E3V 3M8
(506) 735-3331   *SIC* 5511
G & M PLUMBING & HEATING LTD *p* 132
10944 96 AVE, GRANDE PRAIRIE, AB, T8V 3J5
(780) 538-3222   *SIC* 5251
G & M STEEL SERVICE LTD *p* 271
5980 ENTERPRISE WAY, SURREY, BC, V3S 6S8
(604) 530-0117   *SIC* 1791
G & P MILLWORK LTD *p* 878
191 FINCHDENE SQ, SCARBOROUGH, ON, M1X 1E3
(416) 298-4204   *SIC* 2431
G & P WELDING & IRON WORKS *p* 762

See *331265 ONTARIO LIMITED*
G A CHECKPOINT *p* 248
See *GORDON AULENBACK LTD*
G A MASONRY *p* 518
See *GEORGE AND ASMUSSEN LIMITED*
G ADVENTURES INC *p* 980
19 CHARLOTTE ST SUITE 200, TORONTO, ON, M5V 2H5
(416) 260-0999   *SIC* 4725
G AND G WHITE HOWLEY PHARMACY LTD *p* 464
131 KING ST SUITE 148, NORTH SYDNEY, NS, B2A 3S1
(902) 794-7211   *SIC* 5912
G C CUSTOMS BROKERS *p* 759
See *GARDEN CITY CUSTOMS SERVICES INC*
G D AUTO PARTS *p* 808
See *GORD DAVENPORT AUTOMOTIVE INC*
G E MOTEURS D'AVIONS INC *p* 1068
2 BOUL DE L'AEROPORT, BROMONT, QC, J2L 1S6
(450) 534-0917   *SIC* 5599
G F LTD *p* 30
2270 PORTLAND ST SE, CALGARY, AB, T2G 4M6
(403) 287-7111   *SIC* 5999
G F STRONG REHABILITATION CENTRE *p* 294
See *VANCOUVER COASTAL HEALTH AUTHORITY*
G K D INDUSTRIES LTD *p* 16
7939 54 ST SE, CALGARY, AB, T2C 4R7
(403) 279-8087   *SIC* 5084
G N R CAMPING WORLD RV CENTRE *p* 365
See *G N R TRAVEL CENTRE LTD*
G N R TRAVEL CENTRE LTD *p* 365
1370 DUGALD RD, WINNIPEG, MB, R2J 0H2
(204) 233-4478   *SIC* 5561
G PRODUCTION INC *p* 1053
19400 AUT TRANSCANADIENNE, BAIE-D'URFE, QC, H9X 3S4
(514) 457-3366   *SIC* 2834
G R E *p* 806
See *GRAND RIVER ENTERPRISES SIX NATIONS LIMITED*
G T I BROKER GROUP INC *p* 417
177 RUE ST-JEAN, SAINT-LEONARD, NB, E7E 2B3
(506) 423-7777   *SIC* 6411
G&B PORTABLE FABRIC BUILDINGS *p* 349
See *LX CONSTRUCTION INC*
G&F FINANCIAL GROUP *p* 181
See *GULF AND FRASER FISHERMEN'S CREDIT UNION*
G&K SERVICES - WINDSOR *p* 1017
See *G&K SERVICES CANADA INC*
G&K SERVICES CANADA INC *p* 11
2925 10 AVE NE SUITE 7, CALGARY, AB, T2A 5L4
(403) 272-4256   *SIC* 7219
G&K SERVICES CANADA INC *p* 536
205 TURNBULL CRT, CAMBRIDGE, ON, N1T 1W1
(519) 623-7703   *SIC* 7216
G&K SERVICES CANADA INC *p* 688
5935 AIRPORT RD, MISSISSAUGA, ON, L4V 1W5
(905) 677-6161   *SIC* 7213
G&K SERVICES CANADA INC *p* 868
940 WARDEN AVE SUITE 1, SCARBOROUGH, ON, M1L 4C9
(647) 933-2627   *SIC* 2326
G&K SERVICES CANADA INC *p* 1017
9085 TWIN OAKS DR, WINDSOR, ON, N8N 5B8
(519) 979-5913   *SIC* 7213
G&K SERVICES CANADA INC *p* 1170
8400 19E AV, MONTREAL, QC, H1Z 4J3
(514) 723-7666   *SIC* 7213

G&W CANADA CORPORATION p 511
7965 HERITAGE RD, BRAMPTON, ON, L6Y 5X5
(905) 542-2000   SIC 3613

G-MAC'S AGTEAM INC p 1408
908 MAIN ST, KINDERSLEY, SK, S0L 1S0
(306) 463-4769   SIC 5261

G-P DISTRIBUTING INC p 1440
29 MACDONALD RD, WHITEHORSE, YT, Y1A 4L1
(867) 667-4500   SIC 5141

G-SPEK INC p 1147
2039 RUE RENE-PATENAUDE, MAGOG, QC, J1X 7J2
(819) 868-7655   SIC 3089

G-TEK p 1134
See 3427951 CANADA INC

G-TEL ENGINEERING INC p 651
1150 FRANCES ST 2ND FL, LONDON, ON, N5W 5N5
(519) 439-0763   SIC 8748

G-TEL ENGINEERING INC p 1031
200 HANLAN RD, WOODBRIDGE, ON, L4L 3P6
(905) 856-1162   SIC 8748

G-WLG LP p 612
1 MAIN ST W, HAMILTON, ON, L8P 4Z5
(905) 540-8208   SIC 8111

G-WLG LP p 834
160 ELGIN ST SUITE 2600, OTTAWA, ON, K2P 3C3
(613) 233-1781   SIC 8741

G. C. DUKE EQUIPMENT LTD p 531
1184 PLAINS RD E, BURLINGTON, ON, L7S 1W6
(905) 637-5216   SIC 5083

G. C. LOH MERCHANDISING LTD p 580
1530 ALBION RD, ETOBICOKE, ON, M9V 1B4
(416) 745-9070   SIC 5531

G. D. BROKERAGE INC p 446
21 WILLIAMS AVE UNIT 4, DARTMOUTH, NS, B3B 1X3
(902) 468-1777   SIC 5141

G. E. BARBOUR INC p 418
165 STEWART AVE, SUSSEX, NB, E4E 3H1
(506) 432-2300   SIC 2099

G. J. BELL ENTERPISES LTD p 1427
2030 1ST AVE N, SASKATOON, SK, S7K 2A1
(306) 242-1251   SIC 5012

G. PELLERIN C. DESBIENS, PHARMA-CIENS p 1369
1920 105E AV, SHAWINIGAN, QC, G9P 1N4
(819) 537-1869   SIC 5912

G. T. FRENCH PAPER LIMITED p 615
90 GLOVER RD, HAMILTON, ON, L8W 3T7
(905) 574-0275   SIC 5113

G. V. INTERIOR CONTRACTORS LTD p 695
5446 GORVAN DR, MISSISSAUGA, ON, L4W 3E8
SIC 1542

G.A. PAPER p 670
See G.A. PAPER INTERNATIONAL INC

G.A. PAPER INTERNATIONAL INC p 670
327 RENFREW DR SUITE 102, MARKHAM, ON, L3R 9S8
(905) 479-7600   SIC 5099

G.A. VALLANCE HOLDINGS LIMITED p 226
6312 200 ST SUITE 426, LANGLEY, BC, V2Y 1A1
(604) 532-4411   SIC 5541

G.A.L. CANADA ELEVATOR PRODUCTS CORP p 739
6500 GOTTARDO CRT, MISSISSAUGA, ON, L5T 2A2
(905) 564-0838   SIC 5084

G.A.L. POWER SYSTEMS INC p 540
2558 CARP RD, CARP, ON, K0A 1L0
(613) 831-3188   SIC 5063

G.A.R. TREE FARMS LTD p 439
595 FARMINGTON RD, BARSS CORNER,

NS, B0R 1A0
(902) 644-3415   SIC 5199

G.B. BUSINESS ENTERPRISES LTD p 147
8704 100 ST, MORINVILLE, AB, T8R 1K6
(780) 939-3666   SIC 5511

G.B.S. COMMUNICATIONS INC p 456
3480 JOSEPH HOWE DR UNIT 200, HALIFAX, NS, B3L 0B5
(902) 431-1100   SIC 4899

G.C.L. p 1214
See 3731537 CANADA INC

G.C.L. EQUIPEMENTS INC p 1238
35 AV LAGANIERE, MONTREAL-EST, QC, H1B 5T1
(514) 640-0840   SIC 1794

G.C.M. CONSULTANTS INC p 1049
9496 BOUL DU GOLF, ANJOU, QC, H1J 3A1
(514) 351-8350   SIC 8711

G.D. NIRVANA INC p 1339
955 RUE MCCAFFREY, SAINT-LAURENT, QC, H4T 1N3
(514) 739-9111   SIC 5149

G.D.G. ENVIRONNEMENT LTEE p 1384
430 RUE SAINT-LAURENT, TROIS-RIVIERES, QC, G8T 6H3
(819) 373-3097   SIC 8748

G.D.G. INFORMATIQUE ET GESTION INC p 1259
330 RUE DE SAINT-VALLIER E BUREAU 23, QUEBEC, QC, G1K 9C5
(418) 647-0006   SIC 7371

G.E. COWELL HOLDINGS LTD p 254
13611 SMALLWOOD PL, RICHMOND, BC, V6V 1W8
(604) 273-3922   SIC 5511

G.E. FORWARDERS LTD p 685
2797 THAMESGATE DR, MISSISSAUGA, ON, L4T 1G5
(905) 676-9555   SIC 4731

G.E. LOGISTICS p 685
See G.E. FORWARDERS LTD

G.E.'S ALL TRUCKING LIMITED p 441
385 YORK ST, BRIDGEWATER, NS, B4V 3K1
SIC 5084

G.G. TELECOM p 1398
See 9138-4529 QUEBEC INC

G.G.C.S. HOLDINGS LTD p 203
820 CRANBROOK ST N, CRANBROOK, BC, V1C 3R9
(250) 426-5208   SIC 5531

G.H. JOHNSONS FURNITURE INC p 990
950 DUPONT ST, TORONTO, ON, M6H 1Z2
(613) 736-7000   SIC 5021

G.J. CAHILL & COMPANY (1979) LIMITED p 433
240 WATERFORD BRIDGE RD, ST. JOHN'S, NL, A1E 1E2
(709) 368-2125   SIC 1731

G.L.R. INC p 1119
1095 RUE VALETS, L'ANCIENNE-LORETTE, QC, G2E 4M7
(418) 872-3365   SIC 1623

G.M. PACE ENTERPRISES INC p 211
4801 TRANS CANADA HWY SUITE 3, DUNCAN, BC, V9L 6L3
(250) 246-4448   SIC 5541

G.M.I. p 568
See GLUECKLER METAL INC

G.M.R. FREIGHT BROKERS p 1138
See COURTIERS EN TRANSPORT G.M.R. INC, LES

G.N. JOHNSTON EQUIPMENT CO. LTD p 670
See G.N. JOHNSTON EQUIPMENT CO. LTD.

G.N. JOHNSTON EQUIPMENT CO. LTD p 731
See G.N. JOHNSTON EQUIPMENT CO. LTD.

G.N. JOHNSTON EQUIPMENT CO. LTD p 1329
See G.N. JOHNSTON EQUIPMENT CO. LTD.

G.N. JOHNSTON EQUIPMENT CO. LTD. p 670
181 WHITEHALL DR SUITE 2, MARKHAM, ON, L3R 9T1
(416) 798-7195   SIC 3537

G.N. JOHNSTON EQUIPMENT CO. LTD. p 731
5990 AVEBURY RD, MISSISSAUGA, ON, L5R 3R2
(905) 712-6000   SIC 5084

G.N. JOHNSTON EQUIPMENT CO. LTD. p 1329
5000 RUE LEVY, SAINT-LAURENT, QC, H4R 2P1
(514) 956-0020   SIC 5084

G.N. PLASTICS COMPANY LIMITED p 442
345 OLD TRUNK 3, CHESTER, NS, B0J 1J0
(902) 275-3571   SIC 3559

G.O. EQUIPEMENT / VENTES & SERVICE p 1107
See SERVICE DE PNEUS LAVOIE OUTAOUAIS INC

G.P.C.I. p 1053
See G PRODUCTION INC

G.R.R. HOLDINGS LTD p 385
2553 PORTAGE AVE, WINNIPEG, MB, R3J 0P3
(204) 885-5275   SIC 5812

G.R.T. GENESIS INC p 509
173 GLIDDEN RD SUITE 1, BRAMPTON, ON, L6W 3L9
(905) 452-0552   SIC 5162

G.S. HOLDINGS COMPANY LTD p 1
27060 ACHESON RD, ACHESON, AB, T7X 6B1
(780) 962-3544   SIC 1623

G.S. WARK LIMITED p 613
370 YORK BLVD SUITE 101, HAMILTON, ON, L8R 3L1
(905) 529-4717   SIC 1542

G.S.C. CRANE OPERATIONS p 425
See 175042 CANADA INC

G.S.K. MANAGEMENT INC p 771
40 SHEPPARD AVE W SUITE 700, NORTH YORK, ON, M2N 6K9
(416) 225-9400   SIC 6712

G.S.L. MOULD & DIE p 1240
See VESTSHELL INC

G.T. ENTREPOSAGE p 1161
See G.T. SERVICE DE CONTENEURS INC

G.T. MACHINING & FABRICATING LTD p 747
101 RICHMOND BLVD, NAPANEE, ON, K7R 3Z8
(613) 354-6621   SIC 3599

G.T. MACHINING & FABRICATING LTD p 747
7 KELLWOOD CRES, NAPANEE, ON, K7R 4A1
(613) 354-6621   SIC 3443

G.T. SERVICE DE CONTENEURS INC p 1161
10000 BOUL MAURICE-DUPLESSIS, MONTREAL, QC, H1C 2A2
(514) 648-4848   SIC 7692

G.T. TABACCO p 817
See G.T. WHOLESALE LIMITED

G.T. WHOLESALE LIMITED p 817
2480 WALKLEY RD, OTTAWA, ON, K1G 6A9
(613) 521-8222   SIC 5194

G.T.A. WORLD CARGO LTD p 695
2710 BRITANNIA RD E (CARGO 2 TOWER 7), MISSISSAUGA, ON, L4W 2P7
(905) 671-4443   SIC 4581

G.T.C.A. MET-ALL INC p 1333
1215 MONTEE DE LIESSE, SAINT-LAURENT, QC, H4S 1J7
(514) 334-2801   SIC 3444

G.W. ANGLIN MANUFACTURING INC p 902
220 PATILLO RD SUITE 1, TECUMSEH, ON, N8N 2L9
(519) 727-4398   SIC 3499

G2 LOGISTICS INC p 380
944 HENRY AVE, WINNIPEG, MB, R3E 3L2
(204) 633-8989   SIC 4731

G2 OCEAN SHIPPING (CANADA) LTD p 313
1111 HASTINGS ST W SUITE 900, VANCOUVER, BC, V6E 2J3
(604) 661-2020   SIC 4731

G2MC INC p 1225
1215 BOUL CREMAZIE O, MONTREAL, QC, H4N 2W1
(514) 382-1443   SIC 5712

G2MC INC p 1237
2323 DES LAURENTIDES (A-15) E, MONTREAL, QC, H7S 1Z7
(450) 682-3022   SIC 5712

G2S EQUIPEMENT p 1094
See G2S EQUIPEMENT DE FABRICATION ET D'ENTRETIEN INC

G2S EQUIPEMENT DE FABRICATION ET D'ENTRETIEN INC p 1094
1895 CH SAINT-FRANCOIS, DORVAL, QC, H9P 1K3
(514) 683-8665   SIC 5013

G3 CANADA LIMITED p 374
423 MAIN ST SUITE 800, WINNIPEG, MB, R3B 1B3
(204) 983-0239   SIC 4221

G3 GALVANIZING LIMITED p 446
160 JOSEPH ZATZMAN DR, DARTMOUTH, NS, B3B 1P1
(902) 468-1040   SIC 3479

G3 TRANSPORT p 1162
See GROUPE G3 INC, LE

G3 WORLDWIDE (CANADA) INC p 688
3198 ORLANDO DR, MISSISSAUGA, ON, L4V 1R5
(905) 405-8900   SIC 7331

G4S CANADA p 578
See G4S SECURE SOLUTIONS (CANADA) LTD

G4S CASH SOLUTIONS (CANADA) LTD p 23
5040 SKYLINE WAY NE, CALGARY, AB, T2E 6V1
(403) 974-8350   SIC 7381

G4S CASH SOLUTIONS (CANADA) LTD p 286
2743 SKEENA ST, VANCOUVER, BC, V5M 4T1
SIC 7381

G4S CASH SOLUTIONS (CANADA) LTD p 286
2743 SKEENA ST SUITE 200, VANCOUVER, BC, V5M 4T1
SIC 7381

G4S CASH SOLUTIONS (CANADA) LTD p 382
994 WALL ST, WINNIPEG, MB, R3G 2V3
(204) 774-6883   SIC 7381

G4S CASH SOLUTIONS (CANADA) LTD p 595
1303 MICHAEL ST, GLOUCESTER, ON, K1B 3M9
SIC 4212

G4S CASH SOLUTIONS (CANADA) LTD p 639
108 AHRENS ST W, KITCHENER, ON, N2H 4C3
SIC 7381

G4S CASH SOLUTIONS (CANADA) LTD p 779
150 FERRAND DR SUITE 600, NORTH YORK, ON, M3C 3E5
(416) 645-5555   SIC 7381

G4S SECURE SOLUTIONS (CANADA) LTD p 114
9618 42 AVE NW SUITE 100, EDMONTON, AB, T6E 5Y4
(780) 423-4444   SIC 7381

G4S SECURE SOLUTIONS (CANADA) LTD p 145
525 4 ST SE, MEDICINE HAT, AB, T1A 0K7
(403) 526-2001   SIC 7381

G4S SECURE SOLUTIONS (CANADA) LTD
p 384
530 CENTURY ST SUITE 231, WINNIPEG, MB, R3H 0Y4
(204) 774-0005   *SIC* 7381
G4S SECURE SOLUTIONS (CANADA) LTD
p 578
703 EVANS AVE UNIT 103, ETOBICOKE, ON, M9C 5E9
(416) 620-0762   *SIC* 7381
G4S SECURE SOLUTIONS (CANADA) LTD
p 632
2437 PRINCESS ST SUITE 204, KINGSTON, ON, K7M 3G1
(613) 389-1744   *SIC* 7381
G4S SECURE SOLUTIONS (CANADA) LTD
p 638
1448 KING ST E, KITCHENER, ON, N2G 2N7
SIC 7381
G4S SECURE SOLUTIONS (CANADA) LTD
p 653
383 RICHMOND ST SUITE 503, LONDON, ON, N6A 3C4
(647) 678-5111   *SIC* 7381
G4S SECURE SOLUTIONS (CANADA) LTD
p 767
2 LANSING SQ SUITE 204, NORTH YORK, ON, M2J 4P8
(416) 490-8329   *SIC* 7381
G4S SECURE SOLUTIONS (CANADA) LTD
p 812
214 KING ST E, OSHAWA, ON, L1H 1C7
(905) 579-8020   *SIC* 7381
G4S SECURE SOLUTIONS (CANADA) LTD
p 901
1351 D KELLY LAKE RD UNIT 9, SUDBURY, ON, P3E 5P5
(705) 524-1519   *SIC* 7381
G4S SECURE SOLUTIONS (CANADA) LTD
p 913
211 CRAIG ST, TIMMINS, ON, P4N 4A2
(705) 268-7040   *SIC* 7381
G4S SECURE SOLUTIONS (CANADA) LTD
p 1019
3372 MANNHEIM WAY, WINDSOR, ON, N8W 5J9
(519) 255-1441   *SIC* 7381
G4S SECURICOR   *p 779*
See G4S CASH SOLUTIONS (CANADA) LTD
G4S SOLUTION VALEURS   *p 1248*
See CORPORATION GARDAWORLD SERVICES TRANSPORT DE VALEURS CANADA
GA INTERNATIONAL INC   *p 1236*
3208 AV JACQUES-BUREAU, MONTREAL, QC, H7P 0A9
(450) 973-9420   *SIC* 5131
GABBY'S RESTAURANT GROUP   *p 976*
See URBAN DINING GROUP INC
GABLES LODGE   *p 438*
See GEM HEALTH CARE GROUP LIMITED
GABRIEL CONSTRUCTION LTD   *p 1*
234 E 11TH AVE, REGINA, SK, S4N 6G8
(306) 757-1399   *SIC* 1542
GABRIEL COUTURE & FILS LTEE   *p 1081*
2 CH ST-ONGE, CLEVELAND, QC, J0B 2H0
(819) 826-3777   *SIC* 5211
GABRIEL HONDA   *p 1239*
See HANI AUTO INC
GABRIEL KIA   *p 1239*
See GABRIEL MONTREAL-NORD, S.E.C.
GABRIEL MILLER INC   *p 1264*
1850 RUE PROVINCIALE, QUEBEC, QC, G1N 4A2
(418) 628-5550 · *SIC* 1542
GABRIEL MONTREAL-NORD, S.E.C.   *p 1239*
6464 BOUL HENRI-BOURASSA E, MONTREAL-NORD, QC, H1G 5W9
(514) 323-7777   *SIC* 5511
GABRIEL RESOURCES LTD   *p 1440*
204 LAMBERT ST SUITE 200, WHITEHORSE, YT, Y1A 1Z4

SIC 1041
GABRIELE FLOOR & HOME   *p 644*
55 TALBOT ST W, LEAMINGTON, ON, N8H 1M5
(519) 326-5786   *SIC* 5211
GABRIELLA'S KITCHEN INC   *p 203*
910 FITZGERALD AVE UNIT 301, COURTENAY, BC, V9N 2R5
(250) 334-3209   *SIC* 5149
GACEQ   *p 1278*
See GROUPE D'APPROVISIONNEMENT EN COMMUN DE L'EST DU QUEBEC
GADAR PROMOTIONS   *p 832*
See 7786395 CANADA INC
GAETAN VERREAULT FUELS LIMITED   *p 913*
HIGHWAY 101 W, TIMMINS, ON, P4N 7H9
(705) 268-4199   *SIC* 5172
GAGE-BABCOCK & ASSOCIATES LTD   *p 319*
1195 BROADWAY W SUITE 228, VANCOUVER, BC, V6H 3X5
(604) 732-3751   *SIC* 7389
GAGNE, ISABELLE, PATRY, LAFLAMME & ASSOCIES NOTAIRES INC   *p 1106*
188 RUE MONTCALM BUREAU 300, GATINEAU, QC, J8Y 3B5
(819) 771-3231   *SIC* 7389
GAGNON CANTIN LACHAPELLE & ASSOCIES (SENCRL)   *p 1359*
2484 RUE CARTIER, SAINTE-JULIENNE, QC, J0K 2T0
(450) 831-2171   *SIC* 7389
GAGNON FRERES INC   *p 1079*
1460 BOUL TALBOT, CHICOUTIMI, QC, G7H 4C2
(418) 690-3366   *SIC* 5712
GAGNON IMAGE INC   *p 1285*
70 MONTEE INDUSTRIELLE-ET-COMMERCIALE BUREAU F, RIMOUSKI, QC, G5M 1B1
(418) 723-2394   *SIC* 5099
GAGNON SENECHAL COULOMBE & ASSOCIES   *p 1257*
800 BOUL DES CAPUCINS, QUEBEC, QC, G1J 3R8
(418) 648-1717   *SIC* 7389
GAGNON, CANTIN, LACHAPELLE, SASSEVILLE, ETHIER, RIOPEL, HEBERT, LORD (SENCRL) NOTAIRES   *p 1114*
37 PLACE BOURGET S BUREAU 301, JOLIETTE, QC, J6E 5G1
(450) 755-4535   *SIC* 7389
GAIN ENERGY LTD   *p 50*
520 3 AVE SW 30TH FL, CALGARY, AB, T2P 0R3
(403) 294-1336   *SIC* 1382
GAL AVIATION INC   *p 1394*
264 RUE ADRIEN-PATENAUDE, VAUDREUIL-DORION, QC, J7V 5V5
(514) 418-0033   *SIC* 3429
GALA SYSTEMES INC   *p 1308*
3185 1RE RUE, SAINT-HUBERT, QC, J3Y 8Y6
(450) 678-7226   *SIC* 3423
GALANE GOLD LTD   *p 962*
181 BAY ST SUITE 1800, TORONTO, ON, M5J 2T9
(647) 987-7663   *SIC* 1041
GALATA CHEMICALS (CANADA) INC   *p 497*
10 REAGEN'S INDUSTRIAL PKY, BRADFORD, ON, L3Z 0Z8
(905) 775-5000   *SIC* 5169
GALATI BROS SUPERMARKETS   *p 794*
See GALATI SUPERMARKETS (FINCH) LIMITED
GALATI BROS. SUPERMARKETS (JANE) LIMITED   *p 787*
4734 JANE ST, NORTH YORK, ON, M3N 2L2
SIC 5411
GALATI MARKET FRESH   *p 764*

See A & F GALATI LIMITED
GALATI MARKET FRESH INC   *p 765*
5845 LESLIE ST, NORTH YORK, ON, M2H 1J8
(416) 747-1899   *SIC* 5411
GALATI SUPERMARKETS (FINCH) LIMITED   *p 794*
2592 FINCH AVE W, NORTH YORK, ON, M9M 2G3
SIC 5411
GALAXY CINEMAS   *p 925*
See CINEPLEX ODEON CORPORATION
GALAXY CINEMAS   *p 925*
See GALAXY ENTERTAINMENT INC
GALAXY ENTERTAINMENT INC   *p 925*
1303 YONGE ST SUITE 100, TORONTO, ON, M4T 2Y9
(416) 323-6600   *SIC* 7832
GALAXY HOME FURNISHING INC   *p 739*
455 GIBRALTAR DR, MISSISSAUGA, ON, L5T 2S9
(905) 670-5555   *SIC* 5021
GALAXY SECURITY   *p 675*
See SMARTEYES DIRECT INC
GALDERMA CANADA INC   *p 904*
55 COMMERCE VALLEY DR W SUITE 400, THORNHILL, ON, L3T 7V9
(905) 762-2500   *SIC* 5122
GALE'S FUELS   *p 757*
See GALE'S GAS BARS LIMITED
GALE'S GAS BARS LIMITED   *p 757*
4388 PORTAGE RD, NIAGARA FALLS, ON, L2E 6A4
(905) 356-4820   *SIC* 5541
GALE'S WHOLESALE LTD   *p 1416*
1602 ELLIOTT ST, REGINA, SK, S4N 6L1
(306) 757-8545   *SIC* 5193
GALENOVA INC   *p 1312*
4555 AV BEAUDRY, SAINT-HYACINTHE, QC, J2S 8W2
(450) 778-2837   *SIC* 5122
GALERIE CONFORT   *p 1368*
See CORPORATION ZEDBED INTERNATIONAL INC
GALERIE DU JOUET   *p 1045*
See LA GALERIE DU JOUET JFA INC
GALERIE DU MEUBLE, LA   *p 1225*
See G2MC INC
GALERIE DU SOMMEIL   *p 1079*
See GAGNON FRERES INC
GALERIES DE GRANBY   *p 1200*
See WESTCLIFF MANAGEMENT LTD
GALERIES FORD INC, LES   *p 1116*
3443 BOUL DU ROYAUME, JONQUIERE, QC, G7X 0C5
(418) 542-9551   *SIC* 5511
GALERIES ST HYACINTHE, LES   *p 1311*
See BEAUWARD SHOPPING CENTRES LTD
GALERIES TASCHEREAU   *p 1396*
See CANADIAN AUSTIN GROUP HOLDINGS ULC
GALIAM SECURITY CANADA   *p 934*
See INFINIUM CAPITAL CORPORATION
GALKO HOMES LTD   *p 142*
407 MAYOR MAGRATH DR S, LETHBRIDGE, AB, T1J 3L8
(403) 329-3221   *SIC* 1521
GALL CONSTRUCTION LIMITED   *p 635*
1550 VICTORIA ST N, KITCHENER, ON, N2B 3E2
(519) 743-6357   *SIC* 6519
GALLAGHER BASSETT CANADA INC   *p 774*
4311 YONGE ST SUITE 404, NORTH YORK, ON, M2P 1N6
(416) 861-8212   *SIC* 6411
GALLAGHER BROS CONTRACTORS LTD   *p 279*
19140 28 AVE UNIT 114, SURREY, BC, V3Z 6M3
(604) 531-3156   *SIC* 1742
GALLAGHER, ARTHUR J (CANADA)

GROUP   *p 578*
185 THE WEST MALL SUITE 1710, ETOBICOKE, ON, M9C 5L5
(416) 620-8030   *SIC* 6411
GALLAGHER, ARTHUR J. CANADA LIMITED   *p 951*
181 UNIVERSITY AVE UNIT 1200, TORONTO, ON, M5H 3M7
(416) 260-5333   *SIC* 6411
GALLAGHERS CANYON GOLF COURSE (KELOWNA)   *p 313*
See GOLFBC HOLDINGS INC
GALLANT ENTERPRISES LTD   *p 399*
194 RUE ST-FRANCOIS SUITE 210, EDMUNDSTON, NB, E3V 1E9
(506) 739-9390   *SIC* 5093
GALLANT, RAYMOND & SONS LTD   *p 412*
11055 RUE PRINCIPALE, ROGERSVILLE, NB, E4Y 2L8
(506) 775-2797   *SIC* 5531
GALLERIA SUPERMARKET   *p 906*
See 2024232 ONTARIO INC
GALLIMARD LTEE   *p 1185*
3700A BOUL SAINT-LAURENT, MONTREAL, QC, H2X 2V4
(514) 499-0072   *SIC* 5192
GALLINGER FORD LINCOLN   *p 683*
See GALLINGER MOTORS LIMITED
GALLINGER MOTORS LIMITED   *p 683*
655 MAIN ST E, MILTON, ON, L9T 3J2
(905) 875-3673   *SIC* 5511
GALLOWAY CONSTRUCTION GROUP LTD   *p 152*
431029 RANGE RD 261, PONOKA, AB, T4J 1R4
(403) 783-2599   *SIC* 1623
GALLOWAY LUMBER   *p 214*
See GALLOWAY LUMBER COMPANY LTD
GALLOWAY LUMBER COMPANY LTD   *p 214*
7325 GALLOWAY MILL RD, GALLOWAY, BC, V0B 1T2
(250) 429-3496   *SIC* 2421
GALON INSURANCE BROKERS   *p 1427*
See GALON MANAGEMENT LTD
GALON MANAGEMENT LTD   *p 1427*
909 3RD AVE N, SASKATOON, SK, S7K 2K4
(306) 244-7000   *SIC* 6411
GALT CHRYSLER DODGE LTD   *p 539*
2440 EAGLE ST N, CAMBRIDGE, ON, N3H 4R7
(519) 650-2440   *SIC* 5511
GALT COLLEGIATE INST & VOCATIONAL   *p 535*
See WATERLOO REGION DISTRICT SCHOOL BOARD
GALVAN METAL   *p 1238*
See 3323501 CANADA INC
GALVANIC APPLIED SCIENCES INC   *p 35*
7000 FISHER RD SE, CALGARY, AB, T2H 0W3
(403) 252-8470   *SIC* 3825
GALVANISATION QUEBEC INC   *p 1254*
225 RUE JEREMIE-PACAUD, PRINCEVILLE, QC, G6L 0A1
(819) 505-4440   *SIC* 3479
GALVANIZE   *p 325*
See ACL SERVICES LTD
GALVCAST MANUFACTURING INC   *p 473*
49 COMMERCE CRES, ACTON, ON, L7J 2X2
(519) 853-3540   *SIC* 3479
GAMBLES ONTARIO PRODUCE INC   *p 572*
165 THE QUEENSWAY SUITE 240, ETOBICOKE, ON, M8Y 1H8
(416) 259-6391   *SIC* 5148
GAMBO DRUGS LIMITED   *p 424*
GD, HILLVIEW, NL, A0E 2A0
(709) 546-2460   *SIC* 5961
GAMEHOST INC   *p 128*
9825 HARDIN ST, FORT MCMURRAY, AB, T9H 4G9

(780) 790-9739   *SIC* 7999
GAMEHOST INC   p 157
548 LAURA AVE SUITE 104, RED DEER COUNTY, AB, T4E 0A5
(403) 346-4545   *SIC* 7011
GAMEX INC   p 1113
609 RUE PRINCIPALE, ILE-AUX-NOIX, QC, J0J 1G0
(450) 246-3881   *SIC* 5531
GAMMA FOUNDRIES INC   p 855
115 NEWKIRK RD, RICHMOND HILL, ON, L4C 3G4
(905) 884-9091   *SIC* 3325
GAMMA INDUSTRIES   p 1119
See GAMMA MURS ET FENETRES INTERNATIONAL INC
GAMMA MURS ET FENETRES INTERNATIONAL INC   p 1119
6130 BOUL SAINTE-ANNE, L'ANGE GARDIEN, QC, G0A 2K0
(418) 822-1448   *SIC* 5211
GAMMA SALES INC   p 809
100 HUNTER VALLEY RD, ORILLIA, ON, L3V 0Y7
(705) 325-3088   *SIC* 5013
GAMME SIGNATURE PASSION   p 1114
See 8561567 CANADA INC
GAMSBY AND MANNEROW LIMITED p 603
255 WOODLAWN RD W SUITE 210, GUELPH, ON, N1H 8J1
(519) 824-8150   *SIC* 8711
GANANOQUE BOAT LINE LIMITED   p 592
280 MAIN ST, GANANOQUE, ON, K7G 2M2
(613) 382-2144   *SIC* 4489
GANANOQUE CHEV CADILLAC   p 592
See GANANOQUE MOTORS LTD
GANANOQUE MOTORS LTD   p 592
439 KING ST E, GANANOQUE, ON, K7G 1G9
(613) 382-2168   *SIC* 5511
GANDER ACADEMY   p 423
See NEWFOUNDLAND AND LABRADOR ENGLISH SCHOOL DISTRICT
GANDER CONSUMERS CO-OP   p 423
See GANDER CONSUMERS CO-OPERATIVE SOCIETY LIMITED
GANDER CONSUMERS CO-OPERATIVE SOCIETY LIMITED   p 423
72 ELIZABETH DR, GANDER, NL, A1V 1J8
(709) 256-4843   *SIC* 5411
GANGSTER ENTERPRISES LTD   p 75
600 CROWFOOT CRES NW SUITE 230, CALGARY, AB, T3G 0B4
(403) 241-9494   *SIC* 4212
GANOHKWA SRA FAMILY ASSAULT SUPPORT SERVICES   p 806
1781 CHIEFSWOOD RD, OHSWEKEN, ON, N0A 1M0
(519) 445-4324   *SIC* 8699
GANONG BROS., LIMITED   p 418
1 CHOCOLATE DR, ST STEPHEN, NB, E3L 2X5
(506) 465-5600   *SIC* 2064
GANOTEC INC   p 1247
3777 RUE DOLLARD-DESJARDINS, POINTE-AUX-TREMBLES, QC, H1B 5W9
(819) 377-5533   *SIC* 1541
GANOTEC WEST ULC   p 1
26230 TWP RD 531A UNIT 131, ACHESON, AB, T7X 5A4
(780) 960-7450   *SIC* 1541
GANT PARIS DU CANADA LTEE, LE p 1329
2315 RUE COHEN, SAINT-LAURENT, QC, H4R 2N7
(514) 345-0135   *SIC* 5136
GANTERIE CLOUTIER   p 1351
See ENTREPRISES CLOUTIER, ALBERT LTEE, LES
GANTREX CANADA INC   p 474
12 BARR RD, AJAX, ON, L1S 3X9
(905) 686-0560   *SIC* 5051
GANZ   p 1031

1 PEARCE RD, WOODBRIDGE, ON, L4L 3T2
(905) 851-6661   *SIC* 5199
GANZ CANADA   p 1031
See GANZ
GAP   p 35
See GAP (CANADA) INC
GAP   p 71
See GAP (CANADA) INC
GAP   p 190
See GAP (CANADA) INC
GAP   p 503
See GAP (CANADA) INC
GAP   p 935
See GAP (CANADA) INC
GAP (CANADA) INC   p 35
6455 MACLEOD TRAIL SW SUITE 151, CALGARY, AB, T2H 0K3
(403) 640-1305   *SIC* 5651
GAP (CANADA) INC   p 35
6455 MACLEOD TRAIL SW SUITE 210, CALGARY, AB, T2H 0K8
(403) 640-1303   *SIC* 5651
GAP (CANADA) INC   p 71
3625 SHAGANAPPI TRAIL NW, CALGARY, AB, T3A 0E2
(403) 288-5188   *SIC* 5651
GAP (CANADA) INC   p 190
4700 KINGSWAY SUITE 2138, BURNABY, BC, V5H 4M1
(604) 431-6559   *SIC* 5651
GAP (CANADA) INC   p 503
89 WALKER DR, BRAMPTON, ON, L6T 5K5
(905) 793-8888   *SIC* 5651
GAP (CANADA) INC   p 510
9500 MCLAUGHLIN RD, BRAMPTON, ON, L6X 0B8
(905) 460-2060   *SIC* 5651
GAP (CANADA) INC   p 553
1 BASS PRO MILLS DR, CONCORD, ON, L4K 5W4
(905) 761-7577   *SIC* 5651
GAP (CANADA) INC   p 928
60 BLOOR ST W SUITE 1501, TORONTO, ON, M4W 3B8
(416) 921-2225   *SIC* 5651
GAP (CANADA) INC   p 935
220 YONGE ST, TORONTO, ON, M5B 2H1
(416) 595-6336   *SIC* 5651
GAP (CANADA) INC   p 935
260 YONGE ST, TORONTO, ON, M5B 2L9
(416) 599-8802   *SIC* 5651
GAP CONSTRUCTION CO. LTD   p 763
1310 FRANKLIN ST, NORTH BAY, ON, P1B 2M3
(705) 474-3730   *SIC* 1542
GAP NEUROS   p 1058
See APGN INC
GAP OUTLET   p 553
See GAP (CANADA) INC
GAP WIRELESS INC   p 722
2880 ARGENTIA RD UNIT 8-9, MISSISSAUGA, ON, L5N 7X8
(905) 826-3781   *SIC* 5065
GARAGA INC   p 1305
8500 25E AV, SAINT-GEORGES, QC, G6A 1K5
(418) 227-2828   *SIC* 3442
GARAGE CIVIC LIMITEE   p 1091
3650 BOUL DES SOURCES, DOLLARD-DES-ORMEAUX, QC, H9B 1Z9
(514) 683-5533   *SIC* 5511
GARAGE CLEMENT FOURNIER INC p 1138
4560 BOUL GUILLAUME-COUTURE, LEVIS, QC, G6W 6M7
(418) 837-0859   *SIC* 5541
GARAGE COSSETTE   p 1368
See GARAGE F COSSETTE INC
GARAGE DESHARNAIS & FILS LTEE   p 1279
6055 BOUL PIERRE-BERTRAND, QUEBEC, QC, G2K 1M1
(418) 628-0203   *SIC* 7538
GARAGE DODGE CHRYSLER DE SAINT-

BASILE INC   p 1294
225 BOUL SIR-WILFRID-LAURIER, SAINT-BASILE-LE-GRAND, QC, J3N 1M2
(450) 653-0114   *SIC* 5511
GARAGE F COSSETTE INC   p 1368
10303 BOUL DES HETRES, SHAWINIGAN, QC, G9N 4Y2
(819) 539-5457   *SIC* 5511
GARAGE FLORENT BEGIN INC   p 1124
1483 277 RTE, LAC-ETCHEMIN, QC, G0R 1S0
(418) 625-6101   *SIC* 5511
GARAGE FRANKE INC   p 1354
180 RUE PRINCIPALE E, SAINTE-AGATHE-DES-MONTS, QC, J8C 1K3
(819) 326-4775   *SIC* 5511
GARAGE GHISLAIN LECLERC   p 1287
See 9071-0575 QUEBEC INC
GARAGE JEAN-ROCH THIBEAULT INC   p 1054
909 BOUL MONSEIGNEUR-DE LAVAL, BAIE-SAINT-PAUL, QC, G3Z 2V9
(418) 435-2379   *SIC* 5511
GARAGE MONTPLAISIR LTEE   p 1098
875 BOUL SAINT-JOSEPH, DRUMMONDVILLE, QC, J2C 2C4
(819) 477-2323   *SIC* 7549
GARAGE P VENNE INC   p 1283
94 RUE NOTRE-DAME, REPENTIGNY, QC, J6A 2P3
(514) 343-3428   *SIC* 5511
GARAGE POIRIER & FILS LTEE   p 1390
1780 3E AV, VAL-D'OR, QC, J9P 1W4
(819) 825-5214   *SIC* 5521
GARAGE REJEAN ROY INC   p 1397
465 BOUL DES BOIS-FRANCS N, VICTORIAVILLE, QC, G6P 1H1
(819) 758-8000   *SIC* 5511
GARAGE RENAUD FORTIER INC   p 1375
4320 BOUL BOURQUE, SHERBROOKE, QC, J1N 1S3
(819) 562-1700   *SIC* 5511
GARAGE SAVIGNAC, P E LTEE   p 1114
671 RUE SAINT-THOMAS, JOLIETTE, QC, J6E 3R6
(450) 756-4563   *SIC* 5651
GARAGE TARDIF LTEE   p 1046
1222 111 RTE E, AMOS, QC, J9T 1N1
(819) 732-5314   *SIC* 5521
GARAGE VILLEMAIRE & FILS INC   p 1300
55 RUE GREGOIRE, SAINT-ESPRIT, QC, J0K 2L0
(450) 839-7777   *SIC* 5014
GARAGE WINDSOR LTEE   p 1286
287 RUE TEMISCOUATA, RIVIERE-DU-LOUP, QC, G5R 2Y7
(418) 862-3586   *SIC* 5511
GARANT   p 1377
See GARANT GP
GARANT GP   p 1377
375 CH SAINT-FRANCOIS O, ST-FRANCOIS-DE-LA-RIVIERE-DU-S, QC, G0R 3A0
(418) 259-7711   *SIC* 3423
GARANTIE CONSTRUCTION RESIDENTIELLE   p 1052
See GARANTIE DE CONSTRUCTION RESIDENTIELLE (GCR), LA
GARANTIE DE CONSTRUCTION RESIDENTIELLE (GCR), LA   p 1052
7171 RUE JEAN-TALON E BUREAU 200, ANJOU, QC, H1M 3N2
(514) 657-2333   *SIC* 6351
GARANTIE NATIONALE   p 1236
See GARANTIES NATIONALES MRWV LIMITEE, LES
GARANTIES NATIONALES MRWV LIMITEE, LES   p 1236
4605 RUE LOUIS-B.-MAYER, MONTREAL, QC, H7P 6G5

(450) 688-9496   *SIC* 6399
GARAVENTA (CANADA) LTD   p 279
18920 36 AVE, SURREY, BC, V3Z 0P6
(604) 594-0422   *SIC* 3999
GARBANZO BIKE & BEAN   p 343
See WHISTLER & BLACKCOMB MOUNTAIN RESORTS LIMITED
GARBO CREATIONS   p 791
See GARBO GROUP INC
GARBO GROUP INC   p 791
34 WINGOLD AVE, NORTH YORK, ON, M6B 1P5
(416) 782-9500   *SIC* 5094
GARDA   p 703
See CORPORATION DE SECURITE GARDA CANADA
GARDA CANADA SECURITY CORPORATION   p 88
See CORPORATION DE SECURITE GARDA CANADA
GARDA CANADA SECURITY CORPORATION   p 128
See CORPORATION DE SECURITE GARDA CANADA
GARDA DU CANADA   p 1119
See GROUPE DE SECURITE GARDA INC, LE
GARDA SECURITE   p 1104
See GROUPE DE SECURITE GARDA INC, LE
GARDA SECURITY SERVICES   p 1418
See GROUPE DE SECURITE GARDA INC, LE
GARDEL METAL PRODUCTS INCORPORATED   p 852
140 WEST BEAVER CREEK RD UNIT 1, RICHMOND HILL, ON, L4B 1C2
(905) 881-7992   *SIC* 3499
GARDEN BASKET FOOD MARKETS INCORPORATED, THE   p 670
7676 WOODBINE AVE UNIT 1, MARKHAM, ON, L3R 2N2
(905) 305-8220   *SIC* 5411
GARDEN BASKET FOOD MARKETS INCORPORATED, THE   p 679
9271 MARKHAM RD, MARKHAM, ON, L6E 1A1
(905) 471-0777   *SIC* 5411
GARDEN BASKET, THE   p 670
See GARDEN BASKET FOOD MARKETS INCORPORATED, THE
GARDEN BASKET, THE   p 679
See GARDEN BASKET FOOD MARKETS INCORPORATED, THE
GARDEN CITY CHRYSLER JEEP   p 352
See GARDEN CITY CHRYSLER PLYMOUTH LTD
GARDEN CITY CHRYSLER PLYMOUTH LTD   p 352
220 STEPHEN ST, MORDEN, MB, R6M 1T4
(204) 822-6296   *SIC* 5511
GARDEN CITY CUSTOMS SERVICES INC p 759
6045 PROGRESS ST, NIAGARA FALLS, ON, L2G 7X1
(905) 353-8735   *SIC* 4731
GARDEN CITY GROWERS INC   p 761
405 CONCESSION 5 RD, NIAGARA ON THE LAKE, ON, L0S 1J0
(905) 685-1120   *SIC* 5992
GARDEN CITY WAREHOUSING & DISTRIBUTION LTD   p 233
839 OLD VICTORIA RD, NANAIMO, BC, V9R 5Z9
(250) 754-5447   *SIC* 5141
GARDEN FOODS - BOLTON LTD   p 494
501 QUEEN ST S, BOLTON, ON, L7E 1A1
(905) 857-1227   *SIC* 5411

GARDEN GROVE DISTRIBUTION (2013) LTD p 371
440 JARVIS AVE, WINNIPEG, MB, R2W 3A6
SIC 5148
GARDEN HOME (1986) INCORPORATED p 1039
310 NORTH RIVER RD, CHARLOTTE-TOWN, PE, C1A 3M4
(902) 892-4131 *SIC 8051*
GARDEN TERRACE p 625
See OMNI HEALTH CARE LTD
GARDEN TERRACE LOUNGE p 69
See PASUTTO'S HOTELS (1984) LTD
GARDEN VALLEY COLLEGIATE p 361
See GARDEN VALLEY SCHOOL DIVISION
GARDEN VALLEY SCHOOL DIVISION p 361
750 TRIPLE E BLVD, WINKLER, MB, R6W 0M7
(204) 325-8335 *SIC 8211*
GARDEN VALLEY SCHOOL DIVISION p 361
GARDEN VALLEY COLLEGIATE, WIN-KLER, MB, R6W 4C8
(204) 325-8208 *SIC 8211*
GARDENWORKS p 184
See CANADA GARDENWORKS LTD
GARDERIE DU CENTRE Y CARTIERVILLE p 1214
See YMCA DU QUEBEC, LES
GARDERIE LASALLE DES PETITS p 1214
See COLLEGE LASALLE
GARDEWINE GROUP INC p 369
60 EAGLE DR, WINNIPEG, MB, R2R 1V5
(204) 633-5795 *SIC 4731*
GARDEWINE NORTH p 369
See GARDEWINE GROUP INC
GARDINER DAM TERMINAL JOINT VENTURE p 1436
GD, STRONGFIELD, SK, S0H 3Z0
(306) 857-2134 *SIC 5153*
GARDINER DAM TERMINAL LTD p 1409
HWY 19 OLD HWY SUITE 44, LOREBURN, SK, S0H 2S0
(306) 857-2134 *SIC 5153*
GARDINER ROBERTS LLP p 951
22 ADELAIDE ST W UNIT 3600, TORONTO, ON, M5H 4E3
(416) 865-6600 *SIC 8111*
GARDNER CHEVROLET OLDSMOBILE LTD p 215
945 WATER AVE, HOPE, BC, V0X 1L0
(604) 869-2002 *SIC 5511*
GARDNER CHEVROLET PONTIAC BUICK GMC LTD p 215
945 WATER ST, HOPE, BC, V0X 1L0
(604) 869-9511 *SIC 5511*
GARDNER DENVER CANADA CORP p 803
2390 SOUTH SERVICE RD W, OAKVILLE, ON, L6L 5M9
(905) 847-0688 *SIC 5172*
GARDNER ELECTRIC LTD p 416
875 BAYSIDE DR, SAINT JOHN, NB, E2R 1A3
(506) 634-3918 *SIC 1731*
GARDNER MOTORS (1981) LTD p 146
1500 STRACHAN RD SE, MEDICINE HAT, AB, T1B 4V2
(403) 527-2248 *SIC 5511*
GARDWELL SECURITY AGENCY INC p 787
168 OAKDALE RD SUITE 6B, NORTH YORK, ON, M3N 2S5
(416) 746-6007 *SIC 7381*
GAREAU AUTO INC p 1390
1100 3E AV E, VAL-D'OR, QC, J9P 0J6
(819) 825-6880 *SIC 5511*
GARIBALDI GLASS INDUSTRIES INC p 181
8183 WIGGINS ST, BURNABY, BC, V3N 0C4
(604) 420-4527 *SIC 3231*
GARIBALDI SECONDARY SCHOOL p 231
See SCHOOL DISTRICT NO 42 (MAPLE

RIDGE-PITT MEADOWS)
GARIER INC p 1152
13050 RUE BRAULT UNITE 123, MIRABEL, QC, J7J 0W4
(450) 437-7852 *SIC 3569*
GARLAND CANADA p 695
See GARLAND COMMERCIAL RANGES LIMITED
GARLAND CANADA INC p 584
209 CARRIER DR, ETOBICOKE, ON, M9W 5Y8
(416) 747-7995 *SIC 5211*
GARLAND COMMERCIAL RANGES LIMITED p 695
1177 KAMATO RD, MISSISSAUGA, ON, L4W 1X4
(905) 624-0260 *SIC 3589*
GARLOCK CEALING TECHNOLGY p 1373
See GARLOCK OF CANADA LTD
GARLOCK OF CANADA LTD p 1373
4100 RUE DE LA GARLOCK, SHER-BROOKE, QC, J1L 1W5
(819) 563-8080 *SIC 2299*
GARMIN CANADA INC p 80
30 BOW ST COMMON UNIT 124, COCHRANE, AB, T4C 2N1
(403) 932-9292 *SIC 8731*
GARNEAU MANUFACTURING INC p 147
8806 98 ST, MORINVILLE, AB, T8R 1K7
(780) 939-2129 *SIC 3499*
GARNET INSTRUMENTS LTD p 161
286 KASKA RD, SHERWOOD PARK, AB, T8A 4G7
(780) 467-1010 *SIC 5084*
GARON, LAWRENCE M ENTERPRISES LTD p 846
287 WEST SIDE RD, PORT COLBORNE, ON, L3K 5L2
(905) 835-1155 *SIC 5531*
GAROY CONSTRUCTION INC p 1256
4000 BOUL SAINTE-ANNE, QUEBEC, QC, G1E 3M5
(418) 661-1754 *SIC 1542*
GARRISON ESTATES INC p 197
5905 COWICHAN ST, CHILLIWACK, BC, V2R 0G8
(604) 834-3508 *SIC 1521*
GARRITANO BROS. LTD p 812
881 NELSON ST, OSHAWA, ON, L1H 5N7
(905) 576-8642 *SIC 1542*
GARROD FOOD BROKERS LTD p 23
7777 10 ST NE SUITE 120, CALGARY, AB, T2E 8X2
(403) 291-2818 *SIC 5141*
GARRTECH INC p 892
910 ARVIN AVE, STONEY CREEK, ON, L8E 5Y8
(905) 643-6414 *SIC 3544*
GARRY MACHINE MFG INC p 735
165 STATESMAN DR, MISSISSAUGA, ON, L5S 1X4
(905) 564-5340 *SIC 3569*
GARSON PIPE CONTRACTORS LIMITED p 593
1191 O'NEIL DR W, GARSON, ON, P3L 1L5
(705) 693-1242 *SIC 1623*
GARTH WEBB SECONDARY SCHOOL p 805
See HALTON DISTRICT SCHOOL BOARD
GARY DANIELS PHARMACIES LTD p 606
7 CLAIR RD W SUITE 1213, GUELPH, ON, N1L 0A6
(519) 763-3431 *SIC 5912*
GARY JONAS COMPUTING LTD p 1000
8133 WARDEN AVE SUITE 400, UNIONVILLE, ON, L6G 1B3
(905) 470-4600 *SIC 7371*
GAS ALBERTA INC p 8
2618 HOPEWELL PLACE NE SUITE 350, CALGARY, AB, T1Y 7J7
(403) 509-2600 *SIC 4924*
GAS DRIVE GLOBAL LP p 12
4700 47 ST SE, CALGARY, AB, T2B 3R1

(403) 387-6300 *SIC 7699*
GAS DRIVE GLOBAL LP p 1358
2091 RUE LEONARD-DE VINCI UNITE A, SAINTE-JULIE, QC, J3E 1Z2
(450) 649-3174 *SIC 7699*
GAS KING OIL CO. LTD p 142
1604 2 AVE S, LETHBRIDGE, AB, T1J 0G2
(403) 320-2142 *SIC 5541*
GASPARD p 372
See GASPARD REGALIA INC
GASPARD & SONS (1963) LIMITED p 372
1266 FIFE ST, WINNIPEG, MB, R2X 2N6
(204) 949-5700 *SIC 2389*
GASPARD LP p 372
1266 FIFE ST, WINNIPEG, MB, R2X 2N6
(204) 949-5700 *SIC 2389*
GASPARD REGALIA INC p 372
1266 FIFE ST, WINNIPEG, MB, R2X 2N6
(204) 949-5700 *SIC 5137*
GASPE CURED p 1173
See 150147 CANADA INC
GASPRO, DIVISION OF PRORESP INC p 649
See PRORESP INC
GASTALDO CONCRETE HOLDINGS LTD p 206
482 FRASERVIEW PL, DELTA, BC, V3M 6H4
(604) 525-3636 *SIC 6712*
GASTALDO CONCRETE LTD p 206
482 FRASERVIEW PL, DELTA, BC, V3M 6H4
(604) 526-6262 *SIC 1771*
GASTALDO PUMP SALES LTD p 206
482 FRASERVIEW PL, DELTA, BC, V3M 6H4
(604) 526-6262 *SIC 5084*
GASTEM INC p 1204
1155 BOUL ROBERT-BOURASSA UNITE 1215, MONTREAL, QC, H3B 3A7
SIC 1382
GASTIER M.P. INC p 1049
10400 BOUL DU GOLF, ANJOU, QC, H1J 2Y7
(514) 325-4220 *SIC 1731*
GASTON OUELLETTE & FILS INC p 1240
9960 BOUL SAINT-VITAL, MONTREAL-NORD, QC, H1H 4S6
(514) 388-3927 *SIC 1731*
GASTOPS LTD p 596
1011 POLYTEK ST, GLOUCESTER, ON, K1J 9J3
(613) 744-3530 *SIC 8711*
GASTRONOME ANIMAL INC, LE p 1356
300 RANG DES ECOSSAIS, SAINTE-BRIGIDE-D'IBERVILLE, QC, J0J 1X0
(450) 469-0921 *SIC 5191*
GASTRONOMIA ALIMENTS FINS INC p 1215
1619B RUE WILLIAM, MONTREAL, QC, H3J 1R1
(514) 281-6400 *SIC 5142*
GATE GOURMET CANADA INC p 695
2498 BRITANNIA RD E, MISSISSAUGA, ON, L4W 2P7
(905) 405-4100 *SIC 5812*
GATEBY CARE FACILITY p 332
3000 GATEBY PL, VERNON, BC, V1T 8V8
(250) 545-4456 *SIC 8051*
GATEMAN-MILLOY INC p 637
270 SHOEMAKER ST, KITCHENER, ON, N2E 3E1
(519) 748-6500 *SIC 0781*
GATES CANADA INC p 515
225 HENRY ST BLDG 8, BRANTFORD, ON, N3S 7R4
(519) 759-4141 *SIC 5085*
GATES CANADA INC p 1019
3303 ST ETIENNE BLVD, WINDSOR, ON, N8W 5B1
(519) 945-4200 *SIC 3568*
GATES-WINDSOR OPERATIONS, DIV OF p 1019
See GATES CANADA INC

GATESTONE & CO. INC p 776
180 DUNCAN MILL RD UNIT 300, NORTH YORK, ON, M3B 1Z6
(416) 961-9622 *SIC 7322*
GATEWAY CASINO THUNDER BAY p 908
See GATEWAY CASINOS & ENTERTAIN-MENT LIMITED
GATEWAY CASINOS & ENTERTAINMENT INC p 189
4331 DOMINION ST, BURNABY, BC, V5G 1C7
(604) 412-0166 *SIC 7011*
GATEWAY CASINOS & ENTERTAINMENT INC p 237
350 GIFFORD ST SUITE 1, NEW WEST-MINSTER, BC, V3M 7A3
(604) 777-2946 *SIC 7011*
GATEWAY CASINOS & ENTERTAINMENT LIMITED p 189
4331 DOMINION ST, BURNABY, BC, V5G 1C7
(604) 412-0166 *SIC 7011*
GATEWAY CASINOS & ENTERTAINMENT LIMITED p 908
50 CUMBERLAND ST S, THUNDER BAY, ON, P7B 5L4
(877) 656-4263 *SIC 7999*
GATEWAY CHEVROLET INC p 503
2 GATEWAY BLVD, BRAMPTON, ON, L6T 4A7
(905) 791-7111 *SIC 5511*
GATEWAY CHEVROLET OLDSMOBILE INC p 503
2 GATEWAY BLVD, BRAMPTON, ON, L6T 4A7
(905) 791-7111 *SIC 5511*
GATEWAY CO-OPERATIVE LTD p 1405
707 NORWAY RD, CANORA, SK, S0A 0L0
(306) 563-5637 *SIC 5399*
GATEWAY CONSTRUCTION & ENGINEERING LTD p 365
434 ARCHIBALD ST, WINNIPEG, MB, R2J 0X5
(204) 233-8550 *SIC 1542*
GATEWAY HAVEN p 1016
See CORPORATION OF THE COUNTY OF BRUCE, THE
GATEWAY HOME HOUSE p 274
See FRASER HEALTH AUTHORITY
GATEWAY INSURANCE BROKERS LTD p 457
371 ST MARGARETS BAY RD SUITE 101, HALIFAX, NS, B3N 1J8
(902) 431-9300 *SIC 6411*
GATEWAY INSURANCE GROUP p 457
See GATEWAY INSURANCE BROKERS LTD
GATEWAY LODGE INC p 1405
212 CENTRE AVE E, CANORA, SK, S0A 0L0
(306) 563-5685 *SIC 8051*
GATEWAY MECHANICAL SERVICES INC p 30
4001 16A ST SE, CALGARY, AB, T2G 3T5
(403) 265-0010 *SIC 1711*
GATEWAY MECHANICAL SERVICES INC p 93
14605 118 AVE NW, EDMONTON, AB, T5L 2M7
(780) 426-6055 *SIC 1711*
GATEWAY MOTORS (EDMONTON) LTD p 124
2020 103A ST SW, EDMONTON, AB, T6W 2P6
(780) 439-3939 *SIC 5511*
GATEWAY PETROLEUM p 1038
See J.D. FOX ENTERPRISES INC
GATEWAY PROPERTY MANAGEMENT CORPORATION p 207
11950 80 AVE SUITE 400, DELTA, BC, V4C 1Y2
(604) 635-5000 *SIC 8741*
GATEWAY REPAIRS TRUCK & TRAILER

LTD   p 124
14203 157 AVE NW, EDMONTON, AB, T6V 0K8
(780) 451-3343   *SIC 7539*

GATEWAY SECURITIES INC   p 313
1177 HASTINGS ST W SUITE 168, VANCOUVER, BC, V6E 2K3
SIC 6211

GATEWAY TOYOTA   p 124
See *GATEWAY MOTORS (EDMONTON) LTD*

GATEWAY TUBULARS LTD   p 50
144 4 AVE SW SUITE 2800, CALGARY, AB, T2P 3N4
(403) 457-2288   *SIC 5051*

GATEWAYS INTERNATIONAL   p 852
See *JOY OF TRAVEL LTD, THE*

GATEWAYS INTERNATIONAL INC   p 852
30 WERTHEIM CRT UNIT 20, RICHMOND HILL, ON, L4B 1B9
(905) 889-0483   *SIC 4725*

GATHER INVESTMENTS LIMITED   p 990
172 OSSINGTON AVE, TORONTO, ON, M6J 2Z7
(416) 532-2813   *SIC 5211*

GATINEAU HONDA   p 1104
See *3248224 CANADA INC*

GATINEAU NISSAN   p 1104
See *4544391 CANADA INC*

GATSBY VALET INC   p 688
6900 AIRPORT RD, MISSISSAUGA, ON, L4V 1E8
(416) 239-6998   *SIC 7299*

GATSTEEL   p 589
See *VENTURE STEEL INC*

GATSTEEL INDUSTRIES INC   p 584
361 ATTWELL DR, ETOBICOKE, ON, M9W 5C2
(416) 675-2370   *SIC 5051*

GAUDREAU ENVIRONNEMENT (DIVISION QUEBEC)   p 1399
See *GAUDREAU ENVIRONNEMENT INC*

GAUDREAU ENVIRONNEMENT INC p 1399
365 BOUL DE LA BONAVENTURE, VICTORIAVILLE, QC, G6T 1V5
(819) 758-8378   *SIC 7359*

GAUDREAU, MARC INC   p 394
384 OLD VAL D'AMOUR RD, ATHOLVILLE, NB, E3N 4E3
(506) 789-0220   *SIC 5531*

GAUTHIER CHRYSLER DODGE JEEP   p 362
1375 REGENT AVE W, WINNIPEG, MB, R2C 3B2
(204) 661-8999   *SIC 5511*

GAUTHIER, J C INSURANCE BROKER & ASSOCIATES INC   p 821
428 RIDEAU ST SUITE 101, OTTAWA, ON, K1N 5Z2
(613) 789-4140   *SIC 6411*

GAUTHIER, JIM CHEVROLET LTD   p 370
1400 MCPHILLIPS ST, WINNIPEG, MB, R2V 4G6
(204) 697-1400   *SIC 5511*

GAUTHIER, JIM COLLISION CENTRE, DIV OF   p 370
See *GAUTHIER, JIM PONTIAC BUICK GMC LTD*

GAUTHIER, JIM PONTIAC BUICK GMC LTD p 370
2400 MCPHILLIPS ST, WINNIPEG, MB, R2V 4J6
(204) 633-8833   *SIC 7515*

GAUTHIER, VINCE R. DRUGS LTD   p 1021
500 TECUMSEH RD E, WINDSOR, ON, N8X 2S2
(519) 253-1115   *SIC 5912*

GAUVREAU TOP SOIL   p 1108
See *ENTREPRISES D. GAUVREAU ENR*

GAVILLER & COMPANY LLP   p 835
945 3RD AVE E SUITE 201, OWEN SOUND, ON, N4K 2K8
(519) 376-5850   *SIC 8721*

GAY LEA FOODS   p 603

See *GAY LEA FOODS CO-OPERATIVE LIMITED*

GAY LEA FOODS CO-OPERATIVE LIMITED   p 603
21 SPEEDVALE AVE W, GUELPH, ON, N1H 1J5
(519) 822-5530   *SIC 2021*

GAY LEA FOODS CO-OPERATIVE LIMITED p 609
20 MORLEY ST, HAMILTON, ON, L8H 3R7
(905) 544-6281   *SIC 2021*

GAY LEA FOODS CO-OPERATIVE LIMITED p 695
5200 ORBITOR DR, MISSISSAUGA, ON, L4W 5B4
(905) 283-5300   *SIC 2021*

GAYA   p 295
See *GAYA CANADA ENTERPRISE LTD*

GAYA CANADA ENTERPRISE LTD   p 295
1868 GLEN DR SUITE 232, VANCOUVER, BC, V6A 4K4
(604) 738-0971   *SIC 5137*

GAZ COMPRIME INTERNATIONAL p 1072
1705 RTE DU NORD, BROWNSBURG-CHATHAM, QC, J8G 1E4
(450) 533-5911   *SIC 4925*

GAZ METRO INC   p 1174
1717 RUE DU HAVRE, MONTREAL, QC, H2K 2X3
(514) 598-3444   *SIC 4922*

GAZ METRO PLUS INC   p 1065
1350 RUE NOBEL BUREAU 100, BOUCHERVILLE, QC, J4B 5H3
(450) 641-6300   *SIC 7699*

GAZ METROPOLITAIN   p 1059
1230 BOUL MICHELE-BOHEC, BLAINVILLE, QC, J7C 5S4
(450) 419-5000   *SIC 4924*

GAZ NATUREL RICHARD   p 1373
See *GNR CORBUS INC*

GAZ NATUREL WESTMOUNT   p 1223
325 RUE SAINT-AUGUSTIN, MONTREAL, QC, H4C 2N7
(514) 564-1189   *SIC 4924*

GAZ PROPANE RAINVILLE INC   p 1109
280 RUE SAINT-CHARLES S, GRANBY, QC, J2G 7A9
(450) 378-4108   *SIC 5984*

GAZETTE, LA   p 1207
See *POSTMEDIA NETWORK INC*

GAZIFERE INC   p 1105
706 BOUL GREBER, GATINEAU, QC, J8V 3P8
(819) 771-8321   *SIC 4924*

GAZON SAVARD (SAGUENAY) INC p 1079
3478 RANG SAINT-PAUL, CHICOUTIMI, QC, G7H 0G6
(418) 543-5739   *SIC 0181*

GAZZOLA PAVING LIMITED   p 584
529 CARLINGVIEW DR, ETOBICOKE, ON, M9W 5H2
(416) 675-7007   *SIC 1611*

GBC   p 733
See *ACCO BRANDS CANADA INC*

GBHS LION'S HEAD HOSPITAL   p 835
See *GREY BRUCE HEALTH SERVICES*

GCB LOGISTICS   p 1187
See *COURTIERS EN DOUANES GENERAL INC, LES*

GCIC LTD   p 939
1 ADELAIDE ST E SUITE 2800, TORONTO, ON, M5C 2V9
(416) 350-3250   *SIC 6159*

GCIU   p 695
See *GRAPHIC COMMUNICATIONS BENEFITS ADMINISTRATION COR*

GCO CANADA INC   p 739
6300 DIXIE RD, MISSISSAUGA, ON, L5T 1A7
(905) 670-2514   *SIC 5611*

GCP CANADA INC   p 474
294 CLEMENTS RD W, AJAX, ON, L1S 3C6
(905) 683-8561   *SIC 2819*

GCP CANADA INC   p 1132

255 AV LAFLEUR, LASALLE, QC, H8R 3H4
(514) 366-3362   *SIC 2819*

GCP CANADA INC   p 1365
42 RUE FABRE, SALABERRY-DE-VALLEYFIELD, QC, J6S 4K7
(450) 373-4224   *SIC 2819*

GCQ CANADA INC   p 1379
1450 GRANDE ALLEE, TERREBONNE, QC, J6W 6B7
(450) 471-0044   *SIC 7322*

GCR TIRE CENTRES   p 729
See *BRIDGESTONE CANADA INC*

GCS ENERGY SERVICES LTD   p 135
4411 49TH ST, HARDISTY, AB, T0B 1V0
(780) 888-3845   *SIC 1623*

GCT CANADA LIMITED PARTNERSHIP   p 295
1285 FRANKLIN ST, VANCOUVER, BC, V6A 1J9
(604) 267-5200   *SIC 4491*

GCT REPRESENTITIVE SERVICES   p 628
237 AIRPORT RD, KENORA, ON, P9N 0A2
(807) 548-4214   *SIC 8621*

GDB CONSTRUCTEURS   p 647
See *1468792 ONTARIO INC*

GDC AUTOMOTIVE SERVICES   p 328
See *CANADA DRIVES LTD*

GDI INTEGRATED FACILITY SERVICES   p 818
See *GDI SERVICES (CANADA) LP*

GDI INTEGRATED FACILITY SVC   p 609
See *GDI SERVICES (CANADA) LP*

GDI SERVICES (CANADA) LP   p 30
437 36 AVE SE, CALGARY, AB, T2G 1W5
(403) 232-8402   *SIC 7349*

GDI SERVICES (CANADA) LP   p 95
14588 116 AVE NW, EDMONTON, AB, T5M 3E9
(780) 428-9508   *SIC 7349*

GDI SERVICES (CANADA) LP   p 401
475 WILSEY RD, FREDERICTON, NB, E3B 7K1
(506) 453-1404   *SIC 7349*

GDI SERVICES (CANADA) LP   p 446
202 BROWNLOW AVE, DARTMOUTH, NS, B3B 1T5
(902) 468-3103   *SIC 7349*

GDI SERVICES (CANADA) LP   p 584
60 WORCESTER RD, ETOBICOKE, ON, M9W 5X2
(416) 736-1144   *SIC 7349*

GDI SERVICES (CANADA) LP   p 609
39 DUNBAR AVE, HAMILTON, ON, L8H 3E3
SIC 7349

GDI SERVICES (CANADA) LP   p 639
100 CAMPBELL AVE SUITE 12, KITCHENER, ON, N2H 4X8
SIC 7349

GDI SERVICES (CANADA) LP   p 652
931 LEATHORNE ST UNIT E, LONDON, ON, N5Z 3M7
(519) 681-3330   *SIC 7349*

GDI SERVICES (CANADA) LP   p 818
800 INDUSTRIAL AVE SUITE 12, OTTAWA, ON, K1G 4B8
(613) 247-0065   *SIC 7349*

GDI SERVICES (CANADA) LP   p 997
130 KING ST, TORONTO, ON, M9N 1L5
(416) 364-0643   *SIC 1799*

GDI SERVICES (CANADA) LP   p 1420
1319 HAMILTON ST, REGINA, SK, S4R 2B6
SIC 7349

GDI SERVICES (QUEBEC) S.E.C.   p 1132
695 90E AV, LASALLE, QC, H8R 3A4
(514) 368-1505   *SIC 7349*

GDI SERVICES AUX IMMEUBLES INC   p 1132
695 90E AV, LASALLE, QC, H8R 3A4
(514) 368-1504   *SIC 7349*

GDI SERVICES TECHNIQUES S.E.C.   p 1132
695 90E AV, LASALLE, QC, H8R 3A4
(514) 368-1504   *SIC 7349*

GDLS-C   p 649

See *GENERAL DYNAMICS LAND SYSTEMS - CANADA CORPORATION*

GE   p 1264
See *GENERAL ELECTRIC CANADA COMPANY*

GE AIRCRAFT ENGINES   p 1068
See *GENERAL ELECTRIC CANADA COMPANY*

GE AVIATION   p 1068
See *COMPAGNIE GE AVIATION CANADA, LA*

GE BETZ CANADA   p 722
See *GE BETZDEARBORN CANADA COMPANY*

GE BETZDEARBORN CANADA COMPANY p 722
2300 MEADOWVALE BLVD, MISSISSAUGA, ON, L5N 5P9
(905) 465-3030   *SIC 6712*

GE CANADA   p 841
See *GENERAL ELECTRIC CANADA COMPANY*

GE CANADA EQUIPMENT FINANCING AND CAPITALIST FUNDS   p 304
400 BURRARD ST SUITE 1050, VANCOUVER, BC, V6C 3A6
SIC 6351

GE ENERGIES RENOUVELABLES CANADA INC   p 1071
5005 BOUL LAPINIERE BUREAU 6000, BROSSARD, QC, J4Z 0N5
(450) 746-6500   *SIC 3511*

GE ENERGY   p 722
See *GENERAL ELECTRIC CANADA COMPANY*

GE ENERGY OILFIELD TECHNOLGY CANADA INC   p 12
2880 45 AVE SE SUITE 432, CALGARY, AB, T2B 3M1
SIC 5084

GE ENERGY SERVICES   p 526
See *GENERAL ELECTRIC CANADA COMPANY*

GE FANUC AUTOMATION CANADA COMPANY   p 89
10235 101 ST NW, EDMONTON, AB, T5J 3E9
(780) 420-2000   *SIC 7372*

GE GRID SOLUTIONS   p 1193
See *ALSTOM CANADA INC*

GE INNOVATION CENTER   p 679
See *GE MULTILIN*

GE LIGHTING CANADA   p 803
See *GENERAL ELECTRIC CANADA COMPANY*

GE MULTILIN   p 679
650 MARKLAND ST, MARKHAM, ON, L6C 0M1
(905) 927-7070   *SIC 3625*

GE OIL & GAS   p 116
See *PII (CANADA) LIMITED*

GE OIL & GAS CANADA INC   p 114
3575 97 ST NW, EDMONTON, AB, T6E 5S7
(780) 450-1031   *SIC 1389*

GE VFS CANADA LIMITED PARTNERSHIP p 722
2300 MEADOWVALE BLVD SUITE 200, MISSISSAUGA, ON, L5N 5P9
(905) 858-5100   *SIC 6153*

GEA FARM TECHNOLOGIES CANADA INC p 1096
4591 BOUL SAINT-JOSEPH, DRUMONDVILLE, QC, J2A 0C6
(819) 477-7444   *SIC 3523*

GEA REFRIGERATION CANADA INC p 254
2551 VIKING WAY SUITE 150, RICHMOND, BC, V6V 1N4
(604) 278-4118   *SIC 5078*

GEANT MOTORISE INC, LE   p 1291
173 RTE 172, SAINT-AMBROISE, QC, G7P 2N5
(418) 672-4744   *SIC 5561*

GEAR CENTRE, THE   p 95

See EDMONTON GEAR CENTRE LTD
GEAR ENERGY LTD *p 50*
240 4TH AVE SW SUITE 2600, CALGARY, AB, T2P 4H4
(403) 538-8435   *SIC* 1382
GEAR PELLING INSURANCE LTD *p 260*
7340 WESTMINSTER HWY SUITE 110, RICHMOND, BC, V6X 1A1
(604) 276-2474   *SIC* 6321
GEAR-O-RAMA SUPPLY LTD *p 204*
9300 GOLF COURSE RD, DAWSON CREEK, BC, V1G 4E9
(250) 782-8126   *SIC* 5511
GECKO ALLIANCE GROUP INC *p 1277*
450 RUE DES CANETONS, QUEBEC, QC, G2E 5W6
(418) 872-4411   *SIC* 3625
GECKO ALLIANCE GROUP INC *p 1277*
450 AV SAINT-JEAN-BAPTISTE BUREAU 200, QUEBEC, QC, G2E 6H5
(418) 872-4411   *SIC* 3625
GEDCO *p 30*
See GEOPHYSICAL EXPLORATION & DE-VELOPMENT CORPORATION
GEDCO *p 974*
1033 BAY ST SUITE 212, TORONTO, ON, M5S 3A5
(416) 961-1777   *SIC* 5153
GEDDES ENTERPRISES OF LONDON LIMITED *p 653*
140 FULLARTON ST SUITE 604, LONDON, ON, N6A 5P2
SIC 5994
GEDILEX INC *p 1282*
515 BOUL LACOMBE BUREAU 255, RE-PENTIGNY, QC, J5Z 1P5
(450) 581-6545   *SIC* 5912
GEE BEE CONSTRUCTION CO LTD *p 1408*
HIGHWAY 48, KIPLING, SK, S0G 2S0
(306) 736-2332   *SIC* 1611
GEEK SQUAD *p 1130*
See BEST BUY CANADA LTD
GEEK SQUAD *p 1249*
See BEST BUY CANADA LTD
GEEN'S PRESCRIPTION PHARMACY LIMITED *p 491*
276 FRONT ST, BELLEVILLE, ON, K8N 2Z8
(613) 962-4579   *SIC* 5912
GEEP ALBERTA INC *p 124*
250 AURUM RD NE SUITE 700, EDMONTON, AB, T6S 1G9
(780) 475-6545   *SIC* 4953
GEEP CANADA INC *p 487*
220 JOHN ST, BARRIE, ON, L4N 2L2
(705) 725-1919   *SIC* 4953
GEEP CANADA INC *p 1234*
2995 BOUL LE CORBUSIER, MONTREAL, QC, H7L 3M3
(450) 506-0220   *SIC* 5734
GEEP ECOSYS *p 1234*
See GEEP CANADA INC
GEEP ECOSYS INC *p 1234*
2995 BOUL LE CORBUSIER, MONTREAL, QC, H7L 3M3
(450) 506-0220   *SIC* 5045
GEEP HOLDINGS INC *p 487*
220 JOHN ST, BARRIE, ON, L4N 2L2
(705) 725-1919   *SIC* 6712
GEERLINKS BUILDING CENTRE AND FURNITURE LIMITED *p 890*
295 WELLINGTON ST, ST THOMAS, ON, N5R 2S6
(519) 631-2910   *SIC* 5251
GEERLINKS HOME HARDWARE BUILDING CENTRE AND FURNIT *p 890*
See GEERLINKS BUILDING CENTRE AND FURNITURE LIMITED
GEGL *p 1206*
See LORD'STACE INC
GEKKO SYSTEMS INC *p 313*
1112 PENDER ST W SUITE 908, VANCOU-

VER, BC, V6E 2S1
(604) 681-2288   *SIC* 5082
GELLULE INC *p 1266*
2300 BOUL PERE-LELIEVRE, QUEBEC, QC, G1P 2X5
(418) 681-6351   *SIC* 6712
GELOSO BEVERAGE GROUP *p 1101*
See GROUPE DE COURTAGE OMNI LTEE
GELPAC ROUVILLE SOLUTIONS EMBALLAGE INC *p 1149*
400 RUE HENRI-BOURASSA, MARIEVILLE, QC, J3M 1R9
(450) 460-4466   *SIC* 2674
GEM *p 1374*
See GLOBAL EXCEL MANAGEMENT INC
GEM CABINETS LTD *p 93*
14019 128 AVE NW, EDMONTON, AB, T5L 3H3
(780) 454-8652   *SIC* 5211
GEM CAFE LTD *p 1427*
401 21ST ST E, SASKATOON, SK, S7K 0C5
SIC 6712
GEM HEALTH CARE GROUP LIMITED *p 438*
260 CHURCH ST, AMHERST, NS, B4H 3C9
(902) 667-3501   *SIC* 8051
GEM HEALTH CARE GROUP LIMITED *p 458*
25 ALTON DR, HALIFAX, NS, B3N 1M1
(902) 477-1777   *SIC* 8051
GEM HEALTH CARE GROUP LIMITED *p 458*
15 SHOREHAM LANE SUITE 101, HALIFAX, NS, B3P 2R3
(902) 429-6227   *SIC* 6712
GEM HEALTH CARE GROUP LIMITED *p 458*
15 SHOREHAM LANE SUITE 101, HALIFAX, NS, B3P 2R3
(902) 429-6227   *SIC* 8051
GEM HEALTH CARE GROUP LIMITED *p 469*
426 YOUNG ST, TRURO, NS, B2N 7B1
(902) 895-8715   *SIC* 8059
GEM HEALTH CARE GROUP LIMITED *p 849*
470 RAGLAN ST N, RENFREW, ON, K7V 1P5
(613) 432-5823   *SIC* 8051
GEM MANAGEMENT HOLDINGS *p 458*
See GEM HEALTH CARE GROUP LIMITED
GEM-SEN DISTRIBUTION *p 553*
See GEM-SEN HOLDINGS CORP
GEM-SEN HOLDINGS CORP *p 553*
266 APPLEWOOD CRES, CONCORD, ON, L4K 4B4
(905) 660-3110   *SIC* 5199
GEMALTO CANADA INC *p 522*
5347 JOHN LUCAS DR, BURLINGTON, ON, L7L 6A8
(905) 335-9681   *SIC* 7389
GEMCOM SOFTWARE INTERNATIONAL *p 312*
See DASSAULT SYSTEMES CANADA SOFTWARE INC
GEMINI ENGINEERING LIMITED *p 50*
839 5 AVE SW SUITE 400, CALGARY, AB, T2P 3C8
(403) 255-2916   *SIC* 8711
GEMINI FABRICATION LTD *p 152*
4100 67 ST, PONOKA, AB, T4J 1J8
SIC 3499
GEMINI FIELD SOLUTIONS LTD *p 50*
839 5 AVE SW SUITE 400, CALGARY, AB, T2P 3C8
(403) 255-2006   *SIC* 1629
GEMINI FIELD SOLUTIONS LTD *p 152*
4100 67 ST, PONOKA, AB, T4J 1J8
SIC 7692
GEMINI MOTORS LIMITED *p 636*
26 MANITOU DR, KITCHENER, ON, N2C 1L1
(519) 894-2050   *SIC* 5511

GEMINI PACKAGING LTD *p 258*
12071 JACOBSON WAY UNIT 150, RICHMOND, BC, V6W 1L5
(604) 278-3455   *SIC* 2841
GEMINI SOLUTIONS *p 921*
See 1095086 ONTARIO INC
GEMME CANADIENNE P.A. INC *p 1196*
1002 RUE SHERBROOKE O BUREAU 2525, MONTREAL, QC, H3A 3L6
(514) 287-1951   *SIC* 5094
GEMPERLE INC *p 1196*
1002 RUE SHERBROOKE O BUREAU 2525, MONTREAL, QC, H3A 3L6
(514) 287-9017   *SIC* 5094
GEMSTAR SECURITY SERVICE LTD *p 1031*
4000 STEELES AVE W UNIT 29, WOODBRIDGE, ON, L4L 4V9
(905) 850-8517   *SIC* 7381
GEMTEC LIMITED *p 402*
191 DOAK RD, FREDERICTON, NB, E3C 2E6
(506) 453-1025   *SIC* 8711
GENAIRE LIMITED *p 761*
468 NIAGARA STONE RD UNIT D, NIAGARA ON THE LAKE, ON, L0S 1J0
(905) 684-1165   *SIC* 4581
GENATEC INC *p 1339*
5929 RTE TRANSCANADIENNE BUREAU 240, SAINT-LAURENT, QC, H4T 1Z6
(514) 855-1223   *SIC* 5045
GENCO MARINE LIMITED *p 712*
1008 RANGEVIEW RD, MISSISSAUGA, ON, L5E 1H3
(416) 504-2891   *SIC* 5099
GENDRON & LAMOUREUX *p 1109*
See PETRO MONTESTRIE INC
GENDRON CHRYSLER JEEP DODGE *p 1148*
259 BOUL DESJARDINS, MANIWAKI, QC, J9E 2E4
(819) 449-1611   *SIC* 5511
GENDRON FORD *p 1365*
See PRESTIGE FORD INC
GENDRON STEEL *p 1141*
See ACIER GENDRON LTEE
GENEEN AUTOMOBILES LIMITED *p 989*
740 DUPONT ST, TORONTO, ON, M6G 1Z6
(416) 530-1880   *SIC* 5511
GENEOHM SCIENCES CANADA INC *p 1266*
2555 BOUL DU PARC-TECHNOLOGIQUE, QUEBEC, QC, G1P 4S5
(418) 780-5800   *SIC* 2835
GENEPOC INC *p 1266*
360 RUE FRANQUET BUREAU 100, QUEBEC, QC, G1P 4N3
(418) 650-3535   *SIC* 2835
GENEQ INC *p 1049*
10700 RUE SECANT, ANJOU, QC, H1J 1S5
(514) 354-2511   *SIC* 5049
GENER8 MEDIA CORP *p 291*
177 7TH AVE W SUITE 200, VANCOUVER, BC, V5Y 1L8
(604) 669-8885   *SIC* 7819
GENERAL AUTO PARTS *p 582*
See ALL PARTS AUTOMOTIVE LIMITED
GENERAL BEARING SERVICE INC *p 834*
490 KENT ST, OTTAWA, ON, K2P 2B7
(613) 238-8100   *SIC* 5085
GENERAL BODY & EQUIPMENT LTD *p 114*
8124 DAVIES RD NW, EDMONTON, AB, T6E 4N2
(780) 468-5359   *SIC* 3713
GENERAL BREAKERS CANADA *p 899*
See TRACKS & WHEELS EQUIPMENT BROKERS INC
GENERAL CABLE COMPANY LTD *p 503*
156 PARKSHORE DR, BRAMPTON, ON, L6T 5M1
(905) 791-6886   *SIC* 3315
GENERAL CABLE COMPANY LTD *p 1122*
2600 BOUL DE COMPORTE, LA MALBAIE, QC, G5A 1N4
SIC 3357

GENERAL CABLE COMPANY LTD *p 1320*
800 CH DE LA RIVIERE-DU-NORD, SAINT-JEROME, QC, J7Y 5G2
(450) 436-1450   *SIC* 3357
GENERAL CARTAGE & EXPRESS COMPANY LIMITED *p 574*
48 NORTH QUEEN ST, ETOBICOKE, ON, M8Z 2C4
(416) 236-2460   *SIC* 4212
GENERAL COACH CANADA *p 620*
See CITAIR, INC
GENERAL CREDIT SERVICES INC *p 313*
1201 WEST PENDER ST SUITE 400, VANCOUVER, BC, V6E 2V2
(604) 688-6097   *SIC* 7322
GENERAL DYNAMICS INFORMATION TECHNOLOGY CANADA, LIMITED *p 750*
30 CAMELOT DR, NEPEAN, ON, K2G 5X8
(613) 723-9500   *SIC* 7374
GENERAL DYNAMICS LAND SYSTEMS - CANADA CORPORATION *p 23*
1020 68 AVE NE, CALGARY, AB, T2E 8P2
(403) 295-6700   *SIC* 7371
GENERAL DYNAMICS LAND SYSTEMS - CANADA CORPORATION *p 649*
1991 OXFORD ST E BLDG 15, LONDON, ON, N5V 2Z7
(519) 964-5900   *SIC* 3711
GENERAL DYNAMICS LAND SYSTEMS - CANADA CORPORATION *p 649*
2035 OXFORD ST E, LONDON, ON, N5V 2Z7
(519) 964-5900   *SIC* 3711
GENERAL DYNAMICS LAND SYSTEMS - CANADA CORPORATION *p 751*
1941 ROBERTSON RD, NEPEAN, ON, K2H 5B7
(613) 596-7000   *SIC* 3711
GENERAL DYNAMICS MISSION SYSTEMS-CANADA, DIV OF *p 751*
See GENERAL DYNAMICS LAND SYSTEMS - CANADA CORPORATION
GENERAL DYNAMICS PRODUITS DE DEFENSE ET SYSTEMES TACTIQUES-CANADA INC *p 1282*
5 MONTEE DES ARSENAUX, RE-PENTIGNY, QC, J5Z 2P4
(450) 581-3080   *SIC* 3483
GENERAL DYNAMICS PRODUITS DE DEFENSE ET SYSTEMES TACTIQUES-CANADA VALLEYFIELD INC *p 1365*
55 RUE MASSON, SALABERRY-DE-VALLEYFIELD, QC, J6S 4V9
(450) 371-5520   *SIC* 2899
GENERAL ELECTRIC CANADA COMPANY *p 526*
1150 WALKER'S LINE, BURLINGTON, ON, L7M 1V2
(905) 335-6301   *SIC* 3625
GENERAL ELECTRIC CANADA COMPANY *p 722*
1919 MINNESOTA CRT, MISSISSAUGA, ON, L5N 0C9
(905) 858-5100   *SIC* 3625
GENERAL ELECTRIC CANADA COMPANY *p 803*
1290 SOUTH SERVICE RD W, OAKVILLE, ON, L6L 5T7
(905) 849-5048   *SIC* 3625
GENERAL ELECTRIC CANADA COMPANY *p 841*
107 PARK ST N SUITE 2, PETERBOROUGH, ON, K9J 7B5
(705) 748-8486   *SIC* 3625
GENERAL ELECTRIC CANADA COMPANY *p 1068*
2 BOUL DE L'AEROPORT, BROMONT, QC, J2L 1S6
(450) 534-0917   *SIC* 3625
GENERAL ELECTRIC CANADA COMPANY *p 1264*

1130 BOUL CHAREST O, QUEBEC, QC, G1N 2E2
(418) 682-8500   *SIC* 3625

GENERAL ELECTRIC CANADA INTERNATIONAL INC   *p* 722
2300 MEADOWVALE BLVD SUITE 100, MISSISSAUGA, ON, L5N 5P9
(905) 858-5100   *SIC* 8711

GENERAL ELECTRIC CAPITAL CANADA *p* 722
2300 MEADOWVALE BLVD, MISSISSAUGA, ON, L5N 5P9
(905) 858-5100   *SIC* 6153

GENERAL FASTENERS   *p* 30
See G F LTD

GENERAL FUSION INC   *p* 181
3680 BONNEVILLE PL SUITE 106, BURNABY, BC, V3N 4T5
(604) 420-0920   *SIC* 8731

GENERAL GEAR   *p* 794
See TRIUMPH GEAR SYSTEMS-TORONTO ULC

GENERAL GLASS INDUSTRIES LTD *p* 176
2146 QUEEN ST, ABBOTSFORD, BC, V2T 6J4
(604) 854-5757   *SIC* 3231

GENERAL KINETICS ENGINEERING CORPORATION   *p* 503
110 EAST DR, BRAMPTON, ON, L6T 1C1
(905) 458-0888   *SIC* 3714

GENERAL MAINTENANCE SERVICES 858
See 1075177 ONTARIO LTD

GENERAL METAL FABRICATION LTD   *p* 361
269 MANITOBA RD, WINKLER, MB, R6W 0J8
(204) 325-9374   *SIC* 7692

GENERAL MILLS CANADA CORPORATION   391
1555 CHEVRIER BLVD SUITE B, WINNIPEG, MB, R3T 1Y7
(204) 477-8338   *SIC* 2099

GENERAL MILLS CANADA CORPORATION   *p* 681
111 PILLSBURY DR, MIDLAND, ON, L4R 4L4
(705) 526-6311   *SIC* 2041

GENERAL MILLS CANADA CORPORATION   *p* 695
5825 EXPLORER DR, MISSISSAUGA, ON, L4W 5P6
(905) 212-4000   *SIC* 2041

GENERAL MILLS RESTAURANTS INC   *p* 688
5915 AIRPORT RD SUITE 910, MISSISSAUGA, ON, L4V 1T1
(905) 673-7898   *SIC* 5812

GENERAL MOTORS   *p* 503
See GATEWAY CHEVROLET OLDSMOBILE INC

GENERAL MOTORS ACCEPTANCE CORPORATION OF CANADA, LIMITED   *p* 1096
455 BOUL FENELON BUREAU 310, DORVAL, QC, H9S 5K1
(514) 633-6933   *SIC* 6153

GENERAL MOTORS FINANCIAL OF CANADA, LTD.   *p* 767
2001 SHEPPARD AVE E UNIT 600, NORTH YORK, ON, M2J 4Z8
(416) 753-4000   *SIC* 6159

GENERAL MOTORS OF CANADA   *p* 802
See BUDDS CHEVROLET CADILLAC BUICK

GENERAL MOTORS OF CANADA COMPANY   *p* 101
17707 118 AVE NW, EDMONTON, AB, T5S 1P7
(780) 451-7000   *SIC* 5531

GENERAL MOTORS OF CANADA COMPANY   *p* 229
27475 58 CRES, LANGLEY, BC, V4W 3W3
(604) 857-5277   *SIC* 5013

GENERAL MOTORS OF CANADA COMPANY   *p* 621
300 INGERSOLL ST, INGERSOLL, ON, N5C 3J7
(519) 485-6400   *SIC* 3711

GENERAL MOTORS OF CANADA COMPANY   *p* 670
101 MCNABB ST, MARKHAM, ON, L3R 4H8
(905) 644-5000   *SIC* 7389

GENERAL MOTORS OF CANADA COMPANY   *p* 812
1908 COLONEL SAM DR, OSHAWA, ON, L1H 8P7
(905) 644-5000   *SIC* 3711

GENERAL MOTORS OF CANADA COMPANY   *p* 812
1908 COLONEL SAM DR, OSHAWA, ON, L1H 8P7
(289) 676-0530   *SIC* 3711

GENERAL MOTORS OF CANADA COMPANY   *p* 812
500 WENTWORTH ST E SUITE 1, OSHAWA, ON, L1H 3V9
(905) 644-4716   *SIC* 8711

GENERAL MOTORS OF CANADA COMPANY   *p* 814
461 PARK RD S, OSHAWA, ON, L1J 8R3
(905) 845-5456   *SIC* 3711

GENERAL MOTORS OF CANADA COMPANY   *p* 885
570 GLENDALE AVE, ST CATHARINES, ON, L2R 7B3
(905) 641-6424   *SIC* 3465

GENERAL MOTORS OF CANADA COMPANY   *p* 1019
1550 KILDARE RD, WINDSOR, ON, N8W 2W4
(519) 255-4161   *SIC* 3714

GENERAL MOTORS OF CANADA COMPANY   *p* 1035
1401 PARKINSON RD, WOODSTOCK, ON, N4S 7W3
(519) 539-6136   *SIC* 4226

GENERAL MOTORS OF CANADA COMPANY   *p* 1250
5000 RTE TRANSCANADIENNE, POINTE-CLAIRE, QC, H9R 1B6
(514) 630-6209   *SIC* 5012

GENERAL NOLI CANADA INC   *p* 1344
8000 BOUL LANGELIER BUREAU 514, SAINT-LEONARD, QC, H1P 3K2
(514) 852-6262   *SIC* 4731

GENERAL NUTRITION CENTRES COMPANY   *p* 688
6299 AIRPORT RD SUITE 300, MISSISSAUGA, ON, L4V 1N3
(905) 612-1016   *SIC* 5499

GENERAL PAINT CORP   *p* 1368
5230 BOUL ROYAL, SHAWINIGAN, QC, G9N 4R6
(819) 537-5925   *SIC* 2851

GENERAL RECYCLING INDUSTRIES LTD *p* 109
4120 84 AVE NW, EDMONTON, AB, T6B 3H3
(780) 461-5555   *SIC* 5093

GENERAL SCRAP IRON & METALS LTD *p* 109
4120 84 AVE NW, EDMONTON, AB, T6B 3H3
(780) 452-5865   *SIC* 5093

GENERAL SCRAP PARTNERSHIP   *p* 362
135 BISMARCK ST, WINNIPEG, MB, R2C 2W3
(877) 495-6314   *SIC* 5093

GENERAL SPRINKLERS INC   *p* 794
315 DEERHIDE CRES SUITE 3, NORTH YORK, ON, M9M 2Z2
(416) 748-1175   *SIC* 1711

GENERAL TOWING, DIV OF   *p* 242
See SEASPAN ULC

GENERALI GLOBAL HEALTH SERVICES *p* 904
See CMN GLOBAL INC

GENERATION 5 MATHEMATICAL TECHNOLOGIES INC   *p* 767
515 CONSUMERS RD SUITE 600, NORTH YORK, ON, M2J 4Z2
SIC 8732

GENERATION ADVISORS INC   *p* 925
22 ST CLAIR AVE E, TORONTO, ON, M4T 2S3
(416) 361-1498   *SIC* 6282

GENERATION PORTFOLIO MANAGEMENT CORP   *p* 925
22 ST CLAIR AVE E, TORONTO, ON, M4T 2S3
(416) 361-1498   *SIC* 6282

GENERATRICE DRUMMOND   *p* 1306
See INTEGRATED DISTRIBUTION SYSTEMS LIMITED PARTNERSHIP

GENERATRICE LANAUDIERE   *p* 1114
See BRUNEAU ELECTRIQUE INC

GENESEE & WYOMING CANADA INC   *p* 1226
9001 BOUL DE L'ACADIE BUREAU 904, MONTREAL, QC, H4N 3H5
(514) 948-6999   *SIC* 4011

GENESIS BUILDERS GROUP INC   *p* 23
7315 8 ST NE, CALGARY, AB, T2E 8A2
(403) 265-9237   *SIC* 1521

GENESIS FOODS   *p* 604
See PURESOURCE INC

GENESIS GARDENS INC   *p* 645
1003 LIMOGES RD, LIMOGES, ON, K0A 2M0
(613) 443-5751   *SIC* 8051

GENESIS HOSPITALITY INC   *p* 347
3550 VICTORIA AVE, BRANDON, MB, R7B 2R4
(204) 725-1532   *SIC* 7011

GENESIS INTEGRATION INC   *p* 93
14721 123 AVE NW, EDMONTON, AB, T5L 2Y6
(780) 455-3000   *SIC* 1731

GENESIS LAND DEVELOPMENT CORP *p* 23
7315 8 ST NE, CALGARY, AB, T2E 8A2
(403) 266-0746   *SIC* 6553

GENESIS MEAT PACKERS INC   *p* 993
70 GLEN SCARLETT RD, TORONTO, ON, M6N 1P4
SIC 2011

GENESIS METALS CORP   *p* 304
409 GRANVILLE ST SUITE 1500, VANCOUVER, BC, V6C 1T2
(604) 602-1440   *SIC* 1041

GENESYS LABORATORIES CANADA INC *p* 415
50 SMYTHE ST SUITE 2000, SAINT JOHN, NB, E2L 0B8
(506) 637-3900   *SIC* 7372

GENETEC INC   *p* 1228
2280 ALFRED-NOBEL BLVD, MONTREAL, QC, H4S 2A4
(514) 332-4000   *SIC* 7371

GENEX COMMUNICATIONS INC   *p* 1259
410 BOUL CHAREST E, QUEBEC, QC, G1K 8G3

(418) 266-6166   *SIC* 4832

GENEX SERVICES OF CANADA INC   *p* 695
2800 SKYMARK AVE SUITE 401, MISSISSAUGA, ON, L4W 5A6
SIC 6411

GENFOOT INC   *p* 1082
4945 RUE LEGENDRE, CONTRECOEUR, QC, J0L 1C0
(450) 587-2051   *SIC* 3143

GENFOOT INC   *p* 1127
1940 55E AV, LACHINE, QC, H8T 3H3
(514) 341-3950   *SIC* 5661

GENFOR MACHINERY INC   *p* 209
8320 RIVER RD, DELTA, BC, V4G 1B5
(604) 946-6911   *SIC* 3553

GENIARP INC   *p* 1276
4650 BOUL DE L'AUVERGNE, QUEBEC, QC, G2C 2B5
(418) 847-3333   *SIC* 1389

GENICS INC   *p* 1
27717 ACHESON RD, ACHESON, AB, T7X 6B1
SIC 2491

GENIE AUDIO INC   *p* 1326
125 RUE GAGNON BUREAU 102, SAINT-LAURENT, QC, H4N 1T1
(514) 856-9212   *SIC* 5047

GENIK AUTOMATION   *p* 1321
See CONCEPTION GENIK INC

GENIVAR   *p* 63
See WSP CANADA INC

GENIVAR   *p* 163
See WSP CANADA INC

GENIVAR   *p* 677
See WSP CANADA INC

GENIVAR   *p* 830
See WSP CANADA INC

GENIVAR   *p* 909
See WSP CANADA INC

GENIVAR   *p* 1087
See WSP CANADA INC

GENIVAR INC   *p* 1215
EDIFICE NORTHERN 1600 RENE-LEVESQUE BLVD W, MONTREAL, QC, H3H 1P9
(514) 340-0046   *SIC* 8711

GENNUM   *p* 524
See SEMTECH CANADA CORPORATION

GENOA DESIGN INTERNATIONAL LTD   *p* 426
117 GLENCOE DR SUITE 201, MOUNT PEARL, NL, A1N 4S7
(709) 368-0669   *SIC* 8711

GENOIL INC   *p* 67
1811 4 ST SW SUITE 218, CALGARY, AB, T2S 1W2
(587) 400-0249   *SIC* 1382

GENOLOGICS LIFE SCIENCES SOFTWARE INC   *p* 338
4464 MARKHAM ST SUITE 2302, VICTORIA, BC, V8Z 7X8
(250) 483-7011   *SIC* 7371

GENOME QUEBEC   *p* 1204
630 BOUL RENE-LEVESQUE O BUREAU 2660, MONTREAL, QC, H3B 1S6
(514) 398-0668   *SIC* 8731

GENOR RECYCLING SERVICES LIMITED *p* 515
434 HENRY ST, BRANTFORD, ON, N3S 7W1
(519) 756-5264   *SIC* 5093

GENPAK DIV OF   *p* 480
See GREAT PACIFIC ENTERPRISES LIMITED PARTNERSHIP

GENPAK FLEXIBLE   *p* 480
See GREAT PACIFIC ENTERPRISES LIMITED PARTNERSHIP

GENPAK LP   *p* 1085
See GREAT PACIFIC ENTERPRISES INC

GENPAK, DIV OF   *p* 716
See GREAT PACIFIC ENTERPRISES LIMITED PARTNERSHIP

GENROC DRYWALL LTD   *p* 128

7307 RAILWAY AVE, FORT MCMURRAY, AB, T9H 1B9
SIC 1742

GENRON ENTERPRISES LTD p 128
295 MACDONALD CRES, FORT MCMUR-RAY, AB, T9H 4B7
(780) 743-3445 *SIC 1761*

GENSCI OCF INC p 1237
1105 CHOMEDEY (A-13) E, MONTREAL, QC, H7W 5J8
(450) 688-8699 *SIC 5047*

GENSLER p 951
See GENSLER ARCHITECTURE & DE-SIGN CANDA, INC

GENSLER ARCHITECTURE & DESIGN CANDA, INC p 951
150 KING ST W SUITE 1400, TORONTO, ON, M5H 1J9
(416) 601-3890 *SIC 8712*

GENSOLUTIONS p 50
See GEMINI ENGINEERING LIMITED

GENSTAR DEVELOPMENT COMPANY p 69
280 MIDPARK WAY SE SUITE 100, CAL-GARY, AB, T2X 2B5
(403) 256-4000 *SIC 1629*

GENSTEEL p 498
See AUSTIN STEEL GROUP INC

GENTEC p 665
See 901089 ONTARIO LIMITED

GENTEC ELECTRO-OPTIQUE INC p 1277
445 AV SAINT-JEAN-BAPTISTE BUREAU 160, QUEBEC, QC, G2E 5N7
(418) 651-8003 *SIC 3826*

GENTEC INC p 1266
2625 AV DALTON, QUEBEC, QC, G1P 3S9
(418) 651-8000 *SIC 3625*

GENTEC INTERNATIONAL p 670
90 ROYAL CREST CRT, MARKHAM, ON, L3R 9X6
(905) 513-7733 *SIC 5099*

GENTEK BUILDING PRODUCTS p 13
See ASSOCIATED MATERIALS CANADA LIMITED

GENTES ET BOLDUC PHARMACIENS S.E.N.C p 1312
4555 AV BEAUDRY, SAINT-HYACINTHE, QC, J2S 8W2
(450) 778-2837 *SIC 5912*

GENTHERM CANADA ULC p 1020
3445 WHEELTON DR, WINDSOR, ON, N8W 5A6
(519) 948-4808 *SIC 3714*

GENTHERM GLOBAL POWER TECH-NOLOGIES INC p 16
7875 57 ST SE UNIT 16, CALGARY, AB, T2C 5K7
(403) 236-5556 *SIC 3629*

GENTLE CARE DRAPERY & CARPET CLEANERS LTD p 189
3755 WAYBURNE DR, BURNABY, BC, V5G 3L1
(604) 296-4000 *SIC 7217*

GENTOX LABORATORIES INC p 670
1345 DENISON ST, MARKHAM, ON, L3R 5V2
(416) 798-4988 *SIC 8734*

GENUINE CANADIAN CORP, THE p 744
1 PROLOGIS BLVD, MISSISSAUGA, ON, L5W 0G2
(519) 624-6574 *SIC 5137*

GENUINE HEALTH INC p 989
200-491 COLLEGE ST, TORONTO, ON, M6G 1A5
(877) 500-7888 *SIC 5122*

GENUINE PARTS HOLDINGS LTD p 739
1450 MEYERSIDE DR SUITE 305, MISSIS-SAUGA, ON, L5T 2N5
(905) 696-9301 *SIC 6712*

GENUMARK p 765
See GENUMARK PROMOTIONAL MER-CHANDISE INC

GENUMARK PROMOTIONAL MERCHAN-DISE INC p

765
707 GORDON BAKER RD, NORTH YORK, ON, M2H 2S6
(416) 391-9191 *SIC 5199*

GENWORTH FINANCIAL MORTGAGE IN-SURANCE COMPANY CANADA p
797
2060 WINSTON PARK DR SUITE 300, OAKVILLE, ON, L6H 5R7
(905) 287-5300 *SIC 6351*

GENWORTH MI CANADA INC p 797
2060 WINSTON PARK DR SUITE 300, OAKVILLE, ON, L6H 5R7
(905) 287-5300 *SIC 6351*

GENWORTH MORTGAGE INSURANCE CANADA p 797
See GENWORTH FINANCIAL MORTGAGE INSURANCE COMPANY CANADA

GENZYME CANADA INC p 695
2700 MATHESON BLVD E SUITE 800, MIS-SISSAUGA, ON, L4W 4V9
(905) 625-0011 *SIC 5122*

GEO A. HALL INC p 1049
8800 6E CROISSANT, ANJOU, QC, H1J 1A1
(514) 352-5550 *SIC 4212*

GEO EVERYTHING FOR TRAVEL p 91
See UNIGLOBE GEO TRAVEL LTD

GEO JACK ENTERPRISES INC p 1421
4130 ALBERT ST SUITE 425, REGINA, SK, S4S 3R8
(306) 777-8040 *SIC 5912*

GEO-FOR INC p 1347
633 AV GAGNON, SAINT-LUDGER-DE-MILOT, QC, G0W 2B0
SIC 0851

GEO. A. KELSON COMPANY LIMITED p
880
2 BALES DR W, SHARON, ON, L0G 1V0
(905) 898-3400 *SIC 1711*

GEO. SHEARD FABRICS LTD p 1082
84 RUE MERRILL, COATICOOK, QC, J1A 1X4
(819) 849-6311 *SIC 5949*

GEOCALM INC p 681
478 BAY ST SUITE 216, MIDLAND, ON, L4R 1K9
(705) 528-6888 *SIC 5049*

GEODIGITAL INTERNATIONAL INC p 831
1 ANTARES DR UNIT 140, OTTAWA, ON, K2E 8C4
(613) 820-4545 *SIC 8713*

GEODIS FF CANADA LTD p 688
3061 ORLANDO DR, MISSISSAUGA, ON, L4V 1R4
(905) 677-5266 *SIC 4731*

GEOLOGIC SYSTEMS LTD p 50
401 9 AVE SW SUITE 1500, CALGARY, AB, T2P 3C5
(403) 262-1992 *SIC 7371*

GEOLOGICAL INDUSTRY RESEARCH INC p 939
140 YONGE ST, TORONTO, ON, M5C 1X6
(416) 477-1164 *SIC 8999*

GEOLOGISTICS p 737
See AGILITY LOGISTICS, CO

GEOPAC p 1066
See MENARD CANADA INC

GEOPHYSICAL EXPLORATION & DEVEL-OPMENT CORPORATION p
30
125 9 AVE SE UNIT 200, CALGARY, AB, T2G 0P6
(403) 262-5780 *SIC 8999*

GEOPHYSICS G.P.R. INTERNATIONAL p
1144
See GEOPHYSIQUE G.P.R. INTERNA-TIONAL INC

GEOPHYSIQUE G.P.R. INTERNATIONAL INC p 1144
2545 RUE DE LORIMIER BUREAU 100, LONGUEUIL, QC, J4K 3P7
(450) 679-2400 *SIC 8999*

GEORDY RENTALS INC p 283

2576 KING GEORGE BLVD, SURREY, BC, V4P 1H5
(604) 668-7230 *SIC 5521*

GEORGE A. WRIGHT & SON LIMITED p
630
146 HICKSON AVE, KINGSTON, ON, K7K 2N9
(613) 542-4913 *SIC 3599*

GEORGE AND ASMUSSEN LIMITED p 518
5093 FOUNTAIN ST N, BRESLAU, ON, N0B 1M0
(519) 648-2285 *SIC 1741*

GEORGE BRAUN & SONS FARMS LIMITED p 564
GD LCD MAIN, DELHI, ON, N4B 2W7
(519) 582-1239 *SIC 0191*

GEORGE BROWN COLLEGE p 972
See GEORGE BROWN COLLEGE OF AP-PLIED ARTS AND TECHNOLOGY, THE

GEORGE BROWN COLLEGE OF APPLIED ARTS AND TECHNOLOGY, THE p 972
500 MACPHERSON AVE, TORONTO, ON, M5R 1M3
(416) 415-2000 *SIC 8222*

GEORGE BROWN COLLEGE OF APPLIED ARTS AND TECHNOLOGY, THE p 977
160 KENDAL AVE SUITE 126A, TORONTO, ON, M5T 2T9
(416) 415-5000 *SIC 8221*

GEORGE DERBY CARE SOCIETY p 181
7550 CUMBERLAND ST, BURNABY, BC, V3N 3X5
(604) 521-2676 *SIC 8051*

GEORGE DERBY CENTRE p 181
See GEORGE DERBY CARE SOCIETY

GEORGE SYME COMMUNITY SCHOOL p
994
See TORONTO DISTRICT SCHOOL BOARD

GEORGE WESTON LIMITED p 925
22 ST CLAIR AVE E SUITE 1901, TORONTO, ON, M4T 2S7
(416) 922-2500 *SIC 5141*

GEORGE'S MARINE & SPORTS p 567
See G & L WILCOX LIMITED

GEORGE, JS ENTERPRISES LTD p 418
138 MAIN ST SUITE 17, SUSSEX, NB, E4E 3E1
(506) 433-3201 *SIC 5531*

GEORGES NADEAU p 1277
See ENTREPRISES POL R INC

GEORGETOWN CHEVROLET BUICK GMC LTD p 593
33 MOUNTAINVIEW RD N, GEORGE-TOWN, ON, L7G 4J7
(905) 877-6944 *SIC 5511*

GEORGETOWN DISTRICT HIGH SCHOOL p
593
See HALTON CATHOLIC DISTRICT SCHOOL BOARD

GEORGETOWN HONDA p 593
See 942599 ONTARIO LIMITED

GEORGETOWN TERMINAL WARE-HOUSES LIMITED p
593
34 ARMSTRONG AVE, GEORGETOWN, ON, L7G 4R9
(905) 873-2750 *SIC 4226*

GEORGIA PACIFIC REALTY CORPORA-TION p
293
601 BROADWAY W UNIT 200, VANCOU-VER, BC, V5Z 4C2
(604) 222-8585 *SIC 6531*

GEORGIA-PACIFIC CANADA LP p 274
12509 116 AVE, SURREY, BC, V3V 3S6
(604) 209-6588 *SIC 3275*

GEORGIA-PACIFIC CANADA LP p 907
319 ALLANBURG RD, THOROLD, ON, L2V 5C3
(905) 451-0620 *SIC 2679*

GEORGIAN BAY FIRE & SAFETY LTD p 835
1700 20TH ST E, OWEN SOUND, ON, N4K 5W9

(519) 376-6120 *SIC 5099*

GEORGIAN BAY GENERAL HOSPITAL p
681
1112 ST ANDREWS DR, MIDLAND, ON, L4R 4P4
(705) 526-1300 *SIC 8062*

GEORGIAN BAY HOTEL & CONFERENCE CENTRE p 546
See GEORGIAN MANOR RESORT & COUNTRY CLUB INC, THE

GEORGIAN COLLEGE OF APPLIED ARTS AND TECHNOLOGY, THE p 484
1 GEORGIAN DR, BARRIE, ON, L4M 3X9
(705) 728-1968 *SIC 8222*

GEORGIAN INTERNATIONAL LIMITED p
484
85 BAYFIELD ST SUITE 500, BARRIE, ON, L4M 3A7
(705) 730-5900 *SIC 5511*

GEORGIAN MANOR RESORT & COUNTRY CLUB INC, THE p 546
10 VACATION INN DR, COLLINGWOOD, ON, L9Y 5G4
(800) 696-5487 *SIC 7997*

GEORGINA JOB SKILLS p 628
See JOB SKILLS

GEOSYNTEC CONSULTANTS INTERNA-TIONAL INC p
601
130 STONE RD W, GUELPH, ON, N1G 3Z2
(519) 822-2230 *SIC 8748*

GEOTAB INC p 797
2440 WINSTON PARK DR, OAKVILLE, ON, L6H 7V2
(416) 434-4309 *SIC 3812*

GEOTECH DRILLING SERVICES LTD p 248
5052 HARTWAY DR, PRINCE GEORGE, BC, V2K 5B7
(250) 962-9041 *SIC 1081*

GEOTECH LTD p 480
245 INDUSTRIAL PKY N, AURORA, ON, L4G 4C4
(905) 841-5004 *SIC 8999*

GEOX CANADA INC p 695
2110 MATHESON BLVD E SUITE 100, MIS-SISSAUGA, ON, L4W 5E1
(905) 629-8500 *SIC 5661*

GEP PRODUCTIONS INC p 785
40 CARL HALL RD UNIT 3, NORTH YORK, ON, M3K 2C1
(416) 398-6869 *SIC 7812*

GERALDTON DISTRICT HOSPITAL p 594
500 HOGARTH ST, GERALDTON, ON, P0T 1M0
(807) 854-1862 *SIC 8062*

GERARD BERGERON & FILS INC p 1343
1486 RANG BARTHELEMY, SAINT-LEON, QC, J0K 2W0
(819) 228-3936 *SIC 0134*

GERARD HUBERT AUTOMOBILES LTEE p
1148
241 BOUL DESJARDINS, MANIWAKI, QC, J9E 2E3
(819) 449-2266 *SIC 5511*

GERATEK p 1373
See CONSTRUCTION GERATEK LTEE

GERDAU AMERISTEEL CORPORATION p
356
1 RAILWAY ST, SELKIRK, MB, R1A 2B3
(204) 482-6701 *SIC 5093*

GERDAU AMERISTEEL CORPORATION p
356
27 MAIN ST, SELKIRK, MB, R1A 1P6
(204) 482-3241 *SIC 3312*

GERDAU AMERISTEEL CORPORATION p
536
160 ORION PL, CAMBRIDGE, ON, N1T 1R9
(519) 740-2488 *SIC 3312*

GERDAU AMERISTEEL CORPORATION p
1014
1 GERDAU CRT, WHITBY, ON, L1N 7G8
(905) 668-8811 *SIC 3312*

GERDAU AMERISTEEL METALS RECY-

CLING p
1014
See GERDAU AMERISTEEL CORPORATION

GERDAU AMERSTEEL MANITOBA METALS p
356
See GERDAU AMERISTEEL CORPORATION

GERICO FOREST PRODUCTS LTD p 218
666 ATHABASCA ST W, KAMLOOPS, BC, V2H 1C4
(250) 374-0333 *SIC* 8741

GERMAIN LARIVIERE (1970) LTEE p 1310
4370 BOUL LAURIER E, SAINT-HYACINTHE, QC, J2R 2C1
(450) 799-5522 *SIC* 5712

GERMAIN LARIVIERE INC p 1310
4370 BOUL LAURIER E, SAINT-HYACINTHE, QC, J2R 2C1
(450) 799-5522 *SIC* 5722

GERMAN ADVERTISING ADVANTAGE INC, THE p 224
19770 94A AVE, LANGLEY, BC, V1M 3B7
(604) 888-8008 *SIC* 5199

GERMIPHENE CORPORATION p 517
1379 COLBORNE ST E, BRANTFORD, ON, N3T 5M1
(519) 759-7100 *SIC* 3843

GEROQUIP INC p 1236
4795 RUE LOUIS-B.-MAYER, MONTREAL, QC, H7P 6G5
(450) 978-0200 *SIC* 5039

GERRET ENTERPRISES INCORPORATED p 439
58 BOUNDARY ST, BARRINGTON PASSAGE, NS, B0W 1G0
(902) 745-3899 *SIC* 5146

GERRIE ELECTRIC WHOLESALE LIMITED p 522
4104 SOUTH SERVICE RD, BURLINGTON, ON, L7L 4X5
(905) 681-3660 *SIC* 5063

GERRIE SUPPLY CHAIN SERVICES p 522
See GERRIE ELECTRIC WHOLESALE LIMITED

GERRITY CORRUGATED PAPER PRODUCTS LTD p
553
75 DONEY CRES SUITE 1, CONCORD, ON, L4K 1P6
(416) 798-7758 *SIC* 2653

GERRY GORDON'S MAZDA p 390
See CONVENTRY MOTORS LIMITED

GERRY'S TRUCK CENTRE LTD p 660
4049 EASTGATE CRES, LONDON, ON, N6L 1B7
(519) 652-2100 *SIC* 5511

GERTEX HOSIERY INC p 791
9 DENSLEY AVE, NORTH YORK, ON, M6M 2P5
(416) 241-2345 *SIC* 5137

GERVAIS DUBE INC p 1384
62 2E RANG O, TROIS-PISTOLES, QC, G0L 4K0
(418) 851-2994 *SIC* 1623

GES CANADA p 731
See GES EXPOSITION SERVICES (CANADA) LIMITED

GES CANADA p 1130
See EXPOSERVICE STANDARD INC

GES EXPOSITION SERVICES (CANADA) LIMITED p 731
5675 MCLAUGHLIN RD, MISSISSAUGA, ON, L5R 3K5
(905) 283-0500 *SIC* 7389

GESCA LTEE p 821
47 CLARENCE ST SUITE 222, OTTAWA, ON, K1N 9K1
(613) 562-0111 *SIC* 2711

GESCA LTEE p 1188
750 BOUL SAINT-LAURENT, MONTREAL, QC, H2Y 2Z4
(514) 285-7000 *SIC* 2711

GESCA NUMERIQUE INC p 1188
750 BOUL SAINT-LAURENT, MONTREAL, QC, H2Y 2Z4
(514) 285-7000 *SIC* 7371

GESCLADO INC p 1362
1400 BOUL DAGENAIS O, SAINTE-ROSE, QC, H7L 5C7
(450) 622-1600 *SIC* 6712

GESCO INDUSTRIES INC p 503
50 KENVIEW BLVD, BRAMPTON, ON, L6T 5S8
(905) 789-3755 *SIC* 5023

GESCO LIMITED PARTNERSHIP p 503
50 KENVIEW BLVD, BRAMPTON, ON, L6T 5S8
(905) 789-3755 *SIC* 5023

GESTION 357 DE LA COMMUNE INC p
1188
357 RUE DE LA COMMUNE O, MONTREAL, QC, H2Y 2E2
(514) 499-0357 *SIC* 7389

GESTION 47 LTEE p 1083
1601 BOUL SAINT-MARTIN E, COTE SAINT-LUC, QC, H7G 4R4
(450) 669-7070 *SIC* 5511

GESTION A.D.L. SENC p 1150
1665 RUE NISHK, MASHTEUIATSH, QC, G0W 2H0
(418) 275-6161 *SIC* 2131

GESTION A.J.L.R. INC p 1285
451 RUE DE L'EXPANSION, RIMOUSKI, QC, G5M 1B4
(418) 724-2243 *SIC* 6712

GESTION ACCEO INC p 1210
75 RUE QUEEN BUREAU 4700, MONTREAL, QC, H3C 2N6
(514) 288-7161 *SIC* 7379

GESTION AFINITI p 1275
See 9003-9306 QUEBEC INC

GESTION ALAIN LAFOREST INC p 1045
50 BOUL SAINT-LUC, ALMA, QC, G8B 6K1
(418) 662-6618 *SIC* 5311

GESTION ALCOA CANADA CIE p 1204
1 PLACE VILLE-MARIE BUREAU 2310, MONTREAL, QC, H3B 3M5
(514) 904-5030 *SIC* 3334

GESTION ANDRE R. VAILLANCOURT LTEE p 1160
3500 BOUL DU TRICENTENAIRE BUREAU 303, MONTREAL, QC, H1B 0A3
(514) 645-2761 *SIC* 5399

GESTION ANKABETH INC p 1375
4880 BOUL BOURQUE, SHERBROOKE, QC, J1N 2A7
(819) 823-1400 *SIC* 5511

GESTION ASSELIN INC p 1379
934 RUE SAINT-SACREMENT, TERREBONNE, QC, J6W 3G2
(450) 964-8448 *SIC* 5812

GESTION AUDEM INC p 1204
5 PLACE VILLE-MARIE BUREAU 915, MONTREAL, QC, H3B 2G2
(514) 874-2600 *SIC* 4833

GESTION BBFD INC p 1275
3730 RUE DU CAMPANILE, QUEBEC, QC, G1X 4G6
(418) 658-1337 *SIC* 5912

GESTION BC-A INC p 1348
38 AV DU PONT O, SAINT-MARTIN, QC, G0M 1B0
(418) 382-3930 *SIC* 3089

GESTION BEAUCE-ATLAS INC p 1360
600 1RE AV DU PARC-INDUSTRIEL, SAINTE-MARIE, QC, G6E 1B5
(418) 387-4872 *SIC* 5051

GESTION BELANGER, BERNARD LTEE p
1122
1300 4E AV, LA POCATIERE, QC, G0R 1Z0
(418) 856-3858 *SIC* 6712

GESTION BENOIT GUILLEMETTE INC p
1053
650 RUE DE PARFONDEVAL BUREAU 265, BAIE-COMEAU, QC, G5C 3R3
(418) 589-9924 *SIC* 5531

GESTION BRINEKY INC p 1219
5035 CH MIRA, MONTREAL, QC, H3W 2B9
(514) 282-3300 *SIC* 2842

GESTION C. & L. LAROCHELLE INCp 1382
70 BOUL FRONTENAC E BUREAU 156, THETFORD MINES, QC, G6G 1N4
(418) 338-3535 *SIC* 5531

GESTION C.B.R. LASER INC p 1246
340 RTE 116, PLESSISVILLE, QC, G6L 2Y2
(819) 362-2095 *SIC* 6712

GESTION C.T.M.A. INC p 1073
435 CH AVILA-ARSENEAU, CAP-AUX-MEULES, QC, G4T 1J3
(418) 986-6600 *SIC* 6712

GESTION CAE INTERNATIONAL p 1338
See CAE INTERNATIONAL HOLDINGS LIMITED

GESTION CANADADIRECT INC p 1094
743 AV RENAUD, DORVAL, QC, H9P 2N1
(514) 422-8557 *SIC* 8732

GESTION CANDEREL INC p 1196
2000 RUE PEEL BUREAU 900, MONTREAL, QC, H3A 2W5
(514) 842-8636 *SIC* 6553

GESTION CARBO LTEE p 1076
117 BOUL SAINT-JEAN-BAPTISTE, CHATEAUGUAY, QC, J6K 3B1
(450) 691-4130 *SIC* 5511

GESTION CARMINEX INC p 1358
2255 RUE BOMBARDIER, SAINTE-JULIE, QC, J3E 2J9
(450) 922-0900 *SIC* 6712

GESTION CARRIER, ROBERT INC p 1117
73 RUE DU CHAMBERTIN, KIRKLAND, QC, H9H 5E3
SIC 2542

GESTION CAVEAU DES JEANS INCp 1106
84 RUE LOIS, GATINEAU, QC, J8Y 3R4
SIC 5651

GESTION CBCC INC p 1081
3 RUE AAHPPISAACH, CHISASIBI, QC, J0M 1E0
(819) 855-2977 *SIC* 1521

GESTION CEJEMAR INC p 1057
1040 AV GILLES-VILLENEUVE, BERTHIERVILLE, QC, J0K 1A0
(450) 836-1238 *SIC* 5812

GESTION CENTREVISION p 1262
See GROUPE MARCHAND RENE INC

GESTION CENTRIA COMMERCE INC p
1086
3131 BOUL SAINT-MARTIN O, COTE SAINT-LUC, QC, H7T 2Z5
(514) 874-0122 *SIC* 6712

GESTION CENTURION INC p 1349
555 RUE PANNETON, SAINT-NARCISSE, QC, G0X 2Y0
(418) 328-3361 *SIC* 2515

GESTION CERATEC INC p 1264
414 AV SAINT-SACREMENT, QUEBEC, QC, G1N 3Y3
(418) 681-0101 *SIC* 5032

GESTION CHRISTIAN BASTIEN INCp 1367
770 BOUL LAURE UNITE 270, SEPT-ILES, QC, G4R 1Y5
(418) 962-3333 *SIC* 5912

GESTION CHRISTIAN DUGUAY INCp 1232
3100 BOUL DE LA CONCORDE E BUREAU 50D, MONTREAL, QC, H7E 2B8
(450) 661-7748 *SIC* 5912

GESTION CHRISTIAN J. OUELLET INC p
1255
3333 RUE DU CARREFOUR, QUEBEC, QC, G1C 5Y9
(418) 667-7534 *SIC* 5912

GESTION CLAUDE MEILLEUR INC p 1373
3050 BOUL DE PORTLAND, SHERBROOKE, QC, J1L 1K1
(819) 569-9621 *SIC* 5912

GESTION CLAUDIUS INC p 1317
1000 BOUL DU SEMINAIRE N BUREAU 4, SAINT-JEAN-SUR-RICHELIEU, QC, J3A 1E5
(450) 348-6813 *SIC* 5912

GESTION CLAUMOND INC p 1372

2235 RUE GALT O, SHERBROOKE, QC, J1K 1K6
(819) 569-9349 *SIC* 5912

GESTION CLUDE THIBAUDEAU p 1305
See TAPIS VENTURE INC

GESTION D' ACTIF BURGUNDY p 1194
See BURGUNDY ASSET MANAGEMENT LTD

GESTION D'ACTIFS CIBC INC p 1204
1000 RUE DE LA GAUCHETIERE O BUREAU 3100, MONTREAL, QC, H3B 4W5
(514) 875-7040 *SIC* 6726

GESTION D'ACTIFS GLADU INC p 1149
2115 RUE SAINT-CESAIRE, MARIEVILLE, QC, J3M 1E5
(450) 460-4481 *SIC* 3423

GESTION D'ACTIFS SECTORIELS INC p
1196
1000 RUE SHERBROOKE O BUREAU 2120, MONTREAL, QC, H3A 3G4
(514) 849-8777 *SIC* 6282

GESTION D'ETUDE PPKF (1984) INC p
1188
507 PLACE D'ARMES BUREAU 1300, MONTREAL, QC, H2Y 2W8
(514) 282-1287 *SIC* 7389

GESTION D'INVESTISSEMENT 2300 INC p
1329
2300 RUE EMILE-BELANGER, SAINT-LAURENT, QC, H4R 3J4
(514) 747-2536 *SIC* 6712

GESTION D. PRESSAULT INC p 1150
145 RUE PIUZE, MATANE, QC, G4W 0H7
(418) 562-5144 *SIC* 5531

GESTION DAMIEN MORISSETTE INC p
1135
333 CH DES SABLES, LEVIS, QC, G6C 1B5
(418) 838-7444 *SIC* 6712

GESTION DE FONDS SENTIENT CANADA LTEE p 1196
1010 RUE SHERBROOKE O BUREAU 1512, MONTREAL, QC, H3A 2R7
SIC 6722

GESTION DE PORTEFEUILLE NATCAN INC p 1204
1100 BOUL ROBERT-BOURASSA UNITE 400, MONTREAL, QC, H3B 3A5
SIC 6719

GESTION DELOITTE p 1086
See DELOITTE RESTRUCTURING INC

GESTION DELOITTE S.E.C p 1312
850 BOUL CASAVANT O, SAINT-HYACINTHE, QC, J2S 7S3
(450) 774-4000 *SIC* 8742

GESTION DENISON TH INC p 1369
211 CH SAXBY S, SHEFFORD, QC, J2M 1S3
(450) 775-6845 *SIC* 5812

GESTION DESJARDINS CAPITAL INC p
1230
2 COMPLEXE DESJARDINS BUREAU 1717, MONTREAL, QC, H5B 1B8
(514) 281-7131 *SIC* 6719

GESTION DOMINIC PAQUETTE INC p 627
25 BRUNETVILLE RD SUITE 30, KAPUSKASING, ON, P5N 2E9
(705) 335-6066 *SIC* 5531

GESTION DOMINIQUE BOND INC p 1275
2160 BOUL BASTIEN, QUEBEC, QC, G2B 1B7
(418) 842-3648 *SIC* 5912

GESTION DU GROUPE REDBOURNE INCp
1196
1555 RUE PEEL BUREAU 700, MONTREAL, QC, H3A 3L8
(514) 940-1555 *SIC* 6719

GESTION ESTEREL INC p 1100
39 CH FRIDOLIN-SIMARD, ESTEREL, QC, J0T 1E0
(450) 228-2662 *SIC* 7011

GESTION EXCLUSIVE MAINTENANCE p
1361
See 9320-4048 QUEBEC INC

GESTION F.D. DESHARNAIS INC p 1279

6055 BOUL PIERRE-BERTRAND, QUE-BEC, QC, G2K 1M1

(418) 628-0203 *SIC* 7538

GESTION FAMILLE BUCCI INC *p 1379*
1250 BOUL MOODY BUREAU 312, TERRE-BONNE, QC, J6W 3K9

(450) 961-9011 *SIC* 5531

GESTION FAMILLE DEZIEL INC *p 1343*
1869 CH SAINTE-ANGELIQUE, SAINT-LAZARE, QC, J7T 2X9

(450) 455-6165 *SIC* 5411

GESTION FERIQUE *p 1204*
1010 RUE DE LA GAUCHETIERE O, MON-TREAL, QC, H3B 2N2

(514) 840-9206 *SIC* 6722

GESTION FETIA INC *p 1170*
8400 2E AV, MONTREAL, QC, H1Z 4M6

(514) 722-2324 *SIC* 6712

GESTION FRANCOIS MALTAIS INC *p 1370*
1363 RUE BELVEDERE S, SHERBROOKE, QC, J1H 4E4

(819) 565-9595 *SIC* 5912

GESTION FRP INC *p 1272*
2960 BOUL LAURIER BUREAU 214, QUE-BEC, QC, G1V 4S1

(418) 652-1737 *SIC* 8742

GESTION FSTG INC *p 541*
95 LAFLECHE BLVD, CASSELMAN, ON, K0A 1M0

(613) 764-0401 *SIC* 5014

GESTION G.G.V.M. INC *p 1097*
511 RUE HERIOT, DRUMMONDVILLE, QC, J2B 7R3

(819) 477-3777 *SIC* 5912

GESTION G.S.F. INC *p 1283*
581 RUE NOTRE-DAME BUREAU 302, RE-PENTIGNY, QC, J6A 2V1

(450) 654-5226 *SIC* 8741

GESTION GAETAN BOUCHER *p 1292*
405 273 RTE, SAINT-APOLLINAIRE, QC, G0S 2E0

(418) 881-3112 *SIC* 5411

GESTION GAEVAN INC *p 1280*
625 RUE DE L'ARGON, QUEBEC, QC, G2N 2G7

(418) 841-2001 *SIC* 5511

GESTION GCL INC *p 1159*
1595 RTE 117, MONT-TREMBLANT, QC, J8E 2X9

(819) 425-2711 *SIC* 5999

GESTION GEORGES ABRAHAM INC *p 1079*
433 RUE RACINE E, CHICOUTIMI, QC, G7H 1T5

(418) 543-2875 *SIC* 5812

GESTION GEORGES SZARAZ INC. *p 1301*
311 RUE BOILEAU, SAINT-EUSTACHE, QC, J7R 2V5

SIC 8741

GESTION GERALD SAVARD INC *p 1278*
5500 BOUL DES GRADINS BUREAU 405, QUEBEC, QC, G2J 1A1

(418) 622-7333 *SIC* 5941

GESTION GIACOMO D'AMICO INC *p 403*
383 CH MADAWASKA, GRAND-SAULT/GRAND FALLS, NB, E3Y 1A4

(506) 473-3550 *SIC* 5531

GESTION GILLES CHARTRAND INC *p 394*
520 ST. PETER AVE, BATHURST, NB, E2A 2Y7

(506) 547-8120 *SIC* 5531

GESTION GILLES ST-MICHEL INC *p 1289*
245 BOUL RIDEAU, ROUYN-NORANDA, QC, J9X 5Y6

(819) 762-4375 *SIC* 5399

GESTION GILLES-GENEST INC *p 1082*
35 RUE PRINCIPALE E, COOKSHIRE-EATON, QC, J0B 1M0

(819) 875-5455 *SIC* 5411

GESTION GRATIEN PAQUIN INC *p 1369*
1173 AV DE GRAND-MERE, SHAWINIGAN, QC, G9T 2J4

(819) 538-1707 *SIC* 4899

GESTION GREGOIRE INC *p 1315*

210 RUE MOREAU, SAINT-JEAN-SUR-RICHELIEU, QC, J2W 0E9

(450) 347-2835 *SIC* 5511

GESTION GUY GERVAIS INC *p 1226*
1370 RUE CHABANEL O, MONTREAL, QC, H4N 1H4

(514) 384-5590 *SIC* 5032

GESTION GUY L'HEUREUX INC *p 1101*
544 BOUL CURE-LABELLE BUREAU 690, FABREVILLE, QC, H7P 2P4

(450) 963-8686 *SIC* 5531

GESTION GUYTA INC *p 1097*
4275 BOUL SAINT-JOSEPH, DRUM-MONDVILLE, QC, J2B 1T8

(819) 477-1596 *SIC* 3469

GESTION H. DICKNER LTEE *p 1284*
559 RUE DE LAUSANNE, RIMOUSKI, QC, G5L 4A7

(418) 723-7936 *SIC* 6512

GESTION H. LEVESQUE LTEE *p 1068*
2180 BOUL LAPINIERE, BROSSARD, QC, J4W 1M2

(450) 462-2116 *SIC* 5063

GESTION HEROUX ET SAUCIER INC *p 1247*
12675 RUE SHERBROOKE E, POINTE-AUX-TREMBLES, QC, H1A 3W7

(514) 642-2251 *SIC* 5912

GESTION HOTELLUS CANADA *p 1188*
See *HOTELLUS CANADA HOLDINGS INC*

GESTION IMMOBILIERE LUC MAURICE INC *p 1329*
2400 RUE DES NATIONS BUREAU 137, SAINT-LAURENT, QC, H4R 3G4

(514) 331-2788 *SIC* 6719

GESTION INDUSTRIES INC *p 1305*
9095 25E AV, SAINT-GEORGES, QC, G6A 1A1

(418) 228-8934 *SIC* 6712

GESTION INFILISE INC *p 1394*
3901 RUE F.-X.-TESSIER, VAUDREUIL-DORION, QC, J7V 5V5

(450) 424-0161 *SIC* 5169

GESTION J. M. BRASSEUR INC *p 1065*
1361 RUE GRAHAM-BELL, BOUCHERVILLE, QC, J4B 6A1

(450) 655-3155 *SIC* 2047

GESTION J. M. LEROUX LTEE *p 1262*
30 BOUL WILFRID-HAMEL, QUEBEC, QC, G1M 2P7

(418) 687-2111 *SIC* 5251

GESTION J.C. FAVREAU LTEE *p 1059*
1083 BOUL DU CURE-LABELLE BUREAU 110, BLAINVILLE, QC, J7C 3M9

(450) 435-1981 *SIC* 6712

GESTION J.L.T. UNIVERSELLE INC *p 1098*
915 RUE HAINS, DRUMMONDVILLE, QC, J2C 3A1

(819) 472-2942 *SIC* 7011

GESTION J.M.CLEMENT LTEE *p 1278*
5830 BOUL PIERRE-BERTRAND BUREAU 400, QUEBEC, QC, G2J 1B7

(418) 626-0006 *SIC* 6712

GESTION JACQUES BOURGET INC *p 1232*
2955 BOUL DE LA CONCORDE E BUREAU 76, MONTREAL, QC, H7E 2B5

(450) 661-6921 *SIC* 5912

GESTION JEAN LAFRAMBOISE INC *p 1239*
11450 BOUL ALBERT-HUDON, MONTREAL-NORD, QC, H1G 3J9

SIC 2326

GESTION JEAN PAQUETTE INC *p 1255*
705 RUE CLEMENCEAU BUREAU 184, QUEBEC, QC, G1C 7T9

(418) 663-4334 *SIC* 5311

GESTION JEAN-PIERRE ROBIDOUX INC *p 1353*
320 201 RTE, SAINT-STANISLAS-DE-KOSTKA, QC, J0S 1W0

(450) 377-2535 *SIC* 4213

GESTION JOCELYNE CROTEAU INC *p 1283*
91 RUE OUIMET, REPENTIGNY, QC, J6A

1E1

(450) 581-2092 *SIC* 5621

GESTION JUSTE POUR RIRE INC *p 1185*
2101 BOUL SAINT-LAURENT, MONTREAL, QC, H2X 2T5

(514) 845-3155 *SIC* 7999

GESTION JUSTERO INC *p 1049*
11001 RUE COLBERT, ANJOU, QC, H1J 2S1

(514) 355-7484 *SIC* 3442

GESTION KM INC *p 1224*
5855 BOUL GOUIN O, MONTREAL, QC, H4J 1E5

(514) 334-8641 *SIC* 5912

GESTION L. FECTEAU LTEE *p 1243*
3150 CH ROYAL, NOTRE-DAME-DES-PINS, QC, G0M 1K0

(418) 774-3324 *SIC* 6712

GESTION L.L. LOZEAU LTEE *p 1182*
6229 RUE SAINT-HUBERT, MONTREAL, QC, H2S 2L9

(514) 274-6577 *SIC* 6719

GESTION LABERGE INC *p 1119*
6245 BOUL WILFRID-HAMEL, L'ANCIENNE-LORETTE, QC, G2E 5W2

(418) 667-1313 *SIC* 6712

GESTION LEGALIS INC *p 1272*
1195 AV LAVIGERIE BUREAU 200, QUE-BEC, QC, G1V 4N3

(418) 658-9966 *SIC* 6311

GESTION LISE HAMEL-CHARTRAND INC *p 1219*
4815 AV VAN HORNE, MONTREAL, QC, H3W 1J2

(514) 739-1758 *SIC* 5912

GESTION LITTLE MOUSE INC *p 1264*
1350 RUE CYRILLE-DUQUET, QUEBEC, QC, G1N 2E5

(418) 681-6381 *SIC* 5999

GESTION LJT INC *p 1188*
380 RUE SAINT-ANTOINE O BUREAU 7100, MONTREAL, QC, H2Y 3X7

(514) 842-8891 *SIC* 8741

GESTION LOUMA INC *p 1370*
1325 12E AV N, SHERBROOKE, QC, J1E 3P6

(819) 566-4844 *SIC* 5812

GESTION M A S INC *p 1310*
2890 BOUL LAURIER E, SAINT-HYACINTHE, QC, J2R 1P8

(450) 774-7511 *SIC* 6712

GESTION M.E.W. INC *p 1246*
2255 AV VALLEE, PLESSISVILLE, QC, G6L 3P8

(819) 362-6315 *SIC* 3599

GESTION M.L.B. CARDINAL LTEE *p 1059*
500 BOUL DE LA SEIGNEURIE O BUREAU 649, BLAINVILLE, QC, J7C 5T7

(450) 419-4700 *SIC* 5311

GESTION MADELEINE DE VILLERS INC *p 1173*
4246 RUE SAINT-DENIS, MONTREAL, QC, H2J 2K8

(514) 845-4090 *SIC* 5719

GESTION MAGDI TEBECHRANI INC., LES *p 1239*
6000 BOUL HENRI-BOURASSA E, MONTREAL-NORD, QC, H1G 2T6

(514) 323-5010 *SIC* 5912

GESTION MAHEL INC *p 1300*
130 RUE DUBOIS, SAINT-EUSTACHE, QC, J7P 4W9

(450) 974-0440 *SIC* 5812

GESTION MAISON ETHIER INC *p 1294*
267 BOUL SIR-WILFRID-LAURIER, SAINT-BASILE-LE-GRAND, QC, J3N 1M8

(450) 653-1556 *SIC* 5719

GESTION MAJEAU, MARCEL INC *p 1120*
41 RUE DU COUVENT, L'EPIPHANIE, QC, J5X 0B6

(450) 938-0884 *SIC* 6514

GESTION MAJERO INC *p 1339*
8180 COTE-DE-LIESSE ROAD, SAINT-LAURENT, QC, H4T 1G8

SIC 8741

GESTION MARC DESERRES INC *p 1175*
1265 RUE BERRI BUREAU 1000, MON-TREAL, QC, H2L 4X4

(514) 842-6695 *SIC* 5999

GESTION MARC NADEAU INC *p 1262*
625 RUE DU MARAIS, QUEBEC, QC, G1M 2Y2

(418) 681-0696 *SIC* 2095

GESTION MARC-ANDRE LORD INC *p 1123*
91 2E RUE E BUREAU 233, LA SARRE, QC, J9Z 3J9

SIC 5013

GESTION MARCEL G GAGNE INC *p 1368*
1555 RUE TRUDEL BUREAU 131, SHAW-INIGAN, QC, G9N 8K8

(819) 537-8999 *SIC* 5014

GESTION MARIO CHRISTIN INC *p 1247*
12011 RUE SHERBROOKE E, POINTE-AUX-TREMBLES, QC, H1B 1C6

(514) 640-1050 *SIC* 6712

GESTION MARIO ROY INC *p 1122*
375 BOUL DE COMPORTE BUREAU 118, LA MALBAIE, QC, G5A 1H9

(418) 665-6483 *SIC* 5531

GESTION MARTIN BOUTET INC *p 1303*
1180 RTE 243, SAINT-FELIX-DE-KINGSEY, QC, J0B 2T0

(819) 848-2521 *SIC* 6712

GESTION MASSON, ST-PIERRE INC *p 1385*
165 BOUL SAINTE-MADELEINE, TROIS-RIVIERES, QC, G8T 3L7

(819) 375-4824 *SIC* 5411

GESTION MCNALLY INC *p 1134*
2030 BOUL DAGENAIS O, LAVAL-OUEST, QC, H7L 5W2

(450) 625-4662 *SIC* 3556

GESTION MD MANAGEMENT *p 1204*
1000 RUE DE LA GAUCHETIERE O BU-REAU 650, MONTREAL, QC, H3B 4W5

(514) 392-1434 *SIC* 8741

GESTION METALLURGIE CASTECH INC *p 1382*
500 BOUL FRONTENAC E, THETFORD MINES, QC, G6G 7M8

(418) 338-3171 *SIC* 3325

GESTION MICHAEL KORS (CANADA) *p 1213*
See *MICHAEL KORS (CANADA) HOLD-INGS LTD*

GESTION MICHAEL ROSSY LTEE *p 1326*
450 BOUL LEBEAU, SAINT-LAURENT, QC, H4N 1R7

(514) 335-6255 *SIC* 5311

GESTION MICHEL JULIEN INC *p 1065*
115 RUE DE LAUZON, BOUCHERVILLE, QC, J4B 1E7

(450) 641-3150 *SIC* 6712

GESTION MICHEL LANG INC *p 1131*
8096 BOUL CHAMPLAIN, LASALLE, QC, H8P 1B3

(514) 367-3300 *SIC* 5912

GESTION MICHEL SEGUIN INC *p 1070*
9900 BOUL LEDUC, BROSSARD, QC, J4Y 0B4

(450) 443-0005 *SIC* 5531

GESTION N. AUGER INC *p 1136*
5480 RUE SAINT-GEORGES, LEVIS, QC, G6V 4M6

(418) 833-3241 *SIC* 5812

GESTION NEUF ASSOCIES INC *p 1204*
630 BOUL RENE-LEVESQUE O BUREAU 3200, MONTREAL, QC, H3B 1S6

(514) 847-1117 *SIC* 8712

GESTION ORION LTEE *p 1229*
800 RUE DU SQUARE-VICTORIA BUREAU 3700, MONTREAL, QC, H4Z 1A1

(514) 871-9167 *SIC* 8741

GESTION P. A. T. INC *p 1351*
371 BOUL ST-PIERRE, SAINT-RAPHAEL, QC, G0R 4C0

(418) 243-2022 *SIC* 5149

GESTION PACE INVESTCO *p 1252*
See *PACE INVESTCO LTD*

GESTION PADOMAX INC   p 1365
280 BOUL PIE-XII, SALABERRY-DE-VALLEYFIELD, QC, J6S 6P7
(450) 373-4274   SIC 1794

GESTION PERREAULT ET BEAULIEU INC
p 1072
15 BOUL MONTCALM N, CANDIAC, QC, J5R 3L4
(450) 659-5426   SIC 5912

GESTION PHARMASSO INC   p 1345
9235 BOUL LACORDAIRE, SAINT-LEONARD, QC, H1R 2B6
(514) 324-2600   SIC 5912

GESTION PICARD-DUBUC INC   p 1126
2880 RUE REMEMBRANCE BUREAU 74, LACHINE, QC, H8S 1X8
(514) 637-3578   SIC 5912

GESTION PIERRE BEAUCHESNE INC   p
1400
17 RUE SAINTE-JEANNE-D'ARC, WAR-WICK, QC, J0A 1M0
(819) 358-3400   SIC 6712

GESTION PLACE VICTORIA INC   p 1229
800 RUE DU SQUARE-VICTORIA BUREAU 4120, MONTREAL, QC, H4Z 1A1
(514) 875-6010   SIC 8741

GESTION POMERLEAU PAGE INC   p 1159
205 CH DES POIRIER, MONTMAGNY, QC, G5V 3X7
(418) 241-2102   SIC 6712

GESTION PONTIAC INC   p 1391
91 CH DU FORT, VAL-DES-MONTS, QC, J8N 4H4
SIC 5511

GESTION QUADRATEL INC   p 1218
6000 CH DEACON, MONTREAL, QC, H3S 2T9
(514) 731-5298   SIC 6712

GESTION QUADRIVIUM LTEE   p 1169
2506 RUE BEAUBIEN E, MONTREAL, QC, H1Y 1G2
SIC 5411

GESTION QUEMAR INC   p 1264
194 AV SAINT-SACREMENT, QUEBEC, QC, G1N 3X6
(418) 681-5088   SIC 5099

GESTION R.M.L. RODRIGUE INC   p 1138
1890 1RE RUE, LEVIS, QC, G6W 5M6
(418) 839-0671   SIC 3564

GESTION RACAN INC   p 1152
18101 RUE J.A.BOMBARDIER, MIRABEL, QC, J7J 2H8
(450) 979-1212   SIC 6712

GESTION RAPID INC.   p 1149
321 MONTEE MASSON BUREAU 301, MASCOUCHE, QC, J7K 2L6
SIC 8741

GESTION REJEAN LEGER INC   p 1138
600 RUE DE LA CONCORDE, LEVIS, QC, G6W 8A8
(418) 839-9797   SIC 5251

GESTION REJEAN TROTTIER INC   p 1182
6275 BOUL SAINT-LAURENT BUREAU 343, MONTREAL, QC, H2S 3C3
(514) 273-2428   SIC 5531

GESTION REMI GAUTHIER INC   p 407
1106 MOUNTAIN RD, MONCTON, NB, E1C 2T3
(506) 852-2970   SIC 5531

GESTION RENE FORTIN INC   p 1098
150 BOUL SAINT-JOSEPH, DRUM-MONDVILLE, QC, J2C 2A8
(819) 478-8148   SIC 5511

GESTION RENE J. BEAUDOIN INC   p 1170
2225 BOUL CREMAZIE E, MONTREAL, QC, H1Z 4N4
(514) 729-1861   SIC 5311

GESTION RENE J. BEAUDOIN INC   p 1283
115 BOUL BRIEN, REPENTIGNY, QC, J6A 8J3
(450) 585-9840   SIC 5411

GESTION RESEAU SELECTION II INC   p
1086
2400 BOUL DANIEL-JOHNSON, COTE

SAINT-LUC, QC, H7T 3A4
(450) 902-2000   SIC 6513

GESTION RESTO GRANBY INC   p 1109
940 RUE PRINCIPALE, GRANBY, QC, J2G 2Z4
(450) 378-4656   SIC 5812

GESTION RESTO ST-HYACINTHE INC   p
1312
1315 RUE DANIEL-JOHNSON O, SAINT-HYACINTHE, QC, J2S 8S4
(450) 774-7770   SIC 5812

GESTION RITEAL INC   p 1220
1500 AV ATWATER, MONTREAL, QC, H3Z 1X5
(514) 931-4283   SIC 5912

GESTION ROBERT M. HARVEY INC p 1322
210 BOUL DESAULNIERS, SAINT-LAMBERT, QC, J4P 1M6
(450) 658-8771   SIC 3449

GESTION ROCECO INC   p 1304
2685 121E RUE, SAINT-GEORGES, QC, G5Y 5G2
(418) 227-4402   SIC 6712

GESTION ROGER THERIAULT   p 394
384 OLD VAL D'AMOUR RD, ATHOLVILLE, NB, E3N 4E3
(506) 789-0230   SIC 5531

GESTION RONALD HERTELEER INC   p
1234
3985 BOUL INDUSTRIEL, MONTREAL, QC, H7L 4S3
(514) 384-8300   SIC 6712

GESTION ROSLYN-ALVIN LTEE   p 1106
320 BOUL SAINT-JOSEPH BUREAU 221, GATINEAU, QC, J8Y 3Y8
(819) 770-6668   SIC 5912

GESTION S. BISAILLON INC   p 1308
4645 CH DE CHAMBLY, SAINT-HUBERT, QC, J3Y 3M9
(450) 462-2828   SIC 5511

GESTION S.P.S.   p 1147
See GROUPE KANWAL INC

GESTION SARMASO INC   p 1155
2305 CH ROCKLAND BUREAU 191, MONT-ROYAL, QC, H3P 3E9
(514) 739-5551   SIC 5912

GESTION SETR INC   p 1385
4125 BOUL DES FORGES BUREAU 1, TROIS-RIVIERES, QC, G8Y 1W1
(819) 376-4343   SIC 5699

GESTION SIERA CAPITAL INC   p 1196
1501 AV MCGILL COLLEGE BUREAU 800, MONTREAL, QC, H3A 3M8
(514) 954-3300   SIC 6712

GESTION SINOMONDE INC   p 1191
99 AV VIGER O, MONTREAL, QC, H2Z 1E9
(514) 878-9888   SIC 6712

GESTION SOLENO INC   p 1316
1160 RTE 133, SAINT-JEAN-SUR-RICHELIEU, QC, J2X 4J5
(450) 347-7855   SIC 3498

GESTION SOLUTIONS PLASTIK INC   p
1147
2123 BOUL INDUSTRIEL, MAGOG, QC, J1X 7J7
(819) 847-2466   SIC 3089

GESTION SOROMA (MONT ORFORD) INC
p 1210
640 RUE SAINT-PAUL O, MONTREAL, QC, H3C 1L9
(514) 527-9546   SIC 8742

GESTION SPCRC   p 1341
See SPCRC HOLDINGS INC

GESTION ST-H. INC   p 1275
1294 RUE ROLAND-DESMEULES, QUE-BEC, QC, G1X 4Y3
(450) 836-7201   SIC 6712

GESTION STEFANO ROVER INC   p 1125
3642 RUE LAVAL, LAC-MEGANTIC, QC, G6B 1A4
(819) 583-3332   SIC 5531

GESTION STRUCTURES XL INC   p 1381
3005 RUE DES BATISSEURS, TERRE-BONNE, QC, J6Y 0A2

(450) 968-0800   SIC 3312

GESTION SUMMIT STEPS INC   p 1172
5700 RUE FULLUM, MONTREAL, QC, H2G 2H7
(514) 271-2358   SIC 2387

GESTION SYLVAIN GOUDREAULT INC   p
1399
1768 BOUL DES LAURENTIDES BUREAU 1, VIMONT, QC, H7M 2P6
(450) 663-3197   SIC 5912

GESTION SYNER-PHARM INC   p 1397
141 RUE NOTRE-DAME E, VICTORIAV-ILLE, QC, G6P 3Z8
(819) 752-4554   SIC 5999

GESTION SYREBEC   p 1392
See BESSETTE ET BOUDREAU INC

GESTION TECHNIQUE D'IMMEUBLES   p
1049
9000 RUE DE L'INNOVATION, ANJOU, QC, H1J 2X9
(514) 354-6666   SIC 1542

GESTION TERMICO INC   p 1144
120 PLACE CHARLES-LE MOYNE BU-REAU 300, LONGUEUIL, QC, J4K 2T4
(450) 670-3422   SIC 4729

GESTION TFI, SOCIETE EN COMMANDITE
p 1138
1950 3E RUE, LEVIS, QC, G6W 5M6
SIC 4213

GESTION THERRIEN COUTURE INC   p
1312
1200 RUE DANIEL-JOHNSON O UNITE 7000, SAINT-HYACINTHE, QC, J2S 7K7
(450) 773-6326   SIC 8741

GESTION TREE ROOTS INC   p 1329
2300 RUE EMILE-BELANGER, SAINT-LAURENT, QC, H4R 3J4
(514) 747-2536   SIC 5661

GESTION TREMBLAY ET LAPOINTE INC p
1385
300 RUE BARKOFF BUREAU 302, TROIS-RIVIERES, QC, G8T 2A3
(819) 375-3858   SIC 5699

GESTION TREMBLAY LEBOEUF INC   p
1243
1130 RUE SAINT-CYRILLE, NORMANDIN, QC, G8M 4J7
(418) 274-2009   SIC 5411

GESTION UNIVERSITAS INC   p 1274
3005 AV MARICOURT BUREAU 250, QUE-BEC, QC, G1W 4T8
(418) 651-8975   SIC 6722

GESTION VALBEC INC   p 1129
389 CH DU MOULIN, LANDRIENNE, QC, J0Y 1V0
(819) 732-6404   SIC 2421

GESTION VALEANT CANADA   p 1363
See VALEANT CANADA LIMITEE

GESTION VALLIERES ET PELLETIER INC,
LES   p 1098
275 RUE COCKBURN, DRUMMONDVILLE, QC, J2C 4L5
(819) 475-0545   SIC 8361

GESTION VALMIRA INC   p 1107
25 RUE DE L'EMBELLIE, GATINEAU, QC, J9A 3K3
(819) 595-4989   SIC 5812

GESTION VINNY INC   p 1272
2950 BOUL LAURIER, QUEBEC, QC, G1V 2M4
(418) 659-4484   SIC 5812

GESTION YVON GUILLOTTE INC   p 1318
920 RUE PIERRE-CAISSE, SAINT-JEAN-SUR-RICHELIEU, QC, J3B 7Y5
(450) 349-5801   SIC 5051

GESTIONS ARDOVA LTEE, LES   p 1178
433 RUE CHABANEL O BUREAU 1000, MONTREAL, QC, H2N 2J8
(514) 381-5941   SIC 6712

GESTIONS AZURE INC., LES   p 1342
7909 BOUL ARTHUR-SAUVE, SAINT-LAURENT, QC, H7R 3X8
(450) 969-0150   SIC 6712

GESTIONS BAILLARGEON & OUELLET

INC   p 1299
430 108 RTE O, SAINT-EPHREM-DE-BEAUCE, QC, G0M 1R0
(418) 484-5666   SIC 6712

GESTIONS DOROTHEE MINVILLE INC   p
1204
390 RUE SAINTE-CATHERINE O, MON-TREAL, QC, H3B 1A1
(514) 875-7070   SIC 5912

GESTIONS FERNANDA CIVITELLA INC,
LES   p 1096
330 AV DORVAL BUREAU 11, DORVAL, QC, H9S 3H7
(514) 631-1827   SIC 5912

GESTIONS FORTIER-ALLAN 29 INC p 1175
901 RUE SAINTE-CATHERINE E BUREAU 29, MONTREAL, QC, H2L 2E5
(514) 842-4915   SIC 5912

GESTIONS G H P (1986) INC, LES   p 1304
521 6E AV N, SAINT-GEORGES, QC, G5Y 0H1
(418) 228-6688   SIC 8741

GESTIONS G.D. BERUBE INC, LES p 1398
1111 BOUL JUTRAS E BUREAU 11, VIC-TORIAVILLE, QC, G6S 1C1
(819) 357-3657   SIC 5812

GESTIONS GILBERT ROY INC   p 1224
3180 RUE WELLINGTON, MONTREAL, QC, H4G 1T3
(514) 766-8561   SIC 5531

GESTIONS J.B. GREGOIRE INC   p 1315
96 RUE MOREAU, SAINT-JEAN-SUR-RICHELIEU, QC, J2W 2M4
(450) 348-6835   SIC 5511

GESTIONS JEAN-MARC GAGNE LTEE   p
1130
2221 BOUL ANGRIGNON, LASALLE, QC, H8N 3E3
SIC 5014

GESTIONS LENALCO (CANADA) LTEE   p
1326
455 BOUL DE LA COTE-VERTU, SAINT-LAURENT, QC, H4N 1E8
(514) 334-1510   SIC 6712

GESTIONS LUCAP INC   p 1213
1500 RUE SAINTE-CATHERINE O, MON-TREAL, QC, H3G 1S8
(514) 933-4744   SIC 5912

GESTIONS MILLER CARMICHAEL INC   p
1218
3822 AV DE COURTRAI, MONTREAL, QC, H3S 1C1
(514) 735-4361   SIC 6712

GESTIONS MONIT LTEE, LES   p 1205
1255 RUE UNIVERSITY, MONTREAL, QC, H3B 3X4
(514) 861-9772   SIC 6531

GESTIONS MONK HERITAGE INC   p 1339
255 MONTEE DE LIESSE, SAINT-LAURENT, QC, H4T 1P5
(514) 345-0135   SIC 6712

GESTIONS PARKER-SCOTT INC   p 1131
8080 BOUL CHAMPLAIN BUREAU 1439, LASALLE, QC, H8P 1B3
(514) 368-2114   SIC 5812

GESTIONS PREMIER LION   p 1196
See FIRST LION HOLDINGS INC

GESTIONS REJEAN POITRAS INC, LES   p
1394
50 BOUL DE LA CITE-DES-JEUNES BU-REAU 646, VAUDREUIL-DORION, QC, J7V 9L5
(450) 424-2744   SIC 5311

GESTIONS REJEAN SAVARD LTEE p 1232
4975 BOUL ROBERT-BOURASSA BU-REAU 231, MONTREAL, QC, H7E 0A4
(450) 665-4747   SIC 5531

GESTIONS SYLVAIN BERUBE INC p 1363
500 DESSTE CHOMEDEY (A-13) O, SAINTE-ROSE, QC, H7X 3S9
(450) 969-4141   SIC 5531

GESTIPARC   p 1205
See INDIGO PARC CANADA INC

GESTOFOR INC   p 1351

592 RUE GUYON, SAINT-RAYMOND, QC, G3L 0A5

(418) 337-4621   SIC 2421

GESTOLEX, SOCIETE EN COMMANDITE p 1229

800 RUE DU SQUARE-VICTORIA BUREAU 4300, MONTREAL, QC, H4Z 1H1

(450) 686-8683   SIC 6712

GESTRUDO INC p 1283

34 RUE BELMONT, RICHMOND, QC, J0B 2H0

(819) 826-5941   SIC 6712

GET A BETTER MORTGAGE p 572

642 THE QUEENSWAY, ETOBICOKE, ON, M8Y 1K5

(416) 252-9000   SIC 6162

GET IT DONE DEMOLITION & DISPOSAL p 278

12224 BOUNDARY DR N, SURREY, BC, V3X 1Z5

(604) 916-1388   SIC 1795

GETINGE CANADA LIMITED p 731

90 MATHESON BLVD W SUITE 300, MISSISSAUGA, ON, L5R 3R3

(905) 629-8777   SIC 5047

GETRACAN INC p 1229

130 MONTEE DE LIESSE, MONTREAL, QC, H4T 1N4

(514) 382-4860   SIC 5136

GETTING READY FOR INCLUSION TODAY (THE GRIT PROGRAM) SOCIETY OF EDMONTON p 95

14930 114 AVE NW, EDMONTON, AB, T5M 4G4

(780) 454-9910   SIC 8351

GEVITY p 298

See GEVITY CONSULTING INC

GEVITY CONSULTING INC p 298

375 WATER ST SUITE 350, VANCOUVER, BC, V6B 5C6

(604) 608-1779   SIC 8748

GEXEL TELECOM INTERNATIONAL INC p 1188

507 PLACE D'ARMES BUREAU 1503, MONTREAL, QC, H2Y 2W8

(514) 935-9300   SIC 8732

GEXEL TELECOM INTERNATIONAL INC p 1220

5250 BOUL DECARIE BUREAU 100, MONTREAL, QC, H3X 2H9

(514) 935-9300   SIC 4899

GF p 1088

See 10013340 CANADA INC

GFI p 1248

See ABB PRODUITS D'INSTALLATION LTEE

GFI p 1316

See ABB PRODUITS D'INSTALLATION LTEE

GFL ENVIRONMENTAL CORP p 844

1070 TOY AVE, PICKERING, ON, L1W 3P1

(905) 428-8992   SIC 4959

GFL ENVIRONMENTAL INC p 1002

100 NEW PARK PL SUITE 500, VAUGHAN, ON, L4K 0H9

(905) 326-0101   SIC 4953

GFP LES HOTES DE MONTREAL INC p 1182

6983 RUE DE LA ROCHE, MONTREAL, QC, H2S 2E6

(514) 274-6837   SIC 7381

GFR PHARMA LTD p 200

65 NORTH BEND ST UNIT 65, COQUITLAM, BC, V3K 6N9

(604) 460-8440   SIC 2833

GFS CALGARY p 160

See GORDON FOOD SERVICE CANADA LTD

GFS PARTNERSHIP p 835

See GAVILLER & COMPANY LLP

GG BROADWAY INVESTMENTS LIMITED PARTNERSHIP p 185

3823 HENNING DR UNIT 215, BURNABY,

BC, V5C 6P3

(604) 293-0152   SIC 7999

GGI INTERNATIONAL p 1128

See GROUPE GRAHAM INTERNATIONAL INC

GGP DRUGS LTD p 794

2550 FINCH AVE W SUITE 854, NORTH YORK, ON, M9M 2G3

(416) 749-5271   SIC 5912

GGS STRUCTURES INC p 1003

3559 NORTH SERVICE RD, VINELAND STATION, ON, L0R 2E0

(905) 562-7341   SIC 1542

GHA DESIGN p 1208

See STUDIOS DESIGN GHA INC

GHC p 1314

See PRODUITS CHIMIQUES G.H. LTEE

GHD CONSULTANTS LTEE p 1277

445 AV SAINT-JEAN-BAPTISTE BUREAU 390, QUEBEC, QC, G2E 5N7

(418) 658-0112   SIC 8621

GHD CONSULTANTS LTEE p 1334

4600 BOUL DE LA COTE-VERTU BUREAU 200, SAINT-LAURENT, QC, H4S 1C7

(514) 333-5151   SIC 8621

GHD CONTRACTORS LIMITED p 1008

455 PHILLIP ST, WATERLOO, ON, N2L 3X2

(519) 884-0510   SIC 1629

GHD INC p 722

6705 MILLCREEK DR SUITE 1, MISSISSAUGA, ON, L5N 5M4

(416) 213-7121   SIC 8711

GHD LIMITED p 1008

455 PHILLIP ST, WATERLOO, ON, N2L 3X2

(519) 884-0510   SIC 8711

GHOST TRANSPORTATION SERVICES p 1431

See 594827 SASKATCHEWAN LTD

GHP GROUP ULC p 605

271 MASSEY RD, GUELPH, ON, N1K 1B2

(519) 837-9724   SIC 5074

GHR SYSTEMS INC p 951

11 KING ST W SUITE 600, TORONTO, ON, M5H 4C7

(416) 360-5775   SIC 6159

GHY INTERNATIONAL p 376

See YOUNG, GEO H & CO LTD

GI-OCEAN INTERNATIONAL INC p 1334

9899 RTE TRANSCANADIENNE, SAINT-LAURENT, QC, H4S 1V1

(514) 339-9994   SIC 5146

GIA SHOES p 256

See STERLING SHOES LIMITED PARTNERSHIP

GIAMPAOLO INVESTMENTS LIMITED p 503

471 INTERMODAL DR, BRAMPTON, ON, L6T 5G4

(905) 790-3095   SIC 6719

GIANT STEP SCHOOL p 1229

See INSTITUT CANADIEN POUR DEVELOPPEMENT NEURO-INTEGRATIF, L

GIANT TIGER p 11

See TORA WESTERN CANADA LTD

GIANT TIGER p 107

See NORTH WEST COMPANY LP, THE

GIANT TIGER p 652

See TORA LONDON LIMITED

GIANT TIGER p 897

See TORA STRATFORD LIMITED

GIANT TIGER # 405 p 1420

See NORTH WEST COMPANY LP, THE

GIANT TIGER STORE p 747

See AMBURG LIMITED

GIANT TIGER STORES LIMITED p 818

2480 WALKLEY RD, OTTAWA, ON, K1G 6A9

(613) 521-8222   SIC 5311

GIBBONS MAINTENANCE p 1092

See 132405 CANADA INC

GIBBONS, JOHN AUTOMOTIVE GROUP 2010 LTD p 543

725 RICHMOND ST, CHATHAM, ON, N7M 5J5

(519) 352-6200   SIC 5511

GIBBONS, V. CONTRACTING LTD p 890

1755 STEVENSVILLE RD, STEVENSVILLE, ON, L0S 1S0

(905) 382-2393   SIC 1623

GIBBS GAGE ARCHITECTS p 30

350-140 10 AVE SE, CALGARY, AB, T2G 0R1

(403) 233-2000   SIC 8712

GIBBYS p 1188

See GIBBYS RESTAURANT INC

GIBBYS RESTAURANT INC p 1188

298 PLACE D'YOUVILLE, MONTREAL, QC, H2Y 2B6

(514) 282-1837   SIC 5812

GIBIERS CANABEC INC, LES p 1293

115 RUE DES GRANDS-LACS, SAINT-AUGUSTIN-DE-DESMAURES, QC, G3A 2T9

(418) 843-0782   SIC 5147

GIBRALTAR CONSOLIDATED CORPORATION p 771

4936 YONGE ST SUITE 508, NORTH YORK, ON, M2N 6S3

(416) 819-0644   SIC 6719

GIBRALTAR CONSOLIDATED EQUITY & INVESTMENTS p 771

See GIBRALTAR CONSOLIDATED CORPORATION

GIBRALTAR MINES LTD p 313

1040 GEORGIA ST W, VANCOUVER, BC, V6E 4H1

(778) 373-4533   SIC 1081

GIBSON BUILDING SUPPLIES p 480

See 1959612 ONTARIO INC

GIBSON ENERGY INC p 50

440 2 AVE SW SUITE 1700, CALGARY, AB, T2P 5E9

(403) 206-4000   SIC 1389

GIBSON ENERGY ULC p 50

440 2 AVE SW SUITE 1700, CALGARY, AB, T2P 5E9

(403) 206-4000   SIC 5172

GIBSON ENERGY ULC p 132

9502 42 AVE, GRANDE PRAIRIE, AB, T8V 5N3

(780) 539-4427   SIC 5172

GIBSON HOLDINGS (ONTARIO) LTD p 477

343 AMHERST DR SUITE 133, AMHERSTVIEW, ON, K7N 1X3

(613) 384-4585   SIC 8741

GIBSON LIVESTOCK (1981) LTD p 1411

GD LCD MAIN, MOOSE JAW, SK, S6H 4N6

(306) 692-9668   SIC 5154

GIBSON TRANSPORT p 476

See WARREN GIBSON LIMITED

GIBSON'S, TIM HOLDINGS PARRY SOUND LTD p 837

1 MALL DR, PARRY SOUND, ON, P2A 3A9

(705) 746-8467   SIC 5812

GIBSON, R. W. CONSULTING SERVICES LTD p 96

14713 116 AVE NW, EDMONTON, AB, T5M 3E8

(780) 452-8800   SIC 8741

GIBSONS BUILDING SUPPLIES LTD p 214

924 GIBSONS WAY, GIBSONS, BC, V0N 1V7

(604) 886-8141   SIC 5211

GICLEURS ALERTE INC p 1076

1250 RUE DES CASCADES, CHATEAUGUAY, QC, J6J 4Z2

(450) 692-9098   SIC 1711

GIDDEN MORTON ASSOCIATES INC p 735

7050A BRAMALEA RD UNIT 27A, MISSISSAUGA, ON, L5S 1T1

(905) 671-8111   SIC 5065

GIDNEY FISHERIES LIMITED p 449

136 DAKIN PARK RD, DIGBY, NS, B0V 1A0

(902) 834-2775   SIC 5146

GIENOW CANADA INC p 16

7140 40 ST SE, CALGARY, AB, T2C 2B6

(403) 203-8200   SIC 2431

GIESBRECHT & SONS LTD p 350

GD, GIMLI, MB, R0C 1B0

(204) 642-5133   SIC 5511

GIESECKE+DEVRIENT MOBILE SECURITY CANADA, INC p 679

316 MARKLAND ST, MARKHAM, ON, L6C 0C1

(905) 475-1333   SIC 3089

GIFFELS CORPORATION p 584

2 INTERNATIONAL BLVD, ETOBICOKE, ON, M9W 1A2

(416) 798-5500   SIC 8741

GIGG EXPRESS INC p 695

5355 CREEKBANK RD, MISSISSAUGA, ON, L4W 5L5

(905) 614-0544   SIC 4212

GIGUERE & MORIN INC p 1303

1175 RTE 243, SAINT-FELIX-DE-KINGSEY, QC, J0B 2T0

(819) 848-2525   SIC 2426

GILBERT EQUIMENTS DE SCIERIES p 1287

See PRODUITS GILBERT INC, LES

GILBERT HOLDINGS LTD p 150

201 SOUTHRIDGE DR UNIT 700, OKOTOKS, AB, T1S 2E1

(403) 938-3439   SIC 5411

GILBERT PLAINS HEALTH CENTRE INC p 350

100 CUTFORTH ST N, GILBERT PLAINS, MB, R0L 0X0

(204) 548-2161   SIC 8621

GILBERT SMITH FOREST PRODUCTS LTD p 180

4411 BORTHWICK AVE, BARRIERE, BC, V0E 1E0

(250) 672-9435   SIC 5211

GILBERT STEEL LIMITED p 695

1650 BRITANNIA RD E, MISSISSAUGA, ON, L4W 1J2

(905) 670-5771   SIC 3441

GILBERTSON ENTERPRISES p 850

See BERNT GILBERTSON ENTERPRISES LIMITED

GILDAN p 1196

See GILDAN ACTIVEWEAR INC

GILDAN ACTIVEWEAR INC p 1196

600 BOUL DE MAISONNEUVE O 33EME ETAGE, MONTREAL, QC, H3A 3J2

(514) 735-2023   SIC 2259

GILDAN APPAREL (CANADA) LP p 1170

3701 RUE JARRY E, MONTREAL, QC, H1Z 2G1

(514) 376-3000   SIC 2252

GILEAD ALBERTA ULC p 124

1021 HAYTER RD NW, EDMONTON, AB, T6S 1A1

(780) 701-6400   SIC 2834

GILL TECHNOLOGIES GLOBAL COMMUNICATIONS INC p 841

150 KING ST, PETERBOROUGH, ON, K9J 2R9

(877) 507-6988   SIC 4899

GILLAM FAMILY HOLDINGS LIMITED p 880

725 STEELES ST, SHELBURNE, ON, L9V 3M7

(519) 925-3991   SIC 5251

GILLAM GROUP INC p 916

36 NORTHLINE RD, TORONTO, ON, M4B 3E2

(416) 486-6776   SIC 8742

GILLES COTE EXCAVATION p 1125

See ENVIRONNEMENT ROUTIER NRJ INC

GILLESPIE AUTO CENTRE p 1012

See GILLESPIE PONTIAC BUICK CADILLAC LIMITED

GILLESPIE PONTIAC BUICK CADILLAC LIMITED p 1012

16 LINCOLN ST, WELLAND, ON, L3C 5J1

(905) 735-7151   SIC 5511

GILLESPIE-MUNRO INC p 1210

740 RUE NOTRE-DAME O BUREAU 1120,

MONTREAL, QC, H3C 3X6

(514) 871-1033   *SIC* 4731

GILLIES LUMBER INC   *p* 539

777 INDUSTRIAL RD, CAMBRIDGE, ON, N3H 4W2

(519) 653-3219   *SIC* 5031

GILLIES STAIRCASE & MILLWORK   *p* 539

See *GILLIES LUMBER INC*

GILLILAND GOLD YOUNG CONSULTING INC   *p* 771

5001 YONGE ST SUITE 1300, NORTH YORK, ON, M2N 6P6

(416) 250-6777   *SIC* 7371

GILLIS QUARRIES LIMITED   *p* 357

2895 WENZEL ST, SPRINGFIELD, MB, R2E 1H4

(204) 222-2242   *SIC* 1411

GILLIS, JOHN M MEMORIAL LODGE   *p* 1038

3134 GARFIELD RD, BELFAST, PE, C0A 1A0

(902) 659-2337   *SIC* 8741

GILLONS' INSURANCE BROKERS LTD   *p* 592

326 CHURCH ST, FORT FRANCES, ON, P9A 1E1

(807) 274-7716   *SIC* 6411

GILMAR CONSTRUCTION LTD.   *p* 157

129 CLEARWILL AVE, RED DEER COUNTY, AB, T4E 0A1

(403) 343-1028   *SIC* 1521

GILMAR CRANE SERVICE LTD   *p* 142

3216 3 AVE S, LETHBRIDGE, AB, T1J 4H5

(403) 327-6511   *SIC* 7389

GILMER'S BUILDING CENTRE LIMITED   *p* 847

177 TORONTO RD SUITE 1, PORT HOPE, ON, L1A 3V5

(905) 885-4568   *SIC* 5251

GILMER'S HOME CENTRE   *p* 847

See *GILMER'S BUILDING CENTRE LIMITED*

GILMORE GLOBAL LOGISTICS SERVICES INC   *p* 624

120 HERZBERG RD, KANATA, ON, K2K 3B7

(613) 599-6065   *SIC* 8741

GILMORE PRINTING SERVICES INC   *p* 624

110 HERZBERG RD, KANATA, ON, K2K 3B7

(613) 599-3776   *SIC* 2752

GILMORE REPRODUCTIONS   *p* 624

See *GILMORE, R. E. INVESTMENTS CORP*

GILMORE, R. E. INVESTMENTS CORP   *p* 624

120 HERZBERG RD, KANATA, ON, K2K 3B7

(613) 592-2944   *SIC* 2759

GILMYR TRANSPORT INC   *p* 1159

315 CH DU COTEAU, MONTMAGNY, QC, G5V 3R8

(418) 241-5747   *SIC* 4213

GIMBLE EYE CENTER, THE   *p* 71

See *I CARE SERVICE LTD*

GIMLI COMMUNITY HEALTH CENTRE   *p* 350

120 6TH AVE, GIMLI, MB, R0C 1B0

(204) 642-5116   *SIC* 8062

GIN-COR INDUSTRIES INC   *p* 763

255A FISHER ST, NORTH BAY, ON, P1B 2C8

(705) 744-5543   *SIC* 5012

GINEW WELLNESS CENTRE   *p* 350

GD, GINEW, MB, R0A 2R0

(204) 427-2384   *SIC* 8011

GINGER BEEF EXPRESS LTD   *p* 35

5521 3 ST SE, CALGARY, AB, T2H 1K1

(403) 272-8088   *SIC* 2032

GINGRAS CORRIVEAU   *p* 763

See *GIN-COR INDUSTRIES INC*

GINSBERG GLUZMAN FAGE & LEVITZ, LLP   *p* 829

287 RICHMOND RD, OTTAWA, ON, K1Z

6X4

(613) 728-5831   *SIC* 8721

GINSBERG, GINGRAS & ASSOCIES INC   *p* 1105

145 PROM DU PORTAGE, GATINEAU, QC, J8X 2K4

(819) 776-0283   *SIC* 8111

GIRAFE SANTE INC   *p* 1059

617 BOUL DU CURE-LABELLE BUREAU 100, BLAINVILLE, QC, J7C 2J1

SIC 7361

GIRALDEAU INTER-AUTO INC   *p* 1320

2180 BOUL DU CURE-LABELLE, SAINT-JEROME, QC, J7Y 1T3

(450) 476-0720   *SIC* 5511

GIRARD AUTOMOBILE INC   *p* 1282

283 RUE VALMONT, REPENTIGNY, QC, J5Y 3H5

(450) 581-1490   *SIC* 5511

GIRARD BULK SERVICE LTD   *p* 1406

134 4TH ST, ESTEVAN, SK, S4A 0T4

(306) 637-4370   *SIC* 5171

GIRARD, B & FILS INC   *p* 1303

1199 BOUL SAINT-FELICIEN, SAINT-FELICIEN, QC, G8K 3J1

(418) 679-1304   *SIC* 5411

GIRARDIN MINIBUS   *p* 1100

See *CORPORATION MICRO BIRD INC*

GIRL GUIDES OF CANADA   *p* 924

50 MERTON ST, TORONTO, ON, M4S 1A3

(416) 487-5281   *SIC* 8641

GIRLS INCORPORATED OF DURHAM   *p* 474

398 BAYLY ST W SUITE 1A, AJAX, ON, L1S 1P1

(905) 428-8111   *SIC* 8399

GIRO INC   *p* 1217

75 RUE DE PORT-ROYAL E BUREAU 500, MONTREAL, QC, H3L 3T1

(514) 383-0404   *SIC* 7371

GIROUARD, ANDRE & FILS INC   *p* 1399

650 BOUL PIERRE-ROUX E, VICTORIAV-ILLE, QC, G6T 1T2

(819) 758-0643   *SIC* 5083

GIROUXVILLE PLANT   *p* 127

See *OBSIDIAN ENERGY LTD*

GIRTON MANAGEMENT LTD   *p* 365

157 VERMILLION RD SUITE 266, WIN-NIPEG, MB, R2J 3Z7

(204) 254-5169   *SIC* 5399

GIS   *p* 717

See *GREEN IMAGING SUPPLIES INC*

GISBORNE FIRE PROTECTION   *p* 148

See *GISBORNE INDUSTRIAL CON-STRUCTION LTD*

GISBORNE FIRE PROTECTION ALBERTA LTD   *p* 187

7476 HEDLEY AVE, BURNABY, BC, V5E 2P9

(604) 520-7300   *SIC* 1711

GISBORNE GROUP, THE   *p* 187

See *GISBORNE HOLDINGS LTD*

GISBORNE HOLDINGS LTD   *p* 187

7476 HEDLEY AVE, BURNABY, BC, V5E 2P9

(604) 520-7300   *SIC* 6719

GISBORNE INDUSTRIAL CONSTRUCTION LTD   *p* 148

1201 6 ST, NISKU, AB, T9E 7P1

SIC 1541

GISBORNE INDUSTRIAL CONSTRUCTION LTD   *p* 187

7476 HEDLEY AVE, BURNABY, BC, V5E 2P9

(604) 520-7300   *SIC* 1541

GISELLE'S PROFESSIONAL SKIN CARE LTD   *p* 388

1700 CORYDON AVE UNIT 13, WINNIPEG, MB, R3N 0K1

SIC 7231

GIULIANI, G INC   *p* 1101

3970 BOUL LEMAN, FABREVILLE, QC, H7E 1A1

(450) 661-6519   *SIC* 1611

GIUSTI GROUP   *p* 77

See *GIUSTI GROUP LIMITED PARTNER-SHIP*

GIUSTI GROUP LIMITED PARTNERSHIP   *p* 77

4 INDUSTRY WAY SE, CALGARY, AB, T3S 0A2

(403) 203-0492   *SIC* 1531

GIVAUDAN CANADA CO   *p* 695

2400 MATHESON BLVD E, MISSISSAUGA, ON, L4W 5G9

(905) 282-9808   *SIC* 5149

GIVE AND GO PREPARED FOODS CORP   *p* 584

15 MARMAC DR UNIT 200, ETOBICOKE, ON, M9W 1E7

(416) 675-0114   *SIC* 2051

GIVENS ENGINEERING INC   *p* 661

327 SOVEREIGN RD, LONDON, ON, N6M 1A6

(519) 453-9008   *SIC* 3599

GIVESCO INC   *p* 1344

9495 RUE PASCAL-GAGNON, SAINT-LEONARD, QC, H1P 1Z4

(514) 327-7175   *SIC* 5039

GIVEX CANADA CORP   *p* 980

134 PETER ST SUITE 1400, TORONTO, ON, M5V 2H2

(416) 350-9660   *SIC* 7374

GIYANI METALS CORP   *p* 800

277 LAKESHORE RD E SUITE 403, OAKVILLE, ON, L6J 6J3

(289) 837-0066   *SIC* 1061

GIZELLA PASTRY ULC   *p* 286

3436 LOUGHEED HWY, VANCOUVER, BC, V5M 2A4

(604) 253-5220   *SIC* 2051

GKN SINTER METALS - ST THOMAS LTD   *p* 889

7 MICHIGAN BLVD, ST THOMAS, ON, N5P 1H1

(519) 631-4880   *SIC* 3399

GLACIER BILBOQUET INC, LE   *p* 1217

6833 AV DU PARC, MONTREAL, QC, H3N 1W8

SIC 5143

GLACIER MEDIA INC   *p* 249

150 BRUNSWICK ST, PRINCE GEORGE, BC, V2L 2B3

(250) 562-6666   *SIC* 2711

GLACIER MEDIA INC   *p* 291

2188 YUKON ST, VANCOUVER, BC, V5Y 3P1

(604) 872-8565   *SIC* 2721

GLACIER MEDIA INC   *p* 334

2621 DOUGLAS ST, VICTORIA, BC, V8T 4M2

(250) 380-5211   *SIC* 2711

GLACIER MEDIA INC   *p* 1427

2310 MILLAR AVE, SASKATOON, SK, S7K 2Y2

(306) 665-3500   *SIC* 2711

GLACIER PUBLICATIONS LIMITED PARTNERSHIP   *p*

292

1970 ALBERTA ST, VANCOUVER, BC, V5Y 3X4

(604) 708-3291   *SIC* 2711

GLACIER VIEW LODGE SOCIETY   *p* 203

2450 BACK RD, COURTENAY, BC, V9N 8B5

(250) 338-1451   *SIC* 8051

GLADES LODGE   *p* 458

See *GEM HEALTH CARE GROUP LIMITED*

GLADSTONE AUCTION MART LTD   *p* 350

GD, GLADSTONE, MB, R0J 0T0

(204) 385-2537   *SIC* 5154

GLADWIN FARMS LTD   *p* 178

5327 GLADWIN RD, ABBOTSFORD, BC, V4X 1X8

(604) 859-6820   *SIC* 5159

GLAMORGAN CARE CENTRE   *p* 68

See *TRAVOIS HOLDINGS LTD*

GLANBIA NUTRITIONALS (CANADA) INC   *p* 345

190 MAIN ST S, ANGUSVILLE, MB, R0J 0A0

(204) 773-2575   *SIC* 5191

GLANFORD AVIATION SERVICES LTD   *p* 747

9300 AIRPORT RD SUITE 200, MOUNT HOPE, ON, L0R 1W0

(905) 679-4127   *SIC* 5172

GLASROCK OMI   *p* 892

See *GLASROCK PRODUCTS INC*

GLASROCK PRODUCTS INC   *p* 892

274 SOUTH SERVICE RD SUITE 268, STONEY CREEK, ON, L8E 2N9

(905) 664-5300   *SIC* 5085

GLASS WORLD   *p* 176

See *GENERAL GLASS INDUSTRIES LTD*

GLASSCELL ISOFAB INC   *p* 584

1000 MARTIN GROVE RD SUITE 1, ETOBICOKE, ON, M9W 4V8

(416) 241-8663   *SIC* 5033

GLASSFORD MOTORS LIMITED   *p* 621

30 SAMNAH CRES SUITE 4, INGERSOLL, ON, N5C 3J7

(519) 485-0940   *SIC* 5511

GLASSHOUSE PHARMACEUTICALS LIMITED CANADA   *p* 722

2145 MEADOWPINE BLVD, MISSISSAUGA, ON, L5N 6R8

(905) 821-7600   *SIC* 5122

GLASSHOUSE SYSTEMS INC   *p* 779

885 DON MILLS ROAD, NORTH YORK, ON, M3C 1V9

(416) 229-2950   *SIC* 5045

GLASSINE CANADA INC   *p* 1257

1245 BOUL MONTMORENCY, QUEBEC, QC, G1J 5L6

(418) 522-8262   *SIC* 2621

GLASSMASTERS AUTOGLASS LTD   *p* 35

6221 CENTRE ST SW, CALGARY, AB, T2H 0C7

(403) 692-0934   *SIC* 5031

GLASTECH GLAZING CONTRACTORS LTD   *p* 246

1613 KEBET WAY, PORT COQUITLAM, BC, V3C 5W9

(604) 941-9115   *SIC* 1793

GLASVAN TRAILERS INC   *p* 695

1201 AIMCO BLVD SUITE 625, MISSISSAUGA, ON, L4W 1B3

(905) 625-8441   *SIC* 5012

GLASWEGIAN ENTERPRISES INC   *p* 200

1090 LOUGHEED HWY SUITE 214, COQUITLAM, BC, V3K 6G9

(604) 522-4000   *SIC* 6794

GLATFELTER GATINEAU LTEE   *p* 1103

1680 RUE ATMEC, GATINEAU, QC, J8R 7G7

(819) 669-8100   *SIC* 2621

GLAXOSMITHKLINE BIOLOGICALS NORTH AMERICA   *p* 1267

See *ID BIOMEDICAL CORPORATION OF QUEBEC*

GLAXOSMITHKLINE CONSUMER HEALTHCARE INC   *p* 722

7333 MISSISSAUGA RD, MISSISSAUGA, ON, L5N 6L4

(905) 819-3000   *SIC* 5122

GLAXOSMITHKLINE CONSUMER HEALTHCARE INC   *p* 797

2030 BRISTOL CIR, OAKVILLE, ON, L6H 0H2

(800) 387-7374   *SIC* 5122

GLAXOSMITHKLINE INC   *p* 722

7333 MISSISSAUGA RD, MISSISSAUGA, ON, L5N 6L4

(905) 819-3000   *SIC* 2834

GLAXOSMITHKLINE INC   *p* 797

2030 BRISTOL CIR, OAKVILLE, ON, L6H 0H2

SIC 2834

GLAZERS INC   *p* 1334

7800 BOUL HENRI-BOURASSA O, SAINT-LAURENT, QC, H4S 1P4

(514) 335-1500   *SIC 5099*
GLAZIER MEDICAL CENTER   *p 812*
See LAKERIDGE HEALTH
GLC ASSET MANAGEMENT GROUP LTD *p*
653
255 DUFFERIN AVE, LONDON, ON, N6A
4K1
(519) 432-7229   *SIC 6211*
GLC CONTROLS INC   *p 11*
3300 14 AVE NE SUITE 2, CALGARY, AB,
T2A 6J4
SIC 5063
GLEBE CENTRE INCORPORATED, THE *p*
825
950 BANK ST, OTTAWA, ON, K1S 5G6
(613) 230-5730   *SIC 8361*
GLEBE COLLEGIATE INSTITUTE   *p 826*
*See   OTTAWA-CARLETON   DISTRICT
SCHOOL BOARD*
GLEN AVON SCHOOL   *p 165*
*See ST. PAUL EDUCATION REGIONAL DI-
VISION NO 1*
GLEN DIMPLEX AMERICAS LIMITED *p 539*
1367 INDUSTRIAL RD SUITE 768, CAM-
BRIDGE, ON, N3H 4W3
(519) 650-3630   *SIC 5023*
GLEN HAVEN MANOR CORPORATION   *p*
463
739 EAST RIVER RD, NEW GLASGOW,
NS, B2H 5E9
(902) 752-2588   *SIC 8051*
GLEN SCOTTISH PUB & RESTAURANT *p*
891
See MOR-WEN RESTAURANTS LTD
GLEN STOR DUN LODGE FOUNDATION *p*
562
1900 MONTREAL RD, CORNWALL, ON,
K6H 7L1
(613) 933-3384   *SIC 8361*
GLEN TAY TRANSPORTATION   *p 839*
See CONTRANS GROUP INC
GLEN TRANSPORT, DIV OF   *p 269*
See DCT CHAMBERS TRUCKING LTD
GLENBOW MUSEUM   *p 30*
See GLENBOW-ALBERTA INSTITUTE
GLENBOW-ALBERTA INSTITUTE   *p 30*
130 9 AVE SE, CALGARY, AB, T2G 0P3
(403) 268-4100   *SIC 8412*
GLENBRIAR HOME HARDWARE   *p 1006*
262 WEBER ST N, WATERLOO, ON, N2J
3H6
(519) 886-2950   *SIC 5251*
GLENBROOK FIRE HALL   *p 236*
*See CORPORATION OF THE CITY OF
NEW WESTMINSTER*
GLENCO HOLDINGS LTD   *p 176*
2121 PEARDONVILLE RD, ABBOTSFORD,
BC, V2T 6J7
(604) 850-1499   *SIC 6712*
GLENCOE AGRICULTURAL SOCIETY   *p*
594
268 CURRIE ST, GLENCOE, ON, N0L 1M0
(519) 287-2836   *SIC 8621*
GLENCOE CLUB, THE   *p 67*
636 29 AVE SW, CALGARY, AB, T2S 0P1
(403) 214-0032   *SIC 7997*
GLENCOE FOODLAND   *p 594*
195 MAIN ST, GLENCOE, ON, N0L 1M0
(519) 287-2776   *SIC 5411*
GLENCORE CANADA CORPORATION   *p*
986
100 KING ST W SUITE 6900, TORONTO,
ON, M5X 2A1
(416) 775-1200   *SIC 1021*
**GLENDALE GLENDALE MEADOWS COM-
MUNITY ASSOCIATION**   *p*
73
2405 GLENMOUNT DR SW, CALGARY, AB,
T3E 4C1
(403) 242-2110   *SIC 8611*
GLENDALE GOLF & COUNTRY CLUB LTD
p 105
12410 199 ST NW, EDMONTON, AB, T5V
1T8

(780) 447-3529   *SIC 7997*
GLENDALE HIGH SCHOOL   *p 912*
*See THAMES VALLEY DISTRICT SCHOOL
BOARD*
GLENDYNE INC   *p 1348*
396 RUE PRINCIPALE, SAINT-MARC-DU-
LAC-LONG, QC, G0L 1T0
(418) 893-7221   *SIC 3281*
GLENEAGLE SECONDARY SCHOOL *p 198*
*See SCHOOL DISTRICT NO. 43 (COQUIT-
LAM)*
GLENFOREST SECONDARY SCHOOL   *p*
703
See PEEL DISTRICT SCHOOL BOARD
GLENGARRY BUS LINE INC   *p 476*
104 VIAU ST, ALEXANDRIA, ON, K0C 1A0
(613) 525-1443   *SIC 4151*
GLENGARRY INDUSTRIES LTD   *p 538*
1040 FOUNTAIN ST N SUITE 6, CAM-
BRIDGE, ON, N3E 1A3
(519) 653-1098   *SIC 3634*
GLENGARRY MEMORIAL HOSPITAL *p 476*
20260 COUNTY ROAD 43 RR 3, ALEXAN-
DRIA, ON, K0C 1A0
(613) 525-2222   *SIC 8062*
**GLENGARRY MOTEL AND RESTAURANT
LIMITED**   *p 469*
150 WILLOW ST, TRURO, NS, B2N 4Z6
(902) 893-4311   *SIC 7011*
GLENGARRY NEWS LIMITED, THE *p 476*
3 MAIN ST S, ALEXANDRIA, ON, K0C 1A0
(613) 525-2020   *SIC 7389*
GLENLAWN COLLEGIATE INSTITUTE   *p*
368
See LOUIS RIEL SCHOOL DIVISION
GLENLEVEN CHRYSLER   *p 800*
See GLENLEVEN MOTORS LIMITED
GLENLEVEN MOTORS LIMITED   *p 800*
2388 ROYAL WINDSOR DR, OAKVILLE,
ON, L6J 7Y2
(905) 845-7575   *SIC 5511*
GLENLYON-NORFOLK SCHOOL SOCIETY
p 333
801 BANK ST, VICTORIA, BC, V8S 4A8
(250) 370-6801   *SIC 8211*
GLENMAC CORPORATION LTD   *p 70*
11555 29 ST SE, CALGARY, AB, T2Z 0N4
(403) 250-6300   *SIC 5511*
GLENMORE AUDI   *p 73*
See 923416 ALBERTA LTD
GLENMORE INN   *p 16*
See GLENMORE INN HOLDINGS LTD
GLENMORE INN HOLDINGS LTD   *p 16*
2720 GLENMORE TRAIL SE, CALGARY,
AB, T2C 2E6
(403) 279-8611   *SIC 7011*
GLENN DAVIS GROUP INC   *p 709*
77 CITY CENTRE DR UNIT 2, MISSIS-
SAUGA, ON, L5B 1M5
(905) 270-2501   *SIC 7336*
**GLENORA LUMBER & BUILDING SUP-
PLIES LTD**   *p*
96
14505 116 AVE NW, EDMONTON, AB, T5M
3E8
(780) 453-5691   *SIC 5031*
GLENSTONE CAPITAL CORPORATION   *p*
951
181 UNIVERSITY AVE SUITE 1000,
TORONTO, ON, M5H 3M7
(416) 682-5300   *SIC 6331*
GLENTEL INC   *p 182*
8501 COMMERCE CRT, BURNABY, BC,
V5A 4N3
(604) 415-6500   *SIC 4813*
GLENVIEW PARK SECONDARY SCHOOL *p*
535
*See WATERLOO REGION DISTRICT
SCHOOL BOARD*
GLENWAY COUNTRY CLUB LIMITED *p 754*
470 CROSSLAND GATE, NEWMARKET,
ON, L3X 1B8
(905) 235-5422   *SIC 7997*
GLENWOOD KITCHENS LTD   *p 417*

191 MAIN ST, SHEDIAC, NB, E4P 2A5
(506) 532-4491   *SIC 2434*
GLENWOOD LABEL & BOX MFG. LTD   *p*
236
15 BRAID ST SUITE 117, NEW WESTMIN-
STER, BC, V3L 5N7
(604) 522-6001   *SIC 2679*
GLENWOOD LABELS   *p 236*
See GLENWOOD LABEL & BOX MFG. LTD
GLG LIFE TECH CORPORATION   *p 260*
10271 SHELLBRIDGE WAY SUITE 100,
RICHMOND, BC, V6X 2W8
(604) 285-2602   *SIC 5122*
GLIDER GUARD TOOL & DIE INC   *p 807*
5135 URE ST SUITE 1, OLDCASTLE, ON,
N0R 1L0
(519) 737-7313   *SIC 3544*
GLJ PETROLEUM CONSULTANTS LTD   *p*
50
400 3 AVE SW SUITE 4100, CALGARY, AB,
T2P 4H2
(403) 266-9500   *SIC 1389*
GLM   *p 1142*
See 9102-7045 QUEBEC INC
GLOBAL AEROSPACE CORPORATION   *p*
735
7075 FIR TREE DR, MISSISSAUGA, ON,
L5S 1J7
(905) 678-6311   *SIC 4581*
**GLOBAL AEROSPACE UNDERWRITING
MANAGERS (CANADA) LIMITED**   *p 670*
100 RENFREW DR SUITE 200, MARKHAM,
ON, L3R 9R6
(905) 479-2244   *SIC 6411*
**GLOBAL   AGRICULTURE   TRANS-
LOADING INC**   *p*
270
11678 130 ST, SURREY, BC, V3R 2Y3
(604) 580-1786   *SIC 4789*
GLOBAL ALLOY PIPE AND SUPPLY, INC *p*
122
2125 64 AVE NW, EDMONTON, AB, T6P
1Z4
(780) 469-6603   *SIC 5051*
GLOBAL ASSET MANAGEMENT   *p 970*
*See RBC O'SHAUGHNESSY U.S. VALUE
FUND*
GLOBAL BOTANICAL   *p 487*
See HEALTH4ALL PRODUCTS LIMITED
GLOBAL CATERING   *p 705*
See GLOBAL SEA SERVICES LTD
GLOBAL CITRUS GROUP, INC   *p 527*
3410 SOUTH SERVICE RD SUITE G3,
BURLINGTON, ON, L7N 3T2
(289) 895-8302   *SIC 0723*
GLOBAL COMMERCIAL FINANCIAL INC *p*
852
45B WEST WILMOT ST SUITE 208, RICH-
MOND HILL, ON, L4B 2P3
(905) 470-2127   *SIC 6799*
GLOBAL COMMODITIES TRADERS INC *p*
723
2430 MEADOWPINE BLVD SUITE 103,
MISSISSAUGA, ON; L5N 6S2
(905) 908-0092   *SIC 5159*
GLOBAL CONTRACT INC   *p 783*
565 PETROLIA RD, NORTH YORK, ON,
M3J 2X8
(416) 739-5000   *SIC 2522*
GLOBAL CONVENTION SERVICES LTD *p*
415
48 BROAD ST, SAINT JOHN, NB, E2L 1Y5
(506) 658-0506   *SIC 7389*
GLOBAL CREDIT & COLLECTION INC *p*
670
1490 DENISON ST, MARKHAM, ON, L3R
9T7
(905) 479-2222   *SIC 7322*
GLOBAL CREDIT & COLLECTION INC *p*
1196
2055 RUE PEEL BUREAU 100, MON-
TREAL, QC, H3A 1V4
(514) 284-5533   *SIC 7322*
GLOBAL DISTRIBUTION AND WARE-

HOUSING   *p*
498
See 575636 ONTARIO LIMITED
GLOBAL DRIVER SERVICES INC   *p 739*
1415 BONHILL RD SUITE 16, MISSIS-
SAUGA, ON, L5T 1R2
(905) 564-2309   *SIC 7363*
GLOBAL EGG CORPORATION   *p 574*
283 HORNER AVE, ETOBICOKE, ON, M8Z
4Y4
(416) 231-2309   *SIC 2015*
GLOBAL EXCEL MANAGEMENT INC   *p*
1374
73 RUE QUEEN, SHERBROOKE, QC, J1M
0C9
(819) 566-8833   *SIC 6411*
GLOBAL EXPERT GESTION DE RISQUES
p 1196
*See GLOBALEX GESTION DE RISQUES
INC*
GLOBAL FILE INC   *p 553*
7939 KEELE ST, CONCORD, ON, L4K 1Y6
(905) 761-3284   *SIC 2522*
GLOBAL FUELS INC   *p 531*
1463 ONTARIO ST SUITE C, BURLING-
TON, ON, L7S 1G6
(289) 288-0433   *SIC 5172*
GLOBAL FURS INC   *p 1196*
400 BOUL DE MAISONNEUVE O BUREAU
100, MONTREAL, QC, H3A 1L4
(514) 288-6644   *SIC 5137*
GLOBAL GATEWAY CORP   *p 318*
1400 ROBSON ST, VANCOUVER, BC, V6G
1B9
(604) 566-2688   *SIC 7011*
GLOBAL HEALTH CARE SERVICES INC *p*
596
5450 CANOTEK RD, GLOUCESTER, ON,
K1J 9G7
(613) 230-4104   *SIC 8399*
GLOBAL INDUSTRIAL CANADA   *p 850*
*See AVENUE INDUSTRIAL SUPPLY COM-
PANY LIMITED*
GLOBAL INTERNATIONAL INC   *p 168*
GD STN MAIN, STRATHMORE, AB, T1P
1J5
(403) 934-5046   *SIC 8748*
GLOBAL IQX INC   *p 831*
1111 PRINCE OF WALES DR SUITE 500,
OTTAWA, ON, K2C 3T2
(613) 723-8997   *SIC 7371*
**GLOBAL   KNOWLEDGE   NETWORK
(CANADA) INC**   *p 928*
2 BLOOR ST E UNIT 3100, TORONTO, ON,
M4W 1A8
(613) 254-6530   *SIC 8741*
GLOBAL LINK REALTY GROUP INC *p 670*
351 FERRIER ST UNIT 2351, MARKHAM,
ON, L3R 2Z5
(905) 475-0028   *SIC 6531*
GLOBAL LUMBER RESOURCES INC *p 705*
48 VILLAGE CENTRE PL UNIT 100, MIS-
SISSAUGA, ON, L4Z 1V9
(905) 306-7874   *SIC 5031*
GLOBAL M.J.L. LTEE   *p 1180*
8355 RUE JEANNE-MANCE, MONTREAL,
QC, H2P 2Y1
(514) 858-5566   *SIC 5148*
**GLOBAL MART INTERNATIONAL TECH-
NOLOGY INC**   *p*
826
2821 RIVERSIDE DR, OTTAWA, ON, K1V
8N4
SIC 7373
GLOBAL MATRIX   *p 670*
*See GLOBAL TRAVEL COMPUTER HOLD-
INGS LTD*
GLOBAL MAXFIN CAPITAL INC   *p 939*
15 TORONTO ST SUITE 202, TORONTO,
ON, M5C 2E3
(416) 741-1445   *SIC 6211*
**GLOBAL MINING MANAGEMENT CORPO-
RATION**   *p*
304

999 CANADA PL SUITE 654, VANCOUVER, BC, V6C 3E1
(604) 689-8765 *SIC* 8741

GLOBAL NET TRADE *p* 1027
50 PARISIENNE RD, WOODBRIDGE, ON, L4H 0V4
(905) 417-9470 *SIC* 7389

GLOBAL PACIFIC RESOURCES INC *p* 298
134 ABBOTT ST SUITE 500, VANCOUVER, BC, V6B 2K4
(604) 685-4411 *SIC* 5099

GLOBAL PAYMENT SYSTEMS OF CANADA, LTD *p* 765
3381 STEELES AVE E SUITE 200, NORTH YORK, ON, M2H 3S7
(416) 644-5959 *SIC* 7389

GLOBAL PET FOODS *p* 550
See CAN-PET DISTRIBUTORS INC

GLOBAL PETROLEUM MARKETING INC *p* 50
600 6 AVE SW SUITE 600, CALGARY, AB, T2P 0S5
(403) 237-7828 *SIC* 4924

GLOBAL PLAS INC *p* 553
120 SPINNAKER WAY, CONCORD, ON, L4K 2P6
(905) 760-2800 *SIC* 3089

GLOBAL PLASTICS *p* 271
19440 ENTERPRISE WAY, SURREY, BC, V3S 6J9
(604) 514-0600 *SIC* 3089

GLOBAL PLUMBING & HEATING INC *p* 1031
601 ROWNTREE DAIRY RD SUITE 1, WOODBRIDGE, ON, L4L 5T8
(905) 851-4212 *SIC* 1711

GLOBAL POINT DESIGN INC *p* 800
2861 SHERWOOD HEIGHTS DR UNIT 27, OAKVILLE, ON, L6J 7K1
(905) 829-4424 *SIC* 5013

GLOBAL PRECAST INC *p* 664
2101 TESTON RD, MAPLE, ON, L6A 1R3
(905) 832-4307 *SIC* 3272

GLOBAL RAYMAC SURVEYS INC *p* 30
4000 4 ST SE SUITE 312, CALGARY, AB, T2G 2W3
(403) 283-5455 *SIC* 8713

GLOBAL RELAY *p* 298
See GLOBAL RELAY COMMUNICATIONS INC

GLOBAL RELAY COMMUNICATIONS INC *p* 298
220 CAMBIE ST FL 2, VANCOUVER, BC, V6B 2M9
(604) 484-6630 *SIC* 7371

GLOBAL RESEARCH EPICENTER AGAINST HUMAN TRAFFICKIN *p* 1014
301 SAINT JOHN ST W, WHITBY, ON, L1N 1N6
SIC 8062

GLOBAL RESP CORPORATION *p* 852
100 MURAL ST SUITE 201, RICHMOND HILL, ON, L4B 1J3
(416) 741-7377 *SIC* 6732

GLOBAL RESSOURCES HUMAINES INC *p* 1170
3737 BOUL CREMAZIE E BUREAU 400, MONTREAL, QC, H1Z 2K4
(514) 788-0599 *SIC* 6712

GLOBAL REWARD SOLUTIONS INC *p* 852
38 LEEK CRES 4TH FL, RICHMOND HILL, ON, L4B 4N8
(905) 477-3971 *SIC* 8742

GLOBAL ROYALTIES LIMITED *p* 705
145 TRADERS BLVD E UNIT 1, MISSISSAUGA, ON, L4Z 3L3
(905) 890-3000 *SIC* 5094

GLOBAL SEA SERVICES LTD *p* 705
2 ROBERT SPECK PKY SUITE 750, MISSISSAUGA, ON, L4Z 1H8
(905) 908-2141 *SIC* 5812

GLOBAL SEATING, DIV OF *p* 783
See GLOBAL CONTRACT INC

GLOBAL SECURITIES CORPORATION *p* 328
3 BENTALL CTR SUITE 1100, VANCOUVER, BC, V7X 1C4
(604) 689-5400 *SIC* 6211

GLOBAL SECURITIES CORPORATION *p* 328
595 BURRARD ST, VANCOUVER, BC, V7X 1C4
(604) 689-5400 *SIC* 6211

GLOBAL SERVICES *p* 666
See AMEX CANADA INC

GLOBAL SKILLS INC *p* 951
366 BAY ST 10TH FL, TORONTO, ON, M5H 4B2
(416) 907-8400 *SIC* 7361

GLOBAL TARDIF *p* 1293
See GROUPE TARDIF GLF INC, LE

GLOBAL TELESALES OF CANADA INC *p* 841
1900 FISHER DR, PETERBOROUGH, ON, K9J 6X6
(705) 872-3021 *SIC* 7389

GLOBAL TELEVISION *p* 22
See CORUS MEDIA HOLDINGS INC

GLOBAL TELEVISION *p* 118
See CORUS MEDIA HOLDINGS INC

GLOBAL TELEVISION *p* 445
See CORUS MEDIA HOLDINGS INC

GLOBAL TELEVISION *p* 779
See CORUS MEDIA HOLDINGS INC

GLOBAL TELEVISION *p* 933
See CORUS MEDIA HOLDINGS INC

GLOBAL TOTAL OFFICE *p* 783
See GLOBAL UPHOLSTERY CO. INC

GLOBAL TRAVEL COMPUTER HOLDINGS LTD *p* 670
7550 BIRCHMOUNT RD, MARKHAM, ON, L3R 6C6
(905) 479-4949 *SIC* 7374

GLOBAL UPHOLSTERY CO LIMITED *p* 783
560 SUPERTEST RD, NORTH YORK, ON, M3J 2M6
(416) 661-3660 *SIC* 6719

GLOBAL UPHOLSTERY CO. INC *p* 783
1350 FLINT RD, NORTH YORK, ON, M3J 2J7
(416) 661-3660 *SIC* 6719

GLOBAL UPHOLSTERY CO. INC *p* 783
560 SUPERTEST RD, NORTH YORK, ON, M3J 2M6
(416) 661-3660 *SIC* 2522

GLOBAL UPHOLSTERY CO. INC *p* 783
565 PETROLIA RD, NORTH YORK, ON, M3J 2X8
(416) 739-5000 *SIC* 2522

GLOBAL VILLAGE *p* 301
See WESTCOAST ENGLISH LANGUAGE CENTER LIMITED

GLOBAL VINTNERS *p* 599
See ANDREW PELLER LIMITED

GLOBAL WARRANTY CORPORATION *p* 655
471 WATERLOO ST, LONDON, ON, N6B 2P4
(519) 672-9356 *SIC* 6399

GLOBAL WINDOW SOLUTIONS INC *p* 411
128 RUE INDUSTRIAL, RICHIBUCTO, NB, E4W 4A4
(506) 523-4900 *SIC* 3089

GLOBAL WINDOWS AND DOORS *p* 411
See GLOBAL WINDOW SOLUTIONS INC

GLOBAL WIRELESS SOLUTIONS INC *p* 580
22 DIXON RD SUITE 2, ETOBICOKE, ON, M9P 2L1
(416) 246-1656 *SIC* 5999

GLOBAL WOOD CONCEPTS LTD *p* 783
1300 FLINT RD, NORTH YORK, ON, M3J 2J7
(416) 663-4191 *SIC* 2521

GLOBAL-SKY LOGISTICS INC *p* 1250
81 BOUL HYMUS, POINTE-CLAIRE, QC, H9R 1E2
(514) 223-3399 *SIC* 3944

GLOBALEX GESTION DE RISQUES INC *p* 1196
1130 RUE SHERBROOKE O, MONTREAL, QC, H3A 2M8
(514) 382-9625 *SIC* 6411

GLOBALEX GESTION DE RISQUES INC *p* 1196
999 BOUL DE MAISONNEUVE O, MONTREAL, QC, H3A 3L4
(514) 382-6674 *SIC* 6411

GLOBALEYE *p* 66
See ZEDI INC

GLOBALIVE COMMUNICATIONS CORP *p* 942
48 YONGE ST SUITE 1200, TORONTO, ON, M5E 1G6
(416) 640-1088 *SIC* 4899

GLOBALMED INC *p* 999
155 MURRAY ST N, TRENTON, ON, K8V 5R5
(613) 394-9844 *SIC* 3841

GLOBALSTAR CANADA SATELLITE CO. *p* 731
115 MATHESON BLVD W UNIT 100, MISSISSAUGA, ON, L5R 3L1
(905) 890-1377 *SIC* 5731

GLOBCO INTERNATIONAL INC *p* 1138
1660 BOUL GUILLAUME-COUTURE, LEVIS, QC, G6W 5M6
(418) 834-1844 *SIC* 4213

GLOBE AND MAIL *p* 978
See BELL MEDIA INC

GLOBE AND MAIL INC, THE *p* 933
351 KING ST E SUITE 1600, TORONTO, ON, M5A 0N1
(416) 585-5000 *SIC* 5192

GLOBE ELECTRIC COMPANY INC *p* 1250
150 AV ONEIDA, POINTE-CLAIRE, QC, H9R 1A8
(888) 543-1388 *SIC* 5063

GLOBE METAL *p* 1356
See SERVICES DE RECYCLAGE GLOBE METAL, GMR INC

GLOBE STAR SYSTEMS INC *p* 783
7 KODIAK CRES SUITE 100, NORTH YORK, ON, M3J 3E5
(416) 636-2282 *SIC* 3825

GLOBE UNION (CANADA) INC *p* 1334
4610 CH DU BOIS-FRANC, SAINT-LAURENT, QC, H4S 1A7
(514) 907-8000 *SIC* 5074

GLOBE WHOLESALE MEATS INC *p* 793
61 SIGNET DR, NORTH YORK, ON, M9L 2W5
(416) 745-7000 *SIC* 5147

GLOBEHAUL TRANSPORTATION *p* 1298
See TRANSPORTS DUCAMPRO INC

GLOBESPAN TRAVEL LTD *p* 293
660 LEG IN BOOT SQ UNIT C, VANCOUVER, BC, V5Z 4B3
(604) 879-6466 *SIC* 4724

GLOBESTAR SYSTEMS *p* 783
See GLOBE STAR SYSTEMS INC

GLOBETROTTER LOGISTICS INC *p* 578
35 RAKELY CRT, ETOBICOKE, ON, M9C 5A5
(416) 742-2232 *SIC* 4731

GLOBEWAYS CANADA INC *p* 695
2570 MATHESON BLVD E SUITE 110, MISSISSAUGA, ON, L4W 4Z3
(905) 712-1010 *SIC* 5153

GLOBEX COURRIER EXPRESS INTERNATIONAL INC *p* 1329
2267 RUE GUENETTE, SAINT-LAURENT, QC, H4R 2E9
(514) 739-7977 *SIC* 4512

GLOBOCAM (MONTREAL) INC *p* 1248
155 AV REVERCHON, POINTE-CLAIRE, QC, H9P 1K1
(514) 344-4000 *SIC* 5511

GLOBUS FAMILY OF BRANDS *p* 996
See LONTOURS CANADA LIMITED

GLOGOWSKI EURO FOOD LTD *p* 641

403 HIGHLAND RD W, KITCHENER, ON, N2M 3C6
(519) 584-7190 *SIC* 5411

GLOMAR *p* 705
See COMFORT SYSTEM SOLUTIONS INC

GLOPAK *p* 1345
See HOOD PACKAGING CORPORATION

GLORY GLOBAL SOLUTIONS (CANADA) INC *p* 1237
1111 CHOMEDEY (A-13) E UNITE 200, MONTREAL, QC, H7W 5J8
(450) 686-8800 *SIC* 5044

GLORY SOLUTIONS GLOBALES CANADA *p* 1237
See GLORY GLOBAL SOLUTIONS (CANADA) INC

GLOUCESTER CONSTRUCTION LTD *p* 419
4260 RUE PRINCIPALE, TRACADIE-SHEILA, NB, E1X 1B9
SIC 1542

GLOUCESTER HIGH SCHOOL *p* 596
See OTTAWA-CARLETON DISTRICT SCHOOL BOARD

GLOVERTOWN SHIPYARDS *p* 423
See NORTHSIDE MARINE LTD

GLOVIS CANADA, INC *p* 731
5770 HURONTARIO ST SUITE 700, MISSISSAUGA, ON, L5R 3G5
(905) 361-1642 *SIC* 4212

GLR *p* 1119
See G.L.R. INC

GLR - THIRO S.E.N.C. *p* 1119
1095 RUE VALETS, L'ANCIENNE-LORETTE, QC, G2E 4M7
(418) 872-3365 *SIC* 1623

GLS LOGISTICS SYSTEMS CANADA LTD *p* 1094
10755 CH COTE-DE-LIESSE, DORVAL, QC, H9P 1A7
(888) 463-4266 *SIC* 4212

GLS LOGISTICS SYSTEMS CANADA LTD *p* 1094
10500 AV RYAN, DORVAL, QC, H9P 2T7
(514) 636-8033 *SIC* 4731

GLUECKLER METAL INC *p* 568
13 WILLIAM ST, ELMVALE, ON, L0L 1P0
(705) 737-9486 *SIC* 3499

GLUSKIN SHEFF + ASSOCIATES INC *p* 952
333 BAY ST SUITE 5100, TORONTO, ON, M5H 2R2
(416) 681-6000 *SIC* 6282

GLUTINO *p* 1362
See IMPORTATIONS DE-RO-MA (1983) LTEE

GLYNNWOOD *p* 905
See REVERA INC

GLYNSKAR ENTERPRISES LTD *p* 491
260 ADAM ST, BELLEVILLE, ON, K8N 5S4
(613) 962-5100 *SIC* 4899

GM *p* 1090
See DOLBEAU AUTOMOBILES LTEE

GM *p* 1143
See RIVE SUD PONTIAC BUICK GMC INC

GM *p* 1285
See BOULEVARD CHEVROLET INC

GM CANADA EDMONTON PDC 21 *p* 101
See GENERAL MOTORS OF CANADA COMPANY

GM CANADA WOODSTOCK PDC 36 *p* 1035
See GENERAL MOTORS OF CANADA COMPANY

GM CHEVROLET *p* 1075
See AUTOMOBILES CARMER 1990 INC

GM DEVELOPPEMENT INC *p* 1259
520 BOUL CHAREST E BUREAU 233, QUEBEC, QC, G1K 3J3
(418) 692-7470 *SIC* 6531

GM FINANCIAL *p* 767
See GENERAL MOTORS FINANCIAL OF CANADA, LTD.

GM OF CANADA LANGLEY *p* 229
See GENERAL MOTORS OF CANADA COMPANY

GM RIOUX *p* 416

See RIOUX, GILBERT M & FILS LTEE

GMA p 735
See GIDDEN MORTON ASSOCIATES INC

GMA COVER CORP p 600
965 YORK RD, GUELPH, ON, N1E 6Y9
SIC 3714

GMAC p 1096
See GENERAL MOTORS ACCEPTANCE CORPORATION OF CANADA, LIMITED

GMASJ ONTARIO INC p 793
1290 ORMONT DR, NORTH YORK, ON, M9L 2V4
(416) 241-9151 SIC 5148

GMI p 1094
See GRAPHIQUES MATROX INC

GML MECHANICAL LTD p 209
7355 72 ST SUITE 13, DELTA, BC, V4G 1L5
(604) 940-9686 SIC 1711

GMP p 1065
See GAZ METRO PLUS INC

GMP CAPITAL INC p 952
145 KING ST W SUITE 300, TORONTO, ON, M5H 1J8
(416) 367-8600 SIC 6211

GMP SECURITIES p 952
See GMP CAPITAL INC

GMP SECURITIES L.P. p 952
145 KING ST W SUITE 300, TORONTO, ON, M5H 1J8
(416) 367-8600 SIC 6211

GMRI CANADA, INC p 711
790 BURNHAMTHORPE RD W, MISSISSAUGA, ON, L5C 4G3
(905) 848-8477 SIC 5812

GMS CAPITAL CORP p 1164
3055 BOUL DE L'ASSOMPTION, MONTREAL, QC, H1N 2H1
SIC 5122

GN CORPORATIONS INC p 3
2873 KINGSVIEW BLVD SE, AIRDRIE, AB, T4A 0E1
(403) 948-6464 SIC 3533

GN THERMOFORMING EQUIPMENT p 442
See G.N. PLASTICS COMPANY LIMITED

GNA p 794
See GRAND NATIONAL APPAREL INC

GNC p 688
See GENERAL NUTRITION CENTRES COMPANY

GNR CORBUS INC p 1373
4070 RUE BRODEUR, SHERBROOKE, QC, J1L 1V9
(819) 564-2300 SIC 1711

GNUTTI CARLO CANADA LTD p 621
404 CANADA AVE, HURON PARK, ON, N0M 1Y0
(519) 228-6685 SIC 3714

GO AUTO CORPORATION p 101
10220 184 ST NW, EDMONTON, AB, T5S 0B9
(780) 701-9999 SIC 5511

GO AUTO RED DEER CHRYSLER DODGE JEEP RAM LTD p 153
3115 50 AVE, RED DEER, AB, T4N 3X8
(403) 352-7999 SIC 5511

GO BEE INDUSTRIES INC p 566
1-334 A HATT ST, DUNDAS, ON, L9H 2H9
(289) 238-8829 SIC 7319

GO HONDA p 98
See 1583647 ALBERTA LTD

GO NISSAN p 125
See MILLS NISSAN LTD

GO RESILIENT CANADA p 526
See EII LIMITED

GO RV & MARINE RED DEER LTD p 157
29 PETROLIA DR, RED DEER COUNTY, AB, T4E 1B3
(403) 347-5546 SIC 5571

GO SMOOTH TRANSPORT LTD p 723
7 RIMINI MEWS, MISSISSAUGA, ON, L5N 4K1
(905) 696-7023 SIC 4212

GO TRANSIT p 712
See METROLINX

GO TRANSIT p 920
See METROLINX

GO TRANSIT p 965
See METROLINX

GO TRANSIT, DIV OF p 965
See METROLINX

GOBA SPORTS GROUP INC p 670
151 WHITEHALL DR, MARKHAM, ON, L3R 9T1
(888) 989-4015 SIC 5091

GOBIMIN INC p 952
120 ADELAIDE ST W SUITE 2110, TORONTO, ON, M5H 1T1
(416) 915-0133 SIC 1481

GODERICH-EXETER RAILWAY COMPANY LIMITED p 896
101 SHAKESPEARE ST SUITE 2, STRATFORD, ON, N5A 3W5
(519) 271-4441 SIC 4011

GODFATHER PIZZA p 659
See 1025091 ONTARIO LIMITED

GODFREY-MORROW INSURANCE & FINANCIAL SERVICES LTD p 64
1003 11 AVE SW, CALGARY, AB, T2R 0G2
(403) 244-4945 SIC 6411

GOEASY LTD p 709
33 CITY CENTRE DR SUITE 510, MISSISSAUGA, ON, L5B 2N5
(905) 272-2788 SIC 7359

GOFF FISHERIES p 421
See GOFF FISHERIES LIMITED

GOFF FISHERIES LIMITED p 421
5 BLUEBERRY CRES, CARBONEAR, NL, A1Y 1A6
(709) 596-7155 SIC 7999

GOGO GEEK ENTERPRISES INC p 254
13988 CAMBIE RD SUITE 373, RICHMOND, BC, V6V 2K4
(604) 248-0782 SIC 5045

GOGO QUINOA p 1233
See COMPAGNIE 2 AMERIKS INC, LA

GOGOLD RESOURCES INC p 453
2000 BARRINGTON ST SUITE 1301, HALIFAX, NS, B3J 3K1
(902) 482-1998 SIC 1044

GOJI p 1211
See NUMERIQ INC

GOJIT p 1274
See 4211677 CANADA INC

GOLD EAGLE CASINO p 1413
See SASKATCHEWAN INDIAN GAMING AUTHORITY INC

GOLD FREIGHT p 642
11339 ALBION VAUGHAN LINE, KLEINBURG, ON, L0J 1C0
(905) 893-0700 SIC 4731

GOLD KEY AUTOMOTIVE LTD p 271
19545 LANGEY BYPASS, SURREY, BC, V3S 6K1
(604) 534-7431 SIC 5511

GOLD KEY INSURANCE SERVICES LTD p 287
4038 KNIGHT ST, VANCOUVER, BC, V5N 5Y7
(604) 325-1241 SIC 6411

GOLD KEY PONTIAC BUICK (1984) LTD p 271
19545 LANGLEY BYPASS, SURREY, BC, V3S 6K1
(604) 534-7431 SIC 5511

GOLD KEY SALES & SERVICES LTD p 280
2092 152 ST, SURREY, BC, V4A 4N8
(604) 536-7212 SIC 5511

GOLD KEY SALES AND LEASE LTD p 271
19545 LANGEY BYPASS, SURREY, BC, V3S 6K1
(604) 534-7431 SIC 5511

GOLD KEY VOLKSWAGEN p 280
See GOLD KEY SALES & SERVICES LTD

GOLD LINE p 670
See GOLD LINE TELEMANAGEMENT INC

GOLD LINE SOLUTIONS p 527
3228 SOUTH SERVICE RD SUITE 102, BURLINGTON, ON, L7N 3H8
(905) 633-3835 SIC 8732

GOLD LINE TELEMANAGEMENT INC p 670
300 ALLSTATE PKY, MARKHAM, ON, L3R 0P2
(905) 709-3570 SIC 4899

GOLD SEAL p 294
See CANADIAN FISHING COMPANY LIMITED, THE

GOLD STANDARD VENTURES CORP p 304
815 HASTINGS ST W SUITE 610, VANCOUVER, BC, V6C 1B4
(604) 687-2766 SIC 1041

GOLD STAR TRANSPORT (1975) LTD p 132
11002 89 AVE, GRANDE PRAIRIE, AB, T8V 4W4
(780) 532-0773 SIC 4213

GOLD'S GYM BRITISH COLUMBIA p 185
See GG BROADWAY INVESTMENTS LIMITED PARTNERSHIP

GOLD, A. & SONS LTD p 543
7659 QUEENS LINE, CHATHAM, ON, N7M 5J5
(519) 352-0360 SIC 5093

GOLDBAR CONTRACTORS INC p 122
1415 90 AVE NW SUITE 100, EDMONTON, AB, T6P 0C8
(780) 440-6440 SIC 1711

GOLDCORP CANADA LTD p 304
666 BURRARD ST SUITE 3400, VANCOUVER, BC, V6C 2X8
(604) 696-3000 SIC 1041

GOLDEC HAMMS MANUFACTURING LTD p 155
6760 65 AVE, RED DEER, AB, T4P 1A5
(403) 343-6607 SIC 3443

GOLDEN & DISTRICT GENERAL HOSPITAL p 215
See INTERIOR HEALTH AUTHORITY

GOLDEN ACRE FARMS INC p 633
1451 ROAD 2 E, KINGSVILLE, ON, N9Y 2E4
SIC 0182

GOLDEN ARCH FOOD SERVICES LTD p 487
80 BARRIE VIEW DR, BARRIE, ON, L4N 8V4
(705) 735-1700 SIC 5812

GOLDEN ARROW RESOURCES CORPORATION p 304
837 HASTINGS ST W UNIT 312, VANCOUVER, BC, V6C 3N6
(604) 687-1828 SIC 1081

GOLDEN ARROW SCHOOLBUSES LTD p 101
20204 111 AVE NW, EDMONTON, AB, T5S 2G6
(780) 447-1538 SIC 4151

GOLDEN BOY p 182
See GOLDEN BOY FOODS LTD

GOLDEN BOY FOODS GP (2007) INC p 182
7725 LOUGHEED HWY, BURNABY, BC, V5A 4V8
(778) 373-3800 SIC 2099

GOLDEN BOY FOODS LTD p 182
3151 LAKE CITY WAY, BURNABY, BC, V5A 3A3
(604) 421-4500 SIC 4226

GOLDEN BOY FOODS LTD p 182
7725 LOUGHEED HWY, BURNABY, BC, V5A 4V8
(604) 433-2200 SIC 2068

GOLDEN CLIPPER, THE p 446
See HEAD SHOPPE COMPANY LIMITED, THE

GOLDEN CROSSING CONSTRUCTORS JOINT VENTURE p 224
20100 100A AVE, LANGLEY, BC, V1M 3G4
SIC 1622

GOLDEN CROWN FOODS INC p 797
1154 BALLANTRY RD, OAKVILLE, ON, L6H 5M9
(905) 334-9178 SIC 5146

GOLDEN DOOR GERIATRIC CENTRE p 391
See PEMBINA CARE SERVICES LTD

GOLDEN EAGLE GOLF CLUB p 244
See GOLDEN EAGLE GOLF COURSES INC

GOLDEN EAGLE GOLF COURSES INC p 244
21770 LADNER RD, PITT MEADOWS, BC, V3Y 1Z1
(604) 460-1871 SIC 7992

GOLDEN FIRE JUMPERS LTD p 215
1717 MOBERLY SCHOOL RD, GOLDEN, BC, V0A 1H1
(250) 344-6464 SIC 0851

GOLDEN FLEECE FOOD DISTRIBUTORS AND WHOLESALERS LTD p 503
16 BAKER RD, BRAMPTON, ON, L6T 4E3
(905) 458-1101 SIC 5142

GOLDEN FLOORING ACCESSORIES PS LTD p 96
11662 154 ST NW, EDMONTON, AB, T5M 3N8
(780) 451-4222 SIC 5169

GOLDEN FOOD & MANUFACTURE LTD p 553
241 SNIDERCROFT RD, CONCORD, ON, L4K 2J8
(905) 660-3233 SIC 7389

GOLDEN GATE HIDE & LEATHER LTD p 871
21A COSENTINO DR, SCARBOROUGH, ON, M1P 3A3
(416) 299-7195 SIC 5199

GOLDEN GATE SEAFOOD p 368
See MIDLAND FOODS (WINNIPEG), INC

GOLDEN GLOBE CONSTRUCTION LTD p 290
8380 ST. GEORGE ST UNIT 103, VANCOUVER, BC, V5X 3S7
(604) 261-3936 SIC 1521

GOLDEN INTERNATIONAL TRANSPORT p 1060
See TRANSPORT TFI 16, S.E.C.

GOLDEN LIFE MANAGEMENT CORP p 204
1800 WILLOWBROOK DR, CRANBROOK, BC, V1C 7H9
(250) 489-0667 SIC 6531

GOLDEN LIFE MANAGEMENT CORP p 212
55 COKATO RD SUITE 206, FERNIE, BC, V0B 1M4
(250) 423-4214 SIC 8059

GOLDEN LINKS LODGE p 368
See ODD FELLOWS & REBEKAHS PERSONAL CARE HOMES INC

GOLDEN OPPORTUNITIES FUND INC p 1427
410 22ND ST E SUITE 830, SASKATOON, SK, S7K 5T6
(306) 652-5557 SIC 6282

GOLDEN PHOENIX MEAT COMPANY p 702
See 1376371 ONTARIO INC

GOLDEN PLOUGH LODGE p 545
See CORPORATION OF THE COUNTY OF NORTHUMBERLAND

GOLDEN QUEEN MINING CO. LTD p 304
580 HORNBY ST SUITE 880, VANCOUVER, BC, V6C 3B6
(604) 417-7952 SIC 1041

GOLDEN REIGN RESOURCES LTD p 304
595 HOWE ST SUITE 501, VANCOUVER, BC, V6C 2T5
(604) 685-4655 SIC 1081

GOLDEN STAR RESOURCES LTD p 952
150 KING ST W SUITE 1200, TORONTO, ON, M5H 1J9
(416) 583-3800 SIC 1041

GOLDEN TEACHERS ASSOCIATION p 215
912 11TH AVE S, GOLDEN, BC, V0A 1H0
SIC 8611

GOLDEN TRIANGLE RESTORATION INC p 533
2302 DUMFRIES RD, CAMBRIDGE, ON,

N1R 5S3
(519) 624-4487 *SIC* 6331
GOLDEN TRIM ENTERPRISES INC *p* 182
8411 LOUGHEED HWY, BURNABY, BC,
V5A 1X3
(604) 421-3998 *SIC* 5023
GOLDEN VALLEY *p* 479
See GOLDEN VALLEY FARMS INC
GOLDEN VALLEY FARMS INC *p* 479
50 WELLS ST W, ARTHUR, ON, N0G 1A0
(519) 848-3110 *SIC* 0191
GOLDEN VALLEY FOODS LTD *p* 176
3841 VANDERPOL CRT, ABBOTSFORD,
BC, V2T 5W5
(604) 857-0704 *SIC* 0252
GOLDEN VIEW COLONY *p* 1404
*See HUTTERIAN BRETHREN OF GOLDEN
VIEW INC*
GOLDEN WEST BAKING COMPANY ULC *p*
206
1111 DERWENT WAY, DELTA, BC, V3M
5R4
(604) 525-2491 *SIC* 5461
GOLDEN WEST BROADCASTING *p* 345
125 CENTRE AVE W SUITE 201, ALTONA,
MB, R0G 0B0
(204) 324-6464 *SIC* 4832
GOLDEN WINDOWS LIMITED *p* 639
888 GUELPH ST, KITCHENER, ON, N2H
5Z6
(519) 579-3810 *SIC* 3089
**GOLDEN YEARS NURSING & ASSISTED
LIVING CENTRE** *p* 539
*See GOLDEN YEARS NURSING HOMES
(CAMBRIDGE) INC*
**GOLDEN YEARS NURSING HOMES (CAM-
BRIDGE) INC** *p*
539
704 EAGLE ST N, CAMBRIDGE, ON, N3H
1C3
(519) 653-5493 *SIC* 8051
GOLDENLIFE FINANCIAL CORP *p* 578
555 BURNHAMTHORPE RD SUITE 305,
ETOBICOKE, ON, M9C 2Y3
(416) 620-0615 *SIC* 6282
GOLDER ASSOCIATES CORPORATION *p*
723
6925 CENTURY AVE SUITE 100, MISSIS-
SAUGA, ON, L5N 7K2
(905) 567-4444 *SIC* 8711
GOLDER ASSOCIATES LTD *p* 11
2535 3 AVE SE SUITE 102, CALGARY, AB,
T2A 7W5
(403) 299-5600 *SIC* 8748
GOLDER ASSOCIATES LTD *p* 98
16820 107 AVE NW, EDMONTON, AB, T5P
4C3
(780) 483-3499 *SIC* 8711
GOLDER ASSOCIATES LTD *p* 338
3795 CAREY RD FL 2, VICTORIA, BC, V8Z
6T8
(250) 881-7372 *SIC* 8711
GOLDER ASSOCIATES LTD *p* 723
6925 CENTURY AVE, MISSISSAUGA, ON,
L5N 0E3
(905) 567-4444 *SIC* 8711
GOLDER ASSOCIATES LTD *p* 751
1931 ROBERTSON RD, NEPEAN, ON, K2H
5B7
(613) 592-9600 *SIC* 8711
GOLDER ASSOCIATES LTD *p* 900
33 MACKENZIE ST SUITE 100, SUDBURY,
ON, P3C 4Y1
(705) 524-6861 *SIC* 8711
GOLDER ASSOCIATES LTD *p* 1181
7250 RUE DU MILE END 3E ETAGE, MON-
TREAL, QC, H2R 3A4
(514) 383-0990 *SIC* 8711
GOLDER ASSOCIATES LTD *p* 1424
1721 8TH ST E, SASKATOON, SK, S7H 0T4
(306) 665-7989 *SIC* 8711
GOLDER ASSOCIES *p* 1181
See GOLDER ASSOCIATES LTD
GOLDER ASSOCIES LTEE *p* 1367

690 BOUL LAURE BUREAU 112, SEPT-
ILES, QC, G4R 4N8
(418) 968-6111 *SIC* 8621
GOLDER CONSTRUCTION INC *p* 1226
9200 BOUL DE L'ACADIE BUREAU 10,
MONTREAL, QC, H4N 2T2
(514) 389-1631 *SIC* 8711
GOLDFARB SHULMAN PATEL & CO LLP *p*
553
400 BRADWICK DR SUITE 100, CON-
CORD, ON, L4K 5V9
(416) 226-6800 *SIC* 8721
GOLDGROUP MINING INC *p* 313
1166 ALBERNI ST SUITE 1502, VANCOU-
VER, BC, V6E 3Z3
(604) 682-1943 *SIC* 1041
GOLDILOCKS BAKE SHOP (CANADA) INC
p 321
1606 BROADWAY W, VANCOUVER, BC,
V6J 1X6
(604) 736-2464 *SIC* 5461
GOLDMAN SACHS CANADA INC *p* 969
77 KING ST W SUITE 3400, TORONTO,
ON, M5K 2A1
(416) 343-8900 *SIC* 6211
GOLDMINING INC *p* 313
1030 W GEORGIA ST SUITE 1830, VAN-
COUVER, BC, V6E 2Y3
(604) 630-1000 *SIC* 1041
GOLDMONEY INC *p* 980
334 ADELAIDE ST W UNIT 307,
TORONTO, ON, M5V 0M1
(647) 499-6748 *SIC* 7372
GOLDRAY GLASS *p* 16
See GOLDRAY INDUSTRIES LTD
GOLDRAY INDUSTRIES LTD *p* 16
4605 52 AVE SE, CALGARY, AB, T2C 4N7
(403) 236-1333 *SIC* 3211
GOLDRICH PRINTPAK INC *p* 992
100 INDUSTRY ST, TORONTO, ON, M6M
4L8
(416) 769-9000 *SIC* 2657
GOLDRIDGE FARMING CO. LTD *p* 170
GD, TURIN, AB, T0K 2H0
(403) 359-5111 *SIC* 0119
GOLDSTRIKE RESOURCES LTD *p* 313
1130 W PENDER ST SUITE 1010, VAN-
COUVER, BC, V6E 4A4
(604) 681-1820 *SIC* 1041
GOLDWELL COSMETICS (CANADA) LTD *p*
739
1045 TRISTAR DR, MISSISSAUGA, ON,
L5T 1W5
(905) 670-2844 *SIC* 5999
GOLDWOOD INDUSTRIES LTD *p* 254
12691 MITCHELL RD, RICHMOND, BC,
V6V 1M7
(604) 327-2935 *SIC* 5211
GOLDY METALS INC *p* 878
1216 SEWELLS RD, SCARBOROUGH, ON,
M1X 1S1
(416) 286-8686 *SIC* 5093
GOLF CANADA *p* 806
*See ROYAL CANADIAN GOLF ASSOCIA-
TION*
**GOLF DU BOISE DE LACHENAIE-OUEST,
LE** *p* 1379
See IMMEUBDES MOULINS INC., LES
GOLF DU GRAND PORTNEUF INC, LE *p*
1253
2 RTE 365, PONT-ROUGE, QC, G3H 3R4
(418) 329-2238 *SIC* 7992
GOLF KENOSEE CAPITAL INC *p* 1408
GD, KENOSEE LAKE, SK, S0C 2S0
(306) 577-2044 *SIC* 6712
GOLF TOWN *p* 553
*See GOLF TOWN OPERATING LIMITED
PARTNERSHIP*
GOLF TOWN LIMITED *p* 553
610 APPLEWOOD CRES UNIT 302, CON-
CORD, ON, L4K 0E3
(905) 479-0343 *SIC* 5941
**GOLF TOWN OPERATING LIMITED PART-
NERSHIP** *p*

553
610 APPLEWOOD CRES UNIT 302, CON-
CORD, ON, L4K 0E3
(905) 479-0343 *SIC* 5941
GOLFBC HOLDINGS INC *p* 313
1030 GEORGIA ST W SUITE 1800, VAN-
COUVER, BC, V6E 2Y3
(604) 681-8700 *SIC* 7992
GOLFBC HOLDINGS INC *p* 343
8080 NICKLAUS NORTH BLVD,
WHISTLER, BC, V8E 1J7
(604) 938-9898 *SIC* 5812
GOLIATH TRACTOR SERVICE LTD *p* 8
10 WRANGLER PLACE S.E. SUITE 4, CAL-
GARY, AB, T1X 0L7
(403) 203-7352 *SIC* 4213
GOLLIN HARRIS *p* 935
*See WEBER SHANDWICK WORLDWIDE
(CANADA) INC*
GONDERFLEX INTERNATIONAL INC *p*
1141
530 BOUL GUIMOND, LONGUEUIL, QC,
J4G 1P8
(450) 651-2224 *SIC* 5084
GONTE CONSTRUCTION LTD *p* 503
190 CLARK BLVD, BRAMPTON, ON, L6T
4A8
(905) 456-6488 *SIC* 1521
GOOD FAMILY FOODS *p* 849
2899 CROMARTY DR, PUTNAM, ON, N0L
2B0
(519) 269-3700 *SIC* 0182
GOOD HOPE COLONY FARMS LTD *p* 354
GD LCD MAIN, PORTAGE LA PRAIRIE, MB,
R1N 3A7
(204) 252-2334 *SIC* 0191
**GOOD HOPE COLONY OF HUTTERIAN
BRETHREN-TRUST** *p* 354
See GOOD HOPE COLONY FARMS LTD
GOOD HUMOR BREYERS *p* 881
See UNILEVER CANADA INC
GOOD SAMARITAN SOCIETY *p* 112
*See GOOD SAMARITAN SOCIETY, THE (A
LUTHERAN SOCIAL SERVICE ORGANIZA-
TION)*
GOOD SAMARITAN SOCIETY, THE *p* 146
*See GOOD SAMARITAN SOCIETY, THE (A
LUTHERAN SOCIAL SERVICE ORGANIZA-
TION)*
**GOOD SAMARITAN SOCIETY, THE (A
LUTHERAN SOCIAL SERVICE ORGANIZA-
TION)** *p*
112
8861 75 ST NW, EDMONTON, AB, T6C 4G8
(780) 431-3600 *SIC* 8069
**GOOD SAMARITAN SOCIETY, THE (A
LUTHERAN SOCIAL SERVICE ORGANIZA-
TION)** *p*
146
550 SPRUCE WAY SE, MEDICINE HAT, AB,
T1B 4P1
(403) 528-5050 *SIC* 8699
**GOOD SHEPHERD CENTRE HAMILTON,
THE** *p* 612
143 WENTWORTH ST S SUITE 302,
HAMILTON, ON, L8N 2Z1
(905) 528-5877 *SIC* 8322
GOOD SUITS DON'T JUST HAPPEN *p* 1218
See SAMUELSOHN LIMITEE
GOOD WATER COMPANY LTD, THE *p* 492
163 COLLEGE ST W, BELLEVILLE, ON,
K8P 2G7
(613) 707-8400 *SIC* 7389
GOODALL RUBBER *p* 182
See LEWIS-GOETZ ULC
GOODFELLOW INC *p* 540
9184 TWISS RD, CAMPBELLVILLE, ON,
L0P 1B0
(416) 233-1227 *SIC* 5031
GOODFELLOW INC *p* 1089
225 RUE GOODFELLOW, DELSON, QC,
J5B 1V5
(450) 635-6511 *SIC* 5031
GOODFELLOW INC *p* 1098

1750 RUE HAGGERTY, DRUM-
MONDVILLE, QC, J2C 5P8
(819) 477-6898 *SIC* 2426
GOODFOOD MARKET CORP *p* 1339
4600 RUE HICKMORE, SAINT-LAURENT,
QC, H4T 1K2
(514) 730-9530 *SIC* 8322
**GOODISON INSURANCE & FINANCIAL
SERVICES LTD** *p* 508
36 QUEEN ST E SUITE 200, BRAMPTON,
ON, L6V 1A2
(905) 451-1236 *SIC* 6411
GOODKEY SHOW SERVICES LTD *p* 109
5506-48 ST NW, EDMONTON, AB, T6B 2Z1
(780) 426-2211 *SIC* 7389
GOODLAD, JOHN P. SALES INC *p* 906
8081 DUFFERIN ST, THORNHILL, ON, L4J
8R9
(905) 889-7455 *SIC* 5251
GOODLAW SERVICES INC *p* 935
250 YONGE ST SUITE 2400, TORONTO,
ON, M5B 2L7
(416) 979-2211 *SIC* 8111
GOODLIFE FITNESS CENTRES INC *p* 658
710 PROUDFOOT LANE, LONDON, ON,
N6H 5G5
(519) 661-0190 *SIC* 7991
GOODLIFE FITNESS CENTRES INC *p* 830
2655 QUEENSVIEW DR, OTTAWA, ON,
K2B 8K2
SIC 7991
GOODLIFE FITNESS CENTRES INC *p* 871
1911 KENNEDY RD, SCARBOROUGH, ON,
M1P 2L9
(416) 297-7279 *SIC* 7991
GOODLIFE FITNESS CLUBS *p* 658
See GOODLIFE FITNESS CENTRES INC
**GOODMAN & COMPANY, INVESTMENT
COUNSEL LTD** *p* 939
1 ADELAIDE ST E SUITE 2100, TORONTO,
ON, M5C 2V9
(416) 363-9097 *SIC* 6282
**GOODMAN & GRIFFIN BARRISTERS &
SOLICITORS** *p* 705
44 VILLAGE CENTRE PL 3RD FL SUITE
300, MISSISSAUGA, ON, L4Z 1V9
(905) 276-5050 *SIC* 8111
GOODMAN COMPANY CANADA *p* 553
8305 JANE ST UNIT 3, CONCORD, ON,
L4K 5Y3
(905) 760-2737 *SIC* 5075
GOODMANS LLP *p* 952
333 BAY ST SUITE 3400, TORONTO, ON,
M5H 2S7
(416) 979-2211 *SIC* 8111
GOODMEN ROOFING LTD *p* 155
7700 76 ST CLOSE SUITE 110, RED
DEER, AB, T4P 4G6
(403) 343-0380 *SIC* 1761
GOODNESS ME NATURAL FOOD MARKET
p 614
See ROMARAH INCORPORATED
GOODON INDUSTRIES *p* 346
See GOODON, IRVIN INDUSTRIES LTD
GOODON, IRVIN INDUSTRIES LTD *p* 346
HWY 10, BOISSEVAIN, MB, R0K 0E0
(204) 534-2468 *SIC* 1542
GOODRICH AEROSPACE CANADA LTD *p*
522
5415 NORTH SERVICE RD, BURLINGTON,
ON, L7L 5H7
(905) 319-3006 *SIC* 7699
GOODRICH AEROSPACE CANADA LTD *p*
803
1400 SOUTH SERVICE RD W, OAKVILLE,
ON, L6L 5Y7
(905) 827-7777 *SIC* 3728
GOODRICH LANDING GEAR SERVICES *p*
522
*See GOODRICH AEROSPACE CANADA
LTD*
GOODWILL *p* 374
*See CANADIAN GOODWILL INDUSTRIES
CORP*

GOODWILL CAREER CENTRE, THE p 655
See GOODWILL INDUSTRIES, ONTARIO GREAT LAKES
GOODWILL INDUSTRIES NIAGARA p 885
111 CHURCH ST, ST CATHARINES, ON, L2R 3C9
(905) 641-5285   *SIC 5932*
GOODWILL INDUSTRIES OF ALBERTA (REGISTERED SOCIETY) p 114
8761 51 AVE NW, EDMONTON, AB, T6E 5H1
(780) 944-1414   *SIC 8331*
GOODWILL INDUSTRIES, ONTARIO GREAT LAKES p 655
255 HORTON ST E, LONDON, ON, N6B 1L1
(519) 645-1455   *SIC 5932*
GOODWILL INDUSTRIES, ONTARIO GREAT LAKES p 655
390 KING ST, LONDON, ON, N6B 1S3
(519) 850-9675   *SIC 8331*
GOODWILL INDUSTRIES-ESSEX KENT LAMBTON INC p 860
439 PALMERSTON ST S, SARNIA, ON, N7T 3P4
(519) 332-0440   *SIC 5932*
GOODWILL REHAB. SERVICE p 114
See GOODWILL INDUSTRIES OF ALBERTA (REGISTERED SOCIETY)
GOODYEAR p 426
See CITY TIRE & AUTO CENTRE LIMITED
GOODYEAR CANADA INC p 147
1271 12 ST NW, MEDICINE HAT, AB, T1C 1W8
(403) 527-3353   *SIC 3011*
GOODYEAR CANADA INC p 574
450 KIPLING AVE, ETOBICOKE, ON, M8Z 5E1
(416) 201-4300   *SIC 3011*
GOODYEAR CANADA INC p 747
388 GOODYEAR RD, NAPANEE, ON, K7R 3L2
(613) 354-7411   *SIC 3011*
GOODYEAR CANADA INC p 1365
2600 BOUL MONSEIGNEUR-LANGLOIS, SALABERRY-DE-VALLEYFIELD, QC, J6S 5G6
(450) 377-6800   *SIC 3011*
GOODYEAR FARM LTD p 849
139 RAVENSHOE RD, QUEENSVILLE, ON, L0G 1R0
(905) 478-8388   *SIC 0191*
GOODYEAR NAPANEE TIRE MANUFAC-TURING FACILITY p 747
See GOODYEAR CANADA INC
GOOGLE CANADA CORPORATION p 1205
1253 AV MCGILL COLLEGE BUREAU 150, MONTREAL, QC, H3B 2Y5
(514) 670-8700   *SIC 7375*
GORD & KIM'S NO FRILLS p 631
See 1132145 ONTARIO LIMITED
GORD DAVENPORT AUTOMOTIVE INC p 808
74 FIRST ST, ORANGEVILLE, ON, L9W 2E4
(519) 941-1233   *SIC 5013*
GORDON AULENBACK LTD p 248
3034 ST JOHNS ST, PORT MOODY, BC, V3H 2C5
(604) 461-3434   *SIC 5571*
GORDON BAY MARINE LTD p 663
55A HATHERLEY RD SUITE 1, MACTIER, ON, P0C 1H0
(705) 375-2623   *SIC 5551*
GORDON BELL HIGH SCHOOL p 383
See WINNIPEG SCHOOL DIVISION
GORDON FOOD SERVICE CANADA LTD p 160
290212 TOWNSHIP ROAD 261, ROCKY VIEW COUNTY, AB, T4A 0V6
(403) 235-8555   *SIC 5141*
GORDON FOOD SERVICE CANADA LTD p 389

310 STERLING LYON PKY, WINNIPEG, MB, R3P 0Y2
(204) 224-0134   *SIC 5141*
GORDON FOOD SERVICE CANADA LTD p 683
2999 JAMES SNOW PKY N, MILTON, ON, L9T 5G4
(905) 864-3700   *SIC 5141*
GORDON GRAYDON MEMORIAL SEC-ONDARY SCHOOL p 712
See PEEL DISTRICT SCHOOL BOARD
GORDON HOTELS & MOTOR INNS LTD p 367
1011 HENDERSON HWY, WINNIPEG, MB, R2K 2M2
(204) 334-4355   *SIC 7011*
GORDON HOTELS & MOTOR INNS LTD p 385
1975 PORTAGE AVE, WINNIPEG, MB, R3J 0J9
(204) 888-4806   *SIC 7011*
GORDON LATHAM LIMITED p 319
1060 8TH AVE W SUITE 100, VANCOU-VER, BC, V6H 1C4
(604) 683-2321   *SIC 1711*
GORDON'S STATE SERVICES LTD., BRO-KERAGE p 630
490 DISCOVERY AVE UNIT 7, KINGSTON, ON, K7K 7E9
(613) 542-0963   *SIC 6531*
GORDON, AL ELECTRIC LIMITED p 661
1099 PROGRESS DR, LONDON, ON, N6N 1B7
(519) 672-1273   *SIC 1731*
GORDONS PNEUS MECANIQUE p 1222
See W. GORDON INC
GORE BROTHERS VINTAGE HOMES INC p 196
10805 MCDONALD RD, CHILLIWACK, BC, V2P 6H5
(604) 824-1902   *SIC 1521*
GORE MUTUAL INSURANCE COMPANY p 328
505 BURRARD ST UNIT 1780, VANCOU-VER, BC, V7X 1M6
(604) 682-0998   *SIC 6331*
GORE MUTUAL INSURANCE COMPANY p 533
252 DUNDAS ST S, CAMBRIDGE, ON, N1R 8A8
(519) 623-1910   *SIC 6331*
GOREWAY STATION PARTNERSHIP p 503
8600 GOREWAY DR, BRAMPTON, ON, L6T 0A8
(905) 595-4700   *SIC 4911*
GORF CONTRACTING p 846
See NORMAC EQUIP-MENT/CONSTRUCTION LIMITED
GORF CONTRACTING LTD p 846
6855 HWY 101 E, PORCUPINE, ON, P0N 1C0
(705) 235-3278   *SIC 1522*
GORMAN BROS. LUMBER LTD p 341
3900 DUNFIELD RD, WEST KELOWNA, BC, V4T 1W4
(250) 768-5131   *SIC 2421*
GORRIE ADVERTISING MANAGEMENT LIMITED p 695
2770 MATHESON BLVD E, MISSISSAUGA, ON, L4W 4M5
(905) 238-3466   *SIC 8743*
GORRIE MARKETING SERVICES p 695
See GORRIE ADVERTISING MANAGE-MENT LIMITED
GORRUD LIMITED p 683
410 STEELES AVE E, MILTON, ON, L9T 1Y4
(905) 875-2277   *SIC 5521*
GORRUD'S AUTO CENTRE p 683
See GORRUD'S AUTO GROUP
GORRUD'S AUTO GROUP p 683
410 STEELES AVE E, MILTON, ON, L9T

1Y4
(905) 875-2277   *SIC 5521*
GORSKI BULK TRANSPORT INC p 807
5400 WALKER RD, OLDCASTLE, ON, N0R 1L0
(519) 737-1275   *SIC 4213*
GOSTLIN, K E ENTERPRISES LTD p 220
1655 LECKIE RD, KELOWNA, BC, V1X 6E4
(250) 860-4331   *SIC 5531*
GOTHAM STEAKHOUSE & COCKTAIL BAR LIMITED PARTNERSHIP p 298
615 SEYMOUR ST, VANCOUVER, BC, V6B 3K3
(604) 605-8282   *SIC 5813*
GOTREKKERS INC p 71
4625 VARSITY DR NW SUITE 305, CAL-GARY, AB, T3A 0Z9
(403) 289-6938   *SIC 4725*
GOTTARDO CONSTRUCTION LIMITED p 553
277 PENNSYLVANIA AVE, CONCORD, ON, L4K 5R9
(905) 761-7707   *SIC 6512*
GOUDAS FOOD PRODUCTS AND INVEST-MENTS LIMITED p 553
241 SNIDERCROFT RD, CONCORD, ON, L4K 2J8
SIC 5141
GOUDAS FOOD PRODUCTS CO. LTD p 553
241 SNIDERCROFT RD, CONCORD, ON, L4K 2J8
(905) 660-3233   *SIC 5141*
GOULD FASTENERS p 688
6209 NORTHWEST DR, MISSISSAUGA, ON, L4V 1P6
(905) 677-8253   *SIC 5085*
GOULD PACKAGING DIV OF p 776
See LEPAGES 2000 INC
GOURMET MONDIALE p 1356
See MOSTI MONDIALE INC
GOURMET NANTEL p 1358
See 9252-9064 QUEBEC INC
GOURMET NUTRITION F.B INC p 1358
2121 RUE LEONARD-DE VINCI BUREAU 4, SAINTE-JULIE, QC, J3E 1Z2
(450) 922-2885   *SIC 5149*
GOURMET TRADING p 587
See QUALIFIRST FOODS LTD
GOURMET TRADING CO. LTD p 716
3750A LAIRD RD SUITE 7, MISSISSAUGA, ON, L5L 0A6
(905) 826-6800   *SIC 5149*
GOUTTIERES DES LAURENTIDES, LES p 1302
See MANUFACTURIERS D'ALUMINIUM OTTAWA INC, LES
GOUVERNEMENT DE LA PROVINCE DE QUEBEC p 1055
11000 RUE DES MONTAGNARDS RR 1, BEAUPRE, QC, G0A 1E0
(418) 661-5666   *SIC 8361*
GOUVERNEMENT DE LA PROVINCE DE QUEBEC p 1084
308 BOUL CARTIER O, COTE SAINT-LUC, QC, H7N 2J2
(450) 975-4150   *SIC 8322*
GOUVERNEMENT DE LA PROVINCE DE QUEBEC p 1104
1100 BOUL MALONEY O BUREAU 1600, GATINEAU, QC, J8T 6G3
(819) 994-7739   *SIC 7389*
GOUVERNEMENT DE LA PROVINCE DE QUEBEC p 1106
135 BOUL SAINT-RAYMOND, GATINEAU, QC, J8Y 6X7
(819) 777-6261   *SIC 8011*
GOUVERNEMENT DE LA PROVINCE DE QUEBEC p 1106
116 BOUL LIONEL-EMOND, GATINEAU, QC, J8Y 1W7
SIC 8062
GOUVERNEMENT DE LA PROVINCE DE QUEBEC p 1106

15 RUE GAMELIN, GATINEAU, QC, J8Y 6N5
(819) 778-8600   *SIC 6331*
GOUVERNEMENT DE LA PROVINCE DE QUEBEC p 1108
100 RUE LAURIER, GATINEAU, QC, K1A 0M8
(819) 776-7000   *SIC 8412*
GOUVERNEMENT DE LA PROVINCE DE QUEBEC p 1113
1235 RUE DE LA DIGUE, HAVRE-SAINT-PIERRE, QC, G0G 1P0
(418) 538-2662   *SIC 8211*
GOUVERNEMENT DE LA PROVINCE DE QUEBEC p 1114
245 RUE DU CURE-MAJEAU, JOLIETTE, QC, J6E 8S8
(450) 759-1157   *SIC 8399*
GOUVERNEMENT DE LA PROVINCE DE QUEBEC p 1114
380 BOUL BASE-DE-ROC, JOLIETTE, QC, J6E 9J6
(450) 755-2111   *SIC 8399*
GOUVERNEMENT DE LA PROVINCE DE QUEBEC p 1138
1400 BOUL GUILLAUME-COUTURE UNITE RC, LEVIS, QC, G6W 8K7
(418) 838-5615   *SIC 8748*
GOUVERNEMENT DE LA PROVINCE DE QUEBEC p 1144
1255 RUE BEAUREGARD, LONGUEUIL, QC, J4K 2M3
(450) 928-6777   *SIC 8399*
GOUVERNEMENT DE LA PROVINCE DE QUEBEC p 1146
450 2E RUE, LOUISEVILLE, QC, J5V 1V3
(819) 228-2700   *SIC 8361*
GOUVERNEMENT DE LA PROVINCE DE QUEBEC p 1147
50 RUE SAINT-PATRICE E, MAGOG, QC, J1X 3X3
(819) 843-2572   *SIC 8062*
GOUVERNEMENT DE LA PROVINCE DE QUEBEC p 1151
14 BOUL PERRON E, MATAPEDIA, QC, G0J 1V0
SIC 8399
GOUVERNEMENT DE LA PROVINCE DE QUEBEC p 1168
3730 RUE DE BELLECHASSE, MON-TREAL, QC, H1X 3E5
(514) 374-8665   *SIC 8361*
GOUVERNEMENT DE LA PROVINCE DE QUEBEC p 1174
1000 RUE FULLUM, MONTREAL, QC, H2K 3L7
(514) 521-2424   *SIC 4833*
GOUVERNEMENT DE LA PROVINCE DE QUEBEC p 1175
475 BOUL DE MAISONNEUVE E, MON-TREAL, QC, H2L 5C4
(514) 873-1100   *SIC 8231*
GOUVERNEMENT DE LA PROVINCE DE QUEBEC p 1177
950 RUE DE LOUVAIN E, MONTREAL, QC, H2M 2E8
(514) 385-1232   *SIC 8093*
GOUVERNEMENT DE LA PROVINCE DE QUEBEC p 1185
3535 RUE SAINT-DENIS, MONTREAL, QC, H2X 3P1
(514) 282-5111   *SIC 8249*
GOUVERNEMENT DE LA PROVINCE DE QUEBEC p 1188
1 RUE NOTRE-DAME E BUREAU 4.100, MONTREAL, QC, H2Y 1B6
(514) 393-2703   *SIC 8111*
GOUVERNEMENT DE LA PROVINCE DE QUEBEC p 1188
276 RUE SAINT-JACQUES, MONTREAL, QC, H2Y 1N3
(514) 725-5221   *SIC 8331*
GOUVERNEMENT DE LA PROVINCE DE QUEBEC p 1191

159 RUE SAINT-ANTOINE O BUREAU 900, MONTREAL, QC, H2Z 1H2
(514) 871-8122   *SIC* 7389
GOUVERNEMENT DE LA PROVINCE DE QUEBEC
1080 COTE DU BEAVER HALL BUREAU 1000, MONTREAL, QC, H2Z 1S8
(514) 873-2032   *SIC* 8322
GOUVERNEMENT DE LA PROVINCE DE QUEBEC   p 1222
7005 BOUL DE MAISONNEUVE O BUREAU 620, MONTREAL, QC, H4B 1T3
(514) 487-1770   *SIC* 7352
GOUVERNEMENT DE LA PROVINCE DE QUEBEC   p 1229
800 SQ VICTORIA 22E ETAGE, MONTREAL, QC, H4Z 1G3
(514) 395-0337   *SIC* 8741
GOUVERNEMENT DE LA PROVINCE DE QUEBEC   p 1244
2020 CH D'OKA, OKA, QC, J0N 1E0
(450) 479-8365   *SIC* 7996
GOUVERNEMENT DE LA PROVINCE DE QUEBEC   p 1256
3510 RUE CAMBRONNE, QUEBEC, QC, G1E 7H2
(418) 661-3700   *SIC* 8399
GOUVERNEMENT DE LA PROVINCE DE QUEBEC   p 1256
7843 RUE DES SANTOLINES., QUEBEC, QC, G1G 0G3
(418) 683-2511   *SIC* 8361
GOUVERNEMENT DE LA PROVINCE DE QUEBEC   p 1257
700 RUE 7E, QUEBEC, QC, G1J 2S1
(418) 528-8350   *SIC* 4581
GOUVERNEMENT DE LA PROVINCE DE QUEBEC   p 1259
105 RUE HERMINE, QUEBEC, QC, G1K 1Y5
(418) 529-2501   *SIC* 8051
GOUVERNEMENT DE LA PROVINCE DE QUEBEC   p 1262
525 BOUL WILFRID-HAMEL, QUEBEC, QC, G1M 2S8
(418) 649-3700   *SIC* 8093
GOUVERNEMENT DE LA PROVINCE DE QUEBEC   p 1267
2700 RUE EINSTEIN BUREAU C2105, QUEBEC, QC, G1P 3W8
(418) 643-1632   *SIC* 8731
GOUVERNEMENT DE LA PROVINCE DE QUEBEC   p 1269
179 RUE GRANDE ALLEE O, QUEBEC, QC, G1R 2H1
(418) 643-2150   *SIC* 8412
GOUVERNEMENT DE LA PROVINCE DE QUEBEC   p 1269
150 BOUL RENE-LEVESQUE E, QUEBEC, QC, G1R 2B2
(418) 646-4646   *SIC* 8742
GOUVERNEMENT DE LA PROVINCE DE QUEBEC   p 1269
200 CH SAINTE-FOY 3E ETAGE BUREAU 300, QUEBEC, QC, G1R 5T4
(418) 691-2401   *SIC* 2721
GOUVERNEMENT DE LA PROVINCE DE QUEBEC   p 1269
525 BOUL RENE-LEVESQUE E BUREAU 125, QUEBEC, QC, G1R 5Y4
(418) 643-2688   *SIC* 8111
GOUVERNEMENT DE LA PROVINCE DE QUEBEC   p 1278
700 7E RUE DE L'AEROPORT, QUEBEC, QC, G2G 2S8
(418) 528-8686   *SIC* 8711
GOUVERNEMENT DE LA PROVINCE DE QUEBEC   p 1289
80 AV QUEBEC, ROUYN-NORANDA, QC, J9X 6R1
(819) 763-3237   *SIC* 1611
GOUVERNEMENT DE LA PROVINCE DE QUEBEC   p 1320
25 RUE DE MARTIGNY O, SAINT-JEROME,

QC, J7Y 4Z1
(450) 431-4406   *SIC* 8111
GOUVERNEMENT DE LA PROVINCE DE QUEBEC   p 1321
430 RUE LABELLE, SAINT-JEROME, QC, J7Z 5L3
(450) 431-2221   *SIC* 8399
GOUVERNEMENT DE LA PROVINCE DE QUEBEC   p 1347
521 RUE SAINT-ANTOINE, SAINT-LIN-LAURENTIDES, QC, J5M 3A3
(450) 439-2609   *SIC* 8361
GOUVERNEMENT DE LA PROVINCE DE QUEBEC   p 1351
110 RUE DU COLLEGE, SAINT-REMI, QC, J0L 2L0
(450) 454-4694   *SIC* 8322
GOUVERNEMENT DE LA PROVINCE DE QUEBEC   p 1357
5436 BOUL LEVESQUE E, SAINTE-DOROTHEE, QC, H7C 1N7
(450) 661-5440   *SIC* 8361
GOUVERNEMENT DE LA PROVINCE DE QUEBEC   p 1370
300 RUE KING E BUREAU 300, SHERBROOKE, QC, J1G 1B1
(819) 566-7861   *SIC* 8399
GOUVERNEMENT DE LA PROVINCE DE QUEBEC   p 1372
375 RUE ARGYLL, SHERBROOKE, QC, J1J 3H5
(819) 821-1170   *SIC* 8051
GOUVERNEUR INC   p 1175
1415 RUE SAINT-HUBERT, MONTREAL, QC, H2L 3Y9
(514) 842-4881   *SIC* 7011
GOUVERNEUR INC   p 1196
1000 RUE SHERBROOKE O BUREAU 2300, MONTREAL, QC, H3A 3R3
(514) 875-8822   *SIC* 7011
GOUVERNEUR INC   p 1289
41 6E RUE, ROUYN-NORANDA, QC, J9X 1Y8
(819) 762-2341   *SIC* 7011
GOVAN BROWN & ASSOCIATES LIMITED p 994
108 VINE AVE, TORONTO, ON, M6P 1V7
(416) 703-5100   *SIC* 8741
GOVAN BROWN CONSTRUCTION MANAGERS   p 994
See GOVAN BROWN & ASSOCIATES LIMITED
GOVERNANCEGLOBAL   p 949
See BOARDSUITE CORP
GOVERNING COUNCIL OF THE SALVATION ARMY IN CANADA,   p 86
See GOVERNING COUNCIL OF THE SALVATION ARMY IN CANADA, THE
GOVERNING COUNCIL OF THE SALVATION ARMY IN CANADA,   p 236
See GOVERNING COUNCIL OF THE SALVATION ARMY IN CANADA, THE
GOVERNING COUNCIL OF THE SALVATION ARMY IN CANADA,   p 298
See GOVERNING COUNCIL OF THE SALVATION ARMY IN CANADA, THE
GOVERNING COUNCIL OF THE SALVATION ARMY IN CANADA,   p 339
See GOVERNING COUNCIL OF THE SALVATION ARMY IN CANADA, THE
GOVERNING COUNCIL OF THE SALVATION ARMY IN CANADA,   p 373
See GOVERNING COUNCIL OF THE SALVATION ARMY IN CANADA, THE
GOVERNING COUNCIL OF THE SALVATION ARMY IN CANADA,   p 828
See GOVERNING COUNCIL OF THE SAL-

VATION ARMY IN CANADA, THE
GOVERNING COUNCIL OF THE SALVATION ARMY IN CANADA,   p 919
See GOVERNING COUNCIL OF THE SALVATION ARMY IN CANADA, THE
GOVERNING COUNCIL OF THE SALVATION ARMY IN CANADA,   p 1420
See GOVERNING COUNCIL OF THE SALVATION ARMY IN CANADA, THE
GOVERNING COUNCIL OF THE SALVATION ARMY IN CANADA, THE   p 86
9611 102 AVE NW, EDMONTON, AB, T5H 0E5
(780) 429-4274   *SIC* 8322
GOVERNING COUNCIL OF THE SALVATION ARMY IN CANADA, THE   p 236
409 BLAIR AVE, NEW WESTMINSTER, BC, V3L 4A4
(604) 522-7033   *SIC* 8361
GOVERNING COUNCIL OF THE SALVATION ARMY IN CANADA, THE   p 298
555 HOMER ST SUITE 703, VANCOUVER, BC, V6B 1K8
(604) 681-3405   *SIC* 8322
GOVERNING COUNCIL OF THE SALVATION ARMY IN CANADA, THE   p 339
952 ARM ST, VICTORIA, BC, V9A 4G7
(250) 385-3422   *SIC* 8051
GOVERNING COUNCIL OF THE SALVATION ARMY IN CANADA, THE   p 346
510 6TH ST, BRANDON, MB, R7A 3N9
(204) 727-3636   *SIC* 8051
GOVERNING COUNCIL OF THE SALVATION ARMY IN CANADA, THE   p 373
811 SCHOOL RD, WINNIPEG, MB, R2Y 0S8
(204) 888-3311   *SIC* 8322
GOVERNING COUNCIL OF THE SALVATION ARMY IN CANADA, THE   p 651
1340 DUNDAS ST, LONDON, ON, N5W 3B6
(519) 455-4810   *SIC* 8351
GOVERNING COUNCIL OF THE SALVATION ARMY IN CANADA, THE   p 757
5050 JEPSON ST, NIAGARA FALLS, ON, L2E 1K5
(905) 356-1221   *SIC* 8051
GOVERNING COUNCIL OF THE SALVATION ARMY IN CANADA, THE   p 821
171 GEORGE ST, OTTAWA, ON, K1N 5W5
(613) 241-1573   *SIC* 8399
GOVERNING COUNCIL OF THE SALVATION ARMY IN CANADA, THE   p 828
1156 WELLINGTON ST W SUITE 613, OTTAWA, ON, K1Y 2Z3
(613) 722-8025   *SIC* 8051
GOVERNING COUNCIL OF THE SALVATION ARMY IN CANADA, THE   p 919
1132 BROADVIEW AVE, TORONTO, ON, M4K 2S5
(416) 425-1052   *SIC* 8399
GOVERNING COUNCIL OF THE SALVATION ARMY IN CANADA, THE   p 919
2 OVERLEA BLVD, TORONTO, ON, M4H 1P4
(416) 425-2111   *SIC* 8399
GOVERNING COUNCIL OF THE SALVATION ARMY IN CANADA, THE   p 1420
50 ANGUS RD, REGINA, SK, S4R 8P6
(306) 543-0655   *SIC* 8361

VATION ARMY IN CANADA, THE
GOVERNING COUNCIL OF THE UNIVERSITY OF TORONTO   p 570
See GOVERNING COUNCIL OF THE UNIVERSITY OF TORONTO, THE
GOVERNING COUNCIL OF THE UNIVERSITY OF TORONTO   p 932
See GOVERNING COUNCIL OF THE UNIVERSITY OF TORONTO, THE
GOVERNING COUNCIL OF THE UNIVERSITY OF TORONTO   p 945
See GOVERNING COUNCIL OF THE UNIVERSITY OF TORONTO, THE
GOVERNING COUNCIL OF THE UNIVERSITY OF TORONTO   p 974
See GOVERNING COUNCIL OF THE UNIVERSITY OF TORONTO, THE
GOVERNING COUNCIL OF THE UNIVERSITY OF TORONTO   p 975
See GOVERNING COUNCIL OF THE UNIVERSITY OF TORONTO, THE
GOVERNING COUNCIL OF THE UNIVERSITY OF TORONTO   p 977
See GOVERNING COUNCIL OF THE UNIVERSITY OF TORONTO, THE
GOVERNING COUNCIL OF THE UNIVERSITY OF TORONTO, THE   p 570
84 QUEENS AVE, ETOBICOKE, ON, M8V 2N3
(416) 978-8789   *SIC* 8221
GOVERNING COUNCIL OF THE UNIVERSITY OF TORONTO, THE   p 570
80 QUEENS AVE, ETOBICOKE, ON, M8V 2N3
(416) 978-0414   *SIC* 8221
GOVERNING COUNCIL OF THE UNIVERSITY OF TORONTO, THE   p 570
78 QUEENS AVE, ETOBICOKE, ON, M8V 2N3
(416) 978-0210   *SIC* 8221
GOVERNING COUNCIL OF THE UNIVERSITY OF TORONTO, THE   p 865
1265 MILITARY TRAIL SUITE 303, SCARBOROUGH, ON, M1C 1A4
(416) 287-7033   *SIC* 8221
GOVERNING COUNCIL OF THE UNIVERSITY OF TORONTO, THE   p 932
10 ST MARY ST SUITE 700, TORONTO, ON, M4Y 2W8
(416) 978-1000   *SIC* 8221
GOVERNING COUNCIL OF THE UNIVERSITY OF TORONTO, THE   p 945
123 EDWARD ST SUITE 1200, TORONTO, ON, M5G 1E2
(416) 978-2668   *SIC* 8221
GOVERNING COUNCIL OF THE UNIVERSITY OF TORONTO, THE   p 945
124 EDWARD ST, TORONTO, ON, M5G 1G6
(416) 979-4927   *SIC* 8221
GOVERNING COUNCIL OF THE UNIVERSITY OF TORONTO, THE   p 945
190 ELIZABETH ST, TORONTO, ON, M5G 2C4
(416) 978-8383   *SIC* 8221
GOVERNING COUNCIL OF THE UNIVERSITY OF TORONTO, THE   p 945
100 COLLEGE ST RM 110, TORONTO, ON, M5G 1L5
(416) 978-4059   *SIC* 8221

GOVERNING COUNCIL OF THE UNIVERSITY OF TORONTO, THE *p*
945
500 UNIVERSITY AVE SUITE 160, TORONTO, ON, M5G 1V7
(416) 946-8554 *SIC* 8221

GOVERNING COUNCIL OF THE UNIVERSITY OF TORONTO, THE *p*
945
555 UNIVERSITY AVE RM 1436D, TORONTO, ON, M5G 1X8
(416) 813-6122 *SIC* 8221

GOVERNING COUNCIL OF THE UNIVERSITY OF TORONTO, THE *p*
945
101 COLLEGE ST RM 15-701, TORONTO, ON, M5G 1L7
(416) 634-8755 *SIC* 8221

GOVERNING COUNCIL OF THE UNIVERSITY OF TORONTO, THE *p*
972
170 ST. GEORGE ST, TORONTO, ON, M5R 2M8
(416) 978-3190 *SIC* 8221

GOVERNING COUNCIL OF THE UNIVERSITY OF TORONTO, THE *p*
972
170 ST. GEORGE ST 4 FL, TORONTO, ON, M5R 2M8
(416) 978-3311 *SIC* 8221

GOVERNING COUNCIL OF THE UNIVERSITY OF TORONTO, THE *p*
974
35 ST. GEORGE ST SUITE 173, TORONTO, ON, M5S 1A4
(416) 978-3099 *SIC* 8221

GOVERNING COUNCIL OF THE UNIVERSITY OF TORONTO, THE *p*
974
40 ST. GEORGE ST RM 4113, TORONTO, ON, M5S 2E4
(416) 978-1655 *SIC* 8221

GOVERNING COUNCIL OF THE UNIVERSITY OF TORONTO, THE *p*
975
1 DEVONSHIRE PL, TORONTO, ON, M5S 3K7
(416) 946-8900 *SIC* 8221

GOVERNING COUNCIL OF THE UNIVERSITY OF TORONTO, THE *p*
975
80 ST. GEORGE ST, TORONTO, ON, M5S 3H6
(416) 978-3564 *SIC* 8221

GOVERNING COUNCIL OF THE UNIVERSITY OF TORONTO, THE *p*
975
725 SPADINA AVE, TORONTO, ON, M5S 2J4
(416) 946-4058 *SIC* 8221

GOVERNING COUNCIL OF THE UNIVERSITY OF TORONTO, THE *p*
975
55 HARBORD ST SUITE 1048, TORONTO, ON, M5S 2W6
(416) 978-7375 *SIC* 8221

GOVERNING COUNCIL OF THE UNIVERSITY OF TORONTO, THE *p*
975
40 ST. GEORGE ST RM BA 5165, TORONTO, ON, M5S 2E4
SIC 8221

GOVERNING COUNCIL OF THE UNIVERSITY OF TORONTO, THE *p*
975
1 KING'S COLLEGE CIR RM 4207, TORONTO, ON, M5S 1A8
(416) 978-2728 *SIC* 8221

GOVERNING COUNCIL OF THE UNIVERSITY OF TORONTO, THE *p*
975
1 KING'S COLLEGE CIR RM 4396, TORONTO, ON, M5S 1A8
(416) 978-3730 *SIC* 8221

GOVERNING COUNCIL OF THE UNIVERSITY OF TORONTO, THE *p*
975
1 KING'S COLLEGE CIR SUITE 2109, TORONTO, ON, M5S 1A8
(416) 978-6585 *SIC* 8221

GOVERNING COUNCIL OF THE UNIVERSITY OF TORONTO, THE *p*
975
1 KING'S COLLEGE CIRCLE 3RD FL, TORONTO, ON, M5S 1A8
SIC 8221

GOVERNING COUNCIL OF THE UNIVERSITY OF TORONTO, THE *p*
975
1 KING'S COLLEGE CIRCLE RM 7207, TORONTO, ON, M5S 1A8
SIC 8221

GOVERNING COUNCIL OF THE UNIVERSITY OF TORONTO, THE *p*
975
1 SPADINA CRES, TORONTO, ON, M5S 2J5
(416) 978-5038 *SIC* 8221

GOVERNING COUNCIL OF THE UNIVERSITY OF TORONTO, THE *p*
975
10 KING'S COLLEGE RD RM 1024, TORONTO, ON, M5S 3H5
(416) 978-3112 *SIC* 8221

GOVERNING COUNCIL OF THE UNIVERSITY OF TORONTO, THE *p*
975
10 KING'S COLLEGE RD SUITE 3302, TORONTO, ON, M5S 3G4
(416) 978-6025 *SIC* 8221

GOVERNING COUNCIL OF THE UNIVERSITY OF TORONTO, THE *p*
975
100 ST. GEORGE ST, TORONTO, ON, M5S 3G3
(416) 978-3383 *SIC* 8221

GOVERNING COUNCIL OF THE UNIVERSITY OF TORONTO, THE *p*
975
100 ST. GEORGE ST RM 5047, TORONTO, ON, M5S 3G3
(416) 978-3375 *SIC* 8221

GOVERNING COUNCIL OF THE UNIVERSITY OF TORONTO, THE *p*
975
105 ST. GEORGE ST, TORONTO, ON, M5S 3E6
(416) 978-5703 *SIC* 8221

GOVERNING COUNCIL OF THE UNIVERSITY OF TORONTO, THE *p*
975
105 ST. GEORGE ST SUITE 275, TORONTO, ON, M5S 3E6
(416) 978-4574 *SIC* 8221

GOVERNING COUNCIL OF THE UNIVERSITY OF TORONTO, THE *p*
975
144 COLLEGE ST, TORONTO, ON, M5S 3M2
(416) 978-2889 *SIC* 8221

GOVERNING COUNCIL OF THE UNIVERSITY OF TORONTO, THE *p*
975
150 ST. GEORGE ST, TORONTO, ON, M5S 3G7
(416) 978-4622 *SIC* 8221

GOVERNING COUNCIL OF THE UNIVERSITY OF TORONTO, THE *p*
975
200 COLLEGE ST UNIT 217, TORONTO, ON, M5S 3E5
(416) 978-6204 *SIC* 8221

GOVERNING COUNCIL OF THE UNIVERSITY OF TORONTO, THE *p*
975
25 WILLCOCKS STREET, TORONTO, ON, M5S 3B2
SIC 8221

GOVERNING COUNCIL OF THE UNIVERSITY OF TORONTO, THE *p*
975
27 KING'S COLLEGE CIR, TORONTO, ON, M5S 1A1
(416) 978-2196 *SIC* 8221

GOVERNING COUNCIL OF THE UNIVERSITY OF TORONTO, THE *p*
975
40 ST. GEORGE ST RM 6290, TORONTO, ON, M5S 2E4
(416) 978-3323 *SIC* 8221

GOVERNING COUNCIL OF THE UNIVERSITY OF TORONTO, THE *p*
977
250 COLLEGE ST 8 FL, TORONTO, ON, M5T 1R8
(416) 979-6948 *SIC* 8221

GOVERNING COUNCIL OF THE UNIVERSITY OF TORONTO, THE *p*
977
155 COLLEGE ST SUITE 130, TORONTO, ON, M5T 1P8
(416) 978-2392 *SIC* 8221

GOVERNING COUNCIL OF THE UNIVERSITY OF TORONTO, THE *p*
977
263 MCCAUL ST 3 FL, TORONTO, ON, M5T 1W7
(416) 978-5938 *SIC* 8221

GOVERNING COUNCIL OF THE UNIVERSITY OF TORONTO, THE *p*
977
263 MCCAUL ST, TORONTO, ON, M5T 1W7
(416) 978-6801 *SIC* 8221

GOVERNING COUNCIL OF THE UNIVERSITY OF TORONTO, THE *p*
977
340 COLLEGE ST SUITE 400, TORONTO, ON, M5T 3A9
(416) 978-4321 *SIC* 8221

GOVERNMENT OF ONTARIO *p* 490
29 MAIN ST W, BEETON, ON, L0G 1A0
(905) 729-4004 *SIC* 8069

GOVERNMENT OF ONTARIO *p* 580
101 HUMBER COLLEGE BLVD, ETOBICOKE, ON, M9V 1R8
(416) 747-3400 *SIC* 8062

GOVERNMENT OF ONTARIO *p* 695
5090 COMMERCE BLVD UNIT 100, MISSISSAUGA, ON, L4W 5M4
(416) 622-0748 *SIC* 7381

GOVERNMENT OF ONTARIO *p* 794
1860 WILSON AVE, NORTH YORK, ON, M9M 3A7
(416) 392-6500 *SIC* 8399

GOVERNMENT OF ONTARIO *p* 861
1520 QUEEN ST E, SAULT STE. MARIE, ON, P6A 2G4
(705) 949-2301 *SIC* 8221

GOVERNMENT OF ONTARIO *p* 995
400 UNIVERSITY AVE 14TH FLR, TORONTO, ON, M7A 1T7
(416) 326-7600 *SIC* 8111

GOVERNMENT OF ONTARIO *p* 995
900 BAY ST SUITE 200, TORONTO, ON, M7A 1L2
(866) 797-0000 *SIC* 7299

GOVERNMENT OF ONTARIO *p* 1014
920 CHAMPLAIN CRT, WHITBY, ON, L1N 6K9
(905) 430-3308 *SIC* 8059

GOVERNMENT OF SASKATCHEWAN *p*
1412
1092 107TH ST, NORTH BATTLEFORD, SK, S9A 1Z1
(306) 446-6600 *SIC* 8062

GOVERNMENT OF SASKATCHEWAN *p*
1412
123 JERSEY ST, NORTH BATTLEFORD, SK, S9A 4B4
(306) 446-7819 *SIC* 8322

GOVERNMENT OF THE PROVINCE OF ALBERTA *p*
5
GD, BEAVERLODGE, AB, T0H 0C0
(780) 354-2136 *SIC* 8062

GOVERNMENT OF THE PROVINCE OF ALBERTA *p*
92
9820 106 ST NW SUITE 534, EDMONTON, AB, T5K 2J6
(780) 427-3076 *SIC* 6289

GOVERNMENT OF THE PROVINCE OF ALBERTA *p*
127
744 26TH ST, FORT MACLEOD, AB, T0L 0Z0
(403) 553-5300 *SIC* 8062

GOVERNMENT OF THE PROVINCE OF ALBERTA *p*
138
5718 56 AVE, LACOMBE, AB, T4L 1B1
(403) 782-8309 *SIC* 6159

GOVERNMENT OF THE PROVINCE OF ALBERTA *p*
140
3305 18 AVE N SUITE 107, LETHBRIDGE, AB, T1H 5S1
(403) 381-5543 *SIC* 8322

GOVERNMENT OF THE PROVINCE OF ALBERTA *p*
153
150 N 400 E, RAYMOND, AB, T0K 2S0
(403) 752-5411 *SIC* 8062

GOVERNMENT OF THE PROVINCE OF ALBERTA *p*
165
5025 49 AVE, ST PAUL, AB, T0A 3A4
(780) 645-6210 *SIC* 8741

GOVERNMENT OF THE PROVINCE OF BRITISH COLUMBIA *p* 210
5800 MOUNTAIN VIEW BLVD, DELTA, BC, V4K 3V6
(604) 946-1121 *SIC* 8062

GOVERNOR'S WALK LTD *p* 820
150 STANLEY AVE, OTTAWA, ON, K1M 2J7
(613) 564-9255 *SIC* 6513

GOVERNORS OF ST FRANCIS XAVIER UNIVERSITY *p* 438
1 WEST ST, ANTIGONISH, NS, B2G 2W5
(902) 863-3300 *SIC* 8221

GOVERNORS OF THE UNIVERSITY OF ALBERTA, THE *p*
117
111 89 AVE, EDMONTON, AB, T6G 2H5
(780) 492-3111 *SIC* 8221

GOVERNORS OF THE UNIVERSITY OF ALBERTA, THE *p*
117
11405 87 AVE 5TH FL, EDMONTON, AB, T6G 1C9
(780) 492-5391 *SIC* 8221

GOVERNORS OF THE UNIVERSITY OF ALBERTA, THE *p*
117
116 ST & 85 AVE, EDMONTON, AB, T6G 2R3
(780) 492-3111 *SIC* 8221

GOVERNORS OF THE UNIVERSITY OF ALBERTA, THE *p*
117
5 HUMANITIES CTR UNIT 6, EDMONTON, AB, T6G 2E5
(780) 492-2787 *SIC* 8221

GOVERNORS OF THE UNIVERSITY OF ALBERTA, THE *p*
117
51 UNIVERSITY CAMPUS NW SUITE 632, EDMONTON, AB, T6G 2G1
(780) 492-3396 *SIC* 8221

GOVERNORS OF THE UNIVERSITY OF ALBERTA, THE *p*
117
52 UNIVERSITY CAMPUS NW, EDMONTON, AB, T6G 2J8
(780) 492-3790 *SIC* 8231

GOVERNORS OF THE UNIVERSITY OF AL-

BERTA, THE   p
117
8625 112 ST NW SUITE 222, EDMONTON,
AB, T6G 1K8
(780) 492-5787   SIC 8733
GOVERNORS OF THE UNIVERSITY OF AL-
BERTA, THE   p
117
8900 114 ST NW, EDMONTON, AB, T6G
2V2
(780) 492-4241   SIC 8742
GOVERNORS OF THE UNIVERSITY OF AL-
BERTA, THE   p
118
26 EARTH SCIENCES BLDG UNIT 1, ED-
MONTON, AB, T6G 2E3
(780) 492-3265   SIC 8221
GOVERNORS OF THE UNIVERSITY OF AL-
BERTA, THE   p
118
302 GENERAL SERVICES BLDG, EDMON-
TON, AB, T6G 2E1
(780) 492-9400   SIC 8221
GOVERNORS OF THE UNIVERSITY OF
CALGARY, THE   p 41
2500 UNIVERSITY DR NW, CALGARY, AB,
T2N 1N4
(403) 220-5110   SIC 7389
GOVERNORS OF THE UNIVERSITY OF
CALGARY, THE   p 41
3330 HOSPITAL DR NW SUITE 3330, CAL-
GARY, AB, T2N 4N1
SIC 8733
GOVIEX URANIUM INC   p 305
999 CANADA PL SUITE 654, VANCOUVER,
BC, V6C 3E1
(604) 681-5529   SIC 1094
GOVIRAL INC   p 653
383 RICHMOND ST UNIT 1010, LONDON,
ON, N6A 3C4
(519) 850-1991   SIC 7371
GOW'S HARDWARE LIMITED   p 441
76 HIGH ST, BRIDGEWATER, NS, B4V 1V8
(902) 543-7121   SIC 5251
GOW'S HOME HARDWARE & FURNITURE
p 441
See GOW'S HARDWARE LIMITED
GOWANSTOWN POULTRY LIMITED   p 896
17 PINE ST, STRATFORD, ON, N5A 1W2
(519) 275-2240   SIC 0254
GOWAY TRAVEL LIMITED   p 921
3284 YONGE ST SUITE 500, TORONTO,
ON, M4N 3M7
(416) 322-1034   SIC 4725
GOWLING LAFLEUR AND HENDERSON p
639
See GOWLING WLG (CANADA) LLP
GOWLING WLG (CANADA) LLP   p 50
421 7 AVE SW UNIT 1600, CALGARY, AB,
T2P 4K9
(403) 298-1000   SIC 8111
GOWLING WLG (CANADA) LLP   p 305
550 BURRARD ST SUITE 2300, VANCOU-
VER, BC, V6C 2B5
(604) 683-6498   SIC 8111
GOWLING WLG (CANADA) LLP   p 612
1 MAIN ST W, HAMILTON, ON, L8P 4Z5
(905) 540-8208   SIC 8111
GOWLING WLG (CANADA) LLP   p 639
50 QUEEN ST N SUITE 1020, KITCHENER,
ON, N2H 6P4
(519) 575-7506   SIC 8111
GOWLING WLG (CANADA) LLP   p 639
50 QUEEN ST N SUITE 1020, KITCHENER,
ON, N2H 6P4
(519) 576-6910   SIC 8111
GOWLING WLG (CANADA) LLP   p 639
50 QUEEN ST N UNIT 1020, KITCHENER,
ON, N2H 6P4
(519) 576-6910   SIC 8111
GOWLING WLG (CANADA) LLP   p 823
160 ELGIN ST SUITE 2600, OTTAWA, ON,
K1P 1C3
(613) 233-1781   SIC 8111

GOWLING WLG (CANADA) LLP   p 986
1 FIRST CANADIAN PL 100 KING ST W
SUITE 1600, TORONTO, ON, M5X 1G5
(416) 862-7525   SIC 8111
GOWLING WLG (CANADA) LLP   p 1205
1 PLACE VILLE-MARIE BUREAU 3700,
MONTREAL, QC, H3B 3P4
(514) 878-9641   SIC 8111
GOWLINGS   p 50
See GOWLING WLG (CANADA) LLP
GOWLINGS   p 305
See GOWLING WLG (CANADA) LLP
GOWLINGS   p 639
See GOWLING WLG (CANADA) LLP
GOWLINGS   p 834
See G-WLG LP
GOWLINGS CANADA INC   p 834
160 ELGIN ST SUITE 200, OTTAWA, ON,
K2P 2C4
(613) 233-1781   SIC 8111
GOWLINGS CANADA INC   p 1205
1 PLACE VILLE-MARIE BUREAU 3700,
MONTREAL, QC, H3B 3P4
(514) 878-9641   SIC 8111
GOYER PETROLE HUILE A CHAUFFGE   p
1301
794 BOUL ARTHUR-SAUV?, SAINT-
EUSTACHE, QC, J7R 4K3
(450) 473-4794   SIC 5172
GOYETTE, MAURICE PONTIAC BUICK
1983 INC   p 1392
1623 132 RTE, VARENNES, QC, J3X 1P7
SIC 5511
GP BREWING CO. LTD   p 132
8812 111A ST, GRANDE PRAIRIE, AB, T8V
5L3
(780) 533-4677   SIC 2082
GP INTERNATIONAL INC   p 731
796 FOUR WINDS WAY, MISSISSAUGA,
ON, L5R 3W8
(416) 948-0336   SIC 6799
GP WEALTH MANAGEMENT CORPORA-
TION   p
695
5045 ORBITOR DR SUITE 400 BUILDING
11, MISSISSAUGA, ON, L4W 4Y4
(416) 622-9969   SIC 8742
GPE EQUIPEMENT DE MINE ET SERVICES
p 1152
See GROUPE PROCAN EQUIPEMENT
INC
GPL ASSURANCE INC   p 1086
3131 BOUL SAINT-MARTIN O BUREAU
600, COTE SAINT-LUC, QC, H7T 2Z5
(450) 978-5599   SIC 6411
GPL PROULX ASSURANCE   p 1086
See GPL ASSURANCE INC
GPRC   p 132
See GRANDE PRAIRIE REGIONAL COL-
LEGE
GPRC FAIRVIEW CAMPUS   p 126
11235 98TH AVE, FAIRVIEW, AB, T0H 1L0
(780) 835-6600   SIC 8211
GPS CENTRAL   p 31
See RADIOWORLD CENTRAL INC
GPS PRODUCTS INC   p 1009
622 FRIEBURG DR, WATERLOO, ON, N2T
2Y4
(519) 885-7235   SIC 5015
GPVTL CANADA INC   p 939
1 TORONTO ST SUITE 1100, TORONTO,
ON, M5C 2V6
(416) 907-9470   SIC 7371
GRA HAM ENERGY LIMITED   p 888
88 QUEEN ST W, ST MARYS, ON, N4X 1A9
(519) 284-3420   SIC 5541
GRAB 2 HOLDINGS LTD   p 1431
2405B WHEATON AVE, SASKATOON, SK,
S7L 5Y3
(306) 633-2137   SIC 4731
GRACE FOODS CANADA INC   p 852
70 WEST WILMOT ST, RICHMOND HILL,
ON, L4B 1H8
(905) 886-1002   SIC 5141

GRACE MOTORS   p 564
See 1068827 ONTARIO INC
GRACIOUS LIVING CORPORATION   p 1031
7200 MARTIN GROVE RD, WOODBRIDGE,
ON, L4L 9J3
(905) 264-5660   SIC 3089
GRACIOUS LIVING INNOVATIONS INC   p
744
151 COURTNEYPARK DR W SUITE 201,
MISSISSAUGA, ON, L5W 1Y5
(905) 795-5505   SIC 3089
GRACOM MASONRY, DIV OF   p 70
See GRAHAM CONSTRUCTION AND EN-
GINEERING INC
GRAEME'S AUTO SERVICE   p 81
PO BOX 115, DELBURNE, AB, T0M 0V0
(403) 318-6088   SIC 5541
GRAEMOND HOLDINGS LTD   p 234
2535 BOWEN RD, NANAIMO, BC, V9T 3L2
(250) 758-3361   SIC 5511
GRAF CANADA LTD   p 30
2308 PORTLAND ST SE, CALGARY, AB,
T2G 4M6
(403) 287-8585   SIC 3949
GRAFF COMPANY ULC, THE   p 584
35 PRECISION RD, ETOBICOKE, ON, M9W
5H3
(905) 457-8120   SIC 1771
GRAFTONS CONNOR PROPERTY INC   p
453
1741 GRAFTON ST, HALIFAX, NS, B3J 2C6
(902) 454-9344   SIC 5813
GRAHAM AUCTIONS   p 8
See 620205 ALBERTA LIMITED
GRAHAM AUTOMOTIVE SALES INC   p 751
2185 ROBERTSON RD, NEPEAN, ON, K2H
5Z2
(613) 596-1515   SIC 5511
GRAHAM AUTOMOTIVE SALES LTD   p 751
2195 ROBERTSON RD, NEPEAN, ON, K2H
5Z2
(613) 596-1515   SIC 5511
GRAHAM BROS. CONSTRUCTION LIM-
ITED   p
509
297 RUTHERFORD RD S, BRAMPTON,
ON, L6W 3J8
(905) 453-1200   SIC 1611
GRAHAM CONSTRUCTION   p 70
See GRAHAM INCOME TRUST
GRAHAM CONSTRUCTION AND ENGI-
NEERING INC   p
70
10840 27 ST SE, CALGARY, AB, T2Z 3R6
(403) 570-5000   SIC 1542
GRAHAM CONSTRUCTION AND ENGI-
NEERING LP   p
70
10840 27 ST SE, CALGARY, AB, T2Z 3R6
(403) 570-5000   SIC 1542
GRAHAM CREATIVE DECAL INC   p 1128
1790 55E AV, LACHINE, QC, H8T 3J5
(514) 633-8800   SIC 6712
GRAHAM ENERGY   p 622
See R. BRUCE GRAHAM LIMITED
GRAHAM GROUP LTD   p 70
10840 27 ST SE, CALGARY, AB, T2Z 3R6
(403) 570-5000   SIC 1542
GRAHAM GROUP LTD   p 114
8404 MCINTYRE RD NW, EDMONTON, AB,
T6E 6V3
(780) 430-9600   SIC 1541
GRAHAM GROUP LTD   p 1427
875 57TH ST E, SASKATOON, SK, S7K 5Z2
(306) 934-6644   SIC 1541
GRAHAM INCOME TRUST   p 70
10840 27 ST SE, CALGARY, AB, T2Z 3R6
(403) 570-5000   SIC 1542
GRAHAM INDUSTRIAL SERVICES A JV   p
1427
See GRAHAM GROUP LTD
GRAHAM INDUSTRIAL SERVICES AT J V p
114
See GRAHAM GROUP LTD

GRAHAM PACKAGING CANADA LIMITEDp
711
3174 MAVIS RD, MISSISSAUGA, ON, L5C
1T8
(905) 277-1486   SIC 3089
GRAHAM, L.G. HOLDINGS INC   p 634
1020 OTTAWA ST N SUITE 510, KITCH-
ENER, ON, N2A 3Z3
(519) 894-1499   SIC 5461
GRAHAM, TONY INFINITI NISSAN   p 751
See GRAHAM AUTOMOTIVE SALES INC
GRAHAM, TONY MOTORS (1980) LIMITED
p 750
1855 MERIVALE RD, NEPEAN, ON, K2G
1E3
(613) 225-1212   SIC 5511
GRAIN MILLERS CANADA CORP   p 1438
1 GRAIN MILLERS DR, YORKTON, SK,
S3N 3Z4
(306) 783-2931   SIC 2043
GRAIN PROCESS ENTERPRISES LIMITED
p 874
105 COMMANDER BLVD, SCARBOR-
OUGH, ON, M1S 3M7
(416) 291-3226   SIC 2041
GRAIN ST-LAURENT   p 1188
407 RUE MCGILL BUREAU 315, MON-
TREAL, QC, H2Y 2G3
(514) 871-2037   SIC 5153
GRAINS ELITE S.E.C.   p 1226
9001 BOUL DE L'ACADIE BUREAU 200,
MONTREAL, QC, H4N 3H7
SIC 5153
GRAINSCONNECT CANADA   p 16
See GRAINSCONNECT CANADA OPERA-
TIONS INC
GRAINSCONNECT CANADA OPERA-
TIONS INC   p
16
48 QUARRY PARK BLVD SE SUITE 260,
CALGARY, AB, T2C 5P2
(403) 879-2727   SIC 5153
GRAKON HAMSAR HOLDINGS LTD   p 522
5320 DOWNEY ST, BURLINGTON, ON, L7L
6M2
(905) 332-4094   SIC 3679
GRAN COLOMBIA GOLD CORP   p 952
401 BAY ST SUITE 2400, TORONTO, ON,
M5H 2Y4
(416) 360-4653   SIC 1081
GRAN TIERRA ENERGY INC   p 50
520 3RD AVE SW SUITE 900, CALGARY,
AB, T2P 0R3
(403) 265-3221   SIC 1382
GRANBY INDUSTRIES LIMITED PART-
NERSHIP   p
1111
1020 RUE ANDRE-LINE, GRANBY, QC, J2J
1J9
(450) 378-2334   SIC 3443
GRANBY STEEL TANKS   p 1111
See GRANBY INDUSTRIES LIMITED
PARTNERSHIP
GRAND & TOY   p 1128
See GRAND & TOY LIMITED
GRAND & TOY LIMITED   p 23
37 AERO DR NE, CALGARY, AB, T2E 8Z9
(866) 391-8111   SIC 5021
GRAND & TOY LIMITED   p 96
11522 168 ST NW, EDMONTON, AB, T5M
3T9
(866) 391-8111   SIC 5112
GRAND & TOY LIMITED   p 192
4560 TILLICUM ST, BURNABY, BC, V5J 5L4
(866) 391-8111   SIC 5943
GRAND & TOY LIMITED   p 393
15 SCURFIELD BLVD, WINNIPEG, MB,
R3Y 1V4
(204) 284-5100   SIC 5943
GRAND & TOY LIMITED   p 818
900 BELFAST RD, OTTAWA, ON, K1G 0Z6
(866) 391-8111   SIC 5112
GRAND & TOY LIMITED   p 1031
200 AVIVA PARK DR, WOODBRIDGE, ON,

L4L 9C7
(416) 401-6300   *SIC* 5943
GRAND & TOY LIMITED   *p* 1031
200 AVIVA PARK DR, WOODBRIDGE, ON,
L4L 9C7
(866) 391-8111   *SIC* 5112
GRAND & TOY LIMITED   *p* 1128
2275 52E AV, LACHINE, QC, H8T 2Y8
(866) 391-8111   *SIC* 5943
GRAND ADEX MANAGEMENT   *p* 311
See 462388 BC LTD
GRAND ALARMS LTD   *p* 553
9000 KEELE ST UNIT 12, CONCORD, ON,
L4K 0B3
(416) 657-2100   *SIC* 5065
GRAND BAZAR DE GRANBY INC, AU   *p*
1111
1141 RUE PRINCIPALE BUREAU 378,
GRANBY, QC, J2J 0M3
(450) 378-2022   *SIC* 5941
**GRAND BAZAR LA SOURCE DU SPORT,
AU**   *p* 1111
See GRAND BAZAR DE GRANBY INC, AU
GRAND CANADIAN RESORTS INC   *p* 79
91 THREE SISTERS DR, CANMORE, AB,
T1W 3A1
(403) 678-0018   *SIC* 7011
GRAND COLONY FARMS LTD   *p* 354
20125 ROAD 57N, OAKVILLE, MB, R0H
0Y0
(204) 267-2292   *SIC* 0139
**GRAND COLONY OF HUTTERIAN
BRETHREN TRUST**   *p* 354
See GRAND COLONY FARMS LTD
GRAND CONSTRUCTION LTD   *p* 228
4539 210A ST, LANGLEY, BC, V3A 8Z3
(604) 530-1931   *SIC* 1542
GRAND COUNCIL TREATY #3   *p* 628
See GCT REPRESENTITIVE SERVICES
GRAND ERIE DISTRICT SCHOOL BOARD
p 516
349 ERIE AVE, BRANTFORD, ON, N3S 2H7
(519) 756-6301   *SIC* 8211
GRAND ERIE DISTRICT SCHOOL BOARD
p 516
627 COLBORNE ST, BRANTFORD, ON,
N3S 3M8
(519) 756-1320   *SIC* 8211
GRAND ERIE DISTRICT SCHOOL BOARD
p 517
120 BRANT AVE, BRANTFORD, ON, N3T
3H3
(519) 759-3210   *SIC* 8222
GRAND ERIE DISTRICT SCHOOL BOARD
p 607
70 PARKVIEW RD, HAGERSVILLE, ON,
N0A 1H0
(905) 768-3318   *SIC* 8211
GRAND ERIE DISTRICT SCHOOL BOARD
p 880
40 WILSON AVE, SIMCOE, ON, N3Y 2E5
(519) 426-4664   *SIC* 8211
GRAND FALLS GENERAL HOSPITAL *p* 403
See VITALITE HEALTH NETWORK
**GRAND FOREST HOLDINGS INCORPO-
RATED**   *p*
415
300 UNION ST, SAINT JOHN, NB, E2L 4Z2
(506) 635-6666   *SIC* 2611
**GRAND HALE MARINE PRODUCTS COM-
PANY LIMITED**   *p*
254
11551 TWIGG PL, RICHMOND, BC, V6V
2Y2
(604) 325-9393   *SIC* 5146
**GRAND LODGE DU MONT TREMBLANT,
LE**   *p* 1159
*See COMPAGNIE DE VILLEGIATURE ET
DE DEVELOPEMENT GRAND LODGE INC,
LA*
GRAND MARCHE COL-FAX INC   *p* 1236
3699 NORD LAVAL (A-440) O, MONTREAL,
QC, H7P 5P6
(450) 688-7773   *SIC* 5411

GRAND NATIONAL APPAREL INC   *p* 794
100 MARMORA ST SUITE 3, NORTH
YORK, ON, M9M 2X5
(416) 746-3511   *SIC* 5136
**GRAND PACIFIC TRAVEL & TRADE
(CANADA) CORP**   *p* 260
8877 ODLIN CRES SUITE 100, RICH-
MOND, BC, V6X 3Z7
(604) 276-2616   *SIC* 4724
GRAND POWER LOGISTICS GROUP INC *p*
50
505 6 ST SW SUITE 2806, CALGARY, AB,
T2P 1X5
(403) 237-8211   *SIC* 4731
GRAND PRAIRIE LIVESTOCK MARKET   *p*
132
14809 100 ST, GRANDE PRAIRIE, AB, T8V
7C2
SIC 5154
GRAND PRIX IMPORT INC   *p* 1170
8275 17E AV, MONTREAL, QC, H1Z 4J9
(514) 328-2300   *SIC* 5013
**GRAND RIVER CONSERVATION AUTHOR-
ITY**   *p*
541
GD, CAYUGA, ON, N0A 1E0
(905) 768-3288   *SIC* 8641
**GRAND RIVER ENTERPRISES SIX NA-
TIONS LIMITED**   *p*
806
2176 CHIEFSWOOD RD, OHSWEKEN, ON,
N0A 1M0
(519) 445-0919   *SIC* 2111
GRAND RIVER FOODS   *p* 538
See GRAND RIVER POULTRY LTD
GRAND RIVER FOODS LTD   *p* 538
190 VONDRAU DR, CAMBRIDGE, ON, N3E
1B8
(519) 653-3577   *SIC* 2015
GRAND RIVER FOODS LTD   *p* 538
685 BOXWOOD DR, CAMBRIDGE, ON,
N3E 1B4
(519) 653-3577   *SIC* 2015
GRAND RIVER HOSPITAL CORPORATION
p 638
835 KING ST W, KITCHENER, ON, N2G
1G3
(519) 742-3611   *SIC* 8062
GRAND RIVER POULTRY LTD   *p* 538
190 VONDRAU DR, CAMBRIDGE, ON, N3E
1B8
(519) 653-3577   *SIC* 2015
GRAND RIVER TRANSIT   *p* 638
*See REGIONAL MUNICIPALITY OF WA-
TERLOO, THE*
GRAND TOURING AUTOMOBILES   *p* 921
See PTC AUTOMOTIVE LTD
GRAND TOURING CARS   *p* 659
See 990550 ONTARIO INC
**GRAND TRUNK WESTERN RAILROAD IN-
CORPORATED**   *p*
1205
935 RUE DE LA GAUCHETIERE O BU-
REAU 14, MONTREAL, QC, H3B 2M9
(514) 399-4536   *SIC* 4731
GRAND VALLEY DISTRIBUTORS INC *p* 533
1595 BISHOP ST N, CAMBRIDGE, ON,
N1R 7J4
(519) 621-2260   *SIC* 5013
GRAND VALLEY FORTIFIERS LIMITED   *p*
533
486 MAIN ST, CAMBRIDGE, ON, N1R 5S7
(519) 621-5204   *SIC* 2048
GRAND VALLEY REALTY INC   *p* 641
370 HIGHLAND RD W, KITCHENER, ON,
N2M 5J9
(519) 745-7000   *SIC* 6531
GRAND VIEW MANOR   *p* 441
*See KINGS COUNTY SENIOR CITIZENS
HOME CORP*
GRAND WEST ELECTRIC LTD   *p* 16
2408 91 AVE SE, CALGARY, AB, T2C 5H2
(403) 291-2688   *SIC* 4931
GRAND WOOD PARK APARTMENTS AND

RESIDENCE   *p* 656
See COMMUNITY LIFECARE INC
**GRAND'MAISON HEATING-AIR CONDI-
TIONNING**   *p*
1321
See PAUL GRAND'MAISON INC
GRAND-PORTAGE AUTOMOBILES *p* 1286
*See GRAND-PORTAGE VOLKSWAGEN
INC*
GRAND-PORTAGE VOLKSWAGEN INC   *p*
1286
157 RUE FRASER, RIVIERE-DU-LOUP,
QC, G5R 1C9
(418) 862-3490   *SIC* 5511
**GRAND-PRIX AUTOMOTIVE DISTRIBU-
TORS INC**   *p*
30
4313 MANHATTAN RD SE, CALGARY, AB,
T2G 4B1
(403) 243-5622   *SIC* 5511
GRANDE CACHE COAL CORPORATION   *p*
50
800 5 AVE SW SUITE 1610, CALGARY, AB,
T2P 3T6
(403) 543-7070   *SIC* 1221
GRANDE CACHE COAL CORPORATION   *p*
130
GD, GRANDE CACHE, AB, T0E 0Y0
(780) 827-4646   *SIC* 1221
GRANDE CACHE GENERAL HOSPITAL   *p*
131
*See MISTAHIA REGIONAL HEALTH AU-
THORITY*
GRANDE CHEESE COMPANY LIMITED   *p*
1031
468 JEVLAN DR, WOODBRIDGE, ON, L4L
8L4
(905) 856-6880   *SIC* 2022
GRANDE EPOQUE INC, LA   *p* 1191
1099 RUE CLARK BUREAU 3, MONTREAL,
QC, H2Z 1K3
(514) 954-0756   *SIC* 5963
GRANDE PRAIRIE AIRPORT COMMISSION
p 132
10610 AIRPORT DR SUITE 220, GRANDE
PRAIRIE, AB, T8V 7Z5
(780) 539-5270   *SIC* 4581
**GRANDE PRAIRIE AND DISTRICT ASSO-
CIATION FOR PERSONS WITH DEVELOP-
MENTAL DISABILITIES**   *p*
132
8702 113 ST, GRANDE PRAIRIE, AB, T8V
6K5
(780) 532-0236   *SIC* 8322
**GRANDE PRAIRIE ASSOCIATES REALTY
LTD**   *p* 132
10114 100 ST, GRANDE PRAIRIE, AB, T8V
2L9
(780) 538-4700   *SIC* 6531
**GRANDE PRAIRIE CATHOLIC SCHOOL
DISTRICT 28**   *p* 132
9902 101 ST SUITE 28, GRANDE PRAIRIE,
AB, T8V 2P4
(780) 532-3013   *SIC* 8211
**GRANDE PRAIRIE COMPOSITE HIGH
SCHOOL**   *p* 132
*See GRANDE PRAIRIE PUBLIC SCHOOL
DISTRICT #2357*
GRANDE PRAIRIE HOME HARDWARE   *p*
132
*See MANTO, MARK BUILDING MATERI-
ALS LTD*
GRANDE PRAIRIE INN   *p* 131
See 467935 ALBERTA LTD
GRANDE PRAIRIE MAZDA   *p* 132
See MJY AUTO SALES & LEASING LTD
**GRANDE PRAIRIE PUBLIC SCHOOL DIS-
TRICT #2357**   *p*
132
10127 120 AVE, GRANDE PRAIRIE, AB,
T8V 8H8
(780) 532-4491   *SIC* 8211
**GRANDE PRAIRIE PUBLIC SCHOOL DIS-
TRICT #2357**   *p*

132
11202 104 ST SUITE 2357, GRANDE
PRAIRIE, AB, T8V 2Z1
(780) 532-7721   *SIC* 8211
**GRANDE PRAIRIE PUBLIC SCHOOL DIS-
TRICT #2357**   *p*
132
9351 116 AVE, GRANDE PRAIRIE, AB, T8V
6L5
(780) 830-3384   *SIC* 8211
GRANDE PRAIRIE REGIONAL COLLEGE *p*
132
10726 106 AVE, GRANDE PRAIRIE, AB,
T8V 4C4
(780) 539-2911   *SIC* 8221
**GRANDE WEST TRANSPORTATION
GROUP INC**   *p* 179
3168 262 ST, ALDERGROVE, BC, V4W 2Z6
(604) 607-4000   *SIC* 3711
**GRANDE YELLOWHEAD PUBLIC SCHOOL
DIVISION 77**   *p* 126
3656 1 AVE SUITE 35, EDSON, AB, T7E
1N9
(780) 723-4471   *SIC* 8211
GRANDEUR HOUSING LTD   *p* 361
401 PEMBINA AVE E, WINKLER, MB, R6W
4B9
(204) 325-9558   *SIC* 5211
GRANDI COMPANY LIMITED   *p* 590
870 TOWER ST S, FERGUS, ON, N1M 3N7
(519) 787-5125   *SIC* 5812
GRANDI COMPANY LIMITED   *p* 601
372 STONE RD W, GUELPH, ON, N1G 4T8
(519) 763-8842   *SIC* 5812
GRANDI COMPANY LIMITED   *p* 603
243 WOODLAWN RD W, GUELPH, ON,
N1H 8J1
(519) 826-0507   *SIC* 5812
GRANDIN MEDICAL HOLDINGS LTD *p* 165
1 ST ANNE ST, ST. ALBERT, AB, T8N 2E8
SIC 6712
GRANDMAISON BEEF FARMS   *p* 278
See AGM BEEF FARMS LTD
GRANDMOTHER'S PIE SHOPPE INC *p* 988
65 SAMOR RD, TORONTO, ON, M6A 1J2
(416) 782-9000   *SIC* 5461
GRANDMOTHER'S TOUCH INC   *p* 695
5359 TIMBERLEA BLVD SUITE 20, MISSIS-
SAUGA, ON, L4W 4N5
(905) 361-0485   *SIC* 7349
GRANDOR GROUP   *p* 597
See GRANDOR LUMBER INC
GRANDOR LUMBER INC   *p* 597
5224 BANK ST, GLOUCESTER, ON, K1X
1H2
(613) 822-3390   *SIC* 5211
GRANDVIEW BROKERAGE LIMITED *p* 200
11 BURBIDGE ST SUITE 101, COQUIT-
LAM, BC, V3K 7B2
(604) 461-6779   *SIC* 6712
GRANDVIEW COLONY   *p* 134
*See HUTTERIAN BRETHREN CHURCH
OF GRANDVIEW*
GRANDVIEW LODGE   *p* 567
*See CORPORATION OF HALDIMAND
COUNTY, THE*
**GRANDVIEW LODGE HOME FOR THE
AGED**   *p* 909
200 LILLIE ST N, THUNDER BAY, ON, P7C
5Y2
SIC 8361
GRANDVIEW SALES & DISTRIBUTION LTD
p 874
4630 SHEPPARD AVE E SUITE 264, SCAR-
BOROUGH, ON, M1S 3V5
(416) 291-7791   *SIC* 5531
GRANDWEST ENTERPRISES INC   *p* 1427
815 CIRCLE DR E, SASKATOON, SK, S7K
3S4
(306) 665-7755   *SIC* 5511
GRANFORD   *p* 721
See CONTITECH CANADA, INC
GRANICOR INC   *p* 1293
300 RUE DE ROTTERDAM BUREAU 21,

SAINT-AUGUSTIN-DE-DESMAURES,   QC,
G3A 1T4
(418) 878-3530   *SIC 3281*
GRANIREX   p 1382
1045 RUE MONFETTE E, THETFORD
MINES, QC, G6G 7K7
SIC 5032
GRANIT C. ROULEAU INC   p 1378
140 CH DES URSULINES, STANSTEAD,
QC, J0B 3E0
(819) 876-7171   *SIC 3281*
GRANIT DESIGN   p 1378
See GRANIT DESIGN INC
GRANIT DESIGN INC   p 1378
77 RUE INDUSTRIELLE, STANSTEAD, QC,
J0B 3E0
(819) 876-7111   *SIC 5211*
GRANIT PLUS INC   p 1352
386   RUE   PRINCIPALE,   SAINT-
SEBASTIEN-DE-FRONTENAC, QC, G0Y
1M0
(819) 652-2514   *SIC 5032*
GRANITE CLUB   p 915
2350 BAYVIEW AVE, TORONTO, ON, M2L
1E4
(416) 449-8713   *SIC 8641*
GRANITE COURT   p 408
See ATLANTIC BAPTIST SENIOR CITI-
ZENS HOMES INC
GRANITE DEPARTMENT STORE INC p 433
681 TOPSAIL RD, ST. JOHN'S, NL, A1E 2E3
(709) 368-2416   *SIC 5311*
GRANITE OIL CORP   p 50
308 4 AVE SW SUITE 3230, CALGARY, AB,
T2P 0H7
SIC 1081
GRANITE OIL CORP   p 50
308 4 AVE SW SUITE 3230, CALGARY, AB,
T2P 0H7
(587) 349-9113   *SIC 1311*
GRANITE REIT INC   p 969
77 KING ST W, TORONTO, ON, M5K 2A1
(647) 925-7500   *SIC 6798*
GRANITE WORX   p 39
See ACTIVE MARBLE & TILE LTD
GRANNY'S FINEST   p 362
See GRANNY'S POULTRY COOPERATIVE
(MANITOBA) LTD
**GRANNY'S POULTRY COOPERATIVE
(MANITOBA) LTD**   p 346
4 PENNER, BLUMENORT, MB, R0A 0C0
(204) 452-6315   *SIC 2015*
**GRANNY'S POULTRY COOPERATIVE
(MANITOBA) LTD**   p 362
750 PANDORA AVE E, WINNIPEG, MB,
R2C 4G5
(204) 488-2230   *SIC 2015*
**GRANNY'S POULTRY COOPERATIVE
(MANITOBA) LTD**   p 362
750 PANDORA AVE E, WINNIPEG, MB,
R2C 4G5
(204) 925-6260   *SIC 5144*
**GRANT AGGREGATE & INDUSTRIAL SUP-
PLY INC**   p
898
2578 LASALLE BLVD, SUDBURY, ON, P3A
4R7
(705) 524-2711   *SIC 5084*
GRANT BROTHERS SALES   p 733
See 4213424 CANADA INC
GRANT CORPORATION   p 50
540 5 AVE SW SUITE 1850, CALGARY, AB,
T2P 0M2
(403) 663-0050   *SIC 1389*
GRANT FARMS CORP   p 753
863169 UNO PARK RD, NEW LISKEARD,
ON, P0J 1P0
(705) 647-3129   *SIC 5039*
GRANT FUELS INC.   p 753
251 GRAY RD, NEW LISKEARD, ON, P0J
1P0
(705) 647-6566   *SIC 5171*
GRANT HOME HARDWARE   p 753
See GRANT LUMBER BUILDING CEN-

TRES LTD
**GRANT LUMBER BUILDING CENTRES
LTD**   p 753
GD, NEW LISKEARD, ON, P0J 1P0
(705) 647-9311   *SIC 5211*
GRANT MACEWAN UNIVERSITY   p 89
10700 104 AVE NW, EDMONTON, AB, T5J
4S2
(780) 497-5168   *SIC 8221*
GRANT MACEWAN UNIVERSITY   p 98
10045 156 ST NW RM 402, EDMONTON,
AB, T5P 2P7
(780) 497-4310   *SIC 8299*
GRANT PARK HIGH SCHOOL   p 388
See WINNIPEG SCHOOL DIVISION
GRANT PARK PLAZA SAFEWAY   p 388
See SOBEYS WEST INC
**GRANT PRODUCTION TESTING SER-
VICES LTD**   p
50
505 8 AVE SW SUITE 200, CALGARY, AB,
T2P 1G2
(403) 663-0050   *SIC 1389*
**GRANT PRODUCTION TESTING SER-
VICES LTD**   p
155
6750 GOLDEN WEST AVE, RED DEER,
AB, T4P 1A8
(403) 314-0042   *SIC 8748*
GRANT THORNTON LLP   p 89
10060 JASPER AVE NW SUITE 1701, ED-
MONTON, AB, T5J 3R8
(780) 422-7114   *SIC 8721*
GRANT THORNTON LLP   p 222
1633 ELLIS ST SUITE 200, KELOWNA, BC,
V1Y 2A8
(250) 712-6800   *SIC 8721*
GRANT THORNTON LLP   p 298
333 SEYMOUR ST SUITE 1600, VANCOU-
VER, BC, V6B 0A4
(604) 687-2711   *SIC 8721*
GRANT THORNTON LLP   p 453
2000 BARRINGTON ST SUITE 1100, HALI-
FAX, NS, B3J 3K1
(902) 421-1734   *SIC 8721*
GRANT THORNTON LLP   p 670
15 ALLSTATE PKY SUITE 200, MARKHAM,
ON, L3R 5B4
(416) 607-2656   *SIC 8721*
GRANT THORNTON LLP   p 709
201 CITY CENTRE DR SUITE 501, MISSIS-
SAUGA, ON, L5B 2T4
(416) 369-7076   *SIC 8721*
GRANT THORNTON LLP   p 963
12TH-50 BAY ST, TORONTO, ON, M5J 2Z8
(416) 366-4240   *SIC 8721*
GRANT THORTON   p 908
979 ALLOY DR SUITE 300, THUNDER BAY,
ON, P7B 5Z8
(807) 346-7302   *SIC 8721*
GRANT'S INDEPENDENT   p 617
See 784704 ONTARIO LTD
GRANT'S TRANSPORT LIMITED   p 753
251 GRAY RD, NEW LISKEARD, ON, P0J
1P0
(705) 647-8171   *SIC 4213*
GRANT, JAMIE & BARB SALES LTD   p 683
1210 STEELES AVE E, MILTON, ON, L9T
6R1
(905) 878-2349   *SIC 5531*
GRANTEK CONTROL SYSTEMS   p 522
See GRANTEK SYSTEMS INTEGRATION
INC
GRANTEK SYSTEMS INTEGRATION INC p
522
4480 HARVESTER RD, BURLINGTON, ON,
L7L 4X2
(905) 634-0844   *SIC 7373*
**GRANULES COMBUSTIBLES ENERGEX
INC**   p 1125
3891 RUE DU PRESIDENT-KENNEDY,
LAC-MEGANTIC, QC, G6B 3B8
(819) 583-5131   *SIC 2421*
GRANVILLE WEST GROUP LTD   p 313

1075 GEORGIA ST W SUITE 1425, VAN-
COUVER, BC, V6E 3C9
(604) 687-5570   *SIC 6282*
GRAPE ARBOR CONSTRUCTION LTD   p
670
80 TIVERTON CRT SUITE 300, MARKHAM,
ON, L3R 0G4
(905) 477-7609   *SIC 1522*
**GRAPHIC COMMUNICATIONS BENEFITS
ADMINISTRATION COR**   p 695
5025 ORBITOR DR SUITE 210, MISSIS-
SAUGA, ON, L4W 4Y5
SIC 6371
**GRAPHIC PACKAGING INTERNATIONAL
CANADA CORPORATION**   p 695
1355 AEROWOOD DR, MISSISSAUGA,
ON, L4W 1C2
(905) 602-7877   *SIC 3556*
**GRAPHIC PACKAGING INTERNATIONAL
CANADA ULC**   p 367
531 GOLSPIE ST, WINNIPEG, MB, R2K
2T9
(204) 667-6600   *SIC 2631*
**GRAPHIC PACKAGING INTERNATIONAL
CANADA ULC**   p 545
740 DIVISION ST, COBOURG, ON, K9A
0H6
(905) 372-5199   *SIC 2631*
**GRAPHIC PACKAGING INTERNATIONAL
CANADA ULC**   p 735
7830 TRANMERE DR, MISSISSAUGA, ON,
L5S 1L9
(905) 678-8211   *SIC 2631*
**GRAPHIC PACKAGING INTERNATIONAL
CANADA, ULC**   p 1100
2 RUE ANGUS N, EAST ANGUS, QC, J0B
1R0
(819) 832-5300   *SIC 2621*
GRAPHIQUES MATROX INC   p 1094
1055 BOUL SAINT-REGIS, DORVAL, QC,
H9P 2T4
(514) 822-6000   *SIC 8731*
GRAPHISCAN IMPRIMEUR   p 1262
See GRAPHISCAN QUEBEC INC
GRAPHISCAN QUEBEC INC   p 1262
210 RUE FORTIN BUREAU 100, QUEBEC,
QC, G1M 0A4
(418) 266-0707   *SIC 7389*
GRASCAN CONSTRUCTION LTD   p 584
61 STEINWAY BLVD, ETOBICOKE, ON,
M9W 6H6
(416) 644-8858   *SIC 1629*
GRASS RIVER COLONY FARMS LTD p 350
GD, GLENELLA, MB, R0J 0V0
(204) 352-4286   *SIC 0241*
**GRASS RIVER COLONY OF HUTTERIAN
BRETHREN**   p 350
See GRASS RIVER COLONY FARMS LTD
GRASS VALLEY CANADA   p 1334
3499   RUE   DOUGLAS-B.-FLOREANI,
SAINT-LAURENT, QC, H4S 2C6
(514) 333-1772   *SIC 3679*
**GRASS VALLEY, UNE MARQUE DE
BELDEN**   p 1334
See GRASS VALLEY CANADA
GRASSHOPPER SOLAR CORPORATION p
688
5935 AIRPORT RD SUITE 210, MISSIS-
SAUGA, ON, L4V 1W5
(866) 310-1575   *SIC 1711*
GRASSLANDS PUBLIC SCHOOLS   p 7
See GRASSLANDS REGIONAL DIVISION
6
GRASSLANDS REGIONAL DIVISION 6 p 7
745 2 AVE E SUITE 1, BROOKS, AB, T1R
1L2
(403) 793-6700   *SIC 8211*
GRASSROOTS CO-OPERATIVE LTD p 1407
216 MAIN ST, HAZENMORE, SK, S0N 1C0
(306) 264-5111   *SIC 5171*
GRASSWOOD PETRO CANADA   p 1405
See ENGLISH RIVER ENTERPRISES INC
GRATTON COULEE AGRI PARTS LTD   p
137

HWY 881 S, IRMA, AB, T0B 2H0
(780) 754-2303   *SIC 5093*
GRAVELUNI INC   p 1250
277 BOUL SAINT-JEAN, POINTE-CLAIRE,
QC, H9R 3J1
(514) 695-1122   *SIC 5912*
GRAVITAS FINANCIAL INC   p 952
333 BAY ST SUITE 1700, TORONTO, ON,
M5H 2R2
(647) 252-1674   *SIC 6282*
GRAY EGGS   p 647
See GRAY, L. H. & SON LIMITED
GRAY HAND TOOL SALES LIMITED   p 503
299 ORENDA RD, BRAMPTON, ON, L6T
1E8
(905) 457-3014   *SIC 5072*
GRAY HAWK (1991) CO. LTD   p 619
772 MAIN ST E, HAWKESBURY, ON, K6A
1B4
(613) 632-0921   *SIC 1711*
**GRAY HOME HARDWARE BUILDING CEN-
TRES**   p
1021
See GRAY, TOM BUILDING CENTRES INC
GRAY HOUSE GUILD, THE   p 120
5005 28 AVE NW, EDMONTON, AB, T6L
7G1
(780) 469-2371   *SIC 8051*
GRAY RIDGE EGGS   p 897
See GRAY, L. H. & SON LIMITED
GRAY TOOLS CANADA INC   p 503
299 ORENDA RD, BRAMPTON, ON, L6T
1E8
(800) 567-0518   *SIC 3423*
GRAY, L. H. & SON LIMITED   p 647
955 TREMAINE AVE S, LISTOWEL, ON,
N4W 3G9
(519) 291-5150   *SIC 5995*
GRAY, L. H. & SON LIMITED   p 897
644 WRIGHT ST, STRATHROY, ON, N7G
3H8
(519) 245-0480   *SIC 5144*
GRAY, TOM BUILDING CENTRES INC   p
1021
700 TECUMSEH RD W, WINDSOR, ON,
N8X 1H2
(519) 254-1143   *SIC 5211*
GRAYBAR CANADA   p 456
See GRAYBAR CANADA LIMITED
GRAYBAR CANADA LIMITED   p 456
3600 JOSEPH HOWE DR, HALIFAX, NS,
B3L 4H7
(902) 457-8787   *SIC 5063*
GRAYBAR ELECTRIC CANADA LIMITED p
456
3600 JOSEPH HOWE DR, HALIFAX, NS,
B3L 4H7
(902) 443-8311   *SIC 5063*
GRAYMATTER DIRECT (CANADA) INC   p
945
600 BAY ST SUITE 400, TORONTO, ON,
M5G 1M6
(416) 341-0623   *SIC 7389*
GRAYMONT (NB) INC   p 403
4634 ROUTE 880, HAVELOCK, NB, E4Z
5K8
(506) 534-2311   *SIC 1422*
GRAYMONT (PORTNEUF) INC   p 1348
595 BOUL BONA-DUSSAULT, SAINT-
MARC-DES-CARRIERES, QC, G0A 4B0
(418) 268-3501   *SIC 1481*
GRAYMONT (QC) INC   p 1065
25 RUE DE LAUZON BUREAU 206,
BOUCHERVILLE, QC, J4B 1E7
(450) 449-2262   *SIC 1422*
GRAYMONT (QC) INC   p 1114
1300 RUE NOTRE-DAME, JOLIETTE, QC,
J6E 3Z9
(450) 759-8195   *SIC 1422*
GRAYMONT LIMITED   p 260
10991 SHELLBRIDGE WAY SUITE 200,
RICHMOND, BC, V6X 3C6
(604) 207-4292   *SIC 5032*
GRAYMONT WESTERN CANADA INC p 23

3025 12 ST NE SUITE 190, CALGARY, AB, T2E 7J2
(403) 250-9100   *SIC* 3274

GRAYWOOD ELECTRIC LIMITED   p 593
10783 SIXTH LINE, GEORGETOWN, ON, L7G 4S6
(905) 877-6070   *SIC* 1731

GREAT BLUE HERON CHARITY CASINO, DIV OF   p 848
See BAAGWATING COMMUNITY ASSOCIATION

GREAT CANADIAN BEAN COMPANY INC, THE   p 473
26831 NEW ONTARIO RD, AILSA CRAIG, ON, N0M 1A0
(519) 232-4449   *SIC* 5153

GREAT CANADIAN CASINOS INC   p 201
2080 UNITED BLVD SUITE D, COQUITLAM, BC, V3K 6W3
(604) 523-6888   *SIC* 7999

GREAT CANADIAN CASINOS INC   p 201
95 SCHOONER ST, COQUITLAM, BC, V3K 7A8
(604) 303-1000   *SIC* 7999

GREAT CANADIAN CASINOS INC   p 233
620 TERMINAL AVE, NANAIMO, BC, V9R 5E2
(250) 753-3033   *SIC* 7999

GREAT CANADIAN CASINOS INC   p 260
8811 RIVER RD, RICHMOND, BC, V6X 3P8
(604) 247-8900   *SIC* 7999

GREAT CANADIAN COACHES INC   p 636
353 MANITOU DR, KITCHENER, ON, N2C 1L5
(519) 896-8687   *SIC* 4142

GREAT CANADIAN DOLLAR STORE p 411
See BRODY COMPANY LTD, THE

GREAT CANADIAN GAMING CORPORATION   p 201
95 SCHOONER ST, COQUITLAM, BC, V3K 7A8
(604) 303-1000   *SIC* 7999

GREAT CANADIAN HOLIDAYS INC   p 636
353 MANITOU DR, KITCHENER, ON, N2C 1L5
(519) 896-8687   *SIC* 4725

GREAT CANADIAN OIL CHANGE   p 1424
See WEFF HOLDINGS LTD

GREAT CANADIAN RAILTOUR COMPANY LTD   p 218
525 CN RD, KAMLOOPS, BC, V2H 1K3
(250) 314-0576   *SIC* 4725

GREAT CANADIAN RAILTOUR COMPANY LTD   p 326
980 HOWE ST, VANCOUVER, BC, V6Z 1N9
(604) 606-7200   *SIC* 4725

GREAT CLIPS, INC   p 1002
3100 N RUTHERFORD RD SUITE 201, VAUGHAN, ON, L4K 0G6
SIC 7231

GREAT CONNECTIONS EMPLOYMENT SERVICES INC   p 781
5050 DUFFERIN ST UNIT 109, NORTH YORK, ON, M3H 5T5
(416) 850-5060   *SIC* 7361

GREAT EVENTS CATERING INC   p 35
7207 FAIRMOUNT DR SE, CALGARY, AB, T2H 0X6
(403) 256-7150   *SIC* 5812

GREAT GARB BOUTIQUE (TABER) LTD p 169
5221 48 AVE, TABER, AB, T1G 1S8
SIC 5621

GREAT GULF GROUP OF COMPANIES INC p 877
3751 VICTORIA PARK AVE, SCARBOROUGH, ON, M1W 3Z4
(416) 449-1340   *SIC* 1521

GREAT GULF HOMES   p 877
See GREAT GULF HOMES LIMITED

GREAT GULF HOMES LIMITED   p 877
3751 VICTORIA PARK AVE, SCARBOROUGH, ON, M1W 3Z4

(416) 449-1340   *SIC* 1521

GREAT HOBBIES INC   p 1042
17 GLEN STEWART DR SUITE 1, STRATFORD, PE, C1B 2A8
(902) 569-3289   *SIC* 5945

GREAT LAKES COMMODITIES INC p 952
320 BAY ST, TORONTO, ON, M5H 4A6
(416) 864-0856   *SIC* 6221

GREAT LAKES COPPER LTD   p 649
1010 CLARKE RD, LONDON, ON, N5V 3B2
(519) 455-0770   *SIC* 3351

GREAT LAKES FISH COMPANY   p 542
See 2210961 ONTARIO LIMITED

GREAT LAKES GREENHOUSES INC p 644
834 MERSEA ROAD 4, LEAMINGTON, ON, N8H 3V6
(519) 326-7589   *SIC* 0191

GREAT LAKES PILOTAGE AUTHORITY p 563
202 PITT ST 2ND FL, CORNWALL, ON, K6J 3P7
(613) 933-2991   *SIC* 4499

GREAT LAKES PIPELINE CANADA LTD p 50
450 1 ST SW, CALGARY, AB, T2P 5H1
(403) 920-6852   *SIC* 4922

GREAT LAKES POWER LIMITED   p 862
243 INDUSTRIAL PARK CRES, SAULT STE. MARIE, ON, P6B 5P3
(705) 256-7575   *SIC* 4911

GREAT LAKES SCENIC STUDIOS   p 29
See F & D SCENE CHANGES LTD

GREAT LAKES SCHOONER COMPANY LIMITED   p 963
249 QUEENS QUAY W SUITE 111, TORONTO, ON, M5J 2N5
(416) 260-6355   *SIC* 4489

GREAT LITTLE BOX COMPANY LTD, THE p 254
11300 TWIGG PL, RICHMOND, BC, V6V 3C1
(604) 301-3700   *SIC* 2653

GREAT NORTH EQUIPMENT INC   p 114
8743 50 AVE NW, EDMONTON, AB, T6E 5H4
(780) 461-7400   *SIC* 7353

GREAT NORTHERN AUCTION COMPANY LTD   p 409
2131 ROUTE 128, MONCTON, NB, E1G 4K5
(506) 382-2777   *SIC* 7389

GREAT NORTHERN HYDROPONICS p 634
1507 ROAD 3 E, KINGSVILLE, ON, N9Y 2E5
(519) 322-2000   *SIC* 0182

GREAT NORTHERN MOTOR & PUMP REPAIR   p 862
See ARROW PLUMBING INC

GREAT PACIFIC ENTERPRISES INC p 305
1067 CORDOVA ST W UNIT 1800, VANCOUVER, BC, V6C 1C7
(604) 688-6764   *SIC* 3081

GREAT PACIFIC ENTERPRISES INC p 1085
1890 BOUL FORTIN, COTE SAINT-LUC, QC, H7S 1N8
(450) 662-1030   *SIC* 3081

GREAT PACIFIC ENTERPRISES INC p 1111
700 RUE VADNAIS, GRANBY, QC, J2J 1A7
(450) 378-3995   *SIC* 3081

GREAT PACIFIC ENTERPRISES LIMITED PARTNERSHIP   p 480
325 INDUSTRIAL PKY S, AURORA, ON, L4G 3V8
(905) 727-0121   *SIC* 3081

GREAT PACIFIC ENTERPRISES LIMITED PARTNERSHIP   p 480
285 INDUSTRIAL PKY S, AURORA, ON, L4G 3V8
(905) 727-0121   *SIC* 2671

GREAT PACIFIC ENTERPRISES LIMITED PARTNERSHIP   p 716
3185 PEPPER MILL CRT, MISSISSAUGA, ON, L5L 4X3

(905) 569-3660   *SIC* 3086

GREAT PACIFIC INDUSTRIES INC   p 185
4399 LOUGHEED HWY SUITE 996, BURNABY, BC, V5C 3Y7
(604) 298-8412   *SIC* 5411

GREAT PACIFIC INDUSTRIES INC   p 213
10345 100 ST, FORT ST. JOHN, BC, V1J 3Z2
(250) 785-2985   *SIC* 5411

GREAT PACIFIC INDUSTRIES INC   p 222
1876 COOPER RD SUITE 101, KELOWNA, BC, V1Y 9N6
(250) 860-1444   *SIC* 5411

GREAT PACIFIC INDUSTRIES INC   p 224
19855 92A AVE, LANGLEY, BC, V1M 3B6
(604) 888-1213   *SIC* 5411

GREAT PACIFIC INDUSTRIES INC   p 231
20395 LOUGHEED HWY SUITE 300, MAPLE RIDGE, BC, V2X 2P9
(604) 465-8665   *SIC* 5411

GREAT PACIFIC INDUSTRIES INC   p 232
32555 LONDON AVE SUITE 400, MISSION, BC, V2V 6M7
(604) 826-9564   *SIC* 5411

GREAT PACIFIC INDUSTRIES INC   p 234
3200 ISLAND HWY N, NANAIMO, BC, V9T 1W1
(250) 751-1414   *SIC* 5411

GREAT PACIFIC INDUSTRIES INC   p 243
2111 MAIN ST SUITE 161, PENTICTON, BC, V2A 6W6
(250) 492-2011   *SIC* 5411

GREAT PANTHER MINING LIMITED p 305
200 GRANVILLE ST SUITE 1330, VANCOUVER, BC, V6C 1S4
(604) 608-1766   *SIC* 1081

GREAT PLAINS FORD SALES (1978) LTD p 1437
206 SIMS AVE, WEYBURN, SK, S4H 2H6
(306) 842-2645   *SIC* 5511

GREAT PLAINS RAIL CONTRACTORS INC p 378
GD, WINNIPEG, MB, R3C 2G1
(204) 633-0135   *SIC* 1629

GREAT SLAVE HELICOPTERS LTD p 436
106 DICKENS ST, YELLOWKNIFE, NT, X1A 3T2
(867) 873-2081   *SIC* 4522

GREAT STEAK HOUSE INC, THE   p 249
582 GEORGE ST, PRINCE GEORGE, BC, V2L 1R7
(250) 563-1768   *SIC* 5812

GREAT WAR MEMORIAL   p 839
See PERTH AND SMITHS FALLS DISTRICT HOSPITAL

GREAT WATERWAY, THE   p 631
See REGION 9 REGIONAL TOURISM ORGANIZATION

GREAT WEST CHRYSLER INC   p 101
17817 STONY PLAIN RD NW, EDMONTON, AB, T5S 1B4
(780) 483-5337   *SIC* 5511

GREAT WEST DISTRIBUTION LTD p 1425
201 EDSON ST, SASKATOON, SK, S7J 4C8
(306) 933-0027   *SIC* 4213

GREAT WEST DRUGS (SOUTHGATE) LTD p 114
4484 97 ST NW, EDMONTON, AB, T6E 5R9
(780) 496-9366   *SIC* 5912

GREAT WEST EQUIPMENT LTD   p 331
123 L & A CROSS RD, VERNON, BC, V1B 3S1
(250) 549-4232   *SIC* 5084

GREAT WEST ITALIAN IMPORTERS LTD p 23
5130 SKYLINE WAY NE, CALGARY, AB, T2E 6V1
(403) 275-8222   *SIC* 5141

GREAT WEST KENWORTH LTD   p 35
5909 6 ST SE, CALGARY, AB, T2H 1L8
(403) 253-7555   *SIC* 5511

GREAT WEST LIFE ASSURANCE   p 530
360 TORRANCE ST, BURLINGTON, ON, L7R 2R9

(905) 637-6561   *SIC* 6311

GREAT WEST MARKETING & PENSION DEPARTMENT   p 1196
See GREAT-WEST LIFE ASSURANCE COMPANY, THE

GREAT WEST NEWSPAPERS LIMITED PARTNERSHIP   p 165
340 CARLETON DR, ST. ALBERT, AB, T8N 7L3
(780) 460-5500   *SIC* 2711

GREAT WESTERN BREWING COMPANY LIMITED   p 1427
519 2ND AVE N, SASKATOON, SK, S7K 2C6
(306) 653-4653   *SIC* 2082

GREAT WESTERN CONTAINERS   p 13
See 1942675 ALBERTA LTD

GREAT-WEST LIFE ASSURANCE COMPANY, THE   p 89
10110 104 ST NW SUITE 202, EDMONTON, AB, T5J 4R5
(780) 917-7800   *SIC* 6321

GREAT-WEST LIFE ASSURANCE COMPANY, THE   p 313
1075 GEORGIA ST W SUITE 900, VANCOUVER, BC, V6E 4N4
(604) 646-1200   *SIC* 6321

GREAT-WEST LIFE ASSURANCE COMPANY, THE   p 378
100 OSBORNE ST N, WINNIPEG, MB, R3C 1V3
(204) 946-1190   *SIC* 6324

GREAT-WEST LIFE ASSURANCE COMPANY, THE   p 378
60 OSBORNE ST N, WINNIPEG, MB, R3C 1V3
(204) 946-8100   *SIC* 6311

GREAT-WEST LIFE ASSURANCE COMPANY, THE   p 945
330 UNIVERSITY AVE SUITE 400, TORONTO, ON, M5G 1R7
(416) 552-5050   *SIC* 6311

GREAT-WEST LIFE ASSURANCE COMPANY, THE   p 977
190 SIMCOE ST, TORONTO, ON, M5T 3M3
(416) 597-1440   *SIC* 6311

GREAT-WEST LIFE ASSURANCE COMPANY, THE   p 1196
2001 BOUL ROBERT-BOURASSA UNITE 1000, MONTREAL, QC, H3A 2A6
(514) 350-7975   *SIC* 6411

GREAT-WEST LIFECO INC   p 378
100 OSBORNE ST N, WINNIPEG, MB, R3C 1V3
(204) 946-1190   *SIC* 6311

GREATARIO ENGINEERED STORAGE SYSTEMS   p 622
See GREATARIO INDUSTRIAL STORAGE SYSTEMS LTD

GREATARIO INDUSTRIAL STORAGE SYSTEMS LTD   p 622
715647 COUNTY RD 4, INNERKIP, ON, N0J 1M0
(519) 469-8169   *SIC* 1791

GREATER EDMONTON FOUNDATION p 97
14220 109 AVE NW, EDMONTON, AB, T5N 4B3
(780) 482-6561   *SIC* 8361

GREATER ESSEX COUNTY DISTRICT SCHOOL BOARD   p 490
333 SOUTH ST, BELLE RIVER, ON, N0R 1A0
(519) 728-1212   *SIC* 8211

GREATER ESSEX COUNTY DISTRICT SCHOOL BOARD   p 1018
8465 JEROME ST, WINDSOR, ON, N8S

1W8

(519) 948-4116   *SIC* 8211

GREATER ESSEX COUNTY DISTRICT SCHOOL BOARD   p 1020
1930 ROSSINI BLVD, WINDSOR, ON, N8W 4P5

(519) 944-4700   *SIC* 8211

GREATER ESSEX COUNTY DISTRICT SCHOOL BOARD   p 1021
245 TECUMSEH RD E, WINDSOR, ON, N8X 2R2

(519) 254-6475   *SIC* 8211

GREATER ESSEX COUNTY DISTRICT SCHOOL BOARD   p 1022
2100 RICHMOND ST, WINDSOR, ON, N8Y 1L4

(519) 252-6514   *SIC* 8211

GREATER ESSEX COUNTY DISTRICT SCHOOL BOARD   p 1023
451 PARK ST W, WINDSOR, ON, N9A 5V4

(519) 255-3200   *SIC* 8211

GREATER ESSEX COUNTY DISTRICT SCHOOL BOARD   p 1024
1375 CALIFORNIA AVE, WINDSOR, ON, N9B 2Z8

(519) 253-2481   *SIC* 8211

GREATER ESSEX COUNTY DISTRICT SCHOOL BOARD   p 1025
1800 LIBERTY ST, WINDSOR, ON, N9E 1J2

(519) 969-2530   *SIC* 8211

GREATER MONCTON INTERNATIONAL AIRPORT   p 397
See GREATER MONCTON INTERNATIONAL AIRPORT AUTHORITY INC

GREATER MONCTON INTERNATIONAL AIRPORT AUTHORITY INC   p 397
777 AV AVIATION UNIT 12, DIEPPE, NB, E1A 7Z5

(506) 856-5444   *SIC* 4581

GREATER NAPANEE FIRE DEPARTMENT p 747
66 ADVANCE AVE, NAPANEE, ON, K7R 3Y6

(613) 354-3415   *SIC* 7389

GREATER NORTH FOUNDATION   p 4
5210 47 AVE, ATHABASCA, AB, T9S 1K5

(780) 675-9660   *SIC* 6513

GREATER ST. ALBERT CATHOLIC SCHOOLS   p 165
See GREATER ST. ALBERT ROMAN CATHOLIC SEPARATE SCHOOL DISTRICT NO. 734

GREATER ST. ALBERT ROMAN CATHOLIC SEPARATE SCHOOL DISTRICT NO. 734   p 165
6 ST VITAL AVE, ST. ALBERT, AB, T8N 1K2

(780) 459-7711   *SIC* 8211

GREATER SUDBURY HYDRO INC   p 901
500 REGENT ST, SUDBURY, ON, P3E 3Y2

(705) 675-7536   *SIC* 4911

GREATER SUDBURY TRANSIT   p 900
See CITY OF GREATER SUDBURY, THE

GREATER SUDBURY UTILITIES INC   p 901
500 REGENT ST SUITE 250, SUDBURY, ON, P3E 3Y2

(705) 675-7536   *SIC* 4911

GREATER TORONTO AIRPORTS AUTHORITY   p 729
3111 CONVAIR DR, MISSISSAUGA, ON, L5P 1B2

(416) 776-3000   *SIC* 4581

GREATER VANCOUVER ASSOCIATE STORES LTD   p 287
2220 KINGSWAY, VANCOUVER, BC, V5N 2T7

SIC 5531

GREATER VANCOUVER CONVENTION AND VISITORS BUREAU   p 305
200 BURRARD ST SUITE 210, VANCOUVER, BC, V6C 3L6

(604) 682-2222   *SIC* 7389

GREATER VANCOUVER FOOD BANK SOCIETY   p

295

1150 RAYMUR AVE, VANCOUVER, BC, V6A 3T2

(604) 876-3601   *SIC* 8399

GREATER VANCOUVER REGIONAL DISTRICT   p 206
1299 DERWENT WAY, DELTA, BC, V3M 5V9

(604) 525-5681   *SIC* 4953

GREATER VANCOUVER WATER DISTRICT   p 190
4330 KINGSWAY SUITE 505, BURNABY, BC, V5H 4G8

(604) 432-6200   *SIC* 4941

GREATER VICTORIA VISITORS & CONVENTION BUREAU   p 336
31 BASTION SQ, VICTORIA, BC, V8W 1J1

(250) 414-6999   *SIC* 8611

GREAVETTE CHEVROLET PONTIAC BUICK CADILLAC GMC LTD   p 497
375 ECCLESTONE DR, BRACEBRIDGE, ON, P1L 1T6

(705) 645-2241   *SIC* 5511

GRECO ALUMINUM RAILINGS LTD p 1022
3255 WYANDOTTE ST E, WINDSOR, ON, N8Y 1E9

(519) 966-4210   *SIC* 3446

GRECO MANAGEMENT INC   p 892
21 TEAL AVE, STONEY CREEK, ON, L8E 2P1

(905) 560-0661   *SIC* 8721

GRECO PIZZA & DONAIR   p 469
See GRINNER'S FOOD SYSTEMS LIMITED

GRECO, ROBERTO DRUGS LTD   p 644
269 ERIE ST S SUITE 1117, LEAMINGTON, ON, N8H 3C4

(519) 326-2663   *SIC* 5912

GREDICO FOOTWEAR LIMITED   p 739
415 ANNAGEM BLVD, MISSISSAUGA, ON, L5T 3A7

(866) 855-0755   *SIC* 5139

GREELEY CONTAINMENT AND REWORK INC   p 496
200 BASELINE RD E, BOWMANVILLE, ON, L1C 1A2

(905) 623-5678   *SIC* 7549

GREELY CONSTRUCTION INC   p 595
5689 POWER RD, GLOUCESTER, ON, K1G 3N4

(613) 822-0500   *SIC* 1623

GREELY SAND & GRAVEL INC   p 599
1971 OLD PRESCOTT RD, GREELY, ON, K4P 1L3

(613) 821-3003   *SIC* 5211

GREEN ACRES COLONY LTD   p 360
GD, WAWANESA, MB, R0K 2G0

(204) 824-2627   *SIC* 0191

GREEN ACRES SERVICES   p 1416
See SHAW, JACK ENTERPRISES LIMITED

GREEN AND SPIEGEL, LLP   p 952
150 YORK ST 5TH FL, TORONTO, ON, M5H 3S5

(416) 862-7880   *SIC* 8111

GREEN BELTING INDUSTRIES LIMITED p 739
381 AMBASSADOR DR, MISSISSAUGA, ON, L5T 2J3

(905) 564-6712   *SIC* 2399

GREEN CIRCLE SALONS INC   p 980
401 RICHMOND ST W SUITE 371, TORONTO, ON, M5V 3A8

(647) 341-6812   *SIC* 4953

GREEN CROSS (MD)   p 1334
See GREEN CROSS BIOTHERAPEUTIQUES INC

GREEN CROSS BIOTHERAPEUTIQUES INC   p 1334
2911 AV MARIE-CURIE, SAINT-LAURENT, QC, H4S 0B7

(514) 375-5800   *SIC* 2834

GREEN DIAMOND EQUIPMENT   p 410

70 COMMERCE ST, MONCTON, NB, E1H 0A5

(506) 388-3337   *SIC* 5083

GREEN DROP LTD   p 11
1230 MERIDIAN RD NE, CALGARY, AB, T2A 2N9

(403) 273-9845   *SIC* 2874

GREEN EARTH NANO SCIENCE INC p 952
181 UNIVERSITY AVE SUITE 2200, TORONTO, ON, M5H 3M7

(416) 800-0969   *SIC* 4959

GREEN ESSENTIAL SERVICES INC   p 952
250 UNIVERSITY AVE SUITE 200, TORONTO, ON, M5H 3E5

(866) 820-2284   *SIC* 5999

GREEN FOREST LUMBER DIV OF   p 592
See WEYERHAEUSER COMPANY LIMITED

GREEN GABLES GOLF COURSE, DIV OF p 1039
See ISLAND COASTAL SERVICES LTD

GREEN IMAGING SUPPLIES INC   p 717
3330 RIDGEWAY DR UNIT 17, MISSISSAUGA, ON, L5L 5Z9

(905) 607-2525   *SIC* 5112

GREEN ISLAND DISTRIBUTORS PARTNERSHIP   p 439
616 LOWER RD, ARICHAT, NS, B0E 1A0

(902) 226-2633   *SIC* 2091

GREEN ISLAND G AUTO LTD   p 211
6300 TRANS CANADA HWY, DUNCAN, BC, V9L 0C1

(250) 746-7131   *SIC* 5511

GREEN LAKE PROJECTS INC   p 342
8080 NICKLAUS BLVD N, WHISTLER, BC, V0N 1B0

(604) 938-9898   *SIC* 7997

GREEN LEA AG CENTER INC   p 746
324055 MOUNT ELGIN RD, MOUNT ELGIN, ON, N0J 1N0

(519) 485-6861   *SIC* 5083

GREEN LIGHT COURIER INC   p 867
705 PROGRESS AVE SUITE 26, SCARBOROUGH, ON, M1H 2X1

SIC 7389

GREEN LIGHT GRAPHICS INC   p 802
229 DEANE AVE, OAKVILLE, ON, L6K 1N6

(905) 469-8095   *SIC* 7336

GREEN LINE HOSE & FITTINGS (ALBERTA) LTD   p 109
7003 ROPER RD NW, EDMONTON, AB, T6B 3K3

(780) 465-5216   *SIC* 5251

GREEN LINE HOSE & FITTINGS LTD p 206
1477 DERWENT WAY, DELTA, BC, V3M 6N3

(604) 670-1647   *SIC* 5085

GREEN LINE MANUFACTURING LTD   p 1434
3711 MITCHELMORE AVE, SASKATOON, SK, S7P 0C5

(306) 934-8886   *SIC* 5251

GREEN LINE SALES LTD   p 206
1477 DERWENT WAY, DELTA, BC, V3M 6N3

(604) 525-6800   *SIC* 5085

GREEN PIECE WIRE ART   p 747
See 1520940 ONTARIO LTD

GREEN PRAIRIE INTERNATIONAL INC   p 142
210072 TOWNSHIP RD 90B, LETHBRIDGE, AB, T1J 5P1

(403) 327-9941   *SIC* 5191

GREEN SHIELD CANADA   p 1017
8677 ANCHOR DR, WINDSOR, ON, N8N 5G1

(519) 739-1133   *SIC* 6324

GREEN TRACTORS INC   p 762
6770 KING RD, NOBLETON, ON, L0G 1N0

(905) 859-0581   *SIC* 5999

GREEN'S POP SHOP LTD   p 140
613 13 ST N, LETHBRIDGE, AB, T1H 2S7

(403) 329-4848   *SIC* 5411

GREEN, DON HOLDINGS LTD   p 136
702 11 AVE SE, HIGH RIVER, AB, T1V 1P2

(403) 652-2000   *SIC* 6719

GREEN, E J & COMPANY LTD   p 434
287 MAIN ST, WINTERTON, NL, A0B 3M0

(709) 583-2670   *SIC* 2092

GREEN, ESTHER DRUGS LTD   p 775
6205 BATHURST ST, NORTH YORK, ON, M2R 2A5

(416) 222-5464   *SIC* 5912

GREENBERG NAIMER GROUP   p 834
25 CARTIER ST, OTTAWA, ON, K2P 1J2

(613) 237-2111   *SIC* 6512

GREENER STEEL INC   p 913
352 RAILWAY ST, TIMMINS, ON, P4N 2P6

(705) 268-7197   *SIC* 5051

GREENERGY FUELS CANADA INC   p 415
107 GERMAIN ST SUITE 300, SAINT JOHN, NB, E2L 2E9

(506) 632-1650   *SIC* 6799

GREENFIELD ENERGY CENTRE LP p 998
66 WELLINGTON ST W SUITE 3515, TORONTO, ON, N5K 1H1

(416) 362-0978   *SIC* 4911

GREENFIELD GLOBAL QUEBEC INC p 503
2 CHELSEA LN, BRAMPTON, ON, L6T 3Y4

(905) 790-7500   *SIC* 2869

GREENFIELD GLOBAL, INC   p 939
20 TORONTO ST SUITE 1400, TORONTO, ON, M5C 2B8

(416) 304-1700   *SIC* 2869

GREENFIELD PARK PRIMARY INTERNATIONAL SCHOOL   p 1112
See RIVERSIDE SCHOOL BOARD

GREENFIELD PRODUCE LTD   p 263
12151 HORSESHOE WAY, RICHMOND, BC, V7A 4V4

(604) 272-2551   *SIC* 5148

GREENFIRE OIL AND GAS LTD   p 50
444 5 AVE SW SUITE 1650, CALGARY, AB, T2P 2T8

(403) 681-7377   *SIC* 1382

GREENGROCER INC, THE   p 739
6110 SHAWSON DR, MISSISSAUGA, ON, L5T 1E6

(416) 253-9070   *SIC* 5148

GREENHAWK HARNESS & EQUESTRIAN SUPPLIES   p 731
See GREENHAWK INC

GREENHAWK INC   p 731
5665 MCLAUGHLIN RD, MISSISSAUGA, ON, L5R 3K5

(905) 238-0311   *SIC* 5941

GREENHOUSE GROWN FOODS INC p 210
3660 41B ST, DELTA, BC, V4K 3N2

(604) 940-7700   *SIC* 0182

GREENHOUSE JUICE COMPANY ULC   p 990
9 OSSINGTON AVE, TORONTO, ON, M6J 2Y8

(647) 351-0188   *SIC* 5499

GREENISLE ENVIRONMENTAL INC p 1040
7 SUPERIOR CRES, CHARLOTTETOWN, PE, C1E 2A1

(902) 892-1333   *SIC* 4953

GREENLABS CHEMICAL SOLUTIONS   p 805
See SUPERIOR SOLUTIONS LTD

GREENLAND GARDEN CENTRE   p 161
See GREENLAND NURSERY & LANDSCAPING LTD

GREENLAND NURSERY & LANDSCAPING LTD   p 161
23108 16 HWY, SHERWOOD PARK, AB, T8A 4V2

(780) 467-7557   *SIC* 5261

GREENLAWN, LTD   p 695
2385 MATHESON BLVD E, MISSISSAUGA, ON, L4W 5B3

(905) 290-1844   *SIC* 0782

GREENLIGHT INNOVATION CORPORATION   p

182
3430 BRIGHTON AVE UNIT 104A, BURN-ABY, BC, V5A 3H4
(604) 676-4000   SIC 3821
GREENLITE   p 1249
See   CORPORATION   D'ECLAIRAGE GREENLITE, LA
GREENOUGH, L C CONSTRUCTION LTD p 120
2503 PARSONS RD NW, EDMONTON, AB, T6N 1B8
(780) 463-4977   SIC 1542
GREENP   p 941
See TORONTO PARKING AUTHORITY, THE
GREENPEACE CANADA   p 977
33 CECIL ST, TORONTO, ON, M5T 1N1
(416) 597-8408   SIC 8399
GREENSAVER   p 576
See URBAN ENVIRONMENT CENTRE (TORONTO), THE
GREENSPACE BRANDS INC   p 973
176 ST GEORGE ST, TORONTO, ON, M5R 2M7
(416) 934-5034   SIC 5149
GREENSPAR WHOLESALE LIMITED p 424
125 HARVEY ST, HARBOUR GRACE, NL, A0A 2M0
(709) 596-3538   SIC 5199
GREENSTAR PLANT PRODUCTS INC   p 224
9430 198 ST, LANGLEY, BC, V1M 3C8
(604) 882-7699   SIC 5191
GREENTEC INTERNATIONAL INC   p 533
95 STRUCK CRT, CAMBRIDGE, ON, N1R 8L2
(519) 624-3300   SIC 4953
GREENVALLEY EQUIPMENT INC   p 352
25016 ROAD 25W HIGHWAY 3 E, MOR-DEN, MB, R6M 2B9
(204) 325-7742   SIC 5999
GREENVISION TECHNOLOGIES CORPO-RATION   p 1334
7809 RTE TRANSCANADIENNE, SAINT-LAURENT, QC, H4S 1L3
(514) 745-0310   SIC 5065
GREENWAY FARMS LTD   p 279
5040 160 ST SUITE 5040, SURREY, BC, V3Z 1E8
(604) 574-1564   SIC 0161
GREENWIN INC   p 776
19 LESMILL RD UNIT 100, NORTH YORK, ON, M3B 2T3
(416) 487-3883   SIC 6512
GREENWOOD COLLEGE SCHOOL   p 924
443 MOUNT PLEASANT RD, TORONTO, ON, M4S 2L8
(416) 482-9811   SIC 8211
GREENWOOD CONSTRUCTION COM-PANY LIMITED   p 808
HWY 9, ORANGEVILLE, ON, L9W 2Y9
(519) 941-0732   SIC 3273
GREENWOOD COURT, DIV OF   p 897
See TRI-COUNTY MENNONITE HOMES ASSOCIATION
GREENWOOD MUSHROOM FARM   p 479
9760 HERON RD, ASHBURN, ON, L0B 1A0
(905) 655-3373   SIC 0182
GREENWOOD PAVING (PEMBROKE) LTD p 838
1495 PEMBROKE ST W, PEMBROKE, ON, K8A 7A5
(613) 735-4101   SIC 1611
GREENWOOD PETRO CANADA   p 460
See J.D.I. VENTURES LIMITED
GREENWOOD READY MIX LIMITED   p 808
HWY 9, ORANGEVILLE, ON, L9W 2Y9
(519) 941-0710   SIC 1542
GREENWOODS ELDERCARE SOCIETY p 268
133 BLAIN RD, SALT SPRING ISLAND, BC, V8K 1Z9

(250) 537-5561   SIC 8399
GREENWORLD FOOD EXPRESS INC p 695
5380 MAINGATE DR, MISSISSAUGA, ON, L4W 1R8
(905) 212-7720   SIC 5141
GREER CONTRACTING LTD   p 192
6955 BULLER AVE, BURNABY, BC, V5J 4S1
(604) 438-3550   SIC 1542
GREER, W.E. LIMITED   p 93
14704 119 AVE NW, EDMONTON, AB, T5L 2P1
(780) 451-1516   SIC 5169
GREG KELLY WOOLSTEN CROFT   p 821
60 GEORGE ST SUITE 205, OTTAWA, ON, K1N 1J4
(613) 236-0296   SIC 8732
GREG SAARI MERCHANDISING LTD p 70
4155 126 AVE SE, CALGARY, AB, T2Z 0A1
(403) 257-4729   SIC 5251
GREG VANN NISSAN   p 539
See VANN, GREG NISSAN INC
GREGG DISTRIBUTORS   p 109
See GREGG DISTRIBUTORS CO LTD
GREGG DISTRIBUTORS (FORT MCMUR-RAY) LTD   p 128
325 MACALPINE CRES, FORT MCMUR-RAY, AB, T9H 4Y4
(780) 715-4000   SIC 5085
GREGG DISTRIBUTORS CO LTD   p 109
3611 76 AVE NW, EDMONTON, AB, T6B 2S8
(780) 450-2233   SIC 4225
GREGG DISTRIBUTORS LIMITED PART-NERSHIP   p 35
5755 11 ST SE, CALGARY, AB, T2H 1M7
(403) 253-6463   SIC 5085
GREGG DISTRIBUTORS LIMITED PART-NERSHIP   p 105
16215 118 AVE NW, EDMONTON, AB, T5V 1C7
(780) 447-3447   SIC 5013
GREGG'S PLUMBING & HEATING LTD   p 1427
503 51ST ST E, SASKATOON, SK, S7K 6V4
(306) 373-4664   SIC 1711
GREGOIRE RAKELIAN PHARMACIEN   p 1363
3000 AV JACQUES-BUREAU BUREAU BU-REAU, SAINTE-ROSE, QC, H7P 5P7
(450) 682-0099   SIC 5912
GREGOIRE SPORT INC   p 1147
2061 BOUL BARRETTE, LOURDES-DE-JOLIETTE, QC, J0K 1K0
(450) 752-2201   SIC 5599
GREGORY HERITAGE HOLDING INC   p 1401
23 AV WILLOW, WESTMOUNT, QC, H3Y 1Y3
SIC 6712
GREGSON HOLDINGS LTD   p 235
1920 BALSAM RD, NANAIMO, BC, V9X 1T5
(250) 754-7260   SIC 1794
GREIG ASSOCIATES X-RAY, ULTRA-SOUND AND MAMMOGRAPHY INC   p 287
5732 VICTORIA DR, VANCOUVER, BC, V5P 3W6
(604) 321-6769   SIC 8011
GREINER-PACAUD MANAGEMENT ASSO-CIATES   p 963
70 UNIVERSITY AVE SUITE 1200, TORONTO, ON, M5J 2M4
(416) 864-0040   SIC 6371
GRENCO INDUSTRIES LTD   p 109
3710 78 AVE NW, EDMONTON, AB, T6B 3E5
(780) 468-2000   SIC 3533
GRENHALL INDUSTRIES INC   p 503
1 IMPERIAL CRT, BRAMPTON, ON, L6T

4X4
(905) 458-8549   SIC 5169
GRENIER CHEVROLET BUICK GMC INC p 1379
1325 CAR MASSON, TERREBONNE, QC, J6W 6J7
(450) 471-3746   SIC 5511
GRENIER DODGE CHRYSLER INC   p 1379
1245 MONTEE MASSON, TERREBONNE, QC, J6W 6A6
(450) 471-4111   SIC 5511
GRENIER ELPHEGE INC   p 1057
40 BOUL SIR-WILFRID-LAURIER, BE-LOEIL, QC, J3G 4E8
(450) 467-4279   SIC 5149
GRENIER POPULAIRE DES BASSES LAU-RENTIDES   p 1300
217 RUE SAINT-LAURENT, SAINT-EUSTACHE, QC, J7P 4W4
(450) 623-5891   SIC 5712
GRENIER VOLKSWAGEN   p 1149
See AUTOMOBILES L F B INC, LES
GRENOBLE PUBLIC SCHOOL   p 780
See TORONTO DISTRICT SCHOOL BOARD
GRENVILLE MUTUAL   p 882
See GRENVILLE MUTUAL INSURANCE COMPANY
GRENVILLE MUTUAL INSURANCE COM-PANY   p 882
3005 COUNTY RD 21, SPENCERVILLE, ON, K0E 1X0
(613) 258-9988   SIC 6331
GREWAL FARMS INC   p 175
1088 SUMAS WAY, ABBOTSFORD, BC, V2S 8H2
(604) 832-0083   SIC 0291
GREY ADVERTISING ULC   p 980
46 SPADINA AVE SUITE 500, TORONTO, ON, M5V 2H8
(416) 486-0700   SIC 7311
GREY BRUCE HEALTH SERVICES   p 835
1800 8TH ST E, OWEN SOUND, ON, N4K 6M9
(519) 376-2121   SIC 8062
GREY CANADA   p 980
See GREY ADVERTISING ULC
GREY COUNTY TRANSPORTAION AND PUBLIC SAFETY   p 835
595 9TH AVE E, OWEN SOUND, ON, N4K 3E3
(519) 376-2205   SIC 1611
GREY EAGLE CASINO & BINGO   p 170
See SONCO GAMING LIMITED PARTNER-SHIP
GREY GABLES   p 665
206 TORONTO ST S, MARKDALE, ON, N0C 1H0
(519) 986-3010   SIC 8051
GREY MOTORS AUTOMOTIVE GROUP LTD p 835
717936 HIGHWAY 6 N, OWEN SOUND, ON, N4K 5W9
(519) 376-2240   SIC 5511
GREY SIMCOE SPORTS MED   p 487
See GREY-SIMCOE SPORTS MEDICINE AND REHABILITATION CENTRES INC.
GREY-SIMCOE SPORTS MEDICINE AND REHABILITATION CENTRES INC.   p 487
480 HURONIA RD UNIT 104, BARRIE, ON, L4N 6M2
(705) 734-1588   SIC 8041
GREYBACK CONSTRUCTION LTD   p 243
402 WARREN AVE E, PENTICTON, BC, V2A 3M2
(250) 493-7972   SIC 1542
GREYFIELD CONSTRUCTION CO LTD   p 480
15185 YONGE ST SUITE 200, AURORA, ON, L4G 1L8
(905) 713-0999   SIC 1542
GREYHAWK GOLF CLUB   p 748

See CLUBLINK CORPORATION ULC
GREYHOUND CANADA TRANSPORTA-TION ULC   p 72
877 GREYHOUND WAY SW, CALGARY, AB, T3C 3V8
(403) 218-3000   SIC 4131
GREYHOUND CANADA TRANSPORTA-TION ULC   p 295
1150 STATION ST UNIT 200, VANCOUVER, BC, V6A 4C7
(604) 683-8133   SIC 4131
GREYHOUND CANADA TRANSPORTA-TION ULC   p 487
24 MAPLE AVE UNIT 205, BARRIE, ON, L4N 7W4
SIC 4131
GREYSTOKE HOMES & SUPPORT SER-VICES INC   p 142
701 2 AVE S, LETHBRIDGE, AB, T1J 0C4
(403) 320-0911   SIC 8059
GREYSTONE CAPITAL MANAGEMENT INC   p 1421
1230 BLACKFOOT DR UNIT 300, REGINA, SK, S4S 7G4
(306) 779-6400   SIC 6282
GREYSTONE ENERGY SYSTEMS INC   p 408
150 ENGLISH DR, MONCTON, NB, E1E 4G7
(506) 853-3057   SIC 3822
GREYSTONE INDUSTRIES LTD   p 408
150 ENGLISH DR, MONCTON, NB, E1E 4G7
(506) 853-3057   SIC 3822
GREYSTONE MANAGED INVESTMENTS INC   p 1421
1230 BLACKFOOT DR UNIT 300, REGINA, SK, S4S 7G4
(306) 779-6400   SIC 6282
GREYWOLF PRODUCTION SYSTEMS INC p 81
805 LAUT AVE, CROSSFIELD, AB, T0M 0S0
(403) 946-4445   SIC 1389
GRID LINK CORP   p 910
1499 ROSSLYN RD, THUNDER BAY, ON, P7E 6W1
(807) 683-0350   SIC 1731
GRID METALS CORP   p 921
3335 YONGE ST SUITE 304, TORONTO, ON, M4N 2M1
(416) 955-4773   SIC 1021
GRIEG SEAFOOD B.C. LTD   p 195
1180 IRONWOOD ST SUITE 106, CAMP-BELL RIVER, BC, V9W 5P7
(250) 286-0838   SIC 0912
GRIF & GRAF INC   p 1070
9205 BOUL TASCHEREAU, BROSSARD, QC, J4Y 3B8
(450) 659-6999   SIC 7699
GRIFA, BLAISE LTD   p 73
5200 RICHMOND RD SW SUITE 302, CAL-GARY, AB, T3E 6M9
(403) 246-1961   SIC 5531
GRIFF BUILDING SUPPLIES LTD   p 237
340 EWEN AVE, NEW WESTMINSTER, BC, V3M 5B1
(877) 934-7433   SIC 5031
GRIFFEN MANIMPEX LTD   p 785
945 WILSON AVE SUITE 2, NORTH YORK, ON, M3K 1E8
(416) 630-7007   SIC 5136
GRIFFIN CANADA   p 362
See AMSTED CANADA INC
GRIFFIN CENTRE MENTAL HEALTH SER-VICES   p 916
1126 FINCH AVE W UNIT 16, TORONTO, ON, M3J 3J6
(416) 222-1153   SIC 8361

GRIFFIN JEWELLERY DESIGNS INC p 852
50 WEST WILMOT ST SUITE 201, RICHMOND HILL, ON, L4B 1M5
(905) 882-0004   SIC 5944

GRIFFIN TRANSPORTATION SERVICES INC p 295
873 HASTINGS ST E, VANCOUVER, BC, V6A 1R8
(604) 628-4474   SIC 4119

GRIFFIN, HAROLD T. INC p 739
7491 PACIFIC CIR, MISSISSAUGA, ON, L5T 2A4
(905) 564-1710   SIC 5149

GRIFFITH FOODS LIMITED p 868
757 PHARMACY AVE, SCARBOROUGH, ON, M1L 3J8
(416) 288-3050   SIC 2099

GRIFFITH-MCCONNELL RESIDENCE p 1083
See UNITED CHURCH OF CANADA, THE

GRIFFITHS ENERGY INTERNATIONAL INC p 50
555 4 AVE SW SUITE 2100, CALGARY, AB, T2P 3E7
(403) 724-7200   SIC 1382

GRIFFITHS MCBURNEY CANADA CORP p 952
145 KING ST W SUITE 1100, TORONTO, ON, M5H 1J8
(416) 367-8600   SIC 6211

GRIFFITHS, H. COMPANY LIMITED p 1031
140 REGINA RD SUITE 15, WOODBRIDGE, ON, L4L 8N1
(905) 850-7070   SIC 1711

GRIGG PLUMBING & HEATING LTD p 1358
15739 RUE DE LA CASERNE, SAINTE-GENEVIEVE, QC, H9H 1G3
(514) 631-1148   SIC 1711

GRILLO BARRISTERS p 988
See GRILLO BARRISTERS PROFESSIONAL CORPORATION

GRILLO BARRISTERS PROFESSIONAL CORPORATION p 988
38 APEX RD UNIT A, TORONTO, ON, M6A 2V2
(416) 614-6000   SIC 8111

GRIMARD OPTIQUE INC p 1169
3108 RUE BEAUBIEN E, MONTREAL, QC, H1Y 1H3
(514) 439-0602   SIC 5995

GRIMCO CANADA, INC p 783
680 STEEPROCK DR, NORTH YORK, ON, M3J 2X1
(416) 635-6500   SIC 5085

GRIMCO SIGN SUPPLY p 783
See GRIMCO CANADA, INC

GRIMES WELL SERVICING LTD p 115
4526 97 ST NW, EDMONTON, AB, T6E 5N9
(780) 437-7871   SIC 1381

GRIMM'S FINE FOODS p 226
See PREMIUM BRANDS OPERATING LIMITED PARTNERSHIP

GRIMSBY CHRYSLER DODGE JEEP LTD. p 599
421 SOUTH SERVICE RD, GRIMSBY, ON, L3M 4E8
(905) 945-9606   SIC 5511

GRIMSBY HIGH SECONDARY SCHOOL p 599
See DISTRICT SCHOOL BOARD OF NIAGARA

GRIMSBY UTILITY CONSTRUCTION INC p 599
211 ROBERTS RD, GRIMSBY, ON, L3M 4E8
(905) 945-8878   SIC 1623

GRIMSHAW TRUCKING LP p 96
11510 151 ST NW, EDMONTON, AB, T5M 3N6
(780) 414-2850   SIC 4212

GRINNER'S FOOD SYSTEMS LIMITED p 469
105 WALKER ST, TRURO, NS, B2N 4B1
(902) 893-4141   SIC 6794

GRIP LIMITED p 977
179 JOHN ST, TORONTO, ON, M5T 1X4
(416) 340-7111   SIC 7311

GRIP METAL p 877
See NUCAP INDUSTRIES INC

GRISE, OLIER & CIE LTEE p 1350
1 RUE MARTIN, SAINT-PIE, QC, J0H 1W0
(450) 772-2445   SIC 5191

GRISVERT p 1143
See SPB ORGANIZATIONNAL PSYCHOLOGY

GRIT INDUSTRIES INC p 144
10-50-1-4 AIRPORT RD NW, LLOYDMINSTER, AB, T9V 3A5
(780) 875-5577   SIC 3433

GRIT PROGRAM, THE p 95
See GETTING READY FOR INCLUSION TODAY (THE GRIT PROGRAM) SOCIETY OF EDMONTON

GRIZZLY p 1293
See FUMOIR GRIZZLY INC

GRIZZLY FITNESS ACCESSORIES p 635
See CUSTOM LEATHER CANADA LIMITED

GRIZZLY GRILL INC, THE p 630
395 PRINCESS ST, KINGSTON, ON, K7L 1B9
(613) 544-7566   SIC 5812

GRIZZLY GRILL, THE p 630
See GRIZZLY GRILL INC, THE

GRIZZLY OIL SANDS ULC p 50
605 5 AVE SW SUITE 2700, CALGARY, AB, T2P 3H5
(403) 930-6400   SIC 1311

GRIZZLY RESOURCES p 43
See ARCHEAN ENERGY LTD

GRK CANADA LIMITED p 910
1499 ROSSLYN RD, THUNDER BAY, ON, P7E 6W1
(807) 474-4300   SIC 5085

GRK FASTENERS p 910
See GRK CANADA LIMITED

GRO-BARK (ONTARIO) LTD p 531
816 MAYFIELD RD, CALEDON, ON, L7C 0Y6
(905) 846-1515   SIC 2875

GRO-MEC INC p 1080
1911 RUE DES OUTARDES, CHICOUTIMI, QC, G7K 1C3
(418) 549-5961   SIC 5074

GROBE NURSERY LIMITED p 518
1787 GREENHOUSE RD, BRESLAU, ON, N0B 1M0
(519) 648-2247   SIC 5193

GROBER p 535
See BARTELSE HOLDINGS LIMITED

GROBER p 536
See GROBER NUTRITION INC

GROBER INC p 536
425 DOBBIE DR, CAMBRIDGE, ON, N1T 1S9
(519) 622-2500   SIC 2011

GROBER INC p 536
162 SAVAGE DR, CAMBRIDGE, ON, N1T 1S4
(519) 622-2500   SIC 2048

GROBER INC p 536
425 DOBBIE DR, CAMBRIDGE, ON, N1T 1S9
(519) 622-2500   SIC 5147

GROBER NUTRITION INC p 536
415 DOBBIE DR, CAMBRIDGE, ON, N1T 1S8
(519) 622-2500   SIC 5191

GROENEVELD LUBRICATION SOLUTIONS INC p 683
8450 LAWSON RD UNIT 5, MILTON, ON, L9T 0J8
(905) 875-1017   SIC 1796

GROGAN FORD LINCOLN INC p 1011
5271 NAUVOO RD, WATFORD, ON, N0M 2S0
(519) 876-2730   SIC 5511

GROHE CANADA INC p 731
5900 AVEBURY RD, MISSISSAUGA, ON, L5R 3M3
(905) 271-2929   SIC 3088

GROOMBRIDGE, W. ENTERPRISES INC p 858
1380 LONDON RD, SARNIA, ON, N7S 1P8
SIC 7389

GROOT BROS. CONTRACTING LTD p 215
3377 THIRTEENTH ST UNIT 3, HOUSTON, BC, V0J 1Z0
(250) 845-0093   SIC 2411

GROSNOR DISTRIBUTION INC p 513
4 LOWRY DR, BRAMPTON, ON, L7A 1C4
(416) 744-3344   SIC 5092

GROSNOR INDUSTRIES INC p 584
375 REXDALE BLVD, ETOBICOKE, ON, M9W 1R9
(416) 744-2011   SIC 2782

GROSSI, T. & SON CONSTRUCTION LTD p 644
33 PRINCESS ST UNIT 204, LEAMINGTON, ON, N8H 5C5
(519) 326-9081   SIC 1542

GROSSISTE LE FRIGO p 1261
See VIANDEX INC

GROTE ELECTRONICS, DIV OF p 678
See GROTE INDUSTRIES CO.

GROTE ELECTRONICS, DIV. OF p 1010
See GROTE INDUSTRIES CO.

GROTE INDUSTRIES CO. p 678
230 TRAVAIL RD, MARKHAM, ON, L3S 3J1
(905) 209-9744   SIC 5013

GROTE INDUSTRIES CO. p 1010
95 BATHURST DR, WATERLOO, ON, N2V 1N2
(519) 884-4991   SIC 2821

GROUND EFFECTS LTD p 1020
2775 ST ETIENNE BLVD, WINDSOR, ON, N8W 5B1
(519) 944-3800   SIC 3714

GROUND EFFECTS LTD p 1020
4505 RHODES DR, WINDSOR, ON, N8W 5R8
(519) 944-3800   SIC 3714

GROUNDSTAR EXPRESS LTD p 206
1260 CLIVEDEN AVE, DELTA, BC, V3M 6Y1
(604) 527-1038   SIC 7389

GROUNDSWELL GROUP INC p 64
214 11 AVE SW SUITE 200, CALGARY, AB, T2R 0K1
(403) 262-2041   SIC 7373

GROUP 4 SECURICOR p 286
See G4S CASH SOLUTIONS (CANADA) LTD

GROUP CONNECT LTD, THE p 262
8010 SABA RD SUITE 110, RICHMOND, BC, V6Y 4B2
(604) 821-1852   SIC 5999

GROUP ELEVEN RESOURCES CORP p 305
400 BURRARD ST SUITE 1050, VANCOUVER, BC, V6C 3A6
(604) 630-8839   SIC 1031

GROUP EMPORIO CONSTRUCTION INC p 758
4025 DORCHESTER RD SUITE 338, NIAGARA FALLS, ON, L2E 7K8
SIC 1541

GROUP FIVE INVESTORS LTD p 164
GD LCD MAIN, SPRUCE GROVE, AB, T7X 3A1
(780) 962-5000   SIC 7011

GROUP FOR SUCURICOR p 286
See G4S CASH SOLUTIONS (CANADA) LTD

GROUP GSOFT INC p 1216
1751 RUE RICHARDSON BUREAU 5400, MONTREAL, QC, H3K 1G6
(514) 303-8203   SIC 8742

GROUP HEALTH CENTRE p 863
See SAULT STE MARIE & DISTRICT GROUP HEALTH ASSOCIATION

GROUP HEALTH CENTRE, THE p 862
240 MCNABB ST, SAULT STE. MARIE, ON, P6B 1Y5

(705) 759-5521   SIC 8011

GROUP ISH2OTOP p 735
See EVOQUA WATER TECHNOLOGIES LTD

GROUP MECAER p 1357
See MECAER AMERIQUE INC

GROUP MEDICAL SERVICES p 1417
2055 ALBERT ST, REGINA, SK, S4P 2T8
(306) 352-7638   SIC 6324

GROUP OMEGA II p 1362
See OMEGA II INC

GROUP VOYAGES VP INC p 1175
1259 RUE BERRI BUREAU 600, MONTREAL, QC, H2L 4C7
(514) 939-9999   SIC 4724

GROUPE 3SP - AVENSYS p 1327
See TECHNOLOGIES ITF INC

GROUPE A PLUS p 1247
See BEAUDRY & CADRIN INC

GROUPE A&A SPECIALISTE DU DOCUMENT (MONTREAL) INC, LE p 1049
10985 BOUL LOUIS-H.-LAFONTAINE BUREAU 101, ANJOU, QC, H1J 2E8
(514) 325-7700   SIC 5044

GROUPE A&A, LE p 1049
See GROUPE A&A SPECIALISTE DU DOCUMENT (MONTREAL) INC, LE

GROUPE ABS INC p 1351
17 RUE DE L'INDUSTRIE, SAINT-REMI, QC, J0L 2L0
(450) 454-5644   SIC 8711

GROUPE ACCENT-FAIRCHILD INC p 1329
5151 BOUL THIMENS, SAINT-LAURENT, QC, H4R 2C8
(514) 748-6721   SIC 5023

GROUPE ACCISST INC, LE p 1277
5232 BOUL WILFRID-HAMEL, QUEBEC, QC, G2E 2G9
(418) 864-7432   SIC 6722

GROUPE ADF INC p 1344
8788 RUE AETERNA, SAINT-LEONARD, QC, H1P 2R9
(514) 327-5383   SIC 5039

GROUPE ADF INC p 1381
300 RUE HENRY-BESSEMER, TERREBONNE, QC, J6Y 1T3
(450) 965-1911   SIC 8711

GROUPE ADONIS INC p 1086
2425 BOUL CURE-LABELLE, COTE SAINT-LUC, QC, H7T 1R3
(450) 978-2333   SIC 5411

GROUPE ADONIS INC p 1226
2001 RUE SAUVE O, MONTREAL, QC, H4N 3L6
(514) 382-8606   SIC 5411

GROUPE ADONIS INC p 1290
4601 BOUL DES SOURCES, ROXBORO, QC, H8Y 3C5
(514) 685-5050   SIC 5411

GROUPE AECON QUEBEC LTEE p 1196
2015 RUE PEEL BUREAU 600, MONTREAL, QC, H3A 1T8
(514) 388-8928   SIC 1541

GROUPE AGF ACCES INC p 1120
125 RUE DE L'INDUSTRIE, L'ASSOMPTION, QC, J5W 2T9
(450) 589-8100   SIC 6159

GROUPE AGF INC p 1141
2270 RUE GARNEAU, LONGUEUIL, QC, J4G 1E7
(450) 442-9494   SIC 7353

GROUPE AGRITEX INC, LE p 1296
230 RUE MARQUIS, SAINT-CELESTIN, QC, J0C 1G0
(819) 229-3686   SIC 5999

GROUPE ALDO INC, LE p 1329
2300 RUE EMILE-BELANGER, SAINT-LAURENT, QC, H4R 3J4
(514) 747-2536   SIC 5661

GROUPE ALDO INC, LE p 1329
3665 BOUL POIRIER, SAINT-LAURENT, QC, H4R 3J2
(514) 747-5892   SIC 5139

GROUPE ALERTE SANTE INC p 1143
440 BOUL SAINTE-FOY, LONGUEUIL, QC, J4J 5G5
(450) 670-0911 *SIC* 8741

GROUPE ALFID, LE p 1187
See ALFID SERVICES IMMOBILIERS LTEE

GROUPE ALFRED BOIVIN p 1079
See ENTREPRISES ALFRED BOIVIN INC, LES

GROUPE ALGO INC p 1178
225 RUE CHABANEL O, MONTREAL, QC, H2N 2C9
(514) 384-3551 *SIC* 2335

GROUPE ALGO INC p 1334
5555 RUE CYPIHOT, SAINT-LAURENT, QC, H4S 1R3
(514) 388-8888 *SIC* 2335

GROUPE ALIMENTAIRE NORDIQUE INC, LE p 1172
6569 AV PAPINEAU BUREAU 100, MONTREAL, QC, H2G 2X3
(514) 419-3510 *SIC* 2091

GROUPE ALLAIREGINCE INFRASTRUCTURES INC p 1111
70 RUE DE GATINEAU, GRANBY, QC, J2J 0P1
(450) 378-1623 *SIC* 1794

GROUPE ALPHARD INC p 1183
5570 AV CASGRAIN BUREAU 101, MONTREAL, QC, H2T 1X9
(514) 543-6580 *SIC* 8711

GROUPE ALTUS p 1205
1100 BOUL RENE-LEVESQUE O BUREAU 1600, MONTREAL, QC, H3B 4N4
SIC 6531

GROUPE AMEUBLEMENT FOCUS INC p 1392
1567 BOUL LIONEL-BOULET, VARENNES, QC, J3X 1P7
(514) 644-5551 *SIC* 5021

GROUPE APP (CANADA) INC p 1178
600 RUE CHABANEL O, MONTREAL, QC, H2N 2K6
(514) 388-5287 *SIC* 5699

GROUPE APTAS INC p 1360
1332 BOUL VACHON N, SAINTE-MARIE, QC, G6E 1N3
(418) 387-4003 *SIC* 2653

GROUPE ARCHAMBAULT INC p 1164
5655 AV PIERRE-DE COUBERTIN, MONTREAL, QC, H1N 1R2
(514) 272-4049 *SIC* 5736

GROUPE ARCHAMBAULT INC p 1175
500 RUE SAINTE-CATHERINE E, MONTREAL, QC, H2L 2C6
(514) 849-6201 *SIC* 5735

GROUPE ARCOP S.E.N.C., LE p 1213
1244 RUE SAINTE-CATHERINE O BUREAU 3E, MONTREAL, QC, H3G 1P1
(514) 878-3941 *SIC* 8712

GROUPE ARTITALIA INC p 1162
11755 BOUL RODOLPHE-FORGET, MONTREAL, QC, H1E 7J8
(514) 643-0114 *SIC* 2542

GROUPE ASKIDA INC p 1188
410 RUE SAINT-NICOLAS BUREAU 101, MONTREAL, QC, H2Y 2P5
(514) 286-9366 *SIC* 7371

GROUPE ASPEX INC p 1156
5440 RUE PARE, MONT-ROYAL, QC, H4P 1R3
(514) 938-2020 *SIC* 5049

GROUPE ASSURANCE ELCO INC p 1071
4405 BOUL LAPINIERE, BROSSARD, QC, J4Z 3T5
(450) 672-7070 *SIC* 6411

GROUPE ATALLAH INC p 1178
333 RUE CHABANEL O BUREAU 900, MONTREAL, QC, H2N 2E7
(514) 600-5818 *SIC* 5632

GROUPE ATIS INC p 1144
1111 RUE SAINT-CHARLES O BUREAU 952, LONGUEUIL, QC, J4K 5G4

(450) 928-0101 *SIC* 2591

GROUPE AUBE LTEE p 1390
1908 3E AV, VAL-D'OR, QC, J9P 7B1
(819) 825-6440 *SIC* 5511

GROUPE AUTO STE-FOY INC p 1272
2777 BOUL DU VERSANT-NORD, QUEBEC, QC, G1V 1A4
(418) 658-1340 *SIC* 5511

GROUPE AUTOBUS GIRARDIN LTEE p 1100
4000 RUE GIRARDIN, DRUMMONDVILLE, QC, J2E 0A1
(819) 477-3222 *SIC* 6712

GROUPE AUTOMOBILES LAURUS LTEE p 1086
3670 SUD LAVAL (A-440) O, COTE SAINT-LUC, QC, H7T 2H6
(450) 682-3670 *SIC* 6712

GROUPE AUTOMOTIVE HOLAND LEVIS INC p 1136
5303 RUE LOUIS-H.-LA FONTAINE, LEVIS, QC, G6V 8X4
(418) 830-5000 *SIC* 5521

GROUPE AVIATION ET PUISSANCE INC p 1059
1270 BOUL MICHELE-BOHEC, BLAINVILLE, QC, J7C 5S4
(450) 939-0799 *SIC* 3564

GROUPE AXOR INC p 1196
1555 RUE PEEL BUREAU 1100, MONTREAL, QC, H3A 3L8
(514) 846-4000 *SIC* 1542

GROUPE AXXYS p 1216
See 3469051 CANADA INC

GROUPE B.O.D. p 1119
See SANI-PLUS INC

GROUPE BAO, LE p 1161
See CONSTRUCTION BAO INC

GROUPE BARBE & ROBIDOUX.SAT INC p 1159
991 RUE DE SAINT-JOVITE RM 201, MONT-TREMBLANT, QC, J8E 3J8
(819) 425-2777 *SIC* 3829

GROUPE BBA INC p 1158
375 BOUL SIR-WILFRID-LAURIER, MONT-SAINT-HILAIRE, QC, J3H 6C3
(450) 464-2111 *SIC* 8711

GROUPE BBH INC p 1339
4400 RUE HICKMORE, SAINT-LAURENT, QC, H4T 1K2
(514) 633-6765 *SIC* 5136

GROUPE BC2 p 1187
See BC2 GROUPE CONSEIL INC

GROUPE BE-EXC INC p 1136
870 RUE ARCHIMEDE BUREAU 92, LEVIS, QC, G6V 7M5
(418) 833-8073 *SIC* 1622

GROUPE BEAUDET INC, LE p 1061
6455 RUE DORIS-LUSSIER BUREAU 110, BOISBRIAND, QC, J7H 0E8
(514) 990-5833 *SIC* 7992

GROUPE BEDARD p 1247
See BEACON ROOFING SUPPLY CANADA COMPANY

GROUPE BELLE-ILE INC p 419
3113 RUE PRINCIPALE, TRACADIE-SHEILA, NB, E1X 1A2
(506) 395-3374 *SIC* 5146

GROUPE BFL INC p 1358
2121 RUE NOBEL BUREAU 101, SAINTE-JULIE, QC, J3E 1Z9
(514) 874-9050 *SIC* 6712

GROUPE BIBEAU INC p 1303
4581 RANG CASTLE-D'AUTRAY, SAINT-FELIX-DE-VALOIS, QC, J0K 2M0
(450) 889-5505 *SIC* 3713

GROUPE BIRKS INC p 1196
2020 RUE ROBERT-BOURASSA BUREAU 200, MONTREAL, QC, H3A 2A5
(514) 397-2501 *SIC* 5944

GROUPE BMR INC p 1065
1501 RUE AMPERE BUREAU 200, BOUCHERVILLE, QC, J4B 5Z5
(450) 655-2441 *SIC* 5039

GROUPE BMR INC p 1065
1660 RUE EIFFEL, BOUCHERVILLE, QC, J4B 7W1
(450) 655-2441 *SIC* 5072

GROUPE BMTC INC p 1104
500 BOUL DE LA GAPPE, GATINEAU, QC, J8T 8A8
(819) 561-5007 *SIC* 5712

GROUPE BMTC INC p 1238
8500 PLACE MARIEN, MONTREAL-EST, QC, H1B 5W8
(514) 648-5757 *SIC* 6712

GROUPE BO CONCEPT p 1048
See ENSEIGNES INNOVA INC, LES

GROUPE BONNET INC p 1298
54 RUE PRINCIPALE, SAINT-DAMASE, QC, J0H 1J0
(450) 797-3301 *SIC* 6712

GROUPE BOUCHER SPORT p 1271
See 9023-4451 QUEBEC INC

GROUPE BOUFFARD, DIV DE p 1150
See BOUFFARD SANITAIRE INC

GROUPE BOUTIN INC p 1065
128 CH DU TREMBLAY, BOUCHERVILLE, QC, J4B 6Z6
(450) 449-7373 *SIC* 4213

GROUPE BOUTIN INC p 1246
1397 RUE SAVOIE, PLESSISVILLE, QC, G6L 1J8
(819) 362-7333 *SIC* 6712

GROUPE BUGATTI INC, LE p 1061
1963 BOUL LIONEL-BERTRAND, BOISBRIAND, QC, J7H 1N8
(514) 832-1010 *SIC* 5099

GROUPE BUONANOTTE p 1182
See 3838731 CANADA INC

GROUPE C. & G. BEAULIEU INC p 1294
368 BOUL GRAND E, SAINT-BASILE-LE-GRAND, QC, J3N 1M4
(450) 653-9581 *SIC* 1542

GROUPE C.D.J. INC p 1293
4740 RUE SAINT-FELIX, SAINT-AUGUSTIN-DE-DESMAURES, QC, G3A 1B1
SIC 7349

GROUPE CABICO INC p 1082
677 RUE AKHURST, COATICOOK, QC, J1A 0B4
(819) 849-7969 *SIC* 2434

GROUPE CABRELLI INC p 1178
9200 RUE MEILLEUR BUREAU 300, MONTREAL, QC, H2N 2A9
(514) 384-4750 *SIC* 5137

GROUPE CAFE VIENNE 1998 INC, LE p 1210
1422 RUE NOTRE-DAME O, MONTREAL, QC, H3C 1K9
(514) 935-5553 *SIC* 6794

GROUPE CAMBLI INC p 1318
555 RUE SAINT-LOUIS, SAINT-JEAN-SUR-RICHELIEU, QC, J3B 8X7
(450) 358-4920 *SIC* 7381

GROUPE CANADO/NACAN p 1328
See CANADO/NACAN EQUIPEMENT INC

GROUPE CANALAC LABORATOIRES ABBOTT p 1335
See LABORATOIRES ABBOTT, LIMITEE

GROUPE CANAM INC p 1065
270 CH DU TREMBLAY, BOUCHERVILLE, QC, J4B 5X9
(866) 506-4000 *SIC* 3441

GROUPE CANAM INC p 1065
270 CH DU TREMBLAY, BOUCHERVILLE, QC, J4B 5X9
(418) 251-3152 *SIC* 3531

GROUPE CANAM INC p 1065
200 BOUL INDUSTRIEL, BOUCHERVILLE, QC, J4B 2X4
(450) 641-8770 *SIC* 3441

GROUPE CANAM INC p 1264
1445 RUE DU GRAND-TRONC, QUEBEC, QC, G1N 4G1
(418) 683-2561 *SIC* 3443

GROUPE CANAM INC p 1303
115 BOUL CANAM N, SAINT-GEDEON-DE-BEAUCE, QC, G0M 1T0
(418) 582-3331 *SIC* 3441

GROUPE CANAM INC p 1304
11505 1RE AV BUREAU 500, SAINT-GEORGES, QC, G5Y 7H5
(418) 228-8031 *SIC* 3441

GROUPE CANATAL INC p 1383
2885 BOUL FRONTENAC E, THETFORD MINES, QC, G6G 6P6
(418) 338-6044 *SIC* 6712

GROUPE CANIMEX, LE p 1098
See DUBOIS, ROGER INC

GROUPE CANTREX NATIONWIDE INC p 1324
9900 BOUL CAVENDISH BUREAU 400, SAINT-LAURENT, QC, H4M 2V2
(514) 335-0260 *SIC* 7389

GROUPE CARBUR ST-JEROME AUTO DEPOT p 1320
See ST-JEROME CHEVROLET BUICK GMC INC

GROUPE CARON & CARON INC p 1316
800 BOUL PIERRE-TREMBLAY, SAINT-JEAN-SUR-RICHELIEU, QC, J2X 4W8
(450) 545-7174 *SIC* 3272

GROUPE CARREAUX CERAGRES INC p 1326
825 RUE DESLAURIERS, SAINT-LAURENT, QC, H4N 1X3
(514) 384-5590 *SIC* 5032

GROUPE CD BEDARD INC p 1141
753 RUE BERIAULT, LONGUEUIL, QC, J4G 1X7
(450) 679-7704 *SIC* 6712

GROUPE CDREM INC p 1128
10200 CH DE LA COTE-DE-LIESSE, LACHINE, QC, H8T 1A3
(514) 636-4512 *SIC* 5999

GROUPE CEDRICO INC p 1124
50 RANG DIDIER, LAC-AU-SAUMON, QC, G0J 1M0
SIC 2491

GROUPE CENSEO INC p 1241
1200 BOUL CHOMEDEY BUREAU 1050, MONTREAL-OUEST, QC, H7V 3Z3
(450) 973-8000 *SIC* 6411

GROUPE CHAGALL INC p 1358
2051 RUE LEONARD-DE VINCI, SAINTE-JULIE, QC, J3E 1Z2
(450) 649-1001 *SIC* 7389

GROUPE CHAGNON p 1307
See 9051-4076 QUEBEC INC

GROUPE CHAMPLAIN INC p 1057
1231 RUE DR OLIVIER-M.-GENDRON PR, BERTHIERVILLE, QC, J0K 1A0
(450) 836-6241 *SIC* 8361

GROUPE CHAMPLAIN INC p 1280
791 RUE DE SHERWOOD, QUEBEC, QC, G2N 1X7
(418) 849-1891 *SIC* 8361

GROUPE CHAMPLAIN INC p 1298
199 RUE SAINT-PIERRE, SAINT-CONSTANT, QC, J5A 2N8
(450) 632-4451 *SIC* 8361

GROUPE CHARTEAU MIRAGE p 1361
See 3933849 CANADA INC

GROUPE CHASSE INC p 1173
819 RUE RACHEL E, MONTREAL, QC, H2J 2H7
(514) 527-3411 *SIC* 5511

GROUPE CHINOOK AVENTURE INC p 1312
990 AV DE L'H?TEL-DE-VILLE, SAINT-HYACINTHE, QC, J2S 5B2
(514) 773-1911 *SIC* 8699

GROUPE CIMENT QUEBEC INC p 1294
145 BOUL DU CENTENAIRE, SAINT-BASILE, QC, G0A 3G0
(418) 329-2100 *SIC* 3241

GROUPE CIRQUE DU SOLEIL p 1169
See CIRQUE DU SOLEIL INC

GROUPE CIRTECH INC p 1075

660 RUE NOTRE-DAME BUREAU 100, CHARETTE, QC, G0X 1E0
(819) 221-3400 SIC 1542

GROUPE CLR INC p 1387
7200 BOUL JEAN-XXIII, TROIS-RIVIERES, QC, G9A 5C9
(819) 377-2424 SIC 4899

GROUPE CMA p 1345
See SADERCOM INC

GROUPE COLABOR INC p 1065
1620 BOUL DE MONTARVILLE, BOUCHERVILLE, QC, J4B 8P4
(450) 449-4911 SIC 5141

GROUPE COMMENSAL INC p 1062
3737 BOUL DE LA GRANDE-ALLEE, BOIS-BRIAND, QC, J7H 1J6
(450) 979-5772 SIC 2032

GROUPE COMPTANT QUEBEC INC p 1172
2024 AV DU MONT-ROYAL E, MONTREAL, QC, H2H 1J6
(514) 527-6023 SIC 5932

GROUPE CONFORT GLOBAL p 1255
See GROUPE MACADAM INC

GROUPE CONSEIL AON p 1201
See AON HEWITT INC

GROUPE CONSEIL AON p 1271
See AON HEWITT INC

GROUPE CONSEIL DFM INC, LE p 1272
1175 AV LAVIGERIE BUREAU 580, QUEBEC, QC, G1V 4P1
(418) 650-2266 SIC 6712

GROUPE CONSEIL FXINNOVATION INC p 1143
125 BOUL SAINTE-FOY, LONGUEUIL, QC, J4J 1W7
SIC 8748

GROUPE CONSEIL FXINNOVATION INC p 1196
400 BOUL DE MAISONNEUVE O BUREAU 1100, MONTREAL, QC, H3A 1L4
(514) 525-5777 SIC 8742

GROUPE CONSEIL PARISELLA VINCELLI, ASSOCIES INC p 1060
20865 CH DE LA COTE N UNITE 200, BOISBRIAND, QC, J7E 4H5
(450) 970-1970 SIC 8741

GROUPE CONSEIL RES PUBLICA INC p 1205
1155 RUE METCALFE BUREAU 800, MONTREAL, QC, H3B 0C1
(514) 843-2343 SIC 6712

GROUPE CONSEIL TDA INC p 1052
26 BOUL COMEAU, BAIE-COMEAU, QC, G4Z 3A8
(418) 296-6711 SIC 8711

GROUPE CONTANT INC p 1230
6310 BOUL DES MILLE-ILES, MONTREAL, QC, H7B 1B3
(450) 666-6676 SIC 5599

GROUPE CONTROLE INC p 1305
8800 25E AV, SAINT-GEORGES, QC, G6A 1K5
(418) 227-9141 SIC 6712

GROUPE CORPORATIF OLYMBEC p 1326
See INVESTISSEMENTS OLYMBEC INC

GROUPE COTE REGIS INC p 1210
682 RUE WILLIAM BUREAU 200, MONTREAL, QC, H3C 1N9
(514) 871-8595 SIC 8712

GROUPE COTE-HUOT INC p 1260
165 BOUL DES CEDRES, QUEBEC, QC, G1L 1M8
(418) 626-1142 SIC 5063

GROUPE CREOPACK INC p 1157
See EMBALLAGES CRE-O-PACK CANADA INC

GROUPE CRETE CHERTSEY INC p 1077
8227 RTE 125, CHERTSEY, QC, J0K 3K0
(450) 882-2555 SIC 2421

GROUPE CRETE DIVISION ST-FAUSTIN INC p 1302
1617 RTE 117, SAINT-FAUSTIN-LAC-CARRE, QC, J0T 1J2
(819) 688-5550 SIC 5031

GROUPE CRETE INC p 1302
1617 RTE 117, SAINT-FAUSTIN-LAC-CARRE, QC, J0T 1J2
(418) 365-4457 SIC 5031

GROUPE CSL INC p 1188
759 RUE DU SQUARE-VICTORIA BUREAU 600, MONTREAL, QC, H2Y 2K3
(514) 982-3100 SIC 4424

GROUPE CT INC p 1231
5545 RUE MAURICE-CULLEN, MONTREAL, QC, H7C 2T8
(450) 967-3142 SIC 5044

GROUPE CUISINE IDEALE INC p 1372
980 RUE PANNETON, SHERBROOKE, QC, J1K 2B2
(819) 566-2401 SIC 6712

GROUPE D'ALIMENTATION MTY INC p 1334
8210 RTE TRANSCANADIENNE, SAINT-LAURENT, QC, H4S 1M5
(514) 336-8885 SIC 6794

GROUPE D'APPROVISIONNEMENT EN COMMUN DE L'EST DU QUEBEC p 1278
710 RUE BOUVIER BUREAU 296, QUEBEC, QC, G2J 1C2
(418) 780-8111 SIC 6221

GROUPE D'ASSURANCES VERRIER INC p 1098
430 RUE SAINT-GEORGES BUREAU 121, DRUMMONDVILLE, QC, J2C 4H4
(819) 477-6131 SIC 6411

GROUPE D'ONOFRIO p 1346
See JOSEPH D'ONOFRIO ET ASSOCIES INC

GROUPE D.R.I. INC p 1163
5125 RUE DU TRIANON BUREAU 510, MONTREAL, QC, H1M 2S5
SIC 8742

GROUPE DAGENAIS M.D.C. INC p 1068
117 BOUL DE BROMONT, BROMONT, QC, J2L 2K7
SIC 5712

GROUPE DCM INC p 1059
890 BOUL MICHELE-BOHEC, BLAINVILLE, QC, J7C 5E2
(450) 435-9210 SIC 7371

GROUPE DE COURTAGE OMNI LTEE p 1101
3838 BOUL LEMAN, FABREVILLE, QC, H7E 1A1
(450) 661-0281 SIC 5141

GROUPE DE LA COTE INC p 1053
332 RUE DE PUYJALON, BAIE-COMEAU, QC, G5C 1M5
(418) 589-8397 SIC 2326

GROUPE DE SCIERIES G.D.S. INC p 1089
207 RTE 295, DEGELIS, QC, G5T 1R1
(418) 853-2566 SIC 2421

GROUPE DE SECURITE GARDA INC, LE p 35
8989 MACLEOD TRAIL SW SUITE 118, CALGARY, AB, T2H 0M2
(403) 517-5899 SIC 7381

GROUPE DE SECURITE GARDA INC, LE p 1104
25 RUE DE VILLEBOIS, GATINEAU, QC, J8T 8J7
(819) 770-9438 SIC 7381

GROUPE DE SECURITE GARDA INC, LE p 1119
1160 RUE VALETS, L'ANCIENNE-LORETTE, QC, G2E 5Y9
(418) 627-0088 SIC 7381

GROUPE DE SECURITE GARDA INC, LE p 1210
1390 RUE BARRE, MONTREAL, QC, H3C 5X9
(514) 281-2811 SIC 7381

GROUPE DE SECURITE GARDA INC, LE p 1367
456 AV ARNAUD BUREAU 218, SEPT-ILES, QC, G4R 3B1
(418) 968-8006 SIC 7381

GROUPE DE SECURITE GARDA INC, LE p 1418
2505 11TH AVE SUITE 302, REGINA, SK, S4P 0K6
(306) 352-2099 SIC 7381

GROUPE DE SECURITE MGM INC p 1099
975 RUE CORMIER, DRUMMONDVILLE, QC, J2C 2N5
(819) 478-4558 SIC 3499

GROUPE DE TISSUS NINO MARCELLO INC, LE p 1178
555 RUE CHABANEL O UNITE 902, MONTREAL, QC, H2N 2H7
(514) 441-3555 SIC 5137

GROUPE DERIC INC p 1277
5145 RUE RIDEAU, QUEBEC, QC, G2E 5H5
(418) 781-2228 SIC 6712

GROUPE DESCHENES INC p 1170
3901 RUE JARRY E BUREAU 250, MONTREAL, QC, H1Z 2G1
(514) 253-3110 SIC 6712

GROUPE DESGAGNES INC p 1259
21 RUE DU MARCHE-CHAMPLAIN BUREAU 100, QUEBEC, QC, G1K 8Z8
(418) 692-1000 SIC 6719

GROUPE DESMARAIS PINSONNEAULT & AVARD INC p 1312
3395 RUE PICARD, SAINT-HYACINTHE, QC, J2S 1H3
(450) 250-3321 SIC 6411

GROUPE DESSAU INC p 1237
1200 BOUL SAINT-MARTIN O BUREAU 300, MONTREAL, QC, H7S 2E4
(514) 281-1010 SIC 6712

GROUPE DIMENSION MULTI VETERINAIRE INC, LE p 1128
2300 54E AV, LACHINE, QC, H8T 3R2
(514) 633-8888 SIC 0742

GROUPE DMD CONNEXIONS SANTE NUMERIQUES INC p 1396
2 PLACE DU COMMERCE BUREAU 206, VERDUN, QC, H3E 1A1
(514) 783-1698 SIC 7371

GROUPE DOLBEC p 1353
See PATATES DOLBEC INC

GROUPE DPJL INC p 1076
185 BOUL SAINT-JEAN-BAPTISTE BUREAU 100, CHATEAUGUAY, QC, J6K 3B4
(450) 691-9913 SIC 6411

GROUPE DRUMCO CONSTRUCTION INC, LE p 1096
4825 RTE 139, DRUMMONDVILLE, QC, J2A 4E5
(819) 474-5035 SIC 1542

GROUPE DUTAILIER INC p 1350
299 RUE CHAPUT, SAINT-PIE, QC, J0H 1W0
(450) 772-2403 SIC 2512

GROUPE DYNAMITE INC p 1156
5592 RUE FERRIER, MONT-ROYAL, QC, H4P 1M2
(514) 733-3962 SIC 5621

GROUPE EDGENDA INC p 1262
1751 RUE DU MARAIS BUREAU 300, QUEBEC, QC, G1M 0A2
(418) 626-2344 SIC 8741

GROUPE EDIFIO INC p 1380
3205 BOUL DES ENTREPRISES, TERREBONNE, QC, J6X 4J9
(514) 284-7070 SIC 8322

GROUPE EDUCALIVRES INC p 1234
955 RUE BERGAR, MONTREAL, QC, H7L 4Z6
(514) 334-8466 SIC 2731

GROUPE EMBALLAGE SPECIALISE S.E.C. p 890
140 IBER RD, STITTSVILLE, ON, K2S 1E9
(613) 742-6766 SIC 3086

GROUPE EMBALLAGE SPECIALISE S.E.C. p 1250
3300 RTE TRANSCANADIENNE, POINTE-CLAIRE, QC, H9R 1B1

(514) 636-7951 SIC 3089

GROUPE EN INFORMATIQUE ET RECHERCHE OPERATIONNELLE, LE p 1217
See GIRO INC

GROUPE ENCORE p 1327
See VOYAGES ENCORE TRAVEL INC

GROUPE ENERGIE BDL INC p 1049
10390 BOUL LOUIS-H.-LAFONTAINE, ANJOU, QC, H1J 2T3
(514) 493-3576 SIC 5172

GROUPE ENVIRONNEMENTAL LABRIE INC p 1140
175 RTE MARIE-VICTORIN BUREAU B, LEVIS, QC, G7A 2T3
(418) 831-8250 SIC 3531

GROUPE EPICIERS ANGUS INC p 1100
150 RUE ANGUS S BUREAU 10, EAST ANGUS, QC, J0B 1R0
(819) 832-2449 SIC 5411

GROUPE EQUICONCEPT INC p 1276
2160 RUE DE CELLES, QUEBEC, QC, G2C 1X8
(418) 847-1480 SIC 6712

GROUPE ERA INC p 1329
2500 RUE GUENETTE, SAINT-LAURENT, QC, H4R 2H2
(514) 335-0550 SIC 3083

GROUPE ESTRIE-RICHELIEU, COMPAGNIE D'ASSURANCE, LE p 1109
770 RUE PRINCIPALE, GRANBY, QC, J2G 2Y7
(450) 378-0101 SIC 6331

GROUPE ETHIER INC p 1152
16800 CH CHARLES UNITE 123, MIRABEL, QC, J7J 0V9
(450) 435-9581 SIC 5148

GROUPE ETR p 1266
See EDITION LE TELEPHONE ROUGE INC

GROUPE F.G.B. 2000 INC, LE p 1234
1225 RUE BERGAR, MONTREAL, QC, H7L 4Z7
(514) 967-0076 SIC 5141

GROUPE FACILITE INFORMATIQUE (GFI) INC p 1205
5 PLACE VILLE-MARIE BUREAU 1045, MONTREAL, QC, H3B 2G2
(514) 284-5636 SIC 7371

GROUPE FACILITE INFORMATIQUE (GFI) INC p 1272
1100-2875 BOUL LAURIER, QUEBEC, QC, G1V 5B1
(418) 780-3950 SIC 7371

GROUPE FEDERAL, LE p 1248
See TRANSFORMATEUR FEDERAL LTEE

GROUPE FERTEK INC p 1362
3000 AV FRAN?IS-HUGHES, SAINTE-ROSE, QC, H7L 3J5
(450) 663-8700 SIC 6712

GROUPE FILGO INC p 1360
1133 BOUL VACHON N, SAINTE-MARIE, QC, G6E 1M9
(418) 387-5449 SIC 6712

GROUPE FINANCIER AGA INC p 1402
3500 BOUL DE MAISONNEUVE O BUREAU 2200, WESTMOUNT, QC, H3Z 3C1
(514) 935-5444 SIC 6411

GROUPE FINANCIER FORT INC p 1220
3400 BOUL DE MAISONNEUVE O BUREAU 1115, MONTREAL, QC, H3Z 3B8
(514) 288-6161 SIC 6411

GROUPE FLEURY & ASSOCIES p 1279
See FLAGEC INC

GROUPE FOODAROM INC p 1309
5400 RUE ARMAND-FRAPPIER, SAINT-HUBERT, QC, J3Z 1G5
(450) 443-3113 SIC 5149

GROUPE FORDIA INC p 1091
3 RUE HOTEL-DE-VILLE, DOLLARD-DES-ORMEAUX, QC, H9B 3G4
(514) 336-9211 SIC 5084

GROUPE FORGET, LE p 1329

See FORGET & SAUVE, AUDIOPROTHE-SISTES S.E.N.C.

GROUPE FORTIN, LE   *p 1260*
See FOR-NET INC

GROUPE FOURNIER DIESEL INC *p 1353*
5 CH DE LA COTE-SAINT-PAUL, SAINT-STANISLAS-DE-CHAMPLAIN, QC, G0X 3E0
(418) 668-5040   *SIC 6712*

GROUPE G & G LTEE   *p 1344*
6245 BOUL DES GRANDES-PRAIRIES, SAINT-LEONARD, QC, H1P 1A5
(514) 325-3711   *SIC 7692*

GROUPE G.D.S.   *p 1089*
See GROUPE DE SCIERIES G.D.S. INC

GROUPE G.L.P. HI-TECH INC   *p 1318*
440 RUE SAINT-MICHEL, SAINT-JEAN-SUR-RICHELIEU, QC, J3B 1T4
(450) 348-4918   *SIC 3089*

GROUPE G3 INC, LE   *p 1162*
9135 BOUL HENRI-BOURASSA E, MONTREAL, QC, H1E 1P4
(514) 648-8522   *SIC 4213*

GROUPE GAGNE CONSTRUCTION INC *p 1297*
22 RUE DES AFFAIRES, SAINT-CHRISTOPHE-D'ARTHABASK, QC, G6R 0B2
(819) 809-2270   *SIC 1541*

GROUPE GASTON COTE   *p 1375*
See 9098-0145 QUEBEC INC

GROUPE GAUDREAULT INC, LE   *p 1282*
1500 RUE RAYMOND-GAUDREAULT, REPENTIGNY, QC, J5Y 4E3
(450) 585-1210   *SIC 6712*

GROUPE GERMAIN INC   *p 1270*
1200 RUE DES SOEURS-DU-BON-PASTEUR BUREAU 500, QUEBEC, QC, G1S 0B1
(418) 687-1123   *SIC 7011*

GROUPE GESTION NOR INC   *p 1157*
8550 CH DELMEADE, MONT-ROYAL, QC, H4T 1L7
(514) 342-2744   *SIC 6712*

GROUPE GEYSER INC   *p 1362*
205 BOUL CURE-LABELLE BUREAU 201, SAINTE-ROSE, QC, H7L 2Z9
(450) 625-2003   *SIC 1542*

GROUPE GIROUX MACONNEX INC *p 1080*
2223 BOUL SAINT-PAUL, CHICOUTIMI, QC, G7K 1E5
(418) 549-7345   *SIC 5032*

GROUPE GOYETTE INC   *p 1312*
2825 BOUL CASAVANT O, SAINT-HYACINTHE, QC, J2S 7Y4
(450) 773-9615   *SIC 6712*

GROUPE GRAHAM INTERNATIONAL INC *p 1128*
1455 32E AV, LACHINE, QC, H8T 3J1
(514) 631-6662   *SIC 6712*

GROUPE GUILBAULT LTEE   *p 1264*
435 RUE FARADAY, QUEBEC, QC, G1N 4G6
(418) 681-0575   *SIC 4213*

GROUPE HAMELIN INC   *p 1213*
1328 REDPATH CRES, MONTREAL, QC, H3G 2K2
(514) 934-5577   *SIC 2821*

GROUPE HARNOIS INC, LE   *p 1353*
80 RTE 158, SAINT-THOMAS, QC, J0K 3L0
(450) 756-1660   *SIC 5172*

GROUPE HB   *p 1156*
See HB CONNECTIONS INC

GROUPE HELIE   *p 1055*
See AUTOCAR HELIE INC.

GROUPE HELIOS, GESTION D'INFRASTRUCTURES ET DE SERVICES URBAINS INC *p 1141*
2099 BOUL FERNAND-LAFONTAINE, LONGUEUIL, QC, J4G 2J4
(450) 646-1903   *SIC 8741*

GROUPE HEXAVOGUE INC, LE *p 1184*
4200 BOUL SAINT-LAURENT BUREAU 200, MONTREAL, QC, H2W 2R2
(514) 286-4392   *SIC 5137*

GROUPE HONCO INC   *p 1140*
1190 CH INDUSTRIEL, LEVIS, QC, G7A 1B1
(418) 831-2245   *SIC 1541*

GROUPE HOTELIER GRAND CHATEAU INC *p 1085*
2225 DES LAURENTIDES (A-15) E, COTE SAINT-LUC, QC, H7S 1Z6
(450) 682-2225   *SIC 7011*

GROUPE HOTELIER GRAND CHATEAU INC *p 1086*
2440 DES LAURENTIDES (A-15) O, COTE SAINT-LUC, QC, H7T 1X5
(450) 687-2440   *SIC 7011*

GROUPE HOTELIER GRAND CHATEAU INC *p 1394*
21700 RTE TRANSCANADIENNE, VAUDREUIL-DORION, QC, J7V 8P7
(450) 455-0955   *SIC 7011*

GROUPE HYPERTEC   *p 1334*
See HYPERTEC SYSTEMES INC

GROUPE IBI/DAA INC   *p 1211*
100 RUE PEEL 4E ETAGE, MONTREAL, QC, H3C 0L8
(514) 316-1010   *SIC 8748*

GROUPE IN-RGY CONSULTATION INC *p 1188*
390 RUE LE MOYNE, MONTREAL, QC, H2Y 1Y3
(514) 906-7767   *SIC 7373*

GROUPE INCURSION INC   *p 1278*
815 BOUL LEBOURGNEUF BUREAU 202, QUEBEC, QC, G2J 0C1
(418) 687-2400   *SIC 4724*

GROUPE INDUSTRIEL AMI   *p 1116*
See A.M.I. MECANIQUE INC

GROUPE INDUSTRIES FOURNIER INC *p 1383*
3787 BOUL FRONTENAC O, THETFORD MINES, QC, G6H 2B5
(418) 423-4241   *SIC 6712*

GROUPE INTER CLOTURES   *p 1387*
See INTER CLOTURES INC

GROUPE INTERNATIONAL TRAVELWAY INC *p 1334*
4600 CH DU BOIS-FRANC, SAINT-LAURENT, QC, H4S 1A7
(514) 331-3130   *SIC 5199*

GROUPE INTERSAND CANADA INC, LE *p 1065*
125 RUE DE LA BARRE, BOUCHERVILLE, QC, J4B 2X6
(450) 449-7070   *SIC 3295*

GROUPE INTERTAPE POLYMER INC, LE *p 1324*
9999 BOUL CAVENDISH BUREAU 200, SAINT-LAURENT, QC, H4M 2X5
(514) 731-7591   *SIC 2672*

GROUPE INVESTORS   *p 378*
See INVESTORS GROUP FINANCIAL SERVICES INC

GROUPE ISOLOFOAM INC   *p 1360*
1346 BOUL VACHON N, SAINTE-MARIE, QC, G6E 1N4
(800) 463-8886   *SIC 2493*

GROUPE J.C.F. LTEE   *p 1059*
1083 BOUL DU CURE-LABELLE BUREAU 110, BLAINVILLE, QC, J7C 3M9
(450) 435-1981   *SIC 5912*

GROUPE J.F. NADEAU INC, LE *p 1360*
850 RTE PRINCIPALE, SAINTE-MELANIE, QC, J0K 3A0
(450) 889-7237   *SIC 4213*

GROUPE J.L. LECLERC INC   *p 1292*
4919 RTE MARIE-VICTORIN, SAINT-ANTOINE-DE-TILLY, QC, G0S 2C0
(418) 886-2474   *SIC 3599*

GROUPE J.L.D. LAGUE   *p 1232*
See CENTRE AGRICOLE J.L.D. INC

GROUPE J.S.V. INC, LE   *p 1162*
8015 AV MARCO-POLO, MONTREAL, QC, H1E 5Y8
(514) 842-8351   *SIC 5085*

GROUPE JACOB INC   *p 1339*

6125 CH DE LA COTE-DE-LIESSE, SAINT-LAURENT, QC, H4T 1C8
(514) 731-8877   *SIC 5621*

GROUPE JACOBUS INC   *p 1274*
3175 CH DES QUATRE-BOURGEOIS BUREAU 35, QUEBEC, QC, G1W 2K7
(418) 658-7373   *SIC 5944*

GROUPE JEAN COUTU   *p 1323*
See PHARMA NTK INC

GROUPE JEAN COUTU (PJC) INC, LE *p 1392*
245 RUE JEAN-COUTU, VARENNES, QC, J3X 0E1
(450) 646-9760   *SIC 5122*

GROUPE JETTE ASSURANCES INC *p 1314*
153 RUE SAINT-JACQUES, SAINT-JACQUES, QC, J0K 2R0
(450) 839-3911   *SIC 6411*

GROUPE JLD LAGUE   *p 1082*
544 RUE MAIN O, COATICOOK, QC, J1A 2S5
(819) 849-0300   *SIC 5084*

GROUPE JMI   *p 1337*
See VEOLIA EAU TECHNOLOGIES CANADA INC

GROUPE JOHANNE VERDON INC *p 1181*
1274 RUE JEAN-TALON E BUREAU 200, MONTREAL, QC, H2R 1W3
(514) 272-0018   *SIC 5499*

GROUPE KANWAL INC   *p 1147*
1426 BOUL INDUSTRIEL, MAGOG, QC, J1X 4V9
(819) 868-4156   *SIC 6712*

GROUPE KDA INC   *p 1383*
1351 RUE NOTRE-DAME E BUREAU 300, THETFORD MINES, QC, G6G 0G5
(514) 622-7370   *SIC 6799*

GROUPE KTG   *p 1154*
See 9144-8720 QUEBEC INC

GROUPE L.E.D. LAMARRE, EVANGE-LISTE, DELISLE INC *p 1167*
3006 RUE SAINTE-CATHERINE E, MONTREAL, QC, H1W 2B8
(514) 523-2831   *SIC 6712*

GROUPE LACASSE INC   *p 1350*
99 RUE SAINT-PIERRE, SAINT-PIE, QC, J0H 1W0
(450) 772-2495   *SIC 2521*

GROUPE LAFONTAINE   *p 1136*
See EXCAVATIONS LAFONTAINE INC, LES

GROUPE LAFRANCE   *p 1164*
See ENTREPOTS LAFRANCE INC

GROUPE LALIBERTE SPORTS INC *p 1379*
1185 BOUL MOODY BUREAU 90, TERREBONNE, QC, J6W 3Z5
(450) 824-1091   *SIC 5941*

GROUPE LAURIER   *p 1334*
See IMPRESSION PARAGRAPH INC

GROUPE LAUZON   *p 1215*
See 9278-3455 QUEBEC INC

GROUPE LAUZON INC   *p 1086*
2400 BOUL CHOMEDEY CARTE DES ENVIRONS, COTE SAINT-LUC, QC, H7T 2W3
(450) 434-1120   *SIC 6712*

GROUPE LAVOIE PHARMACY   *p 1276*
See DISTRIBUTION PHARMAPLUS INC

GROUPE LCI CANADA, INC   *p 1111*
850 RUE MOELLER, GRANBY, QC, J2J 1K7
(450) 378-6722   *SIC 3231*

GROUPE LD INC   *p 1115*
2370 RUE BAUMAN, JONQUIERE, QC, G7S 4S4
(418) 699-4350   *SIC 5084*

GROUPE LE MASSIF INC   *p 1272*
2505 BOUL LAURIER BUREAU 200, QUEBEC, QC, G1V 2L2
(418) 948-1725   *SIC 8741*

GROUPE LEBEL (2004)   *p 1286*
See GROUPE LEBEL INC

GROUPE LEBEL INC   *p 1286*
54 RUE AMYOT, RIVIERE-DU-LOUP, QC, G5R 3E9

(877) 567-5910   *SIC 2421*

GROUPE LEDOR INC, MUTUELLE D'ASSURANCE *p 1356*
78 BOUL BEGIN, SAINTE-CLAIRE, QC, G0R 2V0
(418) 883-2251   *SIC 6411*

GROUPE LEFEBVRE M.R.P INC, LE *p 1301*
210 RUE ROY, SAINT-EUSTACHE, QC, J7R 5R6
(450) 491-6444   *SIC 1799*

GROUPE LEG   *p 1124*
See EQUIPEMENTS GAETAN INC, LES

GROUPE LEGARE LTEE   *p 1351*
488 RUE SAINT-PIERRE, SAINT-RAYMOND, QC, G3L 1R5
(418) 337-2286   *SIC 6712*

GROUPE LELYS INC   *p 1362*
3275 AV FRANCIS-HUGHES, SAINTE-ROSE, QC, H7L 5A5
(450) 662-7460   *SIC 2759*

GROUPE LEMUR INC, LE   *p 1326*
275 RUE STINSON BUREAU 201, SAINT-LAURENT, QC, H4N 2E1
(514) 748-6234   *SIC 5137*

GROUPE LEROUX, LE   *p 1176*
See ESTIMATEURS PROFESSIONELS LEROUX, BEAUDRY, PICARD & ASSOCIES INC, LES

GROUPE LES MANOIRS DU QUEBEC INC *p 1352*
See GROUPE LES MANOIRS DU QUEBEC INC, LES

GROUPE LES MANOIRS DU QUEBEC INC, LES *p 1269*
44 COTE DU PALAIS, QUEBEC, QC, G1R 4H8
(418) 692-1030   *SIC 7011*

GROUPE LES MANOIRS DU QUEBEC INC, LES *p 1352*
246 CH DU LAC-MILLETTE, SAINT-SAUVEUR, QC, J0R 1R3
(450) 227-1811   *SIC 7011*

GROUPE LESSARD INC   *p 1362*
2025 BOUL DAGENAIS O, SAINTE-ROSE, QC, H7L 5V1
(514) 636-3999   *SIC 3442*

GROUPE LEV-FAB INC   *p 1320*
640 BOUL MONSEIGNEUR-DUBOIS, SAINT-JEROME, QC, J7Y 3L8
(450) 438-7164   *SIC 3599*

GROUPE LEVASSE INC   *p 1138*
1660 BOUL GUILLAUME-COUTURE, LEVIS, QC, G6W 0R5
(418) 834-1844   *SIC 4213*

GROUPE LEXIS MEDIA INC   *p 1309*
7750 BOUL COUSINEAU BUREAU 103, SAINT-HUBERT, QC, J3Z 0C8
(514) 394-7156   *SIC 2711*

GROUPE LFL   *p 1045*
See LAVAL FORTIN LTEE

GROUPE LINENCORP INC   *p 1339*
6435 CH DE LA COTE-DE-LIESSE, SAINT-LAURENT, QC, H4T 1E5
(514) 335-2120   *SIC 5023*

GROUPE LML LTEE, LE   *p 1318*
360 BOUL DU SEMINAIRE N BUREAU 22, SAINT-JEAN-SUR-RICHELIEU, QC, J3B 5L1
(450) 347-1996   *SIC 1731*

GROUPE LMT INC   *p 1141*
2025 RUE DE LA METROPOLE, LONGUEUIL, QC, J4G 1S9
(450) 640-8700   *SIC 3442*

GROUPE LOU-TEC INC   *p 1049*
8500 RUE JULES-LEGER, ANJOU, QC, H1J 1A7
(514) 356-0047   *SIC 6712*

GROUPE LUMENPULSE INC   *p 1141*
1220 BOUL MARIE-VICTORIN, LONGUEUIL, QC, J4G 2H9
(514) 937-3003   *SIC 3646*

GROUPE LUMENPULSE INC   *p 1277*
445 AV SAINT-JEAN-BAPTISTE BUREAU 120, QUEBEC, QC, G2E 5N7
(418) 871-8039   *SIC 3646*

GROUPE LUMINAIRES INC, LE   p 1180
225 RUE DE LIEGE O BUREAU 200, MON-TREAL, QC, H2P 1H4
(514) 385-3515   *SIC* 3648

GROUPE LUMINAIRES INC, LE   p 1250
260 AV LABROSSE, POINTE-CLAIRE, QC, H9R 5L5
(514) 683-3883   *SIC* 5719

GROUPE M.G.B. INC   p 1350
51 RUE SAINT-PIERRE, SAINT-PIE, QC, J0H 1W0
(450) 772-5608   *SIC* 6712

GROUPE MACADAM INC   p 1255
4550 BOUL SAINTE-ANNE, QUEBEC, QC, G1C 2H9
(418) 661-2400   *SIC* 1622

GROUPE MACHINEX INC   p 1246
2121 RUE OLIVIER, PLESSISVILLE, QC, G6L 3G9
(819) 362-3281   *SIC* 6712

GROUPE MAD SCIENCE INC   p 1227
8360 RUE BOUGAINVILLE BUREAU 201, MONTREAL, QC, H4P 2G1
(514) 344-4181   *SIC* 6794

GROUPE MAILHOT INC   p 1380
3330 BOUL DES ENTREPRISES, TERRE-BONNE, QC, J6X 4J8
(450) 477-6222   *SIC* 6712

GROUPE MANN+HUMMEL   p 483
See MANN+HUMMEL FILTRATION TECH-NOLOGY CANADA ULC

GROUPE   MANUFACTURIER D'ASCENSEURS GLOBAL TARDIF INC, LE   p 1293
120 RUE DE NAPLES, SAINT-AUGUSTIN-DE-DESMAURES, QC, G3A 2Y2
(418) 878-4116   *SIC* 8711

GROUPE MARCELLE INC   p 1128
9200 CH DE LA COTE-DE-LIESSE, LA-CHINE, QC, H8T 1A1
(514) 631-7710   *SIC* 2844

GROUPE MARCELLE INC   p 1157
5600 CH DE LA COTE-DE-LIESSE, MONT-ROYAL, QC, H4T 4L1
(514) 735-2309   *SIC* 2844

GROUPE MARCHAND GIGUERE   p 1262
See FYI SERVICES ET PRODUITS QUE-BEC INC

GROUPE MARCHAND RENE INC   p 1262
1100 AV GALIBOIS BUREAU A200, QUE-BEC, QC, G1M 3M7
(418) 527-6682   *SIC* 5995

GROUPE MARIE CLAIRE   p 1047
See BOUTIQUE MARIE CLAIRE INC

GROUPE MARITIME VERREAULT INC   p 1135
108 RUE DU COLLEGE, LES MECHINS, QC, G0J 1T0
(418) 729-3030   *SIC* 6712

GROUPE MARKETING INTERNATIONAL INC   p 1083
37 BOUL DES LAURENTIDES, COTE SAINT-LUC, QC, H7G 2S3
(450) 972-1540   *SIC* 7389

GROUPE MASKA INC   p 1312
550 AV VAUDREUIL, SAINT-HYACINTHE, QC, J2S 4H2
(450) 372-1676   *SIC* 5084

GROUPE MASTER INC, LE   p 1065
1675 BOUL DE MONTARVILLE, BOUCHERVILLE, QC, J4B 7W4
(514) 527-2301   *SIC* 5075

GROUPE MAURICE INC, LE   p 1329
2400 RUE DES NATIONS BUREAU 137, SAINT-LAURENT, QC, H4R 3G4
(514) 331-2788   *SIC* 1522

GROUPE MDMP INC   p 1272
2960 BOUL LAURIER BUREAU 380, QUE-BEC, QC, G1V 4S1
(418) 657-4444   *SIC* 5146

GROUPE MECANITEC INC   p 1358
2091 RUE LEONARD-DE VINCI, SAINTE-JULIE, QC, J3E 1Z2
SIC 3548

GROUPE MECANITEC INC   p 1387
2300 RUE JULES-VACHON, TROIS-RIVIERES, QC, G9A 5E1
(819) 374-4647   *SIC* 6712

GROUPE MEDICOM   p 1248
See MEDICOM GROUP INC

GROUPE MELOCHE INC   p 1366
491 BOUL DES ERABLES, SALABERRY-DE-VALLEYFIELD, QC, J6T 6G3
(450) 371-4646   *SIC* 3599

GROUPE MEQUALTECH INC   p 1170
8740 BOUL PIE-IX, MONTREAL, QC, H1Z 3V1
(514) 593-5755   *SIC* 6712

GROUPE MICHAUDVILLE INC   p 1158
270 RUE BRUNET, MONT-SAINT-HILAIRE, QC, J3H 0M6
(450) 446-9933   *SIC* 6712

GROUPE MINIER CMAC-THYSSEN INC   p 1390
1254 AV 3E E, VAL-D'OR, QC, J9P 0J6
(819) 874-8303   *SIC* 1794

GROUPE MINIMOME INC   p 1178
225 RUE CHABANEL O BUREAU 800, MONTREAL, QC, H2N 2C9
(514) 383-3408   *SIC* 5137

GROUPE MINT GREEN INC, LE   p 1250
6900 RTE TRANSCANADIENNE, POINTE-CLAIRE, QC, H9R 1C2
(514) 333-1465   *SIC* 5136

GROUPE MIOSIS, S.E.N.C.R.L.   p 1106
425 BOUL SAINT-JOSEPH, GATINEAU, QC, J8Y 3Z8
(819) 771-5600   *SIC* 8042

GROUPE MMI   p 1335
See MACDONALD MAINTENANCE INC

GROUPE MONTEL INC   p 1160
225 4E AV, MONTMAGNY, QC, G5V 4N9
(418) 248-0235   *SIC* 6712

GROUPE MONTONI (1995) DIVISION CON-STRUCTION INC   p 1134
4115 DES LAURENTIDES (A-15) E, LAVAL-OUEST, QC, H7L 5W5
(450) 978-7500   *SIC* 1541

GROUPE MPM   p 1365
See MATERIAUX PONT MASSON INC

GROUPE MTA CONSEILS EN GESTION D'EVENEMENTS PUBLIQUES INC, LE   p 1211
80 RUE QUEEN BUREAU 601, MON-TREAL, QC, H3C 2N5
(514) 982-0835   *SIC* 8742

GROUPE MULTI LUMINAIRE INC, LE   p 1086
2591 BOUL DANIEL-JOHNSON, COTE SAINT-LUC, QC, H7T 1S8
(450) 681-3939   *SIC* 5719

GROUPE MULTI-PAVAGE INC.   p 1161
9855 BOUL HENRI-BOURASSA E, MON-TREAL, QC, H1C 1G5
(514) 723-3000   *SIC* 1611

GROUPE MUNDIAL INC   p 1323
12 RUE NAPOLEON-COUTURE, SAINT-LAMBERT-DE-LAUZON, QC, G0S 2W0
(418) 889-0502   *SIC* 6712

GROUPE NEXIO INC   p 1196
2050 RUE DE BLEURY BUREAU 500, MONTREAL, QC, H3A 2J5
(514) 798-3707   *SIC* 7379

GROUPE NOKAMIC INC   p 1090
115 RUE DE LA FALAISE, DOLBEAU-MISTASSINI, QC, G8L 5A6
(418) 276-0126   *SIC* 1629

GROUPE NORDIA   p 1227
See 9195-4750 QUEBEC INC

GROUPE NORDMEC, LE   p 1159
See NORDMEC CONSTRUCTION INC

GROUPE NORMANDIN INC   p 1256
15021 BOUL HENRI-BOURASSA, QUE-BEC, QC, G1G 3Z2
(418) 626-7216   *SIC* 5812

GROUPE NORMANDIN INC   p 1275
2335 BOUL BASTIEN, QUEBEC, QC, G2B 1B3
(418) 842-9160   *SIC* 8721

GROUPE NORMANDIN INC   p 1286
83 BOUL CARTIER, RIVIERE-DU-LOUP, QC, G5R 2N1
(418) 867-1366   *SIC* 5812

GROUPE NOVATECH INC   p 1358
160 RUE DE MURANO, SAINTE-JULIE, QC, J3E 0C6
(450) 922-1045   *SIC* 3211

GROUPE NUTRI INC   p 1312
6655 RUE PICARD, SAINT-HYACINTHE, QC, J2S 1H3
(514) 745-1045   *SIC* 5144

GROUPE OCEAN INC, LE   p 1259
105 RUE ABRAHAM-MARTIN BUREAU 500, QUEBEC, QC, G1K 8N1
(418) 694-1414   *SIC* 3731

GROUPE OPTEL   p 1267
See OPTEL VISION INC

GROUPE OPTIMUM INC   p 1196
425 BOUL DE MAISONNEUVE O BUREAU 1700, MONTREAL, QC, H3A 3G5
(514) 288-2010   *SIC* 6514

GROUPE ORLEANS   p 1211
See KEOLIS CANADA INC

GROUPE P.BOLDUC   p 1292
See PLATE 2000 INC

GROUPE PAGES JAUNES   p 1396
See PAGES JAUNES SOLUTIONS NU-MERIQUES ET MEDIAS LIMITEE

GROUPE PAGES JAUNES CORP   p 864
325 MILNER AVE SUITE 4, SCARBOR-OUGH, ON, M1B 5N1
(416) 412-5000   *SIC* 2741

GROUPE PAGES JAUNES CORP   p 1396
16 PLACE DU COMMERCE, VERDUN, QC, H3E 2A5
(514) 934-2000   *SIC* 4899

GROUPE PANDA DETAIL INC   p 1059
1060 BOUL MICHELE-BOHEC BUREAU 108, BLAINVILLE, QC, J7C 5E2
(579) 637-9741   *SIC* 5661

GROUPE PAQUETTE MECANIQUE DU BA-TIMENT INC   p 1101
275 BOUL MARC-AURELE-FORTIN, FAB-REVILLE, QC, H7L 2A2
(450) 625-2297   *SIC* 1711

GROUPE PARIMA INC   p 1334
4450 RUE COUSENS, SAINT-LAURENT, QC, H4S 1X6
(514) 338-3780   *SIC* 2834

GROUPE PATRICK MORIN INC   p 1247
11850 RUE SHERBROOKE E, POINTE-AUX-TREMBLES, QC, H1B 1C4
(514) 645-1115   *SIC* 5211

GROUPE PATRICK MORIN INC   p 1282
567 BOUL PIERRE-LE GARDEUR, RE-PENTIGNY, QC, J5Z 5H1
(450) 585-8564   *SIC* 5211

GROUPE PATRICK MORIN INC   p 1350
620 BOUL DE L'INDUSTRIE, SAINT-PAUL, QC, J0K 3E0
(450) 752-4774   *SIC* 5039

GROUPE PATRICK MORIN INC   p 1361
4300 BOUL ROBERT-BOURASSA, SAINTE-ROSE, QC, H7E 0C2
(450) 781-4466   *SIC* 5211

GROUPE PATRICK MORIN INC   p 1376
369 BOUL POLIQUIN, SOREL-TRACY, QC, J3P 7W1
(450) 742-4567   *SIC* 5211

GROUPE PETROLIER OLCO ULC   p 1239
2775 AV GEORGES-V, MONTREAL-EST, QC, H1L 6J7
(514) 645-6526   *SIC* 5172

GROUPE PETROLIER OLCO, LE   p 1239
See GROUPE PETROLIER OLCO ULC

GROUPE PETROSOL   p 1139
See PETROSOL INC

GROUPE PGS 2009 INC   p 1080
1371 RUE DE LA MANIC, CHICOUTIMI, QC, G7K 1G7

(418) 696-1212   *SIC* 1711

GROUPE PHOENICIA INC   p 1334
2605 BOUL PITFIELD, SAINT-LAURENT, QC, H4S 1T2
(514) 389-6363   *SIC* 5149

GROUPE PICHE CONSTRUCTION (2005) INC   p 1061
755 BOUL DU CURE-BOIVIN BUREAU 100, BOISBRIAND, QC, J7G 2J2
(450) 433-0783   *SIC* 8742

GROUPE PICHE CONSTRUCTION INC   p 1102
99 12E RUE BUREAU 204, FERME-NEUVE, QC, J0W 1C0
(819) 587-3193   *SIC* 1542

GROUPE PIXCOM INC   p 1188
444 RUE SAINT-PAUL E, MONTREAL, QC, H2Y 3V1
(514) 931-1188   *SIC* 6712

GROUPE PLASTITEL   p 1237
See PRODUITS PLASTITEL INC, LES

GROUPE PLOMBACTION INC   p 1399
575 BOUL PIERRE-ROUX E, VICTORIAV-ILLE, QC, G6T 1S7
(819) 752-6064   *SIC* 1711

GROUPE PMLC, LE   p 1395
See 9218-4118 QUEBEC INC

GROUPE PNEUTECH-ROUSSEAU   p 1128
See PNEUTECH-ROUSSEAU GROUP INC

GROUPE POLINEX ERA   p 1328
See ALLIANCE HANGER INC

GROUPE POLY-M2 INC, LE   p 1373
4005A RUE DE LA GARLOCK, SHER-BROOKE, QC, J1L 1W9
(819) 562-2161   *SIC* 7349

GROUPE POLYALTO INC   p 1276
3825 RUE JEAN-MARCHAND, QUEBEC, QC, G2C 2J2
(418) 847-8311   *SIC* 3089

GROUPE POLYALTO INC   p 1339
4105 RUE HICKMORE, SAINT-LAURENT, QC, H4T 1S5
(514) 738-6817   *SIC* 5162

GROUPE POLYSTAR   p 1162
See EMBALLAGES POLYSTAR INC

GROUPE POMERLEAU INC   p 1305
521 6E AV N, SAINT-GEORGES, QC, G5Y 0H1
(418) 228-6688   *SIC* 6712

GROUPE POSI-PLUS INC   p 1397
10 RUE DE L'ARTISAN, VICTORIAVILLE, QC, G6P 7E4
(800) 758-5717   *SIC* 6712

GROUPE PPD INC   p 1400
325 RUE PRINCIPALE N, WATERVILLE, QC, J0B 3H0
(819) 837-2491   *SIC* 3089

GROUPE PPP   p 1279
See GROUPE PPP LTEE, LE

GROUPE PPP LTEE, LE   p 1279
1165 BOUL LEBOURGNEUF BUREAU 250, QUEBEC, QC, G2K 2C9
(418) 623-8155   *SIC* 6351

GROUPE PREMIER MEDICAL INC   p 1235
2 PLACE LAVAL BUREAU 250, MON-TREAL, QC, H7N 5N6
(450) 667-7737   *SIC* 6411

GROUPE PREMIERE MOISSON INC   p 1394
189 BOUL HARWOOD, VAUDREUIL-DORION, QC, J7V 1Y3
(450) 455-2827   *SIC* 2051

GROUPE PRO-B INC   p 1389
3535 BOUL L.-P.-NORMAND, TROIS-RIVIERES, QC, G9B 0G8
(819) 377-7218   *SIC* 1711

GROUPE PRO-FAB INC   p 1292
294 RUE LAURIER BUREAU 881, SAINT-APOLLINAIRE, QC, G0S 2E0
(418) 881-2288   *SIC* 2452

GROUPE PRO-JEAN, LE   p 1248
See PLACEMENTS JEAN BEAUDRY INC, LES

GROUPE PROCAN EQUIPEMENT INC   p 1152

11700 RUE DE L'AVENIR BUREAU 204, MIRABEL, QC, J7J 0G7

(450) 420-1119   SIC 5082

GROUPE PRODUCTION JL   p 1301

See SURETE CAVALERIE INC

GROUPE PROMEC INC   p 1289

1300 RUE SAGUENAY, ROUYN-NORANDA, QC, J9X 7C3

(819) 797-7500   SIC 1731

GROUPE PROMUTUEL   p 1046

See PRO MUTUEL L'ABITIBIENNE, SOCIETE MUTUELLE D'ASSURANCE GENERALE

GROUPE PROMUTUEL   p 1279

See GROUPE PROMUTUEL FEDERATION DE SOCIETE MUTUELLES D'ASSURANCES GENERALES

GROUPE PROMUTUEL FEDERATION DE SOCIETE MUTUELLES D'ASSURANCES GENERALES   p 1123

48 BOUL TASCHEREAU, LA PRAIRIE, QC, J5R 6C1

(450) 444-0988   SIC 6411

GROUPE PROMUTUEL FEDERATION DE SOCIETE MUTUELLES D'ASSURANCES GENERALES   p 1279

2000 BOUL LEBOURGNEUF BUREAU 400, QUEBEC, QC, G2K 0B6

(418) 840-1313   SIC 6311

GROUPE PVP   p 1151

See PRODUCTIONS VIC PELLETIER INC, LES

GROUPE QUALITAS   p 1116

See SNC-LAVALIN GEM QUEBEC INC

GROUPE QUALITAS   p 1192

See SNC-LAVALIN GEM QUEBEC INC

GROUPE R.Y. BEAUDOIN INC   p 1399

1400 BOUL PIERRE-ROUX E, VICTORIAVILLE, QC, G6T 2T7

(819) 604-1396   SIC 3531

GROUPE RADIOLOGIE LAVAL LAURENTIDES   p 1070

See IMAGIX IMAGERIE MEDICALE INC

GROUPE RAMACIERI INC   p 1326

660 RUE WRIGHT, SAINT-LAURENT, QC, H4N 1M6

(514) 332-0340   SIC 2032

GROUPE RANDSTAD   p 947

See RANDSTAD INTERIM INC

GROUPE RATTE INC   p 1260

103 3E AV, QUEBEC, QC, G1L 2V3

(418) 683-1518   SIC 6712

GROUPE REFRACO INC   p 1080

1207 RUE ANTONIO-LEMAIRE, CHICOUTIMI, QC, G7K 1J2

(418) 545-4200   SIC 3297

GROUPE RESTAURANTS IMVESCOR INC   p 1228

8150 RTE TRANSCANADIENNE BUREAU 310, MONTREAL, QC, H4S 1M5

(514) 341-5544   SIC 6794

GROUPE RESTAURANTS IMVESCOR INC   p 1279

1875 RUE BOUVIER, QUEBEC, QC, G2K 0B5

(418) 624-2525   SIC 6794

GROUPE RESTOS PLAISIRS INC, LE   p 1259

46 BOUL CHAMPLAIN, QUEBEC, QC, G1K 4H7

(418) 694-0303   SIC 5812

GROUPE RESTOS PLAISIRS INC, LE   p 1259

84 RUE DALHOUSIE BUREAU 140, QUEBEC, QC, G1K 8M5

(418) 692-4455   SIC 5812

GROUPE RESTOS PLAISIRS INC, LE   p 1269

1225 COURS DU GENERAL-DE-MONTCALM BUREAU 419, QUEBEC, QC, G1R 4W6

(418) 694-9222   SIC 5812

GROUPE RHWIZE   p 1250

See DIABSOLUT INC

GROUPE ROBERT INC   p 1065

65 RUE DE VAUDREUIL, BOUCHERVILLE, QC, J4B 1K7

(514) 521-1416   SIC 4225

GROUPE ROBERT INC   p 1065

20 BOUL MARIE-VICTORIN, BOUCHERVILLE, QC, J4B 1V5

(514) 521-1011   SIC 4213

GROUPE ROBERT INC   p 1065

20 BOUL MARIE-VICTORIN, BOUCHERVILLE, QC, J4B 1V5

(514) 521-1011   SIC 4212

GROUPE ROBERT INC   p 1288

500 RTE 112, ROUGEMONT, QC, J0L 1M0

(450) 460-1112   SIC 4213

GROUPE ROUILLIER INC   p 1046

824 AV DES FORESTIERS BUREAU 57, AMOS, QC, J9T 4L4

(819) 727-9269   SIC 6712

GROUPE ROY SANTE INC   p 1051

7351 AV JEAN-DESPREZ BUREAU 103, ANJOU, QC, H1K 5A6

(514) 493-9397   SIC 8051

GROUPE ROYAL INC   p 1379

1085 RUE DES CHEMINOTS, TERREBONNE, QC, J6W 0A1

(450) 492-5080   SIC 5039

GROUPE S S E   p 1164

5948 RUE HOCHELAGA, MONTREAL, QC, H1N 1X1

(514) 254-9492   SIC 7381

GROUPE S.M.   p 1178

See GROUPE S.M. INC, LE

GROUPE S.M. INC, LE   p 1178

433 RUE CHABANEL O 12E ETAGE, MONTREAL, QC, H2N 2J8

(514) 982-6001   SIC 8711

GROUPE S.M. INTERNATIONAL INC, LE   p 1178

433 RUE CHABANEL O BUREAU 1200, MONTREAL, QC, H2N 2J8

(514) 982-6001   SIC 8711

GROUPE S.M. TARDIF INC   p 1281

15971 BOUL RUE DE LA COLLINE, QUEBEC, QC, G3G 3A7

(418) 849-7104   SIC 6712

GROUPE S.T.C.H.   p 1076

See SERVICES EN TRANSPORT S.T.C.H. INC

GROUPE SANFACON INC, LE   p 1138

1980 5E RUE, LEVIS, QC, G6W 5M6

(418) 839-1370   SIC 6712

GROUPE SANI-TECH INC   p 1140

1450 RUE THOMAS-POWERS, LEVIS, QC, G7A 0P9

(418) 836-0616   SIC 5122

GROUPE SANTE MEDISYS INC   p 1197

600 BOUL DE MAISONNEUVE O 22E ETAGE, MONTREAL, QC, H3A 3J2

(514) 845-1211   SIC 8093

GROUPE SANTE PHYSIMED   p 1280

1300 BOUL LEBOURGNEUF BUREAU 300, QUEBEC, QC, G2K 2N1

(418) 624-2001   SIC 6411

GROUPE SANTE PHYSIMED INC   p 1339

6363 RTE TRANSCANADIENNE BUREAU 121, SAINT-LAURENT, QC, H4T 1Z9

(514) 747-8888   SIC 8011

GROUPE SANTE VALEO INC   p 1301

495 RUE BIBEAU, SAINT-EUSTACHE, QC, J7R 0B9

(450) 472-6115   SIC 8361

GROUPE SAPERGY CONSULTATION   p 1188

See GROUPE IN-RGY CONSULTATION INC

GROUPE SAVOIE INC   p 417

251 ROUTE 180, SAINT-QUENTIN, NB, E8A 2K9

(506) 235-2228   SIC 2421

GROUPE SCABRINI INC   p 1172

2700 RUE RACHEL E, MONTREAL, QC, H2H 1S7

SIC 2732

GROUPE SCIENCE EN FOLIE   p 1227

See GROUPE MAD SCIENCE INC

GROUPE SCV INC   p 1398

435 RUE GAMACHE, VICTORIAVILLE, QC, G6P 3T4

(819) 758-5756   SIC 1711

GROUPE SEB CANADA INC   p 876

36 NEWMILL GATE, SCARBOROUGH, ON, M1V 0E2

(416) 297-4131   SIC 5064

GROUPE SECOR INC   p 1191

555 BOUL RENE-LEVESQUE O BUREAU 900, MONTREAL, QC, H2Z 1B1

SIC 8732

GROUPE SEMA STRUCTURE FERROVIAIRES INC   p 1358

125 RUE DE L'EXPANSION, SAINTE-FLAVIE, QC, G0J 2L0

(418) 775-7141   SIC 4789

GROUPE SIGNALISATION   p 1374

See SIGNALISATION DE L'ESTRIE INC

GROUPE SIMONEAU INC, LE   p 1065

1541 RUE DE COULOMB, BOUCHERVILLE, QC, J4B 8C5

(450) 641-9140   SIC 3823

GROUPE SINOX INC   p 1292

16 RUE TURGEON, SAINT-ANSELME, QC, G0R 2N0

(418) 885-8276   SIC 3556

GROUPE SNC-LAVALIN INC   p 1191

455 BOUL RENE-LEVESQUE O BUREAU 202, MONTREAL, QC, H2Z 1Z3

(514) 393-1000   SIC 8711

GROUPE SOGIDES INC   p 1141

2315 RUE DE LA PROVINCE, LONGUEUIL, QC, J4G 1G4

(450) 640-1237   SIC 2731

GROUPE SOGIDES INC   p 1175

955 RUE AMHERST, MONTREAL, QC, H2L 3K4

(514) 523-1182   SIC 2731

GROUPE SOLMAX INC   p 1392

2801 RTE MARIE-VICTORIN, VARENNES, QC, J3X 1P7

(450) 929-1234   SIC 3069

GROUPE SOLUTION COLLECT SOLU INC   p 1217

560 BOUL HENRI-BOURASSA O BUREAU 202, MONTREAL, QC, H3L 1P4

(514) 331-1074   SIC 7322

GROUPE SOMAVRAC INC   p 1387

3450 BOUL GENE-H.-KRUGER, TROIS-RIVIERES, QC, G9A 4M3

(819) 379-3311   SIC 2875

GROUPE SOMITEL INC   p 1269

1026 RUE SAINT-JEAN BUREAU 400, QUEBEC, QC, G1R 1R7

(418) 692-5892   SIC 4899

GROUPE SOTECK   p 1397

See 9027-3459 QUEBEC INC

GROUPE SOUCY INC   p 1385

1060 BOUL THIBEAU, TROIS-RIVIERES, QC, G8T 7B2

(819) 376-3111   SIC 7381

GROUPE SPORTS-INTER PLUS INC, LE   p 1264

420 RUE FARADAY, QUEBEC, QC, G1N 4E5

(418) 527-0244   SIC 5091

GROUPE SPORTSCENE INC   p 1065

1180 PLACE NOBEL BUREAU 102, BOUCHERVILLE, QC, J4B 5L2

(450) 641-3011   SIC 5812

GROUPE SPORTSCENE INC   p 1205

1212 RUE DE LA GAUCHETIERE O, MONTREAL, QC, H3B 2S2

(514) 925-2255   SIC 5812

GROUPE SPORTSCENE INC   p 1227

5485 RUE DES JOCKEYS, MONTREAL, QC, H4P 2T7

(514) 731-2020   SIC 5812

GROUPE ST-HENRI INC   p 1130

8000 RUE SAINT-PATRICK, LASALLE, QC, H8N 1V1

(514) 363-0000   SIC 3715

GROUPE ST-ONGE, LE   p 1307

See EXCAVATIONS GILLES ST-ONGE INC, LES

GROUPE STAVIBEL   p 1391

See SNC-LAVALIN STAVIBEL INC

GROUPE STAVIBEL INC   p 1290

See SNC-LAVALIN STAVIBEL INC

GROUPE STERLING INTIMITE INC, LE   p 1178

9600 RUE MEILLEUR BUREAU 930, MONTREAL, QC, H2N 2E3

(514) 385-0500   SIC 5137

GROUPE STINGRAY INC   p 1211

730 RUE WELLINGTON, MONTREAL, QC, H3C 1T4

(514) 664-1244   SIC 5045

GROUPE SUTTON - ACTUEL INC   p 1143

115 RUE SAINT-CHARLES O, LONGUEUIL, QC, J4H 1C7

(450) 651-1079   SIC 6531

GROUPE SUTTON - AVANTAGE PLUS   p 1143

See GROUPE SUTTON - ACTUEL INC

GROUPE SUTTON EXCELLENCE INC   p 1237

1555 BOUL DE L'AVENIR BUREAU 100, MONTREAL, QC, H7S 2N5

(450) 662-3036   SIC 6531

GROUPE SUTTON LAURENTIDES   p 1352

See SOCIETE IMMOBILIERE M.C.M. INC. LA

GROUPE SUTTON SUR L'ILE INC   p 1396

38 PLACE DU COMMERCE BUREAU 280, VERDUN, QC, H3E 1T8

(514) 769-7010   SIC 6531

GROUPE SUTTON SYNERGIE INC   p 1114

635 RUE BEAUDRY N BUREAU 201, JOLIETTE, QC, J6E 8L7

(450) 585-0999   SIC 6531

GROUPE SUTTON-ACTION INC   p 1068

2190 BOUL LAPINIERE, BROSSARD, QC, J4W 1M2

(450) 462-4414   SIC 6531

GROUPE SUTTON-CLODEM INC   p 1132

9515 BOUL LASALLE, LASALLE, QC, H8R 2M9

(514) 364-3315   SIC 6531

GROUPE SUTTON-OUTAOUAIS   p 1104

See LFM COURTIER IMMOBILIER AGREE INC

GROUPE SWAGELOK QUEBEC   p 1337

See VANNES ET RACCORDS LAURENTIEN LTEE

GROUPE SYNERGIE XPRESS, LE   p 1060

See SYNERGIE CANADA INC

GROUPE TABAC SCANDINAVE CANADA INC   p 1144

1000 RUE DE SERIGNY BUREAU 600, LONGUEUIL, QC, J4K 5B1

(450) 677-1807   SIC 5194

GROUPE TACTIQUE   p 1189

See MARKETEL/MCCANN-ERICKSON LTEE

GROUPE TAQ   p 1277

See ATELIERS T.A.Q. INC

GROUPE TARDIF GLF INC, LE   p 1293

120 RUE DE NAPLES, SAINT-AUGUSTIN-DE-DESMAURES, QC, G3A 2Y2

(418) 878-4116   SIC 3534

GROUPE TECHNOLOGIES DESJARDINS INC   p 1230

ETAGE CP 1 SUCC PL-DESJARDINS, MONTREAL, QC, H5B 1B2

(514) 281-7000   SIC 7376

GROUPE TECNOR   p 1367

See 9356-3609 QUEBEC INC

GROUPE TEL-TECH   p 1282

See GROUPE TELTECH INC

GROUPE TELECON   p 1181

See TELECON INC

GROUPE TELTECH INC   p 1282

345D RUE MARION, REPENTIGNY, QC, J5Z 4W8
(450) 657-2000   *SIC* 4899

GROUPE THOMAS MARINE INC   p 1392
550 BOUL LIONEL-BOULET, VARENNES, QC, J3X 1P7
(877) 652-2999   *SIC* 5551

GROUPE TIRU   p 1170
See *REBUTS SOLIDES CANADIENS INC*

GROUPE TOMAPURE INC   p 1234
1790 PLACE MARTENOT, MONTREAL, QC, H7L 5B5
(450) 663-6444   *SIC* 5148

GROUPE TOP BEAUTE   p 1133
See *BEAUTE STAR BEDARD INC*

GROUPE TOUCHETTE INC   p 1179
9000 BOUL SAINT-LAURENT, MONTREAL, QC, H2N 1M7
(514) 381-1888   *SIC* 5014

GROUPE TRAFIC   p 1267
See *GROUPE TRANSTECK INC*

GROUPE TRANSCOL   p 1116
See *9007-6720 QUEBEC INC*

GROUPE TRANSPORT ST-MICHEL   p 1349
See *REMORQUAGE ST-MICHEL INC*

GROUPE TRANSTECK INC   p 1267
2797 AV WATT, QUEBEC, QC, G1P 3X3
(418) 651-9595   *SIC* 4213

GROUPE TREMBLAY   p 1291
See *SOUDURES J.M. TREMBLAY (1987) INC, LES*

GROUPE TRIUM INC   p 1179
9031 AV DU PARC, MONTREAL, QC, H2N 1Z1
(514) 355-1625   *SIC* 5199

GROUPE TRUDO   p 1082
1999 RTE MARIE-VICTORIN, CONTRE-COEUR, QC, J0L 1C0
(450) 587-2098   *SIC* 1231

GROUPE TVA INC   p 1175
1475 RUE ALEXANDRE-DESEVE, MONTREAL, QC, H2L 2V4
(514) 526-9251   *SIC* 1799

GROUPE TVA INC   p 1175
1600 BOUL DE MAISONNEUVE E, MONTREAL, QC, H2L 4P2
(514) 526-9251   *SIC* 4833

GROUPE TVA INC   p 1262
450 AV BECHARD, QUEBEC, QC, G1M 2E9
(418) 688-9330   *SIC* 4833

GROUPE TVA INC   p 1373
3330 RUE KING O, SHERBROOKE, QC, J1L 1C9
(819) 565-7777   *SIC* 4833

GROUPE TYT INC   p 1097
675 BOUL LEMIRE O, DRUMMONDVILLE, QC, J2B 8A9
(819) 474-4884   *SIC* 4213

GROUPE TYT INC   p 1141
454 RUE JEAN-NEVEU, LONGUEUIL, QC, J4G 1N8
(819) 474-4884   *SIC* 4213

GROUPE ULTIMA INC   p 1052
7100 RUE JEAN-TALON E BUREAU 210, ANJOU, QC, H1M 3S3
(514) 722-0024   *SIC* 6411

GROUPE ULTRAGEN LTEE, LE   p 1065
50 RUE DE LAUZON, BOUCHERVILLE, QC, J4B 1E6
(450) 650-0770   *SIC* 8711

GROUPE UNIGESCO INC   p 1397
3900 RUE COOL, VERDUN, QC, H4G 1B4
(514) 360-1509   *SIC* 1542

GROUPE VARITRON INC   p 1308
4811 CH DE LA SAVANE, SAINT-HUBERT, QC, J3Y 9G1
(450) 926-1778   *SIC* 5065

GROUPE VERDUN   p 1296
See *PORTES ET FENETRES VERDUN LTEE*

GROUPE VETERI MEDIC INC   p 1070
7415 BOUL TASCHEREAU, BROSSARD, QC, J4Y 1A2
(450) 656-3660   *SIC* 0742

GROUPE VEZINA & ASSOCIES LTEE, LE p 1085
999 BOUL SAINT-MARTIN O, COTE SAINT-LUC, QC, H7S 1M5
(450) 663-6880   *SIC* 6411

GROUPE VIAU INC   p 1143
550 CH DE CHAMBLY BUREAU 300, LONGUEUIL, QC, J4H 3L8
SIC 6411

GROUPE VIF INC   p 1312
4000 BOUL CASAVANT O, SAINT-HYACINTHE, QC, J2S 9E3
(450) 774-6953   *SIC* 5085

GROUPE VISION NEW LOOK INC   p 1205
1 PLACE VILLE-MARIE SUITE 3670, MONTREAL, QC, H3B 3P2
(514) 877-4119   *SIC* 5995

GROUPE VOLUMAX   p 1324
See *GROUPE CANTREX NATIONWIDE INC*

GROUPE VOLVO CANADA INC   p 1301
1000 BOUL INDUSTRIEL BUREAU 1160, SAINT-EUSTACHE, QC, J7R 5A5
(450) 472-6410   *SIC* 5012

GROUPE VOLVO CANADA INC   p 1303
155 RTE MARIE-VICTORIN, SAINT-FRANCOIS-DU-LAC, QC, J0G 1M0
(450) 568-3335   *SIC* 3711

GROUPE VOLVO CANADA INC   p 1356
35 BOUL GAGNON, SAINTE-CLAIRE, QC, G0R 2V0
(418) 883-3391   *SIC* 3711

GROUPE VOYAGE SUD   p 1269
See *GROUPE VOYAGES QUEBEC INC*

GROUPE VOYAGES QUEBEC INC   p 1269
174 GRANDE ALLEE O, QUEBEC, QC, G1R 2G9
(418) 525-4585   *SIC* 4725

GROUPE WESTCO INC   p 416
9 RUE WESTCO, SAINT-FRANCOIS-DE-MADAWASKA, NB, E7A 1A5
(506) 992-3112   *SIC* 5499

GROUPE WSP GLOBAL INC   p 1215
1600 BOUL RENE-LEVESQUE O BUREAU 16, MONTREAL, QC, H3H 1P9
(514) 340-0046   *SIC* 8741

GROUPE YELLOW INC   p 1183
5665 BOUL SAINT-LAURENT, MONTREAL, QC, H2T 1S9
(514) 273-0424   *SIC* 5661

GROUPE YVES GAGNON   p 1315
See *2732-3930 QUEBEC INC*

GROUPE YVES GAGNON MONT-TREMBLANT   p 1159
See *COUPAL & FILS INC*

GROUPE ZOOM MEDIA INC   p 1197
999 BOUL DE MAISONNEUVE O BUREAU 1000, MONTREAL, QC, H3A 3L4
(514) 842-1155   *SIC* 6712

GROUPE-CODERR   p 1045
See *CORPORATION REGIONALE DE DEVELOPPEMENT DE LA RECUPERATION ET DU RECYCLAGE REGION 02*

GROUPE-SIP   p 1067
See *SITE INTEGRATION PLUS INC*

GROUPECHO CANADA INC   p 1084
1 PLACE LAVAL BUREAU 400, COTE SAINT-LUC, QC, H7N 1A1
(514) 335-3246   *SIC* 7323

GROUPEGENIE/CEGERTEC   p 1071
See *CEGERTEC INC*

GROUPEMENT DES ASSUREURS AUTOMOBILES   p 1229
800 PLACE-VICTORIA BUREAU 2410, MONTREAL, QC, H4Z 0A2
(514) 288-1537   *SIC* 6411

GROUPEMENT DES ASSUREURS AUTOMOBILES (GAA)   p 1229
See *INSURANCE BUREAU OF CANADA*

GROUPEMENT FORESTIER DE KAMOURASKA INC   p 1291

605 289 RTE, SAINT-ALEXANDRE-DE-KAMOURASKA, QC, G0L 2G0
(418) 495-2054   *SIC* 0851

GROUPEMENT FORESTIER DE L'EST DU LAC TEMISCOUATA INC   p 1052
710 RUE DU CLOCHER, AUCLAIR, QC, G0L 1A0
(418) 899-6673   *SIC* 2411

GROUPEMENT FORESTIER DU HAUT YA-MASKA INC   p 1088
578 RUE DE LA RIVIERE, COWANSVILLE, QC, J2K 3G6
(450) 263-7120   *SIC* 0851

GROUPER EPICIER ANGUS   p 1100
See *GROUPE EPICIERS ANGUS INC*

GROUPEX INC   p 929
3 ROWANWOOD AVE, TORONTO, ON, M4W 1Y5
(416) 968-0000   *SIC* 8748

GROUPEX LIMITED   p 929
3 ROWANWOOD AVE, TORONTO, ON, M4W 1Y5
(416) 968-0000   *SIC* 8748

GROUPEX SERVICE EDM (GPX)   p 105
See *GROUPEX SYSTEMS CANADA INC*

GROUPEX SYSTEMS CANADA INC   p 105
15102 128 AVE NW, EDMONTON, AB, T5V 1A8
(780) 454-3366   *SIC* 7389

GROUPEX-SOLUTIONS   p 929
See *GROUPEX INC*

GROUPHEALTH BENEFIT SOLUTIONS   p 279
2626 CROYDON DR SUITE 200, SURREY, BC, V3Z 0S8
(604) 542-4100   *SIC* 6411

GROUPR CVC   p 1361
See *AERO MECANIQUE TURCOTTE INC*

GROVE CHRYSLER DODGE JEEP RAM   p 164
See *GRV C MOTORS LP*

GROVE MOTOR INN   p 164
See *GROUP FIVE INVESTORS LTD*

GROVE PARK HOME   p 484
See *GROVE PARK HOME FOR SENIOR CITIZENS*

GROVE PARK HOME FOR SENIOR CITIZENS   p 484
234 COOK ST SUITE 1274, BARRIE, ON, L4M 4H5
(705) 726-1003   *SIC* 8051

GROVE PONTIAC BUICK GMC LTD   p 164
HIGHWAY 16A W, SPRUCE GROVE, AB, T7X 3B2
SIC 5511

GROVE SCHOOL   p 812
See *DURHAM DISTRICT SCHOOL BOARD*

GROVES MEMORIAL COMMUNITY HOSPITAL   p 590
235 UNION ST E, FERGUS, ON, N1M 1W3
(519) 843-2010   *SIC* 8062

GROVES PARK LODGE   p 849
See *GEM HEALTH CARE GROUP LIMITED*

GROVES, WM. LIMITED   p 609
800 RENNIE ST, HAMILTON, ON, L8H 3R2
(905) 545-1117   *SIC* 1623

GROWER'S CHOICE LANDSCAPE PRODUCTS INC   p 642
1720 HURON RD, KITCHENER, ON, N2R 1R6
(519) 748-6551   *SIC* 5992

GROWERS GREENHOUSE SUPPLIES INC p 1003
3559 NORTH SERVICE RD, VINELAND STATION, ON, L0R 2E0
(905) 562-7341   *SIC* 5191

GROWERS SUPPLY COMPANY LIMITED p 220
2605 ACLAND RD, KELOWNA, BC, V1X 7J4

(250) 765-4500   *SIC* 5191

GROWING TYKES CHILD CARE   p 867
910 MARKHAM RD, SCARBOROUGH, ON, M1H 2Y2
(416) 438-4088   *SIC* 8351

GROWING TYKES LEARNING CENTRE   p 867
See *GROWING TYKES CHILD CARE*

GROWTH WORKS LTD   p 313
2600-1055 GEORGIA ST W, VANCOUVER, BC, V6E 0B6
(604) 688-9631   *SIC* 6211

GROWTHWORKS CAPITAL LTD   p 313
1055 GEORGIA ST W SUITE 2600, VANCOUVER, BC, V6E 0B6
(604) 633-1418   *SIC* 6799

GROWTHWORKS CAPITAL LTD   p 986
130 KING ST W SUITE 2200, TORONTO, ON, M5X 2A2
SIC 8741

GROWTHWORKS ENTERPRISES LTD   p 453
1801 HOLLIS ST SUITE 310, HALIFAX, NS, B3J 3N4
(902) 423-9367   *SIC* 6211

GRUB BOX   p 359
See *MORRISH HOLDINGS LTD*

GRUES J.M. FRANCOEUR INC   p 1164
6155 RUE LA FONTAINE, MONTREAL, QC, H1N 2B8
(514) 747-5700   *SIC* 7389

GRUNDFOS CANADA INC   p 797
2941 BRIGHTON RD, OAKVILLE, ON, L6H 6C9
(905) 829-9533   *SIC* 5084

GRUNTHAL LIVESTOCK AUCTION MART LIMITED   p 350
GD, GRUNTHAL, MB, R0A 0R0
(204) 434-6519   *SIC* 5154

GRUPPO CAMPARI   p 991
See *FORTY CREEK DISTILLERY LTD*

GRUVEN INC   p 878
19 NEWGALE GATE, SCARBOROUGH, ON, M1X 1B6
(416) 292-7331   *SIC* 2389

GRV C MOTORS LP   p 164
200 ST. MATTHEWS AVE, SPRUCE GROVE, AB, T7X 3A6
(780) 809-9971   *SIC* 5511

GRW TRANSPORT, DIV OF   p 753
See *GRANT'S TRANSPORT LIMITED*

GRYB   p 1399
See *GROUPE R.Y. BEAUDOIN INC*

GS   p 952
See *GLUSKIN SHEFF + ASSOCIATES INC*

GS CONSTRUCTION   p 1
See *G.S. HOLDINGS COMPANY LTD*

GS1 CANADA   p 776
1500 DON MILLS RD SUITE 800, NORTH YORK, ON, M3B 3K4
(416) 510-8039   *SIC* 8611

GSF CANADA INC   p 1236
4705 RUE LOUIS-B.-MAYER, MONTREAL, QC, H7P 6G5
(450) 686-0555   *SIC* 7349

GSH   p 436
See *GREAT SLAVE HELICOPTERS LTD*

GSI ENVIRONNEMENT INC   p 1267
4495 BOUL WILFRID-HAMEL BUREAU 100, QUEBEC, QC, G1P 2J7
(418) 872-4227   *SIC* 8748

GSI ENVIRONNEMENT INC   p 1393
100 RUE JEAN-COUTU BUREAU 101, VARENNES, QC, J3X 0E1
(418) 882-2736   *SIC* 2875

GSK   p 722
See *GLAXOSMITHKLINE INC*

GSL CHEV CITY   p 72
See *GSL CHEVROLET OLDSMOBILE CADILLAC (1986) LIMITED*

GSL CHEVROLET OLDSMOBILE CADILLAC (1986) LIMITED   p 72
1720 BOW TRAIL SW, CALGARY, AB, T3C

2E4
(403) 781-1519   *SIC* 5511
GSL FAMILY TRUST   *p* 334
780 TOPAZ AVE, VICTORIA, BC, V8T 2M1
(250) 384-3003   *SIC* 5211
GSL GROUP   *p* 313
See GSL HOLDINGS LTD
GSL HOLDINGS LTD   *p* 313
1177 W HASTINGS ST SUITE 2088, VAN-
COUVER, BC, V6E 2K3
(604) 688-8999   *SIC* 6531
GSM (CANADA) PTY LTD   *p* 1334
5900 RUE KIERAN, SAINT-LAURENT, QC,
H4S 2B5
(514) 336-6382   *SIC* 5091
GSM PROJECT   *p* 1205
See GSMPRJCT CREATION INC
GSMPRJCT CREATION INC   *p* 1205
355 RUE SAINTE-CATHERINE O BUREAU
500, MONTREAL, QC, H3B 1A5
(514) 288-4233   *SIC* 7389
GSNETWORKS   *p* 831
See 1150018 ONTARIO INC
**GSP GESTION STRATEGIQUE DE PRO-
JETS**   *p*
1276
See MAB PROFIL INC
GSS SECURITY LTD   *p* 610
1219 MAIN ST E, HAMILTON, ON, L8K 1A5
(905) 547-5552   *SIC* 7381
GTA ADANAC CUSTOM SYSTEMS INC   *p*
553
467 EDGELEY BLVD SUITE 4, CONCORD,
ON, L4K 4E9
SIC 5065
GTA GOLF   *p* 195
500 COLWYN ST SUITE 58, CAMPBELL
RIVER, BC, V9W 5J2
(250) 255-8897   *SIC* 7997
GTA GOLF & COUNTRY CLUB   *p* 973
800 BATHURST ST UNIT 1, TORONTO,
ON, M5R 3M8
(416) 762-2530   *SIC* 7997
GTA GOLF & COUNTRY CLUB   *p* 973
800 BATHURST ST UNIT 1, TORONTO,
ON, M5R 3M8
(416) 762-2531   *SIC* 7997
GTA PLUMBING LTD   *p* 717
3995 SLADEVIEW CRES UNIT 6, MISSIS-
SAUGA, ON, L5L 5Y1
(905) 569-7558   *SIC* 1711
GTA SECURITY GUARD SERVICES INC   *p*
553
150 SPINNAKER WAY UNIT 12, CON-
CORD, ON, L4K 4M1
(905) 760-0838   *SIC* 7381
GTC (MEDIA)-HEBDO COURRIER LAVAL *p*
1237
2700 AV FRANCIS-HUGHES BUREAU 200,
MONTREAL, QC, H7S 2B9
(450) 667-4360   *SIC* 5192
GTD   *p* 1230
See GROUPE TECHNOLOGIES DES-
JARDINS INC
GTL TRANSPORTATION INC   *p* 446
115 TRIDER CRES, DARTMOUTH, NS,
B3B 1V6
(902) 468-3100   *SIC* 4213
**GUARANTEE CO OF NORTH AMERICA,
(THE)**   *p* 595
36 PARKRIDGE CRES, GLOUCESTER,
ON, K1B 3E7
SIC 6411
**GUARANTEE COMPANY OF NORTH
AMERICA, THE**   *p* 771
4950 YONGE ST SUITE 1400, NORTH
YORK, ON, M2N 6K1
(416) 223-9580   *SIC* 6411
**GUARANTEE COMPANY OF NORTH
AMERICA, THE**   *p* 1035
954 DUNDAS ST, WOODSTOCK, ON, N4S
7Z9
(519) 539-9868   *SIC* 6411
GUARD RFID SOLUTIONS INC   *p* 206

766 CLIVEDEN PL UNIT 140, DELTA, BC,
V3M 6C7
(604) 998-4018   *SIC* 5065
GUARD-X INC   *p* 1049
10600 BOUL PARKWAY, ANJOU, QC, H1J
1R6
(514) 277-2127   *SIC* 5087
**GUARDIAN ALARM COMPANY OF
CANADA LTD**   *p* 1018
2885 LAUZON PKY SUITE 105, WINDSOR,
ON, N8T 3H5
(519) 258-4646   *SIC* 7382
**GUARDIAN BUILDING PRODUCTS DISTRI-
BUTION CANADA, INC**   *p*
569
300 MAIN ST SS 1, ERIN, ON, N0B 1T0
(519) 833-9645   *SIC* 5039
GUARDIAN CAPITAL GROUP LIMITED   *p*
971
199 BAY ST SUITE 3100, TORONTO, ON,
M5L 1E8
(416) 364-8341   *SIC* 6282
GUARDIAN CAPITAL LP   *p* 971
199 BAY ST SUITE 3100, TORONTO, ON,
M5L 1E8
(416) 364-8341   *SIC* 6282
GUARDIAN CHEMICALS INC   *p* 168
55202 825 HWY SUITE 155, STURGEON
COUNTY, AB, T8L 5C1
(780) 998-3711   *SIC* 2819
GUARDIAN DRUGS   *p* 412
See KENNEBECASIS DRUGS LTD
GUARDIAN DRUGS   *p* 672
See MCKESSON CORPORATION
GUARDIAN DRUGS   *p* 896
See SINCLAIR PHARMACY (1980) LTD
GUARDIAN INDUSTRIES CANADA CORP*p*
584
355 ATTWELL DR, ETOBICOKE, ON, M9W
5C2
(416) 674-6945   *SIC* 3211
GUARDIAN INDUSTRIES CANADA CORP*p*
911
10 ROUSE ST, TILLSONBURG, ON, N4G
5W8
(416) 674-6945   *SIC* 3211
**GUARDIAN INTERLOCK SERVICES, DIV
OF**   *p* 582
See ALCOHOL COUNTERMEASURE SYS-
TEMS CORP
GUARDIAN VAN LINES LIMITED   *p* 844
1051 TOY AVE, PICKERING, ON, L1W 3N9
(905) 686-0002   *SIC* 4212
GUARDIAN, DIV OF   *p* 588
See SHAWCOR LTD
GUARDIAN, THE   *p* 1039
See MEDIAS TRANSCONTINENTAL INC
GUAY BEAUTE INC   *p* 1061
585 BOUL DU CURE-BOIVIN, BOIS-
BRIAND, QC, J7G 2A8
(514) 273-9991   *SIC* 5087
GUAY BUSSIERES & ASSOCIES INC   *p*
1267
3405 BOUL WILFRID-HAMEL BUREAU
200, QUEBEC, QC, G1P 2J3
SIC 6411
GUAY INC   *p* 1049
10801 RUE COLBERT, ANJOU, QC, H1J
2G5
(514) 354-4420   *SIC* 7353
GUAY INC   *p* 1280
1160 RUE BOUVIER, QUEBEC, QC, G2K
1L9
(418) 628-8460   *SIC* 7353
GUCI   *p* 599
See GRIMSBY UTILITY CONSTRUCTION
INC
GUELPH CITY MAZDA   *p* 605
See 699215 ONTARIO LIMITED
**GUELPH COLLEGIATE & VOCATIONAL IN-
STITUTE**   *p*
604
See UPPER GRAND DISTRICT SCHOOL
BOARD, THE

GUELPH COMMUNITY HEALTH CENTRE *p*
603
176 WYNDHAM ST N SUITE 1, GUELPH,
ON, N1H 8N9
(519) 821-6638   *SIC* 8621
GUELPH FIRE DEPARTMENT   *p* 603
See GUELPH, CITY OF
GUELPH GENERAL HOSPITAL   *p* 600
115 DELHI ST, GUELPH, ON, N1E 4J4
(519) 822-5350   *SIC* 8062
**GUELPH HYDRO ELECTRIC SYSTEMS
INC**   *p* 601
395 SOUTHGATE DR, GUELPH, ON, N1G
4Y1
(519) 822-3010   *SIC* 4911
GUELPH MANUFACTURING GROUP INC *p*
603
20 MASSEY RD, GUELPH, ON, N1H 7X8
(519) 822-5401   *SIC* 3465
GUELPH MANUFACTURING GROUP INC *p*
603
39 ROYAL RD, GUELPH, ON, N1H 1G2
(519) 822-5401   *SIC* 3465
GUELPH NISSAN INFINITI INC   *p* 605
805 WOODLAWN RD W, GUELPH, ON,
N1K 1E9
(519) 822-9200   *SIC* 5511
**GUELPH PROFESSIONAL FIRE FIGHTERS
ASSOCIATION**   *p* 603
50 WYNDHAM ST S, GUELPH, ON, N1H
4E1
SIC 7389
GUELPH PUBLIC LIBRARY   *p* 603
See GUELPH, CITY OF
GUELPH SERVICES FOR THE AUTISTIC *p*
600
16 CARIBOU CRES, GUELPH, ON, N1E
1C9
(519) 823-9232   *SIC* 8699
GUELPH TOYOTA   *p* 606
See ROYAL CITY MOTORS LTD
GUELPH VOLKSWAGEN   *p* 602
See 1511905 ONTARIO INC
GUELPH, CITY OF   *p* 603
100 NORFOLK ST, GUELPH, ON, N1H 4J6
(519) 824-6220   *SIC* 8231
GUELPH, CITY OF   *p* 603
19 NORTHUMBERLAND ST, GUELPH, ON,
N1H 3A6
(519) 837-5618   *SIC* 8611
GUELPH, CITY OF   *p* 603
50 WYNDHAM ST S, GUELPH, ON, N1H
4E1
(519) 824-6590   *SIC* 7389
GUERLAIN (CANADA) LTD   *p* 1131
2515 RUE LEGER, LASALLE, QC, H8N 2V9
(514) 363-0432   *SIC* 5122
**GUERTIN COATINGS, SEALANTS AND
POLYMERS LTD**   *p* 365
50 PANET RD, WINNIPEG, MB, R2J 0R9
(204) 237-0241   *SIC* 2851
GUERTIN EQUIPMENT LTD   *p* 392
35 MELNICK RD, WINNIPEG, MB, R3X 1V5
(204) 255-0260   *SIC* 5083
GUESS? CANADA CORPORATION   *p* 1170
8275 19E AV, MONTREAL, QC, H1Z 4K2
(514) 593-4107   *SIC* 5136
GUESS? CANADA DETAIL   *p* 1170
See GUESS? CANADA CORPORATION
**GUEST-TEK INTERACTIVE ENTERTAIN-
MENT LTD**   *p*
50
777 8 AVE SW SUITE 600, CALGARY, AB,
T2P 3R5
(403) 509-1010   *SIC* 4813
GUESTLOGIX INC   *p* 980
111 PETER ST SUITE 407, TORONTO, ON,
M5V 2H1
(647) 317-1517   *SIC* 3577
GUIDELITE FINANCIAL NETWORKS LTD*p*
553
1600 STEELES AVE W SUITE 231, CON-
CORD, ON, L4K 4M2
SIC 8748

GUILBAULT LOGISTIQUE INC   *p* 1276
8000 RUE ARMAND-VIAU BUREAU 300,
QUEBEC, QC, G2C 2E2
(418) 843-5587   *SIC* 4731
GUILBEAULT, R CONSTRUCTION INC   *p*
1099
775 BOUL LEMIRE, DRUMMONDVILLE,
QC, J2C 7X5
(819) 474-6521   *SIC* 1611
GUILD ELECTRIC HOLDINGS LIMITED   *p*
871
470 MIDWEST RD, SCARBOROUGH, ON,
M1P 4Y5
(416) 288-8222   *SIC* 1731
GUILD ELECTRIC LIMITED   *p* 871
470 MIDWEST RD, SCARBOROUGH, ON,
M1P 4Y5
(416) 288-8222   *SIC* 1731
GUILD INSURANCE BROKERS INC   *p* 347
2830 VICTORIA AVE, BRANDON, MB, R7B
3X1
(204) 729-4949   *SIC* 6411
GUILDCREST BUILDING CORPORATION *p*
746
20 MILL ST, MOREWOOD, ON, K0A 2R0
(613) 448-2349   *SIC* 2452
GUILDFORD CAB (1993) LTD   *p* 276
8299 129 ST UNIT 101, SURREY, BC, V3W
0A6
(604) 585-8888   *SIC* 4121
GUILDFORD MOTORS INC   *p* 274
13820 104 AVE, SURREY, BC, V3T 1W9
(604) 584-1304   *SIC* 5511
GUILDFORD VENTURES LTD   *p* 270
15269 104 AVE, SURREY, BC, V3R 1N5
(604) 582-9288   *SIC* 7011
GUILDFORD VOLKSWAGEN   *p* 274
See GUILDFORD MOTORS INC
GUILDFORDS (2005) INC   *p* 446
25 GUILDFORD AVE, DARTMOUTH, NS,
B3B 0H5
(902) 481-7900   *SIC* 1742
GUILDLINE INSTRUMENTS LIMITED *p* 881
21 GILROY ST, SMITHS FALLS, ON, K7A
5B7
(613) 283-3000   *SIC* 3825
GUILDWOOD INN LIMITED, THE   *p* 846
1400 VENETIAN BLVD, POINT EDWARD,
ON, N7T 7W6
(519) 337-7577   *SIC* 7011
GUILDY'S   *p* 373
See VOLUNTEER ENTERPRISES OF THE
HEALTH SCIENCES CENTRE INC
GUILLEMETTE, JEAN-PAUL INC   *p* 1276
4500 RUE ARMAND-VIAU BUREAU 342,
QUEBEC, QC, G2C 2B9
(418) 872-6221   *SIC* 5251
GUILLEMETTE, MAURICE INC   *p* 1056
3635 BOUL DE PORT-ROYAL, BECAN-
COUR, QC, G9H 1Y2
(819) 233-2354   *SIC* 5191
GUILLEVIN INTERNATIONAL CIE   *p* 1344
6555 BOUL METROPOLITAIN E BUREAU
301, SAINT-LEONARD, QC, H1P 3H3
(514) 329-2100   *SIC* 5063
GUILLEVIN SANTE-SECURITE   *p* 1344
See GUILLEVIN INTERNATIONAL CIE
GUINDON ESSO   *p* 563
See GUINDON GLENOCO LIMITED
GUINDON GLENOCO LIMITED   *p* 563
1310 PITT ST, CORNWALL, ON, K6J 3T6
(613) 933-5120   *SIC* 5983
**GUINDON, REJEAN CONSTRUCTION
CORPORATION**   *p* 810
3809 ST. JOSEPH UNIT 12, ORLEANS, ON,
K1C 1T1
SIC 1521
GUINOIS & FRERES LTEE   *p* 1314
1365 RUE SAINT-REGIS, SAINT-ISIDORE-
DE-LAPRAIRIE, QC, J0L 2A0
(450) 454-3196   *SIC* 0181
GUINOIS R. G. R. INC   *p* 1357
522 4E RANG, SAINTE-CLOTILDE-DE-
CHATEAUGUAY, QC, J0L 1W0

▲ Public Company   ■ Public Company Family Member   **HQ** Headquarters   **BR** Branch   **SL** Single Location

(450) 826-3140   *SIC 0161*
GUITABEC INC *p 1053*
19420 AV CLARK-GRAHAM, BAIE-D'URFE, QC, H9X 3R8
(514) 457-7977   *SIC 3931*
GUITARD, CHARLES MERCHANDISING LTD *p 401*
1110 SMYTHE ST, FREDERICTON, NB, E3B 3H6
(506) 450-8920   *SIC 5014*
GUITARES GODIN *p 1053*
See GUITABEC INC
GULF AND FRASER FISHERMEN'S CREDIT UNION *p 181*
7375 KINGSWAY, BURNABY, BC, V3N 3B5
(604) 419-8888   *SIC 6062*
GULF AND FRASER FISHERMEN'S CREDIT UNION *p 181*
7375 KINGSWAY, BURNABY, BC, V3N 3B5
(604) 517-5100   *SIC 6062*
GULF OPERATORS LTD *p 413*
633 BAYSIDE DR, SAINT JOHN, NB, E2J 1B4
(506) 633-0116   *SIC 1629*
GULFSTREAM INC *p 533*
145 SHELDON DR, CAMBRIDGE, ON, N1R 5X5
(519) 622-0950   *SIC 5091*
GULFVIEW CONTRACTING LTD *p 877*
3751 VICTORIA PARK AVE, SCARBOROUGH, ON, M1W 3Z4
(416) 449-1340   *SIC 1521*
GULICK FOREST PRODUCTS LIMITED *p 836*
6216 PALMER RD, PALMER RAPIDS, ON, K0J 2E0
(613) 758-2369   *SIC 5031*
GUNGNIR RESOURCES INC *p 280*
1688 152 ST SUITE 404, SURREY, BC, V4A 4N2
(604) 683-0484   *SIC 1041*
GUNN METAL STAMPINGS COMPANY *606*
32 AIRPARK PL, GUELPH, ON, N1L 1B2
SIC 3429
GUNN'S BAKERY *p 371*
See GUNN'S HOMEMADE CAKES & PASTRY LTD
GUNN'S HOMEMADE CAKES & PASTRY LTD *p 371*
247 SELKIRK AVE, WINNIPEG, MB, R2W 2L5
(204) 582-2364   *SIC 5149*
GUNNAR MANUFACTURING INC *p 70*
3200 118 AVE SE, CALGARY, AB, T2Z 3X1
(403) 236-1828   *SIC 5712*
GUNNAR OFFICE FURNISHINGS *p 70*
See GUNNAR MANUFACTURING INC
GUNNEBO CANADA INC *p 503*
9 VAN DER GRAAF CRT, BRAMPTON, ON, L6T 5E5
(905) 595-4140   *SIC 5065*
GUNTER TRANSPORTATION LTD *p 1034*
445 SPRINGBANK AVE S, WOODSTOCK, ON, N0J 1E4
(519) 539-9222   *SIC 4212*
GUNTHER MELE LIMITED *p 514*
30 CRAIG ST, BRANTFORD, ON, N3R 7J1
(519) 756-4330   *SIC 2657*
GUNTHER'S BUILDING SUPPLIES LIMITED *p 72*
2100 10 AVE SW, CALGARY, AB, T3C 0K5
(403) 245-3311   *SIC 6712*
GURIT AMERICAS INC *p 1147*
555 BOUL POIRIER, MAGOG, QC, J1X 7L1
(819) 847-2182   *SIC 2899*
GURIT OUTILLAGE (AMERICAS) INC *p 1339*
7562 CH DE LA COTE-DE-LIESSE, SAINT-LAURENT, QC, H4T 1E7
(514) 522-6329   *SIC 3523*
GUS' NO FRILLS *p 864*
See 1571921 ONTARIO LIMITED

GUSGO TRANSPORT LP *p 642*
7050 MAJOR MACKENZIE DR, KLEINBURG, ON, L0J 1C0
(905) 893-9930   *SIC 4213*
GUSTAFSON'S AUTO SERVICE LTD *p 344*
122 BROADWAY AVE N, WILLIAMS LAKE, BC, V2G 2X8
(250) 392-2305   *SIC 5511*
GUSTAFSON'S AUTOMOBILE CO LTD *p 344*
122 BROADWAY AVE N, WILLIAMS LAKE, BC, V2G 2X8
(250) 392-3035   *SIC 5511*
GUSTAFSON'S KIA *p 344*
See GUSTAFSON'S AUTOMOBILE CO LTD
GUTHRIE FIANANCIAL SERVICES *p 767*
See GUTHRIE INSURANCE BROKERS LTD
GUTHRIE INSURANCE BROKERS LTD *p 767*
505 CONSUMERS RD SUITE 308, NORTH YORK, ON, M2J 4V8
(416) 487-5200   *SIC 6411*
GUTHRIE INVESTMENTS LTD *p 128*
9912 MANNING AVE, FORT MCMURRAY, AB, T9H 2B9
(780) 791-1367   *SIC 1711*
GUTHRIE MECHANICAL SERVICES LTD *p 128*
9912 MANNING AVE, FORT MCMURRAY, AB, T9H 2B9
(780) 791-1367   *SIC 1711*
GUVERNMENT NIGHT CLUB, THE *p 932*
See 1263528 ONTARIO LIMITED
GUY FRENCHY'S OF DIGBY *p 449*
See LEBLANC, GUY ENTERPRISES (1984) LIMITED
GUY HUBERT ET ASSOCIES INC *p 1143*
80 RUE SAINT-LAURENT O BUREAU 210, LONGUEUIL, QC, J4H 1L8
(579) 721-3252   *SIC 2023*
GUY J BAILEY LTD *p 421*
6 HIGHWAY 412, BAIE VERTE, NL, A0K 1B0
(709) 532-4642   *SIC 1611*
GUY LAROCHE *p 1184*
See MANUFACTURE DE LINGERIE CHATEAU INC
GUYANA GOLDFIELDS INC *p 945*
375 UNIVERSITY AV SUITE 802, TORONTO, ON, M5G 2J5
(416) 628-5936   *SIC 1041*
GUYSBOROUGH ANTIGONISH STRAIT HEALTH AUTHORITY *p 442*
138 HOSPITAL RD, CLEVELAND, NS, B0E 1J0
(902) 625-3230   *SIC 8062*
GV COLONY FARMING CO. LTD *p 134*
723042A RANGE ROAD 74, GRANDE PRAIRIE, AB, T8X 4L1
(780) 539-6513   *SIC 0139*
GVA LIGHTING, INC *p 797*
2771 BRISTOL CIR, OAKVILLE, ON, L6H 6X5
(905) 569-6044   *SIC 3646*
GVIC COMMUNICATIONS CORP *p 292*
303 5TH AVE W, VANCOUVER, BC, V5Y 1J6
(604) 638-2451   *SIC 4813*
GVN STRUCTURES INC *p 158*
1611 BROADWAY AVE E SUITE 1, REDCLIFF, AB, T0J 2P0
(403) 548-3100   *SIC 1541*
GVP HOLDIGS INC *p 305*
200 BURRARD ST SUITE 1200, VANCOUVER, BC, V6C 3L6
(604) 525-3900   *SIC 6712*
GW HONOS SECURITY *p 1210*
See CORPORATION DE SECURITE GARDA WORLD
GWAALAGAA NAAY CORPORATION *p 252*
226 HWY 16, QUEEN CHARLOTTE, BC, V0T 1S1
SIC 5541

GWENAL HOLDINGS LTD *p 235*
6900 ISLAND HWY N, NANAIMO, BC, V9V 1P6
SIC 5531
GWI TELECOM *p 722*
See GAP WIRELESS INC
GWIL INDUSTRIES INC *p 185*
5337 REGENT ST, BURNABY, BC, V5C 4H4
(604) 291-9404   *SIC 7353*
GWL REALTY ADVISORS INC *p 709*
1 CITY CENTRE DR SUITE 300, MISSISSAUGA, ON, L5B 1M2
(905) 275-6600   *SIC 6531*
GWL REALTY ADVISORS INC *p 942*
33 YONGE ST SUITE 1000, TORONTO, ON, M5E 1S9
(416) 507-2929   *SIC 6531*
GWL REALTY ADVISORS INC *p 945*
330 UNIVERSITY AVE SUITE 300, TORONTO, ON, M5G 1R7
(416) 552-5959   *SIC 6282*
GWR VISSER FARMS *p 1043*
See VISSER, GERRIT & SONS (1991) INC
GYM FABRIK INC *p 1378*
281 RUE EDWARD-ASSH, STE-CATHERINE-DE-LA-J-CARTIE, QC, G3N 1A3
(418) 875-2600   *SIC 3949*
GYM-CON LTD *p 487*
93 RAWSON AVE, BARRIE, ON, L4N 6E5
(705) 728-2222   *SIC 5039*
GYMN-EAU LAVAL *p 1234*
2465 RUE HONORE-MERCIER, MONTREAL, QC, H7L 2S9
(450) 625-2674   *SIC 8699*
GYMNASTICS MISSISSAUGA *p 705*
5600 ROSE CHERRY PL, MISSISSAUGA, ON, L4Z 4B6
(905) 270-6161   *SIC 8699*
GYPCO DISTRIBUTION *p 1048*
See DISTRIBUTIONS GYPCO (1988) INC
GYPSUM TECHNOLOGIES INC *p 529*
578 KING FOREST CRT, BURLINGTON, ON, L7P 5C1
(905) 567-2000   *SIC 3599*
GYPTECH *p 529*
See GYPSUM TECHNOLOGIES INC

H

'HORISOL', COOPERATIVE DE TRAVAILLEURS *p 1315*
18 RUE DES SOCIETAIRES, SAINT-JEAN-PORT-JOLI, QC, G0R 3G0
(418) 598-3048   *SIC 2421*
H & A FINANCIAL ADVISORS *p 1418*
2445 13TH AVE SUITE 200, REGINA, SK, S4P 0W1
(306) 584-2523   *SIC 6311*
H & B INVESTMENTS LTD *p 222*
3033 PANDOSY ST, KELOWNA, BC, V1Y 1W3
(250) 763-0819   *SIC 5411*
H & H FISHERIES LIMITED *p 449*
100 GOVERNMENT WHARF RD, EASTERN PASSAGE, NS, B3G 1M5
SIC 5146
H & I ENTERPRISES (VANKLEEK) LTD *p 1001*
21160 SERVICE RD, VANKLEEK HILL, ON, K0B 1R0
(613) 525-2120   *SIC 5541*
H & K CANADA INC *p 553*
50 MCCLEARY CRT, CONCORD, ON, L4K 3L5
(905) 695-0440   *SIC 5046*
H & M *p 553*
See H & M HENNES & MAURITZ INC
H & M *p 1205*
See H&M HENNES & MAURITZ INC
H & M HENNES & MAURITZ INC *p 553*
1 BASS PRO MILLS DR, CONCORD, ON, L4K 5W4
(905) 760-1769   *SIC 5651*

H & O CENTERLESS GRINDING COMPANY LTD *p 1010*
45 BATHURST DR, WATERLOO, ON, N2V 1N2
(519) 884-0322   *SIC 3599*
H & R (U.S.) HOLDINGS INC *p 785*
3625 DEUFFERIN ST SUITE 500, NORTH YORK, ON, M3K 1N4
(416) 635-7520   *SIC 6798*
H & R BLOCK CANADA, INC *p 50*
700 2 ST SW SUITE 2600, CALGARY, AB, T2P 2W2
(403) 254-8689   *SIC 7291*
H & R DEVELOPMENT *p 785*
See ALTONE INVESTMENTS LIMITED
H & R TRANSPORT LIMITED *p 16*
4540 54 AVE SE, CALGARY, AB, T2C 2Y8
(403) 720-8344   *SIC 4731*
H & S BUILDING SUPPLIES LIMITED *p 553*
96 MAPLECRETE RD UNIT 4 5, CONCORD, ON, L4K 2B5
(905) 738-6003   *SIC 5039*
H & S HOLDINGS INC *p 1407*
101 EAST SERVICE RD, HAGUE, SK, S0K 1X0
(306) 225-2288   *SIC 1521*
H & W FOOD COUNTRY *p 233*
82 TWELFTH ST, NANAIMO, BC, V9R 6R6
(250) 753-7545   *SIC 5411*
H & W PRODUCE *p 93*
See H & W PRODUCE CORPORATION
H & W PRODUCE CORPORATION *p 93*
12510 132 AVE NW, EDMONTON, AB, T5L 3P9
(780) 451-3700   *SIC 5431*
H A S MARKETING *p 990*
See H.A.S. NOVELTIES LIMITED
H D F INSURANCE & FINANCIAL GROUP *p 173*
5111 50 AVE, WHITECOURT, AB, T7S 1S8
(780) 778-8828   *SIC 6411*
H E ELECTRIC (SASKATOON), DIV *p 1434*
See HUMBOLDT ELECTRIC LTD
H J CAMBIE SECONDARY SCHOOL *p 253*
See BOARD OF EDUCATION SCHOOL DISTRICT #38 (RICHMOND)
H K STRATEGIES CANADA *p 929*
160 BLOOR ST E SUITE 700, TORONTO, ON, M4W 0A2
(416) 413-1218   *SIC 8743*
H R ASSOCIATES *p 577*
302 THE EAST MALL SUITE 600, ETOBICOKE, ON, M9B 6C7
(416) 237-1500   *SIC 7361*
H S F O *p 922*
See HEART AND STROKE FOUNDATION OF ONTARIO
H W JANITORIAL SUPPLIES *p 696*
See HOODEX INDUSTRIES LIMITED
H&M HENNES & MAURITZ INC *p 945*
1 DUNDAS ST W SUITE 1808, TORONTO, ON, M5G 1Z3
(416) 623-4300   *SIC 5651*
H&M HENNES & MAURITZ INC *p 1205*
1100 RUE SAINTE-CATHERINE O, MONTREAL, QC, H3B 1H4
(514) 788-4590   *SIC 5651*
H&O CYLINDRICAL PRECISION *p 1011*
See ODCO, INC
H&R DEVELOPMENTS *p 785*
3625 DUFFERIN ST SUITE 503, NORTH YORK, ON, M3K 1N4
(416) 635-7520   *SIC 1521*
H&R FINANCE TRUST *p 785*
3625 DUFFERIN ST UNIT 503, NORTH YORK, ON, M3K 1N4
(416) 635-7520   *SIC 6726*
H&R PROPERTY MANAGEMENT LTD *p 785*
3625 DUFFERIN ST SUITE 409, NORTH YORK, ON, M3K 1Z2
(416) 635-0163   *SIC 6531*
H&R REAL ESTATE INVESTMENT TRUST *p 785*
3625 DUFFERIN ST SUITE 500, NORTH

YORK, ON, M3K 1Z2
(416) 635-7520   SIC 6798
H-MART   p 553
See HANAHREUM MART INC
H-S TOOL & PARTS INC   p 260
2560 SIMPSON RD SUITE 140, RICH-
MOND, BC, V6X 2P9
(604) 273-4743   SIC 4581
H. A. VAILLANCOURT INC   p 1089
30 BOUL MARIE-VICTORIN, DELSON, QC,
J5B 1A9
(450) 632-2109   SIC 5147
**H. B. MORNINGSTAR INDUSTRIES LIM-
ITED**   p
794
335 CLAYSON RD, NORTH YORK, ON,
M9M 2H4
(416) 745-3547   SIC 5084
H. CHALUT LTEE   p 1320
2172 BOUL DU CURE-LABELLE, SAINT-
JEROME, QC, J7Y 1T3
(450) 438-4153   SIC 5087
H. COLPRON INC   p 1298
4061 GRAND RANG SAINTE-CATHERINE,
SAINT-CUTHBERT, QC, J0K 2C0
(514) 593-5144   SIC 6712
H. DAGENAIS & FILS INC   p 1352
304 RUE PRINCIPALE, SAINT-SAUVEUR,
QC, J0R 1R0
(450) 227-2649   SIC 5072
H. E. FORESTRY LTD   p 394
1990 ROUTE 380, ANDERSON ROAD, NB,
E7G 4C1
(506) 356-2310   SIC 5989
H. GREGOIRE   p 1300
See 2970-7528 QUEBEC INC
H. J. CRABBE & SONS, LTD   p 399
6   LOCKHARTS   MILL   RD,
FLORENCEVILLE-BRISTOL, NB, E7L 2R2
(506) 392-5563   SIC 5031
H. L. STAEBLER COMPANY LIMITED p 635
871 VICTORIA ST N SUITE 7B, KITCH-
ENER, ON, N2B 3S4
(519) 743-5221   SIC 6411
H. MATTEAU ET FILS (1987) INC   p 1368
1650 RUE TRUDEL, SHAWINIGAN, QC,
G9N 0A2
(819) 539-8328   SIC 5251
H. MATTEAU ET FILS (1987) INC   p 1369
891 7E AV, SHAWINIGAN, QC, G9T 2B9
(819) 538-3381   SIC 5211
H. MATTEAU ET FILS (1987) INC   p 1385
15 RUE PHILIPPE-FRANCOEUR, TROIS-
RIVIERES, QC, G8T 9L7
(819) 374-4735   SIC 5211
H. T. DRYWALL (CLG) LTD   p 23
908 53 AVE NE SUITE F, CALGARY, AB,
T2E 6N9
(403) 295-8404   SIC 1742
H. W. M. STORES LTD   p 214
900 GIBSONS WAY, GIBSONS, BC, V0N
1V7
(604) 886-2424   SIC 5411
H. WILSON INDUSTRIES (2010) LTD p 129
1045 MEMORIAL DR, FORT MCMURRAY,
AB, T9K 0K4
(780) 743-1881   SIC 1521
H.A.S. NOVELTIES LIMITED   p 990
300 GEARY AVE, TORONTO, ON, M6H 2C5
(416) 593-1101   SIC 3993
**H.B. GROUP INSURANCE MANAGEMENT
LTD**   p 731
5600 CANCROSS CRT, MISSISSAUGA,
ON, L5R 3E9
(905) 507-6156   SIC 6331
**H.B. GROUP INSURANCE MANAGEMENT
LTD**   p 731
5600 CANCROSS CRT SUITE A, MISSIS-
SAUGA, ON, L5R 3E9
(905) 507-6156   SIC 6411
H.C. VIDAL LTEE   p 1223
5700 RUE PHILIPPE-TURCOT, MON-
TREAL, QC, H4C 1V6
(514) 937-6187   SIC 7699

H.D.D. WHOLESALE DECKING   p 566
See 6648215 CANADA LTD
H.E.D. INSURANCE AND RISK SERVICESp
382
See WESTERN FINANCIAL GROUP INC
H.E.R.O. PRODUCTS GROUP   p 206
See I.C.T.C. HOLDINGS CORPORATION
H.F. NODES CONSTRUCTION LTD   p 248
5102 50 ST, POUCE COUPE, BC, V0C 2C0
(250) 786-5474   SIC 1389
H.G. CAMPBELL ENTERPRISES LTDp 681
HWY 93 S, MIDLAND, ON, L4R 5K9
(705) 526-9321   SIC 5531
H.I.S. CANADA INC   p 305
636 HORNBY ST, VANCOUVER, BC, V6C
2G2
(604) 685-3524   SIC 4724
H.J. SUTTON INDUSTRIES LIMITED p 553
8701 JANE ST UNIT C, CONCORD, ON,
L4K 2M6
(905) 660-4311   SIC 5064
H.J.R. ASPHALT LP   p 1432
1605 CHAPPELL DR, SASKATOON, SK,
S7M 3X9
(306) 975-0070   SIC 1611
H.L. BLACHFORD, LTD   p 713
2323 ROYAL WINDSOR DR, MISSIS-
SAUGA, ON, L5J 1K5
(905) 823-3200   SIC 2992
H.L.O. HEALTH SERVICES INC   p 603
341 WOOLWICH ST, GUELPH, ON, N1H
3W4
(519) 823-2784   SIC 8011
H.P. CONSTRUCTION LTD   p 175
33386 SOUTH FRASER WAY SUITE 202,
ABBOTSFORD, BC, V2S 2B5
(604) 850-1288   SIC 1771
H.R.A. INVESTMENTS LTD   p 313
1021 HASTINGS ST W UNIT 2300, VAN-
COUVER, BC, V6E 0C3
(604) 669-9562   SIC 5094
H.R.D.A. ENTERPRISES LIMITED   p 456
7071 BAYERS RD SUITE 5009, HALIFAX,
NS, B3L 2C2
(902) 454-2851   SIC 4953
H.S. PIKE HOLDINGS INC   p 564
366 BURKES RD RR 1, DEEP RIVER, ON,
K0J 1P0
(613) 584-3337   SIC 5531
H.S.T. SYNTHETICS LTD   p 739
6630 EDWARDS BLVD, MISSISSAUGA,
ON, L5T 2V6
(905) 670-3432   SIC 3089
H.W. HOLLINGER (CANADA) INC   p 1197
550 RUE SHERBROOKE O BUREAU 2070,
MONTREAL, QC, H3A 1B9
(514) 842-8421   SIC 6411
H.Y. LOUIE CO. LIMITED   p 182
2821 PRODUCTION WAY, BURNABY, BC,
V5A 3G7
(604) 421-4242   SIC 5411
H2O ADVENTURES + FITNESS CENTRE p
219
See YMCA-YWCA OF THE CENTRAL
OKANAGAN
H2O INNOVATION INC   p 1259
330 RUE DE SAINT-VALLIER E BUREAU
340, QUEBEC, QC, G1K 9C5
(418) 688-0170   SIC 3589
H2O INNOVATION USA   p 1259
See H2O INNOVATION INC
H2O PERFORMANCE PADDLES   p 876
See NMC DYNAPLAS LTD
H2O POWER LIMITED PARTNERSHIP   p
814
560 KING ST W UNIT 2, OSHAWA, ON, L1J
7J1
(905) 438-8539   SIC 4911
HA-RA PRODUCTS CANADA   p 228
See EJ ENTERPRISE
HAAKON INDUSTRIES (CANADA) LTD   p
263
11851 DYKE RD, RICHMOND, BC, V7A 4X8
(604) 273-0161   SIC 3585

HAAR, JOHN L. THEATRE   p 98
See GRANT MACEWAN UNIVERSITY
HABCO MANUFACTURING INC   p 765
501 GORDON BAKER RD, NORTH YORK,
ON, M2H 2S6
(416) 491-6008   SIC 3585
HABENDUM HOLDING LTD   p 224
365 DAVIS RD, LADYSMITH, BC, V9G 1V1
(250) 245-3212   SIC 7383
HABITAFLEX CONCEPT INC   p 1160
240 AV DES ATELIERS, MONTMAGNY, QC,
G5V 4G4
(418) 248-8886   SIC 5211
**HABITAT ENTERPRISES UNLIMITED, DIV.
OF**   p 164
See (S.P.A.N.) ST PAUL ABILITIES NET-
WORK (SOCIETY)
**HABITAT FOR HUMANITY EDMONTON SO-
CIETY**   p
83
8210 YELLOWHEAD TRAIL NW, EDMON-
TON, AB, T5B 1G5
(780) 479-3566   SIC 1521
HABITAT METIS DU NORD INC   p 1102
213 RUE HERAULT, FORT-COULONGE,
QC, J0X 1V0
(819) 683-1344   SIC 6531
HABITATIONS BORDELEAU, LES   p 1297
See CONSTRUCTION BERNARD BORDE-
LEAU INC.
HABITATIONS CONSULTANTS H.L. INC   p
1256
104 RUE SEIGNEURIALE, QUEBEC, QC,
G1E 4Y5
(418) 666-1324   SIC 1542
HABITATIONS QUALIPRO   p 1315
See 6138144 CANADA LTEE
HABITATS LAFAYETTE, LES   p 1145
See SOCIETE DE GESTION COGIR
S.E.N.C.
HACHETTE CANADA INC   p 1226
9001 BOUL DE L'ACADIE BUREAU 1002,
MONTREAL, QC, H4N 3H5
(514) 382-3034   SIC 5192
**HACHETTE DISTRIBUTION SERVICES
(CANADA) INC**   p 729
GD, MISSISSAUGA, ON, L5P 1B2
(905) 694-9696   SIC 5994
**HACHETTE DISTRIBUTION SERVICES
(CANADA) INC**   p 981
370 KING ST W SUITE 600, TORONTO,
ON, M5V 1J9
(416) 863-6400   SIC 5947
**HACHETTE DISTRIBUTION SERVICES
(CANADA) INC**   p 1049
8155 RUE LARREY, ANJOU, QC, H1J 2L5
(514) 355-3334   SIC 2721
HACIENDA NORTH FARMS INC   p 1013
2961 TALBOT TRAIL, WHEATLEY, ON, N0P
2P0
(519) 800-5062   SIC 0161
HACKMAN, RICHARD B. DRUGS LTDp 161
2020 SHERWOOD DR UNIT 600, SHER-
WOOD PARK, AB, T8A 3H9
(780) 464-9788   SIC 5912
HADRIAN MANUFACTURING INC   p 522
965 SYSCON RD, BURLINGTON, ON, L7L
5S3
(905) 333-0300   SIC 2542
HAEFELE CANADA INC   p 522
5323 JOHN LUCAS DR, BURLINGTON,
ON, L7L 6A8
(905) 336-6608   SIC 5072
HAEMONETICS CANADA LTD   p 89
10025 102A AVE NW SUITE 500, EDMON-
TON, AB, T5J 2Z2
(780) 425-6560   SIC 7371
HAFELE   p 522
See HAEFELE CANADA INC
HAGEN'S TRAVEL & CRUISES   p 270
See HAGENS TRAVEL (1957 OPERA-
TIONS) LTD
**HAGENS TRAVEL (1957 OPERATIONS)
LTD**   p 270

13606 KELLY AVE, SUMMERLAND, BC,
V0H 1Z0
(250) 494-5202   SIC 4724
HAGERSVILLE FOODLAND   p 607
See 987112 ONTARIO INC
HAGERSVILLE SECONDARY SCHOOL   p
607
See GRAND ERIE DISTRICT SCHOOL
BOARD
HAGGAR CANADA CO.   p 783
777 SUPERTEST RD, NORTH YORK, ON,
M3J 2M9
(416) 652-3777   SIC 5136
HAGO   p 1182
See SCHLAGER HOLDING LTD
**HAHN WELDING & OILFIELD SERVICES
LTD**   p 126
5205 47 ST, ELK POINT, AB, T0A 1A0
(780) 724-3323   SIC 1623
HAILEY MANAGEMENT LTD   p 336
1070 DOUGLAS ST SUITE 800, VICTORIA,
BC, V8W 2C4
(250) 388-5421   SIC 6712
HAIN-CELESTIAL CANADA, ULC   p 584
180 ATTWELL DR SUITE 410, ETOBI-
COKE, ON, M9W 6A9
(416) 849-6210   SIC 2075
HAIRCRAFTERS   p 566
See CURLCO INDUSTRIES INC
HAIRY HILL COLONY   p 135
See HAIRY HILL COLONY LTD
HAIRY HILL COLONY LTD   p 135
GD, HAIRY HILL, AB, T0B 1S0
(780) 768-3770   SIC 0191
HAIVISION NETWORK VIDEO   p 1228
See SYSTEMES HAIVISION INC
HAKIM OPTICAL FACTORY OUTLET p 867
See HAKIM OPTICAL LABORATORY LIM-
ITED
HAKIM OPTICAL LABORATORY LIMITEDp
867
3430 LAWRENCE AVE E, SCARBOR-
OUGH, ON, M1H 1A9
(416) 439-3416   SIC 5995
HALBERG DESIGN   p 1356
See INNOVATION PCM INC
HALDEX LIMITED   p 536
500 PINEBUSH RD UNIT 1, CAMBRIDGE,
ON, N1T 0A5
(519) 621-6722   SIC 5531
HALDIMAND COUNTY HYDRO INC p 532
1 GREENDALE DR SUITE 1, CALEDONIA,
ON, N3W 2J3
(905) 765-5211   SIC 4911
HALDIMAND HEALTH AND SEPTIC INSP p
880
12 GILBERTSON DR, SIMCOE, ON, N3Y
4L1
(519) 426-6170   SIC 8399
HALDIMAND MOTORS LTD   p 541
42 TALBOT ST E, CAYUGA, ON, N0A 1E0
(905) 772-3511   SIC 5521
HALDIMAND NORFOLK HEALTH UNIT   p
880
See HALDIMAND HEALTH AND SEPTIC
INSP
HALDIMAND WAR MEMORIAL HOSPITAL
p 567
206 JOHN ST SUITE 101, DUNNVILLE, ON,
N1A 2P7
(905) 774-7431   SIC 8062
**HALDIMAND-NORFOLK   COMMUNITY
CARE ACCESS CENTRE**   p 880
76 VICTORIA ST, SIMCOE, ON, N3Y 1L5
(519) 426-7400   SIC 8741
**HALDIMAND-NORFOLK COMMUNITY SE-
NIOR SUPPORT SERVICES INC**   p
881
230 VICTORIA ST, SIMCOE, ON, N3Y 4K2
(519) 426-6060   SIC 8611
HALE AND PARTNERS   p 211
See HANCO MANAGEMENT LTD
HALENDA'S FINE FOODS LTD   p 812
915 NELSON ST, OSHAWA, ON, L1H 5N7

▲ Public Company   ■ Public Company Family Member   **HQ** Headquarters   **BR** Branch   **SL** Single Location

(905) 576-6328   *SIC* 5421
HALENDA'S MEATS   *p* 812
See *HALENDA'S FINE FOODS LTD*
HALEY DODGE   *p* 283
See *WHITE ROCK CHRYSLER LTD*
HALEY DODGE SUNSHINE COAST   *p* 214
See *HORIZON EXPORTS INC*
HALEY INDUSTRIES   *p* 607
See *MAGELLAN AEROSPACE LIMITED*
HALEY INDUSTRIES DIV OF   *p* 686
See *MAGELLAN AEROSPACE LIMITED*
HALF, ROBERT CANADA INC   *p* 963
181 BAY ST SUITE 820, TORONTO, ON,
M5J 2T3
(416) 203-7656   *SIC* 7361
HALF, ROBERT CANADA INC   *p* 963
181 BAY ST SUITE 820, TORONTO, ON,
M5J 2T3
(416) 350-2010   *SIC* 7361
HALF, ROBERT INTERNATIONAL   *p* 963
181 BAY ST SUITE 820, TORONTO, ON,
M5J 2T3
(416) 365-3153   *SIC* 7361
HALFORD & VALENTINE (1991) LTD   *p* 73
11 RICHARD WAY SW, CALGARY, AB, T3E
7M8
(403) 217-1722   *SIC* 5511
HALFORD HIDE TRADING CO. LTD   *p* 83
8629 126 AVE NW, EDMONTON, AB, T5B
1G8
(780) 474-4989   *SIC* 5159
**HALIBURTON HIGHLANDS HEALTH SER-
VICES CORPORATION**   *p*
607
7199 GELERT RD RR 3, HALIBURTON,
ON, K0M 1S0
(705) 457-1392   *SIC* 8062
**HALIBURTON HIGHLANDS HEALTH SER-
VICES CORPORATION**   *p*
607
7199 GELERT RD, HALIBURTON, ON, K0M
1S0
(705) 457-1392   *SIC* 8062
HALIBURTON HOSPITAL   *p* 607
See *HALIBURTON HIGHLANDS HEALTH
SERVICES CORPORATION*
**HALIBURTON KAWARTHA PINE RIDGE
DISTRICT HEALTH UNIT**   *p* 646
108 ANGELINE ST S, LINDSAY, ON, K9V
3L5
SIC 7991
**HALIBURTON KAWARTHA PINE RIDGE
DISTRICT HEALTH UNIT**   *p* 847
200 ROSEGLEN RD, PORT HOPE, ON,
L1A 3V6
(905) 885-9100   *SIC* 8621
**HALIBURTON LUMBER & ENTERPRISES
LIMITED**   *p* 607
GD, HALIBURTON, ON, K0M 1S0
(705) 457-2510   *SIC* 5039
HALIDIMAND HILLS SPAS VILLAGE, THE   *p*
598
See *926715 ONTARIO INC*
HALIFAX CHRYSLER DODGE JEEP   *p* 458
See *2178320 CANADA LTD*
HALIFAX DEVELOPMENTS   *p* 452
See *CROMBIE DEVELOPMENTS LIMITED*
HALIFAX DEVELOPMENTS   *p* 453
2000 BARRINGTON ST SUITE 1210, HALI-
FAX, NS, B3J 3K1
(902) 429-3660   *SIC* 8741
**HALIFAX GOLF & COUNTRY CLUB, LIM-
ITED**   *p*
457
3250 JOSEPH HOWE ST, HALIFAX, NS,
B3L 4G1
(902) 443-8260   *SIC* 7997
HALIFAX GRAIN ELEVATOR LIMITED   *p* 451
951 SOUTH BLAND ST, HALIFAX, NS, B3H
4S6
(902) 421-1714   *SIC* 5153
HALIFAX HARBOUR BRIDGES   *p* 444
See *HALIFAX-DARTMOUTH BRIDGE
COMMISSION*

HALIFAX HERALD LIMITED, THE   *p* 440
311 BLUEWATER RD, BEDFORD, NS, B4B
1Z9
(902) 426-2811   *SIC* 2711
HALIFAX HERALD LIMITED, THE   *p* 457
2717 JOSEPH HOWE DR SUITE 101, HAL-
IFAX, NS, B3L 4T9
(902) 426-2811   *SIC* 2711
HALIFAX INFIRMARY   *p* 451
See *NOVA SCOTIA HEALTH AUTHORITY*
**HALIFAX INTERNATIONAL AIRPORT AU-
THORITY**   *p*
450
1 BELL BLVD FL 3, ENFIELD, NS, B2T 1K2
(902) 873-4422   *SIC* 4581
HALIFAX PORT AUTHORITY   *p* 451
1215 MARGINAL RD, HALIFAX, NS, B3H
4P8
(902) 426-8222   *SIC* 4491
HALIFAX REGIONAL MUNICIPALITY   *p* 446
200 ILSLEY AVE, DARTMOUTH, NS, B3B
1V1
(902) 490-6614   *SIC* 4111
HALIFAX REGIONAL SCHOOL BOARD   *p*
440
200 INNOVATION DR, BEDFORD, NS, B4B
0G4
(902) 832-8964   *SIC* 8211
HALIFAX REGIONAL SCHOOL BOARD   *p*
444
95 VICTORIA RD, DARTMOUTH, NS, B3A
1V2
(902) 464-2457   *SIC* 8211
HALIFAX REGIONAL SCHOOL BOARD   *p*
446
33 SPECTACLE LAKE DR, DARTMOUTH,
NS, B3B 1X7
(902) 464-2000   *SIC* 8211
HALIFAX REGIONAL SCHOOL BOARD   *p*
450
148 LOCKVIEW RD, FALL RIVER, NS, B2T
1J1
(902) 860-6000   *SIC* 8211
HALIFAX REGIONAL SCHOOL BOARD   *p*
451
1855 TROLLOPE ST, HALIFAX, NS, B3H
0A4
(902) 491-4444   *SIC* 8211
HALIFAX REGIONAL SCHOOL BOARD   *p*
458
283 THOMAS RADDALL DR, HALIFAX, NS,
B3S 1R1
(902) 457-8900   *SIC* 8211
**HALIFAX REGIONAL WATER COMMIS-
SION**   *p*
458
450 COWIE HILL RD, HALIFAX, NS, B3P
2V3
(902) 490-4840   *SIC* 4941
**HALIFAX SEED COMPANY INCORPO-
RATED**   *p*
455
5860 KANE ST, HALIFAX, NS, B3K 2B7
(902) 454-7456   *SIC* 5191
HALIFAX SHIPYARD, DIV OF   *p* 455
See *IRVING SHIPBUILDING INC*
HALIFAX STUDENT HOUSING SOCIETY   *p*
451
1094 WELLINGTON ST, HALIFAX, NS, B3H
2Z9
(902) 494-6888   *SIC* 8699
HALIFAX WATER   *p* 458
See *HALIFAX REGIONAL WATER COM-
MISSION*
HALIFAX WEST HIGHSCHOOL   *p* 458
See *HALIFAX REGIONAL SCHOOL
BOARD*
**HALIFAX-DARTMOUTH BRIDGE COMMIS-
SION**   *p*
444
125 WYSE RD, DARTMOUTH, NS, B3A 4K9
(902) 463-2800   *SIC* 4785
HALKIN TOOL LTD   *p* 272
17819 66 AVE, SURREY, BC, V3S 7X1

(604) 574-9799   *SIC* 3469
HALL FILTER SERVICE (2013) LTD, LES   *p*
239
338 ESPLANADE E, NORTH VANCOUVER,
BC, V7L 1A4
(604) 986-5366   *SIC* 5085
**HALL TRANSPORTATION GROUP LIM-
ITED**   *p*
483
552 PIPER ST, AYR, ON, N0B 1E0
(519) 632-7429   *SIC* 6712
**HALL, KEITH & SONS TRANSPORT LIM-
ITED**   *p*
520
297 BISHOPSGATE RD, BURFORD, ON,
N0E 1A0
(519) 449-2401   *SIC* 4213
HALLCON CORPORATION   *p* 995
5775 YONGE ST SUITE 1010, TORONTO,
ON, M7A 2E5
(416) 964-9191   *SIC* 4741
HALLCON CREW TRANSPORT INC   *p* 770
5775 YONGE ST SUITE 1010, NORTH
YORK, ON, M2M 4J1
(416) 964-9191   *SIC* 4111
HALLE COUTURE & ASSOCIES LTEE   *p*
1122
475 RUE SAINT-ETIENNE, LA MALBAIE,
QC, G5A 1H5
(418) 665-3978   *SIC* 6311
HALLE SERVICES ALIMENTAIRES   *p* 1268
See *VIANDES P.P. HALLE LTEE, LES*
HALLER GROUP INC   *p* 1021
1537 MCDOUGALL ST, WINDSOR, ON,
N8X 3M9
(519) 254-4635   *SIC* 6712
HALLIBURTON ENERGY SERVICES   *p* 147
See *HALLIBURTON GROUP CANADA INC*
HALLIBURTON ENERGY SERVICES   *p* 155
See *HALLIBURTON GROUP CANADA INC*
**HALLIBURTON ENERGY SERVICES DIVI-
SION**   *p*
50
See *HALLIBURTON GROUP CANADA INC*
HALLIBURTON GROUP CANADA INC   *p* 50
645 7 AVE SW SUITE 1600, CALGARY, AB,
T2P 4G8
(403) 231-9300   *SIC* 1389
HALLIBURTON GROUP CANADA INC   *p* 79
10202 70 AVE SUITE 780, CLAIRMONT,
AB, T8X 5A7
(780) 513-8888   *SIC* 1389
HALLIBURTON GROUP CANADA INC   *p*
147
2175 BRIER PARK PL NW, MEDICINE HAT,
AB, T1C 1S7
(403) 527-8895   *SIC* 1389
HALLIBURTON GROUP CANADA INC   *p*
148
1400 5 ST, NISKU, AB, T9E 7R6
(800) 335-6333   *SIC* 1389
HALLIBURTON GROUP CANADA INC   *p*
155
8145 EDGAR INDUSTRIAL CLOSE, RED
DEER, AB, T4P 3R4
(800) 335-6333   *SIC* 1389
HALLMARK   *p* 751
See *DAVIS AGENCY OF OTTAWA LIMITED*
HALLMARK   *p* 762
See *ABBEY CARDS & GIFTS LIMITED,
THE*
HALLMARK   *p* 1063
See *BEAUDEV GESTIONS INC*
HALLMARK CARD SHOP   *p* 359
See *2982651 MANITOBA LIMITED*
HALLMARK CARDS   *p* 480
See *COUTTS, WILLIAM E. COMPANY, LIM-
ITED*
HALLMARK FORD SALES LIMITED   *p* 270
10025 152 ST, SURREY, BC, V3R 4G6
(604) 584-1222   *SIC* 5511
**HALLMARK HOUSEKEEPING SERVICES
INC**   *p* 584
34 RACINE RD, ETOBICOKE, ON, M9W

2Z3
(416) 748-0330   *SIC* 7349
HALLMARK POULTRY PROCESSORS LTD   *p* 285
1756 PANDORA ST, VANCOUVER, BC, V5L
1M1
(604) 254-9885   *SIC* 2015
**HALLMARK TECHNICAL SERVICES DIV
OF**   *p* 50
See *HALLMARK TUBULARS LTD*
HALLMARK TOYOTA   *p* 807
See *1443237 ONTARIO INC*
HALLMARK TUBULARS LTD   *p* 50
308 4 AVE SW SUITE 400, CALGARY, AB,
T2P 0H7
(403) 266-3807   *SIC* 5051
HALLTECH INC   *p* 866
465 CORONATION DR, SCARBOROUGH,
ON, M1E 0E6
(416) 284-6111   *SIC* 2891
HALO METRICS INC   *p* 258
21320 GORDON WAY UNIT 230, RICH-
MOND, BC, V6W 1J8
(604) 273-4456   *SIC* 5065
HALO PHARMACEUTICAL CANADA INC   *p*
1152
17800 RUE LAPOINTE, MIRABEL, QC, J7J
0W8
(450) 433-7673   *SIC* 2834
HALO SAWMILL LIMITED PARTNERSHIP   *p*
244
17700 FRASER DYKE RD, PITT MEAD-
OWS, BC, V3Y 0A7
(604) 465-0682   *SIC* 2421
HALO SECURITY INC   *p* 920
1574 QUEEN ST E SUITE 1, TORONTO,
ON, M4L 1G1
(416) 360-1902   *SIC* 7381
**HALOW, B. J. & SON CONSTRUCTORS
LTD**   *p* 857
22 WING RD, ROSSLYN, ON, P7K 0L2
(807) 939-2533   *SIC* 5032
HALPENNY INSURANCE BROKERS LTD   *p*
829
1550 LAPERRIERE AVE SUITE 100, OT-
TAWA, ON, K1Z 7T2
(613) 722-7626   *SIC* 6411
HALSE-MARTIN CONSTRUCTION CO. LTD   *p* 241
1636 MCGUIRE AVE, NORTH VANCOU-
VER, BC, V7P 3B1
(604) 980-4811   *SIC* 1542
HALSTEEL   *p* 257
See *TREE ISLAND STEEL LTD*
HALSTON BRIDGE ESSO   *p* 218
See *327989 BC LTD*
HALTE 174   *p* 1403
See *9081-9012 QUEBEC INC*
HALTE DU BOIS INC   *p* 1134
250 AUT FELIX-LECLERC, LAVALTRIE,
QC, J5T 3K4
SIC 5541
HALTERM LIMITED   *p* 451
577 MARGINAL RD, HALIFAX, NS, B3H
4P6
(902) 421-1778   *SIC* 4491
**HALTON ALARM RESPONSE & PROTEC-
TION LTD**   *p*
803
760 PACIFIC RD UNIT 21, OAKVILLE, ON,
L6L 6M5
(905) 827-6655   *SIC* 7382
**HALTON CATHOLIC DISTRICT SCHOOL
BOARD**   *p* 526
2333 HEADON FOREST DR, BURLING-
TON, ON, L7M 3X6
(905) 335-1544   *SIC* 8211
**HALTON CATHOLIC DISTRICT SCHOOL
BOARD**   *p* 530
802 DRURY LANE, BURLINGTON, ON, L7R
2Y2
(905) 632-6300   *SIC* 8211
**HALTON CATHOLIC DISTRICT SCHOOL
BOARD**   *p* 593

161 GUELPH ST, GEORGETOWN, ON,
L7G 4A1
(905) 702-8838   *SIC* 8211
**HALTON CATHOLIC DISTRICT SCHOOL
BOARD**   *p* 593
70 GUELPH ST, GEORGETOWN, ON, L7G
3Z5
(905) 877-6966   *SIC* 8211
**HALTON CATHOLIC DISTRICT SCHOOL
BOARD**   *p* 683
1120 MAIN ST E, MILTON, ON, L9T 6H7
(905) 875-0124   *SIC* 8211
**HALTON CATHOLIC DISTRICT SCHOOL
BOARD**   *p* 802
124 DORVAL DR, OAKVILLE, ON, L6K 2W1
(905) 842-9494   *SIC* 8211
HALTON DISTRICT SCHOOL BOARD *p* 473
69 ACTON BLVD, ACTON, ON, L7J 2H4
(519) 853-3800   *SIC* 8211
HALTON DISTRICT SCHOOL BOARD *p* 522
4181 NEW ST, BURLINGTON, ON, L7L 1T3
(905) 637-3825   *SIC* 8211
HALTON DISTRICT SCHOOL BOARD *p* 522
5151 NEW ST, BURLINGTON, ON, L7L 1V3
(905) 632-5151   *SIC* 8211
HALTON DISTRICT SCHOOL BOARD *p* 526
3290 STEEPLECHASE DR, BURLINGTON,
ON, L7M 0W1
(905) 332-4206   *SIC* 8211
HALTON DISTRICT SCHOOL BOARD *p* 526
1433 HEADON RD, BURLINGTON, ON,
L7M 1V7
(905) 335-0961   *SIC* 8211
HALTON DISTRICT SCHOOL BOARD *p* 529
2050 GUELPH LINE, BURLINGTON, ON,
L7P 5A8
(905) 335-3663   *SIC* 8211
HALTON DISTRICT SCHOOL BOARD *p* 529
2399 MOUNTAINSIDE DR, BURLINGTON,
ON, L7P 1C6
(905) 335-5605   *SIC* 8211
HALTON DISTRICT SCHOOL BOARD *p* 529
2425 UPPER MIDDLE RD, BURLINGTON,
ON, L7P 3N9
(905) 335-5588   *SIC* 8211
HALTON DISTRICT SCHOOL BOARD *p* 593
170 EATON ST, GEORGETOWN, ON, L7G
5V6
(905) 877-0151   *SIC* 8211
HALTON DISTRICT SCHOOL BOARD *p* 682
1110 FARMSTEAD DR, MILTON, ON, L9E
0B5
(905) 864-9641   *SIC* 8211
HALTON DISTRICT SCHOOL BOARD *p* 683
1151 FERGUSON DR, MILTON, ON, L9T
7V8
(905) 878-0575   *SIC* 8211
HALTON DISTRICT SCHOOL BOARD *p* 683
396 WILLIAMS AVE, MILTON, ON, L9T 2G4
(905) 878-2839   *SIC* 8211
HALTON DISTRICT SCHOOL BOARD *p* 683
625 SAUVE ST, MILTON, ON, L9T 8M4
(905) 693-0712   *SIC* 8211
HALTON DISTRICT SCHOOL BOARD *p* 683
650 YATES DR, MILTON, ON, L9T 7P6
(905) 878-2255   *SIC* 8211
HALTON DISTRICT SCHOOL BOARD *p* 683
820 FARMSTEAD DR, MILTON, ON, L9T
8J6
(905) 878-2076   *SIC* 8211
HALTON DISTRICT SCHOOL BOARD *p* 797
1330 MONTCLAIR DR, OAKVILLE, ON,
L6H 1Z5
(905) 845-5200   *SIC* 8211
HALTON DISTRICT SCHOOL BOARD *p* 797
1123 GLENASHTON DR, OAKVILLE, ON,
L6H 5M1
(905) 845-0012   *SIC* 8211
HALTON DISTRICT SCHOOL BOARD *p* 800
1460 DEVON RD, OAKVILLE, ON, L6J 3L6
(905) 845-2875   *SIC* 8211
HALTON DISTRICT SCHOOL BOARD *p* 803
1160 REBECCA ST, OAKVILLE, ON, L6L
1Y9

(905) 827-1158   *SIC* 8211
HALTON DISTRICT SCHOOL BOARD *p* 805
2820 WESTOAK TRAILS BLVD, OAKVILLE,
ON, L6M 4W2
(905) 847-6875   *SIC* 8211
HALTON DISTRICT SCHOOL BOARD *p* 805
2561 VALLEYRIDGE DR, OAKVILLE, ON,
L6M 5H4
(905) 469-1138   *SIC* 8211
HALTON DISTRICT SCHOOL BOARD *p* 805
2071 FOURTH LINE, OAKVILLE, ON, L6M
3K1
(905) 469-6119   *SIC* 8211
HALTON DISTRICT SCHOOL BOARD *p* 805
1455 GLEN ABBEY GATE, OAKVILLE, ON,
L6M 2G5
(905) 827-4101   *SIC* 8211
HALTON FORMING   *p* 683
See HALTON FORMING (1992) LTD
HALTON FORMING (1992) LTD   *p* 683
593 MAIN ST E, MILTON, ON, L9T 3J2
(905) 693-4889   *SIC* 1771
**HALTON HEALTHCARE SERVICES COR-
PORATION**   *p*
806
3001 HOSPITAL GATE, OAKVILLE, ON,
L6M 0L8
(905) 845-2571   *SIC* 8062
HALTON HILLS HYDRO INC   *p* 473
43 ALICE ST, ACTON, ON, L7J 2A9
(519) 853-3700   *SIC* 4911
HALTON HONDA   *p* 520
See 805658 ONTARIO INC
HALTON HONDA   *p* 529
See 226138 ONTARIO INC
**HALTON INDOOR CLIMATE SYSTEMS,
LTD**   *p* 695
1021 BREVIK PL, MISSISSAUGA, ON, L4W
3R7
(905) 624-0301   *SIC* 3564
HALTON INVESTMENTS INC   *p* 603
166 WOOLWICH ST, GUELPH, ON, N1H
3V3
(519) 763-8024   *SIC* 6719
HALTON RECYCLING LTD   *p* 381
1029 HENRY AVE, WINNIPEG, MB, R3E
1V6
(204) 772-0770   *SIC* 4953
HALTON RECYCLING LTD   *p* 526
1122 PIONEER RD SUITE 1, BURLING-
TON, ON, L7M 1K4
(905) 336-9084   *SIC* 4953
HALTON'S CHILDREN'S AID SOCIETY   *p*
521
*See CHILDREN'S AID SOCIETY OF THE
REGIONAL MUNICIPALITY OF HALTON*
HAMAN, B. & A. LIMITED   *p* 1011
36 MISSION RD, WAWA, ON, P0S 1K0
(705) 856-2555   *SIC* 5411
HAMBLET'S ROOFING & SIDING INC *p* 760
7130 KINSMEN CRT, NIAGARA FALLS, ON,
L2H 0Y5
(905) 988-6263   *SIC* 1761
HAMBLET'S ROOFING SIDING WINDOWS
p 760
See HAMBLET'S ROOFING & SIDING INC
**HAMBLIN, WATSA INVESTMENT COUN-
SEL LTD**   *p*
963
95 WELLINGTON ST W SUITE 802,
TORONTO, ON, M5J 2N7
(416) 366-9544   *SIC* 6282
HAMBURGSUD   *p* 303
See COLUMBUS LINE CANADA INC
HAMDANI TEXTILES LTD   *p* 885
55 CATHERINE ST, ST CATHARINES, ON,
L2R 5E9
(905) 682-6666   *SIC* 5131
HAMEL AUTO DIRECT   *p* 1300
See GESTION MAHEL INC
HAMEL AUTOS DE BLAINVILLE INC   *p*
1059
620 BOUL DE LA SEIGNEURIE O BUREAU
517, BLAINVILLE, QC, J7C 5T7

(450) 437-5050   *SIC* 5521
HAMEL AUTOS DE MIRABEL INC   *p* 1152
10000 RUE DU PLEIN-AIR, MIRABEL, QC,
J7J 1S5
(450) 435-1313   *SIC* 5511
HAMEL BMW   *p* 1059
See HAMEL AUTOS DE BLAINVILLE INC
HAMEL CHEVROLET BUICK GMC LTEE *p*
1345
9455 BOUL LACORDAIRE, SAINT-
LEONARD, QC, H1R 3E8
(514) 327-3540   *SIC* 5511
HAMEL CONSTRUCTION INC   *p* 1299
2106 RTE PRINCIPALE, SAINT-EDOUARD-
DE-LOTBINIERE, QC, G0S 1Y0
(418) 796-2074   *SIC* 8711
HAMEL HONDA   *p* 1300
*See AUTOS JEAN-FRANCOIS HAMEL
LTEE*
HAMEL HYUNDAI INC   *p* 1300
130 RUE DUBOIS, SAINT-EUSTACHE, QC,
J7P 4W9
(450) 974-0440   *SIC* 5511
HAMEL INC   *p* 1138
436 AV TANIATA, LEVIS, QC, G6W 5M6
(418) 839-4193   *SIC* 2038
HAMEL, PLACEMENTS GAETAN INC, LES
p 1119
6029 BOUL WILFRID-HAMEL,
L'ANCIENNE-LORETTE, QC, G2E 2H3
(418) 871-6010   *SIC* 0181
HAMEL-CRT S.E.N.C.   *p* 1299
2106 RTE PRINCIPALE, SAINT-EDOUARD-
DE-LOTBINIERE, QC, G0S 1Y0
(418) 796-2074   *SIC* 1611
HAMER TREE SERVICES LTD   *p* 81
GD, DE WINTON, AB, T0L 0X0
(403) 938-6245   *SIC* 5992
HAMILL CREEK TIMBER HOMES INC *p* 232
13440 HWY 31, MEADOW CREEK, BC,
V0G 1N0
(250) 366-4320   *SIC* 1522
HAMILL CREEK TIMBERWRIGHTS INC *p*
232
13440 HWY 31, MEADOW CREEK, BC,
V0G 1N0
(250) 366-4320   *SIC* 6712
HAMILTON & BOURASSA (1988) ENR *p*
1052
See 2630-6241 QUEBEC INC
HAMILTON AND PARTNERS   *p* 51
734 7 AVE SW SUITE 1100, CALGARY, AB,
T2P 3P8
(403) 262-2080   *SIC* 6311
HAMILTON ARTS & CRAFTS   *p* 608
303 HIGHRIDGE AVE, HAMILTON, ON, L8E
3W1
(905) 578-0750   *SIC* 5131
**HAMILTON BEACH BRANDS CANADA,
INC**   *p* 670
7300 WARDEN AVE SUITE 201,
MARKHAM, ON, L3R 9Z6
(905) 513-6222   *SIC* 5064
HAMILTON BUILDERS' SUPPLY INC *p* 615
164 LIMERIDGE RD E, HAMILTON, ON,
L9A 2S3
(905) 388-2352   *SIC* 5211
**HAMILTON COMMUNITY CARE ACCESS
CENTRE**   *p* 616
310 LIMERIDGE RD W, HAMILTON, ON,
L9C 2V2
(905) 523-8600   *SIC* 7363
HAMILTON CONSTRUCTION LTD   *p* 546
7645 POPLAR, COLLINGWOOD, ON, L9Y
3Y9
(705) 445-3220   *SIC* 1794
**HAMILTON EAST KIWANIS BOYS & GIRLS
CLUB INCORPORATED**   *p* 609
45 ELLIS AVE, HAMILTON, ON, L8H 4L8
(905) 543-9994   *SIC* 7997
HAMILTON ELLWOOD BUS LINES   *p* 643
*See HAMILTON, ELLWOOD ENTER-
PRISES LTD*
HAMILTON ENTERTAINMENT AND CON-

VENTION FACILITIES INC, THE   *p*
612
1 SUMMERS LN, HAMILTON, ON, L8P 4Y2
(905) 546-3000   *SIC* 7389
**HAMILTON HEALTH SCIENCES CORPO-
RATION**   *p*
612
100 KING ST W SUITE 2300, HAMILTON,
ON, L8P 1A2
(905) 521-2100   *SIC* 8062
**HAMILTON HEALTH SCIENCES CORPO-
RATION**   *p*
612
1200 MAIN ST W RM 2, HAMILTON, ON,
L8N 3Z5
(905) 521-2100   *SIC* 8699
**HAMILTON HEALTH SCIENCES CORPO-
RATION**   *p*
614
699 CONCESSION ST, HAMILTON, ON,
L8V 5C2
(905) 387-9495   *SIC* 8093
**HAMILTON HEALTH SCIENCES CORPO-
RATION**   *p*
614
711 CONCESSION ST SUITE 201, HAMIL-
TON, ON, L8V 1C3
(905) 389-4411   *SIC* 8062
**HAMILTON HEALTH SCIENCES FOUNDA-
TION**   *p*
613
40 WELLINGTON ST N SUITE 203, HAMIL-
TON, ON, L8R 1M8
(905) 522-3863   *SIC* 7389
**HAMILTON HORNETS RUGBY FOOTBALL
CLUB INC**   *p* 616
1300 GARTH ST, HAMILTON, ON, L9C 4L7
(905) 575-3133   *SIC* 7941
**HAMILTON INTERNATIONAL AIRPORT
LIMITED**   *p* 747
9300 AIRPORT RD SUITE 2206, MOUNT
HOPE, ON, L0R 1W0
(905) 679-1999   *SIC* 4581
HAMILTON JEWISH HOME FOR THE AGED
p 614
70 MACKLIN ST N, HAMILTON, ON, L8S
3S1
(905) 528-5377   *SIC* 8361
HAMILTON KENT INC   *p* 997
77 CARLINGVIEW DR, TORONTO, ON,
M9W 5E6
(416) 675-9873   *SIC* 3053
HAMILTON LINGERIE (1978) LTD   *p* 1170
3565 RUE JARRY E BUREAU 600, MON-
TREAL, QC, H1Z 4K6
(514) 721-2151   *SIC* 2341
HAMILTON METALS CANADA, LLC   *p* 122
3215 76 AVE NW, EDMONTON, AB, T6P
1T4
(587) 881-3921   *SIC* 5051
**HAMILTON NIAGARA HALDIMAND BRANT
COMMUNITY CARE ACCESS CENTRE**   *p*
530
440 ELIZABETH ST, BURLINGTON, ON,
L7R 2M1
(905) 639-5228   *SIC* 8059
**HAMILTON NIAGARA HALDIMAND-
BRANT CCAC**   *p*
880
*See HALDIMAND-NORFOLK COMMUNITY
CARE ACCESS CENTRE*
HAMILTON PUBLIC LIBRARY BOARD, THE
p 614
55 YORK BLVD, HAMILTON, ON, L8R 3K1
(905) 546-3200   *SIC* 8231
**HAMILTON REGION CONSERVATION AU-
THORITY**   *p*
608
585 VAN WAGNERS BEACH RD, HAMIL-
TON, ON, L8E 3L8
(905) 561-2292   *SIC* 7996
HAMILTON SPECTATOR, THE   *p* 612
See METROLAND MEDIA GROUP LTD
HAMILTON STORES LIMITED   *p* 424

445 HAMILTON RIVER RD, HAPPY VALLEY-GOOSE BAY, NL, A0P 1S0
(709) 896-5451 *SIC* 5399

HAMILTON STREET RAILWAY COMPANY, THE *p* 747
2200 UPPER JAMES ST, MOUNT HOPE, ON, L0R 1W0
(905) 528-4200 *SIC* 4111

HAMILTON TECH DRIVE INC *p* 616
1030 UPPER JAMES ST SUITE 308, HAMILTON, ON, L9C 6X6
(888) 723-3183 *SIC* 6289

HAMILTON TOWNSHIP MUTUAL INSURANCE COMPANY *p* 545
1185 ELGIN ST W, COBOURG, ON, K9A 4K5
(905) 372-0186 *SIC* 6411

HAMILTON UTILITIES CORPORATION *p* 614
55 JOHN ST N, HAMILTON, ON, L8R 3M8
(905) 317-4595 *SIC* 4911

HAMILTON VOLKSWAGEN AUDI *p* 616
See *1145678 ONTARIO LIMITED*

HAMILTON VOLVO *p* 616
See *MAR-HAM AUTOMOTIVE INC*

HAMILTON WARD AND CATHERS INSURANCE SERVICE LIMITED *p* 482
75 TALBOT ST E, AYLMER, ON, N5H 1H3
(519) 773-8471 *SIC* 6411

HAMILTON YOUNG WOMEN'S CHRISTIAN ASSOCIATION, THE *p* 613
75 MACNAB ST S, HAMILTON, ON, L8P 3C1
(905) 522-9922 *SIC* 8641

HAMILTON'S IGA *p* 152
See *PONOKA FOODS LTD*

HAMILTON, ELLWOOD ENTERPRISES LTD *p* 643
1325 OLD YOUNG'S POINT RD, LAKEFIELD, ON, K0L 2H0
(705) 652-6090 *SIC* 4151

HAMILTON, T & SON ROOFING INC *p* 864
20 THORNMOUNT DR, SCARBOROUGH, ON, M1B 3J4
(416) 755-5522 *SIC* 1761

HAMILTON-WENTWORTH CATHOLIC CHILD CARE CENTRES INC *p* 609
785 BRITANNIA AVE, HAMILTON, ON, L8H 2B6
(905) 523-2349 *SIC* 8699

HAMILTON-WENTWORTH CATHOLIC SCHOOL BOARD *p* 493
200 WINDWOOD DR, BINBROOK, ON, L0R 1C0
(905) 523-2316 *SIC* 8211

HAMILTON-WENTWORTH CATHOLIC SCHOOL BOARD *p* 614
200 WHITNEY AVE, HAMILTON, ON, L8S 2G7
(905) 528-0214 *SIC* 8211

HAMILTON-WENTWORTH CATHOLIC SCHOOL BOARD *p* 614
90 MULBERRY ST, HAMILTON, ON, L8R 2C8
(905) 525-2930 *SIC* 8211

HAMILTON-WENTWORTH CATHOLIC SCHOOL BOARD *p* 614
90 MULBERRY ST, HAMILTON, ON, L8R 2C8
SIC 8211

HAMILTON-WENTWORTH CATHOLIC SCHOOL BOARD *p* 615
200 ACADIA DR, HAMILTON, ON, L8W 1B8
(905) 388-7020 *SIC* 8211

HAMILTON-WENTWORTH CATHOLIC SCHOOL BOARD *p* 615
150 EAST 5TH ST, HAMILTON, ON, L9A 2Z8
(905) 575-5202 *SIC* 8211

HAMILTON-WENTWORTH CATHOLIC SCHOOL BOARD *p* 616
1045 UPPER PARADISE RD, HAMILTON,

ON, L9B 2N4
(905) 388-1178 *SIC* 8211

HAMILTON-WENTWORTH CATHOLIC SCHOOL BOARD *p* 617
1824 RYMAL RD, HANNON, ON, L0R 1P0
(905) 573-2151 *SIC* 8211

HAMILTON-WENTWORTH CATHOLIC SCHOOL BOARD *p* 894
127 GRAY RD, STONEY CREEK, ON, L8G 3V3
(905) 523-2314 *SIC* 8211

HAMILTON-WENTWORTH DISTRICT SCHOOL BOARD, THE *p* 477
374 JERSEYVILLE RD W, ANCASTER, ON, L9G 3K8
(905) 648-4468 *SIC* 8211

HAMILTON-WENTWORTH DISTRICT SCHOOL BOARD, THE *p* 566
310 GOVERNORS RD, DUNDAS, ON, L9H 5P8
(905) 628-2203 *SIC* 8211

HAMILTON-WENTWORTH DISTRICT SCHOOL BOARD, THE *p* 614
130 YORK BLVD, HAMILTON, ON, L8R 1Y5
(905) 528-8363 *SIC* 8211

HAMILTON-WENTWORTH DISTRICT SCHOOL BOARD, THE *p* 614
75 PALMER RD, HAMILTON, ON, L8T 3G1
(905) 389-2234 *SIC* 8211

HAMILTON-WENTWORTH DISTRICT SCHOOL BOARD, THE *p* 614
700 MAIN ST W, HAMILTON, ON, L8S 1A5
(905) 522-1387 *SIC* 8211

HAMILTON-WENTWORTH DISTRICT SCHOOL BOARD, THE *p* 616
465 EAST 16TH ST, HAMILTON, ON, L9A 4K6
(905) 318-1291 *SIC* 8211

HAMILTON-WENTWORTH DISTRICT SCHOOL BOARD, THE *p* 616
39 MONTCALM DR, HAMILTON, ON, L9C 4B1
(905) 385-5395 *SIC* 8211

HAMILTON-WENTWORTH DISTRICT SCHOOL BOARD, THE *p* 616
20 EDUCATION CRT, HAMILTON, ON, L9A 0B9
(905) 527-5092 *SIC* 8211

HAMILTON-WENTWORTH DISTRICT SCHOOL BOARD, THE *p* 616
145 MAGNOLIA DR, HAMILTON, ON, L9C 5P4
(905) 383-3337 *SIC* 8211

HAMILTON-WENTWORTH DISTRICT SCHOOL BOARD, THE *p* 892
200 DEWITT RD, STONEY CREEK, ON, L8E 4M5
(905) 573-3550 *SIC* 8211

HAMILTON-WENTWORTH DISTRICT SCHOOL BOARD, THE *p* 894
108 HIGHLAND RD W, STONEY CREEK, ON, L8J 2T2
(905) 573-3000 *SIC* 8211

HAMILTON-WENTWORTH DISTRICT SCHOOL BOARD, THE *p* 1005
215 PARKSIDE DR, WATERDOWN, ON, L8B 1B9
(905) 689-6692 *SIC* 8211

HAMLET OF RANKIN *p* 472
GD, RANKIN INLET, NU, X0C 0G0
(867) 645-2895 *SIC* 8611

HAMLETS AT PENTICTON *p* 243
See *HAMLETS AT PENTICTON RESIDENCE INC, THE*

HAMLETS AT PENTICTON RESIDENCE INC, THE *p* 243
103 DUNCAN AVE W, PENTICTON, BC, V2A 2Y3
(250) 490-8503 *SIC* 8059

HAMLETS AT WESTSYDE, THE *p* 216
See *OSPREY CARE INC*

HAMM CONSTRUCTION LTD *p* 1427
126 ENGLISH CRES, SASKATOON, SK, S7K 8A5

(306) 931-6626 *SIC* 1623

HAMM HOLDINGS LTD *p* 1408
130 STEWART CRES, KINDERSLEY, SK, S0L 1S1
(306) 463-7112 *SIC* 6712

HAMMARSKJOLD HIGH SCHOOL *p* 908
See *LAKEHEAD DISTRICT SCHOOL BOARD*

HAMMERHEAD RESOURCES INC *p* 51
525 8 AVE SW SUITE 2700, CALGARY, AB, T2P 1G1
(403) 930-0560 *SIC* 1381

HAMMILL *p* 743
See *UNISYNC GROUP LIMITED*

HAMMOND MANUFACTURING COMPANY LIMITED *p* 603
394 EDINBURGH RD N, GUELPH, ON, N1H 1E5
(519) 822-2960 *SIC* 3469

HAMMOND MUSEUM OF RADIO *p* 1004
15 INDUSTRIAL RD, WALKERTON, ON, N0G 2V0
(519) 881-3552 *SIC* 3612

HAMMOND POWER SOLUTIONS INC *p* 601
595 SOUTHGATE DR, GUELPH, ON, N1G 3W6
(519) 822-2441 *SIC* 3612

HAMMOND TRANSPORTATION LIMITED *p* 497
450 ECCLESTONE DR, BRACEBRIDGE, ON, P1L 1R1
(705) 645-5431 *SIC* 4151

HAMPTON FINANCIAL CORPORATION *p* 952
141 ADELAIDE ST W SUITE 1800, TORONTO, ON, M5H 3L5
(416) 862-7800 *SIC* 8741

HAMPTON INN & SUITES *p* 272
See *NURMANN HOLDINGS LTD*

HAMPTON INN & SUITES *p* 299
See *MAYFAIR PROPERTIES LTD*

HAMPTON INN AND HOMEWOOD SUITES HALIFAX DOWNTOWN, THE *p* 454
See *SILVERBIRCH NO. 15 OPERATIONS LIMITED PARTNERSHIP*

HAMPTON LUMBER MILLS - CANADA, LTD *p* 194
GD, BURNS LAKE, BC, V0J 1E0
(250) 692-7177 *SIC* 6712

HAMPTON POWER SYSTEMS LTD *p* 8
3415 29 ST NE SUITE 200, CALGARY, AB, T1Y 5W4
SIC 5063

HAMPTON SECURITIES LIMITED *p* 952
141 ADELAIDE ST W SUITE 1800, TORONTO, ON, M5H 3L5
(416) 862-7800 *SIC* 6211

HAMPTON TERRACE CARE CENTRE *p* 531
See *UNGER NURSING HOMES LIMITED*

HAMPTONS GOLF COURSE LTD *p* 71
69 HAMPTONS DR NW, CALGARY, AB, T3A 5H7
(403) 239-8088 *SIC* 7999

HAMS MARKETING SERVICES CO-OP INC *p* 365
750 MARION ST, WINNIPEG, MB, R2J 0K4
(204) 233-9491 *SIC* 5154

HAMSAR DIVERSCO *p* 522
See *GRAKON HAMSAR HOLDINGS LTD*

HAMSTER *p* 1231
See *NOVEXCO INC*

HANAHREUM MART INC *p* 201
329 NORTH RD SUITE 100, COQUITLAM, BC, V3K 3V8
(604) 939-0135 *SIC* 5411

HANAHREUM MART INC *p* 553
193 JARDIN DR, CONCORD, ON, L4K 1X5
(416) 792-1131 *SIC* 5411

HANBALI, JEFF DRUGS LTD *p* 613
620 KING ST W SUITE 1458, HAMILTON, ON, L8P 1C2
(905) 522-0599 *SIC* 5912

HANBALI, JEFF DRUGS LTD *p* 616
999 UPPER WENTWORTH ST SUITE 200,

HAMILTON, ON, L9A 4X5
(905) 388-8450 *SIC* 5912

HANCO MANAGEMENT LTD *p* 211
372 CORONATION AVE, DUNCAN, BC, V9L 2T3
(250) 748-3761 *SIC* 6712

HANCOCK PETROLEUM INC *p* 144
5904 44 ST, LLOYDMINSTER, AB, T9V 1V7
(780) 875-2495 *SIC* 5171

HANDA TRAVEL SERVICES LTD *p* 819
2269 RIVERSIDE DR SUITE 135, OTTAWA, ON, K1H 8K2
(613) 731-1111 *SIC* 4724

HANDEE PRODUCTS *p* 1156
See *2920654 CANADA INC*

HANDI FOODS LTD *p* 793
190 NORELCO DR, NORTH YORK, ON, M9L 1S4
(416) 743-6634 *SIC* 2051

HANDLING SPECIALTY *p* 599
See *HANDLING SPECIALTY MANUFACTURING LIMITED*

HANDLING SPECIALTY MANUFACTURING LIMITED *p* 599
219 SOUTH SERVICE RD, GRIMSBY, ON, L3M 1Y6
(905) 945-9661 *SIC* 3599

HANDLING TECHNOLOGIES INC *p* 553
21 CORRINE CRT, CONCORD, ON, L4K 4W2
(905) 739-1350 *SIC* 5084

HANDSWORTH SECONDARY SCHOOL *p* 242
See *SCHOOL DISTRICT NO. 44 (NORTH VANCOUVER)*

HANDTMANN CANADA LIMITED *p* 1010
654 COLBY DR, WATERLOO, ON, N2V 1A2
(519) 725-3666 *SIC* 5084

HANDY & HARMAN OF CANADA, LIMITED *p* 584
290 CARLINGVIEW DR, ETOBICOKE, ON, M9W 5G1
(416) 675-1860 *SIC* 3499

HANDYMAN PERSONNEL *p* 824
See *137077 CANADA INC*

HANDYMAN RENTAL CENTRE *p* 1425
See *303567 SASKATCHEWAN LTD*

HANEY BUILDERS SUPPLIES (1964) LTD *p* 231
22740 DEWDNEY TRUNK RD, MAPLE RIDGE, BC, V2X 3K2
(604) 820-0444 *SIC* 5211

HANEY BUILDERS' SUPPLIES (1971) LTD *p* 231
22740 DEWDNEY TRUNK RD, MAPLE RIDGE, BC, V2X 3K2
(604) 463-6206 *SIC* 5211

HANFENG EVERGREEN INC *p* 926
2 ST CLAIR AVE W SUITE 610, TORONTO, ON, M4V 1L5
SIC 5191

HANFORD LUMBER LIMITED *p* 584
45 BETHRIDGE RD SUITE 1, ETOBICOKE, ON, M9W 1M9
(416) 743-5384 *SIC* 5031

HANGAR FARMS INC *p* 355
RIVERS AIR BASE, RIVERS, MB, R0K 1X0
SIC 0191

HANGER, J. E. OF MONTREAL INC *p* 1221
5545 RUE SAINT-JACQUES, MONTREAL, QC, H4A 2E3
(514) 489-8213 *SIC* 3842

HANI AUTO INC *p* 1239
7000 BOUL HENRI-BOURASSA E, MONTREAL-NORD, QC, H1G 6C4
(514) 327-7777 *SIC* 5511

HANK'S MAINTENANCE & SERVICE COMPANY LTD *p* 1406
410 MISSISSIPPIAN DR, ESTEVAN, SK, S4A 2H7
(306) 634-4872 *SIC* 1389

HANLEY CORPORATION *p* 491
289 FRONT ST, BELLEVILLE, ON, K8N 2Z6

(613) 967-1771   *SIC 5461*
HANLON AG CENTRE LTD   *p* 140
3005 18 AVE N, LETHBRIDGE, AB, T1H
5V2
(403) 329-8686   *SIC 5083*
HANNA HEALTH CENTRE   *p* 135
See ALBERTA HEALTH SERVICES
HANNA PAPER FIBRES LIMITED   *p* 680
70 ADDISCOTT CRT, MARKHAM, ON, L6G
1A6
(905) 475-9844   *SIC 4953*
HANNA, NABIL DRUGS LTD   *p* 826
2515 BANK ST, OTTAWA, ON, K1V 0Y4
(613) 523-9999   *SIC 5912*
HANNAFIN, E.J. ENTERPRISES LIMITED *p*
491
57 CANNIFTON RD, BELLEVILLE, ON, K8N
4V1
(613) 966-7017   *SIC 5541*
HANNIGAN'S HONEY INC   *p* 1435
GD, SHELLBROOK, SK, S0J 2E0
(306) 747-7782   *SIC 5149*
HANON SYSTEMS CANADA INC   *p* 491
360 UNIVERSITY AVE SUITE 2,
BELLEVILLE, ON, K8N 5T6
(613) 969-1460   *SIC 3714*
HANON SYSTEMS CANADA PLANT 2   *p*
491
See HANON SYSTEMS CANADA INC
HANON SYSTEMS EFP CANADA LTD   *p*
553
800 TESMA WAY, CONCORD, ON, L4K 5C2
(905) 303-1689   *SIC 3714*
HANOVER AND DISTRICT HOSPITAL *p* 617
90 7TH AVE SUITE 1, HANOVER, ON, N4N
1N1
(519) 364-2340   *SIC 8062*
**HANOVER HOME HARDWARE BUILDING
CENTRE**   *p* 617
See 1020012 ONTARIO INC
HANOVER HONDA   *p* 617
See 2145150 ONTARIO INC
HANOVER RACEWAY   *p* 617
*See HANOVER, BENTINCK & BRANT
AGRICULTURAL SOCIETY*
HANOVER SCHOOL DIVISION   *p* 358
190 MCKENZIE AVE, STEINBACH, MB,
R5G 0P1
(204) 326-6426   *SIC 8211*
HANOVER SCHOOL DIVISION   *p* 358
5 CHRYSLER GATE, STEINBACH, MB,
R5G 0E2
(204) 326-6471   *SIC 8211*
**HANOVER, BENTINCK & BRANT AGRI-
CULTURAL SOCIETY**   *p*
617
265 5TH ST, HANOVER, ON, N4N 3X3
(519) 364-2860   *SIC 7948*
HANSCOMB LIMITED   *p* 924
40 HOLLY ST SUITE 900, TORONTO, ON,
M4S 3C3
(416) 487-3811   *SIC 8741*
HANSEN AUTOMOTIVE & TOWING   *p* 508
See 389259 ONTARIO LIMITED
HANSEN INDUSTRIES LTD   *p* 260
2871 OLAFSEN AVE, RICHMOND, BC, V6X
2R4
(604) 278-2223   *SIC 3469*
HANSEN'S RELEASING COMPANY   *p* 876
See L. HANSEN'S FORWARDING LTD
HANSLER INDUSTRIES LTD   *p* 519
1385 CALIFORNIA AVE, BROCKVILLE,
ON, K6V 5V5
(613) 342-4408   *SIC 7699*
HANSLER SMITH LIMITED   *p* 519
1385 CALIFORNIA AVE, BROCKVILLE,
ON, K6V 5V5
(613) 342-4408   *SIC 5085*
HANSON HARDWARE LTD   *p* 1407
191 BROADWAY AVE, FORT QU'APPELLE,
SK, S0G 1S0
SIC 5251
HANSON PUBLICATIONS INC.   *p* 981
111 PETER ST,STE 406, TORONTO, ON,

M5V 2H1
SIC 2741
HANSON RESTAURANTS (TB) INC   *p* 101
10114 175 ST NW, EDMONTON, AB, T5S
1L1
(780) 484-2896   *SIC 5812*
HANSON RESTAURANTS INC   *p* 104
9768 170 ST NW SUITE 284, EDMONTON,
AB, T5T 5L4
(780) 484-2896   *SIC 5812*
HANTS COMMUNITY HOSPITAL   *p* 442
See NOVA SCOTIA HEALTH AUTHORITY
**HANTS COUNTY RESIDENCE FOR SE-
NIOR CITIZENS**   *p*
470
124 COTTAGE ST, WINDSOR, NS, B0N 2T0
(902) 798-8346   *SIC 8051*
HANWEI ENERGY SERVICES CORP *p* 305
595 HOWE ST SUITE 902, VANCOUVER,
BC, V6C 2T5
(604) 685-2239   *SIC 2679*
HAPAG-LLOYD (CANADA) INC   *p* 1220
3400 BOUL DE MAISONNEUVE O BU-
REAU 1200, MONTREAL, QC, H3Z 3E7
(514) 934-5133   *SIC 4731*
**HAPPY ADVENTURE SEA PRODUCTS
(1991) LIMITED**   *p* 423
PLANT RD, EASTPORT, NL, A0G 1Z0
(709) 677-2612   *SIC 2092*
HAPPY HOUR CARD'N PARTY SHOPS   *p*
668
*See COUTTS, WILLIAM E. COMPANY, LIM-
ITED*
HAPPY INN   *p* 1412
See PFEIFER HOLDINGS LTD
HAPPY INN   *p* 1413
See UNITED ENTERPRISES LTD
HAPPY KIDS CANADA INC   *p* 1179
8955 BOUL SAINT-LAURENT BUREAU
301, MONTREAL, QC, H2N 1M5
(514) 270-1477   *SIC 5137*
HAPPY TRAILS R.V. INC   *p* 132
15211 100 ST, GRANDE PRAIRIE, AB, T8V
7C2
(780) 538-2120   *SIC 5561*
HARADROS FOOD SERVICES INC *p* 1424
1820 8TH ST E SUITE 200, SASKATOON,
SK, S7H 0T6
(306) 955-5555   *SIC 5812*
**HARBISONWALKER   INTERNATIONAL
CORP**   *p* 882
2689 INDUSTRIAL PARK RD, SMITHVILLE,
ON, L0R 2A0
(905) 957-3311   *SIC 3297*
HARBORD COLLEGIATE INSTITUTE *p* 990
*See   TORONTO   DISTRICT   SCHOOL
BOARD*
HARBORD INSURANCE SERVICES LTD   *p*
337
805 CLOVERDALE AVE SUITE 150, VIC-
TORIA, BC, V8X 2S9
(250) 388-5533   *SIC 6411*
HARBOUR AIR LTD   *p* 264
4760 INGLIS DR, RICHMOND, BC, V7B
1W4
(604) 278-3478   *SIC 4512*
HARBOUR AIR LTD   *p* 305
1055 CANADA PL UNIT 1, VANCOUVER,
BC, V6C 0C3
(604) 233-3501   *SIC 4512*
HARBOUR AIR SEAPLANES   *p* 264
See HARBOUR AIR LTD
HARBOUR INDUSTRIES (CANADA) LTD   *p*
1101
1365 BOUL INDUSTRIEL, FARNHAM, QC,
J2N 2X3
(450) 293-5304   *SIC 3315*
**HARBOUR LINK CONTAINER SERVICES
INC**   *p* 209
7420 HOPCOTT RD, DELTA, BC, V4G 1B6
(604) 940-5522   *SIC 4213*
HARBOUR TOWERS HOTEL AND SUITES
p 335
See HARBOUR TOWERS LIMITED PART-

NERSHIP
**HARBOUR TOWERS LIMITED PARTNER-
SHIP**   *p*
335
345 QUEBEC ST, VICTORIA, BC, V8V 1W4
(250) 385-2405   *SIC 7011*
HARBOUR VIEW HIGH SCHOOL   *p* 414
See SCHOOL DISTRICT 8
HARBOURFRONT CENTRE   *p* 963
*See   HARBOURFRONT   CORPORATION
(1990)*
HARBOURFRONT CORPORATION (1990) *p*
963
235 QUEENS QUAY W, TORONTO, ON,
M5J 2G8
(416) 973-4000   *SIC 7922*
HARBOURSIDE   *p* 968
*See YORK CONDOMINIUM CORPORA-
TION NO. 510*
HARBOURVIEW AUTOHAUS LTD   *p* 234
4921 WELLINGTON RD, NANAIMO, BC,
V9T 2H5
(250) 751-1411   *SIC 5511*
HARBOURVIEW HAVEN   *p* 462
*See LUNENBURG HOME FOR SPECIAL
CARE CORP*
HARBRIDGE & CROSS LIMITED   *p* 553
350 CREDITSTONE RD SUITE 202, CON-
CORD, ON, L4K 3Z2
(905) 738-0051   *SIC 1542*
HARCO AG EQUIPMENT   *p* 618
See HARKNESS, JIM EQUIPMENT LTD
HARCO CO. LTD   *p* 705
5610 MCADAM RD, MISSISSAUGA, ON,
L4Z 1P1
(905) 890-1220   *SIC 5087*
HARCUT ENTERPRISES INC   *p* 1128
10636 CH DE LA COTE-DE-LIESSE, LA-
CHINE, QC, H8T 1A5
(514) 636-8800   *SIC 4731*
HARD FLUSHBY   *p* 153
See 1001511 ALBERTA LTD
HARD ROCK CAFE   *p* 759
5685 FALLS AVE, NIAGARA FALLS, ON,
L2G 3K6
(905) 356-7625   *SIC 5812*
HARD ROCK CAFE   *p* 821
*See ROCK THE BYWARD MARKET COR-
PORATION*
HARD ROCK CAFE CANADA   *p* 935
See HRC CANADA INC
HARD ROCK CAFE MONTREAL   *p* 1213
See HRC CANADA INC
HARD ROCK CASINO   *p* 201
See GREAT CANADIAN CASINOS INC
HARD-CO CONSTRUCTION LTD   *p* 1016
625 CONLIN RD, WHITBY, ON, L1R 2W8
(905) 655-2001   *SIC 1611*
HARD-CO SAND & GRAVEL, DIV OF   *p*
1016
See HARD-CO CONSTRUCTION LTD
HARD-LINE SOLUTIONS   *p* 565
See HLS HARD-LINE SOLUTIONS INC
HARDBOR STEELS INTERNATIONAL   *p*
735
*See HIGH STRENGTH PLATES & PRO-
FILES INC*
HARDCASTLE DESIGNS LTD   *p* 30
1316 9 AVE SE SUITE 200, CALGARY, AB,
T2G 0T3
(403) 250-7733   *SIC 7389*
HARDCO ATLANTIC   *p* 705
See HARCO CO. LTD
**HARDIMAN, MOUNT &ASSOCIATES IN-
SURANCE BROKERS LIMITED**   *p*
1014
1032 BROCK ST S SUITE 5, WHITBY, ON,
L1N 4L8
(905) 668-1477   *SIC 6411*
HARDING DISPLAY CORP   *p* 876
150 DYNAMIC DR, SCARBOROUGH, ON,
M1V 5A5
(416) 754-3215   *SIC 3993*
HARDING FORKLIFT SERVICES LTD *p* 282

18623 96 AVE, SURREY, BC, V4N 3P6
(604) 888-1412   *SIC 5084*
HARDING GROUP LIMITED, THE   *p* 876
150 DYNAMIC DR, SCARBOROUGH, ON,
M1V 5A5
(416) 754-3215   *SIC 8743*
**HARDING HEATING AND AIR CONDITION-
ING**   *p*
540
*See HARDING MECHANICAL CONTRAC-
TORS INC*
**HARDING MECHANICAL CONTRACTORS
INC**   *p* 540
2210 CAVANMORE RD RR 2, CARP, ON,
K0A 1L0
(613) 831-2257   *SIC 1711*
HARDISTY NURSING HOME INC   *p* 107
6420 101 AVE NW, EDMONTON, AB, T6A
0H5
(780) 466-9267   *SIC 8051*
HARDMAN GROUP LIMITED, THE   *p* 453
1226 HOLLIS ST, HALIFAX, NS, B3J 1T6
(902) 429-3743   *SIC 6553*
**HARDROCK BITS & OILFIELD SUPPLIES
LTD**   *p* 158
2200 SOUTH HIGHWAY DR SE, REDCLIFF,
AB, T0J 2P0
(403) 529-2100   *SIC 5084*
HARDWOOD FOREST PRODUCTS CO LTD
p 391
1213 CHEVRIER BLVD, WINNIPEG, MB,
R3T 1Y4
(204) 981-1490   *SIC 5031*
HARDWOODS DISTRIBUTION INC   *p* 225
9440 202 ST UNIT 306, LANGLEY, BC, V1M
4A6
(604) 881-1988   *SIC 5031*
HARDWOODS SPECIALTY PRODUCTS LP
p 225
9440 202 ST SUITE 306, LANGLEY, BC,
V1M 4A6
(604) 881-1988   *SIC 5031*
HARDY RINGUETTE AUTOMOBILE INC   *p*
1390
1842 3E AV BUREAU 610, VAL-D'OR, QC,
J9P 7A9
(819) 874-5151   *SIC 5511*
HARDY SALES   *p* 229
See HARDY SALES LTD
HARDY SALES (ALBERTA) LTD   *p* 229
27417 GLOUCESTER WAY, LANGLEY, BC,
V4W 3Z8
(604) 856-3911   *SIC 5147*
HARDY SALES LTD   *p* 229
27417 GLOUCESTER WAY, LANGLEY, BC,
V4W 3Z8
(604) 856-3911   *SIC 5147*
**HARDY TERRACE LONG-TERM CARE FA-
CILITY**   *p*
517
*See DIVERSICARE CANADA MANAGE-
MENT SERVICES CO. INC*
**HARDY TERRACE LONG-TERM CARE FA-
CILITY**   *p*
517
*See DIVERSICARE CANADA MANAGE-
MENT SERVICES CO., INC*
HARDY TERRACE LTC   *p* 517
*See DIVERSICARE CANADA MANAGE-
MENT SERVICES CO., INC*
**HARDY,   NORMAND   &   ASSOCIES
S.E.N.C.R.L.**   *p* 1051
7875 BOUL LOUIS-H.-LAFONTAINE BU-
REAU 200, ANJOU, QC, H1K 4E4
(514) 355-1550   *SIC 8721*
HARE FOODS LTD   *p* 170
4902 51 AVE, TOFIELD, AB, T0B 4J0
(780) 662-3718   *SIC 5411*
HAREL DROUIN GESTION CONSEILS   *p*
1189
*See   MAZARS   HAREL   DROUIN.
S.E.N.C.R.L.*
**HAREMAR PLASTIC MANUFACTURING
LIMITED**   *p* 553

200 GREAT GULF DR, CONCORD, ON, L4K 5W1
(905) 761-7552   SIC 3081

HARIRI PONTARINI ARCHITECTS LLP p 920
235 CARLAW AVE SUITE 301, TORONTO, ON, M4M 2S1
(416) 929-4901   SIC 8712

HARKEL OFFICE FURNITURE LIMITED p 553
1743 CREDITSTONE RD, CONCORD, ON, L4K 5X7
(905) 417-5335   SIC 5021

HARKEN TOWING CO. LTD p 246
1990 ARGUE ST, PORT COQUITLAM, BC, V3C 5K4
(604) 942-8511   SIC 7549

HARKNESS, JIM EQUIPMENT LTD p 618
5808 HIGHWAY 9 RR 4, HARRISTON, ON, N0G 1Z0
(519) 338-3946   SIC 5083

HARLEQUIN BOOKS p 952
See HARLEQUIN ENTERPRISES LIMITED

HARLEQUIN ENTERPRISES LIMITED p 952
22 ADELAIDE STREET W 41ST FL, TORONTO, ON, M5H 4E3
(416) 445-5860   SIC 2731

HARLEY DAVIDSON MOTORCYCLES OF EDMONTON (1980) LTD p 83
7420 YELLOWHEAD TRAIL NW, EDMONTON, AB, T5B 1G3
(780) 451-7857   SIC 5571

HARLEY DAVIDSON OF KINGSTON p 630
295 DALTON AVE, KINGSTON, ON, K7K 6Z1
(613) 544-4600   SIC 5571

HARLEY-DAVIDSON LAVAL p 1236
See MOTOCYCLETTES & ARTICLES DE SPORTS PONT-VIAU INC

HARLEY-DAVIDSON OF SOUTHERN ALBERTA INC p 23
2245 PEGASUS RD NE, CALGARY, AB, T2E 8C3
(403) 250-3141   SIC 5571

HARLOCK MURRAY UNDERWRITING LTD p 237
960 QUAYSIDE DR UNIT 103, NEW WESTMINSTER, BC, V3M 6G2
(604) 669-7745   SIC 6331

HARMAC PACIFIC, DIV OF p 235
See NANAIMO FOREST PRODUCTS LTD

HARMAC TRANSPORTATION INC p 795
55 ARROW RD, NORTH YORK, ON, M9M 2L4
(416) 642-0515   SIC 4213

HARMAN HEAVY VEHICLE SPECIALISTS LTD p 639
8 SEREDA RD, KITCHENER, ON, N2H 4X7
(519) 743-4378   SIC 5013

HARMAN IMPORTS p 739
See HARMAN INVESTMENTS LTD

HARMAN INVESTMENTS LTD p 739
310 ANNAGEM BLVD, MISSISSAUGA, ON, L5T 2V5
(905) 670-0801   SIC 5023

HARMATTAN GAS PROCESSING LIMITED PARTNERSHIP p 51
355 4 AVE SW SUITE 1700, CALGARY, AB, T2P 0J1
(403) 691-7575   SIC 1389

HARMON INTERNATIONAL INDUSTRIES INC p 1427
2401 MILLAR AVE, SASKATOON, SK, S7K 2Y4
(306) 931-1161   SIC 3523

HARMONIA ASSURANCE INC p 1390
1100 3E AV, VAL-D'OR, QC, J9P 1T6
(819) 825-8673   SIC 6411

HARMONIC MACHINE INC p 197
44365 PROGRESS WAY, CHILLIWACK, BC, V2R 0L1
(604) 823-4479   SIC 3599

HARMONY ACURA p 220

See HARMONY PREMIUM MOTORS LTD

HARMONY AUTO SALES LTD p 220
2550 ENTERPRISE WAY, KELOWNA, BC, V1X 7X5
(250) 860-6500   SIC 5511

HARMONY BEEF COMPANY, LTD p 160
260036 RGE RD 291, ROCKY VIEW COUNTY, AB, T4A 0T8
(587) 230-2060   SIC 2011

HARMONY CANADIAN EQUITY POOL p 969
66 WELLINGTON ST W, TORONTO, ON, M5K 1E9
(905) 214-8203   SIC 6722

HARMONY FUNDS p 969
66 WELLINGTON ST W SUITE 3100, TORONTO, ON, M5K 1E9
(905) 214-8204   SIC 6722

HARMONY GROWTH PLUS PORTFOLIO p 969
66 WELLINGTON ST W SUITE 3100, TORONTO, ON, M5K 1E9
(905) 214-8204   SIC 6722

HARMONY HEALTH CARE p 211
2753 CHARLOTTE RD SUITE 2A, DUNCAN, BC, V9L 5J2
(250) 701-9990   SIC 8621

HARMONY HONDA p 220
See HARMONY AUTO SALES LTD

HARMONY LOGISTICS CANADA INC p 76
1724 115 AVE NE, CALGARY, AB, T3K 0P9
(403) 537-8996   SIC 4731

HARMONY MONEY MARKET POOL p 969
66 WELLINGTON ST W SUITE 3100, TORONTO, ON, M5K 1E9
(905) 214-8204   SIC 6722

HARMONY PREMIUM MOTORS LTD p 220
2552 ENTERPRISE WAY, KELOWNA, BC, V1X 7X5
(250) 861-3003   SIC 5511

HARMONY WHOLE FOODS MARKET p 808
See HARMONY WHOLE FOODS MARKET (ORANGEVILLE) LTD

HARMONY WHOLE FOODS MARKET (ORANGEVILLE) LTD p 808
163 FIRST ST UNIT A, ORANGEVILLE, ON, L9W 3J8
(519) 941-8961   SIC 5149

HARNOIS ENERGIES INC p 1150
1640 BOUL INDUSTRIEL, MATAGAMI, QC, J0Y 2A0
(819) 739-2563   SIC 5172

HARO PARK CENTRE SOCIETY p 313
1233 HARO ST, VANCOUVER, BC, V6E 3Y5
(604) 687-5584   SIC 8361

HAROLD & GRACE BAKER CENTRE p 993
See REVERA INC

HAROLD E. SEEGMILLER HOLDINGS LIMITED p 639
305 ARNOLD ST, KITCHENER, ON, N2H 6G1
(519) 579-6460   SIC 6712

HAROLD'S FOODLINER p 1414
See RAVEN ENTERPRISES INC.

HARP SECURITY p 803
See HALTON ALARM RESPONSE & PROTECTION LTD

HARPER GREY LLP p 298
650 GEORGIA ST W SUITE 3200, VANCOUVER, BC, V6B 4P7
(604) 687-0411   SIC 8111

HARPERCOLLINS CANADA LIMITED p 952
22 ADELAIDE ST W, TORONTO, ON, M5H 4E3
(416) 975-9334   SIC 5192

HARPO ENTERPRISES p 272
17960 56 AVE, SURREY, BC, V3S 1C7
(604) 575-1690   SIC 5812

HARRCO DESIGN AND MANUFACTURING LIMITED p 503
50 DEVON RD, BRAMPTON, ON, L6T 5B5

(905) 564-0577   SIC 5046

HARRIS CANADA SYSTEMS, INC p 723
2895 ARGENTIA RD UNIT 5, MISSISSAUGA, ON, L5N 8G6
(905) 817-8300   SIC 3679

HARRIS CHEV-OLDS p 356
See MORSTAR HOLDINGS LTD

HARRIS COMPUTER SYSTEMS p 749
See N. HARRIS COMPUTER CORPORATION

HARRIS INSTITUTE FOR THE ARTS INCORPORATED, THE p 933
118 SHERBOURNE ST, TORONTO, ON, M5A 2R2
(416) 367-0162   SIC 8249

HARRIS KIA p 235
See VANCOUVER ISLAND AUTO SALES LTD

HARRIS REBAR p 12
See HARRIS STEEL ULC

HARRIS REBAR p 130
See HARRIS STEEL ULC

HARRIS SECURITY AGENCY p 830
2720 QUEENSVIEW DR SUITE 1140, OTTAWA, ON, K2B 1A5
(613) 726-6713   SIC 8748

HARRIS STEEL GROUP INC p 892
318 ARVIN AVE, STONEY CREEK, ON, L8E 2M2
(905) 662-0611   SIC 3499

HARRIS STEEL ULC p 12
3208 52 ST SE, CALGARY, AB, T2B 1N2
(403) 272-8801   SIC 3441

HARRIS STEEL ULC p 130
11215 87 AVE, FORT SASKATCHEWAN, AB, T8L 2S3
(780) 992-0777   SIC 3499

HARRIS STEEL ULC p 522
750 APPLEBY LINE, BURLINGTON, ON, L7L 2Y7
(905) 632-2121   SIC 3446

HARRIS STEEL ULC p 522
5400 HARVESTER RD, BURLINGTON, ON, L7L 5N5
(905) 681-6811   SIC 3312

HARRIS STEEL ULC p 892
318 ARVIN AVE, STONEY CREEK, ON, L8E 2M2
(905) 662-0611   SIC 3449

HARRIS/DECIMA p 922
2345 YONGE ST SUITE 405, TORONTO, ON, M4P 2E5
(416) 716-4903   SIC 8732

HARRISON HOME BUILDING CENTRES p 438
See HARRISON, C. ERNEST & SONS LIMITED

HARRISON HOT SPRINGS RESORT & SPA p 215
See HARRISON HOT SPRINGS RESORT & SPA CORP

HARRISON HOT SPRINGS RESORT & SPA CORP p 215
100 ESPLANADE AVE, HARRISON HOT SPRINGS, BC, V0M 1K0
(604) 796-2244   SIC 7011

HARRISON PENSA LLP p 653
450 TALBOT ST, LONDON, ON, N6A 5J6
(519) 679-9660   SIC 8111

HARRISON, C. ERNEST & SONS LIMITED p 438
404 MACDONALD RD, AMHERST, NS, B4H 3Y4
(902) 667-3306   SIC 5211

HARRY ROSEN INC p 975
82 BLOOR ST W, TORONTO, ON, M5S 1L9
(416) 972-0556   SIC 5611

HARRY ROSEN INC p 975
77 BLOOR ST W SUITE 5, TORONTO, ON, M5S 1M2
(416) 935-9200   SIC 5611

HARRY ROSEN MENS WEAR p 975
See HARRY ROSEN INC

HARSCO CANADA CORPORATION p 109
7030 51 AVE NW, EDMONTON, AB, T6B 2P4
(780) 468-3292   SIC 1799

HARSCO CANADA CORPORATION p 614
151 YORK BLVD, HAMILTON, ON, L8R 3M2
(905) 522-8123   SIC 3295

HARSTER GREENHOUSES INC p 566
250 8 HWY, DUNDAS, ON, L9H 5E1
(905) 628-2430   SIC 0181

HARTCO DISTRIBUTION LP p 1048
See DISTRIBUTION HARTCO SOCIETE EN COMMANDITE

HARTCO INC p 1402
4120 RUE SAINTE-CATHERINE O, WESTMOUNT, QC, H3Z 1P4
(514) 354-0580   SIC 6712

HARTEK HOLDINGS LTD p 143
2920 26 AVE S, LETHBRIDGE, AB, T1K 7K8
(403) 320-2272   SIC 5411

HARTEL FINANCIAL MANAGEMENT CORPORATION p 811
540 LACOLLE WAY, ORLEANS, ON, K4A 0N9
(613) 837-8282   SIC 8721

HARTLAND COMMUNITY SCHOOL p 403
See SCHOOL DISTRICT 14

HARTMANN CANADA INC p 517
58 FRANK ST, BRANTFORD, ON, N3T 5E2
(519) 756-8500   SIC 2675

HARTMANN DOMINION INC p 517
58 FRANK ST, BRANTFORD, ON, N3T 5E2
(519) 756-8500   SIC 3086

HARTMANN NORTH AMERICA p 517
See HARTMANN DOMINION INC

HARTS SYSTEMS LTD p 240
1200 LONSDALE AVE SUITE 304, NORTH VANCOUVER, BC, V7M 3H6
(604) 990-9101   SIC 7372

HARTUNG GLASS CANADA p 182
See LAMI GLASS PRODUCTS, LLC

HARTWICK O'SHEA & CARTWRIGHT LIMITED p 688
3245 AMERICAN DR, MISSISSAUGA, ON, L4V 1B8
(905) 672-5100   SIC 4731

HARTZ CANADA INC p 889
1125 TALBOT ST, ST THOMAS, ON, N5P 3W7
(519) 631-7660   SIC 5199

HARVAN MANUFACTURING LTD p 1036
612 JACK ROSS AVE, WOODSTOCK, ON, N4V 1B6
(519) 537-8311   SIC 5085

HARVARD BROADCASTING INC p 1418
1900 ROSE ST, REGINA, SK, S4P 0A9
(306) 546-6200   SIC 4832

HARVARD DEVELOPMENTS INC p 1418
1874 SCARTH ST SUITE 2000, REGINA, SK, S4P 4B3
(306) 777-0600   SIC 6531

HARVARD WESTERN VENTURES INC p 1418
2151 ALBERT ST, REGINA, SK, S4P 2V1
(306) 757-1633   SIC 6411

HARVEST CROSSING p 518
See HARVEST RETIREMENT

HARVEST BAKERY & DELI p 388
See C & R VENTURES INC

HARVEST BARN OF NIAGARA LTD p 761
1822 NIAGARA STONE RD, NIAGARA ON THE LAKE, ON, L0S 1J0
(905) 468-3224   SIC 5431

HARVEST FRASER RICHMOND ORGANICS LTD p 258
7028 YORK RD, RICHMOND, BC, V6W 0B1
(604) 270-7500   SIC 5093

HARVEST HONDA p 358
See HARVEST INVESTMENTS LTD

HARVEST INSURANCE AGENCY LTD p

358
304 MAIN ST, STEINBACH, MB, R5G 1Z1
(204) 326-2323 *SIC* 6411

HARVEST INVESTMENTS LTD *p* 358
144 PTH 12 N, STEINBACH, MB, R5G 1T4
(204) 326-1311 *SIC* 5511

HARVEST MEATS *p* 261
*See PREMIUM BRANDS OPERATING LIM-
ITED PARTNERSHIP*

HARVEST MEATS *p* 1438
*See PREMIUM BRANDS OPERATING LIM-
ITED PARTNERSHIP*

HARVEST OPERATIONS CORP *p* 51
700 2 ST SW SUITE 1500, CALGARY, AB,
T2P 2W1
(403) 265-1178 *SIC* 1311

HARVEST PORTFOLIOS GROUP INC *p* 802
710 DORVAL DR SUITE 200, OAKVILLE,
ON, L6K 3V7
(416) 649-4541 *SIC* 6722

HARVEST POWER *p* 258
*See HARVEST FRASER RICHMOND OR-
GANICS LTD*

HARVEST RETIREMENT *p* 518
15 HARVEST AVE, BRANTFORD, ON, N4G
0E2
(519) 688-0448 *SIC* 6411

HARVEX AGROMART INC *p* 836
2109B COUNTY ROAD 20 RR 2, OXFORD
STATION, ON, K0G 1T0
(613) 258-3445 *SIC* 5191

HARVEY & COMPANY LIMITED *p* 430
88 KENMOUNT RD, ST. JOHN'S, NL, A1B
3R1
(709) 738-8911 *SIC* 5084

HARVEY WOODS *p* 469
See STANFIELD'S LIMITED

HARVEY'S *p* 652
See RECIPE UNLIMITED CORPORATION

HARVEY'S *p* 847
See EASTON'S 28 RESTAURANTS LTD

HARVEY'S *p* 1228
See RESTAURANT MACGEORGES INC

HARVEY'S AUTO CARRIERS *p* 432
See HARVEY, A. & COMPANY LIMITED

HARVEY'S HOME HEAT *p* 431
See HARVEY'S OIL LIMITED

HARVEY'S OIL LIMITED *p* 431
87 WATER ST, ST. JOHN'S, NL, A1C 1A5
(709) 726-1680 *SIC* 5983

HARVEY'S SWISS CHALET *p* 488
See RECIPE UNLIMITED CORPORATION

HARVEY'S TRAVEL LTD *p* 428
92 ELIZABETH AVE, ST. JOHN'S, NL, A1A
1W7
(709) 726-2900 *SIC* 4724

HARVEY'S/SWISS CHALET *p* 808
See JOPAMAR HOLDINGS INC

HARVEY, A. & COMPANY LIMITED *p* 432
60 WATER ST, ST. JOHN'S, NL, A1C 1A3
(709) 576-4761 *SIC* 4491

HARVEY, AUREL & FILS INC *p* 1122
555 RUE SAINT-ETIENNE, LA MALBAIE,
QC, G5A 1J3
(418) 665-4461 *SIC* 4953

HARVEY, R & J ADVENTURES LTD *p* 1438
205 HAMILTON RD, YORKTON, SK, S3N
4B9
(306) 783-9733 *SIC* 5531

**HARWELL ELECTRIC SUPPLY CO. LIM-
ITED** *p*
503
2 WILKINSON RD, BRAMPTON, ON, L6T
4M3
(905) 848-0060 *SIC* 5063

HARWIL FARMS MOBILE FEEDS LTD *p*
607
4410 HIGHWAY 6 RR 6, HAGERSVILLE,
ON, N0A 1H0
(905) 768-1118 *SIC* 5191

HARWOOD FORD SALES LTD *p* 7
1303 SUTHERLAND DR E, BROOKS, AB,
T1R 1C8
(403) 362-6900 *SIC* 5511

HASBRO *p* 695
See HASBRO CANADA CORPORATION

HASBRO CANADA CORPORATION *p* 695
2645 SKYMARK AVE SUITE 200, MISSIS-
SAUGA, ON, L4W 4H2
(905) 238-3374 *SIC* 5092

HASKINS INDUSTRIAL INC *p* 762
1371 FRANKLIN ST, NORTH BAY, ON, P1A
2W1
(705) 474-4420 *SIC* 5085

HASTECH MANUFACTURING *p* 605
See LINAMAR CORPORATION

HASTECH MFG. PLANT 2 *p* 605
See LINAMAR CORPORATION

**HASTINGS & PRINCE EDWARD COUN-
TIES HEALTH UNIT** *p*
492
*See HASTINGS PRINCE EDWARD PUBLIC
HEALTH*

**HASTINGS AND PRINCE EDWARD DIS-
TRICT SCHOOL BOARD** *p*
484
16 MONCK ST SUITE 14, BANCROFT, ON,
K0L 1C0
(613) 332-1220 *SIC* 8211

**HASTINGS AND PRINCE EDWARD DIS-
TRICT SCHOOL BOARD** *p*
492
160 PALMER RD, BELLEVILLE, ON, K8P
4E1
(613) 962-9233 *SIC* 8211

**HASTINGS AND PRINCE EDWARD DIS-
TRICT SCHOOL BOARD** *p*
492
45 COLLEGE ST W, BELLEVILLE, ON, K8P
2G3
(613) 962-9295 *SIC* 8211

**HASTINGS AND PRINCE EDWARD DIS-
TRICT SCHOOL BOARD** *p*
492
224 PALMER RD, BELLEVILLE, ON, K8P
4E1
(613) 962-2516 *SIC* 8211

**HASTINGS AND PRINCE EDWARD DIS-
TRICT SCHOOL BOARD** *p*
845
41 BARKER ST, PICTON, ON, K0K 2T0
(613) 476-2196 *SIC* 8211

**HASTINGS AND PRINCE EDWARD DIS-
TRICT SCHOOL BOARD** *p*
999
15 FOURTH AVE, TRENTON, ON, K8V 5N4
(613) 392-1227 *SIC* 8211

HASTINGS ENTERTAINMENT INC *p* 284
188 RENFREW ST N, VANCOUVER, BC,
V5K 3N8
(604) 254-1631 *SIC* 7948

**HASTINGS PRINCE EDWARD PUBLIC
HEALTH** *p* 492
179 NORTH PARK ST, BELLEVILLE, ON,
K8P 4P1
(613) 966-5500 *SIC* 8011

HASTINGS RACECOURSE & CASINO *p*
284
See HASTINGS ENTERTAINMENT INC

HASTON, NANCY & ASSOCIATES INC *p*
929
175 BLOOR ST E SUITE 807, TORONTO,
ON, M4W 3R8
SIC 8093

HATCH CORPORATION *p* 522
5035 SOUTH SERVICE RD, BURLINGTON,
ON, L7L 6M9
(905) 315-3500 *SIC* 8711

HATCH CORPORATION *p* 715
2800 SPEAKMAN DR, MISSISSAUGA, ON,
L5K 2R7
(905) 855-2010 *SIC* 8711

HATCH CORPORATION *p* 1205
5 PLACE VILLE-MARIE BUREAU 1400,
MONTREAL, QC, H3B 2G2
(514) 861-0583 *SIC* 8711

HATCH ENERGY *p* 715
See HATCH LTD

HATCH ENERGY *p* 758
See HATCH LTD

HATCH LTD *p* 313
1066 HASTINGS ST W SUITE 400, VAN-
COUVER, BC, V6E 3X1
(604) 689-5767 *SIC* 8711

HATCH LTD *p* 378
500 PORTAGE AVE SUITE 600, WIN-
NIPEG, MB, R3C 3Y8
(204) 786-8751 *SIC* 8711

HATCH LTD *p* 715
2800 SPEAKMAN DR, MISSISSAUGA, ON,
L5K 2R7
(905) 855-7600 *SIC* 8711

HATCH LTD *p* 758
4342 QUEEN ST SUITE 500, NIAGARA
FALLS, ON, L2E 7J7
(905) 374-5200 *SIC* 8711

HATCH LTD *p* 797
2265 UPPER MIDDLE RD E SUITE 300,
OAKVILLE, ON, L6H 0G5
(905) 855-7600 *SIC* 8711

HATCH LTD *p* 1205
5 PLACE VILLE-MARIE BUREAU 1400,
MONTREAL, QC, H3B 2G2
(514) 861-0583 *SIC* 8711

HATCH, ROBERT RETAIL INC *p* 80
320 5 AVE W, COCHRANE, AB, T4C 2E3
(403) 851-0894 *SIC* 5531

HATCHCOS HOLDINGS LTD *p* 715
2800 SPEAKMAN DR, MISSISSAUGA, ON,
L5K 2R7
(905) 855-7600 *SIC* 8711

HATHEWAY (TRACADIE) LIMITED *p* 419
3318 RUE LACHAPELLE, TRACADIE-
SHEILA, NB, E1X 1G5
(506) 395-2208 *SIC* 5511

HATHEWAY FORD *p* 419
See HATHEWAY (TRACADIE) LIMITED

HATHEWAY LIMITED *p* 394
1030 ST. ANNE ST, BATHURST, NB, E2A
6X2
(506) 546-4464 *SIC* 5511

HATHEWAY, JIM FORD SALES LIMITED *p*
438
76 ROBERT ANGUS DR, AMHERST, NS,
B4H 4R7
(902) 667-6000 *SIC* 5511

HATLEY - P'TITE MAISON BLEUE INC *p*
1132
860 90E AV, LASALLE, QC, H8R 3A2
(514) 272-8444 *SIC* 5137

HATZIC SECONDARY SCHOOL *p* 232
See SCHOOL DISTRICT #75 (MISSION)

HAUL-ALL EQUIPMENT LTD *p* 140
4115 18 AVE N, LETHBRIDGE, AB, T1H
5G1
(403) 328-5353 *SIC* 3564

HAUNSLA PHARMACY LTD *p* 705
5035 HURONTARIO ST SUITE 1100, MIS-
SISSAUGA, ON, L4Z 3X7
(905) 890-1313 *SIC* 5912

HAUSER COMPANY STORE *p* 1006
See HAUSER INDUSTRIES INC

HAUSER CONTRACT *p* 1006
See HAUSER INDUSTRIES INC

**HAUSER HOME HARDWARE BUILDING
CENTRE** *p* 78
*See HAUSER, R BUILDING MATERIALS
LTD*

HAUSER INDUSTRIES INC *p* 1006
330 WEBER ST N, WATERLOO, ON, N2J
3H6
(519) 747-1138 *SIC* 2514

HAUSER INDUSTRIES INC *p* 1006
330 WEBER ST N, WATERLOO, ON, N2J
3H6
(800) 268-7328 *SIC* 5712

HAUSER, R BUILDING MATERIALS LTD *p*
78
6809 48 AVE, CAMROSE, AB, T4V 4W1
(780) 672-8818 *SIC* 5211

HAUTS BOISES DU CHATEAUGUAY, LES *p*
1132

See KINGSTON BYERS INC

**HAVANA HOUSE CIGAR AND TOBACCO
MERCHANTS LTD** *p* 920
9 DAVIES AVE SUITE 112, TORONTO, ON,
M4M 2A6
(416) 406-6644 *SIC* 5993

HAVAS CANADA HOLDINGS, INC *p* 981
473 ADELAIDE ST W SUITE 300,
TORONTO, ON, M5V 1T1
(416) 920-6864 *SIC* 7311

HAVAS MEDIA *p* 981
See HAVAS CANADA HOLDINGS, INC

HAVEN SOCIETY *p* 234
*See HAVEN SOCIETYTRANSITION
HOUSE*

HAVEN SOCIETYTRANSITION HOUSE *p*
234
3200 ISLAND HWY UNIT 38, NANAIMO,
BC, V9T 6N4
(250) 756-2452 *SIC* 8699

HAVENTREE BANK *p* 951
*See EQUITY FINANCIAL TRUST COM-
PANY*

HAVER & BOECKER CANADA *p* 886
See W. S. TYLER CANADA LTD

HAVERGAL COLLEGE *p* 788
1451 AVENUE RD, NORTH YORK, ON,
M5N 2H9
(416) 483-3519 *SIC* 8211

HAVRE COMMUNAUTAIRE INC, LE *p* 411
17 COMMERCIALE, RICHIBUCTO, NB,
E4W 3X5
(506) 523-6790 *SIC* 8051

HAWK PLASTICS LTD *p* 1023
5295 BURKE ST, WINDSOR, ON, N9A 6J3
(519) 737-1452 *SIC* 3089

HAWKESBURY HONDA *p* 618
See 4475518 CANADA INC

**HAWKESBURY LUMBER SUPPLY COM-
PANY LIMITED** *p*
619
900 ALEXANDER SIVERSKY ST,
HAWKESBURY, ON, K6A 3N4
(613) 632-4663 *SIC* 5211

HAWKESBURY MAZDA *p* 618
See 845453 ONTARIO LTD

HAWKESBURY TOYOTA *p* 618
See 1055551 ONTARIO INC

HAWKINS TRUCK MART LTD *p* 403
125 GREENVIEW DR, HANWELL, NB, E3C
0E4
(506) 452-7946 *SIC* 5511

HAWORTH, LTD *p* 585
110 CARRIER DR, ETOBICOKE, ON, M9W
5R1
SIC 2542

HAWTHORN PARK *p* 221
*See DIVERSICARE CANADA MANAGE-
MENT SERVICES CO., INC*

**HAWTHORN PK RETIREMENT COMMU-
NITY** *p*
221
*See DIVERSICARE REALTY INVEST-
MENTS LIMITED*

HAWTHORNE PARK INC *p* 270
14476 104 AVE, SURREY, BC, V3R 1L9
(604) 587-1040 *SIC* 5812

**HAWTHORNE SENIORS CARE COMMU-
NITY** *p*
247
*See PORT COQUITLAM SENIOR CITI-
ZENS HOUSING SOCIETY*

HAY GROUP LIMITED *p* 952
121 KING ST W SUITE 700, TORONTO,
ON, M5H 3T9
(416) 868-1371 *SIC* 8741

HAY GROUP, THE *p* 952
See HAY GROUP LIMITED

**HAY RIVER HEALTH & SOCIAL SERVICES
AUTHORITY** *p* 435
3 GAETZ DR, HAY RIVER, NT, X0E 0R8
(867) 874-7100 *SIC* 8399

HAYASHI CANADA INC *p* 895
300 DUNN RD, STRATFORD, ON, N4Z 0A7

(519) 271-5600   *SIC* 3465

HAYDEN DIAMOND BIT INDUSTRIES LTD *p* 263
12020 NO. 5 RD, RICHMOND, BC, V7A 4G1
(604) 341-6941   *SIC* 3532

HAYDUK PICKER SERVICE LTD   *p* 82
GD, DRAYTON VALLEY, AB, T7A 1T1
(780) 542-3217   *SIC* 1389

HAYHOE EQUIPMENT AND SUPPLY LTD *p* 554
45 VILLARBOIT CRES SUITE 2, CONCORD, ON, L4K 4R2
(905) 669-5118   *SIC* 5149

HAYHURST, GEORGE LIMITED   *p* 814
441 GIBB ST, OSHAWA, ON, L1J 1Z4
(905) 728-6272   *SIC* 5531

HAYLEY INDUSTRIAL ELECTRONICS LTD *p* 16
7071 112 AVE SE, CALGARY, AB, T2C 5A5
(403) 259-5575   *SIC* 3569

HAYMAN CONSTRUCTION   *p* 653
See HAYMAN, JOHN AND SONS COMPANY, LIMITED, THE

HAYMAN, JOHN AND SONS COMPANY, LIMITED, THE   *p* 653
636 WELLINGTON ST, LONDON, ON, N6A 3R9
(519) 433-3966   *SIC* 1541

HAYS PERSONNEL   *p* 776
See HAYS SPECIALIST RECRUITMENT (CANADA) INC

HAYS SPECIALIST RECRUITMENT (CANADA) INC   *p* 776
1500 DON MILLS RD SUITE 402, NORTH YORK, ON, M3B 3K4
(416) 203-1925   *SIC* 7299

HAYTER'S FARM   *p* 564
See HAYTER'S TURKEY PRODUCTS INC

HAYTER'S TURKEY PRODUCTS INC *p* 564
37451 DASHWOOD RD, DASHWOOD, ON, N0M 1N0
(519) 237-3561   *SIC* 2015

HAYTON GROUP INC   *p* 605
163 CURTIS DR, GUELPH, ON, N1K 1S9
(519) 822-0577   *SIC* 3499

HAYWARD & WARWICK LIMITED   *p* 415
85 PRINCESS ST, SAINT JOHN, NB, E2L 1K5
(506) 653-9066   *SIC* 5023

HAYWARD GORDON ULC   *p* 593
5 BRIGDEN GATE, GEORGETOWN, ON, L7G 0A3
(905) 873-8595   *SIC* 5084

HAYWARD POOL PRODUCTS CANADA, INC   *p* 797
2880 PLYMOUTH DR, OAKVILLE, ON, L6H 5R4
(905) 829-2880   *SIC* 3949

HAYWOOD SECURITIES INC   *p* 305
200 BURRARD ST SUITE 700, VANCOUVER, BC, V6C 3L6
(604) 697-7100   *SIC* 6211

HAYWORTH EQUIPMENT SALES INC *p* 1
26180 114 AVE, ACHESON, AB, T7X 6R1
(780) 962-9100   *SIC* 5511

HAZEL MCCALLION CAMPUS   *p* 710
See SHERIDAN COLLEGE INSTITUTE OF TECHNOLOGY AND ADVANCED LEARNING

HAZMASTERS ENVIRONMENTAL CONTROLS INC   *p* 182
3131 UNDERHILL AVE, BURNABY, BC, V5A 3C8
(604) 420-0025   *SIC* 5084

HAZMASTERS ENVIRONMENTAL INC *p* 334
575 HILLSIDE AVE, VICTORIA, BC, V8T 1Y8
(250) 384-0025   *SIC* 5099

HAZMASTERS INC   *p* 475
651 HARWOOD AVE N UNIT 4, AJAX, ON, L1Z 0K4
(905) 231-0011   *SIC* 5099

HB CONNECTIONS INC   *p* 1156
8190 CH ROYDEN, MONT-ROYAL, QC, H4P 2T2
(514) 340-4414   *SIC* 3171

HB SEALING PRODUCTS LTD   *p* 487
30 SAUNDERS RD SUITE 1, BARRIE, ON, L4N 9A8
(705) 739-6735   *SIC* 5085

HBC   *p* 952
See HUDSON'S BAY COMPANY

HBC LOGISTICS   *p* 585
See HUDSON'S BAY COMPANY

HBC TRANSPORTATION INC   *p* 509
100 KENNEDY RD S, BRAMPTON, ON, L6W 3E7
(416) 639-6764   *SIC* 4213

HBI - HERITAGE BUSINESS INTERIORS INC   *p* 30
2600 PORTLAND ST SE SUITE 2050, CALGARY, AB, T2G 4M6
(403) 252-2888   *SIC* 5712

HBI OFFICE PLUS INC   *p* 1420
1162 OSLER ST, REGINA, SK, S4R 5G9
(306) 757-5678   *SIC* 5112

HBPO CANADA INC   *p* 1020
2570 CENTRAL AVE, WINDSOR, ON, N8W 4J5
(519) 251-4300   *SIC* 3711

HC CANADA OPERATING COMPANY, LTD, THE   *p* 514
325 WEST ST UNIT B200, BRANTFORD, ON, N3R 3V6
(519) 753-2666   *SIC* 2671

HC-TECH INC   *p* 609
665 PARKDALE AVE N, HAMILTON, ON, L8H 5Z1
(905) 547-5693   *SIC* 5169

HCAREERS.COM   *p* 190
See HOSPITALITY CAREERS ONLINE INC

HCC MINING AND DEMOLITION INC *p* 1427
RR 5 LCD MAIN, SASKATOON, SK, S7K 3J8
(306) 652-4168   *SIC* 1241

HCH LAZERMAN INC   *p* 977
278 BATHURST ST, TORONTO, ON, M5T 2S3
(416) 504-2154   *SIC* 3555

HCL AXON TECHNOLOGIES INC   *p* 709
77 CITY CENTRE DR, MISSISSAUGA, ON, L5B 1M5
(905) 603-4381   *SIC* 7372

HCL LOGISTICS INC   *p* 649
2021 OXFORD ST E, LONDON, ON, N5V 2Z7
(519) 681-4254   *SIC* 4225

HCM CONTRACTORS INC   *p* 77
9777 ENTERPRISE WAY SE, CALGARY, AB, T3S 0A1
(403) 248-4884   *SIC* 1794

HCN MOTORS LTD   *p* 749
275 WEST HUNT CLUB RD, NEPEAN, ON, K2E 1A6
(613) 521-6262   *SIC* 5511

HCR   *p* 577
See HCR PERSONNEL SOLUTIONS INC

HCR PERSONNEL SOLUTIONS INC *p* 577
19 FOUR SEASONS PL 2ND FL, ETOBICOKE, ON, M9B 6E7
(416) 622-1427   *SIC* 7361

HD SUPPLY CONSTRUCTION & INDUSTRIAL - BRAFASCO   *p* 1031
See HDS CANADA, INC

HDI   *p* 313
See HUNTER DICKINSON INC

HDI TECHNOLOGIES INC   *p* 1112
200 RUE DES BATISSEURS, GRAND-MERE, QC, G9T 5K5
(819) 538-3398   *SIC* 3679

HDQ INVESTMENTS LTD   *p* 153
4202 50 AVE, RED DEER, AB, T4N 3Z3
(403) 346-3518   *SIC* 5812

HDR ARCHITECTURE ASSOCIATES, INC *p* 952

255 ADELAIDE ST W, TORONTO, ON, M5H 1X9
(647) 777-4900   *SIC* 8712

HDR CORPORATION   *p* 829
300 RICHMOND DR SUITE 200, OTTAWA, ON, K1Z 6X6
(613) 233-6799   *SIC* 8712

HDR/G&G   *p* 952
See HDR ARCHITECTURE ASSOCIATES, INC

HDS CANADA, INC   *p* 1031
100 GALCAT DR, WOODBRIDGE, ON, L4L 0B9
(905) 850-8085   *SIC* 5072

HEAD SHOPPE COMPANY LIMITED, THE *p* 446
10 THORNE AVE, DARTMOUTH, NS, B3B 1Y5
(902) 455-1504   *SIC* 7231

HEADLINE PROMOTIONAL PRODUCTS *p* 457
See HALIFAX HERALD LIMITED, THE

HEADLINE SPORTS   *p* 983
See SCORE TELEVISION NETWORK LTD, THE

HEADWATER EQUIPMENT   *p* 80
See HEADWATER EQUIPMENT SALES LTD

HEADWATER EQUIPMENT SALES LTD *p* 80
592041 RIVER RIDGE RD UNIT 2, COALHURST, AB, T0L 0V0
(403) 327-3681   *SIC* 5084

HEADWATERS HEALTH CARE CENTRE *p* 808
100 ROLLING HILLS DR, ORANGEVILLE, ON, L9W 4X9
(519) 941-2410   *SIC* 8062

HEALTH ACCESS   *p* 1054
See 9038-5477 QUEBEC INC

HEALTH ASSOCIATION OF NOVA SCOTIA *p* 439
2 DARTMOUTH RD, BEDFORD, NS, B4A 2K7
(902) 832-8500   *SIC* 8621

HEALTH CARE & REHAB SPECIALTY *p* 84
See 301776 ALBERTA LTD

HEALTH CARE CENTRE   *p* 127
See GOVERNMENT OF THE PROVINCE OF ALBERTA

HEALTH CARE OF ONTARIO PENSION PLAN   *p* 963
See HOOPP INVESTMENT MANAGEMENT LIMITED

HEALTH CARE PHARMACY   *p* 898
See 1124980 ONTARIO INC

HEALTH EMPLOYERS ASSOCIATION OF BRITISH COLUMBIA   *p* 286
2889 12TH AVE E SUITE 300, VANCOUVER, BC, V5M 4T5
(604) 736-5909   *SIC* 8621

HEALTH INTEGRATION NETWORK OF WATERLOO WELLINGTON   *p* 1006
141 WEBER ST S, WATERLOO, ON, N2J 2A9
(519) 748-2222   *SIC* 8621

HEALTH MEGAMALL   *p* 341
See BABESKIN BODYCARE INC

HEALTH SCIENCES ASSOCIATION OF BRITISH COLUMBIA   *p* 236
180 COLUMBIA ST E, NEW WESTMINSTER, BC, V3L 0G7
(604) 517-0994   *SIC* 8631

HEALTH SCIENCES CENTRE (DIV OF) *p* 374
See WINNIPEG REGIONAL HEALTH AUTHORITY, THE

HEALTH SCIENCES CENTRE, DIV OF *p* 376
See WINNIPEG REGIONAL HEALTH AUTHORITY, THE

HEALTH SCIENCES NORTH   *p* 901
41 RAMSEY LAKE RD, SUDBURY, ON, P3E 5J1

(705) 523-7100   *SIC* 8062

HEALTH SCIENCES NORTH RESEARCH INSTITUTE   *p* 901
41 RAMSEY LAKE RD, SUDBURY, ON, P3E 5J1
(705) 523-7300   *SIC* 8733

HEALTH SYSTEMS GROUP   *p* 718
See HSG HEALTH SYSTEMS GROUP LIMITED

HEALTH TRANS   *p* 870
See HEALTH TRANS SERVICES INC

HEALTH TRANS SERVICES INC   *p* 870
104 BLANTYRE AVE, SCARBOROUGH, ON, M1N 2R5
SIC 4213

HEALTH UNIT   *p* 138
See ASPEN REGIONAL HEALTH

HEALTH VENTURES LTD   *p* 334
2950 DOUGLAS ST SUITE 180, VICTORIA, BC, V8T 4N4
(250) 384-3388   *SIC* 5499

HEALTH4ALL PRODUCTS LIMITED *p* 487
545 WELHAM RD, BARRIE, ON, L4N 8Z6
(705) 733-2117   *SIC* 5149

HEALTHCARE BENEFIT TRUST   *p* 286
350-2889 12TH AVE E, VANCOUVER, BC, V5M 4T5
(604) 736-2087   *SIC* 8748

HEALTHCARE DIAGNOSTIC SECTOR *p* 799
See SIEMENS HEALTHCARE DIAGNOSTICS LTD

HEALTHCARE EMPLOYEES PENSION PLAN - MANITOBA   *p* 378
200 GRAHAM AVE SUITE 900, WINNIPEG, MB, R3C 4L5
(204) 942-6591   *SIC* 6371

HEALTHCARE FOOD SERVICES   *p* 811
See HEALTHCARE FOOD SERVICES INC

HEALTHCARE FOOD SERVICES INC *p* 811
1010 DAIRY DR, ORLEANS, ON, K4A 3N3
(613) 841-7786   *SIC* 2099

HEALTHCARE INSURANCE RECIPROCAL OF CANADA   *p* 363
1200 ROTHESAY ST, WINNIPEG, MB, R2G 1T7
(204) 943-4125   *SIC* 6411

HEALTHCARE INSURANCE RECIPROCAL OF CANADA   *p* 771
4711 YONGE ST SUITE 1600, NORTH YORK, ON, M2N 6K8
(416) 733-2773   *SIC* 6351

HEALTHCARE MATERIALS MANAGEMENT SERVICES   *p* 649
188 STRONACH CRES SUITE 519, LONDON, ON, N5V 3A1
(519) 453-7888   *SIC* 8742

HEALTHCARE PROPERTIES HOLDINGS LTD   *p* 933
284 KING ST E SUITE 100, TORONTO, ON, M5A 1K4
(416) 366-2000   *SIC* 6719

HEALTHCARE SOLUTIONS   *p* 115
See HOME HEALTH CARE SOLUTIONS INC

HEALTHCARE SPECIAL OPPURTUNITIES FUND   *p* 986
130 KING ST W SUITE 2130, TORONTO, ON, M5X 2A2
(416) 362-4141   *SIC* 6722

HEALTHCONNECT INC   *p* 407
210 JOHN ST SUITE 200, MONCTON, NB, E1C 0B8
(506) 384-8020   *SIC* 7389

HEALTHLINK BC   *p* 224
See EMERGENCY AND HEALTH SERVICES COMMISSION

HEALTHPRO PROCUREMENT SERVICES INC   *p* 731
5770 HURONTARIO ST SUITE 902, MISSISSAUGA, ON, L5R 3G5
(905) 568-3478   *SIC* 7389

HEALTHSOURCE PLUS INC   *p* 767

2225 SHEPPARD AVE E SUITE 1400, NORTH YORK, ON, M2J 5C2
SIC 6321

HEALTHSPACE INFORMATICS LTD *p 215*
417 WALLACE ST UNIT 7, HOPE, BC, V0X 1L0
SIC 7371

HEALY FORD *p 89*
See HEALY FORD SALES LIMITED

HEALY FORD SALES LIMITED *p 89*
10616 103 AVE NW, EDMONTON, AB, T5J 0J2
SIC 5511

HEARING LOSS CLINIC INC, THE *p 41*
1632 14 AVE NW SUITE 251, CALGARY, AB, T2N 1M7
(403) 289-3290   *SIC 5999*

HEARINGLIFE *p 926*
See HEARINGLIFE CANADA LTD

HEARINGLIFE CANADA LTD *p 926*
1 ST CLAIR AVE W SUITE 800, TORONTO, ON, M4V 1K7
(416) 925-9223   *SIC 8093*

HEARN AUTOMOTIVE INC *p 1018*
6630 TECUMSEH RD E, WINDSOR, ON, N8T 1E6
SIC 3714

HEARN INDUSTRIAL SERVICES INC *p 804*
2189 SPEERS RD, OAKVILLE, ON, L6L 2X9
(866) 297-6914   *SIC 4225*

HEARN INDUSTRIAL SERVICES INC *p 1022*
2480 SEMINOLE ST, WINDSOR, ON, N8Y 1X3
(226) 674-3200   *SIC 4225*

HEARST HUSKY RESTAURANT & TRUCK STOP *p 619*
See 1535477 ONTARIO LIMITED

HEART AND STROKE FOUNDATION OF BC & YUKON *p 319*
1212 BROADWAY W UNIT 200, VANCOUVER, BC, V6H 3V2
(604) 736-4088   *SIC 8399*

HEART AND STROKE FOUNDATION OF CANADA *p 829*
1525 CARLING AVE UNIT 110, OTTAWA, ON, K1Z 8R9
(613) 691-4048   *SIC 8399*

HEART AND STROKE FOUNDATION OF MANITOBA INC *p 387*
6 DONALD ST SUITE 200, WINNIPEG, MB, R3L 0K6
(204) 949-2000   *SIC 7389*

HEART AND STROKE FOUNDATION OF ONTARIO *p 922*
2300 YONGE ST SUITE 1300, TORONTO, ON, M4P 1E4
(416) 489-7111   *SIC 8399*

HEART LAKE SECONDARY SCHOOL *p 512*
See PEEL DISTRICT SCHOOL BOARD

HEART LOGISTICS INC *p 740*
6975 PACIFIC CIR UNIT D, MISSISSAUGA, ON, L5T 2H3
(905) 362-1100   *SIC 4731*

HEARTHLAND FIREPLACES LIMITED *p 522*
5450 MAINWAY, BURLINGTON, ON, L7L 6A4
(905) 319-0474   *SIC 5023*

HEARTLAND FARM MUTUAL INC *p 1006*
100 ERB ST E, WATERLOO, ON, N2J 1L9
(519) 886-4530   *SIC 6331*

HEARTLAND FRESH PAK INC *p 361*
GD STN MAIN, WINKLER, MB, R6W 4A3
(204) 325-6948   *SIC 7389*

HEARTLAND MOTORS LIMITED *p 344*
106 BROADWAY AVE N, WILLIAMS LAKE, BC, V2G 2X7
(250) 392-3225   *SIC 5521*

HEARTLAND REGIONAL HEALTH AUTHORITY *p 1438*
GD, WILKIE, SK, S0K 4W0
(306) 843-2531   *SIC 8011*

HEARTLAND SERVICES GROUP LIMITED *p 1031*
40 TROWERS RD UNIT 1, WOODBRIDGE, ON, L4L 7K6
(905) 265-9667   *SIC 7349*

HEARTLAND SHIPPING SUPPLIES INC *p 740*
6690 INNOVATOR DR, MISSISSAUGA, ON, L5T 2J3
(905) 564-9777   *SIC 5113*

HEARTLAND TOYOTA *p 344*
See HEARTLAND MOTORS LIMITED

HEARTSAFE EMS INC *p 495*
159 VICTORIA ST, BOLTON, ON, L7E 3G9
(416) 410-4911   *SIC 8748*

HEARTWOOD MANUFACTURING LTD *p 220*
251 ADAMS RD, KELOWNA, BC, V1X 7R1
(250) 765-4145   *SIC 2521*

HEARX HEARING INC *p 619*
290 MCGILL ST SUITE A, HAWKESBURY, ON, K6A 1P8
(877) 268-1045   *SIC 5999*

HEASLIP FORD SALES LTD *p 607*
18 MAIN ST S, HAGERSVILLE, ON, N0A 1H0
(905) 768-3393   *SIC 5511*

HEAT BY DESIGN *p 537*
See WARM WITH CORN INC

HEATH ST HOUSING CO-OP INC *p 925*
232 HEATH ST E, TORONTO, ON, M4T 1S9
(416) 486-8169   *SIC 6513*

HEATHERBRAE BUILDERS CO. LTD *p 263*
12371 HORSESHOE WAY UNIT 140, RICHMOND, BC, V7A 4X6
(604) 277-2315   *SIC 1542*

HEATHERGLENEAGLES GOLF COMPANY LTD *p 80*
100 GLENEAGLES DR, COCHRANE, AB, T4C 1P5
(403) 932-1100   *SIC 7992*

HEAVY CRUDE HAULING L.P. *p 144*
6601 62 ST, LLOYDMINSTER, AB, T9V 3T6
(780) 875-5358   *SIC 4213*

HEAVY EQUIPMENT REPAIR LTD *p 163*
404 BALSAM RD, SLAVE LAKE, AB, T0G 2A0
(780) 849-3768   *SIC 7699*

HEAVY INDUSTRIES *p 16*
See HEAVY INDUSTRIES THEMING CORPORATION

HEAVY INDUSTRIES THEMING CORPORATION *p 16*
9192 52 ST SE, CALGARY, AB, T2C 5A9
(403) 252-2603   *SIC 1799*

HEAVY METAL EQUIPMENT & RENTALS *p 78*
See 2122256 ALBERTA LTD

HEBDRAULIQUE INC *p 1344*
8410 RUE CHAMP D'EAU, SAINT-LEONARD, QC, H1P 1Y3
(514) 327-5966   *SIC 3492*

HEBERT'S RECYCLING INC *p 405*
53 WALSH AVE, MIRAMICHI, NB, E1N 3A5
(506) 773-1880   *SIC 4953*

HEBREW ACADEMY INC *p 1083*
5700 AV KELLERT, COTE SAINT-LUC, QC, H4W 1T4
(514) 489-5321   *SIC 8211*

HEBREW FOUNDATION SCHOOL OF CONGREGATION BETH TIKVAH *p 1090*
2 RUE HOPE, DOLLARD-DES-ORMEAUX, QC, H9A 2V5
(514) 684-6270   *SIC 8211*

HECLA QUEBEC - CASA BERARDI *p 305*
See HECLA QUEBEC INC

HECLA QUEBEC - CASA BERARDI *p 1390*
See HECLA QUEBEC INC

HECLA QUEBEC INC *p 305*
800 PENDER ST W SUITE 970, VANCOUVER, BC, V6C 2V6
(604) 682-6201   *SIC 1081*

HECLA QUEBEC INC *p 1390*
1010 3E RUE, VAL-D'OR, QC, J9P 4B1
(819) 874-4511   *SIC 1081*

HECTOR LARIVEE INC *p 1174*
1755 RUE BERCY, MONTREAL, QC, H2K 2T9
(514) 521-8331   *SIC 5148*

HEDDLE MARINE SERVICE INC *p 610*
208 HILLYARD ST, HAMILTON, ON, L8L 6B6
(905) 528-2635   *SIC 3731*

HEDLEY IMPROVEMENT DISTRICT *p 215*
825 RUE SCOTT, HEDLEY, BC, V0X 1K0
(250) 292-8637   *SIC 7389*

HEDLEY VOLUNTEER FIRE DEPARTMENT *p 215*
See HEDLEY IMPROVEMENT DISTRICT

HEENAN BLAIKIE S.E.N.C.R.L. *p 963*
200 BAY ST, TORONTO, ON, M5J 2J4
(514) 898-5398   *SIC 8111*

HEER'S DECORATING *p 641*
See HEER'S DECORATING AND DESIGN CENTRES INC

HEER'S DECORATING AND DESIGN CENTRES INC *p 641*
428 GAGE AVE UNIT 4, KITCHENER, ON, N2M 5C9
(519) 578-5330   *SIC 5198*

HEERINGA, J.L. ENTERPRISES LTD *p 203*
278 OLD ISLAND HWY, COURTENAY, BC, V9N 3P1
(250) 338-6553   *SIC 6712*

HEFFEL FINE ART AUCTION HOUSE *p 319*
See HEFFEL GALLERY LIMITED

HEFFEL GALLERY LIMITED *p 319*
2247 GRANVILLE ST, VANCOUVER, BC, V6H 3G1
(604) 732-6505   *SIC 7389*

HEFFLEY CREEK, DIV OF *p 332*
See TOLKO INDUSTRIES LTD

HEFFLEY CREEK, DIVISION OF *p 218*
See TOLKO INDUSTRIES LTD

HEFFNER LEXUS TOYOTA *p 634*
See HEFFNER MOTORS LIMITED

HEFFNER MOTORS LIMITED *p 634*
3121 KING ST E, KITCHENER, ON, N2A 1B1
(519) 748-9666   *SIC 5511*

HEGGIE, R. K. GRAIN LTD *p 153*
GD, RAYMOND, AB, T0K 2S0
SIC 5153

HEICO LIGHTING *p 1301*
See EMD TECHNOLOGIES INCORPORATED

HEIDELBERG CANADA GRAPHIC EQUIPMENT LIMITED *p 740*
6265 KENWAY DR, MISSISSAUGA, ON, L5T 2L3
(905) 362-4400   *SIC 5084*

HEIMSTAED LODGE *p 138*
See MACKENZIE HOUSING MANAGEMENT BOARD

HEINEMANN ELECTRIC CANADA LIMITEE *p 1326*
343 RUE DESLAURIERS, SAINT-LAURENT, QC, H4N 1W2
(514) 332-1163   *SIC 5065*

HEISSIG IMPORT & EXPORT LTD *p 717*
3100 RIDGEWAY DR UNIT 30, MISSISSAUGA, ON, L5L 5M5
SIC 5013

HELA CANADA *p 1001*
See HELA SPICE CANADA INC

HELA SPICE CANADA INC *p 1001*
119 FRANKLIN ST, UXBRIDGE, ON, L9P 1J5
(905) 852-5100   *SIC 5149*

HELCIM INC *p 64*
1300 8 ST SW SUITE 403, CALGARY, AB, T2R 1B2
(403) 291-1172   *SIC 6211*

HELEN BETTY OSBORNE ININIW EDUCATION RESOURCE CENTRE *p 353*
See FRONTIER SCHOOL DIVISION

HELEN HENDERSON CARE CENTRE *p 477*
See GIBSON HOLDINGS (ONTARIO) LTD

HELI-ONE *p 264*
See CHC HELICOPTER HOLDING S.A.R.L.

HELI-ONE CANADA ULC *p 264*
4740 AGAR DR, RICHMOND, BC, V7B 1A3
(604) 276-7500   *SIC 7699*

HELICAL PIER SYSTEMS LTD *p 162*
180 STRATHMOOR DR, SHERWOOD PARK, AB, T8H 2B7
(780) 400-3700   *SIC 3312*

HELICOPTER SURVIVAL RESCUE SERVICES *p 446*
See DSS AVIATION INC

HELICOPTER TRANSPORT SERVICES (CANADA) INC *p 541*
5 HUISSON RD, CARP, ON, K0A 1L0
(613) 839-5868   *SIC 4522*

HELIFOR *p 323*
See HELIFOR INDUSTRIES LIMITED

HELIFOR CANADA CORP *p 326*
815 HORNBY ST SUITE 406, VANCOUVER, BC, V6Z 2E6
SIC 2411

HELIFOR INDUSTRIES LIMITED *p 323*
1200 73RD AVE W SUITE 828, VANCOUVER, BC, V6P 6G5
(604) 269-2000   *SIC 2411*

HELIGEAR CANADA ACQUISITION CORPORATION *p 683*
180 MARKET DR, MILTON, ON, L9T 3H5
(905) 875-4000   *SIC 3728*

HELIJET *p 265*
See HELIJET INTERNATIONAL INC

HELIJET INTERNATIONAL INC *p 265*
5911 AIRPORT RD S, RICHMOND, BC, V7B 1B5
(604) 273-4688   *SIC 4522*

HELIQWEST AVIATION INC *p 168*
27018 SH 633 UNIT 37, STURGEON COUNTY, AB, T8T 0E3
(780) 458-3005   *SIC 4522*

HELIX ADVANCED COMMUNICATIONS & INFRASTRUCTURE, INC *p 93*
12540 129 ST NW, EDMONTON, AB, T5L 4R4
(780) 451-2357   *SIC 5999*

HELIX APPLICATIONS INC *p 939*
82 RICHMOND ST SUITE 203 THE CANADIAN VENTURE BUILDING, TORONTO, ON, M5C 1P1
(416) 848-6865   *SIC 1041*

HELIX HEARING CARE *p 619*
See HEARX HEARING INC

HELIX IT INC *p 101*
18211 105 AVE NW UNIT 101, EDMONTON, AB, T5S 2L5
(780) 454-3549   *SIC 8999*

HELIX IT INC *p 809*
9 ONTARIO ST UNIT 7, ORILLIA, ON, L3V 0T7
(705) 327-6564   *SIC 1731*

HELLENIC HOME FOR THE AGE INC *p 989*
33 WINONA DR, TORONTO, ON, M6G 3Z7
(416) 654-7700   *SIC 8361*

HELLMANN WORLDWIDE LOGISTICS INC *p 735*
1375 CARDIFF BLVD UNIT 1, MISSISSAUGA, ON, L5S 1R1
(905) 564-6620   *SIC 4731*

HELMER, MAX CONSTRUCTION LTD *p 216*
1000 PANORAMA DR RR 7, INVERMERE, BC, V0A 1K7
(250) 342-6767   *SIC 1542*

HELPING LIMITED *p 885*
114 DUNKIRK RD UNIT 1, ST CATHARINES, ON, L2P 3H5
(905) 646-9890   *SIC 7349*

HEMA-QUEBEC *p 1272*

1070 AV DES SCIENCES-DE-LA-VIE, QUE-BEC, QC, G1V 5C3
(418) 780-4362   *SIC* 8099
HEMA-QUEBEC   p 1329
4045 BOUL DE LA COTE-VERTU, SAINT-LAURENT, QC, H4R 2W7
(514) 832-5000   *SIC* 8099
HEMATITE MANUFACTURING INC   p 516
46 PLANT FARM BLVD, BRANTFORD, ON, N3S 7W3
(519) 752-8402   *SIC* 4953
HEMATITE MANUFACTURING, DIV OF   p 606
See PAVACO PLASTICS INC
HEMISPHERE ENERGY CORPORATION   p 313
905 W PENDER ST SUITE 501, VANCOUVER, BC, V6E 2E9
(604) 685-9255   *SIC* 1382
HEMMERA ENVIROCHEM INC   p 190
4730 KINGSWAY 18 FL, BURNABY, BC, V5H 0C6
(604) 669-0424   *SIC* 8748
HEMPHILL GM   p 1042
See HEMPHILL PONTIAC BUICK CHEVROLET GMC LIMITED
HEMPHILL PONTIAC BUICK CHEVROLET GMC LIMITED   p 1042
34 WATER ST, SUMMERSIDE, PE, C1N 4T8
(877) 759-1458   *SIC* 5511
HENAULT & GOSSELIN INC   p 1166
4100 RUE NOTRE-DAME E, MONTREAL, QC, H1V 3T5
(514) 522-0909   *SIC* 1794
HENDERSON CENTRE   p 333
See RECREATION OAK BAY
HENDERSON HOSPITAL   p 614
See HAMILTON HEALTH SCIENCES CORPORATION
HENDERSON RECREATION EQUIPMENT LIMITED   p 881
11 GILBERTSON DR, SIMCOE, ON, N3Y 4K8
(519) 426-9380   *SIC* 3949
HENDERSON SUPERMARKET   p 198
See COQUITLAM SUPERMARKETS LTD
HENDERSON'S PHARMACY LIMITED   p 907
15 FRONT ST S, THOROLD, ON, L2V 1W8
(905) 227-2511   *SIC* 5912
HENDERSON'S PHARMASAVE   p 907
See HENDERSON'S PHARMACY LIMITED
HENDERSON, CW DISTRIBUTION   p 583
See CWH DISTRIBUTION SERVICES INC
HENDRICKSON CANADA ULC   p 896
532 ROMEO ST S, STRATFORD, ON, N5A 4V4
(519) 271-4840   *SIC* 3493
HENDRICKSON SPRING   p 896
See HENDRICKSON CANADA ULC
HENDRIKS INDEPENDENT GROCER   p 839
80 DUFFERIN ST, PERTH, ON, K7H 3A7
SIC 5411
HENDRIKS, ANDREW & SONS GREEN-HOUSES INC   p 489
5095 NORTH SERVICE RD, BEAMSVILLE, ON, L0R 1B3
(905) 563-8132   *SIC* 0181
HENDRIX GENETICS LIMITED   p 640
650 RIVERBEND DR UNIT C, KITCHENER, ON, N2K 3S2
(519) 578-2740   *SIC* 0259
HENDRY SWINTON MCKENZIE INSURANCE SERVICES INC   p 336
830 PANDORA AVE, VICTORIA, BC, V8W 1P4
(250) 388-5555   *SIC* 6411
HENGAB INVESTMENTS LIMITED   p 989
804 DUPONT ST, TORONTO, ON, M6G 1Z6
(416) 531-2401   *SIC* 5211
HENINGER TOYOTA   p 30

3640 MACLEOD TRAIL SE, CALGARY, AB, T2G 2P9
(403) 243-8000   *SIC* 5511
HENKEL CANADA CORPORATION   p 723
2515 MEADOWPINE BLVD UNIT 1, MISSISSAUGA, ON, L5N 6C3
(905) 814-6511   *SIC* 5169
HENKEL LOCTITE   p 723
See HENKEL CANADA CORPORATION
HENLEY DEVELOPMENT CORP   p 266
3560 MONCTON ST, RICHMOND, BC, V7E 3A2
(604) 275-2317   *SIC* 5251
HENLEY HONDA   p 884
See HENLEY MOTORS LIMITED
HENLEY HOUSE LTD, THE   p 884
20 ERNEST ST SUITE 2045, ST CATHARINES, ON, L2N 7T2
(905) 937-9703   *SIC* 8051
HENLEY MOTORS LIMITED   p 884
308 LAKE ST, ST CATHARINES, ON, L2N 4H3
(905) 934-3379   *SIC* 5511
HENNIGES AUTOMOTIVE SCHLEGEL CANADA INC   p 522
4445 FAIRVIEW ST, BURLINGTON, ON, L7L 2A4
(289) 636-4461   *SIC* 3465
HENRI SICOTTE INC   p 1140
779 RUE DE LA BRIQUETERIE, LEVIS, QC, G7A 2N2
(418) 836-8417   *SIC* 1623
HENRIQUEZ PARTNERS   p 298
598 GEORGIA ST W, VANCOUVER, BC, V6B 2A3
(604) 687-5681   *SIC* 8621
HENRIQUEZ PARTNERS ARCHITECTS   p 298
See HENRIQUEZ PARTNERS
HENRY COMPANY CANADA INC   p 866
15 WALLSEND DR, SCARBOROUGH, ON, M1E 3X6
(416) 724-2000   *SIC* 2851
HENRY SCHEIN CANADA, INC   p 206
1619 FOSTER'S WAY, DELTA, BC, V3M 6S7
(604) 527-8888   *SIC* 5047
HENRY SCHEIN CANADA, INC   p 761
345 TOWNLINE RD, NIAGARA ON THE LAKE, ON, L0S 1J0
(905) 646-1711   *SIC* 5047
HENRY SCHEIN CANADA, INC   p 1339
3403 RUE GRIFFITH, SAINT-LAURENT, QC, H4T 1W5
(800) 668-5558   *SIC* 5047
HENRY SINGER   p 89
See HENRY SINGER FASHION GROUP LTD
HENRY SINGER FASHION GROUP LTD   p 89
10180 101 ST NW SUITE 165, EDMONTON, AB, T5J 3S4
(780) 420-0909   *SIC* 5611
HENRY SINGER LTD.   p 89
10180 101 ST NW SUITE 160, EDMONTON, AB, T5J 3S4
(780) 420-0909   *SIC* 6712
HENRY STREET HIGH SCHOOL   p 1014
See DURHAM DISTRICT SCHOOL BOARD
HENRY WISE WOOD HIGH SCHOOL   p 68
See CALGARY BOARD OF EDUCATION
HENRY'S CAMERA   p 937
See CRANBROOK GLEN ENTERPRISES LIMITED
HENRY'S ELECTRIC   p 4
See 567945 ALBERTA LTD
HENRY, KATHERINE PHARMACY LTD   p 812
300 TAUNTON RD E SUITE 2, OSHAWA, ON, L1G 7T4
(905) 579-1900   *SIC* 5912
HENSALL DISTRICT CO-OPERATIVE, INCORPORATED   p 620
1 DAVIDSON DR, HENSALL, ON, N0M 1X0

(519) 262-3002   *SIC* 5153
HENTSCHEL, HART INC   p 860
755 CONFEDERATION ST, SARNIA, ON, N7T 1M8
(519) 344-1123   *SIC* 5511
HENUSET PIPELINE CONSTRUCTION INC   p 68
13024 CANSO PL SW, CALGARY, AB, T2W 3A8
(403) 252-5386   *SIC* 1623
HEPP   p 378
See HEALTHCARE EMPLOYEES PENSION PLAN - MANITOBA
HERB & MAUREEN KLEIN   p 226
See MAUREEN KLEIN
HERB'S TRAVEL PLAZA   p 1001
See H & I ENTERPRISES (VANKLEEK) LTD
HERBALAND NATURALS INC   p 255
13330 MAYCREST WAY, RICHMOND, BC, V6V 2J7
(604) 284-5050   *SIC* 2834
HERBALIFE OF CANADA LTD   p 12
4550 25 ST SE SUITE 120, CALGARY, AB, T2B 3P1
(403) 204-2264   *SIC* 5122
HERBERS AUTO BODY REPAIR LTD   p 120
2721 PARSONS RD NW, EDMONTON, AB, T6N 1B8
(780) 469-8888   *SIC* 7532
HERBLENS MOTORS INC   p 101
11204 170 ST NW, EDMONTON, AB, T5S 2X1
(780) 466-8300   *SIC* 5511
HERBORISTERIE LA CLEF DES CHAMPS INC   p 1391
2205 CH DE LA RIVIERE, VAL-DAVID, QC, J0T 2N0
(819) 322-1561   *SIC* 5149
HERBXTRA   p 1358
See GOURMET NUTRITION F.B INC
HERCULES BULLDOG SEALING PRODUCTS   p 487
See HB SEALING PRODUCTS LTD
HERCULES FORWARDING ULC   p 236
151 SPRUCE ST, NEW WESTMINSTER, BC, V3L 5E6
(604) 517-1331   *SIC* 4731
HERCULES INTERNATIONAL   p 636
See HERCULES TIRE INTERNATIONAL INC
HERCULES SLR INC   p 446
520 WINDMILL RD, DARTMOUTH, NS, B3B 1B3
(902) 482-3125   *SIC* 5051
HERCULES SLR INC   p 522
737 OVAL CRT, BURLINGTON, ON, L7L 6A9
SIC 5051
HERCULES TIRE INTERNATIONAL INC   p 636
155 ARDELT AVE, KITCHENER, ON, N2C 2E1
(519) 885-3100   *SIC* 5014
HERD NORTH AMERICA INC   p 362
2168 SPRINGFIELD RD, WINNIPEG, MB, R2C 2Z2
(204) 222-0880   *SIC* 3714
HERGOTT DUVAL STACK LLP   p 1427
410 22ND ST E SUITE 1200, SASKATOON, SK, S7K 5T6
(306) 934-8000   *SIC* 8721
HERITAGE AUTO LEASING, DIV OF   p 869
See HERITAGE FORD SALES LIMITED
HERITAGE CHRISTIAN ONLINE SCHOOL   p 220
See KELOWNA CHRISTIAN CENTER SOCIETY
HERITAGE CO-OP 1997 LTD   p 352
120 MAIN ST, MINNEDOSA, MB, R0J 1E0
(204) 867-2295   *SIC* 5411
HERITAGE COFFEE CO. LTD   p 657
97 BESSEMER RD UNIT 8, LONDON, ON, N6E 1P9

(519) 686-3620   *SIC* 5149
HERITAGE DESIGN   p 636
227 MANITOU DR SUITE 4, KITCHENER, ON, N2C 1L4
SIC 1521
HERITAGE EDUCATION FUNDS INC   p 767
2005 SHEPPARD AVE E SUITE 700, NORTH YORK, ON, M2J 5B4
(416) 758-4400   *SIC* 6732
HERITAGE FAMILY SERVICES LTD   p 153
4825 47 ST SUITE 300, RED DEER, AB, T4N 1R3
(403) 343-3428   *SIC* 8322
HERITAGE FORD SALES LIMITED   p 869
2660 KINGSTON RD, SCARBOROUGH, ON, M1M 1L6
(416) 261-3311   *SIC* 5511
HERITAGE FROZEN FOODS LTD   p 93
14615 124 AVE NW, EDMONTON, AB, T5L 3B2
(780) 454-7383   *SIC* 2099
HERITAGE GAS LIMITED   p 446
238 BROWNLOW AVE SUITE 200, DARTMOUTH, NS, B3B 1Y2
(902) 466-2003   *SIC* 4924
HERITAGE GROUP OF COMPANIES   p 324
See W.D.I. SERVICES LTD
HERITAGE HARLEY-DAVIDSON LTD   p 124
1616 CALGARY TRAIL SW, EDMONTON, AB, T6W 1A1
(780) 430-7200   *SIC* 5571
HERITAGE HARLEY-DAVIDSON/BUELL   p 124
See HERITAGE HARLEY-DAVIDSON LTD
HERITAGE HILL INSURANCE LTD   p 68
10333 SOUTHPORT RD SW SUITE 355, CALGARY, AB, T2W 3X6
SIC 6411
HERITAGE INN   p 236
See MARBOR HOLDINGS LTD
HERITAGE INN   p 1411
See SASCO DEVELOPMENTS LTD
HERITAGE LODGE PERSONAL CARE   p 386
See REVERA INC
HERITAGE NURSING HOMES INC   p 920
1195 QUEEN ST E SUITE 229, TORONTO, ON, M4M 1L6
SIC 8051
HERITAGE OFFICE FURNISHINGS LTD   p 323
1588 RAND AVE, VANCOUVER, BC, V6P 3G2
(604) 688-2381   *SIC* 5712
HERITAGE PARK HISTORICAL VILLAGE   p 68
See HERITAGE PARK SOCIETY
HERITAGE PARK SOCIETY   p 68
1900 HERITAGE DR SW, CALGARY, AB, T2V 2X3
(403) 268-8526   *SIC* 8412
HERITAGE PLACE CARE FACILITY   p 1004
GD, VIRGIL, ON, L0S 1T0
(905) 468-1111   *SIC* 8059
HERITAGE SALMON   p 395
See TRUE NORTH SALMON CO. LTD
HERITAGE SCHOLARSHIP TRUST PLAN   p 767
See HERITAGE EDUCATION FUNDS INC
HERITAGE SHOP   p 433
See HISTORIC SITES ASSOCIATION OF NEWFOUNDLAND AND LABRADOR INC
HERITAGE SOBEYS   p 119
See SOBEYS CAPITAL INCORPORATED
HERITAGE SURFACE SOLUTIONS   p 23
6815 8 ST NE SUITE 165, CALGARY, AB, T2E 7H7
(403) 291-2804   *SIC* 6211
HERITAGE TRUCK LINES INC   p 483
105 GUTHRIE ST, AYR, ON, N0B 1E0
(519) 632-9052   *SIC* 4213
HERITAGE VILLAGE, DIV OF   p 676
See UNIONVILLE HOME SOCIETY
HERITAGE WOODS SECONDARY

SCHOOL p 248
See SCHOOL DISTRICT NO. 43 (COQUIT-LAM)

HERJAVEC GROUP INC, THE p 624
555 LEGGET DR SUITE 530, KANATA, ON, K2K 2X3
(613) 271-2400   SIC 5045

HERJAVEC GROUP INC, THE p 776
180 DUNCAN MILL RD SUITE 700, NORTH YORK, ON, M3B 1Z6
(416) 639-2193   SIC 7371

HERLE'S HOLDINGS LTD p 144
6214 50 AVE, LLOYDMINSTER, AB, T9V 2C9
(780) 875-3422   SIC 5541

HERLE'S TRUCK & AUTO SPECIALISTS p 144
See HERLE'S HOLDINGS LTD

HERMAN MILLER CANADA, INC p 981
462 WELLINGTON ST W SUITE 200, TORONTO, ON, M5V 1E3
(416) 366-3300   SIC 5021

HERMES ELECTRONICS p 444
See ULTRA ELECTRONICS CANADA INC

HERNICK, J. LIMITED p 585
63 GALAXY BLVD SUITE 5, ETOBICOKE, ON, M9W 5R7
(416) 213-9913   SIC 5013

HERON HOMES p 767
See HURLSTONE HOLDINGS CORP

HERON TERRACE p 1017
See SNR NURSING HOMES LTD

HEROUX-DEVTEK INC p 871
1480 BIRCHMOUNT RD, SCARBOROUGH, ON, M1P 2E3
(416) 757-2366   SIC 3443

HEROUX-DEVTEK INC p 1143
755 RUE THURBER, LONGUEUIL, QC, J4H 3N2
(450) 679-5450   SIC 3728

HEROUX-DEVTEK INC p 1144
1111 RUE SAINT-CHARLES O BUREAU 600, LONGUEUIL, QC, J4K 5G4
(450) 679-3330   SIC 3593

HERRLE FARMS LTD p 883
1253 ERB'S RD, ST AGATHA, ON, N0B 2L0
(519) 886-7576   SIC 0181

HERRLE'S COUNTRY FARM MARKET LTD p 883
1253 ERB'S RD, ST AGATHA, ON, N0B 2L0
(519) 886-7576   SIC 0191

HERRON CHEVROLET PONTIAC BUICK GMC LIMITED p 463
465 WESTVILLE RD, NEW GLASGOW, NS, B2H 2J6
(902) 752-1534   SIC 5511

HERSCHEL SUPPLY COMPANY LTD p 295
611 ALEXANDER ST SUITE 327, VANCOUVER, BC, V6A 1E1
(800) 307-5597   SIC 5199

HERSHEY p 696
See HERSHEY CANADA INC

HERSHEY CANADA INC p 443
375 PLEASANT ST, DARTMOUTH, NS, B2Y 4N4
SIC 2064

HERSHEY CANADA INC p 696
5750 EXPLORER DR SUITE 400, MISSISSAUGA, ON, L4W 0A9
(905) 602-9200   SIC 2064

HERSHEY CANADA INC p 881
1 HERSHEY DR, SMITHS FALLS, ON, K7A 4T8
SIC 2066

HERTZ p 381
See MID CANADIAN INDUSTRIES

HERTZ p 585
See HERTZ CANADA LIMITED

HERTZ p 820
See SURGENOR NATIONAL LEASING LIMITED

HERTZ CANADA p 518
See FLITE LINE SERVICES (KITCHENER) INC

HERTZ CANADA LIMITED p 585
2 CONVAIR DR, ETOBICOKE, ON, M9W 7A1
(416) 674-2020   SIC 7514

HERTZ NORTHERN BUS (2006) LTD p 1433
330 103RD ST E, SASKATOON, SK, S7N 1Z1
(306) 374-5161   SIC 4151

HERVIC ENTERPRISES LTD p 439
2896 MELBOURNE RD RR 1, ARCADIA, NS, B0W 1B0
(902) 742-3981   SIC 5146

HERZING COLLEGE p 935
See HERZING INSTITUTES OF CANADA INC

HERZING INSTITUTES OF CANADA INC p 935
220 YONGE ST SUITE 202, TORONTO, ON, M5B 2H1
(416) 599-6996   SIC 8244

HERZLIAH HIGH SCHOOL p 1220
See TALMUD TORAHS UNIS DE MONTREAL INC

HETTICH CANADA LIMITED PARTNERSHIP p 1339
140 RUE BARR, SAINT-LAURENT, QC, H4T 1Y4
(514) 333-3952   SIC 5072

HEUVELMANS CHEVROLET BUICK GMC CADILLAC LIMITED p 542
755 GRAND AVE E, CHATHAM, ON, N7L 1X5
(519) 352-9200   SIC 5511

HEVECO LTD p 418
4534 ROUTE 11, TABUSINTAC, NB, E9H 1J4
(506) 779-9277   SIC 1499

HEWITT ASSOCIATES CORP p 772
2 SHEPPARD AVE E SUITE 1500, NORTH YORK, ON, M2N 7A4
(416) 225-5001   SIC 8748

HEWITT MATERIAL HANDLING INC p 554
425 MILLWAY AVE, CONCORD, ON, L4K 3V8
(905) 669-6590   SIC 5084

HEWITT MATERIAL HANDLING SYSTEMS p 554
See HEWITT MATERIAL HANDLING INC

HEWITT'S DAIRY LIMITED p 607
128 KING ST E, HAGERSVILLE, ON, N0A 1H0
(905) 768-3500   SIC 5143

HEWLETT PACKARD ENTERPRISE CANADA CO p 696
5150 SPECTRUM WAY SUITE 400, MISSISSAUGA, ON, L4W 5G2
(905) 206-4725   SIC 8731

HEXAVEST INC p 1205
1250 BOUL RENE-LEVESQUE O BUREAU 4200, MONTREAL, QC, H3B 4W8
(514) 390-8484   SIC 8742

HEXCEL CONSTRUCTION LTD p 209
7119 RIVER RD, DELTA, BC, V4G 1A9
(604) 946-8744   SIC 1794

HEXION CANADA INC p 105
12621 156 ST NW, EDMONTON, AB, T5V 1E1
(780) 447-1270   SIC 2821

HEYINK, HENRY CONSTRUCTION LTD p 543
275 COLBORNE ST, CHATHAM, ON, N7M 3M3
(519) 354-4593   SIC 1623

HEYS INTERNATIONAL LTD p 731
333 FOSTER CRES SUITE 1, MISSISSAUGA, ON, L5R 4E5
(905) 565-8100   SIC 5099

HFC PRESTIGE INTERNATIONAL CANADA INC p 1094
1255 RTE TRANSCANADIENNE BUREAU 200, DORVAL, QC, H9P 2V4
(514) 421-5050   SIC 5122

HFH INC p 569

6006 HWY 6, ELORA, ON, N0B 1S0
(519) 821-2040   SIC 1542

HGC MANAGEMENT INC p 517
50 SHAVER ST, BRANTFORD, ON, N3T 5M1
(519) 754-4732   SIC 4953

HGS CANADA INC p 446
250 BROWNLOW AVE SUITE 11, DARTMOUTH, NS, B3B 1W9
(902) 481-9475   SIC 7389

HGS CANADA INC p 838
100 CRANDALL ST SUITE 100, PEMBROKE, ON, K8A 6X8
(613) 633-4600   SIC 7379

HGS CANADA INC p 1040
82 HILLSTROM AVE, CHARLOTTETOWN, PE, C1E 2C6
(902) 370-3200   SIC 7379

HHHS p 607
See HALIBURTON HIGHLANDS HEALTH SERVICES CORPORATION

HHOF p 942
See HOCKEY HALL OF FAME AND MUSEUM

HHS VOLUNTEER ASSOCIATION p 612
See HAMILTON HEALTH SCIENCES CORPORATION

HI LINE FARM EQUIPMENT LTD p 172
4723 39 AVE, WETASKIWIN, AB, T9A 2J4
(780) 352-9244   SIC 5083

HI SIGNS THE FATH GROUP LTD p 115
9570 58 AVE NW, EDMONTON, AB, T6E 0B6
(780) 468-6181   SIC 3993

HI-CORE, DIV OF p 1057
See MATRA PLAST INDUSTRIES INC

HI-CUBE STORAGE PRODUCTS LTD p 209
7363 WILSON AVE, DELTA, BC, V4G 1E5
(604) 946-4838   SIC 5046

HI-HOG FARM & RANCH EQUIPMENT LTD p 8
8447 23 AVE NE, CALGARY, AB, T1Y 7G9
(403) 280-8300   SIC 5191

HI-KALIBRE EQUIPMENT LIMITED p 109
7321 68 AVE NW, EDMONTON, AB, T6B 3T6
(780) 435-1111   SIC 3491

HI-LITE p 740
See JASCO SALES INC

HI-POINT INDUSTRIES (1991) LTD p 421
141 SUNSET DR, BISHOPS FALLS, NL, A0H 1C0
(709) 258-6274   SIC 5159

HI-PRO FEEDS LP p 150
HWY 2A 306 AVE, OKOTOKS, AB, T1S 1A2
(403) 938-8350   SIC 5999

HI-TEC INDUSTRIES INC p 355
1000 6TH AVE NE, PORTAGE LA PRAIRIE, MB, R1N 0B4
(204) 239-4270   SIC 3523

HI-TEC PROFILES INC p 1418
2301 INDUSTRIAL DR, REGINA, SK, S4P 3C6
(306) 721-3800   SIC 5211

HI-TECH BEAUTY SUPPLIES LTD p 35
5718 BURBANK CRES SE, CALGARY, AB, T2H 1Z6
(403) 253-3113   SIC 5087

HI-TECH BUSINESS SYSTEMS LTD p 132
10115 100 AVE, GRANDE PRAIRIE, AB, T8V 0V4
(780) 538-4128   SIC 5044

HI-TECH GEARS CANADA INC, THE p 603
361 SPEEDVALE AVE W SUITE 29, GUELPH, ON, N1H 1C7
(519) 836-3180   SIC 3499

HI-TECH SEALS INC p 115
9211 41 AVE NW, EDMONTON, AB, T6E 6R5
(780) 438-6055   SIC 5085

HI-WAY 13 TRANSPORT LTD p 78
4621 19 ST, CAMROSE, AB, T4V 0Z4
(780) 672-1695   SIC 4212

HI-WAY 9 EXPRESS LTD p 82

711 ELGIN CLOSE, DRUMHELLER, AB, T0J 0Y0
(403) 823-4242   SIC 4212

HI-WAY 9 EXPRESS LTD p 155
4120 78 ST CRES SUITE 4120, RED DEER, AB, T4P 3E3
(403) 342-4266   SIC 4212

HI-WAY SALES AND SERVICE p 5
See KOCA AB SERVICES LTD

HIAB QUEBEC p 916
See ATLAS POLAR COMPANY LIMITED

HIBAR SYSTEMS LIMITED p 852
35 POLLARD ST, RICHMOND HILL, ON, L4B 1A8
(905) 731-2400   SIC 3565

HIBCO CONSTRUCTION p 95
See 1496803 ALBERTA INC

HIBERNIA MANAGEMENT AND DEVELOPMENT COMPANY LTD p 432
100 NEW GOWER ST SUITE 1000, ST. JOHN'S, NL, A1C 6K3
SIC 1382

HIBON INC p 1250
100 RUE VOYAGEUR, POINTE-CLAIRE, QC, H9R 6A8
(514) 631-3501   SIC 5084

HICAT CORPORATION INC p 1283
640 14E AV BUREAU 102, RICHELIEU, QC, J3L 5R5
(450) 982-1494   SIC 3732

HICHAUD INC p 1267
2485 BOUL NEUVIALLE, QUEBEC, QC, G1P 3A6
(418) 682-0782   SIC 3149

HICKMAN MOTORS LIMITED p 430
85 KENMOUNT RD, ST. JOHN'S, NL, A1B 3P8
(709) 726-6990   SIC 5511

HICKMAN MOUNT RECONSTRUCTION INC p 649
562 SOVEREIGN RD UNIT 5, LONDON, ON, N5V 4K6
(519) 457-1970   SIC 6331

HICKS MORLEY HAMILTON STEWART STORIE LLP p 969
77 KING ST W 39TH FL TD CENTRE, TORONTO, ON, M5K 2A1
(416) 362-1011   SIC 8111

HIGGINS & BURKE GOURMET p 704
See MOTHER PARKER'S TEA & COFFEE INC

HIGGINS COHN BRAND MANAGEMENT p 1029
See 2012865 ONTARIO INC

HIGGINS CONSTRUCTION p 468
See HIGGINS, ROBERT (1984) COMPANY LIMITED

HIGGINS FAMILY PHARMACY LTD p 467
1174 KINGS RD SUITE 149, SYDNEY, NS, B1S 1C9
(902) 539-8111   SIC 5912

HIGGINS RENT-ALL LTD p 571
389 HORNER AVE, ETOBICOKE, ON, M8W 2A2
(416) 252-4050   SIC 7359

HIGGINS, PATRICK J ENTERPRISES LTD p 1001
327 TORONTO ST S, UXBRIDGE, ON, L9P 1Z7
(905) 852-3315   SIC 5531

HIGGINS, ROBERT (1984) COMPANY LIMITED p 468
205 MAIN ST, TRENTON, NS, B0K 1X0
(902) 755-5515   SIC 1542

HIGGINSON EQUIPMENT INC p 522
1175 CORPORATE DR UNIT 1, BURLINGTON, ON, L7L 5V5
(905) 335-2211   SIC 5085

HIGH ARCTIC ENERGY SERVICES INC p 51
700 2ND ST SW SUITE 500, CALGARY, AB, T2P 2W1

(403) 508-7836   *SIC* 1381
HIGH COUNTRY CHEVROLET BUICK GMC LTD   *p* 136
702 11 AVE SE, HIGH RIVER, AB, T1V 1M3
(403) 652-2000   *SIC* 5511
HIGH HILL COURIERS   *p* 494
See 429400 ONTARIO LTD
HIGH HOOPS   *p* 730
See CANADIAN MARKETING TEST CASE 200 LIMITED
HIGH KOSHER POULTRY   *p* 920
See CHAI POULTRY INC
HIGH LEVEL LUMBER DIVISION   *p* 135
See TOLKO INDUSTRIES LTD
HIGH LIFE HEATING, AIR CONDITIONING & SECURITY INC   *p* 876
102 PASSMORE AVE, SCARBOROUGH, ON, M1V 4S9
(416) 298-2987   *SIC* 1711
HIGH LINE ELECTRICAL CONSTRUCTORS LTD   *p* 124
2304 119 AVE NE SUITE 200, EDMONTON, AB, T6S 1B3
(780) 452-8900   *SIC* 1731
HIGH LINE NETS & GEAR   *p* 462
See YARMOUTH SEA PRODUCTS LTD
HIGH LINER   *p* 461
See HIGH LINER FOODS INCORPORATED
HIGH LINER FOODS INCORPORATED   *p* 461
100 BATTERY PT, LUNENBURG, NS, B0J 2C0
(902) 634-8811   *SIC* 2092
HIGH OUTPUT SPORTS CANADA INC   *p* 239
1465 CHARLOTTE RD, NORTH VANCOUVER, BC, V7J 1H1
(604) 985-3933   *SIC* 5091
HIGH PRAIRIE & DISTRICT RECREATION BOARD   *p* 135
See HIGH PRAIRIE & DISTRICT REGIONAL RECREATION BOARD
HIGH PRAIRIE & DISTRICT REGIONAL RECREATION BOARD   *p* 135
5209 50TH ST, HIGH PRAIRIE, AB, T0G 1E0
(780) 536-2630   *SIC* 8699
HIGH PRAIRIE DIVISION   *p* 135
See TOLKO INDUSTRIES LTD
HIGH PRAIRIE FORD SALES & SERVICE LTD   *p* 135
5404 40 ST, HIGH PRAIRIE, AB, T0G 1E0
(780) 523-4193   *SIC* 5511
HIGH PRAIRIE SCHOOL DIVISION NO 48 *p* 135
16532 TOWNSHIP RD 744, HIGH PRAIRIE, AB, T0G 1E0
(780) 523-3337   *SIC* 8211
HIGH RIVER AUTOPLEX & RV   *p* 135
See 618382 ALBERTA LTD
HIGH RIVER FORD SALES   *p* 136
1103 11 AVE SE, HIGH RIVER, AB, T1V 1P2
SIC 5511
HIGH RIVER GENERAL HOSPITAL   *p* 135
See ALBERTA HEALTH SERVICES
HIGH ROLLERS CUSTOM MOTOR PARTS *p* 130
11091 86 AVE, FORT SASKATCHEWAN, AB, T8L 3T7
(780) 992-3225   *SIC* 5571
HIGH STRENGTH PLATES & PROFILES INC   *p* 735
7464 TRANMERE DR, MISSISSAUGA, ON, L5S 1K4
(905) 673-5770   *SIC* 3312
HIGH-CREST ENTERPRISES LIMITED   *p* 466
11 SPROUL ST, SPRINGHILL, NS, B0M 1X0
(902) 597-2797   *SIC* 8051
HIGH-CREST SPRINGHILL   *p* 466

See HIGH-CREST ENTERPRISES LIMITED
HIGHBOURNE LIFECARE CENTRE   *p* 577
See EXTENDICARE INC
HIGHBURY CANCO CORPORATION *p* 644
148 ERIE ST S, LEAMINGTON, ON, N8H 0C3
(519) 322-1288   *SIC* 2099
HIGHBURY FORD SALES LIMITED   *p* 651
1365 DUNDAS ST, LONDON, ON, N5W 3B5
(519) 455-1800   *SIC* 5511
HIGHER EDUCATION, DIV OF   *p* 954
See MCGRAW-HILL RYERSON LIMITED
HIGHFIELD HOLDINGS INC   *p* 1031
101 JEVLAN DR SUITE 1, WOODBRIDGE, ON, L4L 8C2
(905) 264-2799   *SIC* 6794
HIGHFIELD SQUARE   *p* 466
See CROMBIE DEVELOPMENTS LIMITED
HIGHGATE RETIREMENT HOMES INC   *p* 477
325 FIDDLER'S GREEN RD SUITE 215, ANCASTER, ON, L9G 1W9
(905) 648-8399   *SIC* 5047
HIGHGATE RETIREMENT RESIDENCE   *p* 477
See HIGHGATE RETIREMENT HOMES INC
HIGHLAND CATERERS LTD   *p* 249
570 3RD AVE, PRINCE GEORGE, BC, V2L 3C3
(250) 563-5332   *SIC* 6712
HIGHLAND CELLULAR   *p* 438
See HOME DOCTOR LIMITED, THE
HIGHLAND CHEVROLET CADILLAC LTD *p* 480
15783 YONGE ST, AURORA, ON, L4G 1P4
(905) 727-1900   *SIC* 5511
HIGHLAND COPPER COMPANY INC   *p* 1144
1111 RUE SAINT-CHARLES O BUREAU 101, LONGUEUIL, QC, J4K 5G4
(450) 677-2455   *SIC* 1021
HIGHLAND EQUIPMENT INC   *p* 574
136 THE EAST MALL, ETOBICOKE, ON, M8Z 5V5
(416) 236-9610   *SIC* 3499
HIGHLAND FARMS INC   *p* 706
50 MATHESON BLVD E, MISSISSAUGA, ON, L4Z 1N5
(905) 501-9545   *SIC* 5411
HIGHLAND FARMS INC   *p* 871
850 ELLESMERE RD, SCARBOROUGH, ON, M1P 2W5
(416) 298-1999   *SIC* 5411
HIGHLAND FARMS SUPERMARKETS   *p* 871
See HIGHLAND FARMS INC
HIGHLAND FEATHER MANUFACTURING INC   *p* 874
171 NUGGET AVE, SCARBOROUGH, ON, M1S 3B1
(416) 754-7443   *SIC* 5023
HIGHLAND FORD SALES LIMITED   *p* 470
35 BALODIS DR, WESTVILLE, NS, B0K 2A0
(902) 396-2020   *SIC* 5511
HIGHLAND FORD SALES LIMITED   *p* 862
68 GREAT NORTHERN RD, SAULT STE. MARIE, ON, P6B 4Y5
(705) 759-5050   *SIC* 5511
HIGHLAND FOUNDRY LTD   *p* 282
9670 187 ST, SURREY, BC, V4N 3N6
(604) 888-8444   *SIC* 3325
HIGHLAND HELICOPTERS LTD   *p* 265
4240 AGAR DR, RICHMOND, BC, V7B 1A3
(604) 273-6161   *SIC* 4522
HIGHLAND MOVING & STORAGE LTD   *p* 124
14490 157 AVE NW, EDMONTON, AB, T6V 0K8
(780) 453-6777   *SIC* 4214
HIGHLAND NATIONAL LEASING, DIV OF *p* 480

See HIGHLAND CHEVROLET CADILLAC LTD
HIGHLAND PACKERS LTD   *p* 894
432 HIGHLAND RD E, STONEY CREEK, ON, L8J 3G4
(905) 662-8396   *SIC* 2011
HIGHLAND SECONDARY SCHOOL   *p* 566
See HAMILTON-WENTWORTH DISTRICT SCHOOL BOARD, THE
HIGHLAND SHORES CHILDREN'S AID SOCIETY   *p* 492
363 DUNDAS ST W, BELLEVILLE, ON, K8P 1B3
(613) 962-9291   *SIC* 8322
HIGHLAND TRANSPORT   *p* 676
See TRANSPORT TFI 3 L.P.
HIGHLANDS BLENDING & PACKAGING G.P.   *p* 415
555 COURTENAY CAUSEWAY, SAINT JOHN, NB, E2L 4E6
(506) 632-7000   *SIC* 2992
HIGHLANDS FUEL DELIVERY G.P.   *p* 415
10 SYDNEY ST, SAINT JOHN, NB, E2L 5E6
(506) 202-2000   *SIC* 4924
HIGHLANDS FUEL DELIVERY G.P.   *p* 415
201 CROWN ST, SAINT JOHN, NB, E2L 5E5
(506) 202-2000   *SIC* 4924
HIGHLANDS GOLF CLUB   *p* 107
6603 ADA BLVD NW, EDMONTON, AB, T5W 4N5
(780) 474-4211   *SIC* 7997
HIGHLANDS SUMMER FESTIVAL, THE *p* 607
5358 COUNTY RD 21, HALIBURTON, ON, K0M 1S0
(705) 457-9933   *SIC* 8699
HIGHLIGHT MOTOR FREIGHT INC   *p* 554
391 CREDITSTONE RD, CONCORD, ON, L4K 1N8
(905) 761-1400   *SIC* 4213
HIGHLINE MANUFACTURING LTD   *p* 1437
HWY 27, VONDA, SK, S0K 4N0
(306) 258-2233   *SIC* 3523
HIGHLINE MUSHROOMS   *p* 81
See HIGHLINE MUSHROOMS WEST LIMITED
HIGHLINE MUSHROOMS WEST LIMITED *p* 81
281090 SERVICE RD, CROSSFIELD, AB, T0M 0S0
(403) 464-4396   *SIC* 0182
HIGHLINE MUSHROOMS WEST LIMITED *p* 227
3392 224 ST, LANGLEY, BC, V2Z 2G8
(604) 534-0278   *SIC* 0191
HIGHLINE PRODUCE LIMITED   *p* 493
339 CONLEY RD, BLOOMFIELD, ON, K0K 1G0
(613) 399-3121   *SIC* 0182
HIGHLINE PRODUCE LIMITED   *p* 644
506 MERSEA ROAD 5, LEAMINGTON, ON, N8H 3V5
(519) 326-8643   *SIC* 0182
HIGHLINER INN   *p* 296
See AQUILINI INVESTMENT GROUP INC
HIGHRISE WINDOW TECHNOLOGIES INC *p* 554
131 CALDARI RD UNIT 1, CONCORD, ON, L4K 3Z9
(905) 738-8600   *SIC* 3442
HIGHTECH SALES COACH INC   *p* 319
1338 BROADWAY W SUITE 305, VANCOUVER, BC, V6H 1H2
(604) 731-1377   *SIC* 7389
HIGHVAIL SYSTEMS INC   *p* 926
1 ST CLAIR AVE W SUITE 1201, TORONTO, ON, M4V 1K6
(416) 867-3000   *SIC* 5045
HIGHWAY 21 FEEDERS LTD   *p* 2
GD, ACME, AB, T0M 0A0
(403) 546-2278   *SIC* 0211
HIGHWAY STERLING WESTERN STAR INC

p 483
1021 INDUSTRIAL RD, AYR, ON, N0B 1E0
(519) 740-2405   *SIC* 5511
HIGHWOOD DISTILLERS LTD   *p* 70
4948 126 AVE SE UNIT 23, CALGARY, AB, T2Z 0A9
(403) 216-2440   *SIC* 5182
HIIYE'YU LELUM FRIENDSHIP   *p* 212
See NATIONAL ASSOCIATION OF FRIENDSHIP CENTRES
HILBAR ENTERPRISES INC   *p* 341
118 BRIDGE RD, WEST VANCOUVER, BC, V7P 3R2
(604) 983-2411   *SIC* 6712
HILDEBRAND MOTORS LTD   *p* 151
6401 46 ST, OLDS, AB, T4H 1L7
(403) 556-3371   *SIC* 5511
HILITE FINE FOODS INC   *p* 571
415 HORNER AVE UNIT 4, ETOBICOKE, ON, M8W 4W3
(416) 503-0499   *SIC* 5148
HILL AND KNOWLTON CANADA, DIV OF *p* 931
See WPP GROUP CANADA COMMUNICATIONS LIMITED
HILL PARK SCHOOL   *p* 616
See HAMILTON-WENTWORTH DISTRICT SCHOOL BOARD, THE
HILL, NORMAN REALTY INC   *p* 679
20 CACHET WOODS CRT SUITE 2, MARKHAM, ON, L6C 3G1
(416) 226-5515   *SIC* 6531
HILL-ROM CANADA LTD   *p* 723
6950 CREDITVIEW RD UNIT 4, MISSISSAUGA, ON, L5N 0A6
(905) 206-1355   *SIC* 5047
HILLATON FOODS LIMITED   *p* 465
1853 SAXON ST, PORT WILLIAMS, NS, B0P 1T0
(902) 582-3343   *SIC* 2034
HILLCREST COLONY INC   *p* 1406
GD, DUNDURN, SK, S0K 1K0
(306) 492-2499   *SIC* 0191
HILLCREST HIGH SCHOOL   *p* 818
See OTTAWA-CARLETON DISTRICT SCHOOL BOARD
HILLCREST PLACE HOLDINGS LTD *p* 347
930 26TH ST SUITE 104, BRANDON, MB, R7B 2B8
(204) 728-6690   *SIC* 8051
HILLCREST PLACE PERSONAL CARE   *p* 347
See HILLCREST PLACE HOLDINGS LTD
HILLCREST VOLKSWAGON (1979) LTD *p* 455
3154 ROBIE ST, HALIFAX, NS, B3K 4P9
(902) 453-2790   *SIC* 5511
HILLEN NURSERY LTD   *p* 746
23078 ADELAIDE RD, MOUNT BRYDGES, ON, N0L 1W0
(519) 264-9057   *SIC* 0181
HILLFIELD-STRATHALLAN COLLEGE   *p* 617
299 FENNELL AVE W, HAMILTON, ON, L9C 1G3
(905) 389-1367   *SIC* 8211
HILLMAN CANADA   *p* 868
See HILLMAN GROUP CANADA ULC, THE
HILLMAN GROUP CANADA ULC, THE   *p* 868
55 MILNE AVE, SCARBOROUGH, ON, M1L 4N3
(416) 694-3351   *SIC* 3452
HILLMAN'S TRANSFER LIMITED   *p* 467
1159 UPPER PRINCE ST, SYDNEY, NS, B1P 5P8
(902) 564-8113   *SIC* 4213
HILLMAR INDUSTRIES LIMITED   *p* 209
7371 VANTAGE WAY, DELTA, BC, V4G 1C9
(604) 946-7115   *SIC* 3499
HILLS FOODS LTD   *p* 201
130 GLACIER ST UNIT 1, COQUITLAM, BC, V3K 5Z6
(604) 472-1500   *SIC* 5149

HILLS OF KERRISDALE   p 322
See REID'S DRY GOODS LTD
HILLSBOROUGH HOSPITAL   p 1039
See PROVINCE OF PEI
HILLSDALE CANADIAN PERFORMANCE EQUITY   p 969
100 WELLINGTON ST W SUITE 2100, TORONTO, ON, M5K 1J3
(416) 913-3900   SIC 6722
HILLSDALE INVESTMENT MANAGEMENT INC   p 969
100 WELLINGTON ST W SUITE 2100, TORONTO, ON, M5K 1J3
(416) 913-3900   SIC 6282
HILLSDALE TERRACES   p 811
See CORPORATION OF THE REGIONAL MUNICIPALITY OF DURHAM, THE
HILLSIDE CELLARS WINERY LTD   p 243
1350 NARAMATA RD, PENTICTON, BC, V2A 8T6
(250) 493-6274   SIC 5921
HILLSIDE GARDENS LIMITED   p 497
1383 RIVER RD, BRADFORD, ON, L3Z 4A6
(905) 775-3356   SIC 5148
HILLSIDE MANOR   p 537
See REVERA LONG TERM CARE INC
HILLSIDE MANOR   p 896
See REVERA LONG TERM CARE INC
HILLSIDE MOTORS (1973) LTD   p 1039
113 ST. PETERS RD, CHARLOTTETOWN, PE, C1A 5P3
(902) 368-2438   SIC 5511
HILLSIDE NISSAN LTD   p 401
580 PROSPECT ST, FREDERICTON, NB, E3B 6G9
(506) 458-9423   SIC 5511
HILLSIDE PINES HOME FOR SPECIAL CARE SOCIETY   p 441
77 EXHIBITION DR, BRIDGEWATER, NS, B4V 3K6
(902) 543-1525   SIC 8051
HILLSIDE WINERY AND BISTRO   p 243
See HILLSIDE CELLARS WINERY LTD
HILLTOP PETRO CANADA   p 343
See CANADIAN METAL AND FIBRE LTD
HILLTOP SALES & SERVICE LTD   p 332
4407 27 ST, VERNON, BC, V1T 4Y5
(250) 542-2324   SIC 5511
HILLTOP SUBARU/VERNON HYUNDAI   p 332
See HILLTOP SALES & SERVICE LTD
HILLVIEW COLONY   p 160
See HUTTERIAN BRETHREN CHURCH OF HILLVIEW COLONY
HILROY   p 733
See ACCO BRANDS CANADA LP
HILTON   p 262
See VANCOUVER AIRPORT CENTRE LIMITED
HILTON   p 415
See HILTON CANADA CO.
HILTON   p 1269
See HILTON CANADA CO.
HILTON CANADA CO.   p 415
1 MARKET SQ, SAINT JOHN, NB, E2L 4Z6
(506) 693-8484   SIC 7011
HILTON CANADA CO.   p 688
5875 AIRPORT RD, MISSISSAUGA, ON, L4V 1N1
(905) 677-9900   SIC 7011
HILTON CANADA CO.   p 952
145 RICHMOND ST W, TORONTO, ON, M5H 2L2
(416) 869-3456   SIC 7011
HILTON CANADA CO.   p 1269
1100 BOUL RENE-LEVESQUE E BUREAU 1797, QUEBEC, QC, G1R 5V2
(418) 647-2411   SIC 7011
HILTON GARDEN INN   p 102
See PLATINUM INVESTMENTS LTD
HILTON GARDEN INN HOTEL AND CONFERENCE CENTRE   p 547
See 1406284 ONTARIO INC

HILTON LONDON   p 656
See LONDON (KING ST.) PURCHASECO INC
HILTON MONTREAL / LAVAL   p 1085
See GROUPE HOTELIER GRAND CHATEAU INC
HILTON SUITES CONFERENCE CENTRE & SPA   p 680
See MARKHAM SUITES HOTEL LIMITED
HILTON TORONTO   p 952
See HILTON CANADA CO.
HILTON TORONTO AIRPORT HOTEL & SUITES   p 688
See HILTON CANADA CO.
HILTON TORONTO, THE   p 955
See NORTHSTAR HOSPITALITY LIMITED PARTNERSHIP
HILTON VANCOUVER METROTOWN   p 190
6083 MCKAY AVE, BURNABY, BC, V5H 2W7
(604) 438-1200   SIC 7011
HILTON VILLA CARE CENTRE   p 270
See PARK PLACE SENIORS LIVING INC
HILTON WHISTLER RESORT & SPA   p 343
See WW HOTELS (WHISTLER) LIMITED PARTNERSHIP
HIMSL LAW OFFICE   p 170
See PORTAGE COLLEGE
HINAN, T.R. CONSTRUCTION LIMITED   p 885
31 CHURCH ST, ST CATHARINES, ON, L2R 3B7
   SIC 1542
HINCKS-DELLCREST TREATMENT CENTRE, THE   p 786
1645 SHEPPARD AVE W, NORTH YORK, ON, M3M 2X4
(416) 633-0515   SIC 8093
HIND, CRAIG DODGE CHRYSLER LIMITED   p 871
2180 LAWRENCE AVE E, SCARBOROUGH, ON, M1P 2P8
   SIC 5511
HINES INDUSTRIAL SITE SERVICES GROUP INC   p 128
8130 MANNING AVE, FORT MCMURRAY, AB, T9H 1V7
(780) 790-3500   SIC 7349
HING LEE MOTORS LIMITED   p 920
601 EASTERN AVE, TORONTO, ON, M4M 1E3
(416) 461-2323   SIC 5511
HINO MOTORS CANADA, LTD   p 723
6975 CREDITVIEW RD UNIT 2, MISSISSAUGA, ON, L5N 8E9
(905) 670-3352   SIC 5012
HINO TRUCK CENTRE   p 690
See 1426195 ONTARIO LIMITED
HINSPERGERS POLY INDUSTRIES LTD   p 708
645 NEEDHAM LANE, MISSISSAUGA, ON, L5A 1T9
(905) 272-0144   SIC 2399
HINTON WOOD PRODUCTS   p 136
See WEST FRASER MILLS LTD
HIP RESTAURANTS LTD   p 797
1011 UPPER MIDDLE RD E SUITE C3, OAKVILLE, ON, L6H 5Z9
(647) 403-2494   SIC 5812
HIPPERSON CONSTRUCTION   p 1418
See HIPPERSON CONSTRUCTION COMPANY (1996) LIMITED
HIPPERSON CONSTRUCTION COMPANY (1996) LIMITED   p 1418
2161 SCARTH ST UNIT 200, REGINA, SK, S4P 2H8
(306) 359-0303   SIC 1542
HIRAM WALKER & SONS LIMITED   p 1022
2072 RIVERSIDE DR E, WINDSOR, ON, N8Y 4S5
(519) 254-5171   SIC 2085
HIRE HUSBAND   p 568
200 QUEEN ST W, ELMVALE, ON, L0L 1P0

(705) 733-6355   SIC 1522
HIRE RITE PERSONNEL LTD   p 835
366 9TH ST E, OWEN SOUND, ON, N4K 1P1
(519) 376-6662   SIC 7381
HIRERIGHT CANADA CORPORATION   p 963
70 UNIVERSITY AVE SUITE 200, TORONTO, ON, M5J 2M4
(416) 956-5000   SIC 7361
HIROC   p 363
See HEALTHCARE INSURANCE RECIPROCAL OF CANADA
HIROC   p 771
See HEALTHCARE INSURANCE RECIPROCAL OF CANADA
HIROC FOUNDATION, THE   p 772
4711 YONGE ST SUITE 1600, NORTH YORK, ON, M2N 6K8
(416) 733-2773   SIC 8699
HIROC INSURANCE SERVICES LIMITED   p 772
4711 YONGE ST SUITE 1600, NORTH YORK, ON, M2N 6K8
(416) 733-2773   SIC 6311
HIS INTERNATIONAL TOURS BC INC   p 305
636 HORNBY ST, VANCOUVER, BC, V6C 2G2
(604) 685-3524   SIC 4724
HISHKOONIKUN EDUCATION AUTHORITY   p 627
GD, KASHECHEWAN, ON, P0L 1S0
(705) 275-4111   SIC 8748
HISTAR MANAGEMENT   p 770
See SUNDER GROUP OF COMPANIES LTD
HISTORIC SITES ASSOCIATION OF NEWFOUNDLAND AND LABRADOR INC   p 433
10 FORBES ST SUITE 204, ST. JOHN'S, NL, A1E 3L5
(709) 753-5515   SIC 8699
HITACHI CAPITAL CANADA CORP   p 528
3390 SOUTH SERVICE RD SUITE 301, BURLINGTON, ON, L7N 3J5
(866) 241-9021   SIC 8741
HITACHI CONSTRUCTION TRUCK MANUFACTURING LTD   p 603
200 WOODLAWN RD W, GUELPH, ON, N1H 1B6
(519) 823-2000   SIC 3532
HITACHI DATA SYSTEMS INC   p 952
11 KING ST W SUITE 1400, TORONTO, ON, M5H 4C7
(416) 494-4114   SIC 7372
HITACHI ID SYSTEMS HOLDING, INC   p 30
1401 1 ST SE SUITE 500, CALGARY, AB, T2G 2J3
(403) 233-0740   SIC 7371
HITACHI ID SYSTEMS, INC   p 30
1401 1 ST SE SUITE 500, CALGARY, AB, T2G 2J3
(403) 233-0740   SIC 7371
HITACHI SOLUTIONS CANADA, LTD   p 64
550 11 AVE SW SUITE 1000, CALGARY, AB, T2R 1M7
(866) 231-4332   SIC 7372
HITACHI SOLUTIONS CANADA, LTD   p 774
36 YORK MILLS RD SUITE 502, NORTH YORK, ON, M2P 2E9
(416) 961-4332   SIC 7372
HITACHI SYSTEMS SECURITY INC   p 1059
955 MICHELE-BOHEC BUREAU 244, BLAINVILLE, QC, J7C 5J6
(450) 430-8166   SIC 7376
HITCH HOUSE INC, THE   p 880
1490 11 HWY S, SHANTY BAY, ON, L0L 2L0
(705) 722-0008   SIC 5571
HITE SERVICES LIMITED   p 898
790 LAPOINTE ST, SUDBURY, ON, P3A 5N8
(705) 524-5333   SIC 7389
HITFAR CONCEPTS LTD   p 182

2999 UNDERHILL AVE SUITE 109, BURNABY, BC, V5A 3C2
(604) 873-8364   SIC 5065
HIVE STRATEGIC MARKETING INC, THE   p 981
544 KING ST W, TORONTO, ON, M5V 1M3
(416) 923-3800   SIC 8743
HIWAY FUEL SERVICES LTD   p 246
1485 COAST MERIDIAN RD SUITE 200, PORT COQUITLAM, BC, V3C 5P1
(604) 552-8586   SIC 5172
HIWAY REFRIGERATION LTD   p 246
1462 MUSTANG PL, PORT COQUITLAM, BC, V3C 6L2
(604) 944-0119   SIC 7623
HJ LINNEN ASSOCIATES   p 1418
2161 SCARTH ST SUITE 200, REGINA, SK, S4P 2H8
(306) 586-9611   SIC 8732
HJV EQUIPMENT   p 476
See VANDER ZAAG, H. J. FARM EQUIPMENT LTD
HKH OPPORTUNITIES INC   p 497
118 HOLLAND ST W, BRADFORD, ON, L3Z 2B4
(905) 775-0282   SIC 5461
HLADY, RONALD H. AUTO SALES LTD   p 69
250 SHAWVILLE WAY SE, CALGARY, AB, T2Y 3J1
   SIC 5531
HLS HARD-LINE SOLUTIONS INC   p 565
53 MAIN ST W, DOWLING, ON, P0M 1R0
(705) 855-1310   SIC 3663
HLS THERAPEUTICS INC   p 585
10 CARLSON CRT UNIT 701, ETOBICOKE, ON, M9W 6L2
(647) 495-9000   SIC 2834
HLS THERAPEUTICS INC   p 814
940 THORNTON RD S, OSHAWA, ON, L1J 7E2
(905) 725-5445   SIC 2834
HM SECURITE   p 1182
See GFP LES HOTES DE MONTREAL INC
HMC COMMUNICATIONS INC   p 455
2829 AGRICOLA ST, HALIFAX, NS, B3K 4E5
(902) 453-0700   SIC 7389
HMI CONSTRUCTION INC   p 1276
6275 BOUL DE L'ORMIERE, QUEBEC, QC, G2C 1B9
(418) 842-3232   SIC 1541
HMMS   p 649
See HEALTHCARE MATERIALS MANAGEMENT SERVICES
HMS HOST   p 773
See SMSI TRAVEL CENTRES INC
HMT CANADA LTD   p 16
11051 50 ST SE UNIT 130, CALGARY, AB, T2C 3E5
(403) 252-4487   SIC 7389
HMU   p 237
See HARLOCK MURRAY UNDERWRITING LTD
HMZ METALS INC   p 939
2 TORONTO ST SUITE 500, TORONTO, ON, M5C 2B6
   SIC 3339
HNA ACQUISITION ULC   p 1065
50 BOUL MARIE-VICTORIN, BOUCHERVILLE, QC, J4B 1V5
(450) 655-0396   SIC 2821
HNHB CCAC   p 530
See HAMILTON NIAGARA HALDIMAND BRANT COMMUNITY CARE ACCESS CENTRE
HOAM LTD   p 1035
525 NORWICH AVE, WOODSTOCK, ON, N4S 9A2
(519) 421-7300   SIC 5812
HOANA DRUGS LTD   p 196
45905 YALE RD UNIT 30, CHILLIWACK, BC, V2P 2M6
(604) 792-7377   SIC 5912
HOBAN CONSTRUCTION LTD   p 268

5121 46 AVE SE, SALMON ARM, BC, V1E 1X2
(250) 832-8831 *SIC 1611*

HOBAN EQUIPMENT p 268
See HOBAN CONSTRUCTION LTD

HOBAN EQUIPMENT LTD p 268
2691 13 AVE SW, SALMON ARM, BC, V1E 3K1
(250) 832-8831 *SIC 1611*

HOBART FOOD EQUIPMENT GROUP (OWEN SOUND) DIV OF p 835
See ITW CANADA INC

HOBBYCRAFT CANADA p 550
See CANADIAN HOBBYCRAFT LIMITED

HOC GLOBAL SOLUTIONS p 688
See HARTWICK O'SHEA & CARTWRIGHT LIMITED

HOCK SHOP INC p 484
400 BAYFIELD ST, BARRIE, ON, L4M 5A1
(705) 728-2274 *SIC 6099*

HOCKEY CANADA p 72
151 CANADA OLYMPIC RD SW SUITE 201, CALGARY, AB, T3B 6B7
(403) 777-3636 *SIC 8699*

HOCKEY CANADA p 821
801 KING EDWARD AVE SUITE N204, OTTAWA, ON, K1N 6N5
(613) 696-0211 *SIC 8699*

HOCKEY HALL OF FAME AND MUSEUM p 942
30 YONGE ST, TORONTO, ON, M5E 1X8
(416) 360-7735 *SIC 8412*

HOCKEY HOUSE 2010 p 984
See VISION GROUP OF COMPANIES LTD, THE

HOCKEY SHOP, THE p 273
See BOLIVAR HOLDINGS LTD

HOCO LIMITED p 759
4960 CLIFTON HILL, NIAGARA FALLS, ON, L2G 3N4
(905) 357-5911 *SIC 5812*

HOCO LIMITED p 759
4960 CLIFTON HILL, NIAGARA FALLS, ON, L2G 3N4
(905) 358-3293 *SIC 7011*

HODDER TUGBOAT CO. LTD p 260
11171 RIVER RD, RICHMOND, BC, V6X 1Z6
(604) 273-2821 *SIC 4492*

HODDOR LIGHTING INC p 992
1461 CASTLEFIELD AVE, TORONTO, ON, M6M 1Y4
(416) 651-6570 *SIC 5719*

HODGEVILLE FARMING CO. LTD p 1407
GD, HODGEVILLE, SK, S0H 2B0
(306) 627-0191 *SIC 0191*

HODGKINSON A & G SALES LTD p 484
320 BAYFIELD ST SUITE M103, BARRIE, ON, L4M 3C1
(705) 726-2861 *SIC 5531*

HODGSCO EQUITIES LTD p 165
5 GALARNEAU PL, ST. ALBERT, AB, T8N 2Y3
(780) 458-7100 *SIC 5511*

HODGSON CUSTOM ROLLING INC p 760
5580 KALAR RD, NIAGARA FALLS, ON, L2H 3L1
(905) 356-8132 *SIC 3449*

HODGSON, KING AND MARBLE LIMITED p 260
4200 VANGUARD RD, RICHMOND, BC, V6X 2P4
(604) 247-2422 *SIC 1542*

HOEKERT GROUP p 850
See 10578959 CANADA INC

HOERBIGER (CANADA) LTD p 706
330 BRUNEL RD, MISSISSAUGA, ON, L4Z 2C2
(905) 568-3013 *SIC 3494*

HOFFMAN, R. J. HOLDINGS LTD p 1436
GD, ST WALBURG, SK, S0M 2T0
(306) 248-3466 *SIC 1389*

HOFFMANN-LA ROCHE LIMITED p 723
7070 MISSISSAUGA RD, MISSISSAUGA,

ON, L5N 5M8
(800) 561-1759 *SIC 2834*

HOFFMANN-LA ROCHE LIMITED p 1092
201 BOUL ARMAND-FRAPPIER, DORVAL, QC, H7V 4A2
(450) 686-7050 *SIC 5122*

HOFLAND, JOHN G LTD. p 740
6695 PACIFIC CIR, MISSISSAUGA, ON, L5T 1V6
(905) 670-8220 *SIC 5992*

HOFMANN, E. PLASTICS, INC p 808
51 CENTENNIAL RD, ORANGEVILLE, ON, L9W 3R1
(519) 943-5050 *SIC 3089*

HOGAN CHEVROLET BUICK GMC LIMITED p 874
5000 SHEPPARD AVE E, SCARBOROUGH, ON, M1S 4L9
(416) 291-5054 *SIC 5511*

HOGEBOOM, PAUL W. HOLDINGS LTD p 659
760 WHARNCLIFFE RD S, LONDON, ON, N6J 2N4
(519) 686-1441 *SIC 5712*

HOGEWONING MOTORS LTD p 514
5 WOODYATT DR, BRANTFORD, ON, N3R 7K3
(519) 752-5010 *SIC 5511*

HOGG FUEL & SUPPLY LIMITED p 639
5 HILL ST, KITCHENER, ON, N2H 5T4
(519) 579-5330 *SIC 5983*

HOGG ROBINSON CANADA INC p 981
370 KING ST W SUITE 700, TORONTO, ON, M5V 1J9
(416) 593-8866 *SIC 8742*

HOGG ROBINSON CANADA INC p 1197
1550 RUE METCALFE BUREAU 700, MONTREAL, QC, H3A 1X6
(514) 286-6300 *SIC 4725*

HOGG SHAIN & SCHECK PROFESSIONAL CORPORATION p 767
2235 SHEPPARD AVE E UNIT 800, NORTH YORK, ON, M2J 5B5
(416) 499-3100 *SIC 8721*

HOIST MASTER p 537
See SCAN-TECH INSPECTION SERVICES LTD

HOKUM, BEN AND SON LIMITED p 598
206 BLACK POINT RD, GOLDEN LAKE, ON, K0J 1X0
(613) 757-2399 *SIC 2421*

HOLCIM CANADA p 541
See CAYUGA MATERIALS & CONSTRUCTION CO. LIMITED

HOLDBEST LTD p 769
24 MELLOWOOD DR, NORTH YORK, ON, M2L 2E3
(905) 831-0100 *SIC 6712*

HOLDECOM INC p 1334
1515 BOUL PITFIELD, SAINT-LAURENT, QC, H4S 1G3
(514) 956-7400 *SIC 6712*

HOLDFAST p 235
See HOLDFAST METALWORKS LTD

HOLDFAST METALWORKS LTD p 235
1061 MAUGHAN RD, NANAIMO, BC, V9X 1J2
(250) 591-7400 *SIC 1799*

HOLDING BELL MOBILITE INC p 1396
1 CARREF ALEXANDER-GRAHAM-BELL BUREAU A-7, VERDUN, QC, H3E 3B3
(514) 420-7700 *SIC 4899*

HOLDING CANADIAN AMERICAN TRANSPORTATION C.A.T. INC p 1088
4 RUE DU TRANSPORT, COTEAU-DU-LAC, QC, J0P 1B0
(450) 763-6363 *SIC 4213*

HOLDING NUERA INTERNATIONAL p 1134
See NUERA INC

HOLDING SECURITE C M LTEE, LE p 1053
19400 AV CRUICKSHANK, BAIE-D'URFE, QC, H9X 3P1

(514) 457-6650 *SIC 6712*

HOLDING SOPREMA CANADA INC p 1099
1688 RUE JEAN-BERCHMANS-MICHAUD, DRUMMONDVILLE, QC, J2C 8E9
(819) 478-8163 *SIC 6712*

HOLE'S GREENHOUSES & GARDENS LTD p 165
101 RIEL DR, ST. ALBERT, AB, T8N 3X4
(780) 651-7355 *SIC 5992*

HOLESHOT MOTORSPORTS LTD p 226
8867 201 ST, LANGLEY, BC, V2Y 0C8
(604) 882-3800 *SIC 5571*

HOLIDAY FABRICS p 554
See HOLIDAY HOME FASHIONS INC

HOLIDAY FORD LINCOLN LTD p 841
1555 LANSDOWNE ST W, PETERBOROUGH, ON, K9J 7M3
(705) 742-5432 *SIC 5521*

HOLIDAY GROUP p 1165
See TP-HOLIDAY GROUP LIMITED

HOLIDAY HOME FASHIONS INC p 554
2740 STEELES AVE W SUITE 2, CONCORD, ON, L4K 4T4
SIC 2221

HOLIDAY INN p 451
See COMMONWEALTH HOSPITALITY LTD

HOLIDAY INN p 527
See COMMONWEALTH HOSPITALITY LTD

HOLIDAY INN p 589
See WESTMONT HOSPITALITY MANAGEMENT LIMITED

HOLIDAY INN p 715
See NOR-SHAM HOTELS INC

HOLIDAY INN p 801
See ROYAL HOST INC

HOLIDAY INN p 804
See INNVEST HOTELS GP LTD

HOLIDAY INN p 884
See FIVE BROTHERS HOSPITALITY PARTNERSHIP

HOLIDAY INN p 935
See 541907 ONTARIO LIMITED

HOLIDAY INN & SUITES SELECT OTTAWA WEST (KANATA) p 626
See INNVEST HOTELS GP VIII LTD

HOLIDAY INN (NIAGARA FALLS) LIMITED p 759
5339 MURRAY ST, NIAGARA FALLS, ON, L2G 2J3
(905) 356-1333 *SIC 7011*

HOLIDAY INN - TORONTO AIRPORT p 584
See FELCOR CANADA CO

HOLIDAY INN AIRPORT WEST p 386
See LADCO COMPANY LIMITED

HOLIDAY INN BY THE FALLS p 759
See HOLIDAY INN (NIAGARA FALLS) LIMITED

HOLIDAY INN CONVENTION CENTRE p 107
See 464161 ALBERTA LTD

HOLIDAY INN EXPRESS HOTEL & SUITES p 39
See STANLEY PARK INVESTMENTS LTD

HOLIDAY INN EXPRESS-MONCTON p 457
See PACRIM DEVELOPMENTS INC

HOLIDAY INN GUELPH p 602
See WESTMONT HOSPITALITY MANAGEMENT LIMITED

HOLIDAY INN HARBOURVIEW p 444
See MANGA HOTELS (DARTMOUTH) INC

HOLIDAY INN HOTEL & CONFERENCE CENTRE p 468
See 3032948 NOVA SCOTIA LIMITED

HOLIDAY INN HOTELS p 693
See COMMONWEALTH HOSPITALITY LTD

HOLIDAY INN LONGUEUIL p 1142
See ATLIFIC INC

HOLIDAY INN MONTREAL AEROPORT p 1339
See HOTELS COTE-DE-LIESSE INC

HOLIDAY INN MONTREAL AEROPORT OUEST p 1249
See COMPAGNIE WW HOTELS (POINTE-CLAIRE)

HOLIDAY INN MONTREAL CENTRE-VILLE p 1191
See GESTION SINOMONDE INC

HOLIDAY INN MONTREAL LONGUEUIL p 1142
See 9003-7755 QUEBEC INC

HOLIDAY INN MONTREAL MIDTOWN p 1192
See 2985420 CANADA INC

HOLIDAY INN THE PALACE p 119
See 742718 ALBERTA LTD

HOLIDAY INN TORONTO AIRPORT EAST p 585
600 DIXON RD, ETOBICOKE, ON, M9W 1J1
(416) 240-7511 *SIC 7011*

HOLIDAY INN TORONTO BRAMPTON HOTEL & CONFERENCE CENTRE p 502
See ESSAG CANADA INC

HOLIDAY INN VANCOUVER DOWNTOWN HOTEL p 325
See 1110 HOWE HOLDINGS INCORPORATED

HOLIDAY INN WINNIPEG SOUTH p 390
See ATLIFIC INC

HOLIDAY NETWORK, THE p 943
See TRAVELBRANDS INC

HOLINSHED RESEARCH GROUP INC p 834
200 ELGIN ST SUITE 1102, OTTAWA, ON, K2P 1L5
SIC 8732

HOLLAND AMERICA LINE p 305
999 CANADA PL SUITE 200, VANCOUVER, BC, V6C 3C1
(604) 683-5776 *SIC 4724*

HOLLAND BLOORVIEW KIDS REHABILITATION HOSPITAL p 918
150 KILGOUR RD, TORONTO, ON, M4G 1R8
(416) 425-6220 *SIC 8069*

HOLLAND BLOORVIEW KIDS REHABILITATION HOSPITAL FOUNDATION p 918
150 KILGOUR RD, TORONTO, ON, M4G 1R8
(416) 424-3809 *SIC 8699*

HOLLAND CHRISTIAN HOMES INC p 511
7900 MCLAUGHLIN RD, BRAMPTON, ON, L6Y 5A7
(905) 463-7002 *SIC 8051*

HOLLAND CLEANING SOLUTIONS LTD p 1020
4590 RHODES DR, WINDSOR, ON, N8W 5C2
(519) 948-4373 *SIC 5169*

HOLLAND COLLEGE p 1039
140 WEYMOUTH ST, CHARLOTTETOWN, PE, C1A 4Z1
(902) 629-4217 *SIC 8221*

HOLLAND COLLEGE p 1039
4 SYDNEY ST, CHARLOTTETOWN, PE, C1A 1E9
(902) 894-6805 *SIC 8221*

HOLLAND IMPORTS INC p 185
2306 MADISON AVE, BURNABY, BC, V5C 4Y9
(604) 299-5741 *SIC 5072*

HOLLAND POWER SERVICES p 404
See HOLLAND, E. CONTRACTING INC

HOLLAND, E. CONTRACTING INC p 404
272 ROUTE 105, MAUGERVILLE, NB, E3A 8G2
(506) 472-0649 *SIC 1731*

HOLLANDIA GREENHOUSES LTD p 244
19731 RICHARDSON RD, PITT MEADOWS, BC, V3Y 1Z1
(604) 460-1866 *SIC 0181*

HOLLINGWORTH, A B & SON CONSTRUCTION LTD p 170
GD, VALLEYVIEW, AB, T0H 3N0

(780) 524-4233   *SIC 1389*
HOLLIS FORD INC   *p 469*
266 ROBIE ST, TRURO, NS, B2N 1L1
(902) 895-5000   *SIC 5511*
HOLLIS INSURANCE INC   *p 1278*
6700 BOUL PIERRE-BERTRAND BUREAU 300, QUEBEC, QC, G2J 0B4
(418) 623-4330   *SIC 6311*
HOLLISTER LIMITED   *p 480*
95 MARY ST, AURORA, ON, L4G 1G3
(905) 727-4344   *SIC 5047*
HOLLISWEALTH INC   *p 875*
2075 KENNEDY RD SUITE 500, SCARBOROUGH, ON, M1T 3V3
(416) 292-0869   *SIC 8742*
HOLLISWEALTH INC   *p 942*
26 WELLINGTON ST E SUITE 700, TORONTO, ON, M5E 1S2
(416) 350-3250   *SIC 6719*
HOLLOWAY LODGING CORPORATION *p* 458
106-145 HOBSON LAKE DR, HALIFAX, NS, B3S 0H9
(902) 404-3499   *SIC 7011*
HOLLSHOP IMPORTS LTD   *p 228*
20215 62 AVE UNIT 102, LANGLEY, BC, V3A 5E6
(604) 533-8822   *SIC 5141*
HOLLYBURN COUNTRY CLUB   *p 341*
950 CROSS CREEK RD, WEST VANCOUVER, BC, V7S 2S5
(604) 922-0161   *SIC 7997*
HOLLYBURN PROPERTIES (ALBERTA) LTD   *p 318*
1640 ALBERNI ST SUITE 300, VANCOUVER, BC, V6G 1A7
(604) 926-7345   *SIC 6513*
HOLLYBURN PROPERTIES LIMITED *p 313*
1160 HARO ST SUITE 101, VANCOUVER, BC, V6E 1E2
(604) 685-8525   *SIC 6513*
HOLLYBURN PROPERTIES LIMITED *p 342*
250 18TH ST, WEST VANCOUVER, BC, V7V 3V5
(604) 926-7345   *SIC 6513*
HOLLYWOOD BEAUTY SUPPLY   *p 862*
44 GREAT NORTHERN RD SUITE 51, SAULT STE. MARIE, ON, P6B 4Y5
(705) 949-9132   *SIC 5087*
HOLMAN EXHIBITS LIMITED   *p 776*
160 LESMILL RD, NORTH YORK, ON, M3B 2T5
SIC 3993
HOLMES & BRAKEL LIMITED   *p 844*
830 BROCK RD, PICKERING, ON, L1W 1Z8
(905) 831-6831   *SIC 7389*
HOLMES FREIGHT LINES INC   *p 499*
70 WARD RD, BRAMPTON, ON, L6S 4L5
(905) 458-1155   *SIC 4213*
HOLMES PLASTIC BINDINGS LTD   *p 671*
200 FERRIER ST, MARKHAM, ON, L3R 2Z5
(905) 513-6211   *SIC 2789*
HOLMES THE FINISHING HOUSE   *p 671*
See HOLMES PLASTIC BINDINGS LTD
HOLOWAYCHUK, L.B. PHARMACY LTD *p* 107
16504 95 ST NW SUITE 375, EDMONTON, AB, T5Z 3L7
(780) 456-5557   *SIC 5912*
HOLSAG CANADA INC   *p 646*
164 NEEDHAM ST, LINDSAY, ON, K9V 5R7
(888) 745-0721   *SIC 2512*
HOLSTEIN ASSOCIATION OF CANADA, THE   *p 514*
20 CORPORATE PL, BRANTFORD, ON, N3R 8A6
(519) 756-8300   *SIC 8611*
HOLSTEIN CANADA   *p 514*
See HOLSTEIN ASSOCIATION OF CANADA, THE
HOLT COLONY   *p 137*
See HUTTERIAN BRETHREN CHURCH OF HOLT
HOLT RENFREW   *p 51*

See HOLT, RENFREW & CIE, LIMITEE
HOLT RENFREW   *p 89*
See HOLT, RENFREW & CIE, LIMITEE
HOLT RENFREW   *p 305*
See HOLT, RENFREW & CIE, LIMITEE
HOLT RENFREW   *p 929*
See HOLT, RENFREW & CIE, LIMITEE
HOLT RENFREW   *p 997*
See HOLT, RENFREW & CIE, LIMITEE
HOLT RENFREW   *p 1213*
See HOLT, RENFREW & CIE, LIMITEE
HOLT RENFREW CANADA   *p 1272*
See HOLT, RENFREW & CIE, LIMITEE
HOLT, RENFREW & CIE, LIMITEE   *p 51*
8 AVE SW UNIT 510, CALGARY, AB, T2P 4H9
(403) 269-7341   *SIC 5651*
HOLT, RENFREW & CIE, LIMITEE   *p 89*
10180 101 ST NW, EDMONTON, AB, T5J 3S4
(780) 425-5300   *SIC 5611*
HOLT, RENFREW & CIE, LIMITEE   *p 305*
737 DUNSMUIR ST, VANCOUVER, BC, V6C 1N5
(604) 681-3121   *SIC 5621*
HOLT, RENFREW & CIE, LIMITEE   *p 305*
737 DUNSMUIR ST, VANCOUVER, BC, V6C 1N5
(604) 681-3121   *SIC 5311*
HOLT, RENFREW & CIE, LIMITEE   *p 929*
50 BLOOR ST W SUITE 200, TORONTO, ON, M4W 1A1
(416) 922-2333   *SIC 5621*
HOLT, RENFREW & CIE, LIMITEE   *p 929*
60 BLOOR ST W SUITE 1100, TORONTO, ON, M4W 3B8
(416) 922-2333   *SIC 5621*
HOLT, RENFREW & CIE, LIMITEE   *p 997*
396 HUMBERLINE DR, TORONTO, ON, M9W 6J7
(416) 675-9200   *SIC 5632*
HOLT, RENFREW & CIE, LIMITEE   *p 1213*
1300 RUE SHERBROOKE O, MONTREAL, QC, H3G 1H9
(514) 842-5111   *SIC 5651*
HOLT, RENFREW & CIE, LIMITEE   *p 1272*
2452 BOUL LAURIER, QUEBEC, QC, G1V 2L1
(514) 842-5111   *SIC 5611*
HOLT-MCDERMOTT MINES   *p 959*
See BARRICK GOLD CORPORATION
HOLTEN IMPEX INTERNATIONAL   *p 480*
See 853569 ONTARIO LIMITED
HOLTMANN, J. HOLDINGS INC   *p 387*
106 OSBORNE ST SUITE 200, WINNIPEG, MB, R3L 1Y5
(204) 984-9561   *SIC 5499*
HOLTZMAN, JACK DRUGS LIMITED   *p 481*
14729 YONGE ST SUITE 970, AURORA, ON, L4G 1N1
(905) 727-4275   *SIC 5912*
HOLWIN TOOLING SYSTEMS INC *p 1023*
5270 BURKE ST, WINDSOR, ON, N9A 6J3
(519) 737-7550   *SIC 5084*
HOLY CROSS CATHOLIC ACADEMY   *p* 1034
See YORK CATHOLIC DISTRICT SCHOOL BOARD
HOLY CROSS CATHOLIC SECONDARY SCHOOL   *p 632*
See ALGONQUIN & LAKESHORE CATHOLIC DISTRICT SCHOOL BOARD
HOLY CROSS ELEMENTARY SCHOOL   *p* 643
See WINDSOR-ESSEX CATHOLIC DISTRICT SCHOOL BOARD, THE
HOLY CROSS SECONDARY SCHOOL   *p* 883
See NIAGARA CATHOLIC DISTRICT SCHOOL BOARD
HOLY FAMILY CATHOLIC REGIONAL DIVISION 37   *p* 152
10307 99 ST, PEACE RIVER, AB, T8S 1K1

(780) 624-3956   *SIC 8211*
HOLY FAMILY CATHOLICS SCHOOLS *p* 152
See HOLY FAMILY CATHOLIC REGIONAL DIVISION 37
HOLY FAMILY HOSPITAL   *p 288*
See PROVIDENCE HEALTH CARE SOCIETY
HOLY FAMILY HOSPITAL   *p 327*
See PROVIDENCE HEALTH CARE SOCIETY
HOLY FAMILY ROMAN CATHOLIC SEPARATE SCHOOL DIVISION 140   *p* 1406
1118 2ND ST, ESTEVAN, SK, S4A 0L9
(306) 634-5995   *SIC 8211*
HOLY FAMILY ROMAN CATHOLIC SEPARATE SCHOOL DIVISION 140   *p* 1437
110 SOURIS AVE SUITE 3, WEYBURN, SK, S4H 2Z8
(306) 842-7025   *SIC 8211*
HOLY JUBILEE   *p 664*
See YORK CATHOLIC DISTRICT SCHOOL BOARD
HOLY NAMES HIGH SCHOOL   *p 1025*
See WINDSOR-ESSEX CATHOLIC DISTRICT SCHOOL BOARD, THE
HOLY TRINITY CATHOLIC HIGH SCHOOL *p* 880
See BRANT HALDIMAND NORFOLK CATHOLIC DISTRICT SCHOOL BOARD
HOLY TRINITY CATHOLIC SECONDARY SCHOOL   *p 564*
See PETERBOROUGH VICTORIA NORTHUMBERLAND AND CLARINGTON CATHOLIC DISTRICT SCHOOL BOARD
HOLY TRINITY ROMAN CATHOLIC SEPARATE SCHOOL DIVISION #22   *p* 1411
502 6TH AVE NE, MOOSE JAW, SK, S6H 6B8
(306) 694-5333   *SIC 8211*
HOLY TRINITY SCHOOL (CO-EDUCATIONAL) RICHMOND HILL   *p* 856
11300 BAYVIEW AVE, RICHMOND HILL, ON, L4S 1L4
(905) 737-1114   *SIC 8211*
HOMAG CANADA INC   *p 740*
5090 EDWARDS BLVD, MISSISSAUGA, ON, L5T 2W3
(905) 670-1700   *SIC 5084*
HOME & COMMUNITY CARE SERVICES *p* 243
See VANCOUVER ISLAND HEALTH AUTHORITY
HOME & GARDEN BY RONA   *p 367*
See RONA INC
HOME AND COMMUNITY CARE ACCESS *p* 334
1947 COOK ST, VICTORIA, BC, V8T 3P7
(250) 388-2273   *SIC 8742*
HOME BUILDING CENTER   *p 645*
See 1439037 ONTARIO LTD
HOME BUILDING CENTRE   *p 639*
See SWANSON, JIM LUMBER LTD
HOME BUILDING CENTRE   *p 1410*
See ALLIED LUMBERLAND LTD
HOME BUILDING CENTRE LEAMINGTON *p* 645
See WIEBE, J. BUILDING MATERIALS LTD
HOME BUILDING CENTRE VERNON *p 331*
See 616536 B.C. LTD
HOME CAPITAL GROUP INC   *p 952*
145 KING ST W SUITE 2300, TORONTO, ON, M5H 1J8
(416) 360-4663   *SIC 7389*
HOME COTTAGE   *p 217*
See ROYAL LEPAGE KAMLOOPS REALTY
HOME DEPOT   *p 3*
See HOME DEPOT OF CANADA INC
HOME DEPOT   *p 11*
See HOME DEPOT OF CANADA INC

HOME DEPOT   *p 69*
See HOME DEPOT OF CANADA INC
HOME DEPOT   *p 76*
See HOME DEPOT OF CANADA INC
HOME DEPOT   *p 77*
See HOME DEPOT OF CANADA INC
HOME DEPOT   *p 83*
See HOME DEPOT OF CANADA INC
HOME DEPOT   *p 96*
See HOME DEPOT OF CANADA INC
HOME DEPOT   *p 104*
See HOME DEPOT OF CANADA INC
HOME DEPOT   *p 118*
See HOME DEPOT OF CANADA INC
HOME DEPOT   *p 120*
See HOME DEPOT OF CANADA INC
HOME DEPOT   *p 124*
See HOME DEPOT OF CANADA INC
HOME DEPOT   *p 125*
See HOME DEPOT OF CANADA INC
HOME DEPOT   *p 132*
See HOME DEPOT OF CANADA INC
HOME DEPOT   *p 143*
See HOME DEPOT OF CANADA INC
HOME DEPOT   *p 144*
See HOME DEPOT OF CANADA INC
HOME DEPOT   *p 150*
See HOME DEPOT OF CANADA INC
HOME DEPOT   *p 157*
See HOME DEPOT OF CANADA INC
HOME DEPOT   *p 162*
See HOME DEPOT OF CANADA INC
HOME DEPOT   *p 164*
See HOME DEPOT OF CANADA INC
HOME DEPOT   *p 175*
See HOME DEPOT OF CANADA INC
HOME DEPOT   *p 185*
See HOME DEPOT OF CANADA INC
HOME DEPOT   *p 201*
See HOME DEPOT OF CANADA INC
HOME DEPOT   *p 203*
See HOME DEPOT OF CANADA INC
HOME DEPOT   *p 204*
See HOME DEPOT OF CANADA INC
HOME DEPOT   *p 211*
See HOME DEPOT OF CANADA INC
HOME DEPOT   *p 218*
See HOME DEPOT OF CANADA INC
HOME DEPOT   *p 220*
See HOME DEPOT OF CANADA INC
HOME DEPOT   *p 226*
See HOME DEPOT OF CANADA INC
HOME DEPOT   *p 234*
See HOME DEPOT OF CANADA INC
HOME DEPOT   *p 245*
See HOME DEPOT OF CANADA INC
HOME DEPOT   *p 250*
See HOME DEPOT OF CANADA INC
HOME DEPOT   *p 255*
See HOME DEPOT OF CANADA INC
HOME DEPOT   *p 274*
See HOME DEPOT OF CANADA INC
HOME DEPOT   *p 276*
See HOME DEPOT OF CANADA INC
HOME DEPOT   *p 279*
See HOME DEPOT OF CANADA INC
HOME DEPOT   *p 293*
See HOME DEPOT OF CANADA INC
HOME DEPOT   *p 295*
See HOME DEPOT OF CANADA INC
HOME DEPOT   *p 333*
See HOME DEPOT OF CANADA INC
HOME DEPOT   *p 340*
See HOME DEPOT OF CANADA INC
HOME DEPOT   *p 346*
See HOME DEPOT OF CANADA INC
HOME DEPOT   *p 362*
See HOME DEPOT OF CANADA INC
HOME DEPOT   *p 368*
See HOME DEPOT OF CANADA INC
HOME DEPOT   *p 370*
See HOME DEPOT OF CANADA INC
HOME DEPOT   *p 382*
See HOME DEPOT OF CANADA INC

HOME DEPOT   p 402
See HOME DEPOT OF CANADA INC
HOME DEPOT   p 407
See HOME DEPOT OF CANADA INC
HOME DEPOT   p 413
See HOME DEPOT OF CANADA INC
HOME DEPOT   p 430
See HOME DEPOT OF CANADA INC
HOME DEPOT   p 475
See HOME DEPOT OF CANADA INC
HOME DEPOT   p 478
See HOME DEPOT OF CANADA INC
HOME DEPOT   p 481
See HOME DEPOT OF CANADA INC
HOME DEPOT   p 487
See HOME DEPOT OF CANADA INC
HOME DEPOT   p 497
See HOME DEPOT OF CANADA INC
HOME DEPOT   p 498
See HOME DEPOT OF CANADA INC
HOME DEPOT   p 509
See HOME DEPOT OF CANADA INC
HOME DEPOT   p 514
See HOME DEPOT OF CANADA INC
HOME DEPOT   p 526
See HOME DEPOT OF CANADA INC
HOME DEPOT   p 533
See HOME DEPOT OF CANADA INC
HOME DEPOT   p 540
See HOME DEPOT OF CANADA INC
HOME DEPOT   p 545
See HOME DEPOT OF CANADA INC
HOME DEPOT   p 563
See HOME DEPOT OF CANADA INC
HOME DEPOT   p 579
See HOME DEPOT OF CANADA INC
HOME DEPOT   p 585
See HOME DEPOT OF CANADA INC
HOME DEPOT   p 595
See HOME DEPOT OF CANADA INC
HOME DEPOT   p 608
See HOME DEPOT OF CANADA INC
HOME DEPOT   p 626
See HOME DEPOT OF CANADA INC
HOME DEPOT   p 651
See HOME DEPOT OF CANADA INC
HOME DEPOT   p 660
See HOME DEPOT OF CANADA INC
HOME DEPOT   p 671
See HOME DEPOT OF CANADA INC
HOME DEPOT   p 678
See HOME DEPOT OF CANADA INC
HOME DEPOT   p 683
See HOME DEPOT OF CANADA INC
HOME DEPOT   p 711
See HOME DEPOT OF CANADA INC
HOME DEPOT   p 723
See HOME DEPOT OF CANADA INC
HOME DEPOT   p 731
See HOME DEPOT OF CANADA INC
HOME DEPOT   p 755
See HOME DEPOT OF CANADA INC
HOME DEPOT   p 758
See HOME DEPOT OF CANADA INC
HOME DEPOT   p 783
See HOME DEPOT OF CANADA INC
HOME DEPOT   p 791
See HOME DEPOT OF CANADA INC
HOME DEPOT   p 797
See HOME DEPOT OF CANADA INC
HOME DEPOT   p 800
See HOME DEPOT OF CANADA INC
HOME DEPOT   p 804
See HOME DEPOT OF CANADA INC
HOME DEPOT   p 808
See HOME DEPOT OF CANADA INC
HOME DEPOT   p 809
See HOME DEPOT OF CANADA INC
HOME DEPOT   p 811
See HOME DEPOT OF CANADA INC
HOME DEPOT   p 814
See HOME DEPOT OF CANADA INC
HOME DEPOT   p 826
See HOME DEPOT OF CANADA INC

HOME DEPOT   p 831
See HOME DEPOT OF CANADA INC
HOME DEPOT   p 835
See HOME DEPOT OF CANADA INC
HOME DEPOT   p 838
See HOME DEPOT OF CANADA INC
HOME DEPOT   p 841
See HOME DEPOT OF CANADA INC
HOME DEPOT   p 852
See HOME DEPOT OF CANADA INC
HOME DEPOT   p 857
See HOME DEPOT OF CANADA INC
HOME DEPOT   p 858
See HOME DEPOT OF CANADA INC
HOME DEPOT   p 862
See HOME DEPOT OF CANADA INC
HOME DEPOT   p 864
See HOME DEPOT OF CANADA INC
HOME DEPOT   p 867
See HOME DEPOT OF CANADA INC
HOME DEPOT   p 884
See HOME DEPOT OF CANADA INC
HOME DEPOT   p 899
See HOME DEPOT OF CANADA INC
HOME DEPOT   p 908
See HOME DEPOT OF CANADA INC
HOME DEPOT   p 913
See HOME DEPOT OF CANADA INC
HOME DEPOT   p 918
See HOME DEPOT OF CANADA INC
HOME DEPOT   p 993
See HOME DEPOT OF CANADA INC
HOME DEPOT   p 1010
See HOME DEPOT OF CANADA INC
HOME DEPOT   p 1014
See HOME DEPOT OF CANADA INC
HOME DEPOT   p 1018
See HOME DEPOT OF CANADA INC
HOME DEPOT   p 1020
See HOME DEPOT OF CANADA INC
HOME DEPOT   p 1031
See HOME DEPOT OF CANADA INC
HOME DEPOT   p 1036
See HOME DEPOT OF CANADA INC
HOME DEPOT   p 1049
See HOME DEPOT OF CANADA INC
HOME DEPOT   p 1103
See HOME DEPOT OF CANADA INC
HOME DEPOT   p 1111
See HOME DEPOT OF CANADA INC
HOME DEPOT   p 1112
See HOME DEPOT OF CANADA INC
HOME DEPOT   p 1182
See HOME DEPOT OF CANADA INC
HOME DEPOT   p 1223
See HOME DEPOT OF CANADA INC
HOME DEPOT   p 1235
See HOME DEPOT OF CANADA INC
HOME DEPOT   p 1250
See HOME DEPOT OF CANADA INC
HOME DEPOT   p 1279
See HOME DEPOT OF CANADA INC
HOME DEPOT   p 1298
See HOME DEPOT OF CANADA INC
HOME DEPOT   p 1320
See HOME DEPOT OF CANADA INC
HOME DEPOT   p 1387
See HOME DEPOT OF CANADA INC
HOME DEPOT   p 1394
See HOME DEPOT OF CANADA INC
HOME DEPOT   p 1398
See HOME DEPOT OF CANADA INC
HOME DEPOT   p 1416
See HOME DEPOT OF CANADA INC
HOME DEPOT   p 1427
See HOME DEPOT OF CANADA INC
HOME DEPOT 7146 L'ACADIE   p 1226
See HOME DEPOT OF CANADA INC
HOME DEPOT LACHENAIE   p 1378
See HOME DEPOT OF CANADA INC
HOME DEPOT OF CANADA INC   p 3
2925 MAIN ST SE, AIRDRIE, AB, T4B 3G5
(403) 945-3865   *SIC 5251*
HOME DEPOT OF CANADA INC   p 11

343 36 ST NE, CALGARY, AB, T2A 7S9
(403) 248-3040   *SIC 5251*
HOME DEPOT OF CANADA INC   p 41
1818 16 AVE NW, CALGARY, AB, T2M 0L8
(403) 284-7931   *SIC 5251*
HOME DEPOT OF CANADA INC   p 69
390 SHAWVILLE BLVD SE, CALGARY, AB, T2Y 3S4
(403) 201-5611   *SIC 5251*
HOME DEPOT OF CANADA INC   p 70
5125 126 AVE SE, CALGARY, AB, T2Z 0B2
(403) 257-8756   *SIC 5251*
HOME DEPOT OF CANADA INC   p 76
388 COUNTRY HILLS BLVD NE UNIT 100, CALGARY, AB, T3K 5J6
(403) 226-7500   *SIC 5251*
HOME DEPOT OF CANADA INC   p 77
11320 SARCEE TRAIL NW, CALGARY, AB, T3R 0A1
(403) 374-3866   *SIC 5211*
HOME DEPOT OF CANADA INC   p 77
5019 NOSE HILL DR NW, CALGARY, AB, T3L 0A2
(403) 241-4060   *SIC 5251*
HOME DEPOT OF CANADA INC   p 83
13304 50 ST NW, EDMONTON, AB, T5A 4Z8
(780) 478-7133   *SIC 5251*
HOME DEPOT OF CANADA INC   p 93
13360 137 AVE NW, EDMONTON, AB, T5L 5C9
(780) 472-4201   *SIC 1521*
HOME DEPOT OF CANADA INC   p 96
1 WESTMOUNT SHOPPING CTR NW SUITE 604, EDMONTON, AB, T5M 3L7
(780) 732-9225   *SIC 5251*
HOME DEPOT OF CANADA INC   p 104
17404 99 AVE NW, EDMONTON, AB, T5T 5L5
(780) 484-5100   *SIC 5251*
HOME DEPOT OF CANADA INC   p 118
6725 104 ST NW, EDMONTON, AB, T6H 2L3
(780) 431-4743   *SIC 5251*
HOME DEPOT OF CANADA INC   p 120
2020 101 ST NW, EDMONTON, AB, T6N 1J2
(780) 433-6370   *SIC 1522*
HOME DEPOT OF CANADA INC   p 124
4430 17 ST NW, EDMONTON, AB, T6T 0B4
(780) 577-3575   *SIC 5251*
HOME DEPOT OF CANADA INC   p 125
6218 CURRENTS DR NW, EDMONTON, AB, T6W 0L8
(780) 989-7460   *SIC 5251*
HOME DEPOT OF CANADA INC   p 132
11222 103 AVE, GRANDE PRAIRIE, AB, T8V 7H1
(780) 831-3160   *SIC 5211*
HOME DEPOT OF CANADA INC   p 143
3708 MAYOR MAGRATH DR S, LETH-BRIDGE, AB, T1K 7V1
(403) 331-3581   *SIC 5251*
HOME DEPOT OF CANADA INC   p 144
7705 44 ST, LLOYDMINSTER, AB, T9V 0X9
(780) 870-9420   *SIC 5251*
HOME DEPOT OF CANADA INC   p 146
1851 STRACHAN RD SE, MEDICINE HAT, AB, T1B 4V7
(403) 581-4300   *SIC 5251*
HOME DEPOT OF CANADA INC   p 150
101 SOUTHBANK BLVD UNIT 10, OKO-TOKS, AB, T1S 0G1
(403) 995-4710   *SIC 5211*
HOME DEPOT OF CANADA INC   p 157
2030 50 AVE, RED DEER, AB, T4R 3A2
(403) 358-7550   *SIC 5251*
HOME DEPOT OF CANADA INC   p 162
390 BASELINE RD SUITE 200, SHER-WOOD PARK, AB, T8H 1X1
(780) 417-7875   *SIC 5251*
HOME DEPOT OF CANADA INC   p 164
168 16A HWY, SPRUCE GROVE, AB, T7X 3X3

(780) 960-5600   *SIC 5251*
HOME DEPOT OF CANADA INC   p 165
750 ST ALBERT TRAIL, ST. ALBERT, AB, T8N 7H5
(780) 458-4026   *SIC 5251*
HOME DEPOT OF CANADA INC   p 175
1956 VEDDER WAY, ABBOTSFORD, BC, V2S 8K1
(604) 851-4400   *SIC 5211*
HOME DEPOT OF CANADA INC   p 185
3950 HENNING DR, BURNABY, BC, V5C 6M2
(604) 294-3077   *SIC 5251*
HOME DEPOT OF CANADA INC   p 201
1900 UNITED BLVD SUITE D, COQUIT-LAM, BC, V3K 6Z1
(604) 540-6277   *SIC 5251*
HOME DEPOT OF CANADA INC   p 203
388 LERWICK RD, COURTENAY, BC, V9N 9E5
(250) 334-5400   *SIC 5211*
HOME DEPOT OF CANADA INC   p 204
2000 MCPHEE RD, CRANBROOK, BC, V1C 0A3
(250) 420-4250   *SIC 5251*
HOME DEPOT OF CANADA INC   p 211
2980 DRINKWATER RD UNIT 1, DUNCAN, BC, V9L 6C6
(250) 737-2360   *SIC 5251*
HOME DEPOT OF CANADA INC   p 218
1020 HILLSIDE DR, KAMLOOPS, BC, V2E 2N1
(250) 371-4300   *SIC 5251*
HOME DEPOT OF CANADA INC   p 220
2515 ENTERPRISE WAY, KELOWNA, BC, V1X 7K2
(250) 979-4501   *SIC 5251*
HOME DEPOT OF CANADA INC   p 226
6550 200 ST, LANGLEY, BC, V2Y 1P2
(604) 514-1788   *SIC 5251*
HOME DEPOT OF CANADA INC   p 234
6555 METRAL DR, NANAIMO, BC, V9T 2L9
(250) 390-9093   *SIC 5251*
HOME DEPOT OF CANADA INC   p 245
1069 NICOLA AVE, PORT COQUITLAM, BC, V3B 8B2
(604) 468-3360   *SIC 5251*
HOME DEPOT OF CANADA INC   p 250
5959 O'GRADY RD, PRINCE GEORGE, BC, V2N 6Z5
(250) 906-3610   *SIC 5251*
HOME DEPOT OF CANADA INC   p 255
2700 SWEDEN WAY, RICHMOND, BC, V6V 2W8
(604) 303-7360   *SIC 5251*
HOME DEPOT OF CANADA INC   p 274
12701 110 AVE, SURREY, BC, V3V 3J7
(604) 580-2159   *SIC 5251*
HOME DEPOT OF CANADA INC   p 276
7350 120 ST, SURREY, BC, V3W 3M9
(604) 590-2796   *SIC 5999*
HOME DEPOT OF CANADA INC   p 279
2525 160 ST, SURREY, BC, V3Z 0C8
(604) 542-3520   *SIC 5251*
HOME DEPOT OF CANADA INC   p 293
2388 CAMBIE ST, VANCOUVER, BC, V5Z 2T8
(604) 675-1260   *SIC 5251*
HOME DEPOT OF CANADA INC   p 295
900 TERMINAL AVE, VANCOUVER, BC, V6A 4G4
(604) 608-1423   *SIC 5251*
HOME DEPOT OF CANADA INC   p 332
5501 ANDERSON WAY, VERNON, BC, V1T 9V1
(250) 550-1600   *SIC 5251*
HOME DEPOT OF CANADA INC   p 333
3986 SHELBOURNE ST, VICTORIA, BC, V8N 3E3
(250) 853-5350   *SIC 5251*
HOME DEPOT OF CANADA INC   p 340
2400 MILLSTREAM RD, VICTORIA, BC, V9B 3R3
(250) 391-6001   *SIC 5251*

HOME DEPOT OF CANADA INC p 341
840 MAIN ST SUITE E1, WEST VANCOU-
VER, BC, V7T 2Z3
(604) 913-2630   *SIC* 5251

HOME DEPOT OF CANADA INC p 346
801 18TH ST N, BRANDON, MB, R7A 7S1
(204) 571-3300   *SIC* 5251

HOME DEPOT OF CANADA INC p 362
1590 REGENT AVE W, WINNIPEG, MB,
R2C 3B4
(204) 654-5400   *SIC* 5251

HOME DEPOT OF CANADA INC p 368
1999 BISHOP GRANDIN BLVD, WINNIPEG,
MB, R2M 5S1
(204) 253-7649   *SIC* 5251

HOME DEPOT OF CANADA INC p 370
845 LEILA AVE, WINNIPEG, MB, R2V 3J7
(204) 336-5530   *SIC* 5251

HOME DEPOT OF CANADA INC p 382
727 EMPRESS ST, WINNIPEG, MB, R3G
3P5
(204) 779-0703   *SIC* 5251

HOME DEPOT OF CANADA INC p 402
1450 REGENT ST, FREDERICTON, NB,
E3C 0A4
(506) 462-9460   *SIC* 5251

HOME DEPOT OF CANADA INC p 407
235 MAPLETON RD, MONCTON, NB, E1C
0G9
(506) 853-8150   *SIC* 5251

HOME DEPOT OF CANADA INC p 413
55 LCD CRT, SAINT JOHN, NB, E2J 5E5
(506) 632-9440   *SIC* 5251

HOME DEPOT OF CANADA INC p 430
70 KELSEY DR, ST. JOHN'S, NL, A1B 5C7
(709) 570-2400   *SIC* 5251

HOME DEPOT OF CANADA INC p 446
40 FINNIAN ROW, DARTMOUTH, NS, B3B
0B6
(902) 460-4700   *SIC* 5251

HOME DEPOT OF CANADA INC p 458
368 LACEWOOD DR, HALIFAX, NS, B3S
1L8
(902) 457-3480   *SIC* 5211

HOME DEPOT OF CANADA INC p 467
50 SYDNEY PORT ACCESS RD, SYDNEY,
NS, B1P 7H2
(902) 564-3250   *SIC* 5251

HOME DEPOT OF CANADA INC p 475
260 KINGSTON RD E, AJAX, ON, L1Z 1G1
(905) 428-7939   *SIC* 5211

HOME DEPOT OF CANADA INC p 478
122 MARTINDALE CRES, ANCASTER, ON,
L9K 1J9
(905) 304-5900   *SIC* 5211

HOME DEPOT OF CANADA INC p 478
122 MARTINDALE CRES, ANCASTER, ON,
L9K 1J9
(905) 304-6826   *SIC* 5211

HOME DEPOT OF CANADA INC p 481
15360 BAYVIEW AVE, AURORA, ON, L4G
7J1
(905) 726-4500   *SIC* 5251

HOME DEPOT OF CANADA INC p 487
10 BARRIE VIEW DR, BARRIE, ON, L4N
8V4
(705) 733-2800   *SIC* 5251

HOME DEPOT OF CANADA INC p 492
210 BELL BLVD, BELLEVILLE, ON, K8P
5L8
(613) 961-5340   *SIC* 5251

HOME DEPOT OF CANADA INC p 497
20 DEPOT DR, BRACEBRIDGE, ON, P1L
0A1
(705) 646-5600   *SIC* 5251

HOME DEPOT OF CANADA INC p 497
470 HOLLAND ST W, BRADFORD, ON, L3Z
0A2
(905) 778-2100   *SIC* 5251

HOME DEPOT OF CANADA INC p 498
60 GREAT LAKES DR, BRAMPTON, ON,
L6R 2K7
(905) 792-5430   *SIC* 5251

HOME DEPOT OF CANADA INC p 509

49 FIRST GULF BLVD, BRAMPTON, ON,
L6W 4R8
(905) 457-1800   *SIC* 5211

HOME DEPOT OF CANADA INC p 510
9515 MISSISSAUGA RD, BRAMPTON, ON,
L6X 0Z8
(905) 453-3900   *SIC* 5251

HOME DEPOT OF CANADA INC p 514
25 HOLIDAY DR, BRANTFORD, ON, N3R
7J4
(519) 757-3534   *SIC* 5251

HOME DEPOT OF CANADA INC p 526
3050 DAVIDSON CRT, BURLINGTON, ON,
L7M 4M9
(905) 331-1700   *SIC* 5211

HOME DEPOT OF CANADA INC p 533
35 PINEBUSH RD, CAMBRIDGE, ON, N1R
8E2
(519) 624-2700   *SIC* 5211

HOME DEPOT OF CANADA INC p 540
570 MCNEELY AVE, CARLETON PLACE,
ON, K7C 0A7
(613) 253-3870   *SIC* 5251

HOME DEPOT OF CANADA INC p 543
8582 PIONEER LINE, CHATHAM, ON, N7M
5J1
(519) 380-2040   *SIC* 5211

HOME DEPOT OF CANADA INC p 545
1050 DEPALMA DR, COBOURG, ON, K9A
0A8
(905) 377-7600   *SIC* 5251

HOME DEPOT OF CANADA INC p 563
1825 BROOKDALE AVE, CORNWALL, ON,
K6J 5X7
(613) 930-4470   *SIC* 5211

HOME DEPOT OF CANADA INC p 579
193 NORTH QUEEN ST, ETOBICOKE, ON,
M9C 1A7
(416) 626-9800   *SIC* 5251

HOME DEPOT OF CANADA INC p 585
1983 KIPLING AVE, ETOBICOKE, ON,
M9W 4J4
(416) 746-1357   *SIC* 5251

HOME DEPOT OF CANADA INC p 595
1616 CYRVILLE RD, GLOUCESTER, ON,
K1B 3L8
(613) 744-1700   *SIC* 5251

HOME DEPOT OF CANADA INC p 603
63 WOODLAWN RD W, GUELPH, ON, N1H
1G8
(519) 780-3400   *SIC* 5251

HOME DEPOT OF CANADA INC p 608
350 CENTENNIAL PKY N, HAMILTON, ON,
L8E 2X4
(905) 561-9755   *SIC* 5251

HOME DEPOT OF CANADA INC p 626
10 FRANK NIGHBOR PL SUITE FRNT,
KANATA, ON, K2V 1B9
(613) 271-7577   *SIC* 5251

HOME DEPOT OF CANADA INC p 632
606 GARDINERS RD, KINGSTON, ON,
K7M 3X9
(613) 384-3511   *SIC* 5251

HOME DEPOT OF CANADA INC p 637
1400 OTTAWA ST S, KITCHENER, ON, N2E
4E2
(519) 569-4300   *SIC* 5211

HOME DEPOT OF CANADA INC p 641
100 GATEWAY PARK DR, KITCHENER,
ON, N2P 2J4
(519) 650-3900   *SIC* 5251

HOME DEPOT OF CANADA INC p 651
448 CLARKE RD, LONDON, ON, N5W 6H1
(519) 457-5800   *SIC* 5251

HOME DEPOT OF CANADA INC p 660
3035 WONDERLAND RD S, LONDON, ON,
N6L 1R4
(519) 691-1400   *SIC* 5251

HOME DEPOT OF CANADA INC p 671
3155 HIGHWAY 7 E, MARKHAM, ON, L3R
0T9
(905) 940-5900   *SIC* 5251

HOME DEPOT OF CANADA INC p 678
50 KIRKHAM DR, MARKHAM, ON, L3S 4K7

(905) 201-2590   *SIC* 5211

HOME DEPOT OF CANADA INC p 679
1201 CASTLEMORE AVE, MARKHAM, ON,
L6E 0G5
(905) 201-5500   *SIC* 5251

HOME DEPOT OF CANADA INC p 683
1013 MAPLE AVE, MILTON, ON, L9T 0A5
(905) 864-1200   *SIC* 5251

HOME DEPOT OF CANADA INC p 711
3065 MAVIS RD, MISSISSAUGA, ON, L5C
1T7
(905) 281-6230   *SIC* 5251

HOME DEPOT OF CANADA INC p 723
2920 ARGENTIA RD, MISSISSAUGA, ON,
L5N 8C5
(905) 814-3860   *SIC* 5251

HOME DEPOT OF CANADA INC p 731
650 MATHESON BLVD W, MISSISSAUGA,
ON, L5R 3T2
SIC 5251

HOME DEPOT OF CANADA INC p 755
17850 YONGE ST, NEWMARKET, ON, L3Y
8S1
(905) 898-0090   *SIC* 5251

HOME DEPOT OF CANADA INC p 758
7190 MORRISON ST, NIAGARA FALLS,
ON, L2E 7K5
(905) 371-7470   *SIC* 5211

HOME DEPOT OF CANADA INC p 763
1275 SEYMOUR ST, NORTH BAY, ON, P1B
9V6
(705) 845-2300   *SIC* 5251

HOME DEPOT OF CANADA INC p 779
1 CONCORDE GATE SUITE 900, NORTH
YORK, ON, M3C 4H9
(416) 609-0852   *SIC* 5251

HOME DEPOT OF CANADA INC p 783
2375 STEELES AVE W, NORTH YORK, ON,
M3J 3A8
(416) 664-9800   *SIC* 5251

HOME DEPOT OF CANADA INC p 786
90 BILLY BISHOP WAY, NORTH YORK, ON,
M3K 2C8
(416) 373-6000   *SIC* 5251

HOME DEPOT OF CANADA INC p 791
825 CALEDONIA RD, NORTH YORK, ON,
M6B 3X8
(416) 780-4730   *SIC* 5251

HOME DEPOT OF CANADA INC p 795
2233 SHEPPARD AVE W, NORTH YORK,
ON, M9M 2Z7
SIC 5251

HOME DEPOT OF CANADA INC p 797
2555 BRISTOL CIR, OAKVILLE, ON, L6H
5W9
(905) 829-5900   *SIC* 5251

HOME DEPOT OF CANADA INC p 800
99 CROSS AVE, OAKVILLE, ON, L6J 2W7
(905) 815-5000   *SIC* 5251

HOME DEPOT OF CANADA INC p 804
3300 SOUTH SERVICE RD W, OAKVILLE,
ON, L6L 0B1
(905) 469-7110   *SIC* 5251

HOME DEPOT OF CANADA INC p 808
49 FOURTH AVE, ORANGEVILLE, ON,
L9W 1G7
(519) 940-9061   *SIC* 5251

HOME DEPOT OF CANADA INC p 809
3225 MONARCH DR, ORILLIA, ON, L3V
7Z4
(705) 327-6500   *SIC* 5261

HOME DEPOT OF CANADA INC p 811
2121 TENTH LINE RD SUITE 1, ORLEANS,
ON, K4A 4C5
(613) 590-2030   *SIC* 5251

HOME DEPOT OF CANADA INC p 814
1481 HARMONY RD N, OSHAWA, ON, L1K
0Z6
(905) 743-5600   *SIC* 5231

HOME DEPOT OF CANADA INC p 826
2056 BANK ST, OTTAWA, ON, K1V 7Z8
(613) 739-5300   *SIC* 5251

HOME DEPOT OF CANADA INC p 831
1900 BASELINE RD, OTTAWA, ON, K2C

3Z6
(613) 723-5900   *SIC* 5211

HOME DEPOT OF CANADA INC p 835
1590 20TH AVE E, OWEN SOUND, ON,
N4K 5N3
(519) 372-3970   *SIC* 5251

HOME DEPOT OF CANADA INC p 838
27 ROBINSON LANE, PEMBROKE, ON,
K8A 0A5
(613) 732-6550   *SIC* 5251

HOME DEPOT OF CANADA INC p 841
500 LANSDOWNE ST W, PETERBOR-
OUGH, ON, K9J 8J7
(705) 876-4560   *SIC* 5211

HOME DEPOT OF CANADA INC p 843
1105A KINGSTON RD, PICKERING, ON,
L1V 1B5
(905) 421-2000   *SIC* 5251

HOME DEPOT OF CANADA INC p 852
50 RED MAPLE RD, RICHMOND HILL, ON,
L4B 4K1
(905) 763-2311   *SIC* 5251

HOME DEPOT OF CANADA INC p 857
1706 ELGIN MILLS RD E, RICHMOND
HILL, ON, L4S 1M6
(905) 787-7200   *SIC* 5251

HOME DEPOT OF CANADA INC p 858
1350 QUINN DR, SARNIA, ON, N7S 6L5
(519) 333-2300   *SIC* 5251

HOME DEPOT OF CANADA INC p 862
530 GREAT NORTHERN RD, SAULT STE.
MARIE, ON, P6B 4Z9
(705) 254-1150   *SIC* 5251

HOME DEPOT OF CANADA INC p 864
60 GRAND MARSHALL DR, SCARBOR-
OUGH, ON, M1B 5N6
(416) 283-3166   *SIC* 5251

HOME DEPOT OF CANADA INC p 867
2911 EGLINTON AVE E, SCARBOROUGH,
ON, M1J 2E5
(416) 289-2500   *SIC* 5231

HOME DEPOT OF CANADA INC p 884
20 YMCA DR, ST CATHARINES, ON, L2N
7R6
(905) 937-5900   *SIC* 5251

HOME DEPOT OF CANADA INC p 899
1500 MARCUS DR, SUDBURY, ON, P3B
4K5
(705) 525-2960   *SIC* 5251

HOME DEPOT OF CANADA INC p 908
359 MAIN ST, THUNDER BAY, ON, P7B 5L6
(807) 624-1100   *SIC* 5251

HOME DEPOT OF CANADA INC p 913
2143 RIVERSIDE DR, TIMMINS, ON, P4R
0A1
(705) 360-8750   *SIC* 5251

HOME DEPOT OF CANADA INC p 918
101 WICKSTEED AVE, TORONTO, ON,
M4G 4H9
(416) 467-2300   *SIC* 5251

HOME DEPOT OF CANADA INC p 993
2121 ST CLAIR AVE W, TORONTO, ON,
M6N 5A8
(416) 766-2800   *SIC* 5251

HOME DEPOT OF CANADA INC p 1010
600 KING ST N, WATERLOO, ON, N2V 2J5
(519) 883-0580   *SIC* 5211

HOME DEPOT OF CANADA INC p 1014
1700 VICTORIA ST E, WHITBY, ON, L1N
9K6
(905) 571-5900   *SIC* 5251

HOME DEPOT OF CANADA INC p 1018
6570 TECUMSEH RD E, WINDSOR, ON,
N8T 1E6
(519) 974-5420   *SIC* 5251

HOME DEPOT OF CANADA INC p 1020
1925 DIVISION RD, WINDSOR, ON, N8W
1Z7
(519) 967-3700   *SIC* 5251

HOME DEPOT OF CANADA INC p 1027
8966 HUNTINGTON RD, WOODBRIDGE,
ON, L4H 3V1
(905) 265-4400   *SIC* 4225

HOME DEPOT OF CANADA INC p 1031

▲ Public Company   ■ Public Company Family Member   **HQ** Headquarters   **BR** Branch   **SL** Single Location

140 NORTHVIEW BLVD, WOODBRIDGE, ON, L4L 8T2
(905) 851-1800   *SIC* 5251
HOME DEPOT OF CANADA INC   *p* 1036
901 JULIANA DR, WOODSTOCK, ON, N4V 1B9
(519) 421-5500   *SIC* 5251
HOME DEPOT OF CANADA INC   *p* 1049
11300 RUE RENAUDE-LAPOINTE, ANJOU, QC, H1J 2V7
(514) 356-3650   *SIC* 5251
HOME DEPOT OF CANADA INC   *p* 1062
2400 BOUL DU FAUBOURG, BOISBRIAND, QC, J7H 1S3
(450) 971-6061   *SIC* 5251
HOME DEPOT OF CANADA INC   *p* 1103
243 MONTEE PAIEMENT, GATINEAU, QC, J8P 6M7
(819) 246-4060   *SIC* 5231
HOME DEPOT OF CANADA INC   *p* 1111
165 RUE SIMONDS N, GRANBY, QC, J2J 0R7
(450) 375-5544   *SIC* 5251
HOME DEPOT OF CANADA INC   *p* 1112
500 AV AUGUSTE, GREENFIELD PARK, QC, J4V 3R4
(450) 462-5020   *SIC* 5251
HOME DEPOT OF CANADA INC   *p* 1138
500 RUE DE LA CONCORDE, LEVIS, QC, G6W 8A8
(418) 834-7050   *SIC* 5251
HOME DEPOT OF CANADA INC   *p* 1182
100 RUE BEAUBIEN O, MONTREAL, QC, H2S 3S1
(514) 490-8030   *SIC* 5211
HOME DEPOT OF CANADA INC   *p* 1223
4625 RUE SAINT-ANTOINE O, MONTREAL, QC, H4C 1E2
(514) 846-4770   *SIC* 5039
HOME DEPOT OF CANADA INC   *p* 1226
1000 RUE SAUVE O BUREAU 1000, MONTREAL, QC, H4N 3L5
(514) 333-6868   *SIC* 5251
HOME DEPOT OF CANADA INC   *p* 1235
1400 BOUL LE CORBUSIER, MONTREAL, QC, H7N 6J5
(450) 680-2225   *SIC* 5251
HOME DEPOT OF CANADA INC   *p* 1250
185 BOUL HYMUS, POINTE-CLAIRE, QC, H9R 1E9
(514) 630-8631   *SIC* 5251
HOME DEPOT OF CANADA INC   *p* 1278
1516 AV JULES-VERNE, QUEBEC, QC, G2G 2R5
(418) 872-8007   *SIC* 5211
HOME DEPOT OF CANADA INC   *p* 1279
300 RUE BOUVIER, QUEBEC, QC, G2J 1R8
(418) 634-8880   *SIC* 5211
HOME DEPOT OF CANADA INC   *p* 1295
901 RUE DE L'ETANG, SAINT-BRUNO, QC, J3V 6N8
(450) 461-2000   *SIC* 5251
HOME DEPOT OF CANADA INC   *p* 1298
490 VOIE DE LA DESSERTE, SAINT-CONSTANT, QC, J5A 2S6
(450) 633-2030   *SIC* 5251
HOME DEPOT OF CANADA INC   *p* 1320
1045 BOUL DU GRAND-HERON, SAINT-JEROME, QC, J7Y 3P2
(450) 565-6020   *SIC* 5251
HOME DEPOT OF CANADA INC   *p* 1373
1355 BOUL DU PLATEAU-SAINT-JOSEPH, SHERBROOKE, QC, J1L 3E2
(819) 348-4481   *SIC* 5251
HOME DEPOT OF CANADA INC   *p* 1378
660 MONTEE DES PIONNIERS, TERREBONNE, QC, J6V 1N9
(450) 657-4400   *SIC* 5211
HOME DEPOT OF CANADA INC   *p* 1387
4500 RUE REAL-PROULX, TROIS-RIVIERES, QC, G9A 6P9
(819) 379-3990   *SIC* 5211
HOME DEPOT OF CANADA INC   *p* 1394

55 BOUL DE LA CITE-DES-JEUNES, VAUDREUIL-DORION, QC, J7V 8C1
(450) 510-2600   *SIC* 5251
HOME DEPOT OF CANADA INC   *p* 1398
160 BOUL ARTHABASKA O, VICTORIAVILLE, QC, G6S 0P2
(819) 752-0700   *SIC* 5251
HOME DEPOT OF CANADA INC   *p* 1416
1867 E VICTORIA AVE, REGINA, SK, S4N 6E6
(306) 761-1919   *SIC* 5251
HOME DEPOT OF CANADA INC   *p* 1423
1030 N PASQUA ST, REGINA, SK, S4X 4V3
(306) 564-5700   *SIC* 5251
HOME DEPOT OF CANADA INC   *p* 1427
707 CIRCLE DR E, SASKATOON, SK, S7K 0V1
(306) 651-6250   *SIC* 5251
HOME DEPOT OF CANADA INC   *p* 1435
3043 CLARENCE AVE S SUITE 1, SASKATOON, SK, S7T 0B5
(306) 657-4100   *SIC* 5251
HOME DEPOT RDC 7275   *p* 1027
See HOME DEPOT OF CANADA INC
HOME DEPOT SHERBROOKE   *p* 1373
See HOME DEPOT OF CANADA INC
HOME DEPOT STORE # 7189   *p* 1138
See HOME DEPOT OF CANADA INC
HOME DEPOT TOOL RENTAL   *p* 446
See HOME DEPOT OF CANADA INC
HOME DEPOT, THE   *p* 93
See HOME DEPOT OF CANADA INC
HOME DOCTOR LIMITED, THE   *p* 438
3067 HIGHWAY 104 UNIT C, ANTIGONISH, NS, B2G 2K5
(902) 735-9100   *SIC* 5999
HOME GAME INC, THE   *p* 554
114B FERNSTAFF CRT, CONCORD, ON, L4K 3L9
SIC 5136
HOME HARDWARE   *p* 250
See CENTRAL BUILDERS' SUPPLY P.G. LIMITED
HOME HARDWARE   *p* 405
See ELMWOOD HARDWARE LTD
HOME HARDWARE   *p* 485
See UNITED LUMBER AND BUILDING SUPPLIES COMPANY LIMITED
HOME HARDWARE   *p* 622
See FINES HOME HARDWARE & BUILDING CENTRE
HOME HARDWARE   *p* 1004
See PENNER BUILDING CENTRE AND BUILDERS SUPPLIES LIMITED
HOME HARDWARE   *p* 1289
See BRETON & THIBAULT LTEE
HOME HARDWARE   *p* 1297
See LAFLAMME, GEORGES INC
HOME HARDWARE   *p* 1391
See VOLUMAT INC
HOME HARDWARE   *p* 1393
See THOMAS, RENE & FILS INC
HOME HARDWARE   *p* 1400
See SURPLUS MALOUIN INC
HOME HARDWARE   *p* 1407
See HANSON HARDWARE LTD
HOME HARDWARE BUILDING CENTRE   *p* 143
See BORDER CITY BUILDING CENTRE LTD
HOME HARDWARE BUILDING CENTRE   *p* 180
See SHEPHERD'S HARDWARE LIMITED
HOME HARDWARE BUILDING CENTRE   *p* 204
See RK SCHEPERS HOLDINGS LTD
HOME HARDWARE BUILDING CENTRE   *p* 204
See QUAD CITY BUILDING MATERIALS LTD
HOME HARDWARE BUILDING CENTRE   *p* 213
9820 108 ST, FORT ST. JOHN, BC, V1J 0A7
(250) 787-0371   *SIC* 5251

HOME HARDWARE BUILDING CENTRE   *p* 218
See RICK KURZAC BUILDING MATERIALS LTD
HOME HARDWARE BUILDING CENTRE   *p* 439
See WILSON'S SHOPPING CENTRE LIMITED
HOME HARDWARE BUILDING CENTRE   *p* 619
See HAWKESBURY LUMBER SUPPLY COMPANY LIMITED
HOME HARDWARE BUILDING CENTRE   *p* 809
See ORILLIA BUILDING SUPPLIES (2001) LIMITED
HOME HARDWARE BUILDING CENTRE   *p* 1410
See MEADOW LAKE HOME HARDWARE BUILDING CENTRE LTD
HOME HARDWARE BUILDING CENTRE   *p* 1412
See CASH & CARRY LUMBER MART LTD
HOME HARDWARE BUILDING CENTRE   *p* 1438
See MYROWICH, A BUILDING MATERIAL LTD
HOME HARDWARE BUILDING CENTRE - WOODSTOCK   *p* 1035
See LAMPREA BUILDING MATERIALS LTD
HOME HARDWARE BUILDING CENTRE LONDON EAST   *p* 651
See TEAHEN & TEAHEN BUILDING SUPPLIES LTD
HOME HARDWARE CHARLOTTETOWN   *p* 1040
See SHERWOOD HARDWARE LTD
HOME HARDWARE DISTRIBUTION CENTRE   *p* 172
See HOME HARDWARE STORES LIMITED
HOME HARDWARE DISTRIBUTION CENTRE   *p* 449
See HOME HARDWARE STORES LIMITED
HOME HARDWARE INVERMERE   *p* 216
See INVERMERE HARDWARE & BUILDING SUPPLIES CO LTD
HOME HARDWARE LINDSAY   *p* 645
See 1254613 ONTARIO LIMITED
HOME HARDWARE STORE #5075-4   *p* 213
See 321124 B.C. LTD
HOME HARDWARE STORES LIMITED   *p* 172
6410 36 ST, WETASKIWIN, AB, T9A 3B6
(780) 352-1984   *SIC* 5211
HOME HARDWARE STORES LIMITED   *p* 449
336 LANCASTER CRES, DEBERT, NS, B0M 1G0
(902) 662-2800   *SIC* 5211
HOME HARDWARE STORES LIMITED   *p* 888
34 HENRY ST, ST JACOBS, ON, N0B 2N0
(519) 664-2252   *SIC* 5211
HOME HARDWARE STORES LIMITED   *p* 1042
14 KINLOCK RD, STRATFORD, PE, C1B 1R1
SIC 5211
HOME HEALTH CARE SOLUTIONS INC   *p* 115
5405 99 ST NW, EDMONTON, AB, T6E 3N8
(780) 434-3131   *SIC* 5047
HOME IMPROVEMENT PEOPLE INC, THE   *p* 988
1120 CASTLEFIELD AVE, TORONTO, ON, M6B 1E9
(905) 760-7607   *SIC* 1521
HOME INSTEAD SENIOR CARE   *p* 917
See 1719094 ONTARIO INC
HOME LUMBER INC   *p* 868
714 BIRCHMOUNT RD, SCARBOROUGH, ON, M1K 1R4

(416) 759-4441   *SIC* 5251
HOME OUTFITTERS   *p* 8
See HUDSON'S BAY COMPANY
HOME OUTFITTERS   *p* 120
See HUDSON'S BAY COMPANY
HOME OUTFITTERS   *p* 190
See HUDSON'S BAY COMPANY
HOME OUTFITTERS   *p* 237
See HUDSON'S BAY COMPANY
HOME PARTNERS   *p* 445
See CANADIAN RED CROSS SOCIETY, THE
HOME PRESENCE   *p* 1068
See TRUDEAU CORPORATION 1889 INC
HOME SOLUTIONS   *p* 70
See HOME SOLUTIONS CORPORATION
HOME SOLUTIONS CORPORATION   *p* 70
11550 40 ST SE, CALGARY, AB, T2Z 4V6
(403) 216-0000   *SIC* 1799
HOME STORE   *p* 201
See MILLWOOD FURNITURE ENT. LTD
HOME SUPPORT CENTRAL SOCIETY   *p* 465
30 WATER ST, PORT HOOD, NS, B0E 2W0
(902) 787-3449   *SIC* 8059
HOME TEXTILES INC   *p* 503
35 COVENTRY RD, BRAMPTON, ON, L6T 4V7
(905) 792-1551   *SIC* 5023
HOME TRUST COMPANY   *p* 952
145 KING ST W SUITE 2300, TORONTO, ON, M5H 1J8
(416) 775-5000   *SIC* 6021
HOME-RAIL (CALGARY) LTD   *p* 35
5520 4 ST SE, CALGARY, AB, T2H 1K7
(403) 202-5493   *SIC* 5051
HOMEBASE MEDIA   *p* 189
See TRADER CORPORATION
HOMEFRONT REALTY INC   *p* 514
245 KING GEORGE RD, BRANTFORD, ON, N3R 7N7
(519) 756-8120   *SIC* 6531
HOMEGUARD FUNDING LTD   *p* 754
83 DAWSON MANOR BLVD, NEWMARKET, ON, L3X 2H5
(905) 895-1777   *SIC* 6163
HOMEGUARD FUNDING VERICO   *p* 754
See HOMEGUARD FUNDING LTD
HOMELAND HOUSING   *p* 147
9922 103 ST, MORINVILLE, AB, T8R 1R7
(780) 939-5116   *SIC* 8741
HOMELIFE   *p* 1031
See HOMELIFE/ROYALCORP REAL ESTATE INC
HOMELIFE ATLANTIC   *p* 457
233 BEDFORD HWY, HALIFAX, NS, B3M 2J9
(902) 457-4000   *SIC* 6531
HOMELIFE BAYVIEW REALTY INC   *p* 904
505 HIGHWAY 7 E SUITE 201, THORNHILL, ON, L3T 7T1
(416) 845-0000   *SIC* 6531
HOMELIFE BENCHMARK REALTY CORP   *p* 226
6323 197 ST, LANGLEY, BC, V2Y 1K8
(604) 530-4141   *SIC* 6531
HOMELIFE BENCHMARK TITUS REALTY   *p* 272
105-5477 152 ST, SURREY, BC, V3S 5A5
(604) 575-5262   *SIC* 6531
HOMELIFE CHOLKAN REALTY CORP   *p* 574
109 JUDGE RD, ETOBICOKE, ON, M8Z 5B5
(416) 236-7711   *SIC* 6531
HOMELIFE EXPERTS REALTY LTD   *p* 499
50 COTTRELLE BLVD SUITE 29, BRAMPTON, ON, L6S 0E1
SIC 6531
HOMELIFE FOUNDATION REALTY INC   *p* 769
648 FINCH AVE E SUITE 12, NORTH YORK, ON, M2K 2E6
(416) 229-0515   *SIC* 6531

HOMELIFE FRONTIER REALTY INC *p* 906
7620 YONGE ST SUITE 400, THORNHILL, ON, L4J 1V9
(416) 218-8800   *SIC* 6531

HOMELIFE GLENAYRE REALTY COMPANY LTD *p* 175
3033 IMMEL ST UNIT 360, ABBOTSFORD, BC, V2S 6S2
(604) 520-6829   *SIC* 6531

HOMELIFE GOLD PACIFIC REALTY INC *p* 877
3601 VICTORIA PARK AVE SUITE 401, SCARBOROUGH, ON, M1W 3Y3
(416) 490-1068   *SIC* 6531

HOMELIFE PROSPERITY LAND REALTY INC *p* 904
2900 STEELES AVE E SUITE 211, THORNHILL, ON, L3T 4X1
(905) 707-8020   *SIC* 6411

HOMELIFE REALTY (GUELPH) LIMITED *p* 601
1027 GORDON ST, GUELPH, ON, N1G 4X1
(519) 836-1072   *SIC* 6531

HOMELIFE SUPERSTARS REAL ESTATE LIMITED *p* 503
2565 STEELES AVE E UNIT 11, BRAMPTON, ON, L6T 4L6
(905) 792-7800   *SIC* 6531

HOMELIFE-KEMPENFELT KELLY REAL ESTATE LTD *p* 622
7886 YONGE ST, INNISFIL, ON, L9S 1L4
(705) 436-5111   *SIC* 6531

HOMELIFE/ACES REALTY & INS. LTD *p* 874
4002 SHEPPARD AVE E UNIT 216, SCARBOROUGH, ON, M1S 4R5
(416) 298-8880   *SIC* 6531

HOMELIFE/GOLDEN EAST REALTY INC *p* 671
200 TOWN CENTRE BLVD SUITE 206, MARKHAM, ON, L3R 8G5
(905) 415-1331   *SIC* 6531

HOMELIFE/KEMPENFELT/KELLY REALTY LTD *p* 487
284 DUNLOP ST W, BARRIE, ON, L4N 1B9
(705) 725-0000   *SIC* 6531

HOMELIFE/LEADER INC *p* 671
3636 STEELES AVE E UNIT 307, MARKHAM, ON, L3R 1K9
(416) 298-6633   *SIC* 6531

HOMELIFE/METROPARK REALTY INC *p* 554
8700A DUFFERIN ST, CONCORD, ON, L4K 4S6
(416) 798-7705   *SIC* 6531

HOMELIFE/MIRACLE REALTY LTD *p* 580
5010 STEELES AVE W SUITE 11A, ETOBICOKE, ON, M9V 5C6
(416) 747-9777   *SIC* 6531

HOMELIFE/RESPONSE REALTY INC *p* 706
4312 VILLAGE CENTRE CRT, MISSISSAUGA, ON, L4Z 1S2
(905) 949-0070   *SIC* 6531

HOMELIFE/ROYALCORP REAL ESTATE INC *p* 1031
4040 STEELES AVE W UNIT 12, WOODBRIDGE, ON, L4L 4Y5
(905) 856-6611   *SIC* 6531

HOMELIFE/VISION REALTY INC *p* 776
1945 LESLIE ST, NORTH YORK, ON, M3B 2M3
(416) 383-1828   *SIC* 6531

HOMEOCAN INC *p* 1164
3025 BOUL DE L'ASSOMPTION, MONTREAL, QC, H1N 2H2
(514) 256-6303   *SIC* 2834

HOMES BY AVI (CALGARY) INC *p* 35
245 FORGE RD SE, CALGARY, AB, T2H 0S9
(403) 536-7000   *SIC* 1521

HOMES BY AVI (CANADA) INC *p* 35
245 FORGE RD SE, CALGARY, AB, T2H 0S9

(403) 536-7000   *SIC* 7514

HOMES FIRST SOCIETY *p* 935
90 SHUTER ST, TORONTO, ON, M5B 2K6
(416) 214-1870   *SIC* 8699

HOMESENSE *p* 245
See *WINNERS MERCHANTS INTERNATIONAL L.P.*

HOMESENSE *p* 733
See *WINNERS MERCHANTS INTERNATIONAL L.P.*

HOMESENSE *p* 1248
See *WINNERS MERCHANTS INTERNATIONAL L.P.*

HOMESERVICE CLUB OF CANADA LTD *p* 925
1255 YONGE ST, TORONTO, ON, M4T 1W6
(416) 925-1111   *SIC* 1522

HOMESTARTS INCORPORATED *p* 723
6537 MISSISSAUGA RD UNIT B, MISSISSAUGA, ON, L5N 1A6
(905) 858-1110   *SIC* 8748

HOMESTEAD LAND HOLDINGS LIMITED *p* 630
80 JOHNSON ST, KINGSTON, ON, K7L 1X7
(613) 546-3146   *SIC* 6513

HOMETOWN COMMUNICATIONS *p* 404
97 PINE ST, LORNE, NB, E8G 1M6
SIC 7389

HOMETOWN SERVICE LTD *p* 361
690 MEMORIAL DR, WINKLER, MB, R6W 0M6
(204) 325-4777   *SIC* 5511

HOMETURF LAWN CARE SERVICES *p* 735
See *HOMETURF LTD*

HOMETURF LTD *p* 735
7123 FIR TREE DR, MISSISSAUGA, ON, L5S 1G4
(905) 791-8873   *SIC* 6331

HOMEWAY COMPANY LIMITED *p* 651
1801 TRAFALGAR ST, LONDON, ON, N5W 1X7
(519) 453-6400   *SIC* 5211

HOMEWOOD HEALTH CENTRE INC *p* 600
150 DELHI ST, GUELPH, ON, N1E 6K9
(519) 824-1010   *SIC* 8063

HOMEWOOD HEALTH INC *p* 600
49 EMMA ST SUITE 100, GUELPH, ON, N1E 6X1
(519) 821-9258   *SIC* 8093

HOMEWOOD SUITES BY HILTON *p* 901
See *SUDBURY REGENT STREET INC*

HOMME ET SA MAISON LTEE, L' *p* 1238
605 AV MARSHALL, MONTREAL, QC, H9P 1E1
(514) 737-1010   *SIC* 7382

HONAJI FOOD LTD *p* 201
42 FAWCETT RD UNIT 109, COQUITLAM, BC, V3K 6X9
(604) 759-2886   *SIC* 5149

HONCO BATIMENT D'ACIER *p* 1140
See *9123-1878 QUEBEC INC*

HONDA *p* 1224
See *LALLIER AUTOMOBILE (MONTREAL) INC*

HONDA CANADA FINANCE INC *p* 679
180 HONDA BLVD SUITE 200, MARKHAM, ON, L6C 0H9
(905) 888-4188   *SIC* 6141

HONDA CANADA INC *p* 241
816 AUTOMALL DR, NORTH VANCOUVER, BC, V7P 3R8
(604) 984-0331   *SIC* 5511

HONDA CANADA INC *p* 476
4700 TOTTENHAM RD, ALLISTON, ON, L9R 1A2
(705) 435-5561   *SIC* 3711

HONDA CANADA INC *p* 679
180 HONDA BLVD SUITE 200, MARKHAM, ON, L6C 0H9
(905) 888-8110   *SIC* 3711

HONDA CANADA INC *p* 1065
1750 RUE EIFFEL, BOUCHERVILLE, QC, J4B 7W1
(450) 641-9062   *SIC* 5012

HONDA CASAVANT *p* 1311
See *AUTOS ECONOMIQUES CASAVANT INC, LES*

HONDA CITY *p* 335
See *ZOMEL HOLDINGS LTD*

HONDA DE BLAINVILLE *p* 1058
See *2848-7403 QUEBEC INC*

HONDA DE LA CAPITALE *p* 1281
See *9180-6166 QUEBEC INC*

HONDA DE MONT-LAURIER *p* 1154
See *AUTOMOBILES BELLEM INC, LES*

HONDA DE SAINT-JEAN *p* 1316
See *DAIGNEAULT & FRERE (1966) INC*

HONDA DE SIGI *p* 1191
See *AUTOMOBILES ROCHMAT INC*

HONDA DE TERREBONNE *p* 1380
See *AUTOMOBILES DONALD BRASSARD INC*

HONDA DES BOIS-FRANC *p* 1399
See *VIC AUTORAMA INC*

HONDA FINANCIAL SERVICES *p* 679
See *HONDA CANADA FINANCE INC*

HONDA ILE-PERROT *p* 1120
See *AUTOMOBILES ILE-PERROT INC*

HONDA LALLIER REPENTIGNY *p* 1379
See *LALLIER AUTOMOBILE (REPENTIGNY) INC*

HONDA OF CANADA MANUFACTURING *p* 679
See *HONDA CANADA INC*

HONDA OF CANADA MFG DIV *p* 476
See *HONDA CANADA INC*

HONDA RED DEER SALES *p* 156
See *307711 ALBERTA LTD*

HONDA TRADING CANADA INC *p* 476
4700 INDUSTRIAL PKWY, ALLISTON, ON, L9R 1W7
(705) 435-0172   *SIC* 5051

HONDA WAY, THE *p* 177
See *PARK AVENUE ENTERPRISES LTD*

HONDA WEST *p* 74
See *SARCEE MOTORS LTD*

HONEST ED'S LIMITED *p* 989
581 BLOOR ST W SUITE 1, TORONTO, ON, M6G 1K3
(416) 537-1574   *SIC* 5311

HONEY BADGER EXPLORATION INC *p* 963
145 WELLINGTON ST W SUITE 101, TORONTO, ON, M5J 1H8
(416) 364-7029   *SIC* 1081

HONEY BEE MANUFACTURING LTD *p* 1407
GD, FRONTIER, SK, S0N 0W0
(306) 296-2297   *SIC* 3523

HONEY ELECTRIC LIMITED *p* 543
400 PARK AVE W, CHATHAM, ON, N7M 1W9
(519) 351-0484   *SIC* 1731

HONEYCOMB HILL HOLDINGS OF MULMUR INC *p* 808
410 RICHARDSON RD, ORANGEVILLE, ON, L9W 4W8
(519) 942-9999   *SIC* 5074

HONEYVIEW FARM *p* 179
See *R.J.T. BLUEBERRY PARK INC*

HONEYWELL *p* 717
See *INTERMEC TECHNOLOGIES CANADA ULC*

HONEYWELL ADVANCED SOLUTIONS *p* 89
See *HONEYWELL LIMITED*

HONEYWELL AEROSPACE TORONTO *p* 717
See *HONEYWELL LIMITED*

HONEYWELL LIFE SAFETY *p* 1050
See *PRODUITS DE SECURITE NORTH LTEE*

HONEYWELL LIMITED *p* 89
10405 JASPER AVE NW SUITE 1800, EDMONTON, AB, T5J 3N4
(780) 448-1010   *SIC* 7371

HONEYWELL LIMITED *p* 239
500 BROOKSBANK AVE, NORTH VAN-

COUVER, BC, V7J 3S4
(604) 980-3421   *SIC* 2679

HONEYWELL LIMITED *p* 717
3333 UNITY DR, MISSISSAUGA, ON, L5L 3S6
(905) 608-6000   *SIC* 3822

HONEYWELL LIMITED *p* 1128
2100 52E AV, LACHINE, QC, H8T 2Y5
(514) 422-3400   *SIC* 3822

HONEYWELL LIMITED *p* 1264
2366 RUE GALVANI BUREAU 4, QUEBEC, QC, G1N 4G4
(418) 688-8320   *SIC* 3822

HONG TAI SUPERMARKET *p* 875
See *2051183 ONTARIO INC*

HONTA TRADING INTERNATIONAL INC *p* 671
110A COCHRANE DR, MARKHAM, ON, L3R 5S7
(905) 305-0688   *SIC* 5099

HOOD LOGGING EQUIPMENT CANADA INCORPORATED *p* 908
GD STN CSC, THUNDER BAY, ON, P7B 5E6
(807) 939-2641   *SIC* 5082

HOOD PACKAGING CORPORATION *p* 16
5615 44 ST SE, CALGARY, AB, T2C 1V2
(403) 279-4000   *SIC* 2674

HOOD PACKAGING CORPORATION *p* 530
2380 MCDOWELL RD, BURLINGTON, ON, L7R 4A1
(905) 637-5611   *SIC* 2674

HOOD PACKAGING CORPORATION *p* 1100
15 RUE DAVID-SWAN, EAST ANGUS, QC, J0B 1R0
(819) 832-4971   *SIC* 2674

HOOD PACKAGING CORPORATION *p* 1345
4755 BOUL DES GRANDES-PRAIRIES, SAINT-LEONARD, QC, H1R 1A6
(514) 323-4517   *SIC* 2673

HOODEX INDUSTRIES LIMITED *p* 696
5650 TOMKEN RD UNIT 4, MISSISSAUGA, ON, L4W 4P1
(905) 624-8668   *SIC* 7349

HOOPER WELDING *p* 804
See *HOOPER WELDING ENTERPRISES LIMITED*

HOOPER WELDING ENTERPRISES LIMITED *p* 804
1390 ADVANCE RD, OAKVILLE, ON, L6L 6L6
(905) 827-2600   *SIC* 3443

HOOPER-HOLMES CANADA LIMITED *p* 877
1059 MCNICOLL AVE, SCARBOROUGH, ON, M1W 3W6
(416) 493-2800   *SIC* 6411

HOOPP INVESTMENT MANAGEMENT LIMITED *p* 963
1 YORK ST SUITE 1900, TORONTO, ON, M5J 0B6
(416) 369-9212   *SIC* 6371

HOOTSUITE INC *p* 289
5 8TH AVE E, VANCOUVER, BC, V5T 1R6
(604) 681-4668   *SIC* 7374

HOOVER ENTERPRISES INC *p* 911
81 LINCOLN ST, TILLSONBURG, ON, N4G 5Y4
(519) 842-2890   *SIC* 3312

HOOVER MECHANICAL PLUMBING & HEATING LTD *p* 16
3640 61 AVE SE SUITE 1, CALGARY, AB, T2C 2J3
(403) 217-5655   *SIC* 1711

HOP CITY BREWING CO *p* 416
See *MOOSEHEAD BREWERIES LIMITED*

HOPE & HARDER INSURANCE BROKERS INC *p* 883
512 WELLAND AVE, ST CATHARINES, ON, L2M 5V5
(905) 935-4667   *SIC* 6411

HOPE AERO PROPELLER & COMPO-

NENTS INC p
685
7605 BATH RD, MISSISSAUGA, ON, L4T 3T1
(905) 677-8747 SIC 5088
HOPE DISTRIBUTION & SALES INC p 245
2125 HAWKINS ST SUITE 609, PORT COQUITLAM, BC, V3B 0G6
(604) 468-6951 SIC 5311
HOPE MISSION SOCIETY p 86
9908 106 AVE NW, EDMONTON, AB, T5H 0N6
(780) 422-2018 SIC 8399
HOPE MISSION SOCIETY p 92
10336 114 ST NW, EDMONTON, AB, T5K 1S3
(780) 453-3877 SIC 8399
HOPEWELL CAPITAL CORPORATION p 67
2020 4 ST SW SUITE 410, CALGARY, AB, T2S 1W3
(403) 232-8821 SIC 1522
HOPEWELL LOGISTICS INC p 499
255 CHRYSLER DR SUITE 3A, BRAMPTON, ON, L6S 6C8
(905) 458-8860 SIC 4225
HOPEWELL LOGISTICS INC p 499
9050 AIRPORT RD SUITE 201, BRAMPTON, ON, L6S 6G6
(905) 458-1041 SIC 4225
HOPEWELL RESIDENTIAL MANAGEMENT LP p 67
2020 4 ST SW SUITE 410, CALGARY, AB, T2S 1W3
(403) 232-8821 SIC 6531
HOPITAL CHINOIS DE MONTREAL (1963) INC, L' p 1185
189 AV VIGER E, MONTREAL, QC, H2X 3Y9
(514) 875-9120 SIC 8051
HOPITAL DE LA MISERICORDE p 1185
See CENTRE INTEGRE UNIVERSITAIRE SANTE ET SERVICES SOCIAUX DU CENTRE-SUD-DE-L'ILE-DE-MONTREAL
HOPITAL DE LAMEQUE p 404
See REGIONAL HEALTH AUTHORITY A
HOPITAL DE MONTREAL POUR ENFANTS, L' p 1215
See MCGILL UNIVERSITY HEALTH CENTRE
HOPITAL DE READAPTATION VILLA MEDICA p
1186
See VILLA MEDICA INC
HOPITAL DE VERDUN p 1223
See CENTRE DE SANTE ET DE SERVICES SOCIAUX DU SUD-OUEST-VERDUN
HOPITAL DE VERDUN p 1396
See CENTRE DE SANTE ET DE SERVICES SOCIAUX DU SUD-OUEST-VERDUN
HOPITAL DU ST-SACREMENT DU CENTRE HOSPITALIER AFFILIE UQ p 1270
1050 CH SAINTE-FOY, QUEBEC, QC, G1S 4L8
(418) 682-7511 SIC 8062
HOPITAL GENERAL DE HAWKESBURY & DISTRICT GENERAL HOSPITAL INC p 619
1111 GHISLAIN ST, HAWKESBURY, ON, K6A 3G5
(613) 632-1111 SIC 8062
HOPITAL GENERAL DU LAKESHORE p
1249
See CENTRE DE SANTE ET DE SERVICES SOCIAUX DE L'OUEST-DE-L'ILE
HOPITAL MARIE-CLARAC DES SOEURS DE CHARITE DE STE-MARIE (1995) INC p
1240
3530 BOUL GOUIN E, MONTREAL-NORD, QC, H1H 1B7
(514) 321-8800 SIC 8069
HOPITAL MONTFORT p 820
713 MONTREAL RD, OTTAWA, ON, K1K 0T2
(613) 746-4621 SIC 8062
HOPITAL POUR ENFANTS DE MONTREAL

p 1220
See FONDATION DE L'HOPITAL DE MONTREAL POUR ENFANTS, LA
HOPITAL PSYCHIATRIQUE DE MALARTIC p 1148
See CENTRE DE SANTE ET DE SERVICES SOCIAUX DE LA VALLEE-DE-L'OR
HOPITAL REGIONAL DE PORTNEUF p
1351
See CENTRE DE SANTE ET DE SERVICES SOCIAUX DE PORTNEUF
HOPITAL SAINT FRANCOIS D'ASSISE p
1260
See CENTRE HOSPITALIER UNIVERSITAIRE DE QUEBEC
HOPITAL SANTA CABRINI p 1165
5655 RUE SAINT-ZOTIQUE E, MONTREAL, QC, H1T 1P7
(514) 252-1535 SIC 8062
HOPITAL ST-JOSEPH p 1286
28 RUE JOLY, RIVIERE-DU-LOUP, QC, G5R 3H2
(418) 862-6385 SIC 8069
HOPITAL VETERINAIRE DAUBIGNY p 1267
3349 BOUL WILFRID-HAMEL, QUEBEC, QC, G1P 2J3
(418) 872-5355 SIC 0742
HOPITEL INC p 1227
8225 RUE LABARRE, MONTREAL, QC, H4P 2E6
(514) 739-2525 SIC 7359
HOPKINS CANADA, INC p 493
281 CHATHAM ST S, BLENHEIM, ON, N0P 1A0
(519) 676-5441 SIC 3714
HOPKINS, H LIMITED p 465
11 BREAKWATER ST, PORT MORIEN, NS, B1B 1Y5
(902) 737-2244 SIC 5146
HOPPER AUTOMOBILES LTD p 763
550 MCKEOWN AVE, NORTH BAY, ON, P1B 7M2
(888) 392-9178 SIC 5511
HOPPER BUICK GMC p 763
See HOPPER AUTOMOBILES LTD
HOPPER INC p 1182
5795 AV DE GASPE BUREAU 100, MONTREAL, QC, H2S 2X3
(514) 276-0760 SIC 7371
HORISOL, COOP DE TRAVAIL p 1315
See 'HORISOL', COOPERATIVE DE TRAVAILLEURS
HORIZON AGRO INC p 352
1086 HORIZON RD, MORRIS, MB, R0G 1K0
(204) 746-2026 SIC 5153
HORIZON CONNEXIONS INC p 1049
9660 BOUL DU GOLF, ANJOU, QC, H1J 2Y7
SIC 1731
HORIZON DISTRIBUTORS LTD p 181
5589 TRAPP AVE, BURNABY, BC, V3N 0B2
(604) 524-6610 SIC 5149
HORIZON DRILLING p 62
See WESTERN ENERGY SERVICES CORP
HORIZON EXPORTS INC p 214
1028 GIBSONS WAY, GIBSONS, BC, V0N 1V7
(604) 886-3433 SIC 5511
HORIZON HEALTH NETWORK p 401
See REGIONAL HEALTH AUTHORITY NB
HORIZON INSURANCE p 386
See HUB INTERNATIONAL MANITOBA
HORIZON MARITIME SERVICES LTD p 444
101 RESEARCH DR, DARTMOUTH, NS, B2Y 4T6
(902) 468-2341 SIC 7361
HORIZON MILLING p 1426
See ARDENT MILLS ULC
HORIZON NORTH CAMP & CATERING PARTNERSHIP p 51
240 4 AVE SW SUITE 900, CALGARY, AB, T2P 4H4

(403) 517-4654 SIC 5812
HORIZON NORTH CAMP & CATERING PARTNERSHIP, DIV OF p 51
See HORIZON NORTH POWER SYTEMS
HORIZON NORTH CAMPS & CATERING p 51
See HORIZON NORTH LOGISTICS INC
HORIZON NORTH CAMPS & CATERING, DIV OF p 51
See HORIZON NORTH CAMP & CATERING PARTNERSHIP
HORIZON NORTH LOGISTICS INC p 51
240 4 AVE SW SUITE 900, CALGARY, AB, T2P 4H4
(403) 517-4654 SIC 4731
HORIZON NORTH LOGISTICS INC p 132
10320 140 AVE SUITE 102, GRANDE PRAIRIE, AB, T8V 8A4
(780) 830-5333 SIC 4731
HORIZON NORTH MODULAR MANUFACTURING INC p
51
240 4 AVE SW SUITE 900, CALGARY, AB, T2P 4H4
(403) 517-4654 SIC 2452
HORIZON NORTH POWER SYTEMS p 51
900-240 4 AVE SW, CALGARY, AB, T2P 4H4
(780) 955-2992 SIC 5063
HORIZON PACKAGING MILTON p 683
See COMMUNITY LIVING NORTH HALTON
HORIZON PLASTICS INTERNATIONAL INC p 545
BLDG 3 NORTHAM INDUSTRIAL PARK, COBOURG, ON, K9A 4L1
(905) 372-2291 SIC 3089
HORIZON POULTRY p 617
See MAPLE LEAF FOODS INC
HORIZON SCHOOL DIVISION NO 205 p 1407
10333 8TH AVE, HUMBOLDT, SK, S0K 2A0
(306) 682-2558 SIC 8211
HORIZON SCHOOL DIVISION NO 67 p 169
See BOARD OF TRUSTEES OF HORIZON SCHOOL DIVISION NO 67
HORIZON UTILITIES p 613
See ALECTRA UTILITIES CORPORATION
HORIZONS ACTIVE CORPORATE BOND ETF p 942
26 WELLINGTON ST E SUITE 700, TORONTO, ON, M5E 1S2
(416) 933-5754 SIC 6722
HORIZONS ACTIVE DIVERSIFIED INCOME ETF INC p 942
26 WELLINGTON ST E SUITE 700, TORONTO, ON, M5E 1S2
(416) 933-5745 SIC 8742
HORIZONS ACTIVE HIGH YIELD BOND ETF p 942
26 WELLINGTON ST E SUITE 700, TORONTO, ON, M5E 1S2
(416) 933-5745 SIC 6722
HORNBY ISLAND NEW HORIZONS p 284
1765 SOLLANS, UNION BAY, BC, V0R 3B0
(250) 335-0385 SIC 7389
HORSESHOE HILL CONSTRUCTION INC p 531
18859 HORSESHOE HILL RD, CALEDON, ON, L7K 2B9
(905) 857-7400 SIC 1622
HORSESHOE RESORT p 484
See HORSESHOE RESORT CORPORATION
HORSESHOE RESORT CORPORATION p 484
1101 HORSESHOE VALLEY RD W, BARRIE, ON, L4M 4Y8
(705) 835-2790 SIC 7011
HORSESHOE VALLEY LIMITED PARTNERSHIP p
484
1101 HORSESHOE VALLEY RD W, BARRIE, ON, L4M 4Y8

(705) 835-2790 SIC 7011
HORST WELDING p 646
See 1708828 ONTARIO LIMITED
HORTICLUB p 1236
See NORSECO INC
HORTICO INC p 1005
723 ROBSON RD, WATERDOWN, ON, L8B 1H2
(905) 689-6984 SIC 0181
HORTICULTURAL SOCIETIES OF PARKDALE & TORONTO p
994
1938 BLOOR ST W, TORONTO, ON, M6P 3K8
(416) 486-0898 SIC 8748
HORTON CBI, LIMITED p 168
55116 HWY 825, STURGEON COUNTY, AB, T8L 5C1
(780) 998-2800 SIC 1791
HORTON HIGH SCHOOL p 471
See ANNAPOLIS VALLEY REGIONAL SCHOOL BOARD
HORTON SPICE MILLS LIMITED p 671
256 STEELCASE RD W, MARKHAM, ON, L3R 1B3
(905) 475-6130 SIC 5149
HORTON TRADING LTD p 298
788 BEATTY ST SUITE 307, VANCOUVER, BC, V6B 2M1
(604) 688-8521 SIC 7374
HOSIE & BROWN AUTO ELECTRIC LTD p
595
1352 GOSSET ST, GLOUCESTER, ON, K1B 3P7
(613) 741-8112 SIC 5013
HOSKIN SCIENTIFIC LIMITED p 185
3735 MYRTLE ST, BURNABY, BC, V5C 4E7
(604) 872-7894 SIC 5049
HOSPICE OF WINDSOR AND ESSEX COUNTY INC, THE p 1018
6038 EMPRESS ST, WINDSOR, ON, N8T 1B5
(519) 974-7100 SIC 8399
HOSPITAL CHISASIBI p 1081
PR, CHISASIBI, QC, J0M 1E0
(819) 855-2844 SIC 8062
HOSPITAL FOR SICK CHILDREN FOUNDATION INC, THE p
945
525 UNIVERSITY AVE 14TH FL, TORONTO, ON, M5G 2L3
(416) 813-5320 SIC 8699
HOSPITAL FOR SICK CHILDREN, THE p
945
555 UNIVERSITY AVE, TORONTO, ON, M5G 1X8
(416) 813-1500 SIC 8069
HOSPITAL LOGISTICS INC p 945
1 DUNDAS ST W SUITE 1700, TORONTO, ON, M5G 1Z3
(416) 673-5600 SIC 5047
HOSPITALITY CAREERS ONLINE INC p
190
4789 KINGSWAY SUITE 400, BURNABY, BC, V5H 0A3
(604) 435-8991 SIC 7311
HOSPITALITY DESIGNS p 264
See VERY JAZZROO ENTERPRISES INCORPORATED
HOSPITALITY FALLSVIEW HOLDINGS INC p 759
6361 FALLSVIEW BLVD, NIAGARA FALLS, ON, L2G 3V9
(905) 354-7887 SIC 6712
HOSPITALITY INNS LTD p 39
135 SOUTHLAND DR SE, CALGARY, AB, T2J 5X5
(403) 278-5050 SIC 7011
HOSPITALITY MOTELS LIMITED p 759
6361 FALLSVIEW BLVD, NIAGARA FALLS, ON, L2G 3V9
(905) 357-3184 SIC 7011
HOST INTERNATIONAL OF CANADA, LTD p 23

2000 AIRPORT RD NE SUITE 160, CAL-
GARY, AB, T2E 6W5
(403) 503-2214   SIC 5812
HOSTESS FOOD PRODUCTS   p 440
230 BLUEWATER RD, BEDFORD, NS, B4B
1G9
(902) 832-2865   SIC 2096
HOSTESS FRITO LAY CANADA, DIV OF p
732
See PEPSICO CANADA ULC
HOSTESS FRITO-LAY   p 141
See PEPSICO CANADA ULC
HOSTESS FRITO-LAY   p 169
See PEPSICO CANADA ULC
HOT 89 9 FM CIHT   p 749
See NEWCAP RADIO OTTAWA
HOT HOUSE RESTAURANT AND BAR   p
942
35 CHURCH ST, TORONTO, ON, M5E 1T3
(416) 366-7800   SIC 5812
HOT OVEN BAKERY LTD, THE   p 577
250 THE EAST MALL SUITE 285, ETOBI-
COKE, ON, M9B 3Y8
(416) 233-6771   SIC 5461
HOT SHOT TRUCKING (1990) LTD p 217
937 LAVAL CRES, KAMLOOPS, BC, V2C
5P4
(250) 372-7651   SIC 7389
HOTEL & GOLF MARIGOT INC   p 1256
7900 RUE DU MARIGOT, QUEBEC, QC,
G1G 6T8
(418) 627-8008   SIC 7011
HOTEL & SUITES LE DAUPHIN   p 1099
See IMMEUBLES J.C. MILOT INC, LES
HOTEL 550 WELLINGTON GP LTD   p 981
550 WELLINGTON ST W, TORONTO, ON,
M5V 2V4
(416) 640-7778   SIC 7011
HOTEL ARTS   p 63
See 1504953 ALBERTA LTD
**HOTEL AUBERGE UNIVERSEL MON-
TREAL**   p
1166
See 2990181 CANADA INC
HOTEL BERNIERES INC   p 1140
535 RUE DE BERNIERES, LEVIS, QC, G7A
1C9
(418) 831-3119   SIC 7011
HOTEL BONAVENTURE   p 1345
See 9312-5581 QUEBEC INC
HOTEL CHATEAU LAURIER QUEBEC   p
1269
See COGIRES INC
HOTEL CHERIBOURG INC   p 1244
2603 CH DU PARC, ORFORD, QC, J1X 8C8
(819) 843-3308   SIC 7011
HOTEL CLARENDON   p 1270
See SOCIETE DE GESTION CAP-AUX-
PIERRES INC
HOTEL CLARION GRAND PACIFIC   p 308
See P SUN'S ENTERPRISES (VANCOU-
VER) LTD
HOTEL COURTENEY BAY   p 431
See CITY HOTELS LIMITED
HOTEL DES GOUVERNEURS   p 1196
See GOUVERNEUR INC
HOTEL DES SEIGNEURS   p 1312
See DELTA HOTELS NO. 12 LIMITED PART-
NERSHIP
HOTEL DIEU HOSPITAL   p 631
See RELIGIOUS HOSPITALLERS OF
SAINT JOSEPH OF THE HOTEL DIEU OF
KINGSTON
HOTEL DOGGY   p 1341
See THREAD COLLECTIVE INC
HOTEL EMBASSY SUITES   p 1187
See AQUILINI PROPERTIES LIMITED
PARTNERSHIP
HOTEL EMOTION   p 1100
See GESTION ESTEREL INC
**HOTEL FORESTEL CENTRE DES CON-
GRES**   p
1390
See HOTEL FORESTEL VAL-D'OR INC

HOTEL FORESTEL VAL-D'OR INC   p 1390
1001 3E AV, VAL-D'OR, QC, J9P 1T4
(819) 825-5660   SIC 7011
HOTEL FORT GARRY   p 376
See 3031632 MANITOBA INC
**HOTEL GEORGIA (OP) LIMITED PART-
NERSHIP**   p
305
801 GEORGIA ST W, VANCOUVER, BC,
V6C 1P7
(604) 682-5566   SIC 7011
HOTEL GOUVERNEUR   p 1175
See GOUVERNEUR INC
HOTEL GOUVERNEUR LE NORANDA
1289
See GOUVERNEUR INC
HOTEL GRAND PACIFIC   p 335
See P SUN'S ENTERPRISES (VANCOU-
VER) LTD
HOTEL HALIFAX   p 453
See LEADON (HALIFAX) OPERATIONS LP
HOTEL HOLIDAY INN POINTE-CLAIRE p
1252
See WEST ISLAND HOTELS INC
**HOTEL   INTER-CONTINENTAL   (MON-
TREAL)**   p
1187
See CORPORATION DES HOTELS INTER-
CONTINENTAL (MONTREAL), LA
HOTEL LE DAUPHIN   p 1097
See 2316-7240 QUEBEC INC
HOTEL LE GERMAIN   p 1270
See GROUPE GERMAIN INC
HOTEL LE MONTAGNAIS   p 1079
See COUTURE, ARMAND & FILS INC
HOTEL LOEWS LE CONCORDE   p 1269
See PLACE MONTCALM HOTEL INC
HOTEL MONT GABRIEL   p 1354
See 9055-8842 QUEBEC INC
HOTEL MORTAGNE   p 1063
See 9164-2033 QUEBEC INC
**HOTEL N.S. OWNERSHIP LIMITED PART-
NERSHIP**   p
451
1181 HOLLIS ST SUITE 1, HALIFAX, NS,
B3H 2P6
(902) 421-1000   SIC 7011
HOTEL NEWFOUNDLAND (1982)   p 432
CAVENDISH SQ, ST. JOHN'S, NL, A1C
5W8
(709) 726-4980   SIC 7011
HOTEL OMNI MONT-ROYAL   p 1192
See 3025235 NOVA SCOTIA ULC
HOTEL PALACE ROYAL INC   p 1269
775 AV HONORE-MERCIER, QUEBEC,
QC, G1R 6A5
(418) 694-2000   SIC 7011
HOTEL PLAZA   p 1271
See 3089-3242 QUEBEC INC
HOTEL PUR   p 1257
See 3072930 NOVA SCOTIA COMPANY
HOTEL SACACOMIE   p 1291
See AUBERGE DU LAC SACACOMIE INC
HOTEL SASKATCHEWAN (1990) LTD p 298
1118 HOMER ST SUITE 425, VANCOU-
VER, BC, V6B 6L5
SIC 7011
HOTEL SASKATCHEWAN (1990) LTD
1418
2125 VICTORIA AVE, REGINA, SK, S4P
0S3
(306) 522-7691   SIC 7011
HOTEL SHERATON LAVAL   p 1086
See GROUPE HOTELIER GRAND
CHATEAU INC
HOTEL W MONTREAL   p 1192
See SOCIETE EN COMMANDITE 901
SQUARE VICTORIA
HOTELLUS CANADA HOLDINGS INC   p
1188
360 RUE SAINT-ANTOINE O, MONTREAL,
QC, H2Y 3X4
(514) 987-9900   SIC 7011
HOTELS CANPRO INC, LES   p 1197

1155 RUE SHERBROOKE O, MONTREAL,
QC, H3A 2N3
(514) 285-9000   SIC 7011
HOTELS COTE-DE-LIESSE INC   p 1339
6500 CH DE LA COTE-DE-LIESSE, SAINT-
LAURENT, QC, H4T 1E3
(514) 739-6440   SIC 7011
HOTSPEX INC   p 922
40 EGLINTON AVE E SUITE 801,
TORONTO, ON, M4P 3A2
(416) 487-5439   SIC 8732
HOTSY CLEANING SYSTEMS   p 106
See WATER BLAST MANUFACTURING LP
HOTTE AUTOMOBILE INC   p 619
640 MAIN ST W, HAWKESBURY, ON, K6A
2J3
(613) 632-1159   SIC 5511
HOTTE FORD   p 619
See HOTTE AUTOMOBILE INC
HOTZ AND SONS COMPANY INC   p 610
239 LOTTRIDGE ST, HAMILTON, ON, L8L
6W1
(905) 545-2665   SIC 5093
HOUDE, WILLIAM LTEE   p 1352
8 3E RANG O, SAINT-SIMON-DE-BAGOT,
QC, J0H 1Y0
(450) 798-2002   SIC 2874
HOUGHTAM ENTERPRISES   p 368
1225 ST MARY'S RD SUITE 49, WIN-
NIPEG, MB, R2M 5E5
(204) 257-1132   SIC 5812
HOULDER FARM SUPPLY   p 135
See ROCKY MOUNTAIN DEALERSHIPS
INC
**HOULE   &   FRERES   GARAGE   (TERRE-
BONNE) LTEE**   p
1149
290 MONTEE MASSON, MASCOUCHE,
QC, J7K 3B5
(450) 474-1110   SIC 5511
HOULE AUTOMOBILE LTEE   p 1163
9080 RUE HOCHELAGA, MONTREAL, QC,
H1L 2N9
(514) 351-5010   SIC 5511
HOULE ELECTRIC LIMITED   p 192
5050 NORTH FRASER WAY, BURNABY,
BC, V5J 0H1
(604) 434-2681   SIC 1731
HOULE ET FRERES (HYUNDAY)   p 1149
See HOULE & FRERES GARAGE (TERRE-
BONNE) LTEE
HOULE TOYOTA   p 1163
See HOULE AUTOMOBILE LTEE
HOULE TOYOTA LTEE   p 1247
12305 RUE SHERBROOKE E, POINTE-
AUX-TREMBLES, QC, H1B 1C8
(514) 640-5010   SIC 5511
HOULE, J.U. LTEE   p 1399
20 RUE FRANCOIS-BOURGEOIS, VICTO-
RIAVILLE, QC, G6T 2G8
(819) 758-5235   SIC 5074
HOUSE INC, THE   p 783
620 SUPERTEST RD UNIT 9, NORTH
YORK, ON, M3J 2M5
SIC 5136
**HOUSE OF ELECTRICAL SUPPLIES LIM-
ITED**   p
671
115 SHIELDS CRT UNIT B, MARKHAM,
ON, L3R 9T5
(905) 752-2323   SIC 5063
HOUSE OF FRIENDSHIP   p 638
51 CHARLES ST E, KITCHENER, ON, N2G
2P3
(519) 742-8327   SIC 8699
**HOUSE OF HOPE SOCIETY INCORPO-
RATED**   p
1005
87 BOUSFIELD RISE, WATERDOWN, ON,
L8B 0T4
SIC 8062
HOUSE OF HORVATH INC   p 991
77 OSSINGTON AVE, TORONTO, ON, M6J
2Z2

(416) 534-4254   SIC 5194
HOUSE OF KNIVES   p 184
See AAA ENTERPRISES INC
HOUSE OF METALS COMPANY LIMITED p
918
45 COMMERCIAL RD, TORONTO, ON,
M4G 1Z3
(416) 421-1572   SIC 5051
HOUSE OF SHER 2018 LTD   p 176
2131 QUEEN ST SUITE 104, ABBOTS-
FORD, BC, V2T 6J3
(604) 859-3030   SIC 5141
HOUWELING NURSERIES LTD   p 211
2776 64 ST, DELTA, BC, V4L 2N7
(604) 946-0844   SIC 0182
HOWARD HUY FARMS LTD   p 644
932 MERSEA ROAD 7, LEAMINGTON, ON,
N8H 3V8
(519) 324-0631   SIC 0181
HOWARD JOHNSON   p 327
See WESTBERG HOLDINGS INC
HOWARD JOHNSON   p 400
See A. K. HOLDINGS INC
HOWARD JOHNSON HOTEL   p 320
See AIRLINER MOTOR HOTEL (1972) LTD
HOWARD MARTEN COMPANY LIMITED p
844
902 DILLINGHAM RD, PICKERING, ON,
L1W 1Z6
(905) 831-2901   SIC 3569
**HOWARD   MARTEN   FLUID   TECHNOLO-
GIES INC**   p
844
902 DILLINGHAM RD, PICKERING, ON,
L1W 1Z6
(905) 831-2901   SIC 5084
HOWARD MOTORS INC   p 430
46 KENMOUNT RD, ST. JOHN'S, NL, A1B
1W2
(709) 726-9900   SIC 5511
HOWARD, R. A. BUS SERVICE LIMITED p
479
31 HENRY ST, ATHENS, ON, K0E 1B0
(613) 924-2720   SIC 4151
HOWE PRECISION INDUSTRIAL INC p 244
11718 HARRIS RD, PITT MEADOWS, BC,
V3Y 1Y6
(604) 460-2892   SIC 3823
**HOWE SOUND PULP & PAPER CORPORA-
TION**   p
248
3838 PORT MELLON HWY, PORT MEL-
LON, BC, V0N 2S0
(604) 884-5223   SIC 2611
**HOWE SOUND PULP & PAPER CORPORA-
TION**   p
290
8501 ONTARIO ST, VANCOUVER, BC, V5X
4W2
(604) 301-3300   SIC 2421
HOWELL DATA SYSTEMS INC   p 554
160 PENNSYLVANIA AVE UNIT 4, CON-
CORD, ON, L4K 4A9
(905) 761-1712   SIC 5044
HOWELL DATA SYSTEMS INC   p 1021
250 TECUMSEH RD E, WINDSOR, ON,
N8X 2R3
SIC 5999
HOWELL PIPE & SUPPLY, DIV OF   p 593
See HOWELL PLUMBING SUPPLIES
DASCO LIMITED
**HOWELL PLUMBING SUPPLIES DASCO
LIMITED**   p 593
11 ARMSTRONG AVE, GEORGETOWN,
ON, L7G 4S1
(905) 877-2293   SIC 5085
HOWMET CANADA COMPANY   p 593
93 MOUNTAINVIEW RD N, GEORGE-
TOWN, ON, L7G 4J6
(905) 877-6936   SIC 3365
HOWMET CANADA COMPANY   p 1234
4001 DES LAURENTIDES (A-15) E, MON-
TREAL, QC, H7L 3H7
(450) 680-2500   SIC 3365

HOWMET GEORGETOWN CASTING *p* 593
See HOWMET CANADA COMPANY

HOWMET LAVAL CASTING LTD *p* 1133
4001 AUT DES LAURENTIDES, LAVAL, QC,
H7L 3H7
(450) 680-2500 *SIC* 3365

HOWSON & HOWSON LIMITED *p* 493
232 WESTMORELAND ST, BLYTH, ON,
N0M 1H0
(519) 523-4241 *SIC* 2041

HOWSON MILLS *p* 493
See HOWSON & HOWSON LIMITED

HOYA LENS CANADA INC *p* 717
3330 RIDGEWAY DR UNIT 21, MISSIS-
SAUGA, ON, L5L 5Z9
(905) 828-3477 *SIC* 5049

HOYA VISION CARE, CANADA *p* 717
See HOYA LENS CANADA INC

HOYT'S MOVING & STORAGE LIMITED *p*
446
320 WRIGHT AVE UNIT 12, DARTMOUTH,
NS, B3B 0B3
(902) 876-8202 *SIC* 4213

HOYT'S SPECIALTY SERVICES, DIV OF *p*
446
*See HOYT'S MOVING & STORAGE LIM-
ITED*

HP CANADA CO *p* 696
5150 SPECTRUM WAY 6 FL, MISSIS-
SAUGA, ON, L4W 5G2
(888) 206-0289 *SIC* 8731

HPG INC *p* 804
2240 SPEERS RD, OAKVILLE, ON, L6L 2X8
(905) 825-1218 *SIC* 3728

HPG INC *p* 804
2250 SPEERS RD, OAKVILLE, ON, L6L 2X8
(905) 825-1218 *SIC* 3728

HPS *p* 601
See HAMMOND POWER SOLUTIONS INC

HR OTTAWA, L.P. *p* 597
4837 ALBION RD, GLOUCESTER, ON, K1X
1A3
(613) 822-8668 *SIC* 7011

HRA DIAMONDS *p* 313
See H.R.A. INVESTMENTS LTD

HRC CANADA INC *p* 935
279 YONGE ST, TORONTO, ON, M5B 1N8
(416) 362-3636 *SIC* 5813

HRC CANADA INC *p* 1213
1458 RUE CRESCENT, MONTREAL, QC,
H3G 2B6
SIC 5812

HRDOWNLOADS INC *p* 653
195 DUFFERIN AVE SUITE 500, LONDON,
ON, N6A 1K7
(519) 438-9763 *SIC* 8999

HRG AMERIQUE DU NORD *p* 1197
See HOGG ROBINSON CANADA INC

HRG NORTH AMERICA *p* 981
See HOGG ROBINSON CANADA INC

HRH *p* 916
See HUMBER RIVER HOSPITAL

HS SPRING OF CANADA LTD *p* 585
25 WORCESTER RD, ETOBICOKE, ON,
M9W 1K9
(416) 675-9072 *SIC* 3493

HS TELECOM *p* 1140
See HENRI SICOTTE INC

HSA *p* 236
*See HEALTH SCIENCES ASSOCIATION
OF BRITISH COLUMBIA*

HSB BI&I *p* 949
*See BOILER INSPECTION AND INSUR-
ANCE COMPANY OF CANADA, THE*

HSBC *p* 963
See HSBC SECURITIES (CANADA) INC

HSBC BANK CANADA *p* 298
401 GEORGIA ST W SUITE 1300, VAN-
COUVER, BC, V6B 5A1
(604) 668-4682 *SIC* 8742

HSBC BANK CANADA *p* 305
885 GEORGIA ST W, VANCOUVER, BC,
V6C 3G1
(604) 685-1000 *SIC* 6021

HSBC BANK CANADA *p* 963
70 YORK ST SUITE 800, TORONTO, ON,
M5J 1S9
(416) 868-8000 *SIC* 6021

HSBC CAPITAL (CANADA) INC *p* 305
885 GEORGIA ST W SUITE 1100, VAN-
COUVER, BC, V6C 3E8
(604) 631-8088 *SIC* 6211

HSBC SECURITIES (CANADA) INC *p* 963
70 YORK ST SUITE 800, TORONTO, ON,
M5J 1S9
(416) 868-8000 *SIC* 6211

HSC MONTREAL *p* 1219
*See CORPORATION DE L'ECOLE DES
HAUTES ETUDES COMMERCIALES DE
MONTREAL*

HSE FIRE SERVICES *p* 6
See HSE INTEGRATED LTD

HSE FIRE SERVICES *p* 51
See HSE INTEGRATED LTD

HSE INTEGRATED LTD *p* 6
5503 50 AVE, BONNYVILLE, AB, T9N 2K9
(780) 826-5300 *SIC* 8748

HSE INTEGRATED LTD *p* 51
630 6 AVE SW SUITE 1000, CALGARY, AB,
T2P 0S8
(403) 266-1833 *SIC* 8748

HSF FOODS LTD *p* 396
741 CENTRAL ST SUITE 501, CENTRE-
VILLE, NB, E7K 2M4
(506) 276-3621 *SIC* 2099

HSG HEALTH SYSTEMS GROUP LIMITED
p 718
51 TANNERY ST, MISSISSAUGA, ON, L5M
1V3
(905) 858-0333 *SIC* 8011

HSL *p* 929
See HUTCHINSON SMILEY LIMITED

HSR *p* 747
*See HAMILTON STREET RAILWAY COM-
PANY, THE*

HSS HELITECH SUPPORT SERVICES LTD
p 176
1640 THRESHOLD DR, ABBOTSFORD,
BC, V2T 6H5
(604) 557-9690 *SIC* 4581

HT GRIFFIN FOOD INGREDIENTS *p* 739
See GRIFFIN, HAROLD T. INC

HT INDUSTRIAL LTD *p* 514
36 CRAIG ST, BRANTFORD, ON, N3R 7J1
(519) 759-3010 *SIC* 3443

HT PRODUCTIONS INC *p* 609
690 RENNIE ST, HAMILTON, ON, L8H 3R2
(905) 544-7575 *SIC* 5199

HTH HEATECH INC *p* 77
61 INDUSTRY WAY SE, CALGARY, AB, T3S
0A2
(403) 279-1990 *SIC* 5074

HTI *p* 553
See HANDLING TECHNOLOGIES INC

HTM INSURANCE *p* 545
*See HAMILTON TOWNSHIP MUTUAL IN-
SURANCE COMPANY*

HTS ENGINEERING LTD *p* 787
115 NORFINCH DR, NORTH YORK, ON,
M3N 1W8
(416) 661-3400 *SIC* 5075

HU-A-KAM ENTERPRISES INC *p* 918
1787 BAYVIEW AVE, TORONTO, ON, M4G
3C5
(416) 292-0459 *SIC* 5812

HUACHANGDA CANADA HOLDINGS INC *p*
305
2800 PARK PL 666 BURRARD ST, VAN-
COUVER, BC, V6C 2Z7
SIC 6712

HUARDIERE, LA *p* 1211
See GROUPE IBI/DAA INC

**HUAWEI TECHNOLOGIES CANADA CO.,
LTD** *p* 671
19 ALLSTATE PKY, MARKHAM, ON, L3R
5A4
(905) 944-5000 *SIC* 4899

HUB CANADA *p* 723

*See HUB PARKING TECHNOLOGY
CANADA LTD*

HUB CITY FISHERIES *p* 233
See 434870 B.C. LTD

HUB FINANCIAL (BC) INC, THE *p* 313
1185 GEORGIA ST W SUITE 800, VAN-
COUVER, BC, V6E 4E6
(604) 684-0086 *SIC* 6411

HUB FINANCIAL INC *p* 1031
3700 STEELES AVE W UNIT 1001, WOOD-
BRIDGE, ON, L4L 8K8
(905) 264-1634 *SIC* 6411

HUB INTERNATIONAL *p* 1197
1010 SHERBROOKE ST W STE 2510,
MONTREAL, QC, H3A 2R7
(514) 787-7200 *SIC* 6411

**HUB INTERNATIONAL BARTON INSUR-
ANCE BROKERS** *p*
196
*See HUB INTERNATIONAL CANADA
WEST ULC*

**HUB INTERNATIONAL CANADA WEST
ULC** *p* 196
8346 NOBLE RD, CHILLIWACK, BC, V2P
6R5
(604) 703-7070 *SIC* 6411

HUB INTERNATIONAL HKMB LIMITED *p*
945
595 BAY ST SUITE 900, TORONTO, ON,
M5G 2E3
(416) 597-0008 *SIC* 6411

**HUB INTERNATIONAL INSURANCE BRO-
KERS** *p*
185
4350 STILL CREEK DR SUITE 400, BURN-
ABY, BC, V5C 0G5
(604) 293-1481 *SIC* 6411

HUB INTERNATIONAL MANITOBA *p* 386
1661 PORTAGE AVE SUITE 500, WIN-
NIPEG, MB, R3J 3T7
(204) 988-4800 *SIC* 6411

HUB INTERNATIONAL ONTARIO LIMITED *p*
797
2265 UPPER MIDDLE RD E SUITE 700,
OAKVILLE, ON, L6H 0G5
(905) 847-5500 *SIC* 6411

HUB INTERNATIONAL QUEBEC LIMITEE *p*
1227
8500 BOUL DECARIE, MONTREAL, QC,
H4P 2N2
(514) 374-9600 *SIC* 6411

**HUB PARKING TECHNOLOGY CANADA
LTD** *p* 723
2900 ARGENTIA RD SUITE 1, MISSIS-
SAUGA, ON, L5N 7X9
(905) 813-1966 *SIC* 5065

HUBBARD, C. FUELS *p* 462
See WEST NOVA FUELS LIMITED

**HUBBERT'S PROCESSING AND SALES
LIMITED** *p* 503
109 EAST DR, BRAMPTON, ON, L6T 1B6
(905) 791-0101 *SIC* 2079

HUBBERTS INDUSTRIES *p* 503
*See HUBBERT'S PROCESSING AND
SALES LIMITED*

HUBER DEVELOPMENT LTD *p* 222
516 LAWRENCE AVE, KELOWNA, BC, V1Y
6L7
(250) 860-5858 *SIC* 1522

HUBER DEVELOPMENT LTD *p* 235
701 LAKESIDE DR, NELSON, BC, V1L 6G3
(250) 352-7222 *SIC* 7011

HUBERGROUP *p* 735
See HUBERGROUP CANADA LIMITED

HUBERGROUP CANADA LIMITED *p* 735
2150A DREW RD, MISSISSAUGA, ON, L5S
1B1
(905) 671-0750 *SIC* 2893

HUBERT AUTO *p* 1148
*See GERARD HUBERT AUTOMOBILES
LTEE*

HUBERT SABOURIN HOLDINGS LTD *p* 476
135 SANDFIELD AVE, ALEXANDRIA, ON,
K0C 1A0

(613) 525-1032 *SIC* 5051

HUBIO SOLUTIONS INC *p* 939
20 VICTORIA ST, TORONTO, ON, M5C 2N8
(416) 364-6306 *SIC* 5045

HUCKLEBERRY MINES LTD *p* 215
GD, HOUSTON, BC, V0J 1Z0
(604) 517-4723 *SIC* 1021

HUDBAY MINERALS INC *p* 350
See HUDBAY MINERALS INC

HUDBAY MINERALS INC *p* 350
GD, FLIN FLON, MB, R8A 1N9
(204) 687-2385 *SIC* 1021

HUDBAY MINERALS INC *p* 350
GD STN MAIN, FLIN FLON, MB, R8A 1N9
(204) 687-2385 *SIC* 1081

HUDBAY MINERALS INC *p* 963
25 YORK ST SUITE 800, TORONTO, ON,
M5J 2V5
(416) 362-8181 *SIC* 1081

HUDSON & CO *p* 64
625 11 AVE SW SUITE 300, CALGARY, AB,
T2R 0E1
(403) 265-4357 *SIC* 8721

HUDSON BAY PORT COMPANY *p* 348
1 AXWORTHY WAY, CHURCHILL, MB, R0B
0E0
(204) 675-8823 *SIC* 4491

HUDSON BAY RAILWAY COMPANY *p* 359
728 BIGNEL AVE, THE PAS, MB, R9A 1L8
(204) 627-2007 *SIC* 4011

HUDSON DUFRY - EDMONTON *p* 126
PO BOX 9898, EDMONTON, AB, T9E 0V3
(780) 890-7263 *SIC* 5441

HUDSON ENERGY CANADA CORP *p* 740
6345 DIXIE RD SUITE 200, MISSISSAUGA,
ON, L5T 2E6
(905) 670-4440 *SIC* 4911

HUDSON GROUP CANADA, INC *p* 450
1 BELL BLVD SUITE 1621, ENFIELD, NS,
B2T 1K2
(902) 873-3282 *SIC* 5947

HUDSON PLATING AND COATING CO. LTD
p 192
3750 NORTH FRASER WAY UNIT 102,
BURNABY, BC, V5J 5E9
(604) 430-8384 *SIC* 3479

HUDSON POWDER COATING *p* 192
*See HUDSON PLATING AND COATING
CO. LTD*

HUDSON VALLEY FARMS (CA) ULC *p* 1347
228 RUE PRINCIPALE, SAINT-LOUIS-DE-
GONZAGUE, QC, J0S 1T0
(450) 377-8766 *SIC* 0259

HUDSON VALLEY PRODUITS DE CANARD
p 1347
See HUDSON VALLEY FARMS (CA) ULC

HUDSON'S BAY COMPANY *p* 8
2525 36 ST NE, CALGARY, AB, T1Y 5T4
(403) 261-0759 *SIC* 5311

HUDSON'S BAY COMPANY *p* 8
3333 SUNRIDGE WAY NE, CALGARY, AB,
T1Y 7H5
SIC 5311

HUDSON'S BAY COMPANY *p* 35
6455 MACLEOD TRAIL SW, CALGARY, AB,
T2H 0K8
(403) 255-6121 *SIC* 5311

HUDSON'S BAY COMPANY *p* 39
100 ANDERSON RD SE, CALGARY, AB,
T2J 3V1
(403) 278-9520 *SIC* 5311

HUDSON'S BAY COMPANY *p* 51
200 8 AVE SW, CALGARY, AB, T2P 1B5
(403) 262-0345 *SIC* 5311

HUDSON'S BAY COMPANY *p* 71
3625 SHAGANAPPI TRAIL NW, CALGARY,
AB, T3A 0E2
(403) 286-1220 *SIC* 5311

HUDSON'S BAY COMPANY *p* 84
1 LONDONDERRY MALL NW UNIT 86, ED-
MONTON, AB, T5C 3C8
(780) 478-2931 *SIC* 5311

HUDSON'S BAY COMPANY *p* 85
650 KINGSWAY GARDEN MALL NW, ED-

MONTON, AB, T5G 3E6
(780) 479-7100   *SIC* 5311
HUDSON'S BAY COMPANY   *p* 104
8882 170 ST NW SUITE 1001, EDMON-
TON, AB, T5T 3J7
(780) 444-1550   *SIC* 5311
HUDSON'S BAY COMPANY   *p* 119
150 SOUTHGATE SHOPPING CTR NW,
EDMONTON, AB, T6H 4M7
(780) 435-9211   *SIC* 5311
HUDSON'S BAY COMPANY   *p* 120
9738 19 AVE NW, EDMONTON, AB, T6N
1K6
(780) 414-5850   *SIC* 5311
HUDSON'S BAY COMPANY   *p* 142
200 4 AVE S SUITE 200, LETHBRIDGE, AB,
T1J 4C9
(403) 329-3131   *SIC* 5311
HUDSON'S BAY COMPANY   *p* 146
3292 DUNMORE RD SE SUITE F7,
MEDICINE HAT, AB, T1B 2R4
(403) 526-7888   *SIC* 5311
HUDSON'S BAY COMPANY   *p* 157
4900 MOLLY BANNISTER DR, RED DEER,
AB, T4R 1N9
(403) 347-2211   *SIC* 5311
HUDSON'S BAY COMPANY   *p* 165
375 ST ALBERT TRAIL SUITE 300, ST. AL-
BERT, AB, T8N 3K8
(780) 458-5800   *SIC* 5311
HUDSON'S BAY COMPANY   *p* 175
32900 SOUTH FRASER WAY SUITE 2, AB-
BOTSFORD, BC, V2S 5A1
(604) 853-7711   *SIC* 5311
HUDSON'S BAY COMPANY   *p* 190
4850 KINGSWAY, BURNABY, BC, V5H 4P2
(604) 436-1196   *SIC* 5311
HUDSON'S BAY COMPANY   *p* 190
4800 KINGSWAY SUITE 118, BURNABY,
BC, V5H 4J2
       SIC 5719
HUDSON'S BAY COMPANY   *p* 198
2929 BARNET HWY SUITE 100, COQUIT-
LAM, BC, V3B 5R9
(604) 468-4453   *SIC* 5311
HUDSON'S BAY COMPANY   *p* 216
1320 TRANS CANADA HWY W SUITE 300,
KAMLOOPS, BC, V1S 1J1
(250) 372-8271   *SIC* 5311
HUDSON'S BAY COMPANY   *p* 222
2271 HARVEY AVE SUITE 1415,
KELOWNA, BC, V1Y 6H3
(250) 860-2483   *SIC* 5311
HUDSON'S BAY COMPANY   *p* 228
19705 FRASER HWY SUITE 320, LANG-
LEY, BC, V3A 7E9
(604) 530-8434   *SIC* 5311
HUDSON'S BAY COMPANY   *p* 234
6631 ISLAND HWY N SUITE 1A, NANAIMO,
BC, V9T 4T7
(250) 390-3141   *SIC* 5311
HUDSON'S BAY COMPANY   *p* 237
805 BOYD ST, NEW WESTMINSTER, BC,
V3M 5X2
(604) 525-7362   *SIC* 5311
HUDSON'S BAY COMPANY   *p* 243
2111 MAIN ST SUITE 160, PENTICTON,
BC, V2A 6V1
(250) 493-1900   *SIC* 5311
HUDSON'S BAY COMPANY   *p* 249
1600 15TH AVE SUITE 140, PRINCE
GEORGE, BC, V2L 3X3
(250) 563-0211   *SIC* 5311
HUDSON'S BAY COMPANY   *p* 258
18111 BLUNDELL RD, RICHMOND, BC,
V6W 1L8
(604) 249-3000   *SIC* 4225
HUDSON'S BAY COMPANY   *p* 262
6060 MINORU BLVD SUITE 100, RICH-
MOND, BC, V6Y 1Y2
(604) 273-3844   *SIC* 5311
HUDSON'S BAY COMPANY   *p* 270
1400 GUILDFORD TOWN CTR, SURREY,
BC, V3R 7B7

(604) 588-2111   *SIC* 5311
HUDSON'S BAY COMPANY   *p* 293
650 41ST AVE W, VANCOUVER, BC, V5Z
2M9
(604) 261-3311   *SIC* 5311
HUDSON'S BAY COMPANY   *p* 305
674 GRANVILLE ST SUITE 9999, VAN-
COUVER, BC, V6C 1Z6
(604) 681-6211   *SIC* 5311
HUDSON'S BAY COMPANY   *p* 332
4900 27 ST SUITE 10, VERNON, BC, V1T
2C7
(250) 545-5331   *SIC* 5311
HUDSON'S BAY COMPANY   *p* 336
1150 DOUGLAS ST SUITE 1, VICTORIA,
BC, V8W 2C8
(250) 385-1311   *SIC* 5311
HUDSON'S BAY COMPANY   *p* 338
3125 DOUGLAS ST, VICTORIA, BC, V8Z
3K3
(250) 386-3322   *SIC* 5311
HUDSON'S BAY COMPANY   *p* 341
725 PARK ROYAL N, WEST VANCOUVER,
BC, V7T 1H9
(604) 925-1411   *SIC* 5311
HUDSON'S BAY COMPANY   *p* 378
450 PORTAGE AVE, WINNIPEG, MB, R3C
0E7
(204) 783-2112   *SIC* 5311
HUDSON'S BAY COMPANY   *p* 382
1485 PORTAGE AVE, WINNIPEG, MB, R3G
0W4
(204) 975-3228   *SIC* 5311
HUDSON'S BAY COMPANY   *p* 407
1100 MAIN ST, MONCTON, NB, E1C 1H4
       SIC 5311
HUDSON'S BAY COMPANY   *p* 457
7067 CHEBUCTO RD SUITE 111, HALI-
FAX, NS, B3L 4R5
       SIC 5311
HUDSON'S BAY COMPANY   *p* 503
25 PEEL CENTRE DR SUITE 3, BRAMP-
TON, ON, L6T 3R5
(905) 793-5100   *SIC* 5311
HUDSON'S BAY COMPANY   *p* 503
8925 TORBRAM RD, BRAMPTON, ON, L6T
4G1
(905) 792-4400   *SIC* 5311
HUDSON'S BAY COMPANY   *p* 530
777 GUELPH LINE UNIT 8, BURLINGTON,
ON, L7R 3N2
(905) 634-8866   *SIC* 5311
HUDSON'S BAY COMPANY   *p* 531
900 MAPLE AVE, BURLINGTON, ON, L7S
2J8
(905) 681-0030   *SIC* 5311
HUDSON'S BAY COMPANY   *p* 533
355 HESPELER RD UNIT 1, CAMBRIDGE,
ON, N1R 6B3
(519) 622-4919   *SIC* 5311
HUDSON'S BAY COMPANY   *p* 579
25 THE WEST MALL, ETOBICOKE, ON,
M9C 1B8
(416) 626-4711   *SIC* 5311
HUDSON'S BAY COMPANY   *p* 585
145 CARRIER DR, ETOBICOKE, ON, M9W
5N5
(416) 798-5755   *SIC* 5099
HUDSON'S BAY COMPANY   *p* 585
500 REXDALE BLVD, ETOBICOKE, ON,
M9W 6K5
(416) 674-6000   *SIC* 5311
HUDSON'S BAY COMPANY   *p* 616
999 UPPER WENTWORTH ST, HAMILTON,
ON, L9A 4X5
(905) 318-8008   *SIC* 5311
HUDSON'S BAY COMPANY   *p* 632
945 GARDINERS RD, KINGSTON, ON,
K7M 7H4
(613) 384-3888   *SIC* 5311
HUDSON'S BAY COMPANY   *p* 657
1105 WELLINGTON RD SUITE 5, LON-
DON, ON, N6E 1V4
(519) 685-4100   *SIC* 5311

HUDSON'S BAY COMPANY   *p* 658
1680 RICHMOND ST, LONDON, ON, N6G
3Y9
(519) 675-0080   *SIC* 5311
HUDSON'S BAY COMPANY   *p* 671
5000 HIGHWAY 7 E, MARKHAM, ON, L3R
4M9
(905) 513-1770   *SIC* 5311
HUDSON'S BAY COMPANY   *p* 710
100 CITY CENTRE DR SUITE 200, MISSIS-
SAUGA, ON, L5B 2C9
(905) 270-7600   *SIC* 5311
HUDSON'S BAY COMPANY   *p* 718
5100 ERIN MILLS PKY UNIT Y001, MISSIS-
SAUGA, ON, L5M 4Z5
(905) 820-8300   *SIC* 5311
HUDSON'S BAY COMPANY   *p* 767
1800 SHEPPARD AVE E SUITE 1, NORTH
YORK, ON, M2J 5A7
(416) 491-2010   *SIC* 5311
HUDSON'S BAY COMPANY   *p* 770
6500 YONGE ST, NORTH YORK, ON, M2M
3X4
(416) 226-4202   *SIC* 5311
HUDSON'S BAY COMPANY   *p* 789
3401 DUFFERIN ST, NORTH YORK, ON,
M6A 2T9
(416) 789-8011   *SIC* 5311
HUDSON'S BAY COMPANY   *p* 797
240 LEIGHLAND AVE, OAKVILLE, ON, L6H
3H6
(905) 842-4811   *SIC* 5311
HUDSON'S BAY COMPANY   *p* 810
110 PLACE D'ORLEANS DR, ORLEANS,
ON, K1C 2L9
(613) 837-8274   *SIC* 5311
HUDSON'S BAY COMPANY   *p* 814
419 KING ST W, OSHAWA, ON, L1J 2K5
(905) 571-1211   *SIC* 5311
HUDSON'S BAY COMPANY   *p* 820
1200 ST. LAURENT BLVD, OTTAWA, ON,
K1K 3B8
(613) 748-6105   *SIC* 5311
HUDSON'S BAY COMPANY   *p* 821
73 RIDEAU ST, OTTAWA, ON, K1N 5W8
(613) 241-7511   *SIC* 5311
HUDSON'S BAY COMPANY   *p* 855
9350 YONGE ST SUITE 1999, RICHMOND
HILL, ON, L4C 5G2
(905) 883-1222   *SIC* 5311
HUDSON'S BAY COMPANY   *p* 868
1 EGLINTON SQ, SCARBOROUGH, ON,
M1L 2K1
(416) 759-4771   *SIC* 5311
HUDSON'S BAY COMPANY   *p* 871
300 BOROUGH DR SUITE 2, SCARBOR-
OUGH, ON, M1P 4P5
(416) 296-0555   *SIC* 5311
HUDSON'S BAY COMPANY   *p* 887
221 GLENDALE AVE, ST CATHARINES,
ON, L2T 2K9
(905) 688-4441   *SIC* 5311
HUDSON'S BAY COMPANY   *p* 929
2 BLOOR ST E SUITE 52, TORONTO, ON,
M4W 3H7
(416) 972-3313   *SIC* 5311
HUDSON'S BAY COMPANY   *p* 929
2 BLOOR ST E SUITE 52, TORONTO, ON,
M4W 3H7
(416) 972-3333   *SIC* 5311
HUDSON'S BAY COMPANY   *p* 939
176 YONGE ST, TORONTO, ON, M5C 2L7
(416) 861-6251   *SIC* 5311
HUDSON'S BAY COMPANY   *p* 952
401 BAY ST SUITE 601, TORONTO, ON,
M5H 2Y4
(866) 225-8251   *SIC* 5311
HUDSON'S BAY COMPANY   *p* 1021
3030 HOWARD AVE, WINDSOR, ON, N8X
4T3
(519) 966-4666   *SIC* 5311
HUDSON'S BAY COMPANY   *p* 1086
3045 BOUL LE CARREFOUR, COTE
SAINT-LUC, QC, H7T 1C7

(450) 687-1540   *SIC* 5311
HUDSON'S BAY COMPANY   *p* 1104
1100 BOUL MALONEY O, GATINEAU, QC,
J8T 6G3
(819) 243-7036   *SIC* 5311
HUDSON'S BAY COMPANY   *p* 1128
2105 23E AV, LACHINE, QC, H8T 1X3
       SIC 8742
HUDSON'S BAY COMPANY   *p* 1155
2435 CH ROCKLAND, MONT-ROYAL, QC,
H3P 2Z3
(514) 739-5521   *SIC* 5331
HUDSON'S BAY COMPANY   *p* 1250
6790 AUT TRANSCANADIENNE, POINTE-
CLAIRE, QC, H9R 1C5
(514) 697-4870   *SIC* 5311
HUDSON'S BAY COMPANY   *p* 1280
5401 BOUL DES GALERIES, QUEBEC,
QC, G2K 1N4
(418) 627-5922   *SIC* 5311
HUDSON'S BAY COMPANY   *p* 1287
401 BOUL LABELLE, ROSEMERE, QC, J7A
3T2
(450) 433-6991   *SIC* 5311
HUDSON'S BAY COMPANY   *p* 1296
800 BOUL DES PROMENADES, SAINT-
BRUNO, QC, J3V 5J9
(450) 653-4455   *SIC* 5311
HUDSON'S BAY COMPANY   *p* 1418
2150 11TH AVE, REGINA, SK, S4P 0J5
(306) 525-8511   *SIC* 5311
HUDSON'S BAY COMPANY   *p* 1427
201 1ST AVE S, SASKATOON, SK, S7K 1J5
(306) 242-7611   *SIC* 5311
**HUDSON, LARRY PONTIAC BUICK GMC
(1995) INC**   *p* 647
1000 WALLACE AVE N, LISTOWEL, ON,
N4W 1M5
(519) 291-3791   *SIC* 5511
HUER FOODS INC   *p* 229
5543 275 ST, LANGLEY, BC, V4W 3X9
(604) 626-4888   *SIC* 5145
HUESTIS INSURANCE   *p* 416
*See HUESTIS INSURANCE & ASSO-
CIATES LTD*
**HUESTIS INSURANCE & ASSOCIATES
LTD**   *p* 416
11 LLOYD ST, SAINT JOHN, NB, E2M 4N4
(506) 635-1515   *SIC* 6411
HUESTIS INSURANCE GROUP   *p* 416
11 LLOYD ST, SAINT JOHN, NB, E2M 4N4
(506) 635-1515   *SIC* 6411
HUETHER HOTEL   *p* 1006
See ADLYS HOTELS INC
HUGH & MCKINNON REALTY LTD   *p* 280
14007 16 AVE, SURREY, BC, V4A 1P9
(604) 531-1909   *SIC* 6531
HUGH WOOD CANADA LTD   *p* 774
4120 YONGE ST SUITE 201, NORTH
YORK, ON, M2P 2B8
(416) 229-6600   *SIC* 6411
HUGH'S ROOM   *p* 995
2261 DUNDAS ST W, TORONTO, ON, M6R
1X6
(416) 533-5483   *SIC* 6512
HUGHES PETROLEUM LTD   *p* 101
10330 178 ST NW, EDMONTON, AB, T5S
1J2
(780) 444-4040   *SIC* 7542
HUGO BOSS CANADA INC   *p* 554
2600 STEELES AVE W SUITE 2, CON-
CORD, ON, L4K 3C8
(905) 739-2677   *SIC* 5136
HUILES A CHAUFFAGE RAYMOND, LES *p*
1103
See 120033 CANADA INC
HUILES BERTRAND INC, LES   *p* 1237
4949 BOUL LEVESQUE O, MONTREAL,
QC, H7W 2R8
(450) 682-2845   *SIC* 5172
HUILES NORCO LTEE, LES   *p* 1125
230 RUE NORMAN, LACHINE, QC, H8R
1A1
(514) 486-9000   *SIC* 5983

HUILES THUOT ET BEAUCHEMIN INC, LES   p 1318
775 RUE GAUDETTE, SAINT-JEAN-SUR-RICHELIEU, QC, J3B 7S7
(450) 359-4440   SIC 5983

HUISH OUTDOORS   p 191
See BARE SPORTS CANADA LTD

HULL CHILD & FAMILY SERVICES   p 68
See HULL SERVICES

HULL GROUP INC, THE   p 963
181 BAY ST SUITE 4200, TORONTO, ON, M5J 2T3
(416) 865-0131   SIC 6712

HULL HYUNDAI   p 1107
See 3595650 CANADA INC

HULL NISSAN   p 1107
959 BOUL SAINT-JOSEPH, GATINEAU, QC, J8Z 1W8
(819) 776-0100   SIC 5511

HULL SERVICES   p 68
2266 WOODPARK AVE SW, CALGARY, AB, T2W 2Z8
(403) 251-8000   SIC 8399

HULLY GULLY AUTOMOBILES INC   p 660
940 WHARNCLIFFE RD S, LONDON, ON, N6L 1K3
(519) 686-3754   SIC 5511

HUMAGADE   p 1259
See FRIMA STUDIO INC

HUMANIA ASSURANCE INC   p 1312
1555 RUE GIROUARD O BUREAU 201, SAINT-HYACINTHE, QC, J2S 2Z6
(514) 866-6051   SIC 6311

HUMBER COLLEGE INSTITUTE OF TECHNOLOGY AND ADVANCE LEARNING, THE   p 570
3199 LAKE SHORE BLVD W, ETOBICOKE, ON, M8V 1K8
(416) 675-6622   SIC 8221

HUMBER COLLEGE INSTITUTE OF TECHNOLOGY AND ADVANCE LEARNING, THE   p 585
205 HUMBER COLLEGE BLVD, ETOBICOKE, ON, M9W 5L7
(416) 675-3111   SIC 8222

HUMBER MOTORS FORD   p 422
See HUMBER MOTORS LIMITED

HUMBER MOTORS LIMITED   p 422
8 MOUNT BERNARD AVE, CORNER BROOK, NL, A2H 0C6
(709) 634-4371   SIC 5511

HUMBER RIVER HOSPITAL   p 916
1235 WILSON AVE, TORONTO, ON, M3M 0B2
(416) 242-1000   SIC 8062

HUMBER RIVER HOSPITAL   p 916
2111 FINCH AVE W, TORONTO, ON, M3N 1N1
(416) 744-2500   SIC 8062

HUMBERVIEW GROUP LTD   p 995
2500 BLOOR ST W, TORONTO, ON, M6S 1R7
SIC 5511

HUMBOLDT DISTRICT HOSPITAL   p 1407
See SASKATCHEWAN HEALTH AUTHORITY

HUMBOLDT ELECTRIC LTD   p 1434
102 GLADSTONE CRES, SASKATOON, SK, S7P 0C7
(306) 665-6551   SIC 1731

HUMFORD MANAGEMENT INC   p 92
10050 112 ST NW SUITE 300, EDMONTON, AB, T5K 2J1
(780) 426-4960   SIC 6531

HUMOUR DU MONDE   p 1263
See AGENCE COMEDIHAU INC

HUMPHREY COSBURN PLASTICS   p 993
See CONSOLIDATED BOTTLE CORPORATION

HUMPTY DUMPTY OLD DUTCH FOODS   p 1043
See OLD DUTCH FOODS LTD

HUMPTY'S CLASSIC CAFES   p 30
See HUMPTY'S RESTAURANTS INTERNA-

TIONAL INC

HUMPTY'S RESTAURANTS INTERNATIONAL INC   p 30
2505 MACLEOD TRAIL SW, CALGARY, AB, T2G 5J4
(403) 269-4675   SIC 6794

HUNCO HOLDINGS LTD   p 172
6010 47 ST, WETASKIWIN, AB, T9A 2R3
(780) 352-6061   SIC 3523

HUNT CHRYSLER LTD   p 684
500 BRONTE ST S, MILTON, ON, L9T 9H5
(905) 876-2580   SIC 5511

HUNT CLUB AUTOMOTIVE LTD   p 826
92 TERRY FOX DR, OTTAWA, ON, K1V 0W8
(613) 733-7500   SIC 5511

HUNT CLUB HONDA   p 597
See 724412 ONTARIO LIMITED

HUNT CLUB MOTORS LIMITED   p 597
2655 BANK ST, GLOUCESTER, ON, K1T 1N1
(613) 521-2300   SIC 5511

HUNT CLUB NISSAN   p 749
See HCN MOTORS LTD

HUNT CLUB VOLKSWAGEN   p 597
See HUNT CLUB MOTORS LIMITED

HUNT PERSONNEL   p 711
See SYNERGIE HUNT INTERNATIONAL INC

HUNT REFRIGERATION (CANADA) INC   p 1164
6360 RUE NOTRE-DAME E, MONTREAL, QC, H1N 2E1
(514) 259-9041   SIC 7623

HUNT'S TRANSPORT LIMITED   p 428
168 MAJOR'S PATH, ST. JOHN'S, NL, A1A 5A1
(709) 747-4868   SIC 4213

HUNTER AMENITIES INTERNATIONAL LTD   p 522
1205 CORPORATE DR, BURLINGTON, ON, L7L 5V5
(905) 331-2855   SIC 2844

HUNTER AMENITIES INTERNATIONAL LTD   p 569
37 YORK ST E, ELORA, ON, N0B 1S0
(519) 846-2489   SIC 2841

HUNTER DICKINSON INC   p 313
1040 GEORGIA ST W SUITE 1500, VANCOUVER, BC, V6E 4H8
(604) 684-6365   SIC 1081

HUNTER DOUGLAS CANADA HOLDINGS INC   p 96
15508 114 AVE NW, EDMONTON, AB, T5M 3S8
(800) 265-1363   SIC 2591

HUNTER DOUGLAS CANADA HOLDINGS INC   p 509
132 FIRST GULF BLVD, BRAMPTON, ON, L6W 4T7
(905) 796-7883   SIC 5023

HUNTER DOUGLAS WINDOW FASHIONS   p 509
See HUNTER DOUGLAS CANADA HOLDINGS INC

HUNTER STEEL SALES LTD   p 896
500 LORNE AVE E, STRATFORD, ON, N5A 6S4
(519) 273-3151   SIC 5051

HUNTER'S DRESSED MEATS   p 567
See 566735 ONTARIO INC

HUNTER'S ONE STOP LTD   p 398
2046 ROUTE 690, DOUGLAS HARBOUR, NB, E4B 1Y7
(506) 385-2292   SIC 5541

HUNTING ENERGY SERVICES (CANADA) LTD   p 23
5550 SKYLINE WAY NE, CALGARY, AB, T2E 7Z7
(403) 543-4477   SIC 1389

HUNTING ENERGY SERVICES (CANADA) LTD   p 23
5550 SKYLINE WAY NE, CALGARY, AB,

T2E 7Z7
(403) 543-4477   SIC 5541

HUNTING HILLS HIGH SCHOOL   p 156
See BOARD OF TRUSTEES OF THE RED DEER PUBLIC SCHOOL DISTRICT NO. 104, THE

HUNTING THREADTECH   p 23
See HUNTING ENERGY SERVICES (CANADA) LTD

HUNTINGDON HOTEL & SUITES   p 335
See FRIENDSHIP DEVELOPMENTS LTD

HUNTINGTON TRAVEL GROUP, THE   p 716
See 734758 ONTARIO LIMITED

HUNTSVILLE DISTRICT MEMORIAL HOSPITAL   p 620
See MUSKOKA ALGONQUIN HEALTHCARE

HUNTSVILLE DISTRICT NURSING HOME INC   p 620
14 MILL ST SUITE 101, HUNTSVILLE, ON, P1H 2A4
(705) 789-4476   SIC 8051

HUOT   p 1267
See HUOT, REAL INC

HUOT, REAL INC   p 1267
2550 AV DALTON, QUEBEC, QC, G1P 3S4
(418) 634-5967   SIC 5085

HURLEY FOODS LTD   p 621
273 KING ST W, INGERSOLL, ON, N5C 2K9
(519) 425-4406   SIC 5411

HURLEY MINING EQUIPMENT & SERVICES INC   p 647
10 NELSON RD, LIVELY, ON, P3Y 1M1
(705) 682-0681   SIC 5082

HURLEY SLATE WORKS COMPANY INC   p 422
250 MINERALS RD, CONCEPTION BAY SOUTH, NL, A1W 5A2
(709) 834-2320   SIC 3281

HURLEY'S INDEPENDENT GROCER   p 621
See HURLEY FOODS LTD

HURLSTONE HOLDINGS CORP   p 767
245 YORKLAND BLVD SUITE 100, NORTH YORK, ON, M2J 4W9
(416) 490-1400   SIC 1521

HURON BAY CO-OPERATIVE INC   p 902
15 HILCREST ST, TEESWATER, ON, N0G 2S0
(519) 392-6862   SIC 5999

HURON CENTRAL RAILWAY INC   p 861
30 OAKLAND AVE, SAULT STE. MARIE, ON, P6A 2T3
(705) 254-4511   SIC 4731

HURON COLONY FARMS LTD   p 349
64082 ROAD 17W, ELIE, MB, R0H 0H0
(204) 353-2704   SIC 0119

HURON COMMODITIES INC   p 544
75 WELLINGTON ST, CLINTON, ON, N0M 1L0
(519) 482-8400   SIC 6799

HURON CONSTRUCTION CO LIMITED   p 543
10785 PINEHURST LINE, CHATHAM, ON, N7M 5J3
(519) 354-0170   SIC 1611

HURON HEIGHTS SECONDARY SCHOOL   p 757
See YORK REGION DISTRICT SCHOOL BOARD

HURON LODGE HOME FOR THE AGED   p 1025
See CORPORATION OF THE CITY OF WINDSOR

HURON MOTOR PRODUCTS LIMITED   p 590
70704 LONDON RD, EXETER, ON, N0M 1S1
(514) 700-0180   SIC 5511

HURON PARK SECONDARY SCHOOL   p 1035
See THAMES VALLEY DISTRICT SCHOOL

BOARD

HURON PERTH CATHOLIC DISTRICT SCHOOL BOARD   p 566
87 MILL ST, DUBLIN, ON, N0K 1E0
(519) 345-2440   SIC 8211

HURON PERTH HEALTHCARE ALLIANCE   p 544
98 SHIPLEY ST, CLINTON, ON, N0M 1L0
(519) 482-3447   SIC 8062

HURON PERTH HEALTHCARE ALLIANCE   p 896
46 GENERAL HOSPITAL DR, STRATFORD, ON, N5A 2Y6
(519) 271-2120   SIC 8742

HURON PERTH HEALTHCARE ALLIANCE-ST MARYS MEMORIAL HOSPITAL   p 888
See ST MARYS MEMORIAL HOSPITAL

HURON PRODUCE LIMITED   p 590
40534 THAMES RD, EXETER, ON, N0M 1S5
(519) 235-2650   SIC 5148

HURON TRACTOR LTD   p 590
39995 HARVEST RD, EXETER, ON, N0M 1S3
(519) 235-1115   SIC 5083

HURON UNIVERSITY COLLEGE   p 658
1349 WESTERN RD, LONDON, ON, N6G 1H3
(519) 679-7905   SIC 8221

HURON WINDOW CORPORATION   p 352
345 MOUNTAIN ST S, MORDEN, MB, R6M 1J5
(204) 822-6281   SIC 5031

HURON-PERTH CHILDREN'S AID SOCIETY   p 896
639 LORNE AVE E, STRATFORD, ON, N5A 6S4
(519) 271-5290   SIC 8322

HURON-SUPERIOR CATHOLIC DISTRICT SCHOOL BOARD   p 863
90 ONTARIO AVE, SAULT STE. MARIE, ON, P6B 6G7
(705) 945-5400   SIC 8211

HURONIA/MED-E-OX LTD   p 597
282 SUNCOAST DR E, GODERICH, ON, N7A 4K4
(519) 524-5363   SIC 5169

HURONVIEW HOME FOR THE AGED   p 544
77722A LONDON RD RR 5, CLINTON, ON, N0M 1L0
(519) 482-3451   SIC 8051

HURONWEB OFFSET PRINTING INC   p 1037
395 BROADWAY ST, WYOMING, ON, N0N 1T0
(519) 845-0821   SIC 2752

HURONWEB PRINTING   p 1037
See HURONWEB OFFSET PRINTING INC

HURST MARINA LTD   p 663
2726 RIVER RD, MANOTICK, ON, K4M 1B4
(613) 692-1234   SIC 5551

HUSBY FOREST PRODUCTS LTD   p 210
6425 RIVER RD, DELTA, BC, V4K 5B9
(604) 940-1234   SIC 4212

HUSH PUPPIES   p 728
See WOLVERINE WORLD WIDE CANADA ULC

HUSKY (U.S.A.), INC   p 51
707 8 AVE SW, CALGARY, AB, T2P 1H5
(403) 298-6111   SIC 6712

HUSKY CAR TRUCK STOP   p 565
See DRYDEN TRUCK STOP INC

HUSKY CAR/TRUCK STOP   p 1437
See XPRESS FOOD AND GAS (MOOSE JAW) LTD

HUSKY ENERGIE   p 1409
See HUSKY OIL OPERATIONS LIMITED

HUSKY ENERGY   p 249
See HUSKY OIL OPERATIONS LIMITED

HUSKY ENERGY   p 432
See HUSKY OIL OPERATIONS LIMITED

HUSKY ENERGY INC   p 51

707 8 AVE SW, CALGARY, AB, T2P 1H5
(403) 298-6111   SIC 1382
HUSKY ENERGY INC   p 144
5650 52 ST, LLOYDMINSTER, AB, T9V 0R7
(780) 871-6571   SIC 5033
HUSKY ENERGY INC   p 248
2542 PRINCE GEORGE PULPMILL RD,
PRINCE GEORGE, BC, V2K 5P5
SIC 1311
HUSKY ENERGY INC   p 1409
4335 44 ST, LLOYDMINSTER, SK, S9V 0Z8
(306) 825-1196   SIC 1311
HUSKY ENERGY INC   p 1409
HWY 16 E UPGRADER RD, LLOYDMIN-
STER, SK, S9V 1M6
(306) 825-1700   SIC 1311
**HUSKY ENERGY INTERNATIONAL SUL-
PHUR CORPORATION**   p
51
707 8 AVE SW, CALGARY, AB, T2P 1H5
(403) 298-6111   SIC 1311
**HUSKY FOOD IMPORTERS & DISTRIBU-
TORS LIMITED**   p
1027
155 RAINBOW CREEK DR, WOOD-
BRIDGE, ON, L4H 0A4
(905) 850-8288   SIC 5145
HUSKY GAS MARKETING INC   p 51
707 8 AVE SW, CALGARY, AB, T2P 1H5
SIC 4923
**HUSKY INJECTION MOLDING SYSTEMS
LTD**   p 495
500 QUEEN ST S, BOLTON, ON, L7E 5S5
(905) 951-5000   SIC 6712
HUSKY OIL   p 144
See HUSKY ENERGY INC
HUSKY OIL   p 1409
See HUSKY ENERGY INC
HUSKY OIL LIMITED   p 51
707 8 AVE SW, CALGARY, AB, T2P 1H5
(403) 298-6111   SIC 1311
HUSKY OIL MARKETING CO   p 51
See HUSKY OIL LIMITED
HUSKY OIL OPERATIONS LIMITED p 51
707 8 AVE SW, CALGARY, AB, T2P 1H5
(403) 298-6111   SIC 1311
HUSKY OIL OPERATIONS LIMITED p 144
5650 52 ST, LLOYDMINSTER, AB, T9V 0R7
SIC 1311
HUSKY OIL OPERATIONS LIMITED p 153
HWY 58 W, RAINBOW LAKE, AB, T0H 2Y0
(780) 956-8000   SIC 1311
HUSKY OIL OPERATIONS LIMITED p 249
2542 PG PULPMILL RD, PRINCE
GEORGE, BC, V2L 4V4
SIC 2911
HUSKY OIL OPERATIONS LIMITED p 432
351 WATER ST, ST. JOHN'S, NL, A1C 1C2
(709) 724-3900   SIC 1311
HUSKY OIL OPERATIONS LIMITED p 1409
4335 44 ST, LLOYDMINSTER, SK, S9V 0Z8
(306) 825-1196   SIC 1311
HUSKY TRAVEL CENTER   p 1435
See M&A ENTERPRISES
HUSKY TRUCK STOP   p 194
See DSM INVESTMENTS INC
HUSKY TRUCK STOP   p 733
See UNIPETRO DIXIE INC
HUSQVARNA CANADA CORP   p 744
850 MATHESON BLVD W SUITE 4, MISSIS-
SAUGA, ON, L5V 0B4
(905) 817-1510   SIC 3425
HUSSMANN CANADA INC   p 539
5 CHERRY BLOSSOM RD SUITE 3, CAM-
BRIDGE, ON, N3H 4R7
(519) 653-9980   SIC 5078
HUSSMANN STORE EQUIPMENT   p 539
See HUSSMANN CANADA INC
HUTCHESON SAND & GRAVEL   p 620
See MUSKOKA MINERALS & MINING INC
**HUTCHINSON AERONAUTIQUE & INDUS-
TRIE LIMITEE**   p
1160
3650 BOUL DU TRICENTENAIRE, MON-

TREAL, QC, H1B 5M8
(514) 640-9006   SIC 3089
HUTCHINSON SMILEY LIMITED   p 929
890 YONGE ST SUITE 1002, TORONTO,
ON, M4W 3P4
SIC 8742
HUTCHISON, W A LTD   p 362
1519 REGENT AVE W, WINNIPEG, MB,
R2C 4M4
(204) 667-2454   SIC 5399
**HUTTERIAN BERTHEREN CHURCH OF
QUILL LAKE INC**   p 1415
GD, QUILL LAKE, SK, S0A 3E0
(306) 383-2989   SIC 0139
**HUTTERIAN BERTHEREN CHURCH OF
STAHLVILLE**   p 160
GD, ROCKYFORD, AB, T0J 2R0
(403) 533-2102   SIC 8661
**HUTTERIAN BERTHERN CHURCH OF
DOWNIE LAKE INC**   p 1409
GD, MAPLE CREEK, SK, S0N 1N0
(306) 662-3462   SIC 8661
**HUTTERIAN BERTHERN CHURCH OF
HILLVIEW COLONY**   p 160
GD, ROSEBUD, AB, T0J 2T0
(403) 677-2360   SIC 8661
**HUTTERIAN BERTHERN CHURCH OF
RAINBOW**   p 158
See RAINBOW COLONY FARMING CO
LTD
**HUTTERIAN BRETHERN OF MIXBURN
LTD**   p 147
GD, MINBURN, AB, T0B 3B0
(780) 628-5147   SIC 0291
HUTTERIAN BRETHERN OF SOVEREIGN p
1423
GD, ROSETOWN, SK, S0L 2V0
(306) 882-2447   SIC 8661
**HUTTERIAN BRETHRAN CHURCH OF
BEISEKER**   p 5
GD, BEISEKER, AB, T0M 0G0
(403) 947-2181   SIC 8661
HUTTERIAN BRETHREN   p 171
GD, WARNER, AB, T0K 2L0
(403) 642-2407   SIC 8211
HUTTERIAN BRETHREN CHURCH   p 1407
See HODGEVILLE FARMING CO. LTD
**HUTTERIAN BRETHREN CHURCH OF
CAMROSE**   p 78
GD LCD MAIN, CAMROSE, AB, T4V 1X1
(780) 672-1553   SIC 8661
**HUTTERIAN BRETHREN CHURCH OF
CASTOR**   p 79
GD, CASTOR, AB, T0C 0X0
(403) 882-3305   SIC 8661
**HUTTERIAN BRETHREN CHURCH OF
CLEARDALE**   p 80
GD, CLEARDALE, AB, T0H 3Y0
(780) 685-2870   SIC 8661
**HUTTERIAN BRETHREN CHURCH OF EA-
GLE CREEK INC**   p
1404
GD, ASQUITH, SK, S0K 0J0
(306) 329-4476   SIC 0191
**HUTTERIAN BRETHREN CHURCH OF
EAST CARDSTON (1977)**   p 79
PO BOX 2520, CARDSTON, AB, T0K 0K0
(403) 653-2451   SIC 0191
**HUTTERIAN BRETHREN CHURCH OF
ELKWATER**   p 137
GD, IRVINE, AB, T0J 1V0
(403) 525-4256   SIC 0191
**HUTTERIAN BRETHREN CHURCH OF
EWELME COLONY**   p 127
GD, FORT MACLEOD, AB, T0L 0Z0
(403) 553-2606   SIC 8661
**HUTTERIAN BRETHREN CHURCH OF
FERRYBANK**   p 152
GD, PONOKA, AB, T4J 1R9
(403) 783-2259   SIC 8661
**HUTTERIAN BRETHREN CHURCH OF
GRANDVIEW**   p 134
723042A RANGE ROAD 74, GRANDE
PRAIRIE, AB, T8X 4L1

(780) 532-6500   SIC 8661
**HUTTERIAN BRETHREN CHURCH OF
HOLT**   p 137
GD, IRMA, AB, T0B 2H0
(780) 754-2175   SIC 8661
**HUTTERIAN BRETHREN CHURCH OF
MOUNTAINVIEW, THE**   p 168
GD STN MAIN, STRATHMORE, AB, T1P
1J5
(403) 935-4210   SIC 8661
**HUTTERIAN BRETHREN CHURCH OF
SANDHILL**   p 5
See SAND HILLS COLONY
**HUTTERIAN BRETHREN CHURCH OF SIM-
MIE INC**   p
1436
GD, SIMMIE, SK, S0N 2N0
(306) 297-6304   SIC 8661
**HUTTERIAN BRETHREN CHURCH OF THE
LITTLE BOW**   p 79
GD, CHAMPION, AB, T0L 0R0
(403) 897-3838   SIC 8661
**HUTTERIAN BRETHREN CHURCH OF
TSCHETTER**   p 137
GD, IRRICANA, AB, T0M 1B0
(403) 935-2362   SIC 8661
**HUTTERIAN BRETHREN CHURCH OF
VALLEYVIEW RANCH**   p 170
GD, TORRINGTON, AB, T0M 2B0
(403) 631-2372   SIC 8661
**HUTTERIAN BRETHREN CHURCH OF VET-
ERAN**   p
171
GD, VETERAN, AB, T0C 2S0
(403) 575-2169   SIC 8661
HUTTERIAN BRETHREN LTD   p 1427
GD STN MAIN, SASKATOON, SK, S7K 3J4
(306) 242-5652   SIC 0119
**HUTTERIAN BRETHREN MANNVILLE
COLONY**   p 145
GD, MANNVILLE, AB, T0B 2W0
(780) 763-3079   SIC 0191
**HUTTERIAN BRETHREN OF ARM RIVER
COLONY LTD**   p 1409
PO BOX 570, LUMSDEN, SK, S0G 3C0
(306) 731-2819   SIC 0119
HUTTERIAN BRETHREN OF BRANT, THE p
7
GD, BRANT, AB, T0L 0L0
(403) 684-3649   SIC 0191
**HUTTERIAN BRETHREN OF ESTUARY
CORP**   p 1409
GD, LEADER, SK, S0N 1H0
(306) 628-4116   SIC 0191
**HUTTERIAN BRETHREN OF GOLDEN
VIEW INC**   p 1404
GD, BIGGAR, SK, S0K 0M0
(306) 948-2716   SIC 0119
HUTTERIAN BRETHREN OF HURON LTD p
1404
GD, BROWNLEE, SK, S0H 0M0
(306) 759-2685   SIC 0259
HUTTERIAN BRETHREN OF KYLE INC   p
1408
GD, KYLE, SK, S0L 1T0
(306) 375-2910   SIC 8661
HUTTERIAN BRETHREN OF MILFORD   p
153
See MILFORD COLONY FARMING CO.
LTD
HUTTERIAN BRETHREN OF MILTOW p 171
GD, WARNER, AB, T0K 2L0
(403) 642-0004   SIC 0191
**HUTTERIAN BRETHREN OF PARKLAND,
THE**   p 148
GD, NANTON, AB, T0L 1R0
(403) 646-5761   SIC 0191
**HUTTERIAN BRETHREN OF PENNANT
INC**   p 1413
GD, PENNANT STATION, SK, S0N 1X0
(306) 626-3369   SIC 8661
HUTTERIAN BRETHREN OF RED WILLOW
p 167
GD, STETTLER, AB, T0C 2L0

(403) 742-3988   SIC 0119
HUTTERIAN BRETHREN OF SOUTH BEND
p 3
1539 12 WEST OF 4TH, ALLIANCE, AB,
T0B 0A0
(780) 879-2170   SIC 0119
**HUTTERIAN BRETHREN OF SPRING
POINT COLONY, THE**   p 127
GD, FORT MACLEOD, AB, T0L 0Z0
(403) 553-2284   SIC 0762
HUTTERIAN BRETHREN OF WINNIFRED p
145
GD LCD 1, MEDICINE HAT, AB, T1A 7E4
SIC 4212
**HUTTERIAN BRETHREN SPRING CREEK
COLONY**   p 171
GD, WALSH, AB, T0J 3L0
(403) 937-2524   SIC 8661
**HUTTERITE BRETHREN CHURCH OF
BELLE PLAINE**   p 1404
GD, BELLE PLAINE, SK, S0G 0G0
(306) 345-2544   SIC 5144
HUTTERVILLE COLONY   p 145
See   HUTTERVILLE   HUTTERIAN
BRETHREN
HUTTERVILLE HUTTERIAN BRETHREN p
145
GD, MAGRATH, AB, T0K 1J0
(403) 758-3143   SIC 0191
HUTTON FOREST PRODUCTS INC   p 536
320 PINEBUSH ROAD UNIT 8, CAM-
BRIDGE, ON, N1T 1Z6
(519) 620-4374   SIC 5031
HUTTON TRANSPORT LIMITED   p 643
962979 19TH LINE, LAKESIDE, ON, N0M
2G0
(519) 349-2233   SIC 4212
HUTTON, B. MARKETING LTD   p 231
11969 200 ST, MAPLE RIDGE, BC, V2X
3M7
(604) 460-4664   SIC 5531
HUY, HOWARD GREENHOUSES   p 643
See 1196977 ONTARIO LTD
HUYNH, KIM DRUGS LTD   p 671
7060 WARDEN AVE, MARKHAM, ON, L3R
5Y2
(905) 474-1414   SIC 5912
HVAC INC   p 1234
2185 RUE LE CHATELIER, MONTREAL,
QC, H7L 5B3
(514) 748-4822   SIC 1711
HVE HEALTHCARE ASSESSMENTS INC p
554
260 EDGELEY BLVD UNIT 22, CONCORD,
ON, L4K 3Y4
(905) 264-2020   SIC 8731
HWC INSURANCE   p 482
See HAMILTON WARD AND CATHERS IN-
SURANCE SERVICE LIMITED
HY'S OF CANADA LTD   p 298
128 PENDER ST W UNIT 303, VANCOU-
VER, BC, V6B 1R8
(604) 684-3311   SIC 5812
HY'S OF CANADA LTD   p 952
120 ADELAIDE ST W SUITE 101,
TORONTO, ON, M5H 1T1
(416) 364-6600   SIC 5812
HY'S STEAKHOUSE   p 952
See HY'S OF CANADA LTD
HY'S STEAKHOUSE & COCKTAIL BAR p
298
See HY'S OF CANADA LTD
HY-SPEC   p 1129
See WAJAX INDUSTRIAL COMPONENTS
LIMITED PARTNERSHIP
HY-TECH DRILLING LTD   p 269
2715 TATLOW RD, SMITHERS, BC, V0J
2N5
(250) 847-9301   SIC 1081
HYATT AUTO GALLERY   p 72
See 587577 ALBERTA LIMITED
HYATT AUTO SALES & LEASING INC p 35
161 GLENDEER CIR SE, CALGARY, AB,
T2H 2S8

▲ Public Company   ■ Public Company Family Member   **HQ** Headquarters   **BR** Branch   **SL** Single Location

(403) 252-8833   *SIC 5511*
HYATT GROUP *p 35*
See HYATT AUTO SALES & LEASING INC
HYATT MITSUBISHI *p 33*
See 998699 ALBERTA LTD
HYCO CANADA LIMITED *p 1354*
1025 RUE PRINCIPALE, SAINT-WENCESLAS, QC, G0Z 1J0
(819) 224-4000   *SIC 3593*
HYD-MECH GROUP LIMITED *p 1035*
1079 PARKINSON RD, WOODSTOCK, ON, N4S 7W3
(519) 539-6341   *SIC 3569*
HYDAC CORPORATION *p 1011*
14 FEDERAL RD, WELLAND, ON, L3B 3P2
(905) 714-9322   *SIC 5084*
HYDAC INTERNATIONAL *p 1369*
83 RUE DU TOURNESOL, SHEFFORD, QC, J2M 1K9
(450) 539-3388   *SIC 5085*
HYDRA DYNE TECHNOLOGY INC *p 621*
55 SAMNAH CRES, INGERSOLL, ON, N5C 3J7
(519) 485-2200   *SIC 3593*
HYDRACO INDUSTRIES LTD *p 145*
2111 9 AVE SW, MEDICINE HAT, AB, T1A 8M9
(403) 528-4400   *SIC 5084*
HYDRAULICS INTEGRATED SYSTEMS *p 887*
See LIFCO HYDRAULICS LTD
HYDRAULICS, RIGGING & RUBBER *p 448*
See SOURCE ATLANTIC LIMITED
HYDRAULIQUE EP *p 1260*
See ENGRENAGE PROVINCIAL INC
HYDRAULIQUE NES *p 1046*
See TRIONEX INC
HYDRAULIQUES R.N.P *p 1145*
See 9071-2670 QUEBEC INC
HYDREXCEL INC *p 1056*
665 AV DUTORD BUREAU 294, BECANCOUR, QC, G9H 2Z6
(819) 294-2728   *SIC 5084*
HYDRIL CANADIAN COMPANY LIMITED PARTNERSHIP *p 148*
2307 8 ST, NISKU, AB, T9E 7Z3
(780) 955-2045   *SIC 5084*
HYDRO ALUMINIUM CANADA INC *p 1197*
2000 AV MCGILL COLLEGE BUREAU 2310, MONTREAL, QC, H3A 3H3
(514) 840-9110   *SIC 3334*
HYDRO DISTRIBUTION INC *p 684*
8069 LAWSON RD, MILTON, ON, L9T 5C4
(905) 876-4611   *SIC 4911*
HYDRO EXTRUSION CANADA INC *p 706*
5675 KENNEDY RD, MISSISSAUGA, ON, L4Z 2H9
(905) 890-8821   *SIC 3354*
HYDRO EXTRUSION CANADA INC *p 1250*
325 AV AVRO, POINTE-CLAIRE, QC, H9R 5W3
(514) 697-5120   *SIC 3354*
HYDRO ONE INC *p 531*
1225 KING RD, BURLINGTON, ON, L7T 0B7
(905) 681-4421   *SIC 4911*
HYDRO ONE INC *p 945*
483 BAY ST SUITE 1000, TORONTO, ON, M5G 2P5
(416) 345-5000   *SIC 4911*
HYDRO ONE LIMITED *p 945*
483 BAY ST 8TH FL SOUTH TOWER, TORONTO, ON, M5G 2P5
(416) 345-5000   *SIC 4911*
HYDRO ONE NETWORKS INC *p 657*
727 EXETER RD, LONDON, ON, N6E 1L3
(519) 668-5800   *SIC 4911*
HYDRO ONE NETWORKS INC *p 680*
185 CLEGG RD, MARKHAM, ON, L6G 1B7
(800) 434-1235   *SIC 7299*
HYDRO ONE NETWORKS INC *p 839*
99 DRUMMOND ST W, PERTH, ON, K7H 3E7
(613) 267-6473   *SIC 4911*

HYDRO ONE NETWORKS INC *p 898*
957 FALCONBRIDGE RD, SUDBURY, ON, P3A 5K8
(705) 566-8955   *SIC 4911*
HYDRO ONE NETWORKS INC *p 945*
483 BAY ST SUITE 1000, TORONTO, ON, M5G 2P5
(416) 345-5000   *SIC 4911*
HYDRO ONE REMOTE COMMUNITIES INC *p 945*
483 BAY ST SUITE 1000, TORONTO, ON, M5G 2P5
SIC 4911
HYDRO ONE SAULT STE. MARIE LP *p 863*
2B SACKVILLE RD, SAULT STE. MARIE, ON, P6B 6J6
(705) 254-7444   *SIC 4911*
HYDRO OTTAWA HOLDING INC *p 827*
3025 ALBION RD N, OTTAWA, ON, K1V 9V9
(613) 738-5499   *SIC 4911*
HYDRO QUEBEC HYDRODIRECT SIEGE REGIONAL TERRITOIRE MONTMORENCY *p 1276*
See HYDRO-QUEBEC
HYDRO SHERBROOKE *p 1372*
See VILLE DE SHERBROOKE
HYDRO-QUEBEC *p 1045*
GD, ALMA, QC, G8B 5V5
(418) 668-1400   *SIC 4911*
HYDRO-QUEBEC *p 1053*
1161 RUE MCCORMICK, BAIE-COMEAU, QC, G5C 2S7
(418) 295-1507   *SIC 4911*
HYDRO-QUEBEC *p 1077*
128 CH MILL, CHELSEA, QC, J9B 1K8
(819) 827-7137   *SIC 4911*
HYDRO-QUEBEC *p 1124*
90 RUE BEAUMONT, LA TUQUE, QC, G9X 3P7
(819) 676-4280   *SIC 4911*
HYDRO-QUEBEC *p 1175*
888 BOUL DE MAISONNEUVE E, MONTREAL, QC, H2L 4S8
(514) 286-2020   *SIC 4911*
HYDRO-QUEBEC *p 1180*
140 BOUL CREMAZIE O, MONTREAL, QC, H2P 1C3
(514) 858-8000   *SIC 8731*
HYDRO-QUEBEC *p 1276*
2625 BOUL LEBOURGNEUF BUREAU 14, QUEBEC, QC, G2C 1P1
(888) 385-7252   *SIC 4911*
HYDRO-QUEBEC *p 1279*
5050 BOUL DES GRADINS BUREAU 200, QUEBEC, QC, G2J 1P8
(418) 624-2811   *SIC 8631*
HYDRO-QUEBEC *p 1390*
1600 RUE DE L'HYDRO, VAL-D'OR, QC, J9P 6Z1
(819) 825-3320   *SIC 4911*
HYDRO-QUEBEC *p 1390*
1600 RUE DE L'HYDRO, VAL-D'OR, QC, J9P 6Z1
(819) 825-4880   *SIC 4911*
HYDRO-QUEBEC *p 1393*
1800 BOUL LIONEL-BOULET, VARENNES, QC, J3X 1P7
(450) 925-2008   *SIC 8731*
HYDRO-QUEBEC INTERNATIONAL INC *p 1191*
75 BOUL RENE-LEVESQUE O BUREAU 101, MONTREAL, QC, H2Z 1A4
(514) 289-2211   *SIC 6719*
HYDROCARBONS AND CHEMICALS DIVISION *p 59*
See SNC-LAVALIN INC
HYDROFORM SOLUTIONS, DIV OF *p 1002*
See MARTINREA INTERNATIONAL INC
HYDROGENICS CORPORATION *p 740*
220 ADMIRAL BLVD, MISSISSAUGA, ON, L5T 2N6
(905) 361-3660   *SIC 5063*

HYDROMAX *p 1221*
See 9264 0085 QUEBEC INC
HYDROPOOL HOT TUBS AND SWIM SPAS *p 740*
See HYDROPOOL INC
HYDROPOOL INC *p 740*
335 SUPERIOR BLVD, MISSISSAUGA, ON, L5T 2L6
(800) 465-2933   *SIC 5999*
HYDROSERRE INC *p 1153*
9200 RUE DESVOYAUX, MIRABEL, QC, J7N 2H4
(450) 475-7924   *SIC 0161*
HYDROSERRE MIRABEL *p 1153*
See HYDROSERRE INC
HYDROTECH MARINE, DIV DE *p 1119*
See EBC INC
HYDRX FARMS LTD *p 1014*
209 DUNDAS ST E, WHITBY, ON, L1N 5R7
(844) 493-7922   *SIC 2834*
HYDUKE DRILLING SOLUTIONS INC *p 149*
2107 6 ST, NISKU, AB, T9E 7X8
(780) 955-0360   *SIC 7692*
HYDUKE ENERGY SERVICES INC *p 149*
2107 6 ST, NISKU, AB, T9E 7X8
(780) 955-0360   *SIC 1389*
HYLAND'S HOMEOPATHIC CANADA INC *p 1378*
381 139 RTE N, SUTTON, QC, J0E 2K0
(450) 538-6636   *SIC 5122*
HYLANDS GOLF CLUB *p 597*
2101 ALERT RD, GLOUCESTER, ON, K1V 1J9
(613) 521-1842   *SIC 7997*
HYLAR METAL PRODUCTS, DIV OF *p 1417*
See DEGELMAN INDUSTRIES LTD
HYLEYS CANADA *p 731*
See GP INTERNATIONAL INC
HYLIFE FOODS LP *p 353*
623 MAIN ST E, NEEPAWA, MB, R0J 1H0
(204) 476-3393   *SIC 2011*
HYLIFE LTD *p 351*
5 FABAS ST, LA BROQUERIE, MB, R0A 0W0
(204) 424-5359   *SIC 0291*
HYLIFE LTD *p 353*
623 MAIN ST E, NEEPAWA, MB, R0J 1H0
(204) 476-3624   *SIC 2011*
HYMOPACK LTD *p 574*
41 MEDULLA AVE, ETOBICOKE, ON, M8Z 5L6
(416) 232-1733   *SIC 2673*
HYMOPACK LTD *p 1326*
1225 RUE HODGE, SAINT-LAURENT, QC, H4N 2B5
SIC 2673
HYNDMAN & COMPANY LTD *p 1039*
57 QUEEN ST, CHARLOTTETOWN, PE, C1A 4A5
(902) 566-4244   *SIC 6411*
HYNDMAN TRANSPORT *p 1036*
See HYNDMAN TRANSPORT (1972) LIMITED
HYNDMAN TRANSPORT (1972) LIMITED *p 1036*
1001 BELMORE LINE, WROXETER, ON, N0G 2X0
(519) 335-3575   *SIC 4213*
HYNDMAN TRANSPORT LIMITED *p 1036*
1001 BELMORE LINE, WROXETER, ON, N0G 2X0
(519) 335-3575   *SIC 4731*
HYP GOLF LTD *p 258*
21320 GORDON WAY UNIT 110, RICHMOND, BC, V6W 1J8
(604) 270-6060   *SIC 5137*
HYPERTEC SYSTEMES INC *p 1334*
9300 RTE TRANSCANADIENNE, SAINT-LAURENT, QC, H4S 1K5
(514) 745-4540   *SIC 3571*
HYPHEN TRANSPORTATION MANAGEMENT INC *p 585*
96 DISCO RD, ETOBICOKE, ON, M9W 0A3

(877) 549-7436   *SIC 4731*
HYS STEAKHOUSE *p 298*
See GOTHAM STEAKHOUSE & COCKTAIL BAR LIMITED PARTNERSHIP
HYUNDAI *p 1075*
See SERAY AUTO INC
HYUNDAI *p 1093*
See AUTOMOBILES ULSAN LTEE
HYUNDAI AUTO CANADA CORP *p 671*
75 FRONTENAC DR, MARKHAM, ON, L3R 6H2
(905) 477-0202   *SIC 5012*
HYUNDAI AUTOMOBILES ULSAN LTEE *p 1094*
1625 BOUL HYMUS, DORVAL, QC, H9P 1J5
(514) 336-4613   *SIC 5511*
HYUNDAI BLAINVILLE *p 1058*
See 2782677 CANADA INC
HYUNDAI CANADA INC *p 772*
5160 YONGE ST SUITE 1003, NORTH YORK, ON, M2N 6L9
(416) 229-6668   *SIC 5051*
HYUNDAI CAPITAL LEASE INC *p 963*
123 FRONT ST W SUITE 1000, TORONTO, ON, M5J 2M3
(647) 943-1887   *SIC 7515*
HYUNDAI CASAVANT *p 1311*
See CARREFOUR DE LA VOITURE IMPORTEE INC
HYUNDAI DE CHATEAUGUAY *p 1075*
See 2948-7659 QUEBEC INC
HYUNDAI DRUMMONDVILLE *p 1098*
See GESTION RENE FORTIN INC
HYUNDAI DU ROYAUME *p 1078*
See AUTOMOBILES ROYAUME LTEE
HYUNDAI GRANBY *p 1111*
See PRINCIPALE AUTOS LTEE
HYUNDAI JEAN-ROCH THIBEAULT *p 1054*
See GARAGE JEAN-ROCH THIBEAULT INC
HYUNDAI LONGUEUIL *p 1141*
See AUTOMOBILE G.R. COREE LONGUEUIL LTEE
HYUNDAI OF OAKVILLE *p 804*
See K.L. FINE CARS LTD
HYUNDAI PRESIDENT *p 1092*
See 3725839 CANADA INC
HYUNDAI REGINA, DIV OF *p 1420*
See 604329 SASKATCHEWAN LTD
HYUNDAI REPENTIGNY *p 1281*
See 168360 CANADA INC
HYUNDAI SAINT-LAURENT *p 1325*
See BOULEVARD METROPOLITAIN AUTOMOBILE INC
HYUNDAI SHERBROOKE *p 1375*
See GARAGE RENAUD FORTIER INC
HYUNDAI VAL-BELAIR *p 1281*
See 9311-9089 QUEBEC INC

I

I & D MCEWEN LTD *p 498*
10 GREAT LAKES DR, BRAMPTON, ON, L6R 2K7
(905) 793-4800   *SIC 5531*
I & G BISMARKATING LTD *p 178*
2054 WHATCOM RD SUITE 1, ABBOTSFORD, BC, V3G 2K8
(604) 855-9655   *SIC 5461*
I & S SEAFOODS *p 1287*
See 9036-4514 QUEBEC INC
I & S WAREHOUSING INC *p 554*
21 STAFFERN DR, CONCORD, ON, L4K 2X2
(905) 761-0250   *SIC 4225*
I B S INTEGRATED BUSINESS SERVICES *p 321*
1632 6TH AVE W, VANCOUVER, BC, V6J 1R3
(604) 714-1100   *SIC 5065*
I C B C *p 228*
See INSURANCE CORPORATION OF BRITISH COLUMBIA
I C B C *p 270*

See INSURANCE CORPORATION OF BRITISH COLUMBIA

I C G PROPANE *p 152*
9504 94 ST, PEACE RIVER, AB, T8S 1J2
SIC 4924

I C G PROPANE *p 783*
3993 KEELE ST, NORTH YORK, ON, M3J 2X6
SIC 4924

I C T GROUP *p 461*
See ICT CANADA MARKETING INC

I CARE SERVICE LTD *p 71*
4935 40 AVE NW SUITE 450, CALGARY, AB, T3A 2N1
(403) 286-3022　*SIC 8011*

I CHECK INC *p 696*
1136 MATHESON BLVD E, MISSISSAUGA, ON, L4W 2V4
(905) 625-5156　*SIC 1522*

I D Q *p 530*
See DAIRY QUEEN CANADA INC

I D R C *p 823*
See INTERNATIONAL DEVELOPMENT RESEARCH CENTRE

I E WELDON SECONDARY SCHOOL *p 646*
See TRILLIUM LAKELANDS DISTRICT SCHOOL BOARD

I G A *p 1060*
See MARCHE MONTEE GAGNON INC

I G A *p 1081*
See MARCHE J.R. GRAVEL INC

I G A *p 1083*
See SUPERMARCHE PAGANO ET SHNAIDMAN INC

I G A *p 1120*
See SUPER MARCHE ST-RAPHAEL INC

I G A *p 1122*
See ALIMENTATION J. G. D. INC

I G A *p 1145*
See SUPERMARCHE SARAZIN, GILLES INC

I G A *p 1146*
See MARCHE D'ALIMENTATION DIANE RODRIGUE INC

I G A *p 1242*
See SUPER MARCHE CLEMENT NICOLET INC

I G A *p 1257*
See BOUCHERIE DENIS COUTURE INC

I G A *p 1280*
See ALIMENTATION A.D.R. INC

I G A *p 1292*
See MAGASIN COOP DE ST-ANSELME

I G A *p 1303*
See GIRARD, B & FILS INC

I G A *p 1307*
See ALIMENTATION ST-ONGE INC

I G A *p 1311*
See ALIMENTATION SOGESCO INC

I G A *p 1342*
See EPICERIE QUINTAL & FRERES 1978 INC

I G A *p 1354*
See MARCHE AU CHALET (1978) INC

I G A DES SOURCES *p 1256*
See 9120-9734 QUEBEC INC

I G A EXTRA LEBOURGNEUF *p 1279*
See SOBEYS CAPITAL INCORPORATED

I G A EXTRA MASCOUCHE *p 1149*
See SOBEYS QUEBEC INC

I G A SUPER MARCHE CLEMENT *p 1096*
See ENTREPRISES CLEMENT RUEL (2000) INC

I G P SPECIALISTES D'INVENTAIRE *p 1345*
See 3812073 CANADA INC

I HAVE A CHANCE SUPPORT SERVICES LTD *p 167*
990 BOULDER BLVD, STONY PLAIN, AB, T7Z 0E5
(780) 962-0433　*SIC 8093*

I LEVEL BY WEYERHAUSER *p 628*
See WEYERHAEUSER COMPANY LIMITED

I O T A INFORMATION MANAGEMENT LTD

p 834
150 METCALFE ST, OTTAWA, ON, K2P 1P1
SIC 7379

I P M HOSE & FITTINGS *p 474*
See INDUSTRIAL, PETROLEUM AND MINING SUPPLIES LIMITED

I R S S T *p 1197*
See INSTITUT DE RECHERCHE ROBERT SAUVE EN SANTE ET EN SECURITE DU TRAVAIL

I T L CIRCUITS *p 671*
See INTEGRATED TECHNOLOGY LIMITED

I T N *p 740*
See INTEGRAL TRANSPORTATION NETWORKS CORP

I VISION *p 658*
See FORWARD VISION GROUP INC.

I-CAR CANADA *p 585*
110 WOODBINE DOWNS BLVD UNIT 4, ETOBICOKE, ON, M9W 5S6
SIC 8742

I-CORP SECURITY SERVICES LTD *p 298*
1040 HAMILTON ST SUITE 303, VANCOUVER, BC, V6B 2R9
(604) 687-8645　*SIC 7381*

I-CUBED INDUSTRY INNOVATORS INC *p 892*
999 BARTON ST, STONEY CREEK, ON, L8E 5H4
(905) 643-8685　*SIC 3569*

I-D BEVERAGES INC *p 1237*
1800 SUD LAVAL (A-440) O, MONTREAL, QC, H7S 2E7
(450) 687-2680　*SIC 5084*

I-L SUCCESSOR CORP *p 509*
31 HANSEN RD S, BRAMPTON, ON, L6W 3H7
SIC 7389

I-SIGHT SOFTWARE *p 830*
See CUSTOMER EXPRESSIONS CORP

I-XL LTD *p 145*
525 2 ST SE, MEDICINE HAT, AB, T1A 0C5
(403) 526-5501　*SIC 3251*

I-XL MASONRY SUPPLIES LTD *p 16*
4900 102 AVE SE, CALGARY, AB, T2C 2X8
(403) 243-6031　*SIC 5032*

I. DEVEAU FISHERIES CSI, DIV OF *p 439*
See I. DEVEAU FISHERIES LIMITED

I. DEVEAU FISHERIES LIMITED *p 439*
508 HWY 330 NE, BARRINGTON PASSAGE, NS, B0W 1G0
(902) 745-2877　*SIC 5146*

I. THIBAULT INC *p 1299*
26 RUE DE L'ENTREPRISE, SAINT-DAMIEN-DE-BUCKLAND, QC, G0R 2Y0
(418) 789-2891　*SIC 3544*

I.A.M. *p 825*
See INTERNATIONAL ASSOCIATION OF MACHINISTS LABOUR MANAGEMENT PENSION FUND (CANADA)

I.A.T.S.E. LOCAL 891 *p 194*
See I.A.T.S.E. LOCAL 891 MOTION PICTURE STUDIO PRODUCTION TECHTIONS

I.A.T.S.E. LOCAL 891 MOTION PICTURE STUDIO PRODUCTION TECHTIONS *p 194*
1640 BOUNDARY RD SUITE 891, BURNABY, BC, V5K 4V4
(604) 664-8910　*SIC 8631*

I.C.C. COMPAGNIE DE CHEMINEES INDUSTRIELLES INC *p 1320*
400 RUE JOHN-F.-KENNEDY, SAINT-JEROME, QC, J7Y 4B7
(450) 565-6336　*SIC 3443*

I.C.C. INTEGRATED CONSTRUCTION CONCEPTS LTD *p 276*
12960 84 AVE SUITE 310, SURREY, BC, V3W 1K7
(604) 599-0706　*SIC 1541*

I.C.T.C. HOLDINGS CORPORATION *p 206*
720 EATON WAY, DELTA, BC, V3M 6J9
(604) 522-6543　*SIC 3821*

I.D.C. COMMUNICATIONS *p 365*

See I.D.C. WHOLESALE INC

I.D.C. WHOLESALE INC *p 365*
1385 NIAKWA RD E, WINNIPEG, MB, R2J 3T3
(204) 254-8282　*SIC 5065*

I.E.I. INC *p 1250*
39 BOUL HYMUS, POINTE-CLAIRE, QC, H9R 4T2
(514) 630-8149　*SIC 5137*

I.G. MACHINE *p 509*
See I.G. MACHINE & FIBERS LTD

I.G. MACHINE & FIBERS LTD *p 509*
87 ORENDA RD, BRAMPTON, ON, L6W 1V8
(905) 457-0745　*SIC 3444*

I.G.A. *p 1220*
See SUPERMARCHE ORNAWKA INC

I.G.A. *p 1282*
See SUPERMARCHE CREVIER (VALMONT) INC

I.G.A. *p 1378*
See ENTREPRISES B J T BOULIANNE INC, LES

I.G.A. COUSINEAU *p 1142*
See SUPERMARCH DJS COUSINEAU INC

I.G.A. EXTRA *p 1120*
See SUPERMARCHE CREVIER L'ASSOMPTION INC

I.G.A. PLUS SUMMERLAND NO 155 *p 270*
7519 PRAIRIE VALLEY RD, SUMMERLAND, BC, V0H 1Z4
(250) 494-4376　*SIC 5411*

I.G.S. SECURITY *p 1220*
See ISRA-GUARD (I.G.S.) SECURITE INC

I.H. ASPER SCHOOL OF BUSINESS *p 392*
See UNIVERSITY OF MANITOBA THE

I.H. MATHERS & SON LIMITED *p 453*
1525 BIRMINGHAM ST, HALIFAX, NS, B3J 2J6
(902) 429-5680　*SIC 4491*

I.M.P. GROUP INTERNATIONAL INCORPORATED *p 457*
2651 JOSEPH HOWE DR, HALIFAX, NS, B3L 4T1
(902) 453-2400　*SIC 4581*

I.M.P. GROUP LIMITED *p 457*
2651 JOSEPH HOWE DR SUITE 400, HALIFAX, NS, B3L 4T1
(902) 453-2400　*SIC 4581*

I.M.P. GROUP LIMITED *p 459*
3101 HAMMONDS PLAINS RD, HAMMONDS PLAINS, NS, B3Z 1H7
(902) 835-4433　*SIC 4581*

I.M.P. GROUP LIMITED *p 1094*
10225 AV RYAN, DORVAL, QC, H9P 1A2
(514) 636-7070　*SIC 4581*

I.M.S. *p 573*
See 1570707 ONTARIO INC

I.M.S. INQUIRY MANAGEMENT SYSTEMS LTD *p 574*
55 HORNER AVE UNIT 1, ETOBICOKE, ON, M8Z 4X6
(416) 620-1965　*SIC 7311*

I.P.A.S *p 1366*
See INVESTIGATION PROTECTION ACCES SECURITE INC

I.R.A.S. PHARMACY LTD *p 577*
5230 DUNDAS ST W, ETOBICOKE, ON, M9B 1A8
(416) 233-3269　*SIC 5912*

I.R.C.M. *p 1184*
See INSTITUT DE RECHERCHES CLINIQUES DE MONTREAL

I.R.D.A. *p 1267*
See INSTITUT DE RECHERCHE ET DEVELOPPEMENT EN AGROENVIRONEMENT INC

I.R.P. INDUSTRIAL RUBBER LTD *p 740*
6300 EDWARDS BLVD UNIT 1, MISSISSAUGA, ON, L5T 2V7
(905) 670-5700　*SIC 5085*

I.S.P.A. GROUP *p 593*
See I.S.P.A. WOODWORKING LIMITED

I.S.P.A. WOODWORKING LIMITED *p 593*
114 ARMSTRONG AVE, GEORGETOWN, ON, L7G 4S2
(905) 702-2727　*SIC 2541*

I.T.B. *p 80*
See INTERCONTINENTAL TRUCK BODY LTD

I.W. KUHN CONSTRUCTION LTD *p 1*
208 RAILWAY AVE E, ACADIA VALLEY, AB, T0J 0A0
(403) 972-3740　*SIC 1629*

I.W.A. FOREST INDUSTRY PENSION & PLAN *p 190*
3777 KINGSWAY SUITE 2100, BURNABY, BC, V5H 3Z7
(604) 433-6310　*SIC 8748*

I.XL INDUSTRIES LTD *p 145*
612 PORCELAIN AVE SE, MEDICINE HAT, AB, T1A 8S4
(403) 526-5901　*SIC 3251*

I24 CALL MANAGEMENT SOLUTIONS *p 1218*
See COMMUNICATIONS METRO-MONTREAL INC

I3 INTERNATIONAL INC *p 868*
780 BIRCHMOUNT RD UNIT 16, SCARBOROUGH, ON, M1K 5H4
(416) 261-2266　*SIC 3699*

I3DVR INTERNATIONAL *p 868*
See I3 INTERNATIONAL INC

IA AUTO AND HOME INSURANCE *p 1270*
See INDUSTRIELLE ALLIANCE, ASSURANCE AUTO ET HABITATION INC

IA CLARINGTON GLOBAL TACTICAL INCOME FUND INC *p 945*
522 UNIVERSITY AVE SUITE 700, TORONTO, ON, M5G 1Y7
(416) 860-9880　*SIC 6722*

IA CLARINGTON INVESTMENTS INC *p 946*
522 UNIVERSITY AVE SUITE 700, TORONTO, ON, M5G 1W7
(416) 860-9880　*SIC 6282*

IA CLARINGTON INVESTMENTS INC *p 946*
522 UNIVERSITY AVE UNIT 700, TORONTO, ON, M5G 1W7
(416) 860-9880　*SIC 6722*

IA CLERINGTON INVESTMENTS INC *p 946*
522 UNIVERSITY AVE SUITE 700, TORONTO, ON, M5G 1W7
(416) 860-9880　*SIC 6722*

IA EXCELLENCE *p 1176*
See EXCELLENCE LIFE INSURANCE COMPANY, THE

IA PACIFIC MARKETING *p 300*
See SAL MARKETING INC

IA VALEURS MOBILIERES *p 1197*
See INDUSTRIELLE ALLIANCE VALEURS MOBILIERES INC

IAC *p 554*
See IAC AUTOMOTIVE COMPONENTS ALBERTA ULC

IAC AUTOMOTIVE COMPONENTS ALBERTA ULC *p 554*
375 BASALTIC RD, CONCORD, ON, L4K 4W8
(905) 879-0292　*SIC 3089*

IAFRATE MACHINE WORKS LIMITED *p 907*
1150 BEAVERDAMS RD, THOROLD, ON, L2V 4T3
(905) 227-6141　*SIC 3499*

IAM *p 963*
See INTEGRATED ASSET MANAGEMENT CORP

IAMGOLD CORPORATION *p 952*
401 BAY ST SUITE 3200, TORONTO, ON, M5H 2Y4
(416) 360-4710　*SIC 1041*

IAMGOLD CORPORATION *p 1046*
118 RTE 109 N, AMOS, QC, J9T 3A3
(819) 732-8268　*SIC 1041*

IAMGOLD CORPORATION *p 1046*
See IAMGOLD CORPORATION

IAMGOLD CORPORATION   p 1307
See IAMGOLD CORPORATION

IAMGOLD CORPORATION   p 1307
3400 CH DU COLUMBIUM, SAINT-HONORE-DE-CHICOUTIMI, QC, G0V 1L0
(418) 673-4694   SIC 1081

IAN MARTIN LIMITED   p 800
610 CHARTWELL RD SUITE 101, OAKVILLE, ON, L6J 4A5
(905) 815-1600   SIC 7361

IAN MARTIN LIMITED   p 1329
3333 BOUL DE LA COTE-VERTU BUREAU 202, SAINT-LAURENT, QC, H4R 2N1
(514) 338-3800   SIC 7361

IATA   p 1229
See ASSOCIATION DU TRANSPORT AERIEN INTERNATIONAL (IATA)

IBA   p 997
See INTEGRATED BUSINESS ANALYSIS, INC

IBC ADVANCED ALLOYS CORP   p 305
570 GRANVILLE ST UNIT 1200, VANCOUVER, BC, V6C 3P1
(604) 685-6263   SIC 3351

IBD   p 1191
See 162013 CANADA INC

IBERDROLA CANADA ENERGY SERVICES LTD   p 73
5 RICHARD WAY SW SUITE 208, CALGARY, AB, T3E 7M8
(403) 206-3160   SIC 4922

IBERVILLE FARMS LTD   p 349
GD, ELIE, MB, R0H 0H0
(204) 864-2058   SIC 0191

IBI GROUP   p 23
611 MEREDITH RD NE SUITE 500, CALGARY, AB, T2E 2W5
(403) 270-5600   SIC 8712

IBI GROUP   p 89
10830 JASPER AVE NW SUITE 300, EDMONTON, AB, T5J 2B3
(780) 428-4000   SIC 8712

IBI GROUP   p 313
1285 PENDER ST W SUITE 700, VANCOUVER, BC, V6E 4B1
(604) 683-8797   SIC 8712

IBI GROUP   p 927
55 ST CLAIR AVE W SUITE 700, TORONTO, ON, M4V 2Y7
(416) 596-1930   SIC 8742

IBI GROUP INC   p 927
55 ST CLAIR AVE W SUITE 700, TORONTO, ON, M4V 2Y7
(416) 596-1930   SIC 8711

IBI GROUP INC   p 927
95 ST CLAIR AVE W SUITE 200, TORONTO, ON, M4V 1N6
(416) 596-1930   SIC 8742

IBM CANADA - USINE DE BROMONT   p 1068
See IBM CANADA LIMITED

IBM CANADA LIMITED   p 51
639 5 AVE SW SUITE 2100, CALGARY, AB, T2P 0M9
SIC 7371

IBM CANADA LIMITED   p 89
10044 108 ST NW SUITE 401, EDMONTON, AB, T5J 3S7
(780) 642-4100   SIC 3571

IBM CANADA LIMITED   p 414
400 MAIN ST SUITE 1000, SAINT JOHN, NB, E2K 4N5
(506) 646-4000   SIC 7389

IBM CANADA LIMITED   p 626
770 PALLADIUM DR, KANATA, ON, K2V 1C8
SIC 7371

IBM CANADA LIMITED   p 655
275 DUNDAS ST, LONDON, ON, N6B 3L1
SIC 7379

IBM CANADA LIMITED   p 671
3600 STEELES AVE E, MARKHAM, ON, L3R 9Z7

(905) 316-5000   SIC 3571

IBM CANADA LIMITED   p 1068
23 BOUL DE L'AEROPORT, BROMONT, QC, J2L 1A3
(450) 534-6000   SIC 3674

IBM CANADA LIMITED   p 1213
1360 BOUL RENE-LEVESQUE O BUREAU 400, MONTREAL, QC, H3G 2W6
(888) 245-5572   SIC 7372

IBM GLOBAL SERVICES   p 671
See IBM CANADA LIMITED

IBM RATIONAL SOFTWARE   p 626
See IBM CANADA LIMITED

IBOX   p 206
See IBOX PACKAGING LTD

IBOX PACKAGING LTD   p 206
620 AUDLEY BLVD, DELTA, BC, V3M 5P2
(604) 522-4269   SIC 2653

IBRAHIM, YASSER PHARMACY LIMITED   p 531
900 MAPLE AVE SUITE 747, BURLINGTON, ON, L7S 2J8
(905) 681-1277   SIC 5912

IC AXON INC   p 1185
3575 BOUL SAINT-LAURENT BUREAU 650, MONTREAL, QC, H2X 2T7
(514) 940-1142   SIC 8742

IC GROUP INC   p 393
383 DOVERCOURT DR, WINNIPEG, MB, R3Y 1G4
(204) 487-5000   SIC 8743

ICAN CONTRACTING LTD   p 182
3131 THUNDERBIRD CRES, BURNABY, BC, V5A 3G1
(604) 299-0146   SIC 5032

ICAN INDEPENDENCE CENTRE AND NETWORK   p 900
765 BRENNAN RD, SUDBURY, ON, P3C 1C4
(705) 673-0655   SIC 8051

ICAN TILE DISTRIBUTORS   p 182
See ICAN CONTRACTING LTD

ICANDA CORPORATION   p 1232
3131 BOUL DE LA CONCORDE E BUREAU 306, MONTREAL, QC, H7E 4W4
(450) 661-2972   SIC 1794

ICBC   p 240
See INSURANCE CORPORATION OF BRITISH COLUMBIA

ICBC   p 276
See INSURANCE CORPORATION OF BRITISH COLUMBIA

ICBC   p 334
See INSURANCE CORPORATION OF BRITISH COLUMBIA

ICBC CENTRAL ESTIMATING FACILITY   p 201
See INSURANCE CORPORATION OF BRITISH COLUMBIA

ICC   p 523
See INTERNATIONAL CORROSION CONTROL INC

ICC IMAGINE COMMUNICATIONS CANADA LTD   p 776
25 DYAS RD, NORTH YORK, ON, M3B 1V7
(416) 445-9640   SIC 3663

ICC TECHNOLOGIES   p 1276
See INFORMATIQUE COTE, COULOMBE INC

ICD INSURANCE BROKERS LTD   p 755
569 STEVEN CRT SUITE 5, NEWMARKET, ON, L3Y 6Z3
(905) 830-9000   SIC 6411

ICE CREAM UNLIMITED INC   p 372
55 PLYMOUTH ST, WINNIPEG, MB, R2X 2V5
SIC 2053

ICE CURRENCY SERVICE   p 264
See EXCHANGE CORPORATION CANADA INC

ICE CURRENCY SERVICE   p 1229
See COOPERATION ECHANGE CANADA INC

ICE NGX CANADA INC   p 51
300 5 AVE SW SUITE 1000, CALGARY, AB, T2P 3C4
(403) 974-1700   SIC 6799

ICE RIVER SPRINGS WATER CO. INC   p 880
485387 COUNTY RD 11, SHELBURNE, ON, L9V 3N5
(519) 925-2929   SIC 5149

ICE SPORTS OSHAWA   p 814
See O & O DEVELOPMENTS INC

ICE WESTERN (BC) SALES   p 16
See ICE WESTERN SALES LTD

ICE WESTERN SALES LTD   p 16
9765 54 ST SE, CALGARY, AB, T2C 5J6
(403) 252-5577   SIC 5084

ICEBREAKER MERINO CLOTHING INC   p 298
21 WATER ST SUITE 502, VANCOUVER, BC, V6B 1A1
(778) 328-9666   SIC 5651

ICEC CANADA   p 52
See INTERNATIONAL COMMODITIES EXPORT COMPANY OF CANADA LIMITED

ICECULTURE INC   p 620
81 BROCK ST, HENSALL, ON, N0M 1X0
(519) 262-3500   SIC 2097

ICES CENTRAL   p 921
See INSTITUTE FOR CLINICAL EVALUATIVE SCIENCES

ICEWATER SEAFOODS INC   p 421
24 HIGH LINER AVE, ARNOLDS COVE, NL, A0B 1A0
(709) 463-2445   SIC 2091

ICG PROPANE   p 136
430 8 ST SW, HIGH RIVER, AB, T1V 1B9
SIC 4924

ICG PROPANE   p 411
63 GOLDSBORO AVE, RIVERVIEW, NB, E1B 4E9
SIC 4924

ICG PROPANE INC.   p 204
10117 17 ST, DAWSON CREEK, BC, V1G 4C1
SIC 4924

ICG PROPANE INC.   p 282
19433 96 AVE SUITE 200, SURREY, BC, V4N 4C4
SIC 4924

ICG PROPANE LTD.   p 749
71 BONGARD AVE, NEPEAN, ON, K2E 6V2
(613) 723-5823   SIC 4924

ICHIBOSHI L.P.C LTD   p 396
24 RUE DU QUAI, CARAQUET, NB, E1W 1B6
(506) 727-0807   SIC 2092

ICI   p 696
See INDEPENDENT CORRUGATOR INC

ICICI BANK CANADA   p 779
150 FERRAND DR SUITE 1200, NORTH YORK, ON, M3C 3E5
(416) 847-7881   SIC 6021

ICOM INFORMATION & COMMUNICATIONS L.P.   p 914
111 GORDON BAKER RD SUITE 300, TORONTO, ON, M2H 3R1
(647) 795-9600   SIC 8732

ICOM PRODUCTIONS INC   p 51
140 8 AVE SW SUITE 400, CALGARY, AB, T2P 1B3
(403) 539-9276   SIC 8748

ICON CONSTRUCTION LTD.   p 1416
480 HENDERSON DR, REGINA, SK, S4N 6E3
(306) 584-1991   SIC 1541

ICON DIGITAL PRODUCTIONS INC   p 671
7495 BIRCHMOUNT RD, MARKHAM, ON, L3R 5G2
(905) 889-2800   SIC 7336

ICON DIRECT   p 361
See ICON TECHNOLOGIES LTD

ICON DU CANADA INC   p 1320
900 RUE DE L'INDUSTRIE, SAINT-JEROME, QC, J7Y 4B8

(450) 565-2955   SIC 5091

ICON INDUSTRIAL CONTRACTORS LTD   p 93
12849 141 ST NW, EDMONTON, AB, T5L 4N1
(780) 455-2299   SIC 1711

ICON INFRASTRUCTURE LLP   p 981
155 WELLINGTON ST W SUITE 2930, TORONTO, ON, M5V 3H1
(416) 649-1331   SIC 6211

ICON INSULATION INC   p 993
935 WESTON RD, TORONTO, ON, M6N 3R4
(647) 945-9648   SIC 1742

ICON MEDIA COMMUNICATIONS INC   p 671
7495 BIRCHMOUNT RD, MARKHAM, ON, L3R 5G2
(905) 889-1944   SIC 5099

ICON PRINT   p 671
See ICON DIGITAL PRODUCTIONS INC

ICON SALON SYSTEMS LTD   p 276
13361 78 AVE SUITE 610, SURREY, BC, V3W 5B9
(604) 591-2339   SIC 5131

ICON STONE & TILE INC   p 30
521 36 AVE SE, CALGARY, AB, T2G 1W5
(403) 532-3383   SIC 5032

ICON TECHNOLOGIES LTD   p 361
925 ROBLIN BLVD E, WINKLER, MB, R6W 0N2
(204) 325-1081   SIC 2821

ICONIC POWER SYSTEMS INC   p 16
11090 48 ST SE, CALGARY, AB, T2C 3E1
(403) 910-3823   SIC 1731

ICONIX WATERWORKS LIMITED PARTNERSHIP   p 255
1128 BURDETTE ST, RICHMOND, BC, V6V 2Z3
(604) 273-4987   SIC 4941

ICORR HOLDINGS INC   p 653
700 RICHMOND ST SUITE 100, LONDON, ON, N6A 5C7
(519) 432-0120   SIC 6712

ICORR PROPERTIES INTERNATIONAL   p 653
See ICORR PROPERTIES MANAGEMENT INC

ICORR PROPERTIES MANAGEMENT INC   p 653
700 RICHMOND ST SUITE 100, LONDON, ON, N6A 5C7
(519) 432-1888   SIC 6513

ICPEI   p 1039
See INSURANCE COMPANY OF PRINCE EDWARD ISLAND, THE

ICS   p 276
See INTERNATIONAL CASTINGS & SUPPLIES LTD

ICS   p 314
See INTERNATIONAL CONFERENCE SERVICES LTD

ICS   p 671
See INNOVATIVE CONTROL SOLUTIONS INC

ICS COURIER SERVICES   p 574
See INFORMATION COMMUNICATION SERVICES (ICS) INC

ICS COURIER SERVICES   p 585
See INFORMATION COMMUNICATION SERVICES (ICS) INC

ICS COURIER SERVICES   p 874
See INFORMATION COMMUNICATION SERVICES (ICS) INC

ICS GROUP   p 1000
See INTERNATIONAL CIGAR STORES LIMITED

ICS GROUP INC   p 78
250081 MOUNTAIN VIEW TRAIL, CALGARY, AB, T3Z 3S3
(403) 247-4440   SIC 5722

ICS SERVICE DE COURIER   p 1094
See INFORMATION COMMUNICATION SERVICES (ICS) INC

ICS UNIVERSAL DRUM RECONDITIONING LIMITED PARTNERSHIP   p 713
2460 ROYAL WINDSOR DR, MISSISSAUGA, ON, L5J 1K7
(905) 822-3280   SIC 5085

ICT   p 120
See INTERNATIONAL COOLING TOWER INC

ICT CANADA MARKETING INC   p 405
408 KING GEORGE HWY, MIRAMICHI, NB, E1V 1L4
(506) 836-9050   SIC 7389

ICT CANADA MARKETING INC   p 405
459 ELMWOOD DR, MONCTON, NB, E1A 2X2
SIC 8732

ICT CANADA MARKETING INC   p 407
1234 MAIN ST SUITE 2001, MONCTON, NB, E1C 1H7
SIC 4899

ICT CANADA MARKETING INC   p 411
720 COVERDALE RD UNIT 9, RIVERVIEW, NB, E1B 3L8
SIC 7389

ICT CANADA MARKETING INC   p 414
400 MAIN ST SUITE 2004, SAINT JOHN, NB, E2K 4N5
(506) 653-9050   SIC 7389

ICT CANADA MARKETING INC   p 421
80 POWELL DR, CARBONEAR, NL, A1Y 1A5
SIC 7389

ICT CANADA MARKETING INC   p 461
800 SACKVILLE DR, LOWER SACKVILLE, NS, B4E 1R8
(902) 869-9050   SIC 7389

ICT CANADA MARKETING INC   p 463
690 EAST RIVER RD, NEW GLASGOW, NS, B2H 3S1
(902) 755-9050   SIC 7389

ICT CANADA MARKETING INC   p 467
325 VULCAN AVE, SYDNEY, NS, B1P 5X1
SIC 7389

ICT CANADA MARKETING INC   p 646
370 KENT ST W UNIT 16, LINDSAY, ON, K9V 6G8
SIC 7389

ICT GROUP   p 839
360 GEORGE ST N SUITE 100, PETERBOROUGH, ON, K9H 7E7
SIC 5963

ICU   p 1334
See ICU MEDICAL CANADA INC

ICU MEDICAL CANADA INC   p 1334
2600 BOUL ALFRED-NOBEL BUREAU 100, SAINT-LAURENT, QC, H4S 0A9
(514) 905-2600   SIC 5047

ICUC MODERATION SERVICES   p 390
See 4665181 MANITOBA LTD

ICYNENE INC   p 723
6747 CAMPOBELLO RD, MISSISSAUGA, ON, L5N 2L7
(905) 363-4040   SIC 3086

ID BIOMEDICAL CORPORATION OF QUEBEC   p 1267
2323 BOUL DU PARC-TECHNOLOGIQUE, QUEBEC, QC, G1P 4R8
(450) 978-4599   SIC 8731

IDC   p 435
See INUVIALUIT DEVELOPMENT CORPORATION

IDC CANADA   p 942
See INTERNATIONAL DATA CORPORATION (CANADA) LTD

IDC DISTRIBUTION SERVICES LTD   p 274
10550 TIMBERLAND RD, SURREY, BC, V3V 7Z1
(604) 812-5048   SIC 4789

IDC WORLDSOURCE INSURANCE NETWORK INC   p 313
1075 GEORGIA ST W, VANCOUVER, BC, V6E 3C9

(604) 689-8289   SIC 6351

IDCAD SERVICES CONSEILS   p 1190
See PCO INNOVATION CANADA INC

IDEA COUTURE   p 977
See COGNIZANT TECHNOLOGY SOLUTIONS CANADA, INC

IDEA PARTNER MARKETING INC, THE   p 322
2799 YEW ST, VANCOUVER, BC, V6K 4W2
(604) 736-1640   SIC 6513

IDEABYTES INC   p 752
142 GOLFLINKS DR, NEPEAN, ON, K2J 5N5
(613) 692-9908   SIC 7371

IDEACA LIMITED   p 774
36 YORK MILLS RD, NORTH YORK, ON, M2P 2E9
(416) 961-4332   SIC 8741

IDEAL CENTRE LOGISTIQUE QUEBEC   p 1276
See GUILBAULT LOGISTIQUE INC

IDEAL CONTRACT SERVICES LTD   p 115
9825 45 AVE NW, EDMONTON, AB, T6E 5C8
(780) 463-2424   SIC 1541

IDEAL DRAIN TILE LIMITED   p 903
1100 IDEAL DR, THORNDALE, ON, N0M 2P0
(519) 473-2669   SIC 6712

IDEAL GEAR AND MACHINE WORKS INC   p 210
6415 RIVER RD, DELTA, BC, V4K 5B9
(604) 952-4327   SIC 5085

IDEAL GLASS   p 383
See BUHLER FURNITURE INC

IDEAL HONDA   p 691
See 4247744 CANADA INC

IDEAL INDUSTRIES (CANADA), CORP   p 474
33 FULLER RD, AJAX, ON, L1S 2E1
(905) 683-3400   SIC 3699

IDEAL MUFFLER, DIV OF   p 408
See MARITIME EXHAUST LTD

IDEAL PIPE   p 903
1100 IDEAL DR, THORNDALE, ON, N0M 2P0
(519) 473-2669   SIC 3498

IDEAL PROTEIN   p 1107
See LABORATOIRES C.O.P. INC

IDEAL ROOFING COMPANY LIMITED   p 816
1418 MICHAEL ST, OTTAWA, ON, K1B 3R2
(613) 746-3206   SIC 3444

IDEAL SUPPLY INC   p 647
1045 WALLACE AVE N SUITE PH519, LISTOWEL, ON, N4W 1M6
(519) 291-1060   SIC 5063

IDEAL WELDERS LTD   p 206
660 CALDEW ST, DELTA, BC, V3M 5S2
(604) 525-5558   SIC 3498

IDEE PRO INC   p 1259
54 RUE DE LA POINTE-AUX-LIEVRES, QUEBEC, QC, G1K 5Y3
(418) 522-4455   SIC 2759

IDENTIFICATION MULTI SOLUTIONS INC   p 1334
9000 BOUL HENRI-BOURASSA O, SAINT-LAURENT, QC, H4S 1L5
(514) 336-3213   SIC 5084

IDEON PACKAGING   p 263
11251 DYKE RD, RICHMOND, BC, V7A 0A1
(604) 524-0524   SIC 2653

IDH INVESTMENTS LTD   p 175
2455 WEST RAILWAY ST, ABBOTSFORD, BC, V2S 2E3
(604) 744-2444   SIC 5812

IDL PROJECTS INC   p 250
1088 GREAT ST, PRINCE GEORGE, BC, V2N 2K8
(250) 649-0561   SIC 1542

IDLEWYLD MANOR   p 617
449 SANATORIUM RD, HAMILTON, ON, L9C 2A7
(905) 574-2000   SIC 8361

IDM MINING LTD   p 328

555 BURRARD ST SUITE 1800, VANCOUVER, BC, V7X 1M9
(604) 681-5672   SIC 1041

IDN CANADA   p 791
See INTERNATIONAL DISTRIBUTION NETWORK CANADA LTD

IDRS - DATA PRINT MAIL   p 209
See INTERNATIONAL DIRECT RESPONSE SERVICES LTD

IEC   p 793
See INTERNATIONAL ELECTRONIC COMPONENTS INC

IEC HOLDEN INC   p 1339
8180 CH DE LA COTE-DE-LIESSE, SAINT-LAURENT, QC, H4T 1G8
(514) 735-4371   SIC 3621

IEG CONSULTANTS   p 9
See KLOHN CRIPPEN BERGER LTD

IEL   p 1356
See INDUSTRIES ET EQUIPEMENTS LALIBERTE LTEE, LES

IEM   p 282
See INDUSTRIAL EQUIPMENT MANUFACTURING LTD

IEM CANADA   p 229
See IEM INDUSTRIAL ELECTRIC MFG. (CANADA) INC

IEM INDUSTRIAL ELECTRIC MFG. (CANADA) INC   p 229
27353 58 CRES UNIT 201, LANGLEY, BC, V4W 3W7
(866) 302-9836   SIC 5063

IESO   p 953
See INDEPENDENT ELECTRICITY SYSTEM OPERATOR

IETICKETS   p 23
See INSTIMAX CORPORATION

IFABRIC CORP   p 671
525 DENISON ST UNIT 2, MARKHAM, ON, L3R 1B8
(905) 752-0566   SIC 6799

IFASTGROUPE 2004 L.P.   p 1149
700 RUE OUELLETTE, MARIEVILLE, QC, J3M 1P6
(450) 658-8741   SIC 3452

IFC NORTH AMERICA INC   p 886
63 CHURCH ST SUITE 301, ST CATHARINES, ON, L2R 3C4
(905) 685-8560   SIC 5169

IFC SEAFOOD INC   p 1362
5584 BOUL DES ROSSIGNOLS, SAINTE-ROSE, QC, H7L 5Z1
(450) 682-9144   SIC 5146

IFDS   p 939
See INTERNATIONAL FINANCIAL DATA SERVICES (CANADA) LIMITED

IFG - INTERNATIONAL FINANCIAL GROUP (US) LTD   p 986
100 KING ST W SUITE 910, TORONTO, ON, M5X 1B1
(416) 645-2434   SIC 7361

IFG - INTERNATIONAL FINANCIAL GROUP   p 986
100 KING ST W SUITE 910, TORONTO, ON, M5X 1B1
(416) 645-2434   SIC 8721

IFS AEROSPACE & DEFENSE LTD   p 833
175 TERENCE MATTHEWS CRES, OTTAWA, ON, K2M 1W8
(613) 576-2480   SIC 7371

IFS INTERNATIONAL FREIGHT SYSTEMS INC   p 911
18900 COUNTY ROAD 42 RR 5, TILBURY, ON, N0P 2L0
(519) 682-3544   SIC 4213

IFT SOLUTIONS   p 186
See INTEGRATED FINANCIAL TECHNOLOGIES INC

IG IMAGE GROUP INC   p 292
34 2ND AVE W, VANCOUVER, BC, V5Y 1B3
(604) 873-3333   SIC 5199

IGA   p 5
See WALKER'S GROCERY LTD

IGA   p 7

See FRESON MARKET LTD

IGA   p 132
See FRESON MARKET LTD

IGA   p 196
See WESTWARD ENTERPRISES LTD

IGA   p 199
See PLATEAU FOODS LTD

IGA   p 247
See PORT MCNEIL FOODS LTD

IGA   p 618
See SOBEYS CAPITAL INCORPORATED

IGA   p 1061
See SUPERMARCHES DAIGLE, JACQUES INC

IGA   p 1063
See MAGASIN CO-OP DE BONAVENTURE

IGA   p 1081
See ALIMENTATION COATICOOK (1986) INC

IGA   p 1090
See SOBEYS QUEBEC INC

IGA   p 1101
See MARCHE LAPLANTE FARNHAM INC

IGA   p 1108
See SUPERMARCHE BERGERON INC

IGA   p 1109
See MARCHE GAOUETTE INC

IGA   p 1112
See SUPERMARCHE GEORGES BADRA INC

IGA   p 1121
See ALIMENTATION CHRISTIAN VERREAULT INC

IGA   p 1131
See SOBEYS QUEBEC INC

IGA   p 1149
See MAGASIN COOP DE MARIA IGA

IGA   p 1151
See MARCHE DUCHEMIN ET LACAS INC

IGA   p 1153
See MARCHE ST-CANUT INC

IGA   p 1154
See MARCHE LEBLANC INC

IGA   p 1154
See ALIMENTATION DE LA MITIS INC

IGA   p 1160
See MAGASIN CO-OP DE MONTMAGNY

IGA   p 1163
See ALIMENTATION HOCHELAGA G.S. INC

IGA   p 1180
See SUPERMARCHE DEZIEL INC

IGA   p 1221
See SUPERMARCHE LEFEBVRE ET FILLES INC

IGA   p 1239
See MARCHE C.D.L. TELLIER INC

IGA   p 1261
See 9085-1379 QUEBEC INC

IGA   p 1270
See SOBEYS CAPITAL INCORPORATED

IGA   p 1275
See COOPERATIVE DES CONSOMMATEURS DE LORETTEVILLE

IGA   p 1281
See ALIMENTATIONS GAREAU INC

IGA   p 1283
See MARCHE MICHEL LEMIEUX INC

IGA   p 1284
See EPICERIE R. CADIEUX & FILS INC

IGA   p 1287
See SUPER MARCHE ROBERVAL INC

IGA   p 1298
See MARCHE LAMBERT ET FRERES INC

IGA   p 1301
See SOBEYS QUEBEC INC

IGA   p 1308
See MARCHE DUBREUIL VEILLETTE INC

IGA   p 1311
See 9165-1588 QUEBEC INC

IGA   p 1316
See SUPER MARCHE LAPLANTE INC

IGA   p 1319
See MARCHE ROBERT TELLIER (1990)

INC

IGA p 1322
See MARCHE PIERRE JOBIDON INC

IGA p 1323
See MARCHE DUCHEMIN ET FRERES INC

IGA p 1359
See MARCHE DU FAUBOURG STE-JULIE INC

IGA p 1362
See MARCHE DES OISEAUX INC

IGA p 1376
See MARCHE ANDRE TELLIER INC

IGA p 1379
See ALIMENTATION LE SIEUR ENR

IGA p 1380
See MARCHE ALIMENTATION THIBAULT INC

IGA p 1385
See IGA EXTRA MARCHE PAQUETTE INC

IGA p 1389
See MARCHE LABRIE & LANDRY INC

IGA p 1393
See SOBEYS QUEBEC INC

IGA p 1396
See CHAMPAGNE, GERARD LTEE

IGA DAIGLE p 1364
220 RUE SAINT-CHARLES, SAINTE-THERESE, QC, J7E 2B4
(450) 435-1370   SIC 5411

IGA #8113 p 1316
435 9E AV, SAINT-JEAN-SUR-RICHELIEU, QC, J2X 1K5
(450) 358-2804   SIC 5411

IGA #8215 p 1323
See MARCHES LOUISE MENARD (PRE-VILLE) INC, LES

IGA 111 p 1083
See ALIMENTATIONS SHNAIDMAN PAGANO INC, LES

IGA 8196 p 1303
See RAINVILLE, ROGER & FILS INC

IGA ALIMENTATION COOP POR p 1253
26 BOUL DES ILES, PORT-CARTIER, QC, G5B 0A4
(418) 766-0008   SIC 5411

IGA BOUCHARD p 1375
See 98946 CANADA INC

IGA BOUCHERIE CHOUINARD p 1354
See CHOUINARD, A. & FILS INC

IGA BUY N' FLY p 425
See BUYNFLY FOOD LIMITED

IGA COUTURE p 1370
See SOBEYS QUEBEC INC

IGA CREVIER JOLIETTE p 1243
See MARCHE CREVIER IGA INC

IGA DE COTRET-BRAZEAU p 1103
See 9084-4622 QUEBEC INC

IGA DES SOURCES p 1280
See 9020-7424 QUEBEC INC

IGA EXTRA p 1084
See ALIMENTATION ST-DENIS INC

IGA EXTRA p 1091
See SUPERMARCHE D.D.O. INC

IGA EXTRA p 1131
See MARCHE D'ALIMENTATION BECK INC

IGA EXTRA p 1138
See SOBEYS QUEBEC INC

IGA EXTRA p 1232
See MARCHE HEBERT SENECAL INC

IGA EXTRA p 1246
See MAGASIN CO-OP DE PLESSISVILLE

IGA EXTRA p 1268
See SOBEYS CAPITAL INCORPORATED

IGA EXTRA p 1280
See COOPERATIVE DES CONSOMA-TEURS DE CHARLESBOURG

IGA EXTRA p 1285
See SOBEYS CAPITAL INCORPORATED

IGA EXTRA p 1287
See SOBEYS CAPITAL INCORPORATED

IGA EXTRA p 1296
See MARCHE LAMBERT ET FRERES INC

IGA EXTRA p 1346
See SOBEYS CAPITAL INCORPORATED

IGA EXTRA p 1363
See MARCHE D'ALIMENTATION CREVIER INC

IGA EXTRA p 1374
See SOBEYS CAPITAL INCORPORATED

IGA EXTRA p 1385
See SOBEYS CAPITAL INCORPORATED

IGA EXTRA # 618 p 1360
See BOUCHERIE VEILLEUX INC

IGA EXTRA 514 p 1371
See SOBEYS CAPITAL INCORPORATED

IGA EXTRA 8533 p 1289
See MARCHE BELANGER INC

IGA EXTRA CONVIVIO p 1276
See 9230-9970 QUEBEC INC

IGA EXTRA DAIGNEAULT p 1088
See L. A. DAIGNEAULT & FILS LTEE

IGA EXTRA GLADU p 1317
See 2747-6761 QUEBEC INC

IGA EXTRA MARCHE p 1097
See MARCHE CLEMENT DEFORGES INC

IGA EXTRA MARCHE LACAS INC p 1365
1366 BOUL MONSEIGNEUR-LANGLOIS, SALABERRY-DE-VALLEYFIELD, QC, J6S 1E3
(450) 373-0251   SIC 5411

IGA EXTRA MARCHE PAQUETTE INC p 1385
3925 BOUL DES FORGES, TROIS-RIVIERES, QC, G8Y 1V9
(819) 379-2397   SIC 5411

IGA EXTRA MONTEE PAIEMENT p 1103
See 169727 CANADA INC

IGA EXTRA ROCHETTE & VEZINA p 1121
See SUPERMARCHE DON QUICHOTTE INC

IGA EXTRA THIBAULT p 1380
See SOBEYS QUEBEC INC

IGA EXTRA VALLEE p 1072
See 9191-7906 QUEBEC INC

IGA FAMILLE RICK DEZIEL. p 1343
See POIRIER & FILS LTEE

IGA GAZAILLE p 1147
See 9128-3820 QUEBEC INC

IGA JEAN XXIII p 1385
See 9045-9827 QUEBEC INC

IGA JODOIN, GUY p 1313
See 9026-4979 QUEBEC INC

IGA LAFLAMME p 1106
See LAFLAMME, HENRI INC

IGA LAMOUREUX p 1322
See 9139-6317 QUEBEC INC

IGA LEBLANC p 1246
See 9093-6907 QUEBEC INC

IGA MARCHE LACOSTE HEBERT p 1143
1401 CH DE CHAMBLY, LONGUEUIL, QC, J4J 3X6
(450) 677-2869   SIC 5411

IGA MARCHE MORIN-HEIGHTS p 1242
See 9181-8153 QUEBEC INC

IGA MARCHE ST PIERRE p 1383
See MARCHE ST-PIERRE & FILS INC

IGA PELLETIER p 1391
See SUPERMARCHE PELLETIER INC

IGA PEPIN p 1057
See MARCHES PEPIN INC, LES

IGA PILON-MCKINON p 1365
See SUPERMARCHE ROBERT PILON LTEE

IGA PLUS STORES NO 56 p 215
See WESDAN HOLDINGS INC

IGA ROY p 1290
See SUPERMARCHE ROY INC

IGA SAINT-LUC p 1315
See MARCHE PERREAULT & GELINAS INC

IGA SAINT-PASCAL & IGA p 1349
See 9190-4144 QUEBEC INC.

IGA ST-AUGUSTIN p 1153
14995 RUE DES SAULES, MIRABEL, QC, J7N 2A3
(450) 475-1118   SIC 5149

IGA STANSTEAD p 1378
See PROVISIONS ROCK ISLAND INC

IGA SUPERMARCHE PIERRE PATRY EX-TRA p 1395
See SOBEYS CAPITAL INCORPORATED

IGA TELLIER p 1346
See MARCHE TELLIER JEAN-TALON INC

IGA VIEUX BEAUPORT p 1256
See MARCHE DU VIEUX BEAUPORT INC

IGA YVON HACHE p 1079
See SOBEYS QUEBEC INC

IGA-MELLON p 1115
See SUPERMARCHE MELLON INC

IGB AUTOMOTIVE LTD p 1021
3090 MARENTETTE AVE, WINDSOR, ON, N8X 4G2
(519) 250-5777   SIC 3714

IGF AXIOM INC p 1134
4125 DES LAURENTIDES (A-15) E, LAVAL-OUEST, QC, H7L 5W5
(514) 645-3443   SIC 8748

IGGH p 868
See INA GRAFTON GAGE HOME OF TORONTO

IGL CANADA (WESTERN) LTD p 101
17515 106A AVE NW, EDMONTON, AB, T5S 1M7
(780) 489-3245   SIC 1623

IGLOO BUILDING SUPPLIES GROUP LTD p 101
21421 111 AVE NW, EDMONTON, AB, T5S 1Y1
(780) 451-0600   SIC 5039

IGLOO ERECTORS LTD p 12
3468 46 AVE SE, CALGARY, AB, T2B 3J2
(403) 253-1121   SIC 1761

IGLOO MANUFACTURING LTD p 101
21421 111 AVE NW, EDMONTON, AB, T5S 1Y1
(780) 451-0600   SIC 5039

IGLOOLIK CO-OPERATIVE LIMITED p 472
GD, IGLOOLIK, NU, X0A 0L0
(867) 934-8958   SIC 5411

IGM FINANCIAL INC p 378
447 PORTAGE AVE, WINNIPEG, MB, R3C 3B6
(204) 943-0361   SIC 6211

IGT CANADA SOLUTIONS ULC p 410
328 URQUHART AVE, MONCTON, NB, E1H 2R6
(506) 878-6000   SIC 0971

IGT CANADA SOLUTIONS ULC p 410
328 URQUHART AVE, MONCTON, NB, E1H 2R6
(506) 878-6000   SIC 3999

IHAUL FREIGHT LTD p 226
105-8047 199 ST, LANGLEY, BC, V2Y 0E2
(604) 594-4100   SIC 4731

IHL p 1031
See INVESTMENTS HARDWARE LIMITED

IHS p 30
See IHS ENERGY (CANADA) LTD

IHS ENERGY (CANADA) LTD p 30
1331 MACLEOD TRAIL SE SUITE 200, CALGARY, AB, T2G 0K3
(403) 532-8175   SIC 8741

IHSA p 696
See INFRASTRUCTURE HEALTH AND SAFETY ASSOCIATION

IIO p 946
See INNOVATION INSTITUTE OF ON-TARIO

IIROC p 953
See INVESTMENT INDUSTRY REGULA-TORY ORGANIZATION OF CANADA

IISD p 374
See INTERNATIONAL INSTITUTE FOR SUSTAINABLE DEVELOPMENT

IKEA p 1065
See IKEA CANADA LIMITED PARTNER-SHIP

IKEA CANADA p 120
See IKEA LIMITED

IKEA CANADA p 531
See IKEA CANADA LIMITED PARTNER-SHIP

IKEA CANADA LIMITED PARTNERSHIP p 531
1065 PLAINS RD E, BURLINGTON, ON, L7T 4K1
(905) 637-9440   SIC 5712

IKEA CANADA LIMITED PARTNERSHIP p 574
1475 THE QUEENSWAY, ETOBICOKE, ON, M8Z 1T3
(866) 866-4532   SIC 5712

IKEA CANADA LIMITED PARTNERSHIP p 1065
586 CH DE TOURAINE, BOUCHERVILLE, QC, J4B 5E4
SIC 5712

IKEA CANADA LIMITED PARTNERSHIP p 1339
9090 BOUL CAVENDISH, SAINT-LAURENT, QC, H4T 1Z8
(514) 904-8619   SIC 5712

IKEA DIRECT p 1339
See IKEA CANADA LIMITED PARTNER-SHIP

IKEA ETOBICOKE p 574
See IKEA CANADA LIMITED PARTNER-SHIP

IKEA LIMITED p 120
1311 102 ST NW, EDMONTON, AB, T6N 1M3
(866) 866-4532   SIC 5712

IKKUMA RESOURCES CORP p 51
605 5 AVE SW SUITE 2700, CALGARY, AB, T2P 3H5
(403) 261-5900   SIC 1382

IKO ENTERPRISES LTD p 30
1600 42 AVE SE, CALGARY, AB, T2G 5B5
(403) 265-6022   SIC 6719

IKO INDUSTRIES LTD p 509
80 STAFFORD DR, BRAMPTON, ON, L6W 1L4
(905) 457-2880   SIC 2952

IKO INDUSTRIES LTD p 619
1451 SPENCE AVE, HAWKESBURY, ON, K6A 3T4
(613) 632-8581   SIC 2952

IKO INDUSTRIES LTD p 663
105084 HWY 7, MADOC, ON, K0K 2K0
(613) 473-0430   SIC 2952

IKON OFFICE SOLUTIONS, ULC p 503
100 WESTCREEK BLVD, BRAMPTON, ON, L6T 5V7
SIC 5044

IL FORNELLO RESTAURANT p 931
See 1094285 ONTARIO LIMITED

ILE-DES-SOEURS HYUNDAI p 1395
See 7255721 CANADA INC

ILER LODGE RETIREMENT HOME p 570
See REVERA INC

ILEVEL p 207
See WEYERHAEUSER COMPANY LIM-ITED

ILF CONSULTANTS INC p 51
833 4 AVE SW SUITE 600, CALGARY, AB, T2P 3T5
(587) 288-2600   SIC 8711

ILLINOIS CENTRAL RAILROAD COMPANY p 1205
935 RUE DE LA GAUCHETIERE O BU-REAU 11, MONTREAL, QC, H3B 2M9
(514) 399-4536   SIC 4011

ILLUMINATIONS LIGHTING SOLUTIONS LTD p 334
2885 QUESNEL ST, VICTORIA, BC, V8T 4K2
(250) 382-5483   SIC 5063

ILLUMITI INC p 904
123 COMMERCE VALLEY DR E SUITE 500, THORNHILL, ON, L3T 7W8
(905) 737-1066   SIC 8748

ILSC (VANCOUVER) INC p 298
555 RICHARDS ST, VANCOUVER, BC, V6B

2Z5
(604) 689-9095   SIC 8299
ILSCO OF CANADA COMPANY   p 708
615 ORWELL ST, MISSISSAUGA, ON, L5A 2W4
(905) 274-2341   SIC 3643
ILTA GRAIN INC   p 282
8427 160 ST, SURREY, BC, V4N 0V6
(604) 597-5060   SIC 5153
IMAC ENTERPRISES CORP   p 255
11488 EBURNE WAY, RICHMOND, BC, V6V 3E1
(604) 324-8288   SIC 5031
IMAFLEX INC   p 1223
5710 RUE NOTRE-DAME O, MONTREAL, QC, H4C 1V2
(514) 935-5710   SIC 3081
IMAGE AUTOMOBILES INC   p 608
155 CENTENNIAL PKY N, HAMILTON, ON, L8E 1H8
(905) 561-4100   SIC 5511
IMAGE GROUP   p 292
See IG IMAGE GROUP INC
IMAGE HOME PRODUCTS INC, L'   p 1205
1175 PLACE DU FRERE-ANDRE, MONTREAL, QC, H3B 3X9
(514) 383-4720   SIC 5063
IMAGE HONDA   p 608
See IMAGE AUTOMOBILES INC
IMAGE PLUS   p 176
31935 SOUTH FRASER WAY UNIT 104, ABBOTSFORD, BC, V2T 5N7
(604) 504-7222   SIC 7384
IMAGE TWIST   p 1187
See AGENCE MIRUM CANADA INC
IMAGEHOUSE LIMITED   p 825
275 BAY ST, OTTAWA, ON, K1R 5Z5
(613) 238-6232   SIC 7389
IMAGES 2000 INC   p 570
33 DRUMMOND ST, ETOBICOKE, ON, M8V 1Y7
(416) 252-9693   SIC 2499
IMAGES TURBO INC, LES   p 1305
1225 107E RUE, SAINT-GEORGES, QC, G5Y 8C3
(418) 227-8872   SIC 7532
IMAGINE COMMUNICATIONS   p 776
See ICC IMAGINE COMMUNICATIONS CANADA LTD
IMAGINE FINANCIAL LTD   p 981
460 RICHMOND ST W SUITE 100, TORONTO, ON, M5V 1Y1
(416) 730-8488   SIC 6411
IMAGINE INSURANCE   p 981
See IMAGINE FINANCIAL LTD
IMAGINE WIRELESS INC   p 74
4550 17 AVE SW UNIT 28, CALGARY, AB, T3E 7B9
(403) 974-3150   SIC 5999
IMAGING AND SENSING TECHNOLOGY   p 536
See MIRION TECHNOLOGIES (IST CANADA) INC
IMAGINIT CANADA INC   p 744
151 COURTNEYPARK DR W SUITE 201, MISSISSAUGA, ON, L5W 1Y5
(905) 602-8783   SIC 7372
IMAGINIT TECHNOLOGIES   p 744
See IMAGINIT CANADA INC
IMAGIX IMAGERIE MEDICALE INC   p 1065
600 BOUL DU FORT-SAINT-LOUIS UNITE 202, BOUCHERVILLE, QC, J4B 1S7
(450) 655-2430   SIC 8011
IMAGIX IMAGERIE MEDICALE INC   p 1070
F-4105 BOUL MATTE, BROSSARD, QC, J4Y 2P4
(514) 866-6622   SIC 8011
IMALIGN   p 1264
See INNOVMETRIC LOGICIELS INC
IMARKETING SOLUTIONS GROUP   p 923
See IMKT DIRECT SOLUTIONS CORPORATION
IMARKETING SOLUTIONS GROUP INC   p 75

3710 WESTWINDS DR NE UNIT 24, CALGARY, AB, T3J 5H3
(403) 531-6157   SIC 8399
IMARKETING SOLUTIONS GROUP INC   p 346
800 ROSSER AVE SUITE D7, BRANDON, MB, R7A 6N5
(204) 727-4242   SIC 8399
IMARKETING SOLUTIONS GROUP INC   p 612
4 HUGHSON ST S SUITE P400, HAMILTON, ON, L8N 3Z1
(905) 529-7896   SIC 8399
IMARKETING SOLUTIONS GROUP INC   p 975
80 BLOOR ST W SUITE 601, TORONTO, ON, M5S 2V1
(416) 646-3128   SIC 8399
IMASCO   p 282
See IMASCO MINERALS INC
IMASCO MINERALS INC   p 282
19287 98A AVE, SURREY, BC, V4N 4C8
(604) 888-3848   SIC 3299
IMAX CORPORATION   p 715
2525 SPEAKMAN DR, MISSISSAUGA, ON, L5K 1B1
(905) 403-6500   SIC 5049
IMAX EXPERIENCE, THE   p 715
See IMAX CORPORATION
IMAXX MONEY MARKET FUND   p 771
See FORESTERS FINANCIAL INVESTMENT MANAGEMENT COMPANY OF CANADA INC
IMCD CANADA LIMITED   p 504
99 SUMMERLEA RD, BRAMPTON, ON, L6T 4V2
(800) 575-3382   SIC 5169
IMERYS GRAPHITE & CARBON CANADA INC   p 1124
585 CH DU GRAPHITE, LAC-DES-ILES, QC, J0W 1J0
(819) 597-2911   SIC 1499
IMERYS GRAPHITE & CARBON CANADA INC   p 1381
990 RUE FERNAND-POITRAS, TERREBONNE, QC, J6Y 1V1
(450) 622-9191   SIC 1499
IMERYS TALC CANADA INC   p 913
100 WATER TOWER RD, TIMMINS, ON, P4N 7J5
(705) 268-2208   SIC 1499
IMEX AGRO INC   p 1106
128 BOUL SAINT-RAYMOND, GATINEAU, QC, J8Y 1T2
(819) 483-1515   SIC 5148
IMEX SYSTEMS INC   p 585
34 GREENSBORO DR 2ND FL, ETOBICOKE, ON, M9W 1E1
(647) 352-7520   SIC 7372
IMG   p 712
See INTERIOR MANUFACTURING GROUP INC
IMKT DIRECT SOLUTIONS CORPORATION   p 923
90 EGLINTON AVE W SUITE 300, TORONTO, ON, M4R 2E4
(416) 633-4646   SIC 7389
IMMACULATA HIGH SCHOOL   p 826
See OTTAWA CATHOLIC DISTRICT SCHOOL BOARD
IMMACULATE CONFECTION LTD   p 186
5284 STILL CREEK AVE, BURNABY, BC, V5C 4E4
(604) 293-1600   SIC 5441
IMMEDIATE DELIVERY & COURIER SERVICE INC   p 475
255 SALEM RD N SUITE D2, AJAX, ON, L1Z 0B1
(905) 427-7733   SIC 7389
IMMEDIATE RESPONSE FORCE INC   p 920
1127 BROADVIEW AVE UNIT B, TORONTO, ON, M4K 2S6
(647) 987-0002   SIC 8748

IMMEDIATE RESPONSE SERVICE   p 920
See IMMEDIATE RESPONSE FORCE INC
IMMEUBDES MOULINS INC., LES   p 1379
689 CH DU COTEAU, TERREBONNE, QC, J6W 5H2
SIC 6553
IMMEUBLE M. & A. CONSTANTIN INC   p 1302
1054 BOUL ARTHUR-SAUVE, SAINT-EUSTACHE, QC, J7R 4K3
(450) 473-2374   SIC 6712
IMMEUBLES CARREFOUR RICHELIEU LTEE, LES   p 1197
600 BOUL DE MAISONNEUVE O BUREAU 2600, MONTREAL, QC, H3A 3J2
(514) 499-8300   SIC 6512
IMMEUBLES CJS RIVEST INC   p 1283
96 BOUL INDUSTRIEL, REPENTIGNY, QC, J6A 4X6
(450) 581-4480   SIC 1521
IMMEUBLES DAUPHIN   p 1139
See MATELAS DAUPHIN INC
IMMEUBLES FAIRWAY INC, LES   p 1218
5858 CH DE LA COTE-DES-NEIGES UNITE 612, MONTREAL, QC, H3S 2S1
(514) 342-2791   SIC 6512
IMMEUBLES GOYETTE INC, LES   p 1313
2825 BOUL CASAVANT O, SAINT-HYACINTHE, QC, J2S 7Y4
(450) 773-9615   SIC 6512
IMMEUBLES J.C. MILOT INC, LES   p 1099
600 BOUL SAINT-JOSEPH, DRUMMONDVILLE, QC, J2C 2C1
(819) 478-4141   SIC 7011
IMMEUBLES JOSEPH PELLETIER INC, LES   p 1106
116 RUE LOIS, GATINEAU, QC, J8Y 3R7
(819) 770-3038   SIC 6719
IMMEUBLES RB LTEE   p 1288
500 RTE 112, ROUGEMONT, QC, J0L 1M0
(450) 469-3153   SIC 4225
IMMEUBLES RICHELIEU N. REON INC, LES   p 1318
550 BOUL DU SEMINAIRE N, SAINT-JEAN-SUR-RICHELIEU, QC, J3B 5L6
(450) 349-5883   SIC 6531
IMMEUBLES ROUSSIN LTEE, LES   p 1279
780 BOUL LEBOURGNEUF, QUEBEC, QC, G2J 1S1
(418) 623-5333   SIC 6512
IMMEUBLES STRUC-TUBE LTEE   p 1340
6000 RTE TRANSCANADIENNE, SAINT-LAURENT, QC, H4T 1X9
(514) 333-9747   SIC 5712
IMMEUBLES TANDEM   p 1263
See CAPITAL TRANSIT INC
IMMEUBLES TRANSFORCE   p 1337
See TRANSPORT TFI 2, S.E.C.
IMMEUBLES TURRET INC   p 1155
1320 BOUL GRAHAM BUREAU 330, MONT-ROYAL, QC, H3P 3C8
(514) 737-7132   SIC 6514
IMMEUBLES VILLAGE D.D.O. INC, LES   p 1091
4000 BOUL SAINT-JEAN BUREAU 2000, DOLLARD-DES-ORMEAUX, QC, H9G 1X1
(514) 684-1141   SIC 6531
IMMEUBLES VILLAGE POINTE-CLAIRE INC   p 1250
263 BOUL SAINT-JEAN, POINTE-CLAIRE, QC, H9R 3J1
(514) 694-2121   SIC 6531
IMMEUBLES YALE LIMITEE, LES   p 1197
2015 RUE PEEL BUREAU 1200, MONTREAL, QC, H3A 1T8
(514) 845-2265   SIC 6719
IMMIGRANT AND REFUGEE COMMUNITY ORGANIZATION OF MANITOBA INC   p 373
95 ELLEN ST, WINNIPEG, MB, R3A 1S8
(204) 943-8765   SIC 6531
IMMIGRANT LANGUAGE & VOCATIONAL ASSESSMENT & REFERAL CENTRE   p 51
See IMMIGRANT SERVICES CALGARY SOCIETY

IMMIGRANT SERVICES ASSOCIATION OF NOVA SCOTIA   p 457
6960 MUMFORD RD SUITE 2120, HALIFAX, NS, B3L 4P1
(902) 423-3607   SIC 8641
IMMIGRANT SERVICES CALGARY SOCIETY   p 51
910 7 AVE SW SUITE 1200, CALGARY, AB, T2P 3N8
(403) 265-1120   SIC 8322
IMMIGRANT SERVICES SOCIETY OF BRITISH COLUMBIA, THE   p 287
2610 VICTORIA DR, VANCOUVER, BC, V5N 4L2
(604) 684-2561   SIC 8399
IMMIGRANT WOMEN'S ASSOCIATION OF MANITOBA INC   p 374
515 PORTAGE AVE, WINNIPEG, MB, R3B 2E9
SIC 6311
IMMOBILIER CARBONLEO INC   p 1070
9160 BOUL LEDUC BUREAU 510, BROSSARD, QC, J4Y 0E3
(450) 550-8080   SIC 6719
IMMOBILIER JACK ASTOR'S (DORVAL) INC   p 1091
3051 BOUL DES SOURCES, DOLLARD-DES-ORMEAUX, QC, H9B 1Z6
(514) 685-5225   SIC 5813
IMMOBILIER SKI BROMONT INC   p 1068
150 RUE CHAMPLAIN, BROMONT, QC, J2L 1A2
(450) 534-2200   SIC 5813
IMMOBILIER SKI BROMONT.COM   p 1068
See IMMOBILIER SKI BROMONT INC
IMMOVEX EVALUATEURS AGREES   p 1068
See IMMOVEX INC
IMMOVEX INC   p 1068
2210 BOUL LAPINIERE, BROSSARD, QC, J4W 1M2
(450) 671-9205   SIC 7389
IMMUNOTEC INC   p 1394
300 RUE JOSEPH-CARRIER, VAUDREUIL-DORION, QC, J7V 5V5
(450) 424-9992   SIC 5149
IMO FOODS LIMITED   p 471
26 WATER ST, YARMOUTH, NS, B5A 1K9
(902) 742-3519   SIC 2091
IMOS   p 671
See INTEGRATED MAINTENANCE & OPERATIONS SERVICES INC
IMP ELECTRONIC SYSTEMS   p 459
See I.M.P. GROUP LIMITED
IMPACT AUTO AUCTIONS LTD   p 710
50 BURNHAMTHORPE RD W SUITE 800, MISSISSAUGA, ON, L5B 3C2
(905) 896-9727   SIC 7389
IMPACT CLEANING SERVICES LTD   p 574
21 GOODRICH RD SUITE 8, ETOBICOKE, ON, M8Z 6A3
(416) 253-1234   SIC 7349
IMPACT DETAIL INC   p 1380
2625 BOUL DES ENTREPRISES, TERREBONNE, QC, J6X 4J9
(514) 767-1555   SIC 6221
IMPACT RESEARCH INC   p 1259
300 RUE SAINT-PAUL BUREAU 300, QUEBEC, QC, G1K 7R1
(418) 647-2727   SIC 8732
IMPACT SECURITY GROUP INC   p 374
456 MAIN ST 2ND FL, WINNIPEG, MB, R3B 1B6
(866) 385-7037   SIC 7381
IMPACT STEEL CANADA COMPANY   p 523
1100 BURLOAK DR SUITE 300, BURLINGTON, ON, L7L 6B2
(905) 336-8939   SIC 5051
IMPACT XM INC   p 798
1303 NORTH SERVICE RD E UNIT 1, OAKVILLE, ON, L6H 1A7
(905) 287-4862   SIC 5046
IMPACTO   p 1370
See ATELIERS B.G. INC, LES

IMPARK   p 89
See IMPERIAL PARKING CANADA COR-
PORATION
IMPARK   p 298
See IMPERIAL PARKING CANADA COR-
PORATION
IMPARK   p 374
See IMPERIAL PARKING CANADA COR-
PORATION
IMPART LITHO   p 1398
See 9049-3347 QUEBEC INC
IMPCO ECOTRANS TECHNOLOIGES, INC
p 640
100 HOLLINGER CRES, KITCHENER, ON,
N2K 2Z3
(519) 576-4270   SIC 6712
IMPENCO LTEE   p 1180
240 RUE GUIZOT O, MONTREAL, QC, H2P
1L5
(514) 383-1200   SIC 3172
IMPERIA HOTEL ET SUITES INC   p 1380
3215 BOUL DE LA PINIERE BUREAU 201,
TERREBONNE, QC, J6X 4P7
(450) 492-3336   SIC 6712
IMPERIAL CAPITAL CORPORATION   p 953
200 KING ST W SUITE 1701, TORONTO,
ON, M5H 3T4
(416) 362-3658   SIC 6211
IMPERIAL COFFEE AND SERVICES INC p
783
12 KODIAK CRES, NORTH YORK, ON, M3J
3G5
(416) 638-7404   SIC 5046
IMPERIAL DISTRIBUTORS CANADA INC p
105
16504 121A AVE NW, EDMONTON, AB,
T5V 1J9
(780) 484-2287   SIC 5122
IMPERIAL FLAVOURS INC   p 685
7550 TORBRAM RD, MISSISSAUGA, ON,
L4T 3L8
(905) 678-6680   SIC 2087
IMPERIAL MANUFACTURING GROUP INC
p 411
40 INDUSTRIAL PARK ST, RICHIBUCTO,
NB, E4W 4A4
(506) 523-9117   SIC 3444
IMPERIAL METALS CORPORATION   p 305
580 HORNBY ST SUITE 200, VANCOU-
VER, BC, V6C 3B6
(604) 669-8959   SIC 1041
IMPERIAL OIL   p 183
See SMITH, M.R. LIMITED
IMPERIAL OIL LIMITED   p 16
505 QUARRY PARK BLVD SE, CALGARY,
AB, T2C 5N1
(800) 567-3776   SIC 2911
IMPERIAL OIL LIMITED   p 860
453 CHRISTINA ST N, SARNIA, ON, N7T
5W3
(519) 339-2712   SIC 2911
IMPERIAL OIL LIMITED   p 860
PO BOX 3004 STN MAIN, SARNIA, ON,
N7T 7M5
(519) 339-4015   SIC 2911
IMPERIAL OIL RESOURCES LIMITED p 51
237 4 AVE SW, CALGARY, AB, T2P 0H6
(800) 567-3776   SIC 1382
IMPERIAL PARKING CANADA CORPORA-
TION   p
89
10239 107 ST NW, EDMONTON, AB, T5J
1K1
(780) 420-1976   SIC 7521
IMPERIAL PARKING CANADA CORPORA-
TION   p
298
601 CORDOVA ST W SUITE 300, VANCOU-
VER, BC, V6B 1G1
(604) 681-7311   SIC 7521
IMPERIAL PARKING CANADA CORPORA-
TION   p
374
136 MARKET AVE SUITE 2, WINNIPEG,

MB, R3B 0P4
(204) 943-3578   SIC 7521
IMPERIAL PARKING CANADA CORPORA-
TION   p
1211
640 RUE SAINT-PAUL O BUREAU 106,
MONTREAL, QC, H3C 1L9
(514) 875-5626   SIC 7521
IMPERIAL ROOFING (SARNIA) LTD   p 860
313 GLADWISH DR, SARNIA, ON, N7T 7H3
(519) 336-6146   SIC 5211
IMPERIAL SURGICAL LTD   p 1094
850 AV HALPERN, DORVAL, QC, H9P 1G6
(514) 631-7988   SIC 5047
IMPERIAL TOBACCO CANADA LIMITEE   p
1223
3711 RUE SAINT-ANTOINE O, MON-
TREAL, QC, H4C 3P6
(514) 932-6161   SIC 2111
IMPERIAL TOBACCO COMPAGNIE LIMI-
TEE   p
603
107 WOODLAWN RD W, GUELPH, ON,
N1H 1B4
SIC 2111
IMPERIAL TOBACCO COMPAGNIE LIMI-
TEE   p
1223
3711 RUE SAINT-ANTOINE O, MON-
TREAL, QC, H4C 3P6
(514) 932-6161   SIC 5194
IMPORT AQUATIQUES ABCEE'S   p 1131
See 2623-4419 QUEBEC INC
IMPORT AUTO PLAZA INC   p 430
475 KENMOUNT RD, ST. JOHN'S, NL, A1B
3P9
(709) 579-6487   SIC 5521
IMPORT AUTO RECYCLING   p 176
See DONALD E. CHARLTON LTD
IMPORT DISTRIBUTION CENTER   p 795
See HOME DEPOT OF CANADA INC
IMPORT EXPORT SEAPASS INC   p 1149
321 MONTEE MASSON BUREAU 301,
MASCOUCHE, QC, J7K 2L6
(450) 918-4300   SIC 6799
IMPORT TOOL CORPORATION LTD   p 115
10340 71 AVE NW, EDMONTON, AB, T6E
0W8
(780) 434-3464   SIC 5084
IMPORTANT AND MECHANT SMALLER
PROJECT   p 96
See RESCOM INC
IMPORTATION BERCHICCI LTEE   p 1344
6205 BOUL COUTURE, SAINT-LEONARD,
QC, H1P 3G7
(514) 325-2020   SIC 5143
IMPORTATION J & F   p 1161
See 9097-4775 QUEBEC INC
IMPORTATIONS & DISTRIBUTIONS B.H.
INC   p 1160
12880 RUE JEAN-GROU, MONTREAL, QC,
H1A 3N5
(514) 356-1276   SIC 5141
IMPORTATIONS CACHERES INC.   p 1334
6600 BOUL THIMENS, SAINT-LAURENT,
QC, H4S 1S5
SIC 5141
IMPORTATIONS CARA INC, LES   p 1383
805 BOUL FRONTENAC E, THETFORD
MINES, QC, G6G 6L5
(418) 335-3593   SIC 5099
IMPORTATIONS DE-RO-MA (1983) LTEE   p
1362
2055 BOUL DAGENAIS O, SAINTE-ROSE,
QC, H7L 5V1
(450) 629-7689   SIC 6111
IMPORTATIONS EXPORTATIONS LAM INC
p 1185
2115 BOUL SAINT-LAURENT, MONTREAL,
QC, H2X 2T5
(514) 843-3030   SIC 5199
IMPORTATIONS INTERNATIONALES BO-
CHITEX INC, LES   p
1340

225 MONTEE DE LIESSE, SAINT-
LAURENT, QC, H4T 1P5
(514) 381-3310   SIC 5137
IMPORTATIONS ITAL-PLUS   p 825
See ITAL-PLUS IMPORTS INC
IMPORTATIONS JACQUES FOURNIER
LTEE, LES   p 1305
2525 127E RUE, SAINT-GEORGES, QC,
G5Y 5G4
(418) 228-8594   SIC 5199
IMPORTATIONS JEREMY D. LIMITED   p
1179
9333 BOUL SAINT-LAURENT BUREAU
200, MONTREAL, QC, H2N 1P6
(514) 385-3898   SIC 2335
IMPORTATIONS KROPS INC   p 1163
9761 BOUL DES SCIENCES, MONTREAL,
QC, H1J 0A6
(514) 525-6464   SIC 5148
IMPORTATIONS MIRDO CANADA INC.,
LES   p 1223
6312 RUE NOTRE-DAME O, MONTREAL,
QC, H4C 1V4
(514) 932-1523   SIC 5199
IMPORTATIONS N & N INC, LES   p 1293
109 RUE D'AMSTERDAM, SAINT-
AUGUSTIN-DE-DESMAURES, QC, G3A
2V5
(418) 878-9555   SIC 5137
IMPORTATIONS NOSTALGIA MARKETING
& DESIGN LTEE   p 1160
20 AV DE LA COUR, MONTMAGNY, QC,
G5V 2V9
(418) 248-2600   SIC 5199
IMPORTATIONS RALLYE INC   p 1179
433 RUE CHABANEL O BUREAU 1000,
MONTREAL, QC, H2N 2J8
(514) 381-5941   SIC 5136
IMPORTATIONS S.M.D. LTEE, LES   p 1179
555 RUE CHABANEL O, MONTREAL, QC,
H2N 2H7
(514) 389-3474   SIC 5137
IMPORTATIONS SUNRISE TRADEX, LES   p
1348
See SUNRISE TRADEX CORPORATION
IMPORTATIONS THIBAULT LTEE   p 1373
165 RUE SAUVE, SHERBROOKE, QC, J1L
1L6
(819) 569-6212   SIC 5013
IMPORTATIONS VENETO LIMITEE   p 1334
2569 RUE DE MINIAC, SAINT-LAURENT,
QC, H4S 1E5
(514) 735-1898   SIC 5137
IMPORTATIONS-EXPORTATIONS BENISTI
INC   p 1226
1650 RUE CHABANEL O, MONTREAL, QC,
H4N 3M8
(514) 384-0140   SIC 5136
IMPORTS DRAGON   p 1061
See 9135-3904 QUEBEC INC
IMPRES PHARMA INC   p 533
1165 FRANKLIN BLVD SUITE J, CAM-
BRIDGE, ON, N1R 8E1
(866) 781-0491   SIC 5122
IMPRESSION ALLIANCE 9000 INC   p 1046
142 RUE DU PONT, AMQUI, QC, G5J 2R3
(418) 629-5256   SIC 2732
IMPRESSION PARAGRAPH INC   p 1334
8150 RTE TRANSCANADIENNE BUREAU
100, SAINT-LAURENT, QC, H4S 1M5
(514) 735-7770   SIC 2752
IMPRIMERIE D'ARTHABASKA INC, L'   p
1398
370 RUE GIROUARD, VICTORIAVILLE, QC,
G6P 5V2
SIC 2711
IMPRIMERIE DUMAINE INC   p 1313
5350 AV TRUDEAU, SAINT-HYACINTHE,
QC, J2S 7Y8
(450) 774-3536   SIC 2752
IMPRIMERIE L'EMPREINTE INC   p 1234
4177 BOUL INDUSTRIEL, MONTREAL,
QC, H7L 0G7
(514) 331-0741   SIC 2752

IMPRIMERIE LE LAURENTIEN   p 1160
See MARQUIS IMPRIMEUR INC
IMPRIMERIE MIRABEL   p 1152
See IMPRIMERIE QUEBECOR MEDIA
(2015) INC
IMPRIMERIE NORECOB INC   p 1322
340 RUE PRINCIPALE, SAINT-JULES, QC,
G0N 1R0
(418) 397-2233   SIC 2731
IMPRIMERIE PRESCOTT & RUSSELL p 619
See COMPAGNIE D'EDITION ANDRE PA-
QUETTE INC, LA
IMPRIMERIE QUEBECOR MEDIA (2015)
INC   p 1152
12800 RUE BRAULT, MIRABEL, QC, J7J
0W4
(514) 380-3600   SIC 2731
IMPRIMERIE SOLISCO INC   p 1366
120 10E RUE, SCOTT, QC, G0S 3G0
(418) 387-8908   SIC 2752
IMPRIMERIE STE-JULIE INC   p 1359
1851 RUE NOBEL, SAINTE-JULIE, QC, J3E
1Z6
(450) 649-5479   SIC 2672
IMPRIMERIES TRANSCONTINENTAL 2005
S.E.N.C   p 1146
750 RUE DEVEAULT, LOUISEVILLE, QC,
J5V 3C2
(819) 228-2766   SIC 7389
IMPRIMERIES TRANSCONTINENTAL 2005
S.E.N.C   p 1162
8000 AV BLAISE-PASCAL, MONTREAL,
QC, H1E 2S7
SIC 2752
IMPRIMERIES TRANSCONTINENTAL 2005
S.E.N.C.   p 835
2049 20TH ST E, OWEN SOUND, ON, N4K
5R2
(519) 376-8330   SIC 2732
IMPRIMERIES TRANSCONTINENTAL 2005
S.E.N.C.   p 1205
1 PLACE VILLE-MARIE BUREAU 3240,
MONTREAL, QC, H3B 0G1
(514) 954-4000   SIC 2752
IMPRIMERIES TRANSCONTINENTAL INCp
35
5516 5 ST SE, CALGARY, AB, T2H 1L3
(403) 258-3788   SIC 2752
IMPRIMERIES TRANSCONTINENTAL INCp
206
725 HAMPSTEAD CLOSE, DELTA, BC,
V3M 6R6
(604) 540-2333   SIC 2752
IMPRIMERIES TRANSCONTINENTAL INCp
372
1615 INKSTER BLVD, WINNIPEG, MB, R2X
1R2
(204) 988-9476   SIC 2752
IMPRIMERIES TRANSCONTINENTAL INCp
481
275 WELLINGTON ST E, AURORA, ON,
L4G 6J9
(905) 841-4400   SIC 2752
IMPRIMERIES TRANSCONTINENTAL INCp
835
1590 20TH ST E, OWEN SOUND, ON, N4K
5R2
(519) 371-5171   SIC 2752
IMPRIMERIES TRANSCONTINENTAL INCp
1027
100 ROYAL GROUP CRES UNIT B, WOOD-
BRIDGE, ON, L4H 1X9
(905) 663-1216   SIC 2711
IMPRIMERIES TRANSCONTINENTAL INCp
1049
10807 RUE MIRABEAU, ANJOU, QC, H1J
1T7
(514) 355-4134   SIC 2711
IMPRIMERIES TRANSCONTINENTAL INCp
1055
150 181E RUE, BEAUCEVILLE, QC, G5X
3P3
(418) 774-3367   SIC 2752
IMPRIMERIES TRANSCONTINENTAL INCp

1065
1603 BOUL DE MONTARVILLE, BOUCHERVILLE, QC, J4B 5Y2
(450) 655-2801 *SIC* 2752

IMPRIMERIES TRANSCONTINENTAL INC *p* 1132
999 AV 90E, LASALLE, QC, H8R 3A4
(514) 861-2411 *SIC* 2752

IMPRIMERIES TRANSCONTINENTAL INC *p* 1205
1 PLACE VILLE-MARIE UNITE 3240, MONTREAL, QC, H3B 3Y2
(514) 954-4000 *SIC* 2752

IMPRIMERIES TRANSCONTINENTAL INC *p* 1313
2700 BOUL CASAVANT O, SAINT-HYACINTHE, QC, J2S 7S4
(450) 773-0289 *SIC* 2752

IMPRIMERIES TRANSCONTINENTAL INC *p* 1373
4001 BOUL DE PORTLAND, SHERBROOKE, QC, J1L 1X9
(819) 563-4001 *SIC* 2752

IMPULSE TECHNOLOGIES LTD *p* 735
920 GANA CRT, MISSISSAUGA, ON, L5S 1Z4
(905) 564-9266 *SIC* 5051

IMS *p* 1006
See INTELLIGENT MECHATRONICS SYSTEMS INC.

IMS *p* 1334
See IDENTIFICATION MULTI SOLUTIONS INC

IMS INNOVATIVE MANUFACTURING SOURCE INC *p* 16
3855 64 AVE SE SUITE 3, CALGARY, AB, T2C 2V5
(403) 279-7702 *SIC* 3679

IMS SANTE CANADA INC *p* 1117
16720 RTE TRANSCANADIENNE, KIRKLAND, QC, H9H 5M3
(514) 428-6000 *SIC* 7363

IMT PARTNERSHIP *p* 636
530 MANITOU DR, KITCHENER, ON, N2C 1L3
(519) 748-0848 *SIC* 3444

IMT PARTNERSHIP *p* 846
837 REUTER RD, PORT COLBORNE, ON, L3K 5V7
(905) 834-7211 *SIC* 3444

IMT STANDEN'S LIMITED PARTNERSHIP *p* 35
1222 58 AVE SE, CALGARY, AB, T2H 2E9
(403) 258-7800 *SIC* 3493

IMW INDUSTRIES LTD *p* 197
44688 SOUTH SUMAS RD UNIT 610, CHILLIWACK, BC, V2R 5M3
(604) 795-9491 *SIC* 3491

IN STORE FOCUS *p* 574
50 QUEEN ELIZABETH BLVD, ETOBICOKE, ON, M8Z 1M1
SIC 7389

IN TEGRATION *p* 1341
See SUSTEMA INC

IN-HOUSE SOLUTIONS INC *p* 537
240 HOLIDAY INN DR UNIT A, CAMBRIDGE, ON, N3C 3X4
(519) 658-1471 *SIC* 5045

IN-PRO CLEANING SYSTEMS LTD *p* 671
570 HOOD RD UNIT 24, MARKHAM, ON, L3R 4G7
(905) 475-2020 *SIC* 7349

IN-SYNC *p* 922
See IN-SYNC CONSUMER INSIGHT CORP

IN-SYNC CONSUMER INSIGHT CORP *p* 922
90 EGLINTON AVE E SUITE 403, TORONTO, ON, M4P 2Y3
(416) 932-0921 *SIC* 8732

INA GRAFTON GAGE HOME OF TORONTO *p* 868
40 BELL ESTATE RD SUITE 402, SCARBOROUGH, ON, M1L 0E2

(416) 422-4890 *SIC* 8741

INA INTERNATIONAL LTD *p* 16
110250 QUARRY PARK BLVD SE, CALGARY, AB, T2C 3E7
(403) 717-1400 *SIC* 5091

INBOX MARKETER CORPORATION *p* 603
2 WYNDHAM ST N, GUELPH, ON, N1H 4E3
(519) 824-6664 *SIC* 4899

INC GROUP INC *p* 789
1185 CALEDONIA RD, NORTH YORK, ON, M6A 2X1
(416) 785-1771 *SIC* 5611

INC RESEARCH *p* 981
See INC RESEARCH TORONTO, INC

INC RESEARCH TORONTO, INC *p* 981
720 KING ST W 7TH FL, TORONTO, ON, M5V 2T3
(416) 963-9338 *SIC* 8733

INCA ONE GOLD CORP *p* 314
1140 WEST PENDER SUITE 850, VANCOUVER, BC, V6E 4G1
(604) 568-4877 *SIC* 3339

INCH FOODS INC *p* 616
20 RYMAL RD E, HAMILTON, ON, L9B 1T7
(905) 387-9282 *SIC* 5812

INCOGNITO SOFTWARE SYSTEMS INC *p* 298
375 WATER ST SUITE 500, VANCOUVER, BC, V6B 5C6
(604) 688-4332 *SIC* 7372

INCOHO *p* 829
1960 SCOTT ST SUITE 202C, OTTAWA, ON, K1Z 8L8
(613) 695-9800 *SIC* 7323

INCOM MANUFACTURING GROUP LTD *p* 477
1259 SANDHILL DR SUITE 76, ANCASTER, ON, L9G 4V5
(905) 648-0774 *SIC* 5085

INCORPORATED SYNOD OF THE DIOCESE OF TORONTO, THE *p* 939
135 ADELAIDE ST E, TORONTO, ON, M5C 1L8
(416) 363-6021 *SIC* 8661

INCORPORATION SYNOD DIOCESE OF OTTAWA *p* 825
71 BRONSON AVE, OTTAWA, ON, K1R 6G6
(613) 232-7124 *SIC* 8661

INCOSPEC COMMUNICATIONS INC *p* 1101
2065 RUE MICHELIN, FABREVILLE, QC, H7L 5B7
(450) 686-0033 *SIC* 5063

INCREDIBLE CLOTHING COMPANY, THE *p* 781
See NISE N KOSY INCORPORATED

INCURSION VOYAGE *p* 1278
See GROUPE INCURSION INC

IND DIAGNOSTIC INC *p* 206
1629 FOSTER'S WAY, DELTA, BC, V3M 6S7
SIC 3841

INDAL TECHNOLOGIES INC *p* 711
3570 HAWKESTONE RD, MISSISSAUGA, ON, L5C 2V8
(905) 275-5300 *SIC* 3728

INDALCO ALLOYS *p* 735
See LINCOLN ELECTRIC COMPANY OF CANADA LP

INDALCO ALLOYS, A DIV OF *p* 918
See LINCOLN ELECTRIC COMPANY OF CANADA LP

INDECK COMBUSTION CORPORATION *p* 1313
4300 AV BEAUDRY, SAINT-HYACINTHE, QC, J2S 8A5
(450) 774-5326 *SIC* 1711

INDEKA GROUP, THE *p* 798
See INDEKA IMPORTS LTD

INDEKA IMPORTS LTD *p* 798
2120 BRISTOL CIR, OAKVILLE, ON, L6H 5R3
(905) 829-3000 *SIC* 5139

INDEPENDANT PLANNING GROUP INC/GROUPE INDEPENDANT DE PLANIFICATION INC *p* 749
35 ANTARES DR, NEPEAN, ON, K2E 8B1
(613) 738-3388 *SIC* 6282

INDEPENDENT ADVOCACY INC *p* 92
10050 112 ST NW SUITE 201, EDMONTON, AB, T5K 2J1
(780) 452-9616 *SIC* 8399

INDEPENDENT ARMOURED TRANSPORT ATLANTIC INC *p* 457
287 LACEWOOD DR UNIT 103, HALIFAX, NS, B3M 3Y7
(902) 450-1396 *SIC* 7381

INDEPENDENT CORRUGATOR INC *p* 696
1177 AEROWOOD DR, MISSISSAUGA, ON, L4W 1Y6
(905) 629-2702 *SIC* 2653

INDEPENDENT COUNSELLING ENTERPRISES INC *p* 16
4888 72 AVE SE SUITE 200E, CALGARY, AB, T2C 3Z2
(403) 219-0503 *SIC* 8322

INDEPENDENT DOCKSIDE GRADING INC *p* 426
19 OLD PLACENTIA RD, MOUNT PEARL, NL, A1N 4P4
(709) 364-5473 *SIC* 7549

INDEPENDENT ELECTRIC SUPPLY INC *p* 874
48 MILNER AVE, SCARBOROUGH, ON, M1S 3P8
(416) 291-0048 *SIC* 5063

INDEPENDENT ELECTRICITY SYSTEM OPERATOR *p* 953
120 ADELAIDE ST W SUITE 1600, TORONTO, ON, M5H 1P9
(905) 855-6100 *SIC* 4911

INDEPENDENT FINANCIAL SERVICES LTD *p* 1428
1001 3RD AVE N, SASKATOON, SK, S7K 2K5
(306) 244-7385 *SIC* 6211

INDEPENDENT JEWELLERS *p* 102
See PUGWASH HOLDINGS LTD

INDEPENDENT MECHANICAL SUPPLY INC *p* 585
310 CARLINGVIEW DR, ETOBICOKE, ON, M9W 5G1
(416) 679-1048 *SIC* 5074

INDEPENDENT ORDER OF FORESTERS, THE *p* 779
789 DON MILLS RD SUITE 1200, NORTH YORK, ON, M3C 1T9
(416) 429-3000 *SIC* 6311

INDEPENDENT PAPER CONVERTERS *p* 600
See CAMERON INDUSTRIES INC

INDEPENDENT PLUMBING & HEATING SUPPLY *p* 213
See 13876 ENTERPRISES LTD

INDEPENDENT REHABILITATION SERVICES INC *p* 715
2155 LEANNE BLVD SUITE 240, MISSISSAUGA, ON, L5K 2K8
(905) 823-8895 *SIC* 6411

INDEPENDENT SECURITY SERVICES ATLANTIC (ISS) INC *p* 457
287 LACEWOOD DR UNIT 103, HALIFAX, NS, B3M 3Y7
(902) 450-1396 *SIC* 7381

INDEPENDENT SUPPLY COMPANY INC *p* 272
19505 56 AVE UNIT 104, SURREY, BC, V3S 6K3
(604) 298-4472 *SIC* 5078

INDEPENDENT SYSTEM OPERATOR *p* 51
2500-330 5 AVE SW, CALGARY, AB, T2P 0L4
(403) 539-2450 *SIC* 4911

INDEPENDENT TRADING GROUP (ITG) INC *p* 953
4 KING ST W SUITE 402, TORONTO, ON, M5H 1B6
(416) 941-0046 *SIC* 6211

INDEPENDENT WELL SERVICING LTD *p* 1406
477 DEVONIAN ST, ESTEVAN, SK, S4A 2A5
(306) 634-2336 *SIC* 1389

INDEX EXCHANGE INC *p* 791
74 WINGOLD AVE, NORTH YORK, ON, M6B 1P5
(416) 785-5908 *SIC* 7311

INDEXABLE CUTTING TOOLS OF CANADA LIMITED *p* 1011
66 CLARK ST, WELLAND, ON, L3B 5W6
(905) 735-8665 *SIC* 5251

INDIA BREWERIES INC *p* 942
1 YONGE ST SUITE 1801, TORONTO, ON, M5E 1W7
(416) 214-1855 *SIC* 5181

INDIAN HEAD CHRYSLER *p* 1408
See INDIAN HEAD CHRYSLER DODGE JEEP RAM LTD

INDIAN HEAD CHRYSLER DODGE JEEP RAM LTD *p* 1408
501 JOHNSTON AVE, INDIAN HEAD, SK, S0G 2K0
(306) 695-2254 *SIC* 5511

INDIAN HEAD CONSUMERS CO-OPERATIVE SOCIETY LTD *p* 434
50 CAROLINA AVE, STEPHENVILLE, NL, A2N 2S3
(709) 643-5675 *SIC* 5411

INDIANLIFE FOOD CORPORATION *p* 186
3835 2ND AVE, BURNABY, BC, V5C 3W7
(604) 205-9176 *SIC* 2032

INDIGO *p* 935
See INDIGO BOOKS & MUSIC INC

INDIGO BOOKS & MUSIC INC *p* 9
2555 32 ST NE SUITE 500, CALGARY, AB, T1Y 7J6
(403) 250-9171 *SIC* 5942

INDIGO BOOKS & MUSIC INC *p* 504
100 ALFRED KUEHNE BLVD, BRAMPTON, ON, L6T 4K4
(905) 789-1234 *SIC* 5192

INDIGO BOOKS & MUSIC INC *p* 929
55 BLOOR ST W, TORONTO, ON, M4W 1A5
(416) 925-3536 *SIC* 5942

INDIGO BOOKS & MUSIC INC *p* 935
220 YONGE ST SUITE 103, TORONTO, ON, M5B 2H1
(416) 591-3622 *SIC* 5942

INDIGO BOOKS & MUSIC INC *p* 981
620 KING ST W, TORONTO, ON, M5V 1M6
(416) 364-4499 *SIC* 5942

INDIGO BOOKS & MUSIC INC *p* 981
82 PETER ST SUITE 300, TORONTO, ON, M5V 2G5
(416) 598-8000 *SIC* 5942

INDIGO BOOKS & MUSIC INC *p* 1205
1171 RUE SAINTE-CATHERINE O BUREAU 777, MONTREAL, QC, H3B 1K4
SIC 5942

INDIGO PARC CANADA INC *p* 1205
1 PLACE VILLE-MARIE BUREAU 1130, MONTREAL, QC, H3B 2A7
(514) 874-1208 *SIC* 7299

INDIGO.CHAPTERS.CA *p* 981
See INDIGO BOOKS & MUSIC INC

INDIX30 *p* 1070
See IMMOBILIER CARBONLEO INC

INDO CANADIAN CENTRE *p* 23
826 EDMONTON TRAIL NE, CALGARY, AB, T2E 3J6
(403) 277-1459 *SIC* 6732

INDULBEC INC *p* 1086
3035 BOUL LE CARREFOUR, COTE SAINT-LUC, QC, H7T 1C8
(450) 687-5083 *SIC* 5149

INDULBEC INC p 1236
3625 BOUL CURE-LABELLE BUREAU 100, MONTREAL, QC, H7P 0A5
(450) 689-5726 *SIC* 5145
INDUSTRIAL ALLIANCE PACIFIC LIFE INSURANCE p 98
See INTEGRATED FINANCIAL GROUP INC
INDUSTRIAL AND COMMERCIAL BANK OF CHINA (CANADA) p 953
333 BAY ST SUITE 3710, TORONTO, ON, M5H 2R2
(416) 366-5588 *SIC* 6021
INDUSTRIAL AUTOMATION SYSTEMS, DIV OF p 789
See ONTOR LIMITED
INDUSTRIAL COLD MILLING, DIV OF p 395
See MILLER PAVING LIMITED
INDUSTRIAL CONSTRUCTION INVESTMENTS INC p 124
11850 28 ST NE, EDMONTON, AB, T6S 1G6
(780) 478-4688 *SIC* 1799
INDUSTRIAL DIVISION p 756
See SNAP-ON TOOLS OF CANADA LTD
INDUSTRIAL DIVISION p 1434
See ACKLANDS - GRAINGER INC
INDUSTRIAL ELECTRIC p 585
See INDUSTRIAL ELECTRICAL CONTRACTORS LIMITED
INDUSTRIAL ELECTRICAL CONTRACTORS LIMITED p 585
7 VULCAN ST, ETOBICOKE, ON, M9W 1L3
(416) 749-9782 *SIC* 1731
INDUSTRIAL EQUIPMENT MANUFACTURING LTD p 282
19433 96 AVE UNIT 109, SURREY, BC, V4N 4C4
(604) 513-9930 *SIC* 3535
INDUSTRIAL FABRICATION INC p 647
240 FIELDING RD, LIVELY, ON, P3Y 1L6
(705) 523-1621 *SIC* 3532
INDUSTRIAL FORESTRY SERVICE LTD p 249
1595 5TH AVE, PRINCE GEORGE, BC, V2L 3L9
(250) 564-4115 *SIC* 0851
INDUSTRIAL MACHINE & MFG. INC p 1428
3315 MINERS AVE, SASKATOON, SK, S7K 7K9
(306) 242-8400 *SIC* 3599
INDUSTRIAL METALS (2011) p 365
550 MESSIER ST, WINNIPEG, MB, R2J 0G5
(204) 233-1908 *SIC* 5093
INDUSTRIAL PARTS SERVICE p 1034
See 990731 ONTARIO INC
INDUSTRIAL PROPERTY SERVICES p 679
See YOUNG, PETER LIMITED
INDUSTRIAL ROOF CONSULTANTS (IRC) GROUP INC p 723
2121 ARGENTIA RD SUITE 401, MISSISSAUGA, ON, L5N 2X4
(905) 607-7244 *SIC* 8711
INDUSTRIAL RUBBER SUPPLY (1995) LTD p 372
55 DUNLOP AVE, WINNIPEG, MB, R2X 2V2
(204) 694-4444 *SIC* 2822
INDUSTRIAL SALES AND SERVICES p 426
See K&D PRATT GROUP INC
INDUSTRIAL SCAFFOLD SERVICES L.P. p 235
2076 BALSAM RD, NANAIMO, BC, V9X 1T5
(250) 591-3535 *SIC* 1799
INDUSTRIAL SECURITY LIMITED p 413
635 BAYSIDE DR, SAINT JOHN, NB, E2J 1B4
(506) 648-3060 *SIC* 7381
INDUSTRIAL SERVICES - SOUTH REGION p 80
See CLEARSTREAM ENERGY SERVICES LIMITED PARTNERSHIP
INDUSTRIAL SUPPLIES p 414
See SOURCE ATLANTIC LIMITED
INDUSTRIAL TRUCK SERVICE LTD p 365
89 DURAND RD, WINNIPEG, MB, R2J 3T1
(204) 663-9325 *SIC* 5084
INDUSTRIAL, DIV OF p 648
See CIE MCCORMICK CANADA CO., LA
INDUSTRIAL, PETROLEUM AND MINING SUPPLIES LIMITED p 474
395 WESTNEY RD S, AJAX, ON, L1S 6M6
(905) 686-4071 *SIC* 5085
INDUSTRIAL-ALLIANCE LIFE INS p 402
See YORK FINANCIAL SERVICES INC.
INDUSTRIAL-ALLIANCE LIFE REAL ESTATE SERVICES p 1275
See L'INDUSTRIELLE-ALLIANCE SERVICES IMMOBILIERS INC
INDUSTRIE DE PALETTES STANDARD (I.P.S.) INC p 1083
2400 RUE DE LIERRE, COTE SAINT-LUC, QC, H7G 4Y4
(450) 661-4000 *SIC* 7699
INDUSTRIE LEMIEUX INC p 1065
1401 RUE GRAHAM-BELL, BOUCHERVILLE, QC, J4B 6A1
(450) 655-7910 *SIC* 3444
INDUSTRIE T.L.T. INC p 1361
144 RUE LAROUCHE, SAINTE-MONIQUE-LAC-SAINT-JEA, QC, G0W 2T0
(418) 347-3355 *SIC* 2421
INDUSTRIEL RPT p 1147
See KANWAL INC
INDUSTRIELLE ALLIANCE ASSURANCE ET SERVICES FINANCE p 1344
See INDUSTRIELLE ALLIANCE, ASSURANCE ET SERVICES FINANCIERS INC
INDUSTRIELLE ALLIANCE VALEURS MOBILIERES INC p 1197
2200 AV MCGILL COLLEGE BUREAU 350, MONTREAL, QC, H3A 3P8
(514) 499-1066 *SIC* 6211
INDUSTRIELLE ALLIANCE, ASSURANCE AUTO ET HABITATION INC p 1270
925 GRANDE ALLEE O BUREAU 230, QUEBEC, QC, G1S 1C1
(418) 650-4600 *SIC* 6331
INDUSTRIELLE ALLIANCE, ASSURANCE ET SERVICES FINANCIERS INC p 898
1210 LASALLE BLVD, SUDBURY, ON, P3A 1Y5
(705) 524-5755 *SIC* 6411
INDUSTRIELLE ALLIANCE, ASSURANCE ET SERVICES FINANCIERS INC p 1071
9935 RUE DE CHATEAUNEUF STE 230, BROSSARD, QC, J4Z 3V4
(450) 672-6410 *SIC* 6411
INDUSTRIELLE ALLIANCE, ASSURANCE ET SERVICES FINANCIERS INC p 1270
1080 GRANDE ALLEE O, QUEBEC, QC, G1S 1C7
(418) 684-5000 *SIC* 6311
INDUSTRIELLE ALLIANCE, ASSURANCE ET SERVICES FINANCIERS INC p 1270
925 GRANDE ALLEE O BUREAU 200, QUEBEC, QC, G1S 4Z4
(418) 686-7738 *SIC* 6411
INDUSTRIELLE ALLIANCE, ASSURANCE ET SERVICES FINANCIERS INC p 1344
6555 BOUL METROPOLITAIN E BUREAU 403, SAINT-LEONARD, QC, H1P 3H3
(514) 324-3811 *SIC* 6411
INDUSTRIELS SIMONDS, LES p 1139
See WOOD FIBER CANADA INC
INDUSTRIES AMISCO LTEE, LES p 1121
33 5E RUE, L'ISLET, QC, G0R 2C0
(418) 247-5025 *SIC* 2514
INDUSTRIES APRIL INC, LES p 1247
12755 BOUL INDUSTRIEL, POINTE-AUX-TREMBLES, QC, H1A 4Z6
(514) 640-5355 *SIC* 3231
INDUSTRIES ASSOCIEES DE L'ACIER LTEE, LES p 1356
7140 132 RTE, SAINTE-CATHERINE, QC, J5C 1B6
(450) 632-1881 *SIC* 5093
INDUSTRIES BLAIS INC, LES p 1289
155 BOUL INDUSTRIEL, ROUYN-NORANDA, QC, J9X 6P2
(819) 764-3284 *SIC* 1542
INDUSTRIES BONIMETAL INC, LES p 1344
9225 RUE LE ROYER, SAINT-LEONARD, QC, H1P 3H7
(514) 325-6151 *SIC* 7389
INDUSTRIES BONNEVILLE LTEE, LES p 1057
601 RUE DE L'INDUSTRIE, BELOEIL, QC, J3G 0S5
(450) 464-1001 *SIC* 2452
INDUSTRIES BONNEVILLE LTEE, LES p 1355
316 RUE PRINCIPALE O, SAINTE-ANNE-DE-LA-ROCHELLE, QC, J0E 2B0
(450) 539-3100 *SIC* 2452
INDUSTRIES C.P.S. INC, LES p 1251
30 CH DE L'AVIATION, POINTE-CLAIRE, QC, H9R 5M6
(514) 695-0400 *SIC* 3728
INDUSTRIES CANATAL INC p 1383
2885 BOUL FRONTENAC E, THETFORD MINES, QC, G6G 6P6
(418) 338-6044 *SIC* 3441
INDUSTRIES CANZIP (2000) INC, LES p 1226
1615 RUE CHABANEL O, MONTREAL, QC, H4N 2T7
(514) 934-0331 *SIC* 3965
INDUSTRIES CAPITOL INC, LES p 1182
5795 AV DE GASPE, MONTREAL, QC, H2S 2X3
(514) 273-0451 *SIC* 3364
INDUSTRIES CARON (MEUBLES) INC, LES p 1160
45 4E RUE, MONTMAGNY, QC, G5V 3K8
(418) 248-0255 *SIC* 2434
INDUSTRIES CENDREX INC, LES p 1162
11303 26E AV, MONTREAL, QC, H1E 6N6
(514) 493-1489 *SIC* 3442
INDUSTRIES CENTURY INC, LES p 1156
5645 AV ROYALMOUNT, MONT-ROYAL, QC, H4P 2P9
(514) 842-3933 *SIC* 3645
INDUSTRIES CHEMI-3 INC p 1340
346 RUE ISABEY, SAINT-LAURENT, QC, H4T 1W1
(514) 365-0050 *SIC* 5169
INDUSTRIES COVER INC p 1049
9300 BOUL RAY-LAWSON, ANJOU, QC, H1J 1Y6
(514) 353-3880 *SIC* 2241
INDUSTRIES CRESSWELL INC p 1109
424 RUE SAINT-VALLIER, GRANBY, QC, J2G 7Y4
(450) 378-4611 *SIC* 3499
INDUSTRIES D'ACIER INOXYDABLE LIMITEE p 1066
1440 RUE GRAHAM-BELL, BOUCHERVILLE, QC, J4B 6H5
(450) 449-4000 *SIC* 3312
INDUSTRIES D'EMBALLAGES STARPAC LTEE, LES p 1247
12105 BOUL INDUSTRIEL, POINTE-AUX-TREMBLES, QC, H1B 5W4
(514) 645-5895 *SIC* 3081
INDUSTRIES DE CABLES D'ACIER LTEE p 1251
5501 RTE TRANSCANADIENNE, POINTE-CLAIRE, QC, H9R 1B7
(800) 565-5501 *SIC* 3496
INDUSTRIES DE CIMENT LA GUADELOUPE INC, LES p 1122
238 14E AV, LA GUADELOUPE, QC, G0M 1G0
(418) 459-3542 *SIC* 3272
INDUSTRIES DE FIBRE DE VERRE PREMIER INC, LES p 1240
3390 RUE DE MONT-JOLI, MONTREAL-NORD, QC, H1H 2X8
(514) 321-6410 *SIC* 1522
INDUSTRIES DE LAVAGE DENTEX INC, LES p 1247
12480 RUE APRIL, POINTE-AUX-TREMBLES, QC, H1B 5N5
SIC 7218
INDUSTRIES DE MAINTENANCE EMPIRE p 1132
See GDI SERVICES (QUEBEC) S.E.C.
INDUSTRIES DE MOULAGE POLYCELL INC, LES p 1109
448 RUE EDOUARD, GRANBY, QC, J2G 3Z3
(450) 378-9093 *SIC* 2821
INDUSTRIES DE MOULAGE POLYMAX INC, LES p 1109
454 RUE EDOUARD, GRANBY, QC, J2G 3Z3
(450) 378-9093 *SIC* 3086
INDUSTRIES DE MOULAGE POLYMAX, LES p 1111
See POLYFORM A.G.P. INC
INDUSTRIES DE MOULAGE POLYTECH INC, LES p 1109
454 RUE EDOUARD, GRANBY, QC, J2G 3Z3
(450) 378-9093 *SIC* 3081
INDUSTRIES DE PLASTIQUE TRANSCO LTEE, LES p 1156
8096 CH MONTVIEW, MONT-ROYAL, QC, H4P 2L7
(514) 733-9951 *SIC* 3081
INDUSTRIES DESORMEAU INC p 1344
8195 RUE PASCAL-GAGNON, SAINT-LEONARD, QC, H1P 1Y5
(514) 321-2432 *SIC* 5072
INDUSTRIES DETTSON INC p 1374
3400 BOUL INDUSTRIEL, SHERBROOKE, QC, J1L 1V8
(819) 346-8493 *SIC* 3634
INDUSTRIES DOREL INC, LES p 562
3305 LOYALIST ST, CORNWALL, ON, K6H 6W6
(613) 937-0711 *SIC* 2511
INDUSTRIES DOREL INC, LES p 1239
12345 BOUL ALBERT-HUDON BUREAU 100, MONTREAL-NORD, QC, H1G 3L1
(514) 323-1247 *SIC* 2511
INDUSTRIES DOREL INC, LES p 1402
1255 AV GREENE BUREAU 300, WEST-MOUNT, QC, H3Z 2A4
(514) 934-3034 *SIC* 2512
INDUSTRIES ELIRA INC p 1356
1600 RUE JEAN-LACHAINE, SAINTE-CATHERINE, QC, J5C 1C2
(450) 638-4694 *SIC* 5084
INDUSTRIES ET EQUIPEMENTS LALIBERTE LTEE, LES p 1356
550 RTE BEGIN, SAINTE-CLAIRE, QC, G0R 2V0
(418) 883-3338 *SIC* 3523
INDUSTRIES F.M. INC p 1109
176 RUE FRONTENAC, GRANBY, QC, J2G 7R4
(450) 378-0148 *SIC* 5199
INDUSTRIES FORESTEEL INC, LES p 1162
9225 BOUL HENRI-BOURASSA E, MONTREAL, QC, H1E 1P6
(514) 645-9251 *SIC* 7692
INDUSTRIES FOURNIER INC, LES p 1383
3787 BOUL FRONTENAC O, THETFORD MINES, QC, G6H 2B5
(418) 423-4241 *SIC* 8711
INDUSTRIES GARANTIES LIMITEE, LES p 1156
5420 RUE PARE, MONT-ROYAL, QC, H4P

1R3
(514) 342-3400 *SIC* 1711
INDUSTRIES GENO INC, LES *p 1334*
5750 CH SAINT-FRANCOIS, SAINT-LAURENT, QC, H4S 1B7
(514) 331-4915 *SIC* 5085
INDUSTRIES GODDARD LTEE *p 1380*
2460 BOUL DES ENTREPRISES, TERREBONNE, QC, J6X 4J8
(514) 353-9141 *SIC* 6712
INDUSTRIES GOODWILL RENAISSANCE MONTREAL INC *p 1181*
7250 BOUL SAINT-LAURENT, MONTREAL, QC, H2R 2X9
(514) 276-3626 *SIC* 5399
INDUSTRIES GRC INC, LES *p 1115*
2681 RUE DE LA SALLE, JONQUIERE, QC, G7S 2A8
(418) 548-1171 *SIC* 1761
INDUSTRIES GRC INC, LES *p 1259*
10C COTE DE LA CANOTERIE BUREAU 7, QUEBEC, QC, G1K 3X4
(418) 692-1112 *SIC* 3444
INDUSTRIES HAGEN LTEE *p 1334*
3235 RUE GUENETTE, SAINT-LAURENT, QC, H4S 1N2
(514) 331-2818 *SIC* 2819
INDUSTRIES HARNOIS INC, LES *p 1353*
1044 RUE PRINCIPALE, SAINT-THOMAS, QC, J0K 3L0
(450) 756-1041 *SIC* 3448
INDUSTRIES HYPERSHELL INC *p 1370*
740 RUE GALT O BUREAU 401, SHERBROOKE, QC, J1H 1Z3
(819) 822-3890 *SIC* 7389
INDUSTRIES INTREPID *p 1374*
See PRO-PAR INC
INDUSTRIES J SUSS INC, LES *p 1397*
3865 RUE LESAGE, VERDUN, QC, H4G 1A3
(514) 769-5666 *SIC* 2431
INDUSTRIES J. HAMELIN INC, LES *p 1320*
690 BOUL ROLAND-GODARD, SAINT-JEROME, QC, J7Y 4C5
(450) 431-3221 *SIC* 3553
INDUSTRIES JAM LTEE, LES *p 1053*
21000 AUT TRANSCANADIENNE, BAIE-D'URFE, QC, H9X 4B7
(514) 457-2555 *SIC* 5099
INDUSTRIES JOHN LEWIS *p 1124*
See INDUSTRIES JOHN LEWIS LTEE
INDUSTRIES JOHN LEWIS LTEE *p 1049*
8545 RUE JULES-LEGER, ANJOU, QC, H1J 1A8
(514) 352-2950 *SIC* 2499
INDUSTRIES JOHN LEWIS LTEE *p 1124*
1101 BOUL DUCHARME, LA TUQUE, QC, G9X 3C3
(819) 523-7636 *SIC* 2499
INDUSTRIES KINGSTON LTEE, LES *p 1132*
9100 RUE ELMSLIE, LASALLE, QC, H8R 1V6
(514) 365-1642 *SIC* 8741
INDUSTRIES LASSONDE INC *p 1288*
705 RUE PRINCIPALE, ROUGEMONT, QC, J0L 1M0
(450) 469-4926 *SIC* 2033
INDUSTRIES LASSONDE INC *p 1288*
755 RUE PRINCIPALE, ROUGEMONT, QC, J0L 1M0
(450) 469-4926 *SIC* 6712
INDUSTRIES LECO INC *p 1329*
3235 RUE SARTELON, SAINT-LAURENT, QC, H4R 1E9
(514) 332-0535 *SIC* 2821
INDUSTRIES LEESTA LTEE, LES *p 1251*
6 AV DU PLATEAU, POINTE-CLAIRE, QC, H9R 5W2
(514) 694-3930 *SIC* 3728
INDUSTRIES LONGCHAMPS LTEE, LES *p 1299*
25 BOUL SAINT-JOSEPH, SAINT-EPHREM-DE-BEAUCE, QC, G0M 1R0
(418) 484-2080 *SIC* 7389

INDUSTRIES LOOP, LES *p 1381*
See LOOP INDUSTRIES, INC
INDUSTRIES LYNX INC *p 1323*
175 RUE UPPER EDISON, SAINT-LAMBERT, QC, J4R 2R3
(514) 866-1068 *SIC* 3442
INDUSTRIES LYSTER INC *p 1147*
2555 RUE BECANCOUR, LYSTER, QC, G0S 1V0
SIC 3369
INDUSTRIES M.K.E. (1984) INC, LES *p 1072*
183 BOUL MONTCALM N, CANDIAC, QC, J5R 3L6
(450) 659-6531 *SIC* 3589
INDUSTRIES MACHINEX INC *p 1246*
2121 RUE OLIVIER, PLESSISVILLE, QC, G6L 3G9
(819) 362-3281 *SIC* 3559
INDUSTRIES MAIBEC *p 1138*
See MAIBEC INC
INDUSTRIES MAILHOT INC *p 1314*
2721 RANG SAINT-JACQUES, SAINT-JACQUES, QC, J0K 2R0
(450) 477-6222 *SIC* 3569
INDUSTRIES MAILHOT INC *p 1314*
2721 RANG SAINT-JACQUES, SAINT-JACQUES, QC, J0K 2R0
(450) 839-3663 *SIC* 3569
INDUSTRIES MAJESTIC (CANADA) LTEE, LES *p 1334*
5905 RUE KIERAN, SAINT-LAURENT, QC, H4S 0A3
(514) 727-2000 *SIC* 5136
INDUSTRIES MANUFACTURIERES MEGANTIC DIV. *p 1125*
See MASONITE INTERNATIONAL CORPORATION
INDUSTRIES MARINE SEAGULF INC *p 1211*
815 RUE MILL, MONTREAL, QC, H3C 1Y5
(514) 935-6933 *SIC* 5088
INDUSTRIES MIDWAY LTEE *p 1170*
8270 BOUL PIE-IX, MONTREAL, QC, H1Z 3T6
(514) 722-1122 *SIC* 5136
INDUSTRIES MONDIALES ARMSTRONG CANADA LTEE, LES *p 1241*
1595 BOUL DANIEL-JOHNSON BUREAU 300, MONTREAL-OUEST, QC, H7V 4C2
(450) 902-3900 *SIC* 3996
INDUSTRIES N.R.C. INC *p 1350*
2430 RUE PRINCIPALE E BUREAU 160, SAINT-PAUL-D'ABBOTSFORD, QC, J0E 1A0
(450) 379-5796 *SIC* 3799
INDUSTRIES OCEAN INC *p 1259*
105 RUE ABRAHAM-MARTIN BUREAU 500, QUEBEC, QC, G1K 8N1
(418) 438-2745 *SIC* 3731
INDUSTRIES PAULYMARK INC *p 1288*
340 LA GRANDE-CAROLINE, ROUGEMONT, QC, J0L 1M0
(514) 861-0180 *SIC* 2679
INDUSTRIES POLYKAR INC, LES *p 1334*
5637 RUE KIERAN, SAINT-LAURENT, QC, H4S 0A3
(514) 335-0059 *SIC* 2673
INDUSTRIES PRO-TAC INC, LES *p 1296*
445 RUE JEAN-CLERMONT, SAINT-CELESTIN, QC, J0C 1G0
(819) 229-1288 *SIC* 3053
INDUSTRIES RAD INC *p 1344*
6363 BOUL DES GRANDES-PRAIRIES, SAINT-LEONARD, QC, H1P 1A5
(418) 228-8934 *SIC* 3751
INDUSTRIES RAINVILLE INC *p 1316*
175 RTE 104, SAINT-JEAN-SUR-RICHELIEU, QC, J2X 5T7
(450) 347-5521 *SIC* 5084
INDUSTRIES REHAU INC *p 1053*
625 AV LEE, BAIE-D'URFE, QC, H9X 3S3
(514) 905-0345 *SIC* 3089
INDUSTRIES ROCAND, LES *p 1265*
See 9184-2518 QUEBEC INC

INDUSTRIES RONDI INC, LES *p 1247*
12425 BOUL INDUSTRIEL, POINTE-AUX-TREMBLES, QC, H1B 5M7
(514) 640-0888 *SIC* 3089
INDUSTRIES SANIMAX INC *p 1161*
9900 BOUL MAURICE-DUPLESSIS, MONTREAL, QC, H1C 1G1
(514) 648-3000 *SIC* 6712
INDUSTRIES SEFINA LTEE, LES *p 1340*
750 RUE MCARTHUR, SAINT-LAURENT, QC, H4T 1W2
(514) 735-5911 *SIC* 2431
INDUSTRIES SHOW CANADA INC, LES *p 1231*
5555 RUE MAURICE-CULLEN, MONTREAL, QC, H7C 2T8
(450) 664-5155 *SIC* 8712
INDUSTRIES SPECTRA PREMIUM INC, LES *p 896*
533 ROMEO ST S, STRATFORD, ON, N5A 4V3
(519) 275-3802 *SIC* 3714
INDUSTRIES SPECTRA PREMIUM, LES *p 1066*
1421 RUE AMPERE, BOUCHERVILLE, QC, J4B 5Z5
(450) 641-3090 *SIC* 3433
INDUSTRIES SPECTRA PREMIUM, LES *p 1363*
1313 CHOMEDEY (A-13) E, SAINTE-ROSE, QC, H7W 5L7
(450) 681-1313 *SIC* 3433
INDUSTRIES SPLEND'OR LTEE, LES *p 1170*
8660 8E AV, MONTREAL, QC, H1Z 2W8
SIC 2253
INDUSTRIES STEMA-PRO INC, LES *p 1369*
2699 5E AV BUREAU 26, SHAWINIGAN, QC, G9T 2P7
(819) 533-4756 *SIC* 2511
INDUSTRIES TANGUAY *p 1065*
See GROUPE CANAM INC
INDUSTRIES TETRA TECH *p 1167*
See TETRA TECH INDUSTRIES INC
INDUSTRIES THERMAFIX ABITIBI *p 1377*
See THERMAFIX A. J. INC
INDUSTRIES THERMOPLUS AIR INC, LES *p 1321*
262 RUE SCOTT, SAINT-JEROME, QC, J7Z 1H1
(450) 436-7555 *SIC* 5075
INDUSTRIES TOURNEBO INC, LES *p 1359*
3611 346 RTE, SAINTE-JULIENNE, QC, J0K 2T0
(450) 831-3229 *SIC* 3593
INDUSTRIES TROVAC LIMITEE, LES *p 1059*
3 RUE MARCEL-AYOTTE, BLAINVILLE, QC, J7C 5L7
(450) 434-2233 *SIC* 3635
INDUSTRIES UNICOR INC *p 1049*
9151 RUE CLAVEAU, ANJOU, QC, H1J 2C8
(514) 353-0857 *SIC* 3089
INDUSTRIES VALTECH *p 1366*
See VALTECH FABRICATION INC
INDUSTRIES WAJAX *p 728*
See WAJAX LIMITED
INDUSTRY TRAINING AUTHORITY *p 262*
8100 GRANVILLE AVE UNIT 800, RICHMOND, BC, V6Y 3T6
(604) 214-8700 *SIC* 7699
INEOS CANADA COMPANY *p 153*
HWY 815, RED DEER, AB, T4N 6A1
(403) 314-4500 *SIC* 6712
INEOS CANADA PARTNERSHIP *p 154*
GD, RED DEER, AB, T4N 6A1
(403) 314-4500 *SIC* 2869
INEOS STYRENICS LTD *p 860*
872 TASHMOO AVE, SARNIA, ON, N7T 7H5
(519) 339-7339 *SIC* 2865
INEOS STYROLUTION CANADA LTD *p 860*
872 TASHMOO AVE, SARNIA, ON, N7T 8A3

(226) 784-2872 *SIC* 2869
INETCO SYSTEMS LTD *p 186*
4664 LOUGHEED HWY SUITE 295, BURNABY, BC, V5C 5T5
(604) 451-1567 *SIC* 5045
INFANCY AND EARLY CHILDHOOD SERVICES *p 912*
See COCHRANE TEMISKAMING RESOURCE CENTRE
INFASCO DISTRIBUTION *p 1149*
See IFASTGROUPE 2004 L.P.
INFECTIO DIAGNOSTIC INC *p 1267*
2555 BOUL DU PARC-TECHNOLOGIQUE, QUEBEC, QC, G1P 4S5
(418) 681-4343 *SIC* 3842
INFINITE CABLES INC *p 671*
3993 14TH AVE, MARKHAM, ON, L3R 4Z6
(905) 477-4433 *SIC* 5045
INFINITE OUTSOURCING SOLUTIONS INC *p 997*
2100 LAWRENCE AVE W UNIT 202A, TORONTO, ON, M9N 3W3
(647) 247-5490 *SIC* 7371
INFINITI LAVAL INC *p 1086*
1950 BOUL CHOMEDEY, COTE SAINT-LUC, QC, H7T 2W3
(514) 382-8550 *SIC* 5511
INFINITI QUEBEC INC *p 1275*
2766 RUE EINSTEIN, QUEBEC, QC, G1X 4N8
(418) 658-3535 *SIC* 5511
INFINITY & ASSOCIATES LLP / INC *p 991*
36 LISGAR ST SUITE 623W, TORONTO, ON, M6J 0C7
(888) 508-6277 *SIC* 7389
INFINITY RUBBER TECHNOLOGY GROUP INC *p 1011*
100 KENNEDY ST, WELLAND, ON, L3B 0B4
(905) 735-6366 *SIC* 3069
INFINITY SPORTS GROUP LTD, THE *p 229*
27452 52 AVE, LANGLEY, BC, V4W 4B2
SIC 5091
INFINUM CAPITAL CORPORATION *p 934*
106 FRONT ST E SUITE 200, TORONTO, ON, M5A 1E1
SIC 6211
INFINUM DEZINE *p 1335*
See QUICKSTYLE INDUSTRIES INC
INFIRMERIE NOTRE DAME DE BON SECOURS *p 1221*
See SOEURS DE LA CONGREGATION DE NOTRE-DAME, LES
INFIRMIERES DE L'HUMANITE *p 1286*
4 RUE DES ORMES, RIVIERE-DU-LOUP, QC, G5R 4W7
SIC 8062
INFLAMAX RESEARCH LIMITED *p 696*
1310 FEWSTER DR, MISSISSAUGA, ON, L4W 1A4
(905) 282-1808 *SIC* 8731
INFLIGHT CANADA INC *p 1334*
4650 BOUL DE LA COTE-VERTU BUREAU 200, SAINT-LAURENT, QC, H4S 1C7
(514) 331-9771 *SIC* 1799
INFLO SOLUTIONS *p 1267*
See OPSENS INC
INFO FINANCIAL CONSULTING GROUP INC *p 852*
350 HIGHWAY 7 E SUITE PH8, RICHMOND HILL, ON, L4B 3N2
(905) 886-8811 *SIC* 6722
INFO-FLEX *p 1048*
See COFORCE INC
INFO-SANTE CLSC *p 1355*
See CENTRE DE SANTE ET DE SERVICES SOCIAUX DE LA HAUTE-GASPESIE
INFO-TECH RESEARCH GROUP INC *p 654*
345 RIDOUT ST N, LONDON, ON, N6A 2N8
(519) 432-3550 *SIC* 7299
INFODEV *p 1264*
See INFODEV ELECTRONIC DESIGNERS INTERNATIONAL INC

INFODEV ELECTRONIC DESIGNERS IN-TERNATIONAL INC *p*
1264
1995 RUE FRANK-CARREL BUREAU 202, QUEBEC, QC, G1N 4H9
(418) 681-3539 *SIC 3571*
INFOLASER *p 1047*
See 9019-4002 QUEBEC INC
INFOR (CANADA), LTD *p 779*
250 FERRAND DR SUITE 1200, NORTH YORK, ON, M3C 3G8
(416) 421-6700 *SIC 7372*
INFORM BROKERAGE INC *p 184*
2286 HOLDOM AVE, BURNABY, BC, V5B 4Y5
(604) 324-0565 *SIC 5141*
INFORMATION BALANCE INC *p 774*
4141 YONGE ST SUITE 205, NORTH YORK, ON, M2P 2A8
(416) 962-5235 *SIC 7379*
INFORMATION BUILDERS (CANADA) INC *p*
953
150 YORK ST SUITE 1000, TORONTO, ON, M5H 3S5
(416) 364-0349 *SIC 5045*
INFORMATION COMMUNICATION SER-VICES (ICS) INC *p*
574
288 JUDSON ST SUITE 1, ETOBICOKE, ON, M8Z 5T6
SIC 7389
INFORMATION COMMUNICATION SER-VICES (ICS) INC *p*
585
96 DISCO RD, ETOBICOKE, ON, M9W 0A3
(416) 642-2477 *SIC 4212*
INFORMATION COMMUNICATION SER-VICES (ICS) INC *p*
874
80 COWDRAY CRT, SCARBOROUGH, ON, M1S 4N1
(416) 642-2477 *SIC 7389*
INFORMATION COMMUNICATION SER-VICES (ICS) INC *p*
1094
81 AV LINDSAY, DORVAL, QC, H9P 2S6
(514) 636-9744 *SIC 4212*
INFORMATION SERVICES AND TECHNOL-OGY *p*
118
See GOVERNORS OF THE UNIVERSITY OF ALBERTA, THE
INFORMATION SERVICES CORPORATION *p 1421*
10 RESEARCH DR SUITE 300, REGINA, SK, S4S 7J7
(306) 787-8179 *SIC 6519*
INFORMATION SERVICES CORPORATION OF SASKATCHEWAN *p 1421*
See ISC SASKATCHEWAN INC
INFORMATION TECHNOLOGY UNIT, COL-LEGE OF MEDICINE *p*
1434
See UNIVERSITY OF SASKATCHEWAN
INFORMATIQUE COTE, COULOMBE INC *p*
1276
3770 RUE JEAN-MARCHAND, QUEBEC, QC, G2C 1Y6
(418) 628-2100 *SIC 7371*
INFORMATIQUE INSIGHT DIRECT *p 1220*
See INSIGHT DIRECT CANADA, INC
INFORMATIQUE PRO-CONTACT INC *p*
1277
1000 AV SAINT-JEAN-BAPTISTE BUREAU 111, QUEBEC, QC, G2E 5G5
(418) 871-1622 *SIC 5045*
INFOROUTE SANTE DU CANADA INC *p*
953
150 KING ST W SUITE 1308, TORONTO, ON, M5H 1J9
(416) 979-4606 *SIC 7338*
INFOROUTE SANTE DU CANADA INC *p*
1197
1000 RUE SHERBROOKE O BUREAU

1200, MONTREAL, QC, H3A 3G4
(514) 868-0550 *SIC 7338*
INFOSAT COMMUNICATIONS LP *p 70*
3130 114 AVE SE, CALGARY, AB, T2Z 3V6
(403) 543-8188 *SIC 5063*
INFOSTREAM, DIV OF *p 851*
See COMPAGNIE DE TELEPHONE BELL DU CANADA OU BELL CANADA, LA
INFOSYS LIMITED *p 51*
888 3 ST SW SUITE 1000, CALGARY, AB, T2P 5C5
(403) 444-6896 *SIC 7379*
INFOSYS LIMITED *p 772*
5140 YONGE ST SUITE 1400, NORTH YORK, ON, M2N 6L7
(416) 224-7400 *SIC 7379*
INFOTEK CONSULTING SERVICES INC *p*
953
80 RICHMOND ST W SUITE 400, TORONTO, ON, M5H 2A4
(416) 365-0337 *SIC 7379*
INFRA PIPE SOLUTIONS LTD *p 723*
6507 MISSISSAUGA RD UNIT A, MISSIS-SAUGA, ON, L5N 1A6
(905) 858-0206 *SIC 3498*
INFRA PIPE SOLUTIONS LTD *p 1425*
348 EDSON ST, SASKATOON, SK, S7J 0P9
(306) 242-0755 *SIC 3498*
INFRA-PSP CANADA INC *p 1205*
1250 BOUL RENE-LEVESQUE O BUREAU 1400, MONTREAL, QC, H3B 4W8
(514) 937-2772 *SIC 6282*
INFRASOURCE SERVICES *p 598*
21 CARDICO DR, GORMLEY, ON, L0H 1G0
SIC 4922
INFRASTRUCTURE HEALTH AND SAFETY ASSOCIATION *p*
5110 CREEKBANK RD SUITE 400, MISSIS-SAUGA, ON, L4W 0A1
(416) 674-2726 *SIC 8611*
INFRASTRUCTURE ONTARIO *p 946*
See ONTARIO INFRASTRUCTURE AND LANDS CORPORATION
INFUSION DEVELOPMENT CANADA *p 981*
See INFUSION DEVELOPMENT INC
INFUSION DEVELOPMENT INC *p 981*
200 WELLINGTON ST W, TORONTO, ON, M5V 3C7
(416) 593-6595 *SIC 7379*
INFYNIA.COM INC *p 1340*
170 MONTEE DE LIESSE, SAINT-LAURENT, QC, H4T 1N6
(514) 332-1999 *SIC 7371*
ING & MCKEE INSURANCE LTD *p 157*
2830 BREMNER AVE, RED DEER, AB, T4R 1M9
(403) 346-5547 *SIC 6411*
ING DIRECT *p 820*
See INTACT INSURANCE COMPANY
ING HALIFAX *p 654*
See INTACT INSURANCE COMPANY
ING INSURANCE *p 286*
See INTACT INSURANCE COMPANY
INGADALE INDUSTRIES INC *p 872*
48 CROCKFORD BLVD, SCARBOROUGH, ON, M1R 3C3
(416) 752-6266 *SIC 3599*
INGENIA POLYMERS CORP *p 517*
565 GREENWICH ST, BRANTFORD, ON, N3T 5M2
(519) 758-8941 *SIC 2821*
INGENIA POLYMERS CORP *p 767*
200 YORKLAND BLVD SUITE 605, NORTH YORK, ON, M2J 5C1
(416) 920-8100 *SIC 2821*
INGENIA TECHNOLOGIES INC *p 1152*
18101 RUE J.A.BOMBARDIER, MIRABEL, QC, J7J 2H8
(450) 979-1212 *SIC 3585*
INGENICO CANADA LTD *p 696*
5180 ORBITOR DR 2ND FL, MISSIS-SAUGA, ON, L4W 5L9
(905) 212-9464 *SIC 3578*
INGENICO GROUP *p 696*

See INGENICO CANADA LTD
INGENIERIE WILTECH FLOW *p 1070*
See EQUIPEMENTS CONTRO VALVE INC, LES
INGENIO, FILALE DE LOTO-QUEBEC INC *p*
1197
500 RUE SHERBROOKE O BUREAU 2000, MONTREAL, QC, H3A 3G6
(514) 282-0210 *SIC 8732*
INGENIOUS PACKAGING, INC *p 865*
999 PROGRESS AVE, SCARBOROUGH, ON, M1B 6J1
(416) 292-6600 *SIC 2672*
INGENIUM GROUP INC *p 585*
2 INTERNATIONAL BLVD, ETOBICOKE, ON, M9W 1A2
(416) 675-5950 *SIC 8712*
INGENUITY DEVELOPMENT INC *p 717*
3800A LAIRD RD UNIT 1, MISSISSAUGA, ON, L5L 0B2
(905) 569-2624 *SIC 1541*
INGENUITY GROUP *p 717*
See INGENUITY DEVELOPMENT INC
INGERSOL TILLAGE GROUP *p 611*
See NATT TOOLS GROUP INC
INGERSOLL AXLES *p 636*
See IMT PARTNERSHIP
INGERSOLL DISTRICT COLLEGIATE IN-STITUTE *p*
622
See THAMES VALLEY DISTRICT SCHOOL BOARD
INGERSOLL PAPER BOX CO. LIMITED *p*
621
327 KING ST W, INGERSOLL, ON, N5C 2K9
(519) 485-1830 *SIC 2657*
INGERSOLL RAND SECURITIES TECH-NOLOGIES *p*
712
See ALLEGION CANADA INC
INGERSOLL SUPPORT SERVICES INC *p*
621
148 THAMES ST S, INGERSOLL, ON, N5C 2T4
(519) 425-0005 *SIC 8361*
INGLASCO INC *p 1372*
2745 RUE DE LA SHERWOOD, SHER-BROOKE, QC, J1K 1E1
(819) 563-2205 *SIC 3949*
INGLE INTERNATIONAL INC. *p 981*
460 RICHMOND ST W SUITE 100, TORONTO, ON, M5V 1Y1
(416) 730-8488 *SIC 6141*
INGLESIDE FARM *p 1038*
See ROBINSON, ERIC C. INC
INGLIS, D.W. LIMITED *p 723*
6670 MEADOWVALE TOWN CENTRE CIR, MISSISSAUGA, ON, L5N 4B7
(905) 821-1087 *SIC 5531*
INGRAM MICRO CANADA *p 731*
See INGRAM MICRO INC
INGRAM MICRO INC *p 258*
7451 NELSON RD, RICHMOND, BC, V6W 1L7
(604) 276-8357 *SIC 5045*
INGRAM MICRO INC *p 731*
55 STANDISH CRT SUITE 1, MISSIS-SAUGA, ON, L5R 4A1
(905) 755-5000 *SIC 5045*
INGREDIENTS ALIMENTAIRES BSA INC, LES *p 1344*
6005 BOUL COUTURE, SAINT-LEONARD, QC, H1P 3E1
(514) 852-2719 *SIC 2099*
INGREDIENTS PLUS DISTRIBUTION INC *p*
245
585 SEABORNE AVE UNIT 2120, PORT COQUITLAM, BC, V3B 0M3
(604) 468-7146 *SIC 5153*
INGREDIENTS PROFESSIONNELS *p 1309*
See PRO INGREDIENTS INC
INGREDIENTS QUADRA *p 1395*
See QUADRA CHIMIE LTEE

INGREDION CANADA CORPORATION *p*
710
90 BURNHAMTHORPE RD W UNIT 1600, MISSISSAUGA, ON, L5B 0H9
(905) 281-7950 *SIC 2046*
INK QUEST *p 104*
See 605494 ALBERTA LTD
INKAS ARMORED VEHICLE MANUFAC-TURING *p*
792
See 2000007 ONTARIO INC
INKAS CORPORATION *p 793*
3605 WESTON RD, NORTH YORK, ON, M9L 1V7
(416) 645-8725 *SIC 5411*
INKAS FINANCE CORP *p 917*
2192 GERRARD ST E, TORONTO, ON, M4E 2C7
(416) 686-4587 *SIC 8742*
INLAND AND MARINE SALVAGE LIMITED *p*
902
4408 YORK RD SUITE 32, SUTTON WEST, ON, L0E 1R0
(905) 473-2600 *SIC 4953*
INLAND AUDIO VISUAL LIMITED *p 378*
422 LUCAS AVE, WINNIPEG, MB, R3C 2E6
(204) 786-6521 *SIC 1731*
INLAND AUTO CENTRE LTD *p 204*
11600 8 ST, DAWSON CREEK, BC, V1G 4R7
(250) 782-5507 *SIC 5511*
INLAND AV *p 378*
See INLAND AUDIO VISUAL LIMITED
INLAND CONTRACTING LTD *p 243*
716 OKANAGAN AVE E, PENTICTON, BC, V2A 3K6
(250) 492-2626 *SIC 1611*
INLAND EQUIPMENT SALES *p 243*
See INLAND CONTRACTING LTD
INLAND INDUSTRIAL SUPPLY LTD *p 120*
9949 29A AVE NW, EDMONTON, AB, T6N 1A9
(780) 413-0029 *SIC 5085*
INLAND IRON & METALS *p 902*
See INLAND AND MARINE SALVAGE LIM-ITED
INLAND KENWORTH LTD *p 186*
2482 DOUGLAS RD, BURNABY, BC, V5C 6C9
(604) 291-6021 *SIC 5082*
INLAND PACIFIC RESOURCES INC *p 314*
1188 GEORGIA ST W SUITE 1160, VAN-COUVER, BC, V6E 4A2
(604) 697-6700 *SIC 1623*
INLAND PACLEASE *p 186*
See INLAND KENWORTH LTD
INLAND PLASTICS LTD *p 160*
201 CENTRE ST, ROSEDALE STATION, AB, T0J 2V0
(403) 823-6252 *SIC 2394*
INLAND STEEL PRODUCTS INC *p 1432*
1520 17TH ST W, SASKATOON, SK, S7M 4A4
(306) 652-5353 *SIC 5211*
INLAND TECHNOLOGIES CANADA IN-CORPORATED *p*
469
14 QUEEN ST, TRURO, NS, B2N 2A8
(902) 895-6346 *SIC 4581*
INLAND/PACIFIC DISTRIBUTORS *p 486*
See BRS CANADA ACQUISITION INC
INLET ELECTRIC LTD *p 201*
169 GOLDEN DR UNIT 2, COQUITLAM, BC, V3K 6T1
(604) 464-3133 *SIC 1731*
INLINE FIBERGLASS LTD *p 585*
30 CONSTELLATION CRT, ETOBICOKE, ON, M9W 1K1
(416) 679-1171 *SIC 3299*
INLINE NURSERIES (2010) INC *p 198*
49944 YALE RD, CHILLIWACK, BC, V4Z 0B3
(604) 794-7096 *SIC 5193*
INMAR PROMOTIONS - CANADA INC. *p*

414
661 MILLIDGE AVE, SAINT JOHN, NB, E2K 2N7
(506) 632-1400   *SIC* 7389
INMARCA HOLDING INC   *p* 706
51 VILLAGE CENTRE PL UNIT 7, MISSISSAUGA, ON, L4Z 1V9
(416) 471-1914   *SIC* 5039
INMARSAT SOLUTIONS (CANADA) INC   *p* 426
34 GLENCOE DR, MOUNT PEARL, NL, A1N 4P6
(709) 724-5400   *SIC* 4899
INMARSAT SOLUTIONS (CANADA) INC   *p* 426
34 GLENCOE DR, MOUNT PEARL, NL, A1N 4S8
SIC 5065
INMET   *p* 853
See MULTIMATIC INC
INMET ANATOLIA LIMITED   *p* 953
330 BAY ST SUITE 1000, TORONTO, ON, M5H 2S8
(416) 361-6400   *SIC* 1081
INN AT THE FORKS LP   *p* 378
75 FORKS MARKET RD, WINNIPEG, MB, R3C 0A2
(204) 942-6555   *SIC* 7011
INN AT THE PARK INC   *p* 72
8220 BOWRIDGE CRES NW, CALGARY, AB, T3B 2V1
(403) 288-4441   *SIC* 7011
INN ON THE TWENTY LTD   *p* 623
3836 MAIN ST, JORDAN STATION, ON, L0R 1S0
(905) 562-7313   *SIC* 5812
INNALIK SCHOOL   *p* 1113
See COMMISSION SCOLAIRE KATIVIK
INNERGEX ENERGIE RENOUVELABEL DEVELOPPEMENT DURABLE   *p* 1144
See INNERGEX RENEWABLE ENERGY INC
INNERGEX INC   *p* 1144
1225 RUE SAINT-CHARLES O 10E ETAGE, LONGUEUIL, QC, J4K 0B9
(450) 928-2550   *SIC* 4931
INNERGEX RENEWABLE ENERGY INC   *p* 305
888 DUNSMUIR ST SUITE 1100, VANCOUVER, BC, V6C 3K4
(604) 669-4999   *SIC* 4911
INNERGEX RENEWABLE ENERGY INC   *p* 1144
1225 RUE SAINT-CHARLES O BUREAU 10, LONGUEUIL, QC, J4K 0B9
(450) 928-2550   *SIC* 4931
INNISFAIL MEAT PACKERS LTD   *p* 137
5107 47 AVE, INNISFAIL, AB, T4G 1P8
(403) 277-5166   *SIC* 5147
INNISFAIL SUNSET MANOR   *p* 137
See SUNSET MANSUNSET MANOR
INNISFIL ENERGY SERVICES LIMITED   *p* 622
7251 YONGE ST, INNISFIL, ON, L9S 0J3
(705) 431-4321   *SIC* 4911
INNOCON INC   *p* 855
50 NEWKIRK RD, RICHMOND HILL, ON, L4C 3G3
(905) 508-7676   *SIC* 3273
INNOMAR STRATEGIES INC   *p* 804
3470 SUPERIOR CRT SUITE 2, OAKVILLE, ON, L6L 0C4
(905) 847-4310   *SIC* 8741
INNOMOTIVE SOLUTIONS GROUP INC   *p* 528
3435 SOUTH SERVICE RD, BURLINGTON, ON, L7N 3W6
(877) 845-3816   *SIC* 3442
INNOPHOS CANADA, INC   *p* 711
3265 WOLFEDALE RD, MISSISSAUGA, ON, L5C 1V8
(905) 270-9328   *SIC* 2819
INNOTECH ALBERTA INC   *p* 120
250 KARL CLARK RD, EDMONTON, AB,

T6N 1E4
(780) 450-5111   *SIC* 8733
INNOTEX INC   *p* 1283
275 RUE GOUIN BUREAU 1010, RICHMOND, QC, J0B 2H0
(819) 826-5971   *SIC* 2311
INNOVA GLOBAL LTD   *p* 30
4000 4 ST SE SUITE 222, CALGARY, AB, T2G 2W3
(403) 292-7804   *SIC* 1541
INNOVA MEDICAL OPHTHALMICS INC   *p* 787
48 CARNFORTH RD, NORTH YORK, ON, M4A 2K7
(416) 615-0185   *SIC* 5049
INNOVADERM RECHERCHES INC   *p* 1174
1851 RUE SHERBROOKE E UNITE 502, MONTREAL, QC, H2K 4L5
(514) 521-3111   *SIC* 8731
INNOVADERM RECHERCHES LAVAL   *p* 1174
See INNOVADERM RECHERCHES INC
INNOVAIR INDUSTRIAL LIMITED   *p* 381
150 MCPHILLIPS ST, WINNIPEG, MB, R3E 2J9
(204) 772-9476   *SIC* 5084
INNOVAK DIRECT   *p* 1251
See INNOVAK GROUP INC, THE
INNOVAK GROUP INC, THE   *p* 1251
62 BOUL HYMUS, POINTE-CLAIRE, QC, H9R 1E1
(514) 695-7221   *SIC* 3546
INNOVAPOST   *p* 815
See CANADA POST CORPORATION
INNOVAPOST INC   *p* 832
365 MARCH RD, OTTAWA, ON, K2K 3N5
(613) 270-6262   *SIC* 7372
INNOVASEA MARINE SYSTEMS CANADA INC   *p* 440
20 ANGUS MORTON DR, BEDFORD, NS, B4B 0L9
(902) 450-1700   *SIC* 3669
INNOVATIA INC   *p* 415
1 GERMAIN ST, SAINT JOHN, NB, E2L 4V1
(506) 640-4000   *SIC* 8748
INNOVATION CLIMAT   *p* 1151
See MAISON USINEX INC
INNOVATION CREDIT UNION LIMITED   *p* 1412
1202 102ND ST, NORTH BATTLEFORD, SK, S9A 1G3
(306) 446-7000   *SIC* 6062
INNOVATION INSTITUTE OF ONTARIO   *p* 946
101 COLLEGE ST STE HL20, TORONTO, ON, M5G 1L7
SIC 8742
INNOVATION MARITIME   *p* 1284
53 RUE SAINT-GERMAIN O, RIMOUSKI, QC, G5L 4B4
(418) 725-3525   *SIC* 7389
INNOVATION PCM INC   *p* 1356
21 RUE INDUSTRIELLE, SAINTE-CLAIRE, QC, G0R 2V0
(418) 883-4009   *SIC* 5085
INNOVATION PEI   *p* 1039
See PROVINCE OF PEI
INNOVATION PLACE   *p* 1433
See SASK OPPORTUNITIES
INNOVATIVE AUTOMATION INC   *p* 487
625 WELHAM RD, BARRIE, ON, L4N 0B7
(705) 733-0555   *SIC* 3569
INNOVATIVE BIOMETRIC TECHNOLOGIES CORP   *p* 772
5000 YONGE ST SUITE 1901, NORTH YORK, ON, M2N 7E9
(416) 222-5000   *SIC* 3663
INNOVATIVE CONTROL SOLUTIONS INC   *p* 671
3115 14TH AVE SUITE 8, MARKHAM, ON, L3R 0H1
(905) 709-4220   *SIC* 5085
INNOVATIVE DETAILING SERVICES INC   *p* 867

695 MARKHAM RD SUITE 29, SCARBOROUGH, ON, M1H 2A5
(416) 438-6004   *SIC* 7389
INNOVATIVE FISHERY PRODUCTS INCORPORATED   *p* 440
3569 1 HWY, BELLIVEAU COVE, NS, B0W 1J0
(902) 837-5163   *SIC* 2091
INNOVATIVE GLOBAL SOLUTIONS INC   *p* 23
320 19 ST SE, CALGARY, AB, T2E 6J6
(403) 204-1198   *SIC* 5136
INNOVATIVE INTERIOR SYSTEMS   *p* 107
2050 227 AVE NE, EDMONTON, AB, T5Y 6H5
(780) 414-0637   *SIC* 7389
INNOVATIVE MANUFACTURING INC   *p* 206
861 DERWENT WAY SUITE 877, DELTA, BC, V3M 5R4
(604) 522-2811   *SIC* 5198
INNOVATIVE PIPELINE CROSSINGS INC   *p* 69
340 MIDPARK WAY SE SUITE 300, CALGARY, AB, T2X 1P1
(403) 455-0380   *SIC* 1623
INNOVATIVE RESIDENTIAL INVESTMENTS INC   *p* 1428
101B ENGLISH CRES, SASKATOON, SK, S7K 8G4
(306) 979-7421   *SIC* 6553
INNOVATIVE SECURITY MANAGEMENT (1998) INC   *p* 654
148 YORK ST SUITE 309, LONDON, ON, N6A 1A9
(519) 858-4100   *SIC* 7381
INNOVATIVE STEAM TECHNOLOGIES   *p* 533
See INNOVATIVE STEAM TECHNOLOGIES INC
INNOVATIVE STEAM TECHNOLOGIES INC   *p* 533
549 CONESTOGA BLVD, CAMBRIDGE, ON, N1R 7P5
(519) 740-0036   *SIC* 3569
INNOVATIVE STEEL GROUP INC   *p* 517
85 MORRELL ST, BRANTFORD, ON, N3T 4J6
(519) 720-9797   *SIC* 5051
INNOVATIVE TRAILER DESIGN INDUSTRIES INC   *p* 996
161 THE WEST MALL, TORONTO, ON, M9C 4V8
(416) 620-7755   *SIC* 3715
INNOVATIVE VISION MARKETING INC   *p* 915
515 CONSUMERS RD 6TH FLOOR, TORONTO, ON, M2J 4Z2
(416) 321-8189   *SIC* 4899
INNOVEX CANADA   *p* 1324
See IQVIA RDS CANADA ULC
INNOVEXPLO   *p* 1390
See 9117-9077 QUEBEC INC
INNOVISION HOLDINGS CORPORATION   *p* 671
55 RENFREW DR, MARKHAM, ON, L3R 8H3
(905) 940-2488   *SIC* 6712
INNOVITE HEALTH   *p* 554
See INOYAN LABORATORIES INC
INNOVMETRIC LOGICIELS INC   *p* 1264
2014 RUE CYRILLE-DUQUET BUREAU 310, QUEBEC, QC, G1N 4N6
(418) 688-2061   *SIC* 7372
INNPOWER CORPORATION   *p* 622
7251 YONGE ST, INNISFIL, ON, L9S 0J3
(705) 431-4321   *SIC* 4911
INNU MIKUN INC   *p* 424
GD STN, HAPPY VALLEY-GOOSE BAY, NL, A0P 1C0
(709) 896-5521   *SIC* 4512
INNVEST HOTELS (LONDON) LTD   *p* 656

325 DUNDAS ST, LONDON, ON, N6B 1T9
(519) 679-6111   *SIC* 7011
INNVEST HOTELS GP LTD   *p* 804
2525 WYECROFT RD, OAKVILLE, ON, L6L 6P8
(905) 847-1000   *SIC* 7011
INNVEST HOTELS GP VIII LTD   *p* 626
101 KANATA AVE, KANATA, ON, K2T 1E6
(613) 271-3057   *SIC* 7011
INNVEST HOTELS LP   *p* 823
100 KENT ST, OTTAWA, ON, K1P 5R7
(613) 238-1122   *SIC* 7011
INNVEST HOTELS LP   *p* 963
200 BAY ST SUITE 2200, TORONTO, ON, M5J 2W4
(416) 607-7100   *SIC* 7011
INNVEST PROPERTIES CORP   *p* 939
111 LOMBARD ST, TORONTO, ON, M5C 2T9
(416) 367-5555   *SIC* 7011
INNVEST PROPERTIES CORP   *p* 963
200 BAY ST SUITE 2200, TORONTO, ON, M5J 2J2
(416) 607-7100   *SIC* 7011
INNVEST PROPERTIES CORP   *p* 1023
277 RIVERSIDE DR W, WINDSOR, ON, N9A 5K4
(519) 973-5555   *SIC* 7011
INNVEST REAL ESTATE INVESTMENT TRUST   *p* 407
750 MAIN ST, MONCTON, NB, E1C 1E6
(506) 854-4344   *SIC* 7011
INNVEST REAL ESTATE INVESTMENT TRUST   *p* 963
200 BAY ST SUITE 3205, TORONTO, ON, M5J 2J1
(416) 607-7100   *SIC* 7011
INO   *p* 1267
See INSTITUT NATIONAL D'OPTIQUE
INOAC CANADA LIMITED   *p* 888
575 JAMES ST S, ST MARYS, ON, N4X 1C6
(519) 349-2170   *SIC* 3089
INOAC INTERIOR SYSTEMS LP   *p* 888
575 JAMES ST S, ST MARYS, ON, N4X 1C6
(519) 349-2170   *SIC* 3089
INOVA SYSTEMS CORPORATION   *p* 76
1769 120 AVE NE, CALGARY, AB, T3K 0S5
(403) 537-2100   *SIC* 3829
INOVACO LTEE   *p* 1104
777 BOUL DE LA CITE, GATINEAU, QC, J8T 8J9
(819) 568-3400   *SIC* 5211
INOVATA FOODS CORP   *p* 93
12803 149 ST NW, EDMONTON, AB, T5L 2J7
(780) 454-8665   *SIC* 2099
INOVATA FOODS CORP   *p* 911
98 SPRUCE ST, TILLSONBURG, ON, N4G 5V3
SIC 2099
INOVATECH EGG PRODUCTS, DIV OF   *p* 391
See MFI FOOD CANADA LTD
INOVESCO   *p* 1243
See TURQUOISE, CABINET EN ASSURANCE DE DOMMAGES INC, LA
INOX   *p* 1066
See INOX DISTRIBUTION INC
INOX DISTRIBUTION INC   *p* 1066
1440 RUE GRAHAM-BELL BUREAU A, BOUCHERVILLE, QC, J4B 6H5
(450) 449-9200   *SIC* 5051
INOX INDUSTRIES INC   *p* 504
60 SUMMERLEA RD, BRAMPTON, ON, L6T 4X3
(905) 799-9996   *SIC* 3312
INOX-TECH CANADA INC   *p* 1356
1905 RUE PASTEUR, SAINTE-CATHERINE, QC, J5C 1B7
(450) 638-5441   *SIC* 3556
INOYAN LABORATORIES INC   *p* 554
97 SARAMIA CRES UNIT 1, CONCORD, ON, L4K 4P7
(905) 267-0721   *SIC* 5122

INPLAY OIL CORP p 51
640 5 AVE SW SUITE 920, CALGARY, AB, T2P 3G4
(587) 955-9570 *SIC* 1311
INPROHEAT INDUSTRIES LIMITED p 295
680 RAYMUR AVE, VANCOUVER, BC, V6A 2R1
(604) 254-0461 *SIC* 5051
INPUT CAPITAL CORP p 1418
1914 HAMILTON ST SUITE 300, REGINA, SK, S4P 3N6
(306) 347-3006 *SIC* 0191
INQUENT TECHNOLOGIES INC p 953
150 YORK ST, TORONTO, ON, M5H 3S5
(416) 645-4600 *SIC* 4813
INQUIRY MANAGEMENT SYSTEMS p 573
See *1325931 CANADA INC*
INRS p 1259
See *INSTITUT NATIONAL DE LA RECHERCHE SCIENTIFIQUE*
INRS ETE INSTITUT NATIONALE DE LA RECHEGE SCIENTIFIQUE p 1260
See *UNIVERSITE DU QUEBEC*
INSCAPE CORPORATION p 620
67 TOLL RD, HOLLAND LANDING, ON, L9N 1H2
(905) 836-7676 *SIC* 2522
INSCRIBER TECHNOLOGY CORPORATION p 1006
26 PEPPLER ST, WATERLOO, ON, N2J 3C4
(519) 570-9111 *SIC* 7371
INSERCO-QUEBEC INC p 1326
674 RUE DESLAURIERS, SAINT-LAURENT, QC, H4N 1W5
(514) 523-1551 *SIC* 7389
INSHORE FISHERIES LIMITED p 461
95 DENNIS POINT RD, LOWER WEST PUBNICO, NS, B0W 2C0
(902) 762-2522 *SIC* 2092
INSIDEOUT BURLINGTON LTD p 529
1515 NORTH SERVICE RD, BURLINGTON, ON, L7P 0A2
(905) 681-7173 *SIC* 5712
INSIGHT CANADA INC p 1220
5410 BOUL DECARIE, MONTREAL, QC, H3X 4B2
(514) 344-3500 *SIC* 5734
INSIGHT DIRECT CANADA, INC p 1220
5410 BOUL DECARIE, MONTREAL, QC, H3X 4B2
(514) 344-3500 *SIC* 8742
INSIGHT MEDICAL HOLDINGS·LTD p 98
200 MEADOWLARK SHOPPING CTR NW, EDMONTON, AB, T5R 5W9
(780) 489-8430 *SIC* 8071
INSIGHT MEDICAL IMAGING p 98
200 MEADOWLARK SHOPPING CTR NW, EDMONTON, AB, T5R 5W9
(780) 489-3391 *SIC* 8011
INSIGHT SPORTS LTD p 953
184 PEARL ST SUITE 302, TORONTO, ON, M5H 1L5
(416) 593-0915 *SIC* 4833
INSIGHT SPORTS NETWORKS p 953
See *INSIGHT SPORTS LTD*
INSIGHT TECHNOLOGIES CONSTRUCTION CORP p 580
6817 STEELES AVE W, ETOBICOKE, ON, M9V 4R9
(416) 745-8228 *SIC* 1542
INSIGHT U p 755
See *INSIGHTU.COM INC*
INSIGHTS LEARNING & DEVELOPMENT LTD p 35
5824 2 ST SW SUITE 302, CALGARY, AB, T2H 0H2
(403) 233-7263 *SIC* 8748
INSIGHTU.COM INC p 755
350 HARRY WALKER PKY N SUITE 14, NEWMARKET, ON, L3Y 8L3
(905) 883-9620 *SIC* 8741

INSITUFORM TECHNOLOGIES LIMITED p 122
7605 18 ST NW, EDMONTON, AB, T6P 1N9
(780) 413-0200 *SIC* 7699
INSPEC-SOL p 1277
See *GHD CONSULTANTS LTEE*
INSPEC-SOL p 1334
See *GHD CONSULTANTS LTEE*
INSPECTEUR EN BATIMENT p 1076
110 RUE ALBERT-SEERS, CHATEAUGUAY, QC, J6K 5E5
(514) 515-2334 *SIC* 8621
INSPECTIONAIR GAUGE LIMITED p 1020
3298 RIBERDY RD, WINDSOR, ON, N8W 3T9
(519) 966-1232 *SIC* 3825
INSPECTIONS GROUP INC, THE p 85
12010 111 AVE NW, EDMONTON, AB, T5G 0E6
(780) 454-5048 *SIC* 7389
INSPIRATION FURNITURE INC p 319
1275 6TH AVE W, VANCOUVER, BC, V6H 1A6
(604) 730-1275 *SIC* 5712
INSTABOX (ALBERTA) INC p 23
1139 40 AVE NE, CALGARY, AB, T2E 6M9
(403) 250-9217 *SIC* 2653
INSTACHANGE DISPLAYS LIMITED p 755
360 HARRY WALKER PKY S UNIT 1-3, NEWMARKET, ON, L3Y 9E9
(289) 279-1100 *SIC* 3993
INSTALL-A-FLOR LIMITED p 446
31 STERNS CRT, DARTMOUTH, NS, B3B 1W7
(902) 468-3111 *SIC* 5713
INSTALLATIONS ELECTRIQUES PICHETTE INC, LES p 1234
3080 RUE PEUGEOT, MONTREAL, QC, H7L 5C5
(450) 682-4411 *SIC* 1731
INSTANT BRANDS INC p 624
495 MARCH RD SUITE 200, KANATA, ON, K2K 3G1
(800) 828-7280 *SIC* 5065
INSTANT COURIER SERVICE p 738
See *DATA PARCEL EXPRESS INCORPORATED*
INSTANT POT COMPANY p 624
See *INSTANT BRANDS INC*
INSTEAD ROBOTIC CORP p 1296
1370 RUE HOCQUART, SAINT-BRUNO, QC, J3V 6E1
(450) 653-7868 *SIC* 8748
INSTIMAX CORPORATION p 23
901 CENTRE ST NW UNIT 303, CALGARY, AB, T2E 2P6
(403) 398-8911 *SIC* 2759
INSTITUE UNIVERSITAIRE GERIATRIE p 1372
See *GOUVERNEMENT DE LA PROVINCE DE QUEBEC*
INSTITUT CANADIEN DE QUEBEC, L' p 1259
350 RUE SAINT-JOSEPH E 4E ETAGE, QUEBEC, QC, G1K 3B2
(418) 529-0924 *SIC* 8231
INSTITUT CANADIEN POUR DEVELOPPEMENT NEURO-INTEGRATIF, L p 1229
5460 AV CONNAUGHT, MONTREAL, QC, H4V 1X7
(514) 935-1911 *SIC* 8211
INSTITUT D' ECHAFAUDAGE-QUEBEC p 1115
See *9020-4983 QUEBEC INC*
INSTITUT DE CARDIOLOGIE DE MONTREAL p 1165
5000 RUE BELANGER, MONTREAL, QC, H1T 1C8
(514) 376-3330 *SIC* 8069
INSTITUT DE LA GESTION DE LA FORMATION p 1134

See *IGF AXIOM INC*
INSTITUT DE LA STATISTIQUE DE QUEBEC p 1269
See *GOUVERNEMENT DE LA PROVINCE DE QUEBEC*
INSTITUT DE PROTECTION CONTRE LES INCENDIES DU QUEBEC (IPIQ), L' p 1232
See *COMMISSION SCOLAIRE DE LAVAL*
INSTITUT DE READAPATION EN DEFICIENCE PHYSIQUE DE QUEBEC p 1262
See *GOUVERNEMENT DE LA PROVINCE DE QUEBEC*
INSTITUT DE READAPTATION EN DEFICIENCE PHYSIQUE DE QUEBEC p 1262
525 BOUL WILFRID-HAMEL, QUEBEC, QC, G1M 2S8
(418) 529-9141 *SIC* 8093
INSTITUT DE RECHERCHE BIOLOGIQUE YVES PONROY (CANADA) INC p 1128
2035 RUE ONESIME-GAGNON, LACHINE, QC, H8T 3M5
(514) 448-4325 *SIC* 5149
INSTITUT DE RECHERCHE DU CENTRE UNIVERSITAIRE DE SANTE MCGILL, L' p 1215
2155 RUE GUY BUREAU 500, MONTREAL, QC, H3H 2R9
(514) 934-8354 *SIC* 8071
INSTITUT DE RECHERCHE ET DEVELOPPEMENT EN AGROENVIRONEMENT INC p 1267
2700 RUE EINSTEIN BUREAU D1110, QUEBEC, QC, G1P 3W8
(418) 643-2380 *SIC* 8731
INSTITUT DE RECHERCHE ROBERT SAUVE EN SANTE ET EN SECURITE DU TRAVAIL p 1197
505 BOUL DE MAISONNEUVE O, MONTREAL, QC, H3A 3C2
(514) 288-1551 *SIC* 8731
INSTITUT DE RECHERCHES CLINIQUES DE MONTREAL p 1184
110 AV DES PINS O, MONTREAL, QC, H2W 1R7
(514) 987-5500 *SIC* 8733
INSTITUT DE TECHNOLOGIE AGROALIMENTAIRE p 1312
See *COOPSCO SAINT-HYACINTHE*
INSTITUT DE TOURISME ET D'HOTELLERIE DU QUEBEC, L' p 1185
See *GOUVERNEMENT DE LA PROVINCE DE QUEBEC*
INSTITUT NATIONAL D'OPTIQUE p 1267
2740 RUE EINSTEIN, QUEBEC, QC, G1P 4S4
(418) 657-7006 *SIC* 8731
INSTITUT NATIONAL DE LA RECHERCHE SCIENTIFIQUE p 1259
490 RUE DE LA COURONNE, QUEBEC, QC, G1K 9A9
(418) 654-4677 *SIC* 8733
INSTITUT NATIONAL DE LA RECHERCHE SCIENTIFIQUE ENERGIE & MATERIAUX p 1393
See *UNIVERSITE DU QUEBEC*
INSTITUT NATIONALDE LA RECHERCHE SCIENTIFIQUE (INR p 1087
See *UNIVERSITE DU QUEBEC*
INSTITUT NATIONALE DE SANTE PUBLIQUE DU QUEBEC p 1272
945 AV WOLFE BUREAU 4, QUEBEC, QC, G1V 5B3
(418) 650-5115 *SIC* 8731
INSTITUT NATIONALE DE SANTE PUBLIQUE DU QUEBEC p 1355
20045 CH SAINTE-MARIE, SAINTE-ANNE-DE-BELLEVUE, QC, H9X 3R5
(514) 457-2070 *SIC* 8731
INSTITUT NAZARETH ET LOUIS-BRAILLE p 1144

1111 RUE SAINT-CHARLES O BUREAU 200, LONGUEUIL, QC, J4K 5G4
(450) 463-1710 *SIC* 8093
INSTITUT NEOMED p 1334
7171 RUE FREDERICK-BANTING, SAINT-LAURENT, QC, H4S 1Z9
(514) 367-1212 *SIC* 5122
INSTITUT RAYMOND-DEWAR p 1175
3600 RUE BERRI BUREAU 469, MONTREAL, QC, H2L 4G9
(514) 284-2214 *SIC* 8361
INSTITUT SERVIER DU DIABETE p 1343
See *SERVIER CANADA INC*
INSTITUT UNIVERSITAIRE EN SANTE MENTALE DOUGLAS p 1397
6875 BOUL LASALLE, VERDUN, QC, H4H 1R3
(514) 761-6131 *SIC* 8062
INSTITUTE FOR CLINICAL EVALUATIVE SCIENCES p 921
2075 BAYVIEW AVE SUITE G106, TORONTO, ON, M4N 3M5
(416) 480-4055 *SIC* 8733
INSTITUTE FOR COMPUTING, INFORMATION & COGNITIVE SYSTEMS p 325
See *UNIVERSITY OF BRITISH COLUMBIA, THE*
INSTITUTE FOR WORK & HEALTH p 946
481 UNIVERSITY AVE SUITE 800, TORONTO, ON, M5G 2E9
(416) 927-2027 *SIC* 8399
INSTITUTE NATIONAL DE LA RECHERCHE SCIENTIFIQUE p 1087
531 BOUL DES PRAIRIES BUREAU 26, COTE SAINT-LUC, QC, H7V 1B7
(450) 687-5010 *SIC* 8221
INSTITUTE OF CHARTERED ACCOUNTANTS OF ALBERTA p 89
10088 102 AVE NW UNIT 1900 TD TOWER, EDMONTON, AB, T5J 2Z1
(780) 424-7391 *SIC* 8621
INSTITUTE OF NATUROPATHIC EDUCATION AND RESEARCH p 769
1255 SHEPPARD AVE E, NORTH YORK, ON, M2K 1E2
(416) 498-1255 *SIC* 8221
INSTITUTE OF PUBLIC ADMINISTRATION OF CANADA, THE p 975
1075 BAY ST SUITE 401, TORONTO, ON, M5S 2B1
(416) 924-8787 *SIC* 8733
INSTITUTION QUEBEC p 1296
1395 RUE MARIE-VICTORIN, SAINT-BRUNO, QC, J3V 6B7
(450) 482-0724 *SIC* 5087
INSTORE FOCUS INC p 841
485 THE PARKWAY, PETERBOROUGH, ON, K9J 0B3
SIC 5963
INSTRUMENTS I.T.M. INC, LES p 1355
20800 BOUL INDUSTRIEL, SAINTE-ANNE-DE-BELLEVUE, QC, H9X 0A1
(514) 457-7280 *SIC* 5084
INSTRUMENTS ISAAC INC p 1074
240 BOUL FRECHETTE, CHAMBLY, QC, J3L 2Z5
(450) 658-7520 *SIC* 3823
INSUL-WEST BUILDING MATERIALS LTD p 220
860 MCCURDY RD, KELOWNA, BC, V1X 2P7
(250) 807-2551 *SIC* 5039
INSULFLEX ELECTRONICS p 1248
See *8885168 CANADA INC*
INSURANCE BANK p 96
16403 111 AVE NW, EDMONTON, AB, T5M 2S2
(780) 439-2265 *SIC* 6411
INSURANCE BUREAU OF CANADA p 767
2235 SHEPPARD AVE E SUITE 1100, NORTH YORK, ON, M2J 5B5

(416) 445-5912 *SIC* 6411
INSURANCE BUREAU OF CANADA *p* 946
777 BAY ST SUITE 2400, TORONTO, ON, M5G 2C8

(416) 362-2031 *SIC* 6411
INSURANCE BUREAU OF CANADA *p* 1229
800 RUE DU SQUARE-VICTORIA BUREAU 2410, MONTREAL, QC, H4Z 0A2

(514) 288-4321 *SIC* 6411
INSURANCE CENTRE INC, THE *p* 630
321 CONCESSION ST, KINGSTON, ON, K7K 2B9

(613) 544-5313 *SIC* 6411
INSURANCE COMPANY OF PRINCE EDWARD ISLAND, THE *p* 1039
14 GREAT GEORGE ST SUITE 3, CHARLOTTETOWN, PE, C1A 4J6

(902) 368-3675 *SIC* 6331
INSURANCE CORPORATION OF BRITISH COLUMBIA *p* 201
1575 HARTLEY AVE, COQUITLAM, BC, V3K 6Z7

(604) 777-4627 *SIC* 6331
INSURANCE CORPORATION OF BRITISH COLUMBIA *p* 228
6000 PRODUCTION WAY, LANGLEY, BC, V3A 6L5

(604) 530-7111 *SIC* 6331
INSURANCE CORPORATION OF BRITISH COLUMBIA *p* 240
151 ESPLANADE W, NORTH VANCOUVER, BC, V7M 3H9

(604) 661-2800 *SIC* 6331
INSURANCE CORPORATION OF BRITISH COLUMBIA *p* 270
10262 152A ST, SURREY, BC, V3R 6T8

(604) 584-3211 *SIC* 6331
INSURANCE CORPORATION OF BRITISH COLUMBIA *p* 276
13665 68 AVE, SURREY, BC, V3W 0Y6

(604) 597-7600 *SIC* 6331
INSURANCE CORPORATION OF BRITISH COLUMBIA *p* 334
425 DUNEDIN ST, VICTORIA, BC, V8T 5H7

(250) 480-5600 *SIC* 6331
INSURANCE COUNCIL OF BRITISH COLUMBIA *p* 314
1040 GEORGIA ST W SUITE 300, VANCOUVER, BC, V6E 4H1

(604) 688-0321 *SIC* 6411
INSURANCE GUYS INC, THE *p* 98
16612 109 AVE NW, EDMONTON, AB, T5P 1C2

(780) 448-2298 *SIC* 6411
INSURANCE INFORMATION DIVISION *p* 946
See INSURANCE BUREAU OF CANADA
INSURANCE INFORMATION SERVICES *p* 770
See EQUIFAX CANADA CO.
INSURANCE INSTITUTE OF CANADA, THE *p* 939
18 KING ST E SUITE 600, TORONTO, ON, M5C 1C4

(416) 362-8586 *SIC* 8621
INSURANCE PORTFOLIO INC *p* 865
10 MILNER BUSINESS CRT SUITE 800, SCARBOROUGH, ON, M1B 3C6

(416) 754-3910 *SIC* 6411
INSURANCE SEARCH BUREAU OF CANADA INC *p* 684
8160 PARKHILL DR, MILTON, ON, L9T 5V7

(905) 875-0556 *SIC* 6411
INSURANCE SUPERMARKET INC *p* 554
A101-8000 JANE ST, CONCORD, ON, L4K 5B8

(888) 818-1963 *SIC* 6411
INSURANCE SYSTEMS INC *p* 575
170 EVANS AVE, ETOBICOKE, ON, M8Z 1J7

(416) 249-2260 *SIC* 7371
INSURANCEHOTLINE COM *p* 981
See KANETIX LTD

INSURANCELAND *p* 696
See INSURANCELAND INC
INSURANCELAND INC *p* 696
2585 SKYMARK AVE UNIT 300, MISSISSAUGA, ON, L4W 4L5

(905) 238-0668 *SIC* 6411
INTACT ASSURANCE *p* 1052
See INTACT INSURANCE COMPANY
INTACT FINANCIAL CORPORATION *p* 946
700 UNIVERSITY AVE SUITE 1500, TORONTO, ON, M5G 0A1

(416) 341-1464 *SIC* 6331
INTACT INSURANCE COMPANY *p* 52
321 6 AVE SW SUITE 1200, CALGARY, AB, T2P 3H3

(403) 269-7961 *SIC* 6331
INTACT INSURANCE COMPANY *p* 286
2955 VIRTUAL WAY SUITE 400, VANCOUVER, BC, V5M 4X6

(604) 891-5400 *SIC* 6411
INTACT INSURANCE COMPANY *p* 305
999 HASTINGS ST W SUITE 1100, VANCOUVER, BC, V6C 2W2

(604) 891-5400 *SIC* 6331
INTACT INSURANCE COMPANY *p* 446
20 HECTOR GATE SUITE 200, DARTMOUTH, NS, B3B 0K3

(902) 420-1732 *SIC* 6331
INTACT INSURANCE COMPANY *p* 654
255 QUEENS AVE SUITE 900, LONDON, ON, N6A 5R8

(519) 432-6721 *SIC* 6331
INTACT INSURANCE COMPANY *p* 723
6925 CENTURY AVE SUITE 900, MISSISSAUGA, ON, L5N 0E3

(905) 858-1070 *SIC* 6331
INTACT INSURANCE COMPANY *p* 820
1400 ST. LAURENT BLVD SUITE 300, OTTAWA, ON, K1K 4H4

(800) 267-1836 *SIC* 6331
INTACT INSURANCE COMPANY *p* 946
700 UNIVERSITY AVE SUITE 1500, TORONTO, ON, M5G 0A1

(416) 341-1464 *SIC* 6331
INTACT INSURANCE COMPANY *p* 1052
7101 RUE JEAN-TALON E BUREAU 1000, ANJOU, QC, H1M 0A5

(514) 388-5466 *SIC* 6331
INTACT INVESTMENT MANAGEMENT, INC *p* 946
700 UNIVERSITY AVE SUITE 1500, TORONTO, ON, M5G 0A1

(416) 341-1464 *SIC* 6282
INTEC BILLING CANADA LTD *p* 904
123 COMMERCE VALLEY DR E, THORNHILL, ON, L3T 7W8

SIC 5045
INTEC INVESTMENT HOLDINGS INC *p* 469
9 COMMERCIAL ST, TRURO, NS, B2N 3H8

(902) 895-6346 *SIC* 4581
INTEGRA CANADA ULC *p* 798
2590 BRISTOL CIR UNIT 1, OAKVILLE, ON, L6H 6Z7

(905) 618-1603 *SIC* 5047
INTEGRA CASTINGS INC *p* 361
200 PACIFIC ST, WINKLER, MB, R6W 0K2

(204) 325-7376 *SIC* 3321
INTEGRA GOLD CORP *p* 314
1055 GEORGIA ST W UNIT 2270, VANCOUVER, BC, V6E 0B6

(604) 629-0891 *SIC* 1081
INTEGRA TIRE *p* 1440
See YUKON TIRE CENTRE LTD
INTEGRAL ENERGY SERVICES LTD *p* 3
2890 KINGSVIEW BLVD SE UNIT 101, AIRDRIE, AB, T4A 0E1

(403) 912-1261 *SIC* 1731
INTEGRAL GROUP INC *p* 306
200 GRANVILLE ST SUITE 180, VANCOUVER, BC, V6C 1S4

(604) 687-1800 *SIC* 1711
INTEGRAL PROPERTY SERVICES LTD *p* 35
343 FORGE RD SE SUITE 9, CALGARY,

AB, T2H 0S9

(403) 296-2206 *SIC* 7349
INTEGRAL TRANSPORTATION NETWORKS CORP *p*
740
6975 PACIFIC CIR UNIT D, MISSISSAUGA, ON, L5T 2H3

(905) 362-1111 *SIC* 4731
INTEGRAL WEALTH SECURITIES LIMITED *p* 953
56 TEMPERANCE ST SUITE 900, TORONTO, ON, M5H 3V5

(416) 203-2000 *SIC* 6211
INTEGRAM-WINDSOR, DIV OF *p* 481
See MAGNA SEATING INC
INTEGRATED ASSET MANAGEMENT CORP *p* 963
70 UNIVERSITY AVE SUITE 1200, TORONTO, ON, M5J 2M4

(416) 360-7667 *SIC* 8741
INTEGRATED BUSINESS ANALYSIS, INC *p* 997
130 KING ST, TORONTO, ON, M9N 1L5

(800) 531-7100 *SIC* 8742
INTEGRATED DEALER SYSTEMS CANADA LTD *p* 844
1730 MCPHERSON CRT UNIT 7, PICKERING, ON, L1W 3E6

(800) 769-7425 *SIC* 4213
INTEGRATED DISTRIBUTION SYSTEMS LIMITED PARTNERSHIP *p* 1
26313 TWP RD 531A, ACHESON, AB, T7X 5A3

(780) 487-6700 *SIC* 5084
INTEGRATED DISTRIBUTION SYSTEMS LIMITED PARTNERSHIP *p* 101
17604 105 AVE NW, EDMONTON, AB, T5S 1G4

(780) 483-6641 *SIC* 5084
INTEGRATED DISTRIBUTION SYSTEMS LIMITED PARTNERSHIP *p* 703
1865 SHARLYN RD, MISSISSAUGA, ON, L4X 1R1

(905) 624-5611 *SIC* 5082
INTEGRATED DISTRIBUTION SYSTEMS LIMITED PARTNERSHIP *p* 703
3280 WHARTON WAY, MISSISSAUGA, ON, L4X 2C5

(905) 212-3300 *SIC* 5084
INTEGRATED DISTRIBUTION SYSTEMS LIMITED PARTNERSHIP *p* 1086
2000 RUE JOHN-MOLSON, COTE SAINT-LUC, QC, H7T 0H4

(450) 682-3737 *SIC* 5084
INTEGRATED DISTRIBUTION SYSTEMS LIMITED PARTNERSHIP *p* 1275
2997 AV WATT, QUEBEC, QC, G1X 3W1

(418) 651-4236 *SIC* 5084
INTEGRATED DISTRIBUTION SYSTEMS LIMITED PARTNERSHIP *p* 1306
243 RUE DES ARTISANS, SAINT-GERMAIN-DE-GRANTHAM, QC, J0C 1K0

(819) 472-4076 *SIC* 5063
INTEGRATED DISTRIBUTION SYSTEMS LIMITED PARTNERSHIP *p* 1306
243 RUE DES ARTISANS, SAINT-GERMAIN-DE-GRANTHAM, QC, J0C 1K0

(819) 472-4076 *SIC* 5084
INTEGRATED FINANCIAL GROUP INC *p* 98
10220 156 ST NW SUITE 200, EDMONTON, AB, T5P 2R1

(780) 454-6505 *SIC* 6411
INTEGRATED FINANCIAL TECHNOLOGIES INC *p*
186
4180 LOUGHEED HWY UNIT 400, BURNABY, BC, V5C 6A7

(844) 303-4899 *SIC* 8742
INTEGRATED MAINTENANCE & OPERATIONS SERVICES INC *p*
671
GD, MARKHAM, ON, L3R 9R8

(905) 475-6660 *SIC* 1611
INTEGRATED MARKET SOLUTIONS INC *p*

892
266 SOUTH SERVICE RD, STONEY CREEK, ON, L8E 2N9

(905) 662-9194 *SIC* 1623
INTEGRATED MESSAGING INC *p* 384
550 BERRY ST, WINNIPEG, MB, R3H 0R9

SIC 4899
INTEGRATED PLANNING GROUP *p* 297
See AVC INSURANCE SERVICES INC
INTEGRATED PROACTION CORP *p* 216
1425 HUGH ALLAN DR, KAMLOOPS, BC, V1S 1J3

(250) 828-7977 *SIC* 7389
INTEGRATED PRODUCTION SERVICES *p*
55
See NINE ENERGY CANADA INC
INTEGRATED PROTECTION *p* 744
See VIPOND INC
INTEGRATED PROTECTIVE COATINGS INC *p* 162
500 STREAMBANK AVE, SHERWOOD PARK, AB, T8H 1N1

(780) 467-3299 *SIC* 3479
INTEGRATED SUSTAINABILITY *p* 52
See INTEGRATED SUSTAINABILITY CONSULTANTS LTD
INTEGRATED SUSTAINABILITY CONSULTANTS LTD *p*
52
1600-400 3 AVE SW, CALGARY, AB, T2P 4H2

SIC 8748
INTEGRATED TECHNOLOGY LIMITED *p*
671
90 DON PARK RD, MARKHAM, ON, L3R 1C4

(905) 475-6658 *SIC* 3672
INTEGRATION RE SOURCE *p* 1103
312 RUE SAINT-LOUIS, GATINEAU, QC, J8P 8B3

(819) 770-2018 *SIC* 8322
INTEGRICO INC *p* 491
199 FRONT ST SUITE 215, BELLEVILLE, ON, K8N 5H5

(613) 966-6466 *SIC* 6794
INTEGRICON PROPERTY RESTORATION AND CONSTRUCTION GROUP INC *p* 1031
219 WESTCREEK DR, WOODBRIDGE, ON, L4L 9T7

(416) 736-0395 *SIC* 1771
INTEGRITY HD INC *p* 1021
3126 DEVON DR, WINDSOR, ON, N8X 4L2

(519) 946-1400 *SIC* 3545
INTEGRITY INSTALLATIONS LTD *p* 240
705 15TH ST W, NORTH VANCOUVER, BC, V7M 1T2

(604) 988-3700 *SIC* 1711
INTEGRITY MECHANICAL *p* 240
See INTEGRITY INSTALLATIONS LTD
INTEGRITY TOOL & MOLD INC *p* 807
5015 O'NEIL DR, OLDCASTLE, ON, N0R 1L0

(519) 737-2650 *SIC* 3089
INTEGRITY WALL SYSTEMS INC *p* 341
1371 COURTLAND AVE, VICTORIA, BC, V9E 2C5

(250) 480-5500 *SIC* 5714
INTEK COMMUNICATIONS INC *p* 665
9 HERITAGE RD, MARKHAM, ON, L3P 1M3

(905) 294-0400 *SIC* 4899
INTEL OF CANADA, LTD *p* 585
200 RONSON DR SUITE 201, ETOBICOKE, ON, M9W 5Z9

(647) 259-0101 *SIC* 5045
INTELCAN TECHNOSYSTEMS INC *p* 749
69 AURIGA DR, NEPEAN, ON, K2E 7Z2

(613) 228-1150 *SIC* 3812
INTELCO *p* 1100
See 9210-7556 QUEBEC INC
INTELCOM COURRIER CANADA INC *p*
1211
1380 RUE WILLIAM, MONTREAL, QC, H3C 1R5

(514) 875-2778 *SIC* 7389

INTELCOM COURRIER CANADA INC   *p* 1211
1380 RUE WILLIAM BUREAU 200, MONTREAL, QC, H3C 1R5
(514) 937-0430   *SIC* 7389

INTELCOM EXPRESS   *p* 1211
See *INTELCOM COURRIER CANADA INC*

INTELERAD   *p* 1176
See *SYSTEMES MEDICAUX INTELERAD INCORPOREE, LES*

INTELEX CORPORATION   *p* 963
70 UNIVERSITY AVE SUITE 800, TORONTO, ON, M5J 2M4
(416) 599-6009   *SIC* 7371

INTELEX TECHNOLOGIES INC   *p* 963
70 UNIVERSITY AVE SUITE 800, TORONTO, ON, M5J 2M4
(416) 599-6009   *SIC* 7371

INTELISPEND   *p* 585
See *IPS OF CANADA, U.L.C.*

INTELLICO - IDS INC   *p* 1340
6830 CH DE LA COTE-DE-LIESSE, SAINT-LAURENT, QC, H4T 2A1
(800) 317-2323   *SIC* 5045

INTELLIGARDE INTERNATIONAL INC   *p* 869
3090 KINGSTON RD SUITE 400, SCARBOROUGH, ON, M1M 1P2
(416) 760-0000   *SIC* 7381

INTELLIGENT IMAGING SYSTEMS, INC   *p* 119
6325 GATEWAY BLVD NW SUITE 170, EDMONTON, AB, T6H 5H6
(780) 461-3355   *SIC* 5099

INTELLIGENT MECHATRONICS SYSTEMS INC.   *p* 1006
435 KING ST N, WATERLOO, ON, N2J 2Z5
(519) 745-8887   *SIC* 4899

INTELLIRESPONSE   *p* 936
See *24/7 CUSTOMER CANADA, INC*

INTELYSIS CORP   *p* 922
2619 YONGE ST SUITE 200, TORONTO, ON, M4P 2J1
(416) 216-6962   *SIC* 7323

INTENSITY SECURITY INC   *p* 823
45 O'CONNOR ST SUITE 1150, OTTAWA, ON, K1P 1A4
(613) 755-4094   *SIC* 5072

INTEPLAST BAGS AND FILMS CORPORATION   *p* 209
7503 VANTAGE PL, DELTA, BC, V4G 1A5
(604) 946-5431   *SIC* 2673

INTEPLAST BAGS AND FILMS CORPORATION   *p* 1130
1 RUE VIFAN, LANORAIE, QC, J0K 1E0
(450) 887-7711   *SIC* 3081

INTER CLOTURES INC   *p* 1387
9200 BOUL PARENT, TROIS-RIVIERES, QC, G9A 5E1
(819) 377-5837   *SIC* 7389

INTER MEDICO   *p* 668
See *D.S.L. DIAGNOSTIC PRODUCTS INCORPORATED*

INTER PIPELINE LTD   *p* 52
215 2 ST SW SUITE 3200, CALGARY, AB, T2P 1M4
(403) 290-6000   *SIC* 1382

INTER PIPELINE US MARKETING LTD *p* 52
215 2ND ST SW SUITE 3200, CALGARY, AB, T2P 1M4
(403) 538-9015   *SIC* 5172

INTER PRO DENTAL LAB   *p* 85
See *EDMONTON DENTAL SUPPLIES LTD*

INTER PROPANE INC   *p* 1149
460 RUE SICARD, MASCOUCHE, QC, J7K 3G5
(450) 474-4000   *SIC* 5169

INTER TRIBAL HEALTH AUTHORITY *p* 233
534 CENTRE ST, NANAIMO, BC, V9R 4Z3
(250) 753-0590   *SIC* 6324

INTER WEST   *p* 1428
See *INTER WEST MECHANICAL LTD*

INTER WEST MECHANICAL LTD   *p* 1428
1839 SASKATCHEWAN AVE, SASKATOON, SK, S7K 1R1
(306) 955-1800   *SIC* 1711

INTER-ALBERTA HOLDINGS CORPORATION   *p* 149
1101 4 ST, NISKU, AB, T9E 7N1
(780) 955-7744   *SIC* 7011

INTER-BEST   *p* 182
See *INTERBEST HOUSEWARES INC*

INTER-BOUCHERVILLE INC   *p* 1066
50 CH DU TREMBLAY, BOUCHERVILLE, QC, J4B 6Z5
(450) 655-5050   *SIC* 5511

INTER-CANADA FISHERIES, DIV OF *p* 555
See *M.B. PRODUCT RESEARCH DISTRIBUTING INC*

INTER-CITE CONSTRUCTION LTEE *p* 1079
205 BOUL DU ROYAUME E, CHICOUTIMI, QC, G7H 5H2
(418) 549-0532   *SIC* 1611

INTER-CITE CONSTRUCTION LTEE *p* 1079
209 BOUL DU ROYAUME O, CHICOUTIMI, QC, G7H 5C2
(418) 549-0532   *SIC* 1611

INTER-CITY PAPERS INTERNATIONAL *p* 26
See *VERITIV CANADA, INC*

INTER-CONTINENTAL GEAR & BRAKE INC   *p* 696
1415 SHAWSON DR SUITE 1, MISSISSAUGA, ON, L4W 1C4
(905) 564-5633   *SIC* 5013

INTER-CONTINENTAL MERCANTILE *p* 1244
See *STEINER & ALEXANDERS INC*

INTER-GROUPE ASSURANCES INC *p* 1272
1175 AV LAVIGERIE BUREAU 475, QUEBEC, QC, G1V 4P1
(418) 682-5666   *SIC* 6411

INTER-MARCHE ST-PROSPER   *p* 1350
See *EPICERIE R. BUTEAU INC*

INTER-MEUBLE   *p* 1348
See *9095-6988 QUEBEC INC*

INTER-POWER, DIV DE   *p* 1328
See *COMPRESSEURS QUEBEC A K ENR*

INTER-PROVINCIAL MECANIQUE MAINTENANCE   *p* 1147
See *9192-2773 QUEBEC INC*

INTER-ROCK MINERALS INC   *p* 939
2 TORONTO ST 5TH FL, TORONTO, ON, M5C 2B6
(416) 367-3003   *SIC* 1481

INTER-TEL   *p* 624
See *MITEL NETWORKS CORPORATION*

INTER-VARSITY CHRISTIAN FELLOWSHIP OF CANADA   *p* 585
1 INTERNATIONAL BLVD, ETOBICOKE, ON, M9W 6H3
(416) 443-1170   *SIC* 8661

INTER.NET   *p* 1221
See *INTER.NET CANADA LTEE*

INTER.NET CANADA LTEE   *p* 1221
5252 BOUL DE MAISONNEUVE O BUREAU 200, MONTREAL, QC, H4A 3S5
(514) 481-2585   *SIC* 4813

INTERAC CORP   *p* 963
200 BAY ST SUITE 2400, TORONTO, ON, M5J 2J1
(416) 362-8550   *SIC* 8742

INTERACTIVE TRACKING SYSTEMS INC *p* 1428
820 51ST ST E SUITE 150, SASKATOON, SK, S7K 0X8
(306) 665-5026   *SIC* 7379

INTERAXON INC   *p* 981
555 RICHMOND ST W, SUITE 900, TORONTO, ON, M5V 3B1
(416) 598-8989   *SIC* 7389

INTERBEST HOUSEWARES INC   *p* 182
7588 WINSTON ST, BURNABY, BC, V5A 4X5

(604) 216-3333   *SIC* 5023

INTERCITY EQUITY CORPORATION *p* 321
1847 BROADWAY W SUITE 104, VANCOUVER, BC, V6J 1Y6
(604) 731-6541   *SIC* 6411

INTERCITY INDUSTRIAL SUPPLY LIMITED *p* 908
669 SQUIER ST, THUNDER BAY, ON, P7B 4A7
(807) 345-2324   *SIC* 5085

INTERCITY PACKERS LTD   *p* 255
1900 NO. 6 RD, RICHMOND, BC, V6V 1W3
(604) 295-2010   *SIC* 5147

INTERCITY REALTY INC   *p* 554
163 BUTTERMILL AVE SUITE 15, CONCORD, ON, L4K 3X8
(905) 738-6644   *SIC* 6531

INTERCOAST TRUSS, DIV OF   *p* 94
See *NELSON LUMBER COMPANY LTD*

INTERCONTINENTAL GOLD AND METALS LTD   *p* 953
365 BAY ST SUITE 400, TORONTO, ON, M5H 2V1
(647) 985-2785   *SIC* 1081

INTERCONTINENTAL TORONTO CENTRE, THE   *p* 981
225 FRONT ST W, TORONTO, ON, M5V 2X3
(416) 597-1400   *SIC* 7011

INTERCONTINENTAL TRUCK BODY *p* 272
See *INTERCONTINENTAL TRUCK BODY (B.C.) INC*

INTERCONTINENTAL TRUCK BODY (B.C.) INC   *p* 272
5285 192 ST, SURREY, BC, V3S 8E5
(604) 576-2971   *SIC* 3713

INTERCONTINENTAL TRUCK BODY LTD *p* 80
1806 11 ST, COALDALE, AB, T1M 1N1
(403) 345-4427   *SIC* 3713

INTERCOSMETICS   *p* 692
See *C. DECICCO AGENCIES INC*

INTERDIGITAL   *p* 1197
See *INTERDIGITAL CANADA LTEE*

INTERDIGITAL CANADA LTEE   *p* 1197
1000 RUE SHERBROOKE O BUREAU 1000, MONTREAL, QC, H3A 3G4
(514) 904-6300   *SIC* 4812

INTERFAST INC   *p* 997
22 WORCESTER RD, TORONTO, ON, M9W 5X2
(416) 674-0770   *SIC* 5072

INTERFOR   *p* 328
See *INTERFOR CORPORATION*

INTERFOR CORPORATION   *p* 195
9200 HOLDING RD SUITE 2, CHASE, BC, V0E 1M2
(250) 679-3234   *SIC* 2421

INTERFOR CORPORATION   *p* 328
1055 DUNSMUIR ST SUITE 3500, VANCOUVER, BC, V7X 1H7
(604) 689-6800   *SIC* 2421

INTERFORUM CANADA INC   *p* 1175
1001 BOUL DE MAISONNEUVE E BUREAU 1001, MONTREAL, QC, H2L 4P9
(514) 281-1050   *SIC* 5192

INTERGRAPH CANADA LTD   *p* 76
10921 14 ST NE, CALGARY, AB, T3K 2L5
(877) 569-5500   *SIC* 5045

INTERGRAPHICS DECAL LIMITED   *p* 365
180 DE BAETS ST, WINNIPEG, MB, R2J 3W6
(204) 958-9570   *SIC* 2759

INTERGY RESERVATION & E-MARKETING SOLUTIONS, DIV OF   *p* 440
See *PACRIM HOSPITALITY SERVICES INC*

INTERHEALTH CANADA LIMITED   *p* 953
357 BAY ST SUITE 600, TORONTO, ON, M5H 2T7
(416) 362-4681   *SIC* 8732

INTERIEURS MOBILIA INC, LES   *p* 1251
2525 BOUL DES SOURCES, POINTE-CLAIRE, QC, H9R 5Z9

(514) 685-7557   *SIC* 5712

INTERIM RESSOURCES HUMAINES INC *p* 1129
50 RUE SIMON, LACHUTE, QC, J8H 3R8
SIC 7361

INTERIM RESSOURCES HUMAINES INC *p* 1132
50 AV LABATT, LASALLE, QC, H8R 3E7
SIC 7361

INTERINFORMA INC   *p* 611
400 WELLINGTON ST N UNIT 1, HAMILTON, ON, L8L 5B1
(905) 526-0701   *SIC* 2731

INTERIOR DELIGHTS   *p* 260
See *FABRICANA IMPORTS LTD*

INTERIOR HEALTH   *p* 253
1200 NEWLANDS RD SUITE 5000, REVELSTOKE, BC, V0E 2S1
(250) 837-2131   *SIC* 8062

INTERIOR HEALTH AUTHORITY   *p* 212
1501 5 AVE, FERNIE, BC, V0B 1M0
(250) 423-4453   *SIC* 8062

INTERIOR HEALTH AUTHORITY   *p* 215
835 9TH ST N, GOLDEN, BC, V0A 1H2
(250) 344-5271   *SIC* 8062

INTERIOR HEALTH AUTHORITY   *p* 222
2255 ETHEL ST, KELOWNA, BC, V1Y 2Z9
(250) 862-4100   *SIC* 8051

INTERIOR HEALTH AUTHORITY   *p* 222
505 DOYLE AVE, KELOWNA, BC, V1Y 0C5
(250) 862-4200   *SIC* 8062

INTERIOR HEALTH AUTHORITY   *p* 230
951 MURRAY ST, LILLOOET, BC, V0K 1V0
(250) 256-1300   *SIC* 8062

INTERIOR HEALTH AUTHORITY   *p* 235
3 VIEW ST SUITE 426, NELSON, BC, V1L 2V1
(250) 352-3111   *SIC* 8062

INTERIOR HEALTH KIMBERLY SPECIAL CARE HOME   *p* 223
386 2ND AVE, KIMBERLEY, BC, V1A 2Z8
(250) 427-4807   *SIC* 8361

INTERIOR IMAGES LIMITED   *p* 346
1440 ROSSER AVE UNIT 1, BRANDON, MB, R7A 0M4
(204) 726-8282   *SIC* 7389

INTERIOR MANUFACTURING GROUP INC *p* 712
974 LAKESHORE RD E, MISSISSAUGA, ON, L5E 1E4
(905) 278-9510   *SIC* 2542

INTERIOR PLUMBING AND HEATING LIMITED   *p* 217
782 LAVAL CRES, KAMLOOPS, BC, V2C 5P3
(250) 372-3441   *SIC* 1711

INTERIOR PROVINCIAL EXHIBITION AND STAMPEDE   *p* 179
See *INTERIOR PROVINCIAL EXHIBITION, THE*

INTERIOR PROVINCIAL EXHIBITION, THE *p* 179
3371 PEASANT VALLEY RD, ARMSTRONG, BC, V0E 1B0
(250) 546-9406   *SIC* 8699

INTERIOR ROADS LTD   *p* 217
1212 MCGILL RD, KAMLOOPS, BC, V2C 6N6
(250) 374-7238   *SIC* 1611

INTERIOR SAVINGS CREDIT UNION *p* 222
678 BERNARD AVE SUITE 300, KELOWNA, BC, V1Y 6P3
(250) 869-8300   *SIC* 6062

INTERLAKE ACQUISITION CORPORATION LIMITED   *p* 887
45 MERRITT ST, ST CATHARINES, ON, L2T 1J4
(905) 680-3000   *SIC* 2621

INTERLAKE COLONY FARMS LTD   *p* 359
GD, TEULON, MB, R0C 3B0
(204) 886-2107   *SIC* 0191

INTERLAKE CONSUMERS CO-OPERATIVE LIMITED   *p*

345
253 MAIN ST, ARBORG, MB, R0C 0A0
(204) 376-5245   *SIC* 5171

INTERLAKE PAPER   *p* 887
*See INTERLAKE ACQUISITION CORPO-
RATION LIMITED*

**INTERLAKE REGIONAL HEALTH AU-
THORITY INC**   *p*
345
233 ST PHILLIPS DR, ARBORG, MB, R0C
0A0
(204) 376-5226   *SIC* 8051

**INTERLAKE REGIONAL HEALTH AU-
THORITY INC**   *p*
345
1 STEENSON DR, ASHERN, MB, R0C 0E0
(204) 768-2461   *SIC* 8062

**INTERLAKE REGIONAL HEALTH AU-
THORITY INC**   *p*
356
120 EASTON DRIVE, SELKIRK, MB, R1A
2M2
(204) 482-5800   *SIC* 8062

**INTERLAKE REGIONAL HEALTH AU-
THORITY INC**   *p*
359
162 3 AVE SE, TEULON, MB, R0C 3B0
(204) 886-2108   *SIC* 8062

**INTERLAKE REGIONAL HEALTH AU-
THORITY INC**   *p*
359
68 MAIN ST, STONEWALL, MB, R0C 2Z0
(204) 378-2460   *SIC* 8062

INTERLAKE SCHOOL DIVISION   *p* 359
192 2ND AVE N, STONEWALL, MB, R0C
2Z0
(204) 467-5100   *SIC* 8211

**INTERLAKES VOLUNTEER FIRE DEPART-
MENT**   *p*
180
7657 LITTLE FORT HWY SUITE 24,
BRIDGE LAKE, BC, V0K 1E0
(250) 593-4266   *SIC* 7389

INTERLANGUES   *p* 833
See CMI INTERLANGUES INC

INTERLINE BRANDS INC   *p* 723
6990 CREDITVIEW RD SUITE 4, MISSIS-
SAUGA, ON, L5N 8R9
(905) 821-8292   *SIC* 5074

INTERLINE MOTOR FREIGHT INC   *p* 255
13562 MAYCREST WAY SUITE 5108,
RICHMOND, BC, V6V 2J7
SIC 4212

**INTERMAP TECHNOLOGIES CORPORA-
TION**   *p*
749
2 GURDWARA RD SUITE 200, NEPEAN,
ON, K2E 1A2
SIC 7389

INTERMARCH LAGORIA, L'   *p* 1161
See 2704242 CANADA INC

INTERMARCHE LAGORIA (BELANGER),L'
p 1346
See 4259238 CANADA INC

INTERMARCHE PALUMBO   *p* 1361
See 9158-7022 QUEBEC INC

INTERMARCHE ST-ROCH   *p* 1257
See 9070-5245 QUEBEC INC

INTERMAT   *p* 1070
See DE LA FONTAINE & ASSOCIES INC

INTERMAT (PORTES & BOISERIES)p 1380
See DE LA FONTAINE & ASSOCIES INC

**INTERMEC TECHNOLOGIES CANADA
ULC**   *p* 717
3333 UNITY DR, MISSISSAUGA, ON, L5L
3S6
(905) 608-3167   *SIC* 5045

INTERNATIONAL AQUATIC SERVICES LTD
p 783
4496 CHESSWOOD DR, NORTH YORK,
ON, M3J 2B9
(416) 665-6400   *SIC* 5999

INTERNATIONAL ASPHALT LEASING INC
p 109

6105 76 AVE NW, EDMONTON, AB, T6B
0A7
(780) 469-7304   *SIC* 6712

**INTERNATIONAL ASSOCIATION OF HEAT
& FROST INSULATORS & ALLIED WORK-
ERS**   *p*
381
946 ELGIN AVE SUITE 99, WINNIPEG, MB,
R3E 1B4
(204) 694-0726   *SIC* 8631

**INTERNATIONAL ASSOCIATION OF MA-
CHINISTS LABOUR MANAGEMENT PEN-
SION FUND (CANADA)**   *p*
825
200 ISABELLA ST UNIT 400, OTTAWA, ON,
K1S 1V7
(613) 567-8259   *SIC* 6371

INTERNATIONAL BEAUTY SERVICES *p* 96
See ROMADOR ENTERPRISES LTD

**INTERNATIONAL BRIDGE ADMINISTRA-
TION**   *p*
861
125 HURON ST, SAULT STE. MARIE, ON,
P6A 1R3
(705) 942-4345   *SIC* 4785

INTERNATIONAL BULK SERVICES   *p* 130
21423 TOWNSHIP ROAD 554, FORT
SASKATCHEWAN, AB, T8L 4A4
(780) 220-9264   *SIC* 4924

**INTERNATIONAL CASTINGS & SUPPLIES
LTD**   *p* 276
12383 83A AVE, SURREY, BC, V3W 9Y7
(604) 596-4961   *SIC* 5051

INTERNATIONAL CELLARS INC   *p* 298
1122 MAINLAND ST SUITE 200, VANCOU-
VER, BC, V6B 5L1
(604) 689-5333   *SIC* 5182

INTERNATIONAL CENTRE, THE   *p* 689
See T.I.C.C. LIMITED

**INTERNATIONAL CHAMPIONSHIP MAN-
AGEMENT LIMITED**   *p*
939
20 TORONTO ST, TORONTO, ON, M5C 2B8
(416) 955-0375   *SIC* 7941

INTERNATIONAL CIGAR STORES LIMITED
p 1000
170 MAIN ST, UNIONVILLE, ON, L3R 2G9
(905) 940-1515   *SIC* 5947

INTERNATIONAL CLOTHIERS   *p* 789
See INC GROUP INC

**INTERNATIONAL COMMODITIES EXPORT
COMPANY OF CANADA LIMITED**   *p* 52
606 4 ST SW SUITE 1020, CALGARY, AB,
T2P 1T1
(403) 264-8954   *SIC* 5191

INTERNATIONAL COMPUTER BROKERSp
510
*See INTERNATIONAL COMPUTER BRO-
KERS INC*

**INTERNATIONAL COMPUTER BROKERS
INC**   *p* 510
9052 CREDITVIEW RD, BRAMPTON, ON,
L6X 0E3
(905) 459-2100   *SIC* 5045

**INTERNATIONAL CONFERENCE SER-
VICES LTD**   *p*
314
1201 PENDER ST W SUITE 300, VANCOU-
VER, BC, V6E 2V2
(604) 681-2153   *SIC* 7389

INTERNATIONAL COOLING TOWER INC *p*
120
3310 93 ST NW, EDMONTON, AB, T6N 1C7
(780) 469-4900   *SIC* 7699

**INTERNATIONAL CORROSION CONTROL
INC**   *p* 523
930 SHELDON CRT, BURLINGTON, ON,
L7L 5K6
(905) 634-7751   *SIC* 5169

**INTERNATIONAL CROWD MANAGEMENT
INC**   *p* 192
6881 RUSSELL AVE, BURNABY, BC, V5J
4R8
(604) 688-0070   *SIC* 6289

**INTERNATIONAL CUSTOMER CARE SER-
VICES INC**   *p*
1031
3800 STEELES AVE W UNIT 100E, WOOD-
BRIDGE, ON, L4L 4G9
(905) 850-4760   *SIC* 4899

**INTERNATIONAL CUTLERY PRODUCTS,
DIV OF**   *p* 677
*See ZWILLING J.A. HENCKELS CANADA
LTD*

**INTERNATIONAL DATA CORPORATION
(CANADA) LTD**   *p* 942
33 YONGE ST SUITE 420, TORONTO, ON,
M5E 1G4
(416) 369-0033   *SIC* 8732

**INTERNATIONAL DATACASTING CORPO-
RATION**   *p*
624
10 BREWER HUNT WAY, KANATA, ON, K2K
2B5
(613) 596-4120   *SIC* 3669

**INTERNATIONAL DEVELOPMENT RE-
SEARCH CENTRE**   *p*
823
150 KENT ST, OTTAWA, ON, K1P 0B2
(613) 236-6163   *SIC* 8732

**INTERNATIONAL DIRECT RESPONSE
SERVICES LTD**   *p* 209
10159 NORDEL CRT, DELTA, BC, V4G 1J8
(604) 951-6855   *SIC* 5961

**INTERNATIONAL DISTRIBUTION NET-
WORK CANADA LTD**   *p*
791
70 FLORAL PKY, NORTH YORK, ON, M6L
2B9
(416) 248-5625   *SIC* 5072

**INTERNATIONAL DODGEBALL ASSOCIA-
TION**   *p*
288
*See VANCOUVER DODGEBALL LEAGUE
SOCIETY*

**INTERNATIONAL ECONOMY SERVICES
INC**   *p* 775
1057 STEELES AVE W SUITE 1, NORTH
YORK, ON, M2R 2S9
(416) 725-1294   *SIC* 8742

**INTERNATIONAL ELECTRONIC COMPO-
NENTS INC**   *p*
793
352 SIGNET DR, NORTH YORK, ON, M9L
1V2
(416) 293-2961   *SIC* 5065

**INTERNATIONAL FASTLINE FORWARD-
ING INC**   *p*
265
5200 MILLER RD SUITE 106, RICHMOND,
BC, V7B 1K5
(604) 278-0191   *SIC* 4731

**INTERNATIONAL FINANCIAL DATA SER-
VICES (CANADA) LIMITED**   *p*
939
30 ADELAIDE ST E SUITE 1, TORONTO,
ON, M5C 3G9
(416) 506-8000   *SIC* 6289

INTERNATIONAL FIREARMS   *p* 1338
*See CENTURY INTERNATIONAL ARMS
LTD*

INTERNATIONAL FITNESS HOLDINGS INC
p 71
7222 EDGEMONT BLVD NW, CALGARY,
AB, T3A 2X7
(403) 278-2499   *SIC* 7991

INTERNATIONAL GENETICS LIMITED   *p*
546
GD STN MAIN, COLLINGWOOD, ON, L9Y
3Z3
(705) 445-2734   *SIC* 5154

INTERNATIONAL GRAPHICS ULC   *p* 896
505 DOURO ST, STRATFORD, ON, N5A
3S9
(519) 271-3010   *SIC* 2678

INTERNATIONAL GRAPHICS ULC   *p* 1084
2135A BOUL DES LAURENTIDES, COTE
SAINT-LUC, QC, H7M 4M2

SIC 2678

INTERNATIONAL GROUP, INC, THE   *p* 874
50 SALOME DR, SCARBOROUGH, ON,
M1S 2A8
(416) 293-4151   *SIC* 2911

INTERNATIONAL HERBS (B.C.) LTD *p* 279
4151 184 ST, SURREY, BC, V3Z 1B7
(604) 576-2345   *SIC* 5149

**INTERNATIONAL INSTITUTE FOR SUS-
TAINABLE DEVELOPMENT**   *p*
374
111 LOMBARD AVE SUITE 325, WIN-
NIPEG, MB, R3B 0T4
(204) 958-7700   *SIC* 8733

INTERNATIONAL KNITTING MILLS, DIV OF
p 562
See MORBERN INC

**INTERNATIONAL LANGUAGE SCHOOLS
OF CANADA**   *p* 298
See ILSC (VANCOUVER) INC

INTERNATIONAL LUMBER INC   *p* 875
3410 SHEPPARD AVE E SUITE 400, SCAR-
BOROUGH, ON, M1T 3K4
(416) 754-1020   *SIC* 5031

INTERNATIONAL MAJESTIC   *p* 1334
*See INDUSTRIES MAJESTIC (CANADA)
LTEE, LES*

INTERNATIONAL MARINE SALVAGE INC *p*
846
17 INVERTOSE DR, PORT COLBORNE,
ON, L3K 5V5
(905) 835-1203   *SIC* 4953

INTERNATIONAL MINICUT INC   *p* 1049
8400 BOUL DU GOLF, ANJOU, QC, H1J
3A1
(514) 352-6464   *SIC* 5251

**INTERNATIONAL NAME PLATE SUPPLIES
LIMITED**   *p* 649
1420 CRUMLIN, LONDON, ON, N5V 1S1
(519) 455-7647   *SIC* 3993

INTERNATIONAL NAVISTAR   *p* 1286
See LE CENTRE ROUTIER (1994) INC

INTERNATIONAL NEON   *p* 1156
See 109578 CANADA LTEE

INTERNATIONAL NEWS   *p* 718
See DAKIN NEWS SYSTEMS INC

**INTERNATIONAL NEWTECH DEVELOP-
MENT INCORPORATED**   *p*
206
1629 FOSTER'S WAY, DELTA, BC, V3M 6S7
SIC 8731

**INTERNATIONAL ORNITHOLOGICAL
CONGRESS 2018 ORGANIZING SOCIETY**p
287
7190 DUFF ST, VANCOUVER, BC, V5P 4B3
(604) 218-9138   *SIC* 8748

INTERNATIONAL PACIFIC SALES LTD   *p*
258
22111 FRASERWOOD WAY, RICHMOND,
BC, V6W 1J5
(604) 273-7035   *SIC* 5141

**INTERNATIONAL PAPER CANADA PULP
HOLDINGS ULC**   *p* 132
GD, GRANDE PRAIRIE, AB, T8V 6V4
(780) 539-8500   *SIC* 2611

**INTERNATIONAL PETROLEUM CORPO-
RATION**   *p*
306
885 GEORGIA ST W SUITE 2000, VAN-
COUVER, BC, V6C 3E8
(604) 689-7842   *SIC* 1311

INTERNATIONAL PLAY COMPANY INC   *p*
229
27353 58 CRES UNIT 215, LANGLEY, BC,
V4W 3W7
(604) 607-1111   *SIC* 3949

**INTERNATIONAL PLAYING CARD COM-
PANY LIMITED**   *p*
504
845 INTERMODAL DR UNIT 1, BRAMP-
TON, ON, L6T 0C6
(905) 488-7102   *SIC* 5092

**INTERNATIONAL PRECAST SOLUTIONS,
DIVISION OF**   *p* 1023

See PRESTRESSED SYSTEMS INCOR-PORATED

INTERNATIONAL QUALITY AND PRODUC-TIVITY CENTRE *p 925*
See IQPC WORLDWIDE COMPANY

INTERNATIONAL ROAD DYNAMICS INC *p 1428*
702 43RD ST E, SASKATOON, SK, S7K 3T9
(306) 653-6600 *SIC 4785*

INTERNATIONAL SEATING & DECOR *p 1020*
See GROUND EFFECTS LTD

INTERNATIONAL SILVER DEVELOPMENT INC *p 712*
1260 LAKESHORE RD E, MISSISSAUGA, ON, L5E 3B8
SIC 5094

INTERNATIONAL STAGE LINES INC *p 260*
4171 VANGUARD RD, RICHMOND, BC, V6X 2P6
(604) 270-6135 *SIC 4142*

INTERNATIONAL SUPPLIERS AND CON-TRACTORS INC *p 1053*
19400 AV CRUICKSHANK, BAIE-D'URFE, QC, H9X 3P1
(514) 457-5362 *SIC 5169*

INTERNATIONAL TELE-FILM *p 547*
See 1642852 ONTARIO LTD

INTERNATIONAL TENTNOLOGY CORP *p 272*
15427 66 AVE, SURREY, BC, V3S 2A1
(604) 597-8368 *SIC 2394*

INTERNATIONAL TRANSACTION SYS-TEMS (CANADA) LTD *p 685*
7415 TORBRAM RD, MISSISSAUGA, ON, L4T 1G8
(905) 677-2088 *SIC 3578*

INTERNATIONAL TRUCKLOAD SERVICES INC *p 491*
107 BELLEVUE DR, BELLEVILLE, ON, K8N 4Z5
(613) 961-5144 *SIC 4213*

INTERNATIONAL UNION OF OPERATING ENGINEERS LOCAL 115 *p 189*
4333 LEDGER AVE SUITE 115, BURNABY, BC, V5G 4G9
(604) 291-8831 *SIC 8742*

INTERNATIONAL UNION OF OPERATING ENGINEERS 793 *p 804*
2245 SPEERS RD, OAKVILLE, ON, L6L 6X8
(905) 469-9299 *SIC 8631*

INTERNATIONAL UNION OF OPERATING ENGINEERS LOCAL 955 *p 101*
17603 114 AVE NW, EDMONTON, AB, T5S 2R9
(780) 483-8955 *SIC 8631*

INTERNATIONAL VINEYARD INC *p 260*
4631 SHELL RD SUITE 165, RICHMOND, BC, V6X 3M4
(604) 303-5778 *SIC 2032*

INTERNATIONAL VISION ORGANIZATION *p 40*
44 COLERIDGE CRES NW, CALGARY, AB, T2K 1X9
SIC 8062

INTERNATIONAL WAXES *p 874*
See INTERNATIONAL GROUP, INC, THE

INTERNATIONALE *p 1109*
See RAINVILLE AUTOMOBILE 1975 INC

INTERNET COURIER MESSENGER SER-VICES *p 362*
1137 PANDORA AVE W, WINNIPEG, MB, R2C 1N4
SIC 7389

INTERNET REALTY LTD *p 222*
1101 HARVEY AVE, KELOWNA, BC, V1Y 6E8
(250) 762-9979 *SIC 6531*

INTERNET SECURE *p 803*
See FUNDS FLOW CANADA INC

INTEROUTE CONSTRUCTION LTD *p 213*
9503 79TH AVE, FORT ST. JOHN, BC, V1J 4J3
(250) 787-7283 *SIC 1611*

INTERPAC CORPORATION INC *p 1340*
6855 CH DE LA COTE-DE-LIESSE, SAINT-LAURENT, QC, H4T 1E5
(514) 340-9440 *SIC 2673*

INTERPAC FOREST PRODUCTS LTD *p 225*
9701 201 ST, LANGLEY, BC, V1M 3E7
(604) 881-2300 *SIC 7389*

INTERPHARM LTD *p 914*
30 NOVOPHARM CRT, TORONTO, ON, M1B 2K9
(800) 663-5903 *SIC 5122*

INTERPHONE MONTREAL *p 1130*
See 2733-8649 QUEBEC INC

INTERPLAST PACKAGING INC *p 1381*
955 BOUL INDUSTRIEL, TERREBONNE, QC, J6Y 1V7
(450) 971-0500 *SIC 2679*

INTERPROVINCIAL MEAT SALES LIMITED *p 446*
65 THORNHILL DR, DARTMOUTH, NS, B3B 1R9
(902) 468-5884 *SIC 5142*

INTERPUBLIC GROUP OF COMPANIES CANADA, INC, THE *p 963*
207 QUEENS QUAY W SUITE 2, TORONTO, ON, M5J 1A7
(647) 260-2116 *SIC 7336*

INTERPUBLIC GROUP OF COMPANIES CANADA, INC, THE *p 986*
100 KING ST W SUITE 6200, TORONTO, ON, M5X 1B8
(416) 545-5563 *SIC 7336*

INTERRENT REAL ESTATE INVESTMENT TRUST *p 834*
485 BANK ST SUITE 207, OTTAWA, ON, K2P 1Z2
(613) 569-5699 *SIC 6726*

INTERROLL CANADA LIMITED *p 755*
1201 GORHAM ST, NEWMARKET, ON, L3Y 8Y2
(905) 953-8510 *SIC 3535*

INTERSAC *p 1053*
See INTERNATIONAL SUPPLIERS AND CONTRACTORS INC

INTERSAND CANADA *p 1065*
See GROUPE INTERSAND CANADA INC, LE

INTERSPORT *p 1363*
See 2173-4108 QUEBEC INC

INTERSPORT NORTH HILL *p 41*
See 1249413 ALBERTA LTD

INTERSTATE BATTERY SYSTEMS OF BRAMPTON *p 1030*
See BAUMAN, T & W ENTERPRISES INC

INTERSTYLE CERAMIC & GLASS LTD *p 182*
3625 BRIGHTON AVE, BURNABY, BC, V5A 3H5
(604) 421-7229 *SIC 3231*

INTERTAIN GROUP LIMITED, THE *p 981*
24 DUNCAN ST 2 FL, TORONTO, ON, M5V 2B8
(647) 641-8404 *SIC 5734*

INTERTAPE POLYMER INC *p 469*
50 ABBEY AVE, TRURO, NS, B2N 6W4
SIC 2221

INTERTAPE POLYMER INC. *p 1229*
800 RUE DU SQUARE-VICTORIA, MON-TREAL, QC, H4Z 1A1
SIC 2221

INTERTEC INSTRUMENTATION LTD *p 860*
255 HENRY DR, SARNIA, ON, N7T 7H5
(519) 337-2773 *SIC 3299*

INTERTEK *p 105*
See INTERTEK INSPECTION SERVICES, LTD

INTERTEK HEALTH SCIENCES INC. *p 723*
2233 ARGENTIA RD SUITE 201, MISSIS-SAUGA, ON, L5N 2X7
(905) 542-2900 *SIC 8748*

INTERTEK INSPECTION SERVICES, LTD *p 105*
14920 135 AVE NW, EDMONTON, AB, T5V 1R9
(780) 482-5911 *SIC 7389*

INTERTEK SCIENTIFIC AND REGULA-TORY CONSULTING SERVICES *p 723*
See INTERTEK HEALTH SCIENCES INC.

INTERTEK TESTING SERVICES (ITS) CANADA LTD *p 1239*
2561 AV GEORGES-V, MONTREAL-EST, QC, H1L 6S4
(514) 640-6332 *SIC 8731*

INTERTEK TESTING SERVICES NA LTD *p 1128*
1829 32E AV, LACHINE, QC, H8T 3J1
(514) 631-3100 *SIC 8734*

INTERURBAIN COOPTEL *p 1392*
See COOPTEL COOP DE TELECOMMUNI-CATION

INTERVISTAS CONSULTING INC *p 323*
1200 73RD AVE W SUITE 550, VANCOU-VER, BC, V6P 6G5
(604) 717-1800 *SIC 8742*

INTERWORX PLANNING AND DESIGN *p 314*
1140 PENDER ST W SUITE 600, VANCOU-VER, BC, V6E 4G1
(604) 806-6255 *SIC 7389*

INTERWRAP INC *p 246*
See INTERWRAP ULC

INTERWRAP INC *p 246*
1650 BROADWAY ST SUITE 101, PORT COQUITLAM, BC, V3C 2M8
SIC 3069

INTERWRAP ULC *p 314*
1177 HASTINGS ST W SUITE 1818, VAN-COUVER, BC, V6E 2K3
(800) 567-9727 *SIC 2671*

INTEVA OSHAWA PLANT *p 1014*
See INTEVA PRODUCTS CANADA, ULC

INTEVA PRODUCTS CANADA, ULC *p 1014*
1555 WENTWORTH ST, WHITBY, ON, L1N 9T6
(905) 666-4600 *SIC 7532*

INTIMODE *p 1183*
See JIMMISS CANADA INC

INTIVID SOLUTIONS *p 1341*
See STANLEY SECURITY SOLUTIONS CANADA INC

INTOUCH INSIGHT INC *p 624*
400 MARCH RD, KANATA, ON, K2K 3H4
(613) 270-7900 *SIC 8732*

INTOUCH INSIGHT LTD *p 624*
400 MARCH RD, KANATA, ON, K2K 3H4
(613) 270-7916 *SIC 7376*

INTRA ENERGY BC INC *p 288*
3665 KINGSWAY SUITE 300, VANCOU-VER, BC, V5R 5W2
SIC 4924

INTRACHEM INDUSTRIES INC *p 995*
476 ARMDALE AVE, TORONTO, ON, M6S 3X9
(416) 760-0929 *SIC 5169*

INTRALEC ELECTRICAL PRODUCTS LTD *p 735*
1200 CARDIFF BLVD UNIT 1, MISSIS-SAUGA, ON, L5S 1P6
(905) 670-0970 *SIC 4731*

INTRAWEST RESORT CLUB GROUP *p 343*
4580 CHATEAU BLVD, WHISTLER, BC, V8E 0Z6
(604) 938-3030 *SIC 7011*

INTRAWEST ULC *p 298*
375 WATER ST SUITE 710, VANCOUVER, BC, V6B 5C6
(604) 695-8200 *SIC 7011*

INTRAWEST ULC *p 493*
108 JOZO WEIDER BLVD, BLUE MOUN-TAINS, ON, L9Y 3Z2
(705) 445-0231 *SIC 7011*

INTRAWEST ULC *p 493*
220 GORD CANNING DR, BLUE MOUN-

TAINS, ON, L9Y 0V9
(705) 443-8080 *SIC 7011*

INTREPIDES A DOMICILE, LES *p 1289*
See INTREPIDES DE ROUYN-NORANDA INC., LES

INTREPIDES DE ROUYN-NORANDA INC., LES *p 1289*
380 AV RICHARD BUREAU 203, ROUYN-NORANDA, QC, J9X 4L3
(819) 762-7217 *SIC 8059*

INTRIA (TM) *p 1131*
See INTRIA ITEMS INC

INTRIA ITEMS INC *p 731*
5705 CANCROSS CT, MISSISSAUGA, ON, L5R 3E9
(905) 755-2400 *SIC 7374*

INTRIA ITEMS INC *p 1131*
8301 RUE ELMSLIE, LASALLE, QC, H8N 3H9
(514) 368-5222 *SIC 7374*

INTRICATE NETWORKS *p 1407*
See SOUTH WEST TERMINAL LTD

INTRINSYC TECHNOLOGIES CORPORA-TION *p 306*
885 DUNSMUIR ST 3RD FL, VANCOUVER, BC, V6C 1N5
(604) 801-6461 *SIC 7371*

INTROTEL COMMUNICATIONS INC *p 696*
5170 TIMBERLEA BLVD UNIT B, MISSIS-SAUGA, ON, L4W 2S5
(905) 625-8700 *SIC 5065*

INTSTITUTE FOR GENDER, RACE, SEXU-ALITY AND SOCIAL JUSTICE *p 325*
See UNIVERSITY OF BRITISH COLUMBIA, THE

INTUIT CANADA ULC *p 696*
5100 SPECTRUM WAY, MISSISSAUGA, ON, L4W 5S2
(888) 843-5449 *SIC 7371*

INUKTUN SERVICES LTD *p 234*
2569 KENWORTH RD SUITE C, NANAIMO, BC, V9T 3M4
(250) 729-8080 *SIC 3569*

INUVIALUIT DEVELOPMENT CORPORA-TION *p 435*
107 MACKENZIE RD 3RD FL, INUVIK, NT, X0E 0T0
(867) 777-7000 *SIC 8741*

INUVIK GAS LTD *p 435*
107 MACKENZIE RD SUITE 102, INUVIK, NT, X0E 0T0
(867) 777-3422 *SIC 4924*

INVACARE CANADA *p 704*
See 1207273 ALBERTA ULC

INVACARE CANADA L.P. *p 706*
570 MATHESON BLVD E SUITE 8, MISSIS-SAUGA, ON, L4Z 4G4
(905) 890-8300 *SIC 5047*

INVAR MANUFACTURING DIV *p 603*
See LINAMAR HOLDINGS INC.

INVENTA *p 319*
See INVENTA SALES & PROMOTIONS INC

INVENTA SALES & PROMOTIONS INC *p 319*
1401 8TH AVE W SUITE 210, VANCOU-VER, BC, V6H 1C9
(604) 687-0544 *SIC 8743*

INVENTAIRES LAPARE INC *p 1152*
11329 MONTEE SAINTE-MARIANNE, MIRABEL, QC, J7J 2B2
(450) 435-2997 *SIC 7389*

INVENTIV CANADA ULC *p 779*
895 DON MILLS RD SUITE 700, NORTH YORK, ON, M3C 1W3
(416) 391-5166 *SIC 8741*

INVENTURE SOLUTIONS INC *p 295*
183 TERMINAL AVE, VANCOUVER, BC, V6A 4G2
(604) 877-7000 *SIC 7379*

INVENTYS *p 192*
See INVENTYS THERMAL TECHNOLO-

GIES INC

INVENTYS THERMAL TECHNOLOGIES INC   p 192
8528 GLENLYON PKY UNIT 143, BURNABY, BC, V5J 0B6
(604) 456-0504   SIC 2813

INVERA INC   p 1402
4333 RUE SAINTE-CATHERINE O BUREAU 201, WESTMOUNT, QC, H3Z 1P9
(514) 935-3535   SIC 7371

INVERARY INN & GLENGHORM RESORT p 439
See MACAULAY, SCOTT INVESTMENTS LIMITED

INVERARY MANOR   p 459
See INVERNESS MUNICIPAL HOUSING CORPORATION

INVERMERE & DISTRICT HOSPITAL p 222
See INTERIOR HEALTH AUTHORITY

INVERMERE HARDWARE & BUILDING SUPPLIES CO LTD   p 216
9980 ARROW RD, INVERMERE, BC, V0A 1K2
(250) 342-6908   SIC 5211

INVERNESS MUNICIPAL HOUSING CORPORATION   p 442
15092 CABOT TRAIL RD, CHETICAMP, NS, B0E 1H0
(902) 224-2087   SIC 8051

INVERNESS MUNICIPAL HOUSING CORPORATION   p 459
72 MAPLE ST, INVERNESS, NS, B0E 1N0
(902) 258-2842   SIC 8051

INVESCO CANDA LTD   p 772
5140 YONGE ST SUITE 800, NORTH YORK, ON, M2N 6X7
(416) 590-9855   SIC 6722

INVESQUE INC   p 953
333 BAY ST SUITE 3400, TORONTO, ON, M5H 2S7
SIC 8361

INVESSA ASSURANCES ET SERVICES FINANCIERS INC   p 1086
225 PROM DU CENTROPOLIS BUREAU 220, COTE SAINT-LUC, QC, H7T 0B3
(450) 781-6560   SIC 6411

INVEST REIT   p 762
700 LAKESHORE DR, NORTH BAY, ON, P1A 2G4
(705) 474-5800   SIC 7011

INVESTIA SERVICES FINANCIERS INC   p 1279
6700 BOUL PIERRE-BERTRAND BUREAU 300, QUEBEC, QC, G2J 0B4
(418) 684-5548   SIC 6282

INVESTIGATION PROTECTION ACCES SECURITE INC   p 1366
283 RUE JACQUES-CARTIER BUREAU 6, SALABERRY-DE-VALLEYFIELD, QC, J6T 4S9
(450) 377-3008   SIC 7389

INVESTIGATIONS RK INC   p 1224
2100 AV DE L'EGLISE, MONTREAL, QC, H4E 1H4
(514) 761-7121   SIC 7381

INVESTIGATIVE RESEARCH GROUP INC p 487
49 TRUMAN RD SUITE 102, BARRIE, ON, L4N 8Y7
(705) 739-4800   SIC 7381

INVESTIGATORS GROUP INC, THE   p 874
2061 MCCOWAN RD SUITE 2, SCARBOROUGH, ON, M1S 3Y6
(416) 955-9450   SIC 7381

INVESTISSEMENT CRB INC   p 1066
585 CH DE TOURAINE, BOUCHERVILLE, QC, J4B 5E4
(450) 655-1340   SIC 5251

INVESTISSEMENT IMMOBILIER CCSM LTEE   p 1169

3200 RUE OMER-LAVALLEE, MONTREAL, QC, H1Y 3P5
(514) 523-1160   SIC 6513

INVESTISSEMENT IMMOBILIER GROUPE MAURICE INC   p 1329
2400 RUE DES NATIONS BUREAU 137, SAINT-LAURENT, QC, H4R 3G4
(514) 331-2788   SIC 6719

INVESTISSEMENT LC   p 1220
See GEXEL TELECOM INTERNATIONAL INC

INVESTISSEMENT PIERRE MARCOTTE LIMITEE, LES   p 1296
900 RUE DE L'ETANG, SAINT-BRUNO, QC, J3V 6K8
(450) 653-0222   SIC 5311

INVESTISSEMENT QUEBEC   p 1188
413 RUE SAINT-JACQUES BUREAU 500, MONTREAL, QC, H2Y 1N9
(514) 873-4375   SIC 8748

INVESTISSEMENTS ALONIM INC, LES   p 1251
237 BOUL HYMUS, POINTE-CLAIRE, QC, H9R 5C7
(514) 694-7710   SIC 6712

INVESTISSEMENTS ALT2 INC   p 1374
73 RUE QUEEN, SHERBROOKE, QC, J1M 0C9
(819) 566-8833   SIC 6411

INVESTISSEMENTS BABE INC   p 1383
374 RUE NOTRE-DAME E, THETFORD MINES, QC, G6G 2S4
SIC 6712

INVESTISSEMENTS CANFAB INC., LES   p 1216
2740 RUE SAINT-PATRICK, MONTREAL, QC, H3K 1B8
(514) 935-5265   SIC 2655

INVESTISSEMENTS CAPESPAN CANADA INC, LES   p 1340
6700 CH DE LA COTE-DE-LIESSE BUREAU 301, SAINT-LAURENT, QC, H4T 2B5
(514) 739-9181   SIC 5148

INVESTISSEMENTS DU HAUT-ST-LAURENT INC, LES   p 1293
4770 RUE SAINT-FELIX, SAINT-AUGUSTIN-DE-DESMAURES, QC, G3A 0K9
(418) 872-4936   SIC 8361

INVESTISSEMENTS IMMOBILIERS KEVLAR INC   p 1197
1800 AV MCGILL COLLEGE BUREAU 1900, MONTREAL, QC, H3A 3J6
(514) 393-8858   SIC 6531

INVESTISSEMENTS ISAAM INC, LES   p 1330
3100 BOUL DE LA COTE-VERTU BUREAU 210, SAINT-LAURENT, QC, H4R 2J8
(514) 335-6606   SIC 6712

INVESTISSEMENTS J.B. GREGOIRE INC p 1069
8450 BOUL TASCHEREAU, BROSSARD, QC, J4X 1C2
(450) 466-0999   SIC 5511

INVESTISSEMENTS JEAN C. LAPIERRE LTEE   p 1147
2135 RUE SHERBROOKE, MAGOG, QC, J1X 2T5
(819) 843-3939   SIC 5014

INVESTISSEMENTS KITZA INC   p 1132
9515 BOUL LASALLE, LASALLE, QC, H8R 2M9
(514) 364-3315   SIC 6531

INVESTISSEMENTS LACORDAIRE INC, LES   p 1361
6625 RUE ERNEST-CORMIER, SAINTE-ROSE, QC, H7C 2V2
(514) 321-8260   SIC 6211

INVESTISSEMENTS MANIOLI, LES   p 1226
See MANIOLI INVESTMENTS INC

INVESTISSEMENTS MICHAEL WILSON INC, LES   p 1401
642 AV MURRAY HILL, WESTMOUNT, QC,

H3Y 2W6
(450) 465-3330   SIC 5085

INVESTISSEMENTS MICHEL DESLAURIERS INC, LES   p 1159
370 117 RTE, MONT-TREMBLANT, QC, J8E 2X3
(819) 425-1110   SIC 5531

INVESTISSEMENTS MONIT INC, LES   p 1197
1000 RUE SHERBROOKE O UNITE 1800, MONTREAL, QC, H3A 3G4
(514) 933-3000   SIC 6531

INVESTISSEMENTS NOLINOR INC, LES   p 1153
11600 RUE LOUIS-BISSON, MIRABEL, QC, J7N 1G9
(450) 476-0018   SIC 4512

INVESTISSEMENTS OLYMBEC INC   p 1326
333 BOUL DECARIE ETAGE 5E, SAINT-LAURENT, QC, H4N 3M9
(514) 344-3334   SIC 6719

INVESTISSEMENTS PELLERIN INC, LES p 1217
8600 AV DE L'EPEE, MONTREAL, QC, H3N 2G6
(514) 273-8855   SIC 6712

INVESTISSEMENTS PENTABEL LIMITEE, LES   p 1239
6868 BOUL MAURICE-DUPLESSIS, MONTREAL-NORD, QC, H1G 1Z6
(514) 327-2800   SIC 6712

INVESTISSEMENTS PROSPA INC   p 1215
1262 RUE SAINT-MATHIEU, MONTREAL, QC, H3H 2H8
SIC 5149

INVESTISSEMENTS PSP   p 1207
See OFFICE D'INVESTISSEMENT DES REGIMES DE PENSIONS DU SECTEUR PUBLIC

INVESTISSEMENTS RAMAN 'S.E.N.C.', LES   p 1197
1110 RUE SHERBROOKE O BUREAU 301, MONTREAL, QC, H3A 1G8
(514) 844-3951   SIC 7011

INVESTISSEMENTS RAYMOND GAGNE, LES   p 1146
See CANADIAN TIRE REAL ESTATE LIMITED

INVESTISSEMENTS RAYPAUL LTEE, LES p 1205
1258 RUE STANLEY, MONTREAL, QC, H3B 2S7
(514) 871-0057   SIC 6531

INVESTISSEMENTS SKYFOLD LTEE   p 1053
325 AV LEE, BAIE-D'URFE, QC, H9X 3S3
(514) 735-5410   SIC 6712

INVESTISSEMENTS SYLNIC INC, LES   p 1172
4351 RUE D'IBERVILLE, MONTREAL, QC, H2H 2L7
(514) 598-8130   SIC 6712

INVESTISSEMENTS TREVI INC   p 1152
12775 RUE BRAULT, MIRABEL, QC, J7J 0C4
(450) 973-1249   SIC 6712

INVESTISSEURS 3 B INC   p 1314
15855 AV HUBERT, SAINT-HYACINTHE, QC, J2T 4C9
(450) 773-5258   SIC 2329

INVESTMENT INDUSTRY REGULATORY ORGANIZATION OF CANADA   p 953
121 KING ST W SUITE 1600, TORONTO, ON, M5H 3T9
(416) 364-0604   SIC 8611

INVESTMENT PLANNING COUNSEL INC p 696
5015 SPECTRUM WAY SUITE 200, MISSISSAUGA, ON, L4W 0E4
(905) 212-9799   SIC 8741

INVESTMENT PLANNING COUNSEL OF CANADA LIMITED   p 696
2680 SKYMARK AVE SUITE 700, MISSIS-

SAUGA, ON, L4W 5L6
SIC 8741

INVESTMENTS HARDWARE LIMITED   p 1031
250 ROWNTREE DAIRY RD, WOODBRIDGE, ON, L4L 9J7
(905) 851-8974   SIC 5072

INVESTORS GROUP   p 222
See INVESTORS GROUP FINANCIAL SERVICES INC

INVESTORS GROUP   p 579
See INVESTORS GROUP FINANCIAL SERVICES INC

INVESTORS GROUP FINANCIAL SERVICE p 767
See INVESTORS GROUP TRUST CO. LTD

INVESTORS GROUP FINANCIAL SERVICES   p 865
See INVESTORS GROUP INC

INVESTORS GROUP FINANCIAL SERVICES INC   p 74
37 RICHARD WAY SW UNIT 100, CALGARY, AB, T3E 7M8
(403) 253-4840   SIC 8742

INVESTORS GROUP FINANCIAL SERVICES INC   p 89
10060 JASPER AVE NW SUITE 2400, EDMONTON, AB, T5J 3R8
(780) 448-1988   SIC 8741

INVESTORS GROUP FINANCIAL SERVICES INC   p 222
1628 DICKSON AVE SUITE 100, KELOWNA, BC, V1Y 9X1
(250) 762-3329   SIC 8742

INVESTORS GROUP FINANCIAL SERVICES INC   p 378
447 PORTAGE AVE, WINNIPEG, MB, R3C 3B6
(204) 943-0361   SIC 8741

INVESTORS GROUP FINANCIAL SERVICES INC   p 386
1661 PORTAGE AVE SUITE 702, WINNIPEG, MB, R3J 3T7
(204) 786-2708   SIC 8741

INVESTORS GROUP FINANCIAL SERVICES INC   p 509
208 COUNTY COURT BLVD, BRAMPTON, ON, L6W 4S9
(905) 450-1500   SIC 8741

INVESTORS GROUP FINANCIAL SERVICES INC   p 579
295 THE WEST MALL SUITE 700, ETOBICOKE, ON, M9C 4Z4
(416) 695-8600   SIC 8742

INVESTORS GROUP FINANCIAL SERVICES INC   p 706
1 ROBERT SPECK PKWY 10 FL, MISSISSAUGA, ON, L4Z 3M3
(905) 306-0031   SIC 8742

INVESTORS GROUP FINANCIAL SERVICES INC   p 767
200 YORKLAND BLVD SUITE 300, NORTH YORK, ON, M2J 5C1
(416) 491-7400   SIC 8741

INVESTORS GROUP FINANCIAL SERVICES INC   p 1014
1614 DUNDAS ST E UNIT 111, WHITBY, ON, L1N 8Y8
(905) 434-8400   SIC 8741

INVESTORS GROUP FINANCIAL SERVICES INC   p 1227
8250 BOUL DECARIE BUREAU 200, MON-

TREAL, QC, H4P 2P5
(514) 733-3950   *SIC* 8742

INVESTORS GROUP FINANCIAL SER-VICES INC   *p*
1251
6500 RTE TRANSCANADIENNE UNITE 600, POINTE-CLAIRE, QC, H9R 0A5
(514) 426-0886   *SIC* 8741

INVESTORS GROUP INC   *p* 378
447 PORTAGE AVE, WINNIPEG, MB, R3C 3B6
(204) 943-0361   *SIC* 6722

INVESTORS GROUP INC   *p* 865
305 MILNER AVE SUITE 701, SCARBOR-OUGH, ON, M1B 3V4
(416) 292-7229   *SIC* 6162

INVESTORS GROUP TRUST CO. LTD *p* 767
200 YORKLAND BLVD UNIT 300, NORTH YORK, ON, M2J 5C1
(647) 456-5160   *SIC* 6282

INVESTORS SALES & SERVICES WEST IS-LAND   *p*
1251
See INVESTORS GROUP FINANCIAL SERVICES INC

INVESTORS TACTICAL ASSET ALLOCA-TION FUND   *p*
378
447 PORTAGE AVE, WINNIPEG, MB, R3C 3B6
(204) 957-7383   *SIC* 6722

INVICTUS GAMES TORONTO 2017   *p* 949
See CANADIAN INTERNATIONAL MILI-TARY GAMES CORPORATION

INVIS CANADA'S MORTGAGES EXPERTS
p 731
See INVIS INC

INVIS INC   *p* 731
5770 HURONTARIO ST SUITE 600, MIS-SISSAUGA, ON, L5R 3G5
(905) 283-3300   *SIC* 7389

INVISTA (CANADA) COMPANY   *p* 489
GD, BATH, ON, K0H 1G0
(613) 634-5124   *SIC* 2299

INVISTA (CANADA) COMPANY   *p* 630
455 FRONT RD, KINGSTON, ON, K7L 4Z6
(613) 544-6000   *SIC* 2299

INVISTA (CANADA) COMPANY   *p* 663
1400 COUNTY RD 2, MAITLAND, ON, K0E 1P0
(613) 348-4204   *SIC* 5169

INVISTA COMPANY CANADA   *p* 563
291 ALBERT ST, CORUNNA, ON, N0N 1G0
(519) 862-6881   *SIC* 2822

INVODANE ENGINEERING LTD   *p* 914
44 METROPOLITAN RD, TORONTO, ON, M1R 2T6
(416) 443-8049   *SIC* 8711

INX INTERNATIONAL INK   *p* 1379
See ENCRES INTERNATIONALE INX CORP

IOC   *p* 415
See IRVING OIL COMMERCIAL G.P.

IOC2018   *p* 287
See INTERNATIONAL ORNITHOLOGICAL CONGRESS 2018 ORGANIZING SOCIETY

IODE BARGAIN SHOP   *p* 64
1320 1 ST SW, CALGARY, AB, T2R 0V7
(403) 266-6855   *SIC* 8699

IOGEN BIO-PRODUCTS CORPORATION *p*
827
310 HUNT CLUB RD, OTTAWA, ON, K1V 1C1
(613) 733-9830   *SIC* 8732

IOGEN BIO-PRODUCTS CORPORATION *p*
827
300 HUNT CLUB RD, OTTAWA, ON, K1V 1C1
(613) 733-9830   *SIC* 2869

IOGEN CORPORATION   *p* 827
310 HUNT CLUB RD, OTTAWA, ON, K1V 1C1
(613) 733-9830   *SIC* 2911

IOGEN CORPORATION   *p* 827

310 HUNT CLUB RD, OTTAWA, ON, K1V 1C1
(613) 733-9830   *SIC* 2869

IOGEN ENERGY CORPORATION   *p* 827
310 HUNT CLUB RD, OTTAWA, ON, K1V 1C1
(613) 733-9830   *SIC* 5122

IONA HOLDINGS CORPORATION   *p* 67
120 17 AVE SW, CALGARY, AB, T2S 2T2
(403) 218-5500   *SIC* 8699

IOOF SENIORS HOMES INC   *p* 487
10 BROOKS ST, BARRIE, ON, L4N 5L3
(705) 728-2389   *SIC* 6513

IOS SERVICES GEOSCIENTIFIQUES INC *p*
1080
1319 BOUL SAINT-PAUL, CHICOUTIMI, QC, G7J 3Y2
(418) 698-4498   *SIC* 1481

IOTRON INDUSTRIES CANADA INC   *p* 246
1425 KEBET WAY, PORT COQUITLAM, BC, V3C 6L3
(604) 945-8838   *SIC* 8734

IOU FINANCIAL INC   *p* 1205
1 PLACE VILLE-MARIE BUREAU 1670, MONTREAL, QC, H3B 2B6
(514) 789-0694   *SIC* 6712

IOVATE HEALTH SCIENCES INTERNA-TIONAL INC   *p*
806
381 NORTH SERVICE RD W, OAKVILLE, ON, L6M 0H4
(905) 678-3119   *SIC* 2833

IP FABRICATIONS LTD   *p* 154
6835 52 AVE, RED DEER, AB, T4N 4L2
(403) 343-1797   *SIC* 1799

IP, JERRY PHARMACY INC   *p* 867
1235 MCCOWAN RD, SCARBOROUGH, ON, M1H 3K3
(416) 412-1353   *SIC* 5912

IPAC   *p* 216
See INTEGRATED PROACTION CORP

IPAC   *p* 975
See INSTITUTE OF PUBLIC ADMINISTRA-TION OF CANADA, THE

IPAC SERVICES CORPORATION   *p* 79
8701 102 ST, CLAIRMONT, AB, T8X 5G8
(780) 532-7350   *SIC* 1623

IPERCEPTIONS INC   *p* 1205
606 RUE CATHCART SUITE 1007, MON-TREAL, QC, H3B 1K9
(514) 488-3600   *SIC* 8732

IPEX GESTION INC   *p* 1396
3 PLACE DU COMMERCE BUREAU 101, VERDUN, QC, H3E 1H7
(514) 769-2200   *SIC* 8741

IPEX INC   *p* 109
4225 92 AVE NW, EDMONTON, AB, T6B 3M7
(780) 415-5300   *SIC* 3089

IPEX INC   *p* 228
20460 DUNCAN WAY, LANGLEY, BC, V3A 7A3
(604) 534-8631   *SIC* 3088

IPEX INC   *p* 661
1055 WILTON GROVE RD, LONDON, ON, N6N 1C9
(519) 681-2140   *SIC* 3089

IPEX INC   *p* 713
2441 ROYAL WINDSOR DR, MISSIS-SAUGA, ON, L5J 4C7
(905) 403-8133   *SIC* 3494

IPEX INC   *p* 868
807 PHARMACY AVE, SCARBOROUGH, ON, M1L 3K2
(416) 445-3400   *SIC* 3088

IPEX INC   *p* 917
11 BERMONDSEY RD, TORONTO, ON, M4B 1Z3
(416) 751-3820   *SIC* 3089

IPEX INC   *p* 1314
247 RUE PRINCIPALE, SAINT-JACQUES, QC, J0K 2R0
(450) 839-2655   *SIC* 3088

IPEX INC   *p* 1334

6665 CH SAINT-FRANCOIS, SAINT-LAURENT, QC, H4S 1B6
(514) 337-2624   *SIC* 3089

IPEX INC   *p* 1396
3 PLACE DU COMMERCE BUREAU 101, VERDUN, QC, H3E 1H7
(514) 769-2200   *SIC* 3494

IPEX MANAGEMENT   *p* 109
See IPEX INC

IPEX MANAGEMENT   *p* 228
See IPEX INC

IPEX MANAGEMENT   *p* 713
See IPEX INC

IPEX MANAGEMENT   *p* 868
See IPEX INC

IPEX MANAGEMENT   *p* 917
See IPEX INC

IPEX MANAGEMENT   *p* 1314
See IPEX INC

IPEX MANAGEMENT   *p* 1334
See IPEX INC

IPEX MANAGEMENT   *p* 1396
See IPEX INC

IPG INSURANCE   *p* 749
See INDEPENDANT PLANNING GROUP INC/GROUPE INDEPENDANT DE PLANIFI-CATION INC

IPL   *p* 1199
See PLASTIQUES IPL INC

IPL INC   *p* 399
20 RUE BOYD, EDMUNDSTON, NB, E3V 4H4
(506) 739-9559   *SIC* 3089

IPL INC   *p* 1299
140 RUE COMMERCIALE, SAINT-DAMIEN-DE-BUCKLAND, QC, G0R 2Y0
(418) 789-2880   *SIC* 3089

IPLAYCO   *p* 229
See INTERNATIONAL PLAY COMPANY INC

IPLAYCO CORPORATION LTD   *p* 229
27353 58 CRES UNIT 215, LANGLEY, BC, V4W 3W7
(604) 607-1111   *SIC* 3949

IPOLY   *p* 1003
See PLASTRUCT CANADA INC

IPPOLITO FRUIT AND PRODUCE LIMITED
p 529
201 NORTH SERVICE RD, BURLINGTON, ON, L7P 5C4
(905) 631-7700   *SIC* 5148

IPPOLITO GROUP INC, THE   *p* 529
201 NORTH SERVICE RD, BURLINGTON, ON, L7P 5C4
(905) 639-1174   *SIC* 6712

IPPOLITO TRANSPORTATION INC   *p* 529
201 NORTH SERVICE RD SUITE 1, BURLINGTON, ON, L7P 5C4
(905) 639-7700   *SIC* 4213

IPROSPECT CANADA INC   *p* 1223
3970 RUE SAINT-AMBROISE, MONTREAL, QC, H4C 2C7
(514) 524-7149   *SIC* 7311

IPS   *p* 214
See NINE ENERGY CANADA INC

IPS OF CANADA, U.L.C.   *p* 585
170 ATTWELL DR UNIT 550, ETOBICOKE, ON, M9W 5Z5
(800) 293-1136   *SIC* 6153

IPS WIRELINE, DIV OF   *p* 158
See NINE ENERGY CANADA INC

IPSOS CORP   *p* 314
1285 PENDER ST W SUITE 200, VANCOU-VER, BC, V6E 4B1
(778) 373-5000   *SIC* 8732

IPSOS LIMITED PARTNERSHIP   *p* 314
1700-1075 GEORGIA ST W, VANCOUVER, BC, V6E 3C9
(778) 373-5000   *SIC* 8732

IPSOS LIMITED PARTNERSHIP   *p* 378
185 CARLTON ST FL 4, WINNIPEG, MB, R3C 3J1
(204) 949-3100   *SIC* 8732

IPSOS LIMITED PARTNERSHIP   *p* 929

160 BLOOR ST E SUITE 300, TORONTO, ON, M4W 1B9
(416) 925-4444   *SIC* 8732

IPSOS REID   *p* 378
See IPSOS LIMITED PARTNERSHIP

IPSOS REID   *p* 929
See IPSOS LIMITED PARTNERSHIP

IPSOS REID   *p* 929
See IPSOS-ASI, LTD

IPSOS-ASI, LTD   *p* 929
160 BLOOR ST E SUITE 300, TORONTO, ON, M4W 1B9
(416) 324-2900   *SIC* 8732

IPSOS-ASI, LTD   *p* 929
160 BLOOR ST E SUITE 300, TORONTO, ON, M4W 1B9
(416) 925-4444   *SIC* 8732

IPSOS-INSIGHT CORPORATION   *p* 314
1075 GEORGIA ST W UNIT 1700, VAN-COUVER, BC, V6E 3C9
(778) 373-5000   *SIC* 8732

IQ OFFICE SUITES   *p* 953
See IQ OFFICE SUITES HOLDINGS INC

IQ OFFICE SUITES HOLDINGS INC   *p* 953
150 KING ST W SUITE 200, TORONTO, ON, M5H 1J9
(888) 744-2292   *SIC* 7389

IQ PARTNERS INC   *p* 963
144 FRONT ST W SUITE 600, TORONTO, ON, M5J 2L7
(416) 599-4700   *SIC* 8748

IQ SOQUIA INC   *p* 1272
1195 AV LAVIGERIE BUREAU 060, QUE-BEC, QC, G1V 4N3
(418) 643-5172   *SIC* 6719

IQBAL FOODS CORPORATION   *p* 919
2 THORNCLIFFE PARK DR UNIT 10, TORONTO, ON, M4H 1H2
(416) 467-0177   *SIC* 5141

IQBAL HALAL FOODS INC   *p* 567
2 THORNCLIFFE PARK DR UNIT 7-15, EAST YORK, ON, M4H 1H2
(416) 467-0177   *SIC* 5149

IQMETRIX SOFTWARE DEVELOPMENT CORP   *p* 306
250 HOWE ST SUITE 1210, VANCOUVER, BC, V6C 3R8
(866) 476-3874   *SIC* 7371

IQPC WORLDWIDE COMPANY   *p* 925
60 ST CLAIR AVE E SUITE 304, TORONTO, ON, M4T 1N5
(416) 597-4700   *SIC* 7389

IQVIA   *p* 1117
See IMS SANTE CANADA INC

IQVIA RDS CANADA ULC   *p* 1324
100 BOUL ALEXIS-NIHON 8E ETAGE, SAINT-LAURENT, QC, H4M 2P4
(514) 855-0888   *SIC* 8731

IRC BUILDING SCIENCES GROUP   *p* 723
2121 ARGENTIA RD SUITE 401, MISSIS-SAUGA, ON, L5N 2X4
(905) 607-7244   *SIC* 8711

IRD   *p* 1428
See INTERNATIONAL ROAD DYNAMICS INC

IRDETO   *p* 624
See IRDETO CANADA CORPORATION

IRDETO CANADA CORPORATION   *p* 624
2500 SOLANDT RD SUITE 300, KANATA, ON, K2K 3G5
(613) 271-9446   *SIC* 7371

IREQ   *p* 1393
See HYDRO-QUEBEC

IRGLM   *p* 1218
See L'INSTITUT DE READAPTATION GINGRAS-LINDSAY-DE-MONTREAL

IRIDIA MEDICAL INC   *p* 321
1644 3RD AVE W, VANCOUVER, BC, V6J 1K2
(604) 685-4747   *SIC* 8049

IRIDIAN SPECTRAL TECHNOLOGIES LIM-ITED   *p*
818
2700 SWANSEA CRES, OTTAWA, ON, K1G

6R8
(613) 741-4513   *SIC* 3081
IRIS TECHNOLOGIES INC   *p* 671
675 COCHRANE DR SUITE 6, MARKHAM,
ON, L3R 0B8
(416) 800-4747   *SIC* 4899
**IRIS THE VISUAL GROUP WESTERN
CANADA INC**   *p* 225
9440 202 ST SUITE 315, LANGLEY, BC,
V1M 4A6
(604) 881-0353   *SIC* 5995
IRIS, GROUPE VISUEL (1990) INC, LE   *p*
1086
3030 BOUL LE CARREFOUR BUREAU
1200, COTE SAINT-LUC, QC, H7T 2P5
(450) 688-9060   *SIC* 5048
IRIS-OPTOMISTRIS & OPTICIANS   *p* 225
*See IRIS THE VISUAL GROUP WESTERN
CANADA INC*
IRISH TIMES PUB   *p* 336
See IRISH TIMES PUB CO LTD
IRISH TIMES PUB CO LTD   *p* 336
1200 GOVERNMENT ST, VICTORIA, BC,
V8W 1Y3
(250) 383-5531   *SIC* 5813
IRISNDT CORP   *p* 115
5311 86 ST NW, EDMONTON, AB, T6E 5T8
(780) 437-2022   *SIC* 8734
IRISTEL   *p* 671
See IRIS TECHNOLOGIES INC
**IRL INTERNATIONAL TRUCK CENTRES
LTD**   *p* 216
1495 IRON MASK RD, KAMLOOPS, BC,
V1S 1C8
(250) 372-1445   *SIC* 4212
**IRL INTERNATIONAL TRUCK CENTRES
LTD**   *p* 331
7156 MEADOWLARK RD, VERNON, BC,
V1B 3R6
(877) 463-0292   *SIC* 5511
IRMA COULSON PUBLIC SCHOOL   *p* 683
See HALTON DISTRICT SCHOOL BOARD
IROC ENERGY SERVICES CORP   *p* 155
8113 49 AVE CLOSE, RED DEER, AB, T4P
2V5
(403) 346-9710   *SIC* 1389
IRON HORSE COILED TUBING INC   *p* 158
1901 DIRKSON DR NE, REDCLIFF, AB, T0J
2P0
(403) 526-4600   *SIC* 1389
IRON HORSE EARTHWORKS INC   *p* 159
235090 WRANGLER DR, ROCKY VIEW
COUNTY, AB, T1X 0K3
(403) 217-2711   *SIC* 1794
IRON HORSE ENERGY SERVICES   *p* 158
See IRON HORSE COILED TUBING INC
**IRON MOUNTAIN CANADA OPERATIONS
ULC**   *p* 504
195 SUMMERLEA RD, BRAMPTON, ON,
L6T 4P6
(905) 792-7099   *SIC* 4226
**IRON MOUNTAIN CANADA OPERATIONS
ULC**   *p* 554
70 TALMAN CRT SUITE 415, CONCORD,
ON, L4K 4L5
(905) 695-0564   *SIC* 4226
**IRON MOUNTAIN CANADA OPERATIONS
ULC**   *p* 1241
1655 RUE FLEETWOOD, MONTREAL-
OUEST, QC, H7N 4B2
(450) 667-5960   *SIC* 4226
IRON ORE COMPANY OF CANADA   *p* 425
See COMPAGNIE MINIERE IOC INC
IRON RANGE BUS LINES INC   *p* 908
1141 GOLF LINKS RD, THUNDER BAY, ON,
P7B 7A3
(807) 345-7387   *SIC* 4142
IRONCLAD DEVELOPMENTS INC   *p* 357
57158 SYMINGTON ROAD 20E UNIT 101,
SPRINGFIELD, MB, R2J 4L6
(204) 777-1972   *SIC* 6553
IRONCLAD METALS INC   *p* 226
6325 204 ST UNIT 312, LANGLEY, BC, V2Y
3B3

(604) 539-0112   *SIC* 1542
IRONHORSE CORPORATION   *p* 749
9 CAPELLA CRT UNIT 200, NEPEAN, ON,
K2E 8A7
(613) 228-2813   *SIC* 7389
IRONHORSE GROUP, THE   *p* 749
See IRONHORSE CORPORATION
**IRONLINE COMPRESSION LIMITED PART-
NERSHIP**   *p*
149
700 15 AVE, NISKU, AB, T9E 7S2
**IRONTECH RIG REPAIR & MANUFACTUR-
ING INC**   *p*
1
53016 HWY 60 UNIT 11, ACHESON, AB,
T7X 5A7
(780) 960-4881   *SIC* 1389
IROQUOIS FALLS FOODLAND   *p* 623
171 AMBRIDGE DR, IROQUOIS FALLS,
ON, P0K 1G0
(705) 232-4071   *SIC* 5411
IROQUOIS PARK SPORTS CENTRE, THE *p*
1014
*See CORPORATION OF THE TOWN OF
WHITBY, THE*
IROQUOIS RIDGE SECONDARY SCHOOL *p*
797
See HALTON DISTRICT SCHOOL BOARD
IRPINIA KITCHENS   *p* 855
See 1118741 ONTARIO LTD
IRSI   *p* 715
*See INDEPENDENT REHABILITATION
SERVICES INC*
**IRVINE CARPET ONE & DECORATING
CENTRE**   *p* 484
See IRVINE, G. ERNEST LIMITED
IRVINE, G. ERNEST LIMITED   *p* 484
514 BAYFIELD ST, BARRIE, ON, L4M 5A2
(705) 728-5566   *SIC* 5023
IRVING CONSUMER PRODUCTS   *p* 398
See IRVING, J. D. LIMITED
IRVING CONSUMER PRODUCTS LIMITED
p 397
100 PROM MIDLAND, DIEPPE, NB, E1A
6X4
(506) 858-7777   *SIC* 2679
IRVING CONSUMER PRODUCTS LIMITED
p 992
1551 WESTON RD, TORONTO, ON, M6M
4Y4
(416) 246-6666   *SIC* 2676
IRVING CONSUMER PRODUCTS LIMITED
p 993
1551 WESTON RD, TORONTO, ON, M6M
4Y4
(416) 246-6666   *SIC* 2676
IRVING ENERGY   *p* 415
See IRVING OIL LIMITED
**IRVING ENERGY DISTRIBUTION & MAR-
KETING**   *p*
415
See HIGHLANDS FUEL DELIVERY G.P.
IRVING ENERGY SERVICES LIMITED *p* 415
10 SYDNEY ST, SAINT JOHN, NB, E2L 5E6
(506) 202-2000   *SIC* 4924
IRVING FOREST PRODUCTS LIMITED *p*
415
300 UNION ST SUITE 5777, SAINT JOHN,
NB, E2L 4Z2
(506) 632-7777   *SIC* 5031
IRVING FOREST SERVICES LIMITED *p* 415
300 UNION ST 11TH FL, SAINT JOHN, NB,
E2L 4Z2
(506) 634-4242   *SIC* 8742
IRVING OIL   *p* 415
See HIGHLANDS FUEL DELIVERY G.P.
IRVING OIL COMMERCIAL G.P.   *p* 415
10 SYDNEY ST, SAINT JOHN, NB, E2L 5E6
(506) 202-2000   *SIC* 4925
IRVING OIL LIMITED   *p* 415
10 SYDNEY ST, SAINT JOHN, NB, E2L 5E6
(506) 202-2000   *SIC* 2911
IRVING PAPER   *p* 412

See 011810 N.B. LIMITED
IRVING PERSONAL CARE LIMITED *p* 397
100 PROM MIDLAND, DIEPPE, NB, E1A
6X4
(506) 857-7713   *SIC* 5137
IRVING PULP & PAPER, LIMITED   *p* 415
300 UNION ST, SAINT JOHN, NB, E2L 4Z2
(506) 632-7777   *SIC* 2621
IRVING SHIPBUILDING INC   *p* 455
3099 BARRINGTON ST, HALIFAX, NS, B3K
2X6
(902) 423-9271   *SIC* 3731
IRVING SHIPBUILDING INC   *p* 455
3099 BARRINGTON ST, HALIFAX, NS, B3K
5M7
(902) 423-9271   *SIC* 3731
IRVING SHIPBUILDING INC   *p* 1041
115 WATER ST, GEORGETOWN, PE, C0A
1L0
SIC 3731
IRVING TISSUE   *p* 398
See IRVING, J. D. LIMITED
**IRVING TRANSPORTATION SERVICES
LIMITED**   *p* 402
71 ALISON BLVD, FREDERICTON, NB,
E3C 2N5
SIC 8721
IRVING WALLBOARD   *p* 412
*See ATLANTIC WALLBOARD LIMITED
PARTNERSHIP*
IRVING, J D   *p* 992
*See IRVING CONSUMER PRODUCTS LIM-
ITED*
IRVING, J. D. LIMITED   *p* 395
28 CH DU COUVENT, BOUCTOUCHE, NB,
E4S 3B9
(506) 743-2481   *SIC* 2452
IRVING, J. D. LIMITED   *p* 396
290 MAIN ST, CHIPMAN, NB, E4A 2M7
(506) 339-7900   *SIC* 5211
IRVING, J. D. LIMITED   *p* 396
290 MAIN ST, CHIPMAN, NB, E4A 2M7
(506) 339-7910   *SIC* 2421
IRVING, J. D. LIMITED   *p* 397
632 RUE PRINCIPALE, CLAIR, NB, E7A
2H2
(506) 992-9068   *SIC* 2426
IRVING, J. D. LIMITED   *p* 398
102 RUE DAWSON, DIEPPE, NB, E1A 0C1
(506) 859-5018   *SIC* 2621
IRVING, J. D. LIMITED   *p* 398
100 PROM MIDLAND, DIEPPE, NB, E1A
6X4
(506) 859-5757   *SIC* 2679
IRVING, J. D. LIMITED   *p* 398
120 SOUTH RD, DOAKTOWN, NB, E9C
1H2
(506) 365-1020   *SIC* 2421
IRVING, J. D. LIMITED   *p* 413
225 THORNE AVE, SAINT JOHN, NB, E2J
1W8
(506) 658-8000   *SIC* 5021
IRVING, J. D. LIMITED   *p* 415
300 UNION ST SUITE 5, SAINT JOHN, NB,
E2L 4Z2
(506) 632-7777   *SIC* 2421
IRVING, J. D. LIMITED   *p* 416
45 GIFFORD RD, SAINT JOHN, NB, E2M
5K7
(506) 635-5555   *SIC* 7353
IRVING, J. D. LIMITED   *p* 419
600 ROUTE 785, UTOPIA, NB, E5C 2K4
(506) 755-3384   *SIC* 2679
IRVING, J. D. LIMITED   *p* 426
60 OLD PLACENTIA RD, MOUNT PEARL,
NL, A1N 4Y1
(709) 748-3500   *SIC* 5211
IRWIN TOGS INC   *p* 1180
8484 AV DE L'ESPLANADE, MONTREAL,
QC, H2P 2R7
(514) 384-7700   *SIC* 5137
IS2 WORKFORCE SOLUTIONS INC *p* 115
8023 ROPER RD NW, EDMONTON, AB,
T6E 6S4

(780) 420-9999   *SIC* 7361
ISA INTERNATIONAL INC   *p* 789
46 DUFFLAW RD, NORTH YORK, ON, M6A
2W1
(416) 782-9100   *SIC* 5021
ISA NORTH AMERICA, DIV OF   *p* 640
See HENDRIX GENETICS LIMITED
ISAAC BEAULIEU MEMORIAL SCHOOL *p*
352
See SANDY BAY SCHOOL
ISANS   *p* 457
*See IMMIGRANT SERVICES ASSOCIA-
TION OF NOVA SCOTIA*
ISAUTE   *p* 1361
See 8542732 CANADA INC
ISB CANADA   *p* 684
*See INSURANCE SEARCH BUREAU OF
CANADA INC*
ISC   *p* 1421
*See INFORMATION SERVICES CORPO-
RATION*
ISC APPLIED SYSTEMS CORP   *p* 1251
290 AV LABROSSE, POINTE-CLAIRE, QC,
H9R 5L8
(514) 782-1400   *SIC* 3699
ISC SASKATCHEWAN INC   *p* 1421
10 RESEARCH DR SUITE 300, REGINA,
SK, S4S 7J7
(306) 787-8179   *SIC* 8713
ISCO CANADA, INC   *p* 373
2901 STURGEON RD, WINNIPEG, MB,
R2Y 2L9
(204) 831-8625   *SIC* 5085
ISE METAL INC   *p* 1369
20 RTE DE WINDSOR, SHERBROOKE,
QC, J1C 0E5
(819) 846-1044   *SIC* 3469
ISE-FERLAND METAL   *p* 1369
See ISE METAL INC
ISECURITY INC   *p* 765
111 GORDON BAKER RD 6TH FL, NORTH
YORK, ON, M2H 3R1
(416) 843-6018   *SIC* 7379
**ISFELD, LOU LINCOLN MERCURY SALES
LTD**   *p* 177
32562 SOUTH FRASER WAY, ABBOTS-
FORD, BC, V2T 1X6
(604) 857-1327   *SIC* 5511
ISG SEARCH INC   *p* 935
229 YONGE ST SUITE 408, TORONTO,
ON, M5B 1N9
(416) 775-4800   *SIC* 7361
ISG TRANSPORTATION INC   *p* 504
7965 GOREWAY DR SUITE 2, BRAMPTON,
ON, L6T 5T5
(905) 799-1300   *SIC* 4731
ISH EQUIPMENT LTD   *p* 52
700 4 AVE SW UNIT 310, CALGARY, AB,
T2P 3J4
SIC 6712
**ISHARES U.S. HIGH YIELD BOND INDEX
ETF (CAD-HEDGED)**   *p* 963
161 BAY ST SUITE 2500, TORONTO, ON,
M5J 2S1
(416) 643-4000   *SIC* 6722
ISKIN INC   *p* 779
3 CONCORDE GATE UNIT 311, NORTH
YORK, ON, M3C 3N7
(416) 924-9607   *SIC* 8731
ISKUETEU, LIMITED PARTNERSHIP *p* 433
240 WATERFORD BRIDGE RD, ST.
JOHN'S, NL, A1E 1E2
(709) 747-4209   *SIC* 1731
**ISL ENGINEERING AND LAND SERVICES
LTD**   *p* 115
7909 51 AVE NW SUITE 100, EDMONTON,
AB, T6E 5L9
(780) 438-9000   *SIC* 8711
ISL HOLDINGS INC   *p* 115
7909 51 AVE NW, EDMONTON, AB, T6E
5L9
(780) 438-9000   *SIC* 8711
ISLAND ABBEY FOOD SCIENCE   *p* 1040
See ISLAND ABBEY FOODS LTD

ISLAND ABBEY FOODS LTD p 1040
20 INNOVATION WAY, CHARLOTTETOWN, PE, C1E 0K4
(902) 367-9722 *SIC* 5149

ISLAND ACOUSTICS (OAK BAY) INC p 336
645 FORT ST UNIT 309, VICTORIA, BC, V8W 1G2
(250) 385-3103 *SIC* 5999

ISLAND BEACH COMPANY CLOTHING & GRAPHICS INCORPORATED p 469
82 PURDY DR, TRURO, NS, B2N 5W8
(902) 897-0560 *SIC* 5651

ISLAND CITY BAKING COMPANY INC p 255
12753 VULCAN WAY SUITE 105, RICHMOND, BC, V6V 3C8
(604) 278-6979 *SIC* 2051

ISLAND COASTAL SERVICES LTD p 1039
155 BELVEDERE AVE, CHARLOTTETOWN, PE, C1A 2Y9
(902) 892-1062 *SIC* 1629

ISLAND EMS INC p 1040
229 SHERWOOD RD, CHARLOTTETOWN, PE, C1E 0E5
(902) 892-9995 *SIC* 4119

ISLAND FARMS p 334
See AGROPUR COOPERATIVE

ISLAND GM p 211
See GREEN ISLAND G AUTO LTD

ISLAND GOLD p 1041
See PRINCE EDWARD AQUA FARMS INC

ISLAND HEALTH p 333
See VANCOUVER ISLAND HEALTH AUTHORITY

ISLAND HEARING SERVICES p 336
See NATIONAL HEARING SERVICES INC

ISLAND HEARING SERVICES p 336
See ISLAND ACOUSTICS (OAK BAY) INC

ISLAND HOLDINGS LTD p 398
100 MIDLAND DR, DIEPPE, NB, E1A 6X4
(506) 858-7777 *SIC* 5148

ISLAND INDEPENDENT BUYING GROUP LTD p 196
3110 HOPE PL, CHEMAINUS, BC, V0R 1K4
(250) 246-1828 *SIC* 5141

ISLAND INKJET p 480
See EQUIPMENT LEASING COMPANY LTD, THE

ISLAND PACIFIC LOGGING LTD p 196
3473 SMILEY RD RR 4, CHEMAINUS, BC, V0R 1K4
(250) 246-1414 *SIC* 2411

ISLAND PUBLISHERS LTD p 336
818 BROUGHTON ST, VICTORIA, BC, V8W 1E4
(250) 480-0755 *SIC* 2711

ISLAND SAVINGS CREDIT UNION p 211
499 CANADA AVE SUITE 300, DUNCAN, BC, V9L 1T7
(250) 748-4728 *SIC* 6062

ISLAND SAVINGS, A DIVISION OF FIRST WEST CREDIT UNION p 211
See ISLAND SAVINGS CREDIT UNION

ISLAND TIMBERLANDS LIMITED PARTNERSHIP p 233
65 FRONT ST, NANAIMO, BC, V9R 5H9
(250) 755-3500 *SIC* 7389

ISLAND TUG AND BARGE LTD p 186
800 GLASGOW AVE, BURNABY, BC, V5C 0C9
(604) 873-4312 *SIC* 4492

ISLAND VIEW CONSTRUCTION LTD p 340
2780 VETERANS MEMORIAL PKY SUITE 210, VICTORIA, BC, V9B 3S6
SIC 1521

ISLAND WEST COAST DEVELOPMENTS LTD p 234
2214 MCCULLOUGH RD, NANAIMO, BC, V9S 4M8
(250) 756-9665 *SIC* 1542

ISLANDS WEST MANUFACTURERS LTD p 337
4247 DOUGLAS ST, VICTORIA, BC, V8X

3Y7
(250) 727-0744 *SIC* 5148

ISLANDSAND HOLDINGS INC p 1039
150 QUEEN ST, CHARLOTTETOWN, PE, C1A 4B5
(902) 368-1728 *SIC* 5812

ISLINGTON CHRYSLER PLYMOUTH (1963) LTD p 577
5476 DUNDAS ST W, ETOBICOKE, ON, M9B 1B6
(416) 239-3541 *SIC* 5511

ISLINGTON FLORIST & GARDEN CENTRE p 575
See ISLINGTON NURSERIES LIMITED

ISLINGTON GOLF CLUB, LIMITED p 576
45 RIVERBANK DR, ETOBICOKE, ON, M9A 5B8
(416) 231-1114 *SIC* 7997

ISLINGTON MOTOR SALES LIMITED p 1031
7625 MARTIN GROVE RD SUITE B, WOODBRIDGE, ON, L4L 2C5
(905) 851-1279 *SIC* 5511

ISLINGTON NURSERIES LIMITED p 575
1000 ISLINGTON AVE SUITE 5, ETOBICOKE, ON, M8Z 4P8
(416) 231-8416 *SIC* 5992

ISM INDUSTRIAL STEEL & MANUFACTURING INC p 209
7690 VANTAGE WAY, DELTA, BC, V4G 1A7
(604) 940-4769 *SIC* 3441

ISM INFORMATION SYSTEMS MANAGEMENT CANADA CORPORATION p 1421
1 RESEARCH DR, REGINA, SK, S4S 7H1
(306) 337-5601 *SIC* 7374

ISM SECURITY p 654
See INNOVATIVE SECURITY MANAGEMENT (1998) INC

ISN CANADA GROUP HOLDINGS INC p 1066
88 CH DU TREMBLAY, BOUCHERVILLE, QC, J4B 6Z6
(514) 327-0222 *SIC* 5013

ISOBAR CANADA INC p 963
1 UNIVERSITY AVE FL 6, TORONTO, ON, M5J 2P1
(416) 646-2340 *SIC* 7311

ISODIAGNOSTIKA, DIV OF p 1324
See PALADIN LABS INC

ISODIOL INTERNATIONAL INC p 306
200 GRANVILLE ST SUITE 2710, VANCOUVER, BC, V6C 1S4
(604) 409-4409 *SIC* 5961

ISOLATION AIR-PLUS INC p 1262
560 AV BECHARD, QUEBEC, QC, G1M 2E9
(418) 683-2999 *SIC* 1742

ISOLATION DISPRO p 1048
See DISPRO INC

ISOLATION EQUIPMENT SERVICES INC p 132
12925 97B ST, GRANDE PRAIRIE, AB, T8V 6K1
(780) 402-3060 *SIC* 3533

ISOLATION EQUIPMENT SERVICES INC p 155
8102 49 AVE CLOSE UNIT B, RED DEER, AB, T4P 2V5
(403) 342-0032 *SIC* 1389

ISOLATION QUATRE SAISONS p 1282
See ACOUSTIQUE ISOLATION QUATRE SAISONS INC

ISOMAG p 1097
See PRODUITS INDUSTRIELS DE HAUTE TEMPERATURE PYROTEK INC

ISON T.H. AUTO SALES INC p 917
2300 DANFORTH AVE, TORONTO, ON, M4C 1K6
(416) 423-2300 *SIC* 5511

ISOPAC p 1360
See GROUPE ISOLOFOAM INC

ISOPORC INC p 1310
652 RTE DU MOULIN, SAINT-HUGUES,

QC, J0H 1N0
(450) 794-2555 *SIC* 0213

ISOTOPE MUSIC INC p 528
3375 NORTH SERVICE RD UNIT B9-B11, BURLINGTON, ON, L7N 3G2
(905) 333-3001 *SIC* 7389

ISOVER p 1262
See MULTIVER LTEE

ISRA-GUARD (I.G.S.) SECURITE INC p 1220
5165 CH QUEEN-MARY BUREAU 512, MONTREAL, QC, H3W 1X7
(514) 489-6336 *SIC* 7381

ISRAEL BONDS p 782
See CANADA-ISRAEL SECURITIES LIMITED

ISS p 287
See IMMIGRANT SERVICES SOCIETY OF BRITISH COLUMBIA, THE

ISS p 457
See INDEPENDENT SECURITY SERVICES ATLANTIC (ISS) INC

ISTOCKPHOTO p 30
See ISTOCKPHOTO L.P.

ISTOCKPHOTO L.P. p 30
1240 20 AVE SE SUITE 200, CALGARY, AB, T2G 1M8
(403) 265-3062 *SIC* 7299

ISTOCKPHOTO ULC p 30
1240 20 AVE SE SUITE 200, CALGARY, AB, T2G 1M8
(403) 265-3062 *SIC* 7299

ISTUARY INNOVATION LABS INC p 326
1125 HOWE ST 8TH FL, VANCOUVER, BC, V6Z 2K8
SIC 7371

ISYARI CANADA INC p 696
5045 ORBITOR DR BUILDING 12 SUITE 400, MISSISSAUGA, ON, L4W 4Y4
(905) 212-2515 *SIC* 4724

IT WEAPONS DIV. p 504
See KONICA MINOLTA BUSINESS SOLUTIONS (CANADA) LTD

IT WEAPONS DIV. p 696
See KONICA MINOLTA BUSINESS SOLUTIONS (CANADA) LTD

IT XCHANGE p 717
See IT XCHANGE (ONTARIO) CORP

IT XCHANGE (ONTARIO) CORP p 717
3500 RIDGEWAY DR UNIT 4, MISSISSAUGA, ON, L5L 0B4
(888) 829-5333 *SIC* 5045

IT/NET GROUP INC p 834
150 ELGIN ST SUITE 1800, OTTAWA, ON, K2P 2P8
(613) 234-8638 *SIC* 6712

ITA p 262
See INDUSTRY TRAINING AUTHORITY

ITAFOS p 946
1 DUNDAS ST W SUITE 2500, TORONTO, ON, M5G 1Z3
(416) 367-2200 *SIC* 1475

ITAL-PLUS IMPORTS INC p 825
925 GLADSTONE AVE, OTTAWA, ON, K1R 6Y3
(613) 230-7166 *SIC* 5141

ITALBEC INTERNATIONAL INC p 1180
375 RUE DE LIEGE O, MONTREAL, QC, H2P 1H6
(514) 383-0668 *SIC* 3281

ITALFOODS p 540
See 1649338 ONTARIO INC

ITALIAN CENTRE SHOP SOUTH LTD p 86
10878 95 ST NW, EDMONTON, AB, T5H 2E4
(780) 424-4869 *SIC* 5411

ITALIAN CENTRE SHOP SOUTH LTD p 119
5028 104A ST NW, EDMONTON, AB, T6H 6A2
(780) 989-4869 *SIC* 5411

ITALIAN CULTURAL CENTRE SOCIETY p 286
See ITALIAN FOLK SOCIETY OF BC, THE

ITALIAN FOLK SOCIETY OF BC, THE p 286

3075 SLOCAN ST, VANCOUVER, BC, V5M 3E4
(604) 430-3337 *SIC* 8641

ITALIAN HOME BAKERY LIMITED p 585
271 ATTWELL DR, ETOBICOKE, ON, M9W 5B9
(416) 674-4555 *SIC* 2051

ITALIAN PRODUCE CO. LIMITED p 572
165 THE QUEENSWAY RM 314, ETOBICOKE, ON, M8Y 1H8
(416) 259-7641 *SIC* 5148

ITALNORD p 1245
See CERAMIQUE ITAL-NORD LTEE

ITALPASTA LIMITED p 504
116 NUGGETT CRT, BRAMPTON, ON, L6T 5A9
(416) 798-7154 *SIC* 2098

ITALPASTA LIMITED p 504
199 SUMMERLEA RD, BRAMPTON, ON, L6T 4E5
(905) 792-9928 *SIC* 2098

ITC CONSTRUCTION CANADA INC p 299
564 BEATTY ST SUITE 800, VANCOUVER, BC, V6B 2L3
(604) 685-0111 *SIC* 1542

ITC CONSTRUCTION GROUP p 299
See ITC CONSTRUCTION CANADA INC

ITC SYSTEMS p 915
See 682770 ONTARIO INC

ITHACA ENERGY INC p 52
333 7 AVE SW SUITE 1600, CALGARY, AB, T2P 2Z1
(403) 234-3338 *SIC* 1382

ITI HYDRAULIK p 1359
See INDUSTRIES TOURNEBO INC, LES

ITIF INC p 993
25 BERTAL RD UNIT 9, TORONTO, ON, M6M 4M7
SIC 5046

ITML HOLDINGS INC p 516
75 PLANT FARM BLVD, BRANTFORD, ON, N3S 7W2
(519) 753-2666 *SIC* 6712

ITN FOOD CORPORATION p 874
40 COMMANDER BLVD, SCARBOROUGH, ON, M1S 3S2
(416) 321-2052 *SIC* 5149

ITN INTERNATIONAL CORP p 23
2915 21 ST NE SUITE 201, CALGARY, AB, T2E 7T1
(403) 219-8440 *SIC* 4731

ITN LOGISTICS p 23
See ITN INTERNATIONAL CORP

ITN LOGISTICS GROUP p 736
See 1341611 ONTARIO INC

ITN TRANSBORDER SERVICES INC p 740
6975 PACIFIC CIR UNIT D, MISSISSAUGA, ON, L5T 2H3
(905) 362-1122 *SIC* 4731

ITRACKS p 1428
See INTERACTIVE TRACKING SYSTEMS INC

ITRAVEL 2000.COM p 691
See 4358376 CANADA INC

ITRAVEL2000 p 699
See RED LABEL VACATIONS INC

ITRON CANADA INC p 1386
3260 RUE DU CHANOINE-CHAMBERLAND, TROIS-RIVIERES, QC, G8Z 2T2
(819) 373-5303 *SIC* 5084

ITS CANADA p 685
See INTERNATIONAL TRANSACTION SYSTEMS (CANADA) LTD

ITS ELECTRONICS INC p 1002
3280 LANGSTAFF RD UNIT B, VAUGHAN, ON, L4K 5B6
(905) 660-0405 *SIC* 3663

ITW CANADA INC p 678
120 TRAVAIL RD, MARKHAM, ON, L3S 3J1
(905) 201-8399 *SIC* 5084

ITW CANADA INC p 835
2875 EAST BAY SHORE ROAD, OWEN SOUND, ON, N4K 5P5

(519) 376-8886   *SIC* 3639

ITW CANADA INVESTMENTS LIMITED PARTNERSHIP *p 678*
120 TRAVAIL RD, MARKHAM, ON, L3S 3J1
(905) 471-4250   *SIC* 1541

ITWAL LIMITED *p 513*
440 RAILSIDE DR, BRAMPTON, ON, L7A 1L1
(905) 840-9400   *SIC* 5145

IUOE *p 189*
See INTERNATIONAL UNION OF OPERATING ENGINEERS LOCAL 115

IVACO ROLLING MILLS *p 643*
See IVACO ROLLING MILLS 2004 L.P.

IVACO ROLLING MILLS 2004 L.P. *p 643*
1040 HWY 17, L'ORIGNAL, ON, K0B 1K0
(613) 675-4671   *SIC* 3312

IVAN ARMSTRONG TRUCKING *p 479*
See 441861 ONTARIO LTD

IVAN B. WALLACE ONTARIO LAND SURVEYOR LTD *p 496*
71 MEARNS CRT UNIT 16, BOWMANVILLE, ON, L1C 4N4
(905) 623-2205   *SIC* 8713

IVAN FRANKO HOME *p 718*
See UKRAINIAN HOME FOR THE AGED

IVANHOE CAMBRIDGE *p 1191*
See IVANHOE CAMBRIDGE I INC.

IVANHOE CAMBRIDGE I INC. *p 1191*
1001 RUE DU SQUARE-VICTORIA BUREAU 500, MONTREAL, QC, H2Z 2B5
(514) 841-7600   *SIC* 6512

IVANHOE CAMBRIDGE II INC. *p 531*
900 MAPLE AVE, BURLINGTON, ON, L7S 2J8
(905) 681-2900   *SIC* 6512

IVANHOE CAMBRIDGE INC *p 1191*
1001 RUE DU SQUARE-VICTORIA BUREAU 500, MONTREAL, QC, H2Z 2B5
(514) 841-7600   *SIC* 6512

IVANHOE CAMBRIDGE S *p 1285*
See 9130-1168 QUEBEC INC

IVANHOE CHEESE INC *p 663*
11301 HWY 62, MADOC, ON, K0K 2K0
(613) 473-4269   *SIC* 2022

IVANHOE MINES LTD *p 306*
999 CANADA PL SUITE 654, VANCOUVER, BC, V6C 3E1
(604) 688-6630   *SIC* 1061

IVARI *p 772*
See IVARI CANADA ULC

IVARI CANADA ULC *p 772*
5000 YONGE ST UNIT 500, NORTH YORK, ON, M2N 7J8
(416) 883-5000   *SIC* 6311

IVEDHA INC *p 779*
18 WYNFORD DR UNIT 306, NORTH YORK, ON, M3C 3S2
(416) 424-6614   *SIC* 7373

IVES INSURANCE BROKERS LTD *p 570*
347 MAIDSTONE AVE E, ESSEX, ON, N8M 2K1
(519) 776-7371   *SIC* 6411

IVEX *p 1250*
See GROUPE EMBALLAGE SPECIALISE S.E.C.

IVEY BUSINESS SCHOOL FOUNDATION *p 651*
551 WINDERMERE RD, LONDON, ON, N5X 2T1
(519) 679-4546   *SIC* 7389

IVEY TANGERINE LEADERSHIP CENTRE *p 986*
See DOLCE INTERNATIONAL (ONTARIO) CO.

IVY FISHERIES LTD *p 465*
3762 OLD SAMBRO RD, SAMBRO, NS, B3V 1G1
SIC 5146

IW RESORTS LIMITED PARTNERSHIP *p 216*
2030 PANORAMA DR, INVERMERE, BC, V0A 1K0

(250) 342-6941   *SIC* 7011

IWA-FOREST INDUSTRY PENSION PLAN *p 286*
2955 VIRTUAL WAY SUITE 150, VANCOUVER, BC, V5M 4X6
(604) 433-6310   *SIC* 6371

IWAM *p 374*
See IMMIGRANT WOMEN'S ASSOCIATION OF MANITOBA INC

IWCD *p 234*
See ISLAND WEST COAST DEVELOPMENTS LTD

IWK HEALTH CENTRE *p 455*
See IZAAK WALTON KILLAM HEALTH CENTRE, THE

IWK HEALTH CENTRE CHARITABLE FOUNDATIONS *p 451*
5855 SPRING GARDEN RD SUITE B220, HALIFAX, NS, B3H 4S2
(902) 470-8085   *SIC* 8699

IWN CONSULTING INC *p 865*
10 MILNER BUSINESS CRT SUITE 300, SCARBOROUGH, ON, M1B 3C6
(416) 827-2727   *SIC* 7371

IYINISIW MANAGEMENT INC *p 260*
10551 SHELLBRIDGE WAY UNIT 100, RICHMOND, BC, V6X 2W9
(604) 249-3969   *SIC* 1541

IZAAK WALTON KILLAM HEALTH CENTRE, THE *p 455*
5980 UNIVERSITY AVE, HALIFAX, NS, B3K 6R8
(902) 470-8888   *SIC* 8069

IZAAK WALTON KILLAM HEALTH CENTRE, THE *p 455*
GD, HALIFAX, NS, B3K 6R8
(902) 470-6682   *SIC* 8731

IZON INDUSTRIES, DIV OF *p 515*
See 1589711 ONTARIO INC

J

J & B CYCLE & MARINE CO. LTD *p 913*
950 RIVERSIDE DR, TIMMINS, ON, P4N 3W2
(705) 267-1417   *SIC* 5599

J & B ENGINEERING INC *p 770*
5734 YONGE ST SUITE 501, NORTH YORK, ON, M2M 4E7
(416) 229-2636   *SIC* 8711

J & D FOOD SERVICES *p 84*
See 394045 ALBERTA LTD

J & D PENNER LTD *p 393*
2560 MCGILLIVRAY BLVD, WINNIPEG, MB, R3Y 1G5
(204) 895-8602   *SIC* 1611

J & F WASTE SYSTEMS INC *p 474*
610 FINLEY AVE, AJAX, ON, L1S 2E3
(905) 427-8064   *SIC* 4953

J & H BUILDERS WAREHOUSE *p 1431*
See J.H. ENTERPRISES (1969) LIMITED

J & K DIE CASTING LIMITED *p 871*
18 GOLDEN GATE CRT, SCARBOROUGH, ON, M1P 3A5
(416) 293-8229   *SIC* 3369

J & K FISHERY (2001) LIMITED *p 462*
GD, MERIGOMISH, NS, B0K 1G0
SIC 5146

J & K POULTRY LTD *p 295*
771 CORDOVA ST E, VANCOUVER, BC, V6A 1M2
(604) 253-8292   *SIC* 5144

J & L SUPPLY CO. LTD *p 30*
4511 MANITOBA RD SE, CALGARY, AB, T2G 4B9
(403) 287-3300   *SIC* 5082

J & M GROUP INC *p 696*
5225 ORBITOR DR UNIT 8, MISSISSAUGA, ON, L4W 4Y8
(905) 766-2157   *SIC* 8742

J & M TIRE INTERNATIONAL INC *p 812*
717 DRAKE ST, OSHAWA, ON, L1H 7R3
(905) 723-3323   *SIC* 5014

J & P FARM SERVICES & SADDLERY *p 468*
See CLARENCE FARM SERVICES LIMITED

J & R HOME PRODUCTS LTD *p 181*
5628 RIVERBEND DR UNIT 1, BURNABY, BC, V3N 0C1
(604) 525-8333   *SIC* 5072

J & S BROKERAGE LTD *p 119*
6040 GATEWAY BLVD NW, EDMONTON, AB, T6H 2H6
(780) 435-5446   *SIC* 5141

J & S DISTRIBUTORS *p 119*
See J & S BROKERAGE LTD

J & S HOLDINGS INC *p 365*
1040 BEAVERHILL BLVD SUITE 1, WINNIPEG, MB, R2J 4B1
(204) 255-8431   *SIC* 5461

J & T VAN ZUTPHEN CONSTRUCTION INCORPORATED *p 465*
10442 SOUTHWEST MABOU, PORT HOOD, NS, B0E 2W0
(902) 945-2300   *SIC* 1623

J + A CLEANING SOLUTIONS *p 795*
See J&A CLEANING SOLUTIONS LTD

J 2 PRODUCTS *p 558*
See SAWILL LTD

J A T INVESTMENTS INC *p 413*
535 WESTMORLAND RD SUITE 3, SAINT JOHN, NB, E2J 3T3
(506) 649-2002   *SIC* 5963

J AHMAD DRUGS LTD *p 703*
700 BURNHAMTHORPE RD E, MISSISSAUGA, ON, L4Y 2X3
(905) 279-1812   *SIC* 5912

J B FOOD SERVICES INC *p 1018*
7605 TECUMSEH RD E, WINDSOR, ON, N8T 3H1
(519) 251-1125   *SIC* 5141

J C INDOOR CLEAN AIR SERVICES INC *p 611*
18 LINDEN ST, HAMILTON, ON, L8L 3H6
(905) 383-7855   *SIC* 4961

J D M PHARMACY LTD *p 203*
310 8TH ST, COURTENAY, BC, V9N 1N3
(250) 334-3134   *SIC* 5912

J D T CONSTRUCTION LTD *p 250*
9407 PENN RD, PRINCE GEORGE, BC, V2N 5T6
(250) 561-2027   *SIC* 1541

J J BARNICKE *p 297*
See CCL PROPERTIES LTD

J J M *p 1217*
See J. J. MARSHALL INC

J J MUGGS GOURMET GRILL *p 976*
See MUGGS, J J INC

J K MARINE SERVICES LIMITED *p 461*
5 COMMERCIAL ST, LOUISBOURG, NS, B1C 1B5
(902) 733-2739   *SIC* 5146

J M S PHARMACY SERVICE INC *p 457*
3430 JOSEPH HOWE DR SUITE 138, HALIFAX, NS, B3L 4H7
(902) 443-6084   *SIC* 5912

J R & S HOLDINGS LTD *p 52*
605 5 AVE SW SUITE 1000, CALGARY, AB, T2P 3H5
(403) 265-5091   *SIC* 1311

J V K *p 886*
See JACK VAN KLAVEREN LIMITED

J V LOGGING LTD *p 250*
9453 ROCK ISLAND RD, PRINCE GEORGE, BC, V2N 5T4
(250) 561-2220   *SIC* 2411

J Y S ENTERPRISE INC *p 740*
1081 MEYERSIDE DR UNIT 8, MISSISSAUGA, ON, L5T 1M4
(905) 565-1472   *SIC* 7389

J&A CLEANING SOLUTIONS LTD *p 795*
785 ARROW RD, NORTH YORK, ON, M9M 2L4
(416) 242-4151   *SIC* 7349

J-AAR EXCAVATING LIMITED *p 649*
3003 PAGE ST, LONDON, ON, N5V 4J1

(519) 652-2104   *SIC* 1794

J-D MARKETING (LEAMINGTON) INC *p 634*
2400 GRAHAM, KINGSVILLE, ON, N9Y 2E5
(519) 733-3663   *SIC* 5148

J-LINE TRANSPORT LIMITED *p 489*
4751 CHRISTIE DR, BEAMSVILLE, ON, L0R 1B4
(905) 945-3122   *SIC* 4213

J-SQUARED TECHNOLOGIES INC *p 624*
4015 CARLING AVE SUITE 101, KANATA, ON, K2K 2A3
(613) 592-9540   *SIC* 5065

J. & R. HALL TRANSPORT INC *p 483*
552 PIPER ST, AYR, ON, N0B 1E0
(519) 632-7429   *SIC* 4213

J. BOND & SONS LTD *p 233*
31413 GILL AVE UNIT 103, MISSION, BC, V4S 0C4
(604) 826-5391   *SIC* 3523

J. C. PAVING LTD *p 360*
3000 MAIN ST UNIT 7, WEST ST PAUL, MB, R2V 4Z3
(204) 989-4700   *SIC* 1611

J. C. VENDING (ONTARIO) LIMITED *p 636*
625 WABANAKI DR UNIT 6, KITCHENER, ON, N2C 2G3
SIC 5962

J. D. DODGE CHRYSLER JEEP *p 1063*
See 9274-8706 QUEBEC INC

J. D. MASONRY *p 603*
5954 WELLINGTON ROAD 7, GUELPH, ON, N1H 6J2
(519) 836-4311   *SIC* 1741

J. DROLET & FILS LTEE *p 1399*
11 RUE DES OBLATS S, VILLE-MARIE, QC, J9V 1J9
(819) 629-2885   *SIC* 5211

J. E. MONDOU LTEE *p 1049*
10400 RUE RENAUDE-LAPOINTE, ANJOU, QC, H1J 2V7
(514) 322-5300   *SIC* 5999

J. EUCLIDE PERRON LTEE *p 1079*
41 RUE JACQUES-CARTIER E, CHICOUTIMI, QC, G7H 5G6
(418) 543-0715   *SIC* 1541

J. FAGEN & FILS INC *p 1322*
201 RUE MONTCALM BUREAU 100, SAINT-JOSEPH-DE-SOREL, QC, J3R 1B9
(450) 742-8880   *SIC* 5093

J. FLORIS CONSTRUCTION LTD *p 175*
2776 BOURQUIN CRES W SUITE 204, ABBOTSFORD, BC, V2S 6A4
(604) 864-6471   *SIC* 1542

J. GRANT WALLACE HOLDINGS LTD *p 346*
1655 18TH ST, BRANDON, MB, R7A 5C6
(204) 728-7120   *SIC* 5399

J. H. MCNAIRN LIMITED *p 1014*
125 CONSUMERS DR, WHITBY, ON, L1N 1C4
(905) 668-7533   *SIC* 2671

J. J. HOME PRODUCTS, DIV OF *p 505*
See RENIN CANADA CORP

J. J. MARSHALL INC *p 1217*
9780 RUE WAVERLY, MONTREAL, QC, H3L 2V5
(514) 381-5647   *SIC* 2657

J. M. LAHMAN MFG. INC *p 646*
3617 LICHTY RD, LINWOOD, ON, N0B 2A0
(519) 698-2440   *SIC* 5169

J. MCEWEN'S PETROLEUMS LTD *p 130*
11141 89 AVE, FORT SASKATCHEWAN, AB, T8L 2S6
(780) 997-4120   *SIC* 5191

J. OSKAM STEEL FABRICATORS LIMITED *p 846*
70 ROSEDALE AVE, PORT COLBORNE, ON, L3K 6G5
(905) 834-7321   *SIC* 3441

J. P. ABBOTT DISTRIBUTION SERVICE LTD *p 600*
534 SPEEDVALE AVE E, GUELPH, ON, N1E 1P6
(519) 821-3206   *SIC* 7319

J. R. BRISSON EQUIPMENT LTD *p* 1002
121 ST PIERRE RD, VARS, ON, K0A 3H0
(613) 443-3300   *SIC* 5082

J. RENE HEBERT LTEE   *p* 1188
300 RUE DU SAINT-SACREMENT BUREAU
28, MONTREAL, QC, H2Y 1X4
(514) 281-0112   *SIC* 4731

J.& F. TRUCKING CORPORATION   *p* 474
610 FINLEY AVE, AJAX, ON, L1S 2E3
(905) 683-7111   *SIC* 4213

J.A. LARUE INC   *p* 1275
3003 AV WATT, QUEBEC, QC, G1X 3W2
(418) 658-3003   *SIC* 3569

J.A. MECANIQUE
See 9051-8127 QUEBEC INC

J.B. GEARS CANADA   *p* 991
See PROVINCIAL PROTECTION INC

J.B. GROUP WAREHOUSE   *p* 337
See J.B. PRECISION ENGINES & PARTS
LTD

J.B. HAND & SONS LIMITED   *p* 433
690 TOPSAIL RD, ST. JOHN'S, NL, A1E 2E2
(709) 364-2300   *SIC* 5099

J.B. LAVERDURE INC   *p* 1180
400 BOUL CREMAZIE O, MONTREAL, QC,
H2P 1C7
(514) 382-7520   *SIC* 5148

J.B. MERCHANDISE DESIGN INC   *p* 681
233 WHITFIELD CRES, MIDLAND, ON, L4R
5E3
(705) 361-2012   *SIC* 7389

J.B. PRECISION ENGINES & PARTS LTD *p*
337
3340 OAK ST, VICTORIA, BC, V8X 1R1
(250) 475-2520   *SIC* 5531

J.B.'S AUTOMOTIVE CENTRE LTD   *p* 101
11670 170 ST NW SUITE 80, EDMONTON,
AB, T5S 1J7
(780) 435-3681   *SIC* 5511

J.B.'S POWER CENTRE   *p* 101
See J.B.'S AUTOMOTIVE CENTRE LTD

J.B.M. ENTERPRISES   *p* 179
5000 256 ST, ALDERGROVE, BC, V4W 1J4
(604) 856-1466   *SIC* 5148

**J.D. COLLINS FIRE PROTECTION COM-
PANY INC**   *p*
1027
101 INNOVATION DR UNIT 1, WOOD-
BRIDGE, ON, L4H 0S3
(905) 660-4535   *SIC* 7389

J.D. FOX ENTERPRISES INC   *p* 1038
141 ABEGWEIT BLVD, BORDEN-
CARLETON, PE, C0B 1X0
(902) 437-2600   *SIC* 5541

J.D. MCARTHUR TIRE SERVICES INC   *p*
835
1066 3RD AVE E, OWEN SOUND, ON, N4K
2L2
(519) 376-3520   *SIC* 5531

J.D.A. VENTURES LTD   *p* 134
713031 RANGE ROAD 64, GRANDE
PRAIRIE, AB, T8W 5E5
(780) 532-5101   *SIC* 1389

J.D.I. VENTURES LIMITED   *p* 460
957 CENTRAL AVE, KINGSTON, NS, B0P
1R0
SIC 5541

J.E. MONDOU   *p* 1047
See 2163-2088 QUEBEC INC

J.E. PERRON - INTER-CITE S.E.N.C *p* 1079
205 BOUL DU ROYAUME E, CHICOUTIMI,
QC, G7H 5H2
(418) 549-0532   *SIC* 1771

J.F. & L. RESTAURANTS LIMITED   *p* 579
25 THE WEST MALL SUITE 1019, ETOBI-
COKE, ON, M9C 1B8
(416) 621-4465   *SIC* 5812

J.F. & L. RESTAURANTS LIMITED   *p* 671
110 DENISON ST UNIT 3, MARKHAM, ON,
L3R 1B6
(905) 479-2402   *SIC* 5812

J.F. & L. RESTAURANTS LIMITED   *p* 765
5941 LESLIE ST, NORTH YORK, ON, M2H
1J8

(416) 493-4444   *SIC* 5812

J.F. & L. RESTAURANTS LIMITED   *p* 906
1 PROMENADE CIR, THORNHILL, ON, L4J
4P8
SIC 5812

J.F.K. SYSTEMS INC   *p* 807
3160 MOYNAHAN ST, OLDCASTLE, ON,
N0R 1L0
(519) 737-1361   *SIC* 3544

J.G. RIVE-SUD FRUITS & LEGUMES INC *p*
1074
1963 RUE PATRICK-FARRAR, CHAMBLY,
QC, J3L 4N7
(450) 447-3092   *SIC* 5148

J.H. ENTERPRISES (1969) LIMITED *p* 1431
2505 AVENUE C N, SASKATOON, SK, S7L
6A6
(306) 652-5322   *SIC* 5211

J.J MCGUIRE GENERAL CONTRACTORS*p*
812
See 723926 ONTARIO LIMITED

J.J.'S HOSPITALITY LIMITED   *p* 863
360 GREAT NORTHERN RD SUITE 787,
SAULT STE. MARIE, ON, P6B 4Z7
(705) 945-7614   *SIC* 7011

J.J.'S HOSPITALITY LIMITED   *p* 863
360 GREAT NORTHERN RD, SAULT STE.
MARIE, ON, P6B 4Z7
(705) 949-8111   *SIC* 7011

J.L. & SONS TRADING COMPANY LTD *p*
182
6990 GREENWOOD ST, BURNABY, BC,
V5A 1X8
(604) 294-2331   *SIC* 7389

J.L. BELISLE BUILDING MATERIALS LTD*p*
603
389 SPEEDVALE AVE W, GUELPH, ON,
N1H 1C7
(519) 822-8230   *SIC* 5211

J.L. BRISSETTE LTEE   *p* 1354
24 RUE BRISSETTE, SAINTE-AGATHE-
DES-MONTS, QC, J8C 1T4
(819) 326-3263   *SIC* 5149

J.L. DESJARDINS AUTO COLLECTION INC
p 1275
3330 AV WATT, QUEBEC, QC, G1X 4S6
(418) 650-0063   *SIC* 5511

J.L. FREEMAN, S.E.C.   *p* 1066
1250 RUE NOBEL BUREAU 200,
BOUCHERVILLE, QC, J4B 5H1
(450) 641-4520   *SIC* 5141

J.L. INTERNATIONAL   *p* 852
21 EAST WILMOT ST UNIT 2, RICHMOND
HILL, ON, L4B 1A3
(905) 763-2929   *SIC* 5141

J.L. RICHARDS & ASSOCIATES LIMITED *p*
829
864 LADY ELLEN PL, OTTAWA, ON, K1Z
5M2
(613) 728-3571   *SIC* 8711

J.M. BASTILLE ACIER INC   *p* 1286
396 RUE TEMISCOUATA, RIVIERE-DU-
LOUP, QC, G5R 2Z2
(418) 862-3346   *SIC* 5093

J.M. CHAMPEAU INC   *p* 1347
491 RTE 253, SAINT-MALO, QC, J0B 2Y0
(819) 658-2245   *SIC* 2421

J.M. CLEMENT LTEE   *p* 1279
5830 BOUL PIERRE-BERTRAND BUREAU
400, QUEBEC, QC, G2J 1B7
(418) 626-0006   *SIC* 5641

J.M. DIE LIMITED   *p* 696
909 PANTERA DR, MISSISSAUGA, ON,
L4W 2R9
(905) 625-9571   *SIC* 3541

J.M. DUBRIS LTEE   *p* 1302
500 BOUL ARTHUR-SAUVE, SAINT-
EUSTACHE, QC, J7R 4Z3
(450) 472-2270   *SIC* 5531

J.M.F. TRANSPORT   *p* 1392
See J.M.F. TRANSPORT (1992) LTEE

J.M.F. TRANSPORT (1992) LTEE   *p* 1392
5609 CH DE L'AEROPORT, VALCOURT,
QC, J0E 2L0

(450) 532-2285   *SIC* 4212

J.M.R. ELECTRIC LTD   *p* 590
301 THAMES RD, EXETER, ON, N0M 1S3
(519) 235-1516   *SIC* 1731

J.M.Y. INC   *p* 1121
480 RUE JOSEPH-GAGNE S, LA BAIE, QC,
G7B 3P6
(418) 544-8442   *SIC* 3599

J.O.T. FREIGHT SYSTEMS   *p* 504
See JUST ON TIME FREIGHT SYSTEMS
INC

J.P. LESSARD CANADA INC   *p* 1170
9455 RUE J.-J.-GAGNIER, MONTREAL,
QC, H1Z 3C8
(514) 384-0660   *SIC* 1711

J.R. MECANIQUE LTEE   *p* 1366
485A BOUL DES ERABLES, SALABERRY-
DE-VALLEYFIELD, QC, J6T 6G3
(450) 377-3615   *SIC* 1541

J.R. CAZA & FRERE INC   *p* 1291
3755 RTE 132, SAINT-ANICET, QC, J0S
1M0
(450) 264-2300   *SIC* 5083

J.R. GIUDICE PHARMACY INC   *p* 614
902 MOHAWK RD E, HAMILTON, ON, L8T
2R8
(905) 387-2300   *SIC* 5912

J.R. SIMPLOT COMPANY (FOOD)   *p* 355
See SIMPLOT CANADA (II) LIMITED

J.R.S. AMENITIES LTD   *p* 263
11151 HORSESHOE WAY UNIT 25, RICH-
MOND, BC, V7A 4S5
(604) 244-7627   *SIC* 5046

J.R.T. FARM LTD   *p* 179
2396 272 ST, ALDERGROVE, BC, V4W 2R1
(604) 856-5552   *SIC* 0119

J.V. DRIVER CORPORATION INC   *p* 149
1205 5 ST, NISKU, AB, T9E 7L6
(780) 980-5837   *SIC* 1629

J.V. DRIVER FABRICATORS INC   *p* 149
706 25 AVE, NISKU, AB, T9E 0G6
(780) 955-4282   *SIC* 3312

J.V. DRIVER PROJECTS INC   *p* 149
1205 5 ST, NISKU, AB, T9E 7L6
(780) 980-5837   *SIC* 1541

J.V. LOGGING LTD   *p* 250
See J V LOGGING LTD

J.W. VENTURES INC   *p* 348
1790 HIGHLAND AVE, BRANDON, MB,
R7C 1A7
(204) 571-3152   *SIC* 5812

J.W.T ENTERPRISES INC   *p* 929
160 BLOOR ST E SUITE 8TH, TORONTO,
ON, M4W 3P7
(416) 926-7300   *SIC* 7311

J.Y. MOREAU ELECTRIQUE INC   *p* 1289
160 BOUL INDUSTRIEL, ROUYN-
NORANDA, QC, J9X 6T3
(819) 797-0088   *SIC* 1799

J/E BEARING & MACHINE LTD   *p* 911
68 SPRUCE ST, TILLSONBURG, ON, N4G
5V3
(519) 842-8476   *SIC* 5085

J2 GLOBAL CANADA, INC   *p* 749
2 GURDWARA RD, NEPEAN, ON, K2E 1A2
(613) 733-0000   *SIC* 4899

J2 MANAGEMENT CORP   *p* 915
200 YORKLAND BLVD SUITE 800,
TORONTO, ON, M2J 5C1
(416) 438-6650   *SIC* 6712

JA CANADA   *p* 579
See JUNIOR ACHIEVEMENT OF CANADA

JABLONSKY AST AND PARTNERS   *p* 779
1129 LESLIE ST, NORTH YORK, ON, M3C
2K5
(416) 447-7405   *SIC* 8711

JACCO TOURS (ONTARIO) INC   *p* 876
633 SILVER STAR BLVD UNIT 122, SCAR-
BOROUGH, ON, M1V 5N1
(416) 332-0808   *SIC* 4724

JACCO TOURS ONTARIO INC   *p* 671
7828 KENNEDY RD SUITE 203,
MARKHAM, ON, L3R 5P1
(905) 305-3888   *SIC* 4724

JACE HOLDINGS LTD   *p* 211
1270 56 ST, DELTA, BC, V4L 2A4
(604) 948-9210   *SIC* 5411

JACE HOLDINGS LTD   *p* 233
650 TERMINAL AVE UNIT 3, NANAIMO,
BC, V9R 5E2
(250) 754-6273   *SIC* 5411

JACE HOLDINGS LTD   *p* 238
1893 MILLS RD, NORTH SAANICH, BC,
V8L 5S9
(250) 483-1709   *SIC* 5141

JACE HOLDINGS LTD   *p* 267
6649 BUTLER CRES, SAANICHTON, BC,
V8M 1Z7
(250) 483-1600   *SIC* 5141

JACE HOLDINGS LTD   *p* 267
6772 KIRKPATRICK CRES, SAANICHTON,
BC, V8M 1Z9
(250) 483-1616   *SIC* 5411

JACE HOLDINGS LTD   *p* 337
3475 QUADRA ST SUITE 13, VICTORIA,
BC, V8X 1G8
(250) 382-2751   *SIC* 5141

JACK ASTOR'S   *p* 711
See SIR CORP

JACK ASTOR'S BAR & GRILL   *p* 459
See SIR CORP

JACK ASTOR'S BAR & GRILL   *p* 478
See SIR CORP

JACK ASTOR'S BAR & GRILL   *p* 626
See SIR CORP

JACK ASTOR'S BAR & GRILL   *p* 657
See SIR CORP

JACK ASTOR'S BAR AND GRILL   *p* 525
See SIR CORP

JACK ASTOR'S BAR AND GRILL   *p* 579
See SIR CORP

JACK ASTOR'S BAR AND GRILL   *p* 588
See SIR CORP

JACK ASTOR'S BAR AND GRILL   *p* 967
See SIR CORP

JACK ASTORS RESTAURANTS   *p* 506
See SIR CORP

**JACK COOPER CANADA 2 LIMITED PART-
NERSHIP**   *p*
1340
8050 BOUL CAVENDISH, SAINT-
LAURENT, QC, H4T 1T1
(514) 731-3016   *SIC* 4213

JACK DOHENY COMPANIES   *p* 495
See VACUUM TRUCKS OF CANADA ULC

JACK FM   *p* 58
See ROGERS MEDIA INC

JACK FRENCH LIMITED   *p* 632
200 BINNINGTON CRT, KINGSTON, ON,
K7M 8R6
(613) 547-6666   *SIC* 5211

JACK FRIDAY'S LIMITED   *p* 453
1740 ARGYLE ST, HALIFAX, NS, B3J 2B6
(902) 454-9344   *SIC* 5812

JACK MACKENZIE SCHOO   *p* 1422
See BOARD OF EDUCATION
REGINA SCHOOL DIVISION NO. 4 OF
SASKATCHEWAN

JACK VAN KLAVEREN LIMITED   *p* 886
1894 SEVENTH ST, ST CATHARINES, ON,
L2R 6P9
(905) 641-5599   *SIC* 5191

JACK VICTOR LIMITED   *p* 1205
1250 RUE SAINT-ALEXANDRE BUREAU
100, MONTREAL, QC, H3B 3H6
(514) 866-4891   *SIC* 2311

JACK- FM 96.9   *p* 293
See ROGERS MEDIA INC

JACKMAN FLOWER SHOP LIMITED *p* 763
157 WORTHINGTON ST E, NORTH BAY,
ON, P1B 1G4
(705) 494-8000   *SIC* 5992

JACKMAN MANOR   *p* 179
See ALDERGROVE LIONS SENIORS
HOUSING SOCIETY

JACKMAN'S   *p* 763
See JACKMAN FLOWER SHOP LIMITED

JACKS   *p* 654

539 RICHMOND ST, LONDON, ON, N6A 3E9

(519) 438-1876   SIC 5813

JACKSON DODGE CHRYSLER   p 146
See GARDNER MOTORS (1981) LTD

JACKSON ROBSON INDUSTRIAL SUPPLY
p 526
See SIMPSON, S. B. GROUP INC

JACKSON SQUARE   p 612
See FIRST REAL PROPERTIES LIMITED

JACKSON, GEORGE N. LIMITED   p 381
1139 MCDERMOT AVE, WINNIPEG, MB, R3E 0V2

(204) 786-3821   SIC 5087

JACKSONS TOYOTA   p 488
See T.R.Y. JACKSON BROTHERS LIMITED

JACOB BROS CONSTRUCTION INC p 279
3399 189 ST, SURREY, BC, V3Z 1A7

(604) 541-0303   SIC 1611

JACOB BROS. ASSET CO. LTD   p 279
3399 189 ST, SURREY, BC, V3Z 1A7

(604) 541-0303   SIC 1611

JACOB HESPELER SECONDARY SCHOOL
p 537
See WATERLOO REGION DISTRICT SCHOOL BOARD

JACOBS & THOMPSON INC   p 793
89 KENHAR DR, NORTH YORK, ON, M9L 2R3

(416) 749-0600   SIC 3053

JACOBS CANADA INC   p 16
205 QUARRY PARK BLVD SE, CALGARY, AB, T2C 3E7

(403) 258-6411   SIC 8711

JACOBS CATERING LTD   p 988
2828 BATHURST ST SUITE 502, TORONTO, ON, M6B 3A7

(905) 886-3832   SIC 5812

JACOBS CONSULTANCY   p 823
See JACOBS CONSULTANCY CANADA INC

JACOBS CONSULTANCY CANADA INC p 823
220 LAURIER AVE W SUITE 500, OTTAWA, ON, K1P 5Z9
   SIC 8742

JACOBS INDUSTRIAL SERVICES   p 122
1104 70 AVE NW, EDMONTON, AB, T6P 1P5

(780) 468-2533   SIC 7349

JACOBS INDUSTRIAL SERVICES ULCp 16
205 QUARRY PARK BLVD SE SUITE 200, CALGARY, AB, T2C 3E7

(403) 258-6899   SIC 7349

JACOBSON FORD SALES LTD   p 268
450 TRANS CANADA HWY SW, SALMON ARM, BC, V1E 1S9

(250) 832-2101   SIC 5511

JACOMAU   p 1273
See PRODUITS FORESTIERS D&G LTEE, LES

JACOS   p 52
See JAPAN CANADA OIL SANDS LIMITED

JACOX HARLEY-DAVIDSON INC   p 723
2815 ARGENTIA RD, MISSISSAUGA, ON, L5N 8G6

(905) 858-0966   SIC 5571

JACQUES CARTIER AND CHAMPLAIN BRIDGES INCORPORATED, THE   p 1144
1225 RUE SAINT-CHARLES O UNITE 500, LONGUEUIL, QC, J4K 0B9

(450) 651-8771   SIC 1622

JACQUES LAFERTE LTEE   p 1099
1650 BOUL LEMIRE, DRUMMONDVILLE, QC, J2C 5A4

(819) 477-8950   SIC 5211

JADACO RECREATION MANAGEMENT p 782
See 806040 ONTARIO LTD

JADE STONE LTD   p 16
6429 79 AVE SE, CALGARY, AB, T2C 5P1

(403) 287-0398   SIC 3281

JADE TOURS   p 857
See JADE TRAVEL LTD

JADE TRANSPORT LTD   p 366
963 DUGALD RD, WINNIPEG, MB, R2J 0G8

(204) 233-3566   SIC 4212

JADE TRAVEL LTD   p 857
1650 ELGIN MILLS RD E UNIT 403, RICHMOND HILL, ON, L4S 0B2

(905) 787-9288   SIC 4725

JADEE MEAT PRODUCTS LIMITED   p 489
4710 BARTLETT RD, BEAMSVILLE, ON, L0R 1B1

(905) 563-5381   SIC 2011

JAFFSONS HOLDINGS LTD   p 341
100 PARK ROYAL S SUITE 300, WEST VANCOUVER, BC, V7T 1A2

(604) 925-2700   SIC 6719

JAGO AUTO LTD   p 422
31 CONFEDERATION DR, CORNER BROOK, NL, A2H 0A6

(709) 639-7575   SIC 5511

JAGUAR BOOK GROUP, DIV OF   p 683
See FRASER DIRECT DISTRIBUTION SERVICES LTD

JAGUAR LAND ROVER EDMONTON   p 99
See BRITISH FINE CARS LTD

JAGUAR LAND ROVER LAVAL   p 1085
See 6304966 CANADA INC

JAGUAR MINING INC   p 987
100 KING ST W 56TH FL, TORONTO, ON, M5X 1C9

(416) 847-1854   SIC 1041

JAKE FRIESEN INC   p 177
2425 TOWNLINE RD, ABBOTSFORD, BC, V2T 6L6

(604) 850-1108   SIC 2048

JAKKS PACIFIC (CANADA), INC   p 511
125 EDGEWARE RD SUITE 15, BRAMPTON, ON, L6Y 0P5

(905) 452-6279   SIC 3944

JALALDIN, NARMIN DRUGS LTD   p 829
1309 CARLING AVE, OTTAWA, ON, K1Z 7L3

(613) 722-4277   SIC 5912

JALO FAUCETS   p 1384
See BARIL MANUFACTURIER INC

JAM FILLED ENTERTAINMENT INC p 831
65 AURIGA DR SUITE 103, OTTAWA, ON, K2E 7W6

(613) 366-2550   SIC 7812

JAM FILLED ENTERTAINMENT INC p 981
364 RICHMOND ST W SUITE 100, TORONTO, ON, M5V 1X6

(613) 366-2550   SIC 7812

JAM-BEC INC   p 1114
380 BOUL DE L'INDUSTRIE, JOLIETTE, QC, J6E 8G2

(450) 759-5130   SIC 5141

JAMAC SALES LIMITED   p 671
141 DON PARK RD, MARKHAM, ON, L3R 1C2

(905) 947-9824   SIC 5039

JAMAL, OME PHARMACY LTD   p 865
265 PORT UNION RD, SCARBOROUGH, ON, M1C 2L3

(416) 284-9229   SIC 5912

JAMBO KITMEER LTD   p 504
1810 STEELES AVE E, BRAMPTON, ON, L6T 1A7

(905) 792-3009   SIC 5136

JAMEI COMPANY LTD   p 874
180 COMMANDER BLVD, SCARBOROUGH, ON, M1S 3C8

(416) 293-8385   SIC 2335

JAMEL METALS INC   p 374
316 NOTRE DAME AVE, WINNIPEG, MB, R3B 1P4

(204) 947-3066   SIC 5093

JAMER MATERIALS LIMITED   p 395
3019 ROUTE 127, BAYSIDE, NB, E5B 2S4

(506) 529-1117   SIC 5032

JAMES BAY GENERAL HOSPITAL   p 591
GD, FORT ALBANY, ON, P0L 1H0

(705) 278-3330   SIC 8062

JAMES BAY GENERAL HOSPITAL   p 746
78 FURGUSON RD, MOOSONEE, ON, P0L

1Y0

(705) 336-2947   SIC 8062

JAMES CAMPBELL SERVICES LTD   p 815
550 TAUNTON RD W, OSHAWA, ON, L1L 0N8

(905) 571-5420   SIC 5511

JAMES CARDINAL MCGUIGAN CATHOLIC SCHOOL   p 785
See TORONTO CATHOLIC DISTRICT SCHOOL BOARD

JAMES ELECTRIC MOTOR SERVICES LTD
p 30
4020 8 ST SE, CALGARY, AB, T2G 3A7

(403) 252-5477   SIC 5084

JAMES EVANS AND ASSOCIATES LTD   p 338
4464 MARKHAM ST SUITE 1205, VICTORIA, BC, V8Z 7X8

(250) 380-3811   SIC 7371

JAMES MOTO ENTERPRISES   p 978
See 601712 ONTARIO INC

JAMES R MODER CRYSTAL CHANDELIER   p 289
See MODER, JAMES R. CRYSTAL CHANDELIER (CANADA) LTD

JAMES RICHARDSON INTERNATIONAL (QUEBEC)   p 1376
See RICHARDSON INTERNATIONAL (QUEBEC) LIMITEE

JAMES VALLEY COLONY FARMS LTD   p 349
100 JAMES VALLEY RD, ELIE, MB, R0H 0H0

(204) 353-2827   SIC 0191

JAMES WESTERN STAR TRUCK & TRAILER LTD   p 250
5239 CONTINENTAL WAY, PRINCE GEORGE, BC, V2N 5S5

(250) 561-0646   SIC 5511

JAMESWAY INCUBATOR COMPANY INC p 533
30 HIGH RIDGE CRT, CAMBRIDGE, ON, N1R 7L3

(519) 624-4646   SIC 3523

JAMIE D. TEMPLE PHARMACY LTD   p 627
2727 HWY 43, KEMPTVILLE, ON, K0G 1J0

(613) 258-2557   SIC 5912

JAMIESON   p 927
See JAMIESON LABORATORIES LTD

JAMIESON LABORATORIES LTD   p 927
2 ST CLAIR AVE W, TORONTO, ON, M4V 1L5

(416) 960-0052   SIC 2833

JAMIESON PHARMACY LTD   p 453
5524 SPRING GARDEN RD, HALIFAX, NS, B3J 1G5

(902) 429-2400   SIC 5912

JAMIESON WELLNESS INC   p 939
1 ADELAIDE ST E SUITE 2200, TORONTO, ON, M5C 2V9

(833) 223-2666   SIC 2833

JAN K. OVERWEEL LIMITED   p 1031
3700 STEELES AVE W SUITE 702, WOODBRIDGE, ON, L4L 8K8

(905) 850-9010   SIC 5141

JAN KELLEY MARKETING   p 529
1005 SKYVIEW DR SUITE 322, BURLINGTON, ON, L7P 5B1

(905) 631-7934   SIC 4899

JAN-MAR SALES LIMITED   p 740
6976 COLUMBUS RD, MISSISSAUGA, ON, L5T 2G1

(416) 255-8535   SIC 5087

JAN-PRO   p 1264
See JAN-PRO CANADA INC

JAN-PRO CANADA EST INC   p 1264
2323 BOUL DU VERSANT-NORD BUREAU 114, QUEBEC, QC, G1N 4P4

(418) 527-1400   SIC 6794

JAN-PRO CANADA INC   p 1264
2323 BOUL DU VERSANT-NORD BUREAU 114, QUEBEC, QC, G1N 4P4

(418) 527-1400   SIC 6794

JAN-PRO DES MARITIMES   p 1264

See JAN-PRO CANADA EST INC

JANA AND COMPANY IMPORTS   p 323
8680 CAMBIE ST, VANCOUVER, BC, V6P 6M9

(604) 688-3657   SIC 5137

JANCO STEEL LTD   p 892
925 ARVIN AVE, STONEY CREEK, ON, L8E 5N9

(905) 643-3535   SIC 5051

JANCOX STAMPINGS   p 505
See NAHANNI STEEL PRODUCTS INC

JANDEL HOMES   p 132
9407 153 AVE, GRANDE PRAIRIE, AB, T8V 0B6

(780) 402-3170   SIC 5271

JANG MO JIB KOREAN RESTAURANT   p 318
See A POWER INTERNATIONAL TRADING COMPANY

JANICK ELECTRIC LIMITED   p 786
1170 SHEPPARD AVE W UNIT 9, NORTH YORK, ON, M3K 2A3

(416) 635-8989   SIC 1731

JANICO INVESTMENTS LTD   p 366
928 MARION ST, WINNIPEG, MB, R2J 0K8

(204) 949-7281   SIC 5171

JANNEX ENTERPRISES (1980) LIMITED p 679
280 HILLMOUNT RD UNIT 7, MARKHAM, ON, L6C 3A1

(905) 284-8484   SIC 5112

JANSEN INTERNATIONAL CANADA LTD p 489
4700 SOUTH SERVICE RD, BEAMSVILLE, ON, L0R 1B1

(905) 563-1822   SIC 5021

JANSSEN INC   p 779
19 GREEN BELT DR, NORTH YORK, ON, M3C 1L9

(416) 449-9444   SIC 2834

JANZEN CHEVROLET BUICK GMC LTD p 361
145 BOUNDARY TRAIL, WINKLER, MB, R6W 0L7

(204) 325-9511   SIC 5511

JANZEN STEEL BUILDINGS   p 1413
See JANZEN, HENRY STEEL BUILDINGS LTD

JANZEN, HENRY STEEL BUILDINGS LTDp 1413
GD, OSLER, SK, S0K 3A0

(306) 242-7767   SIC 1791

JAPAN AUTO LEASING INC   p 1008
545 KING ST N, WATERLOO, ON, N2L 5Z6

(519) 746-4120   SIC 5511

JAPAN CANADA OIL SANDS LIMITED p 52
639 5 AVE SW SUITE 2300, CALGARY, AB, T2P 0M9

(403) 264-9046   SIC 8731

JAPAN OTTAWA TRAVEL INC   p 750
139 CRAIG HENRY DR, NEPEAN, ON, K2G 3Z8

(613) 820-8800   SIC 4725

JARDEN   p 504
See INTERNATIONAL PLAYING CARD COMPANY LIMITED

JARDEN CONSUMER SOLUTIONS   p 512
See SUNBEAM CORPORATION (CANADA) LIMITED

JARDIN BANQUET & CONFERENCE CENTRE INC, LE   p 1032
8440 27 HWY, WOODBRIDGE, ON, L4L 1A5

(905) 851-2200   SIC 7299

JARDIN MERITE DE QUEBEC   p 1293
See METRO RICHELIEU INC

JARDIN MERITE MONTREAL, DIV OF   p 1164
See METRO RICHELIEU INC

JARDINE AUCTIONEERS INC   p 403
1849 ROUTE 640, HANWELL, NB, E3C 2A7

(506) 454-4400   SIC 7389

JARDINE BROOK HOLDINGS LIMITED   p

415
300 UNION ST, SAINT JOHN, NB, E2L 4Z2
(506) 632-5110   SIC 6712

JARDINE LLOYD THOMPSON CANADA INC   p 314
1111 GEORGIA ST W SUITE 1600, VANCOUVER, BC, V6E 4G2
(604) 682-4211   SIC 6411

JARDINE SECURITY LTD   p 405
107 TARDY AVE, MIRAMICHI, NB, E1V 3Y8
(506) 622-2787   SIC 7381

JARDINERIE FERNAND FORTIER INC, LA   p 1254
99 116 RTE E, PRINCEVILLE, QC, G6L 4K6
(819) 364-5009   SIC 5261

JARDINS DE LA CITE, LES   p 1098
See GESTION VALLIERES ET PELLETIER INC, LES

JARDINS DU HAUT-ST-LAURENT 1990   p 1293
See INVESTISSEMENTS DU HAUT-ST-LAURENT INC, LES

JARDINS FMS DAIGNEAULT, LES   p 1376
See PRODUITS FRAIS FMS INC

JARDINS G & R LTEE, LES   p 1347
1043 RUE GARIEPY, SAINT-LIN-LAURENTIDES, QC, J5M 2N1
(450) 439-3425   SIC 5148

JARDINS INTERIEURS DE SAINT-LAMBERT INC, LES   p 1323
1705 AV VICTORIA BUREAU 904, SAINT-LAMBERT, QC, J4R 2T3
(450) 671-1314   SIC 6513

JARDINS M.G. S.E.N.C., LES   p 1359
985 RANG SAINT-SIMON, SAINTE-MADELEINE, QC, J0H 1S0
(450) 795-3459   SIC 5148

JARDINS NELSON INC   p 1188
407 PLACE JACQUES-CARTIER, MONTREAL, QC, H2Y 3B1
(514) 861-5731   SIC 5812

JARDINS PAUL COUSINEAU & FILS INC, LES   p 1298
701 RANG SAINT-PIERRE N, SAINT-CONSTANT, QC, J5A 0R2
(450) 635-9000   SIC 0161

JARDINS QUATRE SAISONS   p 1365
See 2619-0645 QUEBEC INC

JARDINS VAL-MONT INC., LES   p 1359
488 AV JULES-CHOQUET, SAINTE-JULIE, QC, J3E 1W6
(450) 649-1863   SIC 5499

JARDINS VEGIBEC INC, LES   p 1244
171 RANG SAINTE-SOPHIE, OKA, QC, J0N 1E0
(450) 496-0566   SIC 0191

JARISLOWSKY, FRASER LIMITEE   p 1197
1010 RUE SHERBROOKE O BUREAU 2005, MONTREAL, QC, H3A 2R7
(514) 842-2727   SIC 6282

JARJA FLORAL   p 881
See JARJA FLORAL INTERNATIONAL CORP

JARJA FLORAL INTERNATIONAL CORP   p 881
577 CHARLOTTEVILLE ROAD 8, SIMCOE, ON, N3Y 4K5
(519) 582-3930   SIC 0181

JARLETTE LTD   p 542
110 SANDYS ST, CHATHAM, ON, N7L 4X3
(519) 351-1330   SIC 8051

JARLETTE LTD   p 607
100 BRUCE ST, HAILEYBURY, ON, P0J 1K0
(705) 672-2123   SIC 8051

JARLETTE LTD   p 620
65 ROGERS COVE DR, HUNTSVILLE, ON, P1H 2L9
(705) 788-7713   SIC 8051

JARLETTE LTD   p 809
25 MUSEUM DR SUITE 204, ORILLIA, ON, L3V 7T9
(705) 325-9181   SIC 8051

JARLETTE LTD   p 1001
2100 MAIN ST, VAL CARON, ON, P3N 1S7
(705) 897-7695   SIC 8059

JARLETTE LTD   p 1005
329 PARKSIDE DR E, WATERDOWN, ON, L0R 2H0
(905) 689-2662   SIC 8051

JARVIS COLLEGIATE INSTITUTE   p 932
See TORONTO DISTRICT SCHOOL BOARD

JAS CANADA INC   p 686
7685 BATH RD, MISSISSAUGA, ON, L4T 3T1
(905) 677-3497   SIC 4731

JAS DAY INVESTMENTS LTD   p 137
94 GEIKIE ST, JASPER, AB, T0E 1E0
(780) 852-4431   SIC 7011

JAS DAY INVESTMENTS LTD   p 137
96 GEIKIE ST, JASPER, AB, T0E 1E0
(780) 852-5644   SIC 7011

JASCO JERSEY   p 1222
See TRICOTS LIESSE (1983) INC

JASCO SALES INC   p 740
1680 BONHILL RD, MISSISSAUGA, ON, L5T 1C8
(905) 677-4032   SIC 5082

JASON INDUSTRIAL CANADA   p 1095
See SOCIETE INDUSTRIELLE JASON (CANADA) LTEE

JASPER SETON HEALTHCARE CENTRE   p 137
See ALBERTA HEALTH SERVICES

JASSUN HOLDINGS LTD   p 217
874 NOTRE DAME DR, KAMLOOPS, BC, V2C 6L5
(250) 372-1991   SIC 5013

JASTRAM HOLDINGS LTD   p 238
135 RIVERSIDE DR, NORTH VANCOUVER, BC, V7H 1T6
(604) 986-0714   SIC 6712

JASWALL INC   p 513
70 VAN KIRK DR, BRAMPTON, ON, L7A 1B1
(905) 846-3177   SIC 3449

JASZTEX FIBRES INC   p 1251
61 BOUL HYMUS, POINTE-CLAIRE, QC, H9R 1E2
(514) 697-3096   SIC 2297

JATOM SYSTEMS INC   p 626
99 MICHAEL COWPLAND DR, KANATA, ON, K2M 1X3
(613) 591-5910   SIC 7371

JAY CEE ENTERPRISES LIMITED   p 499
165 SUN PAC BLVD UNIT 4, BRAMPTON, ON, L6S 5Z6
(905) 791-1303   SIC 5162

JAY ELECTRIC LIMITED   p 504
21 KENVIEW BLVD UNIT 2, BRAMPTON, ON, L6T 5G7
(905) 793-4000   SIC 1731

JAY'S TRANSPORTATION GROUP LTD   p 1416
555 PARK ST, REGINA, SK, S4N 5B2
(306) 569-9369   SIC 4213

JAYCEE HERB TRADERS LTD   p 606
21 AIRPARK PL, GUELPH, ON, N1L 1B2
(519) 829-3535   SIC 5499

JAYFER AUTOMOTIVE GROUP (MARKHAM) INC   p 665
5426 HIGHWAY 7 E, MARKHAM, ON, L3P 1B7
(905) 294-1210   SIC 7538

JAYMAN BUILDER   p 71
See JAYMAN BUILT LTD

JAYMAN BUILT LTD   p 71
3132 118 AVE SE SUITE 200, CALGARY, AB, T2Z 3X1
(403) 258-3772   SIC 1521

JAYMOR GROUP, THE   p 852
See JAYMOR SECURITIES LTD

JAYMOR SECURITIES LTD   p 852
105 WEST BEAVER CREEK RD UNIT 9-10, RICHMOND HILL, ON, L4B 1C6
(905) 882-1212   SIC 6211

JAYNE INDUSTRIES INC   p 892
550 SEAMAN ST, STONEY CREEK, ON, L8E 3X7
(905) 643-9200   SIC 3297

JAYTEX GROUP   p 791
See JAYTEX OF CANADA LIMITED

JAYTEX OF CANADA LIMITED   p 791
29 GURNEY CRES, NORTH YORK, ON, M6B 1S9
(416) 785-1099   SIC 5136

JAZZ AVIATION LP   p 447
3 SPECTACLE LAKE DR SUITE 100, DARTMOUTH, NS, B3B 1W8
(902) 873-5000   SIC 4512

JAZZWORKS   p 827
1234 RIDGEMONT AVE, OTTAWA, ON, K1V 6E7
(613) 523-0316   SIC 7929

JBE HOME & AUTO LIMITED   p 177
32513 SOUTH FRASER WAY SUITE 434, ABBOTSFORD, BC, V2T 4N5
(604) 870-4125   SIC 5531

JBG MANAGEMENT INC   p 481
28 MILL ST, AURORA, ON, L4G 2R9
SIC 8051

JBI (CANADA) INC   p 848
1783 ALLANPORT RD RR 1, PORT ROBINSON, ON, L0S 1K0
SIC 5172

JBL INTERNATIONAL   p 1180
See J.B. LAVERDURE INC

JBM LOGISTICS   p 1425
See 615315 SASKATCHEWAN LTD

JBS   p 233
See J. BOND & SONS LTD

JBS CANADA INC   p 7
GD STN MAIN, BROOKS, AB, T1R 1E4
(403) 362-3457   SIC 2011

JBS CANADA INC   p 35
5101 11 ST SE, CALGARY, AB, T2H 1M7
SIC 2011

JBT TRANSPORT INC   p 483
235 WAYDOM DR SUITE 1, AYR, ON, N0B 1E0
(519) 622-3604   SIC 4213

JBW PIPE & SUPPLY LTD   p 30
1320 HIGHFIELD CRES SE, CALGARY, AB, T2G 5M3
(403) 259-6671   SIC 5074

JC JULIETTE & CHOCOLAT   p 1185
See COMPAGNIE INTERNATIONALE DE PRODUITS ALIMENTAIRES ET COMMERCE DE DETAIL INC

JC PERREAULT   p 1352
See MEUBLES JCPERREAULT INC

JCA ELECTRONICS   p 384
See JCA INDUSTRIES INC

JCA INDUSTRIES INC   p 384
118 KING EDWARD ST E, WINNIPEG, MB, R3H 0N8
(204) 415-1104   SIC 3625

JCB EDMONTON   p 76
See CERVUS CONTRACTORS EQUIPMENT LTD

JCB ENTREPRENEURS GENERAUX INC   p 1070
3875 RUE ISABELLE, BROSSARD, QC, J4Y 2R2
(450) 444-8151   SIC 1542

JCB INDUSTRIAL INC   p 35
6031 4 ST SE, CALGARY, AB, T2H 2A5
(587) 349-1071   SIC 1796

JCF AUTO SPORT   p 1394
904 RTE HARWOOD, VAUDREUIL-DORION, QC, J7V 8P2
SIC 5541

JCORP INC   p 1326
95 RUE GINCE, SAINT-LAURENT, QC, H4N 1J7
(514) 384-3872   SIC 5136

JCS NURSING & HOME CARE SERVICES INC   p 869
3464 KINGSTON RD SUITE 207A, SCARBOROUGH, ON, M1M 1R5

(416) 265-1687   SIC 8741

JD ANIMA   p 1082
See FORMEDICA LTEE

JD IRVING   p 993
See IRVING CONSUMER PRODUCTS LIMITED

JD SWEID FOODS (2013) LTD   p 225
9696 199A ST, LANGLEY, BC, V1M 2X7
(800) 665-4355   SIC 2015

JDA OILFIELD HAULING   p 134
See J.D.A. VENTURES LTD

JDC #10 LIMITED   p 585
274 HUMBERLINE DR, ETOBICOKE, ON, M9W 5S2
(416) 675-1123   SIC 2653

JDCMI   p 533
See DAOUST, JACQUES COATINGS MANAGEMENT INC

JDS ENERGY & MINING INC   p 219
3200 RICHTER ST UNIT 206, KELOWNA, BC, V1W 5K9
(250) 763-6369   SIC 8741

JDS WHOLESALES & DISTRIBUTION   p 581
See 1531011 ONTARIO INC

JEA PENSION SYSTEMS SOLUTIONS   p 338
See JAMES EVANS AND ASSOCIATES LTD

JEALOUS FRUIT   p 224
See CORAL BEACH FARMS LTD

JEAMAR WINCHES CORPORATION   p 1036
125 BYSHAM PARK DR, WOODSTOCK, ON, N4T 1R2
(519) 537-8855   SIC 3531

JEAN BLEU INC, LE   p 1128
1895 46E AV, LACHINE, QC, H8T 2N9
(514) 631-3300   SIC 5611

JEAN C. DUPONT LTEE   p 399
260 CH CANADA, EDMUNDSTON, NB, E3V 1W1
(506) 739-8343   SIC 5531

JEAN COUTU   p 398
See PHARMACIE DENNIS ABUD PHARMACY INC

JEAN COUTU   p 561
See 837705 ONTARIO LTD

JEAN COUTU   p 1091
See PHARMACIE LOUIS LEGAULT, LYETTE BOULE, PHARMACIENS INC

JEAN COUTU   p 1112
See 9255-8097 QUEBEC INC.

JEAN COUTU   p 1123
See VARIETES LNJF INC

JEAN COUTU   p 1151
See PLACEMENTS JACQUES FELIX THIBEAULT INC, LES

JEAN COUTU   p 1155
See 9223-0846 QUEBEC INC

JEAN COUTU   p 1166
See PLACEMENTS ROBERT SIMARD INC

JEAN COUTU   p 1232
See GESTION JACQUES BOURGET INC

JEAN COUTU   p 1236
See PHARMACIE NICOLAS CARBONNEAU INC

JEAN COUTU   p 1242
See CLEMENT GAGNON ET JACINTHE DESJARDINS, PHARMACIENS (S.E.N.C.)

JEAN COUTU   p 1255
See GESTION HEROUX ET SAUCIER INC

JEAN COUTU   p 1255
See GESTION CHRISTIAN J. OUELLET INC

JEAN COUTU   p 1259
See PAQUET, CHRISTINE ET CHARLES BOISVERT, PHARMACIENS S.E.N.C.

JEAN COUTU   p 1260
See 2737-1822 QUEBEC INC

JEAN COUTU   p 1275
See GESTION DOMINIQUE BOND INC

JEAN COUTU   p 1281
See DEFFOSSES ET VALLEE S.E.N.C

JEAN COUTU   p 1281

See DISTRIBUTIONS JOSEE PERRAULT INC
JEAN COUTU   p 1282
See GEDILEX INC
JEAN COUTU   p 1294
See PHARMACIE SONIA GUIMONT PHAR-MACIENNE INC
JEAN COUTU   p 1304
See DANIEL LAVOIE PHARMACIEN INC
JEAN COUTU   p 1346
See FELBER INC
JEAN COUTU   p 1364
See ENTREPRISES CHRISTIAN CHADI INC, LES
JEAN COUTU   p 1367
See GESTION CHRISTIAN BASTIEN INC
JEAN COUTU   p 1372
See PHARMACIE ANIK BERTRAND INC
JEAN COUTU   p 1375
See PHARMACIE CHRISTIAN BOURQUE, PHAMACIEN INC
JEAN COUTU   p 1386
See PHARMACIE SYLVIE GELINAS ET CHANTAL BELLEMARE PHARMACIENNES INC
JEAN COUTU # 12   p 1068
See ECONOFAR (1988) INC
JEAN COUTU # 253   p 1370
See GESTION FRANCOIS MALTAIS INC
JEAN COUTU # 30   p 1112
See SOCIETE IMMOBILIERE LAFLECHE INC, LA
JEAN COUTU #035 - #305   p 1145
See PHARMACIE JEAN-MICHEL COUTU ET TRISTAN GIGUERE INC
JEAN COUTU #087   p 1057
See SOCIETE PRIBEX LTEE, LA
JEAN COUTU #55   p 1164
See L.J.M. MARKETING INC
JEAN COUTU (MARQUE DE COMMERCE)   p 1241
See PLACEMENTS RABPHAR INC
JEAN COUTU 065   p 1224
See GESTION KM INC
JEAN COUTU 108   p 1046
See DISTRIBUTIONS NORYVE INC
JEAN COUTU 258   p 1229
See MAGASINS D'ESCOMPTE ALMICO INC, LES
JEAN COUTU 30   p 1111
See BELZILE, BEAUMIER ET BELZILE SENC
JEAN COUTU ANNIE LAROCHE & MICHEL ST-GEORGES (AFFILIATED PHARMACIES) p 1171
1221 RUE FLEURY E, MONTREAL, QC, H2C 1R2
   SIC 5912
JEAN COUTU GERMAIN CHARTIER & LIVIO PAROLIN (AFFILIATED PHARMA-CIES)   p 1057
790   AV   GILLES-VILLENEUVE, BERTHIERVILLE, QC, J0K 1A0
   (450) 836-3733   *SIC 5912*
JEAN COUTU GROUP   p 618
See 2058658 ONTARIO INC
JEAN COUTU JACQUES BOUILLON (AF-FILIATED PHARMACIES)   p 1287
253B BOUL LABELLE, ROSEMERE, QC, J7A 2H3
   (450) 437-9151   *SIC 5912*
JEAN COUTU JEAN-PHILIPPE ROY (AF-FILIATED PHARMACIES)   p 1075
3300 BOUL FRECHETTE, CHAMBLY, QC, J3L 6Z6
   (450) 447-5511   *SIC 5912*
JEAN COUTU MARIE-CLAUDE OUELLET & ANNIE SANFACON   p 1275
1221 RUE CHARLES-ALBANEL, QUEBEC, QC, G1X 4Y5
   (418) 874-0275   *SIC 5912*

JEAN COUTU PHARMACY #130   p 417
See PHARMACIE LEBLANC, PIERRE INC
JEAN COUTU PHARMACY #59   p 398
See BREAU, RAYMOND LTD
JEAN JACQUES CAMPEAU INC   p 1072
60   RUE   RENAUD,   BROWNSBURG-CHATHAM, QC, J8G 2E6
   (450) 562-2838   *SIC 4151*
JEAN PERREAULT ET NICOLAS ROMPRE
p 1361
See 9115-7776 QUEBEC INC
JEAN TWEED TREATMENT CENTER, THE
p 575
215 EVANS AVE, ETOBICOKE, ON, M8Z 1J5
   (416) 255-7359   *SIC 8399*
JEAN-COUTU   p 1052
See FRECHETTE, JOSEE PHARMACIE
JEAN-COUTU   p 1110
505 RUE DU RUBIS, GRANBY, QC, J2H 2S3
   (450) 266-3966   *SIC 5912*
JEAN-COUTU   p 1358
See ESCOMPTES C.F.M. INC
JEAN-DEPOT   p 1397
See 9368-1476 QUEBEC INC
JEAN-FRANCOIS GAUTHIER ET ALEXAN-DRE RIVARD, PHARMACIENS S.E.N.C   p 1385
200 RUE FUSEY, TROIS-RIVIERES, QC, G8T 2V8
   (819) 375-8941   *SIC 5912*
JEAN-FRANCOIS ROCHEFORT INC p 1182
6600 RUE SAINT-URBAIN BUREAU 440, MONTREAL, QC, H2S 3G8
   (514) 273-7256   *SIC 2389*
JEAN-PAUL FORTIN (1997) INC   p 1276
2050 RUE DE CELLES, QUEBEC, QC, G2C 1X8
   (418) 845-5369   *SIC 5661*
JEAN-SEBASTIEN CROTEAU ISABELLE ANNE ROBITAILLE INC   p 1398
141 RUE NOTRE-DAME E, VICTORIAV-ILLE, QC, G6P 3Z8
   (819) 752-4554   *SIC 5912*
JEANS DEPOT   p 1357
See 9008-6398 QUEBEC INC
JEANS DEPOT - CHATEAUGUAY   p 1400
See 9028-3409 QUEBEC INC
JEBCO INDUSTRIES INC   p 487
111 ELLIS DR, BARRIE, ON, L4N 8Z3
   (705) 797-8888   *SIC 3499*
JEBCO MANUFACTURING INC   p 546
188 KING ST E RR 2, COLBORNE, ON, K0K 1S0
   (905) 355-3757   *SIC 3599*
JEEM HOLDINGS LTD   p 272
19060 54 AVE, SURREY, BC, V3S 8E5
   (604) 576-1808   *SIC 6712*
JEFF'S NO FRILLS   p 570
53 ARTHUR AVE, ESSEX, ON, N8M 2N1
   (519) 776-4944   *SIC 5411*
JEFFERSON ELORA CORPORATION p 569
60 1ST LINE, ELORA, ON, N0B 1S0
   (519) 846-2728   *SIC 3465*
JEFFERY'S GREENHOUSES INC   p 886
1036   LAKESHORE   RD   W,   ST CATHARINES, ON, L2R 6P9
   (905) 934-0514   *SIC 0181*
JEFFREY BEST MOTORS INCORPO-RATED   p 459
843 PARK ST, KENTVILLE, NS, B4N 3V7
   (902) 678-6000   *SIC 5511*
JEFO NUTRITION INC   p 1310
4900   RUE   MARTINEAU,   SAINT-HYACINTHE, QC, J2R 1K3
   (450) 799-4454   *SIC 5141*
JEFO NUTRITION INC   p 1310
5020 AV JEFO, SAINT-HYACINTHE, QC, J2R 2E7
   (450) 799-2000   *SIC 5191*
JEG ENTERPRISES   p 512
57 CHEVIOT CRES, BRAMPTON, ON, L6Z

4G8
   SIC 5149
JEHOVAH'S WITNESSES EAST ST PAUL CONGREGATION   p 363
3760 ANDREWS RD, WINNIPEG, MB, R2E 1C2
   (204) 654-1829   *SIC 8661*
JELD-WEN OF CANADA LTD   p 367
485 WATT ST, WINNIPEG, MB, R2K 2R9
   (204) 694-6012   *SIC 2431*
JELD-WEN OF CANADA LTD   p 1292
90 RUE INDUSTRIELLE BUREAU 200, SAINT-APOLLINAIRE, QC, G0S 2E0
   (418) 881-3974   *SIC 2431*
JELD-WEN OF CANADA LTD   p 1306
115 RUE DE LA GARE, SAINT-HENRI-DE-LEVIS, QC, G0R 3E0
   (418) 882-2223   *SIC 2431*
JELD-WEN OF CANADA, LTD   p 1292
See JELD-WEN OF CANADA LTD
JELD-WEN OF CANADA, LTD   p 1306
See JELD-WEN OF CANADA LTD
JELD-WEN WINDOWS & DOORS   p 367
See JELD-WEN OF CANADA LTD
JELINEK CORK GROUP   p 804
See JELINEK CORK LIMITED
JELINEK CORK LIMITED   p 804
2260 SPEERS RD, OAKVILLE, ON, L6L 2X8
   (905) 827-4666   *SIC 5099*
JELSCHEN FOODS LTD   p 6
4501 50 AVE, BONNYVILLE, AB, T9N 2N5
   (780) 826-2048   *SIC 5411*
JEM D INTERNATIONAL PARTNERS LP p 634
2400 GRAHAM, KINGSVILLE, ON, N9Y 2E5
   (519) 733-3663   *SIC 5148*
JEM FARMS   p 858
See 617885 ONTARIO LTD
JEMARICA INC   p 857
9040 COUNTY ROAD 17 SUITE 623, ROCKLAND, ON, K4K 1V5
   (613) 446-4410   *SIC 5251*
JEMCO VENTURES INC   p 68
11440 BRAESIDE DR SW SUITE 25, CAL-GARY, AB, T2W 3N4
   (403) 278-7447   *SIC 4724*
JEMPAK GK INC   p 804
1485 SPEERS RD, OAKVILLE, ON, L6L 2X5
   (905) 827-1123   *SIC 2841*
JEMS COATING LIMITED   p 554
210 JACOB KEFFER PKY, CONCORD, ON, L4K 4W3
   (905) 303-7433   *SIC 3479*
JEN-COL CONSTRUCTION LTD.   p 1
9620 266 ST SUITE 100, ACHESON, AB, T7X 6H6
   (780) 963-6523   *SIC 1542*
JENKINS, MALCOLM J. (HOLDINGS) LTD p 1414
3725 2ND AVE W, PRINCE ALBERT, SK, S6W 1A1
   (306) 764-9000   *SIC 6712*
JENKINS, MALCOLM J. MERCHANDISING LTD   p 1414
3725 2ND AVE W, PRINCE ALBERT, SK, S6W 1A1
   (306) 764-9000   *SIC 5531*
JENNER CHEVROLET BUICK GMC LTD p 340
1730 ISLAND HWY, VICTORIA, BC, V9B 1H8
   (250) 474-1211   *SIC 7538*
JENNINGS CAPITAL INC   p 52
308 4 AVE SW SUITE 2700, CALGARY, AB, T2P 0H7
   (403) 292-0970   *SIC 6211*
JENO NEUMAN ET FILS INC   p 1061
95 BOUL DES ENTREPRISES, BOIS-BRIAND, QC, J7G 2T1
   (450) 430-5901   *SIC 5137*
JENSEN HUGHES CONSULTING CANADA LTD   p 255
13900 MAYCREST WAY UNIT 135, RICH-

MOND, BC, V6V 3E2
   (604) 295-4000   *SIC 8711*
JENSEN HUGHES CONSULTING CANADA LTD   p 997
2150   ISLINGTON   AVE   SUITE   100, TORONTO, ON, M9P 3V4
   (647) 559-1251   *SIC 8748*
JEPSON   p 1094
See OUTILLAGES KING CANADA INC
JEPSON PETROLEUM (ALBERTA) LTD p 16
5215 61 AVE SE, CALGARY, AB, T2C 3Y6
   (403) 215-1449   *SIC 5172*
JERICO SPORTSWEAR LTD   p 874
120   COMMANDER   BLVD,   SCARBOR-OUGH, ON, M1S 3H7
   (416) 288-0822   *SIC 2339*
JERITRISH COMPANY LTD   p 628
900 HIGHWAY 17 E, KENORA, ON, P9N 1L9
   (807) 468-3018   *SIC 5812*
JERRY FORD SALES LTD   p 126
5908 4 AVE, EDSON, AB, T7E 1L9
   (780) 723-4441   *SIC 5511*
JERTYNE INTERIOR SERVICES LTD p 78
60 COMMERCIAL DR, CALGARY, AB, T3Z 2A7
   (403) 219-1046   *SIC 1742*
JES CONSTRUCTION INC   p 1277
5145 RUE RIDEAU BUREAU 200, QUE-BEC, QC, G2E 5H5
   (418) 874-0007   *SIC 1542*
JESSE & KELLY'S NO FRILLS   p 591
1135 THOMPSON RD, FORT ERIE, ON, L2A 6T7
   (866) 987-6453   *SIC 5411*
JESSEL, BRIAN AUTOSPORT INC   p 286
2311 BOUNDARY RD, VANCOUVER, BC, V5M 4W5
   (604) 222-7788   *SIC 5511*
JESSEL, BRIAN HOLDINGS INC   p 286
2311 BOUNDARY RD, VANCOUVER, BC, V5M 4W5
   (604) 222-7788   *SIC 6712*
JESTA   p 1188
See JESTA I.S. INC
JESTA I.S. INC   p 1188
755 RUE BERRI BUREAU 200, MON-TREAL, QC, H2Y 3E5
   (514) 925-5100   *SIC 7371*
JET EQUIPMENT & TOOLS LTD   p 182
3260 PRODUCTION WAY, BURNABY, BC, V5A 4W4
   (800) 472-7686   *SIC 5085*
JET EQUIPMENT & TOOLS LTD   p 201
49 SCHOONER ST, COQUITLAM, BC, V3K 0B3
   (604) 523-8665   *SIC 5084*
JET ICE LIMITED   p 755
1091 KERRISDALE BLVD, NEWMARKET, ON, L3Y 8W1
   (905) 853-4204   *SIC 5198*
JET KNITTING   p 871
See MCGREGOR INDUSTRIES INC
JET LABEL   p 109
See JET LABEL AND PACKAGING LTD
JET LABEL AND PACKAGING LTD   p 109
9445 49 ST NW, EDMONTON, AB, T6B 2L8
   (780) 440-5135   *SIC 2679*
JET POWER AND CONTROLS SYSTEMS LTD   p 109
7730 34 ST NW, EDMONTON, AB, T6B 3J6
   (780) 485-1438   *SIC 3621*
JET TRANSPORT LTD   p 598
154 540B HWY RR 1, GORE BAY, ON, P0P 1H0
   (705) 282-2640   *SIC 4213*
JETCO MANUFACTURING LIMITED p 793
36 MILVAN DR, NORTH YORK, ON, M9L 1Z4
   (416) 741-1800   *SIC 3498*
JETCO MECHANICAL   p 95
See ALLDRITT DEVELOPMENT LIMITED
JETCO MECHANICAL LIMITED   p 96

15035 114 AVE NW, EDMONTON, AB, T5M 2Z1

(780) 451-2732   *SIC* 5074

JETPORT INC *p* 747
9300 AIRPORT RD SUITE 520, MOUNT HOPE, ON, L0R 1W0

(905) 679-2400   *SIC* 4512

JETRICH CANADA LIMITED *p* 688
3270 ORLANDO DR SUITE A, MISSISSAUGA, ON, L4V 1C6

(905) 673-3110   *SIC* 5023

JETSTREAM *p* 1334
See GROUPE INTERNATIONAL TRAVELWAY INC

JEUX INFINIS *p* 1213
See EDITION JEUX INFINIS INC

JEWELL, E & R CONTRACTING LIMITED *p* 590
6 CHESSER ST, FALCONBRIDGE, ON, P0M 1S0

(705) 693-3761   *SIC* 1629

JEWISH COMMUNITY CENTRE OF GREATER VANCOUVER *p* 293
950 41ST AVE W, VANCOUVER, BC, V5Z 2N7

(604) 257-5111   *SIC* 8322

JEWISH COMMUNITY COUNCIL OF MONTREAL *p* 1220
6819 BOUL DECARIE, MONTREAL, QC, H3W 3E4

(514) 739-6363   *SIC* 8661

JEWISH FAMILY & CHILD *p* 775
See JEWISH FAMILY AND CHILD SERVICE OF GREATER TORONTO

JEWISH FAMILY AND CHILD SERVICE OF GREATER TORONTO *p* 775
4600 BATHURST ST SUITE 1, NORTH YORK, ON, M2R 3V3

(416) 638-7800   *SIC* 8399

JEWISH FEDERATION OF OTTAWA *p* 829
21 NADOLNY SACHS PVT, OTTAWA, ON, K2A 1R9

(613) 798-4696   *SIC* 7389

JEWISH HOME FOR THE AGED OF BRITISH COLUMBIA *p* 322
1055 41ST AVE W, VANCOUVER, BC, V6M 1W9

(604) 261-9376   *SIC* 8051

JEWISH PEOPLE'S SCHOOLS AND PERETZ SCHOOLS INC *p* 1083
6500 CH KILDARE, COTE SAINT-LUC, QC, H4W 3B8

(514) 731-3841   *SIC* 8211

JEWISH PEOPLE'S SCHOOLS AND PERETZ SCHOOLS INC *p* 1083
6500 CH KILDARE, COTE SAINT-LUC, QC, H4W 3B8

SIC 8211

JEWISH VOCATIONAL SERVICE OF METROPOLITAN TORONTO *p* 791
74 TYCOS DR, NORTH YORK, ON, M6B 1V9

(416) 785-0515   *SIC* 8299

JF FABRICS *p* 800
See JOANNE FABRICS INC

JFC INTERNATIONAL (CANADA) INC *p* 696
1025 KAMATO RD, MISSISSAUGA, ON, L4W 0C1

(905) 629-0993   *SIC* 5141

JHAJ HOLDINGS LTD *p* 252
156 MALCOLM DR, QUESNEL, BC, V2J 1E4

(604) 594-8800   *SIC* 5531

JHL INTERNATIONAL TRADING CO. LTD *p* 181
8168 GLENWOOD DR, BURNABY, BC, V3N 5E9

(604) 421-5520   *SIC* 5023

JIBC *p* 236
See JUSTICE INSTITUTE OF BRITISH COLUMBIA

JIFFY PRODUCTS (N.B.) LTD *p* 418
125 RUE PARC INDUSTRIEL, SHIPPAGAN,

NB, E8S 1X9

(506) 336-2284   *SIC* 2655

JIGGERNAUT TACKLE INC *p* 563
1235 CUMBERLAND ST, CORNWALL, ON, K6J 4K6

(613) 932-3474   *SIC* 5091

JIM BROWN PHARMACY LTD *p* 161
2020 SHERWOOD DR UNIT 600, SHERWOOD PARK, AB, T8A 3H9

(780) 464-9788   *SIC* 5912

JIM E' LEONIE *p* 368
See MOM'S PANTRY PRODUCTS LTD

JIM PATTISON ENTERPRISES LTD *p* 306
1067 CORDOVA ST W UNIT 1800, VANCOUVER, BC, V6C 1C7

(604) 688-6764   *SIC* 5142

JIM PENNEY LIMITED *p* 423
105 LAURELL RD, GANDER, NL, A1V 0A9

(709) 256-4821   *SIC* 5511

JIM TUBMAN CHEVROLET *p* 827
See JIM TUBMAN HOLDINGS LTD

JIM TUBMAN HOLDINGS LTD *p* 827
1770 BANK ST, OTTAWA, ON, K1V 7Y6

(613) 733-4050   *SIC* 5511

JIM WILSON CHEVROLET BUICK GMC INC *p* 809
20 MULCAHY CT, ORILLIA, ON, L3V 6H9

(705) 329-2000   *SIC* 5511

JIM'S BROTHER TRADING CO *p* 878
See EUCLID'S HOLDINGS LTD

JIM'S NO FRILLS *p* 855
See 1023714 ONTARIO LTD

JIMEXS INC *p* 1057
1360 RUE LOUIS-MARCHAND, BELOEIL, QC, J3G 6S3

SIC 5072

JIMMISS CANADA INC *p* 1183
5425 AV CASGRAIN BUREAU 502, MONTREAL, QC, H2T 1X6

(514) 271-3133   *SIC* 2322

JIMSAR BUSINESS SERVICES INC *p* 105
13141 156 ST NW, EDMONTON, AB, T5V 1V2

(780) 476-1600   *SIC* 6331

JINZE (CANADA) CO., LTD *p* 852
9140 LESLIE ST SUITE 311 & 312, RICHMOND HILL, ON, L4B 0A9

(905) 762-9300   *SIC* 6799

JITE TECHNOLOGIES INC *p* 871
11 PROGRESS AVE UNIT 25, SCARBOROUGH, ON, M1P 4S7

(416) 298-6447   *SIC* 3678

JITNEYTRADE INC *p* 1189
360 RUE SAINT-JACQUES, MONTREAL, QC, H2Y 1P5

(514) 985-8080   *SIC* 6231

JJM CONSTRUCTION LTD *p* 209
8218 RIVER WAY, DELTA, BC, V4G 1C4

(604) 946-0978   *SIC* 1611

JJM MANUFACTURING LTD *p* 696
5430 TIMBERLEA BLVD SUITE 2, MISSISSAUGA, ON, L4W 2T7

(905) 206-2150   *SIC* 5137

JKL PROPERTIES LTD *p* 793
32 PENN DR, NORTH YORK, ON, M9L 2A9

(416) 740-5671   *SIC* 8748

JL DESJARDINS AUTO COLLECTION INC *p* 1262
175 RUE DU MARAIS, QUEBEC, QC, G1M 3C8

(418) 683-4450   *SIC* 5511

JLV ENTERPRISES *p* 386
3965 PORTAGE AVE UNIT 10, WINNIPEG, MB, R3K 2G8

(204) 452-0756   *SIC* 5511

JM (RETAIL) INC *p* 585
110 RONSON DR, ETOBICOKE, ON, M9W 1B6

(416) 674-7433   *SIC* 5621

JMAX GLOBAL DISTRIBUTORS INC *p* 323
8680 CAMBIE ST, VANCOUVER, BC, V6P 6M9

(604) 688-3657   *SIC* 5137

JMB CRUSHING SYSTEMS ULC *p* 6

660 RANGE RD 455 1 MILE N AND 1 MILE E, BONNYVILLE, AB, T9N 2H4

(780) 826-1774   *SIC* 4212

JMC MARKETING COMMUNICATIONS CORPORATION *p* 779
789 DON MILLS RD, NORTH YORK, ON, M3C 1T5

(416) 424-6644   *SIC* 8741

JMHI INSURANCE GROUP INC *p* 543
550 RICHMOND ST, CHATHAM, ON, N7M 1R3

(226) 312-2020   *SIC* 6411

JMP ENGINEERING INC *p* 533
1425 BISHOP ST N UNIT 8, CAMBRIDGE, ON, N1R 6J9

(519) 622-2505   *SIC* 8711

JMP ENGINEERING INC *p* 660
4026 MEADOWBROOK DR UNIT 143, LONDON, ON, N6L 1C9

(519) 652-2741   *SIC* 8711

JMX CONTRACTING INC *p* 894
130 RAM FOREST RD, STOUFFVILLE, ON, L4A 2G8

(905) 241-2224   *SIC* 1795

JNE CONSULTING LTD *p* 611
121 SHAW ST, HAMILTON, ON, L8L 3P6

(905) 529-5122   *SIC* 8711

JNE CONSULTING LTD *p* 611
176 SHAW ST, HAMILTON, ON, L8L 3P7

(905) 529-5122   *SIC* 8711

JNE WELDING LIMITED PARTNERSHIP *p* 1435
3915 THATCHER AVE, SASKATOON, SK, S7R 1A3

(306) 242-0884   *SIC* 3441

JO-AL DISTRIBUTING LTD *p* 1161
9900 6E RUE, MONTREAL, QC, H1C 1G2

(514) 643-3391   *SIC* 6712

JOANNE FABRICS INC *p* 800
2610 SHERIDAN GARDEN DR, OAKVILLE, ON, L6J 7Z4

(905) 491-3900   *SIC* 5131

JOANS HOME SUPPORT CARE *p* 419
1815 ROUTE 860 SUITE 860, TITUSVILLE, NB, E5N 3V6

(506) 832-0369   *SIC* 8059

JOB SKILLS *p* 628
155 RIVERGLEN DR SUITE 7, KESWICK, ON, L4P 3M3

(905) 476-8088   *SIC* 7361

JOBAL INDUSTRIES LIMITED *p* 499
2 EDVAC DR, BRAMPTON, ON, L6S 5P2

(905) 799-8555   *SIC* 5251

JOBERT INC *p* 1357
161 RUE PRINCIPALE, SAINTE-EMELIE-DE-L'ENERGIE, QC, J0K 2K0

(450) 886-3851   *SIC* 1611

JOBS UNLIMITED INC *p* 401
1079 YORK ST, FREDERICTON, NB, E3B 3S4

(506) 458-9380   *SIC* 7389

JOCELYN CROTEAU INC *p* 1062
2300 BOUL DU FAUBOURG, BOISBRIAND, QC, J7H 1S3

(450) 435-0216   *SIC* 5311

JODDES LIMITEE *p* 1227
6111 AV ROYALMOUNT BUREAU 100, MONTREAL, QC, H4P 2T4

(514) 340-1114   *SIC* 6719

JODHA PHARMACY INC *p* 718
128 QUEEN ST S SUITE 3, MISSISSAUGA, ON, L5M 1K8

(905) 567-0744   *SIC* 5912

JODOIN LAMARRE PRATTE ARCHITECTES INC *p* 1167
3200 RUE RACHEL E, MONTREAL, QC, H1W 1A4

(514) 527-8821   *SIC* 8712

JOE JOHNSON EQUIPMENT *p* 622
See DE RIGUEUR INC

JOE KOOL'S *p* 654
See JOE KOOL'S RESTAURANTS LIMITED

JOE KOOL'S RESTAURANTS LIMITED *p*

654

595 RICHMOND ST, LONDON, ON, N6A 3G2

(519) 663-5665   *SIC* 5812

JOE MARTIN & SONS LTD *p* 101
18335 105 AVE NW UNIT 201, EDMONTON, AB, T5S 2K9

(780) 455-0550   *SIC* 5172

JOE'S NO FRILLS *p* 484
See 1500451 ONTARIO LIMITED

JOE'S NO FRILLS 796 LIMITED *p* 863
519 KORAH RD, SAULT STE. MARIE, ON, P6C 4J4

(866) 987-6453   *SIC* 5411

JOE'S VALU-MART *p* 857
See 1265767 ONTARIO LIMITED

JOEY CROWFOOT *p* 75
50 CROWFOOT WAY NW, CALGARY, AB, T3G 4C8

(403) 547-5639   *SIC* 5812

JOEY RESTAURANT *p* 162
See JOEY TOMATO'S KITCHENS INC

JOEY TOMATO'S *p* 328
505 BURRARD ST UNIT 950, VANCOUVER, BC, V7X 1M5

(604) 699-5639   *SIC* 5812

JOEY TOMATO'S (EAU CLAIRE) INC *p* 52
208 BARCLAY PARADE SW, CALGARY, AB, T2P 4R4

(403) 263-6336   *SIC* 5812

JOEY TOMATO'S KITCHENS INC *p* 92
11228 JASPER AVE NW, EDMONTON, AB, T5K 2V2

(780) 420-1996   *SIC* 5812

JOEY TOMATO'S KITCHENS INC *p* 162
222 BASELINE RD UNIT 250, SHERWOOD PARK, ON, T8H 1S8

(780) 449-1161   *SIC* 5812

JOEY TOMATO'S KITCHENS INC *p* 201
550 LOUGHEED HWY, COQUITLAM, BC, V3K 3S3

(604) 939-3077   *SIC* 5812

JOEY TOMATO'S RESTAURANT *p* 92
See JOEY TOMATO'S KITCHENS INC

JOEY TOMATO'S RESTAURANT *p* 201
See JOEY TOMATO'S KITCHENS INC

JOEY'S *p* 52
See JOEY TOMATO'S (EAU CLAIRE) INC

JOHN B NEIGHBOURHOOD PUB, THE *p* 201
See JOHN B PUB LTD

JOHN B PUB LTD *p* 201
1000 AUSTIN AVE, COQUITLAM, BC, V3K 3P1

(604) 931-5115   *SIC* 5921

JOHN BEAD CORPORATION LIMITED *p* 868
20 BERTRAND AVE, SCARBOROUGH, ON, M1L 2P4

(416) 757-3287   *SIC* 5092

JOHN BEAR BUICK GMC LTD *p* 884
333 LAKE ST, ST CATHARINES, ON, L2N 7T3

(905) 934-2571   *SIC* 5511

JOHN BOB FARM EQUIPMENT LTD *p* 1437
HWY 3 W, TISDALE, SK, S0E 1T0

(306) 873-4588   *SIC* 5083

JOHN BROOKS COMPANY LIMITED *p* 723
2625 MEADOWPINE BLVD, MISSISSAUGA, ON, L5N 7K5

(905) 624-4200   *SIC* 5084

JOHN BUHLER INC *p* 391
1260 CLARENCE AVE, WINNIPEG, MB, R3T 1T2

(204) 661-8711   *SIC* 3523

JOHN CABOT CATHOLIC SECONDARY *p* 694
See DUFFERIN-PEEL CATHOLIC DISTRICT SCHOOL BOARD

JOHN D. ELECTRIC *p* 27
See ACCU-FLO METER SERVICE LTD

JOHN DEER *p* 1399
See GIROUARD, ANDRE & FILS INC

JOHN DEER DEALER *p* 349

See SYDOR FARM EQUIPMENT LTD
JOHN DEERE p 460
See PLANTERS EQUIPMENT LIMITED
JOHN DEERE p 599
See JOHN DEERE CANADA ULC
JOHN DEERE p 1042
See REDDIN FARM EQUIPMENT LTD
JOHN DEERE p 1392
See EQUIPEMENTS LAGUE & MARTIN INC
JOHN DEERE CANADA ULC p 599
295 HUNTER RD, GRIMSBY, ON, L3M 4H5
(905) 945-9281 SIC 3523
JOHN DEERE FINANCIAL INC p 804
3430 SUPERIOR CRT, OAKVILLE, ON, L6L 0C4
(905) 319-9100 SIC 6153
JOHN FLUEVOG SHOES p 326
See FLUEVOG, JOHN BOOTS & SHOES LTD
JOHN FORSYTH SHIRT COMPANY INC, THE p 696
2645 SKYMARK AVE UNIT 105, MISSISSAUGA, ON, L4W 4H2
(905) 362-4040 SIC 5137
JOHN FRASER SECONDARY SCHOOL p 719
See PEEL DISTRICT SCHOOL BOARD
JOHN G DIEFENBAKER HIGH SCHOOL p 40
See CALGARY BOARD OF EDUCATION
JOHN H. DANIELS FACULTY OF ARCHITECTURE, LANDSCAPE AND DESIGN p 975
See GOVERNING COUNCIL OF THE UNIVERSITY OF TORONTO, THE
JOHN LABATT CENTRE, THE p 654
See LONDON CIVIC CENTRE CORPORATION
JOHN LABATT LIMITED p 654
150 SIMCOE ST, LONDON, ON, N6A 8M3
(519) 663-5050 SIC 2082
JOHN M PARROTT CENTRE p 747
See COUNTY OF LENNOX & ADDINGTON
JOHN MALAND HIGH SCHOOL p 81
See BLACK GOLD REGIONAL DIVISION #18
JOHN MCCRAE SECONDARY SCHOOL p 752
See OTTAWA-CARLETON DISTRICT SCHOOL BOARD
JOHN MCGREGOR SECONDARY SCHOOL p 543
See LAMBTON KENT DISTRICT SCHOOL BOARD
JOHN MUNRO AIRPORT p 747
See HAMILTON INTERNATIONAL AIRPORT LIMITED
JOHN O'S FOODS INC p 1013
827 DROVERS RD, WHEATLEY, ON, N0P 2P0
(519) 825-4673 SIC 5142
JOHN PAUL II COLLEGIATE SCHOOL p 1412
See LIGHT OF CHRIST RCSSD
JOHN PLAYER & FILS LTEE p 1223
3711 RUE SAINT-ANTOINE O, MONTREAL, QC, H4C 3P6
(514) 932-6161 SIC 5194
JOHN POLANYI COLLEGIATE INSTITUTE p 790
See TORONTO DISTRICT SCHOOL BOARD
JOHN RENNIE HIGH SCHOOL p 1251
See LESTER B. PEARSON SCHOOL BOARD
JOHN SANFILIPPO AND CO. LTD p 546
333 PEEL ST, COLLINGWOOD, ON, L9Y 3W3
(705) 445-4200 SIC 5148
JOHN SCOTTI AUTOMOTIVE LTEE p 1345
4315 BOUL METROPOLITAIN E, SAINT-LEONARD, QC, H1R 1Z4
(514) 725-9394 SIC 5521

JOHN SK LTD p 487
151 MAPLEVIEW DR W, BARRIE, ON, L4N 9E8
(705) 734-0819 SIC 5541
JOHN VOLKEN ACADEMY SOCIETY p 276
6911 KING GEORGE BLVD, SURREY, BC, V3W 5A1
(604) 594-1700 SIC 8699
JOHN WILEY & SONS CANADA LIMITED p 922
90 EGLINTON AVE E SUITE 300, TORONTO, ON, M4P 2Y3
(416) 236-4433 SIC 2731
JOHN'S NURSERY p 1006
See MAR-JOHN'S NURSERY LTD
JOHN'S PRIME RIB & STEAK HOUSE p 1427
See GEM CAFE LTD
JOHN'S YOUR INDEPENDENT GROCER p 198
215 PORT AUGUSTA ST UNIT C, COMOX, BC, V9M 3M9
(250) 339-7651 SIC 5141
JOHNNY'S BAKERY (1981) LTD p 235
660 BAKER ST, NELSON, BC, V1L 4J4
SIC 5149
JOHNNY'S FRESH MARKET p 881
See MICHIELI'S SUPERMARKET LIMITED
JOHNS MANVILLE CANADA INC p 137
5301 42 AVE, INNISFAIL, AB, T4G 1A2
(403) 227-7100 SIC 3299
JOHNSON & JOHNSON INC p 605
890 WOODLAWN RD W, GUELPH, ON, N1K 1A5
(519) 826-6226 SIC 2834
JOHNSON & JOHNSON INC p 605
890 WOODLAWN RD W, GUELPH, ON, N1K 1A5
SIC 2834
JOHNSON & JOHNSON INC p 671
200 WHITEHALL DR, MARKHAM, ON, L3R 0T5
(905) 946-8999 SIC 3842
JOHNSON & JOHNSON INC p 671
88 MCNABB ST, MARKHAM, ON, L3R 5L2
(905) 968-2000 SIC 3842
JOHNSON & JOHNSON MEDICAL COMPANIES p 671
See JOHNSON & JOHNSON INC
JOHNSON CONTROLS p 852
See JOHNSON CONTROLS NOVA SCOTIA U.L.C.
JOHNSON CONTROLS p 852
See JOHNSON CONTROLS CANADA LP
JOHNSON CONTROLS CANADA LP p 852
56 LEEK CRES, RICHMOND HILL, ON, L4B 1H1
(866) 468-1484 SIC 8711
JOHNSON CONTROLS NOVA SCOTIA U.L.C. p 684
8205 PARKHILL DR, MILTON, ON, L9T 5G8
(905) 875-2128 SIC 3822
JOHNSON CONTROLS NOVA SCOTIA U.L.C. p 808
120 C LINE, ORANGEVILLE, ON, L9W 3Z8
SIC 2531
JOHNSON CONTROLS NOVA SCOTIA U.L.C. p 852
56 LEEK CRES, RICHMOND HILL, ON, L4B 1H1
(866) 468-1484 SIC 2531
JOHNSON CONTROLS NOVA SCOTIA U.L.C. p 912
100 TOWNLINE RD, TILLSONBURG, ON, N4G 2R7
(519) 842-5971 SIC 2531
JOHNSON CONTROLS NOVA SCOTIA U.L.C. p 1326
395 AV SAINTE-CROIX BUREAU 100, SAINT-LAURENT, QC, H4N 2L3
(514) 747-2580 SIC 1711
JOHNSON CORPORATION, THE p 432
10 FACTORY LANE, ST. JOHN'S, NL, A1C

6H5
(709) 737-1500 SIC 6411
JOHNSON EQUIPMENT p 731
See G.N. JOHNSTON EQUIPMENT CO. LTD.
JOHNSON INC p 97
12220 STONY PLAIN RD NW SUITE 301, EDMONTON, AB, T5N 3Y4
SIC 6331
JOHNSON INC p 430
95 ELIZABETH AVE, ST. JOHN'S, NL, A1B 1R6
(709) 737-1500 SIC 6411
JOHNSON INC p 432
10 FACTORY LANE, ST. JOHN'S, NL, A1C 6H5
(888) 737-1680 SIC 6411
JOHNSON INC p 852
1595 16TH AVE SUITE 700, RICHMOND HILL, ON, L4B 3S5
(905) 764-4900 SIC 6411
JOHNSON MATTHEY MATERIAUX POUR BATTERIES LTEE p 1073
280 AV LIBERTE, CANDIAC, QC, J5R 6X1
(514) 906-1359 SIC 7699
JOHNSON MATTHEY MB p 1073
See JOHNSON MATTHEY MATERIAUX POUR BATTERIES LTEE
JOHNSON MEMORIAL HOSPITAL p 350
See GIMLI COMMUNITY HEALTH CENTRE
JOHNSON PATERSON INC p 481
360 INDUSTRIAL PKY S SUITE 7, AURORA, ON, L4G 3V7
(905) 727-0084 SIC 5074
JOHNSON, O M HOLDINGS INC p 861
311 TRUNK RD, SAULT STE. MARIE, ON, P6A 3S8
(705) 256-7481 SIC 5521
JOHNSON, PAULINE COLLEGIATE VOCATIONAL SCHOOL p 516
See GRAND ERIE DISTRICT SCHOOL BOARD
JOHNSON, S. S. SEEDS LTD p 345
GD, ARBORG, MB, R0C 0A0
(204) 376-5228 SIC 5191
JOHNSON, S.E. MANAGEMENT LTD p 71
4330 122 AVE SE, CALGARY, AB, T2Z 0A6
(403) 291-9600 SIC 1711
JOHNSON-ROSE INC p 723
7300 EAST DANBRO CRES, MISSISSAUGA, ON, L5N 6C2
(905) 817-1470 SIC 5087
JOHNSONS BUSINESS INTERIORS p 990
See G.H. JOHNSONS FURNITURE INC
JOHNSTON & DANIEL p 924
See ROYAL LEPAGE LIMITED
JOHNSTON BUILDERS LTD p 165
265 CARLETON DR UNIT 201, ST. ALBERT, AB, T8N 4J9
(780) 460-0441 SIC 1542
JOHNSTON BUTCHER SHOP p 197
See JOHNSTON PACKERS LTD
JOHNSTON CHRYSLER DODGE JEEP p 617
See JOHNSTON MOTOR SALES CO. LIMITED
JOHNSTON DRUG WHOLESALE LTD p 234
2286 DORMAN RD, NANAIMO, BC, V9S 5G2
(250) 758-3341 SIC 5122
JOHNSTON EQUIPMENT ENGINEERED p 731
5990 AVEBURY RD, MISSISSAUGA, ON, L5R 3R2
(905) 712-6000 SIC 3743
JOHNSTON GROUP INC p 384
1051 KING EDWARD ST, WINNIPEG, MB, R3H 0R4
(204) 774-6677 SIC 8748
JOHNSTON MOTOR SALES CO. LIMITED p 617
1350 UPPER JAMES ST, HAMILTON, ON,

L9C 3B4
(905) 388-5502 SIC 5511
JOHNSTON PACKERS (1995) LTD p 197
5828 PROMONTORY RD, CHILLIWACK, BC, V2R 4M4
(604) 858-4882 SIC 2011
JOHNSTON PACKERS LTD p 197
5828 PROMONTORY RD, CHILLIWACK, BC, V2R 4M4
(604) 858-4121 SIC 2011
JOHNSTON PACKERS LTD p 197
7339 VEDDER RD, CHILLIWACK, BC, V2R 4E4
(604) 824-1985 SIC 2011
JOHNSTON WHOLESALE p 234
See JOHNSTON DRUG WHOLESALE LTD
JOHNSTON, KERV MOTORS (1996) LTD p 487
80 MAPLEVIEW DR W, BARRIE, ON, L4N 9H6
(705) 733-2100 SIC 5511
JOHNSTON, MEIER INSURANCE AGENCIES LTD p 231
22367 DEWDNEY TRUNK RD, MAPLE RIDGE, BC, V2X 3J4
(604) 467-4184 SIC 6411
JOHNSTON, RON INSURANCE LTD p 809
448 WEST ST N, ORILLIA, ON, L3V 5E8
(705) 325-6200 SIC 6411
JOHNSTON-VERMETTE p 1388
See JOHNSTON-VERMETTE GROUPE CONSEIL INC
JOHNSTON-VERMETTE GROUPE CONSEIL INC p 1388
6110 RUE CHRISTOPHE-PELISSIER, TROIS-RIVIERES, QC, G9A 5C9
(819) 373-3550 SIC 8711
JOHNSTONE, T. W. p 660
See JOHNSTONE, T. W. COMPANY LIMITED
JOHNSTONE, T. W. COMPANY LIMITED p 660
284 EXETER RD, LONDON, ON, N6L 1A3
(519) 652-9581 SIC 1623
JOHNVINCE FOODS p 783
555 STEEPROCK DR, NORTH YORK, ON, M3J 2Z6
(416) 636-6146 SIC 5145
JOHNVINCE FOODS p 1066
1630 RUE EIFFEL BUREAU 1, BOUCHERVILLE, QC, J4B 7W1
(450) 645-1999 SIC 4783
JOINT INVESTMENT GROUP INC p 1433
118 VETERINARY RD, SASKATOON, SK, S7N 2R4
(306) 978-2800 SIC 6712
JOINTEMENT INTER p 1292
See BREMO INC
JOINTS ETANCHES R.B. INC, LES p 1334
8585 BOUL HENRI-BOURASSA O, SAINT-LAURENT, QC, H4S 1P7
(514) 334-2220 SIC 5085
JOLERA INC p 929
365 BLOOR ST E 2 FL, TORONTO, ON, M4W 3L4
(416) 410-1011 SIC 5734
JOLI-COEUR LACASSE S.E.N.C.R.L p 1270
1134 GRANDE ALLEE O BUREAU 600, QUEBEC, QC, G1S 1E5
(418) 681-7007 SIC 8111
JOLICOEUR LACASSE AVOCATS p 1270
See JOLI-COEUR LACASSE S.E.N.C.R.L
JOLICOEUR LTEE p 1174
4132 RUE PARTHENAIS, MONTREAL, QC, H2K 3T9
(514) 526-4444 SIC 7218
JOLIETTE DODGE CHRYSLER LTEE p 1114
305 RUE DU CURE-MAJEAU, JOLIETTE, QC, J6E 8S9
(450) 586-6002 SIC 5511
JOLIETTE MITSUBISHI p 1355

661 RUE PRINCIPALE, SAINTE-ANNE-DE-LA-PERADE, QC, G0X 2J0

(418) 325-2444   *SIC* 5511

JOLIETTE TOYOTA   p 1243

See *AUTOMOBILES AUMONT (1977) INC, LES*

JOLINA CAPITAL INC   p 1344

8000 BOUL LANGELIER BUREAU 200, SAINT-LEONARD, QC, H1P 3K2

(514) 328-3541   *SIC* 6712

JOLLY FARMER PRODUCTS INC   p 410

56 CRABBE RD, NORTHAMPTON, NB, E7N 1R6

(506) 325-3850   *SIC* 0181

JOLOWAY LTD   p 1040

40 LOWER MALPEQUE RD, CHARLOTTE-TOWN, PE, C1E 1R3

(902) 566-1101   *SIC* 5511

JOLY, ERNEST & FILS INC   p 1044

1530 RUE D'ACTON, ACTON VALE, QC, J0H 1A0

(450) 546-7733   *SIC* 5411

JOMAR ELECTRIC   p 990

See *960667 ONTARIO LIMITED*

JOMAX DRILLING (1988) LTD   p 52

355 4 AVE SW SUITE 2020, CALGARY, AB, T2P 0J1

(403) 265-5312   *SIC* 1381

JOMEDIA   p 1193

See *7503083 CANADA INC*

JON WOOD   p 248

3137 ST JOHNS ST, PORT MOODY, BC, V3H 2C8

SIC 6531

JONAS SOFTWARE   p 1000

See *GARY JONAS COMPUTING LTD*

JONATHAN G   p 1326

See *JCORP INC*

JONATHAN'S DONUTS LTD   p 751

250 GREENBANK RD, NEPEAN, ON, K2H 8X4

(613) 829-8691   *SIC* 7389

JONELJIM CONCRETE CONSTRUCTION (1994) LIMITED   p 467

90 RIVERVIEW DR, SYDNEY, NS, B1S 1N5

(902) 567-2400   *SIC* 1542

JONELJIM INVESTMENTS LIMITED   p 467

199 TOWNSEND ST, SYDNEY, NS, B1P 5E4

(902) 564-5554   *SIC* 5211

JONES APPAREL CANADA GROUP, LP   p 554

388 APPLEWOOD CRES, CONCORD, ON, L4K 4B4

(888) 880-8730   *SIC* 5137

JONES APPAREL GROUP CANADA ULC   p 554

388 APPLEWOOD CRES, CONCORD, ON, L4K 4B4

(905) 760-6000   *SIC* 2339

JONES BROWN INC   p 963

145 WELLINGTON ST W SUITE 1200, TORONTO, ON, M5J 1H8

(416) 408-1920   *SIC* 6411

JONES CONTRACT PACKAGING SERVICES, DIV OF   p 504

See *JONES PACKAGING INC*

JONES DESLAURIERS INSURANCE MANAGEMENT INC   p 696

2375 SKYMARK AVE, MISSISSAUGA, ON, L4W 4Y6

(416) 259-4625   *SIC* 6411

JONES FEED MILLS LIMITED   p 646

1024 ALFRED ST, LINWOOD, ON, N0B 2A0

(519) 698-2082   *SIC* 5191

JONES FOOD STORE EQUIPMENT LTD   p 184

2896 NORLAND AVE, BURNABY, BC, V5B 3A6

(604) 294-6321   *SIC* 5078

JONES GROUP, THE   p 554

See *JONES APPAREL CANADA GROUP,*

LP

JONES LANG LASALLE REAL ESTATE SERVICES, INC   p 953

22 ADELAIDE ST W 26TH FL EAST TOWER, TORONTO, ON, M5H 4E3

(416) 304-6000   *SIC* 6531

JONES MARINE GROUP LTD   p 196

9871 ESPLANADE ST, CHEMAINUS, BC, V0R 1K1

(250) 246-1100   *SIC* 4492

JONES PACKAGING INC   p 504

55 WALKER DR, BRAMPTON, ON, L6T 5K5

(800) 387-1188   *SIC* 7389

JONES PACKAGING INC   p 605

271 MASSEY RD, GUELPH, ON, N1K 1B2   *SIC* 2657

JONES PACKAGING INC   p 649

3000 PAGE ST SUITE 1, LONDON, ON, N5V 5H3

(519) 451-2100   *SIC* 2657

JONES, CHARLES INDUSTRIAL LIMITED p 892

237 ARVIN AVE, STONEY CREEK, ON, L8E 5S6

(905) 664-8448   *SIC* 5085

JONES, DAVY FOODTOWN   p 858

See *1197283 ONTARIO LIMITED*

JONES, MARV LTD   p 231

20611 LOUGHEED HWY, MAPLE RIDGE, BC, V2X 2P9

(604) 465-5464   *SIC* 5511

JONES, TOM CORPORATION   p 908

560 SQUIER ST, THUNDER BAY, ON, P7B 4A8

(807) 345-0511   *SIC* 1542

JONKER AUTO LTD   p 272

19515 LANGLEY BYPASS, SURREY, BC, V3S 6K1

(604) 530-6281   *SIC* 5511

JONKER HONDA   p 272

See *JONKER AUTO LTD*

JONKER NISSAN   p 273

See *S-304 HOLDINGS LTD*

JONKMAN EQUIPMENT LTD   p 178

28355 FRASER HWY, ABBOTSFORD, BC, V4X 1K9

(604) 857-2000   *SIC* 5083

JONSSON, DENNIS MOTOR PRODUCTS LTD   p 245

3800 JOHNSTON RD, PORT ALBERNI, BC, V9Y 5N7

(250) 723-3541   *SIC* 5511

JONVIEW CANADA INC   p 579

191 THE WEST MALL SUITE 800, ETOBICOKE, ON, M9C 5K8

(416) 323-9090   *SIC* 4725

JONVIEW CANADA TRANSAT   p 579

800-191 THE WEST MALL, ETOBICOKE, ON, M9C 5K8

(416) 323-9090   *SIC* 4724

JOPAMAR HOLDINGS INC   p 808

93 FIRST ST, ORANGEVILLE, ON, L9W 2E8

(519) 941-4009   *SIC* 5812

JORDAHL CANADA INC   p 504

35 DEVON RD, BRAMPTON, ON, L6T 5B6

(905) 458-5855   *SIC* 3548

JORDAN CAPITAL MARKETS INC   p 314

1075 GEORGIA ST W SUITE 1920, VANCOUVER, BC, V6E 3C9

(778) 373-4091   *SIC* 6211

JORDAN ENTERPRISES LIMITED   p 213

9830 100 AVE, FORT ST. JOHN, BC, V1J 1Y5

(250) 787-0521   *SIC* 7011

JORDAN ENTERPRISES LIMITED   p 225

20111 93A AVE SUITE 200, LANGLEY, BC, V1M 4A9

(604) 888-8677   *SIC* 7011

JORDAN LION PARK   p 1003

2769 4 AVE, VINELAND, ON, L0R 2C0   *SIC* 8699

JORDANS   p 319

See *JORDANS INTERIORS LTD*

JORDANS INTERIORS LTD   p 319

1470 BROADWAY W, VANCOUVER, BC, V6H 1H4

(604) 733-1174   *SIC* 5712

JORDANS RUGS LTD   p 319

1470 BROADWAY W, VANCOUVER, BC, V6H 1H4

(604) 733-1174   *SIC* 5713

JORIKI FOOD AND BEVERAGE   p 844

See *JORIKI INC*

JORIKI INC   p 844

885 SANDY BEACH RD, PICKERING, ON, L1W 3N6

(905) 420-0188   *SIC* 2024

JORIKI INC   p 876

3431 MCNICOLL AVE, SCARBOROUGH, ON, M1V 2V3

(416) 754-2747   *SIC* 2033

JOSEPH & COMPANY INC   p 640

257 VICTORIA ST N, KITCHENER, ON, N2H 5C9

(519) 743-0205   *SIC* 5093

JOSEPH & COMPANY INC   p 384

1725 SARGENT AVE, WINNIPEG, MB, R3H 0C5

(204) 775-4451   *SIC* 3991

JOSEPH BRANT HOSPITAL   p 531

1245 LAKESHORE RD, BURLINGTON, ON, L7S 0A2

(905) 632-3730   *SIC* 8062

JOSEPH D'ONOFRIO ET ASSOCIES INC p 1346

5045 RUE JEAN-TALON E BUREAU 201, SAINT-LEONARD, QC, H1S 0B6

(514) 328-2555   *SIC* 6411

JOSEPH ELIE   p 1049

See *GROUPE ENERGIE BDL INC*

JOSEPH L. ROTMAN SCHOOL OF MANAGEMENT   p 975

See *GOVERNING COUNCIL OF THE UNIVERSITY OF TORONTO, THE*

JOSEPH RIBKOFF INC   p 1094

2375 RUE DE L'AVIATION, DORVAL, QC, H9P 2X6

(514) 685-9191   *SIC* 2331

JOSEPH S. CHOW LTD   p 263

11780 HAMMERSMITH WAY SUITE 120, RICHMOND, BC, V7A 5E9

(604) 271-0255   *SIC* 5148

JOSSLIN INSURANCE BROKERS LIMITED p 752

118 PEEL ST, NEW HAMBURG, ON, N3A 1E3

(519) 662-1644   *SIC* 6411

JOSTEN DEVELOPMENTS LIMITED p 789

1020 LAWRENCE AVE W SUITE 300, NORTH YORK, ON, M6A 1C8

(416) 787-1135   *SIC* 6719

JOSTENS CANADA LTD   p 384

1643 DUBLIN AVE, WINNIPEG, MB, R3H 0G9

(204) 783-1310   *SIC* 3961

JOSTLE CORPORATION   p 314

1090 WEST GEORGIA ST SUITE 1200, VANCOUVER, BC, V6E 3V7

(604) 566-9520   *SIC* 7371

JOUET K.I.D. INC   p 1276

4000 RUE JEAN-MARCHAND BUREAU 120, QUEBEC, QC, G2C 1Y6

(418) 627-0101   *SIC* 5092

JOUJAN BROTHERS FLOORING INC p 145

941 SOUTH RAILWAY ST SE UNIT 3, MEDICINE HAT, AB, T1A 2W3

(403) 528-8008   *SIC* 5713

JOULE INC   p 826

1031 BANK ST, OTTAWA, ON, K1S 3W7

(888) 855-2555   *SIC* 8621

JOURNAL L'EVEIL   p 1301

See *EDITIONS BLAINVILLE-DEUX-MONTAGNES INC, LES*

JOURNAL LA RELEVE INC   p 1066

528 RUE SAINT-CHARLES, BOUCHERVILLE, QC, J4B 3M5

(450) 641-4844   *SIC* 5192

JOURNAL LE DEVOIR   p 1195

See *DEVOIR INC, LE*

JOURNAL LE PEUPLE LEVIS   p 1136

5790 BOUL ETIENNE-DALLAIRE, LEVIS, QC, G6V 8V6

(418) 833-9398   *SIC* 5192

JOURNAL PREMIERE EDITION   p 1394

469 AV SAINT-CHARLES, VAUDREUIL-DORION, QC, J7V 2N4

(450) 455-7955   *SIC* 8999

JOURNALISTS FOR HUMAN RIGHTS (JHR)   p 981

147 SPADINA AVE SUITE 206, TORONTO, ON, M5V 2L7

(416) 413-0240   *SIC* 8699

JOURNEE DE LA METROLOGIE EN AEROSPATIALE   p 1138

See *CREAFORM INC*

JOURNEY ENERGY INC   p 64

517 10 AVE SW SUITE 700, CALGARY, AB, T2R 0A8

(403) 294-1635   *SIC* 1382

JOURNEY FREIGHT INTERNATIONAL INC p 1118

18100 RTE TRANSCANADIENNE, KIRK-LAND, QC, H9J 4A1

(514) 344-2202   *SIC* 4731

JOURNEY LOGISTICS   p 1118

See *JOURNEY FREIGHT INTERNATIONAL INC*

JOUVENCE L'AUBERGE   p 1244

See *JOUVENCE, BASE DE PLEIN AIR INC*

JOUVENCE, BASE DE PLEIN AIR INC   p 1244

131 CH DE JOUVENCE, ORFORD, QC, J1X 6R2

(450) 532-3134   *SIC* 7011

JOUVIANCE   p 1212

See *SOSEN INC*

JOVFINANCIAL   p 946

See *IA CLARINGTON INVESTMENTS INC*

JOY GLOBAL (CANADA) LTD   p 9

90-2150 29 ST NE, CALGARY, AB, T1Y 7G4

(403) 730-9851   *SIC* 3532

JOY GLOBAL (CANADA) LTD   p 269

749 DOUGLAS FIR RD SUITE 618, SPARWOOD, BC, V0B 2G0

(250) 433-4100   *SIC* 3532

JOY OF TRAVEL LTD, THE   p 852

30 WERTHEIM CRT UNIT 20, RICHMOND HILL, ON, L4B 1B9

(905) 889-1681   *SIC* 4725

JOYAL, CLAUDE INC   p 1306

1 RUE PRINCIPALE, SAINT-GUILLAUME, QC, J0C 1L0

(819) 396-2161   *SIC* 5083

JOYCE FRUIT MARKETS LIMITED   p 795

28 RIVALDA RD SUITE A, NORTH YORK, ON, M9M 2M3

(416) 745-4411   *SIC* 5148

JOYLYPSO INC   p 1340

4850 RUE BOURG, SAINT-LAURENT, QC, H4T 1J2

(514) 735-4255   *SIC* 5087

JP2G CONSULTANTS INC   p 838

12 INTERNATIONAL DR, PEMBROKE, ON, K8A 6W5

(613) 735-2507   *SIC* 8711

JPDL   p 1197

See *JPDL MULTI MANAGEMENT INC*

JPDL MULTI MANAGEMENT INC   p 1197

1555 RUE PEEL BUREAU 500, MONTREAL, QC, H3A 3L8

(514) 287-1070   *SIC* 7389

JPL APRES SINISTRE INC   p 1106

116 RUE LOIS, GATINEAU, QC, J8Y 3R7

(819) 770-3038   *SIC* 1521

JPMA GLOBAL INC   p 1162

7335 BOUL HENRI-BOURASSA E, MONTREAL, QC, H1E 3T5

(514) 648-1042   *SIC* 2542

JPW ROAD & BRIDGE INC   p 179

2310 KIRTON AVE, ARMSTRONG, BC, V0E

1B0
(250) 546-3765   *SIC* 1611
JPW SYSTEMS INC *p* 643
30 DOAN DR, KOMOKA, ON, N0L 1R0
(519) 474-9797   *SIC* 5072
JR CERTUS CONSTRUCTION CO. LTD *p*
1027
81 ZENWAY BLVD UNIT 3, WOODBRIDGE,
ON, L4H 0S5
(647) 494-0150   *SIC* 1542
JRL HVAC INC *p* 509
278 RUTHERFORD RD S, BRAMPTON,
ON, L6W 3K7
(905) 457-6900   *SIC* 1711
JRP GROUP INSURANCE SOLUTIONS INC
p 915
2 LANSING SQ UNIT 207, TORONTO, ON,
M2J 4P8
(647) 776-0906   *SIC* 6411
JSI TELECOM *p* 626
See *JATOM SYSTEMS INC*
JSK TRAFFIC CONTROL SERVICES INC *p*
235
2005 WARING RD, NANAIMO, BC, V9X 1V1
(250) 618-0232   *SIC* 7389
JSM ELECTRICAL LTD *p* 430
28 DUFFY PL, ST. JOHN'S, NL, A1B 4M5
(709) 754-3666   *SIC* 1731
JTB CANADA *p* 260
See *JTB INTERNATIONAL (CANADA) LTD*
JTB INTERNATIONAL (CANADA) LTD *p*
260
8899 ODLIN CRES, RICHMOND, BC, V6X
3Z7
(604) 276-0300   *SIC* 4725
JTI TRUCKING *p* 358
33 CLEAR SPRINGS RD E, STEINBACH,
MB, R5G 1V2
(866) 346-1673   *SIC* 4213
JTI-MACDONALD CORP *p* 706
1 ROBERT SPECK PKY SUITE 1601, MIS-
SISSAUGA, ON, L4Z 0A2
(905) 804-7300   *SIC* 2111
JTI-MACDONALD CORP *p* 1174
2455 RUE ONTARIO E BUREAU 4, MON-
TREAL, QC, H2K 1W3
(514) 598-2525   *SIC* 2111
JTL GROUP CORP *p* 998
37 ADVANCE RD, TORONTO, ON, T5K 1P2
SIC 4213
JTL INTEGRATED MACHINE LTD. *p* 846
857 REUTER RD, PORT COLBORNE, ON,
L3K 5W1
(905) 834-3992   *SIC* 3569
JUAN DE FUCA RECREATION CENTRE *p*
340
See *WEST SHORE PARKS AND RECRE-
ATION SOCIETY*
JUBILANT DRAXIMAGE INC *p* 1117
16751 RTE TRANSCANADIENNE, KIRK-
LAND, QC, H9H 4J4
(514) 694-8220   *SIC* 2834
**JUBILANT HOLLISTERSTIER CONTRACT
MANUFACTURING** *p* 1117
See *JUBILANT HOLLISTERSTIER GEN-
ERAL PARTNERSHIP*
**JUBILANT HOLLISTERSTIER GENERAL
PARTNERSHIP** *p* 1117
16751 RTE TRANSCANADIENNE, KIRK-
LAND, QC, H9H 4J4
(514) 694-8220   *SIC* 2834
JUBILATIONS DINNER THEATRE *p* 72
See *4359241 MANITOBA INC*
JUBILEE FORD SALES (1983) LTD *p* 1425
419 BRAND PL, SASKATOON, SK, S7J 5L6
(306) 373-4444   *SIC* 5511
JUBILEE LODGE NURSING HOME LTD *p*
107
10333 76 ST NW, EDMONTON, AB, T6A
3A8
(780) 469-4456   *SIC* 8051
JUBILEE RESIDENCES INC *p* 1431
833 AVENUE P N, SASKATOON, SK, S7L
2W5

(306) 382-2626   *SIC* 8051
JUBILEE TOURS & TRAVEL LTD *p* 182
3011 UNDERHILL AVE SUITE 201, BURN-
ABY, BC, V5A 3C2
(604) 669-6607   *SIC* 4724
JUDITH & CHARLES *p* 1177
See *163972 CANADA INC*
JUDITH NYMAN SECONDARY SCHOOL *p*
499
See *PEEL DISTRICT SCHOOL BOARD*
JUDY CREEK OPERATIONS *p* 168
See *PENGROWTH ENERGY CORPORA-
TION*
JULIAN TILE INC *p* 225
9688 203 ST, LANGLEY, BC, V1M 4B9
(604) 299-4085   *SIC* 5211
JULIEN BEAUDOIN LTEE *p* 1089
320 6E RUE, DAVELUYVILLE, QC, G0Z
1C0
(819) 367-2344   *SIC* 2514
JULIEN INC *p* 1267
955 RUE LACHANCE, QUEBEC, QC, G1P
2H3
(418) 687-3630   *SIC* 3914
JULIETTE ET CHOCOLAT *p* 1141
See *91933614 QUEBEC INC*
JUMP PLUS STORES ULC *p* 977
275 COLLEGE ST, TORONTO, ON, M5T
1S2
(416) 927-8000   *SIC* 5734
JUMP.CA *p* 1416
See *JUMP.CA WIRELESS SUPPLY CORP*
JUMP.CA WIRELESS SUPPLY CORP *p*
1416
1845 E VICTORIA AVE UNIT B, REGINA,
SK, S4N 6E6
(306) 545-5867   *SIC* 4899
JUNCTION MOTORS LTD *p* 135
5309 50 ST, GRIMSHAW, AB, T0H 1W0
(780) 332-2886   *SIC* 5511
JUNE WARREN PUBLISHING *p* 23
See *JWP PUBLISHING LIMITED PART-
NERSHIP*
JUNGLE JAC'S PLAY CENTRE *p* 244
19800 LOUGHEED HWY SUITE 115, PITT
MEADOWS, BC, V3Y 2W1
(604) 460-1654   *SIC* 3949
JUNIOR ACHIEVEMENT OF CANADA *p* 579
1 EVA RD SUITE 218, ETOBICOKE, ON,
M9C 4Z5
(416) 622-4602   *SIC* 8299
JUNIPER NETWORKS CANADA INC *p* 624
340 TERRY FOX DR, KANATA, ON, K2K
3A2
(613) 591-2700   *SIC* 4899
**JUNIPER PARK TBWA COMMUNICATIONS
ULC** *p* 929
33 BLOOR ST E, TORONTO, ON, M4W 3H1
(416) 413-7301   *SIC* 7311
JUNISE PLASTIQUE *p* 1234
See *JUNISE VENTES INC*
JUNISE VENTES INC *p* 1234
4001 BOUL INDUSTRIEL, MONTREAL,
QC, H7L 4S3
(514) 858-7777   *SIC* 5113
JUNON *p* 1161
See *174664 CANADA LTEE*
JUNVIR INVESTMENTS LIMITED *p* 929
446 SUMMERHILL AVE, TORONTO, ON,
M4W 2E4
(416) 921-2714   *SIC* 5411
JUPITER JUVENILE *p* 1251
See *JASZTEX FIBRES INC*
JURA ENERGY CORPORATION *p* 52
150-6TH AVE SW SUITE 5100, CALGARY,
AB, T2P 3Y7
(403) 266-6364   *SIC* 1382
JURAVINSKI CANCER CENTRE *p* 614
See *HAMILTON HEALTH SCIENCES COR-
PORATION*
JUS TRADITION, LES *p* 1315
See *VERGERS PAUL JODOIN INC*
JUST CARE *p* 237
See *PROCARE HEALTH SERVICES INC*

JUST COZY *p* 650
See *2518879 ONTARIO INC*
JUST DIRECT ENERGY *p* 48
See *DIRECT ENERGY MARKETING LIM-
ITED*
JUST ENERGY *p* 741
See *MOMENTIS CANADA CORP*
JUST ENERGY GROUP INC *p* 740
6345 DIXIE RD SUITE 400, MISSISSAUGA,
ON, L5T 2E6
(905) 670-4440   *SIC* 4911
JUST ENERGY ONTARIO L.P *p* 740
6345 DIXIE RD SUITE 200, MISSISSAUGA,
ON, L5T 2E6
(905) 670-4440   *SIC* 4911
JUST ON TIME FREIGHT SYSTEMS INC *p*
504
95 HEDGEDALE RD UNIT 3-4, BRAMP-
TON, ON, L6T 5P3
(905) 846-9552   *SIC* 4731
JUST REWARDS MANAGEMENT LTD *p* 332
3009 28 ST SUITE B, VERNON, BC, V1T
4Z7
(250) 542-1177   *SIC* 6712
JUST VACATIONS INC *p* 658
101 CHERRYHILL BLVD, LONDON, ON,
N6H 4S4
(519) 472-2700   *SIC* 4724
**JUSTICE INSTITUTE OF BRITISH
COLUMBIA** *p* 236
715 MCBRIDE BLVD, NEW WESTMIN-
STER, BC, V3L 5T4
(604) 525-5422   *SIC* 8221
JUSTIN & STACEY'S NO FRILLS *p* 478
285 MILL ST, ANGUS, ON, L0M 1B4
(705) 424-7090   *SIC* 5411
JUSTIN'S NO FRILLS *p* 905
See *1290357 ONTARIO LIMITED*
JUTRAS AUTO SALES *p* 899
See *JUTRAS, PHIL & SON LIMITED*
JUTRAS, PHIL & SON LIMITED *p* 899
2042 KINGSWAY, SUDBURY, ON, P3B 4J8
(705) 525-5560   *SIC* 4212
JUTZI, D.H. LIMITED *p* 896
279 LORNE AVE E, STRATFORD, ON, N5A
6S4
(519) 271-9831   *SIC* 5541
JUUSOLA, JACK SALES LTD *p* 218
1441 HILLSIDE DR, KAMLOOPS, BC, V2E
1A9
(250) 374-3115   *SIC* 5251
**JUVENILE DIABETES RESEARCH FOUN-
DATION CANADA** *p*
915
235 YORKLAND BLVD SUITE 600,
TORONTO, ON, M2J 4Y8
(647) 789-2000   *SIC* 8399
JV DRIVER GROUP *p* 149
See *J.V. DRIVER CORPORATION INC*
JVS TORONTO *p* 791
See *JEWISH VOCATIONAL SERVICE OF
METROPOLITAN TORONTO*
JWP PUBLISHING LIMITED PARTNERSHIP
p 23
816 55 AVE NE 2ND FL, CALGARY, AB,
T2E 6Y4
(403) 265-3700   *SIC* 2721
JWT *p* 930
See *THOMPSON, J. WALTER COMPANY
LIMITED*
JYSK LINEN'N FURNITURE INC *p* 201
25 KING EDWARD ST UNIT 101, COQUIT-
LAM, BC, V3K 4S8
(604) 472-0769   *SIC* 5712

K

K & D OILFIELD SERVICES *p* 40
See *EMS CANADA, INC*
K & G APARTMENT HOLDINGS INC *p* 922
305 ROEHAMPTON AVE, TORONTO, ON,
M4P 0B2
(416) 487-3050   *SIC* 6531
K & J FAMILY HOLDINGS LTD *p* 590
100 THAMES RD W SS 3 SUITE 3, EX-

ETER, ON, N0M 1S3
(519) 235-0160   *SIC* 5531
K & J PECK SALES LTD *p* 420
388 CONNELL ST, WOODSTOCK, NB, E7M
5G9
(506) 328-3353   *SIC* 5251
K & K RECYCLING SERVICES *p* 844
See *1023248 ONTARIO INC*
K & R POULTRY LTD *p* 177
31171 PEARDONVILLE RD UNIT 2, AB-
BOTSFORD, BC, V2T 6K6
(604) 850-5808   *SIC* 2015
K & Z INSURANCE *p* 886
See *KANNEGIETER-ZIMMERMAN INSUR-
ANCE BROKERS LIMITED*
K A R INDUSTRIES LIMITED *p* 339
1519 ADMIRALS RD, VICTORIA, BC, V9A
2P8
(250) 381-3111   *SIC* 5531
K AND L CONTRACTING *p* 266
10704 HWY 9, ROSEDALE, BC, V0X 1X1
(604) 794-0107   *SIC* 5032
K C AUTOMOTIVE PARTS INC *p* 835
222 14TH ST W SUITE 130, OWEN
SOUND, ON, N4K 3X8
(519) 376-2501   *SIC* 5531
K C IRVING REGIONAL CENTRE *p* 394
See *BATHURST, CITY OF*
K CRAWFORD PHARMACY INC *p* 1039
403 UNIVERSITY AVE, CHARLOTTE-
TOWN, PE, C1A 4N7
(902) 892-3433   *SIC* 5912
K F C *p* 463
674 EAST RIVER RD, NEW GLASGOW,
NS, B2H 3S1
(902) 752-8184   *SIC* 5963
K L O MIDDLE SCHOOL *p* 219
See *BOARD OF EDUCATION OF SCHOOL
DISTRICT NO. 23 (CENTRAL OKANAGAN),
THE*
K L S CONTRACTING LTD *p* 74
7 GLENBROOK PL SW SUITE 206, CAL-
GARY, AB, T3E 6W4
(403) 240-3030   *SIC* 1794
K N CUSTOMS BROKERS *p* 23
2415 PEGASUS RD NE UNIT 210, CAL-
GARY, AB, T2E 8C3
(403) 250-3075   *SIC* 4731
K P M G MANAGEMENT CONSULTING *p* 89
See *KPMG LLP*
K R T CHRISTIAN SCHOOLS *p* 508
141 KENNEDY RD N, BRAMPTON, ON,
L6V 1X9
(905) 459-2300   *SIC* 8211
K R T KIDDIES KOLLEGE *p* 508
See *K R T CHRISTIAN SCHOOLS*
K RICE RETAILING INC *p* 162
169 ORDZE AVE SUITE 428, SHERWOOD
PARK, AB, T8B 1M6
(780) 449-1577   *SIC* 5941
K&D PRATT GROUP INC *p* 426
126 GLENCOE DR, MOUNT PEARL, NL,
A1N 4S9
(709) 722-5690   *SIC* 5085
**K+S POTASH CANADA GENERAL PART-
NERSHIP** *p*
1404
SW 35-19-25-W2, BETHUNE, SK, S0G 0H0
(306) 638-2800   *SIC* 1474
**K+S POTASH CANADA GENERAL PART-
NERSHIP** *p*
1428
220 WALL ST, SASKATOON, SK, S7K 3Y3
(306) 385-8000   *SIC* 1474
K+S SEL WINDSOR LTEE *p* 126
GD, ELK POINT, AB, T0A 1A0
(780) 724-4180   *SIC* 1479
K+S SEL WINDSOR LTEE *p* 1025
30 PROSPECT AVE, WINDSOR, ON, N9C
3G3
(519) 255-5400   *SIC* 2899
K+S SEL WINDSOR LTEE *p* 1026
200 MORTON DR, WINDSOR, ON, N9J
3W9

---

(519) 972-2201 *SIC* 1479

K+S SEL WINDSOR LTEE *p* 1112
50 CH PRINCIPAL, GROSSE-ILE, QC, G4T 6A6
(418) 985-2931 *SIC* 1479

K+S SEL WINDSOR LTEE *p* 1251
755 BOUL SAINT-JEAN BUREAU 700, POINTE-CLAIRE, QC, H9R 5M9
(514) 630-0900 *SIC* 1479

K-BRO LINEN INC *p* 105
14903 137 AVE NW, EDMONTON, AB, T5V 1R9
(780) 453-5218 *SIC* 7212

K-BRO LINEN SYSTEMS INC *p* 105
14903 137 AVE NW, EDMONTON, AB, T5V 1R9
(780) 453-6855 *SIC* 7218

K-BRO LINEN SYSTEMS INC *p* 105
15253 121A AVE NW, EDMONTON, AB, T5V 1N1
(780) 451-3131 *SIC* 7219

K-BRO LINEN SYSTEMS INC *p* 577
15 SHORNCLIFFE RD, ETOBICOKE, ON, M9B 3S4
(416) 233-5555 *SIC* 7219

K-DAC ENTERPRISES INC *p* 483
3025 SANDHILLS RD, BADEN, ON, N3A 3B8
(519) 634-8223 *SIC* 4213

K-DAC EXPEDITE *p* 483
See K-DAC ENTERPRISES INC

K-DENTAL INC *p* 671
750 COCHRANE DR, MARKHAM, ON, L3R 8E1
(416) 293-8365 *SIC* 5047

K-G SPRAY-PAK INC *p* 554
8001 KEELE ST, CONCORD, ON, L4K 1Y8
(905) 669-9855 *SIC* 2813

K-JAY ELECTRIC LTD *p* 101
10752 178 ST NW, EDMONTON, AB, T5S 1J3
(780) 484-1721 *SIC* 1731

K-LINE INSULATORS LIMITED *p* 876
50 PASSMORE AVE, SCARBOROUGH, ON, M1V 4T1
(416) 292-2008 *SIC* 3644

K-LINE MAINTENANCE & CONSTRUCTION LIMITED *p* 894
12731 HIGHWAY 48, STOUFFVILLE, ON, L4A 4A7
(905) 640-2002 *SIC* 1731

K-LINE MAINTENANCE & CONSTRUCTION LIMITED *p* 1406
5 INDUSTRIAL DR, EMERALD PARK, SK, S4L 1B7
(306) 781-2711 *SIC* 1623

K-LINE TRAILERS LTD *p* 229
27360 58 CRES, LANGLEY, BC, V4W 3W7
(604) 856-7899 *SIC* 3715

K-RIGHT COMMUNICATIONS LIMITED *p* 455
6080 YOUNG ST, HALIFAX, NS, B3K 5L2
(902) 484-2800 *SIC* 4841

K-RITE CONSTRUCTION LTD *p* 93
12849 148 ST NW, EDMONTON, AB, T5L 2H9
(780) 452-6291 *SIC* 1542

K-SCRAP RESOURCES LTD *p* 1025
110 HILL AVE, WINDSOR, ON, N9C 3B8
(519) 254-5188 *SIC* 5093

K-TILBURY FOOD MARKET LTD *p* 911
15 QUEEN ST S, TILBURY, ON, N0P 2L0
(519) 682-3245 *SIC* 5411

K-W HABILITATION SERVICES *p* 638
99 OTTAWA ST S, KITCHENER, ON, N2G 3S8
(519) 744-6307 *SIC* 8361

K-WOOD KITCHENS INC *p* 872
32 CONTINENTAL PL, SCARBOROUGH, ON, M1R 2T4
(416) 335-4027 *SIC* 5021

K. A. S. PERSONNEL SERVICES INC *p* 534

534 HESPELER RD SUITE A2, CAMBRIDGE, ON, N1R 6J7
(519) 622-7788 *SIC* 7361

K. C. AUTO *p* 835
See K. C.'S AUTOMOTIVE INC

K. C.'S AUTOMOTIVE INC *p* 835
222R 14TH ST W, OWEN SOUND, ON, N4K 3X8
(519) 376-2501 *SIC* 5013

K. M. S. TOOLS & EQUIPMENT LTD *p* 201
110 WOOLRIDGE ST, COQUITLAM, BC, V3K 5V4
(604) 522-5599 *SIC* 5251

K. TOOL & DIE *p* 798
See KOZMA'S MANUFACTURING CO. LTD

K.A.S. GROUP OF COMPANIES INC, THE *p* 735
7895 TRANMERE DR SUITE 18, MISSISSAUGA, ON, L5S 1V9
(905) 677-3368 *SIC* 7361

K.A.S.A. HOLDINGS LTD *p* 348
1907 RICHMOND AVE, BRANDON, MB, R7B 0T4
(204) 725-2244 *SIC* 5812

K.B. BORISENKO PHARMACY LTD *p* 382
1485 PORTAGE AVE SUITE 178, WINNIPEG, MB, R3G 0W4
(204) 775-2478 *SIC* 5912

K.B. HEATING & AIR CONDITIONING LTD *p* 140
3569 32 AVE N, LETHBRIDGE, AB, T1H 7C2
(403) 328-0337 *SIC* 1711

K.D.S. CONSTRUCTION LTD *p* 279
16250 20 AVE, SURREY, BC, V3Z 9M8
(604) 535-8152 *SIC* 1542

K.F. CONSTRUCTION INC *p* 1363
1410 RUE DE JAFFA BUREAU 201, SAINTE-ROSE, QC, H7P 4K9
(450) 681-8338 *SIC* 1542

K.F.S. LIMITED *p* 562
27 FIRST ST E, CORNWALL, ON, K6H 1K5
(613) 933-7110 *SIC* 5311

K.G. ENTERPRISES INC *p* 660
2126 JACK NASH DR, LONDON, ON, N6K 5R1
(519) 473-4111 *SIC* 3479

K.J BEAMISH CONSTRUCTION CO. LTD *p* 629
3300 KING VAUGHAN RD, KING CITY, ON, L7B 1B2
(905) 833-4666 *SIC* 1611

K.J. BEAMISH HOLDINGS LIMITED *p* 629
3300 KING VAUGHAN RD, KING CITY, ON, L7B 1B2
(905) 833-4666 *SIC* 3281

K.K. PENNER TIRE CENTERS INC *p* 346
39 PENNER DR, BLUMENORT, MB, R0A 0C0
(204) 326-6419 *SIC* 5531

K.L. FINE CARS LTD *p* 804
2500 SOUTH SERVICE RD W, OAKVILLE, ON, L6L 5M9
(905) 845-7791 *SIC* 5511

K.L.S (2009) INC *p* 1080
1615 BOUL SAINT-PAUL, CHICOUTIMI, QC, G7J 3Y3
(418) 543-1515 *SIC* 3354

K.M. BAKERY *p* 977
438 DUNDAS ST W, TORONTO, ON, M5T 1G7
SIC 5461

K.M. TURNBULL SALES INC *p* 1410
290 PRINCE WILLIAM DR, MELVILLE, SK, S0A 2P0
(306) 728-8810 *SIC* 5999

K.M.K. SALES LTD *p* 1407
HWY 20 S, HUMBOLDT, SK, S0K 2A1
(306) 682-0738 *SIC* 5599

K.O.P.S. SECURITY & INVESTIGATIONS INC
1518 3 AVE S, LETHBRIDGE, AB, T1J 0K8
(403) 331-5677 *SIC* 7382

K.P. BRONZE LIMITED *p* 481

16 ALLAURA BLVD SUITE 20, AURORA, ON, L4G 3S5
(905) 727-8706 *SIC* 5051

K.R.S. TECHNICAL SERVICES LIMITED *p* 86
10660 105 ST NW, EDMONTON, AB, T5H 2W9
(780) 426-7820 *SIC* 6712

K.W. PETROLEUM SERVICES LTD *p* 1428
849 56TH ST E, SASKATOON, SK, S7K 5Y9
(306) 244-4468 *SIC* 5084

K2 & ASSOCIATES INVESTMENT MANAGEMENT INC *p* 929
2 BLOOR ST W SUITE 801, TORONTO, ON, M4W 3E2
(416) 365-2155 *SIC* 6726

K2 WIND ONTARIO LIMITED PARTNERSHIP *p* 597
46 VICTORIA ST N, GODERICH, ON, N7A 2R6
(519) 441-1067 *SIC* 4911

K3 SPECIALTIES *p* 288
See WEYERHAEUSER COMPANY LIMITED

K92 MINING INC *p* 314
1090 GEORGIA ST W SUITE 488, VANCOUVER, BC, V6E 3V7
(236) 521-0584 *SIC* 1041

K93FM *p* 400
See ASTRAL MEDIA RADIO ATLANTIC INC

KA DJORDJEVIC PHARMACY INC *p* 704
1077 NORTH SERVICE RD SUITE 27, MISSISSAUGA, ON, L4Y 1A6
(905) 277-3661 *SIC* 5912

KA'LE BAY SEAFOODS LTD *p* 443
501 MAIN ST, DARTMOUTH, NS, B2W 4K1
(902) 842-9454 *SIC* 2092

KABS PHARMACEUTICAL SERVICES *p* 1308
See LABORATOIRES KABS INC

KABUNI TECHNOLOGIES INC *p* 299
375 WATER ST SUITE 200, VANCOUVER, BC, V6B 0M9
(778) 686-2243 *SIC* 5961

KADANT CANADA CORP *p* 272
15050 54A AVE UNIT 8, SURREY, BC, V3S 5X7
(604) 299-3431 *SIC* 3569

KADANT CARMANAH DESIGN *p* 272
See KADANT CANADA CORP

KADEX AERO SUPPLY LTD *p* 841
925 AIRPORT RD UNIT 211A, PETERBOROUGH, ON, K9J 0E7
(705) 742-9725 *SIC* 5088

KAEFER INTEGRATED SERVICES LTD *p* 165
25 CORRIVEAU AVE, ST. ALBERT, AB, T8N 5A3
(780) 484-4310 *SIC* 1799

KAESER COMPRESSEURS CANADA INC *p* 1062
3760 RUE LA VERENDRYE, BOISBRIAND, QC, J7H 1R5
(450) 971-1414 *SIC* 5084

KAHNAWAKE FIRE BRIGADE AMBULANCE SERVICE *p* 1116
520 RUE OLD MALONE, KAHNAWAKE, QC, J0L 1B0
(450) 632-2010 *SIC* 7389

KAHUNAVERSE SPORTS GROUP INC *p* 279
19036 22 AVE SUITE 101, SURREY, BC, V3Z 3S6
(604) 536-2441 *SIC* 5091

KAISER ALUMINUM *p* 649
See KAISER ALUMINUM CANADA LIMITED

KAISER ALUMINUM CANADA LIMITED *p* 649
3021 GORE RD, LONDON, ON, N5V 5A9

(519) 457-3610 *SIC* 3354

KAITLIN GROUP LTD, THE *p* 894
28 SANDIFORD DR SUITE 201, STOUFFVILLE, ON, L4A 1L8
(905) 642-7050 *SIC* 1521

KAIZEN AUTOMOTIVE GROUP *p* 27
See AUTOPLUS RESOURCES LTD

KAL TIRE *p* 16
See KAL TIRE ALBERTA LTD

KAL TIRE *p* 158
See 381616 ALBERTA LTD

KAL TIRE *p* 172
See CIVIC TIRE & BATTERY (WESTLOCK) LTD

KAL TIRE ALBERTA LTD *p* 16
5375 68 AVE SE, CALGARY, AB, T2C 5A7
(403) 236-7171 *SIC* 5531

KAL TIRE LTD *p* 332
1540 KALAMALKA LAKE RD, VERNON, BC, V1T 6V2
(250) 542-2366 *SIC* 5014

KAL-POLYMERS *p* 711
See KAL-TRADING INC

KAL-TIRE *p* 358
See SPACE AGE TIRE LTD

KAL-TRADING INC *p* 711
3440 WOLFEDALE RD, MISSISSAUGA, ON, L5C 1W4
(905) 273-7400 *SIC* 5162

KALA'S HARDWARE LIMITED *p* 887
1380 FOURTH AVE SUITE 3, ST CATHARINES, ON, L2S 0B8
(905) 688-5520 *SIC* 5072

KALA'S HOME HARDWARE *p* 887
See KALA'S HARDWARE LIMITED

KALAWSKY PONTIAC BUICK G M C (1989) LTD *p* 195
1700 COLUMBIA AVE, CASTLEGAR, BC, V1N 2W4
(250) 365-2155 *SIC* 5511

KALESNIKOFF LUMBER CO. LTD *p* 195
2090 3A HWY, CASTLEGAR, BC, V1N 4N1
(250) 399-4211 *SIC* 2421

KALLES, HARVEY REAL ESTATE LTD *p* 788
2145 AVENUE RD, NORTH YORK, ON, M5M 4B2
(416) 441-2888 *SIC* 6531

KALSHEA COMMODITIES INC *p* 389
42 PARKROYAL BAY, WINNIPEG, MB, R3P 1P2
(204) 272-3773 *SIC* 5153

KAMAN INDUSTRIAL TECHNOLOGIES, LTD *p* 206
746 CHESTER RD, DELTA, BC, V3M 6J1
(604) 523-2356 *SIC* 5085

KAMCO CONSTRUCTION INC *p* 1122
149 RUE DU PARC-DE-L'INNOVATION, LA POCATIERE, QC, G0R 1Z0
(418) 856-5432 *SIC* 1542

KAMIK *p* 1082
See GENFOOT INC

KAMIK *p* 1127
See GENFOOT INC

KAMINS DERMATOLOGIQUE, INC *p* 1251
325 AV STILLVIEW, POINTE-CLAIRE, QC, H9R 2Y6
(514) 428-1628 *SIC* 5122

KAMLOOPS DAILY NEWS, THE *p* 217
See POSTMEDIA NETWORK INC

KAMLOOPS DODGE CHRYSLER JEEP LIMITED *p* 217
2525 TRANS CANADA HWY E, KAMLOOPS, BC, V2C 4A9
(250) 374-4477 *SIC* 5511

KAMLOOPS HOME SUPPORT SERVICES ASSOCIATION *p* 216
396 TRANQUILLE RD, KAMLOOPS, BC, V2B 3G7
(250) 851-7550 *SIC* 8322

KAMLOOPS HYUNDAI *p* 217
948 NOTRE DAME DR, KAMLOOPS, BC, V2C 6J2
(250) 851-9380 *SIC* 5511

KAMLOOPS MILL p 217
See DOMTAR INC
KAMLOOPS PROFESSIONAL MANAGE-MENT GROUP p 217
248 2ND AVE, KAMLOOPS, BC, V2C 2C9
(250) 372-5542 SIC 6712
KAMLOOPS, THE CORPORATION OF THE CITY OF p 217
910 MCGILL RD, KAMLOOPS, BC, V2C 6N6
(250) 828-3655 SIC 7999
KAMSACK HOSPTAL AND NURSING HOME p 1408
See KAMSACK UNION HOSPITAL DISTRICT
KAMSACK UNION HOSPITAL DISTRICT p 1408
341 STEWART ST, KAMSACK, SK, S0A 1S0
(306) 542-2635 SIC 8062
KAMSLEY COLONY FARMS p 357
See KAMSLEY COLONY LTD
KAMSLEY COLONY LTD p 357
GD, SOMERSET, MB, R0G 2L0
(204) 744-2706 SIC 0291
KAMTECH SERVICES INC p 1428
3339 FAITHFULL AVE, SASKATOON, SK, S7K 8H5
(306) 931-9655 SIC 1711
KANA OILFIELD SERVICES LTD p 173
4107 41 ST, WHITECOURT, AB, T7S 0A9
(780) 778-2385 SIC 1389
KANAS p 36
See KANAS HOLDINGS CORPORATION
KANAS HOLDINGS CORPORATION p 36
5312 3 ST SE, CALGARY, AB, T2H 1J8
(403) 283-2566 SIC 5051
KANATA HOLDINGS LTD p 260
11251 RIVER RD UNIT 200, RICHMOND, BC, V6X 1Z6
(604) 273-6005 SIC 5421
KANATA HYDRO ELECTRIC COMMISSION p 626
100 MAPLE GROVE RD, KANATA, ON, K2V 1B8
SIC 4911
KANATA TOYOTA p 627
See TONY GRAHAM KANATA LIMITED
KANDREA INSULATION (1995) LIMITED p 82
5604B 58 AVE, DRAYTON VALLEY, AB, T7A 0B1
(780) 542-6847 SIC 1742
KANE VETERINARY SUPPLIES LTD p 101
11204 186 ST NW, EDMONTON, AB, T5S 2W2
(780) 453-1516 SIC 5047
KANE'S HARLEY-DAVIDSON p 30
See KANE'S MOTOR CYCLE SHOP LTD
KANE'S MOTOR CYCLE SHOP LTD p 30
914 11 ST SE, CALGARY, AB, T2G 3E8
(403) 262-5462 SIC 5571
KANE, BRIAN INSURANCE AGENCIES LTD p 23
6815 8 ST NE SUITE 120, CALGARY, AB, T2E 7H7
(403) 276-8766 SIC 6411
KANE, DAN CHEVROLET BUICK GM p 1023
See PREMIER CHEVROLET CADILLAC BUICK GMC INC
KANE, PAUL HIGH SCHOOL p 166
See ST. ALBERT PUBLIC SCHOOL DISTRICT NO. 5565
KANEFF GROUP OF PROPERTIES p 511
See KANEFF PROPERTIES LIMITED
KANEFF PROPERTIES LIMITED p 511
8501 MISSISSAUGA RD SUITE 200, BRAMPTON, ON, L6Y 5G8
(905) 454-0221 SIC 6553
KANETIX LTD p 981
360 ADELAIDE ST W SUITE 100, TORONTO, ON, M5V 1R7

(416) 599-9779 SIC 6411
KANJEE ENTERPRISES LTD p 71
3625 SHAGANAPPI TRAIL NW SUITE 356, CALGARY, AB, T3A 0E2
(403) 288-0111 SIC 5912
KANJI RX DRUG LTD p 76
600 SADDLETOWNE CIR NE SUITE 101, CALGARY, AB, T3J 5M1
(403) 568-7143 SIC 5912
KANNAMPUZHA HOLDINGS LTD p 902
160 HIGH ST, SUTTON WEST, ON, L0E 1R0
(905) 722-3631 SIC 8051
KANNEGIETER-ZIMMERMAN INSURANCE BROKERS LIMITED p 886
131 ONTARIO ST, ST CATHARINES, ON, L2R 5J9
(905) 688-9170 SIC 6411
KANTAR CANADA INC p 929
2 BLOOR ST E SUITE 900, TORONTO, ON, M4W 3H8
(416) 924-5751 SIC 8732
KANTAR MILLWARD BROWN p 929
See KANTAR CANADA INC
KANTOLA MOTORS LIMITED p 628
200 LAKEVIEW DR, KENORA, ON, P9N 0H2
(807) 468-8984 SIC 5511
KANUK INC p 1173
485 RUE RACHEL E, MONTREAL, QC, H2J 2H1
(514) 284-4494 SIC 2311
KANWAL INC p 1147
1426 BOUL INDUSTRIEL, MAGOG, QC, J1X 4V9
(819) 868-5152 SIC 3089
KAO BRANDS p 745
See KAO CANADA INC
KAO CANADA INC p 745
75 COURTNEYPARK DR W UNIT 2, MISSISSAUGA, ON, L5W 0E3
(905) 670-7890 SIC 5122
KAP COLLISION & AUTOGLASS p 627
See EASTVIEW CHEVROLET BUICK GMC LTD
KAPCO TOOL & DIE LIMITED p 1021
3200 DEVON DR, WINDSOR, ON, N8X 4L4
(519) 966-0320 SIC 3544
KAPOOR, VINAY DRUGS LTD p 910
900 ARTHUR ST E, THUNDER BAY, ON, P7E 5M8
(807) 623-2390 SIC 5912
KAPSCH TRAFFICCOM CANADA INC p 696
6020 AMBLER DR, MISSISSAUGA, ON, L4W 2P1
(905) 624-3020 SIC 3669
KAR INDUSTRIEL INC p 1251
100 AV COLUMBUS, POINTE-CLAIRE, QC, H9R 4K4
(514) 694-4711 SIC 5084
KAR-BASHER MANITOBA LTD p 346
855 49TH ST E, BRANDON, MB, R7A 7R2
(204) 726-8080 SIC 5093
KARABUS MANAGEMENT INC p 789
1 YORKDALE RD SUITE 412, NORTH YORK, ON, M6A 3A1
SIC 8748
KARADON p 209
See FAMA INDUSTRIES CORPORATION
KARAM FRUITS ET LEGUMES INC p 1297
700 RUE DE LA VISITATION, SAINT-CHARLES-BORROMEE, QC, J6E 7S3
(450) 753-5881 SIC 5148
KARAM FRUITS ET LEGUMES L'ENTREPOT p 1297
See KARAM FRUITS ET LEGUMES INC
KARCHER DIRECTION REGIONALE DU QUEBEC p 1085
See LAROSE & FILS LTEE
KARDEL CONSULTING SERVICES INC p 339
2951 TILLICUM RD UNIT 209, VICTORIA, BC, V9A 2A6

(250) 382-5959 SIC 8049
KARDIUM INC p 192
8518 GLENLYON PKY SUITE 155, BURNABY, BC, V5J 0B6
(604) 248-8891 SIC 8731
KARE FOR KIDS INTERNATIONAL p 770
7 BISHOP AVE SUITE 2107, NORTH YORK, ON, M2M 4J4
(416) 226-4111 SIC 8699
KARIS SUPPORT SOCIETY p 222
1849 ETHEL ST, KELOWNA, BC, V1Y 2Z3
(250) 860-9507 SIC 8699
KARISS ENTERPRISES LIMITED p 426
65 CLYDE AVE, MOUNT PEARL, NL, A1N 4R8
(709) 745-3403 SIC 5541
KARL STORZ ENDOSCOPY CANADA LTD p 723
7171 MILLCREEK DR, MISSISSAUGA, ON, L5N 3R3
(905) 816-8100 SIC 3845
KARLO CORPORATION SUPPLY & SERVICES p 1049
10801 BOUL RAY-LAWSON BUREAU 100, ANJOU, QC, H1J 1M5
(514) 255-5017 SIC 5088
KARMA CANDY INC p 611
356 EMERALD ST N, HAMILTON, ON, L8L 8K6
(905) 527-6222 SIC 2064
KARMIN EXPLORATION INC p 987
100 KING ST W SUITE 5700, TORONTO, ON, M5X 1C7
(416) 367-0369 SIC 1081
KARMIN GROUP p 1093
See 167986 CANADA INC
KARO DESIGN VANCOUVER INC p 295
611 ALEXANDER ST SUITE 308, VANCOUVER, BC, V6A 1E1
(604) 255-6100 SIC 7389
KARO GROUP INC p 72
1817 10 AVE SW, CALGARY, AB, T3C 0K2
(403) 266-4094 SIC 7389
KAROB FOODS LTD p 272
17710 56 AVE SUITE 10, SURREY, BC, V3S 1C7
SIC 5411
KARRYS BROS., LIMITED p 740
180 COURTNEYPARK DR E, MISSISSAUGA, ON, L5T 2S5
(905) 565-1000 SIC 5141
KARRYS WHOLESALE DISTRIBUTORS p 740
See KARRYS BROS., LIMITED
KARSON AGGREGATES p 541
See WEST CARLETON SAND & GRAVEL INC
KARVE ENERGY INC p 52
205 5 AVE SW SUITE 1700, CALGARY, AB, T2P 2V7
(403) 809-5896 SIC 1382
KASA SUPPLY LTD p 274
13237 KING GEORGE BLVD, SURREY, BC, V3T 2T3
(604) 581-5815 SIC 5039
KASCO CONSTRUCTION ALTA LTD p 11
2770 3 AVE NE SUITE 117, CALGARY, AB, T2A 2L5
SIC 1611
KASH VENTURES LTD p 101
11403 199 ST NW, EDMONTON, AB, T5S 2C6
(780) 428-3867 SIC 4953
KASHRUTH COUNCIL OF CANADA p 789
3200 DUFFERIN ST SUITE 308, NORTH YORK, ON, M6A 3B2
(416) 635-9550 SIC 8734
KASIAN ARCHITECTURE INTERIOR DESIGN AND PLANNING LTD p 52
1011 9 AVE SW, CALGARY, AB, T2P 1L3
(403) 265-2440 SIC 8712
KASIAN ARCHITECTURE INTERIOR DE-

SIGN AND PLANNING LTD p 318
1500 GEORGIA ST W SUITE 1685, VANCOUVER, BC, V6G 2Z6
(604) 683-4145 SIC 8712
KASSELER FOOD PRODUCTS INC p 696
1031 BREVIK PL, MISSISSAUGA, ON, L4W 3R7
(905) 629-2142 SIC 5141
KAST HOLDINGS INC p 1422
2020 COLEMAN CRES, REGINA, SK, S4V 3B9
(306) 721-3335 SIC 5541
KASTNER AUCTIONS LTD p 96
11205 149 ST NW, EDMONTON, AB, T5M 1W6
(780) 447-0596 SIC 7389
KASTNER METALS p 686
See 105675 ONTARIO LIMITED
KASTNERS, DIV OF p 562
See NATHAR LIMITED
KATALYST DATA MANAGEMENT LP p 52
540 5 AVE SW SUITE 1490, CALGARY, AB, T2P 0M2
(403) 294-5274 SIC 1382
KATERI MEMORIAL HOSPITAL CENTRE p 1117
GD, KAHNAWAKE, QC, J0L 1B0
(450) 638-3930 SIC 8069
KATES' PHARMACY LTD p 132
11801 100 ST SUITE 137, GRANDE PRAIRIE, AB, T8V 3Y2
(780) 357-9301 SIC 5912
KATHDEN SERVICES INC p 504
239 ADVANCE BLVD, BRAMPTON, ON, L6T 4J2
SIC 5074
KATOEN NATIE EDMONTON p 100
See COMPAGNIE KATOEN NATIE CANADA
KATZ GROUP INC p 89
10104 103 AVE NW SUITE 1702, EDMONTON, AB, T5J 0H8
(780) 990-0505 SIC 5912
KAUTEX CORPORATION p 1020
2701 KAUTEX DR, WINDSOR, ON, N8W 5B1
(519) 974-6656 SIC 3714
KAUTEX TEXTRON p 1020
See KAUTEX CORPORATION
KAVANAGH INVESTMENTS LTD p 144
4215 70 AVE, LLOYDMINSTER, AB, T9V 2X2
(780) 875-4410 SIC 5531
KAVCO SALES LTD p 798
2510 HYDE PARK GATE, OAKVILLE, ON, L6H 6M2
(905) 829-5552 SIC 5014
KAWAKI (CANADA) LTD p 255
2500 VISCOUNT WAY, RICHMOND, BC, V6V 1N1
(604) 277-7158 SIC 2092
KAWARTHA CAPITAL CONSTRUCTION p 842
See KAWARTHA CAPITAL CORP
KAWARTHA CAPITAL CORP p 842
580 ASHBURNHAM DR, PETERBOROUGH, ON, K9L 2A2
(705) 750-0440 SIC 1541
KAWARTHA DAIRY LIMITED p 494
3332 COUNTY RD 36 S, BOBCAYGEON, ON, K0M 1A0
(705) 738-5123 SIC 5143
KAWARTHA DOWNS & SPEEDWAY p 592
See KAWARTHA DOWNS LTD
KAWARTHA DOWNS LTD p 592
1382 COUNTY ROAD 28, FRASERVILLE, ON, K0L 1V0
(705) 939-6316 SIC 7948
KAWARTHA LAKES COOPERATIVE AUCTION MARKET INC p 1036
580 WOODVILLE RD, WOODVILLE, ON, K0M 2T0
(705) 439-4444 SIC 5154

KAWARTHA METALS CORP *p* 841
1-1961 FISHER DR, PETERBOROUGH, ON, K9J 6X6
(705) 748-6993 *SIC* 5051

KAWARTHA PARTICIPATION PROJECTS *p* 839
440 WATER ST, PETERBOROUGH, K9H 7K6
(705) 745-9434 *SIC* 6531

KAWARTHA PINE RIDGE DISTRICT SCHOOL BOARD *p* 496
200 CLARINGTON BLVD, BOWMANVILLE, ON, L1C 5N8
(905) 697-9857 *SIC* 8211

KAWARTHA PINE RIDGE DISTRICT SCHOOL BOARD *p* 518
71 DUNDAS ST, BRIGHTON, ON, K0K 1H0
(613) 475-0540 *SIC* 8211

KAWARTHA PINE RIDGE DISTRICT SCHOOL BOARD *p* 539
119 RANNEY ST N UNIT 960, CAMPBELLFORD, ON, K0L 1L0
(705) 653-3060 *SIC* 8211

KAWARTHA PINE RIDGE DISTRICT SCHOOL BOARD *p* 545
335 KING ST E, COBOURG, ON, K9A 1M2
(905) 372-2271 *SIC* 8211

KAWARTHA PINE RIDGE DISTRICT SCHOOL BOARD *p* 563
1717 NASH RD, COURTICE, ON, L1E 2L8
(905) 436-2074 *SIC* 8211

KAWARTHA PINE RIDGE DISTRICT SCHOOL BOARD *p* 841
633 MONAGHAN RD, PETERBOROUGH, ON, K9J 5J2
(705) 743-2181 *SIC* 8211

KAWARTHA-HALIBURTON CHILDREN'S AID SOCIETY, THE *p* 839
1100 CHEMONG RD, PETERBOROUGH, ON, K9H 7S2
(705) 743-9751 *SIC* 8322

KAWNEER COMPANY CANADA LIMITED *p* 141
4000 18 AVE N SUITE SIDE, LETHBRIDGE, AB, T1H 5S8
(403) 320-7755 *SIC* 3442

KAYCAN LTEE *p* 473
See KAYCAN LTEE

KAYCAN LTEE *p* 473
323 MAIN ST N, ACTON, ON, L7J 2L9
(519) 853-1230 *SIC* 5031

KAYCAN LTEE *p* 1251
160 AV ONEIDA, POINTE-CLAIRE, QC, H9R 1A8
(514) 694-7200 *SIC* 5039

KAYCAN LTEE *p* 1251
3075 RTE TRANSCANADIENNE, POINTE-CLAIRE, QC, H9R 1B4
(514) 694-5855 *SIC* 5033

KAYFORE HOLDINGS LTD *p* 144
5310 52ND ST, LLOYDMINSTER, AB, T9V 3B5
(780) 875-2266 *SIC* 5171

KAYTEC VINYL INC *p* 1088
105 RUE DES INDUSTRIES, COWANSVILLE, QC, J2K 3Y4
(450) 263-5368 *SIC* 3089

KB COMPONENTS CANADA INC *p* 1020
2900 ST ETIENNE BLVD, WINDSOR, ON, N8W 5E6
(519) 974-6596 *SIC* 8711

KB HOLDINGS LTD *p* 217
411 10TH AVE, KAMLOOPS, BC, V2C 6J8
(250) 372-1734 *SIC* 5541

KBAL *p* 24
See KENN BOREK AIR LTD

KBK NO 51 VENTURES LTD *p* 314
1128 ALBERNI ST, VANCOUVER, BC, V6E 4R6
(604) 683-1399 *SIC* 6513

KBL ENVIRONMENTAL LTD *p* 436
17 CAMERON RD, YELLOWKNIFE, NT, X1A 0E8
(867) 873-5263 *SIC* 4953

KBM COMMERCIAL FLOOR COVERINGS INC *p* 30
1260 26 AVE SE, CALGARY, AB, T2G 5S2
(403) 274-5292 *SIC* 1752

KBR CANADA LTD *p* 149
1302 10 S, NISKU, AB, T9E 8K2
(780) 468-1341 *SIC* 8741

KBR INDUSTRIAL CANADA CO. *p* 126
1302 10 ST NISKU, EDMONTON, AB, T9E 8K2
(780) 468-1341 *SIC* 1541

KBR INDUSTRIAL CANADA COMPANY *p* 149
See KBR CANADA LTD

KBS+P CANADA INC *p* 929
2 BLOOR ST E SUITE 137, TORONTO, ON, M4W 3J4
(416) 260-7000 *SIC* 7311

KBS+P CANADA LP KBS+P CANADA SEC *p* 934
340 KING ST E 4TH FL SUITE 500, TORONTO, ON, M5A 1K8
(416) 260-7000 *SIC* 7311

KCA DEUTAG DRILLING CANADA INC *p* 428
45 HEBRON WAY SUITE 201, ST. JOHN'S, NL, A1A 0P9
(709) 778-6200 *SIC* 1381

KCI MEDICAL CANADA INC *p* 745
75 COURTNEYPARK DR W SUITE 2, MISSISSAUGA, ON, L5W 0E3
(905) 565-7187 *SIC* 5047

KCICRANE PRO SERVICES *p* 523
See KONECRANES CANADA INC

KCLC PROPERTIES ULC *p* 629
12750 JANE ST, KING CITY, ON, L7B 1A3
(905) 833-3086 *SIC* 7389

KDA GROUP INC *p* 1383
1197 RUE NOTRE-DAME E, THETFORD MINES, QC, G6G 2V2
(418) 334-8767 *SIC* 6712

KDC *p* 212
See KHOWUTZUN DEVELOPMENT CORP

KDC *p* 1143
See KNOWLTON DEVELOPMENT CORPORATION INC

KE MARR SUPERMARKET *p* 906
See 2023649 ONTARIO LIMITED

KEAL COMPUTER SERVICES INC *p* 554
55 ADMINISTRATION RD UNIT 21, CONCORD, ON, L4K 4G9
(905) 738-2112 *SIC* 7371

KEAL TECHNOLOGIES *p* 554
See KEAL COMPUTER SERVICES INC

KEANE COMPLETIONS CN CORP *p* 52
435 4 AVE SW SUITE 380, CALGARY, AB, T2P 2S6
(587) 390-0863 *SIC* 1381

KEARNEY PLANTERS *p* 903
See KEARNEY, B. R. ENTERPRISES LTD

KEARNEY, B. R. ENTERPRISES LTD *p* 903
14232 TURIN LINE, THAMESVILLE, ON, N0P 2K0
(519) 678-3206 *SIC* 5083

KEATING TECHNOLOGIES INC *p* 671
25 ROYAL CREST CRT SUITE 120, MARKHAM, ON, L3R 9X4
(905) 479-0230 *SIC* 8741

KEATS BROTHERS (DIV OF) *p* 385
See SIRCO CLEANERS (1980) LTD

KEAY, JIM FORD LINCOLN SALES LTD *p* 810
1438 YOUVILLE DR, ORLEANS, ON, K1C 2X8
(613) 841-1010 *SIC* 5511

KEB HANA BANK CANADA *p* 772
4950 YONGE ST UNIT 1101, NORTH YORK, ON, M2N 6K1
(416) 536-8046 *SIC* 6021

KEB HANA BANK CANADA *p* 772
4950 YONGE ST SUITE 103, NORTH YORK, ON, M2N 6K1
(416) 222-5200 *SIC* 6021

KECHNIE CHEVROLET OLDSMOBILE LTD

p 597
74 KINGSTON ST, GODERICH, ON, N7A 3K4
SIC 5511

KBR CANADA LTD
(duplicate—not shown)

KEE TRANSPORT GROUP INC *p* 740
6760 DAVAND DR SUITE 9, MISSISSAUGA, ON, L5T 2L9
(905) 670-0835 *SIC* 4731

KEE WEST AUTO CARRIERS INC *p* 378
12-15-2 EPM, WINNIPEG, MB, R3C 2E6
(204) 774-2937 *SIC* 4213

KEELE HOLDINGS INC *p* 554
8001 KEELE ST, CONCORD, ON, L4K 1Y8
(905) 669-9855 *SIC* 7389

KEENA TRUCK LEASING AND TRANSPORT LIMITED *p* 495
27 SIMPSON RD, BOLTON, ON, L7E 1E4
(905) 857-1189 *SIC* 4213

KEEPRITE REFRIGERATION *p* 514
See NATIONAL REFRIGERATION & AIR CONDITIONING CANADA CORP

KEEPSAKE PLANTS LTD *p* 644
268 SEACLIFF DR W, LEAMINGTON, ON, N8H 4C8
(519) 326-6121 *SIC* 5191

KEETHILLS AGGREGATE CO LTD *p* 96
11428 168 ST NW SUITE 100, EDMONTON, AB, T5M 3T9
SIC 5032

KEEWATIN PATRICIA DISTRICT SCHOOL BOARD *p* 628
1400 NINTH ST N, KENORA, ON, P9N 2T7
(807) 468-6401 *SIC* 8211

KEEWATIN PATRICIA DISTRICT SCHOOL BOARD *p* 628
240 VETERANS DR 4TH FL, KENORA, ON, P9N 3Y5
(807) 468-5571 *SIC* 8211

KEFOR LTEE *p* 1314
175 RUE BOYER, SAINT-ISIDORE-DE-LAPRAIRIE, QC, J0L 2A0
(450) 454-4636 *SIC* 2439

KEG AT THE MOUNTAIN *p* 343
See SNOWLINE RESTAURANTS INC

KEG IN THE VALLEY *p* 174
See ABBOTSFORD RESTAURANTS LTD

KEG RESTAURANT *p* 241
800 MARINE DR, NORTH VANCOUVER, BC, V7P 1R8
SIC 5812

KEG RESTAURANT *p* 249
See GREAT STEAK HOUSE INC, THE

KEG RESTAURANTS LTD *p* 36
7104 MACLEOD TRAIL SE, CALGARY, AB, T2H 0L3
(403) 253-2534 *SIC* 5812

KEG RESTAURANTS LTD *p* 41
1923 UXBRIDGE DR NW, CALGARY, AB, T2N 2V2
(403) 282-0020 *SIC* 5812

KEG RESTAURANTS LTD *p* 104
9960 170 ST NW, EDMONTON, AB, T5T 6G7
(780) 414-1114 *SIC* 5812

KEG RESTAURANTS LTD *p* 115
8020 105 ST NW, EDMONTON, AB, T6E 4Z4
SIC 5812

KEG RESTAURANTS LTD *p* 120
1631 102 ST NW, EDMONTON, AB, T6N 1M3
(780) 485-6530 *SIC* 5812

KEG RESTAURANTS LTD *p* 198
2991 LOUGHEED HWY UNIT 130, COQUITLAM, BC, V3B 6J6
(604) 464-5340 *SIC* 5812

KEG RESTAURANTS LTD *p* 260
10100 SHELLBRIDGE WAY, RICHMOND, BC, V6X 2W7
(604) 276-0242 *SIC* 5812

KEG RESTAURANTS LTD *p* 276
7948 120 ST, SURREY, BC, V3W 3N2
(604) 591-6161 *SIC* 5812

KEG RESTAURANTS LTD *p* 279
15180 32 AVE DIVERS, SURREY, BC, V3Z 3M1
(604) 542-9733 *SIC* 5812

KEG RESTAURANTS LTD *p* 319
1499 ANDERSON ST, VANCOUVER, BC, V6H 3R5
(604) 685-4735 *SIC* 5812

KEG RESTAURANTS LTD *p* 378
115 GARRY ST, WINNIPEG, MB, R3C 1G5
(204) 942-7619 *SIC* 5812

KEG RESTAURANTS LTD *p* 393
2034 MCGILLIVRAY BLVD, WINNIPEG, MB, R3Y 1V5
(204) 477-5300 *SIC* 5812

KEG RESTAURANTS LTD *p* 432
135 HARBOUR DR, ST. JOHN'S, NL, A1C 6N6
(709) 726-4534 *SIC* 5812

KEG RESTAURANTS LTD *p* 511
70 GILLINGHAM DR, BRAMPTON, ON, L6X 4X7
(905) 456-3733 *SIC* 5812

KEG RESTAURANTS LTD *p* 585
927 DIXON RD, ETOBICOKE, ON, M9W 1J8
(416) 675-2311 *SIC* 5812

KEG RESTAURANTS LTD *p* 776
1977 LESLIE ST, NORTH YORK, ON, M3B 2M3
(416) 446-1045 *SIC* 5812

KEG RESTAURANTS LTD *p* 798
300 HAYS BLVD, OAKVILLE, ON, L6H 7P3
(905) 257-2700 *SIC* 5812

KEG RESTAURANTS LTD *p* 804
3130 SOUTH SERVICE RD W, OAKVILLE, ON, L6L 6T1
(905) 681-1810 *SIC* 5812

KEG RESTAURANTS LTD *p* 821
75 YORK ST, OTTAWA, ON, K1N 5T2
(613) 241-8514 *SIC* 5812

KEG RESTAURANTS LTD *p* 867
60 ESTATE DR, SCARBOROUGH, ON, M1H 2Z1
(416) 438-1452 *SIC* 5812

KEG RESTAURANTS LTD *p* 887
344 GLENDALE AVE, ST CATHARINES, ON, L2T 4E3
(905) 680-4585 *SIC* 5812

KEG RESTAURANTS LTD *p* 908
735 HEWITSON ST, THUNDER BAY, ON, P7B 6B5
(807) 623-1960 *SIC* 5812

KEG RESTAURANTS LTD *p* 932
515 JARVIS ST, TORONTO, ON, M4Y 2H7
(416) 964-6609 *SIC* 5812

KEG RESTAURANTS LTD *p* 942
56 THE ESPLANADE, TORONTO, ON, M5E 1A7
(416) 367-0685 *SIC* 5812

KEG RESTAURANTS LTD *p* 981
560 KING ST W, TORONTO, ON, M5V 0L5
(416) 364-7227 *SIC* 5812

KEG ROYALTIES INCOME FUND, THE *p* 260
10100 SHELLBRIDGE WAY, RICHMOND, BC, V6X 2W7
(604) 276-0242 *SIC* 6722

KEG SOUTH RICHMOND *p* 264
See STEVESTON RESTAURANTS INC

KEG STEAK HOUSE & BAR, THE *p* 585
See KEG RESTAURANTS LTD

KEG STEAKHOUSE & BAR *p* 385
See G.R.R. HOLDINGS LTD

KEG STEAKHOUSE & BAR *p* 1190
See RESTAURANT SAINT-PAUL (MONTREAL) LTEE

KEG STEAKHOUSE & BAR, THE *p* 36
See KEG RESTAURANTS LTD

KEG STEAKHOUSE & BAR, THE *p* 41
See KEG RESTAURANTS LTD

KEG STEAKHOUSE & BAR, THE *p* 115
See KEG RESTAURANTS LTD

KEG STEAKHOUSE & BAR, THE *p* 120

▲ Public Company ■ Public Company Family Member **HQ** Headquarters **BR** Branch **SL** Single Location

See KEG RESTAURANTS LTD
KEG STEAKHOUSE & BAR, THE   p 198
See KEG RESTAURANTS LTD
KEG STEAKHOUSE & BAR, THE   p 260
See KEG RESTAURANTS LTD
KEG STEAKHOUSE & BAR, THE   p 276
See KEG RESTAURANTS LTD
KEG STEAKHOUSE & BAR, THE   p 319
See KEG RESTAURANTS LTD
KEG STEAKHOUSE & BAR, THE   p 378
See KEG RESTAURANTS LTD
KEG STEAKHOUSE & BAR, THE   p 393
See KEG RESTAURANTS LTD
KEG STEAKHOUSE & BAR, THE   p 432
See KEG RESTAURANTS LTD
KEG STEAKHOUSE & BAR, THE   p 511
See KEG RESTAURANTS LTD
KEG STEAKHOUSE & BAR, THE   p 616
See 718695 ONTARIO INC
KEG STEAKHOUSE & BAR, THE   p 776
See KEG RESTAURANTS LTD
KEG STEAKHOUSE & BAR, THE   p 798
See KEG RESTAURANTS LTD
KEG STEAKHOUSE & BAR, THE   p 821
See KEG RESTAURANTS LTD
KEG STEAKHOUSE & BAR, THE   p 867
See KEG RESTAURANTS LTD
KEG STEAKHOUSE & BAR, THE   p 908
See KEG RESTAURANTS LTD
KEG STEAKHOUSE & BAR, THE   p 932
See KEG RESTAURANTS LTD
KEG STEAKHOUSE & BAR, THE   p 942
See KEG RESTAURANTS LTD
KEG STEAKHOUSE & BAR, THE   p 981
See KEG RESTAURANTS LTD
KEG STEAKHOUSE & BAR, THE   p 1008
'42 NORTHFIELD DR E, WATERLOO, ON,
N2L 6A1
(519) 725-4444   SIC 5812
KEG STEAKHOUSE AND BAR   p 94
13960 137 AVE NW, EDMONTON, AB, T5L
5H1
(780) 472-0707   SIC 5812
KEG STEAKHOUSE AND BAR, THE p 804
See KEG RESTAURANTS LTD
KEG, THE   p 347
See 35790 MANITOBA LTD
KEHO LAKE COLONY   p 4
GD, BARONS, AB, T0L 0G0
(403) 757-2330   SIC 0751
KEIJ ENTERPRISES LTD   p 243
2405 SKAHA LAKE RD, PENTICTON, BC,
V2A 6E8
(250) 493-1107   SIC 5511
KEILHAUER LTD   p 914
1450 BIRCHMOUNT RD, TORONTO, ON,
M1P 2E3
(416) 759-5665   SIC 2521
KEIR SURGICAL LTD   p 290
408 E KENT AVE SOUTH SUITE 126, VAN-
COUVER, BC, V5X 2X7
(604) 261-9596   SIC 5047
KEITH PANEL SYSTEMS CO., LTD   p 240
40 GOSTICK PL SUITE 2, NORTH VAN-
COUVER, BC, V7M 3G3
(604) 987-4499   SIC 8712
KEIZER'S COLLISION CENTRE   p 462
1682   SACKVILLE   DR,   MIDDLE
SACKVILLE, NS, B4E 3A9
(902) 865-7311   SIC 7532
KEL-GOR LIMITED   p 860
1411 PLANK RD, SARNIA, ON, N7T 7H3
(519) 336-9312   SIC 1711
**KELCOM MOBILITY SOLUTIONS WIND-
SOR**   p
1025
See RADIOCO LTD
KELCOM TELEMESSAGING   p 1022
See 1118528 ONTARIO INC
KELDON ELECTRIC & DATA LTD   p 222
1909 BREDIN RD, KELOWNA, BC, V1Y 7S9
(250) 861-4255   SIC 1731
KELK   p 778
See VISHAY PRECISION GROUP CANADA

ULC   p 245
KELLAND FOODS LTD   p 245
See KELLAND PROPERTIES INC
KELLAND PROPERTIES INC   p 234
2350 DELINEA PL, NANAIMO, BC, V9T 5L9
(250) 585-1482   SIC 5411
KELLAND PROPERTIES INC   p 245
2943 10TH AVE, PORT ALBERNI, BC, V9Y
2N5
(250) 723-3397   SIC 5411
KELLEHER FORD SALES   p 348
See 4236009 MANITOBA LTD
KELLER CONSTRUCTION LTD   p 96
11430 160 ST NW, EDMONTON, AB, T5M
3Y7
(780) 484-1010   SIC 1542
KELLER EQUIPMENT SUPPLY LTD   p 30
1228 26 AVE SE, CALGARY, AB, T2G 5S2
(403) 243-8666   SIC 5172
KELLER WILLIAMS COMPLETE REALTY p
610
See 1906351 ONTARIO INC
KELLER WILLIAMS INTEGRITY REALTY p
832
245 MENTEN PL UNIT 100, OTTAWA, ON,
K2H 9E8
(613) 829-1818   SIC 6799
**KELLER WILLIAMS REAL ESTATE ASSO-
CIATES**   p
728
See WILLIAMS, KELLER REALTY
**KELLER WILLIAMS REAL ESTATE SER-
VICES**   p
393
See 10022441 MANITOBA LTD
KELLER WILLIAMS REALTY SOUTH   p 39
See SEVENTH LEVEL MANAGEMENT LTD
KELLER WILLIAMS REFERRED REALTY p
777
See REFERRED REALTY INC
KELLOGG CANADA INC   p 696
5350 CREEKBANK RD, MISSISSAUGA,
ON, L4W 5S1
(905) 290-5200   SIC 2043
KELLOWAY CONSTRUCTION LIMITED   p
427
1388 PORTUGAL COVE RD, PORTUGAL
COVE-ST PHILIPS, NL, A1M 3J9
(709) 895-6532   SIC 7349
KELLY & BELL HOLDINGS LTD   p 1425
819 MELVILLE ST, SASKATOON, SK, S7J
5L2
(306) 242-8688   SIC 5511
KELLY COVE SALMON LTD   p 395
874 MAIN ST, BLACKS HARBOUR, NB,
E5H 1E6
(506) 456-6600   SIC 2092
KELLY FORD   p 423
See JIM PENNEY LIMITED
KELLY ROAD SECONDARY SCHOOL p 248
See BOARD OF EDUCATION OF SCHOOL
DISTRICT NO. 57 (PRINCE GEORGE), THE
KELLY SERVICES   p 622
See KELLY SERVICES (CANADA), LTD
KELLY SERVICES (CANADA), LTD   p 622
70 DICKINSON DR, INGLESIDE, ON, K0C
1M0
(613) 537-8491   SIC 7361
KELLY SERVICES (CANADA), LTD   p 710
77 CITY CENTRE DR, MISSISSAUGA, ON,
L5B 1M5
(416) 368-1058   SIC 7363
KELLY TEMPORARY SERVICES   p 710
See KELLY SERVICES (CANADA), LTD
KELLY WESTERN JET CENTRE   p 386
See KELLY WESTERN SERVICES LTD
KELLY WESTERN SERVICES LTD   p 386
30 HANGAR LINE RD, WINNIPEG, MB, R3J
3Y7
(204) 948-9500   SIC 5172
KELLY'S HOME HEALTH CARE   p 491
See KELLY, PAUL (1993) LIMITED
KELLY, JIM BUILDING MATERIALS LTD   p
82

4221 50 ST, DRAYTON VALLEY, AB, T7A
1S1
(780) 542-4044   SIC 5251
KELLY, MARIA ENTERPRISES INC   p 92
11408 JASPER AVE NW, EDMONTON, AB,
T5K 0M1
(780) 482-1011   SIC 5912
KELLY, PAUL (1993) LIMITED   p 491
411 BRIDGE ST E, BELLEVILLE, ON, K8N
1P7
(613) 962-5387   SIC 5912
KELOWNA AMBASSADORS   p 218
680 VALLEY RD SUITE 25, KELOWNA, BC,
V1V 2J3
(250) 712-1634   SIC 7389
KELOWNA CAPITAL NEWS   p 219
See CARIBOO PRESS PRINTING & PUB-
LISHING LTD
KELOWNA CHEVROLET   p 220
See DFC AUTO LTD
KELOWNA CHRISTIAN CENTER SOCIETY
p 220
907 BADKE RD, KELOWNA, BC, V1X 5Z5
(250) 862-2376   SIC 8661
KELOWNA CHRYSLER DODGE JEEP   p
220
2440 ENTERPRISE WAY, KELOWNA, BC,
V1X 6X6
(250) 763-6121   SIC 5511
KELOWNA CYCLE   p 223
See VAN DEN ELZEN DEVELOPMENTS
LTD
**KELOWNA FLIGHTCRAFT AIR CHARTER
LTD**   p 218
5655 AIRPORT WAY SUITE 1, KELOWNA,
BC, V1V 1S1
(250) 491-5500   SIC 4512
**KELOWNA FLIGHTCRAFT AIR CHARTER
LTD**   p 747
9300 AIRPORT RD, MOUNT HOPE, ON,
L0R 1W0
   SIC 4581
KELOWNA FLIGHTCRAFT LTD   p 218
5655 AIRPORT WAY UNIT 1, KELOWNA,
BC, V1V 1S1
(250) 491-5500   SIC 4581
KELOWNA FLIGHTCRAFT LTD   p 747
9500 AIRPORT RD, MOUNT HOPE, ON,
L0R 1W0
(905) 679-3313   SIC 4581
KELOWNA FORD LINCOLN SALES LTD   p
220
2540 ENTERPRISE WAY, KELOWNA, BC,
V1X 7X5
(250) 868-2330   SIC 5511
**KELOWNA HOME HARDWARE BUILDING
CENTRE**   p 223
See TCB TRI-CITIES BUILDERS SUPPLY
LTD
KELOWNA HYUNDAI   p 219
See 0705507 BC LTD
KELOWNA INTERNATIONAL AIRPORT   p
219
5533 AIRPORT WAY SUITE 1, KELOWNA,
BC, V1V 1S1
(250) 807-4300   SIC 4581
KELOWNA MERCEDES BENZ   p 219
See 435809 B.C. LTD
KELOWNA MOTORS LTD   p 220
2560 ENTERPRISE WAY, KELOWNA, BC,
V1X 7X5
(250) 762-2068   SIC 5511
KELOWNA NISSAN LTD   p 220
2741 HIGHWAY 97 N, KELOWNA, BC, V1X
4J8
(250) 712-0404   SIC 5511
KELOWNA ROCKETS HOCKEY CLUB   p
222
See KELOWNA ROCKETS HOCKEY EN-
TERPRISES LTD
**KELOWNA ROCKETS HOCKEY ENTER-
PRISES LTD**   p
222
1223 WATER ST SUITE 101, KELOWNA,

BC, V1Y 9V1
(250) 860-7825   SIC 7941
KELOWNA RV   p 341
See KELOWNA TRUCK & R.V. LTD
KELOWNA SECONDARY   p 221
See BOARD OF EDUCATION OF SCHOOL
DISTRICT NO. 23 (CENTRAL OKANAGAN),
THE
KELOWNA TOYOTA   p 219
See 0092584 B.C. LTD
KELOWNA TRUCK & R.V. LTD   p 341
1780 BYLAND RD, WEST KELOWNA, BC,
V1Z 1A9
(250) 769-1000   SIC 5571
KELSEY PIPELINES LTD   p 1428
107-3239 FAITHFULL AVE, SASKATOON,
SK, S7K 8H4
(306) 385-6285   SIC 4619
KELSEY SCHOOL DIVISION   p 359
322 EDWARDS AVE, THE PAS, MB, R9A
1R4
(204) 623-6421   SIC 8211
**KELSEY TRAIL REGIONAL HEALTH AU-
THORITY**   p
1410
505 BROADWAY AVE N, MELFORT, SK,
S0E 1A0
(306) 752-8700   SIC 8062
**KELSEY TRAIL REGIONAL HEALTH AU-
THORITY**   p
1412
400 6TH AVE E, NIPAWIN, SK, S0E 1E0
(306) 862-9828   SIC 8051
**KELSEY TRAIL REGIONAL HEALTH AU-
THORITY**   p
1437
GD, TISDALE, SK, S0E 1T0
(306) 873-6600   SIC 8062
**KELSEY TRAIL REGIONAL HEALTH AU-
THORITY**   p
1437
GD, TISDALE, SK, S0E 1T0
   SIC 8062
KELSEY'S   p 608
See RECIPE UNLIMITED CORPORATION
KELSEY'S   p 759
See RECIPE UNLIMITED CORPORATION
KELSEY'S   p 808
See RECIPE UNLIMITED CORPORATION
KELSEY'S   p 831
See RECIPE UNLIMITED CORPORATION
KELSEY'S   p 856
See CARA FOODS INTERNATIONAL LTD
KELSEY'S RESTAURANT   p 563
See RECIPE UNLIMITED CORPORATION
KELSEY'S RESTAURANT   p 1035
See HOAM LTD
KELSEY'S RESTAURANTS INC   p 554
199 FOUR VALLEY DR, CONCORD, ON,
L4K 0B8
(905) 760-2244   SIC 5812
KELSO TECHNOLOGIES INC   p 280
13966 18B AVE, SURREY, BC, V4A 8J1
(250) 764-3618   SIC 3743
KELSON CANADA INC   p 24
2431 37 AVE NE SUITE 430, CALGARY, AB,
T2E 6Y7
(403) 296-1500   SIC 6712
KELT EXPLORATION LTD   p 52
311 SIXTH AVE SW SUITE 300, CALGARY,
AB, T2P 3H2
(403) 294-0154   SIC 1382
KELTIC TRANSPORTATION INC   p 410
90 MACNAUGHTON AVE, MONCTON, NB,
E1H 3L9
(506) 854-1233   SIC 4213
KELTOUR CONTROLS INC   p 523
4375 MAINWAY, BURLINGTON, ON, L7L
5N9
(905) 335-6000   SIC 3613
KELVIN HIGH SCHOOL   p 388
See WINNIPEG SCHOOL DIVISION
KEM CANADA MANUFACTURING   p 736
See RDI CHEMICAL CORPORATION

▲ Public Company   ■ Public Company Family Member   **HQ** Headquarters   **BR** Branch   **SL** Single Location

KEMBER HARDWOOD FLOORING INC p 598
246022 COUNTY RD 16, GRAND VALLEY, ON, L9W 6K2
(289) 804-0032   SIC 1752

KEMBER INTERIORS p 598
See KEMBER HARDWOOD FLOORING INC

KEMIRA WATER SOLUTIONS CANADA INC p 1393
3405 RTE MARIE-VICTORIN, VARENNES, QC, J3X 1P7
(450) 652-0665   SIC 2836

KEMP, JAMES CONSTRUCTION LIMITED p 609
121 VANSITMART AVE, HAMILTON, ON, L8H 3A6
(905) 547-7715   SIC 1541

KEMPENFELT CONFERENCE CENTRE, THE p 622
See CANADIAN AUTOMOTIVE INSTITUTE, THE

KEMPTVILLE BUILDING CENTRE LTD p 627
2540 HWY 43, KEMPTVILLE, ON, K0G 1J0
(613) 258-6000   SIC 5211

KEMPTVILLE COLLEGE CAMPUS p 627
See UNIVERSITY OF GUELPH

KEMPTVILLE DISTRICT HOSPITAL p 627
2675 CONCESSION RD, KEMPTVILLE, ON, K0G 1J0
(613) 258-3435   SIC 8062

KEMPTVILLE HOME FURNITURE, DIV OF p 627
See KEMPTVILLE BUILDING CENTRE LTD

KEMPTVILLE TRUCK CENTRE p 627
See NAVISTAR CANADA, INC

KEN MCMASTER p 649
See MACMASTER CHEVROLET LTD

KEN SARGENT GMC BUICK LTD p 132
12308 100 ST, GRANDE PRAIRIE, AB, T8V 4H7
(780) 532-8865   SIC 5511

KEN SHAW MOTORS LIMITED p 993
2336 ST CLAIR AVE W, TORONTO, ON, M6N 1K8
(416) 766-0055   SIC 5511

KENAIDAN CONTRACTING LTD p 745
7080 DERRYCREST DR, MISSISSAUGA, ON, L5W 0G5
(905) 670-2660   SIC 8711

KENAIDAN GROUP LTD p 745
7080 DERRYCREST DR, MISSISSAUGA, ON, L5W 0G5
(905) 670-2660   SIC 1629

KENAIR APARTMENTS LIMITED p 927
500 AVENUE RD, TORONTO, ON, M4V 2J6
(416) 923-7557   SIC 6513

KENAR CONSULTANTS p 1189
See N F O E & ASSOCIES ARCHITECTS

KENAR CONSULTANTS INC p 1189
511 PLACE D'ARMES BUREAU 100, MONTREAL, QC, H2Y 2W7
(514) 397-2616   SIC 8712

KENASTON SELF STORAGE p 1416
See STORAGEVAULT CANADA INC

KENASTON SOBEYS p 389
See SOBEYS CAPITAL INCORPORATED

KENDALL'S FISHERY LIMITED p 427
GD, PORT AU PORT, NL, A0N 1T0
(709) 642-5711   SIC 5146

KENDRAKYLE INVESTMENTS INC p 1086
2540 BOUL DANIEL-JOHNSON BUREAU 207, COTE SAINT-LUC, QC, H7T 2S3
(450) 682-6227   SIC 8742

KENMAC ENERGY INC p 1039
3 MOUNT EDWARD RD, CHARLOTTETOWN, PE, C1A 5R7
(902) 566-2295   SIC 5983

KENMAR FOOD SERVICES LTD p 378
444 ST MARY AVE SUITE 135, WINNIPEG, MB, R3C 3T1
(204) 942-4414   SIC 5812

KENMORE HOMES p 886
See KENMORE MANAGEMENT INC

KENMORE MANAGEMENT INC p 886
151 JAMES ST, ST CATHARINES, ON, L2R 5C4
SIC 1542

KENMOUNT MOTORS INC p 430
547 KENMOUNT RD, ST. JOHN'S, NL, A1B 3P9
(709) 579-1999   SIC 5511

KENN BOREK AIR LTD p 24
290 MCTAVISH RD NE SUITE 4, CALGARY, AB, T2E 7G5
(403) 291-3300   SIC 4522

KENNAMETAL STELLITE, INC p 491
471 DUNDAS ST E, BELLEVILLE, ON, K8N 1G2
(613) 968-3481   SIC 3369

KENNEBEC DODGE CHRYSLER INC p 1305
10240 BOUL LACROIX, SAINT-GEORGES, QC, G5Y 1K1
(418) 228-5575   SIC 5511

KENNEBEC MANOR INC p 414
475 WOODWARD AVE, SAINT JOHN, NB, E2K 4N1
(506) 632-9628   SIC 8051

KENNEBECASIS DRUGS LTD p 412
1A MARR RD, ROTHESAY, NB, E2E 3L4
(506) 847-7581   SIC 5912

KENNEBECASIS VALLEY FIRE DEPT p 412
7 CAMPBELL DR, ROTHESAY, NB, E2E 5B6
(506) 848-6601   SIC 7389

KENNEBECASIS VALLEY HIGH SCHOOL p 411
See ANGLOPHONE SOUTH SCHOOL DISTRICT (ASD-S)

KENNEDY FORD SALES LIMITED p 802
280 SOUTH SERVICE RD W, OAKVILLE, ON, L6K 3X5
(905) 845-1646   SIC 5511

KENNEDY HOUSE p 286
See CHILDREN'S FOUNDATION, THE

KENNEDY INSURANCE BROKERS INC p 763
414 FRASER ST, NORTH BAY, ON, P1B 3W9
(705) 472-5950   SIC 6411

KENNEDY LODGE NURSING HOME p 872
See REVERA LONG TERM CARE INC

KENNER COLLEGIATE VOCATIONAL SCHOOL p 841
See KAWARTHA PINE RIDGE DISTRICT SCHOOL BOARD

KENNETH E. SPENCER MEMORIAL HOME INC, THE p 408
35 ATLANTIC BAPTIST AVE, MONCTON, NB, E1E 4N3
(506) 858-7870   SIC 8051

KENNEY & ROSS LIMITED p 465
6493 SHORE RD RR 3, SHELBURNE, NS, B0T 1W0
(902) 637-2616   SIC 2899

KENNY ENTERPRISES LIMITED p 433
462 TOPSAIL RD, ST. JOHN'S, NL, A1E 2C2
(709) 364-3207   SIC 5411

KENORA DISTRICT SERVICES BOARD p 565
211 PRINCESS ST SUITE 2, DRYDEN, ON, P8N 3L5
(807) 223-2100   SIC 8611

KENORA ENTERPRISES LTD p 186
4638 HASTINGS ST, BURNABY, BC, V5C 2K5
(604) 294-0038   SIC 1623

KENORA FOREST PRODUCTS LTD p 369
165 RYAN ST, WINNIPEG, MB, R2R 0N9
(204) 989-9600   SIC 2421

KENORA FOREST PRODUCTS LTD p 628
1060 LAKEVIEW DR, KENORA, ON, P9N 3X8
(807) 468-1550   SIC 2421

KENORA SAFEWAY p 628
See SOBEYS WEST INC

KENORA-RAINY RIVER DISTRICTS CHILD AND FAMILY SERVICES p 628
820 LAKEVIEW DR, KENORA, ON, P9N 3P7
(807) 467-5437   SIC 8699

KENPAL FARM PRODUCTS INC p 541
69819 LONDON RD SUITE 1, CENTRALIA, ON, N0M 1K0
(519) 228-6444   SIC 2048

KENPIER INVESTISSEMENTS LIMITEE p 1108
1170 CH D'AYLMER, GATINEAU, QC, J9H 7L3
(819) 778-0000   SIC 6512

KENROC BUILDING MATERIALS CO. LTD p 1420
1275 BROAD ST UNIT 200, REGINA, SK, S4R 1Y2
(306) 525-1415   SIC 5039

KENROD STEEL FABRICATING LIMITED p 836
6 ADAMS ST SUITE A, PARIS, ON, N3L 3X4
(519) 865-7921   SIC 3499

KENSINGTON AGRICULTURAL SERVICES LTD p 1041
15 PARK RD, KENSINGTON, PE, C0B 1M0
(902) 836-3212   SIC 5083

KENSINGTON VILLAGE p 650
See SHARON FARMS & ENTERPRISES LTD

KENSTRUCT LTD p 837
24533 PARK RD, PEFFERLAW, ON, L0E 1N0
(416) 505-9737   SIC 1542

KENT & ESSEX MUTUAL INSURANCE COMPANY p 543
10 CREEK RD, CHATHAM, ON, N7M 5J3
SIC 6331

KENT BUILDING SUPPLIES, DIV OF p 415
See IRVING, J. D. LIMITED

KENT HOME IMPROVEMENT WAREHOUSE p 426
See IRVING, J. D. LIMITED

KENT HOMES p 395
See IRVING, J. D. LIMITED

KENT JB FR COUNCIL 6638 p 426
7 GREENWOOD CRES, MOUNT PEARL, NL, A1N 2C1
(709) 781-6638   SIC 1711

KENT PETROLEUM LIMITED p 543
280 RICHMOND ST, CHATHAM, ON, N7M 1P6
(519) 623-7411   SIC 5172

KENT TRUSSES LIMITED p 902
204 FOREST LAKE RD, SUNDRIDGE, ON, P0A 1Z0
(705) 384-5326   SIC 2439

KENTUCKY BLUE GRASS LTD p 109
6107 34 ST NW, EDMONTON, AB, T6B 2V6
(780) 415-5201   SIC 0181

KENTUCKY FRIED CHICKEN p 1433
See EL-RANCHO FOOD SERVICES LIMITED

KENTUCKY FRIED CHICKEN CANADA COMPANY p 1003
191 CREDITVIEW RD UNIT 100, VAUGHAN, ON, L4L 9T1
(416) 664-5200   SIC 6794

KENTVILLE CHRYSLER DODGE JEEP (2005) INC p 459
800 PARK ST, KENTVILLE, NS, B4N 3V7
(902) 678-2134   SIC 5511

KENTVILLE MAZDA p 459
See 3188192 NOVA SCOTIA INCORPORATED

KENTVILLE PUBLISHING p 464
See TRANSCONTINENTAL INC

KENTVILLE TOYOTA p 459
See JEFFREY BEST MOTORS INCORPORATED

KENTWOOD FORD SALES INC p 84
13344 97 ST NW, EDMONTON, AB, T5E 4C9
(780) 476-8600   SIC 5511

KENWAL CANADA INC p 892
1100 SOUTH SERVICE RD SUITE 317, STONEY CREEK, ON, L8E 0C5
(905) 643-8930   SIC 5051

KENWORTH LONDON p 554
See KENWORTH TORONTO LTD

KENWORTH MASKA p 1348
See CAMIONS MASKA INC

KENWORTH TORONTO LTD p 554
500 CREDITSTONE RD, CONCORD, ON, L4K 3Z3
(905) 695-0740   SIC 5012

KEOLIS CANADA INC p 1211
740 RUE NOTRE-DAME O BUREAU 1000, MONTREAL, QC, H3C 3X6
(514) 395-4000   SIC 6712

KEOPS TECHNOLOGIES p 1209
See ALIZENT CANADA INC

KEPA TRANSPORT INC p 1390
12 RUE FINLAY, VAL-D'OR, QC, J9P 0K9
(819) 874-0262   SIC 4213

KERNAGHAN, S J ADJUSTERS LIMITED p 318
1445 GEORGIA ST W SUITE 300, VANCOUVER, BC, V6G 2T3
(604) 688-5651   SIC 6411

KERNAHAN PARK SECONDARY SCHOOL p 885
See DISTRICT SCHOOL BOARD OF NIAGARA

KERNELS p 922
See KERNELS POPCORN LIMITED

KERNELS POPCORN LIMITED p 922
40 EGLINTON AVE E SUITE 250, TORONTO, ON, M4P 3A2
(416) 487-4194   SIC 5441

KERR BROS. LIMITED p 575
956 ISLINGTON AVE, ETOBICOKE, ON, M8Z 4P6
(416) 252-7341   SIC 2064

KERR CONTROLS LIMITED p 469
125 POLYMER RD, TRURO, NS, B2N 7A7
(902) 895-9285   SIC 5075

KERR GROUP, THE p 243
886 WEMBLEY RD UNIT5, PARKSVILLE, BC, V9P 2E6
(250) 586-1100   SIC 6531

KERR INDUSTRIES LIMITED p 812
635 FAREWELL ST, OSHAWA, ON, L1H 6N2
(905) 725-6561   SIC 7549

KERR INTERIOR SYSTEMS LTD p 115
9335 62 AVE NW, EDMONTON, AB, T6E 0E1
(780) 466-2800   SIC 1742

KERR INVESTMENT HOLDING CORP p 806
381 NORTH SERVICE RD W, OAKVILLE, ON, L6M 0H4
(905) 678-3119   SIC 6712

KERR NORTON p 1393
See 1021076 ONTARIO INC

KERR WOOD LEIDAL ASSOCIATES LTD p 186
4185A STILL CREEK DR SUITE 200, BURNABY, BC, V5C 6G9
(604) 294-2088   SIC 8742

KERR, WILLIAM J LTD p 405
365 WELLINGTON ST, MIRAMICHI, NB, E1N 1P6
SIC 1542

KERRIO CORPORATION p 759
6546 FALLSVIEW BLVD, NIAGARA FALLS, ON, L2G 3W2
(905) 356-6965   SIC 5812

KERRISDALE CAMERAS LTD p 322
2170 41ST AVE W, VANCOUVER, BC, V6M 1Z5
(604) 263-3221   SIC 5946

KERRISDALE LUMBER CO LTD p 322
6191 WEST BOULEVARD, VANCOUVER,

BC, V6M 3X3
(604) 261-4274 SIC 5211
KERRS p 575
See KERR BROS. LIMITED
KERRY (CANADA) INC p 1036
615 JACK ROSS AVE, WOODSTOCK, ON,
N4V 1B7
(519) 537-3461 SIC 2099
KERRY INGREDIENTS AND FLAVORS p
500
See RECTOR FOODS LIMITED
KERRY'S PLACE AUTISM SERVICES p 481
34 BERCZY ST UNIT 190, AURORA, ON,
L4G 1W9
(905) 841-6611 SIC 8399
KESMAC INC p 628
23324 WOODBINE AVE, KESWICK, ON,
L4P 3E9
(888) 341-5113 SIC 3523
KESWICK HIGH SCHOOL p 628
See YORK REGION DISTRICT SCHOOL
BOARD
KESWICK PRICE CHOPPER p 628
See 2144011 ONTARIO INC
KETCHUM CANADA p 948
See 582219 ONTARIO INC
KETCHUM MANUFACTURING INC p 519
1245 CALIFORNIA AVE, BROCKVILLE,
ON, K6V 7N5
(613) 342-8455 SIC 3999
KETER CANADA INC p 684
205 MARKET DR, MILTON, ON, L9T 4Z7
(905) 864-6695 SIC 5712
KETTLE FRIENDSHIP SOCIETY p 285
1725 VENABLES ST, VANCOUVER, BC,
V5L 2H3
(604) 251-2856 SIC 8699
KETTLE VALLEY STONE DIV OF p 220
See L & D PETCH CONTRACTING LTD
KETZA CONSTRUCTION CORP p 1440
107 PLATINUM RD, WHITEHORSE, YT,
Y1A 5M3
(867) 668-5997 SIC 1542
**KETZA PACIFIC CONSTRUCTION (1993)
LTD** p 195
2990 ISLAND HWY, CAMPBELL RIVER,
BC, V9W 2H5
(250) 850-2002 SIC 1542
KEURIG CANADA INC p 1170
3700 RUE JEAN-RIVARD BUREAU 1,
MONTREAL, QC, H1Z 4K3
(514) 593-7711 SIC 2095
KEVCO PIPELINES LTD p 16
5050 54 AVE SE, CALGARY, AB, T2C 2Y8
(403) 279-5050 SIC 1623
KEVIN'S NO FRILLS p 800
See 81918 ONTARIO LTD
KEVLAR - COMPLEXE DE VILLE p 1197
See INVESTISSEMENTS IMMOBILIERS
KEVLAR INC
KEVRIC p 1230
See RIMANESA PROPERTIES INC
KEW MEDIA GROUP INC p 989
672 DUPONT ST, TORONTO, ON, M6G 1Z6
(647) 956-1965 SIC 7812
KEY FOOD EQUIPMENT SERVICES LTD p
193
8528 GLENLYON PKY SUITE 145, BURN-
ABY, BC, V5J 0B6
(800) 665-2655 SIC 5023
KEY INSURANCE SERVICES p 240
See 89536 BC LTD
KEY LEASE CANADA LTD p 249
2005 REDWOOD ST, PRINCE GEORGE,
BC, V2L 2N5
(250) 564-7205 SIC 5511
KEY SEISMIC SOLUTIONS LTD p 52
205 5 AVE SW SUITE 700, CALGARY, AB,
T2P 2V7
(403) 232-6557 SIC 8999
KEY TAG SERVICE p 914
See WAR AMPUTATIONS OF CANADA,
THE
KEY TAG SERVICE, THE p 828

See WAR AMPUTATIONS OF CANADA,
THE
KEY WEST FORD SALES LTD p 237
301 STEWARDSON WAY, NEW WESTMIN-
STER, BC, V3M 2A5
(604) 239-7832 SIC 5511
KEYANO COLLEGE p 128
8115 FRANKLIN AVE, FORT MCMURRAY,
AB, T9H 2H7
(780) 791-4800 SIC 8221
KEYBASE FINANCIAL GROUP INC p 852
1725 16TH AVE SUIT1 101, RICHMOND
HILL, ON, L4B 0B3
(905) 709-7911 SIC 8742
KEYBASE FINANCIAL GROUP INC p 852
1725 16TH AVE SUITE 101, RICHMOND
HILL, ON, L4B 0B3
(905) 709-7911 SIC 8741
KEYBRAND FOODS p 635
See FRESHSTONE BRANDS INC
KEYCONTACT p 649
See PARNALL MAILING CORP
KEYCORP INC p 430
303 THORBURN RD, ST. JOHN'S, NL, A1B
4R1
(709) 753-2284 SIC 6794
KEYENCE CANADA INC p 723
6775 FINANCIAL DR SUITE 202, MISSIS-
SAUGA, ON, L5N 0A4
(905) 366-7655 SIC 5085
KEYERA CORP p 52
144 4 AVE SW SUITE 200, CALGARY, AB,
T2P 3N4
(403) 205-8300 SIC 1389
KEYERA ENERGY LTD p 52
144 4 AVE SW SUITE 600, CALGARY, AB,
T2P 3N4
(403) 205-8300 SIC 4922
KEYERA PARTNERSHIP p 52
144 4 AVE SW 2ND FL SUITE 600, CAL-
GARY, AB, T2P 3N4
(403) 205-8414 SIC 4925
KEYERA PARTNERSHIP p 158
44-01 W5 03-05, RIMBEY, AB, T0C 2J0
(403) 843-7100 SIC 1311
KEYESBURY DISTRIBUTORS LIMITED p
540
99 BRUCE CRES, CARLETON PLACE, ON,
K7C 3T3
(613) 257-8100 SIC 5064
KEYMAY INTERNATIONAL INC p 161
53169 RANGE ROAD 225, SHERWOOD
PARK, AB, T8A 4T7
(780) 417-1955 SIC 5085
KEYNOR SPRING MANUFACTURING p 324
See NORSWAY INVESTMENTS & CON-
SULTANTS INC
KEYRUS p 1189
See KEYRUS CANADA INC
KEYRUS CANADA INC p 1189
759 RUE DU SQUARE-VICTORIA UNIT
420, MONTREAL, QC, H2Y 2J7
(514) 989-2000 SIC 7379
**KEYSTONE AGRICULTURE & RECRE-
ATION CENTRE INC** p
346
1175 18TH ST UNIT 1, BRANDON, MB,
R7A 7C5
(204) 726-3500 SIC 7389
KEYSTONE AUTOMOTIVE p 816
See KEYSTONE AUTOMOTIVE INDUS-
TRIES ON INC
KEYSTONE AUTOMOTIVE INDUSTRIES p
1348
See KEYSTONE AUTOMOTIVE INDUS-
TRIES ON INC
**KEYSTONE AUTOMOTIVE INDUSTRIES
ON INC** p 816
1230 OLD INNES RD SUITE 401, OTTAWA,
ON, K1B 3V3
(613) 745-4088 SIC 5013
**KEYSTONE AUTOMOTIVE INDUSTRIES
ON INC** p 1348
2095 RUE DE L'INDUSTRIE, SAINT-

MATHIEU-DE-BELOEIL, QC, J3G 4S5
(450) 464-2511 SIC 5013
**KEYSTONE AUTOMOTIVE OPERATIONS
OF CANADA INC** p 688
3770 NASHUA DR UNIT 4, MISSISSAUGA,
ON, L4V 1M5
(905) 405-0999 SIC 5013
KEYSTONE CENTRE p 346
See KEYSTONE AGRICULTURE &
RECREATION CENTRE INC
KEYSTONE ENVIRONMENTAL LTD p 189
4400 DOMINION ST SUITE 320, BURN-
ABY, BC, V5G 4G3
(604) 430-0671 SIC 8748
KEYSTONE EXCAVATING LTD p 12
4860 35 ST SE, CALGARY, AB, T2B 3M6
(403) 274-5452 SIC 1794
KEYSTONE WESTERN INC p 350
594 BERNAT RD, GRANDE POINTE, MB,
R5A 1H5
(204) 256-0800 SIC 4213
KF AEROSPACE p 218
See KELOWNA FLIGHTCRAFT LTD
KFC p 524
See PIONEER FOOD SERVICES LIMITED
KFC p 1007
See TWINCORP INC
KFSI p 927
See KINGSWAY FINANCIAL SERVICES
INC
KG GROUP RENTAL OFFICE p 922
See K & G APARTMENT HOLDINGS INC
KGC p 964
See KINROSS GOLD CORPORATION
KGHM AJAX MINING INC p 217
124 SEYMOUR ST SUITE 200, KAM-
LOOPS, BC, V2C 2E1
(250) 374-5446 SIC 1021
KGHM AJAX MINING INC p 306
800 PENDER ST W SUITE 615, VANCOU-
VER, BC, V6C 2V6
(604) 682-0301 SIC 1021
KGHM INTERNATIONAL LTD p 1032
191 CREDITVIEW RD SUITE 400, WOOD-
BRIDGE, ON, L4L 9T1
(647) 265-9191 SIC 1081
KGS GROUP p 391
See KONTZAMANIS GRAUMANN SMITH
MACMILLAN INC
KHALSA SCHOOL p 276
6933 124 ST, SURREY, BC, V3W 3W6
(604) 591-2248 SIC 8299
KHALSA SCHOOL p 277
See SATNAM EDUCATION SOCIETY OF
BRITISH COLUMBIA
KHALSA UNION TRADING COMPANY p
1032
418 HANLAN RD SUITE 17, WOOD-
BRIDGE, ON, L4L 4Z1
(905) 851-7999 SIC 5149
KHANNA TRANSPORT INC p 580
100 WESTMORE DR SUITE 12B, ETOBI-
COKE, ON, M9V 5C3
(416) 675-9388 SIC 4213
KHEERAN INSPECTION SERVICES INC p
149
702 23 AVE, NISKU, AB, T9E 7Y6
(780) 800-6295 SIC 7389
KHEOPS INTERNATIONALE p 1113
See KHEOPS VERRE D'ART INC
KHEOPS VERRE D'ART INC p 1113
541 8E RANG, HAM-NORD, QC, G0P 1A0
(819) 344-2152 SIC 5049
KHETIA PHARMACY INC p 786
1084 WILSON AVE, NORTH YORK, ON,
M3K 1G6
(416) 633-9884 SIC 5912
KHOWUTZUN DEVELOPMENT CORP p 212
200 COWICHAN WAY, DUNCAN, BC, V9L
6P4
SIC 8741
KI CANADA CORPORATION p 838
1000 OLYMPIC DR, PEMBROKE, ON, K8A
0E1

(613) 735-5566 SIC 2514
KIA p 731
See KIA CANADA INC
KIA CANADA INC p 731
180 FOSTER CRES, MISSISSAUGA, ON,
L5R 4J5
(905) 755-6250 SIC 5012
KIA CAP SANTE INC p 1074
5 CH DU BOIS-DE-L'AIL, CAP-SANTE, QC,
G0A 1L0
(418) 285-5555 SIC 5561
KIA CAP-SANTE p 1355
See 9097-8875 QUEBEC INC
KIA LEVIS p 1139
See 9218-8069 QUEBEC INC
KIA MARIO BLAIN p 1151
See CENTRE DE L'AUTO BLAIN, MARIO
INC, LE
KIA MOTORS LP p 94
13634 ST ALBERT TRAIL NW, EDMON-
TON, AB, T5L 4P3
(780) 509-1500 SIC 5511
KIA OF SASKATOON p 1424
See 101013121 SASKATCHEWAN LTD
KIA OF TIMMINS p 913
1285 RIVERSIDE DR, TIMMINS, ON, P4R
1A6
(705) 267-8291 SIC 5511
KIA ON HUNT CLUB p 831
See 2310884 ONTARIO INC
KIA SAINT-LEONARD p 1239
See 9080-3404 QUEBEC INC
KIA SOUTH VANCOUVER p 290
396 MARINE DR SW, VANCOUVER, BC,
V5X 2R6
(604) 326-6868 SIC 5511
KIA STE-FOY p 1263
See 9153-7639 QUEBEC INC
KIA WEST p 202
See WEST AUTO SALES LTD
KIA WEST EDMONTON p 98
See 864475 ALBERTA LTD
KIANGTEX COMPANY LIMITED p 917
46 HOLLINGER RD, TORONTO, ON, M4B
3G5
(416) 750-3771 SIC 5137
KIANI MOTORS LTD p 241
1980 MARINE DR, NORTH VANCOUVER,
BC, V7P 1V6
(604) 987-4490 SIC 5541
KICHTON CONTRACTING LTD p 1
25296 117 AVE, ACHESON, AB, T7X 6C2
(780) 447-1882 SIC 1794
KIDCO CONSTRUCTION LTD p 16
4949 76 AVE SE, CALGARY, AB, T2C 3C6
(403) 730-2029 SIC 1629
KIDD, H.A. AND COMPANY LIMITED p 917
5 NORTHLINE RD, TORONTO, ON, M4B
3P2
(416) 364-6451 SIC 3965
KIDDE CANADA INC p 554
340 FOUR VALLEY DR, CONCORD, ON,
L4K 5Z1
(905) 695-6060 SIC 5099
KIDLOGIC p 684
See KINDERSTAR INC
KIDS CLOTHING WAREHOUSE p 1179
See HAPPY KIDS CANADA INC
KIDS HELP PHONE p 946
439 UNIVERSITY AVE SUITE 300,
TORONTO, ON, M5G 1Y8
(416) 586-5437 SIC 8322
KIDS IN THE HALL BISTRO p 85
See EDMONTON CITY CENTRE CHURCH
CORPORATION
KIDS LINK/ NDSA p 883
1855 NOTRE DAME DR, ST AGATHA, ON,
N0B 2L0
(519) 746-5437 SIC 8699
KIDSINKS HOLDINGS INC p 823
100 ELGIN ST, OTTAWA, ON, K1P 5K8
(613) 235-3333 SIC 6513
**KIDZINC SCHOOL AGE CARE SOCIETY
OF ALBERTA** p 73

4411 10 AVE SW, CALGARY, AB, T3C 0L9
(403) 240-2059   SIC 8699

KIEF MUSIC LTD   p 276
13139 80 AVE SUITE 1, SURREY, BC, V3W 3B1
SIC 5099

KIESWETTER MOTORS INC   p 641
4202 KING ST E, KITCHENER, ON, N2P 2G5
(519) 653-2540   SIC 5521

KIEWIT CONSTRUCTION SERVICES ULC p 68
10333 SOUTHPORT RD SW SUITE 200, CALGARY, AB, T2W 3X6
(403) 693-8701   SIC 1541

KIEWIT ENGINEERING CANADA CO.
1062
4333 BOUL DE LA GRANDE-ALLEE, BOIS-BRIAND, QC, J7H 1M7
(450) 435-5756   SIC 1629

KIEWIT, PETER INFRASTRUCTURE p 186
See PETER KIEWIT INFRASTRUCTURE CO.

KIEWIT-NUVUMIUT, SOCIETE EN COPAR-TICIPATION   p
1062
4333 BOUL DE LA GRANDE-ALLEE, BOIS-BRIAND, QC, J7H 1M7
(450) 435-5756   SIC 1081

KIEWIT-PARSONS, UN PARTENARIAT
1062
4333 BOUL DE LA GRANDE-ALLEE, BOIS-BRIAND, QC, J7H 1M7
(450) 435-5756   SIC 1622

KIEWIT/FLATIRON GENERAL PARTNER-SHIP   p
314
1111 GEORGIA ST W SUITE 1410, VAN-COUVER, BC, V6E 4M3
SIC 1542

KIK   p 1008
See KIK INTERACTIVE INC.

KIK CUSTOM PRODUCTS   p 554
See KIK HOLDCO COMPANY INC

KIK CUSTOM PRODUCTS   p 585
See KIK HOLDCO COMPANY INC

KIK HOLDCO COMPANY INC   p 554
101 MACINTOSH BLVD, CONCORD, ON, L4K 4R5
(905) 660-0444   SIC 6719

KIK HOLDCO COMPANY INC   p 585
2000 KIPLING AVE, ETOBICOKE, ON, M9W 4J6
(416) 743-6255   SIC 2842

KIK HOLDCO COMPANY INC   p 585
13 BETHRIDGE RD, ETOBICOKE, ON, M9W 1M6
(416) 740-7400   SIC 2842

KIK INTERACTIVE INC.   p 1008
420 WEBER ST N SUITE I, WATERLOO, ON, N2L 4E7
(226) 868-0056   SIC 7371

KIL INVESTMENTS LTD   p 401
251 WOODSTOCK RD, FREDERICTON, NB, E3B 2H8
(506) 457-4386   SIC 5812

KILDAIR SERVICE ULC   p 1379
1000 MONTEE DES PIONNIERS BUREAU 110, TERREBONNE, QC, J6V 1S8
(450) 756-8091   SIC 5172

KILDONAN AUTO & TRUCK PARTS p 357
See KILDONAN VENTURES LTD

KILDONAN CROSSING SAFEWAY   p 363
See SOBEYS WEST INC

KILDONAN VENTURES LTD   p 357
2850 DAY ST, SPRINGFIELD, MB, R2C 2Z2
SIC 5013

KILDONAN-EAST COLLEGIATE   p 367
See RIVER EAST TRANSCONA SCHOOL DIVISION

KILIAN CANADA ULC   p 575
75 TORLAKE CRES, ETOBICOKE, ON, M8Z 1B7
(416) 252-5936   SIC 5085

KILKENNY IRISH PUB   p 40
See DOUBLE ARROW VENTURES LTD

KILKENNY REAL ESTATE LTD   p 387
663 STAFFORD ST, WINNIPEG, MB, R3M 2X7
(204) 475-9130   SIC 6531

KILLAM APARTMENT REAL ESTATE IN-VESTMENT TRUST   p
455
3700 KEMPT RD SUITE 100, HALIFAX, NS, B3K 4X8
(902) 453-9000   SIC 6798

KILLAM APARTMENT REIT   p 455
See KILLAM APARTMENT REAL ESTATE INVESTMENT TRUST

KILLAM PROPERTIES INC   p 455
3700 KEMPT RD SUITE 100, HALIFAX, NS, B3K 4X8
(902) 453-9000   SIC 6513

KILLARNEY AUCTION MART LTD   p 351
2 17 W SUITE 27, KILLARNEY, MB, R0K 1G0
(204) 523-8477   SIC 5154

KILLARNEY SECONDARY SCHOOL p 288
See BOARD OF EDUCATION OF SCHOOL DISTRICT NO. 39 (VANCOUVER), THE

KILLICK AEROSPACE HOLDING INC. p 52
855 2 ST SW SUITE 3500, CALGARY, AB, T2P 4J8
SIC 6712

KILO GATEAUX   p 1217
See 138984 CANADA LTEE

KILO GATEAUX LTEE   p 1217
6744 RUE HUTCHISON, MONTREAL, QC, H3N 1Y4
(514) 270-3024   SIC 5149

KIM & CO   p 1179
See KIM-LAUREN & CIE INC

KIM MOON BAKERY   p 977
See K.M. BAKERY

KIM'S FARM   p 279
4186 176 ST, SURREY, BC, V3Z 1C3
(604) 649-7938   SIC 0119

KIM-LAUREN & CIE INC   p 1179
9400 BOUL SAINT-LAURENT BUREAU 402, MONTREAL, QC, H2N 1P3
(514) 385-3582   SIC 5137

KIM-TAM LOGISTICS INC   p 704
2360 DIXIE RD, MISSISSAUGA, ON, L4Y 1Z7
(905) 335-9195   SIC 4212

KIMATSU ENTERPRISES   p 772
5334 YONGE ST, NORTH YORK, ON, M2N 6V1
SIC 6799

KIMATSU INTERNATIONAL   p 772
See KIMATSU ENTERPRISES

KIMBERLEY ALPINE RESORT   p 223
See RESORTS OF THE CANADIAN ROCK-IES INC

KIMBERLEY SEARCH & RESCUE SOCI-ETY   p
223
340 SPOKANE ST, KIMBERLEY, BC, V1A 2E8
(250) 427-5998   SIC 8699

KIMBERLEY SPECIAL CARE HOME p 223
See INTERIOR HEALTH KIMBERLY SPE-CIAL CARE HOME

KIMBERLEY TEACHER'S ASSOCIATION p
223
144 DEER PARK AVE SUITE 201, KIMBER-LEY, BC, V1A 2J4
(250) 427-3113   SIC 8621

KIMBERLY-CLARK INC   p 620
570 RAVENSCLIFFE RD, HUNTSVILLE, ON, P1H 2A1
(705) 788-5200   SIC 2621

KIMBERLY-CLARK INC   p 710
50 BURNHAMTHORPE RD W SUITE 1402, MISSISSAUGA, ON, L5B 3C2
(905) 277-6500   SIC 2676

KIMCOT INC   p 779
29 GERVAIS DR UNIT 203, NORTH YORK,
ON, M3C 1Y9
(416) 854-2772   SIC 4899

KIMMEL SALES LIMITED   p 554
126 EDILCAN DR UNIT 1, CONCORD, ON, L4K 3S5
(905) 669-2083   SIC 5141

KIMPEX ACTION   p 1100
See KIMPEX INC

KIMPEX INC   p 1100
5355 RUE SAINT-ROCH S BUREAU 4, DRUMMONDVILLE, QC, J2E 0B4
(819) 472-3326   SIC 5561

KIN LEM DRUGS LIMITED   p 632
1875 BATH RD, KINGSTON, ON, K7M 4Y3
(613) 384-6990   SIC 5912

KIN PLACE HEALTH COMPLEX   p 354
See NORTH EASTMAN HEALTH ASSOCI-ATION INC

KIN'S FARM LTD   p 263
12151 HORSESHOE WAY, RICHMOND, BC, V7A 4V4
(604) 272-2551   SIC 5141

KIN'S FARM MARKET   p 263
See GREENFIELD PRODUCE LTD

KINARK CHILD AND FAMILY SERVICES p
487
34 SIMCOE ST SUITE 3, BARRIE, ON, L4N 6T4
(888) 454-6275   SIC 8322

KINARK CHILD AND FAMILY SERVICES p
671
500 HOOD RD SUITE 200, MARKHAM, ON, L3R 9Z3
(905) 474-9595   SIC 8322

KINARK CHILD AND FAMILY SERVICES p
798
475 IROQUOIS SHORE RD, OAKVILLE, ON, L6H 1M3
(905) 844-4110   SIC 8322

KINAXIS INC   p 626
700 SILVER SEVEN RD SUITE 500, KANATA, ON, K2V 1C3
(613) 592-5780   SIC 7371

KINCARDINE SOBEYS   p 629
See SOBEYS CAPITAL INCORPORATED

KINCORA COPPER LIMITED   p 314
1199 WEST HASTINGS ST SUITE 800, VANCOUVER, BC, V6E 3T5
(604) 283-1722   SIC 1021

KINCORT BAKERY LIMITED   p 993
8 KINCORT ST, TORONTO, ON, M6M 3E1
(416) 651-7671   SIC 6719

KINDERSLEY AND DISTRICT CO-OPERATIVE LIMITED   p
1408
214 MAIN ST, KINDERSLEY, SK, S0L 1S0
(306) 463-2624   SIC 5171

KINDERSLEY INTERGRATED HEALTH CARE FACILITY   p 1408
See SASKATCHEWAN HEALTH AUTHOR-ITY

KINDERSLEY TRANSPORT LTD   p 16
5515 98 AVE SE, CALGARY, AB, T2C 4L1
(403) 279-8721   SIC 4213

KINDERSLEY TRANSPORT LTD   p 1428
2411 WENTZ AVE, SASKATOON, SK, S7K 3V6
(306) 242-3355   SIC 4213

KINDERSLEY TRANSPORT LTD   p 1428
2411 WENTZ AVE, SASKATOON, SK, S7K 3V6
(306) 975-9367   SIC 4213

KINDERSLEY TRANSPORT TERMINAL p
1428
See KINDERSLEY TRANSPORT LTD

KINDERSTAR INC   p 684
690 AUGER TERR, MILTON, ON, L9T 5M2
(905) 864-4420   SIC 6712

KINDRED CONSTRUCTION LTD   p 322
2150 BROADWAY W UNIT 308, VANCOU-VER, BC, V6K 4L9
(604) 736-4847   SIC 8741

KINDRED HOME CARE   p 418
See CHARLOTTE COUNTY HUMANE RE-

SOURCES INC

KINECTRICS   p 946
See KINECTRICS NSS INC

KINECTRICS INC   p 575
800 KIPLING AVE SUITE 2, ETOBICOKE, ON, M8Z 5G5
(416) 207-6000   SIC 3612

KINECTRICS NCL INC   p 996
800 KIPLING AVE UNIT 2, TORONTO, ON, M8Z 5G5
(416) 592-2102   SIC 1623

KINECTRICS NSS INC   p 946
393 UNIVERSITY AVE 4TH FLR, TORONTO, ON, M5G 1E6
(416) 592-7000   SIC 8999

KINEQUIP   p 1308
See NAUTILUS PLUS INC

KINETIC CAPITAL PARTNERS   p 319
1195 BROADWAY W SUITE 500, VANCOU-VER, BC, V6H 3X5
(604) 692-2530   SIC 6722

KINETIC CONSTRUCTION LTD   p 337
862 CLOVERDALE AVE SUITE 201, VIC-TORIA, BC, V8X 2S8
(250) 381-6331   SIC 1542

KINETIC HEALTH INC   p 939
140 YONGE ST, TORONTO, ON, M5C 1X6
(416) 302-4724   SIC 3842

KINETIC MOTORSPORT   p 281
See ADP DISTRIBUTORS INC

KINETIC PROJECTS   p 50
See GEMINI FIELD SOLUTIONS LTD

KINETICS DRIVE SOLUTIONS INC   p 229
27489 56 AVE, LANGLEY, BC, V4W 3X1
(604) 607-8877   SIC 3714

KING & TOWNLINE FRESHCO   p 563
See 1262510 ONTARIO LIMITED

KING ARCHITECTURAL PRODUCTS, DIV OF   p 496
See WSI SIGN SYSTEMS LTD

KING CAPON LIMITED   p 880
18347 WARDEN AVE, SHARON, ON, L0G 1V0
(905) 478-2382   SIC 5144

KING CITY SECONDARY SCHOOL   p 629
See YORK REGION DISTRICT SCHOOL BOARD

KING COLE DUCKS LIMITED   p 894
15351 WARDEN AVE, STOUFFVILLE, ON, L4A 2V5
(905) 836-9461   SIC 0259

KING CONSTRUCTION ENR   p 1243
84 RUE ONTARIO, NOTRE-DAME-DU-NORD, QC, J0Z 3B0
SIC 1521

KING EDWARD REALTY INC   p 939
37 KING ST E, TORONTO, ON, M5C 1E9
(416) 863-9700   SIC 7011

KING FREIGHT LINES LIMITED   p 464
131 HARRIS RD, PICTOU, NS, B0K 1H0
(902) 485-8077   SIC 4213

KING GEORGE CARRIAGE LTD   p 283
2466 KING GEORGE BLVD, SURREY, BC, V4P 1H5
(604) 536-2884   SIC 5511

KING GEORGE NISSAN   p 283
See BERO INVESTMENTS LTD

KING KOATING ROOFING INC   p 554
41 PEELAR RD, CONCORD, ON, L4K 1A3
(905) 669-1771   SIC 1761

KING MANUFACTURING   p 435
9 ASPEN RD, HAY RIVER, NT, X0E 0R6
(867) 874-2373   SIC 5085

KING MARKETING LTD   p 263
11121 HORSESHOE WAY SUITE 148, RICHMOND, BC, V7A 5G7
(604) 271-3455   SIC 8742

KING MAZDA INC   p 413
440 ROTHESAY AVE, SAINT JOHN, NB, E2J 2C4
(506) 634-8370   SIC 5511

KING METAL SPINNING, A DIV OF   p 786
See CROWN FOOD SERVICE EQUIP-MENT LTD

KING NURSING HOME LIMITED *p 495*
49 STERNE ST, BOLTON, ON, L7E 1B9
(905) 857-4117 *SIC 8051*
KING PAVING & MATERIALS COMPANY *p 804*
See KPM INDUSTRIES LTD
KING'S EMBROIDERY LTD *p 874*
225 NUGGET AVE SUITE 6, SCARBOROUGH, ON, M1S 3L2
(416) 292-7471 *SIC 7389*
KING'S ENERGY SERVICES LTD *p 158*
277 BURNT PARK DR, RED DEER COUNTY, AB, T4S 0K7
(403) 343-2822 *SIC 5085*
KING'S HEALTH CENTRE CORPORATION THE *p 953*
250 UNIVERSITY AVE, TORONTO, ON, M5H 3E5
SIC 8093
KING'S HUSKY
See KAYFORE HOLDINGS LTD *p 144*
KING'S PASTRY *p 729*
See 1721502 ONTARIO INC
KING'S RIDING GOLD CLUB *p 629*
See CLUBLINK CORPORATION ULC
KING'S TRANSFER INTERNATIONAL *p 1211*
See KING'S TRANSFER VAN LINES INC
KING'S TRANSFER VAN LINES INC *p 1211*
287 RUE ELEANOR, MONTREAL, QC, H3C 2C1
(514) 932-2957 *SIC 4212*
KING'S UNIVERSITY COLLEGE AT THE UNIVERSITY OF WESTERN ONTARIO *p 654*
266 EPWORTH AVE, LONDON, ON, N6A 2M3
(519) 433-3491 *SIC 8221*
KING'S UNIVERSITY COLLEGE, THE, *p 109*
9125 50 ST NW, EDMONTON, AB, T6B 2H3
(780) 465-3500 *SIC 8221*
KING'S, ERIC FISHERIES LIMITED *p 421*
17 PLANT RD SUITE 15, BURNT ISLANDS BLP, NL, A0M 1B0
(709) 698-3421 *SIC 2091*
KING-O-MATIC INDUSTRIES LIMITED *p 696*
955 PANTERA DR, MISSISSAUGA, ON, L4W 2T4
(905) 624-1956 *SIC 5531*
KING-REED HOLDINGS LTD *p 776*
85 SCARSDALE RD SUITE 309, NORTH YORK, ON, M3B 2R2
(416) 449-8677 *SIC 6712*
KINGBRIDGE CENTRE, THE *p 629*
See KCLC PROPERTIES ULC
KINGDOM CATS LTD *p 81*
108 CHRISTINA LAKE DR, CONKLIN, AB, T0P 1H1
(780) 715-4356 *SIC 1542*
KINGDOM HALL JEHOVAH'S WITNESS *p 1012*
See WATCH TOWER BIBLE AND TRACT SOCIETY OF CANADA
KINGDOM HALL OF JEHOVAH'S WITNESSES *p 363*
See JEHOVAH'S WITNESSES EAST ST PAUL CONGREGATION
KINGDON LUMBER LIMITED *p 643*
34 DEYNCOURT ST, LAKEFIELD, ON, K0L 2H0
(705) 652-3361 *SIC 5211*
KINGDON TIM-BR MART *p 643*
See KINGDON LUMBER LIMITED
KINGFISHER BOATS INC *p 331*
8160 HIGHLAND RD, VERNON, BC, V1B 3W6
(250) 545-9171 *SIC 3732*
KINGLAND FORD SALES LTD *p 435*
922 MACKENZIE HWY SS 22, HAY RIVER, NT, X0E 0R8
SIC 5511
KINGLAND TRUCK & WELDING *p 435*
See KINGLAND FORD SALES LTD

KINGS COUNTY CONSTRUCTION LIMITED *p 1041*
5284A A MACDONALD HWY, MONTAGUE, PE, C0A 1R0
(902) 838-2191 *SIC 1611*
KINGS COUNTY MEMORIAL HOSPITAL *p 1041*
409 MCINTYRE AVE, MONTAGUE, PE, C0A 1R0
(902) 838-0777 *SIC 8062*
KINGS COUNTY SENIOR CITIZENS HOME CORP *p 441*
110A COMMERCIAL ST RR 1, BERWICK, NS, B0P 1E0
(902) 538-3118 *SIC 8051*
KINGS MUTUAL INSURANCE COMPANY, THE *p 441*
220 COMMERCIAL ST, BERWICK, NS, B0P 1E0
(902) 538-3187 *SIC 6411*
KINGS REGIONAL REHABILITATION CENTRE *p 470*
1349 COUNTY RD, WATERVILLE, NS, B0P 1V0
(902) 538-3103 *SIC 8069*
KINGSCROSS HYUNDAI MOTOR SPORTS INC *p 868*
23 CIVIC RD, SCARBOROUGH, ON, M1L 2K6
(416) 757-7700 *SIC 5511*
KINGSCROSS MOTOR SPORTS INC *p 868*
1957 EGLINTON AVE E, SCARBOROUGH, ON, M1L 2M3
(416) 755-6283 *SIC 5511*
KINGSDOWN CANADA *p 1028*
See OWEN & COMPANY LIMITED
KINGSETT CAPITAL INC *p 953*
40 KING ST W SUITE 3700, TORONTO, ON, M5H 3Y2
(416) 687-6700 *SIC 6798*
KINGSPAN INSULATED PANELS LTD *p 495*
12557 COLERAINE DR, BOLTON, ON, L7E 3B5
(905) 951-5600 *SIC 3448*
KINGSTON AND THE ISLANDS POLITICAL PARTY *p 631*
15 ALAMEIN DR, KINGSTON, ON, K7L 4R5
(613) 546-6081 *SIC 8651*
KINGSTON BYERS INC *p 1132*
9100 RUE ELMSLIE, LASALLE, QC, H8R 1V6
(514) 365-1642 *SIC 1541*
KINGSTON DODGE CHRYSLER (1980) LTD *p 632*
1429 PRINCESS ST, KINGSTON, ON, K7M 3E9
(613) 549-8900 *SIC 5511*
KINGSTON DODGE JEEP EAGLE LTD *p 632*
1429 PRINCESS ST, KINGSTON, ON, K7M 3E9
(613) 549-8900 *SIC 5511*
KINGSTON FUELS LTD *p 405*
249 DUKE ST, MIRAMICHI, NB, E1N 1J5
(506) 773-6426 *SIC 5983*
KINGSTON GENERAL HOSPITAL *p 631*
See KINGSTON HEALTH SCIENCES CENTRE
KINGSTON GENERAL HOSPITAL *p 631*
76 STUART ST, KINGSTON, ON, K7L 2V7
(613) 548-3232 *SIC 8062*
KINGSTON HEALTH SCIENCES CENTRE *p 631*
76 STUART ST, KINGSTON, ON, K7L 2V7
(613) 549-6666 *SIC 8062*
KINGSTON HUSKY CAR & TRUCK STOP *p 623*
See 1085453 ONTARIO LTD
KINGSTON HYUNDAI *p 631*
See 1034020 ONTARIO LTD
KINGSTON INDEPENDENT NYLON WORKERS UNION OFFICE & RECREATION CENTRE *p*

632
725 ARLINGTON PARK PL, KINGSTON, ON, K7M 7E4
(613) 389-5255 *SIC 6371*
KINGSTON NISSAN *p 631*
See 421342 ONTARIO LIMITED
KINGSTON REGIONAL CANCER CENTR *p 630*
See CANCER CARE ONTARIO
KINGSTON ROSS PASNAK LLP *p 89*
9888 JASPER AVE NW SUITE 1500, EDMONTON, AB, T5J 5C6
(780) 424-3000 *SIC 8721*
KINGSTON SUPERCENTRE STORE- #3043 *p 633*
See WAL-MART CANADA CORP
KINGSTON VOLKSWAGEN *p 631*
See 995547 ONTARIO LTD
KINGSTON WHIG STANDARD, THE *p 630*
See OSPREY MEDIA PUBLISHING INC
KINGSVILLE STAMPING LIMITED *p 634*
1931 SETTERINGTON DR, KINGSVILLE, ON, N9Y 2E5
(519) 326-6331 *SIC 3469*
KINGSWAY ARMS MANAGEMENT (AT CARLETON PLACE) INC *p 540*
6 ARTHUR ST, CARLETON PLACE, ON, K7C 4S4
(613) 253-7360 *SIC 6513*
KINGSWAY ARMS MANAGEMENT (AT ELGIN LODGE) INC *p 847*
551 MARY ST, PORT ELGIN, ON, N0H 2C2
(519) 389-5457 *SIC 6513*
KINGSWAY COLLEGE *p 814*
1200 LELAND RD, OSHAWA, ON, L1K 2H4
(905) 433-1144 *SIC 2499*
KINGSWAY FINANCIAL SERVICES INC *p 927*
45 ST CLAIR AVE W STE 400, TORONTO, ON, M4V 1K9
(416) 848-1171 *SIC 6331*
KINGSWAY HONDA *p 289*
See DESTINATION AUTO SALES INC
KINGSWAY LODGE ST. MARYS LTD *p 888*
310 QUEEN ST E, ST MARYS, ON, N4X 1C8
(519) 284-2921 *SIC 8051*
KINGSWAY MOTORS (1982) LTD *p 84*
12820 97 ST NW, EDMONTON, AB, T5E 4C3
(780) 478-8300 *SIC 5511*
KINGSWAY TOYOTA *p 84*
See KINGSWAY MOTORS (1982) LTD
KINGSWAY TRANSPORT *p 701*
See TRANSPORT TFI 5, S.E.C.
KINGSWAY TRANSPORT OF AMERICA *p 1337*
See TRANSPORT TFI 5, S.E.C.
KINGSWAY VRAC *p 1293*
See TRANSPORT TFI 4, S.E.C.
KINGSWOOD FAMILY ENTERTAINMENT *p 403*
See MCFADZEN HOLDINGS LIMITED
KINNEAR INDUSTRIES CORPORATION LIMITED *p 706*
254 MATHESON BLVD E, MISSISSAUGA, ON, L4Z 1P5
(905) 890-1402 *SIC 5031*
KINNIKINNICK FOODS INC *p 86*
10940 120 ST NW, EDMONTON, AB, T5H 3P7
(780) 732-7527 *SIC 5461*
KINOVA INC *p 1062*
4333 BOUL DE LA GRANDE-ALLEE, BOISBRIAND, QC, J7H 1M7
(514) 277-3777 *SIC 3549*
KINOVA ROBOTICS *p 1062*
See KINOVA INC
KINROSS GOLD CORPORATION *p 882*
4315 GOLDMINE RD, SOUTH PORCUPINE, ON, P0N 1H0
SIC 1041
KINROSS GOLD CORPORATION *p 964*

25 YORK ST 17TH FL, TORONTO, ON, M5J 2V5
(416) 365-5123 *SIC 1081*
KINSEY ENTERPRISES INC *p 1*
26650 116 AVE, ACHESON, AB, T7X 6H2
(780) 452-0467 *SIC 1731*
KINSMEN PLACE LODGE *p 274*
See WHALLEY & DISTRICT SENIOR CITIZEN HOUSING SOCIETY
KINSMEN RETIREMENT CENTRE ASSOCIATION *p 211*
5410 10 AVE, DELTA, BC, V4M 3X8
(604) 943-0155 *SIC 8361*
KINTETSU INTERNATIONAL EXPRESS (CANADA) INC *p 314*
1140 PENDER ST W SUITE 910, VANCOUVER, BC, V6E 4G1
(778) 328-9754 *SIC 4724*
KINTETSU WORLD EXPRESS (CANADA) INC *p 688*
6405 NORTHAM DR, MISSISSAUGA, ON, L4V 1J2
(905) 677-8830 *SIC 4731*
KIOV INCORPORATED *p 860*
411 CHRISTINA ST N, SARNIA, ON, N7T 5V8
(519) 336-1320 *SIC 5812*
KIPNESS CENTRE FOR VETERANS INC *p 84*
4470 MCCRAE AVE NW, EDMONTON, AB, T5E 6M8
(780) 442-5700 *SIC 8641*
KIRBY INTERNATIONAL TRUCKS LTD *p 636*
48 ARDELT AVE, KITCHENER, ON, N2C 2C9
(519) 578-6680 *SIC 5511*
KIRCHHOFF AUTOMOTIVE *p 850*
See KIRCHHOFF AUTOMOTIVE CANADA INC
KIRCHHOFF AUTOMOTIVE CANADA INC *p 795*
114 CLAYSON RD, NORTH YORK, ON, M9M 2H2
(416) 740-2656 *SIC 3469*
KIRCHHOFF AUTOMOTIVE CANADA INC *p 850*
25 MURAL ST, RICHMOND, ON, L4B 1J4
(905) 727-8585 *SIC 3465*
KIRIN SEAFOOD RESTAURANT *p 292*
See 360641 BC LTD
KIRK CHITICK PETERBOROUGH AUTO *p 841*
898 FORD ST, PETERBOROUGH, ON, K9J 5V3
(705) 536-0050 *SIC 5511*
KIRKFIELD HOTEL LIMITED *p 386*
3317 PORTAGE AVE, WINNIPEG, MB, R3K 0W8
(204) 837-1314 *SIC 5921*
KIRKFIELD MOTOR HOTEL *p 386*
See KIRKFIELD HOTEL LIMITED
KIRKLAND LAKE DISTRICT COMPOSITE SCHOOL *p 634*
See DISTRICT SCHOOL BOARD ONTARIO NORTH EAST
KIRKLAND LAKE GOLD LTD *p 634*
1350 GOVERNMENT RD W, KIRKLAND LAKE, ON, P2N 3J1
(705) 567-5208 *SIC 1081*
KIRKLAND LAKE GOLD LTD *p 964*
200 BAY ST SUITE 3120, TORONTO, ON, M5J 2J1
(416) 840-7884 *SIC 1041*
KIRKLAND LAKE POWER CORP *p 634*
505 ARCHER DR, KIRKLAND LAKE, ON, P2N 3M7
(705) 567-9501 *SIC 4911*
KIRKWOOD & MURPHY LTD *p 696*
5150 TIMBERLEA BLVD, MISSISSAUGA, ON, L4W 2S5
(905) 602-6900 *SIC 5199*
KIRKWOOD GROUP LTD, THE *p 806*

1155 NORTH SERVICE RD W SUITE 8, OAKVILLE, ON, L6M 3E3
(905) 849-4346   *SIC* 5182
KIRMAC AUTOMOTIVE COLLISION SYSTEMS (CANADA) INC   *p* 198
2714 BARNET HWY SUITE 104, COQUITLAM, BC, V3B 1B8
(604) 461-4494   *SIC* 7532
KIRMAC CARSTAR COLLISION   *p* 198
See KIRMAC AUTOMOTIVE COLLISION SYSTEMS (CANADA) INC
KIRSKA TRANSPORTATION   *p* 740
See KRISKA HOLDINGS LIMITED
KIS   *p* 684
See KETER CANADA INC
KISA ENTERPRISES LTD   *p* 240
2305 LONSDALE AVE, NORTH VANCOUVER, BC, V7M 2K9
(604) 986-0288   *SIC* 5541
KISKO PRODUCTS   *p* 1026
See 329985 ONTARIO LIMITED
KISQUARED CORPORATION   *p* 374
388 DONALD ST SUITE 226, WINNIPEG, MB, R3B 2J4
(204) 989-8002   *SIC* 8732
KISSNER MILLING COMPANY LIMITED   *p* 636
148 MANITOU DR SUITE 301, KITCHENER, ON, N2C 1L3
(519) 279-4860   *SIC* 5169
KISSNER SALTS & CHEMICALS   *p* 636
See KISSNER MILLING COMPANY LIMITED
KITCHEN CRAFT   *p* 362
See KITCHEN CRAFT OF CANADA
KITCHEN CRAFT OF CANADA   *p* 362
1180 SPRINGFIELD RD, WINNIPEG, MB, R2C 2Z2
(204) 224-3211   *SIC* 2434
KITCHEN GROUP, THE   *p* 388
See THE KITCHING GROUP (CANADA) INC.
KITCHEN STUFF PLUS INC   *p* 988
125 TYCOS DR, TORONTO, ON, M6B 1W6
(416) 944-2847   *SIC* 5719
KITCHEN TABLE GROCERY STORES *p* 964
See KITCHEN TABLE INCORPORATED, THE
KITCHEN TABLE INCORPORATED, THE   *p* 964
12 QUEENS QUAY W SUITE 416, TORONTO, ON, M5J 2V7
(416) 778-4800   *SIC* 5411
KITCHENER AERO AVIONICS LIMITED   *p* 518
4881 FOUNTAIN ST N SUITE 6, BRESLAU, ON, N0B 1M0
(519) 648-2921   *SIC* 7629
KITCHENER FOREST PRODUCTS INC   *p* 912
1300 JACKSON, TILLSONBURG, ON, N4G 4G7
(519) 842-7381   *SIC* 5031
KITCHENER HONDA   *p* 641
See PAULTOM MOTORS LIMITED
KITCHENER HYUNDAI   *p* 637
See 982875 ONTARIO LIMITED
KITCHENER MAIL PROCESSING PLANT *p* 637
See CANADA POST CORPORATION
KITCHENER NISSAN   *p* 635
See KITCHENER NISSAN (2009) INC
KITCHENER NISSAN (2009) INC   *p* 635
1450 VICTORIA ST N, KITCHENER, ON, N2B 3E2
(519) 744-1188   *SIC* 5511
KITCHENER PUBLIC LIBRARY BOARD *p* 640
85 QUEEN ST N, KITCHENER, ON, N2H 2H1
(519) 743-0271   *SIC* 8231
KITCHENER STEEL SERVICE CENTRE *p* 651

See MISTEELCO INC
KITCHENER WATERLOO YOUNG MENS CHRISTIAN ASSOCIATION, THE   *p* 640
460 FREDERICK ST SUITE 203, KITCHENER, ON, N2H 2P5
(519) 584-7479   *SIC* 8699
KITCHENER-WATERLOO AND NORTH WATERLOO HUMANE SOCIETY   *p* 635
250 RIVERBEND DR, KITCHENER, ON, N2B 2E9
(519) 745-5615   *SIC* 8699
KITCHENER-WATERLOO YWCA   *p* 640
84 FREDERICK ST, KITCHENER, ON, N2H 2L7
(519) 576-8856   *SIC* 8322
KITCHENER-WILMOT HYDRO INC   *p* 638
301 VICTORIA ST S, KITCHENER, ON, N2G 4L2
(519) 745-4771   *SIC* 4911
KITIMAT GENERAL HOSPITAL   *p* 224
See NORTHERN HEALTH AUTHORITY
KITNUNA CORPORATION   *p* 472
10 OMILIK ST, CAMBRIDGE BAY, NU, X0B 0C0
(867) 983-7500   *SIC* 1541
KITNUNA PROJECTS INC   *p* 472
10 OMILIK ST, CAMBRIDGE BAY, NU, X0B 0C0
(867) 983-7500   *SIC* 4953
KITO CANADA INC   *p* 186
3815 1ST AVE SUITE 309, BURNABY, BC, V5C 3V6
(888) 322-5486   *SIC* 5084
KITSILANO SECONDARY SCHOOL   *p* 322
See BOARD OF EDUCATION OF SCHOOL DISTRICT NO. 39 (VANCOUVER), THE
KITSUMKALUM TEMPLE GAS BAR   *p* 283
14309 HWY 16E, TERRACE, BC, V8G 0A6
(250) 635-0017   *SIC* 5541
KITTSON INVESTMENTS LTD   *p* 381
1450 WELLINGTON AVE, WINNIPEG, MB, R3E 0K5
(204) 772-3999   *SIC* 7231
KIWANIS CARE CENTRE   *p* 236
See KIWANIS CARE SOCIETY (1979) OF NEW WESTMINSTER
KIWANIS CARE SOCIETY (1979) OF NEW WESTMINSTER   *p* 236
35 CLUTE ST, NEW WESTMINSTER, BC, V3L 1Z5
(604) 525-6471   *SIC* 8051
KIWANIS NURSING HOME INC   *p* 418
11 BRYANT DR, SUSSEX, NB, E4E 2P3
(506) 432-3118   *SIC* 8051
KIWANIS PAVILLION, THE   *p* 334
See OAK BAY KIWANIS HEALTH CARE SOCIETY
KIWANIS VILLAGE   *p* 234
See NANAIMO DISTRICTY SENIOR CITIZENS HOUSING DEVELOPMENT SOCIETY
KIWANIS VILLAGE LODGE   *p* 234
1221 KIWANIS CRES, NANAIMO, BC, V9S 5Y1
(250) 753-6471   *SIC* 8051
KJMAL ENTERPRISES LTD   *p* 1413
800 15TH ST E UNIT 800, PRINCE ALBERT, SK, S6V 8E3
(306) 922-6366   *SIC* 5812
KJMAL ENTERPRISES LTD   *p* 1421
4651 ALBERT ST, REGINA, SK, S4S 6B6
(306) 584-5656   *SIC* 5812
KJV COURIER SERVICES   *p* 781
See 1032396 ONTARIO LTD
KK PRECISION INC   *p* 787
104 OAKDALE RD, NORTH YORK, ON, M3N 1V9
(416) 742-5911   *SIC* 3599
KL FOODS INC   *p* 671
235 HOOD RD UNIT 3, MARKHAM, ON, L3R 4N3
(905) 479-9048   *SIC* 5145
KLASSEN BRONZE LIMITED   *p* 752
30 MARVIN ST, NEW HAMBURG, ON, N3A 4H8

(519) 662-1010   *SIC* 3993
KLASSEN JEWELLERS LTD   *p* 1431
2318 AVENUE C N, SASKATOON, SK, S7L 5X5
(306) 652-2112   *SIC* 5094
KLASSEN, P CUSTOM FAB INC   *p* 807
5140 URE ST, OLDCASTLE, ON, N0R 1L0
(519) 737-6631   *SIC* 3443
KLEDO CONSTRUCTION LTD   *p* 213
4301 NAHANNI DR, FORT NELSON, BC, V0C 1R0
(250) 774-2501   *SIC* 1611
KLEEN AIR SOLUTIONS   *p* 485
See 1630389 ONTARIO LTD
KLEEN-FLO HOLDINGS INC   *p* 504
75 ADVANCE BLVD, BRAMPTON, ON, L6T 4N1
(905) 793-4311   *SIC* 6712
KLEEN-FLO TUMBLER INDUSTRIES LIMITED   *p*
75 ADVANCE BLVD, BRAMPTON, ON, L6T 4N1
(905) 793-4311   *SIC* 2992
KLEENZONE LTD   *p* 599
2489 SIXTH CONCESSION RD, GREENWOOD, ON, L0H 1H0
(905) 686-6500   *SIC* 7349
KLEIN INTERNATIONAL LTD   *p* 852
66 WEST WILMOT ST, RICHMOND HILL, ON, L4B 1H8
(905) 889-4881   *SIC* 5074
KLEIN'S FOOD MART   *p* 1422
See KLEIN, ROBERT ENTERPRISES INC
KLEIN, ROBERT ENTERPRISES INC   *p* 1422
1005 PASQUA ST, REGINA, SK, S4T 4K9
(306) 791-6362   *SIC* 5411
KLENZOID CANADA INC   *p* 706
245 MATHESON BLVD E SUITE 2, MISSISSAUGA, ON, L4Z 3C9
(905) 712-4000   *SIC* 2899
KLEWCHUK CONSTRUCTION LTD   *p* 122
503 69 AVE NW, EDMONTON, AB, T6P 0C2
SIC 1521
KLEYSEN GROUP LTD   *p* 353
2800 MCGILLIVRAY BLVD, OAK BLUFF, MB, R4G 0B4
(204) 488-5550   *SIC* 4213
KLICK HEALTH   *p* 929
See KLICK INC
KLICK INC   *p* 929
175 BLOOR ST E SUITE 301, TORONTO, ON, M4W 3R8
(416) 214-4977   *SIC* 7379
KLIENTEL   *p* 1209
See 9182-9978 QUEBEC INC
KLINGSPOR ENGINEERED ABBRASIVES *p* 892
See KLINGSPOR INC
KLINGSPOR INC   *p* 892
1175 BARTON ST UNIT 1, STONEY CREEK, ON, L8E 5H1
(905) 643-0770   *SIC* 5085
KLINIC COMMUNITY HEALTH CENTRE *p* 382
See KLINIC INC
KLINIC INC   *p* 382
870 PORTAGE AVE, WINNIPEG, MB, R3G 0P1
(204) 784-4090   *SIC* 8322
KLOHN CRIPPEN BERGER HOLDINGS LTD   *p* 286
2955 VIRTUAL WAY SUITE 500, VANCOUVER, BC, V5M 4X6
(604) 669-3800   *SIC* 6712
KLOHN CRIPPEN BERGER LTD   *p* 9
2618 HOPEWELL PL NE SUITE 500, CALGARY, AB, T1Y 7J7
(403) 274-3424   *SIC* 8711
KLOHN CRIPPEN BERGER LTD   *p* 286
2955 VIRTUAL WAY SUITE 500, VANCOUVER, BC, V5M 4X6
(604) 669-3800   *SIC* 8711

KLONDIKE LUBRICANTS CORPORATION *p* 179
3078 275 ST, ALDERGROVE, BC, V4W 3L4
(604) 856-5335   *SIC* 5172
KLONDIKE MOTORS LTD   *p* 1440
191 RANGE RD, WHITEHORSE, YT, Y1A 3E5
(867) 668-3362   *SIC* 5511
KLS EARTHWORKS INC   *p* 159
240039 FRONTIER CRES, ROCKY VIEW COUNTY, AB, T1X 0W6
(403) 240-3030   *SIC* 1794
KLUANE DRILLING LIMITED   *p* 1440
14 MACDONALD RD, WHITEHORSE, YT, Y1A 4L2
(867) 633-4800   *SIC* 1781
KMC MINING   *p* 1
See KMC MINING CORPORATION
KMC MINING CORPORATION   *p* 1
28712 114 AVE, ACHESON, AB, T7X 6E6
(780) 454-0664   *SIC* 1311
KMC OILFIELD MAINTENANCE LTD *p* 168
4728 WATSON CRES, SWAN HILLS, AB, T0G 2C0
(780) 333-4300   *SIC* 4212
KML WINDOWS INC   *p* 897
71 SECOND ST, STRATHROY, ON, N7G 3H8
(519) 245-2270   *SIC* 3442
KNAPP, KEN FORD SALES LTD   *p* 570
390 TALBOT ST N, ESSEX, ON, N8M 2W4
(519) 776-6447   *SIC* 5511
KNAUER, CLAIRE PHARMACY LTD   *p* 657
395 SOUTHDALE RD E SUITE 1, LONDON, ON, N6E 1A2
(519) 685-1160   *SIC* 5912
KNEBEL WATTERS & ASSOCIATES INC *p* 964
10 BAY ST SUITE 605, TORONTO, ON, M5J 2R8
(416) 362-4300   *SIC* 8748
KNECHTEL'S FOOD MARKET   *p* 911
15 QUEEN S, TILBURY, ON, N0P 2L0
(519) 682-3245   *SIC* 5411
KNELL DOOR & HARDWARE   *p* 635
See KNELL, WILLIAM AND COMPANY LIMITED
KNELL INVESTMENTS INC   *p* 635
2090 SHIRLEY DR, KITCHENER, ON, N2B 0A3
(519) 578-1000   *SIC* 5072
KNELL, WILLIAM AND COMPANY LIMITED *p* 635
2090 SHIRLEY DR, KITCHENER, ON, N2B 0A3
(519) 578-1000   *SIC* 5072
KNELSEN SAND & GRAVEL LTD   *p* 137
10005 100 ST, LA CRETE, AB, T0H 2H0
(780) 928-3935   *SIC* 5032
KNELSEN RECOVERY SYSTEMS INTERNATIONAL INC   *p* 225
19855 98 AVE, LANGLEY, BC, V1M 2X5
(604) 888-4015   *SIC* 6712
KNIGHT ARCHER INSURANCE LTD *p* 1416
512 E VICTORIA AVE, REGINA, SK, S4N 0N7
(306) 569-2288   *SIC* 6411
KNIGHT PIESOLD LTD   *p* 306
750 PENDER ST W SUITE 1400, VANCOUVER, BC, V6C 2T8
(604) 685-0543   *SIC* 8711
KNIGHT SIGN   *p* 209
See PACIFIC SIGN GROUP INC
KNIGHT'S APPLEDEN FRUIT LIMITED *p* 546
11687 COUNTY ROAD 2 RR 3, COLBORNE, ON, K0K 1S0
(905) 349-2521   *SIC* 5148
KNIGHT, CONTRACTING LTD   *p* 338
37 CADILLAC AVE, VICTORIA, BC, V8Z 1T3
(250) 475-2595   *SIC* 1542
KNIGHTS OF COLUMBUS   *p* 490

1303 COUNTY RD 22, BELLE RIVER, ON,
N0R 1A0
    SIC 8699
KNIGHTS OF COLUMBUS INSURANCE *p*
617
    26 DAVIS CRT, HAMPTON, ON, L0B 1J0
    (905) 263-4212   *SIC* 6311
**KNIGHTS ON GUARD PROTECTIVES SER-
VICES** *p*
845
    *See KNIGHTS ON GUARD SECURITY
    SURVEILLANCE SYSTEMS CORPORATION*
**KNIGHTS ON GUARD SECURITY
SURVEILLANCE SYSTEMS CORPORA-
TION** *p*
845
    1048 TOY AVE SUITE 101, PICKERING,
ON, L1W 3P1
    (905) 427-7863   *SIC* 7381
KNIX TEEN   *p* 991
    See KNIX WEAR INC
KNIX WEAR INC   *p* 991
    70 CLAREMONT ST 2ND FL, TORONTO,
ON, M6J 2M5
    (647) 715-9446   *SIC* 5632
KNOLL NORTH AMERICA CORP   *p* 795
    1000 ARROW RD, NORTH YORK, ON, M9M
2Y7
    (416) 741-5453   *SIC* 2521
KNOLL NORTH AMERICA CORP   *p* 1032
    600 ROWNTREE DAIRY RD, WOOD-
BRIDGE, ON, L4L 5T8
    (416) 741-5453   *SIC* 2514
KNOLLCREST LODGE   *p* 685
    50 WILLIAM ST SUITE 221, MILVERTON,
ON, N0K 1M0
    (519) 595-8121   *SIC* 8361
KNOLLWOOD GOLF CLUB   *p* 477
    See KNOLLWOOD GOLF LIMITED
KNOLLWOOD GOLF LIMITED   *p* 477
    1276 SHAVER RD, ANCASTER, ON, L9G
3L1
    (905) 648-6687   *SIC* 7992
KNORR BRAKE LIMITED   *p* 919
    101 CONDOR AVE, TORONTO, ON, M4J
3N2
    (416) 461-4343   *SIC* 3743
KNOWLEDGE FIRST FINANCIAL INC *p* 710
    50 BURNHAMTHORPE RD W SUITE 1000,
MISSISSAUGA, ON, L5B 4A5
    (905) 270-8777   *SIC* 6732
**KNOWLEDGE MANAGEMENT INNOVA-
TIONS** *p*
801
    *See KNOWLEDGE MANAGEMENT INNO-
VATIONS LTD*
**KNOWLEDGE MANAGEMENT INNOVA-
TIONS LTD** *p*
801
    586 ARGUS RD SUITE 201, OAKVILLE,
ON, L6J 3J3
    (416) 410-4817   *SIC* 5045
**KNOWLTON DEVELOPMENT CORPORA-
TION INC** *p*
1143
    255 BOUL ROLAND-THERRIEN BUREAU
100, LONGUEUIL, QC, J4H 4A6
    (450) 243-2000   *SIC* 6712
KNOWROAMING LTD.   *p* 922
    90 EGLINTON AVE E SUITE 701,
TORONTO, ON, M4P 2Y3
    (416) 482-8193   *SIC* 4899
KNOX INSURANCE BROKERS LTD   *p* 763
    705 CASSELLS ST, NORTH BAY, ON, P1B
4A3
    (705) 474-4000   *SIC* 6411
KNP HEADWEAR INC   *p* 865
    50 MELHAM CRT, SCARBOROUGH, ON,
M1B 2E5
    (416) 298-8516   *SIC* 5136
KNRV INVESTMENTS INC   *p* 767
    515 CONSUMERS RD UNIT 700, NORTH
YORK, ON, M2J 4Z2
    (416) 791-4200   *SIC* 6712

KO ENERGY   *p* 436
    4902 45 ST, YELLOWKNIFE, NT, X1A 1K5
    (867) 447-3457   *SIC* 4924
KO-REC-TYPE (CANADA) LTD   *p* 740
    1100 COURTNEYPARK DR E UNIT 4, MIS-
SISSAUGA, ON, L5T 1L7
    SIC 5084
KOBAY ENSTEL LIMITED   *p* 876
    125 NASHDENE RD UNIT 5, SCARBOR-
OUGH, ON, M1V 2W3
    (416) 292-7088   *SIC* 3469
KOBELT MANUFACTURING CO. LTD *p* 277
    8238 129 ST, SURREY, BC, V3W 0A6
    (604) 572-3935   *SIC* 3732
KOCA AB SERVICES LTD   *p* 5
    610 HWY 9, BEISEKER, AB, T0M 0G0
    (403) 947-0006   *SIC* 5541
KOCH FARMS/AGRI-SALES INC   *p* 567
    LOT 5 CONCESSION 3, EARLTON, ON,
P0J 1E0
    (705) 563-8325   *SIC* 1542
KOCH FERTILIZER CANADA, ULC   *p* 347
    1400 17TH ST E, BRANDON, MB, R7A 7C4
    (204) 729-2900   *SIC* 2873
KOCH FORD LINCOLN SALES LTD *p* 119
    5121 GATEWAY BLVD NW, EDMONTON,
AB, T6H 5W5
    (780) 434-8411   *SIC* 5511
KOCH FUEL PRODUCTS INC   *p* 169
    1221 2ND ST N, THREE HILLS, AB, T0M
2A0
    (403) 443-5770   *SIC* 5171
KOCH STAINLESS PRODUCTS LTD *p* 371
    511 JARVIS AVE, WINNIPEG, MB, R2W
3A8
    (204) 586-8364   *SIC* 3499
KOCH TRANSPORT INC   *p* 536
    151 SAVAGE DR UNIT B, CAMBRIDGE,
ON, N1T 1S6
    SIC 4213
KOCH-GLITSCH CANADA LP   *p* 1001
    18 DALLAS ST, UXBRIDGE, ON, L9P 1C6
    (905) 852-3381   *SIC* 3559
KOCSIS TRANSPORT LTD   *p* 1433
    401 PACKHAM PL, SASKATOON, SK, S7N
2T7
    (306) 664-0025   *SIC* 4213
KODAK CANADA ULC   *p* 189
    4225 KINCAID ST, BURNABY, BC, V5G 4P5
    (604) 451-2700   *SIC* 3861
KODIAK CALL CENTRE LTD   *p* 1023
    525 WINDSOR AVE, WINDSOR, ON, N9A
1J4
    SIC 7389
KODIAK GROUP HOLDINGS CO   *p* 536
    415 THOMPSON DR, CAMBRIDGE, ON,
N1T 2K7
    (519) 620-4000   *SIC* 6719
KODIAK OILFIELD SERVICES   *p* 130
    See 248276 ALBERTA LTD
KODICOM CANADA   *p* 867
    2811 EGLINTON AVE E, SCARBOROUGH,
ON, M1J 2E1
    (416) 261-2266   *SIC* 5063
KOGNITIV CORPORATION   *p* 1006
    187 KING ST S, WATERLOO, ON, N2J 1R1
    (226) 476-1124   *SIC* 7372
KOGNITIVE MARKETING INC   *p* 922
    150 EGLINTON AVE E SUITE 801,
TORONTO, ON, M4P 1E8
    (416) 534-5651   *SIC* 7311
KOHL & FRISCH LIMITED   *p* 554
    7622 KEELE ST, CONCORD, ON, L4K 2R5
    (905) 660-7622   *SIC* 5122
KOHLTECH INTERNATIONAL LIMITED *p*
449
    583 MACELMON RD, DEBERT, NS, B0M
1G0
    (902) 662-3100   *SIC* 2431
KOKANEE FOOD SERVICES INC   *p* 204
    1405 CRANBROOK ST N, CRANBROOK,
BC, V1C 3S7
    (250) 426-7767   *SIC* 5812
KOLANDJIAN, A. PHARMACY LTD *p* 767

4865 LESLIE ST, NORTH YORK, ON, M2J
2K8
    (416) 493-2111   *SIC* 5912
**KOLLBEC GATINEAU CHRYSLER JEEP
INC** *p* 1104
    812 BOUL MALONEY O, GATINEAU, QC,
J8T 3R6
    (819) 568-1414   *SIC* 5511
KOLLONTAI   *p* 1174
    See ATELIER KOLLONTAI INC
KOLOFIS   *p* 1234
    See KOLOSTAT INC
KOLOSTAT INC   *p* 1234
    2005 RUE LE CHATELIER, MONTREAL,
QC, H7L 5B3
    (514) 333-7333   *SIC* 1711
KOLTER PROPERTY COMPANY   *p* 924
    *See KOLTER PROPERTY MANAGEMENT
LIMITED*
**KOLTER PROPERTY MANAGEMENT LIM-
ITED** *p*
924
    2200 YONGE ST SUITE 1600, TORONTO,
ON, M4S 2C6
    SIC 6512
KOMATSU MINING   *p* 269
    See JOY GLOBAL (CANADA) LTD
KOMBI   *p* 1156
    See KOMBI SPORTS INC
KOMBI SPORTS INC   *p* 1156
    5711 RUE FERRIER, MONT-ROYAL, QC,
H4P 1N3
    (514) 341-4321   *SIC* 5137
KOMET INTERNATIONAL   *p* 1058
    See 9323-7055 QUEBEC INC
KOMIENSKI LIMITED   *p* 879
    4665 HIGHWAY 24 RR 3, SCOTLAND, ON,
N0E 1R0
    (519) 446-2315   *SIC* 0161
KONA DRUGS LTD   *p* 250
    737 CENTRAL ST W, PRINCE GEORGE,
BC, V2M 3C6
    (250) 562-2311   *SIC* 5912
**KONAL ENGINEERING AND EQUIPMENT
INC** *p* 493
    1 GRAHAM ST, BLENHEIM, ON, N0P 1A0
    (519) 676-8133   *SIC* 3599
KONCRETE CONSTRUCTION GROUP *p*
1409
    609 MILLER ST, LEADER, SK, S0N 1H0
    (306) 628-3757   *SIC* 1389
KONDRO ELECTRIC 1980 LTD   *p* 144
    6202 50 AVE, LLOYDMINSTER, AB, T9V
2C9
    (780) 875-6226   *SIC* 1731
KONE INC   *p* 206
    1488 CLIVEDEN AVE, DELTA, BC, V3M 6L9
    (604) 777-5663   *SIC* 1799
KONE INC   *p* 723
    6696 FINANCIAL DR SUITE 2, MISSIS-
SAUGA, ON, L5N 7J6
    (905) 858-8383   *SIC* 7699
KONECRANES CANADA INC   *p* 523
    5300 MAINWAY, BURLINGTON, ON, L7L
6A4
    (905) 332-9494   *SIC* 7699
KONGSBERG AUTOMOTIVE   *p* 1369
    See KONGSBERG INC
KONGSBERG GEOSPATIAL LTD   *p* 624
    411 LEGGET DR SUITE 400, KANATA, ON,
K2K 3C9
    (613) 271-5500   *SIC* 7372
KONGSBERG INC   *p* 1112
    2801 3E RUE, GRAND-MERE, QC, G9T
5K5
    (819) 533-3202   *SIC* 3651
KONGSBERG INC   *p* 1369
    2699 5E AV, SHAWINIGAN, QC, G9T 2P7
    (819) 533-4757   *SIC* 3679
KONGSBERG INC   *p* 1369
    90 28E RUE, SHAWINIGAN, QC, G9T·5K7
    (819) 533-3201   *SIC* 3679
KONGSBERG MESOTECH LTD   *p* 247
    1598 KEBET WAY, PORT COQUITLAM, BC,

V3C 5M5
    (604) 464-8144   *SIC* 3812
KONICA MINOLTA   *p* 120
    *See KONICA MINOLTA BUSINESS SOLU-
TIONS (CANADA) LTD*
KONICA MINOLTA   *p* 255
    *See KONICA MINOLTA BUSINESS SOLU-
TIONS (CANADA) LTD*
KONICA MINOLTA   *p* 1334
    *See KONICA MINOLTA BUSINESS SOLU-
TIONS (CANADA) LTD*
**KONICA MINOLTA BUSINESS SOLUTIONS
(CANADA) LTD** *p* 120
    9651 25 AVE NW, EDMONTON, AB, T6N
1H7
    (780) 465-6232   *SIC* 5044
**KONICA MINOLTA BUSINESS SOLUTIONS
(CANADA) LTD** *p* 255
    21500 WESTMINSTER HWY, RICHMOND,
BC, V6V 2V1
    (604) 276-1611   *SIC* 5044
**KONICA MINOLTA BUSINESS SOLUTIONS
(CANADA) LTD** *p* 504
    7965 GOREWAY DR UNIT 1, BRAMPTON,
ON, L6T 5T5
    (905) 494-1040   *SIC* 7379
**KONICA MINOLTA BUSINESS SOLUTIONS
(CANADA) LTD** *p* 696
    5875 EXPLORER DR, MISSISSAUGA, ON,
L4W 0E1
    (905) 890-6600   *SIC* 5044
**KONICA MINOLTA BUSINESS SOLUTIONS
(CANADA) LTD** *p* 1334
    8555 RTE TRANSCANADIENNE, SAINT-
LAURENT, QC, H4S 1Z6
    (514) 335-2157   *SIC* 5044
KONRAD GROUP, INC   *p* 627
    1726 HENDERSON LINE, KEENE, ON, K9J
6X8
    (416) 551-3684   *SIC* 7374
KONTRON CANADA INC   *p* 1062
    4555   RUE   AMBROISE-LAFORTUNE,
BOISBRIAND, QC, J7H 0A4
    (450) 437-5682   *SIC* 8731
KONTRON CANADA INC   *p* 1340
    600 RUE MCCAFFREY, SAINT-LAURENT,
QC, H4T 1N1
    (450) 437-4661   *SIC* 4899
KONTRON COMMUNICATIONS   *p* 1340
    See KONTRON CANADA INC
**KONTZAMANIS   GRAUMANN   SMITH
MACMILLAN INC** *p* 391
    865 WAVERLEY ST SUITE 300, WIN-
NIPEG, MB, R3T 5P4
    (204) 896-1209   *SIC* 8711
KOO, JIM WHOLESALE PRODUCE   *p* 285
    See KOO, JIM M. PRODUCE LTD
KOO, JIM M. PRODUCE LTD   *p* 285
    777 CLARK DR, VANCOUVER, BC, V5L
3J3
    (604) 253-6622   *SIC* 5148
KOOLATRON CORPORATION   *p* 513
    139 COPERNICUS BLVD, BRANTFORD,
ON, N3P 1N4
    (519) 756-3950   *SIC* 3086
KOOLIAN ENTREPRISES INC, LES *p* 1128
    2295 52E AV, LACHINE, QC, H8T 3C3
    (514) 633-9292   *SIC* 5013
KOOLINI EATERY   *p* 1020
    See KOOLINI ITALIAN CUISINI LIMITED
KOOLINI ITALIAN CUISINI LIMITED *p* 1020
    1520 TECUMSEH RD E, WINDSOR, ON,
N8W 1C4
    (519) 254-5665   *SIC* 5812
KOOPMAN RESOURCES, INC   *p* 39
    10919 WILLOWGLEN PL SE, CALGARY,
AB, T2J 1R8
    (403) 271-4564   *SIC* 1311
KOORNNEEF PRODUCE LTD   *p* 572
    165 THE QUEENSWAY SUITE 151, ETOBI-
COKE, ON, M8Y 1H8
    (416) 255-5188   *SIC* 5148
KOOTENAY COUNTRY STORE CO-OP *p*
235

▲ Public Company   ■ Public Company Family Member   **HQ** Headquarters   **BR** Branch   **SL** Single Location

295 BAKER ST, NELSON, BC, V1L 4H4
(250) 354-4077   *SIC* 5411

KOOTENAY LAKE HOSPITAL   *p* 235
See INTERIOR HEALTH AUTHORITY

KOOTENAY MADE NATURAL PRODUCTS *p* 235
377 BAKER ST, NELSON, BC, V1L 4H6
(250) 352-2333   *SIC* 5963

KOOTENAY MARKET LTD   *p* 204
2 CRANBROOK ST N SUITE 320, CRANBROOK, BC, V1C 3P6
(250) 426-1846   *SIC* 5411

KOOTENAY SAVINGS CREDIT UNION   284
1101 DEWDNEY AVE SUITE 106, TRAIL, BC, V1R 4T1
(250) 368-2686   *SIC* 6062

KOOTENAY SILVER INC   *p* 314
1075 W GEORGIA ST SUITE 1650, VANCOUVER, BC, V6E 3C9
(604) 601-5650   *SIC* 1061

KOPEL INC   *p* 1308
3360 2E RUE, SAINT-HUBERT, QC, J3Y 8Y7
(514) 398-9595   *SIC* 5065

KOPPERT CANADA LIMITED   *p* 878
40 IRONSIDE CRES UNIT 3, SCARBOROUGH, ON, M1X 1G4
(416) 291-0040   *SIC* 5122

KOR-ALTA CONSTRUCTION LTD   *p* 122
2461 76 AVE NW, EDMONTON, AB, T6P 1Y8
(780) 440-6661   *SIC* 1542

KORAB MARINE LTD   *p* 1125
255 RUE NORMAN, LACHINE, QC, H8R 1A3
(514) 489-5711   *SIC* 6712

KORAH COLLEGIATE AND VOCATIONAL SCHOOL   *p* 863
See ALGOMA DISTRICT SCHOOL BOARD

KORD   *p* 514
See HC CANADA OPERATING COMPANY, LTD, THE

KORE WIRELES CANADA INC   *p* 375
93 LOMBARD AVE SUITE 412, WINNIPEG, MB, R3B 3B1
(204) 954-2888   *SIC* 4899

KOREA BUSINESS CENTRE   *p* 950
See CONSULATE GENERAL OF THE REPUBLIC OF KOREA COMMERCIAL SECTION

KOREA FOOD TRADING LTD   *p* 1002
8500 KEELE ST, VAUGHAN, ON, L4K 2A6
(905) 532-0325   *SIC* 5149

KOREAN BUSINESSMEN'S COOPERATIVE ASSOCIATION   *p* 187
6373 ARBROATH ST, BURNABY, BC, V5E 1C3
(604) 431-7373   *SIC* 5199

KOREX CANADA COMPANY   *p* 575
104 JUTLAND RD, ETOBICOKE, ON, M8Z 2H1
(416) 259-9214   *SIC* 2842

KOREX CANADA COMPANY   *p* 575
78 TITAN RD, ETOBICOKE, ON, M8Z 2J8
(416) 231-7800   *SIC* 2841

KORHANI MANUFACTURE   *p* 554
See KORHANI OF CANADA INC

KORHANI OF CANADA INC   *p* 554
7500 KEELE ST, CONCORD, ON, L4K 1Z9
(905) 660-0863   *SIC* 2273

KORPACH CONSULTING LTD   *p* 11
611 MALVERN DR NE, CALGARY, AB, T2A 5G8
(403) 219-7481   *SIC* 8748

KORSON FURNITURE IMPORTS LTD   *p* 1027
7933 HUNTINGTON RD UNIT 1, WOODBRIDGE, ON, L4H 0S9
(905) 850-1530   *SIC* 5021

KORTH GROUP LTD   *p* 150
64186 393 LOOP E, OKOTOKS, AB, T1S 0L1

(403) 938-3255   *SIC* 5091

KORZITE COATINGS INC   *p* 603
7134 WELLINGTON RD W, GUELPH, ON, N1H 6J3
(519) 821-1250   *SIC* 2851

KOSKIE MINSKY LLP   *p* 953
20 QUEEN ST W UNIT 900, TORONTO, ON, M5H 3R3
(416) 977-8353   *SIC* 8111

KOSS AEROSPACE   *p* 733
See 333111 ONTARIO LIMITED

KOST FIRE EQUIPMENT LTD   *p* 145
677 14 ST SW, MEDICINE HAT, AB, T1A 4V5
(403) 527-1500   *SIC* 5999

KOST FIRE SAFETY   *p* 145
See KOST FIRE EQUIPMENT LTD

KOST KLIP MANUFACTURING LTD   *p* 247
1611 BROADWAY ST UNIT 119, PORT COQUITLAM, BC, V3C 2M7
(604) 468-1117   *SIC* 3993

KOST KLIP MANUFACTURING LTD   *p* 247
1611 BROADWAY ST UNIT 119, PORT COQUITLAM, BC, V3C 2M7
(604) 468-7917   *SIC* 3993

KOTELES FARMS LIMITED   *p* 912
164700 NEW RD SUITE 2, TILLSONBURG, ON, N4G 4G7
(519) 842-5425   *SIC* 0161

KOTOWICH HARDWARE LTD   *p* 165
4001 50 AVE, ST PAUL, AB, T0A 3A2
(780) 645-3173   *SIC* 5211

KOTSOVOS RESTAURANTS LIMITED *p* 999
35 FRONT ST, TRENTON, ON, K8V 4N3
(613) 392-4333   *SIC* 5812

KOTT INC   *p* 752
3228 MOODIE DR, NEPEAN, ON, K2J 4S8
(613) 838-2775   *SIC* 5031

KOTT LUMBER   *p* 894
14 ANDERSON BLVD, STOUFFVILLE, ON, L4A 7X4
(905) 642-4400   *SIC* 5031

KOTYCK BROS. LIMITED   *p* 509
80 HALE RD SUITE 7, BRAMPTON, ON, L6W 3N9
(905) 595-1127   *SIC* 5051

KOWAL CONSTRUCTION ALTA. LTD   *p* 81
601 MCCOOL ST, CROSSFIELD, AB, T0M 0S0
(403) 946-4450   *SIC* 1794

KOYMAN GALLERIES   *p* 818
See KOYMAN GALLERIES LIMITED

KOYMAN GALLERIES LIMITED   *p* 818
1771 ST. LAURENT BLVD, OTTAWA, ON, K1G 3V4
(613) 526-1562   *SIC* 5999

KOYO BEARINGS CANADA INC   *p* 1056
4 RUE VICTORIA S, BEDFORD, QC, J0J 1A0
(450) 248-3316   *SIC* 5085

KOYO FOODS QUEBEC INC   *p* 1340
4605 RUE HICKMORE, SAINT-LAURENT, QC, H4T 1S5
(514) 744-1299   *SIC* 5149

KOZMA'S MANUFACTURING CO. LTD   *p* 798
2751 PLYMOUTH DR, OAKVILLE, ON, L6H 5R5
(905) 829-3660   *SIC* 3469

KP BUILDING PRODUCTS LTD   *p* 473
323 MAIN ST N SUITE 3, ACTON, ON, L7J 2L9
(519) 853-1230   *SIC* 5051

KPH TURCOT, UN PARTENARIAT S.E.N.C *p* 1062
4333 BOUL DE LA GRANDE-ALLEE, BOISBRIAND, QC, J7H 1M7
(450) 435-5756   *SIC* 8742

KPM INDUSTRIES LTD   *p* 804
555 MICHIGAN DR SUITE 100, OAKVILLE, ON, L6L 0G4
(905) 639-2993   *SIC* 1611

KPMB ARCHITECTS   *p* 981
322 KING ST W, TORONTO, ON, M5V 1J2

(416) 977-5104   *SIC* 8712

KPMG   *p* 190
See KPMG LLP

KPMG INC   *p* 89
10125 102 ST NW, EDMONTON, AB, T5J 3V8
(780) 429-7300   *SIC* 8721

KPMG INC   *p* 554
100 NEW PARK PL SUITE 1400, CONCORD, ON, L4K 0J3
(905) 265-5900   *SIC* 8721

KPMG INC   *p* 837
84 JAMES ST, PARRY SOUND, ON, P2A 1T9
(705) 746-9346   *SIC* 8741

KPMG INC   *p* 953
333 BAY ST SUITE 4600, TORONTO, ON, M5H 2S5
(416) 777-8500   *SIC* 8741

KPMG LLP   *p* 52
205 5 AVENUE SW SUITE 3100, CALGARY, AB, T2P 4B9
(403) 691-8000   *SIC* 8721

KPMG LLP   *p* 89
2200-10175 101 ST NW, EDMONTON, AB, T5J 3V8
(780) 429-7300   *SIC* 8721

KPMG LLP   *p* 190
4720 KINGSWAY SUITE 2400, BURNABY, BC, V5H 4N2
(604) 527-3600   *SIC* 8721

KPMG LLP   *p* 217
206 SEYMOUR ST SUITE 200, KAMLOOPS, BC, V2C 6P5
(250) 372-5581   *SIC* 8721

KPMG LLP   *p* 330
777 DUNSMUIR ST SUITE 900, VANCOUVER, BC, V7Y 1K3
(604) 691-3000   *SIC* 8721

KPMG LLP   *p* 336
730 VIEW ST SUITE 800, VICTORIA, BC, V8W 3Y7
(250) 480-3500   *SIC* 8721

KPMG LLP   *p* 375
1 LOMBARD PL UNIT 2000, WINNIPEG, MB, R3B 0X3
(204) 957-1770   *SIC* 8721

KPMG LLP   *p* 613
21 KING ST W SUITE 700, HAMILTON, ON, L8P 4W7
(905) 523-2259   *SIC* 8721

KPMG LLP   *p* 774
4100 YONGE ST UNIT 200, NORTH YORK, ON, M2P 2B5
(416) 228-7000   *SIC* 8721

KPMG LLP   *p* 834
160 ELGIN ST SUITE 2000, OTTAWA, ON, K2P 2P7
(613) 212-5764   *SIC* 8721

KPMG LLP   *p* 953
333 BAY ST SUITE 4600, TORONTO, ON, M5H 2S5
(416) 777-8500   *SIC* 8721

KPMG LLP   *p* 1006
115 KING ST S SUITE 201, WATERLOO, ON, N2J 5A3
(519) 747-8800   *SIC* 8721

KPMG LLP   *p* 1197
600 BOUL DE MAISONNEUVE O UNITE1500, MONTREAL, QC, H3A 0A3
(514) 840-2100   *SIC* 8721

KPMG MSLP   *p* 336
See KPMG LLP

KPMG-SECOUR   *p* 1192
555 BOUL RENE-LEVESQUE O BUREAU 1700, MONTREAL, QC, H2Z 1B1
SIC 8721

KPS   *p* 240
See KEITH PANEL SYSTEMS CO., LTD

KPSS GOLDWELL   *p* 739
See GOLDWELL COSMETICS (CANADA) LTD

KRAFT HEINZ   *p* 622
See KRAFT HEINZ CANADA ULC

KRAFT HEINZ CANADA ULC   *p* 182
2700 PRODUCTION WAY SUITE 450, BURNABY, BC, V5A 4X1
(604) 420-2511   *SIC* 5149

KRAFT HEINZ CANADA ULC   *p* 570
2150 LAKE SHORE BLVD W, ETOBICOKE, ON, M8V 1A3
(416) 506-6000   *SIC* 2051

KRAFT HEINZ CANADA ULC   *p* 622
70 DICKINSON DR, INGLESIDE, ON, K0C 1M0
(613) 537-2226   *SIC* 2022

KRAFT HEINZ CANADA ULC   *p* 776
95 MOATFIELD DR SUITE 316, NORTH YORK, ON, M3B 3L6
(416) 441-5000   *SIC* 2043

KRAFT HEINZ CANADA ULC   *p* 871
1440 BIRCHMOUNT RD, SCARBOROUGH, ON, M1P 2E3
SIC 2099

KRAFT HEINZ CANADA ULC   *p* 871
370 PROGRESS AVE, SCARBOROUGH, ON, M1P 2Z4
(416) 291-3713   *SIC* 2051

KRAFT HEINZ CANADA ULC   *p* 991
277 GLADSTONE AVE, TORONTO, ON, M6J 3L9
(416) 667-6224   *SIC* 2064

KRAFT HEINZ CANADA ULC   *p* 1156
8600 CH DEVONSHIRE, MONT-ROYAL, QC, H4P 2K9
(514) 343-3300   *SIC* 2022

KRAFT HEINZ CANADA ULC   *p* 1166
3055 RUE VIAU BUREAU 4, MONTREAL, QC, H1V 3J5
(514) 259-6921   *SIC* 2051

KRAFT HEINZ CANADA ULC   *p* 1395
401 RUE MARIE-CURIE, VAUDREUIL-DORION, QC, J7V 0B9
(450) 455-5576   *SIC* 5141

KRAMER AUCTIONS LTD   *p* 1412
GD LCD MAIN, NORTH BATTLEFORD, SK, S9A 2X5
(306) 445-2377   *SIC* 5999

KRAMER MAZDA   *p* 39
See SOUTHSIDE MOTORS LTD

KRAN MANAGEMENT SERVICES LIMITED *p* 545
805 WILLIAM ST, COBOURG, ON, K9A 3A8
(905) 372-6335   *SIC* 5812

KRAUS CANADA LP   *p* 372
1551 CHURCH AVE SUITE 167, WINNIPEG, MB, R2X 1G7
(204) 633-1020   *SIC* 5023

KRAUS CARPET LP   *p* 1008
65 NORTHFIELD DR W, WATERLOO, ON, N2L 0A8
(519) 884-2310   *SIC* 2273

KRAUS FLOORS WITHMORE   *p* 1008
See KRAUS CARPET LP

KRAUS GLOBAL LTD   *p* 366
25 PAQUIN RD, WINNIPEG, MB, R2J 3V9
(204) 663-3601   *SIC* 3728

KRAVET FABRICS CANADA COMPANY   *p* 717
3600B LAIRD RD UNIT 5, MISSISSAUGA, ON, L5L 6A7
(905) 607-0706   *SIC* 5131

KRAWFORD CONSTRUCTION INC   *p* 112
8055 ARGYLL RD NW, EDMONTON, AB, T6C 4A9
(780) 436-4381   *SIC* 1542

KREATOR EQUIPMENT & SERVICES INCORPORATED   *p* 863
473036 COUNTY RD 11, SCARBOROUGH, ON, L9W 0R2
(519) 941-7876   *SIC* 5084

KREMBLO INTERNATIONAL TRADE COMPANY INC   *p* 779
49 THE DONWAY W SUITE 1401, NORTH YORK, ON, M3C 3M9
(416) 445-3474   *SIC* 5149

KREVCO LIFESTYLES INC   p 384
700 BERRY ST, WINNIPEG, MB, R3H 0S6
(204) 786-6957   SIC 5091
KRG INSURANCE BROKERS   p 768
See RRJ INSURANCE GROUP LIMITED
KRG LOGISTICS INC   p 706
170 TRADERS BLVD E, MISSISSAUGA,
ON, L4Z 1W7
(905) 501-7277   SIC 4731
KRIKORIAN, S.H. & CO LTD   p 671
1 VALLEYWOOD DR UNIT 4, MARKHAM,
ON, L3R 5L9
(905) 479-4080   SIC 5122
KRINOS FOODS CANADA LTD   p 554
251 DONEY CRES, CONCORD, ON, L4K
1P6
(905) 669-4414   SIC 5143
KRISINGER DRUG LTD   p 283
4647 LAKELSE AVE SUITE 102, TER-
RACE, BC, V8G 1R3
(250) 635-7261   SIC 5912
KRISKA HOLDINGS LIMITED   p 740
6424A DANVILLE RD, MISSISSAUGA, ON,
L5T 2S6
(905) 795-2770   SIC 4213
KRISKA HOLDINGS LIMITED   p 848
850 SOPHIA ST, PRESCOTT, ON, K0E 1T0
(613) 925-5903   SIC 4213
KRISKA TRANSPORTATION   p 848
See KRISKA HOLDINGS LIMITED
KRISTIAN ELECTRIC LTD   p 17
4215 64 AVE SE, CALGARY, AB, T2C 2C8
(403) 292-9111   SIC 7699
KRISTOFOAM INDUSTRIES INC   p 554
160 PLANCHET RD, CONCORD, ON, L4K
2C7
(905) 669-6616   SIC 3086
KRISTOFOAM INDUSTRIES INC   p 555
120 PLANCHET RD, CONCORD, ON, L4K
2C7
(905) 669-6616   SIC 3086
KRISTUS DARZS LATVIAN HOME   p 1032
11290 PINE VALLEY DR, WOODBRIDGE,
ON, L4L 1A6
(905) 832-3300   SIC 8051
KROEGER INC   p 878
455 FINCHDENE SQ, SCARBOROUGH,
ON, M1X 1B7
(416) 752-4382   SIC 5092
KROEKER FARMS LIMITED   p 361
777 CIRCLE K DR, WINKLER, MB, R6W
0K7
(204) 325-4333   SIC 0134
KROMAR PRINTING LTD   p 382
725 PORTAGE AVE, WINNIPEG, MB, R3G
0M8
(204) 775-8721   SIC 2752
KROMET INTERNATIONAL INC   p 534
200 SHELDON DR, CAMBRIDGE, ON, N1R
7K1
(519) 623-2511   SIC 3469
KROMET INTERNATIONAL INC   p 608
20 MILBURN RD, HAMILTON, ON, L8E 3L9
(905) 561-7773   SIC 3469
KRONES MACHINERY CO. LIMITED   p 688
6285 NORTHAM DR SUITE 108, MISSIS-
SAUGA, ON, L4V 1X5
(905) 364-4900   SIC 5084
**KRONIS, ROTSZTAIN, MARGLES, CAPPEL
LLP**   p 772
25 SHEPPARD AVE W SUITE 700, NORTH
YORK, ON, M2N 6S6
(416) 225-8750   SIC 8111
KRONOPOL MARKETING   p 585
See LAMWOOD PRODUCTS (1990) LIM-
ITED
KRONOS CANADA INC   p 1205
1255 BOUL ROBERT-BOURASSA BU-
REAU 1102, MONTREAL, QC, H3B 3W7
(514) 397-3501   SIC 2816
KRONOS CANADA INC   p 1393
3390 RTE MARIE-VICTORIN, VARENNES,
QC, J3X 1P7
(450) 929-5000   SIC 2816

KRONOS FOODS LTD   p 868
371 DANFORTH RD, SCARBOROUGH,
ON, M1L 3X8
(416) 690-1990   SIC 5141
KROPF INDUSTRIAL INC   p 879
1 QUEBEC DR, SEGUIN, ON, P2A 0B2
(705) 378-2453   SIC 3448
KROPF'S IGA   p 569
See L & M FOOD MARKET (ONTARIO) LIM-
ITED
KROTZ, HARVEY FORD SALES   p 647
See KROTZ, HARVEY LIMITED
KROTZ, HARVEY LIMITED   p 647
1199 WALLACE AVE N, LISTOWEL, ON,
N4W 1M6
(519) 291-3520   SIC 5511
KROWN IMPORTS   p 12
See KROWN PRODUCE INC
KROWN PRODUCE INC   p 12
4923 47 ST SE, CALGARY, AB, T2B 3S5
SIC 5148
KROWN RUST CONTROL SYSTEMS   p 879
See CANADIAN KROWN DEALERS INC
KRUEGER ELECTRICAL LTD   p 222
1027 TRENCH PL UNIT 100, KELOWNA,
BC, V1Y 9Y4
(250) 860-3905   SIC 1731
KRUEGER PEMBROKE LP   p 838
1000 OLYMPIC DR, PEMBROKE, ON, K8A
0E1
SIC 2522
KRUG FURNITURE   p 636
See KRUG INC
KRUG INC   p 636
421 MANITOU DR, KITCHENER, ON, N2C
1L5
(519) 748-5100   SIC 2521
KRUG INC   p 636
421 MANITOU DR, KITCHENER, ON, N2C
1L5
(519) 748-5100   SIC 2522
KRUGER   p 1388
See PAPIERS DE PUBLICATION KRUGER
INC
KRUGER BROMPTON S.E.C   p 1218
3285 CH DE BEDFORD, MONTREAL, QC,
H3S 1G5
(819) 846-2721   SIC 2621
KRUGER BROMPTON S.E.C   p 1369
220 RTE DE WINDSOR, SHERBROOKE,
QC, J1C 0E6
(819) 846-2721   SIC 2621
KRUGER INC   p 504
10 PEDIGREE CRT, BRAMPTON, ON, L6T
5T8
(905) 759-1012   SIC 2653
KRUGER INC   p 1131
7474 RUE CORDNER, LASALLE, QC, H8N
2W3
(514) 366-8050   SIC 2653
KRUGER INC   p 1218
3285 CH DE BEDFORD, MONTREAL, QC,
H3S 1G5
(514) 343-3100   SIC 6712
KRUGER INC   p 1223
5845 PLACE TURCOT, MONTREAL, QC,
H4C 1V9
(514) 934-0600   SIC 2631
KRUGER INDUSTRIES INC   p 75
28 CROWFOOT TERRACE NW, CALGARY,
AB, T3G 5W2
(403) 276-6900   SIC 5211
KRUGER IPI INC   p 1218
3285 CH DE BEDFORD, MONTREAL, QC,
H3S 1G5
(514) 343-3100   SIC 2421
KRUGER PRODUCTS L.P.   p 237
1625 FIFTH AVE, NEW WESTMINSTER,
BC, V3M 1Z7
(604) 522-7893   SIC 2621
KRUGER PRODUCTS L.P.   p 723
1900 MINNESOTA CRT SUITE 200, MIS-
SISSAUGA, ON, L5N 5R5
(905) 812-6900   SIC 2621

KRUGER PRODUCTS L.P.   p 1089
100 1E AV, CRABTREE, QC, J0K 1B0
(450) 754-2855   SIC 2676
KRUGER PRODUCTS L.P.   p 1105
20 RUE LAURIER, GATINEAU, QC, J8X 4H3
(819) 595-5302   SIC 2621
KRUGER RECYCLAGE   p 1218
See KRUGER INC
KRUGER TROIS-RIVIERES S.E.C.   p 1388
3735 BOUL GENE-H.-KRUGER, TROIS-
RIVIERES, QC, G9A 6B1
(819) 375-1691   SIC 2621
KRUGER WAYAGAMACK S.E.C.   p 1218
3285 CH DE BEDFORD, MONTREAL, QC,
H3S 1G5
(514) 343-3100   SIC 2621
**KRUPP, MASHA TRANSLATION GROUP
LTD, THE**   p 750
1547 MERIVALE RD SUITE 500, NEPEAN,
ON, K2G 4V3
(613) 820-4566   SIC 7389
KRYTON CANADA CORPORATION   p 287
1645 E KENT AVE NORTH, VANCOUVER,
BC, V5P 2S8
(604) 324-8280   SIC 5039
KS CENTOCO WHEEL CORPORATION   p
1020
2450 CENTRAL AVE, WINDSOR, ON, N8W
4J3
(519) 974-2727   SIC 3429
KS CIRCUITS INC   p 987
100 KING ST W SUITE 5600, TORONTO,
ON, M5X 1C9
(416) 913-5438   SIC 8731
KSB PUMPS INC   p 696
5205 TOMKEN RD, MISSISSAUGA, ON,
L4W 3N8
(905) 568-9200   SIC 5085
KSD ENTERPRISES LTD   p 585
655 DIXON RD SUITE 1, ETOBICOKE, ON,
M9W 1J3
(416) 244-1711   SIC 7011
KSH   p 1220
See KSH SOLUTIONS INC
KSH SOLUTIONS INC   p 1220
3400 BOUL DE MAISONNEUVE O BU-
REAU 1600, MONTREAL, QC, H3Z 3B8
(514) 932-4611   SIC 8711
KSM INC   p 149
1904 4 ST, NISKU, AB, T9E 7T8
(780) 955-3456   SIC 5084
KSR INTERNATIONAL INC   p 857
172 CENTRE ST, RODNEY, ON, N0L 2C0
(519) 785-0121   SIC 3714
KSR INTERNATIONAL INC   p 857
95 ERIE ST S, RIDGETOWN, ON, N0P 2C0
(519) 674-5413   SIC 3714
KTA OFFICE   p 223
See KIMBERLEY TEACHER'S ASSOCIA-
TION
KTC INDUSTRIAL ENGINEERING LTD   p
277
12877 76 AVE SUITE 218, SURREY, BC,
V3W 1E6
(604) 592-3123   SIC 1541
KTH SHELBURNE MFG. INC   p 880
300 2ND LINE, SHELBURNE, ON, L9V 3N4
(519) 925-3030   SIC 3714
KTI LIMITED   p 481
33 ISAACSON CRES, AURORA, ON, L4G
0A4
(905) 727-8807   SIC 5085
KTS TRADING INC   p 723
3744 TRELAWNY CIR, MISSISSAUGA, ON,
L5N 5J7
(905) 824-5679   SIC 6799
KTW HOLDINGS LTD   p 252
580 HIGHWAY W, PRINCETON, BC, V0X
1W0
(250) 372-0451   SIC 5541
KUBES STEEL INC   p 892
930 ARVIN AVE, STONEY CREEK, ON, L8E
5Y8
(905) 643-1229   SIC 3499

KUBIK INC   p 703
1680 MATTAWA AVE, MISSISSAUGA, ON,
L4X 3A5
(905) 272-2818   SIC 3993
KUBOTA   p 1123
See AUBIN & ST-PIERRE INC
KUBOTA CANADA LTD   p 678
5900 14TH AVE, MARKHAM, ON, L3S 4K4
(905) 294-7477   SIC 5084
**KUBOTA MATERIALS CANADA CORPO-
RATION**   p
809
25 COMMERCE RD, ORILLIA, ON, L3V 6L6
(705) 325-2781   SIC 3317
KUCERA CONSTRUCTION EQUIPMENT   p
477
See KUCERA FARM SUPPLY LIMITED
KUCERA FARM SUPPLY LIMITED   p 477
3212 NAUVOO RD, ALVINSTON, ON, N0N
1A0
(519) 898-2961   SIC 5083
KUDLIK CONSTRUCTION LTD   p 472
1519 FEDERAL RD, IQALUIT, NU, X0A 0H0
(867) 979-1166   SIC 1542
KUDU INDUSTRIES INC   p 17
9112 40 ST SE, CALGARY, AB, T2C 2P3
(403) 279-5838   SIC 5084
KUE PERSONAL CARE PRODUCTS   p 482
See ULLMAN, KEN ENTERPRISES INC
KUEHNE + NAGEL   p 1185
See KUEHNE + NAGEL LTD
KUEHNE + NAGEL LOGISTICS INC   p 1335
2500 AV MARIE-CURIE, SAINT-LAURENT,
QC, H4S 1N1
(514) 683-9630   SIC 4731
KUEHNE + NAGEL LTD   p 723
2300 HOGAN DR, MISSISSAUGA, ON, L5S
0C8
(905) 567-4168   SIC 4731
KUEHNE + NAGEL LTD   p 731
77 FOSTER CRES, MISSISSAUGA, ON,
L5R 0K1
(905) 502-7776   SIC 4731
KUEHNE + NAGEL LTD   p 740
6335 EDWARDS BLVD, MISSISSAUGA,
ON, L5T 2W7
(905) 670-6901   SIC 4731
KUEHNE + NAGEL LTD   p 1185
3510 BOUL SAINT-LAURENT BUREAU
400, MONTREAL, QC, H2X 2V2
(514) 397-9900   SIC 4731
KUEHNE + NAGEO   p 23
See K N CUSTOMS BROKERS
KUM SING POULTRY   p 295
See MAN-KWONG ENTERPRISES LTD
KUMI CANADA CORPORATION   p 497
55 REAGEN'S INDUSTRIAL PKY, BRAD-
FORD, ON, L3Z 0Z9
(905) 778-1464   SIC 3089
KUMON CANADA INC   p 1027
6240 HIGHWAY 7 SUITE 300, WOOD-
BRIDGE, ON, L4H 4G3
(416) 490-1434   SIC 8299
KUMON CENTRE OF BEACON HILL   p 1027
See KUMON CANADA INC
KUNG'S MANUFACTORY LTD   p 289
18 2ND AVE E, VANCOUVER, BC, V5T 1B1
(604) 873-6341   SIC 5094
KUNKEL BUS LINES LTD   p 617
301205 KNAPVILLE RD, HANOVER, ON,
N4N 3T1
(519) 364-2530   SIC 4111
KUNKEL LIMOSINE SERVICES   p 617
See KUNKEL BUS LINES LTD
KUNTZ ELECTROPLATING INC   p 636
851 WILSON AVE, KITCHENER, ON, N2C
1J1
(519) 893-7680   SIC 3471
**KUNY'S LEATHER MANUFACTURING
COMPANY LTD**   p 139
5901 44A ST, LEDUC, AB, T9E 7B8
(780) 986-1151   SIC 5948
KURIYAMA CANADA, INC   p 514
140 ROY BLVD, BRANTFORD, ON, N3R

▲ Public Company   ■ Public Company Family Member   **HQ** Headquarters   **BR** Branch   **SL** Single Location

7K2
(519) 753-6717   *SIC* 3052
KURT RYAN PHARMACY SERVICES LTD *p*
458
315 HERRING COVE RD, HALIFAX, NS,
B3R 1V5
(902) 477-1210   *SIC* 5912
KURT'S IRON WORKS LTD   *p* 146
933 19 ST SW, MEDICINE HAT, AB, T1B
0A2
(403) 527-2844   *SIC* 5084
KUSHIES BABY   *p* 891
See DIANA DOLLS FASHIONS INC
KUTCO INTERNATIONAL INC   *p* 504
275 WALKER DR, BRAMPTON, ON, L6T
3W5
SIC 2015
KUZCO LIGHTING INC   *p* 279
19054 28 AVE SUITE 19054, SURREY, BC,
V3Z 6M3
(604) 538-7162   *SIC* 5063
**KVAERNER   PROCESS   SYSTEMS
CANADA INC**   *p* 36
1209 59 AVE SE SUITE 100, CALGARY, AB,
T2H 2P6
(403) 640-4230   *SIC* 4213
KVAERNER PROCESS SYSTEMS, DIV OF
p 15
See FJORDS PROCESSING CANADA INC
KWA PARTNERS   *p* 964
See KNEBEL WATTERS & ASSOCIATES
INC
KWANTLEN POLYTECHNIC UNIVERSITY *p*
228
See KWANTLEN POLYTECHNIC UNIVER-
SITY FOUNDATION
**KWANTLEN POLYTECHNIC UNIVERSITY
FOUNDATION**   *p* 228
20901 LANGLEY BYPASS, LANGLEY, BC,
V3A 8G9
(604) 599-2100   *SIC* 8222
**KWANTLEN POLYTECHNIC UNIVERSITY
FOUNDATION**   *p* 277
12666 72 AVE, SURREY, BC, V3W 2M8
(604) 599-2000   *SIC* 8221
KWL   *p* 186
See KERR WOOD LEIDAL ASSOCIATES
LTD
KWP INC   *p* 1379
1367 RUE NATIONALE, TERREBONNE,
QC, J6W 6H8
(450) 964-5786   *SIC* 5031
KYLE HUTTERIAN BRETHREN FARM   *p*
1408
See HUTTERIAN BRETHREN OF KYLE
INC
**KYOCERA   DOCUMENT   SOLUTIONS
CANADA, LTD**   *p* 740
6120 KESTREL RD, MISSISSAUGA, ON,
L5T 1S8
(905) 670-4425   *SIC* 5044
KYSY INC   *p* 681
795 BALM BEACH RD E, MIDLAND, ON,
L4R 4K4
(705) 527-4067   *SIC* 5411

L

L R TRUCK CENTRE   *p* 1436
See RAYNARD FARM EQUIPMENT LTD
L & A HOSPITAL   *p* 747
See LENNOX AND ADDINGTON COUNTY
GENERAL HOSPITAL ASSOCIATION
L & A METALWORKS INC   *p* 401
1968 LINCOLN RD, FREDERICTON, NB,
E3B 8M7
(506) 458-1100   *SIC* 3499
L & D PETCH CONTRACTING LTD   *p* 220
204 CAMBRO RD, KELOWNA, BC, V1X 7T3
(250) 491-0405   *SIC* 5032
L & L MCCAW HOLDINGS LTD   *p* 430
50 KELSEY DR, ST. JOHN'S, NL, A1B 5C7
(709) 722-5530   *SIC* 5531
**L & L OILFIELD CONSTRUCTION (1990)
LTD**   *p* 1409

6107 49 AVE, LLOYDMINSTER, SK, S9V
2G2
(306) 825-6111   *SIC* 1389
L & M ENTERPRISES LIMITED   *p* 447
20 MACDONALD AVE, DARTMOUTH, NS,
B3B 1C5
(902) 468-8040   *SIC* 6712
L & M FOOD MARKET (ONTARIO) LIMITED
p 569
181 GEDDES ST, ELORA, ON, N0B 1S0
(519) 846-1188   *SIC* 5411
L & M MERCIER ENTERPRISES INC *p* 1406
200 KING ST SUITE 146, ESTEVAN, SK,
S4A 2W4
(306) 634-6407   *SIC* 5531
L & M PRECISION PRODUCTS INC   *p* 793
150 MILVAN DR, NORTH YORK, ON, M9L
1Z9
(416) 741-0700   *SIC* 3451
L & R DISTRIBUTORS LTD   *p* 155
8120 EDGAR INDUSTRIAL DR, RED
DEER, AB, T4P 3R2
SIC 5171
L B C D INGENIEURS CONSEILS INC   *p*
1366
40 RUE SAINTE-CECILE, SALABERRY-DE-
VALLEYFIELD, QC, J6T 1L7
(450) 371-5722   *SIC* 8621
L C FRUITS & LEGUMES   *p* 1162
See LUC CHARBONNEAU FRUITS &
LEGUMES INC
L E I   *p* 206
See LOCHER EVERS INTERNATIONAL
INC
L J C CLEANING SERVICES INC   *p* 818
740 BELFAST RD UNIT B, OTTAWA, ON,
K1G 0Z5
(613) 244-1997   *SIC* 1542
L'AMOREAUX COLLEGIATE INSTITUTE   *p*
878
See   TORONTO   DISTRICT   SCHOOL
BOARD
L'ANNUAIRE DU TELECOPIEUR   *p* 1212
See TAMEC INC
L'ARCHE ASSOCIATION OF CALGARY   *p*
36
307 57 AVE SW, CALGARY, AB, T2H 2T6
(403) 571-0155   *SIC* 8699
L'ARCHE TORONTO HOMES INC   *p* 919
186 FLOYD AVE, TORONTO, ON, M4J 2J1
(416) 406-2869   *SIC* 8699
L'ARENA DES CANADIENS INC   *p* 1211
1275 RUE SAINT-ANTOINE O, MON-
TREAL, QC, H3C 5L2
(514) 989-2814   *SIC* 7941
L'ART DE VIVRE A SON MEILLEUR *p* 1402
4152A RUE SAINTE-CATHERINE O, WEST-
MOUNT, QC, H3Z 1P4
SIC 6719
**L'ASSOCIATION   TOURISTIQUE   DE
L'OUTAOUAIS**   *p* 1105
103 RUE LAURIER, GATINEAU, QC, J8X
3V8
(819) 778-2222   *SIC* 7389
L'AUBAINERIE   *p* 1106
See DENIS CROTEAU INC
L'AUBAINERIE 14   *p* 1282
See C. CROTEAU INC
L'AVIATIC CLUB INC   *p* 1259
450 RUE DE LA GARE-DU-PALAIS BU-
REAU 104, QUEBEC, QC, G1K 3X2
(418) 522-3555   *SIC* 5812
L'EAU-THENTIQUE   *p* 1097
See 9101-7673 QUEBEC INC
L'ECOLE SELWYN HOUSE   *p* 1401
See SELWYN HOUSE ASSOCIATION
L'EDIFICE 3333 BOUL GRAHAM   *p* 1155
3333 BOUL GRAHAM BUREAU 100,
MONT-ROYAL, QC, H3R 3L5
(514) 341-8182   *SIC* 6531
L'EMPREINTE   *p* 1234
See IMPRIMERIE L'EMPREINTE INC
L'EQUIPEUR   *p* 36
See MARK'S WORK WEARHOUSE LTD

L'EQUIPOULE INC   *p* 1149
2010 AV INDUSTRIELLE, MARIEVILLE,
QC, J3M 1J5
(450) 730-0336   *SIC* 0259
L'HEBDO DU ST-MAURICE   *p* 1368
1672 AV SAINT-MARC BUREAU A, SHAW-
INIGAN, QC, G9N 2H4
(819) 537-4161   *SIC* 6311
L'ILE-PERROT NISSAN   *p* 1120
See 3347818 CANADA INC
**L'INDUSTRIELLE-ALLIANCE   SERVICES
IMMOBILIERS INC**   *p* 1275
3810 RUE DE MARLY, QUEBEC, QC, G1X
4B1
(418) 651-7308   *SIC* 6513
**L'INSTITUT DE READAPTATION GINGRAS-
LINDSAY-DE-MONTREAL**   *p*
1218
6300 AV DE DARLINGTON, MONTREAL,
QC, H3S 2J4
(514) 340-2085   *SIC* 8069
L'OCCITANE CANADA CORP   *p* 988
2700 DUFFERIN ST UNIT 89, TORONTO,
ON, M6B 4J3
(416) 782-0005   *SIC* 5999
**L'ORATOIRE SAINT-JOSEPH DU MONT-
ROYAL**   *p*
1219
3800 CH QUEEN-MARY, MONTREAL, QC,
H3V 1H6
(514) 733-8211   *SIC* 8661
L'OREAL CANADA INC   *p* 1197
1500 BOUL ROBERT-BOURASSA BU-
REAU 600, MONTREAL, QC, H3A 3S7
(514) 287-4800   *SIC* 2844
L'UNION-VIE   *p* 1100
See UNION-VIE, COMPAGNIE MUTUELLE
D'ASSURANCE, L'
L'USINE TAC TIC INC   *p* 1305
2030 127E RUE, SAINT-GEORGES, QC,
G5Y 2W8
(418) 227-4279   *SIC* 7389
**L-3   COMMUNICATIONS   ELECTRONIC
SYSTEMS INC**   *p* 450
249 AEROTECH DR, GOFFS, NS, B2T 1K3
(902) 873-2000   *SIC* 3812
**L-3 COMMUNICATIONS MAS (CANADA)
INC**   *p* 735
See L3 TECHNOLOGIES MAS INC
L-3 TECHNOLOGIES   *p* 529
See WESCAM INC.
L-D TOOL & DIE   *p* 891
See MADIX ENGINEERING INC
L-K METAL PRODUCTS CO. LIMITED   *p*
1022
1595 LINCOLN RD, WINDSOR, ON, N8Y
2J3
(519) 256-1861   *SIC* 5075
L. & G. CLOUTIER INC   *p* 1121
303 BOUL NILUS-LECLERC, L'ISLET, QC,
G0R 2C0
(418) 247-5071   *SIC* 3599
L. & M. LUMBER LTD   *p* 331
1241 HWY 16 W, VANDERHOOF, BC, V0J
3A0
(250) 567-4701   *SIC* 3553
L. & S. MARKETING LTD   *p* 1043
142 DALTON AVE, TIGNISH, PE, C0B 2B0
(902) 882-3105   *SIC* 5146
L. A. DAIGNEAULT & FILS LTEE   *p* 1088
1531 RUE DU SUD, COWANSVILLE, QC,
J2K 2Z4
(450) 263-3686   *SIC* 5411
L. BELANGER METAL INC   *p* 1386
2950 RUE DE LA SIDBEC N, TROIS-
RIVIERES, QC, G8Z 4E1
(819) 375-6600   *SIC* 5093
L. BILODEAU ET FILS LTEE   *p* 1113
366 RUE SAINT-JEAN, HONFLEUR, QC,
G0R 1N0
(418) 885-4495   *SIC* 4212
L. DAVIS TEXTILES (1991) INC   *p* 1111
780 RUE GEORGES-CROS, GRANBY, QC,
J2J 1N2

(450) 375-1665   *SIC* 5137
L. FOURNIER ET FILS INC   *p* 1390
1095 RUE LEO-FOURNIER, VAL-D'OR,
QC, J9P 6X6
(819) 825-4000   *SIC* 1794
L. G. HEBERT & FILS LTEE   *p* 1358
428 RUE HEBERT, SAINTE-HELENE-DE-
BAGOT, QC, J0H 1M0
(450) 791-2630   *SIC* 2011
L. HANSEN'S FORWARDING LTD   *p* 876
105 NASHDENE RD, SCARBOROUGH,
ON, M1V 2W3
(416) 293-9135   *SIC* 4213
L. J. L. MECANIQUE INC   *p* 1358
203 PARC INDUSTRIEL, SAINTE-
GERMAINE-BOULE, QC, J0Z 1M0
(819) 787-6509   *SIC* 7699
L. N. REYNOLDS CO. LIMITED   *p* 513
10160 HURONTARIO ST SUITE 1, BRAMP-
TON, ON, L7A 0E4
(905) 840-3700   *SIC* 5141
L. R. JACKSON FISHERIES LIMITED *p* 848
172 MAIN ST, PORT STANLEY, ON, N5L
1H6
(519) 782-3562   *SIC* 5146
L. SIMARD TRANSPORT LIMITEE   *p* 1128
1212 32E AV, LACHINE, QC, H8T 3K7
(514) 636-9411   *SIC* 4212
L. SIMARD TRANSPORT LIMITEE   *p* 1128
3500 RUE FAIRWAY, LACHINE, QC, H8T
1B4
(514) 636-0852   *SIC* 4212
L.A. DALTON SYSTEMS LP   *p* 532
1435 HIGHWAY 56, CALEDONIA, ON, N3W
1T1
SIC 6712
L.A. HEBERT LTEE   *p* 1070
9700 PLACE JADE, BROSSARD, QC, J4Y
3C1
(450) 444-4847   *SIC* 8711
L.A.M.M. INC   *p* 858
1273 LONDON RD, SARNIA, ON, N7S 1P3
(519) 383-7727   *SIC* 6794
**L.B. FOSTER TECHNOLOGIES FERROVI-
AIRES CANADA LTEE**   *p*
1251
172 BOUL BRUNSWICK, POINTE-CLAIRE,
QC, H9R 5P9
(514) 695-8500   *SIC* 5088
L.C. 2000   *p* 1062
See L.C. ENTREPRENEURS GENERAUX
(2000) LTEE
**L.C. ENTREPRENEURS GENERAUX (2000)
LTEE**   *p* 1062
4045 RUE LAVOISIER, BOISBRIAND, QC,
J7H 1N1
(450) 682-1951   *SIC* 1542
L.C.L. EXCAVATION (2006) INC   *p* 396
214 CRAIG RD, CHARLO, NB, E8E 2J2
(506) 684-3453   *SIC* 1794
L.D. AUTO (1986) INC   *p* 1303
854 BOUL DU SACRE-COEUR, SAINT-
FELICIEN, QC, G8K 1S2
(418) 679-1546   *SIC* 5511
L.E.A.R.N   *p* 1134
See LEADING ENGLISH AND EDUCATION
RESOURCE NETWORK (LEARN)
L.E.S. MECANIQUE INC   *p* 1335
1200 RUE SAINT-AMOUR, SAINT-
LAURENT, QC, H4S 1J2
(514) 333-6968   *SIC* 7538
L.F.OAKES & SONS LTD.   *p* 404
259 MCELROY RD, HOLMESVILLE, NB,
E7J 2J4
SIC 0134
L.H.M. TECHNOLOGIES INC   *p* 1032
446 ROWNTREE DAIRY RD, WOOD-
BRIDGE, ON, L4L 8H2
(905) 856-2466   *SIC* 3541
**L.J. ROBICHEAU & SON FISHERIES LIM-
ITED**   *p*
460
219 SHORE RD, LITTLE RIVER, NS, B0V
1C0

(902) 834-2792   *SIC 2092*
L.J.M. MARKETING INC   *p 1164*
6420 RUE SHERBROOKE E BUREAU 55, MONTREAL, QC, H1N 3P6
(514) 259-6991   *SIC 5912*
L.L. LOZEAU   *p 1182*
See CRANBROOK GLEN ENTERPRISES LIMITED
L.M.B TRANPSORT LIMITED   *p 491*
209 PUTTMAN INDUSTRIAL RD, BELLEVILLE, ON, K8N 4Z6
(613) 968-7541   *SIC 7532*
L.M.B. TRANSPORT INC   *p 540*
209 PUTMAN INDUSTRIAL RD, CANNIFTON, ON, K0K 1K0
(613) 968-7524   *SIC 4212*
L.M.L. AUTOMATISATION   *p 1318*
See GROUPE LML LTEE, LE
L.O.D.A INC   *p 1226*
1200 RUE DE LOUVAIN O, MONTREAL, QC, H4N 1G5
(514) 382-0571   *SIC 7389*
L.P. CUSTOM MACHINING LTD   *p 892*
211 BARTON ST, STONEY CREEK, ON, L8E 2K3
SIC 3599
L.P. ROYER INC   *p 1124*
712 RUE PRINCIPALE, LAC-DROLET, QC, G0Y 1C0
(819) 549-2100   *SIC 3143*
L3 MAPPS INC   *p 1340*
8565 CH DE LA COTE-DE-LIESSE, SAINT-LAURENT, QC, H4T 1G5
(514) 787-5000   *SIC 8748*
L3 TECHNOLOGIES MAS INC   *p 735*
7785 TRANMERE DR, MISSISSAUGA, ON, L5S 1W5
(905) 671-5879   *SIC 4581*
L3 TECHNOLOGIES MAS INC   *p 1153*
10000 RUE HELEN-BRISTOL, MIRABEL, QC, J7N 1H3
(450) 476-4000   *SIC 7699*
LA BAIE   *p 1280*
See HUDSON'S BAY COMPANY
LA BODEGA RESTAURANT   *p 326*
See FERNANDO'S RESTAURANT LTD
LA BONBONNICRE SWEET FACTORY   *p 1086*
See INDULBEC INC
LA CAPITALE - COMPAGNIE D'ASSURANCE   *p 1269*
525 BOUL RENE-LEVESQUE E, QUEBEC, QC, G1R 5S9
(418) 266-1700   *SIC 6411*
LA CAPITALE ASSURANCE ET SERVICES FINANCIERS   *p 1269*
See LA CAPITALE SERVICES CONSEILS INC
LA CAPITALE FINANCIAL SECURITY INSURANCE COMPANY   *p 745*
7150 DERRYCREST DR SUITE 1150, MISSISSAUGA, ON, L5W 0E5
(905) 795-2300   *SIC 6321*
LA CAPITALE SAGUENAY LAC-ST-JEAN   *p 1078*
See 9085-3532 QUEBEC INC
LA CAPITALE SERVICES CONSEILS INC   *p 1269*
625 RUE JACQUES-PARIZEAU, QUEBEC, QC, G1R 2G5
(418) 747-7600   *SIC 6311*
LA CHAUMIERE RETIREMENT RESIDENCE   *p 490*
See 822188 ONTARIO INC
LA COMPAGNIE D'IMPORTATION DE COSMETIQUES LIMITEE   *p 1066*
1380 RUE NEWTON BUREAU 203, BOUCHERVILLE, QC, J4B 5H2
(450) 449-1236   *SIC 5122*
LA CRETE CO-OP LIMITED   *p 137*
10502 100 ST, LA CRETE, AB, T0H 2H0

(780) 928-2900   *SIC 5411*
LA CRETE PELLET   *p 137*
See LA CRETE SAWMILLS LTD
LA CRETE SAWMILLS LTD   *p 137*
GD, LA CRETE, AB, T0H 2H0
(780) 928-2292   *SIC 2421*
LA CREVETTE DU NORD ATLANTIQUE INC   *p 1102*
139 RUE DE LA REINE, GASPE, QC, G4X 1T5
(418) 368-1414   *SIC 2092*
LA FONDATION DE L'INSTITUT MARITIME DU QUEBEC INC   *p 1284*
53 RUE SAINT-GERMAIN O, RIMOUSKI, QC, G5L 4B4
(418) 724-2822   *SIC 8299*
LA FROMAGERIE ALEXIS DE PORTNEUF   *p 1351*
See SAPUTO PRODUITS LAITIERS CANADA S.E.N.C.
LA FURLANE CONSTRUCTION (1999)   *p 360*
See 4001966 MANITOBA LTD
LA GALERIE DU JOUET JFA INC   *p 1045*
1435 AV DU PONT S, ALMA, QC, G8B 2V9
(418) 662-6221   *SIC 5092*
LA GROTTA DEL FORMAGGIO   *p 391*
See MONDO FOODS CO. LTD
LA MAISON DU MEUBLE CORBEIL   *p 1237*
See G2MC INC
LA MAISON SAINTE-MARIE DES ANGES   *p 1257*
See SOEURS DE SAINT-FRANCOIS D'ASSISE, LES
LA MEZCALERIA   *p 285*
See TACORPORATION RESTAURANT LTD
LA NASSA FOODS   *p 634*
See LA NASSA FOODS INC
LA NASSA FOODS INC   *p 634*
215 INDUSTRY RD, KINGSVILLE, ON, N9Y 1K9
(519) 733-9100   *SIC 5146*
LA PANTHERE VERTE   *p 1213*
2153 RUE MACKAY, MONTREAL, QC, H3G 2J2
(514) 903-4744   *SIC 5092*
LA PERSONNELLE   *p 1137*
See PERSONNELLE ASSURANCES GENERALES INC, LA
LA RESIDENCE GIA DE SEVE   *p 1175*
See FONDATION DE LA MAISON DU PERE
LA ROCCA CREATIVE CAKES INC   *p 857*
45 VIA RENZO DR, RICHMOND HILL, ON, L4S 0B4
(905) 884-7275   *SIC 5149*
LA RONGE PETROLEUM LTD   *p 1408*
1420 FINNLAYSON ST, LA RONGE, SK, S0J 1L0
(306) 425-6841   *SIC 5171*
LA ROSA'S NOFRILLS   *p 1016*
See LOBLAWS SUPERMARKETS LIMITED
LA ROSE ITALIAN BAKERY & DELICATESSEN   *p 684*
See LIZZI, C. ENTERPRISES INC
LA ROTISSERIE ST HUBERT BOUCHERVILLE 087   *p 1067*
See ROTISSERIES ST-HUBERT LTEE, LES
LA SALLE SECONDARY SCHOOL   *p 631*
See LIMESTONE DISTRICT SCHOOL BOARD
LA SALLE STEEL CORPORATION   *p 1186*
180 BOUL RENE-LEVESQUE E BUREAU 500, MONTREAL, QC, H2X 1N6
(514) 933-8899   *SIC 5051*
LA SENZA CORPORATION   *p 551*
See CORPORATION SENZA, LA
LA TAQUERIA PINCHE TACO SHOP   *p 303*
See COMEX FOOD PRODUCTION INC
LA TRAPPE A FROMAGE DE L'OUTAOUAIS   *p 1106*
114 BOUL SAINT-RAYMOND, GATINEAU, QC, J8Y 1S9

(819) 243-6411   *SIC 5451*
LA&M   *p 661*
See LONDON AUTOMOTIVE & MANUFACTURING LTD
LA-BIL INC   *p 1262*
895 AV GODIN, QUEBEC, QC, G1M 2X5
(418) 842-3216   *SIC 1711*
LA-Z-BOY FURNITURE   *p 382*
See D & S FURNITURE GALLERIES LTD
LA-Z-BOY FURNITURE GALLERIES   *p 98*
See 648781 ALBERTA LTD
LA-Z-BOY FURNITURE GALLERIES   *p 488*
See REID'S FURNITURE OF BARRIE LIMITED
LA-Z-BOY FURNITURE GALLERIES   *p 659*
See BOOMCO DECOR INC
LA-Z-BOY FURNITURE GALLERIES   *p 659*
See HOGEBOOM, PAUL W. HOLDINGS LTD
LA-Z-BOY FURNITURE GALLERIES OF OTTAWA/KINGSTON   *p 594*
See 7902476 CANADA INC
LA-Z-BOY GALLERIES   *p 100*
See COMFORT FURNITURE GALLERIES
LA-ZY-BOY FURNITURE GALLERIES   *p 549*
See BOOMCO DECOR INC
LAARK ENTERPRISES LIMITED   *p 1014*
516 BROCK ST N, WHITBY, ON, L1N 4J2
(905) 430-3703   *SIC 5461*
LAB-VOLT   *p 1280*
See FESTO DIDACTIQUE LTEE
LABARRE GAUTHIER INC   *p 1186*
3575 BOUL SAINT-LAURENT BUREAU 900, MONTREAL, QC, H2X 2T7
(514) 281-8901   *SIC 7311*
LABATT BREWERIES WESTERN CANADA   *p 115*
See LABATT BREWING COMPANY LIMITED
LABATT BREWERY   *p 654*
See JOHN LABATT LIMITED
LABATT BREWING COMPANY LIMITED   *p 115*
10119 45 AVE NW, EDMONTON, AB, T6E 0G8
(780) 436-6060   *SIC 2082*
LABATT BREWING COMPANY LIMITED   *p 433*
60 LESLIE ST, ST. JOHN'S, NL, A1E 2V8
(709) 579-0121   *SIC 2082*
LABATT BREWING COMPANY LIMITED   *p 964*
207 QUEENS QUAY W SUITE 299, TORONTO, ON, M5J 1A7
(416) 361-5050   *SIC 2082*
LABATT BREWING COMPANY LIMITED   *p 1131*
2505 RUE SENKUS, LASALLE, QC, H8N 2X8
(514) 595-2505   *SIC 5813*
LABATT BREWING COMPANY LIMITED   *p 1132*
50 AV LABATT BUREAU 42, LASALLE, QC, H8R 3E7
(514) 366-5050   *SIC 2082*
LABBE-LEECH INTERIORS LTD   *p 30*
2600 PORTLAND ST SE SUITE 2020, CALGARY, AB, T2G 4M6
(403) 252-9991   *SIC 1799*
LABDARA LITHUANIAN NURSING HOME   *p 576*
5 RESURRECTION RD, ETOBICOKE, ON, M9A 5G1
(416) 232-2112   *SIC 8051*
LABELIX INC   *p 1109*
536 RUE GUY, GRANBY, QC, J2G 7J8
(450) 372-7777   *SIC 7389*
LABELLE, M. J. CO. LTD   *p 545*
109 HIGHWAY 11 W, COCHRANE, ON, P0L 1C0
(705) 272-4201   *SIC 1794*
LABELS UNLIMITED INC   *p 366*
67 ARCHIBALD ST, WINNIPEG, MB, R2J

0V7
(204) 233-4444   *SIC 2679*
LABOPRO P.S. INC   *p 1277*
1405 AV SAINT-JEAN-BAPTISTE BUREAU 115, QUEBEC, QC, G2E 5K2
(418) 681-6128   *SIC 7384*
LABORATOIRE ATLAS INC   *p 1049*
9600 BOUL DES SCIENCES, ANJOU, QC, H1J 3B6
(514) 254-7188   *SIC 2834*
LABORATOIRE COULEUR UNIVERSEL INC   *p 1237*
810 RUE SALABERRY, MONTREAL, QC, H7S 1H3
(514) 384-2251   *SIC 7384*
LABORATOIRE D'ESSAIS MEQUALTECH INC   *p 1170*
8740 BOUL PIE-IX, MONTREAL, QC, H1Z 3V1
(514) 593-5755   *SIC 7389*
LABORATOIRE DE CANALISATIONS SOUTERRAINES (LCS) INC   *p 1264*
255 AV SAINT-SACREMENT, QUEBEC, QC, G1N 3X9
(418) 651-9306   *SIC 7389*
LABORATOIRE DE SANTE PUBLIQUE DU QUEBEC   *p 1355*
See INSTITUT NATIONALE DE SANTE PUBLIQUE DU QUEBEC
LABORATOIRE DU-VAR INC   *p 1066*
1460 RUE GRAHAM-BELL, BOUCHERVILLE, QC, J4B 6H5
(450) 641-4740   *SIC 2844*
LABORATOIRE POULIOT INC   *p 1272*
2815 CH DES QUATRE-BOURGEOIS, QUEBEC, QC, G1V 1X8
(418) 652-0100   *SIC 5999*
LABORATOIRE RIVA INC   *p 1059*
660 BOUL INDUSTRIEL, BLAINVILLE, QC, J7C 3V4
(450) 434-7482   *SIC 2834*
LABORATOIRE VICTHOM INC   *p 1237*
2101 BOUL LE CARREFOUR BUREAU 102, MONTREAL, QC, H7S 2J7
(450) 239-6162   *SIC 8069*
LABORATOIRES ABBOTT, LIMITEE   *p 723*
7115 MILLCREEK DR, MISSISSAUGA, ON, L5N 3R3
(905) 858-2450   *SIC 2834*
LABORATOIRES ABBOTT, LIMITEE   *p 1335*
8625 RTE TRANSCANADIENNE, SAINT-LAURENT, QC, H4S 1Z6
(514) 832-7000   *SIC 2834*
LABORATOIRES BUCKMAN DU CANADA, LTEE   *p 1395*
351 RUE JOSEPH-CARRIER, VAUDREUIL-DORION, QC, J7V 5V5
(450) 424-4404   *SIC 2869*
LABORATOIRES BUG TRACKER INC   *p 1166*
2030 BOUL PIE-IX BUREAU 307, MONTREAL, QC, H1V 2C8
(514) 496-0093   *SIC 8742*
LABORATOIRES C.O.P. INC   *p 1107*
60 RUE JEAN-PROULX, GATINEAU, QC, J8Z 1W1
(819) 772-4447   *SIC 5141*
LABORATOIRES CHARLES RIVER MONTREAL ULC   *p 1366*
22022 AUT FELIX-LECLERC, SENNEVILLE, QC, H9X 3R3
(514) 630-8200   *SIC 8731*
LABORATOIRES CHARLES RIVER MONTREAL ULC   *p 1370*
1580 RUE IDA-METIVIER, SHERBROOKE, QC, J1E 0B5
(819) 346-8200   *SIC 8731*
LABORATOIRES CHARLES RIVER SAINT-CONSTANT S.A.   *p 1298*
324 RANG SAINT-REGIS N, SAINT-CONSTANT, QC, J5A 2E7

(450) 638-1571 *SIC* 0279
LABORATOIRES CHEZ-NOUS INC., LES *p*
1303
606 BOUL DU SACRE-COEUR, SAINT-FELICIEN, QC, G8K 1T5
(418) 679-2694 *SIC* 5122
LABORATOIRES CHOISY LTEE *p* 1146
390 BOUL SAINT-LAURENT E, LOUISEVILLE, QC, J5V 2L7
(819) 228-5564 *SIC* 2842
LABORATOIRES CONFAB INC *p* 1308
4355 BOUL SIR-WILFRID-LAURIER, SAINT-HUBERT, QC, J3Y 3X3
(450) 443-6666 *SIC* 2834
LABORATOIRES D'ANALYSES S.M. INC *p*
1393
1471 BOUL LIONEL-BOULET, VARENNES, QC, J3X 1P7
(514) 332-6001 *SIC* 8731
LABORATOIRES DELON (1990) INC *p* 1091
69 BOUL BRUNSWICK, DOLLARD-DES-ORMEAUX, QC, H9B 2N4
(514) 685-9966 *SIC* 2844
LABORATOIRES DERMO-COSMETIK INC *p*
1326
68 RUE STINSON, SAINT-LAURENT, QC, H4N 2E7
(514) 735-1531 *SIC* 2844
LABORATOIRES G.M.F. (1983) INC *p* 1310
7485 AV DUPLESSIS, SAINT-HYACINTHE, QC, J2R 1S5
(450) 796-4772 *SIC* 5122
LABORATOIRES ITR CANADA INC, LES *p*
1053
19601 AV CLARK-GRAHAM, BAIE-D'URFE, QC, H9X 3T1
(514) 457-7400 *SIC* 8731
LABORATOIRES KABS INC *p* 1308
4500 RUE DE TONNANCOUR, SAINT-HUBERT, QC, J3Y 9G2
(450) 656-4404 *SIC* 8731
LABORATOIRES LALCO INC *p* 1379
1542 RUE NATIONALE, TERREBONNE, QC, J6W 6M1
(450) 492-6435 *SIC* 5122
LABORATOIRES MSA *p* 1393
See *LABORATOIRES MSP INC*
LABORATOIRES MSP INC *p* 1393
2401 MONTEE DE PICARDIE, VARENNES, QC, J3X 0J1
(450) 652-4295 *SIC* 2023
LABORATOIRES NICAR INC, LES *p* 1059
10 RUE GASTON-DUMOULIN BUREAU 500, BLAINVILLE, QC, J7C 0A3
(450) 979-0400 *SIC* 5122
LABORATOIRES ODAN LTEE, LES *p* 1251
325 AV STILLVIEW, POINTE-CLAIRE, QC, H9R 2Y6
(514) 428-1628 *SIC* 2834
LABORATOIRES OMEGA LIMITEE *p* 1217
11177 RUE HAMON, MONTREAL, QC, H3M 3E4
(514) 335-0310 *SIC* 2834
LABORATOIRES PIERRE FABRE *p* 1071
See *PIERRE FABRE DERMO-COSMETIQUE CANADA INC*
LABORATOIRES STRADIGI *p* 1200
See *STRADIGI INC*
LABORATOIRES SUISSE INC, LES *p* 1066
1310 RUE NOBEL, BOUCHERVILLE, QC, J4B 5H3
(450) 444-9808 *SIC* 5122
LABORATOIRES TECH-CITE *p* 1172
See *OPTIQUE NIKON CANADA INC*
LABORATORY SERVICES *p* 602
See *UNIVERSITY OF GUELPH*
LABOS CM *p* 1212
See *SIMULATIONS CMLABS INC*
LABOUR GROUP *p* 1001
See *1799795 ONTARIO LIMITED*
LABOUR READY TEMPORARY SERVICES LTD *p* 841
306 GEORGE ST N UNIT 6, PETERBOROUGH, ON, K9J 3H2

(705) 760-9111 *SIC* 7361
LABOURERS INTERNATIONAL UNION OF NORTH AMERICA-LOCAL 183 *p* 786
1263 WILSON AVE SUITE 200, NORTH YORK, ON, M3M 3G2
(416) 241-1183 *SIC* 8631
LABOURERS' PENSION FUND OF CENTRAL AND EASTERN CANADA *p*
798
1315 NORTH SERVICE RD E, OAKVILLE, ON, L6H 1A7
(289) 291-3663 *SIC* 6371
LABRADOR FISHERMAN'S COMPANY *p*
425
See *LABRADOR FISHERMEN'S UNION SHRIMP COMPANY LIMITED*
LABRADOR FISHERMEN'S UNION SHRIMP COMPANY LIMITED *p* 425
46 WATERFRONT RD, L'ANSE AU LOUP, NL, A0K 3L0
(709) 927-5816 *SIC* 2092
LABRADOR INUIT DEVELOPMENT CORPORATION *p*
424
6 ROYAL ST UNIT 2, HAPPY VALLEY-GOOSE BAY, NL, A0P 1E0
(709) 896-8505 *SIC* 6719
LABRADOR IRON ORE ROYALTY CORPORATION *p*
985
40 KING ST W, TORONTO, ON, M5W 2X6
(416) 863-7133 *SIC* 6211
LABRADOR LAURENTIENNE INC *p* 1242
2540 BOUL LOUIS-FRECHETTE, NICOLET, QC, J3T 1N1
(819) 293-4555 *SIC* 5149
LABRADOR MARINE INC *p* 425
111 MAIN ST SUITE 502, LEWISPORTE, NL, A0G 3A0
(709) 535-0810 *SIC* 4731
LABRADOR MOTORS LIMITED *p* 424
12 LORING DR, HAPPY VALLEY-GOOSE BAY, NL, A0P 1C0
(709) 896-2452 *SIC* 5511
LABRADOR SCHOOL BOARD *p* 424
16 STRATHCONA ST, HAPPY VALLEY-GOOSE BAY, NL, A0P 1E0
(709) 896-7220 *SIC* 8211
LABRADOR-ISLAND LINK LIMITED PARTNERSHIP *p*
430
500 COLUMBUS DR, ST. JOHN'S, NL, A1B 0C9
(709) 737-4860 *SIC* 4911
LABRASH SECURITY SERVICES LTD *p*
922
55 EGLINTON AVE E SUITE 403, TORONTO, ON, M4P 1G8
(416) 487-4864 *SIC* 7381
LABSTAT INTERNATIONAL INC *p* 636
262 MANITOU DR, KITCHENER, ON, N2C 1L3
(519) 748-5409 *SIC* 8734
LABTAG *p* 1236
See *GA INTERNATIONAL INC*
LABTICIAN THEA *p* 799
See *THEA PHARMA INC*
LABWORKS, THE *p* 370
See *DON'S PHOTO SHOP LTD*
LABX *p* 681
See *GEOCALM INC*
LAC *p* 658
See *LONDON AGRICULTURAL COMMODITIES INC*
LAC DES ILES MINES LTD *p* 953
130 ADELAIDE ST W SUITE 2116, TORONTO, ON, M5H 3P5
(807) 448-2000 *SIC* 1099
LAC LA BICHE INN LTD *p* 138
10030 101ST AVE, LAC LA BICHE, AB, T0A 2C0
(780) 623-4427 *SIC* 7011
LAC LA BICHE SOBEY'S *p* 138
See *ABOUGOUCHE BROS ENTERPRISES*

LTD
LAC LA BICHE SPORTING GOODS LTD *p*
138
13337 101 AVE, LAC LA BICHE, AB, T0A 2C0
(780) 623-4145 *SIC* 5571
LAC LA BICHE TRANSPORT LTD *p* 137
66569 RR 143, ISLAY, AB, T0A 2C0
(780) 623-4711 *SIC* 4212
LAC LA BICHE TRANSPORT LTD *p* 138
555 TOWER RD, LAC LA BICHE, AB, T0A 2C0
(780) 623-4711 *SIC* 4212
LAC LA RONGE INDIAN BAND *p* 1404
54 FAR RESERVE RD, AIR RONGE, SK, S0J 3G0
(306) 425-2884 *SIC* 8743
LAC LA RONGE MOTOR HOTEL (1983) LTD *p* 1408
1120 LA RONGE AVE, LA RONGE, SK, S0J 1L0
(306) 425-2190 *SIC* 7011
LACASSE & FILS MAITRES COUVREURS INC *p* 1375
10230 BOUL BOURQUE, SHERBROOKE, QC, J1N 0G2
(819) 843-2681 *SIC* 1761
LACE GOODS CANADA, DIV OF *p* 556
See *NORTHCOTT SILK INC*
LACHANCE, B.D. SALES LTD *p* 143
2720 FAIRWAY RD S, LETHBRIDGE, AB, T1K 7A5
(403) 394-9633 *SIC* 5531
LACKNER MCLENNAN INSURANCE LTD *p*
635
818 VICTORIA ST N, KITCHENER, ON, N2B 3C1
(519) 579-3330 *SIC* 6411
LACOMBE ACTION GROUP FOR THE HANDICAPPED *p* 138
4 IRON WOLF BLVD, LACOMBE, AB, T4L 2K6
(403) 782-5531 *SIC* 8322
LACOMBE FORD SALES LTD *p* 138
5610 HIGHWAY 2A, LACOMBE, AB, T4L 1A3
(403) 782-6811 *SIC* 5511
LACOMBE RV 2000 LTD *p* 138
27211 HIGHWAY 12 SUITE 96, LACOMBE COUNTY, AB, T4L 0E3
(403) 782-4544 *SIC* 5561
LACOSTE *p* 1184
See *LACOSTE CANADA INC*
LACOSTE CANADA INC *p* 1184
4200 BOUL SAINT-LAURENT BUREAU 901, MONTREAL, QC, H2W 2R2
(514) 286-1212 *SIC* 5136
LACROIX CONSTRUCTION CO. (SUDBURY) LTD *p*
898
861 LAPOINTE ST, SUDBURY, ON, P3A 5N8
(705) 566-1294 *SIC* 1541
LACROIX DECOR *p* 1279
See *DESCHENES & FILS LTEE*
LACROIX MEATS *p* 1313
See *VIANDES LACROIX INC, LES*
LADCO COMPANY LIMITED *p* 366
40 LAKEWOOD BLVD SUITE 200, WINNIPEG, MB, R2J 2M7
(204) 982-5959 *SIC* 1629
LADCO COMPANY LIMITED *p* 386
2520 PORTAGE AVE, WINNIPEG, MB, R3J 3T6
(204) 885-4478 *SIC* 7011
LADSON PROPERTIES LIMITED *p* 887
235 MARTINDALE RD UNIT 14, ST CATHARINES, ON, L2W 1A5
(905) 684-6542 *SIC* 1542
LADY DUNN HEALTH CENTRE *p* 1011
17 GOVERNMENT RD, WAWA, ON, P0S 1K0
(705) 856-2335 *SIC* 8062
LADY GODIVA'S *p* 1034

See *A & A ENTERPRISES INC*
LADY ISABELLE NURSING HOME LTD *p*
999
102 CORKERY ST, TROUT CREEK, ON, P0H 2L0
(705) 723-5232 *SIC* 8051
LADY MINTO HOSPITAL AT COCHRANE, THE *p* 545
241 EIGHTH ST, COCHRANE, ON, P0L 1C0
(705) 272-7200 *SIC* 8062
LADY YORK FOODS *p* 791
See *LADY YORK HOLDINGS LTD*
LADY YORK HOLDINGS LTD *p* 791
2939 DUFFERIN ST, NORTH YORK, ON, M6B 3S7
(416) 781-8585 *SIC* 5411
LADYSMITH CHRONICLE *p* 336
See *ISLAND PUBLISHERS LTD*
LADYSMITH SECONDARY SCHOOL *p* 224
See *SCHOOL DISTRICT NO. 68 (NANAIMO-LADYSMITH)*
LAEBON DEVELOPMENTS LTD *p* 158
289 BURNT PARK DR, RED DEER COUNTY, AB, T4S 2L4
(403) 346-7273 *SIC* 1521
LAEBON HOMES *p* 158
See *LAEBON DEVELOPMENTS LTD*
LAFARGE AGGREGATES AND CONCRETE *p*
39
See *LAFARGE CANADA INC*
LAFARGE CANADA INC *p* 39
10511 15 ST SE, CALGARY, AB, T2J 7H7
(403) 292-1555 *SIC* 1442
LAFARGE CANADA INC *p* 441
87 CEMENT PLANT RD, BROOKFIELD, NS, B0N 1C0
(902) 673-2281 *SIC* 2891
LAFARGE CANADA INC *p* 555
7880 KEELE ST UNIT 5, CONCORD, ON, L4K 4G7
(905) 738-7070 *SIC* 5032
LAFARGE CANADA INC *p* 688
6509 AIRPORT RD, MISSISSAUGA, ON, L4V 1S7
(905) 738-7070 *SIC* 2891
LAFARGE CANADA INC *p* 1133
3055 BOUL SAINT-MARTIN O BUREAU 300, LAVAL, QC, H7T 0J3
(438) 265-1010 *SIC* 1522
LAFARGE CANADA INC *p* 1340
4000 RUE HICKMORE, SAINT-LAURENT, QC, H4T 1K2
(514) 344-1788 *SIC* 5032
LAFARGE PAVING & CONSTRUCTION (EASTERN) LIMITED *p* 555
7880 KEELE ST UNIT 5, CONCORD, ON, L4K 4G7
(905) 738-7070 *SIC* 1611
LAFARGEHOLCIM *p* 1133
See *LAFARGE CANADA INC*
LAFCO OUTILLAGE INC *p* 1049
7700 RUE BOMBARDIER, ANJOU, QC, H1J 0A2
(514) 327-7556 *SIC* 5085
LAFERTE *p* 1099
See *JACQUES LAFERTE LTEE*
LAFLAMME PORTES ET FENETRES CORP *p* 1292
39 RUE INDUSTRIELLE, SAINT-APOLLINAIRE, QC, G0S 2E0
(418) 881-3950 *SIC* 2431
LAFLAMME, GEORGES INC *p* 1297
2609 AV ROYALE O RR 1, SAINT-CHARLES-DE-BELLECHASSE, QC, G0R 2T0
(418) 887-3347 *SIC* 5072
LAFLAMME, HENRI INC *p* 1106
425 BOUL SAINT-JOSEPH, GATINEAU, QC, J8Y 3Z8
(819) 770-9131 *SIC* 5411
LAFLECHE ROOFING (1992) LIMITED *p*
661

1100 PROGRESS DR, LONDON, ON, N6N 1B8

(519) 681-7610   *SIC* 1761

LAFLEUR SCHOOL TRANSPORTATION LTD   *p* 544
1546 BASELINE RD, CLARENCE CREEK, ON, K0A 1N0

(613) 488-2337   *SIC* 4151

LAFOND, J.-RENE INC   *p* 1153
3203 CH CHARLES-LEONARD, MIRABEL, QC, J7N 2Y7

(450) 258-2448   *SIC* 5083

LAFRENTZ ROAD MARKING   *p* 1
See CANADIAN ROAD BUILDERS INC

LAGRANGE MECHANICAL SERVICES LTD   *p* 167
970 BOULDER BLVD, STONY PLAIN, AB, T7Z 0E6

(780) 968-1782   *SIC* 1711

LAGUE ET GOYETTE LTEE   *p* 1291
124 RUE AUTHIER, SAINT-ALPHONSE-DE-GRANBY, QC, J0E 2A0

(450) 777-1101   *SIC* 5088

LAHAVE SEAFOODS LIMITED   *p* 460
3371 HWY 331, LAHAVE, NS, B0R 1C0

(902) 688-2773   *SIC* 2091

LAIDLAW CARRIERS BULK GP INC *p* 1035
240 UNIVERSAL RD, WOODSTOCK, ON, N4S 7W3

(519) 539-0471   *SIC* 4731

LAIDLAW CARRIERS BULK LP   *p* 1035
240 UNIVERSAL RD, WOODSTOCK, ON, N4S 7W3

(519) 539-0471   *SIC* 4213

LAIDLAW CARRIERS FLATBED LP   *p* 607
11 6 HWY N, HAGERSVILLE, ON, N0A 1H0

(905) 768-3375   *SIC* 4213

LAIDLAW CARRIERS VAN LP   *p* 416
65 ALLOY DR, SAINT JOHN, NB, E2M 7S9

(506) 648-0499   *SIC* 4213

LAIDLAW CARRIERS VAN LP   *p* 849
21 KERR CRES, PUSLINCH, ON, N0B 2J0

(519) 766-0660   *SIC* 4213

LAIDLAW EDUCATIONAL SERVICES *p* 497
See FIRSTCANADA ULC

LAIDLAW EDUCATIONAL SERVICES *p* 761
See FIRSTCANADA ULC

LAIDLAW EDUCATIONAL SERVICES   *p* 1012
See FIRSTCANADA ULC

LAIDLAW TRANSIT   *p* 862
See FIRSTCANADA ULC

LAINAGES VICTOR LTEE, LES   *p* 1353
260 RTE DE LA STATION BUREAU 218, SAINT-VICTOR, QC, G0M 2B0

(418) 588-6827   *SIC* 2231

LAINCO INC   *p* 1381
1010 RUE FERNAND-POITRAS, TERRE-BONNE, QC, J6Y 1V1

(450) 965-6010   *SIC* 3441

LAIRD CONTROLS CANADA LIMITED   *p* 1340
3950 RUE HICKMORE, SAINT-LAURENT, QC, H4T 1K2

(514) 908-1659   *SIC* 3663

LAIRD ELECTRIC INC   *p* 109
6707 59 ST NW, EDMONTON, AB, T6B 3P8

(780) 450-9636   *SIC* 1731

LAIRD PLASTICS (CANADA) INC   *p* 509
155 ORENDA RD UNIT 4, BRAMPTON, ON, L6W 1W3

(905) 595-4800   *SIC* 5162

LAIS HOTEL PROPERTIES LIMITED *p* 761
48 JOHN ST, NIAGARA ON THE LAKE, ON, L0S 1J0

(888) 669-5566   *SIC* 7011

LAIS HOTEL PROPERTIES LIMITED *p* 761
155 BYRON ST, NIAGARA ON THE LAKE, ON, L0S 1J0

(905) 468-2195   *SIC* 7011

LAIS HOTEL PROPERTIES LIMITED *p* 761
6 PINOT TRAIL, NIAGARA ON THE LAKE, ON, L0S 1J0

(905) 468-3246   *SIC* 7011

LAITERIE BERARDINI   *p* 1325
See BERARDINI, FERNANDO INC

LAITERIE CHAGNON LTEE   *p* 1400
550 RUE LEWIS, WATERLOO, QC, J0E 2N0

(450) 539-3535   *SIC* 0241

LAITERIE CHALIFOUX INC   *p* 1393
1625 BOUL LIONEL-BOULET LOCAL 203, VARENNES, QC, J3X 1P7

(450) 809-0211   *SIC* 2022

LAITERIE DE COATICOOK LIMITEE *p* 1082
1000 RUE CHILD BUREAU 255, COATICOOK, QC, J1A 2S5

(819) 849-2272   *SIC* 2024

LAITUE ST-JACQUES   *p* 1357
See 9329-5558 QUEBEC INC

LAJOIE LEMIEUX NOTAIRES S.E.N.C.R.L *p* 1080
138 RUE PRICE O BUREAU 208, CHICOUTIMI, QC, G7J 1G8

(418) 549-6464   *SIC* 7389

LAJORD COLONY SCHOOL   *p* 1418
See PRAIRIE VALLEY SCHOOL DIVISION NO 208

LAKE CITY FORD SALES INC   *p* 344
800 BROADWAY AVE N, WILLIAMS LAKE, BC, V2G 3P4

(250) 392-4455   *SIC* 5511

LAKE DISTRICT HOSPITAL   *p* 194
See NORTHERN HEALTH AUTHORITY

LAKE ERIE   *p* 747
See STELCO INC

LAKE FOUNDRY LTD   *p* 599
287 SOUTH SERVICE RD, GRIMSBY, ON, L3M 1Y6

(905) 643-1248   *SIC* 3321

LAKE LENORE CO-OPERATIVE ASSOCIATION LIMITED   *p* 1408
300 LAKE DR HWY SUITE 368, LAKE LENORE, SK, S0K 2J0

(306) 368-2255   *SIC* 5171

LAKE LOUISE INN   *p* 138
See ATLIFIC INC

LAKE LOUISE LIMITED PARTNERSHIP *p* 138
210 VILLAGE RD, LAKE LOUISE, AB, T0L 1E0

(403) 522-3791   *SIC* 7011

LAKE LOUISE SKI AREA   *p* 139
See RESORTS OF THE CANADIAN ROCKIES INC

LAKE LOUISE SKI AREA LTD, THE *p* 65
1333 8 ST SW SUITE 908, CALGARY, AB, T2R 1M6

(403) 244-4449   *SIC* 7011

LAKE LOUISE SKI AREA LTD, THE *p* 138
1 WHITEHORN RD, LAKE LOUISE, AB, T0L 1E0

(403) 522-3555   *SIC* 7011

LAKE OF THE WOODS DISTRICT HOSPITAL   *p* 628
21 SYLVAN ST, KENORA, ON, P9N 3W7

(807) 468-9861   *SIC* 8062

LAKE SHORE GOLD CORP   *p* 953
181 UNIVERSITY AVE, TORONTO, ON, M5H 3M7

(416) 703-6298   *SIC* 1382

LAKE SIMCOE REGION CONSERVATION AUTHORITY   *p* 755
120 BAYVIEW PKY, NEWMARKET, ON, L3Y 3W3

(905) 895-1281   *SIC* 8999

LAKE UTOPIA PAPER   *p* 419
See IRVING, J. D. LIMITED

LAKEFIELD IGA SUPERMARKET   *p* 643
See BLETSOE ENTERPRISES INC

LAKEHEAD DISTRICT SCHOOL BOARD *p* 908
174 MARLBOROUGH ST, THUNDER BAY, ON, P7B 4G4

(807) 345-1468   *SIC* 8211

LAKEHEAD DISTRICT SCHOOL BOARD *p* 908

80 CLARKSON ST S, THUNDER BAY, ON, P7B 4W8

(807) 767-1631   *SIC* 8211

LAKEHEAD DISTRICT SCHOOL BOARD *p* 909
130 CHURCHILL DR W, THUNDER BAY, ON, P7C 1V5

SIC 8211

LAKEHEAD MOTORS LIMITED, THE *p* 908
951 MEMORIAL AVE, THUNDER BAY, ON, P7B 4A1

(807) 344-0584   *SIC* 5521

LAKEHEAD PSYCHIATRIC HOSPITAL   *p* 907
See SISTERS OF ST. JOSEPH OF SAULT STE. MARIE, THE

LAKEHEAD UNIVERSITY   *p* 908
955 OLIVER RD, THUNDER BAY, ON, P7B 5E1

(807) 343-8110   *SIC* 8221

LAKEHEAD UNIVERSITY   *p* 908
955 OLIVER RD SUITE 2008, THUNDER BAY, ON, P7B 5E1

(807) 343-8500   *SIC* 8221

LAKEHEAD UNIVERSITY STUDENT UNION   *p* 908
955 OLIVER RD, THUNDER BAY, ON, P7B 5E1

(807) 343-8500   *SIC* 5812

LAKELAND CENTRE F A S D   *p* 81
See LAKELAND FETAL ALCOHOL SPECTRUM DISORDER SOCIETY

LAKELAND COLLEGE   *p* 171
5707 COLLEGE DR, VERMILION, AB, T9X 1K5

(780) 853-8400   *SIC* 8222

LAKELAND COLLEGE   *p* 1409
2602 59TH AVE, LLOYDMINSTER, SK, S9V 1Z3

(780) 871-5700   *SIC* 8221

LAKELAND FETAL ALCOHOL SPECTRUM DISORDER SOCIETY   *p* 81
4823 50 AVE, COLD LAKE, AB, T9M 1Y2

(780) 594-9905   *SIC* 8699

LAKELAND FORD SALES LTD   *p* 1413
3434 2ND AVE W, PRINCE ALBERT, SK, S6V 5G2

(306) 764-3325   *SIC* 5511

LAKELAND INN   *p* 80
See 320364 ALBERTA LTD

LAKELAND MILLS LTD   *p* 249
GD, PRINCE GEORGE, BC, V2L 4V4

(250) 564-7976   *SIC* 2421

LAKELAND MULTI-TRADE INC   *p* 545
566 DURHAM ST, COBOURG, ON, K9A 4A9

(905) 372-7413   *SIC* 3599

LAKELAND ROMAN CATHOLIC SEPARATE SCHOOL DISTRICT NO. 150   *p* 6
4810 46 ST, BONNYVILLE, AB, T9N 2R2

(780) 826-3764   *SIC* 8211

LAKER ENERGY PRODUCTS LTD   *p* 804
835 FOURTH LINE, OAKVILLE, ON, L6L 5B8

(905) 332-3231   *SIC* 3569

LAKERIDGE CHRYSLER DODGE JEEP LTD   *p* 847
152 PETER ST, PORT HOPE, ON, L1A 1C6

(905) 885-6550   *SIC* 5511

LAKERIDGE HEALTH   *p* 496
47 LIBERTY ST S, BOWMANVILLE, ON, L1C 2N4

(905) 623-3331   *SIC* 6324

LAKERIDGE HEALTH   *p* 812
1 HOSPITAL CRT, OSHAWA, ON, L1G 2B9

(905) 576-8711   *SIC* 6324

LAKERIDGE HEALTH   *p* 812
11 GIBB ST, OSHAWA, ON, L1H 2J9

(905) 579-1212   *SIC* 8011

LAKERIDGE HEALTH   *p* 814
850 1/4 CHAMPLAIN AVE, OSHAWA, ON, L1J 8R2

(905) 576-8711   *SIC* 8062

LAKERIDGE HEALTH   *p* 848

451 PAXTON ST, PORT PERRY, ON, L9L 1L9

(905) 985-7321   *SIC* 8062

LAKERIDGE HEALTH   *p* 1014
300 GORDON ST SUITE 779, WHITBY, ON, L1N 5T2

(905) 668-6831   *SIC* 8069

LAKERIDGE HEALTH BOWANVILLE   *p* 496
See LAKERIDGE HEALTH

LAKERIDGE HEALTH OSHAWA   *p* 812
See LAKERIDGE HEALTH

LAKERIDGE HEALTH OSHAWA   *p* 814
See LAKERIDGE HEALTH

LAKERIDGE HEALTH WHITBY   *p* 1014
See LAKERIDGE HEALTH

LAKERS GOLF CLUB INC, THE   *p* 331
7000 CUMMINS RD, VERNON, BC, V1H 1M2

(250) 260-1050   *SIC* 6712

LAKES DISTRICT MAINTENANCE INC   *p* 194
881 16 HWY W, BURNS LAKE, BC, V0J 1E0

(250) 692-7766   *SIC* 1611

LAKESHORE CATHOLIC HIGH SCHOOL *p* 846
See NIAGARA CATHOLIC DISTRICT SCHOOL BOARD

LAKESHORE FISH MARKET INC   *p* 847
1 PASSMORE AVE, PORT DOVER, ON, N0A 1N0

(519) 428-8949   *SIC* 5146

LAKESHORE HEALTH CENTER   *p* 345
See INTERLAKE REGIONAL HEALTH AUTHORITY INC

LAKESHORE HONDA   *p* 571
See AVANTGARD INVESTMENTS INC

LAKESHORE INC   *p* 623
2350 FOURTH AVE RR 1, JORDAN STATION, ON, L0R 1S0

(905) 562-4118   *SIC* 6712

LAKESHORE MILL SUPPLIES LTD   *p* 813
150 WENTWORTH ST E, OSHAWA, ON, L1H 3V5

(905) 579-5222   *SIC* 5085

LAKESHORE RECYCLING   *p* 515
See GENOR RECYCLING SERVICES LIMITED

LAKESHORE SCHOOL DIVISION   *p* 349
23 SECOND AVE, ERIKSDALE, MB, R0C 0W0

(204) 739-2101   *SIC* 8211

LAKESIDE ACADEMY   *p* 1128
See LESTER B. PEARSON SCHOOL BOARD

LAKESIDE AUTOMOTIVE GROUP LTD   *p* 362
950 REGENT AVE W, WINNIPEG, MB, R2C 3A8

(204) 667-9200   *SIC* 5012

LAKESIDE COLONY LTD   *p* 348
5600 ASSINIBOINE RD, CARTIER, MB, R4K 1C3

(204) 864-2710   *SIC* 0762

LAKESIDE GRAIN & FEED LIMITED *p* 591
7858 RAWLINGS RD SUITE 1, FOREST, ON, N0N 1J0

(519) 786-2106   *SIC* 5191

LAKESIDE PACKERS   *p* 7
See JBS CANADA INC

LAKESIDE PERFORMANCE GAS SERVICES LTD   *p* 740
6915 DIXIE RD, MISSISSAUGA, ON, L5T 2G2

(289) 562-0054   *SIC* 1623

LAKESIDE PLASTICS LIMITED   *p* 807
3786 NORTH TALBOT RD SUITE 1, OLDCASTLE, ON, N0R 1L0

(519) 737-1271   *SIC* 3089

LAKESIDE PLASTICS LIMITED   *p* 807
5186 O'NEIL DR RR 1, OLDCASTLE, ON, N0R 1L0

(519) 737-1271   *SIC* 3089

LAKESIDE PROCESS CONTROLS LTD   *p*

723
2475 HOGAN DR, MISSISSAUGA, ON, L5N 0E9
(905) 412-0500   SIC 5084

LAKEVIEW CARE CENTRE   p 287
See REVERA LONG TERM CARE INC

LAKEVIEW CELLARS ESTATE WINERY LIMITED   p 761
1067 NIAGARA STONE RD, NIAGARA ON THE LAKE, ON, L0S 1J0
(905) 641-1042   SIC 2084

LAKEVIEW HOTEL INVESTMENT CORP p 378
185 CARLTON ST SUITE 600, WINNIPEG, MB, R3C 3J1
(204) 947-1161   SIC 6726

LAKEVIEW MANAGEMENT INC   p 378
185 CARLTON ST SUITE 600, WINNIPEG, MB, R3C 3J1
(204) 947-1161   SIC 7011

LAKEVIEW MARKET   p 222
See H & B INVESTMENTS LTD

LAKEVIEW MOTORS LP   p 220
2690 HIGHWAY 97 N, KELOWNA, BC, V1X 4J4
(250) 763-5337   SIC 5511

LAKEVIEW VEGETABLE PROCESSING INC   p 849
21413 LESLIE ST RR 1, QUEENSVILLE, ON, L0G 1R0
(905) 478-2537   SIC 5148

LAKEWOOD AGENCIES   p 366
See LADCO COMPANY LIMITED

LAKEWOOD CHEVROLET LTD   p 115
9150 34 AVE NW, EDMONTON, AB, T6E 5P2
(780) 462-5959   SIC 5511

LAKING MOTORS INC   p 899
695 KINGSWAY, SUDBURY, ON, P3B 2E4
(705) 674-7534   SIC 5511

LAKING TOYOTA   p 899
See LAKING MOTORS INC

LALLEMAND BIO-INGREDIENTS   p 1164
See LALLEMAND INC

LALLEMAND INC   p 1164
5494 RUE NOTRE-DAME E, MONTREAL, QC, H1N 2C4
(514) 255-4887   SIC 2099

LALLEMAND INC   p 1167
1620 RUE PREFONTAINE, MONTREAL, QC, H1W 2N8
(514) 522-2131   SIC 2099

LALLEMAND SOLUTIONS SANTE INC p 1152
17975 RUE DES GOUVERNEURS, MIRABEL, QC, J7J 2K7
(450) 433-9139   SIC 2836

LALLIER AUTOMOBILE (CHARLES-BOURG) INC   p 1256
4650 3E AV O, QUEBEC, QC, G1H 6E7
(418) 627-1010   SIC 5511

LALLIER AUTOMOBILE (HULL) INC p 1107
981 BOUL SAINT-JOSEPH, GATINEAU, QC, J8Z 1W8
(819) 778-1444   SIC 5511

LALLIER AUTOMOBILE (MONTREAL) INC p 1224
12435 BOUL LAURENTIEN, MONTREAL, QC, H4K 2J2
(514) 337-2330   SIC 5511

LALLIER AUTOMOBILE (QUEBEC) INC p 1264
2000 RUE CYRILLE-DUQUET, QUEBEC, QC, G1N 2E8
(418) 687-2525   SIC 5511

LALLIER AUTOMOBILE (REPENTIGNY) INC   p 1379
215 RUE DES MIGRATEURS, TERRE-BONNE, QC, J6V 0A8
(450) 581-7575   SIC 5511

LALLIER SAINTE-FOY   p 1264
See LALLIER AUTOMOBILE (QUEBEC) INC

LALLY FARMS INC   p 178
5327 GLADWIN RD, ABBOTSFORD, BC, V4X 1X8
(604) 859-6820   SIC 0171

LALLY KIA   p 543
725 RICHMOND ST, CHATHAM, ON, N7M 5J5
(519) 352-6200   SIC 5511

LAM IMPORT   p 1185
See IMPORTATIONS EXPORTATIONS LAM INC

LAM, MICHELLE PHARMACY LTD   p 107
3812 118 AVE NW SUITE 318, EDMONTON, AB, T5W 5C7
(780) 474-2424   SIC 5912

LAMANTIA COUNTRY MARKET   p 646
See LAMANTIA, J & B LTD

LAMANTIA, J & B LTD   p 646
50 WILLIAM ST S, LINDSAY, ON, K9V 3A5
(705) 324-6625   SIC 5411

LAMARCHE ELECTRIC INC   p 857
9374 COUNTY ROAD 17, ROCKLAND, ON, K4K 1K9
(613) 747-8882   SIC 1731

LAMB COMPANY, THE   p 577
See NEW ZEALAND AND AUSTRALIAN LAMB COMPANY LIMITED, THE

LAMB FORD SALES LTD   p 78
3771 48 AVE, CAMROSE, AB, T4V 3T4
(780) 672-2411   SIC 5511

LAMB PROPERTIES INC   p 178
36035 NORTH PARALLEL RD, ABBOTSFORD, BC, V3G 2C6
(604) 870-1050   SIC 7011

LAMB WESTON CANADA ULC   p 169
102017 RIDGE RD, TABER, AB, T1G 2E5
(403) 223-3088   SIC 2099

LAMBDA CANADA   p 869
See LAMBDA THERAPEUTIC RESEARCH INC

LAMBDA THERAPEUTIC RESEARCH INC p 869
460 COMSTOCK RD, SCARBOROUGH, ON, M1L 4S4
(416) 752-3636   SIC 8732

LAMBERT & GRENIER INC   p 1063
1244 CH QUATRE-SAISONS, BON-CONSEIL, QC, J0C 1A0
(819) 336-2613   SIC 6719

LAMBERT SOMEC INC   p 1264
1505 RUE DES TANNEURS, QUEBEC, QC, G1N 4S7
(418) 687-1640   SIC 1731

LAMBTON CENTRAL COLLEGIATE & VOCATIONAL INSTITUTE   p 843
See LAMBTON KENT DISTRICT SCHOOL BOARD

LAMBTON COLLEGE   p 858
See LAMBTON COLLEGE OF APPLIED ARTS & TECHNOLOGY, THE

LAMBTON COLLEGE OF APPLIED ARTS & TECHNOLOGY, THE   p 858
1457 LONDON RD, SARNIA, ON, N7S 6K4
(519) 542-7751   SIC 8222

LAMBTON COMMUNICATIONS LIMITED p 860
506 CHRISTINA ST N, SARNIA, ON, N7T 5W4
(519) 332-1234   SIC 1731

LAMBTON CONVEYOR LIMITED   p 1004
102 ARNOLD ST, WALLACEBURG, ON, N8A 3P4
(519) 627-8228   SIC 3535

LAMBTON FORD   p 860
See LAMBTON MOTORS LIMITED, THE

LAMBTON KENT DISTRICT SCHOOL BOARD   p 542
285 MCNAUGHTON AVE E, CHATHAM, ON, N7L 2G7
(519) 352-2870   SIC 8211

LAMBTON KENT DISTRICT SCHOOL BOARD   p 543
300 CECILE AVE, CHATHAM, ON, N7M 2C6
(519) 354-1740   SIC 8211

LAMBTON KENT DISTRICT SCHOOL BOARD   p 843
4141 DUFFERIN AVE, PETROLIA, ON, N0N 1R0
(519) 882-1910   SIC 8211

LAMBTON KENT DISTRICT SCHOOL BOARD   p 858
1257 MICHIGAN AVE, SARNIA, ON, N7S 3Y3
(519) 542-5505   SIC 8211

LAMBTON KENT DISTRICT SCHOOL BOARD   p 858
340 MURPHY RD, SARNIA, ON, N7S 2X1
(519) 332-1140   SIC 8211

LAMBTON KENT DISTRICT SCHOOL BOARD   p 860
200 WELLINGTON ST SUITE 2019, SARNIA, ON, N7T 7L2
(519) 336-1500   SIC 8211

LAMBTON KENT DISTRICT SCHOOL BOARD   p 860
275 WELLINGTON ST, SARNIA, ON, N7T 1H1
(519) 336-6131   SIC 8211

LAMBTON KENT DISTRICT SCHOOL BOARD   p 1005
920 ELGIN ST, WALLACEBURG, ON, N8A 3E1
(519) 627-3368   SIC 8211

LAMBTON LUMBER INC   p 585
170 BROCKPORT DR UNIT 14, ETOBICOKE, ON, M9W 5C8
(416) 798-1994   SIC 5031

LAMBTON MEADOWVIEW VILLA   p 843
3958 PETROLIA LINE SUITE 499, PETROLIA, ON, N0N 1R0
(519) 882-1470   SIC 8361

LAMBTON MOTORS LIMITED, THE   p 860
101 INDIAN RD S, SARNIA, ON, N7T 3W1
(519) 464-4020   SIC 5511

LAMCORP MANAGEMENT LTD   p 115
5708 75 ST NW, EDMONTON, AB, T6E 5X6
(780) 413-8388   SIC 6712

LAMI GLASS PRODUCTS, LLC   p 182
7344 WINSTON ST, BURNABY, BC, V5A 2G9
(604) 420-3600   SIC 3231

LAMKO TOOL & MOLD INCORPORATED p 657
105 TOWERLINE PL, LONDON, ON, N6E 2T3
(519) 686-2643   SIC 3544

LAMMLE'S WESTERN WEAR LTD   p 71
12012 44 ST SE, CALGARY, AB, T2Z 4A2
(403) 255-0272   SIC 5699

LAMON, J.J. INC   p 1412
1007 BATTLEFORD RD, NORTH BATTLEFORD, SK, S9A 2P2
(306) 445-3592   SIC 5171

LAMONT, PAUL AUTOMOTIVE LTD   p 763
890 MCKEOWN AVE, NORTH BAY, ON, P1B 8M1
(705) 472-3000   SIC 5399

LAMOTHE, DIV DE   p 1290
See SINTRA INC

LAMPADAIRES FERALUX INC   p 1359
2250 RUE BOMBARDIER, SAINTE-JULIE, QC, J3E 2J9
(450) 649-4114   SIC 3648

LAMPLIGHTER INNS (LONDON) LIMITED p 654
100 PICCADILLY ST, LONDON, ON, N6A 1R8
(519) 681-7151   SIC 7011

LAMPLIGHTER INNS (LONDON) LIMITED p 656
591 WELLINGTON RD, LONDON, ON, N6C 4R3
(519) 681-7151   SIC 7011

LAMPREA BUILDING MATERIALS LTD p 1035
1147 DUNDAS ST SUITE 1, WOODSTOCK, ON, N4S 8W3
(519) 421-0484   SIC 5211

LAMSAR INC   p 860
608 MCGREGOR RD, SARNIA, ON, N7T 7J2
(519) 332-5010   SIC 1711

LAMWOOD PRODUCTS (1990) LIMITED p 585
44 WOODBINE DOWNS BLVD, ETOBICOKE, ON, M9W 5R2
SIC 5023

LANA DISTRIBUTION   p 1093
See 9256-8971 QUEBEC INC

LANARK COUNTY PARAMEDIC SERVICE p 540
See ALMONTE GENERAL HOSPITAL

LANARK LODGE   p 839
115 CHRISTIE LAKE RD SUITE 223, PERTH, ON, K7H 3C6
(613) 267-4225   SIC 8361

LANAU BUS S.E.C.   p 1380
2450 BOUL DES ENTREPRISES, TERRE-BONNE, QC, J6X 4J8
(450) 968-2450   SIC 4111

LANCASHIRE DISTRIBUTION   p 1420
See LANCASHIRE SAW SALES & SERVICE (CANADA) LTD

LANCASHIRE SAW SALES & SERVICE (CANADA) LTD   p 1420
2413 6TH AVE SUITE 306, REGINA, SK, S4R 1B5
(306) 565-0033   SIC 5251

LANCASTER GROUP INC   p 615
195 HEMPSTEAD DR, HAMILTON, ON, L8W 2E6
(905) 388-3800   SIC 1711

LANCASTER MEDICAL SUPPLIES AND PRESCRIPTIONS LTD   p 181
6741 CARIBOO RD UNIT 203, BURNABY, BC, V3N 4A3
(604) 708-8181   SIC 5122

LANCER GRAPHICS SYSTEMS   p 385
See DISCOVERY CANADA MERCHANDISERS LTD

LANCO WELL SERVICES LTD   p 65
525 11 AVE SW SUITE 201, CALGARY, AB, T2R 0C9
SIC 1389

LANCORP CONSTRUCTION CO. LTD p 555
138 CREDITSTONE RD, CONCORD, ON, L4K 1P2
(905) 660-0778   SIC 1623

LANCTOT   p 1330
See RAYMOND LANCTOT LTEE

LANCTOT COUVRE-SOL DESIGN   p 1314
See LANCTOT, J.C. INC

LANCTOT, J.C. INC   p 1314
148 RUE BOYER, SAINT-ISIDORE-DE-LAPRAIRIE, QC, J0L 2A0
(450) 692-4655   SIC 5713

LAND AIR CONTRACTORS LTD   p 172
10011 106 ST SUITE 205, WESTLOCK, AB, T7P 2K3
SIC 1389

LAND ROVER OF RICHMOND   p 254
See COWELL IMPORTS INC

LANDAU FORD LINCOLN SALES LIMITED p 382
555 EMPRESS ST, WINNIPEG, MB, R3G 3H1
(204) 772-2411   SIC 5511

LANDES CANADA INC   p 1109
400 RUE SAINT-VALLIER, GRANBY, QC, J2G 7Y4
(450) 378-9853   SIC 3199

LANDING GEAR, DIV   p 1143
See HEROUX-DEVTEK INC

LANDIS, DIV OF   p 25
See SIEMENS CANADA LIMITED

LANDMARK   p 1343
See ALIMENTS SAPUTO LIMITEE

LANDMARK CANADA   p 801
2902 SOUTH SHERIDAN WAY SUITE 10, OAKVILLE, ON, L6J 7L6

(905) 829-5511   *SIC* 6411
LANDMARK HOME SOLUTIONS INC *p* 907
3430 SCHMON PKY, THOROLD, ON, L2V
4Y6
(905) 646-8995   *SIC* 2431
LANDMARK HOMES (EDMONTON) INC *p*
125
1103 95 ST SW UNIT 301, EDMONTON,
AB, T6X 0P8
(780) 436-5959   *SIC* 1521
LANDMARK ONTARIO LTD *p* 526
3091 HARRISON CRT, BURLINGTON, ON,
L7M 0W4
(905) 319-7700   *SIC* 3443
LANDMARK STRUCTURES COMPANY *p*
526
See LANDMARK ONTARIO LTD
LANDMART BUILDING CORP *p* 478
911 GOLF LINKS RD SUITE 307, AN-
CASTER, ON, L9K 1H9
(905) 304-6459   *SIC* 1521
LANDROVER JAGUAR THORNHILL *p* 906
See 1633578 ONTARIO LIMITED
LANDRY ASPHALTE LTEE *p* 396
14 RUE DU PORTAGE, CARAQUET, NB,
E1W 1A8
(506) 727-6551   *SIC* 1611
LANDRY, CLAUDE INVESTMENTS INC *p*
420
388 CONNELL ST, WOODSTOCK, NB, E7M
5G9
(506) 328-3353   *SIC* 5531
LANDSCAPE SUPPLY DEPOT *p* 642
*See GROWER'S CHOICE LANDSCAPE
PRODUCTS INC*
LANDSOLUTIONS LP *p* 65
601 10 AVE SW SUITE 200, CALGARY, AB,
T2R 0B2
(403) 290-0008   *SIC* 6211
LANDTRAN LOGISTICS INC *p* 109
4819 90A AVE NW, EDMONTON, AB, T6B
2Y3
(780) 486-8607   *SIC* 4213
LANDTRAN SYSTEMS INC *p* 109
9011 50 ST NW, EDMONTON, AB, T6B 2Y2
(780) 468-4300   *SIC* 4212
LANG'S VENTURES INC *p* 341
3099 SHANNON LAKE RD SUITE 105,
WEST KELOWNA, BC, V4T 2M2
(250) 768-7055   *SIC* 7629
LANGARA COLLEGE *p* 292
100 49TH AVE W, VANCOUVER, BC, V5Y
2Z6
(604) 323-5511   *SIC* 8221
**LANGBANK CO-OPERATIVE ASSOCIA-
TION LIMITED, THE** *p*
1408
1ST AVE W, LANGBANK, SK, S0G 2X0
(306) 538-2125   *SIC* 5171
LANGCO FOODS LTD *p* 1412
9801 TERRITORIAL DR, NORTH BATTLE-
FORD, SK, S9A 3Z8
(306) 445-1934   *SIC* 5411
**LANGDON HALL COUNTRY HOUSE HO-
TEL & SPA** *p*
539
See LANGDON HALL LIMITED
LANGDON HALL LIMITED *p* 539
1 LANGDON DR SUITE 33, CAMBRIDGE,
ON, N3H 4R8
(519) 740-2100   *SIC* 7011
LANGE & FETTER MOTORS LIMITED *p* 999
52 DUNDAS ST E, TRENTON, ON, K8V 1K7
(613) 392-6561   *SIC* 5511
**LANGE TRANSPORTATION & STORAGE
LTD** *p* 688
3965 NASHUA DR, MISSISSAUGA, ON,
L4V 1P3
(905) 362-1290   *SIC* 7389
LANGELIER ASSURANCES INC *p* 1313
2500 BOUL CASAVANT O, SAINT-
HYACINTHE, QC, J2S 7R8
(514) 745-8435   *SIC* 6411
LANGEN PACKAGING INC *p* 723

6500 KITIMAT RD UNIT 1, MISSISSAUGA,
ON, L5N 2B8
(905) 670-7200   *SIC* 5084
LANGEVIN & FOREST LTEE *p* 1170
9995 BOUL PIE-IX, MONTREAL, QC, H1Z
3X1
(514) 322-9330   *SIC* 5211
LANGLEY CARE SOCIETY *p* 228
5451 204 ST, LANGLEY, BC, V3A 5M9
(604) 530-2305   *SIC* 8051
LANGLEY CHRYSLER *p* 271
See FRASER CITY MOTORS LTD
LANGLEY FARM MARKET (1997) INC *p* 190
4820 KINGSWAY SUITE 316, BURNABY,
BC, V5H 4P1
(604) 521-2883   *SIC* 5148
LANGLEY HYUNDAI LTD *p* 272
19459 LANGLEY BYPASS, SURREY, BC,
V3S 6K1
(604) 539-8549   *SIC* 5511
LANGLEY LODGE *p* 228
See LANGLEY CARE SOCIETY
LANGLEY MOTOR SPORTS *p* 272
See LANGLEY HYUNDAI LTD
LANGLEY SCHOOL DISTRICT 35 *p* 227
*See BOARD OF EDUCATION OF SCHOOL
DISTRICT NO. 35 (LANGLEY)*
LANGLEY SECONDARY SCHOOL *p* 227
*See SCHOOL DISTRICT NO. 35 (LANG-
LEY)*
LANGLEY TIMES PUBLISHING CO *p* 228
20258 FRASER HWY, LANGLEY, BC, V3A
4E6
(604) 533-4157   *SIC* 2711
LANGLEY TOYOTATOWN *p* 227
See 414067 B.C. LTD
LANGLEY UTILITIES CONTRACTING LTD *p*
496
71 MEARNS CRT UNIT 1, BOWMANVILLE,
ON, L1C 4N4
(905) 623-5798   *SIC* 4911
LANGLEY VOLKSWAGEN *p* 227
See CROSS & NORMAN (1986) LTD
**LANGLEY, CORPORATION OF THE TOWN-
SHIP OF** *p*
226
22170 50 AVE, LANGLEY, BC, V2Y 2V4
(604) 532-7500   *SIC* 7389
**LANGLEY, CORPORATION OF THE TOWN-
SHIP OF** *p*
227
4700 224 ST, LANGLEY, BC, V2Z 1N4
(604) 532-7300   *SIC* 6111
LANGLOIS AVOCATS S.E.N.C.R.L. *p* 1272
2820 BOUL LAURIER BUREAU 1300, QUE-
BEC, QC, G1V 0C1
(418) 650-7000   *SIC* 8111
LANGLOIS GAUDREAU O'CONNOR *p* 1272
See LANGLOIS AVOCATS S.E.N.C.R.L.
LANGLOIS GAUDREAU S.E.N.C. *p* 1197
1002 RUE SHERBROOKE O BUREAU 27,
MONTREAL, QC, H3A 3L6
(514) 842-9512   *SIC* 8111
**LANGLOIS KRONSTROM DESJARDINS
S.E.N.C.** *p* 1197
1002 RUE SHERBROOKE O BUREAU
2800, MONTREAL, QC, H3A 3L6
(514) 842-9512   *SIC* 8111
LANGS BUS LINES LIMITED *p* 897
66 ZIMMERMAN AVE, STRATHROY, ON,
N7G 2G7
(519) 245-2350   *SIC* 4151
LANGSTAFF SECONDARY SCHOOL *p* 856
*See YORK REGION DISTRICT SCHOOL
BOARD*
LANGUAGES OF LIFE INC *p* 826
99 FIFTH AVE SUITE 14, OTTAWA, ON,
K1S 5K4
(613) 232-9770   *SIC* 7389
LANIEL (CANADA) INC *p* 1340
7101 RTE TRANSCANADIENNE, SAINT-
LAURENT, QC, H4T 1A2
(514) 331-3031   *SIC* 5044
LANKI INVESTIGATIONS INC *p* 270

9547 152 ST SUITE 113, SURREY, BC, V3R
5Y5
(604) 930-0399   *SIC* 6411
LANNICK ASSOCIATES *p* 969
See LANNICK GROUP INC
LANNICK GROUP INC *p* 969
77 KING ST W SUITE 4110, TORONTO,
ON, M5K 2A1
(416) 340-1500   *SIC* 7361
LANOUE, ANDRE ORGANIZATION INC *p*
911
85 MILL ST W, TILBURY, ON, N0P 2L0
(519) 682-2424   *SIC* 5511
LANSDOWNE AUTO SERVICE CENTRE *p*
333
*See UPLANDS MOTORING COMPANY
LTD*
LANSDOWNE CHILDREN'S CENTRE *p* 517
39 MOUNT PLEASANT ST, BRANTFORD,
ON, N3T 1S7
(519) 753-3153   *SIC* 8093
LANSDOWNE CINEMA *p* 924
See ONTARIO CINEMAS INC
LANSDOWNE EQUITY VENTURES LTD *p*
69
295 MIDPARK WAY SE SUITE 350, CAL-
GARY, AB, T2X 2A8
(403) 254-6440   *SIC* 6719
LANSDOWNE I G A *p* 119
5120 122 ST NW, EDMONTON, AB, T6H
3S2
(780) 436-8387   *SIC* 5411
LANSDOWNE MALL INC *p* 841
645 LANSDOWNE ST W, PETERBOR-
OUGH, ON, K9J 7Y5
(705) 748-2961   *SIC* 6512
LANSDOWNE PLACE *p* 841
See LANSDOWNE MALL INC
**LANSDOWNE STADIUM LIMITED PART-
NERSHIP** *p*
818
700 INDUSTRIAL AVE UNIT 220, OTTAWA,
ON, K1G 0Y9
(613) 232-6767   *SIC* 7941
LANTECH DRILLING SERVICES INC *p* 398
398 DOVER CH, DIEPPE, NB, E1A 7L6
(506) 853-9131   *SIC* 1499
LANTHEUS MEDICAL IMAGING *p* 1324
See LANTHEUS MI CANADA INC
LANTHEUS MI CANADA INC *p* 1324
1111 BOUL DR.-FREDERIK-PHILIPS BU-
REAU 100, SAINT-LAURENT, QC, H4M 2X6
(514) 333-1003   *SIC* 3845
LANTHIER BAKERY LTD *p* 476
58 DOMINION ST, ALEXANDRIA, ON, K0C
1A0
(613) 525-2435   *SIC* 2051
LANTIC INC *p* 169
5405 64 ST, TABER, AB, T1G 2C4
(403) 223-3535   *SIC* 5149
LANTIC INC *p* 295
123 ROGERS ST, VANCOUVER, BC, V6A
3N2
(604) 253-1131   *SIC* 2062
LANTIC INC *p* 1167
4026 RUE NOTRE-DAME E, MONTREAL,
QC, H1W 2K3
(514) 527-8686   *SIC* 2062
LANTRAX LOGISTICS LTD *p* 282
19272 96 AVE SUITE 10, SURREY, BC,
V4N 4C1
(604) 526-8729   *SIC* 4731
LANXESS CANADA CO./CIE *p* 568
25 ERB ST, ELMIRA, ON, N3B 3A3
(519) 669-1671   *SIC* 2992
LANYAP TRADE *p* 570
88 PALACE PIER CRT SUITE 603, ETOBI-
COKE, ON, M8V 4C2
(647) 808-2186   *SIC* 6111
LAODAS-WAY HEALING LTD *p* 3
GD, ALDER FLATS, AB, T0C 0A0
(780) 621-0765   *SIC* 5199
LAPALME, GERMAIN & FILS INC *p* 1147
2972 CH MILLETTA, MAGOG, QC, J1X 0R4

(819) 843-2367   *SIC* 1794
**LAPLANTE CHEVROLET PONTIAC BUICK
GMC LTD** *p* 541
632 PRINCIPALE ST, CASSELMAN, ON,
K0A 1M0
(613) 764-2846   *SIC* 5511
LAPOINTE AUTOMOBILES INC *p* 1160
160 BOUL TACHE O, MONTMAGNY, QC,
G5V 3A5
(418) 248-8899   *SIC* 5511
LAPOINTE BROS PEMBROKE LIMITED *p*
838
1398 PEMBROKE ST W, PEMBROKE, ON,
K8A 7M3
(613) 735-0634   *SIC* 5511
LAPOINTE CHRYSLER *p* 838
*See LAPOINTE BROS PEMBROKE LIM-
ITED*
LAPOINTE CHRYSLER BROS JEEP *p* 838
1398 PEMBROKE ST W, PEMBROKE, ON,
K8A 7M3
(613) 735-3128   *SIC* 5511
LAPOINTE FISH LIMITED *p* 825
445 CATHERINE ST, OTTAWA, ON, K1R
5T7
(613) 241-1115   *SIC* 5146
LAPOINTE SPORTS *p* 1243
See 9003-2723 QUEBEC INC
**LAPOINTE-FISHER NURSING HOME, LIM-
ITED** *p*
600
271 METCALFE ST, GUELPH, ON, N1E
4Y8
(519) 821-9030   *SIC* 8051
**LAPOINTE-FISHER NURSING HOME, LIM-
ITED** *p*
1005
1934 DUFFERIN AVE, WALLACEBURG,
ON, N8A 4M2
(519) 627-1663   *SIC* 8051
LAPORTE, MARCEL PHARMACY INC *p*
860
260 INDIAN RD S, SARNIA, ON, N7T 3W4
(519) 337-3300   *SIC* 5912
LAPRAIRIE CRANE LTD *p* 284
GD, TUMBLER RIDGE, BC, V0C 2W0
(250) 242-5561   *SIC* 7389
LAPRAIRIE WORKS INC *p* 135
GD, GRIMSHAW, AB, T0H 1W0
(780) 332-4452   *SIC* 1611
**LAPRAIRIE WORKS OILFIELDS SER-
VICES INC** *p*
52
505 2 ST SW SUITE 702, CALGARY, AB,
T2P 1N8
(403) 767-9942   *SIC* 1389
LAPRISE *p* 1160
See MAISONS LAPRISE INC
LAPRISE FARMS LTD *p* 836
7359 MAPLE LINE SUITE 1, PAIN COURT,
ON, N0P 1Z0
(519) 352-2968   *SIC* 0191
LAQUERRE CHRYSLER INC *p* 1399
34 BOUL ARTHABASKA E, VICTORIAV-
ILLE, QC, G6T 0S7
(819) 752-5252   *SIC* 5511
LAR MACHINERIE INC *p* 1151
1760 169 RTE, METABETCHOUAN-LAC-A-
LA-CROIX, QC, G8G 1B1
(418) 349-2875   *SIC* 3599
LARAMIDE RESOURCES LTD *p* 987
130 KING ST W SUITE 3680, TORONTO,
ON, M5X 2A2
(416) 599-7363   *SIC* 1081
LARCO HOSPITALITY INC *p* 342
100 PARK ROYAL S UNIT 300, WEST VAN-
COUVER, BC, V7T 1A2
(604) 925-2700   *SIC* 7011
LARCO INVESTMENTS LTD *p* 342
100 PARK ROYAL S SUITE 300, WEST
VANCOUVER, BC, V7T 1A2
(604) 925-2700   *SIC* 6719
LARCO INVESTMENTS LTD *p* 981
1 BLUE JAYS WAY SUITE 1, TORONTO,

ON, M5V 1J4

(416) 341-7100   SIC 7011

LAREAU - COURTIERS D'ASSURANCES INC   p 1242
4 RTE 219 BUREAU 707, NAPIERVILLE, QC, J0J 1L0

(450) 245-3322   SIC 6411

LAREAU, FRANK INC   p 1047
150 RUE LAGUE, ANGE-GARDIEN, QC, J0E 1E0

(450) 293-2602   SIC 2421

LAREN HOLDINGS INC   p 752
3228 MOODIE DR, NEPEAN, ON, K2J 4S8

(613) 838-2775   SIC 6712

LARGO RESOURCES LTD   p 964
55 UNIVERSITY AVE SUITE 1105, TORONTO, ON, M5J 2H7

(416) 861-9797   SIC 1094

LARICINA ENERGY LTD   p 52
425 1 ST SW SUITE 800, CALGARY, AB, T2P 3L8

(403) 750-0810   SIC 1311

LARK PROJECTS LTD   p 275
13737 96 AVE SUITE 1500, SURREY, BC, V3V 0C6

(604) 576-2935   SIC 1542

LARLYN PROPERTY MANAGEMENT LIMITED   p 659
540 WHARNCLIFFE RD S SUITE 200, LONDON, ON, N6J 2N4

(519) 690-0600   SIC 6514

LARNY HOLDINGS LIMITED   p 819
2520 ST. LAURENT BLVD SUITE 201, OTTAWA, ON, K1H 1B1

(613) 736-7962   SIC 5411

LARO CONSTRUCTION   p 898
See 343315 ONTARIO LTD

LAROCHE PARK COMMUNITY (SPORTS) ASSOCIATION   p 828
42 STONEHURST AVE, OTTAWA, ON, K1Y 1R4

(613) 722-3944   SIC 8699

LAROCHELLE GROUPE CONSEIL INC   p 1205
1010 RUE DE LA GAUCHETIERE O BUREAU 650, MONTREAL, QC, H3B 2N2

(514) 848-1881   SIC 8742

LAROCQUE PONTIAC BUICK GMC   p 1098
See GARAGE MONTPLAISIR LTEE

LAROCQUE, CHRISTIAN SERVICES LTEE   p 403
5106 ROUTE 113, HAUT-LAMEQUE, NB, E8T 3L4

(506) 344-7077   SIC 4212

LAROSA FINE FOODS INC   p 295
855 TERMINAL AVE, VANCOUVER, BC, V6A 2M9

(604) 688-8306   SIC 5141

LAROSE & FILS LTEE   p 1085
2255 BOUL INDUSTRIEL, COTE SAINT-LUC, QC, H7S 1P8

(514) 382-7000   SIC 2842

LAROUCHE CONSTRUCTION   p 1077
See 2412-8779 QUEBEC INC

LARRIVEE GUITARS   p 295
See LARRIVEE, JEAN GUITARS LTD

LARRIVEE, JEAN GUITARS LTD   p 295
780 CORDOVA ST E, VANCOUVER, BC, V6A 1M3

SIC 3931

LARSEN & SHAW LIMITED   p 1004
575 DURHAM ST W, WALKERTON, ON, N0G 2V0

(519) 881-1320   SIC 3429

LARSON JUHL   p 706
See LARSON-JUHL CANADA LTD

LARSON-JUHL CANADA LTD   p 706
416 WATLINE AVE, MISSISSAUGA, ON, L4Z 1X2

(905) 890-1234   SIC 5023

LARWAY TRAFFIC SYSTEMS   p 485
See 621189 ONTARIO INC

LASALLE CENTRE RECREATIF   p 1132

707 75E AV, LASALLE, QC, H8R 3Y2

(514) 367-1000   SIC 7389

LASALLE SECONDARY SCHOOL   p 899
See RAINBOW DISTRICT SCHOOL BOARD

LASALLE, RAYMOND INC   p 1353
1561 RTE 158, SAINT-THOMAS, QC, J0K 3L0

(450) 756-2121   SIC 5083

LASENZA.COM   p 1093
See CORPORATION SENZA, LA

LASER AMP INC   p 1111
770 RUE GEORGES-CROS, GRANBY, QC, J2J 1N2

(450) 776-6982   SIC 3399

LASER QUEST   p 690
See VERSENT CORPORATION ULC

LASER SALES INC   p 649
1717 OXFORD ST E, LONDON, ON, N5V 2Z5

(519) 452-0501   SIC 5072

LASER TRANSPORT INC   p 1020
3380 WHEELTON DR, WINDSOR, ON, N8W 5A7

(519) 974-3435   SIC 4213

LASER VALLEY TECHNOLOGIES CORP   p 282
9761 192 ST UNIT 1, SURREY, BC, V4N 4C7

(604) 888-7085   SIC 5045

LASERNETWORKS INC   p 688
6300 VISCOUNT RD UNIT 2, MISSISSAUGA, ON, L4V 1H3

(800) 461-4879   SIC 3955

LASERS OSELA, LES   p 1128
See OSELA INC

LASFAM INVESTMENTS INC   p 193
3751 NORTH FRASER WAY SUITE 12, BURNABY, BC, V5J 5G4

(604) 327-7264   SIC 4959

LASSER PRODUCE LTD   p 223
601 KEREMEOS BYPASS RD, KEREMEOS, BC, V0X 1N1

(250) 506-0707   SIC 6799

LASSONDE BEVERAGES CANADA, DIV OF   p 581
See A. LASSONDE INC

LASSONDE SERVICES   p 1288
See A. LASSONDE INC

LASSONDE, A.   p 1288
See INDUSTRIES LASSONDE INC

LAST BEST PLACE CORP, THE   p 981
145 JOHN ST, TORONTO, ON, M5V 2E4

SIC 5812

LAST CALL GROUP   p 112
See 675122 ALBERTA LTD

LAST CLASS, THE   p 484
1 GEORGIAN DR, BARRIE, ON, L4M 3X9

(705) 722-1526   SIC 5812

LATCON LTD   p 818
3387 HAWTHORNE RD, OTTAWA, ON, K1G 4G2

(613) 738-9061   SIC 1795

LATEM INDUSTRIES LIMITED   p 534
90 STRUCK CRT, CAMBRIDGE, ON, N1R 8L2

(519) 740-0292   SIC 3471

LATHAM DISTRIBUTORS   p 885
475 GLENDALE AVE, ST CATHARINES, ON, L2P 3Y2

(905) 682-3344   SIC 5149

LATHAM POOL PRODUCTS INC   p 474
430 FINLEY AVE, AJAX, ON, L1S 2E3

(905) 428-6990   SIC 3949

LATHAM POOL PRODUCTS INC   p 516
383 ELGIN ST, BRANTFORD, ON, N3S 7P5

(800) 638-7422   SIC 3949

LATHAMS   p 319
See GORDON LATHAM LIMITED

LATHS WASKA   p 397
See CLAIR INDUSTRIAL DEVELOPMENT CORPORATION LTD

LATITUDE GEOGRAPHICS GROUP LTD   p 336

1117 WHARF ST UNIT 300, VICTORIA, BC, V8W 1T7

(250) 381-8130   SIC 7371

LATOPLAST LTD   p 713
1661 FINFAR CRT, MISSISSAUGA, ON, L5J 4K1

(905) 823-6150   SIC 5099

LATTANVILLE HOLDINGS CORPORATION   p 656
378 HORTON ST E SUITE 494, LONDON, ON, N6B 1L7

(519) 642-7142   SIC 5531

LATTE DRUMMOND   p 1096
See PATIO DRUMMOND LTEE

LAU, REGINALD DRUGS LTD   p 867
685 MCCOWAN RD, SCARBOROUGH, ON, M1J 1K2

(416) 431-4822   SIC 5912

LAUDERVEST DEVELOPMENTS LTD   p 772
4576 YONGE ST SUITE 500, NORTH YORK, ON, M2N 6N4

(416) 224-1200   SIC 1522

LAUER'S RESTAURANT EQUIPMENT LIMITED   p 809
3823 CAMPBELL RD, ORILLIA, ON, L3V 6H3

(705) 325-9938   SIC 5046

LAUNDRY PEOPLE   p 261
See PHELPS APARTMENT LAUNDRIES LTD

LAURA - LAURA PETITES - LAURA PLUS   p 1104
See MAGASIN LAURA (P.V.) INC

LAURA SECORD   p 1261
See 4542410 CANADA INC

LAURA'S YOUR INDEPENDENT GROCERY   p 626
300 EAGLESON RD, KANATA, ON, K2M 1C9

(613) 592-3850   SIC 5411

LAUREL POINT INN   p 335
See PAUL'S RESTAURANTS LTD

LAUREL STEEL   p 522
See HARRIS STEEL ULC

LAUREN CONCISE   p 53
See LAUREN ENGINEERS & CONSTRUCTORS, ULC

LAUREN ENGINEERS & CONSTRUCTORS, ULC   p 53
736 6 AVE SW UNIT 800, CALGARY, AB, T2P 3T7

(403) 237-7160   SIC 8711

LAURENT LAPOINTE LTEE   p 1080
1150 BOUL SAINT-PAUL BUREAU 400, CHICOUTIMI, QC, G7J 3C5

SIC 5039

LAURENTIAN PILOTAGE AUTHORITY   p 1135
40 RUE DES PILOTES, LES ESCOUMINS, QC, G0T 1K0

(418) 233-2995   SIC 4499

LAURENTIAN PUBLISHING LIMITED   p 901
158 ELGIN ST, SUDBURY, ON, P3E 3N5

(705) 673-5120   SIC 2711

LAURENTIAN REGIONAL HIGH SCHOOL   p 1129
See SIR WILFRID LAURIER SCHOOL BOARD

LAURENTIAN SKI HILL   p 764
See LAURENTIAN SKI HILL SNOWBOARDING CLUB

LAURENTIAN SKI HILL SNOWBOARDING CLUB   p 764
15 JANEY AVE, NORTH BAY, ON, P1C 1N1

(705) 494-7463   SIC 7999

LAURENTIDE PEINTURE   p 1368
See GENERAL PAINT CORP

LAURENTIDE RE-SOURCES INC   p 1399
345 RUE DE LA BULSTRODE, VICTORIAVILLE, QC, G6T 1P7

(819) 758-5497   SIC 5231

LAURENTIDE RESOURCES TM   p 1399
See LAURENTIDE RE-SOURCES INC

LAURENTIDES J'EN MANGES   p 1059
See PRODUITS M.G.D. INC, LES

LAURIA HYUNDAI   p 847
50 BENSON CRT, PORT HOPE, ON, L1A 3V6

(905) 885-2880   SIC 5511

LAURIA VOLKSWAGEN   p 847
See 2508046 ONTARIO LTD

LAURIER MAZDA   p 1274
See 9274-4531 QUEBEC INC

LAURIER SENIOR HIGH SCHOOL   p 1087
See SIR WILFRID LAURIER SCHOOL BOARD

LAURIN & COMPANY   p 748
See 152610 CANADA INC

LAURIN CONTENEURS INC   p 1363
487 RUE PRINCIPALE, SAINTE-ROSE, QC, H7X 1C4

(450) 689-1962   SIC 3523

LAURIN YOUR INDEPENDENT GROCER   p 619
See LOBLAWS SUPERMARKETS LIMITED

LAURION, S. & J. LIMITED   p 139
5402 DISCOVERY WAY, LEDUC, AB, T9E 8L9

(780) 986-5229   SIC 5399

LAURYSEN KITCHENS LTD   p 891
2415 CARP RD, STITTSVILLE, ON, K2S 1B3

(613) 836-5353   SIC 2434

LAUZON   p 1245
See PLACEMENTS LAUZON INC

LAUZON - PLANCHERS DE BOIS EXCLUSIFS INC   p 1244
2101 COTE DES CASCADES, PAPINEAUVILLE, QC, J0V 1R0

(819) 427-5144   SIC 5031

LAUZON - PLANCHERS DE BOIS EXCLUSIFS INC   p 1349
1680 RUE PRINCIPALE RR 5, SAINT-NORBERT, QC, J0K 3C0

(450) 836-4405   SIC 2426

LAUZON-RESSOURCES FORESTIERES INC   p 1148
77 RUE COMMERCIALE, MANIWAKI, QC, J9E 1N8

(819) 449-3636   SIC 2411

LAVAL AUTOS HAMEL INC   p 1086
2500 BOUL CHOMEDEY, COTE SAINT-LUC, QC, H7T 2W1

(450) 682-4050   SIC 5511

LAVAL CABLE ET GRANULATIONS INC   p 1234
270 BOUL SAINT-ELZEAR O, MONTREAL, QC, H7L 3P2

(450) 668-8100   SIC 5051

LAVAL FORTIN ADAMS   p 1044
See 9165-2214 QUEBEC INC

LAVAL FORTIN LTEE   p 1045
130 RUE NOTRE-DAME O, ALMA, QC, G8B 2K1

(418) 668-3321   SIC 1541

LAVAL VOLKSWAGEN LTEE   p 1264
777 BOUL CHAREST O, QUEBEC, QC, G1N 2C6

(418) 687-4451   SIC 5511

LAVE AUTO A LA MAIN STEVE INC   p 1092
4216 BOUL SAINT-JEAN, DOLLARD-DES-ORMEAUX, QC, H9G 1X5

(514) 696-9274   SIC 7542

LAVE CAMION INTER   p 1149
See INTER PROPANE INC

LAVERENDRYE GENERAL HOSPITAL   p 592
See RIVERSIDE HEALTH CARE FACILITIES INC

LAVERGNE   p 1049
See LAVERGNE GROUPE INC

LAVERGNE GROUPE INC   p 1049
8800 1ER CROISSANT, ANJOU, QC, H1J 1C8

(514) 354-5757   SIC 3087

LAVERGNE WESTERN BEEF INC *p* 748
3971 NAVAN RD, NAVAN, ON, K4B 1H9
(613) 824-8175 *SIC* 5147

LAVERY DE BILLY, SOCIETE EN NOM COLLECTIF A RESPONSABILITE LIMITEE *p* 1205
1 PLACE VILLE-MARIE BUREAU 4000, MONTREAL, QC, H3B 4M4
(514) 871-1522 *SIC* 8111

LAVIGUEUR *p* 1310
See *BIJOUTERIE LAVIGUEUR LTEE*

LAVINGTON PLANER DIVISION *p* 198
See *TOLKO INDUSTRIES LTD*

LAVOIE, J. P. & SONS LTD *p* 417
2986 FREDERICTON RD, SALISBURY, NB, E4J 2G1
(506) 372-3333 *SIC* 5812

LAVTOR HOLDINGS (ALBERTA) LTD *p* 85
1 KINGSWAY GARDEN MALL NW SUITE 555, EDMONTON, AB, T5G 3A6
(780) 479-1313 *SIC* 5812

LAVTOR HOLDINGS (ALBERTA) LTD *p* 101
17865 106A AVE NW UNIT 101, EDMONTON, AB, T5S 1V8
(780) 483-7545 *SIC* 5812

LAW CRANBERRY RESORT LIMITED *p* 546
19 KEITH AVE, COLLINGWOOD, ON, L9Y 4T9
(705) 445-6600 *SIC* 7011

LAW SOCIETY OF ALBERTA *p* 65
919 11 AVE SW SUITE 500, CALGARY, AB, T2R 1P3
(403) 229-4700 *SIC* 8621

LAW SOCIETY OF UPPER CANADA, THE *p* 953
130 QUEEN ST W SUITE 100, TORONTO, ON, M5H 2N6
(416) 644-4886 *SIC* 8111

LAW SOCIETY OF UPPER CANADA, THE *p* 953
130 QUEEN ST W SUITE 100, TORONTO, ON, M5H 2N6
(416) 947-3315 *SIC* 8111

LAW-MAROT *p* 1314
See *LAW-MAROT-MILPRO INC*

LAW-MAROT-MILPRO INC *p* 1314
1150 RUE BROUILLETTE, SAINT-HYACINTHE, QC, J2T 2G8
(450) 771-6262 *SIC* 3535

LAWDAN INVESTMENTS LTD *p* 331
683 COMMONAGE RD, VERNON, BC, V1H 1G3
(250) 542-1707 *SIC* 5541

LAWDEPOT *p* 116
See *SEQUITER INC*

LAWLESS, M.J. HOLDINGS LTD *p* 863
200 MCNABB ST, SAULT STE. MARIE, ON, P6B 1Y4
(705) 949-0770 *SIC* 7538

LAWMARK CAPITAL INC *p* 375
179 MCDERMOT AVE UNIT 301, WINNIPEG, MB, R3B 0S1
(204) 942-1138 *SIC* 6531

LAWN MAINTANCE/LANDSCAPING *p* 109
See *KENTUCKY BLUE GRASS LTD*

LAWPRO *p* 935
See *LAWYERS PROFESSIONAL INDEMNITY COMPANY*

LAWRENCE MEAT PACKING CO. LTD *p* 204
11088 4TH ST, DAWSON CREEK, BC, V1G 4H8
(250) 782-5111 *SIC* 5147

LAWRENCE S. BLOOMBERG FACULTY OF NURSING *p* 977
See *GOVERNING COUNCIL OF THE UNIVERSITY OF TORONTO, THE*

LAWRENCE SQUARE EMPLOYMENT & SOCIAL SERVICES *p* 794
See *GOVERNMENT OF ONTARIO*

LAWSON HEALTH RESEARCH INSTITUTE *p* 656
See *LAWSON RESEARCH INSTITUTE*

LAWSON LUNDELL LLP *p* 306

925 GEORGIA ST W SUITE 1600, VANCOUVER, BC, V6C 3L2
(604) 685-3456 *SIC* 8111

LAWSON PRODUCTS INC. (ONTARIO) *p* 724
7315 RAPISTAN CRT, MISSISSAUGA, ON, L5N 5Z4
(905) 567-0089 *SIC* 5085

LAWSON RESEARCH INSTITUTE *p* 656
750 BASE LINE RD E SUITE 300, LONDON, ON, N6C 5Z2
(519) 646-6100 *SIC* 8733

LAWTON'S DRUG STORES LIMITED *p* 447
236 BROWNLOW AVE SUITE 270, DARTMOUTH, NS, B3B 1V5
(902) 468-1000 *SIC* 5912

LAWTON'S DRUG STORES LIMITED *p* 447
81 THORNHILL DR, DARTMOUTH, NS, B3B 1R9
(902) 468-4637 *SIC* 5122

LAWTON'S DRUGS WHOLESALE DIV *p* 447
See *LAWTON'S DRUG STORES LIMITED*

LAWTON'S INCORPORATED *p* 447
236 BROWNLOW AVE SUITE 270, DARTMOUTH, NS, B3B 1V5
(902) 468-1000 *SIC* 5912

LAWTONS HOME HEALTH CARE *p* 447
See *LAWTON'S DRUG STORES LIMITED*

LAWYERS PROFESSIONAL INDEMNITY COMPANY *p* 935
250 YONGE ST SUITE 3101, TORONTO, ON, M5B 2L7
(416) 598-5800 *SIC* 6411

LAYER 7 TECHNOLOGIES INC *p* 306
885 GEORGIA ST W SUITE 500, VANCOUVER, BC, V6C 3E8
(604) 681-9377 *SIC* 7371

LAYFIELD CANADA LTD *p* 263
11131 HAMMERSMITH GATE, RICHMOND, BC, V7A 5E6
(604) 275-5588 *SIC* 3081

LAYFIELD GROUP LIMITED *p* 263
11131 HAMMERSMITH GATE, RICHMOND, BC, V7A 5E6
(604) 275-5588 *SIC* 1731

LAYNE CHRISTENSEN CANADA LIMITED *p* 540
9 REGIONAL RD 84 UNIT 84, CAPREOL, ON, P0M 1H0
SIC 1499

LAZY DAYS RV CENTRE INC *p* 162
137 TURBO DR, SHERWOOD PARK, AB, T8H 2J6
(780) 449-6177 *SIC* 5561

LB LEMIEUX BEDARD *p* 1374
See *LEMIEUX BEDARD COMMUNICATIONS INC*

LBC CAPITAL INC *p* 523
5035 SOUTH SERVICE RD, BURLINGTON, ON, L7L 6M9
(905) 633-2400 *SIC* 6159

LBCO CONTRACTING LTD *p* 24
623 35 AVE NE, CALGARY, AB, T2E 2L2
(403) 277-9555 *SIC* 1629

LCBO *p* 942
See *LIQUOR CONTROL BOARD OF ONTARIO, THE*

LCBO *p* 1014
See *LIQUOR CONTROL BOARD OF ONTARIO, THE*

LCBO FINANCIAL OFFICE *p* 942
See *LIQUOR CONTROL BOARD OF ONTARIO, THE*

LCG FOODS DISTRIBUTION *p* 665
See *2075894 ONTARIO INC*

LCI *p* 546
See *LORAC COMMUNICATIONS INC*

LCI *p* 706
See *LCI LASERCOM CLINICS INTERNATIONAL INC*

LCI GROUP *p* 1093
See *9015-0178 QUÉBEC INC*

LCI LASERCOM CLINICS INTERNATIONAL

INC *p* 706
4310 SHERWOODTOWNE BLVD, MISSISSAUGA, ON, L4Z 4C4
(905) 896-4000 *SIC* 7231

LCL BUILDS CORPORATION *p* 776
98 SCARSDALE RD, NORTH YORK, ON, M3B 2R7
(416) 492-0500 *SIC* 1542

LCL CANADA LIMITED *p* 523
1016B SUTTON DR UNIT 205, BURLINGTON, ON, L7L 6B8
(416) 639-1889 *SIC* 4731

LD ENERGY CANADA LP *p* 53
350 7 AVE SW, CALGARY, AB, T2P 3N9
(403) 410-1199 *SIC* 5153

LDC PRECISION CONCRETE INC *p* 1002
112 CLEMENT ST, VARS, ON, K0A 3H0
(613) 822-2872 *SIC* 1771

LDM FOODS *p* 65
See *LOUIS DREYFUS COMPANY YORKTON TRADING LP*

LE BIFTHEQUE INC *p* 1340
6705 CH DE LA COTE-DE-LIESSE, SAINT-LAURENT, QC, H4T 1E5
SIC 5812

LE BON CROISSANT *p* 711
See *596042 ONTARIO LIMITED*

LE CENTRE JEUNESSE DE MONTREAL - INSTITUT UNIVERSITAIRE *p* 1165
See *CENTRE INTEGRE UNIVERSITAIRE SANTE ET SERVICES SOCIAUX DU CENTRE-SUD-DE-L'ILE-DE-MONTREAL*

LE CENTRE ROUTIER (1994) INC *p* 1286
375 RUE TEMISCOUATA BUREAU 998, RIVIERE-DU-LOUP, QC, G5R 2Y9
SIC 5511

LE CHARBON *p* 1259
See *L'AVIATIC CLUB INC*

LE CSSS DE QUEBEC-NORD *p* 1254
See *CENTRE DE SANTE ET DE SERVICES SOCIAUX DE QUEBEC-NORD*

LE FOND DU PRESIDENT DE MIP *p* 1049
See *MIP INC*

LE GALLANT RESTAURANT *p* 412
See *GALLANT, RAYMOND & SONS LTD*

LE GRENIER *p* 1049
See *MODE LE GRENIER INC*

LE GRENIER D'ART (1987) INC *p* 1070
9205 BOUL TASCHEREAU, BROSSARD, QC, J4Y 3B8
(450) 659-6999 *SIC* 2499

LE GROUP VERRIER COURTIERS D'ASSURANCES *p* 1098
See *GROUPE D'ASSURANCES VERRIER INC*

LE GROUPE ARCOP *p* 1213
See *GROUPE ARCOP S.E.N.C., LE*

LE GROUPE BERNIER DAIGLE *p* 1110
See *3100-8410 QUEBEC INC*

LE GROUPE CONSTRUCTION BRIGIL *p* 1106
See *3223701 CANADA INC*

LE GROUPE DES MARCHANDS DE PETROLES DU QUEBEC *p* 1330
See *PETROLES CREVIER INC*

LE GROUPE IRC *p* 723
See *IRC BUILDING SCIENCES GROUP*

LE GROUPE MARTEL *p* 1234
See *EXCEL PRIX GROSSISTE EN ALIMENTATION INC*

LE HAVRE DES CANTONS *p* 1147
231 DOLLARD, MAGOG, QC, J1X 2M5
(819) 868-1010 *SIC* 2869

LE PETROLES LANAUDIERE *p* 1150
See *HARNOIS ENERGIES INC*

LE PUB *p* 1273
See *LE PUB UNIVERSITAIRE INC*

LE PUB UNIVERSITAIRE INC *p* 1273
2325 RUE DE L'UNIVERSITE BUREAU 1312, QUEBEC, QC, G1V 0B3
(418) 656-7075 *SIC* 5812

LE QUOTIDIEN *p* 1077
See *3834310 CANADA INC*

LE RELAIS CHEVROLET CADILLAC

BUICK GMC LTEE *p* 1177
9411 AV PAPINEAU, MONTREAL, QC, H2M 2G5
(514) 384-6380 *SIC* 5521

LE ROI DANIELS ELEMENTARY SCHOOL *p* 34
See *CALGARY BOARD OF EDUCATION*

LE SYNDICAT DE LA COPROPRIETE LES JARDINS DU HAVRE *p* 1256
25 RUE DES MOUETTES BUREAU 431, QUEBEC, QC, G1E 7G1
(418) 660-6599 *SIC* 6531

LE SYNDICAT DE METALLOS *p* 1177
See *METALLURGISTES UNIS D'AMERIQUE*

LEA CONSULTING LTD *p* 671
625 COCHRANE DR 9TH FLR, MARKHAM, ON, L3R 9R9
(905) 470-0015 *SIC* 8711

LEA GROUP HOLDINGS INC *p* 671
625 COCHRANE DR SUITE 900, MARKHAM, ON, L3R 9R9
(905) 470-0015 *SIC* 8711

LEAB MECANIQUE DE PROCEDE *p* 1254
See *ENTREPRISES ANTONIO BARRETTE INC, LES*

LEACOCK CARE CENTRE *p* 809
See *JARLETTE LTD*

LEADBETTER FOODS INC *p* 809
255 HUGHES RD, ORILLIA, ON, L3V 2M2
(705) 325-9922 *SIC* 2011

LEADEC (CA) CORP *p* 476
4700 INDUSTRIAL PKY, ALLISTON, ON, L9R 1A2
(705) 435-5077 *SIC* 7349

LEADER AUTO RESSOURCES LAR INC *p* 1251
2525 AUT TRANSCANADIENNE BUREAU 937, POINTE-CLAIRE, QC, H9R 4V6
(514) 694-6880 *SIC* 5172

LEADER ENERGY SERVICES LTD *p* 80
7001 96 ST, CLAIRMONT, AB, T8X 5B3
(780) 402-9876 *SIC* 1389

LEADER PLUMBING & HEATING INC *p* 1032
91 HAIST AVE UNIT 3, WOODBRIDGE, ON, L4L 5V5
(905) 264-1162 *SIC* 1711

LEADER POST, THE *p* 1416
See *POSTMEDIA NETWORK INC*

LEADFX INC *p* 939
1 ADELAIDE ST E, TORONTO, ON, M5C 2V9
(416) 867-9298 *SIC* 1081

LEADING BRANDS OF CANADA, INC *p* 292
33 8TH AVE W UNIT 101, VANCOUVER, BC, V5Y 1M8
(604) 685-5200 *SIC* 2086

LEADING EDGE FORMING LTD *p* 201
137 GLACIER ST UNIT 107, COQUITLAM, BC, V3K 5Z1
SIC 1799

LEADING EDGE GEOMATICS LTD *p* 404
2398 ROUTE 102 HWY, LINCOLN, NB, E3B 7G1
(506) 446-4403 *SIC* 7389

LEADING ENGLISH AND EDUCATION RESOURCE NETWORK (LEARN) *p* 1134
2030 BOUL DAGENAIS O BUREAU 2, LAVAL-OUEST, QC, H7L 5W2
(450) 622-2212 *SIC* 8733

LEADING MANUFACTURING GROUP HOLDINGS INC *p* 149
801 25 AVE, NISKU, AB, T9E 7Z4
(780) 955-8895 *SIC* 3443

LEADING MANUFACTURING GROUP HOLDINGS INC *p* 171
3801 48 AVE, VERMILION, AB, T9X 1G9
(780) 854-0004 *SIC* 3443

LEADING MANUFACTURING GROUP INC *p* 149
2313 8 ST, NISKU, AB, T9E 7Z3
(780) 955-8895 *SIC* 3443

LEADON (BARRINGTON) OPERATIONS LP
p 453
1875 BARRINGTON ST, HALIFAX, NS, B3J
3L6
(902) 429-7410   SIC 7011
LEADON (HALIFAX) OPERATIONS LP p
453
1990 BARRINGTON ST, HALIFAX, NS, B3J
1P2
(902) 425-6700   SIC 7011
LEADON (REGINA) OPERATIONS LP p
1418
1975 BROAD ST, REGINA, SK, S4P 1Y2
(306) 525-6767   SIC 7011
LEAGOLD MINING CORPORATION p 328
595 BURRARD ST SUITE 3043, VANCOU-
VER, BC, V7X 1J1
(604) 398-4505   SIC 1041
LEAGUE PROJECTS LTD p 7
311 9TH ST E BAY 3, BROOKS, AB, T1R
1C8
(403) 793-2648   SIC 1389
**LEAGUE SAVINGS & MORTGAGE COM-
PANY**
455
6074 LADY HAMMOND RD, HALIFAX, NS,
B3K 2R7
(902) 453-4220   SIC 6162
LEAMINGTON CHRYSLER (1992) LTD p
644
170 OAK ST W, LEAMINGTON, ON, N8H
2B6
(519) 326-9052   SIC 5511
**LEAMINGTON DISTRICT MEMORIAL HOS-
PITAL**
644
194 TALBOT ST W SUITE 167, LEAMING-
TON, ON, N8H 1N9
(519) 326-2373   SIC 8062
**LEAMINGTON SUPERCENTRE STORE #
3164** p 645
See WAL-MART CANADA CORP
LEAR CONSTRUCTION SERVICES INC p
24
4200 10 ST NE, CALGARY, AB, T2E 6K3
(403) 250-3818   SIC 1542
LEARNING PARTNERSHIP CANADA, THE
p 915
45 SHEPPARD AVE E SUITE 400,
TORONTO, ON, M2N 5W9
(416) 440-5100   SIC 8699
LEASE LINK CANADA CORP p 101
17220 STONY PLAIN RD NW SUITE 201A,
EDMONTON, AB, T5S 1K6
(780) 414-0616   SIC 6159
LEATHEAD INVESTMENTS LTD p 220
2727 HIGHWAY 97 N, KELOWNA, BC, V1X
4J8
(250) 860-7700   SIC 5511
LEAUTEC CRYSTAL-SOLEIL p 1117
See 2895102 CANADA INC
LEAVENS VOLKSWAGEN INC p 649
2360 AUTO MALL AVE, LONDON, ON, N5V
0B4
(519) 455-2580   SIC 5511
LEAVOY ROWE BEEF CO. LTD p 703
3066 JARROW AVE, MISSISSAUGA, ON,
L4X 2C7
(905) 272-2330   SIC 5147
LEBLANC & DAVID MARKETING INC p
1175
425 RUE SHERBROOKE E BUREAU 240,
MONTREAL, QC, H2L 1J9
(514) 982-0180   SIC 5192
**LEBLANC, GERARD   COURTIER
D'ASSURANCES LTEE** p 1082
6920   RTE   LOUIS-S.-SAINT-LAURENT,
COMPTON, QC, J0B 1L0
(819) 823-3311   SIC 6411
**LEBLANC, GUY ENTERPRISES (1984)
LIMITED** p 449
343 CONWAY RD, DIGBY, NS, B0V 1A0
(902) 245-2211   SIC 5932
LEBON p 1059

See MONTOUR LTEE
LEBOVIC ENTERPRISES LIMITED p 894
12045 MCCOWAN RD, STOUFFVILLE, ON,
L4A 4C3
(905) 640-7361   SIC 6712
**LECLERC ASSURANCES ET SERVICES
FINANCIERS** p 1100
See ASSURANCES   JEAN-CLAUDE
LECLERC INC
LECLERC LEVAGE INDUSTRIEL p 1292
See GROUPE J.L. LECLERC INC
LECOURS LUMBER CO. LIMITED p 532
HWY 663 N, CALSTOCK, ON, P0L 1B0
(705) 362-4368   SIC 2421
LECOURS MOTOR SALES p 619
See LECOURS, JEAN PAUL LIMITED
LECOURS, JEAN PAUL LIMITED p 619
733 FRONT ST, HEARST, ON, P0L 1N0
(705) 362-4011   SIC 5511
LECUYER & FILS LTEE p 1351
17 RUE DU MOULIN, SAINT-REMI, QC, J0L
2L0
(514) 861-5623   SIC 3272
LED DENTAL p 306
See LED MEDICAL DIAGNOSTICS INC
LED MEDICAL DIAGNOSTICS INC p 306
580 HORNBY ST SUITE 810, VANCOU-
VER, BC, V6C 3B6
(604) 434-4614   SIC 3843
LED ROADWAY LIGHTING LTD p 458
115 CHAIN LAKE DR SUITE 201, HALIFAX,
NS, B3S 1B3
(902) 450-2222   SIC 3648
LEDCOR ALBERTA p 154
See LEDCOR INDUSTRIES INC
LEDCOR CIVIL/MINING p 306
See LEDCOR CMI LTD
LEDCOR CMI LTD p 306
1067 CORDOVA ST W UNIT 1200, VAN-
COUVER, BC, V6C 1C7
(604) 681-7500   SIC 1481
LEDCOR CONSTRUCTION LIMITED p 306
1067 CORDOVA ST W SUITE 1200, VAN-
COUVER, BC, V6C 1C7
(604) 681-7500   SIC 1542
LEDCOR CONSTRUCTION LIMITED p 314
1055 HASTINGS ST W SUITE 1500, VAN-
COUVER, BC, V6E 2E9
(604) 646-2493   SIC 1542
LEDCOR CONTRACTORS LTD p 109
7008 ROPER RD NW, EDMONTON, AB,
T6B 3H2
(780) 395-5400   SIC 1611
LEDCOR FABRICATION p 149
See LEDCOR INDUSTRIES INC
LEDCOR GROUP p 306
See LEDCOR INDUSTRIES INC
LEDCOR HOLDINGS INC p 306
1067 CORDOVA ST W SUITE 1200, VAN-
COUVER, BC, V6C 1C7
(604) 681-7500   SIC 1611
LEDCOR INDUSTRIAL LIMITED p 115
9910 39 AVE NW, EDMONTON, AB, T6E
5H8
(780) 462-9616   SIC 1541
LEDCOR INDUSTRIES INC p 149
3925 8 ST, NISKU, AB, T9E 8M1
(780) 955-1400   SIC 1611
LEDCOR INDUSTRIES INC p 154
27420 TOWNSHIP RD SUITE 374, RED
DEER, AB, T4N 5H3
(403) 309-7129   SIC 1611
LEDCOR INDUSTRIES INC p 306
1067 CORDOVA ST W SUITE 1200, VAN-
COUVER, BC, V6C 1C7
(604) 681-7500   SIC 1611
LEDCOR SPECIAL PROJECTS p 314
See LEDCOR CONSTRUCTION LIMITED
LEDDARTECH INC p 1267
4535 BOUL WILFRID-HAMEL BUREAU
240, QUEBEC, QC, G1P 2J7
(418) 653-9000   SIC 7389
LEDINGHAM GM p 358
See LEDINGHAM PONTIAC BUICK GMC

LEDINGHAM PONTIAC BUICK GMC p 358
200 PTH 12 N, STEINBACH, MB, R5G 1T6
(204) 326-3451   SIC 5511
**LEDOUX, LEW & PATTERSON INSUR-
ANCE BROKERS LIMITED** p
732
115 MATHESON BLVD W SUITE 202, MIS-
SISSAUGA, ON, L5R 3L1
(905) 890-1877   SIC 6411
**LEDOUX, LEW & PATTERSON INSUR-
ANCE BROKERS LTD** p
672
7030   WOODBINE   AVE   SUITE   100,
MARKHAM, ON, L3R 6G2
(905) 944-1188   SIC 6411
LEDUC CHRYSLER JEEP p 139
See LEDUC CHRYSLER LTD
LEDUC CHRYSLER LTD p 139
6102 46A ST, LEDUC, AB, T9E 7A7
(780) 986-2051   SIC 5511
LEDUC CO-OP LTD p 139
5403 50 ST, LEDUC, AB, T9E 6Z7
(780) 986-3036   SIC 5541
LEDUC TRUSS INC p 139
4507 61 AVE, LEDUC, AB, T9E 7B5
(780) 980-0334   SIC 2439
LEDUC TRUST p 139
See 714638 ALBERTA LTD
LEDVANCE LTD p 696
5450 EXPLORER DR SUITE 100, MISSIS-
SAUGA, ON, L4W 5N1
(905) 361-9333   SIC 3641
LEDVANCE LTD p 1099
1 RUE SYLVAN, DRUMMONDVILLE, QC,
J2C 2S8
(819) 478-6500   SIC 3641
LEDWIDGE LUMBER COMPANY LIMITEDp
464
195 OLD POST RD, OLDHAM, NS, B2T 1E2
(902) 883-9889   SIC 2421
LEE HECHT HARRISON-CANADA CORP p
935
250 YONGE ST SUITE 2800, TORONTO,
ON, M5B 2L7
(416) 922-7561   SIC 8742
LEE LI HOLDINGS INC p 740
299 COURTNEYPARK DR E, MISSIS-
SAUGA, ON, L5T 2T6
(905) 565-5968   SIC 5149
LEE MANOR HOME FOR THE AGED p 835
875 6TH ST E, OWEN SOUND, ON, N4K
5W5
(519) 376-4420   SIC 8051
LEE RIVER TRANSPORT p 363
See SUBURBAN CENTRE & AUTO SER-
VICE LTD
LEE SPECIALTIES INC p 5
27312-68 TWP RD 394, BLACKFALDS, AB,
T0M 0J0
(403) 346-4487   SIC 3533
LEE VALLEY HOLDINGS LIMITED p 832
1090 MORRISON DR, OTTAWA, ON, K2H
1C2
(613) 596-0350   SIC 3423
LEE VALLEY TOOLS LTD p 832
1090 MORRISON DR, OTTAWA, ON, K2H
1C2
(613) 596-0350   SIC 5251
LEE, RON CONSTRUCTION INC p 566
439 8 HWY, DUNDAS, ON, L9H 5E1
(905) 628-4148   SIC 1794
LEEDE JONES GABLE INC p 939
110 YONGE ST SUITE 600, TORONTO,
ON, M5C 1T4
(416) 365-8000   SIC 6211
LEEDE JONES GABLE INC. p 53
421 7 AVE SW SUITE 3415, CALGARY, AB,
T2P 4K9
(403) 531-6800   SIC 6211
LEEDS TRANSIT INC p 568
542 MAIN ST, ELGIN, ON, K0G 1E0
(613) 359-5344   SIC 5012
**LEESE ENTERPRISES INTERNATIONAL
INC** p 988

1210 EGLINTON AVE W, TORONTO, ON,
M6C 2E3
(416) 781-8404   SIC 5145
LEESWOOD CONSTRUCTION p 724
See LEESWOOD DESIGN BUILD LTD
LEESWOOD DESIGN BUILD LTD p 724
7200 WEST CREDIT AVE, MISSISSAUGA,
ON, L5N 5N1
(416) 309-4482   SIC 1542
LEEVILLE CONSTRUCTION LTD p 1411
340 8TH AVE NW, MOOSE JAW, SK, S6H
4E7
(306) 692-0677   SIC 1542
LEFEBVRE & BENOIT S.E.C. p 1231
4500 RUE BERNARD-LEFEBVRE, MON-
TREAL, QC, H7C 0A5
(450) 667-6000   SIC 5039
LEFEBVRE, PAYETTE ET ASSOCIES INC p
1318
170 RUE SAINT-JACQUES, SAINT-JEAN-
SUR-RICHELIEU, QC, J3B 2K5
(514) 856-7751   SIC 6411
LEFKO PRODUITS DE PLASTIQUE INC p
1147
1700 BOUL INDUSTRIEL, MAGOG, QC,
J1X 4V9
(819) 843-9237   SIC 2821
LEGACY FORD PONOKA p 152
6305 42 AVE, PONOKA, AB, T4J 1J8
(403) 783-5501   SIC 5511
LEGACY KITCHEN DESIGN GROUP INC p
9
2980 SUNRIDGE WAY NE, CALGARY, AB,
T1Y 7H9
(403) 291-6868   SIC 5021
LEGACY OIL + GAS INC p 53
525 8 AVE SW SUITE 4400, CALGARY, AB,
T2P 1G1
(403) 206-5035   SIC 1382
LEGACY PERSONNEL SOLUTIONS INC p
1022
2480 SEMINOLE ST, WINDSOR, ON, N8Y
1X3
(519) 419-5073   SIC 7361
**LEGACY TRANSPORTATION SOLUTIONS
INC** p 504
1 KENVIEW BLVD UNIT 210, BRAMPTON,
ON, L6T 5E6
(416) 798-4940   SIC 4731
**LEGACY UNIVERSAL PROTECTION SER-
VICE** p
238
See UNIVERSAL PROTECTION SERVICE
OF CANADA CO
LEGAL AID ONTARIO p 946
LEGAL AID ONTARIO, TORONTO, ON,
M5G 2H1
(416) 979-1446   SIC 8111
**LEGAL AID SERVICES SOCIETY OF MAN-
ITOBA** p
378
294 PORTAGE AVE UNIT 402, WINNIPEG,
MB, R3C 0B9
(204) 985-8500   SIC 8111
LEGAL AID SOCIETY OF ALBERTA p 89
10320 102 AVE NW SUITE 300, EDMON-
TON, AB, T5J 4A1
(780) 427-7575   SIC 8111
LEGAL LINK CORPORATION, THE p 953
333 BAY ST SUITE 400, TORONTO, ON,
M5H 2R2
(416) 348-0432   SIC 8732
LEGAL SERVICES SOCIETY p 306
510 BURRARD ST SUITE 400, VANCOU-
VER, BC, V6C 3A8
(604) 601-6200   SIC 8111
LEGALI AID MANITOBA p 378
See LEGAL AID SERVICES SOCIETY OF
MANITOBA
LEGARE LOCATION D'AUTO p 1167
See LOCATION JEAN LEGARE LTEE
LEGARE, DUPERRE INC p 1346
4250   RUE   JEAN-TALON   E,   SAINT-
LEONARD, QC, H1S 1J7

(514) 723-2233 *SIC* 5531
LEGAULT METAL INC *p* 1384
2 CH BOURGEOIS O, TRECESSON, QC,
J0Y 2S0
(819) 732-8818 *SIC* 5082
LEGEND GROUP *p* 290
See LEGEND REAL ESTATE GROUP LTD
LEGEND REAL ESTATE GROUP LTD *p* 290
4728 MAIN ST, VANCOUVER, BC, V5V 3R7
(604) 879-8989 *SIC* 6531
LEGER MARKETING INC *p* 375
35 KING ST SUITE 5, WINNIPEG, MB, R3B
1H4
(204) 885-7570 *SIC* 8732
LEGER MARKETING INC *p* 1189
507 PLACE D'ARMES BUREAU 700, MON-
TREAL, QC, H2Y 2W8
(514) 845-5660 *SIC* 8732
LEGER, D L SALES INC *p* 619
1525 CAMERON ST, HAWKESBURY, ON,
K6A 3R3
(613) 632-3399 *SIC* 5251
LEGERE INDUSTRIAL SUPPLIES LTD *p*
832
1140 MORRISON DR UNIT 110, OTTAWA,
ON, K2H 8S9
(613) 829-8010 *SIC* 5085
LEGG MASON CANADA INC *p* 964
220 BAY ST SUITE 1400, TORONTO, ON,
M5J 2W4
(416) 860-0616 *SIC* 6282
**LEGG MASON GLOBAL ASSET MANAGE-
MENT** *p*
964
See LEGG MASON CANADA INC
LEGGAT CHEVROLET BUICK GMC LTD *p*
585
360 REXDALE BLVD, ETOBICOKE, ON,
M9W 1R7
(416) 743-1810 *SIC* 5012
LEGGETT & PLATT CANADA CO *p* 1010
195 BATHURST DR, WATERLOO, ON, N2V
2B2
(519) 884-1860 *SIC* 3312
LEGGETT & PLATT, DIV OF *p* 837
See PARIS SPRING LTD
LEGGETT, H. & FILS INC *p* 1242
904 RUE DU CENTENAIRE, NAMUR, QC,
J0V 1N0
(819) 426-2176 *SIC* 6712
LEGION VILLAGE *p* 544
See BRANCH 133 LEGION VILLAGE INC
**LEGOLAND DISCOVERY CENTRE
TORONTO** *p* 555
*See MERLIN ENTERTAINMENTS
(CANADA) INC*
LEGRAND AV CANADA ULC *p* 891
113 IBER RD, STITTSVILLE, ON, K2S 1E7
(613) 836-2501 *SIC* 5046
LEGRAND CANADA INC *p* 1002
9024 KEELE ST, VAUGHAN, ON, L4K 2N2
(905) 738-9195 *SIC* 3643
LEGRESLEY, FRANCOIS LTEE/LTD *p* 410
790 RUE PRINCIPALE, NEGUAC, NB, E9G
1N5
(506) 776-8334 *SIC* 5251
LEGROW, CAL INSURANCE LIMITED *p* 430
189 HIGGINS LINE, ST. JOHN'S, NL, A1B
4N4
(709) 722-3282 *SIC* 6411
LEGS BEAUTIFUL *p* 919
See CONREZ GROUP LTD, THE
LEGUBEC INC *p* 1262
905 RUE FERNAND-DUFOUR, QUEBEC,
QC, G1M 3B2
(418) 681-3531 *SIC* 5148
LEGUM MANAGEMENT *p* 222
See PUSHOR MITCHELL LLP
LEGUMES R. & M. INC, LES *p* 1376
26 RANG CONTANT, SHERRINGTON, QC,
J0L 2N0
(514) 977-3840 *SIC* 5148
LEGUMIERE Y.C. INC, LA *p* 1351
1463 RANG SAINTE-THERESE, SAINT-

REMI, QC, J0L 2L0
(450) 454-9437 *SIC* 0161
LEGUPRO INC *p* 1291
1424 RANG DES CHUTES, SAINT-
AMBROISE, QC, G7P 2V4
(418) 672-4717 *SIC* 5142
LEHIGH CEMENT *p* 105
*See LEHIGH HANSON MATERIALS LIM-
ITED*
LEHIGH HANSON MATERIALS LIMITED *p*
105
12640 INLAND WAY NW, EDMONTON, AB,
T5V 1K2
(780) 420-2500 *SIC* 3241
LEHIGH HANSON MATERIALS LIMITED *p*
323
8955 SHAUGHNESSY ST, VANCOUVER,
BC, V6P 3Y7
(604) 261-6225 *SIC* 5032
LEHIGH MATERIALS *p* 323
*See LEHIGH HANSON MATERIALS LIM-
ITED*
LEHMANN PLUMBING LTD *p* 110
3645 73 AVE NW, EDMONTON, AB, T6B
2T8
(780) 465-4434 *SIC* 1711
LEHNER WOOD PRESERVERS LTD *p* 1414
2690 4TH AVE W, PRINCE ALBERT, SK,
S6V 5Y9
(306) 763-4232 *SIC* 3312
LEI *p* 206
*See LOCHER EVERS INTERNATIONAL
INC*
LEI TECHNOLOGY CANADA LTD *p* 688
3160 ORLANDO DR UNIT A, MISSIS-
SAUGA, ON, L4V 1R5
(877) 813-2132 *SIC* 5045
LEIBEL INSURANCE GROUP CORP *p* 101
17415 102 AVE NW SUITE 102, EDMON-
TON, AB, T5S 1J8
(780) 484-8880 *SIC* 6411
LEICA GEOSYSTEMS LTD *p* 877
3761 VICTORIA PARK AVE UNIT 1, SCAR-
BOROUGH, ON, M1W 3S2
(416) 497-2460 *SIC* 5049
LEIS FEED AND SUPPLY LIMITED *p* 1013
1214 QUEENS BUSH RD, WELLESLEY,
ON, N0B 2T0
(519) 656-2810 *SIC* 5191
LEIS PET DISTRIBUTING INC *p* 1013
1315 HUTCHISON RD, WELLESLEY, ON,
N0B 2T0
(519) 656-3559 *SIC* 5149
LEISURE MANUFACTURING INC *p* 599
317 SOUTH SERVICE RD SUITE 2,
GRIMSBY, ON, L3M 4E8
(905) 309-1800 *SIC* 5999
**LEISURE MART & RV CANADA CORPORA-
TION** *p*
749
2098 PRINCE OF WALES DR, NEPEAN,
ON, K2E 7A5
(613) 226-8228 *SIC* 5561
LEISUREWORLD CAREGIVING CENTER *p*
514
See 2063414 ONTARIO LIMITED
LEISUREWORLD CAREGIVING CENTRE *p*
498
See 2063414 ONTARIO LIMITED
LEISUREWORLD CAREGIVING CENTRE *p*
564
See 2063414 ONTARIO LIMITED
LEISUREWORLD CAREGIVING CENTRE *p*
568
See 2063414 ONTARIO LIMITED
LEISUREWORLD CAREGIVING CENTRE *p*
598
See 2063414 ONTARIO LIMITED
LEISUREWORLD CAREGIVING CENTRE *p*
850
See 2063414 ONTARIO LIMITED
LEISUREWORLD CAREGIVING CENTRE *p*
870
See 2063414 ONTARIO LIMITED

LEISUREWORLD CAREGIVING CENTRE *p*
972
See 2063414 ONTARIO LIMITED
**LEISUREWORLD CAREGIVING CENTRE -
CREEDAN VALLEY** *p* 564
See 2063412 INVESTMENT LP
**LEISUREWORLD CAREGIVING CENTRE
NORFINCH** *p* 786
See 2063414 ONTARIO LIMITED
LEISUREWORLD CAREGIVING CENTRES *p* 665
See 2063414 INVESTMENT LP
LEISUREWORLD SENIOR CARE LP *p* 672
302 TOWN CENTRE BLVD SUITE 200,
MARKHAM, ON, L3R 0E8
(905) 477-4006 *SIC* 8741
LEITH WHEELER *p* 306
*See LEITH WHEELER INVESTMENT
COUNSEL LTD*
LEITH WHEELER FIXED INCOME FUND *p*
306
400 BURRARD ST SUITE 1500, VANCOU-
VER, BC, V6C 3A6
(604) 683-3391 *SIC* 6722
**LEITH WHEELER INVESTMENT COUNSEL
LTD** *p* 306
400 BURRARD ST SUITE 1500, VANCOU-
VER, BC, V6C 3A6
(604) 683-3391 *SIC* 6282
LEITNER, IRVING DRUGS LTD *p* 855
9350 YONGE ST SUITE 966, RICHMOND
HILL, ON, L4C 5G2
(905) 884-0555 *SIC* 5912
LEKIU POULTRY (2006) LTD *p* 295
458 PRIOR ST, VANCOUVER, BC, V6A 2E5
(604) 681-1999 *SIC* 5144
LEKKER FOOD DISTRIBUTORS LTD *p* 340
2670 WILFERT RD, VICTORIA, BC, V9B
5Z3
(250) 388-0377 *SIC* 5147
LEKTER INDUSTRIAL SERVICES INC *p*
490
500 HARVARD DR RR 1, BELLE RIVER,
ON, N0R 1A0
(519) 727-3713 *SIC* 1711
LELAND INDUSTRIES INC *p* 874
95 COMMANDER BLVD, SCARBOROUGH,
ON, M1S 3S9
(416) 291-5308 *SIC* 3429
**LELIEVRE, LELIEVRE & LEMOIGNAN
LTEE** *p* 1364
52 RUE DES VIGNEAUX, SAINTE-
THERESE-DE-GASPE, QC, G0C 3B0
(418) 385-3310 *SIC* 2091
LELY CANADA INC *p* 1036
1015 RIDGEWAY RD, WOODSTOCK, ON,
N4V 1E2
(519) 602-6737 *SIC* 5083
LEMARE LAKE LOGGING LTD *p* 247
3341 MINE RD, PORT MCNEILL, BC, V0N
2R0
(250) 956-3123 *SIC* 2411
LEMAY ARCHITECTURE + DESIGN *p* 1223
See LEMAY CO INC
LEMAY CO INC *p* 1223
3500 RUE SAINT-JACQUES, MONTREAL,
QC, H4C 1H2
(514) 932-5101 *SIC* 7389
LEMAY LAND & LIVESTOCK CO *p* 170
GD, TROCHU, AB, T0M 2C0
(403) 442-3022 *SIC* 5154
LEMAY, G & S HOLDINGS INC *p* 419
450 RUE DU MOULIN SUITE 491,
TRACADIE-SHEILA, NB, E1X 1A4
(506) 395-4313 *SIC* 5531
LEMERVEIL, LAURA *p* 1092
160 AV DU COUVENT, DONNACONA, QC,
G3M 1P5
(418) 462-3325 *SIC* 8999
LEMIEUX ASSURANCES INC *p* 1137
1610 BOUL ALPHONSE-DESJARDINS,
LEVIS, QC, G6V 0H1
(418) 835-0939 *SIC* 6411
LEMIEUX ASSURANCES INC *p* 1306

186 RUE COMMERCIALE, SAINT-HENRI-
DE-LEVIS, QC, G0R 3E0
(418) 882-0801 *SIC* 6411
**LEMIEUX BEDARD COMMUNICATIONS
INC** *p* 1374
2665 RUE KING O BUREAU 315, SHER-
BROOKE, QC, J1L 2G5
(819) 823-0850 *SIC* 4899
**LEMIEUX NOLET COMPTABLES AGREES
S.E.N.C.R.L.** *p* 1160
25 BOUL TACHE O BUREAU 205, MONT-
MAGNY, QC, G5V 2Z9
(418) 248-1910 *SIC* 3578
**LEMIEUX NOLET, COMPTABLES AGREES
S.E.N.C.R.L.** *p* 1137
1610 BOUL ALPHONSE-DESJARDINS BU-
REAU 400, LEVIS, QC, G6V 0H1
(418) 833-2114 *SIC* 8721
LEMIEUX NOLET, CONSULTANTS *p* 1137
*See LEMIEUX NOLET, COMPTABLES
AGREES S.E.N.C.R.L.*
LEMIEUX, JACQUES (GROSSISTE) INC *p*
1160
179 RUE DES INDUSTRIES, MONT-
MAGNY, QC, G5V 4G2
(418) 248-8117 *SIC* 5141
LEMIRE PRECISION INC *p* 1099
3000 RUE POWER, DRUMMONDVILLE,
QC, J2C 6H9
(819) 475-5121 *SIC* 3451
LEMIRE, ERIC ENTERPRISES INC *p* 748
4815B MCNEELY RD, NAVAN, ON, K4B 0J3
(613) 835-4040 *SIC* 1791
LEMMER SPRAY SYSTEMS LTD *p* 24
4624 12 ST NE, CALGARY, AB, T2E 4R4
(403) 250-7735 *SIC* 5084
LENBROOK CORP *p* 845
633 GRANITE CRT, PICKERING, ON, L1W
3K1
(905) 831-6333 *SIC* 5065
LENBROOK GROUP OF COMPANIES, THE
p 845
See LENBROOK CORP
LENBROOK INDUSTRIES LIMITED *p* 845
633 GRANITE CRT, PICKERING, ON, L1W
3K1
(905) 831-6333 *SIC* 3651
LENDCARE CAPITAL INC *p* 843
1315 PICKERING PKWY FL 4, PICKERING,
ON, L1V 7G5
(905) 839-1009 *SIC* 6141
**LENNOX AND ADDINGTON COUNTY GEN-
ERAL HOSPITAL ASSOCIATION** *p*
747
8 RICHMOND PARK DR, NAPANEE, ON,
K7R 2Z4
(613) 354-3301 *SIC* 8062
LENNOX DRUM LIMITED *p* 474
233 FULLER RD, AJAX, ON, L1S 2E1
(905) 427-1441 *SIC* 5085
LENNOX INDUSTRIES (CANADA) LTD *p* 71
11500 35 ST SE SUITE 8002, CALGARY,
AB, T2Z 3W4
(403) 279-4448 *SIC* 5023
LENNOX INDUSTRIES (CANADA) LTD *p*
579
400 NORRIS GLEN RD, ETOBICOKE, ON,
M9C 1H5
(416) 621-9302 *SIC* 3634
LENOVO (CANADA) INC *p* 774
10 YORK MILLS RD SUITE 400, NORTH
YORK, ON, M2P 2G4
(855) 253-6686 *SIC* 3571
LENS & SHUTTER CAMERAS LTD *p* 322
2902 BROADWAY W SUITE 201, VANCOU-
VER, BC, V6K 2G8
SIC 5946
LENS MILL STORE *p* 537
See NORFOLK KNITTERS LIMITED
LENSCRAFTERS *p* 724
See LUXOTTICA CANADA INC
LENWORTH METAL PRODUCTS LIMITED *p*
998
275 CARRIER DR, TORONTO, ON, M9W

5Y8
SIC 3499
LEO AUTOMOBILE LTEE   p 1079
1849 BOUL TALBOT, CHICOUTIMI, QC,
G7H 7Y4
(418) 545-1190   SIC 5511
LEO HARLEY DAVIDSON   p 1069
See CENTRE DE MOTOS INC
LEO HAYES HIGH SCHOOL   p 399
See ANGLOPHONE WEST SCHOOL DIS-
TRICT
LEO PHARMA INC   p 904
123 COMMERCE VALLEY DR E SUITE
400, THORNHILL, ON, L3T 7W8
(905) 886-9822   SIC 5122
**LEO'S DISTRIBUTING COMPANY CANADA
LIMITED**   p 654
149 PICCADILLY ST, LONDON, ON, N6A
1R9
(519) 439-2730   SIC 5141
LEO'S LIVESTOCK EXCHANGE LIMITED p
599
1643 SALE BARN RD, GREELY, ON, K4P
1N6
(613) 821-2634   SIC 5154
LEO'S SALES & SERVICE LTD   p 378
STURGEON RD & HWY 101, WINNIPEG,
MB, R3C 2E6
(204) 694-4978   SIC 5083
LEON AMEUBLEMENT   p 1087
See LEON'S FURNITURE LIMITED
LEON'S   p 795
See LEON'S FURNITURE LIMITED
LEON'S FURNITURE   p 405
See ASHKYLE LTD
LEON'S FURNITURE   p 413
See CLEAR VIEW HOME FURNISHINGS
LTD
LEON'S FURNITURE & APPLIANCES p 633
See MCKERCHER KINGSTON LIMITED
LEON'S FURNITURE LIMITED   p 487
81 BRYNE DR, BARRIE, ON, L4N 8V8
(705) 730-1777   SIC 5712
LEON'S FURNITURE LIMITED   p 706
201 BRITANNIA RD E, MISSISSAUGA, ON,
L4Z 3X8
(905) 501-9505   SIC 5712
LEON'S FURNITURE LIMITED   p 761
440 TAYLOR RD, NIAGARA ON THE LAKE,
ON, L0S 1J0
(905) 682-8519   SIC 5712
LEON'S FURNITURE LIMITED   p 795
10 SUNTRACT RD, NORTH YORK, ON,
M9N 3N9
SIC 5712
LEON'S FURNITURE LIMITED   p 795
45 GORDON MACKAY RD, NORTH YORK,
ON, M9N 3X3
(416) 243-7880   SIC 5712
LEON'S FURNITURE LIMITED   p 830
2600 QUEENSVIEW DR, OTTAWA, ON,
K2B 8H6
(613) 820-6446   SIC 5712
LEON'S FURNITURE LIMITED   p 1087
2000 BOUL DANIEL-JOHNSON, COTE
SAINT-LUC, QC, H7T 1A3
(450) 688-3851   SIC 5712
LEON'S FURNITURE LIMITED   p 1275
2840 RUE EINSTEIN, QUEBEC, QC, G1X
5H3
(418) 683-9600   SIC 5712
LEON'S MFG. COMPANY INC   p 1438
135 YORK RD E, YORKTON, SK, S3N 3Z4
(306) 786-2600   SIC 3499
LEONARDO WORLDWIDE CORPORATION
p 981
111 PETER ST SUITE 530, TORONTO, ON,
M5V 2H1
(416) 593-6634   SIC 7374
LEPAGE MILWORK   p 1286
See LEPAGE, ALPHONSE INC
LEPAGE ON YONGE   p 921
See ROYAL LEPAGE LIMITED
LEPAGE SIGNATURE INC   p 1264

960 RUE RAOUL-JOBIN BUREAU D, QUE-
BEC, QC, G1N 1S9
(418) 476-1678   SIC 1793
LEPAGE, ALPHONSE INC   p 1286
141 CH DES RAYMOND, RIVIERE-DU-
LOUP, QC, G5R 5X9
(418) 862-2611   SIC 3089
LEPAGES 2000 INC   p 776
41 LESMILL RD, NORTH YORK, ON, M3B
2T3
(416) 751-4343   SIC 3086
LEPAGESIGNATURE.COM   p 1264
See LEPAGE SIGNATURE INC
LEPINE-CLOUTIER LTEE   p 1259
715 RUE DE SAINT-VALLIER E, QUEBEC,
QC, G1K 3P9
(418) 529-3371   SIC 7261
LEPROHON INC   p 1375
6171 BOUL BOURQUE, SHERBROOKE,
QC, J1N 1H2
(819) 563-2454   SIC 1711
LERNERS LLP   p 654
80 DUFFERIN AVE, LONDON, ON, N6A
1K4
(519) 672-4510   SIC 8111
LERNERS LLP   p 954
130 ADELAIDE ST W SUITE 2400,
TORONTO, ON, M5H 3P5
(416) 867-3076   SIC 8111
LEROUX COTE & BURROGANO   p 1188
See GESTION D'ETUDE PPKF (1984) INC
LEROUX, K. D. SALES LTD   p 869
1901 EGLINTON AVE E, SCARBOROUGH,
ON, M1L 2L8
(416) 615-2666   SIC 5531
LEROUX, SYLVAIN M. ENTREPRISES LTD
p 1220
1500 AV ATWATER BUREAU G, MON-
TREAL, QC, H3Z 1X5
(514) 939-1820   SIC 5251
LES ALIMENTS LUFA   p 1225
See FERMES LUFA INC, LES
LES ALIMENTS MISS ARACHEW   p 1114
See ALIMENTS TRIOVA INC, LES
LES ALIMENTS SARDO   p 495
See SARDO, MARIO SALES INC
LES BOIS STE-GAU   p 1291
See 2621-9634 QUEBEC INC
**LES CENTRES DE LA JEUNESSE ET DE
LA FAMILLE BATSHAW**   p 1253
See CENTRES DE LA JEUNESSE ET DE
LA FAMILLE BATSHAW, L
LES DISTRIBUTION R.V.I, DIR OF   p 638
See MTD PRODUCTS LIMITED
LES ENTREPRISES GAEVAN   p 1280
See 9231-4897 QUEBEC INC
LES ENTREPRISES PASTENE   p 1050
See PASTENE ENTERPRISES ULC
LES ENTREPRISES ROBERT COTE p 1260
See GROUPE COTE-HUOT INC
LES GALERIES NISSAN   p 1311
See 3286509 CANADA INC
LES GALLERIES ACURA   p 1343
See 9042-0209 QUEBEC INC
LES GROSSISTES P & H   p 1170
See GROUPE DESCHENES INC
LES JARDINS DU PARK LINEAIRE   p 1397
See CONSTRUCTIONS JEL BERGERON
LES JARDINS LEBOURGNEUF   p 1279
See IMMEUBLES ROUSSIN LTEE, LES
LES MARCHES TAU   p 1173
See MARCHES D'ALIMENTS NATURELS
TAU INC, LES
**LES PRODUITS SANITAIRES LEPINE VAL-
D'OR**   p
1105
See PRODUITS SANITAIRES LEPINE INC,
LES
**LES RELIGIEUSES DE JESUS-MARIE
RESIDENCE SOUS-LES-BOIS**   p 1271
See RELIGIEUSES DE JESUS-MARIE,
LES
**LES SERVICES INTERNET QUEST-
ZONE.NET**   p

1364
See QUESTZONE.NET INC
LES SYSTEMES TOMRA   p 1054
See TOMRA CANADA INC
LES TERRASSEMENTS ALLAIRE & GINCE
p 1111
See GROUPE ALLAIREGINCE INFRAS-
TRUCTURES INC
LES VIANDES INTERCITE   p 1051
See VIANDES MONTCALM INC, LES
LESAGE INC   p 1085
817 RUE SALABERRY, COTE SAINT-LUC,
QC, H7S 1H5
(514) 337-3585   SIC 1711
LESAGE, L.T. HOLDINGS LTD   p 4
2913 48 AVE, ATHABASCA, AB, T9S 0A4
(780) 675-3019   SIC 5531
LESLIE MOTORS LTD   p 618
73 ELORA ST, HARRISTON, ON, N0G 1Z0
(519) 338-2310   SIC 5511
LESPERANCE, FRANCOIS INC   p 1083
164 BOUL DES LAURENTIDES, COTE
SAINT-LUC, QC, H7G 4P6
(450) 667-0255   SIC 5211
LESSARD BUICK CHEVROLET GMC
1367
See 9204-6424 QUEBEC INC
LESSARD HYUNDAI   p 1280
See LESSARD, M LTEE
LESSARD, M LTEE   p 1280
300 BOUL LOUIS-XIV, QUEBEC, QC, G2K
1W7
(418) 623-5471   SIC 5511
LESTAGE & FILS LTEE   p 1351
699 RUE NOTRE-DAME, SAINT-REMI, QC,
J0L 2L0
(450) 454-7591   SIC 5511
LESTAGE ST-REMI   p 1351
See LESTAGE & FILS LTEE
**LESTER B PEARSON COLLEGIATE INSTI-
TUTE**   p
865
See TORONTO DISTRICT SCHOOL
BOARD
LESTER B PEARSON HIGH SCHOOL p 526
See HALTON DISTRICT SCHOOL BOARD
LESTER B PEARSON PUBLIC SCHOOL   p
1008
See WATERLOO REGION DISTRICT
SCHOOL BOARD
LESTER B. PEARSON SCHOOL BOARD   p
1054
250 BEAUREPAIRE DR, BEACONSFIELD,
QC, H9W 5G7
(514) 697-7220   SIC 8211
LESTER B. PEARSON SCHOOL BOARD   p
1128
5050 RUE SHERBROOKE, LACHINE, QC,
H8T 1H8
(514) 637-2505   SIC 8211
LESTER B. PEARSON SCHOOL BOARD   p
1131
2241 RUE MENARD, LASALLE, QC, H8N
1J4
(514) 595-2043   SIC 8211
LESTER B. PEARSON SCHOOL BOARD   p
1131
8310 RUE GEORGE, LASALLE, QC, H8P
1E5
(514) 363-6213   SIC 8211
LESTER B. PEARSON SCHOOL BOARD   p
1245
5060 BOUL DES SOURCES, PIERRE-
FONDS, QC, H8Y 3E4
(514) 684-2337   SIC 8211
LESTER B. PEARSON SCHOOL BOARD   p
1251
111 AV BROADVIEW, POINTE-CLAIRE,
QC, H9R 3Z3
(514) 694-2760   SIC 8211
LESTER B. PEARSON SCHOOL BOARD   p
1251
120 AV AMBASSADOR, POINTE-CLAIRE,
QC, H9R 1S8

(514) 694-3770   SIC 8211
LESTER B. PEARSON SCHOOL BOARD   p
1251
501 BOUL SAINT-JEAN, POINTE-CLAIRE,
QC, H9R 3J5
(514) 697-3210   SIC 8211
LESTER B. PEARSON SCHOOL BOARD   p
1355
17 RUE MAPLE, SAINTE-ANNE-DE-
BELLEVUE, QC, H9X 2E5
(514) 457-3770   SIC 8211
LESTER B. PEARSON SCHOOL BOARD   p
1397
6100 BOUL CHAMPLAIN, VERDUN, QC,
H4H 1A5
(514) 766-2357   SIC 8211
**LESTER B. PEARSON SENIOR HIGH
SCHOOL**   p 8
See CALGARY BOARD OF EDUCATION
LETH IRON   p 141
See LETHBRIDGE IRON WORKS COM-
PANY LIMITED
LETHBRIDGE COLLEGE   p 143
3000 COLLEGE DR S, LETHBRIDGE, AB,
T1K 1L6
(403) 320-3200   SIC 8222
LETHBRIDGE COUNTRY CLUB   p 143
101 COUNTRY CLUB RD, LETHBRIDGE,
AB, T1K 7N9
(403) 327-6900   SIC 7997
LETHBRIDGE FAMILY SERVICES   p 143
1410 MAYOR MAGRATH DR S SUITE 106,
LETHBRIDGE, AB, T1K 2R3
(403) 317-4624   SIC 8361
**LETHBRIDGE IRON WORKS COMPANY
LIMITED**   p 141
720 32 ST N, LETHBRIDGE, AB, T1H 5K5
(403) 329-4242   SIC 3321
**LETHBRIDGE LODGE HOTEL AND CON-
FERENECE CENTRE**   p
142
See CHIP REIT NO 18 OPERATIONS LIM-
ITED PARTNERSHIP
LETHBRIDGE SCHOOL DISTRICT NO. 51 p
141
1605 15 AVE N, LETHBRIDGE, AB, T1H
1W4
(403) 328-4723   SIC 8211
LETHBRIDGE SCHOOL DISTRICT NO. 51 p
141
2003 9 AVE N, LETHBRIDGE, AB, T1H 1J3
(403) 329-3144   SIC 8211
LETHBRIDGE SCHOOL DISTRICT NO. 51 p
142
433 15 ST S, LETHBRIDGE, AB, T1J 2Z4
(403) 380-5321   SIC 8211
LETHBRIDGE TOYOTA   p 143
See SILVER RIDGE MOTOR PRODUCTS
LTD
LETHBRIDGE TRANSIT   p 141
See LETHBRIDGE, CITY OF
LETHBRIDGE TRUCK EQUIPMENT, DIV OF
p 141
See SOUTHLAND TRAILER CORP
**LETHBRIDGE YOUNG MEN'S CHRISTIAN
ASSOCIATION, THE**   p 142
74 MAURETANIA RD W UNIT 140, LETH-
BRIDGE, AB, T1J 5L4
(403) 942-5757   SIC 8699
LETHBRIDGE, CITY OF   p 141
619 4 AVE N, LETHBRIDGE, AB, T1H 0K4
(403) 320-3885   SIC 4111
LEUCROTTA EXPLORATION INC   p 53
639 5 AVE SW SUITE 700, CALGARY, AB,
T2P 0M9
(403) 705-4525   SIC 1382
LEVAC PROPANE   p 888
See 1649313 ONTARIO INC
LEVAC SUPPLY LIMITED   p 630
25 RAILWAY ST, KINGSTON, ON, K7K 2L7
(613) 546-6663   SIC 5085
LEVAERO AVIATION INC   p 911
2039 DEREK BURNEY DR, THUNDER
BAY, ON, P7K 0A1

▲ Public Company   ■ Public Company Family Member   **HQ** Headquarters   **BR** Branch   **SL** Single Location

(807) 475-5353   *SIC* 5599
LEVEILLE TOYOTA   *p* 1379
See AUTOMOBILES LEVEILLE INC
LEVEL 1 ACS INC   *p* 1035
225 MAIN ST, WOODSTOCK, ON, N4S 1T1
(519) 539-8619   *SIC* 7389
LEVEL GROUND TRADING LTD   *p* 267
1757 SEAN HTS, SAANICHTON, BC, V8M 0B3
(250) 544-0932   *SIC* 5149
LEVEL IT INSTALLATIONS INC   *p* 247
1515 BROADWAY ST UNIT 804, PORT CO-QUITLAM, BC, V3C 6M2
(604) 942-2022   *SIC* 1751
LEVEL PLATFORMS   *p* 624
See LPI LEVEL PLATFORMS INC
LEVEL-RITE SYSTEMS COMPANY *p* 513
29 REGAN RD, BRAMPTON, ON, L7A 1B2
SIC 3999
LEVELTON CONSULTANTS LTD   *p* 255
12791 CLARKE PL SUITE 150, RICH-MOND, BC, V6V 2H9
(604) 278-1411   *SIC* 8711
LEVESQUE & ASSOCIES CONSTRUCTION INC   *p* 1277
475 RUE DES CANETONS, QUEBEC, QC, G2E 5X6
(418) 263-0982   *SIC* 1541
LEVESQUE PLYWOOD LIMITED   *p* 619
225 PRINCE ST, HEARST, ON, P0L 1N0
(705) 362-4242   *SIC* 2435
LEVESQUE, A. ET S. (1993) INC *p* 1358
430 RUE COUTURE, SAINTE-HELENE-DE-BAGOT, QC, J0H 1M0
(450) 791-2727   *SIC* 5941
LEVI STRAUSS & CO. (CANADA) INC *p* 852
1725 16TH AVE SUITE 200, RICHMOND HILL, ON, L4B 4C6
(905) 763-4400   *SIC* 5632
LEVI-STRAUSS   *p* 852
See LEVI STRAUSS & CO. (CANADA) INC
LEVIN, FISCHER LIMITED   *p* 972
525 EGLINTON AVE W, TORONTO, ON, M5N 1B1
(416) 487-5277   *SIC* 6531
LEVIO   *p* 1264
See LEVIO CONSEILS INC
LEVIO CONSEILS INC   *p* 1264
1995 RUE FRANK-CARREL BUREAU 219, QUEBEC, QC, G1N 4H9
(418) 914-3623   *SIC* 7379
LEVIS DISTRIBUTION CENTRE   *p* 1139
See MULTI-MARQUES INC
LEVIS FOODLAND   *p* 913
See 900261 ONTARIO LTD
LEVIS TOYOTA   *p* 1135
See AUTO METIVIER INC
LEVITT-SAFETY LIMITED   *p* 798
2872 BRISTOL CIR, OAKVILLE, ON, L6H 5T5
(905) 829-3668   *SIC* 5099
LEVITT-SAFETY LIMITED   *p* 918
33 LAIRD DR, TORONTO, ON, M4G 3S8
(416) 425-6659   *SIC* 5999
LEVON RESOURCES LTD   *p* 306
666 BURRARD ST SUITE 500, VANCOU-VER, BC, V6C 2X8
(604) 682-2991   *SIC* 1081
LEVURE FLEISCHMANN, DIV OF *p* 1131
See AB MAURI (CANADA) LIMITEE
LEVY CANADA FASHION COMPANY *p* 1179
225 RUE CHABANEL O BUREAU 200, MONTREAL, QC, H2N 2C9
(514) 908-0104   *SIC* 5136
LEVY PILOTTE S.E.N.C.R.L.   *p* 1220
5250 BOUL DECARIE BUREAU 700, MON-TREAL, QC, H3X 3Z6
(514) 487-1566   *SIC* 8721
LEVY'S LEATHERS LIMITED   *p* 375
190 DISRAELI FWY, WINNIPEG, MB, R3B 2Z4
(204) 957-5139   *SIC* 5948
LEVY, JEFF INVESTMENTS LTD   *p* 781

4400 DUFFERIN ST SUITE 1, NORTH YORK, ON, M3H 6A8
(416) 667-9777   *SIC* 5531
LEWIS CATTLE OILER CO. LTD   *p* 354
GD, OAK LAKE, MB, R0M 1P0
(204) 855-2775   *SIC* 5191
LEWIS MOTOR SALES (NORTH BAY) INC *p* 763
19 HEWITT DR, NORTH BAY, ON, P1B 8K5
(705) 472-7220   *SIC* 5511
LEWIS MOTOR SALES INC   *p* 487
76 MAPLEVIEW DR W, BARRIE, ON, L4N 9H6
(705) 728-3026   *SIC* 5511
LEWIS MOULDINGS & WOOD SPECIAL-TIES LIMITED   *p* 470
134 FORT POINT RD, WEYMOUTH, NS, B0W 3T0
(902) 837-7393   *SIC* 2431
LEWIS, MAITLAND ENTERPRISES LTD *p* 863
1124 GREAT NORTHERN RD, SAULT STE. MARIE, ON, P6B 0B6
(705) 759-4545   *SIC* 5511
LEWIS-GOETZ ULC   *p* 182
3181 THUNDERBIRD CRES, BURNABY, BC, V5A 3G1
(604) 444-4885   *SIC* 5169
LEWIS-PATRICK INVESTMENTS LTD *p* 272
6320 148 ST, SURREY, BC, V3S 3C4
(604) 598-9930   *SIC* 6712
LEWISPORTE AREA CO-OP   *p* 425
See LEWISPORTE AREA CONSUMERS CO-OP SOCIETY LTD
LEWISPORTE AREA CONSUMERS CO-OP SOCIETY LTD   *p* 425
423 MAIN ST SUITE 415, LEWISPORTE, NL, A0G 3A0
(709) 535-6728   *SIC* 5411
LEWISPORTE CO-OP LTD   *p* 425
465 MAIN ST, LEWISPORTE, NL, A0G 3A0
(709) 535-6728   *SIC* 5411
LEXAR INTERNATIONAL LTD   *p* 366
16 MAZENOD RD SUITE 3, WINNIPEG, MB, R2J 4H2
(204) 661-9000   *SIC* 5199
LEXISNEXIS CANADA INC   *p* 765
111 GORDON BAKER RD SUITE 900, NORTH YORK, ON, M2H 3R1
(905) 479-2665   *SIC* 2731
LEXMARK CANADA INC   *p* 904
125 COMMERCE VALLEY DR W UNIT 600, THORNHILL, ON, L3T 7W4
(905) 763-0560   *SIC* 5045
LEXON PROJECTS INC   *p* 122
2327 91 AVE NW, EDMONTON, AB, T6P 1L1
(780) 435-7476   *SIC* 1542
LEXSAN ELECTRICAL INC   *p* 806
3328   BURNHAMTHORPE   RD   W, OAKVILLE, ON, L6M 4H3
(905) 827-1616   *SIC* 1731
LEXSUCO CORP   *p* 688
3275 ORLANDO DR, MISSISSAUGA, ON, L4V 1C5
(905) 792-8800   *SIC* 5211
LEXUS LAVAL   *p* 1085
See AUTO AMBASSADEUR INC
LEXUS OF CALGARY   *p* 33
See 1004907 ALBERTA LTD
LEXUS OF EDMONTON   *p* 101
See HERBLENS MOTORS INC
LEXUS OF KELOWNA   *p* 219
See 0859710 B.C. LTD
LEXUS OF OAKVILLE   *p* 806
See PREMIER AUTOMOTIVE GROUP INC
LEXUS SOUTH POINTE   *p* 125
See 1454615 ALBERTA LTD
LEXUS TRAVEL INC   *p* 1197
1411 RUE PEEL BUREAU 403, MON-TREAL, QC, H3A 1S5
(514) 397-9221   *SIC* 4724
LEXUS-TOYOTA GABRIEL   *p* 1324

See 166606 CANADA INC
LFM COURTIER IMMOBILIER AGREE INC *p* 1104
130 AV GATINEAU, GATINEAU, QC, J8T 4J8
(819) 246-1118   *SIC* 6531
LG ELECTRONICS CANADA, INC   *p* 793
20 NORELCO DR SUITE, NORTH YORK, ON, M9L 2X6
(647) 253-6300   *SIC* 5064
LG2   *p* 1186
See LABARRE GAUTHIER INC
LGL LIMITED   *p* 629
22 FISHER ST, KING CITY, ON, L7B 1G3
(905) 833-1244   *SIC* 8748
LGL RESORTS COMPANY   *p* 1159
2396 RUE LABELLE, MONT-TREMBLANT, QC, J8E 1T8
(819) 425-2734   *SIC* 7011
LGM FINANCIAL SERVICES INC   *p* 314
1021 HASTINGS ST W UNIT 400, VAN-COUVER, BC, V6E 0C3
(604) 806-5300   *SIC* 6411
LGM SOLUTION   *p* 1200
See 9152-2458 QUEBEC INC
LGV QUEBEC INC   *p* 1326
400 AV SAINTE-CROIX BUREAU 100, SAINT-LAURENT, QC, H4N 3L4
(514) 748-2522   *SIC* 4724
LGV QUEBEC INC   *p* 1326
400 AV SAINTE-CROIX BUREAU 110, SAINT-LAURENT, QC, H4N 3L4
(514) 748-2522   *SIC* 4724
LHD EQUIPMENT LIMITED   *p* 763
21 EXETER ST, NORTH BAY, ON, P1B 8G5
(705) 472-5207   *SIC* 3593
LHS ENTERPRISES   *p* 858
2916 COUNTY RD 31, RUSCOM STATION, ON, N0R 1R0
SIC 5963
LIARD CONSTRUCTION INC   *p* 1114
599 BOUL BASE-DE-ROC, JOLIETTE, QC, J6E 5P3
SIC 1796
LIBEO INC   *p* 1280
5700 BOUL DES GALERIES BUREAU 300, QUEBEC, QC, G2K 0H5
(418) 520-0739   *SIC* 7374
LIBERAL PARTY OF CANADA   *p* 823
See FEDERAL LIBERAL AGENCY OF CANADA, THE
LIBERAL PARTY OF ONTARIO   *p* 631
See KINGSTON AND THE ISLANDS POLIT-ICAL PARTY
LIBERTE NATURAL FOODS INC   *p* 1309
5000 RUE J.-A.-BOMBARDIER, SAINT-HUBERT, QC, J3Z 1H1
(450) 926-5222   *SIC* 5499
LIBERTY GOLD CORP   *p* 314
1055 HASTINGS ST W SUITE 1900, VAN-COUVER, BC, V6E 2E9
(604) 632-4677   *SIC* 1041
LIBERTY LINEHAUL INC   *p* 483
214 BOIDA AVE SS 2, AYR, ON, N0B 1E0
(519) 740-8181   *SIC* 4213
LIBERTY REALTY (1998) LTD   *p* 1023
1125 MERCER ST, WINDSOR, ON, N9A 1N8
SIC 6531
LIBERTY REGISTRY MANAGEMENT SER-VICES CO   *p* 773
See AFILIAS CANADA, CORP
LIBERTY SECURITY SYSTEMS INC *p* 119
5640 104 ST NW, EDMONTON, AB, T6H 2K2
(780) 988-7233   *SIC* 6211
LIBERTY SPRING   *p* 1160
See RESSORTS LIBERTE INC
LIBERTY TIRE RECYCLING CANADA (AB) *p* 168
See LIBERTY TIRE RECYCLING CANADA LTD
LIBERTY TIRE RECYCLING CANADA LTD

p 168
57425 RGE RD 253, STURGEON COUNTY, AB, T0G 1L1
(780) 961-2090   *SIC* 4953
LIBERTY TIRE RECYCLING CANADA LTD *p* 516
300 HENRY ST, BRANTFORD, ON, N3S 7R5
(519) 752-7696   *SIC* 4953
LIBERTY WINE MERCHANTS LTD *p* 289
291 2ND AVE E SUITE 100, VANCOUVER, BC, V5T 1B8
(604) 739-7801   *SIC* 5921
LIBRAIRIE GUERIN   *p* 1183
See EDITEUR GUERIN LTEE
LIBRAIRIE LAURENTIENNE   *p* 1323
See ASSOCIATION DES ETUDIANTS DU CEGEP ST-LAURENT INC
LIBRAIRIE MARIALE   *p* 1385
See SANCTUAIRE NOTRE-DAME-DU-CAP
LIBRAIRIE PANPOUPE   *p* 1260
See SOCIETE GESTION LIBRAIRIE INC
LIBRAIRIE RAFFIN   *p* 1282
See 9210-7580 QUEBEC INC
LIBRAIRIE RENAUD-BRAY INC   *p* 1164
5655 AV PIERRE-DE COUBERTIN, MON-TREAL, QC, H1N 1R2
(514) 272-4049   *SIC* 5942
LIBRAIRIES BOYER LTEE   *p* 1366
10 RUE NICHOLSON, SALABERRY-DE-VALLEYFIELD, QC, J6T 4M2
(450) 373-6211   *SIC* 5943
LIBRARY BOUND INC   *p* 1010
100 BATHURST DR UNIT 2, WATERLOO, ON, N2V 1V6
(519) 885-3233   *SIC* 5192
LIBRARY SERVICES CENTRE   *p* 637
131 SHOEMAKER ST, KITCHENER, ON, N2E 3B5
(519) 746-4420   *SIC* 5192
LIBRO CREDIT UNION LIMITED   *p* 654
217 YORK ST SUITE 100, LONDON, ON, N6A 5P9
(519) 672-0124   *SIC* 6062
LIBRO FINANCIAL GROUP   *p* 654
See LIBRO CREDIT UNION LIMITED
LIBURDI AUTOMATION INC   *p* 566
400 6 HWY, DUNDAS, ON, L9H 7K4
(905) 689-0734   *SIC* 3548
LIBURDI ENGINEERING LIMITED *p* 566
400 6 HWY, DUNDAS, ON, L9H 7K4
(905) 689-0734   *SIC* 3511
LIBURDI TURBINE SERVICES INC *p* 566
400 6 HWY, DUNDAS, ON, L9H 7K4
(905) 689-0734   *SIC* 4581
LICAPLAST INDUSTRIES EMBALLAGES INC   *p* 1330
2835 RUE DUCHESNE, SAINT-LAURENT, QC, H4R 1J2
(514) 335-4091   *SIC* 2673
LICENCE VINGT10, LA   *p* 1127
See CIE DANAWARES
LICKMAN TRAVEL CENTRE INC *p* 197
43971 INDUSTRIAL WAY SUITE 2, CHILLI-WACK, BC, V2R 3A4
(604) 795-3828   *SIC* 7011
LID BROKERAGE & REALTY CO. (1977) LTD.   *p* 1424
1171 8TH ST E, SASKATOON, SK, S7H 0S3
(306) 668-3000   *SIC* 5141
LID COMPANY, THE   *p* 1424
See LID BROKERAGE & REALTY CO. (1977) LTD.
LIDC   *p* 424
See LABRADOR INUIT DEVELOPMENT CORPORATION
LIDS   *p* 739
See GCO CANADA INC
LIEBERMAN-TRANCHEMONTAGNE INC *p* 1326
653 RUE HODGE, SAINT-LAURENT, QC, H4N 2A3
(514) 747-5510   *SIC* 5023
LIEBHERR-AEROSPACE CANADA   *p* 523

See LIEBHERR-CANADA LTD
LIEBHERR-CANADA LTD p 523
1015 SUTTON DR, BURLINGTON, ON, L7L 5Z8
(905) 319-9222 *SIC 5082*
LIFCO p 1302
See ESTAMPRO INC
LIFCO HYDRAULICS LTD p 887
250 MARTINDALE RD, ST CATHARINES, ON, L2S 0B2
(905) 641-0033 *SIC 5084*
LIFE & BANC SPLIT CORP p 964
181 BAY ST SUITE 2930, TORONTO, ON, M5J 2T3
(416) 642-6000 *SIC 6722*
LIFE SAFETY SYSTEMS, DIV OF p 445
See ATLANTICA MECHANICAL CONTRACTORS INCORPORATED
LIFE SCIENCE NUTRITINALS INC p 1044
1190 RUE LEMAY, ACTON VALE, QC, J0H 1A0
(450) 546-0101 *SIC 2833*
LIFE SCIENCE NUTRITINALS INCORPORATED p 1044
575 RUE DE ROXTON, ACTON VALE, QC, J0H 1A0
(866) 942-2429 *SIC 8731*
LIFEBRIDGE HEALTH MANAGEMENT INC p 710
90 BURNHAMTHORPE RD W SUITE 206, MISSISSAUGA, ON, L5B 3C3
SIC 6311
LIFELABS INC p 585
100 INTERNATIONAL BLVD, ETOBICOKE, ON, M9W 6J6
(416) 675-4530 *SIC 8071*
LIFELABS LP p 871
1290 ELLESMERE RD, SCARBOROUGH, ON, M1P 2X9
(416) 291-1464 *SIC 8071*
LIFELABS MEDICAL LABORATORY SERVICES p 871
See LIFELABS LP
LIFEMARK HEALTH CORP p 923
20 EGLINTON AVE W SUITE 600, TORONTO, ON, M4R 1K8
(416) 485-1344 *SIC 8093*
LIFEPLAN FINANCIAL SERVICES GROUP INC p 337
3960 QUADRA ST SUITE 101, VICTORIA, BC, V8X 4A3
(250) 727-7197 *SIC 8742*
LIFESTYLE MARKETS p 334
See HEALTH VENTURES LTD
LIFESTYLE OPERATIONS LP p 280
15501 16 AVE, SURREY, BC, V4A 9M5
(604) 538-7227 *SIC 6513*
LIFESTYLES GLOBAL NETWORK p 555
See LIFESTYLES NETWORK SERVICES INC
LIFESTYLES NETWORK SERVICES INC p 555
8100 KEELE ST, CONCORD, ON, L4K 2A3
(905) 761-9342 *SIC 5122*
LIFETOUCH CANADA INC p 372
1410 MOUNTAIN AVE UNIT 1, WINNIPEG, MB, R2X 0A4
(204) 977-3475 *SIC 7384*
LIFEWORKS CANADA LTD p 672
675 COCHRANE DR 5TH FL, MARKHAM, ON, L3R 0B8
(905) 947-7214 *SIC 8748*
LIFT BOSS INC p 84
7912 YELLOWHEAD TRAIL NW, EDMONTON, AB, T5B 1G3
(780) 474-9900 *SIC 5084*
LIFT BOSS MATERIAL HANDLING GROUP p 84
See LIFT BOSS INC
LIFT CO. LTD p 981
77 PETER ST SUITE 200, TORONTO, ON, M5V 2G4

(647) 239-6804 *SIC 5734*
LIFT LINE MACHINERY LTD p 1012
495 PRINCE CHARLES DR S, WELLAND, ON, L3B 5X1
(905) 788-0971 *SIC 5084*
LIFT LOCK COACH LINES p 840
See 564242 ONTARIO LIMITED
LIFT RITE INC p 732
5975 FALBOURNE ST UNIT 3, MISSISSAUGA, ON, L5R 3L8
(905) 456-2603 *SIC 3499*
LIFTING SOLUTIONS INC p 110
3710 78 AVE NW, EDMONTON, AB, T6B 3E5
(780) 784-7725 *SIC 5051*
LIFTKING p 1032
See LIFTKING MANUFACTURING CORP
LIFTKING MANUFACTURING CORP p 1032
7135 ISLINGTON AVE, WOODBRIDGE, ON, L4L 1V9
(905) 851-3988 *SIC 3537*
LIFTLOCK IGA p 839
See ARMSTRONG PLAZA LTD
LIFTOW LIMITED p 740
1400 COURTNEYPARK DR E, MISSISSAUGA, ON, L5T 1H1
(905) 677-3270 *SIC 5084*
LIFTOW LIMITED p 1128
1936 32E AV, LACHINE, QC, H8T 3J7
(514) 633-9360 *SIC 5084*
LIFTSAFE ENGINEERING AND SERVICE GROUP INC. p 483
306 DARRELL DR, AYR, ON, N0B 1E0
(519) 896-2430 *SIC 7389*
LIFTWAY LIMITED p 517
GD LCD MAIN, BRANTFORD, ON, N3T 5M2
(519) 759-5590 *SIC 5084*
LIGHT OF CHRIST RCSSD p 1412
1491 97TH ST, NORTH BATTLEFORD, SK, S9A 0K1
(306) 446-2232 *SIC 8211*
LIGHT OF CHRIST RCSSD p 1412
9301 19TH AVE, NORTH BATTLEFORD, SK, S9A 3N5
(306) 445-6158 *SIC 8211*
LIGHT SPEED LOGISTICS INC p 17
5720 84 AVE SE, CALGARY, AB, T2C 4T6
(403) 208-5441 *SIC 4213*
LIGHTFORM CANADA INC p 97
10545 124 ST NW, EDMONTON, AB, T5N 1R8
(780) 413-9898 *SIC 5063*
LIGHTHEADED LIGHTING LTD p 246
572 NICOLA PL SUITE 1150, PORT COQUITLAM, BC, V3B 6J4
(604) 464-5644 *SIC 3646*
LIGHTHOUSE CAMP SERVICES LTD p 30
714 1 ST SE UNIT 300, CALGARY, AB, T2G 2G8
(403) 265-5190 *SIC 7011*
LIGHTHOUSE LOGISTICS, A DIV OF p 30
See LIGHTHOUSE CAMP SERVICES LTD
LIGHTHOUSE SUPPORTED LIVING p 1428
304 2ND AVE S, SASKATOON, SK, S7K 1L1
(306) 653-0538 *SIC 7363*
LIGHTING WORLD p 433
See MCLOUGHLAN SUPPLIES LIMITED
LIGHTNING CIRCUITS INC p 883
12 SEAPARK DR, ST CATHARINES, ON, L2M 6S6
(905) 984-4006 *SIC 5065*
LIGHTSPEED p 1189
See LIGHTSPEED POS INC
LIGHTSPEED POS INC p 1189
700 RUE SAINT-ANTOINE E BUREAU 300, MONTREAL, QC, H2Y 1A6
(514) 907-1801 *SIC 7372*
LIGNAREX INC p 1121
7700 CH DE LA BATTURE, LA BAIE, QC, G7B 3P6
(418) 306-5049 *SIC 5084*
LIGNE D'AUTOBUS DECOUVERTE p 1278
See AUTOBUS LA QUEBECOISE INC

LIJA p 258
See HYP GOLF LTD
LIKRO PRECISION LIMITED p 717
3150 PEPPER MILL CRT, MISSISSAUGA, ON, L5L 4X4
(905) 828-9191 *SIC 3545*
LILIANNE LINGERIE p 1177
See 168662 CANADA INC
LILOOET HOSPITAL & HEALTH CENTER p 230
See INTERIOR HEALTH AUTHORITY
LILY CUPS INC p 865
2121 MARKHAM RD, SCARBOROUGH, ON, M1B 2W3
(416) 293-2877 *SIC 5113*
LILYDALE FOODS p 177
See LILYDALE INC
LILYDALE FOODS p 1438
See LILYDALE INC
LILYDALE INC p 30
2126 HURST RD SE, CALGARY, AB, T2G 4M5
(403) 265-9010 *SIC 2015*
LILYDALE INC p 177
31894 MARSHALL PL SUITE 5, ABBOTSFORD, BC, V2T 5Z9
(604) 850-2633 *SIC 2015*
LILYDALE INC p 247
1910 KINGSWAY AVE, PORT COQUITLAM, BC, V3C 1S7
(604) 941-4041 *SIC 2015*
LILYDALE INC p 1438
502 BOSWORTH ST, WYNYARD, SK, S0A 4T0
(306) 554-2555 *SIC 2015*
LILYDALE POULTRY p 30
See LILYDALE INC
LIMA'S GARDENS & CONSTRUCTION INC p 793
116 TORYORK DR, NORTH YORK, ON, M9L 1X6
(416) 740-9837 *SIC 1542*
LIMEN GROUP LTD p 783
46 LEPAGE CRT SUITE B, NORTH YORK, ON, M3J 1Z9
(416) 638-8880 *SIC 1741*
LIMESTONE ADVISORY FOR CHILD CARE PROGRAMS p 633
930 WOODBINE RD, KINGSTON, ON, K7P 2X4
(613) 384-5188 *SIC 8699*
LIMESTONE DISTRICT SCHOOL BOARD p 630
145 KIRKPATRICK ST, KINGSTON, ON, K7K 2P4
SIC 8211
LIMESTONE DISTRICT SCHOOL BOARD p 631
773 HIGHWAY 15, KINGSTON, ON, K7L 5H6
(613) 546-1737 *SIC 8211*
LIMESTONE DISTRICT SCHOOL BOARD p 632
153 VAN ORDER DR, KINGSTON, ON, K7M 1B9
(613) 542-9871 *SIC 8211*
LIMESTONE DISTRICT SCHOOL BOARD p 632
1059 TAYLOR-KIDD BLVD, KINGSTON, ON, K7M 6J9
(613) 389-8932 *SIC 8211*
LIMESTONE DISTRICT SCHOOL BOARD p 632
153 VAN ORDER DR, KINGSTON, ON, K7M 1B9
(613) 546-5575 *SIC 8211*
LIMESTONE DISTRICT SCHOOL BOARD p 632
1789 BATH RD, KINGSTON, ON, K7M 4Y3
(613) 389-2130 *SIC 8211*
LIMESTONE DISTRICT SCHOOL BOARD p 747
245 BELLEVILLE RD, NAPANEE, ON, K7R 3M7

(613) 354-3381 *SIC 8211*
LIMESTONE DISTRICT SCHOOL BOARD p 902
2860 RUTLEDGE RD, SYDENHAM, ON, K0H 2T0
(613) 376-3612 *SIC 8211*
LIMOCAR p 1318
See TRANSDEV QUEBEC INC
LIMOCAR BASSES LAURENTIDES ENR p 1061
See 2755-4609 QUEBEC INC
LIMOCAR DE LA VALLEE p 1057
See TRANSDEV QUEBEC INC
LIMPACT INTERNATIONAL LIMITED p 545
569 D'ARCY ST, COBOURG, ON, K9A 4B1
(905) 373-4100 *SIC 3499*
LIMSON CANADA, LTD p 263
12411 HORSESHOE WAY, RICHMOND, BC, V7A 4X6
(604) 529-5275 *SIC 6221*
LIN ROBERT SUTTON GROUP p 262
9100 BLUNDELL RD UNIT 550, RICHMOND, BC, V6Y 3X9
(604) 727-0917 *SIC 6531*
LINA'S ITALIAN MARKET p 20
See 574852 ALBERTA LIMITED
LINAMAR CONSUMER PRODUCTS p 604
See SKYJACK INC
LINAMAR CORPORATION p 478
GD, ARISS, ON, N0B 1B0
(519) 822-4080 *SIC 3531*
LINAMAR CORPORATION p 603
287 SPEEDVALE AVE W, GUELPH, ON, N1H 1C5
(519) 836-7550 *SIC 3714*
LINAMAR CORPORATION p 603
74 CAMPBELL RD, GUELPH, ON, N1H 1C1
(519) 821-1650 *SIC 3714*
LINAMAR CORPORATION p 603
280 SPEEDVALE AVE W, GUELPH, ON, N1H 1C4
(519) 824-8899 *SIC 3714*
LINAMAR CORPORATION p 603
355 SILVERCREEK PKY N, GUELPH, ON, N1H 1E6
(519) 821-7576 *SIC 3714*
LINAMAR CORPORATION p 603
277 SILVERCREEK PKY N, GUELPH, ON, N1H 1E6
(519) 763-0063 *SIC 3714*
LINAMAR CORPORATION p 603
347 SILVERCREEK PKY N, GUELPH, ON, N1H 1E6
(519) 837-3055 *SIC 3714*
LINAMAR CORPORATION p 605
375 MASSEY RD, GUELPH, ON, N1K 1B2
(519) 822-9008 *SIC 3714*
LINAMAR CORPORATION p 605
381 MASSEY RD, GUELPH, ON, N1K 1B2
(519) 767-9711 *SIC 3714*
LINAMAR CORPORATION p 605
355 MASSEY RD, GUELPH, ON, N1K 1B2
(519) 837-0880 *SIC 3714*
LINAMAR CORPORATION p 605
415 ELMIRA RD N, GUELPH, ON, N1K 1H3
(519) 763-5369 *SIC 3714*
LINAMAR CORPORATION p 605
12 INDEPENDENCE PL, GUELPH, ON, N1K 1H8
(519) 827-9423 *SIC 3714*
LINAMAR CORPORATION p 605
148 ARROW RD, GUELPH, ON, N1K 1T4
(519) 780-2270 *SIC 3714*
LINAMAR CORPORATION p 605
150 ARROW RD, GUELPH, ON, N1K 1T4
(519) 822-6627 *SIC 3714*
LINAMAR CORPORATION p 605
285 MASSEY RD, GUELPH, ON, N1K 1B2
(519) 763-0704 *SIC 3714*
LINAMAR CORPORATION p 605
30 MALCOLM RD, GUELPH, ON, N1K 1A9
(519) 767-0219 *SIC 3714*
LINAMAR CORPORATION p 605
30 MINTO RD, GUELPH, ON, N1K 1H5

(519) 821-1429 *SIC* 3714
LINAMAR CORPORATION *p* 605
301 MASSEY RD, GUELPH, ON, N1K 1B2
(519) 767-9711 *SIC* 3714
LINAMAR CORPORATION *p* 605
32 INDEPENDENCE PL, GUELPH, ON, N1K 1H8
(519) 827-9423 *SIC* 3714
LINAMAR CORPORATION *p* 1017
3590 VALTEC CRT, WINDSOR, ON, N8N 5E6
(519) 739-3465 *SIC* 3714
LINAMAR GEAR *p* 605
See LINAMAR CORPORATION
LINAMAR HOLDINGS INC. *p* 603
287 SPEEDVALE AVE W, GUELPH, ON, N1H 1C5
(519) 836-7550 *SIC* 3714
LINAMAR PERFORMANCE CENTRE *p* 605
See LINAMAR CORPORATION
LINAMAR TRANSPORTATION INC *p* 605
32 INDEPENDENCE PL, GUELPH, ON, N1K 1H8
(519) 837-2056 *SIC* 4213
LINCIA CORPORATION *p* 77
11940 SARCEE TRAIL NW, CALGARY, AB, T3R 0A1
(403) 295-0200 *SIC* 5531
LINCLUDEN INVESTMENT MANAGEMENT LIMITED *p* 806
1275 NORTH SERVICE RD W SUITE 607, OAKVILLE, ON, L6M 3G4
(905) 825-9000 *SIC* 6722
LINCOLN ELECTRIC COMPANY OF CANADA LP *p* 735
939 GANA CRT, MISSISSAUGA, ON, L5S 1N9
(905) 564-1151 *SIC* 3548
LINCOLN ELECTRIC COMPANY OF CANADA LP *p* 918
179 WICKSTEED AVE, TORONTO, ON, M4G 2B9
(416) 421-2600 *SIC* 3548
LINCOLN FABRICS HOLDINGS LIMITED *p* 884
63 LAKEPORT RD, ST CATHARINES, ON, L2N 4P6
SIC 2299
LINCOLN HEIGHTS FORD SALES LIMITED *p* 830
1377 RICHMOND RD, OTTAWA, ON, K2B 6R7
(613) 829-2120 *SIC* 5511
LINCOLN M. ALEXANDER SECONDARY SCHOOL *p* 686
See PEEL DISTRICT SCHOOL BOARD
LINCOURT MANOR INC *p* 418
1 CHIPMAN ST, ST STEPHEN, NB, E3L 2W9
(506) 466-7855 *SIC* 8051
LINDEN CHRISTIAN SCHOOL INC *p* 389
877 WILKES AVE, WINNIPEG, MB, R3P 1B8
(204) 989-6730 *SIC* 8211
LINDEN NURSING HOME *p* 143
See ALBERTA HEALTH SERVICES
LINDSAY BUICK *p* 646
150 ANGELINE ST N SUITE 484, LINDSAY, ON, K9V 4N1
(705) 324-2148 *SIC* 5511
LINDSAY COLLEGIATE AND VOCATIONAL INSTITUTE *p* 646
See TRILLIUM LAKELANDS DISTRICT SCHOOL BOARD
LINDSAY CONSTRUCTION LIMITED *p* 447
134 EILEEN STUBBS AVE UNIT 105, DARTMOUTH, NS, B3B 0A9
(902) 468-5000 *SIC* 1541
LINDSAY KENNEY LLP *p* 299
401 GEORGIA ST W SUITE 1800, VANCOUVER, BC, V6B 5A1
(604) 687-1323 *SIC* 8111
LINDSAY LLP *p* 299
564 BEATTY ST SUITE 1000, VANCOU-

VER, BC, V6B 2L3
(778) 945-5188 *SIC* 6311
LINDSAY MONUMENTS, DIV OF *p* 490
See CAMPBELL MONUMENT COMPANY LIMITED
LINDSAY PARK SPORTS SOCIETY *p* 30
2225 MACLEOD TRAIL SE, CALGARY, AB, T2G 5B6
(403) 233-8393 *SIC* 7991
LINDSAY PLACE HIGH SCHOOL *p* 1251
See LESTER B. PEARSON SCHOOL BOARD
LINDSAY SQUARE MALL *p* 646
401 KENT ST W SUITE 20, LINDSAY, ON, K9V 4Z1
(705) 324-1123 *SIC* 6512
LINDSAY THURBER COMPREHENSIVE HIGH SCHOOL *p* 153
See BOARD OF TRUSTEES OF THE RED DEER PUBLIC SCHOOL DISTRICT NO. 104, THE
LINDT & SPRUNGLI (CANADA), INC *p* 954
181 UNIVERSITY AVE SUITE 900, TORONTO, ON, M5H 3M7
(416) 351-8566 *SIC* 5145
LINE CREEK OPERATIONS *p* 269
See TECK COAL LIMITED
LINE MACHINES-OUTILS *p* 1110
See FIVES LINE MACHINES INC
LINEAR GRAIN CROP INPUTS, DIV OF *p* 348
See LINEAR GRAIN INC
LINEAR GRAIN INC *p* 348
67 CENTER AVE W, CARMAN, MB, R0G 0J0
(204) 745-6747 *SIC* 5153
LINEAR LOGISTICS LTD *p* 36
7015 MACLEOD TRAIL SW UNIT 603, CALGARY, AB, T2H 2K6
(587) 353-5454 *SIC* 4213
LINEAR TRANSFER AUTOMATION INC *p* 487
61 RAWSON AVE, BARRIE, ON, L4N 6E5
(705) 735-0000 *SIC* 3569
LINEMAN'S TESTING LABORATORIES OF CANADA LIMITED *p* 586
46 MERIDIAN RD, ETOBICOKE, ON, M9W 4Z7
(416) 742-6911 *SIC* 8734
LINEN CHEST *p* 1155
See BOUTIQUE LINEN CHEST (PHASE II) INC
LINERGY MANUFACTURING INC *p* 603
87 CAMPBELL RD, GUELPH, ON, N1H 1B9
(519) 341-5996 *SIC* 3569
LINEX MANUFACTURING *p* 605
See LINAMAR CORPORATION
LING & LING ENTERPRISES LTD *p* 884
533 LAKE ST, ST CATHARINES, ON, L2N 4H6
(905) 937-7719 *SIC* 5411
LINGERIE HAGO INC *p* 1182
7070 RUE SAINT-URBAIN, MONTREAL, QC, H2S 3H6
(514) 276-2518 *SIC* 5137
LINGERIE LILIANNE *p* 1181
See 168662 CANADA INC
LINGERIE SILHOUETTE *p* 1382
See A. SETLAKWE LIMITEE
LINGERIE ZEBRA - CENTRE DE LIQUIDATION *p* 1178
See B.L. INTIMATE APPAREL CANADA INC
LINK + CORPORATION *p* 660
4151 PERKINS RD, LONDON, ON, N6L 1G8
(519) 681-4002 *SIC* 4731
LINK + CUSTOM BROKERS *p* 660
See LINK + CORPORATION
LINK SCAFFOLD SERVICES INC *p* 122
2102 102 AVE NW, EDMONTON, AB, T6P 1W3
(780) 449-6111 *SIC* 1799

LINK SUSPENSIONS OF CANADA, LIMITED PARTNERSHIP *p* 149
601 18 AVE, NISKU, AB, T9E 7T7
(780) 955-2859 *SIC* 3842
LINK-LINE CONSTRUCTION LTD *p* 487
10 CHURCHILL DR, BARRIE, ON, L4N 8Z5
(705) 721-9284 *SIC* 1521
LINKAGE GROUP INC, THE *p* 672
30 CENTURIAN DR SUITE 200, MARKHAM, ON, L3R 8B8
(905) 415-2300 *SIC* 8742
LINKLETTER'S WELDING LTD *p* 1042
26 AV LINKLETTER SUITE 3, SUMMERSIDE, PE, C1N 4J9
(902) 887-2652 *SIC* 3523
LINKMAX PAPER LTD *p* 801
2904 SOUTH SHERIDAN WAY SUITE 303, OAKVILLE, ON, L6J 7L7
(905) 829-0053 *SIC* 5111
LINKNOW MEDIA *p* 1227
See 9209-5256 QUEBEC INC
LINKS AT QUARRY OAK GOLF & COUNTRY CLUB (2002), THE *p* 358
See 4498411 MANITOBA LTD
LINKS OF GLENEAGLES GOLF CORPORATION LTD, THE *p* 80
100 GLENEAGLES DR, COCHRANE, AB, T4C 1P5
(403) 932-1100 *SIC* 7992
LINSEY FOODS LTD *p* 672
121 MCPHERSON ST, MARKHAM, ON, L3R 3L3
(905) 940-3850 *SIC* 2099
LINVATEC CANADA ULC *p* 724
2330 MILLRACE CRT UNIT 5, MISSISSAUGA, ON, L5N 1W2
(905) 814-8900 *SIC* 5047
LINWOOD *p* 209
See LINWOOD HOMES LTD
LINWOOD HOMES LTD *p* 209
8250 RIVER RD, DELTA, BC, V4G 1B5
(604) 946-5421 *SIC* 2452
LION BRIDGE LTD *p* 398
10 RUE DAWSON, DIEPPE, NB, E1A 6C8
(506) 859-5200 *SIC* 7389
LION HYDRAULICS *p* 366
See MONARCH INDUSTRIES LIMITED
LION INTERNATIONAL TRAVEL SERVICE CO LTD *p* 260
110-4140 NO. 3 RD, RICHMOND, BC, V6X 2C2
(604) 231-8256 *SIC* 4724
LION ONE METALS LIMITED *p* 240
311 1ST ST W, NORTH VANCOUVER, BC, V7M 1B5
(604) 998-1250 *SIC* 1011
LION RAMPANT IMPORTS LTD *p* 513
36 EASTON RD, BRANTFORD, ON, N3P 1J5
(905) 572-6446 *SIC* 5092
LION TOURS *p* 260
See LION INTERNATIONAL TRAVEL SERVICE CO LTD
LIONBRIDGE (CANADA) INC *p* 1069
7900 BOUL TASCHEREAU BUREAU E204, BROSSARD, QC, J4X 1C2
(514) 288-2243 *SIC* 7389
LIONEL VENNES & FILS INC *p* 1112
180 32E AV BUREAU 1, GRAND-MERE, QC, G9T 5K5
(819) 538-2308 *SIC* 1711
LIONHEAD GOLF & COUNTRY CLUB *p* 511
See 351658 ONTARIO LIMITED
LIONS CLUB OF WINNIPEG HOUSING CENTRES *p* 375
320 SHERBROOK ST, WINNIPEG, MB, R3B 2W6
(204) 784-1240 *SIC* 8361
LIONS CLUB OF WINNIPEG PLACE FOR SENIOR CITIZENS INC *p* 378
610 PORTAGE AVE SUITE 1214, WIN-

NIPEG, MB, R3C 0G5
(204) 784-1236 *SIC* 8361
LIONS CLUB OF WINNIPEG SENIOR CITIZENS HOME *p* 375
320 SHERBROOK ST, WINNIPEG, MB, R3B 2W6
(204) 784-1240 *SIC* 8361
LIONS GATE ENTERTAINMENT CORP *p* 306
250 HOWE ST FL 20, VANCOUVER, BC, V6C 3R8
(877) 848-3866 *SIC* 7812
LIONS GATE FISHERIES LTD *p* 210
4179 RIVER RD W, DELTA, BC, V4K 1R9
(604) 946-1361 *SIC* 5146
LIONS GATE HOSPITAL *p* 240
See VANCOUVER COASTAL HEALTH
LIONS MANOR *p* 375
See LIONS CLUB OF WINNIPEG SENIOR CITIZENS HOME
LIONS PLACE *p* 378
See LIONS CLUB OF WINNIPEG PLACE FOR SENIOR CITIZENS INC
LIPTON CHARTERED ACCOUNTANTS LLP *p* 767
245 FAIRVIEW MALL DR SUITE 600, NORTH YORK, ON, M2J 4T1
(416) 496-2900 *SIC* 8721
LIQUI-FORCE SERVICES (ONTARIO) INC *p* 634
2015 SPINKS DR SUITE 2, KINGSVILLE, ON, N9Y 2E5
(519) 322-4600 *SIC* 7699
LIQUID CARGO LINES LIMITED *p* 713
452 SOUTHDOWN RD, MISSISSAUGA, ON, L5J 2Y4
SIC 4212
LIQUID NUTRITION *p* 1401
See LIQUID NUTRITION GROUP INC
LIQUID NUTRITION GROUP INC *p* 1401
60 CH BELVEDERE, WESTMOUNT, QC, H3Y 1P8
(514) 932-7555 *SIC* 2033
LIQUID NUTRITION INC *p* 1213
2007 RUE BISHOP, MONTREAL, QC, H3G 2E8
SIC 5499
LIQUID PARTNERS *p* 618
See 1476482 ONTARIO INC
LIQUOR BOX *p* 41
See 1046809 ALBERTA INC
LIQUOR CONTROL BOARD OF ONTARIO, THE *p* 942
55 LAKE SHORE BLVD E SUITE 876, TORONTO, ON, M5E 1A4
(416) 365-5900 *SIC* 5921
LIQUOR CONTROL BOARD OF ONTARIO, THE *p* 942
1 YONGE ST 13TH FLOOR, TORONTO, ON, M5E 1E5
(416) 365-5778 *SIC* 5921
LIQUOR CONTROL BOARD OF ONTARIO, THE *p* 1014
2000 BOUNDARY RD, WHITBY, ON, L1N 7G4
(905) 723-3417 *SIC* 4225
LIQUOR DEPOT *p* 99
See ALCANNA INC
LIQUOR DEPOT AT WINDERMERE CROSSING *p* 115
10508 82 AVE NW UNIT 300, EDMONTON, AB, T6E 2A4
(780) 702-7400 *SIC* 5921
LIQUOR SOURCE CORPORATION *p* 5
4916 50 AVE, BEAUMONT, AB, T4X 1J9
(780) 851-7336 *SIC* 8742
LIQUOR SOURCE RETAIL LIQUOR OUTLETS *p* 5
See LIQUOR SOURCE CORPORATION
LIQUOR STORE CABARET *p* 1273
2600 BOUL LAURIER BUREAU 180, QUEBEC, QC, G1V 4T3

SIC 5921

LIQUOR STORES GP INC *p* 115
10508 82 AVE NW SUITE 300, EDMONTON, AB, T6E 2A4
(780) 944-9994 *SIC 5921*

LIQUOR STORES LIMITED PARTNERSHIP
p 115
10508 82 AVE NW SUITE 300, EDMONTON, AB, T6E 2A4
(780) 944-9994 *SIC 5921*

LISE WATIER COSMETIQUES, DIV *p* 1157
See *GROUPE MARCELLE INC*

LISETTE L MONTREAL *p* 1177
See *AGENCES LISETTE LIMOGES INC, LES*

LISGAR COLLEGIATE INSTITUTE *p* 834
See *OTTAWA-CARLETON DISTRICT SCHOOL BOARD*

LISI AEROSPACE CANADA CORP *p* 1094
2000 PLACE TRANSCANADIENNE, DORVAL, QC, H9P 2X5
(514) 421-4567 *SIC 3721*

LISI MECHANICAL CONTRACTORS LTD *p* 586
160 DISCO RD, ETOBICOKE, ON, M9W 1M4
(416) 674-8333 *SIC 1711*

LISI SERVICES *p* 586
See *LISI MECHANICAL CONTRACTORS LTD*

LISTEL CANADA LTD *p* 314
1300 ROBSON ST, VANCOUVER, BC, V6E 1C5
(604) 684-8461 *SIC 7011*

LISTEL CANADA LTD *p* 343
4121 VILLAGE GREEN, WHISTLER, BC, V8E 1H2
(604) 932-1133 *SIC 7011*

LISTEL HOTEL *p* 343
See *LISTEL CANADA LTD*

LISTEL WHISTLER HOTEL *p* 314
See *LISTEL CANADA LTD*

LISTER INDUSTRIES LTD *p* 110
7410 68 AVE NW, EDMONTON, AB, T6B 0A1
(780) 468-2040 *SIC 1389*

LISTOWEL & WINGHAM HOSPITALS ALLIANCE *p* 1026
See *WINGHAM AND DISTRICT HOSPITAL*

LISTOWEL COLD STORAGE *p* 646
See *ERIE MEAT PRODUCTS LIMITED*

LISTOWEL DISTRICT SECONDARY SCHOOL *p* 646
See *AVON MAITLAND DISTRICT SCHOOL BOARD*

LISTOWEL MEMORIAL HOSPITAL, THE *p* 647
255 ELIZABETH ST E, LISTOWEL, ON, N4W 2P5
(519) 291-3120 *SIC 8062*

LISTOWEL TECHNOLOGY INC *p* 647
1700 MITCHELL RD S, LISTOWEL, ON, N4W 3H4
(519) 291-9900 *SIC 3089*

LISTRO'S NO FRILLS *p* 677
See *1530431 ONTARIO LIMITED*

LITCHFIELD & CO LTD *p* 247
3046 WESTWOOD ST, PORT COQUITLAM, BC, V3C 3L7
(604) 464-7525 *SIC 1795*

LITE FORM ONTARIO, DIVISION OF *p* 598
See *OKE WOODSMITH BUILDING SYSTEMS INC*

LITE-TECH INDUSTRIES LIMITED *p* 787
161 BARTLEY DR, NORTH YORK, ON, M4A 1E6
(416) 751-5644 *SIC 3646*

LITELINE CORPORATION *p* 852
90 WEST BEAVER CREEK RD, RICHMOND HILL, ON, L4B 1E7
(416) 996-1856 *SIC 3089*

LITENS AUTOMOTIVE GROUP *p* 1032
See *LITENS AUTOMOTIVE PARTNERSHIP*

LITENS AUTOMOTIVE PARTNERSHIP *p* 1032
730 ROWNTREE DAIRY RD, WOODBRIDGE, ON, L4L 5T7
(905) 856-0200 *SIC 3429*

LITERIE PRIMO INC *p* 1164
7000 RUE HOCHELAGA, MONTREAL, QC, H1N 1Y7
(514) 256-7543 *SIC 5021*

LITERIES UNIVERSELLES PAGA INC *p* 1229
6395 CH DE LA COTE-DE-LIESSE, MONTREAL, QC, H4T 1E5
(514) 376-7882 *SIC 6712*

LITHION POWER GROUP LTD *p* 53
333 7 AVE SW UNIT 970, CALGARY, AB, T2P 2Z1
(587) 349-5468 *SIC 2819*

LITHIUM AMERIQUE DU NORD INC *p* 1121
500 RTE DU LITHIUM, LA CORNE, QC, J0Y 1R0
(819) 734-5000 *SIC 1081*

LITHIUM X ENERGY CORP *p* 328
595 BURRARD ST SUITE 3123, VANCOUVER, BC, V7X 1J1
(604) 609-6138 *SIC 1081*

LITHO MILE-ILES *p* 1381
See *9220-9147 QUEBEC INC*

LITHO SERVICE CANADA *p* 1369
See *EGZATEK INC*

LITTELFUSE STARTCO *p* 1434
See *STARTCO ENGINEERING LTD*

LITTLE BOW GAS CO-OP LTD *p* 4
108 MAIN ST, BARONS, AB, T0L 0G0
(403) 757-3888 *SIC 4924*

LITTLE CAESARS *p* 413
See *J A T INVESTMENTS INC*

LITTLE CAESARS PIZZA *p* 858
See *L.A.M.M. INC*

LITTLE MOUNTAIN NEIGHBOURHOOD HOUSE SOCIETY *p* 290
3981 MAIN ST, VANCOUVER, BC, V5V 3P3
(604) 879-7104 *SIC 8399*

LITTLE MOUNTAIN PLACE *p* 290
See *LITTLE MOUNTAIN RESIDENTIAL CARE & HOUSING SOCIETY*

LITTLE MOUNTAIN RESIDENTIAL CARE & HOUSING SOCIETY *p* 284
851 BOUNDARY RD, VANCOUVER, BC, V5K 4T2
(604) 299-7567 *SIC 8051*

LITTLE MOUNTAIN RESIDENTIAL CARE & HOUSING SOCIETY *p* 290
330 36TH AVE E, VANCOUVER, BC, V5W 3Z4
(604) 325-2298 *SIC 8051*

LITTLE OAK REALTY LTD *p* 175
2630 BOURQUIN CRES W SUITE 9, ABBOTSFORD, BC, V2S 5N7
(604) 309-5729 *SIC 6531*

LITTLE POTATO COMPANY LTD, THE *p* 101
11749 180 ST NW, EDMONTON, AB, T5S 2H6
(780) 414-6075 *SIC 5148*

LITTLE RED RIVER CREE NATION BOARD OF EDUCATION *p* 130
GD, FOX LAKE, AB, T0H 1R0
(780) 759-3912 *SIC 8211*

LITTLE REMEDY CENTRE *p* 769
See *711620 ONTARIO LIMITED*

LITTLE ROCK FARM TRUCKING *p* 1004
See *1340560 ONTARIO INC*

LITTLE SHORT STOP STORES LIMITED *p* 539
201B PRESTON PKY, CAMBRIDGE, ON, N3H 5E8
(519) 653-3171 *SIC 5411*

LITZ CRANE RENTALS *p* 381
See *LITZ, R. & SONS COMPANY LIMITED*

LITZ, R. & SONS COMPANY LIMITED *p* 381
277 MCPHILLIPS ST, WINNIPEG, MB, R3E 2K7
(204) 783-7979 *SIC 7359*

LITZEN, T. SPORTS LIMITED *p* 566

433 OFIELD RD S, DUNDAS, ON, L9H 5E2
(905) 628-3344 *SIC 5091*

LIUNA GARDENS LIMITED *p* 611
360 JAMES ST N SUITE 201, HAMILTON, ON, L8L 1H5
(905) 525-2410 *SIC 7299*

LIUNA LOCAL 183 *p* 786
See *LABOURERS INTERNATIONAL UNION OF NORTH AMERICA-LOCAL 183*

LIUNA STATION *p* 611
See *LIUNA GARDENS LIMITED*

LIVANOVA CANADA CORP *p* 193
5005 NORTH FRASER WAY, BURNABY, BC, V5J 5M1
(604) 412-5650 *SIC 3841*

LIVANOVA CANADA CORP *p* 679
280 HILLMOUNT RD UNIT 8, MARKHAM, ON, L6C 3A1
(905) 284-4245 *SIC 3841*

LIVE DIFFERENT *p* 610
1429 MAIN ST E SUITE 111, HAMILTON, ON, L8K 1C2
(905) 777-1662 *SIC 8699*

LIVE NATION CANADA, INC *p* 991
909 LAKE SHORE BLVD W SUITE 300, TORONTO, ON, M6K 3L3
(416) 260-5600 *SIC 7922*

LIVE SCIENCE GROUP *p* 737
See *BIO-RAD LABORATORIES (CANADA) LIMITED*

LIVE TO PLAY SPORTS *p* 247
1465 KEBET WAY, PORT COQUITLAM, BC, V3C 6L3
(604) 552-2930 *SIC 5091*

LIVE TO SECURE PROTECTIVE SERVICES INC *p* 791
15 INGRAM DR UNITS 201-702, NORTH YORK, ON, M6M 2L7
(647) 560-4321 *SIC 7381*

LIVERTON HOTELS INTERNATIONAL INC *p* 306
645 HOWE ST, VANCOUVER, BC, V6C 2Y9
(604) 687-1122 *SIC 7011*

LIVING GROUP OF COMPANIES INC *p* 672
7030 WOODBINE AVE SUITE 300, MARKHAM, ON, L3R 6G2
(905) 474-0500 *SIC 6531*

LIVING GROUPS OF COMPANIES *p* 672
See *LIVING REALTY INC*

LIVING HOPE NATIVE MINISTRIES *p* 849
23 HWY 105 SUITE 1, RED LAKE, ON, P0V 2M0
SIC 8699

LIVING REALTY INC *p* 672
7030 WOODBINE AVE SUITE 300, MARKHAM, ON, L3R 6G2
(905) 474-9856 *SIC 6531*

LIVING REALTY INC *p* 711
1177 CENTRAL PKY W UNIT 32, MISSISSAUGA, ON, L5C 4P3
(905) 896-0002 *SIC 6531*

LIVING SKY SCHOOL DIVISION NO. 202 *p* 1412
See *BOARD OF EDUCATION OF THE LIVING SKY SCHOOL DIVISION NO. 202 SASKATCHEWAN*

LIVING WATERS CATHOLIC REGIONAL DIVISION NO.42 *p* 173
4204 KEPLER ST UNIT 1, WHITECOURT, AB, T7S 0A3
(780) 778-5044 *SIC 8211*

LIVINGSTON CUSTOM BROKERAGE *p* 591
See *LIVINGSTON INTERNATIONAL INC*

LIVINGSTON INTERNATIONAL *p* 686
See *4513380 CANADA INC*

LIVINGSTON INTERNATIONAL INC *p* 579
405 THE WEST MALL SUITE 400, ETOBICOKE, ON, M9C 5K7
(416) 626-2800 *SIC 4731*

LIVINGSTON INTERNATIONAL INC *p* 591
36 QUEEN ST, FORT ERIE, ON, L2A 0B5
(905) 871-6500 *SIC 4731*

LIVINGSTONE COLONY *p* 144

See *LIVINGSTONE HUTTERIAN BRETHREN*

LIVINGSTONE HUTTERIAN BRETHREN *p* 144
GD, LUNDBRECK, AB, T0K 1H0
(403) 628-2226 *SIC 0191*

LIVINGSTONE TERRASSO *p* 489
See *JANSEN INTERNATIONAL CANADA LTD*

LIVRAISON WILLIAM LTEE *p* 1094
610 AV ORLY, DORVAL, QC, H9P 1E9
(514) 526-5901 *SIC 5912*

LIXAR I.T. INC *p* 820
373 COVENTRY RD, OTTAWA, ON, K1K 2C5
(613) 722-0688 *SIC 7374*

LIXIL CANADA INC *p* 732
5900 AVEBURY RD, MISSISSAUGA, ON, L5R 3M3
(905) 949-4800 *SIC 3431*

LIZZI, C. ENTERPRISES INC *p* 684
327 BRONTE ST S UNIT 1, MILTON, ON, L9T 4A4
(905) 875-0303 *SIC 5411*

LJ WELDING AUTOMATION LTD *p* 110
4747 76 AVE NW, EDMONTON, AB, T6B 0A3
(780) 466-6658 *SIC 3544*

LJC DEVELOPMENT CORPORATION *p* 1213
1425 RUE DE LA MONTAGNE, MONTREAL, QC, H3G 1Z3
(514) 285-5555 *SIC 7011*

LJP CORPORATION *p* 808
793522 MONO 3RD LINE, ORANGEVILLE, ON, L9W 2Y8
(519) 942-0754 *SIC 0172*

LK PROTECTION INC *p* 703
1590 DUNDAS ST E SUITE 220, MISSISSAUGA, ON, L4X 2Z2
(905) 566-7008 *SIC 7381*

LKQ SHAW AUTO RECYCLERS INC *p* 651
1765 PENSION LANE, LONDON, ON, N5W 6C7
(519) 455-1200 *SIC 5531*

LKQ UPPER BROOKSIDE INC *p* 470
466 BROOKSIDE RD, UPPER BROOKSIDE, NS, B6L 2B3
(902) 897-0252 *SIC 5531*

LLAP HOLDINGS LTD *p* 39
14939 DEER RIDGE DR SE, CALGARY, AB, T2J 7C4
(403) 278-2626 *SIC 5411*

LLEWELLYN SECURITY INCORPORATED *p* 746
107 QUEEN ST, MORRISTON, ON, N0B 2C0
SIC 7381

LLOYD DOUGLAS SOLUTIONS INC *p* 891
130 IBER RD, STITTSVILLE, ON, K2S 1E9
(613) 369-5189 *SIC 3578*

LLOYD MACDONALD NISSAN *p* 467
See *1015605 SALES LIMITED*

LLOYD REFORESTATION LTD *p* 250
13025 WOODLAND RD, PRINCE GEORGE, BC, V2N 5B4
SIC 0781

LLOYD SADD INSURANCE BROKERS LTD *p* 97
10240 124 ST NW UNIT 700, EDMONTON, AB, T5N 3W6
(780) 483-4544 *SIC 6411*

LLOYDMINSTER AND DISTRICT CO-OPERATIVE LIMITED *p* 1409
4090 41 ST SUITE 101, LLOYDMINSTER, SK, S9V 2J1
(306) 825-2271 *SIC 5411*

LLOYDMINSTER HOSPITAL *p* 1409
See *SASKATCHEWAN HEALTH AUTHORITY*

LLOYDMINSTER PUBLIC SCHOOL DIVISION *p* 144

See *LLOYDMINSTER SCHOOL DIVISION NO 99*

LLOYDMINSTER SAFEWAY   p 144
See *SOBEYS WEST INC*

LLOYDMINSTER SCHOOL DIVISION NO 99 p 144
5017 46 ST SUITE 99, LLOYDMINSTER, AB, T9V 1R4
(780) 875-5541   *SIC* 8211

LM SERVICES LIMITED PARTNERSHIP p 964
181 BAY ST SUITE 2500, TORONTO, ON, M5J 2T3
SIC 8741

LMB AUTOMOBILE INC   p 53
520 3 AVE SW SUITE 1900, CALGARY, AB, T2P 0R3
SIC 5511

LMG   p 149
See *LEADING MANUFACTURING GROUP INC*

LMG INSURANCE BROKERS LTD   p 212
2640 BEVERLY ST SUITE 200, DUNCAN, BC, V9L 5C7
(250) 748-3200   *SIC* 6411

LMI   p 193
See *LMI TECHNOLOGIES INC*

LMI TECHNOLOGIES INC   p 193
9200 GLENLYON PKY UNIT 1, BURNABY, BC, V5J 5J8
(604) 636-1011   *SIC* 3545

LML INDUSTRIAL CONTRACTORS LTD p 1409
4815 50 ST SUITE 302, LLOYDMINSTER, SK, S9V 0M8
(306) 825-6115   *SIC* 1799

LMS LIMITED PARTNERSHIP   p 277
7452 132 ST, SURREY, BC, V3W 4M7
(604) 598-9930   *SIC* 1791

LMS MANAGEMENT LTD   p 272
6320 148 ST, SURREY, BC, V3S 3C4
(604) 598-9930   *SIC* 1791

LMS PROLINK LTD   p 946
480 UNIVERSITY AVE SUITE 800, TORONTO, ON, M5G 1V2
(416) 595-7484   *SIC* 6411

LMT ENTERPRISES LTD   p 83
2235 2 AVE, DUNMORE, AB, T1B 0K3
(403) 527-1562   *SIC* 1629

LN LAND DEVELOPMENT TECHNOLOGIES INC   p 128
9908 FRANKLIN AVE UNIT 4, FORT MCMURRAY, AB, T9H 2K5
(780) 791-0075   *SIC* 8713

LNB INC   p 853
121 GRANTON DR SUITE 14, RICHMOND HILL, ON, L4B 3N4
(905) 882-2500   *SIC* 7389

LNLC INC   p 1280
1100 RUE BOUVIER BUREAU 100, QUEBEC, QC, G2K 1L9
(418) 624-6100   *SIC* 5995

LO-BAR LOG TRANSPORT CO. LTD p 248
8377 HART HWY, PRINCE GEORGE, BC, V2K 3B8
(250) 962-8644   *SIC* 2411

LO-COST PROPANE LTD   p 141
3191 5 AVE N, LETHBRIDGE, AB, T1H 0P2
(403) 380-3536   *SIC* 5984

LO-SE-CA FOUNDATION - A CHRISTIAN SOCIETY FOR PERSONS WITH DISABILITIES   p 166
215 CARNEGIE DR SUITE 1, ST. ALBERT, AB, T8N 5B1
(780) 460-1400   *SIC* 8322

LOAD LINE INCORPORATED   p 361
9081 HWY 32, WINKLER, MB, R6W 4B7
(204) 325-4798   *SIC* 3715

LOAD LINE MANUFACTURING   p 361
See *LOAD LINE INCORPORATED*

LOAD LISTER   p 894
See *MYRSA MANAGEMENT SERVICES*

LTD

LOAD SYSTEMS INTERNATIONAL INC p 1267
2666 BOUL DU PARC-TECHNOLOGIQUE BUREAU 190, QUEBEC, QC, G1P 4S6
(418) 650-2330   *SIC* 3625

LOAD'EM UP PETROLEUMS LTD   p 250
1064 GREAT ST, PRINCE GEORGE, BC, V2N 2K8
(250) 562-8166   *SIC* 5171

LOAN ARRANGER, THE   p 866
See *BLACK PALM AVIARIES OF CANADA INC*

LOBE   p 1293
See *LOBE RESEAU INC*

LOBE RESEAU INC   p 1293
3520 RUE DE L'HETRIERE BUREAU 103, SAINT-AUGUSTIN-DE-DESMAURES, QC, G3A 0B4
(418) 877-7222   *SIC* 8093

LOBLA SAINT SAUVEUR   p 1352
See *PROVIGO DISTRIBUTION INC*

LOBLAW   p 1390
See *LOBLAWS INC*

LOBLAW COMPANIES EAST, DIV OF p 816
See *LOBLAWS INC*

LOBLAW COMPANIES LIMITED   p 24
3225 12 ST NE, CALGARY, AB, T2E 7S9
(403) 291-7700   *SIC* 5411

LOBLAW COMPANIES LIMITED   p 421
GD, BAY ROBERTS, NL, A0A 1G0
(709) 786-6001   *SIC* 5411

LOBLAW COMPANIES LIMITED   p 511
1 PRESIDENTS CHOICE CIR, BRAMPTON, ON, L6Y 5S5
(905) 459-2500   *SIC* 5411

LOBLAW COMPANIES LIMITED   p 697
925 RATHBURN RD E UNIT A, MISSISSAUGA, ON, L4W 4C3
(905) 276-6560   *SIC* 5411

LOBLAW COMPANIES LIMITED   p 826
64 ISABELLA ST, OTTAWA, ON, K1S 1V4
(613) 232-4831   *SIC* 5411

LOBLAW COMPANIES LIMITED   p 1313
2000 BOUL CASAVANT O, SAINT-HYACINTHE, QC, J2S 7K2
(450) 771-6601   *SIC* 5411

LOBLAW FINANCIAL HOLDINGS INC p 434
62 PRINCE RUPERT DR, STEPHENVILLE, NL, A2N 3W7
(709) 643-0862   *SIC* 5411

LOBLAW PROPERTIES LIMITED   p 457
3711 JOSEPH HOWE DR, HALIFAX, NS, B3L 4H8
SIC 5411

LOBLAW PROPERTIES LIMITED   p 469
46 ELM ST, TRURO, NS, B2N 3H6
(902) 895-4306   *SIC* 5411

LOBLAW PROPERTIES LIMITED   p 511
1 PRESIDENTS CHOICE CIR, BRAMPTON, ON, L6Y 5S5
(905) 459-2500   *SIC* 6512

LOBLAW PROPERTIES LIMITED   p 993
605 ROGERS RD SUITE 208, TORONTO, ON, M6M 1B9
(416) 653-1951   *SIC* 5411

LOBLAW QUEBEC LIMITEE   p 1326
330 AV SAINTE-CROIX, SAINT-LAURENT, QC, H4N 3K4
(514) 747-0606   *SIC* 5411

LOBLAW'S   p 1105
See *PROVIGO DISTRIBUTION INC*

LOBLAWS   p 546
See *LOBLAWS SUPERMARKETS LIMITED*

LOBLAWS   p 576
See *LOBLAWS SUPERMARKETS LIMITED*

LOBLAWS   p 596
See *LOBLAWS SUPERMARKETS LIMITED*

LOBLAWS   p 626
200 EARL GREY DR, KANATA, ON, K2T 1B6
(613) 599-9934   *SIC* 5992

LOBLAWS   p 633
See *LOBLAWS SUPERMARKETS LIMITED*

LOBLAWS   p 646
See *LOBLAWS SUPERMARKETS LIMITED*

LOBLAWS   p 713
See *LOBLAWS SUPERMARKETS LIMITED*

LOBLAWS   p 751
See *LOBLAWS INC*

LOBLAWS   p 752
See *LOBLAWS SUPERMARKETS LIMITED*

LOBLAWS   p 787
See *LOBLAWS INC*

LOBLAWS   p 810
See *LOBLAWS SUPERMARKETS LIMITED*

LOBLAWS   p 826
See *LOBLAW COMPANIES LIMITED*

LOBLAWS   p 827
See *LOBLAWS INC*

LOBLAWS   p 831
See *LOBLAWS SUPERMARKETS LIMITED*

LOBLAWS   p 843
See *LOBLAWS SUPERMARKETS LIMITED*

LOBLAWS   p 918
See *LOBLAWS SUPERMARKETS LIMITED*

LOBLAWS   p 920
See *LOBLAWS INC*

LOBLAWS   p 989
See *LOBLAWS SUPERMARKETS LIMITED*

LOBLAWS   p 1001
See *LOBLAWS INC*

LOBLAWS   p 1089
See *PROVIGO DISTRIBUTION INC*

LOBLAWS   p 1107
See *PROVIGO DISTRIBUTION INC*

LOBLAWS   p 1119
See *PROVIGO DISTRIBUTION INC*

LOBLAWS   p 1148
See *PROVIGO DISTRIBUTION INC*

LOBLAWS   p 1165
See *PROVIGO DISTRIBUTION INC*

LOBLAWS   p 1218
See *PROVIGO DISTRIBUTION INC*

LOBLAWS   p 1283
See *LOBLAWS INC*

LOBLAWS   p 1313
See *LOBLAW COMPANIES LIMITED*

LOBLAWS 1066   p 577
See *LOBLAWS SUPERMARKETS LIMITED*

LOBLAWS 190   p 802
See *LOBLAWS SUPERMARKETS LIMITED*

LOBLAWS INC   p 3
1050 YANKEE VALLEY BLVD SE, AIRDRIE, AB, T4A 2E4
(403) 912-3800   *SIC* 5411

LOBLAWS INC   p 9
3575 20 AVE NE, CALGARY, AB, T1Y 6R3
(403) 280-8222   *SIC* 5411

LOBLAWS INC   p 17
6810 40 ST SE, CALGARY, AB, T2C 2A5
(905) 459-2500   *SIC* 5411

LOBLAWS INC   p 24
2928 23 ST NE, CALGARY, AB, T2E 8R7
(403) 291-2810   *SIC* 5141

LOBLAWS INC   p 40
7020 4 ST NW, CALGARY, AB, T2K 1C4
(403) 516-8519   *SIC* 5411

LOBLAWS INC   p 69
10505 SOUTHPORT RD SW SUITE 1, CALGARY, AB, T2W 3N2
(403) 225-6207   *SIC* 5411

LOBLAWS INC   p 70
15915 MACLEOD TRAIL SE UNIT 100, CALGARY, AB, T2Y 3R9
(403) 254-3637   *SIC* 5411

LOBLAWS INC   p 71
5251 COUNTRY HILLS BLVD NW SUITE 1575, CALGARY, AB, T3A 5H8
(403) 241-4027   *SIC* 5411

LOBLAWS INC   p 75
5858 SIGNAL HILL CTR SW SUITE 1577, CALGARY, AB, T3H 3P8
(403) 686-8035   *SIC* 5141

LOBLAWS INC   p 76
3633 WESTWINDS DR NE UNIT 100, CALGARY, AB, T3J 5K3
(403) 590-3347   *SIC* 5411

LOBLAWS INC   p 94
12350 137 AVE NW, EDMONTON, AB, T5L 4X6
(780) 406-3768   *SIC* 5411

LOBLAWS INC   p 96
14740 111 AVE NW, EDMONTON, AB, T5M 2P5
(780) 452-5411   *SIC* 5141

LOBLAWS INC   p 101
17303 STONY PLAIN RD NW SUITE 1573, EDMONTON, AB, T5S 1B5
(780) 486-8452   *SIC* 5141

LOBLAWS INC   p 119
4821 CALGARY TRAIL NW SUITE 1570, EDMONTON, AB, T6H 5W8
(780) 430-2797   *SIC* 5411

LOBLAWS INC   p 121
9711 23 AVE NW, EDMONTON, AB, T6N 1K7
(780) 490-3935   *SIC* 5141

LOBLAWS INC   p 124
4410 17 ST NW, EDMONTON, AB, T6T 0C1
(780) 450-2041   *SIC* 5411

LOBLAWS INC   p 128
9 HAINEAULT ST, FORT MCMURRAY, AB, T9H 1R8
(780) 790-3827   *SIC* 5411

LOBLAWS INC   p 132
12225 99 ST SUITE 1544, GRANDE PRAIRIE, AB, T8V 6X9
(780) 831-3827   *SIC* 5411

LOBLAWS INC   p 144
5031 44 ST, LLOYDMINSTER, AB, T9V 0A6
(780) 871-8060   *SIC* 5411

LOBLAWS INC   p 146
1792 TRANS CANADA WAY SE SUITE 1550, MEDICINE HAT, AB, T1B 4C6
(403) 528-5727   *SIC* 5411

LOBLAWS INC   p 154
5016A 51 AVE, RED DEER, AB, T4N 4H5
(403) 350-3531   *SIC* 5411

LOBLAWS INC   p 163
410 BASELINE RD SUITE 100, SHERWOOD PARK, AB, T8H 2A7
(780) 417-5212   *SIC* 5411

LOBLAWS INC   p 164
100 JENNIFER HEIL WAY SUITE 10, SPRUCE GROVE, AB, T7X 4B8
(780) 960-7400   *SIC* 5411

LOBLAWS INC   p 166
101 ST ALBERT RD SUITE 1, ST. ALBERT, AB, T8N 6L5
(780) 418-6818   *SIC* 5399

LOBLAWS INC   p 179
3100 272 ST, ALDERGROVE, BC, V4W 3N7
(604) 859-6501   *SIC* 5411

LOBLAWS INC   p 195
1424 ISLAND HWY SUITE 1524, CAMPBELL RIVER, BC, V9W 8C9
(250) 830-2736   *SIC* 5411

LOBLAWS INC   p 201
1301 LOUGHEED HWY, COQUITLAM, BC, V3K 6P9
(604) 520-8339   *SIC* 5411

LOBLAWS INC   p 207
8195 120 ST, DELTA, BC, V4C 6P7
(604) 592-5218   *SIC* 5411

LOBLAWS INC   p 212
291 COWICHAN WAY SUITE 1563, DUNCAN, BC, V9L 6P5
(250) 746-0529   *SIC* 5141

LOBLAWS INC   p 217
910 COLUMBIA ST W SUITE 1522, KAMLOOPS, BC, V2C 1L2
(250) 371-6418   *SIC* 5411

LOBLAWS INC   p 239
333 SEYMOUR BLVD SUITE 1560, NORTH VANCOUVER, BC, V7J 2J4
(604) 904-5537   *SIC* 5411

LOBLAWS INC   p 244
19800 LOUGHEED HWY SUITE 201, PITT MEADOWS, BC, V3Y 2W1
(604) 460-4319   *SIC* 5411

LOBLAWS INC   p 250

2155 FERRY AVE, PRINCE GEORGE, BC, V2N 5E8
(250) 960-1300 *SIC* 5411
LOBLAWS INC p 252
2335 MAPLE DR E, QUESNEL, BC, V2J 7J6
(250) 747-2803 *SIC* 5411
LOBLAWS INC p 260
4651 NO. 3 RD SUITE 1557, RICHMOND, BC, V6X 2C4
(604) 233-2418 *SIC* 5141
LOBLAWS INC p 277
7550 KING GEORGE BLVD SUITE 1, SURREY, BC, V3W 2T2
SIC 5141
LOBLAWS INC p 287
3185 GRANDVIEW HWY, VANCOUVER, BC, V5M 2E9
(604) 439-5479 *SIC* 5141
LOBLAWS INC p 344
1000 SOUTH LAKESIDE DR, WILLIAMS LAKE, BC, V2G 3A6
(250) 305-2150 *SIC* 5141
LOBLAWS INC p 347
920 VICTORIA AVE, BRANDON, MB, R7A 1A7
(204) 729-4600 *SIC* 5411
LOBLAWS INC p 358
130 PTH 12 N, STEINBACH, MB, R5G 1T4
(204) 320-4101 *SIC* 5411
LOBLAWS INC p 358
276 MAIN ST, STEINBACH, MB, R5G 1Y8
(204) 346-6304 *SIC* 5411
LOBLAWS INC p 367
1035 GATEWAY RD SUITE 1512, WINNIPEG, MB, R2K 4C1
(204) 987-7534 *SIC* 5141
LOBLAWS INC p 370
2132 MCPHILLIPS ST, WINNIPEG, MB, R2V 3C8
(204) 631-6250 *SIC* 5411
LOBLAWS INC p 381
1385 SARGENT AVE, WINNIPEG, MB, R3E 3P8
(204) 784-7901 *SIC* 5411
LOBLAWS INC p 384
1725 ELLICE AVE, WINNIPEG, MB, R3H 1A6
(204) 775-8280 *SIC* 5141
LOBLAWS INC p 386
3193 PORTAGE AVE, WINNIPEG, MB, R3K 0W4
(204) 831-3528 *SIC* 5399
LOBLAWS INC p 391
80 BISON DR SUITE 1509, WINNIPEG, MB, R3T 4Z7
(204) 275-4118 *SIC* 5411
LOBLAWS INC p 418
195 KING ST, ST STEPHEN, NB, E3L 2E4
(506) 465-1457 *SIC* 5411
LOBLAWS INC p 422
5 MURPHY SQ SUITE 926, CORNER BROOK, NL, A2H 1R4
(709) 634-9450 *SIC* 5411
LOBLAWS INC p 475
30 KINGSTON RD W SUITE 1012, AJAX, ON, L1T 4K8
(905) 683-2272 *SIC* 5411
LOBLAWS INC p 511
1 PRESIDENTS CHOICE CIR, BRAMPTON, ON, L6Y 5S5
(905) 459-2500 *SIC* 5141
LOBLAWS INC p 511
85 STEELES AVE W, BRAMPTON, ON, L6Y 0K3
(905) 451-0917 *SIC* 5411
LOBLAWS INC p 519
1972 PARKEDALE AVE SUITE 1017, BROCKVILLE, ON, K6V 7N4
(613) 498-0994 *SIC* 5411
LOBLAWS INC p 542
791 ST CLAIR ST, CHATHAM, ON, N7L 0E9
(519) 352-4982 *SIC* 5411
LOBLAWS INC p 593
171 GUELPH ST SUITE 2811, GEORGE-

TOWN, ON, L7G 4A1
(905) 877-7005 *SIC* 5411
LOBLAWS INC p 599
336 SOUTH SERVICE RD SUITE 2806, GRIMSBY, ON, L3M 4E8
(905) 309-3911 *SIC* 5411
LOBLAWS INC p 626
760 EAGLESON RD, KANATA, ON, K2M 0A7
(613) 254-6050 *SIC* 5411
LOBLAWS INC p 628
538 PARK ST, KENORA, ON, P9N 1A1
(807) 468-1868 *SIC* 5411
LOBLAWS INC p 641
875 HIGHLAND RD W SUITE 178, KITCHENER, ON, N2N 2Y2
(519) 745-4781 *SIC* 5411
LOBLAWS INC p 644
201 TALBOT ST E, LEAMINGTON, ON, N8H 3X5
(519) 322-1371 *SIC* 5411
LOBLAWS INC p 658
1205 OXFORD ST W, LONDON, ON, N6H 1V9
(519) 641-3653 *SIC* 5411
LOBLAWS INC p 664
2911 MAJOR MACKENZIE DR SUITE 80, MAPLE, ON, L6A 3N9
(905) 417-0490 *SIC* 5411
LOBLAWS INC p 681
9292 93 HWY, MIDLAND, ON, L4R 4K4
(705) 527-0388 *SIC* 5411
LOBLAWS INC p 684
820 MAIN ST E SUITE 2810, MILTON, ON, L9T 0J4
(905) 875-3600 *SIC* 5411
LOBLAWS INC p 711
3045 MAVIS RD SUITE 2841, MISSISSAUGA, ON, L5C 1T7
(905) 275-6171 *SIC* 5411
LOBLAWS INC p 751
2065A ROBERTSON RD, NEPEAN, ON, K2H 5Y9
(613) 829-4680 *SIC* 5141
LOBLAWS INC p 783
51 GERRY FITZGERALD DR SUITE 1033, NORTH YORK, ON, M3J 3N4
(416) 665-7636 *SIC* 5411
LOBLAWS INC p 787
3501 YONGE ST, NORTH YORK, ON, M4N 2N5
(416) 481-8105 *SIC* 5411
LOBLAWS INC p 798
201 OAK PARK BLVD SUITE 1024, OAKVILLE, ON, L6H 7T4
(905) 257-9330 *SIC* 5411
LOBLAWS INC p 814
1385 HARMONY RD N SUITE 1043, OSHAWA, ON, L1K 0Z6
(905) 433-9569 *SIC* 5411
LOBLAWS INC p 816
2625 SHEFFIELD RD, OTTAWA, ON, K1B 1A8
(613) 741-4756 *SIC* 5141
LOBLAWS INC p 827
2210C BANK ST SUITE 1188, OTTAWA, ON, K1V 1J5
(613) 733-1377 *SIC* 5411
LOBLAWS INC p 829
190 RICHMOND RD SUITE 1009, OTTAWA, ON, K1Z 6W6
(613) 722-5890 *SIC* 5411
LOBLAWS INC p 858
600 MURPHY RD, SARNIA, ON, N7S 5T7
(519) 383-8133 *SIC* 5411
LOBLAWS INC p 867
755 BRIMLEY RD, SCARBOROUGH, ON, M1J 1C5
(416) 279-0802 *SIC* 5411
LOBLAWS INC p 889
1063 TALBOT ST UNIT 50, ST THOMAS, ON, N5P 1G4
(519) 637-6358 *SIC* 5411
LOBLAWS INC p 898

1485 LASALLE BLVD, SUDBURY, ON, P3A 5H7
(705) 521-1031 *SIC* 5411
LOBLAWS INC p 908
600 HARBOUR EXPY, THUNDER BAY, ON, P7B 6P4
(807) 343-4500 *SIC* 5411
LOBLAWS INC p 920
17 LESLIE ST, TORONTO, ON, M4M 3H9
(416) 469-2897 *SIC* 5411
LOBLAWS INC p 920
720 BROADVIEW AVE, TORONTO, ON, M4K 2P1
(416) 778-8762 *SIC* 5411
LOBLAWS INC p 997
2549 WESTON RD, TORONTO, ON, M9N 2A7
(416) 246-1906 *SIC* 5411
LOBLAWS INC p 1001
100 MCARTHUR AVE, VANIER, ON, K1L 8H5
(613) 744-0705 *SIC* 5411
LOBLAWS INC p 1005
25 45TH ST S, WASAGA BEACH, ON, L9Z 1A7
(705) 429-4315 *SIC* 5411
LOBLAWS INC p 1016
200 TAUNTON RD W SUITE 1058, WHITBY, ON, L1R 3H8
(905) 665-1164 *SIC* 5411
LOBLAWS INC p 1020
4371 WALKER RD SUITE 567, WINDSOR, ON, N8W 3T6
(519) 972-8335 *SIC* 5411
LOBLAWS INC p 1025
2950 DOUGALL AVE SUITE 18, WINDSOR, ON, N9E 1S2
(519) 969-3087 *SIC* 2051
LOBLAWS INC p 1066
1001 BOUL DE MONTARVILLE BUREAU 1, BOUCHERVILLE, QC, J4B 6P5
(450) 449-0081 *SIC* 5411
LOBLAWS INC p 1087
3500 BOUL SAINT-MARTIN O, COTE SAINT-LUC, QC, H7T 2W4
(450) 688-2969 *SIC* 5421
LOBLAWS INC p 1097
1850 BOUL SAINT-JOSEPH, DRUMMONDVILLE, QC, J2B 1R3
(819) 472-1197 *SIC* 5411
LOBLAWS INC p 1108
375 CH D'AYLMER BUREAU 5, GATINEAU, QC, J9H 1A5
(819) 682-4433 *SIC* 5411
LOBLAWS INC p 1240
10200 BOUL PIE-IX, MONTREAL-NORD, QC, H1H 3Z1
(514) 321-3111 *SIC* 5411
LOBLAWS INC p 1255
699 RUE CLEMENCEAU, QUEBEC, QC, G1C 4N6
(418) 666-0155 *SIC* 5411
LOBLAWS INC p 1279
350 RUE BOUVIER, QUEBEC, QC, G2J 1R8
(418) 623-5475 *SIC* 5411
LOBLAWS INC p 1283
86 BOUL BRIEN, REPENTIGNY, QC, J6A 5K7
(450) 581-8866 *SIC* 5411
LOBLAWS INC p 1385
3725 BOUL DES FORGES, TROIS-RIVIERES, QC, G8Y 4P2
(819) 374-8980 *SIC* 5411
LOBLAWS INC p 1390
502 RUE GIGUERE, VAL-D'OR, QC, J9P 7G6
(819) 825-5000 *SIC* 5141
LOBLAWS INC p 1410
290 PRINCE WILLIAM DR, MELVILLE, SK, S0A 2P0
(306) 728-6615 *SIC* 5411
LOBLAWS INC p 1410
620A SASKETCHEWAN AVE, MELFORT,

SK, S0E 1A0
(306) 752-9725 *SIC* 5411
LOBLAWS INC p 1420
336 N MCCARTHY BLVD, REGINA, SK, S4R 7M2
(306) 924-2620 *SIC* 5912
LOBLAWS INC p 1420
921 BROAD ST, REGINA, SK, S4R 8G9
(306) 525-2125 *SIC* 5411
LOBLAWS INC p 1421
3960 ALBERT ST SUITE 9037, REGINA, SK, S4S 3R1
(306) 584-9444 *SIC* 5411
LOBLAWS INC p 1422
2055 PRINCE OF WALES DR SUITE 1584, REGINA, SK, S4V 3A3
(306) 546-6518 *SIC* 5411
LOBLAWS INC p 1423
4450 ROCHDALE BLVD SUITE 1585, REGINA, SK, S4X 4N9
(306) 546-6618 *SIC* 5399
LOBLAWS INC p 1424
2901 8TH ST E SUITE 1535, SASKATOON, SK, S7H 0V4
(306) 978-7040 *SIC* 5411
LOBLAWS INC p 1428
2815 WANUSKEWIN RD, SASKATOON, SK, S7K 8E6
(306) 249-9200 *SIC* 5411
LOBLAWS INC p 1431
411 CONFEDERATION DR, SASKATOON, SK, S7L 5C3
(306) 683-5634 *SIC* 5141
LOBLAWS INC p 1435
315 HEROLD RD, SASKATOON, SK, S7V 1J7
(306) 664-5033 *SIC* 5411
LOBLAWS NO 105 p 867
See LOBLAWS SUPERMARKETS LIMITED
LOBLAWS SUPERMARKETS LIMITED p 475
30 KINGSTON RD W SUITE 1012, AJAX, ON, L1T 4K8
(905) 683-5573 *SIC* 5411
LOBLAWS SUPERMARKETS LIMITED p 482
657 JOHN ST N, AYLMER, ON, N5H 2R2
(519) 765-2811 *SIC* 5411
LOBLAWS SUPERMARKETS LIMITED p 511
1 PRESIDENTS CHOICE CIR, BRAMPTON, ON, L6Y 5S5
(905) 459-2500 *SIC* 5411
LOBLAWS SUPERMARKETS LIMITED p 546
12 HURONTARIO ST, COLLINGWOOD, ON, L9Y 2L6
(705) 445-0461 *SIC* 5411
LOBLAWS SUPERMARKETS LIMITED p 576
270 THE KINGSWAY, ETOBICOKE, ON, M9A 3T7
(416) 231-0931 *SIC* 5411
LOBLAWS SUPERMARKETS LIMITED p 577
380 THE EAST MALL, ETOBICOKE, ON, M9B 6L5
(416) 695-8990 *SIC* 5411
LOBLAWS SUPERMARKETS LIMITED p 593
300 GUELPH ST, GEORGETOWN, ON, L7G 4B1
(905) 877-4711 *SIC* 5411
LOBLAWS SUPERMARKETS LIMITED p 596
1980 OGILVIE RD, GLOUCESTER, ON, K1J 9L3
(613) 746-5724 *SIC* 5411
LOBLAWS SUPERMARKETS LIMITED p 619
1560 CAMERON ST SUITE 820, HAWKESBURY, ON, K6A 3S5
(613) 632-9215 *SIC* 5411
LOBLAWS SUPERMARKETS LIMITED p

633
1048 MIDLAND AVE, KINGSTON, ON, K7P 2X9
(613) 389-4119   SIC 5411

LOBLAWS SUPERMARKETS LIMITED
646
400 KENT ST W, LINDSAY, ON, K9V 6K2
(705) 878-4605   SIC 5411

LOBLAWS SUPERMARKETS LIMITED
657
635 SOUTHDALE RD E, LONDON, ON, N6E 3W6
(519) 686-8007   SIC 5411

LOBLAWS SUPERMARKETS LIMITED p
713
250 LAKESHORE RD W, MISSISSAUGA, ON, L5H 1G6
(905) 271-9925   SIC 5411

LOBLAWS SUPERMARKETS LIMITED p
749
1460 MERIVALE RD, NEPEAN, ON, K2E 5P2
(613) 226-6001   SIC 5411

LOBLAWS SUPERMARKETS LIMITED p
752
3201 GREENBANK RD SUITE 1035, NEPEAN, ON, K2J 4H9
(613) 825-0812   SIC 5411

,**LOBLAWS SUPERMARKETS LIMITED** p
755
18120 YONGE ST, NEWMARKET, ON, L3Y 4V8
(905) 830-4072   SIC 5411

LOBLAWS SUPERMARKETS LIMITED p
802
173 LAKESHORE RD W, OAKVILLE, ON, L6K 1E7
(905) 845-4946   SIC 5411

LOBLAWS SUPERMARKETS LIMITED p
810
1226 PLACE D'ORLEANS DR SUITE 3935, ORLEANS, ON, K1C 7K3
(613) 834-4074   SIC 5411

LOBLAWS SUPERMARKETS LIMITED p
814
481 GIBB ST, OSHAWA, ON, L1J 1Z4
(905) 743-0043   SIC 5411

LOBLAWS SUPERMARKETS LIMITED p
831
1980 BASELINE RD, OTTAWA, ON, K2C 0C6
(613) 723-3200   SIC 5411

LOBLAWS SUPERMARKETS LIMITED p
843
1792 LIVERPOOL RD, PICKERING, ON, L1V 4G6
(905) 831-6301   SIC 5411

LOBLAWS SUPERMARKETS LIMITED p
867
3401 LAWRENCE AVE E, SCARBOROUGH, ON, M1H 1B2
(416) 438-4392   SIC 5411

LOBLAWS SUPERMARKETS LIMITED p
918
301 MOORE AVE, TORONTO, ON, M4G 1E1
(416) 425-0604   SIC 5411

LOBLAWS SUPERMARKETS LIMITED p
925
12 ST CLAIR AVE E, TORONTO, ON, M4T 1L7
(416) 960-8108   SIC 5411

LOBLAWS SUPERMARKETS LIMITED p
989
650 DUPONT ST SUITE 1029, TORONTO, ON, M6G 4B1
(416) 588-3756   SIC 5141

LOBLAWS SUPERMARKETS LIMITED p
1012
821 NIAGARA ST, WELLAND, ON, L3C 1M4
(905) 732-9010   SIC 5411

LOBLAWS SUPERMARKETS LIMITED p
1016
3100 GARDEN ST UNIT 2, WHITBY, ON,

L1R 2G8
(866) 987-6453   SIC 5411

LOBLAWS SUPERMARKETS LIMITED p
1167
2925 RUE RACHEL E, MONTREAL, QC, H1W 3Z8
(514) 522-4442   SIC 5411

LOBLAWS VICTORIAVILLE p 1398
See PROVIGO DISTRIBUTION INC

LOBLAWS WHITE OAKS p 657
See LOBLAWS SUPERMARKETS LIMITED

LOCAL 252 p 547
See UNITED STEELWORKERS OF AMERICA

LOCAL 98 p 1051
See SYNDICAT CANADIEN DES COMMUNICATIONS DE L'ENERGIE ET DU PAPIER

LOCAL 99 p 381
See INTERNATIONAL ASSOCIATION OF HEAT & FROST INSULATORS & ALLIED WORKERS

LOCAL PUBLIC EATERY LTD p 163
222 BASELINE RD SUITE 330, SHERWOOD PARK, AB, T8H 1S8
(780) 417-3182   SIC 5812

LOCATION 18E RUE INC p 1255
455 RUE CLEMENCEAU, QUEBEC, QC, G1C 7B6
(418) 647-1822   SIC 5511

LOCATION A.L.R. INC p 1045
211 RUE DU MISTRAL, ALMA, QC, G8E 2E2
(418) 347-4665   SIC 1611

LOCATION AUTOLUXE p 1226
See 9155-8593 QUEBEC INC

LOCATION AUTOMAX p 1214
See 3566072 CANADA INC

LOCATION BENCH & TABLE INC p 1220
6999 AV VICTORIA, MONTREAL, QC, H3W 3E9
(514) 738-4755   SIC 7359

LOCATION BLAIS INC p 1289
792 AV QUEBEC, ROUYN-NORANDA, QC, J9X 7B1
(819) 797-9292   SIC 5082

LOCATION BLUE PELICAN p 1074
See ARMAND AUTOMOBILES LTEE

LOCATION BROSSARD INC p 1094
2190 BOUL HYMUS, DORVAL, QC, H9P 1J7
(514) 367-1343   SIC 7513

LOCATION D'AUTO 440, DIV DE p 1086
See COMPLEXE AUTO 440 DE LAVAL INC

LOCATION D'EQUIPEMENTS GUS p 1145
See VAC OXYGENE ULC

LOCATION D'OUTILS BROSSARD INC p
1308
3905 MONTEE SAINT-HUBERT, SAINT-HUBERT, QC, J3Y 4K2
(450) 678-3385   SIC 7359

LOCATION D'OUTILS SIMPLEX SEC p
1380
3505 BOUL DES ENTREPRISES, TERREBONNE, QC, J6X 4J9
(450) 477-5960   SIC 1796

LOCATION DE CAMIONS PENSKE p 1335
See PENSKE TRUCK LEASING CANADA INC

LOCATION DE TENTE ACME p 1247
See CHAPITEAUX CLASSIC INC, LES

LOCATION DUMCO p 1148
See 9222-0201 QUEBEC INC

LOCATION FORTIER DIV p 1052
See FORTIER AUTO (MONTREAL) LTEE

LOCATION GM p 1152
See CENTRE DE LOCATION G.M. INC

LOCATION HEBERT 2000 LTEE p 1246
750 AV SAINT-LOUIS, PLESSISVILLE, QC, G6L 2M1
(819) 362-8816   SIC 5511

LOCATION JEAN LEGARE LTEE p 1167
3035 RUE HOCHELAGA, MONTREAL, QC, H1W 1G1
(514) 522-6466   SIC 5511

LOCATION JEAN MILLER INC p 1159
169 117 RTE, MONT-TREMBLANT, QC, J8E 2X2
(819) 425-3797   SIC 7353

LOCATION LOUIS ANDRE PELLETIER LTEE p 1154
233 BOUL ALBINY-PAQUETTE, MONT-LAURIER, QC, J9L 1K2
(819) 623-4015   SIC 5172

LOCATION MONTFE p 1102
7 RUE DU CAMP, FERMONT, QC, G0G 1J0
(418) 287-9402   SIC 5046

LOCATION OCEAN INC p 1259
105 RUE ABRAHAM-MARTIN BUREAU 500, QUEBEC, QC, G1K 8N1
(418) 694-1414   SIC 4492

LOCATION RADIO TAXI UNION LTEE p
1144
1605 RUE VERCHERES, LONGUEUIL, QC, J4K 2Z6
(450) 679-6262   SIC 4121

LOCATION RAOUL PELLETIER INC p 1138
3650 BOUL GUILLAUME-COUTURE, LEVIS, QC, G6W 7L3
(418) 837-2147   SIC 1623

LOCATION RAOUL PELLETIER INC p 1138
3650 BOUL GUILLAUME-COUTURE, LEVIS, QC, G6W 7L3
(418) 837-2147   SIC 1521

LOCATION SAUVAGEAU INC p 1351
521 COTE JOYEUSE BUREAU 1, SAINT-RAYMOND, QC, G3L 4A9
(418) 692-1315   SIC 7514

LOCATION TO p 1128
See SERVICE TRANS-WEST INC

LOCATION V.A. INC p 1133
156 BOUL LAURIER RR 1, LAURIER-STATION, QC, G0S 1N0
(418) 728-2140   SIC 7513

LOCATIONS NORDIQUES p 1367
See 3471250 CANADA INC

LOCATIONS WEST REALTY INC p 243
484 MAIN ST, PENTICTON, BC, V2A 5C5
(250) 493-2244   SIC 6531

LOCAVAN p 1319
See TRANSPORTS INTER-NORD INC, LES

LOCH LOMOND MITSUBISHI p 413
See DISTINCTIVE AUTOBODY & COLLISON CENTER LTD

LOCH LOMOND SKI AREA LIMITED p 910
1800 LOCH LOMOND RD, THUNDER BAY, ON, P7J 1E9
(807) 475-7787   SIC 6712

LOCH LOMOND VILLA INC p 413
185 LOCH LOMOND RD, SAINT JOHN, NB, E2J 3S3
(506) 643-7175   SIC 8051

LOCH MARCH GOLF & COUNTRY CLUB p 832
See METCALFE REALTY COMPANY LIMITED

LOCH MARCH GOLF & COUNTRY CLUB, DIV OF p 830
See METCALFE REALTY COMPANY LIMITED

LOCHBRIDGE p 1187
See CW PROFESSIONAL SERVICES (CANADA) ULC

LOCHER EVERS INTERNATIONAL INC p
206
456 HUMBER PL, DELTA, BC, V3M 6A5
(604) 523-5100   SIC 4731

LOCHER EVERS INTERNATIONAL INC p
206
456 HUMBER PL, DELTA, BC, V3M 6A5
(604) 525-0577   SIC 4225

LOCHIEL ENTERPRISES LIMITED p 466
8000 HIGHWAY 7, SHERBROOKE, NS, B0J 3C0
(902) 522-2005   SIC 2091

LOCKERBIE & HOLE CONTRACTING LIMITED p
105

14940 121A AVE NW, EDMONTON, AB, T5V 1A3
(780) 452-1250   SIC 1711

LOCKERBIE & HOLE INC p 106
14940 121A AVE NW, EDMONTON, AB, T5V 1A3
SIC 1541

LOCKHEED MARTIN CANADA INC p 447
1000 WINDMILL RD, DARTMOUTH, NS, B3B 1L7
(902) 468-3399   SIC 5065

LOCKHEED MARTIN CANADA INC p 823
45 O'CONNOR ST SUITE 870, OTTAWA, ON, K1P 1A4
(613) 688-0698   SIC 3625

LOCKHEED MARTIN CANADA INC p 1335
7171 BOUL DE LA COTE-VERTU, SAINT-LAURENT, QC, H4S 1Z3
(514) 340-8400   SIC 4581

LOCKHEED MARTIN COMMERCIAL ENGINE SOLUTIONS p
823
See LOCKHEED MARTIN CANADA INC

LOCKHEED MARTIN COMMERCIAL ENGINE SOLUTIONS p
1335
See LOCKHEED MARTIN CANADA INC

LOCKVIEW HIGH SCHOOL p 450
See HALIFAX REGIONAL SCHOOL BOARD

LOCKWOOD INDUSTRIES INC p 523
1100 CORPORATE DR, BURLINGTON, ON, L7L 5R6
(905) 336-0300   SIC 3699

LOCOCO'S FRUITS & VEGTABLES p 758
See LOCOCO, A. WHOLESALE LTD

LOCOCO, A. WHOLESALE LTD p 758
4167 VICTORIA AVE, NIAGARA FALLS, ON, L2E 4B2
(905) 358-3281   SIC 5431

LOCURETT ENTERPRISES LTD p 260
5660 MINORU BLVD, RICHMOND, BC, V6X 2A9
(604) 273-1001   SIC 5521

LOCUSI p 1349
See 9132-8997 QUEBEC INC

LOCWELD INC p 1073
50 AV IBERVILLE, CANDIAC, QC, J5R 1J5
(450) 659-9661   SIC 3441

LODE KING INDUSTRIES, DIV. OF p 361
See TRIPLE E CANADA LTD

LODEN HOTEL p 317
See WENTWORTH HOTELS LTD

LODGE AT VALLEY RIDGE, THE p 72
11479 VALLEY RIDGE DR NW SUITE 332, CALGARY, AB, T3B 5V5
(403) 286-4414   SIC 7041

LODGING COMPANY RESERVATIONS LTD, THE p 222
510 BERNARD AVE SUITE 200, KELOWNA, BC, V1Y 6P1
(250) 979-3939   SIC 7389

LODGING OVATIONS CORP p 299
375 WATER ST SUITE 326, VANCOUVER, BC, V6B 5C6
(604) 938-9999   SIC 8741

LOEB p 519
See METRO INC

LOEB p 752
See METRO ONTARIO INC

LOEB p 827
See METRO ONTARIO INC

LOEB #8094 p 632
See PROVIGO DISTRIBUTION INC

LOEB BAYRIDGE p 633
See PROVIGO DISTRIBUTION INC

LOEB CANADA p 830
See METRO ONTARIO INC

LOEB CLUB PLUS GILLES DIONNE INC p
1104
900 BOUL MALONEY O, GATINEAU, QC, J8T 3R6
(514) 243-5231   SIC 5141

LOEB FALLINGBROOK p 810

See *METRO ONTARIO INC*

LOEB PACKAGING LTD *p* 595
1475 STAR TOP RD SUITE 8, GLOUCESTER, ON, K1B 3W5
(613) 746-8171 *SIC* 2653

LOEWEN WINDOWS *p* 358
See *C.P. LOEWEN ENTERPRISES LTD*

LOEWEN, ONDAATJE, MCCUTCHEON LIMITED *p* 973
148 YORKVILLE AVE SUITE 3, TORONTO, ON, M5R 1C2
(416) 964-4400 *SIC* 6211

LOEWS HOTEL VOGUE *p* 1213
See *LJC DEVELOPMENT CORPORATION*

LOFT COMMUNITY SERVICES *p* 939
15 TORONTO ST SUITE 9, TORONTO, ON, M5C 2E3
SIC 8322

LOFTHOUSE MANUFACTURING, DIV OF *p* 520
See *BRAWO BRASSWORKING LIMITED*

LOGAN COMPLETION SYSTEMS INC *p* 53
635 8 AVE SW SUITE 850, CALGARY, AB, T2P 3M3
(403) 930-6810 *SIC* 1389

LOGAN GROUP PARTNERSHIP *p* 269
6661 SOOKE RD SUITE 103, SOOKE, BC, V9Z 0A1
SIC 5411

LOGAN INDUSTRIES LTD *p* 7
6 BOSWELL CRES, BROOKS, AB, T1R 8B8
(403) 362-3736 *SIC* 1389

LOGAN STEVENS CONSTRUCTION (2000) LTD *p* 1438
200 YORK RD E, YORKTON, SK, S3N 4E4
(306) 782-2266 *SIC* 1542

LOGAN, JOHN CHEVROLET OLDSMOBILE INC *p* 509
241 QUEEN ST E, BRAMPTON, ON, L6W 2B5
(905) 451-2030 *SIC* 5012

LOGGIAS VILLA VAL DES ARBRES, LES *p* 1232
See *CHARTWELL QUEBEC (MEL) HOLDINGS INC*

LOGI-TEC MANAGEMENT LIMITED PARTNERSHIP *p* 101
18110 118 AVE NW, EDMONTON, AB, T5S 2G2
(780) 452-6225 *SIC* 5511

LOGIBEC INC *p* 1211
700 RUE WELLINGTON BUREAU 1500, MONTREAL, QC, H3C 3S4
(514) 766-0134 *SIC* 7372

LOGIBES GROUPE INFORMATIQUE *p* 1211
See *LOGIBEC INC*

LOGIC HOLDINGS LTD *p* 141
1217 39 ST N, LETHBRIDGE, AB, T1H 6Y8
(403) 328-7755 *SIC* 6712

LOGIC LUMBER *p* 141
See *LOGIC HOLDINGS LTD*

LOGIC LUMBER (LETH.) LTD *p* 141
1217 39 ST N, LETHBRIDGE, AB, T1H 6Y8
(403) 328-7755 *SIC* 5211

LOGIC-CONTROLE INC *p* 1049
8002 RUE JARRY, ANJOU, QC, H1J 1H5
(514) 493-1162 *SIC* 7521

LOGIC-CONTROLE INC *p* 1264
2300 RUE LEON-HARMEL BUREAU 101, QUEBEC, QC, G1N 4L2
(418) 686-2300 *SIC* 5065

LOGICAN TECHNOLOGIES INC *p* 121
150 KARL CLARK RD NW, EDMONTON, AB, T6N 1E2
(780) 440-4400 *SIC* 3679

LOGICIELS DTI INC *p* 1197
1800 AV MCGILL COLLEGE UNITE 1800, MONTREAL, QC, H3A 3J6
(514) 499-0910 *SIC* 7371

LOGICIELS INSIGHT CANADA *p* 1220
See *INSIGHT CANADA INC*

LOGICIELS LOC *p* 1233

See *9022-5814 QUEBEC INC*

LOGICIELS TANGERINE INC *p* 1324
555 BOUL DR.-FREDERIK-PHILIPS BUREAU 450, SAINT-LAURENT, QC, H4M 2X4
(514) 748-9309 *SIC* 8742

LOGIHEDRON INC *p* 798
2320 BRISTOL CIR UNIT 1, OAKVILLE, ON, L6H 5S3
(905) 823-5767 *SIC* 8741

LOGIKOR INC *p* 536
290 PINEBUSH RD, CAMBRIDGE, ON, N1T 1Z6
(519) 622-8400 *SIC* 4731

LOGINRADIUS INC *p* 306
815 HASTINGS ST W SUITE 801, VANCOUVER, BC, V6C 1B4
(844) 625-8889 *SIC* 7371

LOGIQ3 CORP *p* 939
60 ADELAIDE ST E UNIT 1300, TORONTO, ON, M5C 3E4
(416) 340-7435 *SIC* 6411

LOGISCO GROUPE IMMOBILIER *p* 1138
See *LOGISCO INC*

LOGISCO INC *p* 1138
950 RUE DE LA CONCORDE BUREAU 302, LEVIS, QC, G6W 8A8
(418) 834-4999 *SIC* 6531

LOGISENSE CORPORATION *p* 536
278 PINEBUSH RD SUITE 102, CAMBRIDGE, ON, N1T 1Z6
(519) 249-0508 *SIC* 7371

LOGISIL *p* 1213
See *CONSEILLERS LOGISIL INC, LES*

LOGISTEC ARRIMAGE INC *p* 1189
360 RUE SAINT-JACQUES BUREAU 1500, MONTREAL, QC, H2Y 3X1
(514) 844-9381 *SIC* 4491

LOGISTEC CORPORATION *p* 1189
360 RUE SAINT-JACQUES BUREAU 1500, MONTREAL, QC, H2Y 3X1
(514) 844-9381 *SIC* 4491

LOGISTEC STEVEDORING (NOVA SCOTIA) INC. *p* 451
1096 MARGINAL RD SUITE 208, HALIFAX, NS, B3H 4N4
(902) 422-7483 *SIC* 4491

LOGISTIC FREIGHT MANAGEMENT *p* 692
See *BUCKLEY CARTAGE LIMITED*

LOGISTICS IN MOTION INC *p* 475
500 BAYLY ST E, AJAX, ON, L1Z 0B2
(905) 427-5880 *SIC* 4731

LOGISTIK UNICORP INC *p* 1315
820 CH DU GRAND-BERNIER N, SAINT-JEAN-SUR-RICHELIEU, QC, J2W 0A6
(450) 349-9700 *SIC* 7213

LOGISTIQUE CANAMEX INC *p* 1062
1933 BOUL LIONEL-BERTRAND, BOISBRIAND, QC, J7H 1N8
(450) 434-1939 *SIC* 4731

LOGISTIQUE HBC *p* 1128
See *HUDSON'S BAY COMPANY*

LOGISTIQUE KERRY (CANADA) INC *p* 1094
1425 RTE TRANSCANADIENNE BUREAU 150, DORVAL, QC, H9P 2W9
(514) 420-0282 *SIC* 4731

LOGISTIQUE MIRABEL *p* 1320
See *PAPINEAU INT, S.E.C.*

LOGISTIQUE TRANS-PRO INC *p* 1189
407 RUE MCGILL BUREAU 910, MONTREAL, QC, H2Y 2G3
(514) 858-6482 *SIC* 4731

LOGISTIQUE UNICORP *p* 1315
See *LOGISTIK UNICORP INC*

LOGISTIQUES TRANS-WEST INC *p* 1128
1900 52E AV BUREAU 100, LACHINE, QC, H8T 2X9
(514) 345-1090 *SIC* 4213

LOGIT GROUP INC, THE *p* 996
302 THE EAST MALL SUITE 400, TORONTO, ON, M9B 6C7
(416) 236-4770 *SIC* 8732

LOGITEK DATA SCIENCES LTD *p* 586

155 REXDALE BLVD SUITE 801, ETOBICOKE, ON, M9W 5Z8
(416) 741-1595 *SIC* 7371

LOGITRANS INC *p* 1302
440 RUE DU PARC, SAINT-EUSTACHE, QC, J7R 7G6
(450) 565-8900 *SIC* 4731

LOGIX ITS INC *p* 1132
992 RUE D'UPTON, LASALLE, QC, H8R 2T9
(514) 448-9660 *SIC* 3069

LOISELLE INC *p* 1103
1679 RUE JEAN-LOUIS-MALETTE, GATINEAU, QC, J8R 0C1
SIC 1794

LOISELLE INC *p* 1365
280 BOUL PIE-XII, SALABERRY-DE-VALLEYFIELD, QC, J6S 6P7
(450) 373-4274 *SIC* 1794

LOKI MANAGEMENT SYSTEMS INC *p* 255
13351 COMMERCE PKY SUITE 1258, RICHMOND, BC, V6V 2X7
(604) 249-5050 *SIC* 7371

LOLACHERS CATERING DIV. OF *p* 815
See *126677 CANADA LIMITED*

LOLE *p* 1187
See *COALISION INC*

LOMBARD PRE-CAST INC *p* 340
661 LOMBARD DR, VICTORIA, BC, V9C 3Y9
(250) 478-9581 *SIC* 5211

LOMBARDI AUTO LTEE *p* 1346
4356 BOUL METROPOLITAIN E, SAINT-LEONARD, QC, H1S 1A2
(514) 728-2222 *SIC* 5511

LOMBARDI HONDA *p* 1346
See *LOMBARDI AUTO LTEE*

LOMBARDI, ALDO SALES INC *p* 566
50 COOTES DR, DUNDAS, ON, L9H 1B6
(905) 627-3534 *SIC* 5531

LONCOR RESOURCES INC *p* 987
100 KING ST W SUITE 7070, TORONTO, ON, M5X 2A1
(416) 361-2510 *SIC* 1041

LONDON & MIDDLESEX HOUSING CORPORATION *p* 652
1299 OXFORD ST E UNIT 5C5, LONDON, ON, N5Y 4W5
(519) 434-2765 *SIC* 6531

LONDON (KING ST.) PURCHASECO INC *p* 656
300 KING ST, LONDON, ON, N6B 1S2
(519) 439-1661 *SIC* 7011

LONDON AGRICULTURAL COMMODITIES INC *p* 658
1615 NORTH ROUTLEDGE PK UNIT 43, LONDON, ON, N6H 5L6
(519) 473-9333 *SIC* 6799

LONDON AIR SERVICES LIMITED *p* 265
4580 COWLEY CRES, RICHMOND, BC, V7B 1B8
(604) 272-8123 *SIC* 4512

LONDON AUTOMOTIVE & MANUFACTURING LTD *p* 661
1477 SISE RD, LONDON, ON, N6N 1E1
(519) 686-0489 *SIC* 5511

LONDON CENTRAL SECONDARY SCHOOL *p* 656
See *THAMES VALLEY DISTRICT SCHOOL BOARD*

LONDON CHILDREN'S CONNECTION INC *p* 660
346 WONDERLAND RD S, LONDON, ON, N6K 1L3
(519) 471-4300 *SIC* 8351

LONDON CIVIC CENTRE CORPORATION *p* 654
99 DUNDAS ST, LONDON, ON, N6A 6K1
(519) 667-5700 *SIC* 7941

LONDON CONVENTION CENTRE CORPORATION, THE *p* 656

300 YORK ST, LONDON, ON, N6B 1P8
(519) 661-6200 *SIC* 7389

LONDON DISTRICT CATHOLIC SCHOOL BOARD *p* 657
5250 WELLINGTON RD S, LONDON, ON, N6E 3X8
(519) 663-2088 *SIC* 8221

LONDON DRUGS *p* 166
See *LONDON DRUGS LIMITED*

LONDON DRUGS EXECUTIVE *p* 263
12151 HORSESHOE WAY, RICHMOND, BC, V7A 4V4
(604) 272-7400 *SIC* 5912

LONDON DRUGS INSURANCE SERVICES LTD *p* 260
5971 NO. 3 RD, RICHMOND, BC, V6X 3Y6
(604) 821-0808 *SIC* 6411

LONDON DRUGS LIMITED *p* 9
3545 32 AVE NE, CALGARY, AB, T1Y 6M6
(403) 571-4931 *SIC* 5912

LONDON DRUGS LIMITED *p* 74
5255 RICHMOND RD SW SUITE 300, CALGARY, AB, T3E 7C4
(403) 571-4932 *SIC* 5912

LONDON DRUGS LIMITED *p* 98
14951 STONY PLAIN RD NW, EDMONTON, AB, T5P 4W1
(780) 944-4522 *SIC* 5912

LONDON DRUGS LIMITED *p* 142
905 1 AVE S SUITE 110, LETHBRIDGE, AB, T1J 4M7
(403) 320-8899 *SIC* 5912

LONDON DRUGS LIMITED *p* 166
19 BELLEROSE DR SUITE 10, ST. ALBERT, AB, T8N 5E1
(780) 944-4548 *SIC* 5912

LONDON DRUGS LIMITED *p* 177
32700 SOUTH FRASER WAY SUITE 26, ABBOTSFORD, BC, V2T 4M5
(604) 852-0936 *SIC* 5912

LONDON DRUGS LIMITED *p* 190
4970 KINGSWAY, BURNABY, BC, V5H 2E2
(604) 448-4806 *SIC* 5912

LONDON DRUGS LIMITED *p* 217
450 LANSDOWNE ST SUITE 68, KAMLOOPS, BC, V2C 1Y3
(250) 372-0028 *SIC* 5912

LONDON DRUGS LIMITED *p* 237
60 TENTH ST, NEW WESTMINSTER, BC, V3M 3X3
(604) 524-1326 *SIC* 5912

LONDON DRUGS LIMITED *p* 263
12251 HORSESHOE WAY, RICHMOND, BC, V7A 4X5
(604) 272-7400 *SIC* 5912

LONDON DRUGS LIMITED *p* 270
2340 GUILDFORD TOWN CTR, SURREY, BC, V3R 7B9
(604) 588-7881 *SIC* 5912

LONDON DRUGS LIMITED *p* 293
525 BROADWAY W, VANCOUVER, BC, V5Z 1E6
(604) 448-4804 *SIC* 5912

LONDON DRUGS LIMITED *p* 318
1650 DAVIE ST, VANCOUVER, BC, V6G 1V9
(604) 448-4850 *SIC* 5912

LONDON DRUGS LIMITED *p* 322
2091 42ND AVE W SUITE 10, VANCOUVER, BC, V6M 2B4
(604) 448-1036 *SIC* 5912

LONDON DRUGS LIMITED *p* 326
710 GRANVILLE ST, VANCOUVER, BC, V6Z 1E4
(604) 448-4002 *SIC* 5912

LONDON DRUGS LIMITED *p* 332
4400 32 ST SUITE 700, VERNON, BC, V1T 9H2
(250) 549-1551 *SIC* 5912

LONDON DRUGS LIMITED *p* 340
1907 SOOKE RD, VICTORIA, BC, V9B 1V8
(250) 474-0900 *SIC* 5912

LONDON FINE CARS LTD *p* 659
560 WHARNCLIFFE RD S, LONDON, ON,

N6J 2N4
(519) 649-0889   *SIC* 5511
LONDON FREE PRESS   *p* 655
See 1032451 B.C. LTD
LONDON HEALTH SCIENCE CENTER UNIVERSITY HOSPITAL   *p* 654
See LONDON HEALTH SCIENCES CENTRE
LONDON HEALTH SCIENCES CENTRE   *p* 654
339 WINDERMERE RD, LONDON, ON, N6A 5A5
(519) 685-8500   *SIC* 8011
LONDON HEALTH SCIENCES CENTRE   *p* 654
375 SOUTH ST, LONDON, ON, N6A 4G5
(519) 685-8500   *SIC* 8062
LONDON HEALTH SCIENCES CENTRE   *p* 654
800 COMMISSIONERS RD E, LONDON, ON, N6A 5W9
(519) 685-8500   *SIC* 8062
LONDON HEALTH SCIENCES CENTRE   *p* 660
790 COMMISSIONERS RD W, LONDON, ON, N6K 1C2
(519) 685-8300   *SIC* 8011
LONDON HONDA CAR SALES   *p* 659
See LONDON FINE CARS LTD
LONDON HOSPITAL LINEN SERVICE INCORPORATED   *p* 656
11 MAITLAND ST, LONDON, ON, N6B 3K7
(519) 438-2925   *SIC* 7213
LONDON HYDRO INC   *p* 656
111 HORTON ST E, LONDON, ON, N6B 3N9
(519) 661-5503   *SIC* 4911
LONDON INSURANCE GROUP INC   *p* 654
255 DUFFERIN AVE SUITE 540, LONDON, ON, N6A 4K1
(519) 432-5281   *SIC* 6311
LONDON INTERCOMMUNITY HEALTH CENTRE   *p* 651
659 DUNDAS ST, LONDON, ON, N5W 2Z1
(519) 660-0874   *SIC* 8399
LONDON LIFE INSURANCE COMPANY   *p* 314
See LONDON LIFE, COMPAGNIE D'ASSURANCE-VIE
LONDON LIFE INSURANCE COMPANY   *p* 596
See LONDON LIFE, COMPAGNIE D'ASSURANCE-VIE
LONDON LIFE INSURANCE COMPANY   *p* 710
See LONDON LIFE, COMPAGNIE D'ASSURANCE-VIE
LONDON LIFE INSURANCE COMPANY   *p* 789
See LONDON LIFE, COMPAGNIE D'ASSURANCE-VIE
LONDON LIFE INSURANCE COMPANY   *p* 875
See LONDON LIFE, COMPAGNIE D'ASSURANCE-VIE
LONDON LIFE INSURANCE COMPANY   *p* 1197
See LONDON LIFE, COMPAGNIE D'ASSURANCE-VIE
LONDON LIFE INSURANCE COMPANY   *p* 1330
See LONDON LIFE, COMPAGNIE D'ASSURANCE-VIE
LONDON LIFE, COMPAGNIE D'ASSURANCE-VIE   *p* 314
1111 GEORGIA ST W SUITE 1200, VANCOUVER, BC, V6E 4M3
(604) 685-6521   *SIC* 6311
LONDON LIFE, COMPAGNIE D'ASSURANCE-VIE   *p* 596
1223 MICHAEL ST N SUITE 300, GLOUCESTER, ON, K1J 7T2

(613) 748-3455   *SIC* 6311
LONDON LIFE, COMPAGNIE D'ASSURANCE-VIE   *p* 654
255 DUFFERIN AVE SUITE 273, LONDON, ON, N6A 4K1
(519) 432-5281   *SIC* 6311
LONDON LIFE, COMPAGNIE D'ASSURANCE-VIE   *p* 710
1 CITY CENTRE DR SUITE 1600, MISSISSAUGA, ON, L5B 1M2
(905) 276-1177   *SIC* 6311
LONDON LIFE, COMPAGNIE D'ASSURANCE-VIE   *p* 789
970 LAWRENCE AVE W SUITE 600, NORTH YORK, ON, M6A 3B6
SIC 6311
LONDON LIFE, COMPAGNIE D'ASSURANCE-VIE   *p* 875
2075 KENNEDY RD SUITE 300, SCARBOROUGH, ON, M1T 3V3
SIC 6411
LONDON LIFE, COMPAGNIE D'ASSURANCE-VIE   *p* 1197
1800 AV MCGILL COLLEGE UNITE 1100, MONTREAL, QC, H3A 3J6
(514) 931-4242   *SIC* 6311
LONDON LIFE, COMPAGNIE D'ASSURANCE-VIE   *p* 1197
2001 BOUL ROBERT-BOURASSA UNITE 800, MONTREAL, QC, H3A 2A6
(514) 350-5500   *SIC* 6411
LONDON LIFE, COMPAGNIE D'ASSURANCE-VIE   *p* 1330
3773 BOUL DE LA COTE-VERTU BUREAU 200, SAINT-LAURENT, QC, H4R 2M3
SIC 6311
LONDON MACHINERY INC   *p* 649
15790 ROBIN'S HILL RD, LONDON, ON, N5V 0A4
(519) 963-2500   *SIC* 3531
LONDON MACK   *p* 662
See WILTON GROVE TRUCK SALES & SERVICES LIMITED
LONDON MITSUBISHI   *p* 660
See COLLINS FAMILY CARS INC
LONDON REGIONAL CANCER CENTRE   *p* 660
See LONDON HEALTH SCIENCES CENTRE
LONDON REINSURANCE GROUP INC   *p* 654
255 DUFFERIN AVE SUITE 540, LONDON, ON, N6A 4K1
(519) 432-2000   *SIC* 6712
LONDON SALVAGE AND TRADING COMPANY LIMITED   *p* 652
333 EGERTON ST, LONDON, ON, N5Z 2H3
(519) 451-0680   *SIC* 5093
LONDON SOUTH SECONDARY SCHOOL   *p* 656
See THAMES VALLEY DISTRICT SCHOOL BOARD
LONDON TIRE SALES LIMITED   *p* 897
290 ELLOR ST, STRATHROY, ON, N7G 2L4
(519) 245-1133   *SIC* 5014
LONDON TRANSIT COMMISSION, THE   *p* 651
450 HIGHBURY AVE N, LONDON, ON, N5W 5L2
(519) 451-1340   *SIC* 4111
LONDON X-RAY ASSOCIATES   *p* 656
450 CENTRAL AVE UNIT 104, LONDON, ON, N6B 2E8
(519) 672-7900   *SIC* 8071
LONDONDERRY DODGE CHRYSLER JEEP LTD   *p* 83
13333 FORT RD NW, EDMONTON, AB, T5A 1C3
(780) 665-4851   *SIC* 5511
LONE PINE RESOURCES INC   *p* 53
640 5 AVE SW SUITE 1100, CALGARY, AB, T2P 3G4
(403) 292-8000   *SIC* 1382

LONE STAR CAFE   *p* 581
See 1561716 ONTARIO LTD
LONE STAR GROUP OF COMPANIES LIMITED   *p*
596
1211 LEMIEUX ST, GLOUCESTER, ON, K1J 1A2
(613) 742-9378   *SIC* 5812
LONE STAR GROUP OF COMPANIES LIMITED   *p*
802
472 MORDEN RD SUITE 101, OAKVILLE, ON, L6K 3W4
(905) 845-5852   *SIC* 5812
LONE STAR INC   *p* 36
10 HERITAGE MEADOWS RD SE, CALGARY, AB, T2H 3C1
(403) 253-1333   *SIC* 5511
LONE STAR MERCEDES-BENZ   *p* 36
See LONE STAR INC
LONE STAR TEXAS GRILL   *p* 843
See 1561716 ONTARIO LTD
LONE WOLF REAL ESTATE TECHNOLOGIES INC   *p*
536
231 SHEARSON CRES SUITE 310, CAMBRIDGE, ON, N1T 1J5
(866) 279-9653   *SIC* 7372
LONESTAR AUTOMOTIVE   *p* 1414
1125 2ND AVE W, PRINCE ALBERT, SK, S6V 5A9
(306) 763-4777   *SIC* 5013
LONESTAR TEXAS GRILL   *p* 596
See LONE STAR GROUP OF COMPANIES LIMITED
LONESTAR WEST INC   *p* 157
105 KUUSAMO DR, RED DEER COUNTY, AB, T4E 2J5
(403) 887-2074   *SIC* 1796
LONG & MCQUADE LIMITED   *p* 295
368 TERMINAL AVE, VANCOUVER, BC, V6A 3W9
(604) 734-4886   *SIC* 5736
LONG & MCQUADE LIMITED   *p* 845
722 ROSEBANK RD, PICKERING, ON, L1W 4B2
(905) 837-9785   *SIC* 5736
LONG & MCQUADE LIMITED   *p* 990
925 BLOOR ST W, TORONTO, ON, M6H 1L5
(416) 588-7886   *SIC* 7359
LONG & MCQUADE MUSICAL INSTRUMENTS   *p*
295
See LONG & MCQUADE LIMITED
LONG & MCQUADE MUSICAL INSTRUMENTS   *p*
990
See LONG & MCQUADE LIMITED
LONG HOLDINGS INC   *p* 845
722 ROSEBANK RD, PICKERING, ON, L1W 4B2
(905) 837-9785   *SIC* 5736
LONG ISLAND DISTRIBUTING CO. LIMITED   *p*
916
425 ALNESS ST, TORONTO, ON, M3J 2H4
SIC 5099
LONG MANUFACTURING LTD   *p* 533
See DANA CANADA CORPORATION
LONG PLAIN FIRST NATION   *p* 349
See ARROWHEAD DEVELOPMENT CORPORATION
LONG RUN EXPLORATION LTD   *p* 53
600 3 AVE SW UNIT 600, CALGARY, AB, T2P 0G5
(403) 261-6012   *SIC* 1382
LONG TALL SALLY   *p* 697
See LTS TG LTD
LONG VIEW SYSTEMS CORPORATION   *p*
53
250 2 ST SW SUITE 2100, CALGARY, AB, T2P 0C1
(403) 515-6900   *SIC* 7379

LONGFORD INTERNATIONAL LTD   *p* 874
41 LAMONT AVE, SCARBOROUGH, ON, M1S 1A8
(416) 298-6622   *SIC* 3565
LONGLAC LUMBER INC   *p* 663
101 BLUEBERRY RD, LONGLAC, ON, P0T 2A0
(807) 876-2626   *SIC* 2421
LONGLIFE OF CANADA   *p* 695
See GAY LEA FOODS CO-OPERATIVE LIMITED
LONGO BROTHERS FRUIT MARKETS INC   *p* 511
7700 HURONTARIO ST SUITE 202, BRAMPTON, ON, L6Y 4M3
(905) 455-3135   *SIC* 5431
LONGO BROTHERS FRUIT MARKETS INC   *p* 526
2900 WALKER'S LINE, BURLINGTON, ON, L7M 4M8
(905) 331-1645   *SIC* 5148
LONGO BROTHERS FRUIT MARKETS INC   *p* 531
1225 FAIRVIEW ST, BURLINGTON, ON, L7S 1Y3
(905) 637-3804   *SIC* 5431
LONGO BROTHERS FRUIT MARKETS INC   *p* 672
3085 HIGHWAY 7 E, MARKHAM, ON, L3R 0J5
(905) 479-8877   *SIC* 5411
LONGO BROTHERS FRUIT MARKETS INC   *p* 686
7085 GOREWAY DR, MISSISSAUGA, ON, L4T 3X6
(905) 677-3481   *SIC* 5411
LONGO BROTHERS FRUIT MARKETS INC   *p* 717
3163 WINSTON CHURCHILL BLVD, MISSISSAUGA, ON, L5L 2W1
(905) 828-0008   *SIC* 5411
LONGO BROTHERS FRUIT MARKETS INC   *p* 718
5636 GLEN ERIN DR UNIT 1, MISSISSAUGA, ON, L5M 6B1
(905) 567-4450   *SIC* 5411
LONGO BROTHERS FRUIT MARKETS INC   *p* 798
338 DUNDAS ST E, OAKVILLE, ON, L6H 6Z9
(905) 257-5633   *SIC* 5431
LONGO BROTHERS FRUIT MARKETS INC   *p* 1027
8800 HUNTINGTON RD, WOODBRIDGE, ON, L4H 3M6
(905) 264-4100   *SIC* 5411
LONGO BROTHERS FRUIT MARKETS INC   *p* 1032
8401 WESTON RD, WOODBRIDGE, ON, L4L 1A6
(905) 850-6161   *SIC* 5411
LONGO'S FRUIT MARKET   *p* 511
See LONGO BROTHERS FRUIT MARKETS INC
LONGO'S FRUIT MARKET   *p* 526
See LONGO BROTHERS FRUIT MARKETS INC
LONGO'S FRUIT MARKET   *p* 531
See LONGO BROTHERS FRUIT MARKETS INC
LONGO'S FRUIT MARKET   *p* 672
See LONGO BROTHERS FRUIT MARKETS INC
LONGO'S FRUIT MARKET   *p* 717
See LONGO BROTHERS FRUIT MARKETS INC
LONGO'S FRUIT MARKET   *p* 718
See LONGO BROTHERS FRUIT MARKETS INC
LONGO'S FRUIT MARKET   *p* 1027
See LONGO BROTHERS FRUIT MARKETS INC
LONGO'S FRUIT MARKET   *p* 1032
See LONGO BROTHERS FRUIT MARKETS

INC

LONGO'S MALTON FRUIT MARKET *p* 686
See *LONGO BROTHERS FRUIT MARKETS INC*

LONGO'S OAKVILLE FRUIT MARKET *p* 798
See *LONGO BROTHERS FRUIT MARKETS INC*

LONGUE POINTE CHRYSLER DODGE (1987) LTEE *p* 1346
6200 BOUL METROPOLITAIN E, SAINT-LEONARD, QC, H1S 1A9
(514) 256-5092 *SIC* 5511

LONGUEUIL HONDA *p* 1145
See *VERCHERES AUTO INC*

LONGUEUIL MAZDA *p* 1142
See *2938286 CANADA INC*

LONGUEUIL NISSAN INC *p* 1143
760 RUE SAINT-CHARLES E, LONGUEUIL, QC, J4H 1C3
(450) 442-2000 *SIC* 5511

LONGUEUIL TOYOTA *p* 1144
See *2972344 CANADA INC*

LONGVIEW SOLUTIONS INC *p* 672
65 ALLSTATE PKY SUITE 200, MARKHAM, ON, L3R 9X1
(905) 940-1510 *SIC* 7372

LONGWORTH RETIREMENT VILLAGE *p* 660
See *SIFTON PROPERTIES LIMITED*

LONGYEAR CANADA, ULC *p* 713
2442 SOUTH SHERIDAN WAY, MISSISSAUGA, ON, L5J 2M7
(905) 822-7922 *SIC* 3532

LONKAR SERVICES *p* 7
See *LONKAR SERVICES LTD*

LONKAR SERVICES LTD *p* 7
BOSWELL CR SUITE 5, BROOKS, AB, T1R 1C2
(403) 362-5300 *SIC* 1389

LONKAR SERVICES LTD *p* 156
8080 EDGAR INDUSTRIAL CRES, RED DEER, AB, T4P 3R3
(403) 347-9727 *SIC* 1389

LONSDALE CHEVRON *p* 240
See *KISA ENTERPRISES LTD*

LONTOURS CANADA LIMITED *p* 996
3280 BLOOR ST W 4 FL SUITE 400, TORONTO, ON, M8X 2X3
(800) 268-3636 *SIC* 4724

LOOBY GROUP INCORPORATED *p* 566
10 MATILDA ST, DUBLIN, ON, N0K 1E0
(519) 345-2800 *SIC* 6712

LOOKOUT THE EMERGENCY AID SOCIETY *p* 295
429 ALEXANDER ST, VANCOUVER, BC, V6A 1C6
(604) 255-2347 *SIC* 8361

LOOMIS EXPRESS *p* 1337
See *TRANSPORT TFI 22 S.E.C.*

LOOP INDUSTRIES, INC *p* 1381
480 RUE FERNAND-POITRAS, TERREBONNE, QC, J6Y 1Y4
(450) 951-8555 *SIC* 4953

LOOP RECYCLED PRODUCTS INC *p* 758
940 CHIPPAWA CREEK RD, NIAGARA FALLS, ON, L2E 6S5
(905) 353-0068 *SIC* 5231

LOOSE MOOSE TAP & GRILL, THE *p* 958
See *979786 ONTARIO LIMITED*

LOPES LIMITED *p* 561
84 SMELTER RD, CONISTON, ON, P0M 1M0
(705) 694-4713 *SIC* 1711

LOPES MECHANICAL & ELECTRICAL *p* 561
See *LOPES LIMITED*

LOR-DON LIMITED *p* 651
485 MCCORMICK BLVD, LONDON, ON, N5W 5N1
(519) 679-2322 *SIC* 3441

LORAAS DISPOSAL SERVICES LTD *p* 1428
805 47TH ST E, SASKATOON, SK, S7K

8G7
(306) 242-2300 *SIC* 4953

LORAC COMMUNICATIONS INC *p* 546
115 FIRST ST SUITE 107, COLLINGWOOD, ON, L9Y 4W3
(905) 457-5350 *SIC* 4899

LORD BEAVERBROOK SENIOR HIGH SCHOOL *p* 34
See *CALGARY BOARD OF EDUCATION*

LORD BYNG SECONDARY SCHOOL *p* 324
See *BOARD OF EDUCATION OF SCHOOL DISTRICT NO. 39 (VANCOUVER), THE*

LORD ELGIN HOTEL *p* 823
See *KIDSINKS HOLDINGS INC*

LORD NELSON HOTEL & SUITES *p* 452
See *CENTENNIAL HOTELS LIMITED*

LORD PLASTIQUE *p* 1303
See *PLASTIQUES G.P.R. INC*

LORD SELKIRK REGIONAL COMPREHENSIVE SECONDARY SCHOOL *p* 356
See *LORD SELKIRK SCHOOL DIVISION, THE*

LORD SELKIRK SCHOOL DIVISION, THE *p* 356
205 MERCY ST, SELKIRK, MB, R1A 2C8
(204) 482-5942 *SIC* 8211

LORD SELKIRK SCHOOL DIVISION, THE *p* 356
221 MERCY ST, SELKIRK, MB, R1A 2C8
(204) 482-6926 *SIC* 8211

LORD SHAUGHNESSY HIGH SCHOOL *p* 73
See *CALGARY BOARD OF EDUCATION*

LORD'STACE INC *p* 1206
1155 BOUL RENE-LEVESQUE O UNITE 4000, MONTREAL, QC, H3B 3V2
(418) 575-4942 *SIC* 5063

LORDCO AUTO PARTS *p* 231
See *LORDCO PARTS LTD*

LORDCO PARTS LTD *p* 231
22866 DEWDNEY TRUNK RD, MAPLE RIDGE, BC, V2X 3K6
(604) 467-1581 *SIC* 5531

LORETTE MARKET PLACE LIMITED *p* 351
11 LARAMEE DR, LORETTE, MB, R0A 0Y0
(204) 878-2510 *SIC* 5411

LORETTO ABBEY HIGHSCHOOL *p* 788
See *TORONTO CATHOLIC DISTRICT SCHOOL BOARD*

LORMIT PROCESS SERVICE *p* 217
See *DESSERT CITY INVESTIGATIONS AND SECURITY INC*

LORNE PARK SECONDARY SCHOOL *p* 713
See *PEEL DISTRICT SCHOOL BOARD*

LORTAP ENTERPRISES DIV OF *p* 253
See *VIC VAN ISLE CONSTRUCTION LTD*

LORTIE & MARTIN LTEE *p* 1354
20 RUE SAINT-PAUL E, SAINTE-AGATHE-DES-MONTS, QC, J8C 3M3
(819) 326-3844 *SIC* 5211

LORTIE AVIATION INC *p* 1378
130 RUE TIBO, STE-CATHERINE-DE-LA-J-CARTIE, QC, G3N 2Y7
(418) 875-5111 *SIC* 7699

LOS ANDES COPPER LTD *p* 306
355 BURRARD ST SUITE 1260, VANCOUVER, BC, V6C 2G8
(604) 681-2802 *SIC* 1021

LOSANI HOMES *p* 892
See *LOSANI HOMES (1998) LTD*

LOSANI HOMES (1998) LTD *p* 892
430 MCNEILLY RD, STONEY CREEK, ON, L8E 5E3
(905) 643-7386 *SIC* 6531

LOSS PREVENTION SERVICES LIMITED *p* 791
2221 KEELE ST SUITE 308, NORTH YORK, ON, M6M 3Z5
(416) 248-1261 *SIC* 8741

LOTEK WIRELESS INC *p* 755
115 PONY DR, NEWMARKET, ON, L3Y 7B5
(905) 836-5329 *SIC* 8711

LOTLINX INC *p* 612

8 MAIN ST E SUITE 200, HAMILTON, ON, L8N 1E8
SIC 5511

LOTUS TERMINALS LTD *p* 272
18833 52 AVE, SURREY, BC, V3S 8E5
(604) 534-1119 *SIC* 4213

LOU ROMANO WATER RECLAMATION PLANT *p* 1025
4155 OJIBWAY PKY, WINDSOR, ON, N9C 4A5
(519) 253-7217 *SIC* 4941

LOU-TEC *p* 1308
See *LOCATION D'OUTILS BROSSARD INC*

LOUBERT, CLAUDINE *p* 1323
See *PHARMAPRIX CLAUDINE LOUBERT INC*

LOUCH NIAGARA *p* 1004
See *NIAGARA ORCHARD & VINEYARD CORP*

LOUCON METAL LIMITED *p* 750
39 GRENFELL CRES SUITE 37, NEPEAN, ON, K2G 0G3
(613) 226-1102 *SIC* 5051

LOUDON BROS. LIMITED *p* 909
830A ATHABASCA ST, THUNDER BAY, ON, P7C 3E6
(807) 623-5458 *SIC* 5194

LOUET NORTH AMERICA *p* 848
See *121409 CANADA INC*

LOUGHEED ACURA *p* 201
See *PACIFIC MAINLAND HOLDINGS LTD*

LOUGHEED HYUNDAI *p* 201
See *LUKANDA HOLDINGS LTD*

LOUIS BRIER HOME & HOSPITAL, DIV OF *p* 322
See *JEWISH HOME FOR THE AGED OF BRITISH COLUMBIA*

LOUIS DREYFUS COMPANY CANADA ULC *p* 65
525 11 AVE SW SUITE 500, CALGARY, AB, T2R 0C9
(403) 205-3322 *SIC* 5153

LOUIS DREYFUS COMPANY YORKTON TRADING LP *p* 65
525 11 AVE SW SUITE 500, CALGARY, AB, T2R 0C9
(403) 205-3322 *SIC* 5153

LOUIS GARNEAU SPORTS INC *p* 1293
30 RUE DES GRANDS-LACS, SAINT-AUGUSTIN-DE-DESMAURES, QC, G3A 2E6
(418) 878-4135 *SIC* 2329

LOUIS LUNCHEONETTE INC *p* 1370
386 RUE KING E, SHERBROOKE, QC, J1G 1A8
(819) 563-5581 *SIC* 5812

LOUIS MAGLIO ENTERPRISES LTD *p* 235
29 GOVERNMENT RD, NELSON, BC, V1L 4L9
(250) 352-6661 *SIC* 5211

LOUIS RIEL SCHOOL DIVISION *p* 366
831 BEAVERHILL BLVD, WINNIPEG, MB, R2J 3K1
(204) 257-0637 *SIC* 8211

LOUIS RIEL SCHOOL DIVISION *p* 368
661 DAKOTA ST, WINNIPEG, MB, R2M 3K3
(204) 256-4366 *SIC* 8211

LOUIS RIEL SCHOOL DIVISION *p* 368
770 ST MARY'S RD, WINNIPEG, MB, R2M 3N7
(204) 233-3263 *SIC* 8211

LOUIS RIEL SCHOOL DIVISION *p* 368
900 ST MARY'S RD, WINNIPEG, MB, R2M 3R3
(204) 257-7827 *SIC* 8211

LOUIS RIEL SCHOOL DIVISION BOARD OFFICE *p* 368
See *LOUIS RIEL SCHOOL DIVISION*

LOUIS ST. LAURENT SCHOOL *p* 119
See *EDMONTON CATHOLIC SEPARATE SCHOOL DISTRICT NO.7*

LOUIS W. BRAY CONSTRUCTION LIMITED *p* 1002
308 CORDUROY RD, VARS, ON, K0A 3H0

(613) 938-6711 *SIC* 1611

LOUIS-HEBERT UNIFORME INC *p* 1083
1963 RUE NOTRE-DAME-DE-FATIMA, COTE SAINT-LUC, QC, H7G 4R9
(450) 668-3766 *SIC* 5136

LOUISBOURG SEAFOODS LTD *p* 461
3 COMMERCIAL ST, LOUISBOURG, NS, B1C 1B5
(902) 733-2079 *SIC* 2091

LOUISE KOOL & GALT LIMITED *p* 874
2123 MCCOWAN RD, SCARBOROUGH, ON, M1S 3Y6
(416) 293-0312 *SIC* 5092

LOUISE MARSHALL HOSPITAL *p* 746
See *NORTH WELLINGTON HEALTH CARE CORPORATION*

LOUISEVILLE AUTOMOBILE LTEE *p* 1146
871 BOUL SAINT-LAURENT O, LOUISEVILLE, QC, J5V 1L3
SIC 5511

LOUISIANA-PACIFIC BUILDING PRODUCTS *p* 215
See *LOUISIANA-PACIFIC CANADA LTD*

LOUISIANA-PACIFIC CANADA LTD *p* 213
8220 259 RD SITE 13 COMP 14, FORT ST. JOHN, BC, V1J 4M6
(250) 263-6600 *SIC* 2431

LOUISIANA-PACIFIC CANADA LTD *p* 215
800 9TH ST N, GOLDEN, BC, V0A 1H0
(250) 344-8800 *SIC* 2436

LOUISIANA-PACIFIC CANADA LTD *p* 442
2005 HIGHWAY 14, CHESTER, NS, B0J 1J0
(902) 275-3556 *SIC* 2493

LOUISIANA-PACIFIC CANADA LTD *p* 1060
1012 CH DU PARC-INDUSTRIEL, BOIS-FRANC, QC, J9E 3A9
(819) 449-7030 *SIC* 2431

LOUISIANA-PACIFIC CANADA LTD *p* 1075
572 155 RTE, CHAMBORD, QC, G0W 1G0
(418) 342-6212 *SIC* 2611

LOUISIANA-PACIFIC CANADA LTD *p* 1189
507 PLACE D'ARMES BUREAU 400, MONTREAL, QC, H2Y 2W8
(514) 861-4724 *SIC* 2431

LOUISIANA-PACIFIQUE CANADA LTEE-DIVISON QUEBEC CHAMBORD OSB *p* 1075
See *LOUISIANA-PACIFIC CANADA LTD*

LOUISVILLE *p* 481
See *LOUISVILLE LADDER CORP*

LOUISVILLE LADDER CORP *p* 481
100 ENGELHARD DR, AURORA, ON, L4G 3V2
(905) 727-0031 *SIC* 3499

LOUKIL, SAID *p* 1300
247 RUE ISABELLE, SAINT-EUSTACHE, QC, J7P 4E9
(450) 491-3366 *SIC* 5111

LOUNSBURY AUTOMOTIVE LIMITED *p* 407
2155 WEST MAIN ST, MONCTON, NB, E1C 9P2
(506) 857-4300 *SIC* 5511

LOUNSBURY CHEV OLDS *p* 407
See *LOUNSBURY COMPANY LIMITED*

LOUNSBURY COMPANY LIMITED *p* 407
2155 MAIN ST W, MONCTON, NB, E1C 9P2
(506) 857-4300 *SIC* 5511

LOUNSBURY COMPANY LIMITED *p* 409
1655 MOUNTAIN RD, MONCTON, NB, E1G 1A5
(506) 857-4385 *SIC* 5511

LOUNSBURY HEAVY-DUTY TRUCK LIMITED *p* 408
725 ST GEORGE BLVD, MONCTON, NB, E1E 2C2
(506) 857-4345 *SIC* 7699

LOVEDAY MUSHROOM FARMS LTD *p* 366
556 MISSION RD, WINNIPEG, MB, R2J 0A2
(204) 233-4378 *SIC* 0182

LOVELL DRUGS LIMITED *p* 812
52 1/2 SIMCOE ST N, OSHAWA, ON, L1G

4S1
(905) 723-2276   *SIC* 5912
LOVELY IMPORTS & RETAILS LTD   *p* 783
3720 KEELE ST, NORTH YORK, ON, M3J 2V9
(416) 636-0568   *SIC* 5541
LOVELY IMPORTS & RETAILS LTD   *p* 786
2205 JANE ST, NORTH YORK, ON, M3M 1A5
(416) 248-9814   *SIC* 5541
LOVEPAC INC   *p* 1340
140 RUE BARR, SAINT-LAURENT, QC, H4T 1Y4
(514) 904-4300   *SIC* 7389
LOVER (1996) LTD   *p* 652
200 ADELAIDE ST S, LONDON, ON, N5Z 3L1
(519) 681-2254   *SIC* 5021
LOVERS ATWORK OFFICE FURNITURE   *p* 652
See LOVER (1996) LTD
LOVSUNS TUNNELING CANADA LIMITED
p 998
441 CARLINGVIEW DR, TORONTO, ON, M9W 5G7
(647) 255-0018   *SIC* 3531
LOW COST PROPANE   *p* 141
See SAVE-X-LP GAS LTD
LOWE FARM CO-OP   *p* 351
See LOWE FARM CO-OP SERVICES (1959) LTD
LOWE FARM CO-OP SERVICES (1959) LTD   *p* 351
78 MAIN ST, LOWE FARM, MB, R0G 1E0
(204) 746-8476   *SIC* 5171
LOWE MECHANICAL SERVICES LTD *p* 369
72 PARK LANE AVE, WINNIPEG, MB, R2R 0K2
(204) 233-3292   *SIC* 1711
LOWE'S 3329   *p* 1420
See LOWE'S COMPANIES CANADA, ULC
LOWE'S COMPANIES CANADA, ULC   *p* 9
2909 SUNRIDGE WAY NE, CALGARY, AB, T1Y 7K7
(403) 277-0044   *SIC* 5211
LOWE'S COMPANIES CANADA, ULC *p* 101
10225 186 ST NW, EDMONTON, AB, T5S 0G5
(780) 486-2508   *SIC* 5211
LOWE'S COMPANIES CANADA, ULC *p* 121
10141 13 AVE NW, EDMONTON, AB, T6N 0B6
(780) 430-1344   *SIC* 5211
LOWE'S COMPANIES CANADA, ULC *p* 160
261199 CROSSIRON BLVD UNIT 300, ROCKY VIEW COUNTY, AB, T4A 0J6
(403) 567-7440   *SIC* 5211
LOWE'S COMPANIES CANADA, ULC *p* 237
1085 TANAKA CRT, NEW WESTMINSTER, BC, V3M 0G2
(604) 527-7239   *SIC* 5211
LOWE'S COMPANIES CANADA, ULC *p* 487
71 BRYNE DR, BARRIE, ON, L4N 8V8
(905) 952-2950   *SIC* 5211
LOWE'S COMPANIES CANADA, ULC *p* 512
10111 HEART LAKE RD, BRAMPTON, ON, L6Z 0E4
(905) 840-2351   *SIC* 5211
LOWE'S COMPANIES CANADA, ULC *p* 664
200 MCNAUGHTON RD E, MAPLE, ON, L6A 4E2
(905) 879-2450   *SIC* 5211
LOWE'S COMPANIES CANADA, ULC *p* 697
5150 SPECTRUM WAY, MISSISSAUGA, ON, L4W 5G2
(905) 219-1000   *SIC* 5211
LOWE'S COMPANIES CANADA, ULC *p* 755
18401 YONGE ST, NEWMARKET, ON, L3Y 4V8
(905) 952-2950   *SIC* 5211
LOWE'S COMPANIES CANADA, ULC *p* 760
7959 MCLEOD RD, NIAGARA FALLS, ON, L2H 0G5
(905) 374-5520   *SIC* 5211

LOWE'S COMPANIES CANADA, ULC *p* 772
5160 YONGE ST SUITE 2, NORTH YORK, ON, M2N 6L9
(416) 730-7300   *SIC* 5211
LOWE'S COMPANIES CANADA, ULC *p* 843
1899 BROCK RD, PICKERING, ON, L1V 4H7
(905) 619-7530   *SIC* 5211
LOWE'S COMPANIES CANADA, ULC *p* 876
6005 STEELES AVE E, SCARBOROUGH, ON, M1V 5P7
(416) 940-4827   *SIC* 5211
LOWE'S COMPANIES CANADA, ULC *p* 899
1199 MARCUS DR, SUDBURY, ON, P3B 4K6
(705) 521-7200   *SIC* 5211
LOWE'S COMPANIES CANADA, ULC   *p* 1016
4005 GARRARD RD, WHITBY, ON, L1R 0J1
(905) 433-2870   *SIC* 5211
LOWE'S COMPANIES CANADA, ULC   *p* 1420
489 N ALBERT ST, REGINA, SK, S4R 3C3
(306) 545-1386   *SIC* 5211
LOWE'S HOLDING CANADA, ULC   *p* 697
5150 SPECTRUM WAY SUITE 200, MISSISSAUGA, ON, L4W 5G2
(905) 219-1000   *SIC* 6712
LOWE'S OF E. GWILLIMBURY   *p* 755
See LOWE'S COMPANIES CANADA, ULC
LOWE'S OF MAPLE   *p* 664
See LOWE'S COMPANIES CANADA, ULC
LOWE'S OF NORTH BRAMPTON   *p* 512
See LOWE'S COMPANIES CANADA, ULC
LOWE-MARTIN COMPANY INC   *p* 732
5990 FALBOURNE ST, MISSISSAUGA, ON, L5R 3S7
(905) 507-8782   *SIC* 2752
LOWE-MARTIN COMPANY INC   *p* 827
400 HUNT CLUB RD, OTTAWA, ON, K1V 1C1
(613) 741-0962   *SIC* 2752
LOWER CANADA COLLEGE   *p* 1221
4090 AV ROYAL, MONTREAL, QC, H4A 2M5
(514) 482-9916   *SIC* 8211
LOWER LAKES TOWING LTD   *p* 847
517 MAIN ST, PORT DOVER, ON, N0A 1N0
(519) 583-0982   *SIC* 4449
LOWER NORTH SHORE COMMUNITY SEAFOOD COOPERATIVE   *p* 1113
2 DOCKSIDE DR, HARRINGTON HARBOUR, QC, G0G 1N0
(418) 795-3244   *SIC* 2092
LOWERYS BASICS   *p* 908
See CHRISTIE, B. L. INVESTMENTS INC
LOWERYS BASICS   *p* 908
See LOWERYS, LIMITED
LOWERYS, LIMITED   *p* 908
540 CENTRAL AVE, THUNDER BAY, ON, P7B 6B4
(807) 344-6666   *SIC* 5943
LOWES HOME IMPROVEMENT WAREHOUSE   *p* 1016
See LOWE'S COMPANIES CANADA, ULC
LOWES PHARMACY LIMITED   *p* 104
6655 178 ST NW UNIT 610, EDMONTON, AB, T5T 4J5
(780) 487-1013   *SIC* 5912
LOXCREEN CANADA LTD   *p* 697
5720 AMBLER DR, MISSISSAUGA, ON, L4W 2B1
(905) 625-3210   *SIC* 3442
LOYALIST COLLEGIATE & VOCATIONAL INSTITUTE   *p* 632
See LIMESTONE DISTRICT SCHOOL BOARD
LOYALIST INSURANCE BROKERS LIMITED   *p* 478
911 GOLF LINKS RD SUITE 111, ANCASTER, ON, L9K 1H9
(905) 648-6767   *SIC* 6411

LOYALIST PROTECTION SERVICE   *p* 490
See 381611 ONTARIO LTD
LOYOLA SCHMIDT LTEE   *p* 1395
243 BOUL HARWOOD, VAUDREUIL-DORION, QC, J7V 1Y3
SIC 5072
LP ENGINEERED WOOD PRODUCTS LTD   *p* 215
1221 10TH AVE N, GOLDEN, BC, V0A 1H2
(250) 344-8800   *SIC* 2436
LP GOLDEN   *p* 215
See LP ENGINEERED WOOD PRODUCTS LTD
LPA GROUPE CONSEIL   *p* 1387
See CONSULTANTS VFP INC
LPI COMMUNICATIONS GROUP INC   *p* 36
253 62 AVE SE SUITE 101, CALGARY, AB, T2H 0R5
(403) 735-0655   *SIC* 8743
LPI GROUP   *p* 36
See LPI COMMUNICATIONS GROUP INC
LPI LEVEL PLATFORMS INC   *p* 624
309 LEGGET DR SUITE 300, KANATA, ON, K2K 3A3
(613) 232-1000   *SIC* 7371
LPL CONTRACTING   *p* 680
See 1685300 ONTARIO INC
LPP MANUFACTURING   *p* 603
See LINAMAR CORPORATION
LRG CONSTRUCTION LTD   *p* 189
5655 MONARCH ST, BURNABY, BC, V5G 2A2
(604) 291-2135   *SIC* 1542
LRI   *p* 954
See LRI ENGINEERING INC
LRI ENGINEERING INC   *p* 954
170 UNIVERSITY AVE 3RD FL, TORONTO, ON, M5H 3B3
(416) 515-9331   *SIC* 7389
LS TRAVEL RETAIL NORTH AMERICA   *p* 729
See HACHETTE DISTRIBUTION SERVICES (CANADA) INC
LS TRAVEL RETAIL NORTH AMERICA   *p* 981
See HACHETTE DISTRIBUTION SERVICES (CANADA) INC
LS TRAVEL RETAIL NORTH AMERICA INC   *p* 981
370 KING ST W SUITE 703, TORONTO, ON, M5V 1J9
(416) 863-6400   *SIC* 5947
LSBC CAPTIVE INSURANCE COMPANY LTD   *p* 299
845 CAMBIE ST SUITE 800, VANCOUVER, BC, V6B 4Z9
(604) 669-2533   *SIC* 6351
LSF   *p* 449
See EAST COAST METAL FABRICATION (2015) INC
LSRCA   *p* 755
See LAKE SIMCOE REGION CONSERVATION AUTHORITY
LT CUSTOM FURNISHINGS INC   *p* 664
10899 KEELE ST, MAPLE, ON, L6A 0K6
(905) 303-0005   *SIC* 2541
LTG RAIL CANADA LTEE   *p* 1122
151 RUE DU PARC-DE-L'INNOVATION, LA POCATIERE, QC, G0R 1Z0
(418) 856-1454   *SIC* 3823
LTP SPORTS GROUP INC   *p* 247
1465 KEBET WAY SUITE B, PORT COQUITLAM, BC, V3C 6L3
(604) 552-2930   *SIC* 3751
LTS PROTECTIVE SERVICES   *p* 791
See LIVE TO SECURE PROTECTIVE SERVICES INC
LTS TG LTD   *p* 697
5045 ORBITOR DR BLDG 12 SUITE 202, MISSISSAUGA, ON, L4W 4Y4
(905) 890-2430   *SIC* 5621
LU & SONS ENTERPRISE LTD   *p* 266
12051 NO. 1 RD SUITE 604, RICHMOND, BC, V7E 1T5

(604) 274-7878   *SIC* 5411
LU-ARD ELECTRIQUE   *p* 1379
See 3175120 CANADA INC
LUBE CITY   *p* 112
See 470858 ALBERTA LTD
LUBEMASTER CONSTRUCTION   *p* 505
See NCH CANADA INC
LUBRICO WARRANTY INC   *p* 649
2124 JETSTREAM RD, LONDON, ON, N5V 3P5
(519) 451-1900   *SIC* 6399
LUBRICOR INC   *p* 1008
475 CONESTOGO RD, WATERLOO, ON, N2L 4C9
(519) 884-8455   *SIC* 5172
LUBRIZOL CANADA   *p* 1032
See LUBRIZOL CANADA LIMITED
LUBRIZOL CANADA LIMITED   *p* 1032
3700 STEELES AVE W SUITE 201, WOODBRIDGE, ON, L4L 8K8
(905) 264-4646   *SIC* 2992
LUC CHARBONNEAU FRUITS & LEGUMES INC   *p* 1162
8135 AV MARCO-POLO, MONTREAL, QC, H1E 5Y8
(514) 337-3955   *SIC* 5148
LUCARA DIAMOND CORP   *p* 306
885 GEORGIA ST W SUITE 2000, VANCOUVER, BC, V6C 3E8
(604) 689-7842   *SIC* 1499
LUCAS & MARCO INC   *p* 575
1000 ISLINGTON AVE, ETOBICOKE, ON, M8Z 4P8
(416) 255-4152   *SIC* 5812
LUCAS CONTRACTING   *p* 748
See 1702660 ONTARIO INC
LUCERNE FOODS   *p* 18
See SOBEYS WEST INC
LUCERNE FOODS BREAD PLANT   *p* 381
See SOBEYS WEST INC
LUCERNE FOODS, DIV OF   *p* 169
See SOBEYS WEST INC
LUCIANI AUTOMOBILES INC   *p* 1227
4040 RUE JEAN-TALON O, MONTREAL, QC, H4P 1V5
(514) 340-1344   *SIC* 5511
LUCIANO'S NO FRILLS   *p* 932
See 1784007 ONTARIO LTD
LUCIANO'S RESTAURANT GROUP   *p* 30
316 3 ST SE, CALGARY, AB, T2G 2S4
SIC 5812
LUCID VISION LABS, INC   *p* 255
13200 DELF PL UNIT 130, RICHMOND, BC, V6V 2A2
(833) 465-8243   *SIC* 3861
LUCIDIA STUDIOS LTD   *p* 861
123 MARCH ST SUITE 301, SAULT STE. MARIE, ON, P6A 2Z5
(705) 941-9828   *SIC* 7389
LUCIEN CHARBONNEAU LIMITEE   *p* 1224
1955 RUE CABOT, MONTREAL, QC, H4E 1E2
(514) 336-2500   *SIC* 1711
LUCIEN DAUNOIS   *p* 1179
See IMPORTATIONS JEREMY D. LIMITED
LUCKETT RETAIL MANAGEMENT INC   *p* 439
1595 BEDFORD HWY SUITE 122, BEDFORD, NS, B4A 3Y4
(902) 835-4997   *SIC* 5411
LUCKHART TRANSPORT LTD   *p* 879
4049 PERTH COUNTY RD 135, SEBRINGVILLE, ON, N0K 1X0
(519) 393-6128   *SIC* 4212
LUDIA INC   *p* 1189
410 RUE SAINT-NICOLAS BUREAU 400, MONTREAL, QC, H2Y 2P5
(514) 313-3370   *SIC* 5092
LUDIK DESIGNER CONFISEUR INC *p* 1297
660 RTE 112, SAINT-CESAIRE, QC, J0L 1T0
(450) 469-0514   *SIC* 5145
LUDLOW TECHNICAL PRODUCTS CANADA, LTD   *p* 593

215 HERBERT ST, GANANOQUE, ON, K7G 2Y7
(613) 382-4733 SIC 3845

LUDWICK CATERING LTD p 349
3184 BIRDS HILL RD, EAST ST PAUL, MB, R2E 1H1
(204) 668-8091 SIC 5812

LUFF INDUSTRIES LTD p 159
235010 WRANGLER RD, ROCKY VIEW COUNTY, AB, T1X 0K3
(403) 279-3555 SIC 3535

LUFKIN INDUSTRIES CANADA ULC p 149
1107 8A ST, NISKU, AB, T9E 7R3
(780) 955-7566 SIC 3561

LUGARO JEWELLERS LTD p 194
3114 BOUNDARY RD, BURNABY, BC, V5M 4A2
(604) 454-1200 SIC 5944

LUKANDA HOLDINGS LTD p 201
1288 LOUGHEED HWY, COQUITLAM, BC, V3K 6S4
(604) 523-3009 SIC 5511

LUKE'S MACHINERY CO. LTD p 375
318 NOTRE DAME AVE, WINNIPEG, MB, R3B 1P5
(204) 943-3421 SIC 5084

LULLABIES OF LONDON DIV OF p 661
See TT GROUP LIMITED

LULULEMON p 321
See LULULEMON ATHLETICA CANADA INC

LULULEMON ATHLETICA CANADA INC p 321
1818 CORNWALL AVE SUITE 400, VANCOUVER, BC, V6J 1C7
(604) 732-6124 SIC 2339

LULUMCO INC p 1359
79 RUE SAINT-ALPHONSE, SAINTE-LUCE, QC, G0K 1P0
(418) 739-4881 SIC 2421

LUM & SON FINE FOODS LTD p 335
1058 PANDORA AVE, VICTORIA, BC, V8V 3P5
(250) 384-3543 SIC 5411

LUMAC BIG SCOOP p 409
See POWER PLUS TECHNOLOGY INC

LUMBER MART LIMITED p 459
751 HERRING COVE RD, HERRING COVE, NS, B3R 1Y9
(902) 477-6500 SIC 5039

LUMEC p 1061
See SIGNIFY CANADA LTD

LUMEN p 500
See SONEPAR CANADA INC

LUMEN p 1236
See SONEPAR CANADA INC

LUMEN p 1252
See SONEPAR CANADA INC

LUMEN p 1398
See SONEPAR CANADA INC

LUMEN DYNAMICS p 724
See LUMEN DYNAMICS GROUP INC

LUMEN DYNAMICS GROUP INC p 724
2260 ARGENTIA RD, MISSISSAUGA, ON, L5N 6H7
(905) 821-2600 SIC 3827

LUMENERA CORPORATION p 749
7 CAPELLA CRT, NEPEAN, ON, K2E 8A7
(613) 736-4077 SIC 3861

LUMENIX p 571
See LUMENIX CORPORATION

LUMENIX CORPORATION p 571
15 AKRON RD, ETOBICOKE, ON, M8W 1T3
(855) 586-3649 SIC 3674

LUMENPULSE p 1141
See GROUPE LUMENPULSE INC

LUMENTUM CANADA LTD p 752
61 BILL LEATHEM DR, NEPEAN, ON, K2J 0P7
(613) 843-3000 SIC 3827

LUMENTUM OTTAWA INC p 752
61 BILL LEATHEM DR, NEPEAN, ON, K2J 0P7
(613) 843-3000 SIC 3669

LUMENWERX ULC p 1326
B-393 RUE SAINTE-CROIX, SAINT-LAURENT, QC, H4N 2L3
(514) 225-4304 SIC 3645

LUMERICAL INC p 314
1095 PENDER ST W SUITE 1700, VANCOUVER, BC, V6E 2M6
(604) 733-9006 SIC 7372

LUMI-AIR DORION p 1294
See BEAULIEU & LAMOUREUX INC

LUMI-O INNOVAPLAS INC p 1096
2257 139 RTE, DRUMMONDVILLE, QC, J2A 2G2
(819) 850-2935 SIC 3999

LUMI-O INTERNATIONAL INC p 1320
370 BOUL LAJEUNESSE O, SAINT-JEROME, QC, J7Y 4E5
(450) 565-5544 SIC 3949

LUMIFY INC p 672
2700 JOHN ST, MARKHAM, ON, L3R 2W4
(905) 474-0555 SIC 3648

LUMINEX MOLECULAR DIAGNOSTICS, INC p 946
439 UNIVERSITY AVE SUITE 900, TORONTO, ON, M5G 1Y8
(416) 593-4323 SIC 5047

LUMINIS p 1250
See GROUPE LUMINAIRES INC, LE

LUMIPRO INC p 1094
640 AV LEPINE, DORVAL, QC, H9P 1G2
(514) 633-9320 SIC 5063

LUMISOLUTION INC p 1264
162 AV DU SACRE-COEUR, QUEBEC, QC, G1N 2W2
(418) 522-5693 SIC 5063

LUNDBECK CANADA INC p 1228
2600 BOUL ALFRED-NOBEL BUREAU 400, MONTREAL, QC, H4S 0A9
(514) 844-8515 SIC 5122

LUNDGREN & YOUNG p 96
See INSURANCE BANK

LUNDGREN & YOUNG INSURANCE LTD p 68
9705 HORTON RD SW SUITE 200C, CALGARY, AB, T2V 2X5
(403) 253-1980 SIC 6411

LUNDIN GOLD INC p 307
885 GEORGIA ST W SUITE 2000, VANCOUVER, BC, V6C 3E8
(604) 689-7842 SIC 1041

LUNDIN MINING CORPORATION p 954
150 KING ST W SUITE 1500, TORONTO, ON, M5H 1J9
(416) 342-5560 SIC 1021

LUNDY FOOD p 484
See 1327187 ONTARIO INC

LUNENBERG INDUSTRIAL FOUNDRY & ENGINEERING p 462
See LUNENBURG FOUNDRY & ENGINEERING LIMITED

LUNENBURG CAMPUS p 441
See NOVA SCOTIA, PROVINCE OF

LUNENBURG FOUNDRY & ENGINEERING LIMITED p 462
53 FALKLAND ST, LUNENBURG, NS, B0J 2C0
(902) 634-8827 SIC 3731

LUNENBURG HOME FOR SPECIAL CARE CORP p 462
25 BLOCKHOUSE HILL RD, LUNENBURG, NS, B0J 2C0
(902) 634-8836 SIC 8051

LUNENBURG SAVE EASY p 461
See FRANCIS FOODSTORE LTD

LUNENFELD RESEARCH INSTITUTE p 946
600 UNIVERSITY AVE RM 850, TORONTO, ON, M5G 1X5
(416) 586-8811 SIC 8733

LUNETTERIE BRANCHES INC., LES p 1321
509 RUE SAINT-GEORGES, SAINT-JEROME, QC, J7Z 5B6
(450) 432-3914 SIC 5995

LUNETTERIE NEW LOOK (CANADA) p 1280

See LNLC INC

LUNG ASSOCIATION OF MANITOBA p 373
See SANATORIUM BOARD OF MANITOBA

LUNG ASSOCIATION OF NOVA SCOTIA p 455
6331 LADY HAMMOND RD SUITE 200, HALIFAX, NS, B3K 2S2
(902) 443-8141 SIC 8699

LUSH FRESH HANDMADE COSMETICS p 323
See LUSH HANDMADE COSMETICS LTD

LUSH HANDMADE COSMETICS LTD p 323
8688 CAMBIE ST, VANCOUVER, BC, V6P 6M6
(604) 638-3632 SIC 2844

LUSH LAWN IRRIGATION p 41
See NUCOR SYSTEMS INC

LUSH MANUFACTURING LTD p 323
8680 CAMBIE ST, VANCOUVER, BC, V6P 6M9
(888) 733-5874 SIC 2844

LUSIGHT RESEARCH p 927
See 6142974 CANADA INC

LUSSIER CENTRE DU CAMION p 1358
See CAMIONS LUSSIER-LUSSICAM INC

LUSSIER DALE PARIZEAU INC p 1269
900 BOUL RENE-LEVESQUE E BUREAU 700, QUEBEC, QC, G1R 2B5
(418) 647-1111 SIC 6411

LUSSIER DALE PARIZEAU INC p 1376
80 RUE AUGUSTA, SOREL-TRACY, QC, J3P 1A5
(450) 746-1000 SIC 6159

LUSSIER PONTIAC BUICK G M C LTEE p 1313
3000 RUE DESSAULLES, SAINT-HYACINTHE, QC, J2S 2V8
(450) 778-1112 SIC 5511

LUSSIER, BERNARD INC p 1302
378 BOUL ARTHUR-SAUVE, SAINT-EUSTACHE, QC, J7R 2J4
(450) 473-3911 SIC 5912

LUSSIER, SIMON LTEE p 1059
16 BOUL DE LA SEIGNEURIE E, BLAINVILLE, QC, J7C 3V5
(450) 435-6591 SIC 5031

LUSTRE ARTCRAFT DE MONTREAL LTEE p 1049
8525 RUE JULES-LEGER, ANJOU, QC, H1J 1A8
(514) 353-7200 SIC 3645

LUTHER COLLEGE p 1422
See UNIVERSITY OF REGINA

LUTHER COLLEGE p 1422
1500 ROYAL ST, REGINA, SK, S4T 5A5
(306) 791-9150 SIC 8221

LUTHER COURT SOCIETY p 333
1525 CEDAR HILL CROSS RD, VICTORIA, BC, V8P 5M1
(250) 477-7241 SIC 8051

LUTHERAN CHURCH-CANADA p 386
3074 PORTAGE AVE, WINNIPEG, MB, R3K 0Y2
(204) 895-3433 SIC 8661

LUTHERAN HOMES KITCHENER-WATERLOO p 636
2727 KINGSWAY DR SUITE 227, KITCHENER, ON, N2C 1A7
(519) 893-6320 SIC 8051

LUTHERN SENIOR CITIZEN HOUSING SOCIETY p 272
5939 180 ST, SURREY, BC, V3S 4L2
(604) 576-2891 SIC 8051

LUTHERWOOD p 1008
139 FATHER DAVID BAUER DR SUITE 1, WATERLOO, ON, N2L 6L1
(519) 783-3710 SIC 8399

LUV 2 PAK p 784
See PROGRESS LUV2PAK INTERNATIONAL LTD

LUX WINDOWS p 24
See LUX WINDOWS AND GLASS LTD

LUX WINDOWS AND GLASS LTD p 24
6875 9 ST NE, CALGARY, AB, T2E 8R9
(403) 276-7770 SIC 2431

LUXE MODERN RENTALS p 787
See SUPERIOR EVENTS GROUP INC

LUXOTTICA CANADA INC p 724
2000 ARGENTIA RD SUITE 2, MISSISSAUGA, ON, L5N 1P7
(905) 858-0008 SIC 5995

LUXOTTICA RETAIL CANADA INC p 724
2000 ARGENTIA RD UNIT 2, MISSISSAUGA, ON, L5N 1P7
(905) 858-0008 SIC 5995

LUXURY HOTELS INTERNATIONAL OF CANADA p 30
110 9 AVE SE, CALGARY, AB, T2G 5A6
(403) 266-7331 SIC 7011

LUXURY HOTELS INTERNATIONAL OF CANADA ULC p 407
600 MAIN ST, MONCTON, NB, E1C 0M6
(506) 854-7100 SIC 7011

LUXURY HOTELS INTERNATIONAL OF CANADA ULC p 685
1050 PAIGNTON HOUSE RD, MINETT, ON, P0B 1G0
(705) 765-1900 SIC 7011

LUXURY HOTELS INTERNATIONAL OF CANADA ULC p 697
2425 MATHESON BLVD E SUITE 100, MISSISSAUGA, ON, L4W 5K4
(905) 366-5200 SIC 7011

LUXURY HOTELS INTERNATIONAL OF CANADA ULC p 858
1337 LONDON RD, SARNIA, ON, N7S 1P6
(519) 346-4551 SIC 7389

LUXURY HOTELS INTERNATIONAL OF CANADA ULC p 946
525 BAY ST, TORONTO, ON, M5G 2L2
(416) 597-9200 SIC 7011

LUXURY HOTELS INTERNATIONAL OF CANADA ULC p 1092
800 PLACE LEIGH-CAPREOL, DORVAL, QC, H4Y 0A5
(514) 636-6700 SIC 7011

LUXURY HOTELS INTERNATIONAL OF CANADA, ULC p 30
See LUXURY HOTELS INTERNATIONAL OF CANADA ULC

LUXURY HOTELS INTERNATIONAL OF CANADA, ULC p 399
102 MAIN ST UNIT 16, FREDERICTON, NB, E3A 9N6
SIC 7389

LUXURY HOTELS INTERNATIONAL OF CANADA, ULC p 407
See LUXURY HOTELS INTERNATIONAL OF CANADA ULC

LUXURY HOTELS INTERNATIONAL OF CANADA, ULC p 685
See LUXURY HOTELS INTERNATIONAL OF CANADA ULC

LUXURY HOTELS INTERNATIONAL OF CANADA, ULC p 858
See LUXURY HOTELS INTERNATIONAL OF CANADA ULC

LUXURY HOTELS INTERNATIONAL OF CANADA, ULC p 946
See LUXURY HOTELS INTERNATIONAL OF CANADA ULC

LUXURY HOTELS INTERNATIONAL OF CANADA, ULC p 1092
See LUXURY HOTELS INTERNATIONAL OF CANADA ULC

LUXURY RETREATS INTERNATIONAL ULC p 1224
5530 RUE SAINT-PATRICK BUREAU 2210, MONTREAL, QC, H4E 1A8
(514) 400-5109 SIC 8741

LUZZI'S VALU-MART p 618
See 2037247 ONTARIO LIMITED

LVI DIGITAL GROUP & LVI TECHNOLOGY GROUP p 341
See LANG'S VENTURES INC

LVM / MARITIME TESTING LIMITED p 447

97 TROOP AVE, DARTMOUTH, NS, B3B
2A7

(902) 468-6486   *SIC* 8711

LVM INC   *p* 1237
1200 BOUL SAINT-MARTIN O BUREAU
300, MONTREAL, QC, H7S 2E4

(514) 281-1010   *SIC* 8742

LVN   *p* 306
See *LEVON RESOURCES LTD*

LX CONSTRUCTION INC   *p* 349
68132 HIGHWAY 212, DUGALD, MB, R0E
0K0

(204) 898-8453   *SIC* 1521

LXR & CO   *p* 1181
See *LXRANDCO, INC*

LXRANDCO INC   *p* 1181
40 JEAN-TALON ST W 17TH FL SUITE 34,
MONTREAL, QC, H2R 2W5

(514) 623-2052   *SIC* 5963

LXRANDCO, INC   *p* 1181
7399 BOUL SAINT-LAURENT, MONTREAL,
QC, H2R 1W7

(514) 654-9993   *SIC* 5632

LYCEE CLAUDEL   *p* 818
1635 RIVERSIDE DR, OTTAWA, ON, K1G
0E5

(613) 733-8522   *SIC* 8211

LYDALE CONSTRUCTION (1983) CO. LTD *p*
1428
859 58TH ST E, SASKATOON, SK, S7K 6X5

(306) 934-6116   *SIC* 1521

LYKKI.COM   *p* 200
See *COST LESS EXPRESS LTD*

LYMAN CONTAINER LINE   *p* 523
See *LCL CANADA LIMITED*

LYNCH BUS LINES LTD   *p* 193
4687 BYRNE RD, BURNABY, BC, V5J 3H6

(604) 439-0842   *SIC* 4151

LYNCH DYNAMICS INC   *p* 724
1799 ARGENTIA RD, MISSISSAUGA, ON,
L5N 3A2

(905) 363-2400   *SIC* 3812

LYNCH FLUID CONTROLS INC   *p* 724
1799 ARGENTIA RD, MISSISSAUGA, ON,
L5N 3A2

(905) 363-2400   *SIC* 3492

LYNCH FOOD   *p* 775
See *LYNCH, W. T. FOODS LIMITED*

LYNCH, W. T. FOODS LIMITED   *p* 775
72 RAILSIDE RD, NORTH YORK, ON, M3A
1A3

(416) 449-5464   *SIC* 2099

LYNDEN CANADA CO   *p* 684
8300 PARKHILL DR UNIT 3, MILTON, ON,
L9T 5V7

(905) 636-2970   *SIC* 4731

LYNDEN TRANSPORT   *p* 1
See *CANADIAN LYNDEN TRANSPORT
LTD*

LYNN VALLEY CARE CENTRE   *p* 239
See *NORTH SHORE PRIVATE HOSPITAL
(1985) LTD*

LYNSOS INC   *p* 898
1463 LASALLE BLVD, SUDBURY, ON, P3A
1Z8

(705) 560-2500   *SIC* 5812

LYNUM MANAGEMENT RESOURCES INC *p*
277
8456 129A ST UNIT 17, SURREY, BC, V3W
1A2

(604) 594-0100   *SIC* 5049

LYNUM PROGRESSIVE INDUSTRIES *p* 277
See *LYNUM MANAGEMENT RESOURCES
INC*

LYNXMOTION   *p* 1153
See *ROBOTSHOP INC*

LYONS AUTO BODY LIMITED   *p* 711
1020 BURNHAMTHORPE RD W, MISSIS-
SAUGA, ON, L5C 2S4

(905) 277-1456   *SIC* 7532

**LYONS GARDEN CENTRE & LANDSCAP-
ING**   *p*
218
See *LYONS LANDSCAPING LTD*

LYONS LANDSCAPING LTD   *p* 218
1271 SALISH RD, KAMLOOPS, BC, V2H
1P6

(250) 374-6965   *SIC* 5261

LYONS LTD   *p* 863
500 WELLINGTON ST W, SAULT STE.
MARIE, ON, P6C 3T5

(705) 759-1555   *SIC* 5211

LYONS TIM-BR MART   *p* 863
See *LYONS LTD*

LYY LIFE INC   *p* 906
147 NER ISRAEL DR, THORNHILL, ON,
L4J 8Z7

(647) 673-8888   *SIC* 8322

M

M & A TILE COMPANY LIMITED   *p* 784
1155 PETROLIA RD, NORTH YORK, ON,
M3J 2X7

(416) 667-8171   *SIC* 1752

M & D DRAFTING LTD   *p* 110
3604 76 AVE NW, EDMONTON, AB, T6B
2N8

(780) 465-1520   *SIC* 7389

M & G STEEL LTD   *p* 804
2285 SPEERS RD, OAKVILLE, ON, L6L 2X9

(905) 469-6442   *SIC* 3441

M & L PHARMACY LTD   *p* 410
1198 ONONDAGA ST SUITE 16, ORO-
MOCTO, NB, E2V 1B8

(506) 357-8435   *SIC* 5912

M & L SUPPLY FIRE & SAFETY   *p* 622
See *3635112 CANADA INC*

M & M FARMS LTD   *p* 644
331 TALBOT ST W, LEAMINGTON, ON,
N8H 4H3

(519) 326-2287   *SIC* 0191

M & M MARKETS LTD   *p* 999
58A VICTORIA ST N, TWEED, ON, K0K 3J0

(613) 478-2014   *SIC* 5411

M & M MEAT SHOPS LTD   *p* 724
2240 ARGENTIA RD SUITE 100, MISSIS-
SAUGA, ON, L5N 2K7

(905) 465-6325   *SIC* 5411

M & M MOTOR PRODUCTS LTD   *p* 1420
1400 TORONTO ST, REGINA, SK, S4R 8S8

(306) 757-2001   *SIC* 5172

M & M OFFSHORE LTD   *p* 428
456 LOGY BAY RD, ST. JOHN'S, NL, A1A
5C6

(709) 726-9112   *SIC* 3443

M & M RESOURCES INC   *p* 213
4901 44TH AVE, FORT NELSON, BC, V0C
1R0

(250) 774-4862   *SIC* 1629

M & N CONSTRUCTION LTD   *p* 81
4511 VICTORIA AVE, CORONATION, AB,
T0C 1C0

(403) 578-2016   *SIC* 1623

**M & N CROWELL PHARMACY SERVICES
LTD**   *p* 438
303 MAIN ST SUITE 143, ANTIGONISH,
NS, B2G 2C3

(902) 863-6522   *SIC* 5912

M & P DIRECTED ELECTRONICS INC   *p*
1089
188 CH SAINT-FRANCOIS-XAVIER, DEL-
SON, QC, J5B 1X9

(450) 635-7777   *SIC* 5063

M & P TOOL PRODUCTS INC   *p* 513
43 REGAN RD, BRAMPTON, ON, L7A 1B2

(905) 840-5550   *SIC* 2542

M & T INSTA-PRINT LIMITED   *p* 635
907 FREDERICK ST SUITE 4, KITCH-
ENER, ON, N2B 2B9

(519) 571-0101   *SIC* 2752

M & T INSTA-PRINT LIMITED   *p* 661
318 NEPTUNE CRES SUITE 1, LONDON,
ON, N6M 1A1

(519) 455-6667   *SIC* 2752

M & T INSTAPRINT   *p* 1010
See *M&T PRINTING GROUP LIMITED*

M & V ENTERPRISES LTD   *p* 107
5515 101 AVE NW, EDMONTON, AB, T6A

3Z7

(780) 465-0771   *SIC* 5812

M & Z INDUSTRIAL SUPPLY LTD   *p* 122
7823 25 ST NW, EDMONTON, AB, T6P 1N4

(780) 440-2737   *SIC* 5085

M AND J WOODCRAFTS LTD   *p* 209
7338 PROGRESS WAY UNIT 1, DELTA, BC,
V4G 1L4

(604) 946-4767   *SIC* 2431

M B CHURCH OF MANITOBA   *p* 388
See *MENNONITE BRETHREN CHURCH
OF MANITOBA, THE*

M BOUTIQUE   *p* 989
See *MENDOCINO CLOTHING COMPANY
LTD*

M C M R PERSONNEL   *p* 1163
See *MULTI-CAISSES ET MULTI-
RESOURCES INC*

M CONSOLIDATION LINES LTD   *p* 688
6300 NORTHWEST DR UNIT 2, MISSIS-
SAUGA, ON, L4V 1J7

(905) 362-0249   *SIC* 4731

M I C A   *p* 935
229 YONGE ST SUITE 400, TORONTO,
ON, M5B 1N9

SIC 8748

M I GROUP   *p* 697
See *MI GROUP LTD, THE*

M J B ENTERPRISES LTD   *p* 145
601 17 ST SW, MEDICINE HAT, AB, T1A
4X6

(403) 527-3600   *SIC* 1541

M J FASHIONS LTD   *p* 261
8571 BRIDGEPORT RD, RICHMOND, BC,
V6X 1R7

(604) 273-9233   *SIC* 5137

M J SYSTEMS   *p* 72
See *EXPLORATION DATA SYSTEMS INC*

M K IMPEX CANADA   *p* 724
6382 LISGAR DR, MISSISSAUGA, ON, L5N
6X1

(416) 509-4462   *SIC* 5172

M LINES   *p* 688
See *M CONSOLIDATION LINES LTD*

M PRIVATE RESIDENCES INC   *p* 65
322 11 AVE SW SUITE 205, CALGARY, AB,
T2R 0C5

(403) 264-0993   *SIC* 6799

M PUTZER HORNSBY NURSERIES   *p* 620
See *PUTZER, M. HORNBY LIMITED*

M S M   *p* 1032
See *MAGNA POWERTRAIN INC*

M T K AUTO WEST LTD   *p* 261
10780 CAMBIE RD, RICHMOND, BC, V6X
1K8

(604) 233-0700   *SIC* 5511

M&A ENTERPRISES   *p* 1435
315 MARQUIS DR W, SASKATOON, SK,
S7R 1B6

(306) 653-2744   *SIC* 5172

M&M FOOD MARKET   *p* 724
See *M & M MEAT SHOPS LTD*

M&T PRINTING GROUP LIMITED   *p* 1010
675 DAVENPORT RD, WATERLOO, ON,
N2V 2E2

(519) 804-0017   *SIC* 7336

M'PLAST INC   *p* 1128
2530 RUE ALPHONSE-GARIEPY, LA-
CHINE, QC, H8T 3M2

(514) 633-8181   *SIC* 2673

M-CON PRODUCTS INC   *p* 541
2150 RICHARDSON SIDE RD RR 3, CARP,
ON, K0A 1L0

(613) 831-1736   *SIC* 3272

M-HEALTH SOLUTIONS INC   *p* 528
3190 HARVESTER RD SUITE 203,
BURLINGTON, ON, L7N 3T1

(289) 636-0102   *SIC* 5047

M-I DRILLING FLUIDS CANADA, INC   *p* 53
700 2 ST SW SUITE 500, CALGARY, AB,
T2P 2W1

(403) 290-5300   *SIC* 1389

M-I SWACO, DIV OF   *p* 53
See *M-I DRILLING FLUIDS CANADA, INC*

M. & A. WRIGHT CO. LIMITED   *p* 481
14700 YONGE ST SUITE 189, AURORA,
ON, L4G 7H8

(905) 727-9484   *SIC* 5014

M. & P. VARLEY ENTERPRISES LTD   *p* 119
2331 66 ST NW UNIT 200, EDMONTON,
AB, T6K 4B4

(780) 450-1800   *SIC* 5014

M. A. S. CHIBOUGAMAU INC   *p* 1077
874 3E RUE, CHIBOUGAMAU, QC, G8P
1P9

(418) 748-7674   *SIC* 5531

M. BLOCK & SONS   *p* 998
See *M. BLOCK CANADA, ULC*

M. BLOCK CANADA, ULC   *p* 998
134 BETHRIDGE RD, TORONTO, ON, M9W
1N3

(705) 252-6471   *SIC* 5023

M. D. STEELE CONSTRUCTION LTD   *p* 393
193 HENLOW BAY, WINNIPEG, MB, R3Y
1G4

(204) 488-7070   *SIC* 1542

M. E. T. UTILITIES MANAGEMENT LTD   *p*
767
2810 VICTORIA PARK AVE SUITE 105,
NORTH YORK, ON, M2J 4A9

(416) 495-9448   *SIC* 7389

M. G. FISHERIES LTD   *p* 402
7 NORMAN RD, GRAND MANAN, NB, E5G
2G5

(506) 662-3696   *SIC* 5146

**M. KOPERNIK (NICOLAUS COPERNICUS)
FOUNDATION**   *p* 288
3150 ROSEMONT DR, VANCOUVER, BC,
V5S 2C9

(604) 438-2474   *SIC* 8361

M. LEMIEUX INC   *p* 1276
5005 RUE HUGUES-RANDIN, QUEBEC,
QC, G2C 0G5

(418) 688-5050   *SIC* 5085

M. O. S. ENTERPRISES LIMITED   *p* 858
1475 COUNTY ROAD 34, RUTHVEN, ON,
N0P 2G0

(519) 326-9067   *SIC* 0182

M. SULLIVAN & SON LIMITED   *p* 479
236 MADAWASKA BLVD SUITE 100, ARN-
PRIOR, ON, K7S 0A3

(613) 623-6584   *SIC* 1541

M. V. OSPREY LTD   *p* 464
P.O. BOX 188 STN MAIN, NORTH SYDNEY,
NS, B2A 3M3

(902) 794-1600   *SIC* 0913

**M. VAN NOORT & SONS BULB COMPANY
LIMITED**   *p* 226
22264 NO 10 HWY, LANGLEY, BC, V2Y 2K6

(604) 888-6555   *SIC* 5193

M. VERNESCU DRUGS LTD   *p* 566
101 OSLER DR SUITE 102, DUNDAS, ON,
L9H 4H4

(905) 628-2251   *SIC* 5912

M.A. STEWART & SONS LTD   *p* 277
12900 87 AVE, SURREY, BC, V3W 3H9

(604) 594-8431   *SIC* 5085

M.A.P WATER AND SEWER SERVICES LTD
p 96
14303 116 AVE NW, EDMONTON, AB, T5M
4G2

(780) 453-6996   *SIC* 1623

**M.A.R.C. MANAGEMENT & ENTERTAIN-
MENT INC**   *p*
755
1135 STELLAR DR, NEWMARKET, ON,
L3Y 7B8

SIC 7374

**M.B. PRODUCT RESEARCH DISTRIBUT-
ING INC**   *p*
555
270 PENNSYLVANIA AVE UNIT 11-13,
CONCORD, ON, L4K 3Z7

(905) 660-1421   *SIC* 5146

M.B.R.P. INC   *p* 620
315 OLD FERGUSON RD SUITE 1,
HUNTSVILLE, ON, P1H 2J2

(705) 788-2845   *SIC* 3714

M.C. FORET INC p 1124
5946 BOUL DU CURE-LABELLE RR 3, LA-BELLE, QC, J0T 1H0
(819) 686-1464   *SIC* 0851

M.C. JANITORIAL SYSTEMS p 903
See 1200839 ONTARIO LIMITED

M.C.P. MCCAUGHEY CONSUMER PRODUCTS MANAGEMENT INC p 528
3365 HARVESTER RD SUITE 204, BURLINGTON, ON, L7N 3N2
(905) 319-2246   *SIC* 5122

M.C.T. FORESTIER p 1243
See M.C.T. PNEUS INC

M.C.T. PNEUS INC p 1243
1293 RUE DU PARC-INDUSTRIEL, NOR-MANDIN, QC, G8M 4C6
(418) 274-3765   *SIC* 5531

M.D. AMBULANCE CARE LTD p 1425
430 MELVILLE ST, SASKATOON, SK, S7J 4M2
(306) 975-8808   *SIC* 4119

M.D. CHARLTON CO. LTD p 267
2200 KEATING CROSS RD SUITE E, SAANICHTON, BC, V8M 2A6
(250) 652-5266   *SIC* 5049

M.D. TRANSPORT CO. LTD p 177
1683 MT LEHMAN RD, ABBOTSFORD, BC, V2T 6H6
(604) 850-1818   *SIC* 4213

M.E POWELL INSURANCE BROKERS LTD p 801
349 DAVIS RD, OAKVILLE, ON, L6J 2X2
(905) 844-3629   *SIC* 6411

M.E. LAZERTE SCHOOL p 84
See EDMONTON SCHOOL DISTRICT NO. 7

M.E.I. ASSAINISSEMENT p 1388
See MATERIAUX ECONOMIQUES INC

M.G. CHEMICALS LTD p 282
9347 193 ST, SURREY, BC, V4N 4E7
(604) 888-3084   *SIC* 5065

M.G.B. ELECTRIQUE p 1350
See GROUPE M.G.B. INC

M.G.M. FORD LINCOLN SALES LTD p 157
3010 50 AVE, RED DEER, AB, T4R 1M5
(403) 346-6621   *SIC* 5511

M.I. VIAU & FILS LIMITEE p 1152
14311   RTE   SIR-WILFRID-LAURIER, MIRABEL, QC, J7J 2G4
(450) 436-8221   *SIC* 5074

M.J. ROOFING & SUPPLY LTD p 372
909 JARVIS AVE, WINNIPEG, MB, R2X 0A1
(204) 586-8411   *SIC* 1761

M.J.M. FURNITURE CENTRE LTD p 277
13570 77 AVE, SURREY, BC, V3W 6Y3
(604) 596-9901   *SIC* 5712

M.M. ROBINSON HIGH SCHOOL p 529
See HALTON DISTRICT SCHOOL BOARD

M.M.H. PRESTIGE HOMES INC p 418
14 INDUSTRIAL DR, SUSSEX, NB, E4E 2R8
(506) 433-9130   *SIC* 2452

M.O.S.A.I.C p 288
See M.O.S.A.I.C. MULTI-LINGUAL ORIENTATION SERVICE ASSOCIATION FOR IMMIGRANT COMMUNITIES

M.O.S.A.I.C. MULTI-LINGUAL ORIENTATION SERVICE ASSOCIATION FOR IMMIGRANT COMMUNITIES p 287
2555 COMMERCIAL DR SUITE 312, VANCOUVER, BC, V5N 4C1
(604) 708-3905   *SIC* 8322

M.O.S.A.I.C. MULTI-LINGUAL ORIENTATION SERVICE ASSOCIATION FOR IMMIGRANT COMMUNITIES p 288
5575 BOUNDARY RD, VANCOUVER, BC, V5R 2P9
(604) 254-9626   *SIC* 8399

M.P.I.Q.C. INC p 562
550 CAMPBELL ST, CORNWALL, ON, K6H 6T7

(613) 936-2000   *SIC* 3679

M.P.S. WELDING INC p 81
GD, COLD LAKE, AB, T9M 1P3
(780) 639-3911   *SIC* 1799

M.R. BAULDIC ENTERPRISES INC p 204
11628 8 ST, DAWSON CREEK, BC, V1G 4R7
(250) 782-9552   *SIC* 5531

M.T.E. CONTROLS CORPORATION p 807
5135 HENNIN DR, OLDCASTLE, ON, N0R 1L0
(519) 737-7555   *SIC* 5084

M2 FINANCIAL SOLUTIONS p 812
See M2 SOLUTIONS INC

M2 SOLUTIONS INC p 812
628 BEECHWOOD ST, OSHAWA, ON, L1G 2R9
(905) 436-1784   *SIC* 8721

M2S ELECTRONIQUE LTEE p 1276
2855 RUE DE CELLES, QUEBEC, QC, G2C 1K7
(418) 842-1717   *SIC* 3669

M30 RETAIL SERVICES INC p 67
332 20 ST W UNIT 415, CALGARY, AB, T2T 6S1
(403) 313-9105   *SIC* 8742

M5 MARKETING COMMUNICATIONS INC p 430
42 O'LEARY AVE, ST. JOHN'S, NL, A1B 2C7
(709) 753-5559   *SIC* 7311

MA FEENER SALES LTD p 416
885 FAIRVILLE BLVD, SAINT JOHN, NB, E2M 5T9
(506) 635-1711   *SIC* 5531

MA MAISON p 1118
See DANESCO INC

MA MAWI-WI-CHI-ITATA CENTRE INC p 371
445 KING ST, WINNIPEG, MB, R2W 2C5
(204) 925-0300   *SIC* 8399

MA MAWI-WI-CHI-ITATA CENTRE INC p 375
443 SPENCE ST, WINNIPEG, MB, R3B 2R8
(204) 925-0348   *SIC* 8699

MA PMGI BROKERAGE INC p 724
6505 MISSISSAUGA RD UNIT A, MISSISSAUGA, ON, L5N 1A6
(905) 542-9100   *SIC* 6163

MAAX BATH INC p 1126
160 BOUL SAINT-JOSEPH, LACHINE, QC, H8S 2L3
(514) 844-4155   *SIC* 3088

MAB PROFIL INC p 1276
2800 RUE JEAN-PERRIN BUREAU 200, QUEBEC, QC, G2C 1T3
(418) 842-4100   *SIC* 5021

MABEL'S LABELS INC p 613
150 CHATHAM ST UNIT 1, HAMILTON, ON, L8P 2B6
(905) 667-0306   *SIC* 2679

MABOU MINING INC p 544
3493 ERRINGTON AVE, CHELMSFORD, ON, P0M 1L0
(705) 855-0796   *SIC* 1629

MAC CHAIN COMPANY LIMITED p 282
9445 193A ST, SURREY, BC, V4N 4N5
(604) 888-1229   *SIC* 5411

MAC COSMETICS p 874
See ESTEE LAUDER COSMETICS LTD

MAC INDUSTRIES LTD p 282
9445 193A ST, SURREY, BC, V4N 4N5
(604) 513-4536   *SIC* 5051

MAC MOR OF CANADA LTD p 791
21 BENTON RD, NORTH YORK, ON, M6M 3G2
(416) 596-8237   *SIC* 2329

MAC'S CONVENIENCE p 563
See CORNWALL IRVING 24 & MAINWAY CENTRE

MAC'S CONVENIENCE STORES INC p 914
305 MILNER AVE SUITE 400, TORONTO, ON, M1B 0A5
(416) 291-4441   *SIC* 6712

MAC'S FOODS LTD p 414
5 WELLESLEY AVE, SAINT JOHN, NB, E2K

2V1
(506) 642-2424   *SIC* 5812

MAC'S II AGENCIES LTD p 201
1851 BRIGANTINE DR UNIT 100, COQUITLAM, BC, V3K 7B4
(604) 540-6646   *SIC* 5063

MAC'S OYSTERS LTD p 212
7162 ISLAND HWY S, FANNY BAY, BC, V0R 1W0
(250) 335-2129   *SIC* 5411

MAC-WELD MACHINING AND MANUFACTURING p 858
See MAC-WELD MACHINING LTD

MAC-WELD MACHINING LTD p 858
1324 LOUGAR AVE, SARNIA, ON, N7S 5N7
(519) 332-1388   *SIC* 3599

MACADAMIAN TECHNOLOGIES INC p 1105
179 PROM DU PORTAGE UNITE 4, GATINEAU, QC, J8X 2K5
(819) 772-0300   *SIC* 7371

MACADEN p 1099
See HOLDING SOPREMA CANADA INC

MACARTNEY FARMS p 594
See 1248671 ONTARIO INC

MACAULAY, SCOTT INVESTMENTS LIMITED p 439
368 SHORE RD, BADDECK, NS, B0E 1B0
(902) 295-3500   *SIC* 6719

MACCARTHY MOTORS (TERRACE) LTD p 283
5004 16 HWY W, TERRACE, BC, V8G 5S5
(250) 635-4941   *SIC* 5511

MACCHIA ENTERPRISES LTD p 389
43 NEWBURY CRES, WINNIPEG, MB, R3P 0V6
(204) 255-7181   *SIC* 7231

MACCO p 1365
See MACCO ORGANIQUES INC

MACCO ORGANIQUES INC p 1365
100 RUE MCARTHUR, SALABERRY-DE-VALLEYFIELD, QC, J6S 4M5
(450) 371-1066   *SIC* 2899

MACCOSHAM INC p 110
7220 68 AVE NW, EDMONTON, AB, T6B 0A1
(780) 448-1910   *SIC* 4225

MACCOUL INVESTMENTS LIMITED p 442
211 DUKE ST, CHESTER, NS, B0J 1J0
(902) 275-3262   *SIC* 6282

MACDEN HOLDINGS LTD p 849
HWY 105, RED LAKE, ON, P0V 2M0
(807) 727-2855   *SIC* 5411

MACDON INDUSTRIES LTD p 386
680 MORAY ST, WINNIPEG, MB, R3J 3S3
(204) 885-5590   *SIC* 3523

MACDONALD BUICK GMC CADILLAC LTD p 408
111 BAIG BLVD, MONCTON, NB, E1E 1C9
(506) 853-6202   *SIC* 5511

MACDONALD CHEVROLET p 592
See MACDONALD, JIM MOTORS LTD

MACDONALD CHISHOLM INC p 471
396 MAIN ST SUITE 100, YARMOUTH, NS, B5A 1E9
(902) 742-3531   *SIC* 6411

MACDONALD CHISHOLM INCORPORATED p 459
6 MASTERS AVE, KENTVILLE, NS, B4N 2N6
(902) 678-6277   *SIC* 6411

MACDONALD CHISHOLM TRASK INSURANCE p 471
See MACDONALD CHISHOLM INC

MACDONALD COMMECIAL REAL ESTATE SERVICES LTD p 321
1827 5TH AVE W, VANCOUVER, BC, V6J 1P5
(604) 736-5611   *SIC* 6531

MACDONALD COMMERCIAL p 321

See MACDONALD REALTY LTD

MACDONALD HIGH SCHOOL p 1355
See LESTER B. PEARSON SCHOOL BOARD

MACDONALD MAINTENANCE INC p 1335
6037 CH SAINT-FRANCOIS, SAINT-LAURENT, QC, H4S 1B6
(514) 637-6453   *SIC* 8741

MACDONALD REALTERS WESTMAR p 266
See WESTMAR REALTY LTD

MACDONALD REALTY (1974) LTD p 322
2105 38TH AVE W SUITE 208, VANCOUVER, BC, V6M 1R8
(604) 263-1911   *SIC* 6531

MACDONALD REALTY LTD p 321
1827 5TH AVE W, VANCOUVER, BC, V6J 1P5
(604) 736-5611   *SIC* 8742

MACDONALD STEEL LIMITED p 534
200 AVENUE RD, CAMBRIDGE, ON, N1R 8H5
(519) 620-0400   *SIC* 3499

MACDONALD YOUTH SERVICES p 360
See MACDONALD, SR JOHN HUGH MEMORIAL HOSTEL

MACDONALD'S RESTAURANT p 514
See BRANTMAC MANAGEMENT LIMITED

MACDONALD, D. ALEX FORD LINCOLN p 1042
See MACDONALD, D. ALEX LIMITED

MACDONALD, D. ALEX LIMITED p 1042
25 WATER ST, SUMMERSIDE, PE, C1N 1A3
(902) 436-6653   *SIC* 5511

MACDONALD, DETTWILER AND ASSOCIATES CORPORATION p 1355
21025   AUT   TRANSCANADIENNE, SAINTE-ANNE-DE-BELLEVUE, QC, H9X 3R2
(514) 457-2150   *SIC* 3663

MACDONALD, DETTWILER AND ASSOCIATES INC p 499
9445 AIRPORT RD SUITE 100, BRAMPTON, ON, L6S 4J3
(905) 790-2800   *SIC* 3769

MACDONALD, J A COMPANY p 1038
4557 WHARF RD, CARDIGAN, PE, C0A 1G0
(902) 583-2020   *SIC* 5146

MACDONALD, JIM MOTORS LTD p 592
1324 KING'S HWY, FORT FRANCES, ON, P9A 2X6
(807) 274-5321   *SIC* 5511

MACDONALD, LARRY CHEVROLET LTD p 897
28380 CENTRE RD, STRATHROY, ON, N7G 3C4
(519) 245-0410   *SIC* 5521

MACDONALD, R & G ENTERPRISES LIMITED p 464
603 REEVES ST, PORT HAWKESBURY, NS, B9A 2R8
(902) 625-1199   *SIC* 5461

MACDONALD, SR JOHN HUGH MEMORIAL HOSTEL p 360
83 CHURCHILL DR SUITE 204, THOMPSON, MB, R8N 0L6
(204) 677-7870   *SIC* 8399

MACDONALDS p 681
See MCAMM ENTERPRIZES LTD

MACDONALDS p 1415
See ALEX MARION RESTAURANTS LTD

MACDONALDS RESTAURANTS p 414
See MCPORT CITY FOOD SERVICES LIMITED

MACDONNELL FUELS LIMITED p 835
317504 HWY 6 & 10, OWEN SOUND, ON, N4K 5N6
(519) 376-1916   *SIC* 5172

MACDOUGALL STEEL ERECTORS INC p

1038
168 INDUSTRIAL DR, BORDEN-CARLETON, PE, C0B 1X0
(902) 855-2100   *SIC* 3441

MACDOUGALL, MACDOUGALL & MAC-TIER INC   *p*
1206
1010 RUE DE LA GAUCHETIERE O BU-REAU 2000, MONTREAL, QC, H3B 4J1
(514) 394-3000   *SIC* 6211

MACEACHERN, K & A HOLDINGS LTD   *p*
1040
202 BUCHANAN DR, CHARLOTTETOWN, PE, C1E 2H8
(902) 892-8586   *SIC* 5311

MACENNA BUSINESS SERVICES CORP   *p*
213
10139 101 AVE 2ND FL, FORT ST. JOHN, BC, V1J 2B4
(250) 785-8367   *SIC* 7361

MACENNA STAFFING SERVICES   *p* 213
See MACENNA BUSINESS SERVICES CORP

MACEWEN AGRICENTRE INC   *p* 680
40 CATHERINE ST W, MAXVILLE, ON, K0C 1T0
(613) 527-2175   *SIC* 5191

MACEWEN PETROLEUM INC   *p* 680
18 ADELAIDE ST, MAXVILLE, ON, K0C 1T0
(613) 527-2100   *SIC* 5172

MACFARLANE CHEVROLET LIMITED   *p*
843
4219 OIL HERITAGE RD RR 1, PETROLIA, ON, N0N 1R0
(519) 882-3804   *SIC* 5511

MACGILLIVRAY, R.C. GUEST HOME SOCIETY   *p*
467
25 XAVIER DR, SYDNEY, NS, B1S 2R9
(902) 539-6110   *SIC* 8051

MACGREGOR SLEEP PRODUCTS   *p* 417
See SPRINGWALL SLEEP PRODUCTS INC

MACGREGORS MEAT & SEAFOOD LTD   *p*
793
265 GARYRAY DR, NORTH YORK, ON, M9L 1P2
(416) 749-5951   *SIC* 2011

MACHAN CONSULTING SERVICES LTD   *p*
121
9330 27 AVE NW, EDMONTON, AB, T6N 1B2
(780) 435-5722   *SIC* 6712

MACHIBRODA, P. ENGINEERING LTD   *p*
1428
806 48TH ST E, SASKATOON, SK, S7K 3Y4
(306) 665-8444   *SIC* 8748

MACHINAGE PICHE INC   *p* 1089
414 RUE INDUSTRIELLE, DAVELUYVILLE, QC, G0Z 1C0
(819) 367-3233   *SIC* 3553

MACHINE-O-MATIC, DIV OF   *p* 754
See BEAVER MACHINE CORPORATION

MACHINERIE C. & H. INC   *p* 1306
12 RTE 122, SAINT-GUILLAUME, QC, J0C 1L0
(819) 396-2185   *SIC* 5083

MACHINERIE CH WOTTON   *p* 1306
See MACHINERIE C. & H. INC

MACHINERIE P.W. INC   *p* 1280
151 BOUL LOUIS-XIV, QUEBEC, QC, G2K 1W6
(418) 622-5155   *SIC* 3599

MACHINERIE WEBER MONTREAL HOLDING INC   *p*
1395
269 RUE ADRIEN-PATENAUDE, VAUDREUIL-DORION, QC, J7V 5V5
(450) 455-0169   *SIC* 3089

MACHINERIES B.V. LTEE   *p* 1097
5555 RUE SAINT-ROCH S, DRUMMONDVILLE, QC, J2B 6V4
(819) 474-4444   *SIC* 5084

MACHINERIES NORDTRAC LTEE   *p* 1294

1060 MONTEE SAINT-LAURENT, SAINT-BARTHELEMY, QC, J0K 1X0
(450) 885-3202   *SIC* 5083

MACHINERIES PROVINCIALES INC   *p* 1280
1160 RUE BOUVIER, QUEBEC, QC, G2K 1L9
(418) 628-8460   *SIC* 7699

MACHINERIES ST-JOVITE INC., LES   *p* 1159
1313 RUE DE SAINT-JOVITE, MONT-TREMBLANT, QC, J8E 3J9
(819) 425-3737   *SIC* 5084

MACHINERIES ST-JOVITE, LES   *p* 1159
See MACHINERIES ST-JOVITE INC., LES

MACHINES ROGER INTERNATIONAL INC   *p*
1390
1161 RUE DES MANUFACTURIERS, VAL-D'OR, QC, J9P 6Y7
(819) 825-4657   *SIC* 5082

MACHINEX   *p* 1246
See INDUSTRIES MACHINEX INC

MACINTYRE CHEVROLET CADILLAC LIMITED   *p*
467
101 DISCO ST, SYDNEY, NS, B1P 5V7
(902) 564-4491   *SIC* 5511

MACIOCIA MARIO & FILS LTEE   *p* 1123
131 RANG DES PETITS-ETANGS, LA PRESENTATION, QC, J0H 1B0
(450) 796-3354   *SIC* 5154

MACIVER DODGE JEEP   *p* 755
See MACIVER DODGE LIMITED

MACIVER DODGE LIMITED   *p* 755
17615 YONGE ST, NEWMARKET, ON, L3Y 5H6
(905) 898-1900   *SIC* 5511

MACIVER DODGE-JEEP LTD   *p* 755
17615 YONGE ST, NEWMARKET, ON, L3Y 5H6
(905) 898-1900   *SIC* 5511

MACK MACKENZIE MOTORS LIMITED   *p*
849
547 NEW ST, RENFREW, ON, K7V 1H1
(613) 432-3684   *SIC* 5511

MACK SALES & SERVICE OF DURHAM INC   *p* 474
610 FINLEY AVE UNIT 9, AJAX, ON, L1S 2E3
(905) 426-6225   *SIC* 5511

MACK SALES & SERVICE OF MANITOBA LTD   *p* 384
385 EAGLE DR, WINNIPEG, MB, R3H 0G7
(204) 772-0316   *SIC* 5511

MACK SALES & SERVICE OF NANAIMO LTD   *p* 234
2213 MCCULLOUGH RD, NANAIMO, BC, V9S 4M7
(250) 758-0185   *SIC* 5511

MACK SALES & SERVICE OF STONEY CREEK LTD   *p* 892
330 SOUTH SERVICE RD, STONEY CREEK, ON, L8E 2R4
(905) 662-4240   *SIC* 5511

MACK STE-FOY INC   *p* 1267
2550 AV WATT, QUEBEC, QC, G1P 3T4
(418) 651-9397   *SIC* 5012

MACKAGE   *p* 1178
See GROUPE APP (CANADA) INC

MACKAY & HUGHES   *p* 522
See EARTHFRESH FOODS CORP

MACKAY METERS   *p* 463
See MACKAY, J. J. CANADA LIMITED

MACKAY'S TRUCK & TRAILER CENTER LIMITED   *p* 469
124 LOWER TRURO RD, TRURO, NS, B2N 5E8
(902) 895-0511   *SIC* 5012

MACKAY'S VOLVO TRUCK CENTER   *p* 469
See MACKAY'S TRUCK & TRAILER CENTER LIMITED

MACKAY, J. J. CANADA LIMITED   *p* 463
1342 ABERCROMBIE ROAD, NEW GLASGOW, NS, B2H 5C6
(902) 752-5124   *SIC* 3824

MACKENZIE FINANCIAL   *p* 981

See MACKENZIE INVESTMENTS

MACKENZIE CONSUMERS CO-OPERATIVE ASSOCIATION   *p*
230
403 MACKENZIE BLVD SUITE 103, MACKENZIE, BC, V0J 2C0
(250) 997-3335   *SIC* 5411

MACKENZIE FINANCIAL CORPORATION   *p*
981
180 QUEEN ST W SUITE 1600, TORONTO, ON, M5V 3K1
(800) 387-0614   *SIC* 6722

MACKENZIE HEALTH   *p* 855
10 TRENCH ST, RICHMOND HILL, ON, L4C 4Z3
(905) 883-1212   *SIC* 8062

MACKENZIE HOUSING MANAGEMENT BOARD   *p* 138
9802 105 ST, LA CRETE, AB, T0H 2H0
(780) 928-3677   *SIC* 6513

MACKENZIE INC   *p* 378
447 PORTAGE AVE, WINNIPEG, MB, R3C 3B6
(204) 943-0361   *SIC* 6719

MACKENZIE INVESTMENTS   *p* 981
180 QUEEN ST W, TORONTO, ON, M5V 3K1
(416) 922-5322   *SIC* 6722

MACKENZIE MAXXUM DIVIDEND GROWTH FUND   *p* 981
See MACKENZIE FINANCIAL CORPORATION

MACKENZIE OIL LIMITED   *p* 860
1486 PLANK RD, SARNIA, ON, N7T 7H3
(519) 336-0521   *SIC* 5172

MACKENZIE PLCE   *p* 756
See REVERA LONG TERM CARE INC

MACKENZIE PLUMBING & HEATING   *p*
1416
See MACKENZIE PLUMBING & HEATING (1989) LTD

MACKENZIE PLUMBING & HEATING (1989) LTD   *p* 1416
915 FLEURY ST, REGINA, SK, S4N 4W7
(306) 522-0777   *SIC* 1731

MACKENZIE PULP MILL CORPORATION   *p*
230
1000 COQUAWALDY RD, MACKENZIE, BC, V0J 2C0
(250) 997-2431   *SIC* 5084

MACKENZIE SAWMILL LTD   *p* 270
11732 130 ST, SURREY, BC, V3R 2Y3
(604) 580-4500   *SIC* 2421

MACKIE GROUP, THE   *p* 814
See MACKIE MOVING SYSTEMS CORPORATION

MACKIE HARLEY-DAVIDSON BUELL   *p* 813
See 1268558 ONTARIO LIMITED

MACKIE MOVING SYSTEMS   *p* 447
30 GURHOLT DR, DARTMOUTH, NS, B3B 1J9
(902) 481-2041   *SIC* 4213

MACKIE MOVING SYSTEMS CORPORATION   *p*
814
933 BLOOR ST W, OSHAWA, ON, L1J 5Y7
(905) 728-2400   *SIC* 4231

MACKIE RESEACH CAPITAL CORPORATION   *p*
971
199 BAY ST SUITE 4500, TORONTO, ON, M5L 1G2
(416) 860-7600   *SIC* 6211

MACKIE TRANSPORTATION HOLDINGS INC   *p* 814
933 BLOOR ST W, OSHAWA, ON, L1J 5Y7
(905) 728-1603   *SIC* 6712

MACKIE TRANSPORTATION INC   *p* 1014
1900 BOUNDARY RD UNIT 2, WHITBY, ON, L1N 8P8
(905) 728-1000   *SIC* 4213

MACKIMMIE MATTHEWS   *p* 53
401 9 AVE SW SUITE 700, CALGARY, AB, T2P 3C5

SIC 8111

MACKINNON RESTAURANTS INC   *p* 476
137 YONGE ST W, ALLISTON, ON, L9R 1V1
(705) 434-0003   *SIC* 5812

MACKINNON TRANSPORT INC   *p* 601
405 LAIRD RD, GUELPH, ON, N1G 4P7
(519) 821-2311   *SIC* 4213

MACKINTOSH, K.J. SALES LTD   *p* 107
9603 162 AVE NW SUITE 397, EDMONTON, AB, T5Z 3T6
(780) 495-9696   *SIC* 5531

MACKOW INDUSTRIES   *p* 381
1395 WHYTE AVE, WINNIPEG, MB, R3E 1V7
(204) 774-8323   *SIC* 3499

MACLAB ENTERPRISES CORPORATION   *p*
89
10205 100 AVE NW SUITE 3400, EDMONTON, AB, T5J 4B5
(780) 420-4000   *SIC* 6513

MACLAI DRUGS LIMITED   *p* 718
5100 ERIN MILLS PKY SUITE 904, MISSISSAUGA, ON, L5M 4Z5
(905) 569-3939   *SIC* 5912

MACLAREN MCCANN INTERACTIVE   *p* 982
See MCCANN WORLDGROUP CANADA INC

MACLEAN ENGINEERING & MARKETING CO. LIMITED   *p* 835
1000 6TH ST E, OWEN SOUND, ON, N4K 1H1
(705) 445-5707   *SIC* 3532

MACLEAN HOLDINGS LTD   *p* 36
7220 FISHER ST SE, CALGARY, AB, T2H 2H8
(403) 640-7400   *SIC* 7538

MACLEAN'S SPORTS LTD   *p* 399
489 UNION ST, FREDERICTON, NB, E3A 3M9
(506) 450-6090   *SIC* 5571

MACLEAN, K. T. (KEN) LIMITED   *p* 157
2510 50 AVE, RED DEER, AB, T4R 1M3
(403) 342-2222   *SIC* 5531

MACLEOD'S FARM MACHINERY LIMITED   *p*
461
12412 HWY 2, LOWER ONSLOW, NS, B6L 5E3
(902) 662-2516   *SIC* 5083

MACLEOD-LORWAY FINANCIAL GROUP LIMITED   *p* 467
215 CHARLOTTE ST, SYDNEY, NS, B1P 1C4
(902) 539-6666   *SIC* 6411

MACLIN FORD   *p* 36
See MACLIN MOTORS LIMITED

MACLIN MOTORS LIMITED   *p* 36
135 GLENDEER CIR SE, CALGARY, AB, T2H 2S8
(403) 252-0101   *SIC* 5511

MACLURES CABS (1984) LTD   *p* 323
1275 75TH AVE W, VANCOUVER, BC, V6P 3G4
(604) 683-6666   *SIC* 4121

MACMARMON FOUNDATION   *p* 776
275 DUNCAN MILL RD, NORTH YORK, ON, M3B 3H9
(416) 443-1030   *SIC* 7032

MACMASTER CHEVROLET LTD   *p* 649
1350 DRIVER LANE, LONDON, ON, N5V 0B4
(519) 455-6200   *SIC* 5511

MACMILLAN HUTTERIAN BRETHREN   *p* 79
658 32 ST SW, CAYLEY, AB, T0L 0P0
(403) 395-2221   *SIC* 8661

MACMILLAN YARD   *p* 1002
See COMPAGNIE DES CHEMINS DE FER NATIONAUX DU CANADA

MACMILLAN, DOUG ENTERPRISES LTD   *p*
243
960 RAILWAY ST, PENTICTON, BC, V2A 8N2
(250) 492-3586   *SIC* 5531

MACMOR INDUSTRIES LTD   *p* 384

1175 SHERWIN RD, WINNIPEG, MB, R3H 0V1

(204) 786-5891   *SIC* 5072

MACNAMARA FUELS   p 755
See *MACNAMARA, SAMUEL P. ENTER-PRISES LIMITED*

MACNAMARA, SAMUEL P. ENTERPRISES LIMITED   p 755
2220 DAVIS DR, NEWMARKET, ON, L3Y 4W1

(905) 898-5678   *SIC* 5172

MACNAUGHTON HERMSEN BRITTON CLARKSON PLANNING LIMITED   p 635
540 BINGEMANS CENTRE DR SUITE 200, KITCHENER, ON, N2B 3X9

(519) 576-3650   *SIC* 8742

MACNO TELECOM INC   p 1247
12655 BOUL INDUSTRIEL, POINTE-AUX-TREMBLES, QC, H1A 4Z6

(514) 498-1555   *SIC* 4899

MACO MECANIQUE INC   p 1388
6595 BOUL JEAN-XXIII, TROIS-RIVIERES, QC, G9A 5C9

(819) 378-7070   *SIC* 1711

MACPEK INC   p 1275
2970 AV WATT, QUEBEC, QC, G1X 4P7

(418) 659-1144   *SIC* 5013

MACPHEE FORD   p 442
See *219 AUTOMOTIVE INC*

MACPHERSON, PAUL & ASSOCIATES LTD   p 342
1010 DUCHESS AVE, WEST VANCOUVER, BC, V7T 1G9

(604) 925-0609   *SIC* 3669

MACQUARIE CAPITAL MARKETS CANADA   p 964
See *MACQUARIE NORTH AMERICA LTD*

MACQUARIE CAPITAL MARKETS CANADA LTD   p 307
550 BURRARD ST SUITE 500, VANCOUVER, BC, V6C 2B5

(604) 605-3944   *SIC* 6211

MACQUARIE CAPITAL MARKETS CANADA LTD   p 964
181 BAY ST SUITE 3100, TORONTO, ON, M5J 2T3

(416) 848-3500   *SIC* 6211

MACQUARIE CAPITAL MARKETS CANADA LTD   p 964
181 BAY ST SUITE 900, TORONTO, ON, M5J 2T3

(416) 848-3500   *SIC* 6211

MACQUARIE NORTH AMERICA LTD   p 964
181 BAY ST SUITE 3100, TORONTO, ON, M5J 2T3

(416) 607-5000   *SIC* 8742

MACQUARRIES DRUGS LIMITED   p 469
920 PRINCE ST SUITE 513, TRURO, NS, B2N 1H5

(902) 896-1600   *SIC* 5912

MACQUARRIES PHARMASAVE   p 469
See *MACQUARRIES DRUGS LIMITED*

MACRI CATERING LIMITED   p 1032
71 WINGES RD, WOODBRIDGE, ON, L4L 6B5

(905) 851-8030   *SIC* 5812

MACRO ENGINEERING   p 706
See *MACRO ENGINEERING & TECHNOLOGY INC*

MACRO ENGINEERING & TECHNOLOGY INC   p 706
199 TRADERS BLVD E, MISSISSAUGA, ON, L4Z 2E5

(905) 507-9000   *SIC* 3559

MACRO ENTERPRISES INC   p 213
6807 100 AVE, FORT ST. JOHN, BC, V1J 4J2

(250) 785-0033   *SIC* 1623

MACRO INDUSTRIES INC   p 213
7904 101 AVE, FORT ST. JOHN, BC, V1J 2A3

(250) 785-0033   *SIC* 1389

MACRO PIPELINES INC   p 214
6807 100 AVE, FORT ST. JOHN, BC, V1J

4J2

(250) 785-0033   *SIC* 4619

MACSWEEN ENTERPRISES LTD   p 1040
161 MAYPOINT RD SUITE 14, CHARLOTTETOWN, PE, C1E 1X6

(902) 892-8002   *SIC* 5411

MACTAQUAC GENERATING STATION   p 404
See *NEW BRUNSWICK POWER CORPORATION*

MACTRANS   p 1027
See *MACTRANS LOGISTICS INC*

MACTRANS LOGISTICS INC   p 1027
81 ZENWAY BLVD UNIT 16, WOODBRIDGE, ON, L4H 0S5

(905) 856-6800   *SIC* 4731

MACY HOLDINGS LIMITED   p 825
435 ALBERT ST, OTTAWA, ON, K1R 7X4

(613) 238-8858   *SIC* 7011

MAD ELEVATOR INC   p 740
6635 ORDAN DR, MISSISSAUGA, ON, L5T 1K6

(416) 245-8500   *SIC* 3534

MADACY MUSIC   p 1402
See *DIVERTISSEMENT SONOMA S.E.C.*

MADALENA ENERGY INC   p 53
333 7 AVE SW, CALGARY, AB, T2P 2Z1

(403) 264-1915   *SIC* 1311

MADAME VANIER CHILDREN'S SERVICES   p 652
871 TRAFALGAR ST, LONDON, ON, N5Z 1E6

(519) 433-3101   *SIC* 8093

MADAWASKA DOORS   p 489
See *PLAINTREE SYSTEMS INC*

MADDIES NATURAL PET PRODUCTS LTD   p 209
6655 DENNETT PL, DELTA, BC, V4G 1N4

(604) 946-7977   *SIC* 5149

MADDOCKS ENGINEERED MACHINERY INC   p 609
663 WOODWARD AVE, HAMILTON, ON, L8H 6P3

(905) 549-9626   *SIC* 5085

MADDOCKS ENGINEERING LTD   p 604
84 ROYAL RD, GUELPH, ON, N1H 1G3

(519) 823-1092   *SIC* 3714

MADDOCKS INDUSTRIAL FILTER DIV   p 609
See *MADDOCKS ENGINEERED MACHINERY INC*

MADE BY MARCUS LTD   p 67
1013 17 AVE SW SUITE 121, CALGARY, AB, T2T 0A7

(403) 452-1692   *SIC* 5451

MADE IN JAPAN JAPANESE RESTAURANTS LIMITED   p 802
700 KERR ST SUITE 100, OAKVILLE, ON, L6K 3W5

(905) 337-7777   *SIC* 6794

MADE IN JAPAN TERIYAKI EXPERIENCE   p 802
See *MADE IN JAPAN JAPANESE RESTAURANTS LIMITED*

MADE-RITE MEAT PRODUCTS INC   p 229
26656 56 AVE, LANGLEY, BC, V4W 3X5

(604) 607-8844   *SIC* 2013

MADELEINE, LE   p 1073
See *C.T.M.A. TRAVERSIER LTEE*

MADERO DOORS & HARDWARE   p 1430
See *WEST FOUR GROUP OF COMPANIES INC*

MADILL, F E SECONDARY SCHOOL   p 1026
See *AVON MAITLAND DISTRICT SCHOOL BOARD*

MADISON AVENUE PUB   p 974
See *VILLAGE MANOR (TO) LTD*

MADISON COUNTY FOOD & BEVERAGE CO. LTD, THE   p 809
43 ONTARIO ST, ORILLIA, ON, L3V 0T7

(705) 326-3586   *SIC* 5149

MADISON PACIFIC PROPERTIES INC   p 292
389 6 AVE W, VANCOUVER, BC, V5Y 1L1

(604) 732-6540   *SIC* 6719

MADISON, LE   p 1345
See *CENTRE DE RECEPTION LE MADISON INC*

MADIX ENGINEERING INC   p 891
139 IBER RD, STITTSVILLE, ON, K2S 1E7

(613) 591-1474   *SIC* 3089

MADSEN DIESEL & TURBINE INC   p 426
141 GLENCOE DR, MOUNT PEARL, NL, A1N 4S7

(709) 726-6774   *SIC* 5084

MADSEN'S CUSTOM CABINETS (1983) LTD   p 94
14504 123 AVE NW, EDMONTON, AB, T5L 2Y3

(780) 454-6790   *SIC* 2431

MADYSTA CONSTRUCTIONS LTEE   p 1389
3600 BOUL L.-P.-NORMAND, TROIS-RIVIERES, QC, G9B 0G2

(819) 377-3336   *SIC* 1799

MADYSTA TELECOM   p 1389
See *MADYSTA CONSTRUCTIONS LTEE*

MADYSTA TELECOM LTEE   p 1389
3600 BOUL L.-P.-NORMAND, TROIS-RIVIERES, QC, G9B 0G2

(819) 377-3336   *SIC* 1623

MADZA CHATEAUGUAY   p 1076
See *AMI AUTO INC*

MAERSK CANADA INC   p 697
2576 MATHESON BLVD E SUITE 101, MISSISSAUGA, ON, L4W 5H1

(905) 624-5585   *SIC* 4731

MAERSK LINE   p 697
See *MAERSK CANADA INC*

MAESTRO TECHNOLOGIES INC   p 1393
1625 BOUL LIONEL-BOULET BUREAU 300, VARENNES, QC, J3X 1P7

(450) 652-6200   *SIC* 7372

MAG AEROSPACE CANADA CORP   p 565
1012 HWY 601 UNIT 10, DRYDEN, ON, P8N 0A2

(807) 937-5544   *SIC* 0851

MAG CANADA   p 565
See *MAG AEROSPACE CANADA CORP*

MAGAL MANUFACTURING LTD   p 106
14940 121A AVE NW, EDMONTON, AB, T5V 1A3

(780) 452-1250   *SIC* 1541

MAGASIN   p 1382
See *CANADIAN TIRE*

MAGASIN CO-OP DE BONAVENTURE   p 1063
168 AV DE GRAND-PRE, BONAVENTURE, QC, G0C 1E0

(418) 534-2020   *SIC* 5411

MAGASIN CO-OP DE MONTMAGNY   p 1160
70 BOUL TACHE O, MONTMAGNY, QC, G5V 3A4

(418) 248-1230   *SIC* 5411

MAGASIN CO-OP DE PLESSISVILLE   p 1246
1971 RUE BILODEAU, PLESSISVILLE, QC, G6L 3J1

(819) 362-6357   *SIC* 5411

MAGASIN CO-OP DE STE-PERPETUE, CTE L'ISLET   p 1361
358 RUE PRINCIPALE S, SAINTE-PERPETUE-DE-L'ISLET, QC, G0R 3Z0

(418) 359-2221   *SIC* 5411

MAGASIN COOP DE MARIA IGA   p 1149
524 BOUL PERRON, MARIA, QC, G0C 1Y0

(418) 759-3440   *SIC* 5411

MAGASIN COOP DE RIVIERE-DU-LOUP   p 1286
298 BOUL ARMAND-THERIAULT BUREAU 60, RIVIERE-DU-LOUP, QC, G5R 4C2

(418) 862-3590   *SIC* 5411

MAGASIN COOP DE ST-ANSELME   p 1292
70 RUE PRINCIPALE, SAINT-ANSELME, QC, G0R 2N0

(418) 885-4461   *SIC* 5411

MAGASIN COOP LA PAIX   p 1315
321 RTE DE L'EGLISE, SAINT-JEAN-PORT-JOLI, QC, G0R 3G0

(418) 598-3385   *SIC* 5411

MAGASIN COOP ST-GEDEON   p 1304
105 BOUL CANAM S, SAINT-GEDEON-DE-BEAUCE, QC, G0M 1T0

(418) 582-3977   *SIC* 5411

MAGASIN DE MUSIQUE STEVE INC   p 1192
51 RUE SAINT-ANTOINE O, MONTREAL, QC, H2Z 1G9

(514) 878-2216   *SIC* 5099

MAGASIN EN LIGNE DIRTNROAD.COM, LE   p 1147
See *GREGOIRE SPORT INC*

MAGASIN FARMAJEM INC   p 1120
405 GRAND BOULEVARD, L'ILE-PERROT, QC, J7V 4X3

(514) 453-2896   *SIC* 5912

MAGASIN GENERAL.CA, LE   p 1301
See *CABANE A SUCRE CONSTANTIN (1992) INC*

MAGASIN I G A   p 399
See *SUPER MARCHE DONAT THERIAULT LIMITEE*

MAGASIN JEAN DUMAS INC   p 1354
50 BOUL NORBERT-MORIN, SAINTE-AGATHE-DES-MONTS, QC, J8C 2V6

(819) 326-8900   *SIC* 5531

MAGASIN LATULIPPE INC   p 1264
637 RUE SAINT-VALLIER O, QUEBEC, QC, G1N 1C6

(418) 529-0024   *SIC* 5311

MAGASIN LAURA (P.V.) INC   p 1104
1076 BOUL MALONEY O, GATINEAU, QC, J8T 3R6

(819) 561-8071   *SIC* 5651

MAGASIN LAURA (P.V.) INC   p 1234
3000 BOUL LE CORBUSIER, MONTREAL, QC, H7L 3W2

(450) 973-6090   *SIC* 5621

MAGASIN MARC-ANDRE ST-JACQUES INC   p 1385
6 RUE FUSEY, TROIS-RIVIERES, QC, G8T 2T1

(819) 376-6866   *SIC* 5531

MAGASIN MYRLANIE INC   p 1226
9050 BOUL DE L'ACADIE, MONTREAL, QC, H4N 2S5

(514) 388-6464   *SIC* 5531

MAGASIN POULIN INC   p 1320
700 BOUL MONSEIGNEUR-DUBOIS, SAINT-JEROME, QC, J7Y 4Y9

(450) 438-3506   *SIC* 5014

MAGASIN PROVIGO   p 1235
See *ALIMENTATION R DENIS INC*

MAGASIN RENE VEILLEUX INC   p 544
3595 144 HWY, CHELMSFORD, ON, P0M 1L0

(705) 855-9011   *SIC* 5014

MAGASIN ST-JEAN, ALAIN INC   p 1099
715 BOUL SAINT-JOSEPH BUREAU 158, DRUMMONDVILLE, QC, J2C 7V2

(819) 478-1471   *SIC* 5531

MAGASIN, LE   p 1353
See *GROUPE HARNOIS INC, LE*

MAGASINS C.P.C. INC, LES   p 1375
4500 BOUL BOURQUE, SHERBROOKE, QC, J1N 1S2

(819) 348-0620   *SIC* 5311

MAGASINS D'ESCOMPTE ALMICO INC, LES   p 1229
6624 AV SOMERLED, MONTREAL, QC, H4V 1T2

(514) 487-6530   *SIC* 5912

MAGASINS HART INC   p 1231
900 PLACE PAUL-KANE, MONTREAL, QC, H7C 2T2

(450) 661-4155   *SIC* 5311

MAGASINS J.L. TAYLOR INC, LES   p 1322
525 AV NOTRE-DAME BUREAU 672, SAINT-LAMBERT, QC, J4P 2K6

(450) 672-9722   *SIC* 5651

MAGASINS J.L. TAYLOR INC, LES   p 1322
556 AV VICTORIA, SAINT-LAMBERT, QC, J4P 2J5

(450) 672-9722   *SIC* 5651

MAGASINS KORVETTE LTEE, LES p 1386
2325 BOUL DES RECOLLETS, TROIS-RIVIERES, QC, G8Z 3X6
(819) 374-4625   SIC 5311

MAGASINS LECOMPTE INC p 1398
119 RUE NOTRE-DAME E, VICTORIAVILLE, QC, G6P 3Z8
(819) 758-2626   SIC 5399

MAGASINS MAXI p 1075
1601 BOUL DE PERIGNY, CHAMBLY, QC, J3L 1W9
(450) 447-7500   SIC 5411

MAGASINS TIGRE GEANT, LES p 818
See GIANT TIGER STORES LIMITED

MAGASINS TREVI INC p 1152
12775 RUE BRAULT, MIRABEL, QC, J7J 0C4
(450) 973-1249   SIC 5999

MAGAUBAINES p 1326
See MICHAEL ROSSY LTEE

MAGCHEM INC p 1066
1271 RUE AMPERE BUREAU 101, BOUCHERVILLE, QC, J4B 5Z5
(450) 641-8500   SIC 5169

MAGEE SECONDARY SCHOOL p 322
See BOARD OF EDUCATION OF SCHOOL DISTRICT NO. 39 (VANCOUVER), THE

MAGELLAN AEROSPACE CORPORATION p 686
3160 DERRY RD E, MISSISSAUGA, ON, L4T 1A9
(905) 677-1889   SIC 6712

MAGELLAN AEROSPACE LIMITED p 384
660 BERRY ST, WINNIPEG, MB, R3H 0S5
(204) 775-8331   SIC 3728

MAGELLAN AEROSPACE LIMITED p 607
634 MAGNESIUM RD, HALEY STATION, ON, K0J 1Y0
(613) 432-8841   SIC 3365

MAGELLAN AEROSPACE LIMITED p 686
3160 DERRY RD E, MISSISSAUGA, ON, L4T 1A9
(905) 677-1889   SIC 3728

MAGELLAN AEROSPACE, WINNIPEG p 383
See BRISTOL AEROSPACE LIMITED

MAGELLAN AEROSPACE, WINNIPEG, A DIV OF p 384
See MAGELLAN AEROSPACE LIMITED

MAGELLAN VACATION INC p 387
730 TAYLOR AVE, WINNIPEG, MB, R3M 2K8
(204) 992-5215   SIC 4724

MAGENTA STUDIO PHOTO INC p 1211
300 RUE DE LA MONTAGNE, MONTREAL, QC, H3C 2B1
(514) 935-2225   SIC 7335

MAGEST INC p 895
25 WRIGHT BLVD, STRATFORD, ON, N4Z 1H3
(519) 272-1001   SIC 8711

MAGI-PRIX INC p 1083
3194 AV DES ARISTOCRATES, COTE SAINT-LUC, QC, H7E 5H8
(450) 963-0410   SIC 5331

MAGIC MAINTENANCE INC p 555
25 EDILCAN DR UNIT 3, CONCORD, ON, L4K 3S4
SIC 7349

MAGIC NORTH AMERICA INC p 678
110 TRAVAIL RD, MARKHAM, ON, L3S 3J1
(905) 471-7780   SIC 5084

MAGIC REALTY INC p 846
805 CHRISTINA ST N, POINT EDWARD, ON, N7V 1X6
SIC 6531

MAGIC REALTY INC p 860
380 LONDON RD, SARNIA, ON, N7T 4W7
(519) 542-4005   SIC 6531

MAGIC TECHNOLOGY p 1166
6635 39E AV, MONTREAL, QC, H1T 2W9
(438) 388-6512   SIC 7378

MAGIC WHITE INC p 872
80 CROCKFORD BLVD, SCARBOROUGH, ON, M1R 3C3
(416) 751-2802   SIC 5169

MAGIC WINDOW p 1030
See CANADIAN THERMO WINDOWS INC

MAGIC WOK p 1040
See MACSWEEN ENTERPRISES LTD

MAGICUTS p 427
See WLB SERVICES LIMITED

MAGIL CONSTRUCTION ONTARIO INC p 649
1665 OXFORD ST E, LONDON, ON, N5V 2Z5
(519) 451-5270   SIC 1542

MAGIL CONSTRUCTION ONTARIO INC p 697
5285 SOLAR DR UNIT 102, MISSISSAUGA, ON, L4W 5B8
(905) 890-9193   SIC 1542

MAGIL LAURENTIENNE GESTION IMMOBILIERE INC p 1229
800 RUE DU SQUARE-VICTORIA BUREAU 4120, MONTREAL, QC, H4Z 1A1
(514) 875-6010   SIC 6512

MAGIL LAURENTIENNE GESTION IMMOBILIERE/TERRAINS ST-JACQUES p 1229
See MAGIL LAURENTIENNE GESTION IMMOBILIERE INC

MAGINDUSTRIES CORP p 767
235 YORKLAND BLVD UNIT 409, NORTH YORK, ON, M2J 4Y8
(416) 491-6088   SIC 3356

MAGLIO BUILDING CENTRE p 235
See LOUIS MAGLIO ENTERPRISES LTD

MAGLIO BUILDING CENTRE LTD p 235
29 GOVERNMENT RD, NELSON, BC, V1L 4L9
(250) 352-6661   SIC 5211

MAGMIC INC p 821
126 YORK ST SUITE 400, OTTAWA, ON, K1N 5T5
(613) 241-3571   SIC 7371

MAGMIC X p 821
See MAGMIC INC

MAGNA CLOSURES INC p 754
521 NEWPARK BLVD, NEWMARKET, ON, L3X 2S2
(905) 898-2665   SIC 5013

MAGNA CLOSURES INC p 838
11 CENTENNIAL DR SUITE 1, PENETANGUISHENE, ON, L9M 1G8
(705) 549-7406   SIC 5013

MAGNA EXTERIORS INC p 555
50 CASMIR CRT, CONCORD, ON, L4K 4J5
(905) 669-2888   SIC 3714

MAGNA INSURANCE CORP p 74
5 RICHARD WAY SW UNIT 104, CALGARY, AB, T3E 7M8
(403) 930-0466   SIC 6411

MAGNA INSURANCE GROUP p 74
See MAGNA INSURANCE CORP

MAGNA INTERNATIONAL INC p 481
337 MAGNA DR, AURORA, ON, L4G 7K1
(905) 726-2462   SIC 3714

MAGNA INTERNATIONAL INC p 555
90 SNIDERCROFT RD, CONCORD, ON, L4K 2K1
(905) 738-3700   SIC 3714

MAGNA INTERNATIONAL INC p 606
65 INDEPENDENCE PL, GUELPH, ON, N1K 1H8
(519) 763-6042   SIC 3714

MAGNA INTERNATIONAL INC p 889
1 COSMA CRT, ST THOMAS, ON, N5P 4J5
(519) 633-8400   SIC 3714

MAGNA MECHANICAL INC p 464
65 MEMORIAL DR, NORTH SYDNEY, NS, B2A 0B9
SIC 3714

MAGNA POWERTRAIN FPC LIMITED PARTNERSHIP p 555
800 TESMA WAY, CONCORD, ON, L4K 5C2
(905) 303-1689   SIC 5085

MAGNA POWERTRAIN INC p 481
245 EDWARD ST, AURORA, ON, L4G 3M7
(905) 713-0746   SIC 3714

MAGNA POWERTRAIN INC p 555
50 CASMIR CRT, CONCORD, ON, L4K 4J5
(905) 532-2100   SIC 3714

MAGNA POWERTRAIN INC p 1032
390 HANLAN RD, WOODBRIDGE, ON, L4L 3P6
(905) 851-6791   SIC 3714

MAGNA SEATING INC p 481
337 MAGNA DR, AURORA, ON, L4G 7K1
(905) 726-2462   SIC 3714

MAGNA SEATING INC p 662
3915 COMMERCE RD, LONDON, ON, N6N 1P4
(519) 808-9035   SIC 3714

MAGNA SEATING INC p 754
564 NEWPARK BLVD, NEWMARKET, ON, L3X 2S2
(905) 853-3604   SIC 3714

MAGNA SEATING INC p 754
550 NEWPARK BLVD, NEWMARKET, ON, L3X 2S2
(905) 895-4701   SIC 3714

MAGNACHARGE BATTERY CORPORATION p 206
1279 DERWENT WAY UNIT 1, DELTA, BC, V3M 5V9
(604) 525-0391   SIC 5999

MAGNASONIC INC. p 672
300 ALDEN RD, MARKHAM, ON, L3R 4C1
SIC 6712

MAGNES GROUP INC, THE p 801
1540 CORNWALL RD SUITE 100, OAKVILLE, ON, L6J 7W5
(905) 845-9793   SIC 6411

MAGNESIUM PRODUCTS p 897
See MERIDIAN LIGHTWEIGHT TECHNOLOGIES INC

MAGNESIUM PRODUCTS DIVISION p 897
See MERIDIAN LIGHTWEIGHT TECHNOLOGIES INC

MAGNETO ELECTRIC SERVICE CO. LIMITED p 697
1150 EGLINTON AVE E, MISSISSAUGA, ON, L4W 2M6
(905) 625-9450   SIC 7694

MAGNETO, HYDRAULIQUE & PNEUMATIQUE INC p 1066
1375 RUE GAY-LUSSAC, BOUCHERVILLE, QC, J4B 7K1
(450) 655-2551   SIC 7699

MAGNOTTA WINERY CORPORATION p 1003
271 CHRISLEA RD, VAUGHAN, ON, L4L 8N6
(905) 738-9463   SIC 2084

MAGNUM 2000 INC p 798
1137 NORTH SERVICE RD E, OAKVILLE, ON, L6H 1A7
(905) 339-1104   SIC 7539

MAGNUM CONCRETE INC p 179
26162 30A AVE SUITE 201, ALDERGROVE, BC, V4W 2W5
(604) 607-6576   SIC 5032

MAGNUM INTEGRATED TECHNOLOGIES INC p 509
200 FIRST GULF BLVD, BRAMPTON, ON, L6W 4T5
(905) 595-1998   SIC 3593

MAGNUM OIL (MB) LTD p 372
450 SHEPPARD ST, WINNIPEG, MB, R2X 2P8
(204) 594-0440   SIC 5172

MAGNUM PROJECTS LTD p 299
128 PENDER ST W SUITE 401, VANCOUVER, BC, V6B 1R8
(604) 569-3900   SIC 6719

MAGNUM PROTECTIVE SERVICES LIMITED p 990
1043 BLOOR ST W, TORONTO, ON, M6H 1M4
(416) 591-1566   SIC 7381

MAGNUM STEEL & TUBE INC p 523
4380 CORPORATE DR, BURLINGTON, ON, L7L 5R3
(905) 319-8852   SIC 5051

MAGNUM TRAILER AND EQUIPMENT INC p 175
660 RIVERSIDE RD, ABBOTSFORD, BC, V2S 7M6
(604) 855-7544   SIC 3715

MAGNUS POIRIER INC p 1346
7388 BOUL VIAU, SAINT-LEONARD, QC, H1S 2N9
(514) 727-2847   SIC 7261

MAGNUSON FORD SALES LTD p 177
32562 SOUTH FRASER WAY, ABBOTSFORD, BC, V2T 1X6
(604) 853-7401   SIC 5511

MAGNUSSEN HOME p 752
See MAGNUSSEN HOME FURNISHINGS LTD

MAGNUSSEN HOME FURNISHINGS LTD p 752
66 HINCKS ST SUITE 1, NEW HAMBURG, ON, N3A 2A3
(519) 662-3040   SIC 5021

MAGOG FORD (2000) INC p 1147
2000 RUE SHERBROOKE, MAGOG, QC, J1X 2T3
(819) 843-3673   SIC 5531

MAGOG HONDA p 1148
See QUALITE PERFORMANCE MAGOG INC

MAGOG TOYOTA INC p 1148
2500 RUE SHERBROOKE, MAGOG, QC, J1X 4E8
(819) 843-9883   SIC 5511

MAGOR COMMUNICATIONS CORP p 749
400-1 ANTARES DR, NEPEAN, ON, K2E 8C4
(613) 686-1731   SIC 5065

MAGOTTEAUX LTEE p 1148
601 RUE CHAMPLAIN, MAGOG, QC, J1X 2N1
(819) 843-0443   SIC 3325

MAGRIS RESOURCES INC p 954
333 BAY ST SUITE 1101, TORONTO, ON, M5H 2R2
(416) 901-9877   SIC 6799

MAGTRON p 871
See HEROUX-DEVTEK INC

MAHEU, GERARD INC p 1347
289 5E RANG, SAINT-LOUIS-DE-GONZAGUE, QC, J0S 1T0
(450) 377-1420   SIC 5191

MAHLE FILTER SYSTEMS CANADA, ULC p 911
16 INDUSTRIAL PARK RD, TILBURY, ON, N0P 2L0
(519) 682-0444   SIC 3089

MAHOGANY SALON & SPA LTD p 891
1261 STITTSVILLE MAIN ST UNIT 1, STITTSVILLE, ON, K2S 2E4
(613) 836-3334   SIC 7991

MAHONE INSURANCE GROUP INC p 462
201 MAIN ST, MAHONE BAY, NS, B0J 2E0
(902) 624-9600   SIC 6411

MAIBEC DIV. SAINT THEOPHILE p 1353
See MAIBEC INC

MAIBEC INC p 1138
1984 5E RUE BUREAU 202, LEVIS, QC, G6W 5M6
(418) 830-8855   SIC 2421

MAIBEC INC p 1349
24 6E RANG BUREAU 6, SAINT-PAMPHILE, QC, G0R 3X0
(418) 356-3331   SIC 2421

MAIBEC INC p 1353
340 RTE DU PRESIDENT-KENNEDY, SAINT-THEOPHILE, QC, G0M 2A0
(418) 597-3388   SIC 2429

MAID OF THE MIST CAMPUS   *p* 759
See NIAGARA COLLEGE OF APPLIED ARTS & TECHNOLOGY
MAIL-O-MATIC SERVICES LIMITED *p* 193
7550 LOWLAND DR, BURNABY, BC, V5J 5A4
(604) 439-9668   *SIC* 7331
MAILLETTE HOLDINGS INC   *p* 606
80 IMPERIAL RD S, GUELPH, ON, N1K 2A1
(519) 822-2175   *SIC* 5541
MAILLOUX BAILLARGEON INC   *p* 1298
222 RUE SAINT-PIERRE, SAINT-CONSTANT, QC, J5A 2A2
(514) 861-8417   *SIC* 3999
MAILLOUX, ROCHON ASSURANCE ET SERVICES FINANCIERS   *p* 1055
See FAVREAU, GENDRON ASSURANCE ET SERVICES FINANCIERS INC
MAILPORT COURIER (1986) INC   *p* 688
3405 AMERICAN DR UNIT 1, MISSISSAUGA, ON, L4V 1T6
(416) 679-1777   *SIC* 7389
MAIN FILTER INC   *p* 863
188 INDUSTRIAL PARK CRES, SAULT STE. MARIE, ON, P6B 5P2
(705) 256-6622   *SIC* 3569
MAIN ST. GROUP INC   *p* 570
2275 LAKE SHORE BLVD W SUITE 318, ETOBICOKE, ON, M8V 3Y3
(519) 537-3513   *SIC* 7389
MAIN STREAM   *p* 283
See CERMAQ CANADA LTD
MAIN STREET IGA   *p* 370
See 61401 MANITOBA LTD
MAIN STREET ULTRAMART   *p* 428
See MAURICE'S SERVICE CENTRE LIMITED
MAINFRAME ENTERTAINMENT INC *p* 321
2025 BROADWAY W SUITE 200, VANCOUVER, BC, V6J 1Z6
(604) 714-2600   *SIC* 7812
MAINIL, JERRY LIMITED   *p* 1437
1530 NEW CITY GARDEN RD, WEYBURN, SK, S4H 2L1
(306) 842-5412   *SIC* 1623
MAINLAND CIVIL SITE SERVICES INC *p* 277
12899 80 AVE UNIT 206, SURREY, BC, V3W 0E6
(604) 591-5599   *SIC* 1623
MAINLAND CONSTRUCTION MATERIALS ULC   *p* 225
9525 201 ST UNIT 317, LANGLEY, BC, V1M 4A5
(604) 882-5650   *SIC* 5211
MAINLAND MACHINERY LTD   *p* 177
2255 TOWNLINE RD, ABBOTSFORD, BC, V2T 6H1
(604) 854-4244   *SIC* 3569
MAINLAND SAWMILL   *p* 291
See TERMINAL FOREST PRODUCTS LTD
MAINLAND SAWMILLS, DIV OF   *p* 256
See TERMINAL FOREST PRODUCTS LTD
MAINLINE EQUIPMENT LTD   *p* 96
14535 114 AVE NW, EDMONTON, AB, T5M 2Y8
(780) 453-3695   *SIC* 5084
MAINLINE FASHIONS INC   *p* 789
42 DUFFLAW RD UNIT 100, NORTH YORK, ON, M6A 2W1
(416) 368-1522   *SIC* 5094
MAINROAD CONTRACTING LTD   *p* 272
17474 56 AVE, SURREY, BC, V3S 1C3
(604) 575-7020   *SIC* 1611
MAINROAD EAST KOOTENAY CONTRACTING LTD   *p* 204
258 INDUSTRIAL ROAD F, CRANBROOK, BC, V1C 6N8
(250) 417-4624   *SIC* 1611
MAINROAD EAST KOOTENAY CONTRACTING LTD   *p* 272
17474 56 AVE, SURREY, BC, V3S 1C3

(604) 575-7020   *SIC* 1611
MAINROAD HOWE SOUND CONTRACTING LTD   *p* 272
17474 56 AVE, SURREY, BC, V3S 1C3
(604) 575-7020   *SIC* 1611
MAINROAD LOWER MAINLAND CONTRACTING LTD   *p* 272
17474 56 AVE, SURREY, BC, V3S 1C3
(604) 575-7021   *SIC* 1611
MAINROAD MID-ISLAND CONSTRUCTING LTD   *p* 243
435 SPRINGHILL RD, PARKSVILLE, BC, V9P 2T2
SIC 1611
MAINSTREAM METALS INC   *p* 523
4350 HARVESTER RD, BURLINGTON, ON, L7L 5S4
(905) 631-5945   *SIC* 5093
MAINSTREET EQUITY CORP   *p* 31
305 10 AVE SE, CALGARY, AB, T2G 0W2
(403) 215-6060   *SIC* 6513
MAINTAINANCE SHOP   *p* 247
See SCHOOL DISTRICT NO. 43 (COQUITLAM)
MAINTAIR AVIATION SERVICES LTD *p* 910
316 HECTOR DOUGALL WAY, THUNDER BAY, ON, P7E 6M6
(807) 475-5915   *SIC* 5172
MAINTENANCE ASSISTANT INC   *p* 995
35 GOLDEN AVE SUITE A-201, TORONTO, ON, M6R 2J5
(647) 317-9055   *SIC* 7372
MAINTENANCE DEPOT   *p* 1016
See CORPORATION OF THE REGIONAL MUNICIPALITY OF DURHAM, THE
MAINTENANCE DIV OF   *p* 21
See AVMAX GROUP INC
MAINTENANCE, DIV OF   *p* 21
See AVMAX GROUP INC
MAINWAY HANDLING SYSTEMS INC *p* 528
3345 NORTH SERVICE RD UNIT 101, BURLINGTON, ON, L7N 3G2
(905) 335-0133   *SIC* 5084
MAINWAY HUNTER CREIGHTON INSURANCE INC   *p* 718
101 QUEEN ST S SUITE 100, MISSISSAUGA, ON, L5M 1K7
(905) 826-3215   *SIC* 6411
MAINWAY MAZDA   *p* 1432
See SOUTHCENTER AUTO INC
MAISON AMI-CO (1981) INC, LA   *p* 1344
8455 BOUL LANGELIER, SAINT-LEONARD, QC, H1P 2C5
(514) 351-7520   *SIC* 5087
MAISON BERGEVIN INC, LA   *p* 1260
199 RUE JOLY, QUEBEC, QC, G1L 1N7
SIC 5149
MAISON BLANCHE DE NORTH HATLEY INC, LA   *p* 1243
977 RUE MASSAWIPPI, NORTH HATLEY, QC, J0B 2C0
(450) 666-1567   *SIC* 7021
MAISON CENTRALE   *p* 1370
See FILLES DE LA CHARITE DU SACRE-COEUR DE JESUS, LES
MAISON CHRYSLER DE CHARLESBOURG LTEE, LA   *p* 1256
15070 BOUL HENRI-BOURASSA, QUEBEC, QC, G1G 3Z4
(418) 622-4700   *SIC* 5511
MAISON CONDELLE   *p* 1229
See LITERIES UNIVERSELLES PAGA INC
MAISON D'AFFINAGE BERGERON INC, LA
p 1140
865 RTE DES RIVIERES, LEVIS, QC, G7A 2V2
(418) 831-0991   *SIC* 5451
MAISON DE JADE   *p* 1256
See 2954-8682 QUEBEC INC
MAISON DE L'AUTO DOLBEAU-MISTASSINI   *p*
17474 56 AVE, SURREY, BC, V3S 1C3

1090
See 9171-1440 QUEBEC INC.
MAISON DE LA POMME DE FRELIGHSBURG INC   *p* 1102
32 RTE 237 N, FRELIGHSBURG, QC, J0J 1C0
(450) 298-5275   *SIC* 5431
MAISON DE MERE D'YOUVILLE   *p* 1190
See SOEURS DE LA CHARITE (SOEURS GRISES) DE MONTREAL, LES
MAISON DE SOINS PALLIATIFS SOURCE BLEUE   *p* 1065
See FONDATION SOURCE BLEU
MAISON DE THE CAMELLIA SINENSIS *p* 1185
See 9104-7332 QUEBEC INC
MAISON DE VIE SUNRISE DE FONTAINEBLEAU   *p* 1058
See SUNRISE NORTH SENIOR LIVING LTD
MAISON DES FLEURS VIVACES, LA *p* 1301
See 2436-3392 QUEBEC INC
MAISON DES FUTAILLES, S.E.C.   *p* 1066
500 RUE D'AVAUGOUR BUREAU 2050, BOUCHERVILLE, QC, J4B 0G6
(450) 645-9777   *SIC* 5182
MAISON DES FUTAILLES, S.E.C.   *p* 1164
2021 RUE DES FUTAILLES, MONTREAL, QC, H1N 3M7
(450) 645-9777   *SIC* 2084
MAISON DES PARENTS DE BORDEAUX-CARTIERVILLE INC   *p* 1224
5680 RUE DE SALABERRY, MONTREAL, QC, H4J 1J7
(514) 745-1144   *SIC* 8699
MAISON DU BAGEL INC   *p* 1184
263 RUE SAINT-VIATEUR O, MONTREAL, QC, H2V 1Y1
(514) 276-8044   *SIC* 5461
MAISON DU GIBIER INC, LA   *p* 1280
585 RUE DE L'ARGON, QUEBEC, QC, G2N 2G7
(418) 849-8427   *SIC* 5147
MAISON DU PEINTRE, LA   *p* 1216
See 2164-1204 QUEBEC INC
MAISON ELIZABETH INC   *p* 1221
2131 AV DE MARLOWE, MONTREAL, QC, H4A 3L4
(514) 482-2488   *SIC* 8699
MAISON JESUS MARIE   *p* 1143
See SOEURS DES SAINTS NOMS DE JESUS ET DE MARIE DU QUEBEC, LES
MAISON JOSEPH BATTAT LTEE   *p* 1158
8440 CH DARNLEY, MONT-ROYAL, QC, H4T 1M4
(866) 665-5524   *SIC* 5092
MAISON LIANG   *p* 1076
177A BOUL SAINT-JEAN-BAPTISTE, CHATEAUGUAY, QC, J6K 3B4
(450) 692-1160   *SIC* 5023
MAISON MERE DES SOEURS GRISES DE MONTREAL   *p* 1215
See SOEURS GRISES DE MONTREAL, LES
MAISON PIACENTE   *p* 1369
805 111E RUE, SHAWINIGAN-SUD, QC, G9P 2T5
SIC 5137
MAISON RUSSET INC   *p* 1113
142 RTE 202 BUREAU 103, HUNTINGDON, QC, J0S 1H0
(450) 264-9449   *SIC* 2037
MAISON S.M.A.R.T.   *p* 1391
See MARQUIS CONCEPT INC, LE
MAISON SAINT-JOSEPH   *p* 1372
See PETITE SOEURS DE LA SAINTE-FAMILLE, LES
MAISON SAMI T.A. FRUITS INC, LA *p* 1226
1505 RUE LEGENDRE O, MONTREAL, QC, H4N 1H6
(514) 858-6363   *SIC* 5431
MAISON SIMONS INC, LA   *p* 1269

20 COTE DE LA FABRIQUE, QUEBEC, QC, G1R 3V9
(418) 692-3630   *SIC* 5651
MAISON SIMONS INC, LA   *p* 1296
600 BOUL DES PROMENADES, SAINT-BRUNO, QC, J3V 6L9
(514) 282-1840   *SIC* 5311
MAISON SIMONS INC, LA   *p* 1374
3050 BOUL DE PORTLAND, SHERBROOKE, QC, J1L 1K1
(819) 829-1840   *SIC* 5651
MAISON ST DENIS BOURGET, LA   *p* 1224
See FONDATION LE PILIER
MAISON ST-JOSEPH   *p* 1165
See CENTRE D'HEBERGEMENT ET DE SOINS DE LONGUE DUREE PROVIDENCE SAINT-JOSEPH INC
MAISON STE-ANNE   *p* 1314
See SOEURS DE CHARITE DE SAINT-HYACINTHE, LES
MAISON USINEX INC   *p* 1151
114 RTE 214, MILAN, QC, G0Y 1E0
(819) 657-4268   *SIC* 1521
MAISONEE D'EVELYNE, LA   *p* 1079
546 BOUL TALBOT, CHICOUTIMI, QC, G7H 4A5
(418) 543-5822   *SIC* 7389
MAISONNEUVE ALUMINIUM INC   *p* 1172
5477 RUE CHABOT BUREAU 100, MONTREAL, QC, H2H 1Z1
(514) 523-1155   *SIC* 1541
MAISONNEUVE LALONDE SOULIGNY COURTIERS D'ASSURANCE LTEE   *p* 888
GD, ST ISIDORE, ON, K0C 2B0
(613) 524-2174   *SIC* 6411
MAISONS LAPRISE INC   *p* 1160
166 4E RUE, MONTMAGNY, QC, G5V 3L5
(418) 248-0401   *SIC* 2452
MAISONS LAPRISE INC   *p* 1273
2700 BOUL LAURIER UNITE 2540, QUEBEC, QC, G1V 2L8
(418) 683-3343   *SIC* 2452
MAISONS SUPREME HOMES   *p* 419
See ENTREPRISES A & R SAVOIE ET FILS LTEE, LES
MAISONS USINEES COTE INC   *p* 1347
388 RUE SAINT-ISIDORE, SAINT-LIN-LAURENTIDES, QC, J5M 2V1
(450) 439-8737   *SIC* 2452
MAITLAND FORD LINCOLN MOTORS   *p* 863
See LEWIS, MAITLAND ENTERPRISES LTD
MAITLAND MANOR   *p* 597
See REVERA INC
MAITRE ES CELSIUS   *p* 1375
See LEPROHON INC
MAITRE SALADIER INC   *p* 1062
1755 BOUL LIONEL-BERTRAND, BOISBRIAND, QC, J7H 1N8
(450) 435-0674   *SIC* 2099
MAJA HOLDINGS LTD   *p* 443
4 FOREST HILLS PKY SUITE 317, DARTMOUTH, NS, B2W 5G7
(902) 462-2032   *SIC* 5461
MAJESTIC CONDOMINIUM SALES   *p* 670
See GRAPE ARBOR CONSTRUCTION LTD
MAJESTIC GOLD CORP   *p* 280
1688 152ND ST SUITE 306, SURREY, BC, V4A 4N2
(604) 560-9060   *SIC* 1041
MAJOLI FURNITURE (1983) LIMITED *p* 697
5510 AMBLER DR UNIT 2, MISSISSAUGA, ON, L4W 2V1
(905) 542-0481   *SIC* 2515
MAJOR DRILLING GROUP INTERNATIONAL INC   *p*
111 ST. GEORGE ST SUITE 100, MONCTON, NB, E1C 1T7
(506) 857-8636   *SIC* 1481
MAJOR HIGH SCHOOL   *p* 1412
See BOARD OF EDUCATION OF THE LIVING SKY SCHOOL DIVISION NO. 202

SASKATCHEWAN
MAKE SCENTS FLOWER DISTRIBUTORS INC p 193
3777 MARINE WAY, BURNABY, BC, V5J 5A7
(604) 433-3552   *SIC* 5193
MAKE-A-WISH FOUNDATION (OF THE) ATLANTIC PROVINCES p 451
5991 SPRING GARDEN RD SUITE 705, HALIFAX, NS, B3H 1Y6
(902) 466-9474   *SIC* 8699
MAKE-A-WISH FOUNDATION OF CANADA p 774
4211 YONGE ST SUITE 520, NORTH YORK, ON, M2P 2A9
(416) 224-9474   *SIC* 8699
MAKITA CANADA INC p 1014
1950 FORBES ST, WHITBY, ON, L1N 7B7
(905) 571-2200   *SIC* 5072
MAKKINGA CONTRACTING & EQUIPMENT RENTAL p 907
See 1204626 ONTARIO INC
MAKLOC BUILDINGS INC p 149
706 17 AVE, NISKU, AB, T9E 7T1
(780) 955-2951   *SIC* 3448
MAKSTEEL CORP p 686
7615 TORBRAM RD, MISSISSAUGA, ON, L4T 4A8
(905) 671-9000   *SIC* 3599
MAKWA AVENTURES INC, LES p 1184
4079 RUE SAINT-DENIS, MONTREAL, QC, H2W 2M7
(514) 285-2583   *SIC* 7389
MAL WHITLOCK ENTERPRISES LTD p 570
300 MAIDSTONE AVE W, ESSEX, ON, N8M 2X6
(519) 776-5224   *SIC* 5531
MALAGA INC p 1206
1 PLACE VILLE-MARIE BUREAU 4000, MONTREAL, QC, H3B 4M4
(514) 393-9000   *SIC* 1081
MALASPINA UNIVERSITY-COLLEGE BOOKSTORE, DIV OF p 233
See VANCOUVER ISLAND UNIVERSITY
MALATEST ASSOCIATES p 336
See MALATEST, R. A. & ASSOCIATES LTD
MALATEST, R. A. & ASSOCIATES LTD p 336
858 PANDORA AVE, VICTORIA, BC, V8W 1P4
(250) 384-2770   *SIC* 8732
MALE YOUTH SERVICES p 392
See BEHAVIOURAL HEALTH FOUNDATION INC, THE
MALENFANT DALLAIRE, S.E.N.C.R.L. p 1273
2600 BOUL LAURIER BUREAU 872, QUEBEC, QC, G1V 4W2
(418) 654-0636   *SIC* 8721
MALFAR MECHANICAL INC p 1032
144 WOODSTREAM BLVD SUITE 7, WOODBRIDGE, ON, L4L 7Y3
(905) 850-1242   *SIC* 1711
MALGA p 1111
See PUBLICITE MALGA INC
MALGO, JA SALES LTD p 170
6623 16A HWY W, VEGREVILLE, AB, T9C 0A3
SIC 5531
MALLETTE S.E.N.C.R.L. p 1274
3075 CH DES QUATRE-BOURGEOIS BUREAU 200, QUEBEC, QC, G1W 5C4
(418) 653-4431   *SIC* 8721
MALMBERG TRUCK TRAILER EQUIPMENT LTD p 816
1621 MICHAEL ST, OTTAWA, ON, K1B 3T3
(613) 741-3360   *SIC* 5082
MALO TRANSPORT (1971) INC p 1350
23 CH SAINT-JACQUES, SAINT-PAUL, QC, J6E 3H2
(450) 756-8008   *SIC* 4213

MALO, GILLES INC p 1243
100 RUE DES ENTREPRISES, NOTRE-DAME-DES-PRAIRIES, QC, J6E 0L9
(450) 757-2424   *SIC* 1542
MALPACK LTD p 474
120 FULLER RD, AJAX, ON, L1S 3R2
(888) 678-0707   *SIC* 2673
MALPACK LTD p 474
510 FINLEY AVE, AJAX, ON, L1S 2E3
(905) 428-3751   *SIC* 2673
MALPACK POLYBAG, DIV OF p 474
See MALPACK LTD
MALTACOURT (CANADA) LTD p 534
150 WATER ST S SUITE 201, CAMBRIDGE, ON, N1R 3E2
(519) 756-6463   *SIC* 4731
MALTACOURT GLOBAL LOGISTICS p 534
See MALTACOURT (CANADA) LTD
MALTON NEIGHBOURHOOD SERVICES p 686
3540 MORNING STAR DR, MISSISSAUGA, ON, L4T 1Y2
(905) 677-6270   *SIC* 8699
MAMMOET CANADA EASTERN LTD p 849
7504 MCLEAN RD E, PUSLINCH, ON, N0B 2J0
(519) 740-0550   *SIC* 4212
MAMMOET CANADA HOLDINGS INC p 849
7504 MCLEAN RD E, PUSLINCH, ON, N0B 2J0
(519) 740-0550   *SIC* 6712
MAMMOET CANADA WESTERN LTD p 124
12920 33 ST NE, EDMONTON, AB, T6S 1H6
(780) 449-0552   *SIC* 4213
MAMMOET CRANE (ASSETS) INC p 604
7504 MCLEAN RD E, GUELPH, ON, N1H 6H9
(519) 740-0550   *SIC* 3537
MAMMOET CRANE INC p 124
12920 33 ST NE, EDMONTON, AB, T6S 1H6
(780) 449-0552   *SIC* 4212
MAN ENERGY SOLUTIONS CANADA LTD p 314
1177 HASTINGS ST W SUITE 1930, VANCOUVER, BC, V6E 2K3
(604) 235-2254   *SIC* 5084
MAN-KWONG ENTERPRISES LTD p 295
1233 GLEN DR, VANCOUVER, BC, V6A 3M8
(604) 254-3688   *SIC* 5144
MAN-SHIELD (ALTA) CONSTRUCTION INC p 161
201 KASKA RD UNIT 167, SHERWOOD PARK, AB, T8A 2J6
(780) 467-2601   *SIC* 1542
MAN-SHIELD CONSTRUCTION p 161
See MAN-SHIELD (ALTA) CONSTRUCTION INC
MANA ENERGY CONNECTION p 239
431 MOUNTAIN HIGHWAY, NORTH VANCOUVER, BC, V7J 2L1
SIC 4924
MANA STEEL p 611
See MAX AICHER (NORTH AMERICA) LIMITED
MANAC INC p 1305
2275 107E RUE, SAINT-GEORGES, QC, G5Y 8G6
(418) 228-2018   *SIC* 3715
MANAGEMENT SIMO INC p 1142
2099 BOUL FERNAND-LAFONTAINE, LONGUEUIL, QC, J4G 2J4
(514) 281-6525   *SIC* 4971
MANAGEMENT SYSTEMS RESOURCES INC p 781
2 TIPPETT RD, NORTH YORK, ON, M3H 2V2
(416) 630-3000   *SIC* 7372
MANASTE INSPECTION QUALITY QUANTITY (CANADA) INC p 1239
9756 RUE NOTRE-DAME E, MONTREAL-

EST, QC, H1L 3R4
(514) 645-5554   *SIC* 4785
MANATOKAN OILFIELD SERVICES INC p 31
237 8 AVE SE SUITE 222, CALGARY, AB, T2G 5C3
(403) 718-9842   *SIC* 1389
MANCAL CORPORATION p 53
530 8 AVE SW SUITE 1600, CALGARY, AB, T2P 3S8
(403) 231-7580   *SIC* 6733
MANCHESTER PRODUCTS p 537
See 963488 ONTARIO LIMITED
MANCHU WOK (CANADA) INC p 680
85 CITIZEN CRT UNIT 9, MARKHAM, ON, L6G 1A8
(905) 946-7200   *SIC* 5812
MANCON HOLDINGS LTD p 1416
504 HENDERSON DR, REGINA, SK, S4N 5X2
(306) 721-4777   *SIC* 1731
MANCOR CANADA INC p 804
2485 SPEERS RD, OAKVILLE, ON, L6L 2X9
(905) 827-3737   *SIC* 3499
MANCOR SPEERS RD p 804
See MANCOR CANADA INC
MANCUSO CHEMICALS LIMITED p 759
5725 PROGRESS ST, NIAGARA FALLS, ON, L2G 0C1
(905) 357-3626   *SIC* 2899
MANDALAY RESOURCES CORPORATION p 939
76 RICHMOND ST E SUITE 330, TORONTO, ON, M5C 1P1
(647) 260-1566   *SIC* 1041
MANDARIN RESTAURANT p 530
See 882547 ONTARIO INC
MANDARIN RESTAURANT p 574
See CCFGLM ONTARIO LIMITED
MANDARIN RESTAURANT p 581
See 939927 ONTARIO LIMITED
MANDARIN RESTAURANT p 704
See 1335270 ONTARIO LTD
MANDARIN RESTAURANT p 715
See 1004839 ONTARIO LIMITED
MANDARIN RESTAURANT p 843
See 1051107 ONTARIO LTD
MANDEL SCIENTIFIC COMPANY INC p 601
2 ADMIRAL PL, GUELPH, ON, N1G 4N4
(888) 883-3636   *SIC* 5049
MANDERLEY TURF PRODUCTS INC p 130
55403 RANGE RD 222, FORT SASKATCHEWAN, AB, T8L 2N9
(780) 998-1995   *SIC* 5261
MANDERLEY TURFGRASS p 130
See MANDERLEY TURF PRODUCTS INC
MANDERO HOSIERY MILLS, DIV OF p 791
See GERTEX HOSIERY INC
MANDEX CORPORATION p 386
3081 PORTAGE AVE, WINNIPEG, MB, R3K 0W4
SIC 5521
MANDRAKE MANAGEMENT CONSULTANTS CORPORATION p 927
55 ST CLAIR AVE W SUITE 401, TORONTO, ON, M4V 2Y7
(416) 922-5400   *SIC* 7361
MANDY'S p 1187
See 9342-6484 QUEBEC INC
MANEL CONTRACTING LTD p 795
41 RIVALDA RD, NORTH YORK, ON, M9M 2M4
(416) 635-0876   *SIC* 1542
MANGA HOTELS (DARTMOUTH) INC p 444
101 WYSE RD, DARTMOUTH, NS, B3A 1L9
(902) 463-1100   *SIC* 7011
MANHAL AL HABBOBI CONSULTANTS p 684
6541 DERRY RD, MILTON, ON, L9T 7W1
(905) 491-6864   *SIC* 8748
MANHATTAN INTERNATIONAL CONCEPTS INC p 1340

6150 RTE TRANSCANADIENNE, SAINT-LAURENT, QC, H4T 1X5
(514) 388-5588   *SIC* 5136
MANHEIM AUTO AUCTIONS COMPANY p 684
8277 LAWSON RD, MILTON, ON, L9T 5C7
(905) 275-3000   *SIC* 7389
MANHEIM TORONTO p 684
See MANHEIM AUTO AUCTIONS COMPANY
MANIOLI INVESTMENTS INC p 1226
1650 RUE CHABANEL O BUREAU 1205, MONTREAL, QC, H4N 3M8
(514) 384-0140   *SIC* 6712
MANION WILKINS & ASSOCIATES LTD p 577
21 FOUR SEASONS PL SUITE 500, ETOBICOKE, ON, M9B 0A5
(416) 234-5044   *SIC* 8748
MANITOBA AGRICULTURAL SERVICES CORPORATION p 355
50 24TH ST NW SUITE 400, PORTAGE LA PRAIRIE, MB, R1N 3V9
(204) 239-3499   *SIC* 6159
MANITOBA BAPTIST HOME SOCIETY INC p 368
577 ST ANNE'S RD, WINNIPEG, MB, R2M 3G5
(204) 257-2394   *SIC* 8051
MANITOBA BLUE CROSS p 382
See UNITED HEALTH SERVICES CORPORATION
MANITOBA CHAMBERS OF COMMERCE, THE p 375
227 PORTAGE AVE, WINNIPEG, MB, R3B 2A6
(204) 948-0100   *SIC* 8611
MANITOBA CLINIC p 373
See MANITOBA CLINIC MEDICAL CORPORATION
MANITOBA CLINIC MEDICAL CORPORATION p 373
790 SHERBROOK ST SUITE 503, WINNIPEG, MB, R3A 1M3
(204) 774-6541   *SIC* 8011
MANITOBA COOPERATIVE HONEY PRODUCERS LIMITED p 384
625 ROSEBERRY ST, WINNIPEG, MB, R3H 0T4
(204) 783-2240   *SIC* 5149
MANITOBA FIRST NATIONS EDUCATION RESOURCE CENTRE INC p 351
4820 PORTAGE AVE, HEADINGLEY, MB, R4H 1C8
(204) 831-1224   *SIC* 8748
MANITOBA GOVERNMENT AND GENERAL EMPLOYEES UNION p 378
275 BROADWAY SUITE 601, WINNIPEG, MB, R3C 4M6
(204) 982-6438   *SIC* 8631
MANITOBA HARVEST p 369
See FRESH HEMP FOODS LTD
MANITOBA HYDRO p 378
See MANITOBA HYDRO-ELECTRIC BOARD, THE
MANITOBA HYDRO INTERNATIONAL LTD p 389
211 COMMERCE DR, WINNIPEG, MB, R3P 1A3
(204) 480-5200   *SIC* 8741
MANITOBA HYDRO UTILITY SERVICES LIMITED p 371
35 SUTHERLAND AVE, WINNIPEG, MB, R2W 3C5
(204) 360-5660   *SIC* 7389
MANITOBA HYDRO-ELECTRIC BOARD, THE p 378
360 PORTAGE AVE SUITE 6, WINNIPEG, MB, R3C 0G8
(204) 360-3311   *SIC* 4911
MANITOBA INSTITUTE OF CELL BIOLOGY

p 381
See UNIVERSITY OF MANITOBA THE
MANITOBA INSTITUTE OF CHILD HEALTH
p 380
See CHILDREN'S HOSPITAL FOUNDA-TION OF MANITOBA INC, TH
MANITOBA JOCKEY CLUB INC   *p 386*
3975 PORTAGE AVE, WINNIPEG, MB, R3K 2E9
(204) 885-3330   *SIC 7948*
MANITOBA METIS FEDERATION INC *p 375*
150 HENRY AVE SUITE 300, WINNIPEG, MB, R3B 0J7
(204) 586-8474   *SIC 8651*
MANITOBA MOTOR LEAGUE, THE   *p 382*
870 EMPRESS ST, WINNIPEG, MB, R3G 3H3
(204) 262-6115   *SIC 8699*
MANITOBA NURSES' UNION   *p 379*
275 BROADWAY UNIT 301, WINNIPEG, MB, R3C 4M6
(204) 942-1320   *SIC 8631*
MANITOBA PUBLIC INSURANCE CORPO-RATION, THE   *p 379*
234 DONALD ST SUITE 912, WINNIPEG, MB, R3C 4A4
(204) 985-7000   *SIC 8743*
MANITOBA SAUSAGE   *p 371*
See WINNIPEG OLD COUNTRY SAUSAGE LTD
MANITOBA TEACHERS' SOCIETY, THE   *p 386*
191 HARCOURT ST, WINNIPEG, MB, R3J 3H2
(204) 888-7961   *SIC 8621*
MANITOBAH MUKLUKS   *p 371*
See BLUE MOOSE CLOTHING COMPANY LTD
MANITOBAN NEWSPAPER PUBLICA-TIONS CORPORATION, THE   *p 391*
105 UNIVERSITY CRES, WINNIPEG, MB, R3T 2N5
(204) 474-6535   *SIC 5192*
MANITOBAN, THE   *p 391*
See MANITOBAN NEWSPAPER PUBLICA-TIONS CORPORATION, THE
MANITOU MECHANICAL LTD   *p 898*
874 LAPOINTE ST, SUDBURY, ON, P3A 5N8
(705) 566-5702   *SIC 1541*
MANITOULIN GLOBAL FORWARDING INC
p 740
7035 ORDAN, MISSISSAUGA, ON, L5T 1T1
(905) 283-1600   *SIC 4731*
MANITOULIN HEALTH CENTRE   *p 647*
11 MERIDETH ST, LITTLE CURRENT, ON, P0P 1K0
(705) 368-2300   *SIC 8062*
MANITOULIN TRANSPORT   *p 598*
See JET TRANSPORT LTD
MANITOULIN TRANSPORT INC   *p 598*
154 540B HWY, GORE BAY, ON, P0P 1H0
(705) 282-2640   *SIC 4213*
MANITOULIN TRANSPORTATION   *p 1*
53114 RGE RD 262 UNIT 402, ACHESON, AB, T7X 5A1
(780) 490-1112   *SIC 4213*
MANITOULIN TRANSPORTATION   *p 251*
9499 MILWAUKEE WAY, PRINCE GEORGE, BC, V2N 5T3
(250) 563-9138   *SIC 4212*
MANITOWABI, ANDREW GROUP   *p 1016*
2174 WIKWEMIKONG WAY, WIK-WEMIKONG, ON, P0P 2J0
(705) 859-3788   *SIC 5541*
MANKOTA STOCKMEN'S WEIGH COM-PANY LIMITED   *p 1409*
178 RAILWAY AVE E, MANKOTA, SK, S0H 2W0
(306) 478-2229   *SIC 5154*
MANLUK GLOBAL MANUFACTURING SO-

LUTIONS   *p 172*
See MANLUK INDUSTRIES (2008) INC
MANLUK INDUSTRIES (2008) INC   *p 172*
4815 42 AVE, WETASKIWIN, AB, T9A 2P6
(780) 352-5522   *SIC 3494*
MANLUK INDUSTRIES INC   *p 172*
4815 42 AVE, WETASKIWIN, AB, T9A 2P6
(780) 352-5522   *SIC 3532*
MANN ENGINEERING LTD   *p 789*
150 BRIDGELAND AVE SUITE 101, NORTH YORK, ON, M6A 1Z5
(416) 201-9109   *SIC 1731*
MANN MARKETING   *p 1157*
See MARKETING MANN, ALBERT INC
MANN+HUMMEL FILTRATION TECHNOL-OGY CANADA ULC   *p 483*
1035 INDUSTRIAL RD, AYR, ON, N0B 1E0
(519) 622-4545   *SIC 5013*
MANN, DON EXCAVATING LTD   *p 337*
4098 LOCHSIDE DR, VICTORIA, BC, V8X 2C8
(250) 479-8283   *SIC 1794*
MANN, R. E. BROKERS LTD   *p 881*
28 COLBORNE ST N, SIMCOE, ON, N3Y 3T9
(519) 426-2551   *SIC 6411*
MANN-NORTHWAY AUTO SOURCE *p 1414*
See MANN-NORTHWAY AUTO SOURCE LTD
MANN-NORTHWAY AUTO SOURCE LTD   *p 1414*
500 MARQUIS RD E, PRINCE ALBERT, SK, S6V 8B3
(306) 765-2200   *SIC 5511*
MANNAH FOODS   *p 1025*
See MCDONALD'S RESTAURANTS OF CANADA LIMITED
MANNARICH FOOD INC   *p 878*
131 FINCHDENE SQ UNIT 10, SCARBOR-OUGH, ON, M1X 1A6
(905) 471-9656   *SIC 5142*
MANNING COMMUNITY HEALTH CENTRE   *p 145*
See ALBERTA HEALTH SERVICES
MANNING ELLIOTT LLP   *p 314*
1050 PENDER ST W 11TH FL, VANCOU-VER, BC, V6E 3S7
(604) 714-3600   *SIC 8721*
MANNING FOREST PRODUCTS LTD *p 145*
GD, MANNING, AB, T0H 2M0
(780) 836-3111   *SIC 2421*
MANO'S FAMILY RESTAURANT   *p 1424*
See HARADROS FOOD SERVICES INC
MANOIR DE LA ROSELIERE   *p 1243*
3055 1E AV BUREAU 259, NOTRE-DAME-DES-PINS, QC, G0M 1K0
(418) 774-6700   *SIC 8361*
MANOIR DES SABLES INC   *p 1244*
90 AV DES JARDINS, ORFORD, QC, J1X 6M6
(819) 847-4747   *SIC 7011*
MANOIR DU LAC DELAGE INC   *p 1124*
40 AV DU LAC, LAC-DELAGE, QC, G3C 5C4
(418) 848-0691   *SIC 7011*
MANOIR DU LAC DELAGE, LE   *p 1124*
See MANOIR DU LAC DELAGE INC
MANOIR ET COURS DE L'ATRIUM INC   *p 1256*
545 RUE FRANCIS-BYRNE, QUEBEC, QC, G1H 7L3
(418) 626-6060   *SIC 8361*
MANOIR HOVEY (1985) INC   *p 1073*
575 CH HOVEY, CANTON-DE-HATLEY, QC, J0B 2C0
(819) 842-2421   *SIC 7011*
MANOIR MONTEFIORE   *p 1083*
See REVERA INC
MANOIR SAINT-JEAN BAPTISTE INC *p 395*
5 AV RICHARD, BOUCTOUCHE, NB, E4S 3T2
(506) 743-7344   *SIC 8361*

MANOIR ST-PATRICE INC   *p 1087*
3615 BOUL PERRON, COTE SAINT-LUC, QC, H7V 1P4
(450) 681-1621   *SIC 8361*
MANOIR ST-SAUVEUR   *p 1269*
See GROUPE LES MANOIRS DU QUEBEC INC, LES
MANOR TOOL AND DIE LTD   *p 807*
5264 PULLEYBANK ST, OLDCASTLE, ON, N0R 1L0
(519) 737-6537   *SIC 3544*
MANORCARE PARTNERS   *p 890*
218 EDWARD ST, STIRLING, ON, K0K 3E0
(613) 395-2596   *SIC 8051*
MANORCORE CONSTRUCTION INC *p 490*
4707 CHRISTIE DR, BEAMSVILLE, ON, L0R 1B4
(905) 563-8888   *SIC 1542*
MANORCORE GROUP INC   *p 490*
4707 CHRISTIE DR, BEAMSVILLE, ON, L0R 1B4
(905) 563-8888   *SIC 1542*
MANOUCHER FINE FOODS INC   *p 795*
703 CLAYSON RD, NORTH YORK, ON, M9M 2H4
(416) 747-1234   *SIC 2051*
MANPOWER   *p 899*
See SUDBURY MANAGEMENT SERVICES LIMITED
MANPOWER   *p 909*
See P & A MANAGEMENT LTD
MANPOWER PROFESSIONAL INC   *p 53*
734 7 AVE SW SUITE 120, CALGARY, AB, T2P 3P8
(403) 269-6936   *SIC 7361*
MANPOWER SERVICES   *p 53*
See MANPOWER PROFESSIONAL INC
MANPOWER SERVICES   *p 89*
See MANPOWER SERVICES (ALBERTA) LTD
MANPOWER SERVICES (ALBERTA) LTD *p 89*
10201 JASPER AVE NW SUITE 102, ED-MONTON, AB, T5J 3N7
(780) 420-0110   *SIC 7363*
MANPOWER SERVICES CANADA LIMITED *p 772*
4950 YONGE ST SUITE 700, NORTH YORK, ON, M2N 6K1
(416) 225-4455   *SIC 7363*
MANPOWER TEMPORARY SERVICES   *p 772*
See MANPOWER SERVICES CANADA LIMITED
MANROC DEVELOPMENTS INC   *p 663*
7 BLACK RD, MANITOUWADGE, ON, P0T 2C0
(807) 826-4564   *SIC 1629*
MANSEAU & PERRON INC   *p 1290*
701 AV DAVY, ROUYN-NORANDA, QC, J9Y 0A8
(819) 762-2818   *SIC 1761*
MANSFIELD MEDICAL DIST   *p 1157*
See 3762530 CANADA INC
MANSFIELD MEDICAL DISTRIBUTORS LTD   *p 1158*
5775 AV ANDOVER, MONT-ROYAL, QC, H4T 1H6
(514) 739-3633   *SIC 5122*
MANSION   *p 1072*
See DISTRIBUTIONS ALIMENTAIRES MANSION INC, LES
MANSONVILLE PLASTICS (B.C.) LIMITED *p 272*
19402 56 AVE, SURREY, BC, V3S 6K4
(604) 534-8626   *SIC 2821*
MANSOUR MINING TECHNOLOGIES INC *p 901*
2502 ELM, SUDBURY, ON, P3E 4R8
(705) 682-0671   *SIC 5082*
MANSTEEL LTD   *p 855*
105 INDUSTRIAL RD SUITE 200, RICH-MOND HILL, ON, L4C 2Y4
(905) 780-1488   *SIC 3441*

MANTEAUX MANTEAUX   *p 1155*
See 157503 CANADA INC
MANTEAUX MOOSE   *p 1178*
See CAPITAL STIKLY INC
MANTECH INC.   *p 601*
2 ADMIRAL PL, GUELPH, ON, N1G 4N4
(519) 763-4245   *SIC 3821*
MANTEI HOLDINGS LTD   *p 40*
5935 6 ST NE, CALGARY, AB, T2K 5R5
(403) 295-0028   *SIC 2431*
MANTEI'S TRANSPORT LTD   *p 17*
8715 44 ST SE, CALGARY, AB, T2C 2P5
(403) 531-1600   *SIC 4212*
MANTEO BEACH CLUB LTD   *p 219*
3766 LAKESHORE RD, KELOWNA, BC, V1W 3L4
(250) 860-1031   *SIC 7011*
MANTEO RESORT   *p 219*
See MANTEO BEACH CLUB LTD
MANTHA INSURANCE BROKERS LTD   *p 1001*
295 MONTREAL RD, VANIER, ON, K1L 6B8
(613) 746-1450   *SIC 6411*
MANTHA REAL ESTATE & INSURANCE INC   *p 1001*
295 MONTREAL RD, VANIER, ON, K1L 6B8
(613) 830-3000   *SIC 6411*
MANTIQUE   *p 289*
See MANTIQUE FASHIONS LTD
MANTIQUE FASHIONS LTD   *p 289*
5 5TH AVE E, VANCOUVER, BC, V5T 1G7
(604) 736-7161   *SIC 5621*
MANTO, MARK BUILDING MATERIALS LTD   *p 132*
10921 100 ST, GRANDE PRAIRIE, AB, T8V 2M9
(780) 532-2092   *SIC 5072*
MANTORIA INCORPOREE   *p 1402*
4492 RUE SAINTE-CATHERINE O, WEST-MOUNT, QC, H3Z 1R7
(514) 488-4004   *SIC 4731*
MANTRA PHARMA INC   *p 1071*
4605B BOUL LAPINIERE BUREAU 250, BROSSARD, QC, J4Z 3T5
(450) 678-7088   *SIC 5122*
MANTRALOGIX INC   *p 706*
267 MATHESON BLVD E SUITE 5, MISSIS-SAUGA, ON, L4Z 1X8
(905) 629-3200   *SIC 8741*
MANU FORTI CORPORATION LTD   *p 474*
222 BAYLY ST W, AJAX, ON, L1S 3V4
(905) 686-2133   *SIC 5812*
MANUALIFE SECURITIES   *p 788*
See 1556890 ONTARIO LTD
MANUFACT LOGISTICS LTD   *p 793*
3655 WESTON RD SUITE 1, NORTH YORK, ON, M9L 1V8
(416) 739-8411   *SIC 5078*
MANUFACTURE D'EQUIPMENT HARDT INC   *p 1128*
1400 50E AV, LACHINE, QC, H8T 2V3
(514) 631-7271   *SIC 3469*
MANUFACTURE DE BAS CULOTTES LAM-OUR INC   *p 1179*
55 RUE DE LOUVAIN O BUREAU 200, MONTREAL, QC, H2N 1A4
(514) 381-7687   *SIC 2251*
MANUFACTURE DE BIJOUX ETOILES D'ARGENT   *p 1241*
See SILVER STAR MANUFACTURING CO INC
MANUFACTURE DE LINGERIE CHATEAU INC   *p 1184*
215 RUE SAINT-ZOTIQUE O, MONTREAL, QC, H2V 1A2
(514) 274-7505   *SIC 5136*
MANUFACTURE DE VETEMENTS EMPIRE INC   *p 1182*
5800 RUE SAINT-DENIS BUREAU 302, MONTREAL, QC, H2S 3L5
(514) 279-7341   *SIC 2311*
MANUFACTURE DOMFOAM INTERNA-TIONAL   *p*

1344
See DOMFOAM INTERNATIONAL INC
MANUFACTURE EXM LTEE   p 1059
870 BOUL MICHELE-BOHEC, BLAINVILLE,
QC, J7C 5E2
(450) 979-4373   *SIC 3613*
MANUFACTURE FRAMECO LTEE   p 1322
230 RUE DU PARC, SAINT-JOSEPH-DE-
BEAUCE, QC, G0S 2V0
(418) 397-6895   *SIC 3443*
**MANUFACTURE LEVITON DU CANADA
LTEE**   p 1251
165 BOUL HYMUS, POINTE-CLAIRE, QC,
H9R 1E9
(514) 954-1840   *SIC 5063*
MANUFACTURE TRIPLE G. INC   p 1134
2705 RUE MICHELIN, LAVAL-OUEST, QC,
H7L 5X6
(450) 681-2700   *SIC 5136*
MANUFACTURE UNIVERSELLE S.B. INC p
1183
5555 AV CASGRAIN BUREAU 300, MON-
TREAL, QC, H2T 1Y1
(514) 271-1177   *SIC 2341*
**MANUFACTURERS LIFE INSURANCE
COMPANY, THE**   p 929
200 BLOOR ST E SUITE 1, TORONTO, ON,
M4W 1E5
(416) 926-3000   *SIC 6311*
**MANUFACTURERS LIFE INSURANCE
COMPANY, THE**   p 1008
500 KING ST N, WATERLOO, ON, N2L 5W6
(519) 747-7000   *SIC 6311*
**MANUFACTURERS LIFE INSURANCE
COMPANY, THE**   p 1198
2000 RUE MANSFIELD UNITE 300, MON-
TREAL, QC, H3A 2Z4
(514) 288-6268   *SIC 6311*
**MANUFACTURIER DE BAS DE NYLON
SPLENDID INC**   p 1179
55 RUE DE LOUVAIN O BUREAU 200,
MONTREAL, QC, H2N 1A4
(514) 381-7687   *SIC 5137*
**MANUFACTURIERS D'ACCESSOIRES
MORTUAIRES LTEE**   p 1101
211 RUE BERARD, FARNHAM, QC, J2N
2L4
(450) 293-1712   *SIC 5072*
**MANUFACTURIERS D'ALUMINIUM OT-
TAWA INC, LES**   p
1302
439   BOUL   INDUSTRIEL,   SAINT-
EUSTACHE, QC, J7R 5R3
(450) 983-3766   *SIC 5051*
MANUFACTURIERS WARWICK LTEE, LES
p 1400
235 RUE SAINT-LOUIS, WARWICK, QC,
J0A 1M0
(819) 358-4100   *SIC 2421*
MANUFACTURING / SALES FACILITIES p
121
See WENZEL DOWNHOLE TOOLS LTD
MANUFACTURING CENTER   p 123
See WEATHERFORD CANADA LTD
MANUGYPSE INC   p 1277
5385 RUE RIDEAU BUREAU 871, QUE-
BEC, QC, G2E 5V9
(418) 871-8088   *SIC 5039*
**MANULIFE ASSET MANAGEMENT LIM-
ITED**   p
929
200 BLOOR ST E SUITE 1, TORONTO, ON,
M4W 1E5
(416) 581-8300   *SIC 6722*
MANULIFE BANK OF CANADA   p 640
500 KING ST N SUITE 500-MA, KITCH-
ENER, ON, N2J 4Z6
· (519) 747-7000   *SIC 6021*
MANULIFE CANADA LTD   p 640
500 KING ST N, KITCHENER, ON, N2J 4Z6
(519) 747-7000   *SIC 6311*
MANULIFE CANADA LTD   p 1198
2000 RUE MANSFIELD UNITE 200, MON-
TREAL, QC, H3A 2Z4

(514) 845-1612   *SIC 8742*
**MANULIFE CANADIAN REAL ESTATE IN-
VESTMENT FUND**   p
929
250 BLOOR ST FL 15, TORONTO, ON,
M4W 1E5
(416) 926-5500   *SIC 6531*
MANULIFE FINANCIAL   p 1008
*See MANUFACTURERS LIFE INSURANCE
COMPANY, THE*
MANULIFE FINANCIAL 1182   p 1198
See MANULIFE CANADA LTD
MANULIFE FINANCIAL CORPORATION p
929
200 BLOOR ST E, TORONTO, ON, M4W
1E5
(416) 926-3000   *SIC 6411*
MANULIFE FINANCIAL SERVICES INC p
929
200 BLOOR ST E SUITE 1, TORONTO, ON,
M4W 1E5
(416) 926-3000   *SIC 8742*
**MANULIFE MFC INVESTMENT MANAGE-
MENT**   p
929
*See MANULIFE FINANCIAL CORPORA-
TION*
MANULIFE MUTUAL FUNDS   p 929
*See MANULIFE ASSET MANAGEMENT
LIMITED*
MANULIFE SECURITIES INSURANCE   p
774
4101 YONGE ST SUITE 700, NORTH
YORK, ON, M2P 1N6
(416) 218-8707   *SIC 6411*
**MANULIFE SECURITIES INVESTMENT
SERVICES INC**   p 806
1235 NORTH SERVICE RD W SUITE 500,
OAKVILLE, ON, L6M 2W2
(905) 469-2100   *SIC 6722*
MANULIFE TRUST SERVICES LIMITED p
1213
1245 RUE SHERBROOKE O BUREAU
1500, MONTREAL, QC, H3G 1G3
(514) 499-7999   *SIC 6722*
MANULIFE US REGIONAL BANK TRUST p
929
200 BLOOR ST E NORTH TOWER,
TORONTO, ON, M4W 1E5
(416) 926-3000   *SIC 6726*
MANULIFT   p 1293
See MANULIFT E.M.I. LTEE
MANULIFT E.M.I. LTEE   p 1293
100 RUE D'ANVERS, SAINT-AUGUSTIN-
DE-DESMAURES, QC, G3A 1S4
(418) 878-5424   *SIC 5084*
MANUS ABRASIVE SYSTEMS INC   p 122
1040 78 AVE NW, EDMONTON, AB, T6P
1L7
(780) 468-2588   *SIC 5085*
MANUS INC   p 53
350 7 AVE SW SUITE 1400, CALGARY, AB,
T2P 3N9
(403) 299-9600   *SIC 8742*
MANUTENTION QUEBEC INC   p 1251
100A BOUL HYMUS, POINTE-CLAIRE, QC,
H9R 1E4
(514) 694-4223   *SIC 5084*
**MANUTENTIONS MARSOLAIS BRENDON
INC**   p 1298
7255 CH DE SAINTE-?M?LIE, SAINT-
DAMIEN, QC, J0K 2E0
SIC 4789
MANUTEX   p 1337
See TRANSPORT TFI 14 S.E.C.
**MANY ISLANDS PIPELINES (CANADA)
LIMITED**   p 1418
1777 VICTORIA AVE SUITE 500, REGINA,
SK, S4P 4K5
(306) 777-9500   *SIC 4922*
**MANY RIVERS COUNSELLING & SUP-
PORT SERVICES**   p
1440
4071 4TH AVE, WHITEHORSE, YT, Y1A

1H3
(867) 667-2970   *SIC 8699*
MANZ CONTRACTING SERVICES INC   p
1020
2680 TEMPLE DR, WINDSOR, ON, N8W
5J5
(519) 974-2899   *SIC 1721*
MANZ DECOR CENTRE   p 1020
*See MANZ CONTRACTING SERVICES
INC*
MAPEI INC   p 504
95 WALKER DR, BRAMPTON, ON, L6T 5K5
(905) 799-2663   *SIC 2891*
MAPEI INC   p 1362
2900 AV FRANCIS-HUGHES, SAINTE-
ROSE, QC, H7L 3J5
(450) 662-1212   *SIC 2891*
MAPLE ACURA   p 664
111 AUTO VAUGHAN DR, MAPLE, ON, L6A
4A1
(289) 342-0185   *SIC 5511*
MAPLE CDB CENTRAL JV   p 724
*See MAPLE REINDERS CONSTRUCTORS
LTD*
MAPLE CITY OFFICE EQUIPMENT LTD p
543
170 QUEEN ST, CHATHAM, ON, N7M 2G8
(519) 352-2940   *SIC 5999*
MAPLE COMPUTERS   p 708
See MAPLE COMPUTERS INC
MAPLE COMPUTERS INC   p 708
20 DUNDAS ST E UNIT 4, MISSISSAUGA,
ON, L5A 1W2
(905) 272-1446   *SIC 5932*
MAPLE DALE CHEESE INC   p 846
2864 HWY 37, PLAINFIELD, ON, K0K 2V0
(613) 477-2454   *SIC 5143*
MAPLE FREIGHT PARTNERSHIP   p 265
4871 MILLER RD UNIT 1162, RICHMOND,
BC, V7B 1K8
(604) 279-2525   *SIC 4731*
MAPLE FUN TOURS LTD   p 299
997 SEYMOUR ST SUITE 610, VANCOU-
VER, BC, V6B 3M1
(604) 683-5244   *SIC 4724*
MAPLE GROVE CARE COMMUNITY   p 498
215 SUNNY MEADOW BLVD, BRAMPTON,
ON, L6R 3B5
(905) 458-7604   *SIC 8361*
MAPLE GROVE SOBEYS   p 801
See SOBEYS CAPITAL INCORPORATED
MAPLE HIGH SCHOOL   p 664
*See YORK REGION DISTRICT SCHOOL
BOARD*
MAPLE HILL MANOR SOCIETY INC p 464
700 KING ST, NEW WATERFORD, NS, B1H
3Z5
(902) 862-6495   *SIC 8051*
MAPLE LEAF   p 406
See CANADA BREAD COMPANY, LIMITED
MAPLE LEAF   p 724
See MAPLE LEAF FOODS INC
MAPLE LEAF BREAD   p 555
See MAPLE LEAF BREAD LTD
MAPLE LEAF BREAD LTD   p 555
144 VICEROY RD, CONCORD, ON, L4K
2L8
(905) 738-1242   *SIC 2041*
MAPLE LEAF CONSTRUCTION LTD   p 382
777 ERIN ST, WINNIPEG, MB, R3G 2W2
(204) 783-7091   *SIC 1611*
MAPLE LEAF CONSUMER FOODS   p 366
See MAPLE LEAF FOODS INC
MAPLE LEAF DISPOSAL LTD   p 228
20380 LANGLEY BYPASS, LANGLEY, BC,
V3A 5E7
(604) 533-4993   *SIC 4953*
MAPLE LEAF DISTRIBUTION CENTRE   p
523
See MAPLE LEAF FOODS INC
MAPLE LEAF FOODS INC   p 122
2619 91 AVE NW, EDMONTON, AB, T6P
1S3
(780) 467-6022   *SIC 2015*

MAPLE LEAF FOODS INC   p 141
2720 2A AVE N, LETHBRIDGE, AB, T1H
5B4
(403) 380-9900   *SIC 5148*
MAPLE LEAF FOODS INC   p 142
4141 1 AVE S, LETHBRIDGE, AB, T1J 4P8
(403) 328-1756   *SIC 2011*
MAPLE LEAF FOODS INC   p 347
6355 RICHMOND AVE E, BRANDON, MB,
R7A 7M5
(204) 571-2500   *SIC 2011*
MAPLE LEAF FOODS INC   p 366
607 DAWSON RD N SUITE 555, WIN-
NIPEG, MB, R2J 0T2
(204) 233-7347   *SIC 2048*
MAPLE LEAF FOODS INC   p 366
870 LAGIMODIERE BLVD SUITE 23, WIN-
NIPEG, MB, R2J 0T9
(204) 233-2421   *SIC 2011*
MAPLE LEAF FOODS INC   p 523
5100 HARVESTER RD, BURLINGTON, ON,
L7L 4X4
(905) 681-5050   *SIC 5147*
MAPLE LEAF FOODS INC   p 575
550 KIPLING AVE, ETOBICOKE, ON, M8Z
5E9
SIC 2011
MAPLE LEAF FOODS INC   p 608
21 BROCKLEY DR, HAMILTON, ON, L8E
3C3
(800) 268-3708   *SIC 2011*
MAPLE LEAF FOODS INC   p 617
90 10TH AVE, HANOVER, ON, N4N 3B8
(519) 364-3200   *SIC 5144*
MAPLE LEAF FOODS INC   p 724
6985 FINANCIAL DR, MISSISSAUGA, ON,
L5N 0A1
(905) 285-5000   *SIC 2011*
MAPLE LEAF FOODS INC   p 724
2626 ARGENTIA RD, MISSISSAUGA, ON,
L5N 5N2
(905) 890-0053   *SIC 2015*
MAPLE LEAF FOODS INC   p 732
30 EGLINTON AVE W SUITE 500, MISSIS-
SAUGA, ON, L5R 3E7
(905) 501-3076   *SIC 2011*
MAPLE LEAF FOODS INC   p 752
70 HERITAGE DR, NEW HAMBURG, ON,
N3A 2J4
(519) 662-1501   *SIC 0254*
MAPLE LEAF FOODS INC   p 801
178 SOUTH SERVICE RD E, OAKVILLE,
ON, L6J 0A5
(905) 815-6500   *SIC 5141*
MAPLE LEAF FOODS INC   p 848
15350 OLD SIMCOE RD, PORT PERRY,
ON, L9L 1L8
(905) 985-7373   *SIC 2038*
MAPLE LEAF FOODS INC   p 888
1865 PERTH ROAD SUITE 139, ST
MARYS, ON, N4X 1C8
(519) 229-8900   *SIC 2015*
MAPLE LEAF FOODS INC   p 894
92 HIGHLAND RD E, STONEY CREEK, ON,
L8J 2W6
(905) 662-8883   *SIC 2015*
MAPLE LEAF FOODS INC   p 993
100 ETHEL AVE, TORONTO, ON, M6N 4Z7
(416) 767-5151   *SIC 2015*
MAPLE LEAF FOODS INC   p 1292
254 RUE PRINCIPALE, SAINT-ANSELME,
QC, G0R 2N0
SIC 5411
MAPLE LEAF FOODS INC   p 1432
100 MCLEOD AVE, SASKATOON, SK, S7M
5V9
(306) 382-2210   *SIC 2011*
MAPLE LEAF FOODS, DIV OF   p 752
See MAPLE LEAF FOODS INC
MAPLE LEAF FOREST PRODUCTS INC p
861
418 FOURTH LINE W, SAULT STE. MARIE,
ON, P6A 0B5
(705) 450-2696   *SIC 5031*

MAPLE LEAF FRESH FOODS   p 801
See MAPLE LEAF FOODS INC
MAPLE LEAF HOMES INC   p 401
655 WILSEY RD, FREDERICTON, NB, E3B
7K3
(506) 459-1335   SIC 2452
MAPLE LEAF INTERNATIONAL CONSULT-ING INC   p
925
27 ST CLAIR AVE E SUITE 1145,
TORONTO, ON, M4T 1L8
(416) 724-6475   SIC 8741
MAPLE LEAF METALS (A PARTNERSHIP)
p 110
4510 68 AVE NW, EDMONTON, AB, T6B
2P3
(780) 468-3951   SIC 5085
MAPLE LEAF PORK   p 142
See MAPLE LEAF FOODS INC
MAPLE LEAF PORK   p 347
See MAPLE LEAF FOODS INC
MAPLE LEAF POTOTOES, DIV OF   p 141
See MAPLE LEAF FOODS INC
MAPLE LEAF POULTRY   p 122
See MAPLE LEAF FOODS INC
MAPLE LEAF POULTRY   p 724
See MAPLE LEAF FOODS INC
MAPLE LEAF SELF STORAGE   p 342
See LARCO INVESTMENTS LTD
MAPLE LEAF SPORTS & ENTERTAIN-MENT LTD   p
964
50 BAY ST SUITE 500, TORONTO, ON, M5J
2L2
(416) 815-5400   SIC 7941
MAPLE LEAF TAXI-CAB LIMITED   p 919
1245 DANFORTH AVE SUITE 203,
TORONTO, ON, M4J 5B5
(416) 465-2445   SIC 4121
MAPLE LEAF WHEELCHAIR MANUFAC-TURING INC   p
740
6540 TOMKEN RD, MISSISSAUGA, ON,
L5T 2E9
(905) 564-2250   SIC 3842
MAPLE LODGE FARMS LTD   p 417
2222 COMMERCIALE ST, SAINT-FRANCOIS-DE-MADAWASKA, NB,   E7A
1B6
(506) 992-2192   SIC 2015
MAPLE LODGE FARMS LTD   p 511
8301 WINSTON CHURCHILL BLVD,
BRAMPTON, ON, L6Y 0A2
(905) 455-8340   SIC 2015
MAPLE LODGE HOLDING CORPORATION
p 511
8301 WINSTON CHURCHILL BLVD,
BRAMPTON, ON, L6Y 0A2
(905) 455-8340   SIC 6712
MAPLE LODGE PET FOOD, DIV OF   p 511
See MAPLE LODGE FARMS LTD
MAPLE MANUFACTURING, DIV OF   p 490
See NIAGARA PISTON INC
MAPLE MUSIC   p 981
See MAPLECORE LTD
MAPLE REINDERS CONSTRUCTORS LTD
p 724
2660 ARGENTIA RD, MISSISSAUGA, ON,
L5N 5V4
(905) 821-4844   SIC 8711
MAPLE REINDERS GROUP LTD   p 724
2660 ARGENTIA RD, MISSISSAUGA, ON,
L5N 5V4
(905) 821-4844   SIC 6712
MAPLE RIDGE CHRYSLER   p 231
See MR MOTORS LP
MAPLE RIDGE COMMUNITY MANAGE-MENT LTD   p
706
5753 COOPERS AVE UNIT A, MISSIS-SAUGA, ON, L4Z 1R9
(905) 507-6726   SIC 6531
MAPLE RIDGE HAUDAI   p 230
See SUPER DAVE'S GOLDEN EARS MO-

TORS LTD
MAPLE RIDGE PITT MEADOWS NEWS p
231
22328 119 AVE, MAPLE RIDGE, BC, V2X
2Z3
(604) 467-1122   SIC 5963
MAPLE RIDGE SECONDARY SCHOOL p
231
See SCHOOL DISTRICT NO 42 (MAPLE
RIDGE-PITT MEADOWS)
MAPLE RIDGE/PITT MEADOWS COMMU-NITY SERVICES   p
231
11907 228 ST, MAPLE RIDGE, BC, V2X
8G8
(604) 467-6911   SIC 8699
MAPLE STONE   p 457
See SHANNEX INCORPORATED
MAPLE TERRAZZO MARBLE & TILE IN-CORPORATED   p
495
16 NIXON RD, BOLTON, ON, L7E 1K3
(905) 850-3006   SIC 3281
MAPLE TERRAZZO MARBLE & TILE IN-CORPORATED   p
555
200 EDGELEY BLVD UNIT 9, CONCORD,
ON, L4K 3Y8
(905) 760-1776   SIC 8631
MAPLE TREAT CORPORATION, THE   p
1111
1037 BOUL INDUSTRIEL, GRANBY, QC,
J2J 2B8
(450) 777-4464   SIC 2099
MAPLE UTILITY   p 479
See 1254561 ONTARIO INC
MAPLE VIEW LODGE   p 479
See UNITED COUNTIES OF LEEDS AND
GRENVILLE
MAPLE VILLA LONG TERM CARE CEN-TRE   p
530
See DALLOV HOLDINGS LIMITED
MAPLE VOLKSWAGEN   p 664
260 SWEETRIVER BLVD, MAPLE, ON, L6A
4V3
(905) 832-5711   SIC 5511
MAPLE-REINDERS INC   p 724
2660 ARGENTIA RD, MISSISSAUGA, ON,
L5N 5V4
(905) 821-4844   SIC 1542
MAPLEBRAINS TECHNOLOGIES   p
398
842 GAUVIN RD, DIEPPE, NB, E1A 1N1
(506) 899-1526   SIC 8748
MAPLECORE LTD   p 981
230 RICHMOND ST W SUITE 11,
TORONTO, ON, M5V 3E5
(416) 961-1040   SIC 7389
**MAPLECREST VILLAGE RETIREMENT
RESIDENCE**   p 599
See REVERA INC
MAPLEHURST BAKERIES INC   p 504
379 ORENDA RD, BRAMPTON, ON, L6T
1G6
(905) 791-7400   SIC 2051
MAPLEHURST BAKERIES INC   p 724
2095 MEADOWVALE BLVD, MISSIS-SAUGA, ON, L5N 5N1
(905) 567-0660   SIC 2053
MAPLEHURST BAKERIES INC   p 1416
1700 PARK ST, REGINA, SK, S4N 6B2
(306) 359-7400   SIC 2051
MAPLEHURST BAKERIES, DIV OF   p 504
See MAPLEHURST BAKERIES INC
MAPLERIDGE MECHANICAL CONTACT-ING INC   p
845
939 DILLINGHAM RD, PICKERING, ON,
L1W 1Z7
(905) 831-0524   SIC 1711
MAPLES COLLEGIATE   p 369
See SEVEN OAKS SCHOOL DIVISION
MAPLES HOME FOR SENIORS, THE p 902

See CARESSANT-CARE NURSING AND
RETIREMENT HOMES LIMITED
**MAPLES PERSONAL CARE HOME (1982)
LTD**   p 369
500 MANDALAY DR, WINNIPEG, MB, R2P
1V4
(204) 632-8570   SIC 8051
MAPLESOFT   p 1011
See WATERLOO MAPLE INC
MAPLEVIEW SHOPPING CENTRE   p 531
See IVANHOE CAMBRIDGE II INC.
MAPLEWOOD HIGH SCHOOL   p 866
See TORONTO DISTRICT SCHOOL
BOARD
MAPLEWOOD NURSING HOME LIMITED p
881
500 QUEENSWAY W SUITE 210, SIMCOE,
ON, N3Y 4R4
(519) 426-8305   SIC 6513
MAPLEWOOD NURSING HOME LIMITED p
912
73 BIDWELL ST, TILLSONBURG, ON, N4G
3T8
(519) 842-3563   SIC 8051
MAR DEVELOPMENTS INC   p 555
237 ROMINA DR UNIT 1, CONCORD, ON,
L4K 4V3
(905) 738-2255   SIC 6712
MAR-CON WIRE BELT INC   p 255
2431 VAUXHALL PL, RICHMOND, BC, V6V
1Z5
(604) 278-8922   SIC 5084
MAR-DEE ENTERPRISES   p 348
See 73502 MANITOBA LIMITED
MAR-HAM AUTOMOTIVE INC   p 616
57 RYMAL RD W, HAMILTON, ON, L9B 1B5
(905) 389-7111   SIC 5511
MAR-JOHN'S NURSERY LTD   p 1006
1060 LOBSINGER LINE, WATERLOO, ON,
N2J 4G8
(519) 664-2482   SIC 5191
MAR-QUINN INDUSTRIES LTD   p 139
7115 SPARROW DR, LEDUC, AB, T9E 7L1
(780) 986-7805   SIC 3533
MAR-SAN EXCAVATING & GRADING LTDp
495
21 HOLLAND DR, BOLTON, ON, L7E 4J6
(905) 857-1616   SIC 1794
**MAR-SPAN HOME HARDWARE BUILDING
CENTRE**   p 565
See MAR-SPAN TRUSS INC
MAR-SPAN TRUSS INC   p 565
7873 WELLINGTON RD 8, DRAYTON, ON,
N0G 1P0
(519) 638-3086   SIC 5211
MARA TECHNOLOGIES INC   p 678
5680 14TH AVE, MARKHAM, ON, L3S 3K8
(905) 201-1787   SIC 3672
MARACIHER   p 1244
See JARDINS VEGIBEC INC, LES
MARACLE PRESS LIMITED   p 813
1156 KING ST E, OSHAWA, ON, L1H 1H8
(905) 723-3438   SIC 2752
MARAICHER A. BARBEAU & FILS INC, LE
p 1349
2430 RUE PRINCIPALE, SAINT-MICHEL,
QC, J0L 2J0
(450) 454-2555   SIC 0182
MARANELLO BMW   p 1032
See MARANELLO MOTORS LIMITED
MARANELLO MOTORS LIMITED   p 1032
55 AUTO PARK CIR, WOODBRIDGE, ON,
L4L 8R1
(416) 213-5699   SIC 5511
MARANELLO SPORTS INC   p 1032
200 AUTO PARK CIR, WOODBRIDGE, ON,
L4L 8R1
(416) 749-5325   SIC 5511
MARANT CONSTRUCTION LIMITED   p 918
200 WICKSTEED AVE, TORONTO, ON,
M4G 2B6
(416) 425-6650   SIC 1542
MARANTZ CANADA INC   p 672
505 APPLE CREEK BLVD UNIT 5,

MARKHAM, ON, L3R 5B1
(905) 415-9292   SIC 5065
MARATHON DRILLING CORPORATION   p
599
6847 HIRAM DR, GREELY, ON, K4P 1A2
(613) 821-4800   SIC 1799
**MARATHON FASTENERS & HARDWARE
INC**   p 717
4170 SLADEVIEW CRES UNIT 7, MISSIS-SAUGA, ON, L5L 0A1
(905) 607-8665   SIC 5072
MARATHON OIL CANADA CORPORATION
p 53
440 2 AVE SW SUITE 2400, CALGARY, AB,
T2P 5E9
(403) 233-1700   SIC 1382
MARATHON UNDERGROUND CON-STRUCTOR CORPORATION   p
599
6847 HIRAM DR, GREELY, ON, K4P 1A2
(613) 821-4800   SIC 1381
MARBLE ELECTRONICS INC   p 606
650 WOODLAWN RD W SUITE 16A,
GUELPH, ON, N1K 1B8
(519) 767-2863   SIC 3647
MARBLE RESTAURANTS LTD   p 115
9054 51 AVE NW SUITE 200, EDMONTON,
AB, T6E 5X4
(780) 462-5755   SIC 5812
MARBLE RIDGE FARMS LTD   p 351
GD, HODGSON, MB, R0C 1N0
(204) 372-6438   SIC 4731
MARBOR HOLDINGS LTD   p 236
422 VERNON ST, NELSON, BC, V1L 4E5
(250) 352-5331   SIC 7011
MARBRO CAPITAL LIMITED   p 568
35 EARL MARTIN DR, ELMIRA, ON, N3B
3L4
(519) 669-5171   SIC 2048
MARC ANTHONY COSMETICS LTD   p 555
190 PIPPIN RD, CONCORD, ON, L4K 4X9
(905) 530-2500   SIC 5122
MARC VILLENEUVE INC   p 1395
2050 RUE CHICOINE, VAUDREUIL-DORION, QC, J7V 8P2
(450) 424-4616   SIC 5143
MARC'S NOFRILLS   p 697
See LOBLAW COMPANIES LIMITED
MARCAN PHARMACEUTICALS INC   p 749
2 GURDWARA RD SUITE 112, NEPEAN,
ON, K2E 1A2
(613) 228-2600   SIC 5122
MARCAN TRANSPORT   p 1331
See 9327-0197 QUEBEC INC
MARCANGELO   p 551
See CONCORD PREMIUM MEATS LTD
MARCATUS QED INC   p 991
43 HANNA AVE UNIT C-424, TORONTO,
ON, M6K 1X1
(416) 255-0099   SIC 5149
MARCEL BARIL LTEE   p 1289
101 AV MARCEL-BARIL, ROUYN-NORANDA, QC, J9X 5P5
(819) 764-3211   SIC 5074
MARCEL CHAREST ET FILS INC   p 1349
997 RTE 230 E, SAINT-PASCAL, QC, G0L
3Y0
(418) 492-5911   SIC 1542
MARCH CONSULTING ASSOCIATES INC p
1428
201 21ST ST E SUITE 200, SASKATOON,
SK, S7K 0B8
(306) 651-6330   SIC 8711
MARCH NETWORKS CORPORATIONp 624
303 TERRY FOX DR SUITE 200, KANATA,
ON, K2K 3J1
(613) 591-8181   SIC 3699
MARCH OF DIMES CANADA   p 919
10 OVERLEA BLVD, TORONTO, ON, M4H
1A4
(416) 425-3463   SIC 8331
MARCH SHIPPING (DIV OF)   p 1190
See NORTEC MARINE AGENCIES INC
MARCH? THURSO   p 1384

▲ Public Company   ■ Public Company Family Member   **HQ** Headquarters   **BR** Branch   **SL** Single Location

See 2875446 CANADA INC
MARCH? TRADITION ST-GEORGES *p* 1306
See 2788331 CANADA INC
MARCHAND CANADIAN TIRE DE BEAU-PORT   *p*
1254
See ENTREPRISES BOULOS,PIERRE L INC, LES
MARCHAND   CANADIAN   TIRE   DE BROSSARD   *p* 1070
See GESTION MICHEL SEGUIN INC
MARCHAND CANADIAN TIRE DE LA SARRE   *p* 1150
See GESTION D. PRESSAULT INC
MARCHAND CANADIAN TIRE DE MON-TREAL   *p*
1226
See MAGASIN MYRLANIE INC
MARCHAND CANADIAN TIRE DE MON-TREAL (MAISONNEUVE)   *p*
1382
See GESTION C. & L. LAROCHELLE INC
MARCHAND CANADIAN TIRE DE RE-PENTIGNY   *p*
1283
See GESTION RENE J. BEAUDOIN INC
MARCHAND CANADIAN TIRE DE SAINT-GEROGES   *p*
1304
See ENTREPRISES J.C. LEVESQUE INC, LES
MARCHAND CANADIAN TIRE DE SHAW-INIGAN   *p*
1368
See ENTREPRISES SYLVIE DROLET INC
MARCHAND CANADIAN TIRE DE SHER-BROOKE   *p*
1106
See PLACEMENTS MICHEL MAYRAND INC, LES
MARCHAND CANADIAN TIRE DE ST-JEROME   *p*
1320
See MAGASIN POULIN INC
MARCHAND CANADIAN TIRE DE STE-AGATHE   *p*
1354
See MAGASIN JEAN DUMAS INC
MARCHAND CANADIAN TIRE DE STE-DOROTHEE   *p*
1363
See GESTIONS SYLVAIN BERUBE INC
MARCHAND CANADIAN TIRE DE STE-FOY
p 1045
See GESTION ALAIN LAFOREST INC
MARCHAND CANADIAN TIRE DE VERDUN
p 1182
See GESTION REJEAN TROTTIER INC
MARCHAND CANADIAN TIRE DE VERDUN
p 1224
See GESTIONS GILBERT ROY INC
MARCHAND ELECTRICAL COMPANY LIM-ITED   *p*
595
1283 ALGOMA RD, GLOUCESTER, ON, K1B 3W7
(613) 749-2279   *SIC* 5063
MARCHAND, PIERRE STORE INC   *p* 898
12011 HIGHWAY 17 E, STURGEON FALLS, ON, P2B 2S7
(705) 753-2630   *SIC* 5531
MARCHANT'S SCHOOL SPORT LIMITED *p*
867
849 PROGRESS AVE, SCARBOROUGH, ON, M1H 2X4
(416) 439-9400   *SIC* 5091
MARCHE A. LAROUCHE LTEE   *p* 1079
992 BOUL DU SAGUENAY E, CHICOUTIMI, QC, G7H 1L5
(418) 543-4521   *SIC* 5411
MARCHE ADONIS   *p* 1290
See GROUPE ADONIS INC
MARCHE ALIMENTATION THIBAULT INC *p*
1380

2120 CH GASCON, TERREBONNE, QC, J6X 3A1
(450) 964-2050   *SIC* 5411
MARCHE ANDRE MARTEL INC   *p* 1301
219 RUE SAINT-LAURENT, SAINT-EUSTACHE, QC, J7P 4W4
(450) 472-7720   *SIC* 5411
MARCHE ANDRE TELLIER INC   *p* 1376
411 BOUL POLIQUIN, SOREL-TRACY, QC, J3P 7V9
(450) 743-3693   *SIC* 5411
MARCHE AU CHALET (1978) INC   *p* 1354
1300 BOUL DE SAINTE-ADELE, SAINTE-ADELE, QC, J8B 0K2
(450) 229-4256   *SIC* 7011
MARCHE AUX PUCES CINE-PARC ST-EUSTACHE   *p*
1300
See CINE-PARC ST-EUSTACHE INC
MARCHE AYLMER INC   *p* 1108
799 BOUL WILFRID-LAVIGNE BUREAU 1098, GATINEAU, QC, J9J 1V2
(819) 685-3490   *SIC* 5411
MARCHE BEAUBIEN INC   *p* 1163
6333 RUE BEAUBIEN E, MONTREAL, QC, H1M 3E6
(514) 254-6081   *SIC* 5411
MARCHE BELANGER INC   *p* 1289
680 AV CHAUSSE, ROUYN-NORANDA, QC, J9X 4B9
(819) 762-2992   *SIC* 5411
MARCHE BELLEMARE INC   *p* 1069
2121 BOUL LAPINIERE, BROSSARD, QC, J4W 1L7
(450) 445-3044   *SIC* 5411
MARCHE BELLEMARE INC   *p* 1308
5350 GRANDE ALLEE BUREAU 1353, SAINT-HUBERT, QC, J3Y 1A3
(450) 676-0220   *SIC* 5411
MARCHE BLAIS INC   *p* 1244
204 BOUL PABOS, PABOS, QC, G0C 2H0
(418) 689-3564   *SIC* 5146
MARCHE BOURGEAULT INC   *p* 1303
160 RUE SAINT-GABRIEL, SAINT-GABRIEL-DE-BRANDON, QC, J0K 2N0
(450) 835-4794   *SIC* 5411
MARCHE C.D.L. TELLIER INC   *p* 1239
6190 BOUL HENRI-BOURASSA E, MONTREAL-NORD, QC, H1G 5X3
(514) 321-0120   *SIC* 5411
MARCHE CENTRAL C.J.C. LTEE   *p* 1145
2642 CH DE CHAMBLY, LONGUEUIL, QC, J4L 1M5
(450) 651-4123   *SIC* 5411
MARCHE CHARLEMAGNE   *p* 1075
See 9157-5548 QUEBEC INC
MARCHE CHEVREFILS SAINT-SAUVEUR INC   *p* 1352
222A CH DU LAC-MILLETTE, SAINT-SAUVEUR, QC, J0R 1R3
(450) 227-8734   *SIC* 5411
MARCHE CHEVREFILS STE-AGATHE INC
p 1354
1050 RUE PRINCIPALE, SAINTE-AGATHE-DES-MONTS, QC, J8C 1L6
(819) 326-2822   *SIC* 5411
MARCHE CLEMENT DEFORGES INC   *p*
1097
1910 BOUL SAINT-JOSEPH, DRUM-MONDVILLE, QC, J2B 1R2
(819) 477-7700   *SIC* 5411
MARCHE COUTURE   *p* 1291
See COUTURE, ALFRED LIMITEE
MARCHE CREVIER   *p* 1282
See   SUPERMARCHE   CREVIER (IBERVILLE) INC
MARCHE CREVIER IGA (S.C.B.) INC   *p*
1297
655 RUE DE LA VISITATION, SAINT-CHARLES-BORROMEE, QC, J6E 4P9
(450) 752-1441   *SIC* 5411
MARCHE CREVIER IGA INC   *p* 1243
17 RUE GAUTHIER N, NOTRE-DAME-DES-PRAIRIES, QC, J6E 1T7

(450) 759-2554   *SIC* 5411
MARCHE CROISETIERE BERTHIER INC *p*
1057
1071   AV   GILLES-VILLENEUVE, BERTHIERVILLE, QC, J0K 1A0
(450) 836-3775   *SIC* 5411
MARCHE D'ALIMENTATION BECK INC *p*
1131
8130 BOUL CHAMPLAIN, LASALLE, QC, H8P 1B4
(514) 364-4777   *SIC* 5411
MARCHE D'ALIMENTATION CREVIER INC
p 1363
550 CHOMEDEY (A-13) O, SAINTE-ROSE, QC, H7X 3S9
(450) 689-3131   *SIC* 5992
MARCHE D'ALIMENTATION DIANE RO-DRIGUE INC   *p*
1146
714 BOUL SAINT-LAURENT O, LOUI-SEVILLE, QC, J5V 1K7
(819) 228-5818   *SIC* 5411
MARCHE D'ALIMENTATION MARCANIO & FILS INC   *p* 1172
1550 RUE BELANGER, MONTREAL, QC, H2G 1A8
(514) 729-1866   *SIC* 5411
MARCHE D'ALIMENTATION MARCANIO (ANJOU) INC   *p* 1049
7172 RUE BOMBARDIER, ANJOU, QC, H1J 2Z9
(514) 352-5447   *SIC* 5411
MARCHE   D'ALIMENTATION   MARTIN DUGUAY   *p* 1242
See 9125-9051 QUEBEC INC.
MARCHE   D'ALIMENTATION   MARTIN LAMARRE   *p* 1071
See 9215-9516 QUEBEC INC
MARCHE D'ANIMAUX DE L'EST   *p* 1314
2020 RANG DE LA RIVIERE, SAINT-ISIDORE, QC, G0S 2S0
(418) 882-6301   *SIC* 5154
MARCHE D'ANIMAUX VIVANTS VEILLEUX & FRERES INC   *p* 1122
1287 14E AV, LA GUADELOUPE, QC, G0M 1G0
(418) 459-6832   *SIC* 5154
MARCHE D. BOUTIN ST-FELICIEN INC   *p*
1090
99 8E AV, DOLBEAU-MISTASSINI, QC, G8L 1Z1
(418) 276-0361   *SIC* 5411
MARCHE DE LA CONCORDE   *p* 1083
See MARCHE J.C. MESSIER INC
MARCHE DE LA PLACE (2000), LE *p* 1153
See MARCHE L. ETHIER & FILS INC
MARCHE DE LA ROUSSELIERE INC   *p*
1247
3000 BOUL DE LA ROUSSELIERE, POINTE-AUX-TREMBLES, QC, H1A 4G3
(514) 498-7117   *SIC* 5411
MARCHE DENIGIL (1984) INC   *p* 1363
555 BOUL SAMSON, SAINTE-ROSE, QC, H7X 1J5
(450) 689-2282   *SIC* 5411
MARCHE DES OISEAUX INC   *p* 1362
580 BOUL CURE-LABELLE, SAINTE-ROSE, QC, H7L 4V6
(450) 963-1072   *SIC* 5411
MARCHE DESSAULLES   *p* 1311
See 3095-0497 QUEBEC INC
MARCHE DOMINIC PICHE INC   *p* 1253
3023 BOUL LABELLE, PREVOST, QC, J0R 1T0
SIC 5411
MARCHE DORE & FILS INC   *p* 1154
939 BOUL ALBINY-PAQUETTE BUREAU 1, MONT-LAURIER, QC, J9L 3J1
(819) 623-6984   *SIC* 5431
MARCHE DU FAUBOURG STE-JULIE INC *p*
1359
2055 RUE PRINCIPALE BUREAU 187, SAINTE-JULIE, QC, J3E 1W1
(450) 649-4078   *SIC* 5411

MARCHE DU VIEUX BEAUPORT INC   *p*
1256
771 AV ROYALE, QUEBEC, QC, G1E 1Z1
(418) 661-9181   *SIC* 5411
MARCHE DUBREUIL VEILLETTE INC   *p*
1308
6250 BOUL COUSINEAU BUREAU 100, SAINT-HUBERT, QC, J3Y 8X9
(450) 462-4420   *SIC* 5411
MARCHE DUCHEMIN ET FRERES INC   *p*
1323
1947 BOUL KELLER, SAINT-LAURENT, QC, H4K 2V6
(514) 336-8085   *SIC* 5411
MARCHE DUCHEMIN ET LACAS INC   *p*
1151
927   BOUL   SAINT-JEAN-BAPTISTE, MERCIER, QC, J6R 2K8
(450) 691-7647   *SIC* 5411
MARCHE ELITE ST-ANTOINE INC   *p* 1321
633 BOUL DES LAURENTIDES, SAINT-JEROME, QC, J7Z 4M4
(450) 432-3433   *SIC* 5411
MARCHE ELITE ST-JEROME INC   *p* 1320
430   BOUL   MONSEIGNEUR-DUBOIS, SAINT-JEROME, QC, J7Y 3L8
(450) 432-3433   *SIC* 5411
MARCHE EMERY & FILS INC   *p* 1146
80 RUE SAINT-MARC, LOUISEVILLE, QC, J5V 2E6
(819) 228-2764   *SIC* 5411
MARCHE FLORAL INTER-PROVINCIAL LTEE   *p* 1245
3600 BOUL PITFIELD, PIERREFONDS, QC, H8Y 3L4
(514) 334-7733   *SIC* 7389
MARCHE FORDHAM   *p* 1354
See 116260 CANADA INC
MARCHE FRAIS DE GATINEAU   *p* 1104
See 964211 ONTARIO LTD
MARCHE FRECHETTE INC   *p* 1089
276 RUE PRINCIPALE, DAVELUYVILLE, QC, G0Z 1C0
(819) 367-2352   *SIC* 5411
MARCHE FRUTTA SI   *p* 1130
See 9094-0594 QUEBEC INC
MARCHE G. CARDINAL INC   *p* 1356
5480 BOUL SAINT-LAURENT, SAINTE-CATHERINE, QC, J5C 1B1
(450) 638-0360   *SIC* 5411
MARCHE GAOUETTE INC   *p* 1109
40 RUE EVANGELINE, GRANBY, QC, J2G 8K1
(450) 378-4447   *SIC* 5411
MARCHE GOODFOOD   *p* 1339
See GOODFOOD MARKET CORP
MARCHE HEBERT SENECAL INC   *p* 1232
5805 BOUL ROBERT-BOURASSA, MON-TREAL, QC, H7E 0A4
(450) 665-4441   *SIC* 5411
MARCHE I G A   *p* 1054
See SUPERMARCHE G.C. INC
MARCHE IGA   *p* 1292
See GESTION GAETAN BOUCHER
MARCHE IGA LOUISE MENARD ST-LAMBERT INC   *p*
1322
371 AV VICTORIA, SAINT-LAMBERT, QC, J4P 2H7
(450) 466-3880   *SIC* 5411
MARCHE IGA ST-HENRI DE LEVIS INC *p*
1306
59 RTE CAMPAGNA, SAINT-HENRI-DE-LEVIS, QC, G0R 3E0
(418) 882-5375   *SIC* 5411
MARCHE J P FONTAINE INC   *p* 1100
382 RUE PRINCIPALE, EASTMAN, QC, J0E 1P0
(450) 297-2815   *SIC* 5411
MARCHE J.C. MESSIER INC   *p* 1066
535 RUE SAMUEL-DE-CHAMPLAIN BU-REAU 200, BOUCHERVILLE, QC, J4B 6B6
(450) 641-3032   *SIC* 5411
MARCHE J.C. MESSIER INC   *p* 1083

155 BOUL DE LA CONCORDE E, COTE SAINT-LUC, QC, H7G 2C6

(450) 667-3277   *SIC* 5411

MARCHE J.C. MESSIER INC   *p* 1149
875 MONT?E MASSON, MASCOUCHE, QC, J7K 3T3

(450) 966-9996   *SIC* 5411

MARCHE J.C. MESSIER INC   *p* 1168
3600 BOUL SAINT-JOSEPH E, MONTREAL, QC, H1X 1W6

(514) 254-2950   *SIC* 5411

MARCHE J.R. GRAVEL INC   *p* 1081
110 BOUL NOTRE-DAME, CLERMONT, QC, G4A 1G3

(418) 439-3922   *SIC* 5411

MARCHE KELLY MALONEY INC   *p* 1103
910 BOUL MALONEY E, GATINEAU, QC, J8P 1H5

(819) 643-2353   *SIC* 5411

MARCHE L. ETHIER & FILS INC   *p* 1153
9300 RUE SAINT-ETIENNE, MIRABEL, QC, J7N 2N2

(450) 258-2084   *SIC* 5411

MARCHE L.V. LTEE   *p* 1074
686 BOUL PERRON GD, CARLETON, QC, G0C 1J0

(418) 364-7380   *SIC* 5411

MARCHE LA PERADE   *p* 1355
See MARCHE LA PERADE INC

MARCHE LA PERADE INC   *p* 1355
185 RUE PRINCIPALE, SAINTE-ANNE-DE-LA-PERADE, QC, G0X 2J0

(418) 325-2233   *SIC* 5411

MARCHE LABRIE & LANDRY INC   *p* 1389
1010 BOUL LAURE, UASHAT, QC, G4R 5P1

(418) 962-7797   *SIC* 5411

MARCHE LAMBERT ET FRERES INC   *p* 1294
2400 BOUL DU MILLENAIRE, SAINT-BASILE-LE-GRAND, QC, J3N 1T8

(450) 441-3800   *SIC* 5411

MARCHE LAMBERT ET FRERES INC   *p* 1296
23 BOUL SEIGNEURIAL O, SAINT-BRUNO, QC, J3V 2G9

(450) 653-4466   *SIC* 5411

MARCHE LAMBERT ET FRERES INC   *p* 1298
400 132 RTE, SAINT-CONSTANT, QC, J5A 2J8

SIC 5411

MARCHE LAPLANTE FARNHAM INC   *p* 1101
999 RUE PRINCIPALE E, FARNHAM, QC, J2N 1M9

(450) 293-4210   *SIC* 5411

MARCHE LAVAL VEILLEUX & FILS   *p* 1304
See 2625-8368 QUEBEC INC

MARCHE LAVAL VEILLEUX & FILS   *p* 1304
See 9155- 5714 QUEBEC INC

MARCHE LEBLANC INC   *p* 1154
101 RUE HEBERT, MONT-LAURIER, QC, J9L 3H9

(819) 623-3200   *SIC* 5411

MARCHE LEBLANC MONTEE PAIEMENT INC   *p* 1103
435 MONTEE PAIEMENT, GATINEAU, QC, J8P 0B1

(819) 561-5478   *SIC* 5411

MARCHE LORD & ASSOCIES IGA   *p* 1319
See 9158-9093 QUEBEC INC

MARCHE LORD DE LAFONTAINE   *p* 1319
See 9023-4683 QUEBEC INC

MARCHE LOUISE MENARD (ILE-DES-SOEURS) INC, LES   *p* 1396
30 PLACE DU COMMERCE, VERDUN, QC, H3E 1V7

(514) 362-6330   *SIC* 5411

MARCHE MARCANIO ET FILS INC   *p* 1172
1550 RUE BELANGER, MONTREAL, QC, H2G 1A8

(514) 729-1866   *SIC* 5411

MARCHE MARIO DOIRON INC   *p* 1075

500 AV DAIGNEAULT UNITE 101, CHANDLER, QC, G0C 1K0

(418) 689-6999   *SIC* 5411

MARCHE METRO   *p* 1077
See ENTREPRISES G.A. LEBLANC INC, LES

MARCHE METRO   *p* 1145
See MARCHE CENTRAL C.J.C. LTEE

MARCHE METRO   *p* 1229
See ALIMENTATIONS GOVANNI ROUSSO 2004 INC

MARCHE METRO   *p* 1303
See MARCHE BOURGEAULT INC

MARCHE METRO   *p* 1360
See BOUCHER RONALD & FILS INC

MARCHE METRO ELITE ST-ANTOINE   *p* 1321
See MARCHE ELITE ST-ANTOINE INC

MARCHE METRO MARCANIO   *p* 1049
See MARCHE D'ALIMENTATION MARCANIO (ANJOU) INC

MARCHE METRO PERRIER ET MARTEL   *p* 1342
See SUPERMARCHE PERRIER ET MARTEL INC

MARCHE METRO PLUS   *p* 1135
See ALIMENTATION LAROCHE & FILS INC

MARCHE MICHEL LEMIEUX INC   *p* 1283
450 CH RICHELIEU, RICHELIEU, QC, J3L 3R8

(450) 658-1831   *SIC* 5411

MARCHE MONTEE GAGNON INC   *p* 1060
50 MONTEE GAGNON, BOIS-DES-FILION, QC, J6Z 2L1

(450) 621-2266   *SIC* 5411

MARCHE MOVENPICK   *p* 971
See RICHTREE MARKET RESTAURANTS INC

MARCHE PERREAULT & GELINAS INC   *p* 1315
318 BOUL SAINT-LUC, SAINT-JEAN-SUR-RICHELIEU, QC, J2W 2A3

(450) 359-4110   *SIC* 5411

MARCHE PIERRE JOBIDON INC   *p* 1322
1021 AV DU PALAIS, SAINT-JOSEPH-DE-BEAUCE, QC, G0S 2V0

(418) 397-5213   *SIC* 5411

MARCHE PLOUFFE GRANBY INC   *p* 1109
65 RUE PRINCIPALE, GRANBY, QC, J2G 2T7

(450) 378-9926   *SIC* 5411

MARCHE PLOUFFE SHERBROOKE INC   *p* 1370
1175 RUE KING E, SHERBROOKE, QC, J1G 1E6

(819) 346-2229   *SIC* 5411

MARCHE PLOUFFE WATERLOO INC   *p* 1400
4615 RUE FOSTER, WATERLOO, QC, J0E 2N0

(450) 534-2648   *SIC* 5411

MARCHE PLUS SHAWINIGAN INC   *p* 1369
4175 12E AV, SHAWINIGAN-SUD, QC, G9P 4G3

(819) 537-3724   *SIC* 5411

MARCHE RAYMOND ET FILS   *p* 1287
See 9222-0524 QUEBEC INC

MARCHE RHEAUME INC   *p* 1281
1501 RUE JACQUES-BEDARD, QUEBEC, QC, G3G 1P9

(418) 849-4416   *SIC* 5411

MARCHE RIENDEAU BELOEIL INC   *p* 1057
1030 RUE SAINT-JEAN-BAPTISTE, BELOEIL, QC, J3G 0J1

(450) 536-1113   *SIC* 5411

MARCHE ROBERT DESROCHERS INC   *p* 1077
7000 125 RTE, CHERTSEY, QC, J0K 3K0

(450) 882-2332   *SIC* 5411

MARCHE ROBERT TELLIER (1990) INC   *p* 1319
872 MONTEE SAINTE-THERESE, SAINT-JEROME, QC, J5L 2L1

(450) 565-5977   *SIC* 5411

MARCHE ROMEO ROY & FILS INC   *p* 1299
108 RTE 108 E, SAINT-EPHREM-DE-BEAUCE, QC, G0M 1R0

(418) 484-2085   *SIC* 5411

MARCHE SABREVOIS INC   *p* 1066
535 RUE SAMUEL-DE-CHAMPLAIN BUREAU 2, BOUCHERVILLE, QC, J4B 6B6

(450) 655-2634   *SIC* 5411

MARCHE SENNETERRE INC   *p* 1366
760 10E AV, SENNETERRE, QC, J0Y 2M0

(819) 737-2232   *SIC* 5411

MARCHE SHAWINIGAN-SUD INC   *p* 1369
2105 105E AV, SHAWINIGAN, QC, G9P 1N9

(819) 537-6997   *SIC* 5411

MARCHE ST RAPHAEL   *p* 1351
See GESTION P. A. T. INC

MARCHE ST-ALPHONSE   *p* 1291
See 9069-7897 QUEBEC INC

MARCHE ST-CANUT INC   *p* 1153
9600 RUE HENRI-PICHE, MIRABEL, QC, J7N 0T4

(450) 431-3244   *SIC* 5411

MARCHE ST-JANVIER INC   *p* 1152
13380 BOUL DU CURE-LABELLE, MIRABEL, QC, J7J 1G9

(450) 971-7881   *SIC* 5411

MARCHE ST-PIERRE & FILS INC   *p* 1383
780 BOUL FRONTENAC E, THETFORD MINES, QC, G6G 6H1

(418) 335-6222   *SIC* 5411

MARCHE ST-PIERRE ET FILS INC   *p* 1110
585 RUE SAINT-HUBERT, GRANBY, QC, J2H 1Y5

(450) 777-0898   *SIC* 5411

MARCHE STE-MADELEINE INC   *p* 1359
30 RUE SAINT-JEAN-BAPTISTE, SAINTE-MADELEINE, QC, J0H 1S0

(450) 795-3355   *SIC* 5411

MARCHE STEPHANE BEAULIEU INC   *p* 1359
1535 125 RTE, SAINTE-JULIENNE, QC, J0K 2T0

(450) 831-2166   *SIC* 5411

MARCHE TELLIER JEAN-TALON INC   *p* 1346
5000 RUE JEAN-TALON E, SAINT-LEONARD, QC, H1S 1K6

(514) 728-3535   *SIC* 5411

MARCHELINO RESTAURANT   *p* 821
See RICHTREE MARKET RESTAURANTS INC

MARCHES D'ALIMENTS NATURELS TAU INC, LES   *p* 1173
4238 RUE SAINT-DENIS, MONTREAL, QC, H2J 2K8

(514) 843-4420   *SIC* 5411

MARCHES LOUISE MENARD (ILE-DES-SOEURS), LES   *p* 1322
See MARCHES LOUISE MENARD INC, LES

MARCHES LOUISE MENARD (ILE-DES-SOEURS), LES   *p* 1396
See MARCHE LOUISE MENARD (ILE-DES-SOEURS) INC, LES

MARCHES LOUISE MENARD (PREVILLE) INC, LES   *p* 1323
299 BOUL SIR-WILFRID-LAURIER BUREAU 201, SAINT-LAMBERT, QC, J4R 2L1

(450) 923-9399   *SIC* 5411

MARCHES LOUISE MENARD INC, LES   *p* 1322
34 AV ARGYLE, SAINT-LAMBERT, QC, J4P 2H4

(514) 843-6116   *SIC* 5411

MARCHES PEPIN INC, LES   *p* 1057
865 BOUL YVON-L'HEUREUX N, BELOEIL, QC, J3G 6P5

(450) 467-3512   *SIC* 5411

MARCHES TRADITION, LES   *p* 1299
See MARCHE ROMEO ROY & FILS INC

MARCHON CANADA INC   *p* 1094
1975 BOUL HYMUS BUREAU 250, DOR-

VAL, QC, H9P 1J8

(800) 956-9290   *SIC* 5048

MARCIL CENTRE DE RENOVATION   *p* 1352
See RONA INC

MARCIL LAVALLEE   *p* 596
1420 BLAIR PL SUITE 400, GLOUCESTER, ON, K1J 9L8

(613) 745-8387   *SIC* 8721

MARCO CORPORATION, THE   *p* 518
470 HARDY RD, BRANTFORD, ON, N3V 6T1

(519) 751-2227   *SIC* 8743

MARCO TRANSPORT   *p* 1035
See LAIDLAW CARRIERS BULK GP INC

MARCOMM INTEGRATED BUSINESS SOLUTIONS   *p* 1029
See 10365289 CANADA INC

MARCON CONSTRUCTION LTD   *p* 228
5645 199 ST, LANGLEY, BC, V3A 1H9

(604) 530-5646   *SIC* 8742

MARCOR AUTOMOTIVE INC   *p* 526
1164 WALKER'S LINE, BURLINGTON, ON, L7M 1V2

(905) 549-6445   *SIC* 5013

MARCOTTE SYSTEMES LTEE   *p* 1393
1471 BOUL LIONEL-BOULET UNITE 28, VARENNES, QC, J3X 1P7

(450) 652-6000   *SIC* 5084

MARCUS EVANS   *p* 939
See INTERNATIONAL CHAMPIONSHIP MANAGEMENT LIMITED

MARCUS, HAROLD LIMITED   *p* 496
15124 LONGWOODS RD SUITE 2, BOTHWELL, ON, N0P 1C0

(519) 695-3734   *SIC* 4213

MAREK HOSPITALITY INC   *p* 801
2898 SOUTH SHERIDAN WAY UNIT 200, OAKVILLE, ON, L6J 7L5

(905) 829-0292   *SIC* 5812

MAREL CONTRACTORS   *p* 556
See MUZZO BROTHERS GROUP INC

MARESCO LIMITED   *p* 555
171 BASALTIC RD UNIT 2, CONCORD, ON, L4K 1G4

(905) 669-5700   *SIC* 1542

MARFOGLIA CONSTRUCTION INC   *p* 1049
9031 BOUL PARKWAY, ANJOU, QC, H1J 1N4

(514) 325-8700   *SIC* 1542

MARGARINE THIBAULT INC   *p* 1388
3000 RUE JULES-VACHON, TROIS-RIVIERES, QC, G9A 5E1

(819) 373-3333   *SIC* 2079

MARGOLIANS MARITIMES LIMITED   *p* 469
65 INGLIS PL SUITE 49, TRURO, NS, B2N 4B5

SIC 5311

MARIANN HOME   *p* 855
See MARIANN NURSING HOME AND RESIDENCE

MARIANN NURSING HOME AND RESIDENCE   *p* 855
9915 YONGE ST, RICHMOND HILL, ON, L4C 1V1

(905) 884-9276   *SIC* 8051

MARIANOPOLIS COLLEGE   *p* 1401
4873 AV WESTMOUNT, WESTMOUNT, QC, H3Y 1X9

(514) 931-8792   *SIC* 8221

MARID INDUSTRIES LIMITED   *p* 470
99 WINDSOR JUNCTION RD, WINDSOR JUNCTION, NS, B2T 1G7

(902) 860-1138   *SIC* 1791

MARIE ESTHER SOCIETY, THE   *p* 335
861 FAIRFIELD RD SUITE 317, VICTORIA, BC, V8V 5A9

(250) 480-3100   *SIC* 8069

MARIE, F. LIMITED   *p* 672
123 DENISON ST, MARKHAM, ON, L3R 1B5

(905) 475-0093   *SIC* 5084

MARIES MINI MART   *p* 433

See KENNY ENTERPRISES LIMITED

MARIETTE CLERMONT MEUBLE *p 1236*
See CLERMONT, MARIETTE INC

MARIGOLD FORD LINCOLN SALES LIMITED *p 1014*
1120 DUNDAS ST E, WHITBY, ON, L1N 2K2
(905) 668-5893 *SIC 5511*

MARILU'S MARKET *p 520*
See 1032002 ONTARIO INC

MARIMAC INC *p 1340*
6395 CH DE LA COTE-DE-LIESSE, SAINT-LAURENT, QC, H4T 1E5
(514) 725-7600 *SIC 2392*

MARINA COMMODITIES INC *p 710*
90 BURNHAMTHORPE RD W SUITE 1102, MISSISSAUGA, ON, L5B 3C3
(905) 828-0777 *SIC 5153*

MARINA DE REPENTIGNY, LA *p 1282*
See 2437-0223 QUEBEC INC

MARINA PORT DE PLAISANCE REAL BOUVIER *p 1142*
See ASSOCIATION SOGERIVE INC

MARINARD BIOTECH *p 1102*
See PECHERIES MARINARD LTEE, LES

MARINDUSTRIAL ONTARIO INC *p 717*
4090 RIDGEWAY DR UNIT 8, MISSISSAUGA, ON, L5L 5X5
(905) 607-5052 *SIC 5084*

MARINDUSTRIEL *p 1157*
See ENTREPRISES ELECTRIQUES NADCO INC

MARINE ATLANTIC INC *p 421*
GD, CHANNEL-PORT-AUX-BASQUES, NL, A0M 1C0
(709) 695-4200 *SIC 4482*

MARINE ATLANTIC INC *p 432*
10 FORT WILLIAM PL SUITE 302, ST. JOHN'S, NL, A1C 1K4
(709) 772-8957 *SIC 4482*

MARINE ATLANTIC INC *p 464*
355 PURVES ST, NORTH SYDNEY, NS, B2A 3V2
(902) 794-5200 *SIC 4482*

MARINE CANADA ACQUISITION INC *p 255*
3831 NO. 6 RD SUITE 100, RICHMOND, BC, V6V 1P6
(604) 270-6899 *SIC 8731*

MARINE CANADA ACQUISITION LIMITED PARTNERSHIP *p 255*
3831 NO. 6 RD, RICHMOND, BC, V6V 1P6
(604) 270-6899 *SIC 3492*

MARINE CHRYSLER DODGE JEEP LTD *p 290*
450 MARINE DR SE, VANCOUVER, BC, V5X 4V2
(604) 321-1236 *SIC 5511*

MARINE DEPOT INC *p 1393*
550 BOUL LIONEL-BOULET, VARENNES, QC, J3X 1P7
(450) 652-2999 *SIC 5551*

MARINE DRIVE IMPORTED CARS LTD *p 323*
850 MARINE DR SW, VANCOUVER, BC, V6P 5Z1
(604) 324-6632 *SIC 5511*

MARINE ENGINEERING, DIV OF *p 1133*
See WEIR CANADA, INC

MARINE HARVEST CANADA INC *p 247*
7200 COHOE RD, PORT HARDY, BC, V0N 2P0
(250) 949-9448 *SIC 2091*

MARINE HARVEST NORTH AMERICA INC *p 195*
1334 ISLAND HWY SUITE 124, CAMPBELL RIVER, BC, V9W 8C9
(250) 850-3276 *SIC 6712*

MARINE PETROBULK LTD *p 241*
10 PEMBERTON AVE, NORTH VANCOUVER, BC, V7P 2R1
(604) 987-4415 *SIC 5172*

MARINE PLAZA TVT *p 809*
1753 DIVISION RD W, ORILLIA, ON, L3V 6H2
(705) 329-1646 *SIC 5551*

MARINE RECYCLING CORPORATION *p 846*
17 INVERTOSE DR, PORT COLBORNE, ON, L3K 5V5
(905) 835-1203 *SIC 4499*

MARINE ROOFING & SHEET METAL LTD *p 193*
4909 BYRNE RD SUITE 4, BURNABY, BC, V5J 3H6
(604) 433-4322 *SIC 1761*

MARINE ROOFING LTD *p 193*
4909 BYRNE RD SUITE 4, BURNABY, BC, V5J 3H6
(604) 433-4322 *SIC 1761*

MARINER NEPTUNE FISH & SEAFOOD COMPANY LTD *p 371*
472 DUFFERIN AVE, WINNIPEG, MB, R2W 2Y6
(204) 589-5341 *SIC 5146*

MARINER PARTNERS INC *p 415*
1 GERMAIN ST 18 FL, SAINT JOHN, NB, E2L 4V1
(506) 642-9000 *SIC 7371*

MARINO'S FINE CARS *p 571*
See D'ALESSANDRO INVESTMENTS LIMITED

MARINO'S MARKET LTD *p 242*
3230 CONNAUGHT CRES, NORTH VANCOUVER, BC, V7R 0A5
SIC 5411

MARIO'S *p 145*
See 415329 ALBERTA LTD

MARIPOSA DAIRY LTD *p 646*
201 ST GEORGE ST, LINDSAY, ON, K9V 5Z9
(705) 324-9306 *SIC 2022*

MARIPOSA MARKET *p 809*
See MARIPOSA MARKET LTD

MARIPOSA MARKET LTD *p 809*
109 MISSISSAGA ST E, ORILLIA, ON, L3V 1V6
(705) 325-8885 *SIC 5947*

MARITIME BEAUTY SUPPLY CO LTD *p 455*
3695 BARRINGTON ST, HALIFAX, NS, B3K 2Y3
(902) 429-8510 *SIC 5087*

MARITIME BROADCASTING SYSTEM LIMITED *p 458*
90 LOVETT LAKE CRT SUITE 101, HALIFAX, NS, B3S 0H6
(902) 425-1225 *SIC 4832*

MARITIME COFFEE SERVICE *p 648*
See ALLIED COFFEE CORP

MARITIME DOOR & WINDOW LTD *p 407*
118 ALBERT ST, MONCTON, NB, E1C 1B2
(506) 857-8108 *SIC 1751*

MARITIME ELECTRIC COMPANY, LIMITED *p 1039*
180 KENT ST, CHARLOTTETOWN, PE, C1A 1N9
(800) 670-1012 *SIC 4911*

MARITIME EXHAUST LTD *p 408*
191 HENRI DUNANT ST UNIT 4, MONCTON, NB, E1E 1E4
(506) 857-8733 *SIC 5511*

MARITIME FIBERGLASS FABRICATORS *p 462*
See RPS COMPOSITES INC

MARITIME HOME IMPROVEMENT LIMITED *p 415*
300 UNION ST, SAINT JOHN, NB, E2L 4Z2
(506) 632-4100 *SIC 5211*

MARITIME HYDRAULIC REPAIR CENTRE (1997) LTD *p 410*
355 MACNAUGHTON AVE, MONCTON, NB, E1H 2J9
(506) 858-0393 *SIC 7699*

MARITIME INNS & RESORTS INCORPORATED *p 463*
174 ARCHIMEDES ST, NEW GLASGOW, NS, B2H 2T6
(902) 752-5644 *SIC 7011*

MARITIME INNS AND RESORTS *p 463*
See MARITIME INNS & RESORTS INCORPORATED

MARITIME PAPER PRODUCTS LIMITED PARTNERSHIP *p 447*
25 BORDEN AVE, DARTMOUTH, NS, B3B 1C7
(902) 468-5353 *SIC 2653*

MARITIME PRESSUREWORKS LIMITED *p 444*
41 ESTATES RD, DARTMOUTH, NS, B2Y 4K3
(902) 468-8461 *SIC 7699*

MARITIME PRIDE EGGS INC *p 438*
50 TANTRAMAR CRES, AMHERST, NS, B4H 0A1
(800) 563-2246 *SIC 5144*

MARITIME RESCUE & MEDICAL ACADEMY INC *p 414*
7 FOSTER THURSTON DR, SAINT JOHN, NB, E2K 5J4
(506) 672-3389 *SIC 8999*

MARITIME SOD LTD *p 413*
1101 BAYSIDE DR, SAINT JOHN, NB, E2J 4Y2
(506) 634-8540 *SIC 0181*

MARITIME STEEL AND FOUNDRIES LIMITED *p 463*
379 GLASGOW ST, NEW GLASGOW, NS, B2H 5C3
SIC 3325

MARITIME TRAVEL INC *p 453*
2000 BARRINGTON ST SUITE 202, HALIFAX, NS, B3J 3K1
(902) 420-1554 *SIC 4724*

MARITIME-ONTARIO FREIGHT LINES LIMITED *p 499*
1 MARITIME ONTARIO BLVD, BRAMPTON, ON, L6S 6G4
(905) 792-6101 *SIC 4213*

MARITIME-ONTARIO FREIGHT LINES LIMITED *p 499*
1 MARITIME ONTARIO BLVD SUITE 100, BRAMPTON, ON, L6S 6G4
(905) 792-6100 *SIC 4212*

MARITIME-ONTARIO PARCEL, DIV OF *p 499*
See MARITIME-ONTARIO FREIGHT LINES LIMITED

MARITZ INC *p 1431*
2318 NORTHRIDGE DR, SASKATOON, SK, S7L 1B9
SIC 8732

MARJAK LEASING *p 332*
See WATKIN MOTORS PARTNERSHIP

MARK ANTHONY GROUP INC *p 206*
465 FRASERVIEW PL, DELTA, BC, V3M 6H4
(604) 519-5370 *SIC 2084*

MARK ANTHONY GROUP INC *p 289*
887 GREAT NORTHERN WAY SUITE 500, VANCOUVER, BC, V5T 4T5
(888) 394-1122 *SIC 2084*

MARK ANTHONY PROPERTIES LTD *p 242*
7151 SIBCO LANDFILL, OLIVER, BC, V0H 1T0
SIC 6531

MARK ANTHONY PROPERTIES LTD *p 289*
887 GREAT NORTHERN WAY 101, VANCOUVER, BC, V5T 4T5
(604) 263-9994 *SIC 6719*

MARK ISFELD SCHOOL *p 203*
See SCHOOL DISTRICT NO. 71 (COMOX VALLEY)

MARK MOTORS OF OTTAWA *p 820*
See MARK MOTORS OF OTTAWA (1987) LIMITED

MARK MOTORS OF OTTAWA (1987) LIMITED *p 820*
611 MONTREAL RD SUITE 1, OTTAWA, ON, K1K 0T8
(613) 749-4275 *SIC 5511*

MARK S. LESLIE APATHECARY LTD *p 519*
2399 PARKEDALE AVE SUITE 27, BROCKVILLE, ON, K6V 3G9
(613) 342-6701 *SIC 5912*

MARK'S ACCOUNTS RECEIVABLE *p 804*
See MARK'S WORK WEARHOUSE LTD

MARK'S WORK WEARHOUSE *p 197*
See BEKAR & ASSOCIATES ENTERPRISES LIMITED

MARK'S WORK WEARHOUSE LTD *p 36*
1035 64 AVE SE SUITE 30, CALGARY, AB, T2H 2J7
(403) 255-9220 *SIC 5136*

MARK'S WORK WEARHOUSE LTD *p 804*
3449 SUPERIOR CRT, OAKVILLE, ON, L6L 0C4
(800) 461-4378 *SIC 5651*

MARK-CREST FOODS LTD *p 225*
19670 92A AVE SUITE 100, LANGLEY, BC, V1M 3B2
(604) 882-2066 *SIC 5411*

MARKALTA DEVELOPMENTS LTD *p 789*
1020 LAWRENCE AVE W SUITE 300, NORTH YORK, ON, M6A 1C8
(416) 787-1135 *SIC 6512*

MARKDALE FOODLAND *p 664*
See 1124029 ONTARIO INC

MARKDOM *p 914*
See MARKDOM PLASTIC PRODUCTS LIMITED

MARKDOM PLASTIC PRODUCTS LIMITED *p 914*
1220 BIRCHMOUNT RD, TORONTO, ON, M1P 2C3
(416) 752-4290 *SIC 3089*

MARKEL CANADA LIMITED *p 981*
200 WELLINGTON ST W UNIT 400, TORONTO, ON, M5V 3C7
(416) 601-1133 *SIC 6712*

MARKEM-IMAJE INC *p 735*
7075 EDWARDS BLVD UNIT 2, MISSISSAUGA, ON, L5S 1Z2
(800) 267-5108 *SIC 5084*

MARKET ENGINES *p 1226*
See 6091636 CANADA INC

MARKET ON YATES, THE *p 335*
See CLACE HOLDINGS LTD

MARKET PLACE IGA *p 323*
3535 41ST AVE W, VANCOUVER, BC, V6N 3E7
(604) 261-2423 *SIC 5411*

MARKET PROBE CANADA COMPANY *p 572*
1243 ISLINGTON AVE SUITE 200, ETOBICOKE, ON, M8X 1Y9
(416) 233-1555 *SIC 8732*

MARKET REGULATION SERVICES INC *p 954*
145 KING ST W UNIT 900, TORONTO, ON, M5H 1J8
(416) 646-7204 *SIC 8742*

MARKET SQUARE LIMITED PARTNERSHIP *p 821*
350 DALHOUSIE ST, OTTAWA, ON, K1N 7E9
(613) 241-1000 *SIC 7011*

MARKET STREET VULCAN *p 171*
See FIRST STREET FOODS LTD

MARKET TIRE (1976) LTD *p 1432*
115 IDYLWYLD DR S, SASKATOON, SK, S7M 1L4
(306) 244-5442 *SIC 5531*

MARKETEL COMMUNICATIONS INC *p 1189*
413 RUE SAINT-JACQUES 10E ETAGE, MONTREAL, QC, H2Y 1N9
(514) 935-9445 *SIC 7311*

MARKETEL/MCCANN-ERICKSON LTEE *p 1189*

413 RUE SAINT-JACQUES BUREAU 10E, MONTREAL, QC, H2Y 1N9
(514) 935-9445   SIC 7311

MARKETING EMS INC   p 1070
7505 BOUL TASCHEREAU BUREAU 100, BROSSARD, QC, J4Y 1A2
(450) 443-0300   SIC 1081

MARKETING MANN, ALBERT INC   p 1157
8191 CH MONTVIEW, MONT-ROYAL, QC, H4P 2P2
(514) 800-6266   SIC 5023

MARKETING STORE WORLDWIDE (CANADA) L.P., THE   p 991
1209 KING ST W, TORONTO, ON, M6K 1G2
(416) 583-3931   SIC 8743

MARKETING STORE, THE   p 991
See MARKETING STORE WORLDWIDE (CANADA) L.P., THE

MARKETING TANBORE   p 1340
See NIVEL INC

MARKETPLACE I G A   p 219
See BAR DEN FOODS LTD

MARKETPLACE IGA 48   p 244
19150 LOUGHEED HWY, PITT MEADOWS, BC, V3Y 2H6
SIC 5411

MARKETPLACE IGA 73   p 272
See KAROB FOODS LTD

MARKETSTAR   p 930
See OMNICOM CANADA CORP

MARKETWEST FOOD GROUP LIMITED PARTNERSHIP   p 201
1580 BRIGANTINE DR SUITE 200, COQUITLAM, BC, V3K 7C1
(604) 526-1788   SIC 5141

MARKHAM ACURA   p 1000
See BRUHAM AUTOMOTIVE INC

MARKHAM CENTENNIAL CENTRE   p 1000
8600 MCCOWAN RD, UNIONVILLE, ON, L3P 3M2
(905) 294-6111   SIC 8322

MARKHAM DISTRICT HIGH SCHOOL   p 665
See YORK REGION DISTRICT SCHOOL BOARD

MARKHAM HONDA   p 1000
See NORTH MARKHAM MOTORS LTD

MARKHAM INFINITI LIMITED   p 1000
4340 HIGHWAY 7 E, UNIONVILLE, ON, L3R 1L9
(905) 752-0881   SIC 5511

MARKHAM MAZDA   p 665
See JAYFER AUTOMOTIVE GROUP (MARKHAM) INC

MARKHAM PHYSIOTHERAPY CLINIC   p 923
See LIFEMARK HEALTH CORP

MARKHAM STOUFFVILLE HOSPITAL   p 665
381 CHURCH ST, MARKHAM, ON, L3P 7P3
(905) 472-7000   SIC 8062

MARKHAM STOUFFVILLE HOSPITAL   p 1001
4 CAMPBELL DR, UXBRIDGE, ON, L9P 1S4
(905) 852-9771   SIC 8062

MARKHAM SUITES HOTEL LIMITED   p 680
8500 WARDEN AVE, MARKHAM, ON, L6G 1A5
(905) 470-8500   SIC 7011

MARKHAM WOODBINE HOSPITALITY LTD   p 672
3100 STEELES AVE E SUITE 601, MARKHAM, ON, L3R 8T3
(905) 940-9409   SIC 7011

MARKIO DESIGNS INC   p 973
1200 BAY ST SUITE 600, TORONTO, ON, M5R 2A5
(416) 929-9629   SIC 5661

MARKO AUDIO POST PRODUCTION INC   p 1175
910 RUE DE LA GAUCHETIERE E BUREAU ENTREE, MONTREAL, QC, H2L 2N4
(514) 282-0961   SIC 7389

MARKS SUPPLY INC   p 640

300 ARNOLD ST, KITCHENER, ON, N2H 6E9
(519) 578-5560   SIC 5074

MARKTRAND MANUFACTURING GROUP   p 392
See SMARTREND SUPPLY LTD

MARKUSSON NEW HOLLAND OF REGINA LTD   p 1000
26 GREAT PLAINS RD, EMERALD PARK, SK, S4L 1B6
(306) 781-2828   SIC 5999

MARKVILLE FORD LINCOLN LIMITED   p 1000
8210 KENNEDY RD, UNIONVILLE, ON, L3R 5X3
(905) 474-1350   SIC 5511

MARKVILLE SECONDARY SCHOOL   p 1000
See YORK REGION DISTRICT SCHOOL BOARD

MARKVILLE TOYOTA   p 665
See DON VALLEY NORTH TOYOTA LIMITED

MARKVILLE TOYOTA   p 677
See WEINS CANADA INC

MARKWINS CANADA CORPORATION   p 706
267 MATHESON BLVD E SUITE 1, MISSISSAUGA, ON, L4Z 1X8
(905) 507-4545   SIC 5122

MARLBORO INC   p 1414
See PRINCE ALBERT DEVELOPMENT CORPORATION

MARLBORO WINDOW AND DOOR MANUFACTURER LTD   p 818
2370 STEVENAGE DR, OTTAWA, ON, K1G 3W3
(613) 736-1441   SIC 5211

MARLER MINI MART (CAMROSE) LTD   p 53
350 7 AVE SW SUITE 2900, CALGARY, AB, T2P 3N9
SIC 5411

MARLER MINI MART GROUP   p 53
See MARLER MINI MART (CAMROSE) LTD

MARLIN CHEVROLET BUICK GMC INC   p 1265
2145 RUE FRANK-CARREL, QUEBEC, QC, G1N 2G2
(418) 688-1212   SIC 5012

MARLIN GOLD MINING LTD   p 328
595 BURRARD ST SUITE 2833, VANCOUVER, BC, V7X 1J1
(604) 646-1580   SIC 1041

MARLU INC   p 1385
300 RUE BARKOFF, TROIS-RIVIERES, QC, G8T 2A3
(819) 373-7921   SIC 5812

MARLU INC   p 1388
4520 BOUL DES RECOLLETS, TROIS-RIVIERES, QC, G9A 4N2
(819) 373-5408   SIC 5812

MARMEN ENERGIE INC   p 1150
1905 AV DU PHARE O, MATANE, QC, G4W 3M6
(418) 562-4569   SIC 3569

MARMEN INC   p 1385
557 RUE DES ERABLES, TROIS-RIVIERES, QC, G8T 8Y8
(819) 379-0453   SIC 3545

MARMEN INC   p 1385
845 RUE BERLINGUET, TROIS-RIVIERES, QC, G8T 8N9
(819) 379-0453   SIC 3545

MARMON/KEYSTONE CANADA INC   p 523
1220 HERITAGE RD, BURLINGTON, ON, L7L 4X9
(905) 319-4646   SIC 5051

MARMORA FOOD MARKET LIMITED   p 680
42 MATHEW ST, MARMORA, ON, K0K 2M0
(613) 472-2706   SIC 5411

MARMOT CONSTRUCTION LTD   p 40
636 BEAVER DAM RD NE, CALGARY, AB, T2K 4W6
(403) 730-8711   SIC 1771

MARNOR HOLDINGS LTD   p 179
3243 264 ST, ALDERGROVE, BC, V4W 2X3
(604) 857-8853   SIC 4213

MAROLINE   p 1216
See DISTRIBUTIONS MAROLINE INC

MAROSTICA MOTORS LIMITED   p 908
1142 ALLOY DR, THUNDER BAY, ON, P7B 6M9
(807) 346-5809   SIC 5511

MARPOLE TRANSPORT LIMITED   p 209
7086 BROWN ST, DELTA, BC, V4G 1G8
(604) 940-7000   SIC 4213

MARQUE CONSTRUCTION LIMITED   p 414
400 CHESLEY DR, SAINT JOHN, NB, E2K 5L6
(506) 634-1144   SIC 8741

MARQUEE ENERGY LTD   p 53
500 4 AVE SW SUITE 1700, CALGARY, AB, T2P 2V6
(403) 384-0000   SIC 1382

MARQUES DE VETEMENTS FREEMARK INC   p 1157
5640 RUE PARE, MONT-ROYAL, QC, H4P 2M1
(514) 341-7333   SIC 5136

MARQUES DE VETEMENTS FREEMARK TEC INC   p 1157
5640 RUE PARE, MONT-ROYAL, QC, H4P 2M1
(514) 341-7333   SIC 5611

MARQUEST 2013-1 MINING SUPER FLOW-THROUGH LIMITED PARTNERSHIP   p 964
161 BAY ST SUITE 4420, TORONTO, ON, M5J 2S1
(416) 777-7350   SIC 6722

MARQUEST INVESTMENT COUNSEL INC   p 964
161 BAY ST SUITE 4420, TORONTO, ON, M5J 2S1
(416) 777-7350   SIC 6722

MARQUETTE CONSUMERS COOPERATIVE LIMITED   p 352
GD, MARQUETTE, MB, R0H 0V0
(204) 375-6570   SIC 5171

MARQUEZ TRANSTECH   p 1160
See HUTCHINSON AERONAUTIQUE & INDUSTRIE LIMITEE

MARQUIS   p 1064
See DISTRIBUTIONS ALIMENTAIRES LE MARQUIS INC

MARQUIS AUTOMOBILES INC   p 1150
1065 AV DU PHARE O, MATANE, QC, G4W 3M6
(418) 562-3333   SIC 5511

MARQUIS BUILDING MAINTENANCE SUPPLIES LIMITED   p 703
1786 MATTAWA AVE UNIT 2, MISSISSAUGA, ON, L4X 1K1
(905) 275-0985   SIC 5039

MARQUIS CONCEPT INC, LE   p 1391
180 AV CHAMPLAIN, VAL-D'OR, QC, J9P 2B6
(819) 825-5515   SIC 1623

MARQUIS DOWNS RACE TRACK   p 1424
See SASKATOON PRAIRIELAND PARK CORPORATION

MARQUIS GAGNE   p 1146
See MARQUIS IMPRIMEUR INC

MARQUIS HYDRAULIQUE & PNEUMATIQUE   p 1375
See EQUIPEMENTS MARQUIS INC

MARQUIS IMPRIMEUR INC   p 1146
750 RUE DEVEAULT, LOUISEVILLE, QC, J5V 3C2
(819) 228-2766   SIC 2732

MARQUIS IMPRIMEUR INC   p 1160
350 RUE DES ENTREPRENEURS, MONT-MAGNY, QC, G5V 4T1
(418) 246-5666   SIC 2732

MARQUISE FACILITIES CORPORATION   p 255

13351 COMMERCE PKY SUITE 1373, RICHMOND, BC, V6V 2X7
(604) 214-8525   SIC 6512

MARQUISE FACILITIES MANAGEMENT   p 255
See MARQUISE FACILITIES CORPORATION

MARRINE EXPERT   p 1071
See APRIL MARINE CANADA INC

MARRIOTT   p 672
See MARKHAM WOODBINE HOSPITALITY LTD

MARRIOTT HALIFAX HARBOURFRONT HOTEL   p 697
See LUXURY HOTELS INTERNATIONAL OF CANADA ULC

MARRIOTT NIAGARA FALLS FALLSVIEW HOTEL & SPA   p 759
See NIAGARA 21ST GROUP INC

MARRIOTT REGIONAL WORLD WIDE RESERVATIONS CANADA ADMINISTRATION OFFICES   p 399
See LUXURY HOTELS INTERNATIONAL OF CANADA, ULC

MARS CANADA INC   p 495
12315 COLERAINE DR, BOLTON, ON, L7E 3B4
(905) 857-5620   SIC 2064

MARS CANADA INC   p 495
37 HOLLAND DR, BOLTON, ON, L7E 5S4
(905) 857-5700   SIC 2064

MARS CANADA INC   p 755
285 HARRY WALKER PKY N, NEWMARKET, ON, L3Y 7B3
(905) 853-6000   SIC 2064

MARSAN FOODS LIMITED   p 869
160 THERMOS RD, SCARBOROUGH, ON, M1L 4W2
(416) 755-9262   SIC 2038

MARSH ADJUSTMENT BUREAU LIMITED   p 439
1550 BEDFORD HWY SUITE 711, BEDFORD, NS, B4A 1E6
(902) 469-3537   SIC 6411

MARSH CANADA LIMITED   p 53
222 3 AVE SW SUITE 1100, CALGARY, AB, T2P 0B4
(403) 290-7900   SIC 6411

MARSH CANADA LIMITED   p 307
550 BURRARD ST SUITE 800, VANCOUVER, BC, V6C 2K1
(604) 685-3765   SIC 6411

MARSH CANADA LIMITED   p 964
120 BREMNER BLVD SUITE 800, TORONTO, ON, M5J 0A8
(416) 868-2600   SIC 6411

MARSH CANADA LIMITED   p 1198
1981 AV MCGILL COLLEGE BUREAU 820, MONTREAL, QC, H3A 3T4
(514) 285-4700   SIC 6411

MARSH CONTROL & AUTOMATION PRODUCTS   p 523
See MARSH INSTRUMENTATION LTD

MARSH INSTRUMENTATION LTD   p 523
1016C SUTTON DR UNIT 1, BURLINGTON, ON, L7L 6B8
(905) 332-1172   SIC 3829

MARSH MOTORS CHRYSLER LIMITED   p 424
GD, GRAND FALLS-WINDSOR, NL, A2A 2J9
(709) 489-2151   SIC 5511

MARSH PRIVATE CLIENT SERVICES   p 101
17420 STONY PLAIN RD NW SUITE 100, EDMONTON, AB, T5S 1K6
SIC 6411

MARSH, GLENDA PHARMACY LTD   p 347
809 18TH ST, BRANDON, MB, R7A 5B8
(204) 729-8100   SIC 5912

MARSHALL & WOODWARK INSURANCE BROKERS LTD   p 579

320 NORTH QUEEN ST SUITE 132, ETO-
BICOKE, ON, M9C 5K4
(416) 626-7831   *SIC* 6411
MARSHALL ANDERSON TOURS LTD *p* 65
1117 1 ST SW SUITE 303, CALGARY, AB,
T2R 0T9
(780) 417-2642   *SIC* 4724
**MARSHALL AUTOMOTIVE (PEACE RIVER)
LTD**   *p* 152
7501 100 AVE, PEACE RIVER, AB, T8S
1M5
(780) 428-0563   *SIC* 5511
MARSHALL FABRICS LTD   *p* 384
575 BERRY ST, WINNIPEG, MB, R3H 0S2
(204) 783-1939   *SIC* 5131
MARSHALL GOWLAND MANOR   *p* 859
*See CORPORATION OF THE COUNTY OF
LAMBTON*
MARSHALL, JAMES B ENTERPRISES LTD
p 428
60 ELIZABETH AVE SUITE 144, ST.
JOHN'S, NL, A1A 1W4
(709) 722-1860   *SIC* 5531
MARSHALL, STEVE FORD LINCOLN LTD *p*
234
3851 SHENTON RD SUITE 3, NANAIMO,
BC, V9T 2H1
(250) 758-7311   *SIC* 5511
MARSHALL, STEVE MOTORS (1996) LTD *p*
195
2300 ISLAND HWY, CAMPBELL RIVER,
BC, V9W 2G8
(250) 287-9171   *SIC* 5511
MARSHALL-BARWICK INC   *p* 772
100 SHEPPARD AVE E UNIT 930, NORTH
YORK, ON, M2N 6N5
(416) 225-6240   *SIC* 3441
MARTEC LIMITED   *p* 453
1888 BRUNSWICK ST SUITE 400, HALI-
FAX, NS, B3J 3J8
(902) 425-5101   *SIC* 8748
MARTECH MARKETING LIMITED   *p* 89
10060 JASPER AVE NW SUITE 1701, ED-
MONTON, AB, T5J 3R8
(780) 454-2006   *SIC* 6221
MARTEL BROS LTD   *p* 362
359 PANDORA AVE W, WINNIPEG, MB,
R2C 1M6
(204) 233-2022   *SIC* 4731
MARTEL FILS INC   *p* 1109
688 RUE PRINCIPALE, GRANBY, QC, J2G
2Y4
(450) 361-6445   *SIC* 5099
MARTEL, DAN PHARMACY LIMITED *p* 484
524 BAYFIELD ST SUITE 650, BARRIE,
ON, L4M 5A2
(705) 722-6300   *SIC* 5912
MARTENS, W. GREENHOUSES INC *p* 644
1812 MERSEA ROAD 5, LEAMINGTON,
ON, N8H 3V6
   SIC 0181
MARTIN & BELZILE INC   *p* 1053
691 BOUL LAFLECHE BUREAU 89, BAIE-
COMEAU, QC, G5C 1C4
(418) 589-4969   *SIC* 5912
**MARTIN AIR HEATING & AIR CONDITION-
ING SERVICES LIMITED**   *p*
575
30 FIELDWAY RD, ETOBICOKE, ON, M8Z
0E3
(416) 247-1777   *SIC* 1711
MARTIN CHRYSLER LTD   *p* 7
879 3 ST W, BROOKS, AB, T1R 1L5
(403) 362-3354   *SIC* 5511
MARTIN DESSERT INC   *p* 1140
500 RUE DE BERNIERES, LEVIS, QC, G7A
1E1
(418) 836-1234   *SIC* 5812
MARTIN DESSERT INC   *p* 1279
665 RUE DES ROCAILLES, QUEBEC, QC,
G2J 1A9
(418) 622-0220   *SIC* 2051
MARTIN HOME & AUTO LTD   *p* 887
300 GLENDALE AVE, ST CATHARINES,

ON, L2T 2L5
(905) 227-7481   *SIC* 5531
MARTIN INC   *p* 1318
285 RUE SAINT-JACQUES BUREAU 2,
SAINT-JEAN-SUR-RICHELIEU, QC, J3B 2L1
(450) 347-2373   *SIC* 7219
MARTIN LEMIRE & FILS   *p* 1099
See LEMIRE PRECISION INC
**MARTIN MARIETTA MATERIALS CANADA
LIMITED**   *p* 463
266 LOWER QUARRIE RD, MULGRAVE,
NS, B0E 2G0
(902) 747-2882   *SIC* 5032
MARTIN MERRY & REID LIMITED *p* 942
3 CHURCH ST SUITE 404, TORONTO, ON,
M5E 1M2
(416) 366-3333   *SIC* 6411
MARTIN MOTOR SPORTS SOUTH   *p* 101
See MMD SALES LTD
**MARTIN SPROCKET & GEAR CANADA
INC**   *p* 740
896 MEYERSIDE DR, MISSISSAUGA, ON,
L5T 1R9
(905) 670-1991   *SIC* 5085
MARTIN'S BUS SERVICE   *p* 747
See MARTIN, C. BUS SERVICE LIMITED
MARTIN'S FAMILY FRUIT FARM LTD *p* 1006
1420 LOBSINGER LINE UNIT 1, WATER-
LOO, ON, N2J 4G8
(519) 664-2750   *SIC* 0175
MARTIN, BOB CONSTRUCTION CO LTD *p*
632
1473 JOHN COUNTER BLVD SUITE 400,
KINGSTON, ON, K7M 8Z6
(613) 548-7136   *SIC* 1521
MARTIN, C. BUS SERVICE LIMITED *p* 747
106 ADVANCE AVE, NAPANEE, ON, K7R
3Y6
(613) 354-7545   *SIC* 4151
MARTIN, CLAUDE & MARCEL INC *p* 1137
49C RTE DU PRESIDENT-KENNEDY,
LEVIS, QC, G6V 6C3
(418) 835-1234   *SIC* 5812
MARTIN, CLAUDE & MARCEL INC *p* 1256
3410 BOUL SAINTE-ANNE, QUEBEC, QC,
G1E 3L7
(418) 663-1234   *SIC* 5812
MARTIN, CLAUDE & MARCEL INC *p* 1256
7352 BOUL HENRI-BOURASSA, QUEBEC,
QC, G1H 3E4
(418) 622-0220   *SIC* 5812
MARTIN, CLAUDE & MARCEL INC *p* 1279
701 RUE DES ROCAILLES, QUEBEC, QC,
G2J 1A9
(418) 622-0220   *SIC* 5812
MARTIN, DENNIS M DRUGS INC   *p* 760
3701 PORTAGE RD UNIT 1, NIAGARA
FALLS, ON, L2J 2K8
(905) 354-6511   *SIC* 5912
**MARTIN, IAN TECHNOLOGY STAFFING
LIMITED**   *p* 801
610 CHARTWELL RD SUITE 101,
OAKVILLE, ON, L6J 4A5
(905) 815-1600   *SIC* 6712
MARTIN, LOUIS MERCHANDISING LTD *p*
482
605 JOHN ST N, AYLMER, ON, N5H 2B6
(519) 773-8424   *SIC* 5531
MARTIN-BROWER   *p* 724
See MARTIN-BROWER OF CANADA CO
MARTIN-BROWER OF CANADA CO   *p* 24
4242 21 ST NE, CALGARY, AB, T2E 9A6
(403) 255-3278   *SIC* 5141
MARTIN-BROWER OF CANADA CO   *p* 724
6985 FINANCIAL DR 3RD FL, MISSIS-
SAUGA, ON, L5N 0G3
(905) 363-7000   *SIC* 5113
MARTIN-BROWER OF CANADA CO *p* 1053
475 AV LEE, BAIE-D'URFE, QC, H9X 3S3
(514) 457-4411   *SIC* 5141
MARTIN-PRODUITS DE BUREAU INC   *p*
1114
576 RUE SAINT-VIATEUR, JOLIETTE, QC,
J6E 3B6

(450) 757-7587   *SIC* 2621
MARTINEAU, REAL INC   *p* 1287
10 BOUL BOUTHILLIER, ROSEMERE, QC,
J7A 4B4
(450) 437-2007   *SIC* 5251
MARTINGROVE COLLEGIATE INSTITUTE *p*
578
*See TORONTO DISTRICT SCHOOL
BOARD*
MARTINI-VISPAK INC   *p* 1117
3535 BOUL SAINT-CHARLES BUREAU
600, KIRKLAND, QC, H9H 5B9
(514) 739-4666   *SIC* 8743
MARTINI-VISPAK INC   *p* 1229
174 RUE MERIZZI, MONTREAL, QC, H4T
1S4
(514) 344-1551   *SIC* 7311
MARTINO CONTRACTORS LTD   *p* 555
150 CONNIE CRES UNIT 16, CONCORD,
ON, L4K 1L9
(905) 760-9894   *SIC* 1711
MARTINO NURSING CENTRES LIMITED *p*
614
39 MARY ST, HAMILTON, ON, L8R 3L8
(905) 523-6427   *SIC* 8051
MARTINREA AUTOMOTIVE INC   *p* 1002
3210 LANGSTAFF RD, VAUGHAN, ON, L4K
5B2
(289) 982-3000   *SIC* 3499
**MARTINREA AUTOMOTIVE SYSTEMS
CANADA (AJAX)**   *p* 474
*See MARTINREA AUTOMOTIVE SYS-
TEMS CANADA LTD*
**MARTINREA AUTOMOTIVE SYSTEMS
CANADA (LONDON)**   *p* 662
*See MARTINREA AUTOMOTIVE SYS-
TEMS CANADA LTD*
**MARTINREA AUTOMOTIVE SYSTEMS
CANADA LTD**   *p* 474
650 FINLEY AVE, AJAX, ON, L1S 6N1
(905) 428-3737   *SIC* 3711
**MARTINREA AUTOMOTIVE SYSTEMS
CANADA LTD**   *p* 662
3820 COMMERCE RD, LONDON, ON, N6N
1P6
(519) 644-1567   *SIC* 3711
MARTINREA INTERNATIONAL INC *p* 1002
3210 LANGSTAFF RD, VAUGHAN, ON, L4K
5B2
(416) 749-0314   *SIC* 3499
MARTINREA INTERNATIONAL INC *p* 1032
30 AVIVA PARK DR, WOODBRIDGE, ON,
L4L 9C7
(905) 264-0149   *SIC* 3499
MARTINREA METALLIC CANADA INC   *p*
1002
3210 LANGSTAFF RD, VAUGHAN, ON, L4K
5B2
(416) 749-0314   *SIC* 3465
MARU GROUP CANADA INC   *p* 929
2 BLOOR ST E SUITE 1600, TORONTO,
ON, M4W 1A8
(647) 258-1416   *SIC* 8732
MARU VCR & C   *p* 929
See MARU GROUP CANADA INC
MARV JONES HONDA   *p* 231
See JONES, MARV LTD
MARVEL BEAUTY SCHOOL   *p* 931
*See TOWLE, RUSSELL L ENTERPRISES
LTD*
MARVID POULTRY CANADA   *p* 1239
See 9020-2516 QUEBEC INC
MARVIN CANDY & DISPLAYS   *p* 1016
See MARVIN ENTERPRISES INC
MARVIN ENTERPRISES INC   *p* 1016
3627 COCHRANE ST, WHITBY, ON, L1R
2T2
(905) 665-5686   *SIC* 5145
MARVIN WINDOWS & DOORS   *p* 740
See MARVIN WINDOWS INC
MARVIN WINDOWS INC   *p* 740
1455 COURTNEYPARK DR E, MISSIS-
SAUGA, ON, L5T 2E3
(905) 670-5052   *SIC* 5211

MARWA HOLDINGS INC   *p* 973
61 YORKVILLE AVE PH 914, TORONTO,
ON, M5R 1B7
   SIC 6211
MARWAL INVESTMENTS INC   *p* 724
2875 ARGENTIA RD UNIT 2, MISSIS-
SAUGA, ON, L5N 8G6
(905) 813-3005   *SIC* 6719
MARWEST GROUP OF COMPANIES LTD *p*
379
360 MAIN ST SUITE 300, WINNIPEG, MB,
R3C 3Z3
(204) 947-1200   *SIC* 6712
MARWICK MANUFACTURING INC   *p* 688
6325 NORTHWEST DR, MISSISSAUGA,
ON, L4V 1P6
(905) 677-0677   *SIC* 2789
MARWOOD INTERNATIONAL INC   *p* 912
35 TOWNLINE RD, TILLSONBURG, ON,
N4G 2R5
(519) 688-1144   *SIC* 3714
MARWOOD LTD   *p* 419
3307 ROUTE 101, TRACYVILLE, NB, E5L
1N7
(506) 459-7777   *SIC* 2499
MARWOOD LTD   *p* 459
1948 HAMMONDS PLAINS RD, HAM-
MONDS PLAINS, NS, B4B 1P4
(902) 835-9629   *SIC* 2421
MARX METALS LIMITED   *p* 686
2520 RENA RD, MISSISSAUGA, ON, L4T
3C9
   SIC 5093
MARY CENTER   *p* 781
*See MARY CENTER OF THE ARCHDIO-
CESE OF TORONTO*
**MARY CENTER OF THE ARCHDIOCESE
OF TORONTO**   *p* 781
530 WILSON AVE SUITE 210, NORTH
YORK, ON, M3H 5Y9
(416) 630-5533   *SIC* 8399
MARY KAY COSMETICS LTD   *p* 724
2020 MEADOWVALE BLVD, MISSIS-
SAUGA, ON, L5N 6Y2
(905) 858-0020   *SIC* 5122
MARY MAXIM   *p* 837
See MISS MARY MAXIM LTD
MARY WARD CATHOLIC HIGH SCHOOL *p*
877
*See TORONTO CATHOLIC DISTRICT
SCHOOL BOARD*
MARYMOUND INC   *p* 370
442 SCOTIA ST, WINNIPEG, MB, R2V 1X4
(204) 338-7971   *SIC* 8399
MARYMOUND SCHOOL   *p* 370
See MARYMOUND INC
MARYN INTERNATIONAL SALES LTD *p* 17
4216 54 AVE SE SUITE 8, CALGARY, AB,
T2C 2E3
(403) 252-2239   *SIC* 5172
MARYNA (PRIVATE) LIMITED   *p* 1003
9926 KEELE ST UNIT 5444, VAUGHAN,
ON, L6A 3Y4
   SIC 6726
**MARYVALE ADOLESCENT FAMILY SER-
VICE**   *p*
1025
3640 WELLS ST, WINDSOR, ON, N9C 1T9
(519) 258-0484   *SIC* 8361
MARZILLI INTERNATIONAL INC *p* 1032
511 CHRISLEA RD, WOODBRIDGE, ON,
L4L 8N6
(289) 268-2040   *SIC* 2512
MAS ENGINEERING, DIV OF   *p* 668
See COLE ENGINEERING GROUP LTD
MASCO CANADA LIMITED   *p* 889
350 SOUTH EDGEWARE RD, ST THOMAS,
ON, N5P 4L1
(519) 633-5050   *SIC* 3432
MASCO CANADA LIMITED   *p* 889
35 CURRAH RD, ST THOMAS, ON, N5P
3R2
   SIC 3432
MASCOT TRUCK PARTS   *p* 736

See 1334869 ONTARIO LIMITED
MASK MANAGEMENT CONSULTANTS LIMITED p 816
2571 LANCASTER RD, OTTAWA, ON, K1B 4L5
(613) 733-7800   SIC 8742

MASKA ELECTIQUE ST-HYACINTHE p 1068
See ELECTRIMAT LTEE

MASKI p 1146
See PANNEAUX MASKI INC

MASKIMO CONSTRUCTION INC p 1388
2500 RUE LEON-TREPANIER, TROIS-RIVIERES, QC, G9A 5E1
(819) 601-2999   SIC 5032

MASKIMO CONSTRUCTION/DIVISON CARRIERES ET SABLIERES p 1388
See MASKIMO CONSTRUCTION INC

MASLACK SUPPLY LIMITED p 898
488 FALCONBRIDGE RD, SUDBURY, ON, P3A 4S4
(705) 566-1270   SIC 5082

MASON GRAPHITE INC p 1087
3030 BOUL LE CARREFOUR BUREAU 600, COTE SAINT-LUC, QC, H7T 2P5
(514) 289-3580   SIC 1499

MASON GROUP OF COMPANIES LIMITED, THE p 697
1205 BRITANNIA RD E, MISSISSAUGA, ON, L4W 1C7
(905) 795-0122   SIC 6712

MASON LIFT LTD p 206
1605 CLIVEDEN AVE, DELTA, BC, V3M 6P7
(604) 517-6500   SIC 7359

MASON RESOURCES CORP p 315
1066 HASTINGS ST W SUITE 1650, VANCOUVER, BC, V6E 3X1
(604) 673-2001   SIC 1021

MASON WINDOWS LIMITED p 845
913 BROCK RD, PICKERING, ON, L1W 2X9
(905) 839-1171   SIC 2431

MASON'S MASONRY SUPPLY LIMITED p 740
6291 NETHERHART RD, MISSISSAUGA, ON, L5T 1A2
(905) 670-1233   SIC 5032

MASON, GREG SERVICES INC p 1014
1505 DUNDAS ST E, WHITBY, ON, L1N 2K6
(905) 668-5100   SIC 5511

MASONIC PARK INC p 426
100 MASONIC DR, MOUNT PEARL, NL, A1N 3K5
SIC 8322

MASONIC TEMPLE p 470
See SIRCOM LODGE #66

MASONITE INTERNATIONAL CORPORATION p 1125
6184 RUE NOTRE-DAME, LAC-MEGANTIC, QC, G6B 3B5
(819) 583-1550   SIC 2435

MASONITE INTERNATIONAL CORPORATION p 1299
430 RTE 108 O BUREAU 489, SAINT-EPHREM-DE-BEAUCE, QC, G0M 1R0
(418) 484-5666   SIC 2431

MASS ELECTRONICS p 853
See MASS ELECTRONICS LTD

MASS ELECTRONICS LTD p 853
45 WEST WILMOT ST UNIT 16-17, RICHMOND HILL, ON, L4B 1K1
(905) 764-9533   SIC 5013

MASS INSURANCE BROKER p 1206
630 BOUL RENE-LEVESQUE O BUREAU 2500, MONTREAL, QC, H3B 1S6
(514) 925-3222   SIC 6411

MASS MANAGEMENT SERVICES p 850
See 459324 ONTARIO INC

MASSCOMP ELECTRONICS LTD p 853
40 EAST PEARCE ST, RICHMOND HILL, ON, L4B 1B7
(905) 764-9533   SIC 6399

MASSEY COLLEGE p 976
See MASTER AND FELLOWS OF MASSEY COLLEGE, THE

MASSEY HALL p 961
See CORPORATION OF MASSEY HALL AND ROY THOMSON HALL, THE

MASSEY VANIER HIGH SCHOOL p 1088
See COMMISSION SCOLAIRE EASTERN TOWNSHIPS

MASSEY WHOLESALE LTD p 680
400 CARLALBERT ST, MASSEY, ON, P0P 1P0
(705) 865-2051   SIC 5194

MASSIF INC, LE p 1245
1350 RUE PRINCIPALE, PETITE-RIVIERE-SAINT-FRANCOIS, QC, G0A 2L0
(877) 536-2774   SIC 7011

MASSINE ENTERPRISES INC p 834
296 BANK ST, OTTAWA, ON, K2P 1X8
(613) 234-8692   SIC 5411

MASSINE'S YOUR INDEPENDENT GROCER p 834
See MASSINE ENTERPRISES INC

MASSON p 1288
See VINS ARTERRA CANADA, DIVISION QUEBEC, INC

MASSTOWN MARKET LIMITED p 449
10622 HIGHWAY 2, DEBERT, NS, B0M 1G0
(902) 662-2816   SIC 5431

MASSULLO MOTORS LIMITED p 248
4493 JOYCE AVE, POWELL RIVER, BC, V8A 3A8
(604) 485-7981   SIC 5511

MASTEC CANADA INC p 53
333 7 AVE SW UNIT 2000, CALGARY, AB, T2P 2Z1
(403) 770-7365   SIC 1541

MASTEC CANADA INC p 147
1010 BRIER PARK DR NW, MEDICINE HAT, AB, T1C 1Z7
(403) 529-6444   SIC 1623

MASTER AND FELLOWS OF MASSEY COLLEGE, THE p 976
4 DEVONSHIRE PL, TORONTO, ON, M5S 2E1
(416) 978-2892   SIC 6514

MASTER BUILDING MATERIALS p 1029
See 1146898 ONTARIO INC

MASTER CRAFTSMAN p 500
See 821373 ONTARIO LTD

MASTER DESIGN JEWELLERY LIMITED p 784
1001 PETROLIA RD, NORTH YORK, ON, M3J 2X7
SIC 5094

MASTER FLO VALVE INC. p 110
4611 74 AVE NW, EDMONTON, AB, T6B 2H5
(780) 468-4433   SIC 3494

MASTER MECHANICAL PLUMBING & HEATING (1986) LTD p 122
2107 87 AVE NW, EDMONTON, AB, T6P 1L5
(780) 449-1400   SIC 1711

MASTER MECHANICAL PLUMBING & HEATING p 36
6025 12 ST SE SUITE 19, CALGARY, AB, T2H 2K1
(403) 243-5880   SIC 1711

MASTER MERCHANT SYSTEMS SOFTWARE LIMITED p 447
202 BROWNLOW AVE SUITE 700, DARTMOUTH, NS, B3B 1T5
(902) 496-9500   SIC 5045

MASTER PACKAGING INC p 398
333 BOUL ADELARD-SAVOIE, DIEPPE, NB, E1A 7G9
(506) 389-3737   SIC 2653

MASTER PACKAGING INC p 1038
23784 TRANS CANADA HIGHWAY, BORDEN-CARLETON, PE, C0B 1X0
(902) 437-3737   SIC 3554

MASTER PACKAGING INC p 1039
60 BELVEDERE AVE, CHARLOTTETOWN, PE, C1A 6B1
(902) 368-3737   SIC 2653

MASTER SECURITY LTD p 266
3580 MONCTON ST SUITE 212, RICHMOND, BC, V7E 3A4
(604) 278-3024   SIC 7382

MASTERBATCHES DIV DE p 1333
See CLARIANT (CANADA) INC

MASTERCARD CANADA, INC p 930
121 BLOOR ST E SUITE 600, TORONTO, ON, M4W 3M5
(416) 365-6655   SIC 6153

MASTERCARD TECHNOLOGIES CANADA ULC p 307
475 HOWE ST SUITE 2000, VANCOUVER, BC, V6C 2B3
(604) 800-3711   SIC 7371

MASTERFEEDS INC p 657
1020 HARGRIEVE RD SUITE 1, LONDON, ON, N6E 1P5
(519) 685-4300   SIC 2048

MASTERFEEDS INC p 657
1020 HARGRIEVE RD SUITE 9, LONDON, ON, N6E 1P5
(519) 685-4300   SIC 6712

MASTERFOODS, DIV OF p 495
See MARS CANADA INC

MASTERMIND EDUCATIONAL p 865
See MASTERMIND LP

MASTERMIND LP p 865
415 MILNER AVE SUITE 4, SCARBOROUGH, ON, M1B 2L1
(416) 321-8984   SIC 5945

MASTERNET LTD p 735
690 GANA CRT, MISSISSAUGA, ON, L5S 1P2
(905) 795-0005   SIC 3089

MASTERS INSURANCE LIMITED p 555
7501 KEELE ST SUITE 400, CONCORD, ON, L4K 1Y2
(905) 738-4164   SIC 6411

MASTERS LIFE INSURANCE AGENTS LIMITED p 555
7501 KEELE ST SUITE 400, CONCORD, ON, L4K 1Y2
SIC 6411

MASTRONARDI PRODUCE LIMITED p 634
2100 ROAD 4 E, KINGSVILLE, ON, N9Y 2E5
(519) 326-3218   SIC 5148

MATAKANA SCAFFOLDING B.C. INC p 290
1085 E KENT AVE NORTH SUITE 122, VANCOUVER, BC, V5X 4V9
(604) 873-5140   SIC 1799

MATALCO INC p 504
850 INTERMODAL DR, BRAMPTON, ON, L6T 0B5
(905) 790-2511   SIC 3291

MATALLURGIE FRONTENAC p 1382
See GESTION METALLURGIE CASTECH INC

MATAPEDIENNE COOPERATIVE AGRICOLE, LA p 1046
90 RUE PROULX BUREAU 550, AMQUI, QC, G5J 3G3
(418) 629-4401   SIC 5999

MATASSA INCORPORATED p 807
5335 WALKER RD, OLDCASTLE, ON, N0R 1L0
(519) 737-1506   SIC 1541

MATCH MARKETING GROUP p 697
See MATCH MG CANADA INC

MATCH MG CANADA INC p 697
5225 SATELLITE DR, MISSISSAUGA, ON, L4W 5P9
(905) 566-2824   SIC 8743

MATCO PACKAGING INC p 1330
2519 RUE COHEN, SAINT-LAURENT, QC, H4R 2N5
(514) 337-6050   SIC 5169

MATCO TRANSPORTATION SYSTEMS p 101
See MID-ARCTIC TRANSPORTATION CO. LTD

MATCOM INDUSTRIAL INSTALLATIONS INC p 555
1531 CREDITSTONE RD, CONCORD, ON, L4K 5V6
(416) 667-0463   SIC 7359

MATCON EXCAVATION & SHORING LTD p 201
2208 HARTLEY AVE, COQUITLAM, BC, V3K 6X3
(604) 520-5909   SIC 1794

MATCOR p 504
See MATSU MANUFACTURING INC

MATCOR AUTOMOTIVE INC p 724
7299 EAST DANBRO CRES, MISSISSAUGA, ON, L5N 6P8
(905) 819-9900   SIC 3465

MATCOR METAL FABRICATION INC p 724
7275 EAST DANBRO CRES, MISSISSAUGA, ON, L5N 6P8
(905) 814-7479   SIC 3699

MATCOR METAL FABRICATION, DIV OF p 594
See MATSU MANUFACTURING INC

MATECH B.T.A. INC p 1099
1570 BOUL SAINT-CHARLES, DRUMMONDVILLE, QC, J2C 4Z5
(819) 478-4015   SIC 5013

MATELAS DAUPHIN INC p 1139
8124 RUE DU BLIZZARD, LEVIS, QC, G6X 1C9
(418) 832-2951   SIC 2515

MATERIAUX AUDET INC p 1348
294 BOUL BONA-DUSSAULT, SAINT-MARC-DES-CARRIERES, QC, G0A 4B0
(418) 268-3525   SIC 5039

MATERIAUX BLANCHET INC p 1046
2771 RTE DE L'AEROPORT, AMOS, QC, J9T 3A8
(819) 732-6581   SIC 2421

MATERIAUX BLANCHET INC p 1119
6019 BOUL WILFRID-HAMEL BUREAU 200, L'ANCIENNE-LORETTE, QC, G2E 2H3
(418) 871-2626   SIC 2421

MATERIAUX BLANCHET INC p 1349
1030 RTE ELGIN S, SAINT-PAMPHILE, QC, G0R 3X0
(418) 356-3344   SIC 2421

MATERIAUX BOMAT INC p 1140
1212 CH INDUSTRIEL, LEVIS, QC, G7A 1B1
(418) 831-4848   SIC 5039

MATERIAUX BONHOMME INC p 1103
225 MONTEE PAIEMENT, GATINEAU, QC, J8P 6M7
(819) 561-5577   SIC 5211

MATERIAUX CAMPAGNA (2003) INC p 1290
1200 RUE MANTHA, ROUYN-NORANDA, QC, J9Y 0G2
(819) 797-1200   SIC 5211

MATERIAUX DE CONSTRUCTION CANADA CONTINENTAL p 1074
See CONTINENTAL BUILDING PRODUCTS CANADA INC

MATERIAUX DE CONSTRUCTION D L INC p 1108
760 RUE DE VERNON, GATINEAU, QC, J9J 3K5
(819) 770-9974   SIC 5039

MATERIAUX DE CONSTRUCTION DERBY p 1293
See PRODUITS DE CONSTRUCTION DERBY INC

MATERIAUX DE CONSTRUCTION KP LTEE p 1251
3075 AUT TRANSCANADIENNE, POINTE-CLAIRE, QC, H9R 1B4
(514) 694-5855   SIC 3089

MATERIAUX DE CONSTRUCTION L&B p 1231
See LEFEBVRE & BENOIT S.E.C.

MATERIAUX DE CONSTRUCTION LE-TOURNEAU INC *p*
1400
4855 143 RTE, WATERVILLE, QC, J0B 3H0
(819) 566-5633 *SIC* 5211

MATERIAUX DE CONSTRUCTION OLD-CASTLE CANADA INC, LES *p*
229
See OLDCASTLE BUILDING PRODUCTS CANADA, INC

MATERIAUX DE CONSTRUCTION OLD-CASTLE CANADA INC, LES *p*
892
See OLDCASTLE BUILDING PRODUCTS CANADA, INC

MATERIAUX DE CONSTRUCTION OLD-CASTLE CANADA INC, LES *p*
1073
See OLDCASTLE BUILDING PRODUCTS CANADA, INC

MATERIAUX DE CONSTRUCTION R OLIGNY LTEE, LES *p* 1073
101 BOUL TASCHEREAU, CANDIAC, QC, J5R 1X4
(450) 659-5444 *SIC* 5031

MATERIAUX ECONOMIQUES INC *p* 1388
2900 RUE JULES-VACHON, TROIS-RIVIERES, QC, G9A 5E1
(819) 374-8577 *SIC* 1799

MATERIAUX LAURENTIENS INC *p* 1320
2159 BOUL DU CURE-LABELLE, SAINT-JEROME, QC, J7Y 1T1
(450) 438-9780 *SIC* 5211

MATERIAUX LAURENTIENS INC *p* 1382
7700 BOUL LAURIER, TERREBONNE, QC, J7M 2K8
(450) 478-7557 *SIC* 5211

MATERIAUX MIRON INC *p* 1365
230 BOUL MONSEIGNEUR-LANGLOIS, SALABERRY-DE-VALLEYFIELD, QC, J6S 0A7
(450) 373-7272 *SIC* 5211

MATERIAUX PARENT, DIV OF *p* 417
See NORTH AMERICAN FOREST PRODUCTS LTD

MATERIAUX PAYSAGERS SAVARIA LTEE *p* 1066
950 CH DE LORRAINE, BOUCHERVILLE, QC, J4B 5E4
(450) 655-6147 *SIC* 5191

MATERIAUX PONT MASSON INC *p* 1365
2715 BOUL MONSEIGNEUR-LANGLOIS, SALABERRY-DE-VALLEYFIELD, QC, J6S 5P7
(450) 371-2041 *SIC* 5211

MATERIAUX RE-SOURCE *p* 1103
See PLASTIVAL INC

MATERIEL INDUSTRIEL LTEE, LE *p* 1288
325 LA GRANDE-CAROLINE RR 5, ROUGEMONT, QC, J0L 1M0
(450) 469-4934 *SIC* 3444

MATERIELLES INDUSTRIELLES, LES *p* 1288
See ENTREPRISES BERNARD SORNIN INC, LES

MATH SPORT INC *p* 1265
1130 BOUL CHAREST O BUREAU 7, QUEBEC, QC, G1N 2E2
(581) 999-7707 *SIC* 3149

MATHESON CONSTRUCTORS LIMITED *p* 481
205 INDUSTRIAL PKWY N UNIT 5, AURORA, ON, L4G 4C4
(905) 669-7999 *SIC* 1542

MATHESON VALVES & FITTINGS LTD *p* 1330
4060 BOUL POIRIER, SAINT-LAURENT, QC, H4R 2A5
(514) 337-1106 *SIC* 5085

MATHEW MCNAIR SECONDARY SCHOOL *p* 262
See BOARD OF EDUCATION SCHOOL DISTRICT #38 (RICHMOND)

MATICAIR SUPPLY AND MANUFACTUR-

ING (1996) LTD *p*
555
99 MCCLEARY CRT, CONCORD, ON, L4K 3Z1
(905) 738-5888 *SIC* 3444

MATISS *p* 1305
See GROUPE CONTROLE INC

MATISS INC *p* 1305
8800 25E AV, SAINT-GEORGES, QC, G6A 1K5
(418) 227-9141 *SIC* 3569

MATONABEE PETROEUM LTD *p* 436
117 KAM LAKE RD, YELLOWKNIFE, NT, X1A 0G3
(867) 873-4001 *SIC* 5171

MATONABEE PETROLEUM LTD *p* 436
PO BOX 2697 STN MAIN, YELLOWKNIFE, NT, X1A 2R1
(867) 873-4001 *SIC* 5171

MATRA PLAST INDUSTRIES INC *p* 1057
420 RUE NOTRE-DAME, BERTHIERVILLE, QC, J0K 1A0
(450) 836-7071 *SIC* 3089

MATRICES CARRITEC INC, LES *p* 1053
575 BOUL MORGAN, BAIE-D'URFE, QC, H9X 3T6
(514) 457-7779 *SIC* 2542

MATRIKON INC *p* 90
10405 JASPER AVE NW SUITE 1800, EDMONTON, AB, T5J 3N4
(780) 448-1010 *SIC* 7371

MATRIKON INTERNATIONAL *p* 90
See MATRIKON INC

MATRIX *p* 410
See MATRIX LOGISTICS SERVICES LIMITED

MATRIX *p* 987
See MAVRIX GLOBAL FUND INC

MATRIX ASSET MANAGEMENT *p* 939
See MAVRIX AMERICAN GROWTH FUND

MATRIX ELECTRONICS LIMITED *p* 740
1124 MID-WAY BLVD, MISSISSAUGA, ON, L5T 2C1
(905) 670-8400 *SIC* 5065

MATRIX GEOSERVICES LTD *p* 53
808 4 AVE SW SUITE 600, CALGARY, AB, T2P 3E8
(403) 294-0707 *SIC* 7374

MATRIX LABOUR LEASING LTD *p* 71
11420 27 ST SE SUITE 204, CALGARY, AB, T2Z 3R6
(403) 201-9520 *SIC* 7361

MATRIX LOGISTICS SERVICES LIMITED *p* 9
2525 29 ST NE, CALGARY, AB, T1Y 7B5
(403) 291-9292 *SIC* 4225

MATRIX LOGISTICS SERVICES LIMITED *p* 410
10 DEWARE DR SUITE 1, MONCTON, NB, E1H 2S6
(506) 863-1300 *SIC* 4225

MATRIX LOGISTICS SERVICES LIMITED *p* 511
2675 STEELES AVE W, BRAMPTON, ON, L6Y 5X3
(905) 451-6792 *SIC* 4225

MATRIX LOGISTICS SERVICES LIMITED *p* 740
6941 KENNEDY RD, MISSISSAUGA, ON, L5T 2R6
(905) 795-2200 *SIC* 4225

MATRIX MOTORSPORTS *p* 76
20 FREEPORT LANDNG NE, CALGARY, AB, T3J 5H6
(403) 265-5000 *SIC* 3089

MATRIX NAC *p* 526
See MATRIX NORTH AMERICAN CONSTRUCTION LTD

MATRIX NORTH AMERICAN CONSTRUCTION LTD *p*
526
3196 MAINWAY SUITE 1, BURLINGTON, ON, L7M 1A5
(289) 313-1600 *SIC* 1629

MATRIX RESEARCH LIMITED *p* 904
55 DONCASTER AVE SUITE 280, THORNHILL, ON, L3T 1L7
(905) 707-1300 *SIC* 8732

MATRIX SERVICE CANADA ULC *p* 139
7105 39 ST UNIT 102, LEDUC, AB, T9E 0R8
(780) 986-4058 *SIC* 1791

MATRIX SOLUTIONS INC *p* 65
214 11 AVE SW SUITE 600, CALGARY, AB, T2R 0K1
(403) 237-0606 *SIC* 8748

MATRIX TECHNOLOGY LTD *p* 679
280 HILLMOUNT RD UNIT 6, MARKHAM, ON, L6C 3A1
(905) 477-4442 *SIC* 5065

MATRIX VIDEO COMMUNICATIONS CORP *p* 76
1626 115 AVE NE UNIT 103, CALGARY, AB, T3K 2E4
(403) 640-4490 *SIC* 5065

MATROX *p* 1095
See SYSTEMES ELECTRONIQUES MATROX LTEE

MATSQUI RECREATION CENTRE *p* 176
See CITY OF ABBOTSFORD

MATSU MANUFACTURING INC *p* 504
7657 BRAMALEA RD, BRAMPTON, ON, L6T 5V3
(905) 291-5000 *SIC* 3465

MATSU MANUFACTURING INC *p* 594
71 TODD RD, GEORGETOWN, ON, L7G 4R8
SIC 8711

MATTAMY (MONARCH) LIMITED *p* 767
2550 VICTORIA PARK AVE SUITE 200, NORTH YORK, ON, M2J 5A9
(416) 491-7440 *SIC* 8741

MATTAMY HAWTHORNE VILLAGE *p* 684
See MATTAMY HOMES LIMITED

MATTAMY HOMES LIMITED *p* 536
605 SHELDON DR, CAMBRIDGE, ON, N1T 2K1
SIC 1522

MATTAMY HOMES LIMITED *p* 684
1550 DERRY RD, MILTON, ON, L9T 1A1
(905) 875-2692 *SIC* 5211

MATTAMY HOMES LIMITED *p* 969
66 WELLINGTON ST W, TORONTO, ON, M5K 1G8
(905) 829-2424 *SIC* 6552

MATTCO SERVICES LIMITED *p* 496
350 WAVERLEY RD, BOWMANVILLE, ON, L1C 4Y4
(905) 623-0175 *SIC* 5461

MATTEL CANADA INC *p* 732
6155 FREEMONT BLVD, MISSISSAUGA, ON, L5R 3W2
(905) 501-0404 *SIC* 5092

MATTHEWS, BILL VOLKSWAGEN AUDI *p* 429
See BILL MATTHEWS' AUTOHAUS LIMITED

MATTHEWS, MARK PHARMACY LTD *p* 546
119 HURONTARIO ST, COLLINGWOOD, ON, L9Y 2L9
(705) 444-6055 *SIC* 5912

MATTINA MECHANICAL LIMITED *p* 608
211 LANARK ST UNIT A, HAMILTON, ON, L8E 2Z9
(905) 544-6380 *SIC* 1711

MAUI JIM CANADA ULC *p* 724
2830 ARGENTIA RD UNIT 3, MISSISSAUGA, ON, L5N 8G4
(905) 286-9714 *SIC* 5099

MAUI JIM SUNGLASSES *p* 724
See MAUI JIM CANADA ULC

MAUREEN KLEIN *p* 226
19925 WILLOWBROOK DR UNIT 110, LANGLEY, BC, V2Y 1A7
(604) 530-0231 *SIC* 6531

MAURICE FOUCAULT INC *p* 1320
260 BOUL ROLAND-GODARD, SAINT-JEROME, QC, J7Y 4P7
(450) 530-3420 *SIC* 4924

MAURICE SIGOUIN REPARATION DE MEUBLES LTEE *p* 1107
142 CH FREEMAN BUREAU 8, GATINEAU, QC, J8Z 2B4
(819) 776-3522 *SIC* 7641

MAURICE'S SERVICE CENTRE LIMITED *p* 428
4 BARN RD, ST. ANTHONY, NL, A0K 4S0
(709) 454-3434 *SIC* 5983

MAURICIE TOYOTA INC *p* 1368
8823 BOUL DES HETRES, SHAWINIGAN, QC, G9N 4X3
(819) 539-8393 *SIC* 5511

MAUSER CANADA LTD *p* 526
1121 PIONEER RD, BURLINGTON, ON, L7M 1K5
(905) 332-4800 *SIC* 3412

MAV BEAUTY BRANDS INC *p* 555
190 PIPPIN RD, CONCORD, ON, L4K 4X9
(905) 530-2500 *SIC* 6712

MAVERICK LAND CONSULTANTS LTD *p* 36
6940 FISHER RD SE SUITE 310, CALGARY, AB, T2H 0W3
(403) 243-7833 *SIC* 1389

MAVERICK OILFIELD SERVICES LTD *p* 77
15 ROYAL VISTA PL NW UNIT 320, CALGARY, AB, T3R 0P3
(403) 234-8822 *SIC* 1389

MAVERIX METALS INC *p* 307
510 BURRARD ST SUITE 575, VANCOUVER, BC, V6C 3A8
(604) 449-9290 *SIC* 1499

MAVI JEANS INC *p* 295
580 INDUSTRIAL AVE, VANCOUVER, BC, V6A 2P3
(604) 708-2373 *SIC* 5136

MAVIRO CATALYST CANADA INC *p* 110
7805 34 ST NW, EDMONTON, AB, T6B 2V5
(780) 430-9696 *SIC* 7363

MAVRIX AMERICAN GROWTH FUND *p* 939
36 LOMBARD ST SUITE 2200, TORONTO, ON, M5C 2X3
(416) 362-3077 *SIC* 6722

MAVRIX FUND MANAGEMENT INC *p* 954
212 KING ST W SUITE 501, TORONTO, ON, M5H 1K5
(416) 362-3077 *SIC* 6282

MAVRIX GLOBAL FUND INC *p* 987
130 KING ST W SUITE 2200, TORONTO, ON, M5X 2A2
(416) 362-3077 *SIC* 6722

MAVRON TRANSPORT INC *p* 697
5758 DIXIE RD, MISSISSAUGA, ON, L4W 1E7
(905) 670-9455 *SIC* 4213

MAWER GLOBAL SMALL CAP FUND LTD *p* 65
517 10 AVE SW SUITE 600, CALGARY, AB, T2R 0A8
(403) 267-1988 *SIC* 6722

MAWER INVESTMENT MANAGEMENT LTD *p* 65
600-517 10 AVE SW, CALGARY, AB, T2R 0A8
(403) 262-4673 *SIC* 6722

MAX AICHER (NORTH AMERICA) LIMITED *p* 611
855 INDUSTRIAL DR, HAMILTON, ON, L8L 0B2
(289) 426-5670 *SIC* 3312

MAX AICHER (NORTH AMERICA) REALTY INC *p* 611
855 INDUSTRIAL DR, HAMILTON, ON, L8L 0B2
(289) 426-5670 *SIC* 3312

MAX AUTO SUPPLY *p* 815
See 1270477 ONTARIO INC

MAX AVIATION INC *p* 1308
6100 RTE DE L'AEROPORT, SAINT-HUBERT, QC, J3Y 8Y9
(450) 462-8511 *SIC* 4512

MAX CANADA INSURANCE COMPANY *p* 640
50 QUEEN ST N UNIT 710, KITCHENER,

ON, N2H 6P4
(519) 634-5267   *SIC* 6331
MAX DIE GROUP   *p* 807
See MANOR TOOL AND DIE LTD
MAX FUEL DISTRIBUTORS (1998) LTD   *p*
173
5503 KEPLER ST, WHITECOURT, AB, T7S
1X7
(780) 778-2346   *SIC* 5172
MAX FUEL DISTRIBUTORS LTD   *p* 163
701 12 AVE NE, SLAVE LAKE, AB, T0G 2A2
(780) 849-3820   *SIC* 5171
MAX RESOURCE CORP   *p* 315
1095 W PENDER ST SUITE 1188, VAN-
COUVER, BC, V6E 2M6
(604) 365-1522   *SIC* 1041
**MAX UNDERHILL'S FARM SUPPLY LIM-
ITED**   *p*
1003
56532 CALTON LINE SUITE 1, VIENNA,
ON, N0J 1Z0
(519) 866-3632   *SIC* 5191
**MAX WRIGHT REAL ESTATE CORPORA-
TION**   *p*
321
1672 2ND AVE W, VANCOUVER, BC, V6J
1H4
(604) 632-3300   *SIC* 6531
MAX'S BAKERY & DELICATESSEN   *p* 261
See REDPATH FOODS INC
MAXAMA PROTECTION INC   *p* 841
234 ROMAINE ST, PETERBOROUGH, ON,
K9J 2C5
(705) 745-7500   *SIC* 7381
MAXAR TECHNOLOGIES LTD   *p* 307
200 BURRARD ST SUITE 1570, VANCOU-
VER, BC, V6C 3L6
(604) 974-5275   *SIC* 7371
MAXFIELD INC   *p* 81
1026 WESTERN DR, CROSSFIELD, AB,
T0M 0S0
(403) 946-5678   *SIC* 3533
**MAXGUARD ALARM AND SECURITY
COMPANY LTD**   *p* 555
8700 DUFFERIN ST UNIT 17, CONCORD,
ON, L4K 4S2
(416) 893-9082   *SIC* 7382
MAXI   *p* 1148
See MAXI MANIWAKI INC
MAXI   *p* 1177
See PROVIGO DISTRIBUTION INC
MAXI   *p* 1240
See LOBLAWS INC
MAXI   *p* 1247
See PROVIGO DISTRIBUTION INC
MAXI   *p* 1288
See PROVIGO DISTRIBUTION INC
MAXI   *p* 1315
See PROVIGO DISTRIBUTION INC
MAXI   *p* 1330
See PROVIGO DISTRIBUTION INC
MAXI   *p* 1363
See PROVIGO DISTRIBUTION INC
MAXI   *p* 1379
See PROVIGO DISTRIBUTION INC
MAXI   *p* 1385
See PROVIGO DISTRIBUTION INC
MAXI   *p* 1386
See PROVIGO DISTRIBUTION INC
MAXI # 8649   *p* 1279
See LOBLAWS INC
MAXI #8630   *p* 1125
See PROVIGO DISTRIBUTION INC
MAXI #8689   *p* 1097
See LOBLAWS INC
MAXI & CIE   *p* 1087
See LOBLAWS INC
MAXI & CIE   *p* 1105
See PROVIGO DISTRIBUTION INC
MAXI 8619   *p* 1121
2100 RUE BAGOT, LA BAIE, QC, G7B 3Z3
(418) 544-2848   *SIC* 5411
MAXI BAIE-COMEAU   *p* 1053
See PROVIGO DISTRIBUTION INC

MAXI BEAUPORT   *p* 1255
See LOBLAWS INC
MAXI CANADA INC   *p* 1347
688 RUE DU PARC, SAINT-LIN-
LAURENTIDES, QC, J5M 3B4
(450) 439-2500   *SIC* 2015
MAXI COMPAGNIE   *p* 1320
See PROVIGO DISTRIBUTION INC
MAXI CRISP INC   *p* 1142
2066 RUE DE LA PROVINCE, LONGUEUIL,
QC, J4G 1R7
(450) 670-4256   *SIC* 5046
MAXI FLEUR DE LYS   *p* 1262
See PROVIGO DISTRIBUTION INC
MAXI JOLIETTE   *p* 1115
See PROVIGO DISTRIBUTION INC
MAXI LA BAIE   *p* 1121
See MAXI 8619
MAXI LES SAULES   *p* 1267
See PROVIGO DISTRIBUTION INC
MAXI MANIWAKI INC   *p* 1148
170 RUE PRINCIPALE S, MANIWAKI, QC,
J9E 1Z7
(819) 449-6822   *SIC* 5411
MAXI PREFONTAINE   *p* 1167
2925 RUE SHERBROOKE E, MONTREAL,
QC, H1W 1B2
(514) 521-0660   *SIC* 5411
MAXI ROBERVAL   *p* 1287
150 AV SAINT-ALPHONSE, ROBERVAL,
QC, G8H 3P8
(418) 275-4471   *SIC* 5411
MAXI-METAL INC   *p* 1305
9345 25E AV, SAINT-GEORGES, QC, G6A
1L1
(418) 228-6637   *SIC* 3713
MAXIM 2000 INC   *p* 414
555 SOMERSET ST UNIT 208, SAINT
JOHN, NB, E2K 4X2
(506) 652-9292   *SIC* 1542
MAXIM CONSTRUCTION INC   *p* 414
555 SOMERSET ST UNIT 208, SAINT
JOHN, NB, E2K 4X2
(506) 652-9292   *SIC* 1542
MAXIM POWER CORP   *p* 53
715 5 AVE SW SUITE 1210, CALGARY, AB,
T2P 2X6
(403) 263-3021   *SIC* 4911
MAXIM TRANSPORTATION SERVICES INC
p 379
1860 BROOKSIDE BLVD, WINNIPEG, MB,
R3C 2E6
(204) 790-6599   *SIC* 5511
MAXIM TRUCK & TRAILER   *p* 379
*See MAXIM TRANSPORTATION SER-
VICES INC*
MAXIMIZER SOFTWARE INC   *p* 299
60 SMITHE ST UNIT 260, VANCOUVER,
BC, V6B 0P5
(604) 601-8000   *SIC* 7372
MAXIMS BAKERY LTD   *p* 287
3596 COMMERCIAL ST, VANCOUVER, BC,
V5N 4E9
(604) 876-8266   *SIC* 5461
MAXIMUM EXPRESS & FREIGHT LTD   *p*
334
576 HILLSIDE AVE UNIT 3, VICTORIA, BC,
V8T 1Y9
(250) 721-5170   *SIC* 7389
MAXIMUM REALTY CORPORATION *p* 1032
7694 ISLINGTON AVE, WOODBRIDGE,
ON, L4L 1W3
(905) 856-7653   *SIC* 6531
MAXPRO MANAGEMENT SERVICES LTD *p*
504
170 WILKINSON RD UNIT 3, BRAMPTON,
ON, L6T 4Z5
(905) 452-9669   *SIC* 8742
MAXRELCO INC   *p* 1284
90 201 RTE, RIGAUD, QC, J0P 1P0
(450) 458-5375   *SIC* 6712
MAXSYS STAFFING & CONSULTING INC *p*
821
173 DALHOUSIE ST SUITE A, OTTAWA,

ON, K1N 7C7
(613) 562-9943   *SIC* 8748
MAXUC TRADING LTD   *p* 784
79 MARTIN ROSS AVE, NORTH YORK,
ON, M3J 2L5
(416) 667-0888   *SIC* 5093
MAXUM DRYWALL INC   *p* 555
1681 LANGSTAFF RD UNIT 18, CON-
CORD, ON, L4K 5T3
(905) 856-4108   *SIC* 1742
MAXVILLE MANOR   *p* 680
80 MECHANIC ST W SUITE 620,
MAXVILLE, ON, K0C 1T0
(613) 527-2170   *SIC* 8051
MAXWELL CAPITAL REALTY   *p* 41
See WESTPOINT MANAGEMENT INC
MAXWELL FABRICS LTD   *p* 323
8811 LAUREL ST UNIT 113, VANCOUVER,
BC, V6P 3V9
(604) 253-7744   *SIC* 5023
MAXWELL FARM ELEVATOR   *p* 544
604 CONCESSION 2, CHESLEY, ON, N0G
1L0
(519) 363-3423   *SIC* 5153
MAXWELL MEDIA PRODUCTS   *p* 491
See MAXWELL PAPER CANADA INC
MAXWELL PAPER CANADA INC   *p* 491
270 FRONT ST, BELLEVILLE, ON, K8N 2Z2
(613) 962-7846   *SIC* 5044
MAXWELL WESTVIEW REALTY   *p* 73
1200 37 ST SW SUITE 41, CALGARY, AB,
T3C 1S2
(403) 256-6015   *SIC* 6531
MAXWELL'S II   *p* 424
See NOR-LAB LIMITED
MAXX NORTH AMERICA SERVICES LTD *p*
110
5311 72A AVE NW, EDMONTON, AB, T6B
2J1
(780) 482-4144   *SIC* 1623
MAXXAM ANALYTICS   *p* 108
*See BUREAU VERITAS CANADA (2019)
INC*
**MAXXAM ANALYTICS INTERNATIONAL
CORPORATION**   *p* 21
*See BUREAU VERITAS CANADA (2019)
INC*
**MAXXAM ANALYTICS INTERNATIONAL
CORPORATION**   *p* 188
*See BUREAU VERITAS CANADA (2019)
INC*
**MAXXAM ANALYTICS INTERNATIONAL
CORPORATION**   *p* 440
*See BUREAU VERITAS CANADA (2019)
INC*
**MAXXAM ANALYTICS INTERNATIONAL
CORPORATION**   *p* 1338
*See BUREAU VERITAS CANADA (2019)
INC*
MAXXIS INTERNATIONAL-CANADA *p* 499
See CHENG SHIN RUBBER CANADA, INC
MAXXIUM CANADA   *p* 572
See BEAM CANADA INC
MAY BALIAN & EMAD GABRA S.E.N.C.R.L.
p 1330
2085 BOUL MARCEL-LAURIN, SAINT-
LAURENT, QC, H4R 1K4
(514) 334-1823   *SIC* 5912
MAY COURT BARGAIN BOX   *p* 821
See MAY COURT CLUB OF OTTAWA, THE
MAY COURT CLUB OF OTTAWA, THE *p* 821
228 LAURIER AVE E, OTTAWA, ON, K1N
6P2
(613) 235-0333   *SIC* 8699
MAY, J. K. INVESTMENTS LTD   *p* 379
149 PIONEER AVE, WINNIPEG, MB, R3C
0H2
(204) 943-8525   *SIC* 5145
**MAY, JACK CHEVROLET BUICK GMC LIM-
ITED**   *p*
748
3788 PRINCE OF WALES DR, NEPEAN,
ON, K2C 3H1
(613) 692-3553   *SIC* 5511

MAY, RON PONTIAC BUICK GMC LTD   *p*
467
303 WELTON ST, SYDNEY, NS, B1P 5S3
(902) 539-6494   *SIC* 5511
**MAY-MCCONVILLE-OMNI INSURANCE
BROKERS LIMITED**   *p* 654
685 RICHMOND ST SUITE 300, LONDON,
ON, N6A 5M1
(519) 673-0880   *SIC* 6311
MAYA   *p* 1402
*See TECHNOLOGIES DE TRANSFERT DE
CHALEUR MAYA LTEE*
MAYA GOLD & SILVER INC   *p* 1206
1 PLACE VILLE-MARIE BUREAU 2901,
MONTREAL, QC, H3B 0E9
(514) 866-2008   *SIC* 1081
MAYCO MIX LTD   *p* 235
1125 CEDAR RD, NANAIMO, BC, V9X 1K9
(250) 722-0064   *SIC* 5032
MAYERS PACKAGING LTD   *p* 372
50 MANDALAY DR, WINNIPEG, MB, R2X
2Z2
(204) 774-1651   *SIC* 5113
MAYES-MARTIN LIMITED   *p* 487
150 VESPRA ST, BARRIE, ON, L4N 2G9
(705) 728-5027   *SIC* 5172
MAYFAIR BUSINESS COLLEGE   *p* 134
*See MAYFAIR PERSONNEL (NORTHERN)
LTD*
MAYFAIR PERSONNEL (NORTHERN) LTD *p*
134
11039 78 AVE SUITE 102, GRANDE
PRAIRIE, AB, T8W 2J7
(780) 539-5090   *SIC* 7361
MAYFAIR PROPERTIES LTD   *p* 299
111 ROBSON ST, VANCOUVER, BC, V6B
6P5
(604) 681-0868   *SIC* 7011
MAYFAIR RAQUET & FITNESS CLUBS   *p*
672
See MAYFAIR TENNIS COURTS LIMITED
MAYFAIR RAQUET & FITNESS CLUBS   *p*
920
See MAYFAIR TENNIS COURTS LIMITED
MAYFAIR TENNIS COURTS LIMITED *p* 672
50 STEELCASE RD E, MARKHAM, ON,
L3R 1E8
(905) 475-6668   *SIC* 7997
MAYFAIR TENNIS COURTS LIMITED *p* 920
801 LAKE SHORE BLVD E, TORONTO, ON,
M4M 1A9
(416) 466-3770   *SIC* 7997
MAYFAIR VILLAGE FOODS   *p* 333
2187 OAK BAY AVE UNIT 101, VICTORIA,
BC, V8R 1G1
(250) 592-8911   *SIC* 5411
MAYFIELD INVESTMENTS LTD   *p* 90
10010 106 ST NW SUITE 1005, EDMON-
TON, AB, T5J 3L8
(780) 424-2921   *SIC* 7011
MAYFIELD INVESTMENTS LTD   *p* 146
1051 ROSS GLEN DR SE, MEDICINE HAT,
AB, T1B 3T8
(403) 502-8185   *SIC* 7011
MAYFIELD SECONDARY SCHOOL   *p* 505
See PEEL DISTRICT SCHOOL BOARD
**MAYFIELD SUITES GENERAL PARTNER
INC**   *p* 697
5400 DIXIE RD, MISSISSAUGA, ON, L4W
4T4
(905) 238-0159   *SIC* 7011
MAYFIELD TOYOTA   *p* 98
See 767405 ALBERTA LTD
MAYFLOWER CANADA   *p* 743
See UNITED VAN LINES (CANADA) LTD
MAYHEW INC   *p* 853
28 SIMS CRES, RICHMOND HILL, ON, L4B
2N9
(905) 707-4747   *SIC* 5021
MAYLAN CONSTRUCTION SERVICES INC
p 619
372 BERTHA ST, HAWKESBURY, ON, K6A
2A8
(613) 632-5553   *SIC* 1542

MAYNARD NURSING HOME   *p 990*
See 341822 ONTARIO INC
MAYNARDS LIQUIDATION GROUP INC   *p 255*
3331 JACOMBS RD, RICHMOND, BC, V6V 1Z6
(604) 876-6787   *SIC 7389*
MAYRAND LIMITEE   *p 1049*
9701 BOUL LOUIS-H.-LAFONTAINE, AN-JOU, QC, H1J 2A3
(514) 255-9330   *SIC 5141*
MAYTREE FOUNDATION, THE   *p 976*
170 BLOOR ST W SUITE 804, TORONTO, ON, M5S 1T9
(416) 944-1101   *SIC 8699*
MAZAK CORPORATION CANADA   *p 537*
50 COMMERCE CRT, CAMBRIDGE, ON, N3C 4P7
(519) 658-2021   *SIC 5084*
MAZARS HAREL DROUIN, S.E.N.C.R.L.   *p 1189*
215 RUE SAINT-JACQUES BUREAU 1200, MONTREAL, QC, H2Y 1M6
(514) 845-9253   *SIC 8721*
MAZARS, S.E.N.C.R.L   *p 1189*
215 RUE SAINT-JACQUES, BUREAU 1200, MONTREAL, QC, H2Y 1M6
(514) 878-2600   *SIC 8721*
MAZAYA CONSTRUCTION   *p 1233*
See 9149-8980 QUEBEC INC
MAZDA   *p 220*
See KELOWNA MOTORS LTD
MAZDA CANADA INC   *p 853*
55 VOGELL RD, RICHMOND HILL, ON, L4B 3K5
(905) 787-7000   *SIC 5012*
MAZDA CHATEL   *p 1261*
See AUTOMOBILES MAURICE PARENT INC
MAZDA DE LAVAL   *p 1087*
See QUERIN, ARMAND AUTOMOBILES LTEE
MAZDA DE SHERBROOKE   *p 1375*
See 9101-2468 QUEBEC INC
MAZDA DUVAL   *p 1063*
See 2945-9344 QUEBEC INC
MAZDA JOLIETTE   *p 1243*
See AUTOMOBILES FRANCOIS ST-JEAN INC, LES
MAZDA OF BRAMPTON   *p 512*
See 1042735 ONTARIO INC
MAZDA OF RICHMOND HILL   *p 855*
See 2489736 ONTARIO LIMITED
MAZDA POINTE-AUX-TREMBLES   *p 1247*
See 8863377 CANADA INC
MAZDA PRESIDENT   *p 1047*
See 3725766 CANADA INC
MAZDA REPENTIGNY   *p 1281*
See 3370160 CANADA INC
MAZENC FUELS LTD   *p 1416*
529 E 1ST AVE, REGINA, SK, S4N 4Z3
(306) 721-6667   *SIC 5541*
MAZER IMPLEMENTS   *p 348*
1908 CURRIE BLVD, BRANDON, MB, R7B 4E7
(204) 728-2244   *SIC 5999*
MAZERGROUP LTD   *p 348*
1908 CURRIE BLVD, BRANDON, MB, R7B 4E7
(204) 728-2244   *SIC 5999*
MAZERGROUP LTD   *p 351*
GD, HARTNEY, MB, R0M 0X0
(204) 858-2000   *SIC 5999*
MAZIN FURNITURE INDUSTRIES LIMITED   *p 555*
8080 KEELE ST, CONCORD, ON, L4K 2A3
(905) 761-1594   *SIC 5023*
MAZIN INVESTMENTS LTD   *p 624*
4015 CARLING AVE SUITE 102, KANATA, ON, K2K 2A3
(613) 831-9943   *SIC 5065*
MAZOUT PROPANE BEAUCHEMIN   *p 1318*
See HUILES THUOT ET BEAUCHEMIN INC, LES

MAZZA INNOVATION LTD   *p 209*
7901 PROGRESS WAY, DELTA, BC, V4G 1A3
(604) 337-1578   *SIC 5149*
MB MISSION   *p 178*
32040 DOWNES RD SUITE 300, ABBOTS-FORD, BC, V4X 1X5
(604) 859-6267   *SIC 8661*
MBA RECHERCHE INC   *p 1198*
1470 RUE PEEL BUREAU 800, MON-TREAL, QC, H3A 1T1
(514) 284-9644   *SIC 8732*
MBC   *p 1116*
See CONSORTIUM PONT MOHAWK CPM
MBC FINANCIAL   *p 846*
See MCAVOY BELAN & CAMPBELL IN-SURANCE AND FINANCIAL SERVICES LTD
MBEC COMMUNICATIONS INC   *p 806*
1115 NORTH SERVICE RD W UNIT 1, OAKVILLE, ON, L6M 2V9
(905) 338-9754   *SIC 6794*
MBG BUILDINGS INC   *p 272*
17957 55 AVE SUITE 102, SURREY, BC, V3S 6C4
(604) 574-6600   *SIC 1541*
MBH AMENAGEMENT + MOBILIER DE BU-REAU   *p 1259*
See MOBILIER DE BUREAU MBH INC
MBI DRILLING PRODUCTS INC   *p 1290*
110 RUE JACQUES-BIBEAU, ROUYN-NORANDA, QC, J9Y 0A3
(819) 762-9645   *SIC 5084*
MBI MANUFACTURE   *p 1290*
See MBI DRILLING PRODUCTS INC
MBI PACIFIC DRILLING PRODUCTS LTD   *p 1428*
3150 FAITHFULL AVE, SASKATOON, SK, S7K 8H3
(306) 955-9560   *SIC 5084*
MBI PLASTIQUE INC   *p 1322*
1335 AV DU PALAIS, SAINT-JOSEPH-DE-BEAUCE, QC, G0S 2V0
(418) 397-8088   *SIC 3089*
MBNA CANADA BANK   *p 595*
1600 JAMES NAISMITH DR SUITE 800, GLOUCESTER, ON, K1B 5N8
(613) 907-4800   *SIC 6021*
MBS RESIDENCE INC   *p 364*
213 ST MARY'S RD SUITE 9, WINNIPEG, MB, R2H 1J2
(204) 233-5363   *SIC 6513*
MBW COURIER INCORPORATED   *p 469*
142 PARKWAY DR, TRURO HEIGHTS, NS, B6L 1N8
(902) 895-5120   *SIC 7389*
MC COMMERCIAL INC   *p 523*
5420 NORTH SERVICE RD SUITE 300, BURLINGTON, ON, L7L 6C7
(905) 315-2300   *SIC 5064*
MC DONALD'S   *p 1421*
See KJMAL ENTERPRISES LTD
MC DONALDS   *p 1313*
See RESTAURANTS MAC-VIC INC, LES
MCA VALEURS MOBILIERES INC   *p 1192*
555 BOUL RENE-LEVESQUE O BUREAU 140, MONTREAL, QC, H2Z 1B1
SIC 6211
MCADAM OUTREACH FOR SENIORS PROGRAM   *p 404*
See WAUKLEHEGAN MANOR INC
MCALLISTER INDUSTRIES LTD   *p 282*
9678 186 ST, SURREY, BC, V4N 3N7
(604) 888-1871   *SIC 5085*
MCALPINE FORD LINCOLN SALES LTD   *p 481*
15815 YONGE ST, AURORA, ON, L4G 1P4
(905) 841-2424   *SIC 5511*
MCAMM ENTERPRIZES LTD   *p 681*
9195 HWY 93, MIDLAND, ON, L4R 4K4
(705) 526-4631   *SIC 5812*
MCAN MORTGAGE CORPORATION   *p 954*
200 KING ST W SUITE 600, TORONTO, ON, M5H 3T4

(416) 572-4880   *SIC 6798*
MCAP COMMERCIAL LP   *p 954*
200 KING ST W SUITE 400, TORONTO, ON, M5H 3T4
(416) 598-2665   *SIC 6162*
MCAP SERVICE CORPORATION   *p 640*
101 FREDERICK ST SUITE 600, KITCH-ENER, ON, N2H 6R2
(519) 743-7800   *SIC 6162*
MCAP SERVICE CORPORATION   *p 954*
200 KING ST W SUITE 400, TORONTO, ON, M5H 3T4
(416) 598-2665   *SIC 6162*
MCARTHUR EXPRESS   *p 1337*
See TRANSPORT TFI 21, S.E.C.
MCASPHALT MARINE TRANSPORTATION LTD   *p 609*
180 PIER 24 GATEWAY, HAMILTON, ON, L8H 0A3
(905) 549-9408   *SIC 4412*
MCAULEY'S NOFRILLS   *p 284*
8100 3B HWY SUITE 142, TRAIL, BC, V1R 4N7
(250) 368-8577   *SIC 5411*
MCAVOY BELAN & CAMPBELL INSUR-ANCE AND FINANCIAL SERVICES LTD   *p 846*
350 KING ST, PORT COLBORNE, ON, L3K 4H3
(905) 834-3666   *SIC 6411*
MCBAIN CAMERA LTD   *p 86*
10805 107 AVE NW, EDMONTON, AB, T5H 0W9
(780) 420-0404   *SIC 5946*
MCBRIDE CAREER GROUP INC   *p 92*
10045 111 ST NW SUITE 910, EDMON-TON, AB, T5K 2M5
(780) 448-1380   *SIC 8741*
MCBRIDE METAL FABRICATING CORPO-RATION   *p 902*
305 PATILLO RD, TECUMSEH, ON, N8N 2L9
(519) 727-6640   *SIC 3465*
MCBUNS BAKERY   *p 405*
122 SHEDIAC RD, MONCTON, NB, E1A 2R9
(506) 858-1700   *SIC 2051*
MCBURL CORP   *p 530*
689 GUELPH LINE, BURLINGTON, ON, L7R 3M7
(905) 639-1661   *SIC 5812*
MCBURL CORP   *p 531*
623 PLAINS RD E, BURLINGTON, ON, L7T 2E8
(905) 632-0072   *SIC 5812*
MCC   *p 664*
See MODULAR & CUSTOM CABINETS LIMITED
MCC   *p 954*
See MORTGAGE CENTRE (CANADA) INC, THE
MCC INDUSTRIAL SERVICES LTD   *p 538*
125 VONDRAU DR SUITE 1, CAMBRIDGE, ON, N3E 1A8
(519) 650-9886   *SIC 8748*
MCC SUPPORTIVE CARE SERVICES   *p 175*
See MENNONITE CENTRAL COMMITTEE CANADA
MCCABE PROMOTIONAL ADVERTISING INC   *p 661*
384 SOVEREIGN RD, LONDON, ON, N6M 1A5
(519) 455-7009   *SIC 5199*
MCCAFFERY GROUP INC   *p 106*
12160 160 ST NW, EDMONTON, AB, T5V 1H5
(780) 452-8375   *SIC 3088*
MCCAGUE BORLACK LLP   *p 987*
130 KING ST W SUITE 2700, TORONTO, ON, M5X 2A2
(416) 860-0001   *SIC 8111*
MCCAIN FERTILIZERS LIMITED   *p 399*
9109 ROUTE 130, FLORENCEVILLE-

BRISTOL, NB, E7L 1Y8
(506) 392-2810   *SIC 5191*
MCCAIN FOODS CANADA   *p 399*
See MCCAIN FOODS GROUP INC
MCCAIN FOODS GROUP INC   *p 399*
8800 MAIN ST, FLORENCEVILLE-BRISTOL, NB, E7L 1B2
(506) 392-5541   *SIC 2037*
MCCAIN FOODS LIMITED   *p 981*
439 KING ST W SUITE 500, TORONTO, ON, M5V 1K4
(416) 955-1700   *SIC 2037*
MCCAIN GLOBAL SOURCING   *p 981*
See MCCAIN FOODS LIMITED
MCCAIN INTERNATIONAL INC   *p 399*
8734 MAIN ST UNIT 3, FLORENCEVILLE-BRISTOL, NB, E7L 3G6
(506) 392-5541   *SIC 2037*
MCCAIN PRODUCE INC   *p 399*
8734 MAIN ST UNIT 1, FLORENCEVILLE-BRISTOL, NB, E7L 3G6
(506) 392-3036   *SIC 5148*
MCCAIN PRODUCE, DIV OF   *p 399*
See MCCAIN FERTILIZERS LIMITED
MCCAINE ELECTRIC LTD   *p 389*
106 LOWSON CRES, WINNIPEG, MB, R3P 2H8
(204) 786-2435   *SIC 1731*
MCCALL CENTRE FOR CONTINUING CARE   *p 578*
See EXTENDICARE INC
MCCALL'S SCHOOL OF CAKE DECORA-TION (1987) INC   *p 577*
3810 BLOOR ST W, ETOBICOKE, ON, M9B 6C2
(416) 231-8040   *SIC 5046*
MCCALLUM PRINTING GROUP INC   *p 86*
11755 108 AVE NW, EDMONTON, AB, T5H 1B8
(780) 455-8885   *SIC 2759*
MCCAM INSURANCE BROKERS LTD   *p 814*
292 KING ST W, OSHAWA, ON, L1J 2J9
(905) 579-0111   *SIC 6411*
MCCANN EQUIPMENT LTD   *p 1094*
10255 CH COTE-DE-LIESSE, DORVAL, QC, H9P 1A3
(514) 636-6344   *SIC 5084*
MCCANN REDI-MIX INC   *p 564*
69478 BRONSON LINE, DASHWOOD, ON, N0M 1N0
(519) 237-3647   *SIC 1771*
MCCANN REDI-MIX INC   *p 590*
140 THAMES RD W SS 3, EXETER, ON, N0M 1S3
(519) 235-0338   *SIC 3273*
MCCANN WORLDGROUP CANADA INC   *p 982*
200 WELLINGTON ST W SUITE 1300, TORONTO, ON, M5V 0N6
(416) 594-6000   *SIC 7311*
MCCARTHY ELLIS MERCANTILE LTD   *p 988*
700 LAWRENCE AVE W, TORONTO, ON, M6A 3B4
(289) 442-2851   *SIC 5531*
MCCARTHY TETARAULT LAW OFFICES   *p 315*
See MT SERVICES LIMITED PARTNER-SHIP
MCCARTHY TETRAULT LLP   *p 53*
421 7 AVE SW SUITE 4000, CALGARY, AB, T2P 4K9
(403) 260-3500   *SIC 8111*
MCCARTHY TETRAULT LLP   *p 969*
66 WELLINGTON ST W SUITE 5300, TORONTO, ON, M5K 1E6
(416) 362-1812   *SIC 8111*
MCCARTHY TETRAULT LLP   *p 1206*
1000 RUE DE LA GAUCHETIERE O BU-REAU 2500, MONTREAL, QC, H3B 0A2
SIC 8111
MCCARTHY'S ROOFING LIMITED   *p 443*
850 MAIN ST, DARTMOUTH, NS, B2W 3V1

(902) 469-2260   *SIC* 1761
MCCG   *p* 660
See MUTUAL CONCEPT COMPUTER GROUP INC
MCCLARY STOCKYARDS LIMITED   *p* 175
34559 MCCLARY AVE, ABBOTSFORD, BC, V2S 7N3
(604) 864-2381   *SIC* 5154
MCCLAY GROUP LTD   *p* 622
132 INGERSOLL ST S, INGERSOLL, ON, N5C 3K1
(519) 485-3088   *SIC* 4212
MCCLELLAN WHEATON CHEVROLET BUICK GMS   *p* 78
See MCCLELLAN WHEATON CHEVROLET LTD
MCCLELLAN WHEATON CHEVROLET LTD   *p* 78
3850 48 AVE, CAMROSE, AB, T4V 3Z8
(780) 672-2355   *SIC* 5511
MCCLOSKEY INTERNATIONAL LIMITED   *p* 627
1 MCCLOSKEY RD, KEENE, ON, K9J 0G6
(705) 295-4925   *SIC* 3531
MCCLURE PLACE ASSOCIATION INC   *p* 1424
1825 MCKERCHER DR SUITE 804, SASKATOON, SK, S7H 5N5
(306) 955-7677   *SIC* 6513
MCCLURE, F. & SONS LTD   *p* 403
55 RUE OUELLETTE, GRAND-SAULT/GRAND FALLS, NB, E3Z 0A6
(506) 473-2024   *SIC* 5521
MCCLUSKEY TRANSPORTATION SERVICES LIMITED   *p* 586
514 CARLINGVIEW DR UNIT 200, ETOBICOKE, ON, M9W 5R3
(416) 246-1422   *SIC* 4151
MCCONNELL TRANSPORT LIMITED   *p* 404
208 ROUTE 590, JACKSONVILLE, NB, E7M 3R7
(506) 325-2211   *SIC* 4213
MCCOPIER (CANADA) INC   *p* 1330
4430 RUE GARAND, SAINT-LAURENT, QC, H4R 2A3
(514) 344-1515   *SIC* 5044
MCCORDICK GLOVE & SAFETY   *p* 537
See BUNZL CANADA INC
MCCORMICK HOME   *p* 660
See WOMEN'S CHRISTIAN ASSOCIATION OF LONDON
MCCORMICK RANKIN CORPORATION   *p* 715
2655 NORTH SHERIDAN WAY SUITE 300, MISSISSAUGA, ON, L5K 2P8
(905) 823-8500   *SIC* 8711
MCCOWAN DESIGN & MANUFACTURING LTD   *p* 871
1760 BIRCHMOUNT RD, SCARBOROUGH, ON, M1P 2H7
(416) 291-7111   *SIC* 5999
MCCOY CORPORATION   *p* 156
See MCCOY GLOBAL INC
MCCOY FOUNDRY   *p* 999
See ARCHIE MCCOY (HAMILTON) LIMITED
MCCOY GLOBAL INC   *p* 110
9910 39TH AVE NW SUITE 201, EDMONTON, AB, T6B 3H2
(780) 453-8451   *SIC* 5013
MCCOY GLOBAL INC   *p* 156
7911 EDGAR INDUSTRIAL DR, RED DEER, AB, T4P 3R2
(780) 453-3277   *SIC* 3533
MCCOY TOURS   *p* 633
566 CATARAQUI WOODS DR, KINGSTON, ON, K7P 2Y5
(613) 384-0347   *SIC* 4724
MCCRAM INC   *p* 419
3458 RUE PRINCIPALE, TRACADIE-SHEILA, NB, E1X 1C8
(506) 394-1111   *SIC* 5812
MCCREARY ALONSA HEALTH CENTRE   *p* 352
613 GOVERNMENT RD, MCCREARY, MB, R0J 1B0
(204) 835-2482   *SIC* 8099
MCCRUM'S DIRECT SALES LTD   *p* 36
5310 1 ST SW, CALGARY, AB, T2H 0C8
(403) 259-4939   *SIC* 5712
MCCRUM'S OFFICE FURNISHINGS   *p* 36
See MCCRUM'S DIRECT SALES LTD
MCCULLOUGH, D.E. ENTERPRISES LTD   *p* 492
101 BELL BLVD, BELLEVILLE, ON, K8P 4V2
(613) 968-6701   *SIC* 5531
MCCURDY CHEVROLET OLSMOBILE PONTIAC BUICK GMC LTD   *p* 999
174 TRENTON-FRANKFORD RD, TRENTON, ON, K8V 5R6
(613) 392-1245   *SIC* 5511
MCDANIEL GROUP HOLDING CORPORATION, THE   *p* 53
255 5 AVE SW SUITE 2200, CALGARY, AB, T2P 3G6
(403) 262-5506   *SIC* 8741
MCDANIEL'S Y.I.G.   *p* 748
See 974475 ONTARIO LIMITED
MCDIARMID LUMBER HOME CENTRES   *p* 387
See MCMUNN & YATES BUILDING SUPPLIES LTD
MCDONALD   *p* 1121
See ENTREPRISES MACBAIE INC, LES
MCDONALD   *p* 1136
See GESTION N. AUGER INC
MCDONALD & BYCHKOWSKI LTD   *p* 125
1430 91 ST SW SUITE 201, EDMONTON, AB, T6X 1M5
(780) 424-2727   *SIC* 6411
MCDONALD CONSOLIDATED   *p* 32
See SOBEYS WEST INC
MCDONALD METALS (1983) LTD   *p* 1414
GD, PRINCE ALBERT, SK, S6V 8A4
(306) 764-9333   *SIC* 5093
MCDONALD SALES MERCHAND   *p* 801
See MCDONALD, D. SALES & MERCHANDISING LIMITED
MCDONALD' S   *p* 1313
See RESTAURANTS MAC-VIC INC, LES
MCDONALD'S   *p* 76
See PASLEY, MAX ENTERPRISES LIMITED
MCDONALD'S   *p* 128
See MCDONALD'S RESTAURANTS OF CANADA LIMITED
MCDONALD'S   *p* 142
See PASLEY, MAX ENTERPRISES LIMITED
MCDONALD'S   *p* 161
See MCDONALD'S RESTAURANTS OF CANADA LIMITED
MCDONALD'S   *p* 186
See MCDONALD'S RESTAURANTS OF CANADA LIMITED
MCDONALD'S   *p* 190
See MCDONALD'S RESTAURANTS OF CANADA LIMITED
MCDONALD'S   *p* 196
See MCDONALD'S RESTAURANTS OF CANADA LIMITED
MCDONALD'S   *p* 212
See MCDONALD'S RESTAURANTS OF CANADA LIMITED
MCDONALD'S   *p* 216
See DAWNAL QUICK SERVE LTD
MCDONALD'S   *p* 236
See ABREY ENTERPRISES INC
MCDONALD'S   *p* 261
See MCDONALD'S RESTAURANTS OF CANADA LIMITED
MCDONALD'S   *p* 272
See HARPO ENTERPRISES
MCDONALD'S   *p* 272
See MCDONALD'S RESTAURANTS OF CANADA LIMITED
MCDONALD'S   *p* 295
See MCDONALD'S RESTAURANTS OF CANADA LIMITED
MCDONALD'S   *p* 362
See MCDONALD'S RESTAURANTS OF CANADA LIMITED
MCDONALD'S   *p* 363
See MCDONALD'S RESTAURANTS OF CANADA LIMITED
MCDONALD'S   *p* 364
See MCDONALD'S RESTAURANTS OF CANADA LIMITED
MCDONALD'S   *p* 369
See MCDONALD'S RESTAURANTS OF CANADA LIMITED
MCDONALD'S   *p* 370
See MCDONALD'S RESTAURANTS OF CANADA LIMITED
MCDONALD'S   *p* 386
See CARTER, DWAYNE ENTERPRISES LTD
MCDONALD'S   *p* 393
See MCDONALD'S RESTAURANTS OF CANADA LIMITED
MCDONALD'S   *p* 401
See MCDONALD'S RESTAURANTS
MCDONALD'S   *p* 473
See BEATTY FOODS LTD
MCDONALD'S   *p* 487
See MCDONALD'S RESTAURANTS OF CANADA LIMITED
MCDONALD'S   *p* 498
See MCDONALD'S RESTAURANTS OF CANADA LIMITED
MCDONALD'S   *p* 508
See MCDONALD'S RESTAURANTS OF CANADA LIMITED
MCDONALD'S   *p* 534
See MCDONALD'S RESTAURANTS OF CANADA LIMITED
MCDONALD'S   *p* 537
See MCDONALD'S RESTAURANTS OF CANADA LIMITED
MCDONALD'S   *p* 561
See MCDONALD'S RESTAURANTS OF CANADA LIMITED
MCDONALD'S   *p* 575
See LUCAS & MARCO INC
MCDONALD'S   *p* 641
See CAVCO FOOD SERVICES LTD
MCDONALD'S   *p* 645
See CAMPBELL, JAMES INC
MCDONALD'S   *p* 652
See MCDONALD'S RESTAURANTS OF CANADA LIMITED
MCDONALD'S   *p* 659
See MCDONALD'S RESTAURANTS OF CANADA LIMITED
MCDONALD'S   *p* 752
See MCDONALD'S RESTAURANTS OF CANADA LIMITED
MCDONALD'S   *p* 753
See WILSON FOODS CENTRE LTD
MCDONALD'S   *p* 756
See MILLER, P.G. ENTERPRISES LIMITED
MCDONALD'S   *p* 769
See MCDONALD'S RESTAURANTS OF CANADA LIMITED
MCDONALD'S   *p* 779
See MCDONALD'S RESTAURANTS OF CANADA LIMITED
MCDONALD'S   *p* 787
See MCDONALD'S RESTAURANTS OF CANADA LIMITED
MCDONALD'S   *p* 808
See MCDONALD'S RESTAURANTS OF CANADA LIMITED
MCDONALD'S   *p* 822
See 7073674 CANADA LTD
MCDONALD'S   *p* 827
See MCDONALD'S RESTAURANTS OF CANADA LIMITED
MCDONALD'S   *p* 840
See CAMPBELL, JAMES INC
MCDONALD'S   *p* 843
See MCDONALD'S RESTAURANTS OF CANADA LIMITED
MCDONALD'S   *p* 902
See MCDONALD'S RESTAURANTS OF CANADA LIMITED
MCDONALD'S   *p* 918
See HU-A-KAM ENTERPRISES INC
MCDONALD'S   *p* 990
See MCDONALD'S RESTAURANTS OF CANADA LIMITED
MCDONALD'S   *p* 993
See MCDONALD'S RESTAURANTS OF CANADA LIMITED
MCDONALD'S   *p* 1007
See QUALIDEC CORPORATION
MCDONALD'S   *p* 1018
See MCDONALD'S RESTAURANTS OF CANADA LIMITED
MCDONALD'S   *p* 1042
See MCKENNCO INC
MCDONALD'S   *p* 1057
See GESTION CEJEMAR INC
MCDONALD'S   *p* 1079
See ENTREPRISES MACBAIE INC, LES
MCDONALD'S   *p* 1107
See GESTION VALMIRA INC
MCDONALD'S   *p* 1143
See RESTAURANTS T.S.N.A. INC
MCDONALD'S   *p* 1144
See EQUIPE PCJ INC
MCDONALD'S   *p* 1189
See MCDONALD'S RESTAURANTS OF CANADA LIMITED
MCDONALD'S   *p* 1272
See GESTION VINNY INC
MCDONALD'S   *p* 1283
See MCDONALD'S RESTAURANTS OF CANADA LIMITED
MCDONALD'S   *p* 1379
See ENTERPRISES MICHEL MARCHAND INC, LES
MCDONALD'S   *p* 1385
See MARLU INC
MCDONALD'S   *p* 1388
See MARLU INC
MCDONALD'S   *p* 1413
See KJMAL ENTERPRISES LTD
MCDONALD'S   *p* 1422
See MCDONALD'S RESTAURANTS OF CANADA LIMITED
MCDONALD'S   *p* 1423
See MCDONALD'S RESTAURANTS OF CANADA LIMITED
MCDONALD'S   *p* 1424
See MCDONALD'S RESTAURANTS OF CANADA LIMITED
MCDONALD'S   *p* 1432
See MCDONALD'S RESTAURANTS OF CANADA LIMITED
MCDONALD'S # 8114   *p* 1104
See MCDONALD'S RESTAURANTS OF CANADA LIMITED
MCDONALD'S #40122 PLAINS RD   *p* 531
See MCBURL CORP
MCDONALD'S #5260   *p* 481
See MILLER, P.G. ENTERPRISES LIMITED
MCDONALD'S #8045   *p* 241
See MCDONALD'S RESTAURANTS OF CANADA LIMITED
MCDONALD'S #8159   *p* 270
See MCDONALD'S RESTAURANTS OF CANADA LIMITED
MCDONALD'S #8187   *p* 228
See MCDONALD'S RESTAURANTS OF CANADA LIMITED
MCDONALD'S #8249   *p* 275
See MCDONALD'S RESTAURANTS OF CANADA LIMITED
MCDONALD'S #8341   *p* 186
See MCDONALD'S RESTAURANTS OF CANADA LIMITED
MCDONALD'S #8386   *p* 519

▲ Public Company   ■ Public Company Family Member   **HQ** Headquarters   **BR** Branch   **SL** Single Location

See MCDONALD'S RESTAURANTS OF CANADA LIMITED

MCDONALD'S #8394 p 366
See MCDONALD'S RESTAURANTS OF CANADA LIMITED

MCDONALD'S #8449 p 120
See MCDONALD'S RESTAURANTS OF CANADA LIMITED

MCDONALD'S #8485 p 270
See MCDONALD'S RESTAURANTS OF CANADA LIMITED

MCDONALD'S #8486 p 241
See MCDONALD'S RESTAURANTS OF CANADA LIMITED

MCDONALD'S #8490 p 811
See MCDONALD'S RESTAURANTS OF CANADA LIMITED

MCDONALD'S #8578 p 318
See MCDONALD'S RESTAURANTS OF CANADA LIMITED

MCDONALD'S #8646 p 299
See MCDONALD'S RESTAURANTS OF CANADA LIMITED

MCDONALD'S 7403 p 813
See WILSON FOODS KINGSWAY LTD

MCDONALD'S 8031 p 387
See MCDONALD'S RESTAURANTS OF CANADA LIMITED

MCDONALD'S 8046 p 1020
See MCDONALD'S RESTAURANTS OF CANADA LIMITED

MCDONALD'S 8065 p 1025
See MCDONALD'S RESTAURANTS OF CANADA LIMITED

MCDONALD'S 8067 p 287
See MCDONALD'S RESTAURANTS OF CANADA LIMITED

MCDONALD'S 8075 p 208
See MCDONALD'S RESTAURANTS OF CANADA LIMITED

MCDONALD'S 8092 p 820
See MCDONALD'S RESTAURANTS OF CANADA LIMITED

MCDONALD'S 8108 p 686
See MCDONALD'S RESTAURANTS OF CANADA LIMITED

MCDONALD'S 8571 p 827
See MCDONALD'S RESTAURANTS OF CANADA LIMITED

MCDONALD'S 8784 p 186
See MCDONALD'S RESTAURANTS OF CANADA LIMITED

MCDONALD'S CANDIAC p 1072
See ENTREPRISES JMC (1973) LTEE, LES

MCDONALD'S RESTAURANT p 195
See UNCLE RAY'S RESTAURANT CO. LTD

MCDONALD'S RESTAURANT p 216
See DAWNAL QUICK SERVE LTD

MCDONALD'S RESTAURANT p 225
See RJMB RESTAURANTS LTD.

MCDONALD'S RESTAURANT p 253
See YESNABY INVESTMENTS LTD

MCDONALD'S RESTAURANT p 419
See MCCRAM INC

MCDONALD'S RESTAURANT p 429
See BENNETT RESTAURANT LTD

MCDONALD'S RESTAURANT p 442
See ANGUS G FOODS INC

MCDONALD'S RESTAURANT p 545
See KRAN MANAGEMENT SERVICES LIMITED

MCDONALD'S RESTAURANT p 603
See GRANDI COMPANY LIMITED

MCDONALD'S RESTAURANT p 748
See TAYLYX LTD

MCDONALD'S RESTAURANT p 784
See MCDONALD'S RESTAURANTS OF CANADA LIMITED

MCDONALD'S RESTAURANT p 795
See MCDONALD'S RESTAURANTS OF CANADA LIMITED

MCDONALD'S RESTAURANT p 810
See PEARN, ROY E. ENTERPRISES LIMITED

MCDONALD'S RESTAURANT p 1025
See MCDONALD'S RESTAURANTS OF CANADA LIMITED

MCDONALD'S RESTAURANT p 1420
525 N ALBERT ST, REGINA, SK, S4R 8E2
(306) 543-0236   SIC 5812

MCDONALD'S RESTAURANT 25004 p 476
See MACKINNON RESTAURANTS INC

MCDONALD'S RESTAURANTS p 40
See PASLEY, MAX ENTERPRISES LIMITED

MCDONALD'S RESTAURANTS p 75
See PASLEY, MAX ENTERPRISES LIMITED

MCDONALD'S RESTAURANTS p 172
See DOPKO FOOD SERVICES LTD

MCDONALD'S RESTAURANTS p 204
See KOKANEE FOOD SERVICES INC

MCDONALD'S RESTAURANTS p 211
See SJR FOOD SERVICES LTD

MCDONALD'S RESTAURANTS p 217
See DAWNAL QUICK SERVE LTD

MCDONALD'S RESTAURANTS p 270
See HAWTHORNE PARK INC

MCDONALD'S RESTAURANTS p 382
See MCDONALD'S RESTAURANTS OF CANADA LIMITED

MCDONALD'S RESTAURANTS p 401
1177 PROSPECT ST, FREDERICTON, NB, E3B 3B9
(506) 444-6231   SIC 5812

MCDONALD'S RESTAURANTS p 513
See MCDONALD'S RESTAURANTS OF CANADA LIMITED

MCDONALD'S RESTAURANTS p 530
See MCBURL CORP

MCDONALD'S RESTAURANTS p 591
See ROWENDA INVESTMENTS LTD

MCDONALD'S RESTAURANTS p 601
See GRANDI COMPANY LIMITED

MCDONALD'S RESTAURANTS p 616
See INCH FOODS INC

MCDONALD'S RESTAURANTS p 628
See JERITRISH COMPANY LTD

MCDONALD'S RESTAURANTS p 657
See MCDONALD'S RESTAURANTS OF CANADA LIMITED

MCDONALD'S RESTAURANTS p 762
See CHISHOLM, R. FOOD SERVICES INC

MCDONALD'S RESTAURANTS p 847
175 ROSE GLEN RD, PORT HOPE, ON, L1A 3V6
(905) 885-2480   SIC 5812

MCDONALD'S RESTAURANTS p 886
385 ONTARIO ST, ST CATHARINES, ON, L2R 5L3
(905) 688-0244   SIC 5812

MCDONALD'S RESTAURANTS p 1000
See MCDONALD'S RESTAURANTS OF CANADA LIMITED

MCDONALD'S RESTAURANTS 13861 p 9
See PASLEY, MAX ENTERPRISES LIMITED

MCDONALD'S RESTAURANTS 7031 p 154
See PASLEY, MAX ENTERPRISES LIMITED

MCDONALD'S RESTAURANTS LTD p 217
1751 TRANS CANADA HWY E, KAMLOOPS, BC, V2C 3Z6
(250) 374-1718   SIC 5812

MCDONALD'S RESTAURANTS LTD p 334
1644 HILLSIDE AVE, VICTORIA, BC, V8T 2C5
SIC 5812

MCDONALD'S RESTAURANTS OF CANADA LIMITED p 120
5360 23 AVE NW, EDMONTON, AB, T6L 6X2
(780) 414-8449   SIC 5812

MCDONALD'S RESTAURANTS OF CANADA LIMITED p 128
450 GREGOIRE DR, FORT MCMURRAY, AB, T9H 3R2
(780) 791-0551   SIC 5812

MCDONALD'S RESTAURANTS OF CANADA LIMITED p 161
950 ORDZE RD, SHERWOOD PARK, AB, T8A 4L8
(780) 467-6490   SIC 5812

MCDONALD'S RESTAURANTS OF CANADA LIMITED p 186
4400 STILL CREEK DR, BURNABY, BC, V5C 6C6
(604) 294-2181   SIC 5812

MCDONALD'S RESTAURANTS OF CANADA LIMITED p 186
4400 STILL CREEK DR, BURNABY, BC, V5C 6C6
(604) 718-1090   SIC 5812

MCDONALD'S RESTAURANTS OF CANADA LIMITED p 186
4805 HASTINGS ST, BURNABY, BC, V5C 2L1
(604) 718-1015   SIC 5812

MCDONALD'S RESTAURANTS OF CANADA LIMITED p 190
4700 KINGSWAY SUITE 1160, BURNABY, BC, V5H 4M1
(604) 718-1005   SIC 5812

MCDONALD'S RESTAURANTS OF CANADA LIMITED p 196
45816 YALE RD, CHILLIWACK, BC, V2P 2N7
(604) 795-5911   SIC 5812

MCDONALD'S RESTAURANTS OF CANADA LIMITED p 208
7005 120 ST, DELTA, BC, V4E 2A9
(604) 592-1330   SIC 5812

MCDONALD'S RESTAURANTS OF CANADA LIMITED p 212
5883 TRANS CANADA HWY, DUNCAN, BC, V9L 3R9
(250) 715-2370   SIC 5812

MCDONALD'S RESTAURANTS OF CANADA LIMITED p 228
19780 FRASER HWY, LANGLEY, BC, V3A 4C9
(604) 514-1820   SIC 5812

MCDONALD'S RESTAURANTS OF CANADA LIMITED p 231
22780 LOUGHEED HWY, MAPLE RIDGE, BC, V2X 2V6
(604) 463-7858   SIC 5812

MCDONALD'S RESTAURANTS OF CANADA LIMITED p 241
925 MARINE DR, NORTH VANCOUVER, BC, V7P 1S2
(604) 985-6757   SIC 5812

MCDONALD'S RESTAURANTS OF CANADA LIMITED p 241
1219 MARINE DR, NORTH VANCOUVER, BC, V7P 1T3
(604) 904-4390   SIC 5812

MCDONALD'S RESTAURANTS OF CANADA LIMITED p 261
8191 ALDERBRIDGE WAY, RICHMOND, BC, V6X 3A9
SIC 5812

MCDONALD'S RESTAURANTS OF CANADA LIMITED p 270
1000 GUILDFORD TOWN CTR, SURREY, BC, V3R 7C3
SIC 5812

MCDONALD'S RESTAURANTS OF CANADA LIMITED p 270
10250 152 ST, SURREY, BC, V3R 6N7
(604) 587-3380   SIC 5812

MCDONALD'S RESTAURANTS OF CANADA LIMITED p 272
15574 FRASER HWY, SURREY, BC, V3S 2V9
(604) 507-7900   SIC 5812

MCDONALD'S RESTAURANTS OF CANADA LIMITED p 275
12930 96 AVE, SURREY, BC, V3V 6A8
(604) 587-3390   SIC 5812

MCDONALD'S RESTAURANTS OF CANADA LIMITED p 287

2021 KINGSWAY, VANCOUVER, BC, V5N 2T2
(604) 718-1060   SIC 5812

MCDONALD'S RESTAURANTS OF CANADA LIMITED p 295
1527 MAIN ST, VANCOUVER, BC, V6A 2W5
(604) 718-1075   SIC 5812

MCDONALD'S RESTAURANTS OF CANADA LIMITED p 299
86 PENDER ST W UNIT 1001, VANCOUVER, BC, V6B 6N8
(604) 718-1165   SIC 5812

MCDONALD'S RESTAURANTS OF CANADA LIMITED p 318
1701 ROBSON ST, VANCOUVER, BC, V6G 1C9
(604) 718-1020   SIC 5812

MCDONALD'S RESTAURANTS OF CANADA LIMITED p 362
15 REENDERS DR, WINNIPEG, MB, R2C 5K5
(204) 949-3221   SIC 5812

MCDONALD'S RESTAURANTS OF CANADA LIMITED p 363
1460 HENDERSON HWY, WINNIPEG, MB, R2G 1N4
(204) 949-6074   SIC 5812

MCDONALD'S RESTAURANTS OF CANADA LIMITED p 364
77 GOULET ST, WINNIPEG, MB, R2H 0R5
(204) 949-6018   SIC 5812

MCDONALD'S RESTAURANTS OF CANADA LIMITED p 366
65 VERMILLION RD, WINNIPEG, MB, R2J 3W7
(204) 949-6015   SIC 5812

MCDONALD'S RESTAURANTS OF CANADA LIMITED p 369
994 KEEWATIN ST, WINNIPEG, MB, R2R 2V1
(204) 949-6079   SIC 5812

MCDONALD'S RESTAURANTS OF CANADA LIMITED p 370
847 LEILA AVE, WINNIPEG, MB, R2V 3J7
(204) 949-6066   SIC 5812

MCDONALD'S RESTAURANTS OF CANADA LIMITED p 382
1440 ELLICE AVE, WINNIPEG, MB, R3G 0G4
(204) 949-5123   SIC 5812

MCDONALD'S RESTAURANTS OF CANADA LIMITED p 387
425 NATHANIEL ST SUITE 1187, WINNIPEG, MB, R3M 3X1
(204) 949-6031   SIC 5812

MCDONALD'S RESTAURANTS OF CANADA LIMITED p 393
1725 KENASTON BLVD, WINNIPEG, MB, R3Y 1V5
(204) 949-5128   SIC 5812

MCDONALD'S RESTAURANTS OF CANADA LIMITED p 487
201 FAIRVIEW RD, BARRIE, ON, L4N 9B1
(905) 823-8500   SIC 5812

MCDONALD'S RESTAURANTS OF CANADA LIMITED p 487
85 DUNLOP ST W, BARRIE, ON, L4N 1A5
(705) 726-6500   SIC 5812

MCDONALD'S RESTAURANTS OF CANADA LIMITED p 498
45 MOUNTAINASH RD, BRAMPTON, ON, L6R 1W4
(905) 458-7488   SIC 5812

MCDONALD'S RESTAURANTS OF CANADA LIMITED p 499
2450 QUEEN ST E, BRAMPTON, ON, L6S 5X9
(905) 793-5295   SIC 5812

MCDONALD'S RESTAURANTS OF CANADA LIMITED p 508
344 QUEEN ST E, BRAMPTON, ON, L6V 1C3
(905) 459-8800   SIC 5812

▲ Public Company   ■ Public Company Family Member   **HQ** Headquarters   **BR** Branch   **SL** Single Location

MCDONALD'S RESTAURANTS OF CANADA LIMITED p 513
30 BRISDALE DR, BRAMPTON, ON, L7A 3G1
(905) 495-1122 *SIC* 5812

MCDONALD'S RESTAURANTS OF CANADA LIMITED p 519
2454 PARKEDALE AVE, BROCKVILLE, ON, K6V 3G8
(613) 342-5551 *SIC* 5812

MCDONALD'S RESTAURANTS OF CANADA LIMITED p 534
GD STN GALT, CAMBRIDGE, ON, N1R 5S8
SIC 5812

MCDONALD'S RESTAURANTS OF CANADA LIMITED p 537
401 WESTBOUND HWY, CAMBRIDGE, ON, N3C 4B1
SIC 5812

MCDONALD'S RESTAURANTS OF CANADA LIMITED p 561
3464 COUNTY RD 89, COOKSTOWN, ON, L0L 1L0
SIC 5812

MCDONALD'S RESTAURANTS OF CANADA LIMITED p 652
1159 HIGHBURY AVE N, LONDON, ON, N5Y 1A6
(519) 451-6830 *SIC* 5812

MCDONALD'S RESTAURANTS OF CANADA LIMITED p 657
1074 WELLINGTON RD, LONDON, ON, N6E 1M2
(519) 691-1042 *SIC* 5812

MCDONALD'S RESTAURANTS OF CANADA LIMITED p 659
462 WHARNCLIFFE RD S, LONDON, ON, N6J 2M9
(519) 673-0680 *SIC* 5812

MCDONALD'S RESTAURANTS OF CANADA LIMITED p 686
3510 DERRY RD E, MISSISSAUGA, ON, L4T 3V7
(905) 677-8711 *SIC* 5812

MCDONALD'S RESTAURANTS OF CANADA LIMITED p 752
3773 STRANDHERD DR, NEPEAN, ON, K2J 4B1
(613) 823-7838 *SIC* 5812

MCDONALD'S RESTAURANTS OF CANADA LIMITED p 769
1125 SHEPPARD AVE E, NORTH YORK, ON, M2K 1C5
SIC 5812

MCDONALD'S RESTAURANTS OF CANADA LIMITED p 779
747 DON MILLS RD SUITE 13, NORTH YORK, ON, M3C 1T2
(416) 429-1266 *SIC* 5812

MCDONALD'S RESTAURANTS OF CANADA LIMITED p 779
1 MCDONALDS PL, NORTH YORK, ON, M3C 3L4
(416) 443-1000 *SIC* 5812

MCDONALD'S RESTAURANTS OF CANADA LIMITED p 784
150 RIMROCK RD, NORTH YORK, ON, M3J 3A6
(416) 630-8381 *SIC* 5812

MCDONALD'S RESTAURANTS OF CANADA LIMITED p 787
1831 FINCH AVE W SUITE 56, NORTH YORK, ON, M3N 2V2
(416) 636-7601 *SIC* 5812

MCDONALD'S RESTAURANTS OF CANADA LIMITED p 795
2020 JANE ST, NORTH YORK, ON, M9N 2V3
(416) 248-6648 *SIC* 5812

MCDONALD'S RESTAURANTS OF CANADA LIMITED p 795
2625F WESTON RD, NORTH YORK, ON, M9N 3X2
(416) 241-5505 *SIC* 5812

MCDONALD'S RESTAURANTS OF CANADA LIMITED p 808
95 FIRST ST, ORANGEVILLE, ON, L9W 2E8
(519) 940-0197 *SIC* 5812

MCDONALD'S RESTAURANTS OF CANADA LIMITED p 811
4416 INNES RD, ORLEANS, ON, K4A 3W3
(613) 841-6633 *SIC* 5812

MCDONALD'S RESTAURANTS OF CANADA LIMITED p 820
594 MONTREAL RD, OTTAWA, ON, K1K 0T9
(613) 741-0093 *SIC* 5812

MCDONALD'S RESTAURANTS OF CANADA LIMITED p 827
2380 BANK ST, OTTAWA, ON, K1V 8S1
(613) 526-1258 *SIC* 5812

MCDONALD'S RESTAURANTS OF CANADA LIMITED p 827
1771 WALKLEY RD, OTTAWA, ON, K1V 1L2
(613) 733-8354 *SIC* 5812

MCDONALD'S RESTAURANTS OF CANADA LIMITED p 843
1300 KINGSTON RD, PICKERING, ON, L1V 3M9
(905) 839-5665 *SIC* 5812

MCDONALD'S RESTAURANTS OF CANADA LIMITED p 869
3150 ST CLAIR AVE E, SCARBOROUGH, ON, M1L 1V6
(416) 751-9014 *SIC* 5812

MCDONALD'S RESTAURANTS OF CANADA LIMITED p 902
1631 MANNING RD, TECUMSEH, ON, N8N 2L9
(519) 735-8122 *SIC* 5812

MCDONALD'S RESTAURANTS OF CANADA LIMITED p 990
1185 DUPONT ST, TORONTO, ON, M6H 2A5
(416) 536-4188 *SIC* 5812

MCDONALD'S RESTAURANTS OF CANADA LIMITED p 993
630 KEELE ST, TORONTO, ON, M6N 3E2
(416) 604-1496 *SIC* 5812

MCDONALD'S RESTAURANTS OF CANADA LIMITED p 1000
5225 HIGHWAY 7 E, UNIONVILLE, ON, L3R 1N3
(905) 477-2891 *SIC* 5812

MCDONALD'S RESTAURANTS OF CANADA LIMITED p 1018
7777 TECUMSEH RD E, WINDSOR, ON, N8T 1G3
(519) 945-4751 *SIC* 5812

MCDONALD'S RESTAURANTS OF CANADA LIMITED p 1020
2780 TECUMSEH RD E, WINDSOR, ON, N8W 1G3
(519) 945-3634 *SIC* 5812

MCDONALD'S RESTAURANTS OF CANADA LIMITED p 1025
3354 DOUGALL AVE, WINDSOR, ON, N9E 1S6
(519) 966-0454 *SIC* 5812

MCDONALD'S RESTAURANTS OF CANADA LIMITED p 1025
883 HURON CHURCH RD, WINDSOR, ON, N9C 2K3
(519) 258-3531 *SIC* 5812

MCDONALD'S RESTAURANTS OF CANADA LIMITED p 1025
5631 OJIBWAY PKY, WINDSOR, ON, N9C 4J5
(519) 250-5311 *SIC* 5812

MCDONALD'S RESTAURANTS OF CANADA LIMITED p 1059
797 BOUL DU CURE-LABELLE, BLAINVILLE, QC, J7C 3P5
(450) 979-7131 *SIC* 5812

MCDONALD'S RESTAURANTS OF CANADA LIMITED p 1104
80 BOUL GR?BER, GATINEAU, QC, J8T 3P8
(819) 561-1436 *SIC* 5812

MCDONALD'S RESTAURANTS OF CANADA LIMITED p 1189
1 RUE NOTRE-DAME E, MONTREAL, QC, H2Y 1B6
(514) 285-8720 *SIC* 5812

MCDONALD'S RESTAURANTS OF CANADA LIMITED p 1283
185 RUE NOTRE-DAME, REPENTIGNY, QC, J6A 2R3
(450) 581-8520 *SIC* 5812

MCDONALD'S RESTAURANTS OF CANADA LIMITED p 1286
100 RUE DES CERISIERS, RIVIERE-DU-LOUP, QC, G5R 6E8
(418) 863-4242 *SIC* 5812

MCDONALD'S RESTAURANTS OF CANADA LIMITED p 1346
7445 BOUL LANGELIER, SAINT-LEONARD, QC, H1S 1V6
(514) 252-1105 *SIC* 5812

MCDONALD'S RESTAURANTS OF CANADA LIMITED p 1422
2620 DEWDNEY AVE, REGINA, SK, S4T 0X3
(306) 525-6611 *SIC* 5812

MCDONALD'S RESTAURANTS OF CANADA LIMITED p 1423
1955 PRINCE OF WALES DR, REGINA, SK, S4Z 1A5
(306) 781-1340 *SIC* 5812

MCDONALD'S RESTAURANTS OF CANADA LIMITED p 1423
6210 ROCHDALE BLVD, REGINA, SK, S4X 4K8
(306) 543-6300 *SIC* 5812

MCDONALD'S RESTAURANTS OF CANADA LIMITED p 1424
1706 PRESTON AVE, SASKATOON, SK, S7H 2V8
(306) 955-8677 *SIC* 5812

MCDONALD'S RESTAURANTS OF CANADA LIMITED p 1432
2225 22ND ST W, SASKATOON, SK, S7M 0V5
(306) 955-8660 *SIC* 5812.

MCDONALD, D. SALES & MERCHANDISING LIMITED p 801
2861 SHERWOOD HEIGHTS DR UNIT 28, OAKVILLE, ON, L6J 7K1
(905) 855-8550 *SIC* 7389

MCDONALD, GRANT P. HOLDINGS INC p 595
2680 OVERTON DR, GLOUCESTER, ON, K1G 6T8
(613) 225-9588 *SIC* 7538

MCDONALD, PHIL ENTERPRISES LTD p 1006
400 WEBER ST N, WATERLOO, ON, N2J 3J3
(519) 885-1050 *SIC* 5251

MCDONALDS p 140
See UNDERHILL FOOD SERVICES LTD

MCDONALDS p 487
See GOLDEN ARCH FOOD SERVICES LTD

MCDONALDS p 756
See MILLER, P.G. ENTERPRISES LIMITED

MCDONALDS p 869
See MCDONALD'S RESTAURANTS OF CANADA LIMITED

MCDONALDS p 912
See AUBE, J.-P. RESTAURANT SERVICES LTD

MCDONALDS p 1130
See ENTREPRISES MICHEL MARCHAND INC, LES

MCDONALDS #10305 p 512
See BEATTY FOODS LTD

MCDONALDS - MAPLE RIDGE p 231
See MCDONALD'S RESTAURANTS OF CANADA LIMITED

MCDONALDS 10731 p 508
See BEATTY FOODS LTD

MCDONALDS FAMILY RESTAURANT p 394
See R. G. MC. GROUP LIMITED

MCDONALDS RESTAURANT p 344
See CPM FOODS LTD

MCDONALDS RESTAURANT p 348
See K.A.S.A. HOLDINGS LTD

MCDONALDS RESTAURANT p 474
See MANU FORTI CORPORATION LTD

MCDONALDS RESTAURANT p 590
See GRANDI COMPANY LIMITED

MCDONALDS RESTAURANT p 860
See KIOV INCORPORATED

MCDONALDS RESTAURANT p 1424
3510 8TH ST E UNIT 1, SASKATOON, SK, S7H 0W6
(306) 955-8674 *SIC* 5812

MCDONALDS RESTAURANT OF CANADA INC p 1028
9200 WESTON RD UNIT E, WOODBRIDGE, ON, L4H 2P8
(905) 832-0424 *SIC* 5812

MCDONALDS RESTAURANTS p 637
See CAVCO FOOD SERVICES LTD

MCDONNELL MOTORS LTD p 897
359 CARADOC ST S, STRATHROY, ON, N7G 2P5
(519) 245-0840 *SIC* 5511

MCDOUGALL AUTO SUPERSTORE p 386
See MANDEX CORPORATION

MCDOUGALL ENERGY INC p 863
900 MCNABB ST, SAULT STE. MARIE, ON, P6B 6J1
(705) 949-6202 *SIC* 5983

MCDOUGALL GAULEY BARRISTERS & SOLICITOR p 1418
See MCDOUGALL GAULEY LLP

MCDOUGALL GAULEY BARRISTERS & SOLICITOR p 1424
See MCDOUGALL GAULEY LLP

MCDOUGALL GAULEY LLP p 1418
1881 SCARTH ST SUITE 1500, REGINA, SK, S4P 4K9
(306) 757-1641 *SIC* 8111

MCDOUGALL GAULEY LLP p 1424
500-616 MAIN ST, SASKATOON, SK, S7H 0J6
(306) 653-1212 *SIC* 8111

MCDOUGALL GAULEY LLP p 1424
616 MAIN ST SUITE 500, SASKATOON, SK, S7H 0J6
(306) 653-1212 *SIC* 8111

MCDOUGALL INSURANCE BROKERS LIMITED p 491
199 FRONT ST SUITE 401, BELLEVILLE, ON, K8N 5H5
(613) 966-7001 *SIC* 6411

MCELHANNEY p 299
See MCELHANNEY CONSULTING SERVICES LTD

MCELHANNEY ASSOCIATES LAND SURVEYING LTD p 214
8808 72 ST, FORT ST. JOHN, BC, V1J 6M2
(250) 787-0356 *SIC* 8713

MCELHANNEY ASSOCIATES LAND SURVEYING LTD p 299
858 BEATTY ST SUITE 200, VANCOUVER, BC, V6B 1C1
(604) 683-8521 *SIC* 8713

MCELHANNEY CONSULTING SERVICES LTD p 274
13450 102 AVE SUITE 2300, SURREY, BC, V3T 5X3
(604) 596-0391 *SIC* 8748

MCELHANNEY CONSULTING SERVICES LTD p 299
858 BEATTY ST SUITE 200, VANCOUVER, BC, V6B 1C1
(604) 683-8521 *SIC* 8748

MCELHANNEY GEOMATICS ENGINEERING LTD p

31

See MCELHANNEY LAND SURVEYS LTD
MCELHANNEY LAND SURVEYORS *p 214*
See MCELHANNEY ASSOCIATES LAND SURVEYING LTD
MCELHANNEY LAND SURVEYS LTD *p 31*
100-402 11 AVE SE, CALGARY, AB, T2G 0Y4
(403) 245-4711 *SIC 8713*
MCELHANNEY LAND SURVEYS LTD *p 94*
14315 118 AVE NW SUITE 138, EDMONTON, AB, T5L 4S6
(780) 451-3420 *SIC 8713*
MCEWEN MINING INC *p 954*
150 KING ST W SUITE 2800, TORONTO, ON, M5H 1J9
(647) 258-0395 *SIC 1041*
MCEWEN'S FUELS & FERTILIZERS *p 130*
See J. MCEWEN'S PETROLEUMS LTD
MCEWEN'S FUELS & FERTILIZERS INC *p 130*
11141 89 AVE, FORT SASKATCHEWAN, AB, T8L 2S6
(780) 998-2058 *SIC 5191*
MCF HIGHRISE FORMING INC *p 1003*
2900 HIGHWAY 7 W, VAUGHAN, ON, L6A 0K9
(416) 988-9235 *SIC 1541*
MCF HOLDINGS LTD *p 166*
101 RIEL DR SUITE 100, ST. ALBERT, AB, T8N 3X4
(780) 477-2233 *SIC 5154*
MCF HOUSING FOR SENIORS *p 36*
See METROPOLITAN CALGARY FOUNDATION
MCFADDEN'S HARDWOOD & HARDWARE INC *p 798*
2323 WINSTON PARK DR SUITE 1, OAKVILLE, ON, L6H 6R7
(416) 674-3333 *SIC 5072*
MCFADZEN HOLDINGS LIMITED *p 403*
31 KINGSWOOD WAY, HANWELL, NB, E3C 2L4
(506) 443-3331 *SIC 6531*
MCFARLAN ROWLANDS INSURANCE BROKERS INC *p 656*
503 YORK ST, LONDON, ON, N6B 1R4
(519) 679-5440 *SIC 6411*
MCFEETERS G., ENTERPRISES INC *p 882*
2825 SOUTH GRIMSBY RD 21, SMITHVILLE, ON, L0R 2A0
(905) 643-6167 *SIC 5099*
MCG RESTAURANTS LTD *p 85*
10628 KINGSWAY NW, EDMONTON, AB, T5G 0W8
(780) 944-0232 *SIC 5812*
MCGARREL PLACE *p 658*
See REVERA INC
MCGAVIN FARM EQUIPMENT LTD *p 1005*
83145 BRUSSELS LINE, WALTON, ON, N0K 1Z0
(519) 887-6365 *SIC 5083*
MCGAVIN FARM SUPPLIES *p 1005*
See MCGAVIN FARM EQUIPMENT LTD
MCGEE MOTORS LTD *p 597*
180 SUNCOAST DR E, GODERICH, ON, N7A 4N4
(519) 524-8391 *SIC 5511*
MCGEE PONTIAC BUICK CADILLAC GMC *p 597*
See MCGEE MOTORS LTD
MCGEE, JACK CHEVROLET CADILLAC LIMITED *p 841*
1053 CLONSILLA AVE, PETERBOROUGH, ON, K9J 5Y2
(705) 741-9000 *SIC 5511*
MCGILL FORMING, DIV OF *p 810*
See STORBURN CONSTRUCTION LTD
MCGILL HOPITAL NEUROLOGIQUE DE MONTREAL *p 1198*
See MCGILL UNIVERSITY HEALTH CENTRE
MCGILL LOGISTICS INC *p 809*
GD LCD MAIN, ORILLIA, ON, L3V 6H8

(705) 329-5891 *SIC 4731*
MCGILL ST-LAURENT INC *p 1189*
407 RUE MCGILL BUREAU 315, MONTREAL, QC, H2Y 2G3
(514) 871-2120 *SIC 5031*
MCGILL UNIVERSITY HEALTH CENTRE *p 1198*
3801 RUE UNIVERSITY BUREAU 548, MONTREAL, QC, H3A 2B4
(514) 398-6644 *SIC 8062*
MCGILL UNIVERSITY HEALTH CENTRE *p 1198*
687 AV DES PINS O BUREAU 1408, MONTREAL, QC, H3A 1A1
(514) 934-1934 *SIC 8062*
MCGILL UNIVERSITY HEALTH CENTRE *p 1213*
1650 AV CEDAR, MONTREAL, QC, H3G 1A4
(514) 934-1934 *SIC 8062*
MCGILL UNIVERSITY HEALTH CENTRE *p 1215*
2300 RUE TUPPER BUREAU F372, MONTREAL, QC, H3H 1P3
(514) 412-4307 *SIC 8069*
MCGILLICKY OILFIELD CONSTRUCTION LTD *p 1406*
6 HWY 39 E, ESTEVAN, SK, S4A 2A7
(306) 634-8737 *SIC 1389*
MCGLINCHEY ENTERPRISES LIMITED *p 534*
275 WATER ST N, CAMBRIDGE, ON, N1R 3B9
(519) 621-2360 *SIC 5461*
MCGOWAN INSULATIONS LTD *p 892*
345 BARTON ST, STONEY CREEK, ON, L8E 2L2
(905) 549-1844 *SIC 1799*
MCGRAIL FARM EQUIPMENT LIMITED PARTNERSHIP *p 547*
8705 COUNTY RD 46 RR 1, COMBER, ON, N0P 1J0
(519) 687-6662 *SIC 5999*
MCGRAW ET FRERE LIMITEE *p 419*
2892 RUE PRINCIPALE, TRACADIE-SHEILA, NB, E1X 1A2
(506) 395-2263 *SIC 5511*
MCGRAW-HILL RYERSON LIMITED *p 954*
145 KING ST WEST SUITE 1501, TORONTO, ON, M5H 1J8
(800) 245-2914 *SIC 2731*
MCGREGOR & THOMPSON HARDWARE LTD *p 295*
1250 GEORGIA ST E, VANCOUVER, BC, V6A 2B1
(604) 253-8252 *SIC 5072*
MCGREGOR AND THOMPSON HARDWARE LTD *p 234*
1920 BOXWOOD RD, NANAIMO, BC, V9S 5Y2
(250) 729-7888 *SIC 5072*
MCGREGOR CONSTRUCTION 2000 LTD *p 115*
9925 62 AVE NW, EDMONTON, AB, T6E 0E7
(780) 437-1340 *SIC 1623*
MCGREGOR HOSIERY MILLS *p 934*
See MCGREGOR INDUSTRIES INC
MCGREGOR INDUSTRIES INC *p 871*
1360 BIRCHMOUNT RD, SCARBOROUGH, ON, M1P 2E3
SIC 2252
MCGREGOR INDUSTRIES INC *p 934*
63 POLSON ST, TORONTO, ON, M5A 1A4
(416) 591-9191 *SIC 5136*
MCGUIRE, J.J. GENERAL CONTRACTORS INC *p 813*
880 FAREWELL ST SUITE 1, OSHAWA, ON, L1H 6N6
(905) 436-2554 *SIC 1542*
MCI ENTREPRENEUR GENERAL *p 1149*
See CONSTRUCTION MARIEVILLE INC
MCI MEDICAL CLINICS INC *p 789*

1 YORKDALE RD SUITE 209, NORTH YORK, ON, M6A 3A1
(416) 440-4040 *SIC 8093*
MCILVEEN LUMBER *p 17*
See MCILVEEN LUMBER INDUSTRIES (ALTA.)(2012) LTD
MCILVEEN LUMBER INDUSTRIES (ALTA.)(2012) LTD *p 17*
9440 48 ST SE, CALGARY, AB, T2C 2R2
(403) 273-5333 *SIC 5031*
MCINNES COOPER *p 453*
1969 UPPER WATER ST SUITE 1300, HALIFAX, NS, B3J 3R7
(902) 425-6500 *SIC 8111*
MCINNIS EXPRESS LTD *p 1040*
2 MACALEER DR, CHARLOTTETOWN, PE, C1E 2A1
(902) 892-9333 *SIC 7389*
MCINTEE , WILFRED & CO. LIMITED *p 1004*
11 DURHAM ST, WALKERTON, ON, N0G 2V0
(519) 881-2270 *SIC 6531*
MCINTOSH PERRY CONSULTING ENGINEERS LTD *p 541*
115 WALGREEN RD RR 3, CARP, ON, K0A 1L0
(613) 836-2184 *SIC 8711*
MCINTOSH PERRY LIMITED *p 555*
7900 KEELE ST SUITE 200, CONCORD, ON, L4K 2A3
(905) 856-5200 *SIC 8742*
MCINTYRE GROUP OFFICE SERVICES INC *p 642*
825 TRILLIUM DR, KITCHENER, ON, N2R 1J9
(519) 740-7636 *SIC 1799*
MCIS NON-PROFIT LANGUAGE SERVICES *p 780*
See MULTILINGUAL COMMUNITY INTERPRETER SERVICES (ONTARIO)
MCKAY GM *p 360*
See ROCK COUNTRY CHEVROLET BUICK GMC LTD
MCKAY PONTIAC BUICK (1979) LTD *p 36*
7711 MACLEOD TRAIL SW, CALGARY, AB, T2H 0M1
(403) 243-0109 *SIC 5511*
MCKAY PONTIAC BUICK GMC *p 36*
See MCKAY PONTIAC BUICK (1979) LTD
MCKAY, W. G. LIMITED *p 964*
40 UNIVERSITY AVE SUITE 602, TORONTO, ON, M5J 1J9
(416) 593-1380 *SIC 4731*
MCKECHNIE, ANDY BUILDING MATERIALS LTD *p 569*
830 CENTRE ST, ESPANOLA, ON, P5E 1J1
(705) 869-2130 *SIC 5211*
MCKEEN GLEBE LOEB *p 826*
See MCKEEN, D & J HOLDINGS (OTTAWA) INC
MCKEEN, D & J HOLDINGS (OTTAWA) INC *p 826*
754 BANK ST, OTTAWA, ON, K1S 3V6
(613) 232-9466 *SIC 5411*
MCKEIL MARINE LIMITED *p 523*
1001 CHAMPLAIN AVE SUITE 401, BURLINGTON, ON, L7L 5Z4
(905) 528-4780 *SIC 4499*
MCKELLAR GROUP *p 601*
See MCKELLAR STRUCTURED SETTLEMENTS INC
MCKELLAR STRUCTURED SETTLEMENTS INC *p 601*
649 SCOTTSDALE DR SUITE 100, GUELPH, ON, N1G 4T7
(519) 836-1672 *SIC 6282*
MCKENNA BROS (1989) LIMITED *p 1038*
4109 48 RD, CARDIGAN, PE, C0A 1G0
(902) 583-2951 *SIC 5148*
MCKENNCO INC *p 1042*

481 GRANVILLE ST, SUMMERSIDE, PE, C1N 4P7
(902) 436-5462 *SIC 5812*
MCKENZIE ASSOCIATED AUCTIONEERS *p 650*
See ASSOCIATED AUCTIONEERS INC
MCKENZIE TOWN CARE CENTRE *p 71*
See REVERA INC
MCKENZIE, C. PHARMACY INC *p 1432*
2410 22ND ST W UNIT 20, SASKATOON, SK, S7M 5S6
(306) 382-5005 *SIC 5912*
MCKENZIE-SMITH BENNETT SCHOOL *p 473*
See HALTON DISTRICT SCHOOL BOARD
MCKEOWN MOTOR SALES *p 883*
See MCKEOWN, WILLIAM MOTOR SALES LIMITED
MCKEOWN MOTORS LIMITED *p 632*
805 GARDINERS RD, KINGSTON, ON, K7M 7E6
(613) 389-4426 *SIC 5511*
MCKEOWN, WILLIAM MOTOR SALES LIMITED *p 883*
2589 SPRINGBROOK RD, SPRINGBROOK, ON, K0K 3C0
(613) 395-3883 *SIC 5541*
MCKERCHER HOLDINGS LIMITED *p 633*
2730 PRINCESS ST, KINGSTON, ON, K7P 2W6
(613) 384-2418 *SIC 6719*
MCKERCHER KINGSTON LIMITED *p 633*
2730 PRINCESS ST, KINGSTON, ON, K7P 2W6
(613) 384-2418 *SIC 5712*
MCKERCHER LLP *p 1428*
374 3RD AVE S, SASKATOON, SK, S7K 1M5
(306) 653-2000 *SIC 8111*
MCKESSON CORPORATION *p 672*
131 MCNABB ST, MARKHAM, ON, L3R 5V7
(905) 943-9499 *SIC 5122*
MCKESSON SERVICES PHARMACEUTIQUES *p 1169*
See CORPORATION MCKESSON CANADA, LA
MCKESSON SPECIALIZED DISTRIBUTION *p 684*
See MCKESSON SPECIALIZED DISTRIBUTION INC
MCKESSON SPECIALIZED DISTRIBUTION INC *p 684*
8449 LAWSON RD UNIT 102, MILTON, ON, L9T 9L1
(905) 827-1300 *SIC 5122*
MCKEVITT TRUCKING LIMITED *p 908*
1200 CARRICK ST, THUNDER BAY, ON, P7B 5P9
(807) 623-0054 *SIC 4213*
MCKILLICAN CANADIAN INC *p 106*
16420 118 AVE NW, EDMONTON, AB, T5V 1C8
(780) 453-3841 *SIC 5039*
MCKILLICAN INTERNATIONAL, INC *p 106*
16420 118 AVE NW, EDMONTON, AB, T5V 1C8
(780) 453-3841 *SIC 5039*
MCKINNON MULTI-SERVICES *p 1263*
See 9300-4901 QUEBEC INC
MCKINSTRY'S *p 565*
See MCKINSTRY, WILLIAM LIMITED
MCKINSTRY, WILLIAM LIMITED *p 565*
176 GOVERNMENT ST, DRYDEN, ON, P8N 2N9
(807) 223-4214 *SIC 5511*
MCL MOTOR CARS 1992 INC *p 321*
1718 3RD AVE W, VANCOUVER, BC, V6J 1K4
(604) 736-7911 *SIC 5511*
MCL POWER INC *p 98*
16821 107 AVE NW, EDMONTON, AB, T5P 0Y8

(780) 440-8775 *SIC* 1731

MCLAREN, P. D. LIMITED *p* 282
9725 192 ST UNIT 104, SURREY, BC, V4N 4C7
(604) 371-3732 *SIC* 1799

MCLAUGHLIN, R S COLLEGIATE & VOCATIONAL INSTITUTE *p*
813
See DURHAM DISTRICT SCHOOL BOARD

MCLEAN & DICKEY LTD *p* 809
174 WEST ST S, ORILLIA, ON, L3V 6L4
(705) 325-4461 *SIC* 6411

MCLEAN & DICKEY LTD *p* 809
390 LACLIE ST, ORILLIA, ON, L3V 4P5
(705) 325-4461 *SIC* 6411

MCLEAN & PARTNERS WEALTH MANAGEMENT LTD *p*
65
801 10 AVE SW, CALGARY, AB, T2R 0B4
(403) 234-0005 *SIC* 6282

MCLEAN BUDDEN HIGH INCOME EQUITY FUND *p* 954
See MCLEAN, BUDDEN LIMITED

MCLEAN HALLMARK INSURANCE GROUP LTD *p* 672
10 KONRAD CRES, MARKHAM, ON, L3R 8T7
(416) 364-4000 *SIC* 6411

MCLEAN HALLMARK INSURANCE GROUP LTD *p* 934
184 FRONT ST E SUITE 601, TORONTO, ON, M5A 4N3
(416) 364-4000 *SIC* 6411

MCLEAN INSURANCE PROTECTION TEAM INC *p* 839
58 FOSTER ST, PERTH, ON, K7H 1S1
(613) 267-5100 *SIC* 6411

MCLEAN KENNEDY INC *p* 1189
368 RUE NOTRE-DAME O BUREAU 100, MONTREAL, QC, H2Y 1T9
(514) 849-6111 *SIC* 4731

MCLEAN TAYLOR CONSTRUCTION LIMITED *p*
888
25 WATER ST N, ST MARYS, ON, N4X 1B1
(519) 284-2580 *SIC* 1622

MCLEAN WATSON INVESTMENTS INC *p*
954
141 ADELAIDE ST W SUITE 1200, TORONTO, ON, M5H 3L5
(416) 363-2000 *SIC* 6211

MCLEAN, BRIAN CHEVROLET LTD *p* 203
2145 CLIFFE AVE, COURTENAY, BC, V9N 2L5
(250) 334-3400 *SIC* 5511

MCLEAN, BUDDEN CANADIAN EQUITY GROWTH FUND *p* 954
145 KING ST W SUITE 2525, TORONTO, ON, M5H 1J8
(416) 862-9800 *SIC* 6722

MCLEAN, BUDDEN LIMITED *p* 954
145 KING ST W SUITE 2525, TORONTO, ON, M5H 1J8
(416) 862-9800 *SIC* 6722

MCLEISH CONTAINERS *p* 547
See 2014767 ONTARIO LIMITED

MCLEISH CORR-A-BOX PACKAGING & DESIGN *p* 585
See JDC #10 LIMITED

MCLELLAN'S SUPERMARKET LTD *p* 315
1255 DAVIE ST, VANCOUVER, BC, V6E 1N4
(604) 688-0911 *SIC* 5411

MCLENNAN ROSS LLP *p* 97
12220 STONY PLAIN RD NW SUITE 600, EDMONTON, AB, T5N 3Y4
(780) 482-9200 *SIC* 8111

MCLEOD & COMPANY LLP *p* 69
14505 BANNISTER RD SE SUITE 300, CALGARY, AB, T2X 3J3
(403) 225-6400 *SIC* 8111

MCLEOD HOME BUILDING CENTRE *p* 164
See MCLEOD MERCANTILE LTD

MCLEOD MERCANTILE LTD *p* 164

135 SOUTH AVE, SPRUCE GROVE, AB, T7X 3A5
(780) 962-2575 *SIC* 5211

MCLEOD SAFETY SERVICES LTD *p* 469
30 UPHAM DR, TRURO, NS, B2N 6W5
(902) 897-7233 *SIC* 3812

MCLOUGHLAN SUPPLIES LIMITED *p* 433
24 BLACKMARSH RD SUITE 22, ST. JOHN'S, NL, A1E 1S3
(709) 576-4091 *SIC* 5063

MCM 2001 *p* 993
See MILLWORKS CUSTOM MANUFACTURING (2001) INC

MCM GROUP LTD *p* 1010
730 BRIDGE ST W SUITE 1, WATERLOO, ON, N2V 2J4
(519) 725-3800 *SIC* 5199

MCMAHON DISTRIBUTEUR PHARMACEUTIQUE *p*
1247
See METRO RICHELIEU INC

MCMAHON DISTRIBUTEUR PHARMACEUTIQUE INC *p*
1247
12225 BOUL INDUSTRIEL BUREAU 100, POINTE-AUX-TREMBLES, QC, H1B 5M7
(514) 355-8350 *SIC* 5122

MCMAN SUPPORTED INDEPENDENT LIVING *p*
96
See MCMAN YOUTH, FAMILY AND COMMUNITY SERVICES ASSOCIATION

MCMAN YOUTH, FAMILY AND COMMUNITY SERVICES ASSOCIATION *p*
36
6712 FISHER ST SE UNIT 80, CALGARY, AB, T2H 2A7
(403) 508-7742 *SIC* 8641

MCMAN YOUTH, FAMILY AND COMMUNITY SERVICES ASSOCIATION *p*
96
11016 127 ST NW, EDMONTON, AB, T5M 0T2
(780) 482-4461 *SIC* 8322

MCMASTER STUDENTS UNION INCORPORATED *p*
614
1280 MAIN ST W RM 1, HAMILTON, ON, L8S 4K1
(905) 525-9140 *SIC* 8631

MCMASTER UNIVERSITY *p* 612
GD, HAMILTON, ON, L8N 3Z5
(905) 521-2100 *SIC* 8221

MCMASTER UNIVERSITY *p* 614
1280 MAIN ST W GH209, HAMILTON, ON, L8S 4L8
(905) 525-9140 *SIC* 8221

MCMASTER, PAT & MARLEEN ENTERPRISES LTD *p*
569
801 CENTRE ST, ESPANOLA, ON, P5E 1N2
(705) 869-3807 *SIC* 5531

MCMATH SECONDARY SCHOOL *p* 266
See BOARD OF EDUCATION SCHOOL DISTRICT #38 (RICHMOND)

MCMICHAEL CANADIAN ART COLLECTION *p*
642
10365 ISLINGTON AVE, KLEINBURG, ON, L0J 1C0
(905) 893-1121 *SIC* 8412

MCMILLAN & SAUNDERS INC *p* 744
797 BANCROFT DR, MISSISSAUGA, ON, L5V 2Y6
(905) 858-0712 *SIC* 5511

MCMILLAN & SAUNDERS VOLVO *p* 744
See MCMILLAN & SAUNDERS INC

MCMILLAN LLP *p* 315
1055 GEORGIA ST W SUITE 1500, VANCOUVER, BC, V6E 4N7
(604) 689-9111 *SIC* 8111

MCMILLAN LLP *p* 964
181 BAY ST SUITE 4400, TORONTO, ON,

M5J 2T3
(416) 865-7000 *SIC* 8111

MCMILLAN LLP *p* 1198
1000 RUE SHERBROOKE O BUREAU 2700, MONTREAL, QC, H3A 3G4
(514) 987-5000 *SIC* 8111

MCMILLAN, J.S. FISHERIES LTD *p* 239
12 ORWELL ST, NORTH VANCOUVER, BC, V7J 2G1
(604) 982-9207 *SIC* 2092

MCMILLAN, J.S. FISHERIES LTD *p* 251
GD STN MAIN, PRINCE RUPERT, BC, V8J 3P3
(250) 624-2146 *SIC* 2092

MCMILLAN-MCGEE CORP *p* 12
4895 35B ST SE, CALGARY, AB, T2B 3M9
(403) 569-5100 *SIC* 8711

MCMULLEN & WARNOCK INC *p* 872
70 CROCKFORD BLVD, SCARBOROUGH, ON, M1R 3C3
SIC 1542

MCMUNN & YATES BUILDING SUPPLIES LTD *p* 348
288 2 AVE NE, DAUPHIN, MB, R7N 0Z9
(204) 638-5303 *SIC* 6712

MCMUNN & YATES BUILDING SUPPLIES LTD *p* 387
600 PEMBINA HWY, WINNIPEG, MB, R3M 2M5
(204) 940-4040 *SIC* 5211

MCNAIRN PACKAGING *p* 1014
See CULINARY PAPERS INC

MCNAIRN PACKAGING *p* 1014
See J. H. MCNAIRN LIMITED

MCNALLY CONSTRUCTION INC *p* 609
1855 BARTON ST E SUITE 4, HAMILTON, ON, L8H 2Y7
(905) 549-6561 *SIC* 1629

MCNALLY INTERNATIONAL INC *p* 609
1855 BARTON ST E, HAMILTON, ON, L8H 2Y7
(905) 549-6561 *SIC* 1629

MCNALLY MARINE, DIV OF *p* 609
See MCNALLY CONSTRUCTION INC

MCNAMARA, MERVIN J. INC *p* 898
1066 BARRYDOWNE RD SUITE 278, SUDBURY, ON, P3A 3V3
(705) 566-9735 *SIC* 5531

MCNAUGHT MOTORS *p* 391
See MCNAUGHT PONTIAC BUICK CADILLAC GMC LTD

MCNAUGHT PONTIAC BUICK CADILLAC GMC LTD *p* 391
1717 WAVERLEY ST UNIT 1000, WINNIPEG, MB, R3T 6A9
(204) 786-3811 *SIC* 5511

MCNAUGHTON AUTOMOTIVE LIMITED *p*
753
22789 HAGERTY RD, NEWBURY, ON, N0L 1Z0
(519) 693-4449 *SIC* 5211

MCNAUGHTON HOME HARDWARE BUILDING CENTRE *p* 753
See MCNAUGHTON AUTOMOTIVE LIMITED

MCNEIL CONSUMER HEALTH CARE *p* 606
See MCNEIL PDI INC

MCNEIL CONSUMER HEALTH CARE DIV OF *p* 605
See JOHNSON & JOHNSON INC

MCNEIL CONSUMER HEALTHCARE *p* 605
See JOHNSON & JOHNSON INC

MCNEIL PDI INC *p* 606
890 WOODLAWN RD W, GUELPH, ON, N1K 1A5
SIC 2834

MCNICOL STEVENSON LIMITED *p* 878
3640 MCNICOLL AVE SUITE B, SCARBOROUGH, ON, M1X 1G5
(416) 291-2933 *SIC* 7389

MCPHAIL'S OF HARRISTON *p* 618
See DON MCPHAIL MOTORS LTD

MCPHILLIPS HOLDINGS (WINNIPEG) LTD
p 370

2425 MCPHILLIPS ST, WINNIPEG, MB, R2V 4J7
(204) 338-7985 *SIC* 5511

MCPHILLIPS LIMITED PARTNERSHIP *p*
366
123 VERMILLION RD, WINNIPEG, MB, R2J 4A9
(204) 253-1928 *SIC* 5812

MCPHILLIPS TOYOTA *p* 370
See MCPHILLIPS HOLDINGS (WINNIPEG) LTD

MCPIKE INVESTMENTS LTD *p* 3
440 EAST LAKE RD NE, AIRDRIE, AB, T4A 2J8
(403) 912-7200 *SIC* 3533

MCPORT CITY FOOD SERVICES LIMITED *p*
414
399 MAIN ST, SAINT JOHN, NB, E2K 1J3
(506) 657-4381 *SIC* 8741

MCQUAID, S. PHARMACY LTD *p* 860
510 EXMOUTH ST, SARNIA, ON, N7T 0A5
(519) 344-2409 *SIC* 5912

MCQUARRIE MOTOR PRODUCTS INC *p*
569
228 CENTRE ST, ESPANOLA, ON, P5E 1G1
(705) 869-1351 *SIC* 5511

MCQUEEN AGENCIES *p* 1423
See 563737 SASKATCHEWAN LTD

MCRAE INTEGRATION LTD *p* 586
34 MERIDIAN RD, ETOBICOKE, ON, M9W 4Z7
(416) 252-8833 *SIC* 8742

MCRAE LUMBER COMPANY LIMITED *p*
1016
384 HAY CREEK RD, WHITNEY, ON, K0J 2M0
(613) 637-2190 *SIC* 2411

MCRAE MILLS *p* 1016
See MCRAE LUMBER COMPANY LIMITED

MCRAE MILLS LIMITED *p* 1016
160 HAY CREEK RD, WHITNEY, ON, K0J 2M0
(613) 637-2977 *SIC* 5211

MCRAE'S ENVIRONMENTAL SERVICES LTD *p* 209
7783 PROGRESS WAY, DELTA, BC, V4G 1A3
(604) 434-8313 *SIC* 1794

MCRAE'S SPEC LIQUID WASTE *p* 209
See MCRAE'S ENVIRONMENTAL SERVICES LTD

MCRAE, W. R. COMPANY LIMITED *p* 630
549 MONTREAL ST, KINGSTON, ON, K7K 3J1
(613) 544-6611 *SIC* 5141

MCROBERT FUELS LIMITED *p* 897
4755 EGREMONT DR SUITE 1, STRATHROY, ON, N7G 3H3
(519) 246-1019 *SIC* 5171

MCTAVISH INSURANCE AGENCIES LTD *p*
337
4430 CHATTERTON WAY, VICTORIA, BC, V8X 5J2
(905) 898-0361 *SIC* 6411

MCW CES *p* 964
See MCW CUSTOM ENERGY SOLUTIONS LTD

MCW CONSULTANTS LTD *p* 964
207 QUEENS QUAY W SUITE 615, TORONTO, ON, M5J 1A7
(416) 598-2920 *SIC* 8711

MCW CUSTOM ENERGY SOLUTIONS LTD *p* 964
207 QUEENS QUAY W SUITE 615, TORONTO, ON, M5J 1A7
(416) 598-2920 *SIC* 8711

MCWILLIAMS CARTAGE LIMITED *p* 841
712 THE KINGSWAY, PETERBOROUGH, ON, K9J 6W6
(800) 461-6464 *SIC* 4213

MCWILLIAMS MOVING & STORAGE *p* 841
See MCWILLIAMS CARTAGE LIMITED

MD EQUITY FUND *p* 818

See MD MANAGEMENT LIMITED
MD FINANCIAL MANAGEMENT INC *p* 818
1870 ALTA VISTA DR SUITE 1, OTTAWA, ON, K1G 6R7
(613) 731-4552 *SIC* 8741
MD FINANCIAL MANAGEMENT LIMITED *p* 946
522 UNIVERSITY AVE SUITE 1100, TORONTO, ON, M5G 1W7
(416) 598-1442 *SIC* 8742
MD FUNDS MANAGEMENT LIMITED *p* 946
See MD FINANCIAL MANAGEMENT LIMITED
MD MANAGEMENT LIMITED *p* 818
1870 ALTA VISTA DR, OTTAWA, ON, K1G 6R7
(613) 731-4552 *SIC* 8741
MD PRIVATE TRUST COMPANY *p* 818
1870 ALTA VISTA DR, OTTAWA, ON, K1G 6R7
(613) 731-8610 *SIC* 6722
MDA *p* 499
See MACDONALD, DETTWILER AND ASSOCIATES INC
MDA GEOSPATIAL SERVICES INC *p* 255
13800 COMMERCE PKWY, RICHMOND, BC, V6V 2J3
(604) 278-3411 *SIC* 7335
MDA SYSTEMS HOLDINGS LTD *p* 255
13800 COMMERCE PKWY, RICHMOND, BC, V6V 2J3
(604) 278-3411 *SIC* 8748
MDA SYSTEMS LTD *p* 255
13800 COMMERCE PKWY, RICHMOND, BC, V6V 2J3
(604) 278-3411 *SIC* 7373
MDA SYSTEMS LTD *p* 749
57 AURIGA DR UNIT 201, NEPEAN, ON, K2E 8B2
(613) 727-1087 *SIC* 7373
MDE ELECTRICAL MECHANICAL CONTRACTORS *p* 284
See MDE ENTERPRISES LTD
MDE ENTERPRISES LTD *p* 284
3947 GRAVELEY ST, VANCOUVER, BC, V5C 3T4
(604) 291-1995 *SIC* 1731
MDF MECHANICAL LIMITED *p* 504
2100 STEELES AVE E, BRAMPTON, ON, L6T 1A7
(905) 789-9944 *SIC* 1711
MDG COMPUTERS CANADA INC *p* 798
2940 BRISTOL CIR, OAKVILLE, ON, L6H 6G4
(905) 829-3538 *SIC* 5045
MDH ENGINEERED SOLUTIONS CORP *p* 1428
216 1ST AVE S, SASKATOON, SK, S7K 1K3
(306) 934-7527 *SIC* 7373
MDINA ENTERPRISES LTD *p* 442
121 DUKE ST SUITE 49, CHESTER, NS, B0J 1J0
(855) 855-3180 *SIC* 8742
MDL *p* 772
See MENKES HOLDINGS INC
MDM INSURANCE SERVICES INC *p* 601
834 GORDON ST, GUELPH, ON, N1G 1Y7
(519) 837-1531 *SIC* 6411
MDS AERO SUPPORT CORPORATION *p* 816
1220 OLD INNES RD SUITE 200, OTTAWA, ON, K1B 3V3
(613) 744-5794 *SIC* 8711
MDS AERO SUPPORT CORPORATION *p* 816
1220 OLD INNES RD SUITE 200, OTTAWA, ON, K1B 3V3
(613) 744-7257 *SIC* 8711
MDS AEROSPACE CORPORATION *p* 816
200-1220 OLD INNES RD, OTTAWA, ON, K1B 3V3
(613) 744-7257 *SIC* 3724
MDS COATING TECHNOLOGIES CORPO-

RATION *p* 1042
60 AEROSPACE BLVD, SLEMON PARK, PE, C0B 2A0
(902) 888-3900 *SIC* 3479
MDS DIAGNOSTIC SERVICES *p* 189
See NORDION (CANADA) INC
MDS INVESTMENTS LTD *p* 86
10914 120 ST NW, EDMONTON, AB, T5H 3P7
(780) 452-3110 *SIC* 5075
MDS LABORATORIES *p* 656
See NORDION (CANADA) INC
MDS PHARMA SERVICES *p* 698
See NORDION (CANADA) INC
ME TO WE RESPONSIBLE STYLE *p* 934
See ME TO WE STYLE INC
ME TO WE SHOP INC *p* 934
145 BERKELEY ST, TORONTO, ON, M5A 2X1
(416) 964-8942 *SIC* 5999
ME TO WE STYLE INC *p* 934
145 BERKELEY ST, TORONTO, ON, M5A 2X1
(416) 964-8942 *SIC* 5651
ME TO WE TRIPS INC *p* 934
145 BERKELEY ST, TORONTO, ON, M5A 2X1
(416) 964-8942 *SIC* 4724
MEAD JOHNSON NUTRITION (CANADA) CO *p* 624
535 LEGGET DR SUITE 900, KANATA, ON, K2K 3B8
(613) 595-4700 *SIC* 5149
MEADE RAY INTERNATIONAL INC *p* 1227
8370 RUE LABARRE, MONTREAL, QC, H4P 2E7
(514) 738-5858 *SIC* 5199
MEADOW CREEK CEDAR LTD *p* 218
GD, KASLO, BC, V0G 1M0
(250) 366-4434 *SIC* 2421
MEADOW LAKE CO-OP *p* 1410
See MEADOW LAKE CO-OPERATIVE ASSOCIATION LIMITED
MEADOW LAKE CO-OPERATIVE ASSOCIATION LIMITED *p* 1410
107 2ND ST W, MEADOW LAKE, SK, S9X 1C6
(306) 236-5678 *SIC* 5399
MEADOW LAKE HOME BUILDING CENTRE *p* 1409
See 581976 SASKATCHEWAN LTD
MEADOW LAKE HOME HARDWARE BUILDING CENTRE LTD *p* 1410
802 1ST ST W, MEADOW LAKE, SK, S9X 1E2
(306) 236-4467 *SIC* 5251
MEADOW LAKE MECHANICAL PULP INC *p* 1410
HWY 55 903, MEADOW LAKE, SK, S9X 1V7
(306) 236-2444 *SIC* 2611
MEADOW LAKE OSB LIMITED PARTNERSHIP *p* 1410
12 KM SOUTH OF HWY 55, MEADOW LAKE, SK, S9X 1Y2
(306) 236-6565 *SIC* 2493
MEADOW LAKE UNION HOSPITAL *p* 1410
See PRAIRIE NORTH REGIONAL HEALTH AUTHORITY
MEADOW PARK (LONDON) INC *p* 657
1210 SOUTHDALE RD E SUITE 9, LONDON, ON, N6E 1B4
(519) 686-0484 *SIC* 8051
MEADOW PARK CHATHAM *p* 542
See JARLETTE LTD
MEADOWLANDS RETIREMENT RESIDENCE *p* 147
See REVERA INC
MEADOWLARK DIAGNOSTIC IMAGING *p*

98
See INSIGHT MEDICAL HOLDINGS LTD
MEADOWOOD MANOR *p* 368
See MANITOBA BAPTIST HOME SOCIETY INC
MEADOWS DORCHESTER, THE *p* 760
See REGIONAL MUNICIPALITY OF NIAGARA, THE
MEADOWS LONG TERM CARE CENTRE, THE *p* 478
See REVERA INC
MEADOWVALE FORD SALES AND SERVICE LIMITED *p* 724
2230 BATTLEFORD RD, MISSISSAUGA, ON, L5N 3K6
(905) 542-3673 *SIC* 5511
MEADOWVALE HONDA *p* 714
See MISSISSAUGA AUTOMOTIVE INC
MEADOWVALE SECONDARY SCHOOL *p* 725
See PEEL DISTRICT SCHOOL BOARD
MEADOWVILLE GARDEN CENTRE INC *p* 604
7767 WELLINGTON ROAD 124, GUELPH, ON, N1H 6H7
(519) 822-0840 *SIC* 0181
MEADWELL MOWAT FENNELL *p* 1014
413 DUNDAS ST E, WHITBY, ON, L1N 2J2
(905) 668-3579 *SIC* 6411
MEAFORD NURSING HOME LTD *p* 681
135 WILLIAM ST, MEAFORD, ON, N4L 1T4
(519) 538-1010 *SIC* 8051
MEALS ON WHEELS *p* 231
See MAPLE RIDGE/PITT MEADOWS COMMUNITY SERVICES
MEALS ON WHEELS *p* 1008
See COMMUNITY SUPPORT CONNECTIONS-MEALS ON WHEELS AND MORE
MEANEY, B. CONSULTING LTD *p* 101
21110 108 AVE NW, EDMONTON, AB, T5S 1X4
SIC 8741
MEARS CANADA CORP *p* 159
235080 RYAN RD, ROCKY VIEW COUNTY, AB, T1X 0K3
(587) 471-2344 *SIC* 1623
MEASURAND INC *p* 403
2111 ROUTE 640, HANWELL, NB, E3C 1M7
(506) 462-9119 *SIC* 3827
MEAT FACTORY LIMITED, THE *p* 892
46 COMMUNITY AVE, STONEY CREEK, ON, L8E 2Y3
(905) 664-2126 *SIC* 2013
MEC *p* 289
See MOUNTAIN EQUIPMENT CO-OPERATIVE
MEC *p* 829
See MOUNTAIN EQUIPMENT CO-OPERATIVE
MEC CANADA *p* 931
See YOUNG & RUBICAM GROUP OF COMPANIES ULC, THE
MEC MONTREAL *p* 1215
See PUBLICITE TAXI MONTREAL INC
MECACHROME CANADA INC *p* 1153
11100 RUE JULIEN-AUDETTE, MIRABEL, QC, J7N 3L3
(450) 476-3939 *SIC* 3728
MECAER AMERIQUE INC *p* 1357
5555 RUE WILLIAM-PRICE, SAINTE-DOROTHEE, QC, H7L 6C4
(450) 682-7117 *SIC* 3728
MECANICACTION INC *p* 1345
6660 RUE P.-E.-LAMARCHE, SAINT-LEONARD, QC, H1P 1J7
(514) 666-9770 *SIC* 1711
MECANICAM AUTO *p* 1172
5612 RUE CARTIER, MONTREAL, QC, H2G 2T9
(514) 495-1007 *SIC* 5511
MECANIQUE CNC (2002) INC *p* 1066

1470 RUE GRAHAM-BELL, BOUCHERVILLE, QC, J4B 6H5
(450) 652-6319 *SIC* 1541
MECANIQUE INDUSTRIELLE FORTIER & FILS INC *p* 1123
1675 RUE INDUSTRIELLE, LA PRAIRIE, QC, J5R 2E4
(450) 619-9292 *SIC* 1711
MECANIQUE PRO-B *p* 1389
See GROUPE PRO-B INC
MECANO-SOUDURE DRUMMOND INC *p* 1142
700 RUE TALON, LONGUEUIL, QC, J4G 1P7
(514) 526-4411 *SIC* 3399
MECAR METAL INC *p* 1296
1560 RUE MARIE-VICTORIN, SAINT-BRUNO, QC, J3V 6B9
(450) 653-1002 *SIC* 3585
MECART INC *p* 1293
110 RUE DE ROTTERDAM, SAINT-AUGUSTIN-DE-DESMAURES, QC, G3A 1T3
(418) 880-7000 *SIC* 3296
MECFAB *p* 1065
See INDUSTRIE LEMIEUX INC
MECFOR BROCHOT *p* 1081
See MECFOR INC
MECFOR INC *p* 1081
1788 RUE MITIS, CHICOUTIMI, QC, G7K 1H5
(418) 543-1632 *SIC* 3569
MECHANICAL SYSTEMS REMANUFACTURING INC *p* 735
1740 DREW RD, MISSISSAUGA, ON, L5S 1J6
(905) 673-5733 *SIC* 5088
MECHANOVA INC *p* 77
2501 BEARSPAW SUMMIT PL, CALGARY, AB, T3R 1B5
SIC 4922
MECHET CHARITIES LIMITED *p* 101
18216 102 AVE NW SUITE 200, EDMONTON, AB, T5S 1S7
(780) 442-3640 *SIC* 8699
MED TECH *p* 662
See MEDICAL TECHNOLOGY (W.B.) INC
MED-ENG HOLDINGS ULC *p* 818
2400 ST. LAURENT BLVD, OTTAWA, ON, K1G 6C4
(613) 482-8835 *SIC* 3842
MEDA *p* 1010
See MENNONITE ECONOMIC DEVELOPMENT ASSOCIATES OF CANADA
MEDA LIMITED *p* 1018
1575 LAUZON RD, WINDSOR, ON, N8S 3N4
(519) 944-7221 *SIC* 8711
MEDALLION CORPORATION *p* 789
970 LAWRENCE AVE W SUITE 304, NORTH YORK, ON, M6A 3B6
(416) 256-3900 *SIC* 6531
MEDALLION DEVELOPMENT *p* 789
See MEDALLION CORPORATION
MEDALLION ENERGY SERVICES INC *p* 132
9516 146 AVE, GRANDE PRAIRIE, AB, T8V 7V9
(780) 357-2164 *SIC* 1389
MEDALLION PROPERTIES INC *p* 789
970 LAWRENCE AVE W SUITE 304, NORTH YORK, ON, M6A 3B6
(416) 256-3900 *SIC* 6531
MEDAVIE BLUE CROSS *p* 407
See MEDAVIE INC
MEDAVIE INC *p* 407
644 MAIN ST, MONCTON, NB, E1C 1E2
(506) 853-1811 *SIC* 6321
MEDAVIE INC *p* 1198
550 RUE SHERBROOKE O BUREAU 1200, MONTREAL, QC, H3A 1B9
(514) 286-7778 *SIC* 6321
MEDBRIDGE INVESTMENTS LTD *p* 141

2835 12 AVE N, LETHBRIDGE, AB, T1H 5K9
(403) 328-0922   SIC 5031

MEDCAN   p 954
See MEDCAN HEALTH MANAGEMENT INC

MEDCAN HEALTH MANAGEMENT INC p 954
150 YORK ST SUITE 1500, TORONTO, ON, M5H 3S5
(416) 350-5900   SIC 8011

MEDEIROS, PAUL ENTERPRISES LIMITED p 634
146 GOVERNMENT RD W, KIRKLAND LAKE, ON, P2N 2E9
(705) 567-9281   SIC 5531

MEDELA CANADA INC   p 717
4160 SLADEVIEW CRES UNIT 8, MISSIS-SAUGA, ON, L5L 0A1
(905) 608-7272   SIC 5047

MEDEX. FISH IMPORTING & EXPORTING CO. LTD   p 1032
189 WESTCREEK DR, WOODBRIDGE, ON, L4L 9N6
(905) 856-8188   SIC 5146

MEDI GROUP MASONRY LIMITED   p 586
56 BROCKPORT DR SUITE 3, ETOBI-COKE, ON, M9W 5N1
(416) 747-5170   SIC 1741

MEDI-PARE LTEE   p 1115
2075 BOUL MELLON BUREAU 100, JON-QUIERE, QC, G7S 5Z8
(418) 548-3188   SIC 5912

MEDI-QUOTE INSURANCE BROKERS INC p 362
505 PANDORA AVE W, WINNIPEG, MB, R2C 1M8
(204) 947-9210   SIC 6411

MEDI-SHARE INC   p 534
1986 CEDAR CREEK RD, CAMBRIDGE, ON, N1R 5S5
(519) 740-3336   SIC 8731

MEDI-TRAN SERVICES (1993) LTD p 193
7125 CURRAGH AVE, BURNABY, BC, V5J 4V6
(604) 872-5293   SIC 7389

MEDI-VAN   p 386
See MEDI-VAN TRANSPORTATION SPE-CIALISTS INC

MEDI-VAN TRANSPORTATION SPECIAL-ISTS INC   p 386
284 ROUGE RD, WINNIPEG, MB, R3K 1K2
(204) 982-0790   SIC 4111

MEDIA BUYING SERVICES ULC   p 946
1 DUNDAS ST W SUITE 2800, TORONTO, ON, M5G 1Z3
(416) 961-1255   SIC 7319

MEDIA CASH REGISTER INC   p 1245
9580 BOUL GOUIN O, PIERREFONDS, QC, H8Y 1R3
(514) 685-3630   SIC 5112

MEDIA NEWAD   p 1184
See NEWAD MEDIA INC

MEDIA PROFILE INC   p 982
579 RICHMOND ST W SUITE 500, TORONTO, ON, M5V 1Y6
(416) 504-8464   SIC 8741

MEDIA RESOURCES   p 801
See MEDIA RESOURCES INTERNA-TIONAL INC

MEDIA RESOURCES INC   p 801
1387 CORNWALL RD, OAKVILLE, ON, L6J 7T5
(905) 337-0993   SIC 3993

MEDIA RESOURCES INTERNATIONAL INC p 801
1387 CORNWALL RD, OAKVILLE, ON, L6J 7T5
(905) 337-0993   SIC 1799

MEDIA5 CORPORATION   p 1374
4229 RUE DE LA GARLOCK, SHER-BROOKE, QC, J1L 2C8
(819) 829-8749   SIC 6712

MEDIACO THE PRESENTATION COMPANY INC   p 193
4595 TILLICUM ST, BURNABY, BC, V5J 5K9
(604) 871-1000   SIC 7359

MEDIACOM CANADA   p 946
1 DUNDAS ST W SUITE 2800, TORONTO, ON, M5G 1Z3
(416) 342-6500   SIC 7319

MEDIAQMI INC   p 1211
612 RUE SAINT-JACQUES, MONTREAL, QC, H3C 4M8
(514) 380-6400   SIC 2711

MEDIAS TRANSCONTINENTAL   p 1200
See TRANSCONTINENTAL INC

MEDIAS TRANSCONTINENTAL INC p 433
430 TOPSAIL RD SUITE 86, ST. JOHN'S, NL, A1E 4N1
(709) 364-6300   SIC 2711

MEDIAS TRANSCONTINENTAL INC p 1039
165 PRINCE ST, CHARLOTTETOWN, PE, C1A 4R7
(902) 629-6000   SIC 2711

MEDIAS TRANSCONTINENTAL INC p 1206
1 PLACE VILLE MARIE BUREAU 3240, MONTREAL, QC, H3B 0G1
(514) 954-4000   SIC 2721

MEDIAS TRANSCONTINENTAL INC p 1206
1155 BOUL RENE-LEVESQUE O UNITE 100, MONTREAL, QC, H3B 4R1
(514) 287-1717   SIC 7389

MEDIAS TRANSCONTINENTAL S.E.N.C. p 467
255 GEORGE ST, SYDNEY, NS, B1P 1J7
(902) 564-5451   SIC 2711

MEDIAS TRANSCONTINENTAL S.E.N.C. p 1206
1 PLACE VILLE-MARIE BUREAU 3315, MONTREAL, QC, H3B 3N2
(514) 392-9000   SIC 2721

MEDIAS TRANSCONTINENTAL S.E.N.C. p 1276
2850 RUE JEAN-PERRIN, QUEBEC, QC, G2C 2C8
SIC 2752

MEDIATRIX   p 1374
See MEDIA5 CORPORATION

MEDICAGO INC   p 1273
1020 RTE DE L'EGLISE BUREAU 600, QUEBEC, QC, G1V 3V9
(418) 658-9393   SIC 8731

MEDICAGO R&D INC   p 1273
1020 RTE DE L'EGLISE BUREAU 600, QUEBEC, QC, G1V 3V9
(418) 658-9393   SIC 8731

MEDICAL COUNCIL OF CANADA   p 818
1021 THOMAS SPRATT PL, OTTAWA, ON, K1G 5L5
SIC 8733

MEDICAL FACILITIES CORPORATION p 927
45 ST CLAIR AVE W SUITE 200, TORONTO, ON, M4V 1K9
(416) 848-7380   SIC 8062

MEDICAL HALL (1978) LIMITED   p 450
135 COMMERCIAL ST, GLACE BAY, NS, B1A 3B9
(902) 849-6552   SIC 5912

MEDICAL HALL PHARMASAVE   p 450
See MEDICAL HALL (1978) LIMITED

MEDICAL IMAGING CONSULTANTS p 86
11010 101 ST NW SUITE 203, EDMON-TON, AB, T5H 4B9
(780) 426-1121   SIC 8011

MEDICAL IMAGING CONSULTANTS p 118
8215 112 ST NW SUITE 700, EDMONTON, AB, T6G 2C8
(780) 432-1121   SIC 8011

MEDICAL MART SUPPLIES LIMITED p 732
6200 CANTAY RD, MISSISSAUGA, ON, L5R 3Y9
(905) 624-6200   SIC 5047

MEDICAL MERCY CANADA SOCIETY p 24
1216 34 AVE NE SUITE 6, CALGARY, AB, T2E 6L9
(403) 717-0933   SIC 8099

MEDICAL PHARMACIES GROUP LIMITED p 672
300 TOWN CENTRE BLVD 4TH FL, MARKHAM, ON, L3R 5Z6
(866) 689-3169   SIC 5912

MEDICAL PHARMACY   p 844
See C H S PHARMACY LIMITED

MEDICAL PLASTIC DEVICES   p 1251
See MEDICAL PLASTIC DEVICES M.P.D. INC

MEDICAL PLASTIC DEVICES M.P.D. INC p 1251
161 AV ONEIDA, POINTE-CLAIRE, QC, H9R 1A9
(514) 694-9835   SIC 3841

MEDICAL SERVICES INCORPORATED p 1428
516 2ND AVE N, SASKATOON, SK, S7K 2C5
(306) 244-1192   SIC 6321

MEDICAL TECHNOLOGY (W.B.) INC p 662
1015 GREEN VALLEY RD, LONDON, ON, N6N 1E4
(519) 686-0028   SIC 3999

MEDICAL TECHNOLOGY (W.B.) INC p 662
1040 WILTON GROVE RD, LONDON, ON, N6N 1C7
(519) 686-0028   SIC 3999

MEDICALE ABBOTT CANADA, INC p 724
6975 CREDITVIEW RD UNIT 1, MISSIS-SAUGA, ON, L5N 8E9
(905) 812-8600   SIC 5047

MEDICANA INC   p 1330
2261 RUE GUENETTE, SAINT-LAURENT, QC, H4R 2E9
(514) 335-2677   SIC 5047

MEDICENTRES CANADA INC   p 98
10458 MAYFIELD RD NW SUITE 204, ED-MONTON, AB, T5P 4P4
(780) 483-7115   SIC 8011

MEDICHAIR   p 413
See APOLLO MEDICAL LTD

MEDICHAIR CALGARY   p 27
See 1253207 ALBERTA LTD

MEDICHAIR VICTORIA   p 334
See 443696 B.C. LTD

MEDICHAIR, DIV OF   p 597
See HURONIA/MED-E-OX LTD

MEDICINE HAT CATHOLIC BOARD OF ED-UCATION p 145
1251 1 AVE SW SUITE 20, MEDICINE HAT, AB, T1A 8B4
(403) 527-2292   SIC 8211

MEDICINE HAT CATHOLIC SEPARATE RE-GIONAL DIVISION NO.20 p 145
See MEDICINE HAT CATHOLIC BOARD OF EDUCATION

MEDICINE HAT CO-OP LIMITED   p 146
3030 13 AVE SE SUITE 100, MEDICINE HAT, AB, T1B 1E3
(403) 528-6604   SIC 5411

MEDICINE HAT EXHIBITION & STAMPEDE CO LTD p 146
2055 21 AVE SE, MEDICINE HAT, AB, T1A 7N1
(403) 527-1234   SIC 7999

MEDICINE HAT FAMILY YMCA   p 146
See MEDICINE HAT FAMILY YOUNG MEN'S CHRISTIAN ASSOCIATION

MEDICINE HAT FAMILY YOUNG MEN'S CHRISTIAN ASSOCIATION p 146
150 ASH AVE SE, MEDICINE HAT, AB, T1A 3A9
(403) 529-8115   SIC 8699

MEDICINE HAT HARLEY-DAVIDSON p 83
1923 2 AVE, DUNMORE, AB, T1B 0K3
(403) 527-9235   SIC 5571

MEDICINE HAT LODGE HOTEL   p 90
See MAYFIELD INVESTMENTS LTD

MEDICINE HAT LODGE HOTEL   p 146

See MAYFIELD INVESTMENTS LTD

MEDICINE HAT MALL   p 147
See SLEEPING BAY BUILDING CORP

MEDICINE HAT MALL   p 789
See MARKALTA DEVELOPMENTS LTD

MEDICINE HAT SCHOOL DISTRICT NO. 76 p 146
1201 DIVISION AVE N, MEDICINE HAT, AB, T1A 5Y8
(403) 527-6641   SIC 8211

MEDICINE HAT SCHOOL DISTRICT NO. 76 p 146
601 1 AVE SW, MEDICINE HAT, AB, T1A 4Y7
(403) 528-6700   SIC 8211

MEDICINE HAT WHOLESALE FOODS LTD p 146
702 INDUSTRIAL AVE SE, MEDICINE HAT, AB, T1A 3L8
(403) 527-4481   SIC 5141

MEDICINE HAT, CITY OF   p 146
364 KIPLING ST SE, MEDICINE HAT, AB, T1A 1Y4
(403) 529-8190   SIC 4925

MEDICINE SHOPPE PHARMACY   p 4
See FRESON MARKET LTD

MEDICOM GROUP INC   p 1248
2555 CH DE L'AVIATION, POINTE-CLAIRE, QC, H9P 2Z2
(514) 636-6262   SIC 3843

MEDICURE INC   p 391
1250 WAVERLEY ST SUITE 2, WINNIPEG, MB, R3T 6C6
(204) 487-7412   SIC 2834

MEDICUS   p 1168
See 2330-2029 QUEBEC INC

MEDIEVAL TIMES DINNER & TOURNA-MENT (TORONTO) INC p 991
10 DUFFERIN ST, TORONTO, ON, M6K 3C3
(416) 260-1170   SIC 5812

MEDIKE BRANDING SOLUTIONS INC p 665
216 MAIN ST W, MARKDALE, ON, N0C 1H0
(519) 986-2072   SIC 3199

MEDIPAC INTERNATIONAL INC   p 776
180 LESMILL RD, NORTH YORK, ON, M3B 2T5
(416) 441-7070   SIC 6321

MEDISCA PHARMACEUTIQUE INC p 1330
6090 BOUL HENRI-BOURASSA O, SAINT-LAURENT, QC, H4R 3A6
(800) 932-1039   SIC 5122

MEDISOLUTION (2009) INC   p 1180
110 BOUL CREMAZIE O BUREAU 1200, MONTREAL, QC, H2P 1B9
(514) 850-5000   SIC 5045

MEDISOLUTIONS INC   p 688
5935 AIRPORT RD SUITE 500, MISSIS-SAUGA, ON, L4V 1W5
(905) 673-7715   SIC 5045

MEDISYS CORPORATE HEALTH LP p 1198
500 RUE SHERBROOKE O BUREAU 1100, MONTREAL, QC, H3A 3C6
(514) 499-2778   SIC 8093

MEDISYSTEM PHARMACY LIMITED p 776
75 LESMILL RD SUITE 3, NORTH YORK, ON, M3B 2T8
(416) 441-2293   SIC 5122

MEDISYSTEM TECHNOLOGIES INC p 776
75 LESMILL RD UNIT 3, NORTH YORK, ON, M3B 2T8
(416) 441-2293   SIC 6712

MEDITERRANEAN BAKERY   p 793
See HANDI FOODS LTD

MEDITERRANEAN SHIPPING COMPANY (CANADA) INC p 1189
7 RUE SAINT-JACQUES, MONTREAL, QC, H2Y 1K9
(514) 844-3711   SIC 4731

MEDLEY, LE   p 1186
1170 RUE SAINT-DENIS, MONTREAL, QC, H2X 3J5

SIC 7389

MEDLINE CANADA, CORPORATION *p 684*
8690 ESCARPMENT WAY UNIT 3, MILTON, ON, L9T 0M1
(905) 636-2100 *SIC 5047*
MEDTECH *p 662*
See MEDICAL TECHNOLOGY (W.B.) INC
MEDTRONIC CRYOCATH LP *p 1251*
9000 RTE TRANSCANADIENNE, POINTE-CLAIRE, QC, H9R 5Z8
(514) 694-1212 *SIC 5047*
MEDTRONIC OF CANADA LTD *p 512*
99 HEREFORD ST, BRAMPTON, ON, L6Y 0R3
(905) 460-3800 *SIC 3845*
MEDWAY HIGH SCHOOL *p 479*
See THAMES VALLEY DISTRICT SCHOOL BOARD
MEDXL INC *p 1251*
285 AV LABROSSE, POINTE-CLAIRE, QC, H9R 1A3
(514) 695-7474 *SIC 5047*
MEEST CORPORATION INC *p 575*
97 SIX POINT RD, ETOBICOKE, ON, M8Z 2X3
(416) 236-2032 *SIC 4731*
MEESTER INSURANCE BROKERS, DIV OF *p 882*
See PEACOCK VANDERHOUT & VANDYK INSURANCE BROKERS LTD
MEETSU SOLUTIONS *p 708*
See 9778233 CANADA INC
MEG ENERGY CORP *p 54*
3 AVE SW SUITE 600 25TH FL, CALGARY, AB, T2P 0G5
(403) 770-0446 *SIC 1311*
MEGA BLUES *p 1128*
See JEAN BLEU INC, LE
MEGA BRANDS INC *p 1340*
4505 RUE HICKMORE, SAINT-LAURENT, QC, H4T 1K4
(514) 333-5555 *SIC 3944*
MEGA CENTRE KUBOTA *p 753*
See PRO-AB EQUIPEMENTS 2003 INC
MEGA CITY TILING *p 547*
See 1249762 ONTARIO INC
MEGA CRANES LTD *p 272*
6330 148 ST, SURREY, BC, V3S 3C4
(604) 599-4200 *SIC 7389*
MEGA FORMULE D'OCCASION *p 1285*
169 BOUL SAINTE-ANNE, RIMOUSKI, QC, G5M 1C3
(418) 723-5955 *SIC 5521*
MEGA GROUP INC *p 1428*
720 1ST AVE N, SASKATOON, SK, S7K 6R9
(306) 242-7366 *SIC 5064*
MEGA HAIR & CARE *p 272*
See MEGA HAIR GROUP INC, THE
MEGA HAIR GROUP INC, THE *p 272*
6448 148 ST SUITE 107, SURREY, BC, V3S 7G7
(604) 599-6800 *SIC 7231*
MEGA PLAS *p 754*
See MAGNA CLOSURES INC
MEGA PLEX *p 1379*
See CINEMAS GUZZO INC
MEGA URANIUM LTD *p 935*
211 YONGE ST SUITE 502, TORONTO, ON, M5B 1M4
(416) 643-7630 *SIC 1094*
MEGABURO INC *p 1045*
440 RUE COLLARD, ALMA, QC, G8B 1N2
(418) 668-4591 *SIC 5712*
MEGABURO INC *p 1383*
236 RUE NOTRE-DAME O, THETFORD MINES, QC, G6G 1J6
(418) 338-8808 *SIC 5712*
MEGAFORTUNE INTERNATIONAL INC *p 40*
3500 VARSITY DR NW UNIT 1608, CALGARY, AB, T2L 1Y3
(403) 261-8881 *SIC 6798*
MEGALEXIS COMMUNICATION INC *p 1198*

666 RUE SHERBROOKE O BUREAU 602, MONTREAL, QC, H3A 1E7
(514) 861-4999 *SIC 7389*
MEGANTIC METAL LTEE *p 1383*
1400 BOUL FRONTENAC E, THETFORD MINES, QC, G6G 6Z2
(418) 338-3188 *SIC 5051*
MEGAPNEU *p 1080*
See PNEUS UNIMAX LTEE
MEGAPOL CANADA *p 708*
833 MISSISSAUGA VALLEY BLVD, MISSISSAUGA, ON, L5A 1Z7
(416) 346-1554 *SIC 5044*
MEGASTAR ELECTRONIQUES INC. *p 1239*
5061 RUE D'AMIENS, MONTREAL-NORD, QC, H1G 3G2
(514) 329-0042 *SIC 5065*
MEGATECH ELECTRO *p 1112*
See KONGSBERG INC
MEGATEL *p 1340*
See MEGATEL INFORMATION SYSTEMS INC
MEGATEL INFORMATION SYSTEMS INC *p 1340*
3930 RUE GRIFFITH, SAINT-LAURENT, QC, H4T 1A7
(514) 333-0717 *SIC 5084*
MEGLAB ELECTRONIQUE INC *p 1391*
281 19E RUE, VAL-D'OR, QC, J9P 0L7
(819) 824-7710 *SIC 7629*
MEGLOBAL CANADA INC *p 130*
BAG 16 HWY 15, FORT SASKATCHEWAN, AB, T8L 2P4
(780) 992-4250 *SIC 5169*
MEGLOBAL CANADA INC *p 154*
HWY 597 PRENTISS RD, RED DEER, AB, T4N 6N1
(403) 885-7000 *SIC 5169*
MEGLOBAL CANADA ULC *p 130*
HWY 15 BAG 16, FORT SASKATCHEWAN, AB, T8L 2P4
(877) 885-7237 *SIC 2819*
MEGLOBAL CANADA ULC *p 154*
HWY 597 & PRENTISS RD, RED DEER, AB, T4N 6N1
SIC 2819
MEGSON FITZPATRICK INC *p 333*
3561 SHELBOURNE ST, VICTORIA, BC, V8P 4G8
(250) 595-5212 *SIC 6411*
MEGTEC TURBOSONIC INC *p 1008*
550 PARKSIDE DR UNIT A14, WATERLOO, ON, N2L 5V4
(519) 885-5513 *SIC 5084*
MEGTEC TURBOSONIC TECHNOLOGIES INC *p 1008*
550 PARKSIDE DR UNIT A14, WATERLOO, ON, N2L 5V4
(519) 885-5513 *SIC 5084*
MEI *p 178*
See MENNONITE EDUCATIONAL INSTITUTE SOCIETY
MEI MILLER ENTERPRISES INC *p 36*
7523 FLINT RD SE, CALGARY, AB, T2H 1G3
SIC 5085
MEIDL HONDA *p 1425*
See 591226 SASKATCHEWAN LTD
MEIER INSURANCE AGENCIES LTD *p 237*
602 TWELFTH ST, NEW WESTMINSTER, BC, V3M 4J2
(604) 777-9999 *SIC 6411*
MEIKLE AUTOMATION INC *p 637*
975 BLEAMS RD UNIT 5-10, KITCHENER, ON, N2E 3Z5
(519) 896-0800 *SIC 3599*
MEILLEUR, LE *p 1160*
See LEMIEUX, JACQUES (GROSSISTE) INC
MEILLEURES MARQUES *p 1050*
See ROTISSERIES ST-HUBERT LTEE, LES
MEILLEURES MARQUES LTEE *p 1062*
1755 BOUL LIONEL-BERTRAND, BOIS-BRIAND, QC, J7H 1N8

(450) 435-0674 *SIC 5142*
MEINHARDT FINE FOODS INC *p 319*
3002 GRANVILLE ST, VANCOUVER, BC, V6H 3J8
(604) 732-4405 *SIC 5411*
MEJURI INC *p 991*
18 MOWAT AVE UNIT C, TORONTO, ON, M6K 3E8
(416) 731-2600 *SIC 5944*
MEJURI INC *p 991*
18 MOWAT AVE, TORONTO, ON, M6K 3E8
(416) 731-2600 *SIC 5632*
MELANGE DES BOIS *p 1336*
See TOOTSI IMPEX INC
MELBOURNE FARM AUTOMATION LTD *p 681*
6687 LONGWOODS RD, MELBOURNE, ON, N0L 1T0
(519) 289-5256 *SIC 5083*
MELBURN TRUCK LINES CORP *p 714*
2215 ROYAL WINDSOR DR, MISSISSAUGA, ON, L5J 1K5
(905) 823-7800 *SIC 4213*
MELCHERS CONSTRUCTION LIMITED *p 643*
22662 KOMOKA RD, KOMOKA, ON, N0L 1R0
(519) 473-4149 *SIC 1521*
MELCO CAPITAL INC *p 1379*
1000 MONTEE DES PIONNIERS BUREAU 212, TERREBONNE, QC, J6V 1S8
(514) 564-7600 *SIC 7361*
MELCOR DEVELOPMENTS LTD *p 90*
10310 JASPER AVE NW SUITE 900, EDMONTON, AB, T5J 1Y8
(780) 423-6931 *SIC 6553*
MELCOR REAL ESTATE INVESTMENT TRUST *p 90*
10310 JASPER AVE SUITE 900, EDMONTON, AB, T5J 1Y8
(780) 423-6931 *SIC 6722*
MELDRUM THE MOVER INC *p 1222*
6645 RUE SHERBROOKE O, MONTREAL, QC, H4B 1N4
(514) 400-0182 *SIC 4213*
MELET PLASTICS INC *p 366*
34 DE BAETS ST, WINNIPEG, MB, R2J 3S9
(204) 667-6635 *SIC 3089*
MELITA HEALTH CENTER *p 352*
See PRAIRIE MOUNTAIN HEALTH
MELITRON CORPORATION *p 604*
404 SILVERCREEK PKWY N, GUELPH, ON, N1H 1E8
(519) 763-6660 *SIC 3499*
MELLOUL-BLAMEY CONSTRUCTION INC *p 1010*
700 RUPERT ST, WATERLOO, ON, N2V 2B5
(519) 886-8850 *SIC 1542*
MELLOUL-BLAMEY ENTERPRISES INC *p 1010*
700 RUPERT ST UNIT A, WATERLOO, ON, N2V 2B5
(519) 886-8850 *SIC 6712*
MELLOW WALK FOOTWEAR INC *p 791*
17 MILFORD AVE, NORTH YORK, ON, M6M 2W1
(416) 241-1312 *SIC 3143*
MELLOY INDUSTRIAL SERVICES INC *p 149*
2305 5 ST, NISKU, AB, T9E 7X1
(780) 955-8500 *SIC 3569*
MELLOY MANAGEMENT *p 969*
See FOGLER, RUBINOFF LLP
MELLOY MANAGEMENT LIMITED *p 970*
77 KING ST W SUITE 3000, TORONTO, ON, M5K 1G8
(416) 864-9700 *SIC 8741*
MELMART DISTRIBUTORS INC *p 688*
6100 INDIAN LINE, MISSISSAUGA, ON, L4V 1G5
(905) 677-7600 *SIC 5023*
MELNICK MOTORS LTD *p 345*
1012 PARK AVE, BEAUSEJOUR, MB, R0E

0C0
(204) 268-1514 *SIC 5511*
MELO, J.S. INC *p 631*
285 KING ST E, KINGSTON, ON, K7L 3B1
(613) 544-4434 *SIC 7011*
MELOCHE MONNEX ASSURANCE ET SERVICES FINANCIERS INC *p 90*
See MELOCHE MONNEX FINANCIAL SERVICES INC
MELOCHE MONNEX FINANCIAL SERVICES INC *p 90*
10115 100A ST NW SUITE 600, EDMONTON, AB, T5J 2W2
(780) 429-1112 *SIC 6411*
MELOCHE MONNEX FINANCIAL SERVICES INC *p 672*
101 MCNABB ST, MARKHAM, ON, L3R 4H8
(416) 484-1112 *SIC 6411*
MELOCHE MONNEX INC *p 457*
6940 MUMFORD RD SUITE 301, HALIFAX, NS, B3L 0B7
(902) 420-1112 *SIC 6331*
MELOCHE MONNEX INC *p 1180*
50 BOUL CREMAZIE O BUREAU 1200, MONTREAL, QC, H2P 1B6
(514) 382-6060 *SIC 6712*
MELOCHE'S NO FRILLS *p 477*
See 1144257 ONTARIO LIMITED
MELOCHE, DIVISION DE SINTRA *p 1118*
See SINTRA INC
MELROSE CAFE & BAR *p 66*
See 599515 ALBERTA LTD
MELROSE DRUGS LTD *p 3*
209 CENTRE AVE SW UNIT 100, AIRDRIE, AB, T4B 3L8
(403) 948-0010 *SIC 5912*
MELTWATER NEWS CANADA INC *p 964*
25 YORK ST SUITE 1200, TORONTO, ON, M5J 2V5
(416) 641-4902 *SIC 7372*
MELVILLE LODGE LIMITED PARTNERSHIP *p 458*
50 SHOREHAM LANE, HALIFAX, NS, B3P 2R3
(902) 479-1030 *SIC 8051*
MELVIN HARTMAN ENTERPRISES LIMITED *p 818*
3150 HAWTHORNE RD SUITE B-1, OTTAWA, ON, K1G 5H5
(613) 247-0099 *SIC 5148*
MEMBER OF TTM TECHNOLOGIES *p 914*
See VIASYSTEMS TORONTO INC
MEMME CONSTRUCTION *p 697*
See MEMME EXCAVATION COMPANY LIMITED
MEMME EXCAVATION COMPANY LIMITED *p 697*
1315 SHAWSON DR, MISSISSAUGA, ON, L4W 1C4
(905) 564-7972 *SIC 1623*
MEMORIAL UNIVERSITY OF NEWFOUNDLAND *p 430*
234 ELIZABETH AVE, ST. JOHN'S, NL, A1B 3Y1
(709) 864-8000 *SIC 8231*
MEMORIAL UNIVERSITY OF NEWFOUNDLAND *p 432*
155 RIDGE ROAD, ST. JOHN'S, NL, A1C 5R3
(709) 778-0483 *SIC 8222*
MEMORIAL UNIVERSITY OF NEWFOUNDLAND *p 432*
208 ELIZABETH AVE, ST. JOHN'S, NL, A1C 5S7
(709) 637-6298 *SIC 8221*
MEMORIAL UNIVERSITY OF NEWFOUNDLAND STUDENTS UNION *p*

432
1 ARCTIC PL, ST. JOHN'S, NL, A1C 5S7
SIC 8641
MEMORY EXPRESS INC *p 9*
3333 34 AVE NE, CALGARY, AB, T1Y 6H2
(403) 398-4533 *SIC* 5734
MEMOTEC INC *p 1335*
7755 BOUL HENRI-BOURASSA O, SAINT-LAURENT, QC, H4S 1P7
(514) 738-4781 *SIC* 4899
MEMTRONIK INNOVATIONS INC *p 1170*
8648 BOUL PIE-IX, MONTREAL, QC, H1Z 4G2
(514) 374-1010 *SIC* 3613
MEN'S DEN, THE *p 171*
4902 50 AVE, VERMILION, AB, T9X 1A4
(780) 581-0100 *SIC* 5136
MENAGEZ-VOUS LES FORGES *p 1388*
See MENAGEZ-VOUS TERRITOIRE LES FORGES
MENAGEZ-VOUS TERRITOIRE LES FORGES *p 1388*
749 BOUL DU SAINT-MAURICE, TROIS-RIVIERES, QC, G9A 3P5
SIC 8699
MENARD CANADA INC *p 1066*
1590 RUE AMPERE BUREAU 202, BOUCHERVILLE, QC, J4B 7L4
(450) 449-2633 *SIC* 1794
MENARD, J. R. LIMITED *p 888*
5 RANGER AVE, ST ISIDORE, ON, K0C 2B0
(613) 524-2885 *SIC* 5039
MENASHA PACKAGING CANADA L.P. *p 499*
35 PRECIDIO CRT, BRAMPTON, ON, L6S 6B7
(905) 792-7092 *SIC* 2653
MENASHA PACKAGING CANADA L.P. *p 732*
5875 CHEDWORTH WAY, MISSISSAUGA, ON, L5R 3L9
(905) 507-3042 *SIC* 2653
MENDOCINO CLOTHING COMPANY LTD *p 989*
496 GILBERT AVE, TORONTO, ON, M6E 4X5
(416) 847-0590 *SIC* 5621
MENDRINOS, B. DRUGS LTD *p 659*
467 WHARNCLIFFE RD S, LONDON, ON, N6J 2M8
(519) 672-4970 *SIC* 5912
MENKES CONSTRUCTION LIMITED *p 772*
4711 YONGE ST SUITE 1400, NORTH YORK, ON, M2N 7E4
(416) 491-2222 *SIC* 6553
MENKES HOLDINGS INC *p 772*
4711 YONGE ST SUITE 1400, NORTH YORK, ON, M2N 7E4
(416) 491-2222 *SIC* 6553
MENKES PROPERTY MANAGEMENT SERVICES LTD *p 772*
4711 YONGE ST SUITE 1400, NORTH YORK, ON, M2N 7E4
(416) 491-2222 *SIC* 6553
MENNO HOME *p 175*
See MENNONITE BENEVOLENT SOCIETY
MENNO HOME FOR THE AGED *p 350*
235 PARK ST, GRUNTHAL, MB, R0A 0R0
(204) 434-6496 *SIC* 8361
MENNO TRAVEL SERVICE CANADA LTD *p 177*
GD, ABBOTSFORD, BC, V2T 0A1
(604) 853-0751 *SIC* 4724
MENNONITE BENEVOLENT SOCIETY *p 175*
32910 BRUNDIGE AVE SUITE 257, ABBOTSFORD, BC, V2S 1N2
(604) 853-2411 *SIC* 8059
MENNONITE BRETHREN CHURCH OF MANITOBA, THE *p 388*
1310 TAYLOR AVE, WINNIPEG, MB, R3M 3Z6

MENNONITE CENTRAL COMMITTEE CANADA *p 175*
2776 BOURQUIN CRES W SUITE 103, ABBOTSFORD, BC, V2S 6A4
(604) 850-6608 *SIC* 8399
MENNONITE CENTRAL COMMITTEE CANADA *p 347*
414 PACIFIC AVE, BRANDON, MB, R7A 0H5
(204) 727-1162 *SIC* 5932
MENNONITE CENTRAL COMMITTEE CANADA *p 391*
134 PLAZA DR, WINNIPEG, MB, R3T 5K9
(204) 261-6381 *SIC* 8399
MENNONITE ECONOMIC DEVELOPMENT ASSOCIATES OF CANADA *p 1010*
155 FROBISHER DR SUITE I-106, WATERLOO, ON, N2V 2E1
(519) 725-1633 *SIC* 8699
MENNONITE EDUCATIONAL INSTITUTE SOCIETY *p 178*
4081 CLEARBROOK RD, ABBOTSFORD, BC, V4X 2M8
(604) 859-3700 *SIC* 8211
MENNONITE INTERMEDIATE CARE HOME SOCIETY OF RICHMOND *p 261*
11331 MELLIS DR, RICHMOND, BC, V6X 1L8
(604) 278-1296 *SIC* 8051
MENNONITE MUTUAL INSURANCE CO. (ALBERTA) LTD *p 9*
2946 32 ST NE SUITE 300, CALGARY, AB, T1Y 6J7
(403) 275-6996 *SIC* 6331
MENNONITE NURSING HOMES INCORPORATED *p 1423*
GD, ROSTHERN, SK, S0K 3R0
(306) 232-4861 *SIC* 8051
MENNONITE TRUST LTD *p 1437*
3005 CENTRAL AVE, WALDHEIM, SK, S0K 4R0
(306) 945-2080 *SIC* 6733
MENTAL HEALTH COMMISSION OF CANADA *p 17*
110 QUARRY PARK BLVD SE SUITE 320, CALGARY, AB, T2C 3G3
(403) 255-5808 *SIC* 8699
MENTAL HEALTH SERVICES *p 154*
4733 49 ST, RED DEER, AB, T4N 1T6
(403) 340-5466 *SIC* 8093
MENTHES RITO LTEE, LES *p 1388*
1055 RUE LA VERENDRYE, TROIS-RIVIERES, QC, G9A 2T1
(819) 379-1449 *SIC* 5145
MENTHOLATUM COMPANY OF CANADA LIMITED, THE *p 887*
45 HANNOVER DR UNIT 2, ST CATHARINES, ON, L2W 1A3
(905) 688-1665 *SIC* 5122
MENTOR ENGINEERING INC *p 9*
2175 29 ST NE SUITE 10, CALGARY, AB, T1Y 7H8
(403) 777-3760 *SIC* 3669
MENU FOODS INCOME FUND *p 724*
8 FALCONER DR UNIT 1, MISSISSAUGA, ON, L5N 1B1
(905) 826-3870 *SIC* 6722
MENU-MER LTEE *p 1102*
153 BOUL RENARD E, GASPE, QC, G4X 5K9
(418) 269-7714 *SIC* 5146
MENUISERIE DES PINS LTEE *p 1243*
3150 CH ROYAL, NOTRE-DAME-DES-PINS, QC, G0M 1K0
(418) 774-3324 *SIC* 2431
MENUISEROX INC *p 1055*
159 181E RUE, BEAUCEVILLE, QC, G5X 2S9
(418) 774-9019 *SIC* 2431
MENZIES AVIATION (CANADA) LTD *p 24*
175 AERO WAY NE UNIT 130, CALGARY, AB, T2E 6K2

(403) 250-2033 *SIC* 4111
MENZIES AVIATION FUELING CANADA LIMITED *p 586*
10 CARLSON CT UNIT 301, ETOBICOKE, ON, M9W 6A2
(647) 798-3890 *SIC* 5172
MENZIES CHRYSLER *p 1013*
See AJAX JEEP EAGLE LTD
MEP TECHNOLOGIES INC *p 1234*
3100 RUE PEUGEOT, MONTREAL, QC, H7L 5C6
(450) 682-0804 *SIC* 3444
MEQUIPCO LTD *p 71*
5126 126 AVE SE UNIT 101, CALGARY, AB, T2Z 0H2
(403) 259-8333 *SIC* 3589
MERANGUE INTERNATIONAL LIMITED *p 678*
55 TRAVAIL RD UNIT 2, MARKHAM, ON, L3S 3J1
(905) 209-0955 *SIC* 5112
MERCANA FURNITURE & DECOR LTD *p 279*
3250 189 ST, SURREY, BC, V3Z 1A7
(604) 596-1668 *SIC* 5023
MERCANTILE EXCHANGE CORPORATION *p 939*
8 KING ST E 14TH FL, TORONTO, ON, M5C 1B5
(416) 368-3680 *SIC* 6099
MERCATO INTERNATIONAL LTD *p 67*
2224 4 ST SW, CALGARY, AB, T2S 1W9
(403) 263-5535 *SIC* 5812
MERCATUS TECHNOLOGIES INC *p 982*
545 KING ST W SUITE 500, TORONTO, ON, M5V 1M1
(416) 603-3406 *SIC* 7371
MERCEDES BENZ *p 1015*
See STAR ONE MOTOR CO
MERCEDES BENZ OF REGINA *p 1421*
See REGINA SPORT & IMPORT AUTOMOTIVE GROUP LTD
MERCEDES BENZ PETERBOROUGH INC *p 841*
995 CRAWFORD DR, PETERBOROUGH, ON, K9J 3X1
(705) 742-9000 *SIC* 5511
MERCEDES BENZ RIVE-SUD *p 1112*
See 8421722 CANADA INC
MERCEDES BENZ WINNIPEG *p 389*
See PINNACLE AUTO SALES
MERCEDES CORP *p 888*
1386 KING ST N, ST JACOBS, ON, N0B 2N0
(519) 664-2293 *SIC* 5712
MERCEDES TEXTILES LIMITED *p 1335*
5838 RUE CYPIHOT, SAINT-LAURENT, QC, H4S 1Y5
(514) 335-4337 *SIC* 3429
MERCEDES TROIS-RIVIERES *p 1389*
See AUTOMOBILES VIEILLES FORGES LTEE
MERCEDES-BENZ BLAINVILLE *p 1152*
See HAMEL AUTOS DE MIRABEL INC
MERCEDES-BENZ BURLINGTON *p 529*
See QUANTUM AUTOMOTIVE GROUP INCORPORATED
MERCEDES-BENZ CANADA INC *p 918*
98 VANDERHOOF AVE, TORONTO, ON, M4G 4C9
(416) 425-3550 *SIC* 5012
MERCEDES-BENZ ET SMART *p 1110*
See 9106-3644 QUEBEC INC
MERCEDES-BENZ FINANCIAL SERVICES CANADA CORPORATION *p 697*
2680 MATHESON BLVD E SUITE 500, MISSISSAUGA, ON, L4W 0A5
(800) 532-7362 *SIC* 8741
MERCEDES-BENZ HERITAGE VALLEY *p 124*
See ERICKSEN M-B LTD
MERCEDES-BENZ LAVAL *p 1363*
See AUTO CLASSIQUE DE LAVAL INC
MERCEDES-BENZ LONDON *p 656*

See 2275510 ONTARIO LTD
MERCEDES-BENZ SURREY *p 270*
15508 104 AVE, SURREY, BC, V3R 1N8
(604) 581-7662 *SIC* 5511
MERCEDES-BENZ WINDSOR *p 1018*
See OVERSEAS MOTORS (WINDSOR) INC
MERCER *p 964*
See MERCER (CANADA) LIMITED
MERCER (CANADA) LIMITED *p 54*
222 3 AVE SW SUITE 1200, CALGARY, AB, T2P 0B4
(403) 269-4945 *SIC* 8999
MERCER (CANADA) LIMITED *p 307*
550 BURRARD ST SUITE 900, VANCOUVER, BC, V6C 3S8
(604) 683-6761 *SIC* 8999
MERCER (CANADA) LIMITED *p 964*
70 UNIVERSITY AVE SUITE 900, TORONTO, ON, M5J 2M4
(416) 868-2000 *SIC* 8742
MERCER (CANADA) LIMITED *p 964*
120 BREMNER BLVD SUITE 800, TORONTO, ON, M5J 0A8
(416) 868-2000 *SIC* 6411
MERCER (CANADA) LIMITED *p 1198*
1981 AV MCGILL COLLEGE BUREAU 800, MONTREAL, QC, H3A 3T5
(514) 285-1802 *SIC* 8999
MERCER CELGAR PULP LTD *p 195*
1921 ARROW LAKES DR, CASTLEGAR, BC, V1N 3H9
(250) 365-7211 *SIC* 2611
MERCER INTERNATIONAL INC *p 307*
700 PENDER ST W SUITE 1120, VANCOUVER, BC, V6C 1G8
(604) 684-1099 *SIC* 2611
MERCER INVESTMENT CONSULTING *p 1198*
See MERCER (CANADA) LIMITED
MERCER PEACE RIVER PULP LTD *p 307*
510 BURRARD ST SUITE 700, VANCOUVER, BC, V6C 3A8
(604) 684-4326 *SIC* 2611
MERCER TRUCKING *p 741*
See MERCER, GARRY TRUCKING INC
MERCER'S MARINE EQUIPMENT *p 422*
See MERCER'S MARINE EQUIPMENT LIMITED
MERCER'S MARINE EQUIPMENT LIMITED *p 422*
210 MARINE DR, CLARENVILLE, NL, A5A 1L8
(709) 466-7430 *SIC* 5088
MERCER, GARRY TRUCKING INC *p 741*
1140 MID-WAY BLVD, MISSISSAUGA, ON, L5T 2C1
(905) 670-4721 *SIC* 4213
MERCHANT'S EXPRESS LIMITED *p 244*
19981 RICHARDSON RD, PITT MEADOWS, BC, V3Y 1Z1
(604) 460-1971 *SIC* 4212
MERCHANTS PAPER COMPANY WINDSOR LIMITED *p 1023*
975 CRAWFORD AVE, WINDSOR, ON, N9A 5C8
(519) 977-9977 *SIC* 5113
MERCI ALIMENTS EN VRAC *p 1239*
See DIMA IMPORT-EXPORT INC
MERCIER, INDUSTRIES EN MECANIQUE LTEE *p 1115*
2035 RUE FAY, JONQUIERE, QC, G7S 2N5
(418) 548-7141 *SIC* 3599
MERCK *p 1118*
See SCHERING-PLOUGH CANADA INC
MERCK CANADA INC *p 1117*
16750 RTE TRANSCANADIENNE, KIRKLAND, QC, H9H 4M7
(514) 428-7920 *SIC* 5122
MERCK SHARP & DOHME *p 1117*
See MERCK CANADA INC
MERCOR LIGHTING *p 555*
See MERCURY LIGHTING LIMITED

MERCOR LIGHTING GROUP INC, THE *p 555*
71 ORTONA CRT UNIT 1, CONCORD, ON, L4K 3M2
(905) 738-6161 *SIC 5063*
MERCURY FILMWORKS EAST INC *p 749*
53 AURIGA DR, NEPEAN, ON, K2E 8C3
(613) 482-1814 *SIC 7812*
MERCURY LIGHTING *p 555*
See MERCOR LIGHTING GROUP INC, THE
MERCURY LIGHTING LIMITED *p 555*
71 ORTONA CRT UNIT 1, CONCORD, ON, L4K 3M2
(905) 738-6161 *SIC 5063*
MERCURY MARINE LIMITED *p 684*
8698 ESCARPMENT WAY, MILTON, ON, L9T 0M1
(905) 567-6372 *SIC 5091*
MERCURY PLASTICS OF CANADA INC *p 206*
880 CLIVEDEN AVE, DELTA, BC, V3M 5R5
(604) 525-1061 *SIC 3081*
MERECO *p 1305*
See USINE TAC TIC INC, L'
MERECO *p 1305*
See L'USINE TAC TIC INC
MERFIN PLASTICS *p 271*
See GLOBAL PLASTICS
MERGE HEALTHCARE *p 688*
See MERGE HEALTHCARE CANADA CORP
MERGE HEALTHCARE CANADA CORP *p 688*
6303 AIRPORT RD SUITE 500, MISSISSAUGA, ON, L4V 1R8
(905) 672-2100 *SIC 7371*
MERIAL CANADA INC *p 1053*
20000 AV CLARK-GRAHAM, BAIE-D'URFE, QC, H9X 4B6
(514) 457-1555 *SIC 2834*
MERIDIAN BRICK CANADA LTD *p 530*
5155 DUNDAS ST RR 1, BURLINGTON, ON, L7R 3X4
(800) 263-6229 *SIC 3251*
MERIDIAN BRICK CANADA LTD *p 530*
5155 DUNDAS ST W, BURLINGTON, ON, L7R 3Y2
(905) 335-3401 *SIC 3251*
MERIDIAN CREDIT UNION LIMITED *p 572*
3280 BLOOR ST W, ETOBICOKE, ON, M8X 2X3
(416) 597-4400 *SIC 6062*
MERIDIAN CREDIT UNION LIMITED *p 887*
75 CORPORATE PARK DR SUITE 1, ST CATHARINES, ON, L2S 3W3
(905) 937-4222 *SIC 6062*
MERIDIAN DEVELOPMENT CORP *p 1428*
450 2ND AVE N UNIT 100, SASKATOON, SK, S7K 2C3
(306) 384-0431 *SIC 1522*
MERIDIAN LIGHTWEIGHT TECHNOLOGIES HOLDINGS INC *p 897*
25 MCNAB ST, STRATHROY, ON, N7G 4H6
(519) 246-9600 *SIC 3364*
MERIDIAN LIGHTWEIGHT TECHNOLOGIES INC *p 897*
155 HIGH ST E, STRATHROY, ON, N7G 1H4
(519) 245-4040 *SIC 3364*
MERIDIAN LIGHTWEIGHT TECHNOLOGIES INC *p 897*
800 WRIGHT ST, STRATHROY, ON, N7G 4H7
(519) 246-9620 *SIC 3369*
MERIDIAN LIGHTWEIGHT TECHNOLOGIES INC *p 897*
25 MCNAB ST, STRATHROY, ON, N7G 4H6
(519) 246-9600 *SIC 3364*
MERIDIAN MANUFACTURING INC *p 78*

4232 38 ST, CAMROSE, AB, T4V 4B2
(780) 672-4516 *SIC 3545*
MERIDIAN MANUFACTURING INC *p 141*
3125 24 AVE N, LETHBRIDGE, AB, T1H 5G2
(403) 320-7070 *SIC 3545*
MERIDIAN MANUFACTURING INC *p 1418*
2800 PASQUA ST, REGINA, SK, S4P 2Z4
(306) 545-4044 *SIC 3545*
MERIDIAN ONECAP *p 190*
See MERIDIAN ONECAP CREDIT CORP
MERIDIAN ONECAP CREDIT CORP *p 190*
4710 KINGSWAY SUITE 1500, BURNABY, BC, V5H 4M2
(604) 646-2247 *SIC 6159*
MERIDIAN SURVEYS LTD *p 1428*
3111 MILLAR AVE SUITE 1, SASKATOON, SK, S7K 6N3
(306) 934-1818 *SIC 8713*
MERIDICAN INCENTIVE CONSULTANTS *p 672*
See MERIDICAN TRAVEL INC
MERIDICAN TRAVEL INC *p 672*
16 ESNA PARK DR SUITE 103, MARKHAM, ON, L3R 5X1
(905) 477-7700 *SIC 4724*
MERIDIEN MARITIME REPARATION *p 1150*
See 6318703 CANADA INC
MERIDIEN VERSAILLES- MONTREAL, LE *p 1214*
See 9145-1971 QUEBEC INC
MERIT CONTRACTORS NIAGARA *p 887*
235 MARTINDALE RD SUITE 3, ST CATHARINES, ON, L2W 1A5
(905) 641-2374 *SIC 1542*
MERIT GLASS LTD *p 606*
61 ARROW RD, GUELPH, ON, N1K 1S8
(519) 822-7470 *SIC 1793*
MERIT INSURANCE BROKERS INC *p 765*
111 GORDON BAKER RD SUITE 100, NORTH YORK, ON, M2H 3R1
(416) 497-5556 *SIC 6411*
MERIT PRECISION MOULDING LIMITED *p 841*
2035 FISHER DR, PETERBOROUGH, ON, K9J 6X6
(705) 742-4209 *SIC 3089*
MERIT TRAVEL GROUP INC *p 982*
111 PETER ST SUITE 200, TORONTO, ON, M5V 2H1
(416) 364-3775 *SIC 4724*
MERIT VACATIONS *p 982*
See MERIT TRAVEL GROUP INC
MERITAS CARE CORPORATION *p 1023*
567 VICTORIA AVE, WINDSOR, ON, N9A 4N1
(519) 254-1141 *SIC 8741*
MERITCO INDUSTRIES LTD *p 540*
2675 REID SIDE RD, CAMPBELLVILLE, ON, L0P 1B0
(905) 854-2228 *SIC 5031*
MERITIGROUP LTD *p 672*
7100 WOODBINE AVE SUITE 218, MARKHAM, ON, L3R 5J2
(905) 489-8299 *SIC 6211*
MERITOR AFTERMARKET CANADA INC *p 511*
60 GILLINGHAM DR SUITE 501, BRAMPTON, ON, L6X 0Z9
(905) 454-7070 *SIC 3714*
MERIVALE HIGH SCHOOL *p 750*
See OTTAWA-CARLETON DISTRICT SCHOOL BOARD
MERKLEY SUPPLY LIMITED *p 828*
100 BAYVIEW RD, OTTAWA, ON, K1Y 4L6
(613) 728-2693 *SIC 1542*
MERKS FARMS LIMITED *p 439*
2250 GASPEREAU RIVER RD, AVONPORT, NS, B0P 1B0
(902) 542-4200 *SIC 4213*
MERLIN ENTERTAINMENTS (CANADA) INC *p 555*
1 BASS PRO MILLS DR, CONCORD, ON, L4K 5W4

(905) 761-7066 *SIC 7999*
MERLIN FORD LINCOLN INC *p 1431*
3750 IDYLWYLD DR N, SASKATOON, SK, S7L 6G3
(306) 931-6611 *SIC 5511*
MERLIN MOTORS INC *p 1431*
3750 IDYLWYLD DR N SUITE 107, SASKATOON, SK, S7L 6G3
(306) 931-6611 *SIC 5511*
MERLIN PLASTICS ALBERTA INC *p 36*
616 58 AVE SE, CALGARY, AB, T2H 0P8
(403) 259-6637 *SIC 4953*
MERMAID MARINE PRODUCTS *p 1040*
See 120601 CANADA INC
MEROM FARMS LTD *p 178*
2244 LEFEUVRE RD, ABBOTSFORD, BC, V4X 1C6
(604) 856-3511 *SIC 0181*
MERRETT'S PHARMACY *p 862*
See ORANO LIMITED
MERRIAM SCHOOL OF MUSIC, THE *p 796*
See 1057206 ONTARIO LTD
MERRILL CORPORATION CANADA *p 939*
3000-1 ADELAIDE ST E, TORONTO, ON, M5C 2V9
(416) 214-2448 *SIC 2752*
MERRILL LYNCH & CO., CANADA LTD *p 964*
181 BAY ST SUITE 400, TORONTO, ON, M5J 2V8
(416) 369-7400 *SIC 6211*
MERRILL LYNCH CANADA INC *p 964*
181 BAY ST SUITE 400, TORONTO, ON, M5J 2V8
(416) 369-7400 *SIC 6211*
MERRILL LYNCH CANADA INC *p 1206*
1250 BOUL RENE-LEVESQUE O BUREAU 3100, MONTREAL, QC, H3B 4W8
(514) 846-1050 *SIC 6211*
MERRILL LYNCH FUTURES *p 964*
See MERRILL LYNCH CANADA INC
MERRITHEW CORPORATION *p 924*
2200 YONGE ST SUITE 500, TORONTO, ON, M4S 2C6
(416) 482-4050 *SIC 5091*
MERRITHEW INTERNATIONAL INC *p 924*
2200 YONGE ST SUITE 500, TORONTO, ON, M4S 2C6
(416) 482-4050 *SIC 8299*
MERRY MAIDS *p 700*
See SERVICEMASTER OF CANADA LIMITED
MERSEN CANADA DN LTD *p 571*
496 EVANS AVE, ETOBICOKE, ON, M8W 2T7
(416) 251-2334 *SIC 3624*
MERSEN CANADA TORONTO INC *p 741*
6200 KESTREL RD, MISSISSAUGA, ON, L5T 1Z1
(416) 252-9371 *SIC 3679*
MERSEN CANADA TORONTO INC *p 741*
6220 KESTREL RD, MISSISSAUGA, ON, L5T 1Y9
(647) 846-8684 *SIC 3679*
MERSEN ELECTRICAL POWER *p 741*
See MERSEN CANADA TORONTO INC
MERSEY SEAFOODS LIMITED *p 460*
26 BRISTOL AVE, LIVERPOOL, NS, B0T 1K0
(902) 354-3467 *SIC 5146*
MERTIN CHEVROLET CADILLAC PONTIAC BUICK GMC LTD *p 196*
45930 AIRPORT RD, CHILLIWACK, BC, V2P 1A2
(604) 795-9104 *SIC 5511*
MERTIN G M LEASING *p 196*
See MERTIN CHEVROLET CADILLAC PONTIAC BUICK GMC LTD
MERTIN HYUNDAI *p 196*
45753 YALE RD, CHILLIWACK, BC, V2P 2N5
(604) 702-1000 *SIC 5511*
MERTIN NISSAN *p 196*

8287 YOUNG RD, CHILLIWACK, BC, V2P 4N8
(604) 792-8218 *SIC 5511*
MERUS LABS INTERNATIONAL INC *p 970*
100 WELLINGTON ST W SUITE 2110, TORONTO, ON, M5K 1H1
(905) 726-0995 *SIC 2834*
MERVYN MOTORS LIMITED *p 222*
1717 HARVEY AVE, KELOWNA, BC, V1Y 6G3
(250) 860-6278 *SIC 5511*
MERZ PHARMA CANADA LTD *p 523*
5515 NORTH SERVICE RD SUITE 202, BURLINGTON, ON, L7L 6G4
(905) 315-1193 *SIC 5122*
MESOTEC INC *p 1374*
4705 BOUL DE PORTLAND, SHERBROOKE, QC, J1L 0H3
(819) 822-2777 *SIC 3728*
MESSAGEPOINT INC *p 965*
207 QUEENS QUAY W SUITE 802, TORONTO, ON, M5J 1A7
(416) 410-8956 *SIC 8748*
MESSAGER RAPIDE INC *p 1110*
164 9E RANG E, GRANBY, QC, J2H 0T2
(450) 378-1298 *SIC 7389*
MESSAGERIE PAR TAXI *p 1261*
See TAXI COOP QUEBEC 525-5191
MESSAGERIES A.D.P. INC *p 1176*
955 RUE AMHERST, MONTREAL, QC, H2L 3K4
(514) 523-1182 *SIC 5192*
MESSAGERIES ADP *p 1141*
See GROUPE SOGIDES INC
MESSAGERIES ADP *p 1176*
See MESSAGERIES A.D.P. INC
MESSAGERIES COURRIERTEL INC, LES *p 1364*
148 AV DES MARQUISATS, SAINTE-THERESE, QC, J7E 5J7
(450) 437-9805 *SIC 7389*
MESSENGER FREIGHT SYSTEMS *p 889*
See 1787930 ONTARIO INC
MESSENGER MECHANICAL INCORPORATED *p 801*
1420 CORNWALL RD UNIT 3, OAKVILLE, ON, L6J 7W5
(905) 844-2949 *SIC 1711*
MESSENGERS INTERNATIONAL, THE *p 932*
See 718878 ONTARIO LIMITED
MESSER CANADA INC *p 732*
5860 CHEDWORTH WAY, MISSISSAUGA, ON, L5R 0A2
(905) 501-1700 *SIC 5169*
MESSIER-DOWTY *p 1153*
See SAFRAN LANDING SYSTEMS CANADA INC
MESTEK CANADA INC *p 735*
7555 TRANMERE DR, MISSISSAUGA, ON, L5S 1L4
(905) 670-5888 *SIC 3433*
MET-RECY LTEE *p 1362*
2975 BOUL INDUSTRIEL, SAINTE-ROSE, QC, H7L 3W9
(450) 668-6008 *SIC 5093*
METAFIX INC *p 1128*
1925 46E AV, LACHINE, QC, H8T 2P1
(514) 633-8663 *SIC 3861*
METAFORE *p 1051*
See TECHNOLOGIES METAFORE INC
METAGENICS CANADA, INC *p 712*
851 RANGEVIEW RD SUITE 1, MISSISSAUGA, ON, L5E 1H1
(905) 891-1300 *SIC 5122*
METAL 7 INC *p 1367*
285 RUE DES PIONNIERS, SEPT-ILES, QC, G4R 4X9
(418) 968-5822 *SIC 3479*
METAL ARTECH INC *p 1170*
9455 RUE J.-J.-GAGNIER, MONTREAL, QC, H1Z 3C8
(514) 384-0660 *SIC 3444*

METAL BERNARD INC *p* 1323
12 RUE NAPOLEON-COUTURE, SAINT-LAMBERT-DE-LAUZON, QC, G0S 2W0
(418) 889-0502 *SIC* 7389
METAL BEVERAGE PACKAGING, DIV OF *p* 1013
See BALL PACKAGING PRODUCTS CANADA CORP
METAL CORE ATLANTIC INC *p* 408
180 EDINBURGH DR SUITE 1, MONCTON, NB, E1E 2K7
(506) 854-2673 *SIC* 5051
METAL CRAFT MARINE INCORPORATED *p* 630
347 WELLINGTON ST, KINGSTON, ON, K7K 6N7
(613) 549-7747 *SIC* 3732
METAL EN FEUILLES MURPHCO *p* 1223
See PRODUITS MURPHCO LTEE, LES
METAL FAB *p* 762
See 442527 ONTARIO LIMITED
METAL GOSSELIN LTEE *p* 1154
1591 BOUL ALBINY-PAQUETTE, MONT-LAURIER, QC, J9L 1M8
(819) 623-3369 *SIC* 5051
METAL LEETWO INC *p* 1118
18025 RTE TRANSCANADIENNE, KIRK-LAND, QC, H9J 3Z4
(514) 695-5911 *SIC* 3444
METAL NORGATE 2012 INC *p* 1122
791 8E RUE E, LA GUADELOUPE, QC, G0M 1G0
(418) 459-6988 *SIC* 3441
METAL PERREAULT INC *p* 1092
167 RUE ARMAND-BOMBARDIER, DONNACONA, QC, G3M 1V4
(418) 285-4499 *SIC* 3441
METAL SIGMA INC *p* 1316
750 RUE LUCIEN-BEAUDIN, SAINT-JEAN-SUR-RICHELIEU, QC, J2X 5M3
(450) 348-7333 *SIC* 3499
METAL SUPERMARKETS *p* 1029
See 2261079 ONTARIO LTD
METAL SUPERMARKETS SERVICE COMPANY INC *p* 741
520 ABILENE DR 2ND FL, MISSISSAUGA, ON, L5T 2H7
(905) 362-8226 *SIC* 5051
METAL U.P. INC *p* 1380
3745 RUE PASCAL-GAGNON, TERREBONNE, QC, J6X 4J3
(450) 477-1122 *SIC* 3499
METALAB DESIGN LTD *p* 336
524 YATES ST SUITE 101, VICTORIA, BC, V8W 1K8
SIC 7374
METALCARE GROUP INC *p* 128
291 MACALPINE CRES UNIT A, FORT MC-MURRAY, AB, T9H 4Y4
(780) 715-1889 *SIC* 7389
METALCARE GROUP INC *p* 128
400 MACKENZIE BLVD SUITE 201, FORT MCMURRAY, AB, T9H 4C4
(780) 715-1889 *SIC* 7389
METALCRAFT FASTSHIPS *p* 630
See METAL CRAFT MARINE INCORPORATED
METALIUM INC *p* 1234
4020 RUE GARAND, MONTREAL, QC, H7L 5C9
(450) 963-0411 *SIC* 5051
METALLA ROYALTY & STREAMING LTD *p* 307
543 GRANVILLE ST SUITE 501, VANCOUVER, BC, V6C 1X8
(604) 696-0741 *SIC* 6159
METALLISATION DU NORD INC *p* 1077
876 RUE PERREAULT, CHIBOUGAMAU, QC, G8P 2K3
(418) 748-6442 *SIC* 5093
METALLURGIE CASTECH INC *p* 1383
500 BOUL FRONTENAC E, THETFORD MINES, QC, G6G 7M8

(418) 338-3171 *SIC* 3325
METALLURGIE SYCA INC *p* 1299
500 RUE PRINCIPALE, SAINT-DOMINIQUE, QC, J0H 1L0
(450) 261-0853 *SIC* 2819
METALLURGISTES UNIS D'AMERIQUE *p* 1177
565 BOUL CREMAZIE E BUREAU 5100, MONTREAL, QC, H2M 2V8
(514) 599-2000 *SIC* 6371
METALOGIC INSPECTION SERVICES INC *p* 110
7211 68 AVE NW, EDMONTON, AB, T6B 3T6
(780) 469-6161 *SIC* 7389
METALOGIX SOFTWARE CORP *p* 295
55 CORDOVA ST E SUITE 604, VANCOUVER, BC, V6A 0A5
(604) 677-4636 *SIC* 7372
METALS CREEK RESOURCES CORP *p* 908
945 COBALT CRES, THUNDER BAY, ON, P7B 5Z4
(807) 345-4990 *SIC* 1799
METALS PLUS LTD *p* 1014
1610 MCEWEN DR UNIT 1-3, WHITBY, ON, L1N 8V7
(905) 721-0050 *SIC* 5051
METALSMITH ACCESSORIES *p* 94
PO BOX 3391 STN D, EDMONTON, AB, T5L 4J2
(780) 454-0736 *SIC* 5137
METALSMITHS MASTER ARCHITECTS OF JEWELRY INC *p* 101
17410 107 AVE NW, EDMONTON, AB, T5S 1E9
(780) 454-0736 *SIC* 5944
METALTECH-OMEGA INC *p* 1362
1735 BOUL SAINT-ELZEAR O, SAINTE-ROSE, QC, H7L 3N6
(450) 681-6440 *SIC* 3446
METALUMEN HOLDINGS INC *p* 601
570 SOUTHGATE DR, GUELPH, ON, N1G 4P6
(519) 822-4381 *SIC* 3648
METALUMEN MANUFACTURING INC *p* 601
570 SOUTHGATE DR, GUELPH, ON, N1G 4P6
(519) 822-4381 *SIC* 3646
METAPLAST CIRCUITS LIMITED *p* 914
180 HYMUS RD, TORONTO, ON, M1L 2E1
(416) 285-5000 *SIC* 3672
METARA *p* 1179
See MODE RVING INC
METARIS INC *p* 784
101 CANARCTIC DR, NORTH YORK, ON, M3J 2N7
(416) 638-6000 *SIC* 3714
METASOFT SYSTEMS INC *p* 299
353 WATER ST SUITE 300, VANCOUVER, BC, V6B 1B8
(604) 683-6711 *SIC* 7371
METATUBE (1993) INC *p* 1121
2713 AV DU PORT, LA BAIE, QC, G7B 4S8
(418) 544-3303 *SIC* 3499
METAUX ABSOLUS INC *p* 1152
17550 RUE CHARLES, MIRABEL, QC, J7J 1X9
(450) 437-1777 *SIC* 5051
METAUX AERONAUTIQUE SAMUEL *p* 1054
See SAMUEL, SON & CO., LIMITED
METAUX M.P.I. INC *p* 1152
12695 RUE DU PARC, MIRABEL, QC, J7J 0W5
(450) 420-0858 *SIC* 5051
METAUX PROFUSION INC *p* 1094
2000 BOUL HYMUS, DORVAL, QC, H9P 1J7
(514) 822-0922 *SIC* 5051
METAUX RICHARD, LES *p* 1384
See LEGAULT METAL INC
METAUX TREMBLAY, LES *p* 1141
See GROUPE LMT INC
METCALFE REALTY COMPANY LIMITED *p* 830

2700 QUEENSVIEW DR, OTTAWA, ON, K2B 8H6
(613) 820-6000 *SIC* 6531
METCALFE REALTY COMPANY LIMITED *p* 832
1755 OLD CARP RD, OTTAWA, ON, K2K 1X7
(613) 839-5401 *SIC* 7992
METCALFE'S GARAGE LTD *p* 360
HWY 2 E, TREHERNE, MB, R0G 2V0
(204) 723-2175 *SIC* 5511
METCAP LIVING *p* 932
See 2041098 ONTARIO LIMITED
METCAP LIVING INC *p* 934
260 RICHMOND ST E SUITE 300, TORONTO, ON, M5A 1P4
(416) 340-1600 *SIC* 6531
METCAP LIVING MANAGEMENT INC *p* 934
260 RICHMOND ST E SUITE 300, TORONTO, ON, M5A 1P4
(416) 340-1600 *SIC* 6531
METCON SALES AND ENGINEERING LIMITED *p* 555
15 CONNIE CRES UNIT 3, CONCORD, ON, L4K 1L3
(905) 738-2355 *SIC* 5084
METCREDIT *p* 90
See METROPOLITAN CREDIT ADJUSTERS LTD
METEO FENETRES ET PORTES INC *p* 1323
132C RUE LEON-VACHON, SAINT-LAMBERT-DE-LAUZON, QC, G0S 2W0
SIC 5031
METEO MEDIA *p* 1174
See PELMOREX WEATHER NETWORKS (TELEVISION) INC
METEOR FOUNDRY COMPANY LIMITED *p* 741
1730 BONHILL RD, MISSISSAUGA, ON, L5T 1C8
(905) 670-2890 *SIC* 3365
METEX HEAT TREATING LTD *p* 504
225 WILKINSON RD, BRAMPTON, ON, L6T 4M2
(905) 453-9700 *SIC* 3398
METEX INC *p* 916
789 DON MILLS ROAD, SUITE 218, TORONTO, ON, M3C 1T5
(416) 203-8388 *SIC* 7372
METFIN PROPERTIES LIMITED PARTNERSHIP *p* 982
266 KING ST W SUITE 405, TORONTO, ON, M5V 1H8
(416) 360-0122 *SIC* 6799
METHANEX CORPORATION *p* 307
200 BURRARD ST SUITE 1800, VANCOUVER, BC, V6C 3M1
(604) 661-2600 *SIC* 2869
METHAPHARM INC *p* 516
81 SINCLAIR BLVD, BRANTFORD, ON, N3S 7X6
(519) 751-3602 *SIC* 5122
METHOD STUDIOS *p* 292
50 2ND AVE W, VANCOUVER, BC, V5Y 1B3
(604) 874-8700 *SIC* 7819
METHOD STUDIOS *p* 1193
See ATOMIC FICTION CANADA, INC
METHOT CHEVROLET BUICK GMC *p* 1397
See AUTOMOBILE PIERRE METHOT INC
METIS CHILD, FAMILY AND COMMUNITY SERVICES *p* 386
See METIS CHILD, FAMILY AND COMMUNITY SERVICES AGENCY INC
METIS CHILD, FAMILY AND COMMUNITY SERVICES AGENCY INC *p* 386
2000 PORTAGE AVE, WINNIPEG, MB, R3J 0K1
(204) 927-6960 *SIC* 8699
METIS EDUCATION FOUNDATION OF THE METIS NATION OF ALBERTA ASSOCIATION, THE *p*

85
11738 KINGSWAY NW SUITE 100, EDMONTON, AB, T5G 0X5
(780) 455-2200 *SIC* 8651
METIS NATION BRITISH COLUMBIA *p* 272
See METIS PROVINCIAL COUNCIL OF BRITISH COLUMBIA
METIS NATION OF ONTARIO *p* 934
75 SHERBOURNE ST SUITE 311, TORONTO, ON, M5A 2P9
(416) 977-9881 *SIC* 8399
METIS PROVINCIAL COUNCIL OF BRITISH COLUMBIA *p* 272
103-5668 192 ST, SURREY, BC, V3S 2V7
(604) 557-5851 *SIC* 8748
METLIFE *p* 825
See METROPOLITAN LIFE INSURANCE COMPANY
METOCEAN TELEMATICS LIMITED *p* 447
21 THORNHILL DR, DARTMOUTH, NS, B3B 1R9
(902) 468-2505 *SIC* 3679
METOKOTE CANADA LIMITED *p* 536
50 RAGLIN RD, CAMBRIDGE, ON, N1T 1Z5
(519) 621-2884 *SIC* 3479
METOPOXY INC *p* 1162
7335 BOUL HENRI-BOURASSA E, MONTREAL, QC, H1E 3T5
(514) 648-1042 *SIC* 3479
METOSAK INC *p* 1369
570 RUE JOSEPH-LATOUR, SHERBROOKE, QC, J1C 0W2
(819) 846-0608 *SIC* 3469
METRA ALUMINIUM INC *p* 1237
2000 BOUL FORTIN, MONTREAL, QC, H7S 1P3
(450) 629-4260 *SIC* 3355
METRA SYSTEMS *p* 1237
See METRA ALUMINIUM INC
METRIC CONTRACTING SERVICES CORPORATION *p* 499
34 BRAMTREE CRT, BRAMPTON, ON, L6S 5Z7
(905) 793-4100 *SIC* 1611
METRIC STORAGE SYSTEMS *p* 503
See HARRCO DESIGN AND MANUFACTURING LIMITED
METRICAN MFG. CO. INC *p* 804
2100 WYECROFT RD, OAKVILLE, ON, L6L 5V6
(905) 332-3200 *SIC* 3545
METRICAN STAMPING CO. INC *p* 523
1380 ARTISANS CRT, BURLINGTON, ON, L7L 5Y2
(905) 332-3200 *SIC* 3469
METRIE *p* 328
See METRIE CANADA LTD
METRIE CANADA LTD *p* 17
5367 50 ST SE, CALGARY, AB, T2C 3W1
(403) 543-3260 *SIC* 2431
METRIE CANADA LTD *p* 328
1055 DUNSMUIR ST SUITE 3500, VANCOUVER, BC, V7X 1H3
(604) 691-9100 *SIC* 2431
METRIX READY MIX LTD *p* 793
777 FENMAR DR, NORTH YORK, ON, M9L 1C8
(416) 746-4600 *SIC* 5032
METRO *p* 428
See METRO ONTARIO INC
METRO *p* 479
See METRO ONTARIO INC
METRO *p* 484
See METRO ONTARIO INC
METRO *p* 492
See METRO ONTARIO INC
METRO *p* 497
See METRO ONTARIO INC
METRO *p* 512
See METRO ONTARIO INC
METRO *p* 513
See METRO ONTARIO INC
METRO *p* 514

METRO
See METRO ONTARIO INC

METRO　p 523
See METRO ONTARIO INC

METRO　p 528
See METRO ONTARIO INC

METRO　p 546
See METRO ONTARIO INC

METRO　p 562
See METRO ONTARIO INC

METRO　p 566
See METRO ONTARIO INC

METRO　p 577
See METRO ONTARIO INC

METRO　p 593
See METRO ONTARIO INC

METRO　p 601
See METRO ONTARIO INC

METRO　p 614
See METRO ONTARIO INC

METRO　p 617
See METRO ONTARIO INC

METRO　p 620
See METRO ONTARIO INC

METRO　p 631
See METRO ONTARIO INC

METRO　p 632
See METRO ONTARIO INC

METRO　p 651
See METRO ONTARIO INC

METRO　p 652
See METRO ONTARIO INC

METRO　p 656
See METRO ONTARIO INC

METRO　p 658
See METRO ONTARIO INC

METRO　p 708
See METRO ONTARIO INC

METRO　p 714
See METRO ONTARIO INC

METRO　p 715
See METRO ONTARIO INC

METRO　p 724
See METRO ONTARIO INC

METRO　p 748
See METRO ONTARIO INC

METRO　p 754
See METRO ONTARIO INC

METRO　p 755
See METRO ONTARIO INC

METRO　p 762
See METRO ONTARIO INC

METRO　p 772
See METRO ONTARIO INC

METRO　p 781
See METRO ONTARIO INC

METRO　p 786
See METRO ONTARIO INC

METRO　p 789
See METRO ONTARIO INC

METRO　p 791
See METRO ONTARIO INC

METRO　p 798
See METRO ONTARIO INC

METRO　p 804
See METRO ONTARIO INC

METRO　p 806
See METRO ONTARIO PHARMACIES LIMITED

METRO　p 808
See METRO ONTARIO INC

METRO　p 809
See METRO ONTARIO INC

METRO　p 812
See METRO ONTARIO INC

METRO　p 814
See METRO ONTARIO INC

METRO　p 818
See METRO ONTARIO INC

METRO　p 827
See METRO ONTARIO INC

METRO　p 835
See METRO ONTARIO INC

METRO　p 840
See METRO ONTARIO INC

METRO　p 843
See METRO ONTARIO INC

METRO　p 846
See METRO ONTARIO INC

METRO　p 857
See METRO ONTARIO INC

METRO　p 860
See METRO ONTARIO INC

METRO　p 863
See METRO ONTARIO INC

METRO　p 865
See METRO ONTARIO INC

METRO　p 867
See METRO ONTARIO INC

METRO　p 871
See METRO ONTARIO INC

METRO　p 872
See METRO ONTARIO INC

METRO　p 877
See METRO ONTARIO INC

METRO　p 884
See METRO ONTARIO INC

METRO　p 890
See METRO ONTARIO INC

METRO　p 894
See METRO ONTARIO INC

METRO　p 907
See METRO ONTARIO INC

METRO　p 922
See METRO ONTARIO INC

METRO　p 935
See METRO ONTARIO INC

METRO　p 942
See METRO ONTARIO INC

METRO　p 976
See METRO ONTARIO INC

METRO　p 991
See METRO ONTARIO INC

METRO　p 1001
See METRO ONTARIO INC

METRO　p 1014
See METRO ONTARIO INC

METRO　p 1016
See METRO ONTARIO INC

METRO　p 1017
See METRO ONTARIO INC

METRO　p 1024
See METRO ONTARIO INC

METRO　p 1051
See METRO INC

METRO　p 1056
See SUPER MARCHE PLOUFFE INC

METRO　p 1074
See MARCHE L.V. LTEE

METRO　p 1075
See MARCHE MARIO DOIRON INC

METRO　p 1133
See SUPERMARCHE LAROCHE (1991) INC

METRO　p 1154
See MARCHE DORE & FILS INC

METRO　p 1172
See MARCHE MARCANIO ET FILS INC

METRO　p 1172
See MARCHE D'ALIMENTATION MARCANIO & FILS INC

METRO　p 1181
See BOURDON, EDOUARD & FILS INC

METRO　p 1245
See ALIMENTATION DANIEL INC

METRO　p 1281
See SUPERMARCHE BOUCHER INC

METRO　p 1286
See MAGASIN COOP DE RIVIERE-DU-LOUP

METRO　p 1290
See SUPER MARCHE ROY INC

METRO　p 1301
See MARCHE ANDRE MARTEL INC

METRO　p 1314
See RIENDEAU, GAETAN INC

METRO　p 1354
See ALIMENTS CHEVREFILS INC, LES

METRO　p 1355

METRO　p 1359
See MARCHE STEPHANE BEAULIEU INC

METRO　p 1366
See MARCHE SENNETERRE INC

METRO　p 1402
See METRO RICHELIEU INC

METRO STORES　p 509
See METRO ONTARIO INC

METRO (SUPERMARKETS)　p 910
See METRO ONTARIO INC

METRO 767　p 481
See METRO ONTARIO INC

METRO ACQUISITION 2004, INC　p 555
2600 STEELES AVE W, CONCORD, ON, L4K 3C8
(905) 738-5177　SIC 5198

METRO AU PIEDS DU POND　p 1173
See ALIMENTATION DANIEL BRUYERE INC

METRO AYLMER　p 1108
See MARCHE AYLMER INC

METRO BEAUTY SUPPLY LIMITED　p 1028
315 NEW HUNTINGTON RD, WOOD-BRIDGE, ON, L4H 0R5
(800) 263-2365　SIC 5087

METRO BELLEMARE　p 1069
See MARCHE BELLEMARE INC

METRO BOUCHER　p 1315
See SUPERMARCHE BOUCHER INC

METRO CABANO　p 1378
See SUPERMARCHES GP INC, LES

METRO CHARNY INC　p 1139
8032 AV DES EGLISES, LEVIS, QC, G6X 1X7
(418) 832-5346　SIC 5411

METRO CHRYSLER DODGE JEEP　p 830
See METRO PLYMOUTH CHRYSLER LTD

METRO CHRYSLER LTD　p 1440
5 2 MILE HILL RD, WHITEHORSE, YT, Y1A 0A4
(867) 667-2525　SIC 5511

METRO CHUTE SERVICE INC　p 586
23 RACINE RD, ETOBICOKE, ON, M9W 2Z4
(416) 746-5547　SIC 7699

METRO COMPACTOR SERVICE INC　p 509
145 HEART LAKE RD S, BRAMPTON, ON, L6W 3K3
(416) 743-8484　SIC 7699

METRO CONTINUING EDUCATION　p 111
See EDMONTON SCHOOL DISTRICT NO. 7

METRO DE LA ROUSSELLIERE　p 1246
See ALIMENTATION ANDREA JOLICOEUR INC

METRO DES BOUTIN　p 1302
See 3105-4521 QUEBEC INC

METRO DES FORGES　p 1385
See ALIMENTATION BENOIT ROBERT INC

METRO DES PROMENADES　p 1104
See ALIMENTATION FRANCIS LAMON-TAGNE INC

METRO DUBE　p 1045
See DUBE, R. LTEE

METRO DUFRESNE　p 1391
See DUFRESNE, L. & FILS LTEE

METRO EXCAVATION INC　p 1255
2144 BOUL LOUIS-XIV, QUEBEC, QC, G1C 1A2
(418) 661-5771　SIC 1794

METRO FAMILLE MARTEL　p 1360
See 9128-0453 QUEBEC INC

METRO FAMILLE THIBEAULT ST-JEROME　p 1320
See MARCHE ELITE ST-JEROME INC

METRO FERLAND　p 1263
See ALIMENTATION SERRO INC

METRO FORD SALES LTD　p 54
1111 9 AVE SW, CALGARY, AB, T2P 1L3
(403) 263-4530　SIC 5511

METRO FREIGHTLINER BRANTFORD　p 517
31 GARNET RD, BRANTFORD, ON, N3T 5M1
(519) 750-0055　SIC 4731

METRO FREIGHTLINER HAMILTON INC　p 892
475 SEAMAN ST, STONEY CREEK, ON, L8E 2R2
(905) 561-6110　SIC 5511

METRO G P　p 1151
See SUPERMARCHES GP INC, LES

METRO G P　p 1154
See SUPERMARCHES GP INC, LES

METRO GENERAL INSURANCE CORPO-RATION LIMITED　p 430
20 CROSBIE PL, ST. JOHN'S, NL, A1B 3Y8
SIC 6331

METRO HARDWARE & MAINTENANCE INC　p 784
72 MARTIN ROSS AVE, NORTH YORK, ON, M3J 2L4
(416) 633-4293　SIC 5251

METRO HYUNDAI　p 1131
See METRO NISSAN INC

METRO INC　p 519
237 KING ST W, BROCKVILLE, ON, K6V 3S2
(613) 345-4260　SIC 5411

METRO INC　p 1051
6500 BOUL JOSEPH-RENAUD, ANJOU, QC, H1K 3V4
(514) 354-0282　SIC 5411

METRO INC　p 1052
7151 RUE JEAN-TALON E, ANJOU, QC, H1M 3N8
(514) 356-5800　SIC 5141

METRO INC　p 1083
1600 BOUL SAINT-MARTIN E BUREAU A, COTE SAINT-LUC, QC, H7G 4S7
(514) 643-1000　SIC 5141

METRO INC　p 1161
11011 BOUL MAURICE-DUPLESSIS, MONTREAL, QC, H1C 1V6
(514) 643-1000　SIC 5141

METRO INSURANCE SERVICES　p 416
See HUESTIS INSURANCE GROUP

METRO LA MALBAIE　p 1122
See ALIMENTATION ROBERT DUFOUR INC

METRO LEBEL　p 1122
See ALIMENTATION LEBEL INC

METRO LIMBOUR　p 1105
See 2875448 CANADA INC

METRO LOGISTIQUE INC　p 686
7380 BREN RD UNIT 2, MISSISSAUGA, ON, L4T 1H3
(905) 461-0006　SIC 4225

METRO LOGISTIQUE INC　p 1198
1002 RUE SHERBROOKE O BUREAU 2000, MONTREAL, QC, H3A 3L6
(514) 333-5500　SIC 6512

METRO MARCHE CHEVREFILS MT-TREMBLANT　p 1159
1011 RUE DE SAINT-JOVITE, MONT-TREMBLANT, QC, J8E 3J9
(819) 425-3381　SIC 5411

METRO MARQUIS REPENTIGNY　p 1283
See SUPERMARCHE , MARQUIS RE-PENTIGNY INC

METRO MASSON　p 1385
See GESTION MASSON, ST-PIERRE INC

METRO MEDIA　p 1224
See 10684210 CANADA INC

METRO MORGAN 2024　p 1166
See ALIMENTATION DENIS GODIN INC

METRO MOTORS LTD　p 246
2505 LOUGHEED HWY, PORT COQUIT-LAM, BC, V3B 1B2
(604) 464-6631　SIC 5511

METRO NISSAN INC　p 1131
8686 BOUL NEWMAN, LASALLE, QC, H8N 1Y5
(514) 366-8931　SIC 5511

METRO NORAMCO INC *p* 1335
5855 RUE KIERAN, SAINT-LAURENT, QC, H4S 0A3
(514) 595-9595 *SIC* 5063

METRO NOTRE DAME DU ILE-PERROT *p* 1243
See 9171-2802 QUEBEC INC

METRO ONTARIO *p* 1167
See ALIMENTATION ERIC DA PONTE INC

METRO ONTARIO INC *p* 428
55 STAVANGER DR, ST. JOHN'S, NL, A1A 5E8
(709) 576-3576 *SIC* 5411

METRO ONTARIO INC *p* 474
280 HARWOOD AVE S, AJAX, ON, L1S 2J1
(905) 683-6951 *SIC* 5411

METRO ONTARIO INC *p* 479
375 DANIEL ST S, ARNPRIOR, ON, K7S 3K6
(613) 623-6273 *SIC* 5411

METRO ONTARIO INC *p* 481
1 HENDERSON DR UNIT 1, AURORA, ON, L4G 4J7
(905) 727-0185 *SIC* 5411

METRO ONTARIO INC *p* 484
400 BAYFIELD ST SUITE 1, BARRIE, ON, L4M 5A1
(705) 722-8284 *SIC* 5411

METRO ONTARIO INC *p* 492
110 NORTH FRONT ST, BELLEVILLE, ON, K8P 5J8
(613) 962-0056 *SIC* 5411

METRO ONTARIO INC *p* 497
505 MUSKOKA RD HWY SUITE 118, BRACEBRIDGE, ON, P1L 1T3
(705) 645-8751 *SIC* 5411

METRO ONTARIO INC *p* 498
20 GREAT LAKES DR, BRAMPTON, ON, L6R 2K7
(905) 789-6161 *SIC* 5411

METRO ONTARIO INC *p* 508
227 VODDEN ST E, BRAMPTON, ON, L6V 1N2
(905) 451-7842 *SIC* 5411

METRO ONTARIO INC *p* 509
156 MAIN ST S, BRAMPTON, ON, L6W 2C9
(905) 459-6212 *SIC* 5411

METRO ONTARIO INC *p* 512
180 SANDALWOOD PKY E, BRAMPTON, ON, L6Z 1Y4
(905) 846-2222 *SIC* 5411

METRO ONTARIO INC *p* 513
10088 MCLAUGHLIN RD SUITE 1, BRAMPTON, ON, L7A 2X6
SIC 5411

METRO ONTARIO INC *p* 514
371 ST PAUL AVE, BRANTFORD, ON, N3R 4N5
(519) 758-0300 *SIC* 5411

METRO ONTARIO INC *p* 523
2010 APPLEBY LINE, BURLINGTON, ON, L7L 6M6
(905) 331-7900 *SIC* 5411

METRO ONTARIO INC *p* 523
5353 LAKESHORE RD, BURLINGTON, ON, L7L 1C8
(905) 634-1804 *SIC* 5411

METRO ONTARIO INC *p* 528
3365 FAIRVIEW ST, BURLINGTON, ON, L7N 3N9
(905) 634-1896 *SIC* 5411

METRO ONTARIO INC *p* 534
95 WATER ST N, CAMBRIDGE, ON, N1R 3B5
(519) 623-3652 *SIC* 5141

METRO ONTARIO INC *p* 537
100 JAMIESON PKY, CAMBRIDGE, ON, N3C 4B3
(519) 658-1150 *SIC* 5411

METRO ONTARIO INC *p* 546
640 FIRST ST, COLLINGWOOD, ON, L9Y 4Y7
(705) 444-5252 *SIC* 5411

METRO ONTARIO INC *p* 562
1315 SECOND ST E, CORNWALL, ON, K6H 7C4
(613) 932-0514 *SIC* 5411

METRO ONTARIO INC *p* 566
15 GOVERNORS RD, DUNDAS, ON, L9H 6L9
(905) 627-4791 *SIC* 5411

METRO ONTARIO INC *p* 566
119 OSLER DR, DUNDAS, ON, L9H 6X4
(905) 628-0177 *SIC* 5411

METRO ONTARIO INC *p* 577
5559 DUNDAS ST W, ETOBICOKE, ON, M9B 1B9
(416) 239-7171 *SIC* 5411

METRO ONTARIO INC *p* 577
250 THE EAST MALL, ETOBICOKE, ON, M9B 3Y8
(416) 233-4149 *SIC* 5411

METRO ONTARIO INC *p* 577
25 VICKERS RD, ETOBICOKE, ON, M9B 1C1
(416) 234-6590 *SIC* 5141

METRO ONTARIO INC *p* 577
201 LLOYD MANOR RD, ETOBICOKE, ON, M9B 6H6
(416) 236-3217 *SIC* 5411

METRO ONTARIO INC *p* 579
170 THE WEST MALL, ETOBICOKE, ON, M9C 5L6
(416) 626-4910 *SIC* 4225

METRO ONTARIO INC *p* 593
333 KING ST E, GANANOQUE, ON, K7G 1G6
(613) 382-7090 *SIC* 5411

METRO ONTARIO INC *p* 596
1930 MONTREAL RD, GLOUCESTER, ON, K1J 6N2
(613) 744-2961 *SIC* 5411

METRO ONTARIO INC *p* 600
380 ERAMOSA RD, GUELPH, ON, N1E 6R2
(519) 824-8700 *SIC* 5411

METRO ONTARIO INC *p* 601
500 EDINBURGH RD S, GUELPH, ON, N1G 4Z1
(519) 763-3552 *SIC* 5411

METRO ONTARIO INC *p* 608
2500 BARTON ST E, HAMILTON, ON, L8E 4A2
(905) 578-5454 *SIC* 5411

METRO ONTARIO INC *p* 610
1900 KING ST E, HAMILTON, ON, L8K 1W1
(905) 545-5929 *SIC* 5411

METRO ONTARIO INC *p* 614
845 KING ST W, HAMILTON, ON, L8S 1K4
(905) 523-5044 *SIC* 5411

METRO ONTARIO INC *p* 615
505 RYMAL RD E SUITE 3, HAMILTON, ON, L8W 3X1
(905) 574-5298 *SIC* 5411

METRO ONTARIO INC *p* 615
1070 STONE CHURCH RD E, HAMILTON, ON, L8W 3K8
SIC 5411

METRO ONTARIO INC *p* 617
751 UPPER JAMES ST, HAMILTON, ON, L9C 3A1
(905) 575-5545 *SIC* 5411

METRO ONTARIO INC *p* 620
70 KING WILLIAM ST SUITE 5A, HUNTSVILLE, ON, P1H 2A5
(705) 789-9619 *SIC* 5411

METRO ONTARIO INC *p* 631
310 BARRIE ST, KINGSTON, ON, K7L 5L4
(613) 542-5795 *SIC* 5411

METRO ONTARIO INC *p* 632
1300 BATH RD, KINGSTON, ON, K7M 4X4
(613) 544-9317 *SIC* 5411

METRO ONTARIO INC *p* 632
466 GARDINERS RD, KINGSTON, ON, K7M 7W8
(613) 384-6334 *SIC* 5411

METRO ONTARIO INC *p* 633
775 BAYRIDGE DR, KINGSTON, ON, K7P 2P1
(613) 384-8800 *SIC* 5411

METRO ONTARIO INC *p* 636
655 FAIRWAY RD S, KITCHENER, ON, N2C 1X4
(519) 896-5100 *SIC* 5411

METRO ONTARIO INC *p* 641
851 FISCHER HALLMAN RD, KITCHENER, ON, N2M 5N8
(519) 570-2500 *SIC* 5411

METRO ONTARIO INC *p* 641
370 HIGHLAND RD W SUITE 1, KITCHENER, ON, N2M 5J9
(519) 744-4100 *SIC* 5411

METRO ONTARIO INC *p* 644
288 ERIE ST S, LEAMINGTON, ON, N8H 3C5
(519) 322-1414 *SIC* 5411

METRO ONTARIO INC *p* 646
363 KENT ST W, LINDSAY, ON, K9V 2Z7
(705) 878-3300 *SIC* 5411

METRO ONTARIO INC *p* 651
155 CLARKE RD, LONDON, ON, N5W 5C9
(519) 455-5604 *SIC* 5411

METRO ONTARIO INC *p* 652
1030 ADELAIDE ST N, LONDON, ON, N5Y 2M9
(519) 672-8994 *SIC* 5411

METRO ONTARIO INC *p* 652
1299 OXFORD ST E, LONDON, ON, N5Y 4W5
(519) 453-8510 *SIC* 5411

METRO ONTARIO INC *p* 656
395 WELLINGTON RD, LONDON, ON, N6C 5Z6
(519) 680-2317 *SIC* 5411

METRO ONTARIO INC *p* 658
1225 WONDERLAND RD N, LONDON, ON, N6G 2V9
(519) 472-5601 *SIC* 5411

METRO ONTARIO INC *p* 658
301 OXFORD ST W, LONDON, ON, N6H 1S6
(519) 433-1708 *SIC* 5411

METRO ONTARIO INC *p* 659
509 COMMISSIONERS RD W, LONDON, ON, N6J 1Y5
(519) 473-2857 *SIC* 5411

METRO ONTARIO INC *p* 679
1220 CASTLEMORE AVE, MARKHAM, ON, L6E 0H7
(905) 209-9200 *SIC* 5411

METRO ONTARIO INC *p* 697
4141 DIXIE RD UNIT 2, MISSISSAUGA, ON, L4W 1V5
(905) 238-1366 *SIC* 5411

METRO ONTARIO INC *p* 704
1077 NORTH SERVICE RD SUITE 41, MISSISSAUGA, ON, L4Y 1A6
SIC 5411

METRO ONTARIO INC *p* 708
1585 MISSISSAUGA VALLEY BLVD, MISSISSAUGA, ON, L5A 3W9
(905) 566-9100 *SIC* 5411

METRO ONTARIO INC *p* 708
377 BURNHAMTHORPE RD E, MISSISSAUGA, ON, L5A 3Y1
(905) 270-2143 *SIC* 5411

METRO ONTARIO INC *p* 714
910 SOUTHDOWN RD UNIT 46, MISSISSAUGA, ON, L5J 2Y4
(905) 823-4800 *SIC* 5411

METRO ONTARIO INC *p* 715
2225 ERIN MILLS PKY, MISSISSAUGA, ON, L5K 1T9
(905) 829-3737 *SIC* 5411

METRO ONTARIO INC *p* 717
3476 GLEN ERIN DR, MISSISSAUGA, ON, L5L 3R4
(905) 569-2162 *SIC* 5411

METRO ONTARIO INC *p* 724
3221 DERRY RD W SUITE 16, MISSISSAUGA, ON, L5N 7L7
(905) 785-1844 *SIC* 5411

METRO ONTARIO INC *p* 724
6677 MEADOWVALE TOWN CENTRE CIR, MISSISSAUGA, ON, L5N 2R5
(905) 826-2717 *SIC* 5411

METRO ONTARIO INC *p* 748
35 ALKENBRACK ST, NAPANEE, ON, K7R 4C4
(613) 354-2882 *SIC* 5411

METRO ONTARIO INC *p* 751
1811 ROBERTSON RD, NEPEAN, ON, K2H 8X3
(613) 721-7028 *SIC* 5141

METRO ONTARIO INC *p* 752
900 GREENBANK RD, NEPEAN, ON, K2J 4P6
(613) 823-4458 *SIC* 5411

METRO ONTARIO INC *p* 752
3201 STRANDHERD DR, NEPEAN, ON, K2J 5N1
(613) 823-8825 *SIC* 5411

METRO ONTARIO INC *p* 754
16640 YONGE ST UNIT 1, NEWMARKET, ON, L3X 2N8
(905) 853-5100 *SIC* 5411

METRO ONTARIO INC *p* 755
17725 YONGE ST SUITE 1, NEWMARKET, ON, L3Y 7C1
(905) 895-9700 *SIC* 5411

METRO ONTARIO INC *p* 755
1111 DAVIS DR, NEWMARKET, ON, L3Y 9E5
(905) 853-5355 *SIC* 5411

METRO ONTARIO INC *p* 760
3770 MONTROSE RD, NIAGARA FALLS, ON, L2H 3C8
(905) 371-3200 *SIC* 5411

METRO ONTARIO INC *p* 762
390 LAKESHORE DR, NORTH BAY, ON, P1A 2C7
(705) 840-2424 *SIC* 5411

METRO ONTARIO INC *p* 768
2452 SHEPPARD AVE E, NORTH YORK, ON, M2J 1X1
(416) 756-2513 *SIC* 5411

METRO ONTARIO INC *p* 769
291 YORK MILLS RD, NORTH YORK, ON, M2L 1L3
(416) 444-5809 *SIC* 5411

METRO ONTARIO INC *p* 772
20 CHURCH AVE, NORTH YORK, ON, M2N 0B7
(416) 229-6200 *SIC* 5411

METRO ONTARIO INC *p* 775
1277 YORK MILLS RD, NORTH YORK, ON, M3A 1Z5
(416) 444-7921 *SIC* 5411

METRO ONTARIO INC *p* 781
600 SHEPPARD AVE W, NORTH YORK, ON, M3H 2S1
(416) 636-5136 *SIC* 5411

METRO ONTARIO INC *p* 786
2200 JANE ST, NORTH YORK, ON, M3M 1A4
(416) 241-5732 *SIC* 5411

METRO ONTARIO INC *p* 789
3090 BATHURST ST, NORTH YORK, ON, M6A 2A1
(416) 783-1227 *SIC* 5411

METRO ONTARIO INC *p* 791
1411 LAWRENCE AVE W, NORTH YORK, ON, M6L 1A4
(416) 248-5846 *SIC* 5411

METRO ONTARIO INC *p* 798
1011 UPPER MIDDLE RD E SUITE 412, OAKVILLE, ON, L6H 5Z9
(905) 849-4911 *SIC* 5411

METRO ONTARIO INC *p* 804
1521 REBECCA ST, OAKVILLE, ON, L6L 1Z8
(905) 827-5421 *SIC* 5411

METRO ONTARIO INC *p* 808
150 FIRST ST SUITE 7, ORANGEVILLE, ON, L9W 3T7
(519) 941-6391 *SIC* 5411

METRO ONTARIO INC *p 809*
70 FRONT ST N, ORILLIA, ON, L3V 4R8
(705) 323-9334   *SIC* 5411

METRO ONTARIO INC *p 810*
1675E TENTH LINE RD, ORLEANS, ON, K1E 3P6
(613) 837-2614   *SIC* 5411

METRO ONTARIO INC *p 811*
4510 INNES RD, ORLEANS, ON, K4A 4C5
(613) 824-8850   *SIC* 5141

METRO ONTARIO INC *p 812*
285 TAUNTON RD E SUITE 4, OSHAWA, ON, L1G 3V2
(905) 432-2197   *SIC* 5411

METRO ONTARIO INC *p 814*
149 MIDTOWN DR, OSHAWA, ON, L1J 3Z7
SIC 5411

METRO ONTARIO INC *p 814*
555 ROSSLAND RD E, OSHAWA, ON, L1K 1K8
(905) 579-5862   *SIC* 5411

METRO ONTARIO INC *p 818*
490 INDUSTRIAL AVE, OTTAWA, ON, K1G 0Y9
(613) 737-1300   *SIC* 5141

METRO ONTARIO INC *p 827*
1670 HERON RD, OTTAWA, ON, K1V 0C2
(613) 731-0066   *SIC* 5411

METRO ONTARIO INC *p 827*
2515 BANK ST, OTTAWA, ON, K1V 0Y4
(613) 731-7410   *SIC* 5411

METRO ONTARIO INC *p 827*
3310 MCCARTHY RD, OTTAWA, ON, K1V 9S1
(613) 523-2774   *SIC* 5411

METRO ONTARIO INC *p 830*
1360 RICHMOND RD, OTTAWA, ON, K2B 8L4
(613) 828-4207   *SIC* 5141

METRO ONTARIO INC *p 835*
1070 2ND AVE E, OWEN SOUND, ON, N4K 2H7
(519) 371-0222   *SIC* 5411

METRO ONTARIO INC *p 838*
1100 PEMBROKE ST E SUITE 891, PEMBROKE, ON, K8A 6Y7
(613) 735-1846   *SIC* 5411

METRO ONTARIO INC *p 840*
1154 CHEMONG RD SUITE 9, PETERBOROUGH, ON, K9H 7J6
(705) 745-3381   *SIC* 5411

METRO ONTARIO INC *p 843*
1822 WHITES RD SUITE 11, PICKERING, ON, L1V 4M1
(905) 420-8838   *SIC* 5411

METRO ONTARIO INC *p 846*
124 CLARENCE ST, PORT COLBORNE, ON, L3K 3G3
(905) 834-8800   *SIC* 5411

METRO ONTARIO INC *p 857*
1070 MAJOR MACKENZIE DR E, RICHMOND HILL, ON, L4S 1P3
(905) 770-1400   *SIC* 5411

METRO ONTARIO INC *p 860*
560 EXMOUTH ST, SARNIA, ON, N7T 5P5
(519) 337-8308   *SIC* 5411

METRO ONTARIO INC *p 860*
191 INDIAN RD S, SARNIA, ON, N7T 3W3
(519) 344-1500   *SIC* 5411

METRO ONTARIO INC *p 862*
150 CHURCHILL BLVD, SAULT STE. MARIE, ON, P6A 3Z9
(705) 254-3923   *SIC* 5411

METRO ONTARIO INC *p 862*
625 TRUNK RD, SAULT STE. MARIE, ON, P6A 3T1
(705) 949-7260   *SIC* 5411

METRO ONTARIO INC *p 863*
275 SECOND LINE W, SAULT STE. MARIE, ON, P6C 2J4
(705) 949-0350   *SIC* 5411

METRO ONTARIO INC *p 865*
261 PORT UNION RD, SCARBOROUGH, ON, M1C 2L3

(416) 284-7792   *SIC* 5411

METRO ONTARIO INC *p 866*
2900 ELLESMERE RD SUITE 587, SCARBOROUGH, ON, M1E 4B8
(416) 284-5320   *SIC* 5411

METRO ONTARIO INC *p 867*
3221 EGLINTON AVE E, SCARBOROUGH, ON, M1J 2H7
(416) 261-4204   *SIC* 5411

METRO ONTARIO INC *p 871*
16 WILLIAM KITCHEN RD SUITE 535, SCARBOROUGH, ON, M1P 5B7
(416) 321-0500   *SIC* 5411

METRO ONTARIO INC *p 872*
15 ELLESMERE RD, SCARBOROUGH, ON, M1R 4B7
(416) 391-0626   *SIC* 5411

METRO ONTARIO INC *p 877*
2900 WARDEN AVE, SCARBOROUGH, ON, M1W 2S8
(416) 497-6734   *SIC* 5411

METRO ONTARIO INC *p 881*
150 WEST ST, SIMCOE, ON, N3Y 5C1
(519) 426-2010   *SIC* 5411

METRO ONTARIO INC *p 884*
101 LAKESHORE RD, ST CATHARINES, ON, L2N 2T6
(905) 934-0131   *SIC* 5411

METRO ONTARIO INC *p 890*
417 WELLINGTON ST SUITE 1, ST THOMAS, ON, N5R 5J5
(519) 633-8780   *SIC* 5411

METRO ONTARIO INC *p 894*
5612 MAIN ST, STOUFFVILLE, ON, L4A 8B7
(905) 642-8600   *SIC* 5411

METRO ONTARIO INC *p 900*
400 NOTRE DAME AVE, SUDBURY, ON, P3C 5K5
(705) 675-5845   *SIC* 5411

METRO ONTARIO INC *p 901*
1933 REGENT ST, SUDBURY, ON, P3E 5R2
SIC 5411

METRO ONTARIO INC *p 904*
8190 BAYVIEW AVE, THORNHILL, ON, L3T 2S2
(905) 731-2300   *SIC* 5411

METRO ONTARIO INC *p 907*
640 RIVER ST, THUNDER BAY, ON, P7A 3S4
(807) 345-8342   *SIC* 5411

METRO ONTARIO INC *p 910*
1101 ARTHUR ST W, THUNDER BAY, ON, P7E 5S2
(807) 577-3910   *SIC* 5411

METRO ONTARIO INC *p 910*
505 ARTHUR ST W, THUNDER BAY, ON, P7E 5R5
(807) 475-0276   *SIC* 5411

METRO ONTARIO INC *p 912*
225 BROADWAY ST, TILLSONBURG, ON, N4G 3R2
(519) 842-3625   *SIC* 5411

METRO ONTARIO INC *p 917*
1500 WOODBINE AVE, TORONTO, ON, M4C 4G9
(416) 422-0076   *SIC* 5411

METRO ONTARIO INC *p 919*
45 OVERLEA BLVD SUITE 2, TORONTO, ON, M4H 1C3
(416) 421-1732   *SIC* 5411

METRO ONTARIO INC *p 922*
40 EGLINTON AVE E, TORONTO, ON, M4P 3A2
(416) 759-1952   *SIC* 5411

METRO ONTARIO INC *p 922*
2300 YONGE ST SUITE 752, TORONTO, ON, M4P 1E4
(416) 483-7340   *SIC* 5411

METRO ONTARIO INC *p 922*
656 EGLINTON AVE E, TORONTO, ON, M4P 1P1
(416) 482-7422   *SIC* 5411

METRO ONTARIO INC *p 935*
89 GOULD ST, TORONTO, ON, M5B 2R1
(416) 862-7171   *SIC* 5411

METRO ONTARIO INC *p 942*
80 FRONT ST E SUITE 804, TORONTO, ON, M5E 1T4
(416) 703-9393   *SIC* 5411

METRO ONTARIO INC *p 976*
425 BLOOR ST W, TORONTO, ON, M5S 1X6
(416) 923-9099   *SIC* 5411

METRO ONTARIO INC *p 989*
735 COLLEGE ST, TORONTO, ON, M6G 1C5
(416) 533-2515   *SIC* 5411

METRO ONTARIO INC *p 991*
100 LYNN WILLIAMS ST SUITE 572, TORONTO, ON, M6K 3N6
(416) 588-1300   *SIC* 5411

METRO ONTARIO INC *p 999*
53 QUINTE ST, TRENTON, ON, K8V 3S8
(613) 394-2525   *SIC* 5411

METRO ONTARIO INC *p 1001*
50 BEECHWOOD AVE, VANIER, ON, K1L 8B3
(613) 744-6676   *SIC* 5411

METRO ONTARIO INC *p 1014*
70 THICKSON RD S, WHITBY, ON, L1N 7T2
(905) 668-5334   *SIC* 5411

METRO ONTARIO INC *p 1016*
4111 THICKSON RD N, WHITBY, ON, L1R 2X3
(905) 655-1553   *SIC* 5411

METRO ONTARIO INC *p 1017*
11729 TECUMSEH RD E, WINDSOR, ON, N8N 1L8
(519) 979-9366   *SIC* 5411

METRO ONTARIO INC *p 1018*
2090 LAUZON RD, WINDSOR, ON, N8T 2Z3
(519) 944-7335   *SIC* 5411

METRO ONTARIO INC *p 1018*
6740 WYANDOTTE ST E, WINDSOR, ON, N8S 1P6
(519) 948-5676   *SIC* 5411

METRO ONTARIO INC *p 1023*
880 GOYEAU ST, WINDSOR, ON, N9A 1H8
(519) 258-3064   *SIC* 5411

METRO ONTARIO INC *p 1024*
2750 TECUMSEH RD W, WINDSOR, ON, N9B 3P9
(519) 256-1891   *SIC* 5411

METRO ONTARIO INC *p 1028*
9600 ISLINGTON AVE, WOODBRIDGE, ON, L4H 2T1
(905) 893-1618   *SIC* 5411

METRO ONTARIO INC *p 1035*
868 DUNDAS ST, WOODSTOCK, ON, N4S 1G7
(519) 537-7021   *SIC* 5411

METRO ONTARIO PHARMACIES LIMITED *p 577*
5559 DUNDAS ST W, ETOBICOKE, ON, M9B 1B9
(416) 239-7171   *SIC* 5912

METRO ONTARIO PHARMACIES LIMITED *p 806*
280 NORTH SERVICE RD W, OAKVILLE, ON, L6M 2S2
(905) 337-7694   *SIC* 5411

METRO P.E. PRIX *p 1116*
See 3093-9920 QUEBEC INC

METRO PAPER INDUSTRIES INC *p 869*
111 MANVILLE RD, SCARBOROUGH, ON, M1L 4J2
(416) 757-2737   *SIC* 2676

METRO PARKING LTD *p 315*
1078 PENDER ST W, VANCOUVER, BC, V6E 2N7
(604) 682-6754   *SIC* 7521

METRO PELLETIER CARREFOUR DU NORD-OUEST *p 1389*
See 9093-3789 QUEBEC INC

METRO PLACE SAINTE-FOY *p 1271*

See ALIMENTATION MARIE GIGNAC INC

METRO PLOUFFE *p 1148*
See SUPERMARCHE J.P.V. PLOUFFE INC

METRO PLUS *p 1066*
See MARCHE J.C. MESSIER INC

METRO PLUS *p 1069*
See SUPER MARCHE COLLIN INC

METRO PLUS *p 1076*
105 RUE PRINCIPALE, CHATEAUGUAY, QC, J6K 1G2
(450) 699-8796   *SIC* 5499

METRO PLUS *p 1103*
See MARCHE LEBLANC MONTEE PAIEMENT INC

METRO PLUS *p 1163*
See ALIMENTATION DOMINIC POTVIN INC

METRO PLUS *p 1366*
See METRO RICHELIEU INC

METRO PLUS *p 1369*
See MARCHE PLUS SHAWINIGAN INC

METRO PLUS *p 1377*
See ALIMENTATION SYLVAIN BRIERE INC

METRO PLUS BEACONSFIELD *p 1054*
See METRO RICHELIEU INC

METRO PLUS EMERY LOUISEVILLE *p 1146*
See MARCHE EMERY & FILS INC

METRO PLUS LEVIS *p 1135*
See ALIMENTATION ROBERT DESROCHER INC

METRO PLUS MARIO LAVOIE *p 1079*
1550 BOUL TALBOT, CHICOUTIMI, QC, G7H 4C2
(418) 543-7394   *SIC* 5411

METRO PLUS PLOUFFE *p 1375*
See SUPERMARCHE J C J PLOUFFE INC

METRO PLUS RIENDEAU BELOEIL *p 1057*
See MARCHE RIENDEAU BELOEIL INC

METRO PLUS STE-THERESE *p 1364*
See 9175-6429 QUEBEC INC

METRO PLYMOUTH CHRYSLER LTD *p 830*
1047 RICHMOND RD, OTTAWA, ON, K2B 6R1
(613) 596-1006   *SIC* 5511

METRO POINTE CLAIRE *p 1251*
See METRO RICHELIEU INC

METRO PROTECTIVE SERVICES *p 873*
See 2138894 ONTARIO INC

METRO RACICOT *p 1155*
See SUPER MARCHE RACICOT (1980) INC

METRO RICHELIEU *p 1363*
See MARCHE DENIGIL (1984) INC

METRO RICHELIEU CANDIAC INC *p 1073*
50 BOUL MONTCALM N, CANDIAC, QC, J5R 3L8
(450) 444-2300   *SIC* 5411

METRO RICHELIEU INC *p 614*
967 FENNELL AVE E, HAMILTON, ON, L8T 1R1
(905) 318-7777   *SIC* 5411

METRO RICHELIEU INC *p 1054*
50 BOUL SAINT-CHARLES BUREAU 17, BEACONSFIELD, QC, H9W 2X3
(514) 695-5811   *SIC* 5411

METRO RICHELIEU INC *p 1076*
200 BOUL D'ANJOU BUREAU 626, CHATEAUGUAY, QC, J6K 1C5
(450) 691-2880   *SIC* 5411

METRO RICHELIEU INC *p 1079*
299 RUE DES SAGUENEENS, CHICOUTIMI, QC, G7H 3A5
(418) 696-4114   *SIC* 5411

METRO RICHELIEU INC *p 1083*
1600B BOUL SAINT-MARTIN E BUREAU 300, COTE SAINT-LUC, QC, H7G 4S7
(450) 662-3300   *SIC* 7374

METRO RICHELIEU INC *p 1099*
565 BOUL SAINT-JOSEPH BUREAU 4, DRUMMONDVILLE, QC, J2C 2B6
(819) 474-2702   *SIC* 5411

METRO RICHELIEU INC *p 1104*
720 BOUL MALONEY O, GATINEAU, QC,

J8T 8K7
(819) 243-5117   *SIC* 5411
METRO RICHELIEU INC   p 1106
725A BOUL DE LA CARRIERE, GATINEAU, QC, J8Y 6T9
(819) 595-1344   *SIC* 5411
METRO RICHELIEU INC   p 1112
5012 BOUL TASCHEREAU, GREENFIELD PARK, QC, J4V 2J2
(450) 672-8966   *SIC* 5411
METRO RICHELIEU INC   p 1145
2901 CH DE CHAMBLY, LONGUEUIL, QC, J4L 1M7
(450) 651-6886   *SIC* 5411
METRO RICHELIEU INC   p 1161
11555 BOUL MAURICE-DUPLESSIS BUREAU 1, MONTREAL, QC, H1C 2A1
(514) 643-1000   *SIC* 4225
METRO RICHELIEU INC   p 1161
11011 BOUL MAURICE-DUPLESSIS, MONTREAL, QC, H1C 1V6
(514) 643-1000   *SIC* 5141
METRO RICHELIEU INC   p 1164
5400 AV PIERRE-DE COUBERTIN, MONTREAL, QC, H1N 1P7
SIC 5148
METRO RICHELIEU INC   p 1240
6000 BOUL HENRI-BOURASSA E, MONTREAL-NORD, QC, H1G 2T6
(514) 323-4370   *SIC* 5411
METRO RICHELIEU INC   p 1247
12225 BOUL INDUSTRIEL BUREAU 100, POINTE-AUX-TREMBLES, QC, H1B 5M7
(514) 355-8350   *SIC* 5122
METRO RICHELIEU INC   p 1251
325 BOUL SAINT-JEAN, POINTE-CLAIRE, QC, H9R 3J1
(514) 697-6520   *SIC* 5411
METRO RICHELIEU INC   p 1256
2968 BOUL SAINTE-ANNE, QUEBEC, QC, G1E 3J3
SIC 5431
METRO RICHELIEU INC   p 1267
635 AV NEWTON, QUEBEC, QC, G1P 4C4
(418) 871-7101   *SIC* 5141
METRO RICHELIEU INC   p 1283
85 BOUL BRIEN BUREAU 101, REPENTIGNY, QC, J6A 8B6
(450) 581-3072   *SIC* 5141
METRO RICHELIEU INC   p 1293
60 RUE D'ANVERS, SAINT-AUGUSTIN-DE-DESMAURES, QC, G3A 1S4
SIC 5431
METRO RICHELIEU INC   p 1313
3800 AV CUSSON, SAINT-HYACINTHE, QC, J2S 8V6
(450) 771-1651   *SIC* 5141
METRO RICHELIEU INC   p 1315
61 2E RANG E, SAINT-JEAN-PORT-JOLI, QC, G0R 3G0
(418) 598-3371   *SIC* 5411
METRO RICHELIEU INC   p 1317
600 RUE PIERRE-CAISSE BUREAU 2000, SAINT-JEAN-SUR-RICHELIEU, QC, J3A 1M1
(450) 348-0927   *SIC* 5411
METRO RICHELIEU INC   p 1346
6775 RUE JEAN-TALON E, SAINT-LEONARD, QC, H1S 1N2
(514) 252-0230   *SIC* 5411
METRO RICHELIEU INC   p 1366
398 CH LAROCQUE, SALABERRY-DE-VALLEYFIELD, QC, J6T 4C5
(450) 370-1444   *SIC* 5411
METRO RICHELIEU INC   p 1371
350 RUE BELVEDERE N, SHERBROOKE, QC, J1H 4B1
(819) 564-6014   *SIC* 5411
METRO RICHELIEU INC   p 1376
250 BOUL FISET, SOREL-TRACY, QC, J3P 3P7
(450) 742-4563   *SIC* 5142
METRO RICHELIEU INC   p 1388
750 BOUL DU SAINT-MAURICE, TROIS-RIVIERES, QC, G9A 3P6

(819) 371-1120   *SIC* 5411
METRO RICHELIEU INC   p 1398
601 BOUL JUTRAS E, VICTORIAVILLE, QC, G6P 7H4
(819) 752-6659   *SIC* 5411
METRO RICHELIEU INC   p 1402
4840 RUE SHERBROOKE O, WESTMOUNT, QC, H3Z 1G8
(514) 488-4083   *SIC* 5411
METRO ROSEMERE   p 1287
See 9067-3476 QUEBEC INC
METRO SIROIS   p 1285
See SUPER MARCHE SIROIS INC
METRO ST-JOSEPH   p 1168
See MARCHE J.C. MESSIER INC
METRO ST-RAYMOND   p 1351
See ALIMENTATION ST-RAYMOND INC
METRO SUPERMARKETS   p 610
See METRO ONTARIO INC
METRO SUZUKI   p 444
See 1937225 NOVA SCOTIA LIMITED
METRO TORONTO CONVENTION CENTRE   p 982
See METROPOLITAN TORONTO CONVENTION CENTRE CORPORATION
METRO TRANSIT   p 446
See HALIFAX REGIONAL MUNICIPALITY
METRO TRUCK   p 892
See METRO FREIGHTLINER HAMILTON INC
METRO VAL-EAST   p 1001
See 1011191 ONTARIO INC
METRO VANCOUVER HOUSING CORPORATION   p 190
4330 KINGSWAY SUITE 505, BURNABY, BC, V5H 4G7
(604) 432-6300   *SIC* 6531
METRO WALLCOVERINGS   p 555
See METRO ACQUISITION 2004, INC
METRO WASTE RECYCLING INC   p 816
2811 SHEFFIELD RD, OTTAWA, ON, K1B 3V8
(613) 742-1222   *SIC* 4953
METRO WIDE PERSONNEL INC   p 504
11 BLAIR DR, BRAMPTON, ON, L6T 2H4
SIC 7361
METRO-CAN CONSTRUCTION LTD   p 270
10470 152 ST SUITE 520, SURREY, BC, V3R 0Y3
(604) 583-1174   *SIC* 1522
METROBEC INC   p 1308
5055 RUE RAMSAY, SAINT-HUBERT, QC, J3Y 2S3
(450) 656-6666   *SIC* 4953
METROBUS   p 431
See ST. JOHN'S TRANSPORTATION COMMISSION
METROLAND MEDIA GROUP LTD   p 481
250 INDUSTRIAL PKY N, AURORA, ON, L4G 4C3
SIC 5963
METROLAND MEDIA GROUP LTD   p 523
5046 MAINWAY UNIT 2, BURLINGTON, ON, L7L 5Z1
(905) 632-4444   *SIC* 2711
METROLAND MEDIA GROUP LTD   p 612
44 FRID ST, HAMILTON, ON, L8N 3G3
(905) 526-3333   *SIC* 2711
METROLAND MEDIA GROUP LTD   p 711
3145 WOLFEDALE RD, MISSISSAUGA, ON, L5C 3A9
(905) 281-5656   *SIC* 2711
METROLAND MEDIA GROUP LTD   p 717
3715 LAIRD RD UNIT 6, MISSISSAUGA, ON, L5L 0A3
(905) 281-5656   *SIC* 2711
METROLAND MEDIA GROUP LTD   p 802
467 SPEERS RD SUITE 1, OAKVILLE, ON, L6K 3S4
(905) 845-3824   *SIC* 2711
METROLAND MEDIA GROUP LTD   p 813
865 FAREWELL ST, OSHAWA, ON, L1H 6N8

(905) 579-4400   *SIC* 2711
METROLAND MEDIA GROUP LTD   p 841
884 FORD ST, PETERBOROUGH, ON, K9J 5V3
(705) 749-3383   *SIC* 2711
METROLAND MEDIA GROUP LTD   p 882
65 LORNE ST, SMITHS FALLS, ON, K7A 3K8
(800) 267-7936   *SIC* 2711
METROLINX   p 712
3500 WOLFEDALE RD, MISSISSAUGA, ON, L5C 2V6
SIC 3743
METROLINX   p 784
200 STEEPROCK DR, NORTH YORK, ON, M3J 2T4
SIC 4011
METROLINX   p 920
580 COMMISSIONERS ST, TORONTO, ON, M4M 1A7
(416) 393-4111   *SIC* 4131
METROLINX   p 965
20 BAY ST SUITE 600, TORONTO, ON, M5J 2W3
(416) 869-3200   *SIC* 4011
METROLINX   p 965
97 FRONT ST W SUITE 200, TORONTO, ON, M5J 1E6
(416) 874-5900   *SIC* 4011
METROMEDIA MARKETING LTD   p 24
5774 10 ST NE, CALGARY, AB, T2E 8W7
(403) 291-3912   *SIC* 5199
METROPOLIS   p 1186
59 RUE SAINTE-CATHERINE E, MONTREAL, QC, H2X 1K5
(514) 844-3500   *SIC* 6512
METROPOLITAIN REGIONAL HOUSING AUTHORITY   p 455
2131 GOTTINGEN ST, HALIFAX, NS, B3K 5Z7
(902) 420-6000   *SIC* 6513
METROPOLITAN CALGARY FOUNDATION   p 36
7015 MACLEOD TRAIL SW SUITE 804, CALGARY, AB, T2H 2K6
(403) 276-5541   *SIC* 8361
METROPOLITAN CREDIT ADJUSTERS LTD   p 90
10310 JASPER AVE NW SUITE 400, EDMONTON, AB, T5J 2W4
(780) 423-2231   *SIC* 7322
METROPOLITAN HARDWOOD FLOORS, INC   p 206
811 CLIVEDEN AVE, DELTA, BC, V3M 5R6
(604) 395-2000   *SIC* 5023
METROPOLITAN HOTEL VANCOUVER   p 306
See LIVERTON HOTELS INTERNATIONAL INC
METROPOLITAN LIFE INSURANCE COMPANY   p 825
360 ALBERT ST SUITE 1750, OTTAWA, ON, K1R 7X7
SIC 6311
METROPOLITAN LIFE INSURANCE COMPANY OF CANADA   p 563
55 WATER ST W SUITE 100, CORNWALL, ON, K6J 1A1
SIC 6411
METROPOLITAN MAINTENANCE   p 648
See 469006 ONTARIO INC
METROPOLITAN RUST PROOFING INC   p 1375
4232 BOUL BOURQUE, SHERBROOKE, QC, J1N 1W7
(819) 829-2888   *SIC* 3479
METROPOLITAN TEA COMPANY LTD, THE   p 571
41 BUTTERICK RD, ETOBICOKE, ON, M8W 4W4
(416) 588-0089   *SIC* 5149
METROPOLITAN TORONTO CONVENTION

CENTRE CORPORATION   p 982
255 FRONT ST W, TORONTO, ON, M5V 2W6
(416) 585-8000   *SIC* 7389
METROPOLITAN TORONTO WATERWORKS SYSTEM   p 982
55 JOHN ST, TORONTO, ON, M5V 3C6
(416) 392-8211   *SIC* 4971
METROTOWN MITSUBISHI   p 192
See DEER LAKE SALES & SERVICE LTD
METROTOWN OPTICAL LTD   p 190
6411 NELSON AVE SUITE 105, BURNABY, BC, V5H 4H3
SIC 5995
METROTOWN STORE   p 191
See T & T SUPERMARKET INC
METRUS PROPERTIES LIMITED   p 555
30 FLORAL PKY SUITE 200, CONCORD, ON, L4K 4R1
(416) 798-7173   *SIC* 6512
METSO FLOW CONTROL CANADA LTD   p 1330
4716 BOUL THIMENS, SAINT-LAURENT, QC, H4R 2B2
(514) 908-7045   *SIC* 5084
METSO MINERALS CANADA INC   p 492
161 BRIDGE ST W UNIT 6, BELLEVILLE, ON, K8P 1K2
(613) 962-3411   *SIC* 3569
METSO MINERALS CANADA INC   p 1330
4900 BOUL THIMENS, SAINT-LAURENT, QC, H4R 2B2
(514) 335-5426   *SIC* 5084
METTKO CONSTRUCTION INC   p 768
200 YORKLAND BLVD SUITE 610, NORTH YORK, ON, M2J 5C1
(416) 444-9600   *SIC* 1542
METVIEW REALTY LIMITED   p 823
130 ALBERT ST SUITE 210, OTTAWA, ON, K1P 5G4
(613) 230-5174   *SIC* 6531
MEUBLE IDEAL LTEE   p 1297
6 RUE SAINT-THOMAS, SAINT-CHARLES-DE-BELLECHASSE, QC, G0R 2T0
(418) 887-3331   *SIC* 2511
MEUBLES BDM + INC   p 1150
215 BOUL OUEST, MASKINONGE, QC, J0K 1N0
(819) 227-2284   *SIC* 2511
MEUBLES CATHEDRA INC   p 1398
34 RUE DE L'ARTISAN, VICTORIAVILLE, QC, G6P 7E3
(819) 752-1641   *SIC* 2511
MEUBLES D'AUTRAY INC   p 1057
1180 RUE GREGOIRE, BERTHIERVILLE, QC, J0K 1A0
(450) 836-3187   *SIC* 1751
MEUBLES DENIS RIEL INC   p 1101
1555 BOUL INDUSTRIEL, FARNHAM, QC, J2N 2X3
(450) 293-3605   *SIC* 5712
MEUBLES DOMON   p 1126
See DOMON LTEE
MEUBLES FOLIOT INC   p 1320
721 BOUL ROLAND-GODARD, SAINT-JEROME, QC, J7Y 4C1
(450) 565-9166   *SIC* 2531
MEUBLES JAYMAR CORP   p 1379
75 RUE JAYMAR, TERREBONNE, QC, J6W 1M5
(450) 471-4172   *SIC* 2512
MEUBLES JCPERREAULT INC   p 1352
5 RUE INDUSTRIELLE, SAINT-ROCH-DE-L'ACHIGAN, QC, J0K 3H0
(450) 588-7211   *SIC* 5712
MEUBLES LEON   p 1275
See LEON'S FURNITURE LIMITED
MEUBLES MARCHAND INC, LES   p 1391
1767 3E AV, VAL-D'OR, QC, J9P 1W3
(819) 874-8777   *SIC* 5712
MEUBLES REAL LEVASSEUR & FILS INC   p 1246
1907 RUE PRINCIPALE, POHENEG-

AMOOK, QC, G0L 1J0
(418) 859-3159   *SIC* 5712
MEUBLES RIVE SUD   *p* 1357
See SOUTH SHORE INDUSTRIES LTD
MEUNERIE CHARLEVOIX INC   *p* 1353
31 RANG SAINT-GEORGES, SAINT-URBAIN-DE-CHARLEVOIX, QC, G0A 4K0
(418) 639-2472   *SIC* 5191
MEUNERIE SAINT-DAMASE   *p* 1109
See COOP DES MONTEREGIENNES, LA
MEUNERIE SAWYERVILLE INC   *p* 1082
100 RUE DE LA MEUNERIE, COOKSHIRE-EATON, QC, J0B 1M0
(819) 875-5471   *SIC* 5191
MEVOTECH LP   *p* 988
240 BRIDGELAND AVE, TORONTO, ON, M6A 1Z4
(416) 783-7800   *SIC* 5013
MEX Y CAN TRADING (EAST) INC.   *p* 741
6799 PACIFIC CIR UNIT 4, MISSISSAUGA, ON, L5T 1S6
(905) 670-3355   *SIC* 5193
MEXICAN FLOWER TRADING INC   *p* 741
1240 MID-WAY BLVD UNIT A, MISSISSAUGA, ON, L5T 2B8
(905) 670-0870   *SIC* 5992
MEXICO TOURISM BOARD   *p* 303
See CONSEJO DE PROMOCION TURISTICA DE MEXICO S.A. DE C.A.
MEXX   *p* 1325
See COMPAGNIE MEXX CANADA
MEYER, GENE INSURANCE AGENCIES LTD   *p* 706
315 OXBOW CRES, MISSISSAUGA, ON, L4Z 2S4
(905) 890-0998   *SIC* 6411
MEYERS FRUIT FARMS LTD   *p* 761
1444 IRVINE RD RR 4, NIAGARA ON THE LAKE, ON, L0S 1J0
(905) 934-3925   *SIC* 5193
MEYERS TRANSPORT LIMITED   *p* 491
53 GRILLS RD, BELLEVILLE, ON, K8N 4Z5
(613) 967-8440   *SIC* 4213
MEYKNECHT-LISCHER CONTRACTORS LTD   *p* 541
145 WALGREEN RD, CARP, ON, K0A 1L0
SIC 1521
MFI FOOD CANADA LTD   *p* 391
70 IRENE ST, WINNIPEG, MB, R3T 4E1
(204) 453-6613   *SIC* 2015
MFL MANAGEMENT LIMITED   *p* 987
100 KING ST W, TORONTO, ON, M5X 2A1
(416) 362-0714   *SIC* 6159
MFP RESOURCES CORP   *p* 110
5920 76 AVE NW, EDMONTON, AB, T6B 0A6
(780) 465-9668   *SIC* 5172
MFS INVESTMENT MANAGEMENT CANADA LIMITED   *p* 970
77 KING ST W SUITE 3500, TORONTO, ON, M5K 2A1
(416) 862-9800   *SIC* 6282
MFXCHANGE HOLDINGS INC   *p* 777
225 DUNCAN MILL RD SUITE 320, NORTH YORK, ON, M3B 3K9
(416) 385-4800   *SIC* 6411
MGC SYSTEMS INTERNATIONAL LTD   *p* 555
25 INTERCHANGE WAY, CONCORD, ON, L4K 5W3
(905) 660-4655   *SIC* 3669
MGEU   *p* 378
See MANITOBA GOVERNMENT AND GENERAL EMPLOYEES UNION
MGI SECURITIES INC   *p* 942
26 WELLINGTON ST E SUITE 900, TORONTO, ON, M5E 1S2
(416) 864-6477   *SIC* 6211
MGI TECHNOLOGIES, DIV OF   *p* 253
See ARROW SPEED CONTROLS LIMITED
MGM ELECTRIC LIMITED   *p* 908
724 MACDONELL ST, THUNDER BAY, ON, P7B 4A6
(807) 345-7767   *SIC* 5063

MGN CONSTRUCTORS INC   *p* 85
11760 109 ST NW UNIT W306, EDMONTON, AB, T5G 2T8
(780) 471-4840   *SIC* 1541
MGTP   *p* 1163
See MONTREAL GATEWAY TERMINALS PARTNERSHIP
MHC   *p* 718
See MAINWAY HUNTER CREIGHTON INSURANCE INC
MHD - ROCKLAND INC   *p* 1355
21250 BOUL INDUSTRIEL, SAINTE-ANNE-DE-BELLEVUE, QC, H9X 0B4
(514) 453-1632   *SIC* 5088
MHI CANADA AEROSPACE INC   *p* 688
6390 NORTHWEST DR, MISSISSAUGA, ON, L4V 1S1
(905) 612-6781   *SIC* 3728
MHK INSURANCE INC   *p* 96
12316 107 AVE NW, EDMONTON, AB, T5M 1Z1
(780) 454-9363   *SIC* 6411
MHS   *p* 765
See MULTI-HEALTH SYSTEMS INC
MI CONSTRUCTION SUPPLY   *p* 369
See MOORE INDUSTRIAL LTD
MI GROUP LTD, THE   *p* 697
2425 MATHESON BLVD E, MISSISSAUGA, ON, L4W 5K4
(905) 812-8900   *SIC* 4731
MI5 DIGITAL COMMUNICATIONS INC *p* 703
1550 CATERPILLAR RD, MISSISSAUGA, ON, L4X 1E7
(905) 848-1550   *SIC* 2752
MI5 PRINT & DIGITAL COMMUNICATIONS *p* 702
See 2214264 ONTARIO INC
MI9 RETAIL   *p* 1157
See RAYMARK ULC
MIABC   *p* 292
See MUNICIPAL INSURANCE ASSOCIATION OF BRITISH COLUMBIA
MIALTA COLONY   *p* 171
See MIALTA HUTTERIAN BRETHREN
MIALTA HUTTERIAN BRETHREN   *p* 171
GD, VULCAN, AB, T0L 2B0
SIC 8211
MIAMI COLONY FARMS LTD   *p* 352
GD STN MAIN, MORDEN, MB, R6M 1A1
(204) 435-2447   *SIC* 0191
MIBRO GROUP, THE   *p* 869
See MIBRO PARTNERS
MIBRO PARTNERS   *p* 869
111 SINNOTT RD, SCARBOROUGH, ON, M1L 4S6
(416) 285-9000   *SIC* 5072
MIC-MAC BEVERAGE ROOM LIMITED   *p* 443
219 WAVERLEY RD, DARTMOUTH, NS, B2X 2C3
(902) 434-7600   *SIC* 5411
MICHAEL GARRON HOSPITAL   *p* 917
See TORONTO EAST HEALTH NETWORK
MICHAEL HILL JEWELLER (CANADA) LTD   *p* 315
1090 PENDER ST W SUITE 530, VANCOUVER, BC, V6E 2N7
(604) 913-3114   *SIC* 5944
MICHAEL JACKSON MOTOR SALES LIMITED   *p* 547
480 HUME ST, COLLINGWOOD, ON, L9Y 1W6
(705) 445-2222   *SIC* 5511
MICHAEL KORS (CANADA) CO   *p* 1213
3424 RUE SIMPSON, MONTREAL, QC, H3G 2J3
(514) 737-5677   *SIC* 5632
MICHAEL KORS (CANADA) HOLDINGS LTD   *p* 1213
3424 RUE SIMPSON, MONTREAL, QC, H3G 2J3
(514) 737-5677   *SIC* 5632
MICHAEL ROSSY LTEE   *p* 1326

450 BOUL LEBEAU, SAINT-LAURENT, QC, H4N 1R7
(514) 335-6255   *SIC* 5311
MICHAEL S WONG PHARMACY LTD   *p* 781
1881 STEELES AVE W SUITE 819, NORTH YORK, ON, M3H 5Y4
(416) 665-2631   *SIC* 5912
MICHAEL SMITH LABORATORIES   *p* 324
2185 EAST MALL SUITE 301, VANCOUVER, BC, V6T 1Z4
(604) 822-4838   *SIC* 8731
MICHAEL'S EQUIPMENT LTD   *p* 837
105 SCOTT AVE, PARIS, ON, N3L 3K4
(519) 442-0317   *SIC* 5087
MICHAELS ARTS & CRAFTS STORE   *p* 509
See MICHAELS OF CANADA, ULC
MICHAELS OF CANADA, ULC   *p* 509
547 STEELES AVE E UNIT 3, BRAMPTON, ON, L6W 4S2
(905) 874-9640   *SIC* 5945
MICHANIE CONSTRUCTION INC   *p* 816
2825 SHEFFIELD RD SUITE 201, OTTAWA, ON, K1B 3V8
(613) 737-7717   *SIC* 1542
MICHAUD PETROLEUM INC   *p* 403
866 BOUL EVERARD H DAIGLE, GRAND-SAULT/GRAND FALLS, NB, E3Z 3C8
(506) 473-1197   *SIC* 5983
MICHEL ST ARNEAULT   *p* 1307
See 131638 CANADA INC
MICHEL ST-ARNEAULT INC   *p* 1308
4605 AV THIBAULT, SAINT-HUBERT, QC, J3Y 3S8
(450) 445-0550   *SIC* 2037
MICHEL THIBAUDEAU INC   *p* 1111
70 RUE SIMONDS N, GRANBY, QC, J2J 2L1
(450) 378-9884   *SIC* 5251
MICHEL'S BAGUETTE   *p* 788
See 1456882 ONTARIO LTD
MICHEL'S INDUSTRIES INC   *p* 1436
3 ENTRANCE RD, ST GREGOR, SK, S0K 3X0
(306) 366-2184   *SIC* 3523
MICHEL'S SUPER A FOODS LTD   *p* 131
3100 PINE PLAZA, GRANDE CACHE, AB, T0E 0Y0
(780) 827-2434   *SIC* 5411
MICHELIN AMERIQUE DU NORD (CANADA) INC   *p* 441
233 LOGAN RD, BRIDGEWATER, NS, B4V 3T3
(902) 543-8141   *SIC* 3011
MICHELIN AMERIQUE DU NORD (CANADA) INC   *p* 463
2863 GRANTON RD, NEW GLASGOW, NS, B2H 5C6
(888) 871-4444   *SIC* 5014
MICHELIN AMERIQUE DU NORD (CANADA) INC   *p* 470
866 RANDOLPH RD, WATERVILLE, NS, B0P 1V0
(902) 538-8021   *SIC* 5014
MICHELIN AMERIQUE DU NORD (CANADA) INC   *p* 470
866 RANDOLPH RD, WATERVILLE, NS, B0P 1V0
(902) 535-3675   *SIC* 3089
MICHELIN NORTH AMERICA   *p* 441
See MICHELIN AMERIQUE DU NORD (CANADA) INC
MICHENER INSTITUTE OF EDUCATION AT UHN, THE   *p* 977
222 SAINT PATRICK ST SUITE 414, TORONTO, ON, M5T 1V4
(416) 596-3101   *SIC* 8221
MICHENER-ALLEN AUCTIONEERING LTD   *p* 98
HWY 16 A, EDMONTON, AB, T5P 4V8
(780) 470-5584   *SIC* 7389
MICHIELI'S SUPERMARKET LIMITED *p* 881
79 QUEEN ST, SIOUX LOOKOUT, ON, P8T 1A3

(807) 737-1630   *SIC* 5411
MICK & ANGELO'S EATERY AND BAR *p* 760
See BIAMONTE INVESTMENTS LTD
MICMAC BAR & GRILL   *p* 443
See MIC-MAC BEVERAGE ROOM LIMITED
MICON SPORTS LTD   *p* 811
2085 TENTH LINE RD, ORLEANS, ON, K4A 4C5
(613) 731-6006   *SIC* 5941
MICRALYNE INC   *p* 121
1911 94 ST NW, EDMONTON, AB, T6N 1E6
(780) 431-4400   *SIC* 3674
MICRO BIRD HOLDINGS, INC   *p* 1100
3000 RUE GIRARDIN, DRUMMONDVILLE, QC, J2E 0A1
(819) 477-2012   *SIC* 3713
MICRO COM SYSTEMS LTD   *p* 289
27 7TH AVE E, VANCOUVER, BC, V5T 1M4
(604) 872-6771   *SIC* 7389
MICRO ELECTRONIQUES G.B. INC   *p* 1335
6620 RUE ABRAMS, SAINT-LAURENT, QC, H4S 1Y1
(514) 333-7373   *SIC* 5045
MICRO FORUM SERVICES GROUP   *p* 992
See 1508235 ONTARIO INC
MICRO LOGIC CENTRE DE SERVICE   *p* 1273
See MICRO LOGIC SAINTE-FOY LTEE
MICRO LOGIC SAINTE-FOY LTEE   *p* 1273
2786 CH SAINTE-FOY, QUEBEC, QC, G1V 1V8
(418) 658-6624   *SIC* 5045
MICRO MACHINE & TOOL, DIV OF   *p* 787
See KK PRECISION INC
MICRO-CLAIR INTERNATIONAL INC   *p* 1308
3050 2E RUE, SAINT-HUBERT, QC, J3Y 8Y7
(438) 796-5712   *SIC* 2842
MICRO-ONDES APOLLO LTEE   *p* 1094
1650 RTE TRANSCANADIENNE, DORVAL, QC, H9P 1H7
(514) 421-2211   *SIC* 3663
MICRO-WATT   *p* 76
See MICRO-WATT CONTROL DEVICES LTD
MICRO-WATT CONTROL DEVICES LTD *p* 76
11141 15 ST NE, CALGARY, AB, T3K 0Z5
(403) 250-1594   *SIC* 5084
MICROAGE   *p* 1096
See DRUMMOND INFORMATIQUE LTEE
MICROAGE BASICS   *p* 597
See BLUEWATER OFFICE EQUIPMENT LTD
MICROAGE COMPUTER CENTRES   *p* 862
See 170260 CANADA INC
MICROART SERVICES INC   *p* 680
190 DUFFIELD DR, MARKHAM, ON, L6G 1B5
(905) 752-0800   *SIC* 3679
MICROBYTES   *p* 1251
See ORDINATEURS EN GROS MICROBYTES INC, LES
MICROCEL CORPORATION   *p* 756
1274 RINGWELL DR UNIT 2, NEWMARKET, ON, L3Y 9C7
(905) 853-2568   *SIC* 5065
MICROCOM 'M' INC   *p* 1267
3710 BOUL WILFRID-HAMEL, QUEBEC, QC, G1P 2J2
(418) 871-7676   *SIC* 7382
MICROFLEX 2001 LLC   *p* 1273
2505 BOUL LAURIER BUREAU 300, QUEBEC, QC, G1V 2L2
(418) 694-2300   *SIC* 7371
MICROHARD SYSTEMS INC   *p* 76
150 COUNTRY HILLS LANDNG NW SUITE 101, CALGARY, AB, T3K 5P3
(403) 248-0028   *SIC* 3669
MICROLAND TECHNICAL SERVICES INC *p* 672

170 ALDEN RD UNIT 2, MARKHAM, ON, L3R 4C1
(905) 940-1982   *SIC* 7371

MICROSEMI SEMICONDUCTOR ULC *p* 624
400 MARCH RD, KANATA, ON, K2K 3H4
(613) 592-0200   *SIC* 3674

MICROSERVE BUSINESS COMPUTER SERVICES *p* 187
See *341234 B.C. LTD*

MICROSOFT *p* 724
See *MICROSOFT CANADA INC*

MICROSOFT CANADA INC *p* 54
500 4 AVE SW SUITE 1900, CALGARY, AB, T2P 2V6
(403) 296-6500   *SIC* 7371

MICROSOFT CANADA INC *p* 724
1950 MEADOWVALE BLVD, MISSISSAUGA, ON, L5N 8L9
(905) 568-0434   *SIC* 5045

MICROVITE INVESTMENTS LIMITED *p* 814
1000 THORNTON RD S UNIT B, OSHAWA, ON, L1J 7E2
(905) 619-6565   *SIC* 5192

MICROWAVE COMPONENETS AND SUBSYSTEMS *p* 1002
See *ITS ELECTRONICS INC*

MID CANADIAN INDUSTRIES *p* 381
1577 ERIN ST, WINNIPEG, MB, R3E 2T2
(204) 925-6600   *SIC* 7514

MID EAST FOOD CENTRE *p* 818
See *MIDEAST FOOD DISTRIBUTORS (1987) LTD*

MID SOUTH CONTRACTORS ULC *p* 1021
3110 DEVON DR, WINDSOR, ON, N8X 4L2
(519) 966-6163   *SIC* 1731

MID WEST COAST CANADA INC *p* 892
400 JONES RD SUITE 106, STONEY CREEK, ON, L8E 5P4
(905) 578-9993   *SIC* 4213

MID WESTERN MACHINE WORKS (1987) INC *p* 17
7815 46 ST SE, CALGARY, AB, T2C 2Y5
(403) 279-0727   *SIC* 1389

MID WESTERN REDI-MIX 1980 *p* 347
See *WHEAT CITY CONCRETE PRODUCTS LTD*

MID-ARCTIC TRANSPORTATION CO. LTD *p* 101
18151 107 AVE NW, EDMONTON, AB, T5S 1K4
(780) 484-8800   *SIC* 4213

MID-CANADA MOD CENTER *p* 518
See *KITCHENER AERO AVIONICS LIMITED*

MID-CITY CONSTRUCTION MANAGEMENT INC *p* 110
7103 42 ST NW, EDMONTON, AB, T6B 2T1
(780) 463-0385   *SIC* 1794

MID-LAND GROUP REALTY INC *p* 853
330 HIGHWAY 7 E SUITE 502, RICHMOND HILL, ON, L4B 3P8
(905) 709-0828   *SIC* 6531

MID-NITE SUN TRANSPORTATION LTD *p* 115
5805 98 ST NW, EDMONTON, AB, T6E 3L4
(780) 431-2877   *SIC* 4213

MID-ONTARIO DIESEL LIMITED *p* 487
400 DUNLOP ST W, BARRIE, ON, L4N 1C2
(705) 722-1122   *SIC* 5511

MID-ONTARIO MACK *p* 487
See *MID-ONTARIO DIESEL LIMITED*

MID-RANGE COMPUTER GROUP INC *p* 672
85 IDEMA RD, MARKHAM, ON, L3R 1A9
(905) 940-1814   *SIC* 5734

MID-RANGE TECHNICAL SERVICES *p* 672
See *MID-RANGE COMPUTER GROUP INC*

MID-SCARBOROUGH COMMUNITY RECREATION CENTER *p* 868
2467 EGLINTON AVE E, SCARBOROUGH, ON, M1K 2R1
(416) 267-0714   *SIC* 7999

MID-TOWN FORD SALES LIMITED *p* 391
1717 WAVERLEY ST SUITE 100, WINNIPEG, MB, R3T 6A9
(204) 284-7650   *SIC* 5511

MID-VALLEY CONSTRUCTION (1997) LIMITED *p* 460
15096 HIGHWAY 1, KINGSTON, NS, B0P 1R0
(902) 765-6312   *SIC* 1521

MID-WAY MOTORS (QUINTE) LIMITED *p* 491
48 MILLENNIUM PKY, BELLEVILLE, ON, K8N 4Z5
(613) 968-4538   *SIC* 5511

MID-WEST DESIGN & CONSTRUCTION LTD *p* 146
1065 30 ST SW, MEDICINE HAT, AB, T1B 3N3
(403) 526-0925   *SIC* 1542

MID-WEST GARMENT *p* 381
See *MWG APPAREL CORP*

MIDAS *p* 73
See *CANTELON ENTERPRISES INC*

MIDAS *p* 387
See *3867359 MANITOBA INC*

MIDAS AUTO SERVICE *p* 814
See *WALTON ENTERPRISES LTD*

MIDAS GOLD CORP *p* 307
999 HASTINGS ST W SUITE 890, VANCOUVER, BC, V6C 2W2
(778) 724-4700   *SIC* 1041

MIDAS REALTY CORPORATION OF CANADA INC *p* 874
105 COMMANDER BLVD, SCARBOROUGH, ON, M1S 3M7
(416) 291-4261   *SIC* 6531

MIDBEC LTEE *p* 1099
1725 BOUL LEMIRE, DRUMMONDVILLE, QC, J2C 5A5
(819) 477-1070   *SIC* 5064

MIDDLE ATLANTIC PRODUCTS-CANADA, INC *p* 891
113 IBER RD, STITTSVILLE, ON, K2S 1E7
(613) 836-2501   *SIC* 5046

MIDDLECHURCH HOME OF WINNIPEG INC *p* 360
280 BALDERSTONE RD, WEST ST PAUL, MB, R4A 4A6
(204) 339-1947   *SIC* 8051

MIDDLEFIELD COLLEGIATE INSTITUTE *p* 678
See *YORK REGION DISTRICT SCHOOL BOARD*

MIDDLEFIELD GROUP LIMITED *p* 987
100 KING ST W SUITE 5855, TORONTO, ON, M5X 2A1
(416) 362-0714   *SIC* 6719

MIDDLESEX COMMUNITY LIVING *p* 897
82 FRONT ST W, STRATHROY, ON, N7G 1X7
(519) 245-1301   *SIC* 8399

MIDDLESEX CONCRETE FORMING LTD *p* 628
9644 TOWNSEND LINE SUITE 3, KERWOOD, ON, N0M 2B0
(519) 247-3752   *SIC* 1771

MIDDLESEX LONDON HEALTH UNIT *p* 654
50 KING ST SUITE 101, LONDON, ON, N6A 5L7
(519) 663-5317   *SIC* 8071

MIDDLETON GROUP INC *p* 672
75 DENISON ST SUITE 6, MARKHAM, ON, L3R 1B5
(905) 475-6556   *SIC* 2759

MIDEAST FOOD DISTRIBUTORS (1987) LTD *p* 818
1010 BELFAST RD, OTTAWA, ON, K1G 4A2
(613) 244-2525   *SIC* 5499

MIDFIELD *p* 144
See *EUROPUMP SYSTEMS INC*

MIDISLAND HOLDINGS LTD *p* 234
4750 RUTHERFORD RD SUITE 103, NANAIMO, BC, V9T 4K6

(250) 729-2611   *SIC* 5411

MIDLAND AUTOMOTIVE CORPORATION *p* 681
868 KING ST, MIDLAND, ON, L4R 0B8
(705) 526-1344   *SIC* 5511

MIDLAND COURIER *p* 398
See *MIDLAND TRANSPORT LIMITED*

MIDLAND FOOD PRODUCTS INC *p* 586
195 REXDALE BLVD, ETOBICOKE, ON, M9W 1P7
(416) 741-0123   *SIC* 5146

MIDLAND FOODLAND *p* 681
See *KYSY INC*

MIDLAND FOODS (WINNIPEG), INC *p* 368
900 NAIRN AVE, WINNIPEG, MB, R2L 0X8
(204) 663-3883   *SIC* 5146

MIDLAND GARDENS INC *p* 870
130 MIDLAND AVE SUITE 1006, SCARBOROUGH, ON, M1N 4E6
(416) 264-2301   *SIC* 8741

MIDLAND GROUP *p* 768
See *MIDLAND METALS INTERNATIONAL INC*

MIDLAND HONDA *p* 681
See *MIDLAND AUTOMOTIVE CORPORATION*

MIDLAND LOGISTICS & FREIGHT BROKERAGE, DIV OF *p* 504
See *MIDLAND TRANSPORT LIMITED*

MIDLAND LUMBER & BUILDING SUPPLIES LTD *p* 681
200 THIRD ST, MIDLAND, ON, L4R 3R9
(705) 526-2264   *SIC* 5211

MIDLAND MANUFACTURING LIMITED *p* 355
36 MAIN ST E, ROSENORT, MB, R0G 1W0
(204) 746-2348   *SIC* 3713

MIDLAND METALS *p* 766
See *2023225 ONTARIO LTD*

MIDLAND METALS INTERNATIONAL INC *p* 768
259 YORKLAND RD SUITE 300, NORTH YORK, ON, M2J 5B2
(416) 733-9500   *SIC* 5051

MIDLAND POWER UTILITY CORPORATION *p* 681
16984 12 HWY, MIDLAND, ON, L4R 4P4
(705) 526-9361   *SIC* 4911

MIDLAND SECONDARY SCHOOL *p* 682
See *SIMCOE COUNTY DISTRICT SCHOOL BOARD, THE*

MIDLAND TIM-BR MART *p* 681
See *MIDLAND LUMBER & BUILDING SUPPLIES LTD*

MIDLAND TOYOTA *p* 681
See *894812 ONTARIO INC*

MIDLAND TRANSPORT LIMITED *p* 398
100 MIDLAND DR, DIEPPE, NB, E1A 6X4
(506) 858-5555   *SIC* 4213

MIDLAND TRANSPORT LIMITED *p* 447
31 SIMMONDS DR, DARTMOUTH, NS, B3B 1R4
(902) 494-5555   *SIC* 4212

MIDLAND TRANSPORT LIMITED *p* 504
102 GLIDDEN RD, BRAMPTON, ON, L6T 5N4
(905) 456-5555   *SIC* 4213

MIDLAND TRANSPORT LIMITED *p* 504
102 GLIDDEN RD, BRAMPTON, ON, L6T 5N4
(905) 456-5555   *SIC* 4212

MIDLAND TRANSPORT LIMITED *p* 1094
1560 BOUL HYMUS, DORVAL, QC, H9P 1J6
(888) 643-5263   *SIC* 4212

MIDLITE CONSTRUCTION LTD *p* 129
135 BOREAL AVE, FORT MCMURRAY, AB, T9K 0T4
(780) 714-6559   *SIC* 1623

MIDNIGHT EXPRESS & CARTAGE LTD *p* 697

5355 CREEKBANK RD, MISSISSAUGA, ON, L4W 5L5
(905) 629-0712   *SIC* 4213

MIDNIGHT MECHANICAL LIMITED *p* 435
42099 MACKENZIE HWY, HAY RIVER, NT, X0E 0R9
(867) 874-2201   *SIC* 5172

MIDNIGHT PETROLEUM *p* 435
See *MIDNIGHT MECHANICAL LIMITED*

MIDOME CONSTRUCTION SERVICES LTD *p* 555
665 MILLWAY AVE SUITE 65, CONCORD, ON, L4K 3T8
(905) 738-2211   *SIC* 1542

MIDSTREAM ENERGY PARTNERS (USA), LLC *p* 54
205 5 AVE SW SUITE 3900, CALGARY, AB, T2P 2V7
(403) 296-1660   *SIC* 5172

MIDSTREAM LPG PARTNERSHIP *p* 54
205 5 AVE SW SUITE 3900, CALGARY, AB, T2P 2V7
(403) 266-1985   *SIC* 5172

MIDTOWN HONDA *p* 788
See *1673612 ONTARIO INC*

MIDTOWN PHARMASAVE *p* 464
See *PARAMOUNT PHARMACIES LIMITED*

MIDTOWN SATURN SAAB ISUZU *p* 918
See *ROY FOSS SATURN SAAB OF LEASIDE LTD*

MIDWAY LIVESTOCK *p* 143
See *PERLICH BROS. AUCTION MARKET LTD*

MIDWAY LUMBER MILLS LIMITED *p* 903
41 SHERWOOD RD, THESSALON, ON, P0R 1L0
(705) 842-3246   *SIC* 5211

MIDWAY MOTORS LTD *p* 439
2499 CABOT TRAIL, BADDECK, NS, B0E 1B0
(902) 295-2290   *SIC* 5511

MIDWAY TIRE EXCEL *p* 275
See *0756271 B.C. LTD*

MIDWEST FABRICATORS LTD *p* 101
18073 107 AVE NW SUITE 235, EDMONTON, AB, T5S 1K3
(780) 447-0747   *SIC* 3499

MIDWEST PROPERTY MANAGEMENT *p* 89
See *MACLAB ENTERPRISES CORPORATION*

MIDWEST RESTAURANT INC *p* 1416
2037 PARK ST, REGINA, SK, S4N 6S2
(306) 781-5655   *SIC* 5812

MIDWEST RESTAURANT INC *p* 1424
3134 8TH ST E, SASKATOON, SK, S7H 0W2
(306) 374-9800   *SIC* 5812

MIDWEST SURVEYS INC *p* 9
2827 SUNRIDGE BLVD NE, CALGARY, AB, T1Y 6G1
(403) 244-7471   *SIC* 8713

MIDWESTERN ONTARIO SERVICE EXPERT *p* 1006
826 KING ST N UNIT 14, WATERLOO, ON, N2J 4G8
(519) 664-2974   *SIC* 5722

MIEDEMA'S MOTOR SALES LTD *p* 476
1 ADDISON RD, ALLISTON, ON, L9R 1V2
(705) 435-7609   *SIC* 5511

MIELE ENTERPRISES INC *p* 504
87 WENTWORTH CRT, BRAMPTON, ON, L6T 5L4
(416) 740-1096   *SIC* 1542

MIELE LIMITED *p* 556
161 FOUR VALLEY DR, CONCORD, ON, L4K 4V8
(905) 532-2270   *SIC* 5064

MIELZYNSKI, PETER AGENCIES LIMITED *p* 798
231 OAK PARK BLVD SUITE 400, OAKVILLE, ON, L6H 7S8
(905) 257-2116   *SIC* 5182

MIERAU CONSTRUCTION LTD *p* 177

30444 GREAT NORTHERN AVE SUITE 201, ABBOTSFORD, BC, V2T 6Y6

(604) 850-3536   SIC 1542

MIFF   p 1123
See MECANIQUE INDUSTRIELLE FORTIER & FILS INC

MIFO MOUVEMENT D'IMPLICATION p 810
See MOUVEMENT D'IMPLICATION FRAN-COPHONE D'ORLEANS

MIG HOLDINGS INC   p 801
156 REYNOLDS ST, OAKVILLE, ON, L6J 3K9

(905) 339-0229   SIC 5149

MIGAO CORPORATION   p 954
200 UNIVERSITY AVE SUITE300, TORONTO, ON, M5H 4H1

(416) 869-1108   SIC 1474

MIGHTY ELECTRIC   p 1205
See IMAGE HOME PRODUCTS INC, L'

MIHIR INTERNATIONAL   p 865
531 MEADOWVALE RD, SCARBOROUGH, ON, M1C 1S7

(416) 989-2445   SIC 1542

MIKE AND LORI'S NO FRILLS   p 763
975 MCKEOWN AVE, NORTH BAY, ON, P1B 9P2

(866) 987-6453   SIC 5411

MIKE AND MIKE'S INC   p 1032
1 ROYAL GATE BLVD UNIT F, WOOD-BRIDGE, ON, L4L 8Z7

(416) 987-2772   SIC 5149

MIKE DEAN BUTCHER LIMITED   p 544
19 KING ST, CHESTERVILLE, ON, K0C 1H0

(613) 448-2822   SIC 5411

MIKE DEAN'S SUPER FOOD STORES   p 544
See MIKE DEAN BUTCHER LIMITED

MIKE DOYLE DODGE CHRYSLER INC   p 901
2555 REGENT ST, SUDBURY, ON, P3E 6K6

(705) 523-1101   SIC 5511

MIKE JACKSON GM   p 547
See MICHAEL JACKSON MOTOR SALES LIMITED

MIKE KNAPP FORD SALES LIMITED   p 1012
607 NIAGARA ST, WELLAND, ON, L3C 1L9

(905) 732-3673   SIC 5511

MIKE PRIESTNER AUTOMOTIVE GROUP LTD   p 115
3603 99 ST NW SUITE 780, EDMONTON, AB, T6E 6K6

(780) 450-1021   SIC 5511

MIKE WIEGELE HELICOPTER SKIING   p 180
See CARIBOO HELICOPTER SKIING (88) LTD

MIKE'S FISH MARKET   p 573
See ALLSEAS FISHERIES INC

MIKE'S NO FRILLS   p 860
889 EXMOUTH ST, SARNIA, ON, N7T 5R3

(866) 987-6453   SIC 5411

MIKE'S ONE STOP INC   p 607
229 RORKE AVE S, HAILEYBURY, ON, P0J 1K0

(705) 672-3667   SIC 5541

MIKEY'S GENERAL SALES & REPAIR LTD   p 913
1301 AIRPORT RD, TIMMINS, ON, P4P 0A8

(705) 268-6050   SIC 5571

MIKISEW MIDDLE SCHOOL   p 348
See CROSS LAKE EDUCATION AUTHOR-ITY

MIKKELSEN-COWARD & CO LTD   p 372
1615 INKSTER BLVD, WINNIPEG, MB, R2X 1R2

(204) 694-8900   SIC 1711

MILACRON CANADA CORP   p 523
1175 APPLEBY LINE UNIT B1, BURLING-TON, ON, L7L 5H9

(905) 319-1919   SIC 5169

MILANI PLUMBING DRAINAGE & HEATING LTD   p 190

5526 KINGSWAY, BURNABY, BC, V5H 2G2

(604) 453-1234   SIC 5999

MILBORNE REAL ESTATE INC   p 927
385 MADISON AVE, TORONTO, ON, M4V 2W7

(416) 928-9998   SIC 6531

MILEPOST MANUFACTURING, DIV OF   p 168
See MILEPOST OILFIELD SERVICES LTD

MILEPOST OILFIELD SERVICES LTD p 168
26004 TWP RD 544 UNIT 43, STURGEON COUNTY, AB, T8T 0B6

(780) 459-1030   SIC 3443

MILES INDUSTRIES LTD   p 238
2255 DOLLARTON HWY SUITE 190, NORTH VANCOUVER, BC, V7H 3B1

(604) 984-3496   SIC 3429

MILES MACDONELL COLLEGIATE   p 367
See RIVER EAST TRANSCONA SCHOOL DIVISION

MILES NADAL JEWISH COMMUNITY CEN-TRE   p 976
750 SPADINA AVE, TORONTO, ON, M5S 2J2

(416) 944-8002   SIC 8322

MILES PRODUCE LTD   p 1006
1701 OLD HIGHWAY 24, WATERFORD, ON, N0E 1Y0

(519) 443-7227   SIC 0161

MILESTEP PHARMACY SERVICES INC   p 251
5240 DOMANO BLVD UNIT 470, PRINCE GEORGE, BC, V2N 4A1

(250) 964-1888   SIC 5912

MILESTONE GRILL AND BAR   p 573
See CARA OPERATIONS QUEBEC LTD

MILESTONE'S GRILL AND BAR   p 983
See RECIPE UNLIMITED CORPORATION

MILESTONES GRILL & BAR   p 1000
See RECIPE UNLIMITED CORPORATION

MILESTONES RESTAURANT   p 336
See CAUSEWAY RESTAURANTS LTD

MILFORA DAIRY SUPPLIES INC   p 620
743 SKYHILLS RD, HUNTSVILLE, ON, P1H 2N5

(705) 789-4557   SIC 5149

MILFORD COLONY FARMING CO. LTD   p 153
GD, RAYMOND, AB, T0K 2S0

(403) 752-4478   SIC 0111

MILITEX COATINGS INC   p 649
1881 HURON ST, LONDON, ON, N5V 3A5

(519) 659-0528   SIC 3471

MILK MARC VARIETY   p 860
See ROMAX VARIETY LIMITED

MILL & TIMBER PRODUCTS LTD   p 275
12770 116 AVE, SURREY, BC, V3V 7H9

(604) 580-2781   SIC 5211

MILL BAY FIRE DEPARTMENT   p 232
2675 LODGEPOLE RD, MILL BAY, BC, V0R 2P1

(250) 743-5563   SIC 7389

MILL COVE NURSING HOME INC   p 405
5647 ROUTE 105, MILL COVE, NB, E4C 3A5

SIC 8051

MILL CREEK MOTOR FREIGHT L.P.   p 483
101 EARL THOMPSON RD SS 2, AYR, ON, N0B 1E0

(519) 623-6632   SIC 4213

MILL CREEK MOTOR FREIGHT LTD   p 483
101 EARL THOMPSON RD, AYR, ON, N0B 1E0

(519) 623-6632   SIC 4731

MILL LANE ENTERPRISES   p 433
807 WATER ST, ST. JOHN'S, NL, A1E 1C4

SIC 4953

MILL STREET BREWERY   p 787
See TRILLIUM BEVERAGE INC

MILL-FAB   p 490
See 1203130 ONTARIO INC

MILLAR WESTERN FOREST PRODUCT   p 96

See MILLAR WESTERN INDUSTRIES LTD

MILLAR WESTERN FOREST PRODUCTS LTD   p 96
16640 111 AVE NW, EDMONTON, AB, T5M 2S5

(780) 486-8200   SIC 2611

MILLAR WESTERN FOREST PRODUCTS LTD   p 173
5501 50 AVE, WHITECOURT, AB, T7S 1N9

(780) 778-2036   SIC 2611

MILLAR WESTERN INDUSTRIES LTD   p 96
16640 111 AVE NW, EDMONTON, AB, T5M 2S5

(780) 486-8200   SIC 2819

MILLAR WESTERN INDUSTRIES LTD p 173
5004 52 ST, WHITECOURT, AB, T7S 1N2

(780) 778-2221   SIC 2421

MILLAR, HUGH FAMILY HOLDINGS INC   p 96
16640 111 AVE NW, EDMONTON, AB, T5M 2S5

(780) 486-8200   SIC 1611

MILLARD, ROUSE & ROSEBRUGH LLP   p 517
96 NELSON ST, BRANTFORD, ON, N3T 2N1

(519) 759-3511   SIC 8721

MILLBOURNE SAFEWAY   p 120
See SOBEYS WEST INC

MILLEDGEVILLE SUPERSTORE   p 413
See ATLANTIC WHOLESALERS LTD

MILLENIA RESOURCE CONSULTING   p 65
628 11 AVE SW SUITE 200, CALGARY, AB, T2R 0E2

(403) 571-0510   SIC 8711

MILLENIUM PRINTING INC   p 556
139 BASALTIC RD, CONCORD, ON, L4K 1G4

(905) 760-5522   SIC 2752

MILLENNIUM 1 SOLUTIONS   p 586
See MILLENNIUM PROCESS GROUP, INC

MILLENNIUM EMS SOLUTIONS LTD p 163
2257 PREMIER WAY UNIT 148, SHER-WOOD PARK, AB, T8H 2M8

(780) 496-9048   SIC 8748

MILLENNIUM III PROPERTIES CORPORA-TION   p 1431
2612 KOYL AVE, SASKATOON, SK, S7L 5X9

(306) 955-4174   SIC 6211

MILLENNIUM INSURANCE CORPORATION   p 161
340 SIOUX RD, SHERWOOD PARK, AB, T8A 3X6

(780) 467-1500   SIC 6411

MILLENNIUM PACIFIC GREENHOUSES PARTNERSHIP   p 210
3752 ARTHUR DR, DELTA, BC, V4K 3N2

(604) 940-4440   SIC 0182

MILLENNIUM PLACE STRATHCONA COUNTY   p 163
See STRATHCONA COUNTY

MILLENNIUM PROCESS GROUP, INC p 586
251 ATTWELL DR, ETOBICOKE, ON, M9W 7G2

(416) 503-1800   SIC 8741

MILLENNIUM RESEARCH GROUP INC   p 930
175 BLOOR ST E SUITE 400, TORONTO, ON, M4W 3R8

(416) 364-7776   SIC 8748

MILLENNIUM1 PROMOTIONAL SERVICES   p 414
See INMAR PROMOTIONS - CANADA INC.

MILLENNUIM MANAGEMENT CORP   p 330
609 GRANVILLE ST SUITE 1600, VAN-COUVER, BC, V7Y 1C3

(604) 669-1322   SIC 6211

MILLER & SMITH FOODS INC   p 575
33 CONNELL CRT, ETOBICOKE, ON, M8Z 1E8

(416) 253-2000   SIC 5141

MILLER & SMITH FOODS INCORPORATED

p 575
33 CONNELL CRT, ETOBICOKE, ON, M8Z 1E8

(416) 253-2000   SIC 5142

MILLER BROS. ROOFING & SHEET METAL CO LIMITED   p 590
206 VICTORIA ST W, EXETER, ON, N0M 1S2

(519) 235-3643   SIC 1761

MILLER CAPILANO MAINTENANCE COR-PORATION   p 269
38921 MIDWAY, SQUAMISH, BC, V8B 0J5

(604) 892-1010   SIC 1611

MILLER COMPREHENSIVE HIGH SCHOOL   p 1417
See BOARD OF EDUCATION OF THE REGINA ROMAN CATHOLIC SEPARATE SCHOOL DIVISION NO. 81

MILLER CROSSING CARE CENTRE   p 83
See REVERA LONG TERM CARE INC

MILLER ENVIRONMENTAL CORPORA-TION   p 369
1803 HEKLA AVE, WINNIPEG, MB, R2R 0K3

(204) 925-9600   SIC 4953

MILLER EQUIPMENT LTD   p 1411
1604 PARK AVE, MOOSOMIN, SK, S0G 3N0

(306) 435-3866   SIC 5083

MILLER FAMILY SALES AND SERVICE LTD   p 3
202 VETERANS BLVD NE SUITE 300, AIR-DRIE, AB, T4B 3P2

(403) 948-3993   SIC 5014

MILLER FARM EQUIPMENT 2005 INC   p 1411
GD, MOOSOMIN, SK, S0G 3N0

(306) 435-3866   SIC 5083

MILLER GROUP INC   p 680
505 MILLER AVE, MARKHAM, ON, L6G 1B2

(905) 475-6660   SIC 1611

MILLER INSURANCE BROKERS INC p 629
1115 SUTTON ST, KINCARDINE, ON, N2Z 2C5

SIC 6411

MILLER MAINTENANCE LIMITED   p 875
2064 KENNEDY RD, SCARBOROUGH, ON, M1T 3V1

(416) 332-1360   SIC 1611

MILLER NORTHWEST LIMITED   p 565
351 KENNEDY RD, DRYDEN, ON, P8N 2Z2

(807) 223-2844   SIC 1611

MILLER PAVING LIMITED   p 395
2276 ROUTE 128, BERRY MILLS, NB, E1G 4K4

(506) 857-0112   SIC 1611

MILLER PAVING LIMITED   p 680
505 MILLER AVE, MARKHAM, ON, L6G 1B2

(905) 475-6660   SIC 1611

MILLER PAVING LIMITED   p 753
704024 ROCKLEY RD, NEW LISKEARD, ON, P0J 1P0

(705) 647-4331   SIC 1611

MILLER PAVING LIMITED   p 816
1815 BANTREE ST, OTTAWA, ON, K1B 4L6

(613) 749-2222   SIC 4953

MILLER PAVING LTD   p 753
883316 HWY 65, NEW LISKEARD, ON, P0J 1P0

(877) 842-0543   SIC 1611

MILLER PAVING NORTHERN   p 753
See MILLER PAVING LIMITED

MILLER ROAD HOLDINGS LTD   p 265
6380 MILLER RD, RICHMOND, BC, V7B 1B3

(604) 270-9395   SIC 7521

MILLER SUPPLY LTD.   p 150
48223 338 AVE E, OKOTOKS, AB, T1S 1B2

(403) 995-4797   SIC 5171

MILLER THOMSON LLP   p 54

700 9 AVE SW SUITE 3000, CALGARY, AB,
T2P 3V4
(403) 298-2400   *SIC* 8111

MILLER THOMSON LLP   *p* 90
10155 102 ST NW SUITE 2700, EDMONTON, AB, T5J 4G8
(780) 429-1751   *SIC* 8111

MILLER THOMSON LLP   *p* 326
840 HOWE ST SUITE 1000, VANCOUVER, BC, V6Z 2M1
(604) 687-2242   *SIC* 8111

MILLER THOMSON LLP   *p* 672
60 COLUMBIA WAY SUITE 600, MARKHAM, ON, L3R 0C9
(905) 415-6700   *SIC* 8111

MILLER THOMSON LLP   *p* 954
40 KING ST W UNIT 5800, TORONTO, ON, M5H 3S1
(416) 595-8500   *SIC* 8111

MILLER THOMSON LLP   *p* 1008
295 HAGEY BLVD SUITE 300, WATERLOO, ON, N2L 6R5
(519) 579-3660   *SIC* 8111

MILLER THOMSON LLP   *p* 1206
1000 RUE DE LA GAUCHETIERE O BUREAU 3700, MONTREAL, QC, H3B 4W5
(514) 875-5210   *SIC* 8111

MILLER TIRE SERVICES LTD   *p* 447
16 GLORIA MCCLUSKEY AVE, DARTMOUTH, NS, B3B 2C2
(902) 431-7733   *SIC* 5014

MILLER TRANSIT LIMITED   *p* 672
8050 WOODBINE AVE, MARKHAM, ON, L3R 2N8
(905) 475-1367   *SIC* 4111

MILLER WASTE SYSTEMS   *p* 816
See MILLER PAVING LIMITED

MILLER WASTE SYSTEMS DIV OF   *p* 680
See MILLER PAVING LIMITED

MILLER WASTE SYSTEMS INC   *p* 395
2276 ROUTE 128, BERRY MILLS, NB, E1G 4K4
(506) 855-9783   *SIC* 4953

MILLER WASTE SYSTEMS INC   *p* 672
8050 WOODBINE AVE, MARKHAM, ON, L3R 2N8
(905) 475-6356   *SIC* 4953

MILLER'S AUTO RECYCLING (1992) LTD *p* 591
1557 BOWEN RD, FORT ERIE, ON, L2A 5M4
(800) 263-8104   *SIC* 5932

MILLER'S COLLISION & CAR SALES *p* 591
1557 BOWEN RD, FORT ERIE, ON, L2A 5M4
(905) 871-5105   *SIC* 5521

MILLER, P.G. ENTERPRISES LIMITED   *p* 481
2 ALLAURA BLVD, AURORA, ON, L4G 3S5
(905) 713-1850   *SIC* 5812

MILLER, P.G. ENTERPRISES LIMITED   *p* 756
1100 DAVIS DR, NEWMARKET, ON, L3Y 8W8
(905) 853-0118   *SIC* 5812

MILLER, P.G. ENTERPRISES LIMITED   *p* 756
17760 YONGE ST, NEWMARKET, ON, L3Y 8P4
(905) 895-1222   *SIC* 5812

MILLER-HUGHES FORD SALES LIMITED *p* 563
711 PITT ST, CORNWALL, ON, K6J 3S1
(613) 932-2584   *SIC* 5511

MILLERS LANDING PUB LTD   *p* 247
1979 BROWN ST, PORT COQUITLAM, BC, V3C 2N4
(604) 941-8822   *SIC* 5813

MILLETTE & FILS LTEE   *p* 1134
2105 RUE DE L'EGLISE, LAWRENCEVILLE, QC, J0E 1W0
(450) 535-6305   *SIC* 2441

MILLIGANS FISHERIES LTD   *p* 1042
1968 CARDIGAN ROAD, ST-PETERS BAY,

PE, C0A 2A0
(902) 961-2651   *SIC* 7389

MILLIPORE (CANADA) LTD   *p* 586
109 WOODBINE DOWNS BLVD UNIT 5, ETOBICOKE, ON, M9W 6Y1
(416) 675-1598   *SIC* 8731

MILLRISE PLACE   *p* 70
See TRIPLE A LIVING COMMUNITIES INC

MILLS AQUACULTURE INC   *p* 395
5 RUE MILLS, BOUCTOUCHE, NB, E4S 3S3
SIC 5146

MILLS BASICS   *p* 285
See MILLS PRINTING & STATIONERY CO. LTD

MILLS COMPANY LIMITED   *p* 453
5486 SPRING GARDEN RD, HALIFAX, NS, B3J 1G4
SIC 5621

MILLS GROUP INC, THE   *p* 509
285 QUEEN ST E, BRAMPTON, ON, L6W 2C2
(905) 453-5818   *SIC* 5812

MILLS NISSAN LTD   *p* 125
1275 101 ST SW, EDMONTON, AB, T6X 1A1
(780) 463-5700   *SIC* 5511

MILLS PONTIAC BUICK GMC LTD   *p* 812
240 BOND ST E, OSHAWA, ON, L1G 1B5
(905) 432-7333   *SIC* 5511

MILLS PRINTING & STATIONERY CO. LTD *p* 285
1111 CLARK DR, VANCOUVER, BC, V5L 3K5
(604) 254-7211   *SIC* 5112

MILLS SEA FOOD LTD   *p* 395
5 RUE MILLS, BOUCTOUCHE, NB, E4S 3S3
SIC 2092

MILLS, BRYAN IRODESSO CORP   *p* 779
1129 LESLIE ST, NORTH YORK, ON, M3C 2K5
(416) 447-4740   *SIC* 8748

MILLS-ROY ENTERPRISES LIMITED *p* 591
240 GARRISON RD, FORT ERIE, ON, L2A 1M7
(905) 871-8081   *SIC* 5251

MILLSAP FUEL DISTRIBUTORS LTD   *p* 1432
905 AVENUE P S, SASKATOON, SK, S7M 2X3
(306) 244-7916   *SIC* 5172

MILLSTREAM NURSERY   *p* 413
See MARITIME SOD LTD

MILLTECH MILLWORK LTD   *p* 94
12410 142 ST NW, EDMONTON, AB, T5L 4K2
(780) 455-6655   *SIC* 5211

MILLTOWN COLONY FARMS LTD   *p* 349
GD, ELIE, MB, R0H 0H0
(204) 353-2838   *SIC* 5153

MILLTOWN METAL SHOP LTD   *p* 349
GD, ELIE, MB, R0H 0H0
(204) 353-2741   *SIC* 5153

MILLTOWN MOTORS LIMITED   *p* 493
237 CAUSLEY ST, BLIND RIVER, ON, P0R 1B0
(705) 356-2207   *SIC* 5511

MILLWOOD FURNITURE ENT. LTD   *p* 201
1365 UNITED BLVD, COQUITLAM, BC, V3K 6Y3
(604) 777-1365   *SIC* 5712

MILLWOODS BOTTLE DEPOT   *p* 120
See 338802 ALBERTA LTD

MILLWOODS SHEPARD'S CARE CENTRE *p* 120
See SHEPHERD'S CARE FOUNDATION

MILLWORKS CUSTOM MANUFACTURING (2001) INC   *p* 993
25 BERTAL RD UNIT 9, TORONTO, ON, M6M 4M7
(416) 760-0222   *SIC* 2431

MILMAN INDUSTRIES INC   *p* 901
2502 ELM ST, SUDBURY, ON, P3E 4R6

(705) 682-9277   *SIC* 6512

MILNCO INSURANCE   *p* 379
See MILNE, D. R. & COMPANY LTD

MILNE & NICHOLLS LIMITED   *p* 672
7270 WOODBINE AVE SUITE 200, MARKHAM, ON, L3R 4B9
(905) 513-9700   *SIC* 1542

MILNE, D. R. & COMPANY LTD   *p* 379
330 ST MARY AVE SUITE 210, WINNIPEG, MB, R3C 3Z5
(204) 949-7000   *SIC* 6411

MILNER POWER INC   *p* 54
715 5 AVE SW SUITE 1220, CALGARY, AB, T2P 2X6
(403) 750-9300   *SIC* 4911

MILNER POWER LIMITED PARTNERHSIP *p* 54
715 5 AVE SW SUITE 1210, CALGARY, AB, T2P 2X6
(403) 263-3021   *SIC* 4911

MILNER-RIGSBY CO. LIMITED, THE *p* 1013
139 ELM ST, WEST LORNE, ON, N0L 2P0
(519) 768-1250   *SIC* 3713

MILOMA INVESTMENTS LTD   *p* 556
3280 STEELES AVE W UNIT 18, CONCORD, ON, L4K 2Y2
(905) 738-4545   *SIC* 5961

MILPLEX CIRCUIT (CANADA) INC   *p* 876
70 MAYBROOK DR, SCARBOROUGH, ON, M1V 4B6
(416) 292-8645   *SIC* 3672

MILRON METAL FABRICATORS INC *p* 106
12145 156 ST NW, EDMONTON, AB, T5V 1N4
(780) 451-3258   *SIC* 5084

MILTEX CONSTRUCTION LIMITED   *p* 586
31 RACINE RD SUITE 416, ETOBICOKE, ON, M9W 2Z4
SIC 5084

MILTOM MANAGEMENT LP   *p* 954
40 KING ST W SUITE 5800, TORONTO, ON, M5H 3S1
(416) 595-8500   *SIC* 6712

MILTON CHRYSLER DODGE LIMITED   *p* 684
81 ONTARIO ST N, MILTON, ON, L9T 2T2
(905) 878-8877   *SIC* 5511

MILTON DIST HOSPITAL GIFT SHOP *p* 684
See MILTON DISTRICT HOSPITAL AUXILIARY

MILTON DISTRICT HIGH SCHOOL   *p* 683
See HALTON DISTRICT SCHOOL BOARD

MILTON DISTRICT HOSPITAL   *p* 806
See HALTON HEALTHCARE SERVICES CORPORATION

MILTON DISTRICT HOSPITAL AUXILIARY *p* 684
GD LCD MAIN, MILTON, ON, L9T 2Y2
(905) 878-2383   *SIC* 8399

MILTON HARDWARE & BUILDING SUPPLIES LTD   *p* 684
385 STEELES AVE E, MILTON, ON, L9T 3G6
(905) 878-9222   *SIC* 5251

MILTON HOME HARDWARE BUILDING CENTRE   *p* 684
See MILTON HARDWARE & BUILDING SUPPLIES LTD

MILTON HYDRO   *p* 684
See HYDRO DISTRIBUTION INC

MILTON HYDRO DISTRIBUTION INC *p* 684
200 CHISHOLM DR, MILTON, ON, L9T 3G9
(905) 876-4611   *SIC* 4911

MILTON MANAGEMENT   *p* 54
See MILLER THOMSON LLP

MILTON TOYOTA   *p* 682
See 1341805 ONTARIO INC

MILTOW COLONY   *p* 171
See HUTTERIAN BRETHREN OF MILTOW

MIMERI INVESTMENTS LTD   *p* 925
1220 YONGE ST, TORONTO, ON, M4T 1W1
(416) 961-3700   *SIC* 8741

MIMI FOOD PRODUCTS INC   *p* 556

1260 CREDITSTONE RD UNIT 2-3, CONCORD, ON, L4K 5T7
(905) 660-0010   *SIC* 5142

MIMRAN, JOSEPH & ASSOCIATES INC *p* 994
1485 DUPONT ST, TORONTO, ON, M6P 3S2
(416) 516-0641   *SIC* 5699

MIN-CHEM CANADA LTD   *p* 802
460 WYECROFT RD, OAKVILLE, ON, L6K 2G7
(905) 842-8300   *SIC* 5169

MINARD'S LEISURE WORLD LTD   *p* 1437
921 GOVERNMENT RD S, WEYBURN, SK, S4H 3R3
(306) 842-3288   *SIC* 5561

MINAS BASIN PULP AND POWER COMPANY LIMITED   *p* 440
3 BEDFORD HILLS RD, BEDFORD, NS, B4A 1J5
(902) 835-7100   *SIC* 2631

MINCAVI (1986) INC   *p* 1089
88 CH DU PINACLE, DANVILLE, QC, J0A 1A0
(819) 839-2747   *SIC* 8093

MINCO GAS CO-OP LTD   *p* 137
4907 51 ST, INNISFREE, AB, T0B 2G0
(780) 592-3911   *SIC* 4923

MINCORE INC   *p* 954
80 RICHMOND ST W SUITE 1502, TORONTO, ON, M5H 2A4
(416) 214-1766   *SIC* 1081

MIND GAMES   *p* 667
See BRAIN BUSTER INC

MINDEN GROSS LLP   *p* 954
145 KING ST W SUITE 2200, TORONTO, ON, M5H 4G2
(416) 362-3711   *SIC* 8111

MINDEN HARDWARE LTD   *p* 685
16 BOBCAYGION RD, MINDEN, ON, K0M 2K0
(705) 286-1351   *SIC* 5251

MINDEN HOME HARDWARE & BUILDING SUPPLIES   *p* 685
See MINDEN HARDWARE LTD

MINDORO RESOURCES LTD   *p* 54
639 5 AVE SW SUITE 1250, CALGARY, AB, T2P 0M9
(780) 413-8187   *SIC* 1081

MINDSHARE CANADA   *p* 930
160 BLOOR ST E SUITE 700, TORONTO, ON, M4W 0A2
(416) 987-5100   *SIC* 7311

MINE AND MILL INSTALLATIONS LTD   *p* 682
524 6TH CONCESSION RD W, MILLGROVE, ON, L0R 1V0
SIC 6712

MINE BOUCHARD-HEBERT   *p* 1288
See BREAKWATER RESOURCES LTD

MINE CANADIAN MALARTIC   *p* 1148
See CANADIAN MALARTIC GP

MINE NIOBEC, LA   *p* 1307
See NIOBEC INC

MINE RAGLAN   *p* 986
See GLENCORE CANADA CORPORATION

MINE WESTWOOD   *p* 952
See IAMGOLD CORPORATION

MINECAT   *p* 647
See INDUSTRIAL FABRICATION INC

MINERAI DE FER QUEBEC INC   *p* 1102
556 RTE 389, FERMONT, QC, G0G 1J0
(418) 287-2000   *SIC* 1011

MINERAI DE FER QUEBEC INC   *p* 1206
1100 BOUL RENE-LEVESQUE O BUREAU 610, MONTREAL, QC, H3B 4N4
(514) 316-4858   *SIC* 1011

MINERAL SPRINGS HOSPITAL   *p* 4
See ALBERTA HEALTH SERVICES

MINERAUX MART INC   *p* 1322
201 RUE MONTCALM BUREAU 213, SAINT-JOSEPH-DE-SOREL, QC, J3R 1B9

(450) 746-1126   *SIC* 5051
MINERAUX METSO (CANADA)   *p* 492
See METSO MINERALS CANADA INC
MINERS CONSTRUCTION CO. LTD *p* 1425
440 MELVILLE ST, SASKATOON, SK, S7J
4M2
(306) 934-4703   *SIC* 1542
MINES ABCOURT INC   *p* 1158
506 RUE DES FALAISES, MONT-SAINT-
HILAIRE, QC, J3H 5R7
(450) 446-5511   *SIC* 1081
MINES AGNICO EAGLE LIMITEE   *p* 1288
10200 RTE DE PREISSAC, ROUYN-
NORANDA, QC, J0Y 1C0
(819) 759-3644   *SIC* 1241
MINES D'OR DYNACOR INC   *p* 1206
625 RENE-LEVESQUE BOUL O BUREAU
1105, MONTREAL, QC, H3B 1R2
(514) 393-9000   *SIC* 1041
MINES D'OR WESDOME   *p* 968
See WESDOME GOLD MINES LTD
MINES DE LA VALLEE DE L'OR LTEE   *p*
1391
152 CH DE LA MINE-ECOLE, VAL-D'OR,
QC, J9P 7B6
(819) 824-2808   *SIC* 1081
MINES OPINACA LTEE, LES   *p* 1077
333 3E RUE BUREAU 2, CHIBOUGAMAU,
QC, G8P 1N4
(418) 748-6449   *SIC* 1241
MINES OPINACA LTEE, LES   *p* 1290
853 BOUL RIDEAU BUREAU 764, ROUYN-
NORANDA, QC, J9Y 0G3
(819) 764-6400   *SIC* 8741
MINES SELEINE   *p* 1112
See K+S SEL WINDSOR LTEE
MINES WABUSH   *p* 1367
1505 CH POINTE-NOIRE, SEPT-ILES, QC,
G4R 4L4
(418) 962-5131   *SIC* 1011
MINET INC   *p* 1206
700 RUE DE LA GAUCHETIERE O BU-
REAU 1800, MONTREAL, QC, H3B 0A5
(514) 288-2273   *SIC* 6411
MINEWORX   *p* 182
See MINEWORX TECHNOLOGIES LTD
MINEWORX TECHNOLOGIES LTD   *p* 182
8331 EASTLAKE DR UNIT 114, BURNABY,
BC, V5A 4W2
(250) 751-3661   *SIC* 1081
MING PAO DAILY NEWS   *p* 982
*See MING PAO NEWSPAPERS (CANADA)
LIMITED*
**MING PAO NEWSPAPERS (CANADA) LIM-
ITED**   *p*
255
5368 PARKWOOD PL, RICHMOND, BC,
V6V 2N1
(604) 231-8998   *SIC* 2711
**MING PAO NEWSPAPERS (CANADA) LIM-
ITED**   *p*
982
23 SPADINA AVE, TORONTO, ON, M5V
3M5
(416) 321-0088   *SIC* 2711
MINI CALGARY   *p* 33
See 975002 ALBERTA INC
MINI DIG CORP   *p* 31
2222 ALYTH PL SE, CALGARY, AB, T2G
3K9
(403) 274-0090   *SIC* 1795
MINI DOWNTOWN   *p* 920
See 2232556 ONTARIO INC
MINI OTTAWA EAST (6125)   *p* 596
1020 OGILVIE RD, GLOUCESTER, ON, K1J
8G9
(613) 728-8888   *SIC* 5511
MINI-MICRO SUPPLY INC. CANADA *p* 915
524 GORDON BAKER RD, TORONTO, ON,
M2H 3B4
(905) 305-7671   *SIC* 5045
MINI-SKOOL A CHILD'S PLACE INC *p* 712
1100 CENTRAL PKY W SUITE 17, MISSIS-
SAUGA, ON, L5C 4E5

(905) 275-2378   *SIC* 8351
MINIGOO FISHERIES INC   *p* 1041
195 EAGLE FEATHER TRAIL, LENNOX IS-
LAND, PE, C0B 1P0
SIC 5146
MINING ASSOCIATION OF CANADA, THE*p*
823
275 SLATER ST SUITE 1100, OTTAWA, ON,
K1P 5H9
(613) 233-9391   *SIC* 8611
**MINING TECHNOLOGIES INTERNA-
TIONAL**   *p*
763
See LHD EQUIPMENT LIMITED
**MINISTERE DE LA JUSTICE DIRECTION
REGIONAL DES LAURENTIDES**   *p* 1320
*See GOUVERNEMENT DE LA PROVINCE
DE QUEBEC*
**MINISTERE DES TRANSPORT DU QUE-
BEC**   *p*
1289
*See GOUVERNEMENT DE LA PROVINCE
DE QUEBEC*
MINISTRY OF HEALTH   *p* 580
See GOVERNMENT OF ONTARIO
**MINISTRY OF HEALTH AND LONG TERM
CARE**   *p* 977
*See MICHENER INSTITUTE OF EDUCA-
TION AT UHN, THE*
MINOR BROS. FARM & COUNTRY   *p* 567
See MINOR BROS. FARM SUPPLY LTD
MINOR BROS. FARM SUPPLY LTD   *p* 567
9 MILL AVE, DUNNVILLE, ON, N1A 2W1
(905) 774-7591   *SIC* 5999
MINOTERIES P&H, LES   *p* 375
See PARRISH & HEIMBECKER, LIMITED
MINTECH CANADA INC   *p* 1251
1870 BOUL DES SOURCES BUREAU 100,
POINTE-CLAIRE, QC, H9R 5N4
(514) 697-8260   *SIC* 5211
MINTEQ INTERNATIONAL DIV OF *p* 1251
See MINTECH CANADA INC
MINTO   *p* 823
See MINTO MANAGEMENT LIMITED
MINTO APARTMENTS LIMITED   *p* 772
90 SHEPPARD AVE E SUITE 500, NORTH
YORK, ON, M2N 3A1
(416) 977-0777   *SIC* 6531
MINTO COMMERCIAL   *p* 823
See MINTO PROPERTIES INC
MINTO FURNISH SUITE   *p* 825
See MINTO GROUP INC
MINTO FURNISHED SUITES   *p* 973
61 YORKVILLE AVE SUITE 200,
TORONTO, ON, M5R 1B7
(416) 923-1000   *SIC* 7389
MINTO GROUP INC   *p* 774
4101 YONGE ST UNIT 600, NORTH YORK,
ON, M2P 1N6
(416) 977-0777   *SIC* 1521
MINTO GROUP INC   *p* 825
221 LYON ST N SUITE 806, OTTAWA, ON,
K1R 7X5
SIC 6513
MINTO HOLDINGS INC   *p* 823
180 KENT ST SUITE 200, OTTAWA, ON,
K1P 0B6
(613) 230-7051   *SIC* 6712
MINTO MANAGEMENT   *p* 774
See MINTO GROUP INC
MINTO MANAGEMENT LIMITED   *p* 823
180 KENT ST UNIT 200, OTTAWA, ON, K1P
0B6
(613) 230-7051   *SIC* 6513
MINTO PROPERTIES INC   *p* 823
180 KENT ST SUITE 200, OTTAWA, ON,
K1P 0B6
(613) 786-3000   *SIC* 6512
MINTO TRUCK CENTRE LIMITED   *p* 618
5196 HWY 23 N, HARRISTON, ON, N0G
2P0
(519) 510-2120   *SIC* 4212
MINTZ GLOBAL SCREENING INC   *p* 1211
1303 RUE WILLIAM BUREAU 200, MON-

TREAL, QC, H3C 1R4
(514) 587-6200   *SIC* 8732
MINUS FORTY TECHNOLOGIES CORP *p*
594
30 ARMSTRONG AVE, GEORGETOWN,
ON, L7G 4R9
(905) 702-1441   *SIC* 3585
MINUTE MAID   *p* 841
*See MINUTE MAID COMPANY CANADA
INC, THE*
**MINUTE MAID COMPANY CANADA INC,
THE**   *p* 841
781 LANSDOWNE ST W, PETERBOR-
OUGH, ON, K9J 1Z2
(705) 742-8011   *SIC* 2037
**MINUTE MAID COMPANY CANADA INC,
THE**   *p* 841
781 LANSDOWNE ST W, PETERBOR-
OUGH, ON, K9J 1Z2
(705) 742-8011   *SIC* 2086
**MIOVISION TECHNOLOGIES INCORPO-
RATED**   *p*
638
137 GLASGOW ST SUITE 110, KITCH-
ENER, ON, N2G 4X8
(519) 513-2407   *SIC* 7371
MIP INC   *p* 1049
9100 BOUL RAY-LAWSON, ANJOU, QC,
H1J 1K8
(514) 356-1224   *SIC* 2392
MIQ LOGISTICS, LLC   *p* 725
6580 MILLCREEK DR SUITE 905, MISSIS-
SAUGA, ON, L5N 8B3
(905) 542-7525   *SIC* 4213
MIRA NURSING HOME   *p* 458
See GEM HEALTH CARE GROUP LIMITED
MIRA, THE   *p* 469
See GEM HEALTH CARE GROUP LIMITED
MIRABEL AEROSPACE CENTRE   *p* 1153
See PRATT & WHITNEY CANADA CIE
MIRACLE MART   *p* 565
See MOHAWK IMPERIAL SALES
MIRAGE   *p* 1304
See BOA-FRANC INC
MIRALIS INC   *p* 1291
200 RUE DES FABRICANTS, SAINT-
ANACLET, QC, G0K 1H0
(418) 723-6686   *SIC* 2434
MIRAMICHI CHRYSLER DODGE JEEP INC
p 405
1155 KING GEORGE HWY, MIRAMICHI,
NB, E1V 5J7
(506) 622-3900   *SIC* 5511
MIRAMICHI LODGE   *p* 838
725 PEMBROKE ST W SUITE 735, PEM-
BROKE, ON, K8A 8S6
(613) 735-0175   *SIC* 8051
MIRAMICHI SENIOR CITIZENS HOME INC
p 405
1400 WATER ST, MIRAMICHI, NB, E1N 1A4
(506) 778-6810   *SIC* 8051
MIRATEL SOLUTIONS INC   *p* 784
2501 STEELES AVE W SUITE 200, NORTH
YORK, ON, M3J 2P1
(416) 650-7850   *SIC* 7389
MIRAZED INC   *p* 1308
3715 BOUL LOSCH, SAINT-HUBERT, QC,
J3Y 5T7
(450) 656-6320   *SIC* 2759
MIRCOM GROUP HOLDINGS INC   *p* 556
25 INTERCHANGE WAY, CONCORD, ON,
L4K 5W3
(905) 660-4655   *SIC* 3669
MIRCOM TECHNOLOGIES LTD   *p* 556
25 INTERCHANGE WAY UNIT 1, CON-
CORD, ON, L4K 5W3
(905) 660-4655   *SIC* 3669
**MIRION TECHNOLOGIES (IST CANADA)
INC**   *p* 536
465 DOBBIE DR, CAMBRIDGE, ON, N1T
1T1
(519) 623-4880   *SIC* 3829
MIROIRS LAURIER LTEE   *p* 1133
153 BOUL LAURIER BUREAU 300,

LAURIER-STATION, QC, G0S 1N0
(418) 728-2023   *SIC* 3231
MIROLIN INDUSTRIES CORP   *p* 575
200 NORSEMAN ST, ETOBICOKE, ON,
M8Z 2R4
(416) 231-9030   *SIC* 3431
MIROLIN INDUSTRIES CORP   *p* 575
60 SHORNCLIFFE RD, ETOBICOKE, ON,
M8Z 5K1
(416) 231-5790   *SIC* 3089
MIRROR NOVA SCOTIA LIMITED   *p* 460
600 OTTER LAKE DR, LAKESIDE, NS, B3T
2E2
(902) 453-3490   *SIC* 1629
MIRTREN CONTRACTORS LIMITED *p* 999
18 STOCKDALE RD, TRENTON, ON, K8V
5P6
(613) 392-6511   *SIC* 1542
MIRVISH PRODUCTIONS LTD   *p* 982
284 KING ST W SUITE 400, TORONTO,
ON, M5V 1J2
(416) 593-0351   *SIC* 7922
MIRVISH, ED ENTERPRISES LIMITED *p*
982
284 KING ST W SUITE 400, TORONTO,
ON, M5V 1J2
(416) 593-0351   *SIC* 7922
MISERICORDIA GENERAL HOSPITAL *p*
379
99 CORNISH AVE SUITE 370, WINNIPEG,
MB, R3C 1A2
(204) 774-6581   *SIC* 8011
MISERICORDIA HEALTH CENTRE   *p* 379
See MISERICORDIA GENERAL HOSPITAL
MISS MARY MAXIM LTD   *p* 837
75 SCOTT AVE, PARIS, ON, N3L 3G5
(519) 442-2266   *SIC* 5961
MISSFRESH INC   *p* 1340
4220 RUE GRIFFITH, SAINT-LAURENT,
QC, H4T 4L6
(844) 647-7373   *SIC* 5421
**MISSION ASSOCIATION FOR COMMUNITY
LIVING**   *p* 232
33345 2ND AVE, MISSION, BC, V2V 1K4
(604) 826-9080   *SIC* 8361
MISSION COMMUNITY FOUNDATION*p* 232
GD LCD MAIN, MISSION, BC, V2V 4J2
(604) 826-5322   *SIC* 8699
**MISSION COMMUNITY SERVICES SOCI-
ETY**   *p*
232
33179 2ND AVE, MISSION, BC, V2V 1J9
(604) 826-3634   *SIC* 8399
MISSION GROUP ENTERPRISES LTD *p*
222
1631 DICKSON AVE SUITE 1000,
KELOWNA, BC, V1Y 0B5
(250) 448-8810   *SIC* 1521
MISSION HILL FAMILY ESTATE   *p* 242
See MARK ANTHONY PROPERTIES LTD
MISSION HILL FAMILY ESTATE   *p* 289
See MARK ANTHONY GROUP INC
MISSION OLD BREWERY   *p* 1192
902 BOUL SAINT-LAURENT, MONTREAL,
QC, H2Z 1J2
(514) 866-6591   *SIC* 8361
MISSION PUBLIC SCHOOLS   *p* 232
See SCHOOL DISTRICT #75 (MISSION)
MISSION RACE WAY PARK   *p* 232
See B.C. CUSTOM CAR ASSOCIATION
MISSION SECONDARY SCHOOL   *p* 232
See SCHOOL DISTRICT #75 (MISSION)
MISSION SERVICES OF HAMILTON, INC *p*
611
196 WENTWORTH ST N, HAMILTON, ON,
L8L 5V7
(905) 528-4211   *SIC* 8399
MISSION SERVICES OF LONDON   *p* 652
415 HAMILTON RD, LONDON, ON, N5Z
1S1
(519) 433-2807   *SIC* 8399
MISSION, THE   *p* 822
See UNION MISSION FOR MEN, THE
MISSISQUOI COMPAGNIE D'ASSURANCE,

LA p 1273
1175 AV LAVIGERIE BUREAU 30, QUE-BEC, QC, G1V 4P1
SIC 6411

MISSISSAGI POWER TRUST p 903
4917 129 HWY, THESSALON, ON, P0R 1L0
(705) 842-3377 SIC 4911

MISSISSAUGA ACCOUNTING p 709
See BDO CANADA LLP

MISSISSAUGA AUTOMOTIVE INC p 714
1800 LAKESHORE RD W, MISSISSAUGA, ON, L5J 1J7
(905) 567-8881 SIC 5511

MISSISSAUGA BUS GROUP OF COMPANIES p 741
See MISSISSAUGA BUS, COACH & TRUCK REPAIRS INC

MISSISSAUGA BUS, COACH & TRUCK REPAIRS INC p 741
6625 KESTREL RD, MISSISSAUGA, ON, L5T 1P4
(905) 696-8328 SIC 7538

MISSISSAUGA CITY CENTRE OFFICE BUILDING p 710
See MORGUARD INVESTMENTS LIMITED

MISSISSAUGA CRUISE SHIP CENTRE p 725
6465 MILLCREEK DR SUITE 170, MISSISSAUGA, ON, L5N 5R3
(905) 821-7447 SIC 4724

MISSISSAUGA HALTON CCAC p 579
See MISSISSAUGA HALTON COMMUNITY CARE ACCESS CENTRE

MISSISSAUGA HALTON COMMUNITY CARE ACCESS CENTRE p 579
401 THE WEST MALL SUITE 1001, ETOBICOKE, ON, M9C 5J5
(905) 855-9090 SIC 8011

MISSISSAUGA HONDA p 716
See ERINMOTORWAY INVESTMENTS LIMITED

MISSISSAUGA HOSPITAL GIFT SHOP p 711
See TRILLIUM HEALTH PARTNERS VOLUNTEERS

MISSISSAUGA HYUNDAI p 716
See 982874 ONTARIO LIMITED

MISSISSAUGA KAR KARE CENTRE p 708
See QUEENSWAY CAWTHRA HOLDINGS LTD

MISSISSAUGA NEWS, THE p 711
See METROLAND MEDIA GROUP LTD

MISSISSAUGA PAPER FIBRES LTD p 741
1111 TRISTAR DR UNIT 1, MISSISSAUGA, ON, L5T 1W5
(905) 564-7260 SIC 5093

MISSISSAUGA SECONDARY SCHOOL p 745
See PEEL DISTRICT SCHOOL BOARD

MISSISSAUGA TOYOTA INC p 703
2215 DUNDAS ST E, MISSISSAUGA, ON, L4X 2X2
(905) 625-3420 SIC 5511

MISSISSAUGA YMCA p 711
See YMCA OF GREATER TORONTO

MISSISSAUGUA GOLF AND COUNTRY CLUB p 713
See MISSISSAUGUA GOLF AND COUNTRY CLUB, THE

MISSISSAUGUA GOLF AND COUNTRY CLUB, THE p 713
1725 MISSISSAUGA RD, MISSISSAUGA, ON, L5H 2K4
(905) 278-4857 SIC 7997

MISTAHIA REGIONAL HEALTH AUTHORITY p 131
10200 SHAND AVE, GRANDE CACHE, AB, T0E 0Y0
(780) 827-3701 SIC 6712

MISTEELCO INC p 651
850 DUNDAS ST, LONDON, ON, N5W 2Z7

(519) 679-1939 SIC 5051

MISTER CHEMICAL LTD p 556
101 JACOB KEFFER PKY, CONCORD, ON, L4K 5N8
(905) 761-9995 SIC 5087

MISTER COFFEE & SERVICES INC p 871
2045 MIDLAND AVE SUITE 1, SCARBOROUGH, ON, M1P 3E2
(416) 293-3333 SIC 7389

MISTER PRODUCE LTD p 575
50 JUTLAND RD, ETOBICOKE, ON, M8Z 2H1
(416) 252-9191 SIC 5148

MISTER TIRE p 203
See G.G.C.S. HOLDINGS LTD

MISTEREL INC p 562
201 NINTH ST E, CORNWALL, ON, K6H 2V1
(613) 933-0592 SIC 5251

MISTRAS p 1359
See MISTRAS SERVICES INC

MISTRAS CANADA, INC p 156
8109 EDGAR INDUSTRIAL DR, RED DEER, AB, T4P 3R2
(403) 556-1350 SIC 7389

MISTRAS SERVICES INC p 1138
765 RUE DE SAINT-ROMUALD, LEVIS, QC, G6W 5M6
(418) 837-4664 SIC 8734

MISTRAS SERVICES INC p 1359
2161 RUE LEONARD-DE VINCI, SAINTE-JULIE, QC, J3E 1Z3
(450) 922-3515 SIC 8734

MISTY HARBOUR SEAFOOD p 398
See COASTAL ENTERPRISES LTD

MISTY MOUNTAIN INDUSTRIES LTD p 255
13900 MAYCREST WAY SUITE 130, RICHMOND, BC, V6V 3E2
(604) 273-8299 SIC 5148

MISTY MOUNTAIN SPECIALTIES p 255
See MISTY MOUNTAIN INDUSTRIES LTD

MITCHEL-LINCOLN PACKAGING LTD p 1099
925 RUE ROCHELEAU, DRUMMONDVILLE, QC, J2C 6L8
(819) 477-9700 SIC 2653

MITCHEL-LINCOLN PACKAGING LTD p 1330
3737 BOUL THIMENS, SAINT-LAURENT, QC, H4R 1V1
(514) 332-3480 SIC 2653

MITCHELL & ABBOTT GROUP INSURANCE BROKERS LIMITED, p 616
2000 GARTH ST SUITE 101, HAMILTON, ON, L9B 0C1
(905) 385-6383 SIC 6411

MITCHELL AGENCIES LIMITED p 447
55 WESTON CRT, DARTMOUTH, NS, B3B 2C8
(902) 468-8990 SIC 5141

MITCHELL GROUP ALBERTA INC p 76
2500 48 AVE NE, CALGARY, AB, T3J 4V8
(403) 238-1000 SIC 7011

MITCHELL MCCONNELL INSURANCE LIMITED p 412
660 ROTHESAY AVE SUITE 344, SAINT JOHN, NB, E2H 2H4
(506) 634-7200 SIC 6411

MITCHELL PARTNERSHIP INC, THE p 768
285 YORKLAND BLVD, NORTH YORK, ON, M2J 1S5
(416) 499-8000 SIC 8711

MITCHELL PLASTIC, DIV OF p 642
See ULTRA MANUFACTURING LIMITED

MITCHELL PRESS LIMITED p 181
8328 RIVERBEND CRT, BURNABY, BC, V3N 5C9
(604) 528-9882 SIC 2752

MITCHELL SANDHAM INC p 946
438 UNIVERSITY AVE SUITE 2000, TORONTO, ON, M5G 2K8
(416) 862-1750 SIC 6411

MITCHELL SANDHAM PASTOR DIV p 946

See MITCHELL SANDHAM INC

MITEC TECHNOLOGIES INC p 715
2333 NORTH SHERIDAN WAY SUITE 200, MISSISSAUGA, ON, L5K 1A7
(905) 822-8170 SIC 5065

MITEK CANADA, INC p 497
100 INDUSTRIAL RD, BRADFORD, ON, L3Z 3G7
(905) 952-2900 SIC 3448

MITEL NETWORKS CORPORATION p 624
350 LEGGET DR, KANATA, ON, K2K 2W7
(613) 592-2122 SIC 3661

MITO SUSHI p 1168
See 9138-1616 QUEBEC INC

MITRI, S HAULAGE LTD p 741
6855 INVADER CRES, MISSISSAUGA, ON, L5T 2B7
(905) 564-1200 SIC 4212

MITRUX SERVICES LTD p 177
2160 PEARDONVILLE RD, ABBOTSFORD, BC, V2T 6J8
(604) 746-1008 SIC 4213

MITSUBISHI CANADA LIMITED p 307
200 GRANVILLE ST SUITE 2800, VANCOUVER, BC, V6C 1G6
(604) 654-8000 SIC 5051

MITSUBISHI ELECTRIC SALES CANADA INC p 672
4299 14TH AVE, MARKHAM, ON, L3R 0J2
(905) 475-7728 SIC 5075

MITSUBISHI HITACHI POWER SYSTEMS CANADA, LTD p 1434
3903 BRODSKY AVE SUITE 100, SASKATOON, SK, S7P 0C9
(306) 242-9222 SIC 3699

MITSUBISHI MOTOR SALES OF CANADA, INC p 697
2090 MATHESON BLVD E, MISSISSAUGA, ON, L4W 5P8
(905) 214-9000 SIC 4731

MITSUI & CO. (CANADA) LTD p 970
66 WELLINGTON ST W SUITE 3510, TORONTO, ON, M5K 1K2
(416) 365-3800 SIC 5051

MITSUI HOME CANADA INC p 225
19680 94A AVE, LANGLEY, BC, V1M 3B7
(604) 882-8415 SIC 4731

MITTAL CANADA p 1145
See ARCELORMITTAL PRODUITS LONGS CANADA S.E.N.C.

MITTEN INC p 516
225 HENRY ST UNIT 5A, BRANTFORD, ON, N3S 7R4
(519) 805-4701 SIC 3089

MITTEN VINYL p 516
See MITTEN INC

MITTON, V CO LTD p 1039
365 UNIVERSITY AVE, CHARLOTTETOWN, PE, C1A 4N2
(902) 892-1892 SIC 5812

MITUTOYO CANADA INC p 725
2121 MEADOWVALE BLVD, MISSISSAUGA, ON, L5N 5N1
(905) 821-1261 SIC 5084

MIXBURN COLONY p 147
See HUTTERIAN BRETHERN OF MIXBURN INC

MIXCOR AGGREGATES p 139
See MIXCOR HOLDINGS INC

MIXCOR HOLDINGS INC p 139
6303 43 ST, LEDUC, AB, T9E 0G8
(780) 986-6721 SIC 6712

MIXOLOGY CANADA INC p 504
45 ARMTHORPE RD, BRAMPTON, ON, L6T 5M4
(905) 793-9100 SIC 5149

MIYO WAHKOHTOWIN COMMUNITY EDUCATION AUTHORITY p 136
GD, HOBBEMA, AB, T0C 1N0
(780) 585-2118 SIC 8211

MIZUNO CANADA LTD p 697
5206 TIMBERLEA BLVD, MISSISSAUGA, ON, L4W 2S5

(905) 629-0500 SIC 5091

MJS MECHANICAL LTD p 77
2401 144 AVE NE, CALGARY, AB, T3P 0T3
(403) 250-1355 SIC 1711

MJY AUTO SALES & LEASING LTD p 132
12709 100 ST, GRANDE PRAIRIE, AB, T8V 4H2
(780) 532-5005 SIC 5511

MK SAFETY NET CANADA p 1017
1038 WINDHAM CENTRE RD, WINDHAM CENTRE, ON, N0E 2A0
SIC 8062

MKRT MANAGEMENT p 69
See MCLEOD & COMPANY LLP

MKTG p 750
See KRUPP, MASHA TRANSLATION GROUP LTD, THE

ML ENTRETIEN MULTI SERVICES p 1264
See ENTREPRISES DE NETTOYAGE MARCEL LABBE INC

MLG BLOCKCHAIN CONSULTING LTD p 954
214 KING ST W SUITE 210, TORONTO, ON, M5H 3S6
(647) 377-3489 SIC 8741

MLP p 1428
See MLT AIKINS LLP

MLS INSURANCE BROKERS INC p 888
4741 ST CATHERINE ST, ST ISIDORE, ON, K0C 2B0
(613) 524-2174 SIC 6411

MLT p 1418
See MLT MANAGEMENT INC

MLT AIKINS LLP p 1418
1874 SCARTH ST SUITE 1500, REGINA, SK, S4P 4E9
(306) 347-8000 SIC 8111

MLT AIKINS LLP p 1428
410 22ND ST E SUITE 1500, SASKATOON, SK, S7K 5T6
(306) 975-7100 SIC 8111

MLT MANAGEMENT INC p 1418
1874 SCARTH ST SUITE 1500, REGINA, SK, S4P 4E9
(306) 347-8000 SIC 8741

MLTH HOLDINGS INC p 897
25 MCNAB ST, STRATHROY, ON, N7G 4H6
(519) 246-9600 SIC 6712

MM&T PACKAGING COMPANY p 697
5485 TOMKEN RD, MISSISSAUGA, ON, L4W 3Y3
(800) 651-5951 SIC 2752

MMC p 307
See MERCER (CANADA) LIMITED

MMCC SOLUTIONS CANADA COMPANY p 922
75 EGLINTON AVE E, TORONTO, ON, M4P 3A4
(416) 922-3519 SIC 7389

MMCC SOLUTIONS CANADA COMPANY p 1166
2030 BOUL PIE-IX BUREAU 330, MONTREAL, QC, H1V 2C8
(514) 287-1717 SIC 7389

MMD SALES LTD p 101
17104 118 AVE NW, EDMONTON, AB, T5S 2L7
(780) 452-2790 SIC 5083

MME MULTIURETHANES LTD p 697
5245 CREEKBANK RD, MISSISSAUGA, ON, L4W 1N3
(905) 564-7650 SIC 5039

MMG CANADA LIMITED p 575
10 VANSCO RD, ETOBICOKE, ON, M8Z 5J4
(416) 251-2831 SIC 5995

MMI p 9
See MENNONITE MUTUAL INSURANCE CO. (ALBERTA) LTD

MML CLUB SERVICES LTD p 382
870 EMPRESS ST, WINNIPEG, MB, R3G 3H3
(204) 262-6131 SIC 4724

MMP OFFICE INTERIORS INCORPO-

RATED p 447
656 WINDMILL RD SUITE 1, DARTMOUTH, NS, B3B 1B8
(902) 422-4011   SIC 5712

MMR CANADA LIMITED p 17
11083 48 ST SE, CALGARY, AB, T2C 1G8
(403) 720-9000   SIC 1731

MMTI p 901
See MANSOUR MINING TECHNOLOGIES INC

MNAASGED CHILD AND FAMILY SERVICES p 747
311 JUBILEE DR, MUNCEY, ON, N0L 1Y0
(519) 289-1117   SIC 8699

MNGI p 1002
See MODERN/NIAGARA GROUP INC

MNM HOCKEY p 1240
See 9208-3179 QUEBEC INC

MNM INC p 795
2473 FINCH AVE W, NORTH YORK, ON, M9M 2G1
(416) 744-9675   SIC 7361

MNP p 142
See MNP LLP

MNP LLP p 54
330 5 AVE SW SUITE 2000, CALGARY, AB, T2P 0L4
(403) 444-0150   SIC 8721

MNP LLP p 90
10235 101 ST NW SUITE 1600, EDMONTON, AB, T5J 3G1
(780) 451-4406   SIC 8721

MNP LLP p 142
3425 2 AVE S SUITE 1, LETHBRIDGE, AB, T1J 4V1
(403) 380-1600   SIC 8721

MNP LLP p 328
1055 DUNSMUIR SUITE 2300, VANCOUVER, BC, V7X 1J1
(604) 639-0001   SIC 8721

MNP LLP p 347
1401 PRINCESS AVE, BRANDON, MB, R7A 7L7
(204) 727-0661   SIC 8721

MNP LLP p 954
111 RICHMOND ST W SUITE 300, TORONTO, ON, M5H 2G4
(416) 596-1711   SIC 8721

MNP LLP p 1206
1155 BOUL RENE-LEVESQUE O BUREAU 2300, MONTREAL, QC, H3B 2K2
(514) 932-4115   SIC 8721

MNP LLP p 1418
2010 11TH AVE SUITE 900, REGINA, SK, S4P 0J3
(306) 790-7900   SIC 8721

MNP S.E.N.C.R.L., S.R.L. p 1206
See MNP LLP

MNZ GLOBAL INC p 904
300 JOHN ST SUITE 503, THORNHILL, ON, L3T 5W4
(905) 597-0207   SIC 5051

MOA NICKLE S.A. DIV OF p 130
See SHERRITT INTERNATIONAL CORPORATION

MOBIA TECHNOLOGY INNOVATIONS INCORPORATED p 447
340 WRIGHT AVE UNIT 13, DARTMOUTH, NS, B3B 0B3
(902) 468-8000   SIC 4899

MOBIFY RESEARCH AND DEVELOPMENT INC p 330
725 GRANVILLE ST SUITE 420, VANCOUVER, BC, V7Y 1C6
(866) 502-5880   SIC 7371

MOBIL SHRED INC p 206
588 ANNANCE CRT UNIT 4, DELTA, BC, V3M 6Y8
(604) 526-2622   SIC 7389

MOBILE 1 MESSENGERS INC p 186
3737 NAPIER ST SUITE 200, BURNABY, BC, V5C 3E4
(604) 681-4227   SIC 7389

MOBILE CLIMATE CONTROL, INC p 556
7540 JANE ST, CONCORD, ON, L4K 0A6
(905) 482-2750   SIC 3714

MOBILE INSURANCE SERVICE LTD p 85
11356 119 ST NW UNIT 201, EDMONTON, AB, T5G 2X4
(780) 477-8838   SIC 6411

MOBILE KLINIK p 972
See 9580166 CANADA INC

MOBILE KLINIK p 1105
See MOBILE SERVICE CENTER CANADA LIMITED

MOBILE MIX CONCRETE p 653
See CO-FO CONCRETE FORMING CONSTRUCTION LIMITED

MOBILE PARTS INC p 1001
2472 EVANS RD, VAL CARON, ON, P3N 1P5
(705) 897-4955   SIC 5082

MOBILE SERVICE & CONSTRUCTION p 1235
See SERVICE & CONSTRUCTION MOBILE LTEE

MOBILE SERVICE CENTER CANADA LIMITED p 1105
169 BOUL GREBER, GATINEAU, QC, J8T 3R1
(819) 568-3846   SIC 4812

MOBILICITY p 962
See DATA & AUDIO-VISUAL ENTERPRISES HOLDINGS INC

MOBILIER BOOMRANG p 1282
See 3496252 CANADA INC

MOBILIER DAGENAIS, PHILIPPE p 1068
See GROUPE DAGENAIS M.D.C. INC

MOBILIER DE BUREAU LOGIFLEX INC p 1375
1235 CH SAINT-ROCH N, SHERBROOKE, QC, J1N 0H2
(877) 864-9323   SIC 2521

MOBILIER DE BUREAU MBH INC p 1259
25 RUE SAINT-JOSEPH E, QUEBEC, QC, G1K 3A6
(418) 647-1332   SIC 5021

MOBILIER M.E.Q. LTEE p 1122
22 RUE OLIVIER-MOREL, LA DURANTAYE, QC, G0R 1W0
(418) 884-3050   SIC 2511

MOBILIER RUSTIQUE (BEAUCE) INC p 1348
50 1E RUE O, SAINT-MARTIN, QC, G0M 1B0
(418) 382-5987   SIC 2511

MOBIS PART CANADA CORPORATION p 679
10 MOBIS DR, MARKHAM, ON, L6C 0Y3
(905) 927-3350   SIC 5012

MODASUITE INC p 1183
160 RUE SAINT-VIATEUR E BUREAU 610, MONTREAL, QC, H2T 1A8
(438) 384-0824   SIC 5136

MODE CAPITAL INC, LA p 1326
1200 BOUL JULES-POITRAS BUREAU 200, SAINT-LAURENT, QC, H4N 1X7
(514) 337-4444   SIC 5137

MODE CHOC p 1045
See MODE CHOC (ALMA) LTEE

MODE CHOC p 1305
See MODE CHOC (ALMA) LTEE

MODE CHOC (ALMA) LTEE p 1045
1055 AV DU PONT S BUREAU 50, ALMA, QC, G8B 2V7
(418) 668-2346   SIC 5651

MODE CHOC (ALMA) LTEE p 1305
610 RUE 90E, SAINT-GEORGES, QC, G5Y 3L2
(418) 221-6850   SIC 5651

MODE CHOC (DOLBEAU) LTEE p 1090
361 BOUL VEZINA, DOLBEAU-MISTASSINI, QC, G8L 3K6
(418) 276-7189   SIC 5651

MODE F17 p 1378
See BOUTIQUE LE PENTAGONE INC

MODE LE GRENIER INC p 1049
8501 BOUL RAY-LAWSON, ANJOU, QC, H1J 1K6
(514) 354-0650   SIC 5621

MODE LEVY CANADA p 1179
See LEVY CANADA FASHION COMPANY

MODE PETIT BOUFFON INC, LA p 1183
5425 AV CASGRAIN BUREAU 401, MONTREAL, QC, H2T 1X6
(514) 276-9828   SIC 5137

MODE RVING INC p 1179
555 RUE CHABANEL O BUREAU M42B, MONTREAL, QC, H2N 2J2
(514) 577-2172   SIC 2389

MODER, JAMES R. CRYSTAL CHANDELIER (CANADA) LTD p 289
106 7TH AVE E, VANCOUVER, BC, V5T 1M6
(604) 879-0934   SIC 3645.

MODERCO INC p 1066
115 RUE DE LAUZON, BOUCHERVILLE, QC, J4B 1E7
(450) 641-3150   SIC 2542

MODERN BEAUTY SUPPLIES INC p 31
415 MANITOU RD SE, CALGARY, AB, T2G 4C2
(403) 259-4442   SIC 5087

MODERN BUSINESS EQUIPMENT LIMITED p 433
172 HAMILTON AVE, ST. JOHN'S, NL, A1E 1J5
(709) 579-2147   SIC 5999

MODERN CONSTRUCTION (1983) LTD p 408
275 SALISBURY RD, MONCTON, NB, E1E 4N1
(506) 853-8853   SIC 1429

MODERN FURNACE CLEANERS p 1412
See MODERN JANITORIAL SERVICES (1978) LTD

MODERN GROUNDS MAINTENANCE LTD p 225
9702 216 ST, LANGLEY, BC, V1M 3J2
(604) 888-4999   SIC 1542

MODERN HOUSEWARE IMPORTS INC p 186
2300 MADISON AVE, BURNABY, BC, V5C 4Y9
(604) 299-5132   SIC 5023

MODERN JANITORIAL SERVICES (1978) LTD p 1412
2521 COMMERCE DR, NORTH BATTLEFORD, SK, S9A 2X5
(306) 445-4774   SIC 5087

MODERN MOSAIC LIMITED p 759
8620 OAKWOOD DR, NIAGARA FALLS, ON, L2G 0J2
(905) 356-3045   SIC 5211

MODERN NIAGARA DESIGN SERVICES INC p 626
85 DENZIL DOYLE COURT, KANATA, ON, K2M 2G8
(613) 591-7505   SIC 1711

MODERN NIAGARA HVAC SERVICES p 1028
See MODERN NIAGARA TORONTO INC

MODERN NIAGARA HVAC SERVICES INC p 626
85 DENZIL DOYLE CRT, KANATA, ON, K2M 2G8
(613) 591-7505   SIC 1711

MODERN NIAGARA OTTAWA INC p 626
85 DENZIL DOYLE CRT, KANATA, ON, K2M 2G8
(613) 591-7505   SIC 1711

MODERN NIAGARA TORONTO INC p 1028
8125 HIGHWAY 50, WOODBRIDGE, ON, L4H 4S6
(416) 749-6031   SIC 1711

MODERN NIAGARA VANCOUVER INC p 241
788 HARBOURSIDE DR SUITE 200, NORTH VANCOUVER, BC, V7P 3R7
(604) 980-4891   SIC 1711

MODERN POWER PRODUCTS, DIV OF p 638
See MTD PRODUCTS LIMITED

MODERN REQUIREMENTS p 850
See 2101440 ONTARIO INC

MODERN SALES CO-OP p 487
87 CAPLAN AVE, BARRIE, ON, L4N 9J3
(705) 733-1771   SIC 5013

MODERN TOOL LTD p 17
11488 70 ST SE, CALGARY, AB, T2C 4Y3
(403) 236-1150   SIC 5084

MODERN/NIAGARA GROUP INC p 1002
8125 HWY 50, VAUGHAN, ON, L4H 4S6
(613) 591-1338   SIC 1711

MODES CAZZA INC p 1179
433 RUE CHABANEL O UNITE 801, MONTREAL, QC, H2N 2J7
(514) 383-0026   SIC 5621

MODES CORWIK INC p 1179
225 RUE CHABANEL O BUREAU 200, MONTREAL, QC, H2N 2C9
(514) 381-5393   SIC 5137

MODES DO-GREE LTEE, LES p 1218
3205 CH DE BEDFORD, MONTREAL, QC, H3S 1G3
(514) 904-2109   SIC 5136

MODES ET SPORTS 3050 INC p 1374
3050 BOUL DE PORTLAND BUREAU 528, SHERBROOKE, QC, J1L 1K1
(819) 346-5286   SIC 5941

MODES HOW INTERNATIONAL INC, LES p 1182
6595 RUE SAINT-URBAIN, MONTREAL, QC, H2S 3G6
(514) 904-0055   SIC 5137

MODES I AM JE SUIS p 1338
See COMMERCE INTERNATIONAL MANHATTAN INC

MODES J & X LTEE, LES p 1217
7101 AV DU PARC BUREAU 301, MONTREAL, QC, H3N 1X9
SIC 7389

MODES KNIT SET (2010) LTEE, LES p 1179
9500 RUE MEILLEUR BUREAU 510, MONTREAL, QC, H2N 2B7
SIC 5137

MODES MAISON HERITAGE INC p 1227
5000 RUE JEAN-TALON O BUREAU 150, MONTREAL, QC, H4P 1W9
(514) 341-1311   SIC 5023

MODES MORSAM INC p 1179
350 RUE DE LOUVAIN O BUREAU 101, MONTREAL, QC, H2N 2E8
(514) 383-0033   SIC 5137

MODES ZERO II 60 INC p 1179
9400 BOUL SAINT-LAURENT BUREAU 200, MONTREAL, QC, H2N 1P3
(514) 383-3580   SIC 5137

MODIS CANADA INC p 965
10 BAY ST SUITE 700, TORONTO, ON, M5J 2R8
(416) 367-2020   SIC 7361

MODSPACE FINANCIAL SERVICES CANADA, LTD p 499
2300 NORTH PARK DR, BRAMPTON, ON, L6S 6C6
(905) 794-3900   SIC 7519

MODU-LOC FENCE RENTALS LTD p 219
240 NEAVE RD, KELOWNA, BC, V1V 2L9
(250) 491-4110   SIC 7353

MODULAR & CUSTOM CABINETS LIMITED p 664
10721 KEELE ST, MAPLE, ON, L6A 3Y9
(905) 832-8311   SIC 3843

MODULAR BUILDING SYSTEMS p 599
See NRB INC

MODULE DU NORD QUEBECOIS p 1221
See REGIE REGIONALE DE LA SANTE ET DES SERVICES SOCIAUX NUNAVIK

MODULEX AMERICAS INC p 11
3200 14 AVE NE SUITE 1, CALGARY, AB, T2A 6J4
(403) 272-0597   *SIC 3993*

MODUS STRUCTURES INC p 81
34 MCCOOL CRES, CROSSFIELD, AB, T0M 0S0
(403) 274-2422   *SIC 3448*

MOE'S CLASSIC RUGS & HOME ACCESSORIES LTD p 295
1728 GLEN DR, VANCOUVER, BC, V6A 4L5
(604) 688-0633   *SIC 5963*

MOE'S HOME COLLECTION p 295
See MOE'S CLASSIC RUGS & HOME ACCESSORIES LTD

MOE'S MENS WEAR p 562
See K.F.S. LIMITED

MOE'S TRANSPORT TRUCKING INC p 1024
1333 COLLEGE AVE, WINDSOR, ON, N9B 1M8
(519) 253-8442   *SIC 4213*

MOE, GARY VOLKSWAGEN p 157
See 388010 ALBERTA LTD

MOEN INC p 798
2816 BRISTOL CIR, OAKVILLE, ON, L6H 5S7
(905) 829-3400   *SIC 5074*

MOFFATT & POWELL LIMITED p 658
1282 HYDE PARK RD, LONDON, ON, N6H 5K5
(519) 472-2000   *SIC 5211*

MOFFATT & POWELL RONA p 658
See MOFFATT & POWELL LIMITED

MOFFATT SCRAP IRON & METAL INC p 540
9620 GUELPH LINE, CAMPBELLVILLE, ON, L0P 1B0
(905) 854-2792   *SIC 5093*

MOFFATT SUPPLY & SPECIALTIES p 909
See R.C. MOFFATT SUPPLY LIMITED

MOFFATTS NORTHWOOD MAZDA p 485
See 650124 ONTARIO LIMITED

MOFFITT DODGE CHRYSLER LTD p 410
205 ROUTE 170, OAK BAY, NB, E3L 3X7
(506) 466-3061   *SIC 5511*

MOGO p 299
See MOGO FINANCE TECHNOLOGY INC

MOGO ELECTRICAL SERVICES LTD p 110
5663 70 ST NW, EDMONTON, AB, T6B 3P6
(780) 438-3440   *SIC 1731*

MOGO FINANCE TECHNOLOGY INC p 299
401 GEORGIA ST W SUITE 2100, VANCOUVER, BC, V6B 5A1
(604) 659-4380   *SIC 6153*

MOHAWK COLLEGE OF APPLIED ARTS AND TECHNOLOGY, THE p 617
135 FENNELL AVE W, HAMILTON, ON, L9C 0E5
(905) 575-1212   *SIC 8222*

MOHAWK COLLEGE OF APPLIED ARTS AND TECHNOLOGY, THE p 892
481 BARTON ST, STONEY CREEK, ON, L8E 2L7
(905) 662-9796   *SIC 8222*

MOHAWK COLLEGE STARRT INSTITUTE p 892
See MOHAWK COLLEGE OF APPLIED ARTS AND TECHNOLOGY, THE

MOHAWK COUNCIL OF AKWESASNE p 475
169 AKWESASNE INTERNATIONAL RD, AKWESASNE, ON, K6H 0G5
(613) 933-0409   *SIC 8211*

MOHAWK FORD SALES LIMITED p 617
930 UPPER JAMES ST, HAMILTON, ON, L9C 3A5
(905) 388-1711   *SIC 5511*

MOHAWK IMPERIAL SALES p 565
406 HWY 2 & HWY SUITE 49, DESERONTO, ON, K0K 1X0
(613) 396-3700   *SIC 5411*

MOHAWK INTERNET TECHNOLOGIES p 1206
1250 BOUL RENE-LEVESQUE O BUREAU 4100, MONTREAL, QC, H3B 4W8
(450) 638-4007   *SIC 4899*

MOHAWK STUDENT'S ASSOCIATION p 612
135 FENNEL AVE W RM G109, HAMILTON, ON, L8N 3T2
(905) 575-2393   *SIC 8399*

MOHWAK MEDBUY CORPORATION p 660
4056 MEADOWBROOK DR UNIT 135, LONDON, ON, N6L 1E4
(519) 652-1688   *SIC 7389*

MOIRS DIV OF p 443
See HERSHEY CANADA INC

MOISAN, ELOI INC p 1306
20 354 RTE, SAINT-GILBERT, QC, G0A 3T0
(418) 268-3232   *SIC 5211*

MOLD-MASTERS (2007) LIMITED p 594
233 ARMSTRONG AVE, GEORGETOWN, ON, L7G 4X5
(905) 877-0185   *SIC 3559*

MOLDEX p 1285
See CENTRE TECHNO-PNEU INC

MOLESWORTH FARM SUPPLY LTD p 647
44743 PERTH LINE 86, LISTOWEL, ON, N4W 3G6
(519) 291-3740   *SIC 5191*

MOLINARO'S FINE ITALIAN FOODS LTD p 704
2345 STANFIELD RD UNIT 50, MISSISSAUGA, ON, L4Y 3Y3
(905) 281-0352   *SIC 2038*

MOLISANA IMPORTS p 792
See 996660 ONTARIO LIMITED

MOLL BERCZY HAUS p 878
See TENDERCARE NURSING HOMES LIMITED

MOLSOM AMPHITHEATRE p 991
See LIVE NATION CANADA, INC

MOLSON BREWERIES p 321
See MOLSON CANADA 2005

MOLSON BREWERIES OF CANADA LIMITED p 321
1550 BURRARD ST, VANCOUVER, BC, V6J 3G5
(604) 664-1786   *SIC 2082*

MOLSON BREWERIES OF CANADA LIMITED p 586
33 CARLINGVIEW DR, ETOBICOKE, ON, M9W 5E4
(416) 679-1786   *SIC 5181*

MOLSON CANADA p 586
See MOLSON CANADA 2005

MOLSON CANADA 2005 p 321
1550 BURRARD ST, VANCOUVER, BC, V6J 3G5
(604) 664-1786   *SIC 2082*

MOLSON CANADA 2005 p 432
131 CIRCULAR RD, ST. JOHN'S, NL, A1C 2Z9
(709) 726-1786   *SIC 2082*

MOLSON CANADA 2005 p 586
1 CARLINGVIEW DR, ETOBICOKE, ON, M9W 5E5
(416) 675-1786   *SIC 2082*

MOLSON CANADA 2005 p 586
33 CARLINGVIEW DR SUITE 2005, ETOBICOKE, ON, M9W 5E4
(416) 679-1786   *SIC 2082*

MOLSON COORS BREWING COMPANY p 321
See MOLSON BREWERIES OF CANADA LIMITED

MOLSON COORS BREWING COMPANY p 586
See MOLSON BREWERIES OF CANADA LIMITED

MOLSON COORS CANADA p 432
See MOLSON CANADA 2005

MOLSON COORS CANADA INC p 586

33 CARLINGVIEW DR, ETOBICOKE, ON, M9W 5E4
(416) 679-1786   *SIC 2082*

MOLSON INC p 1176
1555 RUE NOTRE-DAME E, MONTREAL, QC, H2L 2R5
(514) 521-1786   *SIC 5181*

MOLSON SASKATCHEWAN BREWERY LTD p 1416
395 PARK ST SUITE 2, REGINA, SK, S4N 5B2
(306) 359-1786   *SIC 2082*

MOLY-COP ALTASTEEL LTD p 110
9401 34 ST NW, EDMONTON, AB, T6B 2X6
(780) 468-1133   *SIC 3312*

MOM'S PANTRY PRODUCTS LTD p 368
3241 ST MARY'S RD, WINNIPEG, MB, R2N 4B4
(204) 954-2060   *SIC 5142*

MOMENT FACTORY p 1184
See STUDIOS MOMENT FACTORY INC, LES

MOMENTIS CANADA CORP p 741
6345 DIXIE RD SUITE 200, MISSISSAUGA, ON, L5T 2E6
(905) 670-4440   *SIC 4924*

MOMENTIS INFORMATIQUE INC p 1157
5500 AV ROYALMOUNT BUREAU 250, MONT-ROYAL, QC, H4P 1H7
(514) 939-2306   *SIC 7372*

MOMENTUM DISTRIBUTION INC p 1310
2045 RUE FRANCIS BUREAU 200, SAINT-HUBERT, QC, J4T 0A6
(450) 466-5115   *SIC 5091*

MOMENTUM HEALTHWARE, INC p 364
131 PROVENCHER BLVD SUITE 308, WINNIPEG, MB, R2H 0G2
(204) 231-3836   *SIC 7372*

MOMENTUM REALTY INC p 884
353 LAKE ST, ST CATHARINES, ON, L2N 7G4
(905) 935-8001   *SIC 6531*

MOMENTUM TRAVEL GROUP p 1328
See 7513283 CANADA INC

MOMETAL STRUCTURES INC p 1393
201 CH DE L'ENERGIE, VARENNES, QC, J3X 1P7
(450) 929-3999   *SIC 1791*

MOMMA.COM p 1258
See COPERNIC INC

MOMO SPORTS INC p 1374
530 RUE JEAN-PAUL-PERRAULT, SHERBROOKE, QC, J1L 3A6
(819) 822-3077   *SIC 5699*

MON 3047 INC p 626
140 EARL GREY DR, KANATA, ON, K2T 1B6
(613) 270-0518   *SIC 5812*

MON SHEONG FOUNDATION p 876
2030 MCNICOLL AVE, SCARBOROUGH, ON, M1V 5P4
(416) 291-3898   *SIC 8051*

MONAGHAN MUSHROOMS LTD p 540
7345 GUELPH LINE, CAMPBELLVILLE, ON, L0P 1B0
(905) 878-9375   *SIC 0182*

MONAHAN AGENCY LTD p 332
2506 41 ST, VERNON, BC, V1T 6J9
(250) 545-3235   *SIC 5192*

MONAHAN FORD KAWASAKI p 135
See HIGH PRAIRIE FORD SALES & SERVICE LTD

MONARCH INDUSTRIES LIMITED p 361
280 MONARCH DR, WINKLER, MB, R6W 0J6
(204) 325-4393   *SIC 3321*

MONARCH INDUSTRIES LIMITED p 366
51 BURMAC RD, WINNIPEG, MB, R2J 4J3
(204) 786-7921   *SIC 3593*

MONARCH INVESTMENTS LTD p 366
51 BURMAC RD, WINNIPEG, MB, R2J 4J3
(204) 786-7921   *SIC 3369*

MONARCH OIL (KITCHENER) LIMITED p 635

808 VICTORIA ST N, KITCHENER, ON, N2B 3C1
(519) 743-8241   *SIC 5172*

MONARCH PARK COLLEGIATE p 919
See TORONTO DISTRICT SCHOOL BOARD

MONARCH PLASTICS LIMITED p 804
2335 SPEERS RD, OAKVILLE, ON, L6L 2X9
(905) 791-8805   *SIC 3089*

MONARCH WEALTH CORPORATION p 697
5090 EXPLORER DR SUITE 200, MISSISSAUGA, ON, L4W 4X6
(416) 640-2285   *SIC 6722*

MONAS & CIE LTEE p 1184
4575 AV DU PARC, MONTREAL, QC, H2V 4E4
(514) 842-1421   *SIC 5046*

MONASHEE MANUFACTURING CORPORATION LTD p 222
1247 ELLIS ST, KELOWNA, BC, V1Y 1Z6
(250) 762-2646   *SIC 3599*

MONBURO p 1159
See BUREAUTIQUE COTE-SUD INC

MONCION GROCERS PEMBROKE MARKET p 837
See 113559 ONTARIO LIMITED

MONCION GROCERS RIVERSIDE MARKET p 837
See 1048271 ONTARIO INC

MONCTON CRUSHED STONE p 408
See MODERN CONSTRUCTION (1983) LTD

MONCTON FIRE DEPT ADMINISTRATION OFFICE p 408
See MONCTON, CITY OF

MONCTON HIGH SCHOOL p 407
See SCHOOL DISTRICT 2

MONCTON HONDA p 408
See BAIG BLVD MOTORS INC

MONCTON YOUTH RESIDENCES INC p 407
536 MOUNTAIN RD, MONCTON, NB, E1C 2N5
(506) 869-6333   *SIC 8641*

MONCTON, CITY OF p 408
140 MILLENNIUM BLVD, MONCTON, NB, E1E 2G8
(506) 857-2008   *SIC 4131*

MONCTON, CITY OF p 408
800 ST GEORGE BLVD, MONCTON, NB, E1E 2C7
(506) 857-8800   *SIC 7389*

MONDART HOLDINGS LIMITED p 409
1543 MOUNTAIN RD, MONCTON, NB, E1G 1A3
(506) 857-2309   *SIC 7514*

MONDELEZ CANADA INC p 572
3300 BLOOR ST W SUITE 1801, ETOBICOKE, ON, M8X 2X2
SIC 2032

MONDELEZ CANADA INC p 614
45 EWEN RD, HAMILTON, ON, L8S 3C3
(905) 526-7212   *SIC 2032*

MONDELEZ INTERNATIONAL p 572
See MONDELEZ CANADA INC

MONDELEZ INTERNATIONAL CANADA p 614
See MONDELEZ CANADA INC

MONDETTA CANADA, INC p 381
1109 WINNIPEG AVE, WINNIPEG, MB, R3E 0S2
(204) 786-1700   *SIC 5136*

MONDETTA CLOTHING CO p 381
See MONDETTA CANADA, INC

MONDIALE DES CULTURES DE DRUMMONDVILLE p 1096
See FESTIVAL MONDIAL DE FOLKLORE (DRUMMOND)

MONDIV, DIV DE SPECIALITES LASSONDE p

1062
See SPECIALITES LASSONDE INC
MONDO AMERICA *p 1362*
See SOCIETE MONDO AMERICA INC
MONDO FOODS CO. LTD *p 391*
40 OTTER ST, WINNIPEG, MB, R3T 4J7
(204) 453-7722 *SIC 5143*
MONDO PRODUCTS COMPANY LIMITED *p 474*
695 WESTNEY RD S UNIT 1, AJAX, ON, L1S 6M9
(800) 465-5676 *SIC 2842*
MONDOFIX INC *p 1059*
99 RUE EMILIEN-MARCOUX BUREAU 101, BLAINVILLE, QC, J7C 0B4
(450) 433-1414 *SIC 6794*
MONDOR LTEE *p 1316*
785 RUE HONORE-MERCIER, SAINT-JEAN-SUR-RICHELIEU, QC, J2X 3S2
(450) 347-5321 *SIC 2339*
MONDOU, REAL INC *p 1153*
12429 RTE ARTHUR-SAUVE, MIRABEL, QC, J7N 2C2
(450) 258-2817 *SIC 2048*
MONERIS SOLUTIONS CORPORATION *p 412*
2 CHARLOTTE ST, SACKVILLE, NB, E4L 3S8
(506) 364-1920 *SIC 8231*
MONERIS SOLUTIONS CORPORATION *p 572*
3300 BLOOR ST W 10TH FLR, ETOBICOKE, ON, M8X 2X2
(416) 734-1000 *SIC 7389*
MONETTE, EUGENE INC *p 1391*
2650 1ER RANG DE DONCASTER, VAL-DAVID, QC, J0T 2N0
(819) 322-3833 *SIC 5211*
MONEY MART *p 334*
See NATIONAL MONEY MART COMPANY
MONGOOSE *p 54*
See NCS MULTISTAGE INC
MONIDEX DISTRIBUTION INTERNATIONAL INC *p 1050*
10700 RUE COLBERT, ANJOU, QC, H1J 2H8
(514) 323-9932 *SIC 5013*
MONITEURS ANGELCARE INC *p 1073*
201 BOUL DE L'INDUSTRIE LOCAL 104, CANDIAC, QC, J5R 6A6
(450) 462-2000 *SIC 3699*
MONITOR COMPANY CANADA *p 954*
8 ADELAIDE ST W STE 20, TORONTO, ON, M5H 0A9
(416) 408-4800 *SIC 8741*
MONITROL R & D INC *p 1066*
1291 RUE AMPERE, BOUCHERVILLE, QC, J4B 5Z5
(450) 641-4810 *SIC 5063*
MONK OFFICE SUPPLY LTD *p 339*
800 VIEWFIELD RD, VICTORIA, BC, V9A 4V1
(800) 735-3433 *SIC 5712*
MONKLAND EGG GRADING, DIV OF *p 1312*
See GROUPE NUTRI INC
MONKMAN GRACIE & JOHNSTON *p 841*
261 GEORGE ST N, PETERBOROUGH, ON, K9J 3G9
(705) 742-8863 *SIC 6411*
MONSANTO CANADA INC *p 391*
1 RESEARCH RD SUITE 900, WINNIPEG, MB, R3T 6E3
(204) 985-1000 *SIC 0181*
MONSIGNOR DOYLE *p 535*
See WATERLOO CATHOLIC DISTRICT SCHOOL BOARD
MONSTER HOLLOWEEN *p 751*
See 8603600 CANADA INC
MONSTER WORLDWIDE CANADA INC *p 1198*
2020 BOUL ROBERT-BOURASSA BUREAU 2000, MONTREAL, QC, H3A 2A5

(514) 284-0231 *SIC 6712*
MONSTERCAT *p 295*
See MONSTERCAT INC
MONSTERCAT INC *p 295*
380 RAILWAY ST, VANCOUVER, BC, V6A 4E3
(519) 729-2179 *SIC 7389*
MONT SAINT-SAUVEUR INTERNATIONAL INC *p 1352*
350 AV SAINT-DENIS RR 3, SAINT-SAUVEUR, QC, J0R 1R3
(450) 227-4671 *SIC 7011*
MONT ST. JOSEPH HOME INC *p 1414*
777 28TH ST E, PRINCE ALBERT, SK, S6V 8C2
(306) 953-4500 *SIC 8051*
MONT-ROYAL DEVELOPPEMENT *p 1155*
20 AV ROOSEVELT, MONT-ROYAL, QC, H3R 1Z4
(514) 734-3034 *SIC 8748*
MONTAGE SAINT-LAURENT INC *p 1237*
807 RUE MARSHALL, MONTREAL, QC, H7S 1J9
(450) 786-1792 *SIC 1791*
MONTAGE TECHNOLOGIES INC *p 54*
GD LCD 1, CALGARY, AB, T2P 2G8
(403) 263-4089 *SIC 8741*
MONTAGUE REGIONAL HIGH SCHOOL *p 1041*
See EASTERN SCHOOL DISTRICT
MONTALCO CABINETS (1991) LTD *p 261*
2700 SIMPSON RD UNIT 125, RICHMOND, BC, V6X 2P9
(604) 273-5105 *SIC 5211*
MONTANA *p 981*
See LAST BEST PLACE CORP, THE
MONTANA KAMLOOPS *p 219*
See OKANAGAN GENERAL PARTNER LIMITED
MONTANA'S *p 554*
See KELSEY'S RESTAURANTS INC
MONTANA'S COOK HOUSE *p 626*
See MON 3047 INC
MONTANA'S COOKHOUSE *p 338*
315 BURNSIDE RD W, VICTORIA, BC, V8Z 7L6
(250) 978-9333 *SIC 5812*
MONTANA'S COOKHOUSE *p 751*
See RECIPE UNLIMITED CORPORATION
MONTANA'S COOKHOUSE *p 905*
See RECIPE UNLIMITED CORPORATION
MONTANA'S COOKHOUSE SALOON *p 121*
1720 99 ST NW, EDMONTON, AB, T6N 1M5
(780) 466-8520 *SIC 5812*
MONTANA'S COOKHOUSE SALOON *p 368*
See CARA FOODS
MONTANA'S COOKHOUSE SALOON *p 487*
66 BARRIE VIEW DR, BARRIE, ON, L4N 8V4
(705) 726-3375 *SIC 5812*
MONTCALM SECONDARY SCHOOL *p 652*
See THAMES VALLEY DISTRICT SCHOOL BOARD
MONTCALM SERVICES TECHNIQUES INC *p 1132*
695 90E AV, LASALLE, QC, H8R 3A4
SIC 7349
MONTCALM VENTURES LTD *p 324*
1404 MARINE DR SW, VANCOUVER, BC, V6P 5Z9
(604) 261-3343 *SIC 5521*
MONTE CARLO HOTEL-MOTEL INTERNATIONAL INC *p 735*
7045 EDWARDS BLVD FL 5, MISSISSAUGA, ON, L5S 1X2
(905) 564-6194 *SIC 7011*
MONTE CARLO INNS *p 735*
See MONTE CARLO HOTEL-MOTEL INTERNATIONAL INC
MONTE CRISTO BAKERY *p 208*
See 327494 B.C. LTD
MONTEBELLO *p 1112*
See SOURCES VEO INC, LES

MONTECO LTD *p 927*
55 ST CLAIR AVE W SUITE 408, TORONTO, ON, M4V 2Y7
(416) 960-9968 *SIC 3299*
MONTEFERRO AMERICA *p 349*
See CANADIAN GUIDE RAIL CORPORATION
MONTEITH VENTURES INC *p 402*
433 BISHOP DR, FREDERICTON, NB, E3C 2M6
(506) 455-2277 *SIC 5511*
MONTEL INC *p 1160*
225 4E AV, MONTMAGNY, QC, G5V 4N9
(418) 248-0235 *SIC 2542*
MONTEREGIE ST-HYACINTHE CSN- CONSTRUCTION *p 1312*
See FEDERATION DE LA CSN-CONSTRUCTION
MONTESTRIE AUTORAMA INC *p 1111*
6 RUE IRWIN, GRANBY, QC, J2J 2P1
(450) 378-8404 *SIC 5511*
MONTEVA AVIATION *p 1207*
See PLACEMENTS MONTEVA INC
MONTFORT RENAISSANCE INC *p 821*
162 MURRAY ST, OTTAWA, ON, K1N 5M8
(613) 789-5144 *SIC 6531*
MONTGOMERY FORD SALES LIMITED *p 663*
701 CAMPBELL ST, LUCKNOW, ON, N0G 2H0
(519) 528-2813 *SIC 5511*
MONTGOMERY PHARMA PACKAGING *p 730*
See CANADIAN TEST CASE 145
MONTIGO DELRAY *p 229*
See CANADIAN HEATING PRODUCTS INC
MONTMAGNY HYUNDAI *p 1159*
See CARON AUTOMOBILES INC
MONTMAGNY TOYOTA *p 1159*
See ARMANEAU AUTOS INC
MONTMARTRE CO-OPERATIVE ASSOCIATION LIMITED *p 1410*
104 CENTRAL AVE, MONTMARTRE, SK, S0G 3M0
(306) 424-2144 *SIC 5171*
MONTMORENCY FORD (1997) INC *p 1070*
7225 BOUL TASCHEREAU, BROSSARD, QC, J4Y 1A1
(450) 678-9940 *SIC 5511*
MONTOUR LTEE *p 1059*
1080 BOUL MICHELE-BOHEC, BLAINVILLE, QC, J7C 5N5
(450) 433-1312 *SIC 2099*
MONTPAK INTERNATIONAL INC *p 1342*
5730 RUE MAURICE-CULLEN, SAINT-LAURENT, QC, H7C 2V1
(450) 665-9524 *SIC 2011*
MONTREAL ACCOUNTING *p 1201*
See BDO CANADA LLP
MONTREAL AUTO PRIX INC *p 1346*
4900 BOUL METROPOLITAIN E, SAINT-LEONARD, QC, H1S 3A4
(514) 593-9020 *SIC 5521*
MONTREAL BRIQUE ET PIERRE *p 1231*
See 2321-1998 QUEBEC INC
MONTREAL CENTRE SPORTS INC *p 1206*
930 RUE SAINTE-CATHERINE O, MONTREAL, QC, H3B 1E2
(514) 866-1914 *SIC 5941*
MONTREAL CONVENTION CENTRE *p 1191*
See GOUVERNEMENT DE LA PROVINCE DE QUEBEC
MONTREAL GATEWAY TERMINALS PARTNERSHIP *p 1163*
305 RUE CURATTEAU, MONTREAL, QC, H1L 6R6
(514) 257-3040 *SIC 4491*
MONTREAL INTERNATIONAL *p 1189*
380 RUE SAINT-ANTOINE O BUREAU 8000, MONTREAL, QC, H2Y 3X7
(514) 987-8191 *SIC 8748*

MONTREAL PHOTOCOPIEUR *p 1231*
See GROUPE CT INC
MONTREAL PITA INC *p 1218*
654 AV BEAUMONT, MONTREAL, QC, H3N 1V5
(514) 495-4513 *SIC 5461*
MONTREAL PORT ADMINISTRATION *p 1168*
See TRANSPORT CANADA
MONTREAL PORT ADMINISTRATION *p 1211*
2100 AV PIERRE-DUPUY BUREAU 1, MONTREAL, QC, H3C 3R5
(514) 283-7011 *SIC 4491*
MONTREAL PORT AUTHORITY *p 1211*
See MONTREAL PORT ADMINISTRATION
MONTREAL STUDIOS ET EQUIPMENTS S.E.N.C *p 1211*
1777 RUE CARRIE-DERICK, MONTREAL, QC, H3C 6G2
(514) 866-2170 *SIC 7812*
MONTREAL TRACTEUR INC *p 1053*
21601 AV CLARK-GRAHAM, BAIE-D'URFE, QC, H9X 3T5
(514) 457-8100 *SIC 5084*
MONTRES BIG TIME INC *p 1226*
9250 BOUL DE L'ACADIE BUREAU 340, MONTREAL, QC, H4N 3C5
(514) 384-6464 *SIC 5944*
MONTRES ORA, LES *p 1331*
See WENGER LTEE
MONTRIUM HOSTED SOLUTIONS INC *p 1189*
507 PLACE D'ARMES BUREAU 1050, MONTREAL, QC, H2Y 2W8
(514) 223-9153 *SIC 8742*
MONTROSE INTERNATIONAL GROUP *p 801*
See MIG HOLDINGS INC
MONTROSE MORTGAGE CORPORATION LTD *p 379*
200 GRAHAM AVE SUITE 1110, WINNIPEG, MB, R3C 4L5
(204) 982-1110 *SIC 6162*
MONTSHIP INC *p 1189*
360 RUE SAINT-JACQUES BUREAU 1000, MONTREAL, QC, H2Y 1R2
(514) 286-4646 *SIC 4731*
MONTY COULOMBE S.E.N.C *p 1371*
234 RUE DUFFERIN BUREAU 200, SHERBROOKE, QC, J1H 4M2
(819) 566-4466 *SIC 8111*
MONTY PHARMACY LTD *p 917*
812 O'CONNOR DR, TORONTO, ON, M4B 2S9
(416) 285-5822 *SIC 5912*
MONUMENT COMMUNITY ECONOMIC DEVELOPMENT SOCIETY *p 11*
2936 RADCLIFFE DR SE SUITE 16, CALGARY, AB, T2A 6M8
(403) 272-9323 *SIC 8699*
MONUMENT MINING LIMITED *p 315*
1100 MELVILLE ST SUITE 1580, VANCOUVER, BC, V6E 4A6
(604) 638-1661 *SIC 1081*
MOOD MEDIA ENTERTAINMENT LTD *p 556*
99 SANTE DR SUITE B, CONCORD, ON, L4K 3C4
(905) 761-4300 *SIC 7389*
MOODY'S ANALYTICS GLOBAL EDUCATION (CANADA), INC *p 982*
200 WELLINGTON ST W, TORONTO, ON, M5V 3C7
(416) 364-9130 *SIC 8299*
MOODY'S EQUIPMENT LP *p 1428*
71ST ST HWY 16, SASKATOON, SK, S7K 3K1
(306) 934-4686 *SIC 5083*
MOODY'S EQUIPMENT LTD *p 1428*
71 ST & HWY SUITE 16, SASKATOON, SK, S7K 3K1
(306) 934-4686 *SIC 5083*

MOOG COMPONENTS GROUP *p 446*
See FOCAL TECHNOLOGIES CORPORATION
MOONEY INSURANCE AGENCY LTD *p 154*
4910 45 ST, RED DEER, AB, T4N 1K6
SIC 6411
MOORE CANADA CORPORATION *p 102*
18330 102 AVE NW, EDMONTON, AB, T5S 2J9
(780) 452-5592 *SIC 2761*
MOORE CANADA CORPORATION *p 590*
650 VICTORIA TERR, FERGUS, ON, N1M 1G7
(519) 843-2510 *SIC 2761*
MOORE CANADA CORPORATION *p 732*
333 FOSTER CRES SUITE 2, MISSISSAUGA, ON, L5R 3Z9
(905) 890-1080 *SIC 2782*
MOORE CANADA CORPORATION *p 741*
6100 VIPOND DR, MISSISSAUGA, ON, L5T 2X1
(905) 362-3100 *SIC 6712*
MOORE CANADA CORPORATION *p 777*
180 BOND AVE, NORTH YORK, ON, M3B 3P3
(416) 445-8800 *SIC 2752*
MOORE CANADA CORPORATION *p 999*
8 DOUGLAS RD, TRENTON, ON, K8V 5R4
(613) 392-1205 *SIC 2761*
MOORE CANADA CORPORATION *p 1050*
11150 AV L.-J.-FORGET, ANJOU, QC, H1J 2K9
(514) 353-9090 *SIC 2782*
MOORE CANADA CORPORATION *p 1216*
1500 RUE SAINT-PATRICK, MONTREAL, QC, H3K 0A3
(514) 415-7300 *SIC 2759*
MOORE CANADA CORPORATION *p 1326*
395 AV SAINTE-CROIX BUREAU 100, SAINT-LAURENT, QC, H4N 2L3
SIC 2731
MOORE ENTERPRISES INC *p 401*
1050 WOODSTOCK RD, FREDERICTON, NB, E3B 7R8
(506) 450-3778 *SIC 5812*
MOORE INDUSTRIAL LTD *p 369*
169 OMANDS CREEK BLVD, WINNIPEG, MB, R2R 1V9
(204) 632-4092 *SIC 5084*
MOORE MATHESON CONSTRUCTION *p 481*
See MATHESON CONSTRUCTORS LIMITED
MOORE PACKAGING CORPORATION *p 487*
191 JOHN ST, BARRIE, ON, L4N 2L4
(705) 737-1023 *SIC 2653*
MOORE PACKAGING CORPORATION *p 487*
191 JOHN ST SUITE 12, BARRIE, ON, L4N 2L4
(705) 737-1023 *SIC 4783*
MOORE'S INDUSTRIAL SERVICE LTD *p 24*
3333 23 ST NE, CALGARY, AB, T2E 6V8
(403) 219-7160 *SIC 7699*
MOORE, BENJAMIN & CO., LIMITED *p 556*
8775 KEELE ST, CONCORD, ON, L4K 2N1
(905) 761-4800 *SIC 2851*
MOORE, MIKE & SONS CONSTRUCTION LTD *p 863*
167 INDUSTRIAL COURT B UNIT A, SAULT STE. MARIE, ON, P6B 5Z9
(705) 759-3173 *SIC 1542*
MOORES CLOTHING FOR MEN *p 586*
See MOORES THE SUIT PEOPLE INC
MOORES THE SUIT PEOPLE INC *p 586*
129 CARLINGVIEW DR, ETOBICOKE, ON, M9W 5E7
(416) 675-1900 *SIC 5611*
MOOSE BAND DEVELOPMENT CORPORATION *p 746*
22 JONATHAN THETHOO, MOOSE FACTORY, ON, P0L 1W0

(705) 658-4335 *SIC 1542*
MOOSE JAW CO-OP *p 1411*
See MOOSE JAW CO-OPERATIVE ASSOCIATION LIMITED, THE
MOOSE JAW CO-OPERATIVE ASSOCIATION LIMITED, THE *p 1411*
500 1ST AVE NW SUITE B10, MOOSE JAW, SK, S6H 3M5
(306) 692-2351 *SIC 5171*
MOOSE JAW REFINERY ULC *p 54*
440 2 AVE SW SUITE 1700, CALGARY, AB, T2P 5E9
(403) 206-4000 *SIC 5032*
MOOSE JAW SAFEWAY *p 1411*
See SOBEYS WEST INC
MOOSE JAW TIMES HERALD *p 1206*
See MEDIAS TRANSCONTINENTAL INC
MOOSE JAW TOYOTA *p 1411*
See 617274 SASKATCHEWAN LTD
MOOSE WINOOSKI'S *p 641*
See RESTAURANT INNOVATIONS INC
MOOSEHEAD BREWERIES LIMITED *p 416*
89 MAIN ST W, SAINT JOHN, NB, E2M 3H2
(506) 635-7000 *SIC 2082*
MOOSEHORN CONSUMERS COOPERATIVE LTD *p 352*
1 MAIN ST, MOOSEHORN, MB, R0C 2E0
(204) 768-2770 *SIC 5171*
MOPAC AUTO SUPPLY LTD *p 226*
19950 84 AVE SUITE 596, LANGLEY, BC, V2Y 3C2
(604) 881-4900 *SIC 7538*
MOPAC PERFORMANCE DISTRIBUTERS *p 226*
See MOPAC AUTO SUPPLY LTD
MOR-WEN RESTAURANTS LTD *p 891*
1010   STITTSVILLE   MAIN   ST, STITTSVILLE, ON, K2S 1B9
(613) 831-2738 *SIC 5812*
MORAN MINING & TUNNELLING LTD *p 647*
159 FIELDING RD, LIVELY, ON, P3Y 1L7
(705) 682-4070 *SIC 1241*
MORAND INDUSTRIES LTD *p 151*
5502 LAC SUITE ANNE, ONOWAY, AB, T0E 1V0
(780) 967-2500 *SIC 5191*
MORASH INSURANCE *p 467*
See   MACLEOD-LORWAY   FINANCIAL GROUP LIMITED
MORBERN INC *p 562*
80 BOUNDARY RD, CORNWALL, ON, K6H 6M1
(613) 932-8811 *SIC 2295*
MORDEN DIVISION *p 352*
See BUHLER INDUSTRIES INC
MORE CORE DIAMOND DRILLING SERVICES LTD *p 269*
2511 HWY 37A, STEWART, BC, V0T 1W0
(250) 636-9156 *SIC 1799*
MOREAU INDUSTRIEL *p 1289*
See 2950-0519 QUEBEC INC
MOREL ET FILS *p 1347*
See 2950-4602 QUEBEC INC
MORELCO *p 1281*
See SM CONSTRUCTION INC
MORELLO'S INDEPENDANT GROCER *p 842*
See 1426159 ONTARIO LIMITED
MORENCY *p 1344*
See ECO-LOGIXX - GROSSISTE ALIMENTAIRE ET PRODUITS D'EMBALLAGES INC
MORGAN CANADA CORPORATION *p 504*
12 CHELSEA LANE, BRAMPTON, ON, L6T 3Y4
(905) 791-8130 *SIC 3713*
MORGAN CONSTRUCTION AND ENVIRONMENTAL LTD *p 102*
17303 102 AVE NW, EDMONTON, AB, T5S 1J8
(780) 733-9100 *SIC 1623*

MORGAN CREEK KEG *p 279*
See KEG RESTAURANTS LTD
MORGAN CREEK TROPICALS LTD *p 279*
4148 184 ST, SURREY, BC, V3Z 1B7
(604) 576-1156 *SIC 5193*
MORGAN ESSO *p 881*
See 13089980 ONTARIO LTD
MORGAN MEIGHEN & ASSOCIATES LIMITED *p 939*
10 TORONTO ST, TORONTO, ON, M5C 2B7
(416) 366-2931 *SIC 6726*
MORGAN SCHAFFER LTEE *p 1131*
8300 RUE SAINT-PATRICK BUREAU 150, LASALLE, QC, H8N 2H1
(514) 739-1967 *SIC 8734*
MORGAN SOLAR INC *p 993*
100 SYMES RD UNIT 100A, TORONTO, ON, M6N 0A8
(416) 203-1655 *SIC 8731*
MORGAN STANLEY CANADA LIMITED *p 965*
181 BAY ST SUITE 3700, TORONTO, ON, M5J 2T3
(416) 943-8400 *SIC 6211*
MORGAN, W. S. CONSTRUCTION LIMITED *p 837*
19 BOWES ST, PARRY SOUND, ON, P2A 2K7
(705) 746-9686 *SIC 1542*
MORGUARD CORPORATION *p 824*
See CORPORATION MORGUARD
MORGUARD INVESTMENTS LIMITED *p 710*
55 CITY CENTRE DR SUITE 800, MISSISSAUGA, ON, L5B 1M3
(905) 281-3800 *SIC 6531*
MORGUARD INVESTMENTS LIMITED *p 710*
55 CITY CENTRE DR SUITE 800, MISSISSAUGA, ON, L5B 1M3
(905) 281-3800 *SIC 6798*
MORGUARD   NORTH   AMERICAN   RESIDENTIAL   REAL   ESTATE   INVESTMENT TRUST *p 710*
55 CITY CENTRE DR SUITE 1000, MISSISSAUGA, ON, L5B 1M3
(905) 281-3800 *SIC 6798*
MORGUARD REAL ESTATE INVESTMENT TRUST *p 710*
55 CITY CENTRE DR SUITE 800, MISSISSAUGA, ON, L5B 1M3
(905) 281-3800 *SIC 6726*
MORI LEE ASSOCIATES (CANADA) *p 789*
1293 CALEDONIA RD, NORTH YORK, ON, M6A 2X7
(416) 789-9911 *SIC 5131*
MORI NURSERIES LIMITED *p 761*
1695 NIAGARA STONE RD, NIAGARA ON THE LAKE, ON, L0S 1J0
(905) 468-3217 *SIC 5193*
MORIN, JEAN-GUY INC *p 1164*
5955 RUE SHERBROOKE E, MONTREAL, QC, H1N 1B7
(514) 254-7513 *SIC 5912*
MORINVILLE COLONY LTD *p 147*
GD, MORINVILLE, AB, T8R 1A1
(780) 939-2118 *SIC 8748*
MORINVILLE SOBEYS *p 147*
See RADCO FOOD STORES LTD
MORISSETTE, MARCEL INC *p 1356*
171 BOUL BEGIN, SAINTE-CLAIRE, QC, G0R 2V0
(418) 883-3388 *SIC 5451*
MORISTAR PERRENIALS, DIV OF *p 761*
See MORI NURSERIES LIMITED
MORIYAMA & TESHIMA ARCHITECTS *p 934*
117 GEORGE ST, TORONTO, ON, M5A 2N4
(416) 925-4484 *SIC 8712*
MORLEY HOPPER LIMITED *p 541*
1818 BRADLEY SIDE RD, CARP, ON, K0A 1L0

(613) 831-5490 *SIC 1522*
MORMAK INVESTMENTS LTD *p 331*
8140 BECKETTS RD, VERNON, BC, V1B 3V3
(250) 542-7350 *SIC 5084*
MORNEAU ESKIMO *p 1277*
See ESKIMO EXPRESS INC
MORNEAU SHEPELL INC *p 780*
895 DON MILLS RD SUITE 700, NORTH YORK, ON, M3C 1W3
(416) 445-2700 *SIC 6722*
MORNEAU SHEPELL LTD *p 328*
505 BURRARD ST UNIT 1070, VANCOUVER, BC, V7X 1M5
(604) 642-5200 *SIC 8999*
MORNEAU SHEPELL LTD *p 780*
895 DON MILLS RD, NORTH YORK, ON, M3C 1W3
(416) 445-2700 *SIC 8999*
MORNEAU SHEPELL LTD *p 1229*
800 SQUARE VICTORIA BUREAU 4000, MONTREAL, QC, H4Z 0A4
(514) 878-9090 *SIC 8999*
MORNEAU TRANSPORT *p 1292*
See TRANSPORT MORNEAU INC
MORNINGSTAR *p 794*
See H. B. MORNINGSTAR INDUSTRIES LIMITED
MORNINGSTAR AIR EXPRESS INC *p 134*
3759 60 AVE E, GRANDE PRAIRIE, AB, T9E 0V4
(780) 453-3022 *SIC 4522*
MOROCCANOIL CANADA INC *p 1157*
5742 RUE FERRIER, MONT-ROYAL, QC, H4P 1M7
(514) 448-8967 *SIC 5122*
MORREY AUTO GROUP LTD *p 241*
818 AUTOMALL DR, NORTH VANCOUVER, BC, V7P 3R8
(604) 984-9211 *SIC 5511*
MORREY INFINITY NISSAN OF COQUITLAM *p 246*
See MORREY NISSAN OF COQUITLAM LTD
MORREY MAZDA *p 241*
See MORREY AUTO GROUP LTD
MORREY NISSAN OF COQUITLAM LTD *p 246*
2710 LOUGHEED HWY, PORT COQUITLAM, BC, V3B 6P2
(604) 464-1216 *SIC 5511*
MORRICE TRANSPORTATION *p 1021*
See 882819 ONTARIO LTD
MORRIS GENERAL HOSPITAL *p 353*
See R H A CENTRAL MANITOBA INC.
MORRIS INDUSTRIES LTD *p 352*
284 6TH AVE NW, MINNEDOSA, MB, R0J 1E0
(204) 867-2713 *SIC 3523*
MORRIS INDUSTRIES LTD *p 1423*
85 YORK RD W, ROKEBY, SK, S0A 3N0
(306) 783-8585 *SIC 3523*
MORRIS INDUSTRIES LTD *p 1431*
2131 AIRPORT DR, SASKATOON, SK, S7L 7E1
(306) 933-8585 *SIC 3523*
MORRIS NATIONAL INC *p 556*
100 JACOB KEFFER PKY, CONCORD, ON, L4K 4W3
(905) 879-7777 *SIC 5145*
MORRIS NATIONAL INC *p 1131*
2235 RUE LAPIERRE, LASALLE, QC, H8N 1B7
(514) 368-1000 *SIC 5145*
MORRIS WHOLESALE LTD *p 405*
125 PETRIE ST, MIRAMICHI, NB, E1V 1S4
(506) 836-9012 *SIC 5141*
MORRIS, ALWIN *p 1117*
1470 RTE 138, KAHNAWAKE, QC, J0L 1B0
(450) 633-5100 *SIC 8741*
MORRIS, DAVID FINE CARS LTD *p 102*
17407 111 AVE NW, EDMONTON, AB, T5S 0A1

(780) 484-9000   *SIC 5511*
MORRISH HOLDINGS LTD   *p 359*
GD STN MAIN, THE PAS, MB, R9A 1K2
(204) 623-6469   *SIC 5411*
MORRISON CONSTRUCTION (1983) LTD *p 17*
11158 42 ST SE, CALGARY, AB, T2C 0J9
(403) 279-7600   *SIC 1521*
MORRISON HERSHFIELD GROUP INC   *p 904*
125 COMMERCE VALLEY DR W SUITE 300, THORNHILL, ON, L3T 7W4
(416) 499-3110   *SIC 6712*
MORRISON HERSHFIELD LIMITED   *p 36*
6807 RAILWAY ST SE SUITE 300, CALGARY, AB, T2H 2V6
(403) 246-4500   *SIC 8711*
MORRISON HERSHFIELD LIMITED   *p 904*
125 COMMERCE VALLEY DR W UNIT 300, THORNHILL, ON, L3T 7W4
(416) 499-3110   *SIC 8711*
MORRISON HOMES   *p 17*
See *MORRISON CONSTRUCTION (1983) LTD*
MORRISON LAMOTHE INC   *p 878*
141 FINCHDENE SQ, SCARBOROUGH, ON, M1X 1A7
(416) 291-9121   *SIC 2038*
MORRISON LAMOTHE INC   *p 914*
825 MIDDLEFIELD RD UNIT 1, TORONTO, ON, M1V 4Z7
(416) 291-6762   *SIC 2038*
MORRISON LAMOTHE INC   *p 996*
399 EVANS AVE, TORONTO, ON, M8Z 1K9
(416) 255-7731   *SIC 2038*
MORRISON, DAVID W. ENTERPRISES LTD *p 1024*
2650 TECUMSEH RD W, WINDSOR, ON, N9B 3R1
(519) 252-7743   *SIC 5531*
MORSKATE MANUFACTURING LTD *p 152*
431053 RANGE RD SUITE 261, PONOKA, AB, T4J 1R4
(403) 783-6140   *SIC 7692*
MORSTAR HOLDINGS LTD   *p 356*
230 MAIN ST, SELKIRK, MB, R1A 1R9
   SIC 5511
MORTERM LIMITED   *p 1022*
1601 LINCOLN RD, WINDSOR, ON, N8Y 2J3
(519) 973-8200   *SIC 4491*
MORTGAGE 1 CORPORATION   *p 54*
700 4 AVE SW SUITE 1700, CALGARY, AB, T2P 3J4
   SIC 6163
MORTGAGE BROKERS CITY INC   *p 828*
788 ISLAND PARK DR, OTTAWA, ON, K1Y 0C2
(613) 274-3490   *SIC 6163*
MORTGAGE BROKERS OTTAWA   *p 828*
See *MORTGAGE BROKERS CITY INC*
MORTGAGE CENTRE (CANADA) INC, THE *p 954*
123 QUEEN ST W SUITE 403, TORONTO, ON, M5H 3M9
(416) 865-9750   *SIC 6798*
MORTGAGE INTELLIGENCE INC   *p 732*
5770 HURONTARIO ST SUITE 600, MISSISSAUGA, ON, L5R 3G5
(905) 283-3600   *SIC 6163*
MORTGAGEATLANTIC   *p 458*
14 MCQUADE LAKE CRES UNIT 202, HALIFAX, NS, B3S 1B6
(902) 493-3326   *SIC 6211*
MORTIMER'S FINE FOODS   *p 883*
See *CANAFRIC INC*
MORTON CLARKE & CO. LTD   *p 255*
2551 NO. 6 RD UNIT 1105, RICHMOND, BC, V6V 1P3
(604) 273-1055   *SIC 5099*
MORTON METALS   *p 809*
See *1124178 ONTARIO INC*
MORTON WHOLESALE LTD   *p 1023*
5188 WALKER RD, WINDSOR, ON, N9A

6J3
(519) 737-6961   *SIC 5411*
MORZOC INVESTMENT INC   *p 884*
275 GENEVA ST, ST CATHARINES, ON, L2N 2E9
(905) 935-0071   *SIC 5461*
MOSAIC   *p 697*
See *MOSAIC SALES SOLUTIONS CANADA OPERATING CO.*
MOSAIC CANADA ULC   *p 1404*
3 KALIUM RD, BELLE PLAINE, SK, S0G 0G0
(306) 345-8067   *SIC 1474*
MOSAIC CANADA ULC   *p 1418*
2010 12TH AVE SUITE 1700, REGINA, SK, S4P 0M3
(306) 523-2800   *SIC 1474*
MOSAIC CAPITAL CORPORATION   *p 67*
2424 4 ST SW SUITE 400, CALGARY, AB, T2S 2T4
(403) 218-6500   *SIC 6719*
MOSAIC ESTERHAZY HOLDINGS ULC *p 1406*
HWY 80 E, ESTERHAZY, SK, S0A 0X0
(306) 745-4200   *SIC 6712*
MOSAIC POTASH   *p 1418*
See *MOSAIC CANADA ULC*
MOSAIC POTASH BELLE PLAINE MINE *p 1404*
See *MOSAIC CANADA ULC*
MOSAIC POTASH ESTERHAZY LIMITED PARTNERSHIP   *p 1406*
80 PLANT HWY, ESTERHAZY, SK, S0A 0X0
(306) 745-4400   *SIC 1474*
MOSAIC SALES SOLUTIONS   *p 1087*
2500 BOUL DANIEL-JOHNSON BUREAU 203, COTE SAINT-LUC, QC, H7T 2P6
(450) 686-1013   *SIC 8743*
MOSAIC SALES SOLUTIONS CANADA OPERATING CO.   *p 697*
2700 MATHESON BLVD E UNIT 101, MISSISSAUGA, ON, L4W 4V9
(905) 238-8058   *SIC 8743*
MOSAIC SIMON FRASER HOLDINGS LTD *p 319*
2609 GRANVILLE ST UNIT 500, VANCOUVER, BC, V6H 3H3
(604) 685-3888   *SIC 6553*
MOSAKAHIKAN SCHOOL   *p 365*
See *FRONTIER SCHOOL DIVISION*
MOSCONE TILE LTD   *p 556*
8830 JANE ST SUITE 1, CONCORD, ON, L4K 2M9
(905) 761-5722   *SIC 5211*
MOSER, K.G. LIMITED   *p 620*
77 KING WILLIAM ST, HUNTSVILLE, ON, P1H 1E5
(705) 789-5569   *SIC 5531*
MOSLIM, M. PHARMACY LTD   *p 531*
484 PLAINS RD E, BURLINGTON, ON, L7T 2E1
(905) 632-3365   *SIC 5912*
MOSTI MONDIALE INC   *p 1356*
6865 RTE 132, SAINTE-CATHERINE, QC, J5C 1B6
(450) 638-6380   *SIC 5149*
MOTEL BOULEVARD CARTIER INC *p 1286*
80 BOUL CARTIER, RIVIERE-DU-LOUP, QC, G5R 2M9
(418) 867-1830   *SIC 5812*
MOTEURS DECARIE INC, LES   *p 1227*
8255 RUE BOUGAINVILLE, MONTREAL, QC, H4P 2T3
(514) 334-9910   *SIC 5511*
MOTEURS P.M.   *p 1368*
See *SOLUTIONS TECHNIQUES INTELLIGENTES CB INC*
MOTEYO INC   *p 789*
3111 DUFFERIN ST, NORTH YORK, ON, M6A 2S7
(416) 785-3031   *SIC 5999*
MOTHER PARKER'S TEA & COFFEE INC *p 704*
2530 STANFIELD RD, MISSISSAUGA, ON,

L4Y 1S4
(905) 279-9100   *SIC 2095*
MOTHER PARKER'S TEA & COFFEE INC *p 704*
2531 STANFIELD RD, MISSISSAUGA, ON, L4Y 1S4
(905) 279-9100   *SIC 2095*
MOTHER TERESA HIGH SCHOOL   *p 752*
See *OTTAWA CATHOLIC DISTRICT SCHOOL BOARD*
MOTHERS MUSIC   *p 116*
See *PRICE, GORDON MUSIC LTD*
MOTION & CONTROL DIV   *p 684*
See *PARKER HANNIFIN CANADA*
MOTION CANADA   *p 193*
See *MOTION INDUSTRIES (CANADA), INC*
MOTION FITNESS   *p 1435*
See *SS STONEBRIDGE DEL FITNESS CORPORATION*
MOTION INDUSTRIES (CANADA), INC *p 193*
8985 FRASERWOOD CT, BURNABY, BC, V5J 5E8
(604) 521-3207   *SIC 5085*
MOTION MAZDA   *p 808*
753007 2ND LINE E, ORANGEVILLE, ON, L9W 2Z2
(519) 943-1100   *SIC 5511*
MOTION METRICS INTERNATIONAL CORP *p 324*
2389 HEALTH SCIENCES MALL UNIT 101, VANCOUVER, BC, V6T 1Z3
(604) 822-5848   *SIC 1081*
MOTION MICRO SOLUTIONS INC   *p 624*
300 MARCH RD SUITE 400, KANATA, ON, K2K 2E2
(613) 667-9157   *SIC 6211*
MOTION SPECIALTIES WINDSOR   *p 1018*
See *1363199 ONTARIO LIMITED*
MOTO DAYTONA   *p 1222*
See *MOTO M.T.L. INTERNATIONAL INC*
MOTO INTERNATIONAL   *p 1221*
See *136562 CANADA INC*
MOTO M.T.L. INTERNATIONAL INC *p 1222*
6695 RUE SAINT-JACQUES, MONTREAL, QC, H4B 1V3
(514) 483-6686   *SIC 5571*
MOTOCYCLETTES & ARTICLES DE SPORTS PONT-VIAU INC   *p 1236*
4501 NORD LAVAL (A-440) O, MONTREAL, QC, H7P 4W6
(450) 973-4501   *SIC 5571*
MOTOR COACH INDUSTRIES LIMITED *p 391*
1475 CLARENCE AVE, WINNIPEG, MB, R3T 1T5
(204) 284-5360   *SIC 3711*
MOTOR COILS MFG. LTD   *p 519*
1879 PARKEDALE AVE E, BROCKVILLE, ON, K6V 5T2
(613) 345-3580   *SIC 3621*
MOTOR DEALER COUNCIL OF BRITISH COLUMBIA   *p 226*
8029 199 ST SUITE 280, LANGLEY, BC, V2Y 0E2
(604) 574-5050   *SIC 8699*
MOTOR MART   *p 471*
See *2231737 NOVA SCOTIA LIMITED*
MOTOR VEHICLE PERSONNEL (MVP) *p 686*
See *1453633 ONTARIO INC*
MOTOR VEHICLE SALES AUTHORITY OF BRITISH COLUMBIA   *p 226*
See *MOTOR DEALER COUNCIL OF BRITISH COLUMBIA*
MOTOR WORKS ONE HOLDINGS INC *p 835*
510 MOTOR WORKS PVT, OTTAWA, ON, K2R 0A5
(613) 656-6526   *SIC 5511*
MOTOR WORKS TWO HOLDINGS INC *p 835*
520 MOTOR WORKS PVT, OTTAWA, ON, K2R 0A5

(613) 656-6536   *SIC 5511*
MOTORCADE AUTO PARTS   *p 993*
See *MOTORCADE INDUSTRIES INC*
MOTORCADE INDUSTRIES INC   *p 993*
90 KINCORT ST, TORONTO, ON, M6M 5G1
(416) 614-6118   *SIC 5013*
MOTORCITY MITSUBISHI   *p 1013*
See *715837 ONTARIO INC*
MOTORCYCLE INSURANCE BROKERS INC   *p 853*
105 WEST BEAVER CREEK RD SUITE 1, RICHMOND HILL, ON, L4B 1C6
(905) 764-7868   *SIC 6411*
MOTOROLA SOLUTIONS CANADA INC *p 680*
8133 WARDEN AVE, MARKHAM, ON, L6G 1B3
(905) 948-5200   *SIC 5065*
MOTOS DAYTONA INC   *p 1222*
6695 RUE SAINT-JACQUES, MONTREAL, QC, H4B 1V3
(514) 483-6686   *SIC 5571*
MOTOS ILLIMITEES INC   *p 1380*
3250 BOUL DES ENTREPRISES, TERREBONNE, QC, J6X 4J8
(450) 477-4000   *SIC 5599*
MOTOSEL INDUSTRIAL GROUP INC *p 201*
204 CAYER ST UNIT 407, COQUITLAM, BC, V3K 5B1
(604) 629-8733   *SIC 5172*
MOTOSPORT PLUS   *p 629*
See *127897 CANADA LTD*
MOTOVAN CORPORATION   *p 1066*
1391 RUE GAY-LUSSAC BUREAU 100, BOUCHERVILLE, QC, J4B 7K1
(450) 449-3903   *SIC 5013*
MOTT   *p 517*
See *MOTT MANUFACTURING LIMITED*
MOTT ELECTRIC GENERAL PARTNERSHIP   *p 193*
4599 TILLICUM ST SUITE 100, BURNABY, BC, V5J 3J9
(604) 522-5757   *SIC 1731*
MOTT MANUFACTURING LIMITED   *p 517*
452 HARDY RD, BRANTFORD, ON, N3T 5L8
(519) 752-7825   *SIC 6712*
MOTTLAB INC   *p 523*
5230 SOUTH SERVICE RD, BURLINGTON, ON, L7L 5K2
(905) 331-1877   *SIC 5049*
MOTUS BANK   *p 996*
3280 BLOOR ST W CENTRE TOWER SUITE 700, TORONTO, ON, M8X 2X3
(905) 988-1000   *SIC 6021*
MOUAT'S HOME HARDWARE   *p 268*
See *MOUAT'S TRADING CO. LTD*
MOUAT'S TRADING CO. LTD   *p 268*
106 FULFORD-GANGES RD, SALT SPRING ISLAND, BC, V8K 2S3
(250) 537-5551   *SIC 5399*
MOULAGE D'ALUMINIUM HOWMET LTEE *p 1234*
4001 DESSTE DES LAURENTIDES (A-15) E, MONTREAL, QC, H7L 3H7
(450) 680-2500   *SIC 3355*
MOULAGE RANGER   *p 1111*
See *L. DAVIS TEXTILES (1991) INC*
MOULAGE SOUS PRESSION A.M.T. INC *p 1298*
106 RUE COTE, SAINT-CYPRIEN, QC, G0L 2P0
(418) 963-3227   *SIC 3365*
MOULES INDUSTRIELS (C.H.F.G.) INC *p 1374*
3100 BOUL INDUSTRIEL, SHERBROOKE, QC, J1L 1V8
(819) 822-3697   *SIC 3544*
MOULES INDUTRIELS   *p 1374*
See *MOULES INDUSTRIELS (C.H.F.G.) INC*
MOULES MIRPLEX INC, LES   *p 1318*
765 RUE PIERRE-CAISSE, SAINT-JEAN-

SUR-RICHELIEU, QC, J3B 8C6

(450) 348-6611   SIC 5085

MOULES PLASTICOR INC, LES   p 1128

1170 50E AV, LACHINE, QC, H8T 2V3

(514) 636-9630   SIC 5085

MOULEURS DE BEAUCE   p 1322

See MBI PLASTIQUE INC

MOULIN HUBERT LACOSTE INC   p 1356

114 RTE SAINT-JEAN N, SAINTE-CLAIRE, QC, G0R 2V0

(418) 883-3688   SIC 5149

MOULTON, RALPH HOLDINGS LTD   p 545

1125 ELGIN ST W, COBOURG, ON, K9A 5T9

(905) 372-8781   SIC 5541

MOULURE ALEXANDRIA MOULDING INC

p 476

20352 POWER DAM RD, ALEXANDRIA, ON, K0C 1A0

(613) 525-2784   SIC 2431

MOULURES M. WARNET INC   p 1059

100 RUE MARIUS-WARNET, BLAINVILLE, QC, J7C 5P9

(450) 437-1209   SIC 5211

MOULURES WARNET   p 1059

See MOULURES M. WARNET INC

MOUNT ALLISON UNIVERSITY   p 412

65 YORK ST, SACKVILLE, NB, E4L 1E4

(506) 364-2269   SIC 8221

MOUNT BAKER SENIOR SECONDARY SCHOOL   p 204

See SCHOOL DISTRICT NO 5 (SOUTH-EAST KOOTENAY)

MOUNT CARMEL CLINIC   p 371

886 MAIN ST, WINNIPEG, MB, R2W 5L4

(204) 582-2311   SIC 8011

MOUNT DOUGLAS SECONDARY SCHOOL

p 332

See BOARD OF EDUCATION OF SCHOOL DISTRICT NO. 61 (GREATER VICTORIA)

MOUNT EDWARDS COURT CARE HOME p 335

See BAPTIST HOUSING MINISTRIES SOCIETY, THE

MOUNT HOPE CENTRE FOR LONG TERM CARE   p 655

See ST. JOSEPH'S HEALTH CARE, LONDON

MOUNT HOPE CENTRE FOR LONG-TERM CARE   p 655

See ST. JOSEPH'S HEALTH CARE, LONDON

MOUNT NEMO CHRISTIAN NURSING HOME   p 529

See CANADIAN REFORMED SOCIETY FOR A HOME FOR THE AGED INC

MOUNT PLEASANT GROUP OF CEMETERIES   p 919

65 OVERLEA BLVD SUITE 500, TORONTO, ON, M4H 1P1

(416) 696-7866   SIC 6553

MOUNT PLEASANT IGA #7607   p 923

See 1365992 ONTARIO LTD

MOUNT PLEASANT SIMMONS & MCBRIDE CHAPEL   p 285

See SERVICE CORPORATION INTERNATIONAL (CANADA) LIMITED

MOUNT POLLEY MINING CORPORATION p 230

5720 MOOREHEAD-BOOTJACK RD, LIKELY, BC, V0L 1N0

(250) 790-2215   SIC 1041

MOUNT ROYAL COLLEGIATE   p 1431

See BOARD OF EDUCATION OF SASKATOON SCHOOL DIVISION NO. 13 OF SASKATCHEWAN, THE

MOUNT ROYAL HOTEL   p 4

See BREWSTER INC

MOUNT ROYAL UNIVERSITY   p 74

4825 MOUNT ROYAL GATE SW, CALGARY, AB, T3E 6K6

(403) 440-6111   SIC 8222

MOUNT SAINT JOSEPH HOSPITAL   p 289

See PROVIDENCE HEALTH CARE SOCIETY

MOUNT SAINT JOSEPH NURSING HOMEp 405

51 LOBBAN AVE, MIRAMICHI, NB, E1N 2W8

(506) 622-5091   SIC 8051

MOUNT SAINT VINCENT   p 457

See MOUNT SAINT VINCENT UNIVERSITY

MOUNT SAINT VINCENT UNIVERSITY   p 457

166 BEDFORD HWY, HALIFAX, NS, B3M 2J6

(902) 457-6788   SIC 8221

MOUNT SICKER LUMBER COMPANY LTD

p 212

7795 MAYS RD, DUNCAN, BC, V9L 6A8

(250) 746-4121   SIC 2411

MOUNT SINAI HOSPITAL   p 947

See SINAI HEALTH SYSTEM

MOUNT ST MARY HOSPITAL   p 335

See MARIE ESTHER SOCIETY, THE

MOUNT ST VINCENT MOTHER HOUSE p 457

See SISTERS OF CHARITY

MOUNTAIN CREEK FARMS   p 166

See MCF HOLDINGS LTD

MOUNTAIN EQUIPMENT CO-OPERATIVE p 65

830 10 AVE SW, CALGARY, AB, T2R 0A9

(403) 269-2420   SIC 5941

MOUNTAIN EQUIPMENT CO-OPERATIVE p 289

1077 GREAT NORTHERN WAY, VANCOUVER, BC, V5T 1E1

(604) 707-3300   SIC 5941

MOUNTAIN EQUIPMENT CO-OPERATIVE p 829

366 RICHMOND RD, OTTAWA, ON, K2A 0E8

(613) 729-2700   SIC 5941

MOUNTAIN PARK LODGES   p 137

See JAS DAY INVESTMENTS LTD

MOUNTAIN PROVINCE DIAMONDS INC p 965

161 BAY ST SUITE 1410, TORONTO, ON, M5J 2S1

(416) 361-3562   SIC 1499

MOUNTAIN TOP FOODS LTD   p 148

2301 18 AVE, NANTON, AB, T0L 1R0

(403) 646-0038   SIC 5421

MOUNTAIN VIEW CREDIT UNION LTD   p 151

4920 50 AVE, OLDS, AB, T4H 1P5

(403) 556-3306   SIC 6062

MOUNTAIN VIEW LEASING INC   p 119

4916 WHITEMUD RD NW, EDMONTON, AB, T6H 5M3

(780) 462-9600   SIC 2452

MOUNTAIN VIEW MUSHROOMS LTD p 178

38061 ATKINSON RD, ABBOTSFORD, BC, V3G 2G6

SIC 0182

MOUNTAIN VIEW PACKERS LTD   p 399

9112 ROUTE 130, FLORENCEVILLE-BRISTOL, NB, E7K 2R2

(506) 392-6017   SIC 5148

MOUNTAIN VIEW PUBLISHING INC   p 151

5021 51 ST, OLDS, AB, T4H 1P6

(403) 556-7510   SIC 5192

MOUNTAIN VIEW RELOAD INC   p 175

419 SUMAS WAY, ABBOTSFORD, BC, V2S 8E5

SIC 4789

MOUNTAIN VIEW SCHOOL DIVISIONp 348

182519 SW, DAUPHIN, MB, R7N 3B3

(204) 638-3001   SIC 8211

MOUNTAIN VIEW SCHOOL DIVISIONp 349

330 MOUNTAIN RD, DAUPHIN, MB, R7N 2V6

(204) 638-4629   SIC 8211

MOUNTAIN VIEW SENIORS HOUSING p 82

1100A 20 AVE, DIDSBURY, AB, T0M 0W0

(403) 335-8404   SIC 8361

MOUNTAIN VIEW SPECIALTY PRODUCTS INC   p 175

3013 TURNER ST, ABBOTSFORD, BC, V2S 7T9

(604) 850-2070   SIC 5031

MOUNTAIN WEST SERVICES LTD   p 169

14 THEVENAZ IND. TRAIL UNIT 3, SYLVAN LAKE, AB, T4S 2J5

(403) 887-3562   SIC 1389

MOUNTAINVIEW RESIDENCE   p 594

222 MOUNTAINVIEW RD N SUITE 233, GEORGETOWN, ON, L7G 3R2

(905) 877-1800   SIC 6513

MOUNTAINVIEW TURF   p 1281

See MOUNTAINVIEW TURF FARM LTD

MOUNTAINVIEW TURF FARM LTD   p 1281

4790 5E CONC, QUYON, QC, J0X 2V0

(819) 458-2632   SIC 5261

MOURELATOS SUPERMAKET   p 1237

See 4128001 CANADA INC

MOUVEMENT D'IMPLICATION FRANCOPHONE D'ORLEANS   p

6600 CARRIERE ST, ORLEANS, ON, K1C 1J4

(613) 830-6436   SIC 8399

MOUVEMENT DU GRAAL-CANADA p 1077

See FONDATION DU MOUVEMENT DU GRAAL-CANADA INC

MOVATI ATHLETIC   p 514

See MOVATI ATHLETIC (LONDON SOUTH) INC.

MOVATI ATHLETIC (BRANTFORD) INC. p 514

595 WEST ST, BRANTFORD, ON, N3R 7C5

(519) 756-0123   SIC 7991

MOVATI ATHLETIC (LONDON NORTH) INC.

p 659

755 WONDERLAND RD N, LONDON, ON, N6H 4L1

(519) 471-7181   SIC 7991

MOVATI ATHLETIC (LONDON SOUTH) INC.

p 514

595 WEST ST, BRANTFORD, ON, N3R 7C5

(519) 756-0123   SIC 7991

MOVATI ATHLETIC (THUNDER BAY) INC. p 910

1185 ARTHUR ST W, THUNDER BAY, ON, P7E 6E2

(807) 623-6223   SIC 7991

MOVELINE INC   p 804

1317 SPEERS RD, OAKVILLE, ON, L6L 2X5

(905) 814-1700   SIC 1522

MOVEUP   p 190

See OFFICE AND PROFESSIONAL EMPLOYEES INTERNATIONAL UNION

MOWI CANADA WEST INC   p 195

1334 ISLAND HWY SUITE 124, CAMPBELL RIVER, BC, V9W 8C9

(250) 850-3276   SIC 0273

MOXIE'S   p 772

See MOXIE'S RESTAURANTS, LIMITED PARTNERSHIP

MOXIE'S BAR AND GRILL   p 362

See MOXIE'S RESTAURANTS, LIMITED PARTNERSHIP

MOXIE'S CLASIC GROW RESTAURANT p 250

See MOXIE'S RESTAURANTS, LIMITED PARTNERSHIP

MOXIE'S CLASSIC GRILL   p 76

See MOXIE'S RESTAURANTS, LIMITED PARTNERSHIP

MOXIE'S CLASSIC GRILL   p 382

1485 PORTAGE AVE SUITE 234, WINNIPEG, MB, R3G 0W4

(204) 783-1840   SIC 5812

MOXIE'S CLASSIC GRILL   p 484

509 BAYFIELD ST, BARRIE, ON, L4M 4Z8

(705) 733-5252   SIC 5812

MOXIE'S CLASSIC GRILL   p 748

See WAHA ENTERPRISES INC

MOXIE'S CLASSIC GRILL   p 1021

3100 HOWARD AVE UNIT 20, WINDSOR, ON, N8X 3Y8

(519) 250-3390   SIC 5812

MOXIE'S CLASSIC GRILL   p 1416

See MIDWEST RESTAURANT INC

MOXIE'S CLASSIC GRILL RESTAURANTS

p 85

See MCG RESTAURANTS LTD

MOXIE'S RESTAURANT   p 142

See MOXIE'S RESTAURANTS, LIMITED PARTNERSHIP

MOXIE'S RESTAURANT   p 368

See HOUGHTAM ENTERPRISES

MOXIE'S RESTAURANT   p 1424

See MIDWEST RESTAURANT INC

MOXIE'S RESTAURANTS INC   p 146

3090 DUNMORE RD SE, MEDICINE HAT, AB, T1B 2X2

(403) 528-8628   SIC 5812

MOXIE'S RESTAURANTS, LIMITED PARTNERSHIP   p 71

3625 SHAGANAPPI TRAIL NW, CALGARY, AB, T3A 0E2

(403) 288-2663   SIC 5812

MOXIE'S RESTAURANTS, LIMITED PARTNERSHIP   p 76

25 HOPEWELL WAY NE, CALGARY, AB, T3J 4V7

(403) 291-4636   SIC 5812

MOXIE'S RESTAURANTS, LIMITED PARTNERSHIP   p 142

1621 3 AVE S, LETHBRIDGE, AB, T1J 0L1

(403) 320-1102   SIC 5812

MOXIE'S RESTAURANTS, LIMITED PARTNERSHIP   p 250

1804 CENTRAL ST E, PRINCE GEORGE, BC, V2M 3C3

(250) 564-4700   SIC 5812

MOXIE'S RESTAURANTS, LIMITED PARTNERSHIP   p 362

1615 REGENT AVE W SUITE 200, WINNIPEG, MB, R2C 5C6

(204) 654-3345   SIC 5812

MOXIE'S RESTAURANTS, LIMITED PARTNERSHIP   p 710

100 CITY CENTRE DR UNIT 2-730, MISSISSAUGA, ON, L5B 2C9

(905) 276-6555   SIC 5812

MOXIE'S RESTAURANTS, LIMITED PARTNERSHIP   p 772

4950 YONGE ST SUITE 105, NORTH YORK, ON, M2N 6K1

SIC 5812

MOXY MEDIA   p 604

See ORION FOUNDRY (CANADA), ULC

MOYER DIEBEL LIMITED   p 623

2674 NORTH SERVICE RD, JORDAN STATION, ON, L0R 1S0

(905) 562-4195   SIC 3589

MP DESIGN INC   p 292

16 4TH AVE W, VANCOUVER, BC, V5Y 1G3

(604) 708-1184   SIC 3648

MP LIGHTING   p 292

See MP DESIGN INC

MP REPRODUCTIONS INC   p 1192

1030 RUE CHENNEVILLE, MONTREAL, QC, H2Z 1V8

(514) 861-8541   SIC 7384

MP2B INC   p 1084

1600A BOUL SAINT-MARTIN E BUREAU 110, COTE SAINT-LUC, QC, H7G 4R8

(450) 668-5555   SIC 6411

MPAC   p 843

See MUNICIPAL PROPERTY ASSESSMENT CORPORATION

MPAC LANGEN   p 723

See LANGEN PACKAGING INC

MPB COMMUNICATIONS INC   *p* 1251
147 BOUL HYMUS, POINTE-CLAIRE, QC, H9R 1E9
(514) 694-8751   *SIC* 8731

MPE ENGINEERING LTD   *p* 142
714 5 AVE S SUITE 300, LETHBRIDGE, AB, T1J 0V1
(403) 329-3442   *SIC* 8711

MPF MEUBLES PACIFIQUE   *p* 1048
See CONCORDIA FURNITURE LTD

MPI MATCO   *p* 1330
See MATCO PACKAGING INC

MPI MOULIN A PAPIER DE PORTNEUF, INC   *p* 1253
200 RUE DU MOULIN, PORTNEUF, QC, G0A 2Y0
(418) 286-3461   *SIC* 3089

MPI PACKAGING INC   *p* 735
7400B BRAMALEA RD, MISSISSAUGA, ON, L5S 1W9
(905) 673-6447   *SIC* 3085

MPI PAPER MILLS   *p* 869
See METRO PAPER INDUSTRIES INC

MPI PRINT   *p* 556
See MILLENIUM PRINTING INC

MPX INTERNATIONAL CORPORATION   *p* 772
5255 YONGE ST STE 701, NORTH YORK, ON, M2N 6P4
(416) 840-6632   *SIC* 5122

MQM QUALITY MANUFACTURING LTD   *p* 419
2676 COMMERCE ST, TRACADIE-SHEILA, NB, E1X 1G5
(506) 395-7777   *SIC* 1791

MQN INTERIORS LTD   *p* 332
3313 32 AVE SUITE 100, VERNON, BC, V1T 2E1
(250) 542-1199   *SIC* 7389

MR IMAGING CORP   *p* 36
5920 1A ST SW UNIT 301, CALGARY, AB, T2H 0G3
(403) 253-4666   *SIC* 8099

MR LUBE   *p* 31
See PRAIRIE LUBE LTD

MR MIKE STEAKHOUSE   *p* 214
See STONEWATER GROUP OF FRANCHISES

MR MIKE'S   *p* 318
See FULMER DEVELOPMENT CORPORATION, THE

MR MIKES STEAK HOUSE & BAR   *p* 199
See STONEWATER GROUP OF FRANCHISES

MR MOTORS LP   *p* 231
11911 WEST ST, MAPLE RIDGE, BC, V2X 3M6
(604) 465-8931   *SIC* 5511

MR P'S & MR PET'S LTD   *p* 232
33560 1ST AVE, MISSION, BC, V2V 1H4
(604) 814-2994   *SIC* 5999

MR TOMATO   *p* 412
See FINNIGAN GREENHOUSE PRODUCE LTD

MR. GAS LIMITED   *p* 810
1420 YOUVILLE DR SUITE 1, ORLEANS, ON, K1C 7B3
(613) 824-6777   *SIC* 5541

MR. GOUDAS   *p* 553
See GOLDEN FOOD & MANUFACTURE LTD

MR. GREEK RESTAURANTS INC   *p* 780
49 THE DONWAY W SUITE 402, NORTH YORK, ON, M3C 3M9
(416) 444-3266   *SIC* 6794

MR. LUBE CANADA LIMITED PARTNERSHIP   *p* 258
6900 GRAYBAR RD SUITE 2330, RICHMOND, BC, V6W 0A5
(604) 759-4300   *SIC* 6794

MR. PET'S   *p* 232
See MR P'S & MR PET'S LTD

MR. SNACK (1997) INC   *p* 119

6551 GATEWAY BLVD NW, EDMONTON, AB, T6H 2J1
(780) 414-0505   *SIC* 5149

MR. SPORT HOTEL HOLDINGS LTD   *p* 288
3484 KINGSWAY SUITE 101, VANCOUVER, BC, V5R 5L6
(604) 433-8255   *SIC* 7011

MR. SUB   *p* 772
See MR. SUBMARINE LIMITED

MR. SUBMARINE LIMITED   *p* 772
4576 YONGE ST SUITE 600, NORTH YORK, ON, M2N 6N4
(416) 225-5545   *SIC* 6794

MRA ABATEMENT, DIV OF   *p* 571
See MURRAY DEMOLITION CORP

MRC CANADA ULC   *p* 110
4103 53 AVE NW SUITE 726, EDMONTON, AB, T6B 3R5
(780) 466-0328   *SIC* 5085

MRC GLOBAL (CANADA) LTD   *p* 54
255 5 AVE SW SUITE 910, CALGARY, AB, T2P 3G6
(403) 233-7166   *SIC* 3519

MRCC   *p* 971
See MACKIE RESEACH CAPITAL CORPORATION

MRDC   *p* 410
See MRDC OPERATIONS CORPORATION

MRDC OPERATIONS CORPORATION*p* 410
203 AV BLACK WATCH, OROMOCTO, NB, E2V 4L7
(506) 357-1240   *SIC* 1611

MRO ELECTRONIC SUPPLY LTD   *p* 24
2240 PEGASUS RD NE, CALGARY, AB, T2E 8G8
(403) 291-0501   *SIC* 5065

MRS. DUNSTER'S (1996) INC   *p* 418
30 LEONARD DR, SUSSEX, NB, E4E 5T5
(506) 433-9333   *SIC* 2051

MRS. TIGGY WINKLE'S LTD   *p* 828
75 BREEZEHILL AVE N, OTTAWA, ON, K1Y 2H6
(613) 523-3663   *SIC* 5945

MRS. WHYTE'S PRODUCTS   *p* 1233
See ALIMENTS WHYTE'S INC, LES

MRS. WILLMAN'S BAKING LIMITED   *p* 24
4826 11 ST NE UNIT 4, CALGARY, AB, T2E 2W7
SIC 2051

MRT   *p* 1289
See 9064-4287 QUEBEC INC

MRT ENTERPRISES INC   *p* 24
817 19 ST NE SUITE 109, CALGARY, AB, T2E 4X5
(403) 216-8800   *SIC* 5411

MS   *p* 995
See MULTIPLE SCLEROSIS SOCIETY OF CANADA

MS ELITE HOLDINGS INC.   *p* 1087
1811 BOUL CURE-LABELLE, COTE SAINT-LUC, QC, H7T 1L1
(450) 681-0060   *SIC* 6712

MS MEDIA GP HOLDING LIMITED   *p* 965
25 YORK ST SUITE 900, TORONTO, ON, M5J 2V5
(416) 362-0885   *SIC* 7383

MSA   *p* 612
See MOHAWK STUDENT'S ASSOCIATION

MSA FORD SALES LTD   *p* 177
30295 AUTOMALL DR, ABBOTSFORD, BC, V2T 5M1
(604) 856-9000   *SIC* 5511

MSA INFRASTRUCTURES INC   *p* 1318
800 RUE DES CARRIERES, SAINT-JEAN-SUR-RICHELIEU, QC, J3B 2P2
(450) 346-4441   *SIC* 3273

MSB PLASTICS MANUFACTURING (PLANT 2)   *p* 581
See ABC INTERIOR SYSTEMS INC

MSB RESOURCES GLOBALES   *p* 1067
See RESSOURCES GLOBALES AERO INC

MSC INDUSTRIAL SUPPLY ULC   *p* 697
2595 SKYMARK AVE SUITE 202, MISSIS-

SAUGA, ON, L4W 4L5
(905) 219-6300   *SIC* 5085

MSC REHABILITATION INC   *p* 1234
2145 RUE MICHELIN, MONTREAL, QC, H7L 5B8
(450) 687-5610   *SIC* 7389

MSCM LLP   *p* 579
701 EVANS AVE SUITE 800, ETOBICOKE, ON, M9C 1A3
(416) 626-6000   *SIC* 8721

MSI STONE ULC   *p* 725
2140 MEADOWPINE BLVD, MISSISSAUGA, ON, L5N 6H6
(905) 812-6100   *SIC* 5032

MSM CONSTRUCTION SERVICES LTD   *p* 459
12575 HIGHWAY 4, HAVRE BOUCHER, NS, B0H 1P0
(902) 234-3202   *SIC* 1761

MSO CONSTRUCTION LIMITED   *p* 586
175 BETHRIDGE RD, ETOBICOKE, ON, M9W 1N4
(416) 743-3224   *SIC* 1611

MSR LOCATION SCENE MOBILE   *p* 1120
See STAGELINE SCENE MOBILE INC

MSS CANADA   *p* 1052
See WULFTEC INTERNATIONAL INC

MSSC CANADA INC   *p* 543
105 ST GEORGE ST, CHATHAM, ON, N7M 4P3
(519) 354-1100   *SIC* 3493

MSSC CANADA INC   *p* 543
201 PARK AVE E, CHATHAM, ON, N7M 3V7
(905) 878-2395   *SIC* 3492

MSSI   *p* 1352
See MONT SAINT-SAUVEUR INTERNATIONAL INC

MSSI   *p* 1352
See SOMMETS DE LA VALLEE INC, LES

MT BECHER SKI RENTALS LTD   *p* 203
267 6TH ST, COURTENAY, BC, V9N 1L9
(250) 334-2537   *SIC* 6712

MT SERVICES LIMITED PARTNERSHIP   *p* 315
745 THURLOW ST UNIT 2400, VANCOUVER, BC, V6E 0C5
(604) 643-7100   *SIC* 8111

MT SERVICES LIMITED PARTNERSHIP   *p* 970
66 WELLINGTON ST W RD SUITE 5300, TORONTO, ON, M5K 1E6
(416) 601-8200   *SIC* 8111

MT-U OPERATING COMPANY INC   *p* 150
31 SOUTHRIDGE DR SUITE 121A, OKOTOKS, AB, T1S 2N3
(403) 995-5217   *SIC* 6712

MT. BRYDGES FORD SALES LTD   *p* 746
8791 GLENDON DR, MOUNT BRYDGES, ON, N0L 1W0
(519) 264-1912   *SIC* 5511

MT. WASHINGTON ALPINE RESORT   *p* 202
See MT. WASHINGTON SKI RESORT LTD

MT. WASHINGTON SKI RESORT LTD   *p* 202
1 STRATHCONA PKY, COURTENAY, BC, V9J 1L0
(250) 338-1386   *SIC* 7011

MTB TRANSIT SOLUTIONS   *p* 684
See MTB TRUCK & BUS COLLISION INC

MTB TRUCK & BUS COLLISION INC   *p* 684
8170 LAWSON RD, MILTON, ON, L9T 5C4
(905) 876-0669   *SIC* 7538

MTD METRO TOOL & DIE LIMITED   *p* 697
1065 PANTERA DR, MISSISSAUGA, ON, L4W 2X4
(905) 625-8464   *SIC* 4225

MTD PRODUCTS LIMITED   *p* 638
97 KANT AVE, KITCHENER, ON, N2G 4J1
(519) 579-5500   *SIC* 5083

MTD PRODUCTS LIMITED   *p* 638
97 KENT AVE, KITCHENER, ON, N2G 3R2
(519) 579-5500   *SIC* 5083

MTE CONSULTANTS INC   *p* 635
520 BINGEMANS CENTRE DR, KITCHENER, ON, N2B 3X9

(519) 743-6500   *SIC* 8711

MTE LOGISTIX EDMONTON INC   *p* 94
14627 128 AVE NW, EDMONTON, AB, T5L 3H3
(780) 944-9009   *SIC* 4225

MTE LOGISTIX EDMONTON INC   *p* 102
11250 189 ST NW, EDMONTON, AB, T5S 2V6
(780) 944-9009   *SIC* 4225

MTF MAINLAND DISTRIBUTORS INC*p* 229
26868 56 AVE UNIT 101, LANGLEY, BC, V4W 1N9
(604) 626-4465   *SIC* 5399

MTF PRICE MATTERS   *p* 229
See MTF MAINLAND DISTRIBUTORS INC

MTI   *p* 193
See MOTT ELECTRIC GENERAL PARTNERSHIP

MTI   *p* 647
See RCR INDUSTRIAL INC

MTI CANADA INC   *p* 1138
1720 BOUL GUILLAUME-COUTURE, LEVIS, QC, G6W 5M6
(418) 839-4127   *SIC* 5083

MTI POLYFAB INC   *p* 741
7381 PACIFIC CIR, MISSISSAUGA, ON, L5T 2A4
(800) 265-1840   *SIC* 5199

MTL   *p* 1437
See MENNONITE TRUST LTD

MTL GROUP   *p* 101
See METALSMITHS MASTER ARCHITECTS OF JEWELRY INC

MTL RECYCLING   *p* 784
See MAXUC TRADING LTD

MTO METAL PRODUCTS LTD   *p* 1035
1205 WELFORD PL SUITE 54, WOODSTOCK, ON, N4S 7W3
(519) 537-8257   *SIC* 3429

MTP INSTRUMENT, LES   *p* 1240
See PRIMO INSTRUMENT INC

MTS CENTRE   *p* 380
See TRUE NORTH SPORTS & ENTERTAINMENT LIMITED

MTS ICEPLEX   *p* 387
See TN ICEPLEX LIMITED PARTNERSHIP

MTS LOGISTICS   *p* 193
See MEDI-TRAN SERVICES (1993) LTD

MTTL COENTREPRISE   *p* 1260
See TESSIER LTEE

MTU MAINTENANCE CANADA LTD   *p* 265
6020 RUSS BAKER WAY, RICHMOND, BC, V7B 1B4
(604) 233-5700   *SIC* 7699

MUCCI FARMS LTD   *p* 634
1876 SEACLIFF DR, KINGSVILLE, ON, N9Y 2N1
(519) 326-8881   *SIC* 0182

MUCHALAT CONSTRUCTION LTD   *p* 202
3326 DOVE CREEK RD, COURTENAY, BC, V9J 1P3
(250) 338-0995   *SIC* 1531

MUD BAY NURSERIES LTD   *p* 279
4391 KING GEORGE BLVD, SURREY, BC, V3Z 1G6
(604) 596-9201   *SIC* 5261

MUEHLSTEIN CANADA, DIV OF   *p* 587
See RAVAGO CANADA CO

MUELLER CANADA LTD   *p* 487
82 HOOPER RD, BARRIE, ON, L4N 8Z9
(705) 719-9965   *SIC* 5085

MUELLER CANADA LTD   *p* 1320
230 RUE CASTONGUAY, SAINT-JEROME, QC, J7Y 2J7
SIC 5999

MUELLER FLOW CONTROL, DIV OF   *p* 487
See MUELLER CANADA LTD

MUFFLERMAN INC, THE   *p* 657
3480 WHITE OAK RD, LONDON, ON, N6E 2Z9
(519) 685-0002   *SIC* 7533

MUFG BANK, LTD., CANADA BRANCH   *p* 965
200 BAY ST SUITE 1700, TORONTO, ON,

M5J 2J1
(416) 865-0220   *SIC* 6211
MUGGS, J J INC   *p* 976
500 BLOOR ST W, TORONTO, ON, M5S 1Y3
(416) 531-7638   *SIC* 5812
MUHC   *p* 1213
See *MCGILL UNIVERSITY HEALTH CENTRE*
MUIR TAPES & ADHESIVES LTD   *p* 798
2815 BRISTOL CIR, OAKVILLE, ON, L6H 6X5
(905) 820-6847   *SIC* 5085
MULDER'S MEAT MARKET (1983) LTD   *p* 410
1400 ONONDAGA ST, OROMOCTO, NB, E2V 2H6
(506) 357-8862   *SIC* 5147
MULDOON'S OWN AUTHENTIC COFFEE CORP   *p* 697
5680 TIMBERLEA BLVD, MISSISSAUGA, ON, L4W 4M6
(905) 712-2233   *SIC* 5149
MULDOWNEY HOLDINGS LTD   *p* 81
GD, DE WINTON, AB, T0L 0X0
(403) 253-0399   *SIC* 5084
MULGRAVE INDEPENDENT SCHOOL SOCIETY   *p* 341
2330 CYPRESS BOWL LANE, WEST VANCOUVER, BC, V7S 3H9
(604) 922-3223   *SIC* 8211
MULGRAVE SCHOOL   *p* 341
See *MULGRAVE INDEPENDENT SCHOOL SOCIETY*
MULLEN GROUP LTD   *p* 150
31 SOUTHRIDGE DR SUITE 121A, OKOTOKS, AB, T1S 2N3
(403) 995-5200   *SIC* 1389
MULLEN OILFIELD SERVICES LP   *p* 65
333 11 AVE SW SUITE 600, CALGARY, AB, T2R 1L9
(403) 213-4715   *SIC* 1389
MULLEN OILFIELD SERVICES LP, DIV OF   *p* 213
See *FSJ OILFIELD SERVICES*
MULLEN TRANSPORTATION   *p* 150
See *MULLEN GROUP LTD*
MULLEN TRUCKING CORP   *p* 3
80079 MAPLE LEAF RD E UNIT 100, ALDERSYDE, AB, T0L 0A0
(403) 652-8888   *SIC* 4213
MULLER MARTINI CANADA INC   *p* 556
20 CALDARI RD SUITE 2, CONCORD, ON, L4K 4N8
(905) 660-9595   *SIC* 5085
MULRONEY, CAROLINE LEADERSHIP CAMPAIGN   *p* 925
1491 YONGE ST SUITE 201, TORONTO, ON, M4T 1Z4
(416) 922-0573   *SIC* 8651
MULTI BOOKBINDING   *p* 1368
See *MULTI-RELIURE S.F. INC*
MULTI FITTINGS   *p* 661
See *IPEX INC*
MULTI LUMINAIRE   *p* 1086
See *GROUPE MULTI LUMINAIRE INC, LE*
MULTI MEUBLES   *p* 1428
See *MEGA GROUP INC*
MULTI RECYCLAGE S.D. INC   *p* 1232
3030 MONTEE SAINT-FRANCOIS, MONTREAL, QC, H7E 4P2
(450) 625-9191   *SIC* 4212
MULTI RECYCLAGE S.D. INC   *p* 1342
140 RUE SAULNIER, SAINT-LAURENT, QC, H7M 1S8
(450) 975-9952   *SIC* 4953
MULTI X INC   *p* 1082
60 RUE SHEARD, COATICOOK, QC, J1A 0B2
(819) 849-7036   *SIC* 3053
MULTI-CAISSES ET MULTI-RESOURCES INC   *p* 1163
5125 RUE DU TRIANON BUREAU 560,

MONTREAL, QC, H1M 2S5
(514) 848-1845   *SIC* 7363
MULTI-CHOIX   *p* 1260
See *UNIQUE ASSURANCES GENERALES INC, L'*
MULTI-FOODS   *p* 424
See *NEWFOUNDLAND MULTI-FOODS LIMITED*
MULTI-GLASS INSULATION LTD   *p* 504
3925 STEELES AVE E UNIT 1 & 2, BRAMPTON, ON, L6T 5W5
(416) 798-3900   *SIC* 5033
MULTI-HEALTH SYSTEMS INC   *p* 765
3770 VICTORIA PARK AVE, NORTH YORK, ON, M2H 3M6
(416) 492-2627   *SIC* 8748
MULTI-LINE FASTENER SUPPLY CO. LTD   *p* 741
1100 COURTNEYPARK DR E UNIT 5, MISSISSAUGA, ON, L5T 1L7
(905) 677-5088   *SIC* 5085
MULTI-MARQUES INC   *p* 1139
845 RUE JEAN-MARCHAND, LEVIS, QC, G6Y 9G4
(418) 837-3611   *SIC* 5461
MULTI-MARQUES INC   *p* 1166
3265 RUE VIAU, MONTREAL, QC, H1V 3J5
(514) 255-9492   *SIC* 2051
MULTI-MARQUES INC   *p* 1256
553 AV ROYALE, QUEBEC, QC, G1E 1Y4
(418) 661-4400   *SIC* 2051
MULTI-MARQUES INC   *p* 1297
1295 1E AV O, SAINT-COME-LINIERE, QC, G0M 1J0
(418) 685-3351   *SIC* 2051
MULTI-MARQUES INC   *p* 1357
3443 AV FRANCIS-HUGHES BUREAU 1, SAINTE-DOROTHEE, QC, H7L 5A6
(450) 629-9444   *SIC* 5149
MULTI-METAL G. BOUTIN INC   *p* 1276
6500 RUE ROLAND-BEDARD, QUEBEC, QC, G2C 0J2
(418) 842-5888   *SIC* 3446
MULTI-PISCINE   *p* 1370
See *9047-6334 QUEBEC INC*
MULTI-PLASTICS CANADA CO   *p* 1014
55 MOORE CRT, WHITBY, ON, L1N 9Z8
(905) 430-7511   *SIC* 5162
MULTI-PORTIONS INC   *p* 1317
815 RUE PLANTE, SAINT-JEAN-SUR-RICHELIEU, QC, J3A 1M8
(450) 347-6152   *SIC* 2011
MULTI-PRETS HYPOTHEQUES   *p* 1395
See *2786591 CANADA INC*
MULTI-RELIURE S.F. INC   *p* 1368
2112 AV DE LA TRANSMISSION, SHAWINIGAN, QC, G9N 8N8
(819) 537-6008   *SIC* 2789
MULTI-SECTOR NON PROFIT   *p* 904
105 COMMERCE VALLEY DR W UNIT 310, THORNHILL, ON, L3T 7W3
(905) 889-6200   *SIC* 6411
MULTI-TECH SYSTEMS INTERNATIONAL INC   *p* 1010
592 COLBY DRIVE, WATERLOO, ON, N2V 1A2
(905) 825-3825   *SIC* 5084
MULTIBOND INC   *p* 1094
550 AV MARSHALL, DORVAL, QC, H9P 1C9
(514) 636-6230   *SIC* 2891
MULTICHAIR INC   *p* 741
6900 DAVAND DR, MISSISSAUGA, ON, L5T 1J5
SIC 3312
MULTIFORCE   *p* 1273
See *MULTIFORCE TECHNOLOGIES INC*
MULTIFORCE TECHNOLOGIES INC   *p* 1273
2954 BOUL LAURIER UNITE 320, QUEBEC, QC, G1V 4T2
(418) 780-8020   *SIC* 5045
MULTILINGUAL COMMUNITY INTERPRETER SERVICES (ONTARIO)   *p* 780

789 DON MILLS RD SUITE 1010, NORTH YORK, ON, M3C 1T5
(416) 426-7051   *SIC* 7389
MULTIMATIC INC   *p* 556
300 BASALTIC RD SUITE 1, CONCORD, ON, L4K 4Y9
(905) 879-0500   *SIC* 3429
MULTIMATIC INC   *p* 556
301 JACOB KEFFER PKY, CONCORD, ON, L4K 4V6
(905) 879-0200   *SIC* 3465
MULTIMATIC INC   *p* 567
125 CORCORAN CRT, EAST GWILLIMBURY, ON, L9N 0M8
(905) 853-8820   *SIC* 3429
MULTIMATIC INC   *p* 672
8688 WOODBINE AVE SUITE 200, MARKHAM, ON, L3R 8B9
(905) 470-9149   *SIC* 3429
MULTIMATIC INC   *p* 853
35 WEST WILMOT ST, RICHMOND HILL, ON, L4B 1L7
(905) 764-5120   *SIC* 3429
MULTIMATIC MANUFACTURING   *p* 556
See *MULTIMATIC INC*
MULTIMATIC NICHE VEHICLES INC   *p* 672
8688 WOODBINE AVE, MARKHAM, ON, L3R 8B9
(905) 470-9149   *SIC* 3429
MULTIMATIC TECHNICAL CENTRE   *p* 672
See *MULTIMATIC INC*
MULTIPAK LTEE   *p* 689
6417 VISCOUNT RD, MISSISSAUGA, ON, L4V 1K8
SIC 2759
MULTIPLE AWNINGS   *p* 1056
See *AUVENTS MULTIPLES INC*
MULTIPLE REALTY LTD   *p* 287
2298 KINGSWAY, VANCOUVER, BC, V5N 5M9
(604) 434-8843   *SIC* 6531
MULTIPLE SCLEROSIS SOCIETY OF CANADA   *p* 995
250 DUNDAS ST W UNIT 500, TORONTO, ON, M7A 1G1
(416) 922-6065   *SIC* 8399
MULTIPLEX CANADA HSP HOLDINGS LIMITED   *p* 987
130 KING ST W SUITE 2350, TORONTO, ON, M5X 2A2
(416) 359-8559   *SIC* 8741
MULTIPLEX CONSTRUCTION CANADA LIMITED   *p* 987
130 KING ST W SUITE 2350, TORONTO, ON, M5X 2A2
(416) 359-8559   *SIC* 8741
MULTIPLUS D.M. INC   *p* 1094
10389 CH COTE-DE-LIESSE, DORVAL, QC, H9P 2Z3
(514) 422-8881   *SIC* 5199
MULTIPLY   *p* 178
See *MB MISSION*
MULTIRIM INC   *p* 556
226 JARDIN DR SUITE 7, CONCORD, ON, L4K 1Y1
(905) 669-3566   *SIC* 2822
MULTISAC   *p* 1339
See *EMBALLAGE WORKMAN INC*
MULTISEAL INC   *p* 997
4255 WESTON RD, TORONTO, ON, M9L 1W8
(416) 743-6017   *SIC* 1799
MULTISERV   *p* 614
See *HARSCO CANADA CORPORATION*
MULTITUBE   *p* 741
See *MULTICHAIR INC*
MULTIVER DIVISION ISOVER   *p* 1265
See *MULTIVER LTEE*
MULTIVER LTEE   *p* 1262
436 RUE BERUBE, QUEBEC, QC, G1M 1C8
(418) 687-0770   *SIC* 3231
MULTIVER LTEE   *p* 1265
1950 RUE LEON-HARMEL, QUEBEC, QC,

G1N 4K3
(418) 687-0770   *SIC* 3211
MULTIVIEW CANADA   *p* 904
See *CONTENT MANAGEMENT CORPORATION*
MULTIWOOD   *p* 71
See *MULTIWOOD INC*
MULTIWOOD INC   *p* 71
11580 40 ST SE, CALGARY, AB, T2Z 4V6
(403) 279-7789   *SIC* 5712
MULTY HOME LP   *p* 556
7900 KEELE ST UNIT 100, CONCORD, ON, L4K 2A3
(905) 760-3737   *SIC* 5023
MULVEY & BANANI INTERNATIONAL INC   *p* 787
44 MOBILE DR, NORTH YORK, ON, M4A 2P2
(416) 751-2520   *SIC* 8711
MULVIHILL DRUG MART LIMITED   *p* 838
1231 PEMBROKE ST W, PEMBROKE, ON, K8A 5R3
(613) 735-1079   *SIC* 5912
MUN BOOK STORE   *p* 432
See *MEMORIAL UNIVERSITY OF NEWFOUNDLAND*
MUNDO MEDIA LTD   *p* 853
120 EAST BEAVER CREEK RD SUITE 200, RICHMOND HILL, ON, L4B 4V1
(416) 342-5646   *SIC* 7311
MUNICH COMPAGNIE DE REASSURANCE, LA   *p* 1206
630 BOUL RENE-LEVESQUE O BUREAU 2630, MONTREAL, QC, H3B 1S6
(514) 866-6825   *SIC* 6411
MUNICH LIFE MANAGEMENT CORPORATION LTD   *p* 954
390 BAY ST SUITE 2600, TORONTO, ON, M5H 2Y2
(416) 359-2200   *SIC* 6311
MUNICH REINSURANCE COMPANY OF CANADA   *p* 954
390 BAY ST SUITE 2300, TORONTO, ON, M5H 2Y2
(416) 366-9206   *SIC* 6331
MUNICIPAL CAPITAL INCORPORATED   *p* 468
19 MACRAE AVE, SYDNEY, NS, B1S 1M1
(902) 564-4541   *SIC* 1422
MUNICIPAL CONTRACTING LIMITED   *p* 470
927 ROCKY LAKE DR, WAVERLEY, NS, B2R 1S1
(902) 835-3381   *SIC* 1611
MUNICIPAL ENTERPRISES LIMITED   *p* 440
927 ROCKY LAKE DR, BEDFORD, NS, B4A 2T3
(902) 835-3381   *SIC* 2951
MUNICIPAL INSURANCE ASSOCIATION OF BRITISH COLUMBIA   *p* 292
429 2ND AVE W UNIT 200, VANCOUVER, BC, V5Y 1E3
(604) 683-6266   *SIC* 6351
MUNICIPAL PENSION PLAN   *p* 334
See *BC PENSION CORPORATION*
MUNICIPAL PROPERTY ASSESSMENT CORPORATION   *p* 843
1340 PICKERING PKY SUITE 101, PICKERING, ON, L1V 0C4
(905) 831-4433   *SIC* 7389
MUNICIPAL READY-MIX LIMITED   *p* 468
19 MACRAE AVE, SYDNEY, NS, B1S 1M1
(902) 564-4541   *SIC* 3273
MUNICIPAL TANK LINES LIMITED   *p* 54
800 5 AVE SW SUITE 1700, CALGARY, AB, T2P 3T6
(403) 298-5100   *SIC* 4213
MUNICIPALITY OF KINCARDINE, THE   *p* 913
3145 HWY 21 N, TIVERTON, ON, N0G 2T0
(519) 368-2000   *SIC* 4813
MUNK SCHOOL OF GLOBAL AFFAIRS   *p* 975
See *GOVERNING COUNCIL OF THE UNI-*

VERSITY OF TORONTO, THE

MUNN ENTERPRISES LTD *p 186*
1969 WILLINGDON AVE, BURNABY, BC, V5C 5J3
(604) 299-1124   *SIC 5541*

MUNN'S INSURANCE LIMITED *p 430*
121 KELSEY DR SUITE 100, ST. JOHN'S, NL, A1B 0L2
(709) 726-8627   *SIC 6411*

MUNRO AGROMART LTD *p 643*
6011 34 HWY, LANCASTER, ON, K0C 1N0
(613) 347-3063   *SIC 5153*

MUNRO FARM SUPPLIES LTD *p 355*
GD LCD MAIN, PORTAGE LA PRAIRIE, MB, R1N 3A7
(204) 857-8741   *SIC 5261*

MUNRO, HUGH CONSTRUCTION LTD *p 362*
61053 HWY 207, WINNIPEG, MB, R2C 2Z2
(204) 224-9218   *SIC 1794*

MUNSU *p 432*
See MEMORIAL UNIVERSITY OF NEW-FOUNDLAND STUDENTS UNION

MUNVO *p 1199*
See SOLUTIONS MUNVO INC

MURAFLEX INC *p 1165*
5502 RUE NOTRE-DAME E, MONTREAL, QC, H1N 2C4
(450) 462-3632   *SIC 2522*

MURCHIE'S TEA & COFFEE (2007) LTD *p 209*
8028 RIVER WAY, DELTA, BC, V4G 1K9
(604) 231-7501   *SIC 5499*

MURDERS TASTEFULLY EXECUTED INC *p 761*
128 WILLIAM ST, NIAGARA ON THE LAKE, ON, L0S 1J0
(905) 468-0007   *SIC 7922*

MURDOCH MACKAY COLLEGIATE *p 363*
See RIVER EAST TRANSCONA SCHOOL DIVISION

MUROX *p 1065*
See GROUPE CANAM INC

MURPHY BUS LINES *p 479*
See MURPHY, J & T LIMITED

MURPHY FORD SALES LTD *p 838*
1341 PEMBROKE ST W, PEMBROKE, ON, K8A 5R3
(613) 735-6861   *SIC 5511*

MURPHY OIL COMPANY LTD *p 54*
520 3 AVE SW SUITE 4000, CALGARY, AB, T2P 0R3
(403) 294-8000   *SIC 1311*

MURPHY'S KENSINGTON PHARM DIV *p 1039*
See MURPHY'S PHARMACIES INC

MURPHY'S PHARMACIES INC *p 1039*
41 ST. PETERS RD, CHARLOTTETOWN, PE, C1A 5N1
(902) 894-4447   *SIC 6531*

MURPHY'S VALU-MART *p 1004*
1200 YOUNGE ST S, WALKERTON, ON, N0G 2V0
(519) 881-2280   *SIC 5411*

MURPHY, D.P. INC *p 1039*
250 BRACKLEY POINT RD, CHARLOTTE-TOWN, PE, C1A 6Y9
(902) 368-3727   *SIC 5461*

MURPHY, DAN FORD SALES LTD *p 663*
1346 BANKFIELD RD, MANOTICK, ON, K4M 1A7
(613) 692-3594   *SIC 5511*

MURPHY, J & T LIMITED *p 479*
21588 RICHMOND ST, ARVA, ON, N0M 1C0
(519) 660-8200   *SIC 4151*

MURPHY, R & K ENTERPRISES LIMITED *p 461*
2871 HIGHWAY 334, LOWER WEDGE-PORT, NS, B0W 2B0
(902) 663-2503   *SIC 5146*

MURRAY & ASSOCIATES *p 275*
See APLIN & MARTIN CONSULTANTS LTD

MURRAY AUTO GROUP BRANDON LTD *p 347*
1500 RICHMOND AVE, BRANDON, MB, R7A 7E3
(204) 728-0130   *SIC 5511*

MURRAY AUTO GROUP FORT ST. JOHN LTD *p 214*
11204 ALASKA RD, FORT ST. JOHN, BC, V1J 5T5
(250) 785-8005   *SIC 5511*

MURRAY AUTO GROUP LETHBRIDGE LTD *p 143*
2815 26 AVE S, LETHBRIDGE, AB, T1K 7K7
(403) 328-1101   *SIC 5511*

MURRAY AUTO GROUP POCK LP *p 283*
3150 KING GEORGE BLVD, SURREY, BC, V4P 1A2
(604) 538-7022   *SIC 5511*

MURRAY AUTO GROUP WINNIPEG LTD *p 391*
1700 WAVERLEY ST SUITE C, WINNIPEG, MB, R3T 5V7
(204) 261-6200   *SIC 5511*

MURRAY BROS. LUMBER COMPANY LIMITED *p 663*
24749 HWY 60, MADAWASKA, ON, K0J 2C0
(613) 637-2840   *SIC 2421*

MURRAY BUICK GMC PENTICTON *p 243*
1010 WESTMINSTER AVE W, PENTIC-TON, BC, V2A 1L6
(250) 493-7121   *SIC 5511*

MURRAY CHEV OLDS CADILLAC SALES *p 146*
See MURRAY CHEVROLET OLDSMOBILE CADILLAC LTD

MURRAY CHEVROLET CADILLAC *p 347*
See MURRAY AUTO GROUP BRANDON LTD

MURRAY CHEVROLET CADILLAC BUICK GMC MOOSE JAW *p 1411*
15 CHESTER RD, MOOSE JAW, SK, S6J 1N3
(306) 693-4605   *SIC 5511*

MURRAY CHEVROLET CADILLAC LETH-BRIDGE *p 143*
See MURRAY AUTO GROUP LETH-BRIDGE LTD

MURRAY CHEVROLET HUMMER *p 391*
See MURRAY AUTO GROUP WINNIPEG LTD

MURRAY CHEVROLET OLDSMOBILE CADILLAC LTD *p 146*
1270 TRANS CANADA WAY SE, MEDICINE HAT, AB, T1B 1J5
(403) 527-1141   *SIC 7532*

MURRAY CHEVROLET OLDSMOBILE CADILLAC LTD *p 146*
1270 TRANS CANADA WAY SE, MEDICINE HAT, AB, T1B 1J5
(403) 527-5544   *SIC 5511*

MURRAY CHEVROLET PONTIAC BUICK GMC ESTEVAN *p 1406*
801 13TH AVE, ESTEVAN, SK, S4A 2L9
(306) 634-3661   *SIC 5511*

MURRAY CHEVROLET PONTIAC BUICK GMC MERRITT LIMITED PARTNERSHIP *p 232*
2049 NICOLA AVE, MERRITT, BC, V1K 1B8
(250) 378-9255   *SIC 5511*

MURRAY CHRYSLER DODGE JEEP RAM *p 387*
See MURRAY MOTOR SALES WINNIPEG LIMITED PARTNERSHIP

MURRAY DEMOLITION CORP *p 571*
345 HORNER AVE SUITE 300, ETOBI-COKE, ON, M8W 1Z6
(416) 253-6000   *SIC 1795*

MURRAY GM *p 177*
See MURRAY PONTIAC BUICK GMC LIMITED PARTNERSHIP

MURRAY GM *p 214*
See MURRAY AUTO GROUP FORT ST. JOHN LTD

MURRAY GM *p 471*
See MURRAY MOTORS YARMOUTH LIMITED PARTNERSHIP

MURRAY GM *p 1406*
See MURRAY CHEVROLET PONTIAC BUICK GMC ESTEVAN

MURRAY GM *p 1411*
See MURRAY CHEVROLET CADILLAC BUICK GMC MOOSE JAW

MURRAY GM MERRITT *p 232*
See MURRAY CHEVROLET PONTIAC BUICK GMC MERRITT LIMITED PARTNER-SHIP

MURRAY HILL DEVELOPMENTS LTD *p 92*
9833 110 ST NW, EDMONTON, AB, T5K 2P5
(780) 488-0287   *SIC 6531*

MURRAY HONDA CHILLIWACK *p 197*
See MURRAY MOTORS CHILLIWACK LIMITED PARTNERSHIP

MURRAY HYUNDAI WHITE ROCK *p 283*
See MURRAY AUTO GROUP POCK LP

MURRAY LAKE COLONY FARMING CO. LTD *p 81*
6517 TOWNSHIP RD 110, CYPRESS COUNTY, AB, T1A 7N3
(587) 824-2004   *SIC 0191*

MURRAY LATTA PROGRESSIVE MACHINE INC *p 277*
8717 132 ST, SURREY, BC, V3W 4P1
(604) 599-9598   *SIC 3569*

MURRAY MOTOR SALES WINNIPEG LIMITED PARTNERSHIP *p 387*
300 PEMBINA HWY, WINNIPEG, MB, R3L 2E2
(204) 284-6650   *SIC 5511*

MURRAY MOTORS CHILLIWACK LIMITED PARTNERSHIP *p 197*
44954 YALE RD W, CHILLIWACK, BC, V2R 4H1
(604) 792-2724   *SIC 5511*

MURRAY MOTORS FORT ST. JOHN LTD *p 214*
11204 ALASKA RD, FORT ST. JOHN, BC, V1J 5T5
(250) 785-6661   *SIC 5511*

MURRAY MOTORS THE PAS LIMITED PARTNERSHIP *p 359*
212 LAROSE AVE, THE PAS, MB, R9A 1L1
(204) 623-3481   *SIC 5511*

MURRAY MOTORS YARMOUTH LIMITED PARTNERSHIP *p 471*
45 STARRS RD, YARMOUTH, NS, B5A 2T2
(902) 742-7191   *SIC 5511*

MURRAY OK TIRE & TOWING *p 1001*
See VAL RITA TIRE SALES LTD

MURRAY PONTIAC BUICK GMC LIMITED PARTNERSHIP *p 177*
30355 AUTOMALL DR, ABBOTSFORD, BC, V2T 5M1
(604) 857-0742   *SIC 5511*

MURRAY TOWNSHIP FARMS LTD *p 999*
GD LCD MAIN, TRENTON, ON, K8V 5P9
(613) 392-8068   *SIC 0191*

MURRAY'S FARM SUPPLIES *p 356*
See SOLOMON, M.J. LTD

MURRAY'S TRUCKING INC *p 110*
6211 76 AVE NW, EDMONTON, AB, T6B 0A7
(780) 439-2222   *SIC 4213*

MURRAY, DON A. HOLDINGS LTD *p 154*
6380 50 AVE SUITE 300, RED DEER, AB, T4N 4C6
(403) 346-1497   *SIC 5311*

MURRICK INSURANCE SERVICES LTD *p 326*
1045 HOWE ST SUITE 925, VANCOUVER, BC, V6Z 2A9
(604) 688-5158   *SIC 6411*

MURSKA MANAGEMENT (1969) LTD *p 90*
10180 101 ST NW SUITE 3200, EDMON-TON, AB, T5J 3W8
(780) 425-9510   *SIC 8741*

MURTRON HAULING, DIV OF *p 134*
See PETROWEST TRANSPORTATION LP

MUSASHI AUTO PARTS CANADA INC *p 479*
333 DOMVILLE ST, ARTHUR, ON, N0G 1A0
(519) 848-2800   *SIC 3714*

MUSASHI AUTO PARTS CANADA INC *p 479*
500 DOMVILLE ST, ARTHUR, ON, N0G 1A0
(519) 848-2800   *SIC 3714*

MUSCLETECH *p 806*
See IOVATE HEALTH SCIENCES INTER-NATIONAL INC

MUSEE CANADIEN DE L'HISTOIRE *p 1108*
100 RUE LAURIER, GATINEAU, QC, K1A 0M8
(819) 776-7000   *SIC 8412*

MUSEE CANADIEN DES CIVILISATIONS *p 1108*
See GOUVERNEMENT DE LA PROVINCE DE QUEBEC

MUSEE D'ART CONTEMPORAIN DE MON-TREAL *p 1186*
185 RUE SAINTE-CATHERINE O, MON-TREAL, QC, H2X 3X5
(514) 847-6226   *SIC 8412*

MUSEE DE LA CIVILISATION *p 1259*
85 RUE DALHOUSIE, QUEBEC, QC, G1K 8R2
(418) 643-2158   *SIC 8412*

MUSEE DES BEAUX-ARTS DE MONTREAL *p 1213*
1380 RUE SHERBROOKE O, MONTREAL, QC, H3G 1J5
(514) 285-2000   *SIC 8412*

MUSEE DES BEAUX-ARTS DE MONTREAL *p 1214*
1379 RUE SHERBROOKE O, MONTREAL, QC, H3G 1J5
(514) 285-1600   *SIC 8412*

MUSEE NATIONAL DES BEAUX ARTS DU QUEBEC *p 1269*
See GOUVERNEMENT DE LA PROVINCE DE QUEBEC

MUSEE PIERRE-BOUCHER *p 1388*
See SEMINAIRE DES TROIS-RIVIERES

MUSIQUE SELECT INC *p 1211*
612 RUE SAINT-JACQUES, MONTREAL, QC, H3C 4M8
(514) 380-1999   *SIC 3861*

MUSIQUE STEVE *p 1192*
See MAGASIN DE MUSIQUE STEVE INC

MUSIQUEPLUS INC *p 1206*
355 RUE SAINTE-CATHERINE O, MON-TREAL, QC, H3B 1A5
(514) 284-7587   *SIC 4833*

MUSKET EQUIPMENT LEASING LTD *p 714*
2215 ROYAL WINDSOR DR, MISSIS-SAUGA, ON, L5J 1K5
(905) 823-7800   *SIC 4213*

MUSKET MELBURN *p 714*
See MUSKET EQUIPMENT LEASING LTD

MUSKET TRANSPORT LTD, THE *p 714*
2215 ROYAL WINDSOR DR, MISSIS-SAUGA, ON, L5J 1K5
(905) 823-7800   *SIC 4213*

MUSKOKA *p 1304*
See BOA-FRANC, S.E.N.C.

MUSKOKA ALGONQUIN HEALTHCARE *p 620*
100 FRANK MILLER DR, HUNTSVILLE, ON, P1H 1H7
(705) 789-2311   *SIC 8062*

MUSKOKA ALGONQUIN HEALTHCARE *p 620*
8 CRESCENT RD, HUNTSVILLE, ON, P1H 0B3
(705) 789-6451   *SIC 8099*

MUSKOKA AUTO PARTS LIMITED *p 620*
11 KING WILLIAM ST, HUNTSVILLE, ON, P1H 1G6

(705) 789-2321   *SIC* 5531
MUSKOKA BAY GOLF CORPORATION *p* 598
1217 NORTH MULDREW LAKE RD, GRAVENHURST, ON, P1P 1T9
(705) 687-4900   *SIC* 7992
MUSKOKA BAY RESORT   *p* 598
See MUSKOKA BAY GOLF CORPORATION
MUSKOKA CHRYSLER SALES   *p* 496
See 547121 ONTARIO LTD
MUSKOKA DELIVERY SERVICES INC 497
581 ECCLESTONE DR, BRACEBRIDGE, ON, P1L 1R2
(705) 645-1258   *SIC* 4212
MUSKOKA GROWN LIMITED   *p* 497
50 KEITH RD UNIT A, BRACEBRIDGE, ON, P1L 0A1
(705) 645-2295   *SIC* 2833
MUSKOKA LANDING CARE CENTRE *p* 620
See JARLETTE LTD
MUSKOKA LUMBER AND BUILDING SUPPLIES CENTRE LIMITED 846
3687 HWY 118, PORT CARLING, ON, P0B 1J0
(705) 765-3105   *SIC* 5211
MUSKOKA MINERALS & MINING INC *p* 620
1265 ASPDIN RD, HUNTSVILLE, ON, P1H 2J2
(705) 789-4457   *SIC* 1442
MUSKOKA SPRINGS   *p* 598
See MUSKOKA SPRINGS NATURAL SPRING WATER INC
MUSKOKA SPRINGS NATURAL SPRING WATER INC   *p* 598
220 BAY ST, GRAVENHURST, ON, P1P 1H1
(705) 687-8852   *SIC* 5149
MUSKOKA TIMBER MILLS LTD   *p* 497
2152 MANITOBA ST, BRACEBRIDGE, ON, P1L 1X4
(705) 645-7757   *SIC* 5099
MUSKOKA TRANSPORT LIMITED   *p* 497
456 ECCLESTONE DR, BRACEBRIDGE, ON, P1L 1R1
(705) 645-4481   *SIC* 4213
MUSSELWHITE MINES   *p* 304
See GOLDCORP CANADA LTD
MUSTANG DRINKWARE INC   *p* 889
35 CURRAH RD, ST THOMAS, ON, N5P 3R2
(519) 631-3030   *SIC* 3949
MUSTANG HELICOPTERS INC   *p* 5
237-27312 TOWNSHIP RD 394, BLACKFALDS, AB, T0M 0J0
(403) 885-5220   *SIC* 4512
MUSTANG PRODUCTS   *p* 889
See MUSTANG DRINKWARE INC
MUSTANG SURVIVAL HOLDINGS CORPORATION   *p* 255
3810 JACOMBS RD, RICHMOND, BC, V6V 1Y6
(604) 270-8631   *SIC* 6712
MUSTANG SURVIVAL ULC   *p* 193
7525 LOWLAND DR, BURNABY, BC, V5J 5L1
(604) 270-8631   *SIC* 3069
MUSTEL RESEARCH GROUP LTD   *p* 319
1505 2ND AVE W UNIT 402, VANCOUVER, BC, V6H 3Y4
(604) 733-4213   *SIC* 8732
MUTH ELECTRICAL MANAGEMENT INC *p* 115
9850 41 AVE NW, EDMONTON, AB, T6E 5L6
(780) 414-0980   *SIC* 1731
MUTH ENERGY MANAGEMENT   *p* 115
See MUTH ELECTRICAL MANAGEMENT INC
MUTUAL CONCEPT COMPUTER GROUP INC   *p* 660

785 WONDERLAND RD S SUITE 253, LONDON, ON, N6K 1M6
(519) 432-8553   *SIC* 7372
MUTUAL FIRE INSURANCE COMPANY OF BRITISH COLUMBIA, THE   *p* 225
9366 200A ST SUITE 201, LANGLEY, BC, V1M 4B3
(604) 881-1250   *SIC* 6331
MUTUAL FUND DEALERS ASSOCIATION OF CANADA   *p* 955
121 KING ST W SUITE 1000, TORONTO, ON, M5H 3T9
(416) 361-6332   *SIC* 8621
MUTUAL PROPANE LIMITED   *p* 96
16203 114 AVE NW, EDMONTON, AB, T5M 2Z3
(780) 451-4454   *SIC* 5984
MUTUAL SUPPORT SYSTEMS   *p* 590
See MUTUAL SUPPORT SYSTEMS OF THE NIAGARA REGION
MUTUAL SUPPORT SYSTEMS OF THE NIAGARA REGION   *p* 590
792 CANBORO RD, FENWICK, ON, L0S 1C0
(905) 892-4332   *SIC* 8699
MUTUAL TANKS LTD   *p* 96
16203 114 AVE NW, EDMONTON, AB, T5M 2Z3
(780) 451-4454   *SIC* 5984
MUZYK, D.J. DRUGS LTD   *p* 770
1515 STEELES AVE E, NORTH YORK, ON, M2M 3Y7
(416) 226-1313   *SIC* 5912
MUZZO BROTHERS GROUP INC   *p* 556
50 CONFEDERATION PKY, CONCORD, ON, L4K 4T8
(905) 326-4000   *SIC* 1742
MVA STRATFORD INC   *p* 896
753 ONTARIO ST, STRATFORD, ON, N5A 7Y2
(519) 275-2203   *SIC* 3089
MVHC   *p* 190
See METRO VANCOUVER HOUSING CORPORATION
MVR CASH AND CARRY   *p* 793
See MANUFACT LOGISTICS LTD
MW CANADA LTD   *p* 534
291 ELGIN ST N, CAMBRIDGE, ON, N1R 7H9
(519) 621-5460   *SIC* 2591
MWG APPAREL CORP   *p* 381
1147 NOTRE DAME AVE, WINNIPEG, MB, R3E 3G1
(204) 774-2561   *SIC* 2321
MY APARTMENT   *p* 453
See JACK FRIDAY'S LIMITED
MY BROADCASTING CORPORATION *p* 849
321B RAGLAN ST S SUITE B, RENFREW, ON, K7V 1R6
(613) 432-6936   *SIC* 4832
MY FM 96.1 RENFREW   *p* 849
See MY BROADCASTING CORPORATION
MY INSURANCE BROKER HAMILTON CORP   *p* 608
163 CENTENNIAL PKY N SUITE 2, HAMILTON, ON, L8E 1H8
(905) 528-2886   *SIC* 6411
MYANT INC   *p* 586
100 RONSON DR, ETOBICOKE, ON, M9W 1B6
(416) 423-7906   *SIC* 3552
MYE CANADA INC   *p* 110
7115 GIRARD RD NW, EDMONTON, AB, T6B 2C5
(780) 486-6663   *SIC* 2899
MYER SALIT LIMITED   *p* 759
7771 STANLEY AVE, NIAGARA FALLS, ON, L2G 0C7
(905) 354-5691   *SIC* 5051
MYERS BARRHAVEN NIS INC   *p* 752
530 MOTOR WORKS PVT, NEPEAN, ON, K2R 0A5
(613) 778-8893   *SIC* 5511

MYERS BARRHAVEN NISSAN   *p* 752
See MYERS BARRHAVEN NIS INC
MYERS CADILLAC CHEVROLET BUICK GMC INC   *p* 831
1200 BASELINE RD, OTTAWA, ON, K2C 0A6
(613) 225-2277   *SIC* 5511
MYERS HY WEST INC   *p* 752
4115 STRANDHERD DR, NEPEAN, ON, K2J 6H8
(613) 714-8888   *SIC* 5511
MYERS HYUNDAI   *p* 752
See MYERS HY WEST INC
MYERS KANATA CHEV BUICK GMC INC *p* 626
2500 PALLADIUM DR SUITE 200, KANATA, ON, K2V 1E2
(613) 592-9221   *SIC* 5511
MYERS KANATA NISSAN INC   *p* 751
2185 ROBERTSON RD, NEPEAN, ON, K2H 5Z2
(613) 596-1515   *SIC* 5511
MYERS KEMPTVILLE CHEVROLET BUICK GMC INC   *p* 627
104 ELVIRA ST E, KEMPTVILLE, ON, K0G 1J0
(613) 258-3403   *SIC* 5511
MYERS ORLEANS CHEVROLET BUICK GMC INC   *p* 810
1875 ST. JOSEPH BLVD, ORLEANS, ON, K1C 7J2
(613) 834-6397   *SIC* 5511
MYERS VOLKSWAGEN   *p* 626
2500 PALLADIUM DR SUITE 501, KANATA, ON, K2V 1E2
(613) 592-8484   *SIC* 5511
MYERS, BOB CHEVROLET OLDSMOBILE LTD   *p* 474
425 BAYLY ST W, AJAX, ON, L1S 6M3
(905) 427-2500   *SIC* 5511
MYFAX   *p* 749
See J2 GLOBAL CANADA, INC
MYHOSTING.COM   *p* 967
See SOFTCOM INC
MYLAN PHARMACEUTICALS ULC   *p* 575
85 ADVANCE RD, ETOBICOKE, ON, M8Z 2S6
(416) 236-2631   *SIC* 2834
MYLEX LIMITED   *p* 575
1460 THE QUEENSWAY, ETOBICOKE, ON, M8Z 1S7
(416) 259-5595   *SIC* 2517
MYLEX LIMITED   *p* 586
37 BETHRIDGE RD, ETOBICOKE, ON, M9W 1M8
(416) 745-1733   *SIC* 2517
MYRON MANUFACTURING   *p* 864
See ADLER INTERNATIONAL, LTD
MYRON MANUFACTURING CORP (USA) *p* 865
5610 FINCH AVE E, SCARBOROUGH, ON, M1B 6A6
(647) 288-5300   *SIC* 5199
MYROWICH, A BUILDING MATERIAL LTD *p* 1438
145 BROADWAY ST E, YORKTON, SK, S3N 3K5
(306) 783-3608   *SIC* 5211
MYRSA MANAGEMENT SERVICES LTD *p* 894
3 ANDERSON BLVD SUITE 1, STOUFFVILLE, ON, L4A 7X4
(416) 291-9756   *SIC* 6712
MYSHAK CRANE AND RIGGING LTD *p* 1
53016 HWY 60 SUITE 42B, ACHESON, AB, T7X 5A7
(780) 960-9790   *SIC* 7389
MYSHAK SALES & RENTALS LTD   *p* 1
28527 ACHESON RD, ACHESON, AB, T7X 6A8
(780) 960-9255   *SIC* 7359
MYSTICAL DISTRIBUTING COMPANY LTD *p* 999
6 FOSTER STEARNS RD, TRENTON, ON,

K8V 5R5
(613) 394-7056   *SIC* 5092
MYSTIQUE MECHANICAL LTD   *p* 9
3605 29 ST NE SUITE 300, CALGARY, AB, T1Y 5W4
SIC 1711
MYTON PROJECT MANAGEMENT LIMITED   *p* 455
5555 YOUNG ST, HALIFAX, NS, B3K 1Z7
SIC 1542

N

/N SPRO INC   *p* 1186
465 RUE SAINT-JEAN BUREAU 601, MONTREAL, QC, H2Y 2R6
(514) 907-2505   *SIC* 8741
N C HUTTON   *p* 426
See N.C.H. HOLDINGS LIMITED
N F O E & ASSOCIES ARCHITECTS *p* 1189
511 PLACE D'ARMES BUREAU 100, MONTREAL, QC, H2Y 2W7
(514) 397-2616   *SIC* 8712
N K S HEALTH   *p* 708
See N.K.S. PHARMACY LIMITED
N R G MANAGEMENT   *p* 380
See 3075487 MANITOBA LTD
N R MOTORS LTD   *p* 249
805 1ST AVE, PRINCE GEORGE, BC, V2L 2Y4
(250) 563-8891   *SIC* 5271
N R S WESTBURN REALTY LTD   *p* 190
5489 KINGSWAY, BURNABY, BC, V5H 2G1
(604) 209-1225   *SIC* 6531
N T A   *p* 315
See NIPPON TRAVEL AGENCY CANADA LTD
N WELCH PHARMACY SERVICES INC *p* 889
107 EDWARD ST SUITE 101, ST THOMAS, ON, N5P 1Y8
(519) 633-4402   *SIC* 5912
N-ABLE TECHNOLOGIES INTERNATIONAL INC   *p* 624
450 MARCH RD, KANATA, ON, K2K 3K2
(613) 592-6676   *SIC* 7372
N. HARRIS COMPUTER CORPORATION *p* 749
1 ANTARES DR SUITE 400, NEPEAN, ON, K2E 8C4
(613) 226-5511   *SIC* 7371
N. M. BARTLETT INC   *p* 490
4509 BARTLETT RD, BEAMSVILLE, ON, L0R 1B1
(905) 563-8261   *SIC* 5191
N. YANKE TRANSFER LTD   *p* 1432
1359 FLETCHER RD, SASKATOON, SK, S7M 5H5
SIC 4213
N.A.P. WINDOWS & DOORS LTD   *p* 223
8775 JIM BAILEY CRES UNIT B1, KELOWNA, BC, V4V 2L7
(250) 762-5343   *SIC* 3089
N.C.H. HOLDINGS LIMITED   *p* 426
14 CLYDE AVE, MOUNT PEARL, NL, A1N 4S1
(709) 368-2131   *SIC* 6512
N.K.S. PHARMACY LIMITED   *p* 708
130 DUNDAS ST E SUITE 500, MISSISSAUGA, ON, L5A 3V8
(905) 232-2322   *SIC* 8742
N.P.A. LTD   *p* 132
4201 93 RD ST, GRANDE PRAIRIE, AB, T8V 6T4
(780) 532-4600   *SIC* 1611
N.S.M. AUTO LTD   *p* 85
9670 125A AVE NW SUITE SIDE, EDMONTON, AB, T5G 3E5
(780) 479-5700   *SIC* 5511
NABORS DRILLING   *p* 149
See NABORS DRILLING CANADA LIMITED
NABORS DRILLING CANADA LIMITED *p* 7

GD STN MAIN, BROOKS, AB, T1R 1E4
  SIC 1389
NABORS DRILLING CANADA LIMITED p
54
500 4 AVE SW SUITE 2800, CALGARY, AB,
T2P 2V6
  (403) 263-6777   SIC 1381
NABORS DRILLING CANADA LIMITED p
132
HWY 40 W, GRANDE PRAIRIE, AB, T8V
3A1
  SIC 1389
NABORS DRILLING CANADA LIMITED p
149
902 20 AVE, NISKU, AB, T9E 7Z6
  (780) 955-2381   SIC 1381
NABORS DRILLING CANADA LIMITED p
156
8112 EDGAR INDUSTRIAL DR, RED
DEER, AB, T4P 3R2
  SIC 1389
NABORS PRODUCTION SERVICES p 156
  See NABORS DRILLING CANADA LIM-
ITED
**NABORS PRODUCTION SERVICES, DIV
OF** p 7
  See NABORS DRILLING CANADA LIM-
ITED
**NABORS PRODUCTION SERVICES, DIV
OF** p 132
  See NABORS DRILLING CANADA LIM-
ITED
NACEL PROPERTIES LTD p 307
925 GEORGIA ST W SUITE 800, VANCOU-
VER, BC, V6C 3L2
  (604) 685-7789   SIC 6513
NACORA INSURANCE BROKERS LTD p
732
77 FOSTER CRES, MISSISSAUGA, ON,
L5R 0K1
  (905) 507-1551   SIC 6411
NADEAU FERME AVICOLE p 417
  See MAPLE LODGE FARMS LTD
NADEAU, MARCEL MANAGEMENT INC p
197
7560 VEDDER RD, CHILLIWACK, BC, V2R
4E7
  (604) 858-7230   SIC 5531
NADEL ENTERPRISES INC p 689
3320 CAROGA DR, MISSISSAUGA, ON,
L4V 1L4
  (416) 745-2622   SIC 5099
**NADG U.S. CORE PLUS ACQUISITION
FUND (CANADIAN) L.P.** p 673
2851 JOHN ST SUITE 1, MARKHAM, ON,
L3R 5R7
  (905) 477-9200   SIC 6722
NADINE INTERNATIONAL INC p 697
2325 SKYMARK AVE, MISSISSAUGA, ON,
L4W 5A9
  (905) 602-1850   SIC 7371
NADON SPORT p 1301
  See NADON SPORT SAINT-EUSTACHE
INC
NADON SPORT INC p 1302
62 RUE SAINT-LOUIS, SAINT-EUSTACHE,
QC, J7R 1X7
  (450) 473-2381   SIC 5571
NADON SPORT SAINT-EUSTACHE INC p
1301
645 RUE DUBOIS, SAINT-EUSTACHE, QC,
J7P 3W1
  (450) 473-2381   SIC 5571
NAGEOIRE LTEE, LA p 404
144 CH DU HAVRE, LE GOULET, NB, E8S
2H1
  (506) 336-8808   SIC 5146
NAGLE LEASING & RENTALS p 412
  See BAYVIEW TRUCKS & EQUIPMENT
LTD
NAHANNI CONSTRUCTION LTD p 436
100 NAHANNI DR, YELLOWKNIFE, NT,
X1A 0E8
  (867) 873-2975   SIC 1542

NAHANNI STEEL PRODUCTS INC p 505
38 DEERHURST DR, BRAMPTON, ON, L6T
5R8
  (905) 791-2100   SIC 3469
NAILOR INDUSTRIES INC p 793
98 TORYORK DR, NORTH YORK, ON, M9L
1X6
  (416) 744-3300   SIC 3822
NAILOR INTERNATIONAL p 793
  See NAILOR INDUSTRIES INC
NAIRN VACUUM & APPLIANCE p 368
929 NAIRN AVE, WINNIPEG, MB, R2L 0X9
  (204) 668-4901   SIC 5722
NAIT p 85
  See NORTHERN ALBERTA INSTITUTE OF
TECHNOLOGY
NAKA HERBS & VITAMINS p 586
  See NAKA SALES LIMITED
NAKA SALES LIMITED p 586
252 BROCKPORT DR, ETOBICOKE, ON,
M9W 5S1
  (416) 748-3073   SIC 5149
NAKINA AIR SERVICE p 747
  See NAKINA OUTPOST CAMPS & AIR
SERVICE LTD
**NAKINA OUTPOST CAMPS & AIR SER-
VICE LTD** p
747
GD, NAKINA, ON, P0T 2H0
  (807) 329-5341   SIC 4512
NAKISA INC p 1206
733 RUE CATHCART, MONTREAL, QC,
H3B 1M6
  (514) 228-2000   SIC 7371
NAL RESOURCES LIMITED p 54
550 6 AVE SW SUITE 600, CALGARY, AB,
T2P 0S2
  (403) 294-3600   SIC 5171
**NAL RESOURCES MANAGEMENT LIM-
ITED** p
54
550 6 AVE SW SUITE 600, CALGARY, AB,
T2P 0S2
  (403) 294-3600   SIC 8741
NALCO CANADA CO. p 530
1055 TRUMAN ST, BURLINGTON, ON, L7R
3V7
  (905) 632-8791   SIC 5074
NALCO CANADA CO. p 530
1055 TRUMAN ST, BURLINGTON, ON, L7R
3V7
  (905) 633-1000   SIC 2819
NALCO CANADA ULC p 54
815 8 AVE SW SUITE 1400, CALGARY, AB,
T2P 3P2
  (403) 234-7881   SIC 5169
**NALCO CHAMPION, AN ECOLAB COM-
PANY** p
54
  See NALCO CANADA ULC
NALCOR ENERGY p 430
500 COLUMBUS DR, ST. JOHN'S, NL, A1B
4K7
  (709) 737-1440   SIC 4911
**NALCOR ENERGY MARKETING CORPO-
RATION** p
430
500 COLUMBUS DR, ST. JOHN'S, NL, A1B
0P5
  (709) 737-1491   SIC 4911
NALEWAY FOODS LTD. p 372
233 HUTCHINGS ST, WINNIPEG, MB, R2X
2R4
  (204) 633-6535   SIC 2038
NAMAKA FARMS INC p 168
GD STN MAIN, STRATHMORE, AB, T1P
1J5
  (403) 934-6122   SIC 0212
NAMASCO BLANKING CENTER p 516
  See SAMUEL METAL BLANKING
NAMIBIA CRITICAL METALS INC p 440
1550 BEDFORD HWY SUITE 802, BED-
FORD, NS, B4A 1E6
  (902) 835-8760   SIC 1081

NANAIMO CHRYSLER LTD p 234
4170 WELLINGTON RD, NANAIMO, BC,
V9T 2H3
  (250) 758-1191   SIC 5511
NANAIMO DAILY NEWS p 234
  See POSTMEDIA NETWORK INC
**NANAIMO DISTRICTY SENIOR CITIZENS
HOUSING DEVELOPMENT SOCIETY** p 234
1233 KIWANIS CRES, NANAIMO, BC, V9S
5Y1
  (250) 740-2815   SIC 6531
NANAIMO FOREST PRODUCTS LTD p 235
1000 WAVE PL, NANAIMO, BC, V9X 1J2
  (250) 722-3211   SIC 2611
NANAIMO HONDA CARS p 234
  See GRAEMOND HOLDINGS LTD
NANAIMO REALTY CO LTD p 234
2000 ISLAND HWY N SUITE 275,
NANAIMO, BC, V9S 5W3
  (250) 713-0494   SIC 6531
NANAIMO SAWMILL p 234
  See WESTERN FOREST PRODUCTS INC
**NANAIMO SENIORS VILLAGE VENTURES
LTD** p 235
6085 UPLANDS DR, NANAIMO, BC, V9V
1T8
  (250) 729-9524   SIC 6513
NANAIMO TRAVELLERS LODGE SOCIETY
p 234
1917 NORTHFIELD RD, NANAIMO, BC,
V9S 3B6
  (250) 758-4676   SIC 8361
NANCY LOPEZ GOLF p 1006
185 WEBER ST S, WATERLOO, ON, N2J
2B1
  (866) 649-1759   SIC 3949
NANOMETRICS INC p 624
250 HERZBERG RD, KANATA, ON, K2K
2A1
  (613) 592-6776   SIC 3829
NANOOSE BAY PETRO-CANADA p 235
  See PC 96 HOLDINGS LTD
NANOOSE BAY PETRO-CANADA p 235
  See S.A.D.E HOLDINGS LTD
NANOWAVE TECHNOLOGIES INC p 571
425 HORNER AVE SUITE 1, ETOBICOKE,
ON, M8W 4W3
  (416) 252-5602   SIC 3812
NAP GLADU p 1149
  See GESTION D'ACTIFS GLADU INC
NAP STEEL p 209
  See NORTH AMERICAN PIPE & STEEL
LTD
NAPA p 1124
  See PIECES D'AUTOS G. G. M. INC
NAPA AUTO PARTS p 128
  See PARAMOUNT PARTS INC
NAPA AUTO PARTS p 136
  See 389987 ALBERTA LTD
NAPA AUTO PARTS p 225
  See UAP INC
NAPA AUTO PARTS p 633
  See UNIVERSAL INDUSTRIAL SUPPLY
GROUP INC
NAPA AUTO PARTS p 1005
  See WALLACEBURG AUTOMOTIVE INC
NAPA AUTO PARTS p 1131
7214 BOUL NEWMAN, LASALLE, QC, H8N
1X2
  (514) 365-5116   SIC 5531
NAPA AUTO PARTS p 1234
2999 BOUL LE CORBUSIER, MONTREAL,
QC, H7L 3M3
  (450) 681-6495   SIC 5531
NAPA AUTO PARTS p 1414
  See UNIFIED AUTO PARTS INC
NAPA AUTOPARTS DIV OF p 38
  See UAP INC
NAPA AUTOPRO p 600
  See SLESSOR AUTO WORLD
NAPA PIECES D'AUTO p 1057
  See PIECES D'AUTOS M.R. INC., LES
NAPA PIECES D'AUTO p 1165
  See UAP INC

NAPA PIECES D'AUTO p 1283
  See PIECES D'AUTOS CHAMBLY RICHE-
LIEU INC
NAPA PIECES D'AUTO p 1347
557 RUE SAINT-LOUIS, SAINT-LIN-
LAURENTIDES, QC, J5M 2X2
  (450) 439-2006   SIC 5531
**NAPANEE DISTRICT SECONDARY
SCHOOL** p 747
  See LIMESTONE DISTRICT SCHOOL
BOARD
**NAPANEE HOME HARDWARE BUILDING
CENTRE** p 747
  See BEEBE, D LUMBER CO LTD
NAPCO p 1033
  See ROYAL GROUP, INC
NAPEC p 1399
  See THIRAU INC
NAPG EQUITIES INC p 673
2851 JOHN ST SUITE 1, MARKHAM, ON,
L3R 5R7
  (905) 477-9200   SIC 6531
NAPOLEON p 484
  See NAPOLEON SYSTEMS & DEVELOP-
MENTS LTD
NAPOLEON FIREPLACES p 485
  See WOLF STEEL LTD
**NAPOLEON SYSTEMS & DEVELOP-
MENTS LTD** p
484
24 NAPOLEON RD, BARRIE, ON, L4M 0G8
  (705) 721-1212   SIC 3433
NAPP p 499
  See NORTH AMERICAN PAPER INCOR-
PORATED
NARANG FARMS & PROCESSORS LTD p
178
351 BRADNER RD, ABBOTSFORD, BC,
V4X 2J5
  (604) 856-2020   SIC 0171
NARDEI FABRICATORS LTD p 17
8915 44 ST SE, CALGARY, AB, T2C 2P5
  (403) 279-3301   SIC 3498
NARMCO GROUP p 543
  See RUSSELL TOOL & DIE LIMITED
NARMCO GROUP p 807
  See J.F.K. SYSTEMS INC
NARMCO GROUP p 1019
  See CENTRAL STAMPINGS LIMITED
NARMCO GROUP p 1024
  See CANADIAN ELECTROCOATING LTD
NARROFLEX p 893
  See WENTWORTH TEXTILES INC
NARROFLEX INC p 892
590 SOUTH SERVICE RD, STONEY
CREEK, ON, L8E 2W1
  (905) 643-6066   SIC 2241
NART DRUGS INC p 973
292 DUPONT ST, TORONTO, ON, M5R 1V9
  (416) 972-0232   SIC 5912
NARTEL p 405
  See AGROPUR COOPERATIVE
NARTEL p 1063
  See AGROPUR COOPERATIVE
NARTEL p 1108
  See AGROPUR COOPERATIVE
NARTEL p 1325
  See AGROPUR COOPERATIVE
NASCO SERVICES INC p 299
128 PENDER ST W SUITE 205, VANCOU-
VER, BC, V6B 1R8
  (604) 683-2512   SIC 7361
NASG CANADA INC p 1035
975 PATTULO AVE E, WOODSTOCK, ON,
N4S 7W3
  (519) 539-7491   SIC 3469
NASHA METAL EXPORT INC p 878
88 MISTY HILLS TRAIL, SCARBOROUGH,
ON, M1X 1T3
  (647) 765-8952   SIC 5093
NASITTUQ CORPORATION p 825
360 ALBERT ST UNIT 1830, OTTAWA, ON,
K1R 7X7
  (613) 234-9033   SIC 8741

NASON CONTRACTING GROUP LTD p 102
18304 105 AVE NW SUITE 205, EDMONTON, AB, T5S 0C6
(780) 460-7142 *SIC* 1541

NASRI INTERNATIONAL INC p 1326
500 BOUL LEBEAU, SAINT-LAURENT, QC, H4N 1R5
(514) 334-8282 *SIC* 5137

NATART JUVENILE INC p 1254
289 BOUL BARIL O, PRINCEVILLE, QC, G6L 3V8
SIC 5021

NATCO CANADA, LTD p 17
9423 SHEPARD RD SE, CALGARY, AB, T2C 4R6
(403) 203-2119 *SIC* 3443

NATCO PHARMA (CANADA) INC p 725
2000 ARGETIA RD PLAZA 1 SUITE 200, MISSISSAUGA, ON, L5N 1P7
(905) 997-3353 *SIC* 5122

NATHAR LIMITED p 562
27 FIRST ST E, CORNWALL, ON, K6H 1K5
(613) 932-8854 *SIC* 5611

NATION-WIDE HOME SERVICES CORP p 96
11228 142 ST NW, EDMONTON, AB, T5M 1T9
(780) 454-1937 *SIC* 6712

NATIONAL 4WD CENTRE INC p 523
5379 HARVESTER RD, BURLINGTON, ON, L7L 5K4
(905) 634-0001 *SIC* 5531

NATIONAL ARTS CENTRE CORPORATION p 824
1 ELGIN ST, OTTAWA, ON, K1P 5W1
(613) 947-7000 *SIC* 8742

NATIONAL ASSOCIATION OF FRIENDSHIP CENTRES p 212
5462 TRANS CANADA HWY UNIT 205, DUNCAN, BC, V9L 6W4
(250) 748-2242 *SIC* 8322

NATIONAL BAIT INC p 712
946 LAKESHORE RD E, MISSISSAUGA, ON, L5E 1E4
(905) 278-0180 *SIC* 5199

NATIONAL BALLET OF CANADA, THE p 982
470 QUEENS QUAY W, TORONTO, ON, M5V 3K4
(416) 345-9686 *SIC* 7922

NATIONAL BANK FINANCIAL p 304
See FINANCIERE BANQUE NATIONALE INC

NATIONAL BANK INDEPENDENT NETWORK p 987
See NBF INC

NATIONAL BANK INDEPENDENT NETWORK DIV. p 1204
See FINANCIERE BANQUE NATIONALE INC

NATIONAL BANK QUEBEC GROWTH FUND p 1206
See NATIONAL BANK SECURITIES INC.

NATIONAL BANK SECURITIES INC. p 1206
1100 BOUL ROBERT-BOURASSA UNITE 10 E, MONTREAL, QC, H3B 3A5
(514) 394-6282 *SIC* 6722

NATIONAL BANK TRUST INC p 1206
600 RUE DE LA GAUCHETIERE O BUREAU 2800, MONTREAL, QC, H3B 4L2
(514) 871-7100 *SIC* 6021

NATIONAL BRANDS p 1381
See 10167819 CANADA INC

NATIONAL BROKERS INSURANCE SERVICES INC p 741
6725 EDWARDS BLVD, MISSISSAUGA, ON, L5T 2V9
SIC 6411

NATIONAL CABLE SPECIALIST, DIV OF p 201
See NCS INTERNATIONAL CO

NATIONAL CANCER INSTITUTE OF CANADA p 927
10 ALCORN AVE SUITE 200, TORONTO, ON, M4V 3B1
(416) 961-7223 *SIC* 8733

NATIONAL CAR RENTAL p 29
See ENTERPRISE RENT-A-CAR CANADA COMPANY

NATIONAL CAR RENTAL p 645
See ECONOMY WHEELS LTD

NATIONAL CAR RENTAL p 902
See SPADONI MOTORS LIMITED

NATIONAL CELLULAR INC p 798
2679 BRISTOL CIR SUITE 8, OAKVILLE, ON, L6H 6Z8
(905) 828-9200 *SIC* 5999

NATIONAL CHEESE COMPANY p 548
See ARLA FOODS INC

NATIONAL CLUB, THE p 955
303 BAY ST, TORONTO, ON, M5H 2R1
(416) 364-3247 *SIC* 8621

NATIONAL COMMITTEE FOR THE NATIONAL PILGRIM VIRGIN OF CANADA, THE p 591
452 KRAFT RD, FORT ERIE, ON, L2A 4M7
(905) 871-7607 *SIC* 2721

NATIONAL CONCRETE ACCESSORIES CANADA INC p 96
14760 116 AVE NW, EDMONTON, AB, T5M 3G1
(780) 451-1212 *SIC* 5032

NATIONAL CONCRETE ACCESSORIES COMPANY INC p 586
172 BETHRIDGE RD, ETOBICOKE, ON, M9W 1N3
(416) 245-4720 *SIC* 3272

NATIONAL CORPORATE HOUSEKEEPING SERVICES INC p 717
3481 KELSO CRES, MISSISSAUGA, ON, L5L 4R3
(905) 608-8004 *SIC* 7349

NATIONAL DEVELOPMENTS LTD p 386
220 SAULTEAUX CRES, WINNIPEG, MB, R3J 3W3
(204) 889-5430 *SIC* 6512

NATIONAL EGG INC p 897
644 WRIGHT ST, STRATHROY, ON, N7G 3H8
(519) 245-0480 *SIC* 5144

NATIONAL ENERGY EQUIPMENT INC p 735
1850 DERRY RD E, MISSISSAUGA, ON, L5S 1Y6
(905) 564-2422 *SIC* 5084

NATIONAL ENGINEERED FASTENERS INC p 518
1747 GREENHOUSE RD, BRESLAU, ON, N0B 1M0
(519) 886-0919 *SIC* 5085

NATIONAL ENVIRONMENTAL PRODUCTS LTD p 1326
400 BOUL LEBEAU, SAINT-LAURENT, QC, H4N 1R6
(514) 333-1433 *SIC* 3585

NATIONAL EXHAUST SYSTEMS INC p 509
38 HANSEN RD S, BRAMPTON, ON, L6W 3H4
(905) 453-4111 *SIC* 5013

NATIONAL FILM BOARD OF CANADA p 1326
3155 CH DE LA COTE-DE-LIESSE, SAINT-LAURENT, QC, H4N 2N4
(514) 283-9000 *SIC* 7812

NATIONAL FIRE EQUIPMENT LIMITED p 556
40 EDILCAN DR, CONCORD, ON, L4K 3S6
(905) 761-6355 *SIC* 5087

NATIONAL FOCUS DISTRIBUTION/LOGISTICS INC p 476
151 CHURCH ST S, ALLISTON, ON, L9R 1E5
(705) 434-9995 *SIC* 5112

NATIONAL GALLERY OF CANADA p 821

380 SUSSEX DR, OTTAWA, ON, K1N 9N4
(613) 990-1985 *SIC* 8412

NATIONAL GLASS LTD p 228
5744 198 ST, LANGLEY, BC, V3A 7J2
(604) 530-2311 *SIC* 3231

NATIONAL GYPSUM (CANADA) LTD p 466
1707 HIGHWAY 2, SPRINGHILL, NS, B0M 1X0
(902) 758-3256 *SIC* 1499

NATIONAL HEARING SERVICES p 640
50 QUEEN ST N, KITCHENER, ON, N2H 6M2
SIC 5999

NATIONAL HEARING SERVICES INC p 336
1007 LANGLEY ST SUITE 301, VICTORIA, BC, V8W 1V7
(250) 413-2100 *SIC* 5999

NATIONAL HEARING SERVICES INC p 637
20 BEASLEY DR, KITCHENER, ON, N2E 1Y6
(519) 895-0100 *SIC* 8731

NATIONAL HERRING H.J.S. p 1050
See NATIONAL HERRING IMPORTING COMPANY LTD

NATIONAL HERRING IMPORTING COMPANY LTD p 1050
9820 BOUL RAY-LAWSON, ANJOU, QC, H1J 1L1
(514) 274-4774 *SIC* 5146

NATIONAL HOCKEY LEAGUE PLAYERS ASSOCIATION, THE p 965
20 BAY ST SUITE 1700, TORONTO, ON, M5J 2N8
(416) 313-2300 *SIC* 8621

NATIONAL HOME WARRANTY PROGRAMS LTD p 125
9808 12 AVE SW, EDMONTON, AB, T6X 0J5
(780) 425-2981 *SIC* 6351

NATIONAL HYDRONICS LTD p 277
12178 86 AVE, SURREY, BC, V3W 3H7
(604) 591-6106 *SIC* 1711

NATIONAL IMPORTERS CANADA LTD p 255
13100 MITCHELL RD SUITE 120, RICHMOND, BC, V6V 1M8
(604) 324-1551 *SIC* 5141

NATIONAL INCOME PROTECTION PLAN INC p 698
2595 SKYMARK AVE UNIT 206, MISSISSAUGA, ON, L4W 4L5
(905) 219-0096 *SIC* 8748

NATIONAL INDIAN BROTHERHOOD p 825
473 ALBERT ST SUITE 810, OTTAWA, ON, K1R 5B4
(613) 241-6789 *SIC* 8611

NATIONAL INFO-TECH CENTRE p 1192
See 3619842 CANADA INC

NATIONAL LEASING p 390
See CWB NATIONAL LEASING INC

NATIONAL LOGISTICS SERVICES (2006) INC p 745
150 COURTNEYPARK DR W, MISSISSAUGA, ON, L5W 1Y6
(905) 364-0033 *SIC* 5137

NATIONAL MERCHANDISING CORPORATION p 1244
400 AV ATLANTIC BUREAU 705, OUTREMONT, QC, H2V 1A5
(514) 764-0141 *SIC* 8748

NATIONAL MONEY MART COMPANY p 334
401 GARBALLY RD, VICTORIA, BC, V8T 5M3
(250) 595-5211 *SIC* 6099

NATIONAL OIL WELL VARCO p 148
See DRECO ENERGY SERVICES ULC

NATIONAL OILWELL VARCO p 10
See DNOW CANADA ULC

NATIONAL OILWELL VARCO p 109
See DNOW CANADA ULC

NATIONAL OILWELL VARCO p 139

See DNOW CANADA ULC

NATIONAL OILWELL VARCO p 144
See DNOW CANADA ULC

NATIONAL PHARMACY p 865
70 MELFORD DR SUITE 7, SCARBOROUGH, ON, M1B 1Y9
(416) 265-9000 *SIC* 5912

NATIONAL PHILATELIC CENTRE p 438
75 ST NINIAN ST, ANTIGONISH, NS, B2G 2R8
(902) 863-6550 *SIC* 5961

NATIONAL PILGRIM p 591
See NATIONAL COMMITTEE FOR THE NATIONAL PILGRIM VIRGIN OF CANADA, THE

NATIONAL PINES GOLF CLUB p 622
See CLUBLINK CORPORATION ULC

NATIONAL PORT SECURITY SERVICES INC p 1039
379 QUEEN ST, CHARLOTTETOWN, PE, C1A 4C9
(902) 892-9977 *SIC* 8748

NATIONAL PROCESS EQUIPMENT INC p 17
5409 74 AVE SE, CALGARY, AB, T2C 3C9
(403) 724-4300 *SIC* 3561

NATIONAL PRODUCE MARKETING INC p 575
55 PLYWOOD PL UNIT 102, ETOBICOKE, ON, M8Z 5J3
(416) 259-0833 *SIC* 5148

NATIONAL PUBLIC RELATIONS INC p 979
See CABINET DE RELATIONS PUBLIQUES NATIONAL INC, LE

NATIONAL RECYCLING INC p 505
5 COPPER RD, BRAMPTON, ON, L6T 4W5
(905) 790-2828 *SIC* 5399

NATIONAL REFRIGERATION & AIR CONDITIONING CANADA CORP p 514
159 ROY BLVD, BRANTFORD, ON, N3R 7K1
(519) 751-0444 *SIC* 3585

NATIONAL REFRIGERATION HEATING p 787
See AINSWORTH INC

NATIONAL RENT A CAR p 1440
See NORCAN LEASING LTD

NATIONAL RESEARCH COUNCIL CANADA p 430
GD, ST. JOHN'S, NL, A1B 3T5
(709) 772-4939 *SIC* 8732

NATIONAL RESEARCH COUNCIL CANADA p 815
1200 MONTREAL RD BUILDING M-58, OTTAWA, ON, K1A 0R6
(613) 993-9200 *SIC* 8741

NATIONAL RUBBER TECHNOLOGIES CORP p 993
35 CAWTHRA AVE, TORONTO, ON, M6N 5B3
(416) 657-1111 *SIC* 2822

NATIONAL RUBBER TECHNOLOGIES CORP p 993
394 SYMINGTON AVE, TORONTO, ON, M6N 2W3
(416) 657-1111 *SIC* 2822

NATIONAL SAFETY ASSOCIATES OF CANADA INC / NSA CANADA INC p 698
2785 SKYMARK AVE SUITE 15, MISSISSAUGA, ON, L4W 4Y3
(905) 624-6368 *SIC* 5149

NATIONAL SERVICES p 775
See 2179321 ONTARIO LIMITED

NATIONAL SHIPPERS & RECEIVERS INC p 366
45 BEGHIN AVE SUITE 7, WINNIPEG, MB, R2J 4B9
(204) 222-6289 *SIC* 4731

NATIONAL SHOE SPECIALTIES LIMITED p 876
3015 KENNEDY RD UNIT 8-18, SCARBOROUGH, ON, M1V 1E7
(416) 292-7181 *SIC* 5047

NATIONAL SIGNCORP INVESTMENTS LTD *p 206*
1471 DERWENT WAY, DELTA, BC, V3M 6N2
(604) 525-4300   *SIC 3993*

NATIONAL SILICATES *p 575*
See NATIONAL SILICATES PARTNERSHIP

NATIONAL SILICATES PARTNERSHIP *p 575*
429 KIPLING AVE, ETOBICOKE, ON, M8Z 5C7
(416) 255-7771   *SIC 2819*

NATIONAL STEEL CAR LIMITED *p 612*
600 KENILWORTH AVE N, HAMILTON, ON, L8N 3J4
(905) 544-3311   *SIC 3743*

NATIONAL TIME EQUIPMENT CO LTD *p 996*
31 CORONET RD, TORONTO, ON, M8Z 2L8
(416) 252-2293   *SIC 5094*

NATIONAL TIRE DISTRIBUTORS *p 622*
311 INGERSOLL ST S, INGERSOLL, ON, N5C 3J7
(519) 425-1228   *SIC 5531*

NATIONAL TIRE DISTRIBUTORS INC *p 523*
5035 SOUTH SERVICE RD 4TH FL, BURLINGTON, ON, L7L 6M9
(877) 676-0007   *SIC 5014*

NATIONAL TRUCK CENTRE INC *p 225*
9758 203 ST, LANGLEY, BC, V1M 4B9
(604) 888-5577   *SIC 5511*

NATIONAL UTILITY SERVICE (CANADA) LIMITED *p 765*
111 GORDON BAKER RD SUITE 500, NORTH YORK, ON, M2H 3R2
(416) 490-9922   *SIC 4724*

NATIONAL-OILWELL VARCO *p 114*
See DNOW CANADA ULC

NATIONAL-STANDARD COMPANY OF CANADA, LTD *p 604*
20 CAMPBELL RD, GUELPH, ON, N1H 1C1
SIC 3496

NATIONEX *p 1307*
See COLISPRO INC

NATIONEX INC *p 1308*
3505 BOUL LOSCH, SAINT-HUBERT, QC, J3Y 5T7
(450) 445-7171   *SIC 7389*

NATIONWIDE LOGISTICS *p 444*
See 3307862 NOVA SCOTIA LIMITED

NATIVE CHILD AND FAMILY SERVICES OF TORONTO *p 946*
30 COLLEGE ST, TORONTO, ON, M5G 1K2
(416) 969-8510   *SIC 8399*

NATIVE COUNCIL OF NOVA SCOTIA *p 469*
129 TRURO HEIGHTS RD, TRURO HEIGHTS, NS, B6L 1X2
(902) 895-1523   *SIC 8651*

NATIVE COUNSELLING SERVICES OF ALBERTA *p 106*
14904 121A AVE NW, EDMONTON, AB, T5V 1A3
(780) 451-4002   *SIC 8322*

NATPRO *p 17*
See NATIONAL PROCESS EQUIPMENT INC

NATRA CHOCOLATE AMERICA INC *p 662*
2800 ROXBURGH RD, LONDON, ON, N6N 1K9
(519) 681-9494   *SIC 5149*

NATREL *p 811*
See AGROPUR COOPERATIVE

NATSCO *p 684*
See NORTH AMERICAN TRANSIT SUPPLY CORPORATION

NATT TOOLS GROUP INC *p 611*
460 SHERMAN AVE N, HAMILTON, ON, L8L 8J6
(905) 549-7433   *SIC 3523*

NATUR+L XTD INC *p 1313*
2905 AV JOSE-MARIA-ROSELL, SAINT-HYACINTHE, QC, J2S 0J9

(450) 250-4981   *SIC 8731*

NATURA NATURALS INC *p 644*
279 TALBOT ST W, LEAMINGTON, ON, N8H 4H3
(877) 786-6286   *SIC 0182*

NATURAL BAKERY LTD *p 381*
769 HENRY AVE, WINNIPEG, MB, R3E 1V2
(204) 783-7344   *SIC 5461*

NATURAL FACTORS *p 200*
See FACTORS GROUP OF NUTRITIONAL COMPANIES INC

NATURAL FACTORS NUTRITIONAL PRODUCTS LTD *p 201*
1550 UNITED BLVD, COQUITLAM, BC, V3K 6Y2
(604) 777-1757   *SIC 5122*

NATURAL GAS AND PETROLEUM RESOURCES *p 146*
See MEDICINE HAT, CITY OF

NATURAL GAS CUSTOM PIPING *p 1014*
244 BROCK ST S, WHITBY, ON, L1N 4K1
SIC 4925

NATURAL GLACIAL WATERS INC *p 212*
8430 BERRAY RD RR 1, FANNY BAY, BC, V0R 1W0
(250) 335-9119   *SIC 2899*

NATURAL GOURMET *p 595*
See NORTH HOUSE FOODS LTD

NATURAL LIFE NUTRITION INC *p 193*
7337 NORTH FRASER WAY UNIT 108, BURNABY, BC, V5J 0G7
(604) 207-0493   *SIC 5149*

NATURAL RESOURCES CANADA *p 613*
183 LONGWOOD RD S, HAMILTON, ON, L8P 0A5
(905) 645-0683   *SIC 2861*

NATURALIMENT *p 1356*
See GASTRONOME ANIMAL INC, LE

NATURALIZER *p 839*
See CALERES CANADA, INC

NATURALLY FIT SUPPLEMENTS INC *p 404*
125 ROUTE 105, LOWER ST MARYS, NB, E3A 8P8
(506) 451-8707   *SIC 5149*

NATURE 3M INC *p 1243*
943 RUE SAINT-CYRILLE, NORMANDIN, QC, G8M 4H9
(418) 274-2511   *SIC 5199*

NATURE CONSERVANCY OF CANADA, THE *p 922*
245 EGLINTON AVE E SUITE 410, TORONTO, ON, M4P 3J1
(416) 932-3202   *SIC 8999*

NATURE FRESH FARMS INC *p 644*
634 MERSEA ROAD 7, LEAMINGTON, ON, N8H 3V8
(519) 326-8603   *SIC 0182*

NATURE FRESH FARMS SALES INC *p 644*
4 SENECA RD, LEAMINGTON, ON, N8H 5H7
(519) 326-1111   *SIC 5148*

NATURE PET CENTER *p 1248*
See 144503 CANADA INC

NATURE TRUST OF BRITISH COLUMBIA, THE *p 307*
888 DUNSMUIR ST SUITE 500, VANCOUVER, BC, V6C 3K4
(604) 924-9771   *SIC 8999*

NATURE'S CALL, DIV OF *p 3*
See THORLAKSON FEEDYARDS INC

NATURE'S COIN GROUP LTD *p 4*
225A BEAR ST, BANFF, AB, T1L 1B4
(403) 762-3018   *SIC 5944*

NATURE'S EMPORIUM BULK & HEALTH FOODS LTD *p 754*
16655 YONGE ST SUITE 27, NEWMARKET, ON, L3X 1V6
(905) 898-1844   *SIC 5499*

NATURE'S EMPORIUM WHOLISTIC MARKET *p 754*
See NATURE'S EMPORIUM BULK &

HEALTH FOODS LTD

NATURE'S FARE NATURAL FOODS INC *p 217*
1350 SUMMIT DR SUITE 5, KAMLOOPS, BC, V2C 1T8
(250) 314-9560   *SIC 5499*

NATURE'S FINEST PRODUCE LTD *p 836*
6874 PAIN COURT LINE RR 1, PAIN COURT, ON, N0P 1Z0
(519) 380-9520   *SIC 5431*

NATURE'S PATH BAKING INC *p 261*
9100 VAN HORNE WAY, RICHMOND, BC, V6X 1W3
(604) 248-8806   *SIC 5149*

NATURE'S PATH FOODS INC *p 261*
9100 VAN HORNE WAY, RICHMOND, BC, V6X 1W3
(604) 248-8777   *SIC 5149*

NATURE'S SUNSHINE PRODUCTS OF CANADA LTD *p 505*
44 PEEL CENTRE DR UNIT 402, BRAMPTON, ON, L6T 4B5
(905) 458-6100   *SIC 5149*

NATURE'S TOUCH FROZEN FOODS (WEST) INC *p 177*
31122 SOUTH FRASER WAY, ABBOTSFORD, BC, V2T 6L5
(604) 854-1191   *SIC 0723*

NATURE'S TOUCH FROZEN FOODS INC *p 1340*
5105-M RUE FISHER, SAINT-LAURENT, QC, H4T 1J8
(514) 737-7790   *SIC 5142*

NATURE'S VINE PRODUCE INC. *p 793*
5601 STEELES AVE W UNIT 11, NORTH YORK, ON, M9L 1S7
SIC 5148

NATURE'S WAY OF CANADA LIMITED *p 447*
15 GARLAND AVE UNIT 4, DARTMOUTH, NS, B3B 0A6
(902) 334-1468   *SIC 5122*

NATUREL HPP *p 1313*
See NATUR+L XTD INC

NATURES FORMULAE *p 222*
See NATURES FORMULAE HEALTH PRODUCTS LTD

NATURES FORMULAE HEALTH PRODUCTS LTD *p 222*
2130 LECKIE PL SUITE 300, KELOWNA, BC, V1Y 7W7
(250) 717-5700   *SIC 2023*

NATURISTE INC *p 1330*
5900 BOUL HENRI-BOURASSA O, SAINT-LAURENT, QC, H4R 1V9
(514) 336-2244   *SIC 5149*

NAUD, PIERRE INC *p 1369*
405 AV DU CAPITAINE-VEILLEUX, SHAWINIGAN, QC, G9P 1Z7
(819) 537-1877   *SIC 5211*

NAUTEL LIMITED *p 451*
10089 PEGGYS COVE RD HWY 333, HACKETTS COVE, NS, B3Z 3J4
(902) 823-3900   *SIC 3663*

NAUTICAL LANDS GROUP *p 540*
See CHARLAMARA HOLDINGS INC

NAUTILUS MINERALS INC *p 995*
2100 BLOOR ST W SUITE 6125, TORONTO, ON, M6S 5A5
(416) 551-1100   *SIC 1081*

NAUTILUS PLUS INC *p 1308*
3550 1RE RUE, SAINT-HUBERT, QC, J3Y 8Y5
(514) 666-5814   *SIC 5941*

NAV CANADA *p 134*
4396 34 ST E, GRANDE PRAIRIE, AB, T9E 0V4
(780) 890-8360   *SIC 4581*

NAV CANADA *p 277*
7421 135 ST, SURREY, BC, V3W 0M8
(604) 775-9534   *SIC 4899*

NAV CANADA *p 386*
777 MORAY ST, WINNIPEG, MB, R3J 3W8

(204) 983-8566   *SIC 3812*

NAV CANADA *p 411*
222 OLD COACH RD, RIVERVIEW, NB, E1B 4G2
(613) 563-5588   *SIC 7389*

NAV CANADA *p 562*
1950 MONTREAL RD, CORNWALL, ON, K6H 6L2
(613) 936-5050   *SIC 8249*

NAV CANADA *p 597*
1600 TOM ROBERTS AVE, GLOUCESTER, ON, K1V 1E6
(800) 876-4693   *SIC 4899*

NAV CANADA *p 698*
6055 MIDFIELD RD, MISSISSAUGA, ON, L4W 2P7
(905) 676-5045   *SIC 4899*

NAV CANADA *p 824*
77 METCALFE ST, OTTAWA, ON, K1P 5L6
(613) 563-5588   *SIC 4899*

NAV CANADA *p 1094*
1750 CH SAINT-FRANCOIS, DORVAL, QC, H9P 2P6
(514) 633-2884   *SIC 4522*

NAV CANADA *p 1278*
515 RUE PRINCIPALE, QUEBEC, QC, G2G 2T8
(418) 871-7032   *SIC 4899*

NAV CENTRE *p 562*
See NAV CANADA

NAVACON CONSTRUCTION INC *p 517*
415 HARDY RD, BRANTFORD, ON, N3T 5L8
(519) 754-4646   *SIC 1623*

NAVADA LTEE *p 1142*
675 RUE HERELLE, LONGUEUIL, QC, J4G 2M8
(450) 679-3370   *SIC 1711*

NAVAL ENGINEERING TEST ESTABLISHMENT *p 1132*
See DEPARTMENT OF NATIONAL DEFENCE AND THE CANADIAN ARMED FORCES

NAVANTIS INC *p 994*
21 RANDOLPH AVE SUITE 200, TORONTO, ON, M6P 4G4
(416) 532-5554   *SIC 7379*

NAVBLUE INC *p 1008*
295 HAGEY BLVD SUITE 200, WATERLOO, ON, N2L 6R5
(519) 747-1170   *SIC 7371*

NAVELLI DWELLINGS INC *p 556*
1681 LANGSTAFF RD UNIT 1, CONCORD, ON, L4K 5T3
(416) 987-5500   *SIC 1531*

NAVIGANT *p 940*
See NAVIGANT CONSULTING LTD

NAVIGANT CONSULTING LTD *p 940*
1 ADELAIDE ST E SUITE 1250, TORONTO, ON, M5C 2V9
(416) 777-2440   *SIC 8742*

NAVIGATA COMMUNICATIONS 2009, INC *p 241*
949 3RD ST W SUITE 121, NORTH VANCOUVER, BC, V7P 3P7
(604) 998-4490   *SIC 4899*

NAVIGATA COMMUNICATIONS LIMITED *p 318*
1550 ALBERNI ST SUITE 300, VANCOUVER, BC, V6G 1A5
(604) 990-2000   *SIC 4899*

NAVIGATION CP LIMITEE *p 1220*
3400 BOUL DE MAISONNEUVE O BUREAU 1200, MONTREAL, QC, H3Z 3E7
(514) 934-5133   *SIC 4731*

NAVIGATION DES ETATS INDEPENDANTS DU COMMONWEALTH INC *p 1189*
478 RUE MCGILL, MONTREAL, QC, H2Y 2H2
(514) 499-1999   *SIC 4731*

NAVIGATION GILLSHIP *p 1210*
See GILLESPIE-MUNRO INC

NAVIGATION MADELEINE INC *p 1073*

435 CH AVILA-ARSENEAU, CAP-AUX-MEULES, QC, G4T 1J3
(418) 986-6600   *SIC 4432*
NAVIGATORS INSURANCE BROKERS LTD
p 768
4 LANSING SQ SUITE 100, NORTH YORK, ON, M2J 5A2
SIC 6411
NAVISTAR   *p 1373*
See CAMIONS INTER-ESTRIE (1991) INC, LES
NAVISTAR CANADA, INC   *p 627*
405 VAN BUREN ST, KEMPTVILLE, ON, K0G 1J0
(613) 258-1126   *SIC 3711*
NAVSTAR AVIATION INC   *p 729*
6500 SILVER DART DR SUITE 205, MISSISSAUGA, ON, L5P 1A5
(905) 673-7827   *SIC 4581*
NAVTECH INC   *p 1008*
295 HAGEY BLVD SUITE 200, WATERLOO, ON, N2L 6R5
(519) 747-1170   *SIC 8711*
NAYLOR (CANADA), INC   *p 382*
1200 PORTAGE AVE SUITE 200, WINNIPEG, MB, R3G 0T5
(204) 975-0415   *SIC 2721*
NAYLOR GROUP INCORPORATED   *p 798*
455 NORTH SERVICE RD E, OAKVILLE, ON, L6H 1A5
(905) 338-8000   *SIC 1711*
NB SOUTHERN   *p 416*
See NEW BRUNSWICK SOUTHERN RAILWAY COMPANY LIMITED
NBF INC   *p 987*
130 KING ST W SUITE 3000, TORONTO, ON, M5X 1J9
(416) 869-3707   *SIC 6722*
NBFG AUTO LTD   *p 1412*
2501 99TH ST, NORTH BATTLEFORD, SK, S9A 2X6
(306) 445-3300   *SIC 5511*
NCAC REGIONAL TRAINING CENTRE, DIV OF   *p 884*
See ABSOLUTE PALLET & CRATE INC
NCE RESOURCES   *p 940*
See SENTRY INVESTMENTS
NCH CANADA INC   *p 505*
247 ORENDA RD, BRAMPTON, ON, L6T 1E6
(905) 457-5220   *SIC 5169*
NCH CANADA INC   *p 1226*
9001 BOUL DE L'ACADIE BUREAU 800, MONTREAL, QC, H4N 3H5
(514) 733-4572   *SIC 5169*
NCH SERVICES   *p 717*
See NATIONAL CORPORATE HOUSEKEEPING SERVICES INC
NCI CANADA INC   *p 804*
2305 WYECROFT ROAD, OAKVILLE, ON, L6L 6R2
(905) 727-5545   *SIC 5085*
NCIC   *p 927*
See NATIONAL CANCER INSTITUTE OF CANADA
NCIC CLINICAL TRIALS GROUP   *p 631*
10 STUART ST, KINGSTON, ON, K7L 2V5
(613) 533-6430   *SIC 8733*
NCO GROUP   *p 516*
See SERVICES FINANCIERS NCO, INC
NCR CANADA CORP   *p 640*
580 WEBER ST E, KITCHENER, ON, N2H 1G8
SIC 3578
NCR CANADA CORP   *p 1010*
50 NORTHLAND RD, WATERLOO, ON, N2V 1N3
(519) 880-7700   *SIC 5044*
NCR WATERLOO   *p 640*
See NCR CANADA CORP
NCS FLUID HANDLING SYSTEMS INC   *p 163*
280 PORTAGE CLOSE UNIT 530, SHERWOOD PARK, AB, T8H 2R6

(780) 910-7951   *SIC 5084*
NCS INTERNATIONAL CO   *p 201*
70 GLACIER ST, COQUITLAM, BC, V3K 5Y9
(604) 472-6980   *SIC 5063*
NCS INTERNATIONAL CO   *p 735*
7635 TRANMERE DR, MISSISSAUGA, ON, L5S 1L4
(905) 673-0660   *SIC 5063*
NCS MULTISTAGE INC   *p 54*
333 7 AVE SW SUITE 700, CALGARY, AB, T2P 2Z1
(403) 984-7674   *SIC 1389*
NCSG ACQUISITION LTD   *p 1*
53016 HWY 60 UNIT 817, ACHESON, AB, T7X 5A7
(780) 960-6300   *SIC 8732*
NCSG CRANE & HEAVY HAUL SERVICES LTD   *p 1*
28765 ACHESON RD, ACHESON, AB, T7X 6A8
(780) 960-6300   *SIC 7353*
NCSG CRANE & HEAVY HAUL TRANS TECH INC   *p 1*
28765 ACHESON RD, ACHESON, AB, T7X 6A8
(780) 960-6300   *SIC 4212*
NCSG HAULING & RIGGING LTD   *p 160*
261106 WAGON WHEEL CRES SUITE 3, ROCKY VIEW COUNTY, AB, T4A 0E2
(403) 276-9955   *SIC 7389*
NCSG HOLDINGS CANADA LTD   *p 2*
28765 ACHESON RD, ACHESON, AB, T7X 6A8
(780) 960-6300   *SIC 6712*
ND GRAPHICS INC   *p 556*
55 INTERCHANGE WAY UNIT 1, CONCORD, ON, L4K 5W3
(416) 663-6416   *SIC 5084*
NDI   *p 1010*
See NORTHERN DIGITAL INC
NDL CONSTRUCTION LTD   *p 357*
83 SYMINGTON LN S, SPRINGFIELD, MB, R2J 3R8
(204) 255-7300   *SIC 1542*
NDT TECHNOLOGIES INC   *p 1054*
20275 AV CLARK-GRAHAM, BAIE-D'URFE, QC, H9X 3T5
(514) 457-7650   *SIC 3825*
NDX GROWTH & INCOME FUND   *p 955*
121 KING ST W SUITE 2600, TORONTO, ON, M5H 3T9
(416) 681-3966   *SIC 6726*
NEAL BROTHERS INC   *p 853*
50 VOGELL RD UNIT 6, RICHMOND HILL, ON, L4B 3K6
(905) 738-7955   *SIC 5149*
NEAR NORTH CUSTOMS BROKERS INC   *p 487*
20 ELLIOTT AVE, BARRIE, ON, L4N 4V7
(705) 739-0024   *SIC 4731*
NEAR NORTH DISTRICT SCHOOL BOARD   *p 764*
963 AIRPORT RD, NORTH BAY, ON, P1C 1A5
(705) 472-8170   *SIC 8211*
NEARING, ROBERT C. HOLDINGS INC   *p 908*
939 FORT WILLIAM RD SUITE 83, THUNDER BAY, ON, P7B 3A6
(807) 623-1999   *SIC 5015*
NEATFREAK GROUP INC   *p 698*
5320 TIMBERLEA BLVD, MISSISSAUGA, ON, L4W 2S6
(905) 624-6262   *SIC 3089*
NEBB FORMING LTD   *p 556*
41 RITIN LANE, CONCORD, ON, L4K 4W6
(905) 761-6100   *SIC 1799*
NEBRASKA COLLISION CENTRE INC   *p 865*
6511 KINGSTON RD, SCARBOROUGH, ON, M1C 1L5
(416) 282-5794   *SIC 7532*
NEBS   *p 681*

See NEBS BUSINESS PRODUCTS LIMITED
NEBS BUSINESS PRODUCTS LIMITED   *p 681*
330 CRANSTON CRES, MIDLAND, ON, L4R 4V9
(705) 526-4233   *SIC 2761*
NEC CANADA, INC.   *p 36*
7260 12 ST SE UNIT 110, CALGARY, AB, T2H 2S5
(403) 640-6400   *SIC 5065*
NECHAKO BOTTLE DEPOT   *p 249*
See NUMBER EIGHTY-EIGHT HOLDINGS LTD
NECHAKO LUMBER CO. LTD   *p 331*
1241 HWY 16 W, VANDERHOOF, BC, V0J 3A0
(250) 567-4701   *SIC 2421*
NECHAKO NORTHCOAST CONSTRUCTION TERRACE   *p 283*
See 141187 VENTURES LTD
NECHAKO REAL ESTATE LTD   *p 326*
421 PACIFIC ST, VANCOUVER, BC, V6Z 2P5
(604) 685-5951   *SIC 6531*
NEDCO   *p 732*
See REXEL CANADA ELECTRICAL INC
NEDCO, DIV OF   *p 733*
See REXEL CANADA ELECTRICAL INC
NEDLAW ROOFING LIMITED   *p 518*
232 WOOLWICH ST S, BRESLAU, ON, N0B 1M0
(519) 648-2218   *SIC 1761*
NEE   *p 735*
See NATIONAL ENERGY EQUIPMENT INC
NEEDEMPTY   *p 1183*
See CARTOUCHES CERTIFIEES INC
NEEGAN DEVELOPMENT CORPORATION LTD   *p 128*
GD LCD MAIN, FORT MCMURRAY, AB, T9H 3E2
(780) 791-0654   *SIC 1611*
NEELANDS GROUP LIMITED   *p 526*
4131 PALLADIUM WAY, BURLINGTON, ON, L7M 0V9
(905) 332-4555   *SIC 1711*
NEEPAWA HEALTH CENTRE   *p 353*
500 HOSPITAL ST, NEEPAWA, MB, R0J 1H0
(204) 476-2394   *SIC 8062*
NEEPAWA-GLADSTONE COOPERATIVE LIMITED   *p 353*
32 MAIN ST E, NEEPAWA, MB, R0J 1H0
(204) 476-2328   *SIC 5541*
NEFAB INC   *p 841*
211 JAMESON DR, PETERBOROUGH, ON, K9J 6X6
(705) 748-4888   *SIC 2441*
NEFF KITCHEN MANUFACTURERS LIMITED   *p 505*
151 EAST DR, BRAMPTON, ON, L6T 1B5
(905) 791-7770   *SIC 2434*
NEGOCIANT CHASSE & PECHE DUPONT   *p 1264*
See MAGASIN LATULIPPE INC
NEGOCIANTS DE GRAINS OCCIDENTAUX INC   *p 1117*
16766 RTE TRANSCANADIENNE BUREAU 400, KIRKLAND, QC, H9H 4M7
(514) 509-2119   *SIC 5153*
NEGUAC HOME HARDWARE BUILDING CENTRE   *p 410*
See LEGRESLEY, FRANCOIS LTEE/LTD
NEIGHBORHOOD RECYCLING   *p 409*
See RAYAN INVESTMENTS LTD
NEIGHBOURHOOD DOMINION LENDING CENTRES   *p 484*
39 COLLIER ST SUITE 300, BARRIE, ON, L4M 1G5
(705) 720-1001   *SIC 6162*
NEIGHBOURHOOD GROUP COMMUNITY SERVICES, THE   *p 917*

11 COATSWORTH CRES, TORONTO, ON, M4C 5P8
(416) 691-7407   *SIC 8322*
NEIGHBOURHOOD GROUP COMMUNITY SERVICES, THE   *p 917*
3036 DANFORTH AVE, TORONTO, ON, M4C 1N2
(416) 691-7407   *SIC 8322*
NEIL VANDER KRUK HOLDINGS INC   *p 566*
1155 HWY 5, DUNDAS, ON, L9H 5E2
(905) 628-0112   *SIC 5193*
NEILSON INC   *p 1140*
578 CH OLIVIER, LEVIS, QC, G7A 2N6
(418) 831-2141   *SIC 1622*
NEILSON-EBC (7) S.E.N.C.   *p 1140*
578 CH OLIVIER, LEVIS, QC, G7A 2N6
(418) 831-2141   *SIC 1622*
NEILSON-EBC (R3-01-02) S.E.N.C   *p 1140*
578 CH OLIVIER, LEVIS, QC, G7A 2N6
(418) 831-2141   *SIC 1622*
NEKISON ENGINEERING & CONTRACTORS LIMITED   *p 575*
17 SAINT LAWRENCE AVE, ETOBICOKE, ON, M8Z 5T8
(416) 259-4631   *SIC 1711*
NEL-TEKK INDUSTRIAL SPECIALTIES INC   *p 860*
254 TECUMSEH ST, SARNIA, ON, N7T 2K9
(519) 332-6813   *SIC 1742*
NELCO INC   *p 1221*
5510 RUE SAINT-JACQUES, MONTREAL, QC, H4A 2E2
(514) 481-5614   *SIC 5074*
NELCO MECHANICAL LIMITED   *p 640*
77 EDWIN ST, KITCHENER, ON, N2H 4N7
(519) 744-6511   *SIC 1711*
NELLA CUTLERY & FOOD EQUIPMENT INC   *p 698*
1255 FEWSTER DR, MISSISSAUGA, ON, L4W 1A2
(905) 823-1110   *SIC 5046*
NELLA CUTLERY (HAMILTON) INC   *p 608*
2775 BARTON ST E, HAMILTON, ON, L8E 2J8
(905) 561-3456   *SIC 5023*
NELLA CUTLERY (TORONTO) INC   *p 787*
148 NORFINCH DR, NORTH YORK, ON, M3N 1X8
(416) 740-2424   *SIC 5087*
NELLSON   *p 1047*
See ALIMENTS MULTIBAR INC, LES
NELLSON NUTRACEUTIQUE CANADA, INC   *p 1128*
1125 50E AV, LACHINE, QC, H8T 3P3
(514) 380-8383   *SIC 2064*
NELRO SERVICES   *p 95*
See 792259 ALBERTA LTD
NELSON AGGREGATE CO   *p 529*
2433 NO 2 SIDE RD, BURLINGTON, ON, L7P 0G8
(905) 335-5250   *SIC 1442*
NELSON BROS. OILFIELD SERVICES 1997 LTD   *p 82*
5399 JUBILEE AVE, DRAYTON VALLEY, AB, T7A 1R9
(780) 542-5777   *SIC 1389*
NELSON BROS. OILFIELD SERVICES LTD   *p 82*
5399 JUBILEE AVE, DRAYTON VALLEY, AB, T7A 1R9
(780) 542-5777   *SIC 1389*
NELSON BUILDING CENTRE LTD   *p 236*
101 MCDONALD DR, NELSON, BC, V1L 6B9
(250) 352-1919   *SIC 5251*
NELSON CARES SOCIETY   *p 236*
521 VERNON ST, NELSON, BC, V1L 4E9
(250) 352-6011   *SIC 8399*
NELSON CHEVROLET OLDSMOBILE PONTIAC BUICK GMC LTD   *p 1404*
201 1ST AVE W, ASSINIBOIA, SK, S0H 0B0
(306) 642-5995   *SIC 5511*
NELSON CHRYSLER   *p 235*

See *CITY AUTO SERVICE LTD*
NELSON EDUCATION LTD   *p 914*
1120 BIRCHMOUNT RD, TORONTO, ON,
M1K 5G4
(416) 752-9100   *SIC* 2731
NELSON ENVIRONMENTAL REMEDIA-
TION LTD   *p*
2
30541 100 AVE, ACHESON, AB, T7X 6L8
(780) 960-3660   *SIC* 4959
NELSON FORD SALES (2003) INC *p 236*
623 RAILWAY ST, NELSON, BC, V1L 1H5
(250) 352-7202   *SIC* 5511
NELSON GM   *p 1404*
See *NELSON CHEVROLET OLDSMOBILE*
PONTIAC BUICK GMC LTD
NELSON HOME HARDWARE BUILDING
CENTRE   *p 236*
See *NELSON BUILDING CENTRE LTD*
NELSON HOUSE EDUCATION AUTHOR-
ITY, INC   *p*
353
8 BAY RD, NELSON HOUSE, MB, R0B 1A0
(204) 484-2095   *SIC* 8211
NELSON INDUSTRIAL INC   *p 845*
1155 SQUIRES BEACH RD, PICKERING,
ON, L1W 3T9
(905) 428-2240   *SIC* 3499
NELSON LUMBER COMPANY LTD *p 94*
12727 ST ALBERT TRAIL NW, EDMON-
TON, AB, T5L 4H5
(780) 452-9151   *SIC* 5211
NELSON MONUMENTS LTD   *p 418*
23 WESTERN ST, SUSSEX, NB, E4E 1E7
(506) 432-9000   *SIC* 5999
NELSON MOTORS & EQUIPMENT (1976)
LTD   *p 1404*
HWY 334, AVONLEA, SK, S0H 0C0
(306) 868-5000   *SIC* 5999
NELSON RIVER CONSTRUCTION INC *p*
366
101 DAWSON RD N, WINNIPEG, MB, R2J
0S6
(204) 949-8700   *SIC* 1611
NELSON SECONDARY SCHOOL *p 522*
See *HALTON DISTRICT SCHOOL BOARD*
NELSON STEEL   *p 893*
See *SAMUEL, SON & CO., LIMITED*
NELSON, NELSON FOODS INC   *p 881*
15 QUEENSWAY E, SIMCOE, ON, N3Y 4Y2
(519) 428-0101   *SIC* 5461
NELVANA LIMITED   *p 934*
25 DOCKSIDE DR, TORONTO, ON, M5A
0B5
(416) 479-7000   *SIC* 7812
NEMAK OF CANADA CORPORATION *p*
1025
4600 G N BOOTH DR, WINDSOR, ON, N9C
4G8
(519) 250-2500   *SIC* 3334
NEMASKA LITHIUM INC   *p 1259*
450 RUE DE LA GARE-DU-PALAIS, QUE-
BEC, QC, G1K 3X2
(418) 704-6038   *SIC* 1479
NEMASKA LITHIUM SHAWINIGAN TRANS-
FORMATION   *p*
1259
See *NEMASKA LITHIUM INC*
NEMATO CORP   *p 1014*
1605 MCEWEN DR, WHITBY, ON, L1N 7L4
   SIC 3299
NEMCOR INC   *p 534*
501 FRANKLIN BLVD, CAMBRIDGE, ON,
N1R 8G9
(519) 740-0595   *SIC* 5131
NEMETZ, ARNOLD & ASSOCIATES LTD *p*
321
2009 4TH AVE W, VANCOUVER, BC, V6J
1N3
(604) 736-6562   *SIC* 8711
NEMO PRODUCTIONS - CAN, INC *p 181*
8035 GLENWOOD DR, BURNABY, BC, V3N
5C8
   SIC 7829

NEO CAFE   *p 1239*
See *160841 CANADA INC*
NEO PERFORMANCE MATERIALS INC *p*
955
121 KING ST W SUITE 1740, TORONTO,
ON, M5H 3T9
(416) 367-8588   *SIC* 3499
NEO PERFORMANCE MATERIALS ULC *p*
955
121 KING ST W SUITE 1740, TORONTO,
ON, M5H 3T9
(416) 367-8588   *SIC* 2819
NEOCHEM (DIV OF)   *p 140*
See *ENERCON WATER TREATMENT LTD*
NEOCON INTERNATIONAL   *p 446*
See *EXCO TECHNOLOGIES LIMITED*
NEOLECT INC   *p 1073*
104 BOUL MONTCALM N, CANDIAC, QC,
J5R 3L8
(514) 382-1550   *SIC* 1731
NEOPHARM LABS INC   *p 1059*
865 BOUL MICHELE-BOHEC, BLAINVILLE,
QC, J7C 5J6
(450) 435-8864   *SIC* 8734
NEOPOST CANADA LIMITED   *p 673*
150 STEELCASE RD W, MARKHAM, ON,
L3R 3J9
(905) 475-3722   *SIC* 5044
NEOS CANADA SERVICES ULC *p 307*
355 BURRARD ST SUITE 1800, VANCOU-
VER, BC, V6C 2G8
(604) 682-7737   *SIC* 1382
NEOVA TECHNOLOGIES INC   *p 177*
31212 PEARDONVILLE RD, ABBOTS-
FORD, BC, V2T 6K8
(604) 504-0695   *SIC* 2899
NEPCO   *p 1168*
See *ALIMENTATION TRACY INC*
NEPCO INC   *p 1172*
6569 AV PAPINEAU, MONTREAL, QC, H2G
2X3
(514) 729-0404   *SIC* 5144
NEPEAN HIGH SCHOOL   *p 829*
See   *OTTAWA-CARLETON   DISTRICT*
SCHOOL BOARD
NEPTEC DESIGN GROUP LTD   *p 625*
302 LEGGET DR UNIT 202, KANATA, ON,
K2K 1Y5
(613) 599-7602   *SIC* 8711
NEPTRONIC   *p 1326*
See *NATIONAL ENVIRONMENTAL PROD-*
UCTS LTD
NEPTUNE BIOTECHNOLOGIES *p 1087*
See   *NEPTUNE   TECHNOLOGIES   &*
BIORESSOURCES INC
NEPTUNE BULK TERMINALS (CANADA)
LTD   *p 239*
1001 LOW LEVEL RD, NORTH VANCOU-
VER, BC, V7L 1A7
(604) 985-7461   *SIC* 4491
NEPTUNE INTERNATIONAL   *p 1313*
See *PRODUITS NEPTUNE INC, LES*
NEPTUNE TECHNOLOGIES & BIORES-
SOURCES INC   *p*
1087
545 PROM DU CENTROPOLIS SUITE 100,
COTE SAINT-LUC, QC, H7T 0A3
(450) 687-2262   *SIC* 8731
NEPTUNE   TECHNOLOGY   GROUP
(CANADA) LIMITED   *p 725*
7275 WEST CREDIT AVE, MISSISSAUGA,
ON, L5N 5M9
(905) 858-4211   *SIC* 3824
NEPTUNUS YACHTS INTERNATIONAL INC
p 883
8 KEEFER RD, ST CATHARINES, ON, L2M
7N9
(905) 937-3737   *SIC* 3731
NERIUM BIOTECHNOLOGY, INC *p 965*
220 BAY ST UNIT 500, TORONTO, ON, M5J
2W4
(416) 862-7330   *SIC* 8731
NERO BIANCO   *p 1378*
See *9264-6231 QUEBEC INC*

NERO BIANCO GROUP   *p 1378*
See *2169-5762 QUEBEC INC*
NERON INC   *p 1218*
550 AV BEAUMONT BUREAU 500, MON-
TREAL, QC, H3N 1V1
(514) 759-8672   *SIC* 3961
NESA   *p 875*
See *683949 ONTARIO LIMITED*
NESBITT BURNS   *p 44*
See *BMO NESBITT BURNS INC*
NESEL FAST FREIGHT INCORPORATED *p*
495
20 HOLLAND DR, BOLTON, ON, L7E 1G6
(905) 951-7770   *SIC* 4213
NESEL FAST FREIGHT INCORPORATED *p*
901
19216 HAY RD, SUMMERSTOWN, ON,
K0C 2E0
   SIC 4213
NESPRESSO   *p 772*
See *NESTLE CANADA INC*
NESPRESSO CANADA   *p 1214*
See *NESTLE CANADA INC*
NESSCAP ENERGY INC   *p 955*
40 KING ST W SUITE 5800, TORONTO,
ON, M5H 3S1
(416) 596-2127   *SIC* 3675
NESTERS MARKET LTD   *p 343*
7019 NESTERS RD, WHISTLER, BC, V8E
0X1
(604) 932-3545   *SIC* 5411
NESTLE CANADA INC   *p 137*
5128 54 ST, INNISFAIL, AB, T4G 1S1
(403) 227-3777   *SIC* 2047
NESTLE CANADA INC   *p 215*
66700 OTHELLO RD, HOPE, BC, V0X 1L1
(604) 860-4888   *SIC* 5149
NESTLE CANADA INC   *p 544*
171 MAIN ST N, CHESTERVILLE, ON, K0C
1H0
(613) 448-2338   *SIC* 2095
NESTLE CANADA INC   *p 586*
65 CARRIER DR, ETOBICOKE, ON, M9W
5V9
(416) 675-1300   *SIC* 5149
NESTLE CANADA INC   *p 662*
980 WILTON GROVE RD, LONDON, ON,
N6N 1C7
(519) 686-0182   *SIC* 2023
NESTLE CANADA INC   *p 714*
2500 ROYAL WINDSOR DR, MISSIS-
SAUGA, ON, L5J 1K8
(905) 822-1611   *SIC* 2047
NESTLE CANADA INC   *p 772*
25 SHEPPARD AVE W SUITE 1700,
NORTH YORK, ON, M2N 6S6
(416) 512-9000   *SIC* 2095
NESTLE CANADA INC   *p 849*
101 BROCK RD S, PUSLINCH, ON, N0B
2J0
(519) 763-9462   *SIC* 5149
NESTLE CANADA INC   *p 995*
72 STERLING RD, TORONTO, ON, M6R
2B6
(416) 535-2181   *SIC* 2064
NESTLE CANADA INC   *p 999*
1 DOUGLAS RD, TRENTON, ON, K8V 5S7
(613) 394-4712   *SIC* 2037
NESTLE CANADA INC   *p 1214*
2060 RUE DE LA MONTAGNE BUREAU
304, MONTREAL, QC, H3G 1Z7
(514) 350-5754   *SIC* 3634
NESTLE FOOD SERVICES, DIV OF *p 586*
See *NESTLE CANADA INC*
NESTLE PURINA PET CARE DIV OF *p 137*
See *NESTLE CANADA INC*
NESTLE PURINA PET CARE DIV OF *p 714*
See *NESTLE CANADA INC*
NESTLE WATERS CANADA DIV *p 215*
See *NESTLE CANADA INC*
NESTLE WATERS CANADA DIV *p 849*
See *NESTLE CANADA INC*
NET ELECTRIC LIMITED   *p 855*
120 NEWKIRK RD UNIT 8, RICHMOND

HILL, ON, L4C 9S7
(905) 737-7760   *SIC* 1731
NET SAFETY MONITORING INC *p 9*
2721 HOPEWELL PL NE, CALGARY, AB,
T1Y 7J7
(403) 219-0688   *SIC* 3829
NET-LINX AMERICAS, INC   *p 97*
12431 STONY PLAIN RD NW SUITE 200,
EDMONTON, AB, T5N 3N3
   SIC 2741
NETCHEM INC   *p 514*
35 ROY BLVD, BRANTFORD, ON, N3R 7K1
(519) 751-4700   *SIC* 5169
NETGOVERN INC   *p 1211*
180 RUE PEEL BUREAU 333, MONTREAL,
QC, H3C 2G7
(514) 392-9220   *SIC* 7372
NETLEY COLONY LTD   *p 354*
897 HENRY RD, PETERSFIELD, MB, R0C
2L0
(204) 738-2828   *SIC* 0213
NETLEY MILL WORK   *p 354*
See *NETLEY COLONY LTD*
NETMAIL   *p 1211*
See *NETGOVERN INC*
NETNATION COMMUNICATIONS INC *p 307*
550 BURRARD ST SUITE 200, VANCOU-
VER, BC, V6C 2B5
(604) 688-8946   *SIC* 4899
NETOOK CONSTRUCTION LTD *p 151*
GD STN MAIN, OLDS, AB, T4H 1R4
(403) 556-2166   *SIC* 1389
NETSET COMMUNICATION   *p 347*
See *XPLORNET COMMUNICATIONS INC*
NETSET COMMUNICATIONS   *p 347*
See *XPLORNET COMMUNICATIONS INC*
NETSUITE INC   *p 698*
5800 EXPLORER DR SUITE 100, MISSIS-
SAUGA, ON, L4W 5K9
(905) 219-8534   *SIC* 5734
NETTLEWOODS INC   *p 717*
4060 RIDGEWAY DR UNIT 16, MISSIS-
SAUGA, ON, L5L 5X9
(905) 608-1919   *SIC* 2844
NETVERSITY SOLUTIONS   *p 756*
See *NUVU CORPORATION*
NETWORK MECHANICAL INC   *p 556*
73 CORSTATE AVE UNIT 1, CONCORD,
ON, L4K 4Y2
(905) 761-1417   *SIC* 1711
NETWORK MESSENGER INC   *p 995*
34 MAGWOOD CRT, TORONTO, ON, M6S
2M5
(416) 777-2278   *SIC* 7389
NETWORK SOUTH ENTERPRISES *p 364*
188 GOULET ST, WINNIPEG, MB, R2H 0R8
(204) 474-1959   *SIC* 7389
NEUCEL SPECIALTY CELLULOSE LTD *p*
245
300 MARINE DRIVE, PORT ALICE, BC,
V0N 2N0
(250) 284-3331   *SIC* 3081
NEUCEL SPECIALTY CELLULOSE LTD *p*
263
11331 COPPERSMITH WAY SUITE 305,
RICHMOND, BC, V7A 5J9
   SIC 3081
NEUDORF COLONY EQUIPMENT CO LTD
p 81
GD, CROSSFIELD, AB, T0M 0S0
(403) 946-4801   *SIC* 0191
NEUF ARCHITECTS   *p 1204*
See *GESTION NEUF ASSOCIES INC*
NEUFELD, C. M. PHARMACY LTD *p 41*
1632 14 AVE NW UNIT 1790, CALGARY,
AB, T2N 1M7
(403) 289-6761   *SIC* 5912
NEUMAN HOLDING CANADA INC *p 1372*
2205 RUE ROY, SHERBROOKE, QC, J1K
1B8
(819) 563-3589   *SIC* 3341
NEUMAN, THOMAS J LIMITED *p 836*
6421 PALMER RD, PALMER RAPIDS, ON,
K0J 2E0

(613) 758-2555   *SIC* 5031
NEUMANN CANADA   p 1091
See SENNHEISER (CANADA) INC
NEURORX RESEARCH INC   p 1186
3575 AV DU PARC BUREAU 5322, MON-TREAL, QC, H2X 3P9
(514) 906-0062   *SIC* 8731
NEUTRONICS COMPONENTS LTD   p 751
245 MENTEN PL SUITE 301, NEPEAN, ON, K2H 9E8
(613) 599-1263   *SIC* 7389
NEVADA ENERGY METALS INC   p 307
789 PENDER ST W SUITE 1220, VANCOU-VER, BC, V6C 1H2
(604) 428-5690   *SIC* 1479
NEVSUN RESOURCES LTD   p 315
1066 HASTINGS ST W SUITE 1750, VAN-COUVER, BC, V6E 3X1
(604) 623-4700   *SIC* 1081
NEW AGE MARKETING & BRAND MAN-AGEMENT INC   p 36
7210H 5 ST SE, CALGARY, AB, T2H 2L9
(403) 212-1055   *SIC* 5149
NEW AGE ROBOTICS AND CONTROLS INC   p 483
515 WAYDOM DR, AYR, ON, N0B 1E0
(519) 621-3333   *SIC* 5084
NEW AGE SPORTS INC   p 290
8206 ONTARIO ST SUITE 200, VANCOU-VER, BC, V5X 3E3
(604) 324-9943   *SIC* 5941
NEW B INNOVATION CANADA   p 193
See NEW B INNOVATION LIMITED
NEW B INNOVATION LIMITED   p 193
8508 GLENLYON PKY UNIT 168, BURN-ABY, BC, V5J 0B6
(604) 421-7308   *SIC* 8731
NEW BALANCE TORONTO   p 925
See 1404136 ONTARIO LIMITED
NEW BRUNSWICK COMMUNITY COL-LEGE   p 398
See PROVINCE OF NEW BRUNSWICK
NEW BRUNSWICK COMMUNITY COL-LEGE   p 405
See PROVINCE OF NEW BRUNSWICK
NEW BRUNSWICK COMMUNITY COL-LEGE (NBCC)   p 401
284 SMYTHE ST, FREDERICTON, NB, E3B 3C9
(888) 796-6222   *SIC* 8221
NEW BRUNSWICK EMS FLEET CENTRE   p 406
See AMBULANCE NEW BRUNSWICK INC
NEW BRUNSWICK EXTRA MURAL PRO-GRAM   p 401
See REGIONAL HEALTH AUTHORITY NB
NEW BRUNSWICK LIQUOR CORPORA-TION   p 401
170 WILSEY RD, FREDERICTON, NB, E3B 5J1
(506) 452-6826   *SIC* 5921
NEW BRUNSWICK MUNICIPAL FINANCE CORPORATION   p 401
670 KING ST RM 376, FREDERICTON, NB, E3B 1G1
(506) 453-2515   *SIC* 6111
NEW BRUNSWICK OIL BURNER TECH   p 408
555 EDINBURGH DR SUITE 4, MONCTON, NB, E1E 4E3
SIC 4924
NEW BRUNSWICK POWER CORPORA-TION   p 399
239 GILBERT ST, FREDERICTON, NB, E3A 0J6
(506) 458-4308   *SIC* 4911
NEW BRUNSWICK POWER CORPORA-

TION   p 401
515 KING ST, FREDERICTON, NB, E3B 1E7
(506) 458-4444   *SIC* 4911
NEW BRUNSWICK POWER CORPORA-TION   p 404
451 ROUTE 105, KESWICK RIDGE, NB, E6L 1B2
(506) 462-3800   *SIC* 4911
NEW BRUNSWICK SOUTHERN RAILWAY COMPANY LIMITED   p 416
11 GIFFORD RD, SAINT JOHN, NB, E2M 4X8
(506) 632-6314   *SIC* 4011
NEW BRUNSWICK WIRE FENCE COM-PANY LIMITED   p 409
80 HENRI DUNANT ST, MONCTON, NB, E1E 1E6
(506) 857-8141   *SIC* 5039
NEW CANADIANS LUMBER & BUILDING SUPPLIES   p 989
See HENGAB INVESTMENTS LIMITED
NEW CASTLE FARM LTD   p 644
414 MERSEA ROAD 3, LEAMINGTON, ON, N8H 3V5
(519) 322-5411   *SIC* 0191
NEW CIRCUITS LIMITED   p 673
399 DENISON ST, MARKHAM, ON, L3R 1B7
(905) 474-9227   *SIC* 3672
NEW CITY SERVICES GROUP INC.   p 186
4170 STILL CREEK DR SUITE 200, BURN-ABY, BC, V5C 6C6
(604) 473-7769   *SIC* 1542
NEW DAWN ENTERPRISES LIMITED   p 467
106 TOWNSEND ST, SYDNEY, NS, B1P 5E1
(902) 539-9560   *SIC* 8399
NEW DEMOCRATIC PARTY OF B.C.   p 186
4180 LOUGHEED HWY UNIT 301, BURN-ABY, BC, V5C 6A7
(604) 430-8600   *SIC* 8651
NEW DIRECTIONS AROMATICS INC   p 741
6781 COLUMBUS RD, MISSISSAUGA, ON, L5T 2G9
(905) 362-1915   *SIC* 5122
NEW ELECTRIC ENTERPRISES INC   p 806
3185 DUNDAS ST W, OAKVILLE, ON, L6M 4J4
(905) 827-2555   *SIC* 1731
NEW FLYER INDUSTRIES CANADA ULC   p 362
711 KERNAGHAN AVE SUITE 3, WIN-NIPEG, MB, R2C 3T4
(204) 224-1251   *SIC* 3711
NEW FLYER INDUSTRIES CANADA ULC   p 366
25 DE BAETS ST, WINNIPEG, MB, R2J 4G5
(204) 982-8400   *SIC* 3711
NEW FLYER PARTS & PUBLICATIONS   p 366
See NEW FLYER INDUSTRIES CANADA ULC
NEW FRONTIERS SCHOOL BOARD   p 1076
See COMMISSION SCOLAIRE NEW FRONTIER
NEW GLASGOW LOBSTER SUPPERS   p 1041
See NEW GLASGOW RECREATION CEN-TRE (1980) INC
NEW GLASGOW RECREATION CENTRE (1980) INC   p 1041
604 RTE 258 RR 3, HUNTER RIVER, PE, C0A 1N0
(902) 964-2870   *SIC* 5812
NEW GOLD INC   p 965
181 BAY ST SUITE 3320, TORONTO, ON, M5J 2T3
(416) 324-6000   *SIC* 1481
NEW GUINEA GOLD CORPORATION   p 307
595 HOWE ST SUITE 900, VANCOUVER,

BC, V6C 2T5
(604) 689-1515   *SIC* 1081
NEW HAVEN COLONY FARMS LTD   p 345
82080 RD 1 E, ARGYLE, MB, R0C 0B0
(204) 467-8790   *SIC* 8661
NEW HOMEMANDE KOSHER BAKERY, THE   p 1217
See 176061 CANADA INC
NEW HOPE TRANSPORT LTD   p 353
170 AGRI PARK RD, OAK BLUFF, MB, R4G 0A5
SIC 4213
NEW HORIZON CO-OPERATIVE LTD   p 132
9831 100 AVE, GRANDE PRAIRIE, AB, T8V 0T7
(780) 539-6111   *SIC* 5411
NEW HORIZON SYSTEM SOLUTIONS INC   p 575
800 KIPLING AVE SUITE 8, ETOBICOKE, ON, M8Z 5G5
(416) 207-6800   *SIC* 8741
NEW HORIZON SYSTEM SOLUTIONS INC   p 946
700 UNIVERSITY AVE SUITE 200, TORONTO, ON, M5G 1X6
SIC 7374
NEW HORIZONS CAR & TRUCK RENTALS LTD   p 795
720 ARROW RD, NORTH YORK, ON, M9M 2M1
(416) 744-0123   *SIC* 4212
NEW HORIZONS TOWER   p 990
See DOVERCOURT BAPTIST FOUNDA-TION
NEW LISKEARD KENWORTH   p 913
See TIMMINS KENWORTH LTD
NEW MARKET GROUP   p 754
See 1221271 ONTARIO INC
NEW MARKET HONDA   p 756
See NEW MARKET INVESTMENT LIM-ITED
NEW MARKET INVESTMENT LIMITED   p 756
75 MULOCK DR, NEWMARKET, ON, L3Y 8V2
(416) 798-7854   *SIC* 5511
NEW MARKET MEAT PACKERS LTD   p 756
15452 WARDEN AVE, NEWMARKET, ON, L3Y 4W1
(905) 836-7001   *SIC* 5147
NEW MILLENIUM TIRE CENTRE   p 508
See 1519950 ONTARIO INC
NEW ORLEANS PIZZA   p 870
See 2281445 ONTARIO INC
NEW PACIFIC METALS CORP   p 307
200 GRANVILLE ST SUITE 1378, VAN-COUVER, BC, V6C 1S4
(604) 633-1368   *SIC* 1021
NEW PALACE CABARET LIMITED, THE   p 453
1721 BRUNSWICK ST, HALIFAX, NS, B3J 2G4
(902) 420-0015   *SIC* 5813
NEW PL, THE   p 659
See BELL MEDIA INC
NEW ROCKPORT HUTTERIAN BRETHREN   p 148
GD, NEW DAYTON, AB, T0K 1P0
(403) 733-2122   *SIC* 0191
NEW ROOTS HERBAL INC   p 1395
3405 RUE F.-X.-TESSIER, VAUDREUIL-DORION, QC, J7V 5V5
(800) 268-9486   *SIC* 2023
NEW ROSEDALE COLONY FARMS LTD   p 355
GD LCD MAIN, PORTAGE LA PRAIRIE, MB, R1N 3B7
(204) 252-2727   *SIC* 0191
NEW ROSEDALE FEED MILL   p 355
See NEW ROSEDALE COLONY FARMS LTD
NEW STAR REAL ESTATE LTD   p 871
1450 MIDLAND AVE UNIT 206, SCARBOR-OUGH, ON, M1P 4Z8

(416) 288-0800   *SIC* 6531
NEW TOWN BAKERY & RESTAURANT   p 296
See S & K NG ENTERPRISES LTD
NEW UNITED GODERICH INC   p 621
403 CANADA AVE, HURON PARK, ON, N0M 1Y0
(519) 228-6052   *SIC* 4581
NEW VENTURES REALTY INC   p 732
20 KINGSBRIDGE GARDEN CIR SUITE 2004, MISSISSAUGA, ON, L5R 3K7
(905) 507-3030   *SIC* 6513
NEW VILLAGE RETIREMENT HOME   p 894
See THOMAS HEALTH CARE CORPORA-TION, THE
NEW VISTA SOCIETY, THE   p 187
7550 ROSEWOOD ST SUITE 235, BURN-ABY, BC, V5E 3Z3
(604) 521-7764   *SIC* 8361
NEW WATERFORD HOMECARE SERVICE SOCIETY   p 464
3390 PLUMMER AVE, NEW WATERFORD, NS, B1H 1Y9
(902) 862-7554   *SIC* 8399
NEW WAVE CRUISE SHIP CENTRES   p 282
15957 84 AVE SUITE 102, SURREY, BC, V4N 0W7
(604) 572-9500   *SIC* 4724
NEW WAVE ENERGY SERVICES LTD   p 54
140 4 AVE SW SUITE 1955, CALGARY, AB, T2P 3N3
(403) 453-2925   *SIC* 1389
NEW WEST ENERGY SERVICES INC   p 54
435 4 AVE SW SUITE 500, CALGARY, AB, T2P 3A8
(403) 984-9798   *SIC* 1389
NEW WEST FREIGHTLINER INC   p 12
3444 44 AVE SE, CALGARY, AB, T2B 3J9
(403) 569-4800   *SIC* 5511
NEW WEST METALS INC   p 375
13 HIGGINS AVE, WINNIPEG, MB, R3B 0A3
(204) 949-0967   *SIC* 5051
NEW WESTMINSTER BOAT HOUSE   p 238
See SPECTRA GROUP OF GREAT RESTAURANTS INC, THE
NEW WESTMINSTER SCHOOL DISTRICT #40   p 237
See BOARD OF SCHOOL TRUSTEES OF SCHOOL DISTRICT #40 (NEW WESTMIN-STER), THE
NEW WORLD FRICTION CORP   p 534
539 COLLIER MACMILLAN DR UNIT B, CAMBRIDGE, ON, N1R 7P3
(519) 623-0011   *SIC* 3714
NEW WORLD HOTELS LTD   p 315
1133 HASTINGS ST W, VANCOUVER, BC, V6E 3T3
(604) 689-9211   *SIC* 7011
NEW WORLD TECHNOLOGIES INCORPO-RATED   p 177
30580 PROGRESSIVE WAY, ABBOTS-FORD, BC, V2T 6Z2
(604) 852-0405   *SIC* 5251
NEW ZEALAND AND AUSTRALIAN LAMB COMPANY LIMITED, THE   p 577
10 SHORNCLIFFE RD UNIT 1, ETOBI-COKE, ON, M9B 3S3
(416) 231-5262   *SIC* 5147
NEW-LINE HOSE & FITTINGS   p 282
See NEW-LINE PRODUCTS LTD
NEW-LINE PRODUCTS LTD   p 282
9415 189 ST UNIT 1, SURREY, BC, V4N 5L8
(604) 455-5400   *SIC* 5085
NEW-WAY IRRIGATION LTD   p 169
6003 54 AVE, TABER, AB, T1G 1X4
(403) 223-3591   *SIC* 5083
NEWAD MEDIA INC   p 1184
4200 BOUL SAINT-LAURENT BUREAU 1440, MONTREAL, QC, H2W 2R2
(514) 278-3222   *SIC* 7312
NEWCAP INC   p 104

▲ Public Company   ■ Public Company Family Member   **HQ** Headquarters   **BR** Branch   **SL** Single Location

2394 WEST EDMONTON MALL, EDMONTON, AB, T5T 4M2

(780) 432-3165   SIC 4832

NEWCAP INC   p 104
8882 170 ST NW SUITE 2394, EDMONTON, AB, T5T 4M2

(780) 451-8097   SIC 4832

NEWCAP INC   p 447
8 BASINVIEW DR, DARTMOUTH, NS, B3B 1G4

(902) 468-7557   SIC 4832

NEWCAP RADIO   p 447
See NEWCAP INC

NEWCAP RADIO ALBERTA   p 104
See NEWCAP INC

NEWCAP RADIO OTTAWA   p 749
6 ANTARES DR SUITE 100, NEPEAN, ON, K2E 8A9

(613) 723-8990   SIC 4832

NEWCASTLE FOODLAND INC   p 753
131 KING AVE E, NEWCASTLE, ON, L1B 1H3

(905) 987-4627   SIC 5411

NEWCASTLE GOLD LTD   p 307
800 PENDER ST W SUITE 730, VANCOUVER, BC, V6C 2V6

(250) 925-2713   SIC 1041

NEWCO CONSTRUCTION LTD   p 409
50 ROONEY CRES, MONCTON, NB, E1E 4M3

(506) 857-8710   SIC 1542

NEWCO GRAIN LTD   p 80
GD, COALDALE, AB, T1M 1K8

(403) 345-3335   SIC 5153

NEWCOM MEDIA INC   p 734
See ACTION TRAILER SALES INC

NEWCOM MEDIA INC   p 996
5353 DUNDAS ST W SUITE 400, TORONTO, ON, M9B 6H8

(416) 614-2200   SIC 2721

NEWCON INTERNATIONAL LTD   p 765
105 SPARKS AVE, NORTH YORK, ON, M2H 2S5

(416) 663-6963   SIC 5049

NEWCON OPTIK   p 765
See NEWCON INTERNATIONAL LTD

NEWDALE HOLDINGS INC   p 326
1335 HOWE ST, VANCOUVER, BC, V6Z 1R7

SIC 6719

NEWDOCK   p 433
See ST. JOHN'S DOCKYARD LIMITED

NEWELL BRANDS CANADA ULC   p 801
586 ARGUS RD SUITE 400, OAKVILLE, ON, L6J 3J3

(866) 595-0525   SIC 5099

NEWFORCE ENERGY SERVICES LTD p 82
5710 - 57 AVE, DRAYTON VALLEY, AB, T7A 1S7

(780) 514-7882   SIC 1623

NEWFOUND TRADING LIMITED   p 447
11 MORRIS DR SUITE 206, DARTMOUTH, NS, B3B 1M2

(902) 468-7100   SIC 4731

NEWFOUNDLAND & LABRADOR CENTRE FOR HEALTH INFORMATION   p 430
70 O'LEARY AVE, ST. JOHN'S, NL, A1B 2C7

(709) 752-6000   SIC 8011

NEWFOUNDLAND & LABRADOR CREDIT UNION LIMITED   p 432
240 WATER ST, ST. JOHN'S, NL, A1C 1B7

(709) 722-5824   SIC 6062

NEWFOUNDLAND & LABRADOR HYDRO p 424
1 THERMAL PLANT RD, HOLYROOD, NL, A0A 2R0

(709) 229-7441   SIC 4911

NEWFOUNDLAND & LABRADOR HYDRO p 425
1 KEMP BOGGY ROAD, MILLTOWN, NL, A0H 1W0

(709) 882-2551   SIC 4911

NEWFOUNDLAND & LABRADOR HYDRO p

430
500 COLUMBUS DR, ST. JOHN'S, NL, A1B 4K7

(709) 737-1400   SIC 4911

NEWFOUNDLAND & LABRADOR LEGAL AID COMMISSION   p 432
251 EMPIRE AVE SUITE 200, ST. JOHN'S, NL, A1C 3H9

(709) 753-7860   SIC 8111

NEWFOUNDLAND & LABRADOR SAFETY COUNCIL INC   p 426
3 MOFFATT RD, MOUNT PEARL, NL, A1N 5B9

(709) 754-0210   SIC 8748

NEWFOUNDLAND & LABRADOR YOUTH CENTRE   p 434
See PROVINCE OF NEWFOUNDLAND & LABRADOR

NEWFOUNDLAND AND LABRADOR ENGLISH SCHOOL DISTRICT   p 423
55 FRASER RD, GANDER, NL, A1V 1K8

(709) 256-8531   SIC 8211

NEWFOUNDLAND AND LABRADOR HOUSING CORPORATION   p 433
2 CANADA DR, ST. JOHN'S, NL, A1E 0A1

(709) 724-3000   SIC 6531

NEWFOUNDLAND CAPITAL CORPORATION LIMITED   p
430
391 KENMOUNT RD, ST. JOHN'S, NL, A1B 3P9

(709) 726-5590   SIC 4832

NEWFOUNDLAND CAPITAL CORPORATION LIMITED   p
447
8 BASINVIEW DR, DARTMOUTH, NS, B3B 1G4

(902) 468-7557   SIC 4832

NEWFOUNDLAND EGGS, INC   p 422
1 ROACHES LINE, CLARKES BEACH, NL, A0A 1W0

(709) 528-4595   SIC 5144

NEWFOUNDLAND HVAC LIMITED   p 426
16 THOMAS BYRNE DR, MOUNT PEARL, NL, A1N 0E1

(709) 738-7700   SIC 1711

NEWFOUNDLAND LABRADOR HOUSING p 433
See NEWFOUNDLAND AND LABRADOR HOUSING CORPORATION

NEWFOUNDLAND LABRADOR LIQUOR CORPORATION   p 430
90 KENMOUNT RD, ST. JOHN'S, NL, A1B 3R1

(709) 724-1100   SIC 5921

NEWFOUNDLAND MULTI-FOODS LIMITED p 424
43 ASPEN RD, HAPPY VALLEY-GOOSE BAY, NL, A0P 1C0

(709) 896-3543   SIC 5142

NEWFOUNDLAND PERSONNEL INC p 432
3 QUEEN ST, ST. JOHN'S, NL, A1C 4K2

(709) 579-3400   SIC 7363

NEWFOUNDLAND POWER INC   p 430
55 KENMOUNT RD, ST. JOHN'S, NL, A1B 3P8

(709) 737-5600   SIC 4911

NEWFOUNDLAND SALES & MARKETING INC   p 428
18 ARGYLE ST UNIT 201, ST. JOHN'S, NL, A1A 1V3

(709) 722-6706   SIC 5141

NEWGEN RESTAURANT SERVICES INC p
586
15 CARLSON CRT, ETOBICOKE, ON, M9W 6A2

(416) 675-8818   SIC 5812

NEWGEN RESTAURANT SERVICES INC p
732
5975 MAVIS RD, MISSISSAUGA, ON, L5R 3T7

(905) 502-8555   SIC 5812

NEWGEN RESTAURANT SERVICES INC p

780
895 DON MILLS RD SUITE 208, NORTH YORK, ON, M3C 1W3

(416) 751-8731   SIC 5812

NEWGEN RESTAURANT SERVICES INC p
821
61 YORK ST, OTTAWA, ON, K1N 5T2

(613) 241-6525   SIC 5812

NEWGIOCO GROUP INC   p 955
130 ADELAIDE ST W SUITE 701, TORONTO, ON, M5H 2K4

(647) 229-0136   SIC 7999

NEWLANDS GOLF & COUNTRY CLUB LTD p 228
21025 48 AVE, LANGLEY, BC, V3A 3M3

(604) 534-3205   SIC 7299

NEWLY WEDS FOODS   p 121
See NEWLY WEDS FOODS CO.

NEWLY WEDS FOODS CO.   p 121
9110 23 AVE NW, EDMONTON, AB, T6N 1H9

(780) 414-9500   SIC 2099

NEWLY WEDS FOODS CO.   p 741
450 SUPERIOR BLVD, MISSISSAUGA, ON, L5T 2R9

(905) 670-7776   SIC 2099

NEWLY WEDS FOODS CO.   p 1066
1381 RUE AMPERE, BOUCHERVILLE, QC, J4B 5Z5

(450) 641-2200   SIC 2099

NEWMAN BROS. LIMITED   p 886
72 WELLAND AVE, ST CATHARINES, ON, L2R 2M9

(905) 641-8111   SIC 1541

NEWMAN'S VALVE LIMITED   p 484
92 DAVIDSON ST, BARRIE, ON, L4M 3R8

(705) 737-4216   SIC 5085

NEWMAN, OLIVER & MCCARTEN INSURANCE BROKERS LTD   p
539
35 FRONT ST N, CAMPBELLFORD, ON, K0L 1L0

SIC 6411

NEWMAR WINDOW MANUFACTURING INC   p 686
7630 AIRPORT RD, MISSISSAUGA, ON, L4T 4G6

(905) 672-1233   SIC 3089

NEWMARK CONSTRUCTION INC   p 225
9525 201 ST UNIT 219, LANGLEY, BC, V1M 4A5

(604) 371-3963   SIC 1521

NEWMARK GROUP   p 225
See NEWMARK CONSTRUCTION INC

NEWMARK GROUP INC   p 226
20780 WILLOUGHBY TOWN CENTRE DR UNIT 300, LANGLEY, BC, V2Y 0M7

(604) 371-3963   SIC 1531

NEWMARK KNIGHT FRANK - DEVENCORE   p
1203
See DEVENCORE LTEE

NEWMARKET GROUP   p 754
See 87029 CANADA LTD

NEWMARKET HEALTH CENTRE, THE   p
756
See REGIONAL MUNICIPALITY OF YORK, THE

NEWMARKET HIGH SCHOOL   p 757
See YORK REGION DISTRICT SCHOOL BOARD

NEWMARKET HYDRO HOLDINGS INC   p
756
590 STEVEN CRT, NEWMARKET, ON, L3Y 6Z2

(905) 895-2309   SIC 4911

NEWMARKET HYUNDAI   p 754
See 953866 ONTARIO LIMITED

NEWMARKET TOYOTA   p 754
See AUTO GROUP NEWMARKET INC

NEWMARKET-TAY POWER DISTRIBUTION LTD   p 756
590 STEVEN CRT, NEWMARKET, ON, L3Y 6Z2

(905) 895-2309   SIC 4911

NEWPARK CANADA INC   p 54
635 6 AVE SW SUITE 300, CALGARY, AB, T2P 0T5

(403) 266-7383   SIC 1381

NEWPARK CANADA INVESTMENTS LIMITED PARTNERSHIP   p
54
635 6 AVE SW SUITE 300, CALGARY, AB, T2P 0T5

(403) 266-7383   SIC 6712

NEWPARK MAT & INTEGRATED SERVICES, DIV OF   p
54
See NEWPARK CANADA INC

NEWPORT CUSTOM METAL FABRICATIONS INC   p
449
114 LANCASTER CRES LOT 208, DEBERT, NS, B0M 1G0

(902) 662-3840   SIC 3585

NEWPORT HARBOUR CARE CENTRE p 77
See SUMMIT CARE CORPORATION LTD

NEWPORT PARTNERS HOLDINGS LP   p
982
469 KING ST W, TORONTO, ON, M5V 3M4

(416) 867-7555   SIC 6722

NEWPORT PRIVATE WEALTH INC   p 982
469 KING ST W SUITE C, TORONTO, ON, M5V 1K4

(416) 867-7555   SIC 6282

NEWPORT REALTY LTD   p 335
1144 FORT ST, VICTORIA, BC, V8V 3K8

(250) 385-2033   SIC 6531

NEWS 1130   p 293
See CKWX NEWS

NEWS MARKETING CANADA CORP p 987
100 KING ST W SUITE 7000, TORONTO, ON, M5X 1A4

(416) 775-3000   SIC 8743

NEWS THE CLASSIFIED   p 272
5450 152 ST, SURREY, BC, V3S 5J9

(604) 575-5555   SIC 5192

NEWS-GLOBAL SOURCING COMPANY p
698
1109 BRITANNIA RD E, MISSISSAUGA, ON, L4W 3X1

(905) 564-2100   SIC 5191

NEWSCO INTERNATIONAL ENERGY SERVICES INC   p
17
4855 102 AVE SE SUITE 11, CALGARY, AB, T2C 2X7

(403) 243-2331   SIC 1381

NEWSWEST INC   p 36
5716 BURBANK RD SE, CALGARY, AB, T2H 1Z4

(403) 253-8856   SIC 5192

NEWTERRA GROUP LTD   p 519
1291 CALIFORNIA AVE, BROCKVILLE, ON, K6V 7N5

(613) 498-1876   SIC 6712

NEWTERRA LTD   p 519
1291 CALIFORNIA AVE, BROCKVILLE, ON, K6V 7N5

(613) 498-1876   SIC 3589

NEWTON ENTERPRISES (1983)   p 353
1 MAIN ST, NEWTON SIDING, MB, R0H 0X0

(204) 267-2211   SIC 5211

NEWTON GROUP LTD   p 604
41 MASSEY RD, GUELPH, ON, N1H 7M6

(519) 822-5281   SIC 1541

NEWTON REGENCY CARE HOME   p 277
See REGENCY INTERMEDIATE CARE FACILITIES INC

NEWTON SQUARE BINGO COUNTRY   p
275
See 428675 BC LTD

NEWTON'S HI QUALITY MEATS LTD p 277
12481 80 AVE, SURREY, BC, V3W 3A4

(604) 596-1528   SIC 5147

NEWTON, ALAN REAL ESTATE LTD p 906
370 STEELES AVE W SUITE 102, THORN-

HILL, ON, L4J 6X1
(905) 764-7200   *SIC* 6531
NEWTON-TRELAWNEY PROPERTY MAN-AGEMENT SERVICES INC   *p* 474
253 LAKE DRIVEWAY W, AJAX, ON, L1S 5B5
(905) 619-2886   *SIC* 6531
NEWTONBROOK SECONDARY SCHOOL *p* 770
See TORONTO DISTRICT SCHOOL BOARD
NEWTOWN   *p* 1214
See RESTAURANT NEWTOWN INC
NEWTRON GROUP   *p* 498
See 1192901 ONTARIO LTD
NEWTYPE MOTORS LTD   *p* 261
9200 BRIDGEPORT RD, RICHMOND, BC, V6X 1S1
(604) 231-9200   *SIC* 5511
NEWTYPE RICHMOND MITSUBISHI   *p* 261
See NEWTYPE MOTORS LTD
NEWWAY CONCRETE FORMING LTD*p* 186
3750 1ST AVE, BURNABY, BC, V5C 3V9
(604) 299-3709   *SIC* 1799
NEXACOR   *p* 1185
See BGIS O&M SOLUTIONS INC
NEXANS CANADA INC   *p* 590
670 GZOWSKI ST, FERGUS, ON, N1M 2W9
(519) 843-3000   *SIC* 3312
NEXANS CANADA INC   *p* 673
140 ALLSTATE PKY SUITE 300, MARKHAM, ON, L3R 0Z7
(905) 944-4300   *SIC* 3312
NEXANS CANADA INC   *p* 1238
460 AV DUROCHER, MONTREAL-EST, QC, H1B 5H6
(514) 645-2301   *SIC* 3366
NEXANS CANADA INC   *p* 1262
1081 BOUL PIERRE-BERTRAND, QUE-BEC, QC, G1M 2E8
   SIC 3643
NEXANS CANADA INC   *p* 1438
1770 EAST AVE, WEYBURN, SK, S4H 0B8
(306) 842-7451   *SIC* 3312
NEXCYCLE CANADA LTD   *p* 505
235 WILKINSON RD, BRAMPTON, ON, L6T 4M2
(905) 454-2666   *SIC* 4953
NEXCYCLE PLASTICS INC   *p* 505
235 WILKINSON RD, BRAMPTON, ON, L6T 4M2
(905) 454-2666   *SIC* 4953
NEXEN CHEMICALS CANADA LTD PART-NERSHIP   *p* 238
See CHEMTRADE ELECTROCHEM INC
NEXEN HOLDINGS (USA) INC   *p* 54
801 7 AVE SW SUITE 200, CALGARY, AB, T2P 3P7
(403) 234-6700   *SIC* 1311
NEXEN PETROLEUM INTERNATIONAL LTD   *p* 55
801 7 AVE SW SUITE 2900, CALGARY, AB, T2P 3P7
(403) 234-6700   *SIC* 1311
NEXEO SOLUTIONS CANADA CORP *p* 798
2450 BRISTOL CIR, OAKVILLE, ON, L6H 6P6
(800) 387-2376   *SIC* 5169
NEXGEN ENERGY LTD   *p* 315
1021 HASTINGS ST W SUITE 3150, VAN-COUVER, BC, V6E 0C3
(604) 428-4112   *SIC* 1094
NEXGEN FINANCIAL LIMITED PARTNER-SHIP   *p* 940
36 TORONTO ST SUITE 1070, TORONTO, ON, M5C 2C5
(416) 775-3700   *SIC* 6282
NEXIA FRIEDMAN S.E.N.C.R.L.   *p* 1228
8000 BOUL DECARIE BUREAU 500, MON-TREAL, QC, H4P 2S4
(514) 731-7901   *SIC* 8721

NEXIA HEALTH TECHNOLOGIES INC*p* 673
15 ALLSTATE PRKWY 6TH FL, MARKHAM, ON, L3R 5B4
(905) 415-3063   *SIC* 7372
NEXICOM   *p* 682
See NEXICOM TELECOMMUNICATIONS INC
NEXICOM COMMUNICATIONS INC   *p* 682
5 KING ST E, MILLBROOK, ON, L0A 1G0
(888) 639-4266   *SIC* 1731
NEXICOM GROUP   *p* 682
See NEXICOM COMMUNICATIONS INC
NEXICOM TELECOMMUNICATIONS INC *p* 682
9 BANK ST N, MILLBROOK, ON, L0A 1G0
(705) 775-6394   *SIC* 4899
NEXIO.COM   *p* 1196
See GROUPE NEXIO INC
NEXJ SYSTEMS INC   *p* 774
10 YORK MILLS RD SUITE 700, NORTH YORK, ON, M2P 2G4
(416) 222-5611   *SIC* 7379
NEXONIA TECHNOLOGIES INC   *p* 925
2 ST CLAIR AVE E SUITE 750, TORONTO, ON, M4T 2T5
(416) 480-0688   *SIC* 7374
NEXSOURCE POWER INC   *p* 169
40 INDUSTRIAL DR, SYLVAN LAKE, AB, T4S 1P4
(403) 887-3654   *SIC* 4911
NEXT CYCLE INC   *p* 641
275 GAGE AVE, KITCHENER, ON, N2M 2C9
(519) 747-7776   *SIC* 5136
NEXT GENERATION REFORESTATION LTD   *p* 5
GD, BEAVERLODGE, AB, T0H 0C0
(780) 532-2220   *SIC* 0851
NEXT LEVEL GAMES INC   *p* 299
208 ROBSON ST, VANCOUVER, BC, V6B 6A1
(604) 484-6111   *SIC* 3944
NEXT PLUMBING & HYDRONICS SUPPLY INC   *p* 1032
300 GALCAT DR, WOODBRIDGE, ON, L4L 0B9
(289) 304-2000   *SIC* 5074
NEXT SUCCESS INC   *p* 1335
8086 RTE TRANSCANADIENNE, SAINT-LAURENT, QC, H4S 1M5
(514) 343-5544   *SIC* 5065
NEXTRUSION INC   *p* 1050
10500 RUE COLBERT, ANJOU, QC, H1J 2H8
(514) 355-6868   *SIC* 3089
NEXUS ENERGY TECHNOLOGIES INC *p* 157
175 CLEARVIEW DR UNIT 100, RED DEER COUNTY, AB, T4E 0A1
(403) 314-0607   *SIC* 5084
NEXUS PROTECTIVE SERVICES LIMITED *p* 943
56 THE ESPLANADE SUITE 510, TORONTO, ON, M5E 1A7
(416) 815-7575   *SIC* 7381
NEXUS REAL ESTATE INVESTMENT TRUST   *p* 801
340 CHURCH ST, OAKVILLE, ON, L6J 1P1
(416) 613-1262   *SIC* 6798
NEXXSOURCE RECYCLING INC   *p* 516
300 HENRY ST, BRANTFORD, ON, N3S 7R5
(519) 752-7696   *SIC* 7534
NEZIOL GROUP, THE   *p* 514
See NEZIOL INSURANCE BROKERS LTD
NEZIOL INSURANCE BROKERS LTD *p* 514
53 CHARING CROSS ST SUITE 1, BRANT-FORD, ON, N3R 7K9
(519) 759-2110   *SIC* 6411
NFI CANADA   *p* 698
See NFI IPD, LLC
NFI DOMINION CANADA, ULC   *p* 586
1920 ALBION RD, ETOBICOKE, ON, M9W 5T2

(416) 744-2438   *SIC* 4225
NFI GROUP INC   *p* 363
711 KERNAGHAN AVE, WINNIPEG, MB, R2C 3T4
(204) 224-1251   *SIC* 3711
NFI IPD, LLC   *p* 698
2800 SKYMARK AVE SUITE 501, MISSIS-SAUGA, ON, L4W 5A6
(905) 625-2300   *SIC* 4731
NFOE INC   *p* 1189
511 PLACE D'ARMES BUREAU 100, MON-TREAL, QC, H2Y 2W7
(514) 397-2616   *SIC* 8712
NGEX RESOURCES INC   *p* 307
885 GEORGIA ST W SUITE 2000, VAN-COUVER, BC, V6C 3E8
(604) 689-7842   *SIC* 1021
NGK SPARK PLUGS CANADA LIMITED *p* 673
275 RENFREW DR SUITE 101, MARKHAM, ON, L3R 0C8
(905) 477-7780   *SIC* 5013
NGL SUPPLY CO. LTD   *p* 55
435 4 AVE SW SUITE 550, CALGARY, AB, T2P 3A8
(403) 265-1977   *SIC* 5172
NGX   *p* 51
See ICE NGX CANADA INC
NHI   *p* 875
See NURSING & HOMEMAKERS INC
NHLPA   *p* 965
See NATIONAL HOCKEY LEAGUE PLAY-ERS ASSOCIATION, THE
NI-MET METALS INC   *p* 798
2939 PORTLAND DR SUITE 300, OAKVILLE, ON, L6H 5S4
(289) 291-1111   *SIC* 5093
NIAGARA 21ST GROUP INC   *p* 759
6740 FALLSVIEW BLVD, NIAGARA FALLS, ON, L2G 3W6
(905) 357-7300   *SIC* 7011
NIAGARA 21ST GROUP INC   *p* 759
5950 VICTORIA AVE, NIAGARA FALLS, ON, L2G 3L7
(905) 353-4044   *SIC* 7011
NIAGARA ACQUISITION GP INC   *p* 970
66 WELLINGTON ST W SUITE 4400, TORONTO, ON, M5K 1H6
(416) 687-6700   *SIC* 6531
NIAGARA AIR BUS INC   *p* 760
8626 LUNDY'S LANE, NIAGARA FALLS, ON, L2H 1H4
(905) 374-8111   *SIC* 4111
NIAGARA BATTERY & TIRE   *p* 757
See A-A-A BATTERIES LTD
NIAGARA BATTERY & TIRE LTD   *p* 885
79 HARTZEL RD, ST CATHARINES, ON, L2P 1M9
(905) 682-1844   *SIC* 5531
NIAGARA BREWING COMPANY   *p* 587
See PREMIUM BEER COMPANY INC, THE
NIAGARA CATHOLIC DISTRICT SCHOOL BOARD   *p* 760
8699 MCLEOD RD, NIAGARA FALLS, ON, L2H 0Z2
(905) 356-5155   *SIC* 8211
NIAGARA CATHOLIC DISTRICT SCHOOL BOARD   *p* 760
3834 WINDERMERE RD, NIAGARA FALLS, ON, L2J 2Y5
(905) 356-4313   *SIC* 8211
NIAGARA CATHOLIC DISTRICT SCHOOL BOARD   *p* 846
150 JANET ST, PORT COLBORNE, ON, L3K 2E7
(905) 835-2451   *SIC* 8211
NIAGARA CATHOLIC DISTRICT SCHOOL BOARD   *p* 883
460 LINWELL RD, ST CATHARINES, ON, L2M 2P9
(905) 937-6446   *SIC* 8211
NIAGARA CATHOLIC DISTRICT SCHOOL BOARD   *p* 887
40 GLEN MORRIS DR, ST CATHARINES,

ON, L2T 2M9
(905) 684-8731   *SIC* 8211
NIAGARA CATHOLIC DISTRICT SCHOOL BOARD   *p* 1012
64 SMITH ST, WELLAND, ON, L3C 4H4
(905) 788-3060   *SIC* 8211
NIAGARA CATHOLIC DISTRICT SCHOOL BOARD   *p* 1012
427 RICE RD, WELLAND, ON, L3C 7C1
(905) 562-1321   *SIC* 8211
NIAGARA COLLEGE CANADA   *p* 1012
See NIAGARA COLLEGE OF APPLIED ARTS & TECHNOLOGY
NIAGARA COLLEGE OF APPLIED ARTS & TECHNOLOGY   *p* 759
5881 DUNN ST, NIAGARA FALLS, ON, L2G 2N9
(905) 735-2211   *SIC* 8221
NIAGARA COLLEGE OF APPLIED ARTS & TECHNOLOGY   *p* 1012
100 NIAGARA COLLEGE BLVD, WELLAND, ON, L3C 7L3
(905) 735-2211   *SIC* 8222
NIAGARA CONVENTION & CIVIC CENTER *p* 759
6815 STANLEY AVE, NIAGARA FALLS, ON, L2G 3Y9
(905) 357-6222   *SIC* 7299
NIAGARA EMPLOYMENT AGENCY INC *p* 760
4935 KENT AVE, NIAGARA FALLS, ON, L2H 1J5
(905) 356-4141   *SIC* 4953
NIAGARA FALLS BRIDGE COMMISSION *p* 759
5781 RIVER RD, NIAGARA FALLS, ON, L2G 3K9
(905) 354-5641   *SIC* 4785
NIAGARA GORGE JET BOATING LTD*p* 761
61 MELVILLE ST, NIAGARA ON THE LAKE, ON, L0S 1J0
(905) 468-4800   *SIC* 4724
NIAGARA HEALTH SYSTEM   *p* 759
5546 PORTAGE RD, NIAGARA FALLS, ON, L2G 5X8
(905) 378-4647   *SIC* 8062
NIAGARA HEALTH SYSTEM   *p* 761
176 WELLINGTON ST, NIAGARA ON THE LAKE, ON, L0S 1J0
(905) 378-4647   *SIC* 8062
NIAGARA HEALTH SYSTEM   *p* 847
260 SUGARLOAF ST, PORT COLBORNE, ON, L3K 2N7
(905) 834-4501   *SIC* 8062
NIAGARA HEALTH SYSTEM   *p* 886
142 QUEENSTON ST, ST CATHARINES, ON, L2R 2Z7
(905) 684-7271   *SIC* 8062
NIAGARA HEALTH SYSTEM   *p* 887
1200 FOURTH AVE, ST CATHARINES, ON, L2S 0A9
(905) 378-4647   *SIC* 8062
NIAGARA HOSPITALITY HOTELS INC *p* 759
6546 FALLSVIEW BLVD, NIAGARA FALLS, ON, L2G 3W2
(905) 358-4666   *SIC* 7011
NIAGARA ICEDOGS HOCKEY CLUB INC *p* 886
35 QUEEN ST, ST CATHARINES, ON, L2R 5G4
(905) 687-3641   *SIC* 7941
NIAGARA INA GRAFTON GAGE HOME OF THE UNITED CHURCH   *p* 883
413 LINWELL RD SUITE 4212, ST CATHARINES, ON, L2M 7Y2
(905) 935-6822   *SIC* 8361
NIAGARA INA GRAFTON GAGE VILLAGE*p* 883
See NIAGARA INA GRAFTON GAGE HOME OF THE UNITED CHURCH
NIAGARA KANKO TOURS INC   *p* 759
5719 STANLEY AVE, NIAGARA FALLS, ON, L2G 3X6

(905) 356-2025　SIC 4725
NIAGARA MOTORS LIMITED　p 1004
1537 NIAGARA STONE RD, VIRGIL, ON,
L0S 1T0
(905) 468-2145　SIC 5511
**NIAGARA ON THE LAKE GENERAL HOS-
PITAL**　p
761
See NIAGARA HEALTH SYSTEM
NIAGARA ORCHARD & VINEYARD CORPp
1004
1550 HWY 55, VIRGIL, ON, L0S 1T0
(905) 468-3297　SIC 5148
NIAGARA PARKS COMMISSION, THE　p
758
6345 NIAGARA PKWY, NIAGARA FALLS,
ON, L2E 6T2
(905) 356-2217　SIC 5812
NIAGARA PARKS COMMISSION, THE　p
758
6650 NIAGARA PKY, NIAGARA FALLS, ON,
L2E 6T2
(877) 642-7275　SIC 5812
NIAGARA PARKS COMMISSION, THE　p
759
7400 PORTAGE RD, NIAGARA FALLS, ON,
L2G 0E5
(905) 356-2241　SIC 5947
**NIAGARA PENINSULA CHILDREN'S CEN-
TRE**　p
887
567 GLENRIDGE AVE, ST CATHARINES,
ON, L2T 4C2
(905) 688-3553　SIC 8069
NIAGARA PENINSULA ENERGY INC p 758
7447 PIN OAK DR, NIAGARA FALLS, ON,
L2E 6S9
(905) 356-2681　SIC 4911
NIAGARA PISTON INC　p 490
4708 ONTARIO ST, BEAMSVILLE, ON, L0R
1B4
(905) 563-4981　SIC 3714
NIAGARA RECYCLING　p 760
See NIAGARA EMPLOYMENT AGENCY
INC
NIAGARA STRUCTURAL STEEL, DIV OF p
885
See CANERECTOR INC
NIAGARA-ON-THE-LAKE HYDRO INC　p
1004
8 HENEGAN RD, VIRGIL, ON, L0S 1T0
(905) 468-4235　SIC 4911
NIC　p 110
See NORTHERN INDUSTRIAL CARRIERS
LTD
NICA　p 622
See NIFAST CANADA CORPORATION
NICAR INTERNATIONAL　p 1152
See LALLEMAND SOLUTIONS SANTE INC
NICASTRO'S BROS FOOD　p 750
See 1350950 ONTARIO LTD
NICHOLLS, DAVE TOYOTA　p 788
See 1076634 ONTARIO INC
NICHOLS, ROY MOTORS LIMITED　p 564
2728 COURTICE RD, COURTICE, ON, L1E
2M7
(905) 436-2228　SIC 5511
NICHOLSON AND CATES LIMITED　p 526
3060 MAINWAY SUITE 300, BURLINGTON,
ON, L7M 1A3
(905) 335-3366　SIC 5031
NICHOLSON CATHOLIC COLLEGE　p 490
See ALGONQUIN & LAKESHORE
CATHOLIC DISTRICT SCHOOL BOARD
NICHOLSON MANUFACTURING LTD p 268
9896 GALARAN RD, SIDNEY, BC, V8L 4K4
(250) 656-3131　SIC 3553
NICK'S WOODCRAFT INDUSTRIES LTD p
40
112 SKYLINE CRES NE, CALGARY, AB,
T2K 5X7
(403) 275-6432　SIC 6712
NICKEL CENTRE PHARMACY INC p 1001
3140 OLD HWY 69 N SUITE 17, VAL

CARON, ON, P3N 1G3
(705) 897-1867　SIC 5947
NICKLAUS NORTH GOLF COURSE　p 342
See GREEN LAKE PROJECTS INC
NICO METAL INC　p 1388
1005 RUE DU PERE-DANIEL, TROIS-
RIVIERES, QC, G9A 2W9
(819) 375-6426　SIC 3441
NICOL AUTO INC　p 1123
400 2E RUE E, LA SARRE, QC, J9Z 2J1
(819) 333-5467　SIC 5511
NICOL PONTIAC BUICK GMC　p 1123
See NICOL AUTO INC
NICOLA MINING INC　p 307
355 BURRARD ST SUITE 1000, VANCOU-
VER, BC, V6C 2G8
(604) 683-8604　SIC 1044
NICOLA TRIBAL ASSOCIATION INC p 232
2090 COUTLEE AVE UNIT 202, MERRITT,
BC, V1K 1B8
(250) 378-4235　SIC 8741
NICOLA VALLEY DIVISION　p 232
See TOLKO INDUSTRIES LTD
NICOLANI SERVICES LTD　p 216
995 ARLINGTON CRT, KAMLOOPS, BC,
V2B 8T5
(250) 372-0451　SIC 5541
NICOMEKL ENHANCEMENT SOCIETY　p
227
5263 232 ST, LANGLEY, BC, V2Z 2P8
(604) 539-2486　SIC 0273
NIEBOER FARM SUPPLIES (1977) LTD p
150
233016 HWY 519, NOBLEFORD, AB, T0L
1S0
(403) 824-3404　SIC 5083
NIEDNER INC　p 1082
675 RUE MERRILL, COATICOOK, QC, J1A
2S2
(819) 849-2751　SIC 3569
NIELSEN　p 673
See NIELSEN MEDIA RESEARCH LIM-
ITED
NIELSEN　p 1198
See OPINION SEARCH INC
NIELSEN MEDIA RESEARCH LIMITED　p
673
160 MCNABB ST, MARKHAM, ON, L3R 4B8
(905) 475-1131　SIC 8732
**NIENKAMPER FURNITURE & ACCES-
SORIES INC**　p
914
257 FINCHDENE SQUARE, TORONTO,
ON, M1X 1B9
(416) 298-5700　SIC 2522
NIEUWLAND FEED & SUPPLY LIMITED p
565
96 WELLINGTON ST, DRAYTON, ON, N0G
1P0
(519) 638-3008　SIC 5191
NIFAST CANADA CORPORATION　p 622
12 UNDERWOOD RD, INGERSOLL, ON,
N5C 3J9
(519) 485-1050　SIC 5085
NIGHT HAWK SECURITY LTD　p 331
9095 TRONSON RD, VERNON, BC, V1H
1E2
　SIC 7381
NIGHT HAWK TECHNOLOGIES　p 818
See NIGHT HAWK TECHNOLOGIESTM
INC
NIGHT HAWK TECHNOLOGIESTM INC　p
818
25 GREAT OAK PVT, OTTAWA, ON, K1G
6P7
(613) 795-8262　SIC 8731
**NIGHT SHIFT ANSWERING SERVICE LTD,
THE**　p 414
600 MAIN ST SUITE 201, SAINT JOHN, NB,
E2K 1J5
(506) 637-7010　SIC 7389
NIGHTHAWK GOLD CORP　p 955
141 ADELAIDE ST W SUITE 301,
TORONTO, ON, M5H 3L5

(647) 794-4313　SIC 1041
NIGHTINGALE ELECTRICAL LTD　p 263
11121 HORSESHOE WAY SUITE 143,
RICHMOND, BC, V7A 5G7
(604) 275-0500　SIC 1731
NIGHTINGALE FARMS LIMITED　p 643
1492 WINDHAM RD 19, LA SALETTE, ON,
N0E 1H0
(519) 582-2461　SIC 0191
NIGHTINGALE NURSING REGISTRY LTDp
841
2948 LAKEFIELD RD, PETERBOROUGH,
ON, K9J 6X5
(705) 652-6118　SIC 8059
NII NORTHERN INTERNATIONAL INCp 201
1 BURBIDGE ST SUITE 101, COQUITLAM,
BC, V3K 7B2
(604) 464-8606　SIC 5063
NIIGON MACHINES LTD　p 1028
372 NEW ENTERPRISE WAY, WOOD-
BRIDGE, ON, L4H 0S8
(905) 265-0277　SIC 3569
**NIIT LEARNING SOLUTIONS (CANADA)
LTD**　p 698
5045 ORBITOR DR UNIT 100, MISSIS-
SAUGA, ON, L4W 4Y4
(905) 572-1664　SIC 8742
NIKE　p 290
See NEW AGE SPORTS INC
NIKE CANADA CORP　p 869
260 BRIMLEY RD, SCARBOROUGH, ON,
M1M 3H8
(416) 264-8505　SIC 5091
NIKE CANADA CORP　p 982
200 WELLINGTON ST W, TORONTO, ON,
M5V 3C7
(416) 581-1585　SIC 5091
NIKO COSMETICS INC　p 998
397 HUMBERLINE DR UNIT 7, TORONTO,
ON, M9W 5T5
　SIC 7231
NIKO RESOURCES LTD　p 55
800 6 AVE SW SUITE 510, CALGARY, AB,
T2P 3G3
(403) 262-1020　SIC 1311
NIKOLAOS FINE FOODS INC.　p 615
225 NEBO RD UNIT 5, HAMILTON, ON,
L8W 2E1
(905) 388-8074　SIC 5144
NIKON CANADA INC　p 698
1366 AEROWOOD DR, MISSISSAUGA,
ON, L4W 1C1
(905) 625-9910　SIC 5043
NILEX CONSTRUCTION INC　p 115
9304 39 AVE NW, EDMONTON, AB, T6E
5T9
(780) 463-9535　SIC 1799
NILEX INC　p 122
6810 8 ST NW, EDMONTON, AB, T6P 0C5
(780) 463-9535　SIC 5131
NILFISK CANADA COMPANY　p 741
240 SUPERIOR BLVD, MISSISSAUGA, ON,
L5T 2L2
(905) 696-4840　SIC 5087
NILSSON BROS. INC　p 166
101 RIEL DR SUITE 100, ST. ALBERT, AB,
T8N 3X4
(780) 477-2233　SIC 2011
NILSSON BROS. LIVESTOCK EXCHANGE
p 92
See 324007 ALBERTA LTD
NIM DISPOSAL LTD　p 898
2755 LASALLE BLVD, SUDBURY, ON, P3A
4R7
(705) 566-9363　SIC 5093
NIMA VANI ENTERPRISES LIMITED p 443
1 MATTHEW FRANCIS CRT, DARTMOUTH,
NS, B2W 6A1
　SIC 5399
NINE ENERGY CANADA INC　p 55
840 7 AVE SW SUITE 1840, CALGARY, AB,
T2P 3G2
(403) 266-0908　SIC 1389
NINE ENERGY CANADA INC　p 158

37337 BURNT LAKE TRAIL UNIT 30, RED
DEER COUNTY, AB, T4S 2K5
(403) 340-4218　SIC 1389
NINE ENERGY CANADA INC　p 214
9404 73 AVE, FORT ST. JOHN, BC, V1J
4H7
(250) 785-4210　SIC 1389
NINEPOINT PARTNERS　p 967
See SPROTT CANADIAN EQUITY FUND
NINEPOINT PARTNERS LP　p 965
200 BAY ST SUITE 2700, TORONTO, ON,
M5J 2J1
(416) 362-7172　SIC 6282
NINTENDO OF CANADA LTD　p 287
2925 VIRTUAL WAY SUITE 150, VANCOU-
VER, BC, V5M 4X5
(604) 279-1600　SIC 5092
NIOBEC INC　p 955
333 BAY ST SUITE 1101, TORONTO, ON,
M5H 2R2
(416) 901-9877　SIC 1081
NIOBEC INC　p 1307
3400 CH DU COLUMBIUM, SAINT-
HONORE-DE-CHICOUTIMI, QC, G0V 1L0
(418) 673-4694　SIC 1081
NIPAWIN CHRYSLER DODGE LTD p 1412
301 1 AVE W, NIPAWIN, SK, S0E 1E0
(306) 862-4755　SIC 5511
NIPIGON DISTRICT MEMORIAL HOSPITAL
p 761
125 HOGAN RD, NIPIGON, ON, P0T 2J0
(807) 887-3026　SIC 8062
NIPISSING GAME FARM INC　p 532
367 BIRCHGROVE DR W, CALLANDER,
ON, P0H 1H0
(705) 752-2226　SIC 0259
NIPISSING MANOR　p 561
See 913096 ONTARIO LIMITED
NIPISSING TRANSITION HOUSE　p 763
547 JOHN ST, NORTH BAY, ON, P1B 2M9
(705) 476-2429　SIC 7381
NIPISSING UNIVERSITY　p 763
100 COLLEGE DR, NORTH BAY, ON, P1B
8L7
(705) 474-3450　SIC 8221
**NIPPON CABLE (CANADA) HOLDINGS
LTD**　p 270
1280 ALPINE RD RR 1, SUN PEAKS, BC,
V0E 5N0
(250) 578-7232　SIC 7011
NIPPON EXPRESS CANADA LTD　p 741
6250 EDWARDS BLVD, MISSISSAUGA,
ON, L5T 2X3
(905) 565-7525　SIC 4731
NIPPON TRAVEL AGENCY CANADA LTD p
315
1199 PENDER ST W SUITE 370, VANCOU-
VER, BC, V6E 2R1
(604) 685-4663　SIC 4725
NIRADIA ENTERPRISES INC　p 206
460 FRASERVIEW PL, DELTA, BC, V3M
6H4
(604) 523-6188　SIC 6712
NIS NORTHERN INDUSTRIAL SALES LTD
p 96
11440 163 ST NW, EDMONTON, AB, T5M
3T3
(780) 454-2682　SIC 5085
NISBET LODGE　p 920
740 PAPE AVE, TORONTO, ON, M4K 3S7
(416) 469-1105　SIC 8361
NISE N KOSY INCORPORATED　p 781
120 OVERBROOK PL SUITE 100, NORTH
YORK, ON, M3H 4P8
(416) 665-8802　SIC 2321
NISK CONSTRUCTION　p 1077
See 9130-6381 QUEBEC INC
NISKA GAS STORAGE　p 42
See AECO GAS STORAGE PARTNERSHIP
NISKU INN & CONFERENCE CENTRE　p
149
See INTER-ALBERTA HOLDINGS CORPO-
RATION
NISKU TRUCK STOP　p 139

▲ Public Company　■ Public Company Family Member　　**HQ** Headquarters　　**BR** Branch　　**SL** Single Location

See NISKU TRUCK STOP LTD
NISKU TRUCK STOP LTD   p 139
8020 SPARROW DR SUITE 201, LEDUC, AB, T9E 7G3
(780) 986-5312   *SIC 5541*
NISSAN   p 1346
See ST-LEONARD NISSAN INC
NISSAN CANADA INC   p 698
5290 ORBITOR DR, MISSISSAUGA, ON, L4W 4Z5
(905) 602-0792   *SIC 5012*
NISSAN GABRIEL   p 1047
See COMMERCE AUTOMOBILE S.G.C. CORPORATION
NISSAN HALIFAX   p 456
See O'REGAN I-N LIMITED
NISSAN OF NANAIMO   p 234
See 1049054 B.C. LTD.
NISSEN FASTENERS   p 1395
See P.R. NISSEN & CIE LTEE
NITE TOURS INTERNATIONAL   p 85
67 AIRPORT RD NW, EDMONTON, AB, T5G 0W6
   SIC 4725
NITEK LASER INC   p 1242
305 RTE DU PORT, NICOLET, QC, J3T 1R7
(819) 293-4887   *SIC 3398*
NITREX METAL INC   p 1330
3474 BOUL POIRIER, SAINT-LAURENT, QC, H4R 2J5
(514) 335-7191   *SIC 3625*
NITROCHEM CORP   p 725
6733 MISSISSAUGA RD SUITE 306, MISSISSAUGA, ON, L5N 6J5
(905) 814-6665   *SIC 2899*
NITTA CASINGS (CANADA) INC   p 673
57 STEELCASE RD W, MARKHAM, ON, L3R 2M4
(905) 475-6441   *SIC 5149*
NITTA GELATIN CANADA, INC   p 990
60 PATON RD, TORONTO, ON, M6H 1R8
(416) 532-5111   *SIC 2899*
NIVEL INC   p 1340
4850 RUE BOURG, SAINT-LAURENT, QC, H4T 1J2
(514) 735-4251   *SIC 5046*
NIVTOP HOLDINGS LTD   p 863
105 BLACK RD, SAULT STE. MARIE, ON, P6B 0A3
(705) 253-3251   *SIC 1521*
NIXON WENGER LLP   p 332
2706 30 AVE SUITE 301, VERNON, BC, V1T 2B6
(250) 542-5353   *SIC 8111*
NJM CLI   p 1333
See CHARLES LAPIERRE INC
NJM EMBALLAGE   p 1335
See NJM PACKAGING INC
NJM PACKAGING INC   p 1335
5600 RUE KIERAN, SAINT-LAURENT, QC, H4S 2B5
(514) 337-6990   *SIC 5084*
NK'MIP VINEYARDS LTD   p 242
7357 VINEYARD RD, OLIVER, BC, V0H 1T0
(250) 498-3552   *SIC 0172*
NKC OF CANADA INC   p 706
55 VILLAGE CENTRE PL SUITE 213, MISSISSAUGA, ON, L4Z 1V9
(905) 273-4011   *SIC 5084*
NL NOVALINK   p 606
See NOVA-LINK LIMITED
NL TECHNOLOGIES   p 918
See LEVITT-SAFETY LIMITED
NL TECHNOLOGIES, DIV OF   p 798
See LEVITT-SAFETY LIMITED
NLS   p 745
See NATIONAL LOGISTICS SERVICES (2006) INC
NLSD 113   p 1408
See NORTHERN LIGHTS SCHOOL DIVISION 113
NMC DYNAPLAS LTD   p 876
380 PASSMORE AVE, SCARBOROUGH, ON, M1V 4B4

(416) 293-3855   *SIC 3089*
NMP DENEIGEMENT   p 1359
See NMP GOLF CONSTRUCTION INC
NMP GOLF CONSTRUCTION INC   p 1359
2674 CH PLAMONDON BUREAU 201, SAINTE-MADELEINE, QC, J0H 1S0
(450) 795-3373   *SIC 1629*
NMT MACHINING GROUP INC   p 637
290 SHOEMAKER ST, KITCHENER, ON, N2E 3E1
(519) 748-5459   *SIC 3499*
NO 1 COLLISION (1993) INC   p 255
20 VULCAN WAY SUITE 124, RICHMOND, BC, V6V 1J8
(604) 231-9614   *SIC 7532*
NO FIXED ADDRESS INC   p 920
50 CARROLL ST, TORONTO, ON, M4M 3G3
(416) 947-8584   *SIC 7311*
NO FRILLS   p 168
900 PINE RD SUITE 101, STRATHMORE, AB, T1P 0A2
(403) 934-6500   *SIC 5912*
NO FRILLS   p 482
See LOBLAWS SUPERMARKETS LIMITED
NO FRILLS   p 1412
11403 RAILWAY AVENUE E, NORTH BATTLEFORD, SK, S9A 0A1
(306) 445-3375   *SIC 5411*
NO LIMITS SPORTSWEAR INC   p 292
68 5TH AVE W, VANCOUVER, BC, V5Y 1H6
(604) 431-7330   *SIC 5137*
NOBEL BIOCARE CANADA INC   p 853
9133 LESLIE ST UNIT 100, RICHMOND HILL, ON, L4B 4N1
(905) 762-3500   *SIC 5047*
NOBEL DIRECT   p 1333
See EDICIBLE LTEE
NOBLE ACCEPTANCE LTD   p 102
21216 113 AVE NW, EDMONTON, AB, T5S 1Y6
   SIC 3448
NOBLE CONSTRUCTION CORP   p 1406
215 SUMNER ST, ESTERHAZY, SK, S0A 0X0
(306) 745-6984   *SIC 1541*
NOBLE HOMES   p 102
See NOBLE ACCEPTANCE LTD
NOBUL CORPORATION   p 982
200 WELLINGTON ST W, TORONTO, ON, M5V 3C7
(416) 543-3710   *SIC 7371*
NOCO CANADA COMPANY   p 577
5468 DUNDAS ST W SUITE 401, ETOBICOKE, ON, M9B 6E3
(416) 232-6626   *SIC 5172*
NOCO CANADA INC   p 579
133 THE WEST MALL UNIT 11, ETOBICOKE, ON, M9C 1C2
(416) 232-6626   *SIC 5541*
NOCO PETROLEUM DIV   p 579
See NOCO CANADA INC
NOKIA CANADA INC   p 832
600 MARCH RD, OTTAWA, ON, K2K 2T6
(613) 591-3600   *SIC 4899*
NOKIA NETWORKS   p 832
See ALCATEL-LUCENT CANADA INC
NOLAN LOGISTICS GROUP INC   p 499
9150 AIRPORT RD UNIT 10, BRAMPTON, ON, L6S 6G1
(800) 387-5148   *SIC 4731*
NOLINOR AVIATION   p 1153
See INVESTISSEMENTS NOLINOR INC, LES
NOLRAD INTERNATIONAL INC   p 556
1380 CREDITSTONE RD UNIT 5, CONCORD, ON, L4K 0J1
(905) 738-4646   *SIC 5051*
NONUTS BAKING CO INC   p 793
1295 ORMONT DR, NORTH YORK, ON, M9L 2W6
(905) 532-9517   *SIC 2051*
NOODLEBOX   p 175
See IDH INVESTMENTS LTD

NOOELEC   p 756
See NOOELEC INC
NOOELEC INC   p 756
250 HARRY WALKER PKY N UNIT 3, NEWMARKET, ON, L3Y 7B4
(888) 653-3532   *SIC 5065*
NOOTKA SOUND DRYLAND   p 215
See WESTERN FOREST PRODUCTS INC
NOR ARC STEEL FABRICATORS   p 567
See 462673 ONTARIO INC
NOR CLIFF FARMS INC   p 847
888 BARRICK RD, PORT COLBORNE, ON, L3K 6H2
(905) 835-0808   *SIC 2037*
NOR'WEST CO-OP COMMUNITY HEALTH CENTRE, INC   p 372
785 KEEWATIN ST, WINNIPEG, MB, R2X 3B9
(204) 938-5900   *SIC 8011*
NOR-COM INVESTMENT ENTERPRISES LTD   p 132
10525 100 AVE SUITE 200, GRANDE PRAIRIE, AB, T8V 0V8
(780) 539-6080   *SIC 5149*
NOR-LAB LIMITED   p 424
8 LONDON ST, HAPPY VALLEY-GOOSE BAY, NL, A0P 1E0
(709) 896-3795   *SIC 5145*
NOR-LAN CHRYSLER DODGE JEEP   p 133
See NOR-LAN CHRYSLER INC
NOR-LAN CHRYSLER INC   p 133
12517 100 ST, GRANDE PRAIRIE, AB, T8V 4H2
(780) 978-9335   *SIC 5511*
NOR-MAR INDUSTRIES LTD   p 243
682 OKANAGAN AVE E, PENTICTON, BC, V2A 3K6
(250) 492-7866   *SIC 7389*
NOR-SHAM HOLDINGS INC   p 715
2125 NORTH SHERIDAN WAY, MISSISSAUGA, ON, L5K 1A3
(905) 305-5503   *SIC 6712*
NOR-SHAM HOTELS INC   p 715
2125 NORTH SHERIDAN WAY, MISSISSAUGA, ON, L5K 1A3
(905) 855-2000   *SIC 7011*
NORAC SYSTEMS INTERNATIONAL INC   p 1434
3702 KINNEAR PL, SASKATOON, SK, S7P 0A6
(306) 664-6711   *SIC 3625*
NORAG RESOURCES INC   p 847
4476 COUNTY 10 RD, PORT HOPE, ON, L1A 3V5
(905) 753-1180   *SIC 5153*
NORAL MOTORS (1983) LTD   p 128
10129 MACDONALD AVE, FORT MCMURRAY, AB, T9H 1T2
(780) 743-5444   *SIC 5511*
NORAL TOYOTA   p 128
See NORAL MOTORS (1983) LTD
NORALTA LODGE LTD   p 128
7210 CLIFF AVE SUITE 7202, FORT MCMURRAY, AB, T9H 1A1
(780) 791-3334   *SIC 7041*
NORALTA TECHNOLOGIES INC   p 55
808 4 AVE SW UNIT 100, CALGARY, AB, T2P 3E8
(403) 269-4237   *SIC 7629*
NORAM ENTERPRISES INC   p 698
1325 AIMCO BLVD, MISSISSAUGA, ON, L4W 1B4
(905) 238-0470   *SIC 5023*
NORAM GLASS   p 698
See NORAM ENTERPRISES INC
NORAMA ENTERPRISES INC   p 2
53016 HWY 60 SUITE 2, ACHESON, AB, T7X 5A7
(780) 960-7171   *SIC 1611*
NORAMCO WIRE & CABLE   p 735
See NCS INTERNATIONAL CO
NORAMPAC   p 1378
See CASCADES CANADA ULC
NORAMPAC ST. MARYS   p 888

See CASCADES CANADA ULC
NORAMPAC, DIV OF   p 382
See CASCADES CANADA ULC
NORAMPAC, DIV OF   p 408
See CASCADES CANADA ULC
NORAMPAC- VAUGHAN   p 550
See CASCADES CANADA ULC
NORAMPAC-CALGARY, DIV OF   p 34
See CASCADES CANADA ULC
NORAMPAC-JONQUIERE   p 1116
See CASCADES CANADA ULC
NORAMPAC-LITHOTECH   p 864
See CASCADES CANADA ULC
NORAMPAC-SPB   p 1166
See CASCADES CANADA ULC
NORAMPAC-VAUDREUIL, DIV OF   p 1394
See CASCADES CANADA ULC
NORAMPAC-VICTORIAVILLE   p 1399
See CASCADES CANADA ULC
NORAMTEC CONSULTANTS INC   p 750
1400 CLYDE AVE SUITE 217, NEPEAN, ON, K2G 3J2
(613) 727-3997   *SIC 7361*
NORANCO INC   p 1032
710 ROWNTREE DAIRY RD, WOODBRIDGE, ON, L4L 5T7
(905) 264-2050   *SIC 3499*
NORANDA INCOME FUND   p 987
100 KING ST W SUITE 6900, TORONTO, ON, M5X 2A1
(416) 775-1500   *SIC 6722*
NORBEC ARCHITECTURAL INC   p 1066
97 RUE DE VAUDREUIL, BOUCHERVILLE, QC, J4B 1K7
(450) 449-1499   *SIC 3446*
NORBEL METAL SERVICE LIMITED   p 580
100 GUIDED CRT, ETOBICOKE, ON, M9V 4K6
(416) 744-9988   *SIC 7389*
NORBORD INC   p 133
6700 HWY 40 S, GRANDE PRAIRIE, AB, T8V 6Y9
(780) 831-2500   *SIC 2493*
NORBORD INC   p 174
995 EXETER STN RD, 100 MILE HOUSE, BC, V0K 2E0
(250) 395-6246   *SIC 2435*
NORBORD INC   p 940
1 TORONTO ST SUITE 600, TORONTO, ON, M5C 2W4
(416) 365-0705   *SIC 2435*
NORBORD INDUSTRIES INC   p 404
137 JUNIPER RD, JUNIPER, NB, E7L 1G8
(506) 246-1125   *SIC 2431*
NORBORD INDUSTRIES INC   p 546
4 BOISVERT CRES, COCHRANE, ON, P0L 1C0
(705) 272-4210   *SIC 2435*
NORBORD INDUSTRIES INC   p 940
1 TORONTO ST UNIT 600, TORONTO, ON, M5C 2W4
(416) 365-0705   *SIC 2431*
NORBORD INDUSTRIES INC   p 1123
210 9E AV E, LA SARRE, QC, J9Z 2L2
(819) 333-5464   *SIC 2499*
NORBRO HOLDINGS LTD   p 562
1515 VINCENT MASSEY DR, CORNWALL, ON, K6H 5R6
(613) 932-0451   *SIC 7011*
NORBULK SHIPPING NB LTD   p 413
120 MCDONALD ST UNIT 135, SAINT JOHN, NB, E2J 1M5
(506) 657-7555   *SIC 8611*
NORBURN LIGHTING & BATH CENTRE   p 382
See ROBINSON LIGHTING LTD
NORCAN ALUMINUM INC   p 1066
61 CH DU TREMBLAY, BOUCHERVILLE, QC, J4B 7L6
(450) 449-6207   *SIC 2819*
NORCAN ELECTRIC INC   p 128
380 MACKENZIE BLVD SUITE 6B, FORT MCMURRAY, AB, T9H 4C4
(780) 799-3292   *SIC 1731*

NORCAN FLUID POWER 84 *p 225*
See NORCAN FLUID POWER LTD
NORCAN FLUID POWER LTD *p 225*
19650 TELEGRAPH TRAIL, LANGLEY, BC,
V1M 3E5
(604) 881-7877 *SIC 7699*
NORCAN LEASING LTD *p 1440*
213 RANGE RD, WHITEHORSE, YT, Y1A
3E5
(867) 668-2137 *SIC 5521*
NORCARD ENTERPRISES LTD *p 657*
444 NEWBOLD ST, LONDON, ON, N6E 1K3
(519) 690-1717 *SIC 7389*
NORCLAIR *p 1064*
See EBENISTERIE NORCLAIR INC
NORCO MANAGEMENT LTD *p 247*
1465 KEBET WAY SUITE B, PORT CO-
QUITLAM, BC, V3C 6L3
(604) 552-2930 *SIC 3751*
NORCO PERFORMANCE BIKES *p 247*
See LTP SPORTS GROUP INC
NORCRAFT CANADA CORPORATION *p 363*
1980 SPRINGFIELD RD, WINNIPEG, MB,
R2C 2Z2
(204) 222-9888 *SIC 3429*
NORCRAFT COMPANIES LP *p 363*
See NORCRAFT CANADA CORPORATION
NORDA STELO INC *p 1079*
159 RUE SALABERRY, CHICOUTIMI, QC,
G7H 4K2
(418) 549-6471 *SIC 8711*
NORDA STELO INC *p 1189*
33 RUE SAINT-JACQUES BUREAU 400,
MONTREAL, QC, H2Y 1K9
(514) 282-4181 *SIC 8711*
NORDA STELO INC *p 1206*
630 BOUL RENE-LEVESQUE O BUREAU
1500, MONTREAL, QC, H3B 1S6
(800) 463-2839 *SIC 7363*
NORDA STELO INC *p 1274*
1015 AV WILFRID-PELLETIER, QUEBEC,
QC, G1W 0C4
(418) 654-9600 *SIC 8711*
NORDEN AUTOHAUS *p 102*
See NORDEN VOLKSWAGEN LIMITED
NORDEN VOLKSWAGEN LIMITED *p 102*
17820 STONY PLAIN RD NW, EDMONTON,
AB, T5S 1A4
(780) 426-3000 *SIC 5511*
NORDEST VOLKSWAGEN INC *p 1240*
10395 BOUL PIE-IX, MONTREAL-NORD,
QC, H1H 3Z7
(514) 325-3422 *SIC 5511*
NORDEX ENR *p 1044*
See 130395 CANADA INC
NORDIA INC *p 638*
160 KING ST E SUITE 400, KITCHENER,
ON, N2G 4L3
(519) 579-8906 *SIC 4899*
NORDIA INC *p 1177*
255 BOUL CREMAZIE E, MONTREAL, QC,
H2M 1L5
(514) 387-1285 *SIC 7389*
NORDIA INC *p 1236*
3020 AV JACQUES-BUREAU 2E ETAGE,
MONTREAL, QC, H7P 6G2
(514) 415-7088 *SIC 7389*
NORDIA INC *p 1267*
5200 BOUL DE L'ORMIERE, QUEBEC, QC,
G1P 1K7
(418) 864-7359 *SIC 4899*
NORDIC EQUITY LIMITED *p 698*
2800 SKYMARK AVE, MISSISSAUGA, ON,
L4W 5A6
(905) 629-8530 *SIC 4725*
NORDIC HOLDINGS LTD *p 125*
2303 91 ST SW, EDMONTON, AB, T6X 1V8
(780) 437-1527 *SIC 5712*
**NORDIC INSURANCE COMPANY OF
CANADA, THE** *p 946*
700 UNIVERSITY AVE SUITE 1500,
TORONTO, ON, M5G 0A1
(416) 932-0044 *SIC 6331*

NORDIC MECHANICAL SERVICES LTD *p 110*
4143 78 AVE NW, EDMONTON, AB, T6B
2N3
(780) 469-7799 *SIC 7623*
NORDIC MINESTEEL TECHNOLOGIES INC *p 763*
373 MAIN ST W UNIT 1, NORTH BAY, ON,
P1B 2T9
(705) 474-2777 *SIC 3532*
NORDIC NURSERIES LTD *p 178*
29386 HAVERMAN RD, ABBOTSFORD,
BC, V4X 2P3
(604) 607-7074 *SIC 0181*
NORDIC RESORT *p 280*
See ALLDRITT DEVELOPMENT LIMITED
NORDIC TRAVEL GROUP *p 698*
See NORDIC EQUITY LIMITED
NORDIK-SPA EN NATURE, LE *p 1077*
See AUBERGE & SPA LE NORDIK INC
NORDION *p 625*
See NORDION (CANADA) INC
NORDION (CANADA) INC *p 189*
3680 GILMORE WAY, BURNABY, BC, V5G
4V8
(604) 431-5005 *SIC 8071*
NORDION (CANADA) INC *p 625*
447 MARCH RD, KANATA, ON, K2K 1X8
(613) 592-2790 *SIC 2819*
NORDION (CANADA) INC *p 656*
746 BASE LINE RD E SUITE 11, LONDON,
ON, N6C 5Z2
(877) 849-3637 *SIC 8071*
NORDION (CANADA) INC *p 698*
1980 MATHESON BLVD E SUITE 1, MIS-
SISSAUGA, ON, L4W 5R7
(905) 206-8887 *SIC 8071*
NORDIQUE FOOD GROUP *p 1172*
*See GROUPE ALIMENTAIRE NORDIQUE
INC, LE*
NORDMEC CONSTRUCTION INC *p 1159*
390 RUE SIMEON BUREAU 3, MONT-
TREMBLANT, QC, J8E 2R2
(819) 429-5555 *SIC 1542*
NORDMEC INDUSTRIELS & MINES INC *p 1366*
850 BOUL DES ERABLES, SALABERRY-
DE-VALLEYFIELD, QC, J6T 6G4
(450) 373-3739 *SIC 7699*
NORDSON CANADA, LIMITED *p 673*
1211 DENISON ST, MARKHAM, ON, L3R
4B3
(905) 475-6730 *SIC 5084*
NORDSTROM *p 315*
See NORDSTROM CANADA RETAIL, INC
NORDSTROM CANADA RETAIL, INC *p 36*
6455 MACLEOD TRAIL SW, CALGARY, AB,
T2H 0K8
(780) 291-2000 *SIC 5311*
NORDSTROM CANADA RETAIL, INC *p 315*
745 THURLOW ST SUITE 2400, VANCOU-
VER, BC, V6E 0C5
SIC 5311
NORDSTROM CANADA RETAIL, INC *p 330*
799 ROBSON ST, VANCOUVER, BC, V7Y
0A2
(604) 699-2100 *SIC 5311*
NORDSTROM CANADA RETAIL, INC *p 579*
25 THE WEST MALL UNIT 1150A, ETOBI-
COKE, ON, M9C 1B8
(647) 798-4200 *SIC 5311*
NORDSTROM CANADA RETAIL, INC *p 789*
3401 DUFFERIN ST UNIT 500, NORTH
YORK, ON, M6A 2T9
(416) 780-6630 *SIC 5311*
NORDSTROM CANADA RETAIL, INC *p 821*
50 RIDEAU ST SUITE 500, OTTAWA, ON,
K1N 9J7
(613) 567-7005 *SIC 5311*
NORDSTROM CHINOOK CENTRE *p 36*
See NORDSTROM CANADA RETAIL, INC
NORDSTROM PACIFIC CENTRE *p 330*
See NORDSTROM CANADA RETAIL, INC
NORDSTROM RIDEAU CENTRE *p 821*

See NORDSTROM CANADA RETAIL, INC
NORDSTROM SHERWAY GARDENS *p 579*
See NORDSTROM CANADA RETAIL, INC
**NORDSTROM YORKDALE SHOPPING
CENTRE** *p 789*
See NORDSTROM CANADA RETAIL, INC
NORDSTRONG EQUIPMENT LIMITED *p 368*
5 CHESTER ST, WINNIPEG, MB, R2L 1W5
(204) 667-1553 *SIC 5083*
NORECOB IMPRIMEUR *p 1322*
See IMPRIMERIE NORECOB INC
NORELCO CABINETS LTD *p 220*
677 WILLOW PARK RD UNIT 2, KELOWNA,
BC, V1X 5H9
(250) 765-2121 *SIC 2434*
NORFAB MFG. (1993) INC *p 106*
16425 130 AVE NW, EDMONTON, AB, T5V
1K5
(780) 447-5454 *SIC 3441*
**NORFOLK FRUIT GROWERS' ASSOCIA-
TION, THE** *p 881*
99 QUEENSWAY E, SIMCOE, ON, N3Y
4M5
(519) 426-6931 *SIC 5148*
NORFOLK GENERAL HOSPITAL *p 881*
365 WEST ST, SIMCOE, ON, N3Y 1T7
(519) 426-0130 *SIC 8062*
NORFOLK KNITTERS LIMITED *p 537*
50 GROH AVE, CAMBRIDGE, ON, N3C 1Y9
(519) 743-4672 *SIC 5949*
NORFOLK MOBILITY BENEFITS INC *p 65*
999 8 ST SW SUITE 300, CALGARY, AB,
T2R 1N7
(403) 232-8545 *SIC 6321*
NORFOLK POWER DISTRIBUTION INC *p 881*
70 VICTORIA ST, SIMCOE, ON, N3Y 1L5
(519) 426-4440 *SIC 4911*
**NORJOHN CONTRACTING AND PAVING
LIMITED** *p 760*
9101 BROWN RD, NIAGARA FALLS, ON,
L2H 0X1
(905) 371-0809 *SIC 1611*
NORLITE INC *p 495*
5 SIMPSON RD, BOLTON, ON, L7E 1E4
(905) 857-5955 *SIC 5063*
NORLON BUILDERS LONDON LIMITED *p 654*
151 YORK ST, LONDON, ON, N6A 1A8
(519) 672-7590 *SIC 1542*
NORMA DONUTS LIMITED *p 591*
141 GARRISON RD, FORT ERIE, ON, L2A
1M3
(905) 871-1743 *SIC 5812*
NORMAC EQUIPMENT SALES LTD *p 198*
8409 KALAVISTA DR, COLDSTREAM, BC,
V1B 1K4
(250) 542-4726 *SIC 5083*
**NORMAC EQUIPMENT/CONSTRUCTION
LIMITED** *p 846*
6855 HWY 101 E, PORCUPINE, ON, P0N
1C0
(705) 235-3277 *SIC 7359*
NORMAC KITCHENS LIMITED *p 905*
59 GLEN CAMERON RD, THORNHILL, ON,
L3T 5W2
(905) 889-1342 *SIC 2434*
NORMAN ROGERS AIRPORT *p 632*
*See CORPORATION OF THE CITY OF
KINGSTON, THE*
NORMAND MACHINERY *p 1140*
See NORMAND, J.R. INC
NORMAND NADEAU COMMUNICATIONS *p 1360*
See NORMAND NADEAU T.V. INC
NORMAND NADEAU T.V. INC *p 1360*
500 BOUL VACHON N, SAINTE-MARIE,
QC, G6E 1M1
(418) 387-3242 *SIC 7378*
NORMAND, J.R. INC *p 1140*
752 CH OLIVIER, LEVIS, QC, G7A 2N2
(418) 831-3226 *SIC 5084*

NORMANDIN BDJ *p 1256*
See GROUPE NORMANDIN INC
NORMANDIN BEAUDRY *p 1206*
*See NORMANDIN BEAUDRY, ACTUAIRES
CONSEIL INC*
**NORMANDIN BEAUDRY, ACTUAIRES
CONSEIL INC** *p 1206*
630 BOUL RENE-LEVESQUE O SUITE
30E, MONTREAL, QC, H3B 1S6
(514) 285-1122 *SIC 8999*
NORMANDIN INC *p 1377*
931 CH DE MILTON, ST-VALERIEN, QC,
J0H 2B0
(450) 549-2949 *SIC 7389*
NORMANDIN TRANSIT INC *p 1242*
151 BOUL INDUSTRIEL, NAPIERVILLE,
QC, J0J 1L0
(450) 245-0445 *SIC 4213*
NORMANNA REST HOME *p 181*
*See NORWEGIAN OLD PEOPLE'S HOME
ASSOCIATION*
NORMARK INC *p 814*
1350 PHILLIP MURRAY AVE, OSHAWA,
ON, L1J 6Z9
(905) 571-3001 *SIC 5091*
NORMERICA CAPITAL CORPORATION *p 713*
1599 HURONTARIO ST SUITE 300, MIS-
SISSAUGA, ON, L5G 4S1
(416) 626-0556 *SIC 6712*
NORMERICA INC *p 515*
46 MORTON AVE E, BRANTFORD, ON,
N3R 7J7
(519) 756-8414 *SIC 3999*
NORMERICA INC *p 713*
1599 HURONTARIO ST SUITE 300, MIS-
SISSAUGA, ON, L5G 4S1
(416) 626-0556 *SIC 3295*
NORONT RESOURCES LTD *p 955*
212 KING ST W SUITE 501, TORONTO,
ON, M5H 1K5
(416) 367-1444 *SIC 1041*
NORPAC CONSTRUCTION INC *p 217*
5520 CAMPBELL CREEK RD, KAMLOOPS,
BC, V2C 6V4
(778) 696-2434 *SIC 1541*
NORPINE AUTO SUPPLY (96) LTD *p 138*
10533 100 ST, LA CRETE, AB, T0H 2H0
(780) 928-3912 *SIC 5084*
**NORQUAY CO-OPERATIVE ASSOCIATION
LIMITED, THE** *p 1412*
13 HWY 49, NORQUAY, SK, S0A 2V0
(306) 594-2215 *SIC 5211*
NORQUAY HOLDING CO LTD *p 354*
23042 ROAD 68N, OAKVILLE, MB, R0H
0Y0
(204) 267-2139 *SIC 5154*
NORQUAY NURSERIES LTD *p 355*
GD LCD MAIN 28168 1 HWY E, PORTAGE
LA PRAIRIE, MB, R1N 3B2
(204) 239-6507 *SIC 5193*
NORQUEST COLLEGE *p 167*
*See NORQUEST COLLEGE FOUNDATION,
THE*
NORQUEST COLLEGE FOUNDATION, THE *p 90*
10215 108 ST NW, EDMONTON, AB, T5J
1L6
(780) 644-6300 *SIC 8221*
NORQUEST COLLEGE FOUNDATION, THE *p 167*
3201 43 AVE, STONY PLAIN, AB, T7Z 1L1
(780) 968-6489 *SIC 8221*
NORQUEST INDUSTRIES INC *p 110*
3911 74 AVE NW, EDMONTON, AB, T6B
2Z7
(780) 434-3322 *SIC 3599*
NORR LIMITED *p 930*
175 BLOOR ST E, TORONTO, ON, M4W
3R8
(416) 929-0200 *SIC 8712*
NORREF FISHERIES QUEBEC *p 1169*
*See PECHERIES NORREF QUEBEC INC,
LES*

NORREP CAPITAL MANAGEMENT LTD *p* 55
333 7 AVE SW SUITE 1850, CALGARY, AB, T2P 2Z1
(403) 531-2650   *SIC* 8741

NORRIS FORD SALES LTD *p* 171
2929 15 AVE, WAINWRIGHT, AB, T9W 0A4
(780) 842-4400   *SIC* 5511

NORRIZON *p* 1086
See KENDRAKYLE INVESTMENTS INC

NORSASK FARM EQUIPMENT LTD *p* 1412
HWY 16 EAST, NORTH BATTLEFORD, SK, S9A 2M4
(306) 445-8128   *SIC* 5083

NORSASK FOREST PRODUCTS INC *p* 1410
HWY 55 E, MEADOW LAKE, SK, S9X 1V7
(306) 236-5601   *SIC* 2421

NORSAT INTERNATIONAL INC *p* 255
4020 VIKING WAY UNIT 110, RICHMOND, BC, V6V 2N2
(604) 821-2800   *SIC* 3669

NORSECO INC *p* 1236
2914 BOUL CURE-LABELLE, MONTREAL, QC, H7P 5R9
(514) 332-2275   *SIC* 5191

NORSEMAN GROUP LTD *p* 96
14545 115 AVE NW, EDMONTON, AB, T5M 3B8
(780) 451-6939   *SIC* 2394

NORSEMAN INC *p* 96
14545 115 AVE NW, EDMONTON, AB, T5M 3B8
(780) 451-6828   *SIC* 1791

NORSEMAN INC *p* 1434
3815 WANUSKEWIN RD, SASKATOON, SK, S7P 1A4
(306) 385-2888   *SIC* 3448

NORSEMAN STRUCTURES *p* 96
See NORSEMAN INC

NORSEMAN STRUCTURES *p* 1434
See NORSEMAN INC

NORSEMEN INN CAMROSE CORPORATION *p* 78
6505 48 AVE, CAMROSE, AB, T4V 3K3
(780) 672-9171   *SIC* 7011

NORSON CONSTRUCTION LLP *p* 241
949 3RD ST W SUITE 221, NORTH VANCOUVER, BC, V7P 3P7
(604) 986-5681   *SIC* 1542

NORSPEX LTD *p* 673
290 FERRIER ST SUITE 1, MARKHAM, ON, L3R 2Z5
(905) 513-8889   *SIC* 3089

NORSTAN CANADA LTD *p* 768
2225 SHEPPARD AVE E SUITE 1600, NORTH YORK, ON, M2J 5C2
(416) 490-9500   *SIC* 5065

NORSTAN SALES LTD *p* 247
1530 KINGSWAY AVE SUITE 201, PORT COQUITLAM, BC, V3C 6N6
(604) 257-5555   *SIC* 5172

NORSTAR INDUSTRIES LTD *p* 352
27157 HWY 422, MORRIS, MB, R0G 1K0
(204) 746-8200   *SIC* 3532

NORSTAR WINDOWS & DOORS LTD *p* 892
944 SOUTH SERVICE RD, STONEY CREEK, ON, L8E 6A2
(905) 643-9333   *SIC* 3442

NORSTONE FINANCIAL CORPORATION *p* 997
130 KING ST, TORONTO, ON, M9N 1L5
(416) 860-6245   *SIC* 6211

NORSWAY INVESTMENTS & CONSULTANTS INC *p* 324
8563 SELKIRK ST, VANCOUVER, BC, V6P 4J1
(604) 267-1307   *SIC* 3495

NORTAK SOFTWARE LTD *p* 596
1105 CADBORO RD, GLOUCESTER, ON, K1J 7T8
(613) 234-7212   *SIC* 7379

NORTEC MARINE AGENCIES INC *p* 1190
465 RUE SAINT-JEAN BUREAU 708, MONTREAL, QC, H2Y 2R6
(514) 985-2329   *SIC* 4731

NORTEK AIR SOLUTIONS CANADA, INC *p* 1347
200 RUE CARTER, SAINT-LEONARD-D'ASTON, QC, J0C 1M0
(819) 399-2175   *SIC* 1711

NORTEK AIR SOLUTIONS CANADA, INC *p* 1428
1502D QUEBEC AVE, SASKATOON, SK, S7K 1V7
(306) 242-3663   *SIC* 3564

NORTEL NETWORKS LIMITED *p* 492
250 SIDNEY ST, BELLEVILLE, ON, K8P 3Z3
SIC 4899

NORTEX ROOFING LTD *p* 586
40 BETHRIDGE RD, ETOBICOKE, ON, M9W 1N1
(416) 236-6090   *SIC* 1761

NORTH ALBION COLLEGIATE INSTITUTE *p* 581
See TORONTO DISTRICT SCHOOL BOARD

NORTH AMERICA CONSTRUCTION (1993) LTD *p* 746
21 QUEEN ST, MORRISTON, ON, N0B 2C0
(519) 821-8000   *SIC* 1629

NORTH AMERICA STAMPING GROUP *p* 1035
See NASG CANADA INC

NORTH AMERICAN AIR TRAVEL INSURANCE AGENTS LTD *p* 262
6081 NO. 3 RD 11 FL SUITE 1101, RICHMOND, BC, V6Y 2B2
(604) 276-9900   *SIC* 6321

NORTH AMERICAN BOTTLING *p* 292
See LEADING BRANDS OF CANADA, INC

NORTH AMERICAN CLOTHING INC *p* 795
22 LIDO RD, NORTH YORK, ON, M9M 1M6
(416) 741-2626   *SIC* 5137

NORTH AMERICAN CONSTRUCTION GROUP LTD *p* 2
100 AVE ACHESON SUITE 27287, ACHESON, AB, T7X 6H8
(780) 960-7171   *SIC* 1629

NORTH AMERICAN CONSTRUCTION GROUP LTD *p* 2
27287 100 AVE, ACHESON, AB, T7X 6H8
(780) 960-7171   *SIC* 1629

NORTH AMERICAN CONSTRUCTION MANAGEMENT LTD *p* 2
26550 ACHESON RD, ACHESON, AB, T7X 6B2
(780) 960-7171   *SIC* 1629

NORTH AMERICAN CONSTRUCTION MANAGEMENT LTD *p* 128
GD, FORT MCMURRAY, AB, T9H 3E2
(780) 791-1997   *SIC* 1629

NORTH AMERICAN FINANCIAL 15 SPLIT CORP *p* 982
200 FRONT ST WEST SUITE 2510, TORONTO, ON, M5V 3K2
(416) 304-4440   *SIC* 6722

NORTH AMERICAN FOREST PRODUCTS LTD *p* 417
40 LABRIE CH, SAINT-QUENTIN, NB, E8A 2E1
(506) 235-2873   *SIC* 2421

NORTH AMERICAN FUR AUCTIONS *p* 586
See NORTH AMERICAN FUR PRODUCERS INC

NORTH AMERICAN FUR AUCTIONS INC *p* 586
65 SKYWAY AVE, ETOBICOKE, ON, M9W 6C7
(416) 675-9320   *SIC* 5159

NORTH AMERICAN FUR PRODUCERS INC *p* 586
65 SKYWAY AVE, ETOBICOKE, ON, M9W 6C7

(416) 675-9320   *SIC* 6712

NORTH AMERICAN GREENHOUSE SUPPLIES *p* 20
See 489425 ALBERTA LTD

NORTH AMERICAN IMPEX INCORPORATED *p* 673
600 HOOD RD, MARKHAM, ON, L3R 3K9
SIC 5149

NORTH AMERICAN KILN SERVICES INC *p* 910
960 WALSH ST W, THUNDER BAY, ON, P7E 4X4
(807) 622-7728   *SIC* 1629

NORTH AMERICAN LUMBER LIMITED *p* 379
205 FORT ST SUITE 200, WINNIPEG, MB, R3C 1E3
(204) 942-8121   *SIC* 5211

NORTH AMERICAN METALS OF CANADA LTD *p* 756
130 HARRY WALKER PKY N, NEWMARKET, ON, L3Y 7B2
(905) 898-2291   *SIC* 3469

NORTH AMERICAN MINING DIVISION *p* 128
See NORTH AMERICAN CONSTRUCTION MANAGEMENT LTD

NORTH AMERICAN NICKEL INC *p* 315
1055 WEST HASTINGS ST SUITE 2200, VANCOUVER, BC, V6E 2E9
(604) 770-4334   *SIC* 1061

NORTH AMERICAN PALLADIUM LTD *p* 965
ONE UNIVERSITY AVE SUITE 1601, TORONTO, ON, M5J 2P1
(416) 360-7590   *SIC* 1099

NORTH AMERICAN PAPER INCORPORATED *p* 499
16 AUTOMATIC RD, BRAMPTON, ON, L6S 5N3
(905) 793-8202   *SIC* 2679

NORTH AMERICAN PIPE & STEEL LTD *p* 209
7449 RIVER RD, DELTA, BC, V4G 1B9
(604) 946-0916   *SIC* 5051

NORTH AMERICAN PRODUCE BUYERS LIMITED *p* 572
165 THE QUEENSWAY SUITE 336, ETOBICOKE, ON, M8Y 1H8
(416) 255-5544   *SIC* 5148

NORTH AMERICAN PRODUCE SALES *p* 294
See 480412 B.C. LTD

NORTH AMERICAN ROCK & DIRT INC *p* 1414
4271 5TH AVE E, PRINCE ALBERT, SK, S6W 0A5
(306) 764-5337   *SIC* 1629

NORTH AMERICAN STEEL EQUIPMENT INC *p* 1014
300 HOPKINS ST, WHITBY, ON, L1N 2B9
(905) 668-3300   *SIC* 2542

NORTH AMERICAN TEA & COFFEE INC *p* 209
7861 82 ST, DELTA, BC, V4G 1L9
(604) 940-7861   *SIC* 5141

NORTH AMERICAN TRANSIT SUPPLY CORPORATION *p* 684
375 BRONTE ST N, MILTON, ON, L9T 3N7
(905) 876-0255   *SIC* 5088

NORTH AMERICAN TUNGSTEN CORPORATION LTD *p* 307
400 BURRARD ST SUITE 1680, VANCOUVER, BC, V6C 3A6
(604) 638-7440   *SIC* 1081

NORTH ARM TRANSPORTATION LTD *p* 288
2582 E KENT AVE SOUTH, VANCOUVER, BC, V5S 2H8
(604) 321-9171   *SIC* 5172

NORTH ATLANTIC *p* 430

86 THORBURN RD, ST. JOHN'S, NL, A1B 3M3
(709) 738-5542   *SIC* 5172

NORTH ATLANTIC INTERNATIONAL LOGISTICS INC *p* 620
22 DAIRY LANE SUITE 291, HUNTSVILLE, ON, P1H 1T4
(416) 291-2688   *SIC* 4731

NORTH ATLANTIC PETROLEUM *p* 430
See NORTH ATLANTIC REFINING LIMITED

NORTH ATLANTIC PETROLEUM LIMITED *p* 430
29 PIPPY PL, ST. JOHN'S, NL, A1B 3X2
(709) 579-5831   *SIC* 5074

NORTH ATLANTIC REFINING LIMITED *p* 430
29 PIPPY PL, ST. JOHN'S, NL, A1B 3X2
(709) 463-8811   *SIC* 2911

NORTH BATTLEFORD YOUTH CENTER *p* 1412
See GOVERNMENT OF SASKATCHEWAN

NORTH BAY CHRYSLER LTD *p* 762
352 LAKESHORE DR, NORTH BAY, ON, P1A 2C2
(705) 472-0820   *SIC* 5511

NORTH BAY FIRE DEPARTMENT, THE *p* 763
See CORPORATION OF THE CITY OF NORTH BAY, THE

NORTH BAY HYDRO DISTRIBUTION LIMITED *p* 762
74 COMMERCE CRES, NORTH BAY, ON, P1A 0B4
(705) 474-8100   *SIC* 4911

NORTH BAY NUGGET *p* 763
See OSPREY MEDIA PUBLISHING INC

NORTH BAY PARRY SOUND DISTRICT HEALTH UNIT *p* 763
345 OAK ST W, NORTH BAY, ON, P1B 2T2
(705) 474-1400   *SIC* 8621

NORTH BLENHEIM MUTUAL INSURANCE COMPANY *p* 518
11 BAIRD ST N, BRIGHT, ON, N0J 1B0
(519) 454-8661   *SIC* 6331

NORTH CARIBOO AIR *p* 214
See NORTH CARIBOO FLYING SERVICE LTD

NORTH CARIBOO FLYING SERVICE LTD *p* 214
9945 CARIBOU WAY, FORT ST. JOHN, BC, V1J 4J2
(250) 787-0311   *SIC* 4512

NORTH CENTENNIAL MANOR INC *p* 627
2 KIMBERLY DR, KAPUSKASING, ON, P5N 1L5
(705) 335-6125   *SIC* 8051

NORTH CENTRAL CO-OPERATIVE ASSOCIATION LTD *p* 167
4917 50 AVE, STONY PLAIN, AB, T7Z 1W6
(780) 963-2272   *SIC* 5411

NORTH COUNTRY LIVESTOCK LTD *p* 107
24040 17 ST NE, EDMONTON, AB, T5Y 6J6
(780) 478-2333   *SIC* 5154

NORTH DELTA SEAFOODS LTD *p* 209
7857 HUSTON RD, DELTA, BC, V4G 1M1
(604) 582-8268   *SIC* 5146

NORTH DELTA SENIOR SECONDARY SCHOOL *p* 207
See DELTA SCHOOL DISTRICT NO.37

NORTH DOUGLAS SYSCO *p* 340
See SYSCO CANADA, INC

NORTH EAST COMMUNITY CARE ACCESS CENTRE *p* 763
1164 DEVONSHIRE AVE, NORTH BAY, ON, P1B 6X7
(705) 474-5885   *SIC* 8059

NORTH EAST COMMUNITY CARE ACCESS CENTRE *p* 862

▲ Public Company   ■ Public Company Family Member   **HQ** Headquarters   **BR** Branch   **SL** Single Location

390 BAY ST, SAULT STE. MARIE, ON, P6A 1X2

(705) 949-1650 SIC 8322

NORTH EAST COMMUNITY CARE ACCESS CENTRE *p* 900

40 ELM ST SUITE 41-C, SUDBURY, ON, P3C 1S8

(705) 522-3461 SIC 8059

NORTH EAST OUTREACH AND SUPPORT SERVICES, INC *p* 1410

128 MCKENDRY AVE W, MELFORT, SK, S0E 1A0

(306) 752-9464 SIC 8699

NORTH EAST SCHOOL DIVISION *p* 1410

402 MAIN ST, MELFORT, SK, S0E 1A0

(306) 752-5741 SIC 8211

NORTH EASTERN CHRISTMAS TREE ASSOCIATION *p* 450

799 SOUTH RIVER LAKE RD, GOSHEN, NS, B0H 1M0

(902) 783-2430 SIC 5199

NORTH EASTMAN HEALTH ASSOCIATION INC *p* 345

151 1 ST S, BEAUSEJOUR, MB, R0E 0C0

(204) 268-1076 SIC 8062

NORTH EASTMAN HEALTH ASSOCIATION INC *p* 354

689 MAIN ST, OAKBANK, MB, R0E 1J2

(204) 444-2227 SIC 8011

NORTH EDMONTON KIA *p* 94

See KIA MOTORS LP

NORTH ENDERBY TIMBER LTD *p* 212

6261 HWY 97A RR 3, ENDERBY, BC, V0E 1V3

(250) 838-9668 SIC 2421

NORTH FIELD OFFICE *p* 505

See PEEL DISTRICT SCHOOL BOARD

NORTH FRONT MOTORS INC *p* 492

239 NORTH FRONT ST, BELLEVILLE, ON, K8P 3C3

(613) 966-3333 SIC 5511

NORTH FRONT PRICE CHOPPER *p* 492

305 NORTH FRONT ST SUITE 5, BELLEVILLE, ON, K8P 3C3

(613) 966-0270 SIC 5411

NORTH HAMILTON COMMUNITY HEALTH CENTRE *p* 611

438 HUGHSON ST N, HAMILTON, ON, L8L 4N5

(905) 523-1184 SIC 8011

NORTH HASTINGS *p* 484

See QUINTE HEALTHCARE CORPORATION

NORTH HASTINGS HIGH SCHOOL *p* 484

See HASTINGS AND PRINCE EDWARD DISTRICT SCHOOL BOARD

NORTH HERITAGE REALTY INC *p* 898

860 LASALLE BLVD, SUDBURY, ON, P3A 1X5

(705) 688-0007 SIC 6531

NORTH HILL INN *p* 153

See DJ WILL HOLDINGS LIMITED

NORTH HILL MAZDA *p* 20

See 771922 ALBERTA INC

NORTH HILL MOTORS (1975) LTD *p* 3

139 EAST LAKE CRES NE, AIRDRIE, AB, T4A 2H7

(403) 948-2600 SIC 5511

NORTH HOUSE FOODS LTD *p* 595

1169 PARISIEN ST, GLOUCESTER, ON, K1B 4W4

(613) 746-6662 SIC 5148

NORTH INC *p* 638

27 GAUKEL ST, KITCHENER, ON, N2G 1Y6

(888) 777-2546 SIC 7371

NORTH ISLAND COLLEGE *p* 195

1685 DOGWOOD ST S, CAMPBELL RIVER, BC, V9W 8C1

(250) 923-9700 SIC 8221

NORTH KEE TRADING COMPANY *p* 875

See 1519694 ONTARIO INC

NORTH KEY CONSTRUCTION *p* 747

See 1652472 ONTARIO INC

NORTH LAMBTON LODGE *p* 591

See CORPORATION OF THE COUNTY OF LAMBTON

NORTH MARKHAM MOTORS LTD *p* 1000

8220 KENNEDY RD, UNIONVILLE, ON, L3R 5X3

(905) 477-2451 SIC 5511

NORTH OKANAGAN REGIONAL HEALTH BOARD *p* 331

1440 14 AVE, VERNON, BC, V1B 2T1

(250) 549-5700 SIC 8011

NORTH OKANAGAN SHUSWAP SCHOOL DISTRICT 83 *p* 179

2365 PLEASANT VALLEY RD, ARMSTRONG, BC, V0E 1B2

(250) 546-3114 SIC 8211

NORTH PARK NURSING HOME LIMITED *p* 791

450 RUSTIC RD, NORTH YORK, ON, M6L 1W9

(416) 247-0531 SIC 8051

NORTH PARK SECONDARY SCHOOL *p* 499

See PEEL DISTRICT SCHOOL BOARD

NORTH PEACE GAS CO-OPERATIVE LTD *p* 126

10908 92 AVE, FAIRVIEW, AB, T0H 1L0

(780) 835-5444 SIC 4924

NORTH PEACE HOUSING FOUNDATION *p* 135

4918 49 AVE, GRIMSHAW, AB, T0H 1W0

SIC 6531

NORTH PEACE SAVINGS AND CREDIT UNION *p* 214

10344 100 ST, FORT ST. JOHN, BC, V1J 3Z1

(250) 787-0361 SIC 6062

NORTH PEACE SECONDARY SCHOOL *p* 214

See SCHOOL DISTRICT NO. 60 (PEACE RIVER NORTH)

NORTH PORTAL DUTY FREE SHOP, DIV OF *p* 1413

See DAVIS, PERCY H. LIMITED

NORTH QUEENS NURSING HOME INC *p* 441

9565 HIGHWAY 8, CALEDONIA, NS, B0T 1B0

(902) 682-2553 SIC 8361

NORTH RIDGE DEVELOPMENT CORPORATION *p* 1428

3037 FAITHFULL AVE, SASKATOON, SK, S7K 8B3

(306) 242-2434 SIC 1522

NORTH ROCK CONSTRUCTION PROJECTS *p* 545

See 1835755 ONTARIO LIMITED

NORTH SHORE ACURA *p* 241

See DENNISON AUTO LTD

NORTH SHORE HEALTH NETWORK *p* 493

525 CAUSLEY ST, BLIND RIVER, ON, P0R 1B0

(705) 356-1220 SIC 8062

NORTH SHORE PRIVATE HOSPITAL (1985) LTD *p* 239

1070 LYNN VALLEY RD SUITE 321, NORTH VANCOUVER, BC, V7J 1Z8

(604) 988-4181 SIC 8051

NORTH SIDE MITSUBISHI *p* 85

See N.S.M. AUTO LTD

NORTH STAR CONTRACTING INC *p* 77

64 TECHNOLOGY WAY SE, CALGARY, AB, T3S 0B9

(403) 228-3421 SIC 1623

NORTH STAR MANUFACTURING (LONDON) LTD *p* 889

40684 TALBOT LINE, ST THOMAS, ON, N5P 3T2

(519) 637-7899 SIC 3089

NORTH STAR PATROL (1996) LTD *p* 277

12981 80 AVE, SURREY, BC, V3W 3B1

NORTH STAR VINYL WINDOWS AND DOORS *p* 889

See NORTH STAR MANUFACTURING (LONDON) LTD

NORTH TORONTO AUCTION *p* 622

See NORTHERN AUTO AUCTIONS OF CANADA INC

NORTH TORONTO BASEBALL ASSOCIATION *p* 922

2708 YONGE ST, TORONTO, ON, M4P 3J4

(519) 740-3900 SIC 8699

NORTH TORONTO COLLEGIATE INSTITUTE *p* 923

See TORONTO DISTRICT SCHOOL BOARD

NORTH TORONTO MAZDA *p* 903

See 1263815 ONTARIO INC

NORTH VANCOUVER FIRE HALL OFFICE *p* 239

See DISTRICT OF NORTH VANCOUVER MUNICIPAL PU

NORTH VANCOUVER SCHOOL DISTRICT *p* 240

See SCHOOL DISTRICT NO. 44 (NORTH VANCOUVER)

NORTH WELLINGTON CO-OPERATIVE SERVICES *p* 618

56 MARGARET ST, HARRISTON, ON, N0G 1Z0

(519) 338-2331 SIC 5191

NORTH WELLINGTON HEALTH CARE CORPORATION *p* 746

630 DUBLIN ST, MOUNT FOREST, ON, N0G 2L3

(519) 323-2210 SIC 8062

NORTH WEST COMPANY INC, THE *p* 379

77 MAIN ST, WINNIPEG, MB, R3C 1A3

(204) 943-0881 SIC 5311

NORTH WEST COMPANY LP, THE *p* 107

14097 VICTORIA TRAIL NW, EDMONTON, AB, T5Y 2B6

(780) 472-7780 SIC 5411

NORTH WEST COMPANY LP, THE *p* 353

GD, NORWAY HOUSE, MB, R0B 1B0

(204) 359-6258 SIC 5411

NORTH WEST COMPANY LP, THE *p* 379

77 MAIN ST, WINNIPEG, MB, R3C 1A3

(204) 943-0881 SIC 6712

NORTH WEST COMPANY LP, THE *p* 1420

2735 AVONHURST DR, REGINA, SK, S4R 3J3

(306) 789-3155 SIC 5411

NORTH WEST CRANE ENTERPRISES LTD *p* 139

7015 SPARROW DR, LEDUC, AB, T9E 7L1

(780) 980-2227 SIC 7389

NORTH WEST GEOMATICS LTD *p* 24

245 AERO WAY NE, CALGARY, AB, T2E 6K2

(403) 295-0694 SIC 7389

NORTH WEST GROUP *p* 24

See NORTH WEST GEOMATICS LTD

NORTH WEST PAVING LTD *p* 163

20 TURBO DR, SHERWOOD PARK, AB, T8H 2J6

(780) 468-4144 SIC 1611

NORTH WEST REDWATER PARTNERSHIP *p* 55

140 4 AVE SW SUITE 2800, CALGARY, AB, T2P 3N3

(403) 398-0900 SIC 2911

NORTH WEST RUBBER LTD *p* 175

33850 INDUSTRIAL AVE, ABBOTSFORD, BC, V2S 7J9

(604) 859-2002 SIC 3496

NORTH WEST WHOLESALE FLORISTS LTD *p* 193

8580 GREENALL AVE, BURNABY, BC, V5J 3M6

(604) 430-0593 SIC 5193

NORTH WOOD CARPET & TILE COMPANY LTD *p* 495

16 NIXON RD, BOLTON, ON, L7E 1K3

(905) 790-0085 SIC 5023

NORTH YORK CHEVROLET OLDSMOBILE LTD *p* 906

7200 YONGE ST, THORNHILL, ON, L4J 1V8

(905) 881-5000 SIC 5511

NORTH YORK CHRYSLER JEEP DODGE *p* 906

See TORONTO SMART CARS LTD

NORTH YORK EARLY CHILDHOOD *p* 782

See COMMUNITY LIVING TORONTO

NORTH YORK GENERAL HOSPITAL *p* 769

4001 LESLIE ST, NORTH YORK, ON, M2K 1E1

(416) 756-6000 SIC 8062

NORTH YORK GENERAL HOSPITAL *p* 775

555 FINCH AVE W SUITE 262, NORTH YORK, ON, M2R 1N5

(416) 633-9420 SIC 8062

NORTH YORK IRON CORPORATION *p* 784

1100 FLINT RD, NORTH YORK, ON, M3J 2J5

(416) 661-2888 SIC 5051

NORTH YORK MEDICAL BUILDING INC *p* 786

1017 WILSON AVE UNIT 304, NORTH YORK, ON, M3K 1Z1

(416) 783-5100 SIC 8011

NORTH YORK REHABILITATION CENTRE CORP *p* 915

2255 SHEPPARD AVE E SUITE 300, TORONTO, ON, M2J 4Y1

(416) 497-4477 SIC 6321

NORTH-EAST TUBES INC *p* 505

29 NUGGETT CRT, BRAMPTON, ON, L6T 5A9

(905) 792-1200 SIC 5051

NORTH-ED (1994) LTD *p* 83

12996 50 ST NW, EDMONTON, AB, T5A 4L2

(780) 457-0221 SIC 5812

NORTH-WRIGHT AIRWAYS LTD *p* 435

2200, NORMAN WELLS, NT, X0E 0V0

(867) 587-2288 SIC 4724

NORTH/SOUTH CONSULTANTS INC *p* 393

83 SCURFIELD BLVD, WINNIPEG, MB, R3Y 1G4

(204) 284-3366 SIC 8748

NORTHAM BEVERAGES LTD *p* 217

965 MCGILL PL, KAMLOOPS, BC, V2C 6N9

(250) 851-2543 SIC 2085

NORTHAM BEVERAGES LTD *p* 299

68 WATER ST UNIT 501, VANCOUVER, BC, V6B 1A4

(604) 731-2900 SIC 2085

NORTHAM REALTY ADVISORS LIMITED *p* 935

2 CARLTON ST SUITE 909, TORONTO, ON, M5B 1J3

(416) 977-7151 SIC 6531

NORTHAMPTON GROUP INC *p* 698

2601 MATHESON BLVD E SUITE 212, MISSISSAUGA, ON, L4W 5A8

(905) 629-9992 SIC 7011

NORTHBRIDGE FINANCIAL CORPORATION *p* 955

105 ADELAIDE ST W SUITE 700, TORONTO, ON, M5H 1P9

(416) 350-4400 SIC 6411

NORTHBRIDGE FINANCIAL CORPORATION *p* 1206

1000 RUE DE LA GAUCHETIERE O, MONTREAL, QC, H3B 4W5

(514) 843-1111 SIC 6411

NORTHBRIDGE GENERAL INSURANCE CORPORATION *p* 955

105 ADELAIDE ST W 4TH FL, TORONTO, ON, M5H 1P9

(416) 350-4400 SIC 6331

NORTHBRIDGE GENERAL INSURANCE

CORPORATION *p 955*
105 ADELAIDE ST W UNIT 700, TORONTO, ON, M5H 1P9
(416) 350-4300   *SIC* 6331
NORTHBRIDGE INDEMNITY INSURANCE CORPORATION *p 329*
595 BURRARD ST SUITE 1500, VANCOUVER, BC, V7X 1G4
(604) 683-5511   *SIC* 6411
NORTHBRIDGE INDEMNITY INSURANCE CORPORATION *p 955*
105 ADELAIDE ST W UNIT 700, TORONTO, ON, M5H 1P9
(855) 620-6262   *SIC* 6411
NORTHBRIDGE PERSONAL INSURANCE CORPORATION *p 955*
105 ADELAIDE ST W, TORONTO, ON, M5H 1P9
(416) 350-4400   *SIC* 6331
NORTHBUD DISTRIBUTORS LTD *p 732*
6030 FREEMONT BLVD, MISSISSAUGA, ON, L5R 3X4
SIC 5147
NORTHCOAST BUILDING PRODUCTS LTD *p 272*
14682 66 AVE, SURREY, BC, V3S 1Z9
(604) 597-8884   *SIC* 5039
NORTHCOTT SILK INC *p 556*
101 COURTLAND AVE, CONCORD, ON, L4K 3T5
(905) 760-0072   *SIC* 5199
NORTHCREST CARE CENTRE LTD *p 208*
6771 120 ST, DELTA, BC, V4E 2A7
(604) 597-7878   *SIC* 8051
NORTHDOWN INDUSTRIES *p 713*
See NORMERICA INC
NORTHEAST COMMUNITY HEALTH CENTRE *p*
83
See ALBERTA HEALTH SERVICES
NORTHEAST EQUIPMENT LIMITED *p 447*
135 JOSEPH ZATZMAN DR, DARTMOUTH, NS, B3B 1W1
(902) 468-7473   *SIC* 5074
NORTHEAST NUTRITION INC *p 469*
494 WILLOW ST, TRURO, NS, B2N 6X8
(902) 893-9449   *SIC* 2048
NORTHEASTERN CATHOLIC DISTRICT SCHOOL BOARD *p 913*
383 BIRCH ST N, TIMMINS, ON, P4N 6E8
(705) 268-7443   *SIC* 8211
NORTHEASTERN INVESTIGATIONS INCORPORATED *p*
447
202 BROWNLOW AVE SUITE 1, DARTMOUTH, NS, B3B 1T5
(902) 435-1336   *SIC* 7381
NORTHEASTERN PROTECTION SERVICE *p 447*
See NORTHEASTERN INVESTIGATIONS INCORPORATED
NORTHEASTERN SWIMMING POOL DISTRIBUTORS INC *p*
556
282 NORTH RIVERMEDE RD, CONCORD, ON, L4K 3N6
(905) 761-7946   *SIC* 5091
NORTHEC CONSTRUCTION INC *p 913*
2401 AIRPORT RD, TIMMINS, ON, P4N 7C3
(705) 531-3370   *SIC* 1629
NORTHEND PHARMACY LTD *p 409*
1633 MOUNTAIN RD, MONCTON, NB, E1G 1A5
(506) 858-0055   *SIC* 5912
NORTHERN *p 379*
See NORTH WEST COMPANY INC, THE
NORTHERN *p 379*
See NORTH WEST COMPANY LP, THE
NORTHERN ACREAGE SUPPLY LTD *p 251*
4870 CONTINENTAL WAY, PRINCE GEORGE, BC, V2N 5S5
(250) 596-2273   *SIC* 5083
NORTHERN ALBERTA DIVISION *p 97*

See CANADIAN CORPS OF COMMISSIONAIRES (NORTHERN ALBERTA)
NORTHERN ALBERTA INSTITUTE OF TECHNOLOGY *p 85*
10504 PRINCESS ELIZABETH AVE NW, EDMONTON, AB, T5G 3K4
(780) 471-6248   *SIC* 8222
NORTHERN ALBERTA INSTITUTE OF TECHNOLOGY *p 85*
11762 106 ST NW UNIT 108, EDMONTON, AB, T5G 3H2
(780) 471-6248   *SIC* 8222
NORTHERN ALBERTA INSTITUTE OF TECHNOLOGY *p 106*
12204 149 ST NW, EDMONTON, AB, T5V 1A2
(780) 378-7200   *SIC* 8222
NORTHERN ALLIED STEEL SERVICE CENTRE *p 913*
See NORTHERN ALLIED SUPPLY COMPANY LIMITED
NORTHERN ALLIED SUPPLY COMPANY LIMITED *p 913*
352 RAILWAY ST, TIMMINS, ON, P4N 2P6
(705) 264-5291   *SIC* 5051
NORTHERN AUTO AUCTIONS OF CANADA INC *p 622*
3230 THOMAS ST, INNISFIL, ON, L9S 3W5
(705) 436-4111   *SIC* 7389
NORTHERN BLIZZARD *p 55*
440 2 AVE SW, CALGARY, AB, T2P 5E9
(403) 930-3000   *SIC* 6792
NORTHERN BLOWER INC *p 363*
901 REGENT AVE W, WINNIPEG, MB, R2C 2Z8
(204) 222-4216   *SIC* 5084
NORTHERN BOTTLING DISTRUTORS *p*
134
See NORTHERN BOTTLING LTD
NORTHERN BOTTLING LTD *p 134*
15415 91 ST, GRANDE PRAIRIE, AB, T8X 0B4
(780) 532-4222   *SIC* 2086
NORTHERN BREEZE COLONY *p 355*
See NORTHERN BREEZE FARMS LTD
NORTHERN BREEZE FARMS LTD *p 355*
GD LCD MAIN, PORTAGE LA PRAIRIE, MB, R1N 3A7
(204) 239-4396   *SIC* 0212
NORTHERN BUILDALL TIMBER MART *p*
629
See DOIDGE BUILDING CENTRES LTD
NORTHERN BUILDING SUPPLY LTD *p 288*
1640 E KENT AVE SOUTH, VANCOUVER, BC, V5P 2S7
(604) 321-6141   *SIC* 5031
NORTHERN CABLES INC *p 519*
50 CALIFORNIA AVE, BROCKVILLE, ON, K6V 6E6
(613) 345-1594   *SIC* 3357
NORTHERN CARTAGE LIMITED *p 369*
60 EAGLE DR SUITE 204, WINNIPEG, MB, R2R 1V5
(204) 633-5795   *SIC* 4213
NORTHERN CASKET (1976) LIMITED *p 646*
165 ST PETER ST, LINDSAY, ON, K9V 5A7
(705) 324-6164   *SIC* 3995
NORTHERN COLLEGE OF APPLIED ARTS & TECHNOLOGY *p 634*
140 GOVERNMENT RD W, KIRKLAND LAKE, ON, P2N 2E9
(705) 567-9291   *SIC* 8221
NORTHERN COMMUNICATION SERVICES INC *p 900*
230 ALDER ST, SUDBURY, ON, P3C 4J2
(705) 677-6744   *SIC* 7389
NORTHERN CONSTRUCTION AND SUPPLIERS LTD *p*
403
534 WEST RIVER RD, GRANDSAULT/GRAND FALLS, NB, E3Z 3E7
(506) 473-1822   *SIC* 1611
NORTHERN CONSTRUCTION INC *p 403*
554 WEST RIVER RD, GRAND-

SAULT/GRAND FALLS, NB, E3Z 3E7
(506) 473-1822   *SIC* 1611
NORTHERN CREDIT UNION LIMITED *p 863*
280 MCNABB ST, SAULT STE. MARIE, ON, P6B 1Y6
(705) 949-2644   *SIC* 6062
NORTHERN CREDIT UNION LTD *p 863*
681 PINE ST, SAULT STE. MARIE, ON, P6B 3G2
(705) 253-9868   *SIC* 6062
NORTHERN DIABETES HEALTH NETWORK INC *p*
908
1204 ROLAND ST UNIT A, THUNDER BAY, ON, P7B 5M4
(807) 624-1720   *SIC* 8699
NORTHERN DIGITAL INC *p 1010*
103 RANDALL DR, WATERLOO, ON, N2V 1C5
(519) 884-5142   *SIC* 3841
NORTHERN DOCK SYSTEMS INC *p 741*
415 AMBASSADOR DR, MISSISSAUGA, ON, L5T 2J3
(905) 625-1758   *SIC* 5082
NORTHERN DYNASTY MINERALS LTD *p 315*
1040 WEST GEORGIA ST 15TH FL, VANCOUVER, BC, V6E 4H1
(604) 684-6365   *SIC* 1021
NORTHERN ENERGY CONSTRUCTORS LTD *p 251*
9368 MILWAUKEE WAY SUITE 101, PRINCE GEORGE, BC, V2N 5T3
(250) 562-8100   *SIC* 5211
NORTHERN FEATHER CANADA LTD *p 209*
8088 RIVER WAY, DELTA, BC, V4G 1K9
(604) 940-8283   *SIC* 2221
NORTHERN FIBRE TERMINAL INCORPORATED *p*
453
1869 UPPER WATER ST, HALIFAX, NS, B3J 1S9
(902) 422-3030   *SIC* 2611
NORTHERN FOOD SERVICES *p 435*
See 994421 N.W.T. LTD
NORTHERN FORCE SECURITY *p 556*
1750 STEELES AVE W, CONCORD, ON, L4K 2L7
(647) 982-1385   *SIC* 7381
NORTHERN FREEDOM INC *p 359*
PO BOX 510, TEULON, MB, R0C 3B0
(204) 886-2552   *SIC* 2015
NORTHERN GATEWAY PUBLIC SCHOOLS *p 173*
See NORTHERN GATEWAY REGIONAL DIVISION #10
NORTHERN GATEWAY REGIONAL DIVISION #10 *p*
173
4816 49 AVE, WHITECOURT, AB, T7S 0E8
(780) 778-2800   *SIC* 8211
NORTHERN GOLD FOODS LTD *p 247*
1725 COAST MERIDIAN RD, PORT COQUITLAM, BC, V3C 3T7
(604) 941-0731   *SIC* 2043
NORTHERN HARDWARE & FURNITURE CO., LTD *p 249*
1386 3RD AVE, PRINCE GEORGE, BC, V2L 3E9
(250) 563-7161   *SIC* 5251
NORTHERN HARDWARE LTD *p 31*
549 CLEVELAND CRES SE, CALGARY, AB, T2G 4R8
(403) 243-5401   *SIC* 5072
NORTHERN HARVEST SEA FARMS NEWFOUNDLAND LTD *p*
428
183 MAIN ST, ST ALBANS, NL, A0H 2E0
(709) 538-3231   *SIC* 2092
NORTHERN HEALTH AUTHORITY *p 194*
741 CTR ST, BURNS LAKE, BC, V0J 1E0
(250) 692-2400   *SIC* 6324
NORTHERN HEALTH AUTHORITY *p 224*
920 LAHAKAS BLVD S, KITIMAT, BC, V8C

2S3
(250) 632-2121   *SIC* 8062
NORTHERN HEALTH AUTHORITY *p 249*
299 VICTORIA ST SUITE 600, PRINCE GEORGE, BC, V2L 5B8
(250) 565-2649   *SIC* 8062
NORTHERN HEALTH AUTHORITY *p 250*
1000 LIARD DR, PRINCE GEORGE, BC, V2M 3Z3
(250) 649-7293   *SIC* 8742
NORTHERN HEALTH AUTHORITY *p 251*
1305 SUMMIT AVE, PRINCE RUPERT, BC, V8J 2A6
(250) 624-2171   *SIC* 8062
NORTHERN HEALTH AUTHORITY *p 252*
543 FRONT ST, QUESNEL, BC, V2J 2K7
(250) 985-5600   *SIC* 8062
NORTHERN ICE SUPPLY LTD *p 249*
1835 1ST AVE, PRINCE GEORGE, BC, V2L 2Y8
(778) 763-0945   *SIC* 5199
NORTHERN IMAGES, THE *p 371*
See ARCTIC CO-OPERATIVES LIMITED
NORTHERN INDUSTRIAL CARRIERS LTD *p 110*
7823 34 ST NW, EDMONTON, AB, T6B 2V5
(780) 465-0341   *SIC* 4213
NORTHERN INDUSTRIAL SALES *p 251*
See NORTHERN INDUSTRIAL SALES B.C. LTD
NORTHERN INDUSTRIAL SALES B.C. LTD *p 251*
3526 OPIE CRES, PRINCE GEORGE, BC, V2N 2P9
(250) 562-4435   *SIC* 5085
NORTHERN INTERIOR WOODWORKERS HOLDING SOCIETY *p 249*
1777 3RD AVE SUITE 100, PRINCE GEORGE, BC, V2L 3G7
(250) 563-7771   *SIC* 6371
NORTHERN INTERNATIONAL *p 201*
See NII NORTHERN INTERNATIONAL INC
NORTHERN LIFE NEWSPAPER *p 901*
See LAURENTIAN PUBLISHING LIMITED
NORTHERN LIGHTS AVIATION LTD *p 134*
3795 56 AVE E, GRANDE PRAIRIE, AB, T9E 0V4
(780) 890-1300   *SIC* 8748
NORTHERN LIGHTS CASINO *p 1414*
See SASKATCHEWAN INDIAN GAMING AUTHORITY INC
NORTHERN LIGHTS COLLEGE *p 204*
11401 8 ST, DAWSON CREEK, BC, V1G 4G2
(250) 782-5251   *SIC* 8222
NORTHERN LIGHTS FITNESS PRODUCTS INCORPORATED *p 563*
700 WALLRICH AVE, CORNWALL, ON, K6J 5X4
(613) 938-8196   *SIC* 3949
NORTHERN LIGHTS GAS CO-OP LTD *p 138*
10205 101 ST, LA CRETE, AB, T0H 2H0
(780) 928-3881   *SIC* 4923
NORTHERN LIGHTS SCHOOL DIVISION 113 *p 1408*
108 FINLAYSON ST, LA RONGE, SK, S0J 1L0
(306) 425-3302   *SIC* 8211
NORTHERN LIGHTS SCHOOL DIVISION NO. 69 *p 6*
6005 50 AVE, BONNYVILLE, AB, T9N 2L4
(780) 826-3145   *SIC* 8211
NORTHERN LIGHTS SEAFOOD INC *p 425*
44 WATERS ST SUITE 40, MAIN BROOK, NL, A0K 3N0
(709) 865-3333   *SIC* 5146
NORTHERN LINKWELL CONSTRUCTION LTD *p 251*
2011 PG PULP MILL RD, PRINCE GEORGE, BC, V2N 2K3
(250) 563-2844   *SIC* 1622
NORTHERN LOGISTICS, DIV OF *p 369*
See NORTHERN CARTAGE LIMITED

NORTHERN MARKETING & SALES INC *p* 652
11 BUCHANAN CRT, LONDON, ON, N5Z 4P9
(519) 680-0385 *SIC* 5063

NORTHERN MAT & BRIDGE *p* 80
See NORTHERN MAT & BRIDGE LIMITED PARTNERSHIP

NORTHERN MAT & BRIDGE LIMITED PARTNERSHIP *p* 80
8001 99 ST, CLAIRMONT, AB, T8X 5B1
(780) 538-4135 *SIC* 7353

NORTHERN MEAT SERVICE *p* 369
See RUSS PATERSON LTD

NORTHERN METALIC SALES (ALTA) *p* 144
See WEATHERFORD CANADA LTD

NORTHERN METALIC SALES (ALTA) LTD *p* 133
10625 WEST SIDE DR UNIT 206, GRANDE PRAIRIE, AB, T8V 8E6
(780) 513-6095 *SIC* 6719

NORTHERN METALIC SALES (F.S.J.) LTD *p* 214
10407 ALASKA RD, FORT ST. JOHN, BC, V1J 1B1
(250) 787-0717 *SIC* 5085

NORTHERN METALIC SALES (G.P.) LTD *p* 133
9708 108 ST, GRANDE PRAIRIE, AB, T8V 4E2
(780) 539-9555 *SIC* 5251

NORTHERN MICRO INC *p* 818
3155 SWANSEA CRES, OTTAWA, ON, K1G 3J3
(613) 226-1117 *SIC* 3571

NORTHERN MICRO INC *p* 1274
3107 AV DES HOTELS BUREAU 2, QUEBEC, QC, G1W 4W5
(418) 654-1733 *SIC* 5734

NORTHERN NEWS SERVICES LTD *p* 436
5108 50 ST, YELLOWKNIFE, NT, X1A 1S2
(867) 873-4031 *SIC* 2711

NORTHERN NISHNAWBE EDUCATION COUNCIL *p* 881
21 KING ST, SIOUX LOOKOUT, ON, P8T 1B9
(807) 737-2002 *SIC* 8299

NORTHERN OASIS MARKETING & DIRECT SALES *p* 910
701 MONTREAL ST, THUNDER BAY, ON, P7E 3P2
(807) 623-5249 *SIC* 5085

NORTHERN ONTARIO SCHOOL OF MEDICINE *p* 901
935 RAMSEY LAKE RD, SUDBURY, ON, P3E 2C6
(705) 675-4883 *SIC* 8221

NORTHERN ONTARIO SCHOOL OF MEDICINE *p* 908
955 OLIVER RD SUITE 2005, THUNDER BAY, ON, P7B 5E1
(807) 766-7300 *SIC* 8062

NORTHERN RECREATION *p* 249
See N R MOTORS LTD

NORTHERN REFLECTIONS LTD *p* 577
21 FOUR SEASONS PL 2ND FLR, ETOBICOKE, ON, M9B 6J8
(416) 626-2500 *SIC* 5621

NORTHERN REFLECTIONS LTD *p* 995
2198 BLOOR ST W, TORONTO, ON, M6S 1N4
(416) 769-8378 *SIC* 5621

NORTHERN REFORESTATION INC *p* 163
1312 TAMARACK RD NE, SLAVE LAKE, AB, T0G 2A0
(780) 849-1980 *SIC* 0851

NORTHERN REGIONAL HEALTH AUTHORITY *p* 350
84 CHURCH ST, FLIN FLON, MB, R8A 1L8
(204) 687-1300 *SIC* 8062

NORTHERN RESOURCE TRUCKING LIMITED PARTNERSHIP *p* 1428

2945 MILLAR AVE, SASKATOON, SK, S7K 6P6
(306) 933-3010 *SIC* 4213

NORTHERN RESPONSE (INTERNATIONAL) LTD *p* 853
50 STAPLES AVE, RICHMOND HILL, ON, L4B 0A7
(866) 584-1694 *SIC* 5963

NORTHERN SAVINGS CREDIT UNION 251
138 3RD AVE W, PRINCE RUPERT, BC, V8J 1K8
(250) 627-3612 *SIC* 6062

NORTHERN SAWMILLS INC *p* 909
490 MAUREEN ST, THUNDER BAY, ON, P7B 6T2
SIC 2491

NORTHERN SECONDARY SCHOOL *p* 923
See TORONTO DISTRICT SCHOOL BOARD

NORTHERN SHRIMP COMPANY LTD *p* 424
GD, JACKSONS ARM, NL, A0K 3H0
SIC 2092

NORTHERN STORES *p* 353
See NORTH WEST COMPANY LP, THE

NORTHERN STRANDS CO. LTD *p* 1428
3235 MILLAR AVE, SASKATOON, SK, S7K 5Y3
(306) 242-7073 *SIC* 5051

NORTHERN SUNSET MOTEL *p* 1407
See SAKITAWAK DEVELOPMENT CORPORATION

NORTHERN SUPPLY CHAIN *p* 909
See THUNDER BAY REGIONAL HEALTH SCIENCES CENTRE

NORTHERN TAXI *p* 913
See NORTHERN TRANSPORT SERVICES INC

NORTHERN THUNDERBIRD AIR INC *p* 251
4245 HANGER RD UNIT 100, PRINCE GEORGE, BC, V2N 4M6
(250) 963-9611 *SIC* 4522

NORTHERN TOYOTA *p* 249
See KEY LEASE CANADA LTD

NORTHERN TRAFFIC SERVICE *p* 184
See CANADIAN UTILITY CONSTRUCTION CORP

NORTHERN TRANSFORMER CORPORATION *p* 664
245 MCNAUGHTON RD E, MAPLE, ON, L6A 4P5
(905) 669-1853 *SIC* 3612

NORTHERN TRANSPORT SERVICES INC *p* 913
36 PINE ST S SUITE 200, TIMMINS, ON, P4N 2J8
(705) 268-6868 *SIC* 7389

NORTHERN TRUST COMPANY, CANADA *p* 955
145 KING ST W SUITE 1910, TORONTO, ON, M5H 1J8
(416) 365-7161 *SIC* 6722

NORTHERN TRUST GLOBAL ADVISORS *p* 955
See NORTHERN TRUST COMPANY, CANADA

NORTHERN VERTEX MINING CORP *p* 315
1075 W GEORGIA ST SUITE 1650, VANCOUVER, BC, V6E 3C9
(604) 601-3656 *SIC* 1081

NORTHERN VOICE & DATA INC *p* 901
174 DOUGLAS ST, SUDBURY, ON, P3E 1G1
(705) 674-2729 *SIC* 5065

NORTHERN WELD ARC LTD *p* 163
141 STRATHMOOR WAY, SHERWOOD PARK, AB, T8H 1Z7
(780) 467-1522 *SIC* 3441

NORTHERN WOOD *p* 909
See NORTHERN SAWMILLS INC

NORTHERN YOUTH SERVICES INC *p* 899
3200 BANCROFT DR, SUDBURY, ON, P3B

1V3
(705) 524-3354 *SIC* 8399

NORTHFIELD METAL PRODUCTS *p* 1010
See LEGGETT & PLATT CANADA CO

NORTHFORGE INNOVATIONS INC *p* 1105
72 RUE LAVAL, GATINEAU, QC, J8X 3H3
(819) 776-6066 *SIC* 7371

NORTHGATE CHEVROLET BUICK GMC LIMITED PARTNERSHIP *p* 84
13215 97 ST NW, EDMONTON, AB, T5E 4C7
(780) 476-3371 *SIC* 5511

NORTHGATE HONDA *p* 131
See 530664 ALBERTA LTD

NORTHGATE INDUSTRIES LTD *p* 94
12345 121 ST NW, EDMONTON, AB, T5L 4Y7
(780) 448-9222 *SIC* 2452

NORTHGATE SAFEWAY *p* 133
See SOBEYS WEST INC

NORTHLAND CHRYSLER DODGE JEEP RAM *p* 251
See NORTHTOWN AUTO LP

NORTHLAND FLORAL INC *p* 886
1703 SOUTH SERVICE RD, ST CATHARINES, ON, L2R 6P9
(905) 646-2828 *SIC* 5193

NORTHLAND FORD SALES LTD *p* 359
HIGHWAY 10 S, THE PAS, MB, R9A 1K9
(204) 623-4350 *SIC* 5511

NORTHLAND HYUNDAI *p* 249
See NORTHLAND MOTORS LP

NORTHLAND MOTORS LP *p* 249
2021 HIGHWAY 16 W, PRINCE GEORGE, BC, V2L 0A4
(250) 564-6663 *SIC* 5511

NORTHLAND POWER INC *p* 927
30 ST CLAIR AVE W 12 FL, TORONTO, ON, M4V 3A1
(416) 962-6262 *SIC* 4911

NORTHLAND PROPERTIES CORPORATION *p* 36
8001 11 ST SE, CALGARY, AB, T2H 0B8
(403) 252-7263 *SIC* 7011

NORTHLAND PROPERTIES CORPORATION *p* 222
2130 HARVEY AVE, KELOWNA, BC, V1Y 6G8
(250) 860-6409 *SIC* 7011

NORTHLAND PROPERTIES CORPORATION *p* 321
1755 BROADWAY W SUITE 310, VANCOUVER, BC, V6J 4S5
(604) 730-6610 *SIC* 7011

NORTHLAND SCHOOL DIVISION 61 *p* 152
9809 77 AVE, PEACE RIVER, AB, T8S 1C9
(780) 624-2060 *SIC* 8211

NORTHLAND UTILITIES (YELLOWKNIFE) LTD *p* 436
481 RANGE LAKE RD, YELLOWKNIFE, NT, X1A 3R9
(867) 873-4865 *SIC* 4911

NORTHLAND VOLKSWAGEN *p* 40
See 588388 ALBERTA LTD

NORTHLAND VOLKSWAGEN *p* 40
See CALGARY V MOTORS LP

NORTHLANDER INDUSTRIES *p* 589
See 533438 ONTARIO LIMITED

NORTHLANDS PARK *p* 162
See EDMONTON NORTHLANDS

NORTHLANDS SPECTRUM *p* 83
See EDMONTON NORTHLANDS

NORTHLEA ELEMENTARY & MIDDLE SCHOOL *p* 918
See TORONTO DISTRICT SCHOOL BOARD

NORTHLEAF CAPITAL ADVISERS *p* 970
See NORTHLEAF CAPITAL PARTNERS (CANADA) LTD

NORTHLEAF CAPITAL PARTNERS (CANADA) LTD *p* 970

79 WELLINGTON ST W, TORONTO, ON, M5K 1N9
(866) 964-4141 *SIC* 6282

NORTHLEAF INFRASTRUCTURE CAPITAL PARTNERS II LP *p* 970
79 WELLINGTON ST W FL 6, TORONTO, ON, M5K 1N9
(866) 964-4141 *SIC* 6282

NORTHPOINT ENERGY SOLUTIONS INC *p* 1418
2025 VICTORIA AVE, REGINA, SK, S4P 0S1
(306) 566-2103 *SIC* 4911

NORTHPOINT TECHNICAL SERVICES ULC *p* 12
4920 43 ST SE, CALGARY, AB, T2B 3N3
(403) 279-2211 *SIC* 7694

NORTHQUIP INC *p* 393
141 RAILWAY AVE, WOODLANDS, MB, R0C 3H0
(866) 383-7827 *SIC* 5083

NORTHRIDGE ENERGY DEVELOPMENT GROUP INC *p* 31
1509 CENTRE ST SW SUITE 500, CALGARY, AB, T2G 2E6
SIC 8742

NORTHRIDGE LONGTERM CARE CENTER *p* 798
496 POSTRIDGE DR, OAKVILLE, ON, L6H 7A2
(905) 257-9882 *SIC* 8059

NORTHRIVER MIDSTREAM INC *p* 55
425 1 ST SW SUITE 2200, CALGARY, AB, T2P 3L8
(403) 699-1955 *SIC* 4923

NORTHROP FRYE HALL *p* 976
See VICTORIA UNIVERSITY

NORTHSHORE SUDBURY LTD *p* 115
8113 CORONET RD NW, EDMONTON, AB, T6E 4N7
(780) 455-5177 *SIC* 3714

NORTHSIDE COMMUNITY GUEST HOME SOCIETY *p* 464
11 QUEEN ST, NORTH SYDNEY, NS, B2A 1A2
(902) 794-4733 *SIC* 8051

NORTHSIDE MARINE LTD *p* 423
300 MAIN ST N, GLOVERTOWN, NL, A0G 2L0
(709) 533-6792 *SIC* 6712

NORTHSTAR AEROSPACE (MILTON) *p* 683
See HELIGEAR CANADA ACQUISITION CORPORATION

NORTHSTAR DRILLSTEM TESTERS INC *p* 55
440 2 AVE SW UNIT 750, CALGARY, AB, T2P 5E9
(403) 265-8987 *SIC* 1389

NORTHSTAR HOSPITALITY LIMITED PARTNERSHIP *p* 698
5090 EXPLORER DR SUITE 700, MISSISSAUGA, ON, L4W 4T9
(905) 629-3400 *SIC* 7011

NORTHSTAR HOSPITALITY LIMITED PARTNERSHIP *p* 955
145 RICHMOND ST W SUITE 212, TORONTO, ON, M5H 2L2
(416) 869-3456 *SIC* 7011

NORTHSTAR HYUNDAI *p* 94
See NORTHSTAR MOTORS LTD

NORTHSTAR INDUSTRIES *p* 532
See BANBRICO LIMITED

NORTHSTAR MOTORS LTD *p* 94
13634 ST ALBERT TRAIL NW, EDMONTON, AB, T5L 4P3
(780) 478-7669 *SIC* 5511

NORTHSTAR REALTY LTD *p* 279
15272 CROYDON DR SUITE 118, SURREY, BC, V3Z 0Z5
(604) 597-1664 *SIC* 6531

NORTHSTAR RESEARCH PARTNERS INC *p* 940
18 KING ST E SUITE 1500, TORONTO, ON, M5C 1C4

(416) 907-7100   *SIC* 8732
NORTHSTAR SCAFFOLD SERVICES INC *p*
575
362 OLIVEWOOD RD, ETOBICOKE, ON,
M8Z 2Z7
(416) 231-1610   *SIC* 1799
**NORTHSTAR SHARP'S FOUNDATION
SPECIALISTS LTD** *p* 149
1511 SPARROW DR, NISKU, AB, T9E 8H9
(780) 955-2108   *SIC* 1622
NORTHTOWN AUTO LP *p* 251
2844 RECPLACE DR, PRINCE GEORGE,
BC, V2N 0G2
(250) 562-5254   *SIC* 5511
NORTHTOWN STRUCTURAL LTD *p* 495
18 SIMPSON RD, BOLTON, ON, L7E 1G9
(905) 951-6317   *SIC* 1542
**NORTHUMBERLAND BUILDING MATERI-
ALS LTD** *p*
847
205 PETER ST SUITE 368, PORT HOPE,
ON, L1A 3V6
(416) 759-8542   *SIC* 5211
**NORTHUMBERLAND COOPERATIVE LIM-
ITED** *p*
405
256 LAWLOR LANE, MIRAMICHI, NB, E1V
3Z9
(506) 627-7720   *SIC* 2026
NORTHUMBERLAND DAIRY *p* 405
*See NORTHUMBERLAND COOPERATIVE
LIMITED*
NORTHUMBERLAND FERRIES LIMITED *p*
1039
94 WATER ST, CHARLOTTETOWN, PE,
C1A 1A6
(902) 566-3838   *SIC* 4449
NORTHUMBERLAND HILLS HOSPITAL *p*
545
1000 DEPALMA DR, COBOURG, ON, K9A
5W6
(905) 372-6811   *SIC* 8062
**NORTHVIEW APARTMENT REAL ESTATE
INVESTMENT TRUST** *p* 36
6131 6 ST SE SUITE 200, CALGARY, AB,
T2H 1L9
(403) 531-0720   *SIC* 6722
NORTHVIEW APARTMENT REIT *p* 36
See NPR LIMITED PARTNERSHIP
NORTHWATER CAPITAL INC *p* 965
181 BAY ST SUITE 4700, TORONTO, ON,
M5J 2T3
(416) 360-5435   *SIC* 6712
NORTHWAY AVIATION LTD *p* 357
501 AIRLINE RD, ST ANDREWS, MB, R1A
3P4
(204) 339-2310   *SIC* 4522
**NORTHWAY CHEVROLET OLDSMOBILE
LTD** *p* 1414
500 MARQUIS RD E, PRINCE ALBERT, SK,
S6V 8B3
(306) 765-2200   *SIC* 5511
NORTHWAY FORD LINCOLN *p* 517
See NORTHWAY FORD LINCOLN LTD
NORTHWAY FORD LINCOLN LTD *p* 517
388 KING GEORGE RD, BRANTFORD, ON,
N3T 5L8
(519) 753-8691   *SIC* 5511
NORTHWELL OILFIELD HAULING (09) INC
p 2
26318 TOWNSHIP RD 531A UNIT 3, ACHE-
SON, AB, T7X 5A3
(780) 960-4900   *SIC* 1389
NORTHWEST ACURA *p* 74
See 724053 ALBERTA LIMITED
**NORTHWEST CATHOLIC DISTRICT
SCHOOL BOARD, THE** *p* 592
555 FLINDERS AVE, FORT FRANCES, ON,
P9A 3L2
(807) 274-2931   *SIC* 8211
NORTHWEST FABRICS *p* 384
See MARSHALL FABRICS LTD
NORTHWEST FUELS LIMITED *p* 283
5138 KEITH AVE, TERRACE, BC, V8G 1K9

(250) 635-2066   *SIC* 5172
**NORTHWEST HEALTHCARE PROPERTIES
REAL ESTATE INVESTMENT TRUST** *p* 946
180 DUNDAS ST W SUITE 1100,
TORONTO, ON, M5G 1Z8
(416) 366-2000   *SIC* 6798
**NORTHWEST HEALTHCARE PROPERTIES
REIT** *p* 946
*See NORTHWEST HEALTHCARE PROP-
ERTIES REAL ESTATE INVESTMENT
TRUST*
**NORTHWEST HYDRAULIC CONSULTANTS
LTD** *p* 125
9819 12 AVE SW, EDMONTON, AB, T6X
0E3
(780) 436-5868   *SIC* 8711
NORTHWEST LEXUS *p* 498
See 1470754 ONTARIO INC
NORTHWEST LOGISTICS INC *p* 322
2906 BROADWAY W SUITE 260, VANCOU-
VER, BC, V6K 2G8
(604) 731-8001   *SIC* 4785
**NORTHWEST MOTORS (RED DEER) LIM-
ITED** *p*
154
3115 50 AVE, RED DEER, AB, T4N 3X8
(403) 346-2035   *SIC* 5511
**NORTHWEST MUTUAL FUNDS
INC/NORDOUEST FONDS MUTUELS INC** *p*
955
155 UNIVERSITY AVE SUITE 400,
TORONTO, ON, M5H 3B7
(416) 594-6633   *SIC* 6722
**NORTHWEST PROTECTION SERVICES
LTD** *p* 989
1951 EGLINTON AVE W UNIT 201,
TORONTO, ON, M6E 2J7
(416) 787-1448   *SIC* 7381
NORTHWEST SHEET METAL LTD *p* 279
19159 33 AVE, SURREY, BC, V3Z 1A1
(604) 542-9536   *SIC* 1761
NORTHWEST TANK LINES INC *p* 229
7025 272 ST, LANGLEY, BC, V4W 1R3
(604) 856-6666   *SIC* 4213
**NORTHWEST TERRITORIES HYDRO COR-
PORATION** *p*
435
4 CAPITAL DR SS 98 SUITE 98, HAY
RIVER, NT, X0E 1G2
(867) 874-5200   *SIC* 4911
**NORTHWEST TERRITORIES LIQUOR
COMMISSION** *p* 435
31 CAPITAL DR SUITE 201, HAY RIVER,
NT, X0E 1G2
(867) 874-8700   *SIC* 5921
**NORTHWEST TERRITORIES NON-PROFIT
HOUSING CORPORATION** *p* 436
GD LCD MAIN, YELLOWKNIFE, NT, X1A
2L8
(867) 873-7873   *SIC* 6531
**NORTHWEST TERRITORIES POWER COR-
PORATION** *p*
435
4 CAPITAL DR SS 98 SUITE 98, HAY
RIVER, NT, X0E 1G2
(867) 874-5200   *SIC* 4911
**NORTHWEST TERRITORY HEALTH AND
SOCIAL SERVICES AUTHORITY-BDR** *p* 435
285 MACKENZIE RD, INUVIK, NT, X0E 0T0
(867) 777-8000   *SIC* 8062
NORTHWEST TRANSPORT *p* 1
See MANITOULIN TRANSPORTATION
NORTHWEST WASTE SYSTEMS INC *p* 272
19500 56 AVE, SURREY, BC, V3S 6K4
(604) 539-1900   *SIC* 4953
NORTHWEST WOOD TREATERS LP *p* 251
10553 WILLOW CALE FOREST, PRINCE
GEORGE, BC, V2N 4T7
(250) 963-9628   *SIC* 5039
NORTHWEST-ATLANTIC (CANADA) INC *p*
777
864 YORK MILLS RD, NORTH YORK, ON,
M3B 1Y4
(416) 391-3900   *SIC* 6531

NORTHWESTEL INC *p* 436
5201 50 AVE SUITE 300, YELLOWKNIFE,
NT, X1A 3S9
(867) 920-3500   *SIC* 4899
NORTHWESTEL INC *p* 1440
301 LAMBERT ST SUITE 2727, WHITE-
HORSE, YT, Y1A 1Z5
(888) 423-2333   *SIC* 4899
NORTHWESTEL INC *p* 1440
301 LAMBERT ST SUITE 2727, WHITE-
HORSE, YT, Y1A 1Z5
(867) 668-5300   *SIC* 4899
NORTHWESTEL INC *p* 1440
183 RANGE RD, WHITEHORSE, YT, Y1A
3E5
(867) 668-5475   *SIC* 4899
NORTHWESTERN AIR LEASE LTD *p* 435
HANGAR 1, FORT SMITH, NT, X0E 0P0
(867) 872-2216   *SIC* 4512
**NORTHWESTERN ONTARIO REGIONAL
CANCER CENTRE** *p* 908
See CANCER CARE ONTARIO
**NORTHWESTERN SYSTEMS CORPORA-
TION** *p*
209
7601 MACDONALD RD, DELTA, BC, V4G
1N3
(604) 952-0925   *SIC* 3499
NORTHWOOD DIVISION *p* 250
See CANFOR PULP LTD
NORTHWOOD HOMECARE LTD *p* 447
130 EILEEN STUBBS AVE SUITE 19N,
DARTMOUTH, NS, B3B 2C4
(902) 425-2273   *SIC* 8082
NORTHWOOD MORTGAGE LTD *p* 673
7676 WOODBINE AVE SUITE 300,
MARKHAM, ON, L3R 2N2
(416) 969-8130   *SIC* 6163
NORTON MCMULLEN & CO. LLP *p* 673
1 VALLEYWOOD DR SUITE 200,
MARKHAM, ON, L3R 5L9
(905) 479-7001   *SIC* 8721
NORTON ROSE FULBRIGHT *p* 824
*See NORTON ROSE FULBRIGHT CANADA
S.E.N.C.R.L., S.R.L.*
NORTON ROSE FULBRIGHT *p* 1273
*See NORTON ROSE FULBRIGHT CANADA
S.E.N.C.R.L., S.R.L.*
NORTON ROSE FULBRIGHT CANADA LLP
p 55
400 3 AVE SW SUITE 3700, CALGARY, AB,
T2P 4H2
(403) 267-8222   *SIC* 8111
**NORTON ROSE FULBRIGHT CANADA
S.E.N.C.R.L. S.R.L.** *p* 1273
2828 BOUL LAURIER BUREAU 1500, QUE-
BEC, QC, G1V 0B9
(418) 640-7414   *SIC* 8111
**NORTON ROSE FULBRIGHT CANADA
S.E.N.C.R.L., S.R.L.** *p* 824
45 O'CONNOR ST SUITE 1600, OTTAWA,
ON, K1P 1A4
(613) 780-8661   *SIC* 8111
**NORTON ROSE FULBRIGHT CANADA
S.E.N.C.R.L., S.R.L.** *p* 965
200 BAY ST SUITE 3800, TORONTO, ON,
M5J 2Z4
(416) 216-4000   *SIC* 8111
**NORTON ROSE FULBRIGHT CANADA
S.E.N.C.R.L., S.R.L.** *p* 1206
1 PLACE VILLE-MARIE BUREAU 2500,
MONTREAL, QC, H3B 4S2
(514) 847-4747   *SIC* 8111
**NORTON ROSE FULBRIGHT CANADA
S.E.N.C.R.L., S.R.L.** *p* 1273
2828 BOUL LAURIER BUREAU 1500, QUE-
BEC, QC, G1V 0B9
(418) 640-5000   *SIC* 8111
**NORTOWN ELECTRICAL CONTRACTORS
ASSOCIATES** *p* 781
3845 BATHURST ST SUITE 102, NORTH
YORK, ON, M3H 3N2
(416) 638-6700   *SIC* 1731
NORTOWN ELECTRICAL CONTRACTORS

LIMITED *p* 781
3845 BATHURST ST UNIT 102, NORTH
YORK, ON, M3H 3N2
(416) 638-6700   *SIC* 1731
NORTOWN FOODS LIMITED *p* 988
892 EGLINTON AVE W, TORONTO, ON,
M6C 2B6
(416) 789-2921   *SIC* 5411
NORTRAX *p* 1342
See NORTRAX QUEBEC INC
NORTRAX CANADA INC *p* 698
1655 BRITANNIA RD E SUITE 155, MISSIS-
SAUGA, ON, L4W 1S5
(905) 670-1655   *SIC* 5082
NORTRAX QUEBEC INC *p* 1342
4500 DESSTE CHOMEDEY (A-13) O,
SAINT-LAURENT, QC, H7R 6E9
(450) 625-3221   *SIC* 5084
NORTRUX INC *p* 102
18110 118 AVE NW, EDMONTON, AB, T5S
2G2
(780) 452-6225   *SIC* 5012
NORVAN ENTERPRISES (1982) LTD *p* 368
246 DUNKIRK DR, WINNIPEG, MB, R2M
3W9
(204) 257-0373   *SIC* 5812
NORVIEW LODGE *p* 880
*See CORPORATION OF NORFOLK
COUNTY*
NORWALL GROUP INC *p* 505
150 DELTA PARK BLVD, BRAMPTON, ON,
L6T 5T6
(905) 791-2700   *SIC* 5198
**NORWEGIAN OLD PEOPLE'S HOME AS-
SOCIATION** *p*
181
7725 4TH ST, BURNABY, BC, V3N 5B6
(604) 522-5812   *SIC* 8361
**NORWELD MECHANICAL INSTALLA-
TIONS INC** *p*
251
1416 SANTA FE RD, PRINCE GEORGE,
BC, V2N 5T5
(250) 562-6660   *SIC* 1711
NORWELL DAIRY SYSTEMS LTD *p* 565
37 DRAYTON INDUSTRIAL DR, DRAYTON,
ON, N0G 1P0
(519) 638-3535   *SIC* 5083
**NORWELL DISTRICT SECONDARY
SCHOOL** *p* 836
*See UPPER GRAND DISTRICT SCHOOL
BOARD, THE*
NORWESCO INDUSTRIES (1983) LTD *p* 36
6908 6 ST SE BAY SUITE L, CALGARY, AB,
T2H 2K4
(403) 258-3883   *SIC* 3492
NORWEST CONSTRUCTION, DIV OF *p* 108
See 669021 ALBERTA LTD
NORWEST CORPORATION *p* 31
411 1 ST SE SUITE 2700, CALGARY,
T2G 4Y5
(403) 237-7763   *SIC* 8748
NORWEST MANUFACTURING *p* 389
See PRENDIVILLE INDUSTRIES LTD
NORWEST PRECISION LIMITED *p* 793
460 SIGNET DR, NORTH YORK, ON, M9L
2T6
(416) 742-8082   *SIC* 3499
NORWEST REAL ESTATE LTD *p* 40
3604 52 AVE NW SUITE 114, CALGARY,
AB, T2L 1V9
(403) 282-7770   *SIC* 6531
NORWICH REAL ESTATE SERVICES INC *p*
222
1553 HARVEY AVE SUITE 100, KELOWNA,
BC, V1Y 6G1
(250) 717-5000   *SIC* 6531
NORWOOD FOUNDRY LIMITED *p* 149
605 18 AVE, NISKU, AB, T9E 7T7
(780) 955-8844   *SIC* 3365
NORWOOD HOTEL CO LTD *p* 364
112 MARION ST, WINNIPEG, MB, R2H 0T1
(204) 233-4475   *SIC* 7011
NORWOOD MANUFACTURING CANADA

▲ **Public Company**   ■ **Public Company Family Member**   **HQ** Headquarters   **BR** Branch   **SL** Single Location

INC *p* 277
8519 132 ST, SURREY, BC, V3W 4N8
SIC 2844
NORWOOD WINDOW & DOOR, DIV. OF *p* 417
See WEST-WOOD INDUSTRIES LTD
NORZINC LTD *p* 299
650 GEORGIA ST W SUITE 1710, VANCOUVER, BC, V6B 4N9
(604) 688-2001 *SIC 1031*
NOSE CREEK FOREST PRODUCTS CORP *p* 68
184 MALIBOU RD SW, CALGARY, AB, T2V 1X9
SIC 2431
NOSSACK DISTRIBUTION CENTRE *p* 156
7240 JOHNSTONE DR SUITE 100, RED DEER, AB, T4P 3Y6
(403) 346-5006 *SIC 2099*
NOSSACK FINE MEATS LTD *p* 156
7240 JOHNSTONE DR SUITE 100, RED DEER, AB, T4P 3Y6
(403) 346-5006 *SIC 5147*
NOSSACK GOURMET FOODS LTD *p* 137
5804 37 ST, INNISFAIL, AB, T4G 1S8
(403) 227-2121 *SIC 2099*
NOSSO TALHO PARTNERSHIP *p* 990
See 887252 ONTARIO LIMITED
NOTARIUS *p* 1190
See NOTARIUS - TECHNOLGIES ET SYSTEMES D'INFORMATION NOTARIALE INC
NOTARIUS - TECHNOLGIES ET SYSTEMES D'INFORMATION NOTARIALE INC *p* 1190
465 RUE MCGILL BUREAU 300, MONTREAL, QC, H2Y 2H1
(514) 281-1577 *SIC 7389*
NOTHING BUT NATURE INC *p* 973
176 ST. GEORGE ST, TORONTO, ON, M5R 2M7
(416) 934-5034 *SIC 5149*
NOTMAN CHRYSLER DODGE JEEP *p* 562
See NOTMAN MOTOR SALES LTD
NOTMAN MOTOR SALES LTD *p* 562
2205 VINCENT MASSEY DR, CORNWALL, ON, K6H 5R6
(613) 938-0934 *SIC 5511*
NOTRA INC *p* 830
2725 QUEENSVIEW DR SUITE 200, OTTAWA, ON, K2B 0A1
(613) 738-0887 *SIC 8748*
NOTRE DAME AGENCIES LIMITED *p* 425
391 MAIN ST, LEWISPORTE, NL, A0G 3A0
(709) 535-8691 *SIC 5712*
NOTRE DAME BAY MEMORIAL HEALTH CENTER *p* 434
GD, TWILLINGATE, NL, A0G 4M0
(709) 884-2131 *SIC 8062*
NOTRE DAME CASTLE BUILDING CENTRES *p* 425
See NOTRE DAME AGENCIES LIMITED
NOTRE DAME COLLEGE *p* 1438
See ATHOL MURRAY COLLEGE OF NOTRE DAME
NOTRE DAME HIGH SCHOOL *p* 76
11900 COUNTRY VILLAGE LINK NE, CALGARY, AB, T3K 6E4
(403) 500-2109 *SIC 8661*
NOTRE DAME HIGH SCHOOL *p* 1012
See NIAGARA CATHOLIC DISTRICT SCHOOL BOARD
NOTRE DAME INTERMEDIATE SCHOOL *p* 829
See OTTAWA CATHOLIC DISTRICT SCHOOL BOARD
NOTRE DAME ROMAN CATHOLIC SECONDARY SCHOOL *p* 526
See HALTON CATHOLIC DISTRICT SCHOOL BOARD
NOTRE DAME SEAFOODS INC *p* 430
88 KENMOUNT RD, ST. JOHN'S, NL, A1B 3R1

(709) 758-0034 *SIC 2092*
NOTRE DAME SECONDARY SCHOOL *p* 512
See DUFFERIN-PEEL CATHOLIC DISTRICT SCHOOL BOARD
NOTREDAME CATHOLIC SECONDARY SCHOOL *p* 475
See DURHAM CATHOLIC DISTRICT SCHOOL BOARD
NOTTAWASAGA INN, DIV OF *p* 476
See CABLE BRIDGE ENTERPRISES LIMITED
NOURYON PATE ET PERFORMANCE CANADA INC *p* 1148
1900 RUE SAINT-PATRICE E BUREAU 25, MAGOG, QC, J1X 3W5
(819) 843-8942 *SIC 2899*
NOUVEAU TASTE INC *p* 920
38 MCGEE ST, TORONTO, ON, M4M 2K9
(416) 778-6300 *SIC 5142*
NOV COILED TUBING PRESSURE PUMPING CANADA *p* 12
See NOV ENERFLOW ULC
NOV ENERFLOW *p* 17
See NOV ENERFLOW ULC
NOV ENERFLOW ULC *p* 12
4800 27 ST SE, CALGARY, AB, T2B 3M4
(403) 279-9696 *SIC 3533*
NOV ENERFLOW ULC *p* 17
4910 80 AVE SE, CALGARY, AB, T2C 2X3
(403) 569-2222 *SIC 1389*
NOV ENERFLOW ULC *p* 17
8625 68 ST SE, CALGARY, AB, T2C 2R6
(403) 695-3189 *SIC 3533*
NOV ENERFLOW ULC *p* 149
2201 9 ST, NISKU, AB, T9E 7Z7
(780) 955-7675 *SIC 1389*
NOV HYDRA RIG *p* 17
See NOV ENERFLOW ULC
NOVA BUILDERS INC *p* 94
14020 128 AVE NW UNIT 200, EDMONTON, AB, T5L 4M8
(780) 702-6682 *SIC 6552*
NOVA BUS *p* 1303
See GROUPE VOLVO CANADA INC
NOVA BUS *p* 1356
See GROUPE VOLVO CANADA INC
NOVA CAPITAL INCORPORATED *p* 467
530 GRAND LAKE RD, SYDNEY, NS, B1P 5T4
(902) 562-7000 *SIC 5211*
NOVA CHEMICALS *p* 154
See NOVA CHEMICALS (CANADA) LTD
NOVA CHEMICALS (CANADA) LTD *p* 24
2928 16 ST NE, CALGARY, AB, T2E 7K7
SIC 2869
NOVA CHEMICALS (CANADA) LTD *p* 55
1000 7 AVE SW SUITE 1000, CALGARY, AB, T2P 5L5
(403) 750-3600 *SIC 2869*
NOVA CHEMICALS (CANADA) LTD *p* 154
GD, RED DEER, AB, T4N 5E6
(403) 314-8611 *SIC 2821*
NOVA CHEMICALS (CANADA) LTD *p* 156
4940 81 ST SUITE 6, RED DEER, AB, T4P 3V3
(403) 314-8611 *SIC 2869*
NOVA CHEMICALS (CANADA) LTD *p* 563
785 PETROLIA LINE RR 2, CORUNNA, ON, N0N 1G0
(519) 862-2911 *SIC 2821*
NOVA CHEMICALS (CANADA) LTD *p* 745
510 MOORE LINE, MOORETOWN, ON, N0N 1M0
(519) 862-2961 *SIC 2869*
NOVA CHEMICALS (CANADA) LTD *p* 860
872 TASHMOO AVE, SARNIA, ON, N7T 7H5
(519) 332-1212 *SIC 2869*
NOVA CHEMICALS CORPORATION *p* 9
3620 32 ST NE, CALGARY, AB, T1Y 6G7
(403) 291-8444 *SIC 2822*
NOVA CHEMICALS CORPORATION *p* 55

1000 7 AVE SW SUITE 1000, CALGARY, AB, T2P 5L5
(403) 750-3600 *SIC 2821*
NOVA CHEMICALS CORPORATION *p* 563
285 ALBERT ST, CORUNNA, ON, N0N 1G0
(519) 862-1445 *SIC 3089*
NOVA CHEMICALS CORPORATION *p* 745
510 MOORE LINE, MOORETOWN, ON, N0N 1M0
(519) 862-2961 *SIC 2821*
NOVA CHEMICALS RESEARCH CENTER *p* 24
See NOVA CHEMICALS (CANADA) LTD
NOVA COLD LOGISTICS ULC *p* 505
745 INTERMODAL DR, BRAMPTON, ON, L6T 5W2
(905) 791-8585 *SIC 4222*
NOVA CONSTRUCTION *p* 1255
See NOVA CONSTRUCTION C.P. INC
NOVA CONSTRUCTION C.P. INC *p* 1255
1259 RUE PAUL-EMILE-GIROUX, QUEBEC, QC, G1C 0K9
(418) 660-8111 *SIC 1521*
NOVA CONSTRUCTION CO. LTD *p* 438
3098 HIGHWAY 104, ANTIGONISH, NS, B2G 2K3
(902) 863-4004 *SIC 1521*
NOVA ENTERPRISES LIMITED *p* 447
670 AV WILKINSON, DARTMOUTH, NS, B3B 0J4
(902) 468-5900 *SIC 5511*
NOVA EXPRESS MILLENNIUM INC *p* 255
14271 KNOX WAY SUITE 105, RICHMOND, BC, V6V 2Z4
(604) 278-8044 *SIC 7389*
NOVA GAS TRANSMISSION LTD *p* 55
450 1 ST SW, CALGARY, AB, T2P 5H1
(403) 920-2000 *SIC 4923*
NOVA GRAIN INC *p* 1318
800 RUE BOUCHER, SAINT-JEAN-SUR-RICHELIEU, QC, J3B 7Z8
(450) 348-0976 *SIC 5153*
NOVA INDUSTRIAL SUPPLIES LIMITED *p* 464
1006 NOVA DR, NEW MINAS, NS, B4N 3X7
(902) 681-1665 *SIC 5084*
NOVA INTERNATIONAL LIMITED *p* 470
4449 HIGHWAY 1 RR 2, WINDSOR, NS, B0N 2T0
(902) 798-9544 *SIC 5082*
NOVA LEAP HEALTH CORP *p* 457
7071 BAYERS RD SUITE 5003, HALIFAX, NS, B3L 2C2
(902) 401-9480 *SIC 8059*
NOVA MAGNETICS *p* 683
See EAGLEBURGMANN CANADA INC
NOVA METRIX GROUND MONITORING (CANADA) LTD *p* 308
666 BURRARD ST SUITE 1700, VANCOUVER, BC, V6C 2X8
(604) 430-4272 *SIC 6712*
NOVA NETWORKS INC *p* 831
1700 WOODWARD DR SUITE 100, OTTAWA, ON, K2C 3R8
(613) 563-6682 *SIC 7373*
NOVA PERMIS & ESCORTES ROUTIERES *p* 1277
See 9100-9647 QUEBEC INC
NOVA PETROCHEMICALS LTD *p* 55
1000 7 AVE SW, CALGARY, AB, T2P 5L5
(403) 750-3600 *SIC 6712*
NOVA POLE INTERNATIONAL INC *p* 279
2579 188 ST, SURREY, BC, V3Z 2A1
(604) 881-0090 *SIC 2499*
NOVA SCOTIA BUILDING SUPPLIES (1982) LIMITED *p* 441
459 HWY 3, BLOCKHOUSE, NS, B0J 1E0
(902) 624-8328 *SIC 5039*
NOVA SCOTIA BUSINESS INC *p* 453
1800 ARGYLE ST SUITE 701, HALIFAX, NS, B3J 3N8
(902) 424-6650 *SIC 6111*
NOVA SCOTIA COLLEGE OF ART AND DESIGN *p*

453
5163 DUKE ST, HALIFAX, NS, B3J 3J6
(902) 444-9600 *SIC 8221*
NOVA SCOTIA COMMUNITY COLLEGE *p* 455
5685 LEEDS ST, HALIFAX, NS, B3K 2T3
(902) 491-3387 *SIC 8221*
NOVA SCOTIA COMMUNITY COLLEGE *p* 456
5685 LEEDS ST, HALIFAX, NS, B3K 2T3
(902) 491-6701 *SIC 8222*
NOVA SCOTIA COMMUNITY COLLEGE *p* 460
See NOVA SCOTIA, PROVINCE OF
NOVA SCOTIA COMMUNITY COLLEGE *p* 466
39 ACADIA AVE, STELLARTON, NS, B0K 1S0
(902) 752-2002 *SIC 8222*
NOVA SCOTIA COMMUNITY COLLEGE MARCONI CAMPUS *p* 466
1240 GRAND LAKE RD, SYDNEY, NS, B1M 1A2
(902) 563-2450 *SIC 8221*
NOVA SCOTIA COMMUNITY COLLEGE PICTOU CAMPUS *p* 466
See NOVA SCOTIA COMMUNITY COLLEGE
NOVA SCOTIA HEALTH AUTHORITY *p* 438
18 ALBION ST S, AMHERST, NS, B4H 2W3
(902) 661-1090 *SIC 8062*
NOVA SCOTIA HEALTH AUTHORITY *p* 442
89 PAYZANT, CURRYS CORNER, NS, B0N 2T0
(902) 798-8351 *SIC 8062*
NOVA SCOTIA HEALTH AUTHORITY *p* 449
75 WARWICK ST, DIGBY, NS, B0V 1A0
(902) 245-2501 *SIC 8062*
NOVA SCOTIA HEALTH AUTHORITY *p* 451
1276 SOUTH PARK ST SUITE 1278, HALIFAX, NS, B3H 2Y9
(902) 473-5117 *SIC 8062*
NOVA SCOTIA HEALTH AUTHORITY *p* 451
1278 TOWER RD, HALIFAX, NS, B3H 2Y9
(902) 473-1787 *SIC 8062*
NOVA SCOTIA HEALTH AUTHORITY *p* 460
5 CHIPMAN DR, KENTVILLE, NS, B4N 3V7
(902) 365-1700 *SIC 8062*
NOVA SCOTIA HEALTH AUTHORITY *p* 465
1606 LAKE RD, SHELBURNE, NS, B0T 1W0
(902) 875-3011 *SIC 8062*
NOVA SCOTIA HEARING AND SPEECH CENTRES *p* 453
5657 SPRING GARDEN RD SUITE 401, HALIFAX, NS, B3J 3R4
(902) 492-8289 *SIC 8099*
NOVA SCOTIA LIQUOR CORPORATION *p* 459
93 CHAIN LAKE DR, HALIFAX, NS, B3S 1A3
(902) 450-6752 *SIC 5921*
NOVA SCOTIA PENSION SERVICES CORPORATION *p* 453
1949 UPPER WATER ST SUITE 400, HALIFAX, NS, B3J 3N3
(902) 424-5070 *SIC 6371*
NOVA SCOTIA POWER INCORPORATED *p* 453
1223 LOWER WATER ST, HALIFAX, NS, B3J 3S8
(902) 428-6221 *SIC 4911*
NOVA SCOTIA POWER INCORPORATED *p* 468
108 POWER PLANT RD, TRENTON, NS, B0K 1X0
(902) 755-5811 *SIC 4911*
NOVA SCOTIA SOCIETY FOR THE PREVENTION OF CRUELTY *p* 440
1600 BEDFORD HWY SUITE 422, BEDFORD, NS, B4A 1E8
(902) 835-4798 *SIC 8699*

NOVA SCOTIA SPCA p 440
See NOVA SCOTIA SOCIETY FOR THE PREVENTION OF CRUELTY
NOVA SCOTIA, PROVINCE OF p 441
75 HIGH ST, BRIDGEWATER, NS, B4V 1V8
(902) 543-4608 SIC 8221
NOVA SCOTIA, PROVINCE OF p 460
50 ELLIOTT RD SUITE 1, LAWRENCE-TOWN., NS, B0S 1M0
(902) 584-2226 SIC 8222
NOVA STEEL INC p 1034
See ACIER NOVA INC
NOVA STEEL PROCESSING p 891
See ACIER NOVA INC
NOVA TRUCK CENTRES p 447
See NOVA ENTERPRISES LIMITED
NOVA TUBE INC p 1224
5870 RUE SAINT-PATRICK, MONTREAL, QC, H4E 1B3
(514) 762-5220 SIC 3441
NOVA WELDING SUPPLIES, DIV OF p 464
See NOVA INDUSTRIAL SUPPLIES LIMITED
NOVA-LINK LIMITED p 606
935A SOUTHGATE DR UNIT 5, GUELPH, ON, N1L 0B9
(905) 858-3500 SIC 2522
NOVABUS p 1303
See SYNDICAT NATIONAL TCA
NOVACAP TMT V, S.E.C p 1071
3400 RUE DE L'ECLIPSE BUREAU 700, BROSSARD, QC, J4Z 0P3
(450) 651-5000 SIC 6162
NOVACOS BUILDING CLEANING LTD p 454
1505 BARRINGTON ST SUITE 1310, HALIFAX, NS, B3J 3K5
SIC 7349
NOVAFLEX PLASTICS p 852
See FLEXMASTER CANADA LIMITED
NOVAGOLD RESOURCES INC p 308
789 W PENDER ST SUITE 720, VANCOUVER, BC, V6C 1H2
(604) 669-6227 SIC 1041
NOVAKS UNIFORMS SOLUTIONS p 661
See TALBOT MARKETING INC
NOVALI GOURMET INC p 1066
14 RUE DE MONTGOLFIER, BOUCHERVILLE, QC, J4B 7Y4
(450) 655-7790 SIC 2045
NOVANNI STAINLESS INC p 546
2978 SOUTHORN RD, COLDWATER, ON, L0K 1E0
(705) 686-3301 SIC 3469
NOVARTIS ANIMAL HEALTH CANADA INC p 725
2000 ARGENTIA RD SUITE 400, MISSISSAUGA, ON, L5N 1P7
(905) 814-0840 SIC 5122
NOVARTIS PHARMA CANADA INC p 725
2150 TORQUAY MEWS, MISSISSAUGA, ON, L5N 2M6
SIC 5048
NOVATECH CANADA INC p 1359
160 RUE DE MURANO, SAINTE-JULIE, QC, J3E 0C6
(450) 922-1045 SIC 3211
NOVATECH ENGINEERING CONSULTANTS LTD p 626
240 MICHAEL COWPLAND DR SUITE 200, KANATA, ON, K2M 1P6
(613) 254-9643 SIC 8711
NOVATEK INTERNATIONAL PHARMACEUTICAL SOFTWARE p 1224
See 3965546 CANADA LIMITEE
NOVATEL INC p 76
10921 14 ST NE, CALGARY, AB, T3K 2L5
(403) 295-4500 SIC 3812
NOVATEL WIRELESS TECHNOLOGIES LTD p 24
6715 8 ST NE SUITE 200, CALGARY, AB, T2E 7H7

SIC 4899
NOVATRONICS INC p 895
789 ERIE ST, STRATFORD, ON, N4Z 1A2
(519) 271-3880 SIC 3812
NOVEL MECHANICAL INC p 1028
111 ZENWAY BLVD UNIT 23, WOODBRIDGE, ON, L4H 3H9
SIC 1711
NOVELION THERAPEUTICS INC p 299
510 WEST GEORGIA ST SUITE 1800, VANCOUVER, BC, V6B 0M3
(877) 764-3131 SIC 2834
NOVERCO INC p 1192
1000 PLACE JEAN-PAUL-RIOPELLE BUREAU A12, MONTREAL, QC, H2Z 2B3
(514) 847-2126 SIC 6712
NOVEX INSURANCE COMPANY p 770
5775 YONGE ST SUITE 600, NORTH YORK, ON, M2M 4J1
(416) 228-2618 SIC 6331
NOVEX NOVA EXPRESS p 255
See NOVA EXPRESS MILLENNIUM INC
NOVEXCO INC p 1231
950 PLACE PAUL-KANE, MONTREAL, QC, H7C 2T2
(450) 686-1212 SIC 5044
NOVIPRO EST DU CANADA p 1206
See NOVIPRO INC
NOVIPRO INC p 1206
1010 RUE DE LA GAUCHETIERE O BUREAU 1900, MONTREAL, QC, H3B 2N2
(514) 744-5353 SIC 5734
NOVITEX ENTERPRISE SOLUTIONS CANADA, INC p 915
2225 SHEPPARD AVE E SUITE 1008, TORONTO, ON, M2J 5C2
(416) 886-2540 SIC 8741
NOVLAN BROS SALES INC p 1413
GD, PARADISE HILL, SK, S0M 2G0
(877) 344-4433 SIC 5083
NOVLAN BROTHERS SALES PARTNERSHIP p 1413
47 FIRST AVE, PARADISE HILL, SK, S0M 2G0
(306) 344-4448 SIC 5083
NOVO NORDISK CANADA INC p 725
2476 ARGENTIA RD UNIT 101, MISSISSAUGA, ON, L5N 6M1
(905) 629-4222 SIC 5122
NOVO PLASTICS INC p 679
388 MARKLAND ST, MARKHAM, ON, L6C 1Z6
(905) 887-8818 SIC 3089
NOVOCOL PHARMACEUTICAL OF CANADA, INC p 534
25 WOLSELEY CRT, CAMBRIDGE, ON, N1R 6X3
(519) 623-4800 SIC 2834
NOVOLEX p 808
See DIRECT PLASTICS LTD
NOVOTEL HOTELS p 709
See ACCOR CANADA INC
NOVOTEL OTTAWA p 820
See ACCOR CANADA INC
NOVOTEL TORONTO CENTRE HOTEL p 943
See OLDE YORKE ESPLANADE HOTELS LTD
NOVOTEL TORONTO NORTH YORK p 915
See ACCOR CANADA INC
NOVOZYMES BIOAG LIMITED p 1435
3935 THATCHER AVE, SASKATOON, SK, S7R 1A3
(306) 657-8200 SIC 8731
NOVUS ENERGY INC. p 55
700 4 AVE SW UNIT 1700, CALGARY, AB, T2P 3J4
(403) 263-4310 SIC 1382
NOW COMMUNICATIONS INC p 935
189 CHURCH ST, TORONTO, ON, M5B 1Y7
(416) 364-1300 SIC 2721
NOW MAGAZINE p 935
See NOW COMMUNICATIONS INC

NOW NEWSPAPERS p 183
See ROYAL CITY RECORDS NOW
NOWPAC INC p 878
780 TAPSCOTT RD UNIT 5, SCARBOROUGH, ON, M1X 1A3
(416) 321-5799 SIC 8743
NOXENT INC p 1069
6400 BOUL TASCHEREAU BUREAU 200, BROSSARD, QC, J4W 3J2
(450) 926-0662 SIC 8742
NOXS INC p 1179
9500 RUE MEILLEUR BUREAU 200, MONTREAL, QC, H2N 2B7
(514) 385-0636 SIC 5136
NOYE ENTERPRISES INC p 1043
87 OTTAWA ST, SUMMERSIDE, PE, C1N 1W2
SIC 1542
NOYEN CONSTRUCTION LTD p 130
8309 113 ST, FORT SASKATCHEWAN, AB, T8L 4K7
(780) 998-3974 SIC 1611
NPD GROUP p 777
See NPD INTELECT CANADA INC
NPD GROUP CANADA INC, THE p 777
1500 DON MILLS RD SUITE 502, NORTH YORK, ON, M3B 3K4
(647) 723-7700 SIC 8732
NPD INTELECT CANADA INC p 777
1500 DON MILLS RD SUITE 502, NORTH YORK, ON, M3B 3K4
(647) 723-7700 SIC 8732
NPI p 505
See NEXCYCLE PLASTICS INC
NPI GROUP p 1305
See POULIN, NIKOL INC
NPL CANADA LTD p 725
7505 DANBRO CRES, MISSISSAUGA, ON, L5N 6P9
(905) 821-8383 SIC 1623
NPLH DRILLING p 912
See 2355291 ONTARIO IN
NPR LIMITED PARTNERSHIP p 36
6131 6 ST SE SUITE 200, CALGARY, AB, T2H 1L9
(403) 531-0720 SIC 6531
NPS ALLELIX CORP p 689
6850 GOREWAY DR, MISSISSAUGA, ON, L4V 1V7
(905) 677-0831 SIC 5912
NPS PHARMACEUTICALS p 689
See NPS ALLELIX CORP
NRB INC p 599
183 SOUTH SERVICE RD BUREAU 1, GRIMSBY, ON, L3M 4H6
(905) 945-9622 SIC 3448
NRC-FINANCE BRANCH p 815
See NATIONAL RESEARCH COUNCIL CANADA
NRCS INC p 901
31 LARCH ST SUITE 200, SUDBURY, ON, P3E 1B7
(705) 688-1288 SIC 8093
NRG RESEARCH GROUP INC p 315
1100 MELVILLE ST SUITE 1380, VANCOUVER, BC, V6E 4A6
(604) 681-0381 SIC 8732
NRG RESEARCH GROUP INC p 379
360 MAIN ST SUITE 1910, WINNIPEG, MB, R3C 3Z3
(204) 989-8999 SIC 8732
NRT p 1428
See NORTHERN RESOURCE TRUCKING LIMITED PARTNERSHIP
NRT TECHNOLOGY CORP p 874
10 COMPASS CRT, SCARBOROUGH, ON, M1S 5R3
(416) 646-5232 SIC 3944
NRZ INVESTMENTS INC p 659
491 OXFORD ST W, LONDON, ON, N6H 1T2
(519) 472-5410 SIC 5541
NS POWER ENERGY MARKETING INCORPORATED p

454
1223 LOWER WATER ST, HALIFAX, NS, B3J 3S8
(902) 428-6496 SIC 4911
NSA p 698
See NATIONAL SAFETY ASSOCIATES OF CANADA INC / NSA CANADA INC
NSC MINERALS LTD p 1431
2241 SPEERS AVE, SASKATOON, SK, S7L 5X6
(306) 934-6477 SIC 5169
NSCAD UNIVERSITY p 453
See NOVA SCOTIA COLLEGE OF ART AND DESIGN
NSCC ONLINE LEARNING p 455
See NOVA SCOTIA COMMUNITY COLLEGE
NSE AUTOMATECH INC p 1109
520 RUE RUTHERFORD, GRANBY, QC, J2G 0B2
(450) 378-7207 SIC 3545
NSF CANADA p 601
125 CHANCELLORS WAY, GUELPH, ON, N1G 0E7
(519) 821-1246 SIC 8731
NSF INTERNATIONAL p 601
See NSF CANADA
NSG p 547
See PILKINGTON GLASS OF CANADA LTD
NSHN p 493
See NORTH SHORE HEALTH NETWORK
NSK CANADA INC p 706
5585 MCADAM RD, MISSISSAUGA, ON, L4Z 1N4
(905) 890-0740 SIC 5085
NSM ACQUISITION COMPANY LIMITED p 459
12575 HIGHWAY 4, HAVRE BOUCHER, NS, B0H 1P0
(902) 234-3202 SIC 6712
NSP CANADA p 781
See DOT BENEFITS CORP
NT AIR p 251
See NORTHERN THUNDERBIRD AIR INC
NT GLOBAL ADVISORS INC p 955
145 KING ST W SUITE 1910, TORONTO, ON, M5H 1J8
(416) 366-2020 SIC 6282
NT HYDRO p 435
See NORTHWEST TERRITORIES HYDRO CORPORATION
NT SERVICES LIMITED p 24
215 16 ST SE 3RD FL, CALGARY, AB, T2E 7P5
(403) 769-3600 SIC 6099
NTI INSURANCE BROKERS p 673
800 DENISON ST SUITE 200, MARKHAM, ON, L3R 5M9
SIC 6411
NTN BEARING CORPORATION OF CANADA LIMITED p 725
6740 KITIMAT RD, MISSISSAUGA, ON, L5N 1M6
(905) 826-5500 SIC 3562
NTN BEARING CORPORATION OF CANADA LIMITED p 745
305 COURTNEYPARK DR W, MISSISSAUGA, ON, L5W 1Y4
(905) 564-2700 SIC 5085
NTN BEARING MANUFACTURING CANADA p 725
See NTN BEARING CORPORATION OF CANADA LIMITED
NTP/STAG CANADA INC p 1296
1545 RUE MARIE-VICTORIN, SAINT-BRUNO, QC, J3V 6B7
(450) 441-2707 SIC 4213
NTT DATA CANADA, INC p 454
2000 BARRINGTON ST SUITE 300, HALIFAX, NS, B3J 3K1
(902) 422-6036 SIC 7379
NTT DATA CANADA, INC p 853
30 EAST BEAVER CREEK RD SUITE 206,

RICHMOND HILL, ON, L4B 1J2
 SIC 7371
NTT DATA CANADA, INC. p 853
 See NTT DATA CANADA, INC
NU BODY EQUIPMENT SALES LTD p 245
5211 COMPTON RD, PORT ALBERNI, BC, V9Y 7B5
(778) 552-4540 SIC 3845
NU EDGE CONSTRUCTION LTD p 78
3815A 47 AVE, CAMROSE, AB, T4V 4S4
(780) 679-7825 SIC 1623
NU PLAST p 505
 See NEXCYCLE PLASTICS INC
NU SEA PRODUCTS INC p 427
MAIN RD, PORT DE GRAVE, NL, A0A 3J0
(709) 786-6302 SIC 2091
NU SKIN CANADA, INC p 717
4085 SLADEVIEW CRES, MISSISSAUGA, ON, L5L 5X3
(905) 569-5100 SIC 5122
NU TREND CONSTRUCTION CO p 1029
 See 706017 ONTARIO CORP
NU-FAB p 1415
 See ALL-FAB BUILDING COMPONENTS INC
NU-WALL p 615
 See DIVAL DEVELOPMENTS LTD
NU-WAY POTATO PRODUCTS p 793
 See GMASJ ONTARIO INC
NUANCE GROUP (CANADA) INC, THE p 689
5925 AIRPORT RD SUITE 300, MISSISSAUGA, ON, L4V 1W1
(905) 673-7299 SIC 5399
NUBODY'S FITNESS CENTRES INC p 447
51 RADDALL AVE, DARTMOUTH, NS, B3B 1T6
(902) 468-8920 SIC 7991
NUCAP INDUSTRIES INC p 877
3370 PHARMACY AVE, SCARBOROUGH, ON, M1W 3K4
(416) 494-1444 SIC 3714
NUCASA MILLING COMPANY LIMITED p 184
6150 LOUGHEED HWY, BURNABY, BC, V5B 2Z9
(604) 294-3232 SIC 5211
NUCLEAR WASTE MANAGEMENT ORGANIZATION (NWMO) p 925
22 ST CLAIR AVE E 6TH FL, TORONTO, ON, M4T 2S3
(416) 934-9814 SIC 8999
NUCLEUS DISTRIBUTION INC p 698
5220 GENERAL RD, MISSISSAUGA, ON, L4W 1G8
(800) 263-4283 SIC 5084
NUCLEUS INDEPENDENT LIVING p 798
3030 BRISTOL CIR SUITE 110, OAKVILLE, ON, L6H 0H2
(905) 829-0555 SIC 8051
NUCLEUS INDEPENDENT LIVING p 993
30 DENARDA ST SUITE 309, TORONTO, ON, M6M 5C3
(416) 244-1234 SIC 8361
NUCO NETWORKS INC p 982
129 SPADINA AVE SUITE 200, TORONTO, ON, M5V 2L3
(647) 290-3419 SIC 7371
NUCO SERVICES p 364
 See 6089585 CANADA LTD
NUCOR CANADA INC p 531
1455 LAKESHORE RD SUITE 204N, BURLINGTON, ON, L7S 2J1
(905) 634-6868 SIC 5051
NUCOR ENVIRONMENTAL SOLUTIONS LTD p 272
5250 185A ST SUITE 2, SURREY, BC, V3S 7A4
(604) 575-4721 SIC 8748
NUCOR SYSTEMS INC p 41
918 16 AVE NW SUITE 349, CALGARY, AB, T2M 0K3
(403) 236-2824 SIC 5083

NUCORGRATING p 524
 See PENSION PLAN - F & L
NUCRO-TECHNICS p 867
 See VIMY RIDGE GROUP LTD, THE
NUERA INC p 1134
1980 BOUL DAGENAIS O, LAVAL-OUEST, QC, H7L 5W2
(514) 955-1024 SIC 5085
NUEST SERVICES LTD p 272
17858 66 AVE, SURREY, BC, V3S 7X1
(604) 888-1588 SIC 7349
NUFARM AGRICULTURE INC p 77
333 96 AVE NE SUITE 5101, CALGARY, AB, T3K 0S3
(403) 692-2500 SIC 2879
NUFORM BUILDING TECHNOLOGIES INC. p 1032
100 GALCAT DR UNIT 2, WOODBRIDGE, ON, L4L 0B9
(905) 652-0001 SIC 3089
NUGALE PHARMACEUTICAL INC p 914
41 PULLMAN CRT, TORONTO, ON, M1X 1E4
(416) 298-7275 SIC 2834
NUHEAT INDUSTRIES LIMITED p 258
6900 GRAYBAR RD SUITE 3105, RICHMOND, BC, V6W 0A5
(800) 778-9276 SIC 3567
NULOGX INC p 725
2233 ARGENTIA RD SUITE 202, MISSISSAUGA, ON, L5N 2X7
(905) 486-1162 SIC 8742
NULOGX MANAGE TRANSPORTATION SOLUTIONS p 725
 See NULOGX INC
NUMAGE TRADING INC p 556
894 EDGELEY BLVD, CONCORD, ON, L4K 4V4
(905) 660-4172 SIC 5149
NUMBER 7 HONDA p 1032
 See NUMBER 7 HONDA SALES LIMITED
NUMBER 7 HONDA SALES LIMITED p 1032
5555 HIGHWAY 7, WOODBRIDGE, ON, L4L 1T5
(905) 851-2258 SIC 7538
NUMBER EIGHTY-EIGHT HOLDINGS LTD p 249
1922 1ST AVE, PRINCE GEORGE, BC, V2L 2Y9
(250) 562-3871 SIC 7389
NUMED CANADA INC p 563
45 SECOND ST W, CORNWALL, ON, K6J 1G3
(613) 936-2592 SIC 3841
NUMERIQ INC p 1211
612 RUE SAINT-JACQUES, MONTREAL, QC, H3C 4M8
(514) 380-1827 SIC 4899
NUMERIS p 407
1234 MAIN ST SUITE 600, MONCTON, NB, E1C 1H7
(506) 859-7700 SIC 8732
NUMERIS p 777
1500 DON MILLS RD SUITE 305, NORTH YORK, ON, M3B 3L7
(416) 445-9800 SIC 8621
NUMESH INC p 1362
3000 AV FRANCIS-HUGHES, SAINTE-ROSE, QC, H7L 3J5
(450) 663-8700 SIC 3496
NUNA CONTRACTING LTD p 121
9839 31 AVE NW, EDMONTON, AB, T6N 1C5
(780) 434-9114 SIC 1794
NUNASI CORPORATION p 472
1104 INUKSUGAIT PLAZA SUITE 210, IQALUIT, NU, X0A 0H0
(867) 979-8920 SIC 8741
NUNASTAR PROPERTIES INC p 125
1281 91 ST SW SUITE 200, EDMONTON, AB, T6X 1H1
(780) 452-4333 SIC 6512
NUNASTAR PROPERTIES INC p 436
4825 49TH AVE, YELLOWKNIFE, NT, X1A

2R3
(867) 873-3531 SIC 7011
NUNATTA CAMPUS p 472
 See NUNAVUT ARCTIC COLLEGE
NUNAVIK NICKEL PROJECT p 1202
 See CANADIAN ROYALTIES INC
NUNAVIT TEST CASE 1 CANADA p 472
PO BOX 1211, IQALUIT, NU, X0A 0H0
(867) 979-1000 SIC 6712
NUNAVUT ARCTIC COLLEGE p 472
GD, ARVIAT, NU, X0C 0E0
(867) 857-8600 SIC 8221
NUNAVUT ARCTIC COLLEGE p 472
GD, IQALUIT, NU, X0A 0H0
(867) 979-7200 SIC 8211
NUNAVUT ENERGY CENTRE p 472
 See QULLIQ ENERGY CORPORATION
NUNAVUT POWER CORPORATION p 472
2ND FLOOR GN BUILDING, BAKER LAKE, NU, X0C 0A0
(867) 793-4200 SIC 4911
NUNAVUT TUNNGAVIK INCORPORATED p 472
921 QUEEN ELIZABETH WAY II SUITE 301, IQALUIT, NU, X0A 0H0
(867) 975-4900 SIC 8399
NURAN WIRELESS INC p 1265
2150 CYRILLE-DUQUET, QUEBEC, QC, G1N 2G3
(418) 914-7484 SIC 3679
NURKKALA, HJ INVESTMENTS p 358
131 PTH 12 N, STEINBACH, MB, R5G 1T5
(204) 326-3436 SIC 5531
NURMANN HOLDINGS LTD p 272
19500 LANGLEY BYPASS, SURREY, BC, V3S 7R2
(604) 530-6545 SIC 7011
NURSE CHEVROLET CADILLAC LTD p 1014
1530 DUNDAS ST E, WHITBY, ON, L1N 2K7
(905) 668-4044 SIC 5511
NURSES OFFICE p 203
 See FW GREEN HOME, THE
NURSING & HOMEMAKERS INC p 875
2347 KENNEDY RD SUITE 204, SCARBOROUGH, ON, M1T 3T8
(416) 754-0700 SIC 8399
NURUN INC p 1184
358 RUE BEAUBIEN O, MONTREAL, QC, H2V 4S6
(514) 392-1900 SIC 7371
NURUN INC p 1259
330 RUE DE SAINT-VALLIER E BUREAU 120, QUEBEC, QC, G1K 9C5
(418) 627-2001 SIC 7371
NURUN SERVICES CONSEILS p 1184
 See NURUN INC
NUS CONSULTING GROUP p 765
 See NATIONAL UTILITY SERVICE (CANADA) LIMITED
NUSTEF FOODS LIMITED p 708
2440 CAWTHRA RD, MISSISSAUGA, ON, L5A 2X1
(905) 896-3060 SIC 2051
NUT MAN COMPANY INC, THE p 31
4112 8 ST SE, CALGARY, AB, T2G 3A7
(403) 287-1983 SIC 5441
NUTANA MACHINE LTD p 1428
2615 1ST AVE N, SASKATOON, SK, S7K 6E9
(306) 242-3822 SIC 3532
NUTECH FIRE PROTECTION CO. LTD p 608
2814 BARTON ST E, HAMILTON, ON, L8E 2J9
(905) 662-9991 SIC 7389
NUTRABLEND FOODS INC p 536
415 DOBBIE DR, CAMBRIDGE, ON, N1T 1S8
(519) 622-4178 SIC 3556
NUTRACELLE p 1042
9 CARRIAGE LANE, STRATFORD, PE, C1B 2G9

(877) 229-1207 SIC 5149
NUTRAFARMS INC p 487
261 KING ST, BARRIE, ON, L4N 6B5
(705) 739-0669 SIC 5149
NUTRALAB CANADA CORP p 878
980 TAPSCOTT RD, SCARBOROUGH, ON, M1X 1C3
(905) 752-1823 SIC 2834
NUTRASUN FOODS LIMITED PARTNERSHIP p 1422
6201 E PRIMROSE GREEN DR, REGINA, SK, S4V 3L7
(306) 751-2040 SIC 2041
NUTRI-DYN PRODUCTS LTD p 137
4307 49 ST, INNISFAIL, AB, T4G 1P3
(403) 227-3926 SIC 5122
NUTRI-NATION FUNCTIONAL FOODS INC p 247
1560 BROADWAY ST SUITE 1110, PORT COQUITLAM, BC, V3C 2M8
(604) 552-5549 SIC 2032
NUTRIAG LTD p 997
62 ARROW RD, TORONTO, ON, M9M 2L8
(416) 636-1555 SIC 2874
NUTRIART INC p 1262
550 AV GODIN, QUEBEC, QC, G1M 2K2
(418) 687-5320 SIC 2066
NUTRIEN AG SOLUTIONS (CANADA) INC p 1422
2625 VICTORIA AVE 6TH FL, REGINA, SK, S4T 1Z8
(306) 569-4379 SIC 5261
NUTRIEN LTD p 1428
122 1ST AVE S SUITE 500, SASKATOON, SK, S7K 7G3
(306) 933-8500 SIC 2873
NUTRINOR COOPERATIVE p 1296
425 RUE MELANCON, SAINT-BRUNO-LAC-SAINT-JEAN, QC, G0W 2L0
(418) 343-3636 SIC 6712
NUTRIPLUS p 1351
 See SALADEXPRESS INC
NUTRITION & FOOD SERVICES p 367
 See WINNIPEG REGIONAL HEALTH AUTHORITY, THE
NUTRITION & FOOD SERVICES p 474
 See SCARBOROUGH AND ROUGE HOSPITAL
NUTRITION HOUSE p 853
 See NUTRITION HOUSE CANADA INC
NUTRITION HOUSE CANADA INC p 853
80 WEST BEAVER CREEK RD UNIT 12, RICHMOND HILL, ON, L4B 1H3
(905) 707-7633 SIC 6794
NUTRITION INTERNATIONAL p 834
180 ELGIN ST 10 FL, OTTAWA, ON, K2P 2K3
(613) 782-6800 SIC 7389
NUTTER'S BULK & NATURAL FOODS p 145
 See D & L CRANSTON HOLDINGS LTD
NUTTER'S BULK & NATURAL FOODS INC p 146
1601 DUNMORE RD SE SUITE 107, MEDICINE HAT, AB, T1A 1Z8
(403) 529-1664 SIC 5149
NUTTY CHOCOLATIER CO LTD, THE p 848
182 QUEEN ST, PORT PERRY, ON, L9L 1B8
(905) 985-2210 SIC 5441
NUTTY CHOCOLATIER, THE p 848
 See NUTTY CHOCOLATIER CO LTD, THE
NUTTY CLUB p 379
 See SCOTT-BATHGATE LTD
NUUN DIGITAL INC p 31
1206 20 AVE SE, CALGARY, AB, T2G 1M8
(403) 907-0997 SIC 7371
NUVIA CANADA INC p 556
222 SNIDERCROFT RD, CONCORD, ON, L4K 2K1
(647) 800-1319 SIC 8999
NUVISION COMMODITIES INC p 357
49 ELEVATOR RD, ST JEAN BAPTISTE,

MB, R0G 2B0

(204) 758-3401 *SIC 5153*

NUVISTA ENERGY LTD *p 55*
525 8 AVE SW SUITE 2500, CALGARY, AB, T2P 1G1

(403) 538-8500 *SIC 1382*

NUVISTA ENERGY LTD *p 82*
5219 53 AVE, DRAYTON VALLEY, AB, T7A 1R9

SIC 1389

NUVO NETWORK MANAGEMENT INC *p 625*
400 MARCH RD SUITE 190, KANATA, ON, K2K 3H4

SIC 7376

NUVO PHARMACEUTICALS *p 725*
See NUVO PHARMACEUTICALS INC

NUVO PHARMACEUTICALS INC *p 725*
6733 MISSISSAUGA RD UNIT 610, MISSISSAUGA, ON, L5N 6J5

(905) 673-6980 *SIC 2834*

NUVU CORPORATION *p 756*
450 HARRY WALKER PKY S, NEWMARKET, ON, L3Y 8E3

(905) 952-2288 *SIC 5051*

NVENT THERMAL CANADA LTD *p 999*
250 WEST ST, TRENTON, ON, K8V 5S2

(613) 392-6571 *SIC 3315*

NVENTIVE INC *p 1190*
215 RUE SAINT-JACQUES BUREAU 500, MONTREAL, QC, H2Y 1M6

(514) 312-4969 *SIC 7371*

NVI *p 1223*
See IPROSPECT CANADA INC

NWD MICROAGE *p 1134*
See NWD SYSTEMS (MONTREAL) INC

NWD SYSTEMS (MONTREAL) INC *p 1134*
4209 DES LAURENTIDES (A-15) E, LAVAL-OUEST, QC, H7L 5W5

(450) 973-6678 *SIC 5045*

NWI PRECISION TUBE ULC *p 997*
9 FENMAR DR, TORONTO, ON, M9L 1L5

(416) 743-4417 *SIC 3728*

NWMO *p 925*
See NUCLEAR WASTE MANAGEMENT ORGANIZATION (NWMO)

NWP INDUSTRIES LP *p 137*
4017 60 AVE, INNISFAIL, AB, T4G 1S9

(403) 227-4100 *SIC 3443*

NYACK TECHNOLOGY INC *p 1318*
160 RUE VANIER, SAINT-JEAN-SUR-RICHELIEU, QC, J3B 3R4

(450) 245-0373 *SIC 2821*

NYGARD FASHIONS *p 372*
See NYGARD INTERNATIONAL PARTNERSHIP

NYGARD INTERNATIONAL PARTNERSHIP *p 372*
1771 INKSTER BLVD, WINNIPEG, MB, R2X 1R3

(204) 982-5000 *SIC 5621*

NYGH *p 769*
See NORTH YORK GENERAL HOSPITAL

NYLENE CANADA INC *p 479*
200 MCNAB ST, ARNPRIOR, ON, K7S 2C7

(613) 623-3191 *SIC 2824*

NYRSTAR LANGLOIS *p 1134*
See BREAKWATER RESOURCES LTD

NYRSTAR MYRA FALLS LTD. *p 195*
1 BOLIDEN MINE ST, CAMPBELL RIVER, BC, V9W 5E2

(250) 287-9271 *SIC 1481*

O

O & O DEVELOPMENTS INC *p 814*
1401 PHILLIP MURRAY AVE, OSHAWA, ON, L1J 8C4

(905) 725-6951 *SIC 7941*

O & P SUPERMARKETS LTD *p 333*
3829 CADBORO BAY RD, VICTORIA, BC, V8N 4G1

(250) 477-6513 *SIC 5411*

O & Y ENTERPRISE *p 377*
See ENTERPRISE PROPERTY GROUP

(MAN) INC

O A C HOLDINGS LIMITED *p 816*
2525 LANCASTER RD, OTTAWA, ON, K1B 4L5

(613) 523-1540 *SIC 7991*

O D A *p 973*
See ONTARIO DENTAL ASSOCIATION, THE

O I S E *p 976*
See ONTARIO INSTITUTE FOR STUDIES IN EDUCATION OF THE UNIVERSITY OF TORONTO

O K TIRE *p 79*
See 893278 ALBERTA LTD

O M B PARTS & INDUSTRIAL LTD *p 422*
7 BLACKMORE AVE SUITE 1, CLARENVILLE, NL, A5A 1B8

(709) 466-6491 *SIC 5531*

O P G *p 843*
See ONTARIO POWER GENERATION INC

O P G *p 947*
See ONTARIO POWER GENERATION INC

O R H L S *p 750*
See OTTAWA REGIONAL HOSPITAL LINEN SERVICES INCORPORATED

O S Q *p 1269*
See ORCHESTRE SYMPHONIQUE DE QUEBEC, L'

O S S T F DISTRICT 1 *p 913*
111 WILSON AVE SUITE E, TIMMINS, ON, P4N 2S8

SIC 8631

O W L *p 543*
See ONE WORLD LOGISTICS OF AMERICA INC

O'BRIAIN DRUGS LTD *p 406*
320 ELMWOOD DR, MONCTON, NB, E1A 6V2

(506) 383-8303 *SIC 5912*

O'BRIEN ELECTRIC CO LTD *p 415*
79 MARSH ST, SAINT JOHN, NB, E2L 5R1

SIC 1731

O'BRIEN LIFTING SOLUTIONS INC *p 523*
4435 CORPORATE DR, BURLINGTON, ON, L7L 5T9

(905) 336-8245 *SIC 3536*

O'CONNELL, ANN INTERIOR DESIGN LTD *p 673*
7321 VICTORIA PARK AVE SUITE 2, MARKHAM, ON, L3R 2Z8

(905) 477-4695 *SIC 7389*

O'CONNELL, THOMAS INC *p 1223*
5700 RUE NOTRE-DAME O, MONTREAL, QC, H4C 1V1

(514) 932-2145 *SIC 1711*

O'CONNOR DODGE CHRYSLER JEEP *p 196*
See O'CONNOR MOTORS LTD

O'CONNOR ELECTRIC LTD *p 635*
9 CENTENNIAL RD UNIT 2, KITCHENER, ON, N2B 3E9

(519) 745-8886 *SIC 1731*

O'CONNOR MOTORS LTD *p 196*
45730 HOCKING AVE, CHILLIWACK, BC, V2P 1B3

(604) 792-2754 *SIC 5511*

O'CONNOR RV CENTRES *p 197*
44430 YALE RD, CHILLIWACK, BC, V2R 4H1

(604) 792-2747 *SIC 5561*

O'DELL ELECTRIC LTD *p 31*
3827 15A ST SE, CALGARY, AB, T2G 3N7

(403) 266-2935 *SIC 1731*

O'DONNELL SPECIALTY ADVERTISING LTD *p 474*
487 WESTNEY RD S UNIT 16, AJAX, ON, L1S 6W8

(905) 427-8818 *SIC 5199*

O'HANLON PAVING LTD *p 96*
16511 116 AVE NW, EDMONTON, AB, T5M 3V1

(780) 434-8555 *SIC 1611*

O'HARA TECHNOLOGIES INC *p 853*
20 KINNEAR CRT, RICHMOND HILL, ON,

L4B 1K8

(905) 707-3286 *SIC 3559*

O'LEARY BUICK GMC LTD *p 402*
1135 HANWELL RD, FREDERICTON, NB, E3C 1A5

(506) 453-7000 *SIC 5511*

O'LEARY POTATO PACKERS LTD *p 1042*
85 ELLIS AVE, O'LEARY, PE, C0B 1V0

SIC 5148

O'NEIL ELECTRIC SUPPLY *p 1029*
See 972683 ONTARIO INC

O'NEIL ELECTRIC SUPPLY *p 1032*
See O'NEIL, EARL ELECTRIC SUPPLY LIMITED

O'NEIL FISHERIES *p 449*
See SCOTIA HARVEST INC

O'NEIL'S FARM EQUIPMENT (1971) LIMITED *p 493*
2461 HWY 56, BINBROOK, ON, L0R 1C0

(905) 572-6714 *SIC 5083*

O'NEIL, EARL ELECTRIC SUPPLY LIMITED *p 1032*
150 CREDITVIEW RD, WOODBRIDGE, ON, L4L 9N4

(416) 798-7722 *SIC 5063*

O'NEILL COLLEGIATE & VOCATIONAL *p 811*
See DURHAM DISTRICT SCHOOL BOARD

O'NEILL, RAYMOND & SON FISHERIES LTD *p 399*
221 CH ESCUMINAC POINT, ESCUMINAC, NB, E9A 1V6

(506) 228-4794 *SIC 2091*

O'REGAN HALIFAX LIMITED *p 456*
3575 KEMPT RD, HALIFAX, NS, B3K 4X6

(902) 453-2331 *SIC 5511*

O'REGAN I-N LIMITED *p 456*
3461 KEMPT RD, HALIFAX, NS, B3K 5T7

(902) 453-2020 *SIC 5521*

O'REGAN PROPERTIES LIMITED *p 443*
60 BAKER DR UNIT A, DARTMOUTH, NS, B2W 6L4

(902) 464-9550 *SIC 6719*

O'REGAN'S AUTOMOTIVE GROUP *p 443*
See O'REGAN PROPERTIES LIMITED

O'REGAN'S NISSAN DARTMOUTH LTD *p 443*
60 BAKER DR UNIT C, DARTMOUTH, NS, B2W 6L4

(902) 469-8484 *SIC 5511*

O'REGAN'S TOYOTA HALIFAX *p 456*
See O'REGAN HALIFAX LIMITED

O'REILLY'S INDEPENDENT GROCER *p 848*
150 PRESCOTT CENTRE DR, PRESCOTT, ON, K0E 1T0

(613) 925-4625 *SIC 5411*

O'ROURKE ENGINEERING LTD *p 9*
2711 39 AVE NE, CALGARY, AB, T1Y 4T8

(403) 261-4991 *SIC 8711*

O'SHANTER DEVELOPMENT COMPANY LTD *p 920*
245 CARLAW AVE SUITE 107, TORONTO, ON, M4M 2S1

(416) 466-2642 *SIC 6513*

O-I *p 505*
See O-I CANADA CORP

O-I CANADA CORP *p 505*
100 WEST DR, BRAMPTON, ON, L6T 2J5

(905) 457-2423 *SIC 3221*

O-TWO SYSTEMS INTERNATIONAL INC *p 735*
7575 KIMBEL ST UNIT 5, MISSISSAUGA, ON, L5S 1C8

SIC 3842

O. J. COMPANY *p 1376*
See COMPAGNIE OTTO JANGL LTEE

O.B.N. CONSULTANTS INC *p 575*
78 QUEEN ELIZABETH BLVD, ETOBICOKE, ON, M8Z 1M3

(416) 253-7416 *SIC 8748*

O.B.N. SECURITY & INVESTIGATIONS *p 575*
See O.B.N. CONSULTANTS INC

O.C. TANNER RECOGNITION COMPANY LIMITED *p 523*
4200 FAIRVIEW ST, BURLINGTON, ON, L7L 4Y8

(905) 632-7255 *SIC 3911*

O.C. TANNER RECOGNITION COMPANY LIMITED *p 523*
4200 FAIRVIEW ST, BURLINGTON, ON, L7L 4Y8

(905) 632-7255 *SIC 6351*

O.C.P. CONSTRUCTION SUPPLIES INC *p 900*
1072 WEBBWOOD DR, SUDBURY, ON, P3C 3B7

(705) 674-7073 *SIC 5032*

O.E.M. REMANUFACTURING COMPANY INC *p 106*
13315 156 ST NW, EDMONTON, AB, T5V 1V2

(780) 468-6220 *SIC 7538*

O.J. PIPELINES CANADA *p 149*
1409 4 ST, NISKU, AB, T9E 7M9

(780) 955-3900 *SIC 1623*

O.K. INDUSTRIES LTD *p 267*
6702 RAJPUR PL, SAANICHTON, BC, V8M 1Z5

(250) 652-9211 *SIC 1611*

O.K. KIDS *p 1325*
See 9071-7851 QUEBEC INC

O.K. TIRE STORES INC *p 279*
19082 21 AVE, SURREY, BC, V3Z 3M3

(604) 542-7999 *SIC 5531*

O.L.E.G. ENERGY CORPORATION *p 915*
1319 STEELES AVENUE W, TORONTO, ON, M2R 3N2

(416) 886-4798 *SIC 4924*

O.M.H.M. *p 1192*
See OFFICE MUNICIPAL D'HABITATION DE MONTREAL

O.S.I. MACHINERIE INC *p 1305*
2510 98E RUE, SAINT-GEORGES, QC, G6A 1E4

(418) 228-6868 *SIC 3553*

O.T.T. LEGAL SERVICES PROFESSIONAL CORPORATION *p 865*
1504 MARKHAM RD, SCARBOROUGH, ON, M1B 2V9

(416) 292-2022 *SIC 7389*

O/L ENTERPRISES INC *p 425*
GD, LA SCIE, NL, A0K 3M0

(709) 675-2085 *SIC 4832*

OACAS *p 943*
See ONTARIO ASSOCIATION OF CHILDREN'S AID SOCIETIES

OACIQ *p 1071*
See ORGANISME D'AUTOREGLEMENTATION DU COUTAGE IMMOBILERS DU QUEBEC, L'

OAK + FORT *p 289*
See OAK AND FORT CORP

OAK ACRES CHILDREN'S CAMP *p 1039*
See MURPHY, D.P. INC

OAK AND FORT CORP *p 289*
7 6TH AVE E UNIT 200, VANCOUVER, BC, V5T 1J3

(604) 559-6911 *SIC 5651*

OAK BAY BEACH HOTEL LIMITED *p 333*
1175 BEACH DR, VICTORIA, BC, V8S 2N2

(250) 598-4556 *SIC 7011*

OAK BAY HATCHERY *p 395*
See KELLY COVE SALMON LTD

OAK BAY KIWANIS HEALTH CARE SOCIETY *p 334*
3034 CEDAR HILL RD, VICTORIA, BC, V8T 3J3

(250) 598-2022 *SIC 8011*

OAK BAY MARINA LTD *p 284*
1943 PENINSULA RD, UCLUELET, BC, V0R 3A0

(250) 726-7771 *SIC 7011*

OAK BAY MARINA LTD *p 333*
1327 BEACH DR, VICTORIA, BC, V8S 2N4

(250) 370-6509 *SIC 4493*

OAK BLUFF COLONY FARMS LTD *p 353*
GD, MORRIS, MB, R0G 1K0
(204) 746-2122   *SIC 0191*
OAK BLUFF COLONY OF HUTTERIAN BRETHREN *p 353*
See OAK BLUFF COLONY FARMS LTD
OAK CREEK DEVELOPMENTS *p 17*
3816 64 AVE SE, CALGARY, AB, T2C 2B4
(403) 279-2904   *SIC 5599*
OAK LANE ENTERPRISES LTD *p 338*
4420 WEST SAANICH RD, VICTORIA, BC, V8Z 3E9
(250) 708-3900   *SIC 5411*
OAK LEAF CONFECTIONS CO. *p 869*
440 COMSTOCK RD, SCARBOROUGH, ON, M1L 2H6
(416) 751-0740   *SIC 2064*
OAK MARITIME (CANADA) INC *p 315*
1111 GEORGIA ST W SUITE 1500, VAN-COUVER, BC, V6E 4M3
(604) 689-8083   *SIC 4731*
OAK POINT SERVICE *p 369*
272 OAK POINT HWY, WINNIPEG, MB, R2R 1V1
(204) 633-9435   *SIC 7538*
OAK RIDGE MEATS LIMITED *p 352*
1055 BOUNDARY RD, MCCREARY, MB, R0J 1B0
(204) 835-2365   *SIC 5147*
OAK RIVER COLONY FARMS LTD *p 354*
GD, OAK RIVER, MB, R0K 1T0
(204) 566-2359   *SIC 0213*
OAK TERRACE *p 810*
See REVERA INC
OAK-LAND FORD LINCOLN SALES LIMITED *p 801*
570 TRAFALGAR RD, OAKVILLE, ON, L6J 3J2
(905) 844-3273   *SIC 5511*
OAK-LANE PARK INVESTMENTS LIMITED *p 801*
570 TRAFALGAR RD, OAKVILLE, ON, L6J 3J2
(905) 844-3273   *SIC 6712*
OAKCREEK GOLF & TURF LP *p 17*
3816 64 AVE SE, CALGARY, AB, T2C 2B4
(403) 279-2907   *SIC 5091*
OAKEN HOLDINGS INC *p 505*
241 DEERHURST DR, BRAMPTON, ON, L6T 5K3
(416) 679-4172   *SIC 5082*
OAKGROUP AUTOMOTIVE CORPORATION *p 698*
1035 RONSA CRT, MISSISSAUGA, ON, L4W 2N6
(905) 614-0777   *SIC 5511*
OAKHAM HOUSE *p 936*
See PALIN FOUNDATION, THE
OAKLANE COLONY *p 169*
See OAKLANE HUTTERIAN BRETHREN
OAKLANE HUTTERIAN BRETHREN *p 169*
GD STN MAIN, TABER, AB, T1G 2E5
(403) 223-2950   *SIC 0111*
OAKRIDGE ACCOUNTING SERVICES LTD *p 220*
2604 ENTERPRISE WAY UNIT 1, KELOWNA, BC, V1X 7Y5
(250) 712-3800   *SIC 8721*
OAKRIDGE FORD SALES (1981) LIMITED *p 659*
601 OXFORD ST W, LONDON, ON, N6H 1T8
(519) 472-0944   *SIC 5511*
OAKRIDGE LUTHERAN CHURCH *p 293*
See EVANGELICAL LUTHERAN CHURCH IN CANADA
OAKRIDGE SAFEWAY *p 293*
See SOBEYS WEST INC
OAKRIDGE SECONDARY SCHOOL *p 659*
See THAMES VALLEY DISTRICT SCHOOL BOARD
OAKS CONCRETE PRODUCTS *p 513*

See BRAMPTON BRICK LIMITED
OAKS RETIREMENT VILLAGE INC *p 1005*
80 MCNAUGHTON AVE SUITE 114, WAL-LACEBURG, ON, N8A 1R9
(519) 627-9292   *SIC 6513*
OAKVILLE AUTOMOTIVE GROUP INC *p 804*
2375 WYECROFT RD, OAKVILLE, ON, L6L 6L4
(905) 842-8400   *SIC 5511*
OAKVILLE BEAVER *p 802*
See METROLAND MEDIA GROUP LTD
OAKVILLE ENTERPRISES CORPORATION *p 804*
861 REDWOOD SQ SUITE 1900, OAKVILLE, ON, L6L 6R6
(905) 825-9400   *SIC 4911*
OAKVILLE FAMILY YMCA *p 802*
410 REBECCA ST, OAKVILLE, ON, L6K 1K7
(905) 845-3417   *SIC 8351*
OAKVILLE GYMNASTIC CLUB *p 806*
1415 THIRD LINE, OAKVILLE, ON, L6M 3G2
(905) 847-7747   *SIC 7999*
OAKVILLE HYDRO ELECTRICITY DISTRIBUTION INC *p 804*
861 REDWOOD SQ SUITE 1900, OAKVILLE, ON, L6L 6R6
(905) 825-9400   *SIC 4911*
OAKVILLE HYDRO ELECTRICITY, DIV OF *p 803*
See EL CON
OAKVILLE INFINITI *p 802*
See 2507246 ONTARIO INC
OAKVILLE MAZDA *p 805*
See W.J.B. MOTORS LIMITED
OAKVILLE TOYOTA *p 804*
See OAKVILLE AUTOMOTIVE GROUP INC
OAKVILLE TRAFALGAR HIGH SCHOOL *p 800*
See HALTON DISTRICT SCHOOL BOARD
OAKVILLE VOLKSWAGEN INC *p 806*
1345 NORTH SERVICE RD W, OAKVILLE, ON, L6M 2W2
(905) 844-3285   *SIC 5511*
OAKWOOD COLLEGIATE INSTITUTE *p 989*
See TORONTO DISTRICT SCHOOL BOARD
OAKWOOD CONSTRUCTION SERVICES LTD *p 363*
20 BURNETT AVE, WINNIPEG, MB, R2G 1C1
(204) 661-8415   *SIC 8741*
OAKWOOD MOTORS INC *p 1425*
635 BRAND CRT, SASKATOON, SK, S7J 5L3
(306) 664-3333   *SIC 5511*
OAKWOOD NISSAN *p 1425*
See OAKWOOD MOTORS INC
OAKWOOD PARK LODGE *p 759*
6747 OAKWOOD DR, NIAGARA FALLS, ON, L2G 0J3
(905) 356-8732   *SIC 8051*
OAKWOOD PUBLIC SCHOOL *p 846*
See DISTRICT SCHOOL BOARD OF NIA-GARA
OAKWOOD ROOFING AND SHEET METAL CO. LTD *p 363*
20 BURNETT AVE, WINNIPEG, MB, R2G 1C1
(204) 237-8361   *SIC 1761*
OAKWOOD TERRACE *p 443*
See DARTMOUTH SENIOR CARE SOCI-ETY
OASIS ESTHETIQUE DISTRIBUTION INC *p 1214*
1231 RUE SAINTE-CATHERINE O BU-REAU 303, MONTREAL, QC, H3G 1P5
(514) 286-9148   *SIC 5122*
OASIS SURF *p 1069*
See CENTRE OASIS SURF INC
OASIS TECHNOLOGY HOLDINGS LTD *p*

772
90 SHEPPARD AVE E SUITE 100, NORTH YORK, ON, M2N 3A1
(416) 228-8000   *SIC 7371*
OASIS WINDOWS LTD *p 277*
7677 134 ST, SURREY, BC, V3W 9E9
(604) 597-5033   *SIC 5031*
OATH (CANADA) CORP *p 982*
99 SPADINA AVE SUITE 200, TORONTO, ON, M5V 3P8
(416) 263-8100   *SIC 4899*
OBERSON *p 1070*
See SKI MOJO INC
OBERSON *p 1241*
See SKI MOJO INC
OBI PARTS INC *p 714*
350 HAZELHURST RD, MISSISSAUGA, ON, L5J 4T8
(905) 403-7800   *SIC 5012*
OBJECTIF LUNE INC *p 1166*
2030 BOUL PIE-IX BUREAU 500, MON-TREAL, QC, H1V 2C8
(514) 875-5863   *SIC 5112*
OBOR HOLDINGS LTD *p 216*
228 TRANQUILLE RD, KAMLOOPS, BC, V2B 3G1
(250) 376-1710   *SIC 5541*
OBRIANS *p 1429*
2112 MILLAR AVE, SASKATOON, SK, S7K 6P4
(306) 955-5626   *SIC 5521*
OBSCO BEAUTY SUPPLY *p 720*
See BEAUTY SYSTEMS GROUP (CANADA) INC
OBSERVATOIRE DES TOUT-PETITS *p 1196*
See FONDATION LUCIE & ANDRE CHAGNON
OBSERVER, THE *p 860*
See OSPREY MEDIA PUBLISHING INC
OBSI *p 955*
See OMBUDSMAN FOR BANKING SER-VICES AND INVESTMENTS
OBSIDIAN ENERGY LTD *p 55*
207 9 AVE SW SUITE 200, CALGARY, AB, T2P 1K3
(403) 777-2500   *SIC 1311*
OBSIDIAN ENERGY LTD *p 127*
GD, FALHER, AB, T0H 1M0
(780) 837-2929   *SIC 2911*
OBSIDIAN GROUP INC *p 725*
1770 ARGENTIA RD, MISSISSAUGA, ON, L5N 3S7
(905) 814-8030   *SIC 6794*
OC *p 222*
See OKANAGAN COLLEGE
OC CANADA HOLDINGS COMPANY *p 124*
831 HAYTER RD NW, EDMONTON, AB, T6S 1A1
(780) 472-6644   *SIC 5033*
OC CANADA HOLDINGS COMPANY *p 517*
11 SPALDING DR, BRANTFORD, ON, N3T 6B7
(519) 752-5436   *SIC 3296*
OC CANADA HOLDINGS COMPANY *p 876*
3450 MCNICOLL AVE, SCARBOROUGH, ON, M1V 1Z5
(416) 292-4000   *SIC 3296*
OC CANADA HOLDINGS COMPANY *p 1073*
131 BOUL MONTCALM N, CANDIAC, QC, J5R 3L6
(450) 619-2000   *SIC 3296*
OCAD UNIVERSITY *p 977*
See ONTARIO COLLEGE OF ART & DE-SIGN UNIVERSITY
OCASI *p 923*
See OCASI - ONTARIO COUNCIL OF AGENCIES SERVING IMMIGRANTS
OCASI - ONTARIO COUNCIL OF AGEN-CIES SERVING IMMIGRANTS *p 923*
110 EGLINTON AVE W SUITE 200, TORONTO, ON, M4R 1A3
(416) 322-4950   *SIC 8699*
OCC *p 75*

See OPEN CALL CENTRE INC
OCEAN BEACH HOTEL, THE *p 343*
See 527758 B.C. LTD
OCEAN CARGO DIVISION *p 741*
See NIPPON EXPRESS CANADA LTD
OCEAN CHOICE INTERNATIONAL *p 421*
28 CAMPBELL ST SUITE 10, BONAVISTA, NL, A0C 1B0
(709) 468-7840   *SIC 5421*
OCEAN CHOICE INTERNATIONAL *p 427*
7476 FISHER ST, PORT AU CHOIX, NL, A0K 4C0
(709) 861-3506   *SIC 2092*
OCEAN CHOICE INTERNATIONAL *p 428*
69 WATER ST W, ST LAWRENCE, NL, A0E 2V0
(709) 873-2798   *SIC 2092*
OCEAN CHOICE INTERNATIONAL *p 430*
1315 TOPSAIL RD, ST. JOHN'S, NL, A1B 3N4
(709) 782-6244   *SIC 5421*
OCEAN CHOICE INTERNATIONAL L.P. *p 428*
See OCEAN CHOICE INTERNATIONAL
OCEAN CONTRACTORS LIMITED *p 444*
204 CONO DR, DARTMOUTH, NS, B2Y 3Y9
(902) 435-1291   *SIC 1611*
OCEAN LEADER FISHERIES LIMITED *p 461*
138 JACQUARD RD, LOWER WEDGE-PORT, NS, B0W 2B0
(902) 663-4579   *SIC 2092*
OCEAN MIRACLE SEAFOOD *p 1032*
See MEDEX. FISH IMPORTING & EX-PORTING CO. LTD
OCEAN PACIFIC HOTELS LTD *p 308*
999 CANADA PL SUITE 300, VANCOUVER, BC, V6C 3B5
(604) 662-8111   *SIC 7011*
OCEAN PACIFIC MARINE SUPPLY LTD *p 195*
1370 ISLAND HWY SUITE 102, CAMPBELL RIVER, BC, V9W 8C9
(250) 286-1011   *SIC 5088*
OCEAN PARK FORD SALES LTD *p 283*
3050 KING GEORGE BLVD, SURREY, BC, V4P 1A2
(604) 531-8883   *SIC 5511*
OCEAN PARK MECHANICAL INC *p 283*
2428 KING GEORGE BLVD SUITE 102, SURREY, BC, V4P 1H5
(604) 536-2363   *SIC 1711*
OCEAN PIER INC *p 417*
20 PATTISON ST, SCOUDOUC, NB, E4P 3R4
(506) 532-3010   *SIC 2092*
OCEAN SEAFOOD COMPANY *p 873*
See 602390 ONTARIO LIMITED
OCEAN STATE EMBLEM *p 1252*
See SOUVENIRS AVANTI INC
OCEAN STEEL & CONSTRUCTION LTD *p 414*
400 CHESLEY DR, SAINT JOHN, NB, E2K 5L6
(506) 632-2600   *SIC 3441*
OCEAN TRAILER *p 208*
See C. KEAY INVESTMENTS LTD
OCEAN VIEW MANOR SOCIETY *p 449*
1909 CALDWELL RD, EASTERN PAS-SAGE, NS, B3G 1M4
SIC 8051
OCEAN WAVE IMPORTS INC *p 689*
6295 NORTHAM DR UNIT 14, MISSIS-SAUGA, ON, L4V 1W8
(905) 672-5050   *SIC 6799*
OCEAN WEST CONSTRUCTION LTD *p 291*
1083 E KENT AVE NORTH UNIT 113, VAN-COUVER, BC, V5X 4V9
(604) 324-3531   *SIC 1522*
OCEAN WISE CONSERVATION ASSOCIA-TION *p 318*
845 STANLEY PARK DR, VANCOUVER,

BC, V6G 3E2
(604) 659-3400   *SIC* 8422
OCEANAGOLD CORPORATION   *p 326*
777 HORNBY STREET SUITE 1910, VANCOUVER, BC, V6Z 1S4
(604) 235-3360   *SIC* 1081
OCEANEERING CANADA LIMITED   *p 426*
23 DUNDEE AVE, MOUNT PEARL, NL, A1N 4R6
(709) 570-7072   *SIC* 8711
OCEANEX GLOBAL LOGISTICS   *p 432*
See *OCEANEX INC*
OCEANEX GLOBAL LOGISTICS   *p 1206*
See *OCEANEX INC*
OCEANEX INC   *p 432*
10 FORT WILLIAM PL SUITE 701, ST. JOHN'S, NL, A1C 1K4
(709) 758-0382   *SIC* 4424
OCEANEX INC   *p 432*
701 KENT FORT WILLIAM PLACE, ST. JOHN'S, NL, A1C 1K4
(709) 722-6280   *SIC* 4424
OCEANEX INC   *p 1206*
630 BOUL RENE-LEVESQUE O BUREAU 2550, MONTREAL, QC, H3B 1S6
SIC 4424
OCEANFOOD INDUSTRIES LIMITED *p 255*
11520 EBURNE WAY, RICHMOND, BC, V6V 2G7
(604) 324-1666   *SIC* 5146
OCEANFOOD SALES LIMITED   *p 285*
1909 HASTINGS ST E, VANCOUVER, BC, V5L 1T5
(604) 255-1414   *SIC* 5146
OCEANMAMA SEAFOOD   *p 205*
See *FROBISHER INTERNATIONAL ENTERPRISE LTD*
OCEANS RETAIL INVESTMENTS INC *p 177*
2096 CLEARBROOK RD, ABBOTSFORD, BC, V2T 2X2
(604) 852-1950   *SIC* 5541
OCEANSIDE EQUIPMENT LIMITED *p 447*
181 JOSEPH ZATZMAN DR UNIT 12, DARTMOUTH, NS, B3B 1R5
(902) 468-4844   *SIC* 5085
OCEANWIDE CANADA INC   *p 1221*
3400 BOUL DE MAISONNEUVE O BUREAU 1450, MONTREAL, QC, H3Z 3B8
(514) 289-9090   *SIC* 7371
OCEANWORKS INTERNATIONAL CORPORATION   *p 315*
100-535 THURLOW ST, VANCOUVER, BC, V6E 0C8
(604) 398-4998   *SIC* 3429
OCFLINK   *p 261*
See *OVERSEAS CONTAINER FORWARDING, INC*
OCI   *p 427*
See *OCEAN CHOICE INTERNATIONAL*
OCI   *p 430*
See *OCEAN CHOICE INTERNATIONAL*
OCI HOLDINGS INC   *p 1042*
20 HOPE ST, SOURIS, PE, C0A 2B0
(902) 687-1245   *SIC* 5146
OCIMAC INC   *p 1114*
504 BOUL MANSEAU BUREAU 25, JOLIETTE, QC, J6E 3E2
(450) 759-2560   *SIC* 5912
OCL GROUP INC   *p 151*
325 WOODGATE RD, OKOTOKS, AB, T1S 2A5
(403) 982-9090   *SIC* 1623
OCP COMMUNICATIONS INC   *p 530*
2319 FAIRVIEW ST UNIT 601, BURLINGTON, ON, L7R 2E3
(289) 337-5994   *SIC* 1731
OCTAGON DISTRIBUTION COMPANY LIMITED   *p 698*
5220 GENERAL RD, MISSISSAUGA, ON, L4W 1G8
SIC 5084
OCTASIC INC   *p 1168*

2901 RUE RACHEL E BUREAU 30, MONTREAL, QC, H1W 4A4
(514) 282-8858   *SIC* 3679
OCTASIC SEMICONDUCTOR   *p 1168*
See *OCTASIC INC*
OCTOPUS PRODUCTS LIMITED   *p 791*
23 GURNEY CRES, NORTH YORK, ON, M6B 1S9
(416) 531-5051   *SIC* 5162
OCULUS TRANSPORT LTD.   *p 55*
444 5 AVE SW SUITE 650, CALGARY, AB, T2P 2T8
(403) 262-0006   *SIC* 4213
OCWA   *p 943*
See *ONTARIO CLEAN WATER AGENCY*
ODC TOOLING & MOLDS   *p 1006*
See *ONTARIO DIE COMPANY LIMITED*
ODCO, INC   *p 1011*
45 BATHURST DR, WATERLOO, ON, N2V 1N2
(519) 884-0322   *SIC* 3599
ODD FELLOWS & REBEKAH HOMES *p 487*
See *IOOF SENIORS HOMES INC*
ODD FELLOWS & REBEKAHS PERSONAL CARE HOMES INC   *p 368*
2280 ST MARY'S RD, WINNIPEG, MB, R2N 3Z6
(204) 257-9947   *SIC* 8051
ODEM INTERNATIONAL INC   *p 1288*
483 CH DE LA GRANDE-COTE, ROSEMERE, QC, J7A 1M1
(450) 965-1412   *SIC* 5149
ODENZA MARKETING GROUP INC   *p 189*
4370 DOMINION ST SUITE 600, BURNABY, BC, V5G 4L7
(604) 451-1414   *SIC* 4724
ODESSA   *p 1172*
See *POISSONERIE ODESSA INC., LES*
ODLUM BROWN LIMITED   *p 308*
250 HOWE ST SUITE 1100, VANCOUVER, BC, V6C 3S9
(604) 669-1600   *SIC* 6211
ODYSSEY DISTRIBUTION GROUP INC   *p 780*
60 PRINCE ANDREW PL, NORTH YORK, ON, M3C 2H4
(647) 288-2222   *SIC* 6712
ODYSSEY HEALTH SERVICES   *p 523*
1100 BURLOAK DR SUITE 603, BURLINGTON, ON, L7L 6B2
(905) 319-0202   *SIC* 6321
ODYSSEY TIME INC   *p 780*
60 PRINCE ANDREW PL, NORTH YORK, ON, M3C 2H4
(647) 288-2222   *SIC* 5094
OEC CANADA/GOE CANADA   *p 1340*
See *OVERSEAS EXPRESS CONSOLIDATORS (CANADA) INC*
OEC GROUP   *p 1340*
See *OEC GROUPAGE OUTREMER EXPRESS (MONTREAL) INC*
OEC GROUPAGE OUTREMER EXPRESS (MONTREAL) INC   *p 1340*
725 MONTEE DE LIESSE, SAINT-LAURENT, QC, H4T 1P5
(514) 633-1246   *SIC* 4731
OECTA   *p 926*
See *ONTARIO ENGLISH CATHOLIC TEACHERS' ASSOCIATION, THE*
OERLIKON METCO (CANADA) INC *p 130*
10108 114 ST, FORT SASKATCHEWAN, AB, T8L 4R1
(780) 992-5100   *SIC* 3399
OES INC   *p 660*
4056 BLAKIE RD, LONDON, ON, N6L 1P7
(519) 652-5833   *SIC* 3625
OETIKER LIMITED   *p 476*
203 DUFFERIN ST S, ALLISTON, ON, L9R 1E9
(705) 435-4394   *SIC* 3429
OEUFS BRETON, LES   *p 1287*
See *VIANDES DU BRETON INC, LES*
OEUFS OVALE S.E.C., LES   *p 1323*
205 RUE DAMASE-BRETON, SAINT-

LAMBERT-DE-LAUZON, QC, G0S 2W0
(418) 889-8088   *SIC* 5144
OFAH   *p 841*
See *ONTARIO FEDERATION OF ANGLERS AND HUNTERS, THE*
OFC DISTRIBUTION INC   *p 708*
580 ORWELL ST, MISSISSAUGA, ON, L5A 3V7
(905) 270-2009   *SIC* 5141
OFCP   *p 791*
See *ONTARIO FEDERATION FOR CEREBRAL PALSY*
OFFBEAT OUTFITTERS I O D E SHOP *p 64*
See *IODE BARGAIN SHOP*
OFFICE AND PROFESSIONAL EMPLOYEES INTERNATIONAL UNION   *p 190*
4501 KINGSWAY UNIT 301, BURNABY, BC, V5H 0E5
(604) 299-0378   *SIC* 8631
OFFICE COFFEE SOLUTIONS LTD   *p 993*
82 INDUSTRY ST, TORONTO, ON, M6M 4L7
(416) 516-9333   *SIC* 5046
OFFICE D'INVESTISSEMENT DES REGIMES DE PENSIONS DU SECTEUR PUBLIC   *p 1207*
1250 BOUL RENE-LEVESQUE O BUREAU 900, MONTREAL, QC, H3B 4W8
(514) 937-2772   *SIC* 6411
OFFICE DES CONGRES ET DU TOURISME DU GRAND MONTREAL INC, L'   *p 1207*
800 BOUL RENE-LEVESQUE O BUREAU 2450, MONTREAL, QC, H3B 1X9
(514) 844-5400   *SIC* 8743
OFFICE DES TELECOMMUNICATIONS EDUCATIVES DE LANGUE FRANCAISE DE L'ONTARIO   *p 946*
21 COLLEGE ST SUITE 600, TORONTO, ON, M5G 2B3
(416) 968-3536   *SIC* 7812
OFFICE DU TOURISME DE LAVAL INC *p 1087*
480 PROM DU CENTROPOLIS, COTE SAINT-LUC, QC, H7T 3C2
(450) 682-5522   *SIC* 7389
OFFICE INTERIORS   *p 447*
See *MMP OFFICE INTERIORS INCORPORATED*
OFFICE INTERIORS   *p 447*
656 WINDMILL RD, DARTMOUTH, NS, B3B 1B8
(902) 422-4011   *SIC* 5044
OFFICE MUNICIPAL D'HABITATION DE MONTREAL   *p 1192*
415 RUE SAINT-ANTOINE O 2E ETAGE, MONTREAL, QC, H2Z 2B9
(514) 872-6442   *SIC* 6531
OFFICE MUNICIPAL D'HABITATION DE QUEBEC   *p 1265*
110 RUE DE COURCELETTE, QUEBEC, QC, G1N 4T4
(418) 780-5200   *SIC* 8631
OFFICE MUNICIPAL D'HABITATION KATIVIK   *p 1119*
1105 RUE AKIANUT, KUUJJUAQ, QC, J0M 1C0
(819) 964-2000   *SIC* 6531
OFFICE OF THE CHIEF INFORMATION OFFICER   *p 995*
See *GOVERNMENT OF ONTARIO*
OFFICE OF THE FIRE COMMISSIONER *p 379*
401 YORK AVE UNIT 508, WINNIPEG, MB, R3C 0P8
(204) 945-3322   *SIC* 8711
OFFICE OF THE VICE PRESIDENT RESEARCH   *p 1434*
See *UNIVERSITY OF SASKATCHEWAN*
OFFICE PRODUCTS GROUP, DIV OF *p 676*
See *TOSHIBA OF CANADA LIMITED*

OFFICE SOURCE INCORPORATED, THE *p 698*
4800 EASTGATE PKY UNIT 1, MISSISSAUGA, ON, L4W 3W6
(905) 602-7090   *SIC* 5021
OFFICE SPECIALTY   *p 620*
See *INSCAPE CORPORATION*
OFFICEMAXMD GRAND&TOY   *p 1031*
See *GRAND & TOY LIMITED*
OFI L.P.   *p 595*
3985 BELGREEN DR, GLOUCESTER, ON, K1G 3N2
(613) 736-1215   *SIC* 3296
OFIELD, CRAIG GROUP LTD   *p 853*
55 LEEK CRES, RICHMOND HILL, ON, L4B 3Y2
(905) 726-5000   *SIC* 5141
OFIS SYSTEMS INC   *p 556*
452 MILLWAY AVE SUITE 2, CONCORD, ON, L4K 3V7
SIC 2521
OFRIGIDAIRE ALIMENTATION INC *p 1124*
1575 RTE 277, LAC-ETCHEMIN, QC, G0R 1S0
(418) 625-6301   *SIC* 5411
OFS   *p 488*
See *OUGH FIRE SYSTEMS LTD*
OGESCO CONSTRUCTION INC   *p 1274*
3070 CH DES QUATRE-BOURGEOIS, QUEBEC, QC, G1W 2K4
(418) 651-8774   *SIC* 1542
OGI GROUP CORPORATION   *p 55*
888 3 ST SW UNIT 1000, CALGARY, AB, T2P 5C5
(403) 233-7777   *SIC* 1382
OGILVIE MOTORS LTD   *p 596*
1020 OGILVIE RD, GLOUCESTER, ON, K1J 8G9
(613) 745-9191   *SIC* 5511
OGILVIE SUBARU   *p 816*
1040 PARISIEN ST, OTTAWA, ON, K1B 3M8
(613) 745-9191   *SIC* 5511
OGILVIE, BRIAN HOLDING LTD   *p 154*
88 HOWARTH ST SUITE 5, RED DEER, AB, T4N 6V9
(403) 342-6307   *SIC* 5541
OGILVY & ACTION DIV   *p 943*
See *WPP GROUP CANADA COMMUNICATIONS LIMITED*
OGILVY & OGILVY INC   *p 1402*
4115 RUE SHERBROOKE O BUREAU 500, WESTMOUNT, QC, H3Z 1K9
(514) 932-8660   *SIC* 6411
OGILVY ASSURANCE   *p 1402*
See *OGILVY & OGILVY INC*
OGILVY CANADA   *p 943*
See *WPP GROUP CANADA COMMUNICATIONS LIMITED*
OGILVY MONTREAL INC   *p 1190*
215 RUE SAINT-JACQUES BUREAU 333, MONTREAL, QC, H2Y 1M6
(514) 861-1811   *SIC* 7311
OGILVY RENAULT   *p 1273*
See *NORTON ROSE FULBRIGHT CANADA S.E.N.C.R.L. S.R.L.*
OGILVYONE WORLDWIDE LTD   *p 943*
33 YONGE ST SUITE 1100, TORONTO, ON, M5E 1X6
(416) 363-9514   *SIC* 8743
OGO FIBERS INC   *p 853*
9140 LESLIE ST SUITE 312, RICHMOND HILL, ON, L4B 0A9
(905) 762-9300   *SIC* 5093
OH ENVIRONMENTAL INC   *p 706*
311 MATHESON BLVD E, MISSISSAUGA, ON, L4Z 1X8
(905) 890-9000   *SIC* 8748
OHA   *p 982*
See *ONTARIO HOSPITAL ASSOCIATION*
OHE CONSULTANTS   *p 706*
See *OH ENVIRONMENTAL INC*
OHR WHISTLER MANAGEMENT LTD *p 342*
4090 WHISTLER WAY, WHISTLER, BC, V0N 1B4

▲ Public Company   ■ Public Company Family Member   **HQ** Headquarters   **BR** Branch   **SL** Single Location

(604) 905-5000   *SIC 7011*
OII OWNERSHIP IDENTIFICATION INC   *p 217*
1402 MCGILL RD SUITE 102, KAMLOOPS, BC, V2C 1L3
(250) 314-9686   *SIC 7389*
OIL AND GAS   *p 728*
See *WEIR CANADA, INC*
OIL CITY EXPRESS   *p 127*
See *1172895 ALBERTA LTD*
OIL GAS DISTRIBUTION   *p 130*
See *INTERNATIONAL BULK SERVICES*
OIL LIFT TECHNOLOGY INC   *p 24*
950 64 AVE NE, CALGARY, AB, T2E 8S8
(403) 291-5300   *SIC 3533*
OIL SANDS GROUP   *p 129*
See *SUNCOR ENERGY INC*
OIL STATES ENERGY SERVICES (CANADA) INCORPORATED   *p 158*
28042 HIGHWAY 11 SUITE 334, RED DEER COUNTY, AB, T4S 2L4
(403) 340-0716   *SIC 1389*
OIL-DRI CANADA ULC   *p 1237*
730 RUE SALABERRY, MONTREAL, QC, H7S 1H3
(450) 663-5750   *SIC 5085*
OILERSNATION.COM LTD   *p 90*
10020 100 ST NW, EDMONTON, AB, T5J 0N3
(780) 909-2445   *SIC 7941*
OILFIELDS GENERAL HOSPITAL   *p 5*
717 GOVERNMENT RD, BLACK DIAMOND, AB, T0L 0H0
(403) 933-2222   *SIC 8062*
OJEKA GALLERY INC   *p 886*
212 WELLAND AVE, ST CATHARINES, ON, L2R 2P3
(905) 682-4129   *SIC 5461*
OK TIRE   *p 104*
See *WESTERN STERLING TRUCKS LTD*
OK TIRE   *p 422*
See *O M B PARTS & INDUSTRIAL LTD*
OK TIRE ETOBICOKE   *p 573*
See *822099 ONTARIO LIMITED*
OKA COMPUTER SYSTEMS LTD   *p 1198*
2075 RUE UNIVERSITY BUREAU 750, MONTREAL, QC, H3A 2L1
SIC 7379
OKANAGAN CHRYSLER JEEP DODGE   *p 220*
See *LAKEVIEW MOTORS LP*
OKANAGAN COLLEGE   *p 222*
1000 K.L.O. RD, KELOWNA, BC, V1Y 4X8
(250) 762-5445   *SIC 8221*
OKANAGAN COLLEGE   *p 222*
1000 K.L.O. RD UNIT A108, KELOWNA, BC, V1Y 4X8
(250) 862-5480   *SIC 7371*
OKANAGAN COLLEGE   *p 243*
583 DUNCAN AVE W, PENTICTON, BC, V2A 8E1
(250) 492-4305   *SIC 8748*
OKANAGAN GENERAL PARTNER LIMITED   *p 219*
3333 UNIVERSITY WAY, KELOWNA, BC, V1V 1V7
(250) 807-9851   *SIC 5812*
OKANAGAN LANDING ELEMENTARY   *p 332*
See *SCHOOL DISTRICT NO 22 (VERNON)*
OKANAGAN NATION AQUATIC ENTERPRISES LTD   *p 342*
3535 OLD OKANAGAN HWY UNIT 104, WESTBANK, BC, V4T 3L7
(778) 754-8001   *SIC 0921*
OKANAGAN NORTH GROWERS CO-OPERATIVE   *p 223*
9751 BOTTOM WOOD LAKE RD, KELOWNA, BC, V4V 1S7
SIC 0723
OKANAGAN REGIONAL LIBRARY DIS-

TRICT   *p 219*
1430 K.L.O. RD, KELOWNA, BC, V1W 3P6
(250) 860-4652   *SIC 8231*
OKANAGAN RESTORATION SERVICES LTD   *p 331*
6236 PLEASANT VALLEY RD, VERNON, BC, V1B 3R3
(250) 542-3470   *SIC 1629*
OKANAGAN SPRING BREWERY   *p 332*
See *SLEEMAN BREWERIES LTD*
OKANAGAN SPRING BREWERY   *p 602*
See *SLEEMAN BREWERIES LTD*
OKANAGAN TREE FRUIT COOPERATIVE *p 222*
880 VAUGHAN AVE, KELOWNA, BC, V1Y 7E4
(250) 763-7003   *SIC 0723*
OKANAGAN TREE FRUIT COOPERATIVE *p 224*
9751 BOTTOM WOOD LAKE RD, LAKE COUNTRY, BC, V4V 1S7
SIC 0723
OKANAGAN VALLEY NEWSPAPER GROUP, THE   *p 221*
See *CONTINENTAL NEWSPAPERS (CANADA) LTD*
OKE WOODSMITH BUILDING SYSTEMS INC   *p 598*
70964 BLUEWATER HWY SUITE 9, GRAND BEND, ON, N0M 1T0
(519) 238-8893   *SIC 1521*
OKOTOKS FORD   *p 151*
See *OKOTOKS LINCOLN MERCURY*
OKOTOKS HEALTH AND WELLNESS CENTRE   *p 150*
See *ALBERTA HEALTH SERVICES*
OKOTOKS HONDA   *p 150*
See *425507 ALBERTA LTD*
OKOTOKS LINCOLN MERCURY   *p 151*
4 WESTLAND RD, OKOTOKS, AB, T1S 1N1
(403) 938-2255   *SIC 5511*
OKOTOKS SAFEWAY   *p 151*
See *SOBEYS WEST INC*
OL ' GRANDAD'S SNACKS (1992) INC   *p 534*
1680 BISHOP ST N, CAMBRIDGE, ON, N1R 7J3
(519) 624-9992   *SIC 2096*
OLAM CANADA COMPANY   *p 741*
1100 MID-WAY BLVD UNIT 7, MISSISSAUGA, ON, L5T 1V8
(905) 795-8871   *SIC 5149*
OLAMETER INC   *p 1198*
2000 AV MCGILL COLLEGE BUREAU 500, MONTREAL, QC, H3A 3H3
(514) 982-6664   *SIC 7389*
OLD CO-OPERATIVE   *p 151*
See *WESTVIEW CO-OPERATIVE ASSOCIATION LIMITED*
OLD DUTCH FOODS LTD   *p 3*
215 EAST LAKE BLVD NE, AIRDRIE, AB, T4A 2G1
(403) 948-3339   *SIC 2096*
OLD DUTCH FOODS LTD   *p 17*
3103 54 AVE SE, CALGARY, AB, T2C 0A9
(403) 279-2771   *SIC 2096*
OLD DUTCH FOODS LTD   *p 102*
18027 114 AVE NW, EDMONTON, AB, T5S 1T8
(780) 453-2341   *SIC 4225*
OLD DUTCH FOODS LTD   *p 372*
100 BENTALL ST, WINNIPEG, MB, R2X 2Y5
(204) 632-0249   *SIC 2096*
OLD DUTCH FOODS LTD   *p 1043*
4 SLEMON PARK DR, SUMMERSIDE, PE, C1N 4K4
(902) 888-5160   *SIC 2096*
OLD DUTCH FOODS LTD   *p 1335*
6525 RUE ABRAMS, SAINT-LAURENT, QC, H4S 1X9
(514) 745-4449   *SIC 2096*
OLD HIPPY WOOD PRODUCTS INC   *p 122*

2415 80 AVE NW, EDMONTON, AB, T6P 1N3
(780) 448-1163   *SIC 5021*
OLD MILL PONTIAC BUICK CADILLAC LIMITED   *p 994*
2595 ST CLAIR AVE W, TORONTO, ON, M6N 4Z5
(416) 766-2443   *SIC 5511*
OLD MILL TORONTO HOTEL   *p 572*
See *OMT HOSPITALITY INC*
OLD NAVY (CANADA) INC   *p 710*
100 CITY CENTRE DR UNIT E6, MISSISSAUGA, ON, L5B 2C9
(905) 275-5155   *SIC 5651*
OLD NAVY (CANADA) INC   *p 789*
1 YORKDALE RD, NORTH YORK, ON, M6A 3A1
(416) 787-9384   *SIC 5651*
OLD NAVY (CANADA) INC   *p 930*
60 BLOOR ST W SUITE 1501, TORONTO, ON, M4W 3B8
(416) 921-2711   *SIC 5651*
OLD OAK PROPERTIES INC   *p 654*
465 RICHMOND ST SUITE 600, LONDON, ON, N6A 5P4
(519) 661-0215   *SIC 6512*
OLD ORCHARD INN LIMITED   *p 471*
153 GREENWICH RD S, WOLFVILLE, NS, B4P 2R2
(902) 542-5751   *SIC 7011*
OLD REPUBLIC INSURANCE COMPANY OF CANADA   *p 613*
100 KING ST W UNIT 1100, HAMILTON, ON, L8P 1A2
(905) 523-5936   *SIC 6331*
OLD SPAGHETTI FACTORY (EDMONTON) LTD   *p 104*
8882 170 ST NW SUITE 1632, EDMONTON, AB, T5T 4M2
(780) 444-2181   *SIC 5812*
OLD SPAGHETTI FACTORY (WHISTLER) LTD   *p 343*
4154 VILLAGE GREEN, WHISTLER, BC, V8E 1H1
(604) 938-1015   *SIC 5812*
OLD SPAGHETTI FACTORY, THE   *p 104*
See *OLD SPAGHETTI FACTORY (EDMONTON) LTD*
OLD SPAGHETTI FACTORY, THE   *p 337*
See *WATER STREET (VANCOUVER) SPAGHETTI CORP*
OLD SPAGHETTI FACTORY, THE   *p 942*
See *ESPLANADE (TORONTO) SPAGHETTI CORP*
OLD STEELCO INC   *p 862*
105 WEST ST, SAULT STE. MARIE, ON, P6A 7B4
(705) 945-2351   *SIC 3312*
OLD STEELCO INC   *p 862*
GD, SAULT STE. MARIE, ON, P6A 5P2
(705) 945-3172   *SIC 3312*
OLD STEELCO INC   *p 862*
GD, SAULT STE. MARIE, ON, P6A 5P2
(705) 945-3301   *SIC 3312*
OLDCASTLE BUILDING PRODUCTS CANADA, INC   *p 2*
28234 ACHESON RD, ACHESON, AB, T7X 6A9
(780) 962-4010   *SIC 5039*
OLDCASTLE BUILDING PRODUCTS CANADA, INC   *p 229*
5075 275 ST, LANGLEY, BC, V4W 0A8
(604) 607-1300   *SIC 3211*
OLDCASTLE BUILDING PRODUCTS CANADA, INC   *p 684*
8375 NO 5 SIDE RD, MILTON, ON, L9T 2X7
(905) 875-4215   *SIC 5039*
OLDCASTLE BUILDING PRODUCTS CANADA, INC   *p 892*
682 ARVIN AVE, STONEY CREEK, ON, L8E 5R4
SIC 3272
OLDCASTLE BUILDING PRODUCTS CANADA, INC   *p 1073*

2 AV D'INVERNESS, CANDIAC, QC, J5R 4W5
(450) 444-5214   *SIC 2822*
OLDCASTLE BUILDING PRODUCTS CANADA, INC   *p 1073*
2 AV D'INVERNESS, CANDIAC, QC, J5R 4W5
(450) 444-5214   *SIC 5039*
OLDCASTLE BUILDINGENVELOPE CANADA INC   *p 556*
210 GREAT GULF DR, CONCORD, ON, L4K 5W1
(905) 660-4520   *SIC 3211*
OLDE YORK POTATO CHIPS   *p 506*
See *SARATOGA POTATO CHIP COMPANY INC*
OLDE YORKE ESPLANADE HOTELS LTD *p 943*
45 THE ESPLANADE, TORONTO, ON, M5E 1W2
(416) 367-8900   *SIC 7011*
OLDS ALBERTAN, THE   *p 151*
See *MOUNTAIN VIEW PUBLISHING INC*
OLDS AUCTION MART LTD   *p 151*
4613 54 ST, OLDS, AB, T4H 1E9
(403) 556-3655   *SIC 7389*
OLDS DODGE CHRYSLER JEEP   *p 151*
See *551546 ALBERTA LTD*
OLDS GARDENS MARKET IGA   *p 151*
See *DELLA SIEGA ENTERPRISES LTD*
OLDS HOSPITAL & CARE CENTRE   *p 151*
See *ALBERTA HEALTH SERVICES*
OLE MEDIA MANAGEMENT (GP) L.P. *p 965*
120 BREMNER BLVD SUITE 2900, TORONTO, ON, M5J 0A8
(416) 850-1163   *SIC 2741*
OLG   *p 774*
See *ONTARIO LOTTERY AND GAMING CORPORATION*
OLIFRUITS LTEE   *p 1084*
290 BOUL DE LA CONCORDE E, COTE SAINT-LUC, QC, H7G 2E6
(450) 667-4031   *SIC 5431*
OLIGEL DISTRIBUTION INC   *p 1313*
2775 AV BOURDAGES N, SAINT-HYACINTHE, QC, J2S 5S3
SIC 5142
OLIN CANADA ULC   *p 1056*
675 BOUL ALPHONSE-DESHAIES, BE-CANCOUR, QC, G9H 2Y8
(819) 294-6633   *SIC 2819*
OLIN CANADA ULC   *p 1198*
2020 BOUL ROBERT-BOURASSA BUREAU 2190, MONTREAL, QC, H3A 2A5
(514) 397-6100   *SIC 2819*
OLIN PRODUITS CHLORALCALIS   *p 1056*
See *OLIN CANADA ULC*
OLIVE DEVAUD RESIDENCE   *p 248*
See *VANCOUVER COASTAL HEALTH AUTHORITY*
OLIVE GARDEN   *p 102*
See *RED LOBSTER HOSPITALITY LLC*
OLIVE GARDEN   *p 363*
See *RED LOBSTER HOSPITALITY LLC*
OLIVE GARDEN   *p 382*
See *RED LOBSTER HOSPITALITY LLC*
OLIVE GARDEN ITALIAN RESTAURANT *p 228*
20080 LANGLEY BYPASS, LANGLEY, BC, V3A 9J7
(604) 514-3499   *SIC 5812*
OLIVE GARDEN RESTAURANT   *p 119*
See *RED LOBSTER HOSPITALITY LLC*
OLIVE THE SENSES   *p 336*
1701 DOUGLAS ST UNIT 9, VICTORIA, BC, V8W 0C1
(250) 590-8418   *SIC 5149*
OLIVER & ASSOCIATES REAL ESTATE BROKERAGE INC   *p 659*
99 HORTON ST W, LONDON, ON, N6J 4Y6
(519) 657-2020   *SIC 6531*
OLIVER & BONACINI HOSPITALITY INC *p 922*
2323 YONGE ST SUITE 303, TORONTO,

ON, M4P 2C9
(416) 485-8047   *SIC* 5812
OLIVER LODGE   *p* 1431
1405 FAULKNER CRES, SASKATOON, SK,
S7L 3R5
(306) 382-4111   *SIC* 8361
OLIVER LUMBER   *p* 540
See GOODFELLOW INC
**OLIVER LUMBER COMPANY OF
TORONTO**   *p* 540
See 3235 ONTARIO INC
OLIVER OLIVES INC   *p* 495
99 PILLSWORTH RD, BOLTON, ON, L7E
4E4
(905) 951-9096   *SIC* 2033
OLIVER SAFEWAY   *p* 92
See SOBEYS WEST INC
OLIVER, PETER M SALES LTD   *p* 920
1015 LAKE SHORE BLVD E SUITE 654,
TORONTO, ON, M4M 1B4
(416) 778-0102   *SIC* 5531
OLIVER, WYMAN LIMITED   *p* 965
120 BREMNER BLVD SUITE 800,
TORONTO, ON, M5J 0A8
(416) 868-2200   *SIC* 8741
OLIVIER CHRYSLER   *p* 1367
*See OLIVIER SEPT-ILES CHRYSLER
DODGE JEEP RAM INC*
OLIVIER FORD   *p* 1308
See OLIVIER, JACQUES FORD INC
OLIVIER FORD SEPT-ILES   *p* 1367
See FERRO AUTOMOBILES INC
**OLIVIER KAMOURASKA CHRYSLER
DODGE JEEP RAM**   *p* 1349
*See AUTOMOBILE KAMOURASKA (1992)
INC*
**OLIVIER SEPT-ILES CHRYSLER DODGE
JEEP RAM INC**   *p* 1367
119 RUE MONSEIGNEUR-BLANCHE,
SEPT-ILES, QC, G4R 3G7
(418) 962-2555   *SIC* 5511
OLIVIER'S CANDIES LTD   *p* 17
2828 54 AVE SE BAY CTR, CALGARY, AB,
T2C 0A7
(403) 266-6028   *SIC* 5149
OLIVIER, JACQUES FORD INC   *p* 1308
4405 CH DE CHAMBLY, SAINT-HUBERT,
QC, J3Y 3M7
(450) 445-3673   *SIC* 5511
OLIVIERI FOODS DIV   *p* 205
See CATELLI FOODS CORPORATION
OLIVIERI FOODS DIV   *p* 607
See CATELLI FOODS CORPORATION
OLOINGSIGH DRUGS LIMITED   *p* 428
141 TORBAY RD, ST. JOHN'S, NL, A1A 2H1
(709) 722-6270   *SIC* 5912
OLON INDUSTRIES   *p* 593
See ERRION GROUP INC
OLS   *p* 446
See HGS CANADA INC
OLSEN FASHION CANADA INC   *p* 698
5112 TIMBERLEA BLVD, MISSISSAUGA,
ON, L4W 2S5
(905) 290-1919   *SIC* 5621
OLSENS MEAT & PRODUCE LTD   *p* 416
391 LANCASTER AVE, SAINT JOHN, NB,
E2M 2L3
(506) 657-0000   *SIC* 5147
OLSON INTERNATIONAL   *p* 182
*See OLSON INTERNATIONAL TRADING
LTD*
OLSON INTERNATIONAL TRADING LTD   *p*
182
4098 MCCONNELL DR, BURNABY, BC,
V5A 3Y9
(604) 420-8022   *SIC* 5141
OLY-ROBI TRANSFORMATION S.E.C.   *p*
1403
212 CH DU CANTON S, YAMACHICHE, QC,
G0X 3L0
(819) 296-1754   *SIC* 2011
OLYMBEC   *p* 1325
*See DEVELOPPEMENTS REKERN INC,
LES*

OLYMEL   *p* 1064
See COOP FEDEREE, LA
OLYMEL   *p* 1066
See OLYMEL S.E.C.
OLYMEL   *p* 1097
See ALIMENTS PRINCE, S.E.C.
OLYMEL   *p* 1298
See COOP FEDEREE, LA
OLYMEL   *p* 1385
See OLYMEL S.E.C.
OLYMEL DRUMMONDVILLE   *p* 1099
See OLYMEL S.E.C.
OLYMEL FLAMINGO SAINT DAMASE   *p*
1298
See OLYMEL S.E.C.
OLYMEL FLAMINGO, DIV OF   *p* 1310
See COOP FEDEREE, LA
OLYMEL S.E.C.   *p* 505
14 WESTWYN CRT, BRAMPTON, ON, L6T
4T5
(905) 796-6947   *SIC* 2011
OLYMEL S.E.C.   *p* 505
318 ORENDA RD, BRAMPTON, ON, L6T
1G1
(905) 793-5757   *SIC* 2015
OLYMEL S.E.C.   *p* 1050
7770 RUE GRENACHE, ANJOU, QC, H1J
1C3
(514) 353-2830   *SIC* 2011
OLYMEL S.E.C.   *p* 1057
580 RUE LAFERRIERE, BERTHIERVILLE,
QC, J0K 1A0
(450) 836-1651   *SIC* 2011
OLYMEL S.E.C.   *p* 1059
1020 BOUL MICHELE-BOHEC,
BLAINVILLE, QC, J7C 5E2
(450) 979-0001   *SIC* 2013
OLYMEL S.E.C.   *p* 1066
1580 RUE EIFFEL, BOUCHERVILLE, QC,
J4B 5Y1
(514) 858-9000   *SIC* 2011
OLYMEL S.E.C.   *p* 1066
1580 RUE EIFFEL, BOUCHERVILLE, QC,
J4B 5Y1
(514) 858-9000   *SIC* 5147
OLYMEL S.E.C.   *p* 1099
255 RUE ROCHELEAU, DRUM-
MONDVILLE, QC, J2C 7G2
(819) 475-3030   *SIC* 2011
OLYMEL S.E.C.   *p* 1254
155 RUE SAINT-JEAN-BAPTISTE N,
PRINCEVILLE, QC, G6L 5C9
(819) 364-5501   *SIC* 2011
OLYMEL S.E.C.   *p* 1298
249 RUE PRINCIPALE, SAINT-DAMASE,
QC, J0H 1J0
(450) 797-2691   *SIC* 2015
OLYMEL S.E.C.   *p* 1300
125 RUE SAINT-ISIDORE, SAINT-ESPRIT,
QC, J0K 2L0
(450) 839-7258   *SIC* 2011
OLYMEL S.E.C.   *p* 1300
25 RTE 125 E, SAINT-ESPRIT, QC, J0K 2L0
(450) 839-7258   *SIC* 2011
OLYMEL S.E.C.   *p* 1300
57 125 RTE, SAINT-ESPRIT, QC, J0K 2L0
(450) 839-7258   *SIC* 4212
OLYMEL S.E.C.   *p* 1313
1425 AV ST-JACQUES, SAINT-
HYACINTHE, QC, J2S 6M7
(450) 778-2211   *SIC* 7299
OLYMEL S.E.C.   *p* 1313
2200 AV PRATTE BUREAU 400, SAINT-
HYACINTHE, QC, J2S 4B6
(450) 771-0400   *SIC* 2011
OLYMEL S.E.C.   *p* 1315
3380 RUE PRINCIPALE, SAINT-JEAN-
BAPTISTE, QC, J0L 2B0
(450) 467-2875   *SIC* 2015
OLYMEL S.E.C.   *p* 1318
770 RUE CLAUDE, SAINT-JEAN-SUR-
RICHELIEU, QC, J3B 2W5
(450) 347-2241   *SIC* 2011
OLYMEL S.E.C.   *p* 1385

531 RUE DES ERABLES, TROIS-
RIVIERES, QC, G8T 7Z7
(819) 376-3770   *SIC* 5147
OLYMEL S.E.C.   *p* 1392
568 CH DE L'ECORE S, VALLEE-
JONCTION, QC, G0S 3J0
(418) 253-5437   *SIC* 2011
OLYMEL SAINT-ESPRIT   *p* 1300
See OLYMEL S.E.C.
OLYMEL/FLAMINGO   *p* 1057
See OLYMEL S.E.C.
OLYMPE CONSULTANTS   *p* 1280
1500 RUE MIGNERON, QUEBEC, QC, G2K
1X5
SIC 8748
OLYMPIA FINANCIAL GROUP INC   *p* 31
125 9 AVE SE SUITE 2300, CALGARY, AB,
T2G 0P6
(403) 261-0900   *SIC* 6091
OLYMPIA JEWELLERY CORP   *p* 784
312 DOLOMITE DR SUITE 208, NORTH
YORK, ON, M3J 2N2
SIC 5094
OLYMPIA TILE + STONE   *p* 988
See OLYMPIA TILE INTERNATIONAL INC
OLYMPIA TILE INTERNATIONAL INC   *p* 988
1000 LAWRENCE AVE W, TORONTO, ON,
M6A 1C6
(416) 785-6666   *SIC* 5032
OLYMPIA TRUST COMPANY   *p* 31
125 9 AVE SE SUITE 2300, CALGARY, AB,
T2G 0P6
(403) 261-0900   *SIC* 6091
OLYMPIC BUILDING SUPPLIES, DIV OF   *p*
364
*See ALL-FAB BUILDING COMPONENTS
INC*
OLYMPIC BUILDING SYSTEMS LTD   *p* 366
1783 DUGALD RD, WINNIPEG, MB, R2J
0H3
(204) 661-8600   *SIC* 5039
OLYMPIC HONDA   *p* 605
See BREWIS, CHARLES LIMITED
OLYMPIC INDUSTRIES ULC   *p* 240
221 ESPLANADE W SUITE 402, NORTH
VANCOUVER, BC, V7M 3J8
(604) 985-2115   *SIC* 5031
OLYMPIC INTEGRATED SERVICES INC   *p*
31
2226 PORTLAND ST SE, CALGARY, AB,
T2G 4M6
(587) 955-9977   *SIC* 5075
**OLYMPIC INTERNATIONAL AGENCIES
LTD**   *p* 239
344 HARBOUR AVE, NORTH VANCOU-
VER, BC, V7J 2E9
(604) 986-1400   *SIC* 5075
OLYMPIC MATERIAL HANDLING LTD   *p* 556
300 BRADWICK DR, CONCORD, ON, L4K
1K8
(416) 661-4609   *SIC* 5084
OLYMPIC WHOLESALE CO   *p* 474
*See OLYMPIC WHOLESALE COMPANY
LIMITED*
**OLYMPIC WHOLESALE COMPANY LIM-
ITED**   *p*
474
75 GREEN CRT, AJAX, ON, L1S 6W9
(905) 426-5188   *SIC* 5149
OLYMPUS CANADA INC   *p* 853
25 LEEK CRES, RICHMOND HILL, ON, L4B
4B3
(289) 269-0100   *SIC* 5047
OLYMPUS NDT CANADA INC   *p* 1267
3415 RUE PIERRE-ARDOUIN, QUEBEC,
QC, G1P 0B3
(418) 872-1155   *SIC* 3829
OLYSKY LIMITED PARTNERSHIP   *p* 1407
10333 8 AVE, HUMBOLDT, SK, S0K 2A0
(306) 682-5041   *SIC* 0213
**OMBUDSMAN FOR BANKING SERVICES
AND INVESTMENTS**   *p* 955
401 BAY ST SUITE 1505, TORONTO, ON,
M5H 2Y4

(416) 287-2877   *SIC* 6282
OMBUDSPERSON OF B C   *p* 335
947 FORT ST, VICTORIA, BC, V8V 3K3
(250) 387-5855   *SIC* 7389
OMCAN   *p* 717
*See OMCAN MANUFACTURING & DIS-
TRIBUTING COMPANY INC*
**OMCAN MANUFACTURING & DISTRIBUT-
ING COMPANY INC**   *p*
717
3115 PEPPER MILL CRT, MISSISSAUGA,
ON, L5L 4X5
(905) 828-0234   *SIC* 5084
OMD CANADA   *p* 955
67 RICHMOND ST W SUITE 2, TORONTO,
ON, M5H 1Z5
(416) 681-5600   *SIC* 7319
OMEGA FOOD IMPORTERS CO. LTD   *p* 741
395 PENDANT DR UNIT 2, MISSISSAUGA,
ON, L5T 2W9
(905) 212-9252   *SIC* 5149
OMEGA II INC   *p* 1362
1735 BOUL SAINT-ELZEAR O, SAINTE-
ROSE, QC, H7L 3N6
(450) 681-6440   *SIC* 3446
OMEGA JOIST   *p* 149
See SAMUEL, SON & CO., LIMITED
OMEGA PACKING COMPANY LIMITED   *p*
231
2040 HARRISON, MASSET, BC, V0T 1M0
(250) 626-3391   *SIC* 2092
OMEGA TOOL CORP   *p* 807
2045 SOLAR CRES, OLDCASTLE, ON,
N0R 1L0
(519) 737-1201   *SIC* 3544
OMEGACHEM INC   *p* 1138
480 RUE PERREAULT, LEVIS, QC, G6W
7V6
(418) 837-4444   *SIC* 2834
OMER DESERRES INC   *p* 1176
1265 RUE BERRI BUREAU 1000, MON-
TREAL, QC, H2L 4X4
(514) 842-6695   *SIC* 5999
OMERS   *p* 955
*See OMERS ADMINISTRATION CORPO-
RATION*
**OMERS ADMINISTRATION CORPORA-
TION**   *p*
955
100 ADELAIDE ST W SUITE 900,
TORONTO, ON, M5H 0E2
(416) 369-2400   *SIC* 6371
OMERS PRIVATE EQUITY INC   *p* 955
100 ADELAIDE ST W SUITE 900,
TORONTO, ON, M5H 0E2
(416) 864-3200   *SIC* 6282
OMERS REALTY CORPORATION   *p* 955
130 ADELAIDE ST W SUITE 1100,
TORONTO, ON, M5H 3P5
(416) 369-2400   *SIC* 6719
OMEX MANUFACTURING ULC   *p* 896
251 LORNE AVE W, STRATFORD, ON, N5A
6S4
(519) 273-5760   *SIC* 5962
OMF INTERNATIONAL   *p* 877
*See OVERSEAS MISSIONARY FELLOW-
SHIP*
**OMICRON ARCHITECTURE ENGINEER-
ING CONSTRUCTION LTD**   *p*
329
595 BURRARD ST, VANCOUVER, BC, V7X
1M7
(604) 632-3350   *SIC* 8712
OMICRON CANADA INC   *p* 329
595 BURRARD ST, VANCOUVER, BC, V7X
1M7
(604) 632-3350   *SIC* 8712
**OMICRON CONSTRUCTION MANAGE-
MENT LTD**   *p*
329
595 BURRARD ST, VANCOUVER, BC, V7X
1L4
(604) 632-3350   *SIC* 1542
OMICRON CONSULTING GROUP   *p* 329

595 BURRARD ST, VANCOUVER, BC, V7X 1L4
(604) 632-3350   SIC 1541

OMNI FLOORCOVERINGS LTD   p 741
6310 KESTREL RD, MISSISSAUGA, ON, L5T 1Z3
SIC 5023

OMNI HEALTH CARE LIMITED PARTNER-SHIP   p 840
1155 WATER ST, PETERBOROUGH, ON, K9H 3P8
(705) 748-6706   SIC 8051

OMNI HEALTH CARE LTD   p 481
13837 YONGE ST, AURORA, ON, L4G 0N9
(905) 727-0128   SIC 8051

OMNI HEALTH CARE LTD   p 625
100 AIRD PL, KANATA, ON, K2L 4H8
(613) 254-9702   SIC 8051

OMNI HEALTH CARE LTD   p 625
6501 CAMPEAU DR SUITE 353, KANATA, ON, K2K 3E9
(613) 599-1991   SIC 8051

OMNI HEALTH CARE LTD   p 646
225 MARY ST W, LINDSAY, ON, K9V 5K3
(705) 324-8333   SIC 8361

OMNI HEALTH CARE LTD   p 662
30 MILLE ROCHES RD SUITE 388, LONG SAULT, ON, K0C 1P0
(613) 534-2276   SIC 8051

OMNI HEALTH CARE LTD   p 841
2020 FISHER DR, PETERBOROUGH, ON, K9J 6X6
(705) 742-8811   SIC 8051

OMNI HEALTH CARE LTD   p 841
2020 FISHER DR SUITE 1, PETERBOROUGH, ON, K9J 6X6
(705) 748-6631   SIC 8051

OMNI HEALTH COUNTRY TERRACE NURSING HOME   p 643
10072 OXBOW DR, KOMOKA, ON, N0L 1R0
(519) 657-2955   SIC 8051

OMNI HEALTH INVESTMENTS INC   p 841
2020 FISHER DR, PETERBOROUGH, ON, K9J 6X6
(705) 748-6631   SIC 6712

OMNI INSURANCE BROKERS   p 654
560 WELLINGTON ST, LONDON, ON, N6A 3R4
(519) 667-1100   SIC 6411

OMNI KING EDWARD   p 939
See KING EDWARD REALTY INC

OMNI WARRANTY CORP   p 308
355 BURRARD ST SUITE 350, VANCOUVER, BC, V6C 2G8
(604) 806-5300   SIC 6351

OMNICOM CANADA CORP   p 326
777 HORNBY ST SUITE 1600, VANCOUVER, BC, V6Z 2T3
(604) 687-7911   SIC 7311

OMNICOM CANADA CORP   p 930
2 BLOOR ST W SUITE 2900, TORONTO, ON, M4W 3E2
(416) 972-7571   SIC 8743

OMNICOM CANADA CORP   p 930
33 BLOOR ST E SUITE 1300, TORONTO, ON, M4W 3H1
(416) 960-3830   SIC 7311

OMNICOM CANADA CORP   p 982
96 SPADINA AVE 7TH FLOOR, TORONTO, ON, M5V 2J6
(416) 922-0217   SIC 7319

OMNICOM LANGUAGE SERVICES   p 42
See 744648 ALBERTA LTD

OMNIFLEX HOSE & EQUIPMENT LTD   p 534
78 COWANSVIEW RD SUITE 3, CAMBRIDGE, ON, N1R 7N3
(519) 622-0261   SIC 5084

OMNIPLAN DESIGN GROUP LIMITED   p 564
1748 BASELINE RD SUITE 200D, COURTICE, ON, L1E 2T1

(905) 421-9129   SIC 7389

OMNIPLAN PROJECT SERVICES   p 564
See OMNIPLAN DESIGN GROUP LIMITED

OMNIPLAST INC   p 1308
5350 RUE RAMSAY, SAINT-HUBERT, QC, J3Y 2S4
(450) 656-9272   SIC 2673

OMNITEX INC   p 575
120 THE EAST MALL, ETOBICOKE, ON, M8Z 5V5
SIC 5136

OMNITOUR   p 1259
See ORBITOUR LTEE

OMNITRACK   p 359
See HUDSON BAY RAILWAY COMPANY

OMNITRANS INC   p 1228
4300 RUE JEAN-TALON O, MONTREAL, QC, H4P 1W3
(514) 288-6664   SIC 4731

OMNITRAX CANADA INC   p 379
155 CARLTON ST SUITE 300, WINNIPEG, MB, R3C 3H8
(204) 947-0033   SIC 4011

OMRON CANADA INC   p 867
100 CONSILIUM PL SUITE 802, SCARBOROUGH, ON, M1H 3E3
(416) 986-6766   SIC 5065

OMRON ELECTRONIC COMPONENTS CANADA, INC   p 867
100 CONSILIUM PL SUITE 802, SCARBOROUGH, ON, M1H 3E3
(416) 286-6465   SIC 5065

OMS EXPRESS   p 485
See 1430819 ONTARIO LIMITED

OMSAC DEVELOPMENTS, DIV OF   p 381
See BIRD CONSTRUCTION COMPANY

OMSTEAD FOODS LIMITED   p 1013
303 MILO RD, WHEATLEY, ON, N0P 2P0
(519) 825-4611   SIC 4222

OMT HOSPITALITY INC   p 572
21 OLD MILL RD, ETOBICOKE, ON, M8X 1G5
(416) 236-2641   SIC 7011

OMTRANS LOGISTICS INC   p 1028
111 ZENWAY BLVD UNIT 5, WOODBRIDGE, ON, L4H 3H9
(416) 921-2255   SIC 4731

OMYA CANADA INC   p 839
18595 HWY 7 W, PERTH, ON, K7H 3E4
(613) 267-5367   SIC 1499

ON CALL CENTRE INC   p 818
2405 ST. LAURENT BLVD UNIT B, OTTAWA, ON, K1G 5B4
(613) 238-3262   SIC 7389

ON PATH BUSINESS SOLUTIONS INC   p 595
1165 KENASTON ST, GLOUCESTER, ON, K1B 3N9
(613) 564-6565   SIC 4899

ON SEMICONDUCTOR   p 525
See SOUND DESIGN TECHNOLOGIES LTD

ON SIDE RESTORATION SERVICES LTD   p 287
3157 GRANDVIEW HWY, VANCOUVER, BC, V5M 2E9
(604) 293-1596   SIC 1799

ON THE VINE MEAT & PRODUCE   p 412
See 616813 N.B. LTD

ON TRACK SAFETY LTD   p 905
29 RUGGLES AVE, THORNHILL, ON, L3T 3S4
(905) 660-5969   SIC 7389

ON TRADUIT A QUEBEC   p 1257
See ANGLOCOM INC

ON-TRACK RAILWAY OPERATIONS LTD   p 168
55024 RGE RD 234, STURGEON COUNTY, AB, T8T 2A7
(780) 973-6003   SIC 4011

ONACTUATE   p 327
See ONACTUATE CONSULTING INC.

ONACTUATE CONSULTING INC.   p 327
777 HORNBY ST SUITE 600, VANCOU-

VER, BC, V6Z 2H7
(604) 506-3435   SIC 8748

ONBELAY AUTOMOTIVE INC   p 543
540 PARK AVE E, CHATHAM, ON, N7M 5J4
(519) 354-6515   SIC 3479

ONCAP II L.P.   p 965
161 BAY ST, TORONTO, ON, M5J 2S1
(416) 214-4300   SIC 6719

ONCIDIUM HEALTH GROUP   p 698
See NATIONAL INCOME PROTECTION PLAN INC

ONE FLORAL GROUP   p 623
See FLOWER GROUP OPERATING LP

ONE FOR FREIGHT   p 684
See ONTARIO NEW ENGLAND EXPRESS INC

ONE KID'S PLACE   p 621
100 FRANK MILLER DR SUITE 2, HUNTSVILLE, ON, P1H 1H7
(705) 789-9985   SIC 8322

ONE PROPERTIES CORPORATION   p 90
10111 104 AVE NW SUITE 2500, EDMONTON, AB, T5J 0J4
(780) 423-5525   SIC 6531

ONE SOURCE BUSINESS SERVICE   p 784
3991 CHESSWOOD DR, NORTH YORK, ON, M3J 2R8
(416) 398-0863   SIC 7361

ONE SOURCE METAL   p 500
See 1373744 ONTARIO INC

ONE WEST HOLDINGS LTD   p 315
1095 PENDER ST W SUITE 900, VANCOUVER, BC, V6E 2M6
(604) 681-8882   SIC 6553

ONE WIND SERVICES INC   p 447
4 MACDONALD AVE, DARTMOUTH, NS, B3B 1C5
(902) 482-8687   SIC 7699

ONE WORLD LOGISTICS OF AMERICA INC   p 543
400 NATIONAL RD, CHATHAM, ON, N7M 5J5
(519) 380-0800   SIC 4213

ONE-EIGHTY CORP   p 1008
20 ERB ST W SUITE 803, WATERLOO, ON, N2L 1T2
(519) 884-2003   SIC 5521

ONE10 CANADA HOLDINGS ULC   p 987
130 KING ST W SUITE 1600, TORONTO, ON, M5X 2A2
(905) 214-8699   SIC 8741

ONE10 CANADA HOLDINGS ULC   p 1190
759 RUE DU SQUARE-VICTORIA BUREAU 105, MONTREAL, QC, H2Y 2J7
(514) 288-9889   SIC 8732

ONEC CONSTRUCTION INC   p 110
3811 78 AVE NW, EDMONTON, AB, T6B 3N8
(780) 440-0400   SIC 7363

ONEC ENGINEERING INC   p 110
3821 78 AVE NW, EDMONTON, AB, T6B 3N8
(780) 485-5375   SIC 8711

ONEIL MOTORS INC   p 597
1493 SIEVERIGHT RD, GLOUCESTER, ON, K1T 1M5
SIC 7515

ONEMETHOD INC   p 982
225 WELLINGTON ST W, TORONTO, ON, M5V 3G7
(416) 649-0180   SIC 8732

ONEPOINT CANADA INC   p 1207
606 RUE CATHCART BUREAU 400, MONTREAL, QC, H3B 1K9
(514) 989-3116   SIC 7379

ONESPAN CANADA INC   p 1228
8200 BOUL DECARIE BUREAU 300, MONTREAL, QC, H4P 2P5
(514) 337-5255   SIC 7371

ONEX CORPORATION   p 965
161 BAY ST, TORONTO, ON, M5J 2S1
(416) 362-7711   SIC 6282

ONEX PARTNERS ADVISOR GP INC   p 965
161 BAY ST SUITE 4900, TORONTO, ON,

M5J 2S1
(416) 362-7711   SIC 6282

ONF   p 1326
See NATIONAL FILM BOARD OF CANADA

ONFREIGHT LOGISTICS   p 902
See 1266192 ONTARIO LTD

ONGWANADA HOSPITAL   p 632
191 PORTSMOUTH AVE, KINGSTON, ON, K7M 8A6
(613) 548-4417   SIC 8361

ONION LAKE HEALTH BOARD INC   p 1413
GD, ONION LAKE, SK, S0M 2E0
(306) 344-2330   SIC 8021

ONION LAKE RESERVE   p 1413
See ONION LAKE HEALTH BOARD INC

ONIX LAZER CORPORATION   p 818
645 BELFAST RD UNIT 1, OTTAWA, ON, K1G 4V3
SIC 5112

ONLIA HOLDINGS INC   p 934
351 KING ST E SUITE 801, TORONTO, ON, M5A 1L1
(416) 479-2260   SIC 6411

ONLINE BUSINESS SYSTEMS   p 375
See ONLINE ENTERPRISES INC

ONLINE ENTERPRISES INC   p 375
115 BANNATYNE AVE SUITE 200, WINNIPEG, MB, R3B 0R3
(204) 982-0200   SIC 7371

ONLINE SUPPORT   p 838
1200 PEMBROKE ST W SUITE 25, PEMBROKE, ON, K8A 7T1
(613) 633-4200   SIC 7379

ONLINE SUPPORT   p 838
See HGS CANADA INC

ONNI AIRWAYS LTD   p 299
550 ROBSON ST UNIT 300, VANCOUVER, BC, V6B 2B7
(604) 602-7711   SIC 4512

ONTARIO AG EQUIPMENT SALES AGENCY, A DIVISION OF   p 888
See FARM-FLEET INC

ONTARIO ASSOCIATION OF CHILDREN'S AID SOCIETIES   p 546
187 2ND AVE, COCHRANE, ON, P0L 1C0
(705) 272-2449   SIC 8699

ONTARIO ASSOCIATION OF CHILDREN'S AID SOCIETIES   p 943
75 FRONT ST E SUITE 308, TORONTO, ON, M5E 1V9
(416) 987-7725   SIC 8611

ONTARIO BAKERY SUPPLIES LIMITED   p 787
84 OAKDALE RD, NORTH YORK, ON, M3N 1V9
(416) 742-6741   SIC 5149

ONTARIO BELTING & POWER TRANSMISSION CO. LTD   p 1032
371 HANLAN RD, WOODBRIDGE, ON, L4L 3T1
(416) 798-7333   SIC 5085

ONTARIO CENTRES OF EXCELLENCE INC   p 982
325 FRONT ST SUITE 300, TORONTO, ON, M5V 2Y1
(416) 861-1092   SIC 8732

ONTARIO CHRYSLER   p 698
See ONTARIO CHRYSLER JEEP DODGE INC

ONTARIO CHRYSLER JEEP DODGE INC   p 698
5280 DIXIE RD, MISSISSAUGA, ON, L4W 2A7
(905) 625-8801   SIC 5511

ONTARIO CINEMAS INC   p 924
745 MOUNT PLEASANT RD SUITE 300, TORONTO, ON, M4S 2N4
(416) 481-1186   SIC 7832

ONTARIO CLEAN WATER AGENCY   p 943
1 YONGE ST SUITE 1700, TORONTO, ON, M5E 1E5
(416) 314-5600   SIC 4941

ONTARIO COLLEGE OF ART & DESIGN

UNIVERSITY *p 977*
100 MCCAUL ST SUITE 500, TORONTO, ON, M5T 1W1
(416) 977-6000 *SIC 8221*

ONTARIO COLLEGE OF PHARMA- CISTS ORDRE DES PHARMACIENS DE L'ONTARIO *p 973*
483 HURON ST, TORONTO, ON, M5R 2R4
(416) 962-4861 *SIC 8621*

ONTARIO CONFERENCE OF THE SEVENTH-DAY ADVENTISTS CHURCH *p 813*
1110 KING ST E, OSHAWA, ON, L1H 1H8
(905) 571-1022 *SIC 8661*

ONTARIO CONSERVATORY OF MUSIC INC *p 725*
2915 ARGENTIA RD UNIT 3, MISSIS- SAUGA, ON, L5N 8G6
(905) 286-1133 *SIC 8299*

ONTARIO COUNCIL OF ALTERNATIVE BUSINESSES *p 994*
See CONSUMER/SURVIVOR BUSINESS COUNCIL OF ONTARIO

ONTARIO DAIRY HERD IMPROVEMENT CORPORATION *p 606*
660 SPEEDVALE AVE W SUITE 101, GUELPH, ON, N1K 1E5
(519) 824-2320 *SIC 8611*

ONTARIO DENTAL ASSOCIATION, THE *p 973*
4 NEW ST, TORONTO, ON, M5R 1P6
(416) 922-3900 *SIC 8621*

ONTARIO DIAGNOSTIC CENTRES *p 709*
See 2539393 ONTARIO INC

ONTARIO DIE COMPANY LIMITED *p 1006*
119 ROGER ST, WATERLOO, ON, N2J 1A4
(519) 576-8950 *SIC 3423*

ONTARIO DIVISION *p 926*
See CANADIAN CANCER SOCIETY

ONTARIO DOOR SALES LTD *p 684*
8400 LAWSON RD UNIT 2, MILTON, ON, L9T 0J8
(905) 876-1290 *SIC 3089*

ONTARIO DRIVE & GEAR LIMITED *p 752*
3551 BLEAMS RD, NEW HAMBURG, ON, N3A 2J1
(519) 662-2840 *SIC 3711*

ONTARIO EAST INSURANCE AGENCY/ BFG FINANCIAL *p 769*
1210 SHEPPARD AVE E SUITE 401, NORTH YORK, ON, M2K 1E3
(416) 498-1444 *SIC 6411*

ONTARIO ECONOMIC DEVELOPMENT *p 640*
30 DUKE ST W SUITE 906, KITCHENER, ON, N2H 3W5
(519) 571-6074 *SIC 6211*

ONTARIO EDUCATIONAL COMMUNICA- TIONS AUTHORITY, THE *p 924*
2180 YONGE ST, TORONTO, ON, M4S 2B9
(416) 484-2600 *SIC 8733*

ONTARIO ENGLISH CATHOLIC TEACH- ERS ASSOCIATION, THE *p 860*
See ONTARIO ENGLISH CATHOLIC TEACHERS' ASSOCIATION, THE

ONTARIO ENGLISH CATHOLIC TEACH- ERS' ASSOCIATION, THE *p 860*
281 EAST ST N, SARNIA, ON, N7T 6X8
(519) 332-4550 *SIC 8641*

ONTARIO ENGLISH CATHOLIC TEACH- ERS' ASSOCIATION, THE *p 926*
65 ST CLAIR AVE E SUITE 400, TORONTO, ON, M4T 2Y8
(416) 925-2493 *SIC 8621*

ONTARIO FAMILY GROUP HOMES INC *p 995*
146 WESTMINSTER AVE, TORONTO, ON, M6R 1N7
(416) 532-6234 *SIC 8361*

ONTARIO FEDERATION FOR CEREBRAL

PALSY *p 791*
1630 LAWRENCE AVE W UNIT 104, NORTH YORK, ON, M6L 1C5
(416) 244-0899 *SIC 8322*

ONTARIO FEDERATION OF ANGLERS AND HUNTERS, THE *p 841*
4601 GUTHRIE DR, PETERBOROUGH, ON, K9J 0C9
(705) 748-6324 *SIC 8699*

ONTARIO FINNISH RESTHOME ASSOCIA- TION, THE *p 863*
725 NORTH ST SUITE 209, SAULT STE. MARIE, ON, P6B 5Z3
(705) 945-9987 *SIC 8322*

ONTARIO FLOWER GROWERS CO- OPERATIVE LIMITED *p 741*
910 MID-WAY BLVD, MISSISSAUGA, ON, L5T 1T9
(905) 670-9556 *SIC 8611*

ONTARIO HARVESTORE SYSTEMS *p 622*
See ONTARIO HARVESTORE SYSTEMS SERVICES INC

ONTARIO HARVESTORE SYSTEMS SER- VICES INC *p 622*
715647 COUNTY RD NW SUITE 4, IN- NERKIP, ON, N0J 1M0
(519) 469-8200 *SIC 1541*

ONTARIO HEALTHY COMMUNITY COALI- TION *p 936*
2 CARLTON ST SUITE 1810, TORONTO, ON, M5B 1J3
SIC 8699

ONTARIO HIV TREATMENT NETWORK, THE *p 926*
1300 YONGE ST SUITE 600, TORONTO, ON, M4T 1X3
(416) 642-6486 *SIC 8621*

ONTARIO HOME HEALTH *p 896*
See ONTARIO HOME OXYGEN AND RES- PIRATORY SERVICES INC

ONTARIO HOME OXYGEN AND RESPIRA- TORY SERVICES INC *p 896*
29 MONTEITH AVE, STRATFORD, ON, N5A 7J9
(519) 273-1744 *SIC 5047*

ONTARIO HOSE SPECIALTIES LIMITED *p 741*
7245 PACIFIC CIR, MISSISSAUGA, ON, L5T 1V1
(905) 670-0113 *SIC 5085*

ONTARIO HOSPITAL ASSOCIATION *p 982*
200 FRONT ST W SUITE 2800, TORONTO, ON, M5V 3L1
(416) 205-1300 *SIC 8742*

ONTARIO HUMANE SOCIETY *p 756*
See ONTARIO SOCIETY FOR THE PRE- VENTION OF CRUELTY TO ANIMALS, THE

ONTARIO HYUNDAI *p 1014*
See MASON, GREG SERVICES INC

ONTARIO INFRASTRUCTURE AND LANDS CORPORATION *p 946*
1 DUNDAS ST W SUITE 2000, TORONTO, ON, M5G 2L5
(416) 327-3937 *SIC 8748*

ONTARIO INSTITUTE FOR CANCER RE- SEARCH *p 947*
661 UNIVERSITY AVE SUITE 510, TORONTO, ON, M5G 0A3
(416) 977-7599 *SIC 8733*

ONTARIO INSTITUTE FOR STUDIES IN EDUCATION OF THE UNIVERSITY OF TORONTO *p 976*
252 BLOOR ST W SUITE 100, TORONTO, ON, M5S 1V6
(416) 978-0005 *SIC 8733*

ONTARIO LINE CLEARING & TREE EX- PERTS INC *p 545*

7790 TELEPHONE RD, COBOURG, ON, K9A 4J7
(905) 372-6706 *SIC 0783*

ONTARIO LOTTERY AND GAMING COR- PORATION *p 569*
7445 WELLINGTON RD 21, ELORA, ON, N0B 1S0
(519) 846-2022 *SIC 7999*

ONTARIO LOTTERY AND GAMING COR- PORATION *p 774*
4120 YONGE ST SUITE 500, NORTH YORK, ON, M2P 2B8
(416) 224-1772 *SIC 7999*

ONTARIO LUNG ASSOCIATION *p 916*
18 WYNFORD DR SUITE 401, TORONTO, ON, M3C 0K8
(416) 864-9911 *SIC 8399*

ONTARIO MAZDA *p 691*
See 765620 ONTARIO INC

ONTARIO MEDICAL ASSOCIATION *p 976*
150 BLOOR ST W SUITE 900, TORONTO, ON, M5S 3C1
(416) 599-2580 *SIC 8621*

ONTARIO MEDICAL SUPPLY INC *p 595*
1100 ALGOMA RD, GLOUCESTER, ON, K1B 0A3
(613) 244-8620 *SIC 5047*

ONTARIO MINISTRY OF LABOUR *p 995*
See GOVERNMENT OF ONTARIO

ONTARIO MISSION FOR THE DEAF, THE *p 769*
2395 BAYVIEW AVE, NORTH YORK, ON, M2L 1A2
(416) 449-9651 *SIC 8361*

ONTARIO MORTGAGE ACTION CENTRE LTD *p 848*
288 BRIDGE ST, PORT STANLEY, ON, N5L 1C3
SIC 6162

ONTARIO MOTOR SALES LIMITED *p 814*
140 BOND ST W, OSHAWA, ON, L1J 8M2
(905) 725-6501 *SIC 5511*

ONTARIO NATURAL FOOD COMPANY INC *p 732*
5800 KEATON CRES, MISSISSAUGA, ON, L5R 3K2
(905) 507-2021 *SIC 5149*

ONTARIO NATURE *p 951*
See FEDERATION OF ONTARIO NATU- RALISTS

ONTARIO NEW ENGLAND EXPRESS INC *p 684*
8450 LAWSON RD UNIT 2, MILTON, ON, L9T 0J8
(905) 876-3996 *SIC 4213*

ONTARIO NORTHLANC *p 569*
See ONTARIO NORTHLAND TRANS- PORTATION COMMISSION

ONTARIO NORTHLAND RAILWAY *p 763*
See ONTARIO NORTHLAND TRANS- PORTATION COMMISSION

ONTARIO NORTHLAND TRANSPORTA- TION COMMISSION *p 569*
3RD ST, ENGLEHART, ON, P0J 1H0
(705) 544-2292 *SIC 4111*

ONTARIO NORTHLAND TRANSPORTA- TION COMMISSION *p 763*
555 OAK ST E, NORTH BAY, ON, P1B 8E3
(705) 472-4500 *SIC 4731*

ONTARIO NURSES' ASSOCIATION *p 976*
85 GRENVILLE ST SUITE 400, TORONTO, ON, M5S 3A2
(416) 964-8833 *SIC 8631*

ONTARIO NUTRI LAB INC *p 590*
6589 FIRST LINE SUITE 3, FERGUS, ON, N1M 2W4
(519) 843-5669 *SIC 8734*

ONTARIO PC PARTY *p 996*
56 ABERFOYLE CRES UNIT 400, TORONTO, ON, M8X 2W4

(416) 861-0020 *SIC 8651*

ONTARIO PENSION BOARD *p 955*
200 KING ST W SUITE 2200, TORONTO, ON, M5H 3X6
(416) 364-8558 *SIC 6371*

ONTARIO PHARMACISTS' ASSOCIATION *p 955*
155 UNIVERSITY AVE SUITE 600, TORONTO, ON, M5H 3B7
(416) 441-0788 *SIC 8621*

ONTARIO PODIATRIC MEDICAL ASSOCI- ATION *p 772*
45 SHEPPARD AVE E SUITE 900, NORTH YORK, ON, M2N 5W9
(416) 927-9111 *SIC 8621*

ONTARIO POLICE COLLEGE *p 482*
10716 HACIENDA RD, AYLMER, ON, N5H 2T2
(519) 773-5361 *SIC 8221*

ONTARIO POTATO DIST. (ALLISTON) INC. *1991*
GD STN MAIN, ALLISTON, ON, L9R 1T8
(705) 435-6902 *SIC 5148*

ONTARIO POWER CONTRACTING LIM- ITED *p 556*
340 BOWES RD, CONCORD, ON, L4K 1K1
SIC 1623

ONTARIO POWER GENERATION INC *p 489*
7263 HWY 33, BATH, ON, K0H 1G0
(613) 352-3525 *SIC 4911*

ONTARIO POWER GENERATION INC *p 843*
1675 MONTGOMERY PARK RD, PICKER- ING, ON, L1V 2R5
(905) 839-1151 *SIC 4911*

ONTARIO POWER GENERATION INC *p 947*
700 UNIVERSITY AVE, TORONTO, ON, M5G 1X6
(416) 592-2555 *SIC 4911*

ONTARIO PUBLIC SERVICE EMPLOYEES UNION *p 777*
100 LESMILL RD, NORTH YORK, ON, M3B 3P8
(416) 443-8888 *SIC 8631*

ONTARIO PUBLIC SERVICE EMPLOYEES UNION PENSION PLAN TRUST FUND *p 940*
1 ADELAIDE ST E SUITE 1200, TORONTO, ON, M5C 3A7
(416) 681-6161 *SIC 6371*

ONTARIO RACING COMMISSION *p 586*
10 CARLSON CRT SUITE 400, ETOBI- COKE, ON, M9W 6L2
SIC 7948

ONTARIO RACQUET SPORT ENTER- PRISES LTD *p 714*
884 SOUTHDOWN RD, MISSISSAUGA, ON, L5J 2Y4
(905) 822-5240 *SIC 6512*

ONTARIO REAL ESTATE ASSOCIATION *p 777*
99 DUNCAN MILL RD, NORTH YORK, ON, M3B 1Z2
(416) 445-9910 *SIC 8611*

ONTARIO REALTY CORPORATION *p 947*
1 DUNDAS ST W SUITE 2000, TORONTO, ON, M5G 1Z3
(416) 327-3937 *SIC 6531*

ONTARIO REDIMIX LTD *p 586*
21 GOODMARK PL UNIT 3, ETOBICOKE, ON, M9W 6P9
(416) 674-8237 *SIC 3271*

ONTARIO REGIONAL COMMON GROUND ALLIANCE *p 556*
102-545 NORTH RIVERMEDE RD, CON- CORD, ON, L4K 4H1
(905) 532-9836 *SIC 7389*

ONTARIO RIBS INC *p 943*
56 THE ESPLANADE SUITE 201, TORONTO, ON, M5E 1A7
(416) 864-9775 *SIC 5812*

ONTARIO SCHOOL BOARDS' INSURANCE EXCHANGE *p 604*

▲ Public Company   ■ Public Company Family Member   **HQ** Headquarters   **BR** Branch   **SL** Single Location

91 WESTMOUNT RD, GUELPH, ON, N1H 5J2
(519) 767-2182   SIC 6411

ONTARIO SCIENCE CENTRE   p 779
See CENTENNIAL CENTRE OF SCIENCE AND TECHNOLOGY

ONTARIO SECONDARY SCHOOL TEACHERS' FEDERATION, THE   p 787
60 MOBILE DR SUITE 100, NORTH YORK, ON, M4A 2P3
(416) 751-8300   SIC 8621

ONTARIO SECURITIES COMMISSION   p 955
20 QUEEN ST W 22 FLR, TORONTO, ON, M5H 3R3
(416) 593-8314   SIC 8111

ONTARIO SEED CO LIMITED   p 639
77 WELLINGTON ST S, KITCHENER, ON, N2G 2E6
(519) 886-0557   SIC 5191

ONTARIO SHORES CENTRE FOR MENTAL HEALTH SCIENCES   p 1015
700 GORDON ST, WHITBY, ON, L1N 5S9
(905) 668-5881   SIC 8063

ONTARIO SOCCER   p 1032
See ONTARIO SOCCER ASSOCIATION INCORPORATED, THE

ONTARIO SOCCER ASSOCIATION INCORPORATED, THE   p 1032
7601 MARTIN GROVE RD, WOODBRIDGE, ON, L4L 9E4
(905) 264-9390   SIC 8699

ONTARIO SOCIETY FOR THE PREVENTION OF CRUELTY TO ANIMALS, THE   p 756
16586 WOODBINE AVE SUITE 3, NEWMARKET, ON, L3Y 4W1
(905) 898-7122   SIC 8699

ONTARIO TEACHERS GROUP INVESTMENT FUND   p 787
See OTG FINANCIAL

ONTARIO TEACHERS' INSURANCE PLAN INC   p 1008
125 NORTHFIELD DR W SUITE 100, WATERLOO, ON, N2L 6K4
(519) 888-9683   SIC 6371

ONTARIO TEACHERS' PENSION PLAN BOARD   p 770
5650 YONGE ST SUITE 300, NORTH YORK, ON, M2M 4H5
(416) 228-5900   SIC 6371

ONTARIO TELEMEDICINE NETWORK   p 947
438 UNIVERSITY AVE SUITE 200, TORONTO, ON, M5G 2K8
(416) 446-4110   SIC 7363

ONTARIO TIRE RECOVERY INC   p 607
2985 CONCESSION 12 WALPOLE, HAGERSVILLE, ON, N0A 1H0
SIC 5531

ONTARIO TRAP ROCK, DIV OF   p 832
See TOMLINSON, R. W. LIMITED

ONTARIO TRAP ROCK, DIV OF   p 1002
See TOMLINSON, R. W. LIMITED

ONTARIO TRILLIUM FOUNDATION   p 976
800 BAY ST SUITE 2, TORONTO, ON, M5S 3A9
(416) 963-4927   SIC 6111

ONTARIO WEST INSURANCE BROKERS   p 657
1069 WELLINGTON RD SUITE 208, LONDON, ON, N6E 2H6
(519) 657-1400   SIC 6411

ONTARIO WORKS   p 837
See PARRY SOUND DISTRICT SOCIAL SERVICES ADMINISTRATION BOARD, THE

ONTOR LIMITED   p 789
12 LESWYN RD, NORTH YORK, ON, M6A 1K3
(416) 781-5286   SIC 5075

ONWARD CLUTHE HARDWARE PROD-

UCTS INC   p 635
10 CENTENNIAL RD, KITCHENER, ON, N2B 3G1
(519) 742-8446   SIC 5251

ONWARD MANUFACTURING COMPANY LIMITED   p 1011
585 KUMPF DR, WATERLOO, ON, N2V 1K3
(519) 885-4540   SIC 3631

ONWARD MULTI-CORP INC   p 1011
585 KUMPF DR, WATERLOO, ON, N2V 1K3
(519) 885-4540   SIC 3631

ONX ENTERPRISE SOLUTIONS LTD   p 905
165 COMMERCE VALLEY DR W SUITE 300, THORNHILL, ON, L3T 7V8
(905) 881-4414   SIC 5045

ONYX-FIRE PROTECTION SERVICES INC   p 586
42 SHAFT RD, ETOBICOKE, ON, M9W 4M2
(416) 674-5633   SIC 7382

OOCL (CANADA) INC   p 579
703 EVANS AVE SUITE 300, ETOBICOKE, ON, M9C 5E9
(416) 620-4040   SIC 4731

OOLAGEN COMMUNITY SERVICES   p 932
65 WELLESLEY ST E SUITE 500, TORONTO, ON, M4Y 1G7
(416) 395-0660   SIC 8699

OP PROMOTIONS INC   p 917
1017 WOODBINE AVE UNIT 408, TORONTO, ON, M4C 4C3
(416) 425-0363   SIC 8743

OPAL OPTICAL LTD   p 725
10 FALCONER DR UNIT 11, MISSISSAUGA, ON, L5N 3L8
SIC 5049

OPAL-RT TECHNOLOGIES INC   p 1216
1751 RUE RICHARDSON BUREAU 2525, MONTREAL, QC, H3K 1G6
(514) 935-2323   SIC 7371

OPALIS SOFTWARE INC   p 698
2680 MATHESON BLVD E SUITE 202, MISSISSAUGA, ON, L4W 0A5
(905) 670-8180   SIC 7371

OPAWIKOSCIKEN SCHOOL   p 1413
GD, PELICAN NARROWS, SK, S0P 0E0
(306) 632-2161   SIC 8211

OPEN ACCESS LIMITED   p 956
1 RICHMOND ST W SUITE 800, TORONTO, ON, M5H 3W4
(416) 364-4444   SIC 6411

OPEN CALL CENTRE INC   p 75
600 CROWFOOT CRES NW SUITE 340, CALGARY, AB, T3G 0B4
(888) 582-4515   SIC 4899

OPEN HANDS   p 562
See OTTAWA-CARLETON ASSOCIATION FOR PERSONS WITH DEVELOPMENTAL DISABILITIES

OPEN ROAD   p 70
See BOUTIQUE OF LEATHERS LTD, THE

OPEN ROAD AUTO GROUP LTD   p 299
1039 HAMILTON ST, VANCOUVER, BC, V6B 5T4
SIC 5511

OPEN ROAD BMW   p 756
See OPEN ROAD MOTORS INC

OPEN ROAD MOTORS INC   p 756
87 MULOCK DR, NEWMARKET, ON, L3Y 8V2
(905) 895-8700   SIC 5511

OPEN SOLUTIONS CANADA INC   p 802
700 DORVAL DR SUITE 202, OAKVILLE, ON, L6K 3V3
(905) 849-1390   SIC 8741

OPEN SOLUTIONS DATAWEST INC   p 321
1770 BURRARD ST SUITE 300, VANCOUVER, BC, V6J 3G7
(604) 734-7494   SIC 8742

OPEN SOLUTIONS DTS INC   p 321
1441 CREEKSIDE DR SUITE 300, VANCOUVER, BC, V6J 4S7
(604) 714-1848   SIC 7372

OPEN TEXT CORPORATION   p 1009

275 FRANK TOMPA DR, WATERLOO, ON, N2L 0A1
(519) 888-7111   SIC 7372

OPENAIRE SALES INC   p 801
2360 CORNWALL RD UNIT B, OAKVILLE, ON, L6J 7T9
(905) 901-8535   SIC 3446

OPENLANE / ADESA CANADA   p 982
See OPENLANE CANADA INC

OPENLANE CANADA INC   p 943
11 CHURCH ST SUITE 200, TORONTO, ON, M5E 1W1
(416) 861-1366   SIC 5012

OPENLANE CANADA INC   p 982
370 KING ST W SUITE 500, TORONTO, ON, M5V 1J9
(416) 861-5777   SIC 5521

OPENROAD AUTO GROUP LIMITED   p 255
13251 SMALLWOOD PL, RICHMOND, BC, V6V 1W8
(604) 273-3766   SIC 5511

OPENROAD AUTO GROUP LIMITED   p 255
5631 PARKWOOD WAY, RICHMOND, BC, V6V 2M6
(604) 273-5533   SIC 5511

OPENROAD LEXUS - RICHMOND   p 255
See OPENROAD AUTO GROUP LIMITED

OPENROAD RICHMOND AUTO BODY   p 261
See RICHMOND AUTO BODY LTD

OPERATING ENGINEERS BENEFITS & PENSION PLANS   p 189
4333 LEDGER AVE SUITE 402, BURNABY, BC, V5G 4G9
(604) 299-8341   SIC 6411

OPERATION SPRINGBOARD   p 936
2 CARLTON ST SUITE 800, TORONTO, ON, M5B 1J3
(416) 977-0089   SIC 8322

OPERATIONS NETWORK CENTRE   p 618
See TELESAT CANADA

OPINION SEARCH (OSI)   p 922
See DECIMA INC

OPINION SEARCH INC   p 1198
1080 RUE BEAVERHALL BUREAU 400, MONTREAL, QC, H3A 1E4
(514) 288-0199   SIC 8732

OPMA   p 772
See ONTARIO PODIATRIC MEDICAL ASSOCIATION

OPP ART   p 652
See COMMUNITY LIVING LONDON INC

OPP FOODS   p 932
See 709528 ONTARIO LTD

OPPENHEIMER   p 200
See DAVID OPPENHEIMER & ASSOCIATES GENERAL PARTNERSHIP

OPPENHEIMER GROUP, THE   p 200
See GRANDVIEW BROKERAGE LIMITED

OPPENHEIMER GROUP, THE   p 201
See OPPENHEIMER, DAVID AND COMPANY I, LLC

OPPENHEIMER, DAVID AND COMPANY I, LLC   p 201
11 BURBIDGE ST SUITE 101, COQUITLAM, BC, V3K 7B2
(604) 461-6779   SIC 5148

OPPLAST INC   p 490
4743 CHRISTIE DR, BEAMSVILLE, ON, L0R 1B4
(905) 563-1462   SIC 3089

OPPORTUNITY PLASTIC PACKAGING   p 652
See COMMUNITY LIVING LONDON INC

OPSENS INC   p 1267
750 BOUL DU PARC-TECHNOLOGIQUE, QUEBEC, QC, G1P 4S3
(418) 781-0333   SIC 3827

OPSEU   p 777
See ONTARIO PUBLIC SERVICE EMPLOYEES UNION

OPSEU PENSION TRUST   p 940
See ONTARIO PUBLIC SERVICE EMPLOYEES UNION PENSION PLAN TRUST FUND

OPSIS GESTION D'INFRASTRUCTURES INC   p 1142
2099 BOUL FERNAND-LAFONTAINE, LONGUEUIL, QC, J4G 2J4
(514) 982-6774   SIC 8741

OPSMOBIL INC   p 55
815 8 AVE SW SUITE 1200, CALGARY, AB, T2P 3P2
(877) 926-5558   SIC 1389

OPTA MINERALS INC   p 1005
407 PARKSIDE DR, WATERDOWN, ON, L0R 2H0
(905) 689-7361   SIC 3291

OPTAGEX INC   p 1371
243 RUE KING O, SHERBROOKE, QC, J1H 1P8
(819) 563-1191   SIC 5995

OPTEL VISION INC   p 1267
2680 BOUL DU PARC-TECHNOLOGIQUE, QUEBEC, QC, G1P 4S6
(418) 688-0334   SIC 5044

OPTELIAN   p 625
See OPTELIAN ACCESS NETWORKS CORPORATION

OPTELIAN ACCESS NETWORKS CORPORATION   p 625
1 BREWER HUNT WAY, KANATA, ON, K2K 2B5
(613) 287-2000   SIC 5049

OPTIC SOLUTIONS   p 125
See CONNECTRA TECHNOLOGIES INC

OPTICASET INC   p 1157
5440 RUE PARE BUREAU 101, MONTROYAL, QC, H4P 1R3
(514) 739-6993   SIC 5049

OPTIMA CELL   p 1194
See COMMUNICATIONS LMT INC

OPTIMA COMMUNICATIONS INC   p 1015
1615 DUNDAS ST E SUITE 300, WHITBY, ON, L1N 2L1
(905) 448-2300   SIC 5999

OPTIMA COMMUNICATIONS INTERNATIONAL INC   p 965
144 FRONT ST W SUITE 200, TORONTO, ON, M5J 2L7
(416) 581-1236   SIC 4899

OPTIMA MANUFACTURING INC   p 24
2480 PEGASUS RD NE, CALGARY, AB, T2E 8G8
(403) 291-2007   SIC 3599

OPTIMAL SERVICE GROUP, THE   p 687
See CORPORATION SERVICES MONERIS

OPTIMAX EYEWEAR INCORPORATED   p 513
55 REGAN RD UNIT 2, BRAMPTON, ON, L7A 1B2
(905) 846-6103   SIC 5099

OPTIMIL MACHINERY INC   p 209
8320 RIVER RD, DELTA, BC, V4G 1B5
(604) 946-6911   SIC 3553

OPTIMONT INC   p 1071
9995 RUE DE CHATEAUNEUF, BROSSARD, QC, J4Z 3V7
(450) 465-1818   SIC 5065

OPTIMOULE INC   p 1383
275 RUE MONFETTE E, THETFORD MINES, QC, G6G 7H4
(418) 338-6106   SIC 5085

OPTIMUM ACTUAIRES & CONSEILLERS INC   p 1198
425 BOUL DE MAISONNEUVE O BUREAU 1120, MONTREAL, QC, H3A 3G5
(514) 288-1620   SIC 8999

OPTIMUM ASSURANCE AGRICOLE INC   p 1388
25 RUE DES FORGES BUREAU 422, TROIS-RIVIERES, QC, G9A 6A7
(819) 373-2040   SIC 6331

OPTIMUM GENERAL INC   p 1198
425 BOUL DE MAISONNEUVE O BUREAU 1500, MONTREAL, QC, H3A 3G5
(514) 288-8725   SIC 6331

OPTIMUM GESTION DE PLACEMENTS INC *p* 1198
425 BOUL DE MAISONNEUVE O BUREAU 1620, MONTREAL, QC, H3A 3G5
(514) 288-7545   *SIC* 6282

OPTIMUM GESTION DE RISQUES *p* 1198
See *OPTIMUM ACTUAIRES & CONSEILLERS INC*

OPTIMUM HEALTH CHOICES INC *p* 118
7115 109 ST NW SUITE 2, EDMONTON, AB, T6G 1B9
(780) 432-5464   *SIC* 5499

OPTIMUM HEALTH VITAMINS & MORE *p* 118
See *OPTIMUM HEALTH CHOICES INC*

OPTIMUM HYDROPONIX *p* 1361
See *COMPAGNIE D'ENTRETIEN BRITE-LITE LTEE*

OPTIMUM PLACEMENTS *p* 1198
See *OPTIMUM GESTION DE PLACEMENTS INC*

OPTIMUM REASSURANCE *p* 1073
8 PLACE AVILA, CANDIAC, QC, J5R 5R5
(450) 984-1462   *SIC* 6311

OPTIMUM REASSURANCE INC *p* 1198
425 BOUL DE MAISONNEUVE O BUREAU 1200, MONTREAL, QC, H3A 3G5
(514) 288-1900   *SIC* 6411

OPTIMUM SOCIETE D'ASSURANCE INC *p* 1198
425 BOUL DE MAISONNEUVE O BUREAU 1500, MONTREAL, QC, H3A 3G5
(514) 288-8711   *SIC* 6411

OPTIMUM SOLUTIONS *p* 1281
See *9223-4202 QUEBEC INC*

OPTIMUM WEST INSURANCE COMPANY INC *p* 190
4211 KINGSWAY SUITE 600, BURNABY, BC, V5H 1Z6
(604) 688-1541   *SIC* 6331

OPTIMUS SBR INC *p* 940
30 ADELAIDE ST E SUITE 600, TORONTO, ON, M5C 3G8
(416) 962-7500   *SIC* 8741

OPTIONS FOR SEXUAL HEALTH *p* 284
3550 HASTINGS ST E, VANCOUVER, BC, V5K 2A7
(604) 731-4252   *SIC* 8093

OPTIONS NON TRADITIONNELLES INC. *p* 1143
125 BOUL SAINTE-FOY BUREAU 300, LONGUEUIL, QC, J4J 1W7
(450) 646-1030   *SIC* 8748

OPTIONS NORTHWEST PERSONAL SUPPORT SERVICES *p* 907
95 CUMBERLAND ST N, THUNDER BAY, ON, P7A 4M1
(807) 344-4994   *SIC* 8399

OPTIQ LTD *p* 556
344 NORTH RIVERMEDE RD UNIT 2, CONCORD, ON, L4K 3N2
(905) 669-6251   *SIC* 5049

OPTIQUE NIKON CANADA INC *p* 1172
5075 RUE FULLUM BUREAU 100, MONTREAL, QC, H2H 2K3
(514) 521-6565   *SIC* 3851

OPTIQUE PERFECT INC *p* 1244
1265 AV DUCHARME, OUTREMONT, QC, H2V 1E6
(514) 274-9407   *SIC* 5049

OPTIQUE WESTERN *p* 1331
See *108786 CANADA INC*

OPTIVA CANADA INC *p* 725
2233 ARGENTIA RD SUITE 302, MISSISSAUGA, ON, L5N 2X7
(905) 625-2622   *SIC* 7371

OPTIVA INC *p* 725
2233 ARGENTIA RD SUITE 302, MISSISSAUGA, ON, L5N 2X7
(905) 625-2622   *SIC* 7371

OPTMQ *p* 1183
See *ORDRE PROFESSIONEL DES TECHNOLOGISTES MEDICAUX DU QUEBEC, L'*

OPTO-PLUS INC *p* 1396
4 PLACE DU COMMERCE BUREAU 460, VERDUN, QC, H3E 1J4
(514) 762-2020   *SIC* 5049

OPTUM *p* 566
See *OPTUMINSIGHT (CANADA) INC*

OPTUMINSIGHT (CANADA) INC *p* 566
4 INNOVATION DR, DUNDAS, ON, L9H 7P3
(905) 689-3980   *SIC* 8748

OPUS CORPORATION *p* 68
5119 ELBOW DR SW UNIT 500, CALGARY, AB, T2V 1H2
(403) 209-5555   *SIC* 1542

OPUS FRAMING & ART SUPPLIES *p* 321
See *OPUS FRAMING LTD*

OPUS FRAMING LTD *p* 321
1677 2ND AVE W, VANCOUVER, BC, V6J 1H3
(604) 736-7535   *SIC* 5999

OPUS HOTEL *p* 298
See *DAVIE STREET MANAGEMENT SERVICES LTD*

OPUS ONE DESIGN BUILD & CONSTRUCTION PROJECT MANAGEMENT *p* 768
6 LANSING SQ SUITE 237, NORTH YORK, ON, M2J 1T5
SIC 1541

ORACLE CANADA ULC *p* 732
100 MILVERTON DR SUITE 100, MISSISSAUGA, ON, L5R 4H1
(905) 890-8100   *SIC* 7371

ORACLE CANADA ULC *p* 824
45 O'CONNOR ST SUITE 400, OTTAWA, ON, K1P 1A4
(613) 569-0001   *SIC* 7371

ORACLE CANADA ULC *p* 1198
600 BOUL DE MAISONNEUVE O BUREAU 1900, MONTREAL, QC, H3A 3J2
(514) 843-6762   *SIC* 7372

ORACLE CORPORATION CANADA INC *p* 732
100 MILVERTON DR SUITE 100, MISSISSAUGA, ON, L5R 4H1
SIC 7372

ORACLE INSURANCE RISK MANAGEMENT SERVICES INC *p* 557
100 DRUMLIN CIRCLE, CONCORD, ON, L4K 3E6
(905) 660-9740   *SIC* 6411

ORACLE MINING CORP *p* 315
1090 GEORGIA ST W SUITE 250, VANCOUVER, BC, V6E 3V7
(604) 689-9282   *SIC* 1041

ORACLEPOLL RESEARCH LTD *p* 900
130 ELM ST SUITE 102, SUDBURY, ON, P3C 1T6
(705) 674-9591   *SIC* 8732

ORANGE DOOR DIRECT *p* 32
See *WEST CANADIAN INDUSTRIES GROUP LTD*

ORANGE JULIUS *p* 321
See *SPEEDI GOURMET CO LTD*

ORANGE JULIUS CANADA LIMITED *p* 523
5045 SOUTH SERVICE RD SUITE 3000, BURLINGTON, ON, L7L 5Y7
(905) 639-1492   *SIC* 6794

ORANGE MAISON INC *p* 1110
904 RUE DUFFERIN, GRANBY, QC, J2H 0T8
SIC 5149

ORANGE MAISON, DIV DE *p* 1343
See *A. LASSONDE INC*

ORANGE PASTRIES INC *p* 1028
39 TURNING LEAF DR, WOODBRIDGE, ON, L4H 2J5
(289) 236-0270   *SIC* 2051

ORANGE STORE *p* 430
See *NORTH ATLANTIC*

ORANGE TRAFFIC INC *p* 1152
18195 RUE J.A.BOMBARDIER, MIRABEL, QC, J7J 0E7
(800) 363-5913   *SIC* 5046

ORANGELINE FARMS LIMITED *p* 644
627 ESSEX ROAD 14, LEAMINGTON, ON, N8H 3V8
(519) 322-0400   *SIC* 0161

ORANGEVILLE CHRYSLER LIMITED *p* 808
207 163 HWY SUITE 9, ORANGEVILLE, ON, L9W 2Z7
(519) 942-8400   *SIC* 5511

ORANGEVILLE HOME HARDWARE BUILDING CENTRE *p* 808
See *891934 ONTARIO LIMITED*

ORANGEVILLE HONDA *p* 808
See *CARRUS INVESTMENTS LTD*

ORANO CANADA INC *p* 1431
817 45TH ST W, SASKATOON, SK, S7L 5X2
(306) 343-4500   *SIC* 1094

ORANO LIMITED *p* 862
625 TRUNK RD, SAULT STE. MARIE, ON, P6A 3T1
(705) 945-8088   *SIC* 5912

ORATOIRE SAINT-JOSEPH DU MONT-ROYAL *p* 1219
See *L'ORATOIRE SAINT-JOSEPH DU MONT-ROYAL*

ORB FACTORY LIMITED, THE *p* 458
225 HERRING COVE RD, HALIFAX, NS, B3P 1L3
(902) 477-9570   *SIC* 5092

ORB TOYS *p* 458
See *ORB FACTORY LIMITED, THE*

ORBCOMM *p* 627
See *SKYWAVE MOBILE COMMUNICATIONS INC*

ORBIS CANADA LIMITED *p* 580
39 WESTMORE DR, ETOBICOKE, ON, M9V 3Y6
(416) 745-6980   *SIC* 3089

ORBIS INVESTMENTS (CANADA) LIMITED *p* 190
4710 KINGSWAY SUITE 2600, BURNABY, BC, V5H 4M2
(778) 331-3000   *SIC* 6282

ORBITE *p* 1242
See *TECHNOLOGIES ORBITE INC*

ORBITOUR LTEE *p* 1259
105 COTE DE LA MONTAGNE BUREAU 601, QUEBEC, QC, G1K 4E4
(418) 692-1223   *SIC* 4724

ORCA BAY ARENA LIMITED PARTNERSHIP *p* 299
800 GRIFFITHS WAY, VANCOUVER, BC, V6B 6G1
(604) 899-7400   *SIC* 6512

ORCA BAY SPORTS & ENTERTAINMENT *p* 299
See *ORCA BAY ARENA LIMITED PARTNERSHIP*

ORCA GOLD INC *p* 308
885 GEORGIA ST W SUITE 2000, VANCOUVER, BC, V6C 3E8
(604) 689-7842   *SIC* 1041

ORCA SEAFOODS *p* 260
See *KANATA HOLDINGS LTD*

ORCA SPECIALTY FOODS LTD *p* 272
17350 56 AVE SUITE 4, SURREY, BC, V3S 1C3
(604) 574-6722   *SIC* 2091

ORCHARD FORD SALES LTD *p* 220
911 STREMEL RD, KELOWNA, BC, V1X 5E6
(250) 860-1000   *SIC* 5511

ORCHARD INTERNATIONAL INC *p* 741
275 SUPERIOR BLVD UNIT 1, MISSISSAUGA, ON, L5T 2L6
(905) 564-9848   *SIC* 5122

ORCHARD PARK CAR WASH *p* 220
See *DASKO HOLDINGS LTD*

ORCHARD PARK SECONDARY SCHOOL *p* 892
See *HAMILTON-WENTWORTH DISTRICT SCHOOL BOARD, THE*

ORCHARD, VALI PHARMACY INC *p* 909
1186 MEMORIAL AVE UNIT 1, THUNDER BAY, ON, P7B 5K5
(807) 623-3601   *SIC* 5912

ORCHESTRE SYMPHONIQUE DE MONTREAL *p* 1186
1600 RUE SAINT-URBAIN, MONTREAL, QC, H2X 0S1
(514) 842-9951   *SIC* 7929

ORCHESTRE SYMPHONIQUE DE QUEBEC, L' *p* 1269
437 GRANDE ALLEE E BUREAU 250, QUEBEC, QC, G1R 2J5
(418) 643-8486   *SIC* 7929

ORCHIDEE BLANCHE CENTRE D'HEBERGEMENT SOINS LONGUE DUREE INC, L *p* 1232
2577 BOUL RENE-LAENNEC, MONTREAL, QC, H7K 3V4
(450) 629-1200   *SIC* 8361

ORDINATEURS EN GROS MICROBYTES INC, LES *p* 1251
940 BOUL SAINT-JEAN BUREAU 15, POINTE-CLAIRE, QC, H9R 5N8
(514) 426-2586   *SIC* 5045

ORDRE DES DENTISTES DU QUEBEC *p* 1198
2020 BOUL ROBERT-BOURASSA BUREAU 2160, MONTREAL, QC, H3A 2A5
(514) 281-0300   *SIC* 6324

ORDRE DES DENTISTES DU QUEBEC *p* 1207
800 BOUL RENE-LEVESQUE O BUREAU 1640, MONTREAL, QC, H3B 1X9
(514) 281-0300   *SIC* 6411

ORDRE DES INGENIEURS DU QUEBEC *p* 1207
1100 AV DES CANADIENS-DE-MONTREAL BUREAU 350, MONTREAL, QC, H3B 2S2
(514) 845-6141   *SIC* 8621

ORDRE DES TRAVAILLEURS SOCIAUX ET DES THERAPEUTES CONJUGAUX ET FAMILIAUX DU QUEBEC *p* 1177
255 BOUL CREMAZIE E BUREAU 520, MONTREAL, QC, H2M 1L5
(514) 731-3925   *SIC* 8621

ORDRE FRATERNEL DES AIGLES DE MONT-LAURIER INC *p* 1154
742 RUE DE LA MADONE, MONT-LAURIER, QC, J9L 1S9
SIC 8641

ORDRE PROFESSIONEL DES TECHNOLOGISTES MEDICAUX DU QUEBEC, L' *p* 1183
281 AV LAURIER E BUREAU 162, MONTREAL, QC, H2T 1G2
(514) 527-9811   *SIC* 8631

OREA *p* 777
See *ONTARIO REAL ESTATE ASSOCIATION*

ORENDA CORPORATE FINANCE *p* 969
See *ERNST & YOUNG LLP*

OREZONE GOLD CORPORATION *p* 829
290 PICTON AVE SUITE 201, OTTAWA, ON, K1Z 8P8
(613) 241-3699   *SIC* 1041

ORFORD SALES LTD *p* 587
2025 KIPLING AVE, ETOBICOKE, ON, M9W 4J8
(416) 743-6950   *SIC* 5531

ORGANIC BOX LTD *p* 110
5712 59 ST NW, EDMONTON, AB, T6B 3L4
(780) 469-1900   *SIC* 5431

ORGANIC GARAGE LTD *p* 802
579 KERR ST, OAKVILLE, ON, L6K 3E1
(905) 849-1648   *SIC* 5411

ORGANIC MEADOW INC *p* 601
335 LAIRD RD UNIT 1, GUELPH, ON, N1G 4P7
(519) 767-9694   *SIC* 5149

ORGANIC MEADOW LIMITED PARTNER-SHIP p
601
335 LAIRD RD UNIT 1, GUELPH, ON, N1G 4P7
(519) 767-9694   SIC 5143

ORGANIKA HEALTH PRODUCTS INC p 255
13480 VERDUN PL, RICHMOND, BC, V6V 1V2
(604) 277-3302   SIC 5122

ORGANISATION CATHOLIQUE CANADI-ENNE POUR LE DEVELOPPEMENT ET LA PAIX p 1214
1425 BOUL RENE-LEVESQUE O BUREAU 300, MONTREAL, QC, H3G 1T7
(514) 257-8711   SIC 8699

ORGANISME D'AUTOREGLEMENTATION DU COUTAGE IMMOBILERS DU QUEBEC, L' p 1071
4905 BOUL LAPINIERE BUREAU 2200, BROSSARD, QC, J4Z 0G2
(450) 676-4800   SIC 8611

ORGANIZATIONAL SOLUTIONS INC p 523
5360 SOUTH SERVICE RD, BURLINGTON, ON, L7L 5L1
(905) 315-7179   SIC 8741

ORGANIZED INTERIORS p 1003
See ORGANIZED INTERIORS INC

ORGANIZED INTERIORS INC p 1003
201 CHRISLEA RD, VAUGHAN, ON, L4L 8N6
(905) 264-5678   SIC 5072

ORGANIZING UNION LOCAL 204 p 558
See SERVICE EMPLOYEES INTERNA-TIONAL UNION LOCAL 204

ORGUES LETOURNEAU LTEE p 1314
16355 AV SAVOIE, SAINT-HYACINTHE, QC, J2T 3N1
(450) 774-2698   SIC 5736

ORIANA FINANCIAL GROUP OF CANADA LTD p 1032
4300 STEELES AVE W UNIT 34, WOOD-BRIDGE, ON, L4L 4C2
(905) 265-8315   SIC 6163

ORICA CANADA INC p 1072
301 RUE DE L'HOTEL-DE-VILLE, BROWNSBURG-CHATHAM, QC, J8G 3B5
(450) 533-4201   SIC 2892

ORICA CANADA INC p 1072
342 RUE MCMASTER, BROWNSBURG-CHATHAM, QC, J8G 3A8
(450) 533-4201   SIC 2892

ORICOM INTERNET INC p 1262
400 RUE NOLIN BUREAU 150, QUEBEC, QC, G1M 1E7
(418) 683-4557   SIC 4813

ORIENCE INTEGRATION, DIV OF p 31
See NORTHERN HARDWARE LTD

ORIENTEX IND. INC p 673
155 TORBAY RD, MARKHAM, ON, L3R 1G7
(905) 475-8540   SIC 5136

ORIGINAL BAKED QUALITY PITA DIPS INC, L' p 1106
320 BOUL SAINT-JOSEPH, GATINEAU, QC, J8Y 3Y8
(819) 525-6555   SIC 2051

ORIGINAL CAKERIE, THE p 205
See 0429746 B.C. LTD

ORIGINAL CHIMNEYS INC p 871
300 BOROUGH DR, SCARBOROUGH, ON, M1P 4P5
(416) 697-8884   SIC 2051

ORIGINAL JOE'S p 139
5411 DISCOVERY WAY UNIT 101, LEDUC, AB, T9E 8N4
(780) 986-6965   SIC 5149

ORIGINAL RNW p 1218
See MONTREAL PITA INC

ORIGINAL ROOF MAINTAINER INC p 255
16020 RIVER RD, RICHMOND, BC, V6V 1L6
SIC 1761

ORILLIA ASSOCIATION FOR THE HANDI-CAPPED p

809
See 126074 ONTARIO INC

ORILLIA BUILDING SUPPLIES (2001) LIM-ITED p
809
5 KING ST, ORILLIA, ON, L3V 1R2
(705) 326-7371   SIC 5251

ORILLIA DISTRICT COLLEGIATE & VOCA-TIONAL INSTITUTE p
810
See SIMCOE COUNTY DISTRICT SCHOOL BOARD, THE

ORILLIA DODGE CHRYSLER JEEP INC p
809
450 MEMORIAL AVE, ORILLIA, ON, L3V 0T7
(705) 325-1331   SIC 5511

ORILLIA POWER p 809
See ORILLIA POWER DISTRIBUTION CORPORATION

ORILLIA POWER CORPORATION p 809
360 WEST ST S, ORILLIA, ON, L3V 5G8
(705) 326-7315   SIC 4911

ORILLIA POWER DISTRIBUTION CORPO-RATION p
809
360 WEST ST S, ORILLIA, ON, L3V 5G8
(705) 326-7315   SIC 4911

ORION BUILDING MAINTENANCE (OBM) LTD p 110
5503 76 AVE NW, EDMONTON, AB, T6B 0A7
(780) 440-0136   SIC 5999

ORION FOUNDRY (CANADA), ULC p 604
503 IMPERIAL RD N, GUELPH, ON, N1H 6T9
(519) 827-1999   SIC 7374

ORION MANAGEMENT & CONSTRUCTION INC p 415
479 ROTHESAY AVE, SAINT JOHN, NB, E2L 4G7
(506) 634-5717   SIC 1542

ORION MANAGEMENT INC p 31
4015 1 ST SE UNIT 3A, CALGARY, AB, T2G 4X7
(403) 243-8292   SIC 6531

ORION PLASTICS INC p 166
35 CALDER PL, ST. ALBERT, AB, T8N 5A6
(780) 431-2112   SIC 3089

ORION SECURITY AND INVESTIGATION SERVICES p 508
See ORION SECURITY INCORPORATED

ORION SECURITY INCORPORATED p 508
284 QUEEN ST E UNIT 229, BRAMPTON, ON, L6V 1C2
(905) 840-0400   SIC 7381

ORION TRAVEL INSURANCE COMPANY COMPAGNIE D'ASSURANCE VOYAGE ORION p 905
60 COMMERCE VALLEY DR E, THORN-HILL, ON, L3T 7P9
(905) 771-3000   SIC 6321

ORKIN CANADA CORPORATION p 732
5840 FALBOURNE ST, MISSISSAUGA, ON, L5R 4B5
(905) 502-9700   SIC 7342

ORKIN PCO SERVICES p 732
See ORKIN CANADA CORPORATION

ORLANDO CORPORATION p 689
6205 AIRPORT RD SUITE 500, MISSIS-SAUGA, ON, L4V 1E1
(905) 677-5480   SIC 6512

ORLEANS BAKERY p 810
See BEAULIEU BAKERY LTD

ORLEANS DODGE CHRYSLER INC p 810
1465 YOUVILLE DR, ORLEANS, ON, K1C 4R1
(613) 830-1777   SIC 5511

ORLEANS FRESH FRUIT p 816
See 927912 ONTARIO LIMITED

ORLICK INDUSTRIES LIMITED p 609
411 PARKDALE AVE N, HAMILTON, ON, L8H 5Y4
(905) 544-1997   SIC 3365

ORLICK INDUSTRIES LIMITED p 893
500 SEAMAN ST, STONEY CREEK, ON, L8E 2V9
(905) 662-5954   SIC 3365

ORNGE p 698
See ORNGE

ORNGE p 698
5310 EXPLORER DR, MISSISSAUGA, ON, L4W 5H8
(647) 428-2005   SIC 4522

ORNGE ROTOR WING p 691
See 7506406 CANADA INC

OROMOCTO HIGH SCHOOL p 410
See SCHOOL DISTRICT 17

OROS p 1127
See DISTRIBUTION EPICERIE C.T.S. INC

ORPHAN INDUSTRIES LIMITED p 428
45 PEPPERRELL RD, ST. JOHN'S, NL, A1A 5N8
(709) 726-6820   SIC 3312

ORR INSURANCE BROKERS INC p 896
50 COBOURG ST, STRATFORD, ON, N5A 3E5
(519) 271-4340   SIC 6411

ORR'S LITTLE CURRENT VALUE MART p
647
40 MEREDITH, LITTLE CURRENT, ON, P0P 1K0
(705) 368-0617   SIC 5411

ORTHAIDE p 1289
See CENTRE DE READAPTATION LA MAI-SON

ORTHESES BIONICK p 1135
See 9137-0080 QUEBEC INC

ORTHO BIOTECH DIV p 779
See JANSSEN INC

ORTHOFAB INC p 1276
2160 RUE DE CELLES, QUEBEC, QC, G2C 1X8
(418) 847-5225   SIC 3842

ORTHOPAEDIC & ATHRITIC CAMPUS p
932
See SUNNYBROOK HEALTH SCIENCES CENTRE

ORTHOPEDIC SPORTS & MEDICINE OF WEST ISLAND p 1221
See HANGER, J. E. OF MONTREAL INC

ORTHOTIC GROUP INC, THE p 679
160 MARKLAND ST, MARKHAM, ON, L6C 0C6
(800) 551-3008   SIC 3842

ORTYNSKY AUTOMOTIVE COMPANY LTD p 368
980 NAIRN AVE, WINNIPEG, MB, R2L 0Y2
(204) 654-0440   SIC 5511

ORTYNSKY NISSAN LTD p 368
980 NAIRN AVE, WINNIPEG, MB, R2L 0Y2
(204) 669-0791   SIC 5511

ORTYNSKY, TERRY KIA p 368
See ORTYNSKY AUTOMOTIVE COMPANY LTD

ORUS INTEGRATION INC p 1238
1109 CHOMEDEY (A-13) E, MONTREAL, QC, H7W 5J8
SIC 3823

ORVANA MINERALS CORP p 956
170 UNIVERSITY AVE SUITE 900, TORONTO, ON, M5H 3B3
(416) 369-1629   SIC 1081

ORXESTRA INC p 576
5 HEATHROW CRT, ETOBICOKE, ON, M9A 3A2
(416) 233-9318   SIC 8741

ORYX PETROLEUM CORPORATION LIM-ITED p
55
350 7 AVE SW SUITE 3400, CALGARY, AB, T2P 3N9
(403) 261-5350   SIC 1381

OSAKA SUPERMARKET p 258
See T & T SUPERMARKET INC

OSBIE p 604
See ONTARIO SCHOOL BOARDS' INSUR-ANCE EXCHANGE

OSBORN & LANGE INC p 1117
17001 RTE TRANSCANADIENNE BUREAU 300, KIRKLAND, QC, H9H 0A7
(514) 694-4161   SIC 6411

OSBORNE & KYLEMORE SAFEWAY p 387
See SOBEYS WEST INC

OSBORNE HOUSE INC p 379
GD, WINNIPEG, MB, R3C 2H6
(204) 942-7373   SIC 8399

OSC CONSTRUCTORS ULC p 698
5149 BRADCO BLVD, MISSISSAUGA, ON, L4W 2A6
(905) 458-1005   SIC 1795

OSCAN ELECTRICAL SUPPLIES LTD p 813
209 BLOOR ST E, OSHAWA, ON, L1H 3M3
(905) 728-3800   SIC 5063

OSCO p 414
See OCEAN STEEL & CONSTRUCTION LTD

OSELA INC p 1128
1869 32E AV, LACHINE, QC, H8T 3J1
(514) 631-2227   SIC 3841

OSGOODE PROPERTIES LTD p 828
1284 WELLINGTON ST W, OTTAWA, ON, K1Y 3A9
(613) 729-0656   SIC 6531

OSGOODE TOWNSHIP HIGH SCHOOL p
681
See OTTAWA-CARLETON DISTRICT SCHOOL BOARD

OSHAWA CENTRAL COLLEGIATE p 813
See DURHAM DISTRICT SCHOOL BOARD

OSHAWA CLINIC p 813
117 KING ST E, OSHAWA, ON, L1H 1B9
(905) 723-8551   SIC 8011

OSHAWA FIRE SERVICES p 813
See CORPORATION OF THE CITY OF OS-HAWA

OSHAWA PLANT p 812
See A.G. SIMPSON AUTOMOTIVE INC

OSHAWA PUC NETWORKS INC p 813
100 SIMCOE ST S, OSHAWA, ON, L1H 7M7
(905) 723-4623   SIC 4911

OSHAWA THIS WEEK p 813
See METROLAND MEDIA GROUP LTD

OSHAWA THIS WEEK NEWSPAPER p 813
See TORSTAR CORPORATION

OSHAWA YOUNG WOMEN CHRISTIAN AS-SOCIATION, THE p
813
33 MCGRIGOR ST, OSHAWA, ON, L1H 1X8
(905) 576-6356   SIC 3272

OSI p 523
See ORGANIZATIONAL SOLUTIONS INC

OSI GEOSPATIAL INC p 189
4585 CANADA WAY SUITE 400, BURNABY, BC, V5G 4L6
(778) 373-4600   SIC 5088

OSI MACHINERIE p 1305
See O.S.I. MACHINERIE INC

OSI MARITIME SYSTEMS p 189
See OSI GEOSPATIAL INC

OSI MARITIME SYSTEMS LTD p 189
4585 CANADA WAY SUITE 400, BURNABY, BC, V5G 4L6
(778) 373-4600   SIC 3812

OSI-WORLDWIDE INC p 932
10 ST MARY ST SUITE 602, TORONTO, ON, M4Y 1P9
(416) 960-9752   SIC 6311

OSIRIS INC p 505
1 WILKINSON RD, BRAMPTON, ON, L6T 4M6
(905) 452-0392   SIC 5399

OSISKO GOLD ROYALTIES LTD p 1207
1100 AV DES CANADIENS-DE-MONTREAL BUREAU 300, MONTREAL, QC, H3B 2S2
(514) 940-0670   SIC 6282

OSISKO METALS INCORPORATED p 1207
1100 AV DES CANADIENS-DE-MONTREAL BUREAU 300, MONTREAL, QC, H3B 2S2
(514) 861-4441   SIC 1081

▲ Public Company   ■ Public Company Family Member   **HQ** Headquarters   **BR** Branch   **SL** Single Location

OSISKO MINING INC   *p* 956
155 UNIVERSITY AVE SUITE 1440, TORONTO, ON, M5H 3B7
(416) 848-9504   *SIC* 1081

OSLER HOSKIN & HARCOURT   *p* 1202
See CARTHOS SERVICES LP

OSLER, HOSKIN & HARCOURT LLP   *p* 55
450 1 ST SW SUITE 2500, CALGARY, AB, T2P 5H1
(403) 260-7000   *SIC* 8111

OSLER, HOSKIN & HARCOURT LLP   *p* 825
340 ALBERT ST SUITE 1900, OTTAWA, ON, K1R 7Y6
(613) 235-7234   *SIC* 8111

OSLER, HOSKIN & HARCOURT LLP   *p* 987
100 KING ST W SUITE 4600 FIRST CANADIAN PLACE, TORONTO, ON, M5X 1B8
(416) 362-2111   *SIC* 8111

OSLER, HOSKIN & HARCOURT LLP *p* 1207
1000 RUE DE LA GAUCHETIERE O BUREAU 2100, MONTREAL, QC, H3B 4W5
(514) 904-8100   *SIC* 8111

OSM TUBULAR CAMROSE   *p* 78
See CANADIAN NATIONAL STEEL CORPORATION

OSMAN GLOBAL TRADING LTD   *p* 119
3214 82 ST NW, EDMONTON, AB, T6K 3Y3
(780) 757-8100   *SIC* 6799

OSMOCO EMERGENCY TEAM   *p* 1253
See OSMOCO LABORATORIES INC

OSMOCO LABORATORIES INC   *p* 1253
260 CH DU BORD-DU-LAC LAKESHORE, POINTE-CLAIRE, QC, H9S 4K9
(514) 694-4567   *SIC* 5099

OSP DIVISION   *p* 1407
See WEYERHAEUSER COMPANY LIMITED

OSPREY CARE INC   *p* 216
3255 OVERLANDER DR, KAMLOOPS, BC, V2B 0A5
(250) 579-9061   *SIC* 8059

OSPREY MEDIA PUBLISHING INC   *p* 517
53 DALHOUSIE ST SUITE 306, BRANTFORD, ON, N3T 2H9
(519) 756-2020   *SIC* 2711

OSPREY MEDIA PUBLISHING INC   *p* 630
6 CATARAQUI ST SUITE 427, KINGSTON, ON, K7K 1Z7
(613) 544-5000   *SIC* 2711

OSPREY MEDIA PUBLISHING INC   *p* 673
100 RENFREW DR SUITE 110, MARKHAM, ON, L3R 9R6
(905) 752-1132   *SIC* 2711

OSPREY MEDIA PUBLISHING INC   *p* 763
259 WORTHINGTON ST W, NORTH BAY, ON, P1B 3B5
(705) 472-3200   *SIC* 2711

OSPREY MEDIA PUBLISHING INC   *p* 860
140 FRONT ST S, SARNIA, ON, N7T 7M8
(519) 344-3641   *SIC* 2711

OSPREY MEDIA PUBLISHING INC   *p* 860
140 FRONT ST S SUITE FRONT, SARNIA, ON, N7T 7M8
(519) 344-3641   *SIC* 2711

OSPREY MEDIA PUBLISHING INC   *p* 886
17 QUEEN ST, ST CATHARINES, ON, L2R 5G4
(905) 684-7251   *SIC* 2711

OSPREY TRUCK STOP   *p* 399
2 MARTIN DR, EEL RIVER BAR FIRST NATION, NB, E8C 3C7
(506) 685-8210   *SIC* 5541

OSPREY VALLEY RESORTS INC   *p* 477
18821 MAIN ST SUITE 2, ALTON, ON, L7K 1R1
(519) 927-0586   *SIC* 7992

OSSO HOLDINGS LTD   *p* 814
725 BLOOR ST W, OSHAWA, ON, L1J 5Y6
(905) 576-1700   *SIC* 5063

OSSTF   *p* 787
See ONTARIO SECONDARY SCHOOL TEACHERS' FEDERATION, THE

OSSUR CANADA INC   *p* 258
6900 GRAYBAR RD UNIT 2150, RICH-

MOND, BC, V6W 0A5
(604) 241-8152   *SIC* 3842

OSTACO 2000 WINDOORS INC   *p* 557
248 BOWES RD, CONCORD, ON, L4K 1J9
(905) 660-5021   *SIC* 3089

OSTACO WINDOWS   *p* 557
See OSTACO 2000 WINDOORS INC

OSTIC GROUP   *p* 590
See OSTIC INSURANCE BROKERS LIMITED

OSTIC INSURANCE BROKERS LIMITED *p* 590
210 ST PATRICK ST W, FERGUS, ON, N1M 1L7
(519) 843-2540   *SIC* 6411

OSTIGUY ET FRERES INC   *p* 1075
1000 BOUL INDUSTRIEL, CHAMBLY, QC, J3L 6Z7
(450) 658-4371   *SIC* 5039

OSTREM CHEMICAL COMPANY LTD *p* 122
2310 80 AVE NW, EDMONTON, AB, T6P 1N2
(780) 440-1911   *SIC* 2842

OT GROUP   *p* 491
See DCB BUSINESS SYSTEMS GROUP INC

OTEFLO   *p* 946
See OFFICE DES TELECOMMUNICATIONS EDUCATIVES DE LANGUE FRANCAISE DE L'ONTARIO

OTFC   *p* 224
See OKANAGAN TREE FRUIT COOPERATIVE

OTG FINANCIAL   *p* 787
57 MOBILE DR, NORTH YORK, ON, M4A 1H5
(416) 752-9410   *SIC* 6722

OTHODENT LTD   *p* 813
311 VIOLA AVE, OSHAWA, ON, L1H 3A7
(905) 436-3731   *SIC* 3843

OTICON CANADA   *p* 719
See AUDMET CANADA LTD

OTIP/RAEO   *p* 1008
See ONTARIO TEACHERS' INSURANCE PLAN INC

OTIS CANADA, INC   *p* 36
777 64 AVE SE SUITE 7, CALGARY, AB, T2H 2C3
(403) 244-1040   *SIC* 7699

OTIS CANADA, INC   *p* 287
2788 RUPERT ST, VANCOUVER, BC, V5M 3T7
(604) 412-3400   *SIC* 3534

OTIS CANADA, INC   *p* 523
4475 NORTH SERVICE RD SUITE 200, BURLINGTON, ON, L7L 4X7
(905) 332-9919   *SIC* 7699

OTIS CANADA, INC   *p* 1221
5311 BOUL DE MAISONNEUVE O, MONTREAL, QC, H4A 1Z5
(514) 489-9781   *SIC* 7699

OTIS ELEVATORS   *p* 36
See OTIS CANADA, INC

OTN   *p* 947
See ONTARIO TELEMEDICINE NETWORK

OTONABEE MARKETPLACE   *p* 842
See ARAMARK CANADA LTD.

OTPP   *p* 770
See ONTARIO TEACHERS' PENSION PLAN BOARD

OTR WHEEL ENGINEERING CANADA   *p* 115
See NORTHSHORE SUDBURY LTD

OTSTCFQ   *p* 1177
See ORDRE DES TRAVAILLEURS SOCIAUX ET DES THERAPEUTES CONJUGAUX ET FAMILIAUX DU QUEBEC

OTSUKA CANADA PHARMACEUTICAL INC   *p* 1335
2250 BOUL ALFRED-NOBEL BUREAU 301, SAINT-LAURENT, QC, H4S 2C9
(514) 332-3001   *SIC* 5912

OTTAWA ARGO SALES AND SERVICE   *p* 628

See PAROUSIA INVESTMETS LTD

OTTAWA ATHLETIC CLUB   *p* 816
See O A C HOLDINGS LIMITED

OTTAWA BAGEL SHOP INC   *p* 828
1321 WELLINGTON ST W, OTTAWA, ON, K1Y 3B6
(613) 722-8753   *SIC* 5461

OTTAWA BAGELSHOP AND DELI   *p* 828
See OTTAWA BAGEL SHOP INC

OTTAWA CATHOLIC DISTRICT SCHOOL BOARD   *p* 596
2072 JASMINE CRES, GLOUCESTER, ON, K1J 8M5
(613) 741-4525   *SIC* 8211

OTTAWA CATHOLIC DISTRICT SCHOOL BOARD   *p* 625
5115 KANATA AVE, KANATA, ON, K2K 3K5
(613) 271-4254   *SIC* 8211

OTTAWA CATHOLIC DISTRICT SCHOOL BOARD   *p* 663
1040 DOZOIS RD, MANOTICK, ON, K4M 1B2
(613) 692-2551   *SIC* 8211

OTTAWA CATHOLIC DISTRICT SCHOOL BOARD   *p* 750
570 WEST HUNT CLUB RD, NEPEAN, ON, K2G 3R4
(613) 224-2222   *SIC* 8211

OTTAWA CATHOLIC DISTRICT SCHOOL BOARD   *p* 752
3333 GREENBANK RD, NEPEAN, ON, K2J 4J1
(613) 823-4797   *SIC* 8211

OTTAWA CATHOLIC DISTRICT SCHOOL BOARD   *p* 752
440 LONGFIELDS DR, NEPEAN, ON, K2J 4T1
(613) 823-1663   *SIC* 8211

OTTAWA CATHOLIC DISTRICT SCHOOL BOARD   *p* 810
6550 BILBERRY DR, ORLEANS, ON, K1C 2S9
(613) 837-3161   *SIC* 8211

OTTAWA CATHOLIC DISTRICT SCHOOL BOARD   *p* 811
750 CHARLEMAGNE BLVD, ORLEANS, ON, K4A 3M4
(613) 837-9377   *SIC* 8211

OTTAWA CATHOLIC DISTRICT SCHOOL BOARD   *p* 826
140 MAIN ST, OTTAWA, ON, K1S 5P4
(613) 237-2001   *SIC* 8211

OTTAWA CATHOLIC DISTRICT SCHOOL BOARD   *p* 829
710 BROADVIEW AVE, OTTAWA, ON, K2A 2M2
(613) 722-6565   *SIC* 8211

OTTAWA CATHOLIC DISTRICT SCHOOL BOARD   *p* 831
1481 FISHER AVE, OTTAWA, ON, K2C 1X4
(613) 225-8105   *SIC* 8211

OTTAWA CATHOLIC DISTRICT SCHOOL BOARD   *p* 832
2675 DRAPER AVE, OTTAWA, ON, K2H 7A1
(613) 820-9705   *SIC* 8211

OTTAWA CATHOLIC DISTRICT SCHOOL BOARD   *p* 891
SACRED HEART CATHOLIC HIGH SCHOOL, STITTSVILLE, ON, K2S 1X4
(613) 831-6643   *SIC* 8211

OTTAWA CATHOLIC SCHOOL BOARD   *p* 750
See OTTAWA CATHOLIC DISTRICT SCHOOL BOARD

OTTAWA CHILDREN'S TREATMENT CENTRE   *p* 818
2211 THURSTON DR, OTTAWA, ON, K1G 6C9
(613) 688-2126   *SIC* 8322

OTTAWA CITIZEN, THE   *p* 831
See POSTMEDIA NETWORK INC

OTTAWA COMMUNITY HOUSING CORPO-

RATION   *p* 749
39 AURIGA DR, NEPEAN, ON, K2E 7Y8
(613) 731-1182   *SIC* 6531

OTTAWA COMMUNITY HOUSING CORPORATION   *p* 749
39 AURIGA DR, NEPEAN, ON, K2E 7Y8
(613) 731-7223   *SIC* 6531

OTTAWA COMMUNITY IMMIGRANT SERVICES ORGANIZATION   *p* 828
959 WELLINGTON ST W, OTTAWA, ON, K1Y 2X5
(613) 725-5671   *SIC* 8699

OTTAWA CONVENTION CENTRE CORPORATION   *p* 821
55 COLONEL BY DR, OTTAWA, ON, K1N 9J2
(613) 563-1984   *SIC* 7389

OTTAWA EQUIPMENT & HYDRAULIC INC *p* 816
2628 EDINBURGH PL, OTTAWA, ON, K1B 5M1
(613) 748-9000   *SIC* 5084

OTTAWA FASTENER SUPPLY LTD   *p* 751
2205 ROBERTSON RD, NEPEAN, ON, K2H 5Z2
(613) 828-5311   *SIC* 5072

OTTAWA FIBRE   *p* 595
See OFI L.P.

OTTAWA FIBRE L.P.   *p* 827
1365 JOHNSTON RD, OTTAWA, ON, K1V 8Z1
(613) 247-7116   *SIC* 3296

OTTAWA FOOD BANK, THE   *p* 595
1317 MICHAEL ST, GLOUCESTER, ON, K1B 3M9
(613) 745-7001   *SIC* 8399

OTTAWA GOODTIME CENTRE LIMITED   *p* 749
450 WEST HUNT CLUB RD, NEPEAN, ON, K2E 1B2
(613) 731-9071   *SIC* 5571

OTTAWA HEALTH RESEARCH INSTITUTE *p* 828
See OTTAWA HOSPITAL, THE

OTTAWA HEART INSTITUTE RESEARCH CORPORATION   *p* 828
40 RUSKIN ST, OTTAWA, ON, K1Y 4W7
SIC 8733

OTTAWA HONDA   *p* 830
See 501548 ONTARIO LTD

OTTAWA HOSPITAL, THE   *p* 819
1967 RIVERSIDE DR SUITE 323, OTTAWA, ON, K1H 7W9
(613) 798-5555   *SIC* 8062

OTTAWA HOSPITAL, THE   *p* 819
501 SMYTH RD, OTTAWA, ON, K1H 8L6
(613) 737-8899   *SIC* 8011

OTTAWA HOSPITAL, THE   *p* 828
1053 CARLING AVE, OTTAWA, ON, K1Y 4E9
(613) 798-5555   *SIC* 8062

OTTAWA HOSPITAL, THE   *p* 828
1053 CARLING AVE SUITE 119, OTTAWA, ON, K1Y 4E9
(613) 722-7000   *SIC* 8062

OTTAWA HOSPITAL, THE   *p* 828
200 MELROSE AVE S, OTTAWA, ON, K1Y 4K7
(613) 737-7700   *SIC* 8069

OTTAWA HOSPITAL, THE   *p* 828
725 PARKDALE AVE, OTTAWA, ON, K1Y 4E9
(613) 761-4395   *SIC* 8733

OTTAWA HUMANE SOCIETY   *p* 750
245 WEST HUNT CLUB RD, NEPEAN, ON, K2E 1A6
(613) 725-3166   *SIC* 8699

OTTAWA INTERNATIONAL AIRPORT AUTHORITY   *p* 827

See OTTAWA MACDONALD-CARTIER INTERNATIONAL AIRPORT AUTHORITY

OTTAWA JEWISH HOME FOR THE AGED p 829
10 NADOLNY SACHS PVT, OTTAWA, ON, K2A 4G7
(613) 728-3900   *SIC* 8361

OTTAWA LIVESTOCK EXCHANGE   p 599
See LEO'S LIVESTOCK EXCHANGE LIMITED

OTTAWA MACDONALD-CARTIER INTERNATIONAL AIRPORT AUTHORITY   p 827
1000 AIRPORT PARKWAY PVT SUITE 2500, OTTAWA, ON, K1V 9B4
(613) 248-2000   *SIC* 4581

OTTAWA MARRIOTT   p 823
See INNVEST HOTELS LP

OTTAWA MOTOR SALES (1987) LIMITED p 827
2496 BANK ST SUITE 40010, OTTAWA, ON, K1V 8S2
(613) 733-6931   *SIC* 5511

OTTAWA MOULD CRAFT LIMITED   p 819
2510 DON REID DR, OTTAWA, ON, K1H. 1E1
(613) 521-6402   *SIC* 3089

OTTAWA NETWORK FOR BORDERLINE PERSONALITY DISORDER   p 626
412 ROSINGDALE ST, KANATA, ON, K2M 0L8
   SIC 8062

OTTAWA PUBLIC LIBRARY BOARD p 824
120 METCALFE ST, OTTAWA, ON, K1P 5M2
(613) 580-2940   *SIC* 8231

OTTAWA REGIONAL CANCER CENTRE p 828
See OTTAWA HOSPITAL, THE

OTTAWA REGIONAL HOSPITAL LINEN SERVICES INCORPORATED   p 750
45 GURDWARA RD, NEPEAN, ON, K2E 7X6
(613) 842-3000   *SIC* 7218

OTTAWA RIVER POWER CORPORATION p 838
283 PEMBROKE ST E, PEMBROKE, ON, K8A 3K2
(613) 732-3687   *SIC* 4911

OTTAWA RIVER WHITE WATER RAFTING LIMITED   p 489
1260 GRANT SETTLEMENT RD, BEACHBURG, ON, K0J 1C0
(613) 646-2501   *SIC* 7999

OTTAWA SUN, THE   p 748
See 1032451 B.C. LTD

OTTAWA TOURISM   p 834
150 ELGIN ST SUITE 1405, OTTAWA, ON, K2P 1L4
(613) 237-5150   *SIC* 7389

OTTAWA VALLEY FUELS   p 849
See OTTAWA VALLEY GRAIN PRODUCTS INC

OTTAWA VALLEY GRAIN PRODUCTS INC p 849
558 RAGLAN ST S, RENFREW, ON, K7V 1R8
   SIC 5172

OTTAWA VALLEY RAILWAY   p 763
See RAILLINK CANADA LTD

OTTAWA VETERINARY HOSPITAL p 829
See AFFILIATED ANIMAL SERVICES

OTTAWA X PRESS PUBLISHING INC p 834
309 COOPER ST SUITE 401, OTTAWA, ON, K2P 0G5
(613) 237-8226   *SIC* 5192

OTTAWA YOUNG MEN'S AND YOUNG WOMEN'S CHRISTIAN ASSOCIATION p 834
180 ARGYLE AVE SUITE 1622, OTTAWA, ON, K2P 1B7
(613) 237-1320   *SIC* 8621

OTTAWA-CARLETON ASSOCIATION FOR PERSONS WITH DEVELOPMENTAL DISABILITIES   p

562
1141 SYDNEY ST UNIT 1, CORNWALL, ON, K6H 7C2
(613) 933-9520   *SIC* 8322

OTTAWA-CARLETON ASSOCIATION FOR PERSONS WITH DEVELOPMENTAL DISABILITIES   p
825
250 CITY CENTRE AVE SUITE 200, OTTAWA, ON, K1R 6K7
(613) 569-8993   *SIC* 8322

OTTAWA-CARLETON DISTRICT SCHOOL BOARD   p 567
3088 DUNROBIN RD, DUNROBIN, ON, K0A 1T0
(613) 832-0126   *SIC* 8211

OTTAWA-CARLETON DISTRICT SCHOOL BOARD   p 596
2060 OGILVIE RD, GLOUCESTER, ON, K1J 7N8
(613) 745-7176   *SIC* 8211

OTTAWA-CARLETON DISTRICT SCHOOL BOARD   p 625
150 ABBEYHILL DR, KANATA, ON, K2L 1H7
(613) 836-2527   *SIC* 8211

OTTAWA-CARLETON DISTRICT SCHOOL BOARD   p 625
4 PARKWAY THE, KANATA, ON, K2K 1Y4
(613) 592-3361   *SIC* 8211

OTTAWA-CARLETON DISTRICT SCHOOL BOARD   p 681
2800 8TH LINE RD, METCALFE, ON, K0A 2P0
(613) 821-2241   *SIC* 8211

OTTAWA-CARLETON DISTRICT SCHOOL BOARD   p 750
1755 MERIVALE RD, NEPEAN, ON, K2G 1E2
(613) 224-1807   *SIC* 8211

OTTAWA-CARLETON DISTRICT SCHOOL BOARD   p 751
131 GREENBANK RD, NEPEAN, ON, K2H 8R1
(613) 721-1820   *SIC* 8211

OTTAWA-CARLETON DISTRICT SCHOOL BOARD   p 751
40 CASSIDY RD, NEPEAN, ON, K2H 6K1
(613) 828-9101   *SIC* 8211

OTTAWA-CARLETON DISTRICT SCHOOL BOARD   p 751
133 GREENBANK RD, NEPEAN, ON, K2H 6L3
(613) 721-1820   *SIC* 8211

OTTAWA-CARLETON DISTRICT SCHOOL BOARD   p 752
103 MALVERN DR, NEPEAN, ON, K2J 4T2
(613) 823-0367   *SIC* 8211

OTTAWA-CARLETON DISTRICT SCHOOL BOARD   p 818
1900 DAUPHIN RD, OTTAWA, ON, K1G 2L7
(613) 733-1755   *SIC* 8211

OTTAWA-CARLETON DISTRICT SCHOOL BOARD   p 818
900 CANTERBURY AVE, OTTAWA, ON, K1G 3A7
(613) 731-1191   *SIC* 8211

OTTAWA-CARLETON DISTRICT SCHOOL BOARD   p 820
815 ST. LAURENT BLVD, OTTAWA, ON, K1K 3A7
   SIC 8211

OTTAWA-CARLETON DISTRICT SCHOOL BOARD   p 825
300 ROCHESTER ST SUITE 302, OTTAWA, ON, K1R 7N4
(613) 239-2416   *SIC* 8211

OTTAWA-CARLETON DISTRICT SCHOOL BOARD   p 826
212 GLEBE AVE, OTTAWA, ON, K1S 2C9
(613) 239-2424   *SIC* 8211

OTTAWA-CARLETON DISTRICT SCHOOL BOARD   p 827
2597 ALTA VISTA DR, OTTAWA, ON, K1V

7T3
(613) 733-4860   *SIC* 8211

OTTAWA-CARLETON DISTRICT SCHOOL BOARD   p 827
824 BROOKFIELD RD, OTTAWA, ON, K1V 6J3
(613) 733-0610   *SIC* 8211

OTTAWA-CARLETON DISTRICT SCHOOL BOARD   p 829
574 BROADVIEW AVE, OTTAWA, ON, K2A 3V8
(613) 722-6551   *SIC* 8211

OTTAWA-CARLETON DISTRICT SCHOOL BOARD   p 829
590 BROADVIEW AVE, OTTAWA, ON, K2A 2L8
(613) 728-1721   *SIC* 8211

OTTAWA-CARLETON DISTRICT SCHOOL BOARD   p 830
2410 GEORGINA DR, OTTAWA, ON, K2B 7M8
(613) 820-7186   *SIC* 8211

OTTAWA-CARLETON DISTRICT SCHOOL BOARD   p 831
55 CENTREPOINTE DR, OTTAWA, ON, K2G 5L4
(613) 723-5136   *SIC* 8211

OTTAWA-CARLETON DISTRICT SCHOOL BOARD   p 834
29 LISGAR ST, OTTAWA, ON, K2P 0B9
(613) 239-2696   *SIC* 8211

OTTAWA-CARLETON DISTRICT SCHOOL BOARD   p 850
3673 MCBEAN ST, RICHMOND, ON, K0A 2Z0
(613) 838-2212   *SIC* 8211

OTTAWA-CARLETON MORTGAGE INC   p 830
381 RICHMOND RD, OTTAWA, ON, K2A 0E7
(613) 563-3447   *SIC* 6211

OTTAWA-CARLETON REGIONAL TRANSIT COMMISSION   p 817
See CITY OF OTTAWA

OTTAWAY MOTOR EXPRESS (2010) INC   p 1035
520 BEARDS LANE UNIT B, WOODSTOCK, ON, N4S 7W3
(519) 602-3026   *SIC* 4212

OTTER CO-OP   p 229
See OTTER FARM & HOME CO-OPERATIVE

OTTER FARM & HOME CO-OPERATIVE   p 229
3650 248 ST, LANGLEY, BC, V4W 1X7
(604) 607-6924   *SIC* 5191

OTTER POINT FIRE DEPARTMENT p 269
3727 OTTER POINT RD, SOOKE, BC, V9Z 0K1
(250) 642-6211   *SIC* 7389

OTTO BOCK HEALTHCARE CANADA LTD p 798
2897 BRIGHTON RD, OAKVILLE, ON, L6H 6C9
   SIC 5047

OTTO BOCK HEALTHCARE CANADA LTD p 845
901 DILLINGHAM RD, PICKERING, ON, L1W 2Y5
   SIC 3842

OTTO MOBILE VANCOUVER   p 272
17535 55B AVE, SURREY, BC, V3S 5V2
   SIC 5561

OTTO'S COLLISION CENTER   p 829
1551 LAPERRIERE AVE, OTTAWA, ON, K1Z 7T1
(613) 728-7032   *SIC* 5511

OTTO'S SERVICE CENTRE LIMITED p 827
660 HUNT CLUB RD, OTTAWA, ON, K1V 1C1
(613) 725-3048   *SIC* 5511

OTTO'S SUBARU   p 829
See OTTO'S COLLISION CENTER

OTWA N MOTORS LTD   p 595

1599 STAR TOP RD SUITE 417, GLOUCESTER, ON, K1B 5P5
(613) 749-9417   *SIC* 5511

OUAT LED & JOBIN INC   p 994
2844 DUNDAS ST W, TORONTO, ON, M6P 1Y7
(416) 492-1595   *SIC* 4833

OUELLET & JOBIN INC   p 1303
50 RTE DE TADOUSSAC BUREAU 2, SAINT-FULGENCE, QC, G0V 1S0
(418) 674-2811   *SIC* 5541

OUELLET CANADA INC   p 1121
180 3E AV, L'ISLET, QC, G0R 2C0
(418) 247-3947   *SIC* 3567

OUELLET, PATRICK 1843 INC   p 1254
1 RUE GUYON BUREAU 1843, QUEBEC, QC, G1B 1T1
(418) 666-1410   *SIC* 5912

OUELLETTE, RONALD INC   p 399
160 BOUL HEBERT, EDMUNDSTON, NB, E3V 2S7
(506) 735-8459   *SIC* 5912

OUGH FIRE SYSTEMS LTD   p 488
16 LENNOX DR, BARRIE, ON, L4N 9V8
(705) 720-0570   *SIC* 5087

OUGHTRED COFFEE & TEA LTD   p 338
723B VANALMAN AVE, VICTORIA, BC, V8Z 3B6
(250) 384-7444   *SIC* 7389

OULTON FUELS LTD   p 470
1699 KING ST, WINDSOR, NS, B0N 2T0
(902) 798-1118   *SIC* 5172

OUR CHILDREN, OUR FUTURE   p 569
273 MEAD BLVD, ESPANOLA, ON, P5E 1B3
(705) 869-5545   *SIC* 8351

OUR LADY OF LOURDES CATHOLIC HIGH SCHOOL   p 605
See WELLINGTON CATHOLIC DISTRICT SCHOOL BOARD

OUR LADY OF THE LAKE CATHOLIC COLLEGE SCHOOL   p 628
See YORK CATHOLIC DISTRICT SCHOOL BOARD

OUR LADY OF VICTORY CATHOLIC SCHOOL   p 994
See TORONTO CATHOLIC DISTRICT SCHOOL BOARD

OUR NEIGHBOURHOOD LIVING SOCIETY p 440
15 DARTMOUTH RD SUITE 210, BEDFORD, NS, B4A 3X6
(902) 835-8826   *SIC* 8361

OUR PLACE FAMILY RESOURCE AND EARLY YEARS CENTRE   p 641
154 GATEWOOD RD, KITCHENER, ON, N2M 4E4
(519) 571-1626   *SIC* 8699

OUTBACK STEAKHOUSE   p 104
See CHIRO FOODS LIMITED

OUTDOOR GEAR CANADA   p 1332
See ACCESSOIRES POUR VELOS O.G.D. LTEE

OUTDOOR OUTFITS LIMITED   p 982
372 RICHMOND ST W SUITE 400, TORONTO, ON, M5V 1X6
(416) 598-4111   *SIC* 5136

OUTFRONT MEDIA CANADA LP   p 571
377 HORNER AVE, ETOBICOKE, ON, M8W 1Z6
(416) 255-1392   *SIC* 7312

OUTFRONT MEDIA CANADA LP   p 710
309 RATHBURN RD W, MISSISSAUGA, ON, L5B 4C1
(905) 275-4969   *SIC* 7832

OUTIL MAG INC   p 1398
10 BOUL LABBE S, VICTORIAVILLE, QC, G6S 1B5
(819) 751-2424   *SIC* 5084

OUTIL-PAC (ESTRIE)   p 1158
See OUTIL-PAC INC

OUTIL-PAC INC   p 1158
5895 AV ANDOVER, MONT-ROYAL, QC,

H4T 1H8

(514) 733-3555   *SIC* 5084

OUTILLAGE DE PRECISION DRUMMOND INC   *p* 1097

5250 RUE SAINT-ROCH S, DRUMMONDVILLE, QC, J2B 6V4

(819) 474-2622   *SIC* 3499

OUTILLAGE INDUSTRIEL QUEBEC LTEE *p* 1265

395 AV MARCONI, QUEBEC, QC, G1N 4A5

(418) 683-2527   *SIC* 5084

OUTILLAGE PLACIDE MATHIEU INC *p* 1057

670 RUE PICARD, BELOEIL, QC, J3G 5X9

(450) 467-3565   *SIC* 5084

OUTILLAGE SUMMIT   *p* 1321

803 RUE SAINT-GEORGES, SAINT-JEROME, QC, J7Z 5E1

(450) 592-0747   *SIC* 5072

OUTILLAGES KING CANADA INC   *p* 1094

700 AV MELOCHE, DORVAL, QC, H9P 2Y4

(514) 636-5464   *SIC* 5084

OUTILLEUR AGRICOLE, L'   *p* 1314

See *OUTILLEUR S.E.C., L'*

OUTILLEUR S.E.C., L'   *p* 1314

236 RUE SAINTE-GENEVIEVE, SAINT-ISIDORE, QC, G0S 2S0

(418) 882-5656   *SIC* 5251

OUTILLEURS, S.E.C., L'   *p* 1323

1325 RUE DU PONT, SAINT-LAMBERT-DE-LAUZON, QC, G0S 2W0

(418) 889-9521   *SIC* 5072

OUTILS A. RICHARD CO   *p* 1057

120 RUE JACQUES-CARTIER, BERTHIERVILLE, QC, J0K 1A0

(450) 836-3766   *SIC* 5251

OUTILS DE COUPE DRILLMEX INC *p* 1359

2105 RUE BOMBARDIER, SAINTE-JULIE, QC, J3E 2N1

(450) 922-1929   *SIC* 5084

OUTILTECH ORLEANS   *p* 1359

See *OUTILS DE COUPE DRILLMEX INC*

OUTLAWS GROUP INC   *p* 36

7400 MACLEOD TRAIL SE SUITE 24, CALGARY, AB, T2H 0L9

(403) 255-4646   *SIC* 5813

OUTLAWS NIGHTCLUB   *p* 36

See *OUTLAWS GROUP INC*

OUTLOOK & DISTRICT PIONEER HOME INC   *p* 1413

500 SEMPLE ST, OUTLOOK, SK, S0L 2N0

(306) 867-8676   *SIC* 8051

OUTLOOK EYEWEAR CANADA LIMITED *p* 706

290 BRUNEL RD, MISSISSAUGA, ON, L4Z 2C2

(905) 890-1391   *SIC* 5099

OUTLOOK HEALTH CENTRE   *p* 1413

See *OUTLOOK & DISTRICT PIONEER HOME INC*

OUTLOOK PORK LTD   *p* 150

GD, NOBLEFORD, AB, T0L 1S0

SIC 0213

OUTOTEC (CANADA) LTD   *p* 524

1551 CORPORATE DR, BURLINGTON, ON, L7L 6M3

(905) 335-0002   *SIC* 3569

OUTPOST, THE   *p* 908

See *LAKEHEAD UNIVERSITY STUDENT UNION*

OUTSET MEDIA CORPORATION   *p* 338

4226 COMMERCE CIR UNIT 106, VICTORIA, BC, V8Z 6N6

(250) 592-7374   *SIC* 5092

OVALE SEC   *p* 1323

205 RUE DAMASE-BRETON, SAINT-LAMBERT-DE-LAUZON, QC, G0S 2W0

(418) 889-8088   *SIC* 5144

OVATION LOGISTIQUE INC   *p* 1374

531 RUE PEPIN, SHERBROOKE, QC, J1L 1X3

(819) 569-9923   *SIC* 4215

OVER THE RAINBOW PACKAGING SERVICE INC   *p*

499

2165 WILLIAMS PKY, BRAMPTON, ON, L6S 6B8

SIC 7389

OVERHEAD DOOR COMPANY   *p* 141

See *MEDBRIDGE INVESTMENTS LTD*

OVERHEAD DOOR COMPANY OF EDMONTON   *p* 97

See *STORDOR INVESTMENTS LTD*

OVERLAND LEARNING CENTRE   *p* 780

See *TORONTO DISTRICT SCHOOL BOARD*

OVERLAND WEST FREIGHT LINES LTD *p* 270

11398 BRIDGEVIEW DR, SURREY, BC, V3R 0C2

(604) 888-6300   *SIC* 4213

OVERLANDERS MANUFACTURING LP *p* 178

30320 FRASER HWY, ABBOTSFORD, BC, V4X 1G1

(604) 856-6815   *SIC* 1761

OVERSEAS AIR CARGO   *p* 261

10451 SHELLBRIDGE WAY SUITE 100, RICHMOND, BC, V6X 2W8

(604) 734-8155   *SIC* 4729

OVERSEAS CONTAINER FORWARDING, INC   *p* 261

10451 SHELLBRIDGE WAY UNIT 100, RICHMOND, BC, V6X 2W8

(604) 734-8155   *SIC* 4731

OVERSEAS EXPRESS CONSOLIDATORS (CANADA) INC   *p* 1340

725 MONTEE DE LIESSE, SAINT-LAURENT, QC, H4T 1P5

(514) 905-1246   *SIC* 4731

OVERSEAS MISSIONARY FELLOWSHIP *p* 877

10 HUNTINGDALE BLVD, SCARBOROUGH, ON, M1W 2S5

(905) 568-9971   *SIC* 8661

OVERSEAS MOTORS (WINDSOR) INC *p* 1018

9225 TECUMSEH RD E, WINDSOR, ON, N8R 1A1

(519) 254-0358   *SIC* 5511

OVERWAITEA FOOD GROUP   *p* 213

See *GREAT PACIFIC INDUSTRIES INC*

OVERWAITEA FOOD GROUP   *p* 224

See *GREAT PACIFIC INDUSTRIES INC*

OVERWAITEA FOOD GROUP   *p* 234

See *GREAT PACIFIC INDUSTRIES INC*

OVIVO INC   *p* 1198

1010 RUE SHERBROOKE O BUREAU 1700, MONTREAL, QC, H3A 2R7

(514) 284-2224   *SIC* 3569

OWASCO CANADIAN CAR & CAMPER RENTAL LTD   *p* 1015

2030 CHAMPLAIN AVE, WHITBY, ON, L1N 6A7

(905) 579-7573   *SIC* 5561

OWEN & COMPANY LIMITED   *p* 1028

51 STONE RIDGE RD SUITE LBBY, WOODBRIDGE, ON, L4H 0A5

(905) 265-9203   *SIC* 2515

OWEN BIRD LAW CORPORATION   *p* 329

595 BURRARD ST SUITE 2900, VANCOUVER, BC, V7X 1J5

(604) 688-0401   *SIC* 8111

OWEN CORNING   *p* 124

See *OC CANADA HOLDINGS COMPANY*

OWEN OIL TOOLS   *p* 158

See *CORE LABORATORIES CANADA LTD*

OWEN SOUND LEDGEROCK LIMITED *p* 836

138436 LEDGEROCK RD, OWEN SOUND, ON, N4K 5P7

(519) 376-0366   *SIC* 3281

OWEN SOUND MOTORS LIMITED   *p* 836

202423 SUNSET STRIP HWY 6&21, OWEN SOUND, ON, N4K 5N7

(519) 376-5580   *SIC* 5511

OWENS CORNING   *p* 876

See *OC CANADA HOLDINGS COMPANY*

OWENS CORNING SOLUTIONS GROUP *p* 517

See *OC CANADA HOLDINGS COMPANY*

OWENS, R S & COMPANY INCORPORATED   *p* 680

271 YORKTECH DR, MARKHAM, ON, L6G 1A6

(905) 754-3355   *SIC* 6531

OWL   *p* 1172

See *EDITIONS NOVALIS INC, LES*

OWL DISTRIBUTION INC   *p* 1035

220 UNIVERSAL RD, WOODSTOCK, ON, N4S 7W3

(519) 539-8115   *SIC* 5031

OWL RAFTING INC   *p* 826

39 FIRST AVE, OTTAWA, ON, K1S 2G1

(613) 238-7238   *SIC* 7999

OWN INC   *p* 965

181 BAY ST SUITE 1630, TORONTO, ON, M5J 2T3

(416) 642-3770   *SIC* 4833

OWS RAILROAD CONSTRUCTION & MAINTENANCE LTD   *p* 843

4320 DISCOVERY LINE, PETROLIA, ON, N0N 1R0

(519) 882-4996   *SIC* 1629

OXFAM CANADA   *p* 820

39 MCARTHUR AVE, OTTAWA, ON, K1L 8L7

(613) 237-5236   *SIC* 8399

OXFORD DODGE CHRYSLER (1992) LTD *p* 659

1249 HYDE PARK RD, LONDON, ON, N6H 5K6

(519) 473-1010   *SIC* 5511

OXFORD FROZEN FOODS LIMITED   *p* 464

4881 MAIN ST, OXFORD, NS, B0M 1P0

(902) 447-2320   *SIC* 2037

OXFORD MILKWAY TRANSPORT CO-OPERATIVE   *p* 1036

103 LONGWORTH LANE, WOODSTOCK, ON, N4V 1G6

(519) 539-2302   *SIC* 5963

OXFORD MILLS HOME FASHION FACTORY OUTLET INC, THE   *p* 534

425 HESPELER RD UNIT 1C, CAMBRIDGE, ON, N1R 6J2

(519) 342-3026   *SIC* 5719

OXFORD PROPERTIES GROUP INC *p* 956

100 ADELAIDE ST W SUITE 900, TORONTO, ON, M5H 0E2

(416) 865-8300   *SIC* 6512

OXFORD REGIONAL NURSING HOME *p* 621

See *DIVERSICARE CANADA MANAGEMENT SERVICES CO., INC*

OXFORD SEMINARS   *p* 90

162221-10405 JASPER AVE NW, EDMONTON, AB, T5J 3N4

(780) 428-8700   *SIC* 8621

OXFORD STREET VALUE-MART   *p* 652

See *2018775 ONTARIO LIMITED*

OXOID COMPANY   *p* 750

See *OXOID INC*

OXOID INC   *p* 750

1926 MERIVALE RD SUITE 100, NEPEAN, ON, K2G 1E8

(613) 226-1318   *SIC* 2835

OXVILLE HOMES LTD   *p* 557

2220 HIGHWAY 7 UNIT 5, CONCORD, ON, L4K 1W7

(416) 667-0447   *SIC* 1522

OXY VINYLS CANADA CO   *p* 758

8800 THOROLD TOWN LINE, NIAGARA FALLS, ON, L2E 6V9

(905) 357-3131   *SIC* 2821

OZ OPTICS LIMITED   *p* 815

219 WESTBROOK RD, OTTAWA, ON, K0A 1L0

(613) 831-0981   *SIC* 3827

OZAWA AGENCIES   *p* 853

See *OZAWA CANADA INC*

OZAWA CANADA INC   *p* 853

100 EAST BEAVER CREEK RD UNIT 2, RICHMOND HILL, ON, L4B 1J6

(905) 731-5088   *SIC* 5046

OZBURN-HESSEY LOGISTICS   *p* 509

300 KENNEDY RD S UNIT B, BRAMPTON, ON, L6W 4V2

(905) 450-1151   *SIC* 4731

OZERY'S PITA BREAK   *p* 1032

See *OZERY'S PITA BREAK PARTNERSHIP*

OZERY'S PITA BREAK PARTNERSHIP *p* 1032

11 DIRECTOR CRT, WOODBRIDGE, ON, L4L 4S5

(905) 265-1143   *SIC* 5149

OZZ ELECTRIC   *p* 557

20 FLORAL PKY SUITE A, CONCORD, ON, L4K 4R1

(416) 637-7237   *SIC* 1731

OZZ ELECTRIC INC   *p* 557

20 FLORAL PKY SUITE A, CONCORD, ON, L4K 4R1

(416) 637-7237   *SIC* 1731

O'CONNOR RV CENTRES   *p* 197

See *O'CONNOR RV CENTRES*

P

P & A MANAGEMENT LTD   *p* 909

1205 AMBER DR UNIT 106, THUNDER BAY, ON, P7B 6M4

(807) 346-8367   *SIC* 7363

P & E MANUFACTURING LTD   *p* 394

1524 ROUTE 950, BAS-CAP-PELE, NB, E4N 1A9

(506) 577-4356   *SIC* 5551

P & P PROJECTS INC   *p* 793

233 SIGNET DR SUITE 1, NORTH YORK, ON, M9L 1V3

(416) 398-6197   *SIC* 7389

P & R HOFSTATTER SALES LTD   *p* 839

45 DUFFERIN ST, PERTH, ON, K7H 3A5

(613) 267-3412   *SIC* 5531

P & R TRUCK CENTRE LTD   *p* 267

2005 KEATING CROSS RD, SAANICHTON, BC, V8M 2A5

(250) 652-9139   *SIC* 7538

P & R WESTERN STAR TRUCKS   *p* 267

See *P. & R. REPAIRS LTD*

P & WC   *p* 1142

See *PRATT & WHITNEY CANADA CIE*

P A BEVERAGE SALES   *p* 1414

See *P A BOTTLERS LTD*

P A BOTTLERS LTD   *p* 1414

85 11TH ST NW, PRINCE ALBERT, SK, S6V 5T2

(306) 922-7777   *SIC* 2086

P D G (MILLWOODS GOOD SAMARITAN) *p* 120

101 YOUVILLE DRIVE EAST NW, EDMONTON, AB, T6L 7A4

(780) 485-0816   *SIC* 8322

P G BIG   *p* 249

See *BRAIN INJURED GROUP SOCIETY*

P I B   *p* 568

See *PROGRAMMED INSURANCE BROKERS INC*

P M L INSPECTION SERVICES LTD *p* 130

11110 88 AVE SUITE 2, FORT SASKATCHEWAN, AB, T8L 3K8

(780) 992-9360   *SIC* 7389

P O MACK   *p* 741

See *PERFORMANCE EQUIPMENT LTD*

P P I FINANCIAL GROUP (EASTERN) LTD *p* 982

200 FRONT ST W SUITE 2400, TORONTO, ON, M5V 3K5

(416) 494-7707   *SIC* 6411

P SUN'S ENTERPRISES (VANCOUVER) LTD   *p* 308

885 GEORGIA ST W, VANCOUVER, BC, V6C 3E8

(604) 643-7939   *SIC* 7011
P SUN'S ENTERPRISES (VANCOUVER) LTD   *p* 335
463 BELLEVILLE ST, VICTORIA, BC, V8V 1X3
(250) 386-0450   *SIC* 7011

P&C GENERAL CONTRACTING LTD *p* 673
250 SHIELDS CRT SUITE 24, MARKHAM, ON, L3R 9W7
(905) 479-3015   *SIC* 1542

P'TIT GRAND CAFE, LE   *p* 1305
See *PERES NATURE INC, LES*

P. & R. DESJARDINS CONSTRUCTION INC *p* 1330
1777 RUE BEGIN, SAINT-LAURENT, QC, H4R 2B5
(514) 748-1234   *SIC* 1542

P. & R. REPAIRS LTD   *p* 267
2005 KEATING CROSS RD, SAANICHTON, BC, V8M 2A5
(250) 652-9139   *SIC* 4212

P. A. FINE FOODS AND DISTRIBUTORS LTD   *p* 1414
3850 5TH AVE E, PRINCE ALBERT, SK, S6W 0A1
(306) 763-7061   *SIC* 5145

P. BAILLARGEON LTEE   *p* 1318
800 RUE DES CARRIERES, SAINT-JEAN-SUR-RICHELIEU, QC, J3B 2P2
(514) 866-8333   *SIC* 1611

P. G. DISPOSAL SERVICE LTD   *p* 921
9 DIBBLE ST SUITE 1, TORONTO, ON, M4M 2E7
(416) 467-8717   *SIC* 4953

P.B.E. DISTRIBUTORS INC   *p* 115
5308 97 ST NW, EDMONTON, AB, T6E 5W5
(780) 438-0303   *SIC* 5013

P.C. OILFIELD SUPPLIES LTD   *p* 205
501 ROLLA RD, DAWSON CREEK, BC, V1G 4E9
(250) 782-5134   *SIC* 3272

P.C.P. CANADA   *p* 1121
See *6482066 CANADA INC*

P.D.G. MECANIQUE-SOUDURE   *p* 1389
See *9089-8131 QUEBEC INC*

P.E. PAGEAU INC   *p* 1262
460 RUE METIVIER, QUEBEC, QC, G1M 2T8
(418) 681-8080   *SIC* 1611

P.E.I. LIQUOR CONTROL COMMISSION *p* 1039
See *PRINCE EDWARD ISLAND LIQUOR CONTROL COMMISSION*

P.E.I. MUSSEL KING (1994) INC   *p* 1041
318 RED HEAD RD, MORELL, PE, C0A 1S0
(902) 961-3300   *SIC* 0913

P.E.I. VEGETABLE GROWERS CO-OPERATIVE ASSOCIATION, LIMITED   *p* 1040
280 SHERWOOD RD, CHARLOTTETOWN, PE, C1E 0E4
(902) 892-5361   *SIC* 5148

P.E.T. PROCESSING INC   *p* 206
917 CLIVEDEN AVE UNIT 105, DELTA, BC, V3M 5R6
(604) 522-6727   *SIC* 4953

P.F. COLLINS CUSTOMS BROKER LIMITED   *p* 428
251 EAST WHITE HILLS RD UNIT 100, ST. JOHN'S, NL, A1A 5X7
(709) 726-7596   *SIC* 4731

P.F. COLLINS INTERNATIONAL TRADE SOLUTIONS   *p* 428
See *P.F. COLLINS CUSTOMS BROKER LIMITED*

P.G. HOTEL LTD   *p* 454
1725 MARKET ST, HALIFAX, NS, B3J 3N9
(902) 425-1986   *SIC* 7011

P.H. TECH INC   *p* 1137
8650 BOUL GUILLAUME-COUTURE BUREAU 220, LEVIS, QC, G6V 9G9
(418) 833-3231   *SIC* 3089

P.H. VITRES D'AUTOS INC   *p* 1361

2635 RANG SAINT-JOSEPH, SAINTE-PERPETUE, QC, J0C 1R0
(819) 336-6660   *SIC* 5013

P.J. DALY CONTRACTING LIMITED   *p* 615
1320 STONE CHURCH RD E, HAMILTON, ON, L8W 2C8
(905) 575-1525   *SIC* 1742

P.J. IMPEX INC   *p* 1224
5532 RUE SAINT-PATRICK BUREAU 300, MONTREAL, QC, H4E 1A8
(514) 369-2035   *SIC* 5141

P.J. PUB   *p* 1131
See *PLACEMENTS SERGAKIS INC*

P.K. DOUGLASS INC   *p* 698
1033 JAYSON CRT, MISSISSAUGA, ON, L4W 2P4
(905) 624-3300   *SIC* 5099

P.L.E.A.   *p* 287
See *PACIFIC LEGAL EDUCATION ASSOCIATION*

P.O.S CANADA   *p* 691
See *887804 ONTARIO INC*

P.R. DEVELOPMENTS LTD   *p* 24
2828 23 ST NE, CALGARY, AB, T2E 8T4
(403) 291-2003   *SIC* 7011

P.R. DISTRIBUTIONS INC   *p* 1276
6500 RUE ZEPHIRIN-PAQUET, QUEBEC, QC, G2C 0M3
(418) 872-6018   *SIC* 5084

P.R. ENTRETIEN D'EDIFICES INC   *p* 1379
1180 RUE LEVIS BUREAU 2, TERREBONNE, QC, J6W 5S6
(450) 492-5999   *SIC* 7349

P.R. NISSEN & CIE LTEE   *p* 1395
102B BOUL DE LA CITE-DES-JEUNES UNITE 54, VAUDREUIL-DORION, QC, J7V 8B9
(514) 694-0250   *SIC* 5072

P.R. ST-GERMAIN INC   *p* 1376
50 RUE VICTORIA, SOREL-TRACY, QC, J3P 1Y6
(450) 743-5738   *SIC* 5411

P.S. ATLANTIC LIMITED   *p* 426
102 CLYDE AVE, MOUNT PEARL, NL, A1N 4S2
(709) 747-5432   *SIC* 5198

P.T.I.   *p* 201
See *P.T.I. PUNCH TOOLS INC*

P.T.I. PUNCH TOOLS INC   *p* 201
211 SCHOOLHOUSE ST SUITE 11, COQUITLAM, BC, V3K 4X9
(604) 521-3143   *SIC* 5084

P.Y.A. IMPORTER LTD   *p* 789
15 APEX RD, NORTH YORK, ON, M6A 2V6
(416) 929-3300   *SIC* 5136

P2 ENERGY SOLUTIONS ALBERTA ULC *p* 55
639 5 AVE SW SUITE 2100, CALGARY, AB, T2P 0M9
(403) 774-1000   *SIC* 7371

PA - SOUTH HILL BRANCH   *p* 1413
See *CONEXUS CREDIT UNION 2006*

PABER ALUMINIUM INC   *p* 1074
296 CH VINCELOTTE, CAP-SAINT-IGNACE, QC, G0R 1H0
(418) 246-5626   *SIC* 3365

PAC BRAKE MANUFACTURING   *p* 282
19594 96 AVE, SURREY, BC, V4N 4C3
(604) 882-0183   *SIC* 5531

PACA INDUSTRIAL DISTRIBUTION LTD *p* 642
84 MCBRINE PL, KITCHENER, ON, N2R 1H3
(519) 748-5650   *SIC* 5084

PACBLUE DIGITAL IMAGING INC   *p* 256
3551 VIKING WAY UNIT 109, RICHMOND, BC, V6V 1W1
(604) 714-3288   *SIC* 7334

PACBRAKE COMPANY   *p* 282
19594 96 AVE, SURREY, BC, V4N 4C3
(604) 882-0183   *SIC* 3714

PACCAR LEASING   *p* 1340
See *PACCAR OF CANADA LTD*

PACCAR LEASING   *p* 1364

See *PACCAR OF CANADA LTD*

PACCAR OF CANADA LTD   *p* 725
6711 MISSISSAUGA RD SUITE 500, MISSISSAUGA, ON, L5N 4J8
(905) 858-7000   *SIC* 5012

PACCAR OF CANADA LTD   *p* 1340
7500 RTE TRANSCANADIENNE, SAINT-LAURENT, QC, H4T 1A5
(514) 735-2581   *SIC* 5511

PACCAR OF CANADA LTD   *p* 1364
10 RUE SICARD, SAINTE-THERESE, QC, J7E 4K9
(450) 435-6171   *SIC* 3711

PACE CHEMICALS LTD   *p* 206
1597 DERWENT WAY FL 2, DELTA, BC, V3M 6K8
(604) 520-6211   *SIC* 5169

PACE INDEPENDENT LIVING   *p* 789
970 LAWRENCE AVE W SUITE 210, NORTH YORK, ON, M6A 3B6
(416) 789-7806   *SIC* 8399

PACE INVESTCO LTD   *p* 1252
193 BOUL BRUNSWICK, POINTE-CLAIRE, QC, H9R 5N2
(514) 630-6820   *SIC* 5085

PACE LAW FIRM PROFESSIONAL CORPORATION   *p* 578
300 THE EAST MALL UNIT 500, ETOBICOKE, ON, M9B 6B7
(416) 236-3060   *SIC* 8111

PACE PROCESSING AND PRODUCT DEVELOPMENT LTD   *p* 272
19495 55 AVE SUITE 107, SURREY, BC, V3S 8P7
(604) 539-9201   *SIC* 5149

PACE SAVINGS & CREDIT UNION LIMITED *p* 557
8111 JANE ST UNIT 1, CONCORD, ON, L4K 4L7
(905) 738-8900   *SIC* 6062

PACEKIDS SOCIETY FOR CHILDREN WITH SPECIAL NEEDS   *p* 24
808 55 AVE NE, CALGARY, AB, T2E 6Y4
(403) 234-7876   *SIC* 8322

PACESETTER HOMES   *p* 37
See *STERLING HOMES LTD*

PACESETTER PETROLEUM LIMITED   *p* 1440
126 INDUSTRIAL RD, WHITEHORSE, YT, Y1A 2T9
(867) 633-5908   *SIC* 5172

PACESETTER TRAVEL   *p* 921
See *GOWAY TRAVEL LIMITED*

PACESETTER TRAVEL LIMITED   *p* 921
3284 YONGE ST SUITE 300, TORONTO, ON, M4N 3M7
(416) 322-1031   *SIC* 4724

PACIFIC & WESTERN PUBLIC SECTOR FINANCING CORP   *p* 654
140 FULLARTON ST, LONDON, ON, N6A 5P2
(519) 645-1919   *SIC* 6159

PACIFIC ACADEMY   *p* 282
See *PACIFIC PENTECOSTAL EDUCATION AND COMMUNICATION SOCIETY*

PACIFIC BINDERY SERVICES LTD   *p* 324
870 KENT AVE SOUTH W, VANCOUVER, BC, V6P 6Y6
(604) 873-4291   *SIC* 2789

PACIFIC BIOENERGY CORPORATION *p* 315
1111 HASTINGS ST W SUITE 780, VANCOUVER, BC, V6E 2J3
(604) 602-1099   *SIC* 5099

PACIFIC BLASTING & DEMOLITION LTD *p* 184
3183 NORLAND AVE, BURNABY, BC, V5B 3A9
(604) 291-1255   *SIC* 1629

PACIFIC BLENDS LTD   *p* 247
1625 KEBET WAY UNIT 100, PORT CO-

QUITLAM, BC, V3C 5W9
(604) 945-4600   *SIC* 5149

PACIFIC BLUE CROSS   *p* 189
See *PBC HEALTH BENEFITS SOCIETY*

PACIFIC BUILDERS SUPPLIES   *p* 198
3730 TRANS CANADA HWY, COBBLE HILL, BC, V0R 1L7
(250) 743-5584   *SIC* 2452

PACIFIC BUILDING SYSTEMS INC   *p* 198
3730 TRANS CANADA HWY, COBBLE HILL, BC, V0R 1L7
(250) 743-5584   *SIC* 1541

PACIFIC COAST DISTRIBUTION LTD *p* 229
27433 52 AVE, LANGLEY, BC, V4W 4B2
(604) 888-8489   *SIC* 4731

PACIFIC COAST EXPRESS LIMITED *p* 275
10299 GRACE RD, SURREY, BC, V3V 3V7
(604) 582-3230   *SIC* 4213

PACIFIC COAST FRUIT PRODUCTS LTD *p* 175
34352 INDUSTRIAL WAY, ABBOTSFORD, BC, V2S 7M6
(604) 850-3505   *SIC* 2037

PACIFIC COAST TERMINALS CO. LTD *p* 248
2300 COLUMBIA ST, PORT MOODY, BC, V3H 5J9
(604) 939-7371   *SIC* 4491

PACIFIC COASTAL AIRLINES LIMITED *p* 265
4440 COWLEY CRES SUITE 204, RICHMOND, BC, V7B 1B8
(604) 273-8666   *SIC* 4512

PACIFIC COMMUNITY RESOURCES SOCIETY   *p* 287
2830 GRANDVIEW HWY SUITE 201, VANCOUVER, BC, V5M 2C9
(604) 412-7950   *SIC* 8322

PACIFIC COMPANION ENTERPRISES INC *p* 180
7083 SILVERDALE PL, BRENTWOOD BAY, BC, V8M 1G9
SIC 6324

PACIFIC CUSTOMS BROKERS LTD *p* 279
17637 1 AVE SUITE 101, SURREY, BC, V3Z 9S1
(604) 538-1566   *SIC* 4731

PACIFIC DAIRY CENTRE LTD   *p* 197
8558 CHILLIWACK MOUNTAIN RD, CHILLIWACK, BC, V2R 3W8
(604) 852-9020   *SIC* 5083

PACIFIC DOCUMENT EXCHANGE LTD *p* 299
111 SMITHE ST, VANCOUVER, BC, V6B 4Z8
(604) 684-3336   *SIC* 7389

PACIFIC EMERGENCY PRODUCTS   *p* 479
See *PACIFIC SAFETY PRODUCTS INC*

PACIFIC ENERGY FIREPLACE PRODUCTS LTD   *p* 212
2975 ALLENBY RD, DUNCAN, BC, V9L 6V8
(250) 748-1184   *SIC* 3433

PACIFIC ENVIRONMENTAL CONSULTING *p* 239
See *TOTAL SAFETY SERVICES INC*

PACIFIC FIRST   *p* 186
3993 HENNING DR UNIT 215, BURNABY, BC, V5C 6P7
(604) 293-1974   *SIC* 6321

PACIFIC HONDA   *p* 241
See *HONDA CANADA INC*

PACIFIC INLAND RESOURCES, DIV OF *p* 269
See *WEST FRASER MILLS LTD*

PACIFIC INSIGHT   *p* 236
See *PACIFIC INSIGHT ELECTRONICS CORP*

PACIFIC INSIGHT ELECTRONICS CORP *p* 236
1155 INSIGHT DR, NELSON, BC, V1L 5P5
(250) 354-1155   *SIC* 3694

PACIFIC INSURANCE BROKER INC *p* 853
120 EAST BEAVER CREEK RD SUITE 101,

RICHMOND HILL, ON, L4B 4V1
(416) 494-1268   *SIC* 6411
PACIFIC LEGAL EDUCATION ASSOCIATION   *p* 287
3894 COMMERCIAL ST, VANCOUVER, BC, V5N 4G2
(604) 871-0450   *SIC* 8399
PACIFIC LINK MINING CORP   *p* 315
1055 GEORGIA ST W SUITE 2772, VANCOUVER, BC, V6E 0B6
SIC 6799
PACIFIC MAINLAND HOLDINGS LTD *p* 201
1288 LOUGHEED HWY, COQUITLAM, BC, V3K 6S4
(604) 522-6140   *SIC* 5511
PACIFIC MAZDA   *p* 335
See *PACIFIC MOTOR SALES AND SERVICE LTD*
PACIFIC METALS LIMITED   *p* 291
8360 ONTARIO ST, VANCOUVER, BC, V5X 3E5
(604) 327-1148   *SIC* 5093
PACIFIC METALS RECYCLING INTERNATIONAL   *p* 291
See *PACIFIC METALS LIMITED*
PACIFIC MOTOR SALES AND SERVICE LTD   *p* 335
1060 YATES ST, VICTORIA, BC, V8V 3M6
(250) 385-5747   *SIC* 5511
PACIFIC NATIONAL EXHIBITION   *p* 284
2901 HASTINGS ST E, VANCOUVER, BC, V5K 5J1
(604) 253-2311   *SIC* 7999
PACIFIC NET & TWINE LTD   *p* 266
3731 MONCTON ST, RICHMOND, BC, V7E 3A5
(604) 274-7238   *SIC* 5091
PACIFIC NEWSPAPER GROUP DIV OF   *p* 308
See *POSTMEDIA NETWORK INC*
PACIFIC NORTHERN CARRIERS LTD *p* 282
15760 110 AVE, SURREY, BC, V4N 4Z1
(604) 592-9630   *SIC* 4923
PACIFIC NORTHERN GAS (N.E.) LTD *p* 315
1185 GEORGIA ST W SUITE 950, VANCOUVER, BC, V6E 4E6
(604) 691-5680   *SIC* 4924
PACIFIC NORTHERN GAS LTD   *p* 315
SUITE 2550 1066 HASTINGS ST W, VANCOUVER, BC, V6E 3X2
(604) 697-9221   *SIC* 4923
PACIFIC NORTHERN RAIL CONTRACTORS CORP   *p* 497
251 HOLLAND STREET W, BRADFORD, ON, L3Z 1H9
(905) 775-6564   *SIC* 4923
PACIFIC NORTHWEST FREIGHT SYSTEM   *p* 1440
See *PACIFIC NORTHWEST MOVING (YUKON) LIMITED*
PACIFIC NORTHWEST MOVING (YUKON) LIMITED   *p* 1440
3 BURNS RD, WHITEHORSE, YT, Y1A 4Z3
(867) 668-2511   *SIC* 4731
PACIFIC PARTS LTD   *p* 292
110 5TH AVE W, VANCOUVER, BC, V5Y 1H7
(604) 879-1481   *SIC* 5013
PACIFIC PAVING OF MARKHAM LIMITED *p* 698
5845 LUKE RD SUITE 204, MISSISSAUGA, ON, L4W 2K5
(905) 670-7730   *SIC* 6719
PACIFIC PENTECOSTAL EDUCATION AND COMMUNICATION SOCIETY   *p* 282
10238 168 ST, SURREY, BC, V4N 1Z4
(604) 581-0132   *SIC* 8211
PACIFIC RADIATOR MFG   *p* 228
See *PACIFIC RADIATOR MFG. LTD*
PACIFIC RADIATOR MFG. LTD   *p* 228
20579 LANGLEY BYPASS SUITE 203, LAN-

GLEY, BC, V3A 5E8
(604) 534-7555   *SIC* 3714
PACIFIC REALM INVESTMENT GROUP INC.   *p* 831
20E CASTLEBROOK LANE, OTTAWA, ON, K2G 5G3
SIC 6282
PACIFIC RESTAURANT SUPPLY, INC *p* 295
1020 CORDOVA ST E, VANCOUVER, BC, V6A 4A3
(604) 216-2566   *SIC* 5046
PACIFIC RIM CABINETS LTD   *p* 206
640 BELGRAVE WAY, DELTA, BC, V3M 5R7
(604) 515-7377   *SIC* 5712
PACIFIC RIM EXTERIORS   *p* 337
831 SHAMROCK ST, VICTORIA, BC, V8X 2V1
(250) 686-8738   *SIC* 1521
PACIFIC RIM FLOOR SUPPLIES   *p* 277
See *PACIFIC RIM FLOORING LTD*
PACIFIC RIM FLOORING LTD   *p* 277
13375 76 AVE SUITE 101, SURREY, BC, V3W 6J3
(604) 591-3431   *SIC* 5023
PACIFIC RIM INDUSTRIAL INSULATION LTD   *p* 272
19510 55 AVE UNIT 2, SURREY, BC, V3S 8P7
(604) 543-8178   *SIC* 1742
PACIFIC SAFETY PRODUCTS INC   *p* 479
124 FOURTH AVE, ARNPRIOR, ON, K7S 0A9
(613) 623-6001   *SIC* 3842
PACIFIC SALMON INDUSTRIES INC   *p* 277
8305 128 ST, SURREY, BC, V3W 4G1
(604) 501-7600   *SIC* 5146
PACIFIC SEAFOODS INTERNATIONAL LTD *p* 247
9300 TRUSTEE RD, PORT HARDY, BC, V0N 2P0
(250) 949-8781   *SIC* 5146
PACIFIC SIGN GROUP INC   *p* 209
7462 PROGRESS WAY, DELTA, BC, V4G 1E1
(604) 940-2211   *SIC* 3993
PACIFIC SPECIALTY BRANDS CO. ULC *p* 193
7595 LOWLAND DR, BURNABY, BC, V5J 5L1
(604) 430-5253   *SIC* 5064
PACIFIC SURGICAL HOLDINGS LTD *p* 291
408 E KENT AVE SOUTH SUITE 126, VANCOUVER, BC, V5X 2X7
(604) 261-9596   *SIC* 5047
PACIFIC TOWING SERVICES LTD   *p* 239
14 ORWELL ST, NORTH VANCOUVER, BC, V7J 2G1
(604) 990-0591   *SIC* 4492
PACIFIC TRUCK & EQUIPMENT   *p* 215
2226 NORTH NADINA AVE, HOUSTON, BC, V0J 1Z0
(250) 845-0061   *SIC* 5084
PACIFIC TRUSS   *p* 198
See *PACIFIC BUILDERS SUPPLIES*
PACIFIC TUBULARS LTD   *p* 55
734 7 AVE SW SUITE 600, CALGARY, AB, T2P 3P8
(403) 269-7600   *SIC* 5051
PACIFIC VEND DISTRIBUTORS LTD   *p* 291
8250 FRASER ST, VANCOUVER, BC, V5X 3X6
(604) 324-2164   *SIC* 5099
PACIFIC VETERINARY SALES LIMITED   *p* 175
34079 GLADYS AVE, ABBOTSFORD, BC, V2S 2E8
(604) 850-1510   *SIC* 5149
PACIFIC WELLFARE RESOURCE INVESTMENT INC   *p* 181
8218 NORTH FRASER WAY, BURNABY, BC, V3N 0E9
(778) 989-6678   *SIC* 5149
PACIFIC WEST SYSTEMS SUPPLY LTD   *p*

228
20109 LOGAN AVE, LANGLEY, BC, V3A 4L5
(604) 530-7489   *SIC* 5039
PACIFIC WESTERN BREWING COMPANY LTD   *p* 189
3876 NORLAND AVE, BURNABY, BC, V5G 4T9
(604) 421-2119   *SIC* 2082
PACIFIC WESTERN TRANSPORTATION   *p* 248
See *DIVERSIFIED TRANSPORTATION LTD*
PACIFIC WESTERN TRANSPORTATION LTD   *p* 24
1857 CENTRE AVE SE, CALGARY, AB, T2E 6L3
(403) 248-4300   *SIC* 4111
PACIFIC WILDCAT RESOURCES CORP *p* 341
2300 CARRINGTON RD SUITE 110, WEST KELOWNA, BC, V4T 2N6
(250) 768-0009   *SIC* 1081
PACIFIC WINE & SPIRITS INC   *p* 74
2505 17 AVE SW UNIT 208, CALGARY, AB, T3E 7V3
(403) 226-0214   *SIC* 5182
PACIFICA HOUSING ADVISORY ASSOCIATION   *p* 336
827 FISGARD ST, VICTORIA, BC, V8W 1R9
(250) 385-2131   *SIC* 6531
PACIFICA RESORT LIVING RETIREMENT, THE   *p* 283
2525 KING GEORGE BLVD, SURREY, BC, V4P 0C8
(604) 535-9194   *SIC* 6513
PACK FRESH FOODS LTD   *p* 272
17350 56 AVE SUITE 3, SURREY, BC, V3S 1C3
(604) 574-6720   *SIC* 2091
PACKAGE TOURS, A DIV OF   *p* 4
See *BREWSTER INC*
PACKAGING DIVISION   *p* 794
See *DOW CHEMICAL CANADA ULC*
PACKAGING DIVISION   *p* 1131
See *KRUGER INC*
PACKAGING TECHNOLOGIES INC   *p* 557
310A COURTLAND AVE, CONCORD, ON, L4K 4Y6
(905) 738-8226   *SIC* 2653
PACKALL CONSULTANTS (1981) LIMITED *p* 505
2 SHAFTSBURY LANE, BRAMPTON, ON, L6T 3X7
(905) 793-0177   *SIC* 3081
PACKALL PACKAGING INC   *p* 505
2 SHAFTSBURY LANE, BRAMPTON, ON, L6T 3X7
(905) 793-0177   *SIC* 3081
PACKALL PACKAGING INC   *p* 1087
3470 BOUL DE CHENONCEAU, COTE SAINT-LUC, QC, H7T 3B6
SIC 3089
PACKERS LOGISTICS SOLUTIONS, DIV OF   *p* 892
See *MID WEST COAST CANADA INC*
PACKERS PLUS ENERGY SERVICES INC *p* 55
205 5 AVE SW SUITE 2200, CALGARY, AB, T2P 2V7
(403) 263-7587   *SIC* 1382
PACNET SERVICES LTD   *p* 308
595 HOWE ST 4 FL, VANCOUVER, BC, V6C 2T5
(604) 689-0399   *SIC* 6099
PACO   *p* 1078
See *ALBERT, PAUL CHEVROLET BUICK CADILLAC GMC LTEE*
PACO LTEE   *p* 1079
870 BOUL TALBOT, CHICOUTIMI, QC, G7H 4B4
(418) 696-4444   *SIC* 5531
PACRIM DEVELOPMENTS INC   *p* 457
117 KEARNEY LAKE RD SUITE 11, HALI-

FAX, NS, B3M 4N9
(902) 457-0144   *SIC* 6552
PACRIM HOSPITALITY SERVICES INC   *p* 440
30 DAMASCUS RD SUITE 201, BEDFORD, NS, B4A 0C1
(902) 404-7474   *SIC* 8741
PACRIM PIPES (CANADA) ULC   *p* 55
505 4 AVE SW SUITE 1610, CALGARY, AB, T2P 0J8
(403) 234-8228   *SIC* 5051
PACTIV CANADA INC   *p* 853
33 STAPLES AVE, RICHMOND HILL, ON, L4B 4W6
(905) 770-8810   *SIC* 5113
PACTIV CANADA INC   *p* 901
6870 RICHMOND RD, SUMMERSTOWN, ON, K0C 2E0
(613) 931-1439   *SIC* 3089
PAD-CAR MECHANICAL LTD   *p* 147
3271 17 AVE SW, MEDICINE HAT, AB, T1B 4B1
(403) 528-3353   *SIC* 1711
PADDLE PRAIRIE GAS CO-OP LTD   *p* 151
GD, PADDLE PRAIRIE, AB, T0H 2W0
(780) 981-2467   *SIC* 4925
PADDOCK WOOD BREWING SUPPLIES LTD   *p* 1433
116 103RD ST E SUITE B1, SASKATOON, SK, S7N 1Y7
(306) 477-5632   *SIC* 5999
PADDON + YORKE INC   *p* 708
95 DUNDAS ST E, MISSISSAUGA, ON, L5A 1W7
(905) 272-3204   *SIC* 6282
PADERNO   *p* 1038
See *3237681 CANADA INC*
PADERNO COOKWEAR   *p* 1038
See *PADINOX INC*
PADINOX INC   *p* 1038
489 BRACKLEY POINT RD RTE 15, BRACKLEY, PE, C1E 1Z3
(902) 629-1500   *SIC* 3631
PAFCO INSURANCE   *p* 1052
7100 RUE JEAN-TALON E BUREAU 300, ANJOU, QC, H1M 3S3
(514) 351-8711   *SIC* 6411
PAGE, CHRIS AND ASSOCIATES LTD *p* 94
14435 124 AVE NW, EDMONTON, AB, T5L 3B2
(780) 451-4373   *SIC* 5172
PAGE, MARCEL ELECTRICIEN   *p* 1280
See *9089-3470 QUEBEC INC*
PAGEAU MOREL INC   *p* 1180
210 BOUL CREMAZIE O BUREAU 110, MONTREAL, QC, H2P 1C6
(514) 382-5150   *SIC* 6712
PAGENET   *p* 698
See *PAGING NETWORK OF CANADA INC*
PAGES JAUNES LIMITEE   *p* 1216
1751 RUE RICHARDSON BUREAU 2300, MONTREAL, QC, H3K 1G6
(514) 934-2611   *SIC* 2741
PAGES JAUNES SOLUTIONS NUMERIQUES ET MEDIAS LIMITEE   *p* 1396
16 PLACE DU COMMERCE, VERDUN, QC, H3E 2A5
(514) 934-2611   *SIC* 4899
PAGGOS, MARIO DRUGS LTD   *p* 1032
4000 HIGHWAY 7, WOODBRIDGE, ON, L4L 8Z2
(905) 851-2199   *SIC* 5912
PAGING NETWORK OF CANADA INC *p* 698
1685 TECH AVE SUITE 1, MISSISSAUGA, ON, L4W 0A7
(905) 614-3100   *SIC* 5065
PAGUI INC   *p* 1281
15971 BOUL DE LA COLLINE, QUEBEC, QC, G3G 3A7
(418) 849-1832   *SIC* 1731
PAIEMENTS ALERTES   *p* 1215
See *ALERTPAY INCORPORATED*
PAINE, J. R. & ASSOCIATES LTD   *p* 102

17505 106 AVE NW, EDMONTON, AB, T5S
1E7
  (780) 489-0700   *SIC 8734*
PAINT SHOP, THE   *p 426*
  See P.S. ATLANTIC LIMITED
PAINT SUNDRY PRODUCTS   *p 721*
  See DYNAMIC PAINT PRODUCTS INC
PAINTED HAND CASINO   *p 1433*
  *See SASKATCHEWAN INDIAN GAMING
  AUTHORITY INC*
PAINTED HAND CASINO   *p 1438*
  *See SASKATCHEWAN INDIAN GAMING
  AUTHORITY INC*
PAINTED PONY   *p 55*
  See PAINTED PONY ENERGY LTD
PAINTED PONY ENERGY LTD   *p 55*
  520 3RD AVE SW SUITE 1200, CALGARY,
  AB, T2P 0R3
  (403) 475-0440   *SIC 1311*
PAISLEY MANOR INSURANCE GROUP   *p
777*
  *See PAISLEY-MANOR INSURANCE BRO-
KERS INC*
**PAISLEY PRODUCTS OF CANADA INCOR-
PORATED**   *p
869*
  40 UPTON RD, SCARBOROUGH, ON, M1L
2B9
  (416) 751-3700   *SIC 5063*
**PAISLEY-MANOR INSURANCE BROKERS
INC**   *p 777*
  1446 DON MILLS RD SUITE 110, NORTH
YORK, ON, M3B 3N3
  (416) 510-1177   *SIC 6411*
PAJ CANADA COMPANY   *p 673*
  168 KONRAD CRES UNIT 1, MARKHAM,
ON, L3R 9T9
  (905) 752-2080   *SIC 5094*
PAJAR DISTRIBUTION LTD   *p 1183*
  4509 AV COLONIALE, MONTREAL, QC,
H2T 1V8
  (514) 844-3067   *SIC 5139*
PAJAR HOLDINGS INC   *p 1183*
  4509 AV COLONIALE, MONTREAL, QC,
H2T 1V8
  (514) 844-3067   *SIC 6712*
PAL AERO SERVICES LTD   *p 428*
  HANGAR NO 4 ST JOHN'S INTERNA-
TIONAL AIRPORT, ST. JOHN'S, NL, A1A 5B5
  (709) 576-4615   *SIC 5172*
PAL AEROSPACE LTD   *p 428*
  ST. JOHNS INTERNATIONAL AIRPORT,
HANGAR 1, ST. JOHN'S, NL, A1A 5B5
  (709) 576-1800   *SIC 4581*
PAL AIRLINES LTD.   *p 428*
  ST JOHNS INTERNATIONAL AIRPORT, ST.
JOHN'S, NL, A1A 5B5
  (709) 576-1800   *SIC 4512*
PALACE PIER   *p 571*
  *See YORK CONDOMINIUM CORPORA-
TION NO 382*
PALADIN LABS INC   *p 1324*
  100 BOUL ALEXIS-NIHON BUREAU 600,
SAINT-LAURENT, QC, H4M 2P2
  (514) 340-1112   *SIC 2834*
PALADIN SECURITY   *p 36*
  See PALADIN TECHNOLOGIES INC
PALADIN SECURITY SYSTEMS LTD   *p 186*
  4664 LOUGHEED HWY SUITE 295, BURN-
ABY, BC, V5C 5T5
  (416) 591-1745   *SIC 5065*
PALADIN TECHNOLOGIES INC   *p 36*
  6455 MACLEOD TRAIL SW UNIT 701, CAL-
GARY, AB, T2H 0K9
  (403) 508-1888   *SIC 7381*
PALADIN TECHNOLOGIES INC   *p 128*
  604 SIGNAL RD, FORT MCMURRAY, AB,
T9H 4Z4
  (780) 743-1422   *SIC 7381*
PALADIN TECHNOLOGIES INC   *p 189*
  3001 WAYBURNE DR SUITE 201, BURN-
ABY, BC, V5G 4W3
  (604) 677-8700   *SIC 7381*
PALADIN VANCOUVER SECURITY SYS-

TEMS LTD   *p
197*
  4691 WILSON RD, CHILLIWACK, BC, V2R
5C4
  (604) 823-2428   *SIC 7382*
PALADIUM   *p 1142*
  See CENTRE SPORTIF PALADIUM INC
PALASAD BILLIARDS LIMITED   *p 660*
  141 PINE VALLEY BLVD, LONDON, ON,
N6K 3T6
  (519) 685-1390   *SIC 5044*
PALEMERSTON AND DISTRICT HOSPITAL
p 836
  500 WHITES RD RR 3, PALMERSTON, ON,
N0G 2P0
  (519) 343-2030   *SIC 8062*
PALERMO PUBLIC SCHOOL   *p 805*
  See HALTON DISTRICT SCHOOL BOARD
PALES D'EOLIENNE LM (CANADA) INC *p
1102*
  7 RUE DES CERISIERS, GASPE, QC, G4X
2M1
  (418) 361-3486   *SIC 3523*
PALFINGER INC   *p 759*
  7942 DORCHESTER RD, NIAGARA FALLS,
ON, L2G 7W7
  (905) 374-3363   *SIC 5084*
PALIN FOUNDATION, THE   *p 936*
  63 GOULD ST, TORONTO, ON, M5B 1E9
  (416) 979-5250   *SIC 7299*
PALL (CANADA) ULC   *p 717*
  3450 RIDGEWAY DR UNIT 6, MISSIS-
SAUGA, ON, L5L 0A2
  (905) 542-0330   *SIC 5085*
PALLET MANAGEMENT GROUP INC *p 540*
  9148 TWISS RD, CAMPBELLVILLE, ON,
L0P 1B0
  (905) 857-7939   *SIC 7699*
PALLETSOURCE INC   *p 545*
  755 DIVISION ST, COBOURG, ON, K9A
3T1
  (905) 373-0761   *SIC 2448*
PALLISER CHEVROLET LTD   *p 137*
  4604 42 AVE, INNISFAIL, AB, T4G 1P6
  (403) 227-1434   *SIC 5511*
PALLISER FURNITURE HOLDINGS LTD *p
363*
  70 LEXINGTON PK, WINNIPEG, MB, R2G
4H2
  (866) 444-0777   *SIC 6712*
**PALLISER FURNITURE UPHOLSTERY
HOLDINGS LTD**   *p 363*
  70 LEXINGTON PK, WINNIPEG, MB, R2G
4H2
  (204) 988-5600   *SIC 2512*
PALLISER FURNITURE UPHOLSTERY LTD *p
364*
  70 LEXINGTON PK, WINNIPEG, MB, R2G
4H2
  (204) 988-5600   *SIC 2512*
PALLISER LUMBER SALES LTD   *p 81*
  16 MCCOOL CRES, CROSSFIELD, AB,
T0M 0S0
  (403) 946-5494   *SIC 2421*
PALLISER REGIONAL CARE CENTRE   *p
1436*
  See CYPRESS HEALTH REGION
PALLISER RV SALES   *p 137*
  See PALLISER CHEVROLET LTD
PALLISER, THE   *p 49*
  See FAIRMONT HOTELS & RESORTS INC
PALM COMMUNICATION MARKETING INC
p 1207
  1253 AV MCGILL COLLEGE, MONTREAL,
QC, H3B 2Y5
  (514) 845-7256   *SIC 7311*
PALMA BRAVA   *p 665*
  See 1692246 ONTARIO INC
PALMER ATLANTIC   *p 403*
  See PALMER ATLANTIC INSURANCE LTD
PALMER ATLANTIC INSURANCE LTD   *p
403*
  538 MAIN ST UNIT 1, HARTLAND, NB, E7P
2N5

  (506) 375-7500   *SIC 6411*
PALMER CONSTRUCTION GROUP INC *p
862*
  845 OLD GOULAIS BAY RD, SAULT STE.
MARIE, ON, P6A 0B5
  (705) 254-1644   *SIC 1611*
PALMER PAVING   *p 863*
  1121 PEOPLES RD, SAULT STE. MARIE,
ON, P6C 3W4
  (705) 254-1644   *SIC 1611*
PALMER, JACKIE DISTRIBUTORS LTD   *p
17*
  6957 48 ST SE, CALGARY, AB, T2C 5A4
  SIC 5192
PALMETER'S COUNTRY HOME (1986) LTD
p 460
  655 PARK ST, KENTVILLE, NS, B4N 3V7
  (902) 678-7355   *SIC 8051*
PALS GEOMATICS CORP   *p 102*
  10704 176 ST NW, EDMONTON, AB, T5S
1G7
  (780) 455-3177   *SIC 8713*
PAMENSKY, V.J. CANADA INC   *p 789*
  64 SAMOR RD, NORTH YORK, ON, M6A
1J6
  (416) 781-4617   *SIC 5063*
PAMI   *p 1407*
  *See PRAIRIE AGRICULTURAL MACHIN-
ERY INSTITUTE*
**PAN AMERICAN NURSERY PRODUCTS
INC**   *p 279*
  5151 152 ST, SURREY, BC, V3Z 1G9
  (604) 576-8641   *SIC 5193*
PAN AMERICAN SILVER CORP   *p 308*
  625 HOWE ST SUITE 1440, VANCOUVER,
BC, V6C 2T6
  (604) 684-1175   *SIC 1044*
PAN CHANCHO BAKERY   *p 630*
  See CHEZ PIGGY RESTAURANT LIMITED
PAN ORIENT ENERGY CORP   *p 56*
  505 3RD ST SW SUITE 1505, CALGARY,
AB, T2P 3E6
  (403) 294-1770   *SIC 1311*
PAN PACIFIC HOTEL   *p 310*
  See TOKYU CANADA CORPORATION
PAN PACIFIC NISSAN RICHMOND   *p 256*
  See RICHMOND NISSAN LTD
PAN PACIFIC PET LIMITED   *p 175*
  34079 GLADYS AVE, ABBOTSFORD, BC,
V2S 2E8
  (604) 850-1510   *SIC 5149*
PAN PACIFIC VANCOUVER HOTEL   *p 308*
  See OCEAN PACIFIC HOTELS LTD
PAN-GLO CANADA PAN COATINGS INC *p
513*
  84 EASTON RD, BRANTFORD, ON, N3P
1J5
  (519) 756-2800   *SIC 7699*
PAN-OSTON LTD   *p 841*
  660 NEAL DR, PETERBOROUGH, ON, K9J
6X7
  (705) 748-4811   *SIC 2542*
PANABO SALES LTD   *p 239*
  233 1ST ST E, NORTH VANCOUVER, BC,
V7L 1B4
  (604) 988-5051   *SIC 5023*
PANACHE ROTISSEURS (1990) INC *p 575*
  1633 THE QUEENSWAY, ETOBICOKE, ON,
M8Z 1T8
  (416) 251-3129   *SIC 5812*
PANAGO PIZZA INC   *p 175*
  33149 MILL LAKE RD, ABBOTSFORD, BC,
V2S 2A4
  (604) 859-6621   *SIC 6794*
PANALPINA INC   *p 732*
  6350 CANTAY RD, MISSISSAUGA, ON, L5R
4E2
  (905) 755-4500   *SIC 4731*
PANALPINA INC   *p 1335*
  2520 AV MARIE-CURIE, SAINT-LAURENT,
QC, H4S 1N1
  (514) 421-7444   *SIC 4731*
PANASONIC   *p 698*
  See PANASONIC CANADA INC

PANASONIC CANADA INC   *p 698*
  5770 AMBLER DR SUITE 70, MISSIS-
SAUGA, ON, L4W 2T3
  (905) 624-5010   *SIC 5064*
PANASONIC CANADA INC   *p 698*
  5810 AMBLER DR UNIT 4, MISSISSAUGA,
ON, L4W 4J5
  SIC 5065
**PANASONIC ECO SOLUTIONS CANADA
INC**   *p 699*
  5770 AMBLER DR UNIT 70, MISSIS-
SAUGA, ON, L4W 2T3
  (905) 624-5010   *SIC 8731*
PANAXIS INC   *p 791*
  70 WINGOLD AVE, NORTH YORK, ON,
M6B 1P5
  (416) 256-5800   *SIC 5137*
PANCAP PHARMA INC   *p 673*
  50 VALLEYWOOD DR SUITE 6,
MARKHAM, ON, L3R 6E9
  (905) 470-6844   *SIC 2834*
PANCOR   *p 736*
  See 540731 ONTARIO LIMITED
PANDA PROPANE-REPAIR CO DIV OF   *p
620*
  See CARLING PROPANE INC
PANDORA JEWELRY LTD   *p 579*
  5535 EGLINTON AVE W SUITE 234, ETO-
BICOKE, ON, M9C 5K5
  (416) 626-1211   *SIC 5094*
PANEL & FIBER, DIV OF   *p 236*
  See CANADIAN FOREST PRODUCTS LTD
PANEL PRODUCTS   *p 256*
  See RICHELIEU CANADA LTD
PANELS.CA ONTARIO INC   *p 1012*
  123 CENTRE ST, WELLAND, ON, L3B 0E1
  (905) 734-6060   *SIC 2426*
PANERA BREAD ULC   *p 780*
  1066 DON MILLS RD, NORTH YORK, ON,
M3C 0H8
  (416) 384-1116   *SIC 5461*
PANGEO CORPORATION   *p 1020*
  3000 TEMPLE DR, WINDSOR, ON, N8W
5J6
  (519) 737-1678   *SIC 5013*
PANGEO HOLDINGS LTD   *p 1020*
  3000 TEMPLE DR, WINDSOR, ON, N8W
5J6
  (519) 737-1678   *SIC 6712*
PANIER & CADEAU INC, LE   *p 1253*
  274 CH DU BORD-DU-LAC LAKESHORE,
POINTE-CLAIRE, QC, H9S 4K9
  (514) 695-7038   *SIC 5947*
PANIER SANTE   *p 1384*
  See 9051-1916 QUEBEC INC
**PANNEAUX ET QUINCAILLERIE MCFAD-
DENS**   *p
798*
  *See MCFADDEN'S HARDWOOD & HARD-
WARE INC*
PANNEAUX MASKI INC   *p 1146*
  50 10E AV, LOUISEVILLE, QC, J5V 0A5
  (819) 228-8461   *SIC 2421*
PANNEX   *p 1278*
  See SIGNALISATION VER-MAC INC
PANNU BROS. TRUCKING LTD   *p 178*
  30260 FRASER HWY, ABBOTSFORD, BC,
V4X 1G2
  (604) 857-2213   *SIC 4213*
PANO CAP (CANADA) LIMITED   *p 637*
  55 WEBSTER RD, KITCHENER, ON, N2C
2E7
  (519) 893-6055   *SIC 3089*
PANOLAM INDUSTRIES LTD   *p 621*
  61 DOMTAR RD, HUNTSVILLE, ON, P1H
2J7
  (705) 789-9683   *SIC 2436*
PANOPTIC AUTOMATION SOLUTIONS INC
p 71
  3320 114 AVE SE, CALGARY, AB, T2Z 3V6
  (587) 315-1450   *SIC 5962*
PANORAMA BUILDING SYSTEMS LTD   *p
206*
  460 FRASERVIEW PL, DELTA, BC, V3M

6H4
(604) 522-4980 *SIC* 1771
PANORAMA MOUNTAIN RESORT p 242
See PANORAMA MOUNTAIN VILLAGE INC
PANORAMA MOUNTAIN VILLAGE p 216
See IW RESORTS LIMITED PARTNER-SHIP
PANORAMA MOUNTAIN VILLAGE INC p 242
2000 PANORAMA DR, PANORAMA, BC, V0A 1T0
(250) 342-6941 *SIC* 7011
PANTHER DRILLING CORPORATION 1438
GD LCD MAIN, WEYBURN, SK, S4H 2J7
(306) 842-7370 *SIC* 1799
PANTHER INDUSTRIES INC p 1405
108 INTERNAL RD, DAVIDSON, SK, S0G 1A0
(306) 567-2814 *SIC* 7389
PANTHERA DENTAL INC p 1265
2035 RUE DU HAUT-BORD, QUEBEC, QC, G1N 4R7
(418) 527-0388 *SIC* 3843
PANTHERE VERTE, LA p 1183
See ENTREPRISES PANTHERE VERTE INC
PANTORAMA INDUSTRIES INC, LES p 1091
2 RUE LAKE, DOLLARD-DES-ORMEAUX, QC, H9B 3H9
(514) 421-1850 *SIC* 5611
PANTRY SHELF FOOD CORPORATION p 689
3983 NASHUA DR UNIT B, MISSISSAUGA, ON, L4V 1P3
(905) 677-7200 *SIC* 5141
PANZEX VANCOUVER INC p 343
4270 MOUNTAIN SQ, WHISTLER, BC, V0N 1B4
(604) 932-6945 *SIC* 5812
PANZINI DEMOLITION p 1295
See 175784 CANADA INC
PAPE I G A p 919
See 602726 ONTARIO LTD
PAPER EXCELLENCE CANADA p 1410
See MEADOW LAKE MECHANICAL PULP INC
PAPER EXCELLENCE CANADA HOLD-INGS CORPORATION p 261
10551 SHELLBRIDGE WAY SUITE 95, RICHMOND, BC, V6X 2W9
(604) 232-2453 *SIC* 2611
PAPER FIBRES INC p 689
6405 NORTHWEST DR, MISSISSAUGA, ON, L4V 1K2
(905) 672-7222 *SIC* 5093
PAPERCON CANADA HOLDING CORP p 1238
200 AV MARIEN, MONTREAL-EST, QC, H1B 4V2
(514) 645-4571 *SIC* 6712
PAPERTECH p 239
See PT PAPERTECH INC
PAPERWORKS INDUSTRIES p 1054
See ROS-MAR LITHO INC
PAPETERIE ST-REMI INC p 1351
725 RUE NOTRE-DAME, SAINT-REMI, QC, J0L 2L0
(450) 454-6065 *SIC* 5112
PAPIER DOMTAR (CANADA) INC p 1198
395 BOUL DE MAISONNEUVE O BUREAU 200, MONTREAL, QC, H3A 1L6
(514) 848-5555 *SIC* 2611
PAPIER REBUT CENTRAL INC p 1173
4270 RUE HOGAN, MONTREAL, QC, H2H 2N4
(514) 526-4965 *SIC* 5093
PAPIER ROUVILLE p 1149
See GELPAC ROUVILLE SOLUTIONS EM-BALLAGE INC
PAPIERS ATLAS INC, LES p 1162
9000 RUE PIERRE-BONNE, MONTREAL,

QC, H1E 6W5
(514) 494-1931 *SIC* 2657
PAPIERS C.C.T. INC p 1057
830 RUE SAINT-VIATEUR, BERTHIERVILLE, QC, J0K 1A0
(450) 836-3846 *SIC* 2821
PAPIERS CODERR p 1045
See PAPIERS SOLIDERR INC, LES
PAPIERS DE PUBLICATION KRUGER INC p 1218
3285 CH DE BEDFORD, MONTREAL, QC, H3S 1G5
(514) 737-1131 *SIC* 2611
PAPIERS DE PUBLICATION KRUGER INC p 1388
3735 BOUL GENE-H.-KRUGER, TROIS-RIVIERES, QC, G9A 6B1
(819) 375-1691 *SIC* 2611
PAPIERS DOMTAR p 1403
See DOMTAR INC
PAPIERS ET EMBALLAGES ARTEAU INC p 1162
11420 BOUL ARMAND-BOMBARDIER, MONTREAL, QC, H1E 2W9
(514) 494-2222 *SIC* 5113
PAPIERS SOLIDERR INC, LES p 1045
1025 RUE DES PINS O, ALMA, QC, G8B 7V7
(418) 668-1234 *SIC* 4212
PAPIERS SOLIDERR INC, LES p 1045
525 AV DU PONT S, ALMA, QC, G8B 2T9
(418) 668-5377 *SIC* 2679
PAPINEAU INT, S.E.C. p 1320
851 BOUL ROLAND-GODARD, SAINT-JEROME, QC, J7Y 4C2
(450) 432-7555 *SIC* 4213
PAPP PLASTICS AND DISTRIBUTING LIM-ITED p 643
6110 MORTON INDUSTRIAL PKY, LASALLE, ON, N9J 3W3
(519) 734-0700 *SIC* 3089
PAPP PLASTICS AND DISTRIBUTING LIM-ITED p 1026
6110 MORTON INDUSTRIAL PKY, WIND-SOR, ON, N9J 3W3
(519) 734-1112 *SIC* 3089
PAPRICAN p 1250
See FPINNOVATIONS
PAQUET & FILS LTEE p 1137
4 RUE DU TERROIR, LEVIS, QC, G6V 9J3
(418) 833-9602 *SIC* 5172
PAQUET NISSAN INC p 1138
3580 BOUL GUILLAUME-COUTURE, LEVIS, QC, G6W 6N7
(418) 838-3838 *SIC* 5511
PAQUET, CHRISTINE ET CHARLES BOISVERT, PHARMACIENS S.E.N.C. p 1259
138 RUE SAINT-VALLIER O BUREAU 175, QUEBEC, QC, G1K 1K1
(418) 525-4981 *SIC* 5912
PAQUETTE ET ASSOCIES HUISSIERS DE JUSTICE S.E.N.C.R.L. p 1190
511 PLACE D'ARMES BUREAU 800, MON-TREAL, QC, H2Y 2W7
(514) 937-5500 *SIC* 8111
PAQUETTE, GERALD ENTREPRENEUR ELECTRICIEN ET ASSOCIES INC p 1153
17820 RUE CHARLES, MIRABEL, QC, J7J 1J5
(450) 430-9323 *SIC* 1731
PAQUETTE, ROBERT AUTOBUS & FILS INC p 1301
222 25E AV, SAINT-EUSTACHE, QC, J7P 4Z8
(450) 473-4526 *SIC* 4151
PAQUIN ENTERTAINMENT GROUP INC, THE p 387
468 STRADBROOK AVE, WINNIPEG, MB, R3L 0J9
(204) 988-1120 *SIC* 7389
PAQUIN FORD LTEE p 1289
1155 AV LARIVIERE, ROUYN-NORANDA,

QC, J9X 4K9
(819) 797-3673 *SIC* 5511
PAQUIN MAZDA p 1289
See PAQUIN FORD LTEE
PAR NADO INC p 1303
821 RUE DU PARC, SAINT-FREDERIC, QC, G0N 1P0
(418) 426-3666 *SIC* 3799
PAR-S DRUGS LTD p 932
465 YONGE ST, TORONTO, ON, M4Y 1X4
(416) 408-4000 *SIC* 5912
PARA-MED HEALTH SERVICES INC p 947
480 UNIVERSITY AVE SUITE 708, TORONTO, ON, M5G 1V2
(416) 977-5008 *SIC* 8611
PARA-NET BUANDERIE & NETTOYAGE A SEC INC p 1265
1105 RUE VINCENT-MASSEY, QUEBEC, QC, G1N 1N2
(418) 688-0889 *SIC* 7219
PARACHUTE p 922
See PARACHUTE LEADERS IN INJURY PREVENTION
PARACHUTE LEADERS IN INJURY PRE-VENTION p 922
150 EGLINTON AVE E SUITE 300, TORONTO, ON, M4P 1E8
(647) 776-5100 *SIC* 8699
PARADIGM CAPITAL INC p 965
95 WELLINGTON ST W SUITE 2101, TORONTO, ON, M5J 2N7
(416) 361-9892 *SIC* 6211
PARADIGM CONSULTING GROUP INC p 1418
1881 SCARTH ST UNIT 1200, REGINA, SK, S4P 4K9
(306) 522-8588 *SIC* 8742
PARADIGM ELECTRONICS INC p 741
205 ANNAGEM BLVD, MISSISSAUGA, ON, L5T 2V1
(905) 564-1994 *SIC* 3651
PARADIGM QUEST INC p 956
390 BAY ST SUITE 1800, TORONTO, ON, M5H 2Y2
(416) 366-8606 *SIC* 6162
PARADIS AMENAGEMENT URBAIN INC p 1255
436 RUE DES ADIRONDACKS, QUEBEC, QC, G1C 7E8
(418) 660-4060 *SIC* 4959
PARADISE FARMS p 915
See BAGHAI DEVELOPMENT LIMITED
PARADISE HOMES CORP p 915
1 HERONS HILL WAY, TORONTO, ON, M2J 0G2
(416) 756-1972 *SIC* 1521
PARADISE ISLAND CHEESE p 235
See PARADISE ISLAND FOODS INC
PARADISE ISLAND FOODS INC p 235
6451 PORTSMOUTH RD, NANAIMO, BC, V9V 1A3
(800) 889-3370 *SIC* 2022
PARADISE PET CENTER LTD p 166
580 ST ALBERT TRAIL SUITE 50, ST. AL-BERT, AB, T8N 6M9
(780) 459-6896 *SIC* 5999
PARADISE RV p 157
See RED DEER RV COUNTRY LTD
PARADOX ACCESS SOLUTIONS INC p 2
11246 261 ST, ACHESON, AB, T7X 6C7
(587) 461-1500 *SIC* 1611
PARAGON HEALTH CARE INC p 784
3595 KEELE ST, NORTH YORK, ON, M3J 1M7
(416) 633-3431 *SIC* 8361
PARAGON REMEDIATION GROUP LTD p 282
8815 HARVIE RD, SURREY, BC, V4N 4B9
(604) 513-1324 *SIC* 1542
PARALLEL 55 p 230
See EAST FRASER FIBER CO LTD
PARAMED HOME HEALTH CARE p 8
See EXTENDICARE (CANADA) INC

PARAMED HOME HEALTH CARE p 514
See EXTENDICARE (CANADA) INC
PARAMED HOME HEALTH CARE p 563
See EXTENDICARE (CANADA) INC
PARAMED HOME HEALTH CARE p 565
See EXTENDICARE (CANADA) INC
PARAMED HOME HEALTH CARE p 572
See EXTENDICARE (CANADA) INC
PARAMED HOME HEALTH CARE p 615
See EXTENDICARE (CANADA) INC
PARAMED HOME HEALTH CARE p 633
See EXTENDICARE (CANADA) INC
PARAMED HOME HEALTH CARE p 646
See EXTENDICARE (CANADA) INC
PARAMED HOME HEALTH CARE p 755
See EXTENDICARE (CANADA) INC
PARAMED HOME HEALTH CARE p 761
See EXTENDICARE (CANADA) INC
PARAMED HOME HEALTH CARE p 763
See EXTENDICARE (CANADA) INC
PARAMED HOME HEALTH CARE p 796
See EXTENDICARE (CANADA) INC
PARAMED HOME HEALTH CARE p 802
See EXTENDICARE (CANADA) INC
PARAMED HOME HEALTH CARE p 838
See EXTENDICARE (CANADA) INC
PARAMED HOME HEALTH CARE p 907
See EXTENDICARE (CANADA) INC
PARAMED HOME HEALTH CARE p 1021
See EXTENDICARE (CANADA) INC
PARAMITA ENTERPRISES LIMITED p 902
538 BLANCHARD PK, TECUMSEH, ON, N8N 2L9
(519) 727-2323 *SIC* 7011
PARAMOUNT FINE FOODS p 577
See 1726837 ONTARIO INC
PARAMOUNT FURNITURE p 261
See PARAMOUNT INDUSTRIES LTD
PARAMOUNT INDUSTRIES LTD p 261
5520 MINORU BLVD, RICHMOND, BC, V6X 2A9
(604) 273-0155 *SIC* 5712
PARAMOUNT PALLET LP p 587
1330 MARTIN GROVE RD, ETOBICOKE, ON, M9W 4X3
(416) 742-6006 *SIC* 2448
PARAMOUNT PARTS INC p 128
36 RIEDEL ST SUITE 1, FORT MCMUR-RAY, AB, T9H 3E1
(780) 791-3000 *SIC* 5531
PARAMOUNT PHARMACIES LIMITED p 464
3435 PLUMMER AVE SUITE 529, NEW WATERFORD, NS, B1H 1Z4
(902) 862-7186 *SIC* 5912
PARAMOUNT RESOURCES (ACL) LTD p 56
421 7 AVE SW SUITE 2800, CALGARY, AB, T2P 4K9
(403) 261-1200 *SIC* 1382
PARAMOUNT RESOURCES (ACL) LTD p 79
5018 50 AVE, CASTOR, AB, T0C 0X0
(403) 882-3751 *SIC* 1311
PARAMOUNT RESOURCES (TEC) LTD p 56
332 6 AVE SW SUITE 1400, CALGARY, AB, T2P 0B2
(403) 290-2900 *SIC* 1311
PARAMOUNT RESOURCES LTD p 56
421-7TH AVE SW SUITE 2800, CALGARY, AB, T2P 4K9
(403) 290-3600 *SIC* 1311
PARAMOUNT STRUCTURES LTD p 495
46 NIXON RD, BOLTON, ON, L7E 1W2
(905) 951-7528 *SIC* 1799
PARAMOUNT WINDOWS INC p 366
105 PANET RD, WINNIPEG, MB, R2J 0S1
(204) 233-4966 *SIC* 3089
PARASOURCE MARKETING AND DISTRI-BUTION LIMITED p 837
55 WOODSLEE AVE, PARIS, ON, N3L 3E5
(519) 442-7853 *SIC* 5192
PARATEX p 1265
See PARA-NET BUANDERIE & NETTOY-AGE A SEC INC

PARAZA PHARMA INC *p* 1228
2525 AV MARIE-CURIE, MONTREAL, QC, H4S 2E1
(514) 337-7200 *SIC* 5122

PARC NATIONAL DES GRANDS JARDINS ET LE PARC NATIONAL HAUTES GORGES DE LA RIVIERE MALBAIE *p* 1081
See SOCIETE DES ETABLISSEMENTS DE PLEIN AIR DU QUEBEC

PARC NATIONAL DES ILES-DE-BOUCHERVILLE *p*
1067
See SOCIETE DES ETABLISSEMENTS DE PLEIN AIR DU QUEBEC

PARC SIX FLAGS MONTREAL S.E.C. *p*
1211
22 CH MACDONALD, MONTREAL, QC, H3C 6A3
(514) 397-0402 *SIC* 7996

PARCOBEC *p* 1212
See STATIONNEMENT & DEVELOPPE-MENT INTERNATIONAL INC

PARE CENTRE DU CAMION VOLVO *p* 1137
See PARE CENTRE DU CAMION WHITE GMC INC

PARE CENTRE DU CAMION WHITE GMC INC *p* 1137
250 RTE DU PRESIDENT-KENNEDY, LEVIS, QC, G6V 9J6
(418) 833-5333 *SIC* 5511

PARE CHEVROLET OLDSMOBILE INC *p*
1292
1239 RTE BEGIN, SAINT-ANSELME, QC, G0R 2N0
SIC 5511

PARENT, ALAIN INC *p* 1057
640 RUE NOTRE-DAME, BERTHIERVILLE, QC, J0K 1A0
(450) 836-4480 *SIC* 5143

PARENTS FOR COMMUNITY LIVING KITCHENER WATERLOO INC *p* 640
82 WEBER ST E, KITCHENER, ON, N2H 1C7
(519) 742-5849 *SIC* 8399

PARENTY REITMEIER INC *p* 364
123B MARION ST, WINNIPEG, MB, R2H 0T3
(204) 237-3737 *SIC* 7389

PAREX RESOURCES INC *p* 56
2700 EIGHTH AVE PL WEST TOWER 585, 8 AVE SW, CALGARY, AB, T2P 1G1
(403) 265-4800 *SIC* 1382

PARFUMERIES DANS UN JARDIN CANADA *p* 1064
See DANS UN JARDIN CANADA INC

PARIAN LOGISTICS INC *p* 391
1530 GAMBLE PL, WINNIPEG, MB, R3T 1N6
(204) 885-4200 *SIC* 4212

PARIS JEWELLERS CANADA *p* 102
See PARIS JEWELLERS LTD

PARIS JEWELLERS LTD *p* 102
18913 111 AVE NW, EDMONTON, AB, T5S 2X4
(780) 930-1418 *SIC* 5944

PARIS KITCHENS *p* 854
See SANDERSON-HAROLD COMPANY LIMITED, THE

PARIS LADOUCEUR & ASSOCIES INC *p*
1234
63 RUE DE LA POINTE-LANGLOIS, MON-TREAL, QC, H7L 3J4
(450) 963-2777 *SIC* 6531

PARIS MARINE LIMITED *p* 841
2980 LAKEFIELD RD, PETERBOROUGH, ON, K9J 6X5
(705) 652-6444 *SIC* 5551

PARIS ORTHOTICS LTD *p* 287
3630 1ST AVE E, VANCOUVER, BC, V5M 1C3
(604) 301-2150 *SIC* 3842

PARIS SOUTHERN LIGHTS INC *p* 837
6 ADAMS ST SUITE A, PARIS, ON, N3L 3X4
(519) 442-2988 *SIC* 5199

PARIS SPRING LTD *p* 837
41 WOODSLEE AVE, PARIS, ON, N3L 3T5
(519) 442-1502 *SIC* 5085

PARISIEN, J.W. ENTERPRISES LTD *p* 882
10 FERRARA DR SUITE 98, SMITHS FALLS, ON, K7A 5K4
(613) 283-3906 *SIC* 5531

PARK 'N' FLY *p* 689
See PNF HOLDINGS LIMITED

PARK AVENUE ENTERPRISES LTD *p* 177
30360 AUTOMALL DR, ABBOTSFORD, BC, V2T 5M1
(604) 857-1430 *SIC* 5511

PARK AVENUE TOYOTA *p* 1345
See COMPLEXE DE L'AUTO PARK AV-ENUE INC

PARK DEROCHIE INC *p* 124
11850 28 ST NE, EDMONTON, AB, T6S 1G6
(780) 478-4688 *SIC* 1799

PARK GEORGIA INSURANCE AGENCIES LTD *p* 295
180 PENDER ST E UNIT 200, VANCOU-VER, BC, V6A 1T3
(604) 688-2323 *SIC* 6411

PARK GEORGIA REALTY LTD *p* 322
5701 GRANVILLE ST SUITE 201, VAN-COUVER, BC, V6M 4J7
(604) 261-7275 *SIC* 6531

PARK LANE CHEVROLET CADILLAC LTD *p* 858
1290 LONDON RD, SARNIA, ON, N7S 1P5
(519) 541-8883 *SIC* 5511

PARK LANE TERRACE LIMITED *p* 837
295 GRAND RIVER ST N, PARIS, ON, N3L 2N9
(519) 442-2753 *SIC* 8051

PARK LAWN CORPORATION *p* 927
2 ST CLAIR AVE W SUITE 1300, TORONTO, ON, M4V 1L5
(416) 231-1462 *SIC* 7261

PARK LIGHTING AND FURNITURE LTD *p*
98
10353 170 ST NW, EDMONTON, AB, T5P 4V4
(780) 434-9600 *SIC* 5719

PARK MEADOWS SAFEWAY *p* 141
See SOBEYS WEST INC

PARK N FLY *p* 265
See MILLER ROAD HOLDINGS LTD

PARK N JET *p* 32
See STEINBOCK DEVELOPMENT COR-PORATION LTD

PARK NATIONAL D'OKA *p* 1244
See GOUVERNEMENT DE LA PROVINCE DE QUEBEC

PARK PACIFIC LUMBERWORLD LTD *p* 337
3955 QUADRA ST, VICTORIA, BC, V8X 1J7
(250) 479-7151 *SIC* 5211

PARK PLACE CENTRE LIMITED *p* 447
240 BROWNLOW AVE, DARTMOUTH, NS, B3B 1X6
(902) 468-8888 *SIC* 7011

PARK PLACE LODGE *p* 212
See 357672 B.C. LTD

PARK PLACE RAMADA PLAZA HOTEL *p*
447
See PARK PLACE CENTRE LIMITED

PARK PLACE RETIREMENT RESIDENCE *p*
830
See 1230172 ONTARIO INC

PARK PLACE SENIORS LIVING INC *p* 270
13525 HILTON RD, SURREY, BC, V3R 5J3
(604) 588-3424 *SIC* 8051

PARK PROPERTY MANAGEMENT INC *p*
673
16 ESNA PARK DR SUITE 200, MARKHAM, ON, L3R 5X1
(905) 940-1718 *SIC* 6531

PARK ROYAL KEG *p* 241
See KEG RESTAURANT

PARK SHORE MOTORS LTD *p* 241
835 AUTOMALL DR, NORTH VANCOU-VER, BC, V7P 3R8

(604) 985-9344 *SIC* 5511

PARK STREET COLLEGIATE INST *p* 810
See SIMCOE COUNTY DISTRICT SCHOOL BOARD, THE

PARK TOWN ENTERPRISES LTD *p* 1429
924 SPADINA CRES E, SASKATOON, SK, S7K 3H5
(306) 244-5564 *SIC* 7011

PARK TOWN HOTEL *p* 1429
See PARK TOWN ENTERPRISES LTD

PARK VIEW COLONY FARMS LTD *p* 355
GD, RIDING MOUNTAIN, MB, R0J 1T0
(204) 967-2492 *SIC* 6513

PARK WEST SCHOOL DIVISION *p* 345
1161 ST CLARE ST N, BIRTLE, MB, R0M 0C0
(204) 842-2100 *SIC* 8211

PARKBRIDGE LIFESTYLE COMMUNITIES INC *p* 56
500 4 AVE SW SUITE 1500, CALGARY, AB, T2P 2V6
(403) 215-2100 *SIC* 6719

PARKDALE COLLEGIATE INSTITUTE *p* 992
See TORONTO DISTRICT SCHOOL BOARD

PARKDALE GUARDIAN DRUGS *p* 992
See WELCOME PHARMACY (QUEEN) LTD

PARKDALE PRICE CHOPPER *p* 990
See 1476182 ONTARIO LIMITED

PARKER CONSTRUCTION *p* 1018
See 782659 ONTARIO LTD

PARKER FILTERATION CANADA DIV OF *p*
1234
See PARKER HANNIFIN CANADA

PARKER FILTRATION CANADA *p* 893
See PARKER HANNIFIN CANADA

PARKER HANNIFIN CANADA *p* 391
1305 CLARENCE AVE, WINNIPEG, MB, R3T 1T4
(204) 452-6776 *SIC* 3625

PARKER HANNIFIN CANADA *p* 490
4635 DURHAM RD RR 3, BEAMSVILLE, ON, L0R 1B3
SIC 3714

PARKER HANNIFIN CANADA *p* 684
160 CHISHOLM DR SUITE 1, MILTON, ON, L9T 3G9
(905) 693-3000 *SIC* 3593

PARKER HANNIFIN CANADA *p* 893
1100 SOUTH SERVICE RD UNIT 318, STONEY CREEK, ON, L8E 0C5
(905) 309-8230 *SIC* 3593

PARKER HANNIFIN CANADA *p* 1234
2785 AV FRANCIS-HUGHES, MONTREAL, QC, H7L 3J6
(450) 629-3030 *SIC* 3569

PARKER PAD AND PRINTING LIMITED *p*
678
208 TRAVAIL RD, MARKHAM, ON, L3S 3J1
(905) 294-7997 *SIC* 2752

PARKER REALTY LTD *p* 1040
535 NORTH RIVER RD SUITE 1, CHAR-LOTTETOWN, PE, C1E 1J6
(902) 566-4663 *SIC* 6531

PARKER'S CHRYSLER DODGE JEEP LTD *p* 244
1765 MAIN ST, PENTICTON, BC, V2A 5H1
(250) 492-2839 *SIC* 5511

PARKHOLME SCHOOL *p* 513
See PEEL DISTRICT SCHOOL BOARD

PARKHURST KNITWEAR *p* 919
See DOROTHEA KNITTING MILLS LIM-ITED

PARKHURST, AL TRANSPORTATION LTD *p*
492
125 COLLEGE ST E, BELLEVILLE, ON, K8P 5A2
(613) 969-0606 *SIC* 4151

PARKING AND ACCESS CONTROL SER-VICES *p*
325
See U B C TRAFFIC OFFICE

PARKING CORPORATION OF VANCOU-VER, THE *p*

308
700 PENDER ST W SUITE 209, VANCOU-VER, BC, V6C 1G8
(604) 682-6744 *SIC* 7521

PARKINSON COACH LINES 2000 INC *p* 508
10 KENNEDY RD N, BRAMPTON, ON, L6V 1X4
(416) 451-4776 *SIC* 4151

PARKINSON SOCIETY CANADA *p* 774
4211 YONGE ST SUITE 316, NORTH YORK, ON, M2P 2A9
(416) 227-9700 *SIC* 8699

PARKLAND *p* 268
See PARKLAND BUILDING SUPPLIES (1998) LTD

PARKLAND BUILDING SUPPLIES (1998) LTD *p* 268
1125 EAGLE PA WAY RR 2, SICAMOUS, BC, V0E 2V2
(250) 836-2514 *SIC* 5039

PARKLAND C.L.A.S.S. *p* 154
See PARKLAND COMMUNITY LIVING AND SUPPORTS SOCIETY

PARKLAND CO-OPERATIVE ASSOCIA-TION LIMITED, THE *p*
1413
108 ASH ST, PORCUPINE PLAIN, SK, S0E 1H0
(306) 278-2022 *SIC* 5171

PARKLAND COLLEGE *p* 1410
See PARKLAND REGIONAL COLLEGE

PARKLAND COLONY *p* 148
See HUTTERIAN BRETHREN OF PARK-LAND, THE

PARKLAND COMMUNITY LIVING AND SUPPORTS SOCIETY *p* 154
6010 45 AVE, RED DEER, AB, T4N 3M4
(403) 347-3333 *SIC* 8322

PARKLAND FARM EQUIPMENT (1990) LTD *p* 167
34 BOULDER BLVD, STONY PLAIN, AB, T7Z 1V7
(780) 963-7411 *SIC* 5999

PARKLAND FUEL CORPORATION *p* 77
333 96 AVE NE SUITE 6302, CALGARY, AB, T3K 0S3
(403) 567-2500 *SIC* 2873

PARKLAND INDUSTRIES LIMITED PART-NERSHIP *p*
154
4919 59 ST SUITE 236, RED DEER, AB, T4N 6C9
(403) 343-1515 *SIC* 2911

PARKLAND LIVESTOCK MARKET LTD *p*
1408
GD, KELLIHER, SK, S0A 1V0
SIC 5154

PARKLAND LODGE *p* 136
See EVERGREENS FOUNDATION

PARKLAND PULSE GRAIN CO. LTD *p* 1412
GD LCD MAIN, NORTH BATTLEFORD, SK, S9A 2X5
(306) 445-4199 *SIC* 5153

PARKLAND REGIONAL COLLEGE *p* 1410
200 BLOCK 9 AVE E, MELVILLE, SK, S0A 2P0
(306) 728-4471 *SIC* 8221

PARKLAND REGIONAL HEALTH AUTHOR-ITY INC *p*
349
625 3RD ST SW, DAUPHIN, MB, R7N 1R7
(204) 638-2118 *SIC* 8062

PARKLAND REGIONAL HEALTH AUTHOR-ITY INC *p*
355
GD, ROBLIN, MB, R0L 1P0
(204) 937-2142 *SIC* 8062

PARKLAND REGIONAL HEALTH AUTHOR-ITY INC *p*
359
1011 MAIN ST E, SWAN RIVER, MB, R0L 1Z0
(204) 734-3441 *SIC* 8062

PARKLAND RESPIRATORY CARE LTD *p*

121
3152 PARSONS RD NW, EDMONTON, AB, T6N 1L6
(780) 430-8999   *SIC* 5169
PARKLAND SCHOOL DIVISION NO. 70   *p* 164
505 MCLEOD AVE SUITE 505, SPRUCE GROVE, AB, T7X 2Y5
(780) 962-0212   *SIC* 8211
PARKLAND SCHOOL DIVISION NO. 70   *p* 164
1000 CALAHOO RD, SPRUCE GROVE, AB, T7X 2T7
(780) 962-0800   *SIC* 8211
PARKLAND SCHOOL DIVISION NO. 70   *p* 167
4603 48 ST, STONY PLAIN, AB, T7Z 2A8
(780) 963-4010   *SIC* 8211
PARKLANE HOMES   *p* 329
See PARKLANE VENTURES LTD
PARKLANE VENTURES LTD   *p* 329
1055 DUNSMUIR ST SUITE 2000, VANCOUVER, BC, V7X 1L5
(604) 648-1800   *SIC* 6553
PARKS BLUEBERRIES & COUNTRY STORE LTD   *p* 496
14815 LONGWOODS RD, BOTHWELL, ON, N0P 1C0
(519) 692-5373   *SIC* 0191
PARKS STORE   *p* 424
See HAMILTON STORES LIMITED
PARKSIDE COLLEGIATE INSTITUTE *p* 890
See THAMES VALLEY DISTRICT SCHOOL BOARD
PARKSIDE FORD LINCOLN LTD   *p* 370
2000 MAIN ST, WINNIPEG, MB, R2V 2B8
(204) 339-2000   *SIC* 5511
PARKSIDE HOME BUILDING CENTRE   *p* 361
See 3490051 MANITOBA LTD
PARKSVILLE CHRYSLER   *p* 243
230 SHELLY RD, PARKSVILLE, BC, V9P 1V6
(250) 248-3281   *SIC* 5511
PARKVIEW BMW   *p* 778
See 1971041 ONTARIO LTD
PARKVIEW HEALTH CARE PARTNERSHIP *p* 613
545 KING ST W SUITE 412, HAMILTON, ON, L8P 1C1
(905) 525-5903   *SIC* 8051
PARKVIEW NURSING CENTRE   *p* 613
See PARKVIEW HEALTH CARE PARTNERSHIP
PARKVIEW PLACE-CENTRAL PARK LODGES   *p* 375
See REVERA INC
PARKVIEW TRANSIT INC   *p* 619
5 SMALL CRES, HAWKESTONE, ON, L0L 1T0
(705) 327-7100   *SIC* 4151
PARKWAY AUTOMOTIVE SALES LIMITED *p* 787
1681 EGLINTON AVE E, NORTH YORK, ON, M4A 1J6
SIC 7515
PARKWAY FORD SALES (1996) LTD *p* 1007
455 KING ST N, WATERLOO, ON, N2J 2Z5
(519) 884-5110   *SIC* 5511
PARKWAY HONDA   *p* 787
See 2585693 ONTARIO INC
PARKWAY HOTELS AND CONVENTION CENTRE INC   *p* 853
600 HIGHWAY 7 E, RICHMOND HILL, ON, L4B 1B2
(905) 881-2121   *SIC* 7011
PARKWAY LEASING   *p* 787
See PARKWAY AUTOMOTIVE SALES LIMITED
PARKWAY MOTORS   *p* 608
See RED HILL TOYOTA
PARKWAY PLYMOUTH CHRYSLER LTD *p* 725
2260 BATTLEFORD RD, MISSISSAUGA,

ON, L5N 3K6
(905) 567-1700   *SIC* 5511
PARKWAY VEHICLE LEASING   *p* 1007
See PARKWAY FORD SALES (1996) LTD
PARKWEST PROJECTS LTD   *p* 357
1077 OXFORD ST W, SPRINGFIELD, MB, R2C 2Z2
(204) 654-9314   *SIC* 1542
PARKWOOD CONSTRUCTION LTD   *p* 199
1404 ROSS AVE, COQUITLAM, BC, V3J 2K1
(604) 936-2792   *SIC* 1542
PARKWOOD MENNONITE HOME   *p* 1007
See PARKWOOD MENNONITE HOME INC
PARKWOOD MENNONITE HOME INC   *p* 1007
726 NEW HAMPSHIRE ST, WATERLOO, ON, N2K 4M1
(519) 885-4810   *SIC* 8051
PARLEE MCLAWS LLP   *p* 56
421 7 AVE SW UNIT 3300, CALGARY, AB, T2P 4K9
(403) 294-7000   *SIC* 8111
PARLEE MCLAWS LLP   *p* 90
10175 101 ST NW, EDMONTON, AB, T5J 0H3
(780) 423-8500   *SIC* 8111
PARLIAMENT, ART FOODS LIMITED *p* 592
54 FRANKFORD RD, FOXBORO, ON, K0K 2B0
(613) 968-5721   *SIC* 5411
PARLIAMENTARY CENTRE   *p* 824
255 ALBERT ST SUITE 802, OTTAWA, ON, K1P 6A9
(613) 237-0143   *SIC* 8699
PARM'S PRESCRIPTIONS LTD   *p* 277
12080 NORDEL WAY SUITE 101, SURREY, BC, V3W 1P6
(604) 543-8155   *SIC* 5912
PARMALAT CANADA INC   *p* 357
9 PROVINCIAL RD SUITE 240, ST CLAUDE, MB, R0G 1Z0
(204) 379-2571   *SIC* 2026
PARMALAT CANADA INC   *p* 366
330 MAZENOD RD, WINNIPEG, MB, R2J 4L7
(204) 654-6455   *SIC* 2026
PARMALAT CANADA INC   *p* 505
16 SHAFTSBURY LANE, BRAMPTON, ON, L6T 4G7
(905) 791-6100   *SIC* 2026
PARMALAT CANADA INC   *p* 579
405 THE WEST MALL 10TH FL, ETOBICOKE, ON, M9C 5J1
(416) 626-1973   *SIC* 2023
PARMALAT CANADA INC   *p* 579
405 THE WEST MALL, ETOBICOKE, ON, M9C 5J1
(416) 626-1973   *SIC* 2023
PARMALAT CANADA INC   *p* 1016
490 GORDON ST, WINCHESTER, ON, K0C 2K0
(613) 774-2310   *SIC* 2022
PARMALAT CANADA INC   *p* 1149
2350 RUE SAINT-CESAIRE, MARIEVILLE, QC, J3M 1E1
SIC 2022
PARMALAT CANADA INC   *p* 1222
7470 RUE SAINT-JACQUES, MONTREAL, QC, H4B 1W4
(514) 484-8401   *SIC* 2026
PARMALAT CANADA INC   *p* 1222
1900 AV WESTMORE, MONTREAL, QC, H4B 1Z3
(514) 369-3534   *SIC* 5143
PARMALAT CANADA INC   *p* 1399
75 BOUL PIERRE-ROUX E, VICTORIAVILLE, QC, G6T 1S8
(819) 758-6245   *SIC* 2023
PARMALAT DAIRY & BAKERY   *p* 1222
See PARMALAT CANADA INC
PARMALAT DAIRY & BAKERY INC   *p* 579
405 THE WEST MALL 10TH FL, ETOBICOKE, ON, M9C 5J1

SIC 2026
PARMALAT FOOD INC   *p* 996
405 THE WEST MALL 10TH FLOOR, TORONTO, ON, M9C 5J1
SIC 2023
PARMALAT HOLDINGS LIMITED   *p* 579
405 THE WEST MALL 10TH FLOOR, ETOBICOKE, ON, M9C 5J1
(416) 626-1973   *SIC* 2026
PARMED ACADEMY   *p* 927
See ALL HEALTH SERVICES INC
PARMX CHEESE CO. LTD   *p* 31
4117 16A ST SE, CALGARY, AB, T2G 3T7
(403) 237-0707   *SIC* 5143
PARNALL MAILING CORP   *p* 649
555 ADMIRAL DR SUITE 6, LONDON, ON, N5V 4L6
(519) 452-3000   *SIC* 5963
PAROUSIA INVESTMETS LTD   *p* 628
3152 DONALD B MUNRO DR, KINBURN, ON, K0A 2H0
(613) 254-6599   *SIC* 6282
PARQUET DE LUXE LASALLE INC *p* 1132
8801 RUE ELMSLIE, LASALLE, QC, H8R 1V4
(514) 364-9760   *SIC* 5031
PARQUET DELUXE LASALLE   *p* 1132
See PARQUET DE LUXE LASALLE INC
PARR METAL FABRICATORS LTD   *p* 371
717 JARVIS AVE, WINNIPEG, MB, R2W 3B4
(204) 586-8121   *SIC* 5085
PARRISH & HEIMBECKER, LIMITED *p* 375
201 PORTAGE AVE SUITE 1400, WINNIPEG, MB, R3B 3K6
(204) 956-2030   *SIC* 5153
PARROT LABEL, DIV OF   *p* 254
See GREAT LITTLE BOX COMPANY LTD, THE
PARRY AUTOMOTIVE LIMITED   *p* 809
84 DUNEDIN ST, ORILLIA, ON, L3V 5T6
(705) 325-1345   *SIC* 5013
PARRY SOUND DISTRICT SOCIAL SERVICES ADMINISTRATION BOARD, THE *p* 837
1 BEECHWOOD DR, PARRY SOUND, ON, P2A 1J2
(705) 746-7777   *SIC* 8399
PARSEC INTERMODAL OF CANADA LIMITED   *p* 557
751 BOWES RD SUITE 2, CONCORD, ON, L4K 5C9
(905) 669-7901   *SIC* 1629
PARSEC INTERMODAL OF CANADA LIMITED   *p* 642
6830 RUTHERFORD RD, KLEINBURG, ON, L0J 1C0
(888) 333-8111   *SIC* 1629
PARSONS INC   *p* 673
625 COCHRANE DR SUITE 500, MARKHAM, ON, L3R 9R9
(905) 943-0500   *SIC* 8711
PARSONS PRECAST INC   *p* 615
1315 RYMAL RD E, HAMILTON, ON, L8W 3N1
(905) 387-0810   *SIC* 5032
PARSONS TRUCKING LIMITED   *p* 427
1 MAIN ST, SOUTHERN HARBOUR PB, NL, A0B 3H0
(709) 463-8540   *SIC* 4212
PARSONS UNIT STEP   *p* 615
See PARSONS PRECAST INC
PARTAGE VANIER FOOD BANK   *p* 1001
161 MARIER AVE, VANIER, ON, K1L 5R8
(613) 747-2839   *SIC* 8399
PARTAGEC INC   *p* 1255
1299 RUE PAUL-EMILE-GIROUX, QUEBEC, QC, G1C 0K9
(418) 647-1428   *SIC* 7218
PARTENAIRE TOTAL LOGISTIQUES (TLP) AIR EXPRESS   *p* 1094
See LOGISTIQUE KERRY (CANADA) INC

PARTENAIRES EN VOYAGES INC   *p* 1324
100 BOUL ALEXIS-NIHON, STE 110, SAINT-LAURENT, QC, H4M 2N6
SIC 4724
PARTHENON SUPERMARKET   *p* 322
See 0561768 B.C. LTD
PARTICIPATION HOUSE PROJECT (DURHAM REGION), THE   *p* 814
1255 TERWILLEGAR AVE UNIT 9, OSHAWA, ON, L1J 7A4
(905) 579-5267   *SIC* 8399
PARTICIPATION HOUSE SUPPORT SERVICES - LONDON AND AREA   *p* 656
633 COLBORNE ST SUITE 101, LONDON, ON, N6B 2V3
(519) 660-6635   *SIC* 8399
PARTICIPATION HOUSE, MARKHAM *p* 678
See CEREBRAL PALSY PARENT COUNCIL OF TORONTO
PARTITION SYSTEMS   *p* 123
See PSL PARTITION SYSTEMS LTD
PARTNER AG SERVICES LTD   *p* 902
3694 BRUCE RD 10, TARA, ON, N0H 2N0
(519) 934-2343   *SIC* 5083
PARTNER TECHNOLOGIES INCORPORATED   *p* 1416
1155 PARK ST, REGINA, SK, S4N 4Y8
(306) 721-3114   *SIC* 3612
PARTNERS CONSTRUCTION LIMITED   *p* 464
GD, PICTOU, NS, B0K 1H0
(902) 485-4576   *SIC* 7353
PARTNERS IN COMMUNITY NURSING   *p* 1015
1001 BURNS ST E UNIT 2, WHITBY, ON, L1N 6A6
(905) 665-1711   *SIC* 8741
PARTNERS IN CREDIT INC   *p* 905
50 MINTHORN BLVD SUITE 700, THORNHILL, ON, L3T 7X8
(905) 886-0555   *SIC* 7322
PARTNERS INDEMNITY INSURANCE BROKERS LTD   *p* 940
10 ADELAIDE ST E SUITE 400, TORONTO, ON, M5C 1J3
(416) 366-5243   *SIC* 6411
PARTNERS INDUSTRIAL CRANE RENTAL *p* 464
See PARTNERS CONSTRUCTION LIMITED
PARTNERS REAL ESTATE INVESTMENT TRUST   *p* 488
249 SAUNDERS RD UNIT 3, BARRIE, ON, L4N 9A3
(705) 725-6020   *SIC* 6798
PARTNERS VALUE INVESTMENTS LP *p* 965
181 BAY ST SUITE 210, TORONTO, ON, M5J 2T3
(647) 503-6513   *SIC* 6719
PARTNERS YOUR SECRETARIAL SOLUTIONS   *p* 270
14680 110 AVE, SURREY, BC, V3R 2A8
(604) 588-9926   *SIC* 7338
PARTROSE DRUGS LIMITED   *p* 579
666 BURNHAMTHORPE RD, ETOBICOKE, ON, M9C 2Z4
(416) 621-2330   *SIC* 5912
PARTS CANADA DEVELOPMENT CO. *p* 24
2916 21 ST NE, CALGARY, AB, T2E 6Z2
(403) 250-6611   *SIC* 5013
PARTS DEPARTMENT   *p* 632
See KINGSTON DODGE JEEP EAGLE LTD
PARTS DISTRIBUTION CENTRE   *p* 1250
See GENERAL MOTORS OF CANADA COMPANY
PARTS FOR TRUCKS SERVICE CENTRE *p* 447
See PARTS FOR TRUCKS, INC
PARTS FOR TRUCKS, INC   *p* 447

15 MACDONALD AVE, DARTMOUTH, NS, B3B 1C6
(902) 468-6100   SIC 5013

PARTS ON THE HART   p 249
See YRB MANAGEMENT CORP

PARTSMAN INC, THE   p 814
278 PARK RD S, OSHAWA, ON, L1J 4H5
(905) 436-3227   SIC 5531

PARTSMAN, THE   p 814
See PARTSMAN INC, THE

PARTSOURCE   p 924
See CANADIAN TIRE CORPORATION, LIMITED

PARTY CITY CANADA INC   p 784
1225 FINCH AVE W, NORTH YORK, ON, M3J 2E8
(416) 631-8455   SIC 5947

PARTY TIME RENTS, DIV OF   p 1220
See LOCATION BENCH & TABLE INC

PARTYLITE GIFTS, LTD   p 853
55 EAST BEAVER CREEK RD UNIT A, RICHMOND HILL, ON, L4B 1E8
(905) 881-6161   SIC 5199

PAS HEALTH COMPLEX INC, THE   p 360
67 1ST ST W, THE PAS, MB, R9A 1K4
(204) 623-6431   SIC 8062

PAS IGA 1979 FOOD PRODUCTS LTD, THE   p 354
HWY 10 N, OPASKWAYAK, MB, R0B 2J0
SIC 5411

PAS IGA, THE   p 354
See PAS IGA 1979 FOOD PRODUCTS LTD, THE

PASCAL CHEVROLET LTEE   p 1253
80 BOUL DU PORTAGE-DES-MOUSSES, PORT-CARTIER, QC, G5B 1E1
(418) 766-4343   SIC 5511

PASCAN   p 1307
See 9736140 CANADA INC

PASKWAYAK BUSINESS DEVELOMENT CORPORATION LTD   p 354
HWY 10 N, OPASKWAYAK, MB, R0B 2J0
(204) 627-7200   SIC 8732

PASLEY, MAX ENTERPRISES LIMITED   p 9
1920 68 ST, CALGARY, AB, T1Y 6Y7
(403) 280-6388   SIC 5812

PASLEY, MAX ENTERPRISES LIMITED   p 40
6820 4 ST NW, CALGARY, AB, T2K 1C2
(403) 295-1004   SIC 5812

PASLEY, MAX ENTERPRISES LIMITED   p 75
100 STEWART GREEN SW UNIT 100, CALGARY, AB, T3H 3C8
(403) 246-1577   SIC 5812

PASLEY, MAX ENTERPRISES LIMITED   p 76
5219 FALSBRIDGE DR NE, CALGARY, AB, T3J 3C1
(403) 293-4052   SIC 5812

PASLEY, MAX ENTERPRISES LIMITED   p 142
217 3 AVE S, LETHBRIDGE, AB, T1J 4L6
(403) 328-8844   SIC 5812

PASLEY, MAX ENTERPRISES LIMITED   p 154
7149 50 AVE, RED DEER, AB, T4N 4E4
(403) 342-2226   SIC 5812

PASLODE CANADA DIV OF   p 678
See ITW CANADA INVESTMENTS LIMITED PARTNERSHIP

PASLOSKI, DARRELL PHARMACY LTD   p 1440
303 OGILVIE ST SUITE 2, WHITEHORSE, YT, Y1A 2S3
(867) 667-6633   SIC 5912

PASON SYSTEMS CORP   p 36
6130 3 ST SE, CALGARY, AB, T2H 1K4
(403) 301-3400   SIC 3699

PASON SYSTEMS INC   p 37
6130 3 ST SE, CALGARY, AB, T2H 1K4
(403) 301-3400   SIC 1389

PASQUIER   p 1315
See SOCIETE EN COMMANDITE

PASQUIER
PASSEPORTAYLOR   p 1322
See MAGASINS J.L. TAYLOR INC, LES

PASSION CUISINE ET GOURMET   p 1393
2020 BOUL RENE-GAULTIER BUREAU 36, VARENNES, QC, J3X 1N9
(450) 929-2942   SIC 5719

PASTA KITCHEN LP   p 557
350 CREDITSTONE RD UNIT 103, CONCORD, ON, L4K 3Z2
(905) 760-0000   SIC 2098

PASTENE ENTERPRISES ULC   p 1050
9101 RUE DE L'INNOVATION, ANJOU, QC, H1J 2X9
(514) 353-7997   SIC 5141

PASTRY SELECTIONS   p 1253
See SELECTION DU PATISSIER INC

PASTWAY PLANING LIMITED   p 547
2916 ROCKINGHAM RD, COMBERMERE, ON, K0J 1L0
(613) 756-2742   SIC 2421

PASUTTO'S HOTELS (1984) LTD   p 69
400 MIDPARK WAY SE, CALGARY, AB, T2X 3S4
(403) 514-0099   SIC 7011

PASWORD COMMUNICATIONS INC   p 612
122 HUGHSON ST S, HAMILTON, ON, L8N 2B2
(905) 974-1683   SIC 7389

PASWORD GROUP INC, THE   p 612
122 HUGHSON ST S, HAMILTON, ON, L8N 2B2
(905) 645-1162   SIC 7389

PAT & MARIO'S RESTAURANT   p 587
See RICMAR ENTERPRISES LTD

PAT & MARIO'S RESTAURANT   p 898
See LYNSOS INC

PAT POLLOCK FARM   p 493
10972 TALBOT TRAIL, BLENHEIM, ON, N0P 1A0
(519) 380-5940   SIC 0132

PAT'S AUTO BUMPER TO BUMPER   p 131
See 4475470 CANADA INC

PAT'S DRIVE LINE SPECIALTY & MACHINE EDMONTON LTD   p 96
14715 116 AVE NW, EDMONTON, AB, T5M 3E8
(780) 453-5105   SIC 3714

PAT'S DRIVELINE, DIV OF   p 96
See GIBSON, R. W. CONSULTING SERVICES LTD

PAT'S NAME CHANGE   p 730
See CANADIAN TEST CASE 27 LTD

PATATES DINO INC   p 1109
71 RUE FOCH, GRANBY, QC, J2G 6B4
(450) 372-3373   SIC 5148

PATATES DOLBEC INC   p 1353
295 363 RTE S, SAINT-UBALDE, QC, G0A 4L0
(418) 277-2442   SIC 5148

PATEL, SAMIR PHARMACY LTD   p 905
298 JOHN ST, THORNHILL, ON, L3T 6M8
(905) 886-3711   SIC 5912

PATENE BUILDING SUPPLIES LTD   p 606
641 SPEEDVALE AVE W, GUELPH, ON, N1K 1E6
(519) 824-4030   SIC 5039

PATENT CONSTRUCTION SYSTEMS CANADA   p 109
See HARSCO CANADA CORPORATION

PATENT PENDING IDEAS   p 343
1200 ALPHA LAKE RD SUITE 205C, WHISTLER, BC, V0N 1B1
(604) 905-6485   SIC 7336

PATERSON GLOBALFOODS INC   p 379
333 MAIN ST 22ND FL, WINNIPEG, MB, R3C 4E2
(204) 956-2090   SIC 5153

PATERSON GRAIN   p 379
See PATERSON GLOBALFOODS INC

PATES A TOUT INC   p 1273
2500 CH DES QUATRE-BOURGEOIS, QUEBEC, QC, G1V 4P9
(418) 651-8284   SIC 2098

PATHEON INC   p 524
977 CENTURY DR, BURLINGTON, ON, L7L 5J8
(905) 639-5254   SIC 2834

PATHEON INC   p 725
2100 SYNTEX CRT, MISSISSAUGA, ON, L5N 7K9
(905) 821-4001   SIC 2834

PATHEON INC   p 1015
111 CONSUMERS DR, WHITBY, ON, L1N 5Z5
(905) 668-3368   SIC 2834

PATHER PLASTICS CANADA INC   p 673
7400 VICTORIA PARK AVE SUITE 1, MARKHAM, ON, L3R 2V4
(905) 475-6549   SIC 2542

PATHER PLASTICS INTERNATIONALp 673
See PATHER PLASTICS CANADA INC

PATHFACTORY INC   p 977
174 SPADINA AVE SUITE 600, TORONTO, ON, M5T 2C2
(416) 304-9400   SIC 7372

PATHWAY DESIGN & MANUFACTURING INC   p 193
7400 MACPHERSON AVE SUITE 111, BURNABY, BC, V5J 5B6
(604) 603-1053   SIC 3089

PATHWAY HYUNDAI   p 810
1375 YOUVILLE DR, ORLEANS, ON, K1C 4R1
(613) 837-4222   SIC 5521

PATHWAYS HEALTH CENTRE FOR CHILDREN   p 858
1240 MURPHY RD, SARNIA, ON, N7S 2Y6
(519) 542-3471   SIC 8322

PATHWAYS TO EDUCATION CANADA   p 947
439 UNIVERSITY AVE SUITE 1600, TORONTO, ON, M5G 1Y8
(416) 646-0123   SIC 8211

PATHWAYS TO INDEPENDENCE   p 491
289 PINNACLE ST, BELLEVILLE, ON, K8N 3B3
(613) 962-2541   SIC 8399

PATIENT HOME MONITORING   p 322
See PROTECH HOME MEDICAL CORP

PATIENT NEWS PUBLISHING LTD   p 607
5152 COUNTY RD 121, HALIBURTON, ON, K0M 1S0
(705) 457-4030   SIC 2741

PATIO DRUMMOND LTEE   p 1096
8435 BOUL SAINT-JOSEPH, DRUMMONDVILLE, QC, J2A 3W8
(819) 394-2505   SIC 3272

PATISSERIE BRUXELLOISE   p 1393
See 2871149 CANADA INC

PATISSERIE CHEVALIER INC   p 1368
155 RUE DU PARC-INDUSTRIEL, SHAWINIGAN, QC, G9N 6T5
(819) 537-8807   SIC 2051

PATISSERIE GAUDET INC   p 1044
1048 RUE MACDONALD, ACTON VALE, QC, J0H 1A0
(450) 546-3221   SIC 2051

PATISSERIE L'ARC-EN-CIEL   p 1349
See BONNES GATERIES 2007 INC

PATISSERIE MONACO   p 1029
See 2443499 ONTARIO INC

PATISSERIE ST-MARTIN (2005)   p 1084
See 9154-4742 QUEBEC INC

PATISSIERE, LA   p 1232
See ENTREPRISES LA CHARCUTERIE LAVAL INC

PATLON AIRCRAFT & INDUSTRIES LIMITED   p 594
8130 FIFTH LINE, GEORGETOWN, ON, L7G 0B8
(905) 864-8706   SIC 5088

PATMAN LTD   p 347
927 DOUGLAS ST, BRANDON, MB, R7A 7B3
(204) 728-1188   SIC 8721

PATRICE INDEPENDENT GROCER INC   p 477
401 OTTAWA ST, ALMONTE, ON, K0A 1A0
(613) 256-2080   SIC 5411

PATRICK MORIN   p 1350
See GROUPE PATRICK MORIN INC

PATRICK MORIN INC   p 1247
See GROUPE PATRICK MORIN INC

PATRICK MORIN INC   p 1282
See GROUPE PATRICK MORIN INC

PATRICK MORIN INC   p 1361
See GROUPE PATRICK MORIN INC

PATRICK MORIN INC   p 1376
See GROUPE PATRICK MORIN INC

PATRICK MORIN SUPER CENTRE   p 1114
See 3100-6588 QUEBEC INC

PATRICK PLASTICS   p 558
See SEASON TECHNOLOGY INC

PATRICK PLASTICS INC   p 673
1495 DENISON ST, MARKHAM, ON, L3R 5H1
(905) 660-9066   SIC 3829

PATRIK'S WATER HAULING LTD   p 149
504 19 AVE, NISKU, AB, T9E 7W1
(780) 955-8878   SIC 4212

PATRIMOINE HOLLIS   p 956
See SCOTIA CAPITAL INC

PATRIOT FORGE CO.   p 516
280 HENRY ST, BRANTFORD, ON, N3S 7R5
(519) 758-8100   SIC 3499

PATRIOT FORGE OF PARIS INC   p 837
100 CONSOLIDATED DR, PARIS, ON, N3L 3T6
(519) 720-1033   SIC 3499

PATRO DE LEVIS INC, LE   p 1137
6150 RUE SAINT-GEORGES, LEVIS, QC, G6V 4J8
(418) 833-4477   SIC 8322

PATRO LE PREVOST INC   p 1181
7355 AV CHRISTOPHE-COLOMB, MONTREAL, QC, H2R 2S5
(514) 273-8535   SIC 8322

PATROLMAN SECURITY SERVICES INC   p 587
680 REXDALE BLVD SUITE 205, ETOBICOKE, ON, M9W 0B5
(416) 748-3202   SIC 7381

PATTERSON DENTAIRE CANADA INC   p 1217
1205 BOUL HENRI-BOURASSA O, MONTREAL, QC, H3M 3E6
(514) 745-4040   SIC 5047

PATTERSON GRAIN LIMITED   p 888
23364 WELLBURN RD SUITE 3, ST MARYS, ON, N4X 1C6
(519) 461-1829   SIC 5153

PATTERSON-UTI DRILLING CO. CANADAp 56
734 7 AVE SW SUITE 720, CALGARY, AB, T2P 3P8
(403) 269-2858   SIC 1381

PATTISON AGRICULTURE LIMITED   p 1436
2777 NORTH SERVICE RD W, SWIFT CURRENT, SK, S9H 5M1
(306) 773-9351   SIC 5999

PATTISON AGRICULTURE LIMITED   p 1438
580 YORK RD W HWY 16, YORKTON, SK, S3N 2V7
(306) 783-9459   SIC 5083

PATTISON OUTDOOR ADVERTISING LIMITED PARTNERSHIP   p 699
2700 MATHESON BLVD E SUITE 500, MISSISSAUGA, ON, L4W 4V9
(905) 282-6800   SIC 7312

PATTISON SIGN GROUP DIV OF   p 308
See PATTISON, JIM INDUSTRIES LTD

PATTISON SIGN GROUP, DIV OF   p 872
See PATTISON, JIM INDUSTRIES LTD

PATTISON, JIM BROADCAST GROUP LTD   p 158
10 BOUNDARY RD SE, REDCLIFF, AB, T0J 2P0

(403) 548-8282   *SIC 4832*

PATTISON, JIM BROADCAST GROUP LTD
p 217
460 PEMBERTON TER, KAMLOOPS, BC,
V2C 1T5
(250) 372-3322   *SIC 4832*

PATTISON, JIM ENTERTAINMENT LTD   *p*
308
1067 CORDOVA ST W SUITE 1800, VAN-
COUVER, BC, V6C 1C7
(604) 688-6764   *SIC 8412*

PATTISON, JIM GROUP INC   *p* 308
1067 CORDOVA ST W SUITE 1800, VAN-
COUVER, BC, V6C 1C7
(604) 688-6764   *SIC 5511*

PATTISON, JIM INDUSTRIES LTD   *p* 308
1067 CORDOVA ST W SUITE 1800, VAN-
COUVER, BC, V6C 1C7
(604) 688-6764   *SIC 5511*

PATTISON, JIM INDUSTRIES LTD   *p* 872
555 ELLESMERE RD, SCARBOROUGH,
ON, M1R 4E8
(416) 759-1111   *SIC 3993*

PATUREL INTERNATIONAL COMPANY   *p*
410
349 NORTHERN HARBOUR RD, NORTH-
ERN HARBOUR, NB, E5V 1G6
(506) 747-1888   *SIC 2092*

PAUKTUUTIT INUIT WOMEN OF CANADA*p*
821
1 NICHOLAS ST SUITE 520, OTTAWA, ON,
K1N 7B7
(613) 238-3977   *SIC 8699*

PAUL GOLDMAN DRUGS LTD   *p* 936
220 YONGE ST SUITE 824, TORONTO,
ON, M5B 2H1
(416) 979-9373   *SIC 5912*

PAUL GRAND'MAISON INC   *p* 1321
200 BOUL LACHAPELLE, SAINT-JEROME,
QC, J7Z 7L2
(450) 438-1266   *SIC 5983*

PAUL LAKE HUSKY MARKET   *p* 216
See NICOLANI SERVICES LTD

PAUL'S HAULING LTD   *p* 347
1515 RICHMOND AVE E, BRANDON, MB,
R7A 7A3
(204) 728-5785   *SIC 4213*

PAUL'S HAULING LTD   *p* 369
250 OAK POINT HWY, WINNIPEG, MB,
R2R 1V1
(204) 633-4330   *SIC 4213*

PAUL'S MARINE   *p* 470
See D'ENTREMONT, PAUL MARINE LTD

PAUL'S RESTAURANTS LTD   *p* 335
680 MONTREAL ST, VICTORIA, BC, V8V
1Z8
(250) 412-3194   *SIC 7011*

PAUL'S RESTORATIONS INC   *p* 615
1640 UPPER OTTAWA ST, HAMILTON, ON,
L8W 3P2
(905) 388-7285   *SIC 1521*

PAULDONLAM INVESTMENTS INC   *p* 865
2240 MARKHAM RD, SCARBOROUGH,
ON, M1B 2W4
(416) 754-4555   *SIC 5511*

PAULTOM MOTORS LIMITED   *p* 641
3800 KING ST E, KITCHENER, ON, N2P
2G5
(519) 744-4119   *SIC 5511*

PAVACO PLASTICS INC   *p* 606
659 SPEEDVALE AVE W, GUELPH, ON,
N1K 1E6
(519) 823-1383   *SIC 3714*

PAVAGE BOISVERT INC   *p* 1300
180 BOUL DE LA GABELLE, SAINT-
ETIENNE-DES-GRES, QC, G0X 2P0
(819) 374-8277   *SIC 2951*

PAVAGE C.S.F. INC   *p* 1050
11101 RUE MIRABEAU, ANJOU, QC, H1J
2S2
(514) 352-7430   *SIC 1611*

PAVAGE DE LA VALLEE   *p* 1150
See PAVAGES DES MONTS INC, LES

PAVAGE DION INC   *p* 1060

20855 CH DE LA COTE N, BOISBRIAND,
QC, J7E 4H5
(450) 435-0333   *SIC 1794*

PAVAGE ROUTEK, DIV OF   *p* 1348
*See CONSTRUCTION ET PAVAGE PORT-
NEUF INC*

PAVAGE SARTIGAN LTEE   *p* 1305
2125 98E RUE, SAINT-GEORGES, QC,
G5Y 8J5
(418) 228-3875   *SIC 1611*

PAVAGES ABENAKIS LTEE   *p* 1305
11380 79E AV, SAINT-GEORGES, QC, G5Y
5B9
(418) 228-8116   *SIC 1611*

PAVAGES D'AMOUR 2000   *p* 1094
See PAVAGES D'AMOUR INC

PAVAGES D'AMOUR INC   *p* 1094
1635 CROIS NEWMAN, DORVAL, QC, H9P
2R6
(514) 631-4570   *SIC 1611*

PAVAGES DES MONTS INC, LES   *p* 1150
2245 RUE DU PHARE O, MATANE, QC,
G4W 3N1
(418) 562-4343   *SIC 3273*

PAVAGES DORVAL, LES   *p* 1058
See CONSTRUCTION BAU-VAL INC

PAVAGES MASKA INC   *p* 1313
3450 BOUL CHOQUETTE, SAINT-
HYACINTHE, QC, J2S 8V9
(450) 773-2591   *SIC 1611*

PAVILION FINANCIAL CORPORATION   *p*
388
1001 CORYDON AVE SUITE 300, WIN-
NIPEG, MB, R3M 0B6
(204) 954-5103   *SIC 8741*

PAVILION, THE   *p* 863
See J.J.'S HOSPITALITY LIMITED

PAVILLION BOURGEOIS   *p* 1386
*See CENTRE JEUNESSE DE LA
MAURICIE ET DU CENTRE-DU-QUEBEC,
LE*

PAVILLON ALEXANDRE TACHE   *p* 1108
See UNIVERSITE DU QUEBEC

PAVILLON BOIS-JOLI   *p* 1390
*See CENTRE DE SANTE ET DE SER-
VICES SOCIAUX DE LA VALLEE-DE-L'OR*

PAVILLON DENTAIRE   *p* 1166
See DENTAL WINGS INC

PAVILLON J HENRI-CHARBONNEAU   *p*
1167
*See CENTRE DE SANTE ET DE SER-
VICES SOCIAUX LUCILLE-TEASDALE*

PAVILLON LE CLASSIQUE   *p* 1144
*See COLLEGE CHARLES-LEMOYNE DE
LONGUEUIL INC*

PAVILLON MITCHELL   *p* 1370
*See COMMISSION SCOLAIRE DE LA
REGION-DE-SHERBROOKE*

PAVILLON SAINT-DOMINIQUE   *p* 1271
1045 BOUL RENE-LEVESQUE O, QUE-
BEC, QC, G1S 1V3
(418) 681-3561   *SIC 8322*

PAVILLONS LASALLE, LES   *p* 1131
See 4489161 CANADA INC

PAVING BUILDING ROADS   *p* 468
*See DEXTER CONSTRUCTION COMPANY
LIMITED*

PAWS CRESTON   *p* 204
*See CRESTON PET ADOPTION & WEL-
FARE SOCIETY*

PAX CONSTRUCTION LTD   *p* 186
4452 JUNEAU ST, BURNABY, BC, V5C 4C8
(604) 291-8885   *SIC 1542*

PAY A DOLLAR STORE   *p* 443
See NIMA VANI ENTERPRISES LIMITED

PAYLESS SHOESOURCE CANADA INC   *p*
579
191 THE WEST MALL SUITE 1100, ETOBI-
COKE, ON, M9C 5K8
(416) 626-3666   *SIC 5661*

PAYLESS SHOESOURCE GP INC   *p* 971
4000-199 ST BAY, COMMERCE COURT W,
TORONTO, ON, M5L 1A9
SIC 5661

PAYLESS SHOESOURCE LP   *p* 971
4000-199 ST BAY, TORONTO, ON, M5L 1A9
SIC 5661

PAYMENTECH CANADA DEBIT, INC   *p* 868
888 BIRCHMOUNT RD SUITE 7, SCAR-
BOROUGH, ON, M1K 5L1
(416) 288-3027   *SIC 6211*

PAYMENTS CANADA   *p* 824
*See CANADIAN PAYMENTS ASSOCIA-
TION*

PAYNE MACHINE COMPANY LTD   *p* 646
46 MOUNT HOPE ST, LINDSAY, ON, K9V
5G4
(705) 324-8990   *SIC 5088*

PAYNE TRANSPORTATION LTD   *p* 369
435 LUCAS AVE, WINNIPEG, MB, R2R 2S9
(204) 953-1400   *SIC 6712*

PAYNES MARINE   *p* 334
See 260304 BC LTD

PAYPROP CANADA LIMITED   *p* 956
357 BAY ST UNIT 500, TORONTO, ON,
M5H 2T7
(416) 735-7600   *SIC 7371*

PAYS DE LA SAGOUINE INC, LE   *p* 395
57 RUE ACADIE, BOUCTOUCHE, NB, E4S
2T7
(506) 743-1400   *SIC 7999*

PAYSAFE GROUP   *p* 24
See NT SERVICES LIMITED

PAYSAGES LAGAN   *p* 1238
See G.C.L. EQUIPEMENTS INC

PAYSANNE FRUITS & LEGUMES, LA   *p*
1169
See 9058-7239 QUEBEC INC

PAYSTATION INC   *p* 741
6345 DIXIE RD UNIT 4, MISSISSAUGA,
ON, L5T 2E6
(905) 364-0700   *SIC 5044*

PAYTECH LTD   *p* 777
1500 DON MILLS RD SUITE 400, NORTH
YORK, ON, M3B 3K4
(888) 263-1938   *SIC 3578*

PAYTM   *p* 956
See PAYTM LABS INC

PAYTM LABS INC   *p* 956
220 ADELAIDE ST W, TORONTO, ON, M5H
1W7
(647) 360-8331   *SIC 7372*

PAYWORKS INC   *p* 391
1565 WILLSON PL, WINNIPEG, MB, R3T
4H1
(204) 779-0537   *SIC 8721*

PAYZANT BUILDING PRODUCTS LIMITED
p 461
250 SACKVILLE DR, LOWER SACKVILLE,
NS, B4C 2R4
(902) 864-0000   *SIC 5211*

PAYZANT HOME CENTRE   *p* 461
*See PAYZANT BUILDING PRODUCTS LIM-
ITED*

PAZMAC ENTERPRISES LTD   *p* 229
26777 GLOUCESTER WAY, LANGLEY, BC,
V4W 3X6
(604) 857-8838   *SIC 3599*

PBAS   *p* 587
*See PRUDENT BENEFITS ADMINISTRA-
TION SERVICES INC*

PBC HEALTH BENEFITS SOCIETY   *p* 189
4250 CANADA WAY, BURNABY, BC, V5G
4W6
(604) 419-2200   *SIC 6321*

**PBCN P.A. FUEL AND CONVENIENCE LIM-
ITED PARTNERSHIP**   *p*
1414
3451 2ND AVE W, PRINCE ALBERT, SK,
S6V 5G1
(306) 953-1490   *SIC 5541*

PBF PITA BREAD FACTORY LTD   *p* 182
8000 WINSTON ST, BURNABY, BC, V5A
2H5
(604) 528-6111   *SIC 2051*

PBL   *p* 1021
See PBL INSURANCE LIMITED

PBL INSURANCE LIMITED   *p* 1021

150 OUELLETTE PL SUITE 100, WIND-
SOR, ON, N8X 1L9
(519) 254-1633   *SIC 6411*

PBL PROJECTS LP   *p* 393
405 FORT WHYTE WAY UNIT 100, WIN-
NIPEG, MB, R4G 0B1
(204) 633-2515   *SIC 1542*

PBR AUCTIONS   *p* 1435
*See ROY, ROB TRADING & SAMCO HOLD-
INGS*

PC 96 HOLDINGS LTD   *p* 235
2345 ISLAND HWY E, NANOOSE BAY, BC,
V9P 9E2
(250) 468-7441   *SIC 5541*

PC CORP INC   *p* 92
9947 109 ST NW, EDMONTON, AB, T5K
1H6
(780) 428-3000   *SIC 5045*

PC FLOORING   *p* 261
See PRO-CLAIM RESTORATION LTD

PC FORGE   *p* 846
See IMT PARTNERSHIP

PC MEDIC INCORPORATED   *p* 447
50 AKERLEY BLVD SUITE 12, DART-
MOUTH, NS, B3B 1R8
(902) 468-7237   *SIC 5045*

PC OUTLET INC   *p* 853
45A WEST WILMOT ST SUITE 17, RICH-
MOND HILL, ON, L4B 2P2
SIC 5045

PC PARTS NOW INC   *p* 678
5990 14TH AVE, MARKHAM, ON, L3S 4M4
(905) 752-0222   *SIC 5112*

PCAS CANADA INC   *p* 1318
725 RUE TROTTER, SAINT-JEAN-SUR-
RICHELIEU, QC, J3B 8J8
(450) 348-0901   *SIC 2899*

PCC AEROSTRUCTURES DORVAL INC   *p*
1094
123 AV AVRO, DORVAL, QC, H9P 2Y9
(514) 421-0344   *SIC 3728*

**PCC AEROSTRUCTURES GTA WOOD-
BRIDGE**   *p*
1032
See NORANCO INC

PCCA CORP   *p* 649
744 THIRD ST, LONDON, ON, N5V 5J2
(519) 455-0690   *SIC 5122*

PCI GEOMATICS ENTERPRISES INC *p* 673
90 ALLSTATE PKY SUITE 501, MARKHAM,
ON, L3R 6H3
(905) 764-0614   *SIC 7371*

PCL CONSTRUCTION GROUP INC   *p* 115
9915 56 AVE NW SUITE 1, EDMONTON,
AB, T6E 5L7
(780) 733-5000   *SIC 1541*

PCL CONSTRUCTION HOLDINGS LTD   *p*
115
9915 56 AVE NW, EDMONTON, AB, T6E
5L7
(780) 733-5000   *SIC 6159*

PCL CONSTRUCTION MANAGEMENT INC
p 24
2882 11 ST NE, CALGARY, AB, T2E 7S7
(403) 250-4800   *SIC 8741*

PCL CONSTRUCTION MANAGEMENT INC
p 115
5400 99 ST NW, EDMONTON, AB, T6E 3P4
(780) 733-6000   *SIC 8741*

PCL CONSTRUCTION RESOURCES INC *p*
115
5410 99 ST NW, EDMONTON, AB, T6E 3P4
(780) 733-5400   *SIC 6159*

PCL CONSTRUCTORS CANADA INC *p* 750
49 AURIGA DR, NEPEAN, ON, K2E 8A1
(613) 225-6130   *SIC 1542*

PCL CONSTRUCTORS CANADA INC *p* 798
2201 BRISTOL CIR SUITE 500, OAKVILLE,
ON, L6H 0J8
(905) 276-7600   *SIC 1542*

PCL CONSTRUCTORS EASTERN INC   *p*
115
9915 56 AVE NW, EDMONTON, AB, T6E
5L7

SIC 1521
PCL CONSTRUCTORS INC p 116
9915 56 AVE NW SUITE 1, EDMONTON, AB, T6E 5L7
(780) 733-5000   SIC 1541

PCL CONSTRUCTORS NORTHERN INC p 116
9915 56 AVE NW SUITE 1, EDMONTON, AB, T6E 5L7
(780) 733-5000   SIC 1542

PCL CONSTRUCTORS WESTCOAST INC p 256
13911 WIRELESS WAY SUITE 310, RICHMOND, BC, V6V 3B9
(604) 241-5200   SIC 1629

PCL EMPLOYEES HOLDINGS LTD p 116
9915 56 AVE NW, EDMONTON, AB, T6E 5L7
(780) 733-5000   SIC 6712

PCL INDUSTRIAL CONSTRUCTORS INC p 116
9915 56 AVE NW, EDMONTON, AB, T6E 5L7
(780) 733-5500   SIC 1541

PCM CANADA p 98
See ACRODEX INC

PCM FABRICATING p 1265
See QUALTECH INC

PCM POMERY CONSTRUCTION & MAINTENANCE LTD p 184
3060 NORLAND AVE SUITE 109, BURNABY, BC, V5B 3A6
(604) 294-6700   SIC 1521

PCM VENTES CANADA INC p 1207
1100 BOUL ROBERT-BOURASSA, MONTREAL, QC, H3B 3A5
(514) 373-8700   SIC 5734

PCO INNOVATION CANADA INC p 1190
384 RUE SAINT-JACQUES, MONTREAL, QC, H2Y 1S1
(514) 866-3000   SIC 8711

PCS CORY, DIV p 1429
See POTASH CORPORATION OF SASKATCHEWAN INC

PCS LANIGAN, DIV p 1409
See POTASH CORPORATION OF SASKATCHEWAN INC

PCS POTASH ALLAN p 1404
See POTASH CORPORATION OF SASKATCHEWAN INC

PCS POTASH, DIV OF p 1423
See POTASH CORPORATION OF SASKATCHEWAN INC

PCS SALES (CANADA) INC p 1429
122 1ST AVE S SUITE 500, SASKATOON, SK, S7K 7G3
(306) 933-8500   SIC 1474

PCSL p 429
See PUGLISEVICH CREWS & SERVICES LIMITED

PCT p 248
See PACIFIC COAST TERMINALS CO. LTD

PD KANCO LP p 689
5945 AIRPORT RD SUITE 360, MISSISSAUGA, ON, L4V 1R9
(416) 234-8444   SIC 6513

PDADMIN GROUP p 768
See PLANDIRECT INSURANCE SERVICES INC

PDI p 600
See POLYMER DISTRIBUTION INC

PDI p 1118
See PHIPPS DICKSON INTEGRIA (PDI) INC

PDL CALL CENTRES p 11
See SURECALL CONTACT CENTERS LTD

PDL MOBILITY LIMITED p 24
2420 42 AVE NE, CALGARY, AB, T2E 7T6
(403) 291-5400   SIC 5999

PDSCL p 244
See PENTICTON AND DISTRICT SOCIETY FOR COMMUNITY LIVING

PDX COURIER p 299

See PACIFIC DOCUMENT EXCHANGE LTD

PEACE ARCH MOTORS LTD p 283
3174 KING GEORGE BLVD, SURREY, BC, V4P 1A2
(604) 531-2916   SIC 5511

PEACE ARCH TOYOTA p 283
See PEACE ARCH MOTORS LTD

PEACE BRIDGE AUTHORITY p 591
See BUFFALO AND FORT ERIE PUBLIC BRIDGE COMPANY

PEACE BRIDGE DUTY FREE INC p 592
1 PEACE BRIDGE PLAZA, FORT ERIE, ON, L2A 5N1
(905) 871-5400   SIC 5399

PEACE COUNTRY CO-OP LIMITED p 152
9714 96 AVE, PEACE RIVER, AB, T8S 1H8
(780) 624-1096   SIC 5411

PEACE FUEL DISTRIBUTORS p 79
See 1673594 ALBERTA LTD

PEACE FUEL DISTRIBUTORS LTD p 152
7510 99 AVE, PEACE RIVER, AB, T8S 1M5
(780) 624-3003   SIC 5172

PEACE HILLS GENERAL INSURANCE COMPANY p 90
10709 JASPER AVE NW SUITE 300, EDMONTON, AB, T5J 3N3
(780) 424-3986   SIC 6411

PEACE HILLS INSURANCE p 90
See PEACE HILLS GENERAL INSURANCE COMPANY

PEACE HILLS INVESTMENTS LTD p 139
5207 50 AVE, LEDUC, AB, T9E 6V3
(780) 986-2241   SIC 7011

PEACE HILLS INVESTMENTS LTD p 172
4103 56 ST, WETASKIWIN, AB, T9A 1V2
(780) 312-7300   SIC 7011

PEACE HILLS TRUST COMPANY p 90
10011 109 ST NW 10TH FL, EDMONTON, AB, T5J 3S8
(780) 421-1606   SIC 6021

PEACE LIBRARY SYSTEM p 134
8301 110 ST, GRANDE PRAIRIE, AB, T8W 6T2
(780) 538-4656   SIC 5192

PEACE RIVER COAL INC p 315
1055 HASTINGS ST W SUITE 1900, VANCOUVER, BC, V6E 2E9
SIC 1221

PEACE RIVER HYDRO PARTNERS CONSTRUCTION LTD p 214
7007 269 RD, FORT ST. JOHN, BC, V1J 4M7
(250) 263-9920   SIC 1629

PEACE RIVER SCHOOL DIVISION 10 p 152
10018 101 ST SUITE 10, PEACE RIVER, AB, T8S 2A5
(780) 624-3601   SIC 8211

PEACE TRANSPORTATION p 735
7370 BRAMALEA RD SUITE 22, MISSISSAUGA, ON, L5S 1N6
(905) 405-1002   SIC 4731

PEACE VALLEY INDUSTRIES p 196
See PEACE VALLEY INDUSTRIES (2016) LTD

PEACE VALLEY INDUSTRIES (2016) LTD p 196
4311 46TH ST, CHETWYND, BC, V0C 1J0
(250) 788-2922   SIC 7692

PEACE WAPITI SCHOOL DIVISION NO.76 p 133
8611A 108 ST, GRANDE PRAIRIE, AB, T8V 4C5
(780) 532-8133   SIC 8211

PEACHLAND FIRE & RESCUE SERVICE p 243
4401 3RD ST, PEACHLAND, BC, V0H 1X7
(250) 767-2841   SIC 7389

PEACOCK PARADE INC, THE p 991
828 RICHMOND ST W, TORONTO, ON, M6J 1C9
SIC 5961

PEACOCK VANDERHOUT & VANDYK IN-

SURANCE BROKERS LTD p 882
HWY 20 VILLAGE SQUARE MALL, SMITHVILLE, ON, L0R 2A0
(905) 957-2333   SIC 6411

PEAK p 1009
See PEAK REALTY LTD

PEAK ENERGY SERVICES LTD p 56
222 3 AVE SW SUITE 900, CALGARY, AB, T2P 0B4
(403) 543-7325   SIC 1389

PEAK ENGINEERING & CONSTRUCTION LTD p 546
13580 COUNTY ROAD 2, COLBORNE, ON, K0K 1S0
(905) 355-1500   SIC 1629

PEAK INNOVATIONS INC p 263
11782 HAMMERSMITH WAY UNIT 203, RICHMOND, BC, V7A 5E2
(604) 448-8000   SIC 5039

PEAK MECHANICAL LTD p 1429
409 45TH A ST E, SASKATOON, SK, S7K 0W6
(306) 249-4814   SIC 1711

PEAK MECHANICAL PARTNERSHIP p 1429
See PEAK MECHANICAL LTD

PEAK POTENTIALS TRAINING INC p 238
2155 DOLLARTON HWY SUITE 130, NORTH VANCOUVER, BC, V7H 3B2
(604) 083-3344   SIC 8742

PEAK POWER INC p 956
214 KING ST W SUITE 414, TORONTO, ON, M5H 3S6
(647) 226-1834   SIC 4911

PEAK PRODUCTS p 263
See PEAK PRODUCTS MANUFACTURING INC

PEAK PRODUCTS INTERNATIONAL INC p 263
11782 HAMMERSMITH WAY SUITE 203, RICHMOND, BC, V7A 5E2
(604) 448-8000   SIC 6712

PEAK PRODUCTS MANUFACTURING INC p 263
11782 HAMMERSMITH WAY UNIT 203, RICHMOND, BC, V7A 5E2
(604) 448-8000   SIC 5039

PEAK REALTY LTD p 1009
139 NORTHFIELD DR W SUITE 104, WATERLOO, ON, N2L 5A6
(519) 662-4900   SIC 6531

PEAK REALTY LTD p 1009
410 CONESTOGO RD SUITE 210, WATERLOO, ON, N2L 4E2
(519) 747-0231   SIC 6411

PEAK SPORTS MANAGEMENT INC p 772
2996 BAYVIEW AVE, NORTH YORK, ON, M2N 5K9
SIC 7941

PEARL FEVER TEA HOUSE p 200
See CROSS PACIFIC INVESTMENT GROUP INC

PEARL RIVER HOLDINGS LIMITED p 654
383 RICHMOND ST SUITE 502, LONDON, ON, N6A 3C4
(519) 679-1200   SIC 3089

PEARL VILLA HOMES LTD p 94
14315 118 AVE NW SUITE 140, EDMONTON, AB, T5L 4S6
(780) 499-2337   SIC 8059

PEARLE VISION p 724
See LUXOTTICA RETAIL CANADA INC

PEARLON BEAUTY SUPPLIES p 741
See PEARLON PRODUCTS INC

PEARLON PRODUCTS INC p 741
6290 SHAWSON DR, MISSISSAUGA, ON, L5T 1H5
(905) 670-1040   SIC 2844

PEARN, ROY E. ENTERPRISES LIMITED p 810
320 MEMORIAL AVE, ORILLIA, ON, L3V 5X6
(705) 325-9851   SIC 5812

PEARSON CANADA HOLDINGS INC p 756
195 HARRY WALKER PKY N SUITE A, NEWMARKET, ON, L3Y 7B3
(905) 853-7888   SIC 2731

PEARSON CANADA HOLDINGS INC p 780
26 PRINCE ANDREW PL, NORTH YORK, ON, M3C 2H4
(416) 447-5101   SIC 2731

PEARSON CANADA INC p 756
195 HARRY WALKER PKY N SUITE A, NEWMARKET, ON, L3Y 7B3
(905) 853-7888   SIC 2731

PEARSON CANADA INC p 780
26 PRINCE ANDREW PL, NORTH YORK, ON, M3C 2H4
(416) 447-5101   SIC 2731

PEARSON DUNN INSURANCE INC p 893
435 MCNEILLY RD SUITE 103, STONEY CREEK, ON, L8E 5E3
(905) 575-1122   SIC 6411

PEARSON EDUCATION CANADA p 780
See PEARSON CANADA INC

PEARSON EDUCATION CANADA p 780
See PEARSON CANADA HOLDINGS INC

PEARSON INTERNATIONAL FUEL FACILITIES CORPORATION p 689
5915 AIRPORT RD UNIT 110, MISSISSAUGA, ON, L4V 1T1
(905) 677-1020   SIC 5172

PEARSON, GEORGE CENTRE p 324
See VANCOUVER COASTAL HEALTH AUTHORITY

PEARSON, LESTER B CATHOLIC HIGH SCHOOL p 596
See OTTAWA CATHOLIC DISTRICT SCHOOL BOARD

PEAVEY INDUSTRIES LIMITED p 156
7740 40 AVE, RED DEER, AB, T4P 2H9
(403) 346-8991   SIC 5251

PEAVEY MART p 156
See PEAVEY INDUSTRIES LIMITED

PECB GROUP INC p 1346
6683 RUE JEAN-TALON E BUREAU 336, SAINT-LEONARD, QC, H1S 0A5
(514) 814-2548   SIC 7379

PECHERIES BAS-CARAQUET FISHERIES INC p 394
2270 INDUSTRIELLE ST, BAS-CARAQUET, NB, E1W 5Z2
(506) 727-3632   SIC 2092

PECHERIES DE CHEZ-NOUS, LES p 419
See THAI UNION CANADA INC

PECHERIES F.N. FISHERIES LTD p 418
99 15E RUE, SHIPPAGAN, NB, E8S 1E2
SIC 2092

PECHERIES MARINARD LTEE, LES p 1102
41 RUE DE L'ENTREPOT, GASPE, QC, G4X 5L3
(418) 269-3381   SIC 2092

PECHERIES NORREF QUEBEC INC, LES p 1169
4900 RUE MOLSON, MONTREAL, QC, H1Y 3J8
(514) 593-9999   SIC 5146

PEDDIE ROOFING & WATERPROOFING LTD p 12
3352 46 AVE SE, CALGARY, AB, T2B 3J2
(403) 273-7000   SIC 1761

PEDERSEN CONSTRUCTION INC p 753
11 & 65 HWY W, NEW LISKEARD, ON, P0J 1P0
(705) 647-6223   SIC 1623

PEDERSON FAMILY PHARMACY LTD p 129
8600 FRANKLIN AVE SUITE 501, FORT MCMURRAY, AB, T9H 4G8
(780) 743-1251   SIC 5912

PEDIATRICS DEPARTMENT p 1434
See UNIVERSITY OF SASKATCHEWAN

PEDIGRAIN p 1353
See SYNAGRI S.E.C.

PEDLER, BOB REAL ESTATE LIMITED p 1021
280 EDINBOROUGH ST, WINDSOR, ON.

N8X 3C4
(519) 966-3750   *SIC* 6531
PEDNO   *p 1133*
See SCP 89 INC
PEDRE CONTRACTORS LTD   *p 229*
26620 56 AVE UNIT 101, LANGLEY, BC,
V4W 3X5
(604) 881-2411   *SIC* 1623
PEDS CHAUSSETTES & CIE   *p 1198*
See PEDS LEGWEAR INC
PEDS LEGWEAR INC   *p 1198*
1501 AV MCGILL COLLEGE BUREAU 914,
MONTREAL, QC, H3A 3M8
(514) 875-5575   *SIC* 5136
PEEKABOO BEANS INC   *p 325*
11120 BRIDGEPORT RD UNIT 170, VAN-
COUVER, BC, V6X 1T2
(604) 279-2326   *SIC* 2369
PEEL CAS   *p 721*
*See CHILDREN'S AID SOCIETY OF THE
REGION OF PEEL, THE*
PEEL CHILDREN'S CENTRE   *p 741*
85 AVENTURA CRT UNIT A, MISSIS-
SAUGA, ON, L5T 2Y6
(905) 795-3500   *SIC* 8999
PEEL CHRYSLER PLYMOUTH (1991) INC *p 713*
212 LAKESHORE RD W, MISSISSAUGA,
ON, L5H 1G6
(905) 278-6181   *SIC* 5511
PEEL DISTRICT SCHOOL BOARD   *p 498*
275 FERNFOREST DR, BRAMPTON, ON,
L6R 1L9
(905) 793-6157   *SIC* 8211
PEEL DISTRICT SCHOOL BOARD   *p 499*
10 NORTH PARK DR, BRAMPTON, ON,
L6S 3M1
(905) 456-1906   *SIC* 8211
PEEL DISTRICT SCHOOL BOARD   *p 499*
1370 WILLIAMS PKY, BRAMPTON, ON,
L6S 1V3
(905) 791-2400   *SIC* 8211
PEEL DISTRICT SCHOOL BOARD   *p 499*
1305 WILLIAMS PKY, BRAMPTON, ON,
L6S 3J8
(905) 791-6770   *SIC* 8211
PEEL DISTRICT SCHOOL BOARD   *p 505*
215 ORENDA RD, BRAMPTON, ON, L6T
5L1
(905) 451-2862   *SIC* 8211
PEEL DISTRICT SCHOOL BOARD   *p 505*
5000 MAYFIELD RD RR 4, BRAMPTON,
ON, L6T 3S1
(905) 846-6060   *SIC* 8211
PEEL DISTRICT SCHOOL BOARD   *p 508*
32 KENNEDY RD N, BRAMPTON, ON, L6V
1X4
(905) 451-0432   *SIC* 8211
PEEL DISTRICT SCHOOL BOARD   *p 510*
7935 KENNEDY RD, BRAMPTON, ON, L6W
0A2
(905) 453-9220   *SIC* 8211
PEEL DISTRICT SCHOOL BOARD   *p 512*
251 MCMURCHY AVE S, BRAMPTON, ON,
L6Y 1Z4
(905) 451-2860   *SIC* 8211
PEEL DISTRICT SCHOOL BOARD   *p 512*
296 CONESTOGA DR, BRAMPTON, ON,
L6Z 3M1
(905) 840-2328   *SIC* 8211
PEEL DISTRICT SCHOOL BOARD   *p 513*
10750 CHINGUACOUSY RD, BRAMPTON,
ON, L7A 2Z7
(905) 451-1263   *SIC* 8211
PEEL DISTRICT SCHOOL BOARD   *p 513*
370 BRISDALE DR, BRAMPTON, ON, L7A
3K7
(905) 840-2135   *SIC* 8211
PEEL DISTRICT SCHOOL BOARD   *p 686*
3545 MORNING STAR DR, MISSISSAUGA,

ON, L4T 1Y3
(905) 676-1191   *SIC* 8211
PEEL DISTRICT SCHOOL BOARD   *p 703*
3575 FIELDGATE DR, MISSISSAUGA, ON,
L4X 2J6
(905) 625-7731   *SIC* 8211
PEEL DISTRICT SCHOOL BOARD   *p 712*
1490 OGDEN AVE, MISSISSAUGA, ON,
L5E 2H8
(905) 274-2391   *SIC* 8211
PEEL DISTRICT SCHOOL BOARD   *p 712*
3225 ERINDALE STATION RD, MISSIS-
SAUGA, ON, L5C 1Y5
(905) 279-0575   *SIC* 8211
PEEL DISTRICT SCHOOL BOARD   *p 713*
1305 CAWTHRA RD, MISSISSAUGA, ON,
L5G 4L1
(905) 274-1271   *SIC* 8211
PEEL DISTRICT SCHOOL BOARD   *p 713*
1324 LORNE PARK RD, MISSISSAUGA,
ON, L5H 3B1
(905) 278-6177   *SIC* 8211
PEEL DISTRICT SCHOOL BOARD   *p 714*
2524 BROMSGROVE RD, MISSISSAUGA,
ON, L5J 1L8
(905) 822-6700   *SIC* 8211
PEEL DISTRICT SCHOOL BOARD   *p 715*
2021 DUNDAS ST W, MISSISSAUGA, ON,
L5K 1R2
(905) 828-7206   *SIC* 8211
PEEL DISTRICT SCHOOL BOARD   *p 719*
2665 ERIN CENTRE BLVD, MISSISSAUGA,
ON, L5M 5H6
(905) 858-5910   *SIC* 8211
PEEL DISTRICT SCHOOL BOARD   *p 719*
72 JOYMAR DR, MISSISSAUGA, ON, L5M
1G3
(905) 826-1195   *SIC* 8211
PEEL DISTRICT SCHOOL BOARD   *p 725*
6325 MONTEVIDEO RD, MISSISSAUGA,
ON, L5N 4G7
(905) 858-3087   *SIC* 8211
PEEL DISTRICT SCHOOL BOARD   *p 725*
6700 EDENWOOD DR, MISSISSAUGA,
ON, L5N 3B2
(905) 824-1790   *SIC* 8211
PEEL DISTRICT SCHOOL BOARD   *p 732*
5650 HURONTARIO ST SUITE 106, MIS-
SISSAUGA, ON, L5R 1C6
(905) 890-1099   *SIC* 8211
PEEL DISTRICT SCHOOL BOARD   *p 744*
1150 DREAM CREST RD, MISSISSAUGA,
ON, L5V 1N6
(905) 567-4260   *SIC* 8211
PEEL DISTRICT SCHOOL BOARD   *p 745*
550 COURTNEYPARK DR W, MISSIS-
SAUGA, ON, L5W 1L9
(905) 564-1033   *SIC* 8211
PEEL FIAT   *p 713*
*See PEEL CHRYSLER PLYMOUTH (1991)
INC*
**PEEL HALTON ACQUIRED BRAIN IN-
JURIES SERVICES**   *p
713*
1048 CAWTHRA RD, MISSISSAUGA, ON,
L5G 4K2
(905) 891-8384   *SIC* 8093
PEEL HOUSING CORPORATION   *p 510*
5 WELLINGTON ST E, BRAMPTON, ON,
L6W 1Y1
(905) 453-1300   *SIC* 6531
PEEL LIVING   *p 510*
See PEEL HOUSING CORPORATION
PEEL MUTUAL INSURANCE COMPANY   *p
512*
103 QUEEN ST W, BRAMPTON, ON, L6Y
1M3
(905) 451-2386   *SIC* 6331
PEEL PLASTIC PRODUCTS LIMITED *p 510*
49 RUTHERFORD RD S, BRAMPTON, ON,
L6W 3J3
(905) 456-3660   *SIC* 2673
PEEL TRUCK & TRAILER EQUIPMENT INC
p 699

1715 BRITANNIA RD E, MISSISSAUGA,
ON, L4W 2A3
(905) 670-1780   *SIC* 7539
PEELLE COMPANY LIMITED, THE   *p 513*
195 SANDALWOOD PKY W, BRAMPTON,
ON, L7A 1J6
(905) 846-4545   *SIC* 5031
PEEPERS INTERNATIONAL LTD   *p 611*
360 WENTWORTH ST N, HAMILTON, ON,
L8L 5W3
SIC 5137
PEER GROUP HOLDINGS INC   *p 639*
72 VICTORIA ST S SUITE 400, KITCH-
ENER, ON, N2G 4Y9
(519) 749-9554   *SIC* 6712
PEER GROUP INC, THE   *p 639*
72 VICTORIA ST S SUITE 400, KITCH-
ENER, ON, N2G 4Y9
(519) 749-9554   *SIC* 7372
PEERLESS ENGINEERING SALES LTD *p
186*
4015 1ST AVE, BURNABY, BC, V5C 3W5
(604) 659-4100   *SIC* 5084
PEERLESS FISH COMPANY LIMITED *p 427*
GD, PETTY HARBOUR, NL, A0A 3H0
(709) 747-1521   *SIC* 5146
PEERLESS GARMENTS LTD   *p 375*
515 NOTRE DAME AVE, WINNIPEG, MB,
R3B 1R9
SIC 2325
PEERLESS GROUP   *p 1000*
See PEERLESS SECURITY LTD
PEERLESS LIMITED   *p 244*
575 PAGE AVE, PENTICTON, BC, V2A 6P3
(250) 492-0408   *SIC* 3715
PEERLESS SECURITY INC   *p 621*
21 HIGH ST, HUNTSVILLE, ON, P1H 1N9
(705) 789-6253   *SIC* 5065
PEERLESS SECURITY LTD   *p 1000*
544 GREER RD, UTTERSON, ON, P0B
1M0
(705) 645-4108   *SIC* 1731
PEERLESS, E.B. LTD   *p 265*
6651 ELMBRIDGE WAY SUITE 130, RICH-
MOND, BC, V7C 5C2
(604) 279-9907   *SIC* 5088
PEETERS' MUSHROOM FARM   *p 542*
*See PEETERS, WIET FARM PRODUCTS
LIMITED*
**PEETERS, WIET FARM PRODUCTS LIM-
ITED**   *p
542*
LOT 11 CONC 23, CHARING CROSS, ON,
N0P 1G0
(519) 351-1945   *SIC* 0182
PEFOND INC   *p 1376*
170 BOUL FISET, SOREL-TRACY, QC, J3P
3P4
(450) 742-8295   *SIC* 5461
PEGASUS COMMUNITY PROJECT   *p 917*
931 KINGSTON RD, TORONTO, ON, M4E
1S6
(416) 691-5651   *SIC* 8699
PEGASUS PAPER WAREHOUSE   *p 121*
See 1688150 ALBERTA LTD
PEGGY HILL & ASSOCIATES REALTY INC
p 488
11 VICTORIA ST UNIT B3, BARRIE, ON,
L4N 6T3
(705) 739-4455   *SIC* 6531
PEGGY HILL TEAM   *p 488*
*See PEGGY HILL & ASSOCIATES REALTY
INC*
PEGUIS SCHOOL BOARD   *p 354*
GD, PEGUIS, MB, R0C 3J0
(204) 645-2648   *SIC* 8211
PEI BUSINESS DEVELOPMENT INC *p 1039*
94 EUSTON ST, CHARLOTTETOWN, PE,
C1A 1W4
(902) 368-5800   *SIC* 8731
PEI VEGETABLE GROWERS   *p 1040*
*See P.E.I. VEGETABLE GROWERS CO-
OPERATIVE ASSOCIATION, LIMITED*
PEINTURE & PIECES D.R. INC   *p 1148*

2509 RUE SHERBROOKE, MAGOG, QC,
J1X 4E7
(819) 843-0550   *SIC* 5531
PEINTURE CAN-LAK   *p 1089*
See CANLAK INC
**PEINTURE EN POUDRE MONTEREGIE
(PPM)**   *p 1316*
See METAL SIGMA INC
PEINTURE SYLTECK INC   *p 1399*
1521 BOUL JUTRAS O, VICTORIAVILLE,
QC, G6T 2A9
(819) 758-3662   *SIC* 5198
PEINTURE UCP INC   *p 1054*
19500 AUT TRANSCANADIENNE, BAIE-
D'URFE, QC, H9X 3S4
(514) 457-1512   *SIC* 2851
PEINTURES M.F. INC   *p 1234*
1605 BOUL DAGENAIS O, MONTREAL,
QC, H7L 5A3
(450) 628-3831   *SIC* 2851
PEINTURES PROLUX INC   *p 1162*
11430 56E AV, MONTREAL, QC, H1E 2L5
(514) 648-4911   *SIC* 5198
PEKES HOLDINGS INC   *p 1330*
4045 BOUL POIRIER, SAINT-LAURENT,
QC, H4R 2G9
(514) 735-6111   *SIC* 6712
PEKUAKAMIULNUATSH TAKUHIKAN   *p
1150*
65 RUE UAPAKALU, MASHTEUIATSH, QC,
G0W 2H0
(418) 275-2473   *SIC* 6512
PELANGIO EXPLORATION INC   *p 940*
82 RICHMOND ST E, TORONTO, ON, M5C
1P1
(905) 336-3828   *SIC* 1041
PELECANUS HOLDINGS LTD   *p 289*
887 GREAT NORTHERN WAY SUITE 101,
VANCOUVER, BC, V5T 4T5
(604) 263-9994   *SIC* 5169
**PELEE ISLAND WINERY & VINEYARDS
INC**   *p 634*
455 SEACLIFF DR, KINGSVILLE, ON, N9Y
2K5
(519) 733-6551   *SIC* 2084
PELICAN INTERNATIONAL INC   *p 1231*
1000 PLACE PAUL-KANE, MONTREAL,
QC, H7C 2T2
(450) 664-1222   *SIC* 3732
PELICAN NARROWS SCHOOL   *p 1413*
See OPAWIKOSCIKEN SCHOOL
PELLEMON   *p 1280*
See SNC-LAVALIN INC
PELLEMON INC   *p 1192*
455 BOUL RENE-LEVESQUE O, MON-
TREAL, QC, H2Z 1Z3
(514) 735-5651   *SIC* 8711
PELLETIER, D'AMOURS   *p 1136*
*See   DESJARDINS   GROUPE
D'ASSURANCES GENERALES INC*
PELLETIER, RICHARD & FILS INC *p 1377*
4 RUE SAINT-MARC, SQUATEC, QC, G0L
4H0
(418) 855-2951   *SIC* 5031
PELLY BANKS TRADING CO. LTD   *p 1440*
1406 CENTENNIAL ST, WHITEHORSE, YT,
Y1A 3Z3
(867) 633-2265   *SIC* 5411
PELMOREX CORP   *p 798*
2655 BRISTOL CIR, OAKVILLE, ON, L6H
7W1
(905) 829-1159   *SIC* 8999
**PELMOREX   WEATHER   NETWORKS
(TELEVISION) INC**   *p 798*
2655 BRISTOL CIR, OAKVILLE, ON, L6H
7W1
(905) 829-1159   *SIC* 4833
**PELMOREX   WEATHER   NETWORKS
(TELEVISION) INC**   *p 1174*
1205 AV PAPINEAU BUREAU 251, MON-
TREAL, QC, H2K 4R2
(514) 597-0232   *SIC* 8999
**PELMOREX   WEATHER   NETWORKS
(TELEVISION) INC**   *p 1174*

▲ Public Company   ■ Public Company Family Member   **HQ** Headquarters   **BR** Branch   **SL** Single Location

1755 BOUL RENE-LEVESQUE E BUREAU 251, MONTREAL, QC, H2K 4P6

(514) 597-1700   SIC 4833

PELMOREX WEATHER NETWORKS INC p 798

2655 BRISTOL CIR, OAKVILLE, ON, L6H 7W1

(905) 829-1159   SIC 4833

PELP LIMITED PARTNERSHIP p 524

1122 INTERNATIONAL BLVD SUITE 700, BURLINGTON, ON, L7L 6Z8

(905) 639-2060   SIC 5541

PELUCHE ET TARTINE p 1293

See IMPORTATIONS N & N INC, LES

PEM BRAND DIVISION p 387

See PEMBINA PROMOTIONS INC

PEMBINA CARE SERVICES LTD p 391

1679 PEMBINA HWY, WINNIPEG, MB, R3T 2G6

(204) 269-6308   SIC 8361

PEMBINA COLONY FARMS LTD p 348

GD, DARLINGFORD, MB, R0G 0L0

(204) 246-2182   SIC 7389

PEMBINA CONSUMERS CO-OP (2000) LTD p 357

61 MAIN ST, ST LEON, MB, R0G 2E0

(204) 744-2228   SIC 5251

PEMBINA HILLS REGIONAL DIVISION 7 p 4

5307 53 AVE, BARRHEAD, AB, T7N 1P2

(780) 674-8521   SIC 8211

PEMBINA HILLS REGIONAL DIVISION 7 p 4

5310 49 ST, BARRHEAD, AB, T7N 1P3

(780) 674-8500   SIC 8211

PEMBINA NGL CORPORATION p 56

525 8 AVE SW SUITE 3800, CALGARY, AB, T2P 1G1

(403) 231-7500   SIC 4922

PEMBINA PIPELINE p 56

585 8 AVE SW UNIT 4000, CALGARY, AB, T2P 1G1

(403) 231-7500   SIC 4619

PEMBINA PIPELINE CORPORATION p 56

585 8 AVE SW UNIT 4000, CALGARY, AB, T2P 1G1

(403) 231-7500   SIC 4612

PEMBINA PROMOTIONS INC p 387

421 MULVEY AVE, WINNIPEG, MB, R3L 0R6

(204) 453-4132   SIC 5199

PEMBINA TRAILS SCHOOL DIVISION, THE p 389

2240 GRANT AVE, WINNIPEG, MB, R3P 0P7

(204) 888-5898   SIC 8211

PEMBINA TRAILS SCHOOL DIVISION, THE p 391

175 KILLARNEY AVE, WINNIPEG, MB, R3T 3B3

(204) 269-6210   SIC 8211

PEMBINA TRAILS SCHOOL DIVISION, THE p 393

181 HENLOW BAY, WINNIPEG, MB, R3Y 1M7

(204) 488-1757   SIC 8211

PEMBRIDGE INSURANCE COMPANY p 673

27 ALLSTATE PKWY SUITE 100, MARKHAM, ON, L3R 5P8

(905) 513-4013   SIC 6331

PEMBROKE IRVING BIG STOP p 837

See 868971 ONTARIO INC

PEMBROKE MDF INC p 838

777 FIBREBOARD DR, PEMBROKE, ON, K8A 6W4

(613) 732-3939   SIC 2621

PEMBROKE OLD TIME FIDDLING ASSOCIATION INCORPORATED p 564

GD, DEEP RIVER, ON, K0J 1P0

(613) 635-7200   SIC 8699

PEMBROKE REGIONAL HOSPITAL INC p 838

705 MACKAY ST SUITE 732, PEMBROKE, ON, K8A 1G8

(613) 732-2811   SIC 8062

PEMCO CONSTRUCTION LTD p 85

50 AIRPORT RD NW, EDMONTON, AB, T5G 0W7

(780) 414-5410   SIC 8742

PEN PLAST p 592

See PENINSULA PLASTICS LIMITED

PENDER NDI LIFE SCIENCES FUND (VCC) INC p 308

885 GEORGIA ST W SUITE 200, VANCOUVER, BC, V6C 3E8

(604) 688-1511   SIC 6211

PENDOPHARM p 1180

See PHARMASCIENCE INC

PENEQUITY REALTY CORPORATION p 943

33 YONGE ST SUITE 901, TORONTO, ON, M5E 1G4

(416) 408-3080   SIC 6722

PENETANGUISHENE GENERAL HOSPITAL INC, THE p 838

25 JEFFERY ST SUITE 670, PENETANGUISHENE, ON, L9M 1K6

(705) 549-7442   SIC 8062

PENFINANCIAL CREDIT UNION LIMITED p 1012

247 EAST MAIN ST, WELLAND, ON, L3B 3X1

(905) 735-4801   SIC 6062

PENFOLDS ROOFING INC p 295

1262 VERNON ST, VANCOUVER, BC, V6A 4C9

(604) 254-4663   SIC 1761

PENGLAD FARMS INC p 886

3930 NINTH ST, ST CATHARINES, ON, L2R 6P9

(905) 684-7861   SIC 5992

PENGROWTH ENERGY CORPORATION p 56

222 3 AVE SW SUITE 2100, CALGARY, AB, T2P 0B4

(403) 233-0224   SIC 1311

PENGROWTH ENERGY CORPORATION p 168

GD, SWAN HILLS, AB, T0G 2C0

(780) 333-7100   SIC 1311

PENGUIN BOOKS CANADA p 756

See PEARSON CANADA INC

PENGUIN MEAT SUPPLY LTD p 279

19195 33 AVE UNIT 1, SURREY, BC, V3Z 1A1

(604) 531-1447   SIC 5147

PENGUIN PICK-UP LIMITED PARTNERSHIP p 1002

700 APPLEWOOD CRES UNIT 1, VAUGHAN, ON, L4K 5X3

(905) 760-6200   SIC 4215

PENGUIN POWER SOLAR p 1026

2118 HURON BRUCE RD, WINGHAM, ON, N0G 2W0

(519) 274-2179   SIC 1711

PENGUIN RANDOM HOUSE CANADA LIMITED p 982

320 FRONT ST W SUITE 1400, TORONTO, ON, M5V 3B6

(416) 364-4449   SIC 2731

PENGUINPICKUP p 1002

See PENGUIN PICK-UP LIMITED PARTNERSHIP

PENINSULA CO-OP p 267

See PENINSULA CONSUMER SERVICES CO-OPERATIVE

PENINSULA CONSUMER SERVICES CO-OPERATIVE p 267

2132 KEATING CROSS RD UNIT 1, SAANICHTON, BC, V8M 2A6

(250) 652-5752   SIC 5541

PENINSULA FORD LINCOLN p 836

See PENINSULA MOTOR SALES LTD

PENINSULA MOTOR SALES LTD p 836

202392 SUNSET STRIP, OWEN SOUND, ON, N4K 5N7

(519) 376-3252   SIC 5511

PENINSULA PLASTICS LIMITED p 592

620 INDUSTRIAL DR, FORT ERIE, ON, L2A 5M4

(905) 871-4766   SIC 3089

PENINSULA RETIREMENT RESIDENCE p 280

See ROYAL WEST COAST PENINSULA, THE

PENINSULA RIDGE ESTATES WINERY LIMITED p 490

5600 KING ST RR 3, BEAMSVILLE, ON, L0R 1B3

(905) 563-0900   SIC 5182

PENINSULA SECURITY SERVICES LTD p 1012

50 DIVISION ST, WELLAND, ON, L3B 3Z6

(905) 732-2337   SIC 7381

PENN ENGINEERED FASTENERS CORPORATION p 557

590 BASALTIC RD, CONCORD, ON, L4K 5A2

(905) 879-0433   SIC 5085

PENN WEST ENERGY TRUST p 55

See OBSIDIAN ENERGY LTD

PENN-CO CONSTRUCTION CANADA LTD p 346

25 PENNER DR, BLUMENORT, MB, R0A 0C0

(204) 326-1341   SIC 1542

PENN-CO CONSTRUCTION INT'L LTD p 346

16 CENTRE AVE, BLUMENORT, MB, R0A 0C0

(204) 326-1341   SIC 1542

PENN-CO CONSTRUCTION LTD p 346

24 CENTRE AVE, BLUMENORT, MB, R0A 0C0

(204) 326-1341   SIC 6712

PENN-CO TOOL RENTALS p 358

See E.G. PENNER BUILDING CENTRES LTD

PENNECON ENERGY HYDRAULIC SYSTEMS LIMITED p 427

2 MAVERICK PL, PARADISE, NL, A1L 0H6

(709) 726-3490   SIC 7699

PENNECON ENERGY LTD p 433

650 WATER ST, ST. JOHN'S, NL, A1E 1B9

(709) 726-5888   SIC 8741

PENNECON ENERGY MARINE BASE LTD p 433

650 WATER ST, ST. JOHN'S, NL, A1E 1B9

(709) 334-2820   SIC 4491

PENNECON LIMITED p 431

1309 TOPSAIL RD, ST. JOHN'S, NL, A1B 3N4

(709) 782-3404   SIC 6159

PENNECON TECHNICAL SERVICES LTD p 433

650 WATER ST, ST. JOHN'S, NL, A1E 1B9

(709) 726-4554   SIC 7694

PENNER BUILDING CENTRE p 1004

See PENNER LUMBER & BUILDERS' SUPPLIES LIMITED

PENNER BUILDING CENTRE AND BUILDERS SUPPLIES LIMITED p 1004

700 PENNER ST, VIRGIL, ON, L0S 1T0

(905) 468-3242   SIC 5251

PENNER FARM SERVICES p 598

See PENNER FARM SERVICES (AVONBANK) LTD

PENNER FARM SERVICES (AVONBANK) LTD p 598

15456 ELGINFIELD RD RR 3, GRANTON, ON, N0M 1V0

(519) 225-2507   SIC 5083

PENNER INTERNATIONAL INC p 358

20 PTH 12 N, STEINBACH, MB, R5G 1B7

(204) 326-3487   SIC 4213

PENNER LUMBER & BUILDERS' SUPPLIES LIMITED p 1004

700 PENNER ST, VIRGIL, ON, L0S 1T0

(905) 468-3242   SIC 5211

PENNER OIL p 379

See PENNER, LARRY ENTERPRISES INC

PENNER PROPERTIES WEST p 346

See PENN-CO CONSTRUCTION LTD

PENNER, LARRY ENTERPRISES INC p 379

29 MOUNTAIN VIEW, WINNIPEG, MB, R3C 2E6

(204) 989-4300   SIC 5172

PENNER, P & A SALES INC p 1410

300 STONEGATE 500 HWY SUITE 6, MELFORT, SK, S0E 1A0

(306) 752-7277   SIC 5531

PENNEY MAZDA p 431

See SUPERCARS INC

PENNISULA FOODS p 418

514 ROUTE 365, TILLEY ROAD, NB, E8M 1P4

(506) 358-6366   SIC 2037

PENNY POWER HARDWARE LTD p 356

917 MANITOBA AVE, SELKIRK, MB, R1A 3T7

(204) 785-2773   SIC 5251

PENNZOIL ST-LEONARD p 1343

See 2618-7922 QUEBEC INC

PENSA AND ASSOCIATES p 654

450 TALBOT ST, LONDON, ON, N6A 5J6

(519) 679-9660   SIC 8111

PENSION FUNDS p 822

See CBC PENSION BOARD OF TRUSTEES

PENSION PLAN - F & L p 524

750 APPLEBY LINE, BURLINGTON, ON, L7L 2Y7

(905) 632-2121   SIC 1611

PENSIONAT ST NOM DE MARIE p 1143

See SOEURS DES SAINTS NOMS DE JESUS ET DE MARIE DU QUEBEC, LES

PENSKE LOGISTICS CANADA LTD p 634

3065 KING ST E, KITCHENER, ON, N2A 1B1

(519) 650-0123   SIC 4213

PENSKE TRUCK LEASING CANADA INC p 725

7405 EAST DANBRO CRES, MISSISSAUGA, ON, L5N 6P8

(905) 819-7900   SIC 7513

PENSKE TRUCK LEASING CANADA INC p 1335

2500 BOUL PITFIELD, SAINT-LAURENT, QC, H4S 1Z7

(514) 333-4080   SIC 7513

PENTA EQUIPMENT INC p 843

4480 PROGRESS DR, PETROLIA, ON, N0N 1R0

(519) 882-3350   SIC 5083

PENTA TILLAGE p 594

See 1777621 ONTARIO INC

PENTAGON FARM CENTRE LTD p 138

4950 HARRINGTON RIDGE UNIT 1, LACOMBE, AB, T4L 1A8

(403) 782-6873   SIC 5999

PENTAGON GRAPHICS LTD p 1252

271 AV LABROSSE, POINTE-CLAIRE, QC, H9R 1A3

(514) 339-5995   SIC 2752

PENTAGON-RAYMOND INSURANCE BROKERS INC p 810

3009 ST. JOSEPH BLVD UNIT 101, ORLEANS, ON, K1E 1E1

(613) 837-1060   SIC 6411

PENTAIR CANADA, INC p 637

269 TRILLIUM DR, KITCHENER, ON, N2E 1W9

(519) 748-5470   SIC 5084

PENTALIFT EQUIPMENT CORPORATION p 849

21 NICHOLAS BEAVER RD, PUSLINCH,

ON, N0B 2J0
(519) 763-3625 *SIC* 3537
PENTAX CANADA INC *p 725*
6715 MILLCREEK DR UNIT 1, MISSISSAUGA, ON, L5N 5V2
(905) 286-5570 *SIC* 5043
PENTAX MEDICAL *p 725*
See PENTAX CANADA INC
PENTCO INDUSTRIES INC *p 282*
9274 194 ST, SURREY, BC, V4N 4E9
(604) 888-0508 *SIC* 1751
PENTECOSTAL ASSEMBLIES OF CANADA, THE *p 725*
2450 MILLTOWER CRT, MISSISSAUGA, ON, L5N 5Z6
(905) 542-7400 *SIC* 8661
PENTECOSTAL ASSEMBLIES OF NEWFOUNDLAND AND LABRADOR CORPORATION *p 431*
57 THORBURN RD, ST. JOHN'S, NL, A1B 3M2
(709) 753-6314 *SIC* 8661
PENTEL STATIONERY OF CANADA LIMITED *p 265*
5900 NO. 2 RD SUITE 140, RICHMOND, BC, V7C 4R9
(604) 270-1566 *SIC* 5112
PENTICTON & DISTRICT COMMUNITY RESOURCES SOCIETY *p 244*
330 ELLIS ST, PENTICTON, BC, V2A 4L7
(250) 492-5814 *SIC* 8399
PENTICTON AND DISTRICT SOCIETY FOR COMMUNITY LIVING *p 244*
180 INDUSTRIAL AVE W, PENTICTON, BC, V2A 6X9
(250) 493-0312 *SIC* 8322
PENTICTON COURTYARD INN LTD *p 244*
1050 ECKHARDT AVE W, PENTICTON, BC, V2A 2C3
(250) 492-8926 *SIC* 7011
PENTICTON FOUNDRY LTD *p 244*
568 DAWSON AVE, PENTICTON, BC, V2A 3N8
(250) 492-7043 *SIC* 3322
PENTICTON HOME HARDWARE BUILDING CENTRE *p 244*
See PRO BUILDERS LTD
PENTICTON HONDA *p 243*
See 0769510 B.C. LTD
PENTICTON HYUNDAI *p 243*
See 0794856 B.C. LTD
PENTICTON KIA *p 244*
550 DUNCAN AVE W, PENTICTON, BC, V2A 7N1
(250) 276-1200 *SIC* 5511
PENTICTON TOYOTA *p 243*
See KEIJ ENTERPRISES LTD
PEO CANADA LTD *p 56*
805 5 AVE SW SUITE 100, CALGARY, AB, T2P 0N6
(403) 237-5577 *SIC* 7361
PEO CANADA LTD *p 56*
805 5 AVE SW SUITE 100, CALGARY, AB, T2P 0N6
(403) 237-5577 *SIC* 8721
PEOPLE CARE CENTRES INC *p 902*
28 WILLIAM ST N, TAVISTOCK, ON, N0B 2R0
(519) 655-2031 *SIC* 8051
PEOPLE CARE TAVISTOCK *p 902*
See PEOPLE CARE CENTRES INC
PEOPLE CORPORATION *p 389*
1403 KENASTON BLVD, WINNIPEG, MB, R3P 2T5
(204) 940-3933 *SIC* 8742
PEOPLE IN MOTION *p 705*
See CANADIAN NATIONAL SPORTSMEN'S SHOWS (1989) LIMITED
PEOPLE PLACE, THE *p 56*
805 5 AVE SW, CALGARY, AB, T2P 0N6
(403) 705-2353 *SIC* 7361

PEOPLE PLAYERS INC *p 575*
343 EVANS AVE, ETOBICOKE, ON, M8Z 1K2
(416) 532-1137 *SIC* 8699
PEOPLES CHURCH *p 772*
See PEOPLES MINISTRIES INC
PEOPLES FINANCIAL CORPORATION *p 965*
95 WELLINGTON ST W SUITE 915, TORONTO, ON, M5J 2N7
(416) 861-1315 *SIC* 6162
PEOPLES MINISTRIES INC *p 772*
374 SHEPPARD AVE E, NORTH YORK, ON, M2N 3B6
(416) 222-3341 *SIC* 8661
PEOPLES PARK TOWER INC *p 409*
960 ST GEORGE BLVD SUITE 144, MONCTON, NB, E1E 3Y3
(506) 857-8872 *SIC* 6513
PEOPLES TRUST COMPANY/COMPAGNIE DE FIDUCIE PEOPLES *p 308*
888 DUNSMUIR ST SUITE 1400, VANCOUVER, BC, V6C 3K4
(604) 683-2881 *SIC* 6021
PEOPLESOURCE STAFFING SOLUTIONS INC *p 991*
67 MOWAT AVE SUITE 411, TORONTO, ON, M6K 3E3
(905) 277-4455 *SIC* 7361
PEOPLETOGO INC *p 673*
201 WHITEHALL DR UNIT 4, MARKHAM, ON, L3R 9Y3
(905) 940-9292 *SIC* 7363
PEPCO *p 1050*
See PEPCO ENERGY CORP
PEPCO CORP *p 619*
25 GASPESIE RD, HEARST, ON, P0L 1N0
(844) 362-4523 *SIC* 5172
PEPCO ENERGY CORP *p 619*
25 CH. GASPESIE RD, HEARST, ON, P0L 1N0
(844) 362-4523 *SIC* 5172
PEPCO ENERGY CORP *p 1050*
10220 BOUL LOUIS-H.-LAFONTAINE, ANJOU, QC, H1J 2T3
(514) 493-7000 *SIC* 5172
PEPES MEXICAN FOODS INC *p 587*
122 CARRIER DR, ETOBICOKE, ON, M9W 5R1
(416) 674-0882 *SIC* 2099
PEPIN FORTIN CONSTRUCTION *p 1398*
See CONSTRUCTIONS PEPIN ET FORTIN INC, LES
PEPINIERE ABBOTSFORD INC *p 1350*
605 RUE PRINCIPALE E BUREAU 112, SAINT-PAUL-D'ABBOTSFORD, QC, J0E 1A0
(450) 379-5777 *SIC* 0181
PEPINIERE BOUCHER DIVISION PLANTS FORESTIERS INC *p 1291*
94 RANG DES AULNAIES, SAINT-AMBROISE, QC, G7P 2B4
(418) 672-4779 *SIC* 0181
PEPINIERE CHARLEVOIX INC *p 1122*
2375 BOUL DE COMPORTE, LA MALBAIE, QC, G5A 3C6
(418) 439-4646 *SIC* 5261
PEPINIERE CRAMER INC *p 1135*
1002 CH SAINT-DOMINIQUE, LES CEDRES, QC, J7T 1P4
(450) 452-2121 *SIC* 0181
PEPINIERE LEMAY INC *p 1130*
256 RANG SAINT-HENRI, LANORAIE, QC, J0K 1E0
(450) 887-2761 *SIC* 0181
PEPINIERE PIERREFONDS INC *p 1290*
11409 BOUL GOUIN O, ROXBORO, QC, H8Y 1X7
(514) 684-5051 *SIC* 5261
PEPPERS FOOD STORE *p 333*
See O & P SUPERMARKETS LTD
PEPPERS HIGHWAY SERVICE INC *p 171*
HIGHWAY 28, WASKATENAU, AB, T0A 3P0
(780) 358-2644 *SIC* 5541
PEPPERS, SAMMY J GOURMET GRILL

AND BAR *p 226*
19925 WILLOWBROOK DR SUITE 101, LANGLEY, BC, V2Y 1A7
(604) 514-0224 *SIC* 5812
PEPSI BOTTLING GROUP *p 102*
See PEPSI BOTTLING GROUP (CANADA), ULC, THE
PEPSI BOTTLING GROUP *p 141*
2400 31 ST N, LETHBRIDGE, AB, T1H 5K8
(403) 327-1310 *SIC* 5149
PEPSI BOTTLING GROUP (CANADA), ULC, THE *p 17*
4815 78 AVE SE, CALGARY, AB, T2C 2Y9
(403) 279-1500 *SIC* 2086
PEPSI BOTTLING GROUP (CANADA), ULC, THE *p 102*
11315 182 ST NW, EDMONTON, AB, T5S 1R3
(780) 930-7700 *SIC* 2086
PEPSI BOTTLING GROUP (CANADA), ULC, THE *p 206*
747 CHESTER RD, DELTA, BC, V3M 6E7
(604) 520-8000 *SIC* 2086
PEPSI BOTTLING GROUP (CANADA), ULC, THE *p 384*
1850 ELLICE AVE, WINNIPEG, MB, R3H 0B8
(204) 784-0600 *SIC* 2086
PEPSI BOTTLING GROUP (CANADA), ULC, THE *p 409*
220 HENRI DUNANT ST, MONCTON, NB, E1E 1E6
(506) 853-4010 *SIC* 2086
PEPSI BOTTLING GROUP (CANADA), ULC, THE *p 608*
2799 BARTON ST E, HAMILTON, ON, L8E 2J8
(905) 560-7774 *SIC* 2086
PEPSI BOTTLING GROUP (CANADA), ULC, THE *p 662*
40 ENTERPRISE DR SUITE 1, LONDON, ON, N6N 1A7
(519) 681-0030 *SIC* 5149
PEPSI BOTTLING GROUP (CANADA), ULC, THE *p 699*
5205 SATELLITE DR, MISSISSAUGA, ON, L4W 5J7
(905) 212-7377 *SIC* 2086
PEPSI BOTTLING GROUP (CANADA), ULC, THE *p 732*
5900 FALBOURNE ST, MISSISSAUGA, ON, L5R 3M2
(905) 568-8787 *SIC* 2086
PEPSI BOTTLING GROUP (CANADA), ULC, THE *p 818*
869 BELFAST RD, OTTAWA, ON, K1G 0Z4
(613) 244-9961 *SIC* 5149
PEPSI BOTTLING GROUP (CANADA), ULC, THE *p 898*
801 LAPOINTE ST, SUDBURY, ON, P3A 5N8
(705) 525-4000 *SIC* 2086
PEPSI BOTTLING GROUP (CANADA), ULC, THE *p 1079*
1800 BOUL TALBOT, CHICOUTIMI, QC, G7H 7Y1
(418) 549-3135 *SIC* 5149
PEPSI BOTTLING GROUP (CANADA), ULC, THE *p 1330*
3700 BOUL THIMENS, SAINT-LAURENT, QC, H4R 1T8
(514) 332-3770 *SIC* 2086
PEPSI COLA CANADA LTEE *p 1285*
401 BOUL DE LA RIVIERE, RIMOUSKI, QC, G5L 7R1
(418) 722-8080 *SIC* 5149
PEPSI QTG CANADA *p 841*
See PEPSICO CANADA ULC
PEPSICO BEVERAGES CANADA *p 17*
See PEPSI BOTTLING GROUP (CANADA), ULC, THE
PEPSICO BEVERAGES CANADA *p 206*
See PEPSI BOTTLING GROUP (CANADA), ULC, THE

PEPSICO BEVERAGES CANADA *p 384*
See PEPSI BOTTLING GROUP (CANADA), ULC, THE
PEPSICO BEVERAGES CANADA *p 409*
See PEPSI BOTTLING GROUP (CANADA), ULC, THE
PEPSICO BEVERAGES CANADA *p 608*
See PEPSI BOTTLING GROUP (CANADA), ULC, THE
PEPSICO BEVERAGES CANADA *p 662*
See PEPSI BOTTLING GROUP (CANADA), ULC, THE
PEPSICO BEVERAGES CANADA *p 699*
See PEPSI BOTTLING GROUP (CANADA), ULC, THE
PEPSICO BEVERAGES CANADA *p 732*
See PEPSI BOTTLING GROUP (CANADA), ULC, THE
PEPSICO BEVERAGES CANADA *p 818*
See PEPSI BOTTLING GROUP (CANADA), ULC, THE
PEPSICO BEVERAGES CANADA *p 898*
See PEPSI BOTTLING GROUP (CANADA), ULC, THE
PEPSICO BEVERAGES CANADA *p 1079*
See PEPSI BOTTLING GROUP (CANADA), ULC, THE
PEPSICO BEVERAGES CANADA *p 1330*
See PEPSI BOTTLING GROUP (CANADA), ULC, THE
PEPSICO CANADA ULC *p 13*
2867 45 AVE SE, CALGARY, AB, T2B 3L8
(403) 571-9530 *SIC* 2096
PEPSICO CANADA ULC *p 141*
2200 31 ST N, LETHBRIDGE, AB, T1H 5K8
(403) 380-5775 *SIC* 2096
PEPSICO CANADA ULC *p 169*
5904 54 AVE, TABER, AB, T1G 1X3
(403) 223-3574 *SIC* 2096
PEPSICO CANADA ULC *p 275*
11811 103A AVE, SURREY, BC, V3V 0B5
(604) 587-8300 *SIC* 5145
PEPSICO CANADA ULC *p 460*
GD, KENTVILLE, NS, B4N 3W9
(902) 681-6183 *SIC* 2096
PEPSICO CANADA ULC *p 460*
59 WAREHOUSE RD, KENTVILLE, NS, B4N 3W9
(902) 681-2923 *SIC* 2096
PEPSICO CANADA ULC *p 510*
12 CLIPPER CRT, BRAMPTON, ON, L6W 4T9
(905) 460-2400 *SIC* 5145
PEPSICO CANADA ULC *p 539*
1001 BISHOP ST N, CAMBRIDGE, ON, N3H 4V8
(519) 653-5721 *SIC* 2096
PEPSICO CANADA ULC *p 662*
40 ENTERPRISE DR SUITE 2, LONDON, ON, N6N 1A7
(519) 668-4004 *SIC* 5145
PEPSICO CANADA ULC *p 699*
5550 EXPLORER DR, MISSISSAUGA, ON, L4W 0C3
(289) 374-5000 *SIC* 2096
PEPSICO CANADA ULC *p 732*
55 STANDISH CRT SUITE 700, MISSISSAUGA, ON, L5R 4B2
SIC 2096
PEPSICO CANADA ULC *p 841*
14 HUNTER ST E, PETERBOROUGH, ON, K9J 7B2
(705) 743-6330 *SIC* 2043
PEPSICO CANADA ULC *p 865*
1 WATER TOWER GATE, SCARBOROUGH, ON, M1B 6C5
(416) 284-3200 *SIC* 5145
PEPSICO CANADA ULC *p 1111*
855 RUE J.-A.-BOMBARDIER, GRANBY, QC, J2J 1E9
(450) 375-5555 *SIC* 2086
PEPSICO CANADA ULC *p 1137*
8450 BOUL GUILLAUME-COUTURE, LEVIS, QC, G6V 7L7

(418) 833-2121   *SIC* 2096
PEPSICO CANADA ULC *p* 1231
6755 RUE ERNEST-CORMIER, MON-TREAL, QC, H7C 2T4
(450) 664-5800   *SIC* 2096
PERADE FORD INC, LA *p* 1355
727 RUE PRINCIPALE BUREAU 512, SAINTE-ANNE-DE-LA-PERADE, QC, G0X 2J0
(418) 325-2244   *SIC* 5511
PERATON CANADA CORP *p* 24
6732 8 ST NE, CALGARY, AB, T2E 8M4
(403) 295-4770   *SIC* 7699
PERCON CONSTRUCTION INC *p* 587
20 AIRVIEW RD, ETOBICOKE, ON, M9W 4P2
(416) 744-9967   *SIC* 1542
PERENNIAL INC *p* 579
15 WAULRON ST, ETOBICOKE, ON, M9C 1B4
(416) 251-2180   *SIC* 7336
PERES BLANCS, LES *p* 1176
See SOCIETE DES MISSIONAIRES D'AFRIQUE (PERES BLANCS) PROVINCE DE L'AMERIQUE DU NORD
PERES NATURE INC, LES *p* 1305
10735 1RE AV, SAINT-GEORGES, QC, G5Y 2B8
(418) 227-4444   *SIC* 5431
PERFECT OPTICAL HOLDINGS LTD *p* 1244
1265 AV DUCHARME, OUTREMONT, QC, H2V 1E6
(514) 274-9407   *SIC* 5049
PERFECT PLACEMENT SYSTEMS, DIV OF *p* 374
See 4659555 MANITOBA LTD
PERFECT POULTRY INC *p* 793
239 TORYORK DR, NORTH YORK, ON, M9L 1Y2
(416) 656-9666   *SIC* 2011
PERFEXIA INC *p* 637
111 BLEAMS RD, KITCHENER, ON, N2C 2G2
(519) 884-8650   *SIC* 5084
PERFIX INC *p* 1061
645 BOUL DU CURE-BOIVIN, BOIS-BRIAND, QC, J7G 2J2
(450) 435-0540   *SIC* 2522
PERFORMA LUBRICANTS INTERNA-TIONAL INC *p* 1016
42 MONTROSE CRES, WHITBY, ON, L1R 1C5
(905) 668-1440   *SIC* 5172
PERFORMANCE CARS (ST CATHARINES) LIMITED *p* 886
371 ONTARIO ST, ST CATHARINES, ON, L2R 5L3
(905) 685-3838   *SIC* 5511
PERFORMANCE CHRYSLER DODGE JEEP *p* 885
See CHECKPOINT CHRYSLER LTD
PERFORMANCE DE L'EXTRA-PORTEE, LA *p* 1302
See SCHOKBETON QUEBEC INC
PERFORMANCE DRIVER SERVICES INC *p* 37
5925 12 ST SE SUITE 220, CALGARY, AB, T2H 2M3
SIC 7361
PERFORMANCE DRYWALL *p* 101
See IGLOO BUILDING SUPPLIES GROUP LTD
PERFORMANCE EQUIPMENT LTD *p* 741
6950 TOMKEN RD, MISSISSAUGA, ON, L5T 2S3
(905) 564-8333   *SIC* 5511
PERFORMANCE FORD SALES INC *p* 1020
1150 PROVINCIAL RD, WINDSOR, ON, N8W 5W2
(519) 972-6500   *SIC* 5511
PERFORMANCE GROUP 262 LAKE INC *p* 884
262 LAKE ST, ST CATHARINES, ON, L2N

4H1
(905) 934-7246   *SIC* 5511
PERFORMANCE HONDA *p* 197
See FREEBORN MOTORS LTD
PERFORMANCE HYUNDAI *p* 884
268 LAKE ST, ST CATHARINES, ON, L2N 4H1
(905) 937-7000   *SIC* 5511
PERFORMANCE IMPROVEMENTS SPEED SHOPS LIMITED *p* 575
87 ADVANCE RD, ETOBICOKE, ON, M8Z 2S6
(416) 259-9656   *SIC* 5531
PERFORMANCE LAURENTIDES INC *p* 1155
1435 BOUL ALBINY-PAQUETTE, MONT-LAURIER, QC, J9L 1M8
(819) 623-6331   *SIC* 5511
PERFORMANCE LEXUS TOYOTA *p* 884
See PERFORMANCE GROUP 262 LAKE INC
PERFORMANCE LOCATION *p* 1155
See PERFORMANCE LAURENTIDES INC
PERFORMANCE MAZDA *p* 810
See PERFORMANCE MOTORS (OTTAWA) INC
PERFORMANCE MERCEDES-BENZ *p* 886
See PERFORMANCE CARS (ST CATHARINES) LIMITED
PERFORMANCE MOTORS *p* 907
See 1191460 ONTARIO INC
PERFORMANCE MOTORS (OTTAWA) INC *p* 810
1469 YOUVILLE DR, ORLEANS, ON, K1C 4R1
(613) 830-6320   *SIC* 5511
PERFORMANCE ORTHOTICS INC *p* 474
291 CLEMENTS RD W, AJAX, ON, L1S 3W7
(905) 428-2692   *SIC* 3842
PERFORMANCE POLYMERS INC *p* 534
36 RAGLIN PL, CAMBRIDGE, ON, N1R 7J2
(519) 622-1792   *SIC* 5085
PERFORMANCE PRINTING *p* 882
See METROLAND MEDIA GROUP LTD
PERFORMANCE PRINTING LIMITED *p* 882
65 LORNE ST, SMITHS FALLS, ON, K7A 3K8
(613) 283-5650   *SIC* 2711
PERFORMANCE PRINTING SPECIALTY PUBLICATIONS *p* 882
See PERFORMANCE PRINTING LIMITED
PERFORMANCE REALTY LTD *p* 819
1500 BANK ST, OTTAWA, ON, K1H 1B8
(613) 733-9100   *SIC* 6531
PERFORMANCE SCIENCE MATERIALS COMPANY *p* 563
291 ALBERT ST, CORUNNA, ON, N0N 1G0
(519) 862-5700   *SIC* 2821
PERFORMANCE WELL SERVICING LTD *p* 56
604 8 AVE SW SUITE 510, CALGARY, AB, T2P 1G4
SIC 1389
PERFORMANCE WINDOWS & DOORS, DI-VISION OF *p* 787
See VINYL WINDOW DESIGNS LTD
PERFUMES ETC. LTD *p* 742
6880 COLUMBUS RD UNIT 2, MISSIS-SAUGA, ON, L5T 2G1
(905) 850-8060   *SIC* 5122
PERHOL CONSTRUCTION LTD *p* 910
1450 ROSSLYN RD, THUNDER BAY, ON, P7E 6W1
(807) 474-0930   *SIC* 1542
PERI FORMWORK SYSTEMS INC *p* 495
45 NIXON RD, BOLTON, ON, L7E 1K1
(905) 951-5400   *SIC* 7353
PERICHEM TRADING INC *p* 915
4711 YONGE ST 10F, TORONTO, ON, M2N 6K8
(416) 479-5498   *SIC* 6799
PERIMETER AVIATION LP *p* 384

626 FERRY RD, WINNIPEG, MB, R3H 0T7
(204) 786-7031   *SIC* 4522
PERIMETER INDUSTRIES LTD *p* 357
2262 SPRINGFIELD RD SUITE 5, SPRING-FIELD, MB, R2C 2Z2
(204) 988-2140   *SIC* 2653
PERIMETER INSTITUTE *p* 1009
31 CAROLINE ST N, WATERLOO, ON, N2L 2Y5
(519) 569-7600   *SIC* 8733
PERIMETER INSTITUTE FOR THEORETI-CAL PHYSICS *p* 1009
See PERIMETER INSTITUTE
PERKIN'S FAMILY RESTAURANT *p* 366
See MCPHILLIPS LIMITED PARTNERSHIP
PERKINELMER *p* 1032
See PERKINELMER HEALTH SCIENCES CANADA, INC
PERKINELMER HEALTH SCIENCES CANADA, INC *p* 495
32 NIXON RD UNIT 1, BOLTON, ON, L7E 1W2
(905) 857-5665   *SIC* 3826
PERKINELMER HEALTH SCIENCES CANADA, INC *p* 1032
501 ROWNTREE DAIRY RD UNIT 6, WOODBRIDGE, ON, L4L 8H1
(905) 851-4585   *SIC* 5049
PERKINS + WILL ARCHITECTS CO *p* 299
1220 HOMER ST, VANCOUVER, BC, V6B 2Y5
(604) 684-5446   *SIC* 8712
PERKINS FAMILY RESTAURANT *p* 820
See CANADIAN DINERS (1995) L.P. LTD
PERKINS FARMS INC *p* 171
GD STN MAIN, WAINWRIGHT, AB, T9W 1M3
(780) 842-3642   *SIC* 5154
PERL'S MEAT PRODUCTS LIMITED *p* 791
3015 BATHURST ST, NORTH YORK, ON, M6B 3B5
SIC 5421
PERLAW HOLDINGS LIMITED *p* 825
340 ALBERT ST, OTTAWA, ON, K1R 7Y6
(613) 238-2022   *SIC* 6712
PERLE SYSTEMS LIMITED *p* 673
60 RENFREW DR SUITE 100, MARKHAM, ON, L3R 0E1
(905) 475-8885   *SIC* 7371
PERLEY-ROBERTSON, HILL & MC-DOUGALL LLP/S.R.L. *p* 825
340 ALBERT ST SUITE 1400, OTTAWA, ON, K1R 0A5
(613) 238-2022   *SIC* 8111
PERLICH BROS. AUCTION MARKET LTD *p* 143
GD, LETHBRIDGE, AB, T1K 4P4
(403) 329-3101   *SIC* 7389
PERM-A-TEM INC *p* 1145
45 PLACE CHARLES-LE MOYNE BUREAU 100, LONGUEUIL, QC, J4K 5G5
SIC 7361
PERMA INSURANCE ANGENCY *p* 24
See PERMA INSURANCE CONTINENTAL INC
PERMA INSURANCE CONTINENTAL INC *p* 24
901 CENTRE ST NW SUITE 200, CAL-GARY, AB, T2E 2P6
(403) 230-0808   *SIC* 6411
PERMACON GROUP *p* 684
See OLDCASTLE BUILDING PRODUCTS CANADA, INC
PERMANENT SASH & DOOR COMPANY LTD *p* 662
1040 WILTON GROVE RD, LONDON, ON, N6N 1C7
(519) 686-6020   *SIC* 6712
PERMASTEEL *p* 102
See PERMASTEEL PROJECTS LTD
PERMASTEEL PROJECTS LTD *p* 102
17430 103 AVE NW, EDMONTON, AB, T5S

2K8
(780) 452-7281   *SIC* 1542
PERMICOM PERMITS SERVICES INC *p* 557
161 PENNSYLVANIA AVE UNIT 5, CON-CORD, ON, L4K 1C3
SIC 4731
PEROGY - POLISH HALL *p* 909
818 SPRING ST, THUNDER BAY, ON, P7C 3L6
SIC 8699
PEROXYCHEM CANADA LTD *p* 249
2147 PRINCE GEORGE PULPMILL RD, PRINCE GEORGE, BC, V2K 5P5
(250) 561-4200   *SIC* 2819
PERPETUAL ENERGY INC *p* 56
605 5 AVE SW SUITE 3200, CALGARY, AB, T2P 3H5
(403) 269-4400   *SIC* 1311
PERPETUAL HOLDINGS LTD *p* 290
3473 FRASER ST, VANCOUVER, BC, V5V 4C3
(604) 874-4228   *SIC* 6712
PERPETUAL INSURANCE SERVICES LTD *p* 290
3479 FRASER ST SUITE 3473, VANCOU-VER, BC, V5V 4C3
(604) 606-8118   *SIC* 6411
PERPETUAL SECURITY CORPORATION *p* 401
880 HANWELL RD UNIT 203, FREDERIC-TON, NB, E3B 6A3
(506) 457-1458   *SIC* 7382
PERREAULT, YVAN & FILS INC *p* 1154
235 AV PERREAULT, MONT-JOLI, QC, G5H 3K6
(418) 775-7743   *SIC* 5142
PERRI'S LEATHERS LTD *p* 557
45 CASMIR CRT UNIT 11 & 15, CONCORD, ON, L4K 4H5
(905) 761-8549   *SIC* 3199
PERRIN INC *p* 1157
5711 RUE FERRIER, MONT-ROYAL, QC, H4P 1N3
(514) 341-4321   *SIC* 5136
PERRY MECHANICAL INC *p* 814
285 BLOOR ST W, OSHAWA, ON, L1J 1R1
(905) 725-3582   *SIC* 5075
PERRY'S CONSTRUCTION & READY MIX LTD *p* 1043
190 CENTENNIAL DR, TIGNISH, PE, C0B 2B0
(902) 882-3166   *SIC* 1522
PERSE-TECHNOLOGIE INC *p* 1370
2555 RUE DES FRENES BUREAU 100, SHERBROOKE, QC, J1G 4R3
SIC 7372
PERSIAN MAN *p* 907
See BENNETT'S BAKERY LIMITED
PERSISTA POLYURETHANE PRODUCTS DIV *p* 738
See CLARKE ROLLER & RUBBER LIM-ITED
PERSONA COMMUNICATIONS INC *p* 431
17 DUFFY PL, ST. JOHN'S, NL, A1B 4M7
(709) 754-3775   *SIC* 4841
PERSONA COMMUNICATIONS INC *p* 899
500 BARRYDOWNE RD UNIT 15, SUD-BURY, ON, P3A 3T3
(705) 560-1560   *SIC* 4841
PERSONAL TOUCH COURIER *p* 821
See PERSONAL TOUCH INC
PERSONAL TOUCH INC *p* 821
174 COBOURG ST SUITE 100, OTTAWA, ON, K1N 8H5
(613) 723-5891   *SIC* 7389
PERSONNEL DEPARTMENT LTD, THE *p* 90
10665 JASPER AVE NW SUITE 850, ED-MONTON, AB, T5J 3S9
(780) 421-1811   *SIC* 7361
PERSONNEL DEPARTMENT LTD, THE *p* 327
980 HOWE ST UNIT 201, VANCOUVER, BC, V6Z 0C8
(604) 685-3530   *SIC* 7361

PERSONNEL OUTAOUAIS INC p 1106
92 BOUL SAINT-RAYMOND BUREAU 400, GATINEAU, QC, J8Y 1S7
(819) 778-7020 SIC 7361

PERSONNEL SEARCH LTD p 407
883 MAIN ST, MONCTON, NB, E1C 1G5
(506) 857-2156 SIC 7361

PERSONNEL UNIQUE CANADA INC p 1096
455 BOUL FENELON BUREAU 210, DORVAL, QC, H9S 5T8
(514) 633-6220 SIC 8741

PERSONNELLE ASSURANCES GENERALES INC, LA p 1137
6300 BOUL DE LA RIVE-SUD, LEVIS, QC, G6V 6P9
(418) 835-4850 SIC 6331

PERSONNELLE, COMPAGNIE D'ASSURANCES, LA p 706
3 ROBERT SPECK PKY SUITE 550, MISSISSAUGA, ON, L4Z 3Z9
(905) 306-5252 SIC 6331

PERSONNELLE, LA p 706
See PERSONNELLE, COMPAGNIE D'ASSURANCES, LA

PERSTA RESOURCES INC p 56
888 3 ST SW SUITE 3600, CALGARY, AB, T2P 5C5
(403) 355-6623 SIC 1382

PERTH AND SMITHS FALLS DISTRICT HOSPITAL p 839
33 DRUMMOND ST W, PERTH, ON, K7H 2K1
(613) 267-1500 SIC 8062

PERTH AND SMITHS FALLS DISTRICT HOSPITAL p 882
60 CORNELIA ST W, SMITHS FALLS, ON, K7A 2H9
(613) 283-2330 SIC 8062

PERTH COUNTRY INGREDIENTS INC p 888
20 THAMES RD, ST MARYS, ON, N4X 1C4
(519) 284-3449 SIC 0254

PERTH HOME HARDWARE BUILDING CENTRE p 839
See ELLARD ENTERPRISES LIMITED

PERTH SERVICES LTD p 381
765 WELLINGTON AVE SUITE 1, WINNIPEG, MB, R3E 0J1
(204) 697-6100 SIC 7211

PERTH SOAP MANUFACTURING INC p 839
5 HERRIOTT ST, PERTH, ON, K7H 3E5
(613) 267-1881 SIC 2841

PERTH SOAP, DIV OF p 839
See PERTH SOAP MANUFACTURING INC

PERTH'S p 381
See PERTH SERVICES LTD

PESE PECHE INC p 418
140 1RE RUE, SHIPPAGAN, NB, E8S 1A4
(506) 336-1400 SIC 7389

PESTALTO ENVIRONMENTAL HEALTH SERVICES INC p 600
400 ELIZABETH ST UNIT I, GUELPH, ON, N1E 2Y1
SIC 4959

PESTELL MINERALS & INGREDIENTS INC p 752
141 HAMILTON RD, NEW HAMBURG, ON, N3A 2H1
(519) 662-2877 SIC 5191

PESTELL SHAVINGS LIMITED p 752
141 HAMILTON RD SUITE 794, NEW HAMBURG, ON, N3A 2H1
(519) 662-6565 SIC 5191

PESTELL WOOD SHAVINGS p 752
See PESTELL SHAVINGS LIMITED

PET FOOD WAREHOUSE p 383
See BEST WEST PET FOODS INC

PET PLANET LTD p 31
600 MANITOU RD SE, CALGARY, AB, T2G 4C5
(403) 777-4664 SIC 5999

PET SCIENCE LTD p 513
14 REGAN RD UNIT 1, BRAMPTON, ON,

L7A 1B9
(905) 840-1300 SIC 5149

PET VALU p 673
See PET VALU CANADA INC

PET VALU p 1001
See 994794 ONTARIO INC

PET VALU CANADA INC p 673
130 ROYAL CREST CRT, MARKHAM, ON, L3R 0A1
(905) 946-1200 SIC 6712

PETALS WEST INC p 384
975 SHERWIN RD UNIT 1, WINNIPEG, MB, R3H 0T8
(204) 786-1801 SIC 5193

PETAQUILLA MINERALS LTD p 327
777 HORNBY ST SUITE 1230, VANCOUVER, BC, V6Z 1S4
SIC 1041

PETE'S p 439
See LUCKETT RETAIL MANAGEMENT INC

PETE'S AUTOMOTIVE p 883
See BICKNELL, PETER AUTOMOTIVE INC

PETE'S EUROPEAN DELI p 452
See ATRIUM GROUP INC, THE

PETER A. ALLARD SCHOOL OF LAW p 325
See UNIVERSITY OF BRITISH COLUMBIA, THE

PETER ANTHONY DESIGNS INC p 1021
2700 OUELLETTE AVE, WINDSOR, ON, N8X 1L7
(519) 969-7332 SIC 2599

PETER BENNINGER REALTY LTD p 640
508 RIVERBEND DR SUITE 352, KITCHENER, ON, N2K 3S2
(519) 743-5211 SIC 6531

PETER BILT OF HOUSTON BC p 215
See PACIFIC TRUCK & EQUIPMENT

PETER CHARLES ANSLEY HOLDINGS LIMITED p 858
1380 LONDON RD UNIT 300, SARNIA, ON, N7S 1P8
(519) 542-3403 SIC 5531

PETER HODGE TRANSPORT LIMITED p 683
See CONTRANS GROUP INC

PETER IGEL GROUP INC p 768
2235 SHEPPARD AVE E SUITE 909, NORTH YORK, ON, M2J 5B5
(416) 493-8800 SIC 5141

PETER IGEL WINES & SPIRITS p 768
See PETER IGEL GROUP INC

PETER KIEWIT INFRASTRUCTURE CO. p 77
9500 100 ST SE, CALGARY, AB, T3S 0A2
SIC 1611

PETER KIEWIT INFRASTRUCTURE CO. p 102
11211 WINTERBURN RD NW, EDMONTON, AB, T5S 2B2
(780) 447-3509 SIC 1611

PETER KIEWIT INFRASTRUCTURE CO. p 186
4350 STILL CREEK DR SUITE 310, BURNABY, BC, V5C 0G5
(604) 629-5419 SIC 1629

PETER KOHLER WINDOWS & ENTRANCE SYSTEMS p 449
See KOHLTECH INTERNATIONAL LIMITED

PETER THE CHEF FINE FOOD LIMITED p 587
401 HUMBERLINE DR SUITE 4, ETOBICOKE, ON, M9W 6Y4
(416) 674-5800 SIC 2038

PETER THE PLANTMAN INC p 78
250010 MOUNTAIN VIEW TRAIL, CALGARY, AB, T3Z 3S3
(403) 270-8451 SIC 0181

PETER'S BROS. CONSTRUCTION LTD p 244
716 OKANAGAN AVE E, PENTICTON, BC, V2A 3K6
(250) 492-2626 SIC 1611

PETER'S FOOD & DRUG BASICS p 872
2131 LAWRENCE AVE E, SCARBOROUGH, ON, M1R 5G4
(416) 759-7625 SIC 5411

PETERBILT p 910
See THUNDER BAY TRUCK CENTRE INC

PETERBILT ATLANTIC p 403
See HAWKINS TRUCK MART LTD

PETERBILT MANITOBA LTD p 369
1895 BROOKSIDE BLVD, WINNIPEG, MB, R2R 2Y3
(204) 633-0071 SIC 5511

PETERBILT MANITOBA PACLEASE p 369
See PETERBILT MANITOBA LTD

PETERBILT OF LONDON p 652
See PETERBILT OF ONTARIO INC

PETERBILT OF ONTARIO INC p 652
31 BUCHANAN CRT, LONDON, ON, N5Z 4P9
(519) 686-1000 SIC 5511

PETERBILT PACIFIC INC p 282
19470 96 AVE, SURREY, BC, V4N 4C2
(604) 888-1411 SIC 5511

PETERBILT QUEBEC EAST LTD p 1349
195 AV DU PARC, SAINT-PASCAL, QC, G0L 3Y0
(418) 492-7383 SIC 5511

PETERBOROUGH AUTOMOTIVE & MACHINE LTD p 841
898 FORD ST, PETERBOROUGH, ON, K9J 5V3
(705) 742-2446 SIC 5013

PETERBOROUGH BEARINGS p 834
See GENERAL BEARING SERVICE INC

PETERBOROUGH CLINIC, THE p 841
26 HOSPITAL DR SUITE 204, PETERBOROUGH, ON, K9J 7C3
(705) 743-2040 SIC 8011

PETERBOROUGH HYUNDAI SUBARU p 839
See 564205 ONTARIO INC

PETERBOROUGH MEMORIAL CENTRE p 840
See CORPORATION OF THE CITY OF PETERBOROUGH, THE

PETERBOROUGH THIS WEEK p 841
See METROLAND MEDIA GROUP LTD

PETERBOROUGH UTILITIES SERVICES INC p 842
1867 ASHBURNHAM DR, PETERBOROUGH, ON, K9L 1P8
(705) 748-9300 SIC 4941

PETERBOROUGH VICTORIA NORTHUMBERLAND AND CLARINGTON CATHOLIC DISTRICT SCHOOL BOARD p 496
300 SCUGOG ST, BOWMANVILLE, ON, L1C 6Y8
(905) 623-3990 SIC 8211

PETERBOROUGH VICTORIA NORTHUMBERLAND AND CLARINGTON CATHOLIC DISTRICT SCHOOL BOARD p 545
1050 BIRCHWOOD TRAIL, COBOURG, ON, K9A 5S9
(905) 372-4339 SIC 8211

PETERBOROUGH VICTORIA NORTHUMBERLAND AND CLARINGTON CATHOLIC DISTRICT SCHOOL BOARD p 564
2260 COURTICE RD, COURTICE, ON, L1E 2M8
(905) 404-9349 SIC 8211

PETERBOROUGH VICTORIA NORTHUMBERLAND AND CLARINGTON CATHOLIC DISTRICT SCHOOL BOARD p 564
1355 LANSDOWNE ST W, PETERBOROUGH, ON, K9J 7M3
(705) 748-4861 SIC 8211

PETERS & CO. LIMITED p 56
308 4 AVE SW SUITE 2300, CALGARY, AB, T2P 0H7
(403) 261-4850 SIC 6211

PETERS DAIRY BAR LTD p 143
1152 MAYOR MAGRATH DR S, LETHBRIDGE, AB, T1K 2P8

(403) 327-6440 SIC 5812

PETERS' DRIVE INN p 24
219 16 AVE NE, CALGARY, AB, T2E 1J9
(403) 277-2747 SIC 5812

PETERSEN PONTIAC BUICK GMC (ALTA) INC p 163
10 AUTOMALL RD, SHERWOOD PARK, AB, T8H 2N1
(587) 805-0959 SIC 5511

PETERSON SPRING OF CANADA LIMITED p 634
208 WIGLE AVE, KINGSVILLE, ON, N9Y 2J9
(519) 733-2358 SIC 3492

PETHEALTH INC p 802
710 DORVAL DR SUITE 400, OAKVILLE, ON, L6K 3V7
(905) 842-2615 SIC 6411

PETIT DE GRAT PACKERS LIMITED p 464
24 HWY 206, PETIT DE GRAT, NS, B0E 2L0
(902) 226-0029 SIC 2091

PETIT LEM p 1326
See GROUPE LEMUR INC, LE

PETITE BRETONNE (DISTRIBUTION) INC, LA p 1059
1210 BOUL MICHELE-BOHEC, BLAINVILLE, QC, J7C 5S4
(450) 420-9159 SIC 5149

PETITE BRETONNE INC, LA p 1059
1210 BOUL MICHELE-BOHEC, BLAINVILLE, QC, J7C 5S4
(450) 435-3381 SIC 2051

PETITE SOEURS DE LA SAINTE-FAMILLE, LES p 1372
1820 RUE GALT O, SHERBROOKE, QC, J1K 1H9
(819) 823-0345 SIC 8661

PETITS DELICES G.T. INC, AUX p 1265
2022 RUE LAVOISIER BUREAU 198, QUEBEC, QC, G1N 4L5
(418) 683-8099 SIC 5451

PETLAND p 160
See 1009833 ALBERTA LTD

PETO MACCALLUM LTD p 789
165 CARTWRIGHT AVE, NORTH YORK, ON, M6A 1V5
(416) 785-5110 SIC 8711

PETRELLA TRANSPORT LIMITED p 531
12404 AIRPORT RD, CALEDON, ON, L7C 2W1
(905) 951-0584 SIC 4212

PETRELOCATE p 943
See VIP SITTERS INC

PETRIE FORD SALES (KINGSTON) LTD p 632
1388 BATH RD, KINGSTON, ON, K7M 4X6
(613) 544-6203 SIC 5511

PETRIE RAYMOND S.E.N.C.R.L p 1177
255 BOUL CREMAZIE E BUREAU 1000, MONTREAL, QC, H2M 1L5
(514) 342-4740 SIC 8721

PETRIFOND FONDATION COMPAGNIE LIMITEE p 1180
8320 BOUL SAINT-LAURENT, MONTREAL, QC, H2P 2M3
(514) 387-2838 SIC 1794

PETRIN MECHANICAL LTD p 106
12180 152 ST NW, EDMONTON, AB, T5V 1S1
(780) 451-4943 SIC 1711

PETRO ASSETS INC p 997
130 KING ST SUITE 2850, TORONTO, ON, M9N 1L5
(416) 364-8788 SIC 6712

PETRO CANADA p 16
See JEPSON PETROLEUM (ALBERTA) LTD

PETRO CANADA p 18
See S MALIK INVESTMENTS LTD

PETRO CANADA p 60
See SUNCOR ENERGY INC

PETRO CANADA p 84
See 963618 ALBERTA LTD

PETRO CANADA p 165

See 846840 ALBERTA LTD
PETRO CANADA   p 171
See PEPPERS HIGHWAY SERVICE INC
PETRO CANADA   p 177
See OCEANS RETAIL INVESTMENTS INC
PETRO CANADA   p 186
See MUNN ENTERPRISES LTD
PETRO CANADA   p 214
See PETRO-CANADA HIBERNIA PART-
NERSHIP
PETRO CANADA   p 216
See CASTLE FUELS (2008) INC
PETRO CANADA   p 220
See SPRING FUEL DISTRIBUTORS INC
PETRO CANADA   p 241
See KIANI MOTORS LTD
PETRO CANADA   p 243
See CO DARA VENTURES LTD
PETRO CANADA   p 250
See LOAD'EM UP PETROLEUMS LTD
PETRO CANADA   p 340
See DARVIC ENTERPRISES LTD
PETRO CANADA   p 356
See RPM ENTERPRISES LTD
PETRO CANADA   p 361
See CENTENNIAL SUPPLY LTD
PETRO CANADA   p 366
See JANICO INVESTMENTS LTD
PETRO CANADA   p 369
See 625056 SASKATCHEWAN LTD
PETRO CANADA   p 409
See BTK INVESTMENTS LIMITED
PETRO CANADA   p 456
See 3025906 NOVA SCOTIA LIMITED
PETRO CANADA   p 487
See JOHN SK LTD
PETRO CANADA   p 490
See 1211084 ONTARIO LTD
PETRO CANADA   p 496
See 1435207 ONTARIO INC
PETRO CANADA   p 497
See SIMSAK CORPORATION
PETRO CANADA   p 498
See TAKBRO ENTERPRISES LIMITED
PETRO CANADA   p 511
See 2124964 ONTARIO INC
PETRO CANADA   p 528
See 1126194 ONTARIO LIMITED
PETRO CANADA   p 547
See 1249932 ONTARIO INC
PETRO CANADA   p 547
See 1475541 ONTARIO LTD
PETRO CANADA   p 594
See SIX PILLARS LTD
PETRO CANADA   p 597
See 1197767 ONTARIO LTD
PETRO CANADA   p 606
See MAILLETTE HOLDINGS INC
PETRO CANADA   p 632
See 1195149 ONTARIO LIMITED
PETRO CANADA   p 651
See 1319691 ONTARIO INCORPORATED
PETRO CANADA   p 652
See 1553690 ONTARIO INC
PETRO CANADA   p 685
See TUNCER TRADE INC
PETRO CANADA   p 718
See 4-HOWELL BROTHERS INC
PETRO CANADA   p 718
See 2041188 ONTARIO INC
PETRO CANADA   p 753
See GRANT FUELS INC.
PETRO CANADA   p 783
See LOVELY IMPORTS & RETAILS LTD
PETRO CANADA   p 786
See LOVELY IMPORTS & RETAILS LTD
PETRO CANADA   p 796
See 1491222 ONTARIO LTD
PETRO CANADA   p 832
See 1460932 ONTARIO LIMITED
PETRO CANADA   p 869
See V.H. FUELS INC
PETRO CANADA   p 884
See LING & LING ENTERPRISES LTD

PETRO CANADA   p 907
See 1670747 ONTARIO INC
PETRO CANADA   p 918
See 1461148 ONTARIO CORP
PETRO CANADA   p 1000
See 1008803 ONTARIO LTD
PETRO CANADA   p 1006
See 1579149 ONTARIO LTD
PETRO CANADA   p 1015
See VIRGIN & ALL SAINTS CO. LTD, THE
PETRO CANADA   p 1018
See 1498403 ONTARIO INC
PETRO CANADA   p 1061
See 9109-9861 QUEBEC INC
PETRO CANADA   p 1260
See ENTREPRISES ELAINE ROY INC, LES
PETRO CANADA   p 1281
See ENTREPRISES CD VARIN INC, LES
PETRO CANADA   p 1283
See RESEAU GLP & CIE INC
PETRO CANADA   p 1358
See 9035-2022 QUEBEC INC
PETRO CANADA   p 1406
See GIRARD BULK SERVICE LTD
PETRO CANADA   p 1414
See PBCN P.A. FUEL AND CONVENIENCE
LIMITED PARTNERSHIP
PETRO CANADA   p 1416
See MAZENC FUELS LTD
PETRO CANADA   p 1422
See KAST HOLDINGS INC
PETRO CANADA   p 1432
See MILLSAP FUEL DISTRIBUTORS LTD
PETRO CANADA BULK   p 1412
See LAMON, J.J. INC
PETRO CANADA GRASSLAND   p 134
See 413877 ALBERTA LTD
PETRO CANADA RELAIS   p 1083
See 9050-6015 QUEBEC INC
PETRO CANADA, DIV OF   p 152
See PEACE FUEL DISTRIBUTORS LTD
PETRO FIELD INDUSTRY   p 167
See DYNAMIC ATTRACTIONS LTD
PETRO MONTESTRIE INC   p 1109
619 RUE LAURENT, GRANBY, QC, J2G 8Y3
(450) 378-9771   SIC 5172
PETRO SERVICE LIMITED   p 413
11 MCILVEEN DR, SAINT JOHN, NB, E2J
4Y6
(506) 632-1000   SIC 5085
PETRO-CANADA   p 169
See KOCH FUEL PRODUCTS INC
PETRO-CANADA   p 199
See ABHAY ENTERPRISES LTD
PETRO-CANADA   p 217
See KB HOLDINGS LTD
PETRO-CANADA   p 431
See SUNCOR ENERGY INC
PETRO-CANADA   p 436
See MATONABEE PETROLEUM LTD
PETRO-CANADA   p 486
See BOWMAN FUELS LTD
PETRO-CANADA   p 685
See 2116160 ONTARIO INC
PETRO-CANADA   p 747
4663 6 HWY S, MOUNT HOPE, ON, L0R
1W0
(905) 679-1445   SIC 4925
PETRO-CANADA ALBERTA   p 144
See HANCOCK PETROLEUM INC
PETRO-CANADA BUSINESS CENTER   p
715
See SUNCOR ENERGY INC
**PETRO-CANADA HIBERNIA PARTNER-
SHIP**   p
214
11527 ALASKA RD, FORT ST. JOHN, BC,
V1J 6N2
(250) 787-8200   SIC 1311
PETRO-CANADA LUBRICANTS INC p 714
2310 LAKESHORE RD W, MISSISSAUGA,
ON, L5J 1K2
(866) 335-3369   SIC 5172
PETRO-CANADA WHOLESALE MARKET-

ING   p
163
See MAX FUEL DISTRIBUTORS LTD
PETRO-PASS CARDLOCK   p 126
See DOUBLE C. DISTRIBUTORS LTD
PETROCAPITA INCOME TRUST   p 56
717 7 AVE SW SUITE 1400, CALGARY, AB,
T2P 0Z3
(587) 393-3450   SIC 1382
**PETROCARE SERVICES LIMITED PART-
NERSHIP**   p
126
4515 2 AVE, EDSON, AB, T7E 1C1
(780) 723-4237   SIC 1623
PETROCHINA CANADA LTD   p 56
707 5 ST SW SUITE 2700, CALGARY, AB,
T2P 1V8
(403) 265-6635   SIC 1382
**PETROCHINA INTERNATIONAL (CANADA)
TRADING LTD**   p 56
111 5 AVE SW SUITE 1800, CALGARY, AB,
T2P 3Y6
(587) 233-1200   SIC 4924
PETROCOM CONSTRUCTION LTD   p 102
17505 109A AVE NW, EDMONTON, AB,
T5S 2W4
(780) 481-5181   SIC 1542
PETROCORP GROUP INC   p 123
14032 23 AVE NW SUITE 166, EDMON-
TON, AB, T6R 3L6
(780) 910-9436   SIC 1731
PETROFF PARTNERSHIP ARCHITECTS p
674
260 TOWN CENTRE BLVD SUITE 300,
MARKHAM, ON, L3R 8H8
(905) 470-7000   SIC 8712
PETROFIELD INDUSTRIES INC   p 167
4102 44TH AVE, STETTLER, AB, T0C 2L0
(403) 883-2400   SIC 3533
PETROGAS ENERGY CORP   p 56
205 5 AVE SW SUITE 3900, CALGARY, AB,
T2P 2V7
(403) 266-1985   SIC 5172
PETROKAZAKHSTAN INC   p 56
140 4 AVE SW SUITE 1460, CALGARY, AB,
T2P 3N3
(403) 221-8435   SIC 1311
PETROLE CAMPBELL PETROLEUM 2001p
618
See 1443635 ONTARIO INC
PETROLE J.M.B INC   p 1072
85 RUE COMMERCIALE, CABANO, QC,
G0L 1E0
(418) 854-2267   SIC 5172
PETROLE LEGER INC   p 1120
460 GRAND BOULEVARD, L'ILE-PERROT,
QC, J7V 4X5
(514) 453-5766   SIC 5541
PETROLE PAGE INC   p 1253
2899 BOUL DU CURE-LABELLE BUREAU
100, PREVOST, QC, J0R 1T0
(450) 224-1795   SIC 5983
PETROLE XTREME   p 1123
See PETROLES CARUFEL INC, LES
PETROLES ALCASYNA (1993) INC, LES p
1046
511 RUE PRINCIPALE S, AMOS, QC, J9T
2J8
(819) 732-5334   SIC 5172
PETROLES C.L. INC, LES   p 1316
25   104   RTE,   SAINT-JEAN-SUR-
RICHELIEU, QC, J2X 1H2
(450) 346-7555   SIC 5541
PETROLES CADEKO INC   p 1262
455 RUE DES ENTREPRENEURS BU-
REAU 652, QUEBEC, QC, G1M 2V2
(418) 688-9188   SIC 5172
PETROLES CARUFEL INC, LES   p 1123
78 8E AV O, LA SARRE, QC, J9Z 1N3
(819) 762-0765   SIC 5172
PETROLES COULOMBE & FILS INC, LESp
1109
226 RUE ROBINSON S BUREAU 1,
GRANBY, QC, J2G 7M6

(450) 375-2080   SIC 5172
PETROLES CREVIER INC   p 1330
2025 RUE LUCIEN-THIMENS, SAINT-
LAURENT, QC, H4R 1K8
(514) 331-2951   SIC 5172
PETROLES J.C. TRUDEL INC   p 1366
1220 10E AV, SENNETERRE, QC, J0Y 2M0
(819) 737-2477   SIC 5172
PETROLES J.D. INC   p 1151
60 RUE DU PORT, MATANE, QC, G4W 3M6
(418) 562-0969   SIC 5172
PETROLES R.L. INC, LES   p 1079
460 RUE RACINE E, CHICOUTIMI, QC,
G7H 1T7
(418) 543-0775   SIC 5172
PETROLES R.TURMEL INC, LES   p 1125
4575 RUE LATULIPPE, LAC-MEGANTIC,
QC, G6B 3H1
(819) 583-3838   SIC 5172
PETROLES SHERBROOKE INC, LES   p
1372
125 RUE DES QUATRE-PINS, SHER-
BROOKE, QC, J1J 2L5
(819) 565-1770   SIC 5983
**PETROLEUM TANK MANAGEMENT ASSO-
CIATION OF ALBERTA**   p
90
10303 JASPER AVE NW SUITE 980, ED-
MONTON, AB, T5J 3N6
(780) 425-8265   SIC 4922
PETRONAS ENERGY CANADA LTD   p 57
215 2 ST SW SUITE 1600, CALGARY, AB,
T2P 1M4
(403) 216-2510   SIC 1311
PETRONOR INC   p 1391
1401 CH SULLIVAN. VAL-D'OR, QC, J9P
6V6
(819) 824-5505   SIC 5172
PETRONOVA INC   p 57
144 4 AVE SW SUITE 1600, CALGARY, AB,
T2P 3N4
(403) 398-2152   SIC 1311
PETROSHALE INC   p 57
421 7TH AVE SW SUITE 3230, CALGARY,
AB, T2P 4K9
(403) 266-1717   SIC 1381
PETROSOL INC   p 1139
1023 RUE RENAULT BUREAU 100, LEVIS,
QC, G6Z 1B6
(418) 647-3800   SIC 5541
PETROTAL CORP   p 57
421 7TH AVE SW SUITE 4000, CALGARY,
AB, T2P 4K9
(403) 813-4237   SIC 1382
PETROVALUE PRODUCTS CANADA INC p
273
19402 54 AVE UNIT 104, SURREY, BC, V3S
7H9
(604) 576-0004   SIC 5172
PETROWEST CORPORATION   p 57
407 2 ST SW SUITE 800, CALGARY, AB,
T2P 2Y3
(403) 237-0881   SIC 4213
PETROWEST TRANSPORTATION LP p 134
9201 163 AVE, GRANDE PRAIRIE, AB, T8X
0B6
(780) 402-0383   SIC 1382
PETRUS RESOURCES LTD   p 57
240 4 AVE SW SUITE 2400, CALGARY, AB,
T2P 4H4
(403) 984-4014   SIC 1382
PETTIPIECE HELEN SUTTON GROUP   p
262
9100 BLUNDELL RD UNIT 550, RICH-
MOND, BC, V6Y 3X9
(604) 341-7997   SIC 6531
PEXAL-TECALUM CANADA   p 1045
See 9283-9034 QUEBEC INC
**PEYTO EXPLORATION & DEVELOPMENT
CORP**   p 57
600 3 AVE SW SUITE 300, CALGARY, AB,
T2P 0G5
(403) 261-6081   SIC 1311
PF CONSUMER HEALTHCARE CANADA

▲ Public Company   ■ Public Company Family Member   **HQ** Headquarters   **BR** Branch   **SL** Single Location

ULC *p 732*
55 STANDISH CRT SUITE 450, MISSISSAUGA, ON, L5R 4B2
(905) 507-7000 *SIC 2834*

PF CONSUMER HEALTHCARE CANADA ULC *p 1330*
1025 BOUL MARCEL-LAURIN, SAINT-LAURENT, QC, H4R 1J6
(514) 695-0500 *SIC 2834*

PF CUSTOM COUNTERTOPS LTD *p 102*
10417 174 ST NW, EDMONTON, AB, T5S 1H1
(780) 484-0831 *SIC 2541*

PF MEDIA GROUP INC *p 236*
319 GOVERNORS CRT, NEW WESTMINSTER, BC, V3L 5S5
(604) 599-3876 *SIC 7389*

PF RESOLU CANADA INC *p 592*
427 MOWAT AVE, FORT FRANCES, ON, P9A 1Y8
(807) 274-5311 *SIC 2611*

PF RESOLU CANADA INC *p 887*
2 ALLANBURG RD S, ST CATHARINES, ON, L2T 3W9
(905) 227-5000 *SIC 2621*

PF RESOLU CANADA INC *p 910*
2001 NEEBING AVE, THUNDER BAY, ON, P7E 6S3
(807) 475-2110 *SIC 2421*

PF RESOLU CANADA INC *p 910*
2001 NEEBING AVE, THUNDER BAY, ON, P7E 6S3
(807) 475-2400 *SIC 2621*

PF RESOLU CANADA INC *p 1045*
1100 RUE MELANCON O, ALMA, QC, G8B 7G2
(418) 668-9400 *SIC 2621*

PF RESOLU CANADA INC *p 1046*
801 RUE DES PAPETIERS, AMOS, QC, J9T 3X5
(819) 727-1515 *SIC 2621*

PF RESOLU CANADA INC *p 1052*
20 AV MARQUETTE, BAIE-COMEAU, QC, G4Z 1K6
(418) 296-3371 *SIC 2679*

PF RESOLU CANADA INC *p 1053*
1 CH DE LA SCIERIE, BAIE-COMEAU, QC, G5C 2S9
(418) 589-9229 *SIC 5099*

PF RESOLU CANADA INC *p 1075*
7499 BOUL SAINTE-ANNE, CHATEAU-RICHER, QC, G0A 1N0
(418) 824-4233 *SIC 2421*

PF RESOLU CANADA INC *p 1081*
100 RUE DE LA DONOHUE, CLERMONT, QC, G4A 1A7
(418) 439-5300 *SIC 2621*

PF RESOLU CANADA INC *p 1090*
1 4E AV, DOLBEAU-MISTASSINI, QC, G8L 2R4
(418) 239-2350 *SIC 2621*

PF RESOLU CANADA INC *p 1090*
200 RUE DE QUEN, DOLBEAU-MISTASSINI, QC, G8L 5M8
(418) 679-1010 *SIC 2621*

PF RESOLU CANADA INC *p 1103*
79 RUE MAIN, GATINEAU, QC, J8P 4X6
(819) 643-7500 *SIC 4911*

PF RESOLU CANADA INC *p 1108*
2250 RANG SAINT-JOSEPH N, GIRARDVILLE, QC, G0W 1R0
(418) 630-3433 *SIC 2421*

PF RESOLU CANADA INC *p 1116*
3750 RUE DE CHAMPLAIN, JONQUIERE, QC, G7X 1M1
(418) 695-9100 *SIC 2621*

PF RESOLU CANADA INC *p 1121*
5850 AV DES JARDINS, LA DORE, QC, G8J 1B4
(418) 256-3816 *SIC 2421*

PF RESOLU CANADA INC *p 1134*
2050 RTE 805 N, LEBEL-SUR-QUEVILLON, QC, J0Y 1X0
(819) 755-2500 *SIC 2439*

PF RESOLU CANADA INC *p 1148*
200 CH DE MONTCERF, MANIWAKI, QC, J9E 1A1
(819) 449-2100 *SIC 2421*

PF RESOLU CANADA INC *p 1211*
111 BOUL ROBERT-BOURASSA UNITE 5000, MONTREAL, QC, H3C 2M1
(514) 875-2160 *SIC 0831*

PF RESOLU CANADA INC *p 1303*
900 BOUL HAMEL, SAINT-FELICIEN, QC, G8K 2X4
(418) 679-0552 *SIC 2421*

PF RESOLU CANADA INC *p 1353*
300 AV DU MOULIN, SAINT-THOMAS-DIDYME, QC, G0W 1P0
(418) 274-3340 *SIC 2421*

PF RESOLU CANADA INC *p 1366*
40 CH SAINT-PIERRE, SENNETERRE, QC, J0Y 2M0
(819) 737-2300 *SIC 2621*

PFAFF AUTOMOTIVE PARTNERS INC *p 557*
9088 JANE ST, CONCORD, ON, L4K 2M9
(905) 907-2834 *SIC 5511*

PFAFF BMW *p 691*
See *2410147 ONTARIO INC*

PFAFF LEASING *p 557*
See *PFAFF MOTORS INC*

PFAFF MOTORS INC *p 557*
220 CALDARI RD, CONCORD, ON, L4K 4L1
(905) 761-7890 *SIC 5511*

PFB CORPORATION *p 9*
2891 SUNRIDGE WAY NE SUITE 300, CALGARY, AB, T1Y 7K7
(403) 569-4300 *SIC 3086*

PFC FLEXIBLE CIRCUITS LIMITED *p 873*
11 CANADIAN RD SUITE 7, SCARBOROUGH, ON, M1R 5G1
(416) 750-8433 *SIC 3679*

PFEIFER HOLDINGS LTD *p 1412*
992 101ST ST, NORTH BATTLEFORD, SK, S9A 0Z3
(306) 445-9425 *SIC 6712*

PFENNING'S ORGANIC VEGETABLES INC *p 753*
1209 WATERLOO ST, NEW HAMBURG, ON, N3A 1T1
(519) 662-3468 *SIC 5148*

PFIZER CANADA INC *p 1330*
See *PFIZER CANADA SRI*

PFIZER CANADA SRI *p 347*
720 17TH ST E, BRANDON, MB, R7A 7H2
(204) 728-1511 *SIC 2834*

PFIZER CANADA SRI *p 1118*
17300 RTE TRANSCANADIENNE, KIRKLAND, QC, H9J 2M5
(514) 695-0500 *SIC 2834*

PFIZER CANADA SRI *p 1330*
1025 BOUL MARCEL-LAURIN, SAINT-LAURENT, QC, H4R 1J6
(514) 744-6771 *SIC 2834*

PFIZER CANADA ULC *p 347*
See *PFIZER CANADA SRI*

PFIZER CONSUMER HEALTHCARE CANADA *p 732*
See *PF CONSUMER HEALTHCARE CANADA ULC*

PG MOTORS *p 250*
See *PRINCE GEORGE MOTORS LTD*

PG SOLUTIONS INC *p 1285*
217 AV LEONIDAS S BUREAU 13, RIMOUSKI, QC, G5L 2T5
(418) 724-5037 *SIC 7371*

PG4 CONSTRUCTION CORP. *p 1247*
3777 RUE DOLLARD-DESJARDINS, POINTE-AUX-TREMBLES, QC, H1B 5W9
(514) 354-5533 *SIC 1541*

PGC SERVICES INC *p 598*
180 RAM FOREST RD, GORMLEY, ON, L0H 1G0
(905) 900-0010 *SIC 7699*

PGI HOLDINGS INC *p 534*
555 CONESTOGA BLVD, CAMBRIDGE, ON, N1R 7P5
(519) 622-5520 *SIC 1796*

PGSAR *p 249*
See *PRINCE GEORGE SEARCH AND RESCUE SOCIETY*

PHAETON AUTOMOTIVE GROUP INC *p 660*
1065 WHARNCLIFFE RD S, LONDON, ON, N6L 1J9
(519) 680-1800 *SIC 5511*

PHANTOM CABLES *p 671*
See *INFINITE CABLES INC*

PHANTOM INDUSTRIES INC *p 994*
207 WESTON RD, TORONTO, ON, M6N 4Z3
(416) 762-7177 *SIC 2251*

PHANTOM MFG. (INT'L) LTD *p 177*
30451 SIMPSON RD, ABBOTSFORD, BC, V2T 6C7
SIC 5211

PHANTOM SCREENS *p 177*
See *PHANTOM MFG. (INT'L) LTD*

PHARE DES SERVICES COMMUNAUTAIRES INC, LE *p 395*
68 AV DE LA RIVIERE, BOUCTOUCHE, NB, E4S 3A7
(506) 743-7377 *SIC 8322*

PHARLEM INC *p 1316*
795 BOUL D'IBERVILLE, SAINT-JEAN-SUR-RICHELIEU, QC, J2X 4S7
(450) 347-2000 *SIC 5912*

PHARM ESCOMPTE JEAN COUTU *p 1302*
See *LUSSIER, BERNARD INC*

PHARMA MEDICA RESEARCH INC *p 732*
6100 BELGRAVE RD, MISSISSAUGA, ON, L5R 0B7
(905) 624-9115 *SIC 8731*

PHARMA MEDICA RESEARCH INC *p 874*
4770 SHEPPARD AVE E SUITE 2, SCARBOROUGH, ON, M1S 3V6
(416) 759-5554 *SIC 8731*

PHARMA NTK INC *p 1323*
740 BOUL DE LA COTE-VERTU, SAINT-LAURENT, QC, H4L 5C8
(514) 744-2555 *SIC 5912*

PHARMA PLUS DRUGMARTS LTD *p 706*
5965 COOPERS AVE, MISSISSAUGA, ON, L4Z 1R9
(905) 501-7800 *SIC 5912*

PHARMA PRIX *p 1220*
See *GESTION RITEAL INC*

PHARMA-SANTE JONQUIERE INC *p 1116*
2340 RUE SAINT-HUBERT BUREAU 23, JONQUIERE, QC, G7X 5N4
(418) 547-5795 *SIC 5912*

PHARMACIE ANIK BERTRAND INC *p 1372*
1470 RUE KING O, SHERBROOKE, QC, J1J 2C2
(819) 564-3111 *SIC 5912*

PHARMACIE BEDARD LYNE PHARMACIENNE INC *p 1322*
490 AV VICTORIA, SAINT-LAMBERT, QC, J4P 2J4
(450) 671-5563 *SIC 5912*

PHARMACIE BRUNET *p 1397*
See *GESTION SYNER-PHARM INC*

PHARMACIE BRUNET-CANTIN INC *p 619*
4 NINTH ST, HEARST, ON, P0L 1N0
(705) 372-1212 *SIC 5912*

PHARMACIE CAROLINE MILETTE *p 1166*
5700 RUE SAINT-ZOTIQUE E BUREAU 100, MONTREAL, QC, H1T 3Y7
(514) 255-5797 *SIC 5912*

PHARMACIE CHRISTIAN BOURQUE, PHAMACIEN INC *p 1375*
4870 BOUL BOURQUE, SHERBROOKE, QC, J1N 3S5
(819) 820-0222 *SIC 5912*

PHARMACIE CHRISTINE LEGER & MARTIN COTE INC *p 1242*
1693 BOUL LOUIS-FRECHETTE, NICOLET, QC, J3T 1Z6

PHARMACIE DENNIS ABUD PHARMACY INC *p 398*
123 RUE CHAMPLAIN, DIEPPE, NB, E1A 1N5
(506) 859-1990 *SIC 5912*

PHARMACIE FATIMA AIT ADDI *p 1180*
See *FATIMA AIT ADDI*

PHARMACIE GAETAN, JACQUES ET MARCOT, JULIE *p 1253*
196 1RE AV, PORTNEUF, QC, G0A 2Y0
(418) 286-3301 *SIC 5122*

PHARMACIE JEAN COUTU *p 396*
See *056186 N.B. INC*

PHARMACIE JEAN COUTU *p 1059*
See *GROUPE J.C.F. LTEE*

PHARMACIE JEAN COUTU *p 1076*
See *PLACEMENTS JACQUES FELIX THIBAULT INC., LES*

PHARMACIE JEAN COUTU *p 1084*
See *2965-6311 QUEBEC INC*

PHARMACIE JEAN COUTU *p 1090*
See *DUOPHARM INC*

PHARMACIE JEAN COUTU *p 1097*
See *2310-3393 QUEBEC INC*

PHARMACIE JEAN COUTU *p 1106*
See *153927 CANADA INC*

PHARMACIE JEAN COUTU *p 1114*
See *OCIMAC INC*

PHARMACIE JEAN COUTU *p 1119*
See *2759-1106 QUEBEC INC*

PHARMACIE JEAN COUTU *p 1125*
See *VARIETES CHARRON & LECLERC, SENC*

PHARMACIE JEAN COUTU *p 1130*
See *ENTREPRISES MICHEL CAPLETTE INC*

PHARMACIE JEAN COUTU *p 1143*
See *DTS PHARMA INC*

PHARMACIE JEAN COUTU *p 1162*
See *R.D.-PHAR INC*

PHARMACIE JEAN COUTU *p 1168*
See *PHARMACIE RAYMOND BEAUCAIRE PHARMACIEN INC*

PHARMACIE JEAN COUTU *p 1182*
See *RAMVAL INC*

PHARMACIE JEAN COUTU *p 1182*
See *PHARMACIEN A. LAJEUNESSE & ASSOCIES*

PHARMACIE JEAN COUTU *p 1184*
See *2741-3327 QUEBEC INC*

PHARMACIE JEAN COUTU *p 1229*
See *PHARMACIE QUOC HUY HOANG INC*

PHARMACIE JEAN COUTU *p 1235*
See *3097-8217 QUEBEC INC*

PHARMACIE JEAN COUTU *p 1240*
See *PHARMACIE KANOU & YOUSSEF S.E.N.C.*

PHARMACIE JEAN COUTU *p 1242*
See *PHARMACIE CHRISTINE LEGER & MARTIN COTE INC*

PHARMACIE JEAN COUTU *p 1245*
See *VALERIO, TOMASELLI*

PHARMACIE JEAN COUTU *p 1261*
See *BOUCHER, MARC PHARMACIEN*

PHARMACIE JEAN COUTU *p 1270*
See *TALBOT, JOHANNE PHARMACIENNE*

PHARMACIE JEAN COUTU *p 1282*
155 BOUL LACOMBE UNITE 160, REPENTIGNY, QC, J5Z 3C4
(450) 654-6747 *SIC 5912*

PHARMACIE JEAN COUTU *p 1287*
See *JEAN COUTU JACQUES BOUILLON (AFFILIATED PHARMACIES)*

PHARMACIE JEAN COUTU *p 1308*
See *ESCOPHAR INC*

PHARMACIE JEAN COUTU *p 1319*
See *123273 CANADA INC*

PHARMACIE JEAN COUTU *p 1330*
2085 BOUL MARCEL-LAURIN, SAINT-LAURENT, QC, H4R 1K4
(514) 745-3003 *SIC 5912*

PHARMACIE JEAN COUTU *p 1376*

See ANDRE ROY ET SYLVAIN BOISSELLE
PHARMACIENS INC

PHARMACIE JEAN COUTU   p 1382
See ENTREPRISES JULIE LESSARD INC,
LES

PHARMACIE JEAN COUTU   p 1391
See ROYMICK INC

PHARMACIE JEAN COUTU   p 1396
See 153924 CANADA INC

PHARMACIE JEAN COUTU # 159   p 619
See PHARMACIE SYRHAK PHARMACY
INC

PHARMACIE JEAN COUTU #156   p 1120
See MAGASIN FARMAJEM INC

PHARMACIE JEAN COUTU #62 (PJC)   p
1317
See ESCOMPTES FERNAND LACHANCE
INC.

PHARMACIE JEAN COUTU #89   p 1053
See MARTIN & BELZILE INC

PHARMACIE JEAN COUTU M C   p 1219
See DOLARIAN, STEPHAN

PHARMACIE JEAN-COUTU   p 1057
See TREMBLAY, ANDREE P. PHARMA-
CIEN ENR

PHARMACIE JEAN-COUTU   p 1071
See ESCOMPTE CHEZ LAFORTUNE INC

PHARMACIE JEAN-COUTU   p 1171
See RIVET, PATRICE & MANON ST-JEAN
PHARMACIENS SENC

PHARMACIE JEAN-COUTU   p 1295
See ARCHAMBAULT, J. L. PHARMACIEN

PHARMACIE JEAN-COUTU # 237   p 1084
See POTVIN, PIERRE INC

PHARMACIE JEAN-COUTU 163   p 1149
See RONPIEN INC

**PHARMACIE JEAN-MICHEL COUTU ET
TRISTAN GIGUERE INC**   p 1145
3245 CH DE CHAMBLY BUREAU 305,
LONGUEUIL, QC, J4L 4K5
(450) 670-2496   SIC 5912

PHARMACIE KANOU & YOUSSEF S.E.N.C.
p 1240
6405 BOUL LEGER BUREAU 38,
MONTREAL-NORD, QC, H1G 1L4
(514) 323-6270   SIC 5912

PHARMACIE LEBLANC, PIERRE INC p 417
338 MAIN ST, SHEDIAC, NB, E4P 2E5
(506) 532-4410   SIC 5912

**PHARMACIE LOUIS LEGAULT, LYETTE
BOULE, PHARMACIENS INC**   p 1091
3353 BOUL DES SOURCES, DOLLARD-
DES-ORMEAUX, QC, H9B 1Z8
(514) 683-5460   SIC 5912

PHARMACIE MARIE BLAIS GIROUXp 1354
See 9214-1142 QUEBEC INC

**PHARMACIE MARTINE CLAVEAU ET
KEVIN MARK KIRKCALDY INC**   p 1076
103 RUE PRINCIPALE, CHATEAUGUAY,
QC, J6K 1G2
(450) 691-3636   SIC 5912

PHARMACIE MORIN INC   p 1165
5955 RUE SHERBROOKE E, MONTREAL,
QC, H1N 1B7
(514) 254-7513   SIC 5912

PHARMACIE NICOLAS CARBONNEAU INC
p 1236
4515 BOUL ARTHUR-SAUVE, MONTREAL,
QC, H7R 5P8
(450) 962-7455   SIC 5912

PHARMACIE NOVENA   p 619
See PHARMACIE BRUNET-CANTIN INC

PHARMACIE PIERRE GRAVEL   p 1250
See GRAVELUNI INC

PHARMACIE QUOC HUY HOANG INC   p
1229
6624 AV SOMERLED BUREAU 258, MON-
TREAL, QC, H4V 1T2
(514) 487-6530   SIC 5912

**PHARMACIE RAYMOND BEAUCAIRE
PHARMACIEN INC**   p 1168
3452 RUE ONTARIO E, MONTREAL, QC,
H1W 1R2
(514) 522-1126   SIC 5912

PHARMACIE RENE RIVARD   p 1171
2330 RUE FLEURY E, MONTREAL, QC,
H2B 1K9
(514) 387-7102   SIC 5912

**PHARMACIE S GAGNON & L MARMEN
S.E.N.C**   p 1273
2766 CH SAINTE-FOY, QUEBEC, QC, G1V
1V5
(418) 657-2956   SIC 5912

**PHARMACIE SONIA GUIMONT PHARMA-
CIENNE INC**   p
1294
275 BOUL SIR-WILFRID-LAURIER BU-
REAU 100, SAINT-BASILE-LE-GRAND, QC,
J3N 1V6
(450) 441-1944   SIC 5912

**PHARMACIE SYLVIE GELINAS ET CHAN-
TAL BELLEMARE PHARMACIENNES INC** p
1386
940 BOUL DES RECOLLETS, TROIS-
RIVIERES, QC, G8Z 3W9
(819) 379-1444   SIC 5912

PHARMACIE SYRHAK PHARMACY INC   p
619
80 MAIN ST E SUITE 159, HAWKESBURY,
ON, K6A 1A3
(613) 632-2743   SIC 5912

**PHARMACIE UNIPRIX GENEVIEVE BRE-
TON**   p
1372
See GESTION CLAUMOND INC

**PHARMACIEN A. LAJEUNESSE & ASSO-
CIES**   p
1182
6461 AV CHRISTOPHE-COLOMB, MON-
TREAL, QC, H2S 2G5
(514) 273-7373   SIC 5912

PHARMACIEN MARTIN GAGNON INC   p
1102
39 MONTEE DE SANDY BEACH BUREAU
31, GASPE, QC, G4X 2A9
(418) 368-3341   SIC 5912

PHARMACIES AFFILIEES A PROXIM   p
1370
624 RUE BOWEN S, SHERBROOKE, QC,
J1G 2E9
(819) 569-5561   SIC 5912

PHARMACY AND DRUG BASICS   p 577
See METRO ONTARIO PHARMACIES LIM-
ITED

PHARMALAB INC   p 1137
8750 BOUL GUILLAUME-COUTURE,
LEVIS, QC, G6V 9G9
(418) 833-7603   SIC 2834

PHARMAPAR INC   p 1393
1565 BOUL LIONEL-BOULET, VARENNES,
QC, J3X 1P7
(514) 731-2003   SIC 5122

PHARMAPLUS #4950   p 356
366 MAIN ST, SELKIRK, MB, R1A 2J7
(204) 482-6003   SIC 5961

PHARMAPRIX   p 1054
See 9007-8361 QUEBEC INC

PHARMAPRIX   p 1066
100 BOUL DE MONTARVILLE UNITE 120,
BOUCHERVILLE, QC, J4B 5M4
(450) 655-3010   SIC 5961

PHARMAPRIX   p 1067
See SERVICE SANTE CLAUDE GERVAIS
INC, LES

PHARMAPRIX   p 1090
See 9180-9582 QUEBEC INC

PHARMAPRIX   p 1092
See 9029-0917 QUEBEC INC

PHARMAPRIX   p 1096
See GESTIONS FERNANDA CIVITELLA
INC, LES

PHARMAPRIX   p 1106
See GESTION ROSLYN-ALVIN LTEE

PHARMAPRIX   p 1115
See SOCIETE DE GESTION RENE
RAINVILLE LTEE

PHARMAPRIX   p 1116
See PHARMA-SANTE JONQUIERE INC

PHARMAPRIX   p 1117
See 9072-3917 QUEBEC INC

PHARMAPRIX   p 1126
See GESTION PICARD-DUBUC INC

PHARMAPRIX   p 1130
See 9051-8051 QUEBEC INC

PHARMAPRIX   p 1131
See GESTION MICHEL LANG INC

PHARMAPRIX   p 1155
See GESTION SARMASO INC

PHARMAPRIX   p 1161
See 9080-0822 QUEBEC INC

PHARMAPRIX   p 1167
See 9026-2437 QUEBEC INC

PHARMAPRIX   p 1175
See GESTIONS FORTIER-ALLAN 29 INC

PHARMAPRIX   p 1204
See GESTIONS DOROTHEE MINVILLE
INC

PHARMAPRIX   p 1213
See GESTIONS LUCAP INC

PHARMAPRIX   p 1218
See 9070-4701 QUEBEC INC

PHARMAPRIX   p 1219
See GESTION LISE HAMEL-CHARTRAND
INC

PHARMAPRIX   p 1219
See CAROPHIL INC

PHARMAPRIX   p 1221
See CORPORATION DE GESTION E.A. MI-
CHOT, LA

PHARMAPRIX   p 1221
See 9013-5617 QUEBEC INC

PHARMAPRIX   p 1232
See GESTION CHRISTIAN DUGUAY INC

PHARMAPRIX   p 1239
See GESTION MAGDI TEBECHRANI INC.,
LES

PHARMAPRIX   p 1240
See ENTREPRISES KIM LUU INC, LES

PHARMAPRIX   p 1246
See 2968-4305 QUEBEC INC

PHARMAPRIX   p 1248
See 9159-9159 QUEBEC INC

PHARMAPRIX   p 1254
See OUELLET, PATRICK 1843 INC

PHARMAPRIX   p 1287
See 9141-9721 QUEBEC INC

PHARMAPRIX   p 1317
See GESTION CLAUDIUS INC

PHARMAPRIX   p 1319
See ENTREPRISES ISABELLE DES-
JARDINS INC, LES

PHARMAPRIX   p 1323
See 2970-9177 QUEBEC INC

PHARMAPRIX   p 1346
4420 RUE JEAN-TALON E, SAINT-
LEONARD, QC, H1S 1J7
(514) 723-1000   SIC 5912

PHARMAPRIX   p 1368
See SANTE-BEAUTE DANMOR INC

PHARMAPRIX   p 1373
See GESTION CLAUDE MEILLEUR INC

PHARMAPRIX   p 1395
See TRANSPHARM INC

PHARMAPRIX   p 1395
See 9100-9720 QUEBEC INC

PHARMAPRIX   p 1398
See 9132-9326 QUEBEC INC

PHARMAPRIX   p 1399
See GESTION SYLVAIN GOUDREAULT
INC

PHARMAPRIX CAVENDISH   p 1083
See 139273 CANADA INC

PHARMAPRIX CLAUDINE LOUBERT INC p
1323
1031 AV VICTORIA, SAINT-LAMBERT, QC,
J4R 1P6
(450) 671-8367   SIC 5912

PHARMAPRIX INC   p 1226
400 AV SAINTE-CROIX BUREAU 200, MON-
TREAL, QC, H4N 3L4
(514) 933-9331   SIC 6794

PHARMASAVE   p 226

See PHARMASAVE DRUGS (NATIONAL)
LTD

PHARMASAVE   p 395
See BOUCTOUCHE PHARMACY LTD

PHARMASAVE   p 449
See ASSOCIATED MARITIME PHARMA-
CIES LIMITED

PHARMASAVE   p 458
See CROWELLS PHARMACY LTD

PHARMASAVE   p 491
See GEEN'S PRESCRIPTION PHARMACY
LIMITED

PHARMASAVE   p 579
See PARTROSE DRUGS LIMITED

PHARMASAVE   p 880
See CLARK, H. PHARMACY INC

PHARMASAVE #214   p 342
See SERVICE DRUG LTD

PHARMASAVE #338   p 3
See MELROSE DRUGS LTD

PHARMASAVE #519   p 471
See SPEARS & MACLEOD PHARMACY
LIMITED

PHARMASAVE 354   p 135
See STEWART DRUGS HANNA (1984) LTD

PHARMASAVE DRUGS (NATIONAL) LTD p
226
8411 200 ST SUITE 201, LANGLEY, BC,
V2Y 0E7
(604) 455-2400   SIC 6794

PHARMASAVE DRUGS, DIV OF   p 228
See FOREWEST HOLDINGS INC

PHARMASCIENCE INC   p 1073
100 BOUL DE L'INDUSTRIE, CANDIAC,
QC, J5R 1J1
(450) 444-9989   SIC 2834

PHARMASCIENCE INC   p 1180
8580 AV DE L'ESPLANADE, MONTREAL,
QC, H2P 2R8
(514) 384-6516   SIC 2834

PHARMASCIENCE INC   p 1228
6111 AV ROYALMOUNT BUREAU 100,
MONTREAL, QC, H4P 2T4
(514) 340-1114   SIC 2834

PHARMASYSTEMS INC   p 674
151 TELSON RD, MARKHAM, ON, L3R 1E7
(905) 475-2500   SIC 5122

PHARMESCOMPTE JEAN COUTU p 1076
See THIBAULT, JACQUES ENTREPRISES
INC

PHARWAHA DRUGS LIMITED   p 686
7205 GOREWAY DR SUITE B1, MISSIS-
SAUGA, ON, L4T 2T9
(905) 677-7181   SIC 5912

PHASE ANALYZER COMPANY LTD   p 263
11168 HAMMERSMITH GATE, RICH-
MOND, BC, V7A 5H8
(604) 241-9568   SIC 3821

PHASE TWO DOORS, DIV OF   p 282
See PENTCO INDUSTRIES INC

PHASON INC   p 366
2 TERRACON PL, WINNIPEG, MB, R2J
4G7
(204) 233-1400   SIC 5065

PHC PROPERTY MANAGEMENT CORP   p
988
875 EGLINTON AVE W SUITE 300,
TORONTO, ON, M6C 3Z9
(416) 789-2664   SIC 6513

PHD CANADA, DIV OF   p 982
See OMNICOM CANADA CORP

PHD MONTREAL   p 1186
See XLR8 MEDIA INC

PHELPS APARTMENT LAUNDRIES LTD p
261
3640 NO. 4 RD SUITE 1, RICHMOND, BC,
V6X 2L7
(604) 257-8200   SIC 7359

PHELPS HOMES LTD   p 599
166 MAIN ST W, GRIMSBY, ON, L3M 1S3
(905) 945-5451   SIC 1521

PHELPS LEASING LTD   p 261
3640 NO. 4 RD, RICHMOND, BC, V6X 2L7
(604) 257-8230   SIC 7514

PHEROMONE INTERACTIF INC *p* 1211
75 RUE QUEEN BUREAU 3100, MONTREAL, QC, H3C 2N6
SIC 4899

PHIL MAUER & ASSOCIATES INC *p* 567
56954 EDEN LINE, EDEN, ON, N0J 1H0
(519) 866-5677 *SIC* 3569

PHIL'S CAR WASH & GAS BAR *p* 811
See 1213475 ONTARIO INC

PHIL'S VALU-MART *p* 1003
See 2079421 ONTARIO LIMITED

PHILBROOK'S BOATYARD LTD *p* 268
2324 HARBOUR RD, SIDNEY, BC, V8L 2P6
(250) 656-1157 *SIC* 3732

PHILCOS ENTERPRISER LTD *p* 706
120 BRUNEL RD, MISSISSAUGA, ON, L4Z 1T5
(905) 568-1823 *SIC* 5136

PHILIP BUSINESS DEVELOPMENT & INVESTMENT LTD. *p*
742
1680 COURTNEYPARK DR E UNIT 5, MISSISSAUGA, ON, L5T 1R4
(905) 366-8999 *SIC* 5044

PHILIPPE DANDURAND WINES LIMITED *p*
699
1660 TECH AVE SUITE 3, MISSISSAUGA, ON, L4W 5S7
(416) 368-3344 *SIC* 5182

PHILIPPE GOSSELIN & ASSOCIES LIMITEE *p*
1360
1133 BOUL VACHON N, SAINTE-MARIE, QC, G6E 1M9
(418) 387-5449 *SIC* 5172

PHILIPS CANADA LTD *p* 679
281 HILLMOUNT RD, MARKHAM, ON, L6C 2S3
(905) 201-4100 *SIC* 6712

PHILIPS ELECTRONICS LTD *p* 679
281 HILLMOUNT RD, MARKHAM, ON, L6C 2S3
(905) 201-4100 *SIC* 5064

PHILIPS HEALTH CARE, DIV OF *p* 679
See PHILIPS ELECTRONICS LTD

PHILLIPS ENGINEERING TECHNOLOGIES CORP *p* 557
385 CONNIE CRES, CONCORD, ON, L4K 5R2
SIC 3569

PHILPOT & DELGATY LTD *p* 909
800 VICTORIA AVE E, THUNDER BAY, ON, P7C 0A2
(807) 623-9022 *SIC* 6411

PHIPPS DESSERTS LTD *p* 777
1875 LESLIE ST UNIT 21, NORTH YORK, ON, M3B 2M5
(416) 391-5800 *SIC* 5143

PHIPPS DICKSON INTEGRIA (PDI) INC *p*
1118
18103 RTE TRANSCANADIENNE, KIRKLAND, QC, H9J 3Z4
(514) 695-1333 *SIC* 2752

PHLYN HOLDINGS LTD *p* 391
199 HAMELIN ST, WINNIPEG, MB, R3T 0P2
(204) 452-8379 *SIC* 5144

PHN INNOVATIONS *p* 1093
See ENTREPRISES PNH INC, LES

PHOENIX A.M.D. INTERNATIONAL INC *p*
496
41 BUTLER CRT, BOWMANVILLE, ON, L1C 4P8
(905) 427-7440 *SIC* 5023

PHOENIX BUILDING COMPONENTS INC *p*
882
93 OTTAWA AVE, SOUTH RIVER, ON, P0A 1X0
(705) 386-0007 *SIC* 2439

PHOENIX BUILDING COMPONENTS INC *p*
1000
5650 SIDEROAD 30, UTOPIA, ON, L0M 1T0
(705) 733-3843 *SIC* 2439

PHOENIX CONSTRUCTION INC *p* 156

7887 50 AVE SUITE 8, RED DEER, AB, T4P 1M8
(403) 342-2225 *SIC* 1542

PHOENIX CONTACT LTD *p* 684
8240 PARKHILL DR, MILTON, ON, L9T 5V7
(905) 864-8700 *SIC* 5065

PHOENIX EDT *p* 742
See PHOENIX/PMA INC

PHOENIX ENTERPRISES LTD *p* 382
500 ST JAMES ST, WINNIPEG, MB, R3G 3J4
(204) 956-2233 *SIC* 6531

PHOENIX FENCE CORP *p* 106
12816 156 ST NW, EDMONTON, AB, T5V 1E9
(780) 447-1919 *SIC* 3315

PHOENIX FLOOR & WALL PRODUCTS INC *p* 580
111 WESTMORE DR, ETOBICOKE, ON, M9V 3Y6
(416) 745-4200 *SIC* 5023

PHOENIX GEOPHYSICS LIMITED *p* 877
3781 VICTORIA PARK AVE UNIT 3, SCARBOROUGH, ON, M1W 3K5
(416) 491-7340 *SIC* 3829

PHOENIX GLASS INC *p* 209
8166 92 ST, DELTA, BC, V4G 0A4
(604) 525-2800 *SIC* 5031

PHOENIX GRILL LTD, THE *p* 70
16061 MACLEOD TRAIL SE SUITE 335, CALGARY, AB, T2Y 3S5
(403) 509-9111 *SIC* 5812

PHOENIX HOMES *p* 748
See 1120919 ONTARIO LTD

PHOENIX HUMAN SERVICES ASSOCIATION *p*
335
1824 STORE ST, VICTORIA, BC, V8T 4R4
(250) 383-4821 *SIC* 8361

PHOENIX INDUSTRIAL *p* 149
See PHOENIX INDUSTRIAL MAINTENANCE LTD

PHOENIX INDUSTRIAL MAINTENANCE LTD *p* 149
903 9 AVE, NISKU, AB, T9E 1C8
(780) 428-3130 *SIC* 1541

PHOENIX PERFORMANCE PRODUCTS INC *p* 557
100 BASS PRO MILLS DR UNIT 32, CONCORD, ON, L4K 5X1
(905) 539-0370 *SIC* 3949

PHOENIX PETROLEUM LTD *p* 400
400 THOMPSON DR, FREDERICTON, NB, E3A 9X2
(506) 459-6260 *SIC* 1542

PHOENIX RESTORATION INC *p* 1015
1100 BURNS ST E, WHITBY, ON, L1N 6M6
(905) 665-7600 *SIC* 1541

PHOENIX SERVICES ENVIRONNEMENTAUX INC. *p*
1306
144 RTE DU PRESIDENT-KENNEDY, SAINT-HENRI-DE-LEVIS, QC, G0R 3E0
(418) 882-0014 *SIC* 7389

PHOENIX TECHNOLOGY SERVICES INC *p*
57
250 2 ST SW SUITE 1400, CALGARY, AB, T2P 0C1
(403) 543-4466 *SIC* 1381

PHOENIX TECHNOLOGY SERVICES LP *p*
57
250 2 ST SW SUITE 1400, CALGARY, AB, T2P 0C1
(403) 543-4466 *SIC* 1381

PHOENIX TRANSPORTATION *p* 496
See 1429634 ONTARIO LIMITED

PHOENIX/PMA INC *p* 742
1080 MEYERSIDE DR, MISSISSAUGA, ON, L5T 1J4
(905) 678-9400 *SIC* 5051

PHONE EXPERTS COMMUNICATIONS LTD, THE *p* 154
4724 60 ST, RED DEER, AB, T4N 7C7
(403) 343-1122 *SIC* 4899

PHONETIME *p* 914
See TELLZA INC

PHOTO DE LA CAPITALE *p* 1277
See LABOPRO P.S. INC

PHOTO SERVICE LTEE *p* 1190
222 RUE NOTRE-DAME O, MONTREAL, QC, H2Y 1T3
(514) 849-2291 *SIC* 5043

PHOTON CONTROL INC *p* 256
13500 VERDUN PL SUITE 130, RICHMOND, BC, V6V 1V2
(604) 900-3155 *SIC* 3841

PHOTON DYNAMICS CANADA INC *p* 674
221 WHITEHALL DR, MARKHAM, ON, L3R 9T1
SIC 3599

PHQ GLOBAL INC *p* 524
1175 APPLEBY LINE UNIT C2, BURLINGTON, ON, L7L 5H9
(905) 332-3271 *SIC* 5082

PHX ENERGY SERVICES CORP *p* 57
250 2 ST SW SUITE 1400, CALGARY, AB, T2P 0C1
(403) 543-4466 *SIC* 1381

PHYSICAL PLANT *p* 401
See UNIVERSITY OF NEW BRUNSWICK

PHYSICAL PLANT SERVICES *p* 631
See QUEEN'S UNIVERSITY AT KINGSTON

PHYSIO CONTROL CANADA SALES LTD *p*
745
45 INNOVATION DR, MISSISSAUGA, ON, L9H 7L8
(800) 895-5896 *SIC* 5047

PHYSIO-ERGO PLUS INC *p* 1380
3395 BOUL DE LA PINIERE BUREAU 200, TERREBONNE, QC, J6X 4N1
(450) 492-9999 *SIC* 8049

PHYTOBIOMARIN *p* 1326
See LABORATOIRES DERMO-COSMETIK INC

PHYTODERM *p* 1327
See SOINS ESTHETIQUES PHYTODERM INC

PI FINANCIAL CORP *p* 308
666 BURRARD ST SUITE 1900, VANCOUVER, BC, V6C 3N1
(604) 664-2900 *SIC* 6211

PIC CANADA LTD *p* 393
99 SCURFIELD BLVD UNIT 161, WINNIPEG, MB, R3Y 1Y1
(204) 927-7120 *SIC* 2834

PIC GROUP HOLDINGS LIMITED, THE *p*
812
111 SIMCOE ST N, OSHAWA, ON, L1G 4S4
(905) 743-4600 *SIC* 6712

PIC GROUP LTD, THE *p* 843
1305 PICKERING PKWY, PICKERING, ON, L1V 3P2
(905) 743-4600 *SIC* 7549

PIC GROUP LTD, THE *p* 1015
202 SOUTH BLAIR ST UNIT 12, WHITBY, ON, L1N 8X9
(416) 576-6659 *SIC* 4225

PIC GROUP LTD, THE *p* 1021
1303 MCDOUGALL ST, WINDSOR, ON, N8X 3M6
(519) 252-1611 *SIC* 7549

PIC INVESTMENT GROUP INC *p* 1429
70 24TH ST E, SASKATOON, SK, S7K 4B8
(306) 664-3955 *SIC* 6712

PICCIONI BROS MUSHROOM FARM LIMITED *p*
566
355 ROCK CHAPEL RD, DUNDAS, ON, L9H 5E2
(905) 628-3090 *SIC* 0182

PICCOLI, N. CONSTRUCTION LTD *p* 651
1933 GORE RD SUITE 2, LONDON, ON, N5W 6B9
(519) 473-9665 *SIC* 1611

PICHE, R DYNAMITAGE INC *p* 1363
2591 BOUL SAINTE-SOPHIE, SAINTE-SOPHIE, QC, J5J 2V3
(819) 212-0744 *SIC* 1795

PICIS CLINICAL SOLUTIONS, INC *p* 750
1 ANTARES DR SUITE 400, NEPEAN, ON, K2E 8C4
(613) 226-5511 *SIC* 7371

PICIS ENVISION *p* 750
See PICIS CLINICAL SOLUTIONS, INC

PICKERING CAR CORP *p* 843
557 KINGSTON RD, PICKERING, ON, L1V 3N7
(416) 798-4800 *SIC* 5511

PICKERING COLLEGE *p* 756
16945 BAYVIEW AVE, NEWMARKET, ON, L3Y 4X2
(905) 895-1700 *SIC* 8211

PICKERING HOME DEPOT *p* 843
See HOME DEPOT OF CANADA INC

PICKERING TOYOTA *p* 843
See PICKERING CAR CORP

PICKFORD GROUP LTD, THE *p* 151
1237-200 SOUTHRIDGE DR, OKOTOKS, AB, T1S 0N8
(403) 571-0571 *SIC* 5084

PICKLE BARREL RESTAURANT *p* 906
See J.F. & L. RESTAURANTS LIMITED

PICKLE BARREL RESTAURANT, THE *p* 765
See J.F. & L. RESTAURANTS LIMITED

PICKLE BARREL, THE *p* 579
See J.F. & L. RESTAURANTS LIMITED

PICKLE BARREL, THE *p* 671
See J.F. & L. RESTAURANTS LIMITED

PICO OF CANADA LTD *p* 183
7590 CONRAD ST, BURNABY, BC, V5A 2H7
(604) 438-7571 *SIC* 5013

PICOLEUR, LE *p* 1311
See BRASSEURS DU MONDE INC

PICOV DOWNS INC *p* 475
380 KINGSTON RD E, AJAX, ON, L1Z 1W4
(905) 686-8001 *SIC* 7948

PICTET CANADA S.E.C. *p* 1207
1000 RUE DE LA GAUCHETIERE O BUREAU 3100, MONTREAL, QC, H3B 4W5
(514) 288-8161 *SIC* 6211

PICTON MAHONEY LONG SHORT EQUITY FUND *p* 943
33 YONGE ST SUITE 830, TORONTO, ON, M5E 1G4
(416) 955-4108 *SIC* 6722

PICTON MANOR NURSING HOME LIMITED *p* 845
9 HILL ST, PICTON, ON, K0K 2T0
SIC 8051

PICTURE BUTTE AUCTION MARKET 2001 LTD *p* 152
GD, PICTURE BUTTE, AB, T0K 1V0
(403) 732-4400 *SIC* 5154

PICTURE DEPOT *p* 782
See ASKAN ARTS LIMITED

PICTURE PICTURE COMPANY LTD., THE *p*
789
122 CARTWRIGHT AVE, NORTH YORK, ON, M6A 1V2
(416) 787-9827 *SIC* 5023

PICTURE PICTURE, THE *p* 789
See PICTURE PICTURE COMPANY LTD., THE

PIDHERNEY'S INC *p* 159
HWY 11 RANGE RD 70, ROCKY MOUNTAIN HOUSE, AB, T4T 1A7
(403) 845-3072 *SIC* 1629

PIE IX DODGE CHRYSLER 2000 INC *p* 1170
9350 BOUL PIE-IX, MONTREAL, QC, H1Z 4E9
(514) 342-8500 *SIC* 5511

PIE IX TOYOTA INC *p* 1240
6767 BOUL HENRI-BOURASSA E, MONTREAL-NORD, QC, H1G 2V6
(514) 329-0909 *SIC* 5511

PIECES D'AUTO P. & B. GAREAU (2012) *p* 1158
See 9268-8241 QUEBEC INC

PIECES D'AUTO ALAIN COTE INC *p* 1119
6315 BOUL WILFRID-HAMEL, L'ANCIENNE-LORETTE, QC, G2E 5W2

(418) 780-4770   *SIC 5531*
PIECES D'AUTO AT-PAC INC   *p 1161*
10700 BOUL HENRI-BOURASSA E, MON-
TREAL, QC, H1C 1G9
(514) 881-8888   *SIC 5013*
PIECES D'AUTO DE BEDFORD   *p 1318*
See PIECES D'AUTO ST-JEAN INC
PIECES D'AUTO LACROIX INC   *p 1302*
825 BOUL ARTHUR-SAUVE, SAINT-
EUSTACHE, QC, J7R 4K3
(450) 473-0661   *SIC 5013*
PIECES D'AUTO LAVIGNE   *p 1163*
*See PIECES D'AUTOS PAUL LAVIGNE INC,
LES*
**PIECES D'AUTO LEON GRENIER (1987)
INC, LES**   *p 1155*
1260 BOUL ALBINY-PAQUETTE, MONT-
LAURIER, QC, J9L 1M7
(819) 623-3740   *SIC 5013*
PIECES D'AUTO PINCOURT INC, LES   *p
1245*
35 CH DUHAMEL, PINCOURT, QC, J7W
4C6
(514) 453-5610   *SIC 5013*
PIECES D'AUTO ST-JEAN INC   *p 1318*
650 RUE DE DIJON, SAINT-JEAN-SUR-
RICHELIEU, QC, J3B 8G3
(450) 348-3871   *SIC 5013*
PIECES D'AUTO SUPER INC   *p 1308*
7803 CH DE CHAMBLY, SAINT-HUBERT,
QC, J3Y 5K2
(450) 676-1850   *SIC 5531*
PIECES D'AUTO TRANSIT INC, LES *p 1139*
1100 RUE JEAN-MARCHAND, LEVIS, QC,
G6Y 9G8
(866) 937-8916   *SIC 5013*
PIECES D'AUTO VALLEYFIELD INC *p 1365*
940 BOUL MONSEIGNEUR-LANGLOIS,
SALABERRY-DE-VALLEYFIELD, QC, J6S
1C3
(450) 373-9505   *SIC 5015*
**PIECES D'AUTOS CHAMBLY RICHELIEU
INC**   *p 1283*
2000 CH DES PATRIOTES BUREAU 299,
RICHELIEU, QC, J3L 6M1
(450) 658-7474   *SIC 5531*
PIECES D'AUTOS FERNAND BEGIN INC *p
1350*
416 RANG F.-BEGIN, SAINT-PHILIBERT,
QC, G0M 1X0
(418) 228-2413   *SIC 5531*
PIECES D'AUTOS G. M. INC   *p 1124*
1564 277 RTE, LAC-ETCHEMIN, QC, G0R
1S0
(418) 625-3132   *SIC 5013*
PIECES D'AUTOS JEAN LEBLANC LTEE *p
1388*
3780 BOUL GENE-H.-KRUGER, TROIS-
RIVIERES, QC, G9A 4M3
(819) 370-1212   *SIC 5531*
PIECES D'AUTOS JMR ALMA   *p 1044*
See 2742-7608 QUEBEC INC
PIECES D'AUTOS LE PORTAGE LTEE   *p
1120*
1059 BOUL DE L'ANGE-GARDIEN N,
L'ASSOMPTION, QC, J5W 1N7
(450) 589-5735   *SIC 5013*
PIECES D'AUTOS M.R. INC., LES   *p 1057*
125 RUE D'IBERVILLE, BERTHIERVILLE,
QC, J0K 1A0
(450) 836-7001   *SIC 5531*
PIECES D'AUTOS O. FONTAINE INC *p 1359*
415 CH DE TOURAINE, SAINTE-JULIE,
QC, J3E 1Y2
(450) 649-1489   *SIC 5013*
PIECES D'AUTOS PAUL LAVIGNE INC, LES
p 1163
3087 RUE DES ORMEAUX, MONTREAL,
QC, H1L 4Y1
(514) 351-4210   *SIC 5013*
PIECES D'AUTOS SELECT   *p 1284*
See 9183-9530 QUEBEC INC
PIECES D'AUTOS TRANSBEC, LES *p
1231*

5505 RUE ERNEST-CORMIER, MON-
TREAL, QC, H7C 0A1
(450) 665-4440   *SIC 5531*
**PIECES DE TRANSMISSION UNITRANS
LTEE, LES**   *p 1380*
3795 RUE GEORGES-CORBEIL, TERRE-
BONNE, QC, J6X 4J5
(450) 968-2000   *SIC 5013*
**PIECES POUR AUTOMOBILE JEAN-
TALON (1993) LTEE**   *p
1346*
7655 BOUL VIAU, SAINT-LEONARD, QC,
H1S 2P4
(514) 374-2113   *SIC 5013*
**PIECES UNIVERSELLES AUTO
CHICOUTIMI**   *p 1077*
See ENTREPRISES R.E.R. INC
PIED-MONT DORA INC   *p 1355*
176 RUE SAINT-JOSEPH, SAINTE-ANNE-
DES-PLAINES, QC, J0N 1H0
(450) 478-0801   *SIC 2033*
PIER-C PRODUCE INC   *p 644*
7R M C R DR, LEAMINGTON, ON, N8H 3N2
(519) 326-8807   *SIC 0722*
PIERCE FISHERIES   *p 461*
See THORNVALE HOLDINGS LIMITED
PIERCON LTEE   *p 1063*
387 RUE NOTRE-DAME, BON-CONSEIL,
QC, J0C 1A0
(819) 336-3777   *SIC 3281*
PIERRE BELVEDERE INC   *p 1131*
2555 AV DOLLARD, LASALLE, QC, H8N
3A9
(514) 286-2880   *SIC 5092*
PIERRE BROSSARD (1981) LTEE   *p 1070*
9595 RUE IGNACE, BROSSARD, QC, J4Y
2P3
(450) 659-9641   *SIC 1731*
**PIERRE ELLIOTT TRUDEAU HIGH
SCHOOL**   *p 679*
*See YORK REGION DISTRICT SCHOOL
BOARD*
**PIERRE ET MAURICE DE LA FONTAINE
INC**   *p 1102*
1000 RUE DOLLARD, GATINEAU, QC, J8L
3H3
(819) 986-8601   *SIC 5031*
**PIERRE FABRE DERMO-COSMETIQUE
CANADA INC**   *p 1071*
9955 RUE DE CHATEAUNEUF UNITE 115,
BROSSARD, QC, J4Z 3V5
(450) 676-9035   *SIC 5122*
PIERRES STONEDGE, LES   *p 1309*
See TECHO-BLOC INC
PIFFC   *p 689*
*See PEARSON INTERNATIONAL FUEL FA-
CILITIES CORPORATION*
PIGEON BRANDING + DESIGN   *p 977*
See PIGEON BRANDS INC
PIGEON BRANDS INC   *p 977*
179 JOHN ST 2ND FL, TORONTO, ON, M5T
1X4
(416) 532-9950   *SIC 7336*
PIHOKKER FARMS INC   *p 1003*
58126 CALTON LINE RR 1, VIENNA, ON,
N0J 1Z0
(519) 866-5030   *SIC 0161*
PII (CANADA) LIMITED   *p 116*
3575 97 ST NW, EDMONTON, AB, T6E 5S7
(780) 450-1031   *SIC 7389*
PIKANGIKUM EDUCATION AUTHORITY *p
846*
1 SCHOOL RD, PIKANGIKUM, ON, P0V
2L0
(807) 773-1093   *SIC 8211*
PIKE LAKE GOLF CENTRE LIMITED *p 544*
GD, CLIFFORD, ON, N0G 1M0
(519) 338-3010   *SIC 7011*
**PIKE WHEATON CHEVROLET OLDSMO-
BILE LTD**   *p
157*
3110 50 AVE, RED DEER, AB, T4R 1M6
(403) 343-8918   *SIC 5511*
PILAROS   *p 1363*

*See PILAROS INTERNATIONAL TRADING
INC*
PILAROS INTERNATIONAL TRADING INC
p 1363
755 CHOMEDEY (A-13) E, SAINTE-ROSE,
QC, H7W 5N4
(450) 681-6900   *SIC 5141*
PILKINGTON GLASS OF CANADA LTD *p
547*
1000 26 HWY, COLLINGWOOD, ON, L9Y
4V8
(705) 445-4780   *SIC 3231*
PILLAR FABRICATORS, DIV OF   *p 65*
See PILLAR RESOURCE SERVICES INC
PILLAR OILFIELD PROJECTS   *p 110*
See PILLAR RESOURCE SERVICES INC
PILLAR RESOURCE SERVICES INC   *p 65*
550 11 AVE SW, CALGARY, AB, T2R 1M7
(403) 266-7070   *SIC 1389*
PILLAR RESOURCE SERVICES INC *p 110*
4155 84 AVE NW, EDMONTON, AB, T6B
2Z3
(780) 440-2212   *SIC 1629*
PILLAR SECURITY   *p 994*
*See AUTHENTIC CONCIERGE AND SE-
CURITY SERVICES INC*
PILLAR5 PHARMA INC   *p 479*
365 MADAWASKA BLVD, ARNPRIOR, ON,
K7S 0C9
(613) 623-4221   *SIC 2834*
PILLER SAUSAGES   *p 1008*
See WISMER DEVELOPMENTS INC
PILLITTERI ESTATES WINERY INC *p 761*
1696 NIAGARA STONE RD, NIAGARA ON
THE LAKE, ON, L0S 1J0
(905) 468-3147   *SIC 0172*
PILON LTEE   *p 1106*
5 BOUL MONTCLAIR, GATINEAU, QC, J8Y
2E3
(819) 771-5841   *SIC 5039*
PILON MARINE   *p 1392*
See GROUPE THOMAS MARINE INC
PILON, RAYMOND J. ENTERPRISES LTD *p
542*
575 GRAND AVE W, CHATHAM, ON, N7L
1C5
(519) 351-9510   *SIC 5311*
PILOT COFFEE CORP   *p 920*
50 WAGSTAFF DR, TORONTO, ON, M4L
3W9
(416) 546-4006   *SIC 5149*
PILOT DIAMOND TOOLS LIMITED   *p 762*
1851 SEYMOUR ST, NORTH BAY, ON, P1A
0C7
(705) 497-3715   *SIC 3545*
PILOTES DU SAINT-LAURENT CENTRAL *p
1387*
*See CORPORATION DES PILOTES DU
SAINT-LAURENT CENTRAL INC*
PIMEE WELL SERVICING LTD   *p 137*
GD, KEHEWIN, AB, T0A 1C0
(780) 826-6392   *SIC 1389*
PIMM PRODUCTION SERVICES INC *p 214*
10924 ALASKA RD, FORT ST. JOHN, BC,
V1J 5T5
(250) 787-0808   *SIC 6712*
PIN PALACE   *p 66*
See EARL'S RESTAURANTS LTD
**PINCHER CREEK CO-OPERATIVE ASSO-
CIATION LIMITED**   *p
152*
GD, PINCHER CREEK, AB, T0K 1W0
(403) 627-2607   *SIC 5411*
PINCHER CREEK HOSPITAL   *p 152*
See ALBERTA HEALTH SERVICES
**PINCHIN LEBLANC ENVIRONMENTAL
LIMITED**   *p 448*
42 DOREY AVE, DARTMOUTH, NS, B3B
0B1
(902) 461-9999   *SIC 8748*
PINCHIN LTD   *p 725*
2470 MILLTOWER CRT, MISSISSAUGA,
ON, L5N 7W5
(905) 363-0678   *SIC 8748*

PINDER'S LOCK & SECURITY INC *p 884*
25 NIHAN DR, ST CATHARINES, ON, L2N
1L2
(905) 934-6333   *SIC 5065*
PINDER'S SECURITY PRODUCTS *p 884*
See PINDER'S LOCK & SECURITY INC
PINE ACRES (HAMPTON) LIMITED *p 1041*
24965 ROUTE 2, KENSINGTON, PE, C0B
1M0
(902) 836-5040   *SIC 5561*
PINE ACRES HOME   *p 342*
*See WESTBANK FIRST NATION PINE
ACRES HOME*
PINE ACRES RV   *p 1041*
See PINE ACRES (HAMPTON) LIMITED
PINE CLIFF ENERGY LTD   *p 65*
1015 4 ST SW SUITE 850, CALGARY, AB,
T2R 1J4
(403) 269-2289   *SIC 1381*
PINE CREEK CANADA PARTNERSHIP *p 91*
See CAPITAL MANAGEMENT LTD
PINE CREEK SCHOOL DIVISION   *p 350*
25 BROWN ST, GLADSTONE, MB, R0J 0T0
(204) 385-2216   *SIC 8211*
PINE ENVIRONMENTAL CANADA, INC *p
750*
159 COLONNADE RD S UNITS 3 AND 4,
NEPEAN, ON, K2E 7J4
(343) 682-1470   *SIC 5999*
PINE GROVE NURSING HOME   *p 401*
*See FREDERICTON SOUTH NURSING
HOME INC*
PINE RIDGE GARDEN GALLERY   *p 843*
See 1044912 ONTARIO LIMITED
PINE RIDGE SECONDARY SCHOOL *p 845*
See DURHAM DISTRICT SCHOOL BOARD
PINE VALLEY PACKAGING   *p 1001*
See 643487 ONTARIO LIMITED
PINE VALLEY PACKAGING GROUP INC *p
1001*
1 PARRATT RD, UXBRIDGE, ON, L9P 1R1
(905) 862-0830   *SIC 5199*
PINE VIEW ALL NATURAL MEATS INC *p
1413*
GD, OSLER, SK, S0K 3A0
(306) 239-4763   *SIC 0259*
PINE VIEW AUTO SALES INC   *p 1033*
3790 HIGHWAY 7, WOODBRIDGE, ON, L4L
9C3
(905) 851-2851   *SIC 6712*
PINE VIEW FARMS   *p 1413*
See PINE VIEW ALL NATURAL MEATS INC
PINE VIEW HYUNDAI   *p 1033*
See PINE VIEW AUTO SALES INC
PINECORE ENTERPRISES INC   *p 241*
828 HARBOURSIDE DR SUITE 117,
NORTH VANCOUVER, BC, V7P 3R9
(604) 990-9679   *SIC 5199*
PINECREST NURSING HOME   *p 846*
See 656955 ONTARIO LIMITED
PINEDALE PROPERTIES LTD   *p 789*
970 LAWRENCE AVE W SUITE 303,
NORTH YORK, ON, M6A 3B6
(416) 256-2900   *SIC 6531*
PINEGROVE PLACE   *p 261*
*See MENNONITE INTERMEDIATE CARE
HOME SOCIETY OF RICHMOND*
PINEHILL MANAGEMENT CORP   *p 9*
2121 36 ST NE, CALGARY, AB, T1Y 5S3
SIC 5812
PINEHURST GROUP, INC   *p 808*
120 C LINE, ORANGEVILLE, ON, L9W 3Z8
(519) 943-0100   *SIC 2541*
PINEHURST STORE FIXTURES INC *p 808*
120 C LINE, ORANGEVILLE, ON, L9W 3Z8
(519) 943-0100   *SIC 2542*
**PINELAND CO-OPERATIVE ASSOCIATION
LIMITED**   *p 1412*
1511 8 ST W, NIPAWIN, SK, S0E 1E0
(306) 862-4668   *SIC 5411*
PINEO, P. PHARMACEUTICALS INC *p 752*
3151 STRANDHERD DR SUITE 1302, NE-
PEAN, ON, K2J 5N1
(613) 825-8717   *SIC 5912*

PINES LONG TERM CARE RESIDENCE p 496
See DISTRICT MUNICIPALITY OF MUSKOKA, THE

PINES LONG TERM CARE RESIDENCE, THE p 497
98 PINE ST SUITE 610, BRACEBRIDGE, ON, P1L 1N5
(705) 645-4488 SIC 8361

PINES LONG-TERM CARE RESIDENCE p 496
See EXTENDICARE INC

PINESTONE REGIONAL SALES OFFICE p 607
4252 COUNTY RD 21, HALIBURTON, ON, K0M 1S0
SIC 7389

PINEVIEW LODGE p 1412
See KELSEY TRAIL REGIONAL HEALTH AUTHORITY

PINEWOOD COURT p 910
See REVERA LONG TERM CARE INC

PINEWOOD FORD LIMITED p 909
640 MEMORIAL AVE, THUNDER BAY, ON, P7B 3Z5
(807) 344-9611 SIC 5511

PING CANADA p 799
See PING CANADA CORPORATION

PING CANADA CORPORATION p 799
2790 BRIGHTON RD, OAKVILLE, ON, L6H 5T4
(905) 829-8004 SIC 5091

PINGLE'S FARM MARKET p 617
1805 TAUNTON RD, HAMPTON, ON, L0B 1J0
(905) 725-6089 SIC 0191

PINK ELEPHANT INC p 524
5575 NORTH SERVICE RD SUITE 200, BURLINGTON, ON, L7L 6M1
(905) 331-5060 SIC 8741

PINK TARTAN p 994
See MIMRAN, JOSEPH & ASSOCIATES INC

PINKERTON'S OF CANADA p 1018
See SECURITAS CANADA LIMITED

PINKHAM & SONS BUILDING MAINTE-NANCE INC p 816
1181 NEWMARKET ST UNIT M, OTTAWA, ON, K1B 3V1
(613) 745-7753 SIC 7349

PINKHAM & SONS BUILDING MAINTE-NANCE INC p 1330
2449 RUE GUENETTE, SAINT-LAURENT, QC, H4R 2E9
(514) 332-4522 SIC 7349

PINKONLINE p 524
See PINK ELEPHANT INC

PINKWOOD LTD p 40
5929 6 ST NE, CALGARY, AB, T2K 5R5
(403) 279-3700 SIC 2499

PINNACLE AUTO SALES p 389
23 ROTHWELL RD, WINNIPEG, MB, R3P 2M5
(204) 667-2467 SIC 5511

PINNACLE CATERERS LTD p 965
40 BAY ST SUITE 300, TORONTO, ON, M5J 2X2
(416) 815-6036 SIC 5812

PINNACLE CHRYSLER JEEP DODGE INC p 1020
2300 TECUMSEH RD E, WINDSOR, ON, N8W 1E5
(519) 254-1196 SIC 5511

PINNACLE INTERNATIONAL MANAGE-MENT INC p 299
911 HOMER ST SUITE 300, VANCOUVER, BC, V6B 2W6
(604) 602-7747 SIC 7011

PINNACLE PHARMACEUTICS LTD p 1033
7611 PINE VALLEY DR SUITE 31, WOOD-BRIDGE, ON, L4L 0A2

(905) 430-7541 SIC 5122

PINNACLE RENEWABLE ENERGY INC p 265
3600 LYSANDER LN SUITE 350, RICH-MOND, BC, V7B 1C3
(604) 270-9613 SIC 2448

PINNACLE WEALTH BROKERS INC p 77
15 ROYAL VISTA PL NW SUITE 250, CAL-GARY, AB, T3R 0P3
(855) 628-4286 SIC 6211

PINO ALEJANDRO p 924
1867 YONGE ST SUITE 100, TORONTO, ON, M4S 1Y5
(416) 960-9995 SIC 6531

PINPOINT CAREERS INC p 510
181 QUEEN ST E, BRAMPTON, ON, L6W 2B3
(905) 454-1144 SIC 7361

PINTO-PACKAGING LTD p 649
148 STRONACH CRES, LONDON, ON, N5V 3A1
(519) 455-5790 SIC 2653

PINTY'S DELICIOUS FOODS INC p 524
5063 NORTH SERVICE RD SUITE 101, BURLINGTON, ON, L7L 5H6
(905) 835-8575 SIC 2015

PINTY'S DELICIOUS FOODS INC p 799
2714 BRISTOL CIR, OAKVILLE, ON, L6H 6A1
(905) 829-1130 SIC 2015

PIONEER BALLOON CANADA LIMITED p 608
333 KENORA AVE, HAMILTON, ON, L8E 2W3
(905) 560-6534 SIC 3069

PIONEER BUILDING SUPPLIES LTD p 196
45754 YALE RD, CHILLIWACK, BC, V2P 2N4
(604) 795-7238 SIC 5211

PIONEER CAMP p 585
See INTER-VARSITY CHRISTIAN FEL-LOWSHIP OF CANADA

PIONEER CHRYSLER JEEP p 232
See PIONEER GARAGE LIMITED

PIONEER CO-OP p 1436
See PIONEER CO-OPERATIVE ASSOCIA-TION LIMITED, THE

PIONEER CO-OPERATIVE ASSOCIATION LIMITED, THE p 1436
1150 CENTRAL AVE N SUITE 2000, SWIFT CURRENT, SK, S9H 0G1
(306) 778-8800 SIC 5311

PIONEER CONSTRUCTION INC p 762
175 PROGRESS RD, NORTH BAY, ON, P1A 0B8
(705) 472-0890 SIC 1611

PIONEER CONSTRUCTION INC p 901
1 CEASAR RD, SUDBURY, ON, P3E 5P3
(705) 560-7200 SIC 1611

PIONEER CONSTRUCTION INC p 910
1344 OLIVER RD, THUNDER BAY, ON, P7G 1K4
(807) 345-2338 SIC 1611

PIONEER ELECTRONICS OF CANADA, INC p 495
2 MARCONI CRT UNIT 15, BOLTON, ON, L7E 1E5
(905) 479-4411 SIC 5064

PIONEER ENVIRO GROUP LTD p 73
1711 10 AVE SW SUITE 200, CALGARY, AB, T3C 0K1
(403) 229-3969 SIC 6712

PIONEER FOOD COURTS INC p 1015
1 PAISLEY CRT, WHITBY, ON, L1N 9L2
(905) 665-1217 SIC 6512

PIONEER FOOD SERVICES LIMITED p 477
1180 2 HWY SUITE 2, ANCASTER, ON, L9G 3K9
(905) 648-5222 SIC 5812

PIONEER FOOD SERVICES LIMITED p 524
5100 SOUTH SERVICE RD SUITE 1, BURLINGTON, ON, L7L 6A5
(905) 333-9887 SIC 5461

PIONEER GARAGE LIMITED p 232

33320 1ST AVE, MISSION, BC, V2V 1G8
(604) 462-7333 SIC 5511

PIONEER HI-BRED LIMITED p 726
1919 MINNESOTA CRT, MISSISSAUGA, ON, L5N 0C9
(905) 821-3300 SIC 2824

PIONEER HI-BRED LIMITED p 1383
1045 RUE MONFETTE E, THETFORD MINES, QC, G6G 7K7
SIC 3299

PIONEER HI-BRED PRODUCTION LTD p 543
7399 COUNTY RD 2 W, CHATHAM, ON, N7M 5L1
(519) 352-2700 SIC 0181

PIONEER HOUSING FOUNDATION p 161
495 WOODBRIDGE WAY, SHERWOOD PARK, AB, T8A 4P1
SIC 6531

PIONEER LAND & ENVIROMENTAL SER-VICES p 73
See PIONEER ENVIRO GROUP LTD

PIONEER LAND SERVICES LTD p 133
10537 98 AVE SUITE 201, GRANDE PRAIRIE, AB, T8V 4L1
(780) 532-7707 SIC 5172

PIONEER LOG HOMES OF BRITISH COLUMBIA LTD p 344
351 HODGSON RD, WILLIAMS LAKE, BC, V2G 3P7
(250) 392-5577 SIC 1521

PIONEER MANOR DIVISION p 898
See CITY OF GREATER SUDBURY, THE

PIONEER MEATS LTD p 79
104 ELK RUN BLVD, CANMORE, AB, T1W 1L1
(403) 678-4109 SIC 5147

PIONEER PETROLEUMS p 524
See PELP LIMITED PARTNERSHIP

PIONEER RIDGE HOME FOR THE AGED p 909
750 TUNGSTEN ST, THUNDER BAY, ON, P7B 6R1
(807) 684-3910 SIC 8361

PIONEER STANDARD CANADA INC p 689
3415 AMERICAN DR, MISSISSAUGA, ON, L4V 1T4
SIC 5065

PIONEER STEEL LIMITED p 706
355 TRADERS BLVD E, MISSISSAUGA, ON, L4Z 2E5
(905) 890-0209 SIC 5051

PIONEER TIM-BR MART p 196
See PIONEER BUILDING SUPPLIES LTD

PIONEER TRANSPORT INC p 404
208 ROUTE 590, JACKSONVILLE, NB, E7M 3R7
(506) 325-2211 SIC 4131

PIONEER TRUCK LINES LTD p 122
8321 1 ST NW, EDMONTON, AB, T6P 1X2
(780) 467-8880 SIC 1389

PIONEER'S PUB LTD, THE p 263
10111 NO. 3 RD SUITE 200, RICHMOND, BC, V7A 1W6
(604) 271-6611 SIC 5921

PIONEERS CANADA p 565
See SPRINT-PIONEERS MINISTRIES INC

PIONEERS HOUSING p 1411
See SASKATCHEWAN HEALTH AUTHOR-ITY

PIPE & PILING SUPPLIES (WESTERN) LTD p 17
5515 40 ST SE, CALGARY, AB, T2C 2A8
(403) 236-1332 SIC 5051

PIPE QUEST PROJECTS LTD p 4
GD STN MAIN, ATHABASCA, AB, T9S 1A2
(780) 689-9568 SIC 1623

PIPE-ALL PLUMBING & HEATING LTD p 1033
141 STRADA DR, WOODBRIDGE, ON, L4L 5V9
(905) 851-1927 SIC 1711

PIPE-LINES MONTREAL LIMITEE, LES p 1238

10803 RUE SHERBROOKE E, MONTREAL-EST, QC, H1B 1B3
(514) 645-8797 SIC 4612

PIPEFLO CONTRACTING CORP p 613
111 FRID ST, HAMILTON, ON, L8P 4M3
(905) 572-7767 SIC 5032

PIPERS DEPARTMENT STORES p 433
See GRANITE DEPARTMENT STORE INC

PIPETEK INFRASTRUCTURE SERVICES INC p 529
2250 INDUSTRIAL ST, BURLINGTON, ON, L7P 1A1
(905) 319-0500 SIC 7389

PIPEWORX LTD p 2
11122 255 ST, ACHESON, AB, T7X 6C9
(780) 960-2730 SIC 1623

PIPSC p 818
See PROFESSIONAL INSTITUTE OF THE PUBLIC SERVICE OF CANADA, THE

PIQUETTE, ROGER L. INSURANCE AGENCY INC p 899
1210 LASALLE BLVD, SUDBURY, ON, P3A 1Y5
(705) 524-5755 SIC 6411

PIRAMAL HEALTHCARE (CANADA) LIM-ITED p 481
110 INDUSTRIAL PKY N, AURORA, ON, L4G 4C3
(905) 727-9417 SIC 2899

PIRATE GROUP INC p 934
260 KING ST E SUITE 507, TORONTO, ON, M5A 4L5
(416) 594-3784 SIC 8999

PIRET p 956
See PURE INDUSTRIAL REAL ESTATE TRUST

PIROCHE PLANTS INC p 244
20542 MCNEIL RD, PITT MEADOWS, BC, V3Y 2T9
(604) 465-7101 SIC 5193

PISCES EXOTICA PET EMPORIUM LTD p 24
4921 SKYLINE WAY NE, CALGARY, AB, T2E 4G5
(403) 274-3314 SIC 5999

PISCES PET EMPORIUM p 24
See PISCES EXOTICA PET EMPORIUM LTD

PISCINES JOVITEL p 1159
See GESTION GCL INC

PISCINES LAUNIER INC p 1388
5825 BOUL GENE-H.-KRUGER, TROIS-RIVIERES, QC, G9A 4P1
(819) 375-7771 SIC 5999

PISCINES PRO ET PATIOS N.V. INC p 1261
See 9378-7471 QUEBEC INC

PISCINES SOUCY INC p 1267
3605 BOUL WILFRID-HAMEL, QUEBEC, QC, G1P 2J4
(418) 872-4440 SIC 1799

PISCINES TREVI p 1152
See MAGASINS TREVI INC

PISTON RING SERVICE SUPPLY p 381
See 3600106 MANITOBA INC

PITBLADO LLP p 379
360 MAIN ST SUITE 2500, WINNIPEG, MB, R3C 4H6
(204) 956-0560 SIC 8111

PITBULL ENERGY SERVICES INC p 122
2424 91 AVE NW, EDMONTON, AB, T6P 1K9
(780) 757-1688 SIC 1389

PITEAU ASSOCIATES ENGINEERING LTD p 240
788 COPPING ST SUITE 300, NORTH VANCOUVER, BC, V7M 3G6
(604) 986-8551 SIC 8999

PITMAN, WAYNE FORD LINCOLN INC p 606
895 WOODLAWN RD W, GUELPH, ON, N1K 1B7
(519) 824-6400 SIC 5511

PITNEY BOWES GLOBAL CREDIT SERVICES p 699
See PITNEY BOWES OF CANADA LTD

PITNEY BOWES OF CANADA LTD p 189
3001 WAYBURNE DR SUITE 125, BURNABY, BC, V5G 4W3
(778) 328-8900 SIC 5044

PITNEY BOWES OF CANADA LTD p 431
31 PIPPY PL, ST. JOHN'S, NL, A1B 3X2
SIC 5044

PITNEY BOWES OF CANADA LTD p 474
314 HARWOOD AVE S SUITE 200, AJAX, ON, L1S 2J1
(905) 619-7700 SIC 7389

PITNEY BOWES OF CANADA LTD p 699
5500 EXPLORER DR SUITE 1, MISSISAUGA, ON, L4W 5C7
(905) 219-3000 SIC 5044

PITNEY BOWES OF CANADA LTD p 699
5500 EXPLORER DR UNIT 2, MISSISAUGA, ON, L4W 5C7
(800) 672-6937 SIC 5044

PITNEY BOWES OF CANADA LTD p 769
1200 SHEPPARD AVE E SUITE 400, NORTH YORK, ON, M2K 2S5
SIC 5044

PITT MEADOWS SECONDARY SCHOOL p 244
See SCHOOL DISTRICT NO 42 (MAPLE RIDGE-PITT MEADOWS)

PIVAL INTERNATIONAL INC p 1094
1600 RTE TRANSCANADIENNE BUREAU 100, DORVAL, QC, H9P 1H7
(514) 684-1600 SIC 4226

PIVOT CENTRE-DU-QUEBEC p 1099
795 RUE CORMIER, DRUMMONDVILLE, QC, J2C 6P7
(819) 478-3134 SIC 8699

PIVOT FURNITURE TECHNOLOGIES INC p 1429
142 ENGLISH CRES UNIT 20, SASKATOON, SK, S7K 8A5
(306) 220-4557 SIC 7379

PIVOT TECHNOLOGY SOLUTIONS INC p 674
55 RENFREW DR SUITE 200, MARKHAM, ON, L3R 8H3
(416) 360-4777 SIC 8731

PIVOTAL POWER INC p 440
150 BLUEWATER RD, BEDFORD, NS, B4B 1G9
(902) 835-7268 SIC 3621

PIVOTAL SOFTWARE p 939
See GPVTL CANADA INC

PIXINTER p 1188
See GROUPE PIXCOM INC

PIZZA DELIGHT p 398
See ALIMENTATION LIGILICA LTEE

PIZZA HOTLINE p 388
See T.F.G. (1987) LTD

PIZZA HUT p 115
See MARBLE RESTAURANTS LTD

PIZZA HUT p 1424
See CONCORDE FOOD SERVICES (1996) LTD

PIZZA NOVA RESTAURANTS LIMITED p 871
2247 MIDLAND AVE SUITE 12, SCARBOROUGH, ON, M1P 4R1
(416) 439-0051 SIC 5812

PIZZA NOVA TAKE-OUT p 871
See PIZZA NOVA RESTAURANTS LIMITED

PIZZA PIZZA LIMITED p 575
500 KIPLING AVE, ETOBICOKE, ON, M8Z 5E5
(416) 967-1010 SIC 5812

PIZZA PIZZA ROYALTY CORP p 575
500 KIPLING AVE, ETOBICOKE, ON, M8Z 5E5
(416) 967-1010 SIC 6722

PIZZAVILLE INC p 1033
741 ROWNTREE DAIRY RD UNIT 1, WOODBRIDGE, ON, L4L 5T9

(905) 850-0070 SIC 6794

PIZZERIA DEMERS INC p 1370
936 RUE DU CONSEIL, SHERBROOKE, QC, J1G 1L7
(819) 564-2811 SIC 5812

PIZZEY'S NUTRITIONAL p 345
See GLANBIA NUTRITIONALS (CANADA) INC

PJ'S PET CENTRE p 578
See 3499481 CANADA INC

PJ'S PET CENTRE, DIV OF p 716
See 3499481 CANADA INC

PJB-PRIMELINE p 201
See PRIMELINE FOOD PARTNERS LTD

PJC JEAN COUTU p 1330
See MAY BALIAN & EMAD GABRA S.E.N.C.R.L.

PJC JEAN COUTU SANTE p 1392
See GROUPE JEAN COUTU (PJC) INC, LE

PL NOUVELLE FRANCE INC p 1393
1625 BOUL LIONEL-BOULET LOCAL 203, VARENNES, QC, J3X 1P7
(450) 809-0211 SIC 6712

PLACAGE JAY GE LTEE p 1085
1800 BOUL FORTIN, COTE SAINT-LUC, QC, H7S 1N8
(450) 663-7070 SIC 3471

PLACAGES ST-RAYMOND INC p 1351
595 RUE GUYON, SAINT-RAYMOND, QC, G3L 1Z1
(418) 337-4607 SIC 2435

PLACE BONAVENTURE p 1230
See 9161-5781 QUEBEC INC

PLACE CONCORDE p 1018
See CENTRE COMMUNAUTAIRE FRANCOPHONE WINDSOR-ESSEX-KENT INC

PLACE DES ARTS p 200
See COQUITLAM, CITY OF

PLACE DES ARTS p 1186
See SOCIETE DE LA PLACE DES ARTS DE MONTREAL

PLACE DU CENTRE p 1193
See AMENAGEMENT GRANRIVE INC

PLACE DU VILLAGE p 1125
See PETROLES R.TURMEL INC, LES

PLACE KENSINGTON p 1402
See FAIRWAY MANAGEMENT CORPORATION LTD

PLACE MONTCALM HOTEL INC p 1269
1225 COURS DU GENERAL-DE MONTCALM, QUEBEC, QC, G1R 4W6
(418) 647-2222 SIC 7011

PLACE TEVERE INC p 1345
8610 RUE DU CREUSOT, SAINT-LEONARD, QC, H1P 2A7
(514) 322-9762 SIC 5812

PLACEMENT CO-ORDINATION SVC p 884
See COMMUNITY CARE ACCESS CENTRE NIAGARA

PLACEMENT POTENTIEL INC p 1252
111 AV DONEGANI, POINTE-CLAIRE, QC, H9R 2W3
(514) 694-0315 SIC 7361

PLACEMENTS A. LAJEUNESSE INC p 1182
6500 RUE SAINT-HUBERT, MONTREAL, QC, H2S 2M3
(514) 272-8233 SIC 6712

PLACEMENTS ARDEN INC, LES p 1335
2575 BOUL PITFIELD, SAINT-LAURENT, QC, H4S 1T2
(514) 383-4442 SIC 5621

PLACEMENTS BARAKAT INC, LES p 1335
5637 RUE KIERAN, SAINT-LAURENT, QC, H4S 0A3
(514) 335-0059 SIC 6712

PLACEMENTS BERIVES INC, LES p 1286
101 BOUL CARTIER, RIVIERE-DU-LOUP, QC, G5R 2N3
(418) 862-6324 SIC 5511

PLACEMENTS BITUMAR INC, LES p 1238
11155 RUE SAINTE-CATHERINE E, MONTREAL-EST, QC, H1B 0A4
(514) 645-4561 SIC 2911

PLACEMENTS BOIVAIN INC p 1293
149 RUE D'AMSTERDAM, SAINT-AUGUSTIN-DE-DESMAURES, QC, G3A 2V5
(418) 878-3373 SIC 5142

PLACEMENTS C. D. F. G. INC p 1393
59 RUE DE L'AQUEDUC, VARENNES, QC, J3X 2J3
SIC 7389

PLACEMENTS CAMBRIDGE INC p 1252
340 BOUL HYMUS BUREAU 640, POINTE-CLAIRE, QC, H9R 6B3
(514) 694-8383 SIC 6531

PLACEMENTS CHRISTIAN BERGERON INC p 1280
655 RUE DE L'ARGON, QUEBEC, QC, G2N 2G7
(418) 849-7997 SIC 6712

PLACEMENTS CLAUDE GOSSELIN INC p 1383
680 RUE DES ERABLES, THETFORD MINES, QC, G6G 1H7
(418) 335-7552 SIC 6712

PLACEMENTS E.G.B. INC., LES p 1335
9000 BOUL HENRI-BOURASSA O, SAINT-LAURENT, QC, H4S 1L5
(514) 336-3213 SIC 6712

PLACEMENTS EXCELITAS CANADA p 1394
See EXCELITAS CANADA INC

PLACEMENTS FRANCOIS PICHETTE LTEE, LES p 1234
3080 RUE PEUGEOT, MONTREAL, QC, H7L 5C5
(450) 682-4411 SIC 1731

PLACEMENTS GILLES ARNOLD INC p 1115
2595 RUE GODBOUT, JONQUIERE, QC, G7S 5S9
(418) 548-0821 SIC 5511

PLACEMENTS HEBDEN INC p 1070
9700 PLACE JADE, BROSSARD, QC, J4Y 3C1
(450) 444-4847 SIC 8711

PLACEMENTS JACQUES FELIX THIBAULT INC., LES p 1076
237 BOUL SAINT-JEAN-BAPTISTE BUREAU 124, CHATEAUGUAY, QC, J6K 3C3
(450) 692-7981 SIC 5912

PLACEMENTS JACQUES FELIX THIBEAULT INC, LES p 1151
777 BOUL SAINT-JEAN-BAPTISTE, MERCIER, QC, J6R 1G1
(450) 692-5990 SIC 5912

PLACEMENTS JACQUES GOULET LTEE, LES p 1322
830 AV BELAND, SAINT-JOSEPH-DE-BEAUCE, QC, G0S 2V0
SIC 2431

PLACEMENTS JACQUES LAFERTE INC, LES p 1099
1650 BOUL LEMIRE, DRUMMONDVILLE, QC, J2C 5A4
(819) 477-8950 SIC 5211

PLACEMENTS JEAN BEAUDRY INC, LES p 1248
12305 BOUL METROPOLITAIN E, POINTE-AUX-TREMBLES, QC, H1B 5R3
(514) 640-4440 SIC 6712

PLACEMENTS JULES CHAMBERLAND LTEE p 1096
2540 139 RTE, DRUMMONDVILLE, QC, J2A 2P9
(819) 478-4967 SIC 5113

PLACEMENTS LALLEMAND INC p 1168
1620 RUE PREFONTAINE, MONTREAL, QC, H1W 2N8
(514) 522-2133 SIC 2099

PLACEMENTS LAUZON INC p 1245
2101 COTE DES CASCADES, PAPINEAUVILLE, QC, J0V 1R0
(819) 427-5144 SIC 6712

PLACEMENTS LUC CHAMBERLAND INC, LES p 1096

2540 139 RTE, DRUMMONDVILLE, QC, J2A 2P9
(819) 478-4967 SIC 2673

PLACEMENTS M DROUIN INC, LES p 1305
14920 BOUL LACROIX, SAINT-GEORGES, QC, G5Y 1R6
(418) 228-0051 SIC 5541

PLACEMENTS MICHEL MAYRAND INC, LES p 1106
355 BOUL DE LA CARRIERE BUREAU 176, GATINEAU, QC, J8Y 6W4
(819) 777-4381 SIC 5311

PLACEMENTS MONTEVA INC p 1207
1134 RUE SAINTE-CATHERINE O BUREAU 800, MONTREAL, QC, H3B 1H4
(438) 796-8990 SIC 6719

PLACEMENTS MONTRUSCO BOLTON INC p 1198
1501 AV MCGILL COLLEGE BUREAU 1200, MONTREAL, QC, H3A 3M8
(514) 842-6464 SIC 6282

PLACEMENTS PLACEVIC LTEE, LES p 1229
800 RUE DU SQUARE-VICTORIA BUREAU 4120, MONTREAL, QC, H4Z 1A1
(514) 875-6010 SIC 6712

PLACEMENTS RABPHAR INC p 1241
610 BOUL CURE-LABELLE, MONTREAL-OUEST, QC, H7V 2T7
(450) 687-5910 SIC 5912

PLACEMENTS ROBERT PHANEUF INC p 1158
270 RUE BRUNET, MONT-SAINT-HILAIRE, QC, J3H 0M6
(450) 446-9933 SIC 6712

PLACEMENTS ROBERT SIMARD INC p 1166
4466 RUE BEAUBIEN E, MONTREAL, QC, H1T 3Y8
(514) 728-3674 SIC 5912

PLACEMENTS ROCKHILL LTEE, LES p 1219
4858 CH DE LA COTE-DES-NEIGES BUREAU 503, MONTREAL, QC, H3V 1G8
(514) 738-4704 SIC 6513

PLACEMENTS ROGERCAN INC, LES p 1134
2010 BOUL DAGENAIS O, LAVAL-OUEST, QC, H7L 5W2
(450) 963-5080 SIC 5149

PLACEMENTS ROLAND LAVOIE LTEE, LES p 1106
5 BOUL MONTCLAIR, GATINEAU, QC, J8Y 2E3
(819) 771-5841 SIC 6712

PLACEMENTS RRJ INC, LES p 1335
5800 RUE KIERAN, SAINT-LAURENT, QC, H4S 2B5
SIC 5191

PLACEMENTS SERGAKIS INC p 1131
7373 RUE CORDNER, LASALLE, QC, H8N 2R5
(514) 937-0531 SIC 5812

PLACEMENTS YVON GAREAU INC, LES p 1391
1100 3E AV, VAL-D'OR, QC, J9P 1T6
(819) 825-6880 SIC 6712

PLACENTIA HEALTH CENTRE p 427
See EASTERN REGIONAL INTEGRATED HEALTH AUTHORITY

PLACETECO INC p 1368
3763 RUE BURRILL BUREAU 2, SHAWINIGAN, QC, G9N 0C4
(819) 539-8808 SIC 3728

PLAD EQUIPEMENT LTEE p 1060
680 RUE DE LA SABLIERE, BOIS-DES-FILION, QC, J6Z 4T7
(450) 965-0224 SIC 3561

PLAINS MIDSTREAM CANADA ULC p 57
607 8 AVE SW SUITE 1400, CALGARY, AB, T2P 0A7
(403) 298-2100 SIC 4612

PLAINS MIDSTREAM CANADA ULC p 860
1182 PLANK RD, SARNIA, ON, N7T 7H9

(519) 336-4270   SIC 4923

PLAINSMAN MFG. INC   p 116
8305 MCINTYRE RD NW, EDMONTON, AB, T6E 5J7
(780) 496-9800   SIC 3533

PLAINTREE SYSTEMS INC   p 489
14 CONWAY ST, BARRYS BAY, ON, K0J 1B0
(613) 756-7066   SIC 2431

PLAISIRS GASTRONOMIQUES INC   p 1062
3740 RUE LA VERENDRYE, BOISBRIAND, QC, J7H 1R5
(450) 433-1970   SIC 2099

PLAK-IT   p 742
See ROKAN LAMINATING CO LTD

PLAN DE PROTECTION MECANIQUE P.P.M. INC   p 1252
2525 AUT TRANSCANADIENNE, POINTE-CLAIRE, QC, H9R 4V6
SIC 6351

PLAN GROUP INC   p 557
2740 STEELES AVE W, CONCORD, ON, L4K 4T4
(416) 635-9040   SIC 1731

PLANCHERS BELLEFEUILLE   p 1319
See COMPAGNIE DU BOIS FRANC DZD INC, LA

PLANCHERS DAVA INC, LES   p 1388
3400 BOUL GENE-H.-KRUGER, TROIS-RIVIERES, QC, G9A 4M3
(418) 338-0888   SIC 5023

PLANCHERS DE BOIS-FRANC WICKHAM, LES   p 1402
See 2639-1862 QUEBEC INC

PLANCHERS DES APPALACHES LTEE   p 1088
454 RUE DE LA RIVIERE, COWANSVILLE, QC, J2K 3G6
(450) 266-3999   SIC 2426

PLANCHERS EN GROS 2009   p 1116
See 9214-6489 QUEBEC INC

PLANCHERS GROLEAU INC   p 1147
541 AV DALCOURT, LOUISEVILLE, QC, J5V 2Z7
(819) 228-4446   SIC 3996

PLANCHERS MERCIER (DRUM-MONDVILLE) INC, LES   p 1099
1125 RUE ROCHELEAU, DRUM-MONDVILLE, QC, J2C 6L8
(819) 472-1670   SIC 2426

PLANCHERS MERCIER INC, LES   p 1160
330 RUE DES ENTREPRENEURS, MONT-MAGNY, QC, G5V 4T1
(418) 248-1785   SIC 2426

PLANCHERS SEQUOIA INC, LES   p 1357
2800 RUE ETIENNE-LENOIR, SAINTE-DOROTHEE, QC, H7R 0A3
(450) 622-8899   SIC 5211

PLANCY'S BAR & GRILL   p 237
See ROYAL TOWERS HOTEL INC

PLANDIRECT INSURANCE SERVICES INC   p 768
211 CONSUMERS RD SUITE 200, NORTH YORK, ON, M2J 4G8
(416) 490-0072   SIC 6411

PLANET BEAN   p 600
See PLANET BEAN INC

PLANET BEAN INC   p 600
259 GRANGE RD UNIT 2, GUELPH, ON, N1E 6R5
(519) 837-1040   SIC 5149

PLANET DRUGS DIRECT INC   p 277
7455 132 ST SUITE 100, SURREY, BC, V3W 1J8
(604) 501-6902   SIC 5961

PLANET ENERGY CORP   p 772
5525 YONGE ST SUITE 1500, NORTH YORK, ON, M2N 5S3
SIC 8748

PLANET FOODS INC   p 17
4040E 80 AVE SE, CALGARY, AB, T2C 2J7
(403) 281-7911   SIC 5149

PLANET GASTRONOMIE   p 1190

465 RUE SAINT-JEAN, MONTREAL, QC, H2Y 2R6
SIC 5099

PLANET PAPER BOX INC   p 557
2841 LANGSTAFF RD UNIT 1, CONCORD, ON, L4K 4W7
(905) 669-9363   SIC 2653

PLANETE MAZDA   p 1151
See 156023 CANADA INC

PLANNING ALLIANCE INC   p 983
317 ADELAIDE ST W SUITE 205, TORONTO, ON, M5V 1P9
(416) 593-6499   SIC 8712

PLANT 1   p 604
See SKYJACK INC

PLANT HOPE ADJUSTERS LTD   p 409
16 CORONATION DR, MONCTON, NB, E1E 2X1
(506) 853-8500   SIC 6411

PLANT NO. 4   p 483
See BEND ALL AUTOMOTIVE ULC

PLANT PRODUCTS INC   p 644
50 HAZELTON ST, LEAMINGTON, ON, N8H 1B8
(519) 326-9037   SIC 5191

PLANTA YORKVILLE   p 972
See CHG BLOOR HOLDINGS INC

PLANTBEST, INC   p 680
170 DUFFIELD DR UNIT 200, MARKHAM, ON, L6G 1B5
(905) 470-0724   SIC 2879

PLANTE SPORTS   p 1385
See GESTION TREMBLAY ET LAPOINTE INC

PLANTE, PAT AUTOS LTEE   p 1107
850 BOUL SAINT-JOSEPH, GATINEAU, QC, J8Z 1S9
(819) 770-0220   SIC 5511

PLANTERRA LTEE   p 1095
2275 CH SAINT-FRANCOIS, DORVAL, QC, H9P 1K3
(514) 684-0310   SIC 5992

PLANTERS   p 1064
See DISTRIBUTIONS ALIMENTAIRES LE MARQUIS INC

PLANTERS EQUIPMENT LIMITED   p 460
GD, KENTVILLE, NS, B4N 3V6
(902) 678-5555   SIC 5999

PLANTERS PEANUTS   p 783
See JOHNVINCE FOODS

PLANTES D'INTERIEUR VERONNEAU INC, LES   p 1234
2965 BOUL LE CORBUSIER, MONTREAL, QC, H7L 3M3
(450) 680-1989   SIC 5193

PLANTES ET DECORS VERONNEAU, LES   p 1234
See PLANTES D'INTERIEUR VERON-NEAU INC, LES

PLANVIEW UTILITY SERVICES LIMITED   p 674
7270 WOODBINE AVE SUITE 201, MARKHAM, ON, L3R 4B9
(289) 800-7110   SIC 7363

PLANWAY POULTRY INC   p 575
26 CANMOTOR AVE, ETOBICOKE, ON, M8Z 4E5
(416) 252-7676   SIC 5144

PLASP CHILD CARE SERVICES   p 745
60 COURTNEYPARK DR W UNIT 5, MISSISSAUGA, ON, L5W 0B3
(905) 890-1711   SIC 8351

PLASSEIN INTERNATIONAL OF NEWMARKET INC   p 756
175 DEERFIELD RD, NEWMARKET, ON, L3Y 2L8
(905) 895-2308   SIC 3081

PLASTECH INC   p 1374
370 RUE LEGER, SHERBROOKE, QC, J1L 1Y5
(819) 822-1590   SIC 2821

PLASTECH INTERNATIONAL   p 1374
See PLASTECH INC

PLASTER FORM INC   p 712
1180 LAKESHORE RD E, MISSISSAUGA, ON, L5E 1E9
(905) 891-9500   SIC 3275

PLASTI-FAB LTD   p 9
300-2891 SUNRIDGE WAY NE, CALGARY, AB, T1Y 7K7
(403) 569-4300   SIC 2821

PLASTI-FAB LTD   p 81
802 MCCOOL ST, CROSSFIELD, AB, T0M 0S0
(403) 946-4576   SIC 2821

PLASTIC PLUS LIMITED   p 789
14 LESWYN RD, NORTH YORK, ON, M6A 1K2
(416) 789-4307   SIC 3851

PLASTICASE INC   p 1381
1059 BOUL DES ENTREPRISES, TERRE-BONNE, QC, J6Y 1V2
(450) 628-1006   SIC 3089

PLASTICO INDUSTRIES, DIV OF   p 534
See LATEM INDUSTRIES LIMITED

PLASTICON CANADA INC   p 1135
1395 MONTEE CHENIER, LES CEDRES, QC, J7T 1L9
(450) 452-1104   SIC 3299

PLASTICS PLUS   p 609
See 600956 ONTARIO LTD

PLASTIPAK INDUSTRIES   p 1082
See PLASTIPAK INDUSTRIES INC

PLASTIPAK INDUSTRIES INC   p 587
260 REXDALE BLVD, ETOBICOKE, ON, M9W 1R2
(416) 744-4220   SIC 3089

PLASTIPAK INDUSTRIES INC   p 1067
150 BOUL INDUSTRIEL, BOUCHERVILLE, QC, J4B 2X3
(450) 650-2200   SIC 3089

PLASTIPAK INDUSTRIES INC   p 1082
345 RUE BIBEAU, COOKSHIRE-EATON, QC, J0B 1M0
(819) 875-3355   SIC 3089

PLASTIQUE AGE   p 1165
See PRODUITS DE PLASTIQUE AGE INC, LES

PLASTIQUE ALTO   p 1276
See GROUPE POLYALTO INC

PLASTIQUE CADUNA INC   p 1223
5655 RUE PHILIPPE-TURCOT, MONTREAL, QC, H4C 3K8
(514) 932-7821   SIC 3089

PLASTIQUE D.C.N. INC   p 1400
250 RUE SAINT-LOUIS, WARWICK, QC, J0A 1M0
(819) 358-3700   SIC 3089

PLASTIQUE MICRON INC   p 1356
21 BOUL BEGIN BUREAU 190, SAINTE-CLAIRE, QC, G0R 2V0
(418) 883-3333   SIC 3089

PLASTIQUES ANCHOR LTEE   p 1120
730 RUE SAINT-ETIENNE, L'ASSOMPTION, QC, J5W 1Z1
(450) 589-5627   SIC 3089

PLASTIQUES BALCAN LIMITEE, LES   p 1345
9340 RUE DE MEAUX, SAINT-LEONARD, QC, H1R 3H2
(514) 326-0200   SIC 3081

PLASTIQUES BERRY CANADA INC   p 810
301 FOREST AVE, ORILLIA, ON, L3V 3Y7
(705) 326-8921   SIC 3081

PLASTIQUES BERRY CANADA INC   p 1400
33 RUE TAYLOR, WATERLOO, QC, J0E 2N0
(450) 539-2772   SIC 3089

PLASTIQUES DURA (1977) LIMITEE, LES   p 1125
110 RUE RICHER, LACHINE, QC, H8R 1R2
(514) 369-8980   SIC 5162

PLASTIQUES DURA, LES   p 1125
See PLASTIQUES DURA (1977) LIMITEE, LES

PLASTIQUES G PLUS INC   p 1288
180 RUE D'EVAIN, ROUYN-NORANDA,

QC, J0Z 1Y0
(819) 768-8888   SIC 3089

PLASTIQUES G.P.R. INC   p 1303
5200 CH DE SAINT-GABRIEL, SAINT-FELIX-DE-VALOIS, QC, J0K 2M0
(450) 889-7277   SIC 3089

PLASTIQUES GAGNON INC   p 1315
117 AV DE GASPE O, SAINT-JEAN-PORT-JOLI, QC, G0R 3G0
(418) 598-3361   SIC 3089

PLASTIQUES IPL INC   p 1199
1000 SHERBROOKE W ST SUITE 700, MONTREAL, QC, H3A 3G4
(438) 320-6188   SIC 3089

PLASTIQUES JOLIETTE   p 1134
190 CH DES INDUSTRIES, LAVALTRIE, QC, J5T 3R2
SIC 2821

PLASTIQUES MULTICAP INC, LES   p 1234
3232 RUE DELAUNAY, MONTREAL, QC, H7L 5E1
(450) 681-1661   SIC 2821

PLASTIQUES VIF   p 1312
See GROUPE VIF INC

PLASTIVAL INC   p 1103
312 RUE SAINT-LOUIS, GATINEAU, QC, J8P 8B3
(819) 770-2018   SIC 5162

PLASTREC INC   p 1115
1461 RUE LEPINE, JOLIETTE, QC, J6E 4B7
(450) 760-3830   SIC 4953

PLASTRUCT CANADA INC   p 1003
4305 SPRING CREEK RD, VINELAND, ON, L0R 2C0
(905) 563-4000   SIC 5162

PLASTUBE INC   p 1111
590 RUE SIMONDS S, GRANBY, QC, J2J 1E1
(450) 378-2633   SIC 2821

PLASTUBE NORTH AMERICA   p 1111
See PLASTUBE INC

PLATE 2000 INC   p 1292
1239 RTE BEGIN, SAINT-ANSELME, QC, G0R 2N0
(418) 885-0085   SIC 5082

PLATEAU FOODS LTD   p 199
1410 PARKWAY BLVD UNIT A, COQUIT-LAM, BC, V3E 3J7
(604) 464-8506   SIC 5411

PLATFORM INSURANCE MANAGEMENT INC   p 940
20 TORONTO ST SUITE 440, TORONTO, ON, M5C 2B8
(416) 434-4322   SIC 6411

PLATINUM ELECTRICAL CONTRACTORS INC   p 557
270 DRUMLIN CIR UNIT 5, CONCORD, ON, L4K 3E2
(905) 761-7647   SIC 1731

PLATINUM EQUITIES INC   p 65
906 12 AVE SW SUITE 910, CALGARY, AB, T2R 1K7
(403) 228-4799   SIC 6799

PLATINUM FASHIONS   p 1169
See 3727513 CANADA INC

PLATINUM FASHIONS 2000   p 1169
See 3727513 CANADA INC

PLATINUM GROUP METALS LTD   p 308
550 BURRARD ST SUITE 788, VANCOUVER, BC, V6C 2B5
(604) 899-5450   SIC 1041

PLATINUM HEALTH BENEFITS SOLUTIONS INC   p 699
5090 EXPLORER DR SUITE 501, MISSISSAUGA, ON, L4W 4T9
(905) 602-0404   SIC 6324

PLATINUM INVESTMENTS LTD   p 102
17610 STONY PLAIN RD NW, EDMONTON, AB, T5S 1A2
(780) 443-2233   SIC 7011

PLATINUM MITSUBISHI   p 9
See PLATINUM MOTOR CARS INC

PLATINUM MOTOR CARS INC *p 9*
2720 BARLOW TRAIL NE, CALGARY, AB, T1Y 1A1
(403) 276-4878 *SIC 5521*

PLATINUM NATURALS LTD *p 853*
11 SIMS CRES SUITE 2, RICHMOND HILL, ON, L4B 1C9
(905) 731-8097 *SIC 5122*

PLATINUM PRODUCE COMPANY *p 493*
21037 COMMUNICATION RD, BLENHEIM, ON, N0P 1A0
(519) 676-1772 *SIC 0182*

PLATINUM PROPERTIES GROUP CORP *p 293*
777 BROADWAY W SUITE 707, VANCOUVER, BC, V5Z 4J7
(604) 638-3300 *SIC 6211*

PLATINUM RAIL *p 610*
See BARTONAIR FABRICATIONS INC

PLATO *p 401*
See PROFESSIONAL ABORIGINAL TESTING ORGANIZATION INC

PLATS DU CHEF ULC, LES *p 1091*
51 RUE KESMARK, DOLLARD-DES-ORMEAUX, QC, H9B 3J1
(514) 685-9955 *SIC 2038*

PLAY GOLF CALGARY *p 80*
See HEATHERGLENEAGLES GOLF COMPANY LTD

PLAY IT AGAIN SPORTS *p 811*
See MICON SPORTS LTD

PLAYER ONE AMUSEMENT GROUP INC *p 689*
6420 VISCOUNT RD, MISSISSAUGA, ON, L4V 1H3
(416) 251-2122 *SIC 5087*

PLAYER ONE AMUSEMENT GROUP INC *p 710*
99 RATHBURN RD W, MISSISSAUGA, ON, L5B 4C1
(905) 273-9000 *SIC 7999*

PLAYIT INCORPORATED *p 845*
831 BROCK RD UNIT 1, PICKERING, ON, L1W 3L8
(905) 837-7650 *SIC 5945*

PLAYTIME COMMUNITY GAMING CENTRES INC *p 277*
7445 132 ST SUITE 1001, SURREY, BC, V3W 1J8
(604) 590-2577 *SIC 7999*

PLAZA 500 HOTELS LTD *p 293*
500 12TH AVE W, VANCOUVER, BC, V5Z 1M2
(604) 873-1811 *SIC 7011*

PLAZA 69 PHARMACY *p 900*
See 4 CORNERS PHARMACYSTEMS INC

PLAZA AUTO GROUP LTD *p 855*
9144 YONGE ST SUITE 200, RICHMOND HILL, ON, L4C 7A1
(613) 890-4078 *SIC 5511*

PLAZA CHEVROLET HUMMER CADILLAC INC *p 1335*
10480 BOUL HENRI-BOURASSA O, SAINT-LAURENT, QC, H4S 1N6
(514) 332-1673 *SIC 5511*

PLAZA CONSULTING INC *p 770*
5700 YONGE ST SUITE 1400, NORTH YORK, ON, M2M 4K2
(416) 238-5333 *SIC 8742*

PLAZA FORD SALES LIMITED *p 467*
33 TERMINAL RD, SYDNEY, NS, B1P 7B3
(902) 567-1616 *SIC 5511*

PLAZA II CORPORATION, THE *p 930*
90 BLOOR ST E, TORONTO, ON, M4W 1A7
(416) 922-9155 *SIC 7011*

PLAZA KIA *p 855*
See 2394748 ONTARIO INC

PLAZA NATIONAL LEASING *p 789*
See PLAZA PONTIAC BUICK LIMITED

PLAZA NISSAN LIMITED *p 616*
1545 UPPER JAMES ST, HAMILTON, ON, L9B 1K2
(905) 389-3588 *SIC 5511*

PLAZA PONTIAC BUICK LIMITED *p 789*
3400 DUFFERIN ST, NORTH YORK, ON, M6A 2V1
(416) 781-5271 *SIC 5511*

PLAZA RETAIL REIT *p 400*
See PLAZACORP RETAIL PROPERTIES LTD

PLAZA VOLARE *p 1337*
See 9052-9975 QUEBEC INC

PLAZACORP RETAIL PROPERTIES LTD *p 400*
98 MAIN ST, FREDERICTON, NB, E3A 9N6
(506) 451-1826 *SIC 6719*

PLB INTERNATIONAL INC *p 1067*
1361 RUE GRAHAM-BELL, BOUCHERVILLE, QC, J4B 6A1
(450) 655-3155 *SIC 2047*

PLEASANT VALLEY SECONDARY SCHOOL *p 179*
See NORTH OKANAGAN SHUSWAP SCHOOL DISTRICT 83

PLEASANT VALLEY LODGE *p 4*
See GREATER NORTH FOUNDATION

PLEASANT VIEW CARE HOME *p 232*
See PLEASANT VIEW HOUSING SOCIETY 1980

PLEASANT VIEW HOUSING SOCIETY 1980 *p 232*
7540 HURD ST UNIT 101, MISSION, BC, V2V 3H9
(604) 826-2176 *SIC 8051*

PLEASE HOLD CANADA INC *p 860*
775 EXMOUTH ST, SARNIA, ON, N7T 5P7
(519) 339-8842 *SIC 4899*

PLEASURE-WAY INDUSTRIES LTD *p 1425*
302 PORTAGE AVE, SASKATOON, SK, S7J 4C6
(306) 934-6578 *SIC 3716*

PLEIN AIR BRUCHESI INC *p 1307*
50 365E AV, SAINT-HIPPOLYTE, QC, J8A 2Y6
(450) 563-3056 *SIC 7032*

PLENTY *p 295*
See PLENTY STORES INC

PLENTY STORES INC *p 295*
1352 VERNON DR, VANCOUVER, BC, V6A 3P7
(604) 733-4484 *SIC 5651*

PLESSITECH INC *p 1246*
2250 AV VALLEE, PLESSISVILLE, QC, G6L 2Y6
(819) 362-6315 *SIC 7692*

PLEXPACK CORP *p 871*
1160 BIRCHMOUNT RD UNIT 2, SCARBOROUGH, ON, M1P 2B8
(416) 291-8085 *SIC 5084*

PLEXTRON HOLDINGS INC *p 871*
2045 MIDLAND AVE, SCARBOROUGH, ON, M1P 3E2
(416) 293-1156 *SIC 3089*

PLEXUS CONNECTIVITY SOLUTIONS LTD *p 407*
225 BARKER ST, MONCTON, NB, E1C 0M4
(506) 859-1514 *SIC 1731*

PLEXXIS SOFTWARE *p 505*
See PLEXXIS SOFTWARE INC

PLEXXIS SOFTWARE INC *p 505*
14 ABACUS RD, BRAMPTON, ON, L6T 5B7
(905) 889-8979 *SIC 7372*

PLEXXUS LOGISTICS *p 945*
See HOSPITAL LOGISTICS INC

PLIMETAL INC *p 1238*
8555 PLACE MARIEN, MONTREAL-EST, QC, H1B 5W6
(514) 648-2260 *SIC 3469*

PLOMBCO INC *p 1365*
66 RUE EDMOND, SALABERRY-DE-VALLEYFIELD, QC, J6S 3E8
(450) 371-8800 *SIC 3369*

PLOMBERI DERITEC *p 1358*
See GRIGG PLUMBING & HEATING LTD

PLOMBERIE & CHAUFFAGE ALAIN DAIGLE INC *p 1282*
310 RUE CHARLES-MARCHAND, RE-PENTIGNY, QC, J5Z 4P1
(450) 657-1499 *SIC 1711*

PLOMBERIE C.A. BOUCLIN *p 1308*
See EXCEL CLIMATISATION INC

PLOMBERIE DANIEL COTE INC *p 1234*
3000 MONTEE SAINT-AUBIN, MONTREAL, QC, H7L 3N8
(450) 973-2545 *SIC 1711*

PLOMBERIE DE LA CAPITALE INC *p 1119*
6345 BOUL WILFRID-HAMEL UNITE 102, L'ANCIENNE-LORETTE, QC, G2E 5W2
(418) 847-2818 *SIC 1711*

PLOMBERIE GOYER INC *p 1088*
150 RUE DE SHERBROOKE, COWANSVILLE, QC, J2K 3Y9
(450) 263-2226 *SIC 1711*

PLOMBERIE JUBINVILLE *p 1335*
See PLOMBERIE RICHARD JUBINVILLE INC

PLOMBERIE PHCB INC *p 1297*
4 RUE DES AFFAIRES, SAINT-CHRISTOPHE-D'ARTHABASK, QC, G6R 0B2
(819) 260-4422 *SIC 1711*

PLOMBERIE RICHARD JUBINVILLE INC *p 1335*
5600 CH DU BOIS-FRANC, SAINT-LAURENT, QC, H4S 1A9
(514) 333-0856 *SIC 1711*

PLOMBERIE SUTTON *p 1221*
See FOURNITURES DE PLOMBERIE ET CHAUFFAGE SUTTON LTEE

PLOYMAX *p 1345*
See PLASTIQUES BALCAN LIMITEE, LES

PLP *p 536*
See PREFORMED LINE PRODUCTS (CANADA) LIMITED

PLUG CANADA INC *p 256*
13120 VANIER PL, RICHMOND, BC, V6V 2J2
(604) 303-0050 *SIC 8731*

PLUM *p 285*
See PLUM CLOTHING LTD

PLUM CLOTHING LTD *p 285*
1543 VENABLES ST, VANCOUVER, BC, V5L 2G8
(604) 254-5034 *SIC 5651*

PLUMBERS AND STEAMFITTERS UNION LOCAL 46 *p 869*
936 WARDEN AVE SUITE 46, SCARBOROUGH, ON, M1L 4C9
(416) 759-6791 *SIC 8631*

PLUMBING SHOWPLACE *p 1006*
See GLENBRIAR HOME HARDWARE

PLURITEC *p 1368*
See PLURITEC CIVIL LTEE

PLURITEC CIVIL LTEE *p 1368*
585 AV DES CEDRES, SHAWINIGAN, QC, G9N 1N6
(819) 537-1882 *SIC 8711*

PLUSONE INC *p 956*
347 BAY ST SUITE 506, TORONTO, ON, M5H 2R7
(416) 861-1662 *SIC 8741*

PLUTO INVESTMENTS LTD *p 102*
10152 179 ST NW, EDMONTON, AB, T5S 1S1
(780) 486-1780 *SIC 5511*

PLY GEM *p 16*
See GIENOW CANADA INC

PM CANADA INC *p 391*
135 INNOVATION DR UNIT 300, WINNIPEG, MB, R3T 6A8
(204) 889-5320 *SIC 5045*

PMA ASSURANCES INC *p 1112*
632 6E AV, GRAND-MERE, QC, G9T 2H5
(819) 538-8626 *SIC 6411*

PMA ASSURANCES INC *p 1388*
6405 RUE CHRISTOPHE-PELISSIER, TROIS-RIVIERES, QC, G9A 5C9
(819) 379-3508 *SIC 6411*

PMA BRETHOUR REAL ESTATE CORPORATION INC *p 674*

250 SHIELDS CRT UNIT 1, MARKHAM, ON, L3R 9W7
(905) 415-2720 *SIC 6531*

PMA CANADA *p 798*
See MIELZYNSKI, PETER AGENCIES LIMITED

PMA GROUP OF COMPANIES *p 674*
See PMA BRETHOUR REAL ESTATE CORPORATION INC

PMC BUILDERS & DEVELOPERS LTD *p 273*
19414 ENTERPRISE WAY, SURREY, BC, V3S 6J9
(604) 534-1822 *SIC 1521*

PMCL *p 487*
See GREYHOUND CANADA TRANSPORTATION ULC

PMD RETAIL SALES INC *p 604*
10 WOODLAWN RD E SUITE 260, GUELPH, ON, N1H 1G7
(519) 821-2244 *SIC 5531*

PME INC *p 130*
8402 116 ST, FORT SASKATCHEWAN, AB, T8L 0G8
(780) 992-2280 *SIC 1541*

PME INTER NOTAIRES *p 1321*
See RUEL VENNE LEONARD ASSOCIES

PME INTER NOTAIRES INC *p 1370*
2140 RUE KING E UNITE 201, SHERBROOKE, QC, J1G 5G6
(819) 563-3344 *SIC 7389*

PMP SOLUTIONS *p 1264*
See FPINNOVATIONS

PMR INC *p 1062*
4640 BOUL DE LA GRANDE-ALLEE, BOISBRIAND, QC, J7H 1S7
(450) 420-7361 *SIC 3339*

PMT *p 1420*
See PRAIRIE MICRO-TECH (1996) INC

PMT INDUSTRIES LIMITED *p 515*
32 BODINE DR, BRANTFORD, ON, N3R 7M4
(519) 758-5505 *SIC 3479*

PMT INDUSTRIES LIMITED *p 587*
369 ATTWELL DR, ETOBICOKE, ON, M9W 5C2
(416) 675-3352 *SIC 3479*

PMT ROY ASSURANCE ET SERVICES FINANCIERS INC *p 1262*
955 BOUL PIERRE-BERTRAND BUREAU 140, QUEBEC, QC, G1M 2E8
(418) 780-0808 *SIC 6411*

PMU OVL INC *p 599*
1491 MANOTICK STATION RD, GREELY, ON, K4P 1P6
(613) 821-2233 *SIC 6513*

PNB NATION LLC *p 1326*
95 RUE GINCE, SAINT-LAURENT, QC, H4N 1J7
(514) 384-3872 *SIC 5651*

PNB REMITTANCE COMPANY (CANADA) *p 710*
3050 CONFEDERATION PKY UNIT 104, MISSISSAUGA, ON, L5B 3Z6
(905) 897-9600 *SIC 6099*

PNC *p 214*
See POINTS NORTH CONTRACTING LTD

PNE *p 284*
See PACIFIC NATIONAL EXHIBITION

PNE CORPORATION *p 1002*
279 ENTREPRISE RD, VARS, ON, K0A 3H0
(613) 443-2181 *SIC 5169*

PNEU ACTION *p 1145*
See PNEUS CHARTRAND DISTRIBUTION INC

PNEU-HYD INDUSTRIES LIMITED *p 893*
375 GREEN RD UNIT 1, STONEY CREEK, ON, L8E 4A5
(905) 664-5540 *SIC 5531*

PNEUS A RABAIS *p 1357*
See 9215-0770 QUEBEC INC

PNEUS BEAUCERONS INC, LES *p 1055*
538 BOUL RENAULT, BEAUCEVILLE, QC,

G5X 1N2
(418) 774-3404   *SIC* 5531
PNEUS BERNARD, ROBERT, LES   *p* 1398
900 RUE NOTRE-DAME E, VICTORIAV-ILLE, QC, G6P 4B7
(819) 752-4567   *SIC* 5531
PNEUS CHARTRAND DISTRIBUTION INC*p* 1145
1060 BOUL LA FAYETTE, LONGUEUIL, QC, J4K 3B1
(450) 670-1585   *SIC* 5014
PNEUS DU BOULEVARD LTEE   *p* 396
461 BOUL ST-PIERRE O, CARAQUET, NB, E1W 1A3
(506) 727-7488   *SIC* 5531
PNEUS G.B.M.   *p* 1289
See PNEUS G.B.M., S.E.N.C.
PNEUS G.B.M., S.E.N.C.   *p* 1289
1000 RUE SAGUENAY, ROUYN-NORANDA, QC, J9X 7B6
(819) 762-0854   *SIC* 5014
PNEUS MIRACO, DIV DE   *p* 399
See PROVINCIAL BANDAG TIRES LTD
PNEUS RATTE   *p* 1260
See 9022-9097 QUEBEC INC
PNEUS RATTE INC   *p* 1261
103 3E AV, QUEBEC, QC, G1L 2V3
(418) 529-5378   *SIC* 5531
PNEUS ROBERT BERNARD LTEE, LES   *p* 1350
765 RUE PRINCIPALE E, SAINT-PAUL-D'ABBOTSFORD, QC, J0E 1A0
(450) 379-5757   *SIC* 5014
PNEUS SP INC   *p* 1050
9135 RUE EDISON, ANJOU, QC, H1J 1T4
(514) 354-7444   *SIC* 5531
PNEUS UNIMAX LTEE   *p* 1067
235 RUE J.-A.-BOMBARDIER, BOUCHERVILLE, QC, J4B 8P1
(450) 449-0362   *SIC* 5014
PNEUS UNIMAX LTEE   *p* 1080
255 RUE SAINTE-ANNE, CHICOUTIMI, QC, G7J 2M2
(418) 549-1210   *SIC* 5014
PNEUTECH-ROUSSEAU GROUP INC *p* 1128
1475 32E AV, LACHINE, QC, H8T 3J1
(514) 635-7000   *SIC* 5084
PNF HOLDINGS LIMITED   *p* 689
5815 AIRPORT RD, MISSISSAUGA, ON, L4V 1C8
(905) 677-9143   *SIC* 7521
PNI DIGITAL MEDIA ULC   *p* 299
425 CARRALL ST SUITE 100, VANCOU-VER, BC, V6B 6E3
(604) 893-8955   *SIC* 7371
PNL INTERNATIONAL TRADING INC *p* 440
1496 BEDFORD HWY SUITE 212, BED-FORD, NS, B4A 1E5
(902) 307-2117   *SIC* 5146
PNP PHARMACEUTICALS INC   *p* 193
9388 NORTH FRASER CRES, BURNABY, BC, V5J 0E3
(604) 435-6200   *SIC* 2023
PNR   *p* 177
See PNR RAILWORKS INC
PNR RAILWORKS INC   *p* 177
2595 DEACON ST, ABBOTSFORD, BC, V2T 6L4
(604) 850-9166   *SIC* 1629
PNR RAILWORKS INC   *p* 714
2380 ROYAL WINDSOR DR UNIT 11, MIS-SISSAUGA, ON, L5J 1K7
(519) 515-1219   *SIC* 1629
PNR RAILWORKS QUEBEC INC   *p* 1089
100 RUE GOODFELLOW, DELSON, QC, J5B 1V4
(450) 632-6241   *SIC* 4789
POCKAR MASONRY LTD   *p* 24
4632 5 ST NE, CALGARY, AB, T2E 7C3
(403) 276-5591   *SIC* 1741
POCO BUILDING SUPPLIES   *p* 247
See PORT COQUITLAM BUILDING SUP-PLIES LTD

POCZO MANUFACTURING COMPANY LIM-ITED   *p* 505
215 WILKINSON RD, BRAMPTON, ON, L6T 4M2
(905) 452-0567   *SIC* 3599
PODOLINSKY EQUIPMENT LTD   *p* 843
6057 PETROLIA LINE, PETROLIA, ON, N0N 1R0
(519) 844-2360   *SIC* 5999
PODOLLAN'S CONSTRUCTION LTD *p* 332
2201 11 AVE SUITE 205, VERNON, BC, V1T 8V7
(250) 545-7752   *SIC* 6512
PODOLSKY HONEY FARMS   *p* 349
119 MAIN ST W, ETHELBERT, MB, R0L 0T0
(204) 742-3555   *SIC* 0279
POI BUSINESS INTERIORS INC   *p* 674
120 VALLEYWOOD DR, MARKHAM, ON, L3R 6A7
(905) 479-1123   *SIC* 5021
POINT FOUR SYSTEMS INC   *p* 201
16 FAWCETT RD UNIT 103, COQUITLAM, BC, V3K 6X9
SIC 5084
POINT PLUS RESTAURANT-BAR INC, AU *p* 1398
192 BOUL DES BOIS-FRANCS S, VICTO-RIAVILLE, QC, G6P 4S7
(819) 758-9927   *SIC* 5812
POINT S ROBERT BERNARD   *p* 1350
See PNEUS ROBERT BERNARD LTEE, LES
POINT ZERO   *p* 1226
See POINT ZERO GIRLS CLUB INC
POINT ZERO GIRLS CLUB INC   *p* 1226
1650 RUE CHABANEL O, MONTREAL, QC, H4N 3M8
(514) 384-0140   *SIC* 5137
POINT2 TECHNOLOGIES INC   *p* 1424
3301 8TH ST E SUITE 500, SASKATOON, SK, S7H 5K5
(866) 977-1777   *SIC* 7371
POINTCLICKCARE CORP   *p* 699
5570 EXPLORER DR, MISSISSAUGA, ON, L4W 0C4
(905) 858-8885   *SIC* 7372
POINTCLICKCARE TECHNOLOGIES INC *p* 699
5570 EXPLORER DR, MISSISSAUGA, ON, L4W 0C4
(905) 858-8885   *SIC* 7372
POINTE OF VIEW MARKETING & MAN-AGEMENT INC   *p* 25
1121 CENTRE ST NW SUITE 500, CAL-GARY, AB, T2E 7K6
(403) 571-8400   *SIC* 1531
POINTE-CLAIRE STEEL INC   *p* 611
408 WENTWORTH ST N, HAMILTON, ON, L8L 5W3
(905) 544-5604   *SIC* 5051
POINTE-CLAIRE/GREEN VALLEY STEEL GROUP INC   *p* 611
408 WENTWORTH ST N, HAMILTON, ON, L8L 5W3
(905) 544-5604   *SIC* 5051
POINTONE GRAPHICS INC   *p* 575
14 VANSCO RD, ETOBICOKE, ON, M8Z 5J4
(416) 255-8202   *SIC* 2752
POINTS ATHABASCA CONTRACTING LP*p* 1433
401 PACKHAM PL, SASKATOON, SK, S7N 2T7
(306) 242-4927   *SIC* 1541
POINTS INTERNATIONAL LTD   *p* 956
111 RICHMOND ST W SUITE 700, TORONTO, ON, M5H 2G4
(416) 595-0000   *SIC* 8742
POINTS NORTH CONTRACTING LTD *p* 214
8011 93 ST, FORT ST. JOHN, BC, V1J 6X1
(250) 787-5525   *SIC* 1389
POINTS NORTH FREIGHT FORWARDING*p*

1431
See GRAB 2 HOLDINGS LTD
POINTS NORTH FREIGHT FORWARDING INC   *p* 1431
2405B WHEATON AVE, SASKATOON, SK, S7L 5Y3
(306) 633-2137   *SIC* 5172
POINTS WEST LIVING GP INC   *p* 133
11460 104 AVE SUITE 403, GRANDE PRAIRIE, AB, T8V 3G9
(780) 357-5700   *SIC* 8051
POINTS.COM INC   *p* 977
171 JOHN ST SUITE 500, TORONTO, ON, M5T 1X3
(416) 595-0000   *SIC* 7371
POIRIER & FILS LTEE   *p* 1113
484 RUE PRINCIPALE, HUDSON, QC, J0P 1H0
(450) 458-5573   *SIC* 5411
POIRIER & FILS LTEE   *p* 1343
1869 CH SAINTE-ANGELIQUE, SAINT-LAZARE, QC, J7T 2X9
(450) 455-6165   *SIC* 5411
POIRIER CHRYSLER JEEP DODGE LTEE*p* 1289
1265 AV LARIVIERE, ROUYN-NORANDA, QC, J9X 6M6
(819) 764-7437   *SIC* 5511
POIRIER DODGE CHRYSLER   *p* 1390
See GARAGE POIRIER & FILS LTEE
POIRIER IGA   *p* 1113
See POIRIER & FILS LTEE
POIRIER, RICHARD ET FRERES ELEC-TRIQUE   *p* 1366
See RPF LTEE
POIRIER, ROGER AUTOMOBILE INC   *p* 1377
2325 RUE LAPRADE, SOREL-TRACY, QC, J3R 2C1
(450) 742-2743   *SIC* 5511
POIRIER-BERARD LTEE   *p* 1303
4401 RUE CREPEAU, SAINT-FELIX-DE-VALOIS, QC, J0K 2M0
(450) 889-5541   *SIC* 0259
POISSON SALE GASPESIEN LTEE   *p* 1112
39 RUE DU PARC, GRANDE-RIVIERE, QC, G0C 1V0
(418) 385-2424   *SIC* 2091
POISSONERIE ARSENEAU FISH MARKET LTEE/LTD   *p* 410
221 RUE PRINCIPALE, NIGADOO, NB, E8K 3S8
(506) 783-2195   *SIC* 5142
POISSONNERIE ODESSA INC., LES *p* 1172
6569 AV PAPINEAU BUREAU 100, MON-TREAL, QC, H2G 2X3
(450) 743-9999   *SIC* 5421
POISSONNERIE BLANCHETTE INC *p* 1355
150 BOUL PERRON E, SAINTE-ANNE-DES-MONTS, QC, G4V 3A4
(418) 763-9494   *SIC* 5146
POISSONNERIE COWIE (1985) INC, LA *p* 1111
660 RUE BERNARD, GRANBY, QC, J2J 0H6
(450) 375-7500   *SIC* 5142
POISSONNERIE DU HAVRE LTEE   *p* 1113
968 RUE DE LA BERGE, HAVRE-SAINT-PIERRE, QC, G0G 1P0
(418) 538-2515   *SIC* 5421
POISSONNERIE UNIMER INC   *p* 1273
2500 CH DES QUATRE-BOURGEOIS, QUEBEC, QC, G1V 4P9
(418) 654-1880   *SIC* 5146
POISSONNERIE VERSEAU II   *p* 1384
152 132 RTE O, TROIS-PISTOLES, QC, G0L 4K0
(418) 851-1516   *SIC* 5146
POKA INC   *p* 1265
214 AV SAINT-SACREMENT BUREAU 240, QUEBEC, QC, G1N 3X6
(418) 476-2188   *SIC* 7372
POKA TECHNOLOGIES   *p* 1265

See POKA INC
POLANE INC   *p* 1108
621 RUE DE VERNON, GATINEAU, QC, J9J 3K4
(819) 772-4949   *SIC* 1542
POLAR BEAR WATER GROUP (1978) LTD *p* 152
1 MAIN ST, PICKARDVILLE, AB, T0G 1W0
(780) 349-4872   *SIC* 5084
POLAR CAPITAL CORPORATION   *p* 956
372 BAY ST, TORONTO, ON, M5H 2W9
(416) 367-4364   *SIC* 6211
POLAR ELECTRIC INC   *p* 175
2236 WEST RAILWAY ST UNIT 1, ABBOTS-FORD, BC, V2S 2E2
(604) 850-7522   *SIC* 1731
POLAR EXPLOSIVES LTD   *p* 436
349 OLD AIRPORT RD SUITE 104, YEL-LOWKNIFE, NT, X1A 3X6
(867) 880-4613   *SIC* 5169
POLAR FOODS INC   *p* 350
GD, FISHER BRANCH, MB, R0C 0Z0
(204) 372-6132   *SIC* 5149
POLAR MOBILITY RESEARCH LTD   *p* 17
7860 62 ST SE, CALGARY, AB, T2C 5K2
(403) 279-3633   *SIC* 5075
POLAR RAY-O-MAX WINDOWS LTD *p* 367
672 KIMBERLY AVE, WINNIPEG, MB, R2K 0Y2
(204) 956-6555   *SIC* 3089
POLAR, DIV   *p* 180
See CANADIAN FOREST PRODUCTS LTD
POLARIS   *p* 1414
See RALLY MOTORS LTD
POLARIS INDUSTRIES LTD   *p* 366
50 PRAIRIE WAY, WINNIPEG, MB, R2J 3J8
(204) 925-7100   *SIC* 5012
POLARIS INFRASTRUCTURE INC   *p* 930
2 BLOOR ST W SUITE 2700IT, TORONTO, ON, M4W 3E2
(416) 849-2587   *SIC* 1731
POLARIS INTERNATIONAL CARRIERS INC   *p* 686
7099 TORBRAM RD, MISSISSAUGA, ON, L4T 1G7
(905) 672-7952   *SIC* 4731
POLARIS MATERIALS CORPORATION   *p* 315
1055 GEORGIA ST W SUITE 2740, VAN-COUVER, BC, V6E 4N4
(604) 915-5000   *SIC* 1442
POLARIS REALTY (CANADA) LIMITED   *p* 699
2605 SKYMARK AVE SUITE 105, MISSIS-SAUGA, ON, L4W 4L5
(905) 238-8363   *SIC* 6512
POLARIS TRADING CORP   *p* 261
2030-10013 RIVER DR, RICHMOND, BC, V6X 0N2
(778) 834-2701   *SIC* 5199
POLARIS TRANSPORT CARRIERS INC   *p* 686
7099 TORBRAM RD, MISSISSAUGA, ON, L4T 1G7
(905) 671-3100   *SIC* 4731
POLARIS TRANSPORTATION GROUP   *p* 686
See POLARIS TRANSPORT CARRIERS INC
POLE STAR LONG HAUL   *p* 409
See POLE STAR TRANSPORT INCORPO-RATED
POLE STAR TRANSPORT INCORPO-RATED   *p* 409
689 EDINBURGH DR, MONCTON, NB, E1E 2L4
(506) 859-7025   *SIC* 4213
POLE STAR TRANSPORT INCORPO-RATED   *p* 448
80 GUILDFORD AVE, DARTMOUTH, NS, B3B 0G3
(902) 468-8855   *SIC* 4213

POLEY MOUNTAIN RESORTS LTD *p* 419
69 POLEY MOUNTAIN RD, WATERFORD, NB, E4E 4Y2
(506) 433-7653   *SIC* 7011
POLICARO BMW   *p* 498
See 1911661 ONTARIO INC
POLICARO INVESTMENTS LIMITED *p* 500
2 MARITIME ONTARIO BLVD, BRAMPTON, ON, L6S 0C2
(905) 791-3500   *SIC* 5511
POLISH WAR VETERAN'S SOCIETY*p* 1186
63 RUE PRINCE-ARTHUR E, MONTREAL, QC, H2X 1B4
(514) 842-7551   *SIC* 8641
POLITO FORD LINCOLN SALES LTD *p* 646
2 HARVEST ST, LINDSAY, ON, K9V 4S5
(705) 328-3673   *SIC* 5511
POLLARD BANKNOTE   *p* 5
See POLLARD EQUITIES LIMITED
POLLARD BANKNOTE INCOME FUND *p* 5
6203 46 ST, BARRHEAD, AB, T7N 1A1
(780) 674-4750   *SIC* 7999
POLLARD BANKNOTE INCOME FUND *p* 391
140 OTTER ST, WINNIPEG, MB, R3T 0M8
(204) 474-2323   *SIC* 3999
POLLARD BANKNOTE LIMITED   *p* 391
140 OTTER ST, WINNIPEG, MB, R3T 0M8
(204) 474-2323   *SIC* 2679
POLLARD EQUITIES LIMITED   *p* 5
GD STN MAIN, BARRHEAD, AB, T7N 1B8
(780) 674-4750   *SIC* 2759
POLLARD WINDOWS INC   *p* 531
1217 KING RD, BURLINGTON, ON, L7T 0B7
(905) 634-2365   *SIC* 2431
POLLITT & CO. INC   *p* 956
330 BAY ST SUITE 405, TORONTO, ON, M5H 2S8
(416) 365-3313   *SIC* 6211
POLLITT, R. OILFIELD CONSTRUCTION LTD   *p* 140
GD, LESLIEVILLE, AB, T0M 1H0
(403) 588-1230   *SIC* 1623
POLLOCK, PAUL S. ENTERPRISES LTD *p* 637
1400 OTTAWA ST S, KITCHENER, ON, N2E 4E2
(519) 743-1113   *SIC* 5531
POLO PARK SAFEWAY   *p* 382
See SOBEYS WEST INC
POLO SECURITY SERVICES LTD   *p* 291
7251 FRASER ST, VANCOUVER, BC, V5X 3V8
(604) 321-4046   *SIC* 7381
POLTEC   *p* 1309
See CICAME ENERGIE INC
POLY BALENPE WA LOSOER   *p* 419
See DISTRICT SCOLAIRE FRANCO-PHONE NORD-EST
POLY EXCAVATION INC   *p* 1084
295 AV DES TERRASSES, COTE SAINT-LUC, QC, H7H 2A7
(450) 622-4100   *SIC* 1623
POLY-CEL PACKAGING PRODUCTS *p* 743
See ST. SHREDDIES CELLO CO. LTD
POLY-NOVA TECHNOLOGIES INC *p* 601
125 SOUTHGATE DR, GUELPH, ON, N1G 3M5
(519) 822-2109   *SIC* 3069
POLY-NOVA TECHNOLOGIES LIMITED PARTNERSHIP   *p* 601
125 SOUTHGATE DR, GUELPH, ON, N1G 3M5
(519) 822-2109   *SIC* 3069
POLY-TECH M.P   *p* 1050
See PRODUITS & SERVICES DE LA CON-STRUCTION (MONTREAL) INC
POLYCAST INDUSTRIAL PRODUCTS LTD *p* 372
486 SHEPPARD ST, WINNIPEG, MB, R2X 2P8
(204) 632-5428   *SIC* 3677
POLYCAST INTERNATIONAL   *p* 372

See POLYCAST INDUSTRIAL PRODUCTS LTD
POLYCELLO   *p* 438
See EPC INDUSTRIES LIMITED
POLYCLINIC PROFESSIONAL CENTRE INC   *p* 1039
199 GRAFTON ST SUITE 307, CHARLOT-TETOWN, PE, C1A 1L2
(902) 629-8810   *SIC* 8011
POLYCLINIC, THE   *p* 1039
See POLYCLINIC PROFESSIONAL CEN-TRE INC
POLYCOL, UNE DIVISION DE HALLTECH*p* 866
See HALLTECH INC
POLYCOM CANADA LTD   *p* 189
3605 GILMORE WAY SUITE 200, BURN-ABY, BC, V5G 4X5
(604) 453-9400   *SIC* 5065
POLYCON INDUSTRIES   *p* 606
See MAGNA INTERNATIONAL INC
POLYCOR INC   *p* 1259
76 RUE SAINT-PAUL BUREAU 100, QUE-BEC, QC, G1K 3V9
(418) 692-4695   *SIC* 1423
POLYCORE TUBULAR LININGS CORPO-RATION   *p* 65
1011 1 ST SW SUITE 510, CALGARY, AB, T2R 1J2
(403) 444-5554   *SIC* 3443
POLYCORP LTD   *p* 569
33 YORK ST W, ELORA, ON, N0B 1S0
(519) 846-2075   *SIC* 3069
POLYCORP LTD   *p* 965
123 FRONT ST W SUITE 905, TORONTO, ON, M5J 2M2
(416) 364-2241   *SIC* 3069
POLYCOTE INC   *p* 557
8120 KEELE ST, CONCORD, ON, L4K 2A3
(905) 660-7552   *SIC* 3479
POLYCULTURAL IMMIGRANT AND COM-MUNITY SERVICES   *p* 578
17 FOUR SEASONS PL SUITE 102, ETO-BICOKE, ON, M9B 6E6
(416) 233-1655   *SIC* 8641
POLYCULTURE PLANTE (1987) INC *p* 1361
8683 CH ROYAL, SAINTE-PETRONILLE, QC, G0A 4C0
(418) 828-9603   *SIC* 5431
POLYEXPERT INC   *p* 1342
850 AV MUNCK, SAINT-LAURENT, QC, H7S 1B1
(514) 384-5060   *SIC* 3081
POLYFORM A.G.P. INC   *p* 1111
870 BOUL INDUSTRIEL, GRANBY, QC, J2J 1A4
(450) 378-9093   *SIC* 3081
POLYGON HOMES LTD   *p* 319
1333 BROADWAY W SUITE 900, VANCOU-VER, BC, V6H 4C2
(604) 877-1131   *SIC* 6712
POLYGON INTERNATIONAL TECHNOL-OGY INC   *p* 57
400 5 AVE SW SUITE 300, CALGARY, AB, T2P 0L6
(403) 984-2759   *SIC* 5085
POLYMAC MAINTENANCE   *p* 1116
See AMIMAC (2002) LTEE
POLYMER DISTRIBUTION INC   *p* 600
256 VICTORIA RD S, GUELPH, ON, N1E 5R1
(519) 837-4535   *SIC* 4225
POLYMERSHAPES   DISTRIBUTION CANADA INC   *p* 500
9150 AIRPORT RD, BRAMPTON, ON, L6S 6G1
(905) 789-3111   *SIC* 5162
POLYMOS INC   *p* 1378
150 5E BOUL, TERRASSE-VAUDREUIL, QC, J7V 5M3
(514) 453-1920   *SIC* 3086

POLYNOVA INDUSTRIES INC   *p* 263
11480 BLACKSMITH PL UNIT 101, RICH-MOND, BC, V7A 4X1
(604) 277-1274   *SIC* 3086
POLYNT COMPOSITES CANADA INC*p* 513
29 REGAN RD, BRAMPTON, ON, L7A 1B2
(905) 495-0606   *SIC* 3087
POLYONE CANADA INC   *p* 758
940 CHIPPAWA CREEK RD, NIAGARA FALLS, ON, L2E 6S5
(905) 353-4200   *SIC* 2821
POLYONE DSS CANADA INC   *p* 1109
440 RUE ROBINSON S, GRANBY, QC, J2G 9R3
(450) 378-8433   *SIC* 3089
POLYTAINERS INC   *p* 575
197 NORSEMAN ST, ETOBICOKE, ON, M8Z 2R5
(416) 239-7311   *SIC* 3089
POLYTARP PRODUCTS   *p* 782
See ALROS PRODUCTS LIMITED
POLYTECH CANADA INC   *p* 1017
5505 RHODES DR, WINDSOR, ON, N8N 2M1
SIC 5169
POLYTUBES (MAN) INC   *p* 369
1803 HEKLA AVE, WINNIPEG, MB, R2R 0K3
SIC 5074
POLYTUBES 2009 INC   *p* 106
16221 123 AVE NW, EDMONTON, AB, T5V 1N9
(780) 453-2211   *SIC* 3084
POLYTUBES 2009 INC   *p* 841
416 PIDO RD, PETERBOROUGH, ON, K9J 6X7
(705) 740-2872   *SIC* 3084
POLYTUBES INC   *p* 106
12160 160 ST NW, EDMONTON, AB, T5V 1H5
(780) 453-2211   *SIC* 3088
POLYTUBES PETERBOROUGH   *p* 841
See POLYTUBES 2009 INC
POLYVALENTE BELANGER   *p* 1348
See COMMISSION SCOLAIRE DE LA BEAUCE-ETCHEMIN
POLYVALENTE CHAMOINE ARMAND RACICOT   *p* 1316
See COMMISSION SCOLAIRE DES HAUTES-RIVIERES
POLYVALENTE DE LA FORET   *p* 1046
See COMMISSION SCOLAIRE HARRI-CANA
POLYVALENTE HYACINTHE-DELORME *p* 1312
See COMMISSION SCOLAIRE DE SAINT-HYACINTHE, LA
POLYVALENTE JEAN DOLBEAU   *p* 1090
See COMMISSION SCOLAIRE DU PAYS-DES-BLEUETS
POLYVALENTE L'ACHIGAN   *p* 1303
See COMMISSION SCOLAIRE DES SAMARES
POLYVALENTE MARCEL LANDRY *p* 1316
See COMMISSION SCOLAIRE DES HAUTES-RIVIERES
POLYVALENTE MONTIGNAC   *p* 1125
See COMMISSION SCOLAIRE DES HAUTS-CANTONS
POLYVALENTE NICHOLAS GATINEAU *p* 1103
See COMMISSION SCOLAIRE DES DRAVEURS
POLYVALENTE ROBERT OUIMET *p* 1044
See COMMISSION SCOLAIRE DE SAINT-HYACINTHE, LA
POLYVALENTE ROLAND-PEPIN HIGH SCHOOL   *p* 396
See CONSEIL SCOLAIRE DISTRICT NO 5
POLYWEST LTD   *p* 389
3700 MCGILLIVRAY BLVD UNIT B, WIN-NIPEG, MB, R3P 5S3
(204) 924-8265   *SIC* 5084
POLYWHEELS MANUFACTURING LTD   *p*

799
1455 NORTH SERVICE RD E, OAKVILLE, ON, L6H 1A7
SIC 3089
POMAS FARMS INC   *p* 890
1057 HWY 77, STAPLES, ON, N0P 2J0
(519) 326-4410   *SIC* 0161
POMERLEAU INC   *p* 1305
521 6E AV N, SAINT-GEORGES, QC, G5Y 0H1
(418) 228-6688   *SIC* 1542
POMEROY HOTEL LIMITED   *p* 173
4121 KEPLER ST, WHITECOURT, AB, T7S 0A3
(780) 778-8908   *SIC* 7021
POMEROY INN & SUITES FORT ST JOHN*p* 133
See POMEROY LODGING LP
POMEROY LODGING LP   *p* 133
9820 100 AVE, GRANDE PRAIRIE, AB, T8V 0T8
(780) 814-5295   *SIC* 7011
POMMES ENDERLE INC, LES   *p* 1113
514 CH JAMES-FISHER, HEMMINGFORD, QC, J0L 1H0
(450) 247-2463   *SIC* 7389
POMPACTION INC   *p* 1252
119 BOUL HYMUS, POINTE-CLAIRE, QC, H9R 1E5
(514) 697-8600   *SIC* 5084
POMPES ET FILTRATIONS DE THETFORD INC   *p* 1383
221 RUE JALBERT O, THETFORD MINES, QC, G6G 7W1
(418) 335-9348   *SIC* 5084
PONG GAME STUDIOS LIMITED   *p* 1033
201 CREDITVIEW RD, WOODBRIDGE, ON, L4L 9T1
(905) 264-3555   *SIC* 7371
PONOKA CHEVROLET   *p* 152
See PONOKA CHEVROLET OLDSMOBILE LTD
PONOKA CHEVROLET OLDSMOBILE LTD *p* 152
6305 44 AVE, PONOKA, AB, T4J 1J8
(403) 783-4494   *SIC* 5511
PONOKA FOODS LTD   *p* 152
4502 50 ST UNIT 1, PONOKA, AB, T4J 1J5
(403) 783-4528   *SIC* 5411
PONOKA HOSPITAL & CARE CENTRE *p* 152
See ALBERTA HEALTH SERVICES
PONTEIX   COLONY OF HUTTERIAN BRETHREN   *p* 1413
GD, PONTEIX, SK, S0N 1Z0
(306) 625-3652   *SIC* 8741
PONTIAC BUICK GMC   *p* 419
See MCGRAW ET FRERE LIMITEE
PONTIAC BUICK GMC   *p* 1379
See GRENIER CHEVROLET BUICK GMC INC
PONY CORRAL RESTAURANT & BAR *p* 378
See KENMAR FOOD SERVICES LTD
POOL OF EXPERTS   *p* 783
See INTERNATIONAL AQUATIC SER-VICES LTD
POP ENVIRO BAGS & PRODUCTS *p* 708
615 ORWELL ST, MISSISSAUGA, ON, L5A 2W4
(905) 272-2247   *SIC* 2673
POPEYES   *p* 987
See RESTAURANT BRANDS INTERNA-TIONAL INC
POPLAR POINT COLONY FARMS LTD *p* 355
94 RIVER RD W, PORTAGE LA PRAIRIE, MB, R1N 3C4
(204) 267-2560   *SIC* 0191
POPOW & SONS BODY SHOP LTD *p* 138
5017 49 ST, LACOMBE, AB, T4L 1Y2
(403) 782-6941   *SIC* 5093
POPPA CORN CORP   *p* 699
5135 CREEKBANK RD UNIT C, MISSIS-

SAUGA, ON, L4W 1R3

(905) 212-9855   *SIC* 5145

PORCHLIGHT DEVELOPMENTS LTD *p* 170
414 MAIN ST NW, TURNER VALLEY, AB, T0L 2A0

(403) 933-3440   *SIC* 8742

PORSCHE CANADIAN INVESTMENT ULC *p* 456
3367 KEMPT RD, HALIFAX, NS, B3K 4X5

(902) 453-8800   *SIC* 5511

PORSCHE CENTRE CALGARY   *p* 37
5512 MACLEOD TRAIL SW, CALGARY, AB, T2H 0J5

(403) 243-8101   *SIC* 5511

PORSCHE PRESTIGE   *p* 1324
See 6202667 CANADA INC

PORT ALBERNI ASSOCIATION FOR COMMUNITY LIVING   *p* 245
3008 2ND AVE, PORT ALBERNI, BC, V9Y 1Y9

(250) 724-7155   *SIC* 8699

PORT ALBERNI MARINE INDUSTRIES, DIV OF   *p* 239
See PACIFIC TOWING SERVICES LTD

PORT ALBERNI MILL   *p* 245
See CATALYST PAPER CORPORATION

PORT ALICE SPECIALTY CELLULOSE INC *p* 245
PO BOX 2000, PORT ALICE, BC, V0N 2N0
SIC 2611

PORT ARTHUR HEALTH CENTRE INC, THE   *p* 907
194 COURT ST N, THUNDER BAY, ON, P7A 4V7

(807) 345-2332   *SIC* 8011

PORT CITY WATER PARTNERS   *p* 413
380 BAYSIDE DR SUITE 101, SAINT JOHN, NB, E2J 4Y8

(506) 645-9070   *SIC* 1629

PORT COLBORNE GENERAL HOSPITAL *p* 847
See NIAGARA HEALTH SYSTEM

PORT COLBORNE REFINERY   *p* 847
See VALE CANADA LIMITED

PORT COQUITLAM BUILDING SUPPLIES LTD   *p* 247
2650 MARY HILL RD, PORT COQUITLAM, BC, V3C 3B3

(604) 942-7282   *SIC* 5039

PORT COQUITLAM SENIOR CITIZENS HOUSING SOCIETY   *p* 247
2111 HAWTHORNE AVE SUITE 406, PORT COQUITLAM, BC, V3C 1W3

(604) 941-4051   *SIC* 8361

PORT CREDIT HARBOUR MARINA   *p* 712
See CENTRE CITY CAPITAL LIMITED

PORT DE QUEBEC   *p* 1257
See ADMINISTRATION PORTUAIRE DU QUEBEC

PORT HARDY INSURANCENTRE   *p* 195
See WAYPOINT INSURANCE SERVICES INC

PORT HAWKESBURY PAPER LIMITED PARTNERSHIP   *p* 464
120 PULP MILL RD POINT TUPPER INDUSTRIAL PARK, PORT HAWKESBURY, NS, B9A 1A1

(902) 625-2460   *SIC* 2621

PORT KELLS NURSERIES LTD   *p* 282
18730 88 AVE, SURREY, BC, V4N 5T1

(604) 882-1344   *SIC* 0161

PORT MCNEIL FOODS LTD   *p* 247
1705 CAMPBELL WAY UNIT 44, PORT MCNEILL, BC, V0N 2R0

(250) 956-4404   *SIC* 5411

PORT METRO VANCOUVER   *p* 310
See VANCOUVER FRASER PORT AUTHORITY

PORT MOODY SECONDARY SCHOOL   *p* 248
See SCHOOL DISTRICT NO. 43 (COQUITLAM)

PORT O'CALL SAFEWAY   *p* 154

See SOBEYS WEST INC

PORT PERRY HIGH SCHOOL   *p* 848
See DURHAM DISTRICT SCHOOL BOARD

PORTABLE PACKAGING   *p* 732
See MENASHA PACKAGING CANADA L.P.

PORTABLES EXHIBIT SYSTEMS LIMITED, THE   *p* 256
3551 VIKING WAY SUITE 109, RICHMOND, BC, V6V 1W1

(604) 276-2366   *SIC* 3993

PORTAGE AVENUE FAMILY FOODS *p* 385
See CLEMENT FOODS LTD

PORTAGE COLLEGE   *p* 138
9531 94 AVE, LAC LA BICHE, AB, T0A 2C0

(780) 623-5511   *SIC* 8221

PORTAGE COLLEGE   *p* 170
5005 50 AVE, VEGREVILLE, AB, T9C 1T1
SIC 8221

PORTAGE DISTRICT GENERAL HOSPITAL *p* 355
See REGIONAL HEALTH AUTHORITY - CENTRAL MANITOBA INC

PORTAGE LA PRAIRIE MUTUAL INSURANCE CO, THE   *p* 355
749 SASKATCHEWAN AVE E, PORTAGE LA PRAIRIE, MB, R1N 0L3

(204) 857-3415   *SIC* 6411

PORTAGE MUTUAL INSURANCE   *p* 355
See PORTAGE LA PRAIRIE MUTUAL INSURANCE CO, THE

PORTAGE TRANSPORT 1998   *p* 355
See PORTAGE TRANSPORT INC

PORTAGE TRANSPORT INC   *p* 355
1450 LORNE AVE E, PORTAGE LA PRAIRIE, MB, R1N 4A2

(204) 239-6451   *SIC* 7538

PORTAMEDIC   *p* 877
See HOOPER-HOLMES CANADA LIMITED

PORTE DE LA MAURICIE INC, LA *p* 1403
4 RUE SAINTE-ANNE, YAMACHICHE, QC, G0X 3L0

(819) 228-9434   *SIC* 5812

PORTE EVOLUTION INC   *p* 1045
1500 BOUL SAINT-JUDE, ALMA, QC, G8B 3L4

(418) 668-6688   *SIC* 5712

PORTEFEUILLE SOUCY INC   *p* 1097
5450 RUE SAINT-ROCH S, DRUMMONDVILLE, QC, J2B 6V4

(819) 474-6666   *SIC* 3795

PORTENGEN, R. HOME AND AUTO INC *p* 568
50 HILLSIDE DR S, ELLIOT LAKE, ON, P5A 1M7

(705) 848-3663   *SIC* 5531

PORTEOUS LODGE   *p* 1431
See JUBILEE RESIDENCES INC

PORTER AIRLINES INC   *p* 983
4 TORONTO ISLAND AIRPORT, TORONTO, ON, M5V 1A1

(416) 203-8100   *SIC* 4581

PORTER CREEK SECONDARY SCHOOL *p* 1440
1405 HICKORY ST, WHITEHORSE, YT, Y1A 4M4

(867) 667-8044   *SIC* 8211

PORTES & FENETRES ABRITEK INC *p* 1305
5195 127E RUE, SAINT-GEORGES, QC, G5Y 5B9

(418) 228-3293   *SIC* 3089

PORTES & FENETRES NOUVEL HORIZON INC   *p* 1388
1135 RUE LA VERENDRYE, TROIS-RIVIERES, QC, G9A 2T1

(819) 694-0783   *SIC* 3442

PORTES A R D INC, LES   *p* 1129
755 BOUL CRISTINI, LACHUTE, QC, J8H 4N6

(450) 562-2624   *SIC* 5031

PORTES BAILLARGEON, LES   *p* 1299
See MASONITE INTERNATIONAL CORPORATION

PORTES DE GARAGE CEDO INC   *p* 1283
605 BOUL IBERVILLE BUREAU 2061, REPENTIGNY, QC, J6A 5H9

(450) 585-4224   *SIC* 5211

PORTES DECKO INC   *p* 1381
2375 RUE EDOUARD-MICHELIN, TERREBONNE, QC, J6Y 4P2

(450) 477-0199   *SIC* 3231

PORTES DUSCO LTEE, LES   *p* 1162
11825 AV J.-J.-JOUBERT, MONTREAL, QC, H1E 7J5

(514) 355-4877   *SIC* 3231

PORTES ET CADRES METALEC   *p* 1263
See 2972-6924 QUEBEC INC

PORTES ET CHASSIS BOULET, EDDY INC *p* 1377
10700 RTE MARIE-VICTORIN, SOREL-TRACY, QC, J3R 0K2

(450) 742-9424   *SIC* 3442

PORTES ET FENETRES BOULET   *p* 1377
See PORTES ET CHASSIS BOULET, EDDY INC

PORTES ET FENETRES M.P.M. INC *p* 1293
167 RUE D'AMSTERDAM, SAINT-AUGUSTIN-DE-DESMAURES, QC, G3A 2V5

(418) 870-1544   *SIC* 5031

PORTES ET FENETRES ROYALTY *p* 1393
17 BOULEVARD CITE DES JEUNES, VAUDREUIL-DORION, QC, G7V 9E8

(450) 218-4411   *SIC* 5211

PORTES ET FENETRES VERDUN LTEE *p* 1296
1305 RUE MARIE-VICTORIN BUREAU 300, SAINT-BRUNO, QC, J3V 6B7

(450) 441-0472   *SIC* 5039

PORTES ET MOULURES ELEGANCE *p* 1133
See CUISINES LAURIER INC

PORTES GARAGA: STANDARD + INC *p* 1306
8500 25E AV, SAINT-GEORGES, QC, G6A 1K5

(418) 227-2828   *SIC* 6712

PORTES GENSTEEL INC   *p* 1340
4950 RUE HICKMORE, SAINT-LAURENT, QC, H4T 1K6

(514) 733-3562   *SIC* 3442

PORTES JPR INC, LES   *p* 1087
4800 SUD LAVAL (A-440) O UNITE 1, COTE SAINT-LUC, QC, H7T 2Z8

(450) 661-5110   *SIC* 1751

PORTES LAMBTON   *p* 1129
See 2843-5816 QUEBEC INC

PORTES MILETTE INC   *p* 1295
100 AV INDUSTRIELLE, SAINT-BONIFACE-DE-SHAWINIGAN, QC, G0X 2L0

(819) 535-5588   *SIC* 2431

PORTES PATIO NOVATECH INC   *p* 1055
100 181E RUE, BEAUCEVILLE, QC, G5X 2T1

(418) 774-2949   *SIC* 3231

PORTES PATIO RESIVER   *p* 1055
See PORTES PATIO NOVATECH INC

PORTES SAINT-GEORGES INC, LES *p* 1356
2 RUE DES CERISIERS, SAINTE-AURELIE, QC, G0M 1M0

(418) 593-3784   *SIC* 2431

PORTES STANDARD INC   *p* 1085
2300 AV FRANCIS-HUGHES, COTE SAINT-LUC, QC, H7S 2C1

(514) 634-8911   *SIC* 3442

PORTEX MINERALS INC   *p* 971
199 BAY ST W SUITE 2901, TORONTO, ON, M5L 1G1

(416) 786-3876   *SIC* 1041

PORTFOLIO ENTERTAINMENT   *p* 979
See CARL SQUARED PRODUCTIONS INC

PORTFOLIO MANAGEMENT SOLUTIONS INC   *p* 654
200 QUEENS AVE SUITE 700, LONDON, ON, N6A 1J3

(519) 432-0075   *SIC* 7322

PORTIA LEARNING CENTRE INC. *p* 831
1770 COURTWOOD CRES SUITE 201, OTTAWA, ON, K2C 2B5

(613) 221-9777   *SIC* 6411

PORTLAND INVESTMENT COUNCIL *p* 529
See AIC RSP AMERICAN FOCUSED FUND

PORTLAND INVESTMENT COUNSEL INC *p* 529
1375 KERNS RD SUITE 100, BURLINGTON, ON, L7P 4V7

(905) 331-4242   *SIC* 6282

PORTLAND STREET HONDA   *p* 443
See WILKINS LIMITED

PORTOLA PACKAGING CANADA LTD. *p* 263
12431 HORSESHOE WAY, RICHMOND, BC, V7A 4X6

(604) 272-5000   *SIC* 2821

PORTS TORONTO   *p* 967
See TORONTO PORT AUTHORITY

PORTSMOUTH ATLANTIC LIMITED *p* 1039
20 GREAT GEORGE ST SUITE 103, CHARLOTTETOWN, PE, C1A 4J6

(902) 978-1400   *SIC* 8748

POS BIO SCIENCES   *p* 1433
See POS MANAGEMENT CORP

POS MANAGEMENT CORP   *p* 1433
118 VETERINARY RD, SASKATOON, SK, S7N 2R4

(306) 978-2800   *SIC* 8731

POSCOR METAL GROUP   *p* 498
See POSCOR METAL RECOVERY CORP

POSCOR METAL RECOVERY CORP *p* 498
10095 BRAMALEA RD SUITE 201, BRAMPTON, ON, L6R 0K1

(647) 641-3928   *SIC* 5093

POSEIDON 'LES POISSONS ET CRUSTACES' INC   *p* 1140
259 RUE DU BORD-DE-LA-MER, LONGUE-POINTE-DE-MINGAN, QC, G0G 1V0

(418) 949-2331   *SIC* 5421

POSEIDON CARE CENTRE   *p* 388
See REVERA INC

POSI-PLUS TECHNOLOGIES INC *p* 1398
10 RUE DE L'ARTISAN, VICTORIAVILLE, QC, G6P 7E4

(819) 758-5717   *SIC* 7389

POSIMAGE INC   *p* 1119
6285 BOUL WILFRID-HAMEL, L'ANCIENNE-LORETTE, QC, G2E 5W2

(418) 877-2775   *SIC* 3993

POSITOR INC.   *p* 1067
1356 RUE NEWTON, BOUCHERVILLE, QC, J4B 5H2

(450) 449-0327   *SIC* 5561

POSITRON INC   *p* 1228
5101 RUE BUCHAN SUITE 220, MONTREAL, QC, H4P 2R9

(514) 345-2220   *SIC* 3661

POSNER METALS LIMITED   *p* 609
610 BEACH RD, HAMILTON, ON, L8H 3L1

(905) 544-1881   *SIC* 5093

POSSCAN SYSTEMS INC   *p* 338
4243 GLANFORD AVE SUITE 100, VICTORIA, BC, V8Z 4B9

(250) 380-5020   *SIC* 5065

POST FARM STRUCTURES INCORPORATED   *p* 476
80 PEEL ST, ALMA, ON, N0B 1A0

(519) 846-5988   *SIC* 1542

POST FOODS CANADA INC   *p* 759
5651 LEWIS AVE, NIAGARA FALLS, ON, L2G 3R8

(905) 374-7111   *SIC* 2043

POST HOTEL   *p* 139
See SKI CLUB OF THE CANADIAN ROCKIES LIMITED, THE

POST MODERN SOUND INC   *p* 321
1722 2ND AVE W, VANCOUVER, BC, V6J 1H6

(604) 736-7474 *SIC 7389*
POST ROAD HEALTH & DIET INC *p 777*
21 KERN RD, NORTH YORK, ON, M3B 1S9
(416) 447-3438 *SIC 8093*
POST-PROD CMJ TECH INC *p 1322*
5000 RUE D'IBERVILLE BUREAU 332, SAINT-LAMBERT, QC, H2H 2S6
(514) 731-4242 *SIC 7384*
POSTCARD FACTORY, THE *p 677*
See WEISDORF GROUP OF COMPANIES INC, THE
POSTE CANADA *p 1061*
See CANADA POST CORPORATION
POSTE DE LIVRAISON VAUDREUIL *p 1395*
972 AV SAINT-CHARLES, VAUDREUIL-DORION, QC, J7V 8P5
(450) 455-8325 *SIC 4924*
POSTE EXPRESS INC *p 1267*
2659 AV WATT BUREAU 5, QUEBEC, QC, G1P 3T2
(418) 653-1045 *SIC 7389*
POSTLINX *p 868*
See PRINTLINX CORPORATION
POSTMEDIA BUSINESS TECHNOLOGY *p 375*
See POSTMEDIA NETWORK INC
POSTMEDIA INTEGRATED ADVERTISING *p 930*
See POSTMEDIA NETWORK INC
POSTMEDIA NETWORK *p 1429*
See POSTMEDIA NETWORK INC
POSTMEDIA NETWORK CANADA CORP *p 930*
365 BLOOR ST E, TORONTO, ON, M4W 3L4
(416) 383-2300 *SIC 2711*
POSTMEDIA NETWORK INC *p 25*
215 16 ST SE, CALGARY, AB, T2E 7P5
(403) 235-7168 *SIC 2711*
POSTMEDIA NETWORK INC *p 90*
10006 101 ST NW, EDMONTON, AB, T5J 0S1
(780) 429-5100 *SIC 2711*
POSTMEDIA NETWORK INC *p 217*
393 SEYMOUR ST, KAMLOOPS, BC, V2C 6P6
SIC 2711
POSTMEDIA NETWORK INC *p 234*
2575 MCCULLOUGH RD SUITE B1, NANAIMO, BC, V9S 4M9
SIC 2711
POSTMEDIA NETWORK INC *p 261*
7280 RIVER RD SUITE 110, RICHMOND, BC, V6X 1X5
SIC 7374
POSTMEDIA NETWORK INC *p 308*
200 GRANVILLE ST SUITE 1, VANCOUVER, BC, V6C 3N3
(604) 605-2000 *SIC 2711*
POSTMEDIA NETWORK INC *p 335*
780 KINGS RD, VICTORIA, BC, V8T 5A2
(250) 383-2435 *SIC 4833*
POSTMEDIA NETWORK INC *p 375*
300 CARLTON ST 6TH FL, WINNIPEG, MB, R3B 2K6
(204) 926-4600 *SIC 7299*
POSTMEDIA NETWORK INC *p 831*
1101 BAXTER RD, OTTAWA, ON, K2C 3M4
(613) 829-9100 *SIC 2711*
POSTMEDIA NETWORK INC *p 930*
365 BLOOR ST E SUITE 1601, TORONTO, ON, M4W 3L4
(416) 383-2300 *SIC 2711*
POSTMEDIA NETWORK INC *p 1023*
167 FERRY ST, WINDSOR, ON, N9A 0C5
(519) 255-5720 *SIC 2711*
POSTMEDIA NETWORK INC *p 1207*
1010 RUE SAINTE-CATHERINE O BUREAU 200, MONTREAL, QC, H3B 5L1
(514) 284-0040 *SIC 2711*
POSTMEDIA NETWORK INC *p 1416*
1964 PARK ST, REGINA, SK, S4N 7M5
(306) 781-5211 *SIC 2711*
POSTMEDIA NETWORK INC *p 1429*

204 5TH AVE N, SASKATOON, SK, S7K 2P1
(306) 657-6206 *SIC 2711*
POTAGER MONTREALAIS LTEE, LE *p 1357*
1803 CH DE LA RIVIERE, SAINTE-CLOTILDE-DE-CHATEAUGUAY, QC, J0L 1W0
(450) 826-3191 *SIC 0161*
POTAGER RIENDEAU INC, LE *p 1351*
1729 RANG SAINT-ANTOINE, SAINT-REMI, QC, J0L 2L0
(450) 454-9091 *SIC 0161*
POTASH CORPORATION OF SASKATCHEWAN INC *p 1404*
GD, ALLAN, SK, S0K 0C0
(306) 257-3312 *SIC 1474*
POTASH CORPORATION OF SASKATCHEWAN INC *p 1409*
GD, LANIGAN, SK, S0K 2M0
(306) 365-2030 *SIC 1474*
POTASH CORPORATION OF SASKATCHEWAN INC *p 1423*
GD, ROCANVILLE, SK, S0A 3L0
(306) 645-2870 *SIC 1474*
POTASH CORPORATION OF SASKATCHEWAN INC *p 1429*
7 MILES WEST ON HWY 7, SASKATOON, SK, S7K 3N9
(306) 382-0525 *SIC 1474*
POTASH CORPORATION OF SASKATCHEWAN INC *p 1429*
122 1ST AVE S SUITE 500, SASKATOON, SK, S7K 7G3
(306) 933-8500 *SIC 1474*
POTENTIA RENEWABLES INC *p 983*
200 WELLINGTON ST W SUITE 1102, TORONTO, ON, M5V 3G2
(416) 703-1911 *SIC 8748*
POTHIER MOTORS LTD *p 450*
18 FALMOUTH BACK RD, FALMOUTH, NS, B0P 1L0
(877) 286-0154 *SIC 5511*
POTTERS *p 279*
See POTTERS FARM & NURSERY INC
POTTERS FARM & NURSERY INC *p 279*
19158 48 AVE, SURREY, BC, V3Z 1B2
(604) 576-5011 *SIC 5261*
POTTERY BARN *p 790*
See WILLIAMS-SONOMA CANADA, INC
POTTIER'S GENERAL STORES LIMITED *p 469*
8175 HWY 3, TUSKET, NS, B0W 3M0
(902) 648-2212 *SIC 5411*
POTTINGER GAHERTY ENVIRONMENTAL CONSULTANTS LTD *p 315*
1185 GEORGIA ST W SUITE 1200, VANCOUVER, BC, V6E 4E6
(604) 682-3707 *SIC 8748*
POTTRUFF & SMITH INVESTMENTS INC *p 1033*
8001 WESTON RD SUITE 300, WOODBRIDGE, ON, L4L 9C8
(905) 265-7470 *SIC 6719*
POTVIN, A. CONSTRUCTION LTD *p 857*
8850 COUNTY ROAD 17, ROCKLAND, ON, K4K 1L6
(613) 446-5181 *SIC 1521*
POTVIN, PIERRE INC *p 1084*
1859 BOUL RENE-LAENNEC BUREAU 101, COTE SAINT-LUC, QC, H7M 5E2
(450) 662-6064 *SIC 5912*
POTZUS PAVING & ROAD MAINTENANCE LTD *p 1438*
16 W HWY, YORKTON, SK, S3N 2X1
(306) 782-7423 *SIC 1611*
POULETS RIVERVIEW INC *p 1364*
287 RUE MASSON, SAINTE-SOPHIE-DE-LEVRARD, QC, G0X 3C0
(450) 431-1140 *SIC 5144*
POULIN, NIKOL INC *p 1305*
3100 BOUL DIONNE, SAINT-GEORGES, QC, G5Y 3Y4
(418) 228-3267 *SIC 5141*
POULIOT - ORTHESE - CHAUSSURE *p 1272*
See LABORATOIRE POULIOT INC
POULTRY HUT, THE *p 566*
See 1426420 ONTARIO INC
POUTRELLES INTERNATIONALES INC *p 1246*
480 RUE JOCELYN-BASTILLE, POHENEGAMOOK, QC, G0L 1J0
(418) 893-1515 *SIC 2448*
POUTRELLES MODERNES *p 1133*
See STRUCTURES ULTRATEC INC, LES
POUTRELLES VESCOM CANADA *p 1306*
See T.M.S. SYSTEME INC
POW CITY MECHANICAL PARTNERSHIP *p 1425*
2920 JASPER AVE S, SASKATOON, SK, S7J 4L7
(306) 933-3133 *SIC 1711*
POWDER TECH LIMITED *p 488*
699 BAYVIEW DR, BARRIE, ON, L4N 9A5
(705) 726-4580 *SIC 3479*
POWELL (RICHMOND HILL) CONTRACTING LIMITED *p 894*
180 RAM FOREST RD, STOUFFVILLE, ON, L4A 2G8
(905) 727-2518 *SIC 1611*
POWELL CANADA INC *p 2*
10960 274 ST, ACHESON, AB, T7X 6P7
(780) 948-3300 *SIC 1731*
POWELL MOTORS LTD *p 359*
804 MAIN ST E, SWAN RIVER, MB, R0L 1Z0
(204) 734-3464 *SIC 5511*
POWELL RIVER ASSOCIATION FOR COMMUNITY LIVING *p 248*
4675 MARINE AVE UNIT 201, POWELL RIVER, BC, V8A 2L2
(604) 485-4628 *SIC 8699*
POWELL RIVER BUILDING SUPPLY LTD *p 248*
4750 JOYCE AVE, POWELL RIVER, BC, V8A 3B6
(604) 485-2791 *SIC 5211*
POWELL RIVER MILL *p 248*
See CATALYST PAPER CORPORATION
POWELL'S SUPERMARKET LIMITED *p 421*
160 CONCEPTION BAY HWY SUITE 152, BAY ROBERTS, NL, A0A 1G0
(709) 786-2101 *SIC 5411*
POWELL-MAY INTERNATIONAL *p 692*
See C.B. POWELL LIMITED
POWER & TELEPHONE SUPPLY OF CANADA LTD *p 531*
1141 KING RD UNIT 1, BURLINGTON, ON, L7T 0B4
(289) 288-3260 *SIC 5065*
POWER BATTERY SALES LTD *p 475*
165 HARWOOD AVE N, AJAX, ON, L1Z 1L9
(905) 427-2718 *SIC 5013*
POWER BATTERY SALES LTD *p 475*
165 HARWOOD AVE N, AJAX, ON, L1Z 1L9
(905) 427-3035 *SIC 5013*
POWER COMMISSION OF THE CITY OF SAINT JOHN *p 416*
325 SIMMS ST, SAINT JOHN, NB, E2M 3L6
(506) 658-5252 *SIC 4911*
POWER CORPORATION DU CANADA *p 1190*
751 RUE DU SQUARE-VICTORIA, MONTREAL, QC, H2Y 2J3
(514) 286-7400 *SIC 6211*
POWER DRYWALL (2005) LTD *p 225*
19855 98 AVE, LANGLEY, BC, V1M 2X5
(604) 626-4900 *SIC 1742*
POWER ENVIRONMENT ALSTOM HYDRO CANADA *p 1377*
See ALSTOM CANADA INC
POWER EXPRESS *p 122*
303 69 AVE NW, EDMONTON, AB, T6P 0C2
(780) 461-4000 *SIC 4731*
POWER EXPRESS INC *p 116*
4182 93 ST NW, EDMONTON, AB, T6E 5P5

(780) 461-4000 *SIC 7389*
POWER FINANCIAL CORPORATION *p 1190*
751 RUE DU SQUARE-VICTORIA, MONTREAL, QC, H2Y 2J3
(514) 286-7400 *SIC 6712*
POWER LINK *p 1309*
See ENGRENAGES POWER-LINK2 INC. LES
POWER MEASUREMENT LTD *p 267*
2195 KEATING CROSS RD, SAANICHTON, BC, V8M 2A5
(250) 652-7100 *SIC 3825*
POWER MEASUREMENT, INC *p 267*
2195 KEATING CROSS RD, SAANICHTON, BC, V8M 2A5
(250) 652-7100 *SIC 3825*
POWER PLUS TECHNOLOGY INC *p 409*
2731 MOUNTAIN RD, MONCTON, NB, E1G 2W5
(506) 857-9212 *SIC 5541*
POWER SOURCE CANADA *p 806*
See PSC-POWER SOURCE CANADA LTD
POWER SPORTS CANADA INC *p 750*
1 LASER ST, NEPEAN, ON, K2E 7V1
(613) 224-7899 *SIC 5551*
POWER SUPPLY GRAND RAPIDS GS *p 350*
GD, GRAND RAPIDS, MB, R0C 1E0
(204) 639-4138 *SIC 4911*
POWER TECHNOLOGIES GROUP *p 746*
See DANA CANADA CORPORATION
POWER TO CHANGE MINISTRIES *p 226*
20385 64 AVE, LANGLEY, BC, V2Y 1N5
(604) 514-2000 *SIC 8661*
POWER TRADING INC *p 1252*
2555 BOUL DES SOURCES, POINTE-CLAIRE, QC, H9R 5Z3
(514) 421-2225 *SIC 5099*
POWER UP *p 17*
See MARYN INTERNATIONAL SALES LTD
POWER VAC DISASTER KLEENUP *p 427*
See ENVIRO CLEAN (NFLD.) LIMITED
POWER WORKERS UNION *p 922*
244 EGLINTON AVE E, TORONTO, ON, M4P 1K2
(416) 481-4491 *SIC 8631*
POWERADE CENTRE *p 510*
See REAL ICE SPORTS FACILITY MANAGEMENT SERVICES LTD
POWERBEV INC *p 512*
60 HEREFORD ST, BRAMPTON, ON, L6Y 0N3
(905) 453-2855 *SIC 5149*
POWERCAST INC *p 1302*
540 BOUL INDUSTRIEL, SAINT-EUSTACHE, QC, J7R 5V3
(450) 473-1517 *SIC 3365*
POWERFUL ELECTRICAL SERVICES *p 699*
See POWERFUL GROUP OF COMPANIES INC
POWERFUL GROUP OF COMPANIES INC *p 699*
5155 SPECTRUM WAY SUITE 8, MISSISSAUGA, ON, L4W 5A1
(416) 674-8046 *SIC 1711*
POWERLAND COMPUTERS LTD *p 364*
170 MARION ST, WINNIPEG, MB, R2H 0T4
(204) 237-3800 *SIC 5734*
POWERNODE COMPUTER INC *p 674*
35 RIVIERA DR SUITE 11-12, MARKHAM, ON, L3R 8N4
(905) 474-1040 *SIC 5045*
POWERSMITHS INTERNATIONAL CORP *p 505*
8985 AIRPORT RD, BRAMPTON, ON, L6T 5T2
(905) 791-1493 *SIC 3677*
POWERSONIC CONNECT *p 495*
See POWERSONIC INDUSTRIES INC
POWERSONIC INDUSTRIES INC *p 495*
13 SIMPSON RD, BOLTON, ON, L7E 1E4
(905) 951-6399 *SIC 3679*
POWERSPORTS RV CANADA *p 749*

See LEISURE MART & RV CANADA COR-
PORATION

POWERTECH LABS INC   p 277
12388 88 AVE, SURREY, BC, V3W 7R7
(604) 590-7500   SIC 8734

POWERTRADE ELECTRIC LTD   p 871
255 MIDWEST RD, SCARBOROUGH, ON,
M1P 3A6
(416) 757-3008   SIC 5063

POWRMATIC DU CANADA LTEE   p 1050
9530 BOUL RAY-LAWSON, ANJOU, QC,
H1J 1L1
(514) 493-6400   SIC 5075

POYRY (MONTREAL) INC   p 1228
5250 RUE FERRIER BUREAU 700, MON-
TREAL, QC, H4P 1L4
(514) 341-3221   SIC 8711

PP DESLANDES INC   p 1313
4775 AV TRUDEAU, SAINT-HYACINTHE,
QC, J2S 7W9
(450) 778-2426   SIC 1731

PPD   p 1400
See GROUPE PPD INC
PPD   p 1400
See PPD HOLDING INC
PPD   p 1400
See PPD SOLUTION DE MOUSSE INC
PPD FOAM SOLUTION INC   p 1099
See PPD SOLUTION DE MOUSSE INC
PPD HOLDING INC   p 1371
1649 RUE BELVEDERE S, SHERBROOKE,
QC, J1H 4E4
(819) 837-2491   SIC 3089

PPD HOLDING INC   p 1400
325 RUE PRINCIPALE N, WATERVILLE,
QC, J0B 3H0
(819) 837-2491   SIC 3089

PPD HOLDING INC   p 1400
400 RUE RAYMOND, WATERVILLE, QC,
J0B 3H0
SIC 2822

PPD RUBTECH   p 1400
See PPD HOLDING INC

PPD SOLUTION DE MOUSSE INC   p 1099
1275 RUE JANELLE, DRUMMONDVILLE,
QC, J2C 3E4
(819) 850-0159   SIC 2531

PPD SOLUTION DE MOUSSE INC   p 1400
325 RUE PRINCIPALE N, WATERVILLE,
QC, J0B 3H0
(819) 837-2491   SIC 2531

PPFD   p 1015
See PROMOTIONAL PRODUCTS FUL-
FILLMENT & DISTRIBUTION LT

**PPG ARCHITECTURAL COATINGS
CANADA INC**   p 1067
500 - 1550 RUE AMPERE,
BOUCHERVILLE, QC, J4B 7L4
(450) 655-3121   SIC 2851

PPG CANADA INC   p 557
8200 KEELE ST, CONCORD, ON, L4K 2A5
(905) 669-1020   SIC 2851

PPG CANADA INC   p 714
2301 ROYAL WINDSOR DR, MISSIS-
SAUGA, ON, L5J 1K5
SIC 2851

PPG CANADA INC   p 836
1799 20TH ST E, OWEN SOUND, ON, N4K
2C3
SIC 3211

PPHC NORTH LTD   p 1025
1965 AMBASSADOR DR, WINDSOR, ON,
N9C 3R5
(519) 969-4632   SIC 6712

PPI   p 534
See PERFORMANCE POLYMERS INC
PPI CANADA   p 280
See PRECISION PULLEY & IDLER INC
PPI FINANCIAL GROUP   p 63
See 4211596 CANADA INC
PPI QUEBEC ADVISORY INC   p 1396
3000 BOUL RENE-LEVESQUE BUREAU
340, VERDUN, QC, H3E 1T9
(514) 765-7400   SIC 6311

PPI SOLUTIONS INC   p 31
340 50 AVE SE SUITE 1340, CALGARY, AB,
T2G 2B1
(403) 243-6163   SIC 6311

**PPL AQUATIC, FITNESS & SPA GROUP
INC**   p 699
5170 TIMBERLEA BLVD UNIT A, MISSIS-
SAUGA, ON, L4W 2S5
(905) 501-7210   SIC 5091

PPSG DIVISION   p 511
See CANON CANADA INC
PQA   p 401
See PROFESSIONAL QUALITY ASSUR-
ANCE LTD
**PR POMEROY RESTORATION & CON-
STRUCTION LTD**   p
201
2075 BRIGANTINE DR UNIT 18, COQUIT-
LAM, BC, V3K 7B8
(604) 529-9200   SIC 1522

**PR SENIORS HOUSING MANAGEMENT
LTD**   p 203
4640 HEADQUARTERS RD SUITE 227,
COURTENAY, BC, V9N 7J3
(250) 331-1183   SIC 8322

**PR SENIORS HOUSING MANAGEMENT
LTD**   p 287
1880 RENFREW ST, VANCOUVER, BC,
V5M 3H9
(604) 255-7723   SIC 8051

PR-BEL GROUP OF COMPANIES   p 474
See PRO-BEL ENTERPRISES LIMITED
PRACL   p 248
See POWELL RIVER ASSOCIATION FOR
COMMUNITY LIVING
**PRACTICAL ELECTRIC CONTRACTING
INC.**   p 557
527 EDGELEY BLVD UNIT 12, CONCORD,
ON, L4K 4G6
(416) 663-1500   SIC 1731

**PRAIRIE AGRICULTURAL MACHINERY IN-
STITUTE**   p
1407
2215 8 AVE, HUMBOLDT, SK, S0K 2A1
(306) 682-2555   SIC 8734

PRAIRIE BUS LINES LTD   p 154
5310 54 ST, RED DEER, AB, T4N 6M1
(403) 342-6390   SIC 4151

PRAIRIE CO-OPERATIVE LIMITED   p 1410
304 1ST AVE E, MELVILLE, SK, S0A 2P0
(306) 728-5497   SIC 5399

PRAIRIE COMMUNICATIONS LTD   p 384
1305 KING EDWARD ST, WINNIPEG, MB,
R3H 0R6
(204) 632-7800   SIC 5999

PRAIRIE FINANCIAL GROUP LTD   p 735
2355 DERRY RD E UNIT 29, MISSIS-
SAUGA, ON, L5S 1V6
(905) 612-0800   SIC 6311

PRAIRIE FUELS   p 170
4744 51 AVE, VEGREVILLE, AB, T9C 1S1
(780) 632-4987   SIC 5171

PRAIRIE HARLEY-DAVIDSON   p 1420
See PRAIRIE MOTORCYCLE LTD
PRAIRIE HERITAGE SEEDS INC   p 1415
HIGHWAY 28 N MILE 4, RADVILLE, SK,
S0C 2G0
(306) 869-2926   SIC 5153

PRAIRIE HERITAGE SEEDS ORGANICS   p
1415
See PRAIRIE HERITAGE SEEDS INC
PRAIRIE HYDRAULIC EQUIPMENT LTD   p
17
7824 56 ST SE, CALGARY, AB, T2C 4S9
(403) 279-2070   SIC 5084

PRAIRIE LIVESTOCK LTD   p 1411
GD, MOOSOMIN, SK, S0G 3N0
(306) 435-3327   SIC 5154

PRAIRIE LUBE LTD   p 31
5040 12A ST SE UNIT B, CALGARY, AB,
T2G 5K9
(403) 243-7800   SIC 7549

**PRAIRIE MACHINE & PARTS MFG. - PART-
NERSHIP**   p

1429
3311 MILLAR AVE, SASKATOON, SK, S7K
5Y5
(306) 933-4812   SIC 3532

PRAIRIE MEATS   p 1429
2326 MILLAR AVE, SASKATOON, SK, S7K
2Y2
(306) 244-4024   SIC 5147

PRAIRIE METAL INDUSTRIES INC   p 106
16420 130 AVE NW, EDMONTON, AB, T5V
1J8
(780) 447-1400   SIC 1711

PRAIRIE MICRO-TECH (1996) INC   p 1420
2641 ALBERT ST N, REGINA, SK, S4R 8R7
(306) 721-6066   SIC 5191

PRAIRIE MINES & ROYALTY ULC   p 126
GD, EDSON, AB, T7E 1W1
(780) 794-8100   SIC 1221

PRAIRIE MINES & ROYALTY ULC   p 127
GD, FORESTBURG, AB, T0B 1N0
(403) 884-3000   SIC 1221

PRAIRIE MINES & ROYALTY ULC   p 135
GD, HANNA, AB, T0J 1P0
(403) 854-5200   SIC 1221

PRAIRIE MINES & ROYALTY ULC   p 171
GD, WARBURG, AB, T0C 2T0
(780) 848-7786   SIC 1221

PRAIRIE MINES & ROYALTY ULC   p 1404
GD, BIENFAIT, SK, S0C 0M0
(306) 388-2272   SIC 1221

PRAIRIE MINES & ROYALTY ULC   p 1405
GD, CORONACH, SK, S0H 0Z0
(306) 267-4200   SIC 1221

PRAIRIE MOBILE COMMUNICATIONS   p
384
See PRAIRIE COMMUNICATIONS LTD
PRAIRIE MOTORCYCLE LTD   p 1420
1355 MCINTYRE ST, REGINA, SK, S4R
2M9
(306) 522-1747   SIC 5571

PRAIRIE MOUNTAIN HEALTH   p 347
525 VICTORIA AVE E, BRANDON, MB, R7A
6S9
(204) 578-2670   SIC 8059

PRAIRIE MOUNTAIN HEALTH   p 351
86 ELLICE DR, KILLARNEY, MB, R0K 1G0
(204) 523-4661   SIC 8062

PRAIRIE MOUNTAIN HEALTH   p 352
147 SUMMIT ST, MELITA, MB, R0M 1L0
(204) 522-8197   SIC 8062

PRAIRIE MOUNTAIN HEALTH   p 352
334 1ST ST SW, MINNEDOSA, MB, R0J
1E0
(204) 867-2701   SIC 8062

PRAIRIE MOUNTAIN HEALTH   p 357
192 1ST AVE W, SOURIS, MB, R0K 2C0
(204) 483-5000   SIC 8011

PRAIRIE MOUNTAIN HEALTH   p 360
480 KING ST E, VIRDEN, MB, R0M 2C0
(204) 748-1230   SIC 8062

**PRAIRIE MOUNTAIN OILFIELD CON-
STRUCTION INC**   p
82
4002 62 ST, DRAYTON VALLEY, AB, T7A
1S1
(780) 542-3995   SIC 1389

PRAIRIE MUD SERVICE   p 1406
738 6TH ST, ESTEVAN, SK, S4A 1A4
(306) 634-3411   SIC 1389

**PRAIRIE NATURALS HEALTH PRODUCTS
INC**   p 201
56 FAWCETT RD, COQUITLAM, BC, V3K
6V5
(800) 931-4247   SIC 5122

PRAIRIE NORTH CO-OPERATIVE LIMITED
p 1410
1141 MAIN ST, MELFORT, SK, S0E 1A0
(306) 752-9381   SIC 5411

PRAIRIE NORTH CONST. LTD   p 116
4936 87 ST NW SUITE 280, EDMONTON,
AB, T6E 5W3
(780) 463-3363   SIC 1611

PRAIRIE NORTH HEALTH REGION   p 1412
See PRAIRIE NORTH REGIONAL HEALTH

AUTHORITY
**PRAIRIE NORTH REGIONAL HEALTH AU-
THORITY**   p
1410
711 CENTRE ST SUITE 7, MEADOW
LAKE, SK, S9X 1E6
(306) 236-1550   SIC 8062

**PRAIRIE NORTH REGIONAL HEALTH AU-
THORITY**
1412
1092 107TH ST, NORTH BATTLEFORD,
SK, S9A 1Z1
(306) 446-6600   SIC 8062

PRAIRIE PETRO-CHEM HOLDINGS LTD   p
1406
738 6TH ST, ESTEVAN, SK, S4A 1A4
(306) 634-5808   SIC 5169

PRAIRIE PRIDE   p 389
See WESTLAND PLASTICS LTD
PRAIRIE PRIDE NATURAL FOODS LTD   p
1434
3535 MILLAR AVE, SASKATOON, SK, S7P
0A2
(306) 653-1810   SIC 2015

**PRAIRIE PROVIDENT RESOURCES
CANADA LTD**   p 57
640 5 AVE SW SUITE 1100, CALGARY, AB,
T2P 3G4
(403) 292-8000   SIC 1311

PRAIRIE PROVIDENT RESOURCES INC   p
57
640 5 AVE SW SUITE 1100, CALGARY, AB,
T2P 3G4
(403) 292-8000   SIC 1382

PRAIRIE PULSE INC   p 1437
700 CAMPBELL DR, VANSCOY, SK, S0L
3J0
(306) 249-9236   SIC 5153

**PRAIRIE RESEARCH ASSOCIATES PRA
INC**   p 379
363 BROADWAY UNIT 500, WINNIPEG,
MB, R3C 3N9
(204) 987-2030   SIC 8732

PRAIRIE SOIL SERVICES LTD   p 1412
1 MILE W HWY 49, NORQUAY, SK, S0A
2V0
(306) 594-2330   SIC 5261

**PRAIRIE SOUTH SCHOOL DIVISION NO
210**   p 1411
1075 9TH AVE NW, MOOSE JAW, SK, S6H
1V7
(306) 694-1200   SIC 8211

**PRAIRIE SOUTH SCHOOL DIVISION NO
210**   p 1411
145 ROSS ST E, MOOSE JAW, SK, S6H
0S3
(306) 693-4626   SIC 8211

PRAIRIE STEEL PRODUCTS LTD   p 1405
GD, CLAVET, SK, S0K 0Y0
(306) 933-1141   SIC 5191

PRAIRIE SWINE CENTRE INC   p 1424
2105 8TH ST E, SASKATOON, SK, S7H 0T8
(306) 373-9922   SIC 8733

PRAIRIE TRUCK LTD   p 133
9916 108 ST, GRANDE PRAIRIE, AB, T8V
4E2
(780) 532-3541   SIC 5511

**PRAIRIE VALLEY SCHOOL DIVISION NO
208**   p 1418
3080 ALBERT ST N, REGINA, SK, S4P 3E1
(306) 949-3366   SIC 8211

PRAIRIE VIEW HOLDINGS LTD   p 31
140 6 AVE SE, CALGARY, AB, T2G 0G2
(403) 232-4725   SIC 7514

PRAIRIECOAST EQUIPMENT INC   p 133
15102 101 ST, GRANDE PRAIRIE, AB, T8V
0P7
(780) 532-8402   SIC 5083

PRAIRIECOAST EQUIPMENT INC   p 197
44158 PROGRESS WAY, CHILLIWACK, BC,
V2R 0W3
(604) 792-1516   SIC 5083

PRAIRIESKY ROYALTY LTD   p 57
350 7TH AVE SW SUITE 1700, CALGARY,

AB, T2P 3N9
  (587) 293-4000   *SIC* 1382
PRAIRIEVIEW SEED POTATOES LTD *p* 170
162035 TOWNSHIP RD 125, VAUXHALL,
AB, T0K 2K0
  (403) 654-2475   *SIC* 0139
PRANA BIOVEGETALIENS INC *p* 1327
1440 BOUL JULES-POITRAS, SAINT-
LAURENT, QC, H4N 1X7
  (514) 276-4864   *SIC* 5149
PRATT & WHITNEY CANADA CIE *p* 141
4045 26 AVE N, LETHBRIDGE, AB, T1H
6G2
  (403) 380-5100   *SIC* 3519
PRATT & WHITNEY CANADA CIE *p* 450
189 PRATT WHITNEY PK, ENFIELD, NS,
B2T 1L1
  (902) 873-4241   *SIC* 3724
PRATT & WHITNEY CANADA CIE *p* 742
1801 COURTNEYPARK DR E, MISSIS-
SAUGA, ON, L5T 1J3
  (905) 564-7500   *SIC* 3519
PRATT & WHITNEY CANADA CIE *p* 1142
1000   BOUL   MARIE-VICTORIN,
LONGUEUIL, QC, J4G 1A1
  (450) 677-9411   *SIC* 3519
PRATT & WHITNEY CANADA CIE *p* 1153
11155 RUE JULIEN-AUDETTE, MIRABEL,
QC, J7N 0G6
  (450) 476-0049   *SIC* 3519
PRATT MCGARRY INC *p* 379
305 BROADWAY SUITE 500, WINNIPEG,
MB, R3C 3J7
  (204) 943-1600   *SIC* 6531
PRATTS FOOD SERVICE (ALBERTA) LTD *p* 160
291196 WAGON WHEEL RD SUITE 403,
ROCKY VIEW COUNTY, AB, T4A 0E2
  (403) 476-7728   *SIC* 5141
PRATTS LIMITED *p* 372
101 HUTCHINGS ST, WINNIPEG, MB, R2X
2V4
  (204) 949-2800   *SIC* 5194
PRATTS WHOLESALE *p* 372
  See PRATTS LIMITED
PRATTS WHOLESALE (SASK.) LTD *p* 1420
1616 4TH AVE, REGINA, SK, S4R 8C8
  (306) 522-0101   *SIC* 5141
PRAXAIR *p* 659
1435 HYDE PARK RD, LONDON, ON, N6H
0B5
  (519) 473-7834   *SIC* 5169
PRAXAIR CANADA INC *p* 207
1470 DERWENT WAY, DELTA, BC, V3M
6H9
  (604) 527-0700   *SIC* 5169
PRAXAIR CANADA INC *p* 505
80 WESTCREEK BLVD UNIT 1, BRAMP-
TON, ON, L6T 0B8
  (905) 595-3788   *SIC* 2813
PRAXAIR CANADA INC *p* 510
165 BISCAYNE CRES, BRAMPTON, ON,
L6W 4R3
  (905) 450-9353   *SIC* 5169
PRAXAIR CANADA INC *p* 710
1 CITY CENTRE DR SUITE 1200, MISSIS-
SAUGA, ON, L5B 1M2
  (905) 803-1600   *SIC* 2813
PRAXAIR CANADA INC *p* 1050
8151 BOUL METROPOLITAIN E, ANJOU,
QC, H1J 1X6
  (514) 353-3340   *SIC* 5169
PRAXAIR CANADA INC *p* 1429
834 51ST ST E SUITE 5, SASKATOON, SK,
S7K 5C7
  (306) 242-3325   *SIC* 2813
**PRAXAIR SURFACE TECHNOLOGIES
MONTREAL L.P.** *p* 1331
  *See TECHNOLOGIES SURFACE PRAXAIR
MONTREAL S.E.C.*
PRAXAIR TECHNOLOGIES DE SURFACE *p* 1095
  *See TECHNOLOGIES SURFACE PRAXAIR
MONTREAL S.E.C.*

PRAXIS SANTE *p* 1122
  See ACCES SERVICES SANTE GSS INC
PRAXIS TECHNICAL GROUP, INC *p* 234
1618 NORTHFIELD RD, NANAIMO, BC,
V9S 3A9
  (250) 756-7971   *SIC* 7371
PRC BOOKS OF LONDON LIMITED *p* 657
1112 DEARNESS DR UNIT 15, LONDON,
ON, N6E 1N9
  SIC 7389
PRE-CON BUILDERS LTD *p* 353
405 FORT WHYTE WAY SUITE 100, OAK
BLUFF, MB, R4G 0B1
  (204) 633-2515   *SIC* 1541
PRE-CON INC *p* 510
35 RUTHERFORD RD S, BRAMPTON, ON,
L6W 3J4
  (905) 457-4140   *SIC* 3272
PREBILT STEEL *p* 1040
  See PREBILT STRUCTURES LTD
PREBILT STRUCTURES LTD *p* 1040
423 MOUNT EDWARD RD, CHARLOTTE-
TOWN, PE, C1E 2A1
  (902) 892-8577   *SIC* 3441
PRECIMOLD INC *p* 1073
9 BOUL MARIE-VICTORIN, CANDIAC, QC,
J5R 4S8
  (450) 659-2921   *SIC* 5085
PRECIMOULE *p* 1073
  See PRECIMOLD INC
PRECISION BIOLOGIC INC *p* 448
140 EILEEN STUBBS AVE, DARTMOUTH,
NS, B3B 0A9
  (800) 267-2796   *SIC* 5049
**PRECISION COMMUNICATION SERVICES
CORP** *p* 793
99 SIGNET DR UNIT 200, NORTH YORK,
ON, M9L 1T6
  (416) 749-0110   *SIC* 8748
PRECISION CONTRACTORS LTD *p* 144
5912 50 AVE SUITE 101, LLOYDMINSTER,
AB, T9V 0X6
  (780) 875-1962   *SIC* 1389
PRECISION COUNTERTOPS *p* 407
  See WILDWOOD CABINETS LTD
PRECISION DRILLING CORPORATION *p* 57
525 8 AVE SW SUITE 800, CALGARY, AB,
T2P 1G1
  (403) 716-4500   *SIC* 1381
PRECISION DRILLING, DIV OF *p* 57
  *See PRECISION DRILLING CORPORA-
TION*
PRECISION ELECTRONIC COMPONENTS *p* 795
  *See PRECISION ELECTRONICS CORPO-
RATION*
PRECISION ELECTRONIC CORPORATION *p* 997
70 BARTOR RD, TORONTO, ON, M9M 2G5
  (416) 744-8840   *SIC* 3679
**PRECISION ELECTRONICS CORPORA-
TION** *p* 795
70 BARTOR RD, NORTH YORK, ON, M9M
2G5
  (416) 744-8840   *SIC* 3679
PRECISION FAB INC *p* 482
259 ELM ST, AYLMER, ON, N5H 3H3
  (519) 773-5244   *SIC* 3499
PRECISION FINISHED COMPONENTS *p* 464
  See MAGNA MECHANICAL INC
PRECISION GEOMATICS INC *p* 102
17403 105 AVE NW, EDMONTON, AB, T5S
2G8
  (780) 470-4000   *SIC* 8713
PRECISION GIANT SYSTEMS INC *p* 110
7217 GIRARD RD NW, EDMONTON, AB,
T6B 2C5
  (780) 463-0026   *SIC* 5046
PRECISION HOLDINGS LTD *p* 347
404 18TH ST N, BRANDON, MB, R7A 7P3
  (204) 725-0508   *SIC* 5511

PRECISION HYUNDAI *p* 37
  See PRECISION MOTORS LTD
PRECISION INDUSTRIAL LTD *p* 1414
1020 1ST AVE NW, PRINCE ALBERT, SK,
S6V 6J9
  SIC 3535
PRECISION LIMITED PARTNERSHIP *p* 57
150 6 AVE SW SUITE 4200, CALGARY, AB,
T2P 3Y7
  (403) 781-5555   *SIC* 1389
PRECISION MOTORS LTD *p* 37
130 GLENDEER CIR SE, CALGARY, AB,
T2H 2V4
  (403) 243-8344   *SIC* 5511
PRECISION PLASTICS, DIV OF *p* 477
  See WINDSOR MOLD INC
PRECISION PROFILES PLUS *p* 1436
  See BOURGAULT INDUSTRIES LTD
**PRECISION PROPERTY MANAGEMENT
INC** *p* 587
22 GOODMARK PL UNIT 22, ETOBICOKE,
ON, M9W 6R2
  (416) 675-2223   *SIC* 6531
PRECISION PULLEY & IDLER INC *p* 280
3388 190 ST, SURREY, BC, V3Z 1A7
  (604) 560-8188   *SIC* 3429
PRECISION RESOURCE CANADA LTD *p* 539
4 CHERRY BLOSSOM RD, CAMBRIDGE,
ON, N3H 4R7
  (519) 653-7777   *SIC* 3469
PRECISION SCALE *p* 110
  See PRECISION GIANT SYSTEMS INC
PRECISION TOYOTA *p* 347
  See PRECISION HOLDINGS LTD
**PRECISION TRANSFER TECHNOLOGIES
INC** *p* 831
1750 COURTWOOD CRES SUITE 104, OT-
TAWA, ON, K2C 2B5
  (613) 729-8987   *SIC* 5099
PRECISION TRUCK ACCESSORIES *p* 172
9024 100 ST, WESTLOCK, AB, T7P 2L4
  (780) 349-3010   *SIC* 5531
PRECISION TRUCK LINES INC *p* 1028
8111 HUNTINGTON RD, WOODBRIDGE,
ON, L4H 0S6
  (905) 851-1996   *SIC* 4213
PRECISIONERP INCORPORATED *p* 821
12 YORK ST 4TH FL, OTTAWA, ON, K1N
5S6
  (613) 226-9900   *SIC* 8748
PRECO FONDATIONS *p* 1095
  See ROXBORO EXCAVATION INC
PRECO-MSE INC *p* 1395
1885   MONTEE   LABOSSIERE,
VAUDREUIL-DORION, QC, J7V 8P2
  (514) 780-1280   *SIC* 1741
PREDATOR DRILLING *p* 157
  See PREDATOR DRILLING INC
PREDATOR DRILLING INC *p* 157
210 CLEARSKYE WAY, RED DEER
COUNTY, AB, T4E 0A1
  (403) 346-0870   *SIC* 1381
**PREFERRED INSURANCE GROUP LIM-
ITED** *p* 659
778 WHARNCLIFFE RD S, LONDON, ON,
N6J 2N4
  (519) 661-0200   *SIC* 6411
PREFERRED POLYMER COATINGS LTD *p* 572
31 PORTLAND ST, ETOBICOKE, ON, M8Y
1A6
  (416) 201-9003   *SIC* 5085
**PREFERRED SERVICE CUSTOM BRO-
KERS INC** *p* 265
5980 MILLER RD UNIT 115, RICHMOND,
BC, V7B 1K2
  (604) 270-6607   *SIC* 4731
**PREFORMED LINE PRODUCTS (CANADA)
LIMITED** *p* 536
1711 BISHOP ST N, CAMBRIDGE, ON,
N1T 1N5

  (519) 740-6666   *SIC* 3644
PRELCO INC *p* 1286
94 BOUL CARTIER, RIVIERE-DU-LOUP,
QC, G5R 2M9
  (418) 862-2274   *SIC* 3211
PRELSECUR INC *p* 1286
94 BOUL CARTIER, RIVIERE-DU-LOUP,
QC, G5R 2M9
  (418) 862-2274   *SIC* 3211
PREMIER AUTOMOTIVE GROUP INC *p* 806
1453 NORTH SERVICE RD W, OAKVILLE,
ON, L6M 2W2
  (905) 847-8400   *SIC* 5511
PREMIER AVIATION QUEBEC INC *p* 1276
800 8E RUE DE L'AEROPORT, QUEBEC,
QC, G2C 2S6
  (418) 800-1325   *SIC* 4581
PREMIER BATHROOMS CANADA LTD *p* 270
14716 104 AVE, SURREY, BC, V3R 1M3
  (604) 588-9688   *SIC* 5211
PREMIER BRANDS CANADA LTD *p* 845
680 GRANITE CRT, PICKERING, ON, L1W
4A3
  (416) 750-8807   *SIC* 5145
PREMIER CANDLE CORP *p* 699
960 BRITANNIA RD E, MISSISSAUGA, ON,
L4W 5M7
  (905) 795-8833   *SIC* 3999
PREMIER CARE IN BATHING *p* 270
  See PREMIER BATHROOMS CANADA LTD
**PREMIER CHEVROLET CADILLAC BUICK
GMC INC** *p* 1023
500 DIVISION RD, WINDSOR, ON, N9A
6M9
  (519) 969-6000   *SIC* 5511
**PREMIER CHOIX SOLUTIONS DE
PAIEMENT S.E.N.C.** *p* 1211
1000 RUE SAINT-ANTOINE O BUREAU
333, MONTREAL, QC, H3C 3R7
  (866) 437-3189   *SIC* 7389
**PREMIER ELECTION SOLUTIONS
CANADA ULC** *p* 324
1200 73RD AVE W SUITE 350, VANCOU-
VER, BC, V6P 6G5
  (604) 261-6313   *SIC* 7371
PREMIER EQUIPMENT LTD. *p* 568
275 CHURCH ST W, ELMIRA, ON, N3B 1N3
  (519) 669-5453   *SIC* 5999
PREMIER EVENT TENT RENTALS INC *p* 505
10 CARSON CRT, BRAMPTON, ON, L6T
4P8
  (416) 225-7500   *SIC* 7389
PREMIER FASTENERS (DIV OF) *p* 724
  *See LAWSON PRODUCTS INC. (ON-
TARIO)*
PREMIER GOLD MINES LIMITED *p* 909
1100 RUSSELL ST SUITE 200, THUNDER
BAY, ON, P7B 5N2
  (807) 346-1390   *SIC* 1481
PREMIER HORTICULTURE LTD *p* 355
302 NORTH, RICHER, MB, R0E 1S0
  (204) 422-8805   *SIC* 5159
PREMIER HORTICULTURE LTEE *p* 1286
1 AV PREMIER BUREAU 101, RIVIERE-
DU-LOUP, QC, G5R 6C1
  (418) 862-6356   *SIC* 1499
**PREMIER INTEGRATED TECHNOLOGIES
LTD** *p* 156
14 BURNT VALLEY AVE UNIT 210, RED
DEER, AB, T4P 0M5
  (403) 887-1200   *SIC* 1389
**PREMIER MARINE INSURANCE MAN-
AGERS GROUP (WEST) INC** *p* 308
625 HOWE ST SUITE 300, VANCOUVER,
BC, V6C 2T6
  (604) 669-5211   *SIC* 6331
**PREMIER OPERATING CORPORATION
LIMITED** *p* 777
1262 DON MILLS RD SUITE 92, NORTH
YORK, ON, M3B 2W7
  (416) 443-1645   *SIC* 6512

PREMIER PRINTING LTD *p 366*
1 BEGHIN AVE, WINNIPEG, MB, R2J 3X5
(204) 663-9000   *SIC 2752*

PREMIER QUEBEC INC *p 1280*
6655 BOUL PIERRE-BERTRAND BUREAU
101, QUEBEC, QC, G2K 1M1
(418) 681-4733   *SIC 5072*

PREMIER SCHOOL AGENDAS LTD *p 226*
20230 64 AVE UNIT 103, LANGLEY, BC,
V2Y 1N3
(604) 857-1707   *SIC 5999*

PREMIER SECURITY INC *p 320*
1055 BROADWAY W SUITE 603, VANCOU-
VER, BC, V6H 1E2
(604) 739-1893   *SIC 7381*

PREMIER TECH HOME & GARDEN INC *p*
726
1900 MINNESOTA CRT SUITE 125, MIS-
SISSAUGA, ON, L5N 3C9
(905) 812-8556   *SIC 5199*

PREMIER TECH LTEE *p 1286*
1 AV PREMIER BUREAU 101, RIVIERE-
DU-LOUP, QC, G5R 6C1
(418) 867-8883   *SIC 6712*

PREMIER TECH SYSTEMS *p 1286*
*See PREMIER TECH TECHNOLOGIES
LIMITEE*

PREMIER TECH TECHNOLOGIES LIMITEE
p 1286
1 AV PREMIER, RIVIERE-DU-LOUP, QC,
G5R 6C1
(418) 867-8883   *SIC 3565*

PREMIER THEATRES *p 777*
*See PREMIER OPERATING CORPORA-
TION LIMITED*

**PREMIER TRUCK GROUP OF MISSIS-
SAUGA** *p*
742
7035 PACIFIC CIR, MISSISSAUGA, ON,
L5T 2A8
(905) 564-8270   *SIC 5511*

PREMIERE CABLE CONSTRUCTION *p 597*
See AECON UTILITIES INC

**PREMIERE CONFERENCING (CANADA)
LIMITED** *p 983*
225 KING ST W SUITE 900, TORONTO,
ON, M5V 3M2
(416) 516-5170   *SIC 4899*

**PREMIERE EXECUTIVE SUITES ATLANTIC
LIMITED** *p 448*
250 BROWNLOW AVE, DARTMOUTH, NS,
B3B 1W9
(902) 420-1333   *SIC 6512*

PREMIERE INSURANCE *p 986*
*See EVEREST INSURANCE COMPANY OF
CANADA*

**PREMIERE SOCIETE EN COMMANDITE
NATIONALE ALARMCAP** *p 1293*
4780 RUE SAINT-FELIX, SAINT-
AUGUSTIN-DE-DESMAURES, QC, G3A
2J9
(418) 864-7924   *SIC 7382*

PREMIERE VAN LINES *p 595*
See 3705391 CANADA LIMITED

PREMIERE VAN LINES INC *p 699*
5800 AMBLER DR UNIT 210, MISSIS-
SAUGA, ON, L4W 4J4
(905) 712-8960   *SIC 6794*

PREMILEC *p 1060*
See DEMILEC INC

PREMIUM BEER COMPANY INC, THE *p*
587
275 BELFIELD RD, ETOBICOKE, ON, M9W
7H9
(905) 855-7743   *SIC 5181*

PREMIUM BRANDS BAKERY GROUP INC
p 261
10991 SHELLBRIDGE WAY, RICHMOND,
BC, V6X 3C6
(604) 656-3100   *SIC 5149*

**PREMIUM BRANDS HOLDINGS CORPO-
RATION** *p*
84
12251 WILLIAM SHORT RD NW, EDMON-

TON, AB, T5B 2B7
(780) 474-5201   *SIC 2099*

**PREMIUM BRANDS HOLDINGS CORPO-
RATION** *p*
261
10991 SHELLBRIDGE WAY UNIT 100,
RICHMOND, BC, V6X 3C6
(604) 656-3100   *SIC 2099*

**PREMIUM BRANDS OPERATING LIMITED
PARTNERSHIP** *p 226*
8621 201 ST SUITE 120, LANGLEY, BC,
V2Y 0G9
(866) 663-4746   *SIC 2013*

**PREMIUM BRANDS OPERATING LIMITED
PARTNERSHIP** *p 261*
10991 SHELLBRIDGE WAY SUITE 100,
RICHMOND, BC, V6X 3C6
(604) 656-3100   *SIC 2099*

**PREMIUM BRANDS OPERATING LIMITED
PARTNERSHIP** *p 1438*
501 YORK RD W, YORKTON, SK, S3N 2V6
(306) 783-9446   *SIC 2011*

PREMIUM CANADA *p 224*
See SNOWLINE ENTERPRISES LTD

PREMIUM LINE TRANSPORT INC *p 505*
11 WEST DR, BRAMPTON, ON, L6T 4T2
(905) 454-2222   *SIC 4731*

PREMIUM SEAFOOD GROUP *p 439*
See PREMIUM SEAFOODS LIMITED

PREMIUM SEAFOODS LIMITED *p 439*
449 VETERANS MEMORIAL DR, ARICHAT,
NS, B0E 1A0
(902) 226-3474   *SIC 5146*

PREMIUM TRUCK & TRAILER INC *p 251*
1015 GREAT ST, PRINCE GEORGE, BC,
V2N 2K8
(250) 563-0696   *SIC 5511*

PREMONT HARLEY DAVIDSON *p 1266*
*See ATELIER DE MECANIQUE PREMONT
INC*

PREMONTEX *p 1401*
597 RUE CHEF-MAX-GROS-LOUIS, WEN-
DAKE, QC, G0A 4V0
(418) 847-3630   *SIC 1751*

PREMOULE COMPTOIRS *p 1293*
See PREMOULE INC

PREMOULE INC *p 1267*
2375 AV DALTON BUREAU 200, QUEBEC,
QC, G1P 3S3
(418) 652-7777   *SIC 3083*

PREMOULE INC *p 1267*
2375 AV DALTON UNITE 200, QUEBEC,
QC, G1P 3S3
(418) 652-1422   *SIC 2434*

PREMOULE INC *p 1293*
270 RUE DES GRANDS-LACS, SAINT-
AUGUSTIN-DE-DESMAURES, QC, G3A 2K1
(418) 878-5384   *SIC 3083*

PREMSTEEL FABRICATORS INC *p 57*
GD LCD 1, CALGARY, AB, T2P 2G8
(403) 720-6907   *SIC 3441*

PRENDIVILLE CORPORATION *p 369*
165 RYAN ST, WINNIPEG, MB, R2R 0N9
(204) 989-9600   *SIC 5211*

PRENDIVILLE INDUSTRIES LTD *p 389*
986 LORIMER BLVD UNIT 5, WINNIPEG,
MB, R3P 0Z8
(204) 989-9600   *SIC 2431*

PREPAC MANUFACTURING LTD *p 209*
6705 DENNETT PL, DELTA, BC, V4G 1N4
(604) 940-2300   *SIC 2541*

PRESAGIS CANADA INC *p 1228*
4700 RUE DE LA SAVANE BUREAU 300,
MONTREAL, QC, H4P 1T7
(514) 341-3874   *SIC 5045*

**PRESBYTERIAN CHURCH IN CANADA,
THE** *p 780*
50 WYNFORD DR, NORTH YORK, ON,
M3C 1J7
(416) 441-1111   *SIC 8661*

PRESCOTT & RUSSEL RESIDENCE *p 619*
1020 CARTIER BLVD, HAWKESBURY, ON,
K6A 1W7
(613) 632-2755   *SIC 8361*

PRESCOTT FINISHING INC *p 848*
823 WALKERS ST, PRESCOTT, ON, K0E
1T0
(613) 925-2859   *SIC 2258*

PRESENCE *p 1257*
See PRESENCE INFORMATIQUE INC

PRESENCE INFORMATIQUE INC *p 1257*
4600 BOUL HENRI-BOURASSA LOCAL
130, QUEBEC, QC, G1H 3A5
(418) 681-2470   *SIC 5099*

**PRESENTATION SERVICES AUDIO VI-
SUAL** *p*
1029
*See AUDIO VISUAL SERVICES (CANADA)
CORPORATION*

PRESENTATION ULTIMA INC *p 1067*
55 RUE DE MONTGOLFIER,
BOUCHERVILLE, QC, J4B 8C4
(450) 641-0670   *SIC 3161*

PRESENTOIR FILOTECH INC *p 1321*
234 RUE DE SAINTE-PAULE, SAINT-
JEROME, QC, J7Z 1A8
(450) 432-2266   *SIC 3993*

PRESENTOIRES ROCKTENN *p 1247*
*See WESTROCK COMPANY OF CANADA
CORP*

PRESENTOIRES ROCKTENN *p 1360*
*See WESTROCK COMPANY OF CANADA
CORP*

PRESENTOIRS POINT 1 INC *p 1157*
8479 PLACE DEVONSHIRE BUREAU 100,
MONT-ROYAL, QC, H4P 2K1
(514) 344-4888   *SIC 2653*

PRESIDENT'S CHOICE BANK *p 965*
25 YORK ST SUITE 7FL, TORONTO, ON,
M5J 2V5
(416) 204-2600   *SIC 8742*

PRESIDENTS CHOICE FINANCIAL *p 965*
See PRESIDENT'S CHOICE BANK

PRESIMA INC *p 1192*
1000 PLACE JEAN-PAUL-RIOPELLE
UNITE 400, MONTREAL, QC, H2Z 2B6
(514) 673-1375   *SIC 6722*

PRESSE (2018) INC, LA *p 1190*
750 BOUL SAINT-LAURENT, MONTREAL,
QC, H2Y 2Z4
(514) 285-7000   *SIC 2711*

PRESSE (2018) INC, LA *p 1248*
12300 BOUL METROPOLITAIN E, POINTE-
AUX-TREMBLES, QC, H1B 5Y2
(514) 640-1840   *SIC 7319*

PRESSE, LTEE, LA *p 1248*
See PRESSE (2018) INC, LA

PRESSTEK CANADA CORP *p 742*
400 AMBASSADOR DR, MISSISSAUGA,
ON, L5T 2J3
(905) 362-0610   *SIC 5084*

PRESTEVE FOODS LIMITED *p 1013*
20954 ERIE ST S, WHEATLEY, ON, N0P
2P0
(519) 825-4677   *SIC 5146*

**PRESTIGE DESIGNS & CONSTRUCTION
(OTTAWA) LTD** *p 751*
50 CAMELOT DR, NEPEAN, ON, K2G 5X8
(613) 224-9437   *SIC 1611*

PRESTIGE FORD INC *p 1365*
1275 BOUL MONSEIGNEUR-LANGLOIS,
SALABERRY-DE-VALLEYFIELD, QC, J6S
1C1
(450) 371-0711   *SIC 5511*

PRESTIGE GLASS (2002) LTD *p 247*
1353 KEBET WAY, PORT COQUITLAM, BC,
V3C 6G1
(604) 464-5015   *SIC 1793*

PRESTIGE HOMES *p 418*
See M.M.H. PRESTIGE HOMES INC

PRESTIGE INN *p 222*
See HUBER DEVELOPMENT LTD

**PRESTIGE LAKESIDE RESORT & CON-
VENTION CENTRE** *p*
235
See HUBER DEVELOPMENT LTD

PRESTIGE LANDSCAPE GROUP *p 31*
105-1212 34 AVE SE, CALGARY, AB, T2G

1V7
(403) 280-5400   *SIC 0781*

PRESTIGE MOTORS *p 988*
See 970910 ONTARIO INC

PRESTILUX INC *p 1234*
3537 BOUL LE CORBUSIER, MONTREAL,
QC, H7L 4Z4
(450) 963-5096   *SIC 5122*

PRESTOLAM INC *p 1306*
2766 RTE DU PRESIDENT-KENNEDY,
SAINT-HENRI-DE-LEVIS, QC, G0R 3E0
(418) 882-2242   *SIC 2541*

**PRESTON CHEVROLET BUICK GMC
CADILLAC LTD** *p 228*
19990 LANGLEY BYPASS, LANGLEY, BC,
V3A 4Y1
(604) 534-4154   *SIC 5511*

PRESTON HARDWARE (1980) LIMITED *p*
825
248 PRESTON ST UNIT 234, OTTAWA, ON,
K1R 7R4
(613) 230-7166   *SIC 5251*

PRESTON HIGH SCHOOL *p 539*
*See WATERLOO REGION DISTRICT
SCHOOL BOARD*

PRESTON PARK *p 1425*
114 ARMISTICE WAY, SASKATOON, SK,
S7J 3K9
(306) 933-0515   *SIC 6513*

PRESTON PHIPPS INC *p 1335*
6400 RUE VANDEN-ABEELE, SAINT-
LAURENT, QC, H4S 1R9
(514) 333-5340   *SIC 5074*

**PRESTRESSED SYSTEMS INCORPO-
RATED** *p*
1023
4955 WALKER RD, WINDSOR, ON, N9A
6J3
(519) 737-1216   *SIC 3272*

**PRESVAC SYSTEMS (BURLINGTON) LIM-
ITED** *p*
524
4131 MORRIS DR, BURLINGTON, ON, L7L
5L5
(905) 637-2353   *SIC 3443*

PRETIUM CANADA COMPANY *p 1252*
3300 RTE TRANSCANADIENNE, POINTE-
CLAIRE, QC, H9R 1B1
(514) 428-0002   *SIC 3089*

PRETIUM CANADA COMPANY *p 1335*
2800 RUE HALPERN, SAINT-LAURENT,
QC, H4S 1R2
(514) 336-8210   *SIC 3089*

PRETIUM EXPLORATION INC *p 329*
1055 DUNSMUIR ST SUITE 2300, VAN-
COUVER, BC, V7X 1L4
(604) 558-1784   *SIC 1041*

PRETIUM PACKAGING *p 1335*
See PRETIUM CANADA COMPANY

PRETIUM RESOURCES INC *p 329*
1055 DUNSMUIR ST SUITE 2300 FOUR
BENTALL CTR, VANCOUVER, BC, V7X 1L4
(604) 558-1784   *SIC 1041*

PRETTY ESTATES LTD *p 215*
14282 MORRIS VALLEY RD, HARRISON
MILLS, BC, V0M 1L0
(604) 796-1000   *SIC 7011*

**PREVENTION INCENDIE SAFETY FIRST
QUEBEC** *p 1307*
See 1638-2723 QUEBEC INC.

PREVERCO INC *p 1293*
285 RUE DE ROTTERDAM, SAINT-
AUGUSTIN-DE-DESMAURES, QC, G3A
2E5
(800) 667-2725   *SIC 2426*

PREVOST *p 1301*
See GROUPE VOLVO CANADA INC

PREVOST ALUMINIUM ARCHITECTURAL
p 1283
See A. & D. PREVOST INC

PRGX CANADA CORP *p 745*
60 COURTNEY PARK DR W UNIT 4, MIS-
SISSAUGA, ON, N5W 0B3
(905) 670-7879   *SIC 8721*

PRICE CHOPPER p 618
See 2004104 ONTARIO LIMITED
PRICE CHOPPER p 775
See SOBEYS CAPITAL INCORPORATED
PRICE CHOPPER p 999
See SOBEYS CAPITAL INCORPORATED
PRICE CLUB SCARBOROUGH p 872
See COSTCO WHOLESALE CANADA LTD
PRICE INDUSTRIES LIMITED p 367
638 RALEIGH ST, WINNIPEG, MB, R2K 3Z9
(204) 669-4220 SIC 3496
PRICE MECHANICAL LIMITED p 369
404 EGESZ ST, WINNIPEG, MB, R2R 1X5
(204) 633-4808 SIC 1711
PRICE STEEL LTD p 106
13500 156 ST NW, EDMONTON, AB, T5V 1L3
(780) 447-9999 SIC 5051
PRICE'S ALARM SYSTEMS (2009) LTD p 338
4243 GLANFORD AVE UNIT 100, VICTORIA, BC, V8Z 4B9
(250) 384-4104 SIC 5999
PRICE'S BURGLAR STOP p 338
See PRICE'S ALARM SYSTEMS (2009) LTD
PRICE, GORDON MUSIC LTD p 116
10828 82 AVE NW, EDMONTON, AB, T6E 2B3
(780) 439-0007 SIC 5736
PRICEMETRIX p 978
See 3798143 CANADA INC
PRICEPRO p 276
See JOHN VOLKEN ACADEMY SOCIETY
PRICEWATERHOUSECOOPERS LLP p 90
10088 102 AVE NW SUITE 1501, EDMONTON, AB, T5J 3N5
(780) 441-6700 SIC 8721
PRICEWATERHOUSECOOPERS LLP p 308
250 HOWE ST SUITE 700, VANCOUVER, BC, V6C 3S7
(604) 806-7000 SIC 8721
PRICEWATERHOUSECOOPERS LLP p 375
1 LOMBARD PL SUITE 2300, WINNIPEG, MB, R3B 0X6
(204) 926-2400 SIC 8721
PRICEWATERHOUSECOOPERS LLP p 454
1601 LOWER WATER ST SUITE 400, HALIFAX, NS, B3J 3P6
(902) 491-7400 SIC 8721
PRICEWATERHOUSECOOPERS LLP p 613
21 KING ST W SUITE 100, HAMILTON, ON, L8P 4W7
SIC 8721
PRICEWATERHOUSECOOPERS LLP p 655
465 RICHMOND ST SUITE 300, LONDON, ON, N6A 5P4
(519) 640-8000 SIC 8721
PRICEWATERHOUSECOOPERS LLP p 824
99 BANK ST SUITE 800, OTTAWA, ON, K1P 1E4
(613) 237-3702 SIC 8721
PRICEWATERHOUSECOOPERS LLP p 966
18 YORK ST SUITE 2600, TORONTO, ON, M5J 0B2
(416) 863-1133 SIC 8721
PRICEWATERHOUSECOOPERS LLP p 1207
1250 BOUL RENE-LEVESQUE O BUREAU 2800, MONTREAL, QC, H3B 4W8
(514) 866-8409 SIC 8721
PRICEWATERHOUSECOOPERS LLP p 1273
2640 BOUL LAURIER BUREAU 1700, QUEBEC, QC, G1V 5C2
(418) 522-7001 SIC 8721
PRICEWATERHOUSECOOPERS, A DIV OF p 789
See KARABUS MANAGEMENT INC
PRIDE GROUP LOGISTICS LTD p 742
6050 DIXIE RD, MISSISSAUGA, ON, L5T 1A6
(905) 564-7458 SIC 4212
PRIDE OF MUSKOKA MARINE LIMITED p 497
1785 BEAUMONT DR RR 4, BRACEBRIDGE, ON, P1L 1X2
(705) 645-9151 SIC 5551
PRIDE PAK CANADA LTD p 726
6768 FINANCIAL DR, MISSISSAUGA, ON, L5N 7J6
(905) 828-8280 SIC 0723
PRIDE PAK NFLD LTD p 427
107 MCNAMARA DR, PARADISE, NL, A1L 0A7
(709) 782-8000 SIC 5148
PRIDE SIGNS LIMITED p 536
255 PINEBUSH RD UNIT I, CAMBRIDGE, ON, N1T 1B9
(519) 622-4040 SIC 3993
PRIESTLY DEMOLITION INC p 629
3200 LLOYDTOWN-AURORA RD, KING CITY, ON, L7B 0G3
(905) 841-3735 SIC 1795
PRIMA AUTO SALES LIMITED p 1033
7635 MARTIN GROVE RD, WOODBRIDGE, ON, L4L 2C5
(905) 850-8111 SIC 5511
PRIMA AUTOMOBILES INC p 1287
136 CH DES RAYMOND, RIVIERE-DU-LOUP, QC, G5R 5X6
(418) 867-1420 SIC 5511
PRIMA ENTERPRISES LTD p 216
1103 12TH ST UNIT 102, KAMLOOPS, BC, V2B 8A6
(250) 376-9554 SIC 8741
PRIMA MAZDA p 1033
See PRIMA AUTO SALES LIMITED
PRIMA MODA p 1334
See IMPORTATIONS VENETO LIMITEE
PRIMARIS MANAGEMENT INC p 940
1 ADELAIDE ST E SUITE 900, TORONTO, ON, M5C 2V9
(416) 642-7800 SIC 8741
PRIMARIS RETAIL REAL ESTATE INVESTMENT TRUST p 940
1 ADELAIDE ST E SUITE 900, TORONTO, ON, M5C 2V9
(416) 642-7800 SIC 6726
PRIMARY ENGINEERING AND CONSTRUCTION CORPORATION p 25
207 39 AVE NE, CALGARY, AB, T2E 7E3
(403) 873-0400 SIC 8711
PRIMCORP SECURITY LTD p 295
211 GEORGIA ST E SUITE 303, VANCOUVER, BC, V6A 1Z6
(604) 801-6899 SIC 6211
PRIME BOILER SERVICES LTD p 156
155 QUEENS DR, RED DEER, AB, T4P 0R3
(403) 314-2140 SIC 1711
PRIME BUILDING MAINTENANCE LTD p 256
12800 BATHGATE WAY UNIT 13, RICHMOND, BC, V6V 1Z4
(604) 270-7766 SIC 7349
PRIME COMMUNICATIONS CANADA INC p 665
9275 HIGHWAY 48 UNIT 1B3, MARKHAM, ON, L3P 3J3
(647) 848-1388 SIC 4812
PRIME FASTENERS (MANITOBA) LIMITED p 384
1501 KING EDWARD ST, WINNIPEG, MB, R3H 0R8
(204) 633-6624 SIC 5084
PRIME FASTENERS LTD p 17
5940 30 ST SE SUITE 6, CALGARY, AB, T2C 1X8
(403) 279-1043 SIC 5072
PRIME GRAPHIC RESOURCES LTD p 186
3988 STILL CREEK AVE, BURNABY, BC, V5C 6N9
(604) 437-5800 SIC 2759
PRIME MATERIAL HANDLING EQUIPMENT LIMITED p 444

1 CANAL ST, DARTMOUTH, NS, B2Y 2W1
(902) 468-1210 SIC 5084
PRIME PASTRIES p 547
See 1360548 ONTARIO LIMITED
PRIME PLAY SYSTEMS, DIV OF p 259
See WHITEWATER WEST INDUSTRIES LTD
PRIME QUADRANT CORP p 926
2 ST CLAIR AVE E SUITE 800, TORONTO, ON, M4T 2T5
(647) 749-4118 SIC 6282
PRIME QUADRANT FOUNDATION p 926
2 ST CLAIR AVE E SUITE 800, TORONTO, ON, M4T 2T5
(647) 749-4118 SIC 8699
PRIME RESTAURANTS p 601
370 STONE RD W SUITE SIDE, GUELPH, ON, N1G 4V9
(519) 763-7861 SIC 5812
PRIME RESTAURANTS INC p 616
1389 UPPER JAMES ST SUITE SIDE, HAMILTON, ON, L9B 1K2
(905) 574-3890 SIC 5812
PRIME RESTAURANTS INC p 732
10 KINGSBRIDGE GARDEN CIR SUITE 600, MISSISSAUGA, ON, L5R 3K6
(905) 568-0000 SIC 5812
PRIME RESTAURANTS INC p 869
12 LEBOVIC AVE SUITE 9, SCARBOROUGH, ON, M1L 4V9
(416) 285-6631 SIC 5812
PRIME TIME COURIER p 99
See ALZAC HOLDINGS LTD
PRIMELINE FOOD PARTNERS LTD p 201
1580 BRIGANTINE DR SUITE 200, COQUITLAM, BC, V3K 7C1
(604) 526-1788 SIC 5141
PRIMEMAX ENERGY INC p 483
2558 CEDAR CREEK RD SUITE 1, AYR, ON, N0B 1E0
(519) 740-8209 SIC 5984
PRIMERICA p 726
See PRIMERICA LIFE INSURANCE COMPANY OF CANADA
PRIMERICA FINANCIAL p 557
See PRIMERICA FINANCIAL SERVICES LTD
PRIMERICA FINANCIAL SERVICES p 154
See PRIMERICA LIFE INSURANCE COMPANY OF CANADA
PRIMERICA FINANCIAL SERVICES p 636
See BAST, PAUL & ASSOCIATES
PRIMERICA FINANCIAL SERVICES LTD p 557
8555 JANE ST SUITE 101, CONCORD, ON, L4K 5N9
(416) 495-0200 SIC 6411
PRIMERICA FINANCIAL SERVICES LTD p 596
839 SHEFFORD RD SUITE 200, GLOUCESTER, ON, K1J 9K8
(613) 742-0768 SIC 6282
PRIMERICA FINANCIAL SERVICES LTD p 703
1425 DUNDAS ST E SUITE 207, MISSISSAUGA, ON, L4X 2W4
(905) 602-1167 SIC 6282
PRIMERICA FINANCIAL SERVICES LTD p 887
251 ST. PAUL ST W SUITE 1, ST CATHARINES, ON, L2S 2E4
(905) 687-9374 SIC 6411
PRIMERICA FINANCIAL SERVICES LTD p 1015
1615 DUNDAS ST E SUITE 200, WHITBY, ON, L1N 2L1
(905) 436-8499 SIC 6411
PRIMERICA LIFE INSURANCE COMPANY OF CANADA p 154
5580 45 ST UNIT C 8, RED DEER, AB, T4N 1L1
(403) 347-2829 SIC 8741
PRIMERICA LIFE INSURANCE COMPANY OF CANADA p 726

2000 ARGENTIA RD SUITE 5, MISSISSAUGA, ON, L5N 1P7
(905) 812-3520 SIC 6311
PRIMERO GOLD CANADA INC p 454
1969 UPPER WATER ST SUITE 2001, HALIFAX, NS, B3J 3R7
(902) 422-1421 SIC 1041
PRIMERO MINING CORP p 970
79 WELLINGTON ST W TD SOUTH TOWER SUITE 2100, TORONTO, ON, M5K 1H1
(416) 814-3160 SIC 1041
PRIMESOURCE BUILDING PRODUCTS CANADA CORPORATION p 258
7431 NELSON RD SUITE 110, RICHMOND, BC, V6W 1G3
(604) 231-0473 SIC 5085
PRIMEX MANUFACTURING LTD p 225
20160 92A AVE, LANGLEY, BC, V1M 3A4
(604) 881-7875 SIC 3089
PRIMMUM INSURANCE COMPANY p 1180
50 BOUL CREMAZIE O BUREAU 1200, MONTREAL, QC, H2P 1B6
(514) 382-6060 SIC 6331
PRIMO FOODS INC p 795
56 HUXLEY RD, NORTH YORK, ON, M9M 1H2
(416) 741-9300 SIC 2098
PRIMO INSTRUMENT INC p 1240
4407 RUE DE CHARLEROI, MONTREAL-NORD, QC, H1H 1T6
(514) 329-3242 SIC 5084
PRIMO INTERNATIONAL p 1164
See LITERIE PRIMO INC
PRIMO MECHANICAL INC p 1033
253 JEVLAN DR UNIT 15, WOODBRIDGE, ON, L4L 7Z6
(905) 851-6718 SIC 1711
PRIMUS CANADA p 699
See PRIMUS MANAGEMENT ULC
PRIMUS MANAGEMENT ULC p 699
2680 SKYMARK AVE UNIT 100, MISSISSAUGA, ON, L4W 5L6
(416) 236-3636 SIC 4813
PRINCE ALBERT CO-OPERATIVE ASSOCIATION LIMITED, THE p 1414
801 15TH ST E SUITE 791, PRINCE ALBERT, SK, S6V 0C7
(306) 764-9393 SIC 5399
PRINCE ALBERT CO-OPERATIVE HEALTH CENTRE/COMMUNITY CLINIC p 1414
110 8TH ST E, PRINCE ALBERT, SK, S6V 0V7
(306) 763-6464 SIC 8011
PRINCE ALBERT DEVELOPMENT CORPORATION p 1414
67 13TH ST E, PRINCE ALBERT, SK, S6V 1C7
(306) 763-2643 SIC 7011
PRINCE ALBERT DEVELOPMENT CORPORATION p 1414
3680 2ND AVE W, PRINCE ALBERT, SK, S6V 5G2
(306) 763-1362 SIC 5812
PRINCE ALBERT INN p 1414
See PRINCE ALBERT DEVELOPMENT CORPORATION
PRINCE ALBERT TURBO p 1414
See UNIFIED HOLDINGS LTD
PRINCE COUNTY HORSEMAN'S CLUB INC p 1043
477 NOTRE DAME ST, SUMMERSIDE, PE, C1N 1T2
SIC 7948
PRINCE COUNTY HOSPITAL p 1043
65 ROY BOATES AVE, SUMMERSIDE, PE, C1N 6M8
(902) 438-4200 SIC 8062
PRINCE EDWARD AND COLLEGIATE p 845
See HASTINGS AND PRINCE EDWARD DISTRICT SCHOOL BOARD

PRINCE EDWARD AQUA FARMS INC   p
1041
    GD, KENSINGTON, PE, C0B 1M0
    (902) 886-2220   SIC 2092
PRINCE EDWARD ISLAND GRAIN ELEVA-
TORS CORPORATION
1041
    62 VICTORIA ST, KENSINGTON, PE, C0B
1M0
    (902) 836-8935   SIC 5153
PRINCE EDWARD ISLAND LIQUOR CON-
TROL COMMISSION   p
1039
    3 GARFIELD ST, CHARLOTTETOWN, PE,
C1A 6A4
    (902) 368-5710   SIC 5921
PRINCE EDWARD ISLAND MUTUAL IN-
SURANCE COMPANY   p
1043
    116 WALKER AVE, SUMMERSIDE, PE,
C1N 6V9
    (902) 436-2185   SIC 6331
PRINCE EDWARD ISLAND UNION OF PUB-
LIC SECTOR EMPLOYEES   p
1040
    4 ENMAN CRES, CHARLOTTETOWN, PE,
C1E 1E6
    (902) 892-5335   SIC 8631
PRINCE GEORGE CASINO SUPPLY COM-
PANY INC   p
251
    2003 HIGHWAY 97 S, PRINCE GEORGE,
BC, V2N 7A3
    (250) 564-7070   SIC 7999
PRINCE GEORGE CITIZENS NEWSPAPER
p 249
    See GLACIER MEDIA INC
PRINCE GEORGE HOSPICE SOCIETY   p
249
    3089   CLAPPERTON   ST,   PRINCE
GEORGE, BC, V2L 5N4
    (250) 563-2551   SIC 8699
PRINCE GEORGE HOTEL   p 454
    See P.G. HOTEL LTD
PRINCE GEORGE MOTORS LTD   p 250
    1331 CENTRAL ST W, PRINCE GEORGE,
BC, V2M 3E2
    (250) 563-8111   SIC 5511
PRINCE GEORGE PULP & PAPER   p 250
    See CANADIAN FOREST PRODUCTS LTD
PRINCE GEORGE REGIONAL HOSPITAL p
249
    See NORTHERN HEALTH AUTHORITY
PRINCE GEORGE SEARCH AND RESCUE
SOCIETY   p 249
    4057 HART HWY, PRINCE GEORGE, BC,
V2K 2Z5
    (250) 962-5544   SIC 8699
PRINCE GEORGE SECONDARY SCHOOLp
250
    See BOARD OF EDUCATION OF SCHOOL
DISTRICT NO. 57 (PRINCE GEORGE), THE
PRINCE METAL PRODUCTS LTD   p 1025
    945 PRINCE RD, WINDSOR, ON, N9C 2Z4
    (519) 977-5333   SIC 3714
PRINCE MOVING   p 1125
    See 2701545 CANADA INC
PRINCE OF WALES HOTEL   p 761
    See LAIS HOTEL PROPERTIES LIMITED
PRINCE OF WALES MANOR HOME   p 750
    See 1716530 ONTARIO INC
PRINCE RUPERT GRAIN LTD   p 251
    GD STN MAIN, PRINCE RUPERT, BC, V8J
3P3
    (250) 627-8777   SIC 4221
PRINCE RUPERT REGIONAL HOSPITAL p
251
    See NORTHERN HEALTH AUTHORITY
PRINCE RUPERT SCHOOL DISTRICT 52 p
251
    634 6TH AVE E, PRINCE RUPERT, BC, V8J
1X1
    (250) 624-6717   SIC 8211
PRINCEBELLA   p 1203

See DIAMANTS BASAL INC
PRINCESS AUTO LTD   p 363
    475 PANET RD, WINNIPEG, MB, R2C 2Z1
    (204) 667-4630   SIC 5251
PRINCESS GROUP INC   p 363
    475 PANET RD, WINNIPEG, MB, R2C 2Z1
    (204) 667-4630   SIC 5251
PRINCESS MARGARET CANCER FOUN-
DATION, THE   p
947
    610 UNIVERSITY AVE, TORONTO, ON,
M5G 2M9
    (416) 946-6560   SIC 8069
PRINCESS MARGARET CANCER FOUN-
DATION, THE   p
947
    700 UNIVERSITY AVE 10TH FLOOR,
TORONTO, ON, M5G 1Z5
    (416) 946-6560   SIC 8399
PRINCETON DEVELOPMENTS LTD   p 92
    9915 108 ST NW SUITE 1400, EDMON-
TON, AB, T5K 2G8
    (780) 423-7775   SIC 6553
PRINCETON REVIEW CANADA INC, THE p
973
    1255 BAY ST SUITE 550, TORONTO, ON,
M5R 2A9
    (416) 944-8001   SIC 8748
PRINCETON REVIEW, THE   p 973
    See PRINCETON REVIEW CANADA INC,
THE
PRINCIPALE AUTOS LTEE   p 1111
    1196 RUE PRINCIPALE, GRANBY, QC, J2J
0M2
    (450) 378-4666   SIC 5511
PRINGLE CREEK I G A   p 1015
    728 ANDERSON ST UNIT 4, WHITBY, ON,
L1N 3V6
    (905) 668-5538   SIC 5411
PRINGLE INSURANCE BROKERS   p 212
    380 TRUNK RD UNIT 1, DUNCAN, BC, V9L
2P6
    (250) 748-3242   SIC 6411
PRINOTH LTD   p 1111
    1001 RUE J.-A.-BOMBARDIER, GRANBY,
QC, J2J 1E9
    (450) 776-3600   SIC 5013
PRINT MINT, THE   p 1070
    See LE GRENIER D'ART (1987) INC
PRINTERON INC   p 642
    221 MCINTYRE DR, KITCHENER, ON, N2R
1G1
    (519) 748-2848   SIC 2711
PRINTERS TO THE WORLD   p 730
    See CANADIAN MARKETING TEST CASE
206 LIMITED
PRINTING HOUSE LIMITED, THE   p 973
    1403 BATHURST ST, TORONTO, ON, M5R
3H8
    (416) 536-6113   SIC 2752
PRINTLINX CORPORATION   p 868
    1170 BIRCHMOUNT RD SUITE 1, SCAR-
BOROUGH, ON, M1K 5M1
    (416) 752-8100   SIC 7331
PRINTWORKS LTD   p 116
    3850 98 ST NW, EDMONTON, AB, T6E 3L2
    (780) 452-8921   SIC 2752
PRIORITE EXPRESS   p 1092
    See 148274 CANADA INC
PRIORITY ELECTRONICS LTD   p 391
    55 TROTTIER BAY, WINNIPEG, MB, R3T
3R3
    (204) 284-0164   SIC 5065
PRIORITY MECHANICAL LTD   p 116
    9259 35 AVE NW, EDMONTON, AB, T6E
5Y1
    (780) 435-3636   SIC 1711
PRIORITY MECHANICAL SERVICES LTD p
483
    3160 ALPS RD, AYR, ON, N0B 1E0
    (519) 632-7116   SIC 1711
PRIORITY RESTORATION SERVICES LTDp
372
    1300 CHURCH AVE, WINNIPEG, MB, R2X

1G4
    (204) 786-3344   SIC 1541
PRIORY, THE   p 340
    See VANCOUVER ISLAND HEALTH AU-
THORITY
PRISM CONSTRUCTION LTD   p 207
    1525 CLIVEDEN AVE SUITE 201, DELTA,
BC, V3M 6L2
    (604) 526-3731   SIC 1542
PRISM FARMS LIMITED   p 644
    731 MERSEA ROAD 6, LEAMINGTON, ON,
N8H 3V8
    (519) 324-9009   SIC 0191
PRISM MEDICAL LTD   p 557
    485 MILLWAY AVE UNIT 2, CONCORD, ON,
L4K 3V4
    (416) 260-2145   SIC 6712
PRISM POWDER COATINGS LTD   p 557
    321 EDGELEY BLVD, CONCORD, ON, L4K
3Y2
    (905) 660-5361   SIC 2851
PRISTINE LED INC   p 1018
    3215 JEFFERSON BLVD SUITE 100,
WINDSOR, ON, N8T 2W7
    SIC 5063
PRITCHARD ENGINEERING   p 389
    See PRITCHARD METALFAB INC
PRITCHARD ENGINEERING COMPANY
LIMITED   p 391
    100 OTTER ST, WINNIPEG, MB, R3T 0M8
    (204) 452-2344   SIC 5084
PRITCHARD INDUSTRIAL, DIV OF   p 391
    See PRITCHARD ENGINEERING COM-
PANY LIMITED
PRITCHARD METALFAB INC   p 389
    110 LOWSON CRES, WINNIPEG, MB, R3P
2H8
    (204) 784-7600   SIC 3499
PRIVA BUILDING INTELLIGENCE   p 1003
    See PRIVA NORTH AMERICA INC
PRIVA NORTH AMERICA INC   p 1003
    3468   SOUTH   SERVICE   RD   SS   1,
VINELAND STATION, ON, L0R 2E0
    (905) 562-7351   SIC 3823
PRIVALAB   p 1393
    See PHARMAPAR INC
PRIVATE CLIENT SERVICES, DIV OF p 596
    See ENCON GROUP INC
PRIVATE RECIPES LIMITED   p 505
    12 INDELL LANE, BRAMPTON, ON, L6T
3Y3
    (905) 799-1022   SIC 2038
PRO AUTO LTD   p 391
    1761 PEMBINA HWY UNIT 3, WINNIPEG,
MB, R3T 2G6
    (204) 982-3020   SIC 5013
PRO AUTOMATION INC   p 1293
    243   RUE   DE   BORDEAUX,   SAINT-
AUGUSTIN-DE-DESMAURES,   QC,   G3A
2M8
    (418) 878-4500   SIC 5962
PRO BODY PARTS   p 391
    See PRO AUTO LTD
PRO BUILDERS LTD   p 244
    150 FAIRVIEW PL, PENTICTON, BC, V2A
6A5
    (250) 493-7844   SIC 5251
PRO BUILDING SUPPLY LTD   p 244
    150 FAIRVIEW PL, PENTICTON, BC, V2A
6A5
    (250) 492-6635   SIC 5211
PRO CANADA WEST ENERGY INC p 1410
    HWY 39 S, MIDALE, SK, S0C 1S0
    (306) 458-2232   SIC 1623
PRO COUNT STAFFING INC   p 970
    77 KING ST W SUITE 4110, TORONTO,
ON, M5K 2A1
    (416) 340-1500   SIC 7361
PRO CYCLE LIMITED   p 448
    360 HIGNEY AVE, DARTMOUTH, NS, B3B
0L4
    (902) 468-2518   SIC 5571
PRO DRAFT INC   p 270
    14727 108 AVE UNIT 205, SURREY, BC,

V3R 1V9
    (604) 589-6425   SIC 7389
PRO ELECTRIC INC   p 661
    347 SOVEREIGN RD, LONDON, ON, N6M
1A6
    (519) 451-8740   SIC 1731
PRO FAB SUNROOMS LTD   p 368
    342 NAIRN AVE, WINNIPEG, MB, R2L 0W9
    (204) 668-3544   SIC 3448
PRO GAZON   p 1350
    See PEPINIERE ABBOTSFORD INC
PRO INGREDIENTS INC   p 1309
    7750 BOUL COUSINEAU BUREAU 402,
SAINT-HUBERT, QC, J3Z 0C8
    (450) 632-1199   SIC 5159
PRO INSUL LIMITED   p 893
    468 ARVIN AVE, STONEY CREEK, ON, L8E
2M9
    (905) 662-6161   SIC 1799
PRO IT PLUS INC.   p 571
    16 BROOKERS LANE SUITE 2908, ETOBI-
COKE, ON, M8V 0A5
    (905) 977-8168   SIC 5045
PRO KONTROL   p 1101
    See 3100-7669 QUEBEC INC
PRO LINE MANAGEMENT   p 872
    See 1451805 ONTARIO LTD
PRO MUTUEL L'ABITIBIENNE, SOCIETE
MUTUELLE D'ASSURANCE GENERALE p
1046
    282 1RE AV E, AMOS, QC, J9T 1H3
    (819) 732-1531   SIC 6411
PRO ORGANICS, DIV OF   p 187
    See UNFI CANADA, INC
PRO PAK PACKAGING   p 1027
    See BURNAC PRODUCE LIMITED
PRO PAK PACKAGING LIMITED   p 587
    51 KELFIELD ST, ETOBICOKE, ON, M9W
5A3
    (416) 246-0550   SIC 7389
PRO QUINCAILLERIE   p 1081
    See GABRIEL COUTURE & FILS LTEE
PRO WELLNESS HEALTH SERVICES INCp
887
    110 HANNOVER DR SUITE B107, ST
CATHARINES, ON, L2W 1A4
    (905) 682-1059   SIC 8082
PRO-AB EQUIPEMENTS 2003 INC   p 753
    883304 HWY 65, NEW LISKEARD, ON, P0J
1P0
    (705) 647-6065   SIC 5084
PRO-AMINO INTERNATIONAL INC   p 1153
    12700 BOUL HENRI-FABRE E, MIRABEL,
QC, J7N 0A6
    (800) 555-2170   SIC 2032
PRO-BEL ENTERPRISES LIMITED   p 474
    765 WESTNEY RD S, AJAX, ON, L1S 6W1
    (905) 427-0616   SIC 5084
PRO-BEL THE SAFETY ROOF ANCHOR
CO   p 474
    765 WESTNEY RD S, AJAX, ON, L1S 6W1
    (905) 427-0616   SIC 2842
PRO-CHECK HOME SERVICES   p 685
    See TSYCCO LTD
PRO-CLAIM RESTORATION LTD   p 261
    5811 CEDARBRIDGE WAY UNIT 150,
RICHMOND, BC, V6X 2A8
    (604) 276-2483   SIC 6411
PRO-DATA INC   p 385
    1560 ST JAMES ST, WINNIPEG, MB, R3H
0L2
    (204) 779-9960   SIC 5045
PRO-KING   p 696
    See KING-O-MATIC INDUSTRIES LIMITED
PRO-LINE AUTOMATION SYSTEMS LTD p
1028
    303 VAUGHAN VALLEY BLVD, WOOD-
BRIDGE, ON, L4H 3B5
    (905) 264-6230   SIC 5084
PRO-LINE BUILDING MATERIALS LTDp 31
    4910 BUILDERS RD SE, CALGARY, AB,
T2G 4C6
    (403) 262-1008   SIC 1623
PRO-LINE CONSTRUCTION MATERIALS

LTD p 228
20109 LOGAN AVE, LANGLEY, BC, V3A 4L5
(604) 534-2060 SIC 5033

PRO-LINE MANUFACTURING INC p 6
27323 TOWNSHIP RD 394 LOT 48, BLACK-FALDS, AB, T0M 0J0
(403) 885-2527 SIC 5084

PRO-METAL PLUS INC p 1090
12 BOUL DES SOURCES, DESCHAM-BAULT, QC, G0A 1S0
(418) 286-4949 SIC 3599

PRO-MEUBLES INC p 1111
800 RUE VADNAIS BUREAU 450, GRANBY, QC, J2J 1A7
(450) 378-0189 SIC 2521

PRO-PAR INC p 1374
65 RUE WINDER, SHERBROOKE, QC, J1M 1L5
(819) 566-8211 SIC 3443

PRO-PERFORMANCE G. P. L. INC p 1063
5750 BOUL SAINTE-ANNE, BOISCHATEL, QC, G0A 1H0
(418) 822-3838 SIC 5599

PRO-PLY CUSTOM PLYWOOD INC p 505
1195 CLARK BLVD SUITE 905, BRAMP-TON, ON, L6T 3W4
(905) 564-2327 SIC 2435

PRO-ROD INC p 123
3201 84 AVE NW SUITE 3201, EDMON-TON, AB, T6P 1K1
(780) 449-7101 SIC 3354

PRO-SHIELD CORPORATION p 575
33 CORONET RD, ETOBICOKE, ON, M8Z 2L8
(800) 561-4272 SIC 5169

PRO-SOIN p 1273
See SERVICES INFIRMIERS PRO-SOIN INC

PRO-SYSTEMES APX INC p 1111
1050 BOUL INDUSTRIEL, GRANBY, QC, J2J 1A4
(450) 378-0189 SIC 2542

PRO-TECH VALVE SALES INC p 110
5880 56 AVE NW, EDMONTON, AB, T6B 3E4
(780) 466-4405 SIC 5085

PRO-WESTERN PLASTICS LTD p 166
30 RIEL DR, ST. ALBERT, AB, T8N 3Z7
(780) 459-4491 SIC 3089

PRO-X EXHIBIT INC p 686
7621 BATH RD, MISSISSAUGA, ON, L4T 3T1
(905) 696-0993 SIC 7389

PROACTION GROUPE CONSEILS INC p 1186
257 RUE SHERBROOKE E BUREAU 100, MONTREAL, QC, H2X 1E3
(514) 284-7447 SIC 7311

PROACTIVE SUPPLY CHAIN SOLUTIONS INC p 689
3909 NASHUA DRIVE UNIT 4-9, MISSIS-SAUGA, ON, L4V 1R3
(416) 798-3303 SIC 4731

PROALL INTERNATIONAL MFG. INC p 151
5810 47 AVE, OLDS, AB, T4H 1V1
(403) 335-9500 SIC 3531

PROALLIANCE REALTY CORPORATION p 491
357 FRONT ST, BELLEVILLE, ON, K8N 2Z9
(613) 966-6060 SIC 6531

PROAX TECHNOLOGIES LTD p 799
2552 BRISTOL CIR, OAKVILLE, ON, L6H 5S1
(905) 829-2006 SIC 5084

PROAX TECHNOLOGIES LTEE p 1236
3505 RUE JOHN-PRATT, MONTREAL, QC, H7P 0C9
(450) 902-5900 SIC 7389

PROBART MAZDA p 659
See PROBART MOTORS LIMITED

PROBART MOTORS LIMITED p 659
652 WHARNCLIFFE RD S, LONDON, ON, N6J 2N4

(519) 649-1800 SIC 5511

PROBE INVESTIGATION AND SECURITY SERVICES LTD p 781
3995 BATHURST ST SUITE 301, NORTH YORK, ON, M3H 5V3
(416) 636-7000 SIC 7381

PROBE SECURITY p 781
See PROBE INVESTIGATION AND SECU-RITY SERVICES LTD

PROBYN LOG LTD p 236
601 SIXTH ST UNIT 350, NEW WESTMIN-STER, BC, V3L 3C1
(604) 526-8545 SIC 7389

PROCALL MARKETING INC p 57
100 4 AVE SW UNIT 200, CALGARY, AB, T2P 3N2
(403) 265-4014 SIC 7389

PROCAM CONSTRUCTION INC p 1067
1220 RUE MARCONI, BOUCHERVILLE, QC, J4B 8G8
(450) 449-5121 SIC 1542

PROCAM INTERNATIONAL INC p 1362
2035 BOUL DAGENAIS O BUREAU 200, SAINTE-ROSE, QC, H7L 5V1
(450) 963-4442 SIC 4731

PROCARE HEALTH SERVICES INC p 237
624 COLUMBIA ST SUITE 201, NEW WESTMINSTER, BC, V3M 1A5
(604) 525-1234 SIC 8049

PROCASE CONSULTING INC p 1033
180 CASTER AVE SUITE 55, WOOD-BRIDGE, ON, L4L 5Y7
(905) 856-7479 SIC 8741

PROCECO LTEE p 1165
7300 RUE TELLIER, MONTREAL, QC, H1N 3T7
(514) 254-8494 SIC 3569

PROCEED SOLUTIONS INC p 65
906 12 AVE SW SUITE 600, CALGARY, AB, T2R 1K7
(403) 685-8390 SIC 8748

PROCEPT ASSOCIATES LTD p 936
250 YONGE ST SUITE 2201-49, TORONTO, ON, M5B 2L7
(416) 693-5559 SIC 8741

PROCESS & PIPELINE SEVICES, DIV OF p 108
See BAKER HUGHES CANADA COMPANY

PROCESS AND STEAM SPECIALTIES p 805
See VALTROL EQUIPMENT LIMITED

PROCESS AUTOMATION OIL, GAS & PETROCHEMICAL p 13
See ABB INC

PROCESS GROUP p 534
See PGI HOLDINGS INC

PROCESS GROUP INC p 534
555 CONESTOGA BLVD, CAMBRIDGE, ON, N1R 7P5
(519) 622-5520 SIC 1796

PROCESS PRODUCTS LIMITED p 557
50 LOCKE ST UNIT 1, CONCORD, ON, L4K 5R4
(416) 781-3399 SIC 5085

PROCHLOR p 1389
See UBA INC

PROCOM p 923
See PROFESSIONAL COMPUTER CON-SULTANTS GROUP LTD

PROCOM p 924
See PROCOM CONSULTANTS GROUP LTD

PROCOM CONSULTANTS GROUP LTD p 924
2200 YONGE ST SUITE 700, TORONTO, ON, M4S 2C6
(416) 483-0766 SIC 8748

PROCON CONSTRUCTORS INC p 1012
401 ENTERPRISE DR, WELLAND, ON, L3B 6H8
(905) 732-0322 SIC 1731

PROCON EST DU CANADA LTEE p 1391
1400 4E AV, VAL-D'OR, QC, J9P 5Z9
(819) 824-2074 SIC 1081

PROCON GROUP OF COMPANIES, THE p 186
See PROCON MINING & TUNNELLING LTD

PROCON MINING & TUNNELLING LTD p 186
4664 LOUGHEED HWY UNIT 108, BURN-ABY, BC, V5C 5T5
(604) 291-8292 SIC 1081

PROCON SYSTEMS (2013) INC p 68
9504 HORTON RD SW, CALGARY, AB, T2V 2X4
(403) 255-2921 SIC 5084

PROCON SYSTEMS INC p 42
1403 29 ST NW, CALGARY, AB, T2N 2T9
(780) 499-7088 SIC 5084

PROCONTACT STRATEGIES CONSEILS p 1277
See INFORMATIQUE PRO-CONTACT INC

PROCOR LIMITED p 804
585 MICHIGAN DR UNIT 2, OAKVILLE, ON, L6L 0G1
(905) 827-4111 SIC 4741

PROCRANE INC p 123
2440 76 AVE NW, EDMONTON, AB, T6P 1J5
(780) 440-4434 SIC 7353

PROCTER & GAMBLE INC p 491
355 UNIVERSITY AVE, BELLEVILLE, ON, K8N 5T8
(613) 966-5130 SIC 2676

PROCTER & GAMBLE INC p 520
1475 CALIFORNIA AVE, BROCKVILLE, ON, K6V 6K4
(613) 342-9592 SIC 2841

PROCTER & GAMBLE INC p 773
4711 YONGE ST, NORTH YORK, ON, M2N 6K8
(416) 730-4711 SIC 2841

PROCTER & GAMBLE INC p 773
4711 YONGE ST, NORTH YORK, ON, M2N 6K8
(416) 730-4711 SIC 5169

PROCTER & GAMBLE INVESTMENT COR-PORATION p 520
1475 CALIFORNIA AVE, BROCKVILLE, ON, K6V 6K4
(613) 342-9592 SIC 2841

PROCUPINE JOINT VENTURES p 882
See KINROSS GOLD CORPORATION

PROCURA p 335
See DEVELUS SYSTEMS INC

PROCYK FARMS (1994) LIMITED p 1016
GD, WILSONVILLE, ON, N0E 1Z0
(519) 443-4516 SIC 0161

PRODESIGN LIMITED p 587
375 REXDALE BLVD, ETOBICOKE, ON, M9W 1R9
(416) 744-2011 SIC 2782

PRODESIGN SOLUTIONS p 584
See GROSNOR INDUSTRIES INC

PRODIGY GRAPHICS GROUP p 500
See 1627880 ONTARIO INC

PRODIGY VENTURES INC p 966
161 BAY ST SUITE 4420, TORONTO, ON, M5J 2S1
(416) 488-7700 SIC 6799

PRODIMAX INC p 1399
1050 15E AV, VIMONT, QC, H7R 4N9
(450) 627-6068 SIC 8361

PRODOMAX p 486
See DCSR INVESTMENT CORP

PRODUCE DEPOT p 827
See SOUTHBANK FRUIT INC

PRODUCE DEPOT p 829
See CARLING FRUIT INC

PRODUCE TERMINAL, THE p 296
See TERMINAL FRUIT & PRODUCE LTD

PRODUCT EXCELLENCE p 972
See 1561109 ONTARIO INC

PRODUCTEUR DE LAIT QUEBECOIS, LE p 1143
See PRODUCTEURS DE LAIT DU QUE-

BEC, LES

PRODUCTEURS DE LAIT DU QUEBEC, LES p 1143
555 BOUL ROLAND-THERRIEN BUREAU 415, LONGUEUIL, QC, J4H 4G3
(450) 679-0530 SIC 8631

PRODUCTION ACYPOL INC p 1226
1350 RUE MAZURETTE BUREAU 409, MONTREAL, QC, H4N 1H2
(514) 388-8888 SIC 5136

PRODUCTION PAJAR LTEE p 1183
4509 AV COLONIALE, MONTREAL, QC, H2T 1V8
(514) 844-3067 SIC 5139

PRODUCTIONS AGRICOLES OUELLET, LES p 404
1119 ROUTE 280, MCLEODS, NB, E3N 5W6
(506) 753-3736 SIC 5144

PRODUCTIONS ARCHY'S INC, LES p 1271
1457 AV OAK, QUEBEC, QC, G1T 1Z5
(418) 688-3553 SIC 7389

PRODUCTIONS ATLAN INC., LES p 1293
120 RUE DE ROTTERDAM, SAINT-AUGUSTIN-DE-DESMAURES, QC, G3A 1T3
(418) 878-5881 SIC 3069

PRODUCTIONS HORTICOLES DEMERS INC, LES p 1140
1196 RUE DES CARRIERES, LEVIS, QC, G7A 0R7
(418) 831-2489 SIC 0171

PRODUCTIONS LOUNAK, LES p 1124
See ATTRACTION INC

PRODUCTIONS MARAICHERES BOUR-GET & FRERES INC, LES p 1151
410 BOUL SAINTE-MARGUERITE, MERCIER, QC, J6R 2L1
(450) 691-0468 SIC 0139

PRODUCTIONS MIGHTY MAC CANADA INC, LES p 1335
5555 RUE CYPIHOT, SAINT-LAURENT, QC, H4S 1R3
(514) 388-8888 SIC 5137

PRODUCTIONS PIXCOM INC p 1216
1720 RUE DU CANAL, MONTREAL, QC, H3K 3E6
(514) 931-1188 SIC 7812

PRODUCTIONS TMV INC p 1223
642 RUE DE COURCELLE BUREAU 209, MONTREAL, QC, H4C 3C5
(514) 228-8740 SIC 7374

PRODUCTIONS VENDOME II INC, LES p 1216
1751 RUE RICHARDSON BUREAU 5 105, MONTREAL, QC, H3K 1G6
(514) 369-4834 SIC 7922

PRODUCTIONS VIC PELLETIER INC, LES p 1151
296 RUE SAINT-PIERRE, MATANE, QC, G4W 2B9
(514) 667-0787 SIC 7812

PRODUCTIVE SECURITY INC p 990
940 LANSDOWNE AVE, TORONTO, ON, M6H 3Z4
(416) 535-9341 SIC 7381

PRODUCTIVE SPACE INC p 31
3632 BURNSLAND RD SE, CALGARY, AB, T2G 3Z2
SIC 7389

PRODUCTS & CHEMICALS, DIV OF p 860
See IMPERIAL OIL LIMITED

PRODUIT FIELDTURF p 1341
See TARKETT SPORTS CANADA INC

PRODUIT FORESTIERS RESOLU SECTEUR LA DORE p 1121
See PF RESOLU CANADA INC

PRODUIT MOBICAB CANADA p 1044
See EQUIPEMENTS PIERRE CHAMPIGNY LTEE

PRODUITS & BASES DE SOUPE MAJOR DU CANADA INC, LES p 1335
7171 BOUL THIMENS, SAINT-LAURENT,

QC, H4S 2A2

(514) 745-1163 *SIC* 5149

PRODUITS & SERVICES DE LA CON-STRUCTION (MONTREAL) INC *p* 1050

9711 RUE COLBERT, ANJOU, QC, H1J 1Z9

(514) 355-9650 *SIC* 5039

PRODUITS ALBA LTEE *p* 1121

300 BOUL DE LA GRANDE-BAIE N BU-REAU 3, LA BAIE, QC, G7B 3K3

(418) 544-3361 *SIC* 3251

PRODUITS ALIMENTAIRES ANCO LTEE, LES *p* 1309

4700 RUE ARMAND-FRAPPIER, SAINT-HUBERT, QC, J3Z 1G5

(450) 443-4838 *SIC* 5143

PRODUITS ALIMENTAIRES BERTHELET INC *p* 1234

1805 RUE BERLIER, MONTREAL, QC, H7L 3S4

(514) 334-5503 *SIC* 2034

PRODUITS ALIMENTAIRES SA-GER INC, LES *p* 1330

6755 BOUL HENRI-BOURASSA O, SAINT-LAURENT, QC, H4R 1E1

(514) 643-4887 *SIC* 2079

PRODUITS ALIMENTAIRES SAGER, LES *p* 1330

See PRODUITS ALIMENTAIRES SA-GER INC, LES

PRODUITS ALIMENTAIRES VIAU INC, LES *p* 1240

See 9387-0616 QUEBEC INC

PRODUITS ALIMENTAIRES VIAU INC, LES *p* 1361

6625 RUE ERNEST-CORMIER, SAINTE-ROSE, QC, H7C 2V2

(450) 665-6100 *SIC* 5147

PRODUITS AMERICAN BILTRITE (CANADA) LTEE *p* 1371

200 RUE BANK, SHERBROOKE, QC, J1H 4K3

(819) 829-3300 *SIC* 3069

PRODUITS AMERICAN BILTRITE (CANADA) LTEE *p* 1374

635 RUE PEPIN, SHERBROOKE, QC, J1L 2P8

(819) 823-3300 *SIC* 3069

PRODUITS ANDALOS INC *p* 1327

230 BOUL LEBEAU, SAINT-LAURENT, QC, H4N 1R4

(514) 832-1000 *SIC* 5149

PRODUITS AUTOMOBILES LAURENTIDE INC *p* 1162

9355 BOUL HENRI-BOURASSA E, MON-TREAL, QC, H1E 1P4

(514) 643-1917 *SIC* 3089

PRODUITS B.C.M. LTEE *p* 1079

340 RUE EMILE-COUTURE, CHICOUTIMI, QC, G7H 8B6

(418) 545-1698 *SIC* 5198

PRODUITS BATH & BODY WORKS (CANADA) *p* 1093

See BATH & BODY WORKS (CANADA) CORP

PRODUITS BEL INC *p* 1240

6868 BOUL MAURICE-DUPLESSIS, MONTREAL-NORD, QC, H1G 1Z6

(514) 327-2800 *SIC* 3644

PRODUITS BELT-TECH INC *p* 1109

386 RUE DORCHESTER, GRANBY, QC, J2G 3Z7

(450) 372-5826 *SIC* 2399

PRODUITS BREATHER INC *p* 1183

5605 AV DE GASPE BUREAU 610, MON-TREAL, QC, H2T 2A4

(514) 574-8059 *SIC* 6531

PRODUITS CANNEBERGES BECANCOUR *p* 1347

See CANNEBERGES BECANCOUR MAN-AGEMENT INC

PRODUITS CHIMIQUES AMPLEX LTEE, LES *p* 1252

600 AV DELMAR, POINTE-CLAIRE, QC,

H9R 4A8

(514) 630-3309 *SIC* 5169

PRODUITS CHIMIQUES G.H. LTEE *p* 1314

1550 RUE BROUILLETTE, SAINT-HYACINTHE, QC, J2T 2G8

(450) 774-9151 *SIC* 2816

PRODUITS CHIMIQUES MAGNUS LIMITEE *p* 1067

1271 RUE AMPERE, BOUCHERVILLE, QC, J4B 5Z5

(450) 655-1344 *SIC* 2899

PRODUITS CLAIR DE LUNE INC *p* 1340

361 RUE LOCKE, SAINT-LAURENT, QC, H4T 1X7

(514) 389-5757 *SIC* 5719

PRODUITS D'ACIER HASON INC, LES *p* 1130

7 RUE PINAT, LANORAIE, QC, J0K 1E0

(450) 887-0800 *SIC* 3443

PRODUITS D'ACIER ROGER INC, LES *p* 1379

1350 GRANDE ALLEE, TERREBONNE, QC, J6W 4M4

(450) 471-2000 *SIC* 3569

PRODUITS D'ENTREPOSAGE PEDLEX LTEE, LES *p* 1050

10000 BOUL DU GOLF, ANJOU, QC, H1J 2Y7

(514) 324-5310 *SIC* 5046

PRODUITS DALMEN PRODUCTS LTD *p* 888

5630 ST CATHERINE ST, ST ISIDORE, ON, K0C 2B0

(613) 524-2268 *SIC* 3442

PRODUITS DE BATIMENT FUSION BUILD-ING PRODUCTS INC *p* 1231

4500 RUE BERNARD-LEFEBVRE, MON-TREAL, QC, H7C 0A5

(514) 381-7456 *SIC* 3441

PRODUITS DE BATIMENT GENTEK *p* 1249

See ASSOCIATED MATERIALS CANADA LIMITED

PRODUITS DE BATIMENT RESIDENTIEL *p* 1323

See ROYAL GROUP, INC

PRODUITS DE BEAUTE IRIS INC *p* 1091

69 BOUL BRUNSWICK, DOLLARD-DES-ORMEAUX, QC, H9B 2N4

(514) 685-9966 *SIC* 2844

PRODUITS DE BETON CASAUBON INC, LES *p* 1357

2145 RANG DE LA RIVIERE S, SAINTE-ELISABETH, QC, J0K 2J0

(450) 753-3565 *SIC* 3272

PRODUITS DE BOIS CANADIENS - MON-TREAL INC *p* 1190

407 RUE MCGILL BUREAU 315, MON-TREAL, QC, H2Y 2G3

(514) 871-2120 *SIC* 5031

PRODUITS DE CONSTRUCTION DERBY INC *p* 1293

160 RUE DES GRANDS-LACS, SAINT-AUGUSTIN-DE-DESMAURES, QC, G3A 2K1

(418) 878-6161 *SIC* 2822

PRODUITS DE FIL DE FER LAURENTIEN LTEE *p* 1050

10500 RUE SECANT, ANJOU, QC, H1J 1S3

(514) 351-8814 *SIC* 3499

PRODUITS DE FIL ET DE METAL COGAN LTEE *p* 1380

2460 BOUL DES ENTREPRISES, TERRE-BONNE, QC, J6X 4J8

(514) 353-9141 *SIC* 3446

PRODUITS DE L'ERABLE BOLDUC & FILS INC, LES *p* 1353

292 3E RANG N, SAINT-VICTOR, QC, G0M 2B0

(418) 588-3315 *SIC* 5149

PRODUITS DE MARQUE LIBERTE, LES *p* 1069

See YOPLAIT LIBERTE CANADA CIE

PRODUITS DE METAL VULCAIN INC *p*

1320

31 RUE JOHN-F.-KENNEDY, SAINT-JEROME, QC, J7Y 4B4

(450) 436-5355 *SIC* 3469

PRODUITS DE PAPIER LAPACO LTEE, LES *p* 1309

5200 RUE J.-A.-BOMBARDIER, SAINT-HUBERT, QC, J3Z 1H1

(450) 632-5140 *SIC* 2679

PRODUITS DE PATISSERIE MICHAUD INC *p* 1281

1520 AV DES AFFAIRES, QUEBEC, QC, G3J 1Y8

(418) 843-3712 *SIC* 5149

PRODUITS DE PISCINE TRENDIUM INC *p* 1131

2673 BOUL ANGRIGNON, LASALLE, QC, H8N 3J3

(514) 363-7001 *SIC* 3949

PRODUITS DE PISCINE TRENDIUM INC *p* 1131

7050 RUE SAINT-PATRICK, LASALLE, QC, H8N 1V2

(514) 363-3232 *SIC* 3949

PRODUITS DE PLASTIQUE AGE INC, LES *p* 1165

7295 RUE TELLIER, MONTREAL, QC, H1N 3S9

(514) 251-9550 *SIC* 3089

PRODUITS DE PREMIERS SOINS EMER-GENCY (2011) INC *p* 1327

700 BOUL LEBEAU, SAINT-LAURENT, QC, H4N 1R5

SIC 5199

PRODUITS DE SECURITE INDUSTRIELLE CHECKERS CANADA INC *p* 1132

990 RUE D'UPTON, LASALLE, QC, H8R 2T9

(514) 366-6116 *SIC* 6712

PRODUITS DE SECURITE NORTH LTEE *p* 1050

10550 BOUL PARKWAY, ANJOU, QC, H1J 2K4

(514) 351-7233 *SIC* 3842

PRODUITS DE VIANDE PAC-RITE INC, LES *p* 1162

9090 RUE PIERRE-BONNE, MONTREAL, QC, H1E 6W5

(514) 524-3557 *SIC* 5147

PRODUITS DESIGNER ALLIANCE INC *p* 1362

225 BOUL BELLEROSE O, SAINTE-ROSE, QC, H7L 6A1

(450) 624-1611 *SIC* 5039

PRODUITS DIVINE *p* 1158

See SUPERTEK CANADA INC

PRODUITS EXCELDOR, LES *p* 1292

See EXCELDOR COOPERATIVE

PRODUITS EXCELDOR, LES *p* 1298

See EXCELDOR COOPERATIVE

PRODUITS FLEURCO INC, LES *p* 1330

4575 RUE BOUL POIRIER, SAINT-LAURENT, QC, H4R 2A4

(514) 326-2222 *SIC* 5211

PRODUITS FORESTIER TEMREX USINE NOUVELLE *p* 1244

See PRODUITS FORESTIERS TEMREX, SOCIETE EN COMMANDITE

PRODUITS FORESTIERS AMPRO INC *p* 1313

3025 RUE CARTIER, SAINT-HYACINTHE, QC, J2S 1L4

(450) 250-7888 *SIC* 5031

PRODUITS FORESTIERS ARBEC INC *p* 1345

8000 BOUL LANGELIER BUREAU 210, SAINT-LEONARD, QC, H1P 3K2

(514) 327-3350 *SIC* 6712

PRODUITS FORESTIERS ARBEC S.E.N.C. *p* 1119

5005 RTE UNIFORET, L'ASCENSION-DE-NOTRE-SEIGNEUR, QC, G0W 1Y0

(418) 347-4900 *SIC* 2421

PRODUITS FORESTIERS ARBEC S.E.N.C. *p* 1253

175 BOUL PORTAGE DES MOUSSES, PORT-CARTIER, QC, G5B 2V9

(418) 766-2299 *SIC* 2421

PRODUITS FORESTIERS ARBEC S.E.N.C. *p* 1345

8770 BOUL LANGELIER BUREAU 216, SAINT-LEONARD, QC, H1P 3C6

(514) 327-3350 *SIC* 2421

PRODUITS FORESTIERS ARBEC S.E.N.C. *p* 1369

775 CH DE TURCOTTE, SHAWINIGAN, QC, G9T 5K7

(819) 538-0735 *SIC* 2421

PRODUITS FORESTIERS D&G LTEE, LES *p* 1273

2590 BOUL LAURIER BUREAU 500, QUE-BEC, QC, G1V 4M6

(418) 657-6505 *SIC* 2421

PRODUITS FORESTIERS D&G LTEE, LES *p* 1356

313 RANG SAINT-JOSEPH, SAINTE-AURELIE, QC, G0M 1M0

(418) 593-3516 *SIC* 2431

PRODUITS FORESTIERS D. G. LTEE *p* 1356

See PRODUITS FORESTIERS D&G LTEE, LES

PRODUITS FORESTIERS DU CANADA *p* 1190

See PRODUITS DE BOIS CANADIENS - MONTREAL INC

PRODUITS FORESTIERS J.V. *p* 1400

See ROLAND BOULANGER & CIE, LTEE

PRODUITS FORESTIERS LEGARGE *p* 1351

See GROUPE LEGARE LTEE

PRODUITS FORESTIERS M.E.S. INC, LES *p* 1296

590 RUE SAGARD, SAINT-BRUNO, QC, J3V 6C2

(450) 461-1767 *SIC* 5031

PRODUITS FORESTIERS MAURICIE S.E.C. *p* 1144

2419 155 RTE S, LA TUQUE, QC, G9X 3N8

(819) 523-5626 *SIC* 2421

PRODUITS FORESTIERS PETIT PARIS INC *p* 1347

75 CH DE CHUTES-DES-PASSES, SAINT-LUDGER-DE-MILOT, QC, G0W 2B0

(418) 373-2801 *SIC* 2491

PRODUITS FORESTIERS RESOLU *p* 1212

See RESOLUTE FOREST PRODUCTS INC

PRODUITS FORESTIERS RESOLU USINE ALMA *p* 1045

See PF RESOLU CANADA INC

PRODUITS FORESTIERS RESOLUT SCI-ERIE OUTARDES *p* 1053

See PF RESOLU CANADA INC

PRODUITS FORESTIERS ST-RAYMOND, LES *p* 1351

See PLACAGES ST-RAYMOND INC

PRODUITS FORESTIERS TEMREX, SOCI-ETE EN COMMANDITE *p* 1244

521 RTE 132 O, NOUVELLE-OUEST, QC, G0C 2G0

(418) 794-2211 *SIC* 2421

PRODUITS FORESTIERS UNIVERSELLES DU CANADA *p* 1294

See UFP CANADA INC

PRODUITS FRACO LTEE, LES *p* 1348

91 CH DES PATRIOTES, SAINT-MATHIAS-SUR-RICHELIEU, QC, J3L 6B6

(514) 990-7750 *SIC* 3446

PRODUITS FRAIS FMS INC *p* 1376

298 RANG SAINTE-MELANIE, SHERRING-TON, QC, J0L 2N0

(450) 454-6499 *SIC* 5148

PRODUITS GILBERT INC, LES *p* 1287

1840 BOUL MARCOTTE, ROBERVAL, QC, G8H 2P2

(418) 275-5041   SIC 3553
PRODUITS GRISSPASTA LTEE   p 1142
805 BOUL GUIMOND, LONGUEUIL, QC,
J4G 1M1
(450) 651-4150   SIC 2098
PRODUITS IDEALTFC INC   p 1374
4460 RUE HECTOR-BRIEN, SHER-
BROOKE, QC, J1L 0E2
(819) 566-5696   SIC 1711
**PRODUITS INDUSTRIELS DE BEAUCE
(2013)**   p 1284
See DICKNER INC
**PRODUITS INDUSTRIELS DE HAUTE TEM-
PERATURE PYROTEK INC**   p
1097
2400 BOUL LEMIRE, DRUMMONDVILLE,
QC, J2B 6X9
(819) 477-0734   SIC 3569
PRODUITS INDUSTRIELS MITCHELL   p
1323
See ROBERT MITCHELL INC
PRODUITS INTEGRES AVIOR INC   p 1235
1001 NORD LAVAL (A-440) O BUREAU
200, MONTREAL, QC, H7L 3W3
(450) 629-6200   SIC 3728
PRODUITS JUPITER INC, LES   p 1321
338 RUE SAINT-GEORGES, SAINT-
JEROME, QC, J7Z 5A5
(450) 436-7500   SIC 2082
PRODUITS KRUGER S.E.C.   p 1105
See KRUGER PRODUCTS L.P.
PRODUITS KRUGER SHERBROOKE INC p
1218
3285 CH DE BEDFORD, MONTREAL, QC,
H3S 1G5
(514) 737-1131   SIC 2221
PRODUITS LA GULF QUEEN, LES   p 1120
See RENAISSANCE DES ILES INC, LA
PRODUITS LABELINK INC, LES   p 1050
9201 RUE CLAVEAU, ANJOU, QC, H1J 2C8
(514) 328-1887   SIC 2759
PRODUITS M.G.D. INC, LES   p 1059
680 BOUL INDUSTRIEL, BLAINVILLE, QC,
J7C 3V4
(450) 437-1414   SIC 5113
PRODUITS MARINS ST-GODEFROI INC   p
1306
157 RUE PRINCIPALE, SAINT-GODEFROI,
QC, G0C 3C0
(418) 752-5578   SIC 5146
PRODUITS MATRA INC   p 1348
21 11E RUE O, SAINT-MARTIN, QC, G0M
1B0
(418) 382-5151   SIC 2431
**PRODUITS MENAGERS FREUDENBERG
INC**   p 674
15 ALLSTATE PKY, MARKHAM, ON, L3R
5B4
(905) 669-9949   SIC 5199
**PRODUITS MENAGERS FREUDENBERG
INC**   p 1084
666 BOUL SAINT-MARTIN O BUREAU 220,
COTE SAINT-LUC, QC, H7M 5G4
(450) 975-4535   SIC 5199
PRODUITS METALIQUES PMI   p 1285
See PRODUITS METALLIQUES POULIOT
MACHINERIE INC
**PRODUITS METALLIQUES POULIOT MA-
CHINERIE INC**   p
1285
261 AV DU HAVRE, RIMOUSKI, QC, G5M
0B3
(418) 723-2610   SIC 1541
PRODUITS METALLIQUES ROY INC, LES p
1377
52 CH DE MORIGEAU, ST-FRANCOIS-DE-
LA-RIVIERE-DU-S, QC, G0R 3A0
(418) 259-2711   SIC 2542
PRODUITS MICROZINC INC, LES   p 1314
1375 RUE BROUILLETTE, SAINT-
HYACINTHE, QC, J2T 2G7
(450) 774-9151   SIC 3339
PRODUITS MOBILICAB CANADA INC   p
1044

280 RUE BONIN, ACTON VALE, QC, J0H
1A0
(450) 546-0999   SIC 5088
PRODUITS MURPHCO LTEE, LES   p 1223
5363 RUE NOTRE-DAME O BUREAU 117,
MONTREAL, QC, H4C 1T7
(514) 937-3275   SIC 5033
PRODUITS NEPTUNE INC, LES   p 1313
6835 RUE PICARD, SAINT-HYACINTHE,
QC, J2S 1H3
(450) 773-7058   SIC 3431
PRODUITS NEW ROOTS HERBAL, LES   p
1395
See NEW ROOTS HERBAL INC
**PRODUITS NON FERREUX GAUTHIER
INC, LES**   p 1248
12355 RUE APRIL, POINTE-AUX-
TREMBLES, QC, H1B 5L8
(514) 642-4090   SIC 3356
PRODUITS OLIN CHLOR ALKALI   p 1198
See OLIN CANADA ULC
PRODUITS ORAPI-DRY SHINE INC., LES p
1162
7521 BOUL HENRI-BOURASSA E, MON-
TREAL, QC, H1E 1N9
(514) 735-3272   SIC 5172
PRODUITS PBM LTEE, LES   p 1350
130 RUE DU MOULIN, SAINT-PIERRE-DE-
LAMY, QC, G0L 4B0
(418) 497-3927   SIC 2439
**PRODUITS PETROLIERS HARRICANA
(1993)**   p 1391
See PETRONOR INC
**PRODUITS PETROLIERS NORCAN
S.E.N.C., LES**   p 1165
6370 RUE NOTRE-DAME E, MONTREAL,
QC, H1N 2E1
(514) 253-2222   SIC 5172
**PRODUITS PHARMACEUTIQUES
VALEANT INTERNATIONAL**   p 1361
See BAUSCH HEALTH COMPANIES INC
PRODUITS PHOENICIA   p 1334
See GROUPE PHOENICIA INC
PRODUITS PLASTIQUES JAY INC   p 1345
8875 BOUL LANGELIER, SAINT-
LEONARD, QC, H1P 2C8
(514) 321-7272   SIC 3089
PRODUITS PLASTITEL INC, LES   p 1237
2604 RUE DEBRAY, MONTREAL, QC, H7S
2J8
(450) 687-0060   SIC 3089
**PRODUITS POLYWRAP DU CANADA
LTEE, LES**   p 1223
5590 BOUL MONK, MONTREAL, QC, H4C
3R8
(514) 933-2121   SIC 2673
PRODUITS POUR ANIMAUX YAMAS INC p
1313
3175 BOUL CHOQUETTE, SAINT-
HYACINTHE, QC, J2S 7Z8
(418) 771-4622   SIC 5033
**PRODUITS POUR TOITURES FRANSYL
LTEE**   p 1379
See PRODUITS POUR TOITURES FRAN-
SYL LTEE
**PRODUITS POUR TOITURES FRANSYL
LTEE**   p 1379
671 RUE LEVEILLE, TERREBONNE, QC,
J6W 1Z9
(450) 492-2392   SIC 5033
**PRODUITS POUR TOITURES FRANSYL
LTEE**   p 1381
1845 RUE JEAN-MONNET, TERRE-
BONNE, QC, J6X 4L7
(450) 477-4423   SIC 5033
**PRODUITS RECREATIFS FUTURE BEACH
INC**   p 1318
160 RUE VANIER, SAINT-JEAN-SUR-
RICHELIEU, QC, J3B 3R4
(450) 245-0373   SIC 3732
PRODUITS SAINT-HENRI INC, LES   p 1067
91 RUE DE LA BARRE BUREAU 2,
BOUCHERVILLE, QC, J4B 2X6
(450) 449-9799   SIC 5143

PRODUITS SANITAIRES CLOUTIER INC   p
1102
11 BOUL DE GASPE, GASPE, QC, G4X
1A1
(418) 368-7376   SIC 5169
PRODUITS SANITAIRES LEPINE INC, LES
p 1081
1105 RUE BERSIMIS, CHICOUTIMI, QC,
G7K 1A4
(418) 545-0794   SIC 5074
PRODUITS SANITAIRES LEPINE INC, LES
p 1105
134 AV GATINEAU, GATINEAU, QC, J8T
4J8
(819) 205-1626   SIC 5122
**PRODUITS SANITAIRES LEPINE VAL-
D'OR, LES**   p
1081
See PRODUITS SANITAIRES LEPINE INC,
LES
PRODUITS SANITAIRES NORFIL INC   p
1289
320 AV TURPIN, ROUYN-NORANDA, QC,
J9X 7E1
(819) 762-8129   SIC 5169
PRODUITS SEATPLY INC   p 1340
150 RUE MERIZZI, SAINT-LAURENT, QC,
H4T 1S4
(514) 340-1513   SIC 2426
PRODUITS SHELL CANADA   p 1238
See SHELL CANADA LIMITED
PRODUITS STANDARD INC   p 1341
5905 CH DE LA COTE-DE-LIESSE, SAINT-
LAURENT, QC, H4T 1C3
(514) 342-1199   SIC 5063
PRODUITS STAR APPETIZING INC, LES p
1224
1685 RUE CABOT, MONTREAL, QC, H4E
1C9
(514) 765-0614   SIC 5181
PRODUITS THERMOVISION INC   p 1318
680 BOUL INDUSTRIEL, SAINT-JEAN-
SUR-RICHELIEU, QC, J3B 7X4
(450) 348-4970   SIC 3083
PRODUITS VEGKISS INC   p 1115
1400 CH LASALLE, JOLIETTE, QC, J6E
0L8
(450) 752-2250   SIC 5148
PRODUITS ZINDA CANADA INC   p 1073
104 AV LIBERTE, CANDIAC, QC, J5R 6X1
(450) 635-6664   SIC 2041
PROFAB ENERGY SERVICES INC   p 102
17303 102 AVE NW SUITE 200, EDMON-
TON, AB, T5S 1J8
(780) 236-2450   SIC 1541
**PROFESSIONAL ABORIGINAL TESTING
ORGANIZATION INC**   p 401
231 REGENT ST SUITE 301, FREDERIC-
TON, NB, E3B 3W4
(506) 455-7725   SIC 8742
**PROFESSIONAL COMPUTER CONSUL-
TANTS GROUP LTD**   p
923
2323 YONGE ST SUITE 400, TORONTO,
ON, M4P 2C9
(416) 483-0766   SIC 7379
PROFESSIONAL EXCAVATORS LTD   p 17
10919 84 ST SE, CALGARY, AB, T2C 5A6
(403) 236-5686   SIC 1794
**PROFESSIONAL GARDENER CO. LTD,
THE**   p 31
915 23 AVE SE, CALGARY, AB, T2G 1P1
(403) 263-4200   SIC 1542
PROFESSIONAL GROUP INC, THE   p 116
9222 51 AVE NW, EDMONTON, AB, T6E
5L8
(780) 439-9818   SIC 6531
PROFESSIONAL GROUP INC, THE   p 116
9920 63 AVE NW SUITE 130, EDMONTON,
AB, T6E 0G9
(780) 439-9818   SIC 6531
PROFESSIONAL HEALTH PRODUCTS   p
137
See NUTRI-DYN PRODUCTS LTD

**PROFESSIONAL INSTITUTE OF THE PUB-
LIC SERVICE OF CANADA, THE**   p
818
250 TREMBLAY RD, OTTAWA, ON, K1G
3J8
(613) 228-6310   SIC 8631
PROFESSIONAL INSURANCE   p 633
See PROFESSIONAL INVESTMENTS
(KINGSTON) INC
**PROFESSIONAL INVESTMENTS
(KINGSTON) INC**   p 633
1180 CLYDE CRT, KINGSTON, ON, K7P
2E4
(613) 384-7511   SIC 6211
**PROFESSIONAL QUALITY ASSURANCE
LTD**   p 401
231 REGENT ST SUITE 104, FREDERIC-
TON, NB, E3B 3W8
(506) 455-7725   SIC 8742
PROFESSIONAL REALTY GROUP   p 116
See PROFESSIONAL GROUP INC, THE
**PROFESSIONAL REALTY GROUP, THE
DIV OF**   p 116
See PROFESSIONAL GROUP INC, THE
PROFESSIONAL TARGETED MARKETING
p 669
See DIRECT MULTI-PAK MAILING LTD
**PROFESSIONAL WAREHOUSE DEMON-
STRATIONS**   p
143
3200 MAYOR MAGRATH DR S, LETH-
BRIDGE, AB, T1K 6Y6
SIC 7389
PROFESSIONALS' FINANCIAL INC. p 1230
2 COMPLEXE DESJARDINS E, MON-
TREAL, QC, H5B 1C2
(514) 350-5075   SIC 6282
**PROFESSIONNEL(LE)S EN SOINS DE
SANTE UNIS LES**   p 1165
5630 RUE HOCHELAGA, MONTREAL, QC,
H1N 3L7
(514) 932-4417   SIC 8621
PROFILE DRILLING INC   p 689
6525 NORTHAM DR, MISSISSAUGA, ON,
L4V 1J2
(416) 650-6444   SIC 5084
PROFILE INDUSTRIES LIMITED   p 793
201 GARYRAY DR, NORTH YORK, ON,
M9L 2T2
(416) 748-2505   SIC 2522
**PROFILES POUR PORTES ET FENETRES
ROYAL**   p 1101
See ROYAL GROUP, INC
PROFITMASTER CANADA   p 391
See PM CANADA INC
**PROFLASH TECHNOLOGIES INTERNA-
TIONAL INC**   p
1123
904 CH SAINT-JOSE, LA PRAIRIE, QC, J5R
6A9
(450) 444-1384   SIC 5043
PROFORMANCE ADJUSTING SOLUTIONS
p 843
1101 KINGSTON RD SUITE 280, PICKER-
ING, ON, L1V 1B5
SIC 6321
PROFOUND MEDICAL INC   p 699
2400 SKYMARK AVE UNIT 6, MISSIS-
SAUGA, ON, L4W 5K5
(647) 476-1350   SIC 8731
PROG-DIE TOOL & STAMPING LTD   p 712
3161 WOLFEDALE RD, MISSISSAUGA,
ON, L5C 1V8
(905) 277-4651   SIC 3544
PROGAS ENTERPRISES LIMITED   p 57
240 4 AVE SW SUITE 2400, CALGARY, AB,
T2P 4H4
(403) 233-1301   SIC 4924
PROGAS USA INC   p 57
240 4 AVE SW SUITE 2400, CALGARY, AB,
T2P 4H4
(403) 233-1301   SIC 4923
PROGESYS INC   p 1235
4020 BOUL LE CORBUSIER BUREAU 201,

MONTREAL, QC, H7L 5R2
(450) 667-7646 *SIC* 8742
PROGISTIX-SOLUTIONS INC *p* 997
99 SIGNET DR SUITE 300, TORONTO, ON, M9L 0A2
(416) 401-7000 *SIC* 8742
PROGRAIN *p* 1297
See SEMENCES PROGRAIN INC
PROGRAM DE PORTAGE INC, LE *p* 1215
2455 AV LIONEL-GROULX, MONTREAL, QC, H3J 1J6
(514) 935-3431 *SIC* 8322
PROGRAM FOR MENTALLY ILL CHEMICAL ABUSERS (MICA) *p* 1215
See PROGRAM DE PORTAGE INC, LE
PROGRAMME D'ACCREDITATION PROFESSIONNELLE DE GESTION D'AEROPORT *p* 1229
See CONSEIL INTERNATIONAL DES AEROPORTS
PROGRAMME DE L'HEBERGEMENT *p* 1382
See CENTRE DE SANTE ET DE SERVICE SOCIAUX DE LA REGION DE THETFORD
PROGRAMME DE PORTAGE RELATIF A LA DEPENDENCE DE LA DROGUE INC, LE *p* 1215
865 PLACE RICHMOND, MONTREAL, QC, H3J 1V8
(514) 939-0202 *SIC* 8069
PROGRAMMED INSURANCE BROKERS INC *p* 568
49 INDUSTRIAL DR, ELMIRA, ON, N3B 3B1
(519) 669-1631 *SIC* 6411
PROGRESS LUV2PAK INTERNATIONAL LTD *p* 784
20 TANGIERS RD, NORTH YORK, ON, M3J 2B2
(416) 638-1221 *SIC* 7389
PROGRESS RAIL TRANSCANADA CORPORATION *p* 372
478 MCPHILLIPS ST SUITE 300, WINNIPEG, MB, R2X 2G8
(204) 934-4307 *SIC* 3462
PROGRESSIVE ALTERNATIVES SOCIETY OF CALGARY *p* 31
4014 MACLEOD TRAIL SE SUITE 211, CALGARY, AB, T2G 2R7
(403) 262-8515 *SIC* 8399
PROGRESSIVE ANODIZERS INC *p* 873
41 CROCKFORD BLVD, SCARBOROUGH, ON, M1R 3B7
(416) 751-5487 *SIC* 3471
PROGRESSIVE CONTRACTING LTD *p* 261
5591 NO. 3 RD, RICHMOND, BC, V6X 2C7
(604) 273-6655 *SIC* 1623
PROGRESSIVE RUBBER INDUSTRIES INC *p* 218
597A CHILCOTIN RD, KAMLOOPS, BC, V2H 1G6
(250) 851-0611 *SIC* 5085
PROHOME HEALTH SERVICES INC DIVISION *p* 708
See WE CARE HEALTH SERVICES INC
PROJEAN *p* 1355
See INSTRUMENTS I.T.M. INC, LES
PROJOY SPORTSWEAR (DIV) *p* 603
See HALTON INVESTMENTS INC
PROLAB TECHNOLOGIES INC *p* 1383
4531 RUE INDUSTRIELLE, THETFORD MINES, QC, G6H 2J1
(418) 423-2777 *SIC* 5172
PROLAM *p* 1074
See SOCIETE EN COMMANDITE PROLAM
PROLIFIC GRAPHICS INC *p* 372
150 WYATT RD, WINNIPEG, MB, R2X 2X6
(204) 694-2300 *SIC* 2752
PROLIFIC GROUP *p* 372
See PROLIFIC GRAPHICS INC
PROLIFIO INVESTMENT & ASSET MAN-

AGEMENT CORP *p* 966
161 BAY ST, TORONTO, ON, M5J 2S1
(416) 948-5505 *SIC* 6282
PROLINE PIPE EQUIPMENT *p* 110
See PROLINE RESOURCES INC
PROLINE PIPE EQUIPMENT INC *p* 110
7141 67 ST NW, EDMONTON, AB, T6B 3L7
(780) 465-6161 *SIC* 7389
PROLINE RESOURCES INC *p* 110
7141 67 ST NW, EDMONTON, AB, T6B 3L7
(780) 465-6161 *SIC* 6712
PROLINK BROKER NETWORK INC *p* 947
480 UNIVERSITY AVE SUITE 800, TORONTO, ON, M5G 1V2
(416) 595-7484 *SIC* 6411
PROLLENIUM MEDICAL TECHNOLOGIES INC *p* 481
138 INDUSTRIAL PKY N, AURORA, ON, L4G 4C3
(905) 508-1469 *SIC* 3841
PROLOGIC SYSTEMS LIMITED *p* 818
2255 ST. LAURENT BLVD SUITE 320, OTTAWA, ON, K1G 4K3
(613) 238-1376 *SIC* 8741
PROLOGIX DISTRIBUTION SERVICES *p* 869
120 SINNOTT RD, SCARBOROUGH, ON, M1L 4N1
(416) 615-3064 *SIC* 5192
PROLOGUE INC *p* 1062
1650 BOUL LIONEL-BERTRAND, BOISBRIAND, QC, J7H 1N7
(450) 434-0306 *SIC* 5192
PROLUXON INC *p* 1169
5549 BOUL SAINT-MICHEL, MONTREAL, QC, H1Y 2C9
(514) 374-4993 *SIC* 1731
PROMAC INDUSTRIES LIMITED PARTNERSHIP *p* 17
7150 112 AVE SE, CALGARY, AB, T2C 4Z1
(403) 279-8333 *SIC* 5084
PROMAG DISPLAYCORR CANADA INC *p* 1050
11150 AV L.-J.-FORGET, ANJOU, QC, H1J 2K9
(514) 352-9511 *SIC* 3577
PROMARK UTILITY LOCATORS INC *p* 31
4538 MANILLA RD SE, CALGARY, AB, T2G 4B7
(403) 243-1993 *SIC* 4931
PROMARK-TELECON INC *p* 750
203 COLONNADE RD S UNIT 10, NEPEAN, ON, K2E 7K3
(613) 723-9888 *SIC* 1623
PROMARK-TELECON INC *p* 1181
7450 RUE DU MILE END, MONTREAL, QC, H2R 2Z6
(514) 644-2214 *SIC* 4899
PROMAT INC *p* 1035
594711 COUNTY RD 59 S, WOODSTOCK, ON, N4S 7V8
(519) 456-2284 *SIC* 3496
PROMATION ENGINEERING LTD *p* 799
2767 BRIGHTON RD, OAKVILLE, ON, L6H 6J4
(905) 625-6093 *SIC* 3569
PROMAX TRANSPORT LTD *p* 137
4215 52 STREET CLOSE, INNISFAIL, AB, T4G 1P9
(403) 227-2852 *SIC* 4731
PROMAXIS SYSTEMS INC *p* 818
2385 ST. LAURENT BLVD, OTTAWA, ON, K1G 6C3
(613) 737-2112 *SIC* 8742
PROMEL *p* 1387
See GROUPE SOMAVRAC INC
PROMENADE KIA *p* 1104
See 3617581 CANADA INC
PROMENADES DE L'OUTAOUAIS LTD, LES *p* 1105
1100 BOUL MALONEY O, GATINEAU, QC, J8T 6G3

(819) 205-1340 *SIC* 6512
PROMENADES DE LA CATHEDRALE, LES *p* 955
See OMERS REALTY CORPORATION
PROMENADES DU PARC, LES *p* 1146
See SOCIETE EN COMMANDITE LES PROMENADES DU PARC
PROMETEK INC *p* 1255
1005 AV NORDIQUE, QUEBEC, QC, G1C 0C7
(418) 527-4445 *SIC* 3441
PROMETIC *p* 1241
See PROMETIC SCIENCES DE LA VIE INC
PROMETIC BIOSCIENCES INC *p* 1241
500 BOUL CARTIER O BUREAU 150, MONTREAL-OUEST, QC, H7V 5B7
(450) 781-0115 *SIC* 2834
PROMETIC SCIENCES DE LA VIE INC *p* 1241
440 BOUL ARMAND-FRAPPIER BUREAU 300, MONTREAL-OUEST, QC, H7V 4B4
(450) 781-0115 *SIC* 2834
PROMEX DATA PUBLISHING INC *p* 557
37 STAFFERN DR, CONCORD, ON, L4K 2X2
(905) 738-0288 *SIC* 5112
PROMINENT FLUID CONTROLS LTD *p* 601
490 SOUTHGATE DR, GUELPH, ON, N1G 4P5
(519) 836-5692 *SIC* 5074
PROMOBOIS G.D.S. INC *p* 1089
207 295 RTE, DEGELIS, QC, G5T 1R1
(418) 853-5050 *SIC* 5099
PROMOTION LEPINE INC *p* 1267
2800 BOUL WILFRID-HAMEL, QUEBEC, QC, G1P 2J1
(418) 687-0084 *SIC* 5169
PROMOTION SAGUENAY INC *p* 1079
295 RUE RACINE E, CHICOUTIMI, QC, G7H 1S7
(418) 698-3157 *SIC* 4725
PROMOTIONAL PRODUCTS FULFILLMENT & DISTRIBUTION *p* 1013
See 1257391 ONTARIO LIMITED
PROMOTIONAL PRODUCTS FULFILLMENT & DISTRIBUTION LT *p* 1015
80 WILLIAM SMITH DR, WHITBY, ON, L1N 9W1
(905) 668-5060 *SIC* 7389
PROMOTIONAL SPECIALISTS, THE *p* 666
See 987217 ONTARIO LIMITED
PROMOTIONS *p* 878
See T & L FOOD MERCHANDISING SERVICES LTD
PROMOTIONS AZUR, LES *p* 1195
See EQUIPE SPECTRA INC, L'
PROMOTIONS C.D. INC *p* 1067
165 RUE JULES-LEGER, BOUCHERVILLE, QC, J4B 7K8
(450) 641-1161 *SIC* 5199
PROMOTIONS V P S *p* 1224
See 2842-3861 QUEBEC INC
PROMPTON REAL ESTATE SERVICES INC *p* 327
179 DAVIE ST SUITE 201, VANCOUVER, BC, V6Z 2Y1
(604) 899-2333 *SIC* 6531
PROMUTUEL ASSURANCE *p* 1055
See PROMUTUEL BEAUCE-ETCHEMINS, SOCIETE MUTUELLE D'ASSURANCE GENERALE
PROMUTUEL ASSURANCE *p* 1113
See PROMUTUEL DU LAC AU FLEUVE
PROMUTUEL ASSURANCE *p* 1113
See PROMUTUEL DU LAC AU FJORD
PROMUTUEL ASSURANCE *p* 1115
See PROMUTUEL LANAUDIERE, SOCIETE MUTUELLE D'ASSURANCE GENERALE
PROMUTUEL ASSURANCE *p* 1125
See PROMUTUEL MONTS ET RIVES, SOCIETE MUTUELLE D'ASSURANCE GEN-

ERALE
PROMUTUEL ASSURANCE *p* 1160
See PROMUTUEL MONTMAGNY-L'ISLET, SOCIETE MUTUELLE D'ASSURANCE GENERALE
PROMUTUEL ASSURANCE *p* 1301
See PROMUTUEL DEUX-MONTAGNES, SOCIETE MUTUELLE D'ASSURANCE GENERALE
PROMUTUEL ASSURANCE DU LAC AU FLEUVE *p* 1054
See PROMUTUEL DU LAC AU FLEUVE, SOCIETE MUTUELLE D'ASSURANCE GENERALE
PROMUTUEL ASSURANCE VALLEE DU ST-LAURENT *p* 1123
See GROUPE PROMUTUEL FEDERATION DE SOCIETE MUTUELLES D'ASSURANCES GENERALES
PROMUTUEL BEAUCE SOCIETE MUTUELLE D'ASSURANCE GENERALE *p* 1055
60 BOUL RENAULT, BEAUCEVILLE, QC, G5X 3P2
(418) 774-3621 *SIC* 6411
PROMUTUEL BEAUCE-ETCHEMINS, SOCIETE MUTUELLE D'ASSURANCE GENERALE *p* 1055
650 BOUL RENAULT, BEAUCEVILLE, QC, G5X 3P2
SIC 6411
PROMUTUEL CAPITAL, SOCIETE DE FIDUCIE *p* 1280
2000 BOUL LEBOURGNEUF BUREAU 400, QUEBEC, QC, G2K 0B6
SIC 6722
PROMUTUEL CHARLEVOIX-MONTMORENCY *p* 1054
951 BOUL MONSEIGNEUR-DE LAVAL, BAIE-SAINT-PAUL, QC, G3Z 2W3
(418) 435-2793 *SIC* 6331
PROMUTUEL DEUX-MONTAGNES, SOCIETE MUTUELLE D'ASSURANCE GENERALE *p* 1301
200 RUE DUBOIS, SAINT-EUSTACHE, QC, J7P 4W9
(450) 623-5774 *SIC* 6411
PROMUTUEL DU LAC AU FJORD *p* 1045
790 AV DU PONT S, ALMA, QC, G8B 2V4
(418) 662-6595 *SIC* 6411
PROMUTUEL DU LAC AU FJORD *p* 1113
11 RUE COMMERCIALE, HEBERTVILLE, QC, G8N 1N3
(418) 344-1565 *SIC* 6411
PROMUTUEL DU LAC AU FLEUVE *p* 1113
11 RUE COMMERCIALE, HEBERTVILLE, QC, G8N 1N3
(418) 344-1565 *SIC* 6331
PROMUTUEL DU LAC AU FLEUVE, SOCIETE MUTUELLE D'ASSURANCE GENERALE *p* 1054
951 BOUL MONSEIGNEUR-DE LAVAL, BAIE-SAINT-PAUL, QC, G3Z 2W3
(418) 435-2793 *SIC* 6411
PROMUTUEL L'OUTAOUAIS *p* 1291
See PROMUTUEL L'OUTAOUAIS SOCIETE MUTUELLE D'ASSURANCE GENERALE
PROMUTUEL L'OUTAOUAIS SOCIETE MUTUELLE D'ASSURANCE GENERALE *p* 1291
629 321 RTE N RR 3, SAINT-ANDRE-AVELLIN, QC, J0V 1W0
(819) 983-6141 *SIC* 6411
PROMUTUEL LANAUDIERE, SOCIETE MUTUELLE D'ASSURANCE GENERALE *p* 1115
1075 BOUL FIRESTONE BUREAU 4100, JOLIETTE, QC, J6E 6X6
(450) 755-5555 *SIC* 6331
PROMUTUEL LOTBINIERE S.M.A.G. *p* 1133

See PROMUTUEL LOTNINIERE SOCIETE MUTUELLE D'ASSURANCE GENERALE

PROMUTUEL LOTNINIERE SOCIETE MUTUELLE D'ASSURANCE GENERALE *p* 1133
175 BOUL LAURIER RR 1, LAURIER-STATION, QC, G0S 1N0
(418) 728-4110   *SIC* 6411

PROMUTUEL MONTMAGNY-L'ISLET, SOCIETE MUTUELLE D'ASSURANCE GENERALE *p* 1160
124 BOUL TACHE O, MONTMAGNY, QC, G5V 3A5
(418) 248-7940   *SIC* 6411

PROMUTUEL MONTS ET RIVES, SOCIETE MUTUELLE D'ASSURANCE GENERALE *p* 1125
5240 BOUL DES VETERANS, LAC-MEGANTIC, QC, G6B 2G5
(819) 583-4555   *SIC* 6411

PROMUTUEL PORTNEUF-CHAMPLAIN SOCIETE, MUTUAL D'ASSURANCE GENERALE *p* 1294
257 BOUL DU CENTENAIRE RR 1, SAINT-BASILE, QC, G0A 3G0
(418) 329-3330   *SIC* 6411

PROMUTUEL VAUDREUIL-SOULANGES, SOCIETE MUTUELLE D'ASSURANCE GENERALE *p* 1135
245 338 RTE, LES COTEAUX, QC, J7X 1A2
(450) 267-9297   *SIC* 6411

PRONGHORN CONTROLS LTD *p* 17
4919 72 AVE SE SUITE 101, CALGARY, AB, T2C 3H3
(403) 720-2526   *SIC* 7629

PRONGHORN CONTROLS LTD *p* 17
4919 72 AVE SE UNIT 101, CALGARY, AB, T2C 3H3
(403) 720-2526   *SIC* 5084

PRONORTH EQUIPMENT *p* 762
See 618717 ONTARIO INC

PRONORTH TRANSPORTATION *p* 762
See 682439 ONTARIO INC

PRONTOFORMS CORPORATION *p* 832
2500 SOLANDT SUITE 250, OTTAWA, ON, K2K 3G5
(613) 599-8288   *SIC* 7371

PROOF INC *p* 930
33 BLOOR ST E SUITE 900, TORONTO, ON, M4W 3H1
(416) 920-9000   *SIC* 8743

PROPAIR INC *p* 1290
20 RUE PRONOVOST, ROUYN-NORANDA, QC, J9Y 0G1
(819) 762-0811   *SIC* 4512

PROPAK COMPRESSION *p* 3
See PROPAK SYSTEMS LTD

PROPAK PLASTICS (1979) LTD *p* 1118
16817 BOUL HYMUS, KIRKLAND, QC, H9H 3L4
(514) 695-9520   *SIC* 3081

PROPAK SYSTEMS LTD *p* 3
440 EAST LAKE RD NE, AIRDRIE, AB, T4A 2J8
(403) 912-7000   *SIC* 3533

PROPANE DU SUROIT *p* 1360
See 9049-1135 QUEBEC INC

PROPANE NORD-OUEST INC *p* 1391
2701 BOUL JEAN-JACQUES-COSSETTE, VAL-D'OR, QC, J9P 6Y3
(819) 824-6778   *SIC* 5984

PROPER FORD LINCOLN *p* 476
See MIEDEMA'S MOTOR SALES LTD

PROPERTIES GROUP LTD, THE *p* 834
236 METCALFE ST, OTTAWA, ON, K2P 1R3
(613) 237-2425   *SIC* 6719

PROPERTIES TERRA INCOGNITA INC *p* 1186
3530 BOUL SAINT-LAURENT BUREAU 500, MONTREAL, QC, H2X 2V1
(514) 847-3536   *SIC* 6531

PROPERTY VALUATION SERVICES COR-

PORATION *p* 448
238 BROWNLOW AVE SUITE 200, DARTMOUTH, NS, B3B 1Y2
(902) 476-2748   *SIC* 7389

PROPHARM LIMITED *p* 674
131 MCNABB ST, MARKHAM, ON, L3R 5V7
(905) 943-9736   *SIC* 7371

PROPHECY DEVELOPMENT CORP *p* 308
409 GRANVILLE ST SUITE 1610, VANCOUVER, BC, V6C 1T2
(604) 569-3661   *SIC* 1221

PROPHIT MANAGEMENT LTD *p* 18
4540 54 AVE SE UNIT 200, CALGARY, AB, T2C 2Y8
(403) 640-0200   *SIC* 8741

PROPHIX SOFTWARE INC *p* 710
350 BURNHAMTHORPE RD W SUITE 1000, MISSISSAUGA, ON, L5B 3J1
(905) 279-8711   *SIC* 7371

PROPIPE GROUP LTD *p* 134
15201 91 ST, GRANDE PRAIRIE, AB, T8X 0B3
(780) 830-0955   *SIC* 1389

PROPIPE MANUFACTURING DIV OF *p* 131
See 1089243 ALBERTA LTD

PROPORTION PETITE *p* 1178
See COLLECTION CONRAD C INC

PROPRIETES BELCOURT INC, LES *p* 1341
6500 RTE TRANSCANADIENNE BUREAU 210, SAINT-LAURENT, QC, H4T 1X4
(514) 344-1300   *SIC* 1531

PROPUR INC *p* 1277
5185 RUE RIDEAU, QUEBEC, QC, G2E 5S2
(418) 862-7739   *SIC* 5148

PRORESP INC *p* 649
1909 OXFORD ST E SUITE 1, LONDON, ON, N5V 4L9
(519) 686-2615   *SIC* 7352

PROS DE LA PHOTO (QUEBEC) INC, LES *p* 1182
90 RUE BEAUBIEN O BUREAU 101, MONTREAL, QC, H2S 1V6
(514) 322-7476   *SIC* 7335

PROS DE LA PHOTO (QUEBEC) INC, LES *p* 1182
90 RUE BEAUBIEN O BUREAU 201, MONTREAL, QC, H2S 1V6
(514) 273-1588   *SIC* 7384

PROSCAFF NORTH AMERICA INC *p* 988
148 DEWBOURNE AVE, TORONTO, ON, M6C 1Z2
(416) 783-7500   *SIC* 5049

PROSERVIN INC *p* 1059
1250 BOUL MICHELE-BOHEC UNITE 400, BLAINVILLE, QC, J7C 5S4
(450) 433-1002   *SIC* 1542

PROSHRED *p* 726
See REDISHRED CAPITAL CORP

PROSLIDE TECHNOLOGY INC *p* 830
2650 QUEENSVIEW DR SUITE 150, OTTAWA, ON, K2B 8H6
(613) 526-5522   *SIC* 5091

PROSNACK NATURAL FOODS INC *p* 244
19100 AIRPORT WAY UNIT 108, PITT MEADOWS, BC, V3Y 0E2
(604) 465-0548   *SIC* 2032

PROSOL INC *p* 1327
165 RUE DESLAURIERS BUREAU 254, SAINT-LAURENT, QC, H4N 2S4
(514) 745-1212   *SIC* 5169

PROSON UTILITY SOLUTIONS INC *p* 606
355 ELMIRA RD N UNIT 138, GUELPH, ON, N1K 1S5
(519) 767-2643   *SIC* 5084

PROSPECT CALGARY *p* 11
See PROSPECT HUMAN SERVICES SOCIETY

PROSPECT HUMAN SERVICES SOCIETY *p* 11
915 33 ST NE, CALGARY, AB, T2A 6T2
(403) 273-2822   *SIC* 5912

PROSPECT POINT HOLDINGS LTD *p* 318
2099 BEACH AVE, VANCOUVER, BC, V6G

1Z4
(604) 669-2737   *SIC* 6712

PROSPER CANADA *p* 926
60 ST CLAIR AVENUE E SUITE 700, TORONTO, ON, M4T 1N5
(416) 665-2828   *SIC* 6733

PROSYS TECH CORPORATION *p* 1050
7751 RUE JARRY, ANJOU, QC, H1J 1H3
(450) 681-7744   *SIC* 3571

PROTAGON DISPLAY INC *p* 878
719 TAPSCOTT RD, SCARBOROUGH, ON, M1X 1A2
(416) 293-9500   *SIC* 2653

PROTEC DENTAL LABORATORIES LTD *p* 289
38 1ST AVE E, VANCOUVER, BC, V5T 1A1
(604) 873-8000   *SIC* 8072

PROTEC INSTALLATIONS GROUP *p* 261
11720 VOYAGEUR WAY SUITE 9, RICHMOND, BC, V6X 3G9
(604) 278-3200   *SIC* 1731

PROTEC INVESTIGATION AND SECURITY INC *p* 1222
3333 BOUL CAVENDISH BUREAU 200, MONTREAL, QC, H4B 2M5
(514) 485-3255   *SIC* 7381

PROTEC ORTHODONTIC LABORATORIES LTD *p* 289
38 1ST AVE E, VANCOUVER, BC, V5T 1A1
(604) 734-8966   *SIC* 8072

PROTECH BUSINESS SOLUTIONS INC *p* 1241
1200 BOUL CHOMEDEY BUREAU 720, MONTREAL-OUEST, QC, H7V 3Z3
(450) 934-9800   *SIC* 7361

PROTECH CHIMIE LTEE *p* 1335
7600 BOUL HENRI-BOURASSA O, SAINT-LAURENT, QC, H4S 1W3
(514) 745-0200   *SIC* 2851

PROTECH HOME MEDICAL CORP *p* 322
5626 LARCH ST SUITE 202, VANCOUVER, BC, V6M 4E1
(877) 811-9690   *SIC* 3845

PROTECH SOLUTIONS *p* 1241
See PROTECH BUSINESS SOLUTIONS INC

PROTECT AIR CO *p* 674
2751 JOHN ST, MARKHAM, ON, L3R 2Y8
(905) 944-8877   *SIC* 8748

PROTECT-YU SECURITY & TECHNOLOGIES INC *p* 1133
3055 BOUL SAINT-MARTIN O BUREAU 5, LAVAL, QC, H7T 0J3
(514) 916-7280   *SIC* 8731

PROTECTA *p* 734
See CAPITAL SAFETY GROUP CANADA ULC

PROTECTEUR DU CITOYEN *p* 1191
See GOUVERNEMENT DE LA PROVINCE DE QUEBEC

PROTECTEUR DU CITOYEN, LE *p* 1269
See GOUVERNEMENT DE LA PROVINCE DE QUEBEC

PROTECTION DE LA JEUNESSE *p* 1319
See CENTRE JEUNESSE DES LAURENTIDES

PROTECTION INCENDIE L.P.G. INC *p* 1355
260 RUE CLEMENT, SAINTE-ANNE-DES-PLAINES, QC, J0N 1H0
(514) 915-5913   *SIC* 1711

PROTECTION INCENDIE POLYGON INC *p* 1062
1935 BOUL LIONEL-BERTRAND, BOIS-BRIAND, QC, J7H 1N8
(450) 430-7516   *SIC* 5087

PROTECTION INCENDIE ROBERTS LTEE *p* 1252
26A BOUL HYMUS BUREAU 49, POINTE-CLAIRE, QC, H9R 1C9
(514) 695-7070   *SIC* 5084

PROTECTION INCENDIE VIKING INC *p* 1062
1935 BOUL LIONEL-BERTRAND, BOIS-

BRIAND, QC, J7H 1N8
(450) 430-7516   *SIC* 5063

PROTECTION INCENDIE VIKING INC *p* 1335
3005 BOUL PITFIELD, SAINT-LAURENT, QC, H4S 1H4
(514) 332-5110   *SIC* 5063

PROTECTIVE TROOPS RESPONSE FORCE *p* 879
15 WEAVER DR, SCARBOROUGH, ON, M1X 1V2
(905) 233-4873   *SIC* 7381

PROTECTOLITE COMPOSITES INC *p* 775
84 RAILSIDE RD, NORTH YORK, ON, M3A 1A3
(416) 444-4484   *SIC* 3569

PROTECTORS GROUP INSURANCE AGENCIES (1985) LTD, THE *p* 842
215 GEORGE ST N, PETERBOROUGH, ON, K9J 3G7
(705) 748-5181   *SIC* 6411

PROTEGRA INC *p* 84
12031 76 ST NW, EDMONTON, AB, T5B 2C9

SIC 8741

PROTEKITE *p* 557
380 SPINNAKER WAY, CONCORD, ON, L4K 4W1
(905) 738-1221   *SIC* 7389

PROTELEC LTD *p* 372
1450 MOUNTAIN AVE UNIT 200, WINNIPEG, MB, R2X 3C4
(204) 949-1417   *SIC* 7382

PROTEM HEALTH SERVICES INC *p* 409
2069 MOUNTAIN RD, MONCTON, NB, E1G 1B1
(506) 852-9652   *SIC* 8099

PROTEMP GLASS INC *p* 557
360 APPLEWOOD CRES, CONCORD, ON, L4K 4V2
(905) 760-0701   *SIC* 3211

PROTENERGY NATURAL FOODS CORP *p* 853
125 EAST BEAVER CREEK RD, RICHMOND HILL, ON, L4B 4R3
(905) 707-6223   *SIC* 2032

PROTOCASE INCORPORATED *p* 467
46 WABANA CRT, SYDNEY, NS, B1P 0B9
(866) 849-3911   *SIC* 3499

PROTOPLAST INC *p* 545
210 WILLMOTT ST UNIT 2, COBOURG, ON, K9A 0E9
(905) 372-6451   *SIC* 3089

PROTOS SHIPPING LTD *p* 579
701 EVANS AVE SUITE 700, ETOBICOKE, ON, M9C 1A3
(416) 621-4381   *SIC* 4731

PROTOTECH SERVICES LTD *p* 110
6916 68 AVE NW, EDMONTON, AB, T6B 3C5
(780) 433-2133   *SIC* 5084

PROTOTIER-1 INC *p* 490
3690 ADJALA-TECUMSETH TOWNLINE SUITE 2, BEETON, ON, L0G 1A0
(705) 434-0457   *SIC* 5084

PROTOTYPES STEPONE *p* 1318
See GROUPE G.L.P. HI-TECH INC

PROTRANS BC OPERATIONS LTD *p* 261
9851 VAN HORNE WAY, RICHMOND, BC, V6X 1W4
(604) 247-5757   *SIC* 4111

PROUDFOOTS HOME HARDWARE *p* 466
See PROUDFOOTS INCORPORATED

PROUDFOOTS HOME HARDWARE BUILDING CENTER *p*
466
See PROUDFOOTS INCORPORATED

PROUDFOOTS INCORPORATED *p* 466
130 VISTA DR, STELLARTON, NS, B0K 1S0
(902) 752-4600   *SIC* 5251

PROUDFOOTS INCORPORATED *p* 466
130 VISTA DR, STELLARTON, NS, B0K 0A2
(902) 752-1500   *SIC* 5251

PROULX, G. INC *p* 1076

2800 BOUL FORD, CHATEAUGUAY, QC, J6J 4Z2
(450) 691-7110   *SIC 5039*

PROULX, GRATIEN BUILDING MATERIALS LTD   *p 595*
1499 STAR TOP RD SUITE A, GLOUCESTER, ON, K1B 3W5
(613) 749-3344   *SIC 5039*

PROULX, MICHEL STORE INC   *p 746*
12329 COUNTY RD 2, MORRISBURG, ON, K0C 1X0
(613) 543-2845   *SIC 5531*

PROVEER   *p 781*
See *1669051 NOVA SCOTIA LIMITED*

PROVENCHER ROY   *p 1190*
See *PROVENCHER ROY + ASSOCIES ARCHITECTES INC*

PROVENCHER ROY + ASSOCIES ARCHITECTES INC   *p 1190*
276 RUE SAINT-JACQUES BUREAU 700, MONTREAL, QC, H2Y 1N3
(514) 844-3938   *SIC 8621*

PROVENT HCE INC   *p 1345*
6150 BOUL DES GRANDES-PRAIRIES, SAINT-LEONARD, QC, H1P 1A2
(514) 643-0642   *SIC 5064*

PROVIDENCE CARE CENTRE   *p 631*
340 UNION ST, KINGSTON, ON, K7L 5A2
(613) 548-7222   *SIC 8051*

PROVIDENCE CARE CENTRE   *p 631*
752 KING ST W, KINGSTON, ON, K7L 4X3
(613) 548-5567   *SIC 8063*

PROVIDENCE HEALTH CARE SOCIETY   *p 288*
7801 ARGYLE ST, VANCOUVER, BC, V5P 3L6
(604) 321-2661   *SIC 8062*

PROVIDENCE HEALTH CARE SOCIETY   *p 289*
3080 PRINCE EDWARD ST, VANCOUVER, BC, V5T 3N4
(604) 877-8302   *SIC 8062*

PROVIDENCE HEALTH CARE SOCIETY   *p 293*
4950 HEATHER ST SUITE 321, VANCOUVER, BC, V5Z 3L9
(604) 261-9371   *SIC 8059*

PROVIDENCE HEALTH CARE SOCIETY   *p 327*
1081 BURRARD ST, VANCOUVER, BC, V6Z 1Y6
(604) 682-2344   *SIC 8062*

PROVIDENCE HEALTHCARE   *p 869*
3276 ST CLAIR AVE E, SCARBOROUGH, ON, M1L 1W1
(416) 285-3666   *SIC 8069*

PROVIDENCE UNIVERSITY COLLEGE AND THEOLOGICAL SEMINARY   *p 354*
10 COLLEGE CRES, OTTERBURNE, MB, R0A 1G0
(204) 433-7488   *SIC 8221*

PROVIDENT SECURITY CORP   *p 322*
2309 41ST AVE W SUITE 400, VANCOUVER, BC, V6M 2A3
(604) 664-1087   *SIC 7381*

PROVIDER TRANSPORTATION & LOGISTICS INC   *p 483*
3184 ALPS RD, AYR, ON, N0B 1E0
SIC 4731

PROVIGO   *p 1044*
See *JOLY, ERNEST & FILS INC*

PROVIGO   *p 1077*
See *MARCHE ROBERT DESROCHERS INC*

PROVIGO   *p 1084*
See *SUPERMARCHE N.G. INC*

PROVIGO   *p 1096*
See *127113 CANADA INC*

PROVIGO   *p 1102*
See *PROVIGO DISTRIBUTION INC*

PROVIGO   *p 1108*
See *LOBLAWS INC*

PROVIGO   *p 1134*
See *ALIMENTATION GAETAN PLANTE INC*

PROVIGO   *p 1167*
See *LOBLAWS SUPERMARKETS LIMITED*

PROVIGO   *p 1274*
See *PROVIGO DISTRIBUTION INC*

PROVIGO   *p 1327*
See *PROVIGO DISTRIBUTION INC*

PROVIGO   *p 1349*
See *ALIMENTATION D.M. ST-GEORGES INC*

PROVIGO   *p 1351*
See *VOYER & JOBIN LTEE*

PROVIGO   *p 1356*
See *PROVIGO DISTRIBUTION INC*

PROVIGO BOUCHERVILLE   *p 1066*
See *LOBLAWS INC*

PROVIGO CORRIVEAU   *p 1046*
See *SUPERMARCHE GUY CORRIVEAU INC*

PROVIGO DISTRIBUTION INC   *p 632*
1225 PRINCESS ST, KINGSTON, ON, K7M 3E1
(613) 544-8202   *SIC 5411*

PROVIGO DISTRIBUTION INC   *p 633*
775 BAYRIDGE DR, KINGSTON, ON, K7P 2P1
(613) 384-8800   *SIC 5141*

PROVIGO DISTRIBUTION INC   *p 1053*
570 BOUL LAFLECHE, BAIE-COMEAU, QC, G5C 1C3
(418) 589-9020   *SIC 5411*

PROVIGO DISTRIBUTION INC   *p 1067*
180 CH DU TREMBLAY, BOUCHERVILLE, QC, J4B 7W3
(450) 449-8000   *SIC 5148*

PROVIGO DISTRIBUTION INC   *p 1089*
31 BOUL GEORGES-GAGNE S, DELSON, QC, J5B 2E4
(450) 638-5041   *SIC 5411*

PROVIGO DISTRIBUTION INC   *p 1102*
130 AV LEPINE, GATINEAU, QC, J8L 4M4
(819) 281-5232   *SIC 5411*

PROVIGO DISTRIBUTION INC   *p 1105*
800 BOUL MALONEY O, GATINEAU, QC, J8T 3R6
(819) 561-9244   *SIC 5411*

PROVIGO DISTRIBUTION INC   *p 1105*
800 BOUL MALONEY O, GATINEAU, QC, J8T 3R6
(819) 561-9244   *SIC 5499*

PROVIGO DISTRIBUTION INC   *p 1107*
1 BOUL DU PLATEAU, GATINEAU, QC, J9A 3G1
(819) 777-2747   *SIC 5411*

PROVIGO DISTRIBUTION INC   *p 1107*
775 BOUL SAINT-JOSEPH, GATINEAU, QC, J8Y 4C1
(819) 771-7701   *SIC 5411*

PROVIGO DISTRIBUTION INC   *p 1115*
909 BOUL FIRESTONE, JOLIETTE, QC, J6E 2W4
(450) 755-2781   *SIC 5411*

PROVIGO DISTRIBUTION INC   *p 1119*
1201 AUT DUPLESSIS, L'ANCIENNE-LORETTE, QC, G2G 2B4
(418) 872-2400   *SIC 5411*

PROVIGO DISTRIBUTION INC   *p 1125*
3560 RUE LAVAL, LAC-MEGANTIC, QC, G6B 2X4
(819) 583-4001   *SIC 5141*

PROVIGO DISTRIBUTION INC   *p 1146*
1150 RUE KING-GEORGE, LONGUEUIL, QC, J4N 1P3
(450) 647-1717   *SIC 5411*

PROVIGO DISTRIBUTION INC   *p 1148*
1350 RUE SHERBROOKE, MAGOG, QC, J1X 2T3
(819) 868-8630   *SIC 5411*

PROVIGO DISTRIBUTION INC   *p 1165*
7600 RUE SHERBROOKE E, MONTREAL, QC, H1N 3W1
(514) 257-4511   *SIC 5411*

PROVIGO DISTRIBUTION INC   *p 1177*

8305 AV PAPINEAU, MONTREAL, QC, H2M 2G2
(514) 376-6457   *SIC 5411*

PROVIGO DISTRIBUTION INC   *p 1186*
3421 AV DU PARC, MONTREAL, QC, H2X 2H6
(514) 281-0488   *SIC 5411*

PROVIGO DISTRIBUTION INC   *p 1218*
375 RUE JEAN-TALON O, MONTREAL, QC, H3N 2Y8
(514) 948-2600   *SIC 5411*

PROVIGO DISTRIBUTION INC   *p 1237*
2700 AV FRANCIS-HUGHES BUREAU 2172, MONTREAL, QC, H7S 2B9
(514) 383-8800   *SIC 4225*

PROVIGO DISTRIBUTION INC   *p 1247*
12780 RUE SHERBROOKE E, POINTE-AUX-TREMBLES, QC, H1A 4Y3
(514) 498-2675   *SIC 5411*

PROVIGO DISTRIBUTION INC   *p 1262*
552 BOUL WILFRID-HAMEL, QUEBEC, QC, G1M 3E5
(418) 640-1700   *SIC 5411*

PROVIGO DISTRIBUTION INC   *p 1267*
5150 BOUL DE L'ORMIERE, QUEBEC, QC, G1P 4B2
(418) 872-3866   *SIC 5411*

PROVIGO DISTRIBUTION INC   *p 1274*
3440 CH DES QUATRE-BOURGEOIS BUREAU 8143, QUEBEC, QC, G1W 4T3
(418) 653-6241   *SIC 5411*

PROVIGO DISTRIBUTION INC   *p 1288*
339 BOUL LABELLE, ROSEMERE, QC, J7A 2H7
(450) 437-0471   *SIC 5411*

PROVIGO DISTRIBUTION INC   *p 1315*
200 BOUL OMER-MARCIL, SAINT-JEAN-SUR-RICHELIEU, QC, J2W 2V1
(450) 348-0998   *SIC 5411*

PROVIGO DISTRIBUTION INC   *p 1320*
900 BOUL GRIGNON, SAINT-JEROME, QC, J7Y 3S7
(450) 436-3824   *SIC 5411*

PROVIGO DISTRIBUTION INC   *p 1327*
400 AV SAINTE-CROIX, SAINT-LAURENT, QC, H4N 3L4
(514) 383-3000   *SIC 5141*

PROVIGO DISTRIBUTION INC   *p 1330*
1757 BOUL MARCEL-LAURIN, SAINT-LAURENT, QC, H4R 1J5
(514) 747-2203   *SIC 5411*

PROVIGO DISTRIBUTION INC   *p 1352*
50 AV SAINT-DENIS, SAINT-SAUVEUR, QC, J0R 1R4
(450) 227-2827   *SIC 5411*

PROVIGO DISTRIBUTION INC   *p 1356*
480 BOUL SAINTE-ANNE, SAINTE-ANNE-DES-PLAINES, QC, J0N 1H0
(450) 478-1864   *SIC 5141*

PROVIGO DISTRIBUTION INC   *p 1363*
444 BOUL CURE-LABELLE, SAINTE-ROSE, QC, H7P 4W7
(450) 625-4221   *SIC 5411*

PROVIGO DISTRIBUTION INC   *p 1379*
1345 BOUL MOODY, TERREBONNE, QC, J6W 3L1
(450) 471-1009   *SIC 5411*

PROVIGO DISTRIBUTION INC   *p 1385*
320 RUE BARKOFF, TROIS-RIVIERES, QC, G8T 2A3
(819) 378-4932   *SIC 5411*

PROVIGO DISTRIBUTION INC   *p 1386*
5875 BOUL JEAN-XXIII, TROIS-RIVIERES, QC, G8Z 4N8
(819) 378-8759   *SIC 5411*

PROVIGO DISTRIBUTION INC   *p 1398*
60 RUE CARIGNAN, VICTORIAVILLE, QC, G6P 4Z6
SIC 5141

PROVIGO GAGNON   *p 1088*
See *SUPERMARCHE A R G INC*

PROVIGO GAGNON   *p 1110*
See *SUPER MARCHE FRONTENAC INC*

PROVIGO LAROUCHE FLEURIMONT   *p 1369*

See *ALIMENTATION DANIEL LAROUCHE INC*

PROVIGO LE MARCHE   *p 1385*
See *LOBLAWS INC*

PROVIGO LE MARCHE LONGUEUIL   *p 1146*
See *PROVIGO DISTRIBUTION INC*

PROVIGO MARC BOUGIE   *p 1168*
See *ALIMENTATION MARC BOUGIE INC*

PROVIGO MARCHE   *p 1077*
See *2037247 ONTARIO LIMITED*

PROVIGO MONT BLEU   *p 1107*
See *PROVIGO DISTRIBUTION INC*

PROVIGO ST-GERMAIN   *p 1376*
See *P.R. ST-GERMAIN INC*

PROVIGO THOMASSIN, STEPHANE   *p 1271*
See *ALIMENTATION THOMASSIN, STEPHANE INC*

PROVIMI CANADA ULC   *p 1377*
557 CH DE SAINT-DOMINIQUE BUREAU 1, ST-VALERIEN, QC, J0H 2B0
(450) 549-2629   *SIC 5122*

PROVINCE DU QUEBEC DE L'UNION CANADIENNE DES MONIALES DE L'ORDRE DE SAINTE-URSULE   *p 1275*
20 RUE DES DAMES-URSULINES, QUEBEC, QC, G2B 2V1
(418) 692-2523   *SIC 8661*

PROVINCE ELECTRIC SUPPLY LTD   *p 742*
425 SUPERIOR BLVD UNIT 6, MISSISSAUGA, ON, L5T 2W5
(905) 795-1795   *SIC 5063*

PROVINCE OF NEW BRUNSWICK   *p 398*
505 RUE DU COLLEGE, DIEPPE, NB, E1A 6X2
(506) 856-2200   *SIC 8221*

PROVINCE OF NEW BRUNSWICK   *p 405*
80 UNIVERSITY AVE, MIRAMICHI, NB, E1N 0C6
(506) 778-6000   *SIC 8221*

PROVINCE OF NEWFOUNDLAND & LABRADOR   *p 434*
BOND RD, WHITBOURNE, NL, A0B 3K0
(709) 759-2471   *SIC 8322*

PROVINCE OF PEI   *p 1039*
115 DACON GROVE LANE, CHARLOTTETOWN, PE, C1A 7N5
(902) 368-5400   *SIC 8063*

PROVINCE OF PEI   *p 1039*
60 RIVERSIDE DR, CHARLOTTETOWN, PE, C1A 8T5
(902) 894-2111   *SIC 8062*

PROVINCE OF PEI   *p 1039*
94 EUSTON ST, CHARLOTTETOWN, PE, C1A 1W4
(902) 368-6300   *SIC 6111*

PROVINCE OF PEI   *p 1040*
165 JOHN YEO DR, CHARLOTTETOWN, PE, C1E 3J3
(902) 368-4790   *SIC 8059*

PROVINCE OF PEI   *p 1040*
200 BEACH GROVE RD, CHARLOTTETOWN, PE, C1E 1L3
(902) 368-6750   *SIC 8051*

PROVINCE OF PEI   *p 1042*
20 MACPHEE AVE, SOURIS, PE, C0A 2B0
(902) 687-7090   *SIC 8051*

PROVINCE OF PEI   *p 1043*
15 FRANK MELLISH ST, SUMMERSIDE, PE, C1N 0H3
(902) 888-8310   *SIC 8052*

PROVINCIAL AEROSPACE LTD   *p 428*
HANGAR NO 1 ST JOHN'S INTERNATIONAL AIRPORT, ST JOHN'S, NL, A1A 5B5
(709) 576-1800   *SIC 3721*

PROVINCIAL AIRLINES   *p 428*
See *PAL AIRLINES LTD.*

PROVINCIAL AIRLINES LIMITED   *p 429*
HANGAR NO 4 ST JOHN'S INTERNATIONAL AIRPORT, ST. JOHN'S, NL, A1A 5B5
(709) 576-1800   *SIC 4512*

PROVINCIAL BANDAG TIRES LTD   *p 399*
410 RUE ST-FRANCOIS, EDMUNDSTON, NB, E3V 1G6

---

(506) 735-6136 *SIC* 7534
PROVINCIAL CAPITAL CORP *p* 699
1611 BRITANNIA RD E, MISSISSAUGA,
ON, L4W 1S5
(905) 670-7077 *SIC* 7519
PROVINCIAL CHRYSLER LTD *p* 1020
1001 PROVINCIAL RD, WINDSOR, ON,
N8W 5V9
(519) 250-5500 *SIC* 5511
PROVINCIAL ELECTRICAL SERVICES INC
p 110
7429 72A ST NW, EDMONTON, AB, T6B
1Z3
(780) 490-1183 *SIC* 1731
PROVINCIAL FRUIT CO. LIMITED *p* 572
165 THE QUEENSWAY, ETOBICOKE, ON,
M8Y 1H8
(416) 259-5001 *SIC* 5148
**PROVINCIAL HEALTH SERVICES AU-
THORITY** *p*
275
13750 96 AVE, SURREY, BC, V3V 1Z2
(604) 930-2098 *SIC* 8069
**PROVINCIAL HEALTH SERVICES AU-
THORITY** *p*
293
570 7TH AVE W SUITE 100, VANCOUVER,
BC, V5Z 4S6
(604) 707-5800 *SIC* 8731
**PROVINCIAL HEALTH SERVICES AU-
THORITY** *p*
293
600 10TH AVE W, VANCOUVER, BC, V5Z
4E6
(604) 675-8251 *SIC* 8069
**PROVINCIAL HEALTH SERVICES AU-
THORITY** *p*
327
1380 BURRARD ST SUITE 700, VANCOU-
VER, BC, V6Z 2H3
(604) 675-7400 *SIC* 8099
**PROVINCIAL HEALTH SERVICES AU-
THORITY** *p*
333
2410 LEE AVE, VICTORIA, BC, V8R 6V5
(250) 519-5500 *SIC* 8399
**PROVINCIAL INDUSTRIAL ROOFING AND
SHEET METAL COMPANY LIMITED** *p* 557
166 BOWES RD, CONCORD, ON, L4K 1J6
(905) 669-2569 *SIC* 1761
PROVINCIAL INVESTMENTS INC *p* 431
88 KENMOUNT RD, ST. JOHN'S, NL, A1B
3R1
(709) 758-0002 *SIC* 6719
PROVINCIAL LAB FOR PUBLIC HEALTH *p*
42
3030 HOSPITAL DR NW, CALGARY, AB,
T2N 4W4
(403) 944-1200 *SIC* 8071
PROVINCIAL LONG TERM CARE INC *p* 620
100 QUEEN ST E, HENSALL, ON, N0M 1X0
(519) 262-2830 *SIC* 8051
**PROVINCIAL NURSING HOME LIMITED
PARTNERSHIP** *p* 879
100 JAMES ST, SEAFORTH, ON, N0K 1W0
(519) 527-0030 *SIC* 8051
PROVINCIAL PROTECTION INC *p* 991
36 LISGAR ST SUITE 623W, TORONTO,
ON, M6J 0C7
(888) 508-6277 *SIC* 7389
PROVINCIAL READY MIX INC *p* 427
36 PRINCE WILLIAM DR, PLACENTIA, NL,
A0B 2Y0
(709) 227-2727 *SIC* 1522
PROVINCIAL SIGN SERVICE LIMITED *p*
845
1655 FELDSPAR CRT, PICKERING, ON,
L1W 3R7
(905) 837-1791 *SIC* 3993
PROVINCIAL SIGN SYSTEMS *p* 845
See PROVINCIAL SIGN SERVICE LIMITED
PROVINCIAL STORE FIXTURES LTD *p* 712
910 CENTRAL PKY W, MISSISSAUGA, ON,
L5C 2V5

(905) 564-6700 *SIC* 2431
PROVINCIAL TIRE DISTRIBUTORS INC *p*
488
466 WELHAM RD, BARRIE, ON, L4N 8Z4
(705) 726-5510 *SIC* 5014
PROVINCIAL TRAILER RENTALS *p* 699
See PROVINCIAL CAPITAL CORP
PROVISIONS ROCK ISLAND INC *p* 1378
14 CH DE FAIRFAX RR 1, STANSTEAD,
QC, J0B 3E0
(819) 876-7262 *SIC* 5411
PROVO LTD *p* 1033
620 ROWNTREE DAIRY RD, WOOD-
BRIDGE, ON, L4L 5T8
(905) 851-8520 *SIC* 5051
PROVOST HEALTH CENTRE *p* 153
See ALBERTA HEALTH SERVICES
PROWATT INC *p* 1115
2361 RUE BAUMAN BUREAU 1, JON-
QUIERE, QC, G7S 5A9
(418) 548-1184 *SIC* 1731
PROWEST SHIPPING & PACKAGING LTD *p*
102
21635 115 AVE NW, EDMONTON, AB, T5S
2N6
(780) 455-5026 *SIC* 7389
PROXIMED *p* 1346
*See CORPORATION GROUPE PHARMES-
SOR*
PROXIMITY CANADA, DIV OF *p* 928
See BBDO CANADA CORP
PROXIN *p* 1322
*See PHARMACIE BEDARD LYNE PHAR-
MACIENNE INC*
PRSD *p* 152
See PEACE RIVER SCHOOL DIVISION 10
PRT GROWING SERVICES LTD *p* 308
355 BURRARD ST SUITE 410, VANCOU-
VER, BC, V6C 2G8
SIC 7389
PRT GROWING SERVICES LTD *p* 335
1006 FORT ST UNIT 101, VICTORIA, BC,
V8V 3K4
(250) 381-1404 *SIC* 2068
**PRUDENT BENEFITS ADMINISTRATION
SERVICES INC** *p* 587
61 INTERNATIONAL BLVD SUITE 110,
ETOBICOKE, ON, M9W 6K4
(416) 674-8581 *SIC* 8748
PRUDENTIAL ELITE REALTY *p* 694
See ELITE REALTY T. W. INC
PRUDENTIAL KELOWNA PROPERTY *p* 222
See INTERNET REALTY LTD
PRUDENTIAL RELOCATION CANADA LTD
p 770
5700 YONGE ST SUITE 1110, NORTH
YORK, ON, M2M 4K2
SIC 7389
PRUDENTIAL SADIE MORANIS REALTY *p*
777
*See PRUDENTIAL SADIE MORANIS RE-
ALTY LIMITED*
**PRUDENTIAL SADIE MORANIS REALTY
LIMITED** *p* 777
35 LESMILL RD, NORTH YORK, ON, M3B
2T3
(416) 960-9995 *SIC* 6531
PRUDENTIAL STEEL ULC *p* 18
8919 BARLOW TRAIL SE, CALGARY, AB,
T2C 2N7
(403) 279-4401 *SIC* 3312
PRUDENTIAL SUSSEX REALTY *p* 342
2397 MARINE DR, WEST VANCOUVER,
BC, V7V 1K9
(604) 913-4068 *SIC* 6531
PRUDENTIAL TRANSPORTATION LTD *p*
277
8138 128 ST UNIT 239, SURREY, BC, V3W
1R1
(604) 543-2147 *SIC* 4212
**PRYCON CUSTOM BUILDING & RENOVA-
TIONS INC** *p*
488
36 MORROW RD SUITE 100, BARRIE, ON,

L4N 3V8
(705) 739-0023 *SIC* 1541
PRYOR METALS LIMITED *p* 597
2683 FENTON RD, GLOUCESTER, ON,
K1T 3T8
(613) 822-0953 *SIC* 3469
PS INTERNATIONAL CANADA CORP *p*
1422
2595 E QUANCE ST SUITE 201, REGINA,
SK, S4V 2Y8
(306) 565-3904 *SIC* 6799
PS TRAVEL INSURANCE BROKERS INC *p*
1033
8001 WESTON RD SUITE 300, WOOD-
BRIDGE, ON, L4L 9C8
(416) 798-8001 *SIC* 6411
PSA INSURANCE SERVICES, DIV OF *p* 801
See MAGNES GROUP INC, THE
PSB *p* 1112
See POISSON SALE GASPESIEN LTEE
PSB BOISJOLI S.E.N.R.C.L *p* 1155
3333 BOUL GRAHAM BUREAU 400,
MONT-ROYAL, QC, H3R 3L5
(514) 341-5511 *SIC* 8721
PSB INTERNATIONAL *p* 845
See LENBROOK INDUSTRIES LIMITED
PSC NATURAL FOODS LTD *p* 340
2924 JACKLIN RD SUITE 117, VICTORIA,
BC, V9B 3Y5
(250) 386-3880 *SIC* 5141
PSC-POWER SOURCE CANADA LTD *p* 806
8400 PARKHILL DR, OAKVILLE, ON, L9T
5V7
(289) 851-6690 *SIC* 5084
PSEUDIO *p* 459
See SHERLOCK CLOTHING LIMITED
PSHCP ADMINISTRATION AUTHORITY *p*
824
100 SPARKS ST SUITE 1010, OTTAWA,
ON, K1P 5B7
(613) 565-1762 *SIC* 6411
PSI ENGINEERING *p* 717
See PSI PERIPHERAL SOLUTIONS INC
PSI PERIPHERAL SOLUTIONS INC *p* 717
3535 LAIRD RD UNIT 9, MISSISSAUGA,
ON, L5L 5Z4
(905) 858-3600 *SIC* 5045
PSI PROLEW INC *p* 1252
975 AV SELKIRK, POINTE-CLAIRE, QC,
H9R 4S4
(514) 697-7867 *SIC* 5084
PSION INC *p* 1341
7575 RTE TRANSCANADIENNE BUREAU
500, SAINT-LAURENT, QC, H4T 1V6
SIC 3571
PSION TEKLOGIX *p* 728
*See ZEBRA TECHNOLGIES CANADA,
ULC*
PSL PARTITION SYSTEMS LTD *p* 123
1105 70 AVE NW, EDMONTON, AB, T6P
1N5
(780) 465-0001 *SIC* 3275
PSP USA LLC *p* 853
35 EAST BEAVER CREEK RD UNIT 6,
RICHMOND HILL, ON, L4B 1B3
(905) 764-1121 *SIC* 5023
PT ENTERPRISES INC *p* 1040
54 HILLSTROM AVE, CHARLOTTETOWN,
PE, C1E 2C6
(902) 628-6900 *SIC* 3556
PT HEALTH *p* 613
See PT HEALTHCARE SOLUTIONS CORP
PT HEALTHCARE SOLUTIONS CORP *p*
613
70 FRID ST UNIT 2, HAMILTON, ON, L8P
4M4
(877) 734-9887 *SIC* 8049
PT INDUSTRIAL ELECTRIC CO *p* 548
See 372103 ONTARIO LTD
PT PAPERTECH INC *p* 239
219 1ST ST E, NORTH VANCOUVER, BC,
V7L 1B4
(604) 990-1600 *SIC* 5084
PTC AUTOMOTIVE LTD *p* 921

777 DUNDAS ST E, TORONTO, ON, M4M
0E2
(416) 530-1366 *SIC* 5511
PTI *p* 206
See P.E.T. PROCESSING INC
PTI *p* 557
See PACKAGING TECHNOLOGIES INC
PTI *p* 1416
*See PARTNER TECHNOLOGIES INCOR-
PORATED*
PTMAA *p* 90
*See PETROLEUM TANK MANAGEMENT
ASSOCIATION OF ALBERTA*
PTW ENERGY SERVICES LTD *p* 57
355 4 AVE SW SUITE 600 CALGARY
PLACE II, CALGARY, AB, T2P 0J1
(403) 956-8600 *SIC* 6712
PUBCO PRODUITS INTERNATIONALS INC
p 1059
32 BOUL DE LA SEIGNEURIE E,
BLAINVILLE, QC, J7C 3V5
(450) 433-4272 *SIC* 3083
**PUBL TRANS CANADA ADVERTISING
(QUEBEC) LTD** *p* 1142
625 BOUL GUIMOND, LONGUEUIL, QC,
J4G 1L9
SIC 5199
**PUBLIC GENERAL HOSPITAL SOCIETY
OF CHATHAM, THE** *p* 542
80 GRAND AVE W SUITE 301, CHATHAM,
ON, N7L 1B7
(519) 352-6400 *SIC* 8062
**PUBLIC GUARDIAN TRUSTEE OF
SASKATCHEWAN** *p* 1418
1871 SMITH ST SUITE 100, REGINA, SK,
S4P 4W4
(306) 787-5424 *SIC* 8748
**PUBLIC GUARDIAN AND TRUSTEE OF
BRITISH COLUMBIA** *p* 308
808 HASTINGS ST W SUITE 700, VAN-
COUVER, BC, V6C 3L3
(604) 660-4444 *SIC* 6733
PUBLIC HISTORY INC *p* 834
331 COOPER ST SUITE 500, OTTAWA,
ON, K2P 0G5
(613) 236-0713 *SIC* 8732
PUBLIC METAL SUPPLY DIV OF *p* 883
See SAM ADELSTEIN & CO. LIMITED
PUBLIC OUTREACH CONSULTANCY INC *p*
299
207 HASTINGS ST W SUITE 1005, VAN-
COUVER, BC, V6B 1H7
(604) 800-3730 *SIC* 7389
PUBLIC SERVICE ALLIANCE OF CANADA
p 834
233 GILMOUR ST SUITE 402, OTTAWA,
ON, K2P 0P2
(613) 560-2560 *SIC* 8631
PUBLIC SERVICE PENSION PLAN *p* 125
5103 WINDERMERE BLVD SW, EDMON-
TON, AB, T6W 0S9
(800) 358-0840 *SIC* 6371
**PUBLIC SERVICES HEALTH AND SAFETY
ASSOCIATION** *p* 773
4950 YONGE ST SUITE 1800, NORTH
YORK, ON, M2N 6K1
(416) 250-2131 *SIC* 8099
PUBLIC STORAGE *p* 720
*See CANADIAN MINI-WAREHOUSE
PROPERTIES COMPANY*
PUBLIC TRUSTEE OFFICE *p* 379
155 CARLTON ST SUITE 500, WINNIPEG,
MB, R3C 5R9
(204) 945-2700 *SIC* 6733
**PUBLIC UTILITIES COMMISSION FOR THE
MUNICIPALITY OF CHATHAM-KENT** *p* 543
320 QUEEN ST, CHATHAM, ON, N7M 2H6
(519) 352-6300 *SIC* 4911
PUBLICATIONS HANSON *p* 1209
See 9069-5057 QUEBEC INC
PUBLICIS CANADA INC *p* 940
111 QUEEN ST E SUITE 200, TORONTO,
ON, M5C 1S2
(416) 925-7733 *SIC* 7311

PUBLICIS CANADA INC   p 1184
358 RUE BEAUBIEN O BUREAU 500, MONTREAL, QC, H2V 4S6
(514) 285-1414   SIC 7311

PUBLICIS MEDIA CANADA INC   p 930
175 BLOOR ST E 9TH FLOOR, TORONTO, ON, M4W 3R8
(437) 222-5200   SIC 7311

PUBLICITE MALGA INC   p 1111
625 RUE GEORGES-CROS, GRANBY, QC, J2J 1B4
(450) 378-4448   SIC 5199

PUBLICITE TAXI MONTREAL INC   p 1215
1600 BOUL RENE-LEVESQUE O BUREAU 1200, MONTREAL, QC, H3H 1P9
(514) 935-6375   SIC 7311

PUBNICO TRAWLERS LIMITED   p 461
155 HWY 3, LOWER EAST PUBNICO, NS, B0W 2A0
(902) 762-3202   SIC 5141

PUC SERVICES INC   p 862
765 QUEEN ST E, SAULT STE. MARIE, ON, P6A 2A8
(705) 759-6500   SIC 4971

PUDDIFOOT, W. H. LTD   p 324
1566 RAND AVE, VANCOUVER, BC, V6P 3G2
(604) 263-0971   SIC 5023

PUDDISTER TRADING COMPANY LIMITED   p 433
23 SPRINGDALE ST, ST. JOHN'S, NL, A1E 2P9
(709) 722-4000   SIC 4424

PUDDY BROS. LIMITED   p 735
7120 EDWARDS BLVD, MISSISSAUGA, ON, L5S 1Z1
(289) 541-7875   SIC 2015

PUGABOOS   p 242
See SUNTECH OPTICS INC

PUGLIA, P. M. SALES LTD   p 1411
1350 MAIN ST N, MOOSE JAW, SK, S6H 8B9
(306) 693-0888   SIC 5399

PUGLISEVICH CREWS & SERVICES LIMITED   p 429
611 TORBAY RD UNIT 1, ST. JOHN'S, NL, A1A 5J1
(709) 722-2744   SIC 7361

PUGWASH HOLDINGS LTD   p 102
11248 170 ST NW, EDMONTON, AB, T5S 2X1
(780) 484-6342   SIC 5944

PULAARVIK KABLU FRIENDSHIP CENTRE   p 472
GD, RANKIN INLET, NU, X0C 0G0
(867) 645-2600   SIC 8399

PULP & FIBER INC   p 991
822 RICHMOND ST W SUITE 400, TORONTO, ON, M6J 1C9
(416) 361-0030   SIC 8743

PULTRALL INC   p 1383
700 9E RUE N, THETFORD MINES, QC, G6G 6Z5
(418) 335-3202   SIC 5085

PUMA CANADA INC   p 998
175 BOUL GALAXY SUITE 201, TORONTO, ON, M9W 0C9
(416) 481-7862   SIC 5091

PUMP HOUSE BREWERY LTD   p 406
131 MILL RD, MONCTON, NB, E1A 6R1
(506) 854-2537   SIC 2082

PUMPCRETE CORPORATION   p 759
6000 PROGRESS ST, NIAGARA FALLS, ON, L2G 0C4
(905) 354-3855   SIC 7353

PUMPING SERVICES, DIV OF   p 158
See BAKER HUGHES CANADA COMPANY

PUMPS & PRESSURE INC   p 156
7018 JOHNSTONE DR, RED DEER, AB, T4P 3Y6
(403) 340-3666   SIC 5084

PUNA OPERATIONS INC   p 329

1055 DUNSMUIR ST, VANCOUVER, BC, V7X 1G4
(604) 689-3846   SIC 1031

PUNJAB MILK FOODS INC   p 273
6308 146 ST, SURREY, BC, V3S 3A4
(604) 594-9190   SIC 2021

PUPO'S SUPERMARKET LIMITED   p 1012
195 MAPLE AVE, WELLAND, ON, L3C 5G6
(905) 735-5615   SIC 5411

PUR BRANDS INC   p 287
2642 NOOTKA ST, VANCOUVER, BC, V5M 3M5
(604) 299-5045   SIC 5149

PUR COMPANY INC, THE   p 784
23 KODIAK CRES, NORTH YORK, ON, M3J 3E5
(416) 941-7557   SIC 5145

PURATOS CANADA INC   p 742
520 SLATE DR, MISSISSAUGA, ON, L5T 0A1
(905) 362-3668   SIC 2052

PURDUE PHARMA   p 845
575 GRANITE CRT, PICKERING, ON, L1W 3W8
(905) 420-6400   SIC 2834

PURDY'S CHOCOLATES   p 291
See PURDY, R.C. CHOCOLATES LTD

PURDY, R.C. CHOCOLATES LTD   p 291
8330 CHESTER ST, VANCOUVER, BC, V5X 3Y7
(604) 454-2777   SIC 2066

PURE BEAUTY   p 679
See BEAUTY EXPRESS CANADA INC

PURE CANADIAN GAMING CORP   p 106
12464 153RD ST, EDMONTON, AB, T5V 3C5
(780) 424-9467   SIC 7999

PURE CANADIAN GAMING CORP   p 112
7055 ARGYLL RD NW, EDMONTON, AB, T6C 4A5
(780) 465-5377   SIC 7999

PURE CANADIAN GAMING CORP   p 142
1251 3 AVE S, LETHBRIDGE, AB, T1J 0K1
(403) 381-9467   SIC 7999

PURE ENERGY MINERALS LIMITED   p 316
1111 GEORGIA ST SUITE 1400, VANCOUVER, BC, V6E 3M3
(604) 608-6611   SIC 1479

PURE ENERGY REIKI   p 81
16 WILD HAY DR, DEVON, AB, T9G 1S4
(780) 405-7606   SIC 4924

PURE FREEDOM YYOGA WELLNESS INC   p 293
575 8TH AVE W SUITE 500, VANCOUVER, BC, V5Z 0C4
(604) 736-6002   SIC 7999

PURE HOTHOUSE FOODS INC   p 644
459 HIGHWAY 77, LEAMINGTON, ON, N8H 3V6
(519) 326-8444   SIC 5148

PURE INDUSTRIAL REAL ESTATE TRUST   p 956
121 KING ST W SUITE 2100, TORONTO, ON, M5H 3T9
(416) 479-8590   SIC 6722

PURE METAL GALVANIZING, DIV OF   p 515
See PMT INDUSTRIES LIMITED

PURE METAL GALVANIZING, DIV OF   p 587
See PMT INDUSTRIES LIMITED

PURE MULTI-FAMILY REIT LP   p 308
925 GEORGIA ST W SUITE 910, VANCOUVER, BC, V6C 3L2
(604) 681-5959   SIC 6531

PURE TECHNOLOGIES LTD   p 65
705 11 AVE SW SUITE 300, CALGARY, AB, T2R 0E3
(403) 266-6794   SIC 7371

PURESOURCE INC   p 604
5068 WHITELAW RD UNIT 5, GUELPH, ON, N1H 6J3
(519) 837-2140   SIC 5149

PURETAP WATER DISTILLERS LTD   p 742
950 VERBENA RD, MISSISSAUGA, ON, L5T 1T6

(905) 670-7400   SIC 5149

PUREWAL BLUEBERRY FARMS LTD p 244
13753 HALE RD, PITT MEADOWS, BC, V3Y 1Z1
SIC 0171

PUREWOOD INCORPORATED   p 510
341 HEART LAKE RD, BRAMPTON, ON, L6W 3K8
(905) 874-9797   SIC 1751

PURIBEC INC   p 1285
177 RUE DE L'EVECHE O, RIMOUSKI, QC, G5L 4H8
(418) 722-7326   SIC 5074

PURITY FACTORIES LIMITED   p 433
96 BLACKMARSH RD, ST. JOHN'S, NL, A1E 1S8
(709) 579-2035   SIC 2051

PURITY LIFE HEALTH PRODUCTS LP   p 473
6 COMMERCE CRES, ACTON, ON, L7J 2X3
(519) 853-3511   SIC 5122

PURKINJE INC   p 1211
614 RUE SAINT-JACQUES BUREAU 200, MONTREAL, QC, H3C 1E2
(514) 355-0888   SIC 5045

PURNELL ENERGY SERVICES LTD p 133
10502 123 ST, GRANDE PRAIRIE, AB, T8V 8B8
(587) 259-9600   SIC 4911

PUROLATOR COURIER   p 526
See PUROLATOR INC

PUROLATOR FREIGHT   p 587
See PUROLATOR INC

PUROLATOR HOLDINGS LTD   p 732
5995 AVEBURY RD SUITE 100, MISSISSAUGA, ON, L5R 3T8
(905) 712-1251   SIC 4731

PUROLATOR INC   p 25
30 AERO DR NE, CALGARY, AB, T2E 8Z9
(403) 516-6200   SIC 4731

PUROLATOR INC   p 121
3104 97 ST NW, EDMONTON, AB, T6N 1K3
(780) 408-2420   SIC 7389

PUROLATOR INC   p 431
16 DUFFY PL, ST. JOHN'S, NL, A1B 4M5
(709) 579-5671   SIC 4731

PUROLATOR INC   p 448
220 JOSEPH ZATZMAN DR, DARTMOUTH, NS, B3B 1P4
(902) 468-1611   SIC 7389

PUROLATOR INC   p 526
3455 MAINWAY, BURLINGTON, ON, L7M 1A9
(905) 336-3230   SIC 4731

PUROLATOR INC   p 557
1550 CREDITSTONE RD, CONCORD, ON, L4K 5N1
(905) 660-6007   SIC 7389

PUROLATOR INC   p 587
1151 MARTIN GROVE RD SUITE 7, ETOBICOKE, ON, M9W 0C1
(416) 614-0300   SIC 4731

PUROLATOR INC   p 587
62 VULCAN ST, ETOBICOKE, ON, M9W 1L2
(416) 241-4496   SIC 4731

PUROLATOR INC   p 606
147 MASSEY RD, GUELPH, ON, N1K 1B2
(905) 660-6007   SIC 4731

PUROLATOR INC   p 608
21 WARRINGTON ST, HAMILTON, ON, L8E 3L1
(888) 744-7123   SIC 7389

PUROLATOR INC   p 732
5995 AVEBURY RD, MISSISSAUGA, ON, L5R 3P9
(905) 712-1084   SIC 4731

PUROLATOR INC   p 742
6520 KESTREL RD, MISSISSAUGA, ON, L5T 1Z6
(905) 565-9306   SIC 7389

PUROLATOR INC   p 747
9300 AIRPORT RD, MOUNT HOPE, ON,

L0R 1W0
(905) 679-5722   SIC 7389

PUROLATOR INC   p 795
1100 ARROW RD, NORTH YORK, ON, M9M 2Z1
(416) 241-4496   SIC 4731

PUROLATOR INC   p 845
1075 SQUIRES BEACH RD, PICKERING, ON, L1W 3S3
(888) 744-7123   SIC 4731

PUROLATOR INC   p 876
90 SILVER STAR BLVD, SCARBOROUGH, ON, M1V 4V8
(888) 744-7123   SIC 4731

PUROLATOR INC   p 921
20 MORSE ST, TORONTO, ON, M4M 2P6
(416) 461-9031   SIC 4731

PUROLATOR INC   p 1020
4520 NORTH SERVICE RD E, WINDSOR, ON, N8W 5X2
(519) 945-1363   SIC 7389

PUROLATOR INC   p 1067
1330 RUE GRAHAM-BELL, BOUCHERVILLE, QC, J4B 6H5
(450) 641-2430   SIC 4731

PUROLATOR INC   p 1116
3479 RUE DE L'ENERGIE, JONQUIERE, QC, G7X 0C1
(418) 695-1235   SIC 7389

PUROLATOR INC   p 1277
7000 RUE ARMAND-VIAU, QUEBEC, QC, G2C 2C4
(888) 744-7123   SIC 4731

PUROLATOR INC   p 1330
1305 RUE TEES, SAINT-LAURENT, QC, H4R 2A7
(514) 337-6710   SIC 4731

PUROLATOR INC   p 1362
2005 BOUL DAGENAIS O, SAINTE-ROSE, QC, H7L 5V1
(450) 963-3050   SIC 7389

PUROLATOR INC   p 1420
702 TORONTO ST, REGINA, SK, S4R 8L1
(306) 359-0313   SIC 7389

PUROLATOR LOGISTICS   p 732
See PUROLATOR INC

PURVES REDMOND LIMITED   p 966
70 UNIVERSITY AVE SUITE 400, TORONTO, ON, M5J 2M4
(416) 362-4246   SIC 6411

PURVIS HOLDINGS LTD   p 86
11420 107 AVE NW, EDMONTON, AB, T5H 0Y5
(780) 423-4330   SIC 6712

PUSATERI'S FINE FOODS   p 976
See PUSATERI'S LIMITED

PUSATERI'S LIMITED   p 788
1539 AVENUE RD, NORTH YORK, ON, M5M 3X4
(416) 785-9124   SIC 5411

PUSATERI'S LIMITED   p 976
77 BLOOR ST W SUITE 1803, TORONTO, ON, M5S 1M2
(416) 785-9100   SIC 5411

PUSHOR MITCHELL LLP   p 222
1665 ELLIS ST SUITE 301, KELOWNA, BC, V1Y 2B3
(250) 869-1100   SIC 8111

PUTZER, M. HORNBY LIMITED   p 620
7314 SIXTH LINE, HORNBY, ON, L0P 1E0
(905) 878-7226   SIC 0181

PVA CONSULTING GROUP   p 1060
See GROUPE CONSEIL PARISELLA VINCELLI, ASSOCIES INC

PVH CANADA, INC   p 744
775 BRITANNIA RD W UNIT 1, MISSISSAUGA, ON, L5V 2Y1
(905) 826-9645   SIC 5136

PVH CANADA, INC   p 983
555 RICHMOND ST W SUITE 1106, TORONTO, ON, M5V 3B1
(416) 309-7200   SIC 5136

PVH CANADA, INC   p 1341
7445 CH DE LA COTE-DE-LIESSE, SAINT-

LAURENT, QC, H4T 1G2
(514) 278-6000   *SIC* 5136
PVK DRUGS LIMITED   *p* 894
5710 MAIN ST UNIT 3, STOUFFVILLE, ON,
L4A 8A9
(905) 640-2700   *SIC* 5912
**PVNC CATHOLIC DISTRICT SCHOOL
BOARD**   *p* 841
*See   PETERBOROUGH   VICTORIA
NORTHUMBERLAND AND CLARINGTON
CATHOLIC DISTRICT SCHOOL BOARD*
PVS CHEMICALS   *p* 592
See FANCHEM LTD
PVS CONTRACTORS INC   *p* 883
113   CUSHMAN   RD   UNIT   5,   ST
CATHARINES, ON, L2M 6S9
(905) 984-5414   *SIC* 1623
PWC   *p* 655
See PRICEWATERHOUSECOOPERS LLP
PWC   *p* 966
See PRICEWATERHOUSECOOPERS LLP
PWC DEBT SOLUTIONS   *p* 454
See PRICEWATERHOUSECOOPERS LLP
PWC MANAGEMENT SERVICES LP *p* 270
10190 152A ST 3 FL, SURREY, BC, V3R
1J7
(604) 806-7000   *SIC* 8721
PWO CANADA INCORPORATED   *p* 642
255 MCBRINE DR, KITCHENER, ON, N2R
1G7
(519) 893-6880   *SIC* 3469
PWS ONTARIO LTD   *p* 793
155 FENMAR DR, NORTH YORK, ON, M9L
1M7
(416) 665-8377   *SIC* 4953
PYE CONSTRUCTION LTD   *p* 341
1647 LITTLE RD, VICTORIA, BC, V9E 2E3
(250) 384-2662   *SIC* 1541
PYLON ELECTRONICS INC   *p* 742
6355 DANVILLE RD UNIT 10, MISSIS-
SAUGA, ON, L5T 2L4
(905) 362-1395   *SIC* 7629
PYRAMID CORPORATION   *p* 144
6304 56 ST, LLOYDMINSTER, AB, T9V 3T7
(780) 875-6644   *SIC* 1731
PYRAMID FARMS LIMITED   *p* 645
209 ERIE ST N, LEAMINGTON, ON, N8H
3A5
(519) 326-4989   *SIC* 0181
**PYRAMID PROCESS FABRICATORS COR-
PORATION**   *p*
149
2308 8 ST, NISKU, AB, T9E 7Z2
(780) 955-2708   *SIC* 3312
PYRO-AIR LTEE   *p* 1076
2575 BOUL FORD, CHATEAUGUAY, QC,
J6J 4Z2
(450) 691-3460   *SIC* 1711
PYRO-AIR LTEE   *p* 1148
2301 RUE PRINCIPALE O, MAGOG, QC,
J1X 0J4
(819) 847-2014   *SIC* 1711
PYROSPEC   *p* 1062
See PROTECTION INCENDIE VIKING INC
PYROTECH BEI INC   *p* 1362
1455 RUE MICHELIN, SAINTE-ROSE, QC,
H7L 4S2
(450) 967-1515   *SIC* 6331
PYROTENAX   *p* 999
See NVENT THERMAL CANADA LTD
PYTHIAN GROUP INC, THE   *p* 829
319 MCRAE AVE UNIT 700, OTTAWA, ON,
K1Z 0B9
(613) 565-8696   *SIC* 7371
PYXIS REAL ESTATE EQUITIES INC *p* 940
95 KING ST E SUITE 201, TORONTO, ON,
M5C 1G4
(416) 815-0201   *SIC* 5311

Q

Q CONTACTS   *p* 237
640 CLARKSON ST, NEW WESTMINSTER,
BC, V3M 1C8
(604) 717-4500   *SIC* 7389

Q M PLASTICS, DIV OF   *p* 1017
See QUALITY MODELS LIMITED
Q'MAX SOLUTIONS INC   *p* 57
585 8 AVE SW SUITE 1210, CALGARY, AB,
T2P 1G1
(403) 269-2242   *SIC* 1389
Q-LINE TRUCKING LTD   *p* 1429
101 WURTZ AVE, SASKATOON, SK, S7K
3J7
(306) 651-3540   *SIC* 4213
Q-PHARM INC   *p* 536
180 WERLICH DR, CAMBRIDGE, ON, N1T
1N6
(519) 650-9850   *SIC* 7389
Q2 ARTIFICIAL LIFT SERVICES ULC *p* 156
7883 EDGAR INDUSTRIAL WAY, RED
DEER, AB, T4P 3R2
(403) 343-8802   *SIC* 5082
Q4 ARCHITECTS   *p* 788
See QUADRA DESIGN STUDIOS INC
Q4 INC   *p* 983
A-469 KING ST W, TORONTO, ON, M5V
1K4
(416) 626-7829   *SIC* 7374
Q9 NETWORKS   *p* 969
*See COMPAGNIE DE TELEPHONE BELL
DU CANADA OU BELL CANADA, LA*
QA CONSULTANTS   *p* 770
See PLAZA CONSULTING INC
QA LABS, DIV OF   *p* 300
See USTRI CANADA INC
QARROT   *p* 1184
See FRIENDEFI INC
QBD COOLING SYSTEMS INC   *p* 510
31 BRAMSTEELE RD, BRAMPTON, ON,
L6W 3K6
(905) 459-0709   *SIC* 1711
QBD MODULAR SYSTEMS INC   *p* 510
31 BRAMSTEELE RD, BRAMPTON, ON,
L6W 3K6
(905) 459-0709   *SIC* 1711
QCE CANADA (ONTARIO) LTD   *p* 648
56 R2, LOMBARDY, ON, K0G 1L0
(905) 424-4403   *SIC* 1711
**QEII HEALTH SCIENCES CENTRE FOUN-
DATION**   *p*
454
*See QUEEN ELIZABETH II HEALTH SCI-
ENCES CENTRE FOUNDATION*
QHC   *p* 491
*See QUINTE HEALTHCARE CORPORA-
TION*
QIKIQTANI INUIT ASSOCIATION   *p* 472
GD, IQALUIT, NU, X0A 0H0
(867) 975-8400   *SIC* 8699
QINETIQ GROUP CANADA INC   *p* 147
1735 BRIER PARK RD NW UNIT 3,
MEDICINE HAT, AB, T1C 1V5
(403) 528-8782   *SIC* 3728
QINETIQ TARGET SYSTEMS   *p* 147
See QINETIQ GROUP CANADA INC
QIT - FER ET TITANE   *p* 1377
See RIO TINTO FER ET TITANE INC
QLOGITEK   *p* 586
See LOGITEK DATA SCIENCES LTD
**QM BEARINGS & POWER TRANSMISSION
LTD**   *p* 207
1511 DERWENT WAY SUITE 205, DELTA,
BC, V3M 6N4
(604) 521-7226   *SIC* 5084
QM ENVIRONMENTAL   *p* 717
See QM LP
QM LP   *p* 717
3580 LAIRD RD UNIT 1, MISSISSAUGA,
ON, L5L 5Z7
(416) 253-6000   *SIC* 1795
QMS COURIER   *p* 978
See 3119696 CANADA INC
QMX GOLD CORPORATION   *p* 956
65 QUEEN ST W SUITE 800, TORONTO,
ON, M5H 2M5
(416) 861-5899   *SIC* 1081
QMX GOLD CORPORATION   *p* 1391
1900 CH BRADOR, VAL-D'OR, QC, J9P

0A4
(819) 825-3412   *SIC* 1081
QNX SOFTWARE SYSTEMS LIMITED*p* 625
1001 FARRAR RD, KANATA, ON, K2K 0B3
(613) 591-0931   *SIC* 7372
QOC HEALTH INC   *p* 983
436 WELLINGTON ST W UNIT 601,
TORONTO, ON, M5V 1E3
(647) 725-9660   *SIC* 6321
QPS   *p* 587
See QPS EVALUATION SERVICES INC
QPS EVALUATION SERVICES INC   *p* 587
81 KELFIELD ST UNIT 8, ETOBICOKE, ON,
M9W 5A3
(416) 241-8857   *SIC* 7389
QRC LOGISTICS (1978) LTD   *p* 594
8020 FIFTH LINE, GEORGETOWN, ON,
L7G 0B8
(905) 791-9000   *SIC* 7389
QRX TECHNOLOGY GROUP   *p* 547
See 2172004 ONTARIO INC
QRX TECHNOLOGY GROUP INC   *p* 557
200 CONNIE CRES UNIT 4, CONCORD,
ON, L4K 1M1
(905) 738-1688   *SIC* 5112
QSG INC   *p* 1335
8102 RTE TRANSCANADIENNE, SAINT-
LAURENT, QC, H4S 1M5
(514) 744-1000   *SIC* 2759
QSI   *p* 615
See TARESCO LTD
QSI INTERIORS LTD   *p* 102
10240 180 ST NW, EDMONTON, AB, T5S
1E2
(780) 489-4462   *SIC* 1742
QSI INTERIORS LTD   *p* 366
120 TERRACON PL, WINNIPEG, MB, R2J
4G7
(204) 235-0710   *SIC* 1742
QSI INTERIORS LTD   *p* 368
975 THOMAS AVE UNIT 1, WINNIPEG, MB,
R2L 1P7
(204) 953-1200   *SIC* 1742
QSL CANADA INC   *p* 1259
961 BOUL CHAMPLAIN, QUEBEC, QC,
G1K 4J9
(418) 522-4701   *SIC* 4491
QSL QUEBEC INC   *p* 1138
765 RUE DE SAINT-ROMUALD, LEVIS, QC,
G6W 5M6
(418) 837-4664   *SIC* 8734
QTA CIRCUITS LTD   *p* 674
144 GIBSON DR, MARKHAM, ON, L3R 2Z3
(905) 477-4400   *SIC* 3672
QTRADE CANADA INC   *p* 329
505 BURRARD ST SUITE 1920, VANCOU-
VER, BC, V7X 1M6
(604) 605-4111   *SIC* 6211
QTRADE FINANCIAL GROUP   *p* 329
See QTRADE CANADA INC
QTRADE SECURITIES INC   *p* 329
505 BURRARD ST SUITE 1920, VANCOU-
VER, BC, V7X 1M6
(604) 605-4199   *SIC* 7389
QUAD CITY BUILDING MATERIALS LTD *p*
204
1901 MCPHEE RD, CRANBROOK, BC, V1C
7J2
(250) 426-6288   *SIC* 5251
QUAD LOGISTIX INC   *p* 505
5 PAGET RD, BRAMPTON, ON, L6T 5S2
(905) 789-6225   *SIC* 4225
QUADCO INC   *p* 1302
30 BOUL INDUSTRIEL, SAINT-EUSTACHE,
QC, J7R 5C1
(450) 623-3340   *SIC* 5082
QUADRA CHIMIE LTEE   *p* 1395
3901 RUE F.-X.-TESSIER, VAUDREUIL-
DORION, QC, J7V 5V5
(450) 424-0161   *SIC* 5169
QUADRA DESIGN STUDIOS INC   *p* 788
2171 AVENUE RD SUITE 302, NORTH
YORK, ON, M5M 4B4
(416) 322-6334   *SIC* 7389

QUADRA WOOD PRODUCTS LTD   *p* 175
34371 INDUSTRIAL WAY, ABBOTSFORD,
BC, V2S 7M6
(604) 854-1835   *SIC* 5031
QUADRAD MANUFACTURING   *p* 605
See LINAMAR CORPORATION
QUADRANT COSMETICS CORP   *p* 853
20 WEST BEAVER CREEK RD, RICH-
MOND HILL, ON, L4B 3L6
(416) 921-2913   *SIC* 5999
QUADRANT INDUSTRIES INC   *p* 557
1800 STEELES AVE W, CONCORD, ON.
L4K 2P3
(905) 761-9110   *SIC* 3499
QUADRAS INVESTMENT SERVICES LTD *p*
655
255 DUFFERIN AVE, LONDON, ON, N6A
4K1
(519) 435-4826   *SIC* 6282
**QUADREAL PROPERTY GROUP LIMITED
PARTNERSHIP**   *p* 308
666 BURRARD ST SUITE 800, VANCOU-
VER, BC, V6C 2X8
(604) 975-9500   *SIC* 6531
QUADRO ENGINEERING CORP   *p* 1011
613 COLBY DR, WATERLOO, ON, N2V 1A1
(226) 270-6017   *SIC* 3541
QUALI DESSERTS INC   *p* 1166
5067 RUE ONTARIO E, MONTREAL, QC,
H1V 3V2
(514) 259-2415   *SIC* 2051
QUALI-T-FAB   *p* 1068
See QUALI-T-GROUP ULC
QUALI-T-GROUP ULC   *p* 1068
22 BOUL DE L'AEROPORT, BROMONT,
QC, J2L 1S6
(450) 534-2032   *SIC* 3446
**QUALICARE HEALTH SERVICES CORPO-
RATION**   *p*
166
25 ERIN RIDGE RD, ST. ALBERT, AB, T8N
7K8
(780) 458-3044   *SIC* 8051
QUALICARE INC   *p* 781
3910 BATHURST ST SUITE 304, NORTH
YORK, ON, M3H 5Z3
(416) 630-0202   *SIC* 8059
QUALICO   *p* 392
*See QUALICO DEVELOPMENTS CANADA
LTD*
QUALICO DEVELOPMENT WEST   *p* 121
See RANCHO REALTY (EDMONTON) LTD
**QUALICO DEVELOPMENTS (WINNIPEG)
LTD**   *p* 392
1 DR. DAVID FRIESEN DR, WINNIPEG,
MB, R3X 0G8
(204) 233-2451   *SIC* 6712
**QUALICO DEVELOPMENTS CALGARY
LTD**   *p* 37
5709 2 ST SE SUITE 200, CALGARY, AB,
T2H 2W4
(403) 253-3311   *SIC* 1521
QUALICO DEVELOPMENTS CANADA LTD
p 392
1 DR. DAVID FRIESEN DR, WINNIPEG,
MB, R3X 0G8
(204) 233-2451   *SIC* 6712
QUALICO DEVELOPMENTS WEST LTD *p*
37
5716 1 ST SE UNIT 100, CALGARY, AB,
T2H 1H8
(403) 253-3311   *SIC* 6553
QUALICOM INNOVATIONS INC   *p* 765
3389 STEELES AVE E SUITE 401, NORTH
YORK, ON, M2H 3S8
(416) 492-3833   *SIC* 8742
QUALICUM BEACH SHELL   *p* 252
See 470695 BC LTD
QUALIDEC CORPORATION   *p* 1007
55 NORTHFIELD DR E, WATERLOO, ON,
N2K 3T6
SIC 5812
QUALIFAB INC   *p* 1139
2256 AV DE LA ROTONDE, LEVIS, QC,

G6X 2L8
(418) 832-9193 SIC 3498
QUALIFIED CONTRACTORS LTD p 275
12788 ROSS PL, SURREY, BC, V3V 6E1
(604) 951-8677 SIC 1522
QUALIFIED METAL FABRICATORS LTD p 587
55 STEINWAY BLVD, ETOBICOKE, ON, M9W 6H6
(416) 675-7777 SIC 3444
QUALIFIRST FOODS LTD p 587
89 CARLINGVIEW DR, ETOBICOKE, ON, M9W 5E4
(416) 244-1177 SIC 5141
QUALITE CONSTRUCTION (CDN) LTEE p 1293
155 RUE D'AMSTERDAM, SAINT-AUGUSTIN-DE-DESMAURES, QC, G3A 2V5
(418) 878-4044 SIC 1542
QUALITE PERFORMANCE MAGOG INC p 1148
2400 RUE SHERBROOKE, MAGOG, QC, J1X 4E6
(819) 843-0099 SIC 5088
QUALITREE PROPAGATORS INC p 266
51546 FERRY RD, ROSEDALE, BC, V0X 1X2
(604) 794-3375 SIC 5193
QUALITY & COMPANY INC p 557
67 JACOB KEFFER PKY, CONCORD, ON, L4K 5N8
(905) 660-6996 SIC 2599
QUALITY ALLIED ELEVATOR p 679
See 965046 ONTARIO INC
QUALITY AUTO WHOLESALERS p 872
See 1249592 ONTARIO LTD
QUALITY CLASSROOMS INC p 385
840 BRADFORD ST, WINNIPEG, MB, R3H 0N5
(204) 775-6566 SIC 5112
QUALITY CONCRETE INC p 448
20 MACDONALD AVE, DARTMOUTH, NS, B3B 1C5
(902) 468-8040 SIC 3273
QUALITY CONTINUOUS IMPROVEMENT CENTRE FOR COMMUNITY EDUCATION AND TRAINING p 710
90 BURNHAMTHORPE RD W SUITE 210, MISSISSAUGA, ON, L5B 3C3
(905) 949-0049 SIC 8331
QUALITY CRAFT LTD p 273
17750 65A AVE UNIT 301, SURREY, BC, V3S 5N4
(604) 575-5550 SIC 5023
QUALITY EDGE CONVERTING LTD p 366
94 DURAND RD, WINNIPEG, MB, R2J 3T2
(204) 256-4115 SIC 5049
QUALITY ENGINEERED HOMES LTD p 628
7307 HWY 6, KENILWORTH, ON, N0G 2E0
(519) 323-4208 SIC 2452
QUALITY FAST FOOD p 84
See PREMIUM BRANDS HOLDINGS CORPORATION
QUALITY FOODS p 234
See KELLAND PROPERTIES INC
QUALITY FOODS LTD p 212
1581 ALBERNI HWY, ERRINGTON, BC, V0R 1V0
(250) 248-4004 SIC 5411
QUALITY GREENS CANADA LTD p 222
1889 SPALL RD UNIT 101, KELOWNA, BC, V1Y 4R2
(250) 763-8200 SIC 5431
QUALITY HARDWOODS LTD p 848
196 LATOUR CRES RR 3, POWASSAN, ON, P0H 1Z0
(705) 724-2424 SIC 5031
QUALITY HOME PRODUCTS p 553
See H.J. SUTTON INDUSTRIES LIMITED
QUASIR HOTEL p 326
See NEWDALE HOLDINGS INC
QUALITY HOTEL p 939
See INNVEST PROPERTIES CORP

QUALITY HVAC PRODUCTS LTD p 110
3904 53 AVE NW, EDMONTON, AB, T6B 3N7
(780) 643-3215 SIC 5075
QUALITY INN p 267
See BALMORAL INVESTMENTS LTD
QUALITY INN & CONFERENCE CENTRE p 153
See DEER PARK HOLDINGS LTD
QUALITY INN AIRLINER p 383
See AIRLINER MOTOR HOTEL (1972) LTD
QUALITY INN AIRPORT p 290
See BLUE BOY MOTOR HOTEL LTD
QUALITY INN NORTHERN GRAND HOTEL p 213
See JORDAN ENTERPRISES LIMITED
QUALITY INN NORTHERN GRAND, THE p 225
See JORDAN ENTERPRISES LIMITED
QUALITY INSERTIONS LTD p 247
1560 BROADWAY ST UNIT 2, PORT COQUITLAM, BC, V3C 2M8
(604) 941-1942 SIC 7319
QUALITY KNITTING LIMITED p 914
1210 BIRCHMOUNT RD, TORONTO, ON, M1P 2C3
(416) 598-2422 SIC 2253
QUALITY MARKET (THUNDER BAY) INC p 910
146 CENTENNIAL SQ, THUNDER BAY, ON, P7E 1H3
SIC 5411
QUALITY MECHANICAL p 490
See 995451 ONTARIO INC
QUALITY MODELS LIMITED p 1017
478 SILVER CREEK INDUSTRIAL DR SUITE 1, WINDSOR, ON, N8N 4Y3
(519) 727-4255 SIC 3089
QUALITY MOVE MANAGEMENT INC p 209
7979 82 ST, DELTA, BC, V4G 1L7
(604) 952-3650 SIC 7389
QUALITY NATURAL FOODS CANADA INC p 874
420 NUGGET AVE SUITE 1, SCARBOROUGH, ON, M1S 4A4
(416) 261-8700 SIC 5149
QUALITY PACKAGING SOLUTIONS INC p 845
1420 BAYLY ST UNIT 7, PICKERING, ON, L1W 3R4
SIC 7389
QUALITY SAFETY SYSTEMS COMPANY p 902
See TRQSS, INC
QUALITY SEAFOODS LIMITED p 471
306 HILTON RD, YARMOUTH, NS, B5A 4A6
(902) 742-9238 SIC 5146
QUALITY SERVICES INC p 604
497 WOOLWICH ST UNIT 2, GUELPH, ON, N1H 3X9
(519) 827-1147 SIC 8742
QUALITY STORES LTD p 732
5770 HURONTARIO ST, MISSISSAUGA, ON, L5R 3G5
SIC 5311
QUALITY TIRE SERVICE LTD p 1416
2150 E VICTORIA AVE SUITE 201, REGINA, SK, S4N 7B9
(306) 721-2155 SIC 5531
QUALITY TUBING p 154
See QUALITY TUBING CANADA INC
QUALITY TUBING CANADA INC p 154
4610 49 AVE SUITE 103, RED DEER, AB, T4N 6M5
(403) 342-1000 SIC 5051
QUALITY UNDERWRITING SERVICES LTD p 853
111 GRANTON DR SUITE 105, RICHMOND HILL, ON, L4B 1L5
(905) 335-8783 SIC 7323
QUALITY VENDING & COFFEE SERVICES LTD p 372
91 PLYMOUTH ST, WINNIPEG, MB, R2X 2V5

(204) 633-2405 SIC 5962
QUALTECH INC p 1265
1880 RUE LEON-HARMEL, QUEBEC, QC, G1N 4K3
(418) 686-3802 SIC 7373
QUALTECH SEATING SYSTEMS DIV OF p 662
See MAGNA SEATING INC
QUANSER CONSULTING INC p 674
119 SPY CRT, MARKHAM, ON, L3R 5H6
(905) 940-3575 SIC 3821
QUANTA TELECOM CANADA LTD p 77
9595 ENTERPRISE WAY SE, CALGARY, AB, T3S 0A1
(587) 620-0201 SIC 1623
QUANTEC GEOSCIENCE LIMITED p 765
146 SPARKS AVE, NORTH YORK, ON, M2H 2S4
(416) 306-1941 SIC 6712
QUANTRILL, CHEVROLET BUICK GMC CADILLAC LTD p 847
265 PETER ST, PORT HOPE, ON, L1A 3V6
(905) 885-4573 SIC 5511
QUANTUM AUTOMOTIVE GROUP INCORPORATED p 529
441 NORTH SERVICE RD, BURLINGTON, ON, L7P 0A3
(905) 632-4222 SIC 5511
QUANTUM CAPITAL CORPORATION p 1207
615 BOUL RENE LEVESQUE, STE 460, MONTREAL, QC, H3B 1P5
SIC 5045
QUANTUM INTERNATIONAL INCOME CORP p 970
79 WELLINGTON ST W SUITE 1630, TORONTO, ON, M5K 1H1
(416) 477-3400 SIC 0971
QUANTUM MURRAY-NWDD PARTNERSHIP p 256
3600 VIKING WAY SUITE 100, RICHMOND, BC, V6V 1N6
(604) 270-7388 SIC 4959
QUANTUM PLUS LTD p 1028
500 NEW ENTERPRISE WAY, WOODBRIDGE, ON, L4H 0R3
(905) 264-3700 SIC 5099
QUANTUM WINCH p 6
See JMB CRUSHING SYSTEMS ULC
QUARRY INTEGRATED COMMUNICATIONS INC p 888
1440 KING ST N SUITE 1, ST JACOBS, ON, N0B 2N0
(877) 723-2999 SIC 7311
QUARRY INTEGRATED COMMUNICATIONS INC p 888
1440 KING ST N UNIT 1, ST JACOBS, ON, N0B 2N0
(877) 723-2999 SIC 7311
QUARTECH SYSTEMS LIMITED p 287
2889 12TH AVE E SUITE 650, VANCOUVER, BC, V5M 4T5
(604) 291-9686 SIC 7371
QUARTERBACK TRANSPORTATION INC p 769
1210 SHEPPARD AVE E SUITE 114, NORTH YORK, ON, M2K 1E3
(416) 385-2713 SIC 4731
QUARTERDECK BREWING CO LTD p 299
601 CORDOVA ST W, VANCOUVER, BC, V6B 1G1
(604) 689-9151 SIC 5812
QUARTERHILL INC p 640
30 DUKE ST W SUITE 604, KITCHENER, ON, N2H 3W5
(613) 688-1693 SIC 4899
QUASAR, DIV OF p 683
See CWB GROUP - INDUSTRY SERVICES CORP
QUATERRA RESOURCES INC p 316

1199 HASTINGS ST W SUITE 1100, VANCOUVER, BC, V6E 3T5
(855) 681-9059 SIC 1021
QUATIC CONSUMER PRODUCTS p 803
See ARCH CHEMICALS CANADA, INC
QUATRE GLACES (1994) INC, LES p 1069
5880 BOUL TASCHEREAU, BROSSARD, QC, J4W 1M6
(450) 462-2113 SIC 7999
QUATREX ENVIRONNEMENT INC p 1381
2085 BOUL DES ENTREPRISES, TERREBONNE, QC, J6Y 1W9
(450) 963-4747 SIC 5099
QUATTROCCHI, JOSEPH & COMPANY LIMITED p 882
63 CHURCH ST W, SMITHS FALLS, ON, K7A 1R2
(613) 283-4980 SIC 5148
QUE PASA MEXICAN FOODS LTD p 261
9100 VAN HORNE WAY, RICHMOND, BC, V6X 1W3
(866) 880-7284 SIC 2032
QUEBEC AMERIQUE p 1181
See EDITIONS QUEBEC-AMERIQUE INC, LES
QUEBEC EN FORME p 1322
668 AV VICTORIA, SAINT-LAMBERT, QC, J4P 2J6
SIC 8399
QUEBEC LINGE p 184
See CANADIAN LINEN AND UNIFORM SERVICE CO
QUEBEC LINGE p 445
See CANADIAN LINEN AND UNIFORM SERVICE CO
QUEBEC LINGE p 486
See CANADIAN LINEN AND UNIFORM SERVICE CO
QUEBEC LINGE p 573
See CANADIAN LINEN AND UNIFORM SERVICE CO
QUEBEC LINGE p 1166
See QUEBEC LINGE CO
QUEBEC LINGE p 1415
See CANADIAN LINEN AND UNIFORM SERVICE CO
QUEBEC LINGE CO p 1166
4375 RUE DE ROUEN, MONTREAL, QC, H1V 1H2
(514) 670-2005 SIC 7213
QUEBEC LOISIRS ULC p 1327
253 BOUL DECARIE, SAINT-LAURENT, QC, H4N 2L7
(514) 340-2932 SIC 5192
QUEBEC MULTIPLANTS p 1262
755 RUE DU MARAIS, QUEBEC, QC, G1M 3R7
(418) 687-1616 SIC 5193
QUEBEC RECHERCHES p 1169
See RESEARCH HOUSE INC
QUEBEC STEVEDORING COMPANY LTD p 1259
961 BOUL CHAMPLAIN, QUEBEC, QC, G1K 4J9
(418) 522-4701 SIC 4491
QUEBECOR INC p 1211
612 RUE SAINT-JACQUES BUREAU 700, MONTREAL, QC, H3C 4M8
(514) 380-1999 SIC 6712
QUEBECOR MEDIA INC p 934
See QUEBECOR MEDIA INC
QUEBECOR MEDIA INC p 934
333 KING ST E SUITE 1, TORONTO, ON, M5A 3X5
(416) 947-2222 SIC 7319
QUEBECOR MEDIA INC p 1153
See QUEBECOR MEDIA INC
QUEBECOR MEDIA INC p 1153
12800 RUE BRAULT, MIRABEL, QC, J7J 0W4
(450) 663-9000 SIC 5994
QUEBECOR MEDIA INC p 1207
1100 BOUL RENE-LEVESQUE O SUITE 20E, MONTREAL, QC, H3B 4N4

(514) 380-1999   *SIC* 7311
QUEBECOR MEDIA INC   *p* 1212
612 RUE SAINT-JACQUES, MONTREAL, QC, H3C 4M8
(514) 380-1999   *SIC* 2711
QUEBECOR NUMERIQUE   *p* 1207
See QUEBECOR MEDIA INC
QUEEN ALEXANDRA CENTRE FOR CHILDREN   *p* 333
See VANCOUVER ISLAND HEALTH AUTHORITY
QUEEN CITY TAXI & BURNABBY ELI*p* 192
See BONNY'S TAXI LTD
QUEEN ELIZABETH COLLEGIATE   *p* 630
See LIMESTONE DISTRICT SCHOOL BOARD
QUEEN ELIZABETH HIGH SCHOOL   *p* 41
See CALGARY BOARD OF EDUCATION
QUEEN ELIZABETH HOSPITAL   *p* 1039
See PROVINCE OF PEI
QUEEN ELIZABETH II HEALTH SCIENCES CENTRE   *p* 451
See NOVA SCOTIA HEALTH AUTHORITY
QUEEN ELIZABETH II HEALTH SCIENCES CENTRE FOUNDATION   *p* 454
5657 SPRING GARDEN RD SUITE 3005, HALIFAX, NS, B3J 3R4
(902) 334-1546   *SIC* 8399
QUEEN ELIZABETH LL LIBRARY   *p* 430
See MEMORIAL UNIVERSITY OF NEWFOUNDLAND
QUEEN ELIZABETH TWO HOSPITAL *p* 133
10409 98 ST, GRANDE PRAIRIE, AB, T8V 2E8
(780) 538-7100   *SIC* 8742
QUEEN MARGARET'S SCHOOL   *p* 212
660 BROWNSEY AVE, DUNCAN, BC, V9L 1C2
(250) 746-4185   *SIC* 8211
QUEEN OF ANGELS ACADEMY INC*p* 1096
100 BOUL BOUCHARD, DORVAL, QC, H9S 1A7
(514) 636-0900   *SIC* 8211
QUEEN REGION HOME CARE   *p* 1040
See PROVINCE OF PEI
QUEEN STREET MENTAL HEALTH   *p* 918
See CENTRE FOR ADDICTION AND MENTAL HEALTH
QUEEN VICTORIA HOSPITAL   *p* 253
See INTERIOR HEALTH
QUEEN VICTORIA PLACE   *p* 758
See NIAGARA PARKS COMMISSION, THE
QUEEN VICTORIA PUBLIC SCHOOL *p* 992
See TORONTO DISTRICT SCHOOL BOARD
QUEEN WEST COMMUNITY HEALTH CENTRE   *p* 979
See CENTRAL TORONTO COMMUNITY HEALTH CENTRES
QUEEN'S HOUSE RETREATS & RENEWAL CENTRE   *p* 1433
601 TAYLOR ST W, SASKATOON, SK, S7M 0C9
(306) 242-1916   *SIC* 7389
QUEEN'S HOUSING & ANCILLARY SERVICES   *p* 631
See QUEEN'S UNIVERSITY AT KINGSTON
QUEEN'S SCHOOL OF BUSINESS   *p* 534
355 HESPELER RD, CAMBRIDGE, ON, N1R 6B3
(613) 533-2330   *SIC* 8221
QUEEN'S UNIVERSITY   *p* 631
See QUEEN'S UNIVERSITY AT KINGSTON
QUEEN'S UNIVERSITY AT KINGSTON   *p* 631
207 STUART ST, KINGSTON, ON, K7L 2V9
(613) 533-6075   *SIC* 7349
QUEEN'S UNIVERSITY AT KINGSTON   *p* 631
99 UNIVERSITY AVE, KINGSTON, ON, K7L 3N5

(613) 533-2000   *SIC* 8221
QUEEN'S UNIVERSITY AT KINGSTON *p* 631
25 UNION ST, KINGSTON, ON, K7L 3N5
(613) 533-6050   *SIC* 8221
QUEEN'S UNIVERSITY AT KINGSTON *p* 631
75 BADER LANE RM D015, KINGSTON, ON, K7L 3N8
(613) 533-2529   *SIC* 8221
QUEENS GENERAL HOSPITAL   *p* 461
See SOUTH SHORE DISTRICT HEALTH AUTHORITY
QUEENS HOME FOR SPECIAL CARE SOCIETY   *p* 460
20 HOLLANDS DR, LIVERPOOL, NS, B0T 1K0
(902) 354-3451   *SIC* 8361
QUEENS LANDING HOTEL AND CONFERENCE RESORT   *p* 761
See LAIS HOTEL PROPERTIES LIMITED
QUEENS MANOR   *p* 460
See QUEENS HOME FOR SPECIAL CARE SOCIETY
QUEENSDALE SUPERMARKET LTD *p* 240
3030 LONSDALE AVE, NORTH VANCOUVER, BC, V7N 3J5
(604) 987-6644   *SIC* 5411
QUEENSTON CHEVROLET INC   *p* 608
282 CENTENNIAL PKY N, HAMILTON, ON, L8E 2X4
(905) 560-2020   *SIC* 5511
QUEENSTON HEIGHTS RESTAURANT   *p* 759
See NIAGARA PARKS COMMISSION, THE
QUEENSTON LEASING   *p* 608
See SETAY MOTORS INC
QUEENSTON ON THE MOUNTAIN-BUICK-CHEVROLET-GMC   *p* 617
See 4259891 CANADA LTD
QUEENSWAY CAWTHRA HOLDINGS LTD*p* 708
655 QUEENSWAY E, MISSISSAUGA, ON, L5A 3X6
(905) 273-9357   *SIC* 6712
QUEENSWAY HEALTH CENTRE   *p* 996
See TRILLIUM HEALTH PARTNERS
QUEENSWAY MACHINE PRODUCTS LIMITED, THE   *p* 576
8 RANGEMORE RD, ETOBICOKE, ON, M8Z 5H7
(416) 259-4261   *SIC* 3599
QUEENSWAY NURSING & RETIREMENT HOME   *p* 620
See PROVINCIAL LONG TERM CARE INC
QUEENSWAY REAL ESTATE BROKERAGE INC   *p* 996
8 HORNELL ST, TORONTO, ON, M8Z 1X2
(416) 259-4000   *SIC* 6531
QUEENSWAY TANK LINES   *p* 1137
See TRANSPORT JACQUES AUGER INC
QUEENSWAY VOLKSWAGEN AUDI *p* 576
See QUEENSWAY VOLKSWAGEN INC
QUEENSWAY VOLKSWAGEN INC   *p* 576
1306 THE QUEENSWAY, ETOBICOKE, ON, M8Z 1S4
(416) 259-7656   *SIC* 7538
QUEENSWAY-CARLETON HOSPITAL*p* 751
QUEENSWAY-CARLETON HOSPITAL, NEPEAN, ON, K2H 8P4
(613) 721-2000   *SIC* 8062
QUELS SONT VOS GOUTS   *p* 1328
See BOUTIQUE UNISEXE JOVEN INC
QUERIN, ARMAND AUTOMOBILES LTEE *p* 1087
2385 BOUL CHOMEDEY, COTE SAINT-LUC, QC, H7T 2W5
(450) 688-4787   *SIC* 5511
QUESNEL CRAFTERS SOCIETY   *p* 252
102 CARSON AVE, QUESNEL, BC, V2J

2A8
(250) 991-0419   *SIC* 5947
QUESNEL MILL PLYWOOD   *p* 252
See WEST FRASER MILLS LTD
QUESNEL PLYWOOD   *p* 252
See WEST FRASER MILLS LTD
QUESNEL RIVER PULP   *p* 253
See WEST FRASER TIMBER CO. LTD
QUESNEL SCHOOL DISTRICT   *p* 252
See SCHOOL DISTRICT #28
QUESNEL SECONDARY SCHOOL   *p* 252
See SCHOOL DISTRICT #28
QUEST - A SOCIETY FOR ADULT SUPPORT AND REHABILITATION   *p* 456
2131 GOTTINGEN ST SUITE 101, HALIFAX, NS, B3K 5Z7
(902) 490-7200   *SIC* 8361
QUEST AUTOMOTIVE LEASING SERVICES *p* 874
See QUEST AUTOMOTIVE LEASING SERVICES LTD
QUEST AUTOMOTIVE LEASING SERVICES LTD   *p* 874
4960 SHEPPARD AVE E, SCARBOROUGH, ON, M1S 4A7
(416) 298-7600   *SIC* 5511
QUEST BRANDS INC   *p* 505
1 VAN DER GRAAF CRT, BRAMPTON, ON, L6T 5E5
(905) 789-6868   *SIC* 5211
QUEST ENTERPRISES, DIV   *p* 568
See CHEMNORTH SYSTEMS AND SERVICES COMPANY LTD
QUEST METAL PRODUCTS LTD   *p* 382
889 ERIN ST, WINNIPEG, MB, R3G 2W6
(204) 786-2403   *SIC* 3589
QUEST SOFTWARE   *p* 625
See QUEST SOFTWARE CANADA INC
QUEST SOFTWARE CANADA INC   *p* 454
5151 GEORGE ST, HALIFAX, NS, B3J 1M5
(902) 442-5800   *SIC* 7372
QUEST SOFTWARE CANADA INC   *p* 625
515 LEGGET DR SUITE 1001, KANATA, ON, K2K 3G4
(613) 270-1500   *SIC* 7371
QUEST SOFTWARE CANADA INC   *p* 934
260 KING ST E, TORONTO, ON, M5A 4L5
(416) 933-5000   *SIC* 7371
QUEST WINDOW SYSTEMS INC   *p* 689
6811 GOREWAY DR UNIT 1, MISSISSAUGA, ON, L4V 1L9
(905) 851-8588   *SIC* 3442
QUEST WOOD DIVISION   *p* 252
See TOLKO INDUSTRIES LTD
QUEST-TECH PRECISION INC   *p* 491
193 JAMIESON BONE RD, BELLEVILLE, ON, K8N 5T4
(613) 966-7551   *SIC* 3444
QUESTERRE ENERGY CORPORATION *p* 57
801 6 AVE SW SUITE 1650, CALGARY, AB, T2P 3W2
(403) 777-1185   *SIC* 1382
QUESTFIRE ENERGY CORP   *p* 57
350 7 AVE SW SUITE 1100, CALGARY, AB, T2P 3N9
(403) 263-6688   *SIC* 1381
QUESTRADE, INC   *p* 770
5650 YONGE ST SUITE 1700, NORTH YORK, ON, M2M 4G3
(416) 227-9876   *SIC* 6211
QUESTZONE.NET INC   *p* 1364
8 RUE ROUX BUREAU 200, SAINTE-THERESE, QC, J7E 1L3
(450) 979-3339   *SIC* 5065
QUICK AS A WINK COURIER SERVICE LTD *p* 261
9300 VAN HORNE WAY, RICHMOND, BC, V6X 1W3
(604) 276-8686   *SIC* 4212
QUICK LANE TIRE AND AUTO CENTRE *p* 1413
2222 100TH ST, NORTH BATTLEFORD,

SK, S9A 0X6
(306) 445-4495   *SIC* 5012
QUICK SPORTS   *p* 242
4740 CAPILANO RD, NORTH VANCOUVER, BC, V7R 4K3
SIC 5941
QUICK TRANSFER LTD   *p* 363
766 PANDORA AVE E UNIT 200, WINNIPEG, MB, R2C 3A6
(204) 786-6011   *SIC* 4214
QUICK TRANSFER LTD   *p* 385
1680 SARGENT AVE, WINNIPEG, MB, R3H 0C2
(204) 786-6011   *SIC* 4214
QUICK TRANSLOAD   *p* 261
See QUICK AS A WINK COURIER SERVICE LTD
QUICKCARE   *p* 197
See TEKSMED SERVICES INC
QUICKIE CONVENIENCE STORES   *p* 819
See LARNY HOLDINGS LIMITED
QUICKLANE   *p* 874
See EAST-COURT FORD LINCOLN SALES LIMITED
QUICKLOAD CEF INC   *p* 252
1220 RIDLEY ISLAND, PRINCE RUPERT, BC, V8J 4P8
(250) 627-5623   *SIC* 4731
QUICKMOBILE INC   *p* 316
1177 HASTINGS ST W SUITE 2600, VANCOUVER, BC, V6E 2K3
(604) 875-0403   *SIC* 7371
QUICKPLAY MEDIA CO   *p* 983
901 KING ST W UNIT 200, TORONTO, ON, M5V 3H5
(416) 586-6200   *SIC* 4813
QUICKSERVICE TECHNOLOGIES INC   *p* 883
610 WELLAND AVE, ST CATHARINES, ON, L2M 5V6
(905) 687-8440   *SIC* 5044
QUICKSERVICE TECHNOLOGY SYSTEMS *p* 883
See QUICKSERVICE TECHNOLOGIES INC
QUICKSTYLE INDUSTRIES INC   *p* 1335
4505 RUE COUSENS, SAINT-LAURENT, QC, H4S 1V5
(514) 956-9711   *SIC* 5023
QUIET HARMONY INC   *p* 505
30 INTERMODAL DR UNIT 43, BRAMPTON, ON, L6T 5K1
(905) 794-0622   *SIC* 7349
QUIK X LOGISTICS   *p* 699
See QUIK X TRANSPORTATION INC
QUIK X TRANSPORTATION INC   *p* 699
5425 DIXIE RD BLDG B, MISSISSAUGA, ON, L4W 1E6
(905) 238-8584   *SIC* 4213
QUIK'S FARM LIMITED   *p* 198
8340 PREST RD, CHILLIWACK, BC, V4Z 0A6
(604) 795-4651   *SIC* 0181
QUIKRETE   *p* 183
See TARGET PRODUCTS LTD
QUIKRETE CANADA HOLDINGS, LIMITED *p* 183
8535 EASTLAKE DR, BURNABY, BC, V5A 4T7
(604) 444-3620   *SIC* 6712
QUILCHENA GOLF & COUNTRY CLUB *p* 265
3551 GRANVILLE AVE, RICHMOND, BC, V7C 1C8
(604) 277-1101   *SIC* 7997
QUILTS ETC   *p* 180
See 429149 B.C. LTD
QUINAN CONSTRUCTION LIMITED *p* 810
55 PROGRESS DR UNIT 1, ORILLIA, ON, L3V 0T7
(705) 325-7704   *SIC* 1541
QUINCAILLERIE BEAUBIEN INC   *p* 1169
3194 RUE BEAUBIEN E, MONTREAL, QC, H1Y 1H4

(514) 727-0525 *SIC* 5072

QUINCAILLERIE FUTURA, DIV DE *p* 1243
See MENUISERIE DES PINS LTEE

QUINCAILLERIE NOTRE-DAME DE ST-HENRI INC *p*
1215
2371 RUE NOTRE-DAME O BUREAU 1, MONTREAL, QC, H3J 1N3
(514) 932-5616 *SIC* 5251

QUINCAILLERIE RICHELIEU LTEE *p* 1142
See QUINCAILLERIE RICHELIEU LTEE

QUINCAILLERIE RICHELIEU LTEE *p* 1142
800 RUE BERIAULT, LONGUEUIL, QC, J4G 1R8
(514) 259-3737 *SIC* 5072

QUINCAILLERIE RICHELIEU LTEE *p* 1335
7900 BOUL HENRI-BOURASSA O BUREAU 200, SAINT-LAURENT, QC, H4S 1V4
(514) 336-4144 *SIC* 5072

QUINCO & CIE INC *p* 1148
2035 RUE RENE-PATENAUDE, MAGOG, QC, J1X 7J2
(819) 847-4001 *SIC* 2679

QUINLAN BROTHERS LIMITED *p* 432
215 WATER ST SUITE 302, ST. JOHN'S, NL, A1C 6C9
(709) 739-9960 *SIC* 2092

QUINN CONTRACTING LTD *p* 6
27123 1 HWY, BLACKFALDS, AB, T0M 0J0
(403) 885-4788 *SIC* 1541

QUINN DRILLING INC *p* 156
788 ST EDGAR INDUSTRIAL WAY, RED DEER, AB, T4P 3R2
(403) 343-8802 *SIC* 1629

QUINN'S MARINA LTD *p* 837
25 QUINN RD, PEFFERLAW, ON, L0E 1N0
(705) 437-1122 *SIC* 5551

QUINN'S PHARMACY LIMITED (1987) *p*
646
74 KENT ST W SUITE 948, LINDSAY, ON, K9V 2Y4
(705) 324-7400 *SIC* 5912

QUINN'S PRODUCTION SERVICES INC *p*
154
6798 52 AVE, RED DEER, AB, T4N 4K9
(780) 499-0299 *SIC* 3533

QUINTAIN DEVELOPMENTS INC *p* 742
6720 COLUMBUS RD, MISSISSAUGA, ON, L5T 2G1
(905) 670-3599 *SIC* 6531

QUINTAINE, P & SON LTD *p* 347
GD, BRANDON, MB, R7A 5Y5
(204) 729-8565 *SIC* 5154

QUINTE BROADCASTING COMPANY LIMITED *p*
491
10 SOUTH FRONT ST, BELLEVILLE, ON, K8N 2Y3
(613) 969-5555 *SIC* 4832

QUINTE HEALTHCARE CORPORATION *p*
484
1H MANOR LANE, BANCROFT, ON, K0L 1C0
(613) 332-2825 *SIC* 8069

QUINTE HEALTHCARE CORPORATION *p*
491
265 DUNDAS ST E, BELLEVILLE, ON, K8N 5A9
(613) 969-7400 *SIC* 8062

QUINTE HEALTHCARE CORPORATION *p*
845
403 PICTON MAIN ST, PICTON, ON, K0K 2T0
(613) 476-1008 *SIC* 8621

QUINTE HEALTHCARE CORPORATION *p*
999
242 KING ST, TRENTON, ON, K8V 5S6
(613) 392-2540 *SIC* 8062

QUINTE HEALTHCARE PRINCE EDWARD COUNTY MEMORIAL *p* 845
See QUINTE HEALTHCARE CORPORATION

QUINTE SECONDARY SCHOOL *p* 492
See HASTINGS AND PRINCE EDWARD

DISTRICT SCHOOL BOARD

QUINTERRA PROPERTY MAINTENANCE INC *p* 321
1681 CHESTNUT ST SUITE 400, VANCOUVER, BC, V6J 4M6
(604) 689-1800 *SIC* 7349

QUINTERRA PROPERTY MAINTENANCE INC *p* 726
6535 MILLCREEK DR UNIT 63, MISSISSAUGA, ON, L5N 2M2
(905) 821-7171 *SIC* 7349

QUINTEX SERVICES LTD *p* 387
332 NASSAU ST N, WINNIPEG, MB, R3L 0R8
(204) 477-6600 *SIC* 7213

QUINTEX UNIFORM & MAT RENTAL SERVICE *p*
387
See QUINTEX SERVICES LTD

QUINTINMANUS MARKETING GROUP INC *p* 934
258 ADELAIDE ST E SUITE 400, TORONTO, ON, M5A 1N1
SIC 8743

QUISITIVE TECHNOLOGY SOLUTIONS, INC *p* 966
161 BAY ST SUITE 2325, TORONTO, ON, M5J 2S1
(519) 574-5520 *SIC* 7372

QUIZNO'S CANADA RESTAURANT CORPORATION *p*
983
355 KING ST W SUITE 300, TORONTO, ON, M5V 1J6
(647) 259-0333 *SIC* 6794

QULLIQ ENERGY CORPORATION *p* 472
GD, BAKER LAKE, NU, X0C 0A0
(866) 710-4200 *SIC* 4911

QUNARA INC *p* 375
136 MARKET AVE SUITE 8, WINNIPEG, MB, R3B 0P4
(204) 925-0050 *SIC* 4813

QUOREX CONSTRUCTION SERVICES LTD *p* 1421
1630 8TH AVE UNIT A, REGINA, SK, S4R 1E5
(306) 761-2222 *SIC* 1542

QUOREX CONSTRUCTION SERVICES LTD *p* 1432
142 CARDINAL CRES, SASKATOON, SK, S7L 6H6
(306) 244-3717 *SIC* 1542

QUORUM FUNDING CORPORATION *p* 966
70 YORK ST SUITE 1720, TORONTO, ON, M5J 1S9
SIC 6726

QUORUM INFORMATION SYSTEMS INC *p*
37
7500 MACLEOD TRAIL SE SUITE 200, CALGARY, AB, T2H 0L9
(403) 777-0036 *SIC* 7371

QUORUM INFORMATION TECHNOLOGIES INC *p* 37
7500 MACLEOD TRAIL SE SUITE 200, CALGARY, AB, T2H 0L9
(403) 777-0036 *SIC* 7371

QUOTIDIEN DROIT DIV OF *p* 821
See GESCA LTEE

QVELLA CORPORATION *p* 853
9133 LESLIE ST UNIT 110, RICHMOND HILL, ON, L4B 4N1
(289) 317-0414 *SIC* 8731

QWINSTAR CANADA INC *p* 736
1040 CARDIFF BLVD, MISSISSAUGA, ON, L5S 1P3
(905) 696-8102 *SIC* 8741

QX LTD *p* 717
4140 SLADEVIEW CRES UNIT 4, MISSISSAUGA, ON, L5L 6A1
(905) 828-9055 *SIC* 1541

QX TECHNICAL SERVICES *p* 717
See QX LTD

QZINA SPECIALTY FOODS INC *p* 94
12547 129 ST NW, EDMONTON, AB, T5L

1H7
(780) 447-4499 *SIC* 5149

R

?ROS & COMPAGNIE *p* 1233
See AJPRO DISTRIBUTION INC

R & D AUTO SALES *p* 1421
979 WINNIPEG ST SUITE C, REGINA, SK, S4R 1J1
(306) 565-2929 *SIC* 5521

R & D DRYWALL INC *p* 1429
211A 47TH ST E, SASKATOON, SK, S7K 5H1
(306) 933-9328 *SIC* 1742

R & F CONSTRUCTION *p* 810
See R & F CONSTRUCTION INC

R & F CONSTRUCTION INC *p* 810
73 PATTERSON RD, ORILLIA, ON, L3V 6H1
(705) 325-5746 *SIC* 1521

R & G TRANSPORT LTD *p* 412
16 MILK BOARD RD, ROACHVILLE, NB, E4G 2G8
(506) 432-9128 *SIC* 4213

R & L CONVENIENCE ENTERPRISES INC *p*
412
1 ELLIS DR, ROTHESAY, NB, E2E 1A1
(506) 847-1603 *SIC* 5411

R & P FUELS *p* 568
See R & P PETROLEUM INC

R & P PETROLEUM INC *p* 568
2236 COUNTY ROAD 92, ELMVALE, ON, L0L 1P0
(705) 429-5179 *SIC* 5172

R & R TRADING CO. LTD *p* 209
7449 RIVER RD, DELTA, BC, V4G 1B9
(604) 946-0916 *SIC* 5051

R & T PHARMACY LTD *p* 1413
11412 RAILWAY AVE E UNIT 12, NORTH BATTLEFORD, SK, S9A 3P7
(306) 445-6253 *SIC* 5912

R 870 HOLDINGS LTD *p* 220
171 COMMERCIAL DR SUITE 203, KELOWNA, BC, V1X 7W2
SIC 1794

R B & W CORPORATION OF CANADA *p*
500
10 SUN PAC BLVD, BRAMPTON, ON, L6S 4R5
(905) 595-9700 *SIC* 3452

R B D MARKETING INC *p* 910
230 WATERLOO ST S, THUNDER BAY, ON, P7E 2C3
(807) 622-3366 *SIC* 7514

R D I *p* 524
See RETAIL DIMENSIONS INCORPORATED

R D I REFORESTATION & DEVELOPMENTS INC *p*
222
534 CHRISTLETON AVE, KELOWNA, BC, V1Y 5J2
(250) 470-1842 *SIC* 0851

R E LINE TRUCKING (COLEVILLE) LTD *p*
1405
4TH AVE, COLEVILLE, SK, S0L 0K0
(306) 965-2472 *SIC* 1389

R F CONTRACTING INC *p* 863
116 INDUSTRIAL PARK CRES, SAULT STE. MARIE, ON, P6B 5P2
(705) 253-1151 *SIC* 1711

R G MAZER GROUP *p* 348
See MAZER IMPLEMENTS

R H A CENTRAL MANITOBA INC. *p* 353
215 RAILROAD AVE E, MORRIS, MB, R0G 1K0
(204) 746-2301 *SIC* 8062

R HOME SECURITY LTD *p* 913
28 COLUMBUS AVE, TIMMINS, ON, P4N 3H3
(705) 267-5547 *SIC* 7389

R J J HOLDINGS LTD *p* 599
44 LIVINGSTON AVE SUITE 40, GRIMSBY, ON, L3M 1L1
(905) 945-5441 *SIC* 5531

R K R FOODS LTD *p* 135
5023 54 AVE, GRIMSHAW, AB, T0H 1W0
(780) 332-4495 *SIC* 5411

R M H INDUSTRIE INC *p* 1293
130 RUE DE ROTTERDAM, SAINT-AUGUSTIN-DE-DESMAURES, QC, G3A 1T3
(418) 878-0875 *SIC* 3599

R M KOMAR ENTERPRISES LIMITED *p* 368
1621 ST MARY'S RD, WINNIPEG, MB, R2M 3W8
(204) 254-4955 *SIC* 5541

R P B HOLDINGS LTD *p* 331
See BEST WESTERN SANDS HOTEL

R ROBITAILLE ET FILS INC *p* 1315
4000 CH BENOIT, SAINT-JEAN-BAPTISTE, QC, J0L 2B0
(450) 795-3915 *SIC* 0119

R S CABINET DOORS LTD *p* 1433
1102 17TH ST W, SASKATOON, SK, S7M 3Y3
SIC 2431

R T PLASTICS *p* 784
See R.T. RECYCLING TECHNOLOGY INC

R T S I *p* 1372
See TREMBLAY, RODRIGUE (SHERBROOKE) INC

R V OUTFITTERS *p* 662
6068 COLONEL TALBOT RD, LONDON, ON, N6P 1J1
(519) 652-3284 *SIC* 5561

R&R REAL ESTATE INVESTMENT TRUST *p*
699
5090 EXPLORER DR SUITE 700, MISSISSAUGA, ON, L4W 4X6
(905) 206-7100 *SIC* 6798

R'OHAN RIG SERVICES LTD *p* 144
GD, LLOYDMINSTER, AB, T9V 3C1
(780) 872-7887 *SIC* 8748

R-FOUR CONTRACTING LTD *p* 181
7185 11TH AVE, BURNABY, BC, V3N 2M5
(604) 522-4402 *SIC* 1542

R-MAG 118 INC *p* 1148
1615 CH DE LA RIVIERE-AUX-CERISES BUREAU 2, MAGOG, QC, J1X 3W3
(819) 847-3366 *SIC* 5812

R. B. BELL (SUPPLIES) LIMITED *p* 500
2850 QUEEN ST E, BRAMPTON, ON, L6S 6E8
(905) 792-9301 *SIC* 5251

R. BRUCE GRAHAM LIMITED *p* 622
203 BELL ST, INGERSOLL, ON, N5C 2P2
SIC 5172

R. CROTEAU RIMOUSKI INC *p* 1285
400 BOUL JESSOP, RIMOUSKI, QC, G5L 1N1
(418) 723-1614 *SIC* 5651

R. D. M. *p* 481
See RICOH DOCUMENT MANAGEMENT LIMITED PARTNERSHIP

R. DIAMOND GROUP OF COMPANIES LTD, THE *p* 277
13350 COMBER WAY, SURREY, BC, V3W 5V9
(604) 591-8641 *SIC* 4731

R. G. MC. GROUP LIMITED *p* 394
620 ST. PETER AVE, BATHURST, NB, E2A 2Y7
(506) 548-9555 *SIC* 5812

R. GREEN SUPERMARKETS INC *p* 651
1595 ADELAIDE ST N, LONDON, ON, N5X 4E8
(519) 645-8868 *SIC* 5411

R. H. KING ACADEMY *p* 869
See TORONTO DISTRICT SCHOOL BOARD

R. KIDD FUELS CORP *p* 784
3993 KEELE ST, NORTH YORK, ON, M3J 2X6
(416) 741-2343 *SIC* 5171

R. P. OIL LIMITED *p* 1015
1111 BURNS ST E UNIT 3, WHITBY, ON, L1N 6A6
(905) 666-2313 *SIC* 5172

▲ Public Company ■ Public Company Family Member **HQ** Headquarters **BR** Branch **SL** Single Location

R. R. PLETT TRUCKING LTD p 225
19675 98 AVE, LANGLEY, BC, V1M 2X5
(604) 513-9920 SIC 4213

R. ROBITAILLE & FILS INC p 1318
486 RUE DE VERSAILLES, SAINT-JEAN-SUR-RICHELIEU, QC, J3B 4H3
(450) 347-7494 SIC 0191

R. V. ANDERSON ASSOCIATES LIMITED p 768
2001 SHEPPARD AVE E SUITE 400, NORTH YORK, ON, M2J 4Z8
(416) 497-8600 SIC 8711

R.A.C.E. MECHANICAL SYSTEMS INC p 811
9 COBBLEDICK ST, ORONO, ON, L0B 1M0
(905) 983-9800 SIC 1711

R.A.F. HOLDINGS LTD p 474
1 HARWOOD AVE S, AJAX, ON, L1S 2C1
(905) 683-6497 SIC 5812

R.B. INC p 791
79 WINGOLD AVE UNIT 10, NORTH YORK, ON, M6B 1P8
(416) 787-4998 SIC 5091

R.C. MOFFATT SUPPLY LIMITED p 909
1135 RUSSELL ST, THUNDER BAY, ON, P7B 5M6
(807) 626-0040 SIC 5082

R.C. PHARMACY LTD p 600
380 ERAMOSA RD, GUELPH, ON, N1E 6R2
(519) 822-2480 SIC 5912

R.C.I. p 1052
See RENALD COTE 2007 INC

R.C.M. MODULAIRE INC p 1294
28 RUE INDUSTRIELLE, SAINT-BENOIT-LABRE, QC, G0M 1P0
(418) 227-4044 SIC 2452

R.C.R INVESTMENTS LIMITED p 456
6009 QUINPOOL RD SUITE 300, HALIFAX, NS, B3K 5J7
(902) 454-8533 SIC 6712

R.D.-PHAR INC p 1162
8315 BOUL MAURICE-DUPLESSIS, MONTREAL, QC, H1E 3B5
(514) 643-2808 SIC 5912

R.D.M. ENTERPRISES LTD p 228
20436 FRASER HWY UNIT 207, LANGLEY, BC, V3A 4G2
(604) 530-6310 SIC 1794

R.D.M. MANAGEMENT COMPANY (1987) LTD p 175
33695 SOUTH FRASER WAY, ABBOTSFORD, BC, V2S 2C1
SIC 8741

R.E.M. TRANSPORT LTD p 410
4 HALL RD, OLD RIDGE, NB, E3L 5E1
(506) 466-2918 SIC 4213

R.F.G. CANADA INC p 587
50A CLAIREPORT CRES, ETOBICOKE, ON, M9W 6P4
(416) 798-9900 SIC 2038

R.G. HENDERSON & SON LIMITED p 919
100 THORNCLIFFE PARK DR SUITE 416, TORONTO, ON, M4H 1L9
(416) 422-5580 SIC 7699

R.J. BONNEVILLE ENTERPRISES INC p 751
1820 MERIVALE RD DOOR # 258, NEPEAN, ON, K2G 1E6
(613) 224-9330 SIC 5399

R.J. BURNSIDE & ASSOCIATES LIMITED p 808
15 TOWN LINE, ORANGEVILLE, ON, L9W 3R4
(519) 941-5331 SIC 8711

R.J. HOFFMAN HOLDINGS LTD p 144
GD RPO 10, LLOYDMINSTER, AB, T9V 2H2
(780) 871-0723 SIC 1389

R.J. MCCARTHY p 576
See RJM56 INVESTMENTS INC

R.J. O'BRIEN & ASSOCIATES CANADA INC p 389
195 COMMERCE DR, WINNIPEG, MB, R3P 1A2
(204) 594-1440 SIC 6211

R.J.R. INVESTMENTS LTD p 385
670 CENTURY ST, WINNIPEG, MB, R3H 0A1
(204) 788-1100 SIC 5511

R.J.T. BLUEBERRY PARK INC p 179
25990 48 AVE, ALDERGROVE, BC, V4W 1J2
(604) 381-4562 SIC 5142

R.J.V. GAS FIELD SERVICES p 170
See TERRAVEST INDUSTRIES LIMITED PARTNERSHIP

R.K. MACDONALD NURSING HOME CORPORATION p 438
64 PLEASANT ST, ANTIGONISH, NS, B2G 1W7
(902) 863-2578 SIC 8051

R.K. PACKAGING p 665
See T.FLEXO CORPORATION

R.M. & S. COMPANY LIMITED p 434
1 COMMERCIAL ST, WABUSH, NL, A0R 1B0
(709) 282-3644 SIC 5085

R.M. FERGUSON & COMPANY INC p 505
235 ADVANCE BLVD SUITE 1, BRAMPTON, ON, L6T 4J2
(905) 458-5553 SIC 5169

R.M.P. ATHLETIC LOCKER LIMITED p 706
135 MATHESON BLVD UNIT 201, MISSISSAUGA, ON, L4Z 1R2
(905) 361-2390 SIC 5137

R.M.R REAL ESTATE LIMITED p 813
179 KING ST E, OSHAWA, ON, L1H 1C2
(905) 728-9414 SIC 6531

R.O.E. LOGISTICS INC p 1252
195 RUE VOYAGEUR, POINTE-CLAIRE, QC, H9R 6B2
(514) 396-0000 SIC 4731

R.O.E. LOGISTIQUES p 1252
See R.O.E. LOGISTICS INC

R.O.M CONTRACTORS LIMITED p 917
25 CURITY AVE UNIT 4, TORONTO, ON, M4B 3M2
(416) 285-0190 SIC 6712

R.P. JOHNSON CONSTRUCTION LTD p 268
360 TRANS CANADA HWY SW SUITE 317, SALMON ARM, BC, V1E 1B6
(250) 832-9731 SIC 6512

R.P.C. LONGUEUIL p 1142
See REFRIGERATION, PLOMBERIE & CHAUFFAGE LONGUEUIL INC

R.P.M. TECH INC p 1377
1318 RUE PRINCIPALE, ST-VALERIEN, QC, J0H 2B0
(418) 285-1811 SIC 3599

R.R. DONNELLEY p 102
See MOORE CANADA CORPORATION

R.R. DONNELLEY p 590
See MOORE CANADA CORPORATION

R.R. DONNELLEY p 741
See MOORE CANADA CORPORATION

R.R. DONNELLEY p 999
See MOORE CANADA CORPORATION

R.R. DONNELLEY p 1216
See MOORE CANADA CORPORATION

R.R. DONNELLEY p 1326
See MOORE CANADA CORPORATION

R.S. HARRIS TRANSPORT LTD p 391
555 HERVO ST UNIT 15, WINNIPEG, MB, R3T 3L6
(204) 255-2700 SIC 4213

R.S. LINE CONTR. CO. p 125
See FORBES BROS. LTD

R.S.T. INSTRUMENTS LTD p 231
11545 KINGSTON ST, MAPLE RIDGE, BC, V2X 0Z5
(604) 540-1100 SIC 3826

R.T. RECYCLING TECHNOLOGY INC p 784
801 FLINT RD, NORTH YORK, ON, M3J 2J6
(416) 650-1498 SIC 3089

R.T.A. HOLDINGS LTD p 84
12029 75 ST NW, EDMONTON, AB, T5B 0X3
(780) 436-9949 SIC 5013

R3D p 1190
See R3D CONSEIL INC

R3D CONSEIL INC p 1190
485 RUE MCGILL BUREAU 1110, MONTREAL, QC, H2Y 2H4
(514) 879-9000 SIC 8742

RA SKI CLUB p 819
See RECREATION ASSOCIATION OF THE PUBLIC SERVICE OF CANADA, THE

RABAIS CAMPUS p 1175
See LEBLANC & DAVID MARKETING INC

RABBA, J. COMPANY LIMITED, THE p 706
5820 KENNEDY RD, MISSISSAUGA, ON, L4Z 2C3
(905) 890-2436 SIC 5411

RABCON CONTRACTORS LTD p 598
9 GORMLEY, INDUSTRIAL AVE, GORMLEY, ON, L0H 1G0
(905) 888-6281 SIC 1623

RABER GLOVE MFG. CO. LTD p 373
560 MCDERMOT AVE, WINNIPEG, MB, R3A 0C1
(204) 786-2469 SIC 3111

RACETTE, J. P. INC p 1347
557 RUE SAINT-LOUIS, SAINT-LIN-LAURENTIDES, QC, J5M 2X2
(450) 439-2006 SIC 5531

RACEWAY CHRYSLER DODGE JEEP p 587
See RACEWAY PLYMOUTH CHRYSLER LTD

RACEWAY PLYMOUTH CHRYSLER LTD p 587
150 REXDALE BLVD, ETOBICOKE, ON, M9W 1P6
(416) 743-9900 SIC 5511

RACHELLE-BERY PRODUITS NATURELS p 1169
See GESTION QUADRIVIUM LTEE

RACINE & CHAMBERLAND INC p 1170
4001 BOUL CREMAZIE E BUREAU 100, MONTREAL, QC, H1Z 2L2
(514) 722-3501 SIC 6411

RACINE CHEVROLET BUICK GMC LTEE p 1317
1080 RUE DOUGLAS, SAINT-JEAN-SUR-RICHELIEU, QC, J3A 0A2
(450) 359-5900 SIC 5511

RACING FORENSICS INC p 876
3015 KENNEDY RD UNIT 2, SCARBOROUGH, ON, M1V 1E7
(416) 479-4489 SIC 7319

RACK PETROLEUM LTD p 1404
901 HWY 4 S, BIGGAR, SK, S0K 0M0
(306) 948-1800 SIC 5191

RAD TECHNOLOGIES INC p 1383
2835 CH DE L'AEROPORT BUREAU 3, THETFORD MINES, QC, G6G 5R7
(418) 338-4499 SIC 3524

RAD TORQUE SYSTEMS p 177
See NEW WORLD TECHNOLOGIES INCORPORATED

RADAR AUTO PARTS p 544
See RADAR AUTO PARTS INC

RADAR AUTO PARTS INC p 544
20 KING ST, CLINTON, ON, N0M 1L0
(519) 482-3445 SIC 5531

RADCO FOOD STORES LTD p 147
10003 100 ST, MORINVILLE, AB, T8R 1R5
(780) 939-4418 SIC 5411

RADIAL ENGINEERING INC p 247
1588 KEBET WAY, PORT COQUITLAM, BC, V3C 5M5
(604) 942-1001 SIC 3861

RADIANT COMMUNICATIONS CORP p 316
1050 PENDER ST W SUITE 1600, VANCOUVER, BC, V6E 4T3
(604) 257-0500 SIC 4813

RADIANT GLOBAL LOGISTICS (CANADA) INC p 742
1280 COURTNEYPARK DR E, MISSISSAUGA, ON, L5T 1N6
(905) 602-2700 SIC 4731

RADIATEUR MONTREAL RADIATOR p 1184
See RADIATEURS MONTREAL INC

RADIATEURS MONTREAL INC p 1184
270 RUE BEAUBIEN O, MONTREAL, QC, H2V 1C4
(514) 276-8521 SIC 3714

RADIATION SOLUTIONS INC p 706
5875 WHITTLE RD, MISSISSAUGA, ON, L4Z 2H4
(905) 890-1111 SIC 3829

RADICAL ENTERTAINMENT INC p 295
369 TERMINAL AVE, VANCOUVER, BC, V6A 4C4
(604) 688-0606 SIC 7371

RADICALS CAR CLUB INC p 594
14 TODD RD, GEORGETOWN, ON, L7G 4R7
(905) 877-9937 SIC 8699

RADIO 1540 LIMITED p 990
622 COLLEGE ST SUITE 2, TORONTO, ON, M6G 1B6
(416) 531-9991 SIC 4832

RADIO CANADA p 87
See CANADIAN BROADCASTING CORPORATION

RADIO CANADA p 1268
See CANADIAN BROADCASTING CORPORATION

RADIO-ONDE INC p 1280
6655 BOUL PIERRE-BERTRAND BUREAU 643, QUEBEC, QC, G2K 1M1
(418) 527-1602 SIC 4899

RADIOCO LTD p 1025
1983 AMBASSADOR DR, WINDSOR, ON, N9C 3R5
(519) 250-9100 SIC 5065

RADIOLOGY CONSULTANTS ASSOCIATED p 3
110 MAYFAIR CLOSE SE, AIRDRIE, AB, T4A 1T6
(403) 777-3040 SIC 8748

RADIOLOGY CONSULTANTS ASSOCIATED p 68
6707 ELBOW DR SW SUITE 120, CALGARY, AB, T2V 0E3
(403) 777-3007 SIC 8011

RADION LABORATORIES LTD p 210
7198 PROGRESS WAY, DELTA, BC, V4G 1J2
(604) 946-7712 SIC 5047

RADIOWORLD CENTRAL INC p 31
711 48 AVE SE UNIT 8, CALGARY, AB, T2G 4X2
(587) 317-2000 SIC 5961

RADISSON FALLSVIEW p 758
See FALLSVIEW NIAGARA LODGING COMPANY

RADISSON HOTEL p 702
See WW HOTELS CORP

RADISSON HOTEL CALGARY AIRPORT p 25
See SILVERBIRCH NO. 4 OPERATIONS LIMITED PARTNERSHIP

RADISSON HOTEL EDMONTON SOUTH p 119
See SILVERBIRCH NO. 38 OPERATIONS LIMITED PARTNERSHIP

RADISSON HOTEL SASKATOON p 1429
405 20TH ST E, SASKATOON, SK, S7K 6X6
(306) 665-3322 SIC 7011

RADISSON HOTEL SUDBURY p 901
See VISTA SUDBURY HOTEL INC

RADISSON PLAZA HOTEL SASKATCHEWAN p 1418
See HOTEL SASKATCHEWAN (1990) LTD

RADISSONADMIRAL HOTEL p 958
See 1548383 ONTARIO INC

RADISYS p 186
See RADISYS CANADA INC

▲ Public Company ■ Public Company Family Member **HQ** Headquarters **BR** Branch **SL** Single Location

RADISYS CANADA INC p 186
4190 STILL CREEK DR SUITE 300, BURN-ABY, BC, V5C 6C6
(604) 918-6300 *SIC* 4899

RADIUM RESORT INC p 253
8100 GOLF COURSE RD, RADIUM HOT SPRINGS, BC, V0A 1M0
(250) 347-9311 *SIC* 7992

RADIUS GLOBAL SOLUTIONS INC p 280
2455 192 ST SUITE 108, SURREY, BC, V3Z 3X1
(604) 541-1910 *SIC* 4731

RADIUS LOGISTICS p 280
See RADIUS GLOBAL SOLUTIONS INC

RAE ENGINEERING & INSPECTION LTD p 116
4810 93 ST NW, EDMONTON, AB, T6E 5M4
(780) 469-2401 *SIC* 7389

RAF ENTERPRISES INC p 1007
300 WEBER ST N, WATERLOO, ON, N2J 3H6
(519) 885-2000 *SIC* 5511

RAFAT GENERAL CONTRACTOR INC p 495
8850 GEORGE BOLTON PKY, BOLTON, ON, L7E 2Y4
(905) 951-1063 *SIC* 1794

RAFFAN INVESTMENTS LTD p 179
903 HWY 97A RR 7, ARMSTRONG, BC, V0E 1B7
(250) 546-9420 *SIC* 5154

RAFUSE BUILDING SUPPLIES (1977) LTD p 471
200 DYKELAND ST, WOLFVILLE, NS, B4P 1A2
(902) 542-2211 *SIC* 5211

RAFUSE HOME HARDWARE BUILDING CENTRE p 471
See RAFUSE BUILDING SUPPLIES (1977) LTD

RAGLAN INDUSTRIES INC p 813
5151 SIMCOE ST N, OSHAWA, ON, L1H 0S4
(905) 655-3355 *SIC* 3715

RAHR MALTING CANADA LTD p 3
HWY 12 E, ALIX, AB, T0C 0B0
(403) 747-2777 *SIC* 2083

RAI GRANT INSURANCE BROKERS p 674
See RAI INSURANCE BROKERS LTD

RAI INSURANCE BROKERS LTD p 674
140 RENFREW DR SUITE 230, MARKHAM, ON, L3R 6B3
(905) 475-5800 *SIC* 6411

RAICOR CONTRACTING LTD p 186
3993 HENNING DR UNIT 101, BURNABY, BC, V5C 6P7
(604) 293-7702 *SIC* 1742

RAIL CANTECH p 1392
See 2913097 CANADA INC

RAIL-TERM INC p 1095
10765 CH COTE-DE-LIESSE SUITE 201, DORVAL, QC, H9P 2R9
(514) 420-1200 *SIC* 4013

RAILACTION p 1126
See CAD INDUSTRIES FERROVIAIRES LTEE

RAILCRAFT (2010) INTERNATIONAL INC p 277
13272 COMBER WAY, SURREY, BC, V3W 5V9
(604) 543-7245 *SIC* 3446

RAILINK CANADA LTD p 763
445 OAK ST E, NORTH BAY, ON, P1B 1A3
(705) 472-6200 *SIC* 4011

RAIN AND HAIL INSURANCE SERVICE INC p 1421
4303 ALBERT ST SUITE 200, REGINA, SK, S4S 3R6
(306) 584-8844 *SIC* 6331

RAINBOW p 197
See RAINBOW GREENHOUSES INC

RAINBOW BRIDGE p 759
See NIAGARA FALLS BRIDGE COMMISSION

RAINBOW CHRYSALIS p 750
See SAFENET CANADA INC

RAINBOW COLONY FARMING CO LTD p 158
26052 TOWNSHIP ROAD 350, RED DEER COUNTY, AB, T4G 0M4
(403) 227-6465 *SIC* 8661

RAINBOW CONCRETE INDUSTRIES LIMITED p 899
2477 MALEY DR, SUDBURY, ON, P3A 4R7
(705) 566-1740 *SIC* 3271

RAINBOW DAY NURSERY INC p 392
445 ISLAND SHORE BLVD UNIT 11, WINNIPEG, MB, R3X 2B4
(204) 256-0672 *SIC* 8351

RAINBOW DISTRICT SCHOOL BOARD p 899
1545 KENNEDY ST, SUDBURY, ON, P3A 2G1
(705) 566-2280 *SIC* 8211

RAINBOW DISTRICT SCHOOL BOARD p 901
69 YOUNG ST, SUDBURY, ON, P3E 3G5
(705) 377-4615 *SIC* 8211

RAINBOW FORD SALES INC p 159
HWY 11E 42 AVE, ROCKY MOUNTAIN HOUSE, AB, T4T 1A9
(403) 845-3673 *SIC* 5511

RAINBOW GREENHOUSES INC p 197
43756 SOUTH SUMAS RD, CHILLIWACK, BC, V2R 4L6
(604) 858-8100 *SIC* 0181

RAINBOW INTERMEDIATE CARE HOME p 250
See NORTHERN HEALTH AUTHORITY

RAINBOW NATURAL FOODS INC p 830
1487 RICHMOND RD, OTTAWA, ON, K2B 6R9
(613) 726-9200 *SIC* 5411

RAINBOW NURSING REGISTRY LTD p 973
344 DUPONT ST SUITE 402C, TORONTO, ON, M5R 1V9
(416) 922-7616 *SIC* 8049

RAINCITY HOUSING AND SUPPORT SOCIETY p 295
191 ALEXANDER ST, VANCOUVER, BC, V6A 1B8
(604) 662-7023 *SIC* 8699

RAINCOAST BOOK DISTRIBUTION LTD p 256
2440 VIKING WAY, RICHMOND, BC, V6V 1N2
(604) 448-7100 *SIC* 5192

RAINMAKER STUDIOS p 322
See WOW UNLIMITED MEDIA INC

RAINTREE LUMBER SPECIALTIES LTD p 273
5390 192 ST, SURREY, BC, V3S 8E5
(604) 574-0444 *SIC* 2421

RAINVILLE AUTOMOBILE 1975 INC p 1109
15 RUE DUTILLY, GRANBY, QC, J2G 6N6
(450) 378-3943 *SIC* 5511

RAINVILLE, ROGER & FILS INC p 1303
3100 RUE HENRI-L.-CHEVRETTE, SAINT-FELIX-DE-VALOIS, QC, J0K 2M0
(450) 889-4747 *SIC* 5411

RAKUTEN KOBO INC p 992
135 LIBERTY ST SUITE 101, TORONTO, ON, M6K 1A7
(416) 977-8737 *SIC* 5942

RALEIGH CANADA LIMITED p 799
2124 LONDON LANE, OAKVILLE, ON, L6H 5V8
(905) 829-5555 *SIC* 3751

RALEIGH FALLS TIMBER p 621
See 1383791 ONTARIO INC

RALLY MOTOR SPORTS LTD p 1414
10 38TH ST E, PRINCE ALBERT, SK, S6W 1A6
(306) 922-6363 *SIC* 5571

RALLY MOTORS LTD p 1414
60 38TH ST E, PRINCE ALBERT, SK, S6W 1A6
(306) 922-6363 *SIC* 5511

RALLY SUBARU p 118
See DEVONIAN MOTOR CORPORATION

RALLYE MOTORS CHRYSLER p 408
See DAJO HOLDINGS LTD

RALLYE MOTORS HYUNDAI p 407
See RALLYE MOTORS LTD

RALLYE MOTORS LTD p 407
199 CARSON DR, MONCTON, NB, E1C 0K4
(506) 852-8200 *SIC* 5511

RALLYE MOTORS MITSUBISHI p 409
1837 MAIN ST, MONCTON, NB, E1E 1H6
(506) 857-8677 *SIC* 5511

RALPH MCKAY INDUSTRIES INC p 1416
130 HODSMAN RD, REGINA, SK, S4N 5X4
(306) 721-9292 *SIC* 3523

RALPH'S AUTO SUPPLY (B.C.) LTD p 256
12011 MITCHELL RD, RICHMOND, BC, V6V 1M7
(604) 572-5747 *SIC* 5531

RALPH'S RADIO LTD p 289
220 1ST AVE E, VANCOUVER, BC, V5T 1A5
(604) 879-4281 *SIC* 5013

RALSTON FUELS p 1040
See WILBUR, DAVID PRODUCTS LTD

RALSTON METAL PRODUCTS LIMITED p 606
50 WATSON RD S, GUELPH, ON, N1L 1E2
(519) 836-2968 *SIC* 3469

RALY AUTOMOTIVE GROUP LTD p 911
76 MILL ST W, TILBURY, ON, N0P 2L0
(519) 682-3131 *SIC* 5511

RAM CONSTRUCTION INC p 210
8369 RIVER WAY SUITE 101, DELTA, BC, V4G 1G2
(604) 501-5265 *SIC* 1542

RAM DISTRIBUTORS LIMITED p 657
993 ADELAIDE ST S, LONDON, ON, N6E 1R5
(519) 681-1961 *SIC* 5023

RAM FOREST PRODUCTS INC p 598
1 RAM FOREST RD, GORMLEY, ON, L0H 1G0
SIC 2491

RAM HERITAGE LTD p 468
29 GREENS POINT RD, TRENTON, NS, B0K 1X0
(902) 752-6934 *SIC* 6712

RAM INDUSTRIES INC p 1438
33 YORK RD E, YORKTON, SK, S3N 3Z4
(306) 786-2677 *SIC* 5084

RAM IRON & METAL INC p 784
60 ASHWARREN RD, NORTH YORK, ON, M3J 1Z5
(416) 630-4545 *SIC* 4953

RAM MANUFACTURING LTD p 102
10203 184 ST NW, EDMONTON, AB, T5S 2J4
(780) 484-4776 *SIC* 5084

RAMADA HOTEL p 45
See CALGARY RAMADA DOWNTOWN LIMITED PARTNERSHIP

RAMADA HOTEL & CONFERENCE CENTER p 84
See CHIP REIT NO 16 OPERATIONS LIMITED PARTNERSHIP

RAMADA HOTEL & CONFERENCE CENTRE p 601
See D. L. PAGANI LIMITED

RAMADA HOTEL & CONVENTION CENTER p 1417
See 607637 SASKATCHEWAN LTD

RAMADA HOTEL & GOLF DOME p 1431
See 598468 SASKATCHEWAN LTD

RAMADA HOTEL & SUITES p 288
See MR. SPORT HOTEL HOLDINGS LTD

RAMADA INN & SUITES PENTICTON p 244
See PENTICTON COURTYARD INN LTD

RAMADA PLAZA p 178
See LAMB PROPERTIES INC

RAMBLER METALS AND MINING CANADA LIMITED p 421
309 410 WILLIAM CHIPP BLDG HWY, BAIE VERTE, NL, A0K 1B0
(709) 800-1929 *SIC* 1081

RAMBLER MINES p 421
See RAMBLER METALS AND MINING CANADA LIMITED

RAMESH ESSO p 679
550 BUR OAK AVE, MARKHAM, ON, L6C 0C4
(905) 927-0920 *SIC* 4925

RAMJET CONTRACTING LTD p 1416
525 7TH AVE, REGINA, SK, S4N 0G5
(306) 789-6199 *SIC* 1623

RAMKEY COMMUNICATIONS INC p 515
20 ROY BLVD UNIT 2, BRANTFORD, ON, N3R 7K2
(519) 759-0643 *SIC* 4899

RAMP-ART p 1137
See 9050-7641 QUEBEC INC

RAMPF COMPOSITE SOLUTIONS INC p 524
5322 JOHN LUCAS DR, BURLINGTON, ON, L7L 6A6
(905) 331-8042 *SIC* 3728

RAMPION ENTERPRISES LTD p 207
1555 CLIVEDEN AVE, DELTA, BC, V3M 6P7
(604) 395-8225 *SIC* 5091

RAMSAY'S AUTO SALES LIMITED p 468
229 KINGS RD, SYDNEY, NS, B1S 1A5
(902) 539-0112 *SIC* 5511

RAMSAY'S HONDA p 468
See RAMSAY'S AUTO SALES LIMITED

RAMSDEN INDUSTRIES LIMITED p 651
128 OAKLAND AVE, LONDON, ON, N5W 4H6
(519) 451-6720 *SIC* 3365

RAMVAL INC p 1182
6500 RUE SAINT-HUBERT, MONTREAL, QC, H2S 2M3
(514) 272-8233 *SIC* 5912

RAN DON CRANE & LEASING LTD p 763
3736 HIGHWAY 11 N SUITE 2, NORTH BAY, ON, P1B 8G3
(705) 474-4374 *SIC* 1794

RANA MEDICAL p 352
See RIMER ALCO NORTH AMERICA INC

RANCH EHRLO SOCIETY p 1413
GD, PILOT BUTTE, SK, S0G 3Z0
(306) 781-1800 *SIC* 8361

RANCHERS SUPPLY INC p 152
1165 MAIN ST, PINCHER CREEK, AB, T0K 1W0
(403) 627-4451 *SIC* 5083

RANCHMAN'S p 45
See BSL PROPERTY GROUP INC

RANCHO REALTY (EDMONTON) LTD p 121
3203 93 ST NW SUITE 300, EDMONTON, AB, T6N 0B2
(780) 463-2132 *SIC* 6553

RAND & FOWLER INSURANCE LTD p 287
2323 BOUNDARY RD SUITE 101, VANCOUVER, BC, V5M 4V8
(604) 298-4222 *SIC* 6411

RAND A TECHNOLOGY CORPORATION p 745
151 COURTNEYPARK DR W SUITE 201, MISSISSAUGA, ON, L5W 1Y5
(905) 565-2929 *SIC* 8741

RAND ACCESSORIES INC p 1179
9350 AV DE L'ESPLANADE BUREAU 222, MONTREAL, QC, H2N 1V6
(514) 385-3482 *SIC* 5094

RAND AND FOWLER INSURANCE CO-QUITLAM LTD p 198
2918 GLEN DR UNIT 103, COQUITLAM, BC, V3B 2P5
(604) 941-3212 *SIC* 6411

RAND WORLDWIDE p 745
See RAND A TECHNOLOGY CORPORA-

TION
RANDALL'S DECORATION CENTRES p 826
See RANDALL'S PAINTS LIMITED
RANDALL'S PAINTS LIMITED p 826
555 BANK ST, OTTAWA, ON, K1S 5L7
(613) 233-8441 *SIC 5231*
RANDEBAR ENTERPRISES INC p 750
24 GURDWARA RD, NEPEAN, ON, K2E
8B5
(613) 225-9774 *SIC 5075*
RANDHAWA FARMS LTD p 178
33677 HALLERT RD, ABBOTSFORD, BC,
V4X 1W9
(604) 864-8896 *SIC 0191*
RANDON ENTERPRISES LTD p 180
11953 241 RD, ARRAS, BC, V0C 1B0
(250) 843-7394 *SIC 4789*
RANDSTAD CANADA p 534
See RANDSTAD INTERIM INC
RANDSTAD INTERIM INC p 534
1315 BISHOP ST N, CAMBRIDGE, ON,
N1R 6Z2
(519) 740-6944 *SIC 7361*
RANDSTAD INTERIM INC p 947
777 BAY ST SUITE 2000, TORONTO, ON,
M5G 2C8
(800) 540-3594 *SIC 7361*
RANDY RIVER INC p 790
111 ORFUS RD, NORTH YORK, ON, M6A
1M4
(416) 785-1771 *SIC 5611*
RANGELAND ENGINEERING LTD p 65
1520 4 ST SW SUITE 1000, CALGARY, AB,
T2R 1H5
(403) 265-5130 *SIC 8711*
RANGER BOARD p 6
See WEST FRASER MILLS LTD
RANGER EXPRESS FORWARDING INC p
686
7685 BATH RD, MISSISSAUGA, ON, L4T
3T1
(905) 672-3434 *SIC 4731*
RANGER GROUP OF COMPANIES p 686
*See RANGER EXPRESS FORWARDING
INC*
RANGER INSPECTION p 16
See HMT CANADA LTD
RANGER TIRE INC p 31
4020 9 ST SE UNIT 2, CALGARY, AB, T2G
3C4
(403) 723-0777 *SIC 5014*
RANKIN CONSTRUCTION INC p 887
222 MARTINDALE RD, ST CATHARINES,
ON, L2S 0B2
(905) 684-1111 *SIC 1794*
RAPID AID CORP p 717
4120A SLADEVIEW CRES UNIT 1-4, MIS-
SISSAUGA, ON, L5L 5Z3
(905) 820-4788 *SIC 3842*
RAPID ELECTRIC VEHICLES INC p 285
1570 CLARK DR, VANCOUVER, BC, V5L
3L3
SIC 5531
RAPID EQUIPMENT RENTAL LIMITED p
784
5 SAINT REGIS CRES N UNIT 2, NORTH
YORK, ON, M3J 1Y9
(416) 638-7007 *SIC 7353*
RAPID FORMING INC p 473
5 MANSEWOOD CRT, ACTON, ON, L7J
0A1
SIC 1799
RAPID GEAR p 642
*See RAPID PRECISION MACHINING &
GEARING LTD*
**RAPID PRECISION MACHINING & GEAR-
ING LTD** p
642
1596 STRASBURG RD, KITCHENER, ON,
N2R 1E9
(519) 748-4828 *SIC 3566*
**RAPID REFRIGERATION MANUFACTUR-
ING COMPANY LIMITED** p
871

1550 BIRCHMOUNT RD, SCARBOROUGH,
ON, M1P 2H1
(416) 285-8282 *SIC 3585*
RAPIDE INVESTIGATION CANADA LTEE p
1123
114 RUE SAINT-GEORGES, LA PRAIRIE,
QC, J5R 2L9
(514) 879-1199 *SIC 7323*
RAPIDE METAL p 1234
See METALIUM INC
RAPIDGAZ p 1110
*See SERVICE D'ECHANGE RAPIDGAZ
INC*
RAPIDO EQUIPEMENT INC p 1262
735 AV PRUNEAU BUREAU 100, QUEBEC,
QC, G1M 2J9
(418) 684-9000 *SIC 5021*
RAPPORT CREDIT UNION LIMITED p 932
18 GRENVILLE ST SUITE 1, TORONTO,
ON, M4Y 3B3
(416) 314-6772 *SIC 6062*
RAPPORTS PRE-EMPLOI GROUPECHO p
1084
See GROUPECHO CANADA INC
RAPTIM HUMANITARIAN TRAVEL p 177
*See MENNO TRAVEL SERVICE CANADA
LTD*
RAPTOR MINING PRODUCTS INC p 102
18131 AVE NW SUITE 118, EDMONTON,
AB, T5S 1M8
(780) 444-1284 *SIC 5082*
RAPTOR WEAR PARTS p 102
See RAPTOR MINING PRODUCTS INC
RARE METHOD p 67
*See RAREMETHOD INTERACTIVE STU-
DIOS INC*
**RAREMETHOD INTERACTIVE STUDIOS
INC** p 67
1812 4 ST SW SUITE 601, CALGARY, AB,
T2S 1W1
SIC 4899
RASAKTI INC p 1306
148 RUE SYLVESTRE, SAINT-GERMAIN-
DE-GRANTHAM, QC, J0C 1K0
(819) 395-1111 *SIC 3812*
RASSAUN SERVICES INC p 881
22 BOSWELL DR, SIMCOE, ON, N3Y 4N5
(519) 426-0150 *SIC 3441*
RASTALL MINE SUPPLY LIMITED p 900
268 HEMLOCK ST, SUDBURY, ON, P3C
1H9
(705) 675-2431 *SIC 5085*
RASTALL NUT & BOLT CO p 900
See RASTALL MINE SUPPLY LIMITED
RATANA INTERNATIONAL LTD p 291
8310 MANITOBA ST, VANCOUVER, BC,
V5X 3A5
(604) 321-6776 *SIC 5021*
RATCLIFFS/SEVERN LTD p 855
10537 YONGE ST, RICHMOND HILL, ON,
L4C 3C5
SIC 3351
RATH EASTLINK COMMUNITY CENTER p
468
*See CENTRAL NOVA SCOTIA CIVIC CEN-
TER SOCIETY*
RATHI, KANU PRIYA PHARMACY INC p
534
499 HESPELER RD, CAMBRIDGE, ON,
N1R 6J2
(519) 623-6770 *SIC 5912*
RATTRAY, WILLIAM HOLDINGS LTD p 760
3770 MONTROSE RD, NIAGARA FALLS,
ON, L2H 3C8
(905) 354-3848 *SIC 5251*
**RAUFOSS AUTOMOTIVE COMPONENTS
CANADA INC** p 1062
4050 RUE LAVOISIER, BOISBRIAND, QC,
J7H 1R4
(450) 419-4911 *SIC 3714*
RAUFOSS TECHNOLOGY p 1062
*See RAUFOSS AUTOMOTIVE COMPO-
NENTS CANADA INC*
RAVAGO CANADA CO p 587

180 ATTWELL DR SUITE 260, ETOBI-
COKE, ON, M9W 6A9
(416) 977-5456 *SIC 5162*
RAVEN CENTER HOLDINGS LTD p 214
49 ALASKA HWY, FORT ST. JOHN, BC, V1J
4H7
(250) 787-8474 *SIC 7359*
RAVEN ENTERPRISES INC. p 1414
200 28TH ST E, PRINCE ALBERT, SK, S6V
1X2
(306) 922-3663 *SIC 5411*
RAVEN OILFIELD RENTALS p 214
See RAVEN CENTER HOLDINGS LTD
RAVEN ROOFING LTD p 280
18988 34A AVE, SURREY, BC, V3Z 1A7
(604) 531-9619 *SIC 1761*
RAVINE MUSHROOM (1983) LIMITED p
1028
4101 KING-VAUGHAN RD, WOODBRIDGE,
ON, L4H 1E4
(905) 833-5498 *SIC 0182*
RAVINE MUSHROOM FARMS INC p 1033
131 MARYCROFT AVE UNIT 3, WOOD-
BRIDGE, ON, L4L 5Y6
(905) 264-6173 *SIC 7389*
RAW MATERIALS COMPANY INC p 847
17 INVERTOSE DR, PORT COLBORNE,
ON, L3K 5V5
(905) 835-1203 *SIC 4953*
RAWLCO CAPITAL LTD p 37
6807 RAILWAY ST SE SUITE 140, CAL-
GARY, AB, T2H 2V6
(403) 451-9893 *SIC 4832*
RAWLCO CAPITAL LTD p 1418
2401 SASKATCHEWAN DR SUITE 210,
REGINA, SK, S4P 4H8
(306) 525-0000 *SIC 4832*
RAWLCO RADIO p 1418
See RAWLCO CAPITAL LTD
RAWLCO RADIO LTD p 1433
715 SASKATCHEWAN CRES W, SASKA-
TOON, SK, S7M 5V7
(306) 934-2222 *SIC 4832*
RAY AGRO & PETROLEUM LTD p 167
18 BOULDER BLVD, STONY PLAIN, AB,
T7Z 1V7
(780) 963-2078 *SIC 5191*
RAY FRIEL RECREATION COMPLEX p 810
1585 TENTH LINE RD, ORLEANS, ON, K1E
3E8
(613) 830-2747 *SIC 7999*
RAY'S FOOD BASICS p 600
See RJ'S FRUGAL MARKETS INC
**RAY-DONN TOEWS BUILDING MATERI-
ALS LTD** p
1411
506 HIGH ST W, MOOSE JAW, SK, S6H 1T4
(306) 693-0211 *SIC 5211*
RAY-MONT LOGISTIQUES CANADA INC p
1216
1751 RUE RICHARDSON BUREAU 4504,
MONTREAL, QC, H3K 1G6
(514) 933-4449 *SIC 4731*
RAYAN INVESTMENTS LTD p 409
1635 BERRY MILLS RD, MONCTON, NB,
E1E 4R7
(506) 858-1600 *SIC 4953*
RAYBURN'S MARINE WORLD LTD p 220
2330 ENTERPRISE WAY, KELOWNA, BC,
V1X 4H7
(250) 860-4232 *SIC 5551*
RAYDON RENTALS LTD p 102
10235 180 ST NW, EDMONTON, AB, T5S
1C1
(780) 989-1301 *SIC 7353*
RAYDONN CASTLE BUILDING CENTRE p
1411
*See RAY-DONN TOEWS BUILDING MATE-
RIALS LTD*
RAYLINK LTD p 1039
134 KENT ST, CHARLOTTETOWN, PE,
C1A 8R8
(902) 629-8400 *SIC 4724*
RAYMARK ULC p 1157

5460 CH DE LA COTE-DE-LIESSE, MONT-
ROYAL, QC, H4P 1A5
(514) 737-0941 *SIC 7371*
**RAYMOND AND ASSOCIATES ROOFING
INC** p 827
3091 ALBION RD N SUITE 5B, OTTAWA,
ON, K1V 9V9
(613) 274-7508 *SIC 1761*
RAYMOND BEAUSEJOUR (1989) INC p
1391
202 3E AV, VAL-D'OR, QC, J9P 1R5
(819) 824-4185 *SIC 5541*
**RAYMOND CHABOT GRANT THORNTON
RCGT** p 1207
*See RAYMOND CHABOT GRANT THORN-
TON S.E.N.C.R.L.*
**RAYMOND CHABOT GRANT THORNTON
S.E.N.C.R.L.** p 1207
600 RUE DE LA GAUCHETIERE O BU-
REAU 2000, MONTREAL, QC, H3B 4L8
(514) 878-2691 *SIC 8721*
**RAYMOND CHABOT GRANT THORNTON
S.E.N.C.R.L.** p 1371
455 RUE KING O BUREAU 500, SHER-
BROOKE, QC, J1H 6G4
(819) 822-4000 *SIC 8721*
**RAYMOND CHABOT GRANT THORNTON
S.E.N.C.R.L.** p 1371
*See RAYMOND CHABOT GRANT THORN-
TON S.E.N.C.R.L.*
**RAYMOND CHABOT GRANT THORTON
CONSULTING INC.** p 824
116 ALBERT ST, OTTAWA, ON, K1P 5G3
(613) 760-3500 *SIC 8748*
RAYMOND CHABOT INC p 1207
600 RUE DE LA GAUCHETIERE O BU-
REAU 2000, MONTREAL, QC, H3B 4L8
(514) 879-1385 *SIC 8111*
RAYMOND ELEMENTARY SCHOOL p 153
See WESTWIND SCHOOL DIVISION #74
RAYMOND HEALTH CENTRE p 153
*See GOVERNMENT OF THE PROVINCE
OF ALBERTA*
RAYMOND JAMES LTD p 58
525 8 AVE SW SUITE 161, CALGARY, AB,
T2P 1G1
(403) 221-0333 *SIC 6211*
RAYMOND JAMES LTD p 309
925 GEORGIA ST W SUITE 2100, VAN-
COUVER, BC, V6C 3L2
(604) 659-8000 *SIC 6211*
RAYMOND LANCTOT LTEE p 1330
5290 BOUL THIMENS, SAINT-LAURENT,
QC, H4R 2B2
(514) 731-6841 *SIC 5091*
RAYMOND PARENT TEXTILES INC p 1376
33 RUE DU PRINCE, SOREL-TRACY, QC,
J3P 4J5
(450) 743-9666 *SIC 5131*
RAYMOND-CBE MACHINERY INC p 261
11788 RIVER RD SUITE 118, RICHMOND,
BC, V6X 1Z7
SIC 3561
RAYMORE NEW HOLLAND p 1415
See 619020 SASKATCHEWAN LTD
RAYNA PEARL INVESTMENT LTD p 587
19 SHAFT RD, ETOBICOKE, ON, M9W 4M3
(416) 241-1521 *SIC 5621*
RAYNARD FARM EQUIPMENT LTD p 1436
2524 SOUTH SERVICE RD W, SWIFT
CURRENT, SK, S9H 5J9
(306) 773-3030 *SIC 5083*
RAYNOR CANADA CORP p 699
5100 TIMBERLEA BLVD SUITE A, MISSIS-
SAUGA, ON, L4W 2S5
(905) 625-0037 *SIC 3442*
RAYONESE TEXTILE INC p 1320
500 BOUL MONSEIGNEUR-DUBOIS,
SAINT-JEROME, QC, J7Y 3L8
(450) 476-1991 *SIC 2221*
**RAYONIER A.M. CANADA ENTERPRISES
INC** p 1207
4 PLACE VILLE-MARIE BUREAU 100,
MONTREAL, QC, H3B 2E7

---

(514) 871-0137   *SIC 2611*
RAYONIER A.M. CANADA G.P.   *p 542*
175 PLANER RD, CHAPLEAU, ON, P0M 1K0
(705) 864-1060   *SIC 2611*
RAYONIER A.M. CANADA G.P.   *p 546*
70 17TH AVE, COCHRANE, ON, P0L 1C0
(705) 272-4321   *SIC 2421*
RAYONIER A.M. CANADA G.P.   *p 1054*
67 RUE PRINCIPALE S, BEARN, QC, J0Z 1G0
(819) 726-3551   *SIC 2421*
RAYONIER A.M. CANADA G.P.   *p 1151*
400 RUE DU PORT, MATANE, QC, G4W 3M6
(418) 794-2001   *SIC 2611*
RAYONIER A.M. CANADA G.P.   *p 1207*
4 PLACE VILLE-MARIE BUREAU 100, MONTREAL, QC, H3B 2E7
(514) 871-0137   *SIC 2611*
RAYONIER A.M. CANADA G.P.   *p 1378*
10 CH GATINEAU, TEMISCAMING, QC, J0Z 3R0
(819) 627-4387   *SIC 2611*
RAYONIER A.M. CANADA INDUSTRIES INC   *p 1207*
4 PLACE VILLE-MARIE BUREAU 100, MONTREAL, QC, H3B 2E7
(514) 871-0137   *SIC 2421*
RAYONIER A.M. COMPAGNIE DE CONSTRUCTION INC   *p 1207*
4 PLACE VILLE-MARIE BUREAU 100, MONTREAL, QC, H3B 2E7
(514) 871-0137   *SIC 1541*
RAYONIER AM CANADA ENTERPRISES INC   *p 542*
See *RAYONIER A.M. CANADA G.P.*
RAYOVAC DIVISION   *p 745*
See *SPECTRUM BRANDS CANADA, INC*
RAYTHEON CANADA LIMITED   *p 25*
919 72 AVE NE, CALGARY, AB, T2E 8N9
(403) 295-6900   *SIC 3812*
RAYTHEON CANADA LIMITED   *p 681*
450 LEITZ RD SUITE 2, MIDLAND, ON, L4R 5B8
(705) 526-5401   *SIC 3827*
RAYTHEON CANADA LIMITED   *p 825*
360 ALBERT ST SUITE 1640, OTTAWA, ON, K1R 7X7
(613) 233-4121   *SIC 3229*
RAYTHEON CANADA LIMITED   *p 1009*
400 PHILLIP ST, WATERLOO, ON, N2L 6R7
(519) 885-0110   *SIC 3669*
RAYTHEON ELCAN OPTICAL TECHNOLOGIES   *p 681*
See *RAYTHEON CANADA LIMITED*
RAYWAL CABINETS   *p 905*
See *RAYWAL LIMITED PARTNERSHIP, THE*
RAYWAL LIMITED PARTNERSHIP, THE   *p 905*
68 GREEN LANE, THORNHILL, ON, L3T 6K8
(905) 889-6243   *SIC 2434*
RAYWALT CONSTRUCTION CO. LTD   *p 2*
10374 276 ST, ACHESON, AB, T7X 6A5
(780) 962-0030   *SIC 1623*
RAZIR TRANSPORT SERVICES LTD   *p 391*
1460 CLARENCE AVE SUITE 204, WINNIPEG, MB, R3T 1T6
(204) 489-2258   *SIC 4213*
RAZO   *p 25*
See *RAZOR SHARP MAGNETICS INC*
RAZOR ENERGY CORP   *p 58*
500 5 AVE SW SUITE 800, CALGARY, AB, T2P 3L5
(403) 262-0242   *SIC 1311*
RAZOR SHARP MAGNETICS INC   *p 25*
314 11 AVE NE, CALGARY, AB, T2E 0Z1
SIC 5999
RB HEALTH (CANADA) INC   *p 699*
1680 TECH AVE UNIT 2, MISSISSAUGA,

ON, L4W 5S9
(905) 283-7000   *SIC 2833*
RB PROPANE   *p 1303*
See *BELL-GAZ LTEE*
RBC ASSET MANAGEMENT INC   *p 966*
200 BAY ST, TORONTO, ON, M5J 2J5
(416) 974-9419   *SIC 6282*
RBC AUTOMOTIVE FINANCE   *p 572*
See *ROYAL BANK OF CANADA*
RBC AUTOMOTIVE FINANCE   *p 966*
See *ROYAL BANK OF CANADA*
RBC BEARINGS CANADA, INC   *p 1050*
8121 RUE JARRY, ANJOU, QC, H1J 1H6
(514) 352-9425   *SIC 3724*
RBC CAPITAL MARKETS   *p 966*
See *RBC DOMINION SECURITIES INC*
RBC DEXIA INVESTORS SERVICES   *p 58*
335 8 AVE SW, CALGARY, AB, T2P 1C9
(403) 292-3978   *SIC 6211*
RBC DOMINION SECURITIES INC   *p 375*
201 PORTAGE AVE SUITE 3100, WINNIPEG, MB, R3B 3K6
(204) 982-3450   *SIC 6211*
RBC DOMINION SECURITIES INC   *p 966*
200 BAY ST, TORONTO, ON, M5J 2W7
(416) 842-2000   *SIC 6282*
RBC DOMINION SECURITIES LIMITED   *p 966*
200 BAY ST 9TH FLOOR, TORONTO, ON, M5J 2J5
(416) 842-4088   *SIC 6211*
RBC GENERAL INSURANCE COMPANY   *p 726*
6880 FINANCIAL DR SUITE 200, MISSISSAUGA, ON, L5N 7Y5
(905) 816-5400   *SIC 6331*
RBC INSURANCE COMPANY OF CANADA   *p 726*
6880 FINANCIAL DR SUITE 200, MISSISSAUGA, ON, L5N 7Y5
(905) 949-3663   *SIC 6411*
RBC INSURANCE SERVICES INC   *p 726*
6880 FINANCIAL DR WEST TOWER, MISSISSAUGA, ON, L5N 7Y5
(905) 949-3663   *SIC 6311*
RBC INVESTOR SERVICES TRUST   *p 966*
200 BAY ST, TORONTO, ON, M5J 2J5
SIC 6282
RBC INVESTOR SERVICES TRUST   *p 983*
155 WELLINGTON ST W 7 FL, TORONTO, ON, M5V 3H1
(416) 955-6251   *SIC 6282*
RBC LIFE INSURANCE COMPANY   *p 726*
6880 FINANCIAL DR SUITE 1000, MISSISSAUGA, ON, L5N 8E8
(905) 816-2746   *SIC 6311*
RBC O'SHAUGHNESSY U.S. VALUE FUND   *p 970*
77 KING ST W, TORONTO, ON, M5K 2A1
(800) 463-3863   *SIC 6722*
RBC PHILLIPS, HAGER & NORTH INVESTMENT COUNSEL INC   *p 983*
155 WELLINGTON ST W FL 17, TORONTO, ON, M5V 3H1
(416) 956-9618   *SIC 6211*
RBC VENTURES INC   *p 966*
20 BAY ST 17TH FL, TORONTO, ON, M5J 2N8
(416) 846-3465   *SIC 7371*
RBDS RUBBISH BOYS DISPOSAL SERVICE INC   *p 289*
887 GREAT NORTHERN WAY SUITE 301, VANCOUVER, BC, V5T 4T5
(604) 731-5782   *SIC 4953*
RBF INTERNATIONAL LTEE   *p 1321*
780 RUE NOBEL, SAINT-JEROME, QC, J7Z 7A3
(450) 438-4416   *SIC 5169*
RBG SECURITY INC   *p 729*
6500 SILVER DART DR SUITE 228A, MISSISSAUGA, ON, L5P 1A2
(647) 729-2360   *SIC 7381*

RBI DIVISION OF MESTEK CANADA   *p 735*
See *MESTEK CANADA INC*
RBI PLASTIQUE INC   *p 399*
6 AV CRABTREE, EDMUNDSTON, NB, E3V 3K5
(506) 739-9180   *SIC 2821*
RBL WAREHOUSE DISTRIBUTORS   *p 84*
See *R.T.A. HOLDINGS LTD*
RBM   *p 324*
See *RESPONSE BIOMEDICAL CORP*
RBN FISHERIES LIMITED   *p 462*
65 NEWELL RD, MILL VILLAGE, NS, B0J 2H0
(902) 677-2491   *SIC 5146*
RBS BULK SYSTEMS INC   *p 18*
9910 48 ST SE, CALGARY, AB, T2C 2R2
(403) 248-1530   *SIC 4213*
RBS LAWYERS   *p 300*
See *RICHARDS BUELL SUTTON LLP*
RBW GRAPHICS   *p 835*
See *IMPRIMERIES TRANSCONTINENTAL 2005 S.E.N.C.*
RCA DIAGNOSTICS   *p 68*
See *RADIOLOGY CONSULTANTS ASSOCIATED*
RCA RECORDS   *p 780*
See *SONY MUSIC ENTERTAINMENT CANADA INC*
RCAP LEASING INC   *p 524*
5575 NORTH SERVICE RD SUITE 300, BURLINGTON, ON, L7L 6M1
(905) 639-3995   *SIC 6159*
RCBC   *p 300*
See *RECYCLING COUNCIL OF BRITISH COLUMBIA*
RCGT CONSULTING   *p 824*
See *RAYMOND CHABOT GRANT THORTON CONSULTING INC.*
RCI ENVIRONMENT   *p 1051*
See *WM QUEBEC INC*
RCI VENTURES INC.   *p 887*
222 MARTINDALE RD, ST CATHARINES, ON, L2S 0B2
(905) 684-1111   *SIC 1796*
RCM TECHNOLOGIES CANADA CORP   *p 845*
895 BROCK RD, PICKERING, ON, L1W 3C1
(905) 837-8333   *SIC 8999*
RCPEIM   *p 1173*
See *REGROUPEMENT DES CENTRE DE LA PETITE ENFANCE DE L'*
RCR HOSPITALITY GROUP LIMITED   *p 456*
6009 QUINPOOL RD SUITE 300, HALIFAX, NS, B3K 5J7
(902) 454-8533   *SIC 5812*
RCR INDUSTRIAL INC   *p 647*
145 MAGILL ST, LIVELY, ON, P3Y 1K6
(705) 692-3661   *SIC 3532*
RCR INTERNATIONAL INC   *p 793*
89 KENHAR DR, NORTH YORK, ON, M9L 2R3
(416) 749-0600   *SIC 3069*
RCS CONSTRUCTION INCORPORATED   *p 440*
26 TOPSAIL CRT, BEDFORD, NS, B4B 1K5
(902) 468-6757   *SIC 1542*
RCU INSURANCE SERVICES LTD   *p 253*
110 2ND ST W, REVELSTOKE, BC, V0E 2S0
(250) 837-6291   *SIC 6321*
RD ENTERPRISES   *p 587*
See *REAL DEALS ENTERPRISES INC*
RDA INC   *p 1033*
290 ROWNTREE DAIRY RD, WOODBRIDGE, ON, L4L 9J7
(905) 652-8680   *SIC 6411*
RDC   *p 431*
See *RESEARCH & DEVELOPMENT CORPORATION OF NEWFOUNDLAND AND LABRADOR*
RDC CONTROLE LTEE   *p 1059*
1100 BOUL MICHELE-BOHEC, BLAINVILLE, QC, J7C 5N5

(450) 434-0216   *SIC 3823*
RDH BUILDING SCIENCE INC   *p 186*
4333 STILL CREEK DR SUITE 400, BURNABY, BC, V5C 6S6
(604) 873-1181   *SIC 8711*
RDH MINING EQUIPMENT LTD   *p 475*
904 HWY 64, ALBAN, ON, P0M 1A0
(705) 857-2154   *SIC 3532*
RDHR INVESTMENTS & HOLDINGS INC   *p 717*
2187 DUNWIN DR, MISSISSAUGA, ON, L5L 1X2
(905) 820-7887   *SIC 6794*
RDI   *p 156*
See *RED DEER IRONWORKS INC*
RDI CHEMICAL CORPORATION   *p 736*
1875 DREW RD, MISSISSAUGA, ON, L5S 1J5
(905) 673-2556   *SIC 5169*
RDL LEGARE MC NICOLL INC   *p 1280*
1305 BOUL LEBOURGNEUF BUREAU 401, QUEBEC, QC, G2K 2E4
(418) 622-6666   *SIC 8721*
RDP MARATHON INC   *p 1087*
2583 BOUL CHOMEDEY, COTE SAINT-LUC, QC, H7T 2R2
(450) 687-7262   *SIC 5085*
RDS   *p 1174*
See *RESEAU DES SPORTS (RDS) INC, LE*
RE MAX CITE INC   *p 1247*
13150 RUE SHERBROOKE E, POINTE-AUX-TREMBLES, QC, H1A 4B1
(514) 644-0000   *SIC 6531*
RE MAX PROFESSIONALS   *p 576*
See *RE/MAX PROFESSIONALS INC*
RE MAX QUINTE LTD   *p 492*
308 NORTH FRONT ST, BELLEVILLE, ON, K8P 3C4
(613) 969-9907   *SIC 6531*
RE MAX WEST REALTY BROKERAGE INC   *p 994*
1678 BLOOR ST W, TORONTO, ON, M6P 1A9
(416) 769-1616   *SIC 6531*
RE-DOE MOLD COMPANY LIMITED   *p 1026*
665 MORTON DR, WINDSOR, ON, N9J 3T9
(519) 734-6161   *SIC 3544*
RE-MAX IMMO-CONTACT INC   *p 1232*
2820 BOUL SAINT-MARTIN E BUREAU 201, MONTREAL, QC, H7E 5A1
(450) 661-6810   *SIC 6531*
RE-MAX MONTREAL METRO INC   *p 1166*
5136 RUE DE BELLECHASSE, MONTREAL, QC, H1T 2A4
(514) 251-9000   *SIC 6531*
RE/MAX   *p 877*
See *RE/MAX GOLDENWAY REALTY INC*
RE/MAX   *p 1000*
See *RE/MAX ALL-STARS REALTY INC.*
RE/MAX   *p 1322*
See *RE/MAX PERFORMANCE INC*
RE/MAX 2001 INC   *p 1241*
360 BOUL CURE-LABELLE, MONTREAL-OUEST, QC, H7V 2S1
(450) 625-2001   *SIC 6531*
RE/MAX A-B REALTY LTD   *p 896*
88 WELLINGTON ST, STRATFORD, ON, N5A 2L2
(519) 273-2821   *SIC 6531*
RE/MAX ACCORD   *p 119*
See *1140456 ALBERTA LTD*
RE/MAX ACTION (1992) INC   *p 1131*
8280 BOUL CHAMPLAIN, LASALLE, QC, H8P 1B5
(514) 364-3222   *SIC 6531*
RE/MAX ALL-STARS REALTY INC.   *p 1000*
5071 HIGHWAY 7 E, UNIONVILLE, ON, L3R 1N3
(905) 477-0011   *SIC 6531*
RE/MAX BLUE SPRING REALTY (HALTON) CORP   *p 473*
2 MILL ST E, ACTON, ON, L7J 1G9
(519) 853-2086   *SIC 6531*
RE/MAX CADIBEC INC   *p 1118*

3535 BOUL SAINT-CHARLES BUREAU 304, KIRKLAND, QC, H9H 5B9
(514) 694-0840   *SIC* 6531

RE/MAX CAPITALE   *p* 1257
See RE/MAX CAPITALE (1983) INC

RE/MAX CAPITALE (1983) INC   *p* 1257
7385 BOUL HENRI-BOURASSA, QUEBEC, QC, G1H 3E5
(418) 627-3120   *SIC* 6531

RE/MAX CENTRAL   *p* 41
2411 4 ST NW SUITE 206, CALGARY, AB, T2M 2Z8
(403) 241-8199   *SIC* 6411

RE/MAX CENTRE CITY   *p* 652
See RE/MAX CENTRE CITY REALTY INC

RE/MAX CENTRE CITY REALTY   *p* 249
See CENTRE CITY REAL ESTATE INC

RE/MAX CENTRE CITY REALTY INC *p* 652
675 ADELAIDE ST N, LONDON, ON, N5Y 2L4
(519) 667-1800   *SIC* 6531

RE/MAX COLONIAL PACIFIC REALTY   *p* 280
15414 24 AVE, SURREY, BC, V4A 2J3
(604) 541-4850   *SIC* 6531

RE/MAX CONDOS PLUS CORPORATION *p* 966
45 HARBOUR SQ, TORONTO, ON, M5J 2G4
(416) 203-6636   *SIC* 6531

RE/MAX CREST REALTY   *p* 240
See CREST REALTY LTD

RE/MAX CROSSROADS REALTY INC *p* 877
1055 MCNICOLL AVE, SCARBOROUGH, ON, M1W 3W6
(416) 491-4002   *SIC* 6531

RE/MAX CROWN REAL ESTATE LTD   *p* 1421
2350 2ND AVE, REGINA, SK, S4R 1A6
(306) 791-7666   *SIC* 6531

RE/MAX DE FRANCHEVILLE INC   *p* 1368
1000 AV DES CEDRES BUREAU 5, SHAW-INIGAN, QC, G9N 1P6
(819) 537-5000   *SIC* 6531

RE/MAX DE LA POINTE   *p* 1247
See RE/MAX DE LA POINTE INC

RE/MAX DE LA POINTE INC   *p* 1247
13150 RUE SHERBROOKE E BUREAU 201, POINTE-AUX-TREMBLES, QC, H1A 4B1
(514) 644-0000   *SIC* 6531

RE/MAX DU SECTEUR   *p* 1241
See RE/MAX 2001 INC

RE/MAX EAST COAST REALTY   *p* 421
See ROW, TED

RE/MAX EASTERN REALTY INC   *p* 842
64 HASTINGS ST N, PETERBOROUGH, ON, K9J 3G3
(705) 743-9111   *SIC* 6531

RE/MAX ESCARPMENT REALTY INC *p* 616
1595 UPPER JAMES ST UNIT 101, HAMIL-TON, ON, L9B 0H7
(905) 575-5478   *SIC* 6531

RE/MAX EXCELLENCE INC   *p* 1052
7130 RUE BEAUBIEN E, ANJOU, QC, H1M 1B2
(514) 354-6240   *SIC* 6531

RE/MAX EXTRA INC   *p* 1057
365 BOUL SIR-WILFRID-LAURIER BU-REAU 202, BELOEIL, QC, J3G 4T2
(450) 464-1000   *SIC* 6531

RE/MAX FIRST   *p* 39
See REMAX REAL ESTATE CALGARY SOUTH LTD

RE/MAX FIRST CHOICE REALTY LTD *p* 909
846 MACDONELL ST, THUNDER BAY, ON, P7B 5J1
(807) 344-5700   *SIC* 6531

RE/MAX FIRST REALTY LTD   *p* 843
1154 KINGSTON RD, PICKERING, ON, L1V 1B4
(905) 831-3300   *SIC* 6531

RE/MAX FORTIN, DELAGE INC   *p* 1274
3175 CH DES QUATRE-BOURGEOIS BU-REAU 120, QUEBEC, QC, G1W 2K7
(418) 653-5353   *SIC* 6531

RE/MAX GARDEN CITY REALTY INC BRO-KERAGE   *p* 886
161 CARLTON ST SUITE 123, ST CATHARINES, ON, L2R 1R5
(905) 641-1110   *SIC* 6531

RE/MAX GOLDENWAY REALTY INC *p* 877
3390 MIDLAND AVE UNIT 7, SCARBOR-OUGH, ON, M1V 5K3
(416) 299-8199   *SIC* 6531

RE/MAX GRANDE PRAIRIE   *p* 132
See GRANDE PRAIRIE ASSOCIATES RE-ALTY LTD

RE/MAX HALLMARK REALTY LTD   *p* 915
1 DUNCAN MILL RD UNIT 101, TORONTO, ON, M3B 3J5
(416) 424-3170   *SIC* 6531

RE/MAX HALLMARK REALTY LTD   *p* 917
2237 QUEEN ST E, TORONTO, ON, M4E 1G1
(416) 357-1059   *SIC* 6531

RE/MAX HARMONIE INC   *p* 1168
3550 RUE RACHEL E BUREAU 201, MON-TREAL, QC, H1W 1A7
(514) 259-8884   *SIC* 6531

RE/MAX IMPERIAL REALTY INC   *p* 674
3000 STEELES AVE E SUITE 309, MARKHAM, ON, L3R 4T9
(905) 305-0033   *SIC* 6531

RE/MAX KELOWNA   *p* 222
See NORWICH REAL ESTATE SERVICES INC

RE/MAX LONGUEUIL INC   *p* 1143
50 RUE SAINT-CHARLES O BUREAU 100, LONGUEUIL, QC, J4H 1C6
(450) 651-8331   *SIC* 6531

RE/MAX METRO-CITY REALTY LTD   *p* 834
344 FRANK ST, OTTAWA, ON, K2P 0Y1
(613) 288-3300   *SIC* 6531

RE/MAX NIAGARA REALTY LTD   *p* 759
5627 MAIN ST, NIAGARA FALLS, ON, L2G 5Z3
(905) 356-9600   *SIC* 6531

RE/MAX NOVA REAL ESTATE   *p* 448
7 MELLOR AVE UNIT 1, DARTMOUTH, NS, B3B 0E8
(902) 478-0991   *SIC* 6531

RE/MAX ORILLIA REALTY (1996) LTD   *p* 810
97 NEYWASH ST, ORILLIA, ON, L3V 1X4
(705) 325-1373   *SIC* 6531

RE/MAX PERFORMANCE INC   *p* 1322
15 RUE DU PRINCE-ARTHUR, SAINT-LAMBERT, QC, J4P 1X1
(450) 466-4000   *SIC* 6531

RE/MAX PERFORMANCE REALTY   *p* 368
942 ST MARY'S RD, WINNIPEG, MB, R2M 3R5
(204) 255-4204   *SIC* 6531

RE/MAX PERFORMANCE REALTY INC *p* 712
141-1140 BURNHAMTHORPE RD W, MIS-SISSAUGA, ON, L5C 4E9
(905) 270-2000   *SIC* 6531

RE/MAX PERFORMANCE REALTY INC *p* 712
1140 BURNHAMTHORPE RD W SUITE 141, MISSISSAUGA, ON, L5C 4E9
(905) 270-2000   *SIC* 6531

RE/MAX PREFERRED REALTY LTD *p* 1018
6505 TECUMSEH RD E SUITE 1, WIND-SOR, ON, N8T 1E7
(519) 944-5955   *SIC* 6531

RE/MAX PRIVILEGE INC   *p* 1308
5920 BOUL COUSINEAU, SAINT-HUBERT, QC, J3Y 7R9
(450) 678-3150   *SIC* 6531

RE/MAX PRO-COMMERCIAL   *p* 1216
See 9046-6483 QUEBEC INC

RE/MAX PROFESSIONALS INC   *p* 576
270 THE KINGSWAY SUITE 200, ETOBI-COKE, ON, M9A 3T7

(416) 236-1241   *SIC* 6531

RE/MAX PROFESSIONALS INC   *p* 712
1645 DUNDAS ST W, MISSISSAUGA, ON, L5C 1E3
(905) 270-8840   *SIC* 6531

RE/MAX PROFESSIONEL INC   *p* 1111
1050 RUE PRINCIPALE, GRANBY, QC, J2J 2N7
(450) 378-4120   *SIC* 6531

RE/MAX QUEBEC INC   *p* 1085
1500 RUE CUNARD, COTE SAINT-LUC, QC, H7S 2B7
(450) 668-7743   *SIC* 6411

RE/MAX REAL ESTATE (EDMONTON) LTD   *p* 116
4245 97 ST NW SUITE 102, EDMONTON, AB, T6E 5Y7
(780) 434-2323   *SIC* 6531

RE/MAX REAL ESTATE CENTRAL AL-BERTA   *p* 152
6000 48 AVE SUITE 2, PONOKA, AB, T4J 1K2
(403) 783-5007   *SIC* 6799

RE/MAX REAL ESTATE CENTRE INC *p* 510
2 COUNTY COURT BLVD SUITE 150, BRAMPTON, ON, L6W 3W8
(905) 456-1177   *SIC* 6531

RE/MAX REAL ESTATE CENTRE INC *p* 539
766 HESPELER RD SUITE 202, CAM-BRIDGE, ON, N3H 5L8
(519) 740-0001   *SIC* 6531

RE/MAX REAL ESTATE CENTRE INC *p* 539
766 HESPELER RD SUITE 202, CAM-BRIDGE, ON, N3H 5L8
(519) 623-6200   *SIC* 6531

RE/MAX REAL ESTATE SERVICES   *p* 292
See ANDREWS REALTY LTD

RE/MAX REALTRON REALTY INC   *p* 674
88 KONRAD CRES SUITE 1, MARKHAM, ON, L3R 8T7
(905) 944-8800   *SIC* 6531

RE/MAX REALTRON REALTY INC   *p* 773
183 WILLOWDALE AVE, NORTH YORK, ON, M2N 4Y9
(416) 222-8600   *SIC* 6531

RE/MAX REALTRON REALTY INC   *p* 791
2815 BATHURST ST, NORTH YORK, ON, M6B 3A4
(416) 782-8882   *SIC* 6531

RE/MAX REALTRON REALTY INC   *p* 906
7646 YONGE ST, THORNHILL, ON, L4J 1V9
(416) 802-0707   *SIC* 6531

RE/MAX REALTY ENTERPRISES INC *p* 714
1697 LAKESHORE RD W, MISSISSAUGA, ON, L5J 1J4
(905) 823-3400   *SIC* 6531

RE/MAX REALTY ONE INC   *p* 710
50 BURNHAMTHORPE RD W SUITE 102, MISSISSAUGA, ON, L5B 3C2
(905) 277-0771   *SIC* 6531

RE/MAX REALTY SERVICES INC   *p* 510
295 QUEEN ST E SUITE 3, BRAMPTON, ON, L6W 3R1
(905) 456-1000   *SIC* 6531

RE/MAX REALTY SPECIALISTS INC *p* 719
2691 CREDIT VALLEY RD SUITE 101, MIS-SISSAUGA, ON, L5M 7A1
(905) 828-3434   *SIC* 6531

RE/MAX REALTY SPECIALISTS INC *p* 726
6850 MILLCREEK DR UNIT 200, MISSIS-SAUGA, ON, L5N 4J9
(905) 858-3434   *SIC* 6531

RE/MAX ROUGE RIVER REALTY LTD *p* 865
6758 KINGSTON RD UNIT 1, SCARBOR-OUGH, ON, M1B 1G8
(416) 286-3993   *SIC* 6531

RE/MAX ROYAL (JORDAN) INC   *p* 1253
201 AV CARTIER, POINTE-CLAIRE, QC, H9S 4S2
(514) 694-6900   *SIC* 6531

RE/MAX SASKATOON   *p* 1423
See 100% REALTY ASSOCIATES LTD

RE/MAX SASKATOON NORTH   *p* 1429
227 PRIMROSE DR SUITE 200, SASKA-TOON, SK, S7K 5E4
(306) 934-0909   *SIC* 6531

RE/MAX SIGNATURE INC   *p* 1067
130 BOUL DE MORTAGNE BUREAU 200, BOUCHERVILLE, QC, J4B 5M7
(450) 449-5730   *SIC* 6531

RE/MAX SPECIALISTS   *p* 719
See RE/MAX REALTY SPECIALISTS INC

RE/MAX TMS INC   *p* 1364
156 BOUL DU CURE-LABELLE, SAINTE-THERESE, QC, J7E 2X5
(450) 430-4207   *SIC* 6531

RE/MAX TREELAND   *p* 227
See TREELAND REALTY LTD

RE/MAX TREELAND REALTY (1992) LTD *p* 226
6337 198 ST SUITE 101, LANGLEY, BC, V2Y 2E3
(604) 533-3491   *SIC* 6531

RE/MAX TRENT VALLEY REALTY LTD   *p* 999
447 DUNDAS ST W, TRENTON, ON, K8V 3S4
(613) 243-2209   *SIC* 6531

RE/MAX TWIN CITY REALTY INC   *p* 635
842 VICTORIA ST N SUITE 1, KITCHENER, ON, N2B 3C1
(519) 579-4110   *SIC* 6531

RE/MAX TWIN CITY REALTY INC   *p* 1009
83 ERB ST W, WATERLOO, ON, N2L 6C2
(519) 885-0200   *SIC* 6531

RE/MAX UNIQUE INC   *p* 926
1251 YONGE ST, TORONTO, ON, M4T 1W6
(416) 928-6833   *SIC* 6531

RE/MAX VERNON   *p* 331
See FISHER, DEBBIE & LOCHHEAD, DAN

RE/MAX VISION (1990) INC   *p* 1105
225 BOUL DE LA GAPPE BUREAU 102, GATINEAU, QC, J8T 7Y3
(819) 243-3111   *SIC* 6531

RE/MAX WEST REALTY INC   *p* 587
96 REXDALE BLVD SUITE 1, ETOBICOKE, ON, M9W 1N7
(416) 745-2300   *SIC* 6531

RE/MAX YORK GROUP REALTY INC *p* 481
15004 YONGE ST, AURORA, ON, L4G 1M6
(905) 727-1941   *SIC* 6531

RE:SOUND   *p* 973
1235 BAY ST SUITE 900, TORONTO, ON, M5R 3K4
(416) 968-8870   *SIC* 6794

REA INVESTMENTS LIMITED   *p* 795
70 DEERHIDE CRES, NORTH YORK, ON, M9M 2Y6
(905) 264-6481   *SIC* 1542

REACHVIEW VILLAGE   *p* 1001
See REVERA LONG TERM CARE INC

READY HONDA   *p* 708
See READY IMPORT LIMITED

READY IMPORT LIMITED   *p* 708
230 DUNDAS ST E, MISSISSAUGA, ON, L5A 1W9
(905) 896-3500   *SIC* 5511

READY TO PAY   *p* 306
See IQMETRIX SOFTWARE DEVELOP-MENT CORP

REAL ALLOY CANADA LTD   *p* 686
7496 TORBRAM RD, MISSISSAUGA, ON, L4T 1G9
(905) 672-5569   *SIC* 3341

REAL ATLANTIC SUPERSTORE   *p* 409
See ATLANTIC WHOLESALERS LTD

REAL ATLANTIC SUPERSTORE   *p* 438
See ATLANTIC WHOLESALERS LTD

REAL ATLANTIC SUPERSTORE, THE   *p* 394
See ATLANTIC WHOLESALERS LTD

REAL ATLANTIC SUPERSTORE, THE   *p* 408
See ATLANTIC WHOLESALERS LTD

REAL ATLANTIC SUPERSTORE, THE   *p* 410

See ATLANTIC WHOLESALERS LTD
REAL ATLANTIC SUPERSTORE, THE   p
419
See ATLANTIC WHOLESALERS LTD
REAL ATLANTIC SUPERSTORE, THE   p
441
See ATLANTIC WHOLESALERS LTD
REAL ATLANTIC SUPERSTORE, THE   p
442
See ATLANTIC WHOLESALERS LTD
REAL ATLANTIC SUPERSTORE, THE   p
449
See ATLANTIC WHOLESALERS LTD
REAL ATLANTIC SUPERSTORE, THE   p
450
See ATLANTIC WHOLESALERS LTD
REAL ATLANTIC SUPERSTORE, THE   p
458
See ATLANTIC WHOLESALERS LTD
REAL ATLANTIC SUPERSTORE, THE   p
461
See ATLANTIC WHOLESALERS LTD
REAL ATLANTIC SUPERSTORE, THE   p
467
See ATLANTIC WHOLESALERS LTD
REAL ATLANTIC SUPERSTORE, THE   p
1041
See ATLANTIC WHOLESALERS LTD
REAL ATLANTIC SUPERSTORE, THE   p
1042
See ATLANTIC WHOLESALERS LTD
REAL CANADIAN SUPERSTORE   p 9
See LOBLAWS INC
REAL CANADIAN SUPERSTORE   p 40
See LOBLAWS INC
REAL CANADIAN SUPERSTORE   p 69
See LOBLAWS INC
REAL CANADIAN SUPERSTORE   p 70
See LOBLAWS INC
REAL CANADIAN SUPERSTORE   p 71
See LOBLAWS INC
REAL CANADIAN SUPERSTORE   p 75
See LOBLAWS INC
REAL CANADIAN SUPERSTORE   p 76
See LOBLAWS INC
REAL CANADIAN SUPERSTORE   p 96
See LOBLAWS INC
REAL CANADIAN SUPERSTORE   p 124
See LOBLAWS INC
REAL CANADIAN SUPERSTORE   p 128
See LOBLAWS INC
REAL CANADIAN SUPERSTORE   p 132
See LOBLAWS INC
REAL CANADIAN SUPERSTORE   p 154
See LOBLAWS INC
REAL CANADIAN SUPERSTORE   p 163
See LOBLAWS INC
REAL CANADIAN SUPERSTORE   p 164
See LOBLAWS INC
REAL CANADIAN SUPERSTORE   p 166
See LOBLAWS INC
REAL CANADIAN SUPERSTORE   p 195
See LOBLAWS INC
REAL CANADIAN SUPERSTORE   p 207
See LOBLAWS INC
REAL CANADIAN SUPERSTORE   p 217
See LOBLAWS INC
REAL CANADIAN SUPERSTORE   p 239
See LOBLAWS INC
REAL CANADIAN SUPERSTORE   p 244
See LOBLAWS INC
REAL CANADIAN SUPERSTORE   p 260
See LOBLAWS INC
REAL CANADIAN SUPERSTORE   p 287
See LOBLAWS INC
REAL CANADIAN SUPERSTORE   p 347
See LOBLAWS INC
REAL CANADIAN SUPERSTORE   p 368
See WESTFAIR FOODS LTD
REAL CANADIAN SUPERSTORE   p 381
See LOBLAWS INC
REAL CANADIAN SUPERSTORE   p 386
See LOBLAWS INC
REAL CANADIAN SUPERSTORE   p 391

See LOBLAWS INC
REAL CANADIAN SUPERSTORE   p 418
See LOBLAWS INC
REAL CANADIAN SUPERSTORE   p 475
See LOBLAWS SUPERMARKETS LIMITED
REAL CANADIAN SUPERSTORE   p 475
See LOBLAWS INC
REAL CANADIAN SUPERSTORE   p 511
See LOBLAWS INC
REAL CANADIAN SUPERSTORE   p 519
See LOBLAWS INC
REAL CANADIAN SUPERSTORE   p 542
See LOBLAWS INC
REAL CANADIAN SUPERSTORE   p 593
See LOBLAWS INC
REAL CANADIAN SUPERSTORE   p 599
See LOBLAWS INC
REAL CANADIAN SUPERSTORE   p 626
See LOBLAWS INC
REAL CANADIAN SUPERSTORE   p 641
See LOBLAWS INC
REAL CANADIAN SUPERSTORE   p 644
See LOBLAWS INC
REAL CANADIAN SUPERSTORE   p 658
See LOBLAWS INC
REAL CANADIAN SUPERSTORE   p 684
See LOBLAWS INC
REAL CANADIAN SUPERSTORE   p 711
See LOBLAWS INC
REAL CANADIAN SUPERSTORE   p 755
See LOBLAWS SUPERMARKETS LIMITED
REAL CANADIAN SUPERSTORE   p 783
See LOBLAWS INC
REAL CANADIAN SUPERSTORE   p 798
See LOBLAWS INC
REAL CANADIAN SUPERSTORE   p 814
See LOBLAWS INC
REAL CANADIAN SUPERSTORE   p 814
See LOBLAWS SUPERMARKETS LIMITED
REAL CANADIAN SUPERSTORE   p 829
See LOBLAWS INC
REAL CANADIAN SUPERSTORE   p 867
See LOBLAWS INC
REAL CANADIAN SUPERSTORE   p 881
See ZEHRMART INC
REAL CANADIAN SUPERSTORE   p 889
See LOBLAWS INC
REAL CANADIAN SUPERSTORE   p 898
See LOBLAWS INC
REAL CANADIAN SUPERSTORE   p 1005
See LOBLAWS INC
REAL CANADIAN SUPERSTORE   p 1016
See LOBLAWS INC
REAL CANADIAN SUPERSTORE   p 1020
See LOBLAWS INC
REAL CANADIAN SUPERSTORE   p 1025
See LOBLAWS INC
REAL CANADIAN SUPERSTORE   p 1423
See LOBLAWS INC
REAL CANADIAN SUPERSTORE #1505   p
370
See LOBLAWS INC
REAL CANADIAN SUPERSTORE 1504   p
908
See LOBLAWS INC
REAL CANADIAN SUPERSTORE 1521   p
277
See LOBLAWS INC
REAL CANADIAN SUPERSTORE 1536   p
1431
See LOBLAWS INC
REAL CANADIAN SUPERSTORE 1550   p
146
See LOBLAWS INC
REAL CANADIAN SUPERSTORE 1563   p
212
See LOBLAWS INC
REAL CANADIAN SUPERSTORE 1573   p
101
See LOBLAWS INC
REAL CANADIAN SUPERSTORE WESTON
p 997
See LOBLAWS INC
REAL CANADIAN SUPERSTORE, THE   p

119
See LOBLAWS INC
REAL CANADIAN SUPERSTORE, THE   p
250
See LOBLAWS INC
REAL CANADIAN SUPERSTORE, THE   p
681
See LOBLAWS INC
REAL CANADIAN SUPERSTORE, THE   p
858
See LOBLAWS INC
REAL CANADIAN SUPERSTORE, THE   p
1424
See LOBLAWS INC
REAL CANADIAN SUPERSTORES   p 144
See LOBLAWS INC
REAL CANADIAN SUPERSTORES   p 358
See LOBLAWS INC
REAL CANADIAN SUPERSTORES   p 1422
See LOBLAWS INC
REAL CANADIAN WHOLESALE CLUBp 24
See LOBLAWS INC
REAL CANADIAN WHOLESALE CLUB   p
384
See LOBLAWS INC
REAL CANADIAN WHOLESALE CLUB   p
1420
See LOBLAWS INC
**REAL CANADIAN WHOLESALE CLUB,
THE**   p 993
See LOBLAW PROPERTIES LIMITED
REAL CANADIAN-SUPERSTORES   p 121
See LOBLAWS INC
REAL CANADIAN-SUPERSTORES   p 201
See LOBLAWS INC
REAL DEALS ENTERPRISES INC   p 587
18 HUDDERSFIELD RD SUITE 1, ETOBI-
COKE, ON, M9W 5Z6
(416) 248-2020   *SIC* 5023
**REAL ESTATE BOARD OF GREATER VAN-
COUVER**   p
320
2433 SPRUCE ST, VANCOUVER, BC, V6H
4C8
(604) 730-3000   *SIC* 8611
REAL ESTATE COUNCIL OF ONTARIO   p
572
3300 BLOOR ST W UNIT 1200, ETOBI-
COKE, ON, M8X 2X2
(416) 207-4800   *SIC* 8641
REAL ESTATE INVESTMENT TRUST   p 71
80 EDENWOLD DR NW, CALGARY, AB,
T3A 5R9
(403) 241-8990   *SIC* 6513
**REAL ICE SPORTS FACILITY MANAGE-
MENT SERVICES LTD**   p
510
7575 KENNEDY RD, BRAMPTON, ON, L6W
4T2
(905) 459-9340   *SIC* 7999
REAL MATTERS INC   p 905
50 MINTHORN BLVD SUITE 401, THORN-
HILL, ON, L3T 7X8
(905) 739-1212   *SIC* 7371
REAL TRANSPORT   p 1393
See 3235149 CANADA INC
REAL-CANADIAN SUPERSTORES   p 367
See LOBLAWS INC
REALSTAR MANAGEMENT PARTNERSHIP
p 976
77 BLOOR ST W SUITE 2000, TORONTO,
ON, M5S 1M2
(416) 923-2950   *SIC* 8741
**REALSTAR PROPERTY MANAGEMENT
LIMITED**   p 976
77 BLOOR ST W SUITE 2000, TORONTO,
ON, M5S 1M2
(416) 923-2950   *SIC* 6514
REALTORS ASSOCIATION OF EDMONTON
p 95
*See EDMONTON REAL ESTATE BOARD
CO-OPERATIVE LISTING BUREAU LIMITED*
REALTY EXECUTIVE DEVONSHIRE   p 161
See REALTY EXECUTIVES TELOR

REALTY EXECUTIVE SYNERGY INC   p 107
15341 97 ST NW, EDMONTON, AB, T5X
5V3
(780) 699-7347   *SIC* 6531
REALTY EXECUTIVES DEVONSHIREp 161
37 ATHABASCAN AVE SUITE 101, SHER-
WOOD PARK, AB, T8A 4H3
(780) 464-7700   *SIC* 6531
REALTY EXECUTIVES SASKATOON   p
1425
3032 LOUISE ST, SASKATOON, SK, S7J
3L8
(306) 373-7520   *SIC* 6531
REALTY EXECUTIVES TELOR   p 161
37 ATHABASCAN AVE SUITE 101, SHER-
WOOD PARK, AB, T8A 4H3
(780) 464-7700   *SIC* 6531
REALTY NETWORK 100 INC   p 599
263 MAIN ST E, GRIMSBY, ON, L3M 1P7
(905) 945-4555   *SIC* 6531
REASBECK CONSTRUCTION INC   p 901
1085 KELLY LAKE RD, SUDBURY, ON, P3E
5P5
(705) 222-1800   *SIC* 1541
REAUME CHEVROLET BUICK GMCp 1026
See REAUME CHEVROLET LTD
REAUME CHEVROLET LTD   p 1026
500 FRONT RD, WINDSOR, ON, N9J 1Z9
(519) 734-7844   *SIC* 5511
REBOITECH INC   p 1133
112 RUE DE LA PINEDE, LATERRIERE,
QC, G7N 1B8
(418) 545-2893   *SIC* 0783
REBOX CORP   p 1341
7500 CH DE LA COTE-DE-LIESSE, SAINT-
LAURENT, QC, H4T 1E7
(514) 335-1717   *SIC* 5113
REBUTS SOLIDES CANADIENS INCp 1170
2240 RUE MICHEL-JURDANT, MON-
TREAL, QC, H1Z 4N7
(514) 593-9211   *SIC* 7389
REBUTS SOLIDES CANADIENS INCp 1215
1635 RUE SHERBROOKE O BUREAU 300,
MONTREAL, QC, H3H 1E2
(514) 987-5151   *SIC* 4953
RECALL   p 206
See MOBIL SHRED INC
RECHERCHE BCA   p 1193
See BCA RESEARCH INC
RECHERCHE ERICSSON CANADA   p 1156
See ERICSSON CANADA INC
RECHERCHE ERICSSON CANADA   p 1333
See ERICSSON CANADA INC
RECHERCHE NEURORX   p 1186
See NEURORX RESEARCH INC
RECIPE UNLIMITED CORPORATION   p 265
6260 MILLER RD, RICHMOND, BC, V7B
1B3
(604) 278-9144   *SIC* 5812
RECIPE UNLIMITED CORPORATION   p 484
397 BAYFIELD ST, BARRIE, ON, L4M 3C5
(705) 737-5272   *SIC* 5812
RECIPE UNLIMITED CORPORATION   p 488
85 BARRIE VIEW DR, BARRIE, ON, L4N
8V4
(705) 733-0791   *SIC* 5812
RECIPE UNLIMITED CORPORATION   p 515
84 LYNDEN RD SUITE 1771, BRANTFORD,
ON, N3R 6B8
(519) 759-6990   *SIC* 5812
RECIPE UNLIMITED CORPORATION   p 557
199 FOUR VALLEY DR, CONCORD, ON,
L4K 0B8
(905) 760-2244   *SIC* 5812
RECIPE UNLIMITED CORPORATION   p 563
960 BROOKDALE AVE SUITE 18, CORN-
WALL, ON, K6J 4P5
(416) 852-4714   *SIC* 5812
RECIPE UNLIMITED CORPORATION   p 608
200 CENTENNIAL PKY N, HAMILTON, ON,
L8E 4A1
(416) 599-4133   *SIC* 5812
RECIPE UNLIMITED CORPORATION   p 652
1141 HIGHBURY AVE N, LONDON, ON,

N5Y 1A5
(519) 453-8100   SIC 5812
RECIPE UNLIMITED CORPORATION *p* 751
1711 MERIVALE RD, NEPEAN, ON, K2G 3K2
(613) 288-0517   SIC 5812
RECIPE UNLIMITED CORPORATION *p* 759
4960 CLIFTON HILL, NIAGARA FALLS, ON, L2G 3N4
(905) 353-0051   SIC 5812
RECIPE UNLIMITED CORPORATION *p* 808
115 FIFTH AVE, ORANGEVILLE, ON, L9W 5B7
(519) 940-4004   SIC 5812
RECIPE UNLIMITED CORPORATION *p* 831
1100 BAXTER RD, OTTAWA, ON, K2C 4B1
SIC 5812
RECIPE UNLIMITED CORPORATION *p* 875
2555 VICTORIA PARK AVE SUITE 19, SCARBOROUGH, ON, M1T 1A3
(416) 494-9693   SIC 5812
RECIPE UNLIMITED CORPORATION *p* 905
2910 STEELES AVE E, THORNHILL, ON, L3T 7X1
(905) 709-0550   SIC 5812
RECIPE UNLIMITED CORPORATION *p* 983
132 JOHN ST, TORONTO, ON, M5V 2E3
SIC 5812
RECIPE UNLIMITED CORPORATION *p* 994
590 KEELE ST, TORONTO, ON, M6N 3E2
(416) 760-7893   SIC 5812
RECIPE UNLIMITED CORPORATION *p* 1000
3760 HIGHWAY 7 E, UNIONVILLE, ON, L3R 0N2
(905) 760-2244   SIC 5812
RECIPE UNLIMITED CORPORATION *p* 1015
175 CONSUMERS DR, WHITBY, ON, L1N 1C4
(905) 666-1411   SIC 5812
RECIPE UNLIMITED CORPORATION *p* 1092
1185 RUE RODOLPHE-PAGE BUREAU 1, DORVAL, QC, H4Y 1H3
(514) 636-5824   SIC 5812
RECKITT BENCKISER (CANADA) INC *p* 699
1680 TECH AVE UNIT 2, MISSISSAUGA, ON, L4W 5S9
(905) 283-7000   SIC 2842
RECKITT BENCKISER HEALTH *p* 699
See RECKITT BENCKISER (CANADA) INC
RECO *p* 572
See REAL ESTATE COUNCIL OF ONTARIO
RECOCHEM INC *p* 684
8725 HOLGATE CRES, MILTON, ON, L9T 5G7
(905) 878-5544   SIC 3221
RECOCHEM INC *p* 1341
850 MONTEE DE LIESSE, SAINT-LAURENT, QC, H4T 1P4
(514) 341-3550   SIC 2899
RECOGNIA INC *p* 751
301 MOODIE DR SUITE 200, NEPEAN, ON, K2H 9C4
(613) 789-2267   SIC 6282
RECOLTES MARCOTTE, LES *p* 1097
See 3095-6395 QUEBEC INC
RECON *p* 58
See RECON PETROTECHNOLOGIES LTD
RECON PETROTECHNOLOGIES LTD *p* 58
510 5 ST SW UNIT 410, CALGARY, AB, T2P 3S2
(403) 517-3266   SIC 1389
RECONNECT COMMUNITY HEALTH SERVICES *p* 989
1281 ST. CLAIR AVE W, TORONTO, ON, M6E 1B8
(416) 248-2050   SIC 8093
RECORD, THE *p* 639
See TORSTAR CORPORATION
RECORDER AND TIMES, THE *p* 518

See 1032451 B.C. LTD
RECREATION ASSOCIATION OF THE PUBLIC SERVICE OF CANADA, THE *p* 819
2451 RIVERSIDE DR, OTTAWA, ON, K1H 7X7
(613) 733-5100   SIC 7997
RECREATION OAK BAY *p* 333
2291 CEDAR HILL CROSS RD, VICTORIA, BC, V8P 5H9
(250) 370-7200   SIC 7999
RECREGESTION LE GROUPE INC *p* 1084
6010 RUE DE PRINCE-RUPERT, COTE SAINT-LUC, QC, H7H 1C4
(450) 625-0196   SIC 7032
RECTOR FOODS LIMITED *p* 500
2280 NORTH PARK DR, BRAMPTON, ON, L6S 6C6
(905) 789-9691   SIC 2099
RECTOR MACHINE WORKS LTD *p* 863
190 SACKVILLE RD, SAULT STE. MARIE, ON, P6B 4T6
(705) 256-6221   SIC 5084
RECUP ESTRIE *p* 1371
2180 RUE CLAUDE-GREFFARD, SHERBROOKE, QC, J1H 5H1
(819) 346-2111   SIC 5084
RECUPERACTION CENTRE DU QUEBEC INC *p* 1097
5620 RUE SAINT-ROCH S, DRUMMONDVILLE, QC, J2B 6V4
(819) 477-1312   SIC 4953
RECUPERACTION MARRONNIERS INC *p* 1131
2555 AV DOLLARD, LASALLE, QC, H8N 3A9
(514) 595-1212   SIC 5084
RECUPERATION FRONTENAC INC *p* 1383
217 RUE MONFETTE O, THETFORD MINES, QC, G6G 7Y3
(418) 338-8551   SIC 4953
RECUPERATION MAURICIE, SOCIETE EN NOM COLLECTIF *p* 1300
400 BOUL LA GABELLE BUREAU 23, SAINT-ETIENNE-DES-GRES, QC, G0X 2P0
(819) 372-5125   SIC 4953
RECYCAN INC *p* 1054
20500 AV CLARK-GRAHAM, BAIE-D'URFE, QC, H9X 4B6
(514) 457-0322   SIC 4953
RECYCAN INC *p* 1330
3555 RUE ASHBY, SAINT-LAURENT, QC, H4R 2K3
(514) 379-1006   SIC 4953
RECYCLAGE AUTOMOBILES GRAVEL INC *p* 1060
677 BOUL DU CURE-LABELLE, BLAINVILLE, QC, J7C 2J5
(450) 435-8335   SIC 5013
RECYCLAGE DE PAPIER HANNA LTEE *p* 1322
760 AV GUY-POULIN, SAINT-JOSEPH-DE-BEAUCE, QC, G0S 2V0
(418) 397-5859   SIC 5093
RECYCLING COUNCIL OF BRITISH COLUMBIA *p* 300
119 PENDER ST W SUITE 10, VANCOUVER, BC, V6B 1S5
(604) 683-6009   SIC 8999
RECYCLING MATTERS *p* 776
See COMMUNITY LIVING ONTARIO
RECYCLO-CENTRE INC *p* 1376
165 AV DE L'HOTEL-DIEU, SOREL-TRACY, QC, J3P 1M2
(450) 746-4559   SIC 5932
RECYCLO-ENVIRONNEMENT *p* 1376
See RECYCLO-CENTRE INC
RED APPLE STORES INC *p* 689
6877 GOREWAY DR SUITE 3, MISSISSAUGA, ON, L4V 1L9
(905) 293-9700   SIC 5399
RED ARROW EXPRESS, DIV OF *p* 88
See DIVERSIFIED TRANSPORTATION LTD
RED ARROW EXPRESS, DIV OF *p* 114

See DIVERSIFIED TRANSPORTATION LTD
RED BARN COUNTRY MARKET LTD *p* 338
751 VANALMAN AVE, VICTORIA, BC, V8Z 3B8
(250) 479-6817   SIC 5411
RED BARN MARKET *p* 338
See RED BARN COUNTRY MARKET LTD
RED BRANCH EXECUTIVE SEARCH & RECRUITMENT *p* 934
232-366 ADELAIDE ST E, TORONTO, ON, M5A 3X9
(416) 862-2525   SIC 7361
RED BULL CANADA LTD *p* 983
381 QUEEN ST W SUITE 200, TORONTO, ON, M5V 2A5
(416) 593-1629   SIC 2086
RED CAR AIRPORT SERVICE *p* 600
See RED CAR SERVICE INC
RED CAR SERVICE INC *p* 600
530 ELIZABETH ST, GUELPH, ON, N1E 6C3
(519) 824-9344   SIC 4131
RED CARPET REAL WORLD REALTY INC *p* 674
340 FERRIER ST UNIT 218, MARKHAM, ON, L3R 2Z5
(905) 415-8855   SIC 6531
RED CARPET TRANSPORT LTD *p* 123
6303 18 ST NW, EDMONTON, AB, T6P 0B6
(780) 463-3936   SIC 6712
RED DEER ADVOCATE *p* 156
See BLACK PRESS GROUP LTD
RED DEER BOTTLING COCA COLA *p* 156
See RED DEER BOTTLING COMPANY LTD
RED DEER BOTTLING COMPANY LTD *p* 156
6855 EDGAR INDUSTRIAL DR, RED DEER, AB, T4P 3R2
(403) 346-2585   SIC 5149
RED DEER CATHOLIC REGIONAL DIVISION NO. 39 *p* 154
5210 61 ST, RED DEER, AB, T4N 6N8
(403) 343-1055   SIC 8211
RED DEER CHILD CARE SOCIETY *p* 154
5571 45 ST UNIT 2, RED DEER, AB, T4N 1L2
(403) 347-7973   SIC 8351
RED DEER CO-OP LIMITED *p* 154
5118 47 AVE, RED DEER, AB, T4N 3P7
(403) 340-1766   SIC 5411
RED DEER COLLEGE *p* 154
100 COLLEGE BLVD, RED DEER, AB, T4N 5H5
(403) 342-3300   SIC 8222
RED DEER GYMNASTIC ASSOCIATION *p* 157
3031 30 AVE, RED DEER, AB, T4R 2Z7
(403) 342-4940   SIC 8699
RED DEER IRONWORKS INC *p* 156
6430 GOLDEN WEST AVE, RED DEER, AB, T4P 1A6
(403) 343-1141   SIC 3533
RED DEER LODGE LTD *p* 154
4311 49 AVE, RED DEER, AB, T4N 5Y7
(403) 754-5503   SIC 7011
RED DEER MOTORS *p* 155
See 1076528 ALBERTA LTD
RED DEER OVER DOOR *p* 155
See 804652 ALBERTA LTD
RED DEER REBELS *p* 157
See SIMPSON'S SPORTS LIMITED
RED DEER RV COUNTRY LTD *p* 157
1 GASOLINE ALLEY E, RED DEER COUNTY, AB, T4E 1B3
(403) 340-1132   SIC 5561
RED EAGLE MINING CORPORATION *p* 309
666 BURRARD ST SUITE 2348, VANCOUVER, BC, V6C 2X8
(604) 638-2545   SIC 1041
RED FLAME INDUSTRIES INC *p* 156
6736 71 ST, RED DEER, AB, T4P 3Y7
(403) 343-2012   SIC 1389

RED HAT CO-OPERATIVE LTD *p* 158
809 BROADWAY AVE E, REDCLIFF, AB, T0J 2P0
(403) 548-6453   SIC 5148
RED HILL TOYOTA *p* 608
2333 BARTON ST E, HAMILTON, ON, L8E 2W8
(905) 561-1202   SIC 5511
RED ISLE PRIVATE INVESTMENTS INC *p* 1207
1250 BOUL RENE-LEVESQUE O, MONTREAL, QC, H3B 4W8
SIC 6282
RED LABEL VACATIONS INC *p* 699
5450 EXPLORER DR SUITE 400, MISSISSAUGA, ON, L4W 5N1
(905) 283-6020   SIC 4724
RED LAKE HOSPITAL *p* 849
See RED LAKE MARGARET COCHENOUR MEMORIAL HOSPITAL CORPORATION, THE
RED LAKE IGA *p* 849
See MACDEN HOLDINGS LTD
RED LAKE MARGARET COCHENOUR MEMORIAL HOSPITAL CORPORATION, THE *p* 849
51 HWY 105, RED LAKE, ON, P0V 2M0
(807) 727-2231   SIC 8062
RED LOBSTER *p* 711
See GMRI CANADA, INC
RED LOBSTER HOSPITALITY LLC *p* 11
312 35 ST NE, CALGARY, AB, T2A 6S7
(403) 248-8111   SIC 5812
RED LOBSTER HOSPITALITY LLC *p* 37
6100 MACLEOD TRAIL SW SUITE 100, CALGARY, AB, T2H 0K5
(403) 252-8818   SIC 5812
RED LOBSTER HOSPITALITY LLC *p* 102
10111 171 ST NW, EDMONTON, AB, T5S 1S6
(780) 484-0660   SIC 5812
RED LOBSTER HOSPITALITY LLC *p* 102
10121 171 ST NW, EDMONTON, AB, T5S 1S6
(780) 484-0700   SIC 5812
RED LOBSTER HOSPITALITY LLC *p* 119
4111 CALGARY TRAIL NW, EDMONTON, AB, T6J 6S6
(780) 436-8510   SIC 5812
RED LOBSTER HOSPITALITY LLC *p* 119
4110 CALGARY TRL NW, EDMONTON, AB, T6J 6Y6
(780) 437-3434   SIC 5812
RED LOBSTER HOSPITALITY LLC *p* 363
51 REENDERS DR, WINNIPEG, MB, R2C 5E8
(204) 661-8129   SIC 5812
RED LOBSTER HOSPITALITY LLC *p* 382
1544 PORTAGE AVE, WINNIPEG, MB, R3G 0W9
(204) 783-9434   SIC 5812
RED LOBSTER HOSPITALITY LLC *p* 382
1540 PORTAGE AVE, WINNIPEG, MB, R3G 0W9
(204) 783-9434   SIC 5812
RED LOBSTER HOSPITALITY LLC *p* 484
319 BAYFIELD ST, BARRIE, ON, L4M 3C2
(705) 728-2401   SIC 5812
RED LOBSTER HOSPITALITY LLC *p* 515
67 KING GEORGE RD, BRANTFORD, ON, N3R 5K2
(519) 759-7121   SIC 5812
RED LOBSTER HOSPITALITY LLC *p* 579
1790 THE QUEENSWAY, ETOBICOKE, ON, M9C 5H5
(416) 620-9990   SIC 5812
RED LOBSTER HOSPITALITY LLC *p* 656
667 WELLINGTON RD, LONDON, ON, N6C 4R4
(519) 668-0220   SIC 5812
RED LOBSTER HOSPITALITY LLC *p* 751
1595 MERIVALE RD, NEPEAN, ON, K2G 3J4
(613) 727-0035   SIC 5812

RED LOBSTER HOSPITALITY LLC   p 759
6220 LUNDY'S LANE, NIAGARA FALLS, ON, L2G 1T6
(905) 357-1303   SIC 5812

RED LOBSTER HOSPITALITY LLC   p 790
3200 DUFFERIN ST, NORTH YORK, ON, M6A 3B2
(416) 785-7930   SIC 5812

RED LOBSTER HOSPITALITY LLC   p 818
1499 ST. LAURENT BLVD, OTTAWA, ON, K1G 0Z9
(613) 744-7560   SIC 5812

RED LOBSTER HOSPITALITY LLC   p 875
3252 SHEPPARD AVE E, SCARBOR-OUGH, ON, M1T 3K3
(416) 491-2507   SIC 5812

RED LOBSTER HOSPITALITY LLC   p 905
7291 YONGE ST, THORNHILL, ON, L3T 2A9
(905) 731-3550   SIC 5812

RED LOBSTER HOSPITALITY LLC   p 1019
6575 TECUMSEH RD E, WINDSOR, ON, N8T 1E7
(519) 948-7677   SIC 5812

RED LOBSTER HOSPITALITY LLC   p 1424
2501 8TH ST E, SASKATOON, SK, S7H 0V4
(306) 373-8333   SIC 5812

RED LOBSTER RESTAURANTS   p 11
See RED LOBSTER HOSPITALITY LLC

RED LOBSTER RESTAURANTS   p 37
See RED LOBSTER HOSPITALITY LLC

RED LOBSTER RESTAURANTS   p 102
See RED LOBSTER HOSPITALITY LLC

RED LOBSTER RESTAURANTS   p 119
See RED LOBSTER HOSPITALITY LLC

RED LOBSTER RESTAURANTS   p 484
See RED LOBSTER HOSPITALITY LLC

RED LOBSTER RESTAURANTS   p 515
See RED LOBSTER HOSPITALITY LLC

RED LOBSTER RESTAURANTS   p 579
See RED LOBSTER HOSPITALITY LLC

RED LOBSTER RESTAURANTS   p 656
See RED LOBSTER HOSPITALITY LLC

RED LOBSTER RESTAURANTS   p 751
See RED LOBSTER HOSPITALITY LLC

RED LOBSTER RESTAURANTS   p 759
See RED LOBSTER HOSPITALITY LLC

RED LOBSTER RESTAURANTS   p 790
See RED LOBSTER HOSPITALITY LLC

RED LOBSTER RESTAURANTS   p 818
See RED LOBSTER HOSPITALITY LLC

RED LOBSTER RESTAURANTS   p 875
See RED LOBSTER HOSPITALITY LLC

RED LOBSTER RESTAURANTS   p 905
See RED LOBSTER HOSPITALITY LLC

RED LOBSTER RESTAURANTS   p 1019
See RED LOBSTER HOSPITALITY LLC

RED LOBSTER RESTAURANTS   p 1424
See RED LOBSTER HOSPITALITY LLC

RED MOUNTAIN HOLDINGS LTD   p 1418
2800 PASQUA ST N, REGINA, SK, S4P 3E1
(306) 545-4044   SIC 3523

RED OAK CATERING INC   p 433
50 HAMLYN RD SUITE 466, ST. JOHN'S, NL, A1E 5X7
(709) 368-6808   SIC 5812

RED PIN, THE   p 943
See THEREDPIN.COM REALTY INC., BROKERAGE

RED RIBBON PRODUCTS   p 479
See ALL TREAT FARMS LIMITED

RED RIVER AIR BRAKE INC   p 363
171 GUNN RD, WINNIPEG, MB, R2C 2Z8
(204) 231-4111   SIC 4789

RED RIVER CO OPERATIVE   p 392
See 5195684 MANITOBA INC

RED RIVER COOPERATIVE LTD   p 366
10 PRAIRIE WAY, WINNIPEG, MB, R2J 3J8
(204) 631-4600   SIC 5541

RED RIVER MANOR INC   p 356
133 MANCHESTER AVE, SELKIRK, MB, R1A 0B5
(204) 482-3036   SIC 8322

RED RIVER PLACE NURSING HOME p 356

See RED RIVER MANOR INC

RED RIVER VALLEY MUTUAL INSURANCE COMPANY   p 345
245 CENTRE AVE E, ALTONA, MB, R0G 0B0
(204) 324-6434   SIC 6411

RED RIVER VALLEY SCHOOL DIVISION   p 353
233 MAIN ST, MORRIS, MB, R0G 1K0
(204) 746-2317   SIC 8211

RED ROBIN   p 163
See RRGB RESTAURANTS CANADA INC

RED ROBIN   p 337
See RRGB RESTAURANTS CANADA INC

RED ROBIN RESTAURANT   p 103
See RRGB RESTAURANTS CANADA INC

RED ROBIN RESTAURANT (CAPILANO) LTD   p 241
801 MARINE DR SUITE 100, NORTH VAN-COUVER, BC, V7P 3K6
SIC 5812

RED ROCK SEAFOODS LTD   p 1041
546 MAIN ST, MONTAGUE, PE, C0A 1R0
(902) 549-5087   SIC 5146

RED ROSE REALTY INC   p 916
101 DUNCAN MILL RD UNIT G5, TORONTO, ON, M3B 1Z3
(416) 640-0512   SIC 6531

RED SEAL NOTARY INC   p 940
25 ADELAIDE ST E UNIT 100, TORONTO, ON, M5C 3A1
(416) 922-7325   SIC 7389

RED SUCKER LAKE HEALTH AUTHORITY INC   p 355
GD, RED SUCKER LAKE, MB, R0B 1H0
(204) 469-5229   SIC 6324

RED SUN FARMS   p 634
See JEM D INTERNATIONAL PARTNERS LP

RED SUN FARMS CANADA INC   p 634
2400 GRAHAM SIDERD, KINGSVILLE, ON, N9Y 2E5
(519) 733-3663   SIC 6712

RED WILLOW COLONY   p 167
See HUTTERIAN BRETHREN OF RED WILLOW

RED ZOO MARKETING   p 858
See 971016 ONTARIO LIMITED

RED-D-ARC LIMITED   p 599
667 SOUTH SERVICE RD, GRIMSBY, ON, L3M 4E8
(905) 643-4212   SIC 7359

RED-D-ARC WELDER RENTALS   p 599
See RED-D-ARC LIMITED

RED-L DISTRIBUTORS LTD   p 149
3675 13 ST, NISKU, AB, T9E 1C5
(780) 437-2630   SIC 5085

REDA ENTERPRISES LTD   p 6
GD STN MAIN, BONNYVILLE, AB, T9N 2J6
(780) 826-2737   SIC 5032

REDBERRY FRANCHISING CORP   p 579
401 THE WEST MALL SUITE 700, ETOBI-COKE, ON, M9C 5J4
(416) 626-6464   SIC 6794

REDDEN, C. I. LTD   p 442
50 EMPIRE LANE, CURRYS CORNER, NS, B0N 2T0
(902) 798-3222   SIC 5251

REDDIN FARM EQUIPMENT LTD   p 1042
237 MASON RD, STRATFORD, PE, C1B 2G1
(902) 569-2500   SIC 5083

REDFERN ENTERPRISES INC   p 347
922 DOUGLAS ST, BRANDON, MB, R7A 7B2
(204) 725-8580   SIC 6712

REDFERN FARM SERVICES LTD   p 347
922 DOUGLAS ST, BRANDON, MB, R7A 7B2
(204) 725-8580   SIC 5261

REDHEAD EQUIPMENT   p 1418
GD LCD MAIN, REGINA, SK, S4P 2Z4
(306) 721-2666   SIC 7353

REDHEAD EQUIPMENT LTD   p 1416

BOX 32098 HWY 1 E, REGINA, SK, S4N 7L2
(306) 721-2666   SIC 5084

REDHEAD EQUIPMENT LTD   p 1429
9010 NORTH SERVICE ROAD, SASKA-TOON, SK, S7K 7E8
(306) 931-4600   SIC 5571

REDISHRED CAPITAL CORP   p 726
6505 MISSISSAUGA RD SUITE A, MISSIS-SAUGA, ON, L5N 1A6
(416) 490-8600   SIC 7389

REDKEN   p 1101
See CONCEPT JP INC

REDKEN CONCEPT J P INC   p 1101
2089 RUE MICHELIN, FABREVILLE, QC, H7L 5B7
(450) 687-2595   SIC 5122

REDLEN TECHNOLOGIES INC   p 267
1763 SEAN HTS UNIT 123, SAANICHTON, BC, V8M 0A5
(250) 656-5411   SIC 3674

REDLINE COMMUNICATIONS GROUP INC   p 674
302 TOWN CENTRE BLVD 4TH FL, MARKHAM, ON, L3R 0E8
(905) 479-8344   SIC 4899

REDLINE COMMUNICATIONS INC   p 674
302 TOWN CENTRE BLVD SUITE 100, MARKHAM, ON, L3R 0E8
(905) 479-8344   SIC 3661

REDLINE DRAFTING INC   p 58
1000 7 AVE SW SUITE 600, CALGARY, AB, T2P 5L5
(403) 452-3810   SIC 6712

REDLINE INNOVATIONS GROUP   p 674
See REDLINE COMMUNICATIONS GROUP INC

REDMOND/WILLIAMS DISTRIBUTIONS INC   p 699
5605 TIMBERLEA BLVD, MISSISSAUGA, ON, L4W 2S4
(905) 238-8208   SIC 5075

REDPATH CANADA LIMITED   p 763
101 WORTHINGTON ST E, NORTH BAY, ON, P1B 1G5
(705) 474-2461   SIC 1081

REDPATH FOODS INC   p 261
2560 SIMPSON RD, RICHMOND, BC, V6X 2P9
(604) 873-1393   SIC 5461

REDPATH GROUP   p 763
See REDPATH CANADA LIMITED

REDPATH MINING INC   p 763
101 WORTHINGTON ST E 3RD FL, NORTH BAY, ON, P1B 1G5
(705) 474-2461   SIC 1081

REDPATH SUGAR LTD   p 943
95 QUEENS QUAY E, TORONTO, ON, M5E 1A3
(416) 366-3561   SIC 2061

REDROCK CAMPS INC   p 65
322 11 AVENUE SW STE 302, CALGARY, AB, T2R 0C5
(403) 264-7610   SIC 2411

REDSPACE INC   p 440
1595 BEDFORD HWY SUITE 168, BED-FORD, NS, B4A 3Y4
(902) 444-3490   SIC 7371

REDVERS HEALTH CENTRE   p 1415
See SUN COUNTRY REGIONAL HEALTH AUTHORITY

REDVERS ROAD AMBULANCE   p 1415
See SUN COUNTRY REGIONAL HEALTH AUTHORITY

REEBOK-CCM   p 1314
See SPORT MASKA INC

REED ATWOOD BUILDERS (ONTARIO) INC   p 1000
8693 6TH LINE, UTOPIA, ON, L0M 1T0
(705) 797-0553   SIC 1542

REED ATWOOD BUILDERS INC   p 18
5716 35 ST SE, CALGARY, AB, T2C 2G3
SIC 1542

REED ELSEVIER CANADA LTD   p 983

555 RICHMOND ST W SUITE 1100, TORONTO, ON, M5V 3B1
(416) 253-3640   SIC 2731

REED HYCALOG CORING SERVICES   p 149
1507 4 ST, NISKU, AB, T9E 7M9
(780) 955-8929   SIC 1389

REEFER SALES & SERVICE (TORONTO) INCORPORATED   p 742
425 GIBRALTAR DR, MISSISSAUGA, ON, L5T 2S9
(905) 795-0234   SIC 7623

REEL COH INC   p 1061
801 BOUL DU CURE-BOIVIN, BOIS-BRIAND, QC, J7G 2J2
(450) 430-6500   SIC 3531

REENDERS CAR WASH LTD   p 363
85 REENDERS DR, WINNIPEG, MB, R2C 5E8
(204) 669-9700   SIC 7542

REES N.D.T. INSPECTION SERVICES LTDp 133
15612 89 ST, GRANDE PRAIRIE, AB, T8E 2N8
(780) 539-3594   SIC 7389

REFENDOIRS C. R. LTEE, LES   p 1125
300 RUE DE LA BERGE-DU-CANAL BU-REAU 4, LACHINE, QC, H8R 1H3
(514) 366-2222   SIC 7389

REFERRED REALTY INC   p 777
156 DUNCAN MILL RD SUITE 1, NORTH YORK, ON, M3B 3N2
(416) 445-8855   SIC 6531

REFORM ENERGY SERVICES CORP p 58
808 4 AVE SW SUITE 500, CALGARY, AB, T2P 3E8
(403) 262-2181   SIC 1381

REFPLUS INC   p 1310
2777 GRANDE ALLEE, SAINT-HUBERT, QC, J4T 2R4
(450) 641-2665   SIC 3585

REFRESCO CANADA INC   p 689
6525 VISCOUNT RD, MISSISSAUGA, ON, L4V 1H6
(905) 672-1900   SIC 2086

REFRIGERATION ACTAIR INC   p 1067
1370 RUE JOLIOT-CURIE BUREAU 704, BOUCHERVILLE, QC, J4B 7L9
(450) 449-5266   SIC 1711

REFRIGERATION METROPOLITAINE COMMERCIALE   p 1047
See 9272-8781 QUEBEC INC

REFRIGERATION NOEL INC   p 1265
1700 RUE LEON-HARMEL, QUEBEC, QC, G1N 4R9
(418) 663-0879   SIC 7623

REFRIGERATION, PLOMBERIE & CHAUFFAGE LONGUEUIL INC   p 1142
800 RUE JEAN-NEVEU, LONGUEUIL, QC, J4G 2M1
(514) 789-0456   SIC 7623

REFRIGERATIVE SUPPLY   p 193
8028 NORTH FRASER WAY, BURNABY, BC, V5J 0E1
(604) 435-7151   SIC 5075

REGAL ALUMINUM (1993) INC   p 558
177 DRUMLIN CIR SUITE 1, CONCORD, ON, L4K 3E7
(905) 738-4375   SIC 5211

REGAL AUCTIONS LTD   p 11
2600 7 AVE NE, CALGARY, AB, T2A 2L8
(403) 250-1995   SIC 7389

REGAL BELOIT CANADA   p 742
320 SUPERIOR BLVD SUITE 1, MISSIS-SAUGA, ON, L5T 2N7
(905) 670-4770   SIC 5063

REGAL BELOIT CANADA ULC   p 229
4916 275 ST, LANGLEY, BC, V4W 0A3
(604) 888-0110   SIC 3625

REGAL BUILDING MATERIALS LTD   p 37
7131 6 ST SE SUITE D, CALGARY, AB, T2H 2M8
(403) 253-2010   SIC 5211

REGAL CONSOLIDATED VENTURES LIM-

ITED   *p*
940
20 ADELAIDE ST E SUITE 1100, TORONTO, ON, M5C 2T6
(416) 642-0602   *SIC 1081*

REGAL GIFTS CORPORATION   *p 488*
360 SAUNDERS RD, BARRIE, ON, L4N 9Y2
(800) 565-3130   *SIC 5961*

REGAL SECURITY INC   *p 790*
1244 CALEDONIA RD, NORTH YORK, ON, M6A 2X5
(416) 633-8558   *SIC 7381*

REGENCE   *p 1280*
See CHAUSSURES REGENCE INC

REGENCY APPAREL CO LTD   *p 777*
255 DUNCAN MILL RD SUITE 303, NORTH YORK, ON, M3B 3H9
SIC 2329

REGENCY AUTO ENTERPRISE INC   *p 186*
4278 LOUGHEED HWY, BURNABY, BC, V5C 3Y5
(604) 291-8122   *SIC 5511*

REGENCY AUTO INVESTMENTS INC *p 289*
401 KINGSWAY, VANCOUVER, BC, V5T 3K1
(604) 879-8411   *SIC 5511*

REGENCY CHRYSLER   *p 252*
See 330542 BC LTD

REGENCY GROUP CANADA   *p 289*
See REGENCY AUTO INVESTMENTS INC

REGENCY INTERMEDIATE CARE FACILITIES INC   *p*
277
13855 68 AVE, SURREY, BC, V3W 2G9
(604) 597-9333   *SIC 8361*

REGENCY LEXUS TOYOTA INC   *p 289*
401 KINGSWAY, VANCOUVER, BC, V5T 3K1
(604) 879-6241   *SIC 5511*

REGENCY MALL   *p 901*
469 BOUCHARD ST SUITE 203, SUDBURY, ON, P3E 2K8
(705) 522-4722   *SIC 6512*

REGENCY PARK LTC HOME   *p 1023*
See MERITAS CARE CORPORATION

REGENCY PLASTICS COMPANY LIMITED
p 784
50 BRISBANE RD, NORTH YORK, ON, M3J 2K2
(416) 661-3000   *SIC 3081*

REGENCY TOYOTA BURNABY   *p 186*
See REGENCY AUTO ENTERPRISE INC

REGENS DISPOSAL LTD   *p 1406*
500 BOURQUIN RD, ESTEVAN, SK, S4A 2H8
(306) 634-7209   *SIC 4953*

REGENT COLLEGE   *p 325*
5800 UNIVERSITY BLVD, VANCOUVER, BC, V6T 2E4
(604) 224-3245   *SIC 8221*

REGENT HOTEL   *p 779*
See FOUR SEASONS HOTELS LIMITED

REGENT INDUSTRIES   *p 116*
See SIMPLY BOSS INC

REGENT SHELL   *p 363*
See S & L PROPERTIES LTD

REGGIN TECHNICAL SERVICES LTD *p 13*
4550 35 ST SE, CALGARY, AB, T2B 3S4
(403) 287-2540   *SIC 1711*

REGIE DES CLUBS D'EXCELLENCE COLLEGE D'ENSEIGNEMENT GENERAL ET PROFESSIONNEL DE LIMOILOU   *p 1257*
1300 8E AV BUREAU 1400, QUEBEC, QC, G1J 5L5
(418) 647-6600   *SIC 8221*

REGIE DU BATIMENT DU QUEBEC *p 1145*
201 PLACE CHARLES-LE MOYNE BUREAU 310, LONGUEUIL, QC, J4K 2T5
(450) 928-7603   *SIC 7389*

REGIE INTERMUNICIPALE DE SECURITE PUBLIQUE DES CHUTES   *p 1089*
337 RUE PRINCIPALE, DAVELUYVILLE, QC, G0Z 1C0
(819) 367-3395   *SIC 7389*

REGIE REGIONALE DE LA SANTE ET DES SERVICES SOCIAUX NUNAVIK   *p 1221*
4039 RUE TUPPER BUREAU 7, MONTREAL, QC, H3Z 1T5
(514) 932-9047   *SIC 8059*

REGINA ABILITY CENTRE   *p 1425*
See SASKATCHEWAN ABILITIES COUNCIL INC

REGINA AIRPORT AUTHORITY INC *p 1422*
5201 REGINA AVE UNIT 1, REGINA, SK, S4W 1B3
(306) 761-7555   *SIC 4581*

REGINA HUMANE SOCIETY INC   *p 1418*
GD LCD MAIN, REGINA, SK, S4P 2Z4
(306) 543-6363   *SIC 8699*

REGINA INN   *p 1418*
See LEADON (REGINA) OPERATIONS LP

REGINA MOTOR PRODUCTS (1970) LTD *p*
1418
ALBERT ST S HWY 1-6, REGINA, SK, S4P 3A8
(866) 273-5778   *SIC 7538*

REGINA MUNDI CATHOLIC COLLEGE   *p*
657
See LONDON DISTRICT CATHOLIC SCHOOL BOARD

REGINA REALTY SALES LTD   *p 1422*
3889 E ARCOLA AVE, REGINA, SK, S4V 1P5
(306) 359-1900   *SIC 6531*

REGINA RESIDENTIAL RESOURCE CENTRE   *p*
1416
1047 WADEY DR, REGINA, SK, S4N 7J6
(306) 352-3223   *SIC 8399*

REGINA SPORT & IMPORT AUTOMOTIVE GROUP LTD   *p*
755 BROAD ST, REGINA, SK, S4R 8G3
(306) 757-2369   *SIC 5511*

REGINA TRANSIT   *p 1420*
See CITY OF REGINA, THE

REGINA TRAVELODGE HOTEL   *p 1422*
See REGINA TRAVELODGE LTD

REGINA TRAVELODGE LTD   *p 1422*
4177 ALBERT ST, REGINA, SK, S4S 3R6
(306) 586-3443   *SIC 7011*

REGINA VOLVO TRUCKS   *p 1416*
See STERLING TRUCK & TRAILER SALES LTD

REGION 9 REGIONAL TOURISM ORGANIZATION   *p*
631
945 PRINCESS ST SUITE 202, KINGSTON, ON, K7L 5L9
(613) 344-2095   *SIC 6282*

REGION OF DURHAM WORKS DEPARTMENT   *p*
1013
See CORPORATION OF THE REGIONAL MUNICIPALITY OF DURHAM, THE

REGIONAL AUTHORITY OF THE EAST CENTRAL FRANCOPHONE EDUCATION REGION NO.3, THE   *p 165*
4617 50 AVE, ST PAUL, AB, T0A 3A3
(780) 645-3888   *SIC 8211*

REGIONAL CRANE RENTALS LTD   *p 595*
1409 CYRVILLE RD, GLOUCESTER, ON, K1B 3L7
(613) 748-7922   *SIC 7353*

REGIONAL DOORS & HARDWARE (NIAGARA) LIMITED   *p*
886
44 SCOTT ST W, ST CATHARINES, ON, L2R 1C9
(905) 684-8161   *SIC 5031*

REGIONAL FLEET SERVICE   *p 883*
See T R SAND & GRAVEL INC

REGIONAL GROUP OF COMPANIES INC, THE   *p 831*
1737 WOODWARD DR SUITE 200, OTTAWA, ON, K2C 0P9
(613) 230-2100   *SIC 6531*

REGIONAL HEALTH AUTHORITY - CENTRAL MANITOBA INC   *p*
350
24 MILL ST, GLADSTONE, MB, R0J 0T0
(204) 385-2968   *SIC 8062*

REGIONAL HEALTH AUTHORITY - CENTRAL MANITOBA INC   *p*
355
524 5TH ST SE, PORTAGE LA PRAIRIE, MB, R1N 3A8
(204) 239-2211   *SIC 8062*

REGIONAL HEALTH AUTHORITY - CENTRAL MANITOBA INC   *p*
357
180 CENTENNAIRE DR, SOUTHPORT, MB, R0H 1N1
(204) 428-2720   *SIC 8062*

REGIONAL HEALTH AUTHORITY A   *p 394*
1750 SUNSET DR, BATHURST, NB, E2A 4L7
(506) 544-3000   *SIC 8062*

REGIONAL HEALTH AUTHORITY A   *p 394*
275 MAIN ST SUITE 600, BATHURST, NB, E2A 1A9
(506) 544-2188   *SIC 8062*

REGIONAL HEALTH AUTHORITY A   *p 404*
29 RUE DE L'HOPITAL, LAMEQUE, NB, E8T 1C5
(506) 344-2261   *SIC 8062*

REGIONAL HEALTH AUTHORITY A   *p 419*
400 RUE DES HOSPITALIERES, TRACADIE-SHEILA, NB, E1X 1G5
(506) 394-3000   *SIC 8062*

REGIONAL HEALTH AUTHORITY NB *p 401*
180 WOODBRIDGE ST, FREDERICTON, NB, E3B 4R3
(506) 623-5500   *SIC 8062*

REGIONAL HEALTH AUTHORITY NB *p 401*
700 PRIESTMAN ST, FREDERICTON, NB, E3B 3B7
(506) 452-5800   *SIC 8051*

REGIONAL HEALTH AUTHORITY NB *p 412*
8 MAIN ST, SACKVILLE, NB, E4L 4A3
(506) 364-4100   *SIC 8062*

REGIONAL HOSE & EQUIPMENT LTD   *p*
536
175 TURNBULL CRT, CAMBRIDGE, ON, N1T 1C6
(519) 740-1662   *SIC 5084*

REGIONAL HOSE & HYDROLICS   *p 536*
See REGIONAL HOSE & EQUIPMENT LTD

REGIONAL HOSE TORONTO LTD   *p 558*
15 CONNIE CRES UNIT 2223, CONCORD, ON, L4K 1L3
(905) 660-5560   *SIC 5084*

REGIONAL HOSE TORONTO LTD   *p 576*
236 NORSEMAN ST, ETOBICOKE, ON, M8Z 2R4
(416) 239-9555   *SIC 5085*

REGIONAL MENTAL HEALTH CARE, LONDON   *p*
652
See ST. JOSEPH'S HEALTH CARE, LONDON

REGIONAL MENTAL HEALTH CARE, LONDON   *p*
655
See ST. JOSEPH'S HEALTH CARE, LONDON

REGIONAL MENTAL HEALTH CARE, ST THOMAS   *p 889*
See ST. JOSEPH'S HEALTH CARE, LONDON

REGIONAL MUNICIPALITY OF NIAGARA, THE   *p 760*
6623 KALAR RD SUITE 312, NIAGARA FALLS, ON, L2H 2T3
(905) 357-1911   *SIC 8051*

REGIONAL MUNICIPALITY OF NIAGARA, THE   *p 1012*
277 PLYMOUTH RD, WELLAND, ON, L3B 6E3
(905) 714-7428   *SIC 8361*

REGIONAL MUNICIPALITY OF PEEL, THE *p 714*
2460 TRUSCOTT DR, MISSISSAUGA, ON, L5J 3Z8
(905) 791-8668   *SIC 8051*

REGIONAL MUNICIPALITY OF WATERLOO, THE   *p*
638
250 STRASBURG RD, KITCHENER, ON, N2E 3M6
(519) 585-7597   *SIC 4173*

REGIONAL MUNICIPALITY OF YORK, THE
p 756
194 EAGLE ST SUITE 3011, NEWMARKET, ON, L3Y 1J6
(905) 895-2382   *SIC 8051*

REGIONAL POWER INC   *p 726*
6755 MISSISSAUGA RD SUITE 308, MISSISSAUGA, ON, L5N 7Y2
(905) 363-4200   *SIC 4911*

REGIONAL POWER OPCO INC   *p 726*
6755 MISSISSAUGA RD SUITE 308, MISSISSAUGA, ON, L5N 7Y2
(905) 363-4200   *SIC 4911*

REGIONAL RESIDENTIAL SERVICES SOCIETY   *p*
448
202 BROWNLOW AVE SUITE LKD1, DARTMOUTH, NS, B3B 1T5
(902) 465-4022   *SIC 8361*

REGIONAL SECURITY SERVICES LTD   *p*
249
190 VICTORIA ST, PRINCE GEORGE, BC, V2L 2J2
(250) 562-1215   *SIC 7381*

REGIONAL SELLING, DIVISION OF   *p 193*
See LIVANOVA CANADA CORP

REGIONAL WASTE   *p 640*
See JOSEPH & COMPANY INC

REGIONALARCHITECTS   *p 983*
See PLANNING ALLIANCE INC

REGIOPOLIS-NOTRE DAME CATHOLIC HIGH SCHOOL   *p 629*
See ALGONQUIN & LAKESHORE CATHOLIC DISTRICT SCHOOL BOARD

REGIS CANADA   *p 722*
See FIRST CHOICE HAIRCUTTERS LTD

REGIS COTE ET ASSOCIES, ARCHITECTES   *p*
1210
See GROUPE COTE REGIS INC

REGISTERED NURSES ASSOCIATION OF ONTARIO   *p 956*
158 PEARL ST, TORONTO, ON, M5H 1L3
(416) 599-1925   *SIC 8621*

REGITEX INC   *p 1322*
745 AV GUY-POULIN, SAINT-JOSEPH-DE-BEAUCE, QC, G0S 2V0
(418) 397-5775   *SIC 2282*

REGNIER'S YOUR INDEPENDENT GROCERS   *p*
842
See 1401911 ONTARIO LIMITED

REGROUPEMENT DES CENTRE DE LA PETITE ENFANCE DE L'   *p 1173*
4321 AV PAPINEAU, MONTREAL, QC, H2H 1T3
(514) 528-1442   *SIC 8611*

REGROUPEMENT DES ORGANISMES NATIONAUX DE LOISIRS DU QUEBEC   *p*
1166
4545 AV PIERRE-DE COUBERTIN, MONTREAL, QC, H1V 0B2
(514) 252-3126   *SIC 8699*

REGROUPEMENT LOISIR QUEBEC *p 1166*
See REGROUPEMENT DES ORGANISMES NATIONAUX DE LOISIRS DU QUEBEC

REGULVAR INC   *p 1235*
3985 BOUL INDUSTRIEL, MONTREAL, QC, H7L 4S3
(450) 629-0435   *SIC 5084*

REGULVAR INC   *p 1277*
2800 RUE JEAN-PERRIN BUREAU 100, QUEBEC, QC, G2C 1T3
(418) 842-5114   *SIC 1796*

REGUS BUSINESS CENTRE LTD   *p 966*

161 BAY ST, TORONTO, ON, M5J 2S1
(416) 572-2200   *SIC* 7389
REHABILITATION CENTRE FOR CHIL-DREN INC   *p*
381
1155 NOTRE DAME AVE, WINNIPEG, MB, R3E 3G1
(204) 452-4311   *SIC* 8361
REHABILITATION DU O INC   *p* 1087
5270 BOUL CLEROUX, COTE SAINT-LUC, QC, H7T 2E8
(450) 682-2733   *SIC* 1623
REHABILITATION SCIENCES INSTITUTE   *p*
945
See GOVERNING COUNCIL OF THE UNI-VERSITY OF TORONTO, THE
REHO INTERNATIONAL INC   *p* 765
7 EQUESTRIAN CRT, NORTH YORK, ON, M2H 3M9
(416) 269-2950   *SIC* 5169
REHOBOTH A CHRISTIAN ASSOCIATION FOR THE MENTALLY HANDICAPPED OF ALBERTA   *p* 9
3505 29 ST NE SUITE 106, CALGARY, AB, T1Y 5W4
(403) 250-7333   *SIC* 8331
REICHHOLD INDUSTRIES LIMITED   *p* 248
50 DOUGLAS ST, PORT MOODY, BC, V3H 3L9
(604) 939-1181   *SIC* 2821
REID & DELEYE CONTRACTORS LTD   *p*
564
4926 HIGHWAY 59, COURTLAND, ON, N0J 1E0
(519) 688-2600   *SIC* 1541
REID CANDY & NUT SHOP   *p* 533
See DREW-SMITH COMPANY LIMITED, THE
REID CROWTHER & PARTNERS LIMITED*p*
69
340 MIDPARK WAY SE SUITE 300, CAL-GARY, AB, T2X 1P1
    SIC 8711
REID'S DAIRY COMPANY LIMITED, THE   *p*
492
222 BELL BLVD, BELLEVILLE, ON, K8P 5L7
(613) 967-1970   *SIC* 2024
REID'S DRY GOODS LTD   *p* 322
2125 41ST AVE W, VANCOUVER, BC, V6M 1Z3
(604) 266-9177   *SIC* 5651
REID'S FOODLAND   *p* 1003
6145 HIGHWAY 38, VERONA, ON, K0H 2W0
(613) 374-2112   *SIC* 5411
REID'S FURNITURE OF BARRIE LIMITED*p*
488
491 BRYNE DR, BARRIE, ON, L4N 9P7
(705) 735-3337   *SIC* 5963
REID'S HERITAGE CONSTRUCTION   *p* 537
See RHC DESIGN-BUILD
REID'S HERITAGE HOMES LTD   *p* 537
6783 WELLINGTON ROAD 34, CAM-BRIDGE, ON, N3C 2V4
(519) 658-6656   *SIC* 1521
REID'S VALU-MART   *p* 645
See 1543892 ONTARIO LTD
REID-BUILT HOMES LTD   *p* 102
18140 107 AVE NW, EDMONTON, AB, T5S 1K5
(780) 486-3666   *SIC* 1521
REID-WORLD WIDE CORPORATION   *p* 102
18140 107 AVE NW SUITE 200, EDMON-TON, AB, T5S 1K5
(780) 451-7778   *SIC* 6552
REIDER INSURANCE SERVICES   *p* 370
1399 MCPHILLIPS ST, WINNIPEG, MB, R2V 3C4
(204) 334-4319   *SIC* 6411
REILLY'S SECURITY SERVICES   *p* 788
See 1175469 ONTARIO LTD
REIMAR CONSTRUCTION CORPORATION
p 617

328 TRINITY CHURCH RD, HANNON, ON, L0R 1P0
(905) 692-9900   *SIC* 1799
REIMAR FORMING & CONSTRUCTION   *p*
617
See REIMAR CONSTRUCTION CORPO-RATION
REIMER CONSOLIDATED CORP   *p* 375
201 PORTAGE AVE SUITE 2900, WIN-NIPEG, MB, R3B 3K6
(204) 958-5300   *SIC* 6712
REIMER EXPRESS   *p* 1096
See YRC FREIGHT CANADA COMPANY
REIMER EXPRESS ENTERPRISES LTD   *p*
375
201 PORTAGE AVE SUITE 2900, WIN-NIPEG, MB, R3B 3K6
(204) 958-5000   *SIC* 6712
REIMER FARM SUPPLIES LTD   *p* 358
340 PTH 12 N, STEINBACH, MB, R5G 1T6
(204) 326-1305   *SIC* 5083
REIMER HARDWOODS LTD   *p* 177
31135 PEARDONVILLE RD, ABBOTS-FORD, BC, V2T 6K6
(604) 850-9281   *SIC* 5031
REIMER WORLD CORP   *p* 375
201 PORTAGE AVE SUITE 2900, WIN-NIPEG, MB, R3B 3K6
(204) 958-5300   *SIC* 8741
REINDERS GROUP LTD   *p* 726
2660 ARGENTIA RD, MISSISSAUGA, ON, L5N 5V4
(905) 821-4844   *SIC* 8711
REINGOLD, M. DRUGS LIMITED   *p* 926
1507 YONGE ST, TORONTO, ON, M4T 1Z2
(416) 923-7700   *SIC* 5912
REINHART FOODS   *p* 768
See REINHART FOODS LIMITED
REINHART FOODS LIMITED   *p* 768
235 YORKLAND BLVD SUITE 1101, NORTH YORK, ON, M2J 4Y8
(416) 645-4910   *SIC* 2099
REINHART FOODS LIMITED   *p* 890
7449 HWY 26, STAYNER, ON, L0M 1S0
(705) 428-2422   *SIC* 2099
REINSURANCE MANAGEMENT ASSO-CIATES INC   *p*
956
170 UNIVERSITY AVE SUITE 500, TORONTO, ON, M5H 3B3
(416) 408-2602   *SIC* 6311
REIS EQUIPMENT CENTER   *p* 849
See REIS, H.J. INTERNATIONAL LTD
REIS, H.J. INTERNATIONAL LTD   *p* 849
479 O'BRIEN RD, RENFREW, ON, K7V 3Z3
(613) 432-4133   *SIC* 5083
REISER (CANADA) CO.   *p* 529
1549 YORKTON CRT UNIT 4, BURLING-TON, ON, L7P 5B7
(905) 631-6611   *SIC* 5084
REISER CANADA   *p* 529
See REISER (CANADA) CO.
REITMANS (CANADA) LIMITEE   *p* 1217
250 RUE SAUVE O, MONTREAL, QC, H3L 1Z2
(514) 384-1140   *SIC* 5621
REJUDICARE SYNERGY LTD   *p* 1026
6220 WESTAR DR, WINDSOR, ON, N9J 0B5
(519) 734-6600   *SIC* 5122
REKAM   *p* 781
See REKAM IMPORT EXPORT INTERNA-TIONAL INC
REKAM IMPORT EXPORT INTERNA-TIONAL INC   *p*
781
222 FAYWOOD BLVD, NORTH YORK, ON, M3H 6A9
(416) 630-2892   *SIC* 5043
REKO INTERNATIONAL GROUP INC   *p*
1017
469 SILVER CREEK INDUSTRIAL DR, WINDSOR, ON, N8N 4W2
(519) 727-3287   *SIC* 3544

REKO MANUFACTURING GROUP INC   *p*
1017
469 SILVER CREEK INDUSTRIAL DR, WINDSOR, ON, N8N 4W2
(519) 727-3287   *SIC* 3544
RELAIS   *p* 1374
260 RUE LEGER, SHERBROOKE, QC, J1L 1Y5
(819) 566-7317   *SIC* 5531
RELAIS NORDIK INC   *p* 1259
21 RUE DU MARCHE-CHAMPLAIN BU-REAU 100, QUEBEC, QC, G1K 8Z8
(418) 692-1000   *SIC* 4424
RELAIS PNEUS FREINS ET SUSPEN-SIONS INC, LE   *p*
1375
4255 BOUL BOURQUE, SHERBROOKE, QC, J1N 1S4
(819) 566-7722   *SIC* 5531
RELAIS TOYOTA   *p* 1371
See AUTOMOBILES RELAIS 2000 INC
RELAMPING SERVICES CANADA LIMITED   *p* 505
48 WEST DR, BRAMPTON, ON, L6T 3T6
(905) 457-1815   *SIC* 7349
RELANCE OUTAOUAIS INC, LA   *p* 1105
45 BOUL SACRE-COEUR, GATINEAU, QC, J8X 1C6
(819) 776-5870   *SIC* 8399
RELANCE OUTAOUAIS INC, LA   *p* 1105
270 BOUL DES ALLUMETTIERES, GATINEAU, QC, J8X 1N3
(819) 770-5325   *SIC* 8399
RELAXUS PRODUCTS LTD   *p* 285
1590 POWELL ST, VANCOUVER, BC, V5L 1H3
(604) 879-3895   *SIC* 5047
RELCO INC   *p* 558
7700 KEELE ST UNIT 10, CONCORD, ON, L4K 2A1
(416) 740-8632   *SIC* 5084
RELIABLE CLEANING SERVICES   *p* 913
See RELIABLE WINDOW CLEANERS (SUDBURY) LIMITED
RELIABLE CONTROLS   *p* 339
See RELIABLE CONTROLS CORPORA-TION
RELIABLE CONTROLS CORPORATION   *p*
339
120 HALLOWELL RD, VICTORIA, BC, V9A 7K2
(250) 475-2036   *SIC* 3625
RELIABLE CORPORATION   *p* 791
100 WINGOLD AVE UNIT 5, NORTH YORK, ON, M6B 4K7
(416) 785-0200   *SIC* 5084
RELIABLE LIFE INSURANCE COMPANY   *p*
613
100 KING ST W, HAMILTON, ON, L8P 1A2
(905) 525-5031   *SIC* 6311
RELIABLE MAINTENANCE PRODUCT   *p*
900
See RELIABLE WINDOW CLEANERS (SUDBURY) LIMITED
RELIABLE MOTORS LTD   *p* 1041
14 JOHN YEO DR, CHARLOTTETOWN, PE, C1E 3H6
(902) 566-4409   *SIC* 5511
RELIABLE PARTS LTD   *p* 201
85 NORTH BEND ST, COQUITLAM, BC, V3K 6N1
(604) 941-1355   *SIC* 5722
RELIABLE TUBE (EDMONTON) LTD   *p* 2
26936 ACHESON RD, ACHESON, AB, T7X 6B2
(780) 962-0130   *SIC* 5051
RELIABLE TUBE INC   *p* 230
26867 GLOUCESTER WAY, LANGLEY, BC, V4W 3Y3
(604) 857-9861   *SIC* 5051
RELIABLE WINDOW CLEANERS (SUD-BURY) LIMITED   *p*
900
345 REGENT ST, SUDBURY, ON, P3C 4E1

(705) 675-5281   *SIC* 5087
RELIABLE WINDOW CLEANERS (SUD-BURY) LIMITED   *p*
913
167 WILSON AVE, TIMMINS, ON, P4N 2T2
(705) 360-1194   *SIC* 1799
RELIANCE COMFORT LIMITED PARTNER-SHIP   *p*
768
2 LANSING SQ, NORTH YORK, ON, M2J 4P8
(416) 499-7600   *SIC* 1711
RELIANCE FOODS INTERNATIONAL INC*p*
1120
549 GRAND BOULEVARD, L'ILE-PERROT, QC, J7V 4X4
(514) 425-1880   *SIC* 5142
RELIANCE FOUNDRY CO. LTD   *p* 273
6450 148 ST UNIT 207, SURREY, BC, V3S 7G7
(604) 547-0460   *SIC* 5051
RELIANCE HOME COMFORT, DIV OF*p* 768
See RELIANCE COMFORT LIMITED PART-NERSHIP
RELIANCE INDUSTRIAL INVESTMENTS LTD   *p* 149
606 19 AVE, NISKU, AB, T9E 7W1
(780) 955-7115   *SIC* 6712
RELIANCE INSURANCE AGENCIES LTD   *p*
186
4853 HASTINGS ST SUITE 100, BURN-ABY, BC, V5C 2L1
(604) 255-4616   *SIC* 6411
RELIANCE METALS CANADA LIMITED   *p*
123
6925 8 ST NW, EDMONTON, AB, T6P 1T9
(780) 801-4114   *SIC* 5051
RELIANCE OFFSHORE CANADA INC*p* 454
1525 BIRMINGHAM ST, HALIFAX, NS, B3J 2J6
(902) 429-1255   *SIC* 7361
RELIANCE PRODUCTS LTD   *p* 385
1093 SHERWIN RD, WINNIPEG, MB, R3H 1A4
(204) 633-4403   *SIC* 3089
RELIANCE TRADE BROKERS INC   *p* 524
4145 NORTH SERVICE RD, BURLINGTON, ON, L7L 6A3
(289) 201-7841   *SIC* 6531
RELIC ENTERTAINMENT, INC   *p* 300
1040 HAMILTON ST SUITE 400, VANCOU-VER, BC, V6B 2R9
(604) 801-6577   *SIC* 7372
RELIGIEUSES DE JESUS-MARIE, LES   *p*
1271
2049 CH SAINT-LOUIS, QUEBEC, QC, G1T 1P2
(418) 687-9260   *SIC* 8661
RELIGIOUS HOSPITALLERS OF SAINT JOSEPH OF THE HOTEL DIEU OF KINGSTON   *p* 631
166 BROCK ST, KINGSTON, ON, K7L 5G2
(613) 549-2680   *SIC* 8069
RELIGIOUS HOSPITALLERS OF SAINT JOSEPH OF THE HOTEL DIEU OF KINGSTON   *p* 631
166 BROCK ST SUITE 262D, KINGSTON, ON, K7L 5G2
(613) 544-3310   *SIC* 8062
RELY-EX CONTRACTING INC   *p* 1429
516 43RD ST E, SASKATOON, SK, S7K 0V6
(306) 664-2155   *SIC* 1542
REM TEK ENTERPRISES LTD   *p* 320
3195 GRANVILLE ST SUITE 218, VAN-COUVER, BC, V6H 3K2
(604) 733-6345   *SIC* 8741
REM-MEDI HEALTH CARE SERVICES   *p*
1218
See SERVICES DE SOINS A DOMICILE ROYAL TREATMENT INC
REMAI HOLDINGS LTD   *p* 25
2828 23 ST NE, CALGARY, AB, T2E 8T4
(403) 291-2003   *SIC* 7011

REMAI INVESTMENT CORPORATION *p 1429*
500 SPADINA CRES E SUITE 101, SASKA-TOON, SK, S7K 4H9
(306) 244-1119   *SIC 7011*

REMAI VENTURES INC *p 1432*
143 CARDINAL CRES, SASKATOON, SK, S7L 6H5
(306) 934-2799   *SIC 7011*

REMARK FARMS *p 1020*
See 658771 ONTARIO LTD

REMARK FRESH MARKETS *p 658*
See 1594058 ONTARIO LTD

REMATEK INC *p 1335*
8975 BOUL HENRI-BOURASSA O, SAINT-LAURENT, QC, H4S 1P7
(514) 333-6414   *SIC 3544*

REMATEK-ENERGIE *p 1335*
See REMATEK INC

REMAX *p 246*
See REMAX SABRE REAL ESTATE GROUP LTD

REMAX *p 598*
See REMAX NORTH COUNTRY REALTY INC

REMAX 2000 REALTY *p 270*
See CONCEPT 2000 REAL ESTATE (1989) INCORPORATED

REMAX ACTIF INC *p 1296*
1592 RUE MONTARVILLE BUREAU 102, SAINT-BRUNO, QC, J3V 3T7
(450) 461-1708   *SIC 6531*

REMAX ASSOCIATES *p 372*
1060 MCPHILLIPS ST, WINNIPEG, MB, R2X 2K9
(204) 989-9000   *SIC 6531*

REMAX DU CARTIER INC *p 1182*
7085 BOUL SAINT-LAURENT, MONTREAL, QC, H2S 3E3
(514) 278-7170   *SIC 6531*

REMAX EXCELLENCE REALTY INC *p 1033*
3700 STEELES AVE W, WOODBRIDGE, ON, L4L 8K8
(905) 856-1111   *SIC 6531*

REMAX FIRST REALTY *p 39*
9625 MACLEOD TRAIL SW, CALGARY, AB, T2J 0P6
(403) 938-4848   *SIC 6531*

REMAX GATEWAY REALTY LTD *p 830*
2255 CARLING AVE SUITE 101, OTTAWA, ON, K2B 7Z5
(613) 288-0090   *SIC 6531*

REMAX GEORGIAN BAY REALTY LTD *p 682*
833 KING ST, MIDLAND, ON, L4R 0B7
(705) 526-9366   *SIC 6531*

REMAX LITTLE OAK REALTY *p 175*
See LITTLE OAK REALTY LTD

REMAX MEDALTA REAL ESTATE (1989) LTD *p 147*
1235 SOUTHVIEW DR SE UNIT 109, MEDICINE HAT, AB, T1B 4K3
(403) 529-9393   *SIC 6531*

REMAX METRO CITY REALTY *p 830*
See REMAX GATEWAY REALTY LTD

REMAX NORTH COUNTRY REALTY INC *p 598*
405 MUSKOKA RD S UNIT B, GRAVEN-HURST, ON, P1P 1T1
(705) 687-2243   *SIC 6531*

REMAX QUEST REALITY *p 994*
See RE MAX WEST REALTY BROKERAGE INC

REMAX REAL ESTATE 'MOUNTAIN VIEW' LTD *p 71*
4625 VARSITY DR NW SUITE 222, CAL-GARY, AB, T3A 0Z9
(403) 651-4400   *SIC 6531*

REMAX REAL ESTATE CALGARY SOUTH LTD *p 39*
8820 BLACKFOOT TRAIL SE SUITE 115, CALGARY, AB, T2J 3J1
(403) 278-2900   *SIC 6531*

REMAX REALTY SPECIALISTS INC *p 706*

4310 SHERWOODTOWNE BLVD UNIT 200, MISSISSAUGA, ON, L4Z 4C4
(905) 361-4663   *SIC 6531*

REMAX SABRE REAL ESTATE GROUP LTD *p 246*
2748 LOUGHEED HWY SUITE 102, PORT COQUITLAM, BC, V3B 6P2
(604) 942-0606   *SIC 6531*

REMAX SOLID GOLD REALTY (II) LTD *p 1007*
180 WEBER ST S, WATERLOO, ON, N2J 2B2
(519) 888-7110   *SIC 6531*

REMBOS INC *p 517*
60 OLD ONONDAGA RD E, BRANTFORD, ON, N3T 5L4
(519) 770-1207   *SIC 5031*

REMBOURRAGE ANP INC *p 1254*
105 RUE BEAUDET, PRINCEVILLE, QC, G6L 4L3
(819) 364-2645   *SIC 3732*

REMBOURRAGE PRINCEVILLE TECH *p 1254*
105 RUE BEAUDET, PRINCEVILLE, QC, G6L 4L3
(819) 364-2645   *SIC 5551*

REMCAN PROJECTS LIMITED PARTNER-SHIP *p 225*
20075 100A AVE SUITE 2, LANGLEY, BC, V1M 3G4
(604) 882-0840   *SIC 1629*

REMEDY ENERGY SERVICES INC *p 11*
720 28 ST NE UNIT 255, CALGARY, AB, T2A 6R3
(403) 272-0703   *SIC 1389*

REMEDY HOLDINGS INC *p 674*
675 COCHRANE DR SUITE 110, MARKHAM, ON, L3R 0B8
(647) 794-3388   *SIC 5912*

REMEDY'S RX *p 674*
See REMEDY HOLDINGS INC

REMEQ INC *p 1254*
391 RUE SAINT-JEAN-BAPTISTE N, PRINCEVILLE, QC, G6L 5G3
(819) 364-5400   *SIC 3715*

REMINGTON HOMES *p 549*
See CALSPER DEVELOPMENTS INC

REMORQUAGE GOYER *p 1302*
See SAULNIER AUTOMOBILES INC

REMORQUAGE NEW RICHMOND *p 1112*
See AUTOMOBILES MAUGER FORD INC

REMORQUAGE PROFESSIONNEL SAGUENAY INC *p 1116*
2386 RUE CANTIN, JONQUIERE, QC, G7X 8S6
(418) 695-1114   *SIC 7549*

REMORQUAGE ST-MICHEL INC *p 1349*
340 CH PIGEON, SAINT-MICHEL, QC, J0L 2J0
(450) 454-9973   *SIC 7549*

REMORQUES ST-HENRI *p 1130*
See GROUPE ST-HENRI INC

REMPEL BROS. CONCRETE LTD *p 227*
20353 64 AVE UNIT 203, LANGLEY, BC, V2Y 1N5
(604) 525-9344   *SIC 3273*

REMPLE DISPOSAL INC *p 178*
35321 DELAIR RD, ABBOTSFORD, BC, V3G 2C8
(604) 866-9020   *SIC 4953*

REMTEC INC *p 1075*
933 AV SIMARD, CHAMBLY, QC, J3L 4B7
(450) 658-6671   *SIC 3443*

REN'S FEED AND SUPPLIES LIMITED *p 849*
20 BROCK RD N UNIT 3, PUSLINCH, ON, N0B 2J0
(519) 767-5858   *SIC 5999*

REN'S PETS DEPOT *p 849*
See REN'S FEED AND SUPPLIES LIMITED

REN-WIL INC *p 1132*
9181 RUE BOIVIN, LASALLE, QC, H8R 2E8
(514) 367-1741   *SIC 2499*

RENAISSANCE DES ILES INC, LA *p 1120*
521 CH DU GROS-CAP, L'ETANG-DU-NORD, QC, G4T 3M1
(418) 986-2710   *SIC 2092*

RENAISSANCE FALLSVIEW HOTEL *p 758*
See 577793 ONTARIO INC

RENAISSANCE HOTEL *p 981*
See LARCO INVESTMENTS LTD

RENAISSANCE INVESTMENTS *p 1194*
See CIBC ASSET MANAGEMENT INC

RENAISSANCE OIL CORP *p 329*
595 BURRARD ST SUITE 3123, VANCOU-VER, BC, V7X 1J1
(604) 536-3637   *SIC 1382*

RENAISSANCE PRINTING INC *p 845*
1800 IRONSTONE MANOR, PICKERING, ON, L1W 3J9
(905) 831-3000   *SIC 2721*

RENAISSANCE VANCOUVER HOTEL HARBOURSIDE *p 315*
See NEW WORLD HOTELS LTD

RENAISSANCE WINE & SPIRITS *p 31*
See RENAISSANCE WINE MERCHANTS LTD

RENAISSANCE WINE MERCHANTS LTD *p 31*
3303 8 ST SE, CALGARY, AB, T2G 3A4
(403) 296-0170   *SIC 5182*

RENALD COTE 2007 INC *p 1052*
48 AV WILLIAM-DOBELL, BAIE-COMEAU, QC, G4Z 1T7
(418) 296-2854   *SIC 1794*

RENAUD FURNITURE LTD *p 416*
4327 ROUTE 115, SAINT-ANTOINE SUD, NB, E4V 2Z4
(506) 525-2493   *SIC 5021*

RENAUD, LARRY FORD & RV SALES *p 618*
175 KING ST W, HARROW, ON, N0R 1G0
(519) 738-6767   *SIC 5511*

RENCO FOODS LTD *p 909*
161 COURT ST S, THUNDER BAY, ON, P7B 2X7
(807) 345-3947   *SIC 5411*

RENDEZ-VOUS CHRYSLER LTD *p 403*
795 BOUL EVERARD H DAIGLE, GRAND-SAULT/GRAND FALLS, NB, E3Z 3C7
(506) 473-5000   *SIC 5511*

RENE BERNARD INC *p 1055*
88 AV LAMBERT, BEAUCEVILLE, QC, G5X 3N4
(418) 774-3382   *SIC 5031*

RENE ET MARCO DESROCHER CON-STRUCTION INC *p 1391*
1470 4E RUE, VAL-D'OR, QC, J9P 6X2
(819) 825-4279   *SIC 1542*

RENE GOUPIL JESUITS *p 845*
2315 LIVERPOOL RD, PICKERING, ON, L1X 1V4
(905) 839-5155   *SIC 8699*

RENE HENRICHON INC *p 1381*
3160 COTE DE TERREBONNE, TERRE-BONNE, QC, J6Y 1G1
SIC 1542

RENE MATERIAUX COMPOSITES LTEE *p 1300*
55 RTE 271 S, SAINT-EPHREM-DE-BEAUCE, QC, G0M 1R0
(418) 484-5282   *SIC 3714*

RENE ST-CYR (1996) INC *p 1243*
3330 RTE 157, NOTRE-DAME-DU-MONT-CARMEL, QC, G0X 3J0
(819) 379-2202   *SIC 5031*

RENE ST-CYR PLANCHERS ET ES-CALIERS *p 1243*
See RENE ST-CYR (1996) INC

RENEWABLE ENERGY SOLUTIONS THESSALON *p 903*
48 FELTHAM RD, THESSALON, ON, P0R 1L0
(705) 842-6911   *SIC 4924*

RENEX INC *p 443*
73 TACOMA DR SUITE 800, DARTMOUTH,

NS, B2W 3Y6
SIC 7299

RENFREW CARE CENTER *p 287*
See PR SENIORS HOUSING MANAGE-MENT LTD

RENFREW CHRYSLER INC. *p 73*
1920 PUMPHOUSE RD SW, CALGARY, AB, T3C 3N4
(403) 266-1920   *SIC 5511*

RENFREW CHRYSLER JEEP *p 73*
See RENFREW CHRYSLER INC.

RENFREW COUNTY DISTRICT SCHOOL BOARD *p 838*
420 BELL ST, PEMBROKE, ON, K8A 2K5
(613) 735-6858   *SIC 8211*

RENFREW EDUCATIONAL SERVICES SO-CIETY *p 69*
75 SUNPARK DR SE, CALGARY, AB, T2X 3V4
(403) 291-5038   *SIC 8211*

RENFREW HOME HARDWARE BUILDING CENTRE *p 849*
See 697739 ONTARIO INC

RENFREW NATIONAL LEASING LTD *p 73*
1920 PUMPHOUSE RD SW, CALGARY, AB, T3C 3N4
(403) 266-1920   *SIC 5511*

RENFREW PARK COMMUNITY ASSOCIA-TION *p 287*
2929 22ND AVE E, VANCOUVER, BC, V5M 2Y3
(604) 257-8388   *SIC 8322*

RENFREW PARK COMMUNITY CENTRE *p 287*
See RENFREW PARK COMMUNITY AS-SOCIATION

RENFREW TAPE *p 849*
See SCAPA TAPES NORTH AMERICA LTD

RENFREW VICTORIA HOSPITAL *p 849*
499 RAGLAN ST N, RENFREW, ON, K7V 1P6
(613) 432-4851   *SIC 8062*

RENIN CANADA CORP *p 505*
110 WALKER DR, BRAMPTON, ON, L6T 4H6
(905) 791-7930   *SIC 2431*

RENISON UNIVERSITY COLLEGE *p 1009*
265 WESTMOUNT RD N, WATERLOO, ON, N2L 3G7
(519) 884-4404   *SIC 8221*

RENNAT INC *p 1341*
4850 RUE BOURG, SAINT-LAURENT, QC, H4T 1J2
(514) 735-4255   *SIC 6712*

RENNIE MARKETING SYSTEMS *p 294*
See 541823 BC LTD

RENNSTADD PHARMA INC *p 477*
47 WILSON ST W, ANCASTER, ON, L9G 1N1
(905) 648-4493   *SIC 5912*

RENO DEPOT *p 1262*
See RONA INC

RENO FOOD PACKAGING *p 901*
See PACTIV CANADA INC

RENO-DEPOT *p 1309*
See RONA INC

RENO-DEPOT *p 1395*
See RONA INC

RENO-DEPOT DE LAVAL *p 1237*
See RONA INC

RENO-DEPOT DE MARCHE CENTRAL *p 1226*
See RONA INC

RENO-DIRECT INC *p 1362*
1329 BOUL DAGENAIS O, SAINTE-ROSE, QC, H7L 5Z9
(450) 625-2660   *SIC 5072*

RENO-VALLEE INC *p 1046*
358 BOUL SAINT-BENOIT O, AMQUI, QC, G5J 2G3
(418) 629-3800   *SIC 5251*

RENOIR RETIREMENT RESIDENCE *p 68*

See REVERA INC

RENOVAPRIX INC *p 1301*
226 25E AV, SAINT-EUSTACHE, QC, J7P 4Z8
(450) 472-3000 *SIC 5211*

RENOVATEUR REGIONAL *p 1320*
1025 BOUL JEAN-BAPTISTE-ROLLAND O, SAINT-JEROME, QC, J7Y 4Y7
(450) 560-3979 *SIC 5211*

RENOVATEUR RONA *p 1096*
See BROUILLETTE & FRERE INC

RENOVATEUR RONA *p 1123*
See ROBERGE ET FILS INC

RENOVATEUR RONA, LE *p 1150*
See CARON, CAMILLE INC

RENOVATEUR RONA, LE *p 1395*
See LOYOLA SCHMIDT LTEE

RENOVATION EXPO INC *p 1254*
40 RUE SAINT-PIERRE, PRINCEVILLE, QC, G6L 5A9
(819) 364-2616 *SIC 5712*

RENOVATION STE-AGATHE *p 1391*
See MONETTE, EUGENE INC

RENOVATIONEXPERTS.COM *p 443*
See RENEX INC

RENOVATIONS BY AVI *p 35*
See HOMES BY AVI (CANADA) INC

RENOVATIONS ET RESTAURATION APRES-SINISTRE RENOVCO INC *p 1095*
11355 CH COTE-DE-LIESSE, DORVAL, QC, H9P 1B2
(514) 856-9993 *SIC 1541*

RENOVATIONS MARTIN MARTIN INC *p 1173*
5187 AV PAPINEAU, MONTREAL, QC, H2H 1W1
(514) 270-6599 *SIC 5211*

RENOVATIONS OLYMBEC INC *p 1327*
333 BOUL DECARIE 5E ETAGE, SAINT-LAURENT, QC, H4N 3M9
(514) 344-3334 *SIC 1542*

RENOVCO *p 1095*
See RENOVATIONS ET RESTAURATION APRES-SINISTRE RENOVCO INC

RENSERVALL LIMITED *p 834*
116 LISGAR ST SUITE 500, OTTAWA, ON, K2P 0C2
(613) 237-3444 *SIC 6712*

RENSHAW TRAVEL & CRUISE CENTER *p 322*
See RENSHAW TRAVEL LTD

RENSHAW TRAVEL LTD *p 322*
2175 4TH AVE W, VANCOUVER, BC, V6K 1N7
(604) 838-1008 *SIC 4724*

RENT-ALL CENTRE *p 544*
See 348461 ONTARIO LIMITED

RENTAL RIGHT *p 467*
See SCHWARTZ & COMPANY (2006) LIMITED

RENTCO EQUIPMENT LTD *p 133*
11437 97 AVE, GRANDE PRAIRIE, AB, T8V 5R8
(780) 539-7860 *SIC 7353*

RENTCO'S TOOL SHED *p 133*
See RENTCO EQUIPMENT LTD

RENYCO INC *p 1384*
425 GALIPEAU RANG 5 RR 1, THURSO, QC, J0X 3B0
SIC 2426

REPAIR & OVERHAUL DIV OF *p 501*
See AIRCRAFT APPLIANCES AND EQUIPMENT LIMITED

REPAREX *p 891*
See SANI-SOL INC

REPARTITEURS DU RESEAU DE TRANSPORT DE LA CAPITALE *p 1279*
See SYNDICAT DES INSPECTEURS ET DES REPARTITEURS DU RESEAU DE TRANSPORT DE LA CAPITALE (FISA)

REPENTIGNY CHEVROLET BUICK GMC INC *p 1283*
612 RUE NOTRE-DAME, REPENTIGNY, QC, J6A 2T9
(450) 581-9500 *SIC 5511*

REPENTIGNY FIAT *p 1282*
See GIRARD AUTOMOBILE INC

REPERAGE BOOMERANG INC *p 1226*
9280 BOUL DE L'ACADIE, MONTREAL, QC, H4N 3C5
(514) 234-8722 *SIC 5065*

REPIT-RESSOURCE DE L'EST DE MONTREAL *p 1163*
7707 RUE HOCHELAGA BUREAU 100, MONTREAL, QC, H1L 2K4
(514) 353-1479 *SIC 8322*

REPITS DE GABY, LES *p 1089*
51 19E RUE, CRABTREE, QC, J0K 1B0
(450) 754-2782 *SIC 8699*

REPLICON INC *p 58*
910 7 AVE SW SUITE 800, CALGARY, AB, T2P 3N8
(403) 262-6519 *SIC 7371*

REPORT ON BUSINESS TELEVISION *p 978*
See BELL MEDIA INC

REPRESENTATIVE WEBCO BOWES *p 139*
See 1032451 B.C. LTD

REPRODUCTIONS-PHOTOS M.P. LTEE *p 1226*
222 BOUL LEBEAU, MONTREAL, QC, H4N 1R4
(514) 383-4313 *SIC 8741*

REPRODUCTIVE IMAGING *p 906*
See TRUE NORTH IMAGING INC

REPROMATIC SYSTEMS INC *p 558*
60 PIPPIN RD SUITE 34, CONCORD, ON, L4K 4M8
(905) 669-2900 *SIC 7389*

REPSOL CANADA ENERGY PARTNERSHIP *p 58*
888 3 ST SW SUITE 2000, CALGARY, AB, T2P 5C5
(403) 237-1234 *SIC 1382*

REPSOL OIL & GAS CANADA INC *p 58*
888 3 ST SW SUITE 2000, CALGARY, AB, T2P 5C5
SIC 1382

REPUBLIC CANADIAN DRAWN, INC *p 613*
155 CHATHAM ST, HAMILTON, ON, L8P 2B7
(905) 546-5656 *SIC 3316*

REPUBLIC PACKAGING OF CANADA *p 623*
See CRAIG PACKAGING LIMITED

REPUBLIC TECHNOLOGIES CANADA, DIV DE *p 1060*
See COMPAGNIE TOP TUBES

RES CANADA *p 1186*
See SYSTEMES D'ENERGIE RENOUVELABLE CANADA INC

RES PRECAST INC *p 622*
3450 THOMAS ST, INNISFIL, ON, L9S 3W6
(705) 436-7383 *SIC 3272*

RES PUBLICA *p 1205*
See GROUPE CONSEIL RES PUBLICA INC

RES-MAR *p 1102*
478 MONTEE DE WAKEHAM, GASPE, QC, G4X 1Y6
(418) 368-5373 *SIC 7389*

RESCO CANADA, INC *p 1112*
1330 RTE 148, GRENVILLE-SUR-LA-ROUGE, QC, J0V 1B0
(819) 242-2721 *SIC 3312*

RESCOM INC *p 96*
12704 110 AVE NW, EDMONTON, AB, T5M 2L7
(780) 454-6500 *SIC 8741*

RESEARCH & DEVELOPMENT CORPORATION OF NEWFOUNDLAND AND LABRADOR *p 431*
68 PORTUGAL COVE RD, ST. JOHN'S, NL, A1B 2L9
(709) 758-0913 *SIC 8732*

RESEARCH AND MANAGEMENT CORPORATION *p 587*
20 CARLSON CRT SUITE 10, ETOBICOKE, ON, M9W 7K6
(905) 678-7588 *SIC 6794*

RESEARCH HOUSE INC *p 1169*
2953 RUE BELANGER BUREAU 214, MONTREAL, QC, H1Y 3G4
SIC 8732

RESEARCH INSTITUTE *p 294*
See VANCOUVER COASTAL HEALTH AUTHORITY

RESEARCH NOW INC *p 921*
3080 YONGE ST SUITE 2000, TORONTO, ON, M4N 3N1
(800) 599-7938 *SIC 8731*

RESEARCH SERCVICES, DEPARTMENT OF *p 455*
See IZAAK WALTON KILLAM HEALTH CENTRE, THE

RESEARCH SERVICES OFFICE *p 117*
See GOVERNORS OF THE UNIVERSITY OF ALBERTA, THE

RESEARCH UNIVERSITIES' COUNCIL OF BRITISH COLUMBIA, THE *p 336*
880 DOUGLAS ST SUITE 400, VICTORIA, BC, V8W 2B7
(250) 480-4859 *SIC 8742*

RESEAU BUREAUTIQUE *p 1222*
See 2865-8169 QUEBEC INC

RESEAU CANOE *p 932*
See CANOE INC

RESEAU DE TRANSPORT DE LONGUEUIL *p 1142*
1150 BOUL MARIE-VICTORIN, LONGUEUIL, QC, J4G 2M4
(450) 442-8600 *SIC 4111*

RESEAU DES SPORTS (RDS) INC, LE *p 1174*
1755 BOUL RENE-LEVESQUE E BUREAU 300, MONTREAL, QC, H2K 4P6
(514) 599-2244 *SIC 4841*

RESEAU ENCANS QUEBEC (S.E.C) *p 1310*
5110 RUE MARTINEAU, SAINT-HYACINTHE, QC, J2R 1T9
(450) 796-2612 *SIC 7389*

RESEAU GLP & CIE INC *p 1283*
95 BOUL BRIEN, REPENTIGNY, QC, J6A 8B6
(450) 654-8787 *SIC 5541*

RESEAU SANS FIL OTODATA INC *p 1226*
9280 BOUL DE L'ACADIE, MONTREAL, QC, H4N 3C5
(514) 673-0244 *SIC 3663*

RESEAU SOLUTIONS CANADA ULC *p 1123*
1400 RUE INDUSTRIELLE BUREAU 100, LA PRAIRIE, QC, J5R 2E5
(450) 659-8921 *SIC 3569*

RESEAUX ACCEDIAN INC, LES *p 1336*
2351 BOUL ALFRED-NOBEL SUITE N-410, SAINT-LAURENT, QC, H4S 0B2
(514) 331-6181 *SIC 8748*

RESEAUX DE SANTE MEDITEL *p 1227*
See HOPITEL INC

RESERVEAMERICA *p 726*
See RESERVEAMERICA ON INC

RESERVEAMERICA ON INC *p 726*
2480 MEADOWVALE BLVD SUITE 1, MISSISSAUGA, ON, L5N 8M6
(905) 286-6600 *SIC 7371*

RESERVOIRS GIL-FAB INTERNATIONAL INC, LES *p 1149*
1429 AV DE LA GARE, MASCOUCHE, QC, J7K 3G6
(450) 474-7400 *SIC 3443*

RESFORM CONSTRUCTION LTD *p 561*
3761 COUNTY RD 89, COOKSTOWN, ON, L0L 1L0
(705) 458-0600 *SIC 1771*

RESIDENCE *p 1276*
See GENIARP INC

RESIDENCE AND CONFERENCE CENTRE *p 578*
See CAMPUS LIVING CENTRES INC

RESIDENCE AVELLIN DALCOURT *p 1146*
See GOUVERNEMENT DE LA PROVINCE DE QUEBEC

RESIDENCE BERTHIAUME-DU TREMBLAY *p 1171*
1635 BOUL GOUIN E, MONTREAL, QC, H2C 1C2
(514) 381-1841 *SIC 8051*

RESIDENCE COTE JARDINS INC *p 1271*
880 AV PAINCHAUD, QUEBEC, QC, G1S 0A3
(418) 688-1221 *SIC 8361*

RESIDENCE DU COLLEGE CRP (2014) INC *p 1297*
1390 RUE NOTRE-DAME, SAINT-CESAIRE, QC, J0L 1T0
(450) 816-1390 *SIC 6411*

RESIDENCE DU PARC *p 1322*
See REVERA INC

RESIDENCE INN TORONTO DOWNTOWN/ENTERTAINMENT DISTRICT *p 984*
See WELLINGTON WINDSOR HOLDINGS LTD

RESIDENCE L'ARTISAN *p 1301*
See GROUPE SANTE VALEO INC

RESIDENCE LE CITADIN *p 1346*
See CONSTRUCTIONS MAXERA INC, LES

RESIDENCE LE GIBRALTAR INC *p 1271*
1300 CH SAINTE-FOY BUREAU 610, QUEBEC, QC, G1S 0A6
(418) 681-2777 *SIC 8361*

RESIDENCE NOTRE-DAME-DE-LA-PROTECTION *p 1115*
See SOEURS DE LA CONGREGATION DE NOTRE-DAME, LES

RESIDENCE P.F, LES *p 1292*
See GROUPE PRO-FAB INC

RESIDENCE RIVIERA INC *p 1241*
2999 BOUL NOTRE-DAME, MONTREAL-OUEST, QC, H7V 4C4
(450) 682-0111 *SIC 8069*

RESIDENCE SAINT MAURICE *p 1368*
See CENTRE LAFLECHE GRAND-MERE

RESIDENCE SAINT-JOSEPH, LA *p 1286*
See CENTRE DE SANTE ET DE SERVICES SOCIAUX DE RIVIERE-DU-LOUP

RESIDENCE SAINT-LOUIS *p 810*
See SOEURS DE LA CHARITE D'OTTAWA, LES

RESIDENCE SEPHARADE SALOMON (COMMUNAUTE SEPHARADE UNIFIEE DU QUEBEC) *p 1220*
5900 BOUL DECARIE, MONTREAL, QC, H3X 2J7
(514) 733-2157 *SIC 8361*

RESIDENCE SOREL-TRACY INC *p 1377*
4025 RUE FRONTENAC, SOREL-TRACY, QC, J3R 4G8
(450) 742-9427 *SIC 8361*

RESIDENCE ST ANTOINE *p 1261*
See CENTRE DE SANTE ET DE SERVICES SOCIAUX DE LA VIEILLE-CAPITALE

RESIDENCE WALES HOME *p 1081*
See WALES HOME, THE

RESIDENCES AT ICON INC, THE *p 781*
4800 DUFFERIN ST, NORTH YORK, ON, M3H 5S9
(416) 661-9290 *SIC 6531*

RESIDENCES COWANSVILLE (CRP) INC *p 1088*
117 RUE PRINCIPALE, COWANSVILLE, QC, J2K 1J3
(450) 266-3757 *SIC 6514*

RESIDENCES MGR CHIASSON INC, LES *p 418*
130J BOUL J D GAUTHIER, SHIPPAGAN, NB, E8S 1N8
(506) 336-3266 *SIC 8051*

RESIDENCES RICHELOISES, LES *p 1151*
See SOCIETE DE GESTION COGIR INC

RESIDENCES SELECTION S.E.C.- I, LES

1087
2400 BOUL DANIEL-JOHNSON, COTE SAINT-LUC, QC, H7T 3A4
(450) 902-2000 *SIC* 6531

RESIDENTIAL ELECTRICAL CONTRACTOR CORPORATION, THE *p* 25
2616 16 ST NE SUITE 4, CALGARY, AB, T2E 7J8
(403) 735-6120 *SIC* 1731

RESIDENTIAL ENERGY SAVING PRODUCTS INC *p* 893
201 BARTON ST UNIT 3, STONEY CREEK, ON, L8E 2K3
(905) 578-2292 *SIC* 1522

RESISTANT MATERIAL AND SUPPLY *p* 434
See R.M. & S. COMPANY LIMITED

RESMAN MANAGEMENT LIMITED *p* 37
1209 59 AVE SE SUITE 245, CALGARY, AB, T2H 2P6
(403) 259-8826 *SIC* 8741

RESOLUTE BAY HOTEL, DIV *p* 63
See ATCO FRONTEC LTD

RESOLUTE FORCE PRODUCT *p* 910
See PF RESOLU CANADA INC

RESOLUTE FOREST PRODUCTS *p* 1134
See PF RESOLU CANADA INC

RESOLUTE FOREST PRODUCTS *p* 1353
See PF RESOLU CANADA INC

RESOLUTE FOREST PRODUCTS INC *p* 1212
111 BOUL ROBERT-BOURASSA BUREAU 5000, MONTREAL, QC, H3C 2M1
(514) 875-2160 *SIC* 2621

RESOLUTE TECHNOLOGY SOLUTIONS INC *p* 375
433 MAIN ST SUITE 600, WINNIPEG, MB, R3B 1B3
(204) 927-3520 *SIC* 8748

RESOLVE CORPORATION *p* 441
197 DUFFERIN ST SUITE 100, BRIDGEWATER, NS, B4V 2G9
(902) 541-3600 *SIC* 8742

RESOLVE CORPORATION *p* 700
2400 SKYMARK AVE UNIT 6, MISSISSAUGA, ON, L4W 5K5
SIC 8742

RESOLVE CORPORATION *p* 818
2405 ST LAURENT BLVD, OTTAWA, ON, K1G 5B4
SIC 7374

RESOLVE CORPORATION *p* 918
210 WICKSTEED AVE, TORONTO, ON, M4G 2C3
SIC 8743

RESOLVE CORPORATION *p* 1041
50 WATTS AVE, CHARLOTTETOWN, PE, C1E 2B8
(902) 629-3000 *SIC* 7389

RESOLVE CORPORATION *p* 1043
150 INDUSTRIAL CRES, SUMMERSIDE, PE, C1N 5N6
(902) 432-7500 *SIC* 7389

RESOLVE RECRUIT INC *p* 732
30 EGLINTON AVE W SUITE 812, MISSISSAUGA, ON, L5R 3E7
(905) 568-8828 *SIC* 7361

RESOLVER INC *p* 983
111 PETER ST SUITE 804, TORONTO, ON, M5V 2H1
(416) 622-2299 *SIC* 7371

RESORTS OF THE CANADIAN ROCKIES INC *p* 67
1505 17 AVE SW, CALGARY, AB, T2T 0E2
(403) 254-7669 *SIC* 7999

RESORTS OF THE CANADIAN ROCKIES INC *p* 139
1 WHAIT HORN RD, LAKE LOUISE, AB, T0L 1E0
(403) 522-3555 *SIC* 7999

RESORTS OF THE CANADIAN ROCKIES INC *p* 223
301 NORTH STAR BLVD, KIMBERLEY, BC,

V1A 2Y5
(250) 427-4881 *SIC* 7011

RESOUND MUSIC LICENSING COMPANY *p* 973
See RE:SOUND

RESOURCE INDUSTRIAL GROUP INC *p* 483
295 WAYDOM DR SUITE 2, AYR, ON, N0B 1E0
(519) 622-5266 *SIC* 1796

RESOURCE RECOVERY FUND BOARD, INCORPORATED *p* 469
35 COMMERCIAL ST SUITE 400, TRURO, NS, B2N 3H9
(902) 895-7732 *SIC* 4953

RESPONSE BIOMEDICAL CORP *p* 324
1781 75TH AVE W, VANCOUVER, BC, V6P 6P2
(604) 456-6010 *SIC* 5047

RESPONSETEK *p* 327
See RESPONSETEK NETWORKS CORP

RESPONSETEK NETWORKS CORP *p* 327
969 ROBSON ST SUITE 320, VANCOUVER, BC, V6Z 2V7
(604) 484-2900 *SIC* 7372

RESSORTS B L *p* 1111
See SERVICES DE MECANIQUE MOBILE B L INC

RESSORTS LIBERTE INC *p* 1160
173 RUE DES INDUSTRIES, MONTMAGNY, QC, G5V 4G2
(418) 248-8871 *SIC* 3495

RESSORTS LIBERTE MEXIQUE INC *p* 1160
173 RUE DES INDUSTRIES, MONTMAGNY, QC, G5V 4G2
(418) 248-8871 *SIC* 3714

RESSORTS MASKA INC *p* 1310
2890 BOUL LAURIER E, SAINT-HYACINTHE, QC, J2R 1P8
(450) 774-7511 *SIC* 7539

RESSOURCE DE LA MONTAGNE *p* 1217
See 9191-1263 QUEBEC INC

RESSOURCES FALCO LTEE *p* 1207
1100 AV DES CANADIENS-DE-MONTREAL BUREAU 300, MONTREAL, QC, H3B 2S2
(514) 905-3162 *SIC* 6799

RESSOURCES GLOBALES AERO INC *p* 1067
333 CH DU TREMBLAY BUREAU J, BOUCHERVILLE, QC, J4B 7M1
(514) 667-9399 *SIC* 7361

RESSOURCES METANOR INC *p* 1391
2872 CH SULLIVAN BUREAU 2, VAL-D'OR, QC, J9P 0B9
(819) 825-8678 *SIC* 1041

RESSOURCES MSV INC *p* 1207
1155 BOUL ROBERT-BOURASSA UNITE 1405, MONTREAL, QC, H3B 3A7
(418) 748-7691 *SIC* 6519

RESSOURCES ROBEX INC *p* 1269
437 GRANDE ALLEE E BUREAU 100, QUEBEC, QC, G1R 2J5
(581) 741-7421 *SIC* 1081

RESSOURCES SANTE L M INC *p* 1352
21 RUE FORGET, SAINT-SAUVEUR, QC, J0R 1R0
(450) 227-6663 *SIC* 8322

REST HAVEN LODGE *p* 337
See BROADMEAD CARE SOCIETY

REST HAVEN NURSING HOME *p* 358
See REST HAVEN NURSING HOME OF STEINBACH INC

REST HAVEN NURSING HOME OF STEINBACH INC *p* 358
185 WOODHAVEN AVE SUITE 175, STEINBACH, MB, R5G 1K7
(204) 326-2206 *SIC* 8051

REST-WELL MATTRESS COMPANY LTD *p* 273
14922 54A AVE, SURREY, BC, V3S 5X7
(604) 576-2339 *SIC* 2515

RESTAURANT A LA RIVE INC *p* 1160
153 RUE SAINT-LOUIS, MONTMAGNY, QC, G5V 1N4
(418) 248-3494 *SIC* 5812

RESTAURANT AIX INC *p* 1190
711 COTE DE LA PLACE-D'ARMES, MONTREAL, QC, H2Y 2X6
(514) 904-1201 *SIC* 5812

RESTAURANT B.C.L. INC *p* 1398
609 BOUL DES BOIS-FRANCS S, VICTORIAVILLE, QC, G6P 5X1
(819) 357-9226 *SIC* 5812

RESTAURANT BRANDS INTERNATIONAL INC *p* 987
130 KING ST W SUITE 300, TORONTO, ON, M5X 1E1
(905) 339-5724 *SIC* 5812

RESTAURANT BUFFET DES CONTINENTS *p* 1387
See 9122-6910 QUEBEC INC

RESTAURANT CHEZ GEORGES *p* 1079
See GESTION GEORGES ABRAHAM INC

RESTAURANT CHEZ HENRI *p* 1297
See CHEZ HENRI MAJEAU ET FILS INC

RESTAURANT CONTINENTAL INC *p* 1269
26 RUE SAINT-LOUIS, QUEBEC, QC, G1R 3Y9
(418) 694-9995 *SIC* 5812

RESTAURANT DEMERS *p* 1370
See PIZZERIA DEMERS INC

RESTAURANT DU VIEUX PORT INC *p* 1190
39 RUE SAINT-PAUL E, MONTREAL, QC, H2Y 1G2
(514) 866-3175 *SIC* 5812

RESTAURANT FESTIGOUT *p* 1224
See CORBEILLE - BORDEAUX - CARTIERVILLE, LA

RESTAURANT INNOVATIONS INC *p* 641
20 HELDMANN RD, KITCHENER, ON, N2P 0A6
(519) 653-9660 *SIC* 5812

RESTAURANT JACK ASTOR'S BAR & GRILL *p* 1091
See IMMOBILIER JACK ASTOR'S (DORVAL) INC

RESTAURANT L'ESPADON *p* 1285
See AUBERGE DE LA POINTE INC

RESTAURANT LES JARDINS DU BOISE *p* 1218
See ASSOCIES SPORTIFS DE MONTREAL, SOCIETE EN COMMANDITE, LES

RESTAURANT MACGEORGES INC *p* 1228
7475 BOUL DECARIE, MONTREAL, QC, H4P 2G9
(514) 738-3588 *SIC* 5812

RESTAURANT MANGIAMO *p* 1380
See 9030-5582 QUEBEC INC

RESTAURANT MCDONALD'S *p* 1079
See ENTREPRISES MACBAIE INC, LES

RESTAURANT MCDONALD'S *p* 1245
See 175246 CANADA INC

RESTAURANT MCDONALD'S *p* 1281
See RESTAURANTS MIKA INC, LES

RESTAURANT MCDONALD'S *p* 1286
See MCDONALD'S RESTAURANTS OF CANADA LIMITED

RESTAURANT MCDONALD'S *p* 1398
See GESTIONS G.D. BERUBE INC, LES

RESTAURANT MCDONALD'S LACHENAIE *p* 1378
See 9026-7139 QUEBEC INC

RESTAURANT MCDONALDS *p* 1101
See RESTAURANTS DUMAS LTEE, LES

RESTAURANT MONTE CRISTO *p* 1275
See CHATEAU BONNE ENTENTE INC

RESTAURANT NEWTOWN INC *p* 1214
1476 RUE CRESCENT, MONTREAL, QC, H3G 2B6
(514) 284-6555 *SIC* 5812

RESTAURANT NORMANDIN *p* 1275
See BOUVIER INC, LE

RESTAURANT NORMANDIN *p* 1275
See RESTAURANT NORMANDIN (2014) INC

RESTAURANT NORMANDIN (2014) INC *p* 1275
2335 BOUL BASTIEN, QUEBEC, QC, G2B 1B3
(418) 842-9160 *SIC* 5812

RESTAURANT NORMANDIN (2014) INC *p* 1349
530 RTE DU PONT, SAINT-NICOLAS, QC, G7A 2N9
(418) 831-1991 *SIC* 5812

RESTAURANT PANACHE *p* 1257
See 6143580 CANADA INC.

RESTAURANT SAINT-PAUL (MONTREAL) LTEE *p* 1190
25 RUE SAINT-PAUL E, MONTREAL, QC, H2Y 1G2
(514) 871-9093 *SIC* 5812

RESTAURANT SCORES BATON ROUGE *p* 1279
See GROUPE RESTAURANTS IMVESCOR INC

RESTAURANT ST HUBERT *p* 1219
See ROTISSERIES ST-HUBERT LTEE, LES

RESTAURANT TEVERE *p* 1345
See PLACE TEVERE INC

RESTAURANT-BAR LA ROCHELIERE INC *p* 1323
1370 RUE DU PONT, SAINT-LAMBERT-DE-LAUZON, QC, G0S 2W0
(418) 889-0183 *SIC* 5541

RESTAURANTS CANADA *p* 991
1155 QUEEN ST W, TORONTO, ON, M6J 1J4
(416) 923-8416 *SIC* 8611

RESTAURANTS DUMAS LTEE, LES *p* 1101
410 BOUL CURE-LABELLE, FABREVILLE, QC, H7P 2P1
(450) 628-0171 *SIC* 5812

RESTAURANTS IANA INC *p* 1370
975 RUE KING E, SHERBROOKE, QC, J1G 1E3
(819) 571-9623 *SIC* 5812

RESTAURANTS MAC-VIC INC, LES *p* 1313
3005 BOUL LAFRAMBOISE, SAINT-HYACINTHE, QC, J2S 4Z6
(450) 774-5955 *SIC* 5812

RESTAURANTS MAC-VIC INC, LES *p* 1313
3200 BOUL LAFRAMBOISE, SAINT-HYACINTHE, QC, J2S 4Z5
(450) 261-8880 *SIC* 5812

RESTAURANTS MCDONALD'S *p* 1059
See MCDONALD'S RESTAURANTS OF CANADA LIMITED

RESTAURANTS MCDONALD'S *p* 1346
See MCDONALD'S RESTAURANTS OF CANADA LIMITED

RESTAURANTS MIKA INC, LES *p* 1281
1154 RUE DE LA FAUNE, QUEBEC, QC, G3E 1T2
(418) 845-6323 *SIC* 5812

RESTAURANTS P & P INC, LES *p* 1123
170 BOUL TASCHEREAU BUREAU 300, LA PRAIRIE, QC, J5R 5H6
(450) 444-4749 *SIC* 6794

RESTAURANTS SERQUA INC, LES *p* 1381
1415 BOUL MOODY, TERREBONNE, QC, J6X 4C8
(450) 471-1161 *SIC* 5812

RESTAURANTS T.S.N.A. INC *p* 1143
365 RUE SAINT-JEAN, LONGUEUIL, QC, J4H 2X7
(450) 670-5609 *SIC* 5812

RESTAURATION MIMAR INC *p* 1352
725 CH JEAN-ADAM, SAINT-SAUVEUR, QC, J0R 1R3
(450) 227-4664 *SIC* 5812

RESTAURATIONS DYC INC *p* 1089
170 RUE BROSSARD, DELSON, QC, J5B 1X1
(450) 638-5560 *SIC* 1542

RESTER MANAGEMENT HERMES EDIFICE *p* 1200
See 123179 CANADA INC

RESTIGOUCHE HEALTH AUTHORITY   p
396
189 LILY LAKE RD, CAMPBELLTON, NB,
E3N 3H3
(506) 789-5000   SIC 8062
RESTIGOUCHE MOTORS LTD   p 396
388 DOVER ST, CAMPBELLTON, NB, E3N
3M7
(506) 753-5019   SIC 5511
RESTIGOUCHE TOYOTA   p 396
See RESTIGOUCHE MOTORS LTD
RESTO BAR 1909   p 1200
See 10087408 CANADA INC
RESTORERS GROUP INC, THE   p 855
344 NEWKIRK RD, RICHMOND HILL, ON,
L4C 3G7
(905) 770-1323   SIC 1542
**RESULTATS SUR TOUTE LA LIGNE, EN
LIGNE**   p 1241
See CORPORATION XPRIMA.COM
**RESURRECION CATHOLIC SECONDARY
SCHOOL**   p 641
See WATERLOO CATHOLIC DISTRICT
SCHOOL BOARD
RETAIL   p 1428
See NUTRIEN LTD
RETAIL DIMENSIONS INCORPORATED   p
524
4335 MAINWAY, BURLINGTON, ON, L7L
5N9
SIC 5651
RETAIL READY FOODS INC   p 956
130 ADELAIDE ST W SUITE 810,
TORONTO, ON, M5H 3P5
(905) 812-8555   SIC 5147
RETHINK COMMUNICATIONS INC   p 309
470 GRANVILLE ST SUITE 700, VANCOU-
VER, BC, V6C 1V5
(604) 685-8911   SIC 4899
RETIREMENT LIVING CENTRES INC   p 658
1673 RICHMOND ST SUITE 147, LONDON,
ON, N6G 2N3
(519) 858-9889   SIC 6712
**RETIREMENT RESIDENCES REAL ES-
TATE INVESTMENT TRUST**   p
72
See REVERA INC
**RETIREMENT RESIDENCES REAL ES-
TATE INVESTMENT TRUST**   p
628
See REVERA INC
RETOURS.CA   p 1399
See SURPLUS R.D. INC
RETURN ON INNOVATION ADVISORS LTD
p 943
43 FRONT ST E SUITE 301, TORONTO,
ON, M5E 1B3
(416) 361-6162   SIC 6722
REUVEN INTERNATIONAL LIMITED   p 924
1881 YONGE ST SUITE 201, TORONTO,
ON, M4S 3C4
(416) 929-1496   SIC 5142
REV ENGINEERING LTD   p 13
3236 50 AVE SE, CALGARY, AB, T2B 3A3
(403) 287-0156   SIC 7629
REVAY ET ASSOCIES LIMITEE   p 1402
4333 RUE SAINTE-CATHERINE O BU-
REAU 500, WESTMOUNT, QC, H3Z 1P9
(514) 932-2188   SIC 8741
**REVCON OILFIELD CONSTRUCTORS IN-
CORPORATED**   p
125
625 PARSONS RD SW SUITE 201, ED-
MONTON, AB, T6X 0N9
(780) 497-8586   SIC 1623
REVE ALCHIMIQUE INC   p 1216
1751 RUE RICHARDSON, MONTREAL,
QC, H3K 1G6
(514) 904-3700   SIC 5092
REVELL FORD LINCOLN   p 1003
6715 MAIN ST, VERONA, ON, K0H 2W0
(613) 374-2612   SIC 5521
REVELL FORD LINCOLN MERCURY   p
1003

See REVELL MOTORS SALES LIMITED
REVELL MOTORS SALES LIMITED   p 1003
6628 38 HWY, VERONA, ON, K0H 2W0
(613) 374-2133   SIC 5511
**REVELSTOKE MOUNTAIN RESORT LIM-
ITED PARTNERSHIP**   p
253
2950 CAMOZZI RD, REVELSTOKE, BC,
V0E 2S3
(250) 814-0087   SIC 7011
**REVENBERG, GUS PONTIAC BUICK HUM-
MER GMC LTD**   p
1018
10150 TECUMSEH RD E, WINDSOR, ON,
N8R 1A2
(519) 979-2800   SIC 5511
REVENCO (1991) INC   p 1265
1755 RUE PROVINCIALE, QUEBEC, QC,
G1N 4S9
(418) 682-5993   SIC 1731
**REVENUE PROPERTIES COMPANY LIM-
ITED**   p
710
55 CITY CENTRE DR SUITE 1000, MISSIS-
SAUGA, ON, L5B 1M3
(905) 281-5943   SIC 6512
REVENUEWIRE INC   p 333
3962 BORDEN ST SUITE 102, VICTORIA,
BC, V8P 3H8
(250) 590-2273   SIC 6099
REVERA INC   p 68
9229 16 ST SW, CALGARY, AB, T2V 5H3
(403) 255-2105   SIC 8361
REVERA INC   p 71
80 PROMENADE WAY SE, CALGARY, AB,
T2Z 4G4
(403) 508-9808   SIC 8051
REVERA INC   p 72
5927 BOWNESS RD NW, CALGARY, AB,
T3B 0C7
(403) 288-2373   SIC 8051
REVERA INC   p 77
150 SCOTIA LANDNG NW, CALGARY, AB,
T3L 2K1
(403) 208-0338   SIC 8322
REVERA INC   p 90
10015 103 AVE NW SUITE 1208, EDMON-
TON, AB, T5J 0H1
(780) 420-1222   SIC 8361
REVERA INC   p 98
8903 168 ST NW, EDMONTON, AB, T5R
2V6
(780) 489-4931   SIC 8051
REVERA INC   p 146
603 PROSPECT DR SW, MEDICINE HAT,
AB, T1A 4C2
(403) 527-5531   SIC 8051
REVERA INC   p 147
223 PARK MEADOWS DR SE SUITE 127,
MEDICINE HAT, AB, T1B 4K7
(403) 504-5123   SIC 6513
REVERA INC   p 322
4505 VALLEY DR, VANCOUVER, BC, V6L
2L1
(604) 261-4292   SIC 8051
REVERA INC   p 323
2803 41ST AVE W SUITE 110, VANCOU-
VER, BC, V6N 4B4
(604) 263-0921   SIC 8361
REVERA INC   p 348
3015 VICTORIA AVE SUITE 219, BRAN-
DON, MB, R7B 2K2
(204) 728-2030   SIC 8051
REVERA INC   p 375
440 EDMONTON ST, WINNIPEG, MB, R3B
2M4
(204) 942-5291   SIC 8059
REVERA INC   p 386
3555 PORTAGE AVE, WINNIPEG, MB, R3K
0X2
(204) 888-7450   SIC 8051
REVERA INC   p 388
70 POSEIDON BAY SUITE 504, WIN-
NIPEG, MB, R3M 3E5

(204) 452-6204   SIC 8051
REVERA INC   p 478
12 TRANQUILITY AVE SUITE 1, AN-
CASTER, ON, L9G 5C2
(905) 304-1993   SIC 8322
REVERA INC   p 534
614 CORONATION BLVD SUITE 200, CAM-
BRIDGE, ON, N1R 3E8
(519) 622-1840   SIC 8051
REVERA INC   p 570
111 ILER AVE SUITE 1, ESSEX, ON, N8M
1T6
(519) 776-5243   SIC 8051
REVERA INC   p 597
290 SOUTH ST, GODERICH, ON, N7A 4G6
(519) 524-7324   SIC 8361
REVERA INC   p 599
85 MAIN ST E, GRIMSBY, ON, L3M 1N6
(905) 945-7044   SIC 6513
REVERA INC   p 618
101 10TH ST SUITE 2006, HANOVER, ON,
N4N 1M9
(519) 364-4320   SIC 6513
REVERA INC   p 628
237 LAKEVIEW DR, KENORA, ON, P9N
4J7
(807) 468-9532   SIC 8051
REVERA INC   p 658
355 MCGARRELL DR, LONDON, ON, N6G
0B1
(519) 672-0500   SIC 8322
REVERA INC   p 700
1500 RATHBURN RD E, MISSISSAUGA,
ON, L4W 4L7
(905) 238-0800   SIC 6513
REVERA INC   p 700
5015 SPECTRUM WAY SUITE 600, MIS-
SISSAUGA, ON, L4W 0E4
(289) 360-1252   SIC 8051
REVERA INC   p 780
8 THE DONWAY E SUITE 557, NORTH
YORK, ON, M3C 3R7
(416) 445-7555   SIC 8051
REVERA INC   p 810
291 MISSISSAGA ST W SUITE 106, ORIL-
LIA, ON, L3V 3B9
(705) 325-2289   SIC 8051
REVERA INC   p 857
9 MYRTLE ST, RIDGETOWN, ON, N0P 2C0
(519) 674-5427   SIC 8051
REVERA INC   p 857
980 ELGIN MILLS RD E, RICHMOND HILL,
ON, L4S 1M4
(905) 884-9248   SIC 8361
REVERA INC   p 905
7700 BAYVIEW AVE SUITE 518, THORN-
HILL, ON, L3T 5W1
(905) 881-9475   SIC 8051
REVERA INC   p 972
645 CASTLEFIELD AVE SUITE 716,
TORONTO, ON, M5N 3A5
(416) 785-1511   SIC 8051
REVERA INC   p 993
1 NORTHWESTERN AVE, TORONTO, ON,
M6M 2J7
(416) 654-2889   SIC 8051
REVERA INC   p 1083
5885 BOUL CAVENDISH BUREAU 202,
COTE SAINT-LUC, QC, H4W 3H4
(514) 485-5994   SIC 8051
REVERA INC   p 1322
33 AV ARGYLE, SAINT-LAMBERT, QC, J4P
3P5
(450) 465-1401   SIC 8051
REVERA INC   p 1397
GD SUCC BUREAU-CHEF, VERDUN, QC,
H4G 3C9
SIC 8051
REVERA LONG TERM CARE INC   p 83
14251 50 ST NW, EDMONTON, AB, T5A
5J4
(780) 478-9212   SIC 8051
REVERA LONG TERM CARE INC   p 287
3490 PORTER ST, VANCOUVER, BC, V5N

5W4
(604) 874-2803   SIC 8051
REVERA LONG TERM CARE INC   p 475
1020 WESTNEY RD N, AJAX, ON, L1T 4K6
(905) 426-6296   SIC 8059
REVERA LONG TERM CARE INC   p 493
10 MARY ST, BLENHEIM, ON, N0P 1A0
(519) 676-8119   SIC 8051
REVERA LONG TERM CARE INC   p 515
425 PARK RD N, BRANTFORD, ON, N3R
7G5
(519) 759-1040   SIC 8051
REVERA LONG TERM CARE INC   p 534
650 CORONATION BLVD, CAMBRIDGE,
ON, N1R 7S6
(519) 740-3820   SIC 8051
REVERA LONG TERM CARE INC   p 535
200 STIRLING MACGREGOR DR, CAM-
BRIDGE, ON, N1S 5B7
(519) 622-3434   SIC 8051
REVERA LONG TERM CARE INC   p 537
600 JAMIESON PKY, CAMBRIDGE, ON,
N3C 0A6
(519) 622-1840   SIC 8051
REVERA LONG TERM CARE INC   p 540
256 HIGH ST, CARLETON PLACE, ON,
K7C 1X1
(613) 257-4355   SIC 8051
REVERA LONG TERM CARE INC   p 612
330 MAIN ST E, HAMILTON, ON, L8N 3T9
(905) 523-1604   SIC 8051
REVERA LONG TERM CARE INC   p 629
550 PHILIP PL, KINCARDINE, ON, N2Z 3A6
(519) 396-4400   SIC 8051
REVERA LONG TERM CARE INC   p 641
60 WESTHEIGHTS DR, KITCHENER, ON,
N2N 2A8
(519) 576-3320   SIC 8051
REVERA LONG TERM CARE INC   p 659
46 ELMWOOD PL, LONDON, ON, N6J 1J2
(519) 433-7259   SIC 8051
REVERA LONG TERM CARE INC   p 756
52 GEORGE ST, NEWMARKET, ON, L3Y
4V3
(905) 853-3242   SIC 8059
REVERA LONG TERM CARE INC   p 806
2370 THIRD LINE, OAKVILLE, ON, L6M
4E2
(905) 469-3294   SIC 8059
REVERA LONG TERM CARE INC   p 814
186 THORNTON RD S SUITE 1103, OS-
HAWA, ON, L1J 5Y2
(905) 576-5181   SIC 8051
REVERA LONG TERM CARE INC   p 830
2330 CARLING AVE, OTTAWA, ON, K2B
7H1
(613) 820-9328   SIC 8051
REVERA LONG TERM CARE INC   p 836
850 4TH ST E, OWEN SOUND, ON, N4K
6A3
(519) 376-3213   SIC 8051
REVERA LONG TERM CARE INC   p 845
13628 LOYALIST PKY, PICTON, ON, K0K
2T0
(613) 476-4444   SIC 8051
REVERA LONG TERM CARE INC   p 847
501 ST GEORGE ST, PORT DOVER, ON,
N0A 1N0
(519) 583-1422   SIC 8051
REVERA LONG TERM CARE INC   p 857
182 YORKLAND ST SUITE 1, RICHMOND
HILL, ON, L4S 2M9
(905) 737-0858   SIC 8051
REVERA LONG TERM CARE INC   p 858
1464 BLACKWELL RD, SARNIA, ON, N7S
5M4
(519) 542-3421   SIC 8051
REVERA LONG TERM CARE INC   p 872
1400 KENNEDY RD, SCARBOROUGH, ON,
M1P 4V6
(416) 752-8282   SIC 8051
REVERA LONG TERM CARE INC   p 884
168 SCOTT ST, ST CATHARINES, ON, L2N
1H2

(905) 934-3321   *SIC* 8051
REVERA LONG TERM CARE INC   *p* 894
385 HIGHLAND RD W, STONEY CREEK, ON, L8J 3X9
(905) 561-3332   *SIC* 8051
REVERA LONG TERM CARE INC   *p* 896
5066 LINE 34 SUITE 8, STRATFORD, ON, N5A 6S6
(519) 393-5132   *SIC* 8051
REVERA LONG TERM CARE INC   *p* 910
2625 WALSH ST E SUITE 1127, THUNDER BAY, ON, P7E 2E5
(807) 577-1127   *SIC* 8361
REVERA LONG TERM CARE INC   *p* 917
77 MAIN ST, TORONTO, ON, M4E 2V6
(416) 690-3001   *SIC* 8051
REVERA LONG TERM CARE INC   *p* 1001
130 REACH ST SUITE 25, UXBRIDGE, ON, L9P 1L3
(905) 852-5191   *SIC* 8051
REVERSOMATIC MANUFACTURING LTD *p* 1033
790 ROWNTREE DAIRY RD, WOODBRIDGE, ON, L4L 5V3
(905) 851-6701   *SIC* 3564
REVETEMENT R.H.R. INC   *p* 1318
755 RUE BOUCHER, SAINT-JEAN-SUR-RICHELIEU, QC, J3B 8P4
(450) 359-7868   *SIC* 5211
REVETEMENTS AGRO INC, LES   *p* 1111
1195 RUE PRINCIPALE, GRANBY, QC, J2J 0M3
(450) 776-1010   *SIC* 5198
REVETEMENTS ALNORDICA INC   *p* 1323
1230 RUE DES ERABLES, SAINT-LAMBERT-DE-LAUZON, QC, G0S 2W0
(418) 889-9761   *SIC* 1761
REVETEMENTS SCELL-TECH INC, LES *p* 1085
1478 RUE CUNARD, COTE SAINT-LUC, QC, H7S 2B7
(514) 990-7886   *SIC* 1721
REVISION MILITAIRE INC   *p* 1224
3800 RUE SAINT-PATRICK BUREAU 200, MONTREAL, QC, H4E 1A4
(514) 739-4444   *SIC* 3851
REVISION SECURITY INC   *p* 1341
460 RUE ISABEY, SAINT-LAURENT, QC, H4T 1V3
(514) 448-6285   *SIC* 5065
REVITAL POLYMERS INC   *p* 858
1271 LOUGAR AVE, SARNIA, ON, N7S 5N5
(519) 332-0430   *SIC* 4953
REVLON CANADA INC   *p* 700
1590 SOUTH GATEWAY RD, MISSISSAUGA, ON, L4W 0A8
(905) 276-4500   *SIC* 2844
REVOLUTION ENVIRONMENTAL SOLUTIONS ACQUISITION GP INC   *p* 524
1100 BURLOAK DR UNIT 500, BURLINGTON, ON, L7L 6B2
(800) 263-8602   *SIC* 4953
REVOLUTION ENVIRONMENTAL SOLUTIONS LP   *p* 524
1100 BURLOAK DR SUITE 500, BURLINGTON, ON, L7L 6B2
(800) 263-8602   *SIC* 4959
REVOLUTION ENVIRONMENTAL SOLUTIONS LP   *p* 524
1100 BURLOAK DR SUITE 500, BURLINGTON, ON, L7L 6B2
(905) 315-6300   *SIC* 4953
REVOLUTION LANDFILL LP   *p* 524
1100 BURLOAK DR, BURLINGTON, ON, L7L 6B2
(905) 315-6304   *SIC* 2844
REVOLUTION VSC ACQUISITION GP INC *p* 524
1100 BURLOAK DR SUITE 200, BURLINGTON, ON, L7L 6B2
(905) 315-6300   *SIC* 0721

REVOLUTION VSC LP   *p* 524
1100 BURLOAK DR SUITE 500, BURLINGTON, ON, L7L 6B2
(905) 279-9555   *SIC* 3341
REVSTONE PLASTICS CANADA INC *p* 807
2045 SOLAR CRES RR 1, OLDCASTLE, ON, N0R 1L0
(519) 737-1201   *SIC* 3544
REW   *p* 1028
See ROBERTSON ELECTRIC WHOLESALE 2008 LIMITED
REWARD OILFIELD SERVICES LTD *p* 170
SE 15- 70- 22 W 5, VALLEYVIEW, AB, T0H 3N0
(780) 524-5220   *SIC* 1389
REX BEAUTY INC.   *p* 786
3304 KEELE ST, NORTH YORK, ON, M3M 2H7
(416) 398-9494   *SIC* 5087
REX PAK LIMITED   *p* 865
85 THORNMOUNT DR, SCARBOROUGH, ON, M1B 5V3
(416) 755-3324   *SIC* 7389
REX POWER MAGNETICS   *p* 560
See TRANSFACTOR INDUSTRIES INC
REXALL   *p* 706
See PHARMA PLUS DRUGMARTS LTD
REXALL LONG TERM CARE PHARMACY *p* 114
See GREAT WEST DRUGS (SOUTHGATE) LTD
REXALL PHARMACY GROUP LTD   *p* 706
5965 COOPERS AVE, MISSISSAUGA, ON, L4Z 1R9
(905) 501-7800   *SIC* 5912
REXALL PLACE   *p* 83
See EDMONTON NORTHLANDS
REXDALE BRICK   *p* 581
See 1442503 ONTARIO INC
REXEL AMERIQUE DU NORD INC *p* 1341
505 RUE LOCKE BUREAU 202, SAINT-LAURENT, QC, H4T 1X7
(514) 332-5331   *SIC* 6712
REXEL CANADA ELECTRICAL INC *p* 184
5700 KINGSLAND DR, BURNABY, BC, V5B 4W6
(604) 205-2700   *SIC* 5063
REXEL CANADA ELECTRICAL INC *p* 385
1650 NOTRE DAME AVE UNIT 1, WINNIPEG, MB, R3H 0Y7
(204) 954-9900   *SIC* 5063
REXEL CANADA ELECTRICAL INC *p* 732
5600 KEATON CRES, MISSISSAUGA, ON, L5R 3G3
(905) 712-4004   *SIC* 5063
REXEL CANADA ELECTRICAL INC *p* 733
5600 KEATON CRES, MISSISSAUGA, ON, L5R 3G3
(905) 712-4004   *SIC* 5063
REXEL CANADA ELECTRICAL INC *p* 742
1180 COURTNEYPARK DR E, MISSISSAUGA, ON, L5T 1P2
(905) 670-2800   *SIC* 5063
REXEL CANADA ELECTRICAL INC *p* 742
301 AMBASSADOR DR, MISSISSAUGA, ON, L5T 2J3
(905) 565-2985   *SIC* 5063
REXFORET INC   *p* 1148
248 RUE CARTIER, MANIWAKI, QC, J9E 3P5
(819) 449-6088   *SIC* 0851
REXPLAS   *p* 742
See RICHARDS PACKAGING INC
REYNOLDS AND REYNOLDS (CANADA) LIMITED   *p* 707
3 ROBERT SPECK PKY UNIT 600, MISSISSAUGA, ON, L4Z 2G5
(905) 267-6000   *SIC* 5045
REYNOLDS AND REYNOLDS (CANADA) LIMITED   *p* 1050
11075 BOUL LOUIS-H.-LAFONTAINE, ANJOU, QC, H1J 3A3
(514) 355-7550   *SIC* 5045
REYNOLDS MIRTH RICHARDS & FARMER

LLP   *p* 90
10180 101 ST NW SUITE 3200, EDMONTON, AB, T5J 3W8
(780) 425-9510   *SIC* 8111
REYNOLDS SECONDARY   *p* 333
See BOARD OF EDUCATION OF SCHOOL DISTRICT NO. 61 (GREATER VICTORIA)
REZONE WELL OIL AND GAS SERVICE REPAIR   *p* 156
8071 EDGAR INDUSTRIAL DR, RED DEER, AB, T4P 3R2
(403) 342-7772   *SIC* 1381
REREALTY PROFESSIONALS   *p* 33
See ADVANTAGE MANAGEMENT INC
RF-MTL ELECTRONIQUE INC   *p* 1336
1415 RUE SAINT-AMOUR, SAINT-LAURENT, QC, H4S 1T4
(514) 332-9998   *SIC* 5065
RFI CANADA PARTNERSHIP   *p* 1000
178 MAIN ST, UNIONVILLE, ON, L3R 2G9
(905) 534-1044   *SIC* 5149
RG PROPERTIES LTD   *p* 222
1223 WATER ST SUITE 102, KELOWNA, BC, V1Y 9V1
(250) 979-0888   *SIC* 7999
RG PROPERTIES LTD   *p* 316
1177 HASTINGS ST W SUITE 2088, VANCOUVER, BC, V6E 2K3
(604) 688-8999   *SIC* 6553
RGA INTERNATIONAL CORPORATION *p* 966
161 BAY ST SUITE 4600, TORONTO, ON, M5J 2S1
(416) 943-6770   *SIC* 6712
RGA LIFE REINSURANCE COMPANY OF CANADA   *p* 970
77 KING ST W SUITE 2300, TORONTO, ON, M5K 2A1
(416) 682-0000   *SIC* 6311
RGA LIFE REINSURANCE COMPANY OF CANADA   *p* 1199
1981 AV MCGILL COLLEGE UNITE 1300, MONTREAL, QC, H3A 3A8
(514) 985-5260   *SIC* 6311
RGA LIFE REINSURANCE COMPANY OF CANADA   *p* 1208
1255 RUE PEEL BUREAU 1000, MONTREAL, QC, H3B 2T9
(514) 985-5502   *SIC* 6311
RGIS CANADA ULC   *p* 364
196 TACHE AVE UNIT 5, WINNIPEG, MB, R2H 1Z6
(204) 774-0013   *SIC* 7389
RGIS CANADA ULC   *p* 407
236 ST GEORGE ST, MONCTON, NB, E1C 1W1
(506) 382-9146   *SIC* 7389
RGIS CANADA ULC   *p* 478
911 GOLF LINKS RD, ANCASTER, ON, L9K 1H9
(905) 304-9700   *SIC* 7389
RGIS CANADA ULC   *p* 700
2560 MATHESON BLVD E SUITE 224, MISSISSAUGA, ON, L4W 4Y9
(905) 206-1107   *SIC* 7389
RGIS CANADA ULC   *p* 819
2197 RIVERSIDE DR SUITE 305, OTTAWA, ON, K1H 7X3
(613) 226-4086   *SIC* 7389
RGIS CANADA ULC   *p* 1228
8300 RUE BOUGAINVILLE, MONTREAL, QC, H4P 2G1
(514) 521-5258   *SIC* 7389
RGIS CANADA ULC   *p* 1237
1882 BOUL SAINT-MARTIN O BUREAU 200, MONTREAL, QC, H7S 1M9
SIC 7389
RGIS INVENTORY SERVICES LLC *p* 610
1889 KING ST E, HAMILTON, ON, L8K 1V9
(905) 527-8383   *SIC* 7389
RGIS SPECIALISTES EN INVENTAIRE *p* 1228
See RGIS CANADA ULC
RGM CHEMTECH INTERNATIONAL INC *p*

256
14351 BURROWS RD SUITE 100, RICHMOND, BC, V6V 1K9
(604) 270-3320   *SIC* 2841
RGO OFFICE PRODUCTS EDMONTON LTD *p* 85
11624 120 ST NW, EDMONTON, AB, T5G 2Y2
(780) 413-6600   *SIC* 5943
RGO PRODUCTS LTD   *p* 11
229 33 ST NE SUITE 100, CALGARY, AB, T2A 4Y6
(403) 569-4400   *SIC* 5021
RHC DESIGN-BUILD   *p* 537
6783 WELLINGTON ROAD 34, CAMBRIDGE, ON, N3C 2V4
(519) 249-0758   *SIC* 1542
RHCC HOLDINGS LIMITED   *p* 855
8905 BATHURST ST, RICHMOND HILL, ON, L4C 0H4
(905) 731-2800   *SIC* 7997
RHEAUME, MICHEL & ASSOCIES LTEE *p* 1177
800-1611 BOUL CREMAZIE E, MONTREAL, QC, H2M 2P2
(514) 329-3333   *SIC* 6411
RHEEM CANADA LTD   *p* 512
125 EDGEWARE RD UNIT 1, BRAMPTON, ON, L6Y 0P5
(905) 450-4460   *SIC* 5074
RHEINMETALL CANADA INC   *p* 1318
225 BOUL DU SEMINAIRE S, SAINT-JEAN-SUR-RICHELIEU, QC, J3B 8E9
(450) 358-2000   *SIC* 3669
RHEMA HEALTH PRODUCTS LIMITED *p* 244
19055 AIRPORT WAY UNIT 601, PITT MEADOWS, BC, V3Y 0G4
(604) 516-0199   *SIC* 2833
RHI CANADA INC   *p* 524
4355 FAIRVIEW ST, BURLINGTON, ON, L7L 2A4
(905) 633-4500   *SIC* 3297
RHO-CAN MACHINE & TOOL COMPANY LTD   *p* 650
770 INDUSTRIAL RD, LONDON, ON, N5V 3N7
(519) 451-9100   *SIC* 3544
RHODES & WILLIAMS LIMITED   *p* 832
1050 MORRISON DR, OTTAWA, ON, K2H 8K7
(613) 226-6590   *SIC* 6411
RHYASON CONTRACTING LTD   *p* 214
7307 BIPA RD E, FORT ST. JOHN, BC, V1J 4M6
(250) 785-0515   *SIC* 1623
RHYOLITE RESOURCES LTD   *p* 329
595 BURRARD ST SUITE 1703, VANCOUVER, BC, V7X 1J1
(604) 488-8717   *SIC* 1041
RHYTHM & HUES STUDIOS   *p* 300
401 GEORGIA ST W SUITE 500, VANCOUVER, BC, V6B 5A1
(604) 288-8745   *SIC* 7819
RI-GO LIFT TRUCK LIMITED   *p* 558
175 COURTLAND AVE, CONCORD, ON, L4K 4T2
(416) 213-7277   *SIC* 5084
RIAL   *p* 1377
See RIAL ELECTRIQUE INC
RIAL ELECTRIQUE INC   *p* 1377
2205 RUE LAPRADE, SOREL-TRACY, QC, J3R 2C1
(450) 746-7349   *SIC* 1731
RIBAK PHARMA LTD   *p* 894
377 HIGHWAY 8 SUITE 369, STONEY CREEK, ON, L8G 1E7
(905) 662-9996   *SIC* 5912
RICARDA'S INC   *p* 536
240 SHEARSON CRES, CAMBRIDGE, ON, N1T 1J6
(416) 304-9134   *SIC* 5812
RICARDO MEDIA INC   *p* 1323
300 RUE D'ARRAN, SAINT-LAMBERT, QC,

J4R 1K5
(450) 465-4500   SIC 2721
RICCI FOOD GROUP CANADA   p 587
See R.F.G. CANADA INC
RICCI'S TRUCKING   p 621
See 777603 ONTARIO INC
RICE AUTOMOTIVE INVESTMENTS LTD p
203
445 CROWN ISLE BLVD, COURTENAY, BC,
V9N 9W1
(250) 338-6761   SIC 5511
RICE DEVELOPMENT COMPANY INC p 510
7735 KENNEDY RD, BRAMPTON, ON, L6W
0B9
(905) 796-3630   SIC 6712
RICE ENGINEERING & OPERATING LTD p
116
9333 41 AVE NW, EDMONTON, AB, T6E
6R5
(780) 469-1356   SIC 8711
RICE TOOL & MANUFACTURING INC p 529
2247 HAROLD RD, BURLINGTON, ON, L7P
2J7
(905) 335-0181   SIC 1541
**RICH IN TRADITION, FOCUSED ON THE
FUTURE**   p 945
See GWL REALTY ADVISORS INC
RICH PRODUCTS OF CANADA LIMITED p
592
12 HAGEY AVE, FORT ERIE, ON, L2A 1W3
(905) 871-2605   SIC 2053
RICH PRODUCTS OF CANADA LIMITED p
1033
149 ROWNTREE DAIRY RD SUITE 1,
WOODBRIDGE, ON, L4L 6E1
(905) 850-3836   SIC 2024
**RICHARD IVEY SCHOOL OF BUSINESS,
THE**   p 655
See UNIVERSITY OF WESTERN ON-
TARIO, THE
RICHARD REINDERS SALES LTD   p 204
1100 VICTORIA AVE N SUITE 395, CRAN-
BROOK, BC, V1C 6G7
(250) 489-3300   SIC 5531
RICHARD, B. A. LTEE   p 417
374 CH COTE SAINTE-ANNE, SAINTE-
ANNE-DE-KENT, NB, E4S 1M6
(506) 743-6198   SIC 2091
RICHARD, MARIAN ENTERPRISES LTD p
645
262 ERIE ST S, LEAMINGTON, ON, N8H
3C5
(519) 326-8191   SIC 5311
RICHARDS BUELL SUTTON LLP   p 300
401 GEORGIA ST W SUITE 700, VANCOU-
VER, BC, V6B 5A1
(604) 682-3664   SIC 8111
RICHARDS PACKAGING INC   p 742
6095 ORDAN DR, MISSISSAUGA, ON, L5T
2M7
(905) 670-7760   SIC 3221
RICHARDS PACKAGING INCOME FUND p
742
6095 ORDAN DR, MISSISSAUGA, ON, L5T
2M7
(905) 670-7760   SIC 5099
RICHARDS-WILCOX CANADA   p 699
See RAYNOR CANADA CORP
RICHARDSON BROS (OLDS) LIMITED p
151
GD, OLDS, AB, T4H 1P4
(403) 556-6366   SIC 1611
RICHARDSON FOODS GROUP   p 233
See GARDEN CITY WAREHOUSING &
DISTRIBUTION LTD
RICHARDSON GMP LIMITED   p 58
525 8 AVE SW SUITE 4700, CALGARY, AB,
T2P 1G1
(403) 355-7735   SIC 8742
**RICHARDSON HOUSE OF FIXTURES AND
SUPPLIES LTD**   p 1421
2101 7TH AVE, REGINA, SK, S4R 1C3
(306) 525-8301   SIC 5063
RICHARDSON INTERNATIONAL (QUE-

BEC) LIMITEE   p
1376
10 RUE DE LA REINE, SOREL-TRACY, QC,
J3P 4R2
(450) 743-3893   SIC 5083
RICHARDSON INTERNATIONAL LIMITED p
239
375 LOW LEVEL RD, NORTH VANCOU-
VER, BC, V7L 1A7
(604) 987-8855   SIC 5153
RICHARDSON INTERNATIONAL LIMITED p
375
1 LOMBARD PL SUITE 2800, WINNIPEG,
MB, R3B 0X3
(204) 934-5961   SIC 5153
RICHARDSON INTERNATIONAL LIMITED p
799
2835 BRISTOL CIR, OAKVILLE, ON, L6H
6X5
(905) 829-2942   SIC 2079
RICHARDSON LIGHTING   p 1421
See RICHARDSON HOUSE OF FIXTURES
AND SUPPLIES LTD
RICHARDSON MILLING LIMITED   p 5
PO BOX 4615 STN MAIN, BARRHEAD, AB,
T7N 1A5
(780) 674-4669   SIC 2043
RICHARDSON MILLING LIMITED   p 355
1 CAN-OAT DR, PORTAGE LA PRAIRIE,
MB, R1N 3W1
(204) 857-9700   SIC 5153
**RICHARDSON OILSEED EASTERN
CANADA**   p 799
See RICHARDSON INTERNATIONAL LIM-
ITED
RICHARDSON OILSEED LIMITED   p 141
2415 2A AVE N, LETHBRIDGE, AB, T1H
6P5
(403) 329-5500   SIC 2079
RICHARDSON OILSEED LIMITED   p 375
1 LOMBARD PL SUITE 2800, WINNIPEG,
MB, R3B 0X3
(204) 934-5961   SIC 2079
RICHARDSON OILSEED LIMITED   p 1438
HWY 16 3 MILES W, YORKTON, SK, S3N
2W1
(306) 828-2200   SIC 2079
RICHARDSON PIONEER GRAIN   p 375
See RICHARDSON INTERNATIONAL LIM-
ITED
RICHARDSON PIONEER LIMITED   p 375
1 LOMBARD PL SUITE 2700, WINNIPEG,
MB, R3B 0X8
(204) 934-5961   SIC 5153
RICHARDSON, ALISON REALTOR   p 156
47 ROTH CRES, RED DEER, AB, T4P 2Y7
(403) 358-1557   SIC 6531
RICHARDSON, JAMES & SONS, LIMITED p
375
3000 ONE LOMBARD PL, WINNIPEG, MB,
R3B 0Y1
(204) 953-7970   SIC 5153
RICHCRAFT HOMES LTD   p 818
2280 ST. LAURENT BLVD SUITE 201, OT-
TAWA, ON, K1G 4K1
(613) 739-7111   SIC 6553
RICHELIEU CANADA LTD   p 256
2600 VIKING WAY, RICHMOND, BC, V6V
1N2
(604) 273-3108   SIC 5072
RICHELIEU FINANCES LTEE   p 1336
7900 BOUL HENRI-BOURASSA O BU-
REAU 200, SAINT-LAURENT, QC, H4S 1V4
(514) 336-4144   SIC 6719
RICHELIEU HARDWARE CANADA LTD p
1228
7900 BOUL HENRI-BOURASSA O, MON-
TREAL, QC, H4S 1V4
(514) 336-4144   SIC 5072
RICHEMONT CANADA, INC   p 700
4610 EASTGATE PKY UNIT 1, MISSIS-
SAUGA, ON, L4W 3W6
(905) 602-8532   SIC 5094
RICHFORM CONSTRUCTION SUPPLY CO

LTD   p 202
35 LEEDER ST UNIT A, COQUITLAM, BC,
V3K 3V5
(604) 777-9974   SIC 5051
RICHLU MANUFACTURING   p 374
See WINNIPEG PANTS & SPORTSWEAR
MFG. LTD
RICHLU SPORTSWEAR MFG. LTD   p 373
85 ADELAIDE ST, WINNIPEG, MB, R3A
0V9
(204) 942-3494   SIC 2329
RICHMOND ACURA   p 260
See DCH MOTORS LTD
RICHMOND AUTO BODY LTD   p 261
2691 NO. 5 RD, RICHMOND, BC, V6X 2S8
(604) 278-9158   SIC 7532
RICHMOND BUILDING SUPPLIES CO. LTD
p 256
12231 BRIDGEPORT RD, RICHMOND,
V6V 1J4
(604) 278-9865   SIC 5039
**RICHMOND CHRISTIAN SCHOOL ASSOCI-
ATION**   p
263
10200 NO. 5 RD, RICHMOND, BC, V7A 4E5
(604) 272-5720   SIC 8211
RICHMOND CHRYSLER DODGE JEEP LTD
p 256
5491 PARKWOOD WAY, RICHMOND, BC,
V6V 2M9
(604) 273-7521   SIC 5511
RICHMOND COUNTRY CLUB   p 263
9100 STEVESTON HWY, RICHMOND, BC,
V7A 1M5
(604) 277-3141   SIC 7997
**RICHMOND ELEVATOR MAINTENANCE
LTD**   p 264
12091 NO. 5 RD SUITE 5, RICHMOND, BC,
V7A 4E9
(604) 274-8440   SIC 1796
RICHMOND HILL AUTO PARK LIMITED p
857
11240 YONGE ST, RICHMOND HILL, ON,
L4S 1K9
(905) 889-1189   SIC 5511
RICHMOND HILL COUNTRY CLUB   p 855
See RHCC HOLDINGS LIMITED
RICHMOND HILL FINE CARS   p 855
See 898984 ONTARIO INC
RICHMOND HILL GOLF CLUB   p 777
See TECHNOR DEVELOPMENTS LIM-
ITED
RICHMOND HILL HONDA   p 856
See SMALL CAR CENTRE LTD
RICHMOND HILL HYUNDAI   p 856
See 1675001 ONTARIO LIMITED
RICHMOND HILL TOYOTA   p 857
See RICHMOND HILL AUTO PARK LIM-
ITED
RICHMOND HILL WHOLESALE MEAT LTD
p 674
70 DENISON ST SUITE 8, MARKHAM, ON,
L3R 1B6
(905) 513-1817   SIC 5147
RICHMOND HONDA   p 256
See RICHMOND IMPORTS LTD
RICHMOND HOSPITAL, THE   p 261
7000 WESTMINSTER HWY, RICHMOND,
BC, V6X 1A2
(604) 278-9711   SIC 8062
RICHMOND HOSPITAL, THE   p 262
6111 MINORU BLVD, RICHMOND, BC, V6Y
1Y4
(604) 244-5300   SIC 8059
RICHMOND IMPORTS LTD   p 256
13600 SMALLWOOD PL, RICHMOND, BC,
V6V 1W8
(604) 207-1846   SIC 5511
RICHMOND INN HOTEL LTD   p 261
7551 WESTMINSTER HWY, RICHMOND,
BC, V6X 1A3
(604) 273-7878   SIC 7011
**RICHMOND INTERMEDIATE CARE SOCI-
ETY**   p

266
6260 BLUNDELL RD, RICHMOND, BC, V7C
5C4
(604) 271-3590   SIC 8051
**RICHMOND INTERNATIONAL TECHNOL-
OGY CORP**   p
256
4460 JACOMBS RD SUITE 102, RICH-
MOND, BC, V6V 2C5
(604) 273-8248   SIC 5063
RICHMOND LEXUS   p 255
See OPENROAD AUTO GROUP LIMITED
RICHMOND NISSAN LTD   p 256
13220 SMALLWOOD PL, RICHMOND, BC,
V6V 1W8
(604) 273-1661   SIC 5511
**RICHMOND OLYMPIC OVAL CORPORA-
TION**   p
266
6111 RIVER RD, RICHMOND, BC, V7C 0A2
(778) 296-1400   SIC 7999
**RICHMOND PLYWOOD CORPORATION
LIMITED**   p 256
13911 VULCAN WAY, RICHMOND, BC, V6V
1K7
(604) 278-9111   SIC 2436
RICHMOND PUBLIC LIBRARY BOARD p
262
7700 MINORU GATE SUITE 100, RICH-
MOND, BC, V6Y 1R8
(604) 231-6422   SIC 8231
RICHMOND SCHOOL BOARD   p 262
See BOARD OF EDUCATION SCHOOL
DISTRICT #38 (RICHMOND)
RICHMOND SECONDARY   p 262
See BOARD OF EDUCATION SCHOOL
DISTRICT #38 (RICHMOND)
RICHMOND STEEL RECYCLING LIMITED p
256
11760 MITCHELL RD, RICHMOND, BC,
V6V 1V8
(604) 324-4656   SIC 4953
RICHMOND SUBARU   p 259
See COSMO MOTORS LTD
RICHMOND, CITY OF   p 256
12800 CAMBIE RD, RICHMOND, BC, V6V
0A9
(604) 233-8399   SIC 8322
RICHMOND, CITY OF   p 266
9180 NO. 1 RD, RICHMOND, BC, V7E 6L5
(604) 238-8400   SIC 8322
RICHTER & ASSOCIES   p 1402
See RICHTER GROUPE CONSEIL SENC
RICHTER GROUPE CONSEIL SENC p 1402
3500 BOUL DE MAISONNEUVE O UNITE
1800, WESTMOUNT, QC, H3Z 3C1
(514) 934-3497   SIC 8741
RICHTER S.E.N.C.R.L.   p 1199
1981 AV MCGILL COLLEGE SUITE 11E,
MONTREAL, QC, H3A 2W9
(514) 934-3400   SIC 8721
RICHTREE MARKET RESTAURANTS INC p
821
50 RIDEAU ST SUITE 115, OTTAWA, ON,
K1N 9J7
SIC 5812
RICHTREE MARKET RESTAURANTS INC p
956
14 QUEEN ST W, TORONTO, ON, M5H 3X4
(416) 366-8986   SIC 5812
RICHTREE MARKET RESTAURANTS INC p
971
40 YONGE BLVD, TORONTO, ON, M5M
3G5
(416) 366-8986   SIC 5812
RICHVALE YORK BLOCK INC   p 895
5 CARDICO DR, STOUFFVILLE, ON, L4A
2G5
(416) 213-7444   SIC 3271
**RICHWAY ENVIRONMENTAL TECHNOLO-
GIES LTD**   p
264
11300 NO. 5 RD SUITE 100, RICHMOND,
BC, V7A 5J7

(604) 275-2201   *SIC* 5084
RICHWIL TRUCK CENTRE LTD   *p* 404
314 LOCKHART MILL RD, JACKSONVILLE, NB, E7M 3S4

(506) 328-9379   *SIC* 5511
RICK HANSEN FOUNDATION   *p* 265
3820 CESSNA DR SUITE 300, RICHMOND, BC, V7B 0A2

(604) 295-8149   *SIC* 8699
RICK HANSEN MAN IN MOTION FOUNDATION   *p* 265
See RICK HANSEN FOUNDATION

RICK HANSEN SECONDARY SCHOOL   *p* 177
See SCHOOL DISTRICT NO 34 (ABBOTSFORD)

RICK HANSON SECONDARY SCHOOL   *p* 744
See PEEL DISTRICT SCHOOL BOARD

RICK KURZAC BUILDING MATERIALS LTD   *p* 218
1325 JOSEP WAY, KAMLOOPS, BC, V2H 1N6

(250) 377-7234   *SIC* 5211
RICK NICKELL TRUCKING INC   *p* 179
4280 SPALLUMCHEEN DR, ARMSTRONG, BC, V0E 1B6

(250) 546-2566   *SIC* 4213
RICKYS ALL DAY GRILL   *p* 197
See 639809 BC LTD

RICMAR ENTERPRISES LTD   *p* 587
925 DIXON RD, ETOBICOKE, ON, M9W 1J8

(416) 674-3031   *SIC* 5812
RICOH CANADA INC   *p* 700
5560 EXPLORER DR SUITE 100, MISSISSAUGA, ON, L4W 5M3

(905) 795-9659   *SIC* 5044
RICOH CANADA INC   *p* 774
4100 YONGE ST SUITE 600, NORTH YORK, ON, M2P 2B5

(416) 218-4360   *SIC* 5044
RICOH CANADA, DIV OF   *p* 961
See COMMONWEALTH LEGAL INC

RICOH DOCUMENT MANAGEMENT LIMITED PARTNERSHIP   *p* 481
205 INDUSTRIAL PKY N UNIT 2, AURORA, ON, L4G 4C4

(905) 841-8433   *SIC* 2731
RIDEAU AUCTIONS INC   *p* 1016
GD, WINCHESTER, ON, K0C 2K0

(613) 774-2735   *SIC* 7389
RIDEAU BAKERY LIMITED   *p* 827
1666 BANK ST, OTTAWA, ON, K1V 7Y6

(613) 737-3355   *SIC* 5461
RIDEAU CARLTON RACEWAY CASINO   *p* 597
See HR OTTAWA, L.P.

RIDEAU CLUB LIMITED   *p* 824
99 BANK ST SUITE 1500, OTTAWA, ON, K1P 6B9

(613) 233-7787   *SIC* 8699
RIDEAU COMMUNITY HEALTH SERVICES   *p* 681
354 READ ST, MERRICKVILLE, ON, K0G 1N0

(613) 269-3400   *SIC* 8011
RIDEAU COUNCIL   *p* 896
See RIDEAU COUNCIL 2444

RIDEAU COUNCIL 2444   *p* 896
93 MORGAN ST, STRATFORD, ON, N5A 7V2

(519) 272-9700   *SIC* 8641
RIDEAU HIGH SCHOOL   *p* 820
See OTTAWA-CARLETON DISTRICT SCHOOL BOARD

RIDEAU HOME HARDWARE BUILDING CENTRE   *p* 882
See RIDEAU LUMBER (SMITH'S FALLS) LIMITED

RIDEAU LUMBER (SMITH'S FALLS) LIMITED   *p*

882
58 ABBOTT ST N, SMITHS FALLS, ON, K7A 1W5

(613) 283-2211   *SIC* 5211
RIDEAU ORDERS, MEDALS AND DECORATIONS   *p* 1327
See SOLUTIONS DE RECONNAISSANCE RIDEAU INC

RIDEAU PARK PERSONAL CARE HOME   *p* 347
See PRAIRIE MOUNTAIN HEALTH

RIDEAU PIPE & DRILLING SUPPLIES   *p* 839
See 519728 ONTARIO LTD

RIDEAU ST LAWRENCE DISTRIBUTION INC   *p* 848
985 INDUSTRIAL RD, PRESCOTT, ON, K0E 1T0

(613) 925-3851   *SIC* 4911
RIDEAU VALLEY CONSERVATION AUTHORITY   *p* 663
3889 RIDEAU VALLEY DR, MANOTICK, ON, K4M 1A5

(613) 692-3571   *SIC* 8713
RIDEAUCREST HOME FOR THE AGED   *p* 630
See CORPORATION OF THE CITY OF KINGSTON, THE

RIDEOUT LABRADOR LIMITED   *p* 424
GD, HAPPY VALLEY-GOOSE BAY, NL, A0P 1C0

(709) 754-2240   *SIC* 5084
RIDEOUT TOOL & MACHINE   *p* 424
See RIDEOUT LABRADOR LIMITED

RIDEOUT TOOL AND MACHINE INC   *p* 431
222 KENMOUNT RD, ST. JOHN'S, NL, A1B 3R2

(709) 754-2240   *SIC* 5084
RIDETONES INC   *p* 1007
161 ROGER ST, WATERLOO, ON, N2J 1B1

(519) 745-8887   *SIC* 5531
RIDGE DEVELOPMENT CORPORATION   *p* 102
17307 106 AVE NW, EDMONTON, AB, T5S 1E7

(780) 483-7077   *SIC* 1522
RIDGE MEADOWS HOSPITAL   *p* 231
See FRASER HEALTH AUTHORITY

RIDGE MEADOWS RECYCLING SOCIETY   *p* 231
10092 236 ST, MAPLE RIDGE, BC, V2X 7G2

(604) 463-5545   *SIC* 4953
RIDGE NATIONAL INC   *p* 1023
100 OUELLETTE AVE SUITE 1004, WINDSOR, ON, N9A 6T3

(519) 256-2112   *SIC* 1611
RIDGE SHEET METAL LTD   *p* 247
2532 DAVIES AVE, PORT COQUITLAM, BC, V3C 2J9

(604) 942-0244   *SIC* 1761
RIDGE VALLEY COLONY LTD   *p* 81
GD, CROOKED CREEK, AB, T0H 0Y0

(780) 957-2607   *SIC* 0291
RIDGEBACK RESOURCES INC   *p* 58
525 8 AVE SW UNIT 2800, CALGARY, AB, T2P 1G1

(403) 268-7800   *SIC* 1382
RIDGEDALE CO-OPERATIVE ASSOCIATION LTD   *p* 1423
119 MAIN ST, RIDGEDALE, SK, S0E 1L0

(306) 277-2042   *SIC* 5171
RIDGEHILL FORD SALES (1980) LIMITED   *p* 534
217 HESPELER RD SUITE 637, CAMBRIDGE, ON, N1R 3H8

(519) 621-0720   *SIC* 5511
RIDGELINE CANADA INC   *p* 25
3016 19 ST NE SUITE 101, CALGARY, AB, T2E 6Y9

(403) 806-2380   *SIC* 8748
RIDGEMAR   *p* 351

See MARBLE RIDGE FARMS LTD
RIDGEMONT HIGH SCHOOL   *p* 827
See OTTAWA-CARLETON DISTRICT SCHOOL BOARD

RIDGETOWN COLLEGE   *p* 857
See UNIVERSITY OF GUELPH

RIDGEVIEW LONG TERM CARE CENTER   *p* 894
See REVERA LONG TERM CARE INC

RIDGEWAY MECHANICAL LTD   *p* 202
925 SHERWOOD AVE UNIT 1, COQUITLAM, BC, V3K 1A9

(604) 525-0238   *SIC* 1711
RIDLEY COLLEGE   *p* 886
2 RIDLEY RD, ST CATHARINES, ON, L2R 7C3

(905) 684-1889   *SIC* 8221
RIDLEY FEED OPERATIONS   *p* 366
See RIDLEY INC

RIDLEY INC   *p* 366
34 TERRACON PL, WINNIPEG, MB, R2J 4G7

(204) 956-1717   *SIC* 2048
RIDLEY MF INC   *p* 366
715 MARION ST, WINNIPEG, MB, R2J 0K6

(204) 233-1112   *SIC* 2048
RIDLEY TERMINALS INC   *p* 252
2110 RIDLEY RD, PRINCE RUPERT, BC, V8J 4H3

(250) 624-9511   *SIC* 4491
RIDLEY WINDOWS & DOORS   *p* 540
See MERITCO INDUSTRIES LTD

RIDOUT & MAYBEE LLP   *p* 956
250 UNIVERSITY AVE 5TH FL, TORONTO, ON, M5H 3E5

(416) 868-1482   *SIC* 8111
RIDSDALE TRANSPORT LTD   *p* 1435
210 APEX ST, SASKATOON, SK, S7R 0A2

(306) 668-9200   *SIC* 4213
RIEGER   *p* 58
808 4 AVE SW SUITE 600, CALGARY, AB, T2P 3E8

(403) 537-7642   *SIC* 6411
RIELLO CANADA, INC   *p* 726
2165 MEADOWPINE BLVD, MISSISSAUGA, ON, L5N 6H6

(905) 542-0303   *SIC* 3433
RIENDEAU, GAETAN INC   *p* 1314
2030 BOUL LAURIER E, SAINT-HYACINTHE, QC, J2T 1K7

(450) 774-2311   *SIC* 5411
RIESE INVESTMENTS LTD   *p* 1408
1 RIESE BAY, LA RONGE, SK, S0J 1L0

(306) 425-2314   *SIC* 5153
RIESE'S CANADIAN LAKE WILD RICE   *p* 1408
See RIESE INVESTMENTS LTD

RIETER AUTOMOTIVE CANADA CARPET   *p* 648
See AUTONEUM CANADA LTD

RIFCO INC   *p* 154
4909 49 ST SUITE 702, RED DEER, AB, T4N 1V1

(403) 314-1288   *SIC* 6141
RIFCO NATIONAL AUTO FINANCE CORPORATION   *p* 154
4909 49 ST SUITE 702, RED DEER, AB, T4N 1V1

(403) 314-1288   *SIC* 6141
RIFE RESOURCES LTD   *p* 58
144 4 AVE SW SUITE 400, CALGARY, AB, T2P 3N4

(403) 221-0800   *SIC* 1311
RIFF'S LIMITED   *p* 424
2 HARDY AVE, GRAND FALLS-WINDSOR, NL, A2A 2P9

(709) 489-5631   *SIC* 5311
RIG   *p* 483
See RESOURCE INDUSTRIAL GROUP INC

RIG LOGISTICS INC   *p* 159
10 WRANGLER PL UNIT 4, ROCKY VIEW COUNTY, AB, T1X 0L7

(403) 285-1111   *SIC* 4212
RIG SHOP LIMITED, THE   *p* 123
1704 66 AVE NW, EDMONTON, AB, T6P 1M4

(780) 440-4202   *SIC* 3533
RIGA FARMS   *p* 756
See RIGA FARMS LTD

RIGA FARMS LTD   *p* 756
19810 DUFFERIN ST, NEWMARKET, ON, L3Y 4V9

(905) 775-4217   *SIC* 0161
RIGEL SHIPPING CANADA INC   *p* 417
3521 ROUTE 134, SHEDIAC CAPE, NB, E4P 3G6

(506) 533-9000   *SIC* 4213
RIGHT AT HOME REALTY INC   *p* 853
300 WEST BEAVER CREEK RD SUITE 202, RICHMOND HILL, ON, L4B 3B1

(905) 695-7888   *SIC* 6531
RIGHT AT HOME REALTY, INC   *p* 780
895 DON MILLS RD SUITE 202, NORTH YORK, ON, M3C 1W3

(416) 391-3232   *SIC* 4731
RIGHT TO LIFE ASSOCIATION OF WINDSOR AND AREA   *p* 1025
3021 DOUGALL AVE, WINDSOR, ON, N9E 1S3

(519) 969-7555   *SIC* 8699
RIIDE HAIL   *p* 1432
See RIIDE HOLDINGS INC

RIIDE HOLDINGS INC   *p* 1432
225 AVENUE B N, SASKATOON, SK, S7L 1E1

(306) 244-3767   *SIC* 4111
RILEY AND JAMES; DIV OF   *p* 1181
See VETEMENTS MARK-EDWARDS INC

RILLING BUS LTD   *p* 1438
GD STN MAIN, YORKTON, SK, S3N 2V5

(306) 782-2955   *SIC* 4151
RIMANESA PROPERTIES INC   *p* 1230
800 RUE DE LA GAUCHETIERE O BUREAU 240, MONTREAL, QC, H5A 1K6

(514) 397-2211   *SIC* 8741
RIMAR VOLKSWAGON   *p* 1346
See AUTOMOBILES RIMAR INC

RIMBEY AUCTION MART (1996) LTD   *p* 158
4831 47 ST, RIMBEY, AB, T0C 2J0

(403) 843-2439   *SIC* 5154
RIMBEY CO-OP ASSOCIATION LTD   *p* 158
4625 51 ST, RIMBEY, AB, T0C 2J0

(403) 843-2268   *SIC* 5411
RIMBEY GAS PLANT   *p* 158
See KEYERA PARTNERSHIP

RIMER ALCO NORTH AMERICA INC   *p* 352
205 STEPHEN ST, MORDEN, MB, R6M 1V2

(204) 822-6595   *SIC* 5999
RIMEX SUPPLY LTD   *p* 230
5929 274 ST, LANGLEY, BC, V4W 0B8

(604) 888-0025   *SIC* 3714
RIMOKA HOUSING FOUNDATION   *p* 152
5608 57 AVE SUITE 101, PONOKA, AB, T4J 1P2

(403) 783-0128   *SIC* 6531
RINAX COMPUTER SYSTEMS   *p* 37
See RINAX SYSTEMS LTD

RINAX SYSTEMS LTD   *p* 37
5542 1A ST SW, CALGARY, AB, T2H 0E7

(403) 243-4074   *SIC* 5045
RINFRET AUTO INC   *p* 1137
5355 BOUL GUILLAUME-COUTURE, LEVIS, QC, G6V 4Z3

(418) 833-2133   *SIC* 5511
RINFRET VOLKSWAGEN   *p* 1137
See RINFRET AUTO INC

RINGBALL CORPORATION   *p* 726
2160 MEADOWPINE BLVD, MISSISSAUGA, ON, L5N 6H6

(905) 826-1100   *SIC* 5085
RINOX INC   *p* 1381
3155 BOUL DES ENTREPRISES, TERREBONNE, QC, J6X 4J9

(450) 477-7888   *SIC* 3272
RINTALA CONSTRUCTION COMPANY LIM-

ITED
647
377 BLACK LAKE RD, LIVELY, ON, P3Y 1H8
(705) 692-3648   *SIC 5032*

RIO TEXTILES EXPORTERS LTD   *p 867*
1840 ELLESMERE RD, SCARBOROUGH, ON, M1H 2V5
SIC 5932

RIO TINTO   *p 1208*
See *RIO TINTO GESTION CANADA INC*

RIO TINTO ALCAN INC   *p 224*
1 SMELTER SITE RD, KITIMAT, BC, V8C 2H2
(250) 639-8000   *SIC 3334*

RIO TINTO ALCAN INC   *p 1045*
3000 RUE DES PINS O, ALMA, QC, G8B 5W2
(418) 480-6000   *SIC 3399*

RIO TINTO ALCAN INC   *p 1115*
1955 BOUL MELLON, JONQUIERE, QC, G7S 0L4
(418) 699-2002   *SIC 3334*

RIO TINTO ALCAN INC   *p 1115*
1954 RUE DAVIS, JONQUIERE, QC, G7S 3B6
SIC 4911

RIO TINTO ALCAN INC   *p 1121*
5000 RTE DU PETIT PARC, LA BAIE, QC, G7B 4G9
(418) 697-9600   *SIC 3334*

RIO TINTO ALCAN INC   *p 1121*
262 1RE RUE, LA BAIE, QC, G7B 3R1
(418) 544-9660   *SIC 4512*

RIO TINTO ALCAN INC   *p 1208*
1190 AV DES CANADIENS-DE-MONTREAL BUREAU 400, MONTREAL, QC, H3B 0E3
(514) 848-8000   *SIC 3334*

RIO TINTO ALCAN INC   *p 1368*
1100 BOUL SAINT-SACREMENT, SHAWINIGAN, QC, G9N 0E3
(819) 539-0765   *SIC 3334*

RIO TINTO ALCAN INTERNATIONAL LTEE
p 1208
1190 AV DES CANADIENS-DE-MONTREAL BUREAU 400, MONTREAL, QC, H3B 0E3
(514) 848-8000   *SIC 8731*

RIO TINTO FER ET TITANE INC   *p 1377*
1625 RTE MARIE-VICTORIN, SOREL-TRACY, QC, J3R 1M6
(450) 746-3000   *SIC 3399*

RIO TINTO GESTION CANADA INC   *p 1208*
1190 AV DES CANADIENS-DE-MONTREAL BUREAU 400, MONTREAL, QC, H3B 0E3
(514) 288-8400   *SIC 2816*

RIO2 LIMITED   *p 309*
355 BURRARD ST SUITE 1260, VANCOUVER, BC, V6C 2G8
(604) 260-2696   *SIC 1041*

RIOCAN MANAGEMENT INC   *p 923*
2300 YONGE ST SUITE 500, TORONTO, ON, M4P 1E4
(800) 465-2733   *SIC 6531*

RIOCAN PROPERTY SERVICES INC   *p 790*
700 LAWRENCE AVE W SUITE 315, NORTH YORK, ON, M6A 3B4
(416) 256-0256   *SIC 6531*

RIOCAN REAL ESTATE INVESTMENT TRUST   *p 923*
2300 YONGE ST SUITE 500, TORONTO, ON, M4P 1E4
(416) 866-3033   *SIC 6798*

RIOCAN RETAIL VALUE L.P.   *p 923*
2300 YONGE ST SUITE 500, TORONTO, ON, M4P 1E4
(416) 866-3033   *SIC 6799*

RIOUX, GILBERT M & FILS LTEE   *p 416*
855 ROUTE 108, SAINT-ANDRE, NB, E3Y 4A5
(506) 473-1764   *SIC 4731*

RIPLEY'S BELIEVE IT OR NOT   *p 308*
See *PATTISON, JIM ENTERTAINMENT LTD*

RIPPLEPAK, DIV OF   *p 676*
See *UTHANE RESEARCH LTD*

RISE HEALTHWARE   *p 991*
See *3161234 MANITOBA LIMITED*

RISING EDGE TECHNOLOGIES LTD   *p 25*
2620 22 ST NE, CALGARY, AB, T2E 7L9
(403) 202-8751   *SIC 1796*

RISKTECH INSURANCE SERVICES INC   *p 98*
300-14727 87 AVE NW, EDMONTON, AB, T5R 4E5
(780) 732-7129   *SIC 6411*

RISLEY EQUIPMENT, DIV OF   *p 133*
See *RISLEY MANUFACTURING LTD*

RISLEY MANUFACTURING LTD   *p 133*
9024 108 ST, GRANDE PRAIRIE, AB, T8V 4C8
(780) 532-3282   *SIC 3531*

RITCHIE BROS.   *p 193*
See *RITCHIE BROS. AUCTIONEERS INCORPORATED*

RITCHIE BROS. AUCTIONEERS (INTERNATIONAL) LTD   *p*
193
9500 GLENLYON PKY SUITE 300, BURNABY, BC, V5J 0C6
(778) 331-5500   *SIC 5999*

RITCHIE BROS. AUCTIONEERS INCORPORATED   *p*
193
9500 GLENLYON PKY, BURNABY, BC, V5J 0C6
(778) 331-5500   *SIC 7389*

RITCHIE BROS. FINANCIAL SERVICES LTD   *p 193*
9500 GLENLYON PKY, BURNABY, BC, V5J 0C6
(778) 331-5500   *SIC 8742*

RITCHIE FEED & SEED INC   *p 595*
1390 WINDMILL LANE, GLOUCESTER, ON, K1B 4V5
(613) 741-4430   *SIC 5261*

RITCHIE'S CARPET WAREHOUSE   *p 402*
See *RITCHIE, KEVIN A LTD*

RITCHIE, KEVIN A LTD   *p 402*
1250 HANWELL RD, FREDERICTON, NB, E3C 1A7
(506) 458-8588   *SIC 5713*

RITCHIE-SMITH FEEDS INC   *p 175*
33777 ENTERPRISE AVE, ABBOTSFORD, BC, V2S 7T9
(604) 859-7128   *SIC 2048*

RITE CORPORATION   *p 1050*
10250 BOUL PARKWAY, ANJOU, QC, H1J 2K4
(514) 324-8900   *SIC 5085*

RITE-PAK PRODUCE CO. LIMITED   *p 573*
165 THE QUEENSWAY, ETOBICOKE, ON, M8Y 1H8
(416) 252-3121   *SIC 5148*

RITE-WAY FENCING (2000) INC   *p 18*
7710 40 ST SE, CALGARY, AB, T2C 3S4
(403) 243-8733   *SIC 1799*

RITE-WAY METALS LTD   *p 225*
20058 92A AVE, LANGLEY, BC, V1M 3A4
(604) 882-7557   *SIC 1542*

RITTAL SYSTEMS LTD   *p 742*
6485 ORDAN DR, MISSISSAUGA, ON, L5T 1X2
(905) 795-0777   *SIC 5063*

RITZ MACHINE WORKS INC   *p 349*
507 1ST AVE SE, DAUPHIN, MB, R7N 2Z8
(204) 638-1633   *SIC 3443*

RITZ PLASTICS INC   *p 842*
435 PIDO RD, PETERBOROUGH, ON, K9J 6X7
(705) 748-6776   *SIC 3089*

RITZ-CARLTON HOTEL COMPANY OF CANADA LIMITED, THE   *p 983*
181 WELLINGTON ST W, TORONTO, ON, M5V 3G7
(416) 585-2500   *SIC 7011*

RIVE SUD CHRYSLER DODGE INC   *p 1069*
9400 BOUL TASCHEREAU, BROSSARD,

QC, J4X 1C3
(450) 444-9400   *SIC 5511*

RIVE SUD CHRYSLER DODGE JEEP RAM   *p 1069*
See *RIVE SUD CHRYSLER DODGE INC*

RIVE SUD PONTIAC BUICK GMC INC   *p*
1143
395 RUE SAINT-CHARLES O, LONGUEUIL, QC, J4H 1G1
SIC 5511

RIVER BUTTE MANAGEMENT LTD   *p 180*
2866 BRISCO RD, BRISCO, BC, V0A 1B0
(250) 346-3315   *SIC 8741*

RIVER CABLE LTD   *p 270*
11406 132A ST, SURREY, BC, V3R 7S2
(604) 580-4636   *SIC 5051*

RIVER CITY ELECTRIC LTD   *p 102*
11323 174 ST NW, EDMONTON, AB, T5S 0B7
(780) 484-6676   *SIC 1731*

RIVER CITY FORD SALES   *p 386*
See *178011 CANADA INC*

RIVER CITY NISSAN   *p 217*
2405 TRANS CANADA HWY E, KAMLOOPS, BC, V2C 4A9
(250) 377-8850   *SIC 5511*

RIVER CREE RESORT AND CASINO, THE   *p 126*
See *RIVER CREE RESORT LIMITED PARTNERSHIP*

RIVER CREE RESORT LIMITED PARTNERSHIP   *p*
126
300 E LAPOTAC BLVD, ENOCH, AB, T7X 3Y3
(780) 484-2121   *SIC 7011*

RIVER EAST COLLEGIATE   *p 364*
See *RIVER EAST TRANSCONA SCHOOL DIVISION*

RIVER EAST PERSONAL CARE HOME LTD   *p 367*
1375 MOLSON ST, WINNIPEG, MB, R2K 4K8
(204) 668-7460   *SIC 8059*

RIVER EAST TRANSCONA SCHOOL DIVISION   *p*
363
260 REDONDA ST, WINNIPEG, MB, R2C 1L6
(204) 958-6460   *SIC 8211*

RIVER EAST TRANSCONA SCHOOL DIVISION   *p*
364
295 SUTTON AVE, WINNIPEG, MB, R2G 0T1
(204) 338-4611   *SIC 8211*

RIVER EAST TRANSCONA SCHOOL DIVISION   *p*
367
589 ROCH ST, WINNIPEG, MB, R2K 2P7
(204) 667-7130   *SIC 8211*

RIVER EAST TRANSCONA SCHOOL DIVISION   *p*
367
757 ROCH ST, WINNIPEG, MB, R2K 2R1
(204) 667-1103   *SIC 8211*

RIVER EAST TRANSCONA SCHOOL DIVISION   *p*
367
795 PRINCE RUPERT AVE, WINNIPEG, MB, R2K 1W6
(204) 668-9304   *SIC 8211*

RIVER EAST TRANSCONA SCHOOL DIVISION   *p*
367
845 CONCORDIA AVE, WINNIPEG, MB, R2K 2M6
(204) 667-2960   *SIC 8211*

RIVER GLEN HAVEN NURSING HOME   *p 902*
See *KANNAMPUZHA HOLDINGS LTD*

RIVER PARK GARDENS   *p 368*
See *WINNIPEG REGIONAL HEALTH AUTHORITY, THE*

RIVER ROAD CO-OP   *p 416*
See *CONSUMERS COMMUNITY CO-OP*

RIVER ROCK CASINO RESORT   *p 260*
See *GREAT CANADIAN CASINOS INC*

RIVER RUN   *p 489*
See *OTTAWA RIVER WHITE WATER RAFTING LIMITED*

RIVER SEAFOODS INC   *p 237*
522 SEVENTH ST UNIT 320, NEW WESTMINSTER, BC, V3M 5T5
SIC 2092

RIVER SIDE FORD SALES LIMITED   *p 520*
25 ELEANOR ST, BROCKVILLE, ON, K6V 4H9
(613) 342-0234   *SIC 5511*

RIVER VALLEY MASONRY GROUP LTD   *p 704*
2444 HAINES RD, MISSISSAUGA, ON, L4Y 1Y6
(905) 270-0599   *SIC 1741*

RIVER VALLEY SPECIALTY FARMS INC   *p 345*
GD, BAGOT, MB, R0H 0E0
(204) 274-2467   *SIC 0161*

RIVER'S END FARMS LTD   *p 204*
2046 CORN CREEK RD, CRESTON, BC, V0B 1G7
(250) 428-3905   *SIC 0181*

RIVER'S REACH PUB INC   *p 236*
320 SIXTH ST, NEW WESTMINSTER, BC, V3L 3A8
(604) 777-0101   *SIC 5921*

RIVERBEND CO-OPERATIVE LTD   *p 1413*
101 SASKATCHEWAN AVE E, OUTLOOK, SK, S0L 2N0
(306) 867-8614   *SIC 5411*

RIVERBEND COLONY LTD   *p 348*
GD, CARBERRY, MB, R0K 0H0
(204) 834-3141   *SIC 2439*

RIVERBEND FREIGHT SERVICES LIMITED   *p 426*
26 KYLE AVE, MOUNT PEARL, NL, A1N 4R5
(709) 368-1773   *SIC 4731*

RIVERBEND PLACE CAMBRIDGE   *p 534*
See *REVERA LONG TERM CARE INC*

RIVERBEND RETIREMENT RESIDENCE   *p 123*
103 RABBIT HILL CRT NW, EDMONTON, AB, T6R 2V3
(780) 438-2777   *SIC 6513*

RIVERCREST CARE CENTRE   *p 130*
See *RIVERCREST LODGE NURSING HOME LTD*

RIVERCREST LODGE NURSING HOME LTD   *p 130*
10104 101 AVE, FORT SASKATCHEWAN, AB, T8L 2A5
(780) 998-2425   *SIC 8051*

RIVERDALE COLLEGIATE INSTITUTE   *p 921*
See *TORONTO DISTRICT SCHOOL BOARD*

RIVERDALE HEALTH CENTRE   *p 355*
See *RIVERDALE HEALTH SERVICES DISTRICT FOUNDATION INC*

RIVERDALE HEALTH SERVICES DISTRICT FOUNDATION INC   *p 355*
512 QUEBEC ST, RIVERS, MB, R0K 1X0
(204) 328-5321   *SIC 8062*

RIVERDALE HIGH SCHOOL   *p 1245*
See *LESTER B. PEARSON SCHOOL BOARD*

RIVERDALE SUPER A   *p 1440*
See *CELIA HARBOUR HOLDINGS LTD*

RIVERPARK PLACE LIMITED PARTNERSHIP   *p 751*
1 CORKSTOWN RD, NEPEAN, ON, K2H 1B6
(613) 828-8882   *SIC 8361*

RIVERPARK PLACE RETIREMENT RESIDENCE   *p 751*

▲ Public Company   ■ Public Company Family Member   **HQ** Headquarters   **BR** Branch   **SL** Single Location

See RIVERPARK PLACE LIMITED PART-NERSHIP

RIVERSHORE CHRYSLER JEEP   p 218
See SUNRISE VEHICLE SALES LTD

RIVERSIDE SECONDARY SCHOOL p 1018
See GREATER ESSEX COUNTY DISTRICT SCHOOL BOARD

RIVERSIDE ARCTIC CAT   p 1414
See RIVERSIDE DODGE CHRYSLER JEEP LTD

RIVERSIDE BRASS   p 753
See RIVERSIDE BRASS & ALUMINUM FOUNDRY LIMITED

RIVERSIDE BRASS & ALUMINUM FOUNDRY LIMITED   p 753
55 HAMILTON RD, NEW HAMBURG, ON, N3A 2H1
(800) 265-2197   SIC 3369

RIVERSIDE CAMPUS   p 819
See OTTAWA HOSPITAL, THE

RIVERSIDE CAMPUS   p 828
See OTTAWA HOSPITAL, THE

RIVERSIDE DODGE CHRYSLER JEEP LTD p 1414
160 38TH ST E, PRINCE ALBERT, SK, S6W 1A6
(306) 764-4217   SIC 5511

RIVERSIDE DOOR & TRIM INC   p 1009
520 CONESTOGO RD, WATERLOO, ON, N2L 4E2
(519) 578-3265   SIC 1751

RIVERSIDE HEALTH CARE FACILITIES INC   p 592
110 VICTORIA AVE, FORT FRANCES, ON, P9A 2B7
(807) 274-3266   SIC 8062

RIVERSIDE HONDA & SKI-DOO SALES   p 165
See 393346 ALBERTA LTD

RIVERSIDE HONDA & SKIDOO SALES   p 165
See 293564 ALBERTA LTD

RIVERSIDE HUTTERIAN MUTUAL CORPORATION   p 345
GD, ARDEN, MB, R0J 0B0
(204) 368-2444   SIC 8748

RIVERSIDE LOBSTER INTERNATIONAL INC   p 462
11 JOHN THIBODEAU RD, METEGHAN CENTRE, NS, B0W 2K0
(902) 645-3433   SIC 2092

RIVERSIDE LOBSTER INTERNATIONAL INC   p 462
11 JOHN THIBODEAU RD, METEGHAN CENTRE, NS, B0W 2K0
(902) 645-3455   SIC 2092

RIVERSIDE MILLWORK GROUP INC p 662
1275 HUBREY RD SUITE 7, LONDON, ON, N6N 1E2
(519) 686-7573   SIC 5031

RIVERSIDE NATURAL FOODS LTD   p 558
2720 STEELES AVE W, CONCORD, ON, L4K 4S3
(416) 360-8200   SIC 2032

RIVERSIDE OPTICALAB LIMITED   p 816
2485 LANCASTER RD UNIT 10, OTTAWA, ON, K1B 5L1
(613) 523-5765   SIC 3851

RIVERSIDE PONTIAC BUICK LTD   p 848
101 DEVELOPMENT DR, PRESCOTT, ON, K0E 1T0
(613) 925-5941   SIC 5511

RIVERSIDE POULTRY FARM   p 345
See RIVERSIDE HUTTERIAN MUTUAL CORPORATION

RIVERSIDE RENTALS INC   p 149
1807 8 ST, NISKU, AB, T9E 7S8
(780) 955-5051   SIC 1623

RIVERSIDE RETIREMENT CENTRE LTD   p 242
4315 SKYLINE DR, NORTH VANCOUVER, BC, V7R 3G9
(604) 307-1104   SIC 8361

RIVERSIDE SALES LTD   p 166
15 INGLEWOOD DR SUITE 2, ST. ALBERT, AB, T8N 5E2
(780) 458-7272   SIC 5571

RIVERSIDE SCHOOL BOARD   p 1112
880 RUE HUDSON, GREENFIELD PARK, QC, J4V 1H1
(450) 656-6100   SIC 8211

RIVERSIDE SCHOOL BOARD   p 1112
776 RUE CAMPBELL, GREENFIELD PARK, QC, J4V 1Y7
(450) 672-0042   SIC 8211

RIVERSIDE SCHOOL BOARD   p 1308
7445 CH DE CHAMBLY, SAINT-HUBERT, QC, J3Y 3S3
(450) 678-1070   SIC 8211

RIVERSIDE SECONDARY SCHOOL   p 247
See SCHOOL DISTRICT NO. 43 (COQUITLAM)

RIVERSIDE YAMAHA-SUZUKI   p 166
See RIVERSIDE SALES LTD

RIVERTON COMMUNITY HEALTH OFFICE p 359
See INTERLAKE REGIONAL HEALTH AUTHORITY INC

RIVERTON EARLY MIDDLE YEARS SCHOOL p 350
See EVERGREEN SCHOOL DIVISION

RIVERVIEW AUTOMOBILE LIMITED p 1005
854 MURRAY ST, WALLACEBURG, ON, N8A 1W4
(519) 627-6014   SIC 5511

RIVERVIEW CARE CENTRE   p 146
See REVERA INC

RIVERVIEW COLONY   p 1427
See HUTTERIAN BRETHREN LTD

RIVERVIEW HEALTH CENTRE INC   p 387
1 MORLEY AVE, WINNIPEG, MB, R3L 2P4
(204) 478-6203   SIC 8051

RIVERVIEW HOME CORPORATION p 466
24 RIVERVIEW LANE, STELLARTON, NS, B0K 0A2
(902) 755-4884   SIC 8361

RIVERVIEW HOSPITAL   p 199
See BRITISH COLUMBIA MENTAL HEALTH SOCIETY

RIVERVIEW MANOR NURSING HOME   p 840
See OMNI HEALTH CARE LIMITED PARTNERSHIP

RIVERVIEW MOTORS   p 424
See RIVERVIEW MOTORS LIMITED

RIVERVIEW MOTORS LIMITED   p 424
75 LINCOLN RD, GRAND FALLS-WINDSOR, NL, A2A 1N3
(709) 489-2138   SIC 5511

RIVERVIEW POULTRY   p 404
See PRODUCTIONS AGRICOLES OUELLET, LES

RIVERVIEW POULTRY LIMITED   p 541
1560 KOHLER RD, CAYUGA, ON, N0A 1E0
(905) 957-0300   SIC 2015

RIVERVIEW SERVICE CENTRE LIMITED p 543
351 RICHMOND ST, CHATHAM, ON, N7M 1P5
(519) 352-4937   SIC 5511

RIVERVIEW STEEL CO. LTD   p 1017
8165 ANCHOR DR, WINDSOR, ON, N8N 5B7
(519) 979-5576   SIC 5051

RIVERVIEW SUPERSTORE   p 411
See ATLANTIC WHOLESALERS LTD

RIVET CANADA   p 992
219 DUFFERIN ST SUITE 200A, TORONTO, ON, M6K 3J1
(416) 483-3624   SIC 7311

RIVET INSURANCE   p 898
See RIVET, J. G. BROKERS LIMITED

RIVET, J. G. BROKERS LIMITED   p 898
229 MAIN ST SUITE 1, STURGEON FALLS, ON, P2B 1P5
(705) 753-0130   SIC 6411

RIVET, PATRICE & MANON ST-JEAN

PHARMACIENS SENC   p 1171
1465 RUE JEAN-TALON E BUREAU 282, MONTREAL, QC, H2E 1S8
(514) 270-2151   SIC 5912

RIVETT ARCHITECTURAL HARDWARE LTD   p 1015
111 INDUSTRIAL DR UNIT 1, WHITBY, ON, L1N 5Z9
(905) 668-4455   SIC 5072

RIVIERA PARQUE, BANQUET & CONVENTION CENTRE INC   p 558
2800 HIGHWAY 7 SUITE 301, CONCORD, ON, L4K 1W8
(905) 669-4933   SIC 7299

RIZWAN CHAMPSI PHARMACY INC p 923
2345 YONGE ST, TORONTO, ON, M4P 2E5
(416) 487-5411   SIC 5961

RIZZUTO BROS. LIMITED   p 612
160 JOHN ST S, HAMILTON, ON, L8N 2C4
(905) 522-2525   SIC 4121

RJ'S FRUGAL MARKETS INC   p 600
63 MAIN ST W, GRIMSBY, ON, L3M 4H1
(905) 945-3323   SIC 5411

RJAMES MANAGEMENT GROUP LTD   p 217
2072 FALCON RD, KAMLOOPS, BC, V2C 4J3
(250) 374-1431   SIC 5511

RJC ENGINEERS   p 319
See CHRISTOFFERSEN, READ JONES LTD

RJF HEALTHCARE SERVICES LTD p 454
5657 SPRING GARDEN RD UNIT 700, HALIFAX, NS, B3J 3R4
(902) 425-4031   SIC 8049

RJM56 INVESTMENTS INC   p 576
360 EVANS AVE, ETOBICOKE, ON, M8Z 1K5
(416) 593-6900   SIC 5699

RJMB RESTAURANTS LTD   p 225
20394 88 AVE, LANGLEY, BC, V1M 2Y6
(604) 881-6220   SIC 5812

RJO CANADA ONLINE, DIV OF   p 389
See R.J. O'BRIEN & ASSOCIATES CANADA INC

RJP TRAILERS   p 540
See 4452241 CANADA LTD

RJW STONEMASONS LTD   p 816
2563 EDINBURGH PL, OTTAWA, ON, K1B 5M1
(613) 722-7790   SIC 1741

RK SCHEPERS HOLDINGS LTD   p 204
1608 NORTHWEST BLVD, CRESTON, BC, V0B 1G6
(250) 428-9388   SIC 5211

RKO STEEL LIMITED   p 448
85 MACDONALD AVE, DARTMOUTH, NS, B3B 1T8
(902) 468-1322   SIC 3441

RLB LLP   p 604
15 LEWIS RD SUITE 1, GUELPH, ON, N1H 1E9
(519) 822-9933   SIC 8721

RLK REALTY LTD   p 222
1890 COOPER RD UNIT 1, KELOWNA, BC, V1Y 8B7
(250) 860-1100   SIC 6531

RLM MANUFACTURING INC   p 1015
701 ROSSLAND RD E UNIT 370, WHITBY, ON, L1N 8Y9
(905) 434-4567   SIC 3569

RLOGISTICS LIMITED PARTNERSHIP   p 558
501 APPLEWOOD CRES, CONCORD, ON, L4K 4J3
(905) 660-5030   SIC 5734

RLP MACHINE   p 913
See RLP MACHINE & STEEL FABRICATION INC

RLP MACHINE & STEEL FABRICATION INC   p 913
259 RELIABLE LANE, TIMMINS, ON, P4N 7W7

(705) 267-1445   SIC 3441

RM CLASSIC CARS INC   p 493
1 CLASSIC CAR DR RR 5, BLENHEIM, ON, N0P 1A0
(519) 352-4575   SIC 7532

RM SOTHEBY'S   p 493
1 CLASSIC CAR DR, BLENHEIM, ON, N0P 1A0
(519) 352-4575   SIC 5012

RMA   p 956
See REINSURANCE MANAGEMENT ASSOCIATES INC

RMC INTERNATIONAL INC   p 592
505 CENTRAL AVE, FORT ERIE, ON, L2A 3T9
(905) 991-0431   SIC 3825

RMC READY-MIX LTD   p 273
19275 54 AVE, SURREY, BC, V3S 8E5
(604) 574-1164   SIC 3273

RMR BONDING LTD   p 102
17413 107 AVE NW, EDMONTON, AB, T5S 1E5
(780) 465-4422   SIC 7389

RMS BUILDERS INC   p 124
150 WEST RAILWAY ST NW, EDMONTON, AB, T6T 1J1
(780) 414-0330   SIC 1542

RMS WELDING SYSTEMS, DIV OF   p 149
See O.J. PIPELINES CANADA

RMSENERGY DALHOUSIE MOUNTAIN GP INC   p 465
1383 MOUNT THOM RD, SALT SPRINGS, NS, B0K 1P0
(902) 925-9463   SIC 4911

RMW HOLDINGS LTD   p 268
2066 HENRY AVE W, SIDNEY, BC, V8L 5Y1
(250) 656-5314   SIC 3441

RNAO   p 956
See REGISTERED NURSES ASSOCIATION OF ONTARIO

RNC MEDIA INC   p 1107
171A RUE JEAN-PROULX BUREAU 5, GATINEAU, QC, J8Z 1W5
(819) 503-9711   SIC 4833

RNC MEDIA INC   p 1289
380 AV MURDOCH, ROUYN-NORANDA, QC, J9X 1G5
(819) 762-0741   SIC 4832

RNC MEDIA INC   p 1402
1 PL WESTMOUNT SQUARE BUREAU 1405, WESTMOUNT, QC, H3Z 2P9
(514) 866-8686   SIC 4832

RNF VENTURES LTD   p 1414
811 CENTRAL AVE, PRINCE ALBERT, SK, S6V 4V2
(306) 763-3700   SIC 1542

ROACH'S TAXI (1988) LTD   p 907
216 CAMELOT ST, THUNDER BAY, ON, P7A 4B1
(807) 344-8481   SIC 4121

ROAD TRAIN OILFIELD TRANSPORT LTD p 158
39139 HIGHWAY 2A SUITE 4328, RED DEER COUNTY, AB, T4S 2A8
(403) 346-5311   SIC 1389

ROADKING TRAVEL CENTRE STRATHCONA INC   p 163
26 STRATHMOOR DR SUITE 164, SHERWOOD PARK, AB, T8H 2B6
(780) 417-9400   SIC 5541

ROADMASTER RV, DIV OF   p 138
See LACOMBE RV 2000 LTD

ROADRUNNER APPAREL INC   p 1128
2005 23E AV, LACHINE, QC, H8T 1X1
(514) 631-4669   SIC 5137

ROADSHOW ACADEMY, DIV OF   p 941
See BARNES COMMUNICATIONS INC

ROADSIDE PAVING LIMITED   p 793
125A TORYORK DR SUITE A, NORTH YORK, ON, M9L 1X9
(416) 740-3876   SIC 1611

ROADSPORT HONDA   p 872
See ROADSPORT LIMITED

ROADSPORT LIMITED *p* 872
940 ELLESMERE RD, SCARBOROUGH, ON, M1P 2W8
(416) 291-9501 *SIC* 5511

ROADSTAR TRANSPORT COMPANY LTD *p* 207
10064 RIVER RD, DELTA, BC, V4C 2R3
(604) 882-7623 *SIC* 4212

ROADWAY OPERATIONS & MAINTENANCE CORPORATION OF ONTARIO INC *p* 804
1224 SPEERS RD, OAKVILLE, ON, L6L 5B6
(905) 827-4167 *SIC* 1611

ROADWAY SYSTEMS LIMITED *p* 409
64 ROONEY CRES, MONCTON, NB, E1E 4M3
(506) 384-3069 *SIC* 4899

ROAM MOBILITY HOLDINGS, INC *p* 992
96 MOWAT AVE, TORONTO, ON, M6K 3M1
(416) 535-0123 *SIC* 4899

ROB MCINTOSH CHINA INC *p* 882
20369 SOUTH SERVICE RD, SOUTH LANCASTER, ON, K0C 2C0
(613) 347-2461 *SIC* 5719

ROB MCINTOSH CHINA STORES *p* 882
See ROB MCINTOSH CHINA INC

ROB ROLSTON BUILDING MATERIALS LTD *p* 621
35 CRESCENT RD, HUNTSVILLE, ON, P1H 1Y3
(705) 789-4111 *SIC* 5211

ROB WILLITTS SALES LTD *p* 356
1041 MANITOBA AVE SUITE 447, SELKIRK, MB, R1A 3T7
(204) 482-8473 *SIC* 5014

ROB'S NO FRILLS *p* 510
295 QUEEN ST E, BRAMPTON, ON, L6W 3R1
(905) 452-9200 *SIC* 5411

ROBADAIR LTD *p* 816
2400 LANCASTER RD, OTTAWA, ON, K1B 3W9
(613) 731-6019 *SIC* 3499

ROBAR INDUSTRIES LTD *p* 277
12945 78 AVE, SURREY, BC, V3W 2X8
(604) 591-8811 *SIC* 3321

ROBCO INC *p* 1131
7200 RUE SAINT-PATRICK, LASALLE, QC, H8N 2W7
(514) 367-2252 *SIC* 3053

ROBELY TRADING INC *p* 558
20 BARNES CRT SUITE H, CONCORD, ON, L4K 4L4
(905) 881-2222 *SIC* 5023

ROBERGE ET FILS INC *p* 1123
45 7E AV E, LA SARRE, QC, J9Z 1M5
(819) 333-5405 *SIC* 3442

ROBERGE TRANSPORT INC *p* 1411
1750 STADACONA ST W, MOOSE JAW, SK, S6H 4P4
(800) 667-5190 *SIC* 4213

ROBERT ALLEN FABRICS (CANADA) LTD *p* 726
2880 ARGENTIA RD UNIT 11, MISSISSAUGA, ON, L5N 7X8
(905) 826-7750 *SIC* 5131

ROBERT ALLEN GROUP, THE *p* 726
See ROBERT ALLEN FABRICS (CANADA) LTD

ROBERT BATEMAN HIGH SCHOOL *p* 522
See HALTON DISTRICT SCHOOL BOARD

ROBERT BATEMAN SECONDARY SCHOOL *p* 175
See SCHOOL DISTRICT NO 34 (ABBOTSFORD)

ROBERT BOSCH INC *p* 726
6955 CREDITVIEW RD, MISSISSAUGA, ON, L5N 1R1
(905) 826-6060 *SIC* 5085

ROBERT EXCAVATING, DIV OF *p* 569
See 561861 ONTARIO LTD

ROBERT FER ET METEAUX S.E.C. *p* 1368
3206 CH DES BUISSONS, SHAWINIGAN, QC, G9N 6T5

(819) 539-7318 *SIC* 3341

ROBERT G. AYLWARD SALES LTD *p* 422
4 MURPHY SQ UNIT 185, CORNER BROOK, NL, A2H 1R4
(709) 634-8531 *SIC* 5531

ROBERT HALF LEGAL *p* 963
See HALF, ROBERT INTERNATIONAL

ROBERT K. BUZZELL LIMITED *p* 409
254 HORSMAN RD, MONCTON, NB, E1E 0E8
(506) 853-0936 *SIC* 7699

ROBERT LEE LTD *p* 316
1177 HASTINGS ST W SUITE 517, VANCOUVER, BC, V6E 2K3
(604) 669-7733 *SIC* 6512

ROBERT MEDIA *p* 1288
See TRANSPORT ROBERT (1973) LTEE

ROBERT MITCHELL INC *p* 1323
350 BOUL DECARIE, SAINT-LAURENT, QC, H4L 3K5
(514) 747-2471 *SIC* 3498

ROBERT MOTORS (1980) LIMITED *p* 578
5450 DUNDAS ST W, ETOBICOKE, ON, M9B 1B4
(416) 231-1984 *SIC* 5511

ROBERT MOTORS JAGUAR *p* 578
See SCOTT-FISHER ENTERPRISES INC

ROBERT POSITANO'S WOODBINE PONTIAC BUICK GMC *p* 581
See 2154781 CANADA LTD

ROBERT Q AIRBUS *p* 659
See ROBERT Q'S AIRBUS INC

ROBERT Q'S AIRBUS INC *p* 659
105 WHARNCLIFFE RD S, LONDON, ON, N6J 2K2
(519) 673-6804 *SIC* 4131

ROBERT Q'S TRAVEL MART INC *p* 659
105 WHARNCLIFFE RD S, LONDON, ON, N6J 2K2
(519) 672-9020 *SIC* 4724

ROBERT S FRANK HALL *p* 532
See DUFFERIN-PEEL CATHOLIC DISTRICT SCHOOL BOARD

ROBERT THIRSK HIGH SCHOOL *p* 75
8777 NOSE HILL DR NW, CALGARY, AB, T3G 5T3
(403) 817-3400 *SIC* 8211

ROBERT TRANS GAZ ENR *p* 1151
15 RUE GIROUX, MERCIER, QC, J6R 2P3
SIC 4925

ROBERT TRANSPORT *p* 1065
See GROUPE ROBERT INC

ROBERT TRANSPORT SPECIALIZED INC *p* 1288
500 RTE 112, ROUGEMONT, QC, J0L 1M0
(450) 460-1112 *SIC* 4731

ROBERT'S FARM EQUIPMENT SALES INC *p* 544
14945 COUNTY RD 10, CHESLEY, ON, N0G 1L0
(519) 363-3192 *SIC* 5083

ROBERT'S NO FRILLS *p* 484
319 BLAKE ST, BARRIE, ON, L4M 1K7
(705) 725-8607 *SIC* 5411

ROBERTA PLACE *p* 488
503 ESSA RD, BARRIE, ON, L4N 9E4
(705) 733-3231 *SIC* 8741

ROBERTO *p* 1091
See PANTORAMA INDUSTRIES INC, LES

ROBERTS COMPANY CANADA LIMITED *p* 510
34 HANSEN RD S, BRAMPTON, ON, L6W 3H4
(905) 791-4444 *SIC* 2891

ROBERTS ONSITE INC *p* 637
209 MANITOU DR, KITCHENER, ON, N2C 1L4
(519) 578-2230 *SIC* 1731

ROBERTS WELDING & FABRICATING LTD *p* 1035
873 DEVONSHIRE AVE, WOODSTOCK, ON, N4S 8Z4
(519) 421-0036 *SIC* 3531

ROBERTS, DAVID FOOD CORPORATION *p* 799
2351 UPPER MIDDLE RD E, OAKVILLE, ON, L6H 6P7
(905) 502-7700 *SIC* 5145

ROBERTS, WALTER INSURANCE BROKERS INC *p*
110 WEST BEAVER CREEK RD SUITE 22, RICHMOND HILL, ON, L4B 1J9
(905) 764-8061 *SIC* 6411

ROBERTSON BRIGHT INC *p* 726
2875 ARGENTIA RD UNIT 1, MISSISSAUGA, ON, L5N 8G6
(905) 813-3005 *SIC* 1731

ROBERTSON BUILDING SYSTEMS LIMITED *p* 478
1343 SANDHILL DR, ANCASTER, ON, L9G 4V5
(905) 304-1111 *SIC* 3448

ROBERTSON BULK SALES CALGARY LTD *p* 18
6811 52 ST SE, CALGARY, AB, T2C 4J5
(403) 531-5700 *SIC* 5172

ROBERTSON CONSTRUCTION LTD *p* 273
17802 66 AVE UNIT 101A, SURREY, BC, V3S 7X1
(778) 574-4455 *SIC* 1742

ROBERTSON DRYWALL SERVICES *p* 273
See ROBERTSON CONSTRUCTION LTD

ROBERTSON EADIE & ASSOCIATES *p* 802
41 MORDEN RD SUITE 210, OAKVILLE, ON, L6K 3W6
(905) 338-7002 *SIC* 6411

ROBERTSON ELECTRIC WHOLESALE 2008 LIMITED *p* 1028
180 NEW HUNTINGTON RD UNIT 2, WOODBRIDGE, ON, L4H 0P5
(905) 856-9311 *SIC* 5063

ROBERTSON FIRE EQUIPMENT *p* 576
See ROBERTSON PYROTECHEM LIMITED

ROBERTSON HALL INSURANCE *p* 655
See ROBERTSON INSURANCE AND FINANCIAL SERVICES INC

ROBERTSON IMPLEMENTS (1988) LTD *p* 1436
2464 SOUTH SERVICE RD W, SWIFT CURRENT, SK, S9H 5J8
(306) 773-4948 *SIC* 5571

ROBERTSON INC *p* 524
1185 CORPORATE DR SUITE 1, BURLINGTON, ON, L7L 5V5
(905) 332-7776 *SIC* 5085

ROBERTSON INSURANCE AND FINANCIAL SERVICES INC *p* 655
431 RICHMOND ST SUITE 300, LONDON, ON, N6A 6E2
(519) 680-3111 *SIC* 6411

ROBERTSON MOTOR SPORTS *p* 1436
See ROBERTSON IMPLEMENTS (1988) LTD

ROBERTSON PYROTECHEM LIMITED *p* 576
50 CHAUNCEY AVE, ETOBICOKE, ON, M8Z 2Z4
(416) 233-3934 *SIC* 5087

ROBERTSON, SAMUEL TECHNICAL SECONDARY SCHOOL *p* 230
See SCHOOL DISTRICT NO 42 (MAPLE RIDGE-PITT MEADOWS)

ROBIC, S.E.N.C.R.L. *p* 1208
630 BOUL RENE-LEVESQUE O 20E ETAGE, MONTREAL, QC, H3B 1S6
(514) 987-6242 *SIC* 8111

ROBIE & KEMPT SERVICES LIMITED *p* 456
3630 KEMPT RD, HALIFAX, NS, B3K 4X8
(902) 832-2103 *SIC* 5812

ROBIN HOOD MULTIFOODS *p* 675
See SMUCKER FOODS OF CANADA CORP

ROBINS PARKING SERVICES LTD *p* 335
1102 FORT ST SUITE 196, VICTORIA, BC, V8V 3K8
(250) 382-4411 *SIC* 1799

ROBINSON BUICK GMC LTD *p* 606
875 WOODLAWN RD W, GUELPH, ON, N1K 1B7
(519) 821-0520 *SIC* 5511

ROBINSON FORGIONE GROUP INC *p* 700
1200 AEROWOOD DR SUITE 50, MISSISSAUGA, ON, L4W 2S7
(905) 602-1965 *SIC* 5087

ROBINSON GROUP LIMITED *p* 973
263 DAVENPORT RD, TORONTO, ON, M5R 1J9
(416) 960-2444 *SIC* 1521

ROBINSON LEASING AND SALES LIMITED *p* 606
875 WOODLAWN RD W, GUELPH, ON, N1K 1B7
(519) 821-0520 *SIC* 5511

ROBINSON LIGHTING LTD *p* 382
995 MILT STEGALL DR, WINNIPEG, MB, R3G 3H7
(204) 784-0099 *SIC* 5719

ROBINSON PRE-WEIGH SERVICES *p* 633
See ROBINSON SOLUTIONS (KINGSTON) INC

ROBINSON SOLUTIONS (CANADA) INC *p* 633
1456 CENTENNIAL DR, KINGSTON, ON, K7P 0K4
(613) 389-7611 *SIC* 6712

ROBINSON SOLUTIONS (KINGSTON) INC *p* 633
1456 CENTENNIAL DR, KINGSTON, ON, K7P 0K4
(613) 634-7552 *SIC* 7389

ROBINSON SOLUTIONS INC *p* 956
390 BAY ST SUITE 1520, TORONTO, ON, M5H 2Y2
(416) 479-7440 *SIC* 8741

ROBINSON SOLUTIONS INC *p* 1035
715106 OXFORD RD SUITE 4, WOODSTOCK, ON, N4S 7V9
(519) 653-1111 *SIC* 8741

ROBINSON TRANSPORT & WAREHOUSE *p* 618
See 452056 ONTARIO LTD

ROBINSON'S INDEPENDENT GROCER *p* 620
See 2043665 ONTARIO LIMITED

ROBINSON'S YOUR INDEPENDENT GROCER *p* 663
1160 BEAVERWOOD DR, MANOTICK, ON, K4M 1A5
(613) 692-2828 *SIC* 5411

ROBINSON, B.A. CO. LTD *p* 385
619 BERRY ST, WINNIPEG, MB, R3H 0S2
(204) 784-0150 *SIC* 5074

ROBINSON, D. CONTRACTING LTD *p* 234
4341 BOBAN DR, NANAIMO, BC, V9T 5V9
SIC 1542

ROBINSON, ERIC C. INC *p* 1038
1804 RTE 115, ALBANY, PE, C0B 1A0
(902) 437-6666 *SIC* 5148

ROBINSON, SHEPPARD, SHAPIRO, S.E.N.C.R.L. *p* 1229
800 RUE DU SQUARE-VICTORIA BUREAU 4600, MONTREAL, QC, H4Z 1H6
(514) 878-2631 *SIC* 8111

ROBITAILLE R & FILS INC *p* 1081
1051 RANG VICTORIA, CLARENCEVILLE, QC, J0J 1B0
SIC 0191

ROBITAILLE R & FILS INC *p* 1158
522 RANG DE VERSAILLES, MONT-SAINT-GREGOIRE, QC, J0J 1K0
(450) 358-1355 *SIC* 0213

ROBLIN ATHLETIC INC *p* 391
1457 CHEVRIER BLVD SUITE A, WINNIPEG, MB, R3T 1Y7

(204) 477-5100   *SIC* 5139
ROBLIN DISTRICT HEALTH CENTRE *p* 355
See PARKLAND REGIONAL HEALTH AUTHORITY INC
ROBLIN FOOTWEAR *p* 391
See ROBLIN ATHLETIC INC
ROBLIN FOREST PRODUCTS LTD *p* 355
83 N HWY, ROBLIN, MB, R0L 1P0
(204) 937-2103   *SIC* 5031
ROBO CAR WASH *p* 216
See OBOR HOLDINGS LTD
ROBOCUTS INC *p* 1226
1625 RUE CHABANEL O BUREAU 729, MONTREAL, QC, H4N 2S7
(514) 388-8001   *SIC* 7389
ROBOTSHOP INC *p* 1153
18005 RUE LAPOINTE BUREAU 305, MIRABEL, QC, J7J 0G2
(450) 420-1446   *SIC* 5084
ROBOVER INC *p* 1265
1595 BOUL WILFRID-HAMEL, QUEBEC, QC, G1N 3Y7
(418) 682-3580   *SIC* 3231
ROBUCK CONTRACTING (1986) LIMITED *p* 651
2326 FANSHAWE PARK RD E, LONDON, ON, N5X 4A2
(519) 455-1108   *SIC* 6712
ROBYN'S TRANSPORTATION & DISTRIBUTION SERVICES LTD *p* 37
6404 BURBANK RD SE, CALGARY, AB, T2H 2C2
(403) 292-9260   *SIC* 4213
ROCCA, LEE FORMING LTD *p* 802
488 MORDEN RD UNIT 1, OAKVILLE, ON, L6K 3W4
(905) 842-2543   *SIC* 1794
ROCH GAUTHIER ET FILS INC *p* 1350
68   RUE SAINTE-CATHERINE, SAINT-POLYCARPE, QC, J0P 1X0
(450) 265-3256   *SIC* 5251
ROCHE CANADA *p* 723
See HOFFMANN-LA ROCHE LIMITED
ROCHE DIAGNOSTICS *p* 1092
See HOFFMANN-LA ROCHE LIMITED
ROCHEBANYAN *p* 596
5310 CANOTEK RD SUITE 10, GLOUCESTER, ON, K1J 9N5
(613) 749-5027   *SIC* 6411
ROCHEFORT, PERRON, BILLETTE INC *p* 1365
1000   BOUL MONSEIGNEUR-LANGLOIS BUREAU   300,   SALABERRY-DE-VALLEYFIELD, QC, J6S 0J7
(514) 395-8703   *SIC* 6411
ROCHELEAU CHEVROLET & OLDS *p* 1088
434 RUE DE LA RIVIERE, COWANSVILLE, QC, J2K 1N5
(450) 263-1541   *SIC* 5571
ROCHELEAU, PAUL INC *p* 1399
760 BOUL PIERRE-ROUX E, VICTORIAVILLE, QC, G6T 1S6
(819) 758-7525   *SIC* 5072
ROCHESTER MIDLAND LIMITED *p* 804
851 PROGRESS CRT SUITE 1, OAKVILLE, ON, L6L 6K1
(905) 847-3000   *SIC* 2899
ROCHESTER RESOURCES LTD *p* 316
1090 W GEORGIA ST SUITE 1305, VANCOUVER, BC, V6E 3V7
(604) 685-9316   *SIC* 1081
ROCHLING ENGINEERING PLASTICS LTD *p* 808
21   TIDEMAN DR, ORANGEVILLE, ON, L9W 3K3
(519) 941-5300   *SIC* 3083
ROCHON BUILDING CORPORATION *p* 993
74 INDUSTRY ST, TORONTO, ON, M6M 4L7
(416) 638-6666   *SIC* 1542
ROCHON NATIONAL SERVICE *p* 784
37 KODIAK CRES, NORTH YORK, ON, M3J 3E5

(416) 398-2888   *SIC* 1542
ROCHON NATIONAL SMALL PROJECT DIV OF *p* 993
See ROCHON BUILDING CORPORATION
ROCK COUNTRY CHEVROLET BUICK GMC LTD *p* 360
121 NELSON RD, THOMPSON, MB, R8N 0B7
(204) 778-7081   *SIC* 5511
ROCK GLEN CO-OPERATIVE ASSOCIATION LIMITED, THE *p* 1423
150 HWY 2 S, ROCKGLEN, SK, S0H 3R0
(306) 476-2210   *SIC* 5171
ROCK LAKE COLONY *p* 80
See ROCK LAKE HUTTERIAN BRETHREN
ROCK LAKE HEALTH DISTRICT FOUNDATION INC *p* 354
115 BROWN ST APT 27, PILOT MOUND, MB, R0G 1P0
(204) 825-2246   *SIC* 8361
ROCK LAKE HUTTERIAN BRETHREN *p* 80
GD STN MAIN, COALDALE, AB, T1M 1K8
(403) 345-3892   *SIC* 0191
ROCK LAKE PERSONAL CARE HOME *p* 354
See ROCK LAKE HEALTH DISTRICT FOUNDATION INC
ROCK OF AGES CANADA INC *p* 1378
4 RUE ROCK OF AGES, STANSTEAD, QC, J0B 3E2
(819) 876-2745   *SIC* 3281
ROCK SOLID SUPPLY *p* 485
See 1569243 ONTARIO INC
ROCK THE BYWARD MARKET CORPORATION *p* 821
73 YORK ST, OTTAWA, ON, K1N 5T2
(613) 241-2442   *SIC* 5812
ROCKBRUNE BROTHERS LIMITED *p* 474
725 FINLEY AVE, AJAX, ON, L1S 3T1
(905) 683-4321   *SIC* 4214
ROCKHAVEN RESOURCES LTD *p* 300
510 HASTINGS ST W SUITE 1016, VANCOUVER, BC, V6B 1L8
(604) 688-2568   *SIC* 1041
ROCKHILL APARTMENTS *p* 1219
See PLACEMENTS ROCKHILL LTEE, LES
ROCKLAND FLOORING *p* 1013
See MILNER-RIGSBY CO. LIMITED, THE
ROCKLAND HELP CENTRE *p* 857
2815 CHAMBERLAND ST, ROCKLAND, ON, K4K 1M7
(613) 446-7594   *SIC* 8399
ROCKMAN PSYCHOLOGY PROFESSIONAL CORPORATION *p* 905
7191 YONGE ST SUITE 801, THORNHILL, ON, L3T 0C4
(416) 602-3230   *SIC* 8049
ROCKPORT BOAT LINE (1994) LIMITED *p* 857
23 FRONT ST, ROCKPORT, ON, K0E 1V0
(613) 659-3402   *SIC* 4489
ROCKPORT CANADA *p* 1026
See ADIDAS CANADA LIMITED
ROCKPORT HOMES LIMITED *p* 780
170 THE DONWAY W SUITE 307, NORTH YORK, ON, M3C 2G3
(416) 444-7391   *SIC* 1522
ROCKPORT HUTTERIAN BRETHREN CORPORATION *p* 145
GD, MAGRATH, AB, T0K 1J0
(403) 758-3077   *SIC* 0191
ROCKSHIELD ENGINEERED WOOD PRODUCTS *p* 546
See NORBORD INDUSTRIES INC
ROCKTENN *p* 1124
See WESTROCK COMPANY OF CANADA CORP
ROCKTENN MERCHANDISING DISPLAY, DIV OF *p* 576
See WESTROCK COMPANY OF CANADA

CORP
ROCKWELL AUTOMATION CANADA CONTROL SYSTEMS *p* 534
135 DUNDAS ST, CAMBRIDGE, ON, N1R 5N9
(519) 623-1810   *SIC* 3625
ROCKWELL AUTOMATION CANADA CONTROL SYSTEMS *p* 534
12 RAGLIN PL, CAMBRIDGE, ON, N1R 7J2
(519) 740-5500   *SIC* 3613
ROCKWELL AUTOMATION CANADA INC *p* 534
135 DUNDAS ST N, CAMBRIDGE, ON, N1R 5X1
(519) 623-1810   *SIC* 3625
ROCKWELL AUTOMATION CANADA LTD *p* 1071
9975 RUE DE CHATEAUNEUF BUREAU U, BROSSARD, QC, J4Z 3V6
(450) 445-3353   *SIC* 7372
ROCKWELL SERVICING INC *p* 4
440 HWY 28, ARDMORE, AB, T0A 0B0
(780) 826-6464   *SIC* 1389
ROCKWELL SERVICING INC *p* 58
400 5 AVE SW SUITE 1000, CALGARY, AB, T2P 0L6
(403) 265-6361   *SIC* 1389
ROCKWELL SERVICING INC *p* 149
2105 8 ST, NISKU, AB, T9E 7Z1
(780) 955-7066   *SIC* 1389
ROCKWOOD FOREST NURSERIES *p* 539
See 1254711 ONTARIO LIMITED
ROCKWOOD TERRACE *p* 567
See CORPORATION OF THE COUNTY OF GREY
ROCKWOOD TRANSPORTATION CO. LTD *p* 410
909 ROUTE 495, MUNDLEVILLE, NB, E4W 2M8
(506) 523-9813   *SIC* 1794
ROCKWOOL *p* 684
See ROXUL INC
ROCKY CROSS CONSTRUCTION (CALGARY) LIMITED *p* 31
444 42 AVE SE SUITE 4, CALGARY, AB, T2G 1Y4
SIC 1799
ROCKY CROSS CONSTRUCTION (NORTH) LTD *p* 76
1610 104 AVE NE UNIT 145, CALGARY, AB, T3J 0T5
(403) 252-2550   *SIC* 1771
ROCKY GAS CO-OP LTD *p* 159
4920 43 ST, ROCKY MOUNTAIN HOUSE, AB, T4T 1A5
(403) 845-2766   *SIC* 4923
ROCKY LAKE QUARY, DIV OF *p* 440
See MUNICIPAL ENTERPRISES LIMITED
ROCKY MOUNTAIN CHOCOLATE FACTORY *p* 186
See IMMACULATE CONFECTION LTD
ROCKY MOUNTAIN DEALERSHIPS INC *p* 31
3345 8 ST SE SUITE 301, CALGARY, AB, T2G 3A4
(403) 265-7364   *SIC* 5082
ROCKY MOUNTAIN DEALERSHIPS INC *p* 135
4802 57TH AVE, GRIMSHAW, AB, T0H 1W0
(780) 332-4691   *SIC* 5083
ROCKY MOUNTAIN DEALERSHIPS INC *p* 142
3939 1 AVE S, LETHBRIDGE, AB, T1J 4P8
(403) 327-3154   *SIC* 5082
ROCKY MOUNTAIN DEALERSHIPS INC *p* 160
260180 WRITING CREEK CRES, ROCKY VIEW COUNTY, AB, T4A 0M9
(403) 513-7000   *SIC* 5082
ROCKY MOUNTAIN DODGE CHRYSLER

JEEP LTD *p* 159
4415 42ND AVE, ROCKY MOUNTAIN HOUSE, AB, T4T 1B6
(403) 845-2851   *SIC* 5511
ROCKY MOUNTAIN EQUIPMENT *p* 31
See ROCKY MOUNTAIN DEALERSHIPS INC
ROCKY MOUNTAIN EQUIPMENT *p* 142
See ROCKY MOUNTAIN DEALERSHIPS INC
ROCKY MOUNTAIN EQUIPMENT *p* 160
See ROCKY MOUNTAIN DEALERSHIPS INC
ROCKY MOUNTAIN LIQUOR INC *p* 96
11478 149 ST, EDMONTON, AB, T5M 1W7
(780) 483-8183   *SIC* 5921
ROCKY MOUNTAIN TURF CLUB INC *p* 142
3401 PARKSIDE DR S, LETHBRIDGE, AB, T1J 4R3
(403) 380-1905   *SIC* 7948
ROCKY MOUNTAIN VILLAGE *p* 212
See GOLDEN LIFE MANAGEMENT CORP
ROCKY MOUNTAINEER VACATION *p* 218
See GREAT CANADIAN RAILTOUR COMPANY LTD
ROCKY MOUNTAINEER VACATIONS *p* 326
See GREAT CANADIAN RAILTOUR COMPANY LTD
ROCKY ROAD RECYCLING LTD *p* 353
4154 MCGILLIVRAY BLVD, OAK BLUFF, MB, R4G 0B5
(204) 832-7802   *SIC* 1611
ROCKY SUPPORT SERVICES SOCIETY *p* 159
4940 50 AVE, ROCKY MOUNTAIN HOUSE, AB, T4T 1A8
(403) 845-4080   *SIC* 8399
ROCKY VIEW SCHOOL DIVISION NO. 41, THE *p* 3
2651 CHINOOK WINDS DR SW, AIRDRIE, AB, T4B 0B4
(403) 945-4000   *SIC* 8211
ROCKY WOOD PRESERVERS LTD *p* 159
GD STN MAIN, ROCKY MOUNTAIN HOUSE, AB, T4T 1T1
(403) 845-2212   *SIC* 2421
ROCKY'S HARLEY DAVIDSON *p* 662
See ROCKY'S HARLEY DAVIDSON LTD
ROCKY'S HARLEY DAVIDSON LTD *p* 662
900 WILTON GROVE RD, LONDON, ON, N6N 1C7
(519) 438-1450   *SIC* 5571
ROCOTO LTEE *p* 1079
1540 BOUL DU ROYAUME O BUREAU 4, CHICOUTIMI, QC, G7H 5B1
(418) 549-5574   *SIC* 5511
ROCTEL MANUFACTURING *p* 605
See LINAMAR CORPORATION
ROCTEST LTEE *p* 1322
680 AV BIRCH, SAINT-LAMBERT, QC, J4P 2N3
(450) 465-1113   *SIC* 8711
ROD & JOE'S NO FRILLS *p* 870
See 1576610 ONTARIO LTD
RODA DEACO VALVE INC *p* 121
3230 97 ST NW, EDMONTON, AB, T6N 1K4
(780) 465-4429   *SIC* 3491
RODAIR INTERNATIONAL LTD *p* 742
350 PENDANT DR, MISSISSAUGA, ON, L5T 2W6
(905) 671-4655   *SIC* 4731
RODAN ENERGY SOLUTIONS INC *p* 707
165 MATHESON BLVD E SUITE 6, MISSISSAUGA, ON, L4Z 3K2
(905) 625-9900   *SIC* 5084
RODD MANAGEMENT LIMITED *p* 1038
86 DEWARS LN, CARDIGAN, PE, C0A 1G0
(902) 652-2332   *SIC* 7011
RODD-BRUDENELL RIVER RESORT *p* 1038
See RODD MANAGEMENT LIMITED
RODEO FORD SALES LIMITED *p* 147
1788 SAAMIS DR NW, MEDICINE HAT, AB, T1C 1W7

▲ Public Company   ■ Public Company Family Member   **HQ** Headquarters   **BR** Branch   **SL** Single Location

(403) 529-2777   *SIC* 5511
RODFAM HOLDINGS LIMITED   *p* 1020
2575 AIRPORT RD, WINDSOR, ON, N8W
1Z4
(519) 969-3350   *SIC* 6712
RODI DESIGN INC   *p* 1142
1100   BOUL   MARIE-VICTORIN,
LONGUEUIL, QC, J4G 2H9
(450) 679-7755   *SIC* 2512
RODNEY ENTERPRISES LIMITED   *p* 448
20 RADDALL AVE, DARTMOUTH, NS, B3B
1T2
(902) 468-2601   *SIC* 5199
RODRIGUE METAL LTEE   *p* 1138
1890 1RE RUE, LEVIS, QC, G6W 5M6
(418) 839-0400   *SIC* 3569
ROEVIN TECHNICAL PEOPLE   *p* 959
See ADECCO EMPLOYMENT SERVICES
LIMITED
ROGER BISSON INC   *p* 1309
5450 RUE RAMSAY, SAINT-HUBERT, QC,
J3Y 2S4
(514) 990-2519   *SIC* 1522
ROGER OUIMET & FILS   *p* 1072
See ASSURANCIA GROUPE BROSSEAU
INC
ROGER'S COMMUNICATIONS   *p* 653
See GEDDES ENTERPRISES OF LON-
DON LIMITED
ROGER'S ELECTRIC AND MACHINE *p* 394
See ROGER'S ELECTRIC MOTOR SER-
VICE (1998) LTD
ROGER'S ELECTRIC MOTOR SERVICE
(1998) LTD   *p* 394
1990 CONNOLLY AVE, BATHURST, NB,
E2A 4W7
(506) 548-8711   *SIC* 5084
ROGERS AT & T   *p* 74
See IMAGINE WIRELESS INC
ROGERS AT & T   *p* 1425
See ADVANCED 2000 SYSTEMS INC
ROGERS AT & T UPTOWN   *p* 854
See UPTOWN COMMUNICATION HOUSE
INC
ROGERS AUTHORIZED DEALER   *p* 789
See MOTEYO INC
ROGERS BLUE JAYS BASEBALL PART-
NERSHIP   *p*
983
1   BLUE   JAYS   WAY   SUITE   3200,
TORONTO, ON, M5V 1J1
(416) 341-1000   *SIC* 7941
ROGERS COMMUNICATIONS CANADA
INC   *p* 930
333 BLOOR ST E 9TH FL, TORONTO, ON,
M4W 1G9
(416) 935-7777   *SIC* 4841
ROGERS COMMUNICATIONS CANADA
INC   *p* 930
333 BLOOR ST E FL 8, TORONTO, ON,
M4W 1G9
(800) 485-9745   *SIC* 4813
ROGERS COMMUNICATIONS CANADA
INC   *p* 932
1   MOUNT PLEASANT RD SUITE 115,
TORONTO, ON, M4Y 2Y5
(416) 764-2000   *SIC* 6712
ROGERS COMMUNICATIONS INC   *p* 190
4710 KINGSWAY SUITE 1900, BURNABY,
BC, V5H 4M4
(604) 431-1400   *SIC* 4899
ROGERS COMMUNICATIONS INC   *p* 930
333 BLOOR ST E, TORONTO, ON, M4W
1G9
(416) 935-7777   *SIC* 4899
ROGERS COMMUNICATIONS PARTNERS*p*
930
See ROGERS COMMUNICATIONS INC
ROGERS FOODS LTD   *p* 180
4420 LARKIN CROSS RD, ARMSTRONG,
BC, V0E 1B6
(250) 546-8744   *SIC* 2041
ROGERS INSURANCE LTD   *p* 32
1331 MACLEOD TRL SE SUITE 800, CAL-

GARY, AB, T2G 0K3
(403) 296-2400   *SIC* 6411
ROGERS MEDIA INC   *p* 58
535 7 AVE SW, CALGARY, AB, T2P 0Y4
(403) 250-9797   *SIC* 4832
ROGERS MEDIA INC   *p* 293
2440 ASH ST, VANCOUVER, BC, V5Z 4J6
(604) 872-2557   *SIC* 4832
ROGERS MEDIA INC   *p* 930
333 BLOOR ST E, TORONTO, ON, M4W
1G9
(416) 935-8200   *SIC* 2721
ROGERS SHARED OPERATIONS   *p* 190
See ROGERS COMMUNICATIONS INC
ROGERS SPORTS GROUP INC   *p* 930
333 BLOOR ST E, TORONTO, ON, M4W
1G9
(416) 935-8200   *SIC* 4832
ROGERS SPORTSNET INC   *p* 874
9 CHANNEL NINE CRT, SCARBOROUGH,
ON, M1S 4B5
(416) 764-6000   *SIC* 4833
ROGERS SUGAR INC   *p* 1168
4026 RUE NOTRE-DAME E, MONTREAL,
QC, H1W 2K3
(514) 940-4350   *SIC* 6726
ROGERS SUGAR LTD   *p* 295
See LANTIC INC
ROGERS WEST   *p* 375
See ROGERS WEST GROUP INCORPO-
RATED
ROGERS WEST GROUP INCORPORATED
p 375
201 PORTAGE AVE SUITE 1800, WIN-
NIPEG, MB, R3B 3K6
(204) 800-0202   *SIC* 8741
ROGERS WIRELESS   *p* 271
See CELLCOM WIRELESS INC
ROGERS WIRELESS   *p* 893
See COMPLETE COMMUNICATION SYS-
TEMS INC
ROGERS' CHOCOLATES LTD   *p* 338
4253 COMMERCE CIR, VICTORIA, BC,
V8Z 4M2
(250) 384-7021   *SIC* 2064
ROGERS, JOHN C. SHEET METAL LTD   *p*
1015
2300 FORBES ST, WHITBY, ON, L1N 8M3
(905) 571-2422   *SIC* 1711
ROGUE SPECIALTY TRANSPORT   *p* 745
See ROGUE TRANSPORTATION SER-
VICES INC
ROGUE TRANSPORTATION SERVICES
INC   *p* 745
255 COURTNEYPARK DR W UNIT 102,
MISSISSAUGA, ON, L5W 0A5
(905) 362-9401   *SIC* 4212
ROHDE & LIESENFELD CANADA INC *p* 58
144 4 AVE SW SUITE 1600, CALGARY, AB,
T2P 3N4
(403) 514-6907   *SIC* 4731
ROHIT COMMUNITIES INC   *p* 125
550 91 ST SW, EDMONTON, AB, T6X 0V1
(780) 436-9015   *SIC* 6552
ROHIT DEVELOPMENTS LTD   *p* 116
9636 51 AVE NW, EDMONTON, AB, T6E
6A5
(780) 436-9015   *SIC* 1522
ROHM AND HAAS CANADA LP   *p* 866
2 MANSE RD, SCARBOROUGH, ON, M1E
3T9
(416) 284-4711   *SIC* 2899
ROINS FINANCIAL SERVICES LIMITED   *p*
966
18 YORK ST SUITE 410, TORONTO, ON,
M5J 2T8
(416) 366-7511   *SIC* 6331
ROJAC ENTREPRISES INC   *p* 417
1671   CH   NICHOLAS-DENYS,   SAINTE-
ROSETTE, NB, E8K 3J9
SIC 5031
ROKAN LAMINATING CO LTD   *p* 742
1660 TRINITY DR, MISSISSAUGA, ON, L5T
1L6

(905) 564-7525   *SIC* 7389
ROKE TECHNOLOGIES LTD   *p* 11
1220 28 ST NE UNIT 100, CALGARY, AB,
T2A 6A2
(403) 247-3480   *SIC* 1389
ROKSTAD   *p* 202
See RPC HISTORICAL LIMITED PART-
NERSHIP
ROL LIFT   *p* 508
See BLUE GIANT EQUIPMENT CORPO-
RATION
ROL-LAND FARMS MUSHROOMS INC *p* 3
GD, AIRDRIE, AB, T4B 2A2
(403) 946-4395   *SIC* 0161
ROL-LAND FARMS MUSHROOMS INC   *p*
493
19002   COMMUNICATION   RD   RR   4,
BLENHEIM, ON, N0P 1A0
(519) 676-8125   *SIC* 0182
ROLAN INC   *p* 568
63 UNION ST, ELMIRA, ON, N3B 2Y3
(519) 669-1842   *SIC* 5063
ROLAND & FRERES LIMITEE   *p* 1349
22   RUE   FORTIER,   SAINT-PACOME,   QC,
G0L 3X0
(418) 852-2191   *SIC* 5141
ROLAND BOULANGER & CIE, LTEE*p* 1400
235   RUE   SAINT-LOUIS,   WARWICK,   QC,
J0A 1M0
(819) 358-4100   *SIC* 2431
ROLAND CANADA LTD   *p* 256
5480 PARKWOOD WAY, RICHMOND, BC,
V6V 2M4
(604) 270-6626   *SIC* 5099
ROLAND GRENIER CONSTRUCTION LTEE
p 1050
9150 RUE CLAVEAU, ANJOU, QC, H1J 1Z4
(514) 252-1818   *SIC* 1542
ROLAND'S SEA VEGETABLES   *p* 402
174 HILL RD, GRAND MANAN, NB, E5G
4C4
(506) 662-3468   *SIC* 5149
ROLARK STAINLESS STEEL INC   *p* 1028
71   CONAIR   PKWY,   WOODBRIDGE,   ON,
L4H 0S4
(416) 798-7770   *SIC* 5051
ROLEX CANADA LTD   *p* 927
50 ST CLAIR AVE W, TORONTO, ON, M4V
3B7
(416) 968-1100   *SIC* 5094
ROLF C. HAGEN INC   *p* 1054
20500   AUT TRANSCANADIENNE,   BAIE-
D'URFE, QC, H9X 0A2
(514) 457-0914   *SIC* 5199
ROLF C. HAGEN INC   *p* 1336
2450 AV MARIE-CURIE, SAINT-LAURENT,
QC, H4S 1N1
SIC 5199
ROLIPROJECTS   *p* 58
See ROHDE & LIESENFELD CANADA INC
ROLL PACKAGING TECHNOLOGY   *p* 516
See SONOCO CANADA CORPORATION
ROLL'N OILFIELD INDUSTRIES LTD   *p* 154
5208 53 AVE SUITE 305, RED DEER, AB,
T4N 5K2
(403) 343-1710   *SIC* 6719
ROLLED ALLOYS-CANADA, INC   *p* 726
7111   SYNTEX   DR   SUITE   120,   MISSIS-
SAUGA, ON, L5N 8C3
(905) 363-0277   *SIC* 5051
ROLLING MIX CONCRETE   *p* 37
See ROLLING MIX MANAGEMENT LTD
ROLLING MIX CONCRETE (B.C) LTD *p* 251
105 FOOTHILL BLVD, PRINCE GEORGE,
BC, V2N 2J8
(250) 563-9213   *SIC* 3273
ROLLING MIX CONCRETE (EDMONTON)
LTD   *p* 102
22235 115 AVE NW, EDMONTON, AB, T5S
2N6
(780) 434-3736   *SIC* 3273
ROLLING MIX MANAGEMENT LTD   *p* 37
7209 RAILWAY ST SE, CALGARY, AB, T2H
2V6

(403) 253-6426   *SIC* 3273
ROLLINS MACHINERY LIMITED   *p* 227
21869 56 AVE, LANGLEY, BC, V2Y 2M9
(604) 533-0048   *SIC* 5084
ROLLO BAY HOLDINGS LTD   *p* 1042
677 2 RTE RR 4, SOURIS, PE, C0A 2B0
(902) 687-3333   *SIC* 0134
ROLLOVER PREMIUM PET FOOD LTD   *p*
136
12 11 AVE SE, HIGH RIVER, AB, T1V 1E6
SIC 2047
ROLLS RUFINA LINGERIE   *p* 1244
See 163288 CANADA INC
ROLLS-ROYCE CANADA LIMITEE   *p* 1095
9545 CH COTE-DE-LIESSE BUREAU 100,
DORVAL, QC, H9P 1A5
(514) 636-0964   *SIC* 4581
ROLLS-ROYCE CANADA LIMITEE   *p* 1128
9500 CH DE LA COTE-DE-LIESSE, LA-
CHINE, QC, H8T 1A2
(514) 631-3541   *SIC* 4581
ROLLS-ROYCE CIVIL NUCLEAR CANADA
LTD   *p* 842
678 NEAL DR, PETERBOROUGH, ON, K9J
6X7
(705) 743-2708   *SIC* 8711
ROLLSTAMP MANUFACTURING, DIV OF *p*
555
See MAGNA INTERNATIONAL INC
ROLLY'S WHOLESALE LTD   *p* 410
10 MACNAUGHTON AVE, MONCTON, NB,
E1H 3L9
(506) 859-7110   *SIC* 5194
ROLSTON HOME BUILDING CENTRE   *p*
621
See ROB ROLSTON BUILDING MATERI-
ALS LTD
ROLTEK INTERNATIONAL INC   *p* 576
305 EVANS AVE, ETOBICOKE, ON, M8Z
1K2
(416) 252-1101   *SIC* 7389
ROM GOVERNORS   *p* 976
See ROYAL ONTARIO MUSEUM FOUNDA-
TION, THE
ROMA FENCE LIMITED   *p* 495
10 HOLLAND DR, BOLTON, ON, L7E 1G6
(905) 951-9063   *SIC* 5039
ROMA LUBE LTD   *p* 784
3975 KEELE ST, NORTH YORK, ON, M3J
1P1
(416) 656-4189   *SIC* 5172
ROMA MOULDING INC   *p* 1033
360 HANLAN RD, WOODBRIDGE, ON, L4L
3P6
(905) 850-1500   *SIC* 2499
ROMADOR ENTERPRISES LTD   *p* 96
11348 142 ST NW, EDMONTON, AB, T5M
1T9
(780) 454-3388   *SIC* 5087
ROMAN CATHOLIC ARCHDIOCESE OF
VANCOUVER, THE   *p* 293
4885 SAINT JOHN PAUL II WAY, VANCOU-
VER, BC, V5Z 0G3
(604) 683-0281   *SIC* 8661
ROMAN CATHOLIC DIOCESE OF VICTO-
RIA   *p*
337
See BISHOP OF VICTORIA CORPORA-
TION SOLE
ROMAN CATHOLIC EPISCOPAL CORP OF
THE DIOCESE OF PETERBOROUGH *p* 840
350   HUNTER   ST   W,   PETERBOROUGH,
ON, K9H 2M4
(705) 745-5123   *SIC* 8661
ROMAN CATHOLIC EPISCOPAL CORP OF
THE DIOCESE OF SAULT STE MARIE, IN
ONTARIO CANADA   *p* 900
30 STE. ANNE RD, SUDBURY, ON, P3C
5E1
(705) 674-2727   *SIC* 8661
ROMAN CATHOLIC EPISCOPAL CORPO-
RATION FOR THE DIOCESE OF TORONTO,
IN CANADA   *p* 926
1155 YONGE ST, TORONTO, ON, M4T 1W2

(416) 934-3400   *SIC 8661*
ROMAN CATHOLIC EPISCOPAL CORPORATION FOR THE DIOCESE OF TORONTO, IN CANADA *p 926*
1155 YONGE ST SUITE 603, TORONTO, ON, M4T 1W2
(416) 934-0606   *SIC 8661*
ROMAN CATHOLIC EPISCOPAL CORPORATION OF THE DIOCESE OF LONDON IN ONTARIO, THE *p 655*
1070 WATERLOO ST, LONDON, ON, N6A 3Y2
(519) 433-0658   *SIC 8661*
ROMAN CHEESE PRODUCTS LIMITED *p 760*
7770 CANADIAN DR, NIAGARA FALLS, ON, L2H 0X3
(905) 356-2639   *SIC 5141*
ROMAN DELI LTD *p 887*
87 HANNOVER DR SUITE 3, ST CATHARINES, ON, L2W 1A3
(905) 641-5211   *SIC 5147*
ROMANO'S MACARONI GRILL *p 338*
See SPECTRA GROUP OF GREAT RESTAURANTS INC, THE
ROMANO, DOMENIC PHARMACY INC *p 510*
1 KENNEDY RD S UNIT 1, BRAMPTON, ON, L6W 3C9
(905) 454-4464   *SIC 5912*
ROMARAH INCORPORATED *p 614*
1000 UPPER GAGE AVE SUITE 14, HAMILTON, ON, L8V 4R5
(905) 388-8400   *SIC 5499*
ROMAX VARIETY LIMITED *p 860*
900 WELLINGTON ST, SARNIA, ON, N7T 1J5
(519) 336-6660   *SIC 5331*
ROMCO *p 804*
See ROADWAY OPERATIONS & MAINTENANCE CORPORATION OF ONTARIO INC
ROMCO CORPORATION *p 524*
5575 NORTH SERVICE RD SUITE 401, BURLINGTON, ON, L7L 6M1
(905) 339-3555   *SIC 6712*
ROME LOGISTICS *p 640*
See ROME TRANSPORTATION INC
ROME SALES INC *p 640*
100 CAMPBELL AVE UNIT 2, KITCHENER, ON, N2H 4X8
(519) 883-4105   *SIC 7389*
ROME TRANSPORTATION INC *p 640*
100 CAMPBELL AVE UNIT 2, KITCHENER, ON, N2H 4X8
(519) 883-4105   *SIC 4731*
ROMEO BESSETTE & FILS INC *p 1317*
815 RUE PLANTE, SAINT-JEAN-SUR-RICHELIEU, QC, J3A 1M8
(450) 359-1471   *SIC 6411*
ROMET LIMITED *p 700*
5030 TIMBERLEA BLVD, MISSISSAUGA, ON, L4W 2S5
(905) 624-1591   *SIC 3824*
RON CLARK MOTORS *p 1037*
See 1197243 ONTARIO LTD
RON DITTBERNER LTD *p 195*
1444 ISLAND HWY, CAMPBELL RIVER, BC, V9W 8C9
(250) 286-0122   *SIC 5251*
RON EDWARDS FAMILY YMCA *p 530*
See YMCA OF HAMILTON/BURLINGTON/BRANTFORD
RON HODGSON CHEVROLET BUICK GMC LTD *p 166*
5 GALARNEAU PL, ST. ALBERT, AB, T8N 2Y3
(780) 458-7100   *SIC 5511*
RON'S NO FRILLS *p 493*
See 1520202 ONTARIO LTD
RON'S NO FRILLS *p 758*
See 727432 ONTARIO LIMITED
RON'S NO FRILLS *p 883*
525 WELLAND AVE SUITE 1316, ST CATHARINES, ON, L2M 6P3

(905) 685-4096   *SIC 5411*
RONA *p 232*
See FRASER VALLEY BUILDING SUPPLIES INC
RONA *p 1046*
See RENO-VALLEE INC
RONA *p 1129*
See CADIEUX & ASSOCIES S.E.N.C.
RONA *p 1215*
See QUINCAILLERIE NOTRE-DAME DE ST-HENRI INC
RONA *p 1290*
See MATERIAUX CAMPAGNA (2003) INC
RONA *p 1323*
See OUTILLEURS, S.E.C., L'
RONA *p 1380*
See CENTRE DE RENOVATION TERREBONNE INC
RONA BUILDING CENTRE *p 248*
See POWELL RIVER BUILDING SUPPLY LTD
RONA BUILDING CENTRE *p 353*
See NEWTON ENTERPRISES (1983)
RONA CASHWAY *p 847*
See NORTHUMBERLAND BUILDING MATERIALS LTD
RONA CASHWAY BUILDING CENTRE *p 602*
See FILSINGER, W. & SONS LIMITED
RONA DAGENAIS *p 1352*
See H. DAGENAIS & FILS INC
RONA DEPOT - HULL *p 1107*
See RONA INC
RONA H MATTEAU *p 1368*
See H. MATTEAU ET FILS (1987) INC
RONA HOME & GARDEN *p 9*
See RONA INC
RONA HOME & GARDEN *p 566*
See RONA INC
RONA HOME & GARDEN LONDON NORTH *p 659*
See RONA INC
RONA HOME CENTRE FLEETWOOD *p 282*
See RONA INC
RONA HOME CENTRE FORT MCMURRAY *p 129*
See RONA INC
RONA INC *p 9*
2665 32 ST NE, CALGARY, AB, T1Y 6Z7
(403) 219-5800   *SIC 5211*
RONA INC *p 129*
8408 MANNING AVE, FORT MCMURRAY, AB, T9H 5G2
(780) 743-4666   *SIC 5251*
RONA INC *p 282*
16659 FRASER HWY, SURREY, BC, V4N 0E7
(604) 576-2955   *SIC 5211*
RONA INC *p 367*
775 PANET RD, WINNIPEG, MB, R2K 4C6
(204) 663-7389   *SIC 5211*
RONA INC *p 392*
1530 GAMBLE PL SUITE 453, WINNIPEG, MB, R3T 1N6
SIC 5191
RONA INC *p 566*
52 DUNDAS ST E, DUNDAS, ON, L9H 0C2
(905) 689-8700   *SIC 5072*
RONA INC *p 632*
2342 PRINCESS ST, KINGSTON, ON, K7M 3G4
(613) 531-6225   *SIC 5072*
RONA INC *p 659*
820 BLYTHWOOD RD, LONDON, ON, N6H 5T8
(519) 471-6621   *SIC 5072*
RONA INC *p 1067*
220 CH DU TREMBLAY, BOUCHERVILLE, QC, J4B 8H7
(514) 599-5900   *SIC 5072*
RONA INC *p 1074*
1458 CH DE CHAMBLY, CARIGNAN, QC, J3L 0J4
(450) 658-8774   *SIC 5072*

RONA INC *p 1076*
99 RUE PRINCIPALE, CHATEAUGUAY, QC, J6K 1G2
(450) 692-9992   *SIC 5072*
RONA INC *p 1099*
875 RUE HAINS, DRUMMONDVILLE, QC, J2C 7Y8
SIC 5072
RONA INC *p 1107*
95 RUE ATAWE, GATINEAU, QC, J8Y 6W7
(819) 770-7366   *SIC 5072*
RONA INC *p 1226*
1011 RUE DU MARCHE-CENTRAL, MONTREAL, QC, H4N 3J6
(514) 385-6888   *SIC 5251*
RONA INC *p 1237*
1505 BOUL LE CORBUSIER, MONTREAL, QC, H7S 1Z3
(450) 682-2220   *SIC 5251*
RONA INC *p 1245*
3933 BOUL SAINT-CHARLES, PIERREFONDS, QC, H9H 3C7
(514) 624-2332   *SIC 5072*
RONA INC *p 1262*
999 RUE DU MARAIS, QUEBEC, QC, G1M 3T9
(418) 688-2220   *SIC 5251*
RONA INC *p 1309*
5035 BOUL COUSINEAU, SAINT-HUBERT, QC, J3Y 3K7
(450) 656-4422   *SIC 5211*
RONA INC *p 1352*
180 RUE PRINCIPALE, SAINT-SAUVEUR, QC, J0R 1R0
(450) 227-2627   *SIC 5072*
RONA INC *p 1395*
3010 BOUL DE LA GARE, VAUDREUIL-DORION, QC, J7V 0H1
(450) 455-3067   *SIC 5072*
RONA L'ENTREPOT *p 1245*
See RONA INC
RONA L'ENTREPOT LAVAL *p 1086*
See CORPORATION ALLIANCE DYNAMIQUE
RONA L'ENTREPOT GATINEAU *p 1104*
See INOVACO LTEE
RONA L'ENTREPOT MASCOUCHE *p 1149*
See 9027-0653 QUEBEC INC
RONA LE REGIONAL *p 1083*
See 9067-6628 QUEBEC INC
RONA LESPERANCE *p 1083*
See LESPERANCE, FRANCOIS INC
RONA MARCIL & FRERES *p 1076*
See RONA INC
RONA PRINCE GEORGE *p 250*
See CAPITAL BUILDING SUPPLIES LTD
RONALD D. BAILEY GROCERY LIMITED *p 888*
GD, ST MARYS, ON, N4X 1A6
(519) 284-2631   *SIC 5411*
RONAM CONSTRUCTIONS INC *p 1140*
1085 CH INDUSTRIEL, LEVIS, QC, G7A 1B3
(418) 836-5569   *SIC 1542*
RONCO DISPOSABLE PRODUCTS LTD *p 558*
70 PLANCHET RD, CONCORD, ON, L4K 2C7
(905) 660-6700   *SIC 5099*
RONCO PROTECTIVE PRODUCTS *p 558*
See RONCO DISPOSABLE PRODUCTS LTD
RONDAR INC *p 608*
333 CENTENNIAL PKY N, HAMILTON, ON, L8E 2X6
(905) 561-2808   *SIC 7629*
RONDE, LA *p 1211*
See PARC SIX FLAGS MONTREAL S.E.C.
RONDEAU CHRYSLER JEEP DODGE INC *p 1315*
180 RUE MOREAU, SAINT-JEAN-SUR-RICHELIEU, QC, J2W 2M4
(450) 359-7333   *SIC 5511*
RONKAY MANAGEMENT INC *p 787*

2000 SHEPPARD AVE W SUITE 304, NORTH YORK, ON, M3N 1A2
(416) 740-4158   *SIC 6513*
RONPIEN INC *p 1149*
3131 BOUL DE MASCOUCHE, MASCOUCHE, QC, J7K 3B7
(450) 474-6171   *SIC 5912*
RONSCO INC *p 1088*
75 RUE INDUSTRIELLE, COTEAU-DU-LAC, QC, J0P 1B0
(514) 866-1033   *SIC 5088*
RONSONS SHOE STORES LTD *p 264*
12495 HORSESHOE WAY, RICHMOND, BC, V7A 4X6
(604) 270-9974   *SIC 5661*
RONZONI FOODS CANADA *p 1164*
See CATELLI FOODS CORPORATION
ROOF TILE MANAGEMENT INC *p 742*
360 GIBRALTAR DR, MISSISSAUGA, ON, L5T 2P5
(905) 672-9992   *SIC 1761*
ROOFING STORE, THE *p 275*
See ALL WEATHER PRODUCTS LTD
ROOFMART ALBERTA INC *p 37*
6125 11 ST SE SUITE 250, CALGARY, AB, T2H 2L6
(403) 233-8030   *SIC 5033*
ROOFMART HOLDINGS LIMITED *p 510*
305 RUTHERFORD RD S, BRAMPTON, ON, L6W 3R5
(905) 453-9689   *SIC 5033*
ROOFMART PACIFIC LTD *p 37*
6125 11 ST SE SUITE 250, CALGARY, AB, T2H 2L6
(403) 233-8030   *SIC 5033*
ROOFMART WESTERN LTD *p 37*
6125 11 ST SE SUITE 250, CALGARY, AB, T2H 2L6
(403) 233-8030   *SIC 5033*
ROOM, THE *p 939*
See HUDSON'S BAY COMPANY
ROOSTER ENERGY LTD *p 309*
666 BURRARD ST SUITE 1700, VANCOUVER, BC, V6C 2X8
(604) 574-7558   *SIC 7371*
ROOTER OTTAWA *p 815*
See DRAIN-ALL LTD
ROOTS *p 790*
See DON MICHAEL HOLDINGS INC
ROOTS CANADA *p 988*
See DON MICHAEL HOLDINGS INC
ROOTS CORPORATION *p 988*
1400 CASTLEFIELD AVE SUITE 2, TORONTO, ON, M6B 4N4
(416) 781-3574   *SIC 3143*
ROOTS OF EMPATHY *p 780*
250 FERRAND DR SUITE 1501, NORTH YORK, ON, M3C 3G8
(416) 944-3001   *SIC 8699*
ROOTS ORGANIC INC *p 280*
3585 184 ST, SURREY, BC, V3Z 1B8
(604) 576-2567   *SIC 5148*
ROPACK INC *p 1163*
10801 RUE MIRABEAU, MONTREAL, QC, H1J 1T7
(514) 353-7000   *SIC 2834*
ROPACK PHARMA SOLUTIONS *p 1163*
See ROPACK INC
ROPAK CANADA INC *p 230*
5850 272 ST, LANGLEY, BC, V4W 3Z1
(604) 857-1177   *SIC 3089*
ROPAK CANADA INC *p 466*
29 MEMORIAL CRES, SPRINGHILL, NS, B0M 1X0
(902) 597-3787   *SIC 3089*
ROPAK CANADA INC *p 804*
2240 WYECROFT RD, OAKVILLE, ON, L6L 6M1
(905) 827-9340   *SIC 3089*
ROPAK PACKAGING - NORTHEAST DIVISION *p 466*
See ROPAK CANADA INC
ROS-MAR INC *p 1054*

19500 AV CLARK-GRAHAM, BAIE-D'URFE, QC, H9X 3R8
(514) 694-2178   *SIC* 2752
ROS-MAR LITHO INC   *p* 1054
19500 AV CLARK-GRAHAM, BAIE-D'URFE, QC, H9X 3R8
(514) 694-2178   *SIC* 2752
ROSA FLORA GROWERS LIMITED *p* 567
GD LCD MAIN, DUNNVILLE, ON, N1A 2W9
(905) 774-8044   *SIC* 5992
ROSA FLORA LIMITED   *p* 567
717 DILTZ RD SUITE 2, DUNNVILLE, ON, N1A 2W2
(905) 774-8044   *SIC* 0181
ROSALIE HALL   *p* 872
3020 LAWRENCE AVE E, SCARBOROUGH, ON, M1P 2T7
(416) 438-6660   *SIC* 8399
ROSATI CONSTRUCTION INC   *p* 1026
6555 MALDEN RD, WINDSOR, ON, N9H 1T5
(519) 734-6511   *SIC* 1541
ROSBACK, R A ENTERPRISES LTD *p* 248
1700 BROUGHTON BLVD, PORT MC-NEILL, BC, V0N 2R0
(250) 956-3323   *SIC* 5251
ROSCOE CONSTRUCTION LIMITED *p* 441
5765 HIGHWAY 1, CAMBRIDGE, NS, B0P 1G0
(902) 538-8080   *SIC* 1542
ROSCOE POSTLE ASSOCIATES INC *p* 966
55 UNIVERSITY AVE SUITE 501, TORONTO, ON, M5J 2H7
(416) 947-0907   *SIC* 8999
ROSE BUILDING MAINTENANCE LTD *p* 166
7 ST ANNE ST SUITE 223, ST. ALBERT, AB, T8N 2X4
(780) 459-4146   *SIC* 7349
ROSE CITY FORD SALES LIMITED *p* 1019
6333 TECUMSEH RD E, WINDSOR, ON, N8T 1E7
(519) 948-7800   *SIC* 5511
ROSE CORPORATION, THE   *p* 777
156 DUNCAN MILL RD SUITE 12, NORTH YORK, ON, M3B 3N2
(416) 449-3535   *SIC* 3443
ROSE DRUMMOND   *p* 1097
See ROSE DRUMMOND INC
ROSE DRUMMOND INC   *p* 1097
210 BOUL LEMIRE O, DRUMMONDVILLE, QC, J2B 8A9
(819) 474-3488   *SIC* 5992
ROSE MECHANICAL LTD   *p* 562
18060 GLEN RD, CORNWALL, ON, K6H 5T1
(613) 938-9867   *SIC* 1711
ROSE VALLEY COLONY LTD   *p* 350
GD, GRAYSVILLE, MB, R0G 0T0
(204) 828-3338   *SIC* 0191
ROSE WATER SUPER CLUB   *p* 936
See 1174976 ONTARIO INC
ROSEBURN RANCHES LTD   *p* 136
GD STN MAIN, HIGH RIVER, AB, T1V 1M2
(403) 652-3257   *SIC* 0211
ROSEDALE COLONY   *p* 126
See ROSEDALE HUTTERIAN BRETHREN
ROSEDALE GOLF ASSOCIATION LIMITED, THE   *p* 921
1901 MOUNT PLEASANT RD, TORONTO, ON, M4N 2W3
(416) 485-9321   *SIC* 7997
ROSEDALE GOLF CLUB   *p* 921
See ROSEDALE GOLF ASSOCIATION LIMITED, THE
ROSEDALE HEIGHTS SCHOOL OF THE ARTS   *p* 931
See TORONTO DISTRICT SCHOOL BOARD
ROSEDALE HUTTERIAN BRETHREN *p* 126
GD, ETZIKOM, AB, T0K 0W0
(587) 787-2456   *SIC* 0191
ROSEDALE ON ROBSON SUITE HOTEL (2018) INC   *p* 300

838 HAMILTON ST, VANCOUVER, BC, V6B 6A2
(604) 689-8033   *SIC* 6712
ROSEDALE SEATING INC   *p* 791
920 CALEDONIA RD UNIT 3, NORTH YORK, ON, M6B 3Y1
(647) 348-6666   *SIC* 5021
ROSEDALE TRANSPORT LIMITED *p* 742
6845 INVADER CRES, MISSISSAUGA, ON, L5T 2B7
(905) 670-0057   *SIC* 4212
ROSEHILL AUCTION SERVICE   *p* 151
See OLDS AUCTION MART LTD
ROSEHILL AUCTION SERVICE LTD *p* 151
4613 54 ST, OLDS, AB, T4H 1E9
(403) 556-3655   *SIC* 7389
ROSEMERE HIGH SCHOOL   *p* 1288
See SIR WILFRID LAURIER SCHOOL BOARD
ROSENAU TRANSPORT LTD   *p* 116
5805 98 ST NW, EDMONTON, AB, T6E 3L4
(780) 431-2065   *SIC* 4213
ROSENAU TRANSPORT LTD   *p* 123
3300 76 AVE NW, EDMONTON, AB, T6P 1J4
(780) 431-2877   *SIC* 4213
ROSENAU TRANSPORT LTD   *p* 159
234180 WRANGLER RD, ROCKY VIEW COUNTY, AB, T1X 0K2
(403) 279-4800   *SIC* 4212
ROSENBERG SMITH & PARTNERS LLP *p* 558
2000 STEELES AVE W UNIT 200, CONCORD, ON, L4K 3E9
(905) 660-3800   *SIC* 8721
ROSENBLOOM GROUPE INC   *p* 1327
1225 RUE HODGE, SAINT-LAURENT, QC, H4N 2B5
(514) 748-7711   *SIC* 5113
ROSENDALE FARMS LIMITED   *p* 1007
544 SAWMILL RD, WATERLOO, ON, N2J 4G8
(519) 744-4941   *SIC* 5153
ROSENEATH CAPITAL CORP   *p* 853
91 GRANTON DR, RICHMOND HILL, ON, L4B 2N5
(905) 882-4740   *SIC* 6712
ROSENEATH DIRECT OPERATING CORPORATION   *p*
854
91 GRANTON DR, RICHMOND HILL, ON, L4B 2N5
SIC 5963
ROSETOWN FARMING CO. LTD *p* 1423
GD, ROSETOWN, SK, S0L 2V0
(306) 882-1991   *SIC* 0291
ROSETOWN MAINLINE MOTOR PRODUCTS LIMITED   *p*
1423
505 7 HWY W, ROSETOWN, SK, S0L 2V0
(306) 882-2691   *SIC* 5511
ROSEVIEW FLC ELECTRIC INC *p* 855
51 ROSEVIEW AVE, RICHMOND HILL, ON, L4C 1C6
(647) 667-5618   *SIC* 7371
ROSEWAY HOSPITAL   *p* 465
See NOVA SCOTIA HEALTH AUTHORITY
ROSEWAY MANOR INCORPORATED *p* 465
1604 LAKE RD, SHELBURNE, NS, B0T 1W0
(902) 875-4707   *SIC* 8361
ROSEWOOD HOTEL GEORGIA   *p* 305
See HOTEL GEORGIA (OP) LIMITED PARTNERSHIP
ROSEWOOD MANOR   *p* 266
See RICHMOND INTERMEDIATE CARE SOCIETY
ROSKA DBO INC   *p* 133
9715 115 ST, GRANDE PRAIRIE, AB, T8V 5S4
(780) 532-8347   *SIC* 1389
ROSKI   *p* 1290
See ROSKI COMPOSITES INC
ROSKI COMPOSITES INC   *p* 1290

130 RUE DE L'EGLISE BUREAU 3, ROXTON FALLS, QC, J0H 1E0
(450) 548-5821   *SIC* 5561
ROSS AGRI-SUPPLIES (CAMROSE) INC *p* 78
3838 47 AVE, CAMROSE, AB, T4V 3W8
(780) 672-2529   *SIC* 5171
ROSS AND ANGLIN LIMITEE   *p* 1126
45 BOUL SAINT-JOSEPH, LACHINE, QC, H8S 2K9
(514) 364-4220   *SIC* 1522
ROSS DREY LIMITED   *p* 1015
155 CONSUMERS DR, WHITBY, ON, L1N 1C4
(905) 668-5828   *SIC* 5531
ROSS LAND MUSHROOM FARM LTD *p* 178
3555 ROSS RD, ABBOTSFORD, BC, V4X 1M6
SIC 0182
ROSS MEMORIAL HOSPITAL, THE *p* 646
10 ANGELINE ST N, LINDSAY, ON, K9V 4M8
(705) 324-6111   *SIC* 8062
ROSS MORRISON ELECTRICAL LTD *p* 186
3950 1ST AVE, BURNABY, BC, V5C 3W2
(604) 299-0281   *SIC* 1731
ROSS VENTURES LTD   *p* 401
35 COLTER CRT, FREDERICTON, NB, E3B 1X7
(506) 453-1800   *SIC* 6512
ROSS VIDEO LIMITED   *p* 623
8 JOHN ST, IROQUOIS, ON, K0E 1K0
(613) 652-4886   *SIC* 3663
ROSS VIDEO LIMITED   *p* 750
64 AURIGA DR SUITE 1, NEPEAN, ON, K2E 1B8
(613) 228-0688   *SIC* 3663
ROSS, JOHN AND SONS LIMITED *p* 459
171 CHAIN LAKE DR, HALIFAX, NS, B3S 1B3
(902) 450-5633   *SIC* 5093
ROSS, SANDY WELL SERVICING LTD *p* 1408
1004 9TH AVE W, KINDERSLEY, SK, S0L 1S0
(306) 463-3875   *SIC* 1389
ROSSBOROUGH CANADA   *p* 1005
See OPTA MINERALS INC
ROSSCLAIR CONTRACTORS INC *p* 914
59 COMSTOCK RD SUITE 1, TORONTO, ON, M1L 2G6
(416) 285-0190   *SIC* 1542
ROSSDOWN FARMS LTD   *p* 178
2325 BRADNER RD, ABBOTSFORD, BC, V4X 1E2
(604) 856-6698   *SIC* 0259
ROSSDREY LTD   *p* 1422
2965 GORDON RD SUITE 65, REGINA, SK, S4S 6H7
(306) 585-1355   *SIC* 5531
ROTALEC CANADA INC   *p* 1341
900 RUE MCCAFFREY, SAINT-LAURENT, QC, H4T 2C7
(514) 341-3685   *SIC* 5084
ROTALEC INTERNATIONAL INC *p* 1341
900 RUE MCCAFFREY, SAINT-LAURENT, QC, H4T 2C7
(514) 341-3685   *SIC* 5065
ROTARY CHILDREN'S CENTRE   *p* 1007
See TREATMENT CENTRE OF WATERLOO REGION, THE
ROTARY CLUB OF VANCOUVER *p* 309
475 HOWE ST SUITE 315, VANCOUVER, BC, V6C 2B3
(604) 685-0481   *SIC* 8399
ROTATING ENERGY SERVICES CA CORP *p* 158
39139 HIGHWAY 2A SUITE 4016, RED DEER COUNTY, AB, T4S 2A8
(403) 358-5577   *SIC* 4911
ROTERRA PILING LTD   *p* 2
25420 114 AVE, ACHESON, AB, T7X 6M4
(780) 948-8556   *SIC* 1521
ROTEX SUPPLY INC   *p* 94

14360 123 AVE NW, EDMONTON, AB, T5L 2Y3
(780) 465-0637   *SIC* 5085
ROTHENBERG & ROTHENBERG ANNUITIES LTD   *p*
1402
4420 RUE SAINTE-CATHERINE O, WESTMOUNT, QC, H3Z 1R2
(514) 934-0586   *SIC* 6282
ROTHESAY COLLEGIATE SCHOOL, THE *p* 412
40 COLLEGE HILL RD, ROTHESAY, NB, E2E 5H1
(506) 847-8224   *SIC* 8211
ROTHESAY NETHERWOOD SCHOOL *p* 412
See ROTHESAY COLLEGIATE SCHOOL, THE
ROTHMANS, BENSON & HEDGES INC *p* 777
1500 DON MILLS RD SUITE 900, NORTH YORK, ON, M3B 3L1
(416) 449-5525   *SIC* 2111
ROTHSAY   *p* 468
See DARLING INTERNATIONAL CANADA INC
ROTHSAY   *p* 535
See DARLING INTERNATIONAL CANADA INC
ROTHSAY   *p* 566
See DARLING INTERNATIONAL CANADA INC
ROTHSAY   *p* 745
See DARLING INTERNATIONAL CANADA INC
ROTHSAY   *p* 1356
See DARLING INTERNATIONAL CANADA INC
ROTHSAY RENDERING, DIV OF *p* 366
See MAPLE LEAF FOODS INC
ROTHSCHILD (CANADA) INC   *p* 966
161 BAY ST SUITE 4230, TORONTO, ON, M5J 2S1
(416) 369-9600   *SIC* 6211
ROTISSERIE ROUYN-NORANDA INC *p* 1290
60 AV QUEBEC, ROUYN-NORANDA, QC, J9X 6P9
(819) 797-2151   *SIC* 5812
ROTISSERIE ST HUBERT   *p* 1317
See ROTISSERIES DU HAUT RICHELIEU LTEE, LES
ROTISSERIE ST-HUBERT   *p* 1109
See GESTION RESTO GRANBY INC
ROTISSERIE ST-HUBERT   *p* 1148
See R-MAG 118 INC
ROTISSERIE ST-HUBERT   *p* 1167
See COOPERATIVE DES TRAVAILLEUSES ET TRAVAILLEURS EN RESTAURATION LA DEMOCRATE
ROTISSERIE ST-HUBERT   *p* 1256
See MARTIN, CLAUDE & MARCEL INC
ROTISSERIE ST-HUBERT   *p* 1286
See MOTEL BOULEVARD CARTIER INC
ROTISSERIE ST-HUBERT   *p* 1290
See ROTISSERIE ROUYN-NORANDA INC
ROTISSERIE ST-HUBERT   *p* 1312
See GESTION RESTO ST-HYACINTHE INC
ROTISSERIE ST-HUBERT   *p* 1352
See RESTAURATION MIMAR INC
ROTISSERIE ST-HUBERT   *p* 1398
See RESTAURANT B.C.L. INC
ROTISSERIE ST-HUBERT EXPRESS MONTMAGNY   *p* 1159
See GESTION POMERLEAU PAGE INC
ROTISSERIES AU COQ LTEE, LES *p* 1168
3060 RUE HOCHELAGA, MONTREAL, QC, H1W 1G2
(514) 527-8833   *SIC* 6712
ROTISSERIES DE SHERBROOKE INC, LES *p* 1374
3070 RUE KING O, SHERBROOKE, QC, J1L 1C9
(819) 563-5111   *SIC* 5812
ROTISSERIES DU HAUT RICHELIEU LTEE,

LES p 1317
960 BOUL DU SEMINAIRE N, SAINT-JEAN-SUR-RICHELIEU, QC, J3A 1L2
(450) 348-6876 *SIC* 5812
ROTISSERIES ST-HUBERT p 1103
See 139670 CANADA LTEE
ROTISSERIES ST-HUBERT # 19 p 1342
See COOPERATIVE DES TRAVAILLEURS ET TRAVAILLEUSES PREMIER DEFI LAVAL
ROTISSERIES ST-HUBERT LTEE, LES p 1050
9050 IMP DE L'INVENTION, ANJOU, QC, H1J 3A7
(514) 324-5400 *SIC* 5145
ROTISSERIES ST-HUBERT LTEE, LES p 1067
500 RUE ALBANEL, BOUCHERVILLE, QC, J4B 2Z6
(450) 449-9366 *SIC* 5812
ROTISSERIES ST-HUBERT LTEE, LES p 1071
6325 BOUL TASCHEREAU, BROSSARD, QC, J4Z 1A6
SIC 5812
ROTISSERIES ST-HUBERT LTEE, LES p 1087
2500 BOUL DANIEL-JOHNSON BUREAU 700, COTE SAINT-LUC, QC, H7T 2P6
(450) 435-0674 *SIC* 6794
ROTISSERIES ST-HUBERT LTEE, LES p 1165
6225 RUE SHERBROOKE E, MONTREAL, QC, H1N 1C3
(514) 259-6939 *SIC* 5812
ROTISSERIES ST-HUBERT LTEE, LES p 1208
1180 AV DES CANADIENS-DE-MONTREAL, MONTREAL, QC, H3B 2S2
(514) 866-0500 *SIC* 5812
ROTISSERIES ST-HUBERT LTEE, LES p 1219
5235 CH DE LA COTE-DES-NEIGES, MONTREAL, QC, H3T 1Y1
(514) 342-9495 *SIC* 6794
ROTISSERIES ST-HUBERT, LES p 1394
See COJALY INC
ROTLEC AUTOMATION p 1341
See ROTALEC CANADA INC
ROTO FASCO CANADA INC. p 742
6625 ORDAN DR UNIT 1, MISSISSAUGA, ON, L5T 1X2
(905) 670-8559 *SIC* 3364
ROTO FORM, DIV OF p 555
See MAGNA POWERTRAIN INC
ROTOBEC INC p 1359
200 RUE INDUSTRIELLE BUREAU 383, SAINTE-JUSTINE, QC, G0R 1Y0
(418) 383-3002 *SIC* 3531
ROTOFLEX TOOLING, DIV OF p 719
See 383565 ONTARIO INC
ROTOPRECISION INC p 707
304 WATLINE AVE, MISSISSAUGA, ON, L4Z 1P4
(905) 712-3800 *SIC* 5085
ROTORK CONTROLS (CANADA) LTD p 726
6705 MILLCREEK DR UNIT 3, MISSISSAUGA, ON, L5N 5M4
(905) 363-0313 *SIC* 5085
ROTSAERT DENTAL LABORATORY SERVICES INC p 612
71 EMERALD ST S, HAMILTON, ON, L8N 2V4
(905) 527-1422 *SIC* 8072
ROUGE RIVER FARMS INC p 598
24 GORMLEY INDUSTRIAL AVE, GORMLEY, ON, L0H 1G0
(800) 773-9216 *SIC* 0161
ROUGHLEY INSURANCE BROKERS LTD p 812
1000 SIMCOE ST N SUITE 205, OSHAWA, ON, L1G 4W4
(905) 576-7770 *SIC* 6411
ROUGHRIDER CIVIL INFRASTRUCTURE

LTD p 18
7003 30 ST SE BAY 16, CALGARY, AB, T2C 1N6
(403) 243-1666 *SIC* 1611
ROUILLARD & FRERES INC p 1245
21 RUE GEORGES, PIERREVILLE, QC, J0G 1J0
(450) 568-3510 *SIC* 5411
ROULEMENTS KOYO CANADA p 1056
See KOYO BEARINGS CANADA INC
ROULOTTES A & S LEVESQUE p 1358
See LEVESQUE, A. ET S. (1993) INC
ROULOTTES E. TURMEL INC p 1075
7010 BOUL SAINTE-ANNE, CHATEAU-RICHER, QC, G0A 1N0
(418) 824-3401 *SIC* 5561
ROULOTTES LUPIEN (2000) INC p 1298
2700 RTE 122, SAINT-CYRILLE-DE-WENDOVER, QC, J1Z 1C1
(819) 397-4949 *SIC* 5571
ROULOTTES R. G. GAGNON INC p 1120
175 MONTEE DE SAINT-SULPICE, L'ASSOMPTION, QC, J5W 2T3
(450) 589-5718 *SIC* 5561
ROULOTTES R.G. GAGNON p 1120
See 3320235 CANADA INC
ROULOTTES STE-ANNE INC p 1381
3306 BOUL DES ENTREPRISES, TERREBONNE, QC, J6X 4J8
(450) 477-1803 *SIC* 5561
ROULSTON PHARMACY LTD p 896
211 ONTARIO ST UNIT 1, STRATFORD, ON, N5A 3H3
(519) 271-8600 *SIC* 5912
ROULSTON'S DISCOUNT DRUGS LIMITED p 881
17 NORFOLK ST S, SIMCOE, ON, N3Y 2V8
(519) 426-1731 *SIC* 5912
ROULSTON'S PHARMACY p 881
See ROULSTON'S DISCOUNT DRUGS LIMITED
ROUSSE, RAYMOND INC p 1365
569 RUE ELLEN, SALABERRY-DE-VALLEYFIELD, QC, J6S 0B1
(450) 373-5085 *SIC* 5142
ROUSSEAU CONTROLS INC. p 1128
1475 32E AV, LACHINE, QC, H8T 3J1
(506) 859-8992 *SIC* 5085
ROUSSEAU METAL INC p 1315
105 AV DE GASPE O, SAINT-JEAN-PORT-JOLI, QC, G0R 3G0
(418) 598-3381 *SIC* 3499
ROUSSEAU, MARC LTEE p 1241
520 BOUL CURE-LABELLE, MONTREAL-OUEST, QC, H7V 2T2
(450) 688-1170 *SIC* 5211
ROUSSEL MOTORS p 405
See ROUSSEL TOYOTA
ROUSSEL TOYOTA p 405
323 KING GEORGE HWY, MIRAMICHI, NB, E1V 1L2
(506) 622-1867 *SIC* 5511
ROUTE 1 BIGSTOP p 412
See R & L CONVENIENCE ENTERPRISES INC
ROUTE 97 p 1178
See GROUPE DE TISSUS NINO MARCELLO INC, LE
ROUTE1 INC p 940
8 KING ST E SUITE 600, TORONTO, ON, M5C 1B5
(416) 848-8391 *SIC* 7371
ROVA PRODUCTS CANADA INC p 500
30 AUTOMATIC RD, BRAMPTON, ON, L6S 5N8
(905) 793-1955 *SIC* 5065
ROW, TED p 421
164 CONCEPTION BAY HWY, BAY ROBERTS, NL, A0A 1G0
(709) 786-2310 *SIC* 6531
ROWAN WILLIAMS DAVIES & IRWIN INC p 601
600 SOUTHGATE DR, GUELPH, ON, N1G 4P6

(519) 823-1311 *SIC* 8711
ROWE FARM p 995
See ROWE FARM MEATS LIMITED
ROWE FARM MEATS LIMITED p 995
105 RONCESVALLES AVE, TORONTO, ON, M6R 2K9
(416) 532-3738 *SIC* 5147
ROWE'S CONSTRUCTION LTD p 435
25 STUDNEY DR, HAY RIVER, NT, X0E 0R6
(867) 874-3243 *SIC* 1629
ROWENDA INVESTMENTS LTD p 591
124 HWY 20 E, FONTHILL, ON, L0S 1E6
(905) 892-7906 *SIC* 5812
ROWLAND FARMS p 169
See ROWLAND SEEDS INC
ROWLAND SEEDS INC p 169
6210 64 ST, TABER, AB, T1G 1Z3
(403) 223-8164 *SIC* 0119
ROWMONT HOLDINGS LIMITED p 479
5445 MADAWASKA BLVD, ARNPRIOR, ON, K7S 3H4
(613) 623-7361 *SIC* 5013
ROXBORO EXCAVATION INC p 1095
1620 CROIS NEWMAN, DORVAL, QC, H9P 2R8
(514) 631-1888 *SIC* 1794
ROXBOROUGH BUS LINES LIMITED p 680
17504 DYER RD, MAXVILLE, ON, K0C 1T0
(613) 538-2461 *SIC* 4151
ROXBOROUGH POULTRY p 924
See REUVEN INTERNATIONAL LIMITED
ROXGOLD INC p 956
360 BAY ST SUITE 500, TORONTO, ON, M5H 2V6
(416) 203-6401 *SIC* 1041
ROXON MEDI-TECH LTEE p 1345
9400 RUE PASCAL-GAGNON, SAINT-LEONARD, QC, H1P 1Z7
(514) 326-7780 *SIC* 5047
ROXSON ENTERPRISES LIMITED p 479
80 MCGONIGAL ST W, ARNPRIOR, ON, K7S 1M3
SIC 5812
ROXUL INC p 215
6526 INDUSTRIAL PKWY, GRAND FORKS, BC, V0H 1H0
(250) 442-5253 *SIC* 3296
ROXUL INC p 684
8024 ESQUESING LINE, MILTON, ON, L9T 6W3
(905) 878-8474 *SIC* 3296
ROY & BRETON, INC p 1353
577 RTE DE SAINT-VALLIER, SAINT-VALLIER, QC, G0R 4J0
(418) 833-0047 *SIC* 2521
ROY & BRETON, INC p 1353
577 RTE DE SAINT-VALLIER, SAINT-VALLIER, QC, G0R 4J0
(418) 884-4041 *SIC* 2521
ROY CONSULTANTS p 394
See ROY CONSULTANTS GROUP LTD
ROY CONSULTANTS GROUP LTD p 394
548 KING AVE, BATHURST, NB, E2A 1P7
(506) 546-4484 *SIC* 8711
ROY DESROCHERS LAMBERT S.E.N.C.R.L p 1398
450 BOUL DES BOIS-FRANCS N, VICTORIAVILLE, QC, G6P 1H3
(819) 758-1544 *SIC* 8721
ROY FOSS MOTORS LTD p 906
7200 YONGE ST UNIT 1, THORNHILL, ON, L4J 1V8
(905) 886-2000 *SIC* 5511
ROY FOSS SATURN SAAB OF LEASIDE LTD p 918
957 EGLINTON AVE E, TORONTO, ON, M4G 4B5
SIC 5511
ROY NORTHERN LAND AND EVIRONMENTAL p 126
See ROY NORTHERN LAND SERVICE LTD
ROY NORTHERN LAND SERVICE LTD p

126
10912-100F, FAIRVIEW, AB, T0H 1L0
(780) 835-2682 *SIC* 8748
ROY'S CHEVROLET BUICK GMC INC p 599
4000 COUNTY RD 34, GREEN VALLEY, ON, K0C 1L0
(613) 525-2300 *SIC* 5511
ROY, G.R. CONSTRUCTION LTD p 913
GD LCD MAIN, TIMMINS, ON, P4N 7C4
(705) 266-3585 *SIC* 1541
ROY, ROB TRADING & SAMCO HOLDINGS p 1435
105 71ST ST W, SASKATOON, SK, S7R 1B4
(306) 931-7666 *SIC* 5012
ROY, SPEED & ROSS LTD p 524
5500 NORTH SERVICE RD SUITE 300, BURLINGTON, ON, L7L 6W6
(905) 331-3113 *SIC* 6331
ROYAL & SUN ALLIANCE INSURANCE COMPANY OF CANADA p 65
326 11 AVE SW SUITE 300, CALGARY, AB, T2R 0C5
(403) 233-6000 *SIC* 6331
ROYAL & SUN ALLIANCE INSURANCE COMPANY OF CANADA p 448
50 GARLAND AVE SUITE 101, DARTMOUTH, NS, B3B 0A3
(902) 493-1500 *SIC* 6331
ROYAL & SUN ALLIANCE INSURANCE COMPANY OF CANADA p 715
2225 ERIN MILLS PKY SUITE 1000, MISSISSAUGA, ON, L5K 2S9
(905) 403-2333 *SIC* 6331
ROYAL & SUN ALLIANCE INSURANCE COMPANY OF CANADA p 966
18 YORK ST SUITE 800, TORONTO, ON, M5J 2T8
(416) 366-7511 *SIC* 6331
ROYAL & SUN ALLIANCE INSURANCE COMPANY OF CANADA p 1199
1001 BOUL DE MAISONNEUVE O BUREAU 1004, MONTREAL, QC, H3A 3C8
(514) 844-1116 *SIC* 6411
ROYAL & SUN ALLIANCE INSURANCE COMPANY OF CANADA p 1271
2475 BOUL LAURIER, QUEBEC, QC, G1T 1C4
(418) 622-2040 *SIC* 6411
ROYAL ADHESIVES & SEALANTS CANADA LTD p 587
266 HUMBERLINE DR, ETOBICOKE, ON, M9W 5X1
(416) 679-5676 *SIC* 2899
ROYAL ALEXANDRA HOSPITAL p 85
See ALBERTA HEALTH SERVICES
ROYAL ALEXANDRA THEATRE p 982
See MIRVISH, ED ENTERPRISES LIMITED
ROYAL AND MCPHERSON THEATRES SOCIETY p 337
1005 BROAD ST UNIT 302, VICTORIA, BC, V8W 2A1
(250) 361-0800 *SIC* 6512
ROYAL ARCH MASONIC HOME AND SENIORS APARTMENTS p 288
See ROYAL ARCH MASONIC HOMES SOCIETY
ROYAL ARCH MASONIC HOMES SOCIETY p 288
7850 CHAMPLAIN CRES SUITE 252, VANCOUVER, BC, V5S 4C7
(604) 437-7343 *SIC* 8051
ROYAL AUTOMOTIVE GROUP LTD p 1033
30 AVIVA PARK DR, WOODBRIDGE, ON, L4L 9C7
(416) 749-0314 *SIC* 3714
ROYAL BANK HOLDING INC p 966
200 BAY ST 9TH FLOOR, TORONTO, ON, M5J 2J5
(416) 974-7493 *SIC* 6211
ROYAL BANK OF CANADA p 572
3250 BLOOR ST W SUITE 800, ETOBI-

COKE, ON, M8X 2X9
SIC 6159

ROYAL BANK OF CANADA p 966
200 BAY ST, TORONTO, ON, M5J 2J5
(416) 974-3940   SIC 6021

ROYAL BANK OF CANADA p 966
88 QUEENS QUAY W SUITE 300,
TORONTO, ON, M5J 0B8
(416) 955-2777   SIC 6021

ROYAL BUILDING PRODUCTS p 1028
See ROYAL GROUP, INC

**ROYAL CANADIAN AIR FORCE ASSOCIA-
TION** p
860
415 EXMOUTH ST, SARNIA, ON, N7T 8A4
(519) 344-8050   SIC 8641

ROYAL CANADIAN GOLF ASSOCIATION p
806
1333 DORVAL DR UNIT 1, OAKVILLE, ON,
L6M 4X6
(905) 849-9700   SIC 8621

**ROYAL CANADIAN LEGION ONTARIO
COMMAND** p 865
See ROYAL CANADIAN LEGION ONTARIO
COMMAND,THE

**ROYAL CANADIAN LEGION ONTARIO
COMMAND,THE** p 865
45 LAWSON RD, SCARBOROUGH, ON,
M1C 2J1
(416) 281-2992   SIC 8641

ROYAL CANADIAN LEGION, THE p 479
49 DANIEL ST N, ARNPRIOR, ON, K7S 2K6
(613) 623-4722   SIC 8641

ROYAL CANADIAN MINT p 366
520 LAGIMODIERE BLVD, WINNIPEG, MB,
R2J 3E7
(204) 983-6400   SIC 5094

ROYAL CANADIAN MINT p 815
320 SUSSEX DR, OTTAWA, ON, K1A 0G8
(613) 993-8990   SIC 5094

ROYAL CANADIAN SECURITIES LIMITED p
379
240 GRAHAM AVE SUITE 800, WINNIPEG,
MB, R3C 0J7
(204) 947-2835   SIC 5541

ROYAL CANADIAN STEEL INC p 506
70 TITAN RD, BRAMPTON, ON, L6T 4A3
(905) 454-7274   SIC 5051

ROYAL CANADIAN YACHT CLUB, THE p
973
141 ST. GEORGE ST SUITE 218,
TORONTO, ON, M5R 2L8
(416) 967-7245   SIC 7997

ROYAL CANIN CANADA COMPANY p 849
See ROYAL CANIN CANADA INC

ROYAL CANIN CANADA INC p 849
100 BEIBER RD, PUSLINCH, ON, N0B 2J0
(519) 780-6700   SIC 5149

ROYAL CHEVROLET-CADILLAC INC p 808
1 MONORA PARK DR, ORANGEVILLE,
ON, L9W 0E1
(519) 941-0420   SIC 5511

ROYAL CITY AMBULANCE SERVICE LTD p
606
355 ELMIRA RD N SUITE 134, GUELPH,
ON, N1K 1S5
(519) 824-1510   SIC 4119

ROYAL CITY CHARTER COACH LINES LTD
p 210
8730 RIVER RD, DELTA, BC, V4G 1B5
(604) 940-1707   SIC 6712

ROYAL CITY FIRE SUPPLIES LTD p 237
633 TWELFTH ST, NEW WESTMINSTER,
BC, V3M 4J5
(604) 522-4240   SIC 5099

ROYAL CITY MANOR LTD p 236
77 JAMIESON CRT, NEW WESTMINSTER,
BC, V3L 5P8
(604) 522-6699   SIC 8361

ROYAL CITY MOTORS LTD p 606
635 WOODLAWN RD W, GUELPH, ON,
N1K 1E9
(519) 837-3431   SIC 5511

ROYAL CITY RECORDS NOW p 183

3430 BRIGHTON AVE SUITE 201A, BURN-
ABY, BC, V5A 3H4
SIC 5192

ROYAL CITY SOCCER CLUB p 531
336 PLAINS RD E SUITE 2, BURLINGTON,
ON, L7T 2C8
(905) 639-4178   SIC 7941

ROYAL CITY TAXI LTD p 237
436 ROUSSEAU ST, NEW WESTMINSTER,
BC, V3L 3R3
(604) 526-6666   SIC 4212

ROYAL COACHMAN INN LTD, THE p 195
84 DOGWOOD ST, CAMPBELL RIVER, BC,
V9W 2X7
(250) 286-0231   SIC 5921

**ROYAL COLLEGE OF DENTAL SURGEONS
OF ONTARIO** p 930
6 CRESCENT RD, TORONTO, ON, M4W
1T1
(416) 961-6555   SIC 8621

**ROYAL COLLEGE OF PHYSICIANS AND
SURGEONS OF CANADA, THE** p 826
774 ECHO DR, OTTAWA, ON, K1S 5N8
(613) 730-8177   SIC 8621

ROYAL CONTAINERS LTD p 506
80 MIDAIR CRT, BRAMPTON, ON, L6T 5V1
(905) 789-8787   SIC 2653

ROYAL DIGITAL p 558
See ROYAL ENVELOPE LTD

ROYAL DISTRIBUTING p 606
See ROYAL J & M DISTRIBUTING INC

ROYAL DOORS LTD p 409
105 HENRI DUNANT ST, MONCTON, NB,
E1E 1E4
(506) 857-4075   SIC 5211

ROYAL ENVELOPE LTD p 558
111 JACOB KEFFER PKY, CONCORD, ON,
L4K 4V1
(905) 879-0000   SIC 2677

ROYAL FORD p 1438
See ROYAL FORD LINCOLN SALES LTD

ROYAL FORD LINCOLN SALES LTD p 1438
117 BROADWAY ST E, YORKTON, SK, S3N
3B2
(306) 782-2261   SIC 5511

ROYAL GARAGE LIMITED, THE p 426
709 TOPSAIL RD, MOUNT PEARL, NL, A1N
3N4
(709) 748-2110   SIC 5511

ROYAL GARDENS LIMITED p 411
30 ROYAL GARDENS RD, PENOBSQUIS,
NB, E4G 2C5
(506) 433-2030   SIC 5193

ROYAL GLENORA CLUB p 90
11160 RIVER VALLEY RD, EDMONTON,
AB, T5J 2G7
(780) 482-2371   SIC 7997

ROYAL GLENORA PRO SHOP p 90
See ROYAL GLENORA CLUB

ROYAL GROUP TAPESTRY REALTY p 278
See TAPESTRY REALTY LTD

ROYAL GROUP, INC p 1028
10 ROYBRIDGE GATE SUITE 201, WOOD-
BRIDGE, ON, L4H 3M8
(905) 264-1660   SIC 3089

ROYAL GROUP, INC p 1028
71 ROYAL GROUP CRES SUITE 2, WOOD-
BRIDGE, ON, L4H 1X9
(905) 264-5500   SIC 5039

ROYAL GROUP, INC p 1028
30 ROYAL GROUP CRES, WOODBRIDGE,
ON, L4H 1X9
(905) 264-0701   SIC 2519

ROYAL GROUP, INC p 1028
111 ROYAL GROUP CRES, WOOD-
BRIDGE, ON, L4H 1X9
SIC 3089

ROYAL GROUP, INC p 1028
100 ROYAL GROUP CRES UNIT B, WOOD-
BRIDGE, ON, L4H 1X9
(905) 264-2989   SIC 3448

ROYAL GROUP, INC p 1033
131 REGALCREST CRT, WOODBRIDGE,
ON, L4L 8P3

(905) 652-0461   SIC 3084

ROYAL GROUP, INC p 1101
3035 BOUL LE CORBUSIER BUREAU 7,
FABREVILLE, QC, H7L 4C3
(450) 687-5115   SIC 3431

ROYAL GROUP, INC p 1323
1401 RUE BELLEVUE, SAINT-LAMBERT-
DE-LAUZON, QC, G0S 2W0
SIC 3089

ROYAL GROUP, INC p 1380
1085 RUE DES CHEMINOTS BUREAU 10,
TERREBONNE, QC, J6W 0A1
(450) 668-5549   SIC 5031

ROYAL HOMES LIMITED p 1026
213 ARTHUR ST, WINGHAM, ON, N0G
2W0
(519) 357-2606   SIC 2452

ROYAL HOST INC p 41
1804 CROWCHILD TRAIL NW, CALGARY,
AB, T2M 3Y7
(403) 289-0241   SIC 7011

ROYAL HOST INC p 454
1809 BARRINGTON ST SUITE 1108, HALI-
FAX, NS, B3J 3K8 .
(902) 470-4500   SIC 7011

ROYAL HOST INC p 587
925 DIXON RD, ETOBICOKE, ON, M9W
1J8
(416) 674-2222   SIC 7011

ROYAL HOST INC p 801
590 ARGUS RD, OAKVILLE, ON, L6J 3J3
(905) 842-5000   SIC 7011

ROYAL INN NORTH CALGARY p 25
See REMAI HOLDINGS LTD

**ROYAL INSTITUTE FOR ADVANCEMENT
OF LEARNING MCGILL** p 1199
817 RUE SHERBROOKE O BUREAU 382,
MONTREAL, QC, H3A 0C3
(514) 398-7251   SIC 8221

**ROYAL INSTITUTE FOR ADVANCEMENT
OF LEARNING MCGILL** p 1199
845 SHERBROOKE STREET WEST, MON-
TREAL, QC, H3A 0G4
(514) 398-8120   SIC 8221

**ROYAL INTERNATIONAL COLLECTABLES
INC** p 924
2161 YONGE ST SUITE 608, TORONTO,
ON, M4S 3A6
SIC 5094

**ROYAL IRAQI HEAVY EQUIPMENT COR-
PORATION, THE** p
488
55 BROWNING TRAIL, BARRIE, ON, L4N
5A5
(705) 241-0082   SIC 7353

ROYAL J & M DISTRIBUTING INC p 606
925 WOODLAWN RD W, GUELPH, ON,
N1K 1B7
(519) 822-7081   SIC 5699

ROYAL JUBILEE HOSPITAL AUXILIARY p
333
1952 BAY ST, VICTORIA, BC, V8R 1J8
(250) 370-8496   SIC 8742

ROYAL LASER MFG INC p 587
25 CLAIREVILLE DR, ETOBICOKE, ON,
M9W 5Z7
(416) 679-9474   SIC 3499

ROYAL LE PAGE MAXIMUM REALTY p
1033
7694 ISLINGTON AVE, WOODBRIDGE,
ON, L4L 1W3
(416) 324-2626   SIC 6531

ROYAL LE PAGE REAL ESTATE p 992
905 KING ST W, TORONTO, ON, M6K 3G9
(416) 271-1569   SIC 6531

ROYAL LE PAGE SUPREME p 990
1245 DUPONT ST, TORONTO, ON, M6H
2A6
(416) 543-0979   SIC 6531

ROYAL LEGAL SOLUTIONS P.C. INC p 943
1 YONGE ST SUITE 1801, TORONTO, ON,
M5E 1W7
SIC 8111

ROYAL LEPAGE p 222

See RLK REALTY LTD

ROYAL LEPAGE p 478
See STATE REALTY LIMITED

ROYAL LEPAGE p 709
See FS REALTY CENTRE CORPORATION

ROYAL LEPAGE p 894
See STATE REALTY LIMITED

ROYAL LEPAGE p 916
See ROYAL LEPAGE REAL ESTATE SER-
VICES LTD

ROYAL LEPAGE p 1032
See MAXIMUM REALTY CORPORATION

ROYAL LEPAGE p 1256
See COURTIERS INTER-QUEBEC INC,
LES

ROYAL LEPAGE (1598) p 1155
1301 CH CANORA, MONT-ROYAL, QC,
H3P 2J5
(514) 735-2281   SIC 6531

ROYAL LEPAGE ACTION REALTY p 515
See ACTION REALTY LTD

ROYAL LEPAGE ADVANCE p 194
See ADVANCE REALTY LTD

ROYAL LEPAGE ATLANTIC p 413
See 501420 NB INC

ROYAL LEPAGE COMMUNITY REALTY LTD
p 147
1202 SOUTHVIEW DR SE, MEDICINE HAT,
AB, T1B 4B6
(403) 528-4222   SIC 6531

ROYAL LEPAGE COMPLETE REALTY p 476
7 VICTORIA ST W, ALLISTON, ON, L9R
1S9
(705) 435-3000   SIC 6531

**ROYAL LEPAGE CROWN REALTY SER-
VICES INC** p
534
471 HESPELER RD UNIT 4, CAMBRIDGE,
ON, N1R 6J2
(519) 740-6400   SIC 6531

ROYAL LEPAGE DOWNTOWN p 331
See DOWNTOWN REALTY LTD

ROYAL LEPAGE DYNAMIC p 388
See 4395612 MANITOBA LTD

ROYAL LEPAGE ESTATE REALTY p 917
See ESTATE REALTY LTD

ROYAL LEPAGE FACILITY p 652
955 HIGHBURY AVE N, LONDON, ON, N5Y
1A3
(519) 659-9058   SIC 8741

ROYAL LEPAGE FIRST CONTACT REALTY
p 486
See FARIS TEAM CORP, THE

ROYAL LEPAGE FIRST CONTACT REALTY
p 487
See FIRST CONTACT REALTY LTD

ROYAL LEPAGE FOOTHILLS p 74
See Z69115 ALBERTA LTD

ROYAL LEPAGE GALE REAL ESTATE p
663
5510 MANOTICK MAIN ST, MANOTICK,
ON, K4M 0A1
(613) 692-2555   SIC 6531

ROYAL LEPAGE GRAND VALLEY REALTY
p 641
See GRAND VALLEY REALTY INC

ROYAL LEPAGE HAUT-RICHELIEU p 1318
See IMMEUBLES RICHELIEU N. REON
INC, LES

ROYAL LEPAGE IN THE COMOX VALLEY p
203
See SOUP BONE ENTERPRISES INC

ROYAL LEPAGE KAMLOOPS REALTY p
217
322 SEYMOUR ST, KAMLOOPS, BC, V2C
2G2
(250) 374-3022   SIC 6531

**ROYAL LEPAGE KAWARTHA LAKES RE-
ALTY INC** p
646
261 KENT ST W, LINDSAY, ON, K9V 2Z3
(705) 878-3737   SIC 6531

ROYAL LEPAGE LIMITED p 572
3031 BLOOR ST W, ETOBICOKE, ON, M8X

1C5
(416) 236-1871   *SIC* 6531
ROYAL LEPAGE LIMITED   *p* 713
1654 LAKESHORE RD E, MISSISSAUGA,
ON, L5G 1E2
(905) 278-5273   *SIC* 6531
ROYAL LEPAGE LIMITED   *p* 719
5055 PLANTATION PL UNIT 1, MISSIS-
SAUGA, ON, L5M 6J3
(905) 828-1122   *SIC* 6531
ROYAL LEPAGE LIMITED   *p* 780
39 WYNFORD DR, NORTH YORK, ON,
M3C 3K5
(416) 510-5800   *SIC* 6531
ROYAL LEPAGE LIMITED   *p* 801
326 LAKESHORE RD E, OAKVILLE, ON,
L6J 1J6
(905) 845-4267   *SIC* 6531
ROYAL LEPAGE LIMITED   *p* 811
250 CENTRUM BLVD SUITE 107, OR-
LEANS, ON, K1E 3J1
(613) 830-3350   *SIC* 6531
ROYAL LEPAGE LIMITED   *p* 921
3080 YONGE ST SUITE 2060, TORONTO,
ON, M4N 3N1
(416) 487-4311   *SIC* 6531
ROYAL LEPAGE LIMITED   *p* 924
477 MOUNT PLEASANT RD, TORONTO,
ON, M4S 2L9
(416) 489-2121   *SIC* 6531
ROYAL LEPAGE LIMITED   *p* 924
477 MOUNT PLEASANT RD UNIT 210,
TORONTO, ON, M4S 2L9
(416) 489-2121   *SIC* 7389
**ROYAL LEPAGE MARTIN-LIBERTY RE-
ALTY LTD**   *p*
347
920 VICTORIA AVE, BRANDON, MB, R7A
1A7
SIC 6531
**ROYAL LEPAGE NIAGARA REAL ESTATE
CENTRE**   *p* 886
33 MAYWOOD AVE, ST CATHARINES, ON,
L2R 1C5
(905) 688-4561   *SIC* 6531
**ROYAL LEPAGE NORTH HERITAGE RE-
ALTY**   *p*
898
See NORTH HERITAGE REALTY INC
ROYAL LEPAGE NORTHSTAR REALTY   *p*
279
See NORTHSTAR REALTY LTD
ROYAL LEPAGE PERFORMANCE REALTY
p 811
See ROYAL LEPAGE LIMITED
ROYAL LEPAGE PRIME REAL ESTATE   *p*
364
1877 HENDERSON HWY, WINNIPEG, MB,
R2G 1P4
(204) 989-7900   *SIC* 6531
ROYAL LEPAGE PRINCE GEORGE   *p* 251
3166 MASSEY DR, PRINCE GEORGE, BC,
V2N 2S9
(250) 564-4488   *SIC* 6531
ROYAL LEPAGE PROALLIANCE REALTY *p*
491
*See PROALLIANCE REALTY CORPORA-
TION*
ROYAL LEPAGE PROALLIANCE REALTY *p*
545
1111 ELGIN ST W, COBOURG, ON, K9A
5H7
(905) 377-8888   *SIC* 6531
ROYAL LEPAGE REAL ESTATE SERVICES
p 713
See ROYAL LEPAGE LIMITED
**ROYAL LEPAGE REAL ESTATE SERVICES
LTD**   *p* 719
5055 PLANTATION PL UNIT 1, MISSIS-
SAUGA, ON, L5M 6J3
(905) 828-1122   *SIC* 6531
**ROYAL LEPAGE REAL ESTATE SERVICES
LTD**   *p* 819
1500 BANK ST SUITE 201, OTTAWA, ON,

K1H 7Z2
(613) 733-9100   *SIC* 6531
**ROYAL LEPAGE REAL ESTATE SERVICES
LTD**   *p* 826
165 PRETORIA AVE, OTTAWA, ON, K1S
1X1
(613) 238-2801   *SIC* 6531
**ROYAL LEPAGE REAL ESTATE SERVICES
LTD**   *p* 916
39 WYNFORD DR 3 FL, TORONTO, ON,
M3C 3K5
(416) 510-5810   *SIC* 6531
**ROYAL LEPAGE REAL ESTATE SERVICES
LTD**   *p* 927
55 ST CLAIR AVE W, TORONTO, ON, M4V
2Y7
(416) 921-1112   *SIC* 6531
ROYAL LEPAGE REALTY PLUS LTD   *p* 715
2575 DUNDAS ST W SUITE 3, MISSIS-
SAUGA, ON, L5K 2M6
(905) 828-6550   *SIC* 6531
ROYAL LEPAGE REGINA REALTY   *p* 1422
See REGINA REALTY SALES LTD
**ROYAL LEPAGE RESIDENTIAL REAL ES-
TATE SERVICES**   *p*
801
See ROYAL LEPAGE LIMITED
ROYAL LEPAGE ROYAL CITY REALTY LTD
p 590
840 TOWER ST S, FERGUS, ON, N1M 2R3
(519) 843-1365   *SIC* 6531
ROYAL LEPAGE SCHARF REALTY   *p* 1009
See SCHARF REALTY LTD
ROYAL LEPAGE SHOWCASE PLUS   *p* 248
See JON WOOD
ROYAL LEPAGE SIGNATURE REALTY   *p*
780
49 THE DONWAY W, NORTH YORK, ON,
M3C 3M9
(416) 443-0300   *SIC* 6531
ROYAL LEPAGE STERLING REALTY *p* 248
220 BREW ST SUITE 801, PORT MOODY,
BC, V3H 0H6
(604) 421-1010   *SIC* 6531
ROYAL LEPAGE TEAM   *p* 625
484 HAZELDEAN RD SUITE 1, KANATA,
ON, K2L 1V4
(613) 867-2508   *SIC* 6531
ROYAL LEPAGE TEAM REALTY   *p* 829
1335 CARLING AVE SUITE 200, OTTAWA,
ON, K1Z 8N8
(613) 216-1198   *SIC* 6531
ROYAL LEPAGE TOP PRODUCERS   *p* 368
1549 ST MARY'S RD SUITE 6, WINNIPEG,
MB, R2M 5G9
(204) 989-6900   *SIC* 6531
ROYAL LEPAGE TRILAND REALTY   *p* 651
See TRILAND REALTY LTD
ROYAL LEPAGE TRILAND REALTY   *p* 656
See TRILAND REALTY LTD
ROYAL LEPAGE URBAN REALTY   *p* 920
See URBAN REALTY INC
ROYAL LEPAGE VANTAGE REALTY   *p* 604
See VANTAGE REALTY LTD
ROYAL LEPAGE VILLAGE   *p* 1250
*See IMMEUBLES VILLAGE POINTE-
CLAIRE INC*
ROYAL LEPAGE VILLAGE-DOLLARD   *p*
1091
*See IMMEUBLES VILLAGE D.D.O. INC,
LES*
ROYAL LEPAGE WOLLE REALTY   *p* 636
See WOLLE REALTY INC
**ROYAL LEPAGE YOUR COMMUNITY RE-
ALTY**   *p*
856
See YOUR COMMUNITY REALTY INC
**ROYAL LEPAGE-LOCATIONS WEST RE-
ALTY**   *p*
243
See LOCATIONS WEST REALTY INC
ROYAL LEPAGE-NANAIMO REALTY *p* 234
See NANAIMO REALTY CO LTD
ROYAL LEPAGE-WESTWIN REALTY LTD *p*

217
800 SEYMOUR ST, KAMLOOPS, BC, V2C
2H5
(250) 819-3404   *SIC* 6531
ROYAL LEPAGE/STEVENSON ADVISORS*p*
379
See STEVENSON ADVISORS LTD
ROYAL MAT INC   *p* 1055
132 181E RUE, BEAUCEVILLE, QC, G5X
2S8
(418) 774-3694   *SIC* 3069
ROYAL MAYFAIR GOLF CLUB LTD   *p* 90
9450 GROAT RD NW, EDMONTON, AB,
T5J 2G8
(780) 432-0066   *SIC* 7997
ROYAL NICKEL CORPORATION   *p* 956
141 ADELAIDE ST W SUITE 1608,
TORONTO, ON, M5H 3L5
(416) 363-0649   *SIC* 1061
ROYAL OAK COUNTRY GROCERY   *p* 338
See OAK LANE ENTERPRISES LTD
ROYAL OAK LEXUS   *p* 77
7677 112 AVE NW, CALGARY, AB, T3R 1R8
(403) 261-9977   *SIC* 5511
ROYAL OAK LONG TERM CARE CENTER*p*
633
See CSH ROYAL OAK LTC INC
**ROYAL ONTARIO MUSEUM FOUNDATION,
THE**   *p* 976
100 QUEEN'S PK, TORONTO, ON, M5S
2C6
(416) 586-5660   *SIC* 8699
ROYAL ONTARIO MUSEUM, THE   *p* 976
100 QUEEN'S PK, TORONTO, ON, M5S
2C6
(416) 586-8000   *SIC* 8412
ROYAL OUTDOOR PRODUCTS, DIV OF *p*
1028
See ROYAL GROUP, INC
ROYAL PACIFIC REALTY CORP   *p* 288
3107 KINGSWAY, VANCOUVER, BC, V5R
5J9
(604) 439-0068   *SIC* 6531
ROYAL PACIFIC REALTY GROUP   *p* 288
See ROYAL PACIFIC REALTY CORP
ROYAL PHOTO INC   *p* 1172
2106 BOUL ROSEMONT, MONTREAL, QC,
H2G 1T4
(514) 273-1723   *SIC* 5043
ROYAL ROADS UNIVERSITY   *p* 340
2005 SOOKE RD, VICTORIA, BC, V9B 5Y2
(250) 391-2511   *SIC* 8221
ROYAL SPECIALTY SALES   *p* 873
See D & L SALES LIMITED
ROYAL SPORTS SHOP LTD   *p* 367
650 RALEIGH ST, WINNIPEG, MB, R2K 3Z9
(204) 668-4584   *SIC* 5941
ROYAL ST GEORGE'S COLLEGE   *p* 973
120 HOWLAND AVE, TORONTO, ON, M5R
3B5
(416) 533-9481   *SIC* 8211
ROYAL SUPPLY CHAIN INC   *p* 988
65A WINGOLD AVE, TORONTO, ON, M6B
1P8
(647) 344-8142   *SIC* 4731
ROYAL TERRACE   *p* 836
See SHANTI ENTERPRISES LIMITED
ROYAL TOWERS HOTEL INC   *p* 237
140 SIXTH ST, NEW WESTMINSTER, BC,
V3L 2Z9
(604) 524-4689   *SIC* 7011
**ROYAL TRUST CORPORATION OF
CANADA**   *p* 970
77 KING ST W SUITE 3800, TORONTO,
ON, M5K 2A1
(416) 974-1400   *SIC* 6021
ROYAL VANCOUVER YACHT CLUB   *p* 324
3811 POINT GREY RD, VANCOUVER, BC,
V6R 1B3
(604) 224-1344   *SIC* 7997
ROYAL VICTORIA HOSPITAL   *p* 1198
*See MCGILL UNIVERSITY HEALTH CEN-
TRE*
ROYAL WEST COAST PENINSULA, THE *p*

280
2088 152 ST SUITE 402, SURREY, BC, V4A
9Z4
(604) 538-2033   *SIC* 6513
ROYAL WEST EDMONTON INN LTD   *p* 103
10010 178 ST NW, EDMONTON, AB, T5S
1T3
(780) 484-6000   *SIC* 7011
**ROYAL WINDOW & DOOR PROFILES
PLANT 2**   *p* 1028
See ROYAL GROUP, INC
**ROYAL WINDOW & DOOR PROFILES,
PLANT 10**   *p* 1380
See ROYAL GROUP, INC
ROYAL WINNIPEG BALLET, THE   *p* 379
380 GRAHAM AVE, WINNIPEG, MB, R3C
4K2
(204) 956-0183   *SIC* 7922
ROYAL YORK OPERATIONS LP   *p* 966
100 FRONT ST W, TORONTO, ON, M5J
1E3
(416) 368-2511   *SIC* 7011
ROYALGUARD VINYL CO DIV   *p* 1002
See ROYPLAST LIMITED
ROYALMOUNT PHARMACEUTICALS   *p*
1228
See PHARMASCIENCE INC
ROYALPLAST DOOR SYSTEMS CO *p* 1379
See GROUPE ROYAL INC
ROYCE-AYR CUTTING TOOLS INC   *p* 536
405 SHELDON DR, CAMBRIDGE, ON, N1T
2B7
(519) 623-0580   *SIC* 3541
ROYER DEVELOPMENTS 2015 LTD.   *p* 94
14635 134 AVE NW, EDMONTON, AB, T5L
4S9
(780) 454-9677   *SIC* 1794
ROYMICK INC   *p* 1391
823 3E AV BUREAU 31, VAL-D'OR, QC, J9P
1S8
(819) 824-3645   *SIC* 5912
ROYNAT CAPITAL   *p* 1199
See ROYNAT INC
ROYNAT CAPITAL INC   *p* 956
40 KING ST W, TORONTO, ON, M5H 3Y2
(416) 933-2730   *SIC* 6159
ROYNAT EQUITY PARTNERS   *p* 956
See ROYNAT CAPITAL INC
ROYNAT INC   *p* 1199
1002 RUE SHERBROOKE O BUREAU
1100, MONTREAL, QC, H3A 3L6
(514) 987-4947   *SIC* 6159
ROYPLAST LIMITED   *p* 1002
91 ROYAL GROUP CRT, VAUGHAN, ON,
L4H 1X9
SIC 3089
ROZON INSURANCE BROKERS LTD *p* 643
150 MAIN ST N, LANCASTER, ON, K0C
1N0
(613) 347-7600   *SIC* 6411
RP DEBT OPPORTUNITIES FUND   *p* 973
39 HAZELTON AVE, TORONTO, ON, M5R
2E3
(647) 776-1777   *SIC* 6722
RP INVESTMENT AND ADVISOR LP *p* 973
See RP DEBT OPPORTUNITIES FUND
RPA   *p* 966
See ROSCOE POSTLE ASSOCIATES INC
RPC BPI AGRICULTURE   *p* 107
See AT FILMS INC
RPC HISTORICAL LIMITED PARTNERSHIP
p 202
80 GOLDEN DR, COQUITLAM, BC, V3K
6T1
(604) 553-1810   *SIC* 1796
RPF LTEE   *p* 1366
163 RTE 132 O, SAYABEC, QC, G0J 3K0
(418) 536-5453   *SIC* 1731
RPG SUPPLY INC   *p* 1015
40 SUNRAY ST, WHITBY, ON, L1N 8Y3
(905) 430-8170   *SIC* 5013
RPM CANADA   *p* 919
220 WICKSTEED AVE, TORONTO, ON.
M4H 1G7

(416) 421-3300   *SIC* 2851
RPM CANADA   *p* 1015
See *RPM CANADA COMPANY FINANCE ULC*

RPM CANADA COMPANY FINANCE ULC *p* 1015
95 SUNRAY ST, WHITBY, ON, L1N 9C9
(905) 430-3333   *SIC* 2851

RPM CANANDA, DIVISION OF   *p* 1015
See *STONHARD LTD*

RPM ECO   *p* 1060
See *RPM ENVIRONNEMENT LTEE*

RPM ENTERPRISES LTD   *p* 356
395 MAIN ST, SELKIRK, MB, R1A 1T9
(204) 482-4131   *SIC* 5541

RPM ENVIRONNEMENT LTEE   *p* 1060
100 RUE MARIUS-WARNET, BLAINVILLE, QC, J7C 5P9
(450) 435-0777   *SIC* 4953

RPM TECHNOLOGIES CORPORATION   *p* 966
120 BREMNER BLVD SUITE 2300, TORONTO, ON, M5J 0A8
(416) 214-6232   *SIC* 7372

RPS CANADA LIMITED   *p* 58
555 4 AVE SW SUITE 700, CALGARY, AB, T2P 3E7
(403) 691-9717   *SIC* 8999

RPS COMPOSITES INC   *p* 462
740 MAIN ST S, MAHONE BAY, NS, B0J 2E0
(902) 624-8383   *SIC* 3299

RPS ENERGY CANADA LTD   *p* 58
800 5 AVE SW SUITE 1400, CALGARY, AB, T2P 3T6
(403) 265-7226   *SIC* 8711

RPSC HOLDINGS LTD   *p* 1199
2050 RUE DE BLEURY BUREAU 300, MONTREAL, QC, H3A 2J5
(514) 286-2636   *SIC* 4813

RR DONELLEY CANADA FINANCIAL COMPANY   *p* 780
60 GERVAIS DR, NORTH YORK, ON, M3C 1Z3
(416) 445-8800   *SIC* 2752

RR DONNELLEY   *p* 777
See *MOORE CANADA CORPORATION*

RRC   *p* 383
See *BOARD OF GOVERNOR'S OF RED RIVER COLLEGE, THE*

RRFB NOVA SCOTIA   *p* 469
See *RESOURCE RECOVERY FUND BOARD, INCORPORATED*

RRGB RESTAURANTS CANADA INC *p* 103
10010 171 ST NW, EDMONTON, AB, T5S 1S3
(780) 484-6735   *SIC* 5812

RRGB RESTAURANTS CANADA INC *p* 107
4950 137 AVE NW, EDMONTON, AB, T5Y 2V4
(780) 456-8700   *SIC* 5812

RRGB RESTAURANTS CANADA INC *p* 163
8005 EMERALD DR SUITE 250, SHERWOOD PARK, AB, T8H 0P1
(587) 269-4401   *SIC* 5812

RRGB RESTAURANTS CANADA INC *p* 175
33011 SOUTH FRASER WAY, ABBOTSFORD, BC, V2S 2A6
(604) 853-8185   *SIC* 5812

RRGB RESTAURANTS CANADA INC *p* 191
4640 KINGSWAY SUITE 112, BURNABY, BC, V5H 4L9
SIC 5812

RRGB RESTAURANTS CANADA INC *p* 270
10237 152 ST, SURREY, BC, V3R 4G6
(604) 930-2415   *SIC* 5812

RRGB RESTAURANTS CANADA INC *p* 337
800 TOLMIE AVE, VICTORIA, BC, V8X 3W4
(250) 386-4440   *SIC* 5812

RRGG   *p* 1120
See *ROULOTTES R. G. GAGNON INC*

RRJ INSURANCE GROUP LIMITED *p* 768
2450 VICTORIA PARK AVE SUITE 700, NORTH YORK, ON, M2J 4A1

(416) 636-4544   *SIC* 6411
RRU   *p* 340
See *ROYAL ROADS UNIVERSITY*

RS   *p* 1115
See *COMPAGNIE DE CHEMIN DE FER ROBERVAL-SAGUENAY INC, LA*

RS COMPOSITE UTILITY POLES   *p* 40
See *RS TECHNOLOGIES INC*

RS COMPOSITE UTILITY POLES   *p* 911
See *RS TECHNOLOGIES INC*

RS LINE CONSTRUCTION INC   *p* 228
5680 PRODUCTION WAY, LANGLEY, BC, V3A 4N4
(778) 278-7000   *SIC* 1623

RS TECHNOLOGIES INC   *p* 40
3553 31 ST NW, CALGARY, AB, T2L 2K7
(403) 219-8000   *SIC* 2499

RS TECHNOLOGIES INC   *p* 911
22 INDUSTRIAL PARK RD, TILBURY, ON, N0P 2L0
(519) 682-1110   *SIC* 2499

RSA   *p* 966
See *ROYAL & SUN ALLIANCE INSURANCE COMPANY OF CANADA*

RSA   *p* 1271
See *ROYAL & SUN ALLIANCE INSURANCE COMPANY OF CANADA*

RSA GROUP   *p* 65
See *ROYAL & SUN ALLIANCE INSURANCE COMPANY OF CANADA*

RSB LOGISTIC INC   *p* 1432
219 CARDINAL CRES, SASKATOON, SK, S7L 7K8
(306) 242-8300   *SIC* 4212

RSCOM LTD   *p* 481
238 WELLINGTON ST E SUITE 210, AURORA, ON, L4G 1J5
(647) 989-8603   *SIC* 4899

RSL JOINT VENTURE   *p* 262
See *SNC-LAVALIN CONSTRUCTORS (PACIFIC) INC*

RSM US LLP   *p* 713
81 LAKESHORE ROAD E, MISSISSAUGA, ON, L5G 4S7
SIC 8721

RSSW & DESIGN (MC)   *p* 1275
See *MACPEK INC*

RST INDUSTRIES LIMITED   *p* 413
485 MCALLISTER DR, SAINT JOHN, NB, E2J 2S8
(506) 634-8800   *SIC* 4213

RSVP CUSTOMER CARE CENTRES INC *p* 327
1265 HOWE ST SUITE 201, VANCOUVER, BC, V6Z 1R3
(604) 682-2001   *SIC* 7389

RSW INC   *p* 1208
1010 RUE DE LA GAUCHETIERE O BUREAU 1400, MONTREAL, QC, H3B 2N2
(514) 287-8500   *SIC* 8711

RSW-LMB   *p* 1208
See *RSW INC*

RTA INTERNATIONAL   *p* 1208
See *RIO TINTO ALCAN INTERNATIONAL LTEE*

RTD QUALITY SERVICES INC   *p* 110
5504 36 ST NW, EDMONTON, AB, T6B 3P3
(780) 440-6600   *SIC* 7389

RTDS TECHNOLOGIES INC   *p* 392
100-150 INNOVATION DR, WINNIPEG, MB, R3T 2E1
(204) 989-9700   *SIC* 3571

RTG PROTECH INC   *p* 1222
3333 BOUL CAVENDISH BUREAU 270, MONTREAL, QC, H4B 2M5
(514) 868-1919   *SIC* 7389

RTI-CLARO INC   *p* 1232
5515 RUE ERNEST-CORMIER, MONTREAL, QC, H7C 2S9
(450) 786-2001   *SIC* 3599

RTL- ROBINSON ENTERPRISES LTD *p* 103
10821 209 ST NW, EDMONTON, AB, T5S 1Z7
(780) 447-4900   *SIC* 4213

RTL- ROBINSON ENTERPRISES LTD *p* 436
350 OLD AIRPORT RD, YELLOWKNIFE, NT, X1A 3T4
(867) 873-6271   *SIC* 4213

RTM   *p* 742
See *ROOF TILE MANAGEMENT INC*

RTO ASSET MANAGEMENT INC   *p* 710
33 CITY CENTRE DR SUITE 510, MISSISSAUGA, ON, L5B 2N5
(905) 272-2788   *SIC* 7359

RUBBER TECH. INTERNATIONAL LTD *p* 140
GD, LEGAL, AB, T0G 1L0
(780) 961-3229   *SIC* 5199

RUBBERLINE PRODUCTS LIMITED *p* 637
81 BLEAMS RD, KITCHENER, ON, N2C 2G2
(519) 894-0400   *SIC* 5085

RUBICON OILFIELD INTERNATIONAL *p* 123
See *TOP-CO INC*

RUBICON PHARMACIES CANADA INC *p* 1438
117 3RD ST UNIT 206, WEYBURN, SK, S4H 0W3
(306) 848-3855   *SIC* 5912

RUBIE'S COSTUME COMPANY (CANADA) *p* 674
2710 14TH AVE, MARKHAM, ON, L3R 0J1
(905) 470-0300   *SIC* 5099

RUBIN, MARILYN D. SALES & SERVICE INC   *p* 597
35430 HURON RD RR 2 SUITE 2, GODERICH, ON, N7A 3X8
(519) 524-2121   *SIC* 5531

RUBY CORP   *p* 923
20 EGLINTON AVE W SUITE 1200, TORONTO, ON, M4R 1K8
(416) 480-2334   *SIC* 7299

RUBY INTERNATIONAL   *p* 1337
See *109652 CANADA LTD/LTEE*

RUBY SEAS INTERNATIONAL INC *p* 989
1061 EGLINTON AVE W SUITE 202, TORONTO, ON, M6C 2C9
(416) 787-3474   *SIC* 5146

RUCBC   *p* 336
See *RESEARCH UNIVERSITIES' COUNCIL OF BRITISH COLUMBIA, THE*

RUDD SERVICES LTD   *p* 947
123 EDWARD ST SUITE 825, TORONTO, ON, M5G 1E2
(416) 597-1995   *SIC* 8099

RUDSACK   *p* 1173
829 AV DU MONT-ROYAL E, MONTREAL, QC, H2J 1W9
(514) 508-4100   *SIC* 5136

RUDSAK INC   *p* 1179
9160 BOUL SAINT-LAURENT BUREAU 400, MONTREAL, QC, H2N 1M9
(514) 389-9661   *SIC* 2386

RUEL BROS. CONTRACTING   *p* 122
See *E CONSTRUCTION LTD*

RUEL VENNE LEONARD ASSOCIES *p* 1321
100 RUE DE LA GARE, SAINT-JEROME, QC, J7Z 2C1
(450) 432-2661   *SIC* 7389

RUETGERS CANADA INC   *p* 609
725 STRATHEARNE AVE, HAMILTON, ON, L8H 5L3
(905) 544-2891   *SIC* 2865

RUETGERS POLYMERES LTEE   *p* 1073
120 BOUL DE L'INDUSTRIE, CANDIAC, QC, J5R 1J2
(450) 659-9693   *SIC* 2869

RUGGEDCOM SIEMENS   *p* 558
See *SIEMENS CANADA LIMITED*

RULMECA CANADA LIMITED   *p* 1005
75 MASON ST, WALLACEBURG, ON, N8A 4L7
(519) 627-2277   *SIC* 3535

RUMBLE FOUNDATIONS (ONTARIO) LTD *p* 714
580 HAZELHURST RD, MISSISSAUGA,

ON, L5J 2Z7
(905) 822-3000   *SIC* 1741

RUNDLES NO FRILLS   *p* 657
635 SOUTHDALE RD E, LONDON, ON, N6E 3W6
(866) 987-6453   *SIC* 5411

RUNNALLS INDUSTRIES INC   *p* 736
1275 CARDIFF BLVD, MISSISSAUGA, ON, L5S 1R1
(905) 453-4220   *SIC* 5051

RUNNERS CLOTHING INTERNATIONAL *p* 1177
See *9149-5077 QUEBEC INC*

RUNNERS LIGHT HAULING (2006) LTD *p* 110
4320 82 AVE NW, EDMONTON, AB, T6B 2S4
(780) 465-5311   *SIC* 7389

RUNNING ROOM CANADA INC   *p* 116
9750 47 AVE NW SUITE 60, EDMONTON, AB, T6E 5P3
(780) 439-3099   *SIC* 5661

RUNNING ROOM, THE   *p* 116
See *RUNNING ROOM CANADA INC*

RUNNYMEDE HEALTHCARE CENTRE *p* 995
625 RUNNYMEDE RD, TORONTO, ON, M6S 3A3
(416) 762-7316   *SIC* 8051

RUOFF & COMPANY INC   *p* 708
2360 TEDLO ST, MISSISSAUGA, ON, L5A 3V3
(905) 281-9000   *SIC* 7359

RURAL AGRI LEASING, DIV OF   *p* 1004
See *ERNEWEIN, JOHN LIMITED*

RUSCO ENTERPRISES LTD   *p* 342
2410 MARINE DR, WEST VANCOUVER, BC, V7V 1L1
(604) 925-9095   *SIC* 1521

RUSH ELECTRONICS LTD   *p* 686
2738 SLOUGH ST, MISSISSAUGA, ON, L4T 1G3
SIC 5065

RUSH TRUCK CENTRES OF CANADA LIMITED   *p* 686
7450 TORBRAM RD, MISSISSAUGA, ON, L4T 1G9
(905) 671-7600   *SIC* 5511

RUSHTON GAS & OIL EQUIPMENT (1991) LTD   *p* 124
2331 121 AVE NE, EDMONTON, AB, T6S 1B2
(780) 475-8801   *SIC* 5084

RUSKCAST INC   *p* 907
110 ORMOND ST S, THOROLD, ON, L2V 4J6
(905) 227-4011   *SIC* 5051

RUSKIN CONSTRUCTION LTD   *p* 251
2011 PG PULP MILL RD, PRINCE GEORGE, BC, V2N 2K3
(250) 563-2800   *SIC* 1622

RUSORO MINING LTD   *p* 329
595 BURRARD ST SUITE 3123, VANCOUVER, BC, V7X 1J1
(604) 609-6110   *SIC* 1041

RUSS PATERSON LTD   *p* 369
49 OMANDS CREEK BLVD, WINNIPEG, MB, R2R 2V2
(204) 985-5400   *SIC* 5147

RUSSEL METAL PROCESSING   *p* 1429
See *RUSSEL METALS INC*

RUSSEL METALS - ATLANTIC   *p* 460
See *RUSSEL METALS INC*

RUSSEL METALS INC   *p* 18
5724 40 ST SE, CALGARY, AB, T2C 2A1
(403) 279-6600   *SIC* 3312

RUSSEL METALS INC   *p* 116
7016 99 ST NW, EDMONTON, AB, T6E 3R3
SIC 5051

RUSSEL METALS INC   *p* 207
830 CARLISLE RD, DELTA, BC, V3M 5P4
(604) 525-0544   *SIC* 5051

RUSSEL METALS INC   *p* 385

1359 ST JAMES ST, WINNIPEG, MB, R3H 0K9

SIC 5051

RUSSEL METALS INC *p 392*
1510 CLARENCE AVE, WINNIPEG, MB, R3T 1T6
(204) 475-8584 *SIC 1791*

RUSSEL METALS INC *p 460*
28 LAKESIDE PARK DR, LAKESIDE, NS, B3T 1A3
(902) 876-7861 *SIC 5051*

RUSSEL METALS INC *p 726*
1900 MINNESOTA CRT SUITE 210, MISSISSAUGA, ON, L5N 3C9
(905) 567-8500 *SIC 5051*

RUSSEL METALS INC *p 726*
6600 FINANCIAL DR, MISSISSAUGA, ON, L5N 7J6
(905) 819-7777 *SIC 5051*

RUSSEL METALS INC *p 1429*
503 50TH ST E, SASKATOON, SK, S7K 6H3
(306) 244-7511 *SIC 3599*

RUSSEL METALS NORTH WINNIPEG *p 385*
See RUSSEL METALS INC

RUSSELL A. FARROW LIMITED *p 483*
See FARROW, RUSSELL A. LIMITED

RUSSELL FOOD EQUIPMENT (CALGARY) LIMITED *p 37*
5707 4 ST SE, CALGARY, AB, T2H 1K8
(403) 253-1383 *SIC 5046*

RUSSELL FOOD EQUIPMENT LIMITED *p 295*
1255 VENABLES ST, VANCOUVER, BC, V6A 3X6
(604) 253-6611 *SIC 5046*

RUSSELL HEALTH CENTRE *p 356*
426 ALEXANDRIA AVE, RUSSELL, MB, R0J 1W0
(204) 773-2125 *SIC 8742*

RUSSELL HENDRIX FOODSERVICE EQUIPMENT *p 295*
See RUSSELL FOOD EQUIPMENT LIMITED

RUSSELL INDUSTRIES LTD *p 183*
4062 MCCONNELL DR, BURNABY, BC, V5A 3A8
(604) 420-2440 *SIC 5063*

RUSSELL INVESTMENTS CANADA LIMITED *p 987*
100 KING ST W SUITE 5900, TORONTO, ON, M5X 2A1
(416) 362-8411 *SIC 6411*

RUSSELL PETRO-CANADA CENTRE *p 356*
See BRENDONN HOLDINGS LTD

RUSSELL SECURITY SERVICES INC *p 488*
80 BRADFORD ST SUITE 826, BARRIE, ON, L4N 6S7
(705) 721-1480 *SIC 5065*

RUSSELL STEEL *p 1383*
See MEGANTIC METAL LTEE

RUSSELL TOOL & DIE LIMITED *p 543*
381 PARK AVE W, CHATHAM, ON, N7M 1W6
(519) 352-8168 *SIC 3544*

RUSSELL, J.E. PRODUCE LTD *p 573*
165 THE QUEENSWAY SUITE 332, ETOBICOKE, ON, M8Y 1H8
(416) 252-7838 *SIC 5148*

RUSSELLE ENTERPRISES INC *p 842*
1400 LANSDOWNE ST W, PETERBOROUGH, ON, K9J 2A2
(705) 742-4288 *SIC 5511*

RUSSELLE TOYOTA INC *p 842*
1400 LANSDOWNE ST W, PETERBOROUGH, ON, K9J 2A2
(705) 742-4288 *SIC 5511*

RUSTAN METALS LTD *p 295*
630 RAYMUR AVE, VANCOUVER, BC, V6A 3L2
SIC 5052

RUTH'S CHRIS STEAK HOUSE *p 26*
See 1184892 ALBERTA LTD

RUTH'S CHRIS STEAK HOUSE EDMON-

TON *p 90*
10103 100 ST NW, EDMONTON, AB, T5J 0N8
(780) 990-0123 *SIC 5812*

RUTHERFORD CONTRACTING LTD *p 481*
224 EARL STEWART DR, AURORA, ON, L4G 6V7
(905) 726-4888 *SIC 1542*

RUTHERFORD INTERNATIONAL FREIGHT SERVICE *p 689*
See RUTHERFORD, WILLIAM L. LIMITED

RUTHERFORD TERMINALS *p 265*
See RUTHERFORD, WILLIAM L (BC) LTD

RUTHERFORD, WILLIAM L (BC) LTD *p 265*
6086 RUSS BAKER WAY SUITE 125, RICHMOND, BC, V7B 1B4
(604) 273-8611 *SIC 4731*

RUTHERFORD, WILLIAM L. LIMITED *p 689*
3350 AIRWAY DR, MISSISSAUGA, ON, L4V 1T3
(905) 673-2222 *SIC 4731*

RUTLAND SENIOR SECONDARY SCHOOL *p 219*
See BOARD OF EDUCATION OF SCHOOL DISTRICT NO. 23 (CENTRAL OKANAGAN), THE

RUTLEDGE FLOWERS AT YORKDALE INC *p 924*
635 MOUNT PLEASANT RD SUITE A, TORONTO, ON, M4S 2M9
(416) 783-6355 *SIC 5992*

RUTMET INC *p 799*
2939 PORTLAND DR SUITE 300, OAKVILLE, ON, L6H 5S4
(289) 291-1111 *SIC 5093*

RV CITY *p 147*
See G.B. BUSINESS ENTERPRISES LTD

RW CONSUMER PRODUCTS LTD *p 369*
200 OMANDS CREEK BLVD, WINNIPEG, MB, R2R 1V7
(204) 786-6873 *SIC 2834*

RWAM INSURANCE ADMINISTRATORS INC *p 568*
49 INDUSTRIAL DR, ELMIRA, ON, N3B 3B1
(519) 669-1632 *SIC 8741*

RWDI *p 601*
See ROWAN WILLIAMS DAVIES & IRWIN INC

RWDI AIR INC *p 601*
600 SOUTHGATE DR, GUELPH, ON, N1G 4P6
(519) 823-1311 *SIC 8711*

RWDI GROUP INC *p 601*
600 SOUTHGATE DR, GUELPH, ON, N1G 4P6
(519) 823-1311 *SIC 8711*

RX FRASER LTD *p 9*
2525 36 ST NE SUITE 135, CALGARY, AB, T1Y 5T4
(403) 280-6667 *SIC 5912*

RXSOURCE CORP *p 855*
556 EDWARD AVE UNIT 74, RICHMOND HILL, ON, L4C 9Y5
(905) 883-4333 *SIC 5122*

RYAN COMPANY LIMITED *p 338*
723A VANALMAN AVE, VICTORIA, BC, V8Z 3B6
(250) 388-4254 *SIC 5962*

RYAN ENERGY TECHNOLOGIES *p 58*
500 4 AVE SW SUITE 2800, CALGARY, AB, T2P 2V6
(403) 263-6777 *SIC 1381*

RYAN FOREST PRODUCTS, DIV OF *p 369*
See KENORA FOREST PRODUCTS LTD

RYAN ULC *p 726*
6775 FINANCIAL DR SUITE 102, MISSISSAUGA, ON, L5N 0A4
(905) 567-7926 *SIC 8742*

RYAN VENDING *p 338*
See RYAN COMPANY LIMITED

RYAN, D.C. SALES INC *p 567*
1002 BROAD ST E, DUNNVILLE, ON, N1A

2Z2
(905) 774-2545 *SIC 5531*

RYASH COFFEE CORPORATION *p 679*
9251 WOODBINE AVE, MARKHAM, ON, L6C 1Y9
(905) 887-8444 *SIC 5461*

RYCOM INC *p 1028*
6201 7 HWY UNIT 8, WOODBRIDGE, ON, L4H 0K7
(905) 264-4800 *SIC 5065*

RYCOTT FOODSERVICE *p 608*
See RYCOTT WHOLESALE FOODS INC

RYCOTT WHOLESALE FOODS INC *p 608*
504 KENORA AVE, HAMILTON, ON, L8E 3X8
(905) 560-2424 *SIC 5146*

RYCROFT CO-OP *p 132*
See NEW HORIZON CO-OPERATIVE LTD

RYDER CANADA *p 662*
See RYDER TRUCK RENTAL CANADA LTD

RYDER CANADA *p 726*
See RYDER TRUCK RENTAL CANADA LTD

RYDER CONTRACTING LTD *p 245*
5700 SHOEMAKER BAY RD, PORT ALBERNI, BC, V9Y 8X8
(250) 736-1995 *SIC 1611*

RYDER MATERIAL HANDLING ULC *p 742*
210 ANNAGEM BLVD, MISSISSAUGA, ON, L5T 2V5
(905) 565-2100 *SIC 5084*

RYDER TRUCK RENTAL CANADA LTD *p 506*
30 PEDIGREE CRT SUITE 1, BRAMPTON, ON, L6T 5T8
(905) 759-2000 *SIC 8721*

RYDER TRUCK RENTAL CANADA LTD *p 662*
2724 ROXBURGH RD SUITE 7, LONDON, ON, N6N 1K9
SIC 7513

RYDER TRUCK RENTAL CANADA LTD *p 726*
6755 MISSISSAUGA RD SUITE 201, MISSISSAUGA, ON, L5N 7Y2
(905) 826-8777 *SIC 7513*

RYDING-REGENCY MEAT PACKERS LTD *p 994*
70 GLEN SCARLETT RD, TORONTO, ON, M6N 1P4
(416) 763-1611 *SIC 5147*

RYE PATCH GOLD CORP *p 330*
701 WEST GEORGIA ST SUITE 1500, VANCOUVER, BC, V7Y 1C6
(604) 638-1588 *SIC 1041*

RYERSON CANADA, INC *p 524*
1219 CORPORATE DR SUITE 2, BURLINGTON, ON, L7L 5V5
(416) 622-3100 *SIC 5051*

RYERSON CANADA, INC *p 1362*
3399 AV FRANCIS-HUGHES, SAINTE-ROSE, QC, H7L 5A5
(450) 975-7171 *SIC 5051*

RYERSON UNIVERSITY *p 936*
350 VICTORIA ST, TORONTO, ON, M5B 2K3
(416) 979-5000 *SIC 8221*

RYFAN ELECTRIC LTD *p 436*
9 NAHANNI DR, YELLOWKNIFE, NT, X1A 0E8
(867) 765-6100 *SIC 1731*

RYGIEL SUPPORTS FOR COMMUNITY LIVING *p 616*
930 UPPER PARADISE RD UNIT 11, HAMILTON, ON, L9B 2N1
(905) 525-4311 *SIC 8361*

RYKER OILFIELD HAULING LTD *p 146*
1779 9 AVE SW, MEDICINE HAT, AB, T1A 8S2
(403) 529-9090 *SIC 1389*

RYSEN BOBCAT SERVICES LIMITED *p 2*
107-26230 TOWNSHIP RD 531A, ACHESON, AB, T7X 5A4
(780) 470-2085 *SIC 1611*

S

(S.P.A.N.) ST PAUL ABILITIES NETWORK (SOCIETY) *p 164*
4637 45 AVE, ST PAUL, AB, T0A 3A3
(780) 645-3405 *SIC 8331*

S & B KESWICK MOTORS LIMITED *p 628*
475 THE QUEENSWAY S, KESWICK, ON, L4P 2E2
(905) 476-3111 *SIC 5511*

S & B MANAGEMENT *p 879*
See 1090349 ONTARIO INC

S & C ELECTRIC CANADA LTD *p 998*
90 BELFIELD RD, TORONTO, ON, M9W 1G4
(416) 249-9171 *SIC 3613*

S & E LIMITED PARTNERSHIP *p 309*
666 BURRARD ST SUITE 1700, VANCOUVER, BC, V6C 2X8
(604) 631-1300 *SIC 8111*

S & F *p 1353*
See TRANSPORT SYLVESTER & FORGET INC

S & F FOOD IMPORTERS *p 548*
See 340532 ONTARIO LIMITED

S & F FOOD IMPORTERS INC *p 558*
565 EDGELEY BLVD, CONCORD, ON, L4K 4G4
(416) 410-9091 *SIC 5141*

S & K NG ENTERPRISES LTD *p 296*
158 PENDER ST E, VANCOUVER, BC, V6A 1T3
(604) 689-7835 *SIC 5461*

S & L PROPERTIES LTD *p 363*
605 REGENT AVE W, WINNIPEG, MB, R2C 1R9
(204) 222-9431 *SIC 5541*

S & M ENTERPRISES *p 796*
See 1161396 ONTARIO INC

S & S TRUCK PARTS CANADA INC *p 742*
6460 KESTREL RD, MISSISSAUGA, ON, L5T 1Z7
(905) 564-7100 *SIC 5013*

S & T ALLARD FOOD LTD *p 133*
10206 100 ST SUITE 640, GRANDE PRAIRIE, AB, T8V 3K1
(780) 532-6660 *SIC 5812*

S & V PLANNING CORPORATION *p 335*
968 MEARES ST, VICTORIA, BC, V8V 3J4
(250) 388-6774 *SIC 6311*

S B R GLOBAL *p 944*
See 678925 ONTARIO INC

S C I *p 957*
See STADIUM CONSULTANTS INTERNATIONAL INC

S C RESTORATIONS LTD *p 223*
1025 TRENCH PL, KELOWNA, BC, V1Y 9Y4
(250) 763-1556 *SIC 7299*

S C RESTORATIONS LTD *p 223*
1216 ST. PAUL ST SUITE 201, KELOWNA, BC, V1Y 2C8
(250) 832-9818 *SIC 1629*

S C. F P SECTION LOCALE 1500 *p 1290*
75 AV QUEBEC, ROUYN-NORANDA, QC, J9X 7A2
(819) 762-4422 *SIC 8631*

S G L *p 827*
See SANDER GEOPHYSICS LIMITED

S G POWER *p 335*
See S G POWER PRODUCTS LTD

S G POWER PRODUCTS LTD *p 335*
730 HILLSIDE AVE, VICTORIA, BC, V8T 1Z4
(250) 382-8291 *SIC 5551*

S G S MINERALS SERVICES *p 777*
See SGS CANADA INC

S I METRIC MANIFACTURING LTD *p 756*
150 PONY DR, NEWMARKET, ON, L3Y 7B6
(905) 898-6322 *SIC 5049*

S I R SOLUTIONS *p 1169*
See 9013-6573 QUEBEC INC

S M P *p 1429*
See SASKATOON MOTOR PRODUCTS (1973) LTD

S MALIK INVESTMENTS LTD *p 18*
8338 18 ST SE SUITE 432, CALGARY, AB, T2C 4E4
(403) 236-2776 *SIC 5541*

S MITRI TRANSPORT, DIV *p 741*
See MITRI, S HAULAGE LTD

S O S CHILDREN'S VILLAGE SOCIETY *p 266*
3800 MONCTON ST, RICHMOND, BC, V7E 3A6
(604) 274-8866 *SIC 8399*

S O S JANITORIAL SERVICES LTD *p 1421*
2396 2ND AVE, REGINA, SK, S4R 1A6
(306) 757-0027 *SIC 7349*

S O S TREASURE COTTAGE *p 266*
See S O S CHILDREN'S VILLAGE SOCIETY

S P A PLUS *p 1051*
See SERVICES PROFESSIONNELS DES ASSUREURS PLUS INC

S P C A *p 14*
See CALGARY HUMANE SOCIETY FOR PREVENTION OF CRUELTY TO ANIMALS

S P L BRAND *p 848*
See STREEF PRODUCE LIMITED

S R I V O *p 1105*
See SERVICE REGIONAL D'INTERPRETATION VISUELLE DE L'OUTAOUAIS

S S P A *p 1135*
See SYNDICAT DES SALARIES DE PIN-TENDRE AUTO

S SHOWA DENKO *p 1129*
See SHOWA DENKO CARBONE CANADA INC

S TEAM 92 AUTOMATION TECHNOLOGY INC *p 761*
827 LINE 4 RR 2, NIAGARA ON THE LAKE, ON, L0S 1J0
SIC 7373

S TECH DIV *p 673*
See PATRICK PLASTICS INC

S W C RECYCLING *p 401*
760 WILSEY RD, FREDERICTON, NB, E3B 7K4
(506) 453-9931 *SIC 4953*

S&H HEALTH FOODS *p 718*
See 1122630 ONTARIO LIMITED

S&P DATA CORP *p 924*
1920 YONGE ST, TORONTO, ON, M4S 3E2
(844) 877-3282 *SIC 7389*

S&S/BOLTON ELECTRIC INC *p 596*
5411 CANOTEK RD, GLOUCESTER, ON, K1J 9M3
(613) 748-0432 *SIC 1731*

S-304 HOLDINGS LTD *p 273*
19505 LANGLEY BYPASS, SURREY, BC, V3S 6K1
(604) 534-7957 *SIC 5511*

S-A-S PETROLEUM TECHNOLOGIES INC *p 566*
432 MACNAB ST, DUNDAS, ON, L9H 2L3
(905) 627-5451 *SIC 1799*

S. & T. ELECTRICAL CONTRACTORS LIMITED *p 863*
158 SACKVILLE RD SUITE 2, SAULT STE. MARIE, ON, P6B 4T6
(705) 942-3043 *SIC 1731*

S. & T. GROUP *p 863*
See S. & T. ELECTRICAL CONTRACTORS LIMITED

S. A. ARMSTRONG LIMITED *p 869*
23 BERTRAND AVE, SCARBOROUGH, ON, M1L 2P3
(416) 755-2291 *SIC 3561*

S. A. M. (MANAGEMENT) INC *p 382*
200-1080 PORTAGE AVE, WINNIPEG, MB, R3G 3M3
(204) 942-0991 *SIC 6531*

S. BOUDRIAS HORTICOLE INC *p 1342*
29 RUE SAULNIER, SAINT-LAURENT, QC, H7M 1S7
(450) 663-4245 *SIC 2875*

S. BOURASSA (STE-AGATHE) LTEE *p 1354*
680 RUE PRINCIPALE, SAINTE-AGATHE-DES-MONTS, QC, J8C 1L3
(819) 326-1707 *SIC 5141*

S. COHEN INC *p 1341*
153 RUE GRAVELINE, SAINT-LAURENT, QC, H4T 1R4
(514) 342-6700 *SIC 2326*

S. F. PARTNERSHIP LLP *p 773*
4950 YONGE ST SUITE 400, NORTH YORK, ON, M2N 6K1
(416) 250-1212 *SIC 8721*

S. GUMPERT CO. OF CANADA LTD *p 708*
2500 TEDLO ST, MISSISSAUGA, ON, L5A 4A9
(905) 279-2600 *SIC 5461*

S. H. DAYTON LTD *p 356*
144 INDUSTRIAL RD, SHOAL LAKE, MB, R0J 1Z0
(204) 759-2065 *SIC 5083*

S. HUOT INC *p 1265*
108 RUE RAOUL-JOBIN, QUEBEC, QC, G1N 4N3
(418) 681-0291 *SIC 3535*

S. M. HEWITT (SARNIA) LIMITED *p 846*
1555 VENETIAN BLVD SUITE 11 3RD FL, POINT EDWARD, ON, N7T 0A9
(519) 332-4411 *SIC 4731*

S. ROSSY INC *p 1157*
5805 AV ROYALMOUNT, MONT-ROYAL, QC, H4P 0A1
(514) 737-1006 *SIC 6514*

S. SETLAKWE LTEE *p 1383*
493 BOUL FRONTENAC O, THETFORD MINES, QC, G6G 6K2
(418) 338-8511 *SIC 5712*

S.A.D.E HOLDINGS LTD *p 235*
2345 ISLAND HWY E, NANOOSE BAY, BC, V9P 9E2
(250) 468-7441 *SIC 5411*

S.A.Q. *p 1165*
See SOCIETE DES ALCOOLS DU QUE-BEC

S.A.T SOLAR & ALTERNATIVE TECHNOL-OGY *p 736*
1935 DREW RD SUITE 28, MISSISSAUGA, ON, L5S 1M7
(905) 673-6060 *SIC 1711*

S.B. SIMPSON HOLDINGS LIMITED *p 526*
3210 MAINWAY, BURLINGTON, ON, L7M 1A5
(905) 335-6575 *SIC 6712*

S.C. JOHNSON AND SON, LIMITED *p 517*
1 WEBSTER ST, BRANTFORD, ON, N3T 5A3
(519) 756-7900 *SIC 2842*

S.D.R. DISTRIBUTION SERVICES *p 700*
1880 MATHESON BLVD E, MISSISSAUGA, ON, L4W 5N4
(905) 625-7377 *SIC 5137*

S.E.A. 2000 INTERNATIONAL *p 1092*
See 3552047 CANADA INC

S.F. MARKETING INC *p 1096*
325 BOUL BOUCHARD, DORVAL, QC, H9S 1A9
(514) 780-2070 *SIC 5065*

S.G. SPORT MARINE *p 1291*
See LAGUE ET GOYETTE LTEE

S.G.T. 2000 INC *p 1306*
354 CH YAMASKA, SAINT-GERMAIN-DE-GRANTHAM, QC, J0C 1K0
(819) 395-4213 *SIC 4213*

S.H.A.R.E *p 622*
See S.H.A.R.E. AGRICULTURE FOUNDA-TION

S.H.A.R.E. AGRICULTURE FOUNDATION *p 622*
14110 KENNEDY RD, INGLEWOOD, ON, L7C 2G3
(905) 838-0897 *SIC 7389*

S.I. SYSTEMS LTD *p 58*
401 9 AVE SW SUITE 309, CALGARY, AB, T2P 3C5

(403) 263-1200 *SIC 8741*

S.I. SYSTEMS PARTNERSHIP *p 58*
401 9 AVE SW SUITE 309, CALGARY, AB, T2P 3C5
(403) 286-1200 *SIC 8741*

S.I.F. SUPERIOR INDUSTRIAL FRICTIONS LTD *p 96*
11570 154 ST NW, EDMONTON, AB, T5M 3N8
(780) 451-6894 *SIC 3714*

S.I.R.C.O. *p 1240*
See 2969-9899 QUEBEC INC

S.I.T. (SERVICE D'INTEGRATION AU TRA-VAIL) *p 1388*
1090 RUE LA VERENDRYE, TROIS-RIVIERES, QC, G9A 2S8
(819) 694-9971 *SIC 8699*

S.I.T. MAURICIE *p 1388*
See S.I.T. (SERVICE D'INTEGRATION AU TRAVAIL)

S.K.S. NOVELTY COMPANY LTD *p 547*
30 SANDFORD FLEMING RD, COLLING-WOOD, ON, L9Y 4V7
(705) 444-5653 *SIC 5199*

S.L. DEVISON PHARMACIES INC *p 831*
888 MEADOWLANDS DR, OTTAWA, ON, K2C 3R2
(613) 225-6204 *SIC 5912*

S.L. FORD SALES LTD *p 163*
309 1A AVE SE SS 3, SLAVE LAKE, AB, T0G 2A3
(780) 849-4419 *SIC 5511*

S.L.K. MARKETING LIMITED *p 1033*
126 TROWERS RD, WOODBRIDGE, ON, L4L 5Z4
(905) 856-4343 *SIC 5199*

S.M. PRODUCTS (B.C.) LTD *p 210*
3827 RIVER RD W, DELTA, BC, V4K 3N2
(604) 946-7665 *SIC 5146*

S.M.I. QUEBEC CONSTRUCTION *p 1051*
See STEAMATIC METROPOLITAIN INC

S.M.P SPECIALTY METAL PRODUCTS LTD *p 707*
326 WATLINE AVE, MISSISSAUGA, ON, L4Z 1X2
SIC 5051

S.N.S. AUTOMATION PRODUCTS *p 888*
See S.N.S. INDUSTRIAL PRODUCTS LIM-ITED

S.N.S. INDUSTRIAL PRODUCTS LIMITED *p 888*
142 SUGAR MAPLE RD, ST GEORGE BRANT, ON, N0E 1N0
(519) 448-3055 *SIC 5084*

S.O.F. WHITE PAPER COMPANY LTD *p 210*
9990 RIVER WAY, DELTA, BC, V4G 1M9
(604) 951-3900 *SIC 5111*

S.O.M.R. *p 1336*
See SOCIETE D'OUTILLAGE M.R. LTEE

S.O.S. DEPANNAGE GRANBY ET REGION INC *p 1109*
327 RUE MATTON, GRANBY, QC, J2G 7R1
(450) 378-4208 *SIC 8399*

S.P. RICHARDS CO. CANADA INC *p 207*
820 CLIVEDEN PL UNIT 4, DELTA, BC, V3M 6C7
(604) 540-0444 *SIC 5112*

S.P.A. DE QUEBEC *p 1268*
See SOCIETE DE QUEBEC POUR PRE-VENIR LES CRUAUTES CONTRE LES ANI-MAUX, LA

S.P.C.A. DE MONTREAL, LA *p 1228*
See SOCIETE POUR LA PREVENTION DE LA CRUAUTE ENVERS LES ANIMAUX (CANADIENNE), LA

S.R.E.P.E. INC *p 1173*
4837 RUE BOYER BUREAU 240, MON-TREAL, QC, H2J 3E6
(514) 525-3447 *SIC 6211*

S.R.M. PLOMBERIE & CHAUFFAGE *p 1063*
See 2953-6778 QUEBEC INC

S.R.V. INDUSTRIAL SUPPLY INC *p 872*
2500 LAWRENCE AVE E SUITE 12, SCAR-BOROUGH, ON, M1P 2R7
(416) 757-1020 *SIC 5093*

S.S.P. TELECOM *p 1386*
See SERVICES ET SOLUTIONS PROFES-SIONNELS EN TELECOMMUNICATIONS S.S.P. INC

S.T.A.F. INOXYDABLE *p 1063*
See ACIER INOXYDABLE FAFARD INC

S.T.O.P. RESTAURANT SUPPLY LTD *p 635*
206 CENTENNIAL CRT, KITCHENER, ON, N2B 3X2
(519) 749-2710 *SIC 5046*

S.T.R. ELECTRONIQUE INC *p 1255*
610 RUE ARDOUIN, QUEBEC, QC, G1C 7J8
(418) 660-8899 *SIC 5045*

S.U.C.C.E.S.S. *p 300*
See S.U.C.C.E.S.S. (ALSO KNOWN AS UNITED CHINESE COMMUNITY ENRICH-MENT SERVICES SOCIETY)

S.U.C.C.E.S.S. (ALSO KNOWN AS UNITED CHINESE COMMUNITY ENRICHMENT SERVICES SOCIETY) *p 300*
28 PENDER ST W, VANCOUVER, BC, V6B 1R6
(604) 684-1628 *SIC 8399*

S3 *p 1107*
See 6861083 CANADA INC

SAADCO EXPRESS INC *p 674*
300 STEELCASE RD W UNIT 9, MARKHAM, ON, L3R 2W2
(905) 940-1680 *SIC 7389*

SAAM SMIT CANADA INC *p 285*
2285 COMMISSIONER ST, VANCOUVER, BC, V5L 1A8
(604) 255-1133 *SIC 4492*

SAAND DISTRIBUTION *p 587*
See SAAND INC

SAAND INC *p 587*
250 BROCKPORT DR SUITE 3, ETOBI-COKE, ON, M9W 5S1
(416) 798-2345 *SIC 5039*

SAAND INC *p 587*
355 ATTWELL DR, ETOBICOKE, ON, M9W 5C2
(416) 674-6945 *SIC 5039*

SAAND LONDON INC *p 651*
14 FIRESTONE BLVD, LONDON, ON, N5W 5L4
(519) 659-0819 *SIC 3231*

SAAND TORONTO INC *p 587*
250 BROCKPORT DR SUITE 3, ETOBI-COKE, ON, M9W 5S1
(416) 798-2345 *SIC 3231*

SAANICH FIRE DEPARTMENT *p 337*
See CORPORATION OF THE DISTRICT OF SAANICH, THE

SAATCHI & SAATCHI *p 930*
See SAATCHI & SAATCHI ADVERTISING INC

SAATCHI & SAATCHI ADVERTISING INC *p 930*
2 BLOOR ST E SUITE 600, TORONTO, ON, M4W 1A8
(416) 359-9595 *SIC 7311*

SABA SOFTWARE (CANADA) INC *p 625*
495 MARCH RD SUITE 100, KANATA, ON, K2K 3G1
(613) 270-1011 *SIC 7372*

SABEM, SEC *p 1282*
1500 RUE RAYMOND-GAUDREAULT, RE-PENTIGNY, QC, J5Y 4E3
(450) 585-1210 *SIC 4151*

SABIAN LTD *p 405*
219 MAIN ST, MEDUCTIC, NB, E6H 2L5
(506) 272-2019 *SIC 3931*

SABIC INNOVATIVE PLASTICS CANADA INC *p 545*
44 NORMAR RD, COBOURG, ON, K9A 4L7
(905) 372-6801 *SIC 5162*

SABIC INNOVATIVE PLASTICS CANADA INC *p 662*
1 STRUCTURED PRODUCT DR, LONG SAULT, ON, K0C 1P0

(905) 372-6801   *SIC 5162*
SABIC POLYMERSHAPES   *p 662*
See *SABIC INNOVATIVE PLASTICS CANADA INC*
SABLE FISH PACKERS (1988) LIMITED *p 442*
377 DANIELS HEAD RD, CLARKS HARBOUR, NS, B0W 1P0
(902) 745-2500   *SIC 2091*
SABLES OLIMAG INC, LES   *p 1383*
2899 BOUL FRONTENAC E, THETFORD MINES, QC, G6G 6P6
(418) 338-3562   *SIC 5032*
SABLIERE DRAPEAU (1986) INC   *p 1079*
205 BOUL DU ROYAUME E, CHICOUTIMI, QC, G7H 5H2
(418) 549-0532   *SIC 5032*
SABLIERES DEMERS   *p 1381*
See *DEMERS, ROBERT & GILLES INC*
SABON   *p 921*
See *1619214 ONTARIO LIMITED*
SABRE INSTRUMENT SERVICES LTD *p 18*
4460 54 AVE SE, CALGARY, AB, T2C 3A8
(403) 258-0566   *SIC 1796*
SABRE WELL SERVICING INC   *p 58*
435 4 AVE SW SUITE 380, CALGARY, AB, T2P 3A8
(403) 237-0309   *SIC 1389*
SABRINA FOODS   *p 558*
See *SABRINA WHOLESALE FOODS INC*
SABRINA WHOLESALE FOODS INC *p 558*
1950 HIGHWAY 7 UNIT 18, CONCORD, ON, L4K 3P2
(416) 665-1533   *SIC 5141*
SABRITIN HOSPITALITY INC   *p 512*
370 BOVAIRD DR E, BRAMPTON, ON, L6Z 2S8
(905) 846-3321   *SIC 5812*
SAC DRUMMOND INC   *p 1306*
192 CH DE LA STATION, SAINT-GERMAIN-DE-GRANTHAM, QC, J0C 1K0
(819) 395-4286   *SIC 5541*
SACKVILLE MEMORIAL HOSPITAL *p 412*
See *REGIONAL HEALTH AUTHORITY NB*
SACKVILLE SPORTS STADIUM   *p 461*
409 GLENDALE DR, LOWER SACKVILLE, NS, B4C 2T6
(902) 252-4000   *SIC 7999*
SACLA   *p 141*
See *SOUTHERN ALBERTA COMMUNITY LIVING ASSOCIATION*
SACOPAN INC   *p 1290*
652 CH DU MOULIN, SACRE-COEUR-SAGUENAY, QC, G0T 1Y0
(418) 236-1144   *SIC 3544*
SACRE CONSULTANTS LTD   *p 239*
315 MOUNTAIN HWY, NORTH VANCOUVER, BC, V7J 2K7
(604) 983-0305   *SIC 8711*
SACRE-DAVEY INNOVATIONS   *p 239*
See *SACRE CONSULTANTS LTD*
SACRED HEART CATHOLIC HIGH SCHOOL   *p 891*
See *OTTAWA CATHOLIC DISTRICT SCHOOL BOARD*
SACRED HEART CHURCH   *p 926*
See *ROMAN CATHOLIC EPISCOPAL CORPORATION FOR THE DIOCESE OF TORONTO, IN CANADA*
SACRED HEART COMMUNITY HEALTH CENTRE   *p 145*
See *ALBERTA HEALTH SERVICES*
SACRED HEART HIGH SCHOOL   *p 757*
See *YORK CATHOLIC DISTRICT SCHOOL BOARD*
SACRED HEART HIGH SCHOOL   *p 1004*
See *BRUCE-GREY CATHOLIC DISTRICT SCHOOL BOARD*
SADD, LLOYD   *p 102*
See *RMR BONDING LTD*
SADDLE STITCHING SYSTEMS, A DIV *p 556*
See *MULLER MARTINI CANADA INC*
SADE CANADA INC   *p 1267*

1564 AV AMPERE, QUEBEC, QC, G1P 4B9
(581) 300-7233   *SIC 1623*
SADERCOM INC   *p 1345*
4875 BOUL METROPOLITAIN E BUREAU 100, SAINT-LEONARD, QC, H1R 3J2
(514) 326-4100   *SIC 6411*
SADIE MORANIS REALTY CORPORATION *p 777*
35 LESMILL RD, NORTH YORK, ON, M3B 2T3
(416) 449-2020   *SIC 6531*
SADLON, PAUL MOTORS INCORPORATED *p 484*
550 BAYFIELD ST, BARRIE, ON, L4M 5A2
(705) 721-7733   *SIC 5511*
SAE POWER COMPANY   *p 872*
1810 BIRCHMOUNT RD, SCARBOROUGH, ON, M1P 2H7
(416) 298-0560   *SIC 3679*
SAEXPLORATION (CANADA) LTD *p 32*
3333 8 ST SE SUITE 300, CALGARY, AB, T2G 3A4
(403) 776-1950   *SIC 1382*
SAEXPLORATION HOLDINGS INC *p 13*
4860 25 ST SE, CALGARY, AB, T2B 3M2
(403) 776-1950   *SIC 6712*
SAF-HOLLAND CANADA LIMITED *p 796*
20 PHOEBE ST, NORWICH, ON, N0J 1P0
(519) 863-3414   *SIC 3714*
SAF-HOLLAND CANADA LIMITED *p 1035*
595 ATHLONE AVE, WOODSTOCK, ON, N4S 7V8
(519) 537-2366   *SIC 3714*
SAF-T-CAB, INC   *p 621*
7 CANADA AVE, HURON PARK, ON, N0M 1Y0
(519) 228-6538   *SIC 3531*
SAFARI CONDO   *p 1303*
See *PAR NADO INC*
SAFDIE & CO. INC   *p 1157*
8191 CH MONTVIEW, MONT-ROYAL, QC, H4P 2P2
(514) 344-7599   *SIC 5131*
SAFE SOFTWARE INC   *p 274*
9639 137A ST SUITE 1200, SURREY, BC, V3T 0M1
(604) 501-9985   *SIC 7372*
SAFECROSS FIRST AID LTD   *p 784*
21 KODIAK CRES SUITE 200, NORTH YORK, ON, M3J 3E5
(416) 665-0050   *SIC 5199*
SAFEHAVEN NURSING & SERVICES INC *p 340*
3700 RIDGE POND DR, VICTORIA, BC, V9C 4M8
(250) 477-8339   *SIC 8741*
SAFELY HOME   *p 24*
See *PACIFIC WESTERN TRANSPORTATION LTD*
SAFEMAP   *p 309*
See *SAFEMAP INTERNATIONAL INC*
SAFEMAP INTERNATIONAL INC   *p 309*
666 BURRARD ST SUITE 500, VANCOUVER, BC, V6C 3P6
(604) 642-6110   *SIC 8748*
SAFENET CANADA INC   *p 750*
20 COLONNADE RD SUITE 200, NEPEAN, ON, K2E 7M6
(613) 723-5077   *SIC 3699*
SAFESEA-AMI SHIPPING INC   *p 700*
1030 KAMATO RD SUITE 210, MISSISSAUGA, ON, L4W 4B6
SIC 4731
SAFETY BOSS INC   *p 25*
17-2135 32 AVE NE, CALGARY, AB, T2E 6Z3
(403) 261-5075   *SIC 1389*
SAFETY EXPRESS LTD   *p 717*
4190 SLADEVIEW CRES UNIT 1-2, MISSISSAUGA, ON, L5L 0A1
(905) 608-0111   *SIC 5099*
SAFETY FIRST CONTRACTING (1995) LTD *p 448*
116 THORNE AVE, DARTMOUTH, NS, B3B

1Z2
(902) 464-0889   *SIC 3669*
SAFETY FIRST FIRE PREVENTION *p 1002*
See *SAFETY FIRST ONTARIO INC*
SAFETY FIRST ONTARIO INC   *p 1002*
41 COURTLAND AVE UNIT 1, VAUGHAN, ON, L4K 3T3
(905) 738-4999   *SIC 7389*
SAFETY FIRST-SFC   *p 448*
See *SAFETY FIRST CONTRACTING (1995) LTD*
SAFETY INSURANCE SERVICE (1959) LTD *p 674*
8300 WOODBINE AVE SUITE 200, MARKHAM, ON, L3R 9Y7
SIC 6411
SAFETY MART #5 (1994) LTD   *p 198*
74 YOUNG RD, CLEARWATER, BC, V0E 1N2
(250) 674-2213   *SIC 5411*
SAFETY MART FOODS   *p 196*
See *SAFETY MART NO. 7 (2001) LTD*
SAFETY MART FOODS   *p 198*
See *SAFETY MART #5 (1994) LTD*
SAFETY MART NO. 7 (2001) LTD *p 196*
305 BROOK DR UNIT 6, CHASE, BC, V0E 1M0
(250) 679-8515   *SIC 5411*
SAFETY NET SECURITY LTD   *p 909*
857 MAY ST N, THUNDER BAY, ON, P7C 3S2
(807) 623-1844   *SIC 5065*
SAFETY SERVICES NL   *p 426*
See *NEWFOUNDLAND & LABRADOR SAFETY COUNCIL INC*
SAFETY SERVICES NOVA SCOTIA *p 448*
201 BROWNLOW AVE UNIT 1, DARTMOUTH, NS, B3B 1W2
(902) 454-9621   *SIC 8748*
SAFETY-KLEEN CANADA INC   *p 518*
300 WOOLWICH ST S, BRESLAU, ON, N0B 1M0
(519) 648-2291   *SIC 2992*
SAFEWAY   *p 7*
See *SOBEYS WEST INC*
SAFEWAY   *p 18*
See *SOBEYS WEST INC*
SAFEWAY   *p 25*
See *SOBEYS WEST INC*
SAFEWAY   *p 40*
See *SOBEYS WEST INC*
SAFEWAY   *p 41*
See *SOBEYS WEST INC*
SAFEWAY   *p 42*
See *SOBEYS WEST INC*
SAFEWAY   *p 67*
See *SOBEYS WEST INC*
SAFEWAY   *p 68*
See *SOBEYS WEST INC*
SAFEWAY   *p 69*
See *SOBEYS WEST INC*
SAFEWAY   *p 78*
See *SOBEYS WEST INC*
SAFEWAY   *p 83*
See *SOBEYS WEST INC*
SAFEWAY   *p 94*
See *SOBEYS WEST INC*
SAFEWAY   *p 104*
See *SOBEYS WEST INC*
SAFEWAY   *p 107*
See *SOBEYS WEST INC*
SAFEWAY   *p 119*
See *SOBEYS WEST INC*
SAFEWAY   *p 120*
See *SOBEYS WEST INC*
SAFEWAY   *p 123*
See *SOBEYS WEST INC*
SAFEWAY   *p 129*
See *SOBEYS WEST INC*
SAFEWAY   *p 186*
See *SOBEYS WEST INC*
SAFEWAY   *p 238*
See *SOBEYS WEST INC*
SAFEWAY   *p 278*

See *SOBEYS WEST INC*
SAFEWAY   *p 287*
See *SOBEYS WEST INC*
SAFEWAY   *p 293*
See *SOBEYS WEST INC*
SAFEWAY   *p 356*
See *SOBEYS WEST INC*
SAFEWAY   *p 392*
See *SOBEYS WEST INC*
SAFEWAY   *p 565*
See *SOBEYS WEST INC*
SAFEWAY   *p 1434*
See *SOBEYS WEST INC*
SAFEWAY #801   *p 140*
See *SOBEYS WEST INC*
SAFEWAY BONAVISTA SHOPPING PLAZA *p 39*
See *SOBEYS WEST INC*
SAFEWAY FOOD & DRUG   *p 358*
See *SOBEYS WEST INC*
SAFEWAY LOCAL   *p 332*
See *SOBEYS WEST INC*
SAFEWAY PHARMACY   *p 180*
See *SOBEYS WEST INC*
SAFEWAY PHARMACY   *p 227*
See *SOBEYS WEST INC*
SAFEWAY PHARMACY   *p 239*
See *SOBEYS WEST INC*
SAFEWAY PHARMACY   *p 342*
See *SOBEYS WEST INC*
SAFEWAY REGENT PARK   *p 1421*
See *SOBEYS WEST INC*
SAFEWAY SOUTHCENTRE   *p 39*
See *SOBEYS WEST INC*
SAFEWAY STORE #0198   *p 231*
See *SOBEYS WEST INC*
SAFEWAY, DIV   *p 277*
See *SOBEYS WEST INC*
SAFEWAY, DIV OF   *p 9*
See *SOBEYS WEST INC*
SAFEWAY, DIV OF   *p 166*
See *SOBEYS WEST INC*
SAFEWAY, DIV OF   *p 204*
See *SOBEYS WEST INC*
SAFILO CANADA INC   *p 1169*
4800 RUE MOLSON, MONTREAL, QC, H1Y 3J8
(514) 521-2555   *SIC 5049*
SAFRAN CABIN CANADA CO.   *p 1118*
18107 RTE TRANSCANADIENNE, KIRKLAND, QC, H9J 3K1
(514) 697-5555   *SIC 8711*
SAFRAN ELECTRONICS & DEFENSE CANADA INC   *p 842*
2000 FISHER DR, PETERBOROUGH, ON, K9J 6X6
(705) 743-6903   *SIC 3812*
SAFRAN LANDING SYSTEMS CANADA INC   *p 474*
574 MONARCH AVE, AJAX, ON, L1S 2G8
(905) 683-3100   *SIC 3728*
SAFRAN LANDING SYSTEMS CANADA INC   *p 1153*
13000 RUE DU PARC, MIRABEL, QC, J7J 0W6
(450) 434-3400   *SIC 3728*
SAFRAN MOTEURS D'HELICOPTERES CANADA INC   *p 1153*
11800 RUE HELEN-BRISTOL, MIRABEL, QC, J7N 3G8
(450) 476-2550   *SIC 7538*
SAFWAY SERVICES CANADA, ULC *p 129*
1005 MEMORIAL DR UNIT 3, FORT MCMURRAY, AB, T9K 0K4
(780) 791-6473   *SIC 1799*
SAFWAY SERVICES CANADA, ULC *p 130*
11237 87 AVE, FORT SASKATCHEWAN, AB, T8L 2S3
(780) 992-1929   *SIC 1799*
SAFWAY SERVICES CANADA, ULC *p 587*
503 CARLINGVIEW DR, ETOBICOKE, ON, M9W 5H2
(416) 675-2449   *SIC 1799*
SAGAMIE LE DEPANNEUR PLUS *p 1303*

See OUELLET & JOBIN INC

SAGE EXECUTIVE GROUP   p 223
See STATESMEN REALTY CORPORATION

SAGE OTTAWA   p 821
700 SUSSEX DR SUITE 200, OTTAWA, ON,
K1N 1K4
  SIC 6331

SAGE-LINK LTD   p 58
700 4 AVE SW SUITE 1180, CALGARY, AB,
T2P 3J4
  (403) 457-1590   *SIC 1389*

SAGINAW BAKERIES   p 280
See SAGINAW ENTERPRISES LTD

SAGINAW ENTERPRISES LTD   p 280
2520 190 ST SUITE 102, SURREY, BC, V3Z
3W6
  (604) 385-2520   *SIC 2051*

SAGIT INVESTMENT MANAGEMENT LTDp
309
789 PENDER ST W SUITE 900, VANCOU-
VER, BC, V6C 1H2
  SIC 6722

SAGKEENG EDUCATION AUTHORITY   p
354
GD, PINE FALLS, MB, R0E 1M0
  (204) 367-4109   *SIC 8621*

SAHALI MALL SAFEWAY   p 218
See SOBEYS WEST INC

SAHIB FREIGHT SERVICES INC   p 700
1665 ENTERPRISE RD, MISSISSAUGA,
ON, L4W 4L4
  (905) 696-8050   *SIC 4731*

SAHO   p 1419
*See SASKATCHEWAN HEALTH-CARE AS-
SOCIATION*

SAHOTA FARMS LTD   p 178
40990 NO. 3 RD, ABBOTSFORD, BC, V3G
2S1
  (604) 823-2341   *SIC 5148*

SAI GLOBAL INC   p 587
20 CARLSON CRT SUITE 200, ETOBI-
COKE, ON, M9W 7K6
  (416) 401-8700   *SIC 8742*

SAIL PLEIN AIR INC   p 1133
2850 AV JACQUES-BUREAU, LAVAL, QC,
H7P 0B7
  (450) 688-6264   *SIC 5941*

SAINE MARKETING INC   p 1215
2222 BOUL RENE-LEVESQUE O BUREAU
220, MONTREAL, QC, H3H 1R6
  (514) 931-8233   *SIC 8732*

SAINT BRIGID'S HOME INC   p 1271
1645 CH SAINT-LOUIS, QUEBEC, QC, G1S
4M3
  (418) 681-4687   *SIC 8361*

**SAINT CHARLES ADULT EDUCATION
CONTINUING EDUCATION**   p 615
*See HAMILTON-WENTWORTH CATHOLIC
SCHOOL BOARD*

SAINT ELIZABETH HEALTH CARE   p 674
90 ALLSTATE PKY SUITE 300, MARKHAM,
ON, L3R 6H3
  (905) 940-9655   *SIC 8082*

SAINT ELIZABETH HEALTH CARE   p 750
30 COLONNADE RD N SUITE 225, NE-
PEAN, ON, K2E 7J6
  (613) 738-9661   *SIC 8059*

SAINT ELIZABETH HEALTH CARE   p 1015
420 GREEN ST SUITE 202, WHITBY, ON,
L1N 8R1
  (905) 430-6997   *SIC 8361*

SAINT EUGENE MISSION RESORT   p 204
*See SEM RESORT LIMITED PARTNER-
SHIP*

SAINT FRANCIS HIGH SCHOOL (10-12)   p
40
*See CALGARY ROMAN CATHOLIC SEPA-
RATE SCHOOL DISTRICT #1*

**SAINT JOHN AQUATIC CENTRE COMMIS-
SION**   p
415
50 UNION ST, SAINT JOHN, NB, E2L 1A1
  (506) 658-4715   *SIC 7999*

SAINT JOHN ENERGY   p 416

*See POWER COMMISSION OF THE CITY
OF SAINT JOHN*

SAINT JOHN TRANSIT COMMISSIONp 413
55 MCDONALD ST, SAINT JOHN, NB, E2J
0C7
  (506) 658-4710   *SIC 4111*

SAINT JOHN VOLKSWAGEN   p 413
297 ROTHESAY AVE, SAINT JOHN, NB,
E2J 2C1
  (506) 658-1313   *SIC 5511*

SAINT JOHN'S SCHOOL OF ALBERTA   p
167
GD, STONY PLAIN, AB, T7Z 1X5
  (780) 701-5625   *SIC 8699*

**SAINT LEONARD'S SOCIETY OF NOVA
SCOTIA**   p 456
5506 CUNARD ST SUITE 101, HALIFAX,
NS, B3K 1C2
  (902) 406-3631   *SIC 8699*

SAINT LUKE'S PLACE   p 537
1624 FRANKLIN BLVD, CAMBRIDGE, ON,
N3C 3P4
  (519) 658-5183   *SIC 8051*

SAINT MARY'S UNIVERSITY   p 451
923 ROBIE ST SUITE 210, HALIFAX, NS,
B3H 3C3
  (902) 420-5400   *SIC 8221*

SAINT PAUL CATHOLIC HIGH SCHOOL   p
760
*See NIAGARA CATHOLIC DISTRICT
SCHOOL BOARD*

SAINT PAUL UNIVERSITY   p 826
223 MAIN ST SUITE 267, OTTAWA, ON,
K1S 1C4
  (613) 236-1393   *SIC 8221*

SAINT VINCENT'S NURSING HOME   p 456
2080 WINDSOR ST SUITE 509, HALIFAX,
NS, B3K 5B2
  (902) 429-0550   *SIC 8361*

**SAINT-AUGUSTIN CANADA ELECTRIQUE
INC**   p 1293
75 RUE D'ANVERS, SAINT-AUGUSTIN-DE-
DESMAURES, QC, G3A 1S5
  (418) 878-6900   *SIC 1711*

SAINT-CONSTANT AUTO 2010 INC   p 1298
48   RUE   SAINT-PIERRE,   SAINT-
CONSTANT, QC, J5A 1B9
  (450) 632-0700   *SIC 5511*

SAINT-CONSTANT MAZDA   p 1298
See SAINT-CONSTANT AUTO 2010 INC

SAINT-GOBAIN CANADA INC   p 846
28 ALBERT ST W, PLATTSVILLE, ON, N0J
1S0
  (519) 684-7441   *SIC 3291*

SAINT-GOBAIN SOLAR GUARD, INC   p 804
760 PACIFIC RD UNIT 1, OAKVILLE, ON,
L6L 6M5
  (905) 847-2790   *SIC 2899*

SAINT-HYACINTHE, VILLE DE   p 1313
935   RUE   DESSAULLES,   SAINT-
HYACINTHE, QC, J2S 3C4
  (450) 778-8550   *SIC 7389*

SAINT-JEAN HYUNDAI   p 1316
See 9185-9322 QUEBEC INC

SAINT-RAYMOND TOYOTA   p 1351
See FUTUROTO INC

SAINTE REVERA   p 1397
See REVERA INC

SAIPEM CANADA INC   p 58
530 8 AVE SW SUITE 2100, CALGARY, AB,
T2P 3S8
  (403) 441-2793   *SIC 1629*

SAIPEM CONSTRUCTION CANADA   p 58
See SAIPEM CANADA INC

SAJE NATURAL BUSINESS INC   p 289
22 5TH AVE E SUITE 500, VANCOUVER,
BC, V5T 1G8
  (877) 275-7253   *SIC 5169*

SAJE NATURAL WELLNESS   p 289
See SAJE NATURAL BUSINESS INC

SAJO INC   p 1155
1320 BOUL GRAHAM BUREAU 129,
MONT-ROYAL, QC, H3P 3C8
  (514) 385-0333   *SIC 1542*

SAJY COMMUNICATIONS INC   p 1052
7070 RUE BEAUBIEN E, ANJOU, QC, H1M
1B2
  (514) 521-4301   *SIC 2791*

**SAKITAWAK DEVELOPMENT CORPORA-
TION**   p
1407
GD, ILE-A-LA-CROSSE, SK, S0M 1C0
  (306) 833-2466   *SIC 6712*

SAKKIO JAPAN   p 677
See YATSEN GROUP INC

SAKO MATERIALS LIMITED   p 510
71 ORENDA RD, BRAMPTON, ON, L6W
1V8
  (905) 457-5321   *SIC 5033*

SAKS FIFTH AVENUE   p 503
See HUDSON'S BAY COMPANY

SAKS FIFTH AVENUE OFF 5TH CANADAp
503
See HUDSON'S BAY COMPANY

SAKUNDIAK EQUIPMENT   p 1418
See RED MOUNTAIN HOLDINGS LTD

SAL MARKETING INC   p 300
2165 BROADWAY W, VANCOUVER, BC,
V6B 5H6
  (604) 737-3816   *SIC 6351*

SALADE ETCETERA U INC   p 1376
147 RANG SAINT-PAUL, SHERRINGTON,
QC, J0L 2N0
  (450) 454-7712   *SIC 0723*

SALADEXPRESS INC   p 1351
225 RUE SAINT-ANDRE, SAINT-REMI, QC,
J0L 2L0
  (514) 385-3362   *SIC 0723*

SALAISON ALPHA LTEE   p 1050
10800 BOUL DU GOLF, ANJOU, QC, H1J
2Y7
  (514) 593-8430   *SIC 5147*

SALAISON LA MAISON DU ROTI INC   p
1173
1969 AV DU MONT-ROYAL E, MONTREAL,
QC, H2H 1J5
  (514) 521-2448   *SIC 5147*

SALAISON LEVESQUE INC   p 1218
500 AV BEAUMONT, MONTREAL, QC, H3N
1T7
  (514) 273-1702   *SIC 5147*

SALAISONS DESCO, LES   p 1060
See 4525663 CANADA INC

SALAMEH DRUGS LTD   p 713
321 LAKESHORE RD W, MISSISSAUGA,
ON, L5H 1G9
  (905) 271-4581   *SIC 5912*

SALB, H. INTERNATIONAL   p 795
49 RIVALDA RD, NORTH YORK, ON, M9M
2M4
  (416) 746-1944   *SIC 5136*

SALEM CONTRACTING LTD   p 251
9097   MILWAUKEE   WAY,   PRINCE
GEORGE, BC, V2N 5T3
  (250) 564-2244   *SIC 1542*

SALEM HOME INC   p 361
165 15TH ST, WINKLER, MB, R6W 1T8
  (204) 325-4316   *SIC 8051*

SALEM MANOR NURSING HOME   p 139
See SALEM MANOR SOCIETY, THE

SALEM MANOR SOCIETY, THE   p 139
4419 46 ST SUITE 612, LEDUC, AB, T9E
6L2
  (780) 986-8654   *SIC 8051*

SALERNO DAIRY PRODUCTS LIMITED   p
609
20 MORLEY ST, HAMILTON, ON, L8H 3R7
  (905) 544-6281   *SIC 2022*

SALERNO PACKAGING   p 1076
*See EMBALLAGES SALERNO CANADA
INC*

**SALERNO PELLICULE ET SACS DE PLAS-
TIQUE (CANADA) INC**   p
1076
2275 BOUL FORD, CHATEAUGUAY, QC,
J6J 4Z2
  (450) 692-8642   *SIC 2673*

SALERS ASSOCIATION OF CANADA   p 25

5160 SKYLINE WAY NE, CALGARY, AB,
T2E 6V1
  (403) 264-5850   *SIC 8621*

**SALES BEACON PRODUCTIVITY SOLU-
TIONS**   p
442
See MDINA ENTERPRISES LTD

SALES OFFICE   p 980
*See EF INTERNATIONAL LANGUAGE
SCHOOLS (CANADA) LIMITED*

**SALESFORCE.COM CANADA CORPORA-
TION**   p
966
20 BAY ST SUITE 800, TORONTO, ON, M5J
2N8
  (647) 258-3800   *SIC 8741*

SALFLEX POLYMERS LTD   p 795
1925 WILSON AVE, NORTH YORK, ON,
M9M 1A9
  (416) 741-0273   *SIC 2822*

SALISBURY COMPOSITE HIGH SCHOOLp
161
*See ELK ISLAND PUBLIC SCHOOLS RE-
GIONAL DIVISION NO. 14*

SALISBURY HOUSE   p 392
See SALISBURY HOUSE OF CANADA LTD

SALISBURY HOUSE OF CANADA LTD   p
370
787 LEILA AVE, WINNIPEG, MB, R2V 3J7
  (204) 594-7257   *SIC 5812*

SALISBURY HOUSE OF CANADA LTD   p
392
1941 PEMBINA HWY, WINNIPEG, MB, R3T
2G7
  SIC 5812

SALISBURY IRVING BIG STOP   p 417
See LAVOIE, J. P. & SONS LTD

SALISBURY MORSE PLACE SCHOOL   p
367
*See RIVER EAST TRANSCONA SCHOOL
DIVISION*

SALIT STEEL   p 759
See MYER SALIT LIMITED

SALKELD, C. & S. ENTERPRISES LTD   p
842
1200 LANSDOWNE ST W SUITE 81, PE-
TERBOROUGH, ON, K9J 2A1
  (705) 742-0406   *SIC 5531*

SALLE ALBERT-ROUSSEAU   p 1272
*See CORPORATION DE LA SALLE
ALBERT-ROUSSEAU, LA*

SALLE FRED BARRY, LA   p 1167
See THEATRE DENISE PELLETIER INC

SALLE J.-ANTONIO-THOMPSON, LA   p
1387
*See CORPORATION DE DEVELOPMENT
CULTUREL DE TROIS-RIVIERES*

SALLE JEAN-PAUL TARDIF   p 1270
*See   COLLEGE   SAINT-CHARLES-
GARNIER, LE*

SALLY FOURMY & ASSOCIATES   p 28
See CINTAS CANADA LIMITED

SALLY FOURMY & ASSOCIATES   p 716
See CINTAS CANADA LIMITED

SALLY FOURMY & ASSOCIATES   p 755
See CINTAS CANADA LIMITED

SALLY FOURMY & ASSOCIATES   p 786
See CINTAS CANADA LIMITED

SALLY FOURMY & ASSOCIATES   p 1064
See CINTAS CANADA LIMITED

SALMAN PARTNERS INC   p 316
1095 PENDER ST W SUITE 1702, VAN-
COUVER, BC, V6E 2M6
  SIC 6211

SALMEER ENTERPRISES   p 104
17046 90 AVE NW, EDMONTON, AB, T5T
1L6
  (780) 486-6466   *SIC 4925*

SALMON ARM CHEV BUICK GMC LTD   p
268
3901 11 AVE NE, SALMON ARM, BC, V1E
2S2
  (250) 832-6066   *SIC 5511*

SALMON ARM GAS BAR   p 179

See ARMSTRONG REGIONAL CO-OPERATIVE

SALMON ARM GM *p 268*
See SALMON ARM CHEV BUICK GMC LTD

SALMON ARM SAVINGS AND CREDIT UNION *p 268*
370 LAKESHORE DR NE, SALMON ARM, BC, V1E 1E4
(250) 832-8011 *SIC 6062*

SALMON CAPITAL CORPORATION *p 651*
100 KELLOGG LANE, LONDON, ON, N5W 0B4
(519) 266-3400 *SIC 5065*

SALON CENTRE *p 384*
See COSIMO MINNELLA INVESTMENTS INC

SALTFLEET DISTRICT HIGH SCHOOL *p 894*
See HAMILTON-WENTWORTH DISTRICT SCHOOL BOARD, THE

SALTWORKS TECHNOLOGIES INC *p 258*
13800 STEVESTON HWY, RICHMOND, BC, V6W 1A8
(604) 628-6508 *SIC 8748*

SALUMATICS INC. *p 717*
3250 RIDGEWAY DR UNIT 10, MISSISSAUGA, ON, L5L 5Y6
(905) 362-2230 *SIC 7374*

SALVATION ARMY TORONTO GRACE HEALTH CENTER, THE *p 932*
650 CHURCH ST, TORONTO, ON, M4Y 2G5
(416) 925-2251 *SIC 8051*

SALVATORE L. BRIQUETEUR 65 *p 1380*
See 9167-0661 QUEBEC INC

SALVEX INC *p 1232*
2450 MONTEE SAINT-FRANCOIS BUREAU 2, MONTREAL, QC, H7E 4P2
(450) 664-4335 *SIC 1542*

SAM ADELSTEIN & CO. LIMITED *p 883*
492 WELLAND AVE, ST CATHARINES, ON, L2M 5V5
(905) 988-9336 *SIC 5093*

SAM HOLDINGS LTD *p 68*
1623 96 AVE SW, CALGARY, AB, T2V 5E5
(403) 266-1985 *SIC 5172*

SAM KOTZER LIMITED *p 571*
77 FIMA CRES, ETOBICOKE, ON, M8W 3R1
(416) 532-1114 *SIC 5945*

SAM'S DELI *p 338*
See ROGERS' CHOCOLATES LTD

SAM'S NO FRILLS *p 510*
See 1408939 ONTARIO LIMITED

SAMA RESOURCES INC *p 1155*
1320 BOUL GRAHAM BUREAU 132, MONT-ROYAL, QC, H3P 3C8
(514) 747-4653 *SIC 6799*

SAMBRO FISHERIES LIMITED *p 465*
40 LENNYS LANE, SAMBRO, NS, B3V 1L5
(902) 868-2140 *SIC 5146*

SAMCO MACHINERY LIMITED *p 914*
351 PASSMORE AVE, TORONTO, ON, M1V 3N8
(416) 285-0619 *SIC 3542*

SAMEDAY COURIER *p 650*
See TFORCE FINAL MILE CANADA INC

SAMETCO AUTO INC *p 375*
233 PORTAGE AVE SUITE 200, WINNIPEG, MB, R3B 2A7
(204) 925-7278 *SIC 5531*

SAMI FRUITS *p 1226*
See MAISON SAMI T.A. FRUITS INC, LA

SAMKO SALES *p 571*
See SAM KOTZER LIMITED

SAMMI INTERNATIONAL TRADING LTD *p 266*
6191 WESTMINSTER HWY UNIT 150, RICHMOND, BC, V7C 4V4
(778) 938-2277 *SIC 6799*

SAMOSA AND SWEET FACTORY *p 581*
See 1199893 ONTARIO LIMITED

SAMPLER POSTAL OUTLET, THE *p 858*
See GROOMBRIDGE, W. ENTERPRISES

INC

SAMSON CONTROLS INC *p 674*
105 RIVIERA DR UNIT 1, MARKHAM, ON, L3R 5J7
(905) 474-0354 *SIC 5084*

SAMSONITE CANADA INC *p 896*
305 C H MEIER BLVD, STRATFORD, ON, N5A 0H4
(519) 271-5040 *SIC 5099*

SAMSUNG ELECTRONICS CANADA INC *p 726*
2050 DERRY RD W SUITE 1, MISSISSAUGA, ON, L5N 0B9
(905) 542-3535 *SIC 5064*

SAMSUNG RENEWABLE ENERGY INC *p 727*
2050 DERRY RD W 2FL, MISSISSAUGA, ON, L5N 0B9
(905) 501-4934 *SIC 4911*

SAMTACK COMPUTER *p 674*
See SAMTACK INC

SAMTACK INC *p 674*
1100 RODICK RD, MARKHAM, ON, L3R 8C3
(905) 940-1880 *SIC 5045*

SAMUEL & CO. APPAREL LIMITED *p 459*
127 CHAIN LAKE DR UNIT 9, HALIFAX, NS, B3S 1B3
(902) 454-7093 *SIC 5621*

SAMUEL BOTHWELL, DIV OF *p 704*
See SAMUEL, SON & CO., LIMITED

SAMUEL FLAT ROLLED PROCESSING GROUP *p 609*
See SAMUEL, SON & CO., LIMITED

SAMUEL METAL BLANKING *p 516*
See SAMUEL, SON & CO., LIMITED

SAMUEL METAL BLANKING *p 516*
546 ELGIN ST, BRANTFORD, ON, N3S 7P8
(519) 758-1125 *SIC 1791*

SAMUEL PLATE SALES *p 893*
See SAMUEL, SON & CO., LIMITED

SAMUEL, SON & CO., LIMITED *p 149*
1709 8 ST, NISKU, AB, T9E 7S8
(780) 955-7516 *SIC 5051*

SAMUEL, SON & CO., LIMITED *p 516*
546 ELGIN ST, BRANTFORD, ON, N3S 7P8
(519) 758-2710 *SIC 5051*

SAMUEL, SON & CO., LIMITED *p 537*
133 TROH AVE, CAMBRIDGE, ON, N3C 4B1
(416) 777-9554 *SIC 1791*

SAMUEL, SON & CO., LIMITED *p 609*
410 NASH RD N, HAMILTON, ON, L8H 7R9
(800) 263-6553 *SIC 5051*

SAMUEL, SON & CO., LIMITED *p 674*
7455 WOODBINE AVE, MARKHAM, ON, L3R 1A7
(905) 475-6464 *SIC 5051*

SAMUEL, SON & CO., LIMITED *p 704*
2360 DIXIE RD, MISSISSAUGA, ON, L4Y 1Z7
(905) 279-5460 *SIC 6712*

SAMUEL, SON & CO., LIMITED *p 893*
12 TEAL AVE, STONEY CREEK, ON, L8E 3Y5
(800) 263-1316 *SIC 5051*

SAMUEL, SON & CO., LIMITED *p 893*
400 GLOVER RD, STONEY CREEK, ON, L8E 5X1
(905) 662-1404 *SIC 3479*

SAMUEL, SON & CO., LIMITED *p 1054*
21525 AV CLARK-GRAHAM, BAIE-D'URFE, QC, H9X 3T5
(800) 361-3483 *SIC 5051*

SAMUEL, SON & CO., LIMITED *p 1085*
2225 AV FRANCIS-HUGHES, COTE SAINT-LUC, QC, H7S 1N5
(514) 384-5220 *SIC 5051*

SAMUELSOHN LIMITEE *p 1218*
6930 AV DU PARC, MONTREAL, QC, H3N 1W9
(514) 273-7741 *SIC 2311*

SAN FORESTRY LTD *p 152*
9925 100 ST, PLAMONDON, AB, T0A 2T0

SIC 2411

SAN GOLD CORPORATION *p 386*
1661 PORTAGE AVE UNIT 212, WINNIPEG, MB, R3J 3T7
(204) 772-9149 *SIC 1041*

SAN INDUSTRIES, DIV OF *p 225*
See SANGROUP INC

SAN MIGUEL FOODS LTD *p 481*
1 HENDERSON DR UNIT 4, AURORA, ON, L4G 4J7
(905) 727-7918 *SIC 5812*

SAN RUFO HOMES LTD *p 166*
35C RAYBORN CRES, ST. ALBERT, AB, T8N 4A9
(780) 470-4070 *SIC 1531*

SAN-O-PHONE HEALTH CARE DIV. *p 578*
See EMERAUD CANADA LIMITED

SANATORIUM BOARD OF MANITOBA *p 373*
629 MCDERMOT AVE, WINNIPEG, MB, R3A 1P6
(204) 774-5501 *SIC 7389*

SANCON COMMISSIONING *p 395*
See SANCON CONTRACTING LTD

SANCON CONTRACTING LTD *p 395*
4621 MAIN ST, BELLEDUNE, NB, E8G 2L3
(506) 507-2222 *SIC 1521*

SANCTON EQUIPMENT *p 413*
See SANCTON GROUP INC

SANCTON GROUP INC *p 413*
85 MCILVEEN DR, SAINT JOHN, NB, E2J 4Y6
(506) 635-8500 *SIC 5084*

SANCTUAIRE NOTRE-DAME-DU-CAP *p 1385*
626 RUE NOTRE-DAME E, TROIS-RIVIERES, QC, G8T 4G9
(819) 374-2441 *SIC 8661*

SAND BAR, THE *p 318*
See SEQUOIA COMPANY OF RESTAURANTS INC

SAND HILLS COLONY *p 5*
GD, BEISEKER, AB, T0M 0G0
(403) 947-2042 *SIC 5499*

SAND LAKE HUTTERIAN BRETHREN INC *p 1437*
GD, VAL MARIE, SK, S0N 2T0
(306) 298-2068 *SIC 7389*

SANDALE UTILITY PRODUCTS *p 446*
See EMCO CORPORATION

SANDALWOOD SUITES HOTEL *p 693*
See CHIP REIT NO 23 OPERATIONS LIMITED PARTNERSHIP

SANDCASTLE TOURS *p 85*
See NITE TOURS INTERNATIONAL

SANDER GEOPHYSICS LIMITED *p 827*
260 HUNT CLUB RD, OTTAWA, ON, K1V 1C1
(613) 521-9626 *SIC 1382*

SANDERSON MONUMENT COMPANY LIMITED *p 810*
33 PETER ST S, ORILLIA, ON, L3V 5A8
(705) 326-6131 *SIC 3281*

SANDERSON-HAROLD COMPANY LIMITED, THE *p 854*
245 WEST BEAVER CREEK RD UNIT 2, RICHMOND HILL, ON, L4B 1L1
(519) 442-6311 *SIC 2434*

SANDFORD - BLACKSTOCK INVESTMENTS LIMITED *p 895*
37 SANDIFORD DR UNIT 300, STOUFFVILLE, ON, L4A 3Z2
SIC 6282

SANDHER FRUIT PACKERS LTD *p 220*
4525 SCOTTY CREEK RD, KELOWNA, BC, V1X 6N3
(250) 491-9176 *SIC 5431*

SANDMAN HOTEL & SUITES CALGARY SOUTH *p 36*
See NORTHLAND PROPERTIES CORPORATION

SANDMAN HOTEL & SUITES KELOWNA *p 222*
See NORTHLAND PROPERTIES CORPORATION

SANDMAN INNS *p 321*
See NORTHLAND PROPERTIES CORPORATION

SANDOZ *p 1067*
See SANDOZ CANADA INC

SANDOZ CANADA INC *p 1067*
145 RUE JULES-LEGER, BOUCHERVILLE, QC, J4B 7K8
(450) 641-4903 *SIC 2834*

SANDPIPER CONTRACTING LTD *p 282*
9342 194 ST, SURREY, BC, V4N 4E9
(604) 888-8484 *SIC 1623*

SANDPIPER GOLF CLUB/ROWENAS INN ON THE RIVER *p 215*
See PRETTY ESTATES LTD

SANDRA TEA & COFFEE LIMITED *p 474*
144 MILLS RD, AJAX, ON, L1S 2H1
(905) 683-5000 *SIC 2099*

SANDS BULK SALES LTD *p 251*
1059 EASTERN ST, PRINCE GEORGE, BC, V2N 5R8
(250) 563-2855 *SIC 5983*

SANDS BULK TRANSPORT *p 251*
See SANDS BULK SALES LTD

SANDS COMMERCIAL FLOOR COVERINGS INC *p 674*
180 BENTLEY ST, MARKHAM, ON, L3R 3L2
(905) 475-6380 *SIC 5023*

SANDSTORM GOLD LTD *p 309*
400 BURRARD ST SUITE 1400, VANCOUVER, BC, V6C 3G2
(604) 689-0234 *SIC 1041*

SANDTRON AUTOMATION LIMITED *p 526*
1221 DILLON RD, BURLINGTON, ON, L7M 1K6
(905) 827-8230 *SIC 5065*

SANDVIK CANADA, INC *p 479*
425 MCCARTNEY, ARNPRIOR, ON, K7S 3P3
(613) 623-6501 *SIC 3312*

SANDVIK CANADA, INC *p 524*
4445 FAIRVIEW ST, BURLINGTON, ON, L7L 2A4
SIC 3532

SANDVIK CANADA, INC *p 647*
100 MAGILL ST, LIVELY, ON, P3Y 1K7
(705) 692-5881 *SIC 5051*

SANDVIK CANADA, INC *p 727*
2550 MEADOWVALE BLVD UNIT 3, MISSISSAUGA, ON, L5N 8C2
(905) 826-8900 *SIC 3312*

SANDVIK CANADA, INC *p 727*
2550 MEADOWVALE BLVD UNIT 3, MISSISSAUGA, ON, L5N 8C2
(905) 826-8900 *SIC 5084*

SANDVIK CANADA, INC *p 764*
400 KIRKPATRICK ST SUITE B, NORTH BAY, ON, P1B 8G5
SIC 5082

SANDVIK MATERIALS TECHNOLOGY CANADA *p 479*
See SANDVIK CANADA, INC

SANDVIK MINING *p 727*
See SANDVIK CANADA, INC

SANDVIK MINING AND CONSTRUCTION *p 647*
See SANDVIK CANADA, INC

SANDVIK MINING AND CONSTRUCTION *p 764*
See SANDVIK CANADA, INC

SANDVINE INCORPORATED ULC *p 1009*
408 ALBERT ST, WATERLOO, ON, N2L 3V3
(519) 880-2600 *SIC 3825*

SANDVINE LTD *p 1009*
408 ALBERT ST, WATERLOO, ON, N2L 3V3
(519) 880-2600 *SIC 3825*

SANDY BAY SCHOOL *p 352*
GD, MARIUS, MB, R0H 0T0

---

(204) 843-2407 *SIC* 8211
SANDY HILL COMMUNITY HEALTH CENTRE INC *p*
821
221 NELSON ST, OTTAWA, ON, K1N 1C7
(613) 789-6309 *SIC* 8093
SANDY MCTYRE RETAIL LTD *p* 657
1125 WELLINGTON RD, LONDON, ON, N6E 1M1
(519) 681-2655 *SIC* 5531
SANDY'S FURNITURE LTD *p* 202
1335 UNITED BLVD SUITE D, COQUITLAM, BC, V3K 6V3
(604) 520-0800 *SIC* 5712
SANEAL CAMERA *p* 73
See SANEAL CAMERA SUPPLIES LTD
SANEAL CAMERA SUPPLIES LTD *p* 73
1402 11 AVE SW, CALGARY, AB, T3C 0M8
(403) 228-1865 *SIC* 5946
SANEXEN - EXCAVATION, DIV OF *p* 1071
See SANEXEN SERVICES ENVIRONNEMENTAUX INC
SANEXEN SERVICES ENVIRONNEMENTAUX INC *p*
1071
9935 RUE DE CHATEAUNEUF UNITE 200, BROSSARD, QC, J4Z 3V4
(450) 466-2123 *SIC* 4959
SANGOMA TECHNOLOGIES CORPORATION *p*
674
100 RENFREW DR SUITE 100, MARKHAM, ON, L3R 9R6
(905) 474-1990 *SIC* 7372
SANGROUP INC *p* 225
25583 88 AVE, LANGLEY, BC, V1M 3N8
(604) 881-4848 *SIC* 5211
SANI METAL LTEE *p* 1277
5170 RUE RIDEAU, QUEBEC, QC, G2E 5S4
(418) 872-5170 *SIC* 2514
SANI PRO INC *p* 433
99 BLACKMARSH RD, ST. JOHN'S, NL, A1E 1S6
(709) 579-2151 *SIC* 5046
SANI SPORT INC *p* 1069
7777 BOUL MARIE-VICTORIN, BROSSARD, QC, J4W 1B3
(450) 465-7220 *SIC* 7991
SANI-ECO INC *p* 1109
530 RUE EDOUARD, GRANBY, QC, J2G 3Z6
(450) 777-4977 *SIC* 4953
SANI-GEAR FIRE *p* 642
See SANI-GEAR INC
SANI-GEAR INC *p* 642
545 TRILLIUM DR UNIT 4, KITCHENER, ON, N2R 1J4
(519) 893-1235 *SIC* 7389
SANI-MANIC COTE-NORD INC *p* 1246
37 CH DE LA SCIERIE, POINTE-AUX-OUTARDES, QC, G5C 0B7
(418) 589-2376 *SIC* 7699
SANI-MARC INC *p* 1398
42 RUE DE L'ARTISAN, VICTORIAVILLE, QC, G6P 7E3
(819) 758-1541 *SIC* 2841
SANI-PLUS INC *p* 1119
1600 RUE DU PINCELIER, L'ANCIENNE-LORETTE, QC, G2E 6B7
(418) 871-4683 *SIC* 5122
SANI-SERVICE *p* 193
See LASFAM INVESTMENTS INC
SANI-SOL INC *p* 891
149 IBER RD, STITTSVILLE, ON, K2S 1E7
(613) 831-3698 *SIC* 5169
SANIMAX ABP INC *p* 1161
9900 6E RUE, MONTREAL, QC, H1C 1G2
(514) 643-3391 *SIC* 4953
SANIMAX ACI INC *p* 1139
2001 AV DE LA ROTONDE, LEVIS, QC, G6X 2L8
(418) 832-4645 *SIC* 2077
SANIMAX EEI INC *p* 1161
9900 BOUL MAURICE-DUPLESSIS, MON-

TREAL, QC, H1C 1G1
(514) 648-3000 *SIC* 4212
SANIMAX LOM INC *p* 1161
9900 BOUL MAURICE-DUPLESSIS, MONTREAL, QC, H1C 1G1
(514) 648-3000 *SIC* 2077
SANIMAX LTD *p* 604
5068 WHITELAW RD SUITE 6, GUELPH, ON, N1H 6J3
(519) 824-2381 *SIC* 4953
SANIMAX SAN INC *p* 1161
9900 BOUL MAURICE-DUPLESSIS, MONTREAL, QC, H1C 1G1
(514) 648-6001 *SIC* 2077
SANIVAC *p* 1243
See 9363-9888 QUEBEC INC
SANJEL CANADA LTD *p* 18
10774 42 ST SE, CALGARY, AB, T2C 0L5
(403) 215-4420 *SIC* 1389
SANJEL CANADA LTD *p* 58
505 2 ST SW SUITE 200, CALGARY, AB, T2P 1N8
(403) 269-1420 *SIC* 1389
SANJEL CANADA LTD *p* 156
8051 EDGAR INDUSTRIAL DR, RED DEER, AB, T4P 3R2
(403) 357-1616 *SIC* 1389
SANJEL CANADA LTD *p* 158
1901 DIRKSON DR NE, REDCLIFF, AB, T0J 2P0
SIC 1389
SANJEL ENERGY SERVICES *p* 18
See SANJEL CANADA LTD
SANLING ENERGY LTD *p* 58
250 2 ST SW SUITE 1700, CALGARY, AB, T2P 0C1
(403) 303-8500 *SIC* 1311
SANMAR CANADA *p* 323
See AUTHENTIC T-SHIRT COMPANY ULC, THE
SANMINA-SCI NPI *p* 625
See SCI BROCKVILLE CORP
SANOFI PASTEUR LIMITED *p* 775
1755 STEELES AVE W, NORTH YORK, ON, M2R 3T4
(416) 667-2700 *SIC* 2836
SANOFI SANTE GRAND PUBLIC INC *p*
1087
2905 PLACE LOUIS-R.-RENAUD, COTE SAINT-LUC, QC, H7V 0A3
(514) 956-6200 *SIC* 5122
SANOFI-AVENTIS CANADA INC *p* 1087
2905 PLACE LOUIS-R.-RENAUD, COTE SAINT-LUC, QC, H7V 0A3
(514) 331-9200 *SIC* 5122
SANOH CANADA, LTD *p* 808
300 C LINE, ORANGEVILLE, ON, L9W 3Z8
(519) 941-2229 *SIC* 5013
SANOOR INVESTMENT LTD *p* 186
4201 LOUGHEED HWY, BURNABY, BC, V5C 3Y6
(604) 298-2010 *SIC* 8741
SANPAUL INVESTMENTS LIMITED *p* 784
365 FLINT RD UNIT 1, NORTH YORK, ON, M3J 2J2
(416) 667-8929 *SIC* 5661
SANSOM EQUIPMENT LIMITED *p* 469
100 UPHAM DR, TRURO, NS, B2N 6W8
(902) 895-2885 *SIC* 5084
SANT, GEORGE & SONS LTD *p* 642
11831 COLD CREEK RD SUITE 1, KLEINBURG, ON, L0J 1C0
(905) 893-1592 *SIC* 1531
SANTACRUZ SILVER MINING LTD *p* 309
580 HORNBY ST SUITE 880, VANCOUVER, BC, V6C 3B6
(604) 569-1609 *SIC* 1044
SANTE BAUSCH, CANADA INC *p* 1362
2150 BOUL SAINT-ELZEAR O, SAINTE-ROSE, QC, H7L 4A8
(514) 744-6792 *SIC* 2834
SANTE COURVILLE INC *p* 1342
5200 80E RUE, SAINT-LAURENT, QC, H7R 5T6

(450) 627-7990 *SIC* 8361
SANTE MONTREAL COLLECTIF CJV, S.E.C. *p* 1186
1031 RUE SAINT-DENIS, MONTREAL, QC, H2X 3H9
(514) 394-1440 *SIC* 1542
SANTE NATURELLE A.G. LTEE *p* 1070
3555 BOUL MATTE, BROSSARD, QC, J4Y 2P4
(450) 659-7723 *SIC* 2833
SANTE-BEAUTE DANMOR INC *p* 1368
1 RUE LA PLAZA-DE-MAURICIE BUREAU 27, SHAWINIGAN, QC, G9N 7C1
(819) 539-5416 *SIC* 5912
SANTEK INVESTMENTS (1991) INC *p* 578
1 VALHALLA INN RD, ETOBICOKE, ON, M9B 1S9
(416) 233-5554 *SIC* 7011
SANTEREGIE INC *p* 1145
3645 CH DE CHAMBLY, LONGUEUIL, QC, J4L 1N9
SIC 7361
SANTINEL INC *p* 1145
1061 BOUL SAINTE-FOY, LONGUEUIL, QC, J4K 1W5
(450) 679-7801 *SIC* 8748
SANYO CANADA INC *p* 1033
201 CREDITVIEW RD, WOODBRIDGE, ON, L4L 9T1
(905) 760-9944 *SIC* 5064
SANYO CANADIAN MACHINE WORKS INCORPORATED *p*
568
33 INDUSTRIAL DR, ELMIRA, ON, N3B 3B1
(519) 669-1591 *SIC* 3569
SAP *p* 316
See SAP CANADA INC
SAP CANADA INC *p* 316
1095 PENDER ST W SUITE 400, VANCOUVER, BC, V6E 2M6
(604) 647-8888 *SIC* 7371
SAP CANADA INC *p* 774
222 BAY ST SUITE 1800, 1900, 2000, NORTH YORK, ON, M2P 2B8
(416) 229-0574 *SIC* 7372
SAP CANADA INC *p* 1009
445 WES GRAHAM WAY, WATERLOO, ON, N2L 6R2
(519) 886-3700 *SIC* 7371
SAP CANADA INC *p* 1190
380 RUE SAINT-ANTOINE O BUREAU 2000, MONTREAL, QC, H2Y 3X7
(514) 350-7300 *SIC* 7372
SAP SYBASE OFFICES *p* 1009
See SAP CANADA INC
SAPIENT CANADA INC *p* 983
134 PETER ST SUITE 1200, TORONTO, ON, M5V 2H2
(416) 645-1500 *SIC* 7379
SAPPORO CANADA INC *p* 606
551 CLAIR RD W, GUELPH, ON, N1L 1E9
(519) 822-1834 *SIC* 6712
SAPUNJIS ENTERPRISES INC *p* 18
7520 114 AVE SE, CALGARY, AB, T2C 4T3
(403) 216-5150 *SIC* 5051
SAPUTO *p* 902
See ALIMENTS SAPUTO LIMITEE
SAPUTO DAIRY PRODUCTS CANADA G.P. *p* 999
See SAPUTO INC
SAPUTO DAIRY PRODUCTS CANADA GP *p* 1327
See SAPUTO PRODUITS LAITIERS CANADA S.E.N.C.
SAPUTO FOOD *p* 76
See SAPUTO INC
SAPUTO FOODS *p* 175

See SAPUTO INC
SAPUTO FOODS *p* 593
See ALIMENTS SAPUTO LIMITEE
SAPUTO INC *p* 76
5434 44 ST NE, CALGARY, AB, T3J 3Z3
(403) 568-3800 *SIC* 4222
SAPUTO INC *p* 175
1799 RIVERSIDE RD SUITE 48, ABBOTSFORD, BC, V2S 4J8
(604) 853-2225 *SIC* 5143
SAPUTO INC *p* 808
425 RICHARDSON RD, ORANGEVILLE, ON, L9W 4Z4
(519) 941-9206 *SIC* 2022
SAPUTO INC *p* 999
7 RIVERSIDE DRIVE, TRENTON, ON, K8V 5R7
(613) 392-6762 *SIC* 2022
SAPUTO INC *p* 1345
6869 BOUL METROPOLITAIN E, SAINT-LEONARD, QC, H1P 1X8
(514) 328-6662 *SIC* 2022
SAPUTO INC *p* 1435
122 WAKOOMA ST, SASKATOON, SK, S7R 1A8
(306) 668-6833 *SIC* 2023
SAPUTO PRODUITS LAITIERS CANADA S.E.N.C. *p* 97
16110 116 AVE NW, EDMONTON, AB, T5M 3V4
(514) 328-3366 *SIC* 5141
SAPUTO PRODUITS LAITIERS CANADA S.E.N.C. *p* 183
6800 LOUGHEED HWY SUITE 3, BURNABY, BC, V5A 1W2
(604) 420-6611 *SIC* 2023
SAPUTO PRODUITS LAITIERS CANADA S.E.N.C. *p* 1165
6869 BOUL METROPOLITAIN, MONTREAL, QC, H1P 1X8
(514) 328-6662 *SIC* 2022
SAPUTO PRODUITS LAITIERS CANADA S.E.N.C. *p* 1246
1245 AV FORAND, PLESSISVILLE, QC, G6L 1X5
(819) 362-6378 *SIC* 2022
SAPUTO PRODUITS LAITIERS CANADA S.E.N.C. *p* 1313
1195 RUE DANIEL-JOHNSON E UNITE 117, SAINT-HYACINTHE, QC, J2S 7Y6
(450) 773-1004 *SIC* 2023
SAPUTO PRODUITS LAITIERS CANADA S.E.N.C. *p* 1327
100 RUE STINSON, SAINT-LAURENT, QC, H4N 2E7
(514) 328-3312 *SIC* 5143
SAPUTO PRODUITS LAITIERS CANADA S.E.N.C. *p* 1327
2365 CH DE LA COTE-DE-LIESSE, SAINT-LAURENT, QC, H4N 2M7
(514) 328-6663 *SIC* 5143
SAPUTO PRODUITS LAITIERS CANADA S.E.N.C. *p* 1345
7750 RUE PASCAL-GAGNON, SAINT-LEONARD, QC, H1P 3L1
(514) 328-6662 *SIC* 2022
SAPUTO PRODUITS LAITIERS CANADA S.E.N.C. *p* 1351
71 AV SAINT-JACQUES, SAINT-RAYMOND, QC, G3L 3X9
(418) 337-4287 *SIC* 2022
SAPUTO SAINT-HYACINTHE *p* 1313
See SAPUTO PRODUITS LAITIERS CANADA S.E.N.C.
SARA *p* 695
See GLOBEWAYS CANADA INC
SARATOGA POTATO CHIP COMPANY INC *p* 506
230 DEERHURST DR, BRAMPTON, ON, L6T 5R8
(905) 458-4100 *SIC* 2096
SARAZEN REALTY LTD *p* 826
80 ABERDEEN ST SUITE 300, OTTAWA, ON, K1S 5R5

(613) 831-4455   *SIC 6531*
SARCAN RECYCLING   *p 1432*
See SASKATCHEWAN ASSOCIATION OF REHABILITATION CENTRES
SARCEE MOTORS LTD   *p 74*
55 GLENBROOK PL SW, CALGARY, AB, T3E 6W4
(403) 249-9166   *SIC 5511*
SARDIS EXPLOSIVES (2000) LTD   *p 197*
6890 LICKMAN RD, CHILLIWACK, BC, V2R 4A9
(604) 858-6919   *SIC 5169*
SARDIS SECONDARY SCHOOL   *p 197*
See SCHOOL DISTRICT NO 33 CHILLIWACK
SARDO FOODS   *p 494*
See ALIMENTS SARDO INC., LES
SARDO FOODS   *p 495*
See OLIVER OLIVES INC
SARDO, MARIO SALES INC   *p 495*
99 PILLSWORTH RD, BOLTON, ON, L7E 4E4
(905) 951-9096   *SIC 5141*
SARENS CANADA INC   *p 140*
6019 35 ST, LEDUC, AB, T9E 1E6
(780) 612-4400   *SIC 7353*
SARGENT FARMS   *p 685*
See T & R SARGENT FARMS LIMITED
SARGENT FARMS LIMITED   *p 684*
189 MILL ST, MILTON, ON, L9T 1S3
(905) 878-4401   *SIC 5144*
SARGENT PARK SCHOOL   *p 381*
See WINNIPEG SCHOOL DIVISION
SARGENT, T & R   *p 684*
See SARGENT FARMS LIMITED
SARI THERAPEUTIC RIDING   *p 479*
See SPECIAL ABILITY RIDING INSTITUTE
SARJEANT COMPANY LIMITED, THE *p 488*
15 SARJEANT DR, BARRIE, ON, L4N 4V9
(705) 728-2460   *SIC 3273*
SARM   *p 1422*
See SASKATCHEWAN ASSOCIATION OF RURAL MUNICIPALITIES, THE
SARNIA AND DISTRICT ASSOCIATION FOR COMMUNITY LIVING   *p 860*
551 EXMOUTH ST SUITE 202, SARNIA, ON, N7T 5P6
(519) 332-0560   *SIC 8322*
SARNIA CARE-A-VAN   *p 859*
1169 MICHENER RD, SARNIA, ON, N7S 4W3
(519) 336-3789   *SIC 8742*
SARNIA COLLEGIATE INSTITUTE & TECHNICAL SCHOOL   *p 860*
See LAMBTON KENT DISTRICT SCHOOL BOARD
SARNIA EDUCATION CENTRE   *p 860*
See LAMBTON KENT DISTRICT SCHOOL BOARD
SARNIA EMS BASE #2   *p 859*
See CORPORATION OF THE COUNTY OF LAMBTON
SARNIA FINE CARS 2019 INC   *p 860*
799 CONFEDERATION ST, SARNIA, ON, N7T 2E4
(519) 332-2886   *SIC 5012*
SARNIA OBSERVER   *p 860*
See OSPREY MEDIA PUBLISHING INC
SARNIA-LAMBTON CHILDREN'S AID SOCIETY   *p 861*
See CHILDREN'S AID SOCIETY OF THE CITY OF SARNIA AND THE COUNTY OF LAMBTON
SARNIA/LAMBTON COMMUNITY CARE ACCESS CENTRE   *p 859*
1150 PONTIAC DR, SARNIA, ON, N7S 3A7
(519) 337-1000   *SIC 8621*
SARONA ASSET MANAGEMENT INC *p 640*
55 VICTORIA ST N UNIT K, KITCHENER, ON, N2H 5B7
(519) 883-7557   *SIC 6726*
SARTREX POWER CONTROL SYSTEMS

INC   *p 558*
222 SNIDERCROFT RD SUITE 2, CONCORD, ON, L4K 2K1
(905) 669-2278   *SIC 3829*
SAS GOLDMINES   *p 940*
See ST ANDREW GOLDFIELDS LTD
SAS INSTITUTE (CANADA) INC   *p 934*
280 KING ST E UNIT 500, TORONTO, ON, M5A 1K7
(416) 363-4424   *SIC 7372*
SASAGINNIGAK FISHING LODGE   *p 357*
See NORTHWAY AVIATION LTD
SASCO CONTRACTORS LTD   *p 184*
3060 NORLAND AVE SUITE 114, BURNABY, BC, V5B 3A6
(604) 299-1640   *SIC 1731*
SASCO DEVELOPMENTS LTD   *p 1411*
1590 MAIN ST N, MOOSE JAW, SK, S6J 1L3
(306) 693-7550   *SIC 7011*
SASCOPACK INC   *p 1425*
106 MELVILLE ST, SASKATOON, SK, S7J 0R1
SIC 7389
SASK HIGHWAYS MAINTENANCE *p 1436*
1200 SOUTH SERVICE RD W, SWIFT CURRENT, SK, S9H 5G7
(306) 778-8364   *SIC 4785*
SASK OPPORTUNITIES   *p 1433*
1 ACCESS RD N, SASKATOON, SK, S7N 5A2
(306) 933-5485   *SIC 6531*
SASK SPORT INC   *p 1418*
1870 LORNE ST, REGINA, SK, S4P 2L7
(306) 780-9340   *SIC 8699*
SASKATCHEWAN   *p 149*
2510 SPARROW DR, NISKU, AB, T9E 8N5
(780) 955-3639   *SIC 8699*
SASKATCHEWAN ABILITIES COUNCIL INC   *p 1425*
2310 LOUISE AVE, SASKATOON, SK, S7J 2C7
(306) 374-4448   *SIC 8331*
SASKATCHEWAN ABILITIES COUNCIL INC   *p 1436*
1551 NORTH RAILWAY ST W, SWIFT CURRENT, SK, S9H 5G3
(306) 773-2076   *SIC 8331*
SASKATCHEWAN ASSOCIATION OF REHABILITATION CENTRES   *p 1432*
111 CARDINAL CRES, SASKATOON, SK, S7L 6H5
(306) 933-0616   *SIC 4953*
SASKATCHEWAN ASSOCIATION OF RURAL MUNICIPALITIES, THE   *p 1422*
2301 WINDSOR PARK RD, REGINA, SK, S4V 3A4
(306) 757-3577   *SIC 8611*
SASKATCHEWAN BAND ASSOCIATION INC   *p 1438*
34 SUNSET DR N, YORKTON, SK, S3N 3K9
(306) 783-2263   *SIC 8621*
SASKATCHEWAN BLUE CROSS   *p 1417*
See BLUE CROSS LIFE INSURANCE COMPANY OF CANADA
SASKATCHEWAN BLUE CROSS   *p 1428*
See MEDICAL SERVICES INCORPORATED
SASKATCHEWAN CANCER AGENCY   *p 1422*
4101 DEWDNEY AVE SUITE 300, REGINA, SK, S4T 7T1
(306) 766-2213   *SIC 8093*
SASKATCHEWAN CATHOLIC HEALTH CORPORATION, THE   *p 1410*
200 HERITAGE DR, MELVILLE, SK, S0A 2P0
(306) 728-5407   *SIC 8062*
SASKATCHEWAN CENTRE OF THE ARTS FOUNDATION INC   *p 1422*
200A LAKESHORE DR, REGINA, SK, S4S

7L3
(306) 565-4500   *SIC 7922*
SASKATCHEWAN CROP INSURANCE CORPORATION   *p 1410*
484 PRINCE WILLIAM DR, MELVILLE, SK, S0A 2P0
(306) 728-7200   *SIC 6331*
SASKATCHEWAN DRAG RACING ASSOCIATION INC   *p 1424*
133 WESTERN CRES, SASKATOON, SK, S7H 4J4
(306) 373-8148   *SIC 7948*
SASKATCHEWAN GAMING CORPORATION   *p 1418*
1880 SASKATCHEWAN DR, REGINA, SK, S4P 0B2
(306) 565-3000   *SIC 7999*
SASKATCHEWAN GOVERNMENT & GENERAL EMPLOYEES' UNION   *p 1423*
1011 N DEVONSHIRE DR, REGINA, SK, S4X 2X4
(306) 522-8571   *SIC 8631*
SASKATCHEWAN GOVERNMENT INSURANCE   *p 1418*
2260 11TH AVE SUITE 18, REGINA, SK, S4P 0J9
(306) 751-1200   *SIC 6331*
SASKATCHEWAN HEALTH AUTHORITY *p 1406*
300 JAMES ST, ESTERHAZY, SK, S0A 0X0
(306) 745-6444   *SIC 8361*
SASKATCHEWAN HEALTH AUTHORITY *p 1407*
GD, ILE-A-LA-CROSSE, SK, S0M 1C0
(306) 833-2016   *SIC 8011*
SASKATCHEWAN HEALTH AUTHORITY *p 1407*
1210 NINTH ST N, HUMBOLDT, SK, S0K 2A1
(306) 682-2603   *SIC 8062*
SASKATCHEWAN HEALTH AUTHORITY *p 1408*
1003 1ST ST W RR 2, KINDERSLEY, SK, S0L 1S2
SIC 8051
SASKATCHEWAN HEALTH AUTHORITY *p 1409*
3820 43 AVE, LLOYDMINSTER, SK, S9V 1Y5
(306) 820-6000   *SIC 8062*
SASKATCHEWAN HEALTH AUTHORITY *p 1411*
1000 ALBERT ST, MOOSE JAW, SK, S6H 2Y2
(306) 693-4616   *SIC 8051*
SASKATCHEWAN HEALTH AUTHORITY *p 1425*
2003 ARLINGTON AVE, SASKATOON, SK, S7J 2H6
(306) 655-4500   *SIC 8069*
SASKATCHEWAN HEALTH AUTHORITY *p 1429*
701 QUEEN ST, SASKATOON, SK, S7K 0M7
(306) 655-0080   *SIC 8011*
SASKATCHEWAN HEALTH AUTHORITY *p 1433*
1319 COLONY ST, SASKATOON, SK, S7N 2Z1
(306) 655-1070   *SIC 8062*
SASKATCHEWAN HEALTH AUTHORITY *p 1436*
2004 SASKATCHEWAN DR, SWIFT CURRENT, SK, S9H 5M8
(306) 778-9400   *SIC 8062*
SASKATCHEWAN HEALTH AUTHORITY *p 1438*
304 7TH ST E, WILKIE, SK, S0K 4W0
(306) 843-2644   *SIC 8062*
SASKATCHEWAN HEALTH-CARE ASSO-

CIATION   *p 1419*
2002 VICTORIA AVE SUITE 500, REGINA, SK, S4P 0R7
(306) 347-1740   *SIC 6324*
SASKATCHEWAN HEALTHCARE EMPLOYEES' PENSION PLAN   *p 1423*
4581 PARLIAMENT AVE SUITE 201, REGINA, SK, S4W 0G3
(306) 751-8300   *SIC 6371*
SASKATCHEWAN HOUSING CORPORATION   *p 1419*
1920 BROAD ST SUITE 900, REGINA, SK, S4P 3V6
(306) 787-4177   *SIC 6531*
SASKATCHEWAN INDIAN GAMING AUTHORITY INC   *p 1405*
GD, CARLYLE, SK, S0C 0R0
(306) 577-4577   *SIC 7999*
SASKATCHEWAN INDIAN GAMING AUTHORITY INC   *p 1413*
11906 RAILWAY AVE E, NORTH BATTLEFORD, SK, S9A 3K7
(306) 446-3833   *SIC 7999*
SASKATCHEWAN INDIAN GAMING AUTHORITY INC   *p 1414*
44 MARQUIS RD W, PRINCE ALBERT, SK, S6V 7Y5
(306) 764-4777   *SIC 7999*
SASKATCHEWAN INDIAN GAMING AUTHORITY INC   *p 1433*
103C PACKHAM AVE SUITE 250, SASKATOON, SK, S7N 4K4
(306) 477-7777   *SIC 7999*
SASKATCHEWAN INDIAN GAMING AUTHORITY INC   *p 1438*
30 THIRD AVE N, YORKTON, SK, S3N 1B9
(306) 786-6777   *SIC 7993*
SASKATCHEWAN INDIAN INSTITUTE OF TECHNOLOGIES   *p 1429*
229 4TH AVE S SUITE 201, SASKATOON, SK, S7K 4K3
(306) 373-4777   *SIC 8299*
SASKATCHEWAN INTERNATIONAL RACEWAY   *p 1424*
See SASKATCHEWAN DRAG RACING ASSOCIATION INC
SASKATCHEWAN LEGAL AID COMMISSION, THE   *p 1429*
201 21ST ST E SUITE 502, SASKATOON, SK, S7K 0B8
(306) 933-5300   *SIC 8111*
SASKATCHEWAN LIBERAL ASSOCIATION   *p 1419*
2054 BROAD ST, REGINA, SK, S4P 1Y3
SIC 8651
SASKATCHEWAN LOTTERIES   *p 1418*
See SASK SPORT INC
SASKATCHEWAN MOTOR CLUB   *p 1421*
200 ALBERT ST N, REGINA, SK, S4R 2N4
(306) 791-4321   *SIC 8699*
SASKATCHEWAN MOTOR CLUB SERVICES LIMITED   *p 1421*
200 ALBERT ST, REGINA, SK, S4R 2N4
(306) 791-4321   *SIC 6331*
SASKATCHEWAN MUNICIPAL HAIL INSURANCE ASSOCIATION   *p 1419*
2100 CORNWALL ST, REGINA, SK, S4P 2K7
(306) 569-1852   *SIC 6331*
SASKATCHEWAN MUTUAL INSURANCE COMPANY   *p 1429*
279 3RD AVE N, SASKATOON, SK, S7K

2H8

(306) 653-4232   SIC 6331

SASKATCHEWAN OPPORTUNITIES COR-PORATION p

1433

15 INNOVATION BLVD SUITE 114, SASKA-TOON, SK, S7N 2X8

(306) 933-6295   SIC 6519

SASKATCHEWAN PLAYWRIGHTS' CEN-TRE p

1429

601 SPADINA CRES E SUITE 700, SASKA-TOON, SK, S7K 3G8

(306) 665-7707   SIC 8699

SASKATCHEWAN POLYTECHNIC p 1429

119 4TH AVE S SUITE 400, SASKATOON, SK, S7K 5X2

(866) 467-4278   SIC 8222

SASKATCHEWAN POWER CORPORATION p 1405

GD, CORONACH, SK, S0H 0Z0

(306) 267-5200   SIC 4911

SASKATCHEWAN POWER CORPORATION p 1406

18 BOUNDARY DAM HWY W, ESTEVAN, SK, S4A 2A6

(306) 634-1300   SIC 4911

SASKATCHEWAN POWER CORPORATION p 1406

GD LCD MAIN, ESTEVAN, SK, S4A 2A1

(306) 634-1700   SIC 4911

SASKATCHEWAN POWER CORPORATION p 1419

2025 VICTORIA AVE, REGINA, SK, S4P 0S1

(306) 566-2121   SIC 4911

SASKATCHEWAN RESEARCH COUNCIL, THE p 1433

15 INNOVATION BLVD SUITE 125, SASKA-TOON, SK, S7N 2X8

(306) 933-5400   SIC 8733

SASKATCHEWAN RIVER SCHOOL DIVI-SION #119 p

1414

665 28TH ST E, PRINCE ALBERT, SK, S6V 6E9

(306) 922-3115   SIC 8211

SASKATCHEWAN TEACHERS' FEDERA-TION p

1425

2317 ARLINGTON AVE, SASKATOON, SK, S7J 2H8

(306) 373-1660   SIC 8621

SASKATCHEWAN TELECOMMUNICA-TIONS HOLDING CORPORATION p

1419

2121 SASKATCHEWAN DR, REGINA, SK, S4P 3Y2

(800) 992-9912   SIC 4899

SASKATCHEWAN TELECOMMUNICA-TIONS INTERNATIONAL, INC p

1419

2121 SASKATCHEWAN DR, REGINA, SK, S4P 3Y2

(306) 777-2201   SIC 4899

SASKATCHEWAN UNION OF NURSES p

1421

2330 2ND AVE, REGINA, SK, S4R 1A6

(306) 525-1666   SIC 8631

SASKATCHEWAN WATER CORPORATION p 1411

111 FAIRFORD ST E SUITE 400, MOOSE JAW, SK, S6H 7X9

(306) 694-3098   SIC 4941

SASKATCHEWAN WORKERS' COMPEN-SATION BOARD p

1419

1881 SCARTH ST SUITE 200, REGINA, SK, S4P 4L1

(800) 667-7590   SIC 6331

SASKATOON p 1429

See SASKATCHEWAN POLYTECHNIC

SASKATOON AEROCENTRE p 1431

See DEPMAR FLIGHT HOLDINGS INC

SASKATOON AIRPORT AUTHORITY p

1432

2625 AIRPORT DR SUITE 1, SASKATOON, SK, S7L 7L1

(306) 975-4274   SIC 4581

SASKATOON BOILER p 1429

See SASKATOON BOILER MFG CO LTD

SASKATOON BOILER MFG CO LTD p 1429

2011 QUEBEC AVE, SASKATOON, SK, S7K 1W5

(306) 652-7022   SIC 3443

SASKATOON C AUTO LP p 1424

2200 8TH ST E, SASKATOON, SK, S7H 0V3

(306) 374-2120   SIC 5511

SASKATOON CENTENNIAL AUDITORIUM FOUNDATION p 1429

35 22ND ST E, SASKATOON, SK, S7K 0C8

(306) 975-7777   SIC 7922

SASKATOON CO-OP p 1432

See SASKATOON CO-OPERATIVE ASSO-CIATION LIMITED, THE

SASKATOON CO-OP p 1435

See SASKATOON CO-OPERATIVE ASSO-CIATION LIMITED, THE

SASKATOON CO-OPERATIVE ASSOCIA-TION LIMITED, THE p

1432

1624 33RD ST W, SASKATOON, SK, S7L 0X3

(306) 933-3865   SIC 5141

SASKATOON CO-OPERATIVE ASSOCIA-TION LIMITED, THE p

1435

503 WELLMAN CRES SUITE 201, SASKA-TOON, SK, S7T 0J1

(306) 933-3801   SIC 5411

SASKATOON COMMUNITY CLINIC p 1426

See COMMUNITY HEALTH SERVICES (SASKATOON) ASSOCIATION LIMITED

SASKATOON CONVALESCENT HOME p

1432

101 31ST ST W, SASKATOON, SK, S7L 0P6

(306) 244-7155   SIC 8051

SASKATOON DIESEL p 1432

See TURBOTRONICS

SASKATOON FAMILY YOUNG MEN'S CHRISTIAN ASSOCIATION p 1429

25 22ND ST E, SASKATOON, SK, S7K 0C7

(306) 652-7515   SIC 8641

SASKATOON FARM, THE p 81

See HAMER TREE SERVICES LTD

SASKATOON HOT SHOT TRANSPORTER SERVICES (1995) LTD p 1432

2342B HANSELMAN AVE, SASKATOON, SK, S7L 5Z3

(306) 653-5255   SIC 4212

SASKATOON HYUNDAI p 1431

See 625974 SASKATCHEWAN LTD

SASKATOON LIGHT AND POWER p 1425

See SASKATOON, CITY OF

SASKATOON MOTOR PRODUCTS (1973) LTD p 1429

715 CIRCLE DR E, SASKATOON, SK, S7K 0V1

(306) 242-0276   SIC 5511

SASKATOON PRAIRIELAND PARK COR-PORATION p

1424

2615 ST HENRY AVE, SASKATOON, SK, S7H 0A1

(306) 242-6100   SIC 7948

SASKATOON PRAIRIELAND PARK COR-PORATION p

1429

503 RUTH ST W, SASKATOON, SK, S7K 4E4

(306) 931-7149   SIC 8741

SASKATOON PRIVATE INVESTIGATION INC p 1430

333 25TH ST E SUITE 505, SASKATOON, SK, S7K 0L4

(306) 975-0999   SIC 7389

SASKATOON PUBLIC LIBRARY p 1430

311 23RD ST E, SASKATOON, SK, S7K 0J6

(306) 975-7558   SIC 8231

SASKATOON PUBLIC SCHOOLS p 1426

See BOARD OF EDUCATION OF SASKA-TOON SCHOOL DIVISION NO. 13 OF SASKATCHEWAN, THE

SASKATOON RINGETTE ASSOCIATION p

1432

510 CYNTHIA ST SUITE 128, SASKA-TOON, SK, S7L 7K7

(306) 975-0839   SIC 8699

SASKATOON SPECIALTY MEATS LTD p 1425

106 MELVILLE ST, SASKATOON, SK, S7J 0R1

(306) 653-9292   SIC 5147

SASKATOON TRAVELODGE HOTEL p 1431

See DEER LODGE HOTELS LTD

SASKATOON WHOLESALE TIRE LTD p 1430

2705 WENTZ AVE, SASKATOON, SK, S7K 4B6

(306) 244-9512   SIC 5531

SASKATOON, CITY OF p 1425

322 BRAND RD, SASKATOON, SK, S7J 5J3

(306) 975-2414   SIC 4911

SASKATOON, CITY OF p 1433

1030 AVENUE H S, SASKATOON, SK, S7M 1X5

(306) 975-2534   SIC 4953

SASKCAN PULSE TRADING p 1422

See AGT FOOD AND INGREDIENTS INC

SASKENERGY INCORPORATED p 1419

1777 VICTORIA AVE SUITE 1000, REGINA, SK, S4P 4K5

(306) 777-9225   SIC 4923

SASKENERGY INCORPORATED p 1430

408 36TH ST E, SASKATOON, SK, S7K 4J9

(306) 975-8561   SIC 4924

SASKPOWER p 1405

See SASKATCHEWAN POWER CORPO-RATION

SASKPOWER p 1406

See SASKATCHEWAN POWER CORPO-RATION

SASKPOWER p 1419

See SASKATCHEWAN POWER CORPO-RATION

SASKPOWER SHAND POWER STATION p

1406

See SASKATCHEWAN POWER CORPO-RATION

SASKTEL HOLDCO p 1419

See SASKATCHEWAN TELECOMMUNI-CATIONS HOLDING CORPORATION

SASKTEL INTERNATIONAL p 1419

See SASKATCHEWAN TELECOMMUNI-CATIONS INTERNATIONAL, INC

SASKWATER p 1411

111 FAIRFORD ST E SUITE 200, MOOSE JAW, SK, S6H 1C8

SIC 4941

SAT SOCIETE DES ARTS TECH-NOLOGIQUES p

1186

1201 BOUL SAINT-LAURENT, MONTREAL, QC, H2X 2S6

(514) 844-2033   SIC 8699

SAT, LA p 1186

See SAT SOCIETE DES ARTS TECH-NOLOGIQUES

SATAU INC p 1091

71 BOUL BRUNSWICK, DOLLARD-DES-ORMEAUX, QC, H9B 2N4

(514) 631-5775   SIC 5149

SATCOM DIV. p 593

See COMMUNICATIONS & POWER IN-DUSTRIES CANADA INC

SATELITE MECHANICAL SERVICES p 93

See GATEWAY MECHANICAL SERVICES INC

SATIN FINISH HARDWOOD FLOORING, LIMITED p 793

15 FENMAR DR, NORTH YORK, ON, M9L

1L4

(416) 747-9924   SIC 2426

SATISFACTION CHRYSLER DODGE JEEP p 1399

See SATISFACTION PLYMOUTH CHRYLSER INC

SATISFACTION DE BOIS-FRANCS p 1399

See LAQUERRE CHRYSLER INC

SATISFACTION PLYMOUTH CHRYLSER INC p 1399

1475 BOUL JUTRAS O, VICTORIAVILLE, QC, G6T 2A9

(819) 752-5252   SIC 5511

SATISFASHION INC p 874

33 COMMANDER BLVD SUITE 1, SCAR-BOROUGH, ON, M1S 3E7

SIC 2337

SATNAM EDUCATION SOCIETY OF BRITISH COLUMBIA p 277

6933 124 ST, SURREY, BC, V3W 3W6

SIC 8299

SATRANG DESIGNER WEAR INC p 126

2956 ELLWOOD DR SW, EDMONTON, AB, T6X 0A9

(780) 245-0043   SIC 5961

SATURN INDUSTRIES LTD p 369

37 SYLVAN WAY, WINNIPEG, MB, R2R 2B9

(204) 633-1529   SIC 5072

SATURN ISUZU OF REGENT p 363

See SOR HOLDINGS LTD

SATURN OF ST CATHARINES p 884

See 859689 ONTARIO INC

SATURN SAAB CADILLAC DE LAVAL p

1363

See BOURASSA AUTOMOBILES INTER-NATIONAL INC

SATURN SAAB ISUZU OF EDMONTON p 94

14803 137 AVE NW, EDMONTON, AB, T5L 2L5

(780) 484-4455   SIC 5511

SATURN SAAB ISUZU SHERBROOKE p

1375

See GESTION ANKABETH INC

SATURN TERREBONNE p 1379

See AUTO IMPORTATION TERREBONNE INC

SATURN TOOL & DIE (WINDSOR) INC p

807

5175 HENNIN DR, OLDCASTLE, ON, N0R 1L0

SIC 3542

SAUDER MOULDINGS CALGARY p 17

See METRIE CANADA LTD

SAUDER SCHOOL OF BUSINESS p 325

See UNIVERSITY OF BRITISH COLUMBIA, THE

SAUDER SCHOOL OF BUSINESS p 325

2053 MAIN MALL SUITE 402, VANCOU-VER, BC, V6T 1Z2

(604) 822-8391   SIC 8742

SAUGEEN DIST SECONDARY SCHOOL p 847

See BLUEWATER DISTRICT SCHOOL BOARD

SAUGEEN VALLEY NURSING CENTER LTD p 746

465 DUBLIN ST, MOUNT FOREST, ON, N0G 2L3

(519) 323-2140   SIC 8051

SAULNIER AUTOMOBILES INC p 1302

445 BOUL INDUSTRIEL, SAINT-EUSTACHE, QC, J7R 5R3

(450) 623-7446   SIC 5511

SAULT AREA HOSPITAL p 863

750 GREAT NORTHERN RD SUITE 1, SAULT STE. MARIE, ON, P6B 0A8

(705) 759-3434   SIC 8062

SAULT COLLEGE OF APPLIED ARTS & TECHNOLOGY, THE p 863

443 NORTHERN AVE E, SAULT STE. MARIE, ON, P6B 4J3

(705) 759-2554   SIC 8221

SAULT STAR, LIMITED p 862

145 OLD GARDEN RIVER RD, SAULT STE. MARIE, ON, P6A 5M5
(705) 759-3030   *SIC* 2754
SAULT STAR, THE   p 862
See SAULT STAR, LIMITED
SAULT STE MARIE & DISTRICT GROUP HEALTH ASSOCIATION   p 863
240 MCNABB ST, SAULT STE. MARIE, ON, P6B 1Y5
(705) 759-1234   *SIC* 8011
SAULT STE MARIE HOUSING CORPORATION   p 862
180 BROCK ST, SAULT STE. MARIE, ON, P6A 3B7
(705) 946-2077   *SIC* 6531
SAULT STE MARIE MAIN OFFICE   p 862
See NORTH EAST COMMUNITY CARE ACCESS CENTRE
SAULT STE. MARIE INNOVATION CENTRE p 862
1520 QUEEN ST E SUITE 307, SAULT STE. MARIE, ON, P6A 2G4
(705) 942-7927   *SIC* 8732
SAUNDERS AUTOMOTIVE LIMITED p 896
640 LORNE AVE E, STRATFORD, ON, N5A 6S4
(519) 271-9227   *SIC* 5511
SAUNDERS BOOK COMPANY   p 547
See SAUNDERS OFFICE AND SCHOOL SUPPLIES LIMITED
SAUNDERS OFFICE AND SCHOOL SUPPLIES LIMITED   p 547
29 STEWART RD, COLLINGWOOD, ON, L9Y 4M7
(705) 444-1696   *SIC* 5942
SAUNDERS SECONDARY SCHOOL p 660
See THAMES VALLEY DISTRICT SCHOOL BOARD
SAUVETAGE L'ARANEA INC   p 1350
2351 RANG RENVERSY, SAINT-PAULIN, QC, J0K 3G0
(819) 268-3369   *SIC* 8999
SAVAGE ARMS (CANADA) INC   p 643
248 WATER ST, LAKEFIELD, ON, K0L 2H0
(705) 652-8000   *SIC* 3484
SAVAGE CANAC INTERNATIONAL INC p 1341
6505 RTE TRANSCANADIENNE BUREAU 405, SAINT-LAURENT, QC, H4T 1S3
(514) 734-4700   *SIC* 8742
SAVANNA ENERGY SERVICES CORP p 58
311 6 AVE SW SUITE 800, CALGARY, AB, T2P 3H2
(403) 503-9990   *SIC* 1381
SAVANNA WELL SERVICING INC   p 58
311 6 AVE SW SUITE 800, CALGARY, AB, T2P 3H2
(403) 503-0650   *SIC* 1389
SAVARD ORTHO CONFORT INC   p 1265
1350 RUE CYRILLE-DUQUET, QUEBEC, QC, G1N 2E5
(418) 681-6381   *SIC* 5999
SAVARIA   p 1066
See MATERIAUX PAYSAGERS SAVARIA LTEE
SAVARIA CONCORD LIFTS INC   p 506
2 WALKER DR, BRAMPTON, ON, L6T 5E1
(905) 791-5555   *SIC* 3534
SAVARIA SALES INSTALLATION AND SERVICES INC   p 657
85 BESSEMER RD, LONDON, ON, N6E 1P9
(519) 681-3311   *SIC* 1796
SAVE EASY   p 456
See ATLANTIC WHOLESALERS LTD
SAVE ON FOODS   p 268
See SOBEYS WEST INC
SAVE OUR LIVING ENVIRONMENT SOCIETY (S.O.L.E.)   p 296
39 HASTINGS ST E, VANCOUVER, BC, V6A 1M9

(604) 681-0001   *SIC* 7389
SAVE THE CHILDREN CANADA   p 774
4141 YONGE ST SUITE 300, NORTH YORK, ON, M2P 2A8
(416) 221-5501   *SIC* 8399
SAVE-ON-FOODS   p 185
See GREAT PACIFIC INDUSTRIES INC
SAVE-ON-FOODS   p 222
See GREAT PACIFIC INDUSTRIES INC
SAVE-ON-FOODS   p 231
See GREAT PACIFIC INDUSTRIES INC
SAVE-ON-FOODS   p 232
See GREAT PACIFIC INDUSTRIES INC
SAVE-ON-FOODS   p 243
See GREAT PACIFIC INDUSTRIES INC
SAVE-ON-FOODS LIMITED PARTNERSHIP p 225
19855 92A AVE, LANGLEY, BC, V1M 3B6
(604) 888-1213   *SIC* 5411
SAVE-ON-FOODS LIMITED PARTNERSHIP p 239
1199 LYNN VALLEY RD UNIT 1221, NORTH VANCOUVER, BC, V7J 3H2
(604) 980-4857   *SIC* 5411
SAVE-ON-FOODS LIMITED PARTNERSHIP p 316
1133 ALBERNI ST, VANCOUVER, BC, V6E 4T9
(604) 648-2053   *SIC* 5411
SAVE-ON-FOODS LIMITED PARTNERSHIP p 340
759 MCCALLUM RD, VICTORIA, BC, V9B 6A2
(250) 475-3157   *SIC* 5411
SAVE-X-LP GAS LTD   p 141
3195 5 AVE N, LETHBRIDGE, AB, T1H 0P2
(403) 380-3536   *SIC* 5984
SAVERS   p 10
See VALUE VILLAGE STORES, INC
SAVERS   p 181
See VALUE VILLAGE STORES, INC
SAVEUR ULTIME FLAVOUR   p 1074
See J.G. RIVE-SUD FRUITS & LEGUMES INC
SAVIC HOMES LTD   p 634
26 IDLE RIDGE CRT, KITCHENER, ON, N2A 3W3
(519) 954-0370   *SIC* 1521
SAVOIE CLEARING   p 1431
See AUTO CLEARING (1982) LTD
SAVONA SPECIALTY PLYWOOD CO. LTDp 268
7273 KAMLOOPS LAKE DR, SAVONA, BC, V0K 2J0
(250) 373-5600   *SIC* 5031
SAVOURA   p 1253
See SERRES SAVOURA ST-ETIENNE INC, LES
SAVVIS COMMUNICATIONS CANADA, INC p 727
6800 MILLCREEK DR, MISSISSAUGA, ON, L5N 4J9
(905) 363-3737   *SIC* 8741
SAWARNE LUMBER CO. LTD   p 321
1770 BURRARD ST SUITE 280, VANCOUVER, BC, V6J 3G7
(604) 324-4666   *SIC* 2421
SAWCHUK DEVELOPMENTS CO. LTD p 220
486 ADAMS RD, KELOWNA, BC, V1X 7S1
(250) 765-3838   *SIC* 1542
SAWILL LTD   p 558
54 AUDIA CRT UNIT 2, CONCORD, ON, L4K 3N4
(905) 669-0341   *SIC* 5198
SAWMILL RESTAURANT & LOUNGE p 119
See SAWMILL RESTAURANT GROUP LTD
SAWMILL RESTAURANT GROUP LTD p 119
4810 CALGARY TRAIL NW, EDMONTON, AB, T6H 5H5
(780) 463-4499   *SIC* 5812
SAWRIDGE ENTERPRISES LTD   p 90
10104 103 AVE NW UNIT 1910, EDMON-

TON, AB, T5J 0H8
(780) 428-3330   *SIC* 7011
SAWRIDGE INN & CONFERENCE CENTRE JASPER   p 90
See SAWRIDGE ENTERPRISES LTD
SAXON LEATHER LTD   p 373
310 ROSS AVE, WINNIPEG, MB, R3A 0L4
(204) 956-4011   *SIC* 5948
SAYAL ELECTRONICS   p 877
See SAYAL PURCHASING SERVICES INC
SAYAL PURCHASING SERVICES INCp 877
3791 VICTORIA PARK AVE UNIT 1, SCARBOROUGH, ON, M1W 3K6
(416) 494-8999   *SIC* 5065
SAYANI INVESTMENTS LTD   p 202
405 NORTH RD, COQUITLAM, BC, V3K 3V9
(604) 936-9399   *SIC* 7011
SAYBOLT, DIV OF   p 22
See CORE LABORATORIES CANADA LTD
SAYERS & ASSOCIATES LTD.   p 545
1000 DEPALMA DR, COBOURG, ON, K9A 5W6
    SIC 1711
SAYWELL CONTRACTING LTD   p 234
2599 MCCULLOUGH RD UNIT B, NANAIMO, BC, V9S 4M9
(250) 729-0197   *SIC* 1542
SB NAVITAS TUBULAR INC   p 58
435 4 AVE SW SUITE 480, CALGARY, AB, T2P 3A8
(403) 984-9548   *SIC* 5051
SB PHARMACY SERVICES LTD   p 1015
1801 DUNDAS ST E, WHITBY, ON, L1N 7C5
(905) 436-1050   *SIC* 5912
SB SCIENTIFIC   p 670
See ESBE SCIENTIFIC INDUSTRIES INC
SBC   p 1350
See SPECIALISTE DU BARDEAU DE CEDRE INC, LE
SBC FIREMASTER LTD   p 252
275 COPPER MOUNTAIN RD, PRINCETON, BC, V0X 1W0
(250) 295-7685   *SIC* 5099
SBHPP   p 591
See DUREZ CANADA COMPANY LTD
SBI   p 1293
See FABRICANT DE POELES INTERNATIONAL INC
SBI CANADA BANK   p 710
77 CITY CENTRE DR SUITE 106, MISSISSAUGA, ON, L5B 1M5
(905) 896-6540   *SIC* 6021
SBW   p 324
See SMITH BROS. & WILSON (B.C.) LTD
SC 360 INC   p 1336
2425 BOUL PITFIELD, SAINT-LAURENT, QC, H4S 1W8
(514) 735-8557   *SIC* 8748
SC JOHNSON PROFESSIONAL CA INC p 518
1 WEBSTER ST, BRANTFORD, ON, N3T 5R1
(519) 443-8697   *SIC* 2841
SCA HYGIENE PRODUCTS   p 805
See ESSITY CANADA INC
SCA PRODUITS D'HYGIENE   p 1098
See ESSITY CANADA INC
SCADDABUSH ITALIAN KITCHEN & BARp 711
See SIR CORP
SCALAR DECISIONS INC   p 940
1 TORONTO ST 3RD FL, TORONTO, ON, M5C 2V6
(416) 202-0020   *SIC* 7379
SCALE HOUSE MILL YARD   p 396
See IRVING, J. D. LIMITED
SCAMP INDUSTRIES LTD   p 230
26988 GLOUCESTER WAY, LANGLEY, BC, V4W 3Y5
(604) 856-8211   *SIC* 4212
SCAMP TRANSPORT   p 230
See SCAMP INDUSTRIES LTD

SCAN DESIGNS LTD   p 202
1400 UNITED BLVD, COQUITLAM, BC, V3K 6Y2
(604) 524-3444   *SIC* 5712
SCAN-TECH INSPECTION SERVICES LTD p 537
221 HOLIDAY INN DR, CAMBRIDGE, ON, N3C 3T2
(519) 651-1656   *SIC* 7389
SCANDESIGNS   p 202
See SCAN DESIGNS LTD
SCANDINAVIAN BUILDING MAINTENANCE LTD   p 242
245 FELL AVE SUITE 101, NORTH VANCOUVER, BC, V7P 2K1
    SIC 7349
SCANDINAVIAN BUILDING SERVICES LTD p 94
14238 134 AVE NW, EDMONTON, AB, T5L 5V8
(780) 477-3311   *SIC* 7349
SCANDINAVIAN HERITAGE SOCIETY OF EDMONTON   p 94
12336 ST ALBERT TRAIL NW, EDMONTON, AB, T5L 4G8
(780) 451-3868   *SIC* 8699
SCANLINE VFX INC   p 309
580 GRANVILLE ST, VANCOUVER, BC, V6C 1W6
(604) 683-6822   *SIC* 7819
SCANNER ENTERPRISES   p 277
See PACIFIC SALMON INDUSTRIES INC
SCANNER ENTERPRISES (1982) INCp 277
8305 128 ST, SURREY, BC, V3W 4G1
(604) 591-2908   *SIC* 2092
SCANSA CONSTRUCTION LTD   p 340
2089 MILLSTREAM RD UNIT 203, VICTORIA, BC, V9B 6H4
(250) 478-5222   *SIC* 1623
SCANTRADE INTERNATIONAL LIMITED p 742
6685 KENNEDY RD SUITE 7, MISSISSAUGA, ON, L5T 3A5
(905) 795-9380   *SIC* 5023
SCAPA TAPES NORTH AMERICA LTD p 849
609 BARNET BLVD, RENFREW, ON, K7V 0A9
(613) 432-8545   *SIC* 2672
SCAQUAM SECONDARY SCHOOL   p 208
See DELTA SCHOOL DISTRICT NO.37
SCARBORO MAZDA   p 872
See 1123932 ONTARIO INC
SCARBOROUGH AND ROUGE HOSPITAL p 474
580 HARWOOD AVE S SUITE 199, AJAX, ON, L1S 2J4
(905) 683-2320   *SIC* 6324
SCARBOROUGH AND ROUGE HOSPITAL p 872
3050 LAWRENCE AVE E, SCARBOROUGH, ON, M1P 2V5
(416) 438-2911   *SIC* 8062
SCARBOROUGH CENTRE FOR HEALTHY COMMUNITIES   p 867
629 MARKHAM RD UNIT 2, SCARBOROUGH, ON, M1H 2A4
(416) 642-9445   *SIC* 8011
SCARBOROUGH CITY CAB   p 866
See 1210670 ONTARIO INC
SCARBOROUGH KIA   p 867
See 1137283 ONTARIO INC
SCARBOROUGH LEXUS TOYOTA   p 989
See 415841 ONTARIO LIMITED
SCARBOROUGH NISSAN (1989) LIMITEDp 869
1941 EGLINTON AVE E, SCARBOROUGH, ON, M1L 2M4
(416) 751-3511   *SIC* 5511
SCARBOROUGH STATION D   p 870
See CANADA POST CORPORATION
SCARBOROUGH SUBARU AND SUZUKI p 867

See CARMEN & FRANKS GARAGE LTD

SCARBOROUGH TOWN CENTRE HOLD-INGS INC p
966
200 BAY ST SUITE 900, TORONTO, ON, M5J 2J2
(416) 865-8300 *SIC 6512*

SCARBOROUGH TOYOTA NATCO LEAS-ING p
868
See 1216809 ONTARIO LIMITED

SCARBOROUGH TRUCK CENTRE INC p
865
1810 MARKHAM RD, SCARBOROUGH, ON, M1B 2W2
SIC 5511

SCARLETT HOUSE FOOD GROUP INC p
736
7615 KIMBEL ST UNIT 8, MISSISSAUGA, ON, L5S 1A8
(905) 672-6302 *SIC 5812*

SCARPONE'S p 23
See GREAT WEST ITALIAN IMPORTERS LTD

SCARSIN CORPORATION p 1001
2 BROCK ST W SUITE 201, UXBRIDGE, ON, L9P 1P2
(905) 852-0086 *SIC 7371*

SCARSVIEW CHRYSLER DODGE JEEP p
865
See SCARSVIEW MOTORS LTD

SCARSVIEW MOTORS LTD p 865
951 MILNER AVE, SCARBOROUGH, ON, M1B 5X4
(416) 281-6200 *SIC 5511*

SCB PROPERTY MANAGEMENT SER-VICES LP p
819
See FIRST CAPITAL REALTY CORP

SCBD p 1190
See SECRETARIAT DE LA CONVENTION SUR LA DIVERSITE BIOLOGIQUE

SCC GROUP p 298
See HOTEL SASKATCHEWAN (1990) LTD

SCDA (2015) INC p 1214
1245 RUE SHERBROOKE O BUREAU 2100, MONTREAL, QC, H3G 1G3
(514) 499-8855 *SIC 6311*

SCELLTECH p 1085
See REVETEMENTS SCELL-TECH INC, LES

SCENIC ACRES RETIREMENT RESI-DENCE p
77
See REVERA INC

SCENIC TOURS p 309
See ST TOURING CANADA LTD

SCENTS ALIVE p 560
See VEGEWAX CANDLEWORX LTD

SCEPTER CANADA INC p 872
170 MIDWEST RD, SCARBOROUGH, ON, M1P 3A9
(416) 751-9445 *SIC 3089*

SCEPTER DRUGS LTD p 195
1297 SHOPPERS ROW SUITE 209, CAMP-BELL RIVER, BC, V9W 2C7
(250) 286-1166 *SIC 5912*

SCFP (F.T.Q.) p 1180
See SYNDICAT EMPLOYEE-ES DE METIERS D'HYDRO-QUEBEC SECTION LOCALE 1500 SCFP (F.T.Q.)

SCHAAF FOODS INC p 1011
130 FROBISHER DR SUITE 6, WATER-LOO, ON, N2V 1Z9
(519) 747-1655 *SIC 5149*

SCHAAN HEALTH CARE PRODUCTS p
1431
See CARLOU MARKETING INC

SCHAEFER SYSTEM INTERNATIONAL LIMITED p 506
140 NUGGETT CRT, BRAMPTON, ON, L6T 5H4
(905) 458-5399 *SIC 5093*

SCHAEFFER & ASSOCIATES LTD p 558

6 RONROSE DR SUITE 100, CONCORD, ON, L4K 4R3
SIC 8742

SCHAEFFLER AEROSPACE CANADA INC p 895
151 WRIGHT BLVD, STRATFORD, ON, N4Z 1H3
(519) 271-3230 *SIC 3369*

SCHAEFFLER AEROSPACE CANADA INC p 896
801 ONTARIO ST, STRATFORD, ON, N5A 6T2
(519) 271-3230 *SIC 3568*

SCHAEFFLER CANADA INC p 896
801 ONTARIO ST, STRATFORD, ON, N5A 7Y2
(519) 271-3231 *SIC 3562*

SCHARF REALTY LTD p 1009
50 WESTMOUNT RD N, WATERLOO, ON, N2L 2R5
(519) 747-2040 *SIC 6531*

SCHAWK CANADA INC p 700
1620 TECH AVE SUITE 3, MISSISSAUGA, ON, L4W 5P4
(905) 219-1600 *SIC 7336*

SCHAWK TRISTAR, DIV OF p 700
See SCHAWK CANADA INC

SCHECHTER, SOLOMON ACADEMY INC p 1220
5555 CH DE LA COTE-SAINT-LUC, MON-TREAL, QC, H3X 2C9
(514) 485-0866 *SIC 8211*

SCHEFFER ANDREW LTD p 94
12204 145 ST NW, EDMONTON, AB, T5L 4V7
(780) 732-7800 *SIC 8711*

SCHELL COUNTRY DEPOT p 895
See SCHELL LUMBER LIMITED

SCHELL LUMBER LIMITED p 895
33 EDWARD ST, STOUFFVILLE, ON, L4A 1A4
(905) 640-3440 *SIC 5211*

SCHENCK FARMS & GREENHOUSES CO. LIMITED p 886
1396 SOUTH SERVICE RD, ST CATHARINES, ON, L2R 6P9
(905) 684-5478 *SIC 5159*

SCHENDEL MECHANICAL CONTRACTING LTD p 103
20310 107 AVE NW, EDMONTON, AB, T5S 1W9
(780) 447-3400 *SIC 1711*

SCHENKER DISTRIBUTION p 689
See SCHENKER OF CANADA LIMITED

SCHENKER LOGISTICS p 316
See SCHENKER OF CANADA LIMITED

SCHENKER LOGISTICS p 587
See SCHENKER OF CANADA LIMITED

SCHENKER OF CANADA LIMITED p 210
8181 CHURCHILL ST, DELTA, BC, V4K 0C2
(604) 688-8511 *SIC 4731*

SCHENKER OF CANADA LIMITED p 316
1030 GEORGIA ST W SUITE 3A, VANCOU-VER, BC, V6E 2Y3
(604) 688-8511 *SIC 4731*

SCHENKER OF CANADA LIMITED p 495
12315 COLERAINE DR, BOLTON, ON, L7E 3B4
(905) 857-5620 *SIC 4731*

SCHENKER OF CANADA LIMITED p 587
1920 ALBION RD, ETOBICOKE, ON, M9W 5T2
(416) 798-8070 *SIC 4226*

SCHENKER OF CANADA LIMITED p 689
5935 AIRPORT RD SUITE 9, MISSIS-SAUGA, ON, L4V 1W5
(905) 676-0676 *SIC 4731*

SCHENKER OF CANADA LIMITED p 1095
2100 AV REVERCHON BUREAU 257, DORVAL, QC, H9P 2S7
(514) 636-6350 *SIC 4731*

SCHERER, STEVE PONTIAC BUICK GMC LTD p 637
1225 COURTLAND AVE E, KITCHENER,

ON, N2C 2N8
(519) 893-8888 *SIC 7538*

SCHERING-PLOUGH CANADA INC p 1118
16750 RTE TRANSCANADIENNE, KIRK-LAND, QC, H9H 4M7
(514) 426-7300 *SIC 2834*

SCHICKEDANZ BROS. LIMITED p 769
3311 BAYVIEW AVE SUITE 105, NORTH YORK, ON, M2K 1G4
(416) 223-0710 *SIC 6513*

SCHIEDEL CONSTRUCTION INCORPO-RATED p
537
405 QUEEN ST W, CAMBRIDGE, ON, N3C 1G6
(519) 658-9317 *SIC 1541*

SCHILL INSURANCE BROKERS LTD p 271
15127 100 AVE UNIT 302, SURREY, BC, V3R 0N9
(604) 585-4445 *SIC 6411*

SCHINDLER ELEVATOR CORPORATION p
879
3640 MCNICOLL AVE UNIT A, SCARBOR-OUGH, ON, M1X 1G5
(416) 332-8280 *SIC 1796*

SCHINDLER ELEVATOR CORPORATION p
1158
8577 CH DALTON, MONT-ROYAL, QC, H4T 1V5
(514) 737-5507 *SIC 3534*

SCHIPPERS CANADA LTD p 138
27211 HIGHWAY 12 SUITE 120, LACOMBE COUNTY, AB, T4L 0E3
(403) 786-9911 *SIC 5999*

SCHLAGER HOLDING LTD p 1182
7070 RUE SAINT-URBAIN, MONTREAL, QC, H2S 3H6
(514) 276-2518 *SIC 6712*

SCHLEGEL VILLAGES INC p 604
60 WOODLAWN RD E, GUELPH, ON, N1H 8M8
(519) 822-5272 *SIC 6513*

SCHLEGEL VILLAGES INC p 616
1620 UPPER WENTWORTH ST, HAMIL-TON, ON, L9B 2W3
(905) 575-4735 *SIC 8051*

SCHLUETER ACURA OF KITCHENER p
635
See FAIRVIEW IMPORT MOTORS INC

SCHLUETER CHEVROLET OLDSMOBILE LIMITED p 637
2685 KINGSWAY DR, KITCHENER, ON, N2C 1A7
(519) 884-9000 *SIC 5511*

SCHLUMBERGER CANADA LIMITED p 7
419 AQUADUCT DR, BROOKS, AB, T1R 1C5
(403) 362-3437 *SIC 1389*

SCHLUMBERGER CANADA LIMITED p 18
8087 54 ST SE, CALGARY, AB, T2C 4R7
(403) 509-4300 *SIC 1389*

SCHLUMBERGER CANADA LIMITED p 32
125 9 AVE SE SUITE 200, CALGARY, AB, T2G 0P6
(403) 509-4000 *SIC 1389*

SCHLUMBERGER CANADA LIMITED p 65
322 11 AVE SW SUITE 600, CALGARY, AB, T2R 0C5
SIC 1389

SCHLUMBERGER CANADA LIMITED p 80
9602 72 AVE, CLAIRMONT, AB, T8X 5B3
(780) 830-4501 *SIC 1389*

SCHLUMBERGER CANADA LIMITED p 116
5003 93 ST NW, EDMONTON, AB, T6E 5S9
(780) 434-3476 *SIC 3533*

SCHLUMBERGER CANADA LIMITED p 121
9450 17 AVE NW, EDMONTON, AB, T6N 1M9
SIC 3821

SCHLUMBERGER CANADA LIMITED p 126
9803 12 AVE SW, EDMONTON, AB, T6X 0E3
SIC 3533

SCHLUMBERGER CANADA LIMITED p 147

2167 BRIER PARK PL NW, MEDICINE HAT, AB, T1C 1S7
(403) 527-8895 *SIC 1389*

SCHLUMBERGER CANADA LIMITED p 149
1606 8 ST, NISKU, AB, T9E 7S6
(780) 955-2800 *SIC 1389*

SCHLUMBERGER CANADA LIMITED p 149
406 22 AVE, NISKU, AB, T9E 7W8
(780) 979-0627 *SIC 1389*

SCHLUMBERGER CANADA LIMITED p 156
6794 65 AVE, RED DEER, AB, T4P 1A5
(403) 356-4398 *SIC 1389*

SCHLUMBERGER CANADA LIMITED p 426
2 PANTHER PL, MOUNT PEARL, NL, A1N 5B1
(709) 748-7900 *SIC 1389*

SCHLUMBERGER EDMONTON PRODUCT CENTRE p 126
See SCHLUMBERGER CANADA LIMITED

SCHLUMBERGER INFORMATION SOLU-TIONS p
65
See SCHLUMBERGER CANADA LIMITED

SCHLUMBERGER WELL SERVICES p 147
See SCHLUMBERGER CANADA LIMITED

SCHLUMBERGER WELL SERVICES p 156
See SCHLUMBERGER CANADA LIMITED

SCHLUMBERGER-OIL FIELD SERVICES DIV OF p 426
See SCHLUMBERGER CANADA LIMITED

SCHMIDT, JACK SUPPLIES LIMITED p 889
1063 TALBOT ST UNIT 25, ST THOMAS, ON, N5P 1G4
(519) 631-4910 *SIC 5531*

SCHMIDT, WM. MECHANICAL CONTRAC-TORS LTD p
25
4603 13 ST NE SUITE D, CALGARY, AB, T2E 6M3
(403) 250-1157 *SIC 1711*

SCHMOLZ + BICKENBACH CANADA, INC. p 742
6350 VIPOND DR, MISSISSAUGA, ON, L5T 1G2
(416) 675-5941 *SIC 5051*

SCHMUNK GATT SMITH & ASSOCIATES p
228
20334 56 AVE SUITE 204, LANGLEY, BC, V3A 3Y7
(604) 533-9813 *SIC 6311*

SCHNEIDER ELECTRIC p 94
See SCHNEIDER ELECTRIC CANADA INC

SCHNEIDER ELECTRIC p 267
See POWER MEASUREMENT LTD

SCHNEIDER ELECTRIC p 267
See POWER MEASUREMENT, INC

SCHNEIDER ELECTRIC p 733
See SCHNEIDER ELECTRIC CANADA INC

SCHNEIDER ELECTRIC p 1070
See SCHNEIDER ELECTRIC CANADA INC

SCHNEIDER ELECTRIC p 1252
See SCHNEIDER ELECTRIC CANADA INC

SCHNEIDER ELECTRIC CANADA p 18
See SCHNEIDER ELECTRIC SOFTWARE CANADA INC

SCHNEIDER ELECTRIC CANADA INC p 94
12825 144 ST NW, EDMONTON, AB, T5L 4N7
(780) 453-3561 *SIC 5063*

SCHNEIDER ELECTRIC CANADA INC p
258
22171 FRASERWOOD WAY, RICHMOND, BC, V6W 1J5
(604) 273-3711 *SIC 1731*

SCHNEIDER ELECTRIC CANADA INC p
733
5985 MCLAUGHLIN RD, MISSISSAUGA, ON, L5R 1B8
(905) 366-3999 *SIC 3699*

SCHNEIDER ELECTRIC CANADA INC p
1070
4100 PLACE JAVA, BROSSARD, QC, J4Y 0C4
(450) 444-0143 *SIC 3699*

SCHNEIDER ELECTRIC CANADA INC p 1070
4100 PLACE JAVA, BROSSARD, QC, J4Y 0C4
(450) 444-0143 *SIC* 8711

SCHNEIDER ELECTRIC CANADA INC p 1252
825 AV BANCROFT, POINTE-CLAIRE, QC, H9R 4L6
SIC 3699

SCHNEIDER ELECTRIC SOFTWARE CANADA INC p 18
49 QUARRY PARK BLVD SE SUITE 100, CALGARY, AB, T2C 5H9
(403) 253-8848 *SIC* 7371

SCHNEIDER ELECTRIC SYSTEMS CANADA INC p 1091
4 RUE LAKE, DOLLARD-DES-ORMEAUX, QC, H9B 3H9
(514) 421-4210 *SIC* 3556

SCHNEIDER FOODS p 575
See MAPLE LEAF FOODS INC

SCHNEIDER FOODS p 848
See MAPLE LEAF FOODS INC

SCHNEIDER FOODS p 888
See MAPLE LEAF FOODS INC

SCHNITZER STEEL CANADA LTD p 275
12195 MUSQUEAM DR, SURREY, BC, V3V 3T2
(604) 580-0251 *SIC* 5093

SCHOKBETON QUEBEC INC p 1302
430 BOUL ARTHUR-SAUVE BUREAU 6030, SAINT-EUSTACHE, QC, J7R 6V7
(450) 473-6831 *SIC* 3272

SCHOLAR'S CHOICE p 651
See EDUCATOR SUPPLIES LIMITED

SCHOLASTIC CANADA LTD p 679
175 HILLMOUNT RD, MARKHAM, ON, L6C 1Z7
(905) 887-7323 *SIC* 5192

SCHOLLE IPN CANADA LTD p 1054
22000 AV CLARK-GRAHAM, BAIE-D'URFE, QC, H9X 4B6
(514) 457-1569 *SIC* 2673

SCHON, GEORGE MOTORS LIMITED p 1033
7685 MARTIN GROVE RD, WOODBRIDGE, ON, L4L 1B5
(905) 851-3993 *SIC* 5511

SCHONBERGER FAMILY FARMS LIMITED p 643
1412 CONCESSION 1 RD ENR, LANGTON, ON, N0E 1G0
(519) 875-2988 *SIC* 0161

SCHOOL BOARD DISTRICT 01 p 401
715 PRIESTMAN ST, FREDERICTON, NB, E3B 5W7
(506) 453-3991 *SIC* 8211

SCHOOL BUS GARAGE p 205
See SCHOOL DISTRICT #59 PEACE RIVER SOUTH

SCHOOL DISTRICT #28 p 252
850 ANDERSON DR, QUESNEL, BC, V2J 1G4
(250) 992-7007 *SIC* 8211

SCHOOL DISTRICT #28 p 252
585 CALLANAN ST, QUESNEL, BC, V2J 2V3
(250) 992-2131 *SIC* 8211

SCHOOL DISTRICT #28 p 252
401 NORTH STAR RD SUITE 28, QUESNEL, BC, V2J 5K2
(250) 992-8802 *SIC* 8211

SCHOOL DISTRICT #59 PEACE RIVER SOUTH p 205
11600 7 ST, DAWSON CREEK, BC, V1G 4R8
(250) 782-2106 *SIC* 8211

SCHOOL DISTRICT #70 (ALBERNI) SCHOOL BOARD p 245
4000 BURDE ST, PORT ALBERNI, BC, V9Y 3L6
(250) 724-3284 *SIC* 8211

SCHOOL DISTRICT #74 (GOLD TRAIL) p 180
400 HOLLIS RD, ASHCROFT, BC, V0K 1A0
(250) 453-9101 *SIC* 8211

SCHOOL DISTRICT #75 (MISSION) p 232
33046 4TH AVE SUITE 75, MISSION, BC, V2V 1S5
(604) 826-6286 *SIC* 8211

SCHOOL DISTRICT #75 (MISSION) p 232
34800 DEWDNEY TRUNK RD SUITE 1, MISSION, BC, V2V 5V6
(604) 826-3651 *SIC* 8211

SCHOOL DISTRICT #75 (MISSION) p 232
32939 7TH AVE, MISSION, BC, V2V 2C5
(604) 826-7191 *SIC* 8211

SCHOOL DISTRICT #81 (FORT NELSON) p 213
5104 AIRPORT DR, FORT NELSON, BC, V0C 1R0
(250) 774-2591 *SIC* 8211

SCHOOL DISTRICT 14 p 403
217 ROCKLAND RD, HARTLAND, NB, E7P 0A2
(506) 375-3000 *SIC* 8211

SCHOOL DISTRICT 17 p 410
25 MACKENZIE AVE, OROMOCTO, NB, E2V 1K4
(506) 357-4015 *SIC* 8211

SCHOOL DISTRICT 2 p 407
207 CHURCH ST, MONCTON, NB, E1C 5A3
(506) 856-3439 *SIC* 8211

SCHOOL DISTRICT 2 p 409
1077 ST GEORGE BLVD, MONCTON, NB, E1E 4C9
(506) 856-3222 *SIC* 8211

SCHOOL DISTRICT 51 BOUNDARY p 215
1021 CENTRAL AVE, GRAND FORKS, BC, V0H 1H0
(250) 442-8258 *SIC* 8211

SCHOOL DISTRICT 63 (SAANICH) p 180
1101 NEWTON PL, BRENTWOOD BAY, BC, V8M 1G3
(250) 652-1135 *SIC* 8211

SCHOOL DISTRICT 63 (SAANICH) p 267
1627 STELLYS CROSS RD, SAANICHTON, BC, V8M 1S8
(250) 652-4401 *SIC* 8211

SCHOOL DISTRICT 63 (SAANICH) p 338
4980 WESLEY RD, VICTORIA, BC, V8Y 1Y9
(250) 686-5221 *SIC* 8211

SCHOOL DISTRICT 73 (KAMLOOPS/THOMPSON) p 217
710 MCGILL RD, KAMLOOPS, BC, V2C 0A2
(250) 372-5853 *SIC* 4173

SCHOOL DISTRICT 73 (KAMLOOPS/THOMPSON) p 217
821 MUNRO ST, KAMLOOPS, BC, V2C 3E9
(250) 374-1405 *SIC* 8211

SCHOOL DISTRICT 73 (KAMLOOPS/THOMPSON) p 218
1383 9TH AVE, KAMLOOPS, BC, V2C 3X7
(250) 374-0679 *SIC* 8211

SCHOOL DISTRICT 8 p 413
1490 HICKEY RD, SAINT JOHN, NB, E2J 4E7
(506) 658-5367 *SIC* 8211

SCHOOL DISTRICT 8 p 414
305 DOUGLAS AVE, SAINT JOHN, NB, E2K 1E5
(506) 658-5359 *SIC* 8211

SCHOOL DISTRICT NO 22 (VERNON) p 331
2301 FULTON RD, VERNON, BC, V1H 1Y1
(250) 545-1348 *SIC* 8211

SCHOOL DISTRICT NO 22 (VERNON) p 332
1401 15 ST, VERNON, BC, V1T 8S8
(250) 542-3331 *SIC* 8211

SCHOOL DISTRICT NO 22 (VERNON) p 332
2303 18 ST, VERNON, BC, V1T 3Z9
(250) 545-0701 *SIC* 8211

SCHOOL DISTRICT NO 22 (VERNON) p 332
2701 41 AVE, VERNON, BC, V1T 6X3
(250) 542-3361 *SIC* 8211

SCHOOL DISTRICT NO 27 (CARIBOO-CHILCOTIN) p 344
350 SECOND AVE N, WILLIAMS LAKE, BC, V2G 1Z9
(250) 398-3800 *SIC* 8211

SCHOOL DISTRICT NO 33 CHILLIWACK p 196
8430 CESSNA DR, CHILLIWACK, BC, V2P 7K4
(604) 792-1321 *SIC* 8211

SCHOOL DISTRICT NO 33 CHILLIWACK p 197
45460 STEVENSON RD, CHILLIWACK, BC, V2R 2Z6
(604) 858-9424 *SIC* 8211

SCHOOL DISTRICT NO 33 CHILLIWACK p 197
46363 YALE RD, CHILLIWACK, BC, V2P 2P8
(604) 795-7295 *SIC* 8211

SCHOOL DISTRICT NO 34 (ABBOTSFORD) p 175
34620 OLD YALE RD, ABBOTSFORD, BC, V2S 7S6
(604) 853-0778 *SIC* 8211

SCHOOL DISTRICT NO 34 (ABBOTSFORD) p 175
35045 EXBURY AVE, ABBOTSFORD, BC, V2S 7L1
(604) 864-0220 *SIC* 8211

SCHOOL DISTRICT NO 34 (ABBOTSFORD) p 177
31150 BLUERIDGE DR, ABBOTSFORD, BC, V2T 5R2
(604) 864-0011 *SIC* 8211

SCHOOL DISTRICT NO 34 (ABBOTSFORD) p 177
32355 MOUAT DR, ABBOTSFORD, BC, V2T 4E9
(604) 853-7191 *SIC* 8211

SCHOOL DISTRICT NO 36 (SURREY) p 271
See SCHOOL DISTRICT NO. 36 (SURREY)
SCHOOL DISTRICT NO 36 (SURREY) p 273
See SCHOOL DISTRICT NO. 36 (SURREY)
SCHOOL DISTRICT NO 36 (SURREY) p 274
See SCHOOL DISTRICT NO. 36 (SURREY)
SCHOOL DISTRICT NO 36 (SURREY) p 277
See SCHOOL DISTRICT NO. 36 (SURREY)
SCHOOL DISTRICT NO 36 (SURREY) p 278
See SCHOOL DISTRICT NO. 36 (SURREY)
SCHOOL DISTRICT NO 36 (SURREY) p 280
See SCHOOL DISTRICT NO. 36 (SURREY)
SCHOOL DISTRICT NO 36 (SURREY) p 281
See SCHOOL DISTRICT NO. 36 (SURREY)
SCHOOL DISTRICT NO 36 (SURREY) p 282
See SCHOOL DISTRICT NO. 36 (SURREY)

SCHOOL DISTRICT NO 42 (MAPLE RIDGE-PITT MEADOWS) p 230
10445 245 ST SUITE 10445, MAPLE RIDGE, BC, V2W 2G4
(604) 466-8409 *SIC* 8211

SCHOOL DISTRICT NO 42 (MAPLE RIDGE-PITT MEADOWS) p 231
20905 WICKLUND AVE, MAPLE RIDGE, BC, V2X 8E8
(604) 467-3481 *SIC* 8211

SCHOOL DISTRICT NO 42 (MAPLE RIDGE-PITT MEADOWS) p 231
21911 122 AVE, MAPLE RIDGE, BC, V2X 3X2
(604) 463-4175 *SIC* 8211

SCHOOL DISTRICT NO 42 (MAPLE RIDGE-PITT MEADOWS) p 231
22225 BROWN AVE, MAPLE RIDGE, BC, V2X 8N6
(604) 463-4200 *SIC* 8211

SCHOOL DISTRICT NO 42 (MAPLE RIDGE-PITT MEADOWS) p 231
24789 DEWDNEY TRUNK RD, MAPLE RIDGE, BC, V4R 1X2
(604) 463-3500 *SIC* 8211

SCHOOL DISTRICT NO 42 (MAPLE RIDGE-PITT MEADOWS) p 244
19438 116B AVE, PITT MEADOWS, BC, V3Y 1G1
(604) 465-7141 *SIC* 8211

SCHOOL DISTRICT NO 5 (SOUTHEAST KOOTENAY) p 204
940 INDUSTRIAL ROAD 1 SUITE 1, CRANBROOK, BC, V1C 4C6
(250) 426-4201 *SIC* 8211

SCHOOL DISTRICT NO 58 (NICOLA-SIMILKAMEEN) p 232
1550 CHAPMAN ST, MERRITT, BC, V1K 1B0
(250) 378-5161 *SIC* 8211

SCHOOL DISTRICT NO 62 (SOOKE) p 340
3067 JACKLIN RD, VICTORIA, BC, V9B 3Y7
(250) 478-5501 *SIC* 8211

SCHOOL DISTRICT NO 62 (SOOKE) p 340
3143 JACKLIN RD, VICTORIA, BC, V9B 5R1
(250) 474-9800 *SIC* 8211

SCHOOL DISTRICT NO 62 (SOOKE) p 340
3341 PAINTER RD, VICTORIA, BC, V9C 2J1
(250) 478-5548 *SIC* 8211

SCHOOL DISTRICT NO 67 (OKANAGAN SKAHA) p 244
425 JERMYN AVE, PENTICTON, BC, V2A 1Z4
(250) 770-7700 *SIC* 8211

SCHOOL DISTRICT NO 69 (QUALICUM) p 243
135 N PYM RD, PARKSVILLE, BC, V9P 2H4
(250) 248-5721 *SIC* 8211

SCHOOL DISTRICT NO. 20 (KOOTENAY-COLUMBIA) p 284
2001 THIRD AVE, TRAIL, BC, V1R 1R6
(250) 368-6434 *SIC* 8211

SCHOOL DISTRICT NO. 23 (CENTRAL OKANAGAN) p 219
See BOARD OF EDUCATION OF SCHOOL DISTRICT NO. 23 (CENTRAL OKANAGAN), THE

SCHOOL DISTRICT NO. 35 (LANGLEY) p 179
26850 29 AVE, ALDERGROVE, BC, V4W 3C1
(604) 856-2521 *SIC* 8211

SCHOOL DISTRICT NO. 35 (LANGLEY) p 225
8919 WALNUT GROVE DR, LANGLEY, BC, V1M 2N7
(604) 882-0220 *SIC* 8211

SCHOOL DISTRICT NO. 35 (LANGLEY) p 227
21405 56 AVE, LANGLEY, BC, V2Y 2N1
(604) 534-7155 *SIC* 8211

SCHOOL DISTRICT NO. 35 (LANGLEY) p 227
23752 52 AVE, LANGLEY, BC, V2Z 2P3
(604) 530-2151 *SIC* 8211

SCHOOL DISTRICT NO. 36 (SURREY) p 271
10719 150 ST, SURREY, BC, V3R 4C8
(604) 585-2566 *SIC* 8211

SCHOOL DISTRICT NO. 36 (SURREY) p 271
15350 99 AVE, SURREY, BC, V3R 0R9
(604) 581-5500 *SIC* 8211

SCHOOL DISTRICT NO. 36 (SURREY) p 273
6151 180 ST, SURREY, BC, V3S 4L5
(604) 574-7407 *SIC* 8211

SCHOOL DISTRICT NO. 36 (SURREY) p 273
7940 156 ST, SURREY, BC, V3S 3R3

(604) 597-2301 *SIC* 8211
SCHOOL DISTRICT NO. 36 (SURREY) *p*
274
10441 132 ST, SURREY, BC, V3T 3V3
(604) 588-6934 *SIC* 8211
SCHOOL DISTRICT NO. 36 (SURREY) *p*
275
14033 92 AVE, SURREY, BC, V3V 0B7
(604) 596-7733 *SIC* 8211
SCHOOL DISTRICT NO. 36 (SURREY) *p*
277
6700 144 ST, SURREY, BC, V3W 5R5
(604) 572-0500 *SIC* 4173
SCHOOL DISTRICT NO. 36 (SURREY) *p*
277
12600 66 AVE, SURREY, BC, V3W 2A8
(604) 597-5234 *SIC* 8211
SCHOOL DISTRICT NO. 36 (SURREY) *p*
277
12772 88 AVE, SURREY, BC, V3W 3J9
(604) 502-5710 *SIC* 8211
SCHOOL DISTRICT NO. 36 (SURREY) *p*
277
12870 72 AVE, SURREY, BC, V3W 2M9
(604) 594-5458 *SIC* 8211
SCHOOL DISTRICT NO. 36 (SURREY) *p*
278
6248 144 ST, SURREY, BC, V3X 1A1
(604) 543-8749 *SIC* 8211
SCHOOL DISTRICT NO. 36 (SURREY) *p*
280
1785 148 ST, SURREY, BC, V4A 4M6
(604) 536-2131 *SIC* 8211
SCHOOL DISTRICT NO. 36 (SURREY) *p*
280
15751 16 AVE, SURREY, BC, V4A 1S1
(604) 531-8354 *SIC* 8211
SCHOOL DISTRICT NO. 36 (SURREY) *p*
281
13484 24 AVE, SURREY, BC, V4A 2G5
(604) 538-6678 *SIC* 8211
SCHOOL DISTRICT NO. 36 (SURREY) *p*
282
15945 96 AVE, SURREY, BC, V4N 2R8
(604) 581-4433 *SIC* 8211
SCHOOL DISTRICT NO. 36 (SURREY) *p*
282
16060 108 AVE, SURREY, BC, V4N 1M1
(604) 582-9231 *SIC* 8211
SCHOOL DISTRICT NO. 43 (COQUITLAM) *p*
198
1195 LANSDOWNE DR, COQUITLAM, BC,
V3B 7Y8
(604) 464-5793 *SIC* 8211
SCHOOL DISTRICT NO. 43 (COQUITLAM) *p*
199
2525 COMO LAKE AVE, COQUITLAM, BC,
V3J 3R8
(604) 461-5581 *SIC* 8211
SCHOOL DISTRICT NO. 43 (COQUITLAM) *p*
199
570 POIRIER ST, COQUITLAM, BC, V3J
6A8
(604) 939-9201 *SIC* 8211
SCHOOL DISTRICT NO. 43 (COQUITLAM) *p*
199
550 POIRIER ST, COQUITLAM, BC, V3J
6A7
(604) 939-9201 *SIC* 8211
SCHOOL DISTRICT NO. 43 (COQUITLAM) *p*
246
1260 RIVERWOOD GATE, PORT COQUIT-
LAM, BC, V3B 7Z5
(604) 941-5401 *SIC* 8211
SCHOOL DISTRICT NO. 43 (COQUITLAM) *p*
247
1982 KINGSWAY AVE, PORT COQUITLAM,
BC, V3C 1S5
(604) 941-5643 *SIC* 8211
SCHOOL DISTRICT NO. 43 (COQUITLAM) *p*
247
2215 REEVE ST, PORT COQUITLAM, BC,
V3C 6K8
(604) 941-6053 *SIC* 8211

SCHOOL DISTRICT NO. 43 (COQUITLAM) *p*
248
1300 DAVID AVE, PORT MOODY, BC, V3H
5K6
(604) 461-8679 *SIC* 8211
SCHOOL DISTRICT NO. 43 (COQUITLAM) *p*
248
300 ALBERT ST, PORT MOODY, BC, V3H
2M5
(604) 939-6656 *SIC* 8211
**SCHOOL DISTRICT NO. 44 (NORTH VAN-
COUVER)** *p*
238
931 BROADVIEW DR, NORTH VANCOU-
VER, BC, V7H 2E9
(604) 903-3700 *SIC* 8211
**SCHOOL DISTRICT NO. 44 (NORTH VAN-
COUVER)** *p*
239
1131 FREDERICK RD, NORTH VANCOU-
VER, BC, V7K 1J3
(604) 903-3300 *SIC* 8211
**SCHOOL DISTRICT NO. 44 (NORTH VAN-
COUVER)** *p*
240
1860 SUTHERLAND AVE, NORTH VAN-
COUVER, BC, V7L 4C2
(604) 903-3500 *SIC* 8211
**SCHOOL DISTRICT NO. 44 (NORTH VAN-
COUVER)** *p*
240
2121 LONSDALE AVE, NORTH VANCOU-
VER, BC, V7M 2K6
(604) 903-3444 *SIC* 8211
**SCHOOL DISTRICT NO. 44 (NORTH VAN-
COUVER)** *p*
242
1044 EDGEWOOD RD, NORTH VANCOU-
VER, BC, V7R 1Y7
(604) 903-3600 *SIC* 8211
**SCHOOL DISTRICT NO. 45 (WEST VAN-
COUVER)** *p*
342
1075 21ST ST SUITE 45, WEST VANCOU-
VER, BC, V7V 4A9
(604) 981-1000 *SIC* 8211
**SCHOOL DISTRICT NO. 45 (WEST VAN-
COUVER)** *p*
342
1750 MATHERS AVE, WEST VANCOUVER,
BC, V7V 2G7
(604) 981-1100 *SIC* 8211
**SCHOOL DISTRICT NO. 46 (SUNSHINE
COAST)** *p* 214
494 SOUTH FLETCHER RD, GIBSONS,
BC, V0N 1V0
(604) 886-8811 *SIC* 8211
**SCHOOL DISTRICT NO. 48 (HOWE
SOUND)** *p* 269
37866 2ND AVE, SQUAMISH, BC, V8B 0A2
(604) 892-3421 *SIC* 8211
**SCHOOL DISTRICT NO. 54 (BULKLEY
VALLEY)** *p* 269
3377 THIRD AVE, SMITHERS, BC, V0J 2N3
(250) 847-4846 *SIC* 8211
**SCHOOL DISTRICT NO. 60 (PEACE RIVER
NORTH)** *p* 214
10112 105 AVE, FORT ST. JOHN, BC, V1J
4S4
(250) 262-6000 *SIC* 8211
**SCHOOL DISTRICT NO. 60 (PEACE RIVER
NORTH)** *p* 214
9304 86 ST, FORT ST. JOHN, BC, V1J 6L9
(250) 785-4429 *SIC* 8211
**SCHOOL DISTRICT NO. 68 (NANAIMO-
LADYSMITH)** *p*
224
710 6TH AVE, LADYSMITH, BC, V9G 1A1
(250) 245-3043 *SIC* 8211
**SCHOOL DISTRICT NO. 68 (NANAIMO-
LADYSMITH)** *p*
233
395 WAKESIAH AVE, NANAIMO, BC, V9R
3K6

(250) 754-5521 *SIC* 8211
**SCHOOL DISTRICT NO. 68 (NANAIMO-
LADYSMITH)** *p*
234
1270 STRATHMORE ST, NANAIMO, BC,
V9S 2L9
(250) 753-2271 *SIC* 8211
**SCHOOL DISTRICT NO. 68 (NANAIMO-
LADYSMITH)** *p*
234
3135 MEXICANA RD, NANAIMO, BC, V9T
2W8
(250) 758-9191 *SIC* 8211
**SCHOOL DISTRICT NO. 68 (NANAIMO-
LADYSMITH)** *p*
235
6135 MCGIRR RD, NANAIMO, BC, V9V
1M1
(250) 756-4595 *SIC* 8211
**SCHOOL DISTRICT NO. 71 (COMOX VAL-
LEY)** *p*
203
1551 LERWICK RD, COURTENAY, BC, V9N
9B5
(250) 334-2428 *SIC* 8211
**SCHOOL DISTRICT NO. 79 (COWICHAN
VALLEY)** *p* 232
953 SHAWNIGAN-MILL BAY RD, MILL BAY,
BC, V0R 2P2
(250) 743-6916 *SIC* 8211
**SCHOOL DISTRICT NO. 91 (NECHAKO
LAKE)** *p* 330
See *BOARD OF EDUCATION OF SCHOOL
DISTRICT NO. 91 (NECHAKO LAKE), THE*
SCHOOL DISTRICT NO. 92 (NISGA'A) *p*
179
5002 SKATEEN AVE, AIYANSH, BC, V0J
1A0
(250) 633-2228 *SIC* 8211
**SCHOOL DISTRICT NO. 93 (CONSEIL
SCOLAIRE FRANCOPHONE)** *p* 254
See *CONSEIL SCOLAIRE FRANCO-
PHONE DE LA COLOMBIE-BRITANNIQUE*
SCHOOL OF COMPUTING *p* 631
See *QUEEN'S UNIVERSITY AT KINGSTON*
SCHOOL OF DENTISTRY *p* 117
See *GOVERNORS OF THE UNIVERSITY
OF ALBERTA, THE*
**SCHOOL OF ENVIRONMENT AND SUS-
TAINABILITY** *p*
1434
See *UNIVERSITY OF SASKATCHEWAN*
SCHOOL OF KINESIOLOGY *p* 325
See *UNIVERSITY OF BRITISH COLUMBIA,
THE*
SCHOOL OF MANAGEMENT *p* 822
See *UNIVERSITY OF OTTAWA*
SCHOOL OF NURSING *p* 325
See *UNIVERSITY OF BRITISH COLUMBIA,
THE*
**SCHOOL SPECIALTY CANADA PREMIER
AGENDAS** *p* 226
See *PREMIER SCHOOL AGENDAS LTD*
SCHOONER SEAFOODS LIMITED *p* 470
51 DOUCET WHARF RD, WEDGEPORT,
NS, B0W 3P0
(902) 663-2521 *SIC* 2091
SCHOONER TRANSPORT *p* 595
See *MCDONALD, GRANT P. HOLDINGS
INC*
**SCHOTT GEMTRON (CANADA) CORPO-
RATION** *p*
682
125 ALBERT ST, MIDLAND, ON, L4R 4L3
(705) 526-3771 *SIC* 3231
SCHREIBER BROTHERS LIMITED *p* 608
50 BROCKLEY DR, HAMILTON, ON, L8E
3P1
(905) 561-7780 *SIC* 1761
SCHREIBER ROOFING *p* 608
See *SCHREIBER BROTHERS LIMITED*
SCHRIEMER FAMILY FARM LTD *p* 354
33096 RAT RIVER RD, OTTERBURNE, MB,
R0A 1G0

(204) 299-9708 *SIC* 0161
**SCHULICH SCHOOL OF MEDICINE AND
DENTISTRY** *p* 655
See *UNIVERSITY OF WESTERN ON-
TARIO, THE*
SCHULTE INDUSTRIES LTD *p* 1406
1 RAILWAY AVE, ENGLEFELD, SK, S0K
1N0
(306) 287-3715 *SIC* 3549
SCHURE SPORTS INC *p* 558
345 CONNIE CRES, CONCORD, ON, L4K
5R2
(905) 669-6021 *SIC* 5136
SCHWAB TRADING INC *p* 799
2391 CENTRAL PARK DR UNIT 608,
OAKVILLE, ON, L6H 0E4
(905) 827-6298 *SIC* 6799
SCHWAN'S CANADA CORPORATION *p*
1128
2900 RUE LOUIS-A.-AMOS, LACHINE, QC,
H8T 3K6
(514) 631-9275 *SIC* 6712
SCHWARTZ & CO LTD *p* 467
325 VULCAN AVE, SYDNEY, NS, B1P 5X1
(902) 539-4404 *SIC* 5712
SCHWARTZ & COMPANY (2006) LIMITED *p*
467
30 REEVES ST, SYDNEY, NS, B1P 3C5
(902) 539-4404 *SIC* 5712
SCHWARTZ FURNITURE SHOWROOMS *p*
467
See *SCHWARTZ & CO LTD*
SCHWARTZ LEVITSKY FELDMAN LLP *p*
923
2300 YONGE ST SUITE 1500, TORONTO,
ON, M4P 1E4
(416) 785-5353 *SIC* 8721
SCHWARTZ LEVITSKY FELDMAN LLP *p*
1215
1980 RUE SHERBROOKE O ETAGE 10,
MONTREAL, QC, H3H 1E8
(514) 937-6392 *SIC* 8721
**SCHWARTZ LEVITSKY FELDMAN
S.E.N.C.R.L.** *p* 923
See *SCHWARTZ LEVITSKY FELDMAN
LLP*
**SCHWARTZ RELIANCE INSURANCE &
REGISTRIES** *p* 142
See *DAV-BAR-DAL INSURANCE SER-
VICES LTD*
SCHWEITZER-MAUDUIT CANADA, INC *p*
361
340 AIRPORT DR, WINKLER, MB, R6W 0J9
(204) 325-7986 *SIC* 2621
SCI BROCKVILLE CORP *p* 625
500 MARCH RD, KANATA, ON, K2K 0J9
(613) 886-6148 *SIC* 3661
SCI GROUP INC *p* 588
180 ATTWELL DR SUITE 600, ETOBI-
COKE, ON, M9W 6A9
(416) 401-3011 *SIC* 4213
SCI INTERIORS LIMITED *p* 674
11 ALLSTATE PKY SUITE 204, MARKHAM,
ON, L3R 9T8
(905) 479-7007 *SIC* 5021
SCI LOGISTICS LTD *p* 588
180 ATTWELL DR SUITE 600, ETOBI-
COKE, ON, M9W 6A9
(416) 401-3011 *SIC* 4225
SCI SITECAST INTERNATIONAL INC *p* 750
16 CONCOURSE GATE SUITE 200, NE-
PEAN, ON, K2E 7S8
(613) 225-8118 *SIC* 1542
SCI-WHITE GLOVE SERVICES *p* 739
See *FIRST TEAM TRANSPORT INC*
SCICAN LTD *p* 916
1440 DON MILLS RD, TORONTO, ON, M3B
3P9
(416) 445-1600 *SIC* 3843
SCIEMETRIC INSTRUMENTS INC *p* 625
359 TERRY FOX DR SUITE 100, KANATA,
ON, K2K 2E7
(613) 254-7054 *SIC* 3823
SCIENTEK MEDICAL EQUIPMENT *p* 261

▲ Public Company   ■ Public Company Family Member   **HQ** Headquarters   **BR** Branch   **SL** Single Location

11151 BRIDGEPORT RD, RICHMOND, BC, V6X 1T3
   SIC 3841
SCIENTIFIC-ATLANTA CANADA   *p 873*
   See CISCO SYSTEMS CO.
SCIERADE INVESTMENT CORPORATIONp 973
   1235 BAY ST, TORONTO, ON, M5R 3K4
   (647) 244-6707   *SIC 6282*
SCIERIE LEDUC   *p 1257*
   See SOCIETE EN COMMANDITE STADA-CONA WB
SCIERIE LEDUC, DIV OF   *p 1281*
   See SOCIETE EN COMMANDITE STADA-CONA WB
SCIERIE ST-ELZEAR INC   *p 1299*
   215 RTE DE L'EGLISE, SAINT-ELZEAR-DE-BONAVENTURE, QC, G0C 2W0
   (418) 534-2596   *SIC 2421*
SCIERIES ADRIEN ARSENEAULT LTEE   *p 394*
   47 DU MOULIN ST, BALMORAL, NB, E8E 1H6
      SIC 5031
SCINTREX LIMITED   *p 558*
   222 SNIDERCROFT RD SUITE 2, CONCORD, ON, L4K 2K1
   (905) 669-2280   *SIC 3829*
SCISL   *p 1419*
   See SGI CANADA INSURANCE SERVICES LTD
SCITI TRUST   *p 985*
   40 KING ST W, TORONTO, ON, M5W 2X6
   (416) 863-7411   *SIC 6722*
SCM ADJUSTERS CANADA LTD.   *p 392*
   1479 BUFFALO PL SUITE 200, WINNIPEG, MB, R3T 1L7
   (204) 985-1777   *SIC 6411*
SCM CANADA   *p 1177*
   See SCM INSURANCE SERVICES INC
SCM GROUP CANADA INC   *p 736*
   1180 LORIMAR DR, MISSISSAUGA, ON, L5S 1M9
   (905) 670-5110   *SIC 5084*
SCM INSURANCE SERVICES INC   *p 125*
   5083 WINDERMERE BLVD SW SUITE 101, EDMONTON, AB, T6W 0J5
   (780) 430-9012   *SIC 6411*
SCM INSURANCE SERVICES INC   *p 1177*
   255 BOUL CREMAZIE E BUREAU 1070, MONTREAL, QC, H2M 1L5
   (514) 331-1030   *SIC 6411*
SCN INDUSTRIEL INC   *p 1367*
   22555 AUT TRANSCANADIENNE, SENNEVILLE, QC, H9X 3L7
   (514) 457-1709   *SIC 5084*
SCOCHI HOLDINGS INC   *p 228*
   19820 FRASER HWY, LANGLEY, BC, V3A 4C9
   (604) 533-7881   *SIC 5511*
SCOLART   *p 1261*
   See 2961-4765 QUEBEC INC
SCONA ELECTRIC INC   *p 116*
   10003 69 AVE NW, EDMONTON, AB, T6E 0T1
   (780) 433-4247   *SIC 4911*
SCOR CANADA REINSURANCE COMPANY   *p 971*
   199 BAY ST SUITE 2800, TORONTO, ON, M5L 1G1
   (416) 869-3670   *SIC 6331*
SCORE (CANADA) LIMITED   *p 123*
   9192 14 ST NW, EDMONTON, AB, T6P 0B7
   (780) 455-5273   *SIC 1389*
SCORE MEDIA VENTURES INC   *p 983*
   500 KING ST W, TORONTO, ON, M5V 1L9
   (416) 479-8812   *SIC 7371*
SCORE TELEVISION NETWORK LTD, THE   *p 983*
   370 KING ST W SUITE 435, TORONTO, ON, M5V 1J9
   (416) 977-6787   *SIC 4841*
SCORPIO MASONRY (NORTHERN) INC   *p*

103
   20203 113 AVE NW, EDMONTON, AB, T5S 2W1
   (780) 447-1682   *SIC 1741*
SCORPIO STONE   *p 103*
   See SCORPIO MASONRY (NORTHERN) INC
SCORPION OILFIELD SERVICES LTD   *p 1409*
   406 6TH W, LASHBURN, SK, S0M 1H0
   (306) 285-2433   *SIC 1389*
SCOT YOUNG (WESTERN) LIMITED   *p 37*
   413 FORGE RD SE, CALGARY, AB, T2H 0S9
   (403) 259-2293   *SIC 7349*
SCOTCHTOWN VOLUNTEER FIRE DEPARTMENT   *p 465*
   11 CATHERINE ST, SCOTCHTOWN, NS, B1H 3B3
   (902) 862-8362   *SIC 7389*
SCOTFORD COMPLEX   *p 130*
   See SHELL CANADA LIMITED
SCOTIA BANK   *p 302*
   See BANK OF NOVA SCOTIA, THE
SCOTIA CAPITAL INC   *p 59*
   119 6 AVE SW SUITE 300, CALGARY, AB, T2P 0P8
   (403) 298-4000   *SIC 6211*
SCOTIA CAPITAL INC   *p 90*
   10104 103 AVE NW SUITE 2000, EDMONTON, AB, T5J 0H8
   (780) 497-3200   *SIC 6211*
SCOTIA CAPITAL INC   *p 825*
   350 ALBERT ST SUITE 2100, OTTAWA, ON, K1R 1A4
   (613) 563-0991   *SIC 6211*
SCOTIA CAPITAL INC   *p 956*
   40 KING ST W, TORONTO, ON, M5H 3Y2
   (416) 863-7411   *SIC 6211*
SCOTIA CAPITAL INC   *p 1199*
   1002 RUE SHERBROOKE O BUREAU 600, MONTREAL, QC, H3A 3L6
   (514) 287-3600   *SIC 6211*
SCOTIA CHRYSLER INC   *p 467*
   325 WELTON ST, SYDNEY, NS, B1P 5S3
   (902) 539-2280   *SIC 5511*
SCOTIA FOODSERVICE LTD   *p 460*
   4 DOMINION CRES, LAKESIDE, NS, B3T 1M1
   (902) 876-2356   *SIC 5141*
SCOTIA FUELS LIMITED   *p 456*
   6380 LADY HAMMOND RD, HALIFAX, NS, B3K 2S3
   (902) 453-2121   *SIC 5983*
SCOTIA GARDEN SEAFOOD INCORPORATED   *p 471*
   112 WATER ST, YARMOUTH, NS, B5A 1L5
   (902) 742-2411   *SIC 5146*
SCOTIA HARVEST INC   *p 449*
   144 WATER ST, DIGBY, NS, B0V 1A0
   (902) 245-6528   *SIC 5146*
SCOTIA INVESTMENTS LIMITED   *p 440*
   3 BEDFORD HILLS RD, BEDFORD, NS, B4A 1J5
   (902) 835-7100   *SIC 6712*
SCOTIA MCLEOD   *p 59*
   See SCOTIA CAPITAL INC
SCOTIA MCLEOD   *p 90*
   See SCOTIA CAPITAL INC
SCOTIA MCLEOD   *p 825*
   See SCOTIA CAPITAL INC
SCOTIA MORTGAGE AUTHORITY   *p 970*
   79 WELLINGSTON ST W SUITE 3400, TORONTO, ON, M5K 1K7
   (416) 350-7400   *SIC 6162*
SCOTIA PRIVATE CLIENT GROUP   *p 379*
   200 PORTAGE AVE SUITE 845, WINNIPEG, MB, R3C 3X2
   (204) 985-3104   *SIC 6211*
SCOTIA RECYCLING (NL) LIMITED   *p 429*
   55 ELIZABETH AVE STE 49, ST. JOHN'S, NL, A1A 1W9

   (709) 579-7466   *SIC 4953*
SCOTIA RECYCLING LIMITED   *p 448*
   5 BROWN AVE, DARTMOUTH, NS, B3B 1Z7
   (902) 468-5650   *SIC 5093*
SCOTIA TIRE SERVICES LIMITED   *p 457*
   267 BEDFORD HWY, HALIFAX, NS, B3M 2K5
   (902) 443-3150   *SIC 5531*
SCOTIA WATEROUS INC   *p 59*
   225 6 AVE SW STE 1700, CALGARY, AB, T2P 1M2
   (403) 410-9947   *SIC 6211*
SCOTIA WEALTH INSURANCE SERVICES INC   *p 956*
   40 KING ST W, TORONTO, ON, M5H 1H1
   (416) 863-7272   *SIC 6411*
SCOTIA WEALTH MANAGEMENT   *p 937*
   See BANK OF NOVA SCOTIA TRUST COMPANY, THE
SCOTIABANK   *p 302*
   See BANK OF NOVA SCOTIA, THE
SCOTIABANK   *p 377*
   See BANK OF NOVA SCOTIA, THE
SCOTIABANK   *p 1193*
   See BANK OF NOVA SCOTIA, THE
SCOTIABANK   *p 1214*
   See BANK OF NOVA SCOTIA, THE
SCOTIABANK CONVENTION CENTER   *p 759*
   See NIAGARA CONVENTION & CIVIC CENTER
SCOTIABANK THEATER TORONTO   *p 979*
   See CINEPLEX ODEON CORPORATION
SCOTIABANK THEATRE VANCOUVER   *p 326*
   See CINEPLEX ODEON CORPORATION
SCOTIABANK THEATRE WEST EDMONTON MALL   *p 104*
   See CINEPLEX ODEON CORPORATION
SCOTIACAPITAL   *p 956*
   See SCOTIA WEALTH INSURANCE SERVICES INC
SCOTIALIFE FINANCIAL SERVICES INC   *p 940*
   100 YONGE ST SUITE 400, TORONTO, ON, M5C 2W1
   (416) 866-7075   *SIC 6321*
SCOTIAMCLEOD   *p 1193*
   See BANK OF NOVA SCOTIA, THE
SCOTIAMCLEOD   *p 1199*
   See SCOTIA CAPITAL INC
SCOTIAMCLEOD INC   *p 806*
   1235 NORTH SERVICE RD W SUITE 200, OAKVILLE, ON, L6M 2W2
   (905) 637-4962   *SIC 7389*
SCOTIAN GOLD CO-OPERATIVE LIMITED   *p 442*
   2900 LOVETT RD, COLDBROOK, NS, B4R 1A6
   (902) 679-2191   *SIC 5148*
SCOTLYNN INVESTMENTS INC   *p 1004*
   1150 VITTORIA RD, VITTORIA, ON, N0E 1W0
   (519) 426-2700   *SIC 6712*
SCOTLYNN SWEETPAC GROWERS INC   *p 1004*
   1150 VITTORIA RD, VITTORIA, ON, N0E 1W0
   (519) 426-2700   *SIC 0161*
SCOTSBURN   *p 432*
   See BROOKFIELD ICE CREAM LIMITED
SCOTSBURN CO-OPERATIVE SERVICES LIMITED   *p 467*
   1120 UPPER PRINCE ST, SYDNEY, NS, B1P 5P6
      SIC 2026
SCOTSBURN DAIRY GROUP   *p 414*
   See BRAXCO LIMITED
SCOTSBURN DAIRY GROUP   *p 467*
   See SCOTSBURN CO-OPERATIVE SERVICES LIMITED
SCOTSBURN LUMBER LTD   *p 465*

65 CONDON RD, SCOTSBURN, NS, B0K 1R0
   (902) 485-8041   *SIC 2421*
SCOTT AND STEWART FORESTRY CONSULTANTS LIMITED   *p 466*
   2267 ANTIGONISH GUYSBOROUGH RD, ST ANDREWS, NS, B0H 1X0
   (902) 863-5508   *SIC 8748*
SCOTT BADER ATC INC   *p 1099*
   2400 RUE CANADIEN BUREAU 303, DRUMMONDVILLE, QC, J2C 7W3
   (819) 477-1752   *SIC 2891*
SCOTT BATHGATE   *p 379*
   See MAY, J. K. INVESTMENTS LTD
SCOTT BUILDERS INC   *p 156*
   8105 49 AVE CLOSE, RED DEER, AB, T4P 2V5
   (403) 343-7270   *SIC 1541*
SCOTT CANADA LTD   *p 397*
   1571 ROUTE 310, COTEAU ROAD, NB, E8T 3K7
   (506) 344-2225   *SIC 1499*
SCOTT CONSTRUCTION GROUP   *p 191*
   See SCOTT CONSTRUCTION LTD
SCOTT CONSTRUCTION LTD   *p 191*
   3777 KINGSWAY UNIT 1750, BURNABY, BC, V5H 3Z7
   (604) 874-8228   *SIC 1542*
SCOTT INDUSTRIAL, DIV DE   *p 1252*
   See PSI PROLEW INC
SCOTT LAND & LEASE LTD   *p 59*
   202 6 AVE SW SUITE 900, CALGARY, AB, T2P 2R9
   (403) 261-1000   *SIC 6211*
SCOTT PLASTICS LTD   *p 268*
   2065 HENRY AVE W, SIDNEY, BC, V8L 5Z6
   (250) 656-8102   *SIC 3429*
SCOTT SAFETY SUPPLY SERVICES LTD   *p 173*
   3365 33 ST, WHITECOURT, AB, T7S 0A2
   (780) 778-3389   *SIC 5999*
SCOTT SPRINGFIELD MFG. INC   *p 32*
   2234 PORTLAND ST SE, CALGARY, AB, T2G 4M6
   (403) 236-1212   *SIC 3433*
SCOTT STEEL   *p 615*
   See SCOTT STEEL ERECTORS INC
SCOTT STEEL ERECTORS INC   *p 615*
   58 BIGWIN RD, HAMILTON, ON, L8W 3R4
   (905) 631-8708   *SIC 1541*
SCOTT'S DIRECTORIES, DIV OF   *p 292*
   See GLACIER PUBLICATIONS LIMITED PARTNERSHIP
SCOTT'S NURSERY LTD   *p 404*
   2192 ROUTE 102, LINCOLN, NB, E3B 8N1
   (506) 458-9208   *SIC 5193*
SCOTT'S PARABLE CHRISTIAN STORES INC   *p 1430*
   810 CIRCLE DR E SUITE 106B, SASKATOON, SK, S7K 3T8
   (306) 244-3700   *SIC 5961*
SCOTT, GORD NISSAN INC   *p 154*
   6863 50 AVE, RED DEER, AB, T4N 4E2
   (403) 347-2258   *SIC 5511*
SCOTT, KIPP PONTIAC BUICK LTD   *p 154*
   6841 50 AVE, RED DEER, AB, T4N 4E2
   (403) 343-6633   *SIC 5511*
SCOTT, S.F. MANUFACTURING CO. LIMITED   *p 146*
   724 14 ST SW, MEDICINE HAT, AB, T1A 4V7
   (403) 526-9170   *SIC 3949*
SCOTT-BATHGATE LTD   *p 379*
   149 PIONEER AVE, WINNIPEG, MB, R3C 0H2
   (204) 943-8525   *SIC 5145*
SCOTT-DOUGLAS PLASTICS LIMITED   *p 622*
   50 JANES RD, INGERSOLL, ON, N5C 0A9
   (519) 485-1943   *SIC 3089*
SCOTT-FISHER ENTERPRISES INC   *p 578*
   5507 DUNDAS ST W, ETOBICOKE, ON,

M9B 1B8
(416) 207-0565 *SIC 5511*
SCOTTS CANADA LTD *p 727*
2000 ARGENTIA RD SUITE 300, MISSIS-SAUGA, ON, L5N 1P7
(905) 814-7425 *SIC 5199*
SCOULAR CANADA LTD *p 69*
10201 SOUTHPORT RD SW SUITE 1110, CALGARY, AB, T2W 4X9
(403) 720-9050 *SIC 6799*
SCOUT LOGISTICS CORPORATION *p 994*
3351 DUNDAS ST W, TORONTO, ON, M6P 2A6
(416) 630-7268 *SIC 4731*
SCOUTS CANADA *p 831*
1345 BASELINE RD SUITE 200, OTTAWA, ON, K2C 0A7
(613) 224-0139 *SIC 8641*
SCOUTS FRANCOPHONES DIST. DE *p 900*
30 STE. ANNE RD, SUDBURY, ON, P3C 5E1
(705) 560-4499 *SIC 8399*
SCP 89 INC *p 1133*
3641 RUE DES FORGES, LATERRIERE, QC, G7N 1N4
(418) 678-1506 *SIC 3496*
SCP DISTRIBUTORS CANADA INC *p 516*
373 ELGIN ST, BRANTFORD, ON, N3S 7P5
(519) 720-9219 *SIC 5091*
SCP SCIENCE *p 1052*
See SEIGNIORY CHEMICAL PRODUCTS LTD
SCPCN *p 69*
See SOUTH CALGARY PRIMARY CARE NETWORK, THE
SCR *p 983*
See SCORE MEDIA VENTURES INC
SCR MINING & TUNNELLING INC *p 1001*
2797 WHITE ST, VAL CARON, ON, P3N 1B2
(705) 897-1932 *SIC 1629*
SCRAPBOOK, EH WHOLESALE LTD *p 25*
5421 11 ST NE UNIT 109, CALGARY, AB, T2E 6M4
(403) 229-1058 *SIC 5112*
SCRAPMEN *p 610*
See 1650473 ONTARIO INC
SCRIBBLE TECHNOLOGIES INC *p 983*
49 SPADINA AVE UNIT 303, TORONTO, ON, M5V 2J1
(416) 364-8118 *SIC 7372*
SCRIBBLELIVE *p 983*
See SCRIBBLE TECHNOLOGIES INC
SCRIPTECH MEDS INC *p 512*
8965 CHINGUACOUSY RD SUITE 1092, BRAMPTON, ON, L6Y 0J2
(905) 454-1620 *SIC 5912*
SCRIVENS FAMILY OF COMPANIES *p 834*
See W. H. SCRIVENS & SON LIMITED
SCRUTON-EDWARD CORP *p 544*
268 ALBERT ST, CLINTON, ON, N0M 1L0
(519) 482-7381 *SIC 5172*
SCS CANADA *p 1062*
See SECURITE POLYGON INC
SCS SUPPLY GROUP INC *p 652*
145 ADELAIDE ST S, LONDON, ON, N5Z 3K7
(519) 686-2650 *SIC 5085*
SDF ABRASIF INC *p 1388*
8750 BOUL INDUSTRIEL BUREAU 202, TROIS-RIVIERES, QC, G9A 5E1
(819) 697-2408 *SIC 5085*
SDI MARKETING *p 588*
See SECOND DIMENSION INTERNA-TIONAL LIMITED
SDL INTERNATIONAL (CANADA) INC *p 1208*
1155 RUE METCALFE BUREAU 1200, MONTREAL, QC, H3B 2V6
(514) 844-2577 *SIC 7389*
SDM *p 1172*
See SERVICES DOCUMENTAIRES MULTI-MEDIA (S.D.M) INC
SDP TELECOM ULC *p 1095*

1725 RTE TRANSCANADIENNE, DORVAL, QC, H9P 1J1
(514) 421-5959 *SIC 3663*
SDS INDUSTRIAL BUILDING SUPPLIES LTD *p 121*
2920 101 ST NW, EDMONTON, AB, T6N 1A6
(780) 224-8058 *SIC 5039*
SDX ENERGY INC *p 59*
520 3 AVE SW SUITE 1900, CALGARY, AB, T2P 0R3
(403) 457-5035 *SIC 1382*
SDX MECANIQUE *p 1366*
See NORDMEC INDUSTRIELS & MINES INC
SE CE DISTRIBUTION *p 1338*
See CIE D'HABILLEMENT SE CE LTEE, LA
SEA AGRA SEAFOOD BROKERAGE LTD *p 240*
1078 ADDERLEY ST, NORTH VANCOU-VER, BC, V7L 1T3
(604) 984-3303 *SIC 5146*
SEA AGRA SEAFOOD JOINT VENTURE *p 240*
See SEA AGRA SEAFOOD BROKERAGE LTD
SEA AIR INTERNATIONAL FORWARDERS LIMITED *p 742*
1720 MEYERSIDE DR, MISSISSAUGA, ON, L5T 1A3
(905) 677-7701 *SIC 4731*
SEA FRESH FISH LTD *p 230*
23963 LOUGHEED HWY, MAPLE RIDGE, BC, V2W 1J1
(604) 463-9817 *SIC 5411*
SEA GLASS INDUSTRIES, DIV OF *p 448*
See SEAMASTERS SERVICES LIMITED
SEA LIFE FISHERIES *p 465*
See COMEAU'S SEA FOODS LIMITED
SEA MERCHANTS INC *p 576*
55 VANSCO RD, ETOBICOKE, ON, M8Z 5Z8
(416) 255-2700 *SIC 5146*
SEA TIDE GROUND FISH PLANT *p 396*
See SEA TIDE IMPORT & EXPORT LTD
SEA TIDE IMPORT & EXPORT LTD *p 396*
45 RUE CORMIER, CAP-PELE, NB, E4N 1N8
(506) 577-4070 *SIC 2092*
SEA TO SKY *p 343*
See WHISTLER TAXI LTD
SEA TO SKY COMMUNITY HEALTH COUN-CIL *p 269*
38140 BEHRNER DR, SQUAMISH, BC, V8B 0J3
(604) 892-9337 *SIC 8062*
SEA TO SKY COURIER & FREIGHT LTD *p 214*
38922 MID WAY SUITE 1, GARIBALDI HIGHLANDS, BC, V0N 1T0
(604) 892-8484 *SIC 7389*
SEA TO SKY FORD *p 269*
See SEA TO SKY FORD SALES LTD
SEA TO SKY FORD SALES LTD *p 269*
1100 COMMERCIAL PL, SQUAMISH, BC, V8B 0S7
(604) 892-3673 *SIC 5511*
SEA TO SKY HELI RIGGING LTD *p 269*
GD, SQUAMISH, BC, V8B 0J2
SIC 4522
SEABEE MINE, DIV OF *p 1408*
See CLAUDE RESOURCES INC
SEABEE MINE, DIV OF *p 1431*
See CLAUDE RESOURCES INC
SEABIRD ISLAND INDIAN BAND *p 179*
2895 CHOWAT RD RR 2, AGASSIZ, BC, V0M 1A2
(604) 796-2177 *SIC 8299*
SEABOARD LIQUID CARRIERS LIMITED *p 414*
120 ASHBURN RD, SAINT JOHN, NB, E2K 5J5
(506) 652-7070 *SIC 4213*

SEABOARD LIQUID CARRIERS LIMITED *p 448*
721 WILKINSON AVE, DARTMOUTH, NS, B3B 0H4
(902) 468-4447 *SIC 4212*
SEABOARD SPECIAL CROPS *p 1422*
See PS INTERNATIONAL CANADA CORP
SEABOARD SPECIALTY GRAINS & FOOD *p 1407*
See FILL-MORE SEEDS INC
SEABOARD TRANSPORT GROUP *p 414*
See SEABOARD LIQUID CARRIERS LIM-ITED
SEABOARD TRANSPORT GROUP *p 448*
See SEABOARD LIQUID CARRIERS LIM-ITED
SEACORE SEAFOOD INC *p 1033*
81 AVIVA PARK DR, WOODBRIDGE, ON, L4L 9C1
(905) 856-6222 *SIC 5146*
SEAFIRST INSURANCE BROKERS LTD *p 268*
9769 FIFTH ST SUITE A2, SIDNEY, BC, V8L 2X1
(250) 656-9886 *SIC 6411*
SEAFORTH FOOD MARKET *p 879*
See 450252 ONTARIO LTD
SEAFORTH MANOR RETIREMENT LIVING AND LONG TERM CARE *p 879*
See PROVINCIAL NURSING HOME LIM-ITED PARTNERSHIP
SEAGULL COMPANY INCORPORATED, THE *p 588*
20 VOYAGER CRT S SUITE A, ETOBI-COKE, ON, M9W 5M7
(416) 847-4612 *SIC 5199*
SEALAST *p 1248*
See VIBAC CANADA INC
SEALED AIR (CANADA) CO./CIE *p 717*
3755 LAIRD RD UNIT 10, MISSISSAUGA, ON, L5L 0B3
(905) 829-1200 *SIC 3089*
SEALFLEX *p 1298*
See CONDOR CHIMIQUES INC
SEALING PRODUCTS *p 542*
See DANA CANADA CORPORATION
SEALING SYSTEMS GROUP *p 593*
See COOPER-STANDARD AUTOMOTIVE CANADA LIMITED
SEALING SYSTEMS GROUP *p 895*
See COOPER-STANDARD AUTOMOTIVE CANADA LIMITED
SEALY CANADA LTD *p 97*
14550 112 AVE NW, EDMONTON, AB, T5M 2T9
(780) 452-3070 *SIC 2515*
SEALY CANADA LTD *p 875*
145 MILNER AVE, SCARBOROUGH, ON, M1S 3R1
(416) 699-7170 *SIC 2515*
SEAMASTERS SERVICES LIMITED *p 448*
647 WINDMILL RD, DARTMOUTH, NS, B3B 1B7
(902) 468-5967 *SIC 5551*
SEARCH & WEB SERVICES *p 923*
See CORNERSTONE GROUP OF COMPA-NIES LIMITED
SEARCH ENGINE PEOPLE INC *p 843*
1305 PICKERING PKY SUITE 500, PICK-ERING, ON, L1V 3P2
(905) 421-9340 *SIC 4813*
SEARCH REALTY CORP *p 707*
50 VILLAGE CENTRE PL UNIT 100, MIS-SISSAUGA, ON, L4Z 1V9
(416) 993-7653 *SIC 6531*
SEARCHLIGHT SYSTEMS LTD *p 285*
1395 FRANCES ST, VANCOUVER, BC, V5L 1Z1
(604) 255-4620 *SIC 7371*
SEARCHMONT RESORT *p 879*
See SEARCHMONT SKI ASSOCIATION INC
SEARCHMONT SKI ASSOCIATION INC *p 879*

103 SEARCHMONT RESORT RD, SEARCHMONT, ON, P0S 1J0
(705) 781-2340 *SIC 7011*
SEARCY TRUCKING LTD *p 392*
1470 CHEVRIER BLVD, WINNIPEG, MB, R3T 1Y6
(204) 475-8411 *SIC 4213*
SEARLES, DENNIS CHEVROLET LIMITED *p 532*
160 ARGYLE ST S, CALEDONIA, ON, N3W 1K7
(905) 765-4424 *SIC 5511*
SEARS CANADA INC *p 936*
290 YONGE ST SUITE 700, TORONTO, ON, M5B 2C3
SIC 5311
SEARS CATALOGUE, DIV OF *p 936*
See SEARS CANADA INC
SEARS, WC HOLDINGS INC *p 422*
27 MANITOBA DR, CLARENVILLE, NL, A5A 1K3
(709) 466-8080 *SIC 5531*
SEASIA FOODS LTD *p 291*
8310 PRINCE EDWARD ST, VANCOUVER, BC, V5X 3R9
(604) 618-8680 *SIC 5149*
SEASIDE CHEVROLET LIMITED *p 417*
13 HARBOUR VIEW DR, SCOUDOUC, NB, E4P 3L5
(506) 532-6666 *SIC 5511*
SEASIDE PAPER PRODUCTS LTD *p 210*
9999 RIVER WAY, DELTA, BC, V4G 1M8
(604) 930-2700 *SIC 2679*
SEASON TECHNOLOGY INC *p 558*
18 BASALTIC RD SUITE 1, CONCORD, ON, L4K 1G6
(905) 660-9066 *SIC 3829*
SEASPAN FERRIES CORPORATION *p 210*
7700 HOPCOTT RD, DELTA, BC, V4G 1B6
(604) 940-7228 *SIC 4482*
SEASPAN MARINE *p 242*
See SEASPAN ULC
SEASPAN SHIP MANAGEMENT LTD *p 309*
200 GRANVILLE ST SUITE 2600, VAN-COUVER, BC, V6C 1S4
(604) 638-2575 *SIC 8741*
SEASPAN ULC *p 242*
10 PEMBERTON AVE, NORTH VANCOU-VER, BC, V7P 2R1
(604) 988-3111 *SIC 4492*
SEASTAR SOLUTIONS *p 255*
See MARINE CANADA ACQUISITION INC
SEASTAR SOLUTIONS *p 255*
See MARINE CANADA ACQUISITION LIM-ITED PARTNERSHIP
SEATON VILLA *p 184*
See ACTION LINE HOUSING SOCIETY
SEATPLY *p 1340*
See PRODUITS SEATPLY INC
SEAVIEW MANOR CORPORATION *p 450*
275 SOUTH ST, GLACE BAY, NS, B1A 1W6
(902) 849-7300 *SIC 8051*
SEAWAY CHEVROLET CADILLAC BUICK GMC LTD *p 563*
2695 BROOKDALE AVE, CORNWALL, ON, K6J 5X9
(613) 933-3000 *SIC 5511*
SEAWAY INTERNATIONAL BRIDGE COR-PORATION LTD, THE *p 475*
200 AKWESASNE INTERNATIONAL RD, AKWESASNE, ON, K6H 5R7
(613) 932-6601 *SIC 4785*
SEAWAY MALL *p 1012*
See DORAL HOLDINGS LIMITED
SEAWAY MARINE TRANSPORT *p 886*
63 CHURCH ST SUITE 600, ST CATHARINES, ON, L2R 3C4
(905) 988-2600 *SIC 4731*
SEAWAY SELF UNLOADERS *p 886*
63 CHURCH ST SUITE 503, ST CATHARINES, ON, L2R 3C4
(905) 988-2600 *SIC 4424*
SEAWAY YARNS LIMITED *p 562*

▲ Public Company   ■ Public Company Family Member   **HQ** Headquarters   **BR** Branch   **SL** Single Location

3320 LOYALIST ST, CORNWALL, ON, K6H 6C8

(613) 933-2770   *SIC* 2299

SEBJ   *p* 1176
See *SOCIETE D'ENERGIE DE LA BAIE JAMES*

SEC PAPIER MASSON WB   *p* 1103
See *SOCIETE EN COMMANDITE PAPIER MASSON WB*

SECHOIRS DE BEAUCE INC   *p* 1055
201 134E RUE, BEAUCEVILLE, QC, G5X 3H9

(418) 774-3606   *SIC* 2431

SECHOIRS DE LERY   *p* 1055
See *MENUISEROX INC*

SECHOIRS WENDAKE, LES   *p* 1401
See *PREMONTEX*

SECOND CUP LTD, THE   *p* 689
6303 AIRPORT RD FLR 2, MISSISSAUGA, ON, L4V 1R8

(905) 362-1827   *SIC* 5812

SECOND CUP LTD, THE   *p* 773
5095 YONGE ST, NORTH YORK, ON, M2N 6Z4

(416) 227-9332   *SIC* 5812

SECOND DIMENSION INTERNATIONAL LIMITED   *p* 588
175 GALAXY BLVD UNIT 202, ETOBICOKE, ON, M9W 0C9

(416) 674-9010   *SIC* 8743

SECOND NATURE BATH AND BODY PRODUCTS INC   *p* 530
385 SMITH AVE, BURLINGTON, ON, L7R 2T9

SIC 5963

SECOND REAL PROPERTIES LIMITED   *p* 613
100 KING ST W, HAMILTON, ON, L8P 1A2

(905) 522-3501   *SIC* 6512

SECRETARIAT DE LA CONVENTION SUR LA DIVERSITE BIOLOGIQUE   *p* 1190
413 RUE SAINT-JACQUES BUREAU 500, MONTREAL, QC, H2Y 1N9

(514) 288-2220   *SIC* 8641

SECRETARIAT INTEGRALE CAPITALE RESSOURCES HUMAINES   *p* 1273
See *SERVICES DE SECRETARIAT INTEGRALE ENR, LES*

SECTEUR DES CHENAUX   *p* 1358
See *CENTRE DE SANTE ET DE SERVICES SOCIAUX DE LA VALLEE-DE-LA-BATISCAN*

SECUR-ASSURE   *p* 1218
See *191837 CANADA INC*

SECURASSURE CANADA INC   *p* 1218
3901 RUE JEAN-TALON O BUREAU 301, MONTREAL, QC, H3R 2G4

(514) 373-3131   *SIC* 5999

SECURE 724 LTD   *p* 777
1959 LESLIE ST, NORTH YORK, ON, M3B 2M3

(416) 923-6984   *SIC* 3699

SECURE ENERGY SERVICES INC   *p* 59
205 5 AVE SW SUITE 3600, CALGARY, AB, T2P 2V7

(403) 264-1588   *SIC* 1389

SECURE ENERGY SERVICES INC   *p* 59
205 5 AVE SW SUITE 3600, CALGARY, AB, T2P 2V7

(403) 984-6100   *SIC* 1389

SECURE ENERGY SERVICES INC   *p* 133
9516 146 AVE, GRANDE PRAIRIE, AB, T8V 7V9

(780) 357-5600   *SIC* 1389

SECURE FREIGHT   *p* 265
See *SECURE FREIGHT SYSTEMS INC*

SECURE FREIGHT SYSTEMS INC   *p* 265
4871 MILLER RD SUITE 1160, RICHMOND, BC, V7B 1K8

(604) 276-2369   *SIC* 4731

SECURE INSURANCE SOLUTIONS GROUP INC   *p* 665
181 TORONTO ST, MARKDALE, ON, N0C 1H0

(519) 986-3250   *SIC* 6411

SECURE PROTECTION SERVICES   *p* 8
See *1588545 ALBERTA LTD*

SECURE STORE   *p* 489
See *1124965 ONTARIO LTD*

SECURED SECURITY GROUP (INTERNATIONAL) LIMITED   *p*
309
3555 BURRARD ST SUITE 1400, VANCOUVER, BC, V6C 2G8

(604) 385-1555   *SIC* 7381

SECUREKEY TECHNOLOGIES INC   *p* 774
4101 YONGE ST SUITE 501, NORTH YORK, ON, M2P 1N6

(416) 477-5625   *SIC* 3699

SECURIFORT INC   *p* 1384
45 RUE CAYOUETTE, TINGWICK, QC, J0A 1L0

(819) 359-2226   *SIC* 3499

SECURIGLOBE INC   *p* 1199
1450 RUE CITY COUNCILLORS BUREAU 1000, MONTREAL, QC, H3A 2E6

(450) 462-2444   *SIC* 6321

SECURIGUARD SERVICES LIMITED   *p* 234
2520 BOWEN RD SUITE 205, NANAIMO, BC, V9T 3L3

(250) 756-4452   *SIC* 7381

SECURIGUARD SERVICES LIMITED   *p* 318
1445 GEORGIA ST W, VANCOUVER, BC, V6G 2T3

(604) 685-6011   *SIC* 7381

SECURITAS CANADA   *p* 485
See *SECURITAS CANADA LIMITED*

SECURITAS CANADA LIMITED   *p* 191
5172 KINGSWAY SUITE 270, BURNABY, BC, V5H 2E8

(604) 454-3600   *SIC* 7381

SECURITAS CANADA LIMITED   *p* 443
175 MAIN ST SUITE 201, DARTMOUTH, NS, B2X 1S1

(902) 434-2442   *SIC* 5999

SECURITAS CANADA LIMITED   *p* 485
400 BAYFIELD ST SUITE 215, BARRIE, ON, L4M 5A1

(705) 728-7777   *SIC* 7381

SECURITAS CANADA LIMITED   *p* 534
1425 BISHOP ST N SUITE 14, CAMBRIDGE, ON, N1R 6J9

(519) 620-9864   *SIC* 7381

SECURITAS CANADA LIMITED   *p* 707
420 BRITANNIA RD E SUITE 100, MISSISSAUGA, ON, L4Z 3L5

(905) 272-0330   *SIC* 7381

SECURITAS CANADA LIMITED   *p* 768
400-235 YORKLAND BLVD, NORTH YORK, ON, M2J 4Y8

(416) 774-2500   *SIC* 7381

SECURITAS CANADA LIMITED   *p* 813
1908 COLONEL SAM DR, OSHAWA, ON, L1H 8P7

(905) 644-6370   *SIC* 6211

SECURITAS CANADA LIMITED   *p* 840
349A GEORGE ST N SUITE 206, PETERBOROUGH, ON, K9H 3P9

(705) 743-8026   *SIC* 7381

SECURITAS CANADA LIMITED   *p* 899
767 BARRYDOWNE RD SUITE 301, SUDBURY, ON, P3A 3T6

(705) 675-3654   *SIC* 7381

SECURITAS CANADA LIMITED   *p* 1018
11210 TECUMSEH RD E, WINDSOR, ON, N8R 1A8

(519) 979-1317   *SIC* 7381

SECURITAS CANADA LIMITED   *p* 1215
1980 RUE SHERBROOKE O BUREAU 300, MONTREAL, QC, H3H 1E8

(514) 935-2533   *SIC* 7381

SECURITAS CANADA LIMITED   *p* 1341
817 RUE MCCAFFREY, SAINT-LAURENT, QC, H4T 1N3

(514) 938-3433   *SIC* 7381

SECURITAS TRANSPORT AVIATION SECURITY LTD   *p*
1290

100 AV DE L'AEROPORT UNITE 17, ROUYN-NORANDA, QC, J9Y 0G1

(819) 764-3507   *SIC* 7389

SECURITE AVANT-SCENE   *p* 1256
See *SECURITE SIROIS EVENEMENTS SPECIAUX INC*

SECURITE KOLOSSAL INC   *p* 1212
1390 RUE BARRE, MONTREAL, QC, H3C 1N4

(514) 253-4021   *SIC* 5065

SECURITE KOLOSSAL INC   *p* 1262
325 RUE DU MARAIS BUREAU 220, QUEBEC, QC, G1M 3R3

(418) 683-1713   *SIC* 7381

SECURITE NATIONALE COMPAGNIE D'ASSURANCE   *p* 1180
50 BOUL CREMAZIE O BUREAU 1200, MONTREAL, QC, H2P 1B6

(514) 382-6060   *SIC* 6712

SECURITE PLUS MODE PLEIN AIR INC   *p*
1388
5426 BOUL GENE-H.-KRUGER, TROIS-RIVIERES, QC, G9A 4N8

(819) 379-2434   *SIC* 5099

SECURITE POLYGON INC   *p* 1062
1935 BOUL LIONEL-BERTRAND, BOISBRIAND, QC, J7H 1N8

(450) 430-7516   *SIC* 5087

SECURITE PROFESSIONNELLE DU QUEBEC   *p*
1300
See *CONSULTANTS S.P.I. INC*

SECURITE SIROIS EVENEMENTS SPECIAUX INC   *p*
1256
104 RUE SEIGNEURIALE, QUEBEC, QC, G1E 4Y5

(418) 692-4137   *SIC* 7381

SECURITY AND SAFETY, DIV OF   *p* 582
See *ALLEGION CANADA INC*

SECURITY COMPASS INC   *p* 956
257 ADELAIDE ST W SUITE 500, TORONTO, ON, M5H 1X9

(888) 777-2211   *SIC* 7371

SECURITY COMPASS LTD   *p* 983
390 QUEENS QUAY W SUITE 209, TORONTO, ON, M5V 3A6

(888) 777-2211   *SIC* 7371

SECURITY GROUP   *p* 334
See *CENTRAL VICTORIA SECURITY LTD*

SECURITY MANAGEMENT SERVICES   *p*
920
See *HALO SECURITY INC*

SECURITY ONE ALARM SYSTEMS LTD   *p*
645
200 SHERK ST, LEAMINGTON, ON, N8H 0A8

(519) 326-2020   *SIC* 5063

SECURITY RESOURCE GROUP INC   *p* 274
10252 CITY PKY SUITE 301, SURREY, BC, V3T 4C2

(604) 951-3388   *SIC* 7381

SECURO VISION INC   *p* 1142
2285 RUE DE LA METROPOLE, LONGUEUIL, QC, J4G 1E5

(450) 679-2330   *SIC* 5099

SECURTEK MONITORING SOLUTIONS INC   *p* 1439
70 FIRST AVE N, YORKTON, SK, S3N 1J6

(306) 786-4331   *SIC* 7382

SED SYSTEMS   *p* 1433
See *CALIAN LTD*

SED SYSTEMS ENGINEER, A DIV OF   *p*
1202
See *CALIAN LTD*

SEDGWICK CMS CANADA INC   *p* 689
5915 AIRPORT RD SUITE 200, MISSISSAUGA, ON, L4V 1T1

(905) 671-7800   *SIC* 6411

SEE REALTY INC   *p* 976
991 BAY ST, TORONTO, ON, M5S 3C4

SIC 6531

SEED WINNIPEG INC   *p* 371
80 SALTER ST, WINNIPEG, MB, R2W 4J6

(204) 927-9935   *SIC* 8699

SEED-EX   *p* 351
See *SEED-EX INC*

SEED-EX INC   *p* 351
GD, LETELLIER, MB, R0G 1C0

(204) 737-2000   *SIC* 5149

SEENERGY FOODS LIMITED   *p* 558
475 NORTH RIVERMEDE RD, CONCORD, ON, L4K 3N1

(905) 660-0041   *SIC* 2035

SEGAL LLP   *p* 915
502-4101 YONGE ST, TORONTO, ON, M2P 1N6

(416) 391-4499   *SIC* 8721

SEGUE SYSTEMS INC   *p* 116
4504 101 ST NW, EDMONTON, AB, T6E 5G9

(780) 442-2340   *SIC* 5044

SEGUIN NAUD VENTES & MARKETING   *p*
1235
See *4069838 CANADA INC*

SEHC BC   *p* 674
See *SAINT ELIZABETH HEALTH CARE*

SEHDEV PHARMACY INC   *p* 498
51 MOUNTAINASH RD SUITE 1, BRAMPTON, ON, L6R 1W4

(905) 458-5526   *SIC* 5912

SEI   *p* 748
See *6074961 CANADA INC*

SEI INDUSTRIES LTD   *p* 210
7400 WILSON AVE, DELTA, BC, V4G 1H3

(604) 946-3131   *SIC* 0851

SEIGNEURIE BLAINVILLE INC, LA   *p* 1060
9 BOUL DE LA SEIGNEURIE E, BLAINVILLE, QC, J7C 4G6

(450) 434-3313   *SIC* 5411

SEIGNIORY CHEMICAL PRODUCTS LTD   *p*
1052
21800 AV CLARK-GRAHAM, BAIE D URFE, QC, H9X 4B6

(514) 457-0701   *SIC* 5049

SEISLAND SURVEYS LTD   *p* 37
7235 FLINT RD SE, CALGARY, AB, T2H 1G2

(403) 255-2770   *SIC* 8713

SEITEL   *p* 42
See *1334130 ALBERTA LTD*

SEKISUI DIAGNOSTICS P.E.I. INC   *p* 1041
70 WATTS AVE SUITE 24, CHARLOTTETOWN, PE, C1E 2B9

(902) 566-1396   *SIC* 2819

SEKO CANADA LOGISTICS   *p* 742
See *RODAIR INTERNATIONAL LTD*

SEKURE CARD SERVICES   *p* 1211
See *PREMIER CHOIX SOLUTIONS DE PAIEMENT S.E.N.C.*

SEL PLUS, DIV. OF   *p* 1224
See *STAR SALT INC*

SELA INDUSTRIES INC   *p* 1252
755 BOUL SAINT-JEAN BUREAU 305, POINTE-CLAIRE, QC, H9R 5M9

(514) 693-9150   *SIC* 6712

SELBA INDUSTRIES INC   *p* 558
3231 LANGSTAFF RD, CONCORD, ON, L4K 4L2

(905) 660-1614   *SIC* 2434

SELECT BAIT & FISHING SUPPLIES INC   *p*
918
45 RESEARCH RD, TORONTO, ON, M4G 2G8

(416) 429-5656   *SIC* 5199

SELECT CALL CENTRE   *p* 116
See *SELECT COMMUNICATIONS INC*

SELECT CLASSIC CARRIERS INC   *p* 1425
226A PORTAGE AVE, SASKATOON, SK, S7J 4C6

(306) 374-2733   *SIC* 4213

SELECT COMMUNICATIONS INC   *p* 116
10368 82 AVE NW SUITE 201, EDMONTON, AB, T6E 1Z8

(780) 917-5400   *SIC* 7389

SELECT DRYWALL & ACOUSTICS INC   *p*
1033
75 SHARER RD SUITE 2, WOODBRIDGE,

ON, L4L 8Z3
(905) 856-8249   *SIC* 1742
SELECT EQUIPMENT RENTALS LTD *p* 166
4 RIEL DR, ST. ALBERT, AB, T8N 3Z7
(780) 419-6100   *SIC* 7353
SELECT FARM & EXPORT SERVICES INC
p 618
GD LCD MAIN, HANOVER, ON, N4N 3C2
(519) 369-6000   *SIC* 5154
SELECT FINANCIAL SERVICES INC *p* 534
193 PINEBUSH RD SUITE 200, CAM-
BRIDGE, ON, N1R 7H8
(519) 622-9613   *SIC* 6282
SELECT FINISHING   *p* 1004
See 1528593 ONTARIO INC
SELECT FOOD PRODUCTS LIMITED *p* 916
120 SUNRISE AVE, TORONTO, ON, M4A
1B4
(416) 759-9316   *SIC* 2099
SELECT FOOD SERVICES INC   *p* 765
155 GORDON BAKER RD UNIT 214,
NORTH YORK, ON, M2H 3N5
(416) 391-1244   *SIC* 6794
SELECT MORTGAGE CORP   *p* 339
1497 ADMIRALS RD SUITE 205, VICTO-
RIA, BC, V9A 2P8
(250) 483-1373   *SIC* 6162
SELECT PRODUCTION SERVICES   *p* 172
See 878175 ALBERTA LTD
SELECT SANDS CORP   *p* 309
850 HASTINGS ST W SUITE 310, VAN-
COUVER, BC, V6C 1E1
(604) 639-4533   *SIC* 1446
SELECT SANDWICH CO.   *p* 765
See SELECT FOOD SERVICES INC
SELECT SIRES CANADA INC   *p* 627
2 INDUSTRIAL RD, KEMPTVILLE, ON, K0G
1J0
(613) 258-3800   *SIC* 5159
SELECT TOOL INC   *p* 807
3015 NORTH TALBOT RD, OLDCASTLE,
ON, N0R 1L0
(519) 737-6406   *SIC* 3544
SELECT WINE AND SPIRITS   *p* 300
See SELECT WINE MERCHANTS LTD
SELECT WINE MERCHANTS LTD   *p* 300
1122 MAINLAND ST SUITE 470, VANCOU-
VER, BC, V6B 5L1
(604) 687-8199   *SIC* 5182
SELECTCARE WORLDWIDE CORP *p* 947
438 UNIVERSITY AVE SUITE 1201,
TORONTO, ON, M5G 2K8
(416) 340-7265   *SIC* 6321
SELECTION DU PATISSIER INC   *p* 1253
450 2E AV, PORTNEUF, QC, G0A 2Y0
(418) 286-3400   *SIC* 2052
SELECTIONS TANDEM   *p* 1226
*See UNIVINS ET SPIRITUEUX (CANADA)
INC*
SELECTRA CONTROLS   *p* 896
See SELECTRA INC
SELECTRA INC   *p* 896
750 DOURO ST, STRATFORD, ON, N5A
0E3
(519) 271-0322   *SIC* 1731
SELFLAND CO-OP LTD   *p* 1404
409 CENTRE ST, ASSINIBOIA, SK, S0H
0B0
(306) 642-3347   *SIC* 5411
**SELKIRK & DISTRICT GENERAL HOSPI-
TAL**   *p*
356
*See INTERLAKE REGIONAL HEALTH AU-
THORITY INC*
SELKIRK BEVERAGES LTD   *p* 204
604 INDUSTRIAL ROAD C, CRANBROOK,
BC, V1C 4Y8
(250) 426-2731   *SIC* 5962
SELKIRK CANADA CORPORATION *p* 520
1400 CALIFORNIA AVE, BROCKVILLE,
ON, K6V 5V3
(888) 693-9563   *SIC* 3259
SELKIRK CANADA CORPORATION *p* 762
21 WOODS RD, NOBEL, ON, P0G 1G0

(705) 342-5236   *SIC* 3259
SELKIRK CANADA CORPORATION *p* 893
375 GREEN RD SUITE 1, STONEY
CREEK, ON, L8E 4A5
(905) 662-6600   *SIC* 3259
**SELKIRK CHEVROLET PONTIAC BUICK
GMC LTD**   *p* 356
1010 MANITOBA AVE, SELKIRK, MB, R1A
3T7
(204) 482-1010   *SIC* 5541
SELKIRK CHRYSLER (MB) LTD   *p* 356
1011 MANITOBA AVE, SELKIRK, MB, R1A
3T7
(204) 482-4151   *SIC* 5511
SELKIRK CHRYSLER JEEP   *p* 356
See SELKIRK CHRYSLER (MB) LTD
SELKIRK COLLEGE   *p* 195
301 FRANK BEINDER WAY, CASTLEGAR,
BC, V1N 4L3
(250) 365-7292   *SIC* 8221
SELKIRK GM   *p* 356
*See SELKIRK CHEVROLET PONTIAC
BUICK GMC LTD*
**SELKIRK HOME HARDWARE BUILDING
CENTRE**   *p* 356
See PENNY POWER HARDWARE LTD
SELKIRK SIGNS & SERVICES LTD *p* 204
421 PATTERSON ST W, CRANBROOK, BC,
V1C 6T3
(250) 489-3321   *SIC* 3993
SELLICK EQUIPMENT LIMITED   *p* 618
2131 ROSEBOROUGH RD, HARROW, ON,
N0R 1G0
(519) 738-2255   *SIC* 3537
SELLORS, ERIC R. HOLDINGS LIMITED *p*
769
1019 SHEPPARD AVE E SUITE 4, NORTH
YORK, ON, M2K 1C2
(416) 226-4415   *SIC* 5531
SELMA ALTIKUM ALISEZEN   *p* 706
See INMARCA HOLDING INC
SELTECH ELECTRONICS INC   *p* 684
342 BRONTE ST S UNIT 5-6, MILTON, ON,
L9T 5B7
(905) 875-2985   *SIC* 5065
SELWYN HOUSE ASSOCIATION   *p* 1401
95 CH DE LA COTE-SAINT-ANTOINE,
WESTMOUNT, QC, H3Y 2H8
(514) 931-9481   *SIC* 8211
SEM RESORT LIMITED PARTNERSHIP   *p*
204
7777 MISSION RD, CRANBROOK, BC, V1C
7E5
(250) 420-2000   *SIC* 7011
SEMAFO INC   *p* 1324
100 BOUL ALEXIS-NIHON BUREAU 700,
SAINT-LAURENT, QC, H4M 2P3
(514) 744-4408   *SIC* 1081
SEMCAMS   *p* 59
See SEMCAMS MIDSTREAM ULC
SEMCAMS MIDSTREAM ULC   *p* 59
520 3 AVE SUITE 700, CALGARY, AB, T2P
0R3
(403) 536-3000   *SIC* 1389
SEMCAMS MIDSTREAM ULC   *p* 173
GD, WHITECOURT, AB, T7S 1S1
(780) 778-7800   *SIC* 1389
SEMEGEN, MICHEL HOLDINGS LTD *p* 400
75 TWO NATIONS XG SUITE 337, FRED-
ERICTON, NB, E3A 0T3
(506) 450-8933   *SIC* 5531
SEMENCES PROGRAIN INC   *p* 1297
145 RANG DU BAS-DE-LA-RIVIERE N,
SAINT-CESAIRE, QC, J0L 1T0
(450) 469-5744   *SIC* 3999
SEMIAHMOO HOUSE SOCIETY   *p* 281
15306 24 AVE, SURREY, BC, V4A 2J1
(604) 536-1242   *SIC* 8322
SEMICAN   *p* 1246
See SEMICAN INTERNATIONAL INC
SEMICAN ATLANTIC INC   *p* 1246
366 10E RANG, PLESSISVILLE, QC, G6L
2Y2
(819) 362-6759   *SIC* 5191

SEMICAN INTERNATIONAL INC   *p* 1246
366 10E RANG, PLESSISVILLE, QC, G6L
2Y2
(819) 362-6759   *SIC* 5153
SEMINAIRE DE CHICOUTIMI   *p* 1079
602 RUE RACINE E BUREAU 102,
CHICOUTIMI, QC, G7H 1V1
(418) 693-8448   *SIC* 8699
SEMINAIRE DE SHERBROOKE   *p* 1371
195 RUE MARQUETTE BUREAU 116,
SHERBROOKE, QC, J1H 1L6
(819) 563-2050   *SIC* 8222
SEMINAIRE DES TROIS-RIVIERES   *p* 1388
858 RUE LAVIOLETTE, TROIS-RIVIERES,
QC, G9A 5J1
(819) 376-4459   *SIC* 8211
SEMINAIRE DES TROIS-RIVIERES   *p* 1388
858 RUE LAVIOLETTE BUREAU 553,
TROIS-RIVIERES, QC, G9A 5J1
(819) 376-4459   *SIC* 8211
SEMINAIRE SAINT-FRANCOIS   *p* 1293
4900 RUE SAINT-FELIX, SAINT-
AUGUSTIN-DE-DESMAURES, QC, G3A
0L4
(418) 872-0611   *SIC* 8211
**SEMINAIRE SALESIEN DE SHERBROOKE,
LE**   *p* 1374
135 RUE DON-BOSCO N, SHERBROOKE,
QC, J1L 1E5
(819) 566-2222   *SIC* 8211
SEMINOLE CANADA GAS CO   *p* 59
350 7 AVE SW SUITE 2200, CALGARY, AB,
T2P 3N9
SIC 5172
**SEMPLE GOODER ROOFING CORPORA-
TION**   *p*
998
1365 MARTIN GROVE RD, TORONTO, ON,
M9W 4X7
(416) 743-5370   *SIC* 1761
**SEMPLE-GOODER ROOFING CORPORA-
TION**   *p*
483
309 DARRELL DR, AYR, ON, N0B 1E0
(519) 623-3300   *SIC* 1761
SEMTECH CANADA CORPORATION *p* 524
4281 HARVESTER RD, BURLINGTON, ON,
L7L 5M4
(905) 632-2996   *SIC* 3679
SENATOR HOMES INC   *p* 777
250 LESMILL RD, NORTH YORK, ON, M3B
2T5
(416) 445-8552   *SIC* 1521
SENATOR HOTELS LIMITED   *p* 913
14 MOUNTJOY ST S, TIMMINS, ON, P4N
1S4
(705) 267-6211   *SIC* 7011
SENCHUK FORD SALES LTD   *p* 1406
118 SOURIS AVE, ESTEVAN, SK, S4A 1J6
(306) 634-3696   *SIC* 5511
SENCORE COMPANY   *p* 865
See 989116 ONTARIO LIMITED
**SENECA COLLEGE OF APPLIED ARTS &
TECHNOLOGY**   *p* 768
1750 FINCH AVE E, NORTH YORK, ON,
M2J 2X5
(416) 491-5050   *SIC* 8222
SENECHAL, EMILE ET FILS LTEE   *p* 403
190 CH INDUSTRIEL, GRAND-
SAULT/GRAND FALLS, NB, E3Y 3V3
(506) 473-2392   *SIC* 2674
SENES HOLDINGS CORP   *p* 854
121 GRANTON DR UNIT 12, RICHMOND
HILL, ON, L4B 3N4
(905) 764-9380   *SIC* 8748
SENEX PONTIAC BUICK CHEVROLET *p*
1366
See AUTOMOBILES SENEX LTEE
SENIOR CAPITAL CORP LTD   *p* 999
21 ALBERT ST, TRENTON, ON, K8V 4S4
(613) 394-3317   *SIC* 6719
SENIOR DISCOVERY TOURS INC   *p* 923
225 EGLINTON AVE W, TORONTO, ON,
M4R 1A9

(416) 322-1500   *SIC* 4725
**SENIOR PEOPLES' RESOURCES IN
NORTH TORONTO INCORPORATED** *p* 924
140 MERTON ST, TORONTO, ON, M4S 1A1
(416) 481-6411   *SIC* 8322
SENIOR SUPPORT SERVICES   *p* 881
*See HALDIMAND-NORFOLK COMMUNITY
SENIOR SUPPORT SERVICES INC*
SENIORS FOR SENIORS   *p* 609
*See AGE LINK PERSONNEL SERVICES
INC*
SENIORS FOR SENIORS   *p* 926
See 154644 CANADA INC
**SENIORS HEALTH CENTRE OF NORTH
YORK GENERAL HOSPITAL**   *p* 768
2 BUCHAN CRT, NORTH YORK, ON, M2J
5A3
(416) 756-1040   *SIC* 8051
SENNHEISER (CANADA) INC   *p* 1091
275 RUE KESMARK, DOLLARD-DES-
ORMEAUX, QC, H9B 3J1
(514) 426-3013   *SIC* 5065
**SENS LE MASSIF DE CHARLEVOIX MAG-
AZINE**   *p*
1272
See GROUPE LE MASSIF INC
SENSATION THERAPY INC   *p* 1070
See MARKETING EMS INC
SENSE INC   *p* 596
2339 OGILVIE RD SUITE 46095,
GLOUCESTER, ON, K1J 8M6
(877) 556-5268   *SIC* 5047
SENSENBRENNER HOSPITAL   *p* 627
101 PROGRESS CRES, KAPUSKASING,
ON, P5N 3H5
(705) 337-6111   *SIC* 8062
SENSORMATIC CANADA INCORPORATED
p 506
7 PAGET RD, BRAMPTON, ON, L6T 5S2
(905) 792-2858   *SIC* 7382
SENSORS & SOFTWARE INC   *p* 700
1040 STACEY CRT, MISSISSAUGA, ON,
L4W 2X8
(905) 614-1789   *SIC* 3829
SENSTAR CORPORATION   *p* 541
119 JOHN CAVANAUGH DR, CARP, ON,
K0A 1L0
(613) 839-5572   *SIC* 3699
**SENSUS COMMUNICATION SOLUTIONS
INC**   *p* 193
5589 BYRNE RD SUITE 124, BURNABY,
BC, V5J 3J1
(604) 263-9399   *SIC* 5065
**SENTERRE ENTREPRENEUR ELEC-
TRICIEN**   *p*
1142
*See SENTERRE ENTREPRENEUR GEN-
ERAL INC*
**SENTERRE ENTREPRENEUR GENERAL
INC**   *p* 1142
550 BOUL GUIMOND, LONGUEUIL, QC,
J4G 1P8
(450) 655-9301   *SIC* 1542
SENTES CHEVROLET LTD   *p* 244
933 WESTMINSTER AVE W, PENTICTON,
BC, V2A 1L1
(250) 493-2333   *SIC* 5511
SENTIMED MEDICAL CORPORATION *p*
1067
135 BOUL DE MORTAGNE UNIT E,
BOUCHERVILLE, QC, J4B 6G4
SIC 5047
SENTINEL ALARM   *p* 1238
See HOMME ET SA MAISON LTEE, L'
SENTINEL BUSINESS CENTRE (DIV OF) *p*
90
*See SENTINEL SELF-STORAGE CORPO-
RATION*
SENTINEL DRUGS LIMITED   *p* 457
3711 JOSEPH HOWE DR, HALIFAX, NS,
B3L 4H8
(902) 468-8866   *SIC* 5912
**SENTINEL FINANCIAL MANAGEMENT
CORP**   *p* 1430

200-446 2ND AVE N, SASKATOON, SK, S7K 2C3
(306) 652-7225   SIC 6411

SENTINEL LIFE MANAGEMENT CORP p 1430
446 2ND AVE N SUITE 200, SASKATOON, SK, S7K 2C3
(306) 652-7225   SIC 6411

SENTINEL POLYMERS CANADA INC p 651
1105 FRANCES ST, LONDON, ON, N5W 2L9
(519) 451-7677   SIC 5162

SENTINEL PROTECTION SERVICES LTD p 9
3132 26 ST NE SUITE 335, CALGARY, AB, T1Y 6Z1
(403) 237-8485   SIC 7381

SENTINEL SECONDARY SCHOOL p 341
See BOARD OF SCHOOL TRUSTEES OF SCHOOL DISTRICT NO. 45

SENTINEL SELF-STORAGE CORPORATION p 90
10123 99 ST NW SUITE 1970, EDMONTON, AB, T5J 3H1
(780) 424-8945   SIC 4225

SENTON INCORPORATED p 650
1669 OXFORD ST E, LONDON, ON, N5V 2Z5
(519) 455-5500   SIC 2752

SENTON PRINTING & PACKAGING p 650
See SENTON INCORPORATED

SENTREX COMMUNICATIONS INC p 793
25 MILVAN DR, NORTH YORK, ON, M9L 1Y8
(416) 749-7400   SIC 1731

SENTRY ENHANCED CORPORATE BOND FUND p 971
199 BAY ST SUITE 2700, TORONTO, ON, M5L 1E2
(416) 861-8729   SIC 6722

SENTRY FIRE PROTECTION SERVICES p 859
See 2182553 ONTARIO LTD

SENTRY INVESTMENTS p 940
2 QUEEN ST E FL 12, TORONTO, ON, M5C 3G7
(416) 861-8729   SIC 6282

SENTRY PRECISION SHEET METAL LTD p 751
20 ENTERPRISE AVE, NEPEAN, ON, K2G 0A6
(613) 224-4341   SIC 3499

SENTRY SECURITY AND INVESTIGATIONS INC p 442
1225 COXHEATH RD, COXHEATH, NS, B1L 1B4
(902) 574-3276   SIC 7381

SENTRY SELECT p 997
See PETRO ASSETS INC

SENVEST CAPITAL INC p 1199
1000 RUE SHERBROOKE O BUREAU 2400, MONTREAL, QC, H3A 3G4
(514) 281-8082   SIC 6211

SEON DESIGN p 200
See FLEETMIND SEON SOLUTIONS INC

SEPHORA BEAUTY CANADA, INC p 710
100 CITY CENTRE DR UNIT 2-930, MISSISSAUGA, ON, L5B 2C9
(905) 279-4400   SIC 5999

SEPRACOR CANADA, INC p 727
6790 CENTURY AVE SUITE 100, MISSISSAUGA, ON, L5N 2V8
(905) 814-9145   SIC 6712

SEPRO MINERAL SYSTEMS CORP p 225
9850 201 ST UNIT 101A, LANGLEY, BC, V1M 4A3
(604) 888-5568   SIC 3532

SEPT FRERES CONSTRUCTION INC p 1162
7910 AV MARCO-POLO, MONTREAL, QC, H1E 2S5
(514) 648-0935   SIC 1541

SEPTIMATECH GROUP INC p 1011
106 RANDALL DR, WATERLOO, ON, N2V 1K5
(519) 746-7463   SIC 3565

SEPTODONT p 534
See NOVOCOL PHARMACEUTICAL OF CANADA, INC

SEQUEL NATURALS ULC p 189
3001 WAYBURNE DR UNIT 101, BURNABY, BC, V5G 4W3
(866) 839-8863   SIC 5149

SEQUITER INC p 116
9644 54 AVE NW UNIT 209, EDMONTON, AB, T6E 5V1
(780) 437-2410   SIC 7371

SEQUOIA COMPANY OF RESTAURANTS INC p 318
1583 COAL HARBOUR QUAY, VANCOUVER, BC, V6G 3E7
(604) 687-5684   SIC 5812

SERAY AUTO INC p 1075
730 BOUL DE PERIGNY, CHAMBLY, QC, J3L 1W3
(450) 658-4482   SIC 5511

SERCAB p 1331
See STANEX INC

SERCO CANADA INC p 424
271 CANADIAN FORCES, HAPPY VALLEY-GOOSE BAY, NL, A0P 1C0
(709) 896-6946   SIC 8741

SERCO CANADA INC p 957
330 BAY ST SUITE 400, TORONTO, ON, M5H 2S8
(416) 225-3788   SIC 8741

SERCO FACILITIES MANAGEMENT p 424
See SERCO CANADA INC

SERENA FASHIONS (ALBERTA) LTD p 37
6737 FAIRMOUNT DR SE SUITE 60, CALGARY, AB, T2H 0X6
(403) 255-1551   SIC 5621

SERENA FASHIONS LTD p 322
2700 BROADWAY W, VANCOUVER, BC, V6K 2G4
(604) 733-8508   SIC 5621

SERENDIPITY CLOTHING CO p 223
2903 PANDOSY ST SUITE 102, KELOWNA, BC, V1Y 1W1
(250) 861-4166   SIC 5963

SERENITY HOME CARE p 426
See SERENITY NURSING AND HOME SUPPORT SERVICES LTD

SERENITY NURSING AND HOME SUPPORT SERVICES LTD p 426
2 GLENDALE AVE, MOUNT PEARL, NL, A1N 1M9
(709) 364-9688   SIC 8059

SERIGRAPHIE RICHFORD INC p 1252
2001 BOUL DES SOURCES BUREAU 101, POINTE-CLAIRE, QC, H9R 5Z4
(514) 426-8700   SIC 2759

SERKO.CA p 1262
See ORICOM INTERNET INC

SERLAN INC p 1115
957 RUE RAOUL-CHARETTE, JOLIETTE, QC, J6E 8S4
(450) 752-0030   SIC 4783

SERNAS GROUP INC, THE p 1015
110 SCOTIA CRT UNIT 41, WHITBY, ON, L1N 8Y7
(905) 432-7878   SIC 8711

SEROYAL INTERNATIONAL INC p 855
490 ELGIN MILLS RD E, RICHMOND HILL, ON, L4C 0L8
(905) 508-2050   SIC 5122

SERRES DU ST-LAURENT (LES) p 1300
360 BOUL DE LA GABELLE, SAINT-ETIENNE-DES-GRES, QC, G0X 2P0
(819) 694-6944   SIC 0181

SERRES FRANK ZYRONSKI INC, LES p 1287
1853 CH LALIBERTE, RIVIERE-ROUGE, QC, J0T 1T0
(819) 275-5156   SIC 0181

SERRES LEFORT INC, LES p 1357
644 3E RANG, SAINTE-CLOTILDE-DE-CHATEAUGUAY, QC, J0L 1W0
(450) 826-3117   SIC 0182

SERRES PION, ROSAIRE & FILS INC, LES p 1313
8185 GRAND RANG, SAINT-HYACINTHE, QC, J2S 9A8
(450) 796-3193   SIC 0181

SERRES RIEL INC, LES p 1351
1851 RANG NOTRE-DAME, SAINT-REMI, QC, J0L 2L0
(450) 454-9425   SIC 5193

SERRES ROYALES INC, LES p 1321
1954 BOUL SAINT-ANTOINE, SAINT-JEROME, QC, J7Z 7M2
(450) 438-1334   SIC 5148

SERRES SAVOURA PORTNEUF INC, LES p 1363
2743 BOUL SAINTE-SOPHIE, SAINTE-SOPHIE, QC, J5J 2V3
(450) 431-6343   SIC 0182

SERRES SAVOURA ST-ETIENNE INC, LES p 1253
700 RUE LUCIEN-THIBODEAU, PORT-NEUF, QC, G0A 2Y0
(418) 286-6681   SIC 0161

SERRES TOUNDRA INC p 1303
4190 RTE SAINT-EUSEBE, SAINT-FELICIEN, QC, G8K 2N9
(418) 679-1834   SIC 0182

SERSA TOTAL TRACK LTD p 663
68 COUNTY RD 5, MALLORYTOWN, ON, K0E 1R0
(613) 923-5702   SIC 1799

SERTI INFORMATION SOLUTIONS p 1050
See SERTI INFORMATIQUE INC

SERTI INFORMATIQUE INC p 1050
7555 RUE BECLARD, ANJOU, QC, H1J 2S5
(514) 493-1909   SIC 5045

SERTI INFORMATIQUE INC p 1050
10975 BOUL LOUIS-H.-LAFONTAINE UNITE 201, ANJOU, QC, H1J 2E8
(514) 493-1909   SIC 5045

SERUM INTERNATIONAL INC p 1342
4400 DESSTE CHOMEDEY (A-13) O, SAINT-LAURENT, QC, H7R 6E9
(514) 625-8511   SIC 5139

SERV-ALL MECHANICAL SERVICES LTD p 103
18120 107 AVE NW, EDMONTON, AB, T5S 1K5
(780) 484-6681   SIC 1711

SERVA GROUP (CANADA) ULC p 18
7345 110 AVE SE, CALGARY, AB, T2C 3B8
(403) 269-7847   SIC 3533

SERVANTAGE SERVICES INC p 42
4 PARKDALE CRES NW, CALGARY, AB, T2N 3T8
(403) 263-8170   SIC 7349

SERVCON INC p 854
25 WEST BEAVER CREEK RD SUITE 13, RICHMOND HILL, ON, L4B 1K2
(905) 881-4300   SIC 1541

SERVICE & CONSTRUCTION MOBILE LTEE p 1235
1820 PLACE MARTENOT BUREAU 383, MONTREAL, QC, H7L 5B5
(514) 383-5752   SIC 1799

SERVICE & MAINTENANCE DE CASTEL (1997) INC p 1162
11650 AV J.-J.-JOUBERT, MONTREAL, QC, H1E 7E7
(514) 648-5166   SIC 5087

SERVICE & SUPPORT DIVISION p 25
See RAYTHEON CANADA LIMITED

SERVICE AERIEN GOUVERNEMENTAL p 1278
See GOUVERNEMENT DE LA PROVINCE DE QUEBEC

SERVICE AERIEN PFD, DIV OF p 1073
See ENTREPRISES PAUL F. DELANEY INC

SERVICE AGRO MECANIQUE p 1297

See SERVICE AGROMECANIQUE INC

SERVICE AGROMECANIQUE INC p 1297
24 RUE PRINCIPALE O, SAINT-CLEMENT, QC, G0L 2N0
(418) 963-2177   SIC 5083

SERVICE ALIMENTAIRE DESCO INC p 1061
97 RUE PREVOST, BOISBRIAND, QC, J7G 3A1
(450) 437-7182   SIC 2015

SERVICE CONCIERGE MEDISYS p 1197
See GROUPE SANTE MEDISYS INC

SERVICE CORPORATION INTERNATIONAL (CANADA) LIMITED p 285
1835 HASTINGS ST E, VANCOUVER, BC, V5L 1T3
(604) 806-4100   SIC 7261

SERVICE CUISINE G.P. INC p 1060
82 RUE REAL-BENOIT, BLAINVILLE, QC, J7C 5J1
(450) 979-9921   SIC 5812

SERVICE D B p 1223
See SERVICE DE MANUTENTION D.B. INC

SERVICE D'AIDE A LA FAMILLE EDMUNDSTON GRAND SAULT INC p 399
13 RUE DUGAL, EDMUNDSTON, NB, E3V 1X4
(506) 737-8000   SIC 8741

SERVICE D'ECHANGE RAPIDGAZ INC p 1110
241 RUE SAINT-CHARLES S, GRANBY, QC, J2G 7A7
(450) 375-6644   SIC 5172

SERVICE D'ENTRETIEN CLEAN INTERNATIONAL INC p 1140
1006 RUE RENAULT, LEVIS, QC, G6Z 2Y8
(418) 839-0928   SIC 7349

SERVICE D'ENTRETIEN DES PLANTES ALPHA INC p 1212
230 RUE PEEL, MONTREAL, QC, H3C 2G7
(514) 935-1812   SIC 7389

SERVICE D'EQUIPEMENT G.D. INC p 1293
104 RUE D'ANVERS, SAINT-AUGUSTIN-DE-DESMAURES, QC, G3A 1S4
(418) 681-0080   SIC 5082

SERVICE D'IMPARTITION INDUSTRIEL INC p 1388
2300 RUE JULES-VACHON, TROIS-RIVIERES, QC, G9A 5E1
(819) 374-4647   SIC 1796

SERVICE DE COUPAGE DOMINION INC p 1179
99 RUE CHABANEL O BUREAU 104, MONTREAL, QC, H2N 1C3
(514) 270-4118   SIC 5023

SERVICE DE FREINS MONTREAL LTEE p 1162
11650 6E AV BUREAU 151, MONTREAL, QC, H1E 1S1
(514) 648-7403   SIC 5013

SERVICE DE L'ENVIRONNEMENT ET DES TRAVAUX PUBLICS p 1365
See VILLE DE SALABERRY DE VALLEY-FIELD

SERVICE DE L'ESTRIE (VENTE & REPARATION) INC p 1371
225 RUE WELLINGTON S, SHERBROOKE, QC, J1H 5E1
(819) 563-0563   SIC 5722

SERVICE DE MANUTENTION D.B. INC p 1223
3971 RUE NOTRE-DAME O, MONTREAL, QC, H4C 1R2
(514) 934-5681   SIC 7363

SERVICE DE PNEU K & S KELLY INC p 1108
627 RUE AUGUSTE-MONDOUX, GATINEAU, QC, J9J 3K2
(819) 600-1061   SIC 5531

SERVICE DE PNEUS AUCLAIR INC *p* 1268
3755 BOUL WILFRID-HAMEL, QUEBEC, QC, G1P 2J4
(418) 871-6740   *SIC* 5531

SERVICE DE PNEUS LAVOIE OUTAOUAIS INC *p* 1107
27 RUE MANGIN, GATINEAU, QC, J8Y 3L8
(819) 771-2392   *SIC* 5014

SERVICE DE RECYCLAGE GW, LES *p* 1309
See *SERVICES RICOVA INC*

SERVICE DES FINANCES DE HYUNDAI MOTORS / HYUNDAI MOTORS FINANCE DEPARTMENT *p* 963
See *HYUNDAI CAPITAL LEASE INC*

SERVICE DRUG LTD *p* 342
5331 HEADLAND DR, WEST VANCOUVER, BC, V7W 3C6
(604) 926-5331   *SIC* 5912

SERVICE DU DEVELOPPEMENT ECONOMIQUE *p* 1260
295 BOUL CHAREST E, QUEBEC, QC, G1K 3G8
(418) 641-6186   *SIC* 7389

SERVICE EMPLOYEES INTERNATIONAL UNION LOCAL 204 *p* 558
2180 STEELES AVE W SUITE 200, CONCORD, ON, L4K 2Z5
(905) 660-1800   *SIC* 8631

SERVICE INCENDIE SAINT-HYACINTHE *p* 1313
See *SAINT-HYACINTHE, VILLE DE*

SERVICE MASTER *p* 488
See *SIMCOE COUNTY CLEANING LIMITED*

SERVICE MASTER CONTRACT SERVICE ATLANTIC *p* 443
See *COMMERCIAL CLEANING SERVICES LIMITED*

SERVICE MASTER OF CALGARY JMS *p* 20
See *550338 ALBERTA LIMITED*

SERVICE MASTER OF SAULT STE MARIE *p* 863
See *NIVTOP HOLDINGS LTD*

SERVICE MECANESSENCE *p* 1105
See *RELANCE OUTAOUAIS INC, LA*

SERVICE MECANIQUE EXPRESS JOLIETTE *p* 1295
See *ENTREPRISES DUPONT 1972 INC, LES*

SERVICE MOLD + AEROSPACE INC *p* 1020
2711 ST ETIENNE BLVD, WINDSOR, ON, N8W 5B1
(519) 945-3344   *SIC* 3544

SERVICE PARTS DIVISION *p* 489
See *DANA CANADA CORPORATION*

SERVICE PARTS DIVISION *p* 802
See *DANA CANADA CORPORATION*

SERVICE PLUS AQUATICS INC *p* 717
3600B LAIRD RD UNIT 7, MISSISSAUGA, ON, L5L 6A7
(905) 569-7899   *SIC* 5091

SERVICE QUALITY MEASUREMENT GROUP INC *p* 332
3126 31 AVE SUITE 301, VERNON, BC, V1T 2H1
(800) 446-2095   *SIC* 8732

SERVICE RECREATIFS DEMSIS *p* 1077
75 CH BARNES, CHELSEA, QC, J9B 1H7
SIC 1389

SERVICE REGIONAL D'INTERPRETARIAT DE L'EST DU QUEBEC INC *p* 1275
9885 BOUL DE L'ORMIERE, QUEBEC, QC, G2B 3K9
(418) 622-1037   *SIC* 7389

SERVICE REGIONAL D'INTERPRETATION VISUELLE DE L'OUTAOUAIS *p* 1105
115 BOUL SACRE-COEUR BUREAU 212, GATINEAU, QC, J8X 1C5
SIC 7389

SERVICE REMTEC INC *p* 1247
3560 39E AV, POINTE-AUX-TREMBLES, QC, H1A 3V1
(514) 642-6020   *SIC* 5013

SERVICE SANTE CLAUDE GERVAIS INC, LES *p* 1067
520 BOUL DU FORT-SAINT-LOUIS BUREAU 1, BOUCHERVILLE, QC, J4B 1S5
(450) 655-6651   *SIC* 5912

SERVICE TRANS-WEST INC *p* 1128
1900 52E AV BUREAU 100, LACHINE, QC, H8T 2X9
(514) 345-1090   *SIC* 4213

SERVICE USACAN *p* 1331
See *USACAN MEDIA DISTRIBUTION SERVICE INC*

SERVICEMASTER *p* 92
See *961945 ALBERTA LTD*

SERVICEMASTER *p* 272
See *NUEST SERVICES LTD*

SERVICEMASTER CLEAN *p* 402
See *AQUA-POWER CLEANERS (1979) LTD*

SERVICEMASTER CLEAN OF NIAGARA *p* 885
See *HELPING LIMITED*

SERVICEMASTER CONTRACT SERVICES *p* 713
See *STRONG, J.E. LIMITED*

SERVICEMASTER OF CANADA LIMITED *p* 700
5462 TIMBERLEA BLVD, MISSISSAUGA, ON, L4W 2T7
(905) 670-0000   *SIC* 6794

SERVICEMASTER OF DURHAM CONTRACT SERVICES *p* 1016
See *AINSWORTH MANAGEMENT SERVICES INC*

SERVICEMASTER OF OTTAWA *p* 818
See *L J C CLEANING SERVICES INC*

SERVICEMASTER OF OWEN SOUND *p* 836
107 JASON ST UNIT 1, OWEN SOUND, ON, N4K 5N7
SIC 6411

SERVICEMASTER RESTORATION *p* 191
See *305466 B.C. LTD*

SERVICES AAR MRO - CANADA, TROIS RIVIERES *p* 1387
See *AAR AIRCRAFT SERVICES - TROIS RIVIERES ULC*

SERVICES AIRBASE INC, LES *p* 1095
81 AV LINDSAY, DORVAL, QC, H9P 2S6
(514) 735-5260   *SIC* 6211

SERVICES ALIMENTAIRE HALLE *p* 1266
See *ENTREPRISES P.P. HALLE LTEE*

SERVICES ALIMENTAIRES CAMPUS NOTRE-DAME-DE-FOY *p* 1292
See *CAMPUS NOTRE-DAME-DE-FOY*

SERVICES ALIMENTAIRES DELTA DAILY-FOOD (CANADA) INC, LES *p* 1284
26 RUE J.-MARC-SEGUIN, RIGAUD, QC, J0P 1P0
(450) 451-6761   *SIC* 2038

SERVICES ALIMENTAIRES RIVERVIEW *p* 1364
See *POULETS RIVERVIEW INC*

SERVICES ALIMENTAIRES WOLFE INC *p* 1342
2624 BOUL DES OISEAUX, SAINT-LAURENT, QC, H7L 4N9
(450) 628-5760   *SIC* 5149

SERVICES BIOANALYTIQUES BIOTRIAL INC *p* 1235
3885 BOUL INDUSTRIEL, MONTREAL, QC, H7L 4S3
(450) 663-6724   *SIC* 8731

SERVICES CLSC *p* 1193
See *ASSOCIATION QUEBECOISE D'ETABLISSEMENT DE SANTE & DES SERVICES SOCIAUX*

SERVICES COMERCO INC *p* 1087
3300 BOUL SAINT-MARTIN O BUREAU 300, COTE SAINT-LUC, QC, H7T 1A1
(450) 682-9900   *SIC* 6351

SERVICES COMMEMORATIFS CELEBRIS INC *p* 1155

160 BOUL GRAHAM, MONT-ROYAL, QC, H3P 3H9
(514) 735-2025   *SIC* 7261

SERVICES CONSEILS ARBITREX INC, LES *p* 1273
2875 BOUL LAURIER UNITE 200, QUEBEC, QC, G1V 5B1
(418) 651-9900   *SIC* 8111

SERVICES CONSEILS SYSTEMATIX INC, LES *p* 1273
2600 BOUL LAURIER BUREAU 128, QUEBEC, QC, G1V 4Y4
(418) 681-0151   *SIC* 7379

SERVICES D'ENTRETIEN D'EDIFICES ALLIED (QUEBEC) INC *p* 1184
6585 RUE JEANNE-MANCE, MONTREAL, QC, H2V 4L1
(514) 272-1137   *SIC* 7349

SERVICES D'ENTRETIEN MINIERS INDUSTRIELS R.N. 2000 INC *p* 1290
155 BOUL INDUSTRIEL, ROUYN-NORANDA, QC, J9X 6P2
(819) 797-4387   *SIC* 1241

SERVICES D'IMPRESSION ESSENCE DU PAPIER INC *p* 1190
127 RUE SAINT-PIERRE BUREAU 200, MONTREAL, QC, H2Y 2L6
(514) 286-2880   *SIC* 6712

SERVICES DAVID JONES INC, LES *p* 1118
29 RUE DE BONDVILLE, KNOWLTON, QC, J0E 1V0
(450) 955-3600   *SIC* 7389

SERVICES DE CAFE VAN HOUTTE INC *p* 1170
8215 17E AV, MONTREAL, QC, H1Z 4J9
(514) 728-2233   *SIC* 7389

SERVICES DE CAFE VAN HOUTTE INC *p* 1170
3700 RUE JEAN-RIVARD, MONTREAL, QC, H1Z 4K3
(514) 593-7711   *SIC* 5046

SERVICES DE CALECHES & TRAINEAUX LUCKY LUC ENR, LES *p* 1215
1810 RUE BASIN, MONTREAL, QC, H3J 1S3
(514) 934-6105   *SIC* 4789

SERVICES DE CAMIONNAGE VITESSE INC *p* 1128
1111 46E AV, LACHINE, QC, H8T 3C5
(514) 631-2777   *SIC* 4213

SERVICES DE CARTES DESJARDINS *p* 1191
See *FEDERATION DES CAISSES DESJARDINS DU QUEBEC*

SERVICES DE DEFENSE DISCOVERY AIR *p* 1095
See *TOP ACES INC*

SERVICES DE FORAGE ORBIT GARANT INC *p* 1391
3200 BOUL JEAN-JACQUES-COSSETTE, VAL-D'OR, QC, J9P 6Y6
(819) 824-2707   *SIC* 1081

SERVICES DE FRET PATRIOT INC *p* 1336
6800 CH SAINT-FRANCOIS, SAINT-LAURENT, QC, H4S 1B7
(514) 631-2900   *SIC* 4731

SERVICES DE GESTION QUANTUM LIMITEE, LES *p* 1199
2000 AV MCGILL COLLEGE BUREAU 1800, MONTREAL, QC, H3A 3H3
(514) 842-5555   *SIC* 8741

SERVICES DE JEUX BABEL INC *p* 1216
1751 RUE RICHARDSON BUREAU 8400, MONTREAL, QC, H3K 1G6
(514) 904-3700   *SIC* 7371

SERVICES DE LOCALISATION GAT INTERNATIONAL INC *p* 1208
1100 AV DES CANADIENS-DE-MONTREAL BUREAU C25, MONTREAL, QC, H3B 2S2

(514) 288-7818   *SIC* 7389

SERVICES DE LUBRIFIANTS INDUSTRIELS & COMMERCIAUX (SLIC) INC *p* 1371
402 RUE ALEXANDRE, SHERBROOKE, QC, J1H 4T3
(819) 562-1411   *SIC* 5172

SERVICES DE MECANIQUE MOBILE B L INC *p* 1111
50 RUE SAINT-JUDE S, GRANBY, QC, J2J 2N4
(450) 378-0413   *SIC* 5511

SERVICES DE PAIE *p* 1176
See *FEDERATION DES CAISSES DESJARDINS DU QUEBEC*

SERVICES DE PERSONNEL S.M. INC. *p* 1179
433, RUE CHABANEL OUEST 12E ETAGE, MONTREAL, QC, H2N 2J9
(514) 982-6001   *SIC* 7361

SERVICES DE PLACEMENT DE PERSONNEL DURAND & PRATT INC, LES *p* 1199
666 RUE SHERBROOKE O BUREAU 800, MONTREAL, QC, H3A 1E7
(514) 987-1815   *SIC* 7361

SERVICES DE PNEUS DESHARNAIS INC *p* 1265
710 BOUL CHAREST O, QUEBEC, QC, G1N 2C1
(418) 681-6041   *SIC* 5531

SERVICES DE READAPTATION DU SUD-OUEST ET DU RENFORT, LES *p* 1317
See *CENTRE INTEGRE DE SANTE ET DE SERVICES SOCIAUX DE LA MONTEREGIE-OUEST*

SERVICES DE READAPTATION SUD OUEST ET DU RENFORT, LES *p* 1318
315 RUE MACDONALD BUREAU 105, SAINT-JEAN-SUR-RICHELIEU, QC, J3B 8J3
(450) 348-6121   *SIC* 8361

SERVICES DE READAPTATION SUD OUEST ET DU RENFORT, LES *p* 1366
30 RUE SAINT-THOMAS BUREAU 200, SALABERRY-DE-VALLEYFIELD, QC, J6T 4J2
(450) 371-4816   *SIC* 8361

SERVICES DE RECYCLAGE GLOBE METAL, GMR INC *p* 1356
1545 1RE AV, SAINTE-CATHERINE, QC, J5C 1C5
(450) 635-9397   *SIC* 4953

SERVICES DE SANTE LES RAYONS DE SOLEIL INC *p* 1171
2055 RUE SAUVE E BUREAU 100, MONTREAL, QC, H2B 1A8
(514) 383-7555   *SIC* 7363

SERVICES DE SANTE MEDISYS *p* 1198
See *MEDISYS CORPORATE HEALTH LP*

SERVICES DE SECRETARIAT INTEGRALE ENR, LES *p* 1273
2590 BOUL LAURIER BUREAU 1020, QUEBEC, QC, G1V 4M6
(418) 624-4989   *SIC* 7361

SERVICES DE SOINS A DOMICILE ROYAL TREATMENT INC *p* 1218
5757 AV DECELLES, MONTREAL, QC, H3S 2C3
(514) 342-8293   *SIC* 7361

SERVICES DE SOINS DE SANTE OPTI-SOINS *p* 1115
2655 BOUL DU ROYAUME BUREAU 550, JONQUIERE, QC, G7S 4S9
(418) 548-0010   *SIC* 6324

SERVICES DE TRANSPORT FLS, LES *p* 1326
See *FLS TRANSPORTATION SERVICES LIMITED*

SERVICES DE TRANSPORT TRAC-WORLD INC *p* 1356
6565 BOUL HEBERT, SAINTE-CATHERINE, QC, J5C 1B5
(450) 635-8271   *SIC* 4412

SERVICES DE VOYAGES YVES BORDE-LEAU INC, LES p 1385
765 BOUL THIBEAU BUREAU 100, TROIS-RIVIERES, QC, G8T 7A4
(819) 374-0747   SIC 4724

SERVICES DOCUMENTAIRES MULTIMEDIA (S.D.M) INC p 1172
5650 RUE D'IBERVILLE BUREAU 620, MONTREAL, QC, H2G 2B3
(514) 382-0895   SIC 4226

SERVICES EN TRANSPORT S.T.C.H. INC p 1076
248 BOUL INDUSTRIEL, CHATEAUGUAY, QC, J6J 4Z2
(450) 699-2357   SIC 4731

SERVICES ENERGETIQUES ECOSYSTEM INC, LES p 1273
2875 BOUL LAURIER BUREAU 950 EDIFICE DELTA 3, QUEBEC, QC, G1V 2M2
(418) 651-1257   SIC 1731

SERVICES ENVIRONNEMENTAUX CLEAN HARBORS QUEBEC, INC p 1356
6785 RTE 132, SAINTE-CATHERINE, QC, J5C 1B6
(450) 632-6640   SIC 1629

SERVICES ENVIRONNEMENTAUX DELSAN-A.I.M. INC, LES p 1162
7825 BOUL HENRI-BOURASSA E, MONTREAL, QC, H1E 1N9
(514) 494-9898   SIC 1795

SERVICES ET SOLUTIONS PROFESSIONNELS EN TELECOMMUNICATIONS S.S.P. INC p 1386
2535 RUE DE LA SIDBEC S, TROIS-RIVIERES, QC, G8Z 4M6
(819) 693-2535   SIC 5065

SERVICES EXP INC, LES p 1236
4500 RUE LOUIS-B.-MAYER, MONTREAL, QC, H7P 6E4
(450) 682-8013   SIC 8734

SERVICES EXP INC., LES p 1372
150 RUE DE VIMY, SHERBROOKE, QC, J1J 3M7
(819) 780-1868   SIC 8711

SERVICES FAMILIAUX JEANNE SAUVE FAMILY SERVICES p 546
See ONTARIO ASSOCIATION OF CHILDREN'S AID SOCIETIES

SERVICES FERROVIAIRES CANAC INC p 1341
6505 RTE TRANSCANADIENNE BUREAU 405, SAINT-LAURENT, QC, H4T 1S3
(514) 734-4700   SIC 8741

SERVICES FINANCIERS DU CHUQ p 1280
See CENTRE HOSPITALIER UNIVERSITAIRE DE QUEBEC

SERVICES FINANCIERS ETERNA p 1270
See ASSURANCES ETERNA INC

SERVICES FINANCIERS LA LAURENTIENNE p 1286
See CENTRE FINANCIER S.F.L. DU LITTORAL INC

SERVICES FINANCIERS MORRIS MOHAWK p 1117
See MORRIS, ALWIN

SERVICES FINANCIERS NCO, INC p 492
610 DUNDAS ST E, BELLEVILLE, ON, K8N 1G7
SIC 7322

SERVICES FINANCIERS NCO, INC p 516
33 SINCLAIR BLVD UNIT 4, BRANTFORD, ON, N3S 7X6
(519) 750-6000   SIC 7322

SERVICES FINANCIERS NCO, INC p 1217
75 RUE DE PORT-ROYAL E BUREAU 240, MONTREAL, QC, H3L 3T1
(514) 385-4444   SIC 7322

SERVICES FINANCIERS PAQUETTE DUBEAU p 1241
See GROUPE CENSEO INC

SERVICES FINANCIERS PENSON CANADA INC p 1190
360 RUE SAINT-JACQUES BUREAU 1201, MONTREAL, QC, H2Y 1P5
SIC 6289

SERVICES FINANCIERS XN (CANADA) INC p 1199
600 BOUL DE MAISONNEUVE O BUREAU 2310, MONTREAL, QC, H3A 3J2
(514) 908-1835   SIC 6411

SERVICES FMC p 1203
See DENTONS CANADA LLP

SERVICES FORESTIERS DE MONT-LAURIER LTEE p 1124
327 CH DU GOLF RR 1, LAC-DES-ECORCES, QC, J0W 1H0
(819) 623-3143   SIC 5084

SERVICES FORESTIERS ET TERRITORIAUX DE MANAWAN (SFTM) INC p 1148
180 RUE AMISKW, MANOUANE, QC, J0K 1M0
SIC 7999

SERVICES FUSION BPO p 1188
See FUSION BPO SERVICES LIMITED

SERVICES HEALTHMARK LTEE, LES p 1336
8827 BOUL HENRI-BOURASSA O, SAINT-LAURENT, QC, H4S 1P7
(514) 336-0012   SIC 5122

SERVICES INDUSTRIELS SYSTEMEX (S.I.S.) INC p 1157
8260 CH DEVONSHIRE UNITE 240, MONT-ROYAL, QC, H4P 2P7
(514) 738-6323   SIC 5999

SERVICES INFIRMIERS PRO-SOIN INC p 1273
2750 CH SAINTE-FOY BUREAU 240, QUEBEC, QC, G1V 1V6
(418) 653-4471   SIC 8741

SERVICES INFRASPEC INC p 1133
4585 BOUL LITE, LAVAL, QC, H7C 0B8
(450) 937-1508   SIC 7389

SERVICES INTERNATIONALS SKYPORT INC p 1095
400 AV MICHEL-JASMIN BUREAU 200, DORVAL, QC, H9P 1C1
(514) 631-1155   SIC 4111

SERVICES J. SONIC INC p 1330
6869 BOUL HENRI-BOURASSA O, SAINT-LAURENT, QC, H4R 1E1
(514) 341-5789   SIC 5031

SERVICES JAG INC, LES p 1357
425 RUE LAURIER, SAINTE-CROIX, QC, G0S 2H0
(418) 926-2412   SIC 4213

SERVICES KD, LES p 1093
See 3174891 CANADA INC

SERVICES LINGUISTIQUES VERSACOM INC p 1199
1501 AV MCGILL COLLEGE 6E ETAGE, MONTREAL, QC, H3A 3M8
(514) 397-1950   SIC 7389

SERVICES LUMENWERX p 1326
See LUMENWERX ULC

SERVICES MATREC INC p 1067
4 CH DU TREMBLAY BUREAU 625, BOUCHERVILLE, QC, J4B 6Z5
(450) 641-3070   SIC 6712

SERVICES NOLITREX INC p 1116
3462 RUE DE L'ENERGIE, JONQUIERE, QC, G7X 9H3
(418) 542-0386   SIC 4225

SERVICES OPTOMETRIQUES (OPT) INC p 1396
4 PLACE DU COMMERCE BUREAU 460, VERDUN, QC, H3E 1J4
(514) 762-2020   SIC 5049

SERVICES OR LP p 1208
See SERVICES OR LP/SEC

SERVICES OR LP/SEC p 1208
1 PLACE VILLE-MARIE UNITE 2500, MONTREAL, QC, H3B 1R1

(514) 847-4747   SIC 8741

SERVICES PARTAGES METSO LTEE p 1126
795 AV GEORGE-V, LACHINE, QC, H8S 2R9
(877) 677-2005   SIC 7389

SERVICES PHARMACEUTIQUES AVARA BOUCHERVILLE INC p 1067
145 RUE JULES-LEGER, BOUCHERVILLE, QC, J4B 7K8
(450) 650-3050   SIC 2834

SERVICES PHARMACEUTIQUES SOCJETI LTEE p 822
50 RIDEAU ST SUITE 125, OTTAWA, ON, K1N 9J7
(613) 236-2533   SIC 5912

SERVICES PROFESSIONNELS DES ASSUREURS PLUS INC p 1051
8290 BOUL METROPOLITAIN E, ANJOU, QC, H1K 1A2
SIC 7389

SERVICES PROFESSIONNELS INC p 1283
529 RUE NOTRE-DAME BUREAU 300, REPENTIGNY, QC, J6A 2T6
SIC 6411

SERVICES RICOVA INC p 1309
5000 RUE ARMAND-FRAPPIER, SAINT-HUBERT, QC, J3Z 1G5
(450) 466-6688   SIC 4953

SERVICES S & E SOCIETE EN COMMANDITE p 1208
1155 BOUL RENE-LEVESQUE O BUREAU 4100, MONTREAL, QC, H3B 3V2
(514) 397-3318   SIC 8742

SERVICES SANITAIRES MAJ INC p 1077
225 AV DU PROGRES, CHERTSEY, QC, J0K 3K0
(450) 882-9186   SIC 4953

SERVICES TECHNIQUES INDUSTRIELS MARCHAND (STIM) p 1369
See 9208-4144 QUEBEC INC

SERVICES TECHNIQUES LAURENTIDES INC p 1232
3131 BOUL DE LA CONCORDE E BUREAU 410, MONTREAL, QC, H7E 4W4
SIC 7389

SERVICES-CONSEILS EN AFFAIRES IBM p 1208
See SOCIETE CONSEIL GROUPE LGS

SERVIER CANADA INC p 1343
235 BOUL ARMAND-FRAPPIER, SAINT-LAURENT, QC, H7V 4A7
(450) 978-9700   SIC 5122

SERVISAIR p 1324
See SWISSPORT CANADA INC

SERVITANK INC p 1388
3450 BOUL GENE-H.-KRUGER, TROIS-RIVIERES, QC, G9A 4M3
(819) 379-4081   SIC 4226

SERVITANK PLANT p 1388
See SERVITANK INC

SERVOMAX INC p 1330
1790 RUE BEAULAC, SAINT-LAURENT, QC, H4R 1W8
(514) 745-5757   SIC 7389

SERVPRO OF CALGARY SOUTH p 33
See 7648243 CANADA LIMITED

SERVUS CREDIT UNION p 121
See SERVUS CREDIT UNION LTD

SERVUS CREDIT UNION LTD p 121
151 KARL CLARK RD NW, EDMONTON, AB, T6N 1H5
(780) 496-2000   SIC 6062

SERVUS CREDIT UNION LTD p 154
4901 48 ST SUITE 201, RED DEER, AB, T4N 6M4
(403) 342-5533   SIC 6062

SERVUS CREDIT UNION PLACE p 166
400 CAMPBELL RD, ST. ALBERT, AB, T8N 0R8
(780) 418-6088   SIC 8699

SESCOLITE LIGHTING p 992

See HODDOR LIGHTING INC

SESHA ONTARIO INC p 569
476 ROBINSON RD, ENNISMORE, ON, K0L 1T0
(705) 292-6719   SIC 5141

SET DESIGN p 707
See STAGEVISION INC

SETAY HOLDINGS LIMITED p 610
78 QUEENSTON RD, HAMILTON, ON, L8K 6R6
(905) 549-4656   SIC 6712

SETAY MOTORS INC p 608
282 CENTENNIAL PKY N, HAMILTON, ON, L8E 2X4
(905) 549-4656   SIC 5511

SETON CANADA p 677
See W.H.B. IDENTIFICATION SOLUTIONS INC

SETPBHQ SECTION LOCALE 2000, SYNDICAT CANADIEN DE LA FONCTION PUBLIQUE (F.T.Q.) p 1180
See SYNDICAT DES EMPLOYE-E-S DE TECHNIQUES PROFFESSION

SETTLEMENT CO p 1006
See 1928321 ONTARIO INC

SEVEN CONTINENTS CORPORATION p 786
945 WILSON AVE SUITE 1, NORTH YORK, ON, M3K 1E8
(416) 784-3717   SIC 3999

SEVEN GENERATIONS ENERGY LTD p 59
525 8 AVE SW UNIT 4400, CALGARY, AB, T2P 1G1
(403) 718-0700   SIC 1311

SEVEN OAKS GENERAL HOSPITAL p 370
2300 MCPHILLIPS ST, WINNIPEG, MB, R2V 3M3
(204) 632-7133   SIC 8062

SEVEN OAKS HOMES FOR THE AGED p 866
See SEVEN OAKS HOMES INC

SEVEN OAKS HOMES INC p 866
9 NEILSON RD, SCARBOROUGH, ON, M1E 5E1
(416) 392-3500   SIC 8051

SEVEN OAKS MOTOR INN LTD p 1421
777 ALBERT ST, REGINA, SK, S4R 2P6
(306) 757-0121   SIC 7011

SEVEN OAKS SCHOOL DIVISION p 369
1330 JEFFERSON AVE, WINNIPEG, MB, R2P 1L3
(204) 632-6641   SIC 8211

SEVEN OAKS SCHOOL DIVISION p 370
711 JEFFERSON AVE, WINNIPEG, MB, R2V 0P7
(204) 336-5050   SIC 8211

SEVEN OAKS SCHOOL DIVISION p 370
830 POWERS ST, WINNIPEG, MB, R2V 4E7
(204) 586-8061   SIC 8211

SEVEN OAKS SCHOOL DIVISION MET SCHOOL p 370
See SEVEN OAKS SCHOOL DIVISION

SEVEN REGIONS HEALTH CENTRE p 350
See REGIONAL HEALTH AUTHORITY - CENTRAL MANITOBA INC

SEVEN REGIONS HEALTH CENTRE p 357
See REGIONAL HEALTH AUTHORITY - CENTRAL MANITOBA INC

SEVEN SEAS FISH CO. LTD p 256
12411 VULCAN WAY, RICHMOND, BC, V6V 1J7
(604) 247-1266   SIC 5146

SEVEN STAR EXPRESS LINE LTD p 608
36 COVINGTON ST, HAMILTON, ON, L8E 2Y5
SIC 4213

SEVEN VIEW CHRYSLER DODGE JEEP p 558
See SEVEN VIEW PLYMOUTH CHRYSLER LTD

SEVEN VIEW PLYMOUTH CHRYSLER LTD p 558
2685 HIGHWAY 7, CONCORD, ON, L4K

1V8
(905) 669-5051   SIC 5511

SEVENTH LEVEL MANAGEMENT LTD p 39
11012 MACLEOD TRAIL SE SUITE 600,
CALGARY, AB, T2J 6A5
(403) 837-1195   SIC 6531

SEVENTH STREET PLAZA   p 88
See EDON MANAGEMENT

SEVITA INTERNATIONAL CORPORATION p
622
11451 CAMERON RD, INKERMAN, ON,
K0E 1J0
(613) 989-3000   SIC 5153

**SEW-EURODRIVE COMPANY OF CANADA
LTD**   p 506
210 WALKER DR, BRAMPTON, ON, L6T
3W1
(905) 791-1553   SIC 3566

SEXAUER LTD   p 723
See INTERLINE BRANDS INC

SEXAUER LTD   p 727
6990 CREDITVIEW RD UNIT 3, MISSIS-
SAUGA, ON, L5N 8R9
(905) 821-8292   SIC 5074

SEYDACO PACKAGING CORP   p 742
215 COURTNEYPARK DR E, MISSIS-
SAUGA, ON, L5T 2T6
(905) 565-8030   SIC 5045

**SEYEM' QWANTLEN BUSINESS MANAGE-
MENT LTD**   p
225
23684 GABRIEL LANE, LANGLEY, BC, V1M
2S4
(604) 888-5556   SIC 8741

SEYMOUR MEDICAL CLINIC, THE   p 321
1530 7TH AVE W SUITE 200, VANCOU-
VER, BC, V6J 1S3
(604) 738-2151   SIC 8011

SEYMOUR PACIFIC DEVELOPMENTS LTD
p 195
100 ST. ANN'S RD, CAMPBELL RIVER, BC,
V9W 4C4
(250) 286-8045   SIC 1522

SEYMOUR PEOPLE DRUG MART #174   p
195
See CHOO KIN ENTERPRISES LTD

SEYMOUR-CAP PARTNERSHIP   p 239
See FRONTIER-KEMPER CONSTRUC-
TORS ULC

**SF INSURANCE PLACEMENT CORPORA-
TION OF CANADA**   p
481
333 FIRST COMMERCE DR, AURORA,
ON, L4G 8A4
(905) 750-4100   SIC 6331

SFE ENERGY MARYLAND, INC   p 733
100 MILVERTON DR SUITE 608, MISSIS-
SAUGA, ON, L5R 4H1
(905) 366-7037   SIC 4911

SFP CANADA LTD   p 1131
7077 BOUL NEWMAN BUREAU 15,
LASALLE, QC, H8N 1X1
(514) 366-7660   SIC 5947

SFP POINTE-NOIRE   p 1367
See SOCIETE FERROVIAIRE ET PORTU-
AIRE DE POINTE-NOIRE S.E.C.

SFU   p 183
See SIMON FRASER UNIVERSITY

SG CERESCO INC   p 1353
164 CH DE LA GRANDE-LIGNE, SAINT-
URBAIN-PREMIER, QC, J0S 1Y0
(450) 427-3831   SIC 5153

SG TRANSPORT ENERGIE INC   p 1255
520 RUE ADANAC, QUEBEC, QC, G1C 7B7
(418) 660-8888   SIC 6712

SGEU   p 1423
See SASKATCHEWAN GOVERNMENT &
GENERAL EMPLOYEES' UNION

SGGG FUND SERVICES INC.   p 957
121 KING ST W UNIT 300, TORONTO, ON,
M5H 3T9
(416) 967-0038   SIC 8721

SGI CANADA   p 1418
See SASKATCHEWAN GOVERNMENT IN-

SURANCE

SGI CANADA INSURANCE SERVICES LTD
p 1419
2260 11TH AVE SUITE 18, REGINA, SK,
S4P 0J9
(306) 751-1200   SIC 6331

SGS AXYS ANALYTICAL SERVICES LTD p
268
2045 MILLS RD W, SIDNEY, BC, V8L 5X2
(250) 655-5800   SIC 8734

SGS CANADA INC   p 129
235 MACDONALD CRES, FORT MCMUR-
RAY, AB, T9H 4B5
(780) 791-6454   SIC 8734

SGS CANADA INC   p 643
3347 LAKEFIELD RD RR 3, LAKEFIELD,
ON, K0L 2H0
(705) 652-2000   SIC 8734

SGS CANADA INC   p 700
5825 EXPLORER DR, MISSISSAUGA, ON,
L4W 5P6
(905) 364-3757   SIC 8734

SGS CANADA INC   p 743
6490 VIPOND DR, MISSISSAUGA, ON, L5T
1W8
(905) 364-3757   SIC 8734

SGS CANADA INC   p 777
1885 LESLIE ST, NORTH YORK, ON, M3B
2M3
(416) 736-2782   SIC 8734

SGS PHARMACY INC   p 1424
2105 8TH ST E UNIT 42, SASKATOON, SK,
S7H 0T8
(306) 374-4888   SIC 5912

SGS SPORTS INC   p 1341
6400 CH DE LA COTE-DE-LIESSE, SAINT-
LAURENT, QC, H4T 1E3
(514) 737-5665   SIC 5137

SGT TRANSPORT   p 1306
See S.G.T. 2000 INC

SHAAN TRUCK LINES   p 691
See 2350936 ONTARIO INC

**SHADDY INTERNATIONAL MARKETING
LTD**   p 820
373 COVENTRY RD, OTTAWA, ON, K1K
2C5
(613) 749-2053   SIC 5044

SHADOW LINES   p 224
See BRITISH PACIFIC TRANSPORT
HOLDINGS LTD

SHADY LANE GRAIN FACILITY   p 171
GD, WANHAM, AB, T0H 3P0
(780) 694-3005   SIC 5153

SHADY MAPLE FARMS PRODUCTION   p
1246
See CITADELLE COOPERATIVE DE PRO-
DUCTEURS DE SIROP D'ERABLE

SHAEFFERS CONSULTING ENGINEERS p
558
See SCHAEFFER & ASSOCIATES LTD

SHAFER - HAGGART LTD   p 316
1100 MELVILLE ST SUITE 938, VANCOU-
VER, BC, V6E 4A6
(604) 669-5512   SIC 5149

SHAFER COMMODITIES INC   p 316
1100 MELVILLE ST SUITE 938, VANCOU-
VER, BC, V6E 4A6
(604) 669-5512   SIC 5191

SHAFTESBURY HIGH SCHOOL A   p 389
See PEMBINA TRAILS SCHOOL DIVISION,
THE

SHAGANAPPI GM   p 72
See SHAGANAPPI MOTORS (1976) LTD

SHAGANAPPI MOTORS (1976) LTD   p 72
4720 CROWCHILD TRAIL NW, CALGARY,
AB, T3A 2N2
(403) 288-0444   SIC 5511

SHAIR SALES LTD   p 280
3557 190 ST UNIT 101, SURREY, BC, V3Z
0P6
(604) 514-7005   SIC 5087

SHAKLEE CANADA INC   p 528
3100 HARVESTER RD UNIT 7, BURLING-
TON, ON, L7N 3W8

(905) 681-1422   SIC 5122

SHALABY ENTERPRISES LIMITED   p 818
2310 ST. LAURENT BLVD, OTTAWA, ON,
K1G 5H9
(613) 526-5212   SIC 6712

**SHALOM MANOR LONG TERM CARE
HOME**   p 600
12 BARTLETT AVE, GRIMSBY, ON, L3M
0A2
(905) 945-9631   SIC 8051

SHALOM VILLAGE   p 614
See HAMILTON JEWISH HOME FOR THE
AGED

SHAMARAN PETROLEUM CORP   p 309
885 GEORGIA ST W SUITE 2000, VAN-
COUVER, BC, V6C 3E8
(604) 689-7842   SIC 1382

SHAMROCK BUILDING SERVICES LTD   p
94
12673 125 ST NW, EDMONTON, AB, T5L
0T6
(780) 472-7351   SIC 1521

SHAMROCK COLONY   p 6
See SHAMROCK HUTTERIAN BRETHREN

SHAMROCK ELEMENTARY SCHOOL p 366
See LOUIS RIEL SCHOOL DIVISION

**SHAMROCK FLOORING ACCESSORIES
LTD**   p 37
7510 5 ST SE UNIT D, CALGARY, AB, T2H
2L9
(403) 253-5330   SIC 5023

SHAMROCK HUTTERIAN BRETHREN   p 6
GD, BOW ISLAND, AB, T0K 0G0
(403) 545-6190   SIC 8661

SHAMROCK PROPERTY MANAGEMENT p
95
See ALLDRITT DEVELOPMENT LIMITED

SHAN INC   p 1400
4390 SUD LAVAL (A-440) O, VIMONT, QC,
H7T 2P7
(450) 687-7101   SIC 6712

SHAN STUDIO   p 1400
See COLLECTIONS SHAN INC, LES

SHANAHAN CARRIAGE CO. LTD, THE p
756
567 DAVIS DR, NEWMARKET, ON, L3Y
2P5
(416) 798-4858   SIC 5511

SHANAHAN FORD LINCOLN SALES p 756
567 DAVIS DR, NEWMARKET, ON, L3Y
2P5
(905) 853-5000   SIC 6719

**SHANAHAN'S BUILDING SPECIALTIES
LIMITED**   p 18
2808 58 AVE SE SUITE 2, CALGARY, AB,
T2C 0B3
(403) 279-2782   SIC 5039

SHANAHAN'S INDUSTRIES   p 18
See SHANAHAN'S BUILDING SPECIAL-
TIES LIMITED

SHANAHAN'S LIMITED PARTNERSHIP   p
18
2731 57 AVE SE SUITE 1, CALGARY, AB,
T2C 0B2
(403) 279-2890   SIC 3499

SHANAHAN'S LIMITED PARTNERSHIP   p
277
13139 80 AVE, SURREY, BC, V3W 3B1
(604) 591-5111   SIC 5039

SHANAHAN'S MANUFACTURING   p 18
See SHANAHAN'S LIMITED PARTNER-
SHIP

SHANDEX GROUP, THE   p 845
See SHANDEX SALES GROUP LIMITED

**SHANDEX PERSONAL CARE MANUFAC-
TURING INC**   p
839
5 HERRIOTT ST, PERTH, ON, K7H 3E5
(613) 267-1881   SIC 2841

SHANDEX SALES GROUP LIMITED   p 845
1100 SQUIRES BEACH RD, PICKERING,
ON, L1W 3N8
(905) 420-7407   SIC 5137

SHANE HOLDINGS LTD   p 25

5661 7 ST NE, CALGARY, AB, T2E 8V3
(403) 536-2200   SIC 1521

SHANE HOMES LIMITED   p 25
5661 7 ST NE, CALGARY, AB, T2E 8V3
(403) 536-2200   SIC 1521

SHANGHAI ENERGY CORPORATION p 59
605 5 AVE SW UNIT 700, CALGARY, AB,
T2P 3H5
(587) 393-3600   SIC 1311

SHANGRI-LA HOTEL TORONTO   p 948
See 180 UNIVERSITY HOTEL LIMITED
PARTNERSHIP

**SHANNAHAN'S INVESTIGATION SECU-
RITY LIMITED**   p
470
30 BROOKFALLS CRT, WAVERLEY, NS,
B2R 1J2
(902) 873-4536   SIC 7381

SHANNEX INCORPORATED   p 457
245 MAIN AVE, HALIFAX, NS, B3M 1B7
(902) 443-1971   SIC 8051

SHANNEX INCORPORATED   p 459
48 LOVETT LAKE CRT, HALIFAX, NS, B3S
1B8
(902) 454-7499   SIC 8051

SHANNEX INCORPORATED   p 469
378 YOUNG ST, TRURO, NS, B2N 7H2
(902) 895-2891   SIC 8051

SHANNON'S, GREG FOOD BASICS   p 885
149 HARTZEL RD, ST CATHARINES, ON,
L2P 1N6
(905) 684-7439   SIC 5411

**SHANNON, BRENDA CONTRACTS LIM-
ITED**   p
463
130 GEORGE ST, NEW GLASGOW, NS,
B2H 2K6
SIC 7349

SHANTI ENTERPRISES LIMITED   p 836
600 WHITES RD RR 3, PALMERSTON, ON,
N0G 2P0
(519) 343-2611   SIC 8051

SHAPE FOODS, INC   p 347
2001 VICTORIA AVE E, BRANDON, MB,
R7A 7L2
(204) 727-3529   SIC 5141

SHAPE INDUSTRIES INC   p 372
255 HUTCHINGS ST, WINNIPEG, MB, R2X
2R4
(204) 947-0409   SIC 3399

SHAPE MARKETING CORP   p 329
505 BURRARD ST SUITE 2020, VANCOU-
VER, BC, V7X 1M6
(604) 681-2358   SIC 6531

SHAPE PROCESS AUTOMATION   p 525
See TECH-CON AUTOMATION ULC

SHAPE PROPERTIES (BTCR) CORP p 329
505 BURRARD ST SUITE 2020, VANCOU-
VER, BC, V7X 1M6
(604) 681-2358   SIC 6531

SHAPIRO COHEN LLP   p 625
555 LEGGET DR SUITE 830, KANATA, ON,
K2K 2X3
(613) 232-5300   SIC 6794

SHARE CORPORATION CANADA LTD   p
373
1691 CHURCH AVE, WINNIPEG, MB, R2X
2Y7
(204) 633-8553   SIC 5169

SHAREAN DRUGS LTD   p 631
445 PRINCESS ST, KINGSTON, ON, K7L
1C3
(613) 546-3696   SIC 5912

SHARK CLUB   p 133
See SHARK CLUBS OF CANADA INC

SHARK CLUB QUESNEL   p 76
See SHARK CLUBS OF CANADA INC

SHARK CLUBS OF CANADA INC   p 76
31 HOPEWELL WAY NE, CALGARY, AB,
T3J 4V7
(403) 543-2600   SIC 5812

SHARK CLUBS OF CANADA INC   p 133
9898 99 ST, GRANDE PRAIRIE, AB, T8V
2H2

(780) 513-5450   *SIC* 5813
SHARON FARMS & ENTERPRISES LTD *p*
650
1340 HURON ST, LONDON, ON, N5V 3R3
(519) 455-3910   *SIC* 8051
SHARP   *p 707*
See SHARP ELECTRONICS OF CANADA LTD
SHARP BUS LINES LIMITED   *p 518*
567 OAK PARK RD, BRANTFORD, ON, N3T 5L8
(519) 751-3434   *SIC* 4151
SHARP BUS LINES LIMITED   *p 622*
6 SCOTT ST, INNERKIP, ON, N0J 1M0
SIC 4151
SHARP ELECTRONICS OF CANADA LTD *p*
707
335 BRITANNIA RD E, MISSISSAUGA, ON, L4Z 1W9
(905) 890-2100   *SIC* 5064
SHARP'S AUDIO VISUAL   *p 27*
See AUDIO VISUAL SYSTEMS INTEGRATION INC
SHARPE FOODS LTD   *p 540*
85 FRONT ST N, CAMPBELLFORD, ON, K0L 1L0
(705) 653-2326   *SIC* 5411
SHARPE'S IGA   *p 540*
See SHARPE FOODS LTD
SHARPE'S SOIL SERVICES LTD   *p 1411*
205 PARK AVE, MOOSOMIN, SK, S0G 3N0
(306) 435-3319   *SIC* 5191
SHASHI FOODS INC   *p 918*
55 ESANDAR DR, TORONTO, ON, M4G 4H2
(416) 645-0611   *SIC* 2044
SHATO HOLDINGS LTD   *p 293*
4088 CAMBIE ST SUITE 300, VANCOUVER, BC, V5Z 2X8
(604) 874-5533   *SIC* 6712
SHAUGHNESSY GOLF AND COUNTRY CLUB   *p 323*
4300 MARINE DR SW, VANCOUVER, BC, V6N 4A6
(604) 266-4141   *SIC* 7997
SHAUNAVON HOSPITAL & CARE CENTRE
p 1435
GD, SHAUNAVON, SK, S0N 2M0
(306) 297-2644   *SIC* 6324
SHAUNAVON LIVESTOCK SALES (1988) LTD   *p 1435*
GD, SHAUNAVON, SK, S0N 2M0
(306) 297-2457   *SIC* 5154
SHAW ALMEX FUSION CANADA, DIV OF *p*
893
See SHAW-ALMEX INDUSTRIES LIMITED
SHAW AUTO RECYCLERS   *p 651*
See LKQ SHAW AUTO RECYCLERS INC
SHAW CABLE   *p 59*
See SHAW COMMUNICATIONS INC
SHAW CABLE   *p 103*
See SHAW COMMUNICATIONS INC
SHAW CABLE   *p 337*
See SHAW COMMUNICATIONS INC
SHAW CABLESYSTEMS G.P.   *p 59*
630 3 AVE SW, CALGARY, AB, T2P 4L4
(403) 750-4500   *SIC* 4841
SHAW CABLESYSTEMS G.P.   *p 103*
10450 178 ST NW, EDMONTON, AB, T5S 1S2
(780) 490-3555   *SIC* 4841
SHAW CABLESYSTEMS G.P.   *p 592*
1037 FIRST ST E, FORT FRANCES, ON, P9A 1L8
(807) 274-5522   *SIC* 4841
SHAW CABLESYSTEMS LIMITED   *p 25*
2400 32 AVE NE, CALGARY, AB, T2E 9A7
(403) 750-4500   *SIC* 4833
SHAW CENTRE   *p 821*
See OTTAWA CONVENTION CENTRE CORPORATION
SHAW COMMUNICATIONS INC   *p 59*
630 3 AVE SW SUITE 900, CALGARY, AB, T2P 4L4

(403) 750-4500   *SIC* 4813
SHAW COMMUNICATIONS INC   *p 103*
10450 178 ST NW, EDMONTON, AB, T5S 1S2
(780) 490-3555   *SIC* 4841
SHAW COMMUNICATIONS INC   *p 337*
861 CLOVERDALE AVE, VICTORIA, BC, V8X 4S7
(250) 475-5655   *SIC* 4841
SHAW CONFERENCE CENTRE   *p 88*
See EDMONTON ECONOMIC DEVELOPMENT CORPORATION
SHAW FESTIVAL THEATRE FOUNDATION CANADA   *p 761*
10 QUEENS PARADE, NIAGARA ON THE LAKE, ON, L0S 1J0
(905) 468-2172   *SIC* 7922
SHAW FESTIVAL THEATRE, CANADA   *p*
761
See SHAW FESTIVAL THEATRE FOUNDATION CANADA
SHAW GROUP LIMITED, THE   *p 457*
255 LACEWOOD DR SUITE 100C, HALIFAX, NS, B3M 4G2
(902) 457-0689   *SIC* 3251
SHAW GROUP LIMITED, THE   *p 460*
1101 HIGHWAY 2, LANTZ, NS, B2S 1M9
(902) 883-2201   *SIC* 3251
SHAW MANAGEMENT CONSULTANTS INC
p 579
145 THE WEST MALL, ETOBICOKE, ON, M9C 5P5
(416) 767-4200   *SIC* 8741
SHAW PIPE PROTECTION   *p 123*
See SHAWCOR LTD
SHAW SABEY & ASSOCIATES LTD   *p 329*
555 BURRARD ST SUITE 1275, VANCOUVER, BC, V7X 1M9
(604) 689-2441   *SIC* 6411
SHAW SATELLITE SERVICES INC   *p 715*
2055 FLAVELLE BLVD, MISSISSAUGA, ON, L5K 1Z8
(905) 403-2020   *SIC* 4899
SHAW'S ENTERPRISES LTD   *p 149*
2801 5 ST, NISKU, AB, T9E 0C2
(780) 955-7222   *SIC* 5085
SHAW, HERB AND SONS LIMITED   *p 838*
31 SHARON ST, PEMBROKE, ON, K8A 7J5
(613) 732-9989   *SIC* 5031
SHAW, JACK ENTERPRISES LIMITED   *p*
1416
225 E 6TH AVE, REGINA, SK, S4N 6A6
(306) 545-5454   *SIC* 5541
SHAW, K. & SONS CONTRACTING LTD   *p*
133
10424 96 AVE, GRANDE PRAIRIE, AB, T8V 5V2
(780) 539-6960   *SIC* 1542
SHAW, KEN LEXUS TOYOTA   *p 993*
See KEN SHAW MOTORS LIMITED
SHAW-ALMEX INDUSTRIES LIMITED *p 837*
17 SHAW ALMEX DR, PARRY SOUND, ON, P2A 2X4
(705) 746-5884   *SIC* 3535
SHAW-ALMEX INDUSTRIES LIMITED *p 893*
323 GLOVER RD, STONEY CREEK, ON, L8E 5M2
(905) 643-7750   *SIC* 3535
SHAWA ENTERPRISES CANADA   *p 1208*
See SHAWA ENTERPRISES CORP
SHAWA ENTERPRISES CORP   *p 1208*
1250 BOUL ROBERT-BOURASSA UNITE 921, MONTREAL, QC, H3B 3B8
SIC 6512
SHAWCOR LTD   *p 123*
10275 21 ST NW, EDMONTON, AB, T6P 1P3
(780) 467-5501   *SIC* 3479
SHAWCOR LTD   *p 588*
25 BETHRIDGE RD, ETOBICOKE, ON, M9W 1M7
(416) 743-7111   *SIC* 3533
SHAWINIGAN ALUMINIUM INC   *p 1368*
1250 BOUL SAINT-SACREMENT, SHAW-

INIGAN, QC, G9N 0E3
(819) 731-0644   *SIC* 2819
SHAWINIGAN CHRYSLER   *p 1367*
See 9308-3152 QUEBEC INC
SHAWN & ASSOCIATES MANAGEMENT LTD   *p 37*
1209 59 AVE SE SUITE 100, CALGARY, AB, T2H 2P6
(403) 255-5017   *SIC* 8741
SHEARER'S FOODS CANADA, INC   *p 602*
745 SOUTHGATE DR, GUELPH, ON, N1G 3R3
(519) 746-0045   *SIC* 2096
SHEARFORCE EQUIPMENT   *p 177*
2707 PROGRESSIVE WAY SUITE 107, ABBOTSFORD, BC, V2T 0A7
(604) 855-5101   *SIC* 5082
SHEARFORCE EQUIPMENT   *p 230*
See WEST COAST MACHINERY LTD
SHEARS BUILDING SUPPLIES   *p 423*
See SHEARS, W BRYANT LIMITED
SHEARS, W BRYANT LIMITED   *p 423*
201 NICHOLSVILLE RD, DEER LAKE, NL, A8A 1W5
(709) 635-2186   *SIC* 5039
SHEARWALL TRIFORCE INCORPORATED
p 166
340 CIRCLE DR UNIT 200, ST. ALBERT, AB, T8N 7L5
(780) 459-4777   *SIC* 1542
SHEDIAC LOBSTER SHOP LTD   *p 417*
261 MAIN ST, SHEDIAC, NB, E4P 2A6
(506) 532-4302   *SIC* 5146
SHEEHAN & ROSIE LTD   *p 887*
70 ST. PAUL ST W, ST CATHARINES, ON, L2S 2C5
(905) 688-3713   *SIC* 6411
SHEEHAN'S TRUCK CENTRE INC   *p 524*
4320 HARVESTER RD, BURLINGTON, ON, L7L 5S4
(905) 632-0300   *SIC* 5511
SHEEN LEGEND PACKAGING CORP *p 736*
2280 DREW RD SUITE B, MISSISSAUGA, ON, L5S 1B8
(905) 677-2888   *SIC* 2657
SHEFFAR PLANNING AND REFERRAL SERVICES   *p 655*
See SHEFFAR, POTTER, MUCHAN INC
SHEFFAR, POTTER, MUCHAN INC   *p 655*
362 OXFORD ST E, LONDON, ON, N6A 1V7
(519) 432-6199   *SIC* 6411
SHEFFIELD MOVING AND STORAGE INC *p*
596
5499 CANOTEK RD, GLOUCESTER, ON, K1J 9J5
(613) 741-3015   *SIC* 4214
SHEFFIELD MOVING AND STORAGE INC *p*
877
4069 GORDON BAKER RD, SCARBOROUGH, ON, M1W 2P3
(416) 291-1200   *SIC* 4214
SHELBURNE HOME HARDWARE   *p 880*
See GILLAM FAMILY HOLDINGS LIMITED
SHELDRICK, J. W. SANITATION LTD *p 882*
4278 LONDON RD, SMITHVILLE, ON, L0R 2A0
(905) 957-3165   *SIC* 4953
SHELL   *p 359*
See SUPER SPLASH AUTO CLEANING LTD
SHELL   *p 773*
See 1107078 ONTARIO INC
SHELL   *p 826*
See 1514660 ONTARIO INC
SHELL   *p 1072*
See PETROLE J.M.B INC
SHELL AEROCENTRE   *p 238*
See YYJ FBO SERVICES LTD
SHELL CANADA   *p 1408*
See LA RONGE PETROLEUM LTD
SHELL CANADA LIMITED   *p 59*
400 4 AVE SW, CALGARY, AB, T2P 0J4
(403) 691-3111   *SIC* 1311

SHELL CANADA LIMITED   *p 79*
GD, CAROLINE, AB, T0M 0M0
(403) 722-7000   *SIC* 1389
SHELL CANADA LIMITED   *p 130*
55522 RANGE ROAD 214, FORT SASKATCHEWAN, AB, T8L 4A4
(780) 992-3600   *SIC* 2911
SHELL CANADA LIMITED   *p 152*
100 ST, PEACE RIVER, AB, T8S 1V8
(780) 624-6800   *SIC* 1311
SHELL CANADA LIMITED   *p 152*
GD, PINCHER CREEK, AB, T0K 1W0
(403) 627-7200   *SIC* 1311
SHELL CANADA LIMITED   *p 520*
250 LAURIER BLVD, BROCKVILLE, ON, K6V 5V7
(613) 498-5700   *SIC* 5541
SHELL CANADA LIMITED   *p 563*
339 LASALLE LINE RR 1, CORUNNA, ON, N0N 1G0
(519) 481-1369   *SIC* 2992
SHELL CANADA LIMITED   *p 563*
150 ST CLAIR PKY, CORUNNA, ON, N0N 1G0
(519) 481-1245   *SIC* 2911
SHELL CANADA LIMITED   *p 1238*
10501 RUE SHERBROOKE E, MONTREAL-EST, QC, H1B 1B3
(514) 645-1661   *SIC* 2911
SHELL CANADA PRODUCTS   *p 59*
400 4 AVE SW, CALGARY, AB, T2P 0J4
(403) 691-3111   *SIC* 5172
SHELL ENERGY NORTH AMERICA (CANADA) INC   *p 59*
400 4 AVE SW SUITE 212, CALGARY, AB, T2P 0J4
(403) 216-3600   *SIC* 4911
SHELL GLOBAL SOLUTIONS CANADA INC   *p 59*
400 4 AVE SW, CALGARY, AB, T2P 0J4
(403) 691-3540   *SIC* 5169
SHELL O'TRENTE ENR   *p 1290*
630 BOUL RIDEAU, ROUYN-NORANDA, QC, J9X 7G1
(819) 764-3530   *SIC* 5541
SHELL WATERTON COMPLEX   *p 152*
See SHELL CANADA LIMITED
SHELL-RYN MACHINING, DIV OF   *p 7*
See LOGAN INDUSTRIES LTD
SHELLBROOK CHEVROLET OLDSMOBILE LTD   *p*
1435
43 MAIN ST, SHELLBROOK, SK, S0J 2E0
(306) 747-2411   *SIC* 5511
SHELLBROOK CO-OPERATIVE ASSOCIATION LIMITED, THE   *p*
1435
GD, SHELLBROOK, SK, S0J 2E0
(306) 747-2122   *SIC* 5171
SHELLEY AUTOMATION   *p 777*
See SHELLEY INDUSTRIAL AUTOMATION INC
SHELLEY INDUSTRIAL AUTOMATION INC
p 777
41 COLDWATER RD, NORTH YORK, ON, M3B 1Y8
(416) 447-6471   *SIC* 5084
SHELLEY, R G ENTERPRISES (1990) INC *p*
777
41 COLDWATER RD, NORTH YORK, ON, M3B 1Y8
(416) 447-6471   *SIC* 5084
SHELLX COURIER   *p 558*
See REPROMATIC SYSTEMS INC
SHELTER CANADIAN PROPERTIES LIMITED   *p*
387
2600 SEVEN EVERGREEN PLACE, WINNIPEG, MB, R3L 2T3
(204) 475-9090   *SIC* 6282
SHELTER CANADIAN PROPERTIES LIMITED   *p*
387
7 EVERGREEN PL SUITE 2600, WIN-

NIPEG, MB, R3L 2T3
(204) 474-5975   SIC 6513

SHELTER MODULAR INC   p 179
3294 262 ST, ALDERGROVE, BC, V4W 2X2
(604) 856-1311   SIC 1541

SHENGLIN FINANCIAL GROUP   p 773
See SHENGLIN FINANCIAL INC

SHENGLIN FINANCIAL INC   p 773
170 SHEPPARD AVE E SUITE 500, NORTH YORK, ON, M2N 3A4
(416) 789-3691   SIC 6311

SHEPEHERD GROUP, THE   p 795
140 WENDELL AVE SUITE 9, NORTH YORK, ON, M9N 3R2
(416) 249-1700   SIC 6331

SHEPHERD LODGE   p 875
See SHEPHERD VILLAGE INC

SHEPHERD VILLAGE INC   p 875
3760 SHEPPARD AVE E, SCARBOROUGH, ON, M1T 3K9
(416) 609-5700   SIC 8361

SHEPHERD'S CARE FOUNDATION   p 94
12603 135 AVE NW, EDMONTON, AB, T5L 5B2
(780) 447-3840   SIC 8322

SHEPHERD'S CARE FOUNDATION   p 120
6620 28 AVE NW, EDMONTON, AB, T6K 2R1
(780) 463-9810   SIC 8051

SHEPHERD'S CARE FOUNDATION KENSINGTON VILLAGE   p 94
See SHEPHERD'S CARE FOUNDATION

SHEPHERD'S HARDWARE LIMITED   p 180
3525 MILL ST, ARMSTRONG, BC, V0E 1B0
(250) 546-3002   SIC 5211

SHEPHERDS OF GOOD HOPE   p 822
256 KING EDWARD AVE, OTTAWA, ON, K1N 7M1
(613) 789-8210   SIC 8322

SHEPP   p 1423
See SASKATCHEWAN HEALTHCARE EMPLOYEES' PENSION PLAN

SHEPPELL FGI DIV OF   p 328
See MORNEAU SHEPELL LTD

SHEPPELL FGI, DIV OF   p 1229
See MORNEAU SHEPELL LTD

SHERATON CAVALIER HOTEL CALGARY   p 8
See CAVALIER ENTERPRISES LTD

SHERATON CAVALIER SASKATOON   p 1426
See CAVALIER ENTERPRISES LTD

SHERATON HOTEL   p 957
See STARWOOD CANADA ULC

SHERATON LAVAL   p 1394
See GROUPE HOTELIER GRAND CHATEAU INC

SHERATON MONTREAL AIRPORT HOTEL   p 1093
See 9207-4616 QUEBEC INC

SHERATON MONTREAL, LE   p 1208
See STARWOOD HOTELS & RESORTS, INC

SHERATON ON THE FALLS   p 758
See CANADIAN NIAGARA HOTELS INC

SHERATON OTTAWA HOTEL   p 822
See CHATEAU OTTAWA HOTEL INC

SHERATON PARKWAY TORONTO NORTH HOTEL SUITES & CONVENTION CENTRE   p 853
See PARKWAY HOTELS AND CONVENTION CENTRE INC

SHERATON SUITES CALGARY EAU CLAIRE   p 49
See FAIRMONT HOTELS & RESORTS INC

SHERATON TORONTO AIRPORT HOTEL AND CONFERENCE CENTRE   p 581
See 1265534 ONTARIO INC

SHERATON VANCOUVER AIRPORT HOTEL   p 261
See RICHMOND INN HOTEL LTD

SHERATON VANCOUVER GUILDFORD

HOTEL   p 270
See GUILDFORD VENTURES LTD

SHERATON VANCOUVER WALL CENTRE   p 327
See WALL FINANCIAL CORPORATION

SHERBROOKE AUTOMOBILE INC   p 1375
4465 BOUL BOURQUE, SHERBROOKE, QC, J1N 1S4
(819) 569-9111   SIC 5511

SHERBROOKE COMMUNITY CENTRE   p 1424
See SHERBROOKE COMMUNITY SOCIETY INC

SHERBROOKE COMMUNITY SOCIETY INC   p 1424
401 ACADIA DR SUITE 330, SASKATOON, SK, S7H 2E7
(306) 655-3600   SIC 8059

SHERBROOKE FIAT   p 1376
See ELITE CHRYSLER JEEP INC

SHERBROOKE HONDA   p 1371
See ECONAUTO (1985) LTEE

SHERBROOKE IGA   p 840
See ARMSTRONG STORE LIMITED

SHERBROOKE NISSAN INC   p 1375
4280 BOUL BOURQUE, SHERBROOKE, QC, J1N 1W7
(819) 823-8008   SIC 5511

SHERBROOKE O.E.M. LTD   p 1374
3425 BOUL INDUSTRIEL, SHERBROOKE, QC, J1L 2W1
(819) 563-7374   SIC 1796

SHERBROOKE RESTORATION COMMISSION   p 466
42 MAIN ST, SHERBROOKE, NS, B0J 3C0
(902) 522-2400   SIC 8412

SHERBROOKE VILLAGE COMPANY STORE   p 466
See SHERBROOKE RESTORATION COMMISSION

SHERET, ANDREW HOLDINGS LIMITED   p 335
721 KINGS RD, VICTORIA, BC, V8T 1W4
(250) 386-7744   SIC 5074

SHERET, ANDREW LIMITED   p 335
740 HILLSIDE AVE SUITE 401, VICTORIA, BC, V8T 1Z4
(250) 386-7744   SIC 5074

SHERGROUP INC   p 1148
205 RUE DU CENTRE, MAGOG, QC, J1X 5B6
(819) 843-4441   SIC 6712

SHERIDAN COLLEGE INSTITUTE OF TECHNOLOGY AND ADVANCED LEARNING   p 512
7899 MCLAUGHLIN RD, BRAMPTON, ON, L6Y 5H9
(647) 309-6634   SIC 8222

SHERIDAN COLLEGE INSTITUTE OF TECHNOLOGY AND ADVANCED LEARNING   p 710
4180 DUKE OF YORK BLVD, MISSISSAUGA, ON, L5B 0G5
(905) 845-9430   SIC 8222

SHERIDAN COLLEGE INSTITUTE OF TECHNOLOGY AND ADVANCED LEARNING   p 799
1430 TRAFALGAR RD, OAKVILLE, ON, L6H 2L1
(905) 845-9430   SIC 8222

SHERIDAN FORD LINCOLN SALES LTD   p 712
1345 LAKESHORE RD E, MISSISSAUGA, ON, L5E 1G5
SIC 5511

SHERIDAN NURSERIES LIMITED   p 594
12302 TENTH LINE, GEORGETOWN, ON, L7G 4S7
(905) 873-0522   SIC 5261

SHERIDAN NURSERIES LIMITED   p 1000

4077 HIGHWAY 7 E, UNIONVILLE, ON, L3R 1L5
(905) 477-2253   SIC 0181

SHERIDAN RETAIL INC   p 715
2225 ERIN MILLS PKY, MISSISSAUGA, ON, L5K 1T9
(905) 822-0344   SIC 6512

SHERIDAN SPECIALTIES   p 714
See SHERIDAN VENTURES LTD

SHERIDAN VENTURES LTD   p 714
2222 SOUTH SHERIDAN WAY UNIT 210, MISSISSAUGA, ON, L5J 2M4
(905) 823-7780   SIC 5149

SHERIDAN VILLA HOME FOR AGED   p 714
See REGIONAL MUNICIPALITY OF PEEL, THE

SHERLOCK CLOTHING LIMITED   p 459
127 CHAIN LAKE DR UNIT 9, HALIFAX, NS, B3S 1B3
(902) 454-7098   SIC 5651

SHERLOCK RESOURCES INC   p 558
289 BRADWICK DR, CONCORD, ON, L4K 1K5
(905) 669-5888   SIC 6712

SHERMAG IMPORT INC   p 1057
10 RUE BISHOP, BISHOPTON, QC, J0B 1G0
(819) 884-1145   SIC 2511

SHERMAG IMPORT INC   p 1111
825 BOUL INDUSTRIEL, GRANBY, QC, J2J 1A5
(450) 776-6361   SIC 2511

SHERMAN, L.E. MOTORS LTD   p 252
1001 CHAMBERLIN AVE, PRINCE RUPERT, BC, V8J 4J5
(250) 624-9171   SIC 5511

SHERRITT INTERNATIONAL CORPORATION   p 130
10101 114 ST, FORT SASKATCHEWAN, AB, T8L 2T3
(780) 992-7000   SIC 3339

SHERRITT INTERNATIONAL CORPORATION   p 957
22 ADELAIDE ST W SUITE 4220, TORONTO, ON, M5H 4E3
(416) 924-4551   SIC 1081

SHERRITT INTERNATIONAL OIL AND GAS LIMITED   p 59
425 1 ST SW SUITE 2000, CALGARY, AB, T2P 3L8
(403) 260-2900   SIC 1382

SHERWAY FINE CARS LTD   p 579
2000 THE QUEENSWAY, ETOBICOKE, ON, M9C 5H5
(416) 620-1987   SIC 5521

SHERWAY FORD TRUCK SALES   p 576
See THORNCREST SHERWAY INC

SHERWAY NISSAN   p 578
See SHERWAY NISSAN (2000) LIMITED

SHERWAY NISSAN (2000) LIMITED   p 578
5448 DUNDAS ST W, ETOBICOKE, ON, M9B 1B4
(416) 239-1217   SIC 5511

SHERWAY WAREHOUSING INC   p 743
325A ANNAGEM BLVD SUITE 2, MISSISSAUGA, ON, L5T 3A7
(905) 364-3300   SIC 4225

SHERWEB INC   p 1372
95 BOUL JACQUES-CARTIER S BUREAU 400, SHERBROOKE, QC, J1J 2Z3
(819) 562-6610   SIC 4813

SHERWIN-WILLIAMS CANADA INC   p 592
224 CATHERINE ST, FORT ERIE, ON, L2A 0B1
(905) 871-2724   SIC 2851

SHERWIN-WILLIAMS CANADA INC   p 600
13 IROQUOIS TRAIL, GRIMSBY, ON, L3M 5E6
(905) 945-3802   SIC 2851

SHERWIN-WILLIAMS CANADA INC   p 905
8500 LESLIE ST SUITE 220, THORNHILL, ON, L3T 7M8

SIC 5198

SHERWIN-WILLIAMS STORE GROUP INC   p 707
170 BRUNEL RD UNIT B, MISSISSAUGA, ON, L4Z 1T5
(905) 507-0166   SIC 5198

SHERWIN-WILLIAMS STORES GROUP, CANADA   p 707
See SHERWIN-WILLIAMS STORE GROUP INC

SHERWOOD BMR   p 1041
See SHERWOOD TIMBER MART INC

SHERWOOD BUICK GMC   p 163
See PETERSEN PONTIAC BUICK GMC (ALTA) INC

SHERWOOD CARE   p 161
2020 BRENTWOOD BLVD, SHERWOOD PARK, AB, T8A 0X1
(780) 467-2281   SIC 8051

SHERWOOD CHEVEROLET   p 1425
See SHERWOOD INVESTMENTS LIMITED

SHERWOOD CHEVROLET INC   p 1425
550 BRAND RD, SASKATOON, SK, S7J 5J3
(306) 374-6330   SIC 5511

SHERWOOD CO OP   p 1422
See SHERWOOD CO-OPERATIVE ASSOCIATION LIMITED

SHERWOOD CO-OPERATIVE ASSOCIATION LIMITED   p 1415
615 WINNIPEG ST N, REGINA, SK, P0T 2S0
(306) 791-9300   SIC 5171

SHERWOOD CO-OPERATIVE ASSOCIATION LIMITED   p 1422
2925 E QUANCE ST, REGINA, SK, S4V 3B7
(306) 791-9300   SIC 5411

SHERWOOD COURT LONG TERM CARE CENTRE   p 664
300 RAVINEVIEW DR SUITE 1, MAPLE, ON, L6A 3P8
(905) 303-3565   SIC 8052

SHERWOOD ELECTROMOTION INC   p 558
20 BARNES CRT UNIT A-E, CONCORD, ON, L4K 4L4
(289) 695-5555   SIC 7694

SHERWOOD FORD   p 163
2540 BROADMOOR BLVD, SHERWOOD PARK, AB, T8H 1B4
(780) 449-3673   SIC 8742

SHERWOOD HARDWARE LTD   p 1040
115 ST. PETERS RD, CHARLOTTETOWN, PE, C1A 5P3
(902) 892-8509   SIC 5251

SHERWOOD HOCKEY   p 1372
See 1794342 ONTARIO INC

SHERWOOD HONDA   p 162
See 1443803 ALBERTA LTD

SHERWOOD INDUSTRIES LTD   p 267
6782 OLDFIELD RD, SAANICHTON, BC, V8M 2A3
(250) 652-6080   SIC 3433

SHERWOOD INNOVATIONS INC   p 588
125 BETHRIDGE RD, ETOBICOKE, ON, M9W 1N4
(416) 740-2777   SIC 5013

SHERWOOD INVESTMENTS LIMITED   p 1425
550 BRAND RD, SASKATOON, SK, S7J 5J3
(306) 374-6330   SIC 5521

SHERWOOD KIA   p 163
See SHERWOOD PARK AUTO SALES LTD

SHERWOOD MARINE CENTRE LTD   p 267
6771 OLDFIELD RD, SAANICHTON, BC, V8M 2A2
(250) 652-6520   SIC 5551

SHERWOOD NISSAN   p 162
See AUTO-NET AUTOMOBILE SALES LTD

SHERWOOD PARK AUTO SALES LTD   p 163
20 BROADWAY BLVD, SHERWOOD PARK, AB, T8H 2A2
(780) 449-4499   SIC 5521

SHERWOOD PARK DODGE CHRYSLER JEEP LTD p 163
230 PROVINCIAL AVE, SHERWOOD PARK, AB, T8H 0E1
(780) 410-4100 SIC 5511
SHERWOOD PARK HYUNDAI p 163
See SHERWOOD PARK VEHICLES LP
SHERWOOD PARK IGA p 161
688 WYE RD, SHERWOOD PARK, AB, T8A 6G3
(780) 416-7920 SIC 5411
SHERWOOD PARK TOYOTA p 162
See 1185140 ALBERTA LTD
SHERWOOD PARK VEHICLES LP p 163
41 AUTOMALL RD, SHERWOOD PARK, AB, T8H 0C7
(780) 410-2450 SIC 5511
SHERWOOD PARK VOLKSWAGEN p 163
See SPV MOTORS LP
SHERWOOD SAFEWAY p 161
See SOBEYS WEST INC
SHERWOOD STEEL LTD p 123
3303 84 AVE NW, EDMONTON, AB, T6P 1K1
(780) 449-6548 SIC 5051
SHERWOOD TIMBER MART INC p 1041
423 MOUNT EDWARD RD, CHARLOTTE-TOWN, PE, C1E 2A1
(902) 368-3648 SIC 5211
SHERWOOD YACHT SALES p 267
6771 OLDFIELD RD, SAANICHTON, BC, V8M 2A2
(250) 652-5445 SIC 7389
SHEUNG KEE TRADING COMPANY INC p 877
3411 MCNICOLL AVE UNIT 11, SCARBOROUGH, ON, M1V 2V6
(905) 471-4481 SIC 5141
SHIBLEY RIGHTON LLP p 957
250 UNIVERSITY AVE SUITE 700, TORONTO, ON, M5H 3E5
(416) 214-5200 SIC 8111
SHIFT RECYCLING INC p 793
700 ORMONT DR, NORTH YORK, ON, M9L 2V4
(416) 995-4202 SIC 4953
SHIGS ENTERPRISES LTD p 296
450 ALEXANDER ST, VANCOUVER, BC, V6A 1C5
(604) 251-9093 SIC 5421
SHIMANO CANADA LTD p 842
427 PIDO RD, PETERBOROUGH, ON, K9J 6X7
(705) 745-3232 SIC 5091
SHIMMERMAN PENN LLP p 957
111 RICHMOND ST W SUITE 300, TORONTO, ON, M5H 2G4
(416) 964-7200 SIC 8721
SHIPMASTER CONTAINERS LIMITED p 675
380 ESNA PARK DR, MARKHAM, ON, L3R 1G5
(416) 493-9193 SIC 2653
SHIPPAM & ASSOCIATES INC p 385
865 KING EDWARD ST, WINNIPEG, MB, R3H 0P8
(204) 925-3696 SIC 5199
SHIPPERS SUPPLY INC p 110
5219 47 ST NW, EDMONTON, AB, T6B 3N4
(780) 444-7777 SIC 5113
SHIPWAY STAIRS LIMITED p 524
1820 IRONSTONE DR, BURLINGTON, ON, L7L 5V3
(905) 336-1296 SIC 2431
SHIRLEY, STEWART A ENTERPRISES LIMITED p 438
133 CHURCH ST SUITE 1, ANTIGONISH, NS, B2G 2E3
(902) 863-4753 SIC 5531
SHIRLON PLASTIC COMPANY INC p 534
100 PINEBUSH RD, CAMBRIDGE, ON, N1R 8J8
(519) 620-1333 SIC 3089

SHISEIDO (CANADA) INC p 675
303 ALLSTATE PKY, MARKHAM, ON, L3R 5P9
(905) 763-1250 SIC 5122
SHNIER p 503
See GESCO LIMITED PARTNERSHIP
SHOAL LAKE WILD RICE p 362
See 5465461 MANITOBA INC
SHOAL LAKE-STRATHCLAIR HEALTH CENTRE p 356
524 MARY ST, SHOAL LAKE, MB, R0J 1Z0
(204) 759-2336 SIC 8062
SHOCK TRAUMA AIR RESCUE SERVICE p 25
1441 AVIATION PK NE UNIT 570, CALGARY, AB, T2E 8M7
(403) 295-1811 SIC 4522
SHOCK TRAUMA AIR RESCUE SERVICE p 134
1519 35 AVE E SUITE 100, GRANDE PRAIRIE, AB, T9E 0V6
(780) 890-3131 SIC 4522
SHOEBOX AUDIOMETRY p 826
See SHOEBOX LTD
SHOEBOX LTD p 826
80 ABERDEEN ST SUITE 301, OTTAWA, ON, K1S 5R5
(877) 349-9934 SIC 3841
SHOEMAKER DRYWALL SUPPLIES p 121
See SDS INDUSTRIAL BUILDING SUPPLIES LTD
SHOEMAKER DRYWALL SUPPLIES LTD p 25
7012 8 ST NE, CALGARY, AB, T2E 8L8
(403) 291-1013 SIC 1742
SHOES FOR CREWS p 745
199 LONGSIDE DR, MISSISSAUGA, ON, L5W 1Z9
SIC 5139
SHOKER FARMS LTD p 197
46825 BAILEY RD, CHILLIWACK, BC, V2R 4S8
(604) 824-1541 SIC 0139
SHOL DICE INSURANCE p 542
300 GRAND AVE W, CHATHAM, ON, N7L 1C1
(519) 352-9016 SIC 6411
SHOOTING EDGE p 37
See SHOOTING EDGE INC, THE
SHOOTING EDGE INC, THE p 37
510 77 AVE SE SUITE 4, CALGARY, AB, T2H 1C3
(403) 720-4867 SIC 5941
SHOP, LA p 1103
See MATERIAUX BONHOMME INC
SHOP, THE p 900
See 375414 ONTARIO LIMITED
SHOPCO FOOD PROVISIONERS p 866
See BEEFEATERS INC
SHOPIFY INC p 834
150 ELGIN ST 8TH FLOOR, OTTAWA, ON, K2P 1L4
(613) 241-2828 SIC 7374
SHOPLOGIX INC p 524
5100 SOUTH SERVICE RD SUITE 39, BURLINGTON, ON, L7L 6A5
(905) 469-9994 SIC 7371
SHOPPER'S DRUG MART p 363
See SONAL BACHU PHARMACY LTD
SHOPPER'S DRUG MART p 686
See PHARWAHA DRUGS LIMITED
SHOPPER'S DRUG MART p 759
See FERGUSON, N. DRUGS LTD
SHOPPER+ INC p 1128
2210 52E AV, LACHINE, QC, H8T 2Y3
(514) 631-5216 SIC 5734
SHOPPERS DRUG MART p 9
See RX FRASER LTD
SHOPPERS DRUG MART p 33
See BERTOLIN, S. PHARMACY LTD
SHOPPERS DRUG MART p 41
See NEUFELD, C. M. PHARMACY LTD
SHOPPERS DRUG MART p 71
See KANJEE ENTERPRISES LTD

SHOPPERS DRUG MART p 76
See KANJI RX DRUG LTD
SHOPPERS DRUG MART p 92
See KELLY, MARIA ENTERPRISES INC
SHOPPERS DRUG MART p 104
See LOWES PHARMACY LIMITED
SHOPPERS DRUG MART p 107
See LAM, MICHELLE PHARMACY LTD
SHOPPERS DRUG MART p 107
See HOLOWAYCHUK, L.B. PHARMACY LTD
SHOPPERS DRUG MART p 124
See CASPEN DRUGS LTD
SHOPPERS DRUG MART p 143
See D. R. PERRY PHARMACY LTD
SHOPPERS DRUG MART p 150
See BROWN'S GENERAL STORE LTD
SHOPPERS DRUG MART p 161
See HACKMAN, RICHARD B. DRUGS LTD
SHOPPERS DRUG MART p 165
See ELAINE MAH PHARMACY LTD
SHOPPERS DRUG MART p 184
See D'SA, MEL M. INC
SHOPPERS DRUG MART p 190
See DZOMBETA DRUG LTD
SHOPPERS DRUG MART p 195
See SCEPTER DRUGS LTD
SHOPPERS DRUG MART p 196
See HOANA DRUGS LTD
SHOPPERS DRUG MART p 203
See J D M PHARMACY LTD
SHOPPERS DRUG MART p 211
See 653457 B.C. LTD
SHOPPERS DRUG MART p 222
See FWS PHARMACY SERVICES LTD
SHOPPERS DRUG MART p 232
See 662942 BC LTD
SHOPPERS DRUG MART p 243
140 ISLAND HWY E, PARKSVILLE, BC, V9P 2G5
(250) 248-3521 SIC 5912
SHOPPERS DRUG MART p 250
See KONA DRUGS LTD
SHOPPERS DRUG MART p 251
See MILESTEP PHARMACY SERVICES INC
SHOPPERS DRUG MART p 259
See 663353 B.C. LTD
SHOPPERS DRUG MART p 277
See PARM'S PRESCRIPTIONS LTD
SHOPPERS DRUG MART p 283
See KRISINGER DRUG LTD
SHOPPERS DRUG MART p 340
See WARDILL, J.A. ENTERPRISES INC
SHOPPERS DRUG MART p 347
See MARSH, GLENDA PHARMACY LTD
SHOPPERS DRUG MART p 360
See 5043680 MANITOBA INC
SHOPPERS DRUG MART p 382
See K.B. BORISENKO PHARMACY LTD
SHOPPERS DRUG MART p 387
See DELBIGIO, KEN PHARMACY LTD
SHOPPERS DRUG MART p 390
See ECONOMY DRUGS LTD
SHOPPERS DRUG MART p 395
See STEVE DOUCET PHARMACUETICAL INC
SHOPPERS DRUG MART p 398
See WADE, R.S. HEALTH CARE LTD
SHOPPERS DRUG MART p 398
477 RUE PAUL SUITE 181, DIEPPE, NB, E1A 4X5
(506) 857-0820 SIC 5912
SHOPPERS DRUG MART p 399
See OUELLETTE, RONALD INC
SHOPPERS DRUG MART p 399
See E & L DRUGS LTD
SHOPPERS DRUG MART p 400
See BARRY PHARMACY LTD
SHOPPERS DRUG MART p 406
See O'BRIAIN DRUGS LTD
SHOPPERS DRUG MART p 409
See NORTHEND PHARMACY LTD
SHOPPERS DRUG MART p 410

See M & L PHARMACY LTD
SHOPPERS DRUG MART p 413
See COVE VIEW PHARMACY INC
SHOPPERS DRUG MART p 416
See WEST SIDE PHARMACY INC
SHOPPERS DRUG MART p 420
See CUMMINGS PHARMACY LTD
SHOPPERS DRUG MART p 428
See OLOINGSIGH DRUGS LIMITED
SHOPPERS DRUG MART p 434
See VITAL PHARMACY INC
SHOPPERS DRUG MART p 434
See WAY'S PHARMACY LIMITED
SHOPPERS DRUG MART p 438
See M & N CROWELL PHARMACY SERVICES LTD
SHOPPERS DRUG MART p 444
See D.M. SERVANT PHARMACY LIMITED
SHOPPERS DRUG MART p 453
See JAMIESON PHARMACY LTD
SHOPPERS DRUG MART p 457
278 LACEWOOD DR SUITE 136, HALIFAX, NS, B3M 3N8
(902) 443-5214 SIC 5912
SHOPPERS DRUG MART p 457
See J M S PHARMACY SERVICE INC
SHOPPERS DRUG MART p 458
See KURT RYAN PHARMACY SERVICES LTD
SHOPPERS DRUG MART p 464
See G AND G WHITE HOWLEY PHARMACY LTD
SHOPPERS DRUG MART p 475
See SPINA, JOHN DRUGS LTD
SHOPPERS DRUG MART p 477
See WOLFF, MARY ANN DRUGS LTD
SHOPPERS DRUG MART p 477
See RENNSTADD PHARMA INC
SHOPPERS DRUG MART p 481
See HOLTZMAN, JACK DRUGS LIMITED
SHOPPERS DRUG MART p 484
See MARTEL, DAN PHARMACY LIMITED
SHOPPERS DRUG MART p 490
See WILF'S DRUG STORE LTD
SHOPPERS DRUG MART p 492
See SULLIVAN, EVAN PHARMACY LIMITED
SHOPPERS DRUG MART p 498
See SEHDEV PHARMACY INC
SHOPPERS DRUG MART p 500
See TRIPLE J PHARMACY LTD
SHOPPERS DRUG MART p 509
See CHAUHAN PHARMACY SERVICES LTD
SHOPPERS DRUG MART p 510
See ROMANO, DOMENIC PHARMACY INC
SHOPPERS DRUG MART p 512
See SCRIPTECH MEDS INC
SHOPPERS DRUG MART p 516
See BOVE DRUGS LIMITED
SHOPPERS DRUG MART p 519
See MARK S. LESLIE APATHECARY LTD
SHOPPERS DRUG MART p 531
See IBRAHIM, YASSER PHARMACY LIMITED
SHOPPERS DRUG MART p 531
See MOSLIM, M. PHARMACY LTD
SHOPPERS DRUG MART p 534
See RATHI, KANU PRIYA PHARMACY INC
SHOPPERS DRUG MART p 540
315 MCNEELY AVE, CARLETON PLACE, ON, K7C 4S6
(613) 253-5595 SIC 5912
SHOPPERS DRUG MART p 545
See TONA, ALAN PHARMACY LIMITED
SHOPPERS DRUG MART p 546
See MATTHEWS, MARK PHARMACY LTD
SHOPPERS DRUG MART p 566
See M. VERNESCU DRUGS LTD
SHOPPERS DRUG MART p 571
See WEINGARTEN, ALAN DRUGS LTD
SHOPPERS DRUG MART p 572
See BARRY PHILLIPS DRUGS LIMITED
SHOPPERS DRUG MART p 573

See WARRIAN, KAREN PHARMACY
SHOPPERS DRUG MART   p 577
See I.R.A.S. PHARMACY LTD
SHOPPERS DRUG MART   p 580
See FOUZIA AKHTAR DRUGS LTD
SHOPPERS DRUG MART   p 580
See BAJAJ DRUGS LIMITED
SHOPPERS DRUG MART   p 590
See DREVER, S. PHARMACY LIMITED
SHOPPERS DRUG MART   p 592
See AJRAM'S, ANNY PHARMACY LTD
SHOPPERS DRUG MART   p 600
See R.C. PHARMACY LTD
SHOPPERS DRUG MART   p 602
See C.J.W. PHARMACY INCORPORATED
SHOPPERS DRUG MART   p 606
See GARY DANIELS PHARMACIES LTD
SHOPPERS DRUG MART   p 613
See HANBALI, JEFF DRUGS LTD
SHOPPERS DRUG MART   p 614
See J.R. GIUDICE PHARMACY INC
SHOPPERS DRUG MART   p 616
See HANBALI, JEFF DRUGS LTD
SHOPPERS DRUG MART   p 627
See JAMIE D. TEMPLE PHARMACY LTD
SHOPPERS DRUG MART   p 630
See ADAMS PHARMACY LTD
SHOPPERS DRUG MART   p 631
See SHAREAN DRUGS LTD
SHOPPERS DRUG MART   p 632
See KIN LEM DRUGS LIMITED
SHOPPERS DRUG MART   p 633
See FORD'S, SCOTT PHARMACY LTD
SHOPPERS DRUG MART   p 634
See BETTER WELLNESS JMC LTD
SHOPPERS DRUG MART   p 637
See EXUS PHARMACEUTICALS LTD
SHOPPERS DRUG MART   p 644
See GRECO, ROBERTO DRUGS LTD
SHOPPERS DRUG MART   p 646
See QUINN'S PHARMACY LIMITED (1987)
SHOPPERS DRUG MART   p 652
See FESUK, ROBERT S. PHARMACY LTD
SHOPPERS DRUG MART   p 657
See KNAUER, CLAIRE PHARMACY LTD
SHOPPERS DRUG MART   p 658
See DHAMI, TEJI DRUGS LTD
SHOPPERS DRUG MART   p 658
See ABRAHAM, R.J. DRUGS LTD
SHOPPERS DRUG MART   p 659
See MENDRINOS, B. DRUGS LTD
SHOPPERS DRUG MART   p 660
See COULTER'S PHARMACY (LONDON) LTD
SHOPPERS DRUG MART   p 664
See DALIMONTE, M. PHARMACY LTD
SHOPPERS DRUG MART   p 668
See CHRISTOPHER YEE DRUGS LTD
SHOPPERS DRUG MART   p 671
See HUYNH, KIM DRUGS LTD
SHOPPERS DRUG MART   p 682
See TOLMIE, M. B. DRUGS LTD
SHOPPERS DRUG MART   p 703
See J AHMAD DRUGS LTD
SHOPPERS DRUG MART   p 704
See KA DJORDJEVIC PHARMACY INC
SHOPPERS DRUG MART   p 705
See HAUNSLA PHARMACY LTD
SHOPPERS DRUG MART   p 713
See SALAMEH DRUGS LTD
SHOPPERS DRUG MART   p 718
See MACLAI DRUGS LIMITED
SHOPPERS DRUG MART   p 718
See TIRCONNELL PHARMACY LIMITED
SHOPPERS DRUG MART   p 718
See JODHA PHARMACY INC
SHOPPERS DRUG MART   p 727
See TAILOR DRUGS LIMITED
SHOPPERS DRUG MART   p 752
See PINEO, P. PHARMACEUTICALS INC
SHOPPERS DRUG MART   p 757
See ZAHID, M. DRUGS LTD
SHOPPERS DRUG MART   p 760
See MARTIN, DENNIS M DRUGS INC

SHOPPERS DRUG MART   p 767
See KOLANDJIAN, A. PHARMACY LTD
SHOPPERS DRUG MART   p 768
See SHOPPERS DRUG MART CORPORATION
SHOPPERS DRUG MART   p 769
See CHIU, WALLY DRUGS LTD
SHOPPERS DRUG MART   p 770
See MUZYK, D.J. DRUGS LTD
SHOPPERS DRUG MART   p 770
See AHMAD, J DRUGS LTD
SHOPPERS DRUG MART   p 778
See A. JAFFER PHARMACY LTD
SHOPPERS DRUG MART   p 781
See MICHAEL S WONG PHARMACY LTD
SHOPPERS DRUG MART   p 788
See F D PHARMACY INC
SHOPPERS DRUG MART   p 794
See GGP DRUGS LTD
SHOPPERS DRUG MART   p 796
See CHEUNG, ARTHUR PHARMACY LIMITED
SHOPPERS DRUG MART   p 811
See TRIPLE A PHARMACY INC
SHOPPERS DRUG MART   p 812
See HENRY, KATHERINE PHARMACY INC
SHOPPERS DRUG MART   p 822
See SERVICES PHARMACEUTIQUES SOCJETI LTEE
SHOPPERS DRUG MART   p 822
See STEPHEN MACDONALD PHARMACY INC
SHOPPERS DRUG MART   p 824
See SURANI, B. DRUGS LTD
SHOPPERS DRUG MART   p 826
See TEE, FRANK PHARMACIES LTD
SHOPPERS DRUG MART   p 826
See HANNA, NABIL DRUGS LTD
SHOPPERS DRUG MART   p 829
See JALALDIN, NARMIN DRUGS LTD
SHOPPERS DRUG MART   p 831
See S.L. DEVISON PHARMACIES INC
SHOPPERS DRUG MART   p 843
1355 KINGSTON RD SUITE 618, PICKERING, ON, L1V 1B8
(905) 839-4488   SIC 5912
SHOPPERS DRUG MART   p 847
60 ONTARIO ST, PORT HOPE, ON, L1A 2T8
(905) 885-1294   SIC 5912
SHOPPERS DRUG MART   p 855
10660 YONGE ST, RICHMOND HILL, ON, L4C 3C9
(905) 884-5233   SIC 5912
SHOPPERS DRUG MART   p 855
See LEITNER, IRVING DRUGS LTD
SHOPPERS DRUG MART   p 860
See LAPORTE, MARCEL PHARMACY INC
SHOPPERS DRUG MART   p 860
See MCQUAID, S. PHARMACY LTD
SHOPPERS DRUG MART   p 865
See JAMAL, OME PHARMACY LTD
SHOPPERS DRUG MART   p 867
See IP, JERRY PHARMACY INC
SHOPPERS DRUG MART   p 884
See COSTINIUK, D PHARMACY LTD
SHOPPERS DRUG MART   p 889
See N WELCH PHARMACY SERVICES INC
SHOPPERS DRUG MART   p 894
See PVK DRUGS LIMITED
SHOPPERS DRUG MART   p 894
See RIBAK PHARMA LTD
SHOPPERS DRUG MART   p 896
See ROULSTON PHARMACY LTD
SHOPPERS DRUG MART   p 900
See BRISTOW, TERRY DRUGS LTD
SHOPPERS DRUG MART   p 905
See PATEL, SAMIR PHARMACY LTD
SHOPPERS DRUG MART   p 907
See 1548732 ONTARIO LIMITED
SHOPPERS DRUG MART   p 909
See ORCHARD, VALI PHARMACY INC
SHOPPERS DRUG MART   p 910

See KAPOOR, VINAY DRUGS LTD
SHOPPERS DRUG MART   p 911
See COTNAM, DAN DRUGS LTD
SHOPPERS DRUG MART   p 917
See MONTY PHARMACY LTD
SHOPPERS DRUG MART   p 917
See ST. PIERRE, BARRY PHARMACY LTD
SHOPPERS DRUG MART   p 917
See VANDENBURG, ROMEO DRUG COMPANY LTD
SHOPPERS DRUG MART   p 920
See CHEUNG, HARRY PHARMACIES LTD
SHOPPERS DRUG MART   p 923
See RIZWAN CHAMPSI PHARMACY INC
SHOPPERS DRUG MART   p 926
See REINGOLD, M. DRUGS LIMITED
SHOPPERS DRUG MART   p 931
See WANG, MAURICE DRUGS LTD
SHOPPERS DRUG MART   p 932
See PAR-S DRUGS LTD
SHOPPERS DRUG MART   p 933
See D.C. DRUGS LIMITED
SHOPPERS DRUG MART   p 936
See PAUL GOLDMAN DRUGS LTD
SHOPPERS DRUG MART   p 971
See A.D.H. DRUGS LIMITED
SHOPPERS DRUG MART   p 973
See NART DRUGS INC
SHOPPERS DRUG MART   p 976
See TAN, KENNY PHARMACY INC
SHOPPERS DRUG MART   p 984
See WEYLAND, LAURA PHARMACY LTD
SHOPPERS DRUG MART   p 995
See CHUNG, A. T. PHARMACY LIMITED
SHOPPERS DRUG MART   p 998
See A L NEILSON FAMILY PHARMACY LTD
SHOPPERS DRUG MART   p 1000
See DEREK K. HO PHARMACY LTD
SHOPPERS DRUG MART   p 1007
See V.A. HEALTH CARE INC
SHOPPERS DRUG MART   p 1009
See DN PHARMACY INC
SHOPPERS DRUG MART   p 1015
See SB PHARMACY SERVICES LTD
SHOPPERS DRUG MART   p 1017
See BABINEAU, D. DRUGS INC
SHOPPERS DRUG MART   p 1021
See GAUTHIER, VINCE R. DRUGS LTD
SHOPPERS DRUG MART   p 1026
See CRAIG, JAN DRUG STORE LTD
SHOPPERS DRUG MART   p 1035
See SILVERTHORNE PHARMACY LTD
SHOPPERS DRUG MART   p 1039
See K CRAWFORD PHARMACY INC
SHOPPERS DRUG MART   p 1413
See R & T PHARMACY LTD
SHOPPERS DRUG MART   p 1419
See ZABS PHARMACY LTD
SHOPPERS DRUG MART   p 1420
See CONPHARM LTD
SHOPPERS DRUG MART   p 1421
See GEO JACK ENTERPRISES INC
SHOPPERS DRUG MART   p 1424
See CHRISTINE'S HOLDINGS INC
SHOPPERS DRUG MART   p 1424
See SGS PHARMACY INC
SHOPPERS DRUG MART   p 1432
See MCKENZIE, C. PHARMACY INC
SHOPPERS DRUG MART   p 1440
See PASLOSKI, DARRELL PHARMACY LTD
SHOPPERS DRUG MART # 213   p 132
See KATES' PHARMACY LTD
SHOPPERS DRUG MART # 327   p 129
See PEDERSON FAMILY PHARMACY LTD
SHOPPERS DRUG MART # 930   p 1032
See PAGGOS, MARIO DRUGS LTD
SHOPPERS DRUG MART #1089   p 601
See ALAM DRUGS LIMITED
SHOPPERS DRUG MART #149   p 467
See HIGGINS FAMILY PHARMACY LTD
SHOPPERS DRUG MART #501   p 867
See LAU, REGINALD DRUGS LTD
SHOPPERS DRUG MART #919   p 775

See GREEN, ESTHER DRUGS LTD
SHOPPERS DRUG MART - CACHET CENTRE   p 679
See WONG, VICKY C.K. DRUGS LTD
SHOPPERS DRUG MART - GLEN ERIN PLAZA   p 728
See VARTEGEZ SIMONIAN PHARMACY LTD
SHOPPERS DRUG MART - HEART LAKE TOWN CENTRE   p 512
See SILVA, MANUEL J DRUGS LTD
SHOPPERS DRUG MART - PITT MEADOWS   p 244
See TSANG, A.J. PHARMACY LTD
SHOPPERS DRUG MART - YONGE & BIG BAY   p 488
See WIERSEMA, TRACY PHARMACY LTD
SHOPPERS DRUG MART 263   p 292
See 640039 BC LTD
SHOPPERS DRUG MART 545   p 358
See EPP'S PHARMACY LTD
SHOPPERS DRUG MART 669   p 862
See FILEK, STEVE DRUGS LIMITED
SHOPPERS DRUG MART 708   p 684
See SUBIR BAINS PHARMACY LTD
SHOPPERS DRUG MART 820   p 786
See KHETIA PHARMACY INC
SHOPPERS DRUG MART CORPORATION p 768
243 CONSUMERS RD, NORTH YORK, ON, M2J 4W8
(416) 493-1220   SIC 5912
SHOPPERS DRUG MART CORPORATION p 787
104 BARTLEY DR, NORTH YORK, ON, M4A 1C5
(416) 752-8885   SIC 5999
SHOPPERS DRUG MART INC   p 745
60 COURTNEYPARK DR W, MISSISSAUGA, ON, L5W 0B3
(416) 493-1220   SIC 6794
SHOPPERS DRUG MART NO. 333   p 161
See JIM BROWN PHARMACY LTD
SHOPPERS DRUG MART STORE   p 988
See DINOFF, S. DRUGS LIMITED
SHOPPERS HOME HEALTH CARE   p 907
See BARRA HOLDINGS INC
SHOPPERS HOME HEALTH CARE   p 908
See CROOKS, J R HEALTH CARE SERVICES INC
SHOPPERS HOME HEALTH CARE (CANADA) INC   p 768
243 CONSUMERS RD, NORTH YORK, ON, M2J 4W8
(416) 493-1220   SIC 5999
SHOPPERS HOME HEALTH CARE (ONTARIO) INC   p 787
104 BARTLEY DR, NORTH YORK, ON, M4A 1C5
(416) 752-8885   SIC 5999
SHOPPERS HOME HEALTHCARE   p 787
See SHOPPERS DRUG MART CORPORATION
SHOPPERS WHOLESALE FOOD COMPANY   p 251
1959 NICHOLSON ST S, PRINCE GEORGE, BC, V2N 2Z9
(250) 562-6655   SIC 5141
SHOPPERS WORLD BRAMPTON   p 511
See 1388688 ONTARIO LIMITED
SHOPPING WEB PLUS INC   p 1385
450 RUE DES ?RABLES, TROIS-RIVIERES, QC, G8T 5H9
SIC 7389
SHOPRITE STORES   p 248
See ROSBACK, R A ENTERPRISES LTD
SHOPSY'S DELI   p 943
See SHOPSY'S HOSPITALITY INC
SHOPSY'S HOSPITALITY INC   p 943
33 YONGE ST, TORONTO, ON, M5E 1G4

(905) 474-3333   *SIC 5812*
SHORE TO SEA SERVICES LLS   *p 309*
999 CANADA PL, VANCOUVER, BC, V6C 3C1
(604) 775-7200   *SIC 4491*
SHOREFAST SOCIAL ENTERPRISES INC*p* 425
181 MAIN ST, JOE BATTS ARM, NL, A0G 2X0
(709) 658-3444   *SIC 7011*
SHOREHAM VILLAGE HOME FOR SPE-CIAL CARE   *p* 442
See SHOREHAM VILLAGE SENIOR CITI-ZENS ASSOCIATION
SHOREHAM VILLAGE SENIOR CITIZENS ASSOCIATION   *p 442*
50 SHOREHAM VILLAGE CRES, CHESTER, NS, B0J 1J0
(902) 275-5631   *SIC 8322*
SHORELINE LUBE DISTRIBUTION INC   *p* 402
55 CH RAYMEL, GRAND-BARACHOIS, NB, E4P 7M7
(506) 577-4440   *SIC 5172*
SHOREWOOD CARTON CORPORATION LIMITED   *p 873*
44 ROLARK DR, SCARBOROUGH, ON, M1R 4G2
(416) 940-2436   *SIC 2657*
SHOREWOOD PACKAGING CORP. OF CANADA LIMITED   *p 872*
2220 MIDLAND AVE UNIT 50, SCARBOR-OUGH, ON, M1P 3E6
(416) 940-2400   *SIC 2657*
SHOULDICE DESIGNER STONE LTD *p 879*
281227 SHOULDICE BLOCK RD SUITE 281, SHALLOW LAKE, ON, N0H 2K0
(800) 265-3174   *SIC 3271*
SHOULDICE HOSPITAL LIMITED   *p 905*
7750 BAYVIEW AVE SUITE 370, THORN-HILL, ON, L3T 4A3
(905) 889-1125   *SIC 8069*
SHOULDICE SURGERY   *p 905*
See SHOULDICE HOSPITAL LIMITED
SHOW CANADA PRODUCTIONS   *p 1231*
See INDUSTRIES SHOW CANADA INC, LES
SHOW CASE RESTAURANT   *p 317*
See VANCOUVER MARRIOTT PINNACLE DOWNTOWN HOTEL
SHOWA CANADA INC   *p 879*
1 SHOWA CRT, SCHOMBERG, ON, L0G 1T0
(905) 939-0575   *SIC 3714*
SHOWA DENKO CARBONE CANADA INC*p* 1129
505 AV BETHANY BUREAU 202, LACHUTE, QC, J8H 4A6
(450) 409-0727   *SIC 3823*
SHOWCARE SOLUTIONS   *p 666*
See ARSYSTEMS INTERNATIONAL INC
SHOWCASE   *p 505*
See OSIRIS INC
SHRADER CANADA LIMITED   *p 805*
830 PROGRESS CRT, OAKVILLE, ON, L6L 6K1
(905) 847-0222   *SIC 2819*
SHRED-IT AMERICA INC   *p 801*
2794 SOUTH SHERIDAN WAY, OAKVILLE, ON, L6J 7T4
(905) 829-2794   *SIC 6794*
SHRED-IT INTERNATIONAL ULC   *p 799*
1383 NORTH SERVICE RD E, OAKVILLE, ON, L6H 1A7
(905) 829-2794   *SIC 7389*
SHRED-IT JV LP   *p 801*
2794 SOUTH SHERIDAN WAY, OAKVILLE, ON, L6J 7T4
(888) 750-6450   *SIC 7389*
SHRED-TECH CORPORATION   *p 536*
295 PINEBUSH RD, CAMBRIDGE, ON, N1T 1B2
(519) 621-3560   *SIC 3589*

SHUNDA CONSTRUCTION   *p 154*
See SHUNDA CONSULTING & CON-STRUCTION MANAGEMENT LTD
SHUNDA CONSULTING & CONSTRUC-TION MANAGEMENT LTD   *p* 154
6204 46 AVE, RED DEER, AB, T4N 7A2
(403) 347-6931   *SIC 1542*
SHUR LOK PRODUCTS   *p 1024*
See 792716 ONTARIO LTD
SHUR-GAIN   *p 602*
See TROUW NUTRITION CANADA INC
SHUR-GAIN   *p 1310*
See TROUW NUTRITION CANADA INC
SHYLO NURSING SERVICES LTD   *p 240*
1305 ST. GEORGES AVE, NORTH VAN-COUVER, BC, V7L 3J2
(604) 985-6881   *SIC 8049*
SI ALARMS LIMITED   *p 381*
1380 NOTRE DAME AVE UNIT 200, WIN-NIPEG, MB, R3E 0P7
(204) 231-1606   *SIC 6211*
SI MANUFACTURING   *p 756*
See SPECTRUM EDUCATIONAL SUP-PLIES LIMITED
SI VOUS PLAY SPORTS   *p 581*
See 1125151 ONTARIO LIMITED
SIA   *p 1140*
See ABRASIFS J.J.S. INC
SIB ENTERPRISES INC   *p 875*
393 NUGGET AVE, SCARBOROUGH, ON, M1S 4G3
(416) 292-7792   *SIC 5932*
SICARD HOLIDAY CAMPERS LIMITED   *p* 882
7526 REGIONAL ROAD 20, SMITHVILLE, ON, L0R 2A0
(905) 957-3344   *SIC 5561*
SICARD RV   *p 882*
See SICARD HOLIDAY CAMPERS LIM-ITED
SICK KIDS FOUNDATION   *p 945*
See HOSPITAL FOR SICK CHILDREN FOUNDATION INC, THE
SICK KIDS HOSPITAL   *p 945*
See HOSPITAL FOR SICK CHILDREN, THE
SICK LTD   *p 854*
2 EAST BEAVER CREEK RD UNIT 3, RICH-MOND HILL, ON, L4B 2N3
(905) 771-1444   *SIC 5084*
SICOM INDUSTRIES LTD   *p 230*
27385 GLOUCESTER WAY, LANGLEY, BC, V4W 3Z8
(604) 856-3455   *SIC 3599*
SID LEE INC   *p 1212*
75 RUE QUEEN BUREAU 1400, MON-TREAL, QC, H3C 2N6
(514) 282-2200   *SIC 7311*
SIDEL CANADA INC   *p 1238*
1045 CHOMEDEY (A-13) E, MONTREAL, QC, H7W 4V3
(450) 973-3337   *SIC 3535*
SIDENSE CORP   *p 625*
84 HINES RD SUITE 260, KANATA, ON, K2K 3G3
(613) 287-0292   *SIC 3674*
SIDNEY TIRE & AUTO SERVICE   *p 268*
See SIDNEY TIRE LTD
SIDNEY TIRE LTD   *p 268*
9817 RESTHAVEN DR, SIDNEY, BC, V8L 3E7
(250) 656-5544   *SIC 5531*
SIEGWERK CANADA INC   *p 506*
40 WESTWYN CRT, BRAMPTON, ON, L6T 4T5
SIC 2893
SIEGWERK INK PACKAGING   *p 506*
See SIEGWERK CANADA INC
SIEMENS CANADA LIMITED   *p 25*
1930 MAYNARD RD SE UNIT 24, CAL-GARY, AB, T2E 6J8
(403) 259-3404   *SIC 3679*
SIEMENS CANADA LIMITED

1930 MAYNARD RD SE UNIT 24, CAL-GARY, AB, T2E 6J8
(403) 259-3404   *SIC 7382*
SIEMENS CANADA LIMITED   *p 25*
1930 MAYNARD RD SE UNIT 24, CAL-GARY, AB, T2E 6J8
(403) 259-3404   *SIC 1711*
SIEMENS CANADA LIMITED   *p 111*
6652 50 ST NW, EDMONTON, AB, T6B 2N7
(780) 450-6762   *SIC 8742*
SIEMENS CANADA LIMITED   *p 524*
1550 APPLEBY LINE, BURLINGTON, ON, L7L 6X7
(905) 319-3600   *SIC 3625*
SIEMENS CANADA LIMITED   *p 558*
300 APPLEWOOD CRES SUITE 1, CON-CORD, ON, L4K 5C7
(905) 856-5288   *SIC 3625*
SIEMENS CANADA LIMITED   *p 743*
6375 SHAWSON DR, MISSISSAUGA, ON, L5T 1S7
(905) 212-4500   *SIC 8742*
SIEMENS CANADA LIMITED   *p 799*
1577 NORTH SERVICE RD E, OAKVILLE, ON, L6H 0H6
(905) 465-8000   *SIC 3625*
SIEMENS CANADA LIMITED   *p 827*
2435 HOLLY LANE, OTTAWA, ON, K1V 7P2
(613) 733-9781   *SIC 1711*
SIEMENS CANADA LIMITED   *p 842*
1954 TECHNOLOGY DR, PETERBOR-OUGH, ON, K9J 6X7
(705) 745-2431   *SIC 3823*
SIEMENS CANADA LIMITED   *p 905*
55 COMMERCE VALLEY DR W SUITE 400, THORNHILL, ON, L3T 7V9
SIC 7371
SIEMENS CANADA LIMITED   *p 1095*
1425 RTE TRANSCANADIENNE UNITE 400, DORVAL, QC, H9P 2W9
SIC 3625
SIEMENS CANADA LIMITED   *p 1095*
9505 CH COTE-DE-LIESSE BUREAU 9501, DORVAL, QC, H9P 2N9
(514) 828-3400   *SIC 3625*
SIEMENS CANADA LIMITED   *p 1171*
8455 19E AV, MONTREAL, QC, H1Z 4J2
SIC 5063
SIEMENS CANADA LIMITED   *p 1171*
8455 19E AV, MONTREAL, QC, H1Z 4J2
SIC 5999
SIEMENS CANADA LIMITED   *p 1277*
2800 AV SAINT-JEAN-BAPTISTE BUREAU 190, QUEBEC, QC, G2E 6J5
(418) 687-4524   *SIC 3625*
SIEMENS CONSTRUCTION INC   *p 83*
GD, EDBERG, AB, T0B 1J0
(780) 877-2478   *SIC 1542*
SIEMENS FINANCIAL LTD   *p 525*
1550 APPLEBY LINE, BURLINGTON, ON, L7L 6X7
(905) 315-6868   *SIC 6153*
SIEMENS GAMESA RENEWABLE EN-ERGY LIMITED   *p* 799
1577 NORTH SERVICE RD E 4TH FL, OAKVILLE, ON, L6H 0H6
(905) 465-8000   *SIC 3511*
SIEMENS HEALTHCARE DIAGNOSTICS LTD   *p 799*
1577 NORTH SERVICE RD E 2FL, OAKVILLE, ON, L6H 0H6
(905) 564-7333   *SIC 3841*
SIEMENS IT SOLUTIONS AND SERVICES*p* 743
See SIEMENS CANADA LIMITED
SIEMENS MILLTRONICS PROCESS IN-STRUMENTS   *p* 842
See SIEMENS CANADA LIMITED
SIEMENS NETWORK OF CARING   *p 799*
See SIEMENS CANADA LIMITED
SIEMENS PROTECTION INCENDIE   *p 1171*
See SIEMENS CANADA LIMITED

SIEMENS TANGO SOFTWARE   *p 905*
See SIEMENS CANADA LIMITED
SIEMENS TECHNOLOGIES DU BATIMENT   *p 1171*
See SIEMENS CANADA LIMITED
SIEMENS, VERNON CONSTRUCTION INC   *p 83*
GD, EDBERG, AB, T0B 1J0
(780) 877-2478   *SIC 1542*
SIENNA SENIOR LIVING INC   *p 675*
302 TOWN CENTRE BLVD SUITE 300, MARKHAM, ON, L3R 0E8
(905) 477-4006   *SIC 8361*
SIERA YNG CAPITAL   *p 1196*
See GESTION SIERA CAPITAL INC
SIERRA CONSTRUCTION (WOODSTOCK) LIMITED   *p 1035*
1401 DUNDAS ST, WOODSTOCK, ON, N4S 7V9
(519) 421-9689   *SIC 1542*
SIERRA CUSTOM FOODS INC   *p 506*
275 WALKER DR, BRAMPTON, ON, L6T 3W5
(905) 595-2260   *SIC 0254*
SIERRA MESSENGER & COURIER   *p 370*
See SIERRA MESSENGER & COURIER SERVICE LTD
SIERRA MESSENGER & COURIER SER-VICE LTD   *p* 370
165 RYAN ST, WINNIPEG, MB, R2R 0N9
(204) 632-8920   *SIC 7389*
SIERRA METALS INC   *p 966*
161 BAY ST SUITE 4260, TORONTO, ON, M5J 2S1
(416) 366-7777   *SIC 1021*
SIERRA ONCOLOGY, INC   *p 309*
885 WEST GEORGIA ST SUITE 2150, VANCOUVER, BC, V6C 3E8
(604) 558-6536   *SIC 8731*
SIERRA SYSTEMS   *p 957*
See SIERRA SYSTEMS GROUP INC
SIERRA SYSTEMS GROUP INC   *p 91*
10104 103 AVE NW UNIT 1300, EDMON-TON, AB, T5J 0H8
(780) 424-0852   *SIC 7379*
SIERRA SYSTEMS GROUP INC   *p 316*
1177 HASTINGS ST W SUITE 2500, VAN-COUVER, BC, V6E 2K3
(604) 688-1371   *SIC 7379*
SIERRA SYSTEMS GROUP INC   *p 337*
737 COURTNEY ST, VICTORIA, BC, V8W 1C3
(250) 385-1535   *SIC 7379*
SIERRA SYSTEMS GROUP INC   *p 824*
220 LAURIER AVE W SUITE 800, OTTAWA, ON, K1P 5Z9
(613) 236-7888   *SIC 7379*
SIERRA SYSTEMS GROUP INC   *p 957*
150 YORK ST SUITE 1910, TORONTO, ON, M5H 3S5
(416) 777-1212   *SIC 7379*
SIERRA VENTURES CORP   *p 1419*
1810 COLLEGE AVE, REGINA, SK, S4P 1C1
(306) 949-1510   *SIC 7349*
SIERRA WIRELESS, INC   *p 256*
13811 WIRELESS WAY, RICHMOND, BC, V6V 3A4
(604) 231-1100   *SIC 4899*
SIFTO SALT, DIV OF   *p 597*
See COMPASS MINERALS CANADA CORP
SIFTON PROPERTIES LIMITED   *p 660*
1295 RIVERBEND RD SUITE 300, LON-DON, ON, N6K 0G2
(519) 434-1000   *SIC 6553*
SIFTON PROPERTIES LIMITED   *p 660*
600 LONGWORTH RD SUITE 118, LON-DON, ON, N6K 4X9
(519) 472-1115   *SIC 6513*
SIFTON PROPERTIES LIMITED   *p 715*
2132 DUNDAS ST W, MISSISSAUGA, ON, L5K 2K7

▲ Public Company   ■ Public Company Family Member   **HQ** Headquarters   **BR** Branch   **SL** Single Location

(905) 823-7273   *SIC* 8059
SIGA INTERNATIONAL   *p* 784
81 SAINT REGIS CRES S, NORTH YORK, ON, M3J 1Y6
(416) 504-7442   *SIC* 5136
SIGAN INDUSTRIES INC   *p* 506
296 ORENDA RD, BRAMPTON, ON, L6T 4X6
(905) 456-8888   *SIC* 2844
SIGFUSSON NORTHERN LTD   *p* 351
50 SWAN CREEK DR, LUNDAR, MB, R0C 1Y0
(204) 762-5500   *SIC* 1629
SIGMA   *p* 689
See SIGMA CONVECTOR ENCLOSURE CORP
SIGMA ANALYTICS   *p* 1418
See HJ LINNEN ASSOCIATES
SIGMA ASSISTEL INC   *p* 1208
1100 BOUL RENE-LEVESQUE O BUREAU 514, MONTREAL, QC, H3B 4N4
(514) 875-9170   *SIC* 7389
SIGMA BUSINESS SOLUTIONS INC *p* 966
55 YORK ST SUITE 900, TORONTO, ON, M5J 1R7
(416) 368-2000   *SIC* 7371
SIGMA CONVECTOR ENCLOSURE CORP
p 689
3325A ORLANDO DR, MISSISSAUGA, ON, L4V 1C5
(905) 670-3200   *SIC* 3567
SIGMA INDUSTRIES INC   *p* 1300
55 RTE 271 S, SAINT-EPHREM-DE-BEAUCE, QC, G0M 1R0
(418) 484-5282   *SIC* 3089
SIGMA MOULDERS   *p* 865
150 MCLEVIN AVE, SCARBOROUGH, ON, M1B 4Z7
(416) 297-0088   *SIC* 3089
SIGMA SOFTWARE SOLUTIONS INC *p* 966
55 YORK ST SUITE 1100, TORONTO, ON, M5J 1R7
(416) 368-2000   *SIC* 7371
SIGMA SYSTEMS GROUP INC   *p* 966
55 YORK ST SUITE 1100, TORONTO, ON, M5J 1R7
(416) 943-9696   *SIC* 7371
SIGMA-ALDRICH CANADA CO.   *p* 799
2149 WINSTON PARK DR, OAKVILLE, ON, L6H 6J8
(905) 829-9500   *SIC* 5169
SIGMAPAC ENGINEERED SERVICES INC *p* 865
71 MELFORD DR UNIT 1, SCARBOROUGH, ON, M1B 2G6
(866) 805-4256   *SIC* 7389
SIGMAPOINT TECHNOLOGIES INC   *p* 562
2880 MARLEAU AVE, CORNWALL, ON, K6H 6B5
(613) 937-4462   *SIC* 3672
SIGN   *p* 1439
See SOCIETY FOR THE INVOLVEMENT OF GOOD NEIGHBOURS
SIGNA + INC   *p* 1235
975 RUE BERGAR, MONTREAL, QC, H7L 4Z6
(450) 668-0047   *SIC* 7389
SIGNAL HILL EQUITY PARTNERS INC *p* 936
2 CARLTON ST SUITE 1700, TORONTO, ON, M5B 1J3
(416) 847-1502   *SIC* 2434
SIGNALISATION COMO INC   *p* 1345
4325 RUE J.-B.-MARTINEAU, SAINT-LEONARD, QC, H1R 3W9
(514) 327-2875   *SIC* 7359
SIGNALISATION DE L'ESTRIE INC   *p* 1374
520 RUE PEPIN, SHERBROOKE, QC, J1L 2Y8
(819) 822-3828   *SIC* 7359
SIGNALISATION DE MONTREAL INC   *p* 1126
15 BOUL SAINT-JOSEPH, LACHINE, QC, H8S 2K9

(514) 821-7668   *SIC* 0722
SIGNALISATION DES CANTONS INC   *p* 1376
1001 CH DION, SHERBROOKE, QC, J1R 0R8
(819) 987-1483   *SIC* 5149
SIGNALISATION JP INC   *p* 1356
1980 RUE LAURIER, SAINTE-CATHERINE, QC, J5C 1B8
(450) 845-3461   *SIC* 5099
SIGNALISATION SIGNA PRO INC   *p* 1348
700 MONTEE MONETTE, SAINT-MATHIEU-DE-LAPRAIRIE, QC, J0L 2H0
(450) 444-0006   *SIC* 5063
SIGNALISATION VER-MAC INC   *p* 1278
1781 RUE BRESSE, QUEBEC, QC, G2G 2V2
(418) 654-1303   *SIC* 3669
SIGNALTA   *p* 52
See J R & S HOLDINGS LTD
SIGNALTA RESOURCES LIMITED   *p* 59
840 6 AVE SW SUITE 700, CALGARY, AB, T2P 3E5
(403) 265-5091   *SIC* 1311
SIGNATURE   *p* 1402
See 2161-1298 QUEBEC INC
SIGNATURE ALUMINUM CANADA INC   *p* 845
1850 CLEMENTS RD, PICKERING, ON, L1W 3R8
(905) 427-6550   *SIC* 3354
SIGNATURE INTERPRETIVE & TRANSLATIVE SERVICES LTD   *p* 9
4608 26 AVE NE, CALGARY, AB, T1Y 2R8
(403) 590-6382   *SIC* 7389
SIGNATURE MAURICE TANGUAY   *p* 1276
See AMEUBLEMENTS TANGUAY INC
SIGNATURE MUSHROOMS LTD   *p* 4
52557 RANGE ROAD 215, ARDROSSAN, AB, T8E 2H6
(780) 922-2535   *SIC* 0191
SIGNATURE SERVICE D'ENTRETIEN   *p* 1172
See 157971 CANADA INC
SIGNATURE SERVICE GMAC REAL ESTATE   *p* 707
186 ROBERT SPECK PKY, MISSISSAUGA, ON, L4Z 3G1
(905) 896-4622   *SIC* 6531
SIGNATURE SHOWCASE DIV   *p* 560
See UNIQUE STORE FIXTURES LTD
SIGNATURE SUR LE SAINT-LAURENT CONSTRUCTION S.E.N.C.   *p* 1396
8 PLACE DU COMMERCE UNITE 300, VERDUN, QC, H3E 1N3
(514) 876-1020   *SIC* 8742
SIGNATURE TEXTILE PAR VAL-ABEL   *p* 1337
See 2960-2778 QUEBEC INC
SIGNATURE VACATIONS   *p* 588
See SUNWING VACATIONS INC
SIGNATURES CRAFT SHOWS   *p* 920
See SIGNATURES CRAFT SHOWS LTD
SIGNATURES CRAFT SHOWS LTD   *p* 920
37 LANGLEY AVE, TORONTO, ON, M4K 1B4
(416) 465-8055   *SIC* 7389
SIGNCORP   *p* 206
See NATIONAL SIGNCORP INVESTMENTS LTD
SIGNE GARNEAU   *p* 1399
See SIGNE GARNEAU PAYSAGISTE INC
SIGNE GARNEAU PAYSAGISTE INC *p* 1399
29 BOUL ARTHABASKA E, VICTORIAVILLE, QC, G6T 0S5
(819) 758-3887   *SIC* 5992
SIGNEL SERVICES INC   *p* 1348
700 MONTEE MONETTE, SAINT-MATHIEU-DE-LAPRAIRIE, QC, J0L 2H0
(450) 444-0006   *SIC* 3993
SIGNIFY   *p* 679
See SIGNIFY CANADA LTD

SIGNIFY CANADA LTD   *p* 562
525 EDUCATION RD, CORNWALL, ON, K6H 6C7
SIC 3641
SIGNIFY CANADA LTD   *p* 679
281 HILLMOUNT RD, MARKHAM, ON, L6C 2S3
(905) 927-4900   *SIC* 3646
SIGNIFY CANADA LTD   *p* 1061
640 BOUL DU CURE-BOIVIN, BOIS-BRIAND, QC, J7G 2A7
(450) 430-7040   *SIC* 3646
SIGNIFY CANADA LTD   *p* 1129
3015 RUE LOUIS-A.-AMOS, LACHINE, QC, H8T 1C4
(514) 636-0670   *SIC* 3646
SIGNODE CANADA   *p* 675
See SIGNODE PACKAGING GROUP CANADA ULC
SIGNODE PACKAGING GROUP CANADA ULC   *p* 675
241 GOUGH RD, MARKHAM, ON, L3R 5B3
(905) 479-9754   *SIC* 2673
SIGVARIS CORPORATION   *p* 1158
8423 CH DALTON, MONT-ROYAL, QC, H4T 1V5
(514) 336-2362   *SIC* 5047
SIKA CANADA INC   *p* 106
16910 129 AVE NW SUITE 1, EDMONTON, AB, T5V 1L1
(780) 453-3060   *SIC* 2891
SIKA CANADA INC   *p* 1252
601 AV DELMAR, POINTE-CLAIRE, QC, H9R 4A9
(514) 697-2610   *SIC* 2891
SIKA SARNAFIL   *p* 1252
See SIKA CANADA INC
SIKSIKA BOARD OF EDUCATION   *p* 163
PO BOX 1099, SIKSIKA, AB, T0J 3W0
(403) 734-5400   *SIC* 8211
SIL INDUSTRIAL MINERALS   *p* 124
See 543077 ALBERTA LTD
SILANI SWEET CHEESE LIMITED   *p* 879
4205 2ND LINE, SCHOMBERG, ON, L0G 1T0
(416) 324-3290   *SIC* 2022
SILANI SWEET CHEESE LIMITED   *p* 1033
661 CHRISLEA RD UNIT 14, WOODBRIDGE, ON, L4L 0C4
(905) 792-3811   *SIC* 2022
SILCOTECH NORTH AMERICA INC   *p* 495
54 NIXON RD, BOLTON, ON, L7E 1W2
(905) 857-9998   *SIC* 2821
SILENCIEUX FEDERAL MUFFLER   *p* 1126
See 2747-6035 QUEBEC INC
SILENT AIRE MANUFACTURING INC *p* 123
7107 8 ST NW, EDMONTON, AB, T6P 1T9
(780) 456-1061   *SIC* 3585
SILENT-AIRE LIMITED PARTNERSHIP *p* 123
7107 8 ST NW, EDMONTON, AB, T6P 1T9
(780) 456-1061   *SIC* 3585
SILEX INNOVATIONS INC   *p* 743
6659 ORDAN DR, MISSISSAUGA, ON, L5T 1K6
(905) 612-4000   *SIC* 3567
SILFAB ONTARIO   *p* 743
See SILFAB SOLAR INC
SILFAB SOLAR INC   *p* 743
240 COURTNEYPARK DR E, MISSISSAUGA, ON, L5T 2S5
(905) 255-2501   *SIC* 3674
SILGAN PLASTICS CANADA INC   *p* 736
1575 DREW RD, MISSISSAUGA, ON, L5S 1S5
(905) 677-2324   *SIC* 3089
SILGAN PLASTICS CANADA INC   *p* 872
1200 ELLESMERE RD, SCARBOROUGH, ON, M1P 2X4
(416) 293-8233   *SIC* 3089
SILGAN PLASTICS CANADA INC   *p* 1033
400 ROWNTREE DAIRY RD, WOODBRIDGE, ON, L4L 8H2
(416) 746-8300   *SIC* 3089

SILHOUET-TONE CORPORATION   *p* 1235
1985 RUE MONTEREY, MONTREAL, QC, H7L 3T6
(450) 688-0123   *SIC* 3999
SILICA SERVING CHEMISTRY   *p* 1268
See SILICYCLE INC
SILICIUM BECANCOUR   *p* 1056
See SILICIUM QUEBEC SOCIETE EN COMMANDITE
SILICIUM BECANCOUR INC   *p* 1056
6500 RUE YVON-TRUDEAU, BECANCOUR, QC, G9H 2V8
(819) 294-6000   *SIC* 3674
SILICIUM QUEBEC SOCIETE EN COMMANDITE   *p* 1056
6500 RUE YVON-TRUDEAU, BECANCOUR, QC, G9H 2V8
(819) 294-6000   *SIC* 3674
SILICYCLE INC   *p* 1268
2500 BOUL DU PARC-TECHNOLOGIQUE, QUEBEC, QC, G1P 4S6
(418) 874-0054   *SIC* 2819
SILK HOLIDAYS INC   *p* 293
4012 CAMBIE ST, VANCOUVER, BC, V5Z 2X8
SIC 4724
SILKWAY TRAVEL & CRUISE   *p* 293
See SILKWAY TRAVEL & DESTINATION MANAGEMENT INC
SILKWAY TRAVEL & DESTINATION MANAGEMENT INC   *p* 293
4018 CAMBIE ST SUITE 4012, VANCOUVER, BC, V5Z 2X8
SIC 4725
SILLIKER CANADA CO   *p* 675
90 GOUGH RD UNIT 4, MARKHAM, ON, L3R 5V5
(905) 479-5255   *SIC* 8734
SILLIKER JR LABORATORIES, ULC *p* 193
3871 NORTH FRASER WAY UNIT 12, BURNABY, BC, V5J 5G6
(604) 432-9311   *SIC* 8734
SILO SUPERIEUR (1993) INC   *p* 1138
520 2E AV, LEVIS, QC, G6W 5M6
(418) 839-8808   *SIC* 3272
SILONEX INC   *p* 1324
2150 RUE WARD, SAINT-LAURENT, QC, H4M 1T7
SIC 3674
SILTECH CORPORATION   *p* 919
225 WICKSTEED AVE, TORONTO, ON, M4H 1G5
(416) 424-4567   *SIC* 2869
SILVA, MANUEL J DRUGS LTD   *p* 512
180 SANDALWOOD PKY E, BRAMPTON, ON, L6Z 1Y4
(905) 846-4700   *SIC* 5912
SILVACOM LTD   *p* 116
3912 91 ST NW, EDMONTON, AB, T6E 5K7
(780) 462-3238   *SIC* 8741
SILVANO COLOR LABORATORIES LIMITED   *p* 994
355 WESTON RD, TORONTO, ON, M6N 4Y7
SIC 7384
SILVER AUTOMOTIVE   *p* 140
See 612337 ALBERTA LTD.
SILVER AUTOMOTIVE   *p* 141
See SILVER AUTOMOTIVE (LETHBRIDGE) LTD
SILVER AUTOMOTIVE (LETHBRIDGE) LTD   *p* 141
3042 2 AVE N, LETHBRIDGE, AB, T1H 0C6
(403) 328-9621   *SIC* 5013
SILVER CONCRETE LTD   *p* 6
4901 50 AVE, BONNYVILLE, AB, T9N 2J2
(780) 826-5797   *SIC* 1799
SILVER CREEK PUBLIC SCHOOL   *p* 593
See HALTON DISTRICT SCHOOL BOARD
SILVER CROSS   *p* 1342
See CORPORATION SAVARIA

SILVER CROSS AUTOMOTIVE INC *p* 588
14 GOODMARK PL, ETOBICOKE, ON, M9W 6R1
(905) 799-5533 *SIC* 5511

SILVER HILLS BAKERY *p* 175
See VIBRANT HEALTH PRODUCTS INC

SILVER HOTEL (AMBLER) INC *p* 727
2501 ARGENTIA RD, MISSISSAUGA, ON, L5N 4G8
(905) 858-2424 *SIC* 7011

SILVER JEANS CO, DIV OF *p* 373
See WESTERN GLOVE WORKS

SILVER LAKES GOLF & COUNTRY CLUB INC *p* 756
21114 YONGE ST, NEWMARKET, ON, L3Y 4V8
(905) 836-8070 *SIC* 7997

SILVER PACIFIC INVESTMENTS INC *p* 208
7337 120 ST SUITE 245, DELTA, BC, V4C 6P5
(604) 588-0227 *SIC* 4731

SILVER RIDGE MOTOR PRODUCTS LTD *p* 143
3524 2 AVE S, LETHBRIDGE, AB, T1J 4T9
(403) 329-6888 *SIC* 5511

SILVER STAR *p* 1227
See AUTOMOBILES SILVER STAR (MONTREAL) INC

SILVER STAR AUTO MB INC *p* 271
15508 104 AVE, SURREY, BC, V3R 1N8
(604) 581-7806 *SIC* 5511

SILVER STAR MANUFACTURING CO INC *p* 1241
750 BOUL CURE-LABELLE BUREAU 205, MONTREAL-OUEST, QC, H7V 2T9
(450) 682-3381 *SIC* 3911

SILVER STAR MERCEDES-BENZ *p* 271
See SILVER STAR AUTO MB INC

SILVERADO LAND CORP *p* 203
399 CLUBHOUSE DR, COURTENAY, BC, V9N 9G3
(250) 897-0233 *SIC* 6553

SILVERBIRCH HOTELS AND RESORTS LIMITED PARTNERSHIP *p* 316
1188 GEORGIA ST W UNIT 1640, VANCOUVER, BC, V6E 4A2
(604) 646-2447 *SIC* 8742

SILVERBIRCH NO. 15 OPERATIONS LIMITED PARTNERSHIP *p* 454
1960 BRUNSWICK ST, HALIFAX, NS, B3J 2G7
(902) 422-1391 *SIC* 7299

SILVERBIRCH NO. 38 OPERATIONS LIMITED PARTNERSHIP *p* 119
4440 GATEWAY BLVD NW, EDMONTON, AB, T6H 5C2
(780) 437-6010 *SIC* 7011

SILVERBIRCH NO. 4 OPERATIONS LIMITED PARTNERSHIP *p* 25
2120 16 AVE NE, CALGARY, AB, T2E 1L4
(403) 291-4666 *SIC* 7011

SILVERBIRCH NO. 41 OPERATIONS LIMITED PARTNERSHIP *p* 285
2205 COMMISSIONER ST, VANCOUVER, BC, V5L 1A4
SIC 5812

SILVERCITY GLOUCESTER *p* 596
See CINEPLEX ODEON CORPORATION

SILVERCITY POLO PARK *p* 382
See CINEPLEX ODEON CORPORATION

SILVERCORP METALS INC *p* 309
200 GRANVILLE ST SUITE 1378, VANCOUVER, BC, V6C 1S4
(604) 669-9397 *SIC* 1044

SILVERHILL ACURA *p* 37
See SILVERHILL MOTORS LTD

SILVERHILL MOTORS LTD *p* 37
5728 MACLEOD TRAIL SW, CALGARY, AB, T2H 0J6
(403) 253-6060 *SIC* 5511

SILVERSTEIN'S BAKERY LIMITED *p* 977
195 MCCAUL ST, TORONTO, ON, M5T 1W6
(416) 598-3478 *SIC* 2051

SILVERSTEIN'S HOLDINGS INC *p* 977
195 MCCAUL ST, TORONTO, ON, M5T 1W6
(416) 598-3478 *SIC* 2051

SILVERT'S STORE *p* 556
See MILOMA INVESTMENTS LTD

SILVERTHORNE PHARMACY LTD *p* 1035
959 DUNDAS ST SUITE 1, WOODSTOCK, ON, N4S 1H2
(519) 537-2042 *SIC* 5912

SILVERTIP SECURITY LTD *p* 248
7100 ALBERNI ST SUITE 24, POWELL RIVER, BC, V8A 5K9
SIC 6211

SILVERWOOD MOTOR PRODUCTS LTD *p* 144
5103 25 ST, LLOYDMINSTER, AB, T9V 3G2
(780) 870-5166 *SIC* 5511

SILVERWOOD TOYOTA *p* 144
See SILVERWOOD MOTOR PRODUCTS LTD

SIM BUSINESS FURNITURE *p* 820
See SHADDY INTERNATIONAL MARKETING LTD

SIM DIGITAL *p* 992
See SIM VIDEO INTERNATIONAL INC

SIM VIDEO INTERNATIONAL INC *p* 992
1 ATLANTIC AVE SUITE 110, TORONTO, ON, M6K 3E7
(416) 979-9958 *SIC* 7359

SIM'S FURNITURE LIMITED *p* 157
2811 BREMNER AVE UNIT A, RED DEER, AB, T4R 1P7
(403) 342-7467 *SIC* 5712

SIMARD WESTLINK INC *p* 258
16062 PORTSIDE RD, RICHMOND, BC, V6W 1M1
(604) 231-8756 *SIC* 4731

SIMARD-BEAUDRY CONSTRUCTION INC *p* 1232
4230 RANG SAINT-ELZEAR E, MONTREAL, QC, H7E 4P2
(450) 664-5700 *SIC* 1622

SIMARD-BEAUDRY CONSTRUCTION INC *p* 1302
699 BOUL INDUSTRIEL, SAINT-EUSTACHE, QC, J7R 6C3
SIC 1442

SIMARIL INC *p* 373
321 MCDERMOT AVE SUITE 402, WINNIPEG, MB, R3A 0A3
(204) 788-4366 *SIC* 8611

SIMARK CONTROLS LTD *p* 18
10509 46 ST SE, CALGARY, AB, T2C 5C2
(403) 236-0580 *SIC* 5084

SIMBA TECHNOLOGIES INCORPORATED *p* 293
938 8TH AVE W, VANCOUVER, BC, V5Z 1E5
(604) 633-0008 *SIC* 7371

SIMBAS LIMITED *p* 947
330 UNIVERSITY AVE SUITE 504, TORONTO, ON, M5G 1R7
(416) 595-1155 *SIC* 8111

SIMBROW, JEFFREY ASSOCIATES *p* 779
See INVENTIV CANADA ULC

SIMCOE BLOCK (1979) LIMITED *p* 488
140 FERNDALE DR N, BARRIE, ON, L4N 9W1
(705) 728-1773 *SIC* 3271

SIMCOE BUILDING CENTRE *p* 488
See SIMCOE BLOCK (1979) LIMITED

SIMCOE COMPOSITE SCHOOL *p* 880
See GRAND ERIE DISTRICT SCHOOL BOARD

SIMCOE COUNTY AIRPORT SERVICES *p* 486
See ALLANDALE SCHOOL TRANSIT LIMITED

SIMCOE COUNTY CLEANING LIMITED *p* 488
49 MORROW RD UNIT 14, BARRIE, ON,

L4N 3V7
(705) 722-7203 *SIC* 7349

SIMCOE COUNTY DISTRICT SCHOOL BOARD, THE *p* 476
203 VICTORIA ST E, ALLISTON, ON, L9R 1G5
(705) 435-6288 *SIC* 8211

SIMCOE COUNTY DISTRICT SCHOOL BOARD, THE *p* 485
421 GROVE ST E, BARRIE, ON, L4M 5S1
(705) 728-1321 *SIC* 8211

SIMCOE COUNTY DISTRICT SCHOOL BOARD, THE *p* 485
110 GROVE ST E, BARRIE, ON, L4M 2P3
(705) 726-6541 *SIC* 8211

SIMCOE COUNTY DISTRICT SCHOOL BOARD, THE *p* 488
125 DUNLOP ST W, BARRIE, ON, L4N 1A9
SIC 8211

SIMCOE COUNTY DISTRICT SCHOOL BOARD, THE *p* 497
70 PROFESSOR DAY DR, BRADFORD, ON, L3Z 3B9
(905) 775-2262 *SIC* 8211

SIMCOE COUNTY DISTRICT SCHOOL BOARD, THE *p* 547
6 CAMERON ST, COLLINGWOOD, ON, L9Y 2J2
(705) 445-3161 *SIC* 8211

SIMCOE COUNTY DISTRICT SCHOOL BOARD, THE *p* 681
1170 HWY 26, MIDHURST, ON, L0L 1X0
(705) 734-6363 *SIC* 8211

SIMCOE COUNTY DISTRICT SCHOOL BOARD, THE *p* 682
865 HUGEL AVE, MIDLAND, ON, L4R 1X8
(705) 526-7817 *SIC* 8211

SIMCOE COUNTY DISTRICT SCHOOL BOARD, THE *p* 810
2 BORLAND ST E, ORILLIA, ON, L3V 2B4
(705) 728-7570 *SIC* 8211

SIMCOE COUNTY DISTRICT SCHOOL BOARD, THE *p* 810
233 PARK ST, ORILLIA, ON, L3V 5W1
SIC 8211

SIMCOE COUNTY DISTRICT SCHOOL BOARD, THE *p* 810
381 BIRCH ST, ORILLIA, ON, L3V 2P5
(705) 325-1318 *SIC* 8211

SIMCOE ENERGY & TECHNICAL SERVICES INC *p* 497
285 DISSETTE ST, BRADFORD, ON, L3Z 3G9
(905) 778-8105 *SIC* 5984

SIMCOE ESTATES LTD *p* 855
24 TANNERY CRT, RICHMOND HILL, ON, L4C 7V4
(705) 259-1344 *SIC* 1521

SIMCOE MANOR HOME FOR THE AGED *p* 490
5988 8TH LINE, BEETON, ON, L0G 1A0
(905) 729-2267 *SIC* 8361

SIMCOE MUSKOKA CATHOLIC DISTRICT SCHOOL BOARD *p* 485
243 CUNDLES RD E, BARRIE, ON, L4M 6L1
(705) 728-3120 *SIC* 8211

SIMCOE MUSKOKA CATHOLIC DISTRICT SCHOOL BOARD *p* 485
46 ALLIANCE BLVD, BARRIE, ON, L4M 5K3
(705) 722-3555 *SIC* 8211

SIMCOE MUSKOKA CATHOLIC DISTRICT SCHOOL BOARD *p* 488
201 ASHFORD DR, BARRIE, ON, L4N 6A3
(705) 734-0168 *SIC* 8211

SIMCOE MUSKOKA CATHOLIC DISTRICT SCHOOL BOARD *p* 998
2 NOLAN RD, TOTTENHAM, ON, L0G 1W0
(905) 936-4743 *SIC* 8211

SIMCOE MUSKOKA CATHOLIC DISTRICT SCHOOL BOARD SECONDARY SCHOOLS ST JOAN OF ARC *p* 488
See ST. JOAN OF ARC CATHOLIC HIGH SCHOOL

SIMCOE MUSKOKA CHILD, YOUTH AND FAMILY SERVICES *p* 485
60 BELL FARM RD SUITE 7, BARRIE, ON, L4M 5G6
(800) 461-4236 *SIC* 8699

SIMCOE MUSKOKA DISTRICT HEALTH UNIT *p* 485
15 SPERLING DR, BARRIE, ON, L4M 6K9
(705) 721-7520 *SIC* 8011

SIMCOE MUSKOKA FAMILY CONNEXIONS *p* 485
See SIMCOE MUSKOKA CHILD, YOUTH AND FAMILY SERVICES

SIMCOE PARTS SERVICE INC *p* 476
6795 INDUSTRIAL PKY, ALLISTON, ON, L9R 1V4
(705) 435-7814 *SIC* 5013

SIMCONA ELECTRONICS OF CANADA INC *p* 660
3422 WONDERLAND RD S, LONDON, ON, N6L 1A7
(519) 652-1130 *SIC* 5065

SIMDAR INC *p* 1291
500 CH DU LAC-A-L'EAU-CLAIRE, SAINT-ALEXIS-DES-MONTS, QC, J0K 1V0
(819) 265-3185 *SIC* 7011

SIMERRA PROPERTY MANAGEMENT INC *p* 588
89 SKYWAY AVE SUITE 200, ETOBICOKE, ON, M9W 6R4
(416) 293-5900 *SIC* 8741

SIMEX DEFENCE INC *p* 1252
216 BOUL BRUNSWICK, POINTE-CLAIRE, QC, H9R 1A6
(514) 697-7655 *SIC* 5088

SIMEX INC *p* 934
600-210 KING ST E, TORONTO, ON, M5A 1J7
(416) 597-1585 *SIC* 3571

SIMEX-IWERKS ENTERTAINMENT *p* 934
See SIMEX INC

SIMLUC CONTRACTORS LIMITED *p* 816
2550 BLACKWELL ST, OTTAWA, ON, K1B 5R1
(613) 748-0066 *SIC* 1761

SIMMAX CORP *p* 116
8750 58 AVE NW, EDMONTON, AB, T6E 6G6
(780) 437-9315 *SIC* 1731

SIMMLANDS INSURANCE BROKERS DIV OF *p* 963
See JONES BROWN INC

SIMMONS AUTO SALES & SERVICE LIMITED *p* 423
461 JAMES BLVD, GANDER, NL, A1V 2V4
(709) 256-3415 *SIC* 5511

SIMMONS EDECO INC *p* 65
1414 8 ST SW SUITE 500, CALGARY, AB, T2R 1J6
(403) 244-5340 *SIC* 1381

SIMMONS HONDA *p* 423
See SIMMONS AUTO SALES & SERVICE LIMITED

SIMMONS MATTRESS GALLERY *p* 426
See COHEN'S HOME FURNISHINGS LIMITED

SIMMONS PET FOOD ON, INC *p* 727
8 FALCONER DR, MISSISSAUGA, ON, L5N 1B1
(905) 826-3870 *SIC* 2047

SIMMS *p* 414
See T. S. SIMMS & CO. LIMITED

SIMO MANAGEMENT *p* 1061
150 RUE CHAUVIN, BOISBRIAND, QC, J7G 2N5
SIC 5074

SIMON FRASER LODGE INC *p* 250
2410 LAURIER CRES, PRINCE GEORGE, BC, V2M 2B3
(250) 563-3413 *SIC* 8059

SIMON FRASER SOCIETY FOR COMMUNITY LIVING, THE *p*

202
218 BLUE MOUNTAIN ST SUITE 300, CO-QUITLAM, BC, V3K 4H2
(604) 525-9494   *SIC* 8322
SIMON FRASER SOCIETY, THE   *p* 202
See SIMON FRASER SOCIETY FOR COMMUNITY LIVING, THE
SIMON FRASER STUDENT SOCIETY *p* 183
8888 UNIVERSITY DR SUITE 2250, BURNABY, BC, V5A 1S6
(778) 782-3111   *SIC* 8641
SIMON FRASER UNIVERSITY   *p* 183
8888 UNIVERSITY DR SUITE 1200, BURNABY, BC, V5A 1S6
(778) 782-3111   *SIC* 8221
SIMON FRASER UNIVERSITY   *p* 300
555 HASTINGS ST W SUITE 17U, VANCOUVER, BC, V6B 4N5
(778) 782-5235   *SIC* 5942
SIMON FRASER UNIVERSITY   *p* 309
500 GRANVILLE ST, VANCOUVER, BC, V6C 1W6
(778) 782-5013   *SIC* 8244
SIMON FRASER UNIVERSITY BOOKSTORE   *p* 300
See SIMON FRASER UNIVERSITY
SIMONDS HIGH SCHOOL   *p* 413
See SCHOOL DISTRICT 8
SIMPLE CONCEPT INC   *p* 1236
2812 RUE JOSEPH-A.-BOMBARDIER, MONTREAL, QC, H7P 6E2
(450) 978-0602   *SIC* 1751
SIMPLER NETWORKS INC   *p* 1095
1840 RTE TRANSCANADIENNE UNITE 100, DORVAL, QC, H9P 1H7
(514) 684-2112   *SIC* 3669
SIMPLESTRATUS   *p* 1214
See VISION 7 COMMUNICATIONS INC
SIMPLESTRATUS   *p* 1260
See VISION 7 COMMUNICATIONS INC
SIMPLEX GRINNELL   *p* 32
See TYCO INTEGRATED FIRE & SECURITY CANADA, INC
SIMPLEX GRINNELL   *p* 1331
See TYCO INTEGRATED FIRE & SECURITY CANADA, INC
SIMPLEX INDUSTRIES INC   *p* 816
2762 SHEFFIELD RD, OTTAWA, ON, K1B 3V9
(613) 244-0586   *SIC* 4214
SIMPLEXGRINNELL   *p* 26
See TYCO INTEGRATED FIRE & SECURITY CANADA, INC
SIMPLEXGRINNELL   *p* 38
See TYCO INTEGRATED FIRE & SECURITY CANADA, INC
SIMPLEXGRINNELL   *p* 207
See TYCO INTEGRATED FIRE & SECURITY CANADA, INC
SIMPLEXGRINNELL   *p* 781
See TYCO INTEGRATED FIRE & SECURITY CANADA, INC
SIMPLEXGRINNELL   *p* 1331
See TYCO INTEGRATED FIRE & SECURITY CANADA, INC
SIMPLEXGRINNELL, A DIV   *p* 103
See TYCO INTEGRATED FIRE & SECURITY CANADA, INC
SIMPLI HOME   *p* 550
See CCT GLOBAL SOURCING INC
SIMPLOT CANADA (II) LIMITED   *p* 355
HWY 1 W & SIMPLOT RD, PORTAGE LA PRAIRIE, MB, R1N 3A4
(204) 857-1400   *SIC* 2099
SIMPLY BOSS INC   *p* 116
4529 97 ST NW, EDMONTON, AB, T6E 5Y8
SIC 5063
SIMPLY COMFORT INC.   *p* 768
2225 SHEPPARD AVE E SUITE 1501, NORTH YORK, ON, M2J 5C2
(416) 477-0626   *SIC* 1711
SIMPLY COMPUTING INC   *p* 321
1690 BROADWAY W SUITE 203, VANCOU-

VER, BC, V6J 1X6
(604) 714-1450   *SIC* 5734
SIMPLY MOBILE LTD   *p* 650
1920 DUNDAS ST, LONDON, ON, N5V 3P1
(519) 451-5120   *SIC* 5571
SIMPLY THE BEST GOURMET PRODUCTS *p* 273
17665 66A AVE SUITE 110, SURREY, BC, V3S 2A7
(604) 576-9395   *SIC* 5149
SIMPORT SCIENTIFIQUE INC   *p* 1348
2588 RUE BERNARD-PILON BUREAU 1, SAINT-MATHIEU-DE-BELOEIL, QC, J3G 4S5
(450) 464-1723   *SIC* 3089
SIMPRO SOLUTIONS INC   *p* 867
100 CONSILIUM PL UNIT 601, SCARBOROUGH, ON, M1H 3E3
(416) 915-9571   *SIC* 7389
SIMPSON AUTOMOBILES INC   *p* 1102
112 BOUL DE GASPE, GASPE, QC, G4X 1A9
(800) 368-2279   *SIC* 5511
SIMPSON SEEDS INC   *p* 1411
1170 NORTH SERVICE RD, MOOSE JAW, SK, S6H 4P8
(306) 693-2132   *SIC* 5153
SIMPSON STRONG-TIE CANADA LIMITED *p* 506
5 KENVIEW BLVD, BRAMPTON, ON, L6T 5G5
(800) 999-5099   *SIC* 3452
SIMPSON'S FENCE LTD   *p* 543
1030 RICHMOND ST, CHATHAM, ON, N7M 5J5
(519) 354-0540   *SIC* 5039
SIMPSON'S SPORTS LIMITED   *p* 157
4847 19 ST SUITE C, RED DEER, AB, T4R 2N7
(403) 341-6000   *SIC* 7941
SIMPSON, S. B. GROUP INC   *p* 526
3210 MAINWAY, BURLINGTON, ON, L7M 1A5
(905) 335-6575   *SIC* 5251
SIMSAK CORPORATION   *p* 497
133 HOLLAND ST E, BRADFORD, ON, L3Z 2A8
(905) 778-9600   *SIC* 5541
SIMSON MAXWELL   *p* 116
8750 58 AVE NW, EDMONTON, AB, T6E 6G6
(780) 434-6431   *SIC* 5084
SIMULATIONS CMLABS INC   *p* 1212
645 RUE WELLINGTON BUREAU 301, MONTREAL, QC, H3C 1T2
(514) 287-1166   *SIC* 7371
SIMUNITION   *p* 1282
See GENERAL DYNAMICS PRODUITS DE DEFENSE ET SYSTEMES TACTIQUES-CANADA INC
SINAI HEALTH SYSTEM   *p* 947
600 UNIVERSITY AVE, TORONTO, ON, M5G 1X5
(416) 596-4200   *SIC* 8062
SINCERE REALTY INC   *p* 877
1033 MCNICOLL AVE, SCARBOROUGH, ON, M1W 3W6
(416) 497-8900   *SIC* 6531
SINCERE TRADING OF K.B.A. CO-OPERATIVE LTD   *p* 579
169 THE WEST MALL, ETOBICOKE, ON, M9C 1C2
(416) 789-7544   *SIC* 5145
SINCLAIR DENTAL   *p* 242
See SINCLAIR DENTAL CO. LTD
SINCLAIR DENTAL CO. LTD   *p* 242
900 HARBOURSIDE DR, NORTH VANCOUVER, BC, V7P 3T8
(604) 986-1544   *SIC* 5047
SINCLAIR PHARMACY (1980) LTD   *p* 896
12 WELLINGTON ST, STRATFORD, ON, N5A 2L2
(519) 271-8940   *SIC* 5912
SINCLAIR SUPPLY LTD   *p* 86

10914 120 ST NW, EDMONTON, AB, T5H 3P7
(780) 452-3110   *SIC* 5075
SINCLAIR TECHNOLOGIES INC   *p* 481
85 MARY ST, AURORA, ON, L4G 6X5
(905) 727-0165   *SIC* 3663
SING TAO (CANADA) LIMITED   *p* 324
8508 ASH ST, VANCOUVER, BC, V6P 3M2
(604) 321-1111   *SIC* 2711
SING TAO DAILY   *p* 675
See SING TAO NEWSPAPERS (CANADA 1988) LIMITED
SING TAO NEWSPAPERS (CANADA 1988) LIMITED   *p* 324
8508 ASH ST, VANCOUVER, BC, V6P 3M2
(604) 909-1122   *SIC* 5192
SING TAO NEWSPAPERS (CANADA 1988) LIMITED   *p* 675
221 WHITEHALL DR, MARKHAM, ON, L3R 9T1
(416) 596-8140   *SIC* 2711
SINGGA ENTERPRISES INC   *p* 288
3373 KINGSWAY, VANCOUVER, BC, V5R 5K6
SIC 5137
SINGLA BROS. HOLDINGS LTD   *p* 244
567 HEATHER RD SUITE 32860, PENTICTON, BC, V2A 6N8
(250) 490-1700   *SIC* 1521
SINGLETON URQUHART LLP   *p* 309
925 GEORGIA ST W SUITE 1200, VANCOUVER, BC, V6C 3L2
(604) 682-7474   *SIC* 8111
SINGLETONS PROFESSIONAL FAMILY HAIR CARE   *p* 381
See KITTSON INVESTMENTS LTD
SINKING SHIP ENTERTAINMENT INC *p* 992
1179 KING ST W SUITE 302, TORONTO, ON, M6K 3C5
(416) 533-8172   *SIC* 7812
SINNOTT'S YIG   *p* 155
See 8273537 CANADA LIMITED
SINOBEC TRADING INC   *p* 1336
4455 RUE COUSENS, SAINT-LAURENT, QC, H4S 1X5
(514) 339-9333   *SIC* 5719
SINOCANADA PETROLEUM CORPORATION   *p* 59
444 7 AVE SW UNIT 800, CALGARY, AB, T2P 0X8
SIC 5172
SINOPEC CANADA   *p* 59
See SINOPEC DAYLIGHT ENERGY LTD
SINOPEC DAYLIGHT ENERGY LTD   *p* 59
112 4 AVE SW SUITE 2700, CALGARY, AB, T2P 0H3
(403) 266-6900   *SIC* 2911
SINORAMA CORPORATION   *p* 1192
998 BLVD SAINT-LAURENT OFFICE 518, MONTREAL, QC, H2Z 9Y9
(514) 866-6888   *SIC* 4724
SINOX CONCEPT   *p* 1292
See GROUPE SINOX INC
SINTERIS   *p* 493
See 2027844 ONTARIO INC
SINTRA INC   *p* 1073
3600 CH DUNANT, CANTON-DE-HATLEY, QC, J0B 2C0
(819) 346-8634   *SIC* 1611
SINTRA INC   *p* 1118
3125 BOUL SAINT-CHARLES, KIRKLAND, QC, H9H 3B9
(514) 695-3395   *SIC* 1611
SINTRA INC   *p* 1140
678 AV TANIATA UNITE 839, LEVIS, QC, G6Z 2C2
(418) 839-4175   *SIC* 1611
SINTRA INC   *p* 1228
4984 PLACE DE LA SAVANE, MONTREAL, QC, H4P 2M9
(514) 341-5331   *SIC* 1611
SINTRA INC   *p* 1287
105 RUE LOUIS-PHILIPPE-LEBRUN,

RIVIERE-DU-LOUP, QC, G5R 5W5
(418) 862-0000   *SIC* 1611
SINTRA INC   *p* 1290
240 AV MARCEL-BARIL, ROUYN-NORANDA, QC, J9X 7C1
(819) 762-6505   *SIC* 8711
SINTRA INC   *p* 1291
101 RUE DE LA SINTRA, SAINT-ALPHONSE-DE-GRANBY, QC, J0E 2A0
(450) 375-4471   *SIC* 1611
SINTRA INC   *p* 1314
7 RANG SAINT-REGIS S, SAINT-ISIDORE-DE-LAPRAIRIE, QC, J0L 2A0
(450) 638-0172   *SIC* 1611
SIOUX LOOKOUT MENO-YA-WIN HEALTH CENTRE PLANNING CORPORATION *p* 881
1 MENO YA WIN WAY, SIOUX LOOKOUT, ON, P8T 1B4
(807) 737-3030   *SIC* 8062
SIPKENS NURSERIES LTD   *p* 1037
3261 LONDON LINE, WYOMING, ON, N0N 1T0
(519) 542-8353   *SIC* 5193
SIR ALLAN MACNAB   *p* 616
See HAMILTON-WENTWORTH DISTRICT SCHOOL BOARD, THE
SIR CORP   *p* 459
184 CHAIN LAKE DR, HALIFAX, NS, B3S 1C5
(902) 450-1370   *SIC* 5812
SIR CORP   *p* 478
839 GOLF LINKS RD, ANCASTER, ON, L9K 1L5
(905) 304-1721   *SIC* 5812
SIR CORP   *p* 506
154 WEST DR, BRAMPTON, ON, L6T 5P1
(905) 457-5200   *SIC* 5812
SIR CORP   *p* 525
5360 SOUTH SERVICE RD SUITE 200, BURLINGTON, ON, L7L 5L1
(905) 681-2997   *SIC* 5812
SIR CORP   *p* 579
1900 THE QUEENSWAY, ETOBICOKE, ON, M9C 5H5
(416) 626-2700   *SIC* 5813
SIR CORP   *p* 588
25 CARLSON CRT, ETOBICOKE, ON, M9W 6A2
(416) 213-1688   *SIC* 5812
SIR CORP   *p* 626
125 ROLAND MICHENER DR SUITE B1, KANATA, ON, K2T 1G7
(613) 271-1041   *SIC* 5813
SIR CORP   *p* 657
1070 WELLINGTON RD SUITE 1, LONDON, ON, N6E 3V8
(519) 680-3800   *SIC* 5812
SIR CORP   *p* 711
299 RATHBURN RD W, MISSISSAUGA, ON, L5B 4C1
(905) 279-3342   *SIC* 5812
SIR CORP   *p* 711
219 RATHBURN RD W, MISSISSAUGA, ON, L5B 4C1
(905) 566-4662   *SIC* 5812
SIR CORP   *p* 711
209 RATHBURN RD W, MISSISSAUGA, ON, L5B 4C1
(905) 281-1721   *SIC* 5812
SIR CORP   *p* 967
144 FRONT ST W, TORONTO, ON, M5J 2L7
(416) 585-2121   *SIC* 5812
SIR GUY CARLTON SECONDARY SCHOOL *p* 831
See OTTAWA-CARLETON DISTRICT SCHOOL BOARD
SIR JAMES DUNN COLLEGIATE & VOCATIONAL   *p*
861
See ALGOMA DISTRICT SCHOOL BOARD
SIR JAMES WHITNEY SCHOOL FOR THE DEAF   *p* 492
350 DUNDAS ST W, BELLEVILLE, ON, K8P 1B2

(613) 967-2823   *SIC* 8211
SIR JOHN A MACDONALD SECONDARY SCHOOL   p 614
See HAMILTON-WENTWORTH DISTRICT SCHOOL BOARD, THE
SIR OLIVER MOWAT C I   p 865
See TORONTO DISTRICT SCHOOL BOARD
SIR ROBERT BORDEN HIGH SCHOOL p 751
See OTTAWA-CARLETON DISTRICT SCHOOL BOARD
SIR ROYALTY INCOME FUND   p 525
5360 SOUTH SERVICE RD SUITE 200, BURLINGTON, ON, L7L 5L1
(905) 681-2997   *SIC* 6726
SIR SANDFORD FLEMING COLLEGE OF APPLIED ARTS AND TECHNOLOGY p 842
599 BREALEY DR, PETERBOROUGH, ON, K9J 7B1
(705) 749-5530   *SIC* 8222
SIR THOMAS RODDICK HOSPITAL   p 434
See WESTERN REGIONAL INTEGRATED HEALTH AUTHORITY, THE
SIR WILFRID LAURIER COLLEGIATE INSTITUTE   p 866
See TORONTO DISTRICT SCHOOL BOARD
SIR WILFRID LAURIER SCHOOL BOARD p 1087
2323 BOUL DANIEL-JOHNSON, COTE SAINT-LUC, QC, H7T 1H8
(450) 686-6300   *SIC* 8211
SIR WILFRID LAURIER SCHOOL BOARD p 1129
448 AV D'ARGENTEUIL, LACHUTE, QC, J8H 1W9
(450) 562-8571   *SIC* 8211
SIR WILFRID LAURIER SCHOOL BOARD p 1288
530 RUE NORTHCOTE, ROSEMERE, QC, J7A 1Y2
(450) 621-5900   *SIC* 8211
SIR WILFRID LAURIER SECONDARY SCHOOL   p 656
See THAMES VALLEY DISTRICT SCHOOL BOARD
SIR WILLIAM MULOCK SECONDARY SCHOOL   p 754
See YORK REGION DISTRICT SCHOOL BOARD
SIR WILLIAM OSLER HIGH SCHOOL p 875
See TORONTO DISTRICT SCHOOL BOARD
SIR WINSTON CHURCHILL C. & V.I. p 909
See LAKEHEAD DISTRICT SCHOOL BOARD
SIR WINSTON CHURCHILL HIGH SCHOOL p 40
See CALGARY BOARD OF EDUCATION
SIR WINSTON CHURCHILL PUB   p 1212
See 9010-5826 QUEBEC INC
SIR WINSTON CHURCHILL SECONDARY SCHOOL   p 323
See BOARD OF EDUCATION OF SCHOOL DISTRICT NO. 39 (VANCOUVER), THE
SIRCO CLEANERS (1980) LTD   p 385
1393 BORDER ST UNIT 5, WINNIPEG, MB, R3H 0N1
(204) 831-8551   *SIC* 5169
SIRCO MACHINERY COMPANY LIMITED p 576
40 JUTLAND RD, ETOBICOKE, ON, M8Z 2G9
(416) 255-1321   *SIC* 5084
SIRCOM LODGE #66   p 470
GD, WHYCOCOMAGH, NS, B0E 3M0
(902) 756-3262   *SIC* 8641
SIRIUS BENEFIT PLANS INC   p 389
1403 KENASTON BLVD, WINNIPEG, MB, R3P 2T5
(204) 488-7600   *SIC* 6411
SIRIUS XM CANADA HOLDINGS INC p 992

135 LIBERTY ST 4TH FLOOR, TORONTO, ON, M6K 1A7
(416) 408-6000   *SIC* 4832
SIRIUS XM CANADA INC   p 992
135 LIBERTY ST SUITE 400, TORONTO, ON, M6K 1A7
(416) 513-7470   *SIC* 4832
SIROCCO COMMUNICATION   p 1312
See GROUPE CHINOOK AVENTURE INC
SIROIS & SONS GENERAL CONTRACTORS   p 828
38 LYNWOOD AVE, OTTAWA, ON, K1Y 2B3
SIC 1541
SIROTIERE DU SOMMET YAMASKA p 1294
See 132082 CANADA INC
SIRVA CANADA LP   p 103
10403 172 ST NW SUITE 310, EDMONTON, AB, T5S 1K9
(780) 443-6800   *SIC* 4214
SIS STRATEGIC INFORMATION SYSTEMS INC   p 103
11432 WINTERBURN RD NW, EDMONTON, AB, T5S 2Y3
(780) 701-4050   *SIC* 5045
SISCA GESTION D'AFFAIRES INC   p 1132
790 RUE D'UPTON, LASALLE, QC, H8R 2T9
(514) 363-5511   *SIC* 7334
SISKINDS LLP   p 655
680 WATERLOO ST, LONDON, ON, N6A 0B3
(519) 672-2121   *SIC* 8111
SISKINDS, THE LAW FIRM   p 655
See SISKINDS LLP
SISLER HIGH SCHOOL   p 373
See WINNIPEG SCHOOL DIVISION
SISLEY FOR HONDA   p 906
See SISLEY MOTORS LIMITED
SISLEY MOTORS LIMITED   p 906
88 STEELES AVE W, THORNHILL, ON, L4J 1A1
(416) 223-3111   *SIC* 5511
SISTEMALUX INC   p 1179
9320 BOUL SAINT-LAURENT BUREAU 100, MONTREAL, QC, H2N 1N7
(514) 523-1339   *SIC* 5063
SISTERS OF CHARITY   p 457
215 SETON RD, HALIFAX, NS, B3M 0C9
(902) 406-8100   *SIC* 8661
SISTERS OF CHARITY OF OTTAWA p 822
See SOEURS DE LA CHARITE D'OTTAWA, LES
SISTERS OF CHARITY OF OTTAWA, THE p 820
50 MAPLE LANE, OTTAWA, ON, K1M 1G8
(613) 745-1584   *SIC* 8661
SISTERS OF CHARITY OF PROVIDENCE OF WESTERN CANADA, THE   p 119
3005 119 ST NW, EDMONTON, AB, T6J 5R5
(780) 430-9491   *SIC* 8661
SISTERS OF PROVIDENCE   p 119
See SISTERS OF CHARITY OF PROVIDENCE OF WESTERN CANADA, THE
SISTERS OF ST. JOSEPH OF SAULT STE. MARIE, THE   p 907
580 ALGOMA ST N, THUNDER BAY, ON, P7A 8C5
(807) 343-4300   *SIC* 8063
SISTERS OF ST. JOSEPHS OF HAMILTON p 566
574 NORTHCLIFFE AVE, DUNDAS, ON, L9H 7L9
(905) 528-0138   *SIC* 8661
SISTERS OF STE ANNE   p 1126
See SOEURS DE SAINTE-ANNE DU QUEBEC, LES
SISU INC   p 193
7635 NORTH FRASER WAY SUITE 102, BURNABY, BC, V5J 0B8
(604) 420-6610   *SIC* 5122
SITA AIRPORT AND DESKTOP SERVICES TORONTO   p 528

See SITA INFORMATION NETWORKING COMPUTING CANADA INC
SITA INFORMATION NETWORKING COMPUTING CANADA INC   p 528
777 WALKER'S LINE, BURLINGTON, ON, L7N 2G1
(905) 681-6200   *SIC* 7371
SITCONF LIMITED   p 665
160 BULLOCK DR, MARKHAM, ON, L3P 1W2
(905) 554-6029   *SIC* 5021
SITE ENERGY SERVICES LTD   p 163
120 PEMBINA RD SUITE 170, SHERWOOD PARK, AB, T8H 0M2
(780) 400-7483   *SIC* 1389
SITE INTEGRATION PLUS INC   p 1067
1356 RUE NEWTON, BOUCHERVILLE, QC, J4B 5H2
(450) 449-0094   *SIC* 1731
SITE OLIVIER GUIMOND   p 1164
See CENTRE DE SANTE ET DE SERVICES SOCIAUX LUCILLE-TEASDALE
SITEL CANADA CORPORATION   p 409
320C EDINBURGH DR, MONCTON, NB, E1E 2L1
SIC 7389
SITHE GLOBAL CANADIAN POWER SERVICES LTD   p 506
8600 GOREWAY DR, BRAMPTON, ON, L6T 0A8
(905) 595-4700   *SIC* 4911
SITQ   p 1192
See SITQ INTERNATIONAL INC
SITQ INTERNATIONAL INC   p 1192
1001 RUE DU SQUARE-VICTORIA BUREAU 500, MONTREAL, QC, H2Z 2B5
(514) 287-1852   *SIC* 8741
SITQ NATIONAL INC   p 1192
1001 RUE DU SQUARE-VICTORIA BUREAU C 200, MONTREAL, QC, H2Z 2B1
(514) 287-1852   *SIC* 6798
SIVACO ONTARIO   p 622
See SIVACO WIRE GROUP 2004 L.P.
SIVACO QUEBEC   p 1149
See SIVACO WIRE GROUP 2004 L.P.
SIVACO WIRE GROUP 2004 L.P.   p 622
330 THOMAS ST, INGERSOLL, ON, N5C 3K5
(800) 265-0418   *SIC* 3496
SIVACO WIRE GROUP 2004 L.P.   p 1149
800 RUE OUELLETTE, MARIEVILLE, QC, J3M 1P5
(450) 658-8741   *SIC* 3496
SIVEM PHARMACEUTICALS ULC   p 1330
4800 RUE LEVY, SAINT-LAURENT, QC, H4R 2P1
(514) 832-1290   *SIC* 5122
SIX NATIONS NATURAL GAS LIMITED PARTNERSHIP   p 806
1953 FOURTH LINE, OHSWEKEN, ON, N0A 1M0
(519) 445-4213   *SIC* 4924
SIX NATIONS OF THE GRAND RIVER DEVELOPMENT CORPORATION   p 806
2498 CHIEFSWOOD, OHSWEKEN, ON, N0A 1M0
(519) 753-1950   *SIC* 8741
SIX PILLARS LTD   p 594
375 MOUNTAINVIEW RD S, GEORGETOWN, ON, L7G 5X3
(905) 873-9982   *SIC* 5541
SIXPRO INC   p 1063
1576 10E RANG DE SIMPSON, BONCONSEIL, QC, J0C 1A0
(819) 336-2117   *SIC* 3479
SIZELAND EVANS INTERIOR DESIGN INC p 59
441 5 AVE SW SUITE 700, CALGARY, AB, T2P 2V1
SIC 7389
SJ & DESIGN   p 1331

See STELLA-JONES INC
SJ FINE FOODS LTD   p 1430
827 56TH ST E, SASKATOON, SK, S7K 5Y9
(306) 653-1702   *SIC* 2011
SJNFC   p 433
See ST JOHN'S NATIVE FRIENDSHIP CENTRE ASSOCIATION
SJR FOOD SERVICES LTD   p 211
1835 56 ST UNIT 44, DELTA, BC, V4L 2M1
(604) 948-3630   *SIC* 5812
SK SECURITY SERVICES   p 380
See 5126614 MANITOBA INC
SKAHA FORD INC   p 244
198 PARKWAY PL, PENTICTON, BC, V2A 8G8
(250) 492-3800   *SIC* 5511
SKANA FOREST PRODUCTS LTD   p 256
20800 WESTMINSTER HWY SUITE 1303, RICHMOND, BC, V6V 2W3
(604) 273-5441   *SIC* 5031
SKATE ASSET MANAGEMENT   p 957
See SLATE RETAIL REAL ESTATE INVESTMENT TRUST
SKATE CANADA   p 820
1200 ST. LAURENT BLVD SUITE 261, OTTAWA, ON, K1K 3B8
(613) 747-1007   *SIC* 8699
SKECHERS USA CANADA, INC   p 700
5055 SATELLITE DR UNIT 6, MISSISSAUGA, ON, L4W 5K7
(905) 238-7121   *SIC* 5139
SKEENA SAWMILLS LTD   p 316
1030 WEST GEORGIA ST SUITE 1518, VANCOUVER, BC, V6E 2Y3
(604) 800-5990   *SIC* 2421
SKELLY, ROBERT E. LIMITED   p 1019
5415 TECUMSEH RD E, WINDSOR, ON, N8T 1C5
(519) 948-8111   *SIC* 5531
SKF CANADA LIMITED   p 875
40 EXECUTIVE CRT, SCARBOROUGH, ON, M1S 4N4
(416) 299-1220   *SIC* 5085
SKI BROMONT.COM, SOCIETE EN COMMANDITE   p 1068
150 RUE CHAMPLAIN, BROMONT, QC, J2L 1A2
(450) 534-2200   *SIC* 5813
SKI CELLAR SNOWBOARD   p 67
See SPORTSMAN LIMITED, THE
SKI CLUB OF THE CANADIAN ROCKIES LIMITED, THE   p 139
200 PIPESTONE RD, LAKE LOUISE, AB, T0L 1E0
(403) 522-3989   *SIC* 7011
SKI MARMOT BASIN LIMITED PARTNERSHIP   p 137
GD, JASPER, AB, T0E 1E0
(780) 852-3816   *SIC* 7011
SKI MARMOT GP CORP   p 137
GD, JASPER, AB, T0E 1E0
(780) 852-3816   *SIC* 7011
SKI MOJO INC   p 1070
8025 BOUL TASCHEREAU, BROSSARD, QC, J4Y 1A4
(450) 462-4040   *SIC* 5941
SKI MOJO INC   p 1241
1355 BOUL DES LAURENTIDES, MONTREAL-OUEST, QC, H7N 4Y5
(450) 669-5123   *SIC* 5941
SKI MONT SAINT-BRUNO   p 1295
See DOMAINE DU SKI MONT BRUNO INC
SKI MONT-CASCADES   p 1073
See 4094468 CANADA INC
SKI NAKISKA   p 137
See SKI MARMOT GP CORP
SKI TAK HUT   p 203
See MT BECHER SKI RENTALS LTD
SKICAN LIMITED   p 924
745 MOUNT PLEASANT RD SUITE 300, TORONTO, ON, M4S 2N4
(416) 488-1169   *SIC* 4725

SKIDMORE DEVELOPMENT GROUP LTD p 309
837 HASTINGS ST W SUITE 715, VANCOUVER, BC, V6C 3N6
(604) 757-7461   SIC 6159

SKIIS & BIIKES p 703
See SKIIS LTD

SKIIS LTD p 703
1945 DUNDAS ST E SUITE 210, MISSISSAUGA, ON, L4X 2T8
(905) 896-1206   SIC 5941

SKIL BOSCH POWER TOOL, DIV OF p 726
See ROBERT BOSCH INC

SKILLS FOR CHANGE p 989
See SKILLS FOR CHANGE OF METRO TORONTO

SKILLS FOR CHANGE OF METRO TORONTO p 989
791 ST CLAIR AVE W, TORONTO, ON, M6C 1B7
(416) 658-3101   SIC 8331

SKIRON INC p 1260
56 RUE SAINT-PIERRE BUREAU 101, QUEBEC, QC, G1K 4A1
(418) 694-0114   SIC 7311

SKJODT-BARRETT CONTRACT PACKAGING INC p
500
5 PRECIDIO CRT, BRAMPTON, ON, L6S 6B7
(905) 671-2884   SIC 1541

SKJODT-BARRETT FOODS INC p 500
5 PRECIDIO CRT, BRAMPTON, ON, L6S 6B7
(905) 671-2884   SIC 2033

SKOCDOPOLE CONSTRUCTION LTD p 83
GD, ECKVILLE, AB, T0M 0X0
(403) 746-5744   SIC 1623

SKOOKUM ASPHALT LTD p 1440
1 EAR LAKE RD, WHITEHORSE, YT, Y1A 6L4
(867) 668-6326   SIC 1794

SKOOKUMCHUCK PULP INC p 269
4501 FARSTAD WAY, SKOOKUMCHUCK, BC, V0B 2E0
(250) 422-3261   SIC 2611

SKOOKUMCHUCK PULP MILL p 269
See SKOOKUMCHUCK PULP INC

SKOR CULINARY CONCEPTS INC p 700
1330 CRESTLAWN DR, MISSISSAUGA, ON, L4W 1P8
(905) 625-4447   SIC 2099

SKOR FOOD SERVICE LTD p 558
10 RONROSE DR, CONCORD, ON, L4K 4R3
(905) 660-1212   SIC 5142

SKOTIDAKIS GOAT FARM p 888
See 1048547 ONTARIO INC

SKRETTING CANADA INC p 291
1370 E KENT AVE SOUTH, VANCOUVER, BC, V5X 2Y2
(604) 325-0302   SIC 2048

SKRETTING DIV. p 291
See SKRETTING CANADA INC

SKY BAR LTD p 327
938 HOWE ST SUITE 615, VANCOUVER, BC, V6Z 1N9
(604) 697-0990   SIC 5812

SKY REGIONAL AIRLINES INC p 729
6120 MIDFIELD RD, MISSISSAUGA, ON, L5P 1B1
(905) 362-5941   SIC 4512

SKY SERVICE F.B.O. INC. p 729
6120 MIDFIELD RD, MISSISSAUGA, ON, L5P 1B1
(905) 677-3300   SIC 4581

SKY SERVICE F.B.O. INC. p 1095
9785 AV RYAN, DORVAL, QC, H9P 1A2
(514) 636-3300   SIC 4512

SKY TECK LABS INC p 703
3289 LENWORTH DR SUITE B, MISSISSAUGA, ON, L4X 2H1
(905) 602-8007   SIC 5169

SKY WINDOW TECHNOLOGIES INC p 784

40 SAINT REGIS CRES N, NORTH YORK, ON, M3J 1Z2
(416) 633-1881   SIC 3442

SKY-HI SCAFFOLDING LTD p 183
3195 PRODUCTION WAY, BURNABY, BC, V5A 3H2
(604) 291-7245   SIC 1799

SKY-TEC SATELLITE p 405
See SKYCO INC

SKYBOX LABS INC p 186
4190 LOUGHEED HWY SUITE 200, BURNABY, BC, V5C 6A8
(604) 558-4330   SIC 5092

SKYCARE AIR AMBULANCE p 881
17 AIRPORT RD, SIOUX LOOKOUT, ON, P8T 1A3
(807) 737-0038   SIC 4522

SKYCO INC p 405
734 KING GEORGE HWY, MIRAMICHI, NB, E1V 1P8
(506) 622-8890   SIC 7699

SKYFOLD CLASSIC p 1054
See SKYFOLD INC

SKYFOLD INC p 1054
325 AV LEE, BAIE-D'URFE, QC, H9X 3S3
(514) 457-4767   SIC 3449

SKYJACK INC p 604
55 CAMPBELL RD, GUELPH, ON, N1H 1B9
(519) 837-0888   SIC 3531

SKYJACK INC p 604
55 CAMPBELL RD SUITE 1, GUELPH, ON, N1H 1B9
(519) 837-0888   SIC 3531

SKYLAND TRAVEL INC p 292
445 6TH AVE W SUITE 100, VANCOUVER, BC, V5Y 1L3
(604) 685-6885   SIC 4724

SKYLARK LOGISTICS INC p 537
7295 MASON RD, CAMBRIDGE, ON, N3C 2V4
(519) 821-7999   SIC 4212

SKYLINE (PHP) CANADA ULC p 1069
2220 BOUL LAPINIERE BUREAU 205, BROSSARD, QC, J4W 1M2
(450) 461-6366   SIC 5051

SKYLINE DEERHURST RESORT INC p 621
1235 DEERHURST DR, HUNTSVILLE, ON, P1H 2E8
(705) 789-6411   SIC 7011

SKYLINE HOLDINGS INCORPORATED p
414
331 CHESLEY DR, SAINT JOHN, NB, E2K 5P2
    SIC 5085

SKYLINE INVESTMENTS INC p 940
36 KING ST E SUITE 700, TORONTO, ON, M5C 2L9
(416) 368-2565   SIC 6512

SKYLINE SHERATON ON THE FALLS p 757
See CANADIAN NIAGARA HOTELS INC

SKYLINK AVIATION INC p 914
100 SHEPPARD AVE E SUITE 760, TORONTO, ON, M1T 3L3
(416) 924-9000   SIC 4512

SKYLINK EXPRESS INC p 727
2000 ARGENTIA RD PLAZA 4 SUITE 101, MISSISSAUGA, ON, L5N 1W1
(416) 925-4530   SIC 4512

SKYLINK SECURITY INC p 930
1027 YONGE ST, TORONTO, ON, M4W 2K9
(416) 922-5017   SIC 6211

SKYLINK VOYAGES INC p 1199
1450 RUE CITY COUNCILLORS BUREAU 110, MONTREAL, QC, H3A 2E6
(514) 842-6344   SIC 4729

SKYSERVICE BUSINESS AVIATION INC p 25
575 PALMER RD NE, CALGARY, AB, T2E 7G4
(403) 592-3700   SIC 7363

SKYSERVICE BUSINESS AVIATION INC p 729
6120 MIDFIELD RD, MISSISSAUGA, ON, L5P 1B1

(905) 677-3300   SIC 4522

SKYSERVICE BUSINESS AVIATION INC p 1095
9785 AV RYAN, DORVAL, QC, H9P 1A2
(514) 636-3300   SIC 4522

SKYSERVICE INVESTMENTS INC p 729
6120 MIDFIELD RD, MISSISSAUGA, ON, L5P 1B1
(905) 678-5767   SIC 6719

SKYTRAIN p 181
See BRITISH COLUMBIA RAPID TRANSIT COMPANY LTD

SKYVIEW ELECTRIC INC p 106
12850 149 ST NW, EDMONTON, AB, T5V 1A4
    SIC 1731

SKYVIEW KEG p 94
See KEG STEAKHOUSE AND BAR

SKYWAVE MOBILE COMMUNICATIONS INC p 627
750 PALLADIUM DR SUITE 368, KANATA, ON, K2V 1C7
(613) 836-4844   SIC 5065

SKYWAY CANADA LIMITED p 588
170 CLAIREVILLE DR, ETOBICOKE, ON, M9W 5Y3
(416) 744-6000   SIC 5082

SKYWORDS TRAFFIC NETWORK p 676
See TORRES AVIATION INCORPORATED

SL MARKETING p 1012
See SL MARKETING INC

SL MARKETING INC p 1012
555 BROWN RD, WELLAND, ON, L3B 5N4
(905) 714-4000   SIC 5093

SLACAN INDUSTRIES INC p 515
145 ROY BLVD, BRANTFORD, ON, N3R 7K1
(519) 758-8888   SIC 3644

SLALOM CONSULTING ULC p 940
8 KING ST E UNIT 2000, TORONTO, ON, M5C 1B5
(416) 366-5390   SIC 8748

SLATE OFFICE II L.P. p 957
121 KING ST W SUITE 200, TORONTO, ON, M5H 3T9
(416) 644-4264   SIC 6798

SLATE OFFICE MANAGEMENT p 957
See SLATE OFFICE II L.P.

SLATE OFFICE REIT p 957
121 KING ST W SUITE 200, TORONTO, ON, M5H 3T9
(416) 644-4264   SIC 6798

SLATE RETAIL REAL ESTATE INVESTMENT TRUST p
957
121 KING ST W SUITE 200, TORONTO, ON, M5H 3T9
(416) 644-4264   SIC 6798

SLAVE LAKE CHRYSLER p 163
See SLAVE LAKE CHRYSLER DODGE JEEP RAM LTD

SLAVE LAKE CHRYSLER DODGE JEEP RAM LTD p 163
701 15 AVE SW, SLAVE LAKE, AB, T0G 2A4
(780) 849-5225   SIC 5511

SLAVE LAKE EQUITIES INC p 94
13920 YELLOWHEAD TRAIL NW SUITE 1000, EDMONTON, AB, T5L 3C2
(780) 702-6682   SIC 6553

SLAVE LAKE PULP CORPORATION p 163
GD, SLAVE LAKE, AB, T0G 2A0
(780) 849-7777   SIC 2611

SLAVE LAKE PULP CORPORATION p 300
858 BEATTY ST SUITE 501, VANCOUVER, BC, V6B 1C1
(604) 895-2700   SIC 2611

SLAVENS ASSOCIATES p 972
435 EGLINTON AVE W, TORONTO, ON, M5N 1A4
(416) 483-4337   SIC 6531

SLAVENS, PAUL AND ASSOCIATES p 972
See SLAVENS ASSOCIATES

SLE-CO p 648
See 1142024 ONTARIO INC

SLE-CO PLASTICS INC p 650
1425 CREAMERY RD, LONDON, ON, N5V 5B3
(519) 451-3748   SIC 3089

SLEEGERS ENGINEERED PRODUCTS INC. p 650
5 CUDDY BLVD, LONDON, ON, N5V 3Y3
(519) 451-5480   SIC 3441

SLEEMAN BREWERIES LTD p 332
2808 27 AVE, VERNON, BC, V1T 9K4
(250) 542-2337   SIC 2082

SLEEMAN BREWERIES LTD p 602
505 SOUTHGATE DR, GUELPH, ON, N1G 3W6
(519) 822-1834   SIC 2082

SLEEMAN BREWERY p 606
See SAPPORO CANADA INC

SLEEMAN BREWING & MALTING COMPANY LTD, THE p
606
551 CLAIR RD W, GUELPH, ON, N1L 1E9
(519) 822-1834   SIC 2082

SLEEP COUNTRY CANADA HOLDINGS INC p 506
7920 AIRPORT RD, BRAMPTON, ON, L6T 4N8
(289) 748-0206   SIC 5712

SLEEP COUNTRY CANADA INC p 238
805 BOYD ST SUITE 100, NEW WESTMINSTER, BC, V3M 5X2
(604) 515-9711   SIC 5712

SLEEP COUNTRY CANADA INC p 506
7920 AIRPORT RD, BRAMPTON, ON, L6T 4N8
(289) 748-0206   SIC 5712

SLEEP FACTORY, THE p 697
See MAJOLI FURNITURE (1983) LIMITED

SLEEP MANAGEMENT GROUP LIMITED p
802
466 SPEERS RD UNIT 4, OAKVILLE, ON, L6K 3W9
(905) 337-0699   SIC 5047

SLEEPING BAY BUILDING CORP p 147
3292 DUNMORE RD SE SUITE F7, MEDICINE HAT, AB, T1B 2R4
(403) 526-4888   SIC 6512

SLEEVER INTERNATIONAL INC p 743
6815 COLUMBUS RD, MISSISSAUGA, ON, L5T 2G9
(905) 565-0952   SIC 2679

SLEGG CONSTRUCTION p 235
See SLEGG LIMITED PARTNERSHIP

SLEGG DEVELOPMENTS LTD p 341
2901 SOOKE RD, VICTORIA, BC, V9C 3W7
(250) 386-3667   SIC 5031

SLEGG LIMITED PARTNERSHIP p 235
4950 JORDAN AVE, NANAIMO, BC, V9T 2H8
(250) 758-8329   SIC 5031

SLEGG LIMITED PARTNERSHIP p 268
2030 MALAVIEW AVE W, SIDNEY, BC, V8L 5X6
(250) 656-1125   SIC 5031

SLEMON PARK CORPORATION p 1042
30 AEROSPACE BLVD UNIT A, SLEMON PARK, PE, C0B 2A0
(902) 432-1700   SIC 6531

SLESSOR AUTO WORLD p 600
569 MAIN ST W, GRIMSBY, ON, L3M 1V1
(905) 643-1221   SIC 5511

SLF p 1215
See SCHWARTZ LEVITSKY FELDMAN LLP

SLH TRANSPORT p 97
See SLH TRANSPORT INC

SLH TRANSPORT p 440
See SLH TRANSPORT INC

SLH TRANSPORT INC p 97
14525 112 AVE NW, EDMONTON, AB, T5M 2V5
(780) 451-7543   SIC 4212

SLH TRANSPORT INC p 440
347 BLUEWATER RD, BEDFORD, NS, B4B 1Y3

(902) 832-4900   *SIC* 4213
SLH TRANSPORT INC   *p* 633
1585 CENTENNIAL DR, KINGSTON, ON, K7P 0K4
(613) 384-9515   *SIC* 4213
SLH TRANSPORT INC   *p* 700
905 SHAWSON DR, MISSISSAUGA, ON, L4W 1T9
(905) 893-5170   *SIC* 4213
SLH TRANSPORT INC   *p* 1330
3075 BOUL THIMENS, SAINT-LAURENT, QC, H4R 1Y3
(514) 335-4990   *SIC* 4213
SLI MANUFACTURING INC   *p* 765
550 MCNICOLL AVE, NORTH YORK, ON, M2H 2E1
(416) 493-8900   *SIC* 3577
SLIC   *p* 1371
See SERVICES DE LUBRIFIANTS INDUS-TRIELS & COMMERCIAUX (SLIC) INC
SLICED FC LTD   *p* 13
4936 52 ST SE, CALGARY, AB, T2B 3R2
(403) 508-6868   *SIC* 0723
SLII   *p* 799
See SNC-LAVALIN INTERNATIONAL INC
SLING-CHOKER MFG. (HAMILTON) LTD *p* 610
605 RENNIE ST, HAMILTON, ON, L8H 3P8
(905) 545-5025   *SIC* 3536
SLIPP, SCOTT NISSAN LIMITED   *p* 460
975 PARK ST, KENTVILLE, NS, B4N 4H8
(902) 679-4000   *SIC* 5521
SLIZEK INC   *p* 223
1450 ST. PAUL ST, KELOWNA, BC, V1Y 2E6
(250) 861-3446   *SIC* 8049
SLM-LOGISTICS CORPORATION   *p* 506
15 BRAMALEA RD SUITE 101, BRAMP-TON, ON, L6T 2W4
(416) 743-8866   *SIC* 4953
SLOPED CONCRETE SOLUTIONS   *p* 998
See SEMPLE GOODER ROOFING COR-PORATION
SLOVENIAN LINDEN FOUNDATION *p* 580
52 NEILSON DR, ETOBICOKE, ON, M9C 1V7
(416) 621-3820   *SIC* 8051
SLP CUSTOMER SUPPORT   *p* 396
See SNC-LAVALIN INC
SLR CONSULTING (CANADA) LTD   *p* 321
1620 8TH AVE W SUITE 200, VANCOU-VER, BC, V6J 1V4
(604) 738-2500   *SIC* 8748
SLS GROUP INDUSTRIES INC   *p* 292
22 2ND AVE W SUITE 2, VANCOUVER, BC, V5Y 1B3
(604) 874-2226   *SIC* 5063
SM CONSTRUCTION INC   *p* 1281
15971 BOUL DE LA COLLINE, QUEBEC, QC, G3G 3A7
(418) 849-7104   *SIC* 1542
SM FREIGHT INC   *p* 493
25 GRAHAM ST, BLENHEIM, ON, N0P 1A0
(519) 676-5198   *SIC* 4213
SM+I   *p* 915
See VISION TRAVEL DT ONTARIO-WEST INC
SMAEA HOLDINGS INC   *p* 602
570 SOUTHGATE DR, GUELPH, ON, N1G 4P6
(519) 822-4381   *SIC* 3648
SMALL ANIMAL CLINIC   *p* 1434
See USASK SMALL ANIMAL CLINICAL STUD
SMALL CAR CENTRE LTD   *p* 856
77 16TH AVE, RICHMOND HILL, ON, L4C 7A5
(905) 731-8899   *SIC* 5511
SMALL POTATOES URBAN DELIVERY INC *p* 285
1660 HASTINGS ST E, VANCOUVER, BC, V5L 1S6
(604) 215-7783   *SIC* 5149
SMARDT INC   *p* 1095

1800 RTE TRANSCANADIENNE, DORVAL, QC, H9P 1H7
(514) 426-8989   *SIC* 3443
SMART & BIGGAR   *p* 824
55 METCALFE ST SUITE 900, OTTAWA, ON, K1P 6L5
(613) 232-2486   *SIC* 8111
SMART DESIGN & DEVELOPMENT   *p* 37
7130 FISHER RD SE SUITE 10, CALGARY, AB, T2H 0W3
SIC 1521
SMART EMPLOYEE BENEFITS INC   *p* 700
5500 EXPLORER DR 4TH FLR, MISSIS-SAUGA, ON, L4W 5C7
(888) 939-8885   *SIC* 7372
SMART ENTERPRISES CORPORATION   *p* 506
7956 TORBRAM RD UNIT 25, BRAMPTON, ON, L6T 5A2
(416) 798-0168   *SIC* 2759
SMART LASER GRAFIX   *p* 506
See SMART ENTERPRISES CORPORA-TION
SMART TECHNOLOGIES INC   *p* 40
3636 RESEARCH RD NW, CALGARY, AB, T2L 1Y1
(403) 245-0333   *SIC* 3674
SMART TECHNOLOGIES ULC   *p* 40
3636 RESEARCH RD NW, CALGARY, AB, T2L 1Y1
(403) 245-0333   *SIC* 3674
SMART TECHNOLOGIES ULC   *p* 627
501 PALLADIUM DR, KANATA, ON, K2V 0A2
(403) 245-0333   *SIC* 3674
SMART-TEK COMMUNICATIONS INC *p* 264
130-11300 NO. 5 RD, RICHMOND, BC, V7A 5J7
(604) 718-1882   *SIC* 7382
SMARTCENTRES   *p* 1002
See SMARTCENTRES REAL ESTATE IN-VESTMENT TRUST
SMARTCENTRES MANAGEMENT SER-VICES INC   *p* 558
3200 HIGHWAY 7, CONCORD, ON, L4K 5Z5
(905) 326-6400   *SIC* 6512
SMARTCENTRES REAL ESTATE INVEST-MENT TRUST   *p* 1002
3200 HIGHWAY 7, VAUGHAN, ON, L4K 5Z5
(905) 326-6400   *SIC* 6512
SMARTCENTRES REIT   *p* 558
See SMARTCENTRES MANAGEMENT SERVICES INC
SMARTCOVERAGE INSURANCE AGENCY INC   *p* 1020
3600 RHODES DR, WINDSOR, ON, N8W 5A4
(519) 974-7067   *SIC* 6331
SMARTDESIGN GROUP (CANADA) LTD *p* 296
1150 STATION ST SUITE 102, VANCOU-VER, BC, V6A 4C7
(604) 662-7015   *SIC* 7389
SMARTDESIGN GROUP KTBS INC   *p* 321
1788 5TH AVE W SUITE 300, VANCOU-VER, BC, V6J 1P2
(604) 662-7015   *SIC* 7389
SMARTDM   *p* 571
See SOMORICH MARKETING CORPORA-TION
SMARTEYES DIRECT INC   *p* 675
7755 WARDEN AVE UNIT 1, MARKHAM, ON, L3R 0N3
(905) 946-8998   *SIC* 5043
SMARTPRACTICE CANADA ULC   *p* 11
720 28TH STREET NE, STE 210, CAL-GARY, AB, T2A 6R3
(403) 450-9997   *SIC* 5122
SMARTREND SUPPLY LTD   *p* 392
1249 CLARENCE AVE UNIT 9, WINNIPEG, MB, R3T 1T4

(204) 489-7237   *SIC* 5099
SMC PNEUMATICS (CANADA) LTD *p* 799
2715 BRISTOL CIR SUITE 2, OAKVILLE, ON, L6H 6X5
(905) 812-0400   *SIC* 5084
SMG ADVISORS INC   *p* 191
4250 KINGSWAY SUITE 213, BURNABY, BC, V5H 4T7
(604) 419-0455   *SIC* 8742
SMG CANADA ULC   *p* 707
5500 ROSE CHERRY PL, MISSISSAUGA, ON, L4Z 4B6
(905) 502-9100   *SIC* 7999
SMH MANAGEMENT INC   *p* 82
545 HWY 10 E, DRUMHELLER, AB, T0J 0Y0
(403) 823-2030   *SIC* 8741
SMIT MARINE CANADA INC   *p* 285
2285 COMMISSIONER ST, VANCOUVER, BC, V5L 1A8
(604) 255-1133   *SIC* 4492
SMITH & ANDERSEN   *p* 774
See SMITH AND ANDERSEN CONSULT-ING ENGINEERING
SMITH & NEPHEW INC   *p* 1336
2250 BOUL ALFRED-NOBEL BUREAU 300, SAINT-LAURENT, QC, H4S 2C9
(514) 956-1010   *SIC* 5047
SMITH & SCOTT STEAKHOUSE LIMITED *p* 456
6061 YOUNG ST, HALIFAX, NS, B3K 2A3
(902) 454-8814   *SIC* 5812
SMITH AGENCY LIMITED   *p* 388
929 CORYDON AVE SUITE 3, WINNIPEG, MB, R3M 0W8
(204) 287-2872   *SIC* 6531
SMITH AND ANDERSEN CONSULTING EN-GINEERING   *p* 774
4211 YONGE ST SUITE 500, NORTH YORK, ON, M2P 2A9
(416) 487-8151   *SIC* 8711
SMITH AND LONG LIMITED   *p* 675
115 IDEMA RD, MARKHAM, ON, L3R 1A9
(416) 391-0443   *SIC* 1731
SMITH BROS. & WILSON (B.C.) LTD *p* 324
8729 AISNE ST, VANCOUVER, BC, V6P 3P1
(604) 324-1155   *SIC* 1541
SMITH CAMERON PROCESS SOLUTIONS *p* 277
See SMITH CAMERON PUMP SOLUTIONS INC
SMITH CAMERON PUMP SOLUTIONS INC *p* 277
13478 78 AVE UNIT 1, SURREY, BC, V3W 8J6
(604) 596-5522   *SIC* 5084
SMITH CHEVROLET OLDSMOBILE LTD *p* 218
950 NOTRE DAME DR SUITE 3310, KAM-LOOPS, BC, V2C 6J2
(250) 377-3302   *SIC* 5511
SMITH GROUP HOLDINGS LTD   *p* 7
143040 TWP RD 191, BROOKS, AB, T1R 1B6
(403) 362-4071   *SIC* 6712
SMITH INDUSPAC OTTAWA   *p* 890
See GROUPE EMBALLAGE SPECIALISE S.E.C.
SMITH INSURANCE SERVICE   *p* 130
9902 102 ST, FORT SASKATCHEWAN, AB, T8L 2C3
(780) 998-2501   *SIC* 6411
SMITH NIXON   *p* 948
See AUDICO SERVICES LIMITED PART-NERSHIP
SMITH PETRIE CARR & SCOTT INSUR-ANCE BROKERS LTD   *p* 834
359 KENT ST SUITE 600, OTTAWA, ON, K2P 0R6
(613) 237-2871   *SIC* 6411
SMITH QUALITY MEAT & POULTRY INC *p*

1341
125 RUE BARR, SAINT-LAURENT, QC, H4T 1W6
(514) 735-2100   *SIC* 5147
SMITH SERVICES   *p* 149
See SCHLUMBERGER CANADA LIMITED
SMITH'S MARKETS INC   *p* 899
971 LASALLE BLVD, SUDBURY, ON, P3A 1X7
(705) 560-3663   *SIC* 5431
SMITH'S R V CENTRE   *p* 907
See 539290 ONTARIO LTD
SMITH, BYRON FORD SALES INC   *p* 168
1040 WESTRIDGE RD, STRATHMORE, AB, T1P 1H8
(403) 934-2100   *SIC* 5511
SMITH, EMERY FISHERIES LIMITED *p* 465
5309 HWY 3, SHAG HARBOUR, NS, B0W 3B0
(902) 723-2115   *SIC* 5146
SMITH, J.D. & SONS LIMITED   *p* 558
180 BASALTIC RD, CONCORD, ON, L4K 1G6
(905) 669-8980   *SIC* 4225
SMITH, JACK FUELS LTD   *p* 911
351 QUEEN ST N, TILBURY, ON, N0P 2L0
(519) 682-0111   *SIC* 5172
SMITH, L & H FRUIT COMPANY LIMITED *p* 656
22 MAITLAND ST, LONDON, ON, N6B 3L2
(519) 433-4004   *SIC* 5148
SMITH, M.R. LIMITED   *p* 183
3100 UNDERHILL AVE, BURNABY, BC, V5A 3C6
(604) 420-4331   *SIC* 5172
SMITH, PETER CHEVROLET CADILLAC LTD   *p* 492
42 TOWNCENTRE RD, BELLEVILLE, ON, K8N 4Z5
(613) 968-6767   *SIC* 5511
SMITH, TOM CHEVROLET LIMITED *p* 682
824 KING ST, MIDLAND, ON, L4R 0B8
(705) 526-0193   *SIC* 5511
SMITH, WAYNE & HAROLD CONSTRUC-TION LIMITED   *p* 879
55 BIRCH ST, SEAFORTH, ON, N0K 1W0
(519) 527-1079   *SIC* 1542
SMITHERS INTERNATIONAL LIMITED *p* 444
1 CANAL ST, DARTMOUTH, NS, B2Y 2W1
(902) 465-3400   *SIC* 6712
SMITHERS SAFEWAY   *p* 269
See SOBEYS WEST INC
SMITHERS SCHOOL BOARD DISTRICT #54 (BULKLEY VALLEY)   *p* 269
4408 THIRD AVE, SMITHERS, BC, V0J 2N3
(250) 847-2231   *SIC* 8211
SMITHERS SECONDARY SCHOOL   *p* 269
See SMITHERS SCHOOL BOARD DIS-TRICT #54 (BULKLEY VALLEY)
SMITHRITE DISPOSAL LTD   *p* 202
70 GOLDEN DR, COQUITLAM, BC, V3K 6B5
(604) 529-4030   *SIC* 4953
SMITHRITE PORTABLE SERVICES LTD *p* 202
1650 HARTLEY AVE, COQUITLAM, BC, V3K 7A1
(604) 529-4028   *SIC* 7359
SMITHS CONSTRUCTION COMPANY ARN-PRIOR LIMITED   *p* 479
276 MADAWASKA BLVD, ARNPRIOR, ON, K7S 3H4
(613) 623-3144   *SIC* 1611
SMITHS DETECTION MONTREAL INC *p* 727
6865 CENTURY AVE SUITE 3002, MISSIS-SAUGA, ON, L5N 7K2
(905) 817-5990   *SIC* 3812
SMITHS MEDICAL CANADA LTD   *p* 675
301 GOUGH RD, MARKHAM, ON, L3R 4Y8
(905) 477-2000   *SIC* 5047

SMITHVILLE FOODLAND   p 882
See 2408234 ONTARIO INC
SMITTY'S   p 444
See SYDAX DEVELOPMENTS LIMITED
SMITTY'S CANADA INC   p 67
501 18 AVE SW SUITE 600, CALGARY, AB,
T2S 0C7
(403) 229-3838   SIC 5812
SMITTY'S FAMILY RESTAURANT   p 85
See LAVTOR HOLDINGS (ALBERTA) LTD
SMITTY'S FAMILY RESTAURANT   p 101
See LAVTOR HOLDINGS (ALBERTA) LTD
SMITTY'S FINE FURNITURE   p 618
See SMITTY'S SHOPPING CENTRE LIMITED
SMITTY'S KIP IMPORTS   p 515
80 MORTON AVE E SUITE A, BRANT-
FORD, ON, N3R 7J7
SIC 7389
SMITTY'S RESTAURANT   p 348
See J.W. VENTURES INC
SMITTY'S SHOPPING CENTRE LIMITED p
618
170 3RD ST, HANOVER, ON, N4N 1B2
(519) 364-3800   SIC 5712
SML CANADA ACQUISITION CORP p 1331
2328 RUE COHEN, SAINT-LAURENT, QC,
H4R 2N8
(514) 858-7272   SIC 5136
SML ENTERTAINMENT   p 9
See SOUTHERN MUSIC LTD
SML STAINLESS STEEL GROUP   p 1277
See SANI METAL LTEE
SMOKY LAKE COLONY LTD   p 164
GD, SMOKY LAKE, AB, T0A 3C0
(780) 656-2372   SIC 0191
SMOKY OILFIELD RENTALS   p 57
See PRECISION LIMITED PARTNERSHIP
SMOOK CONTRACTORS LTD   p 360
101 HAYES RD, THOMPSON, MB, R8N
1M3
(204) 677-1560   SIC 1629
SMOOK FUELS LTD   p 360
HWY 201, VITA, MB, R0A 2K0
(204) 425-3997   SIC 5171
**SMOOTH ROCK FALLS HOSPITAL COR-
PORATION**   p
882
107 KELLY RD, SMOOTH ROCK FALLS,
ON, P0L 2B0
(705) 338-2781   SIC 8062
SMP MOTOR PRODUCTS LTD   p 889
33 GAYLORD RD, ST THOMAS, ON, N5P
3R9
(519) 633-8422   SIC 3621
SMP SPECIALTY METAL PRODUCTS INCp
707
326 WATLINE AVE, MISSISSAUGA, ON,
L4Z 1X2
(905) 568-4459   SIC 5051
SMRID   p 141
See ST. MARY RIVER IRRIGATION DIS-
TRICT
**SMS CONSTRUCTION AND MINING SYS-
TEMS INC**   p
2
53113 RANGE ROAD 263A, ACHESON,
AB, T7X 5A5
(780) 948-2200   SIC 5082
SMS EQUIPMENT INC   p 2
11285 274 ST, ACHESON, AB, T7X 6P9
(780) 454-0101   SIC 5082
SMS EQUIPMENT INC   p 97
16116 111 AVE NW, EDMONTON, AB, T5M
2S1
(780) 451-2630   SIC 5082
SMS EQUIPMENT INC   p 129
22K HIGHWAY 63 NORTH, FORT MCMUR-
RAY, AB, T9H 3G2
(780) 714-5300   SIC 5082
SMS RENTS   p 2
See SMS CONSTRUCTION AND MINING
SYSTEMS INC
SMSI TRAVEL CENTRES INC   p 773

45 SHEPPARD AVE E SUITE 302, NORTH
YORK, ON, M2N 5W9
(416) 221-4900   SIC 5812
SMSS   p 454
See STEWART MCKELVEY STIRLING
SCALES
SMT DIRECT MARKETING INC   p 773
5255 YONGE ST SUITE 1400, NORTH
YORK, ON, M2N 6P4
SIC 8732
SMT-ASSY ELECTRONIQUE   p 1248
See 3330389 CANADA INC
SMTC   p 675
See SMTC MANUFACTURING CORPORA-
TION OF CANADA
SMTC CORPORATION   p 675
7050 WOODBINE AVE SUITE 300,
MARKHAM, ON, L3R 4G8
(905) 479-1810   SIC 3672
**SMTC MANUFACTURING CORPORATION
OF CANADA**   p 675
7050 WOODBINE AVE SUITE 300,
MARKHAM, ON, L3R 4G8
(905) 479-1810   SIC 3672
SMTC NOVA SCOTIA COMPANY   p 675
7050 WOODBINE AVE SUITE 300,
MARKHAM, ON, L3R 4G8
(905) 479-1810   SIC 3672
SMU   p 451
See SAINT MARY'S UNIVERSITY
SMUCKER FOODS OF CANADA CORP   p
675
80 WHITEHALL DR, MARKHAM, ON, L3R
0P3
(905) 940-9600   SIC 2033
SMUGGLER'S INN   p 33
See 28 AUGUSTA FUND LTD
SMUS   p 333
See ST. MICHAELS UNIVERSITY SCHOOL
SOCIETY
**SMYL CHEVROLET PONTIAC BUICK GMC
LTD**   p 173
3520 KEPLER ST, WHITECOURT, AB, T7S
1N9
(780) 778-2202   SIC 5511
SMYL GM   p 173
See SMYL CHEVROLET PONTIAC BUICK
GMC LTD
SMYL MOTORS LTD   p 165
5015 44 ST SS 2, ST PAUL, AB, T0A 3A2
(780) 645-4414   SIC 5511
SMYL RV CENTRE   p 165
See SMYL MOTORS LTD
SMYLIE'S YOUR INDEPENDENT GROCER
p 999
293 DUNDAS ST E, TRENTON, ON, K8V
1M1
(613) 392-0297   SIC 5411
SMYTHE RATCLIFFE LLP   p 309
355 BURRARD ST SUITE 700, VANCOU-
VER, BC, V6C 2G8
(604) 687-1231   SIC 8721
SNAP HOME FINANCE CORP   p 300
538 CAMBIE ST, VANCOUVER, BC, V6B
2N7
(866) 282-2384   SIC 8742
SNAP LAKE PROJECT   p 22
See DE BEERS CANADA INC
**SNAP TIGHT ALUMINUM RAILING SYS-
TEM INTERNATIONAL LTD**   p
187
7465 CONWAY AVE, BURNABY, BC, V5E
2P7
(604) 438-6261   SIC 5051
SNAP TOGETHER PRODUCTIONS   p 454
5091 TERMINAL RD, HALIFAX, NS, B3J
3Y1
(902) 422-6287   SIC 4833
SNAP-ON TOOLS OF CANADA LTD   p 727
6500A MILLCREEK DR, MISSISSAUGA,
ON, L5N 2W6
(905) 826-8600   SIC 3536
SNAP-ON TOOLS OF CANADA LTD   p 756
See SNAP-ON TOOLS OF CANADA LTD

SNAP-ON TOOLS OF CANADA LTD   p 756
145 HARRY WALKER PKY N, NEWMAR-
KET, ON, L3Y 7B3
(905) 812-5774   SIC 3469
SNAP-ON TOOLS OF CANADA LTD   p 756
195 HARRY WALKER PKY N UNIT A, NEW-
MARKET, ON, L3Y 7B3
(905) 836-8121   SIC 5013
**SNC LAVALIN ENGINEERS & CONSTRUC-
TORS**   p
861
See SNC-LAVALIN INTERNATIONAL INC
SNC-LAVALIN ATP INC   p 59
640 5 AVE SW UNIT 300, CALGARY, AB,
T2P 3G4
(403) 539-4550   SIC 8711
SNC-LAVALIN CONSTRUCTION INCp 1192
455 BOUL RENE-LEVESQUE O BUREAU
202, MONTREAL, QC, H2Z 1Z3
(514) 393-1000   SIC 1542
**SNC-LAVALIN CONSTRUCTORS (PACIFIC)
INC**   p 262
7400 RIVER RD SUITE 160, RICHMOND,
BC, V6X 1X6
SIC 1541
SNC-LAVALIN GEM QUEBEC INC   p 1116
3306 BOUL SAINT-FRANCOIS, JON-
QUIERE, QC, G7X 2W9
(418) 547-5716   SIC 8742
SNC-LAVALIN GEM QUEBEC INC   p 1192
455 BOUL RENE-LEVESQUE O, MON-
TREAL, QC, H2Z 1Z3
(514) 393-8000   SIC 8742
SNC-LAVALIN GTS INC   p 1190
360 RUE SAINT-JACQUES BUREAU 1600,
MONTREAL, QC, H2Y 1P5
(514) 393-1000   SIC 6712
SNC-LAVALIN INC   p 59
605 5 AVE SW SUITE 1400, CALGARY, AB,
T2P 3H5
(403) 294-2100   SIC 8711
SNC-LAVALIN INC   p 91
10235 101 ST NW SUITE 608, EDMON-
TON, AB, T5J 3G1
(780) 426-1000   SIC 8711
SNC-LAVALIN INC   p 316
745 THURLOW ST SUITE 500, VANCOU-
VER, BC, V6E 0C5
(604) 662-3555   SIC 8711
SNC-LAVALIN INC   p 396
88 SR GREEN RD SUITE 101, CAMPBELL-
TON, NB, E3N 3Y6
(506) 759-6350   SIC 6798
SNC-LAVALIN INC   p 426
1090 TOPSAIL RD, MOUNT PEARL, NL,
A1N 5E7
(709) 368-0118   SIC 8711
SNC-LAVALIN INC   p 454
5657 SPRING GARDEN RD SUITE 200,
HALIFAX, NS, B3J 3R4
(902) 492-4544   SIC 8711
SNC-LAVALIN INC   p 580
195 THE WEST MALL, ETOBICOKE, ON,
M9C 5K1
(416) 252-5315   SIC 8711
SNC-LAVALIN INC   p 1192
455 BOUL RENE-LEVESQUE O, MON-
TREAL, QC, H2Z 1Z3
(514) 393-1000   SIC 8711
SNC-LAVALIN INC   p 1280
5500 BOUL DES GALERIES BUREAU 200,
QUEBEC, QC, G2K 2E2
(418) 621-5500   SIC 8711
SNC-LAVALIN INTERNATIONAL INC   p 59
605 5 AVE SW SUITE 1400, CALGARY, AB,
T2P 3H5
(403) 294-2100   SIC 8711
SNC-LAVALIN INTERNATIONAL INC p 799
2275 UPPER MIDDLE RD E, OAKVILLE,
ON, L6H 0C3
(905) 829-8808   SIC 8711
SNC-LAVALIN INTERNATIONAL INC p 861
265 FRONT ST N SUITE 301, SARNIA, ON,
N7T 7X1

(519) 336-0201   SIC 8711
SNC-LAVALIN NUCLEAR INC   p 715
2251 SPEAKMAN DR, MISSISSAUGA, ON,
L5K 1B2
(905) 829-8808   SIC 8999
**SNC-LAVALIN OPERATIONS & MAINTE-
NANCE INC**   p
580
195 THE WEST MALL, ETOBICOKE, ON,
M9C 5K8
(416) 207-4700   SIC 6531
SNC-LAVALIN PHARMA INC   p 1228
8000 BOUL DECARIE 3EME ETAGE, MON-
TREAL, QC, H4P 2S4
(514) 735-5651   SIC 8711
SNC-LAVALIN STAVIBEL INC   p 1290
1375 AV LARIVIERE, ROUYN-NORANDA,
QC, J9X 6M6
(819) 764-5181   SIC 8711
SNC-LAVALIN STAVIBEL INC   p 1391
1271 7E RUE, VAL-D'OR, QC, J9P 3S1
(819) 825-2233   SIC 8711
SNELLING PAPER & SANITATION LTD p
816
1410 TRIOLE ST, OTTAWA, ON, K1B 3M5
(613) 745-7184   SIC 5113
SNJ FORESTERIE   p 394
4016 ROUTE 480, ACADIEVILLE, NB, E4Y
2B7
(506) 775-2895   SIC 0851
SNO-BALL   p 1157
See PERRIN INC
SNOBELEN FARMS LTD   p 663
323 HAVELOCK ST, LUCKNOW, ON, N0G
2H0
(519) 528-2092   SIC 5153
SNOBSHOP   p 1101
See ATTITUDES IMPORT INC
SNOC INC   p 1314
17200 AV CENTRALE, SAINT-HYACINTHE,
QC, J2T 4J7
(450) 774-5238   SIC 3648
SNOLAB   p 647
See SUDBURY NEUTRINO OBSERVA-
TORY
SNOW CAP ENTERPRISES LTD   p 181
5698 TRAPP AVE SUITE 564, BURNABY,
BC, V3N 5G4
(604) 515-3202   SIC 5461
SNOW COVERS   p 321
See SNOW COVERS SPORTS INC
SNOW COVERS SPORTS INC   p 321
1701 3RD AVE W, VANCOUVER, BC, V6J
1K7
(604) 738-3715   SIC 5941
SNOW, DR. V. A. CENTRE INC   p 403
54 DEMILLE CRT SUITE 14, HAMPTON,
NB, E5N 5S7
(506) 832-6210   SIC 8051
SNOWBEAR LIMITED   p 604
155 DAWSON RD, GUELPH, ON, N1H 1A4
SIC 3523
SNOWBEAR TRAILERS   p 604
See SNOWBEAR LIMITED
SNOWBIRD VACATIONS INTERNATIONAL
p 266
See FORUM NATIONAL INVESTMENTS
LTD
**SNOWCAP INTERIOR FOOD SERVICES
LTD**   p 180
4130 SPALLUMCHEEN DR, ARMSTRONG,
BC, V0E 1B6
(250) 546-8781   SIC 5149
SNOWCREST PACKERS   p 1013
See OMSTEAD FOODS LIMITED
SNOWHITE   p 839
See OMYA CANADA INC
SNOWLINE ENTERPRISES LTD   p 224
3121 HILL RD SUITE 214, LAKE COUN-
TRY, BC, V4V 1G1
(250) 766-0068   SIC 5169
SNOWLINE RESTAURANTS INC   p 343
4429 SUNDIAL PL, WHISTLER, BC, V0N
1B4

(604) 932-5151   *SIC* 5812
SNOWSHOE MOUNTAIN RESOURCES CORP   *p* 230
GD, MACKENZIE, BC, V0J 2C0
(250) 988-1325   *SIC* 4924
SNR NURSING HOMES LTD   *p* 1017
11550 MCNORTON ST, WINDSOR, ON, N8P 1T9
(519) 979-6730   *SIC* 8361
SNUBCO GROUP INC   *p* 150
502 23A AVE, NISKU, AB, T9E 8G2
(780) 955-3550   *SIC* 1389
SNUBCO PRESSURE CONTROL LTD *p* 150
502 23A AVE, NISKU, AB, T9E 8G2
(780) 955-3550   *SIC* 1389
SNUG HARBOUR SEAFOOD BAR & GRILL *p* 713
14 STAVEBANK RD S, MISSISSAUGA, ON, L5G 2T1
(905) 274-5000   *SIC* 5812
SNUG PUB   *p* 333
See OAK BAY BEACH HOTEL LIMITED
SO CANADA INC   *p* 768
2005 SHEPPARD AVE E SUITE 100, NORTH YORK, ON, M2J 5B4
SIC 8731
SO, JAMES REALTY LTD   *p* 921
259 BROADVIEW AVE, TORONTO, ON, M4M 2G6
(416) 465-2412   *SIC* 6531
SOARING PHOENIX INC   *p* 1364
15 BOUL DU CURE-LABELLE, SAINTE-THERESE, QC, J7E 2X1
(450) 435-6541   *SIC* 6712
SOBEC   *p* 1137
See PAQUET & FILS LTEE
SOBEY'S   *p* 6
See JELSCHEN FOODS LTD
SOBEY'S   *p* 161
See SHERWOOD PARK IGA
SOBEY'S   *p* 478
See SOBEYS CAPITAL INCORPORATED
SOBEY'S   *p* 500
See SOBEYS CAPITAL INCORPORATED
SOBEY'S   *p* 1015
See PRINGLE CREEK I G A
SOBEY'S 649   *p* 1007
See SOBEYS CAPITAL INCORPORATED
SOBEY'S 861   *p* 422
See SOBEYS CAPITAL INCORPORATED
SOBEY'S READY TO SERVE 640   *p* 1036
See SOBEYS CAPITAL INCORPORATED
SOBEY'S RIVERGROVE   *p* 370
See 3881793 MANITOBA LTD
SOBEY'S STORE 777   *p* 806
See SOBEYS CAPITAL INCORPORATED
SOBEY'S WEST, DIV OF   *p* 18
See SOBEYS CAPITAL INCORPORATED
SOBEYS   *p* 70
See SOBEYS CAPITAL INCORPORATED
SOBEYS   *p* 77
See SOBEYS CAPITAL INCORPORATED
SOBEYS   *p* 106
See SOBEYS CAPITAL INCORPORATED
SOBEYS   *p* 123
See SOBEYS CAPITAL INCORPORATED
SOBEYS   *p* 144
See SOBEYS CAPITAL INCORPORATED
SOBEYS   *p* 151
See SOBEYS CAPITAL INCORPORATED
SOBEYS   *p* 157
See SOBEYS CAPITAL INCORPORATED
SOBEYS   *p* 163
See SOBEYS CAPITAL INCORPORATED
SOBEYS   *p* 166
See SOBEYS CAPITAL INCORPORATED
SOBEYS   *p* 350
See DORING ENTERPRISES INC
SOBEYS   *p* 355
See W.R.A. ENTERPRISES PORTAGE LA PRAIRIE LTD
SOBEYS   *p* 367
See SOBEYS CAPITAL INCORPORATED
SOBEYS   *p* 396

See SOBEYS CAPITAL INCORPORATED
SOBEYS   *p* 400
See SOBEYS CAPITAL INCORPORATED
SOBEYS   *p* 401
See SOBEYS CAPITAL INCORPORATED
SOBEYS   *p* 407
See SOBEYS CAPITAL INCORPORATED
SOBEYS   *p* 417
See SOBEYS CAPITAL INCORPORATED
SOBEYS   *p* 433
See SOBEYS CAPITAL INCORPORATED
SOBEYS   *p* 443
See SOBEYS CAPITAL INCORPORATED
SOBEYS   *p* 457
See SOBEYS CAPITAL INCORPORATED
SOBEYS   *p* 458
See SOBEYS CAPITAL INCORPORATED
SOBEYS   *p* 463
See SOBEYS CAPITAL INCORPORATED
SOBEYS   *p* 464
See SOBEYS CAPITAL INCORPORATED
SOBEYS   *p* 466
See SOBEYS INC
SOBEYS   *p* 475
See SOBEYS CAPITAL INCORPORATED
SOBEYS   *p* 481
See SOBEYS CAPITAL INCORPORATED
SOBEYS   *p* 512
See SOBEYS CAPITAL INCORPORATED
SOBEYS   *p* 600
See SOBEYS CAPITAL INCORPORATED
SOBEYS   *p* 641
See SOBEYS CAPITAL INCORPORATED
SOBEYS   *p* 651
See R. GREEN SUPERMARKETS INC
SOBEYS   *p* 814
See SOBEYS CAPITAL INCORPORATED
SOBEYS   *p* 840
See 1307299 ONTARIO INC.
SOBEYS   *p* 881
See SOBEYS CAPITAL INCORPORATED
SOBEYS   *p* 895
See SOBEYS CAPITAL INCORPORATED
SOBEYS   *p* 902
See 1323339 ONTARIO LIMITED
SOBEYS   *p* 1009
See SOBEYS CAPITAL INCORPORATED
SOBEYS   *p* 1012
See 1847674 ONTARIO INC
SOBEYS   *p* 1041
See SOBEYS CAPITAL INCORPORATED
SOBEYS   *p* 1240
See SOBEYS CAPITAL INCORPORATED
SOBEYS   *p* 1290
See SOBEYS CAPITAL INCORPORATED
SOBEYS # 439   *p* 1076
See SOBEYS CAPITAL INCORPORATED
SOBEYS # 596   *p* 438
See SOBEYS CAPITAL INCORPORATED
SOBEYS #425   *p* 1043
See SOBEYS CAPITAL INCORPORATED
SOBEYS #574   *p* 451
See SOBEYS CAPITAL INCORPORATED
SOBEYS #590   *p* 422
See SOBEYS CAPITAL INCORPORATED
SOBEYS #594   *p* 469
See SOBEYS CAPITAL INCORPORATED
SOBEYS #660   *p* 450
See SOBEYS CAPITAL INCORPORATED
SOBEYS #670   *p* 461
See SOBEYS CAPITAL INCORPORATED
SOBEYS #672   *p* 470
See SOBEYS CAPITAL INCORPORATED
SOBEYS #692   *p* 413
See SOBEYS CAPITAL INCORPORATED
SOBEYS #704   *p* 464
See SOBEYS CAPITAL INCORPORATED
SOBEYS #736   *p* 411
See SOBEYS CAPITAL INCORPORATED
SOBEYS #747   *p* 464
See SOBEYS CAPITAL INCORPORATED
SOBEYS #772   *p* 443
See SOBEYS CAPITAL INCORPORATED
SOBEYS #776   *p* 444

See SOBEYS CAPITAL INCORPORATED
SOBEYS 323   *p* 439
See SOBEYS CAPITAL INCORPORATED
SOBEYS 495   *p* 412
See SOBEYS CAPITAL INCORPORATED
SOBEYS 576   *p* 416
See SOBEYS CAPITAL INCORPORATED
SOBEYS 588   *p* 460
See SOBEYS CAPITAL INCORPORATED
SOBEYS 611   *p* 920
See SOBEYS CAPITAL INCORPORATED
SOBEYS 634   *p* 485
See SOBEYS CAPITAL INCORPORATED
SOBEYS 678   *p* 535
See SOBEYS CAPITAL INCORPORATED
SOBEYS 846   *p* 420
See SOBEYS CAPITAL INCORPORATED
SOBEYS ATLANTIC   *p* 449
See SOBEYS CAPITAL INCORPORATED
SOBEYS CAPITAL INCORPORATED   *p* 5
5700 50 ST, BEAUMONT, AB, T4X 1M8
(780) 929-2749   *SIC* 5411
SOBEYS CAPITAL INCORPORATED   *p* 18
7704 30 ST SE, CALGARY, AB, T2C 1M8
SIC 5141
SOBEYS CAPITAL INCORPORATED   *p* 70
150 MILLRISE BLVD SW UNIT 3109, CALGARY, AB, T2Y 5G7
(403) 873-5085   *SIC* 5411
SOBEYS CAPITAL INCORPORATED   *p* 70
2335 162 AVE SW SUITE 100, CALGARY, AB, T2Y 4S6
(403) 873-0101   *SIC* 5411
SOBEYS CAPITAL INCORPORATED   *p* 71
20 MCKENZIE TOWNE AVE SE, CALGARY, AB, T2Z 3S7
(403) 257-4343   *SIC* 5411
SOBEYS CAPITAL INCORPORATED   *p* 77
11300 TUSCANY BLVD NW SUITE 2020, CALGARY, AB, T3L 2V7
(403) 375-0595   *SIC* 5411
SOBEYS CAPITAL INCORPORATED   *p* 81
6403 51 ST, COLD LAKE, AB, T9M 1C8
(780) 594-3335   *SIC* 5411
SOBEYS CAPITAL INCORPORATED   *p* 94
13140 ST ALBERT TRAIL NW, EDMONTON, AB, T5L 4P6
(780) 486-4800   *SIC* 5411
SOBEYS CAPITAL INCORPORATED *p* 106
12910 156 ST NW, EDMONTON, AB, T5V 1E9
(780) 447-1440   *SIC* 5141
SOBEYS CAPITAL INCORPORATED *p* 107
5119 167 AVE NW, EDMONTON, AB, T5Y 0L2
(780) 478-4740   *SIC* 5411
SOBEYS CAPITAL INCORPORATED *p* 107
15367 CASTLE DOWNS RD NW, EDMONTON, AB, T5X 6C3
(780) 472-0100   *SIC* 5411
SOBEYS CAPITAL INCORPORATED *p* 119
2011 111 ST NW, EDMONTON, AB, T6J 4V9
(780) 435-1224   *SIC* 5411
SOBEYS CAPITAL INCORPORATED *p* 120
5011 23 AVE NW, EDMONTON, AB, T6L 7G5
(780) 485-6622   *SIC* 5411
SOBEYS CAPITAL INCORPORATED *p* 123
2430 RABBIT HILL RD NW, EDMONTON, AB, T6R 3B5
(780) 989-1610   *SIC* 5411
SOBEYS CAPITAL INCORPORATED *p* 129
210 THICKWOOD BLVD, FORT MCMURRAY, AB, T9K 1X9
(780) 743-9339   *SIC* 5411
SOBEYS CAPITAL INCORPORATED *p* 130
10004 99 AVE, FORT SASKATCHEWAN, AB, T8L 3Y1
(780) 998-5429   *SIC* 5411
SOBEYS CAPITAL INCORPORATED *p* 141
327 BLUEFOX BLVD N, LETHBRIDGE, AB, T1H 6T3
(403) 320-5154   *SIC* 5411

SOBEYS CAPITAL INCORPORATED *p* 144
4227 75 AVE, LLOYDMINSTER, AB, T9V 2X4
(780) 871-0955   *SIC* 5411
SOBEYS CAPITAL INCORPORATED *p* 144
4227 75 AVE, LLOYDMINSTER, AB, T9V 2X4
(780) 875-3215   *SIC* 5411
SOBEYS CAPITAL INCORPORATED *p* 151
201 SOUTHRIDGE DR SUITE 700, OKOTOKS, AB, T1S 2E1
(403) 995-4088   *SIC* 5411
SOBEYS CAPITAL INCORPORATED *p* 151
6700 46 ST SUITE 300, OLDS, AB, T4H 0A2
(403) 556-3113   *SIC* 5411
SOBEYS CAPITAL INCORPORATED *p* 157
2110 50 AVE, RED DEER, AB, T4R 2K1
(403) 348-0848   *SIC* 5411
SOBEYS CAPITAL INCORPORATED *p* 159
4419 52 AVE, ROCKY MOUNTAIN HOUSE, AB, T4T 1A3
(403) 846-0038   *SIC* 5411
SOBEYS CAPITAL INCORPORATED *p* 159
5427 52 AVE, ROCKY MOUNTAIN HOUSE, AB, T4T 1S9
(403) 845-3371   *SIC* 5411
SOBEYS CAPITAL INCORPORATED *p* 163
590 BASELINE RD UNIT 100, SHERWOOD PARK, AB, T8H 1Y4
(780) 417-0419   *SIC* 5411
SOBEYS CAPITAL INCORPORATED *p* 166
392 ST ALBERT RD, ST. ALBERT, AB, T8N 5J9
(780) 459-5909   *SIC* 5411
SOBEYS CAPITAL INCORPORATED *p* 167
4607 50 ST, STETTLER, AB, T0C 2L0
(403) 742-5025   *SIC* 5411
SOBEYS CAPITAL INCORPORATED *p* 172
4703 50 ST, WETASKIWIN, AB, T9A 1J6
(780) 352-2227   *SIC* 5411
SOBEYS CAPITAL INCORPORATED *p* 348
3409 VICTORIA AVE, BRANDON, MB, R7B 2L8
(204) 727-3443   *SIC* 5411
SOBEYS CAPITAL INCORPORATED *p* 358
178 PTH 12 N UNIT 1, STEINBACH, MB, R5G 1T7
(204) 326-1316   *SIC* 5411
SOBEYS CAPITAL INCORPORATED *p* 367
965 HENDERSON HWY, WINNIPEG, MB, R2K 2M2
(204) 338-0349   *SIC* 5411
SOBEYS CAPITAL INCORPORATED *p* 368
1939 BISHOP GRANDIN BLVD, WINNIPEG, MB, R2M 5S1
(204) 255-5064   *SIC* 5411
SOBEYS CAPITAL INCORPORATED *p* 368
1500 DAKOTA ST SUITE 1, WINNIPEG, MB, R2N 3Y7
(204) 253-3663   *SIC* 5411
SOBEYS CAPITAL INCORPORATED *p* 373
1870 BURROWS AVE, WINNIPEG, MB, R2X 3C3
(204) 697-1997   *SIC* 5411
SOBEYS CAPITAL INCORPORATED *p* 373
1800 INKSTER BLVD, WINNIPEG, MB, R2X 2Z5
(204) 632-7100   *SIC* 5141
SOBEYS CAPITAL INCORPORATED *p* 387
3635 PORTAGE AVE, WINNIPEG, MB, R3K 2G6
(204) 832-8605   *SIC* 5411
SOBEYS CAPITAL INCORPORATED *p* 389
1660 KENASTON BLVD, WINNIPEG, MB, R3P 2M6
(204) 489-7007   *SIC* 5411
SOBEYS CAPITAL INCORPORATED *p* 396
140 ROSEBERRY ST, CAMPBELLTON, NB, E3N 2G9
(506) 753-5339   *SIC* 5411
SOBEYS CAPITAL INCORPORATED *p* 400
463 BROOKSIDE DR SUITE 349, FREDERICTON, NB, E3A 8V4
(506) 450-7109   *SIC* 5411

▲ Public Company   ■ Public Company Family Member   **HQ** Headquarters   **BR** Branch   **SL** Single Location

SOBEYS CAPITAL INCORPORATED *p* 401
1150 PROSPECT ST, FREDERICTON, NB, E3B 3C1
(506) 458-8891   *SIC* 5411

SOBEYS CAPITAL INCORPORATED *p* 407
1380 MOUNTAIN RD, MONCTON, NB, E1C 2T8
(506) 858-8283   *SIC* 5411

SOBEYS CAPITAL INCORPORATED *p* 411
1 LEWIS ST, OROMOCTO, NB, E2V 4K5
(506) 357-9831   *SIC* 5411

SOBEYS CAPITAL INCORPORATED *p* 411
1160 FINDLAY BLVD, RIVERVIEW, NB, E1B 0J6
(506) 386-4616   *SIC* 5411

SOBEYS CAPITAL INCORPORATED *p* 412
140A HAMPTON RD, ROTHESAY, NB, E2E 2R1
(506) 847-5697   *SIC* 5411

SOBEYS CAPITAL INCORPORATED *p* 413
519 WESTMORLAND RD, SAINT JOHN, NB, E2J 3W9
(506) 633-1187   *SIC* 5411

SOBEYS CAPITAL INCORPORATED *p* 414
149 LANSDOWNE AVE SUITE 233, SAINT JOHN, NB, E2K 2Z9
(506) 652-4470   *SIC* 5411

SOBEYS CAPITAL INCORPORATED *p* 416
1 PLAZA AVE, SAINT JOHN, NB, E2M 0C2
(506) 674-1460   *SIC* 5411

SOBEYS CAPITAL INCORPORATED *p* 417
183 MAIN ST SUITE 738, SHEDIAC, NB, E4P 2A5
(506) 532-0842   *SIC* 5411

SOBEYS CAPITAL INCORPORATED *p* 420
370 CONNELL ST UNIT 11, WOODSTOCK, NB, E7M 5G9
(506) 328-6819   *SIC* 5411

SOBEYS CAPITAL INCORPORATED *p* 422
1 MOUNT BERNARD AVE SUITE 861, CORNER BROOK, NL, A2H 6Y5
(709) 639-7193   *SIC* 5411

SOBEYS CAPITAL INCORPORATED *p* 422
350 CONCEPTION BAY HWY, CONCEPTION BAY SOUTH, NL, A1X 7A3
(709) 834-9052   *SIC* 5411

SOBEYS CAPITAL INCORPORATED *p* 426
10 OLD PLACENTIA RD, MOUNT PEARL, NL, A1N 4P5
(709) 748-1200   *SIC* 5148

SOBEYS CAPITAL INCORPORATED *p* 429
10 ELIZABETH AVE SUITE 744, ST. JOHN'S, NL, A1A 5L4
(709) 753-3402   *SIC* 5411

SOBEYS CAPITAL INCORPORATED *p* 433
45 ROPEWALK LANE, ST. JOHN'S, NL, A1E 4P1
(709) 739-8663   *SIC* 5411

SOBEYS CAPITAL INCORPORATED *p* 433
470 TOPSAIL RD SUITE 340, ST. JOHN'S, NL, A1E 2C3
(709) 748-1250   *SIC* 5411

SOBEYS CAPITAL INCORPORATED *p* 438
151 CHURCH ST, ANTIGONISH, NS, B2G 2E2
(902) 863-6022   *SIC* 5411

SOBEYS CAPITAL INCORPORATED *p* 439
3552 HWY 3, BARRINGTON PASSAGE, NS, B0W 1G0
(902) 637-3063   *SIC* 5411

SOBEYS CAPITAL INCORPORATED *p* 441
349 LAHAVE ST SUITE 322, BRIDGEWATER, NS, B4V 2T6
(902) 543-9244   *SIC* 5411

SOBEYS CAPITAL INCORPORATED *p* 443
100 MAIN ST SUITE 250, DARTMOUTH, NS, B2X 1R5
(902) 434-6696   *SIC* 5411

SOBEYS CAPITAL INCORPORATED *p* 443
612 MAIN ST SUITE 622, DARTMOUTH, NS, B2W 5M5
(902) 433-0140   *SIC* 5411

SOBEYS CAPITAL INCORPORATED *p* 443
4 FOREST HILLS PKY, DARTMOUTH, NS, B2W 5G7
(902) 435-3909   *SIC* 5411

SOBEYS CAPITAL INCORPORATED *p* 444
6 PRIMROSE ST, DARTMOUTH, NS, B3A 4C5
(902) 463-2910   *SIC* 5411

SOBEYS CAPITAL INCORPORATED *p* 444
551 PORTLAND ST, DARTMOUTH, NS, B2Y 4B1
(902) 469-8396   *SIC* 5411

SOBEYS CAPITAL INCORPORATED *p* 449
246 LANCASTER CRES, DEBERT, NS, B0M 1G0
(902) 752-8371   *SIC* 5411

SOBEYS CAPITAL INCORPORATED *p* 450
269 HIGHWAY 214 UNIT 1, ELMSDALE, NS, B2S 1K1
(902) 883-8111   *SIC* 5411

SOBEYS CAPITAL INCORPORATED *p* 451
1120 QUEEN ST, HALIFAX, NS, B3H 2R9
(902) 422-7605   *SIC* 5411

SOBEYS CAPITAL INCORPORATED *p* 456
2651 WINDSOR ST SUITE 554, HALIFAX, NS, B3K 5C7
(902) 455-8508   *SIC* 5411

SOBEYS CAPITAL INCORPORATED *p* 457
287 LACEWOOD DR SUITE 644, HALIFAX, NS, B3M 3Y7
(902) 457-2102   *SIC* 5411

SOBEYS CAPITAL INCORPORATED *p* 458
279 HERRING COVE RD, HALIFAX, NS, B3P 1M2
(902) 477-2817   *SIC* 5411

SOBEYS CAPITAL INCORPORATED *p* 460
180 BRISTOL AVE, LIVERPOOL, NS, B0T 1K0
(902) 354-4225   *SIC* 5411

SOBEYS CAPITAL INCORPORATED *p* 461
752 SACKVILLE DR SUITE 670, LOWER SACKVILLE, NS, B4E 1R7
(902) 865-5057   *SIC* 5411

SOBEYS CAPITAL INCORPORATED *p* 463
38 GEORGE ST SUITE 652, NEW GLASGOW, NS, B2H 2K1
(902) 752-6258   *SIC* 5411

SOBEYS CAPITAL INCORPORATED *p* 464
239 WEST RIVER RD, PICTOU, NS, B0K 1H0
(902) 485-5841   *SIC* 5411

SOBEYS CAPITAL INCORPORATED *p* 464
622 REEVES ST UNIT 1, PORT HAWKESBURY, NS, B9A 2R7
(902) 625-1242   *SIC* 5411

SOBEYS CAPITAL INCORPORATED *p* 464
9256 COMMERCIAL ST, NEW MINAS, NS, B4N 4A9
(902) 681-3723   *SIC* 5411

SOBEYS CAPITAL INCORPORATED *p* 466
115 KING ST, STELLARTON, NS, B0K 0A2
(902) 752-8371   *SIC* 5141

SOBEYS CAPITAL INCORPORATED *p* 467
272B PRINCE ST, SYDNEY, NS, B1P 5K6
(902) 562-1762   *SIC* 5411

SOBEYS CAPITAL INCORPORATED *p* 469
68 ROBIE ST SUITE 594, TRURO, NS, B2N 1L2
(902) 893-9388   *SIC* 5411

SOBEYS CAPITAL INCORPORATED *p* 469
985 PRINCE ST, TRURO, NS, B2N 1H7
(902) 895-9579   *SIC* 5411

SOBEYS CAPITAL INCORPORATED *p* 470
50 EMPIRE LANE WENTWORTH RD, WINDSOR, NS, B0N 2T0
(902) 798-0992   *SIC* 5411

SOBEYS CAPITAL INCORPORATED *p* 475
260 KINGSTON RD W, AJAX, ON, L1T 4E4
(905) 426-7144   *SIC* 5411

SOBEYS CAPITAL INCORPORATED *p* 476
161 YOUNG ST, ALLISTON, ON, L9R 2A9
(705) 434-9512   *SIC* 5411

SOBEYS CAPITAL INCORPORATED *p* 477
83 SANDWICH ST S, AMHERSTBURG, ON, N9V 1Z5
(519) 736-4520   *SIC* 5411

SOBEYS CAPITAL INCORPORATED *p* 478
247 MILL ST, ANGUS, ON, L0M 1B2
(705) 424-1588   *SIC* 5411

SOBEYS CAPITAL INCORPORATED *p* 478
977 GOLF LINKS RD, ANCASTER, ON, L9K 1K1
(905) 648-3534   *SIC* 5411

SOBEYS CAPITAL INCORPORATED *p* 481
15500 BAYVIEW AVE, AURORA, ON, L4G 7J1
(905) 726-2530   *SIC* 5411

SOBEYS CAPITAL INCORPORATED *p* 485
409 BAYFIELD ST SUITE C1, BARRIE, ON, L4M 6E5
(705) 739-1100   *SIC* 5411

SOBEYS CAPITAL INCORPORATED *p* 488
37 MAPLEVIEW DR W, BARRIE, ON, L4N 9H5
(705) 728-9858   *SIC* 5411

SOBEYS CAPITAL INCORPORATED *p* 490
4610 ONTARIO ST, BEAMSVILLE, ON, L0R 1B3
(905) 563-1088   *SIC* 5411

SOBEYS CAPITAL INCORPORATED *p* 500
930 NORTH PARK DR, BRAMPTON, ON, L6S 3Y5
(905) 458-7673   *SIC* 5411

SOBEYS CAPITAL INCORPORATED *p* 512
11965 HURONTARIO ST, BRAMPTON, ON, L6Z 4P7
(905) 846-5658   *SIC* 5411

SOBEYS CAPITAL INCORPORATED *p* 512
380 BOVAIRD DR E SUITE 29, BRAMPTON, ON, L6Z 2S8
(905) 840-0770   *SIC* 5411

SOBEYS CAPITAL INCORPORATED *p* 512
8975 CHINGUACOUSY RD, BRAMPTON, ON, L6Y 0J2
(905) 796-1517   *SIC* 5411

SOBEYS CAPITAL INCORPORATED *p* 534
75 DUNDAS ST, CAMBRIDGE, ON, N1R 6G5
(519) 620-9022   *SIC* 5411

SOBEYS CAPITAL INCORPORATED *p* 535
130 CEDAR ST, CAMBRIDGE, ON, N1S 1W4
(519) 622-8906   *SIC* 5411

SOBEYS CAPITAL INCORPORATED *p* 573
125 THE QUEENSWAY, ETOBICOKE, ON, M8Y 1H6
(416) 259-1758   *SIC* 5411

SOBEYS CAPITAL INCORPORATED *p* 590
15 LINDSAY ST, FENELON FALLS, ON, K0M 1N0
(705) 887-3611   *SIC* 5411

SOBEYS CAPITAL INCORPORATED *p* 591
110 20 HWY E, FONTHILL, ON, L0S 1E0
(905) 892-2570   *SIC* 5411

SOBEYS CAPITAL INCORPORATED *p* 598
55 MAIN ST E, GRAND BEND, ON, N0M 1T0
(519) 238-8944   *SIC* 5411

SOBEYS CAPITAL INCORPORATED *p* 600
44 LIVINGSTON AVE, GRIMSBY, ON, L3M 1L1
(905) 945-9973   *SIC* 5411

SOBEYS CAPITAL INCORPORATED *p* 609
700 QUEENSTON RD UNIT A, HAMILTON, ON, L8G 1A3
(905) 560-8111   *SIC* 5411

SOBEYS CAPITAL INCORPORATED *p* 615
905 RYMAL RD E, HAMILTON, ON, L8W 3M2
(905) 383-9930   *SIC* 5411

SOBEYS CAPITAL INCORPORATED *p* 618
236 10TH ST, HANOVER, ON, N4N 1N9
(519) 364-2891   *SIC* 5411

SOBEYS CAPITAL INCORPORATED *p* 627
840 MARCH RD, KANATA, ON, K2W 0C9
(613) 599-8965   *SIC* 5411

SOBEYS CAPITAL INCORPORATED *p* 629
814 DURHAM ST, KINCARDINE, ON, N2Z 3B9
(519) 395-0022   *SIC* 5411

SOBEYS CAPITAL INCORPORATED *p* 638
1187 FISCHER HALLMAN RD SUITE 852, KITCHENER, ON, N2E 4H9
(519) 576-1280   *SIC* 5411

SOBEYS CAPITAL INCORPORATED *p* 641
274 HIGHLAND RD W, KITCHENER, ON, N2M 3C5
(519) 744-6561   *SIC* 5411

SOBEYS CAPITAL INCORPORATED *p* 686
7205 GOREWAY DR UNIT1, MISSISSAUGA, ON, L4T 2T9
(905) 677-0239   *SIC* 5411

SOBEYS CAPITAL INCORPORATED *p* 719
5602 TENTH LINE W, MISSISSAUGA, ON, L5M 7L9
(905) 858-2899   *SIC* 5411

SOBEYS CAPITAL INCORPORATED *p* 760
3714 PORTAGE RD, NIAGARA FALLS, ON, L2J 2K9
(905) 371-2270   *SIC* 5411

SOBEYS CAPITAL INCORPORATED *p* 764
1899 ALGONQUIN AVE, NORTH BAY, ON, P1B 4Y8
(705) 472-4001   *SIC* 5411

SOBEYS CAPITAL INCORPORATED *p* 764
2555 TROUT LAKE RD, NORTH BAY, ON, P1B 7S8
(705) 495-4221   *SIC* 5141

SOBEYS CAPITAL INCORPORATED *p* 775
6201 BATHURST ST, NORTH YORK, ON, M2R 2A5
SIC 5411

SOBEYS CAPITAL INCORPORATED *p* 801
511 MAPLE GROVE DR SUITE 4, OAKVILLE, ON, L6J 6X8
(905) 849-0691   *SIC* 5411

SOBEYS CAPITAL INCORPORATED *p* 805
2441 LAKESHORE RD W, OAKVILLE, ON, L6L 5V5
(905) 825-2278   *SIC* 5411

SOBEYS CAPITAL INCORPORATED *p* 806
1500 UPPER MIDDLE RD W, OAKVILLE, ON, L6M 0C2
(905) 847-1909   *SIC* 5411

SOBEYS CAPITAL INCORPORATED *p* 809
500 RIDDELL RD, ORANGEVILLE, ON, L9W 5L1
(519) 941-1339   *SIC* 5411

SOBEYS CAPITAL INCORPORATED *p* 813
564 KING ST E, OSHAWA, ON, L1H 1G5
(905) 571-4835   *SIC* 5411

SOBEYS CAPITAL INCORPORATED *p* 814
1377 WILSON RD N, OSHAWA, ON, L1K 2Z5
(905) 440-4687   *SIC* 5411

SOBEYS CAPITAL INCORPORATED *p* 837
307 GRAND RIVER ST N, PARIS, ON, N3L 2N9
(519) 442-4485   *SIC* 5411

SOBEYS CAPITAL INCORPORATED *p* 881
438 NORFOLK ST S, SIMCOE, ON, N3Y 2X3
(519) 426-4799   *SIC* 5411

SOBEYS CAPITAL INCORPORATED *p* 883
400 SCOTT ST, ST CATHARINES, ON, L2M 3W4
(905) 935-9974   *SIC* 5411

SOBEYS CAPITAL INCORPORATED *p* 895
30 QUEENSLAND RD, STRATFORD, ON, N4Z 1H4
(519) 273-2631   *SIC* 5411

SOBEYS CAPITAL INCORPORATED *p* 906
9200 BATHURST ST, THORNHILL, ON, L4J 8W1
(905) 731-7600   *SIC* 5411

SOBEYS CAPITAL INCORPORATED *p* 912
678 BROADWAY ST, TILLSONBURG, ON, N4G 3S9
(519) 688-1734   *SIC* 5411

SOBEYS CAPITAL INCORPORATED *p* 917
2451 DANFORTH AVE SUITE 938, TORONTO, ON, M4C 1L1
(416) 698-6868   *SIC* 5411

SOBEYS CAPITAL INCORPORATED *p* 920

▲ Public Company   ■ Public Company Family Member   **HQ** Headquarters   **BR** Branch   **SL** Single Location

1015 BROADVIEW AVE SUITE 718, TORONTO, ON, M4K 2S1
(416) 421-5906 *SIC* 5141
SOBEYS CAPITAL INCORPORATED *p* 990
840 DUPONT ST, TORONTO, ON, M6G 1Z8
(416) 534-3588 *SIC* 5411
SOBEYS CAPITAL INCORPORATED *p* 998
260 QUEEN ST N, TOTTENHAM, ON, L0G 1W0
(905) 936-1077 *SIC* 5411
SOBEYS CAPITAL INCORPORATED *p* 999
30 ONTARIO ST, TRENTON, ON, K8V 5S9
(613) 394-2791 *SIC* 5411
SOBEYS CAPITAL INCORPORATED *p* 1007
94 BRIDGEPORT RD E, WATERLOO, ON, N2J 2J9
(519) 885-4170 *SIC* 5411
SOBEYS CAPITAL INCORPORATED *p* 1009
450 COLUMBIA ST W, WATERLOO, ON, N2T 2W1
(519) 880-9143 *SIC* 5411
SOBEYS CAPITAL INCORPORATED *p* 1026
19 AMY CROFT DR, WINDSOR, ON, N9K 1C7
(519) 735-4110 *SIC* 5411
SOBEYS CAPITAL INCORPORATED *p* 1036
379 SPRINGBANK AVE N, WOODSTOCK, ON, N4T 1R3
(519) 421-3340 *SIC* 5411
SOBEYS CAPITAL INCORPORATED *p* 1041
GD, MONTAGUE, PE, C0A 1R0
(902) 838-3388 *SIC* 5411
SOBEYS CAPITAL INCORPORATED *p* 1041
679 UNIVERSITY AVE, CHARLOTTE-TOWN, PE, C1E 1E5
(902) 566-3218 *SIC* 5411
SOBEYS CAPITAL INCORPORATED *p* 1042
9 KINLOCK RD SUITE 621, STRATFORD, PE, C1B 1P8
(902) 894-3800 *SIC* 5411
SOBEYS CAPITAL INCORPORATED *p* 1043
868-475 GRANVILLE ST, SUMMERSIDE, PE, C1N 3N9
(902) 436-5795 *SIC* 5411
SOBEYS CAPITAL INCORPORATED *p* 1076
90 BOUL D'ANJOU, CHATEAUGUAY, QC, J6K 1C3
(450) 692-3446 *SIC* 5411
SOBEYS CAPITAL INCORPORATED *p* 1240
11281 BOUL ALBERT-HUDON, MONTREAL-NORD, QC, H1G 3J5
(514) 324-1010 *SIC* 5141
SOBEYS CAPITAL INCORPORATED *p* 1240
11281 BOUL ALBERT-HUDON, MONTREAL-NORD, QC, H1G 3J5
(514) 324-1010 *SIC* 5411
SOBEYS CAPITAL INCORPORATED *p* 1255
969 AV NORDIQUE BUREAU 458, QUEBEC, QC, G1C 7S8
(418) 667-5700 *SIC* 5411
SOBEYS CAPITAL INCORPORATED *p* 1268
5005 BOUL DE L'ORMIERE BUREAU 445, QUEBEC, QC, G1P 1K6
(418) 877-3922 *SIC* 5411
SOBEYS CAPITAL INCORPORATED *p* 1268
950 AV GALILEE BUREAU 2008, QUEBEC, QC, G1P 4B7
(418) 681-1922 *SIC* 5141
SOBEYS CAPITAL INCORPORATED *p* 1270
255 CH SAINTE-FOY, QUEBEC, QC, G1R 1T5
(418) 524-9890 *SIC* 5411
SOBEYS CAPITAL INCORPORATED *p* 1279
5555 BOUL DES GRADINS, QUEBEC, QC, G2J 1C8
(418) 622-5262 *SIC* 5411
SOBEYS CAPITAL INCORPORATED *p* 1285
395 AV SIROIS, RIMOUSKI, QC, G5L 8R2
(418) 724-2244 *SIC* 5411
SOBEYS CAPITAL INCORPORATED *p* 1287
254 BOUL DE L'HOTEL-DE-VILLE BUREAU 451, RIVIERE-DU-LOUP, QC, G5R 1M4
(418) 862-7861 *SIC* 5411
SOBEYS CAPITAL INCORPORATED *p* 1290

333 AV MONTEMURRO, ROUYN-NORANDA, QC, J9X 7C6
(819) 797-1900 *SIC* 5141
SOBEYS CAPITAL INCORPORATED *p* 1346
7150 BOUL LANGELIER, SAINT-LEONARD, QC, H1S 2X6
(514) 254-5454 *SIC* 5141
SOBEYS CAPITAL INCORPORATED *p* 1371
775 RUE GALT O BUREAU 514, SHER-BROOKE, QC, J1H 1Z1
(819) 564-8686 *SIC* 5411
SOBEYS CAPITAL INCORPORATED *p* 1374
3950 RUE KING O BUREAU B, SHER-BROOKE, QC, J1L 1P6
(819) 563-5172 *SIC* 5411
SOBEYS CAPITAL INCORPORATED *p* 1385
645 BOUL THIBEAU, TROIS-RIVIERES, QC, G8T 6Z6
(819) 376-1551 *SIC* 5411
SOBEYS CAPITAL INCORPORATED *p* 1395
585 AV SAINT-CHARLES, VAUDREUIL-DORION, QC, J7V 8P9
(450) 424-3549 *SIC* 5411
SOBEYS CAPITAL INCORPORATED *p* 1406
440 KING ST, ESTEVAN, SK, S4A 2B4
(306) 637-2550 *SIC* 5411
SOBEYS CAPITAL INCORPORATED *p* 1407
2304 QUILL CTR, HUMBOLDT, SK, S0K 2A1
(306) 682-2130 *SIC* 5411
SOBEYS CAPITAL INCORPORATED *p* 1423
4101 ROCHDALE BLVD, REGINA, SK, S4X 4P7
(306) 546-5881 *SIC* 5411
SOBEYS CAPITAL INCORPORATED *p* 1424
1550 8TH ST E, SASKATOON, SK, S7H 0T3
(306) 477-5800 *SIC* 5411
SOBEYS DISTRIBUTION CENTRE *p* 411
See SOBEYS CAPITAL INCORPORATED
SOBEYS ESPIRIT WINE AND COLD BEER *p* 107
See SOBEYS WESTERN CELLARS
SOBEYS ESTEVAN *p* 1406
See SOBEYS CAPITAL INCORPORATED
SOBEYS FENELON FALLS *p* 590
See SOBEYS CAPITAL INCORPORATED
SOBEYS FOOD VILLAGE *p* 478
See SOBEYS CAPITAL INCORPORATED
SOBEYS HOLLICK KENYON *p* 107
See SOBEYS CAPITAL INCORPORATED
SOBEYS INC *p* 466
115 KING ST, SHELBURNE, NS, B0T 1W0
(902) 752-8371 *SIC* 5411
SOBEYS MCKENZIE TOWNE MARKET *p* 71
See SOBEYS CAPITAL INCORPORATED
SOBEYS NORTH BATTLEFORD *p* 1412
See LANGCO FOODS LTD
SOBEYS OKOTOKS *p* 150
See GILBERT HOLDINGS LTD
SOBEYS ONTARIO *p* 990
See SOBEYS CAPITAL INCORPORATED
SOBEYS PHARMACY *p* 130
See SOBEYS CAPITAL INCORPORATED
SOBEYS QUEBEC *p* 1240
See SOBEYS CAPITAL INCORPORATED
SOBEYS QUEBEC *p* 1268
See SOBEYS CAPITAL INCORPORATED
SOBEYS QUEBEC INC *p* 1067
1500 BOUL DE MONTARVILLE, BOUCHERVILLE, QC, J4B 5Y3
(514) 324-1010 *SIC* 5141
SOBEYS QUEBEC INC *p* 1079
1324 BOUL TALBOT, CHICOUTIMI, QC, G7H 4B8
(418) 549-9751 *SIC* 5411
SOBEYS QUEBEC INC *p* 1090
850 CH D'OKA, DEUX-MONTAGNES, QC, J7R 1L7
(450) 473-6280 *SIC* 5411
SOBEYS QUEBEC INC *p* 1131
8130 BOUL CHAMPLAIN, LASALLE, QC, H8P 1B4
(514) 364-4777 *SIC* 5411
SOBEYS QUEBEC INC *p* 1138

1060 BOUL GUILLAUME-COUTURE, LEVIS, QC, G6W 5M6
(418) 834-3811 *SIC* 5411
SOBEYS QUEBEC INC *p* 1149
65 MONTEE MASSON, MASCOUCHE, QC, J7K 3B4
(450) 474-2444 *SIC* 5411
SOBEYS QUEBEC INC *p* 1220
4885 AV VAN HORNE, MONTREAL, QC, H3W 1J2
(514) 731-8336 *SIC* 5141
SOBEYS QUEBEC INC *p* 1301
299 BOUL ARTHUR-SAUVE, SAINT-EUSTACHE, QC, J7P 2B1
(450) 472-1558 *SIC* 5411
SOBEYS QUEBEC INC *p* 1370
2240 RUE KING E, SHERBROOKE, QC, J1G 5G8
(819) 566-8282 *SIC* 5411
SOBEYS QUEBEC INC *p* 1380
675 BOUL DES SEIGNEURS, TERRE-BONNE, QC, J6W 1T5
(450) 492-5580 *SIC* 5411
SOBEYS QUEBEC INC *p* 1393
1777 RTE 132, VARENNES, QC, J3X 1P7
(450) 929-0405 *SIC* 5411
SOBEYS READY TO SERVE LEDUC *p* 139
See BROMLEY FOODS LTD
SOBEYS RIVERBEND *p* 13
See 698004 ALBERTA LTD
SOBEYS ROCKY MOUNTAIN HOUSE *p* 158
See CARRINGTON-O'BRIEN FOODS LTD
SOBEYS ROCKY MOUNTAIN HOUSE *p* 159
See SOBEYS CAPITAL INCORPORATED
SOBEYS SCENIC SQUARE *p* 143
See HARTEK HOLDINGS LTD
SOBEYS STORE *p* 456
See SOBEYS CAPITAL INCORPORATED
SOBEYS STORE 1117 *p* 70
See SOBEYS CAPITAL INCORPORATED
SOBEYS STORE 1130 *p* 151
See SOBEYS CAPITAL INCORPORATED
SOBEYS STORE 3132 *p* 107
See SOBEYS CAPITAL INCORPORATED
SOBEYS STORE 3170 *p* 144
See SOBEYS CAPITAL INCORPORATED
SOBEYS STORE 5104 *p* 387
See SOBEYS CAPITAL INCORPORATED
SOBEYS STORE 6722 *p* 598
See SOBEYS CAPITAL INCORPORATED
SOBEYS STORE 7383 *p* 573
See SOBEYS CAPITAL INCORPORATED
SOBEYS STORE 794 *p* 906
See SOBEYS CAPITAL INCORPORATED
SOBEYS STORE 852 *p* 638
See SOBEYS CAPITAL INCORPORATED
SOBEYS STORE# 3149 *p* 159
See SOBEYS CAPITAL INCORPORATED
SOBEYS STORE# 5138 *p* 348
See SOBEYS CAPITAL INCORPORATED
SOBEYS STORE# 7329 *p* 591
See SOBEYS CAPITAL INCORPORATED
SOBEYS WEST *p* 373
See SOBEYS CAPITAL INCORPORATED
SOBEYS WEST INC *p* 7
550 CASSILS RD W SUITE 100, BROOKS, AB, T1R 0W3
(403) 362-6851 *SIC* 5411
SOBEYS WEST INC *p* 9
3550 32 AVE NE SUITE 286, CALGARY, AB, T1Y 6J2
(403) 291-2035 *SIC* 5411
SOBEYS WEST INC *p* 11
399 36 ST NE, CALGARY, AB, T2A 7R4
(403) 248-0848 *SIC* 5411
SOBEYS WEST INC *p* 18
3440 56 AVE SE, CALGARY, AB, T2C 2C3
(403) 279-2555 *SIC* 2011
SOBEYS WEST INC *p* 18
7740 18 ST SE, CALGARY, AB, T2C 2N5
(403) 236-0559 *SIC* 5411
SOBEYS WEST INC *p* 25
1020 64 AVE NE, CALGARY, AB, T2E 7V8
(403) 730-3500 *SIC* 5411

SOBEYS WEST INC *p* 25
1818 CENTRE ST NE SUITE 20, CALGARY, AB, T2E 2S6
(403) 276-3328 *SIC* 5411
SOBEYS WEST INC *p* 32
203 42 AVE SE, CALGARY, AB, T2G 1Y3
(403) 287-4048 *SIC* 4225
SOBEYS WEST INC *p* 39
11011 BONAVENTURE DR SE, CALGARY, AB, T2J 6S1
(403) 278-5225 *SIC* 5912
SOBEYS WEST INC *p* 39
1755 LAKE BONAVISTA DR SE SUITE 1, CALGARY, AB, T2J 0N3
(403) 271-1616 *SIC* 5411
SOBEYS WEST INC *p* 39
9737 MACLEOD TRAIL SW, CALGARY, AB, T2J 0P6
(403) 252-8199 *SIC* 5411
SOBEYS WEST INC *p* 40
215 42 AVE NW, CALGARY, AB, T2K 0H3
(403) 730-3500 *SIC* 4225
SOBEYS WEST INC *p* 40
3636 BRENTWOOD RD NW, CALGARY, AB, T2L 1K8
(403) 289-1424 *SIC* 5411
SOBEYS WEST INC *p* 40
5607 4 ST NW, CALGARY, AB, T2K 1B3
(403) 730-5080 *SIC* 5411
SOBEYS WEST INC *p* 41
3636 MORLEY TR NW, CALGARY, AB, T2L 1K8
(403) 289-9890 *SIC* 5411
SOBEYS WEST INC *p* 42
1632 14 AVE NW UNIT 1846, CALGARY, AB, T2N 1M7
(403) 210-0002 *SIC* 5411
SOBEYS WEST INC *p* 42
410 10 ST NW, CALGARY, AB, T2N 1V9
(403) 270-3054 *SIC* 5411
SOBEYS WEST INC *p* 65
813 11 AVE SW, CALGARY, AB, T2R 0E6
(403) 264-1375 *SIC* 5411
SOBEYS WEST INC *p* 67
524 ELBOW DR SW, CALGARY, AB, T2S 2H6
(403) 228-6141 *SIC* 5411
SOBEYS WEST INC *p* 68
1600 90 AVE SW, CALGARY, AB, T2V 5A8
(403) 255-2755 *SIC* 5411
SOBEYS WEST INC *p* 69
2525 WOODVIEW DR SW, CALGARY, AB, T2W 4N4
(403) 238-1400 *SIC* 5411
SOBEYS WEST INC *p* 78
6800 48 AVE SUITE 200, CAMROSE, AB, T4V 4T1
(780) 672-1211 *SIC* 5411
SOBEYS WEST INC *p* 79
135 CHESTERMERE STATION WAY UNIT 100, CHESTERMERE, AB, T1X 1V2
(403) 410-9700 *SIC* 5411
SOBEYS WEST INC *p* 83
500 MANNING CROSS NW, EDMONTON, AB, T5A 5A1
(780) 475-2896 *SIC* 5411
SOBEYS WEST INC *p* 91
1858230 82ND AVE, EDMONTON, AB, T5J 2K2
(780) 469-9452 *SIC* 5411
SOBEYS WEST INC *p* 92
11410 104 AVE NW, EDMONTON, AB, T5K 2S5
(780) 424-0666 *SIC* 5411
SOBEYS WEST INC *p* 94
12950 137 AVE NW, EDMONTON, AB, T5L 4Y8
(780) 377-2402 *SIC* 5411
SOBEYS WEST INC *p* 97
601 WESTMOUNT SHOPPING CENTER, EDMONTON, AB, T5M 3L7
(780) 451-1860 *SIC* 5411
SOBEYS WEST INC *p* 104
6655 178 ST NW SUITE 600, EDMONTON,

AB, T5T 4J5
(780) 481-7646   *SIC* 5411
SOBEYS WEST INC   *p* 107
3004 118 AVE NW, EDMONTON, AB, T5W
4W3
(780) 477-6923   *SIC* 5411
SOBEYS WEST INC   *p* 107
8720 156 AVE NW, EDMONTON, AB, T5Z
3B4
(780) 486-0584   *SIC* 5411
SOBEYS WEST INC   *p* 112
8330 82 AVE NW, EDMONTON, AB, T6C
0Y6
(780) 469-9464   *SIC* 5411
SOBEYS WEST INC   *p* 119
2304 109 ST NW, EDMONTON, AB, T6J
3S8
(780) 430-4278   *SIC* 5411
SOBEYS WEST INC   *p* 120
2331 66 ST NW SUITE 341, EDMONTON,
AB, T6K 4B4
(780) 450-8180   *SIC* 5411
SOBEYS WEST INC   *p* 120
38 AVENUE & MILLWOODS RD SUITE 100,
EDMONTON, AB, T6K 3L6
(780) 462-4424   *SIC* 5411
SOBEYS WEST INC   *p* 123
576 RIVERBEND SQ NW SUITE 802, ED-
MONTON, AB, T6R 2E3
(780) 434-6124   *SIC* 5411
SOBEYS WEST INC   *p* 129
131 SIGNAL RD, FORT MCMURRAY, AB,
T9H 4N6
(780) 791-3909   *SIC* 5411
SOBEYS WEST INC   *p* 129
9601 FRANKLIN AVE, FORT MCMURRAY,
AB, T9H 2J8
(780) 790-1988   *SIC* 5411
SOBEYS WEST INC   *p* 133
9925 114 AVE, GRANDE PRAIRIE, AB, T8V
4A9
(780) 532-1627   *SIC* 5411
SOBEYS WEST INC   *p* 140
6112 50 ST SUITE 6112, LEDUC, AB, T9E
6N7
(780) 986-0390   *SIC* 5411
SOBEYS WEST INC   *p* 141
1702 23 ST N, LETHBRIDGE, AB, T1H 5B3
(403) 320-2231   *SIC* 5411
SOBEYS WEST INC   *p* 143
2750 FAIRWAY PLAZA RD S, LETH-
BRIDGE, AB, T1K 6Z3
(403) 328-0330   *SIC* 5411
SOBEYS WEST INC   *p* 144
5211 44 ST, LLOYDMINSTER, AB, T9V 0A7
(780) 875-3448   *SIC* 5411
SOBEYS WEST INC   *p* 151
610 BIG ROCK LN, OKOTOKS, AB, T1S 1L2
(403) 938-9341   *SIC* 5411
SOBEYS WEST INC   *p* 154
4408 50 AVE, RED DEER, AB, T4N 3Z6
(403) 346-1886   *SIC* 5411
SOBEYS WEST INC   *p* 161
2020 SHERWOOD DR, SHERWOOD
PARK, AB, T8A 3H9
(780) 467-3037   *SIC* 5411
SOBEYS WEST INC   *p* 161
985 FIR ST, SHERWOOD PARK, AB, T8A
4N5
(780) 467-0177   *SIC* 5411
SOBEYS WEST INC   *p* 166
2 HEBERT RD SUITE 300, ST. ALBERT, AB,
T8N 5T8
(780) 460-9356   *SIC* 5411
SOBEYS WEST INC   *p* 166
395 ST ALBERT TRAIL, ST. ALBERT, AB,
T8N 5Z9
(780) 458-3620   *SIC* 5411
SOBEYS WEST INC   *p* 169
4926 46 AVE, TABER, AB, T1G 2A4
(403) 223-5749   *SIC* 5411
SOBEYS WEST INC   *p* 179
27566 FRASER HWY, ALDERGROVE, BC,
V4W 3N5

(604) 857-1351   *SIC* 5411
SOBEYS WEST INC   *p* 180
9855 AUSTIN RD, BURNABY, BC, V3J 1N4
(604) 420-8091   *SIC* 5411
SOBEYS WEST INC   *p* 186
4440 HASTINGS ST SUITE E, BURNABY,
BC, V5C 2K2
(604) 205-7497   *SIC* 5411
SOBEYS WEST INC   *p* 199
3051 LOUGHEED HWY SUITE 100, CO-
QUITLAM, BC, V3B 1C6
   SIC 5411
SOBEYS WEST INC   *p* 202
1033 AUSTIN AVE, COQUITLAM, BC, V3K
3P2
(604) 939-2850   *SIC* 5411
SOBEYS WEST INC   *p* 204
1200 BAKER ST, CRANBROOK, BC, V1C
1A8
(250) 417-0221   *SIC* 5411
SOBEYS WEST INC   *p* 218
945 COLUMBIA ST W, KAMLOOPS, BC,
V2C 1L5
(250) 374-2811   *SIC* 5411
SOBEYS WEST INC   *p* 227
6153 200 ST, LANGLEY, BC, V2Y 1A2
(604) 530-6131   *SIC* 5411
SOBEYS WEST INC   *p* 231
20201 LOUGHEED HWY SUITE 300,
MAPLE RIDGE, BC, V2X 2P6
(604) 460-7200   *SIC* 5411
SOBEYS WEST INC   *p* 238
1175 MT SEYMOUR RD, NORTH VANCOU-
VER, BC, V7H 2Y4
(604) 924-1302   *SIC* 5411
SOBEYS WEST INC   *p* 238
800 CARNARVON ST SUITE 220, NEW
WESTMINSTER, BC, V3M 0G3
(604) 522-2019   *SIC* 5411
SOBEYS WEST INC   *p* 239
1170 27TH ST E, NORTH VANCOUVER,
BC, V7J 1S1
(604) 988-7095   *SIC* 5411
SOBEYS WEST INC   *p* 268
2345 BEACON AVE, SIDNEY, BC, V8L 1W9
(250) 656-2735   *SIC* 5411
SOBEYS WEST INC   *p* 268
360 TRANS CANADA HWY SW UNIT 1,
SALMON ARM, BC, V1E 1B4
(250) 832-8086   *SIC* 5411
SOBEYS WEST INC   *p* 269
3664 16 HWY E, SMITHERS, BC, V0J 2N6
(250) 847-4744   *SIC* 5411
SOBEYS WEST INC   *p* 277
7165 138 ST, SURREY, BC, V3W 7T9
(604) 594-4515   *SIC* 5411
SOBEYS WEST INC   *p* 278
7450 120 ST, SURREY, BC, V3W 3M9
(604) 594-7341   *SIC* 5411
SOBEYS WEST INC   *p* 281
12825 16 AVE, SURREY, BC, V4A 1N5
(604) 531-3422   *SIC* 5411
SOBEYS WEST INC   *p* 287
1780 BROADWAY E, VANCOUVER, BC,
V5N 1W3
(604) 873-0225   *SIC* 5411
SOBEYS WEST INC   *p* 293
650 41ST AVE W, VANCOUVER, BC, V5Z
2M9
(604) 263-5502   *SIC* 5411
SOBEYS WEST INC   *p* 293
990 KING EDWARD AVE W, VANCOUVER,
BC, V5Z 2E2
(604) 733-0073   *SIC* 5411
SOBEYS WEST INC   *p* 318
1641 DAVIE ST, VANCOUVER, BC, V6G
1W1
(604) 669-8131   *SIC* 5411
SOBEYS WEST INC   *p* 318
1766 ROBSON ST, VANCOUVER, BC, V6G
1E2
(604) 683-0202   *SIC* 5411
SOBEYS WEST INC   *p* 322
2733 BROADWAY W, VANCOUVER, BC,

V6K 2G5
(604) 732-5030   *SIC* 5411
SOBEYS WEST INC   *p* 332
4300 32 ST, VERNON, BC, V1T 9H1
(250) 542-2627   *SIC* 5411
SOBEYS WEST INC   *p* 342
5385 HEADLAND DR, WEST VANCOU-
VER, BC, V7W 3C7
(604) 926-2034   *SIC* 5411
SOBEYS WEST INC   *p* 356
318 MANITOBA AVE, SELKIRK, MB, R1A
0Y7
(204) 482-5775   *SIC* 5411
SOBEYS WEST INC   *p* 358
143 PTH 12 N, STEINBACH, MB, R5G 1T5
(204) 346-1555   *SIC* 5411
SOBEYS WEST INC   *p* 363
105 PANDORA AVE E, WINNIPEG, MB,
R2C 0A1
(204) 222-6878   *SIC* 5411
SOBEYS WEST INC   *p* 363
1615 REGENT AVE W UNIT 500, WIN-
NIPEG, MB, R2C 5C6
(204) 663-6862   *SIC* 5411
SOBEYS WEST INC   *p* 370
850 KEEWATIN ST SUITE 12, WINNIPEG,
MB, R2R 0Z5
(204) 632-6763   *SIC* 5411
SOBEYS WEST INC   *p* 381
1525 ERIN ST, WINNIPEG, MB, R3E 2T2
(204) 775-0344   *SIC* 2051
SOBEYS WEST INC   *p* 382
1485 PORTAGE AVE SUITE 160E, WIN-
NIPEG, MB, R3G 0W4
(204) 775-6348   *SIC* 5411
SOBEYS WEST INC   *p* 387
655 OSBORNE ST, WINNIPEG, MB, R3L
2B7
(204) 475-0793   *SIC* 5411
SOBEYS WEST INC   *p* 388
1120 GRANT AVE, WINNIPEG, MB, R3M
2A6
(204) 452-7197   *SIC* 5411
SOBEYS WEST INC   *p* 389
2025 CORYDON AVE SUITE 150, WIN-
NIPEG, MB, R3P 0N5
(204) 489-6498   *SIC* 5411
SOBEYS WEST INC   *p* 389
3900 GRANT AVE SUITE 20, WINNIPEG,
MB, R3R 3C2
(204) 837-5339   *SIC* 5411
SOBEYS WEST INC   *p* 392
1319 PEMBINA HWY, WINNIPEG, MB, R3T
2B6
(204) 284-0973   *SIC* 5411
SOBEYS WEST INC   *p* 565
75 WHYTE AVE, DRYDEN, ON, P8N 3E6
(807) 223-3276   *SIC* 5411
SOBEYS WEST INC   *p* 628
400 FIRST AVE S, KENORA, ON, P9N 1W4
(807) 468-5868   *SIC* 5411
SOBEYS WEST INC   *p* 1411
200 1ST AVE NW, MOOSE JAW, SK, S6H
1K9
(306) 693-8033   *SIC* 5411
SOBEYS WEST INC   *p* 1421
3859 SHERWOOD DR, REGINA, SK, S4R
4A8
(306) 949-7488   *SIC* 5411
SOBEYS WEST INC   *p* 1424
3310 8TH ST E, SASKATOON, SK, S7H
5M3
(306) 955-4644   *SIC* 5411
SOBEYS WEST INC   *p* 1430
134 PRIMROSE DR, SASKATOON, SK,
S7K 5S6
(306) 242-6090   *SIC* 5411
SOBEYS WEST INC   *p* 1432
300 CONFEDERATION DR SUITE 100,
SASKATOON, SK, S7L 4R6
(306) 384-9599   *SIC* 5411
SOBEYS WEST INC   *p* 1434
1739 PRESTON AVE N, SASKATOON, SK,
S7N 4V2

(306) 668-9901   *SIC* 5411
SOBEYS WESTEND   *p* 348
See SOBEYS CAPITAL INCORPORATED
SOBEYS WESTERN CELLARS   *p* 107
15353 CASTLE DOWNS RD NW, EDMON-
TON, AB, T5X 6C3
(780) 473-7800   *SIC* 5182
SOBOTEC LTD   *p* 608
67 BURFORD RD, HAMILTON, ON, L8E
3C6
(905) 578-1278   *SIC* 3499
SOCADIS INC   *p* 1327
420 RUE STINSON, SAINT-LAURENT, QC,
H4N 3L7
(514) 331-3300   *SIC* 5192
SOCAN   *p* 777
*See SOCIETY OF COMPOSERS, AU-
THORS AND MUSIC PUBLISHERS OF
CANADA*
SOCAN FOUNDATION, THE   *p* 777
41 VALLEYBROOK DR, NORTH YORK, ON,
M3B 2S6
(416) 445-8700   *SIC* 7389
SOCAR TRADING (CANADA) LTD   *p* 59
118 8 AVE SW UNIT 200, CALGARY, AB,
T2P 1B3
(587) 956-1100   *SIC* 5172
SOCIAL ENTERPRISE FOR CANADA*p* 756
17705A LESLIE ST SUITE 202, NEWMAR-
KET, ON, L3Y 3E3
(905) 895-0809   *SIC* 8699
SOCIAL HOUSING PROGRAMS   *p* 436
*See NORTHWEST TERRITORIES NON-
PROFIT HOUSING CORPORATION*
**SOCIAL SCIENCES AND HUMANITIES RE-
SEARCH COUNCIL OF CANADA**   *p*
825
350 ALBERT ST SUITE 1610, OTTAWA,
ON, K1R 1A4
(613) 992-0691   *SIC* 8732
SOCIETE A PORTEFEUILLE RPSC *p* 1199
See RPSC HOLDINGS LTD
SOCIETE ABITIBI-CONSOLIDATED *p* 1211
See PF RESOLU CANADA INC
SOCIETE AIR FRANCE   *p* 729
6500 SILVER DART DR VISTA, MISSIS-
SAUGA, ON, L5P 1A2
(905) 676-2782   *SIC* 4512
SOCIETE BIBLIQUE CANADIEN   *p* 1173
2700 RUE RACHEL E BUREAU 100, MON-
TREAL, QC, H2H 1S7
(514) 524-7873   *SIC* 5942
**SOCIETE BRISTOL-MYERS SQUIBB
CANADA, LA**   *p* 1336
2344 BOUL ALFRED-NOBEL BUREAU 300,
SAINT-LAURENT, QC, H4S 0A4
(514) 333-3200   *SIC* 2834
SOCIETE CANADIENNE DE MONTREAL *p*
1165
See CANADIAN CANCER SOCIETY
**SOCIETE CO-OPERATIVE DE LAMEQUE
LTEE, LA**   *p* 404
68 RUE PRINCIPALE, LAMEQUE, NB, E8T
1M6
(506) 344-2206   *SIC* 5399
SOCIETE CONSEIL GROUPE LGS *p* 1208
1 PLACE VILLE-MARIE BUREAU 2200,
MONTREAL, QC, H3B 2B2
(514) 964-0939   *SIC* 8741
**SOCIETE COOPERATIVE AGRICOLE DE
LA RIVIERE-DU-SUD**   *p* 1377
34 CH SAINT-FRANCOIS O, ST-
FRANCOIS-DE-LA-RIVIERE-DU-S,   QC,
G0R 3A0
(418) 259-7715   *SIC* 5251
**SOCIETE COOPERATIVE AGRICOLE DE
SAINT-UBALD**   *p* 1353
464 RUE SAINT-PAUL, SAINT-UBALDE,
QC, G0A 4L0
(418) 277-2225   *SIC* 5411
**SOCIETE COOPERATIVE AGRICOLE DES
APPALACHES**   *p* 1133
156 RUE GRENIER, LAURIERVILLE, QC,
G0S 1P0

(819) 365-4372 *SIC* 5251
SOCIETE COOPERATIVE AGRICOLE LA SEIGNEURIE *p* 1349
404 RUE SAINT-FRANCOIS, SAINT-NARCISSE-DE-BEAURIVAGE, QC, G0S 1W0
(418) 475-6645 *SIC* 2041
SOCIETE D'ASSURANCES AUTOMOBILES DE QUEBEC *p* 1336
7575 BOUL HENRI-BOURASSA O BUREAU 66, SAINT-LAURENT, QC, H4S 1Z2
(514) 873-7620 *SIC* 7389
SOCIETE D'ELECTROLYSE ET DE CHIMIE ALCAN LIMITEE *p* 1199
1188 RUE SHERBROOKE O, MONTREAL, QC, H3A 3G2
SIC 3334
SOCIETE D'ENERGIE DE LA BAIE JAMES *p* 1175
See HYDRO-QUEBEC
SOCIETE D'ENERGIE DE LA BAIE JAMES *p* 1176
800 BOUL DE MAISONNEUVE E BUREAU 1100, MONTREAL, QC, H2L 4L8
(514) 286-2020 *SIC* 8741
SOCIETE D'EXPLOITATION DES RESSOURCES DE LA NEIGETTE INC *p* 1124
1 RUE PRINCIPALE O, LA TRINITE-DES-MONTS, QC, G0K 1B0
(418) 779-2095 *SIC* 0851
SOCIETE D'EXPLOITATION DES RESSOURCES DE LA VALLEE *p* 1124
108 RUE DU NOVICIAT, LAC-AU-SAUMON, QC, G0J 1M0
(418) 778-5877 *SIC* 0851
SOCIETE D'EXPLORATION MINIERE D'AFRIQUE DE L'OUEST *p* 1324
See SEMAFO INC
SOCIETE D'EXPLORATION MINIERE VIO *p* 1260
116 RUE SAINT-PIERRE BUREAU 200, QUEBEC, QC, G1K 4A7
(418) 692-2678 *SIC* 1081
SOCIETE D'HABITATION DE ST-ANTOINE INC *p* 416
7 DE L'EGLISE AVE, SAINT-ANTOINE, NB, E4V 1L6
(506) 525-4040 *SIC* 8741
SOCIETE D'HYPOTHEQUE DE LA BANQUE ROYALE *p* 1212
1 PLACE VILLE-MARIE, MONTREAL, QC, H3C 3A9
(514) 874-7222 *SIC* 6162
SOCIETE D'OUTILLAGE M.R. LTEE *p* 1336
8500 BOUL HENRI-BOURASSA O, SAINT-LAURENT, QC, H4S 1P4
(514) 336-5182 *SIC* 3599
SOCIETE DE CHAUDIERES INDECK *p* 1313
4300 AV BEAUDRY, SAINT-HYACINTHE, QC, J2S 8A5
(450) 774-5326 *SIC* 3443
SOCIETE DE COGENERATION *p* 1302
See ENEL GREEN POWER CANADA INC
SOCIETE DE COGENERATION DE ST-FELICIEN, SOCIETE EN COMMANDITE *p* 1303
1250 RUE DE L'ENERGIE, SAINT-FELICIEN, QC, G8K 3J2
(418) 630-3800 *SIC* 4931
SOCIETE DE COMMERCE ACADEX INC *p* 1179
350 RUE DE LOUVAIN O BUREAU 310, MONTREAL, QC, H2N 2E8
(514) 389-7297 *SIC* 5137
SOCIETE DE CONTROLE JOHNSON *p* 1326
See JOHNSON CONTROLS NOVA SCOTIA U.L.C.
SOCIETE DE DEVELOPPEMENT INTERNATIONAL (SDI) INC *p* 1273
2006 RUE RICHER, QUEBEC, QC, G1V

1P1
(418) 264-8188 *SIC* 8748
SOCIETE DE DIAMANT STORNOWAY *p* 1145
See STORNOWAY DIAMOND CORPORATION
SOCIETE DE FIDUCIE BMO *p* 1208
1250 BOUL RENE-LEVESQUE O UNITE 4600, MONTREAL, QC, H3B 5J5
(514) 877-7373 *SIC* 6211
SOCIETE DE GESTION 20 VIC *p* 937
See CUSHMAN & WAKEFIELD ASSET SERVICES ULC
SOCIETE DE GESTION ALI INC *p* 1366
760 BOUL DES ERABLES, SALABERRY-DE-VALLEYFIELD, QC, J6T 6G4
(450) 373-2010 *SIC* 6712
SOCIETE DE GESTION B3CG INTERCONNECT INC *p*
310 BOUL INDUSTRIEL, SAINT-EUSTACHE, QC, J7R 5R4
(450) 491-4040 *SIC* 6712
SOCIETE DE GESTION CAP-AUX-PIERRES INC *p* 1270
57 RUE SAINTE-ANNE, QUEBEC, QC, G1R 3X4
(418) 692-2480 *SIC* 7011
SOCIETE DE GESTION COGIR INC *p* 1069
7250 BOUL TASCHEREAU BUREAU 200, BROSSARD, QC, J4W 1M9
(450) 671-6381 *SIC* 6531
SOCIETE DE GESTION COGIR INC *p* 1151
701 CH DU RICHELIEU BUREAU 139, MCMASTERVILLE, QC, J3G 6T5
(450) 467-7667 *SIC* 6513
SOCIETE DE GESTION COGIR S.E.N.C. *p* 1069
7250 BOUL TASCHEREAU BUREAU 200, BROSSARD, QC, J4W 1M9
(450) 671-6381 *SIC* 6531
SOCIETE DE GESTION COGIR S.E.N.C. *p* 1145
100 BOUL LA FAYETTE UNITE 426, LONGUEUIL, QC, J4K 5H6
(450) 674-8111 *SIC* 6513
SOCIETE DE GESTION DE LA ZONE PORTUAIRE DE CHICOUTIMI INC *p* 1079
49 RUE LA FONTAINE, CHICOUTIMI, QC, G7H 7Y7
(418) 698-3025 *SIC* 8641
SOCIETE DE GESTION DU FONDS POUR LE DEVELOPPEMENT DES JEUNES ENFANTS *p* 1223
4720 RUE DAGENAIS BUREAU 117, MONTREAL, QC, H4C 1L7
(514) 526-2187 *SIC* 8399
SOCIETE DE GESTION DU RESEAU INFORMATIQUE DES COMMISSIONS SCOLAIRES *p* 1167
5100 RUE SHERBROOKE E BUREAU 300, MONTREAL, QC, H1V 3R9
(514) 251-3700 *SIC* 7376
SOCIETE DE GESTION REJEAN & SERGE AUCOIN INTERNATIONAL INC *p* 1174
2359 RUE FRONTENAC, MONTREAL, QC, H2K 2Z8
(514) 356-3545 *SIC* 5172
SOCIETE DE GESTION RENE RAINVILLE LTEE *p* 1115
1075 BOUL FIRESTONE BUREAU 1240, JOLIETTE, QC, J6E 6X6
(450) 759-8800 *SIC* 5912
SOCIETE DE LA PLACE DES ARTS DE MONTREAL *p* 1186
260 BOUL DE MAISONNEUVE O, MONTREAL, QC, H2X 1Y9
(514) 285-4200 *SIC* 6512
SOCIETE DE PLACEMENTS BERNFERST INC *p* 1402

3 CAR WESTMOUNT, WESTMOUNT, QC, H3Z 2S5
(514) 384-7462 *SIC* 6712
SOCIETE DE PORTEFEUILLE ET D'ACQUISITION BANQUE NATIONAL INC *p* 1208
600 RUE DE LA GAUCHETIERE O BUREAU 11E, MONTREAL, QC, H3B 4L2
(514) 394-4385 *SIC* 6712
SOCIETE DE PROTECTION DES FORETS CONTRE LE FEU (SO *p* 1151
See SOCIETE DE PROTECTION DES FORETS CONTRE LE FEU (SOPFEU)
SOCIETE DE PROTECTION DES FORETS CONTRE LE FEU (SOPFEU) *p* 1151
175 105 RTE, MESSINES, QC, J0X 2J0
(819) 449-4271 *SIC* 0851
SOCIETE DE PROTECTION DES FORETS CONTRE LE FEU (SOPFEU) *p* 1278
715 7E RUE DE L'AEROPORT, QUEBEC, QC, G2G 2S7
(418) 871-3341 *SIC* 0851
SOCIETE DE PROTECTION DES FORETS CONTRE LE FEU (SOPFEU) *p* 1287
1230 RTE DE L'AEROPORT, ROBERVAL, QC, G8H 2M9
(418) 275-6400 *SIC* 0851
SOCIETE DE PROTECTION DES FORETS CONTRE LES INSECTES ET MALADIES *p* 1265
1780 RUE SEMPLE, QUEBEC, QC, G1N 4B8
(418) 681-3381 *SIC* 0851
SOCIETE DE QUEBEC POUR PREVENIR LES CRUAUTES CONTRE LES ANIMAUX, LA *p* 1268
1130 AV GALILEE BUREAU 487, QUEBEC, QC, G1P 4B7
(418) 527-9104 *SIC* 8699
SOCIETE DE SAINT-VINCENT DE PAUL DE MONTREAL, LA *p* 1176
1930 RUE DE CHAMPLAIN, MONTREAL, QC, H2L 2S8
(514) 526-5937 *SIC* 8699
SOCIETE DE SERVICES DENTAIRES (A.C.D.Q.) INC *p* 1199
425 BOUL DE MAISONNEUVE O BUREAU 1450, MONTREAL, QC, H3A 3G5
(514) 282-1425 *SIC* 6324
SOCIETE DE TRANSPORT DE MONTREAL *p* 1050
8150 RUE LARREY, ANJOU, QC, H1J 2J5
(514) 280-5913 *SIC* 4111
SOCIETE DE TRANSPORT DE MONTREAL *p* 1131
7770 RUE SAINT-PATRICK, LASALLE, QC, H8N 1V1
(514) 280-6382 *SIC* 4111
SOCIETE DE TRANSPORT DE MONTREAL *p* 1176
2000 RUE BERRI, MONTREAL, QC, H2L 4V7
(514) 786-6876 *SIC* 4111
SOCIETE DE TRANSPORT DE MONTREAL *p* 1230
800 RUE DE LA GAUCHETIERE O BUREAU 8420, MONTREAL, QC, H5A 1J6
(514) 786-4636 *SIC* 4111
SOCIETE DE TRANSPORT DE SHERBROOKE *p* 1372
895 RUE CABANA, SHERBROOKE, QC, J1K 2M3
(819) 564-2687 *SIC* 4111
SOCIETE DE TRANSPORT DU SAGUENAY *p* 1081
1330 RUE BERSIMIS, CHICOUTIMI, QC, G7K 1A5
(418) 545-3683 *SIC* 4131
SOCIETE DE VIN INTERNATIONALE LTEE *p* 1101
3838 BOUL LEMAN, FABREVILLE, QC, H7E 1A1
(450) 661-0281 *SIC* 5182

SOCIETE DES ALCOOLS DU QUEBEC *p* 1165
560 RUE HECTOR-BARSALOU, MONTREAL, QC, H1N 3T2
(514) 254-6000 *SIC* 5921
SOCIETE DES ALCOOLS DU QUEBEC *p* 1165
7500 RUE TELLIER, MONTREAL, QC, H1N 3W5
(514) 254-6000 *SIC* 5921
SOCIETE DES CASINOS DU QUEBEC INC, LA *p* 1122
183 RUE RICHELIEU, LA MALBAIE, QC, G5A 1X8
(418) 665-5300 *SIC* 7032
SOCIETE DES CASINOS DU QUEBEC INC, LA *p* 1199
500 RUE SHERBROOKE O BUREAU 1500, MONTREAL, QC, H3A 3C6
(514) 282-8000 *SIC* 7999
SOCIETE DES CASINOS DU QUEBEC INC, LA *p* 1212
1 AV DU CASINO, MONTREAL, QC, H3C 4W7
(514) 392-2756 *SIC* 7999
SOCIETE DES CASINOS DU QUEBEC INC, LA *p* 1216
325 RUE BRIDGE BUREAU 1178, MONTREAL, QC, H3K 2C7
(514) 409-3111 *SIC* 7311
SOCIETE DES ETABLISSEMENTS DE PLEIN AIR DU QUEBEC *p* 1067
55 ILE-SAINTE-MARGUERITE, BOUCHERVILLE, QC, J4B 5J6
(450) 928-5089 *SIC* 7996
SOCIETE DES ETABLISSEMENTS DE PLEIN AIR DU QUEBEC *p* 1081
25 BOUL NOTRE-DAME, CLERMONT, QC, G4A 1C2
(418) 439-1227 *SIC* 7999
SOCIETE DES ETABLISSEMENTS DE PLEIN AIR DU QUEBEC *p* 1378
140 MONTEE DE L'AUBERGE, STE-CATHERINE-DE-LA-J-CARTIE, QC, G3N 2Y6
(418) 875-2711 *SIC* 7032
SOCIETE DES LOTERIES DU QUEBEC *p* 1199
500 RUE SHERBROOKE O, MONTREAL, QC, H3A 3C6
(514) 282-8000 *SIC* 7999
SOCIETE DES MISSIONAIRES D'AFRIQUE (PERES BLANCS) PROVINCE DE L'AMERIQUE DU NORD *p* 1176
1640 RUE SAINT-HUBERT, MONTREAL, QC, H2L 3Z3
(514) 849-1167 *SIC* 8661
SOCIETE DES TECHNOLOGIES DE L'ALUMINIUM DU SAGUENAY S.T.A.S. *p* 1080
See STAS INC
SOCIETE DES TRAVERSIERS DU QUEBEC *p* 1260
250 RUE SAINT-PAUL, QUEBEC, QC, G1K 9K9
(418) 643-2019 *SIC* 4482
SOCIETE DES TRAVERSIERS DU QUEBEC *p* 1376
9 RUE ELIZABETH, SOREL-TRACY, QC, J3P 4G1
(450) 742-3313 *SIC* 4111
SOCIETE DU CENTRE DES CONGRES DE QUEBEC *p* 1270
1000 BOUL RENE-LEVESQUE E, QUEBEC, QC, G1R 5T8
(418) 644-4000 *SIC* 7389
SOCIETE DU DROIT DE REPRODUCTION DES AUTEURS COMPOSITEURS ET EDITEURS AU CANADA *p*
See SODRAC (2003) INC
SOCIETE DU GRAND THEATRE DE QUEBEC, LA *p* 1270

269 BOUL RENE-LEVESQUE E, QUEBEC, QC, G1R 2B3

(418) 643-8111   *SIC* 7922

SOCIETE DU GROUPE D'EMBOUTEILLAGE PEPSI   *p* 1285

See PEPSI COLA CANADA LTEE

SOCIETE DU PALAIS DES CONGRES DE MONTREAL   *p* 1191

See GOUVERNEMENT DE LA PROVINCE DE QUEBEC

SOCIETE DU VIEUX-PORT DE MONTREAL INC   *p* 1190

333 RUE DE LA COMMUNE O, MONTREAL, QC, H2Y 2E2

(514) 283-5256   *SIC* 8743

SOCIETE EMBALLAGES HOOD   *p* 1100

See HOOD PACKAGING CORPORATION

SOCIETE EN COMMANDITE 901 SQUARE VICTORIA   *p* 1192

901 RUE DU SQUARE-VICTORIA BUREAU 1471, MONTREAL, QC, H2Z 1R1

(514) 395-3100   *SIC* 7011

SOCIETE EN COMMANDITE AIRBUS CANADA   *p* 1153

13100 BOUL HENRI-FABRE E, MIRABEL, QC, J7N 3C6

(514) 855-7110   *SIC* 3721

SOCIETE EN COMMANDITE AUBERGE GODEFROY   *p* 1056

17575 BOUL BECANCOUR, BECANCOUR, QC, G9H 1A5

(819) 233-2200   *SIC* 7011

SOCIETE EN COMMANDITE BROSPEC 2001   *p* 1113

13 RUE MILL, HOWICK, QC, J0S 1G0

SIC 3399

SOCIETE EN COMMANDITE CANADELLE   *p* 1345

4405 BOUL METROPOLITAIN E, SAINT-LEONARD, QC, H1R 1Z4

(514) 376-6240   *SIC* 5137

SOCIETE EN COMMANDITE COULONGE ENERGIE   *p* 1400

GD, WALTHAM, QC, J0X 3H0

(819) 689-5226   *SIC* 4911

SOCIETE EN COMMANDITE FF SOUCY WB   *p* 1287

191 RUE DELAGE, RIVIERE-DU-LOUP, QC, G5R 6E2

(418) 862-6941   *SIC* 2621

SOCIETE EN COMMANDITE FREE 2 PLAY   *p* 1167

4750 RUE SHERBROOKE E, MONTREAL, QC, H1V 3S8

(514) 328-3668   *SIC* 7941

SOCIETE EN COMMANDITE LE FELIX VAUDREUIL-DORION   *p* 1395

3223 BOUL DE LA GARE, VAUDREUIL-DORION, QC, J7V 0L5

(514) 331-2788   *SIC* 6719

SOCIETE EN COMMANDITE LES PROMENADES DU PARC   *p* 1146

1910 RUE ADONCOUR BUREAU 500, LONGUEUIL, QC, J4N 1T3

(450) 448-3448   *SIC* 3993

SOCIETE EN COMMANDITE MANOIR RICHELIEU   *p* 1122

181 RUE RICHELIEU BUREAU 200, LA MALBAIE, QC, G5A 1X7

(418) 665-3703   *SIC* 7011

SOCIETE EN COMMANDITE PAPIER MASSON WB   *p* 1103

2 CH DE MONTREAL E, GATINEAU, QC, J8M 1E9

(819) 986-4300   *SIC* 2621

SOCIETE EN COMMANDITE PASQUIER   *p* 1315

87 BOUL SAINT-LUC BUREAU A, SAINT-JEAN-SUR-RICHELIEU, QC, J2W 1E2

(450) 299-9999   *SIC* 5141

SOCIETE EN COMMANDITE PROLAM   *p* 1074

439 CH VINCELOTTE, CAP-SAINT-IGNACE, QC, G0R 1H0

(418) 246-5101   *SIC* 2426

SOCIETE EN COMMANDITE REVENUE NORANDA   *p* 1366

860 BOUL GERARD-CADIEUX, SALABERRY-DE-VALLEYFIELD, QC, J6T 6L4

(450) 373-9144   *SIC* 3339

SOCIETE EN COMMANDITE SCIERIE OPIT-CIWAN   *p* 1244

DE LA POINTE, OBEDJIWAN, QC, G0W 3B0

(819) 974-1116   *SIC* 2421

SOCIETE EN COMMANDITE STADACONA WB   *p* 1257

10 BOUL DES CAPUCINS, QUEBEC, QC, G1J 0G9

(418) 842-8405   *SIC* 2421

SOCIETE EN COMMANDITE STADACONA WB   *p* 1281

1092 AV LAPIERRE BUREAU 220, QUEBEC, QC, G3E 1Z3

SIC 2421

SOCIETE EN COMMANDITE USINE DE SOUFRE SUNCOR MONTREAL   *p* 1238

11450 RUE CHERRIER, MONTREAL-EST, QC, H1B 1A6

(514) 645-1636   *SIC* 5169

SOCIETE EN COMMENDITE PLACE ALEXANDRA   *p* 1256

2475 RUE ALEXANDRA, QUEBEC, QC, G1E 7A8

(418) 666-7636   *SIC* 6513

SOCIETE FERROVIAIRE ET PORTUAIRE DE POINTE-NOIRE S.E.C.   *p* 1367

1505 CH POINTE-NOIRE, SEPT-ILES, QC, G4R 4L4

(418) 962-5131   *SIC* 4482

SOCIETE GAMMA INC   *p* 834

240 BANK ST SUITE 600, OTTAWA, ON, K2P 1X4

(613) 233-4407   *SIC* 7389

SOCIETE GEEP CANADA   *p* 1234

See GEEP ECOSYS INC

SOCIETE GENERALE (CANADA)   *p* 1199

1501 AV MCGILL COLLEGE BUREAU 1800, MONTREAL, QC, H3A 3M8

(514) 841-6000   *SIC* 6081

SOCIETE GENERALE CORPORATE INVESTMENT   *p* 1199

See SOCIETE GENERALE (CANADA)

SOCIETE GESTION LIBRAIRIE INC   *p* 1260

286 RUE SAINT-JOSEPH E, QUEBEC, QC, G1K 3A9

(418) 692-1175   *SIC* 6712

SOCIETE GRICS   *p* 1167

See SOCIETE DE GESTION DU RESEAU INFORMATIQUE DES COMMISSIONS SCOLAIRES

SOCIETE HOLDING VELAN LTEE   *p* 1341

7007 CH DE LA COTE-DE-LIESSE, SAINT-LAURENT, QC, H4T 1G2

(514) 748-7743   *SIC* 3494

SOCIETE IMMOBILIERE LAFLECHE INC, LA   *p* 1112

765 6E AV, GRAND-MERE, QC, G9T 2H8

(819) 538-8606   *SIC* 5912

SOCIETE IMMOBILIERE M.C.M. INC, LA   *p* 1352

204 RUE PRINCIPALE, SAINT-SAUVEUR, QC, J0R 1R0

(450) 227-2611   *SIC* 6531

SOCIETE INDUSTRIELLE JASON (CANADA) LTEE   *p* 1095

9135 CH COTE-DE-LIESSE, DORVAL, QC, H9P 2N9

(514) 631-6781   *SIC* 5085

SOCIETE LAURENTIDE INC   *p* 1368

4660 BOUL DE SHAWINIGAN-SUD, SHAWINIGAN, QC, G9N 6T5

(819) 537-6636   *SIC* 2851

SOCIETE MAKIVIK   *p* 1324

1111 BOUL DR.-FREDERIK-PHILIPS 3E ETAGE, SAINT-LAURENT, QC, H4M 2X6

(514) 745-8880   *SIC* 4512

SOCIETE MONDO AMERICA INC   *p* 1362

2655 AV FRANCIS-HUGHES, SAINTE-ROSE, QC, H7L 3S8

(450) 967-5800   *SIC* 3069

SOCIETE PARC-AUTO DU QUEBEC   *p* 1270

965 PLACE D'YOUVILLE, QUEBEC, QC, G1R 3P1

(418) 694-9662   *SIC* 7521

SOCIETE POLYONE DSS CANADA   *p* 1109

See POLYONE DSS CANADA INC

SOCIETE POUR LA PREVENTION DE LA CRUAUTE ENVERS LES ANIMAUX (CANADIENNE), LA   *p* 1228

5215 RUE JEAN-TALON O, MONTREAL, QC, H4P 1X4

(514) 735-2711   *SIC* 8699

SOCIETE POUR LES ENFANTS HANDICAPES DU QUEBEC   *p* 1291

210 RUE PAPILLON, SAINT-ALPHONSE-RODRIGUEZ, QC, J0K 1W0

(450) 883-2915   *SIC* 7032

SOCIETE PRIBEX LTEE, LA   *p* 1057

350 BOUL SIR-WILFRID-LAURIER, BELOEIL, QC, J3G 4G7

(450) 467-0296   *SIC* 5912

SOCIETE PROTECTRICE DES ANIMAUX DE L'ESTRIE   *p* 1374

145 RUE SAUVE, SHERBROOKE, QC, J1L 1L6

(819) 821-4727   *SIC* 8699

SOCIETE QUEBECOISE D'EXPLORATION MINIERE   *p* 1391

See SOQUEM INC

SOCIETE QUEBECOISE D'INFORMATION JURIDIQUE   *p* 1190

715 RUE DU SQUARE-VICTORIA BUREAU 600, MONTREAL, QC, H2Y 2H7

(514) 842-8741   *SIC* 2759

SOCIETE QUEBECOISE D'INITIATIVES AGRO-ALIMENTAIRES   *p* 1272

See IQ SOQUIA INC

SOCIETE QUEBECOISE DES INFRASTRUCTURES   *p* 1270

1075 RUE DE L'AMERIQUE-FRANCAISE, QUEBEC, QC, G1R 5P8

(418) 646-1766   *SIC* 6531

SOCIETE SAINT-JEAN BAPTISTE DU CENTRE-DU-QUEBEC INC, LA   *p* 1097

449 RUE NOTRE-DAME, DRUMMONDVILLE, QC, J2B 2K9

(819) 478-2519   *SIC* 6321

SOCIETE SAINT-JEAN-BAPTISTE DE LA MAURICIE OBNL   *p* 1386

3239 RUE PAPINEAU, TROIS-RIVIERES, QC, G8Z 1P4

(819) 375-4881   *SIC* 6311

SOCIETE SPECTRA SCENE INC, LA   *p* 1199

400 BOUL DE MAISONNEUVE O BUREAU 800, MONTREAL, QC, H3A 1L4

(514) 523-3378   *SIC* 7922

SOCIETE SYLVICOLE   *p* 1075

See SOCIETE SYLVICOLE CHAMBORD LTEE

SOCIETE SYLVICOLE CHAMBORD LTEE   *p* 1075

21 RUE DES SOURCES, CHAMBORD, QC, G0W 1G0

(418) 342-6251   *SIC* 0851

SOCIETE SYLVICOLE MISTASSINI LTEE   *p* 1090

245 RUE DE QUEN, DOLBEAU-MISTASSINI, QC, G8L 5M3

(418) 276-8080   *SIC* 0851

SOCIETE TRANSPORT TROIS-RIVIERES   *p* 1388

2000 RUE BELLEFEUILLE, TROIS-RIVIERES, QC, G9A 3Y2

(819) 373-4533   *SIC* 4731

SOCIETE VIA   *p* 1139

See SOCIETE VIA ENVIRONNEMENT

SOCIETE VIA ENVIRONNEMENT   *p* 1139

1200 RUE DES RIVEURS, LEVIS, QC, G6Y 9G2

(418) 833-0421   *SIC* 4953

SOCIETE XYLEM CANADA   *p* 604

55 ROYAL RD, GUELPH, ON, N1H 1T1

(519) 821-1900   *SIC* 5084

SOCIETE XYLEM CANADA   *p* 1252

300 AV LABROSSE, POINTE-CLAIRE, QC, H9R 4V5

(514) 695-0133   *SIC* 6531

SOCIETY CARUSO CLUB OF SUDBURY   *p* 900

385 HAIG ST, SUDBURY, ON, P3C 1C5

(705) 675-1357   *SIC* 8641

SOCIETY FOR MANITOBANS WITH DISABILITIES INC   *p* 373

825 SHERBROOK ST, WINNIPEG, MB, R3A 1M5

(204) 975-3010   *SIC* 8093

SOCIETY FOR THE INVOLVEMENT OF GOOD NEIGHBOURS   *p* 1439

83 NORTH ST, YORKTON, SK, S3N 0G9

(306) 783-9409   *SIC* 8699

SOCIETY OF COMPOSERS, AUTHORS AND MUSIC PUBLISHERS OF CANADA   *p* 777

41 VALLEYBROOK DR, NORTH YORK, ON, M3B 2S6

(416) 445-8700   *SIC* 7313

SOCIETY OF SAINT VINCENT DE PAUL   *p* 426

110 ASHFORD DR, MOUNT PEARL, NL, A1N 3L6

(709) 747-3320   *SIC* 8699

SOCO   *p* 1433

See SASKATCHEWAN OPPORTUNITIES CORPORATION

SODA CREEK DIVISION   *p* 344

See TOLKO INDUSTRIES LTD

SODASTREAM CANADA LTD   *p* 700

5450 EXPLORER DR SUITE 202, MISSISSAUGA, ON, L4W 5N1

(905) 629-4450   *SIC* 5084

SODEM INC   *p* 1073

4765 CH DE CAPELTON, CANTON-DE-HATLEY, QC, J0B 2C0

SIC 7299

SODEM INC   *p* 1183

4750 AV HENRI-JULIEN BUREAU RC 050, MONTREAL, QC, H2T 2C8

(514) 527-9546   *SIC* 8741

SODEM INC   *p* 1238

11111 RUE NOTRE-DAME E, MONTREAL-EST, QC, H1B 2V7

(514) 640-2737   *SIC* 7999

SODEMA   *p* 1206

See MEDIAS TRANSCONTINENTAL INC

SODEXHO   *p* 976

See SODEXO CANADA LTD

SODEXO   *p* 525

See SODEXO CANADA LTD

SODEXO CANADA LTD   *p* 41

1301 16 AVE NW, CALGARY, AB, T2M 0L4

(403) 284-8536   *SIC* 7349

SODEXO CANADA LTD   *p* 227

7600 GLOVER RD, LANGLEY, BC, V2Y 1Y1

(604) 513-2009   *SIC* 5812

SODEXO CANADA LTD   *p* 438

GD, ANTIGONISH, NS, B2G 2W5

(902) 867-2491   *SIC* 5812

SODEXO CANADA LTD   *p* 525

5420 NORTH SERVICE RD SUITE 501, BURLINGTON, ON, L7L 6C7

(905) 632-8592   *SIC* 5812

SODEXO CANADA LTD   *p* 562

1950 MONTREAL RD, CORNWALL, ON, K6H 6L2

(613) 936-5800   *SIC* 5812

SODEXO CANADA LTD *p* 631
75 BADER LANE, KINGSTON, ON, K7L 3N8
(613) 533-2953 *SIC* 5812

SODEXO CANADA LTD *p* 976
21 SUSSEX AVE UNIT 3, TORONTO, ON, M5S 1J6
SIC 5812

SODEXO CANADA LTD *p* 976
41 CLASSIC AVE, TORONTO, ON, M5S 2Z3
SIC 5812

SODEXO QUEBEC LIMITEE *p* 1108
100 RUE LAURIER, GATINEAU, QC, K1A 0M8
(819) 776-8391 *SIC* 5812

SODRAC (2003) INC *p* 1199
1470 RUE PEEL BUREAU 1010, MONTREAL, QC, H3A 1T1
(514) 845-3268 *SIC* 6794

SODROX CHEMICALS LTD *p* 604
7040 WELLINGTON ROAD 124, GUELPH, ON, N1H 6J3
(519) 837-2330 *SIC* 5169

SOEHNER SALES LIMITED *p* 438
152 ALBION ST S, AMHERST, NS, B4H 4H4
(902) 667-7218 *SIC* 5531

SOEURS DE CHARITE DE SAINT-HYACINTHE, LES *p* 1314
16470 AV BOURDAGES S, SAINT-HYACINTHE, QC, J2T 4J8
(450) 773-9785 *SIC* 8661

SOEURS DE LA CHARITE (SOEURS GRISES) DE MONTREAL, LES *p* 1190
138 RUE SAINT-PIERRE, MONTREAL, QC, H2Y 2L7
(514) 842-9411 *SIC* 8661

SOEURS DE LA CHARITE D'OTTAWA, LES *p* 810
879 HIAWATHA PARK RD, ORLEANS, ON, K1C 2Z6
(613) 562-6262 *SIC* 8361

SOEURS DE LA CHARITE D'OTTAWA, LES *p* 822
27 BRUYERE ST, OTTAWA, ON, K1N 5C9
(613) 241-2710 *SIC* 8661

SOEURS DE LA CHARITE D'OTTAWA, LES *p* 822
43 BRUYERE ST, OTTAWA, ON, K1N 5C8
(613) 562-0050 *SIC* 8661

SOEURS DE LA CONGREGATION DE NOTRE-DAME, LES *p* 1115
393 RUE DE LANAUDIERE, JOLIETTE, QC, J6E 3L9
(450) 752-1481 *SIC* 8661

SOEURS DE LA CONGREGATION DE NOTRE-DAME, LES *p* 1215
2330 RUE SHERBROOKE O, MONTREAL, QC, H3H 1G8
(514) 931-5891 *SIC* 8661

SOEURS DE LA CONGREGATION DE NOTRE-DAME, LES *p* 1221
5015 AV NOTRE-DAME-DE-GRACE, MONTREAL, QC, H4A 1K2
(514) 485-1461 *SIC* 8661

SOEURS DE LA PRESENTATION DE MARIE DU QUEBEC *p* 1168
3600 RUE BELANGER, MONTREAL, QC, H1X 1B1
(514) 721-4979 *SIC* 8661

SOEURS DE SAINT-FRANCOIS D'ASSISE, LES *p* 1257
600 60E RUE E, QUEBEC, QC, G1H 3A9
(418) 623-1515 *SIC* 8661

SOEURS DE SAINTE-ANNE DU QUEBEC, LES *p* 1126
1950 RUE PROVOST, LACHINE, QC, H8S 1P7
(514) 637-3783 *SIC* 8661

SOEURS DE SAINTE-CROIX *p* 1323
900 BOUL DE LA COTE-VERTU, SAINT-LAURENT, QC, H4L 4T9
SIC 8661

SOEURS DES SAINTS NOMS DE JESUS ET DE MARIE DU QUEBEC, LES *p* 1143
82 RUE SAINT-CHARLES E, LONGUEUIL, QC, J4H 1A9
(450) 651-3744 *SIC* 8661

SOEURS DES SAINTS NOMS DE JESUS ET DE MARIE DU QUEBEC, LES *p* 1143
86 RUE SAINT-CHARLES E, LONGUEUIL, QC, J4H 1A9
(450) 651-0179 *SIC* 8661

SOEURS FILLES DE JESUS *p* 1386
1193 BOUL SAINT-LOUIS, TROIS-RIVIERES, QC, G8Z 2M8
(819) 376-3741 *SIC* 6411

SOEURS GRISES DE MONTREAL, LES *p* 1215
1190 RUE GUY, MONTREAL, QC, H3H 2L4
SIC 8661

SOFA INTERNATIONAL *p* 1379
See *MEUBLES JAYMAR CORP*

SOFA TO GO *p* 1047
12900 BOUL INDUSTRIELLE, ANJOU, QC, H1A 4Z6
(514) 387-7632 *SIC* 5712

SOFATEC *p* 1355
See *ACIERS SOFATEC INC, LES*

SOFINA FOODS INC *p* 291
8385 FRASER ST, VANCOUVER, BC, V5X 3X8
(604) 668-5800 *SIC* 2011

SOFINA FOODS INC *p* 689
3340 ORLANDO DR, MISSISSAUGA, ON, L4V 1C7
(905) 673-7145 *SIC* 2038

SOFINA FOODS INC *p* 875
170 NUGGET AVE, SCARBOROUGH, ON, M1S 3A7
(416) 297-1062 *SIC* 2013

SOFINA FOODS INC *p* 905
100 COMMERCE VALLEY DR W SUITE 900, THORNHILL, ON, L3T 0A1
(905) 747-3333 *SIC* 2013

SOFITEL HOTEL & RESORTS *p* 1197
See *HOTELS CANPRO INC, LES*

SOFT-MOC INC *p* 1015
1400 HOPKINS ST UNIT 3-4, WHITBY, ON, L1N 2C3
(905) 665-8119 *SIC* 5661

SOFTCHOICE CORPORATION *p* 992
173 DUFFERIN ST SUITE 200, TORONTO, ON, M6K 3H7
(416) 588-9002 *SIC* 7371

SOFTCHOICE LP *p* 992
173 DUFFERIN ST SUITE 200, TORONTO, ON, M6K 3H7
(416) 588-9000 *SIC* 7371

SOFTCOM INC *p* 967
88 QUEENS QUAY W SUITE 2610, TORONTO, ON, M5J 0B8
(416) 957-7400 *SIC* 4813

SOFTINFO *p* 1180
See *MEDISOLUTION (2009) INC*

SOFTLANDING SOLUTIONS INC *p* 300
555 HASTINGS ST W SUITE 1605, VANCOUVER, ON, V6B 4N6
(604) 633-1410 *SIC* 8748

SOFTVOYAGE INC *p* 1183
201 AV LAURIER E BUREAU 630, MONTREAL, QC, H2T 3E6
(514) 273-0008 *SIC* 5045

SOFTWARE MAINTENANCE & DEVELOPMENT *p* 771
See *GILLILAND GOLD YOUNG CONSULTING INC*

SOGEFI AIR & COOLING CANADA CORP *p* 1165
1500 RUE DE BOUCHERVILLE, MONTREAL, QC, H1N 3V3
(514) 764-8806 *SIC* 3599

SOGEL *p* 1190
See *SOGELCO INTERNATIONAL INC*

SOGELCO INTERNATIONAL INC *p* 1190
715 RUE DU SQUARE-VICTORIA BUREAU

400, MONTREAL, QC, H2Y 2H7
(514) 849-2414 *SIC* 5146

SOGEMA TECHNOLOGIES INC *p* 1145
1111 RUE SAINT-CHARLES O BUREAU 700, LONGUEUIL, QC, J4K 5G4
(450) 651-2800 *SIC* 8731

SOGEP INC *p* 1142
2099 BOUL FERNAND-LAFONTAINE, LONGUEUIL, QC, J4G 2J4
(514) 527-9546 *SIC* 8741

SOGETEL *p* 1054
37 RUE VERVILLE, BAIE-DU-FEBVRE, QC, J0G 1A0
(450) 783-1005 *SIC* 4813

SOGETEL INC *p* 1242
111 RUE DU 12-NOVEMBRE, NICOLET, QC, J3T 1S3
(819) 293-6125 *SIC* 4813

SOGO *p* 1216
See *4423038 CANADA INC*

SOIL ENGINEER LTD *p* 854
90 WEST BEAVER CREEK RD SUITE 100, RICHMOND HILL, ON, L4B 1E7
(416) 754-8515 *SIC* 1794

SOINS DIRECT INC *p* 1214
1414 RUE DRUMMOND BUREAU 620, MONTREAL, QC, H3G 1W1
(514) 739-1919 *SIC* 7361

SOINS ESTHETIQUES PHYTODERM INC *p* 1327
68 RUE STINSON, SAINT-LAURENT, QC, H4N 2E7
(514) 735-1531 *SIC* 5122

SOKIL EXPRESS LINES LTD *p* 84
8830 126 AVE NW, EDMONTON, AB, T5B 1G9
(780) 479-1955 *SIC* 4213

SOKIL TRANSPORTATION SERVICES *p* 83
See *EDMONTON TRANSFER LTD*

SOL-R PRODUITS DE FENETRES *p* 1327
50 RUE BENJAMIN-HUDON, SAINT-LAURENT, QC, H4N 1H8
SIC 5023

SOLACE CORPORATION *p* 625
535 LEGGET DR FL 3, KANATA, ON, K2K 3B8
(613) 271-1010 *SIC* 3825

SOLACE POWER INC. *p* 426
1118 TOPSAIL RD SUITE 201, MOUNT PEARL, NL, A1N 5E7
(709) 745-6099 *SIC* 4911

SOLACOM TECHNOLOGIES INC *p* 1107
80 RUE JEAN-PROULX, GATINEAU, QC, J8Z 1W1
(819) 205-8100 *SIC* 3812

SOLAR ERECTORS LTD *p* 893
332 JONES RD UNIT 1, STONEY CREEK, ON, L8E 5N2
(905) 643-1829 *SIC* 1771

SOLAR MODULE MANUFACTURING *p* 605
See *CANADIAN SOLAR INC*

SOLAR TURBINES CANADA LTD *p* 123
2510 84 AVE NW, EDMONTON, AB, T6P 1K3
(780) 464-8900 *SIC* 5084

SOLAR WEST *p* 1436
See *F.P. BOURGAULT TILLAGE TOOLS LTD*

SOLARFECTIVE PRODUCTS LIMITED *p* 869
55 HYMUS RD, SCARBOROUGH, ON, M1L 2C6
(416) 421-3800 *SIC* 3861

SOLARIS INTERNATIONAL INC *p* 1119
6150 BOUL SAINTE-ANNE, L'ANGE GARDIEN, QC, G0A 2K0
(418) 822-0643 *SIC* 5211

SOLARIS PHARMACEUTICALS INC *p* 278
8322 130 ST SUITE 201, SURREY, BC, V3W 8J9
(778) 218-2655 *SIC* 5912

SOLARIS QUEBEC *p* 1119
See *9353-0251 QUEBEC INC*

SOLARIS QUEBEC PORTES ET FENE-

TRES INC *p*
1119
6150 BOUL SAINTE-ANNE, L'ANGE GARDIEN, QC, G0A 2K0
(418) 822-0643 *SIC* 3089

SOLARWINDS MSP CANADA ULC *p* 832
450 MARCH RD 2ND FL, OTTAWA, ON, K2K 3K2
(613) 592-6676 *SIC* 8731

SOLBAKKEN AND ASSOCIATES *p* 335
990 HILLSIDE AVE SUITE 201, VICTORIA, BC, V8T 2A1
(250) 590-5211 *SIC* 8721

SOLCZ GROUP INC *p* 1019
6555 HAWTHORNE DR, WINDSOR, ON, N8T 3G6
(519) 974-5200 *SIC* 6712

SOLE PRODUCE *p* 596
See *1019884 ONTARIO INC*

SOLECTRON GLOBAL SERVICES *p* 197
See *STREAM INTERNATIONAL CANADA ULC*

SOLID CAD *p* 854
See *SOLID CADDGROUP INC*

SOLID CADDGROUP INC *p* 854
25B EAST PEARCE ST, RICHMOND HILL, ON, L4B 2M9
(905) 474-1499 *SIC* 5045

SOLID WALL CONCRETE FORMING LTD *p* 664
45 RODINEA RD SUITE 8, MAPLE, ON, L6A 1R3
(905) 832-4311 *SIC* 1771

SOLID XPERTS INC *p* 1336
2650 AV MARIE-CURIE, SAINT-LAURENT, QC, H4S 2C3
(514) 343-9111 *SIC* 7372

SOLIDEAL *p* 692
See *CAMSO DISTRIBUTION CANADA INC*

SOLIDWEAR ENTERPRISES LIMITED *p* 875
59 MILNER AVE, SCARBOROUGH, ON, M1S 3P6
(416) 298-2667 *SIC* 2253

SOLIGO GRUPPO *p* 1266
See *CERAMIQUE DECORS M.S.F. INC*

SOLINE TRADING LTD *p* 1336
9899 RTE TRANSCANADIENNE, SAINT-LAURENT, QC, H4S 1V1
(514) 339-1818 *SIC* 5146

SOLINST CANADA LTD *p* 594
35 TODD RD, GEORGETOWN, ON, L7G 4R8
(905) 873-2255 *SIC* 3823

SOLIS FOODS CORPORATION INC *p* 513
79 EASTON RD, BRANTFORD, ON, N3P 1J4
(519) 349-2020 *SIC* 2052

SOLISCOM *p* 1366
See *IMPRIMERIE SOLISCO INC*

SOLIUM CAPITAL INC *p* 59
600 3 AVE SW SUITE 1500, CALGARY, AB, T2P 0G5
(403) 515-3910 *SIC* 6211

SOLMAX INTERNATIONAL INC *p* 1393
2801 RTE MARIE-VICTORIN, VARENNES, QC, J3X 1P7
(450) 929-1234 *SIC* 3081

SOLOMON COATINGS LTD *p* 111
6382 50 ST NW, EDMONTON, AB, T6B 2N7
(780) 413-4545 *SIC* 7532

SOLOMON, M.J. LTD *p* 356
124 INDUSTRIAL PARK RD, SHOAL LAKE, MB, R0J 1Z0
(204) 759-2626 *SIC* 5191

SOLOTECH INC *p* 1167
5200 RUE HOCHELAGA BUREAU 100, MONTREAL, QC, H1V 1G3
(514) 526-3094 *SIC* 3645

SOLOTECH INC *p* 1268
935 RUE LACHANCE BUREAU 200, QUEBEC, QC, G1P 2H3
(418) 683-5553 *SIC* 3645

SOLOWAVE DESIGN INC *p* 746

375 SLIGO RD W SS 1 SUITE 1, MOUNT FOREST, ON, N0G 2L0
(519) 323-3833   SIC 3949

SOLOWAVE DESIGN INC   p 1009
103 BAUER PL SUITE 5, WATERLOO, ON, N2L 6B5
(519) 323-3833   SIC 3949

SOLOWAVE INVESTMENTS LIMITED   p 1009
103 BAUER PL SUITE 5, WATERLOO, ON, N2L 6B5
(519) 725-5379   SIC 3949

SOLS CALCO SOILS INC, LES   p 746
17354 ALLAIRE RD, MOOSE CREEK, ON, K0C 1W0
(613) 538-2885   SIC 5159

SOLUS SAFETY   p 1386
See SOLUS SECURITE INC

SOLUS SECURITE INC   p 1386
2545 RUE DE LA SIDBEC S, TROIS-RIVIERES, QC, G8Z 4M6
(819) 373-2053   SIC 5099

SOLUSTAT   p 1075
See SOLUTIONS INHALOSTAT INC, LES

SOLUTIA SDO LTD   p 983
30 DUNCAN ST UNIT 202, TORONTO, ON, M5V 2C3
(416) 204-9797   SIC 8742

SOLUTION BOURASSA BOYER   p 1394
See BOURASSA BOYER SOLUTION INC

SOLUTION CELLULAIRE   p 1372
See 9044-4928 QUEBEC INC

SOLUTION FORD INC   p 1077
117 BOUL SAINT-JEAN-BAPTISTE, CHATEAUGUAY, QC, J6K 3B1
(450) 691-4130   SIC 5511

SOLUTION MORNEAU INC   p 1050
9601 BOUL DES SCIENCES, ANJOU, QC, H1J 0A6
(514) 325-2727   SIC 4212

SOLUTION OCCASION   p 1077
See SOLUTION FORD INC

SOLUTION Q INC   p 777
222 LESMILL RD, NORTH YORK, ON, M3B 2T5
(416) 385-0774   SIC 5045

SOLUTION SHERWEB   p 1372
See SHERWEB INC

SOLUTIONS   p 361
777 NORQUAY DR, WINKLER, MB, R6W 2S2
(204) 325-1006   SIC 5112

SOLUTIONS 2 GO INC   p 506
15 PRODUCTION DR, BRAMPTON, ON, L6T 4N8
(905) 564-1140   SIC 5072

SOLUTIONS 2 GO LATAM INC   p 506
15 PRODUCTION RD, BRAMPTON, ON, L6T 4N8
(905) 564-1140   SIC 5092

SOLUTIONS ABILIS INC   p 1199
1010 RUE SHERBROOKE O BUREAU 1900, MONTREAL, QC, H3A 2R7
(514) 844-4888   SIC 7379

SOLUTIONS APTOS CANADA   p 1332
See APTOS CANADA INC

SOLUTIONS BEYOND TECHNOLOGIES INC   p 1212
111 BOUL ROBERT-BOURASSA BUREAU 3600, MONTREAL, QC, H3C 2M1
(514) 227-7323   SIC 7379

SOLUTIONS CONTACT PHOCUS INC   p 1190
507 PLACE D'ARMES BUREAU 800, MONTREAL, QC, H2Y 2W8
(514) 788-5650   SIC 7389

SOLUTIONS D'AIR DESHUMIDIFIE INC   p 1228
5685 RUE CYPIHOT, MONTREAL, QC, H4S 1R3
(514) 336-3330   SIC 5078

SOLUTIONS D'AIR NORTEK QUEBEC, INC   p 1050
9100 RUE DU PARCOURS, ANJOU, QC,

H1J 2Z1
(514) 354-7776   SIC 3585

SOLUTIONS D'EMBALLAGES PENTAFLEX INC   p 1050
7905 RUE JARRY, ANJOU, QC, H1J 2C3
(514) 353-4330   SIC 7389

SOLUTIONS DE MAINTENANCE APPLIQUEES (AMS) INC   p 816
1470 TRIOLE ST, OTTAWA, ON, K1B 3S6
(613) 241-7794   SIC 7349

SOLUTIONS DE MAINTENANCE APPLIQUEES (AMS) INC   p 1182
7075 RUE MARCONI, MONTREAL, QC, H2S 3K4
(514) 272-8400   SIC 7349

SOLUTIONS DE RECONNAISSANCE RIDEAU INC   p 1327
473 RUE DESLAURIERS, SAINT-LAURENT, QC, H4N 1W2
(514) 336-9200   SIC 8748

SOLUTIONS HEBERGEES MONTRIUM   p 1189
See MONTRIUM HOSTED SOLUTIONS INC

SOLUTIONS INFORMATIQUES INSO INC   p 1184
6615 AV DU PARC, MONTREAL, QC, H2V 4J1
(514) 270-4477   SIC 5734

SOLUTIONS INHALOSTAT INC, LES   p 1075
1697 RUE FELIX-LECLERC, CHAMBLY, QC, J3L 5Z3
(450) 447-2112   SIC 7322

SOLUTIONS MAGNETIQUES TRANSFAB INC   p 1142
2315 RUE DE LA METROPOLE, LONGUEUIL, QC, J4G 1E5
(450) 449-0412   SIC 5063

SOLUTIONS MECANICA INC, LES   p 1336
10000 BOUL HENRI-BOURASSA O, SAINT-LAURENT, QC, H4S 1R5
(514) 340-1818   SIC 7371

SOLUTIONS MEDIAS 360 INC   p 1212
355 RUE PEEL BUREAU 901, MONTREAL, QC, H3C 2G9
(514) 717-9812   SIC 7371

SOLUTIONS MUNVO INC   p 1199
1400 RUE METCALFE SUITE 300, MONTREAL, QC, H3A 1X2
(514) 392-9822   SIC 8731

SOLUTIONS PROCESSIA INC   p 1087
3131 BOUL SAINT-MARTIN O BUREAU 220, COTE SAINT-LUC, QC, H7T 2Z5
(450) 786-0400   SIC 7379

SOLUTIONS TECHNIQUES INTELLIGENTES CB INC   p 1368
75 RUE DU PARC-INDUSTRIEL, SHAWINIGAN, QC, G9N 6T5
(819) 536-2609   SIC 7694

SOLUTIONS VICTRIX INC, LES   p 1199
630 RUE SHERBROOKE O BUREAU 1100, MONTREAL, QC, H3A 1E4
(514) 879-1919   SIC 7379

SOLUTIONS-YOUR ORGANIZED LIVING STORE   p 690
See 1348441 ONTARIO INC

SOLVA-NET   p 1162
See PRODUITS AUTOMOBILES LAURENTIDE INC

SOLVERA SOLUTIONS   p 1419
1853 HAMILTON ST SUITE 201, REGINA, SK, S4P 2C1
(306) 757-3510   SIC 7379

SOLWAY METAL SALES   p 994
See 570026 ONTARIO LIMITED

SOLWAY'S IGA   p 594
See 911803 ONTARIO INC

SOMA AUTO INC   p 1046
42 10E AV O, AMOS, QC, J9T 1W8
(819) 732-3205   SIC 5511

SOMAGEN DIAGNOSTICS INC   p 121

9220 25 AVE NW, EDMONTON, AB, T6N 1E1
(780) 702-9500   SIC 5049

SOMAK INTERNATIONAL INC   p 1235
1985 RUE MONTEREY, MONTREAL, QC, H7L 3T6
(450) 688-0123   SIC 5122

SOMAPHARM   p 1127
See BARIATRIX NUTRITION INC

SOMAVRAC INC   p 1386
2550 RUE DE LA SIDBEC S, TROIS-RIVIERES, QC, G8Z 4M6
(819) 374-7551   SIC 4213

SOMAVRAC INC   p 1388
3450 BOUL GENE-H.-KRUGER, TROIS-RIVIERES, QC, G9A 4M3
(819) 379-3311   SIC 4491

SOMERSET CHEV   p 934
See SOMERSET CHEVROLET CORVETTE LTD

SOMERSET CHEVROLET CORVETTE LTD   p 934
291 LAKE SHORE BLVD E, TORONTO, ON, M5A 1B9
(416) 368-8878   SIC 5511

SOMERSET WEST CHC   p 825
See SOMERSET WEST COMMUNITY HEALTH CENTRE

SOMERSET WEST COMMUNITY HEALTH CENTRE   p 825
55 ECCLES ST, OTTAWA, ON, K1R 6S3
(613) 238-8210   SIC 8322

SOMERVILLE MERCHANDISING INC   p 865
5760 FINCH AVE E, SCARBOROUGH, ON, M1B 5J9
(416) 754-7228   SIC 3993

SOMERVILLE NATIONAL LEASING & RENTALS LTD   p 795
75 ARROW RD, NORTH YORK, ON, M9M 2L4
(416) 747-7576   SIC 7515

SOMERVILLE, ROBERT B. CO., LIMITED   p 629
13176 DUFFERIN ST, KING CITY, ON, L7B 1K5
(905) 833-3100   SIC 1623

SOMI INC   p 744
6160 MAVIS RD, MISSISSAUGA, ON, L5V 2X4
(905) 569-7777   SIC 5511

SOMMERFELD COLONY FARMS LTD   p 351
GD, HIGH BLUFF, MB, R0H 0K0
(204) 243-2453   SIC 0213

SOMMERS MOTOR-GENERATOR SALES LIMITED   p 895
70 PACKHAM AVE, STRATFORD, ON, N4Z 0A6
(519) 655-2396   SIC 5063

SOMMETS DE LA VALLEE INC, LES   p 1352
350 AV SAINT-DENIS, SAINT-SAUVEUR, QC, J0R 1R3
(450) 227-4671   SIC 7011

SOMORICH MARKETING CORPORATION   p 571
324 HORNER AVE UNIT A, ETOBICOKE, ON, M8W 1Z3
(416) 461-9271   SIC 7331

SON'S BAKERY   p 371
See BAGOS BUN BAKERY LTD

SON'S OF ITALY CHARITABLE CORPORATION   p 617
530 UPPER PARADISE RD, HAMILTON, ON, L9C 7W2
(905) 388-4552   SIC 8699

SONACA MONTREAL INC   p 1153
13075 RUE BRAULT, MIRABEL, QC, J7J 0W2
(450) 434-6114   SIC 3728

SONACA NMF CANADA   p 1153
See SONACA MONTREAL INC

SONAL BACHU PHARMACY LTD   p 363
1555 REGENT AVE W UNIT 32T, WINNIPEG, MB, R2C 4J2

(204) 661-8068   SIC 5912

SONAVOX CANADA INC   p 1028
100-261 MILANI BLVD, WOODBRIDGE, ON, L4H 4E3
(905) 265-2060   SIC 8731

SONCO GAMING LIMITED PARTNERSHIP   p 170
377 GREY EAGLE DR, TSUU T'INA, AB, T3E 3X8
(403) 385-3777   SIC 7999

SONCO GAMING NEW BRUNSWICK LIMITED PARTNERSHIP   p 409
21 CASINO DR, MONCTON, NB, E1G 0R7
(506) 859-7770   SIC 7011

SONCO STEEL TUBE DIVISION   p 510
See ARCELORMITTAL TUBULAR PRODUCTS CANADA G.P.

SONDER CANADA INC   p 1184
15 RUE MARIE-ANNE O BUREAU 201, MONTREAL, QC, H2W 1B6
(800) 657-9859   SIC 6531

SONEPAR CANADA INC   p 103
11330 189 ST NW, EDMONTON, AB, T5S 2V6
(780) 944-9331   SIC 5063

SONEPAR CANADA INC   p 275
10449 120 ST, SURREY, BC, V3V 4G4
(604) 528-3700   SIC 5063

SONEPAR CANADA INC   p 500
250 CHRYSLER DR UNIT 4, BRAMPTON, ON, L6S 6B6
(905) 696-2838   SIC 5063

SONEPAR CANADA INC   p 1236
4655 NORD LAVAL (A-440) O, MONTREAL, QC, H7P 5P9
(450) 688-9249   SIC 5063

SONEPAR CANADA INC   p 1252
117 BOUL HYMUS BUREAU 17, POINTE-CLAIRE, QC, H9R 1E5
(514) 426-0629   SIC 5063

SONEPAR CANADA INC   p 1398
415 BOUL LABBE N, VICTORIAVILLE, QC, G6P 9J4
(819) 758-6205   SIC 5063

SONEX CONSTRUCTION GROUP LTD   p 103
21110 108 AVE NW, EDMONTON, AB, T5S 1X4
(780) 447-4409   SIC 1629

SONIGEM PRODUCTS   p 672
See MAGNASONIC INC.

SONIPLASTICS INC   p 1067
1610 RUE EIFFEL, BOUCHERVILLE, QC, J4B 5Y1
(450) 449-6000   SIC 3089

SONNY NAKASHIMA FARMS LTD   p 8
GD, BURDETT, AB, T0K 0J0
(403) 655-2270   SIC 0139

SONOBOARD TMA 26598   p 1241
See INDUSTRIES MONDIALES ARMSTRONG CANADA LTEE, LES

SONOCO CANADA CORPORATION   p 516
33 PARK AVE E, BRANTFORD, ON, N3S 7R9
(905) 823-7910   SIC 2655

SONOCO CANADA CORPORATION   p 543
674 RICHMOND ST, CHATHAM, ON, N7M 5K4
(519) 352-8201   SIC 2655

SONOCO CANADA CORPORATION   p 999
5 BERNARD LONG RD, TRENTON, ON, K8V 5P6
(613) 394-6903   SIC 2631

SONOCO CANADA CORPORATION   p 1385
530 RUE DES ERABLES, TROIS-RIVIERES, QC, G8T 8N6
(819) 374-5222   SIC 2655

SONOCO FLEXIBLE PACKAGING CANADA CORPORATION   p 392
1664 SEEL AVE, WINNIPEG, MB, R3T 4X5
SIC 2759

SONOCO FLEXIBLE PACKAGING CANADA CORPORATION   p 516

33 PARK AVE E, BRANTFORD, ON, N3S 7R9
(519) 752-6591   SIC 3086
SONOCO PLASTICS CANADA ULC   p 707
245 BRITANNIA RD E, MISSISSAUGA, ON, L4Z 4J3
(905) 624-2337   SIC 3089
SONORO ENERGY LTD   p 59
520 5 AVE SW SUITE 900, CALGARY, AB, T2P 3R7
(403) 262-3252   SIC 1382
SONOVA CANADA INC   p 745
80 COURTNEYPARK DR W SUITE 1, MISSISSAUGA, ON, L5W 0B3
(905) 677-1167   SIC 3842
SONOVISION CANADA INC   p 1155
4480 CH DE LA COTE-DE-LIESSE BUREAU 215, MONT-ROYAL, QC, H4N 2R1
(514) 344-5008   SIC 2741
SONS BAKERY   p 33
See BAGOS BUN BAKERY LTD
SONY INTERACTIVE ENTERTAINMENT CANADA INC   p 745
1 PROLOGIS BLVD SUITE 103, MISSISSAUGA, ON, L5W 0G2
(905) 795-5152   SIC 5092
SONY MUSIC ENTERTAINMENT CANADA INC   p 780
150 FERRAND DR SUITE 300, NORTH YORK, ON, M3C 3E5
(416) 589-3000   SIC 5099
SONY OF CANADA LTD   p 768
2235 SHEPPARD AVE E SUITE 700, NORTH YORK, ON, M2J 5B5
(416) 499-1414   SIC 5064
SONY STORES, THE   p 768
See SONY OF CANADA LTD
SOO MILL & LUMBER COMPANY LIMITED p 863
539 GREAT NORTHERN RD, SAULT STE. MARIE, ON, P6B 5A1
(705) 759-0533   SIC 5211
SOO SUZUKI   p 861
See DICK'S GARAGE LIMITED
SOPER'S SUPPLY LTD   p 86
10519 114 ST NW, EDMONTON, AB, T5H 3J6
(780) 423-4066   SIC 5063
SOPFIM   p 1265
See SOCIETE DE PROTECTION DES FORETS CONTRE LES INSECTES ET MALADIES
SOPHOS INC   p 309
580 GRANVILLE ST SUITE 400, VANCOUVER, BC, V6C 1W6
(604) 484-6400   SIC 7371
SOPLEX SOLUTIONS D'ASSURANCE INC p 1087
225 PROM DU CENTROPOLIS BUREAU 215, COTE SAINT-LUC, QC, H7T 0B3
(450) 781-6566   SIC 6411
SOPREMA INC   p 1099
1688 RUE JEAN-BERCHMANS-MICHAUD, DRUMMONDVILLE, QC, J2C 8E9
(819) 478-8163   SIC 2952
SOQUEM INC   p 1391
1740 CH SULLIVAN BUREAU 2000, VAL-D'OR, QC, J9P 7H1
(819) 874-3773   SIC 1081
SOQUIJ   p 1190
See SOCIETE QUEBECOISE D'INFORMATION JURIDIQUE
SOR HOLDINGS LTD   p 363
1364 REGENT AVE W, WINNIPEG, MB, R2C 3A8
(204) 667-9993   SIC 5511
SORBARA SERVICES LIMITED   p 1033
3700 STEELES AVE W SUITE 800, WOODBRIDGE, ON, L4L 8M9
(905) 850-6154   SIC 8741
SORENSEN GREENHOUSES INC   p 645
3 MILL ST E, LEAMINGTON, ON, N8H 1R6
(519) 322-5024   SIC 0181
SORINCO   p 1074

See COVANTA SOLUTIONS ENVIRONNEMENTALES INC
SOROC TECHNOLOGY INC   p 1033
607 CHRISLEA RD, WOODBRIDGE, ON, L4L 8A3
(905) 265-8000   SIC 5045
SOROC TECHNOLOGY INC   p 1085
1800 BOUL LE CORBUSIER BUREAU 132, COTE SAINT-LUC, QC, H7S 2K1
(450) 682-5029   SIC 7378
SORRELL FINANCIAL INC   p 91
10111 104 AVE NW UNIT 2600, EDMONTON, AB, T5J 0J4
(780) 424-1424   SIC 6411
SORRENTINO'S BISTRO BAR   p 85
See 340107 ALBERTA LTD
SOS DEPANNAGE MAGASIN GENERAL   p 1109
See S.O.S. DEPANNAGE GRANBY ET REGION INC
SOSEN INC   p 1212
995 RUE WELLINGTON BUREAU 210, MONTREAL, QC, H3C 1V3
(514) 789-1255   SIC 5122
SOTECH-NITRAM INC   p 1062
3975 BOUL DE LA GRANDE-ALLEE, BOISBRIAND, QC, J7H 1M6
(450) 975-2100   SIC 4731
SOTHEBY'S INTERNATIONAL REALTY CANADA   p
See MAX WRIGHT REAL ESTATE CORPORATION
SOTHEBY'S INTERNATIONAL REALTY CANADA, BROKERAGE   p 924
See PINO ALEJANDRO
SOTI INC   p 733
5770 HURONTARIO ST SUITE 1100, MISSISSAUGA, ON, L5R 3G5
(905) 624-9828   SIC 7371
SOTREM (1993) INC   p 1081
1685 RUE DE LA MANIC, CHICOUTIMI, QC, G7K 1G8
(418) 696-2019   SIC 3398
SOTTO SOTTO RISTORANTE LIMITED   p 973
116 AVENUE RD UNIT A, TORONTO, ON, M5R 2H4
(416) 962-0011   SIC 5812
SOUCIE-SALO SAFETY INC   p 900
1300 LORNE ST, SUDBURY, ON, P3C 5N1
(705) 674-8092   SIC 5136
SOUCY BARON INC   p 1320
851 RUE BARON, SAINT-JEROME, QC, J7Y 4E1
(450) 436-2433   SIC 3069
SOUCY BELGEN INC   p 1097
4475 BOUL SAINT-JOSEPH, DRUMMONDVILLE, QC, J2B 1T8
(819) 477-2434   SIC 3321
SOUCY CAOUTCHOUC   p 1097
See SOUCY INTERNATIONAL INC
SOUCY CAOUTCHOUC   p 1100
See SOUCY INTERNATIONAL INC
SOUCY INDUSTRIEL   p 1285
See ADELARD SOUCY (1975) INC
SOUCY INTERNATIONAL INC   p 1097
5450 RUE SAINT-ROCH S, DRUMMONDVILLE, QC, J2B 6V4
(819) 474-6666   SIC 3714
SOUCY INTERNATIONAL INC   p 1100
5195 RUE RICHARD, DRUMMONDVILLE, QC, J2E 1A7
(819) 474-4522   SIC 3795
SOUCY KOUTOU INC   p 1099
1825 RUE POWER, DRUMMONDVILLE, QC, J2C 5X4
(819) 478-9032   SIC 7389
SOUCY PLASTIQUES INC   p 1097
5755 PLACE KUBOTA, DRUMMONDVILLE, QC, J2B 6V4
(819) 474-4151   SIC 3089
SOUCY RIVALAIR INC   p 1099
650 RUE ROCHELEAU, DRUMMONDVILLE, QC, J2C 7R8

(819) 474-2908   SIC 3499
SOUCY TECHNO INC   p 1375
2550 CH SAINT-ROCH S, SHERBROOKE, QC, J1N 2R6
(819) 864-4284   SIC 3069
SOUDURE COUTURE   p 1310
See SOUDURE M. COUTURE & FILS INC
SOUDURE M. COUTURE & FILS INC p 1310
8020 AV DUPLESSIS, SAINT-HYACINTHE, QC, J2R 1S6
(450) 796-1617   SIC 3446
SOUDURES EXPRESS INC   p 1045
995 AV BOMBARDIER, ALMA, QC, G8B 6H2
(418) 669-1911   SIC 7692
SOUDURES J.M. TREMBLAY (1987) INC, LES   p 1291
1303 RTE 132, SAINT-ANICET, QC, J0S 1M0
(450) 264-5690   SIC 3312
SOUND DESIGN TECHNOLOGIES LTD   p 525
970 FRASER DR, BURLINGTON, ON, L7L 5P5
(905) 635-0800   SIC 3842
SOUND FM   p 1008
See CKMS-FM 100.3
SOUND INSURANCE SERVICES INC p 777
205 LESMILL RD, NORTH YORK, ON, M3B 2V1
(416) 756-3334   SIC 6411
SOUND WAVES ENTERTAINMENT NETWORK LTD   p 223
1-325 BAY AVE, KELOWNA, BC, V1Y 7S3
(250) 868-3333   SIC 7359
SOUNDS FANTASTIC   p 406
See 501479 NB LTD
SOUP BONE ENTERPRISES INC   p 203
750 COMOX RD SUITE 121, COURTENAY, BC, V9N 3P6
(250) 897-1300   SIC 6712
SOURCE (BELL) ELECTRONICS INC, THE p 485
279 BAYVIEW DR, BARRIE, ON, L4M 4W5
(705) 728-2262   SIC 5731
SOURCE ATLANTIC LIMITED   p 414
331 CHESLEY DR, SAINT JOHN, NB, E2K 5P2
(506) 635-7711   SIC 5084
SOURCE ATLANTIC LIMITED   p 414
331 CHESLEY DR, SAINT JOHN, NB, E2K 5P2
(506) 632-1000   SIC 5084
SOURCE ATLANTIC LIMITED   p 448
14 AKERLEY BLVD, DARTMOUTH, NS, B3B 1J3
(902) 494-5377   SIC 5999
SOURCE ENERGY SERVICES CANADA LP GP LTD   p 32
438 11 AVE SE UNIT 500, CALGARY, AB, T2G 0Y4
(403) 262-1312   SIC 1389
SOURCE ENERGY SERVICES LTD   p 32
438 11 AVE SE SUITE 500, CALGARY, AB, T2G 0Y4
(403) 262-1312   SIC 3532
SOURCE SANTE ACTION INC   p 1297
100 RUE JOHANNE, SAINT-COLOMBAN, QC, J5K 2A5
(450) 560-4980   SIC 8741
SOURCE SANTE PLUS   p 767
See HEALTHSOURCE PLUS INC
SOURCE, THE   p 485
See SOURCE (BELL) ELECTRONICS INC, THE
SOURCES 40 WESTT INC   p 1252
2305 RTE TRANSCANADIENNE, POINTE-CLAIRE, QC, H9R 5Z5
(514) 428-9378   SIC 5812
SOURCES VEO INC, LES   p 1112
1335 CH DE LA RIVIERE-ROUGE, GRENVILLE-SUR-LA-ROUGE, QC, J0V 1B0

(819) 242-2882   SIC 5149
SOURIS DISTRICT HOSPITAL & AMBULANCE SERVICE   p 357
155 BRINDLE AVE E, SOURIS, MB, R0K 2C0
(204) 483-2121   SIC 8062
SOURIS MINI   p 1265
See 9381-0596 QUEBEC INC
SOURIS MINI   p 1275
See 9381-0455 QUEBEC INC
SOURIS RIVER COLONY FARMS LTD p 349
GD, ELGIN, MB, R0K 0T0
SIC 7389
SOUS LE COUVERT DES ARBRES   p 1104
See 2734-7681 QUEBEC INC
SOUS-REGION QUEBEC-SUD   p 1258
See FONDATION DU CENTRE JEUNESSE DE QUEBEC
SOUS-TRAITANCE L.B.   p 1082
See 3011933 CANADA INC
SOUS-VETEMENTS U.M. INC, LES   p 1179
9200 BOUL SAINT-LAURENT, MONTREAL, QC, H2N 1M9
(514) 387-3791   SIC 2321
SOUTENEMENT DU SOL MINOVA CANADA   p 1072
See ORICA CANADA INC
SOUTH ALBERTA RIBS (2002) LTD   p 37
6712 MACLEOD TRAIL SE, CALGARY, AB, T2H 0L3
(403) 301-7427   SIC 5812
SOUTH AMERICAN GOLD AND COPPER COMPANY LIMITED   p 943
67 YONGE ST SUITE 1201, TORONTO, ON, M5E 1J8
(416) 369-9115   SIC 1081
SOUTH BEND COLONY   p 3
See HUTTERIAN BRETHREN OF SOUTH BEND
SOUTH BRUCE GREY HEALTH CENTRE p 1004
21 MCGIVERN ST, WALKERTON, ON, N0G 2V0
(519) 881-1220   SIC 8062
SOUTH CALGARY PRIMARY CARE NETWORK, THE   p 69
1800 194 AVE SE SUITE 4000, CALGARY, AB, T2X 0R3
(403) 256-3222   SIC 8011
SOUTH CAMBRIDGE HOME HARDWARE BUILDING CENTRE   p 535
See TROUNCY INC
SOUTH CARIBOO HEALTH CENTRE p 174
See 100 MILE DISTRICT GENERAL HOSPITAL
SOUTH CARLETON HIGH SCHOOL   p 850
See OTTAWA-CARLETON DISTRICT SCHOOL BOARD
SOUTH COAST BRITISH COLUMBIA TRANSPORTATION AUTHORITY   p 237
287 NELSON'S CRT SUITE 300, NEW WESTMINSTER, BC, V3L 0E7
(604) 515-8300   SIC 4111
SOUTH COAST BRITISH COLUMBIA TRANSPORTATION AUTHORITY   p 237
287 NELSON'S CRT SUITE 400, NEW WESTMINSTER, BC, V3L 0E7
(778) 375-7500   SIC 4111
SOUTH COAST FORD SALES LTD   p 268
5606 WHARF RD, SECHELT, BC, V0N 3A0
(604) 885-3281   SIC 5511
SOUTH COAST INSURANCE AGENCY LIMITED   p
227 ATLANTIC ST, MARYSTOWN, NL, A0E 2M0
(709) 279-3200   SIC 6411
SOUTH COCHRANE CHILD AND YOUTH SERVICE INCORPORATED   p 680
507 EIGTH AVE SUITE 15, MATHESON, ON, P0K 1N0
(705) 273-3041   SIC 8399

SOUTH COUNTRY AG LTD   *p* 1412
40 MAIN ST, MOSSBANK, SK, S0H 3G0
SIC 6712

SOUTH COUNTRY AGENCIES   *p* 169
5300 47 AVE, TABER, AB, T1G 1R1
(403) 223-8123   *SIC* 6351

SOUTH COUNTRY CO-OP LIMITED   *p* 146
969 16 ST SW, MEDICINE HAT, AB, T1A 4X5
(403) 528-6600   *SIC* 5171

SOUTH COUNTRY EQUIPMENT LTD *p* 1411
1731 MAIN ST N, MOOSE JAW, SK, S6J 1L6
(306) 642-3366   *SIC* 5999

SOUTH DELTA SECONDARY SCHOOL   *p* 211
See DELTA SCHOOL DISTRICT NO.37

SOUTH EAST COMMUNITY CARE ACCESS CENTRE   *p* 632
1471 JOHN COUNTER BLVD SUITE 200, KINGSTON, ON, K7M 8S8
(613) 544-7090   *SIC* 8011

SOUTH EAST CONSTRUCTION   *p* 1406
600 MAIN ST, ESTERHAZY, SK, S0A 0X0
(306) 745-4830   *SIC* 8748

SOUTH EAST CONSTRUCTION LP *p* 1406
See SOUTH EAST CONSTRUCTION

SOUTH EAST PALLET AND WOOD PRODUCTS   *p* 346
See 4117638 MANITOBA LTD

SOUTH EASTHOPE MUTUAL INSURANCE COMPANY   *p* 902
62 WOODSTOCK ST N, TAVISTOCK, ON, N0B 2R0
(519) 655-2011   *SIC* 6411

SOUTH ESSEX FABRICATING INC   *p* 645
4 SENECA RD, LEAMINGTON, ON, N8H 5H7
(519) 322-5995   *SIC* 5191

SOUTH FORT CHEVROLET LTD   *p* 130
10109 89 AVE, FORT SASKATCHEWAN, AB, T8L 3V5
(780) 998-7881   *SIC* 5511

SOUTH GRANVILLE BUSINESS CENTRE *p* 321
See MACDONALD COMMECIAL REAL ESTATE SERVICES LTD

SOUTH HILL FINE FOODS   *p* 1411
See WATSON HOLDINGS LTD

SOUTH HURON DISTRICT HIGH SCHOOL *p* 589
See AVON MAITLAND DISTRICT SCHOOL BOARD

SOUTH HURON HOSPITAL ASSOCIATION *p* 590
24 HURON ST W, EXETER, ON, N0M 1S2
(519) 235-2700   *SIC* 8062

SOUTH KAMLOOPS SECONDARY SCHOOL   *p* 217
See SCHOOL DISTRICT 73 (KAMLOOPS/THOMPSON)

SOUTH LONDON INFINITI-NISSAN INC   *p* 660
1055 WHARNCLIFFE RD S, LONDON, ON, N6L 1J9
(519) 685-5497   *SIC* 5511

SOUTH OAKVILLE CHRYSLER DODGE JEEP RAM LTD   *p* 802
175 WYECROFT RD, OAKVILLE, ON, L6K 3S3
(905) 845-6653   *SIC* 5511

SOUTH OAKVILLE CHRYSLER FIAT *p* 802
See SOUTH OAKVILLE CHRYSLER DODGE JEEP RAM LTD

SOUTH OKANAGAN GENERAL HOSPITAL *p* 242
7139 362 AVE, OLIVER, BC, V0H 1T0
(250) 498-5000   *SIC* 8062

SOUTH PEACE COMMUNITY RESOURCES SOCIETY   *p* 205
10110 13 ST, DAWSON CREEK, BC, V1G 3W2

(250) 782-9174   *SIC* 8399

SOUTH PEACE DISTRIBUTORS LTD *p* 136
AB-43, HYTHE, AB, T0H 2C0
(780) 356-3970   *SIC* 5172

SOUTH POINT CHEVROLET PONTIAC BUICK GMC LTD   *p* 645
108 ERIE ST N, LEAMINGTON, ON, N8H 0A9
(519) 326-3206   *SIC* 5511

SOUTH RIVERDALE COMMUNITY HEALTH CENTRE   *p* 921
955 QUEEN ST E, TORONTO, ON, M4M 3P3
(416) 461-1925   *SIC* 8011

SOUTH SASKACHEWAN DIVISION   *p* 1420
See CANADIAN CORPS OF COMMISSIONAIRES NATIONAL OFFICE, THE

SOUTH SHORE CHEVROLET   *p* 441
See 3302775 NOVA SCOTIA LTD

SOUTH SHORE DISTRICT HEALTH AUTHORITY   *p* 461
175 SCHOOL ST, LIVERPOOL, NS, B0T 1K0
(902) 354-5785   *SIC* 8069

SOUTH SHORE INDUSTRIES LTD   *p* 1357
6168 RUE PRINCIPALE, SAINTE-CROIX, QC, G0S 2H0
(418) 926-3291   *SIC* 2511

SOUTH SHORE RADIOLOGISTS   *p* 1065
See IMAGIX IMAGERIE MEDICALE INC

SOUTH SHORE READY MIX LIMITED *p* 441
1896 KING ST, BRIDGEWATER, NS, B4V 2W9
(902) 543-4639   *SIC* 3273

SOUTH SHORE REGIONAL SCHOOL BOARD   *p* 441
69 WENTZELL DR, BRIDGEWATER, NS, B4V 0A2
(902) 543-2468   *SIC* 8211

SOUTH SHORE SAND & GRAVEL   *p* 441
See SOUTH SHORE READY MIX LIMITED

SOUTH SHORE SEAFOODS LTD   *p* 1038
6 FOY RD, BLOOMFIELD STATION, PE, C0B 1E0
(902) 853-4052   *SIC* 5146

SOUTH SHORE TRADING CO. LTD   *p* 419
36 JOHN A TRENHOLM RD, UPPER CAPE, NB, E4M 2R6
(506) 538-7619   *SIC* 5146

SOUTH STAMPING PLANT   *p* 812
See GENERAL MOTORS OF CANADA COMPANY

SOUTH STREET HOSPITAL   *p* 654
See LONDON HEALTH SCIENCES CENTRE

SOUTH SURREY HOTEL LTD   *p* 281
1160 KING GEORGE BLVD, SURREY, BC, V4A 4Z2
(604) 535-1432   *SIC* 7011

SOUTH TRAIL CHRYSLER LTD   *p* 71
6103 130 AVE SE, CALGARY, AB, T2Z 5E1
(587) 349-7272   *SIC* 5521

SOUTH WEST AG PARTNERS INC   *p* 543
40 CENTRE ST SUITE 200, CHATHAM, ON, N7M 5W3
(519) 380-0002   *SIC* 5153

SOUTH WEST CHRYSLER DODGE INC   *p* 659
658 WHARNCLIFFE RD S, LONDON, ON, N6J 2N4
(519) 649-2121   *SIC* 5511

SOUTH WEST LOCAL HEALTH INTEGRATION NETWORK   *p* 659
356 OXFORD ST W, LONDON, ON, N6H 1T3
(519) 672-0445   *SIC* 8621

SOUTH WEST TERMINAL LTD   *p* 1407
GD, GULL LAKE, SK, S0N 1A0
(306) 672-4112   *SIC* 4221

SOUTH WESTERN INSURANCE GROUP LIMITED   *p* 580
401 THE WEST MALL SUITE 700, ETOBI-

COKE, ON, M9C 5J4
(416) 620-6604   *SIC* 6411

SOUTHAMPTON CARE CENTRE INC *p* 882
140 GREY ST S, SOUTHAMPTON, ON, N0H 2L0
(519) 797-3220   *SIC* 8051

SOUTHAMPTON INDUSTRIAL MANUFACTURING INC   *p* 18
5605 48 ST SE, CALGARY, AB, T2C 4X8
(403) 930-9299   *SIC* 3494

SOUTHAMPTON TRAIN INDUSTRIAL   *p* 18
See SOUTHAMPTON INDUSTRIAL MANUFACTURING INC

SOUTHAMPTON-TRANE   *p* 18
See SOUTHAMPTON-TRANE AIR CONDITIONING (CALGARY) INC

SOUTHAMPTON-TRANE AIR CONDITIONING (CALGARY) INC   *p* 18
10905 48 ST SE SUITE 157, CALGARY, AB, T2C 1G8
(403) 301-0090   *SIC* 5722

SOUTHBANK DODGE CHRYSLER (1982) LTD   *p* 827
1255 JOHNSTON RD, OTTAWA, ON, K1V 8Z1
(613) 731-1970   *SIC* 5511

SOUTHBANK FRUIT INC   *p* 827
2446 BANK ST UNIT 131, OTTAWA, ON, K1V 1A4
(613) 521-9653   *SIC* 5431

SOUTHBRIDGE HEALTH CARE LP *p* 539
766 HESPELER RD SUITE 301, CAMBRIDGE, ON, N3H 5L8
(519) 621-8886   *SIC* 8741

SOUTHBROOK RETIREMENT COMMUNITY   *p* 511
See 728567 ONTARIO LIMITED

SOUTHCENTER AUTO INC   *p* 1432
321 CIRCLE DR W, SASKATOON, SK, S7L 5S8
(306) 373-3711   *SIC* 5511

SOUTHCOAST MILLWORK LTD   *p* 230
23347 MCKAY AVE, MAPLE RIDGE, BC, V2W 1B9
(604) 467-0111   *SIC* 2431

SOUTHDOWN INSTITUTE, THE   *p* 481
1335 ST. JOHN'S SIDEROAD SUITE 2, AURORA, ON, L4G 0P8
(905) 727-4214   *SIC* 8661

SOUTHDOWN INSTITUTE, THE   *p* 620
18798 OLD YONGE ST, HOLLAND LANDING, ON, L9N 0L1
(905) 727-4214   *SIC* 8699

SOUTHEAST PERSONAL CARE HOME   *p* 392
See SOUTHEAST PERSONAL CARE HOME INC

SOUTHEAST PERSONAL CARE HOME INC   *p* 392
1265 LEE BLVD, WINNIPEG, MB, R3T 2M3
(204) 269-7111   *SIC* 8052

SOUTHEAST RESOURCE DEVELOPMENT COUNCIL CORP   *p* 379
360 BROADWAY, WINNIPEG, MB, R3C 0T6
(204) 956-7500   *SIC* 8399

SOUTHEASTERN FARM EQUIPMENT LTD *p* 358
300 PTH 12 N, STEINBACH, MB, R5G 1T6
(204) 326-9834   *SIC* 5999

SOUTHERN ALBERTA COMMUNITY LIVING ASSOCIATION   *p* 141
401 21A ST N, LETHBRIDGE, AB, T1H 6L6
(403) 329-1525   *SIC* 8699

SOUTHERN ALBERTA WEB PRINTERS *p* 147
3257 DUNMORE RD SE, MEDICINE HAT, AB, T1B 3R2
(403) 528-5674   *SIC* 2759

SOUTHERN FIRST NATIONS NETWORK OF CARE   *p* 382

835 PORTAGE AVE, WINNIPEG, MB, R3G 0N6
(204) 944-4200   *SIC* 8322

SOUTHERN GLAZER'S WINE AND SPIRITS OF CANADA, LLC   *p* 572
3250 BLOOR ST W SUITE 901, ETOBICOKE, ON, M8X 2X9
(647) 347-7711   *SIC* 5149

SOUTHERN GRAPHIC SYSTEMS-CANADA LTD   *p* 576
2 DORCHESTER AVE, ETOBICOKE, ON, M8Z 4W3
(416) 252-9331   *SIC* 3555

SOUTHERN GRAPHICS SYSTEMS-CANADA, CO.   *p* 576
2 DORCHESTER AVE, ETOBICOKE, ON, M8Z 4W3
(416) 252-9331   *SIC* 7336

SOUTHERN HEALTH-SANTE SUD *p* 357
354 PREFONTAINE AVE, ST PIERRE JOLYS, MB, R0A 1V0
(204) 433-7611   *SIC* 8062

SOUTHERN HEALTH-SANTE SUD *p* 358
316 HENRY ST, STEINBACH, MB, R5G 0P9
(204) 326-6411   *SIC* 8062

SOUTHERN HEALTH-SANTE SUD *p* 360
217 1ST AVE, VITA, MB, R0A 2K0
(204) 425-3325   *SIC* 8062

SOUTHERN MANITOBA POTATO CO. LTD *p* 361
375 NORTH RAILWAY AVE, WINKLER, MB, R6W 1J4
(204) 325-4318   *SIC* 0134

SOUTHERN MUSIC LTD   *p* 9
3605 32 ST NE, CALGARY, AB, T1Y 5Y9
(403) 291-1666   *SIC* 7359

SOUTHERN PLAINS CO-OPERATIVE LIMITED   *p* 1406
826 4TH ST, ESTEVAN, SK, S4A 0W1
(306) 637-4300   *SIC* 5399

SOUTHERN RAILWAY OF BRITISH COLUMBIA LIMITED   *p* 238
2102 RIVER DR, NEW WESTMINSTER, BC, V3M 6S3
(604) 521-1851   *SIC* 4011

SOUTHERN SANITATION INC   *p* 790
161 BRIDGELAND AVE, NORTH YORK, ON, M6A 1Z1
(416) 787-5000   *SIC* 4953

SOUTHERN SUPPLIES LIMITED   *p* 814
323 BLOOR ST W, OSHAWA, ON, L1J 6X4
(905) 728-6216   *SIC* 5075

SOUTHGATE AUDI   *p* 125
See 2071848 ALBERTA LTD

SOUTHGATE CHEVROLET BUICK GMC LTD   *p* 39
13103 LAKE FRASER DR SE, CALGARY, AB, T2J 3H5
(403) 256-4960   *SIC* 5511

SOUTHGATE PONTIAC BUICK GMC LTD *p* 116
9751 34 AVE NW, EDMONTON, AB, T6E 5X9
(855) 971-6989   *SIC* 5511

SOUTHGOBI RESOURCES LTD   *p* 309
250 HOWE ST 20TH FLOOR, VANCOUVER, BC, V6C 3R8
(604) 762-6783   *SIC* 1081

SOUTHLAKE REGIONAL HEALTH CENTRE   *p* 756
596 DAVIS DR, NEWMARKET, ON, L3Y 2P9
(905) 895-4521   *SIC* 8062

SOUTHLAND CANADA STORE   *p* 37
6015 4 ST SE, CALGARY, AB, T2H 2A5
(403) 253-6218   *SIC* 5411

SOUTHLAND CO-OPERATIVE LTD *p* 1404
409 CENTRE ST, ASSINIBOIA, SK, S0H 0B0
(306) 642-4128   *SIC* 5411

SOUTHLAND INTERNATIONAL TRUCKS LTD *p 141*
4310 9 AVE N, LETHBRIDGE, AB, T1H 6N1
(403) 328-0808   *SIC 5511*
SOUTHLAND SHELL   *p 762*
See 1530460 ONTARIO INC
SOUTHLAND TRAILER CORP   *p 141*
1405 41 ST N, LETHBRIDGE, AB, T1H 6G3
(403) 327-8212   *SIC 3715*
SOUTHLAND TRANSPORTATION LTD *p 32*
823 HIGHFIELD AVE SE, CALGARY, AB, T2G 4C7
(403) 287-1395   *SIC 4151*
SOUTHLAND TRANSPORTATION LTD *p 80*
216 GRIFFIN RD E, COCHRANE, AB, T4C 2B9
(403) 932-7100   *SIC 4151*
SOUTHLAND VOLKSWAGEN   *p 146*
See 1131898 ALBERTA LTD
SOUTHMEDIC INCORPORATED   *p 485*
50 ALLIANCE BLVD, BARRIE, ON, L4M 5K3
(705) 726-9383   *SIC 3841*
SOUTHRIDGE BUILDING SUPPLIES LTD *p 273*
17444 56 AVE, SURREY, BC, V3S 1C3
(604) 576-2113   *SIC 5039*
SOUTHRIDGE CHRYSLER LTD   *p 151*
12 SOUTHRIDGE DR, OKOTOKS, AB, T1S 1N1
(403) 938-3636   *SIC 5511*
SOUTHSIDE CONSTRUCTION (LONDON) LIMITED   *p 659*
75 BLACKFRIARS ST, LONDON, ON, N6H 1K8
(519) 433-0634   *SIC 1542*
SOUTHSIDE CONSTRUCTION LONDON *p 661*
3089 WONDERLAND RD S, LONDON, ON, N6L 1R4
(519) 657-6583   *SIC 1521*
SOUTHSIDE DODGE CHRYSLER & R.V. CENTRE   *p 157*
See SOUTHSIDE PLYMOUTH CHRYSLER LTD
SOUTHSIDE GROUP OF COMPANIES *p 659*
See SOUTHSIDE CONSTRUCTION (LONDON) LIMITED
SOUTHSIDE INTERNATIONAL TRUCKS, DIV OF   *p 100*
See DIAMOND INTERNATIONAL TRUCKS LTD
SOUTHSIDE MITSUBISHI   *p 112*
See 979094 ALBERTA LTD
SOUTHSIDE MOTORS LTD   *p 39*
11888 MACLEOD TRAIL SE, CALGARY, AB, T2J 7J2
(403) 252-4327   *SIC 5511*
SOUTHSIDE NISSAN LTD   *p 291*
290 MARINE DR SW, VANCOUVER, BC, V5X 2R5
(604) 324-4644   *SIC 5511*
SOUTHSIDE PLYMOUTH CHRYSLER LTD *p 157*
2804 50 AVE, RED DEER, AB, T4R 1M4
(403) 346-5577   *SIC 5511*
SOUTHSTAR EQUIPMENT LTD   *p 218*
728 TAGISH ST, KAMLOOPS, BC, V2H 1B7
(250) 828-7820   *SIC 5082*
SOUTHTOWN CHRYSLER INC   *p 120*
4404 66 ST NW, EDMONTON, AB, T6K 4E7
(780) 490-3200   *SIC 5511*
SOUTHTOWN HYUNDAI   *p 115*
See MIKE PRIESTNER AUTOMOTIVE GROUP LTD
SOUTHVIEW ACURA   *p 112*
See 967530 ALBERTA LTD
SOUTHWEST ALBERTA CHILD & FAMILY SERVICES   *p 140*
See GOVERNMENT OF THE PROVINCE OF ALBERTA
SOUTHWEST AUTO CENTRE LTD   *p 348*
2080 CURRIE BLVD, BRANDON, MB, R7B 4E7

(204) 728-8740   *SIC 5511*
SOUTHWEST BINDING SYSTEMS LTD *p 875*
20 DOVEDALE CRT, SCARBOROUGH, ON, M1S 5A7
(416) 285-7044   *SIC 5084*
SOUTHWEST CONTRACTING LTD   *p 282*
9426 192 ST, SURREY, BC, V4N 3R9
(604) 888-5221   *SIC 1623*
SOUTHWEST HORIZON SCHOOL DIVISION   *p 352*
GD, MELITA, MB, R0M 1L0
(204) 483-6292   *SIC 8211*
SOUTHWEST PLASTIC BINDINGS   *p 875*
See SOUTHWEST BINDING SYSTEMS LTD
SOUTHWEST PROPERTIES   *p 454*
See WINDMILL CROSSING LIMITED
SOUTHWESTERN MANUFACTURING INC *p 1025*
3710 PETER ST, WINDSOR, ON, N9C 1J9
(519) 985-6161   *SIC 3499*
SOUTHWIRE CANADA COMPANY   *p 733*
5705 CANCROSS CRT SUITE 100, MISSISSAUGA, ON, L5R 3E9
(800) 668-0303   *SIC 3357*
SOUTHWOOD SECONDARY SCHOOL *p 535*
See WATERLOO REGION DISTRICT SCHOOL BOARD
SOUTHWORKS OUTLET MALL INC   *p 535*
64 GRAND AVE S, CAMBRIDGE, ON, N1S 2L8
(519) 740-0380   *SIC 6512*
SOUVENIR CITY   *p 757*
See 647802 ONTARIO LIMITED
SOUVENIRS AVANTI INC   *p 1252*
116 AV LEACOCK, POINTE-CLAIRE, QC, H9R 1H1
(514) 694-0707   *SIC 3993*
SOVEA AUTOS LTEE   *p 1262*
125 RUE DU MARAIS, QUEBEC, QC, G1M 3C8
(418) 681-0011   *SIC 5511*
SOVEREIGN GENERAL INSURANCE COMPANY, THE *p 37*
6700 MACLEOD TRAIL SE UNIT 140, CALGARY, AB, T2H 0L3
(403) 298-4200   *SIC 6411*
SOVEREIGN GENERAL INSURANCE COMPANY, THE *p 37*
6700 MACLEOD TRAIL SE SUITE 140, CALGARY, AB, T2H 0L3
SIC 6331
SOWA HOLDINGS LTD   *p 637*
500 MANITOU DR, KITCHENER, ON, N2C 1L3
(519) 748-5750   *SIC 6712*
SOWA TOOL & MACHINE COMPANY *p 637*
See SOWA HOLDINGS LTD
SOWA TOOL AND MACHINE COMPANY LIMITED   *p 637*
500 MANITOU DR, KITCHENER, ON, N2C 1L3
(519) 748-5750   *SIC 5049*
SOYLUTIONS INC   *p 1281*
1629 AV DES AFFAIRES, QUEBEC, QC, G3J 1Y7
(418) 845-9888   *SIC 2035*
SP DATA CAPITAL ULC   *p 613*
110 KING ST W SUITE 500, HAMILTON, ON, L8P 4S6
(905) 645-5610   *SIC 7389*
SP DATA CAPITAL ULC   *p 923*
1 EGLINTON AVE E 8TH FL, TORONTO, ON, M4P 3A1
(416) 915-3300   *SIC 7389*
SPA   *p 1283*
See SERVICES PROFESSIONNELS INC
SPA D' OTTAWA   *p 750*
See OTTAWA HUMANE SOCIETY

SPA DE L'ESTRIE   *p 1374*
See SOCIETE PROTECTRICE DES ANIMAUX DE L'ESTRIE
SPA EASTMAN   *p 1100*
See CENTRE DE SANTE D'EASTMAN INC
SPA UTOPIA & SALON   *p 227*
See UTOPIA DAY SPAS & SALONS LTD
SPA-O   *p 1320*
See LUMI-O INTERNATIONAL INC
SPACE AGE TIRE LTD   *p 358*
8 PTH 52 W, STEINBACH, MB, R5G 1X7
(204) 326-6039   *SIC 5531*
SPACE AID MANUFACTURING   *p 513*
See M & P TOOL PRODUCTS INC
SPACE MAINTAINERS LAB CANADA LTD *p 67*
115 17 AVE SW, CALGARY, AB, T2S 0A1
(403) 228-7001   *SIC 8072*
SPACEBRIDGE INC   *p 1095*
657 AV ORLY, DORVAL, QC, H9P 1G1
(514) 420-0045   *SIC 3679*
SPACEBRIDGE INC   *p 1095*
657 AV ORLY, DORVAL, QC, H9P 1G1
(514) 420-0045   *SIC 4899*
SPACEMAKER LIMITED   *p 712*
3069 WOLFEDALE RD, MISSISSAUGA, ON, L5C 1V9
(905) 279-2632   *SIC 3448*
SPACES INC   *p 111*
9319 47 ST NW, EDMONTON, AB, T6B 2R7
(587) 855-6684   *SIC 5999*
SPACESAVER SOLUTIONS INC   *p 481*
115 ENGELHARD DR, AURORA, ON, L4G 3V1
(905) 726-3933   *SIC 5085*
SPADONI MOTORS LIMITED   *p 902*
HWY 17, TERRACE BAY, ON, P0T 2W0
(807) 825-4561   *SIC 5521*
SPAENAUR INC   *p 635*
815 VICTORIA ST N, KITCHENER, ON, N2B 3C3
(519) 578-0381   *SIC 5085*
SPAFAX CANADA INC   *p 930*
2 BLOOR ST E SUITE 1020, TORONTO, ON, M4W 1A8
(416) 350-2425   *SIC 5199*
SPALDING HARDWARE LTD   *p 73*
1616 10 AVE SW, CALGARY, AB, T3C 0J5
(403) 244-5531   *SIC 5072*
SPALDING HARDWARE SYSTEMS   *p 73*
See SPALDING HARDWARE LTD
SPALDING HARDWARE SYSTEMS INC *p 73*
1616 10 AVE SW, CALGARY, AB, T3C 0J5
(403) 244-5531   *SIC 5072*
SPAMEDICA CANADA   *p 972*
See 924169 ONTARIO LIMITED
SPANISH MOUNTAIN GOLD LTD   *p 316*
1095 PENDER ST W SUITE 1120, VANCOUVER, BC, V6E 2M6
(604) 601-3651   *SIC 1081*
SPAQ   *p 1270*
See SOCIETE PARC-AUTO DU QUEBEC
SPAR CONSTRUCTION (EDMONTON) LTD *p 97*
14415 114 AVE NW, EDMONTON, AB, T5M 2Y8
(780) 453-3555   *SIC 1521*
SPAR ROOFING & METAL SUPPLIES LIMITED *p 990*
1360 BLOOR ST W, TORONTO, ON, M6H 1P2
(416) 534-8421   *SIC 5211*
SPAR-MARATHON ROOFING SUPPLIES *p 990*
See SPAR ROOFING & METAL SUPPLIES LIMITED
SPARK AUTO ELECTRIC CO LTD   *p 868*
401 BIRCHMOUNT RD, SCARBOROUGH, ON, M1K 1N3
(416) 690-3133   *SIC 5013*
SPARLING'S PROPANE CO. LIMITED *p 493*
82948 LONDON RD, BLYTH, ON, N0M 1H0

(519) 523-4256   *SIC 5984*
SPARTA 2002 DESIGNS & PROMOTIONS INC   *p 1132*
9246 RUE BOIVIN, LASALLE, QC, H8R 2E7
(514) 363-5674   *SIC 5199*
SPARTA PEWTER   *p 1132*
See SPARTA 2002 DESIGNS & PROMOTIONS INC
SPARTAN ATHLETIC PRODUCTS LIMITED *p 448*
10 MORRIS DR UNIT 13, DARTMOUTH, NS, B3B 1K8
(902) 482-0330   *SIC 5091*
SPARTAN BIOSCIENCE INC   *p 751*
2934 BASELINE RD SUITE 500, NEPEAN, ON, K2H 1B2
(613) 228-7756   *SIC 3826*
SPARTAN CONTROLS LTD   *p 11*
305 27 ST SE, CALGARY, AB, T2A 7V2
(403) 207-0797   *SIC 5084*
SPARTAN CONTROLS LTD   *p 116*
8403 51 AVE NW, EDMONTON, AB, T6E 5L9
(780) 468-5463   *SIC 5085*
SPARTAN FITNESS EQUIPMENT   *p 448*
See SPARTAN ATHLETIC PRODUCTS LIMITED
SPARTAN INDUSTRIAL MARINE   *p 446*
See HERCULES SLR INC
SPARTEK SYSTEMS INC   *p 169*
1 THEVENAZ IND. TRAIL, SYLVAN LAKE, AB, T4S 2J6
(403) 887-2443   *SIC 3829*
SPASATION SALON & DAY SPA   *p 84*
See EL BASIL GROUP INC
SPATSIZI REMOTE SERVICES CORPORATION *p 205*
GD, DEASE LAKE, BC, V0C 1L0
(250) 771-5484   *SIC 5812*
SPB DIMENSIONS   *p 1143*
See SPB PSYCHOLOGIE ORGANISATIONNELLE INC.
SPB ORGANIZATIONNAL PSYCHOLOGY *p 1143*
555 BOUL ROLAND-THERRIEN UNITE 300, LONGUEUIL, QC, J4H 4E7
(450) 646-1022   *SIC 8049*
SPB PSYCHOLOGIE ORGANISATIONNELLE INC. *p 1143*
555 BOUL ROLAND-THERRIEN BUREAU 300, LONGUEUIL, QC, J4H 4E7
(450) 646-1022   *SIC 8999*
SPB SOLUTIONS INC   *p 1067*
1350 RUE NEWTON, BOUCHERVILLE, QC, J4B 5H2
(450) 655-3505   *SIC 2048*
SPCA   *p 392*
See WINNIPEG HUMANE SOCIETY FOR THE PREVENTION CRUELTY TO ANIMALS
SPCA   *p 1012*
See WELLAND & DISTRICT SOCIETY FOR THE PREVENTION OF CRUELTY TO ANIMALS
SPCRC HOLDINGS INC   *p 1341*
850 MONT?E DE LIESSE, SAINT-LAURENT, QC, H4T 1P4
(514) 341-3550   *SIC 6712*
SPEAKERS' SPOTLIGHT   *p 977*
See SPEAKERS' SPOTLIGHT INC
SPEAKERS' SPOTLIGHT INC   *p 977*
179 JOHN ST SUITE 302, TORONTO, ON, M5T 1X4
(416) 345-1559   *SIC 7389*
SPEARE SEEDS   *p 618*
99 JOHN ST N, HARRISTON, ON, N0G 1Z0
(519) 338-3840   *SIC 5191*
SPEARING SERVICE   *p 1413*
See SPEARING SERVICE (2006) LTD
SPEARING SERVICE (2006) LTD   *p 1413*
41 MARION AVE, OXBOW, SK, S0C 2B0
(306) 483-2848   *SIC 1389*
SPEARS & MACLEOD PHARMACY LIM-

ITED p
471
333 MAIN ST SUITE 519, YARMOUTH, NS, B5A 1E5
(902) 742-7825   *SIC* 5912

SPEC FURNITURE INC p 588
165 CITY VIEW DR, ETOBICOKE, ON, M9W 5B1
(416) 246-5550   *SIC* 2522

SPECIAL SERVICES CATHOLIC EDUCATION CENTRE p
773
See TORONTO CATHOLIC DISTRICT SCHOOL BOARD

SPECIAL ABILITY RIDING INSTITUTE p
479
12659 MEDWAY RD, ARVA, ON, N0M 1C0
(519) 666-1123   *SIC* 8699

SPECIAL D. BAKING LTD p 116
6003 92 ST NW, EDMONTON, AB, T6E 3A5
(780) 436-9650   *SIC* 5149

SPECIAL EDITION MARKETING p 633
See 1362385 ONTARIO LIMITED

SPECIAL EVENT RENTALS p 112
See ALBERTA SPECIAL EVENT EQUIPMENT RENTALS & SALES LTD

SPECIAL INVESTIGATIONS UNIT p 695
See GOVERNMENT OF ONTARIO

SPECIAL OLYMPICS CANADA p 925
See CANADIAN SPECIAL OLYMPICS INC

SPECIAL OLYMPICS MANITOBA, INC p
375
145 PACIFIC AVE SUITE 304, WINNIPEG, MB, R3B 2Z6
(204) 925-5628   *SIC* 8699

SPECIAL OLYMPICS ONTARIO INC p 919
65 OVERLEA BLVD SUITE 200, TORONTO, ON, M4H 1P1
(416) 447-8326   *SIC* 8699

SPECIALISTE DU BARDEAU DE CEDRE INC, LE p 1350
754 8E RUE, SAINT-PROSPER-DE-DORCHESTER, QC, G0M 1Y0
(418) 594-6201   *SIC* 2429

SPECIALISTE DU BUREAU FREDAL INC, LE p 1107
186 RUE JEAN-PROULX, GATINEAU, QC, J8Z 1V8
(819) 205-9555   *SIC* 5044

SPECIALISTES DE L'ELECTROMENAGER, LES p 1371
See SERVICE DE L'ESTRIE (VENTE & REPARATION) INC

SPECIALISTES DE L'ELECTROMENAGER, LES p 1388
3215 BOUL DES RECOLLETS, TROIS-RIVIERES, QC, G9A 6M1
(819) 693-3393   *SIC* 5722

SPECIALITE HYDRAULIQUE COTE NORD p 1367
See WAINBEE S H C N INC

SPECIALITES LASSONDE INC p 1062
3810 RUE ALFRED-LALIBERTE, BOIS-BRIAND, QC, J7H 1P8
(450) 979-0717   *SIC* 2033

SPECIALITES LASSONDE INC p 1288
170 5E AV, ROUGEMONT, QC, J0L 1M0
(450) 469-0856   *SIC* 2033

SPECIALITES M.B. INC p 1313
5450 AV TRUDEAU, SAINT-HYACINTHE, QC, J2S 7Y8
(450) 771-1415   *SIC* 2013

SPECIALITES MONARCH INC, LES p 1236
4155 CHOMEDEY (A-13) E, MONTREAL, QC, H7P 0A8
(450) 628-4488   *SIC* 5021

SPECIALITES PRODAL p 1297
See SPECIALITES PRODAL (1975) LTEE, LES

SPECIALITES PRODAL (1975) LTEE, LES p 1297
251 AV BOYER, SAINT-CHARLES-DE-BELLECHASSE, QC, G0R 2T0
(418) 887-3301   *SIC* 2013

SPECIALIZED PACKAGING (LONDON) COMPANY ULC p 650
5 CUDDY BLVD, LONDON, ON, N5V 3Y3
(519) 659-7011   *SIC* 2679

SPECIALIZED PROPERTY EVALUATION CONTROL SERVICES LIMITED p 225
9525 201 ST SUITE 303, LANGLEY, BC, V1M 4A5
(604) 882-8930   *SIC* 7389

SPECIALTIES GRAPHIC FINISHERS LTD p 869
946 WARDEN AVE, SCARBOROUGH, ON, M1L 4C9
(416) 701-0111   *SIC* 2789

SPECIALTY CARE BRADFORD VALLEY p 497
See SPECIALTY CARE INC

SPECIALTY CARE CASE MANOR INC p 494
18 BOYD ST, BOBCAYGEON, ON, K0M 1A0
(705) 738-2374   *SIC* 8051

SPECIALTY CARE EAST INC p 632
800 EDGAR ST SUITE 114, KINGSTON, ON, K7M 8S4
(613) 547-0040   *SIC* 8051

SPECIALTY CARE FAMILY p 891
See SPECIALTY CARE INC

SPECIALTY CARE INC p 497
2656 LINE 6, BRADFORD, ON, L3Z 2A1
(905) 952-2270   *SIC* 8059

SPECIALTY CARE INC p 512
10260 KENNEDY RD, BRAMPTON, ON, L6Z 4N7
(905) 495-4695   *SIC* 8059

SPECIALTY CARE INC p 558
400 APPLEWOOD CRES SUITE 110, CONCORD, ON, L4K 0C3
SIC 8051

SPECIALTY CARE INC p 628
121 MORTON AVE SUITE 308, KESWICK, ON, L4P 3T5
(905) 476-2656   *SIC* 8051

SPECIALTY CARE INC p 891
5501 ABBOTT ST E, STITTSVILLE, ON, K2S 2C5
(613) 836-0331   *SIC* 8051

SPECIALTY CARE WOODHALL PARK p 512
See SPECIALTY CARE INC

SPECIALTY DISTRIBUTING LTD p 1430
829 48TH ST E, SASKATOON, SK, S7K 0X5
(306) 975-9867   *SIC* 5199

SPECIALTY LAMINATE MANUFACTURING LTD p 18
2624 54 AVE SE BAY SUITE B, CALGARY, AB, T2C 1R5
(403) 273-3800   *SIC* 2493

SPECIALTY METAL PRODUCTS p 707
See S.M.P SPECIALTY METAL PRODUCTS LTD

SPECIALTY POLYMER COATINGS INC p 228
20529 62 AVE SUITE 104, LANGLEY, BC, V3A 8R4
(604) 514-9711   *SIC* 2851

SPECIALTY PRINT p 885
See 407994 ONTARIO LIMITED

SPECIALTY SALES & MARKETING INC p 727
6725 MILLCREEK DR UNIT 5, MISSISSAUGA, ON, L5N 5V3
(905) 816-0011   *SIC* 5013

SPECIALTY STEELS p 523
See MARMON/KEYSTONE CANADA INC

SPECIFIC MECHANICAL SYSTEMS LTD p 267
6848 KIRKPATRICK CRES, SAANICHTON, BC, V8M 1Z9
(250) 652-2111   *SIC* 3556

SPECIFIED CONSTRUCTION MANAGEMENT INC p 481
2 VATA CRT UNIT 4, AURORA, ON, L4G 4B6

(905) 726-2902   *SIC* 1542

SPECIFIED FLOORING CONTRACTORS p 481
See SPECIFIED CONSTRUCTION MANAGEMENT INC

SPECIFIED LIGHTING SYSTEMS p 292
See SLS GROUP INDUSTRIES INC

SPECS p 225
See SPECIALIZED PROPERTY EVALUATION CONTROL SERVICES LIMITED

SPECSAUDIO 1990 INC p 1107
79 RUE CREMAZIE, GATINEAU, QC, J8Y 3P1
(819) 777-3681   *SIC* 5099

SPECTIS MOULDERS INC p 353
100 CEDAR DR, NIVERVILLE, MB, R0A 1E0
(204) 388-6700   *SIC* 2821

SPECTOR & CO. INC p 1336
5700 RUE KIERAN, SAINT-LAURENT, QC, H4S 2B5
(514) 337-7721   *SIC* 5112

SPECTOR & COMPAGNIE p 1336
See SPECTOR & CO. INC

SPECTRA ALUMINUM PRODUCTS LTD p 497
95 REAGEN'S INDUSTRIAL PKY, BRADFORD, ON, L3Z 0Z9
(905) 778-8093   *SIC* 3354

SPECTRA ANODIZING LTD p 1033
201 HANLAN RD, WOODBRIDGE, ON, L4L 3R7
(905) 851-1141   *SIC* 3471

SPECTRA ENERGY p 283
4716 LAZELLE AVE SUITE 210, TERRACE, BC, V8G 1T2
SIC 4924

SPECTRA ENERGY p 592
410 MOWAT AVE, FORT FRANCES, ON, P9A 1Y7
(807) 274-3924   *SIC* 4924

SPECTRA ENERGY EMPRESS L.P. p 60
425 1 ST SW SUITE 2600, CALGARY, AB, T2P 3L8
(403) 699-1999   *SIC* 8732

SPECTRA ENERGY MIDSTREAM CORPORATION p
60
425 1 ST SW SUITE 2200, CALGARY, AB, T2P 3L8
(403) 699-1900   *SIC* 1389

SPECTRA GROUP OF GREAT RESTAURANTS INC, THE p
238
900 QUAYSIDE DR, NEW WESTMINSTER, BC, V3M 6G1
(604) 525-3474   *SIC* 5812

SPECTRA GROUP OF GREAT RESTAURANTS INC, THE p
338
3195 DOUGLAS ST, VICTORIA, ON, V8Z 3K3
SIC 5812

SPECTRIS CANADA INC p 1268
350 RUE FRANQUET BUREAU 45, QUEBEC, QC, G1P 4P3
(418) 656-6453   *SIC* 5049

SPECTRIS CANADA INC p 1331
4921 PLACE OLIVIA, SAINT-LAURENT, QC, H4R 2V6
(514) 956-2132   *SIC* 5049

SPECTRUM BRANDS CANADA, INC p 745
255 LONGSIDE DR UNIT 101, MISSISSAUGA, ON, L5W 0G7
(800) 566-7899   *SIC* 3524

SPECTRUM COMMUNICATIONS INTERNATIONAL INC p
656
79 WELLINGTON ST, LONDON, ON, N6B 2K4
(519) 663-2109   *SIC* 5999

SPECTRUM COMMUNICATIONS LTD p 656
79 WELLINGTON ST, LONDON, ON, N6B 2K4

(519) 663-2109   *SIC* 5065

SPECTRUM COMMUNITY SCHOOL p 338
See BOARD OF EDUCATION OF SCHOOL DISTRICT NO. 61 (GREATER VICTORIA)

SPECTRUM EDUCATIONAL SUPPLIES LIMITED p 756
150 PONY DR, NEWMARKET, ON, L3Y 7B6
(905) 898-0031   *SIC* 5961

SPECTRUM HEALTH AMBULATORY CARE CLINIC p 712
See SPECTRUM HEALTH CARE LTD

SPECTRUM HEALTH CARE LTD p 712
1290 CENTRAL PKY W SUITE 302, MISSISSAUGA, ON, L5C 4R3
(905) 272-2271   *SIC* 8741

SPECTRUM HEALTH CARE LTD p 930
2 BLOOR ST E SUITE 1200, TORONTO, ON, M4W 1A8
(416) 964-0322   *SIC* 8082

SPECTRUM MANAGEMENT LTD p 316
1166 ALBERNI ST SUITE 501, VANCOUVER, BC, V6E 3Z3
(604) 682-1388   *SIC* 7349

SPECTRUM RESOURCE GROUP INC p 251
3810 18TH AVE, PRINCE GEORGE, BC, V2N 4V5
(250) 564-0383   *SIC* 8748

SPECTRUM SIGNAL PROCESSING BY VECIMA, DIV OF p 339
See VECIMA NETWORKS INC

SPECTUBE INC p 1081
1152 RUE DE LA MANIC, CHICOUTIMI, QC, G7K 1A2
(418) 696-2545   *SIC* 3354

SPEED SYSTEM ORTHODONTIC SUPPLIES & PRECISION MACHINING p 537
See STRITE INDUSTRIES LIMITED

SPEEDI GOURMET CO LTD p 321
1650 4TH AVE W, VANCOUVER, BC, V6J 1L9
(604) 731-8877   *SIC* 5812

SPEEDWAY MOTORS LTD p 338
3329 DOUGLAS ST, VICTORIA, BC, V8Z 3L2
(250) 386-6650   *SIC* 5511

SPEEDY AUTOMOTIVE LIMITED p 422
92 BROADWAY, CORNER BROOK, NL, A2H 4C8
(709) 639-8929   *SIC* 5013

SPEEDY CREEK (2011) LTD p 103
17724 102 AVE NW, EDMONTON, AB, T5S 1H5
SIC 5812

SPEEDY CREEK (2011) LTD p 119
10333 34 AVE NW, EDMONTON, AB, T6J 6V1
SIC 5812

SPEEDY CREEK (2011) LTD p 123
514 RONNING ST NW, EDMONTON, AB, T6R 1B7
(780) 486-2882   *SIC* 6794

SPEEDY ELECTRICAL CONTRACTORS LIMITED p 1033
114 CASTER AVE SUITE A, WOODBRIDGE, ON, L4L 5Y9
(905) 264-2344   *SIC* 1731

SPEEDY TRANSPORT p 510
See SPEEDY TRANSPORT GROUP INC

SPEEDY TRANSPORT GROUP INC p 510
265 RUTHERFORD RD S, BRAMPTON, ON, L6W 1V9
(416) 510-2035   *SIC* 4212

SPELMER CHRYSLER JEEP DODGE SALES LTD p 999
51 HIGHWAY 33, TRENTON, ON, K8V 5R1
(613) 394-3945   *SIC* 5511

SPENCE DIAMONDS LTD p 293
550 6TH AVE W SUITE 410, VANCOUVER, BC, V5Z 1A1
(604) 739-9928   *SIC* 5944

SPENCER STEEL LIMITED p 621
200 KING ST, ILDERTON, ON, N0M 2A0
(519) 471-6888   *SIC* 1791

SPENCER STUART & ASSOCIATES (CANADA) LTD p 967
1 UNIVERSITY AVE UNIT 1900, TORONTO, ON, M5J 2P1
(416) 361-0311   SIC 8741
SPENCER SUPPORT p 1377
See EQUIPE H.B. HELLER INC, L'
SPENCER, BILL CHEVROLET OLDSMOBILE LTD p 545
1090 ELGIN ST W SUITE 12, COBOURG, ON, K9A 5V5
(905) 372-8773   SIC 5511
SPENCERARL DIV OF p 1018
See ASSEMBLE-RITE, LTD
SPEQ p 1129
See VCS INVESTIGATION INC
SPEQ LE DEVOIR INC p 1200
2050 RUE DE BLEURY BUREAU 900, MONTREAL, QC, H3A 3M9
(514) 985-3333   SIC 6712
SPEQ PHOTO p 1051
See STUDIO DE PHOTOS DES ECOLES QUEBECOISES INC
SPERIAN VETEMENTS DE PROTECTION LTEE p 1184
4200 BOUL SAINT-LAURENT, MONTREAL, QC, H2W 2R2
SIC 3842
SPERIDIAN TECHNOLOGIES CANADA INC p 957
357 BAY ST SUITE 402, TORONTO, ON, M5H 2T7
(416) 613-1621   SIC 7371
SPERLING INDUSTRIES LTD p 357
51 STATION SR, SPERLING, MB, R0G 2M0
(204) 626-3401   SIC 1711
SPERRY-SUN DRILLING SERVICES p 148
See HALLIBURTON GROUP CANADA INC
SPG HYDRO INTERNATIONAL p 1138
See MISTRAS SERVICES INC
SPG HYDRO INTERNATIONAL INC p 1359
2161 RUE LEONARD-DE VINCI BUREAU 101, SAINTE-JULIE, QC, J3E 1Z3
(450) 922-3515   SIC 7373
SPG INTERNATIONAL LTEE p 1097
4275 BOUL SAINT-JOSEPH, DRUMMONDVILLE, QC, J2B 1T8
(819) 477-1596   SIC 3499
SPHERE 3D CORP p 707
240 MATHESON BLVD E, MISSISSAUGA, ON, L4Z 1X1
(416) 749-5999   SIC 7371
SPI p 896
See INDUSTRIES SPECTRA PREMIUM INC, LES
SPI INTERNATIONAL TRANSPORTATION p 208
See SILVER PACIFIC INVESTMENTS INC
SPI SANTE SECURITE INC p 1060
60 RUE GASTON-DUMOULIN, BLAINVILLE, QC, J7C 0A3
(450) 420-2012   SIC 5999
SPI SECURITE INC p 1060
60 RUE GASTON-DUMOULIN, BLAINVILLE, QC, J7C 0A3
(450) 967-0911   SIC 3842
SPI SECURITY p 1430
See SASKATOON PRIVATE INVESTIGATION INC
SPICERS p 1033
See SPICERS CANADA ULC
SPICERS CANADA ULC p 1033
200 GALCAT DR, WOODBRIDGE, ON, L4L 0B9
(905) 265-5000   SIC 5111
SPIEGEL SOHMER AVOCATS p 1208
See SPIEGEL SOHMER INC
SPIEGEL SOHMER INC p 1208
1255 RUE PEEL BUREAU 1000, MONTREAL, QC, H3B 2T9
(514) 875-2100   SIC 8111
SPIETH-ANDERSON p 811
See SPIETH-ANDERSON INTERNA-

TIONAL INC
SPIETH-ANDERSON INTERNATIONAL INC p 811
135 FORESTVIEW RD, ORO-MEDONTE, ON, L3V 0R4
(705) 325-2274   SIC 3949
SPIKE MARKS INC p 1327
275 RUE STINSON, SAINT-LAURENT, QC, H4N 2E1
(514) 737-0066   SIC 5194
SPILAK TANK TRUCK SERVICE LTD p 164
911 6 AVE NW, SLAVE LAKE, AB, T0G 2A1
(780) 849-2757   SIC 4212
SPIN MASTER CORP p 983
225 KING ST W SUITE 200, TORONTO, ON, M5V 3M2
(416) 364-6002   SIC 6712
SPIN MASTER FILM PRODUCTION p 983
See SPIN MASTER LTD
SPIN MASTER LTD p 983
225 KING ST W SUITE 200, TORONTO, ON, M5V 1B6
(416) 364-6002   SIC 3944
SPINA, JOHN DRUGS LTD p 475
15 WESTNEY RD N SUITE 2, AJAX, ON, L1T 1P5
(905) 426-3355   SIC 5912
SPINDLE FACTORY LTD, THE p 103
11319 199 ST NW, EDMONTON, AB, T5S 2C6
(780) 453-5973   SIC 2431
SPINELLI FAIRVIEW TOYOTA p 1252
See SPINELLI TOYOTA (1981) INC
SPINELLI HONDA p 1126
220 BOUL MONTREAL-TORONTO, LACHINE, QC, H8S 1B8
(514) 637-6565   SIC 5531
SPINELLI MAZDA p 1125
See 3729451 CANADA INC
SPINELLI NISSAN p 1250
See FAIRVIEW NISSAN LIMITEE
SPINELLI TOYOTA (1981) INC p 1126
561 BOUL SAINT-JOSEPH, LACHINE, QC, H8S 2K9
(514) 634-7171   SIC 6712
SPINELLI TOYOTA (1981) INC p 1252
10 AV AUTO PLAZA, POINTE-CLAIRE, QC, H9R 3H9
(514) 694-1510   SIC 5511
SPINELLI TOYOTA (1981) INC p 1252
12 AV AUTO PLAZA, POINTE-CLAIRE, QC, H9R 4W6
(514) 694-1510   SIC 5511
SPINELLI TOYOTA POINTE CLAIRE p 1252
See SPINELLI TOYOTA (1981) INC
SPINIC MANUFACTURING p 605
See LINAMAR CORPORATION
SPINNAKER INDUSTRIES INC p 756
1171 GORHAM ST, NEWMARKET, ON, L3Y 8Y2
(416) 742-0598   SIC 3499
SPINRITE p 647
See SPINRITE LIMITED PARTNERSHIP
SPINRITE CORP p 647
320 LIVINGSTONE AVE S, LISTOWEL, ON, N4W 0C9
(519) 291-3780   SIC 2281
SPINRITE LIMITED PARTNERSHIP p 647
320 LIVINGSTONE AVE S, LISTOWEL, ON, N4W 3H3
(519) 291-3780   SIC 2281
SPIRAL OF CANADA INC p 743
6155 TOMKEN RD UNIT 10, MISSISSAUGA, ON, L5T 1X3
(905) 564-8990   SIC 3089
SPIRAX SARCO p 558
See SPIRAX SARCO CANADA LIMITED
SPIRAX SARCO CANADA LIMITED p 558
383 APPLEWOOD CRES, CONCORD, ON, L4K 4J3
(905) 660-5510   SIC 5075
SPIRE GROUP LIMITED p 774
4110 YONGE ST SUITE 602, NORTH YORK, ON, M2P 2B7

(416) 250-0090   SIC 6712
SPIRENT COMMUNICATIONS OF OTTAWA LTD p 627
750 PALLADIUM DR UNIT 310, KANATA, ON, K2V 1C7
(613) 592-2661   SIC 3669
SPIRIT PIPELINES LTD p 172
GD LCD MAIN, WETASKIWIN, AB, T9A 1W7
(780) 352-7305   SIC 4619
SPIRITUEUX UNGAVA CIE LTEE, LES p 1088
291 RUE MINER, COWANSVILLE, QC, J2K 3Y6
(450) 263-5835   SIC 5182
SPIRO MEGA INC p 1362
1225 RUE MICHELIN, SAINTE-ROSE, QC, H7L 4S2
(450) 663-4457   SIC 5075
SPIROL INDUSTRIES LIMITED p 1020
3103 ST ETIENNE BLVD, WINDSOR, ON, N8W 5B1
(519) 974-3334   SIC 3429
SPIVAK, N-J LIMITED p 661
3334 WONDERLAND RD S SUITE 2, LONDON, ON, N6L 1A6
(519) 652-3276   SIC 3273
SPIVO CANADA INC p 1220
3150 PLACE DE RAMEZAY BUREAU 202, MONTREAL, QC, H3Y 0A3
(514) 726-1749   SIC 3949
SPLASH INTERNATIONAL MARKETING INC p 675
395 COCHRANE DR SUITE 3, MARKHAM, ON, L3R 9R5
(905) 947-4440   SIC 5199
SPLASHES BATH & KITCHEN CENTRE, A DIV OF p 335
See SHERET, ANDREW LIMITED
SPM AUTOMATION (CANADA) INC p 1023
5445 OUTER DR, WINDSOR, ON, N9A 6J3
(519) 737-0320   SIC 3569
SPM FLOW CONTROL LTD p 156
8060 EDGAR INDUSTRIAL CRES UNIT A, RED DEER, AB, T4P 3R3
(403) 341-3410   SIC 1389
SPOLETINI/PALUMBO INC p 32
1308 9 AVE SE, CALGARY, AB, T2G 0T3
(403) 537-1161   SIC 5411
SPOLUMBO'S FINE FOOD & DELI p 32
See SPOLETINI/PALUMBO INC
SPONGEZZ INC p 784
79 SAINT REGIS CRES N, NORTH YORK, ON, M3J 1Y9
(416) 636-6611   SIC 3089
SPORT BY ABILITY NIAGARA p 886
8 NAPIER ST, ST CATHARINES, ON, L2R 6B4
SIC 8699
SPORT CHEK p 1021
See FGL SPORTS LTD
SPORT EXPERT p 1352
See BEAULIEU, CLAUDE SPORT INC
SPORT EXPERT ATMOSPHERE p 1278
See 4094590 CANADA INC
SPORT MASKA INC p 1314
15855 AV HUBERT, SAINT-HYACINTHE, QC, J2T 4C9
(450) 773-5258   SIC 2329
SPORT MASKA INC p 1331
3400 RUE RAYMOND-LASNIER, SAINT-LAURENT, QC, H4R 3L3
(514) 461-8000   SIC 3949
SPORT S.M. INC p 1275
11337 BOUL VALCARTIER, QUEBEC, QC, G2A 2M4
(418) 842-2703   SIC 5571
SPORTBALL p 905
See SPORTBALL LTD
SPORTBALL LTD p 905
39 GLEN CAMERON RD UNIT 8, THORNHILL, ON, L3T 1P1
(905) 882-4473   SIC 7999
SPORTING LIFE INC p 580

25 THE WEST MALL SUITE 7, ETOBICOKE, ON, M9C 1B8
(416) 620-7002   SIC 5941
SPORTING LIFE INC p 924
130 MERTON ST 6TH FL, TORONTO, ON, M4S 1A4
(416) 485-1685   SIC 5941
SPORTING LIFE SHERWAY GARDENS p 580
See SPORTING LIFE INC
SPORTOP MARKETING INC p 909
875 TUNGSTEN ST UNIT C, THUNDER BAY, ON, P7B 6H2
(807) 346-5400   SIC 5199
SPORTS 12345 INC p 1087
3035 BOUL LE CARREFOUR BUREAU T02, COTE SAINT-LUC, QC, H7T 1C8
(450) 682-0032   SIC 5941
SPORTS AND ENTERTAINMENT CENTER p 861
See CORPORATION OF THE CITY OF SAULT STE MARIE, THE
SPORTS DIX 30 INC p 1070
9550 BOUL LEDUC BUREAU 15, BROSSARD, QC, J4Y 0B3
(450) 926-2000   SIC 5311
SPORTS EXCELLENCE p 1374
See MOMO SPORTS INC
SPORTS EXPERTS p 748
See 910259 ONTARIO INC
SPORTS EXPERTS p 1077
See 3100-2504 QUEBEC INC
SPORTS EXPERTS p 1087
See SPORTS 12345 INC
SPORTS EXPERTS p 1155
See DIVERSION P.L. SPORTS INC
SPORTS EXPERTS p 1206
See MONTREAL CENTRE SPORTS INC
SPORTS EXPERTS p 1279
See 2427-9028 QUEBEC INC
SPORTS EXPERTS p 1385
See GESTION SETR INC
SPORTS EXPERTS #526 p 1296
See ST-BRUNO MODES ET SPORTS INC
SPORTS EXPERTS - ATMOSPHERE p 1069
See 4094590 CANADA INC
SPORTS EXPERTS 528 p 1374
See MODES ET SPORTS 3050 INC
SPORTS INTERNATIONAL CSTS INC p 576
221 EVANS AVE, ETOBICOKE, ON, M8Z 1J5
(416) 251-2132   SIC 2329
SPORTS MONTREAL INC p 1177
1000 AV EMILE-JOURNAULT, MONTREAL, QC, H2M 2E7
(514) 872-7177   SIC 7032
SPORTS TRADERS - VICTORIA p 335
See STM SPORTS TRADE MALL LTD
SPORTS-CAN INSURANCE CONSULTANTS LTD p 227
8411 200 ST SUITE 103, LANGLEY, BC, V2Y 0E7
(604) 888-0050   SIC 6351
SPORTSMAN LIMITED, THE p 67
1442 17 AVE SW, CALGARY, AB, T2T 0C8
(403) 245-4311   SIC 5941
SPORTSMANS CORNER GAS 2002 p 223
3162 10TH AVE SS 1, KEREMEOS, BC, V0X 1N1
(250) 499-7192   SIC 4925
SPORTSPHERE p 576
See SPORTS INTERNATIONAL CSTS INC
SPP CANADA AIRCRAFT, INC p 727
2025 MEADOWVALE BLVD UNIT 1, MISSISSAUGA, ON, L5N 5N1
(905) 821-9339   SIC 3728
SPRAGUE FOODS LIMITED p 492
385 COLLEGE ST E, BELLEVILLE, ON, K8N 5S7
(613) 966-1200   SIC 2032
SPRATT AGGREGATES LTD p 541
2300 CARP RD, CARP, ON, K0A 1L0
(613) 831-0717   SIC 5211

SPRAY LAKE SAWMILLS (1980) LTD *p 80*
305 GRIFFIN RD W, COCHRANE, AB, T4C 2C4
(403) 932-2234 *SIC 2491*
SPRAY-PAK INDUSTRIES *p 547*
See 1132694 ONTARIO INC
SPRAY-PAK INDUSTRIES *p 733*
See 1132694 ONTARIO INC
SPRIGGS INSURANCE BROKERS LIMITED *p 801*
159 CHURCH ST, OAKVILLE, ON, L6J 1N1
(905) 844-9232 *SIC 6411*
SPRING AIR *p 273*
See REST-WELL MATTRESS COMPANY LTD
SPRING CREEK COLONY *p 171*
See HUTTERIAN BRETHREN SPRING CREEK COLONY
SPRING FUEL DISTRIBUTORS INC *p 220*
275 CAMPION ST, KELOWNA, BC, V1X 7S9
(250) 491-0427 *SIC 5172*
SPRING GLOBAL MAIL *p 688*
See G3 WORLDWIDE (CANADA) INC
SPRING HILL COLONY FARMS LTD *p 353*
30 TOWNSHIP 15 RG SUITE 15, NEEP-AWA, MB, R0J 1H0
(204) 476-2715 *SIC 2013*
SPRING HONDA *p 203*
See 0889541 BC LTD
SPRING VALLEY COLONY FARMS LTD *p 347*
GD, BRANDON, MB, R7A 5Y4
(204) 728-3830 *SIC 0119*
SPRING VALLEY GARDENS (NIAGARA) INC *p 886*
1330 FIFTH ST LOUTH, ST CATHARINES, ON, L2R 6P9
(905) 935-9002 *SIC 5193*
SPRING VALLEY GARDENS INC *p 886*
1846 SEVENTH ST, ST CATHARINES, ON, L2R 6P9
(905) 682-9002 *SIC 0181*
SPRING VALLEY HUTTERIAN COLONY *p 347*
See SPRING VALLEY COLONY FARMS LTD
SPRINGBANK MECHANICAL SYSTEMS LIMITED *p 717*
3615 LAIRD RD UNIT 1, MISSISSAUGA, ON, L5L 5Z8
(905) 569-8990 *SIC 1711*
SPRINGBOARD *p 936*
See OPERATION SPRINGBOARD
SPRINGDALE COUNTRY MANOR *p 841*
See OMNI HEALTH CARE LTD
SPRINGDALE FOREST RESOURCES INC *p 428*
406 LITTLE BAY RD, SPRINGDALE, NL, A0J 1T0
(709) 673-4695 *SIC 0851*
SPRINGER INVESTMENTS LTD *p 413*
97 LOCH LOMOND RD, SAINT JOHN, NB, E2J 1X6
(506) 847-9168 *SIC 5461*
SPRINGER'S MEATS INC *p 610*
544 PARKDALE AVE N, HAMILTON, ON, L8H 5Y7
(905) 544-0782 *SIC 5147*
SPRINGFIELD HUTTERIAN BRETHREN INC *p 1408*
GD, KINDERSLEY, SK, S0L 1S0
(306) 463-4255 *SIC 8748*
SPRINGFIELD INDUSTRIES LTD *p 364*
125 FURNITURE PARK, WINNIPEG, MB, R2G 1B9
SIC 2821
SPRINGFREE TRAMPOLINE INC *p 675*
151 WHITEHALL DR UNIT 2, MARKHAM, ON, L3R 9T1
(905) 948-0124 *SIC 3949*
SPRINGHILL CONSTRUCTION LIMITED *p 402*

940 SPRINGHILL RD, FREDERICTON, NB, E3C 1R5
(506) 452-0044 *SIC 1541*
SPRINGHILL FARMS *p 351*
See HYLIFE LTD
SPRINGHILL FARMS *p 353*
See HYLIFE LTD
SPRINGHILL GROUND SEARCH AND RESCUE (EMO) *p 466*
GD, SPRINGHILL, NS, B0M 1X0
(902) 597-3866 *SIC 8999*
SPRINGHILL LUMBER WHOLESALE LTD *p 364*
1820 DE VRIES AVE, WINNIPEG, MB, R2G 3S8
(204) 661-1055 *SIC 5039*
SPRINGS CANADA, INC *p 733*
110 MATHESON BLVD W SUITE 200, MISSISSAUGA, ON, L5R 3T4
(905) 890-4994 *SIC 5131*
SPRINGS CHRISTIAN ACADEMY ELEMENTARY SCHOOL CAMPUS *p 364*
See SPRINGS OF LIVING WATER CHRISTIAN ACADEMY INC
SPRINGS CHURCH *p 366*
See SPRINGS OF LIVING WATER CENTRE INC
SPRINGS OF LIVING WATER CENTRE INC *p 366*
595 LAGIMODIERE BLVD SUITE 1, WINNIPEG, MB, R2J 3X2
(204) 233-7003 *SIC 8661*
SPRINGS OF LIVING WATER CHRISTIAN ACADEMY INC *p 364*
261 YOUVILLE ST, WINNIPEG, MB, R2H 2S7
(204) 231-3640 *SIC 8211*
SPRINGSIDE HUTTERIAN BRETHREN LTD *p 83*
GD, DUCHESS, AB, T0J 0Z0
(403) 378-4734 *SIC 8741*
SPRINGWALL SLEEP PRODUCTS INC *p 417*
211 PARKER RD, SCOUDOUC, NB, E4P 3P7
(506) 532-4481 *SIC 2515*
SPRINT *p 924*
See SENIOR PEOPLES' RESOURCES IN NORTH TORONTO INCORPORATED
SPRINT COURIER *p 815*
See 718009 ONTARIO INC
SPRINT MECHANICAL INC *p 588*
50 WOODBINE DOWNS BLVD, ETOBI-COKE, ON, M9W 5R2
(416) 747-6059 *SIC 1711*
SPRINT-PIONEERS MINISTRIES INC *p 565*
51 BYRON AVE SS 2, DORCHESTER, ON, N0L 1G2
(519) 268-8778 *SIC 8661*
SPROTT ASSET MANAGEMENT INC *p 967*
200 BAY ST SUITE 2700, TORONTO, ON, M5J 2J1
(416) 955-5885 *SIC 6282*
SPROTT BULL/BEAR RSP *p 967*
200 BAY ST SUITE 2700, TORONTO, ON, M5J 2J1
(416) 943-6707 *SIC 6722*
SPROTT CANADIAN EQUITY FUND *p 967*
200 BAY ST SUITE 2700, TORONTO, ON, M5J 2J1
(416) 362-7172 *SIC 6722*
SPROTT INC *p 967*
200 BAY ST SUITE 2600, TORONTO, ON, M5J 2J1
(416) 943-8099 *SIC 6282*
SPROTT PHYSICAL GOLD & SILVER TRUST *p 967*
200 BAY ST SUITE 2600, TORONTO, ON, M5J 2J1
(877) 403-2310 *SIC 6726*
SPROTT RESOURCE HOLDINGS INC *p 967*
200 BAY ST SUITE 2600, TORONTO, ON, M5J 2J1

(855) 943-8099 *SIC 1011*
SPROULE ASSOCIATES LIMITED *p 60*
140 4 AVE SW UNIT 900, CALGARY, AB, T2P 3N3
(403) 294-5500 *SIC 8711*
SPROULE HOLDINGS LIMITED *p 60*
140 4 AVE SW SUITE 900, CALGARY, AB, T2P 3N3
(403) 294-5500 *SIC 8711*
SPROULE INTERNATIONAL LIMITED *p 60*
140 4 AVE SW SUITE 900, CALGARY, AB, T2P 3N3
(403) 294-5500 *SIC 8711*
SPROUSE FIRE & SAFETY (1996) CORP *p 18*
5329 72 AVE SE, CALGARY, AB, T2C 4X6
(403) 265-3891 *SIC 5087*
SPROUSE FIRE SAFETY LTD *p 18*
5329 72 AVE SE STE 38, CALGARY, AB, T2C 4X6
SIC 7389
SPRUCE FALLS ACQUISITION CORP *p 627*
1 GOVERNMENT RD, KAPUSKASING, ON, P5N 2Y2
(705) 337-1311 *SIC 6712*
SPRUCE GROVE BUILDING CLEANERS *p 397*
See 041216 NB LTD
SPRUCE GROVE COMPOSITE HIGH SCHOOL *p 164*
See PARKLAND SCHOOL DIVISION NO. 70
SPRUCE GROVE I G A *p 98*
See VANAN FOODS LIMITED
SPRUCE GROVE PIZZA LTD *p 164*
201 CALAHOO RD, SPRUCE GROVE, AB, T7X 1R1
(780) 962-0224 *SIC 5812*
SPRUCE LODGE HOME FOR THE AGED *p 896*
643 WEST GORE ST, STRATFORD, ON, N5A 1L4
(519) 271-4090 *SIC 8361*
SPRUCE MEADOWS *p 69*
See ADVANTAGE DISTRIBUTORS LTD
SPRUCE MEADOWS LTD *p 69*
18011 SPRUCE MEADOWS WAY SW, CALGARY, AB, T2X 4B7
(403) 974-4200 *SIC 7941*
SPRUCE TOP LUMBER SALES LTD *p 359*
11 TONY'S TRAIL, STONEWALL, MB, R0C 2Z0
(204) 467-1915 *SIC 5031*
SPRUCEDALE AGROMART LIMITED *p 902*
291 YOUNG ST, TARA, ON, N0H 2N0
(519) 934-2340 *SIC 5191*
SPRUCEDALE CARE CENTRE INC *p 897*
96 KITTRIDGE AVE E SUITE 115, STRATHROY, ON, N7G 2A8
(519) 245-2808 *SIC 8051*
SPRUCEGROVE INVESTMENT MANAGEMENT LTD *p 957*
181 UNIVERSITY AVE SUITE 1300, TORONTO, ON, M5H 3M7
(416) 363-5854 *SIC 6282*
SPRUCELAND FORD SALES LTD *p 173*
4144 KEPLER ST, WHITECOURT, AB, T7S 0A3
(780) 778-4777 *SIC 5511*
SPRUCELAND MILLWORKS *p 96*
See MILLAR WESTERN FOREST PRODUCTS LTD
SPRUCEWOOD COLONY FARMS LTD *p 348*
GD, BROOKDALE, MB, R0K 0G0
(204) 354-2318 *SIC 0191*
SPUD *p 285*
See SMALL POTATOES URBAN DELIVERY INC
SPUD PLAINS FARMS LTD *p 360*
12 14W NE SUITE 32, WELLWOOD, MB, R0K 2H0
(204) 834-3866 *SIC 5159*

SPV MOTORS LP *p 163*
2365 BROADMOOR BLVD, SHERWOOD PARK, AB, T8H 1B4
(780) 400-4800 *SIC 5511*
SPX CLYDE UNION CANADA *p 521*
See CLYDE UNION CANADA LIMITED
SQI HOLDINGS II INC *p 466*
115 KING ST, STELLARTON, NS, B0K 0A2
(902) 752-8371 *SIC 6712*
SQM GROUP *p 332*
See SERVICE QUALITY MEASUREMENT GROUP INC
SQUAMISH GENERAL HOSPITAL *p 269*
See SEA TO SKY COMMUNITY HEALTH COUNCIL
SQUAMISH TERMINALS LTD *p 269*
37500 THIRD AVE, SQUAMISH, BC, V8B 0B1
(604) 892-3511 *SIC 4491*
SQUARE VICTORIA IMMOBILIER *p 1190*
See POWER CORPORATION DU CANADA
SQUIRREL SYSTEMS OF CANADA, LTD *p 183*
8585 BAXTER PL, BURNABY, BC, V5A 4V7
(604) 412-3300 *SIC 7371*
SQUISHCANDY *p 1227*
See BONBONS OINK OINK INC, LES
SR PACKAGING, DIV OF *p 32*
See VYEFIELD ENTERPRISES LTD
SRA *p 971*
See PORTEX MINERALS INC
SRB EDUCATION SOLUTIONS INC *p 675*
200 TOWN CENTRE BLVD SUITE 400, MARKHAM, ON, L3R 8G5
(877) 772-4685 *SIC 7371*
SRB TECHNOLOGIES (CANADA) INC *p 838*
320 BOUNDARY RD E SUITE 140, PEMBROKE, ON, K8A 6W5
(613) 732-0055 *SIC 3993*
SRH *p 872*
See SCARBOROUGH AND ROUGE HOSPITAL
SRIEQ: SERVICE D'AIDE A LA COMMUNICATION / BAS ST-LAURENT *p 1275*
See SERVICE REGIONAL D'INTERPRETARIAT DE L'EST DU QUEBEC INC
SRIULLI LONG TERM CARE *p 1033*
40 FRIULI CRT, WOODBRIDGE, ON, L4L 9T3
(905) 856-3939 *SIC 8052*
SRK CONSULTING (CANADA) INC *p 316*
1066 HASTINGS ST W SUITE 2200, VANCOUVER, BC, V6E 3X1
(604) 681-4196 *SIC 1081*
SRM ASSOCIATES *p 1015*
See SERNAS GROUP INC, THE
SRS VICTORIA REALTY *p 291*
7291 FRASER ST, VANCOUVER, BC, V5X 3V8
(604) 263-3033 *SIC 6531*
SRW TECHNOLOGIES *p 116*
4521 101 ST NW, EDMONTON, AB, T6E 5C6
(780) 413-4833 *SIC 7692*
SRY *p 238*
See SOUTHERN RAILWAY OF BRITISH COLUMBIA LIMITED
SS LASER TECH LTD *p 256*
13560 MAYCREST WAY UNIT 2115, RICHMOND, BC, V6V 2W9
(604) 821-0058 *SIC 5112*
SS RIG & VAC LTD *p 150*
1801 8 ST, NISKU, AB, T9E 7S8
(780) 979-9987 *SIC 5199*
SS STONEBRIDGE DEL FITNESS CORPORATION *p 1435*
431 NELSON RD, SASKATOON, SK, S7S 1P2
(306) 975-1003 *SIC 7991*
SS&C TECHNOLOGIES CANADA CORP *p*

700
5255 ORBITOR DR UNIT 1, MISSIS-
SAUGA, ON, L4W 5M6
(905) 629-8000   SIC 7371
SSAB SWEDISH STEEL LTD   p 207
1031 CLIVEDEN AVE, DELTA, BC, V3M 5V1
(604) 526-3700   SIC 5051
SSENSE   p 1178
See GROUPE ATALLAH INC
SSH BEDDING CANADA CO   p 32
3636 11A ST SE, CALGARY, AB, T2G 3H3
(403) 287-0600   SIC 2394
SSH BEDDING CANADA CO   p 1118
17400 RTE TRANSCANADIENNE, KIRK-
LAND, QC, H9J 2M5
(514) 694-3030   SIC 2394
SSH BEDDING CANADA CO.   p 32
See SSH BEDDING CANADA CO
SSH BEDDING CANADA CO   p 1118
See SSH BEDDING CANADA CO
**SSI SUSTAINABLE SOLUTIONS INTERNA-
TIONAL PARTNERS**   p
181
8395 RIVERBEND CRT, BURNABY, BC,
V3N 5E7
(604) 430-2020   SIC 5122
SSL   p 537
See SUTHERLAND-SCHULTZ LTD
SSL CONSTRUCTION   p 1396
See SIGNATURE SUR LE SAINT-LAURENT
CONSTRUCTION S.E.N.C.
SSQ ASSURANCE   p 1273
See SSQ, SOCIETE D'ASSURANCE INC
SSQ ASSURANCES GENERALES   p 1273
See SSQ SOCIETE D'ASSURANCES GEN-
ERALES INC
SSQ DISTRIBUTION INC   p 1273
2525 BOUL LAURIER, QUEBEC, QC, G1V
4Z6
(418) 682-1245   SIC 6531
SSQ FINANCIAL GROUP   p 773
See SSQ SOCIETE D'ASSURANCE-VIE
INC
SSQ GROUPE FINANCIER   p 1273
See SSQ SOCIETE D'ASSURANCE-VIE
INC
SSQ SOCIETE D'ASSURANCE-VIE INC p
773
110 SHEPPARD AVE E UNIT 500, NORTH
YORK, ON, M2N 6Y8
(416) 221-3477   SIC 6351
SSQ SOCIETE D'ASSURANCE-VIE INC p
1273
2525 BOUL LAURIER, QUEBEC, QC, G1V
4Z6
(418) 651-7000   SIC 6311
**SSQ SOCIETE D'ASSURANCES GEN-
ERALES INC**   p
1273
2515 BOUL LAURIER, QUEBEC, QC, G1V
2L2
(819) 538-4610   SIC 6411
SSQ, SOCIETE D'ASSURANCE INC p 1273
2525 BOUL LAURIER, QUEBEC, QC, G1V
2L2
(418) 651-7000   SIC 6311
SSR MINING INC   p 329
1055 DUNSMUIR ST SUITE 800, VANCOU-
VER, BC, V7X 1G4
(604) 689-3846   SIC 1044
SST   p 506
See SIMPSON STRONG-TIE CANADA LIM-
ITED
ST ADOLPHE PERSONAL CARE HOME p
392
See ST NORBERT LODGES LTD
**ST AGNES OF ASSISI ELEMENTARY
SCHOOL**   p 1029
See YORK CATHOLIC DISTRICT SCHOOL
BOARD
ST ALBERT FIRE SERVICES   p 166
See ST. ALBERT, CITY OF
ST ALBERT/INGLEWOOD SAFEWAY p 166
See SOBEYS WEST INC

ST AMANT INC   p 368
440 RIVER RD, WINNIPEG, MB, R2M 3Z9
(204) 256-4301   SIC 8059
ST ANDREW GOLDFIELDS LTD   p 940
20 ADELAIDE ST E SUITE 1500,
TORONTO, ON, M5C 2T6
(416) 815-9855   SIC 1041
ST ANDREWS CENTRE   p 97
See ST ANDREWS HOUSING LIMITED
ST ANDREWS HOUSING LIMITED   p 97
12720 111 AVE NW SUITE 345, EDMON-
TON, AB, T5M 3X3
(780) 452-4444   SIC 6513
ST ANDREWS SCHOOL   p 627
See HISHKOONIKUN EDUCATION AU-
THORITY
ST ANN'S HOME   p 1425
See ST ANN'S SENIOR CITIZENS' VIL-
LAGE CORPORATION
**ST ANN'S SENIOR CITIZENS' VILLAGE
CORPORATION**   p 1425
2910 LOUISE ST, SASKATOON, SK, S7J
3L8
(306) 374-8900   SIC 8051
ST ANNES SOBEYS   p 368
See SOBEYS CAPITAL INCORPORATED
ST ANNS LOBSTER GALLEY LIMITED p
439
51943 CABOT TRAIL, BADDECK, NS, B0E
1B0
(902) 295-3100   SIC 5146
ST ANTHONY ELEMENTARY SCHOOL p
499
See DUFFERIN-PEEL CATHOLIC DIS-
TRICT SCHOOL BOARD
ST ANTHONYS GENERAL HOSPITALp 360
See PAS HEALTH COMPLEX INC, THE
ST AUGUSTINE CATHOLIC HIGH SCHOOL
p 679
See YORK CATHOLIC DISTRICT SCHOOL
BOARD
ST BASIL SCHOOL   p 694
See DUFFERIN-PEEL CATHOLIC DIS-
TRICT SCHOOL BOARD
**ST BENEDICT CATHOLIC SECONDARY
SCHOOL**   p 532
See WATERLOO CATHOLIC DISTRICT
SCHOOL BOARD
ST CATHARINES COLLEGIATE   p 885
See DISTRICT SCHOOL BOARD OF NIA-
GARA
ST CATHARINES ENGINE PLANT   p 885
See GENERAL MOTORS OF CANADA
COMPANY
**ST CATHARINES MAINSTREAM NON
PROFIT HOUSING PROJECT**   p 887
263 PELHAM RD, ST CATHARINES, ON,
L2S 1X7
(905) 934-3924   SIC 8699
ST CATHARINES STANDARD, THE   p 886
See OSPREY MEDIA PUBLISHING INC
ST CLAIR MARKET   p 511
See LOBLAWS SUPERMARKETS LIMITED
ST CLAIR MARKET   p 925
See LOBLAWS SUPERMARKETS LIMITED
ST CLAIR WEST SERVICES FOR SENIORS
p 993
2562 EGLINTON AVE W SUITE 202,
TORONTO, ON, M6M 1T4
(416) 787-2114   SIC 8399
ST CLAIRE MERCY HOSPITAL   p 431
See EASTERN REGIONAL INTEGRATED
HEALTH AUTHORITY
**ST COLUMBIA CATHOLIC WOMEN
LEAGUE FAIRFIELD**   p 1041
3849 EAST POINT RD -RTE 16, ELMIRA,
PE, C0A 1K0
(902) 357-2695   SIC 8699
**ST DEMETRIUS (UKRAINIAN CATHOLIC)
DEVELOPMENT CORPORATION, THE**   p
577
60 RICHVIEW RD, ETOBICOKE, ON, M9A
5E4
(416) 243-7653   SIC 8051

ST HUBERT BAR-B-Q   p 575
See PANACHE ROTISSEURS (1990) INC
ST HUBERT CADILLAC   p 1165
See ROTISSERIES ST-HUBERT.LTEE, LES
ST HUBERT ROTISSERIE   p 1395
See YANJACO INC
ST IGNATIUS HIGH SCHOOL   p 907
See THUNDER BAY CATHOLIC DISTRICT
SCHOOL BOARD
ST JEAN DE BREBEUF SCHOOL   p 615
See HAMILTON-WENTWORTH CATHOLIC
SCHOOL BOARD
ST JOHN'S CONVENTION CENTRE   p 432
See ST. JOHN'S SPORTS & ENTERTAIN-
MENT LTD
ST JOHN'S MUSIC LTD   p 373
1570 CHURCH AVE, WINNIPEG, MB, R2X
1G8
(204) 694-1818   SIC 5736
**ST JOHN'S NATIVE FRIENDSHIP CENTRE
ASSOCIATION**   p 433
716 WATER ST, ST. JOHN'S, NL, A1E 1C1
(709) 726-5902   SIC 8399
ST JOHN'S REHAB HOSPITAL   p 770
See ST JOHN'S REHABILITATION HOSPI-
TAL
ST JOHN'S REHABILITATION HOSPITAL p
770
285 CUMMER AVE, NORTH YORK, ON,
M2M 2G1
(416) 226-6780   SIC 8093
ST JOHN'S SCHOOL   p 322
See ST. JOHN'S SCHOOL SOCIETY
ST JOHN'S SCHOOL   p 1406
See HOLY FAMILY ROMAN CATHOLIC
SEPARATE SCHOOL DIVISION 140
ST JOHN'S-RAVENSCOURT SCHOOL p
392
400 SOUTH DR, WINNIPEG, MB, R3T 3K5
(204) 504-3110   SIC 8211
**ST JOHNS COLLEGE SECONDARY
SCHOOL**   p 514
See BRANT HALDIMAND NORFOLK
CATHOLIC DISTRICT SCHOOL BOARD
ST JOSEPH COMMUNICATIONS   p 559
See ST. JOSEPH PRINTING LIMITED
**ST JOSEPH HEALTHCARE CENTRE FOR
AMBULATORY**   p 609
See ST. JOSEPH'S HEALTHCARE FOUN-
DATION, HAMILTON
ST JOSEPH HIGH SCHOOL   p 752
See OTTAWA CATHOLIC DISTRICT
SCHOOL BOARD
ST JOSEPH HIGH SCHOOL   p 1435
See ST. PAUL'S ROMAN CATHOLIC SEPA-
RATE SCHOOL DIVISION NO 20
**ST JOSEPH HOSPITAL AUXILARY GIFT
SHOP**   p 655
See ST JOSEPH'S HEALTH CENTRE AUX-
ILARY
ST JOSEPH PI MEDIA   p 791
See ST. JOSEPH PRINTING LIMITED
ST JOSEPH PRINT GROUP INC   p 595
1165 KENASTON ST, GLOUCESTER, ON,
K1B 3N9
(613) 729-4303   SIC 2752
**ST JOSEPH PRINT GROUP OTTAWA, DIV
OF**   p 595
See ST JOSEPH PRINT GROUP INC
ST JOSEPH SECONDARY SCHOOL   p 744
See DUFFERIN-PEEL CATHOLIC DIS-
TRICT SCHOOL BOARD
ST JOSEPH'S CONVENT   p 566
See SISTERS OF ST. JOSEPHS OF
HAMILTON
ST JOSEPH'S GENERAL HOSPITAL p 170
5241 43RD ST, VEGREVILLE, AB, T9C 1R5
(780) 632-2811   SIC 8062
ST JOSEPH'S GENERAL HOSPITAL p 198
2137 COMOX AVE, COMOX, BC, V9M 1P2
(250) 339-1451   SIC 8062
ST JOSEPH'S HEALTH CENTRE (GUELPH)
p 604
100 WESTMOUNT RD, GUELPH, ON, N1H

5H8
(519) 824-6000   SIC 8051
**ST JOSEPH'S HEALTH CENTRE AUXI-
LARY**   p
655
268 GROSVENOR ST, LONDON, ON, N6A
4L6
(519) 646-6000   SIC 5947
ST JOSEPH'S HOSPITAL   p 1407
See SASKATCHEWAN HEALTH AUTHOR-
ITY
ST JOSEPH'S SECONDARY SCHOOL p
562
See CATHOLIC DISTRICT SCHOOL
BOARD OF EASTERN ONTARIO
ST JOSEPH'S VILLA, DUNDAS   p 566
See ST. JOSEPH'S VILLA FOUNDATION,
DUNDAS
ST JOSEPHS AUXILIARY HOSPITAL p 119
See ALBERTA HEALTH SERVICES
ST JOSEPHS BAKERY (NIAGARA) INC p
884
53 FACER ST, ST CATHARINES, ON, L2M
5H7
(905) 937-4411   SIC 5149
ST JOSEPHS HIGH SCHOOL   p 485
See SIMCOE MUSKOKA CATHOLIC DIS-
TRICT SCHOOL BOARD
ST JUDE'S ANGLICAN HOME SOCIETY p
293
810 27TH AVE W, VANCOUVER, BC, V5Z
2G7
(604) 874-3200   SIC 8051
ST LAWRENCE CASKET   p 398
See CERCUEILS ALLIANCE CASKETS
INC
ST LAWRENCE CENTRE FOR THE ARTSp
943
27 FRONT ST E, TORONTO, ON, M5E 1B4
(416) 366-7723   SIC 6512
ST LAWRENCE COLLEGE/ ONT SKILL p
562
See ST. LAWRENCE COLLEGE OF AP-
PLIED ARTS AND TECHNOLOGY, THE
ST LAWRENCE POOLS (1995) LIMITED p
632
525 DAYS RD, KINGSTON, ON, K7M 3R8
(613) 389-5510   SIC 1799
ST LEONARDS SOCIETY OF TORONTO p
919
779 DANFORTH AVE, TORONTO, ON, M4J
1L2
(416) 462-1596   SIC 8699
ST MARY CATHOLIC HIGH SCHOOL p 519
See CATHOLIC DISTRICT SCHOOL
BOARD OF EASTERN ONTARIO
**ST MARY'S ECONOMIC DEVELOPMENT
CORP**   p 400
150 CLIFFE ST, FREDERICTON, NB, E3A
0A1
(506) 452-9367   SIC 5411
**ST MARY'S ECONOMIC DEVELOPMENT
CORPORATION**   p 400
185 GABRIEL DR, FREDERICTON, NB,
E3A 5V9
(506) 462-9300   SIC 7999
ST MARY'S ENTERTAINMENT CENTRE p
400
See ST MARY'S ECONOMIC DEVELOP-
MENT CORPORATION
ST MARY'S HIGH SCHOOL   p 637
See WATERLOO CATHOLIC DISTRICT
SCHOOL BOARD
ST MARY'S HOSPITAL CAMROSE   p 78
4607 53 ST, CAMROSE, AB, T4V 1Y5
(780) 679-6100   SIC 8062
ST MARY'S RIVER SMOKEHOUSES p 466
See LOCHIEL ENTERPRISES LIMITED
ST MARY'S SUPERMARKET   p 400
See ST MARY'S ECONOMIC DEVELOP-
MENT CORP
ST MARY'S UNIVERSITY   p 69
14500 BANNISTER RD SE 4TH FL, CAL-
GARY, AB, T2X 1Z4

▲ Public Company   ■ Public Company Family Member   **HQ** Headquarters   **BR** Branch   **SL** Single Location

(403) 531-9130   *SIC* 8221
ST MARYS MEMORIAL HOSPITAL   *p* 888
267 QUEEN ST W, ST MARYS, ON, N4X
1B6
(519) 284-1330   *SIC* 8062
ST MARYS OF THE LAKE HOSPITAL *p* 631
See PROVIDENCE CARE CENTRE
**ST MATTHEW CATHOLIC ELEMENTARY
SCHOOL**   *p* 493
*See HAMILTON-WENTWORTH CATHOLIC
SCHOOL BOARD*
ST MATTHEW HIGH SCHOOL   *p* 810
*See OTTAWA CATHOLIC DISTRICT
SCHOOL BOARD*
ST MICHAEL CATHOLIC HIGH SCHOOL *p*
760
*See NIAGARA CATHOLIC DISTRICT
SCHOOL BOARD*
ST MICHAEL'S CENTRE   *p* 193
*See ST MICHAEL'S CENTRE HOSPITAL
SOCIETY*
**ST MICHAEL'S CENTRE HOSPITAL SOCI-
ETY**   *p*
193
7451 SUSSEX AVE, BURNABY, BC, V5J
5C2
(604) 434-1323   *SIC* 8069
**ST MICHAEL'S EXTENDED CARE CENTRE
SOCIETY**   *p* 84
7404 139 AVE NW, EDMONTON, AB, T5C
3H7
(780) 473-5621   *SIC* 8051
ST MICHAEL'S HEALTH GROUP   *p* 84
*See ST MICHAEL'S LONG TERM CARE
CENTRE*
ST MICHAEL'S HOSPITAL FOUNDATION *p*
936
30 BOND ST, TORONTO, ON, M5B 1W8
(416) 864-5000   *SIC* 6732
**ST MICHAEL'S LONG TERM CARE CEN-
TRE**   *p*
84
7404 139 AVE NW, EDMONTON, AB, T5C
3H7
(780) 473-5621   *SIC* 8051
ST NORBERT LODGES LTD   *p* 392
50 ST PIERRE ST, WINNIPEG, MB, R3V
1J6
(204) 269-4538   *SIC* 8051
ST PATRICK HIGH SCHOOL   *p* 910
*See THUNDER BAY CATHOLIC DISTRICT
SCHOOL BOARD*
ST PATRICK'S HOME OF OTTAWA   *p* 827
2865 RIVERSIDE DR, OTTAWA, ON, K1V
8N5
(613) 731-4660   *SIC* 8051
ST PAUL CATHOLIC HIGH SCHOOL *p* 832
*See OTTAWA CATHOLIC DISTRICT
SCHOOL BOARD*
**ST PAUL CO-OP GAS BAR & CONVE-
NIENCE STORE**   *p*
165
See ATRC ENTERPRISES
ST PAUL DODGE LTD   *p* 165
4014 50 AVE, ST PAUL, AB, T0A 3A2
SIC 5511
**ST PAUL HOME HARDWARE BUILDING
CENTRE**   *p* 165
See KOTOWICH HARDWARE LTD
ST PETER'S HOSPITAL   *p* 1410
*See SASKATCHEWAN CATHOLIC HEALTH
CORPORATION, THE*
ST ROBERT CATHOLIC HIGH SCHOOL *p*
905
*See YORK CATHOLIC DISTRICT SCHOOL
BOARD*
**ST STANISLAUS-ST CASIMIR'S POLISH
PARISHES CREDIT UNION LIMITED** *p* 995
220 RONCESVALLES AVE, TORONTO,
ON, M6R 2L7
(416) 537-2181   *SIC* 6062
ST STEPHENS COMMUNITY HOUSE *p* 977
91 BELLEVUE AVE, TORONTO, ON, M5T
2N8

(416) 925-2103   *SIC* 8399
**ST STEPHENS COMMUNITY HOUSE DAY-
CARE**   *p*
977
See ST STEPHENS COMMUNITY HOUSE
ST THERESE HEALTH CENTRE   *p* 164
See ALBERTA HEALTH SERVICES
**ST THOMAS AQUINAS SECONDARY
SCHOOL**   *p* 499
*See DUFFERIN-PEEL CATHOLIC DIS-
TRICT SCHOOL BOARD*
**ST THOMAS AQUINAS SECONDARY
SCHOOL**   *p* 802
*See HALTON CATHOLIC DISTRICT
SCHOOL BOARD*
ST THOMAS CENTRE DE SANTE   *p* 112
8411 91 ST NW SUITE 234, EDMONTON,
AB, T6C 1Z9
(780) 450-2987   *SIC* 8361
ST THOMAS ENERGY INC   *p* 889
135 EDWARD ST, ST THOMAS, ON, N5P
4A8
(519) 631-5550   *SIC* 4911
ST THOMAS FOOD MARKET   *p* 890
See 808269 ONTARIO INC
ST THOMAS HEALTH CENTER   *p* 112
See ST THOMAS CENTRE DE SANTE
ST THOMAS HIGH SCHOOL   *p* 1251
*See LESTER B. PEARSON SCHOOL
BOARD*
**ST THOMAS MORE CATHOLIC SEC-
ONDARY SCHOOL**   *p*
616
*See HAMILTON-WENTWORTH CATHOLIC
SCHOOL BOARD*
ST TOURING CANADA LTD   *p* 309
900 GEORGIA ST W, VANCOUVER, BC,
V6C 2W6
(604) 689-1553   *SIC* 4725
ST VIATEUR NURSING HOME   *p* 645
See GENESIS GARDENS INC
ST VINCENT DE PAUL SOCIETY   *p* 936
240 CHURCH ST, TORONTO, ON, M5B 1Z2
(416) 364-5577   *SIC* 8399
ST VITAL GARDEN MARKET IGA   *p* 368
See SOBEYS CAPITAL INCORPORATED
ST-ALBERT CHEESE CO-OPERATIVE INC
p 883
150 ST PAUL ST, ST ALBERT, ON, K0A 3C0
(613) 987-2872   *SIC* 2022
ST-AMBROISE   *p* 1222
See BRASSERIE MCAUSLAN INC, LA
ST-BASILE TOYOTA   *p* 1294
See 9151-8100 QUEBEC INC
ST-BONIFACE MUNICIPAL GARAGE*p* 1295
500 MUNICIPALE PL, SAINT-BONIFACE-
DE-SHAWINIGAN, QC, G0X 2L0
(819) 535-5443   *SIC* 7538
ST-BRUNO MODES ET SPORTS INC*p* 1296
750 BOUL DES PROMENADES, SAINT-
BRUNO, QC, J3V 6A8
(450) 372-0368   *SIC* 5699
ST-CLAIR INSURANCE BROKERS INC   *p*
902
13340 LANOUE ST, TECUMSEH, ON, N8N
5E1
(519) 259-1955   *SIC* 6411
ST-CONSTANT HONDA   *p* 1297
See ENTOUR AUTOMOBILES INC
ST-FELICIEN DIESEL (1988) INC   *p* 1303
981 BOUL HAMEL, SAINT-FELICIEN, QC,
G8K 2E3
(418) 679-2474   *SIC* 7699
**ST-GEORGES CHEVROLET PONTIAC
BUICK CADILLAC GMC INC**   *p* 1305
520 87E RUE, SAINT-GEORGES, QC, G5Y
7L9
(418) 228-8801   *SIC* 5511
ST-GERMAIN EGOUTS & AQUEDUCS INC
p 1309
3800 BOUL SIR-WILFRID-LAURIER,
SAINT-HUBERT, QC, J3Y 6T1
(450) 671-6171   *SIC* 5032
ST-HUBERT   *p* 1381

See RESTAURANTS SERQUA INC, LES
ST-HUBERT BAR-B-Q   *p* 1256
See MARTIN, CLAUDE & MARCEL INC
ST-HUBERT BAR-B-Q   *p* 1279
See MARTIN, CLAUDE & MARCEL INC
ST-HUBERT EXPRESS   *p* 1087
See ROTISSERIES ST-HUBERT LTEE, LES
ST-HUBERT RESTAURANTS   *p* 1137
See MARTIN, CLAUDE & MARCEL INC
ST-HUBERT RESTAURANTS   *p* 1140
See MARTIN DESSERT INC
**ST-HYACINTHE CHRYSLER JEEP DODGE
INC**   *p* 1313
1155 BOUL CHOQUETTE, SAINT-
HYACINTHE, QC, J2S 0C4
(450) 924-0568   *SIC* 5531
ST-HYACINTHE SUZUKI   *p* 1311
See 3652548 CANADA INC
ST-JEAN PHOTOCHIMIE   *p* 1318
See PCAS CANADA INC
ST-JEROME CHEVROLET BUICK GMC INC
p 1320
265 RUE JOHN-F.-KENNEDY, SAINT-
JEROME, QC, J7Y 4B5
(450) 438-1203   *SIC* 5511
ST-JEROME TOYOTA   *p* 1152
See AGENCES KYOTO LTEE, LES
ST-LAWRENCE BEANS   *p* 1360
See AGROCENTRE BELCAN INC
ST-LAWRENCE CEMENT   *p* 713
See CRH CANADA GROUP INC
ST-LEONARD NISSAN INC   *p* 1346
4400 BOUL METROPOLITAIN E, SAINT-
LEONARD, QC, H1S 1A2
(514) 365-7777   *SIC* 5511
ST-PIERRE, JULES LTEE   *p* 1155
1054 BOUL ALBINY-PAQUETTE, MONT-
LAURIER, QC, J9L 1M1
SIC 5149
ST-VIATEUR BAGEL   *p* 1184
See MAISON DU BAGEL INC
**ST. JOSEPH'S GENERAL HOSPITAL EL-
LIOT LAKE**   *p*
568
70 SPINE RD, ELLIOT LAKE, ON, P5A 1X2
(705) 848-7181   *SIC* 8062
ST. ALBERT DODGE CHRYSLER LTD*p* 166
184 ST ALBERT TRAIL, ST. ALBERT, AB,
T8N 0P7
(780) 238-8787   *SIC* 5511
ST. ALBERT INN & SUITES   *p* 166
See STURGEON HOTEL LTD
**ST. ALBERT PUBLIC SCHOOL DISTRICT
NO. 5565**   *p* 166
12 CUNNINGHAM RD, ST. ALBERT, AB,
T8N 2E9
(780) 459-4405   *SIC* 8211
**ST. ALBERT PUBLIC SCHOOL DISTRICT
NO. 5565**   *p* 166
49 GIROUX RD, ST. ALBERT, AB, T8N 6N4
(780) 460-8490   *SIC* 8211
**ST. ALBERT PUBLIC SCHOOL DISTRICT
NO. 5565**   *p* 166
60 SIR WINSTON CHURCHILL AVE, ST.
ALBERT, AB, T8N 0G4
(780) 460-3712   *SIC* 8211
ST. ALBERT, CITY OF   *p* 166
18 SIR WINSTON CHURCHILL AVE, ST.
ALBERT, AB, T8N 2W5
(780) 459-7021   *SIC* 7389
**ST. ALOYSIUS GONZAGA SECONDARY
SCHOOL**   *p* 718
*See DUFFERIN-PEEL CATHOLIC DIS-
TRICT SCHOOL BOARD*
ST. ANDREW'S COLLEGE   *p* 481
15800 YONGE ST, AURORA, ON, L4G 3H7
(905) 727-3178   *SIC* 8211
ST. BONIFACE GENERAL HOSPITAL *p* 364
409 TACHE AVE, WINNIPEG, MB, R2H 2A6
(204) 233-8563   *SIC* 8062
ST. CATHARINES GENERAL SITE   *p* 886
See NIAGARA HEALTH SYSTEM
ST. CATHARINES NISSAN   *p* 884
See 1991943 ONTARIO INC

ST. CATHARINES STANDARD GROUP INC
p 886
1 ST. PAUL ST SUITE 10, ST CATHARINES,
ON, L2R 7L4
(905) 684-7251   *SIC* 2711
ST. CHARLES COUNTRY CLUB   *p* 387
100 COUNTRY CLUB BLVD, WINNIPEG,
MB, R3K 1Z3
(204) 889-4444   *SIC* 7997
**ST. CLAIR CATHOLIC DISTRICT SCHOOL
BOARD**   *p* 542
85 GRAND AVE W, CHATHAM, ON, N7L
1B6
(519) 351-2987   *SIC* 8221
**ST. CLAIR CATHOLIC DISTRICT SCHOOL
BOARD**   *p* 1005
420 CREEK ST, WALLACEBURG, ON, N8A
4C4
(519) 627-6762   *SIC* 8211
ST. CLAIR MECHANICAL INC   *p* 518
2963 BRIGDEN RD SUITE 1, BRIGDEN,
ON, N0N 1B0
(519) 864-0927   *SIC* 3498
ST. CLAIR O'CONNOR COMMUNITY INC *p*
917
2701 ST CLAIR AVE E SUITE 211,
TORONTO, ON, M4B 1M5
(416) 757-8757   *SIC* 8361
ST. CLAIR SECONDARY SCHOOL   *p* 858
*See LAMBTON KENT DISTRICT SCHOOL
BOARD*
ST. CLAIR TECHNOLOGIES INC   *p* 1005
827 DUFFERIN AVE, WALLACEBURG, ON,
N8A 2V5
(519) 627-1673   *SIC* 3714
ST. CLEMENT'S SCHOOL   *p* 923
21 ST CLEMENTS AVE, TORONTO, ON,
M4R 1G8
(416) 483-4835   *SIC* 8211
ST. DAVIDS HYDROPONICS LTD   *p* 761
822 CONCESSION 7 RD RR 4, NIAGARA
ON THE LAKE, ON, L0S 1J0
(905) 682-7570   *SIC* 0182
**ST. FRANCIS ADVOCATES FOR THE
AUTISTIC & DEVELOPMENTALLY DIS-
ABLED (SARNIA) INC**   *p*
478
7346 ARKONA RD, ARKONA, ON, N0M 1B0
(519) 828-3399   *SIC* 7699
**ST. FRANCIS MEMORIAL HOSPITAL AS-
SOCIATION**   *p*
489
7 ST FRANCIS MEMORIAL DR, BARRYS
BAY, ON, K0J 1B0
(613) 756-3044   *SIC* 8062
ST. FRANCIS XAVIER HIGH SCHOOL *p* 98
*See EDMONTON CATHOLIC SEPARATE
SCHOOL DISTRICT NO.7*
ST. FRANCIS XAVIER UNIVERSITY   *p* 438
5005 CHAPEL SQ, ANTIGONISH, NS, B2G
2W5
(902) 863-3300   *SIC* 8211
ST. GENEVE FINE BEDLINENS LTD   *p* 264
11160 SILVERSMITH PL, RICHMOND, BC,
V7A 5E4
(604) 272-3004   *SIC* 5023
**ST. GEORGE'S GOLF AND COUNTRY
CLUB**   *p* 577
1668 ISLINGTON AVE, ETOBICOKE, ON,
M9A 3M9
(416) 231-3393   *SIC* 7997
ST. HELEN SEAFOODS INC   *p* 990
138 SAINT HELENS AVE, TORONTO, ON,
M6H 0B8
(416) 536-5111   *SIC* 5146
ST. HELEN'S MEAT PACKERS LIMITED   *p*
994
55 GLEN SCARLETT RD, TORONTO, ON,
M6N 1P5
(416) 769-1788   *SIC* 5147
ST. HILDA'S TOWERS, INC   *p* 989
2339 DUFFERIN ST, TORONTO, ON, M6E
4Z5
(416) 781-6621   *SIC* 8361

ST. ISIDORE ASPHALT LTD *p 417*
19 RUE DUCLOS, SAINT-ISIDORE, NB, E8M 1N3
(506) 358-6345 *SIC 1611*

ST. JAMES CATHOLIC HIGH SCHOOL *p 600*
See WELLINGTON CATHOLIC DISTRICT SCHOOL BOARD

ST. JAMES VOLKSWAGEN *p 383*
See 191191 CANADA LTD

ST. JAMES-ASSINIBOIA SCHOOL DIVISION *p 386*
2574 PORTAGE AVE, WINNIPEG, MB, R3J 0H8
(204) 888-7951 *SIC 8211*

ST. JOAN OF ARC CATHOLIC HIGH SCHOOL *p 488*
460 MAPLETON AVE, BARRIE, ON, L4N 9C2
(705) 721-0398 *SIC 8211*

ST. JOAN OF ARC CATHOLIC SECONDARY SCHOOL *p 718*
See DUFFERIN-PEEL CATHOLIC DISTRICT SCHOOL BOARD

ST. JOHN AMBULANCE *p 940*
See ST. JOHN COUNCIL FOR ONTARIO

ST. JOHN COUNCIL FOR ONTARIO *p 940*
15 TORONTO ST SUITE 800, TORONTO, ON, M5C 2E3
(416) 923-8411 *SIC 8611*

ST. JOHN HIGH SCHOOL *p 371*
See WINNIPEG SCHOOL DIVISION

ST. JOHN PAUL LL CATHOLIC SECONDARY SCHOOL *p 866*
See TORONTO CATHOLIC DISTRICT SCHOOL BOARD

ST. JOHN'S DOCKYARD LIMITED *p 433*
475 WATER ST, ST. JOHN'S, NL, A1E 6B5
(709) 758-6800 *SIC 3731*

ST. JOHN'S INTERNATIONAL AIRPORT AUTHORITY *p 429*
100 WORLD PARKWAY SUITE 1, ST. JOHN'S, NL, A1A 5T2
(709) 758-8500 *SIC 4581*

ST. JOHN'S SCHOOL SOCIETY *p 322*
2215 10TH AVE W, VANCOUVER, BC, V6K 2J1
(604) 732-4434 *SIC 8211*

ST. JOHN'S SPORTS & ENTERTAINMENT LTD *p 432*
50 NEW GOWER ST, ST. JOHN'S, NL, A1C 1J3
(709) 758-1111 *SIC 7999*

ST. JOHN'S TRANSPORTATION COMMISSION *p 431*
25 MESSENGER DR, ST. JOHN'S, NL, A1B 0H6
(709) 570-2020 *SIC 4111*

ST. JOHN'S TROPHIES LTD *p 743*
1750 BONHILL RD, MISSISSAUGA, ON, L5T 1C8
(905) 564-2001 *SIC 5094*

ST. JOHN'S YMCA-YWCA *p 429*
See ST. JOHN'S YOUNG MEN'S AND YOUNG WOMEN'S CHRISTIAN ASSOCIATION

ST. JOHN'S YOUNG MEN'S AND YOUNG WOMEN'S CHRISTIAN ASSOCIATION *p 429*
34 NEW COVE RD, ST. JOHN'S, NL, A1A 2B8
(709) 754-2960 *SIC 8641*

ST. JOSEPH COMMUNICATIONS *p 777*
See ST. JOSEPH PRINTING LIMITED

ST. JOSEPH COMMUNICATIONS *p 791*
See 1772887 ONTARIO LIMITED

ST. JOSEPH CORPORATION *p 558*
50 MACINTOSH BLVD, CONCORD, ON, L4K 4P3
(905) 660-3111 *SIC 2752*

ST. JOSEPH HIGH SCHOOL AND ASCEN-

SION COLLEGIATE *p 85*
See EDMONTON CATHOLIC SEPARATE SCHOOL DISTRICT NO.7

ST. JOSEPH MORROW PARK CATHOLIC SECONDARY SCHOOL *p 770*
See TORONTO CATHOLIC DISTRICT SCHOOL BOARD

ST. JOSEPH PRINT GROUP INC *p 775*
135 RAILSIDE RD, NORTH YORK, ON, M3A 1B7
(613) 746-4005 *SIC 2752*

ST. JOSEPH PRINT THORN *p 775*
See ST. JOSEPH PRINT GROUP INC

ST. JOSEPH PRINTING LIMITED *p 559*
50 MACINTOSH BLVD, CONCORD, ON, L4K 4P3
(905) 660-3111 *SIC 2752*

ST. JOSEPH PRINTING LIMITED *p 777*
236 LESMILL RD, NORTH YORK, ON, M3B 2T5
(416) 449-4579 *SIC 2711*

ST. JOSEPH PRINTING LIMITED *p 791*
15 BENTON RD, NORTH YORK, ON, M6M 3G2
(416) 248-4868 *SIC 2752*

ST. JOSEPH'S (GREY NUN'S) OF GRAVELBOURG *p 1407*
216 BETTEZ ST, GRAVELBOURG, SK, S0H 1X0
(306) 648-3185 *SIC 8062*

ST. JOSEPH'S CONTINUING CARE CENTRE *p 901*
See ST. JOSEPH'S CONTINUING CARE CENTRE OF SUDBURY

ST. JOSEPH'S CONTINUING CARE CENTRE OF SUDBURY *p 901*
1140 SOUTH BAY RD, SUDBURY, ON, P3E 0B6
(705) 674-2846 *SIC 8062*

ST. JOSEPH'S HEALTH CARE, LONDON *p 652*
850 HIGHBURY AVE N, LONDON, ON, N5Y 1A4
(519) 455-5110 *SIC 8093*

ST. JOSEPH'S HEALTH CARE, LONDON *p 655*
268 GROSVENOR ST, LONDON, ON, N6A 4V2
(519) 646-6100 *SIC 8361*

ST. JOSEPH'S HEALTH CARE, LONDON *p 655*
268 GROSVENOR ST, LONDON, ON, N6A 4V2
(519) 646-6100 *SIC 8093*

ST. JOSEPH'S HEALTH CARE, LONDON *p 889*
GD, ST THOMAS, ON, N5P 3T4
(519) 631-8510 *SIC 8093*

ST. JOSEPH'S HEALTH CENTRE *p 995*
30 THE QUEENSWAY, TORONTO, ON, M6R 1B5
(416) 530-6000 *SIC 8062*

ST. JOSEPH'S HEALTH SYSTEM *p 612*
50 CHARLTON AVE E, HAMILTON, ON, L8N 4A6
(905) 522-4941 *SIC 8699*

ST. JOSEPH'S HEALTHCARE FOUNDATION, HAMILTON *p 609*
2757 KING ST E, HAMILTON, ON, L8G 5E4
(905) 573-7777 *SIC 8093*

ST. JOSEPH'S HEALTHCARE FOUNDATION, HAMILTON *p 617*
100 WEST 5TH ST, HAMILTON, ON, L9C 0E3
(905) 388-2511 *SIC 8063*

ST. JOSEPH'S HOME CARE *p 616*
1550 UPPER JAMES ST SUITE 201, HAMILTON, ON, L9B 2L6

(905) 522-6887 *SIC 8082*

ST. JOSEPH'S HOSPICE RESOURCE CENTRE OF SARNIA LAMBTON *p 861*
475 CHRISTINA ST N, SARNIA, ON, N7T 5W3
(519) 337-0537 *SIC 8699*

ST. JOSEPH'S HOSPITAL OF ESTEVAN *p 1406*
1176 NICHOLSON RD SUITE 203, ESTEVAN, SK, S4A 0H3
(306) 637-2400 *SIC 8062*

ST. JOSEPH'S HOSPITAL/FOYER D'YOUVILLE *p 1407*
See ST. JOSEPH'S (GREY NUN'S) OF GRAVELBOURG

ST. JOSEPH'S LIFECARE CENTRE, BRANTFORD *p 516*
99 WAYNE GRETZKY PKY, BRANTFORD, ON, N3S 6T6
(519) 751-7096 *SIC 8051*

ST. JOSEPH'S PROVINCE HOUSE INC *p 995*
419 PARKSIDE DR, TORONTO, ON, M6R 2Z7
(416) 604-7992 *SIC 8699*

ST. JOSEPH'S RESIDENCE INC *p 369*
1149 LEILA AVE, WINNIPEG, MB, R2P 1S6
(204) 697-8031 *SIC 8059*

ST. JOSEPH'S VILLA FOUNDATION, DUNDAS *p 566*
56 GOVERNORS RD, DUNDAS, ON, L9H 5G7
(905) 627-3541 *SIC 8051*

ST. JOSEPH'S VILLA OF SUDBURY, INC *p 901*
1250 SOUTHBAY RD, SUDBURY, ON, P3E 6L9
SIC 8059

ST. JOSEPH-SCOLLARD HALL CATHOLIC SECONDARY SCHOOL *p 764*
675 O'BRIEN ST, NORTH BAY, ON, P1B 9R3
(705) 494-8600 *SIC 8211*

ST. LAWRENCE COLLEGE OF APPLIED ARTS AND TECHNOLOGY, THE *p 520*
2288 PARKEDALE AVE, BROCKVILLE, ON, K6V 5X3
(613) 345-0660 *SIC 8222*

ST. LAWRENCE COLLEGE OF APPLIED ARTS AND TECHNOLOGY, THE *p 562*
2 ST LAWRENCE DR, CORNWALL, ON, K6H 4Z1
(613) 933-6080 *SIC 8221*

ST. LAWRENCE COLLEGE OF APPLIED ARTS AND TECHNOLOGY, THE *p 632*
100 PORTSMOUTH AVE, KINGSTON, ON, K7M 1G2
(613) 544-5400 *SIC 8221*

ST. LAWRENCE LODGE *p 520*
1803 HIGHWAY 2 E, BROCKVILLE, ON, K6V 5T1
(613) 345-0255 *SIC 8361*

ST. LAWRENCE SEAWAY MANAGEMENT CORPORATION, THE *p 563*
202 PITT ST, CORNWALL, ON, K6J 3P7
(613) 932-5170 *SIC 4449*

ST. LAWRENCE SEAWAY MANAGEMENT CORPORATION, THE *p 886*
508 GLENDALE AVE, ST CATHARINES, ON, L2R 6V8
(905) 641-1932 *SIC 4432*

ST. LAWRENCE SEAWAY MANAGEMENT CORPORATION, THE *p 1069*
9200 BOUL MARIE-VICTORIN, BROSSARD, QC, J4X 1A3
(450) 672-4115 *SIC 4499*

ST. LEONARD'S COMMUNITY SERVICES *p 516*
133 ELGIN ST, BRANTFORD, ON, N3S 5A4
(519) 759-8830 *SIC 8361*

ST. MARGARET'S SCHOOL *p 338*
1080 LUCAS AVE, VICTORIA, BC, V8X 3P7

(250) 479-7171 *SIC 8211*

ST. MARK CATHOLIC HIGH SCHOOL *p 663*
See OTTAWA CATHOLIC DISTRICT SCHOOL BOARD

ST. MARY RIVER IRRIGATION DISTRICT *p 141*
1210 36 ST N, LETHBRIDGE, AB, T1H 5H8
(403) 380-6152 *SIC 4971*

ST. MARY'S CATHOLIC SECONDARY SCHOOL *p 614*
See HAMILTON-WENTWORTH CATHOLIC SCHOOL BOARD

ST. MARY'S CO-OP *p 368*
See R M KOMAR ENTERPRISES LIMITED

ST. MARY'S GENERAL HOSPITAL *p 641*
911 QUEENS BLVD SUITE 453, KITCHENER, ON, N2M 1B2
(519) 744-3311 *SIC 8011*

ST. MARY'S RETAIL SALES *p 400*
150 CLIFFE ST, FREDERICTON, NB, E3A 0A1
(506) 452-9367 *SIC 5411*

ST. MARY'S SECONDARY SCHOOL *p 545*
See PETERBOROUGH VICTORIA NORTHUMBERLAND AND CLARINGTON CATHOLIC DISTRICT SCHOOL BOARD

ST. MARY'S SENIOR HIGH SCHOOL *p 66*
See CALGARY ROMAN CATHOLIC SEPARATE SCHOOL DISTRICT #1

ST. MARYS CEMENT CO *p 918*
See ST. MARYS CEMENT INC. (CANADA)

ST. MARYS CEMENT INC. (CANADA) *p 496*
400 BOWMANVILLE AVE, BOWMANVILLE, ON, L1C 7B5
(905) 623-3341 *SIC 3241*

ST. MARYS CEMENT INC. (CANADA) *p 889*
585 WATER ST S, ST MARYS, ON, N4X 1B6
(519) 284-1020 *SIC 3241*

ST. MARYS CEMENT INC. (CANADA) *p 918*
55 INDUSTRIAL ST, TORONTO, ON, M4G 3W9
(416) 423-1300 *SIC 3241*

ST. MARYS CEMENT INC. (CANADA) *p 918*
55 INDUSTRIAL ST, TORONTO, ON, M4G 3W9
(416) 423-1300 *SIC 3273*

ST. MICHAEL COLLEGE *p 976*
See UNIVERSITY OF ST MICHAEL'S COLLEGE, THE

ST. MICHAEL'S ARENA *p 972*
See ST. MICHAEL'S COLLEGE SCHOOL

ST. MICHAEL'S COLLEGE SCHOOL *p 972*
1515 BATHURST ST, TORONTO, ON, M5P 3H4
(416) 653-4483 *SIC 8211*

ST. MICHAEL'S HEALTH GROUP *p 84*
See ST MICHAEL'S EXTENDED CARE CENTRE SOCIETY

ST. MICHAELS UNIVERSITY SCHOOL SOCIETY *p 333*
3400 RICHMOND RD, VICTORIA, BC, V8P 4P5
(250) 592-2411 *SIC 8211*

ST. MILDRED'S-LIGHTBOURN SCHOOL *p 801*
1080 LINBROOK RD, OAKVILLE, ON, L6J 2L1
(905) 845-2386 *SIC 8211*

ST. ONGE RECREATION *p 486*
See BARRIE RECREATION LTD

ST. PATRICK CATHOLIC SECONDARY SCHOOL *p 919*
See TORONTO CATHOLIC DISTRICT SCHOOL BOARD

ST. PATRICK SQUARE *p 1082*
See FONDATION D'AMENAGEMENT ST-PATRICK

ST. PATRICK'S ELEMENTARY SCHOOL *p 337*
See CATHOLIC INDEPENDENT SCHOOLS, DIOCESE OF VICTORIA

ST. PAUL EDUCATION REGIONAL DIVI-

SION NO 1 p
165
4313 48 AVE SUITE 1, ST PAUL, AB, T0A 3A3
(780) 645-3323   *SIC* 8211
ST. PAUL EDUCATION REGIONAL DIVISION NO 1 p
165
5201 50 AVE, ST PAUL, AB, T0A 3A0
(780) 645-3237   *SIC* 8211
ST. PAUL'S L'AMOREAUX CENTRE p 878
3333 FINCH AVE E, SCARBOROUGH, ON, M1W 2R9
(416) 493-3333   *SIC* 6513
ST. PAUL'S ROMAN CATHOLIC SEPARATE SCHOOL DIVISION NO 20 p 1432
411 AVENUE M N, SASKATOON, SK, S7L 2S7
(306) 659-7550   *SIC* 8211
ST. PAUL'S ROMAN CATHOLIC SEPARATE SCHOOL DIVISION NO 20 p 1435
115 NELSON RD, SASKATOON, SK, S7S 1H1
(306) 659-7650   *SIC* 8211
ST. PETER CATHOLIC HIGH SCHOOL p
811
See OTTAWA CATHOLIC DISTRICT SCHOOL BOARD
ST. PETER'S SECONDARY SCHOOL p 488
See SIMCOE MUSKOKA CATHOLIC DISTRICT SCHOOL BOARD
ST. PHILLIPS BAKERY p 664
See ST. PHILLIPS FOODS LIMITED
ST. PHILLIPS FOODS LIMITED p 664
2563 MAJOR MACKENZIE DR SUITE 8, MAPLE, ON, L6A 2E8
(905) 832-5688   *SIC* 5141
ST. PIERRE, BARRY PHARMACY LTD p 917
1500 WOODBINE AVE, TORONTO, ON, M4C 4G9
(416) 429-2529   *SIC* 5912
ST. PIUS X HIGH SCHOOL p 831
See OTTAWA CATHOLIC DISTRICT SCHOOL BOARD
ST. RAYMOND SEPARATE SCHOOL p 990
See TORONTO CATHOLIC DISTRICT SCHOOL BOARD
ST. REGIS CRYSTAL INC p 680
271 YORKTECH DR, MARKHAM, ON, L6G 1A6
(905) 754-3355   *SIC* 5099
ST. SHREDDIES CELLO CO. LTD p 743
6141 ATLANTIC DR UNIT 1, MISSISSAUGA, ON, L5T 1L9
(905) 670-2414   *SIC* 3084
ST. STEPHEN CATHOLIC SECONDARY SCHOOL p 496
See PETERBOROUGH VICTORIA NORTHUMBERLAND AND CLARINGTON CATHOLIC DISTRICT SCHOOL BOARD
ST. THOMAS AQUINAS HIGH SCHOOL p 998
See SIMCOE MUSKOKA CATHOLIC DISTRICT SCHOOL BOARD
ST. THOMAS FORD LINCOLN p 889
See ST. THOMAS FORD LINCOLN SALES LIMITED
ST. THOMAS FORD LINCOLN SALES LIMITED p 889
1012 TALBOT ST, ST THOMAS, ON, N5P 1G3
(519) 631-5080   *SIC* 5511
ST. THOMAS OF VILLANOVA SECONDARY SCHOOL p 1024
See WINDSOR-ESSEX CATHOLIC DISTRICT SCHOOL BOARD, THE
ST. THOMAS UNIVERSITY p 401
51 DINEEN DR COLLEGE HILL, FREDERICTON, NB, E3B 5G3
(506) 452-0640   *SIC* 8221
ST. THOMAS-ELGIN GENERAL HOSPITAL, THE p 890

189 ELM ST, ST THOMAS, ON, N5R 5C4
(519) 631-2030   *SIC* 8062
ST. WILLIAMS NURSERY AND ECOLOGY CENTRE INC p 890
885 24 HWY E, ST WILLIAMS, ON, N0E 1P0
(519) 586-9116   *SIC* 0851
STAALDUINEN FLORAL LIMITED p 893
1255 ARVIN AVE, STONEY CREEK, ON, L8E 0H7
(905) 643-2703   *SIC* 5992
STABLEX CANADA INC p 1060
760 BOUL INDUSTRIEL, BLAINVILLE, QC, J7C 3V4
(450) 430-9230   *SIC* 4953
STACE p 1293
See SAINT-AUGUSTIN CANADA ELECTRIQUE INC
STACKPOLE p 478
See STACKPOLE INTERNATIONAL ENGINEERED PRODUCTS, LTD
STACKPOLE INTERNATIONAL p 478
See STACKPOLE INTERNATIONAL ENGINEERED PRODUCTS, LTD
STACKPOLE INTERNATIONAL p 714
See STACKPOLE INTERNATIONAL ENGINEERED PRODUCTS, LTD
STACKPOLE INTERNATIONAL ENGINEERED PRODUCTS, LTD p 478
1310 CORMORANT RD, ANCASTER, ON, L9G 4V5
(905) 304-8533   *SIC* 5013
STACKPOLE INTERNATIONAL ENGINEERED PRODUCTS, LTD p 478
1325 CORMORANT RD, ANCASTER, ON, L9G 4V5
(905) 304-9455   *SIC* 5013
STACKPOLE INTERNATIONAL ENGINEERED PRODUCTS, LTD p 714
2400 ROYAL WINDSOR DR, MISSISSAUGA, ON, L5J 1K7
(905) 403-0550   *SIC* 5013
STACKPOLE INTERNATIONAL POWDER METAL, LTD p 478
See STACKPOLE INTERNATIONAL POWDER METAL, LTD.
STACKPOLE INTERNATIONAL POWDER METAL, LTD p 896
See STACKPOLE INTERNATIONAL POWDER METAL, LTD.
STACKPOLE INTERNATIONAL POWDER METAL, LTD. p 478
1325 CORMORANT RD 2ND FL, ANCASTER, ON, L9G 4V5
(905) 304-9455   *SIC* 3714
STACKPOLE INTERNATIONAL POWDER METAL, LTD. p 478
1325 CORMORANT RD 1ST FL, ANCASTER, ON, L9G 4V5
(905) 304-9455   *SIC* 3714
STACKPOLE INTERNATIONAL POWDER METAL, LTD. p 896
128 MONTEITH AVE, STRATFORD, ON, N5A 2P5
(519) 271-6060   *SIC* 3714
STACKPOLE INTERNATIONAL ULC p 478
1325 CORMORANT RD FL 2, ANCASTER, ON, L9G 4V5
(905) 304-9455   *SIC* 3714
STACKTECK p 506
See STACKTECK SYSTEMS LIMITED
STACKTECK SYSTEMS LIMITED p 506
1 PAGET RD, BRAMPTON, ON, L6T 5S2
(416) 749-0680   *SIC* 3544
STACY'S AUTO RANCH LIMITED p 441
366 DUFFERIN ST, BRIDGEWATER, NS, B4V 2H2
(902) 212-0024   *SIC* 5511
STADIUM CONSULTANTS INTERNATIONAL INC p 957

14 DUNCAN ST, TORONTO, ON, M5H 3G8
(416) 591-6777   *SIC* 8742
STADIUM NISSAN INC p 41
2420 CROWCHILD TRAIL NW, CALGARY, AB, T2M 4N5
(403) 284-4611   *SIC* 5511
STAEBLER INSURANCE p 635
See H. L. STAEBLER COMPANY LIMITED
STAEDTLER-MARS LIMITED p 744
850 MATHESON BLVD W UNIT 4, MISSISSAUGA, ON, L5V 0B4
(905) 501-9008   *SIC* 5199
STAFF p 1173
See STAFF PERSONNEL EVENEMENTIEL INC
STAFF OF THE NON-PUBLIC FUNDS, CANADIAN FORCES p 815
101 COLONEL BY DR, OTTAWA, ON, K1A 0K2
(613) 995-8509   *SIC* 8399
STAFF PERSONNEL EVENEMENTIEL INC p 1173
5000 RUE D'IBERVILLE BUREAU 239, MONTREAL, QC, H2H 2S6
(514) 899-8776   *SIC* 7389
STAFF RELIEF HEALTH CARE SERVICES INC p 854
350 HIGHWAY 7 E UNIT PH4, RICHMOND HILL, ON, L4B 3N2
(905) 709-1767   *SIC* 8621
STAFFORD TEXTILES LIMITED p 580
1 EVA RD SUITE 101, ETOBICOKE, ON, M9C 4Z5
(416) 252-3133   *SIC* 5131
STAFTEX p 580
See STAFFORD TEXTILES LIMITED
STAG SHOP p 932
See TC BIZZ.COM CORP
STAG TIMBER, DIV OF p 282
See TEAL CEDAR PRODUCTS LTD
STAGE WEST THEATRE RESTAURANT p 28
See CHALMERS INVESTMENT CORP LTD
STAGELINE GROUPE INC p 1120
827 BOUL DE L'ANGE-GARDIEN, L'ASSOMPTION, QC, J5W 1T3
(450) 589-1063   *SIC* 6712
STAGELINE SCENE MOBILE INC p 1120
700 RUE MARSOLAIS, L'ASSOMPTION, QC, J5W 2G9
(450) 589-1063   *SIC* 3999
STAGELINE SCENE MOBILE INC p 1120
827 BOUL DE L'ANGE-GARDIEN, L'ASSOMPTION, QC, J5W 1T3
(450) 589-1063   *SIC* 3999
STAGEM DIVISION ENTREPRISE D'INSERTION INC p 1287
150 RTE DE SAINTE-HEDWIDGE, ROBERVAL, QC, G8H 2M9
(418) 275-7241   *SIC* 2421
STAGEVISION INC p 707
5915 COOPERS AVE, MISSISSAUGA, ON, L4Z 1R9
(905) 890-8200   *SIC* 7389
STAGEWEST ALL SUITE HOTEL & THEATRE RESTAURANT p 697
See MAYFIELD SUITES GENERAL PARTNER INC
STAHL PETERBILT INC p 103
18020 118 AVE NW, EDMONTON, AB, T5S 2G2
(780) 483-6666   *SIC* 5511
STAHL PETERBILT PACLEASE p 103
See STAHL PETERBILT INC
STAHLSCHMIDT CABLE SYSTEMS p 700
See STAHLSCHMIDT LTD
STAHLSCHMIDT LTD p 700
5208 EVEREST DR, MISSISSAUGA, ON, L4W 2R4
(905) 629-4568   *SIC* 3465
STAINLESS PROCESS EQUIPMENT INC p 736
1317 CARDIFF BLVD, MISSISSAUGA, ON,

L5S 1R1
(905) 670-1163   *SIC* 5046
STAIRFAB AND RAILINGS INC p 756
450 KENT RD, NEWMARKET, ON, L3Y 4Y9
(905) 895-1050   *SIC* 2431
STALCO INC p 916
64 BAKERSFIELD ST, TORONTO, ON, M3J 2W7
(647) 367-2459   *SIC* 4783
STAMBAUGH HOLDINGS LTD p 130
18 WESTPARK CRT, FORT SASKATCHEWAN, AB, T8L 3W9
(780) 992-1600   *SIC* 6712
STAMCO PLASTICS p 116
See STAMCO SPECIALTY TOOL & MFG. CO. (1979) LTD
STAMCO SPECIALTY TOOL & MFG. CO. (1979) LTD p 116
6048 97 ST NW, EDMONTON, AB, T6E 3J4
(780) 436-2647   *SIC* 3599
STAMP-A-TRON MANUFACTURING, DIV OF p 1033
See ROYAL AUTOMOTIVE GROUP LTD
STAMPEDE CRANE & RIGGING p 177
See TNT CRANE & RIGGING CANADA INC
STAMPEDE DRILLING INC p 60
250 6 AVE SW 22ND FLR, CALGARY, AB, T2P 3H7
(403) 984-5042   *SIC* 7353
STAMPEDE ELECTRIC INC p 71
4300 118 AVE SE, CALGARY, AB, T2Z 4A4
(587) 327-2777   *SIC* 1731
STAMPEDE PONTIAC BUICK (1988) LTD p 60
1110 9 AVE SW, CALGARY, AB, T2P 1M1
SIC 5511
STAMPEDE PONTIAC BUICK GMC p 60
See STAMPEDE PONTIAC BUICK (1988) LTD
STAMPEDE TOYOTA p 9
See STAMPEDE TOYOTA & LEASING LTD
STAMPEDE TOYOTA & LEASING LTD p 9
2508 24 AVE NE, CALGARY, AB, T1Y 6R8
(403) 291-2111   *SIC* 5511
STANCE HEALTHCARE INC p 637
45 GOODRICH DR, KITCHENER, ON, N2C 0B8
(519) 896-2400   *SIC* 5047
STANDARD & POORS'S RATING SERVICES p 987
130 KING ST W SUITE 1100, TORONTO, ON, M5X 2A2
(416) 507-2500   *SIC* 6289
STANDARD AERO LIMITED p 227
21330 56 AVE UNIT 48, LANGLEY, BC, V2Y 0E5
(604) 514-0388   *SIC* 4581
STANDARD AERO LIMITED p 256
20699 WESTMINSTER HWY, RICHMOND, BC, V6V 1B3
(604) 273-6040   *SIC* 4581
STANDARD AERO LIMITED p 265
4551 AGAR DR, RICHMOND, BC, V7B 1A4
(604) 276-7600   *SIC* 4581
STANDARD AERO LIMITED p 385
33 ALLEN DYNE RD, WINNIPEG, MB, R3H 1A1
(204) 775-9711   *SIC* 7538
STANDARD AERO LIMITED p 385
570 FERRY RD SUITE 4, WINNIPEG, MB, R3H 0T7
SIC 7538
STANDARD AUTO WRECKERS p 878
See GOLDY METALS INC
STANDARD BROADCAST PRODUCTIONS LTD p 1215
1411 RUE DU FORT UNITE 300, MONTREAL, QC, H3H 2N7
(514) 989-2523   *SIC* 4832
STANDARD BUILDING SUPPLIES LTD p 187
4925 STILL CREEK AVE, BURNABY, BC, V5C 5V1

(604) 294-4411   *SIC 5031*
STANDARD FIRE PROTECTION INC *p 998*
254 ATTWELL DR, TORONTO, ON, M9W
5B2
(416) 240-7980   *SIC 7389*
STANDARD GENERAL ASPHALT PLANT
INC *p 106*
12230 170 ST NW, EDMONTON, AB, T5V
1L7
(780) 447-1666   *SIC 2951*
STANDARD GENERAL INC *p 166*
250 CARLETON DR, ST. ALBERT, AB, T8N
6W2
(780) 459-6611   *SIC 1611*
STANDARD HEAT TREATING *p 367*
See STANDARD MANUFACTURERS SER-
VICES LTD
STANDARD INSURANCE BROKERS LTD,
THE *p 628*
319 SECOND ST S, KENORA, ON, P9N
1G3
(807) 468-3333   *SIC 6411*
STANDARD LAND COMPANY INC *p 60*
734 7 AVE SW SUITE 1400, CALGARY, AB,
T2P 3P8
(403) 269-3931   *SIC 8741*
STANDARD MACHINE *p 1430*
See TIMKEN CANADA LP
STANDARD MANUFACTURERS SERVICES
LTD *p 367*
691 GOLSPIE ST, WINNIPEG, MB, R2K
2V3
(204) 956-6300   *SIC 5084*
STANDARD MECHANICAL SYSTEMS LIM-
ITED *p*
703
3055 UNIVERSAL DR, MISSISSAUGA, ON,
L4X 2E2
(905) 625-9505   *SIC 1711*
STANDARD MOTORS (77) LTD *p 1436*
44 2ND AVE NW, SWIFT CURRENT, SK,
S9H 0N9
(306) 773-3131   *SIC 5511*
STANDARD PAINT SYSTEMS LTD *p 1033*
80 ASHBRIDGE CIR UNIT 1-4, WOOD-
BRIDGE, ON, L4L 3R5
SIC 1721
STANDARD SECURITIES CAPITAL COR-
PORATION *p*
973
24 HAZELTON AVE, TORONTO, ON, M5R
2E2
SIC 6211
STANDARD TOOL & MOLD INC *p 1024*
5110 HALFORD DR, WINDSOR, ON, N9A
6J3
(519) 737-1778   *SIC 3544*
STANDARD WEST STEEL LTD *p 156*
6749 65 AVE, RED DEER, AB, T4P 1X5
(403) 358-4227   *SIC 3441*
STANDARDBRED CANADA *p 727*
2150 MEADOWVALE BLVD SUITE 1, MIS-
SISSAUGA, ON, L5N 6R6
(905) 858-3060   *SIC 8611*
STANDEN'S MANAGEMENT INC *p 37*
1222 58 AVE SE, CALGARY, AB, T2H 2E9
(403) 258-7800   *SIC 3714*
STANEX INC *p 1331*
2437 RUE GUENETTE, SAINT-LAURENT,
QC, H4R 2E9
(514) 333-5280   *SIC 5065*
STANFIELD'S LIMITED *p 469*
1 LOGAN ST, TRURO, NS, B2N 5C2
(902) 895-5406   *SIC 2322*
STANFORD INN *p 131*
See 287706 ALBERTA LTD
STANG'S AUTOMOTIVE ENTERPRISES
INC *p 9*
3003 32 AVE NE, CALGARY, AB, T1Y 6J1
(403) 291-7060   *SIC 5511*
STANHOPE SIMPSON INSURANCE LIM-
ITED *p*
457
3845 JOSEPH HOWE DR SUITE 300, HAL-

IFAX, NS, B3L 4H9
(902) 454-8641   *SIC 6411*
STANLEY BLACK & DECKER CANADA *p*
519
See BLACK & DECKER CANADA INC
STANLEY BLACK & DECKER CANADA
CORPORATION *p 727*
6275 MILLCREEK DR, MISSISSAUGA, ON,
L5N 7K6
(289) 290-4638   *SIC 3429*
STANLEY DOOR SYSTEMS *p 1162*
See PORTES DUSCO LTEE, LES
STANLEY HARDWARE *p 727*
See STANLEY BLACK & DECKER CANADA
CORPORATION
STANLEY HEALTHCARE SOLUTIONS *p*
625
See XMARK CORPORATION
STANLEY KNOWLES SCHOOL *p 370*
See WINNIPEG SCHOOL DIVISION
STANLEY MUTUAL INSURANCE COM-
PANY *p*
418
32 IRISHTOWN RD, STANLEY, NB, E6B
1B6
(506) 367-2273   *SIC 6331*
STANLEY PARK INVESTMENTS LTD *p 39*
12025 LAKE FRASER DR SE, CALGARY,
AB, T2J 7G5
(403) 225-3000   *SIC 7011*
STANLEY SECURITY SOLUTIONS
CANADA INC *p 1341*
160 RUE GRAVELINE, SAINT-LAURENT,
QC, H4T 1R7
SIC 5065
STANLEY'S OLDE MAPLE LANE FARM *p*
567
See 103190 ONTARIO INC
STANMORE EQUIPMENT LIMITED *p 895*
3 ANDERSON BLVD, STOUFFVILLE, ON,
L4A 7X4
(416) 291-1928   *SIC 5082*
STANPAC INC *p 882*
2790 THOMPSON RD, SMITHVILLE, ON,
L0R 2A0
(905) 957-3326   *SIC 2675*
STANPRO LIGHTING SYSTEMS INC *p 1095*
2233 RUE DE L'AVIATION, DORVAL, QC,
H9P 2X6
(514) 739-9984   *SIC 5063*
STANTEC ARCHITECTURE LTD *p 11*
325 25 ST SE SUITE 200, CALGARY, AB,
T2A 7H8
(403) 716-8000   *SIC 8711*
STANTEC ARCHITECTURE LTD *p 91*
10220 103 AVE NW SUITE 400, EDMON-
TON, AB, T5J 0K4
(780) 917-7000   *SIC 8712*
STANTEC ARCHITECTURE LTD *p 375*
500 / 311 PORTAGE AVE, WINNIPEG, MB,
R3B 2B9
(204) 489-5900   *SIC 8712*
STANTEC ARCHITECTURE LTD *p 748*
1331 CLYDE AVE SUITE 400, NEPEAN,
ON, K2C 3G4
(613) 722-4420   *SIC 8712*
STANTEC ARCHITECTURE QUEBEC LTD *p*
1324
100 BOUL ALEXIS-NIHON BUREAU 110,
SAINT-LAURENT, QC, H4M 2N6
(514) 739-0708   *SIC 8712*
STANTEC CONSULTING *p 375*
See STANTEC ARCHITECTURE LTD
STANTEC CONSULTING INTERNATIONAL
LTD *p 91*
10220 103 AVE NW SUITE 400, EDMON-
TON, AB, T5J 0K4
(780) 917-7000   *SIC 8711*
STANTEC CONSULTING INTERNATIONAL
LTD *p 764*
147 MCINTYRE ST W SUITE 200, NORTH
BAY, ON, P1B 2Y5
(705) 494-8255   *SIC 8711*
STANTEC CONSULTING LTD *p 91*

10220 103 AVE NW SUITE 400, EDMON-
TON, AB, T5J 0K4
(780) 917-7000   *SIC 8711*
STANTEC CONSULTING LTD *p 375*
311 PORTAGE AVE UNIT 500, WINNIPEG,
MB, R3B 2B9
(204) 489-5900   *SIC 8711*
STANTEC CONSULTING LTD *p 431*
141 KELSEY DR, ST. JOHN'S, NL, A1B 0L2
(709) 576-1458   *SIC 8711*
STANTEC CONSULTING LTD *p 655*
171 QUEENS AVE 6TH FLOOR, LONDON,
ON, N6A 5J7
(519) 645-2007   *SIC 8711*
STANTEC CONSULTING LTD *p 675*
675 COCHRANE DR SUITE 300 W,
MARKHAM, ON, L3R 0B8
(905) 944-7777   *SIC 8711*
STANTEC CONSULTING LTD *p 1009*
300 HAGEY BLVD SUITE 100, WATERLOO,
ON, N2L 0A4
(519) 579-4410   *SIC 8711*
STANTEC CONSULTING LTD *p 1079*
255 RUE RACINE E, CHICOUTIMI, QC,
G7H 7L2
(418) 549-6680   *SIC 8711*
STANTEC CONSULTING LTD *p 1208*
1060 BOUL ROBERT-BOURASSA UNITE
600, MONTREAL, QC, H3B 4V3
(514) 281-1033   *SIC 8711*
STANTEC EXPERTS-CONSEILS LTEE *p*
1079
See STANTEC CONSULTING LTD
STANTEC GEOMATICS LTD *p 11*
325 25 ST SE SUITE 200, CALGARY, AB,
T2A 7H8
(403) 716-8000   *SIC 8713*
STANTEC GEOMATICS LTD *p 91*
10220 103 AVE NW SUITE 400, EDMON-
TON, AB, T5J 0K4
(780) 917-7000   *SIC 8713*
STANTEC GEOMATICS LTD *p 1009*
300 HAGEY BLVD SUITE 100, WATERLOO,
ON, N2L 0A4
(519) 579-4410   *SIC 8713*
STANTEC INC *p 91*
10220 103 AVE NW SUITE 400, EDMON-
TON, AB, T5J 0K4
(780) 917-7000   *SIC 8711*
STANTEC LAND SURVEYING LTD. *p 191*
4730 KINGSWAY SUITE 500, BURNABY,
BC, V5H 0C6
(604) 436-3014   *SIC 8713*
STANTON DISTRIBUTING & LIQUOR OP-
ERATIONS *p*
435
See STANTON DISTRIBUTING CO LTD
STANTON DISTRIBUTING CO LTD *p 435*
49 NAVY RD, INUVIK, NT, X0E 0T0
(867) 777-4381   *SIC 5141*
STANTON TERRITORIAL HEALTH AU-
THORITY *p*
436
550 BYRNE RD, YELLOWKNIFE, NT, X1A
2N1
(867) 669-4111   *SIC 8062*
STANTON TERRITORIAL HOSPITAL *p 436*
See STANTON TERRITORIAL HEALTH AU-
THORITY
STAPLES CANADA ULC *p 456*
2003 GOTTINGEN ST, HALIFAX, NS, B3K
3B1
(902) 474-5100   *SIC 5943*
STAPLES CANADA ULC *p 854*
6 STAPLES AVE, RICHMOND HILL, ON,
L4B 4W3
(905) 737-1147   *SIC 5943*
STAPLES PROMOTIONAL PRODUCTS *p*
559
See STAPLES PROMOTIONAL PROD-
UCTS CANADA, LTD
STAPLES PROMOTIONAL PRODUCTS
CANADA, LTD *p 559*
55 INTERCHANGE WAY UNIT 4, CON-

CORD, ON, L4K 5W3
(905) 660-0685   *SIC 8743*
STAPLES THE BUSINESS DEPOT *p 456*
See STAPLES CANADA ULC
STAR ALUMINUM RAILING SYSTEMS INC
p 18
3511 64 AVE SE UNIT 1, CALGARY, AB,
T2C 1N3
(403) 640-7878   *SIC 5051*
STAR BUILDING MATERIALS *p 32*
See STAR BUILDING MATERIALS (AL-
BERTA) LTD
STAR BUILDING MATERIALS (ALBERTA)
LTD *p 32*
2345 ALYTH RD SE, CALGARY, AB, T2G
5T8
(403) 720-0010   *SIC 5211*
STAR BUILDING MATERIALS (ALBERTA)
LTD *p 366*
16 SPEERS RD, WINNIPEG, MB, R2J 1L8
(204) 233-8687   *SIC 5211*
STAR BUILDING MATERIALS LTD *p 367*
16 SPEERS RD SUITE 118, WINNIPEG,
MB, R2J 1L8
(204) 233-8687   *SIC 5211*
STAR CHOICE BUSINESS TELEVISION *p*
25
See STAR CHOICE TELEVISION NET-
WORK INCORPORATED
STAR CHOICE TELEVISION NETWORK IN-
CORPORATED *p*
25
2924 11 ST NE, CALGARY, AB, T2E 7L7
(403) 538-4672   *SIC 4841*
STAR CITY FARMING CO. LTD *p 1436*
GD, STAR CITY, SK, S0E 1P0
(306) 863-2343   *SIC 0119*
STAR EGG CO. LTD *p 1430*
1302 QUEBEC AVE, SASKATOON, SK,
S7K 1V5
(306) 244-4041   *SIC 5144*
STAR LABOUR SUPPLY LTD *p 291*
426E 59TH AVE E, VANCOUVER, BC, V5X
1Y1
(604) 325-1027   *SIC 7361*
STAR LANE *p 526*
See CENTRAL WEST SPECIALIZED DE-
VELOPMENTAL SERVICES
STAR LIMOUSINE SERVICE LTD *p 296*
328 INDUSTRIAL AVE, VANCOUVER, BC,
V6A 2P3
(604) 685-5600   *SIC 7514*
STAR MARKETING LTD *p 280*
3289 190 ST, SURREY, BC, V3Z 1A7
(778) 574-0778   *SIC 5141*
STAR OFFICE INSTALLINS LTD *p 917*
85 NORTHLINE RD, TORONTO, ON, M4B
3E9
(416) 750-1104   *SIC 6712*
STAR ONE MOTOR CO *p 1015*
250 THICKSON RD S, WHITBY, ON, L1N
9Z1
(905) 666-8805   *SIC 5511*
STAR PACKAGING EQUIPMENT LIMITED *p*
743
6935 DAVAND DR, MISSISSAUGA, ON,
L5T 1L5
(905) 564-0092   *SIC 5084*
STAR PLASTICS INC *p 736*
1930 DREW RD UNIT 1, MISSISSAUGA,
ON, L5S 1J6
(905) 672-0298   *SIC 3089*
STAR PRODUCE *p 194*
See SUN PROCESSING LTD
STAR PRODUCE LTD *p 1425*
2941 PORTAGE AVE, SASKATOON, SK,
S7J 3S6
(306) 934-0999   *SIC 5148*
STAR QUALITY OFFICE FURNITURE MFG
LTD *p 1033*
10 WESTCREEK DR SUITE 16, WOOD-
BRIDGE, ON, L4L 9R5
(416) 741-8000   *SIC 5712*
STAR SALT INC *p 1224*

3351 RUE SAINT-PATRICK, MONTREAL, QC, H4E 1A1
(514) 933-1117   SIC 5149

STAR SECURITY INCORPORATED p 714
2351 ROYAL WINDSOR DR SUITE 205, MISSISSAUGA, ON, L5J 4S7
(905) 855-7827   SIC 7381

STAR SUPPLY INC p 884
530 EASTCHESTER AVE E, ST CATHARINES, ON, L2M 7P3
(905) 641-1240   SIC 5084

STAR SYSTEM p 18
See STAR ALUMINUM RAILING SYSTEMS INC

STAR SYSTEM INTERNATIONAL p 187
See SNAP TIGHT ALUMINUM RAILING SYSTEM INTERNATIONAL LTD

STAR TRUSS, DIV OF p 367
See STAR BUILDING MATERIALS LTD

STAR-TECH ENTERPRISES INC p 657
25 INVICTA CRT, LONDON, ON, N6E 2T4
(519) 681-8672   SIC 3544

STARBOARD SEAFOOD (ONTARIO) INC p 869
33 UPTON RD, SCARBOROUGH, ON, M1L 2C1
(416) 752-2828   SIC 5146

STARBRITE HUTTERIAN BRETHREN p 127
GD, FOREMOST, AB, T0K 0X0
(403) 867-2299   SIC 5144

STARBUCKS COFFEE CANADA, INC p 773
5140 YONGE ST SUITE 1205, NORTH YORK, ON, M2N 6L7
(416) 228-7300   SIC 5812

STARBUCKS COFFEE COMPANY p 773
See STARBUCKS COFFEE CANADA. INC

STARCAN CORPORATION p 967
211 QUEENS QUAY W SUITE 908, TORONTO, ON, M5J 2M6
(416) 361-0255   SIC 6712

STARCHOICEONE SOLUTIONS, A DIV p 860
See PLEASE HOLD CANADA INC

STARCOM MEDIAVEST GROUP SMG p 930
175 BLOOR ST E SUITE 1200N, TORONTO, ON, M4W 3R9
(416) 927-3300   SIC 7311

STARCOM WORLDWIDE p 930
See STARCOM MEDIAVEST GROUP SMG

STARCORE INTERNATIONAL MINES LTD p 309
580 HORNBY ST SUITE 750, VANCOUVER, BC, V6C 3B6
(604) 602-4935   SIC 1041

STARFIELD LION COMPANY INC p 791
22 BENTON RD, NORTH YORK, ON, M6M 3G4
(416) 789-4354   SIC 3842

STARFISH MEDICAL p 339
See STARFISH PRODUCT ENGINEERING INC

STARFISH PRODUCT ENGINEERING INC p 339
455 BOLESKINE RD, VICTORIA, BC, V8Z 1E7
(250) 388-3537   SIC 3841

STARK IRON & METAL p 993
See 1222433 ONTARIO INC

STARKEY LABS-CANADA CO p 727
2476 ARGENTIA RD SUITE 301, MISSISSAUGA, ON, L5N 6M1
(905) 542-7555   SIC 3842

STARKMAN HOME HEALTH CARE DEPOT p 974
See STARKMAN SURGICAL SUPPLY INC

STARKMAN SURGICAL SUPPLY INC p 974
1243 BATHURST ST, TORONTO, ON, M5R 3H3
(416) 534-8411   SIC 5047

STARKS PLUMBING AND HEATING LTD p 147
4850 BOX SPRINGS RD NW, MEDICINE HAT, AB, T1C 0C8
(403) 527-2929   SIC 1711

STARKS PLUMBING HEATING & ELECTRICAL p 147
See STARKS PLUMBING AND HEATING LTD

STARLIGHT CASINO p 189
See GATEWAY CASINOS & ENTERTAINMENT INC

STARLIGHT CASINO p 237
See GATEWAY CASINOS & ENTERTAINMENT INC

STARLIGHT INVESTMENTS p 572
3280 BLOOR ST W UNIT 1400, ETOBICOKE, ON, M8X 2X3
(416) 234-8444   SIC 6531

STARLIGHT INVESTMENTS p 996
See STARLIGHT U.S. MULTI-FAMILY (NO.5) CORE FUND

STARLIGHT INVESTMENTS LTD p 572
3280 BLOOR ST W UNIT 1400, ETOBICOKE, ON, M8X 2X3
(416) 234-8444   SIC 6799

STARLIGHT U.S. MULTI-FAMILY (NO.5) CORE FUND p 996
3280 BLOOR ST W SUITE 1400, TORONTO, ON, M8X 2X3
(416) 234-8444   SIC 6722

STARLINE WINDOW p 338
See BOLZANO HOLDINGS LTD

STARLINE WINDOWS (2001) LTD p 280
19091 36 AVE, SURREY, BC, V3Z 0P6
(604) 882-5100   SIC 5031

STARLINE WINDOWS LTD p 280
19091 36 AVE, SURREY, BC, V3Z 0P6
(604) 882-5100   SIC 3442

STARLITE ILLUMINATION INC p 341
81 DEEP DENE RD, WEST VANCOUVER, BC, V7S 1A1
(604) 926-4808   SIC 7389

STARPLEX p 588
See STARPLEX SCIENTIFIC INC

STARPLEX SCIENTIFIC INC p 588
50A STEINWAY BLVD, ETOBICOKE, ON, M9W 6Y3
(416) 674-7474   SIC 3841

STARR CULINARY DELIGHTS INC p 689
3880 NASHUA DR, MISSISSAUGA, ON, L4V 1M5
(905) 612-1958   SIC 5149

STARR, MARVIN PONTIAC BUICK CADILLAC INC p 867
3132 EGLINTON AVE E, SCARBOROUGH, ON, M1J 2H1
SIC 5511

STARS p 134
See SHOCK TRAUMA AIR RESCUE SERVICE

STARS AIR AMBULANCE SERVICE p 25
See SHOCK TRAUMA AIR RESCUE SERVICE

STARS AVIATION CANADA INC p 25
1441 AVIATION PK NE, CALGARY, AB, T2E 8M7
(403) 295-1811   SIC 4522

STARS GROUP INC, THE p 967
200 BAY ST SUITE 3205, TORONTO, ON, M5J 2J3
(437) 371-5742   SIC 3944

STARS MENS SHOPS p 784
See STRAUSSCO HOLDINGS LTD

STARSHIP FREIGHT p 594
See STARSHIP LOGISTICS INC

STARSHIP LOGISTICS INC p 594
36 ARMSTRONG AVE SUITE 200, GEORGETOWN, ON, L7G 4R9
(905) 702-1800   SIC 4731

STARSKY FINE FOODS MISSISSAUGA INC p 703
2040 DUNDAS ST E UNIT 2, MISSISSAUGA, ON, L4X 2X8
(905) 279-8889   SIC 5411

STARSKY FINE FOODS MISSISSAUGA INC p 717

3115 DUNDAS ST W, MISSISSAUGA, ON, L5L 3R8
(905) 363-2000   SIC 5411

STARTCO ENGINEERING LTD p 1434
3714 KINNEAR PL, SASKATOON, SK, S7P 0A6
(306) 373-5505   SIC 3699

STARTEC REFRIGERATION & COMPRESSION p 25
7664 10 ST NE SUITE 11, CALGARY, AB, T2E 8W1
(403) 347-1131   SIC 1711

STARTEC REFRIGERATION SERVICES LTD p 18
9423 SHEPARD RD SE, CALGARY, AB, T2C 4R6
(403) 295-5855   SIC 3563

STARTECH.COM LTD p 650
45 ARTISANS CRES, LONDON, ON, N5V 5E9
(800) 265-1844   SIC 5045

STARWOOD CANADA ULC p 60
320 4 AVE SW, CALGARY, AB, T2P 2S6
(403) 266-1611   SIC 7011

STARWOOD CANADA ULC p 822
11 COLONEL BY DR, OTTAWA, ON, K1N 9H4
(613) 560-7000   SIC 7011

STARWOOD CANADA ULC p 957
123 QUEEN ST W SUITE 100, TORONTO, ON, M5H 2M9
(416) 947-4955   SIC 7011

STARWOOD HOTEL p 727
2501 ARGENTIA RD, MISSISSAUGA, ON, L5N 4G8
(905) 858-2424   SIC 7011

STARWOOD HOTELS & RESORTS, INC p 1208
1201 BOUL RENE-LEVESQUE O BUREAU 217, MONTREAL, QC, H3B 2L7
(514) 878-2046   SIC 7011

STARWOOD MANUFACTURING INC p 714
2370 SOUTH SHERIDAN WAY, MISSISSAUGA, ON, L5J 2M4
SIC 2426

STAS INC p 1080
622 RUE DES ACTIONNAIRES, CHICOUTIMI, QC, G7J 5A9
(418) 696-0074   SIC 3569

STATE p 1002
See STATE WINDOW CORPORATION

STATE BUILDING MAINTENANCE LIMITED p 580
34 ASHMOUNT CRES, ETOBICOKE, ON, M9R 1C7
(416) 247-1290   SIC 7349

STATE CHEMICAL LTD p 743
1745 MEYERSIDE DR SUITE 1, MISSISSAUGA, ON, L5T 1C6
(905) 670-4669   SIC 5169

STATE FARM FINANCE p 482
See STATE FARM INSURANCE

STATE FARM INSURANCE p 481
See SF INSURANCE PLACEMENT CORPORATION OF CANADA

STATE FARM INSURANCE p 482
333 FIRST COMMERCE DR, AURORA, ON, L4G 8A4
(905) 750-4100   SIC 6411

STATE FARM INSURANCE p 525
5420 NORTH SERVICE RD SUITE 400, BURLINGTON, ON, L7L 6C7
(905) 315-3900   SIC 6411

STATE FARM INSURANCE COMPANIES p 9
2611 37 AVE NE SUITE 3, CALGARY, AB, T1Y 5V7
(403) 291-1283   SIC 6411

STATE GROUP INC, THE p 689
3206 ORLANDO DR, MISSISSAUGA, ON, L4V 1R5
(905) 672-2772   SIC 1731

STATE REALTY LIMITED p 478
1122 WILSON ST W, ANCASTER, ON, L9G

3K9
(905) 648-4451   SIC 6531

STATE REALTY LIMITED p 615
987 RYMAL RD E, HAMILTON, ON, L8W 3M2
(905) 574-4600   SIC 6531

STATE REALTY LIMITED p 894
115 HIGHWAY 8, STONEY CREEK, ON, L8G 1C1
(905) 662-6666   SIC 6531

STATE WINDOW CORPORATION p 1002
220 HUNTER'S VALLEY RD, VAUGHAN, ON, L4H 3V9
(416) 646-1421   SIC 3442

STATESMAN CORPORATION p 75
7370 SIERRA MORENA BLVD SW, CALGARY, AB, T3H 4H9
(403) 256-4151   SIC 1522

STATESMAN GROUP OF COMPANIES LTD, THE p 75
7370 SIERRA MORENA BLVD SW SUITE 200, CALGARY, AB, T3H 4H9
(403) 256-4151   SIC 1531

STATESMEN REALTY CORPORATION p 223
1980 COOPER RD SUITE 108, KELOWNA, BC, V1Y 8K5
(250) 861-5122   SIC 6531

STATEVIEW HOMES LTD p 1034
410 CHRISLEA RD UNIT 1, WOODBRIDGE, ON, L4L 8B5
(905) 851-1849   SIC 1521

STATION 50 p 620
2 STATION, HILLSBURGH, ON, N0B 1Z0
SIC 7389

STATION CREEK GOLF CLUB p 598
See CLUBLINK CORPORATION ULC

STATION D'EPURATION p 1161
See VILLE DE MONTREAL

STATION D'EPURATION DES EAU USE, LA JEAN-R-MARCOTTE p 1161
See VILLE DE MONTREAL

STATION DE SKI MONT-ORIGNAL p 1124
See EQUIPE JUNIOR DE SKI DU MONT ORIGNAL INC

STATION INNU ENR p 1389
100 BOUL DES MONTAGNAIS, UASHAT, QC, G4R 5P9
(418) 968-4866   SIC 5541

STATION MONT TREMBLANT INC p 1159
1000 CH DES VOYAGEURS, MONT-TREMBLANT, QC, J8E 1T1
(819) 681-3000   SIC 7011

STATION MONT-SAINTE-ANNE INC p 1055
2000 BOUL DU BEAU-PRE BUREAU 400, BEAUPRE, QC, G0A 1E0
(418) 827-4561   SIC 7011

STATION MONT-TREMBLANT SOCIETE EN COMMANDITE p 1159
1000 CH DES VOYAGEURS, MONT-TREMBLANT, QC, J8E 1T1
(819) 681-2000   SIC 7011

STATION PARK LOGISTICS p 890
28 MAJESTIC CRT, ST THOMAS, ON, N5R 0B9
(519) 207-3399   SIC 4731

STATION SKYSPA INC p 1070
6000 BOUL DE ROME BUREAU 400, BROSSARD, QC, J4Y 0B6
(450) 462-9111   SIC 7991

STATIONNEMENT & DEVELOPPEMENT INTERNATIONAL INC p 1212
544 RUE DE L'INSPECTEUR BUREAU 200, MONTREAL, QC, H3C 2K9
(514) 396-6421   SIC 7521

STATIONNEMENT IMPERIAL p 1211
See IMPERIAL PARKING CANADA CORPORATION

STATTEN, TAYLOR CAMP COMPANY, LIMITED p 924
59 HOYLE AVE, TORONTO, ON, M4S 2X5
(416) 486-6959   SIC 7032

STATTEN, TAYLOR CAMPS p 924

See STATTEN, TAYLOR CAMP COMPANY, LIMITED

STATUM DESIGNS INC p 793
180 NORELCO DR, NORTH YORK, ON, M9L 1S4
(416) 740-4010   *SIC* 2512

STATUS ELECTRICAL CORPORATION p 177
2669 DEACON ST, ABBOTSFORD, BC, V2T 6L4
(604) 859-1892   *SIC* 1731

STAUFFER MOTORS LIMITED p 912
685 BROADWAY ST, TILLSONBURG, ON, N4G 4H1
(519) 842-3646   *SIC* 5511

STAVSTAN INC p 1071
3955 RUE DE LONGFORD, BROSSARD, QC, J4Y 3J6
(450) 445-7390   *SIC* 4225

STAWARM, DIV OF p 278
See AQUIFORM DISTRIBUTORS LTD

STAWNICHY'S HOLDINGS LTD p 148
5212 50 ST, MUNDARE, AB, T0B 3H0
(780) 764-3912   *SIC* 5421

STAWNICHY'S MEAT PROCESSING p 148
See STAWNICHY'S HOLDINGS LTD

STAX PACKAGING SERVICES INC p 650
575 INDUSTRIAL RD, LONDON, ON, N5V 1V2
(519) 455-0119   *SIC* 7389

STAXI CORPORATION LIMITED p 1034
120 JEVLAN DR UNIT 4B, WOODBRIDGE, ON, L4L 8G3
(877) 677-8294   *SIC* 5087

STC STEEL TECHNOLOGIES CANADA LTD p 539
16 CHERRY BLOSSOM RD, CAMBRIDGE, ON, N3H 4R7
(519) 653-2880   *SIC* 7389

STE ANNE'S COUNTRY INN & SPA p 598
See 926715 ONTARIO INC

STE ROSE AUCTION MART LTD p 358
GD, STE ROSE DU LAC, MB, R0L 1S0
(204) 447-2266   *SIC* 5154

STE ROSE GENERAL HOSPITAL p 358
540 3RD AVE E, STE ROSE DU LAC, MB, R0L 1S0
(204) 447-2131   *SIC* 8062

STE-FOY HYUNDAI p 1265
See 2333-2224 QUEBEC INC

STE-FOY TOYOTA p 1272
See GROUPE AUTO STE-FOY INC

STE-MARIE AUTOMOBILES LTEE p 1351
540 RANG NOTRE-DAME, SAINT-REMI, QC, J0L 2L0
(514) 861-5529   *SIC* 5511

STE-MARIE, CLAUDE SPORT INC p 1309
5925 CH DE CHAMBLY, SAINT-HUBERT, QC, J3Y 3R4
(450) 678-4700   *SIC* 5571

STE-THERESE TOYOTA p 1364
See 9146-3000 QUEBEC INC

STEADFAST CEDAR PRODUCTS LTD p 230
27400 LOUGHEED HWY, MAPLE RIDGE, BC, V2W 1L1
(604) 462-7335   *SIC* 5031

STEAK & STEIN RESTAURANT p 443
See CONSOLIDATED RESTAURANTS LIMITED

STEAK AND STEIN STEAK HOUSE p 456
See SMITH & SCOTT STEAKHOUSE LIMITED

STEAM WHISTLE BREWING INC p 983
255 BREMNER BLVD, TORONTO, ON, M5V 3M9
(416) 362-2337   *SIC* 2082

STEAM-ASD p 761
See S TEAM 92 AUTOMATION TECHNOLOGY INC

STEAMATIC METROPOLITAIN INC p 1051
8351 BOUL LOUIS-H.-LAFONTAINE, ANJOU, QC, H1J 3B4
(514) 351-7500   *SIC* 1799

STEAMWORKS BREWING CO p 299
See QUARTERDECK BREWING CO LTD

STEDELBAUER CHEVROLET INC p 84
13145 97 ST NW, EDMONTON, AB, T5E 4C4
(780) 476-6221   *SIC* 5511

STEDFAST INC p 1110
230 RUE SAINT-CHARLES S, GRANBY, QC, J2G 3Y3
(450) 378-8441   *SIC* 2295

STEED & EVANS LIMITED p 887
3000 AMENT LINE, ST CLEMENTS, ON, N0B 2M0
(519) 744-7315   *SIC* 1611

STEEGRAIN INC p 1314
103 RUE SAINTE-GENEVIEVE, SAINT-ISIDORE, QC, G0S 2S0
(418) 882-3731   *SIC* 5153

STEEL - CRAFT DOOR PRODUCTS LTD p 94
13504 ST ALBERT TRAIL NW, EDMONTON, AB, T5L 4P4
(780) 453-3761   *SIC* 3442

STEEL ART SIGNS CORP p 675
37 ESNA PARK DR, MARKHAM, ON, L3R 1C9
(905) 474-1678   *SIC* 3993

STEEL CANADA LIMITED p 707
355 TRADERS BLVD E, MISSISSAUGA, ON, L4Z 2E5
(905) 890-0209   *SIC* 5051

STEEL COMMUNICATION p 430
See NEWFOUNDLAND CAPITAL CORPORATION LIMITED

STEEL FIRE EQUIPMENT LIMITED p 743
150 SUPERIOR BLVD, MISSISSAUGA, ON, L5T 2L2
(905) 564-1500   *SIC* 5087

STEEL MET SUPPLY, DIV OF p 1429
See RELY-EX CONTRACTING INC

STEEL PACIFIC RECYCLING p 334
See 0743398 B.C. LTD

STEEL VIEW ENERGY & INDUSTRIAL SERVICES LTD p 79
222 MAIN ST, CHAUVIN, AB, T0B 0V0
(780) 858-3820   *SIC* 1389

STEELCORE CONSTRUCTION LTD p 865
1295 MORNINGSIDE AVE UNIT 27, SCARBOROUGH, ON, M1B 4Z4
(416) 282-4888   *SIC* 1542

STEELCRAFT INC p 896
904 DOWNIE RD, STRATFORD, ON, N5A 6T3
(519) 271-4750   *SIC* 3443

STEELCRAFT INC p 1009
446 ALBERT ST, WATERLOO, ON, N2L 3V3
(519) 884-4320   *SIC* 3443

STEELE AUTO GROUP LIMITED p 448
8 BASINVIEW DR, DARTMOUTH, NS, B3B 1G4
(902) 454-3185   *SIC* 5511

STEELE CHEVROLET BUICK GMC CADILLAC p 443
636 PORTLAND ST, DARTMOUTH, NS, B2W 2M3
(902) 434-4100   *SIC* 5511

STEELE CHRYSLER PLYMOUTH LIMITED p 457
44 BEDFORD HWY, HALIFAX, NS, B3M 2J2
(902) 454-7341   *SIC* 5511

STEELE DISTRIBUTORS INC p 266
3351 FRANCIS RD, RICHMOND, BC, V7C 1J1
(604) 278-4569   *SIC* 5192

STEELE FORD LINCOLN p 454
See 3041518 NOVA SCOTIA LIMITED

STEELE HYUNDAI p 454
See 3039214 NOVA SCOTIA LIMITED

STEELE MAZDA p 442
See 3067419 NOVA SCOTIA LIMITED

STEELE SECURITY & INVESTIGATION SERVICE DIVISION OF UNITED PROTECTIONS p

116
8055 CORONET RD NW, EDMONTON, AB, T6E 4N7
SIC 7381

STEELE VOLKSWAGEN LIMITED p 448
696 WINDMILL RD, DARTMOUTH, NS, B3B 2A5
(902) 468-6411   *SIC* 5511

STEELHEAD CONTRACTING RENOVATION LTD p 183
4179 MCCONNELL DR, BURNABY, BC, V5A 3J7
(604) 420-9368   *SIC* 1522

STEELHORSE FREIGHT SERVICES INC p 136
82054 466 AVE, HIGH RIVER, AB, T1V 1P3
SIC 4731

STEELITE INTERNATIONAL CANADA LIMITED p 675
26 RIVIERA DR UNIT 2, MARKHAM, ON, L3R 5M1
(905) 752-1074   *SIC* 5023

STEELS CAFE & GRILL p 103
See ROYAL WEST EDMONTON INN LTD

STEELTEC, DIV OF p 913
See BUCKET SHOP INC, THE

STEELTOWN FORD SALES 1980 LTD p 356
933 MANITOBA AVE, SELKIRK, MB, R1A 3T7
(888) 485-3230   *SIC* 5511

STEELWAY BUILDING SYSTEMS p 482
See WHITE, GLEN INDUSTRIES LTD

STEELWOOD DOORS p 1028
See ROYAL GROUP, INC

STEELWORKERS p 249
See NORTHERN INTERIOR WOODWORKERS HOLDING SOCIETY

STEEP ROCK LTD p 81
11524 RANGE ROAD 52 UNIT 1, CYPRESS COUNTY, AB, T1B 0K7
(403) 529-9668   *SIC* 5032

STEERS INSURANCE LIMITED p 429
99 AIRPORT RD UNIT 201, ST. JOHN'S, NL, A1A 4Y3
(709) 722-1532   *SIC* 6411

STEEVES & ROZEMA ENTERPRISES LIMITED p 859
1310 MURPHY RD SUITE 216, SARNIA, ON, N7S 6K5
(519) 542-2939   *SIC* 8059

STEEVES & ROZEMA ENTERPRISES LIMITED p 859
1221 MICHIGAN AVE, SARNIA, ON, N7S 3Y3
(519) 542-5529   *SIC* 8051

STEEVES & ROZEMA ENTERPRISES LIMITED p 861
265 FRONT ST N SUITE 200, SARNIA, ON, N7T 7X1
(519) 344-8829   *SIC* 8051

STEGG LIMITED p 492
294 UNIVERSITY AVE, BELLEVILLE, ON, K8N 5S6
(613) 966-4000   *SIC* 5251

STEIN MONAST S.E.N.C.R.L. p 1260
70 RUE DALHOUSIE BUREAU 300, QUEBEC, QC, G1K 4B2
(418) 529-6531   *SIC* 8111

STEINBACH CREDIT UNION LIMITED p 358
305 MAIN ST, STEINBACH, MB, R5G 1B1
(204) 326-3495   *SIC* 6062

STEINBACH DODGE CHRYSLER LTD p 359
208 MAIN ST, STEINBACH, MB, R5G 1Y6
(204) 326-4461   *SIC* 5511

STEINBACH GARDEN MARKET p 358
See SOBEYS CAPITAL INCORPORATED

STEINBACH REGIONAL SECONDARY SCHOOL p 358
See HANOVER SCHOOL DIVISION

STEINBOCK DEVELOPMENT CORPORATION LTD p 32
140 6 AVE SE, CALGARY, AB, T2G 0G2
(403) 232-4725   *SIC* 7521

STEINER & ALEXANDERS INC p 1244
45 CH BATES BUREAU 200, OUTREMONT, QC, H2V 1A6
(514) 271-1101   *SIC* 5023

STELCO HOLDINGS INC p 611
386 WILCOX ST, HAMILTON, ON, L8L 8K5
(905) 528-2511   *SIC* 6712

STELCO INC p 611
386 WILCOX ST, HAMILTON, ON, L8L 8K5
(905) 528-2511   *SIC* 3312

STELCO INC p 747
2330 HALDIMAND RD 3, NANTICOKE, ON, N0A 1L0
(519) 587-4541   *SIC* 3312

STELFAST INC p 506
5 PARKSHORE DR, BRAMPTON, ON, L6T 5M1
(905) 670-9400   *SIC* 5085

STELIA AERONAUTIQUE CANADA INC p 1153
12000 RUE HENRY-GIFFARD, MIRABEL, QC, J7N 1H4
(450) 595-8300   *SIC* 3721

STELIA AEROSPACE NORTH AMERICA INC p 462
71 HALL ST, LUNENBURG, NS, B0J 2C0
(902) 634-8448   *SIC* 3728

STELIA AMERIQUE DU NORD p 1153
See STELIA AERONAUTIQUE CANADA INC

STELIA NORTH AMERICA p 462
See STELIA AEROSPACE NORTH AMERICA INC

STELLA-JONES INC p 1331
3100 BOUL DE LA COTE-VERTU BUREAU 300, SAINT-LAURENT, QC, H4R 2J8
(514) 934-8666   *SIC* 2491

STELLAR INDUSTRIAL SALES LIMITED p 448
520 WINDMILL RD, DARTMOUTH, NS, B3B 1B3
(902) 468-5499   *SIC* 5085

STELLAR METAL p 1034
See STELLAR METAL PRODUCTS INC

STELLAR METAL PRODUCTS INC p 1034
609 HANLAN RD, WOODBRIDGE, ON, L4L 4R8
(289) 371-0218   *SIC* 5046

STELLARC PRECISION BAR INC p 516
101 WAYNE GRETZKY PKY, BRANTFORD, ON, N3S 7N9
SIC 3316

STELLY'S SECONDARY SCHOOL p 267
See SCHOOL DISTRICT 63 (SAANICH)

STELMASCHUK, W. J. AND ASSOCIATES LTD p 231
22470 DEWDNEY TRUNK RD SUITE 510, MAPLE RIDGE, BC, V2X 5Z6
SIC 8399

STELMASCHUK, W.J. AND ASSOCIATES LTD p 231
11491 KINGSTON ST SUITE 2, MAPLE RIDGE, BC, V2X 0Y6
(604) 465-5515   *SIC* 8741

STELPRO DESIGN INC p 1296
1041 RUE PARENT, SAINT-BRUNO, QC, J3V 6L7
(450) 441-0101   *SIC* 3433

STEMCELL TECHNOLOGIES CANADA INC p 293
570 7TH AVE W SUITE 400, VANCOUVER, BC, V5Z 1B3
(604) 877-0713   *SIC* 8733

STEMCELL TECHNOLOGIES CANADA INC p 296
1618 STATION ST, VANCOUVER, BC, V6A 1B6
(604) 877-0713   *SIC* 2836

STEMMLER MEATS & CHEESE p 619

See STEMMLER MEATS & CHEESE (HEIDELBERG) INCORPORATED

STEMMLER MEATS & CHEESE (HEIDELBERG) INCORPORATED *p*
619
3031 LOBSINGER LINE, HEIDELBERG, ON, N0B 2M1
(519) 699-4590   *SIC 5421*

STEMSOFT SOFTWARE *p 293*
See STEMCELL TECHNOLOGIES CANADA INC

STENEK CORPORATION *p 438*
40 TANTRAMAR CRES, AMHERST, NS, B4H 0A1
SIC 5043

STENTECH *p 679*
See 1359470 ONTARIO INC.

STEP ENERGY SERVICES LTD *p 60*
205 5 AVE SW SUITE 1200, CALGARY, AB, T2P 2V7
(403) 457-1772   *SIC 1731*

STEPAN CANADA INC *p 662*
3800 LONGFORD MILLS RD, LONGFORD MILLS, ON, L0K 1L0
(705) 326-7329   *SIC 2869*

STEPHANI MOTORS LTD *p 5*
4811 53 ST, BARRHEAD, AB, T7N 1G2
(780) 674-2211   *SIC 5511*

STEPHEN GROUP INC., THE *p 381*
765 WELLINGTON AVE, WINNIPEG, MB, R3E 0J1
(204) 697-6100   *SIC 7215*

STEPHEN LEACOCK COLLEGIATE INSTITUTE *p*
875
See TORONTO DISTRICT SCHOOL BOARD

STEPHEN MACDONALD PHARMACY INC *p*
822
334 CUMBERLAND ST, OTTAWA, ON, K1N 7J2
(705) 325-2377   *SIC 5912*

STEPHENS BUILDING SUPPLIES *p 467*
See JONELJIM INVESTMENTS LIMITED

STEPHENSON SENIOR LINK HOME *p 917*
See NEIGHBOURHOOD GROUP COMMUNITY SERVICES, THE

STEPHENSON'S RENTAL SERVICES INC *p*
743
6895 COLUMBUS RD SUITE 502, MISSISSAUGA, ON, L5T 2G9
(905) 507-3650   *SIC 7359*

STERICYCLE COMMUNICATION SOLUTIONS, ULC *p*
777
2 DUNCAN MILL RD, NORTH YORK, ON, M3B 1Z4
SIC 4899

STERICYCLE ULC *p 506*
19 ARMTHORPE RD, BRAMPTON, ON, L6T 5M4
(905) 595-2651   *SIC 4953*

STERICYCLE ULC *p 506*
95 DEERHURST DR SUITE 1, BRAMPTON, ON, L6T 5R7
(905) 789-6660   *SIC 4953*

STERICYCLE, ULC *p 506*
See STERICYCLE ULC

STERINOVA INC *p 1313*
3005 AV JOSE-MARIA-ROSELL, SAINT-HYACINTHE, QC, J2S 0J9
(450) 252-2520   *SIC 2834*

STERIPRO CANADA INC *p 689*
6580 NORTHWEST DR UNIT B, MISSISSAUGA, ON, L4V 1L5
(905) 766-4051   *SIC 8742*

STERIS CANADA INC *p 707*
375 BRITANNIA RD E UNIT 2, MISSISSAUGA, ON, L4Z 3E2
(905) 677-0863   *SIC 5047*

STERIS CANADA ULC *p 1255*
490 BOUL ARMAND-PARIS, QUEBEC, QC, G1C 8A3
(418) 664-1549   *SIC 3431*

STERLING CENTRECORP INC *p 675*
2851 JOHN ST SUITE 1, MARKHAM, ON, L3R 5R7
(905) 477-9200   *SIC 6552*

STERLING CRANE DIV. *p 123*
See PROCRANE INC

STERLING FORD SALES (OTTAWA) INC *p*
596
1425 OGILVIE RD, GLOUCESTER, ON, K1J 7P3
(613) 741-3720   *SIC 5511*

STERLING HEALTH SERVICES CORP *p*
296
1188 QUEBEC ST SUITE 1402, VANCOUVER, BC, V6A 4B3
(604) 261-2616   *SIC 8741*

STERLING HOFFMAN *p 801*
See STERLING IM INC

STERLING HOMES (EDMONTON) LTD *p*
121
3203 93 ST NW, EDMONTON, AB, T6N 0B2
(780) 461-8369   *SIC 1531*

STERLING HOMES LTD *p 37*
5709 2 ST SE SUITE 200, CALGARY, AB, T2H 2W4
(403) 253-7476   *SIC 1522*

STERLING HONDA *p 616*
See 1053038 ONTARIO LIMITED

STERLING IM INC *p 801*
610 CHARTWELL RD SUITE 101, OAKVILLE, ON, L6J 4A5
(416) 979-6701   *SIC 7361*

STERLING KARAMAR PROPERTY MANAGEMENT *p*
774
See STERLING SILVER DEVELOPMENT CORPORATION

STERLING MARINE FUELS *p 1025*
3565 RUSSELL ST, WINDSOR, ON, N9C 1E8
(519) 253-4694   *SIC 5551*

STERLING MARKING PRODUCTS INC *p*
659
1147 GAINSBOROUGH RD, LONDON, ON, N6H 5L5
(519) 434-5785   *SIC 3953*

STERLING MUTUALS INC *p 1024*
880 OUELLETTE AVE, WINDSOR, ON, N9A 1C7
(519) 256-8999   *SIC 6211*

STERLING NEWSPAPERS GROUP *p 324*
1200 73RD AVE W SUITE 920, VANCOUVER, BC, V6P 6G5
(604) 732-4443   *SIC 5192*

STERLING O&G INTERNATIONAL CORPORATION *p*
389
99 ROYAL CREST DR, WINNIPEG, MB, R3P 2R1
(204) 952-1505   *SIC 5984*

STERLING PACKERS LIMITED *p 506*
250 SUMMERLEA RD, BRAMPTON, ON, L6T 3V6
(905) 595-4300   *SIC 4213*

STERLING PLUMBING & HEATING LTD *p*
1421
1625 8TH AVE, REGINA, SK, S4R 1E6
(306) 586-5050   *SIC 1711*

STERLING SHOES LIMITED PARTNERSHIP *p*
256
2580 VISCOUNT WAY, RICHMOND, BC, V6V 1N1
(604) 270-6640   *SIC 5661*

STERLING SILVER DEVELOPMENT CORPORATION *p*
774
53 THE LINKS RD, NORTH YORK, ON, M2P 1T7
(416) 226-9400   *SIC 6553*

STERLING TILE & CARPET *p 1028*
505 CITYVIEW BLVD UNIT 1, WOODBRIDGE, ON, L4H 0L8
(905) 585-4800   *SIC 1743*

STERLING TRUCK & TRAILER SALES LTD *p 1416*
762 MCDONALD ST, REGINA, SK, S4N 7M7
(306) 525-0466   *SIC 5012*

STERLING TRUCKS OF CALGARY LTD *p 9*
2800 BARLOW TRAIL NE SUITE 291, CALGARY, AB, T1Y 1A2
(866) 792-1443   *SIC 5511*

STERLING VALVE AUTOMATION DIV OF *p*
11
See SPARTAN CONTROLS LTD

STERLING VALVE AUTOMATION, DIV. OF *p*
116
See SPARTAN CONTROLS LTD

STERLING WESTERN STAR TRUCKS ALBERTA LTD *p*
18
9115 52 ST SE, CALGARY, AB, T2C 2R4
(403) 720-3400   *SIC 5511*

STERN PARTNERS INC *p 300*
650 GEORGIA ST W UNIT 2900, VANCOUVER, BC, V6B 4N8
(604) 681-8817   *SIC 6211*

STERN REALTY (1994) LTD *p 323*
6272 EAST BOULEVARD, VANCOUVER, BC, V6M 3V7
(604) 266-1364   *SIC 6531*

STERNE ACURA *p 482*
See STERNE MOTORS LTD

STERNE MOTORS LTD *p 482*
625 ST. JOHN'S SIDEROAD E, AURORA, ON, L4G 0Z1
(905) 841-1400   *SIC 5511*

STETSON MOTORS (2000) LTD *p 82*
2451 50TH ST, DRAYTON VALLEY, AB, T7A 1S4
(780) 542-5391   *SIC 5511*

STETTLER AUCTION MART (1990) LTD *p*
167
4305 52 AVE, STETTLER, AB, T0C 2L0
(403) 742-2369   *SIC 5154*

STETTLER DODGE LTD *p 167*
4406 44 AVE, STETTLER, AB, T0C 2L0
(403) 742-3000   *SIC 5511*

STETTLER GM *p 167*
See STETTLER MOTORS (1998) LTD

STETTLER MOTORS (1998) LTD *p 167*
6115 50 AVE SS 2, STETTLER, AB, T0C 2L2
(403) 742-3407   *SIC 5511*

STETTLER SOBEYS *p 167*
See SOBEYS CAPITAL INCORPORATED

STEVE & LIZ'S NO FRILLS 265 *p 894*
See 994731 ONTARIO LTD

STEVE DOUCET PHARMACUETICAL INC *p*
395
939 ST. PETER AVE, BATHURST, NB, E2A 2Z3
(506) 547-8023   *SIC 5912*

STEVE MARSHALL FORD *p 195*
See MARSHALL, STEVE MOTORS (1996) LTD

STEVE NASH SPORTS CLUB *p 310*
See VANCOUVER BAY CLUBS LTD

STEVE'S LIVESTOCK TRANSPORTATION (BLUMENORT) LTD *p 346*
214 CENTER AVE SS 10, BLUMENORT, MB, R0A 0C1
(204) 326-6380   *SIC 4212*

STEVE'S NO FRILLS LTD *p 836*
1020 10TH ST W, OWEN SOUND, ON, N4K 5S1
(866) 987-6453   *SIC 5411*

STEVEN K. LEE AND CO. LTD *p 119*
3803 CALGARY TRAIL NW SUITE 550, EDMONTON, AB, T6J 5M8
(780) 438-4921   *SIC 7538*

STEVENS COMPANY LIMITED, THE *p 513*
425 RAILSIDE DR, BRAMPTON, ON, L7A 0N8
(905) 791-8600   *SIC 5047*

STEVENS GROUP MANAGEMENT *p 447*
See L & M ENTERPRISES LIMITED

STEVENSON ADVISORS LTD *p 379*
260 ST MARY AVE UNIT 200, WINNIPEG, MB, R3C 0M6
(204) 956-1901   *SIC 6531*

STEVENSON INSULATION INC *p 635*
260 SHIRLEY AVE, KITCHENER, ON, N2B 2E1
(519) 743-2857   *SIC 1742*

STEVENSON MEMORIAL HOSPITAL, THE *p 476*
200 FLETCHER CRES, ALLISTON, ON, L9R 1M1
(705) 435-6281   *SIC 8062*

STEVENSON, G & L TRANSPORT LIMITED *p 569*
1244 COUNTY ROAD 22, EMERYVILLE, ON, N0R 1C0
(519) 727-3478   *SIC 4151*

STEVENSVILLE LAWN SERVICE INC *p 890*
2821 STEVENSVILLE RD RR 2, STEVENSVILLE, ON, L0S 1S0
(905) 382-2124   *SIC 1611*

STEVESTON LONDON SECONDARY SCHOOL *p 266*
See BOARD OF EDUCATION SCHOOL DISTRICT #38 (RICHMOND)

STEVESTON MARINE & HARDWARE *p 266*
See HENLEY DEVELOPMENT CORP

STEVESTON RESTAURANTS LTD *p 264*
11151 NO. 5 RD, RICHMOND, BC, V7A 4E8
(604) 272-1399   *SIC 5812*

STEWART & STEVENSON CANADA INC *p*
18
3111 SHEPARD PL SE SUITE 403, CALGARY, AB, T2C 4P1
(403) 215-5300   *SIC 3533*

STEWART BROTHERS NURSERIES LTD *p*
219
4129 SPIERS RD, KELOWNA, BC, V1W 4B5
(250) 764-2121   *SIC 0181*

STEWART DRUGS HANNA (1984) LTD *p*
135
610 2ND AVE W, HANNA, AB, T0J 1P0
(403) 854-4154   *SIC 5411*

STEWART FOODSERVICE INC *p 488*
201 SAUNDERS RD, BARRIE, ON, L4N 9A3
(705) 728-3051   *SIC 5141*

STEWART MCKELVEY STIRLING SCALES *p 415*
44 CHIPMAN HILL SUITE 1000, SAINT JOHN, NB, E2L 2A9
(506) 632-1970   *SIC 8111*

STEWART MCKELVEY STIRLING SCALES *p 454*
1959 UPPER WATER ST SUITE 900, HALIFAX, NS, B3J 3N2
(902) 420-3200   *SIC 8111*

STEWART VEHICLE LEASING *p 913*
See KIA OF TIMMINS

STEWART'S NEW HOLLAND LTD *p 569*
9410 WELLINGTON RD 124, ERIN, ON, N0B 1T0
(519) 833-9384   *SIC 5083*

STEWART'S, ED GARAGE & EQUIPMENT LTD *p 569*
9410 WELLINGTON RD 124 RR 2, ERIN, ON, N0B 1T0
(519) 833-9616   *SIC 5999*

STEWART, J. J. MOTORS LIMITED *p 796*
2239 8 LINE, NORWOOD, ON, K0L 2V0
(705) 639-5383   *SIC 5521*

STEWART, JAMIE D MCLEOD & COMPANY LLP LAWYERS *p 69*
14505 BANNISTER RD SE, CALGARY, AB, T2X 3J3
(403) 225-6412   *SIC 8111*

STI MAINTENANCE INC *p 1115*
1946 RUE DAVIS, JONQUIERE, QC, G7S 3B6
(418) 699-5101   *SIC 8741*

STICKY MEDIA *p 1125*
See 9132-1604 QUEBEC INC

STICS DECO *p 1148*

See QUINCO & CIE INC

STIGAN MEDIA INC p 300
55 WATER STREET, VANCOUVER, BC, V6B 1A1
(778) 379-0888 *SIC 7311*

STIHL LIMITED p 662
1515 SISE RD SUITE 5666, LONDON, ON, N6N 1E1
(519) 681-3000 *SIC 5084*

STIKEMAN ELLIOTT LLP p 971
5300 COMMERCE CRT W SUITE 199, TORONTO, ON, M5L 1B9
(416) 869-5500 *SIC 8111*

STIKEMAN ELLIOTT LLP p 1208
1155 BOUL RENE-LEVESQUE O BUREAU B01, MONTREAL, QC, H3B 4R1
(514) 397-3000 *SIC 8111*

STILES' CLOTHIERS INC p 25
1435 40 AVE NE UNIT 4, CALGARY, AB, T2E 8N6
(403) 230-8515 *SIC 5651*

STILL CREEK PRESS p 186
See PRIME GRAPHIC RESOURCES LTD

STILLWATER CREEK LIMITED PARTNERSHIP p
751
2018 ROBERTSON RD SUITE 353, NEPEAN, ON, K2H 1C6
(613) 828-7575 *SIC 8059*

STILLWATER CREEK RETIREMENT COMMUNITY p
751
See STILLWATER CREEK LIMITED PARTNERSHIP

STILMAS AMERICAS INC p 528
3250 HARVESTER RD UNIT 6, BURLINGTON, ON, L7N 3W9
(905) 639-7025 *SIC 3589*

STIMLINE SERVICES INC p 18
7475 51 ST SE, CALGARY, AB, T2C 4L6
(403) 720-0874 *SIC 3533*

STINCOR PROMOTIONAL SPECIALTIES p
791
See STINCOR SPECIALTIES LTD

STINCOR SPECIALTIES LTD p 791
15 DENSLEY AVE, NORTH YORK, ON, M6M 2P5
(416) 243-0293 *SIC 5199*

STINGRAY COURRIER SERVICE p 978
See 2945-8171 QUEBEC INC

STINGRAY DIGITAL GROUP p 1211
See GROUPE STINGRAY INC

STINSON CREATIVE p 948
See 1 KING WEST INC

STIPSITS HOLDINGS CORP p 525
720 OVAL CRT, BURLINGTON, ON, L7L 6A9
(905) 333-8364 *SIC 1521*

STIR STICKS & PICKS INTERNATIONAL INC p 588
50 FASKEN DR UNIT 9, ETOBICOKE, ON, M9W 1K5
(416) 675-2064 *SIC 5113*

STIRIS RESEARCH INC p 660
1650 BIRCHWOOD PL, LONDON, ON, N6K 4X3
(519) 471-6211 *SIC 8742*

STIRLING HEIGHTS p 535
See REVERA LONG TERM CARE INC

STIRLING MANOR NURSING HOME p 890
See MANORCARE PARTNERS

STITCH IT CANADA'S TAILOR INC p 528
3221 NORTH SERVICE RD SUITE 101, BURLINGTON, ON, L7N 3G2
(905) 335-0922 *SIC 7219*

STITCHES p 790
See YM INC. (SALES)

STITTCO ENERGY LIMITED p 67
255 17 AVE SW UNIT 303, CALGARY, AB, T2S 2T8
(403) 228-5815 *SIC 5984*

STM BG AUTO INC p 889
449 QUEEN ST W, ST MARYS, ON, N4X 1B7

(519) 284-3310 *SIC 5511*

STM SPORTS TRADE MALL LTD p 335
508 DISCOVERY ST, VICTORIA, BC, V8T 1G8
(250) 383-6443 *SIC 5941*

STOBER, AL CONSTRUCTION LTD p 223
1631 DICKSON AVE SUITE 1700, KELOWNA, BC, V1Y 0B5
(250) 763-2305 *SIC 6719*

STOCK ON THE JOURNEY OF LEARNING p 588
See STOCK TRANSPORTATION LTD

STOCK POT, LE p 435
See 994486 N.W.T LTD

STOCK TRANSPORTATION LTD p 103
11454 WINTERBURN RD NW, EDMONTON, AB, T5S 2Y3
(780) 451-9536 *SIC 4151*

STOCK TRANSPORTATION LTD p 448
51 FRAZEE AVE, DARTMOUTH, NS, B3B 1Z4
(902) 481-8400 *SIC 4151*

STOCK TRANSPORTATION LTD p 588
60 MCCULLOCH AVE, ETOBICOKE, ON, M9W 4M6
(416) 244-5341 *SIC 4151*

STOCK TRANSPORTATION LTD p 762
59 COMMERCE CRES, NORTH BAY, ON, P1A 0B3
(705) 474-4370 *SIC 4151*

STOCK TRANSPORTATION LTD p 856
550 EDWARD AVE, RICHMOND HILL, ON, L4C 3K4
(905) 883-6665 *SIC 4151*

STOCK TRANSPORTATION LTD p 869
17 UPTON RD, SCARBOROUGH, ON, M1L 2C1
(416) 754-4949 *SIC 4151*

STOCK TRANSPORTATION LTD p 895
24 CARDICO DR, STOUFFVILLE, ON, L4A 2G5
SIC 4111

STOCK TRANSPORTATION LTD p 901
36 12 HWY, SUNDERLAND, ON, L0C 1H0
(705) 357-3187 *SIC 4151*

STOCKADE INVESTMENTS LTD p 606
785 IMPERIAL RD N, GUELPH, ON, N1K 1X4
(519) 763-1050 *SIC 5961*

STOCKADE WOOD & CRAFT SUPPLIES p 606
See STOCKADE INVESTMENTS LTD

STOCKDALES ELECTRIC MOTOR CORP p 1416
1441 FLEURY ST, REGINA, SK, S4N 7N5
(306) 352-4505 *SIC 5063*

STOCKERYALE CANADA INC p 1091
275 RUE KESMARK, DOLLARD-DES-ORMEAUX, QC, H9B 3J1
SIC 3699

STOCKFISH, GEORGE FORD SALES (1987) LTD p 764
HWY 17 E, NORTH BAY, ON, P1B 8J5
(705) 476-1506 *SIC 5511*

STOCKIE, GARY CHEVROLET LIMITED p 640
20 OTTAWA ST N, KITCHENER, ON, N2H 0A4
SIC 5511

STOCKSY UNITED CO-OP p 337
560 JOHNSON ST SUITE 320, VICTORIA, BC, V8W 3C6
(250) 590-7308 *SIC 6794*

STOGRYN SALES LTD p 111
6808 82 AVE NW, EDMONTON, AB, T6B 0E7
(780) 465-6408 *SIC 5087*

STOKES CANADA INC p 1157
5660 RUE FERRIER, MONT-ROYAL, QC, H4P 1M7
(514) 341-4334 *SIC 5719*

STOKES INC p 1157
5660 RUE FERRIER, MONT-ROYAL, QC, H4P 1M7

(514) 341-4334 *SIC 5719*

STOKES SEEDS LIMITED p 907
296 COLLIER RD S, THOROLD, ON, L2V 5B6
(905) 688-4300 *SIC 0181*

STOLLERY'S p 930
See STOLLERY, FRANK LIMITED

STOLLERY, FRANK LIMITED p 930
1 BLOOR ST W, TORONTO, ON, M4W 1A3
SIC 5611

STOLTZ SALES & SERVICE p 568
See STOLTZ SALES & SERVICE (ELMIRA) LTD

STOLTZ SALES & SERVICE (ELMIRA) LTD p 568
GD LCD MAIN, ELMIRA, ON, N3B 2Z4
(519) 669-1561 *SIC 5083*

STONE HEARTH BAKERY, DIV OF p 456
See H.R.D.A. ENTERPRISES LIMITED

STONE INVESTMENT GROUP LIMITED p 967
40 UNIVERSITY AVE SUITE 901, TORONTO, ON, M5J 1T1
(416) 364-9188 *SIC 6719*

STONE STRAW LIMITED p 516
72 PLANT FARM BLVD, BRANTFORD, ON, N3S 7W3
(519) 756-1974 *SIC 2656*

STONE TILE INTERNATIONAL INC p 791
834 CALEDONIA RD SUITE 1, NORTH YORK, ON, M6B 3X9
(416) 515-9000 *SIC 5032*

STONE TOWN CONSTRUCTION LIMITED p 889
25 WATER ST N, ST MARYS, ON, N4X 1B1
(519) 284-2580 *SIC 1629*

STONE'S R V & HOME CENTRE p 463
See STONE'S SUPERIOR HOMES LIMITED

STONE'S SUPERIOR HOMES LIMITED p 463
2689 WESTVILLE RD, NEW GLASGOW, NS, B2H 5C6
(902) 752-3164 *SIC 5571*

STONE, BRUCE ENTERPRISES LTD p 911
1221 ARTHUR ST W, THUNDER BAY, ON, P7K 1A7
(807) 475-4235 *SIC 5311*

STONELEIGH MOTORS LIMITED p 682
9186 COUNTY ROAD HWY SUITE 93, MIDLAND, ON, L4R 4K6
(705) 526-3724 *SIC 5511*

STONERIDGE INSURANCE BROKERS p 477
See 2158124 ONTARIO INC

STONERIDGE MANOR p 540
See REVERA LONG TERM CARE INC

STONETOWN FOODLAND MARKET p 888
See RONALD D. BAILEY GROCERY LIMITED

STONEWALL FAMILY FOODS p 359
See STONEWALL GROCERS LIMITED, THE

STONEWALL GROCERS LIMITED, THE p 359
330 3RD AVE S UNIT 3, STONEWALL, MB, R0C 2Z0
(204) 467-5553 *SIC 5411*

STONEWATER GROUP OF FRANCHISES p 199
2991 LOUGHEED HWY UNIT 32, COQUITLAM, BC, V3B 6J6
(604) 529-9220 *SIC 6794*

STONEWATER GROUP OF FRANCHISES p 214
9324 ALASKA RD, FORT ST. JOHN, BC, V1J 6L5
(250) 262-4151 *SIC 5812*

STONEWORX MARBLE & GRANITE p 495
See MAPLE TERRAZZO MARBLE & TILE INCORPORATED

STONEY CREEK DISTRIBUTION LTD p 894
135 KING ST E, STONEY CREEK, ON, L8G 0B2

SIC 2024

STONEY CREEK FURNITURE LIMITED p 893
395 LEWIS RD, STONEY CREEK, ON, L8E 5N5
(905) 643-4121 *SIC 5712*

STONEY CREEK LIFECARE CENTRE p 892
See EXTENDICARE INC

STONEY CREEK MACK p 892
See MACK SALES & SERVICE OF STONEY CREEK LTD

STONG'S EXPRESS p 324
See STONG'S MARKETS LTD

STONG'S MARKETS LTD p 324
4560 DUNBAR ST, VANCOUVER, BC, V6S 2G6
(604) 266-1401 *SIC 5411*

STONHARD LTD p 1015
95 SUNRAY ST, WHITBY, ON, L1N 9C9
(705) 749-1460 *SIC 1752*

STONY MOUNTAIN WASTE MANAGEMENT p 27
See 1840807 ALBERTA LTD

STONY PLAIN CHRYSLER LTD p 168
4004 51 ST, STONY PLAIN, AB, T7Z 0A2
(780) 963-2236 *SIC 5511*

STONY VALLEY CONTRACTING LTD p 129
245 TAIGANOVA CRES, FORT MCMURRAY, AB, T9K 0T4
(780) 743-0527 *SIC 5032*

STOODLEY BRIAN p 65
1014 12 AVE SW UNIT A, CALGARY, AB, T2R 0J6
(403) 262-9402 *SIC 4925*

STOP 23 AUTO SALES LTD p 647
910 WALLACE AVE N, LISTOWEL, ON, N4W 1M5
(519) 291-5757 *SIC 5511*

STOP 23 SERVICE LIMITED p 647
910 WALLACE AVE N, LISTOWEL, ON, N4W 1M5
(519) 291-3628 *SIC 5521*

STORAGE & TRANSFER TECHNOLOGIES, INC p 684
8485 PARKHILL DR, MILTON, ON, L9T 5E9
(905) 693-9301 *SIC 8711*

STORAGE APPLIANCE CORPORATION p 854
30 WEST BEAVER CREEK RD UNIT 115, RICHMOND HILL, ON, L4B 3K1
(416) 484-0009 *SIC 5045*

STORAGEVAULT CANADA INC p 1416
6050 DIEFENBAKER AVE, REGINA, SK, S4N 7L2
(306) 546-5999 *SIC 4225*

STORBURN CONSTRUCTION LTD p 810
GD, ORILLIA, ON, L3V 6J3
(705) 326-4140 *SIC 1542*

STORCHEM INC p 528
855 HARRINGTON CRT, BURLINGTON, ON, L7N 3P3
(905) 639-9700 *SIC 5169*

STORCK CANADA INC p 707
2 ROBERT SPECK PKY SUITE 695, MISSISSAUGA, ON, L4Z 1H8
(905) 272-4480 *SIC 5149*

STORDOR INVESTMENTS LTD p 97
11703 160 ST NW, EDMONTON, AB, T5M 3Z3
(780) 451-0060 *SIC 5211*

STORE SUPPORT p 727
See STORESUPPORT CANADA INC

STORECHECK -CONCORD p 559
2180 STEELES AVE W, CONCORD, ON, L4K 2Z5
(905) 660-1334 *SIC 6289*

STOREFRONT HUMBER INCORPORATED p 571
2445 LAKE SHORE BLVD W, ETOBICOKE, ON, M8V 1C5
(416) 259-4207 *SIC 8399*

STORESUPPORT CANADA INC p 727
2000 ARGENTIA RD SUITE 440, MISSIS-

SAUGA, ON, L5N 1P7
(905) 847-6513   *SIC* 2789
STOREX INDUSTRIES CORPORATION *p*
1132
9440 RUE CLEMENT, LASALLE, QC, H8R
3W1
(514) 745-1234   *SIC* 3089
STORK CRAFT MANUFACTURING INC *p*
258
12033 RIVERSIDE WAY SUITE 200, RICH-
MOND, BC, V6W 1K6
(604) 274-5121   *SIC* 5021
STORKCRAFT BABY   *p* 258
*See STORK CRAFT MANUFACTURING
INC*
STORM RESOURCES LTD   *p* 60
215 2 ST SW SUITE 600, CALGARY, AB,
T2P 1M4
(403) 817-6145   *SIC* 1382
**STORMTECH PERFORMANCE APPAREL
LTD**   *p* 187
3773 STILL CREEK AVE, BURNABY, BC,
V5C 4E2
(866) 407-2222   *SIC* 5136
STORNOWAY DIAMOND CORPORATION *p*
1145
111 RUE SAINT-CHARLES O BUREAU 400,
LONGUEUIL, QC, J4K 5G4
(450) 616-5555   *SIC* 1499
STOTHART AUTOMOTIVE INC   *p* 395
335 MURRAY AVE, BATHURST, NB, E2A
1T4
(506) 548-8988   *SIC* 5511
STOTT PILATES   *p* 924
See MERRITHEW CORPORATION
**STOUFFVILLE DISTRICT SECONDARY
SCHOOL**   *p* 895
*See YORK REGION DISTRICT SCHOOL
BOARD*
STOUFFVILLE HONDA   *p* 894
See 2449616 ONTARIO INC
STOUFFVILLE TOYOTA   *p* 894
See 2194747 ONTARIO INC
STOUGHTON FIRE PROTECTION LTD *p* 11
620 MORAINE RD NE, CALGARY, AB, T2A
2P3
(403) 291-0291   *SIC* 7389
STOWE, LESLEY FINE FOODS LTD *p* 321
1685 5TH AVE W, VANCOUVER, BC, V6J
1N5
          SIC 5149
**STP PUBLICATIONS LIMITED PARTNER-
SHIP**   *p*
292
2188 YUKON ST, VANCOUVER, BC, V5Y
3P1
(604) 983-3434   *SIC* 2721
**STP SPECIALTY TECHNICAL PUBLISH-
ERS**   *p*
292
*See STP PUBLICATIONS LIMITED PART-
NERSHIP*
STQ   *p* 1260
*See SOCIETE DES TRAVERSIERS DU
QUEBEC*
STRABAG INC   *p* 727
6790 CENTURY AVE SUITE 401, MISSIS-
SAUGA, ON, L5N 2V8
(905) 353-5500   *SIC* 1541
STRACHAN, ALASTAIR   *p* 733
5770 HURONTARIO ST SUITE 200, MIS-
SISSAUGA, ON, L5R 3G5
(905) 568-9500   *SIC* 6531
**STRAD COMPRESSION AND PRODUC-
TION SERVICES LTD**   *p*
167
HWY 12 W, STETTLER, AB, T0C 2L0
(403) 742-6900   *SIC* 7699
STRAD INC   *p* 60
440 2 AVE SW SUITE 1200, CALGARY, AB,
T2P 5E9
(403) 232-6900   *SIC* 7353
STRAD MANUFACTURING INC   *p* 150
602 25 AVE, NISKU, AB, T9E 0G6

(780) 955-9393   *SIC* 4911
STRADA AGGREGATES INC   *p* 559
30 FLORAL PKY SUITE 400, CONCORD,
ON, L4K 4R1
(905) 738-2200   *SIC* 5032
**STRADA CRUSH AGGREGATE PROCESS-
ING**   *p*
559
See STRADA CRUSH LIMITED
STRADA CRUSH LIMITED   *p* 559
69 CONNIE CRES SUITE 1, CONCORD,
ON, L4K 1L3
(905) 303-6200   *SIC* 5032
STRADIGI INC   *p* 1200
1470 RUE PEEL BUREAU A1050, MON-
TREAL, QC, H3A 1T1
(514) 395-9018   *SIC* 7371
STRAIGHT AWAY MANAGEMENT   *p* 73
See MAXWELL WESTVIEW REALTY
STRAIGHT SHOOTER SAFETY INC   *p* 136
GD, HIGH RIVER, AB, T1V 1M3
(403) 336-1124   *SIC* 5999
STRAIT CROSSING BRIDGE LIMITED *p*
1038
104 ABEGWEIT BLVD SUITE 2032,
BORDEN-CARLETON, PE, C0B 1X0
(902) 437-7300   *SIC* 4785
STRAIT CROSSING DEVELOPMENT INC *p*
1038
104 ABEGWEIT BLVD, BORDEN-
CARLETON, PE, C0B 1X0
(902) 437-7300   *SIC* 4785
**STRAIT REGIONAL CENTRE FOR EDUCA-
TION, THE**   *p*
438
105 BRAEMORE AVE, ANTIGONISH, NS,
B2G 1L3
(902) 863-1620   *SIC* 8211
**STRAIT REGIONAL CENTRE FOR EDUCA-
TION, THE**   *p*
465
304 PITT ST UNIT 2, PORT HAWKESBURY,
NS, B9A 2T9
(902) 625-2191   *SIC* 8211
STRAIT REGIONAL SCHOOL BOARD   *p*
438
*See STRAIT REGIONAL CENTRE FOR ED-
UCATION, THE*
STRAIT RICHMOND HOSPITAL   *p* 442
*See GUYSBOROUGH ANTIGONISH
STRAIT HEALTH AUTHORITY*
**STRANDHERD CROSSING MEDICAL CEN-
TER**   *p*
751
See A 1 MEDICAL CENTRE INC
STRANG'S VALU-MART   *p* 493
See 1179131 ONTARIO LIMITED
STRATA CORPORATION # 962   *p* 337
1234 WHARF ST SUITE 962, VICTORIA,
BC, V8W 3H9
(250) 386-2211   *SIC* 6531
STRATACACHE CANADA INC   *p* 689
5925 AIRPORT RD SUITE 200, MISSIS-
SAUGA, ON, L4V 1W1
(905) 405-6208   *SIC* 7372
STRATAPRIME   *p* 987
See STRATAPRIME SOLUTIONS, INC
STRATAPRIME SOLUTIONS, INC   *p* 987
1 FIRST CANADIAN PLACE SUITE 350,
TORONTO, ON, M5X 1C1
(647) 693-7656   *SIC* 7389
STRATECOM INC   *p* 1134
1940 BOUL TASCHEREAU BUREAU 100A,
LEMOYNE, QC, J4P 3N2
(450) 466-6640   *SIC* 5999
STRATEGIC COACH INC, THE   *p* 992
33 FRASER AVE SUITE 201, TORONTO,
ON, M6K 3J9
(416) 531-7399   *SIC* 8741
STRATEGIC COMMUNICATIONS INC *p* 992
1179 KING ST W SUITE 202, TORONTO,
ON, M6K 3C5
(416) 537-6100   *SIC* 8748
STRATEGIC COUNSEL, THE   *p* 821

See GREG KELLY WOOLSTEN CROFT
STRATEGIC GROUP   *p* 60
*See STRATEGIC REALTY MANAGEMENT
CORP*
STRATEGIC METALS LTD   *p* 300
510 HASTINGS ST W SUITE 1016, VAN-
COUVER, BC, V6B 1L8
(604) 687-2522   *SIC* 1081
STRATEGIC OIL & GAS LTD   *p* 60
645 7 AVE SW SUITE 1100, CALGARY, AB,
T2P 4G8
(403) 767-9000   *SIC* 1382
**STRATEGIC REALTY MANAGEMENT
CORP**   *p* 60
630 8 AVE SW SUITE 400, CALGARY, AB,
T2P 1G6
(403) 770-2300   *SIC* 6531
**STRATEGIC UNDERWRITING MANAGERS
INC**   *p* 940
18 KING ST E SUITE 903, TORONTO, ON,
M5C 1C4
(416) 603-7864   *SIC* 6411
STRATEGIS TECHNOLOGIES   *p* 1145
See SOGEMA TECHNOLOGIES INC
STRATEGY INSTITUTE INC   *p* 983
401 RICHMOND ST W SUITE 401,
TORONTO, ON, M5V 3A8
(416) 944-9200   *SIC* 7389
STRATFORD AUCTION   *p* 896
See DILL, W.C. & COMPANY INC
STRATFORD CHILDREN'S SERVICES INC
p 896
508 ERIE ST, STRATFORD, ON, N5A 2N6
(519) 273-3623   *SIC* 8093
**STRATFORD FESTIVAL THEATRE OF
CANADA**   *p* 897
*See STRATFORD SHAKESPEAREAN FES-
TIVAL OF CANADA, THE*
**STRATFORD HOME HARDWARE BUILD-
ING CENTRE**   *p*
895
See 1441246 ONTARIO INC
STRATFORD HYUNDAI   *p* 896
See SAUNDERS AUTOMOTIVE LIMITED
**STRATFORD MOTOR PRODUCTS (1984)
LTD**   *p* 896
824 ONTARIO ST, STRATFORD, ON, N5A
3K1
(519) 271-5900   *SIC* 5511
**STRATFORD NORTHWESTERN SEC-
ONDARY SCHOOL**   *p*
895
*See AVON MAITLAND DISTRICT SCHOOL
BOARD*
**STRATFORD SHAKESPEAREAN FESTI-
VAL OF CANADA, THE**   *p*
897
55 QUEEN ST, STRATFORD, ON, N5A 4M9
(519) 271-4040   *SIC* 7922
STRATFORD-PERTH FAMILY YMCA *p* 897
204 DOWNIE ST, STRATFORD, ON, N5A
1X4
(519) 271-0480   *SIC* 7997
**STRATHBRIDGE ASSET MANAGEMENT
INC**   *p* 957
121 KING ST W SUITE 2600, TORONTO,
ON, M5H 3T9
(416) 681-3900   *SIC* 6371
STRATHCONA COMMUNITY CENTRE   *p*
296
*See STRATHCONA COMMUNITY CENTRE
ASSOCIATION (1972)*
**STRATHCONA COMMUNITY CENTRE AS-
SOCIATION (1972)**   *p*
296
601 KEEFER ST, VANCOUVER, BC, V6A
3V8
(604) 713-1838   *SIC* 8322
STRATHCONA COUNTY   *p* 163
2000 PREMIER WAY, SHERWOOD PARK,
AB, T8H 2G4
(780) 416-3300   *SIC* 7999
STRATHCONA COUNTY HEALTH CENTER
p 162

See ALBERTA HEALTH SERVICES
STRATHCONA GARDENS RECREATION *p*
195
*See COMOX VALLEY REGIONAL DIS-
TRICT*
STRATHCONA HOTEL   *p* 337
*See STRATHCONA HOTEL OF VICTORIA
LTD*
STRATHCONA HOTEL OF VICTORIA LTD *p*
337
919 DOUGLAS ST, VICTORIA, BC, V8W
2C2
(250) 383-7137   *SIC* 5813
STRATHCONA MECHANICAL LIMITED   *p*
140
6612 44 ST, LEDUC, AB, T9E 7E4
(780) 980-1122   *SIC* 1711
STRATHCONA PAPER LP   *p* 748
77 COUNTY RD 16, NAPANEE, ON, K7R
3L2
(613) 378-6672   *SIC* 2631
STRATHCONA PAPER LP   *p* 748
77 COUNTY RD 16, NAPANEE, ON, K7R
3L2
(613) 378-6676   *SIC* 2631
STRATHCONA SCHOOL   *p* 114
*See EDMONTON SCHOOL DISTRICT NO.
7*
STRATHCONA-TWEEDSMUIR SCHOOL   *p*
151
GD, OKOTOKS, AB, T1S 1A3
(403) 938-4431   *SIC* 8211
STRATHHAVEN LIFECARE CENTRE *p* 496
See EXTENDICARE INC
STRATHMERE LODGE   *p* 897
*See CORPORATION OF THE COUNTY OF
MIDDLESEX*
STRATHMORE HUSKY   *p* 168
See 6842071 CANADA INC
STRATHMORE MOTOR PRODUCTS LTD *p* 168
900 WESTRIDGE RD, STRATHMORE, AB,
T1P 1H8
(403) 934-3334   *SIC* 5511
**STRATHROY MIDDLESEX GENERAL HOS-
PITAL**   *p*
897
395 CARRIE ST SUITE 360, STRATHROY,
ON, N7G 3C9
(519) 245-5295   *SIC* 8062
STRATICOM PLANNING ASSOCIATES INC
p 983
366 ADELAIDE ST W, TORONTO, ON, M5V
1R9
(416) 362-7407   *SIC* 7389
STRATICS NETWORKS   *p* 616
See 7868774 CANADA INC
STRATOS PIZZERIA   *p* 1385
5030 BOUL DES FORGES, TROIS-
RIVIERES, QC, G8Y 1X2
(819) 694-7777   *SIC* 5149
STRATOSPHERE QUALITY, INC   *p* 805
1515 REBECCA ST, OAKVILLE, ON, L6L
1Z8
(877) 224-8584   *SIC* 4785
STRATTY ENTERPRISES LTD   *p* 173
5116 59 ST, WHITECOURT, AB, T7S 1X7
(780) 706-4889   *SIC* 7353
**STRATUS ELECTRICAL & INSTRUMENTA-
TION LTD**   *p*
71
12204 40 ST SE UNIT 12, CALGARY, AB,
T2Z 4K6
(403) 775-7599   *SIC* 7629
STRATUS PIPELINES LTD   *p* 80
10828 99 ST SUITE 3, CLAIRMONT, AB,
T8X 5B4
(780) 897-0605   *SIC* 1623
STRAUSSCO HOLDINGS LTD   *p* 784
601 MAGNETIC DR UNIT 41, NORTH
YORK, ON, M3J 3J2
(416) 650-1404   *SIC* 5611
STRAWBERRY TYME INC   *p* 881
1250 ST JOHN'S RD W, SIMCOE, ON, N3Y

▲ Public Company   ■ Public Company Family Member   **HQ** Headquarters   **BR** Branch   **SL** Single Location

4K1
(519) 426-3099   SIC 5431
STREAM   p 450
See STREAM INTERNATIONAL CANADA ULC
STREAM FLO INDUSTRIES   p 133
15501 89 STREET, GRANDE PRAIRIE, AB, T8V 0V7
(780) 532-1433   SIC 1389
STREAM INTERNATIONAL CANADA ULC p 197
7955 EVANS RD, CHILLIWACK, BC, V2R 5R7
(604) 702-5100   SIC 7389
STREAM INTERNATIONAL CANADA ULC p 450
95 UNION ST, GLACE BAY, NS, B1A 2P6
(902) 842-3800   SIC 7389
STREAM OIL & GAS LTD   p 42
609 14 ST NW SUITE 300, CALGARY, AB, T2N 2A1
(403) 531-2358   SIC 1382
STREAM-FLO INDUSTRIES LTD   p 111
4505 74 AVE NW, EDMONTON, AB, T6B 2H5
(780) 468-6789   SIC 3533
STREAM-FLO RESOURCES LTD   p 60
202 6 AVE SW SUITE 400, CALGARY, AB, T2P 2R9
(403) 269-5531   SIC 6712
STREAMLINE CONSTRUCTION CO. LTD p 103
11030 205 ST NW, EDMONTON, AB, T5S 1Z4
(780) 447-4518   SIC 1623
STREAMLINE FIRE PROTECTION LTD p 97
15695 116 AVE NW, EDMONTON, AB, T5M 3W1
(780) 436-6911   SIC 7382
STREAMLINE FOODS INC.   p 492
315 UNIVERSITY AVE, BELLEVILLE, ON, K8N 5T7
(613) 961-1265   SIC 2061
STREAMLINE INSPECTION LIMITED p 159
240040 FRONTIER PL UNIT 5, ROCKY VIEW COUNTY, AB, T1X 0N2
(403) 454-6630   SIC 7389
STREAMLINE MECHANICAL   p 161
See STREAMLINE MECHANICAL L.P.
STREAMLINE MECHANICAL L.P.   p 161
53113 21 HWY, SHERWOOD PARK, AB, T8A 4T7
(780) 467-6941   SIC 1711
STREEF PRODUCE LIMITED   p 848
447 HWY 2, PRINCETON, ON, N0J 1V0
(519) 458-4311   SIC 5148
STREET CAPITAL BANK OF CANADA p 943
See STREET CAPITAL GROUP INC
STREET CAPITAL GROUP INC   p 943
1 YONGE ST SUITE 2401, TORONTO, ON, M5E 1E5
(647) 259-7873   SIC 6719
STREET KIA   p 882
See STREET MOTOR SALES LTD
STREET MOTOR SALES LTD   p 882
171 LOMBARD ST, SMITHS FALLS, ON, K7A 5B8
(613) 284-0023   SIC 5521
STREETSIDE DEVELOPMENT CORPORATION   p 392
1 DR. DAVID FRIESEN DR, WINNIPEG, MB, R3X 0G8
(204) 233-2451   SIC 1522
STREETSVILLE HYUNDAI   p 727
6225 MISSISSAUGA RD, MISSISSAUGA, ON, L5N 1A4
(905) 812-5401   SIC 5511
STREETSVILLE SECONDARY SCHOOL p 719
See PEEL DISTRICT SCHOOL BOARD
STREIT GROUP   p 682
See STREIT MANUFACTURING INC

STREIT MANUFACTURING INC   p 682
111 PILLSBURY DR, MIDLAND, ON, L4R 4L4
(705) 526-6557   SIC 3711
STRESCON LIMITED   p 414
400 CHESLEY DR SUITE 3, SAINT JOHN, NB, E2K 5L6
(506) 633-8877   SIC 3272
STRESS-CRETE LIMITED   p 528
840 WALKER'S LINE SUITE 7, BURLINGTON, ON, L7N 2G2
(905) 827-6901   SIC 3272
STRICTLAND BUDGET LOT   p 895
See BUY SELL TRADE
STRICTLY HYDRAULICS   p 448
See STRICTLY SALES & SERVICE INC
STRICTLY LOBSTER LIMITED   p 471
72 WATER ST, YARMOUTH, NS, B5A 1K9
(902) 742-6272   SIC 5146
STRICTLY SALES & SERVICE INC   p 448
125 TRIDER CRES, DARTMOUTH, NS, B3B 1V6
(902) 468-5308   SIC 5084
STRIDE MANAGEMENT CORP   p 25
3950 12 ST NE, CALGARY, AB, T2E 8H9
(403) 508-7313   SIC 4899
STRIGHT-MACKAY LIMITED   p 463
209 TERRA COTTA DR, NEW GLASGOW, NS, B2H 6A8
(902) 928-1900   SIC 5088
STRIKE FIRST CORPORATION   p 879
777 TAPSCOTT RD, SCARBOROUGH, ON, M1X 1A2
(416) 299-7767   SIC 7389
STRIKE GROUP INC   p 60
505 3 ST SW SUITE 1300, CALGARY, AB, T2P 3E6
(403) 232-8448   SIC 1389
STRIKE GROUP LIMITED PARTNERSHIP p 60
505 3 ST SW SUITE 1300, CALGARY, AB, T2P 3E6
(403) 232-8448   SIC 1389
STRIKE GROUP LIMITED PARTNERSHIP p 135
10600 94 ST SS 1, HIGH LEVEL, AB, T0H 1Z0
(780) 926-2429   SIC 1389
STRILKIWSKI CONTRACTING LTD   p 349
GD LCD MAIN, DAUPHIN, MB, R7N 2T3
(204) 638-9304   SIC 1611
STRITE INDUSTRIES LIMITED   p 537
298 SHEPHERD AVE, CAMBRIDGE, ON, N3C 1V1
(519) 658-9361   SIC 3843
STRONACH & SONS INC   p 573
165 THE QUEENSWAY SUITE 318, ETOBICOKE, ON, M8Y 1H8
(416) 259-5009   SIC 5148
STRONCO DESIGNS INC   p 703
1510 CATERPILLAR RD, MISSISSAUGA, ON, L4X 2Y1
(905) 270-6767   SIC 7389
STRONCO SHOW SERVICES   p 703
See STRONCO DESIGNS INC
STRONE CORPORATION   p 799
2717 COVENTRY RD, OAKVILLE, ON, L6H 5V9
(905) 829-2766   SIC 1799
STRONG, J.E. LIMITED   p 713
19 ANN ST, MISSISSAUGA, ON, L5G 3E9
(905) 274-2327   SIC 7349
STRONGCO CORPORATION   p 700
1640 ENTERPRISE RD, MISSISSAUGA, ON, L4W 4L4
(905) 670-5100   SIC 7353
STRONGCO ENGINEERED SYSTEMS INC p 700
1640 ENTERPRISE RD, MISSISSAUGA, ON, L4W 4L4
(905) 670-5100   SIC 3541
STRONGCO LIMITED PARTNERSHIP p 700
1640 ENTERPRISE RD, MISSISSAUGA, ON, L4W 4L4

(905) 670-5100   SIC 5082
STRONGEST FAMILIES INSTITUTE   p 461
267 COBEQUID RD SUITE 200, LOWER SACKVILLE, NS, B4C 4E6
(902) 442-9520   SIC 8733
STROUD AGENCIES INSURANCE BROKERS   p 107
See STROUD AGENCIES LTD
STROUD AGENCIES LTD   p 107
9945 50 ST NW UNIT 304, EDMONTON, AB, T6A 0L4
(780) 426-2400   SIC 6311
STRUC-TUBE LTEE   p 1341
6000 RTE TRANSCANADIENNE, SAINT-LAURENT, QC, H4T 1X9
(514) 333-9747   SIC 5712
STRUCT-CON CONSTRUCTION LTD p 500
2051 WILLIAMS PKY UNIT 14, BRAMPTON, ON, L6S 5T3
(905) 791-5445   SIC 1542
STRUCTFORM INTERNATIONAL LIMITED p 598
29 GORMLEY INDUSTRIAL AVE UNIT 6, GORMLEY, ON, L0H 1G0
(416) 291-7576   SIC 1542
STRUCTO NORTH AMERICA INC   p 996
200 EVANS AVE UNIT 11, TORONTO, ON, M8Z 1J7
(877) 787-8286   SIC 2752
STRUCTURAL COMPOSITE TECHNOLOGIES LTD   p 363
100 HOKA ST UNIT 200, WINNIPEG, MB, R2C 3N2
(204) 668-9320   SIC 3299
STRUCTURAL CONTRACTING LTD   p 598
29 GORMLEY INDUSTRIAL AVE UNIT 6, GORMLEY, ON, L0H 1G0
(416) 291-7576   SIC 1791
STRUCTURAL FLOOR FINISHING LIMITED p 598
29 GORMLEY INDUSTRIAL RD, GORMLEY, ON, L0H 1G0
(416) 291-7576   SIC 1771
STRUCTURE LAFERTE INC   p 1097
2300 BOUL LEMIRE, DRUMMONDVILLE, QC, J2B 6X9
(819) 477-7723   SIC 2439
STRUCTURECRAFT BUILDERS INC p 177
1929 FOY ST, ABBOTSFORD, BC, V2T 6B1
(604) 940-8889   SIC 1542
STRUCTURES BARRETTE INC   p 1385
545 RANG SAINT-MALO, TROIS-RIVIERES, QC, G8V 0A8
(819) 374-8784   SIC 5031
STRUCTURES BRETON INC, LES p 1296
500 RUE SAGARD, SAINT-BRUNO, QC, J3V 6C2
(450) 653-9999   SIC 1791
STRUCTURES CPI INC   p 1377
516 RTE 172 O, ST-NAZAIRE-DU-LAC-ST-JEAN, QC, G0W 2V0
(418) 668-3371   SIC 3441
STRUCTURES DE BEAUCE INC, LES p 1349
305 RUE DU PARC RR 1, SAINT-ODILON, QC, G0S 3A0
(418) 464-2000   SIC 1791
STRUCTURES G.B. LTEE, LES   p 1285
105 MONTEE INDUSTRIELLE-ET-COMMERCIALE, RIMOUSKI, QC, G5M 1A8
(418) 724-9433   SIC 3312
STRUCTURES MOMETAL   p 1393
See MOMETAL STRUCTURES INC
STRUCTURES ST-JOSEPH LTEE   p 1322
200 RUE DU PARC, SAINT-JOSEPH-DE-BEAUCE, QC, G0S 2V0
(418) 397-5712   SIC 2439
STRUCTURES ULTRATEC INC, LES p 1133
235 RUE DE LA STATION, LAURIER-STATION, QC, G0S 1N0
(418) 682-2033   SIC 2452

STRUCTURLAM MASS TIMBER CORPORATION   p 244
2176 GOVERNMENT ST, PENTICTON, BC, V2A 8B5
(250) 492-8912   SIC 2439
STRYKER CANADA HOLDING COMPANY p 183
8329 EASTLAKE DR UNIT 101, BURNABY, BC, V5A 4W2
(604) 232-9861   SIC 8731
STRYKER CANADA LP   p 1005
2 MEDICORUM PLACE, WATERDOWN, ON, L8B 1W2
(905) 690-5700   SIC 5047
STRYKER MEDICAL LONDON   p 657
See 1767388 ONTARIO INC
STS   p 151
See STRATHCONA-TWEEDSMUIR SCHOOL
STS   p 1372
See SOCIETE DE TRANSPORT DE SHERBROOKE
STS PETER & PAUL UKRANIAN CATHOLIC CHURCH   p 370
See UKRANIAN CATHOLIC ARCHEPARCHY OF WINNIPEG
STT STANCO   p 684
See STORAGE & TRANSFER TECHNOLOGIES, INC
STU   p 401
See ST. THOMAS UNIVERSITY
STUART OLSON BUILDINGS LTD   p 74
4954 RICHARD RD SW SUITE 400, CALGARY, AB, T3E 6L1
(403) 520-2767   SIC 1522
STUART OLSON BUILDINGS LTD   p 256
13777 COMMERCE PKY SUITE 300, RICHMOND, BC, V6V 2X3
(604) 273-7765   SIC 1522
STUART OLSON CONSTRUCTION LTD   p 74
4820 RICHARD RD SW SUITE 600, CALGARY, AB, T3E 6L1
(403) 520-2767   SIC 1522
STUART OLSON INC   p 74
4820 RICHARD RD SW SUITE 600, CALGARY, AB, T3E 6L1
(403) 685-7777   SIC 1541
STUART OLSON INDUSTRIAL CONSTRUCTORS INC   p 899
670 FALCONBRIDGE RD UNIT 1, SUDBURY, ON, P3A 4S4
(705) 222-4848   SIC 1711
STUART OLSON INDUSTRIAL INC   p 126
2627 ELLWOOD DR SW SUITE 201, EDMONTON, AB, T6X 0P7
(780) 450-9636   SIC 1541
STUART OLSON INDUSTRIAL SERVICES LTD   p 156
8024 EDGAR INDUSTRIAL CRES UNIT 102, RED DEER, AB, T4P 3R3
(780) 481-9600   SIC 1541
STUART, W H HOLDINGS LIMITED   p 675
11 ALLSTATE PKY SUITE 410, MARKHAM, ON, L3R 9T8
(905) 305-0880   SIC 6282
STUART, W H INSURANCE AGENCY p 675
See STUART, W H HOLDINGS LIMITED
STUART, W H MUTUALS LTD   p 1000
16 MAIN ST, UNIONVILLE, ON, L3R 2E4
(905) 305-0880   SIC 6722
STUBBE'S PRECAST   p 618
See STUBBE'S REDI-MIX INC
STUBBE'S PRECAST COMMERCIAL INC p 618
44 MUIR LINE, HARLEY, ON, N0E 1E0
(519) 424-2183   SIC 1791
STUBBE'S REDI-MIX INC   p 618
30 MUIR LINE, HARLEY, ON, N0E 1E0
(519) 424-2183   SIC 3272
STUCCOCONTRACTORS.CA   p 576
2 FIELDWAY RD, ETOBICOKE, ON, M8Z

0B9
(416) 900-8715   *SIC* 1542
STUCOR CONSTRUCTION LTD   *p* 623
2540 SOUTH SERVICE RD, JORDAN STATION, ON, L0R 1S0
(905) 562-1118   *SIC* 1542
STUDENT ASSOCIATION OF GEORGE BROWN COLLEGE   *p* 974
142 KENDAL AVE RM E100, TORONTO, ON, M5R 1M3
(416) 415-5000   *SIC* 8699
STUDENT ASSOCIATION OF THE BCIT   *p* 189
See STUDENT ASSOCIATION OF THE BRITISH COLUMBIA INSTITUTE OF TECHNOLOGY
STUDENT ASSOCIATION OF THE BRITISH COLUMBIA INSTITUTE OF TECHNOLOGY*p* 189
3700 WILLINGDON AVE SUITE 260, BURNABY, BC, V5G 3H2
(604) 432-8847   *SIC* 5411
STUDENT TRANSPORTATION INC   *p* 488
160 SAUNDERS RD UNIT 6, BARRIE, ON, L4N 9A4
(705) 721-2626   *SIC* 4151
STUDENT TRANSPORTATION OF CANADA INC   *p* 488
160 SAUNDERS RD UNIT 6, BARRIE, ON, L4N 9A4
(705) 721-2626   *SIC* 4151
STUDENTGUARD HEALTH INSURANCE *p* 905
See TRAVEL HEALTHCARE INSURANCE SOLUTIONS INC
STUDENTS ASSOCIATION OF MOUNT ROYAL COLLEGE   *p* 74
4825 MOUNT ROYAL GATE SW, CALGARY, AB, T3E 6K6
(403) 440-6077   *SIC* 8651
STUDIO DE PHOTOS DES ECOLES QUEBECOISES INC   *p* 1051
8300 RUE DE L'INDUSTRIE, ANJOU, QC, H1J 1S7
(514) 351-8275   *SIC* 7221
STUDIO MUNGE   *p* 790
See 1279317 ONTARIO LTD
STUDIO NANC   *p* 1182
See PROS DE LA PHOTO (QUEBEC) INC, LES
STUDIO NIKO   *p* 998
See NIKO COSMETICS INC
STUDIO SQUEEZE   *p* 1257
See ANIMATION SQUEEZE STUDIO INC
STUDIO UBISOFT SAINT-ANTOINE *p* 1191
See UBISOFT DIVERTISSEMENTS INC
STUDIOS BKOM   *p* 1278
See 10684651 CANADA INC
STUDIOS DESIGN GHA INC   *p* 1208
1100 AV DES CANADIENS-DE-MONTREAL BUREAU 130, MONTREAL, QC, H3B 2S2
(514) 843-5812   *SIC* 7389
STUDIOS FRAMESTORE INC   *p* 1183
5455 AV DE GASPE BUREAU 900, MONTREAL, QC, H2T 3B3
(514) 277-0004   *SIC* 7812
STUDIOS MARKO   *p* 1175
See MARKO AUDIO POST PRODUCTION INC
STUDIOS MOMENT FACTORY INC, LES *p* 1184
6250 AV DU PARC, MONTREAL, QC, H2V 4H8
(514) 843-8433   *SIC* 7336
STUDON ELECTRIC & CONTROLS INC *p* 156
8024 EDGAR INDUSTRIAL CRES UNIT 102, RED DEER, AB, T4P 3R3
(403) 342-1666   *SIC* 1731
STUDY BREAK LIMITED   *p* 596
5480 CANOTEK RD SUITE 20, GLOUCESTER, ON, K1J 9H7

(613) 745-6389   *SIC* 5812
STURDELL INDUSTRIES INC   *p* 588
1907 ALBION RD, ETOBICOKE, ON, M9W 5S8
(416) 675-2025   *SIC* 7389
STURGEON CREEK COLONY FARMS LTD *p* 351
1069 ROAD 63, HEADINGLEY, MB, R4J 1C1
(204) 633-2196   *SIC* 7692
STURGEON CREEK RETIREMENT RESIDENCE   *p* 373
See ALL SENIORS CARE LIVING CENTRES LTD
STURGEON CREEK RETIREMENT RESIDENCE II   *p* 373
707 SETTER ST SUITE 136, WINNIPEG, MB, R2Y 0A4
(204) 885-0303   *SIC* 6513
STURGEON CREEK WELDING   *p* 351
See STURGEON CREEK COLONY FARMS LTD
STURGEON FOUNDATION   *p* 147
9922 103 ST, MORINVILLE, AB, T8R 1R7
(780) 939-5116   *SIC* 8741
STURGEON HOTEL LTD   *p* 166
156 ST ALBERT TRAIL SUITE 10, ST. ALBERT, AB, T8N 0P5
(780) 459-5551   *SIC* 7011
STURGEON LAKE FINE FOODS & GAS BAR   *p* 1436
1 ECONOMIC LANE, STURGEON LAKE, SK, S0J 2E1
(306) 764-1222   *SIC* 5541
STURGEON PUBLIC SCHOOL DIVISION *p* 147
See STURGEON SCHOOL DIVISION #24
STURGEON SCHOOL DIVISION #24 *p* 147
9820 104 ST, MORINVILLE, AB, T8R 1L8
(780) 939-4341   *SIC* 8211
STURGEON TIRE   *p* 367
See STURGEON TIRE (1993) LTD
STURGEON TIRE (1993) LTD   *p* 367
791 MARION ST, WINNIPEG, MB, R2J 0K6
(204) 987-9566   *SIC* 5014
STURO METAL INC   *p* 1139
600 RUE JEAN-MARCHAND, LEVIS, QC, G6Y 9G6
(418) 833-2107   *SIC* 3441
STUTTERS CONSTRUCTION RESTORATIONS   *p* 223
See S C RESTORATIONS LTD
STUYVER'S BAKESTUDIO   *p* 230
27353 58 CRES UNIT 101, LANGLEY, BC, V4W 3W7
(604) 607-7760   *SIC* 2051
STYLE SOLUTIONS, DIV OF   *p* 319
See JORDANS RUGS LTD
STYLUS MADE TO ORDER SOFAS   *p* 193
See STYLUS SOFAS INC
STYLUS SOFAS INC   *p* 193
7885 RIVERFRONT GATE, BURNABY, BC, V5J 5L6
(604) 436-4100   *SIC* 2512
STYRO RAIL INC   *p* 1400
65 RTE 105, WAKEFIELD, QC, J0X 3G0
(819) 643-4456   *SIC* 5033
STYROCHEM CANADA LTEE   *p* 1054
19250 AV CLARK-GRAHAM, BAIE-D'URFE, QC, H9X 3R8
(514) 457-3226   *SIC* 2821
SUBARU   *p* 920
See HING LEE MOTORS LIMITED
SUBARU AUTHORISED DEALERS *p* 1015
See C & C MOTOR SALES LTD
SUBARU CANADA, INC   *p* 733
560 SUFFOLK CRT, MISSISSAUGA, ON, L5R 4J7
(905) 568-4959   *SIC* 5012
SUBARU CITY   *p* 100
See DEVONIAN MOTOR INCORPORA-

TION
SUBARU DES SOURCES   *p* 1093
See 3588025 CANADA INC
SUBARU OF KINGSTON   *p* 632
399 BATH RD, KINGSTON, ON, K7M 7C9
(613) 546-7000   *SIC* 5511
SUBARU OF MAPLE   *p* 664
250 SWEETRIVER BLVD, MAPLE, ON, L6A 4V3
(289) 342-7800   *SIC* 5521
SUBARU OF MISSISSAUGA   *p* 744
See SOMI INC
SUBARU RIVE-SUD   *p* 1069
See 9119-8523 QUEBEC INC
SUBARU SALES & SERVICE   *p* 816
See OGILVIE SUBARU
SUBARU STE-AGATHE ENR   *p* 1354
See 2625-2106 QUEBEC INC
SUBIR BAINS PHARMACY LTD   *p* 684
265 MAIN ST E UNIT 104, MILTON, ON, L9T 1P1
(905) 878-4492   *SIC* 5961
SUBLIME DESSERT INC   *p* 1336
7777 BOUL THIMENS, SAINT-LAURENT, QC, H4S 2A2
(514) 333-0338   *SIC* 2024
SUBMERSIBLE CONSULTING & ENGINEERING   *p* 162
See 6094376 CANADA LTD
SUBNET SOLUTIONS INC   *p* 32
916 42 AVE SE UNIT 110, CALGARY, AB, T2G 1Z2
(403) 270-8885   *SIC* 7372
SUBTERRANEAN (MANITOBA) LTD *p* 360
6 ST PAUL BLVD, WEST ST PAUL, MB, R2P 2W5
(204) 775-8291   *SIC* 1629
SUBURBAN CENTRE & AUTO SERVICE LTD   *p* 363
130 TRANSPORT RD, WINNIPEG, MB, R2C 2Z2
(204) 953-6200   *SIC* 4213
SUBURBAN CONSTRUCTION LTD *p* 1432
2505 AVENUE C N, SASKATOON, SK, S7L 6A6
(306) 652-5322   *SIC* 6712
SUBURBAN MOTORS   *p* 339
See VICTORIA FORD ALLIANCE LTD
SUBWAY   *p* 607
See MIKE'S ONE STOP INC
SUBWAY   *p* 1039
See ISLANDSAND HOLDINGS INC
SUCCESSION CAPITAL CORPORATION *p* 997
88 ARROW RD, TORONTO, ON, M9M 2L8
(416) 223-1700   *SIC* 6211
SUCCESSION FORAGE GEORGE DOWNING LTEE   *p* 1112
410 RUE PRINCIPALE, GRENVILLE-SUR-LA-ROUGE, QC, J0V 1B0
(819) 242-6469   *SIC* 1081
SUDANESE CANADIAN COMMUNITY ASSOCIATION OF LONDON   *p* 659
360 SPRINGBANK DR SUITE 9, LONDON, ON, N6J 1G5
(519) 681-6719   *SIC* 8699
SUDBURY CATHOLIC DISTRICT SCHOOL BOARD   *p* 900
165A D'YOUVILLE ST, SUDBURY, ON, P3C 5E7
(705) 674-4231   *SIC* 8211
SUDBURY DEVELOPMENTAL SERVICES*p* 899
245 MOUNTAIN ST, SUDBURY, ON, P3B 2T8
(705) 674-1451   *SIC* 8361
SUDBURY HOSPITAL SERVICES   *p* 901
363 YORK ST, SUDBURY, ON, P3E 2A8
(705) 674-2158   *SIC* 7219
SUDBURY MANAGEMENT SERVICES LIMITED   *p*

899
1901 LASALLE BLVD, SUDBURY, ON, P3A 2A3
SIC 7363
SUDBURY NEUTRINO OBSERVATORY   *p* 647
1039 REGIONAL RD 24, LIVELY, ON, P3Y 1N2
(705) 692-7000   *SIC* 8733
SUDBURY REGENT STREET INC   *p* 901
2270 REGENT ST, SUDBURY, ON, P3E 0B4
(705) 523-8100   *SIC* 7011
SUDBURY WINDOW MANUFACTURING LTD   *p* 899
902 NEWGATE AVE, SUDBURY, ON, P3A 5J9
(705) 560-5700   *SIC* 3089
SUDDEN REALTY   *p* 156
See RICHARDSON, ALISON REALTOR
SUDDEN SERVICE TECHNOLOGIES CORPORATION   *p* 193
7635 NORTH FRASER WAY UNIT 103, BURNABY, BC, V5J 0B8
(604) 873-3910   *SIC* 5045
SUDDEN TECHNOLOGIES   *p* 193
See SUDDEN SERVICE TECHNOLOGIES CORPORATION
SUDS   *p* 1007
See SUDS EXPRESS INC
SUDS EXPRESS INC   *p* 1007
130 DEARBORN PL, WATERLOO, ON, N2J 4N5
(519) 886-0561   *SIC* 7542
SUE'S MARKET   *p* 856
See SUE'S PRODUCE WORLD LTD
SUE'S PRODUCE WORLD LTD   *p* 856
205 DON HEAD VILLAGE BLVD SUITE 7, RICHMOND HILL, ON, L4C 7R4
(905) 737-0520   *SIC* 5431
SUEDART   *p* 1318
See MARTIN INC
SUEDE MASTER (1975) INC   *p* 791
25 CONNIE ST, NORTH YORK, ON, M6L 2H8
(416) 614-8000   *SIC* 5087
SUEZ CANADA INC   *p* 1095
1375 RTE TRANSCANADIENNE BUREAU 400, DORVAL, QC, H9P 2W8
(514) 683-1200   *SIC* 1781
SUEZ CANADA WASTE SERIVCES INC *p* 116
9426 51 AVE NW SUITE 307, EDMONTON, AB, T6E 5A6
(780) 391-7303   *SIC* 2875
SUEZ CANADA WASTE SERIVCES INC *p* 117
9426 51 AVE NW SUITE 307, EDMONTON, AB, T6E 5A6
(780) 989-5212   *SIC* 4953
SUEZ CANADA WASTE SERIVCES INC *p* 168
10000 CHRYSTINA LAKE RD, SWAN HILLS, AB, T0G 2C0
(780) 333-4197   *SIC* 4953
SUEZ SOLUTIONS DE TRAITEMENT CANADA   *p* 1228
See SUEZ TREATMENT SOLUTIONS CANADA L.P.
SUEZ TREATMENT SOLUTIONS CANADA L.P.   *p* 478
1295 CORMORANT RD SUITE 200, ANCASTER, ON, L9G 4V5
(289) 346-1000   *SIC* 3589
SUEZ TREATMENT SOLUTIONS CANADA L.P.   *p* 1228
5490 BOUL THIMENS BUREAU 100, MONTREAL, QC, H4R 2K9
(514) 683-1200   *SIC* 1781
SUEZ WATER TECHNOLOGIES & SOLUTIONS CANADA   *p* 806
3239 DUNDAS ST W, OAKVILLE, ON, L6M 4B2

(905) 465-3030   SIC 5169
SUGI CANADA LTEE   p 1236
3255 RUE JULES-BRILLANT, MONTREAL, QC, H7P 6C9
SIC 5139
SUGOI PERFORMANCE APPAREL LIMITED PARTNERSHIP   p
289
144 7TH AVE E, VANCOUVER, BC, V5T 1M6
(604) 875-0887   SIC 2329
SUKI'S BEAUTY BAZAAR LTD   p 320
3157 GRANVILLE ST, VANCOUVER, BC, V6H 3K1
(604) 738-2127   SIC 7231
SUKI'S INTERNATIONAL HAIR DESIGN   p
320
See SUKI'S BEAUTY BAZAAR LTD
SULLIVAN MOTOR PRODUCTS LTD   p 216
2760 YELLOWHEAD HWY SUITE 16, HOUSTON, BC, V0J 1Z0
(250) 845-2244   SIC 5511
SULLIVAN MOTORS   p 216
See SULLIVAN MOTOR PRODUCTS LTD
SULLIVAN, EVAN PHARMACY LIMITED   p
492
150 SIDNEY ST SUITE 1, BELLEVILLE, ON, K8P 5E2
(613) 962-3406   SIC 5912
SULZER PUMPS (CANADA) INC   p 183
4129 LOZELLS AVE, BURNABY, BC, V5A 2Z5
(604) 415-7800   SIC 3561
SUM INSURANCE   p 940
See STRATEGIC UNDERWRITING MANAGERS INC
SUM IT CORPORATION   p 86
10934 120 ST NW, EDMONTON, AB, T5H 3P7
(780) 452-7200   SIC 5131
SUMAC LODGE   p 858
See REVERA LONG TERM CARE INC
SUMAGGO COLLECTION INC   p 707
5715 COOPERS AVE SUITE 7, MISSISSAUGA, ON, L4Z 2C7
(905) 712-9777   SIC 5136
SUMAS   p 193
See SUMAS ENVIRONMENTAL SERVICES INC
SUMAS CEDAR   p 175
See QUADRA WOOD PRODUCTS LTD
SUMAS ENVIRONMENTAL SERVICES INC
p 193
4623 BYRNE RD, BURNABY, BC, V5J 3H6
(604) 682-6678   SIC 4953
SUMITOMO CANADA LIMITED   p 60
350 7 AVE SW SUITE 2400, CALGARY, AB, T2P 3N9
(403) 264-7021   SIC 5051
SUMMA ENGINEERING LIMITED   p 689
6423 NORTHAM DR, MISSISSAUGA, ON, L4V 1J2
(905) 678-3388   SIC 5065
SUMMER STREET INDUSTRIES INC p 463
72 PARK ST, NEW GLASGOW, NS, B2H 5B8
(902) 755-1745   SIC 8331
SUMMERHILL ESTATE WINERY CO p 219
4870 CHUTE LAKE RD SUITE 1, KELOWNA, BC, V1W 4M3
(250) 764-8000   SIC 5921
SUMMERHILL MARKET   p 929
See JUNVIR INVESTMENTS LIMITED
SUMMERHILL PYRAMID WINERY   p 219
See SUMMERHILL ESTATE WINERY CO
SUMMERSET MANOR   p 1043
See PROVINCE OF PEI
SUMMERSIDE CHRYSLER DODGE (1984) LTD   p 1043
3 WATER ST, SUMMERSIDE, PE, C1N 1A2
(902) 436-9141   SIC 5511
SUMMERSIDE LIONS CENTRE   p 422
19 PARK DR, CORNER BROOK, NL, A2H 4T4

(709) 783-2616   SIC 8699
SUMMERSIDE RACEWAY   p 1043
See PRINCE COUNTY HORSEMAN'S CLUB INC
SUMMERWOOD PRODUCTS   p 866
See DECOR STRUCTURES CORP
SUMMIT AIR LTD   p 436
100 DICKENS ST, YELLOWKNIFE, NT, X1A 3T2
(867) 873-4464   SIC 4522
SUMMIT CARE CORPORATION (EDMONTON) LTD   p
124
1808 RABBIT HILL RD NW, EDMONTON, AB, T6R 3H2
(780) 665-8050   SIC 8361
SUMMIT CARE CORPORATION LTD   p 77
10 COUNTRY VILLAGE COVE NE, CALGARY, AB, T3K 6B4
(403) 567-0461   SIC 8051
SUMMIT COMPLETIONS LTD   p 5
4912 50TH ST, BASHAW, AB, T0B 0H0
SIC 1389
SUMMIT CUSTOM BROKERS   p 265
See SUMMIT INTERNATIONAL TRADE SERVICES INC
SUMMIT DODGE CHRYSLER JEEP LIMITED   p
495
10 SIMONA DR, BOLTON, ON, L7E 4C7
SIC 5511
SUMMIT DODGE JEEP CHRYSLER   p 402
See 612111 NB LTD
SUMMIT FOOD   p 817
See COLABOR LIMITED PARTNERSHIP
SUMMIT FOOD SERVICE DISTRIBUTORS p
738
See COLABOR LIMITED PARTNERSHIP
SUMMIT FOOD SERVICE DISTRIBUTORS, DIV OF   p 648
See COLABOR LIMITED PARTNERSHIP
SUMMIT FOOD SERVICE, A DIVISION OF COLABOR   p 648
See COLABOR LIMITED PARTNERSHIP
SUMMIT FORD SALES (1982) LIMITED   p
580
12 CARRIER DR, ETOBICOKE, ON, M9V 2C1
(416) 741-6221   SIC 5511
SUMMIT HELICOPTERS LTD   p 436
27 YELLOWKNIFE AIRPORT 100 DICKINS ST, YELLOWKNIFE, NT, X1A 3T2
(867) 765-5969   SIC 4522
SUMMIT INDUSTRIAL INCOME REIT p 506
75 SUMMERLEA RD UNIT B, BRAMPTON, ON, L6T 4V2
(905) 791-1181   SIC 6722
SUMMIT INTERNATIONAL TRADE SERVICES INC   p
265
5200 MILLER RD SUITE 2060, RICHMOND, BC, V7B 1L1
(604) 278-3551   SIC 4731
SUMMIT MOTORS LTD   p 169
4801 46 AVE, TABER, AB, T1G 2A4
(403) 223-3563   SIC 5012
SUMMIT PIPELINE SERVICES ULC p 857
46 COOPER RD SUITE 13, ROSSLYN, ON, P7K 0E3
(807) 939-1100   SIC 1623
SUMMIT PLACE   p 836
See REVERA LONG TERM CARE INC
SUMMIT SALON SERVICES INC   p 18
10905 48 ST SE SUITE 105, CALGARY, AB, T2C 1G8
(403) 252-6201   SIC 5087
SUMMIT SECURITY GROUP LTD   p 218
GD STN MAIN, KAMLOOPS, BC, V2C 5K2
SIC 7381
SUMMIT SKI LIMITED   p 343
4293 MOUNTAIN SQ UNIT 118, WHISTLER, BC, V8E 1B8
(604) 932-6225   SIC 5941
SUMMIT VETERINARY PHARMACY INC   p

482
25 FURBACHER LANE SUITE 1, AURORA, ON, L4G 6W3
(905) 713-2040   SIC 2834
SUMMITT ENERGY MANAGEMENT INC   p
733
100 MILVERTON DR SUITE 608, MISSISSAUGA, ON, L5R 4H1
(905) 366-7000   SIC 4911
SUMMO MANUFACTURING, DIV OF p 525
See VOESTALPINE ROTEC SUMMO CORP
SUMMUM BEAUTE INTERNATIONAL (DISTRIBUTION)   p
1309
See SUMMUM BEAUTE INTERNATIONAL INC
SUMMUM BEAUTE INTERNATIONAL INC p
1309
4400 BOUL KIMBER, SAINT-HUBERT, QC, J3Y 8L4
(450) 678-3231   SIC 5122
SUMMUM GRANIT INC   p 1352
460 RUE PRINCIPALE, SAINT-SEBASTIEN-DE-FRONTENAC, QC, G0Y 1M0
(819) 652-2333   SIC 3281
SUMWA TRADING CO. LTD   p 11
2710 5 AVE NE, CALGARY, AB, T2A 4V4
(403) 230-8823   SIC 6799
SUN CHEMICAL LIMITED   p 506
10 WEST DR, BRAMPTON, ON, L6T 4Y4
(905) 796-2222   SIC 2893
SUN COUNTRY HIGHWAY LTD   p 520
76000 LONDON RD RR 1, BRUCEFIELD, ON, N0M 1J0
(866) 467-6920   SIC 5531
SUN COUNTRY HOLDINGS LTD   p 164
411 SOUTH AVE, SPRUCE GROVE, AB, T7X 3B5
(780) 962-1030   SIC 1629
SUN COUNTRY REGIONAL HEALTH AUTHORITY   p
1415
18 EICHHORST ST, REDVERS, SK, S0C 2H0
(306) 452-3553   SIC 8062
SUN COUNTRY REGIONAL HEALTH AUTHORITY   p
1415
18 EICHORST ST, REDVERS, SK, S0C 2H0
(306) 452-3553   SIC 4119
SUN COUNTRY REGIONAL HEALTH AUTHORITY   p
1437
201 WILFRED ST, WAWOTA, SK, S0G 5A0
SIC 8051
SUN COUNTRY REGIONAL HEALTH AUTHORITY   p
1438
201 1ST AVE NE, WEYBURN, SK, S4H 0N1
(306) 842-8400   SIC 8062
SUN COUNTRY TOYOTA   p 216
See 646371 B.C. LTD
SUN DISTRIBUTION   p 111
4990 92 AVE NW, EDMONTON, AB, T6B 3A1
SIC 2711
SUN GRO HORTICULTURE CANADA LTD p
160
52130 RANGE RD, SEBA BEACH, AB, T0E 2B0
(780) 797-3019   SIC 5159
SUN GRO HORTICULTURE CANADA LTD p
349
GD, ELMA, MB, R0E 0Z0
(204) 426-2121   SIC 1499
SUN GRO HORTICULTURE CANADA LTD p
403
4492 ROUTE 113, HAUT-LAMEQUE, NB, E8T 3L3
(506) 336-2229   SIC 5159
SUN GRO HORTICULTURE PROCESSING   p 349

See SUN GRO HORTICULTURE CANADA LTD
SUN LIFE ASSURANCE COMPANY OF CANADA   p 967
1 YORK ST, TORONTO, ON, M5J 0B6
(416) 979-9966   SIC 6311
SUN LIFE ASSURANCE COMPANY OF CANADA   p 1208
1001 RUE DU SQUARE-DORCHESTER BUREAU 600, MONTREAL, QC, H3B 1N1
(514) 731-7961   SIC 6311
SUN LIFE ASSURANCE COMPANY OF CANADA   p 1208
1155 RUE METCALFE BUREAU 20, MONTREAL, QC, H3B 2V9
(514) 866-6411   SIC 6311
SUN LIFE ASSURANCES (CANADA) LIMITEE   p
1208
1155 RUE METCALFE BUREAU 1024, MONTREAL, QC, H3B 2V9
(514) 866-6411   SIC 6411
SUN LIFE DU CANADA, COMPAGNIE D'ASSURANCE-VIE   p 1208
1155 RUE METCALFE BUREAU 1410, MONTREAL, QC, H3B 2V9
(514) 393-8820   SIC 6311
SUN LIFE FINANCIAL   p 1208
See SUN LIFE ASSURANCES (CANADA) LIMITEE
SUN LIFE FINANCIAL AND DEPATIE FINANCIAL SERVICES INC   p
138
4906 50 AVE, LACOMBE, AB, T4L 1Y1
(403) 782-3555   SIC 8742
SUN LIFE FINANCIAL INC   p 967
1 YORK ST, TORONTO, ON, M5J 0B6
(416) 979-9966   SIC 6411
SUN LIFE FINANCIAL INVESTMENT SERVICES (CANADA) INC   p
1007
227 KING ST S, WATERLOO, ON, N2J 1R2
(519) 888-2290   SIC 6722
SUN PARLOR HOME   p 645
175 TALBOT ST E, LEAMINGTON, ON, N8H 1L9
(519) 326-5731   SIC 8361
SUN PARLOR HOMES   p 644
See CORPORATION OF THE COUNTY OF ESSEX, THE
SUN PARLOUR GREENHOUSE GROWERS CO-OPERATIVE LIMITED   p 645
230 COUNTY RD 31, LEAMINGTON, ON, N8H 3V5
(519) 326-8681   SIC 5148
SUN PARLOUR GROWER SUPPLY LIMITED   p
645
230 COUNTY RD 31, LEAMINGTON, ON, N8H 3W2
(519) 326-8681   SIC 5191
SUN PEAKS GRAND HOTEL   p 215
See 19959 YUKON INC
SUN PEAKS RESORT   p 270
See NIPPON CABLE (CANADA) HOLDINGS LTD
SUN PROCESSING LTD   p 194
7580 LOWLAND DR, BURNABY, BC, V5J 5A4
(604) 688-8372   SIC 5148
SUN RAY SPAS   p 111
See SUNRAY MANUFACTURING INC
SUN RICH FRESH FOODS INC   p 258
22151 FRASERWOOD WAY, RICHMOND, BC, V6W 1J5
(604) 244-8800   SIC 2033
SUN RICH FRESH FOODS INC   p 500
35 BRAMTREE CRT UNIT 1, BRAMPTON, ON, L6S 6G2
(905) 789-0200   SIC 2033
SUN RIVERS LIMITED PARTNERSHIP   p
218
1000 CLUBHOUSE DR, KAMLOOPS, BC, V2H 1T9

▲ Public Company   ■ Public Company Family Member   **HQ** Headquarters   **BR** Branch   **SL** Single Location

(250) 828-9989   *SIC* 6552

SUN SUI WAH SEAFOOD RESTAURANT *p* 262

4940 NO. 3 RD SUITE 102, RICHMOND, BC, V6X 3A5

(604) 273-8208   *SIC* 5812

SUN TOYOTA LTD   *p* 117

10130 82 AVE NW, EDMONTON, AB, T6E 1Z4

(780) 433-2411   *SIC* 5511

SUN VALLEY FINE FOODS   *p* 920

See SUN VALLEY FRUIT MARKET & GRO-CERIES (DANFORTH) LTD

SUN VALLEY FRUIT MARKET & GRO-CERIES (DANFORTH) LTD   *p* 920

583 DANFORTH AVE, TORONTO, ON, M4K 1P9

(416) 264-2323   *SIC* 5431

SUN VALLEY HONDA   *p* 146

See 636066 ALBERTA LTD

SUN VALLEY SUPERMARKET INCORPO-RATED   *p* 868

468 DANFORTH RD, SCARBOROUGH, ON, M1K 1C6

(416) 264-2323   *SIC* 5411

SUN WEST SCHOOL DIVISION NO 207 SASKATCHEWAN   *p* 1423

501 FIRST ST W, ROSETOWN, SK, S0L 2V0

(306) 882-2677   *SIC* 8211

SUN-BRITE FOODS INC   *p* 858

1532 COUNTY ROAD 34, RUTHVEN, ON, N0P 2G0

(519) 326-9033   *SIC* 2033

SUN-GLO PRODUCTS INC   *p* 743

6681 EXCELSIOR CRT, MISSISSAUGA, ON, L5T 2J2

(905) 678-6456   *SIC* 5199

SUN-RYPE PRODUCTS LTD   *p* 223

1165 ETHEL ST, KELOWNA, BC, V1Y 2W4

(250) 860-7973   *SIC* 2033

SUN-VIEW INDUSTRIES LTD   *p* 270

15915 BENTLEY PL, SUMMERLAND, BC, V0H 1Z3

(250) 494-1327   *SIC* 5561

SUN-VIEW POWDER COATING   *p* 270

See SUN-VIEW INDUSTRIES LTD

SUNAC WOODWORK INC   *p* 94

13030 146 ST NW, EDMONTON, AB, T5L 2H7

SIC 5031

SUNBEAM CENTRE   *p* 637

595 GREENFIELD AVE SUITE 43, KITCH-ENER, ON, N2C 2N7

(519) 894-2098   *SIC* 8059

SUNBEAM CORPORATION (CANADA) LIMITED   *p* 512

20 HEREFORD ST SUITE B, BRAMPTON, ON, L6Y 0M1

(905) 593-6255   *SIC* 5064

SUNBEAM RESIDENTIAL GROUP HOME *p* 637

See SUNBEAM CENTRE

SUNBELT RENTALS OF CANADA INC   *p* 202

93 NORTH BEND ST SUITE 838, COQUIT-LAM, BC, V3K 6N1

(604) 291-8001   *SIC* 7359

SUNBURY CEDAR SALES, DIV OF   *p* 207

See DELTA CEDAR SPECIALTIES LTD

SUNBURY TRANSPORT LIMITED   *p* 413

485 MCALLISTER DR, SAINT JOHN, NB, E2J 2S8

(800) 786-2878   *SIC* 4213

SUNCHEF FARMS   *p* 1047

See ALIMENTS SUNCHEF INC

SUNCO DRYWALL LTD   *p* 38

7835 FLINT RD SE, CALGARY, AB, T2H 1G3

(403) 250-9701   *SIC* 1742

SUNCO DRYWALL LTD   *p* 220

330 HIGHWAY 33 W UNIT 102, KELOWNA,

BC, V1X 1X9

(250) 807-2270   *SIC* 1742

SUNCO FOODS INC   *p* 194

9208 NORTH FRASER CRES, BURNABY, BC, V5J 0E3

(604) 451-9208   *SIC* 5149

SUNCOR ENERGY INC   *p* 60

6 AVE SW SUITE 150, CALGARY, AB, T2P 3Y7

(403) 296-8000   *SIC* 2911

SUNCOR ENERGY INC   *p* 91

GD STN MAIN, EDMONTON, AB, T5J 2G8

(780) 410-5610   *SIC* 2911

SUNCOR ENERGY INC   *p* 124

801 PETROLEUM WAY NW, EDMONTON, AB, T6S 1H5

(780) 410-5681   *SIC* 2911

SUNCOR ENERGY INC   *p* 129

512 SNOW EAGLE DR, FORT MCMURRAY, AB, T9H 0B6

(780) 790-1999   *SIC* 1311

SUNCOR ENERGY INC   *p* 129

GD LCD MAIN, FORT MCMURRAY, AB, T9H 3E2

(780) 743-6411   *SIC* 1311

SUNCOR ENERGY INC   *p* 161

241 KASKA RD, SHERWOOD PARK, AB, T8A 4E8

(780) 449-2100   *SIC* 4613

SUNCOR ENERGY INC   *p* 214

11527 ALASKA RD, FORT ST. JOHN, BC, V1J 6N2

(250) 787-8200   *SIC* 2911

SUNCOR ENERGY INC   *p* 431

140 KELSEY DR, ST. JOHN'S, NL, A1B 0T2

(709) 778-3500   *SIC* 1389

SUNCOR ENERGY INC   *p* 715

2489 NORTH SHERIDAN WAY, MISSIS-SAUGA, ON, L5K 1A8

(905) 804-4500   *SIC* 1389

SUNCOR ENERGY INC   *p* 746

535 ROKEBY LINE RR 1, MOORETOWN, ON, N0N 1M0

(519) 481-0454   *SIC* 2911

SUNCOR ENERGY INC   *p* 805

3275 REBECCA ST, OAKVILLE, ON, L6L 6N5

(905) 804-7152   *SIC* 2911

SUNCOR ENERGY INC   *p* 1248

11701 RUE SHERBROOKE E, POINTE-AUX-TREMBLES, QC, H1B 1C3

(514) 640-8000   *SIC* 2911

SUNCOR ENERGY MARKETING INC *p* 60

150 6 AVE SW, CALGARY, AB, T2P 3Y7

(403) 296-8000   *SIC* 2911

SUNCOR ENERGY OIL SANDS LIMITED PARTNERSHIP   *p* 60

150 6 AVE SW UNIT 2, CALGARY, AB, T2P 3Y7

(403) 296-8000   *SIC* 1311

SUNCOR ENERGY PRODUCTS INC *p* 715

2489 NORTH SHERIDAN WAY, MISSIS-SAUGA, ON, L5K 1A8

(905) 804-4500   *SIC* 2911

SUNCOR ENERGY PRODUCTS INC *p* 774

36 YORK MILLS RD SUITE 110, NORTH YORK, ON, M2P 2E9

(416) 498-7751   *SIC* 2911

SUNCOR ENERGY PRODUCTS INC *p* 861

1900 RIVER RD, SARNIA, ON, N7T 7J3

(519) 337-2301   *SIC* 5172

SUNCOR ENERGY PRODUCTS PARTNER-SHIP   *p* 60

150 6 AVE SW, CALGARY, AB, T2P 3Y7

(403) 296-8000   *SIC* 2911

SUNCOR SOCIAL CLUB   *p* 161

See SUNCOR ENERGY INC

SUNCORP VALUATIONS LTD   *p* 1430

261 1ST AVE N SUITE 300, SASKATOON, SK, S7K 1X2

(306) 652-0311   *SIC* 7389

SUNCREST COLONY FARMS LTD   *p* 360

43051 SUNCREST RD, TOUROND, MB,

R0A 2G0

(204) 433-7853   *SIC* 0191

SUNDANCE MAZDA   *p* 100

See DONMAR CAR SALES LTD

SUNDER GROUP OF COMPANIES LTD *p* 770

5650 YONGE ST, NORTH YORK, ON, M2M 4G3

(416) 226-1809   *SIC* 8741

SUNDERLAND CO-OPERATIVE INC *p* 901

1 RIVER ST, SUNDERLAND, ON, L0C 1H0

(705) 357-3491   *SIC* 5999

SUNDERLAND HOG FARMS LTD   *p* 151

GD, PARADISE VALLEY, AB, T0B 3R0

(780) 745-2214   *SIC* 5154

SUNDIAL HOMES LIMITED   *p* 773

4576 YONGE ST SUITE 500, NORTH YORK, ON, M2N 6N4

(416) 224-1200   *SIC* 1521

SUNDINE PRODUCE INC   *p* 743

6075 KESTREL RD, MISSISSAUGA, ON, L5T 1Y8

(905) 364-1600   *SIC* 5148

SUNDOG DISTRIBUTING INC   *p* 40

83 SKYLINE CRES NE, CALGARY, AB, T2K 5X2

(403) 516-6600   *SIC* 5099

SUNDOG EYEWARE   *p* 40

See SUNDOG DISTRIBUTING INC

SUNDOG PRINTING, DIV OF   *p* 72

See DATA COMMUNICATIONS MANAGE-MENT CORP

SUNDRE FOREST PRODUCTS INC *p* 168

5541 HWY 584 W, SUNDRE, AB, T0M 1X0

(403) 638-4093   *SIC* 2421

SUNDRE HOSPITAL & CARE CENTRE *p* 168

See ALBERTA HEALTH SERVICES

SUNDRE MOTORS LTD   *p* 168

104 MAIN AVE NE, SUNDRE, AB, T0M 1X0

SIC 5511

SUNDRIDGE HAPPY GANG, THE   *p* 902

110 MAIN ST E, SUNDRIDGE, ON, P0A 1Z0

(705) 384-7351   *SIC* 8322

SUNERA   *p* 72

See SUNORA FOODS INC

SUNFORCE PRODUCTS INC   *p* 1241

9015 CH AVON BUREAU 2017, MONTREAL-OUEST, QC, H4X 2G8

(514) 989-2100   *SIC* 5013

SUNFRESH LIMITED   *p* 512

1 PRESIDENTS CHOICE CIR, BRAMP-TON, ON, L6Y 5S5

(905) 459-2500   *SIC* 5141

SUNHILLS MINING LIMITED PARTNER-SHIP   *p* 160

4419 B SUNDANCE RD, SEBA BEACH, AB, T0E 2B0

(780) 731-5300   *SIC* 1221

SUNICE INC   *p* 1341

850 RUE MCCAFFREY, SAINT-LAURENT, QC, H4T 1N1

(514) 341-6767   *SIC* 5136

SUNKATCHERS RV PARK COOPERATIVE *p* 223

4155 HWY 3, KEREMEOS, BC, V0X 1N1

(250) 499-2065   *SIC* 6111

SUNNY CORNER ENTERPRISES INC *p* 405

259 DALTON AVE, MIRAMICHI, NB, E1V 3C4

(506) 622-5600   *SIC* 1711

SUNNY CREST RETIREMENT VILLA   *p* 1015

See SUNNYCREST NURSING HOMES LIMITED

SUNNY CRUNCH FOODS HOLDINGS LTD *p* 675

200 SHIELDS CRT, MARKHAM, ON, L3R 9T5

(905) 475-0422   *SIC* 2043

SUNNY CRUNCH FOODS LIMITED *p* 675

200 SHIELDS CRT, MARKHAM, ON, L3R

9T5

(905) 475-0422   *SIC* 5149

SUNNY FOODMART   *p* 778

See 2169319 ONTARIO INC

SUNNY HOLDINGS LIMITED   *p* 41

1140 16 AVE NW, CALGARY, AB, T2M 0K8

SIC 5812

SUNNY SITE COLONY   *p* 171

See HUTTERIAN BRETHREN

SUNNY VIEW PUBLIC SCHOOL   *p* 787

See TORONTO DISTRICT SCHOOL BOARD

SUNNYBROOK HEALTH SCIENCES CEN-TRE   *p* 921

2075 BAYVIEW AVE, TORONTO, ON, M4N 3M5

(416) 480-6100   *SIC* 8062

SUNNYBROOK HEALTH SCIENCES CEN-TRE   *p* 932

43 WELLESLEY ST E SUITE 327, TORONTO, ON, M4Y 1H1

(416) 967-8500   *SIC* 8069

SUNNYBROOK HOSPITAL   *p* 921

See SUNNYBROOK HEALTH SCIENCES CENTRE

SUNNYBROOK RESEARCH INSTITUTE *p* 921

2075 BAYVIEW AVE, TORONTO, ON, M4N 3M5

(416) 480-6100   *SIC* 8732

SUNNYCREST NURSING HOMES LIMITED *p* 1015

1635 DUNDAS ST E, WHITBY, ON, L1N 2K9

(905) 576-0111   *SIC* 8051

SUNNYHOLME INC   *p* 604

2 WYNDHAM ST N, GUELPH, ON, N1H 4E3

(519) 824-6664   *SIC* 6712

SUNNYSIDE ADVENTIST CARE CENTRE LTD   *p* 1433

2200 ST HENRY AVE, SASKATOON, SK, S7M 0P5

(306) 653-1267   *SIC* 8051

SUNNYSIDE COLONY LTD   *p* 353

GD, NEWTON SIDING, MB, R0H 0X0

(204) 267-2812   *SIC* 0191

SUNNYSIDE COLONY OF HUTTERIAN TRUST   *p* 353

See SUNNYSIDE COLONY LTD

SUNOPTA FOOD DISTRIBUTION GROUP *p* 559

See SUNOPTA INC

SUNOPTA INC   *p* 559

8755 KEELE ST, CONCORD, ON, L4K 2N1

(905) 738-4304   *SIC* 5149

SUNOPTA INC   *p* 727

2233 ARGENTIA RD SUITE 401, MISSIS-SAUGA, ON, L5N 2X7

(905) 821-9669   *SIC* 5149

SUNORA FOODS INC   *p* 72

4616 VALIANT DR NW SUITE 205, CAL-GARY, AB, T3A 0X9

(403) 247-8300   *SIC* 2079

SUNOVA CREDIT UNION LIMITED   *p* 356

233 MAIN ST, SELKIRK, MB, R1A 1S1

(204) 785-7625   *SIC* 6062

SUNOVA CREDIT UNION LIMITED   *p* 359

410 CENTRE AVE, STONEWALL, MB, R0C 2Z0

(204) 467-5574   *SIC* 6062

SUNOVION PHARMACEUTICALS CANADA INC   *p* 727

6790 CENTURY AVE SUITE 100, MISSIS-SAUGA, ON, L5N 2V8

(905) 814-9145   *SIC* 2834

SUNOX INDUSTRIAL GASES INC   *p* 536

440 SHELDON DR, CAMBRIDGE, ON, N1T 2C1

(519) 624-4413   *SIC* 5085

SUNPLY CORPORATION   *p* 385

551 CENTURY ST, WINNIPEG, MB, R3H

0L8
(204) 786-5555   *SIC* 5211
SUNRAY MANUFACTURING INC   *p* 111
7509 72A ST NW, EDMONTON, AB, T6B 1Z3
(780) 440-1595   *SIC* 5999
SUNRIDGE FORAGE LTD   *p* 356
15 2128 NW, RUSSELL, MB, R0J 1W0
SIC 5191
SUNRIDGE MAZDA   *p* 9
See STANG'S AUTOMOTIVE ENTERPRISES INC
SUNRIDGE NISSAN   *p* 9
See SUNRIDGE NISSAN LTD
SUNRIDGE NISSAN LTD   *p* 9
3131 32 AVE NE, CALGARY, AB, T1Y 6J1
(403) 291-2626   *SIC* 5511
SUNRIPE FARMS PRODUCE   *p* 861
See 509334 ONTARIO INC
SUNRISE ASSISTED LIVING & SUNRISE OF VANCOUVER   *p* 324
See SUNRISE NORTH SENIOR LIVING LTD
SUNRISE ASSISTED LIVING OF RICHMOND HILL   *p*
856
See SUNRISE NORTH ASSISTED LIVING LTD
SUNRISE ASSISTED LIVING UNIONVILLE   *p* 1000
See SUNRISE OF MARKHAM LIMITED
SUNRISE BAKERY   *p* 92
See 312407 ALBERTA LTD
SUNRISE BAKERY LTD   *p* 94
14728 119 AVE NW, EDMONTON, AB, T5L 2P2
(780) 454-5797   *SIC* 2051
SUNRISE COLONY   *p* 126
See SUNRISE HUTTERIAN BRETHREN
SUNRISE CREDIT UNION LIMITED   *p* 360
220 7TH AVE S, VIRDEN, MB, R0M 2C0
(204) 748-2907   *SIC* 6062
SUNRISE FARMS   *p* 278
See SUNRISE POULTRY PROCESSORS LTD
SUNRISE FOODS INTERNATIONAL INC   *p* 1430
306 QUEEN ST SUITE 200, SASKATOON, SK, S7K 0M2
(306) 931-4576   *SIC* 5153
SUNRISE FORD SALES LTD   *p* 174
872 ALPINE RD, 100 MILE HOUSE, BC, V0K 2E0
(250) 395-2414   *SIC* 5511
SUNRISE HUTTERIAN BRETHREN   *p* 126
GD, ETZIKOM, AB, T0K 0W0
(403) 666-3787   *SIC* 8748
SUNRISE KITCHENS LTD   *p* 278
13375 COMBER WAY, SURREY, BC, V3W 5V8
(604) 597-0364   *SIC* 2541
SUNRISE MARKETS INC   *p* 296
729 POWELL ST, VANCOUVER, BC, V6A 1H5
(604) 253-2326   *SIC* 2099
SUNRISE MEDICAL CANADA INC   *p* 559
237 ROMINA DR UNIT 3, CONCORD, ON, L4K 4V3
(905) 660-2459   *SIC* 5047
SUNRISE NORTH ASSISTED LIVING LTD *p* 704
1279 BURNHAMTHORPE RD E SUITE 220, MISSISSAUGA, ON, L4Y 3V7
(905) 625-1344   *SIC* 8361
SUNRISE NORTH ASSISTED LIVING LTD *p* 856
9800 YONGE ST SUITE 101, RICHMOND HILL, ON, L4C 0P5
(905) 883-6963   *SIC* 8361
SUNRISE NORTH SENIOR LIVING LTD   *p* 239
980 LYNN VALLEY RD, NORTH VANCOUVER, BC, V7J 3V7
(604) 904-1226   *SIC* 8361

SUNRISE NORTH SENIOR LIVING LTD   *p* 324
999 57TH AVE W, VANCOUVER, BC, V6P 6Y9
(604) 261-5799   *SIC* 8361
SUNRISE NORTH SENIOR LIVING LTD   *p* 482
3 GOLF LINKS DR SUITE 2, AURORA, ON, L4G 7Y4
(905) 841-0022   *SIC* 8361
SUNRISE NORTH SENIOR LIVING LTD   *p* 525
5401 LAKESHORE RD, BURLINGTON, ON, L7L 6S5
(905) 333-9969   *SIC* 8361
SUNRISE NORTH SENIOR LIVING LTD   *p* 717
4046 ERIN MILLS PKY, MISSISSAUGA, ON, L5L 2W7
(905) 569-0004   *SIC* 8322
SUNRISE NORTH SENIOR LIVING LTD   *p* 801
456 TRAFALGAR RD SUITE 312, OAKVILLE, ON, L6J 7X1
(905) 337-1145   *SIC* 8361
SUNRISE NORTH SENIOR LIVING LTD   *p* 906
484 STEELES AVE W, THORNHILL, ON, L4J 0C7
(905) 731-4300   *SIC* 8741
SUNRISE NORTH SENIOR LIVING LTD   *p* 1022
5065 RIVERSIDE DR E SUITE 203, WINDSOR, ON, N8Y 5B3
(519) 974-5858   *SIC* 8059
SUNRISE NORTH SENIOR LIVING LTD   *p* 1058
50 BOUL DES CHATEAUX, BLAINVILLE, QC, J7B 0A3
(450) 420-2727   *SIC* 8361
SUNRISE OF AURORA   *p* 482
See SUNRISE NORTH SENIOR LIVING LTD
SUNRISE OF MARKHAM LIMITED   *p* 1000
38 SWANSEA RD, UNIONVILLE, ON, L3R 5K2
(905) 947-4566   *SIC* 8051
SUNRISE POULTRY PROCESSORS LTD   *p* 273
17565 65A AVE, SURREY, BC, V3S 7B6
(604) 596-9505   *SIC* 5147
SUNRISE POULTRY PROCESSORS LTD   *p* 278
13538 73 AVE, SURREY, BC, V3W 2R6
(604) 596-9505   *SIC* 2015
SUNRISE RECORDS   *p* 477
See 2428391 ONTARIO INC
SUNRISE SCHOOL DIVISION   *p* 345
344 2ND ST N, BEAUSEJOUR, MB, R0E 0C0
(204) 268-6500   *SIC* 8211
SUNRISE SCHOOL DIVISION   *p* 345
85 5TH ST S, BEAUSEJOUR, MB, R0E 0C0
(204) 268-2423   *SIC* 8211
SUNRISE SENIOR LIVING OF BURLINGTON   *p* 525
See SUNRISE NORTH SENIOR LIVING LTD
SUNRISE SENIOR LIVING OF ERIN MILLS *p* 717
See SUNRISE NORTH SENIOR LIVING LTD
SUNRISE SENIOR LIVING OF MISSISSAUGA   *p* 704
See SUNRISE NORTH ASSISTED LIVING LTD
SUNRISE SERVICE ABBOTSFORD LTD   *p* 177
30210 AUTOMALL DR, ABBOTSFORD, BC, V2T 5M1
(604) 857-2658   *SIC* 5511
SUNRISE SOYA FOODS   *p* 296

See SUNRISE MARKETS INC
SUNRISE TOYOTA   *p* 177
See SUNRISE SERVICE ABBOTSFORD LTD
SUNRISE TRADEX CORP   *p* 1082
271 RUE SAINT-JACQUES S, COATICOOK, QC, J1A 2P3
(819) 804-0551   *SIC* 5075
SUNRISE TRADEX CORPORATION   *p* 1348
3122 RUE BERNARD-PILON, SAINT-MATHIEU-DE-BELOEIL, QC, J3G 4S5
(450) 536-2175   *SIC* 5075
SUNRISE VEHICLE SALES LTD   *p* 218
2477 TRANS CANADA HWY E, KAMLOOPS, BC, V2C 4A9
(250) 372-5588   *SIC* 5511
SUNRISE WHIRLPOOL SPAS   *p* 599
See LEISURE MANUFACTURING INC
SUNSELECT PRODUCE INC   *p* 179
349 264 ST, ALDERGROVE, BC, V4W 2K1
(604) 607-7655   *SIC* 0181
SUNSET   *p* 634
See MASTRONARDI PRODUCE LIMITED
SUNSET COMMUNITY   *p* 465
See SUNSET RESIDENTIAL & REHABILITATION SERVICES INCORPORATED
SUNSET MANSUNSET MANOR   *p* 137
3312 52 AVE SUITE 3402, INNISFAIL, AB, T4G 0C3
(403) 227-8200   *SIC* 6513
SUNSET RESIDENTIAL & REHABILITATION SERVICES INCORPORATED   *p* 465
140 SUNSET LANE, PUGWASH, NS, B0K 1L0
(902) 243-2571   *SIC* 8361
SUNSHINE ASPARAGUS FARMS   *p* 903
See 768308 ONTARIO INC
SUNSHINE BUILDING MAINTENANCE INC *p* 529
2500 INDUSTRIAL ST, BURLINGTON, ON, L7P 1A5
(905) 335-2020   *SIC* 7349
SUNSHINE CABS LIMITED   *p* 239
1465 RUPERT ST, NORTH VANCOUVER, BC, V7J 1G1
(604) 988-8888   *SIC* 4121
SUNSHINE COAST ASSOCIATION FOR COMMUNITY LIVING   *p* 268
5711 MERMAID ST SUITE 105, SECHELT, BC, V0N 3A3
(604) 885-7455   *SIC* 8699
SUNSHINE COAST CREDIT UNION   *p* 214
985 GIBSONS WAY RR 8, GIBSONS, BC, V0N 1V8
(604) 740-2662   *SIC* 6062
SUNSHINE HONDA   *p* 331
See 351684 BC LTD
SUNSHINE OILSANDS LTD   *p* 60
903 8 AVE SW UNIT 1020, CALGARY, AB, T2P 0P7
(403) 984-1450   *SIC* 1311
SUNSHINE TOYOTA   *p* 390
See DILAWRI HOLDINGS INC
SUNSHINE VILLAGE CORPORATION   *p* 65
1037 11 AVE SW, CALGARY, AB, T2R 0G1
(403) 705-4000   *SIC* 7011
SUNSPACE MODULAR ENCLOSURES INC *p* 753
300 TORONTO ST, NEWCASTLE, ON, L1B 1C2
(905) 987-4111   *SIC* 3448
SUNSPACE SUNROOMS   *p* 753
See SUNSPACE MODULAR ENCLOSURES INC
SUNSTAR AMERICAS, INC   *p* 606
515 GOVERNORS RD, GUELPH, ON, N1K 1C7
(519) 837-2500   *SIC* 5047
SUNSTRUM, GARRY W. SALES LIMITED *p* 484
341 HASTINGS ST N RR 2 SUITE 130, BANCROFT, ON, K0L 1C0
(613) 332-0145   *SIC* 5531

SUNTASTIC HOTHOUSE INC   *p* 590
40534 THAMES RD E, EXETER, ON, N0M 1S5
(519) 235-3357   *SIC* 0182
SUNTECH OPTICS INC   *p* 242
758 HARBOURSIDE DR, NORTH VANCOUVER, BC, V7P 3R7
(604) 929-8141   *SIC* 5099
SUNTERRA ENTERPRISES INC   *p* 119
5728 111 ST NW, EDMONTON, AB, T6H 3G1
(780) 434-2610   *SIC* 5411
SUNTERRA MARKET PLACE   *p* 119
See SUNTERRA ENTERPRISES INC
SUNTERRA MEATS LTD   *p* 137
4312 51 ST, INNISFAIL, AB, T4G 1A3
(403) 442-4202   *SIC* 5421
SUNTERRA MEATS TROCHU   *p* 170
See TROCHU MEAT PROCESSORS LTD
SUNVIEW PATIO DOORS LTD   *p* 1028
500 ZENWAY BLVD, WOODBRIDGE, ON, L4H 0S7
(905) 851-1006   *SIC* 5039
SUNWEST AUTO CENTRE LTD   *p* 203
401 RYAN RD, COURTENAY, BC, V9N 3R5
(250) 338-7565   *SIC* 5511
SUNWEST FOOD PROCESSORS LTD   *p* 177
31100 WHEEL AVE, ABBOTSFORD, BC, V2T 6H1
(604) 852-3760   *SIC* 5141
SUNWEST FOODS PROCESSORS LTD   *p* 1011
35 NORTHLAND RD, WATERLOO, ON, N2V 1Y8
(519) 747-5546   *SIC* 1541
SUNWEST SCREEN GRAPHICS LTD *p* 386
277 CREE CRES, WINNIPEG, MB, R3J 3X4
(204) 888-0003   *SIC* 2759
SUNWING AIRLINES INC   *p* 588
27 FASKEN DR, ETOBICOKE, ON, M9W 1K6
(416) 620-4955   *SIC* 4522
SUNWING CANADA INC   *p* 588
27 FASKEN DR, ETOBICOKE, ON, M9W 1K6
(416) 695-0500   *SIC* 4522
SUNWING TRAVEL GROUP INC   *p* 588
27 FASKEN DR, ETOBICOKE, ON, M9W 1K6
(416) 620-4955   *SIC* 4724
SUNWING VACATIONS INC   *p* 588
27 FASKEN DR, ETOBICOKE, ON, M9W 1K6
(416) 620-5999   *SIC* 4725
SUPER A FOODS   *p* 135
See R K R FOODS LTD
SUPER A FOODS   *p* 1440
See PELLY BANKS TRADING CO. LTD
SUPER AUTO CENTRE INC   *p* 392
2028 PEMBINA HWY, WINNIPEG, MB, R3T 2G8
(204) 269-8444   *SIC* 7549
SUPER C   *p* 1076
See METRO RICHELIEU INC
SUPER C   *p* 1099
See METRO RICHELIEU INC
SUPER C   *p* 1104
See METRO RICHELIEU INC
SUPER C   *p* 1106
See METRO RICHELIEU INC
SUPER C   *p* 1112
See METRO RICHELIEU INC
SUPER C   *p* 1240
See METRO RICHELIEU INC
SUPER C   *p* 1317
See METRO RICHELIEU INC
SUPER C   *p* 1346
See METRO RICHELIEU INC
SUPER C   *p* 1359
See ALIMENTATION MARQUIS, YVES INC
SUPER C   *p* 1371
See METRO RICHELIEU INC
SUPER C   *p* 1388

See *METRO RICHELIEU INC*
SUPER C   p 1398
See *METRO RICHELIEU INC*
SUPER C REPENTIGNY   p 1283
See *METRO RICHELIEU INC*
SUPER C SOREL   p 1376
See *METRO RICHELIEU INC*
SUPER C ST HYACINTHE   p 1313
See *METRO RICHELIEU INC*
SUPER C, DIV DE   p 1145
See *METRO RICHELIEU INC*
**SUPER DAVE'S GOLDEN EARS MOTORS
LTD**   p 230
23213 LOUGHEED HWY, MAPLE RIDGE,
BC, V2W 1C1
(604) 467-3401   *SIC* 5511
SUPER DISCOUNT STORE INC   p 678
46 NORMAN ROSS DR, MARKHAM, ON,
L3S 2Z1
(416) 939-5451   *SIC* 5311
SUPER FINE   p 1166
See *FRANCE DELICES INC*
SUPER FIX   p 1225
See *BONNETERIE BELLA INC.*
SUPER FRESHMART LTD   p 932
524 CHURCH ST, TORONTO, ON, M4Y 2E1
SIC 5331
SUPER GROCER & PHARMACY   p 266
See *LU & SONS ENTERPRISE LTD*
SUPER LOVE BOUTIQUE   p 103
See *TELFORD INVESTMENTS LTD*
SUPER MARCH? MASCOUCHE   p 1149
See *MARCHE J.C. MESSIER INC*
SUPER MARCHE CLAUDE ST-PIERRE IGA
p 1223
See *132087 CANADA INC*
SUPER MARCHE CLEMENT NICOLET INC
p 1242
2000 BOUL LOUIS-FRECHETTE UNITE
100, NICOLET, QC, J3T 1M9
(819) 293-6937   *SIC* 5411
SUPER MARCHE COLLIN INC   p 1069
2004 BOUL DE ROME, BROSSARD, QC,
J4W 3M7
(450) 671-8885   *SIC* 5411
**SUPER MARCHE DONAT THERIAULT LIM-
ITEE**   p
399
570 RUE VICTORIA, EDMUNDSTON, NB,
E3V 3N1
(506) 735-1860   *SIC* 5411
SUPER MARCHE FRONTENAC INC p 1110
320 BOUL LECLERC O, GRANBY, QC, J2G
1V3
(450) 372-8014   *SIC* 5411
SUPER MARCHE IBERVILLE INC   p 1283
305 BOUL IBERVILLE, REPENTIGNY, QC,
J6A 2A6
(450) 581-2630   *SIC* 5411
SUPER MARCHE IGA   p 1243
See *GESTION TREMBLAY LEBOEUF INC*
SUPER MARCHE J.C. BEDARD LTEE   p
1253
169 RUE DUPONT, PONT-ROUGE, QC,
G3H 1N3
(418) 873-2415   *SIC* 5411
SUPER MARCHE LAPLANTE INC   p 1316
420 2E AV BUREAU 171, SAINT-JEAN-
SUR-RICHELIEU, QC, J2X 2B8
(450) 357-1258   *SIC* 5411
SUPER MARCHE METRO #1571   p 1173
See *SUPER MARCHE MONT-ROYAL
(1988) INC*
SUPER MARCHE MONT-ROYAL (1988) INC
p 1173
2185 AV DU MONT-ROYAL E, MONTREAL,
QC, H2H 1K2
(514) 522-5146   *SIC* 5411
SUPER MARCHE PLOUFFE INC   p 1056
5 AV DES PINS, BEDFORD, QC, J0J 1A0
(450) 248-2968   *SIC* 5411
SUPER MARCHE RACICOT (1980) INC   p
1155
1280 AV BEAUMONT, MONT-ROYAL, QC,

H3P 3E5
(514) 737-3511   *SIC* 5411
SUPER MARCHE ROBERVAL INC   p 1287
1221 BOUL MARCOTTE BUREAU 1,
ROBERVAL, QC, G8H 3B8
(418) 275-4692   *SIC* 5411
SUPER MARCHE ROY INC   p 1290
240 AV LARIVIERE, ROUYN-NORANDA,
QC, J9X 4G8
(819) 762-5783   *SIC* 5411
SUPER MARCHE SIROIS INC   p 1285
465 BOUL SAINT-GERMAIN, RIMOUSKI,
QC, G5L 3P2
(418) 722-0722   *SIC* 5411
SUPER MARCHE ST-RAPHAEL INC p 1120
640 BOUL JACQUES-BIZARD, L'ILE-
BIZARD, QC, H9C 2H2
(514) 620-4443   *SIC* 5411
SUPER SAVE GAS   p 271
See *ACTTON SUPER-SAVE GAS STA-
TIONS LTD*
SUPER SAVE PROPANE   p 273
See *SUPER-SAVE ENTERPRISES LTD*
**SUPER SHINE JANITORIAL SERVICES
LIMITED**   p 718
4161 SLADEVIEW CRES UNIT 21, MISSIS-
SAUGA, ON, L5L 5R3
(905) 607-8200   *SIC* 7349
SUPER SLINGS INC   p 150
505 11 AVE, NISKU, AB, T9E 7N5
(780) 955-7111   *SIC* 5085
SUPER SOIR   p 1360
See *PHILIPPE GOSSELIN & ASSOCIES
LIMITEE*
SUPER SPLASH AUTO CLEANING LTD   p
359
53 PTH 12 N, STEINBACH, MB, R5G 1T3
(204) 326-3474   *SIC* 5541
SUPER THRIFTY DRUGS CANADA LTD   p
347
381 PARK AVE E UNIT F, BRANDON, MB,
R7A 7A5
(204) 728-1522   *SIC* 5912
SUPER VALU   p 242
See *MARINO'S MARKET LTD*
SUPER VALU 23   p 214
See *H. W. M. STORES LTD*
SUPER VALUE 18   p 242
See *DOUBLE O MARKETS LTD*
SUPER-FIT KNITTING MILLS INC   p 974
1191 BATHURST ST, TORONTO, ON, M5R
3H4
(416) 537-2137   *SIC* 5137
SUPER-LITE   p 392
See *SUPER-LITE LIGHTING LTD*
SUPER-LITE LIGHTING LTD   p 392
1040 WAVERLEY ST, WINNIPEG, MB, R3T
0P3
(204) 989-7277   *SIC* 5063
SUPER-PUFFT SNACKS CORP   p 736
880 GANA CRT, MISSISSAUGA, ON, L5S
1N8
(905) 564-1180   *SIC* 2096
SUPER-SAVE ENTERPRISES LTD   p 273
19395 LANGLEY BYPASS, SURREY, BC,
V3S 6K1
(604) 533-4423   *SIC* 5984
SUPERCARS INC   p 431
220 KENMOUNT RD, ST. JOHN'S, NL, A1B
3T2
(709) 726-8555   *SIC* 5511
SUPERCLUB VIDEOTRON   p 1101
See *9341-6246 QUEBEC INC*
SUPERCLUB VIDEOTRON LTEE, LE p 1173
4545 RUE FRONTENAC BUREAU 101,
MONTREAL, QC, H2H 2R7
(514) 259-6000   *SIC* 6794
SUPERFIT   p 1225
See *BELLA HOSIERY MILLS INC*
SUPERFREIGHT TRANSPORTATION INC p
536
445 DOBBIE DR, CAMBRIDGE, ON, N1T
1S9
(519) 650-5555   *SIC* 4731

SUPERHEAT   p 629
See *1797509 ALBERTA ULC*
SUPERHEAT FGH CANADA INC   p 629
1463 HIGHWAY 21, KINCARDINE, ON, N2Z
2X3
(519) 396-1324   *SIC* 8711
SUPERHEAT FGH TECHNOLOGIES INC p
629
1463 HIGHWAY 21, KINCARDINE, ON, N2Z
2X3
(519) 396-1324   *SIC* 3498
SUPERIEUR PROPANE   p 1155
252 AV DU MOULIN, MONT-LAURIER, QC,
J9L 3W1
SIC 5984
SUPERIOR BREAD   p 585
See *ITALIAN HOME BAKERY LIMITED*
SUPERIOR CABINETS   p 1432
See *SUPERIOR MILLWORK LTD*
SUPERIOR CITY SERVICES LTD   p 273
15151 64 AVE, SURREY, BC, V3S 1X9
(604) 591-3434   *SIC* 6712
SUPERIOR CLEANING SYSTEMS   p 568
See *1084408 ONTARIO INC*
SUPERIOR DELIVERY   p 688
See *MAILPORT COURIER (1986) INC*
SUPERIOR DODGE   p 861
See *JOHNSON, O M HOLDINGS INC*
**SUPERIOR DODGE CHRYSLER (1978)
LIMITED**   p 862
311 TRUNK RD, SAULT STE. MARIE, ON,
P6A 3S8
(705) 256-7481   *SIC* 5511
SUPERIOR ESSEX   p 880
See *ESSEX GROUP CANADA INC*
SUPERIOR EVENTS GROUP INC   p 787
430 NORFINCH DR, NORTH YORK, ON,
M3N 1Y4
(416) 249-4000   *SIC* 7359
SUPERIOR FRAMES   p 559
See *SUPERIOR SEATING HOSPITALITY
INC*
SUPERIOR GAS LIQUIDS   p 984
See *SUPERIOR PLUS CORP*
SUPERIOR GENERAL PARTNER INC   p
1102
101 CH DONALDSON, GATINEAU, QC, J8L
3X3
(819) 986-1135   *SIC* 5169
SUPERIOR GLOVE WORKS LIMITED p 473
36 VIMY ST, ACTON, ON, L7J 1S1
(519) 853-1920   *SIC* 2381
SUPERIOR GOLD INC   p 967
70 UNIVERSITY AVE SUITE 1410,
TORONTO, ON, M5J 2M4
(647) 925-1291   *SIC* 1041
**SUPERIOR GREENSTONE DISTRICT
SCHOOL BOARD**   p 664
12 HEMLO DR BAG A, MARATHON, ON,
P0T 2E0
(807) 229-0436   *SIC* 8211
**SUPERIOR HEATING & AIR CONDITION-
ING/ST. JAMES SHEET METAL LTD**   p
373
1600 CHURCH AVE, WINNIPEG, MB, R2X
1G8
(204) 697-5666   *SIC* 1731
SUPERIOR INDUSTRIAL SERVICES p 863
See *1022013 ONTARIO LIMITED*
SUPERIOR MEDICAL LIMITED   p 784
520 CHAMPAGNE DR, NORTH YORK, ON,
M3J 2T9
(416) 635-9797   *SIC* 5047
SUPERIOR MILLWORK LTD   p 1432
747 46TH ST W, SASKATOON, SK, S7L
6A1
(306) 667-6600   *SIC* 2434
SUPERIOR PLUS CORP   p 984
200 WELLINGTON ST W SUITE 401,
TORONTO, ON, M5V 3C7
(416) 345-8050   *SIC* 2819
SUPERIOR PLUS LP   p 578
302 THE EAST MALL SUITE 200, ETOBI-
COKE, ON, M9B 6C7

(416) 239-7111   *SIC* 2819
SUPERIOR PLUS LP   p 604
7022 WELLINGTON RD, GUELPH, ON,
N1H 6H8
(807) 223-2980   *SIC* 5984
SUPERIOR PLUS LP   p 984
200 WELLINGTON ST W SUITE 401,
TORONTO, ON, M5V 3C7
(416) 345-8050   *SIC* 5984
SUPERIOR PLUS LP   p 1102
101 CH DONALDSON, GATINEAU, QC, J8L
3X3
(819) 986-1135   *SIC* 2819
SUPERIOR PLUS LP   p 1430
GD STN MAIN, SASKATOON, SK, S7K 3J4
(306) 931-7767   *SIC* 2819
SUPERIOR POULTRY PROCESSORS LTD p
199
2784 ABERDEEN AVE, COQUITLAM, BC,
V3B 1A3
(604) 464-0533   *SIC* 5144
SUPERIOR PROPANE   p 604
See *SUPERIOR PLUS LP*
SUPERIOR PROPANE   p 984
See *SUPERIOR PLUS LP*
SUPERIOR PROPANE INC   p 94
14820 123 AVE NW, EDMONTON, AB, T5L
2Y3
(780) 732-3636   *SIC* 5984
SUPERIOR PROPANE INC   p 144
6210 44 ST, LLOYDMINSTER, AB, T9V 1V9
SIC 5984
SUPERIOR PROPANE INC.   p 60
425 1 ST SW SUITE 1400, CALGARY, AB,
T2P 3L8
SIC 4924
SUPERIOR SAFETY CODES INC   p 94
14613 134 AVE NW, EDMONTON, AB, T5L
4S9
(780) 489-4777   *SIC* 7389
SUPERIOR SAFETY INC   p 909
782 MACDONELL ST, THUNDER BAY, ON,
P7B 4A6
(807) 344-3473   *SIC* 5099
SUPERIOR SANITATION SERVICES LTD p
1041
7 SUPERIOR CRES, CHARLOTTETOWN,
PE, C1E 2A1
(902) 892-1333   *SIC* 4953
SUPERIOR SEATING HOSPITALITY INC p
559
9000 KEELE ST UNIT 11, CONCORD, ON,
L4K 0B3
(905) 738-7900   *SIC* 2599
SUPERIOR SOLUTIONS LTD   p 805
851 PROGRESS CRT, OAKVILLE, ON, L6L
6K1
(800) 921-5527   *SIC* 5087
SUPERIOR TRUCK AND TRAILER   p 1040
See *GREENISLE ENVIRONMENTAL INC*
SUPERIOR TRUSS CO LTD   p 353
165 INDUSTRIAL RD, OAK BLUFF, MB,
R4G 0A5
(204) 888-7663   *SIC* 2439
SUPERLEC HV SOLUTIONS   p 1376
See *SURPLEC INC*
SUPERLINE FUELS (2009) LIMITED p 456
3479 BARRINGTON ST SUITE 3451, HALI-
FAX, NS, B3K 2X8
(902) 429-0740   *SIC* 5172
SUPERMARCH DJS COUSINEAU INC   p
1142
455 BOUL JEAN-PAUL-VINCENT,
LONGUEUIL, QC, J4G 1R3
(450) 646-4302   *SIC* 5411
SUPERMARCHE A R G INC   p 1088
175 RUE PRINCIPALE, COWANSVILLE,
QC, J2K 3L9
SIC 5411
SUPERMARCHE ANDRE GRASSET INC p
1177
8935 AV ANDRE-GRASSET, MONTREAL,
QC, H2M 2E9
(514) 382-1465   *SIC* 5411

SUPERMARCHE BELSERA INC p 1268
2300 BOUL PERE-LELIEVRE, QUEBEC,
QC, G1P 2X5
(418) 682-4197 *SIC 5411*
SUPERMARCHE BERGERON INC p 1108
2195 CH RIDGE, GODMANCHESTER, QC,
J0S 1H0
(450) 264-2909 *SIC 5411*
SUPERMARCHE BOUCHER INC p 1281
3528 RUE METCALFE, RAWDON, QC, J0K
1S0
(450) 834-2561 *SIC 5411*
SUPERMARCHE BOUCHER INC p 1315
841 RTE LOUIS-CYR, SAINT-JEAN-DE-
MATHA, QC, J0K 2S0
(450) 886-1010 *SIC 5411*
SUPERMARCHE CLAKA INC p 1263
1625 RUE DU MARAIS, QUEBEC, QC, G1M
0A2
(418) 688-1441 *SIC 5411*
**SUPERMARCHE CREVIER (IBERVILLE)
INC** p 1282
1124 BOUL IBERVILLE BUREAU 110, RE-
PENTIGNY, QC, J5Y 3M6
(450) 704-4750 *SIC 5999*
**SUPERMARCHE CREVIER (LACHENAIE)
INC** p 1379
325 MONTEE DES PIONNIERS, TERRE-
BONNE, QC, J6V 1H4
(450) 582-2271 *SIC 5411*
**SUPERMARCHE CREVIER (REPENTIGNY)
INC** p 1283
180 BOUL BRIEN, REPENTIGNY, QC, J6A
7E9
(450) 582-0201 *SIC 5411*
**SUPERMARCHE CREVIER (VALMONT)
INC** p 1282
315 RUE VALMONT, REPENTIGNY, QC,
J5Y 0Y5
(450) 657-5082 *SIC 5411*
**SUPERMARCHE CREVIER
L'ASSOMPTION INC** p 1120
860 BOUL DE L'ANGE-GARDIEN N,
L'ASSOMPTION, QC, J5W 1P1
(450) 589-5738 *SIC 5411*
SUPERMARCHE D.D.O. INC p 1091
11800 BOUL DE SALABERRY, DOLLARD-
DES-ORMEAUX, QC, H9B 2R8
(514) 685-5252 *SIC 5411*
SUPERMARCHE DEZIEL INC p 1180
1155 RUE JARRY E, MONTREAL, QC, H2P
1W9
(514) 725-9323 *SIC 5411*
SUPERMARCHE DON QUICHOTTE INC p
1121
110 BOUL DON-QUICHOTTE, L'ILE-
PERROT, QC, J7V 6L7
(514) 453-3027 *SIC 5411*
SUPERMARCHE FAMILLE ROUSSEAU INC
p 1140
1855 RTE DES RIVIERES, LEVIS, QC, G7A
4X8
(418) 831-5400 *SIC 5411*
SUPERMARCHE G.C. INC p 1054
1020 BOUL MONSEIGNEUR-DE LAVAL
BUREAU 1, BAIE-SAINT-PAUL, QC, G3Z 2W6
(418) 435-5210 *SIC 5411*
SUPERMARCHE GEORGES BADRA INC p
1112
300 AV AUGUSTE, GREENFIELD PARK,
QC, J4V 3R4
(450) 656-7055 *SIC 5411*
SUPERMARCHE GUY CORRIVEAU INC p
1046
511 7E RUE O, AMOS, QC, J9T 2Y3
SIC 5411
SUPERMARCHE I G A p 1281
See MARCHE RHEAUME INC
SUPERMARCHE IBERVILLE p 1282
See 2858-6691 QUEBEC INC
SUPERMARCHE IGA PEPIN p 1139
See 9158-9325 QUEBEC INC
SUPERMARCHE J C J PLOUFFE INC p
1375

4801 BOUL BOURQUE, SHERBROOKE,
QC, J1N 2G6
(819) 564-7733 *SIC 5411*
SUPERMARCHE J.P.V. PLOUFFE INC p
1148
460 RUE SAINT-PATRICE O, MAGOG, QC,
J1X 1W9
(819) 843-9202 *SIC 5411*
SUPERMARCHE LACHUTE INC p 1129
501 AV BETHANY, LACHUTE, QC, J8H 4A6
(450) 562-7919 *SIC 5411*
SUPERMARCHE LAFRANCE INC p 1051
7172 RUE BOMBARDIER, ANJOU, QC, H1J
2Z9
(514) 352-1386 *SIC 5411*
SUPERMARCHE LAROCHE (1991) INC p
1133
122 BOUL LAURIER, LAURIER-STATION,
QC, G0S 1N0
(418) 728-2882 *SIC 5411*
**SUPERMARCHE LEFEBVRE ET FILLES
INC** p 1221
1500 AV ATWATER, MONTREAL, QC, H3Z
1X5
(514) 933-0995 *SIC 5411*
**SUPERMARCHE MARQUIS
L'ASSOMPTION INC** p 1120
790 MONTEE DE SAINT-SULPICE,
L'ASSOMPTION, QC, J5W 0M6
(450) 589-0442 *SIC 5411*
**SUPERMARCHE MARQUIS REPENTIGNY
INC** p 1283
150 RUE LOUVAIN, REPENTIGNY, QC, J6A
8J7
(450) 585-1445 *SIC 5411*
SUPERMARCHE MELLON INC p 1115
2085 BOUL MELLON, JONQUIERE, QC,
G7S 3G4
(418) 548-7557 *SIC 5411*
SUPERMARCHE METRO FERLAND p 1263
See SUPERMARCHE CLAKA INC
SUPERMARCHE MONT ST-HILAIRE p 1158
345 BOUL HONORIUS-CHARBONNEAU,
MONT-SAINT-HILAIRE, QC, J3H 5H6
(450) 467-8977 *SIC 5411*
SUPERMARCHE MOURELATOS p 1323
See 3424626 CANADA INC
**SUPERMARCHE MOURELATOS (PIERRE-
FONDS)** p
1245
See 3183441 CANADA INC
SUPERMARCHE N.G. INC p 1084
1855 BOUL RENE-LAENNEC, COTE
SAINT-LUC, QC, H7M 5E2
(450) 629-1850 *SIC 5411*
SUPERMARCHE ORNAWKA INC p 1220
4885 AV VAN HORNE, MONTREAL, QC,
H3W 1J2
(514) 731-8336 *SIC 5411*
SUPERMARCHE P.A. p 1184
See 3855155 CANADA INC
SUPERMARCHE P.A. p 1214
See 3855155 CANADA INC
SUPERMARCHE PA p 1183
See 167395 CANADA INC
**SUPERMARCHE PAGANO ET SHNAID-
MAN INC** p
1083
7151 CH DE LA COTE-SAINT-LUC BU-
REAU 108, COTE SAINT-LUC, QC, H4V 1J2
(514) 486-3254 *SIC 5411*
SUPERMARCHE PATRY, PIERRE p 1394
See 9008-4013 QUEBEC INC
SUPERMARCHE PELLETIER INC p 1391
1177 8E RUE, VAL-D'OR, QC, J9P 1R1
(819) 825-6608 *SIC 5411*
**SUPERMARCHE PERRIER ET MARTEL
INC** p 1342
6155 BOUL ARTHUR-SAUVE, SAINT-
LAURENT, QC, H7R 3X8
(450) 627-4496 *SIC 5411*
**SUPERMARCHE PIERRE LEDUC ET
FILLES** p 1217
See SUPERMARCHE PIERRE M LEDUC

INC
SUPERMARCHE PIERRE M LEDUC INC p
1217
2820 RUE DE SALABERRY, MONTREAL,
QC, H3M 1L3
(514) 745-1640 *SIC 5411*
SUPERMARCHE RAYMOND MARTIN INC p
1398
11 RUE DE L'AQUEDUC, VICTORIAVILLE,
QC, G6P 1L4
(819) 752-9797 *SIC 5411*
SUPERMARCHE ROBERT PILON LTEE p
1365
1380 BOUL MONSEIGNEUR-LANGLOIS,
SALABERRY-DE-VALLEYFIELD, QC, J6S
1E3
(450) 373-0251 *SIC 5411*
SUPERMARCHE ROY INC p 1290
240 AV LARIVIERE BUREAU 550, ROUYN-
NORANDA, QC, J9X 4G8
(819) 762-7739 *SIC 5411*
SUPERMARCHE SARAZIN, GILLES INC p
1145
825 RUE SAINT-LAURENT O, LONGUEUIL,
QC, J4K 2V1
(450) 677-5237 *SIC 5411*
SUPERMARCHE ST-BRUNO INC p 1296
750 MONTEE MONTARVILLE, SAINT-
BRUNO, QC, J3V 6B1
(450) 461-0792 *SIC 5411*
SUPERMARCHES DAIGLE, JACQUES INC
p 1061
25 BOUL DES ENTREPRISES, BOIS-
BRIAND, QC, J7G 3K6
(450) 430-1396 *SIC 5411*
SUPERMARCHES GP INC, LES p 1151
750 AV DU PHARE O BUREAU 4415,
MATANE, QC, G4W 3W8
(418) 562-4434 *SIC 5411*
SUPERMARCHES GP INC, LES p 1154
40 AV DOUCET, MONT-JOLI, QC, G5H 0B8
(418) 775-8848 *SIC 5411*
SUPERMARCHES GP INC, LES p 1378
633 RUE COMMERCIALE N UNITE 100,
TEMISCOUATA-SUR-LE-LAC, QC, G0L 1E0
(418) 854-2177 *SIC 5411*
SUPERMARCHES QUATRE FRERES ENR p
1184
See 9191-0174 QUEBEC INC
SUPERMETAL DIVISION DE L'OUEST p
1138
See SUPERMETAL STRUCTURES INC
SUPERMETAL QUEBEC INC p 1138
1955 5E RUE, LEVIS, QC, G6W 5M6
(418) 834-1955 *SIC 1791*
SUPERMETAL SHERBROOKE INC p 1371
375 RUE DE COURCELETTE, SHER-
BROOKE, QC, J1H 3X4
(819) 566-2965 *SIC 3441*
SUPERMETAL STRUCTURES INC p 1138
1955 5E RUE, LEVIS, QC, G6W 5M6
(418) 834-1955 *SIC 3441*
SUPERPORT MARINE SERVICES LIMITED
p 465
30 WATER ST, PORT HAWKESBURY, NS,
B9A 3L1
(902) 625-3375 *SIC 1629*
SUPERSTORE p 94
See LOBLAWS INC
SUPERSTYLE FURNITURE LTD p 1034
123 ASHBRIDGE CIR, WOODBRIDGE, ON,
L4L 3R5
(905) 850-6060 *SIC 2512*
SUPERTEK CANADA INC p 1158
8605 CH DARNLEY, MONT-ROYAL, QC,
H4T 1X2
(514) 737-8354 *SIC 5099*
SUPERVALU 48 p 315
See MCLELLAN'S SUPERMARKET LTD
SUPPLEMENTS ALIMENTAIRES LSN, LES
p 1044
*See LIFE SCIENCE NUTRITIONALS IN-
CORPORATED*
SUPPLEMENTS AROMATIK INC p 1393

2334 RTE MARIE-VICTORIN BUREAU 87,
VARENNES, QC, J3X 1R4
(450) 929-1933 *SIC 2833*
SUPPLES LANDING p 837
See 760496 ONTARIO LTD
SUPPLMENTS ALIMENTAIRES LSN, LES p
1044
See LIFE SCIENCE NUTRITIONALS INC
SUPPLY CHAIN MANAGEMENT p 745
See WALMART CANADA LOGISTICS ULC
SUPPORTED LIFESTYLES LTD p 11
495 36 ST NE SUITE 210, CALGARY, AB,
T2A 6K3
(403) 207-5115 *SIC 8322*
SUPRALIMENT S.E.C. p 1300
25 125 RTE E, SAINT-ESPRIT, QC, J0K 2L0
(450) 839-7258 *SIC 2011*
SUPRALIMENT S.E.C. p 1306
183 RTE DU PRESIDENT-KENNEDY,
SAINT-HENRI-DE-LEVIS, QC, G0R 3E0
(418) 882-2282 *SIC 2011*
SUPRALIMENT S.E.C. p 1313
2200 AV PRATTE BUREAU 400, SAINT-
HYACINTHE, QC, J2S 4B6
(450) 771-0400 *SIC 2011*
SUPREM AUTOMOBILE p 1375
See 2955-4201 QUEBEC INC
SUPREME BASICS, DIV OF p 1416
*See SUPREME OFFICE PRODUCTS LIM-
ITED*
SUPREME CHAIN LOGISTICS LTD p 278
8277 129 ST UNIT 201, SURREY, BC, V3W
0A6
(604) 585-1415 *SIC 4731*
SUPREME GROUP INC p 2
28169 96 AVE, ACHESON, AB, T7X 6J7
(780) 483-3278 *SIC 6712*
**SUPREME INTERNATIONAL CO. CANADA
LTD** p 795
100 MARMORA ST SUITE 3, NORTH
YORK, ON, M9M 2X5
(416) 746-3511 *SIC 5136*
SUPREME INTERNATIONAL LIMITED p
172
6010 47 ST, WETASKIWIN, AB, T9A 2R3
(780) 352-6061 *SIC 5191*
**SUPREME LIGHTING & ELECTRIC SUP-
PLY LTD** p
665
9 LAIDLAW BLVD, MARKHAM, ON, L3P
1W5
(905) 477-3113 *SIC 5063*
SUPREME MEAT SUPPLIES LTD p 187
1725 MACDONALD AVE, BURNABY, BC,
V5C 4P3
(604) 299-0541 *SIC 5147*
SUPREME OFFICE PRODUCTS LIMITED p
1416
310 HENDERSON DR, REGINA, SK, S4N
5W7
(306) 566-8800 *SIC 5112*
SUPREME STEEL BRIDGE, DIV OF p 2
See SUPREME STEEL LP
SUPREME STEEL BRIDGE, DIV OF p 123
See SUPREME STEEL LP
SUPREME STEEL LP p 2
28169 96 AVE, ACHESON, AB, T7X 6J7
(780) 483-3278 *SIC 3441*
SUPREME STEEL LP p 123
10496 21 ST NW, EDMONTON, AB, T6P
1W4
(780) 467-2266 *SIC 1622*
SUPREME TANK INCORPORATED p 449
26 HARBOUR DR, EDWARDSVILLE, NS,
B2A 4T4
(902) 564-9504 *SIC 5984*
SUPREME TOOLING GROUP p 792
See ABC PLASTICS LIMITED
SUPREME WINDOWS (CALGARY) INC p 18
4705 102 AVE SE, CALGARY, AB, T2C 2X7
(403) 279-2797 *SIC 3089*
SUPREMEX INC p 588
400 HUMBERLINE DR, ETOBICOKE, ON,
M9W 5T3

(416) 675-9370   *SIC* 2677
SUPREMEX INC   p 700
5300 TOMKEN RD, MISSISSAUGA, ON, L4W 1P2
(905) 624-4973   *SIC* 2677
SUPREMEX INC   p 1131
7213 RUE CORDNER, LASALLE, QC, H8N 2J7
(514) 595-0555   *SIC* 2677
SUPREMEX INC   p 1327
645 RUE STINSON, SAINT-LAURENT, QC, H4N 2E6
(514) 331-7110   *SIC* 2677
SUPTON LAMGRA REALITY   p 324
See WANG, JOHN C
SUR-SEAL PACKAGING   p 380
See 8948399 CANADA INC
SURAL LAMINATED PRODUCTS OF CANADA INC   p 1056
6900 BOUL RAOUL-DUCHESNE, BECAN-COUR, QC, G9H 2V2
(819) 294-2900   *SIC* 3353
SURANI, B. DRUGS LTD   p 824
161 BANK ST, OTTAWA, ON, K1P 5N7
(613) 232-5723   *SIC* 5912
SURATI SWEET MART LIMITED   p 875
300 MIDDLEFIELD RD, SCARBOROUGH, ON, M1S 5B1
(416) 752-3366   *SIC* 2051
SURE CROP FEEDS   p 175
See RITCHIE-SMITH FEEDS INC
SURE FLAME PRODUCTS, DIV OF   p 140
See HAUL-ALL EQUIPMENT LTD
SURE FLOW EQUIPMENT INC   p 525
5010 NORTH SERVICE RD, BURLINGTON, ON, L7L 5R5
(905) 335-1350   *SIC* 3494
SURE FRESH FOODS INC   p 497
3855 LINE 4, BRADFORD, ON, L3Z 0Z1
(905) 939-2962   *SIC* 5144
SURE GOOD FOODS LTD   p 715
2333 NORTH SHERIDAN WAY SUITE 100, MISSISSAUGA, ON, L5K 1A7
(905) 286-1619   *SIC* 5147
SURE-FLOW OILFIELD SERVICES INC p 6
50 AVE BAY SUITE 5506, BONNYVILLE, AB, T9N 2K8
(780) 826-6864   *SIC* 1389
SURECALL CONTACT CENTERS LTD p 11
3030 3 AVE NE SUITE 240, CALGARY, AB, T2A 6T7
(403) 291-5400   *SIC* 4899
SURECAN CONSTRUCTION LTD   p 112
7707 71 AVE NW, EDMONTON, AB, T6C 0A9
(780) 469-3162   *SIC* 1521
SURECOMP INC   p 790
1 YORKDALE RD SUITE 602, NORTH YORK, ON, M6A 3A1
(416) 781-5545   *SIC* 7372
SURELITE   p 703
See SUREWAY INTERNATIONAL ELEC-TRIC INC
SUREPOINT SERVICES INC   p 133
11004 96 AVE, GRANDE PRAIRIE, AB, T8V 3J5
(780) 832-0551   *SIC* 8734
SUREPOINT SERVICES INC   p 150
1211 8A ST, NISKU, AB, T9E 7R3
(780) 955-3939   *SIC* 5084
SUREPOINT TECHNOLOGIES GROUP INC p 150
1211 8A ST, NISKU, AB, T9E 7R3
(780) 955-3939   *SIC* 1381
SURERUS CONSTRUCTION & DEVELOP-MENT LTD   p 214
9312 109 ST, FORT ST. JOHN, BC, V1J 6G9
(250) 785-2423   *SIC* 7359
SURESHOT DISPENSING SYSTEMS p 461
See A.C. DISPENSING EQUIPMENT IN-CORPORATED
SURESPAN CONSTRUCTION LTD   p 242
38 FELL AVE SUITE 301, NORTH VAN-

COUVER, BC, V7P 3S2
(604) 998-1133   *SIC* 1622
SURESPAN INVESTMENTS GROUP INC p 242
38 FELL AVE SUITE 301, NORTH VAN-COUVER, BC, V7P 3S2
(604) 998-1133   *SIC* 1622
SURETE CAVALERIE INC   p 1301
193A BOUL ARTHUR-SAUVE, SAINT-EUSTACHE, QC, J7P 2A7
(450) 983-7070   *SIC* 7381
SURETE DU TRANSPORT AERIEN SECU-RITAS   p 1290
See SECURITAS TRANSPORT AVIATION SECURITY LTD
SURETY, DIV OF   p 52
See INTACT INSURANCE COMPANY
SUREWAY CONSTRUCTION LTD   p 123
9175 14 ST NW, EDMONTON, AB, T6P 0C9
(780) 440-2121   *SIC* 1623
SUREWAY EQUIPMENT LEASING LTD p 123
9175 14 ST NW, EDMONTON, AB, T6P 0C9
(780) 440-2121   *SIC* 1623
SUREWAY INTERNATIONAL ELECTRIC INC   p 703
3151 WHARTON WAY, MISSISSAUGA, ON, L4X 2B6
(905) 624-0077   *SIC* 5063
SUREWAY LOGGING LTD   p 138
GD, LA CRETE, AB, T0H 2H0
(780) 539-0388   *SIC* 5082
SUREWAY METAL SYSTEMS LIMITED p 159
285120 DUFF DR, ROCKY VIEW COUNTY, AB, T1X 0K1
(403) 287-2742   *SIC* 3499
SUREWERX   p 201
See JET EQUIPMENT & TOOLS LTD
SUREWOOD FOREST PRODUCTS, DIV OF p 311
See CANWEL BUILDING MATERIALS LTD
SUREXDIRECT.COM LTD   p 145
6 SOUTH 1ST ST W, MAGRATH, AB, T0K 1J0
(403) 388-2387   *SIC* 6411
SURGE ENERGY INC   p 60
635 8 AVE SW SUITE 2100, CALGARY, AB, T2P 3M3
(403) 930-1010   *SIC* 1382
SURGE GENERAL PARTNERSHIP   p 60
635 8 AVE SW SUITE 2100, CALGARY, AB, T2P 3M3
(403) 930-1010   *SIC* 1382
SURGENOR GATINEAU CHEVROLET CADILLAC LTEE   p 1107
950 BOUL SAINT-JOSEPH, GATINEAU, QC, J8Z 1S9
(819) 777-2731   *SIC* 5511
SURGENOR NATIONAL LEASING LIMITED p 820
881 ST. LAURENT BLVD, OTTAWA, ON, K1K 3B1
(613) 706-4779   *SIC* 7515
SURGENOR PONTIAC BUICK LIMITED p 816
1571 LIVERPOOL CRT, OTTAWA, ON, K1B 4L1
(613) 745-0024   *SIC* 5511
SURGENOR PONTIAC BUICK LIMITED p 820
939 ST. LAURENT BLVD, OTTAWA, ON, K1K 3B1
(613) 741-0741   *SIC* 5511
SURGENOR TRUCK CENTRE   p 816
See SURGENOR PONTIAC BUICK LIM-ITED
SURGENOR TRUCK CENTRE   p 820
See SURGENOR PONTIAC BUICK LIM-ITED
SURGICAL CENTRES INC   p 72
3125 BOWWOOD DR NW, CALGARY, AB, T3B 2E7

(403) 640-1188   *SIC* 8011
SURMONT SAND & GRAVEL LTD   p 129
431 MACKENZIE BLVD UNIT 8, FORT MC-MURRAY, AB, T9H 4C5
(780) 743-2533   *SIC* 5211
SURNET INSURANCE GROUP INC   p 1015
1621 MCEWEN DR SUITE 50, WHITBY, ON, L1N 9A5
(905) 433-2378   *SIC* 6411
SURPLEC INC   p 1376
149 CH GODIN, SHERBROOKE, QC, J1R 0S6
(819) 821-3636   *SIC* 5063
SURPLEC INDUSTRIEL INC   p 1376
155 CH GODIN, SHERBROOKE, QC, J1R 0S6
(819) 821-3634   *SIC* 5084
SURPLUS FREIGHT OF CANADA   p 485
See 1342205 ONTARIO LIMITED
SURPLUS MALOUIN INC   p 1400
6400 RUE FOSTER, WATERLOO, QC, J0E 2N0
(450) 539-3722   *SIC* 5211
SURPLUS R.D. INC   p 1399
500 RUE DE L'ACADIE, VICTORIAVILLE, QC, G6T 1A6
(819) 758-2466   *SIC* 5399
SURRETTE BATTERY COMPANY LIMITED p 466
1 STATION RD, SPRINGHILL, NS, B0M 1X0
(902) 597-3767   *SIC* 3691
SURREY DISTRIBUTION CENTRE   p 274
See CATALYST PAPER CORPORATION
SURREY FARMS COMPANY   p 280
5180 152 ST, SURREY, BC, V3Z 1G9
(604) 574-1390   *SIC* 0191
SURREY GOLF CLUB   p 281
See 1001432 B.C. LTD
SURREY GYMNASTIC SOCIETY   p 278
13940 77 AVE, SURREY, BC, V3W 5Z4
(604) 594-2442   *SIC* 8699
SURREY HONDA   p 271
See SURREY IMPORTS LTD
SURREY IMPORTS LTD   p 271
15291 FRASER HWY, SURREY, BC, V3R 3P3
(604) 583-7421   *SIC* 5511
SURREY LIBRARY   p 274
See SURREY PUBLIC LIBRARY
SURREY METRO TAXI   p 276
See GUILDFORD CAB (1993) LTD
SURREY PLACE CENTRE   p 976
2 SURREY PL, TORONTO, ON, M5S 2C2
(416) 925-5141   *SIC* 8399
SURREY PUBLIC LIBRARY   p 274
10350 UNIVERSITY DR 3RD FLOOR, SUR-REY, BC, V3T 4B8
(604) 598-7300   *SIC* 8231
SURROUND TECHNOLOGIES INC   p 230
27222 LOUGHEED HWY, MAPLE RIDGE, BC, V2W 1M4
(604) 462-8223   *SIC* 3499
SURTECO   p 502
See DOLLKEN WOODTAPE
SURTECO CANADA LTD   p 506
230 ORENDA RD, BRAMPTON, ON, L6T 1E9
(905) 759-1074   *SIC* 2295
SURTEK INDUSTRIES INC   p 278
13018 84 AVE UNIT 4, SURREY, BC, V3W 1L2
(604) 590-2235   *SIC* 3679
SURVITEC GROUP   p 205
See DBC MARINE SAFETY SYSTEMS LTD
SURVIVAL SYSTEMS HOLDING LIMITED p 444
20 ORION CRT SUITE 1, DARTMOUTH, NS, B2Y 4W6
(902) 466-7878   *SIC* 5099
SUSANNE LANG FRAGRANCE INC   p 989
670 CALEDONIA RD UNIT 100, TORONTO, ON, M6E 4V9
(416) 961-1234   *SIC* 2844
SUSSEX FRANCHISE SYSTEMS INC. p 238

173 FORESTER ST UNIT 108, NORTH VANCOUVER, BC, V7H 0A6
(604) 983-6955   *SIC* 6411
SUSSEX INSURANCE   p 238
See SUSSEX FRANCHISE SYSTEMS INC.
SUSSEX REGIONAL HIGH SCHOOL   p 418
See ANGLOPHONE SOUTH SCHOOL DIS-TRICT (ASD-S)
SUSSEX SUPER VALUE   p 418
See ATLANTIC WHOLESALERS LTD
SUSTAINCO INC   p 1003
1 ROYAL GATE BLVD, VAUGHAN, ON, L4L 8Z7
(905) 850-8686   *SIC* 6799
SUSTEMA INC   p 1341
3590 RUE GRIFFITH, SAINT-LAURENT, QC, H4T 1A7
(514) 744-5499   *SIC* 5021
SUTCO CONTRACTING LTD   p 267
8561 HWY 6, SALMO, BC, V0G 1Z0
(250) 357-2612   *SIC* 4212
SUTHERLAND EQUIPMENT LTD   p 401
911 HANWELL RD, FREDERICTON, NB, E3B 9Z1
(506) 452-1155   *SIC* 5511
SUTHERLAND GLOBAL SERVICES CANADA ULC   p 1024
500 OUELLETTE AVE, WINDSOR, ON, N9A 1B3
(800) 591-9395   *SIC* 7361
SUTHERLAND HILLS REST HOME LTD p 219
3081 HALL RD, KELOWNA, BC, V1W 2R5
(250) 860-2330   *SIC* 8051
SUTHERLAND HONDA   p 401
See SUTHERLAND EQUIPMENT LTD
SUTHERLAND INSURANCE   p 600
See SUTHERLAND, JOHN & SONS LIM-ITED
SUTHERLAND SECONDARY SCHOOL p 240
See SCHOOL DISTRICT NO. 44 (NORTH VANCOUVER)
SUTHERLAND UNION INC   p 957
335 BAY ST SUITE 1000, TORONTO, ON, M5H 2R3
SIC 5112
SUTHERLAND, HAROLD CONSTRUCTION LTD   p 627
323545 E LINTON W, KEMBLE, ON, N0H 1S0
(519) 376-5698   *SIC* 5032
SUTHERLAND, JOHN & SONS LIMITED p 600
240 VICTORIA RD N, GUELPH, ON, N1E 6L8
(519) 822-0160   *SIC* 6411
SUTHERLAND-SCHULTZ LTD   p 537
140 TURNBULL CRT, CAMBRIDGE, ON, N1T 1J2
(519) 653-4123   *SIC* 1731
SUTTON CENTRE REALTY   p 194
See ELITE PACIFIC REALTY INC
SUTTON DISTRICT HIGH SCHOOL   p 902
See YORK REGION DISTRICT SCHOOL BOARD
SUTTON GRANITE HILL REALTY INC p 924
2010 YONGE ST SUITE 200, TORONTO, ON, M4S 1Z9
SIC 6531
SUTTON GROUP   p 40
See NORWEST REAL ESTATE LTD
SUTTON GROUP   p 242
See WEST COAST REALTY LTD
SUTTON GROUP   p 526
See APEX RESULTS REALTY INC
SUTTON GROUP   p 712
See SUTTON GROUP REALTY SYSTEMS INC
SUTTON GROUP   p 1274
See 9065-0805 QUEBEC INC
SUTTON GROUP - TOWN AND COUNTRY REALTY LTD   p 895
6209 MAIN ST, STOUFFVILLE, ON, L4A

4H8
(905) 640-0888   *SIC* 6531
SUTTON GROUP - WEST COAST REALTY
p 227
19653 WILLOWBROOK DR UNIT 156, LANGLEY, BC, V2Y 1A5
(604) 533-3939   *SIC* 6361
SUTTON GROUP - WEST LANGARA REALTY   *p*
323
See 0844212 BC LTD
SUTTON GROUP ADMIRAL REALTY INC *p*
781
1881 STEELES AVE W SUITE 12, NORTH YORK, ON, M3H 5Y4
(416) 739-7200   *SIC* 6531
SUTTON GROUP ELITE REALTY INC *p* 708
3643 CAWTHRA RD SUITE 201, MISSISSAUGA, ON, L5A 2Y4
(905) 848-9800   *SIC* 6531
SUTTON GROUP HERITAGE REALTY INC *p*
540
26 CAMERON ST W, CANNINGTON, ON, L0E 1E0
    SIC 6531
SUTTON GROUP HERITAGE REALTY INC *p*
843
1755 PICKERING PKY UNIT 10, PICKERING, ON, L1V 6K5
(416) 678-9622   *SIC* 6531
SUTTON GROUP INCENTIVE REALTY INC
p 488
241 MINET'S POINT RD, BARRIE, ON, L4N 4C4
(705) 739-1300   *SIC* 6531
SUTTON GROUP OLD MILL REALTY INC *p*
572
4237 DUNDAS ST W, ETOBICOKE, ON, M8X 1Y3
(416) 234-2424   *SIC* 6531
SUTTON GROUP PROFESSIONAL REALTY   *p*
443
73 TACOMA DR SUITE 800, DARTMOUTH, NS, B2W 3Y6
(902) 223-1399   *SIC* 6531
SUTTON GROUP QUANTUM REALTY INC *p*
714
1673 LAKESHORE RD W, MISSISSAUGA, ON, L5J 1J4
(905) 822-5000   *SIC* 6531
SUTTON GROUP REALTY SERVICES LTD *p*
300
1080 MAINLAND ST SUITE 206, VANCOUVER, BC, V6B 2T4
(604) 568-1005   *SIC* 6794
SUTTON GROUP REALTY SYSTEMS INC *p*
712
1528 DUNDAS ST W UNIT 1, MISSISSAUGA, ON, L5C 1E4
(905) 896-3333   *SIC* 6531
SUTTON GROUP STATUS REALTY INC   *p*
814
286 KING ST W, OSHAWA, ON, L1J 2J9
(905) 436-0990   *SIC* 6531
SUTTON GROUP-ASSOCIATES REALTY INC   *p* 974
358 DAVENPORT RD, TORONTO, ON, M5R 1K6
(416) 966-0300   *SIC* 6531
SUTTON GROUP-CAPITAL REALTY LTD *p*
431
451 KENMOUNT RD, ST. JOHN'S, NL, A1B 3P9
(709) 726-6262   *SIC* 6531
SUTTON GROUP-KILKENNY REAL ESTATE   *p*
387
See KILKENNY REAL ESTATE LTD
SUTTON GROUP-NEW STANDARD REALTY INC   *p*
854
360 HIGHWAY 7 E UNIT L 1, RICHMOND HILL, ON, L4B 3Y7

(905) 709-8000   *SIC* 6531
SUTTON GROUP-RIGHT WAY REAL ESTATE INC   *p*
1035
28 PERRY ST, WOODSTOCK, ON, N4S 3C2
(519) 539-6194   *SIC* 6531
SUTTON GROUP-SECURITY REAL ESTATE INC   *p*
989
1239 ST CLAIR AVE W, TORONTO, ON, M6E 1B5
(416) 654-1010   *SIC* 6531
SUTTON GROUP-SUMMIT REALTY INC *p*
712
1100 BURNHAMTHORPE RD W UNIT 27, MISSISSAUGA, ON, L5C 4G4
(905) 897-9555   *SIC* 6531
SUTTON PLACE GRANDE LIMITED   *p* 86
See 955 BAY STREET HOSPITALITY INC
SUTTON PLACE GRANDE LIMITED   *p* 974
See 955 BAY STREET HOSPITALITY INC
SUTTON PLACE HOTEL TORONTO, THE *p*
325
See 955 BAY STREET HOSPITALITY INC
SUTTON REALTY   *p* 708
See SUTTON GROUP ELITE REALTY INC
SUTTON WEST REALTY INC   *p* 580
6 DIXON RD, ETOBICOKE, ON, M9P 2L1
(416) 240-1000   *SIC* 6531
SUWILAAWKS COMMUNITY SCHOOL   *p*
283
See BOARD OF EDUCATION OF SCHOOL DISTRICT #82 (COAST M
SUZANNE ROY FORD INC   *p* 1137
61 RTE DU PRESIDENT-KENNEDY, LEVIS, QC, G6V 6C7
(418) 835-1915   *SIC* 5511
SUZUKI CANADA INC   *p* 854
100 EAST BEAVER CREEK RD, RICHMOND HILL, ON, L4B 1J6
(905) 764-1574   *SIC* 5511
SUZUKI CANADA INC.   *p* 488
360 SAUNDERS RD, BARRIE, ON, L4N 9Y2
(705) 999-8600   *SIC* 5012
SUZUKI K/W   *p* 639
See 798983 ONTARIO INC
SUZUKI SUBARU REPENTIGNY INC *p* 1283
575 RUE NOTRE-DAME, REPENTIGNY, QC, J6A 2T6
(514) 891-9950   *SIC* 5511
SVAH TRADERS INC   *p* 208
11322 77 AVE, DELTA, BC, V4C 1L9
(604) 897-8272   *SIC* 5052
SVAT ELECTRONICS   *p* 760
See CIRCUS WORLD DISPLAYS LIMITED
SW AUDIO VISUAL   *p* 223
See SOUND WAVES ENTERTAINMENT NETWORK LTD
SWAD GRAIN EXPORTS   *p* 718
See 1815264 ONTARIO INC
SWAGELOK CENTRAL CANADA   *p* 389
118 COMMERCE DR, WINNIPEG, MB, R3P 0Z6
(204) 633-4446   *SIC* 5085
SWAN DUST CONTROL LIMITED   *p* 1007
35 UNIVERSITY AVE E, WATERLOO, ON, N2J 2V9
(519) 885-4450   *SIC* 7359
SWAN HILLS TREATMENT CENTER   *p* 99
See AECOM CANADA LTD
SWAN HILLS TREATMENT CENTER   *p* 388
See AECOM CANADA LTD
SWAN HILLS TREATMENT CENTRE   *p* 117
See SUEZ CANADA WASTE SERIVCES INC
SWAN HILLS TREATMENT CENTRE   *p* 168
See SUEZ CANADA WASTE SERIVCES INC
SWAN INDUSTRIES, DIV OF   *p* 132
See GRANDE PRAIRIE AND DISTRICT ASSOCIATION FOR PERSONS WITH DEVELOPMENTAL DISABILITIES
SWAN RIVER FRIENDSHIP CENTRE INC *p*

359
1413 MAIN ST, SWAN RIVER, MB, R0L 1Z0
(204) 734-9301   *SIC* 8699
SWAN RIVER HEALTH CENTRE   *p* 359
See PARKLAND REGIONAL HEALTH AUTHORITY INC
SWAN SOURCE   *p* 1016
47 BUTTERFIELD CRES, WHITBY, ON, L1R 1K5
(647) 967-6723   *SIC* 4924
SWAN VALLEY AGENCIES LTD   *p* 359
922 MAIN ST E, SWAN RIVER, MB, R0L 1Z0
(204) 734-9421   *SIC* 6411
SWAN VALLEY CONSUMERS COOPERATIVE LIMITED   *p*
359
811 MAIN ST E, SWAN RIVER, MB, R0L 1Z0
(204) 734-3431   *SIC* 5399
SWAN VALLEY REGIONAL SECONDARY SCHOOL   *p* 359
See SWAN VALLEY SCHOOL DIVISION
SWAN VALLEY SCHOOL DIVISION   *p* 359
1483 3RD ST N, SWAN RIVER, MB, R0L 1Z0
(204) 734-4511   *SIC* 8211
SWAN-E-SET BAY RESORT LTD   *p* 244
16651 RANNIE RD, PITT MEADOWS, BC, V3Y 1Z1
(604) 465-9380   *SIC* 7997
SWANS ENTERPRISES LTD   *p* 337
506 PANDORA AVE SUITE 203, VICTORIA, BC, V8W 1N6
(250) 361-3310   *SIC* 5813
SWANS SUITE HOTELS   *p* 337
See SWANS ENTERPRISES LTD
SWANSON, JIM LUMBER LTD   *p* 639
166 PARK ST, KITCHENER, ON, N2G 1M8
(519) 743-1404   *SIC* 5211
SWAROVSKI CANADA LIMITED   *p* 675
80 GOUGH RD UNIT 2, MARKHAM, ON, L3R 6E8
(905) 752-0498   *SIC* 5944
SWARTZ ENTERPRISES INC   *p* 237
804 WINTHROP ST, NEW WESTMINSTER, BC, V3L 4B1
(778) 859-5040   *SIC* 1771
SWATCH GROUP (CANADA) LTD, THE   *p*
984
555 RICHMOND ST W SUITE 1105, TORONTO, ON, M5V 3B1
(416) 703-1667   *SIC* 5094
SWEDA CANADA INC   *p* 774
4101 YONGE ST SUITE 500, NORTH YORK, ON, M2P 1N6
(416) 614-0199   *SIC* 7371
SWEDA FARMS LTD   *p* 493
3880 EDGERTON RD SS 101, BLACKSTOCK, ON, L0B 1B0
(905) 986-5747   *SIC* 0252
SWEET GALLERY EXCLUSIVE PASTRY & CAFE   *p* 576
See SWEET GALLERY EXCLUSIVE PASTRY LIMITED
SWEET GALLERY EXCLUSIVE PASTRY LIMITED   *p* 576
350 BERING AVE, ETOBICOKE, ON, M8Z 3A9
(416) 232-1539   *SIC* 5461
SWEET PARADISE BAKERY   *p* 616
See 651233 ONTARIO INC
SWEET POTATO INCORPORATED, THE   *p*
994
108 VINE AVE, TORONTO, ON, M6P 1V7
(416) 762-4848   *SIC* 5149
SWEET SAND & GRAVEL   *p* 479
See TACKABERRY, G & SONS CONSTRUCTION COMPANY LIMITED
SWEET YORK DESSERTS   *p* 781
See CATERERS (YORK) LIMITED
SWEGON NORTH AMERICA INC   *p* 675
355 APPLE CREEK BLVD, MARKHAM, ON, L3R 9X7

(416) 291-7371   *SIC* 3625
SWENSON, LARRY ENTERPRISES LTD   *p*
463
689 WESTVILLE RD, NEW GLASGOW, NS, B2H 2J6
(902) 752-6442   *SIC* 5812
SWG   *p* 169
See SOUTH COUNTRY AGENCIES
SWG CANADA   *p* 580
See SOUTH WESTERN INSURANCE GROUP LIMITED
SWIFT CURRENT CARE CENTRE   *p* 1436
700 ABERDEEN ST SUITE 22, SWIFT CURRENT, SK, S9H 3E3
    SIC 8051
SWIFT POWER CORP   *p* 300
55 WATER ST SUITE 608, VANCOUVER, BC, V6B 1A1
(604) 637-6393   *SIC* 4911
SWIFT SWEEPING CO   *p* 730
See CANADIAN MARKETING TEST CASE 201 LIMITED
SWIFT TRADE SECURITIES LTD   *p* 927
55 ST CLAIR AVE W SUITE 900, TORONTO, ON, M4V 2Y7
(416) 351-0000   *SIC* 6211
SWIMCO AQUATIC SUPPLIES LTD   *p* 38
6403 BURBANK RD SE SUITE 1, CALGARY, AB, T2H 2E1
(403) 259-6113   *SIC* 5699
SWIMCO FOR SWIMWEAR   *p* 38
See SWIMCO AQUATIC SUPPLIES LTD
SWINGSTAGE, DIV OF   *p* 873
See TRACTEL LTD
SWISH   *p* 842
See SWISH MAINTENANCE LIMITED
SWISH MAINTENANCE LIMITED   *p* 842
2060 FISHER DR, PETERBOROUGH, ON, K9J 6X6
(705) 745-5763   *SIC* 5999
SWISS CHALET   *p* 484
See RECIPE UNLIMITED CORPORATION
SWISS CHALET   *p* 512
See SABRITIN HOSPITALITY INC
SWISS CHALET   *p* 515
See RECIPE UNLIMITED CORPORATION
SWISS CHALET HARVEY'S   *p* 481
See SAN MIGUEL FOODS LTD
SWISS CHALET ROTISSERIE & GRILL   *p*
1015
See RECIPE UNLIMITED CORPORATION
SWISS CHALET ROTISSERIE GRILL *p* 875
See RECIPE UNLIMITED CORPORATION
SWISS PASTRIES & DELICATESSEN OF OTTAWA LIMITED   *p* 595
1423 STAR TOP RD, GLOUCESTER, ON, K1B 3W5
    SIC 5461
SWISS RE LIFE & HEALTH CANADA *p* 957
150 KING ST W SUITE 1000, TORONTO, ON, M5H 1J9
(416) 947-3800   *SIC* 6321
SWISS REINSURANCE COMPANY CANADA   *p* 957
150 KING ST W SUITE 2200, TORONTO, ON, M5H 1J9
(416) 408-0272   *SIC* 6331
SWISS WATER   *p* 183
See SWISS WATER DECAFFEINATED COFFEE INC
SWISS WATER DECAFFEINATED COFFEE INC   *p* 183
3131 LAKE CITY WAY, BURNABY, BC, V5A 3A3
(604) 420-4050   *SIC* 5149
SWISSMAR LTD   *p* 854
35 EAST BEAVER CREEK RD UNIT 6, RICHMOND HILL, ON, L4B 1B3
(905) 764-6068   *SIC* 5023
SWISSPLAS LIMITED   *p* 506
735 INTERMODAL DR, BRAMPTON, ON, L6T 5W2
(905) 789-9300   *SIC* 3089
SWISSPORT   *p* 827

▲ Public Company   ■ Public Company Family Member   **HQ** Headquarters   **BR** Branch   **SL** Single Location

See SWISSPORT CANADA INC
SWISSPORT CANADA HANDLING INC *p* 729
6500 SILVER DART DR, MISSISSAUGA, ON, L5P 1A2
(905) 676-2888   *SIC* 4581
SWISSPORT CANADA INC *p* 25
1601 AIRPORT RD NE SUITE 810, CALGARY, AB, T2E 6Z8
(403) 221-1660   *SIC* 4581
SWISSPORT CANADA INC *p* 265
GD, RICHMOND, BC, V7B 1Y4
(604) 303-4550   *SIC* 4581
SWISSPORT CANADA INC *p* 827
130 THAD JOHNSON PVT, OTTAWA, ON, K1V 0X1
(613) 521-4730   *SIC* 4581
SWISSPORT CANADA INC *p* 1324
100 BOUL ALEXIS-NIHON UNITE 400, SAINT-LAURENT, QC, H4M 2N8
(514) 748-2277   *SIC* 4581
SWS *p* 58
See SABRE WELL SERVICING INC
SWS STAR WARNING SYSTEMS INC *p* 760
7695 BLACKBURN PKY, NIAGARA FALLS, ON, L2H 0A6
(905) 357-0222   *SIC* 3647
SWSE ATHLETIC TEAMS LTD *p* 899
874 LAPOINTE ST, SUDBURY, ON, P3A 5N8
(705) 675-7973   *SIC* 7941
SYBER CONCRETE FORMING LTD *p* 282
18812 96 AVE UNIT 11, SURREY, BC, V4N 3R1
(604) 513-5717   *SIC* 1771
SYBRON CANADA LP *p* 746
55 LAURIER DR, MORRISBURG, ON, K0C 1X0
(613) 543-3791   *SIC* 3843
SYDAX DEVELOPMENTS LIMITED *p* 444
300 PRINCE ALBERT RD, DARTMOUTH, NS, B2Y 4J2
(902) 468-8817   *SIC* 5812
SYDCO FUELS LIMITED *p* 467
452 GEORGE ST, SYDNEY, NS, B1P 1K3
(902) 539-6444   *SIC* 5983
SYDENHAM HIGH SCHOOL *p* 902
See LIMESTONE DISTRICT SCHOOL BOARD
SYDNEY AUTO PARTS DIVISION *p* 433
See COLONIAL GARAGE & DISTRIBUTORS LIMITED
SYDNEY CALL CENTRE INC, THE *p* 467
90 INGLIS ST UNIT A005, SYDNEY, NS, B1P 1W8
(877) 707-0365   *SIC* 4899
SYDNEY MINES FIRE DEPARTMENT *p* 468
4 ELLIOT ST, SYDNEY MINES, NS, B1V 3G1
(902) 736-2298   *SIC* 7389
SYDOR FARM EQUIPMENT LTD *p* 349
GD, DAUPHIN, MB, R7N 2T3
(204) 638-6443   *SIC* 5083
SYKES *p* 405
See ICT CANADA MARKETING INC
SYKES ASSISTANCE SERVICES CORPORATION *p* 655
248 PALL MALL ST, LONDON, ON, N6A 5P6
(519) 434-3221   *SIC* 7549
SYKES ASSISTANCE SERVICES CORPORATION *p* 764
555 OAK ST E, NORTH BAY, ON, P1B 8E3
SIC 8099
SYKES TELEHEALTH *p* 764
See SYKES ASSISTANCE SERVICES CORPORATION
SYLOGIST LTD *p* 74
5 RICHMOND WAY SW SUITE 102, CALGARY, AB, T3E 7M8
(403) 266-4808   *SIC* 7372
SYLON INC *p* 707

5610 MCADAM RD, MISSISSAUGA, ON, L4Z 1P1
(905) 890-1220   *SIC* 5087
SYLVAN AUTOMATION LTD *p* 863
1018 MCNABB ST, SAULT STE. MARIE, ON, P6B 6J1
(705) 254-4669   *SIC* 5085
SYLVAN LEARNING CENTRE INC *p* 628
205 SECOND ST S, KENORA, ON, P9N 1G1
(807) 467-8374   *SIC* 8299
SYLVANIA LIGHTING SERVICES *p* 696
See LEDVANCE LTD
SYLVITE AGRI-SERVICES LTD *p* 528
3221 NORTH SERVICE RD SUITE 200, BURLINGTON, ON, L7N 3G2
(519) 485-5770   *SIC* 5191
SYLVITE HOLDINGS INC *p* 528
3221 NORTH SERVICE RD SUITE 200, BURLINGTON, ON, L7N 3G2
(905) 331-8365   *SIC* 5191
SYLVITE SALES, DIV OF *p* 528
See SYLVITE HOLDINGS INC
SYLVITE TRANSPORTATION GROUP, DIV OF *p* 528
See SYLVITE AGRI-SERVICES LTD
SYM-CRC INC *p* 1143
174 BOUL SAINTE-FOY BUREAU 101, LONGUEUIL, QC, J4J 1W9
(877) 565-6777   *SIC* 7389
SYM-TECH AUTOMOTIVE PROTECTION *p* 854
See SYM-TECH INC
SYM-TECH INC *p* 854
150 WEST BEAVER CREEK RD SUITE 1, RICHMOND HILL, ON, L4B 1B4
(905) 889-5390   *SIC* 6399
SYMANTEC (CANADA) CORPORATION *p* 60
100 4 AVE SW SUITE 1000, CALGARY, AB, T2P 3N2
SIC 4813
SYMANTEC (CANADA) CORPORATION *p* 765
3381 STEELES AVE E, NORTH YORK, ON, M2H 3S7
(416) 774-0000   *SIC* 7371
SYMBILITY SOLUTIONS INC *p* 984
111 PETER ST SUITE 900, TORONTO, ON, M5V 2H1
(647) 775-8601   *SIC* 5045
SYMBIOSE CUSTOMER CONTACT CENTER *p* 1143
See SYM-CRC INC
SYMBOL TECHNOLOGIES CANADA, ULC *p* 700
5180 ORBITOR DR, MISSISSAUGA, ON, L4W 5L9
(905) 629-7226   *SIC* 5065
SYMBOTIC CANADA ULC *p* 1051
10925 BOUL LOUIS-H.-LAFONTAINE, ANJOU, QC, H1J 2E8
(514) 352-0500   *SIC* 8711
SYMCO 2015 INC *p* 1263
320 BOUL PIERRE-BERTRAND BUREAU 106, QUEBEC, QC, G1M 2C8
(581) 981-4774   *SIC* 1542
SYMCO CONSTRUCTION *p* 1263
See SYMCO 2015 INC
SYMCOR INC *p* 76
3663 63 AVE NE, CALGARY, AB, T3J 0G6
(905) 273-1000   *SIC* 7389
SYMCOR INC *p* 379
195 FORT ST, WINNIPEG, MB, R3C 3V1
(204) 924-5819   *SIC* 7374
SYMCOR INC *p* 454
1580 GRAFTON ST, HALIFAX, NS, B3J 2C2
(902) 404-4606   *SIC* 4226
SYMCOR INC *p* 700
1625 TECH AVE, MISSISSAUGA, ON, L4W 5P5
(289) 360-2000   *SIC* 2752
SYMCOR INC *p* 707

1 ROBERT SPECK PKY SUITE 400, MISSISSAUGA, ON, L4Z 4E7
(905) 273-1000   *SIC* 7374
SYMCOR INC *p* 780
8 PRINCE ANDREW PL, NORTH YORK, ON, M3C 2H4
(905) 273-1000   *SIC* 8741
SYMCOR INC *p* 1216
650 RUE BRIDGE, MONTREAL, QC, H3K 3K9
(514) 787-4325   *SIC* 2621
SYMONS THE BAKER LTD *p* 1406
1305 9TH ST, ESTEVAN, SK, S4A 1J1
(306) 634-6456   *SIC* 5812
SYMPHONY SENIOR LIVING INC *p* 70
2220 162 AVE SW SUITE 210, CALGARY, AB, T2Y 5E3
(403) 201-3555   *SIC* 8361
SYMPHONY SENIOR LIVING INC *p* 940
20 TORONTO ST SUITE 440, TORONTO, ON, M5C 2B8
(416) 366-3888   *SIC* 6513
SYMPLI *p* 183
See WHITE HOUSE DESIGN COMPANY INC
SYMTECH INNOVATIONS LTD *p* 675
35 RIVIERA DR, MARKHAM, ON, L3R 8N4
(905) 940-8044   *SIC* 1731
SYNAGRI S.E.C. *p* 1310
5175 BOUL LAURIER E, SAINT-HYACINTHE, QC, J2R 2B4
(450) 799-3225   *SIC* 3999
SYNAGRI S.E.C. *p* 1353
80 RUE DES ERABLES, SAINT-THOMAS, QC, J0K 3L0
(450) 759-8070   *SIC* 2874
SYNAPSE ELECTRONIQUE INC *p* 1369
1010 7E AV, SHAWINIGAN, QC, G9T 2B8
(819) 533-3553   *SIC* 3822
SYNCA DIRECT *p* 1282
See SYNCA MARKETING INC
SYNCA MARKETING INC *p* 1282
337 RUE MARION, REPENTIGNY, QC, J5Z 4W8
(450) 582-1093   *SIC* 5047
SYNCHRONICA INC *p* 1208
1100 AV DES CANADIENS-DE-MONTREAL, MONTREAL, QC, H3B 2S2
(514) 390-1333   *SIC* 8748
SYNCREON CANADA INC *p* 1362
1340 BOUL DAGENAIS O, SAINTE-ROSE, QC, H7L 5C7
(450) 625-0400   *SIC* 3714
SYNCRUDE CANADA LTD *p* 60
525 3 AVE SW SUITE 525, CALGARY, AB, T2P 0G4
(403) 385-2400   *SIC* 1311
SYNCRUDE CANADA LTD *p* 121
9421 17 AVE NW, EDMONTON, AB, T6N 1H4
(780) 970-6800   *SIC* 8731
SYNCRUDE CANADA LTD *p* 129
9911 MACDONALD AVE SUITE 200, FORT MCMURRAY, AB, T9H 1S7
(780) 790-5911   *SIC* 1311
SYNDICAT CANADIEN DES COMMUNICATIONS DE L'ENERGIE ET DU PAPIER *p* 1051
8290 BOUL METROPOLITAIN E, ANJOU, QC, H1K 1A2
(514) 259-7237   *SIC* 8631
SYNDICAT CANADIEN DES EMPLOYES DU METIER D'HYDRO-QUEBEC *p* 1388
7080 RUE MARION BUREAU 207, TROIS-RIVIERES, QC, G9A 6G4
(819) 693-1500   *SIC* 8631
SYNDICAT DE LA FONCTION PUBLIQUE ET PARAPUBLIQUE DU QUEBEC INC *p* 1279
5100 BOUL DES GRADINS, QUEBEC, QC, G2J 1N4
(418) 623-2424   *SIC* 8631
SYNDICAT DE PROFESSIONNELLES ET PROFESSIONNELS DU GOUVERNEMENT

DU QUEBEC *p* 1176
1001 RUE SHERBROOKE E BUREAU 300, MONTREAL, QC, H2L 1L3
(514) 849-1103   *SIC* 8631
SYNDICAT DES EMPLOYE-E-S DE TECHNIQUES PROFFESSION *p* 1180
2E ETAGE 1010, RUE DE LIEGE E, MONTREAL, QC, H2P 1L2
(514) 381-2000   *SIC* 8631
SYNDICAT DES EMPLOYEES COLS BLANCS DE VILLE DE SAGUENAY *p* 1376
3760 RTE SAINT-LEONARD, SHIPSHAW, QC, G7P 1G9
SIC 8631
SYNDICAT DES EMPLOYEES ET EMPLOYES PROFESSIONNELS-LES ET DE BUREAU-QUEBEC (SEPB-QUEBEC) *p* 1177
565 BOUL CREMAZIE E BUREAU 11100, MONTREAL, QC, H2M 2W2
(514) 522-6511   *SIC* 8631
SYNDICAT DES EMPLOYES EN RADIO TELEDIFFUSION DE TELE-QUEBEC *p* 1174
1000 RUE FULLUM BUREAU 231, MONTREAL, QC, H2K 3L7
(514) 529-2805   *SIC* 8631
SYNDICAT DES INSPECTEURS ET DES REPARTITEURS DU RESEAU DE TRANSPORT DE LA CAPITALE (FISA) *p* 1279
720 RUE DES ROCAILLES, QUEBEC, QC, G2J 1A5
(418) 627-2351   *SIC* 4111
SYNDICAT DES METALLOS SECTION LOCAL 9153 *p* 1305
11780 1RE AV BUREAU 204, SAINT-GEORGES, QC, G5Y 2C8
SIC 8631
SYNDICAT DES PROFESSIONNELLES DE LA SANTE DU RESEAU PAPNEAU, SPSRP-FIQ *p* 1102
617 AV DE BUCKINGHAM, GATINEAU, QC, J8L 2H4
(819) 986-3359   *SIC* 8062
SYNDICAT DES PROFESSIONNELLES EN SOINS DU CENTRE DE SANTE ET SERVICES SOCIAUX DU COEUR DE *p* 1171
1385 RUE JEAN-TALON E, MONTREAL, QC, H2E 1S6
(514) 495-6767   *SIC* 8062
SYNDICAT DES PROFESSIONNELLES EN SOINS DU CENTRE DE SANTE ET SERVICES SOCIAUX DU COEUR DE *p* 1182
6910 RUE BOYER, MONTREAL, QC, H2S 2J7
(514) 272-3011   *SIC* 8322
SYNDICAT DES SALARIES DE PINTENDRE AUTO *p* 1135
914 RTE DU PRESIDENT-KENNEDY, LEVIS, QC, G6C 1A5
(418) 833-8111   *SIC* 8631
SYNDICAT DES TRAVAILLEUSES & TRAVAILLEURS DE LA CSN DU CSSS DU AM-N *p* 1171
2180 RUE FLEURY E, MONTREAL, QC, H2B 1K3
(514) 383-5054   *SIC* 8631
SYNDICAT DES TRAVAILLEUSES ET DES TRAVAILLEURS DE LA CSN *p* 1174
See CONFEDERATION DES SYNDICATS NATIONAUX (C.S.N.)
SYNDICAT DES TRAVAILLEUSES ET TRAVAILLEURS DE SYLVANIA *p* 1099
1 RUE SYLVAN, DRUMMONDVILLE, QC, J2C 2S8
(819) 477-8541   *SIC* 8631
SYNDICAT EMPLOYEE-ES DE METIERS D'HYDRO-QUEBEC SECTION LOCALE

1500 SCFP (F.T.Q.) p 1180
1010 RUE DE LIEGE E BUREAU 1500, MONTREAL, QC, H2P 1L2
(514) 387-1500 *SIC* 8631

SYNDICAT EMPLOYES DE METIERS HYDRO-QUEBEC p 1279
See HYDRO-QUEBEC

SYNDICAT NATIONAL DES EMPLOYES DE L'ALUMINUM D'ARVIDA INC, LE p 1116
1932 BOUL MELLON, JONQUIERE, QC, G7S 3H3
(418) 548-4667 *SIC* 8631

SYNDICAT NATIONAL DES TRAVAILLEURS ET TRAVAILLEUSES DE L'AUTOMOBILE DU CANADA INC p 1364
49 RUE SAINT-LAMBERT BUREAU 728, SAINTE-THERESE, QC, J7E 3J9
(450) 434-9664 *SIC* 8631

SYNDICAT NATIONAL TCA p 1303
155 RTE MARIE-VICTORIN, SAINT-FRANCOIS-DU-LAC, QC, J0G 1M0
(514) 531-5362 *SIC* 8631

SYNDICAT QUEBECOIS DES EMPLOYEES & EMPLOYES DE SERVICE SECTION LOCAL 298 (FTQ) p 1177
565 BOUL CREMAZIE E BUREAU 4300, MONTREAL, QC, H2M 2V6
(514) 727-1696 *SIC* 8631

SYNDICAT REGIONAL DES EMPLOYES DE SOUTIEN (C S Q) ENR p 1079
895 RUE BEGIN, CHICOUTIMI, QC, G7H 4P1
(418) 698-5271 *SIC* 8631

SYNDICAT SCFP DU CSSSRDL p 1287
28 RUE JOLY, RIVIERE-DU-LOUP, QC, G5R 3H2
SIC 8631

SYNEOS HEALTH p 1268
See SYNEOS HEALTH CLINIQUE INC

SYNEOS HEALTH CLINIQUE INC p 1268
2500 RUE EINSTEIN, QUEBEC, QC, G1P 0A2
(418) 527-4000 *SIC* 8071

SYNERGEX CORPORATION p 743
1280 COURTNEYPARK DR E, MISSISSAUGA, ON, L5T 1N6
(905) 565-1212 *SIC* 5045

SYNERGIE CANADA INC p 1060
60 RUE EMILIEN-MARCOUX, BLAINVILLE, QC, J7C 0B5
(450) 939-5757 *SIC* 4731

SYNERGIE HUNT INTERNATIONAL INC p 711
50 BURNHAMTHORPE RD W SUITE 204, MISSISSAUGA, ON, L5B 3C2
(905) 273-3221 *SIC* 7361

SYNERGY BUILDING SOLUTIONS p 166
See SYNERGY PROJECTS LTD

SYNERGY CREDIT UNION LTD p 1409
4907 50 ST, LLOYDMINSTER, SK, S9V 0N1
(306) 825-3301 *SIC* 6062

SYNERGY PROJECTS LTD p 166
110 CARLETON DR SUITE 120, ST. ALBERT, AB, T8N 3Y4
(780) 459-3344 *SIC* 1542

SYNERGY SERVICES INC p 647
515 MAITLAND AVE S, LISTOWEL, ON, N4W 2M7
(519) 291-4638 *SIC* 5154

SYNERGY TRUCKING LTD p 278
7184 120 ST SUITE 190, SURREY, BC, V3W 0M6
(604) 598-3498 *SIC* 4731

SYNERTEK INDUSTRIES INC p 1140
1044 RUE DU PARC-INDUSTRIEL, LEVIS, QC, G6Z 1C6
(418) 835-6264 *SIC* 7389

SYNERVEST HOLDINGS INC p 684
490 MCGEACHIE DR, MILTON, ON, L9T 3Y5
SIC 2851

SYNGENTA CANADA INC p 602
140 RESEARCH LANE, GUELPH, ON, N1G

4Z3
(519) 836-5665 *SIC* 5191

SYNNEX CANADA p 665
See 1371185 ONTARIO INC

SYNNEX CANADA LIMITED p 588
200 RONSON DR SUITE 104, ETOBICOKE, ON, M9W 5Z9
(416) 240-7012 *SIC* 5045

SYNNEX CANADA LIMITED p 604
107 WOODLAWN RD W, GUELPH, ON, N1H 1B4
(519) 837-2444 *SIC* 5045

SYNTAX.NET p 1228
See SYSTEMES SYNTAX LTEE

SYNTEC PROCESS EQUIPMENT LTD p 495
77 PILLSWORTH RD UNIT 12, BOLTON, ON, L7E 4G4
(905) 951-8000 *SIC* 5084

SYNTELLECT CANADA, DIV OF p 669
See ENGHOUSE SYSTEMS LIMITED

SYNTEX-ENERFLEX p 133
See TARPON ENERGY SERVICES LTD

SYS-TECH p 1280
See LIBEO INC

SYSCO CANADA p 578
See SYSCO CANADA, INC

SYSCO CANADA, INC p 18
4639 72 AVE SE, CALGARY, AB, T2C 4H7
(403) 720-1300 *SIC* 5141

SYSCO CANADA, INC p 247
1346 KINGSWAY AVE, PORT COQUITLAM, BC, V3C 6G4
(604) 944-4410 *SIC* 5141

SYSCO CANADA, INC p 340
2881 AMY RD, VICTORIA, BC, V9B 0B2
(250) 475-3333 *SIC* 5141

SYSCO CANADA, INC p 392
1570 CLARENCE AVE, WINNIPEG, MB, R3T 1T6
(204) 478-4000 *SIC* 5411

SYSCO CANADA, INC p 398
611 BOUL FERDINAND, DIEPPE, NB, E1A 7G1
(506) 857-6000 *SIC* 5141

SYSCO CANADA, INC p 410
460 MACNAUGHTON AVE, MONCTON, NB, E1H 2K1
(866) 447-9726 *SIC* 5141

SYSCO CANADA, INC p 427
10 OLD PLACENTIA RD, MOUNT PEARL, NL, A1N 4P5
(709) 748-1200 *SIC* 5142

SYSCO CANADA, INC p 460
1 DUCK POND RD SUITE 1, LAKESIDE, NS, B3T 1M5
(902) 876-2311 *SIC* 5812

SYSCO CANADA, INC p 559
1400 CREDITSTONE RD SUITE B, CONCORD, ON, L4K 0E2
(905) 760-7200 *SIC* 2011

SYSCO CANADA, INC p 578
21 FOUR SEASONS PL SUITE 400, ETOBICOKE, ON, M9B 6J8
(416) 234-2666 *SIC* 5141

SYSCO CANADA, INC p 633
650 CATARAQUI WOODS DR, KINGSTON, ON, K7P 2Y4
(613) 384-6666 *SIC* 5141

SYSCO CANADA, INC p 842
65 ELMDALE RD, PETERBOROUGH, ON, K9J 6X4
(705) 748-6701 *SIC* 5141

SYSCO CANADA, INC p 898
106 BAY ST, STURGEON FALLS, ON, P2B 3G6
(705) 753-4444 *SIC* 5141

SYSCO CANADA, INC p 1162
11625 AV 55E BUREAU 864, MONTREAL, QC, H1E 2K2
(514) 494-5200 *SIC* 5141

SYSCO CANADA, INC p 1416
266 E DEWDNEY AVE, REGINA, SK, S4N 4G2
(306) 347-5200 *SIC* 5141

SYSCO CENTRAL ONTARIO, INC p 842
65 ELMDALE RD, PETERBOROUGH, ON, K9J 0G5
(705) 748-6701 *SIC* 5141

SYSCO FINE MEATS OF TORONTO p 559
See SYSCO CANADA, INC

SYSCO FOOD SERVICES p 898
See SYSCO CANADA, INC

SYSCO FOOD SERVICES ATLANTIC p 426
See SOBEYS CAPITAL INCORPORATED

SYSCO FOOD SERVICES OF ATLANTIC CANADA p 410
See SYSCO CANADA, INC

SYSCO FOOD SERVICES OF ATLANTIC CANADA p 427
See SYSCO CANADA, INC

SYSCO FOOD SERVICES OF ATLANTIC CANADA p 460
See SYSCO CANADA, INC

SYSCO FOOD SERVICES OF CALGARY p 18
See SYSCO CANADA, INC

SYSCO FOOD SERVICES OF ONTARIO p 842
See SYSCO CANADA, INC

SYSCO FOOD SERVICES OF WINNIPEG p 392
See SYSCO CANADA, INC

SYSCO FOUR SEASONS PRODUCE LTD p 291
127 E KENT AVE NORTH, VANCOUVER, BC, V5X 2X5
SIC 5141

SYSCO GUEST SUPPLY CANADA INC p 707
570 MATHESON BLVD E SUITE 8, MISSISSAUGA, ON, L4Z 4G4
(905) 896-1060 *SIC* 5046

SYSCO KINGSTON p 633
See SYSCO CANADA, INC

SYSCO QUEBEC p 1162
See SYSCO CANADA, INC

SYSCO REGINA p 1416
See SYSCO CANADA, INC

SYSCO VANCOUVER p 247
See SYSCO CANADA, INC

SYSCO VICTORIA, INC p 340
2881 AMY RD, VICTORIA, BC, V9B 0B2
(250) 475-3333 *SIC* 5141

SYSCOMAX INC p 1060
1060 BOUL MICHELE-BOHEC BUREAU 106, BLAINVILLE, QC, J7C 5E2
(450) 434-0008 *SIC* 1541

SYSCON JUSTICE SYSTEMS CANADA LTD p 265
3600 LYSANDER LANE SUITE 300, RICHMOND, BC, V7B 1C3
(604) 606-7650 *SIC* 7372

SYSCOR p 1218
6600 CH DE LA COTE-DES-NEIGES BUREAU 600, MONTREAL, QC, H3S 2A9
(514) 737-3201 *SIC* 7371

SYSTECH INSTRUMENTATION INC p 18
3-4351 104 AVE SE, CALGARY, AB, T2C 5C6
(403) 291-3535 *SIC* 5084

SYSTEM ONE MFG INC p 111
4420 76 AVE NW, EDMONTON, AB, T6B 0A5
(780) 485-6006 *SIC* 3713

SYSTEMAIR INC p 395
50 KANALFLAKT WAY ROUTE, BOUCTOUCHE, NB, E4S 3M5
(506) 743-9500 *SIC* 3564

SYSTEMATIC MILL INSTALLATIONS LTD p 223
1226 ST. PAUL ST, KELOWNA, BC, V1Y 2C8
(236) 420-4041 *SIC* 1541

SYSTEMATIX p 1208
See SYSTEMATIX TECHNOLOGIES DE L'INFORMATION INC

SYSTEMATIX TECHNOLOGIES DE L'INFORMATION INC p 1208

1 PLACE VILLE-MARIE UNITE 1601, MONTREAL, QC, H3B 3Y2
(514) 393-1313 *SIC* 7379

SYSTEMATIX TECHNOLOGY CONSULTANTS INC p 707
5975 WHITTLE RD SUITE 120, MISSISSAUGA, ON, L4Z 3N1
(416) 650-9669 *SIC* 7379

SYSTEME DE DISTRIBUTION DE LA CHAINE D'APPROVISIONNEMENT FEDEX DU CANADA p 15
See FEDEX SUPPLY CHAIN DISTRIBUTION SYSTEM OF CANADA, INC

SYSTEME DE DISTRIBUTION DE LA CHAINE D'APPROVISIONNEMENT FEDEX DU CANADA p 1088
See FEDEX SUPPLY CHAIN DISTRIBUTION SYSTEM OF CANADA, INC

SYSTEME DE SECURITE A C DE QUEBEC INC p 1281
1394 RUE DE FRONSAC, QUEBEC, QC, G3E 1A3
(418) 842-7440 *SIC* 1731

SYSTEME INTERIEUR EXCEL + INC p 1060
735 BOUL INDUSTRIEL BUREAU 107, BLAINVILLE, QC, J7C 3V3
(450) 477-4585 *SIC* 1742

SYSTEMES ACCESSAIR INC, LES p 1356
1905 RUE PASTEUR, SAINTE-CATHERINE, QC, J5C 1B7
(450) 638-5441 *SIC* 5084

SYSTEMES ADEX INC, LES p 1113
67 RUE SAINT-PAUL RR 1, HEBERTVILLE-STATION, QC, G0W 1T0
(418) 343-2640 *SIC* 3299

SYSTEMES APPLIQUES ISC p 1251
See ISC APPLIED SYSTEMS CORP

SYSTEMES B.M.H. INC, LES p 1296
1395 RUE RENE-DESCARTES, SAINT-BRUNO, QC, J3V 0B7
(450) 441-1770 *SIC* 3559

SYSTEMES CALE INC p 1071
9005 BOUL DU QUARTIER, BROSSARD, QC, J4Y 0A8
(450) 444-4484 *SIC* 5046

SYSTEMES CANADIEN KRONOS INC p 1219
3535 CH QUEEN-MARY BUREAU 500, MONTREAL, QC, H3V 1H8
(514) 345-0580 *SIC* 7371

SYSTEMES D'AFFAIRES POUR PUBLICATION CANADA INC p 1084
2012 BOUL RENE-LAENNEC BUREAU 275, COTE SAINT-LUC, QC, H7M 4J8
(450) 902-6000 *SIC* 6712

SYSTEMES D'ECLAIRAGE STANPRO p 1095
See STANPRO LIGHTING SYSTEMS INC

SYSTEMES D'ECRAN STRONG/MDI INC, LES p 1115
1440 RUE RAOUL-CHARETTE, JOLIETTE, QC, J6E 8S7
(450) 755-3795 *SIC* 3861

SYSTEMES D'EMBALLAGE AESUS INC p 1252
188 AV ONEIDA, POINTE-CLAIRE, QC, H9R 1A8
(514) 694-3439 *SIC* 3565

SYSTEMES D'EMBALLAGE SECURITAIRE NELMAR INC p 1382
3100 RUE DES BATISSEURS, TERREBONNE, QC, J6Y 0A2
(450) 477-0001 *SIC* 2673

SYSTEMES D'ENERGIE RENOUVELABLE CANADA INC p 1186
300 RUE LEO-PARISEAU BUREAU 2516, MONTREAL, QC, H2X 4B3
(514) 525-2113 *SIC* 4911

SYSTEMES D'ENTRAINEMENT MEGGITT (QUEBEC) INC p 1331
6140 BOUL HENRI-BOURASSA O, SAINT-LAURENT, QC, H4R 3A6

(514) 339-9938   *SIC* 3699
SYSTEMES D'ETIQUETAGE AESUS, LES *p* 1252
See SYSTEMES D'EMBALLAGE AESUS INC
SYSTEMES DE CHENILLES CTC DIV OF *p* 1147
See CAMSO INC
SYSTEMES DE COMMUNICATION TACTIQUES ULTRA ELECTRONICS 1158
See ULTRA ELECTRONICS TCS INC
SYSTEMES DE DETECTION MEGGITT CANADA *p* 1331
See SYSTEMES D'ENTRAINEMENT MEGGITT (QUEBEC) INC
SYSTEMES DE DIFFUSION SPRAYLOGIK INC, LES *p* 1314
17420 AV CENTRALE, SAINT-HYACINTHE, QC, J2T 3L7
(450) 778-1850   *SIC* 5047
SYSTEMES DE FRET MONDIAL GTI *p* 1093
See 8027722 CANADA INC
SYSTEMES DE LIGNES D'EXTRUSION FABE INC *p* 1129
1930 52E AV, LACHINE, QC, H8T 2Y3
(514) 633-5933   *SIC* 3569
SYSTEMES DE SECURITE HITACHI *p* 1059
See HITACHI SYSTEMS SECURITY INC
SYSTEMES DE SECURITE PARADOX LTEE *p* 1302
780 BOUL INDUSTRIEL, SAINT-EUSTACHE, QC, J7R 5V3
(450) 491-7444   *SIC* 3669
SYSTEMES ELECTRONIQUES MATROX LTEE *p* 1095
1055 BOUL SAINT-REGIS, DORVAL, QC, H9P 2T4
(514) 822-6000   *SIC* 3674
SYSTEMES ET CABLES PRYSMIAN CANADA LTEE *p* 623
137 COMMERCE PL, JOHNSTOWN, ON, K0E 1T1
(613) 925-6008   *SIC* 1623
SYSTEMES FONEX DATA INC, LES *p* 1336
5400 CH SAINT-FRANCOIS, SAINT-LAURENT, QC, H4S 1P6
(514) 333-6639   *SIC* 5065
SYSTEMES HAIVISION INC *p* 1228
2600 BOUL ALFRED-NOBEL 5EME ETAGE, MONTREAL, QC, H4S 0A9
(514) 334-5445   *SIC* 3669
SYSTEMES INFORMATIQUES O.G.C. INC, LES *p* 1341
7575 RTE TRANSCANADIENNE BUREAU 403, SAINT-LAURENT, QC, H4T 1V6
(514) 331-7873   *SIC* 5045
SYSTEMES INTERIEURS BERNARD MNJ & ASSOCIES INC *p* 1232
5000 RUE BERNARD-LEFEBVRE, MONTREAL, QC, H7C 0A5
(450) 665-1335   *SIC* 1742
SYSTEMES KANTECH *p* 1071
See TYCO SAFETY PRODUCTS CANADA LTD
SYSTEMES LUMINESCENT CANADA INC *p* 1095
55 AV LINDSAY, DORVAL, QC, H9P 2S6
(514) 636-9921   *SIC* 4213
SYSTEMES MEDICAUX INTELERAD INCORPOREE, LES *p* 1176
800 BOUL DE MAISONNEUVE E 12EME ETAGE, MONTREAL, QC, H2L 4L8
(514) 931-6222   *SIC* 7371
SYSTEMES MINERAUX DE SEPRO *p* 225
See SEPRO MINERAL SYSTEMS CORP
SYSTEMES NORBEC INC *p* 1067
97 RUE DE VAUDREUIL, BOUCHERVILLE, QC, J4B 1K7
(450) 449-1499   *SIC* 3585
SYSTEMES P.B.M. *p* 1350
See PRODUITS PBM LTEE, LES
SYSTEMES PAUL DAVIS RIVE-NORD *p*

1151
See 9091-9101 QUEBEC INC
SYSTEMES PERFORMANTS, LES *p* 1336
See RESEAUX ACCEDIAN INC, LES
SYSTEMES RAILTERM INC, LES *p* 1095
10765 CH COTE-DE-LIESSE BUREAU 201, DORVAL, QC, H9P 2R9
(514) 420-1200   *SIC* 8748
SYSTEMES SCHNEIDER ELECTRIC CANADA *p* 1091
See SCHNEIDER ELECTRIC SYSTEMS CANADA INC
SYSTEMES SYNTAX LTEE *p* 1228
8000 BOUL DECARIE BUREAU 300, MONTREAL, QC, H4P 2S4
(514) 733-7777   *SIC* 7372
SYSTEMES TECHNO-POMPES INC, LES *p* 1279
6055 RUE DES TOURNELLES, QUEBEC, QC, G2J 1P7
(418) 623-2022   *SIC* 1711
SYSTEMES TESTFORCE INC *p* 1336
9450 RTE TRANSCANADIENNE, SAINT-LAURENT, QC, H4S 1R7
(514) 856-0970   *SIC* 5065
SYSTEMES URBAINS INC *p* 1345
8345 RUE PASCAL-GAGNON, SAINT-LEONARD, QC, H1P 1Y5
(514) 321-5205   *SIC* 1731
SYSTEMES VERINT CANADA, INC *p* 1362
1800 RUE BERLIER, SAINTE-ROSE, QC, H7L 4S4
(450) 686-9000   *SIC* 5065
SYSTEMES WESTCON CANADA (WCSI) INC, LES *p* 799
1383 JOSHUAS CREEK DR, OAKVILLE, ON, L6H 7G4
(888) 307-7218   *SIC* 5065
SYSTEMS CISCO CANADA *p* 1194
See CISCO SYSTEMS CANADA CO
SYSTEMS PLUS *p* 483
See 1936100 ONTARIO INC
SYSTEMS VIC INC *p* 1309
5200 RUE ARMAND-FRAPPIER, SAINT-HUBERT, QC, J3Z 1G5
(450) 926-3164   *SIC* 5075
SYSTEMWARE INNOVATIONS *p* 922
See ALITHYA DIGITAL TECHNOLOGY CORPORATION
SYSTRA CANADA INC *p* 1209
1100 BOUL RENE-LEVESQUE O ETAGE 10E, MONTREAL, QC, H3B 4N4
(514) 985-0930   *SIC* 8711
SZE STRAKA ENGINEERS, DIV OF *p* 635
See MTE CONSULTANTS INC

T

(T.P.Q.) TERMINAUX PORTUAIRES DU QUEBEC *p* 1259
See QSL CANADA INC
(T.P.Q.) TERMINAUX PORTUAIRES DU QUEBEC INC *p* 1257
961 BOUL CHAMPLAIN, QUEBEC, QC, G1K 4J9
(418) 529-6521   *SIC* 4491
T & B COMMANDER *p* 1248
See ABB PRODUITS D'INSTALLATION LTEE
T & C STEEL LTD *p* 1424
4032 TAYLOR ST E, SASKATOON, SK, S7H 5J5
(306) 373-5191   *SIC* 5051
T & L FOOD MERCHANDISING SERVICES LTD *p* 878
78 PINEMEADOW BLVD, SCARBOROUGH, ON, M1W 1P2
(416) 497-6573   *SIC* 8743
T & L GREGORINI ENTERPRISES INC *p* 284
8238 3B HWY, TRAIL, BC, V1R 4W4
(250) 364-3333   *SIC* 5531
T & R SARGENT FARMS LIMITED *p* 685
189 MILL ST, MILTON, ON, L9T 1S3
(905) 878-4401   *SIC* 5144

T & T GROUP OF COMPANIES *p* 1425
See 601861 SASKATCHEWAN LTD
T & T HONDA *p* 10
See 502386 ALBERTA LTD
T & T SUPERMARKET INC *p* 11
999 36 ST NE SUITE 800, CALGARY, AB, T2A 7X6
(403) 569-6888   *SIC* 5411
T & T SUPERMARKET INC *p* 104
8882 170 ST NW SUITE 2580, EDMONTON, AB, T5T 4M2
(780) 483-6638   *SIC* 5411
T & T SUPERMARKET INC *p* 191
4800 KINGSWAY SUITE 147, BURNABY, BC, V5H 4J2
(604) 436-4881   *SIC* 5411
T & T SUPERMARKET INC *p* 258
21500 GORDON WAY, RICHMOND, BC, V6W 1J8
(604) 276-9889   *SIC* 5411
T & T SUPERMARKET INC *p* 262
3700 NO. 3 RD SUITE 1000, RICHMOND, BC, V6X 3X2
(604) 276-8808   *SIC* 5411
T & T SUPERMARKET INC *p* 262
8181 CAMBIE RD SUITE 1000, RICHMOND, BC, V6X 3X9
(604) 284-5550   *SIC* 5411
T & T SUPERMARKET INC *p* 300
179 KEEFER PL, VANCOUVER, BC, V6B 6L4
(604) 899-8836   *SIC* 5411
T & T SUPERMARKET INC *p* 906
1 PROMENADE CIR, THORNHILL, ON, L4J 4P8
(905) 763-8113   *SIC* 5411
T & T TRUCKING LTD *p* 1430
855 60TH ST E, SASKATOON, SK, S7K 5Z7
(306) 934-3383   *SIC* 4213
T A F CONSTRUCTION LTD *p* 284
2620 HASTINGS ST E, VANCOUVER, BC, V5K 1Z6
(604) 254-1111   *SIC* 1542
T B W A CHIAT/DAY *p* 984
10 LOWER SPADINA AVE, TORONTO, ON, M5V 2Z2
(416) 642-1380   *SIC* 7311
T BELL TRANSPORT INC *p* 747
231 HWY 17, NAIRN CENTRE, ON, P0M 2L0
(705) 869-5959   *SIC* 4213
T C ENTERPRISES LTD *p* 1437
HWY 6 & 5 SW CORNER, WATSON, SK, S0K 4V0
(306) 287-3636   *SIC* 5541
T E S *p* 531
See CITY ELECTRIC SUPPLY CORPORATION
T F I *p* 507
See TAYLOR FREEZERS INC
T G & G MASTRONARDI *p* 643
See 745926 ONTARIO LIMITED
T K GROUP INC, THE *p* 829
880 LADY ELLEN PL SUITE 100, OTTAWA, ON, K1Z 5L9
(613) 728-7030   *SIC* 6411
T K INSURANCE GROUP *p* 829
See T K GROUP INC, THE
T L D COMPUTERS INC *p* 264
12251 HORSESHOE WAY UNIT 100, RICHMOND, BC, V7A 4V4
(604) 272-6000   *SIC* 5734
T M P CONSULTING ENGINEERS *p* 768
See MITCHELL PARTNERSHIP INC, THE
T MACRAE FAMILY SALES LTD *p* 239
1350 MAIN ST SUITE 601, NORTH VANCOUVER, BC, V7J 1C6
(604) 982-9101   *SIC* 5014
T N L INDUSTRIAL CONTRACTORS LTD *p* 264
12391 HORSESHOE WAY SUITE 130, RICHMOND, BC, V7A 4X6
(604) 278-7424   *SIC* 1731
T N T APPLIANCES *p* 790

See T N T GROUP INC
T N T GROUP INC *p* 790
65 DUFFLAW RD, NORTH YORK, ON, M6A 2W2
(416) 781-9156   *SIC* 5064
T R H GROUP, THE *p* 559
See THOMPSON, ROACH & HUGHES CONSULTING INC
T R SAND & GRAVEL INC *p* 883
1417 NOTRE DAME DR RR 1, ST AGATHA, ON, N0B 2L0
(519) 747-4173   *SIC* 5521
T S MANUFACTURING CO *p* 645
See 381572 ONTARIO LIMITED
T U A C LOCAL 501 *p* 1346
See TRAVAILLEURS & TRAVAILLEUSES UNIS DE L'ALIMENTATION ET DU COMMERCE T U A C LOCAL 501
T U C *p* 427
See TORNGAIT UJAGANNIAVINGIT CORPORATION
T&R SARGENT FARMS LTD *p* 712
3410 SEMENYK CRT SUITE 5, MISSISSAUGA, ON, L5C 4P8
(905) 896-1059   *SIC* 0251
T-BASE COMMUNICATIONS INC *p* 831
885 MEADOWLANDS DR SUITE 401, OTTAWA, ON, K2C 3N2
(613) 236-0866   *SIC* 7389
T-BROTHERS FOOD AND TRADING LTD *p* 202
88 BRIGANTINE DR SUITE 100, COQUITLAM, BC, V3K 6Z6
(604) 540-0306   *SIC* 5141
T. & D. ENTERPRISES LTD *p* 393
1546 SASKATCHEWAN AVE, WINNIPEG, MB, S7K 1P7
(204) 786-3384   *SIC* 1731
T. A. BLAKELOCK HIGH SCHOOL *p* 803
See HALTON DISTRICT SCHOOL BOARD
T. A. BRANNON STEEL LIMITED *p* 506
14 TILBURY CRT, BRAMPTON, ON, L6T 3T4
(905) 453-4730   *SIC* 3398
T. L. PENNER MANAGEMENT LTD *p* 351
HWY 257 E, KOLA, MB, R0M 1B0
(204) 556-2265   *SIC* 1542
T. S. SIMMS & CO. LIMITED *p* 414
560 MAIN ST SUITE 320, SAINT JOHN, NB, E2K 1J5
(506) 635-6330   *SIC* 3991
T.A. MORRISON & CO. INC *p* 891
27 IBER RD, STITTSVILLE, ON, K2S 1E6
(613) 831-7000   *SIC* 3822
T.A.C. CONTROLS & AUTOMATION INC *p* 559
259 EDGELEY BLVD UNIT 5, CONCORD, ON, L4K 3Y5
(905) 660-0878   *SIC* 5962
T.A.C. CORROSION-RESISTANT TECHNOLOGY INC *p* 1155
1255 BOUL LAIRD BUREAU 240, MONT-ROYAL, QC, H3P 2T1
(514) 737-8566   *SIC* 3272
T.B.T. WINDOWS & DOORS EXTRUSION INC. *p* 786
27 TORBARRIE RD UNIT 25, NORTH YORK, ON, M3L 1G5
(416) 244-0000   *SIC* 5031
T.C. BACKHOE & DIRECTIONAL DRILLING LIMITED PARTNERSHIP *p* 161
302 CREE RD, SHERWOOD PARK, AB, T8A 4G2
(780) 467-1367   *SIC* 1629
T.C. ENTERPRISES LTD *p* 436
5013 48 ST, YELLOWKNIFE, NT, X1A 1N4
(867) 669-8300   *SIC* 6519
T.E. FINANCIAL CONSULTANTS LTD *p* 943
26 WELLINGTON ST E SUITE 800, TORONTO, ON, M5E 1S2
(416) 366-1451   *SIC* 6282
T.E. WEALTH *p* 943
See T.E. FINANCIAL CONSULTANTS LTD

T.E.A.M. LOGISTICS SYSTEMS INC *p 483*
118 EARL THOMPSON RD, AYR, ON, N0B
1E0
(519) 622-2473 *SIC 4213*

T.F. LYNN AND ASSOCIATES INC *p 40*
5512 4 ST NW SUITE 224, CALGARY, AB,
T2K 1A9
(403) 215-6880 *SIC 5065*

T.F. WARREN GROUP INC *p 518*
57 OLD ONONDAGA RD W, BRANTFORD,
ON, N3T 5M1
(519) 756-8222 *SIC 5169*

T.F. WARREN GROUP INC *p 518*
57 OLD ONONDAGA RD W, BRANTFORD,
ON, N3T 5M1
(519) 756-8222 *SIC 6712*

T.F.G. (1987) LTD *p 388*
834 CORYDON AVE SUITE 1, WINNIPEG,
MB, R3M 0Y2
SIC 6794

T.FLEXO CORPORATION *p 665*
528 RAYMERVILLE DR, MARKHAM, ON,
L3P 6G4
(647) 477-8482 *SIC 2673*

**T.G.A. GENERAL CONTRACTING (1980)
INC** *p 792*
31 DENSLEY AVE, NORTH YORK, ON,
M6M 2P5
(416) 247-7471 *SIC 1521*

T.I.C.C. LIMITED *p 689*
6900 AIRPORT RD SUITE 120, MISSIS-
SAUGA, ON, L4V 1E8
(905) 677-6131 *SIC 7999*

T.J. TRADING CO. INC *p 787*
260 BARTLEY DR, NORTH YORK, ON,
M4A 1G5
(416) 661-9506 *SIC 5085*

T.J.'S OILFIELD CONTRACTING LTD *p 79*
GD, CHARD, AB, T0P 1G0
SIC 1389

T.M.S. SYSTEME INC *p 1306*
170 RTE DU PRESIDENT-KENNEDY,
SAINT-HENRI-DE-LEVIS, QC, G0R 3E0
(418) 895-6877 *SIC 3272*

T.P.Q. *p 1257*
See *(T.P.Q.) TERMINAUX PORTUAIRES
DU QUEBEC INC*

T.R.Y. JACKSON BROTHERS LIMITED *p
488*
181 MAPLEVIEW DR W, BARRIE, ON, L4N
9E8
(705) 726-0288 *SIC 5511*

T.S. SIMMS & CO *p 569*
300 MAIN ST, ERIN, ON, N0B 1T0
(905) 362-1470 *SIC 3991*

T.T.O.C.S. LIMITED *p 814*
419 KING ST W SUITE SIDE, OSHAWA,
ON, L1J 2K5
SIC 5812

T.T.S. HOLDINGS INC *p 913*
85 PINE ST S, TIMMINS, ON, P4N 2K1
(705) 264-7200 *SIC 6712*

T.W. COMMODITIES *p 1436*
See *DUNNINGTON HOLDINGS LTD*

T4G LIMITED *p 934*
340 KING ST E SUITE 300, TORONTO, ON,
M5A 1K8
(416) 462-4200 *SIC 7379*

TA COGEN *p 66*
See *TRANSALTA GENERATION PART-
NERSHIP*

TAB CANADA *p 765*
See *TAB PRODUCTS OF CANADA, CO.*

TAB PRODUCTS OF CANADA, CO. *p 765*
136 SPARKS AVE, NORTH YORK, ON,
M2H 2S4
(416) 497-1552 *SIC 5044*

TABER SPECIAL NEEDS SOCIETY *p 169*
6005 60 AVE, TABER, AB, T1G 2C1
(403) 223-4941 *SIC 8699*

TABLE ROCK RESTAURANT *p 758*
See *NIAGARA PARKS COMMISSION, THE*
TABLEX *p 1387*
See *ASPASIE INC*

TABOR HOME INC *p 352*
450 LOREN DR, MORDEN, MB, R6M 0E2
(204) 822-4848 *SIC 8051*

TABOR HOME SOCIETY *p 177*
31944 SUNRISE CRES, ABBOTSFORD,
BC, V2T 1N5
(604) 859-8718 *SIC 8059*

TABOR MANOR *p 177*
See *TABOR HOME SOCIETY*

**TABOR MANOR LONG TERM CARE FACIL-
ITY** *p*
884
1 TABOR DR, ST CATHARINES, ON, L2N
1V9
(905) 934-2548 *SIC 6351*

TABOR VIEW HOLDINGS LTD *p 249*
505 4TH AVE, PRINCE GEORGE, BC, V2L
3H2
(250) 563-8250 *SIC 6712*

TAC MECHANICAL INC *p 588*
215 CARLINGVIEW DR SUITE 311, ETOBI-
COKE, ON, M9W 5X8
(416) 798-8400 *SIC 1711*

TACAMOR INC *p 427*
1 AUGUSTA PL, PLACENTIA, NL, A0B 2Y0
SIC 6351

TACC CONSTRUCTION CO. LTD *p 1034*
270 CHRISLEA RD, WOODBRIDGE, ON,
L4L 8A8
(905) 856-8500 *SIC 1623*

TACC CONSTRUCTION LTD *p 1034*
270 CHRISLEA RD, WOODBRIDGE, ON,
L4L 8A8
(905) 856-8500 *SIC 1623*

TACF *p 589*
See *TORONTO AIRPORT CHRISTIAN FEL-
LOWSHIP*

**TACKABERRY HEATING & REFRIGERA-
TION SUPPLIES** *p*
630
See *TACKABERRY HEATING SUPPLIES
LIMITED*

**TACKABERRY HEATING SUPPLIES LIM-
ITED** *p*
630
60 DALTON AVE, KINGSTON, ON, K7K 6C3
(613) 549-3320 *SIC 5722*

**TACKABERRY, G & SONS CONSTRUC-
TION COMPANY LIMITED** *p*
479
109 WASHBURN RD, ATHENS, ON, K0E
1B0
(613) 924-2634 *SIC 1611*

TACKLES *p 415*
See *HAYWARD & WARWICK LIMITED*

TACO BELL OF CANADA *p 101*
See *HANSON RESTAURANTS (TB) INC*

TACORPORATION RESTAURANT LTD *p
285*
1622 COMMERCIAL DR UNIT A, VANCOU-
VER, BC, V5L 3Y4
(604) 559-8226 *SIC 5812*

TADAM *p 1279*
See *MARTIN DESSERT INC*

TAFISA CANADA INC *p 1125*
4660 RUE VILLENEUVE, LAC-MEGANTIC,
QC, G6B 2C3
(819) 583-2930 *SIC 2499*

TAG CONSTRUCTION LTD *p 227*
21869 56 AVE UNIT B, LANGLEY, BC, V2Y
2M9
(604) 534-2685 *SIC 1623*

TAG INTERNATIONAL INC *p 809*
75 FIRST ST SUITE 321, ORANGEVILLE,
ON, L9W 2E7
(519) 943-0074 *SIC 6211*

TAG PROTECTION SERVICE *p 809*
See *TAG INTERNATIONAL INC*

TAGGART CONSTRUCTION LIMITED *p 827*
3187 ALBION RD S, OTTAWA, ON, K1V 8Y3
(613) 521-3000 *SIC 1623*

TAGGEL AUTOMOBILE INC *p 528*
805 WALKER'S LINE, BURLINGTON, ON,
L7N 2G1

(905) 333-0595 *SIC 8699*

TAGISH ENTERPRISES LTD *p 1406*
5A SOUTH PLAINS ROAD W, EMERALD
PARK, SK, S4L 1A1
(306) 585-8480 *SIC 1521*

TAHK PROJECTS LTD *p 161*
296 KASKA RD, SHERWOOD PARK, AB,
T8A 4G7
(780) 416-7770 *SIC 1623*

**TAHLTAN NATION DEVELOPMENT COR-
PORATION** *p*
205
HWY 37 N, DEASE LAKE, BC, V0C 1L0
(250) 771-5482 *SIC 1611*

TAI FOONG INVESTMENTS LTD *p 879*
2900 MARKHAM RD, SCARBOROUGH,
ON, M1X 1E6
(416) 299-7575 *SIC 5146*

TAI PAN VACATIONS INC *p 794*
3668 WESTON RD UNIT A, NORTH YORK,
ON, M9L 1W2
(416) 646-8828 *SIC 4724*

TAIGA BUILDING PRODUCTS LTD *p 191*
4710 KINGSWAY SUITE 800, BURNABY,
BC, V5H 4M2
(604) 438-1471 *SIC 5031*

TAIL RISK SYSTEMS SOLUTIONS LTD *p 60*
202 6 AVE SW SUITE 1110, CALGARY, AB,
T2P 2R9
(587) 352-5071 *SIC 5169*

TAILOR DRUGS LIMITED *p 727*
6975 MEADOWVALE TOWN CENTRE CIR,
MISSISSAUGA, ON, L5N 2V7
(905) 826-7112 *SIC 5912*

TAJ TOURS *p 819*
See *HANDA TRAVEL SERVICES LTD*

TAKARA COMPANY, CANADA, LTD *p 714*
2076 SOUTH SHERIDAN WAY, MISSIS-
SAUGA, ON, L5J 2M4
(905) 822-2755 *SIC 5087*

TAKBRO ENTERPRISES LIMITED *p 498*
10115 BRAMALEA RD, BRAMPTON, ON,
L6R 1W6
(905) 789-0753 *SIC 5541*

TAKE FLIGHT *p 20*
See *AIR PARTNERS CORP*

TAKEDA CANADA INC *p 806*
435 NORTH SERVICE RD W SUITE 101,
OAKVILLE, ON, L6M 4X8
(905) 469-9333 *SIC 5122*

TAKHAR FINANCIAL INSTITUTE *p 534*
See *TAKHAR INVESTMENTS INC*

TAKHAR INVESTMENTS INC *p 534*
202 BEVERLY ST, CAMBRIDGE, ON, N1R
3Z8
(519) 622-3130 *SIC 6712*

TAKNOLOGY (CANADA) INC *p 854*
50 EAST PEARCE ST, RICHMOND HILL,
ON, L4B 1B7
(905) 882-2299 *SIC 5045*

TAKUMI STAMPING CANADA INC *p 890*
100 DENNIS RD, ST THOMAS, ON, N5P
0B6
(519) 633-6070 *SIC 3465*

TALBOT MARKETING INC *p 661*
383 SOVEREIGN RD, LONDON, ON, N6M
1A3
(519) 659-5862 *SIC 5199*

TALBOT SALES LIMITED *p 865*
120 VENTURE DR, SCARBOROUGH, ON,
M1B 3L6
(416) 286-3666 *SIC 5085*

TALBOT, JOHANNE PHARMACIENNE *p
1270*
110 BOUL RENE-LEVESQUE O BUREAU
118, QUEBEC, QC, G1R 2A5
(418) 522-1235 *SIC 5912*

TALENT EMPLOYMENT INC *p 794*
5601 STEELES AVE W UNIT 5, NORTH
YORK, ON, M9L 1S7
(416) 748-3982 *SIC 7361*

TALISKER CORPORATION *p 957*
145 ADELAIDE ST W SUITE 500,
TORONTO, ON, M5H 4E5

(416) 864-0213 *SIC 6799*

TALISKER RESOURCES LTD *p 987*
100 KING STREET W 70 FLOOR,
TORONTO, ON, M5X 1A9
(416) 361-2808 *SIC 6282*

TALISMAN CENTRE *p 30*
See *LINDSAY PARK SPORTS SOCIETY*

TALISMAN MOUNTAIN RESORT LTD *p 628*
150 TALISMAN BLVD, KIMBERLEY, ON,
N0C 1G0
SIC 7011

TALKA ENTERPRISES LTD *p 576*
1608 THE QUEENSWAY, ETOBICOKE, ON,
M8Z 1V1
(416) 255-5531 *SIC 5531*

TALL PINES SCHOOL INC *p 506*
8525 TORBRAM RD, BRAMPTON, ON, L6T
5K4
(905) 458-6770 *SIC 8211*

TALL TIMBER LTD *p 79*
GD, CARDSTON, AB, T0K 0K0
SIC 5531

TALLBOYS GRILL & PUB *p 357*
10 PTH 2, ST CLAUDE, MB, R0G 1Z0
(204) 379-2491 *SIC 5541*

TALLGRASS *p 292*
See *TALLGRASS NATURAL HEALTH LTD*

TALLGRASS NATURAL HEALTH LTD *p 292*
375 5TH AVE W SUITE 201, VANCOUVER,
BC, V5Y 1J6
(604) 709-0101 *SIC 5122*

TALLMAN TRANSPORTS LIMITED *p 1012*
1003 NIAGARA ST, WELLAND, ON, L3C
1M5
(416) 735-1410 *SIC 4213*

TALLMAN TRUCK CENTRE LIMITED *p 686*
7450 TORBRAM RD, MISSISSAUGA, ON,
L4T 1G9
(905) 671-7600 *SIC 5511*

TALLON, DENNIS M. & ASSOCIATES INC *p
476*
400 MAIN ST S, ALEXANDRIA, ON, K0C
1A0
(613) 525-2383 *SIC 5531*

TALLON, TIMOTHY J SALES INC *p 994*
2129 ST CLAIR AVE W SUITE 182,
TORONTO, ON, M6N 5B4
(416) 766-8141 *SIC 5531*

**TALMUD TORAHS UNIS DE MONTREAL
INC** *p 1220*
4840 AV SAINT-KEVIN BUREAU 210, MON-
TREAL, QC, H3W 1P2
(514) 739-2294 *SIC 8661*

TALON ENERGY SERVICES INC *p 432*
215 WATER ST SUITE 301, ST. JOHN'S,
NL, A1C 6C9
(709) 739-8450 *SIC 1389*

TALON SEBEQ INC *p 1142*
555 BOUL GUIMOND, LONGUEUIL, QC,
J4G 1L9
(450) 677-7449 *SIC 1611*

TAM ELECTRIC LTD *p 794*
456 GARYRAY DR, NORTH YORK, ON,
M9L 1P7
(416) 743-6214 *SIC 1731*

TAM-KAL LIMITED *p 598*
34 CARDICO DR UNIT 2, GORMLEY, ON,
L4A 2G5
(905) 888-9200 *SIC 1761*

TAMAGGO INC *p 1200*
2001 AV MCGILL COLLEGE BUREAU 700,
MONTREAL, QC, H3A 1G1
SIC 3651

TAMAR BUILDING PRODUCTS (1981) LTD
p 1020
3957 WALKER RD, WINDSOR, ON, N8W
3T4
(519) 969-7060 *SIC 5039*

TAMARACK CANADA INC *p 1353*
381 153 RTE, SAINT-TITE, QC, G0X 3H0
(819) 694-0395 *SIC 2411*

**TAMARACK DEVELOPMENTS CORPORA-
TION** *p*
827

3187 ALBION RD S, OTTAWA, ON, K1V 8Y3
(613) 739-2919 SIC 1531

TAMARACK FOUNDATION p 1432
510 CYNTHIA ST SUITE 136, SASKATOON, SK, S7L 7K7
(306) 975-0855 SIC 8699

TAMARACK GEOGRAPHIC TECHNOLOGIES LTD. p 431
303 THORBURN RD SUITE 302, ST. JOHN'S, NL, A1B 4R1
(709) 726-1046 SIC 8731

TAMARACK LUMBER INC p 528
3255 SERVICE RD NORTH, BURLINGTON, ON, L7N 3G2
(905) 335-1115 SIC 5211

TAMARACK VALLEY ENERGY LTD p 61
425 1ST ST SW SUITE 600, CALGARY, AB, T2P 3L8
(403) 263-4440 SIC 1311

TAMCO p 891
See T.A. MORRISON & CO. INC

TAMEC INC p 1212
980 RUE SAINT-ANTOINE O BUREAU 400, MONTREAL, QC, H3C 1A8
SIC 2741

TAMODA APPAREL INC p 289
319 2ND AVE E SUITE 315, VANCOUVER, BC, V5T 1B9
(604) 877-2282 SIC 5136

TAMWIN HOLDINGS LIMITED p 1020
3957 WALKER RD, WINDSOR, ON, N8W 3T4
(519) 969-7060 SIC 6712

TAN, KENNY PHARMACY INC p 976
360 BLOOR ST W SUITE 806, TORONTO, ON, M5S 1X1
(416) 961-2121 SIC 5912

TANCO p 351
See TANTALUM MINING CORPORATION OF CANADA LIMITED

TANDET EASTERN LIMITED p 630
191 DALTON AVE, KINGSTON, ON, K7K 6C2
(613) 544-1212 SIC 5511

TANDET KENWORTH, DIV OF p 630
See TANDET EASTERN LIMITED

TANDET LOGISTICS INC p 805
1351 SPEERS RD, OAKVILLE, ON, L6L 2X5
(905) 827-4200 SIC 4213

TANDET MANAGEMENT INC p 805
1351 SPEERS RD, OAKVILLE, ON, L6L 2X5
(905) 827-0501 SIC 4213

TANDET MANAGEMENT INC p 880
2510 DAVIS DR, SHARON, ON, L0G 1V0
(905) 953-5457 SIC 4212

TANDIA FINANCIAL CREDIT UNION LIMITED p 613
75 JAMES ST S, HAMILTON, ON, L8P 2Y9
(800) 598-2891 SIC 6062

TANDUS CENTIVA LIMITED p 469
435 WILLOW ST SUITE 30, TRURO, NS, B2N 6T2
(902) 895-5491 SIC 2273

TANDUS FLOORING LIMITED p 469
GD RPO PRINCE, TRURO, NS, B2N 5B5
(902) 895-5491 SIC 2273

TANG APPAREL CO. LIMITED p 917
50 NORTHLINE RD, TORONTO, ON, M4B 3E2
(416) 603-0021 SIC 2337

TANGERINE BANK p 765
3389 STEELES AVE E, NORTH YORK, ON, M2H 3S8
(416) 497-5157 SIC 6036

TANGO GOLD MINES INCORPORATED p 987
130 KING ST W, TORONTO, ON, M5X 2A2
(416) 479-4433 SIC 1081

TANGRAM SURFACES INC p 448
66 WRIGHT AVE, DARTMOUTH, NS, B3B 1H3
(902) 468-7679 SIC 5032

TANK TRADERS, DIV OF p 351
See VOMAR INDUSTRIES INC

TANK TRUCK TRANSPORT INC p 642
11339 ALBION VAUGHAN RD, KLEINBURG, ON, L0J 1C0
(905) 893-3447 SIC 4213

TANKMART INTERNATIONAL p 1231
See CITERNES EXPERTS INC

TANKMART PARTS & SERVICES p 1247
See SERVICE REMTEC INC

TANN PAPER LIMITED p 420
149 HELLER RD, WOODSTOCK, NB, E7M 1X3
(506) 325-9100 SIC 2621

TANNIS FOOD DISTRIBUTORS p 819
See TANNIS TRADING INC

TANNIS TRADING INC p 819
2390 STEVENAGE DR, OTTAWA, ON, K1G 3W3
(613) 736-6000 SIC 5149

TANSEY INSURANCE SERVICE LTD p 227
4769 222 ST UNIT 103, LANGLEY, BC, V2Z 3C1
(604) 539-7783 SIC 6311

TANTALUM MINING CORPORATION OF CANADA LIMITED p 351
BERNIC LAKE, LAC DU BONNET, MB, R0E 1A0
(204) 884-2400 SIC 1061

TANTALUS SYSTEMS CORP p 189
3555 GILMORE WAY SUITE 200, BURNABY, BC, V5G 0B3
(604) 299-0458 SIC 4899

TANTRAMAR CHEVROLET p 438
See TANTRAMAR CHEVROLET BUICK GMC (2009) LIMITED

TANTRAMAR CHEVROLET BUICK GMC (2009) LIMITED p 438
88 ROBERT ANGUS DR, AMHERST, NS, B4H 4R7
(902) 667-9975 SIC 5511

TANZANIAN ROYALTY EXPLORATION CORPORATION p 940
82 RICHMOND ST W SUITE 208, TORONTO, ON, M5C 1P1
(844) 364-1830 SIC 1081

TAO GROUP HOLDINGS CORP p 957
11 KING ST W SUITE 1600, TORONTO, ON, M5H 4C7
(416) 309-7557 SIC 6712

TAO SOLUTIONS INC p 957
11 KING ST W SUITE 1600, TORONTO, ON, M5H 4C7
(416) 309-7557 SIC 5045

TAOIST TAI CHI SOCIETY OF CANADA p 978
134 D'ARCY ST, TORONTO, ON, M5T 1K3
(416) 656-2110 SIC 8699

TAPESTRY AT THE O'KEEFE - ARBUTUS WALK p 322
See IDEA PARTNER MARKETING INC, THE

TAPESTRY REALTY LTD p 278
13049 76 AVE SUITE 104, SURREY, BC, V3W 2V7
SIC 6531

TAPIS VENTURE INC p 1305
700 120E RUE, SAINT-GEORGES, QC, G5Y 6R6
(418) 227-5955 SIC 2273

TAQA NORTH LTD p 61
308 4 AVE SW SUITE 2100, CALGARY, AB, T2P 0H7
(403) 724-5000 SIC 1311

TAQUANYAH CONSERVATION AREA p 541
See GRAND RIVER CONSERVATION AUTHORITY

TAR INVESTMENTS LIMITED p 448
30 TROOP AVE, DARTMOUTH, NS, B3B 1Z1
(902) 468-3200 SIC 6719

TARA NATURAL p 181
See HORIZON DISTRIBUTORS LTD

TARA OILFIELD SERVICES LTD p 82

1805 19 ST, DIDSBURY, AB, T0M 0W0
(403) 335-9158 SIC 1389

TARANIS CONTRACTING GROUP LTD p 910
1473 ROSSLYN RD, THUNDER BAY, ON, P7E 6W1
(807) 475-5443 SIC 1611

TARDIF, PIERRE INC p 1265
1595 BOUL WILFRID-HAMEL, QUEBEC, QC, G1N 3Y7
(418) 655-1521 SIC 6719

TARESCO LTD p 615
175A NEBO RD, HAMILTON, ON, L8W 2E1
(905) 575-8078 SIC 1751

TARGET EMISSION SERVICES INC p 38
1235 64 AVE SE SUITE 12 B, CALGARY, AB, T2H 2J7
(403) 225-8755 SIC 1799

TARGET EXCAVATING INC p 153
GD, PROVOST, AB, T0B 3S0
(780) 753-3931 SIC 1623

TARGET INVESTIGATION & SECURITY LTD p 559
2900 LANGSTAFF RD UNIT 3, CONCORD, ON, L4K 4R9
(905) 760-9090 SIC 7381

TARGET PARK GROUP INC p 984
525 KING ST W SUITE 300, TORONTO, ON, M5V 1K4
(416) 425-7275 SIC 7521

TARGET PRODUCTS LTD p 183
8535 EASTLAKE DR, BURNABY, BC, V5A 4T7
(604) 444-3620 SIC 3272

TARGET VACATIONS p 559
3175 RUTHERFORD RD UNIT 55, CONCORD, ON, L4K 5Y6
(416) 687-5925 SIC 4724

TARGETED MICROWAVE SOLUTIONS INC p 316
1066 HASTINGS ST W SUITE 2300, VANCOUVER, BC, V6E 3X2
(778) 995-5833 SIC 3822

TARGRAY AMERIQUES INC p 1118
18105 RTE TRANSCANADIENNE, KIRKLAND, QC, H9J 3Z4
(514) 695-8095 SIC 5172

TARGRAY TECHNOLOGIE INTERNATIONALE INC p 1118
18105 RTE TRANSCANADIENNE, KIRKLAND, QC, H9J 3Z4
(514) 695-8095 SIC 5063

TARGUS (CANADA) LTD p 743
6725 EDWARDS BLVD, MISSISSAUGA, ON, L5T 2V9
(905) 564-9300 SIC 5099

TARION WARRANTY CORPORATION p 773
5160 YONGE ST 12TH FL, NORTH YORK, ON, M2N 6L9
(416) 229-3828 SIC 6351

TARKETT INC p 1101
1001 RUE YAMASKA E, FARNHAM, QC, J2N 1J7
(450) 293-3173 SIC 2851

TARKETT SPORTS CANADA INC p 1341
7445 CH DE LA COTE-DE-LIESSE BUREAU 200, SAINT-LAURENT, QC, H4T 1G2
(514) 340-9311 SIC 3523

TARO PHARMACEUTICALS INC p 506
130 EAST DR, BRAMPTON, ON, L6T 1C1
(905) 791-8276 SIC 2834

TAROPHARMA p 506
See TARO PHARMACEUTICALS INC

TARPIN LUMBER INCORPORATED p 622
2267 BOWMAN ST, INNISFIL, ON, L9S 3V5
(705) 436-5373 SIC 5211

TARPON CONSTRUCTION MANAGEMENT LTD p 111
3944 53 AVE NW, EDMONTON, AB, T6B 3N7
(780) 468-6333 SIC 1731

TARPON ENERGY SERVICES p 6
See TARPON ENERGY SERVICES LTD

TARPON ENERGY SERVICES LTD p 6
5001 55 AVE, BONNYVILLE, AB, T9N 0A7
(780) 826-7570 SIC 1389

TARPON ENERGY SERVICES LTD p 19
7020 81 ST SE, CALGARY, AB, T2C 5B8
(403) 234-8647 SIC 1389

TARPON ENERGY SERVICES LTD p 133
11418 91 AVE, GRANDE PRAIRIE, AB, T8V 6K6
(780) 539-9696 SIC 1389

TARPON ENERGY SERVICES(PROCESS SYSTEMS)LTD p 19
7020 81 ST SE, CALGARY, AB, T2C 5B8
(403) 234-8647 SIC 5084

TARRISON PRODUCTS LTD p 799
2780 COVENTRY RD, OAKVILLE, ON, L6H 6R1
(905) 825-9665 SIC 5046

TARTAN CANADA CORPORATION p 61
401 9TH AVE SW SUITE 960, CALGARY, AB, T2P 2H7
(780) 455-3804 SIC 1389

TARTAN FORD p 5
See TARTAN SALES (1973) LTD

TARTAN HOMES CORPORATION p 834
233 METCALFE ST 11, OTTAWA, ON, K2P 2C2
(613) 238-2040 SIC 1521

TARTAN INDUSTRIAL LTD p 158
5007 48 AVE, REDWATER, AB, T0A 2W0
(780) 942-3802 SIC 1389

TARTAN SALES (1973) LTD p 5
202 10 ST, BEAVERLODGE, AB, T0H 0C0
SIC 5511

TAS AVIATION INC p 559
30 MOYAL CRT, CONCORD, ON, L4K 4R8
(905) 669-4812 SIC 5013

TASAR'S p 4
See NATURE'S COIN GROUP LTD

TASCO APPLIANCES p 794
See TASCO DISTRIBUTORS INC

TASCO DISTRIBUTORS INC p 794
84 KENHAR DR, NORTH YORK, ON, M9L 1N2
(416) 642-5600 SIC 5722

TASCO SUPPLIES LTD p 344
336 MACKENZIE AVE N, WILLIAMS LAKE, BC, V2G 1N7
(250) 392-6232 SIC 5085

TASEKO MINES LIMITED p 316
1040 GEORGIA ST W 15TH FL, VANCOUVER, BC, V6E 4H1
(778) 373-4533 SIC 1081

TASK ENGINEERING LTD p 338
5141 CORDOVA BAY RD, VICTORIA, BC, V8Y 2K1
(250) 590-2440 SIC 7363

TASK MICRO-ELECTRIQUES INC p 1118
See TASK MICRO-ELECTRONICS INC

TASK MICRO-ELECTRONICS INC p 1118
16700 RTE TRANSCANADIENNE, KIRKLAND, QC, H9H 4M7
(514) 697-6616 SIC 5065

TASK TOOLS p 208
See CAPLAN INDUSTRIES INC

TASKTOP TECHNOLOGIES INCORPORATED p 318
1500 GEORGIA ST W SUITE 1100, VANCOUVER, BC, V6G 2Z6
(778) 588-6896 SIC 5045

TASLAR TRADING CORP p 1415
100 SHERWOOD FOREST RD, REGINA, SK, S0G 3W0
(306) 500-5522 SIC 5153

TASTE OF NATURE FOODS INC p 675
230 FERRIER ST, MARKHAM, ON, L3R 2Z5
(905) 415-8218 SIC 5149

TASTE OF THE NORTH p 1139
See FRUITS & LEGUMES ERIC FRECHETTE, LES

TASUS CANADA CORPORATION p 608
41A BROCKLEY DR UNIT 1, HAMILTON, ON, L8E 3C3

(905) 560-1337   *SIC* 2759
TAT PROPERTIES LTD   *p* 195
GD STN A, CAMPBELL RIVER, BC, V9W
4Z8
(250) 287-7813   *SIC* 6712
TATA COMMUNICATIONS (CANADA) LTD *p*
1212
1441 RUE CARRIE-DERICK, MONTREAL,
QC, H3C 4S9
(514) 868-7272   *SIC* 4899
**TATA CONSULTANCY SERVICES CANADA
INC**   *p* 947
400 UNIVERSITY AVE 25TH FL,
TORONTO, ON, M5G 1S5
(647) 790-7200   *SIC* 7379
TATA GLOBAL BEVERAGES CANADA INC
p 588
10 CARLSON CRT SUITE 700, ETOBI-
COKE, ON, M9W 6L2
(416) 798-1224   *SIC* 5149
TATE ASP ACCESS FLOORS INC   *p* 805
880 EQUESTRIAN CRT, OAKVILLE, ON,
L6L 6L7
(905) 847-0138   *SIC* 3444
TATHAM, C.C. & ASSOCIATES LTD   *p* 547
115 SANDFORD FLEMING RD SUITE 200,
COLLINGWOOD, ON, L9Y 5A6
(705) 444-2565   *SIC* 8711
TATRO EQUIPMENT SALES LTD   *p* 543
7744 SEVENTH LINE E, CHATHAM, ON,
N7M 5J6
(519) 354-4352   *SIC* 5084
TATRO TRUCKS LTD   *p* 543
7744 SEVENTH LINE E, CHATHAM, ON,
N7M 5J6
(519) 354-4352   *SIC* 5012
TAUB, BERNARD & COMPANY   *p* 790
1167 CALEDONIA RD, NORTH YORK, ON,
M6A 2X1
(416) 785-5353   *SIC* 8721
TAUNTON ENGINEERING COMPANY   *p*
1374
See SHERBROOKE O.E.M. LTD
TAURUS CRACO MACHINERY INC   *p* 507
282 ORENDA RD, BRAMPTON, ON, L6T
4X6
(905) 451-8430   *SIC* 5084
TAURUS SITE SERVICES INC   *p* 130
11401 85 AVE, FORT SASKATCHEWAN,
AB, T8L 0A9
(780) 998-5001   *SIC* 1611
TAX AND DUTY FREE   *p* 689
See NUANCE GROUP (CANADA) INC, THE
TAXELCO INC   *p* 1209
355 RUE SAINTE-CATHERINE O BUREAU
500, MONTREAL, QC, H3B 1A5
(514) 504-8293   *SIC* 4119
TAXI CANADA LTD   *p* 984
495 WELLINGTON ST W SUITE 102,
TORONTO, ON, M5V 1E9
(416) 342-8294   *SIC* 7311
TAXI CANADA LTD   *p* 1200
1435 RUE SAINT-ALEXANDRE BUREAU
620, MONTREAL, QC, H3A 2G4
(514) 842-8294   *SIC* 7311
TAXI COOP QUEBEC 525-5191   *p* 1261
496 2E AV, QUEBEC, QC, G1L 3B1
(418) 525-4953   *SIC* 5541
TAXI L'AGENCE DE PUBLICITE   *p* 1200
See TAXI CANADA LTD
TAYCO PANELINK LTD   *p* 580
400 NORRIS GLEN RD, ETOBICOKE, ON,
M9C 1H5
(416) 252-8000   *SIC* 2521
TAYCO PAVING COMPANY   *p* 267
See O.K. INDUSTRIES LTD
TAYLOR & GRANT SPECIALTIES LIMITED
p 1007
151 WEBER ST S SUITE 2, WATERLOO,
ON, N2J 2A9
SIC 5145
TAYLOR AUTOMALL   *p* 632
*See TAYLOR, JEROME D CHEVROLET
CADILLAC LIMITED*

TAYLOR CHRYSLER DODGE INC   *p* 608
260 CENTENNIAL PKY N, HAMILTON, ON,
L8E 2X4
(905) 561-0333   *SIC* 5511
TAYLOR FLOORING LIMITED   *p* 443
114 WOODLAWN RD SUITE 257, DART-
MOUTH, NS, B2W 2S7
(902) 435-3567   *SIC* 5713
TAYLOR FLUID SYSTEMS INC   *p* 897
81 GRIFFITH RD, STRATFORD, ON, N5A
6S4
(519) 273-2811   *SIC* 5085
TAYLOR FORD LINCOLN   *p* 406
See TAYLOR FORD SALES LTD
TAYLOR FORD SALES LTD   *p* 406
10 LEWISVILLE RD, MONCTON, NB, E1A
2K2
(506) 857-2300   *SIC* 5511
TAYLOR FREEZERS INC   *p* 507
52 ARMTHORPE RD, BRAMPTON, ON,
L6T 5M4
(905) 790-2211   *SIC* 5046
TAYLOR GROUP, THE   *p* 510
*See TAYLOR MANUFACTURING INDUS-
TRIES INC*
TAYLOR HILL DEVELOPMENTS   *p* 492
106 NORTH FRONT ST, BELLEVILLE, ON,
K8P 3B4
(613) 969-9907   *SIC* 1382
TAYLOR INTERNATIONAL   *p* 531
*See TAYLOR MOVING & STORAGE LIM-
ITED*
TAYLOR LUMBER COMPANY LIMITED   *p*
462
12111 HWY 224 RR 4, MIDDLE
MUSQUODOBOIT, NS, B0N 1X0
(902) 384-2444   *SIC* 5211
TAYLOR MADE GOLF CANADA LTD *p* 1028
6240 HIGHWAY 7 SUITE 100, WOOD-
BRIDGE, ON, L4H 4G3
(800) 668-9883   *SIC* 5091
**TAYLOR MANUFACTURING INDUSTRIES
INC**   *p* 510
255 BISCAYNE CRES, BRAMPTON, ON,
L6W 4R2
(905) 451-5800   *SIC* 3993
TAYLOR MOTOR SALES LTD   *p* 1421
655 BROAD ST, REGINA, SK, S4R 1X5
(306) 569-8777   *SIC* 5511
TAYLOR MOVING & STORAGE LIMITED *p*
531
1200 PLAINS RD E, BURLINGTON, ON,
L7S 1W6
(905) 632-8010   *SIC* 4214
TAYLOR MOVING AND STORAGE   *p* 530
See 465439 ONTARIO INC
TAYLOR SHELLFISH CANADA ULC   *p* 212
8260 ISLAND HWY S, FANNY BAY, BC, V0R
1W0
(250) 335-0125   *SIC* 5421
TAYLOR STEEL INC   *p* 893
395 GREEN RD, STONEY CREEK, ON, L8E
5V4
(905) 662-5555   *SIC* 4225
TAYLOR STEEL INC   *p* 893
477 ARVIN AVE, STONEY CREEK, ON, L8E
2N1
(905) 662-4925   *SIC* 5051
TAYLOR VOLKSWAGEN INC   *p* 1421
775 BROAD ST, REGINA, SK, S4R 8G3
(306) 757-9657   *SIC* 5511
TAYLOR'S   *p* 1322
See MAGASINS J.L. TAYLOR INC, LES
**TAYLOR, JEROME D CHEVROLET CADIL-
LAC LIMITED**   *p*
632
2440 PRINCESS ST, KINGSTON, ON, K7M
3G4
(613) 549-1311   *SIC* 5511
TAYLOR, LEIBOW LLP   *p* 612
105 MAIN ST E SUITE 700, HAMILTON,
ON, L8N 1G6
(905) 523-0003   *SIC* 8721
TAYLYX LTD   *p* 748

475 CENTRE ST N, NAPANEE, ON, K7R
3S4
(613) 354-9707   *SIC* 5812
TAYMOR INDUSTRIES LTD   *p* 207
1655 DERWENT WAY, DELTA, BC, V3M
6K8
(604) 540-9525   *SIC* 5072
TBAY TEL MOBILITY   *p* 908
*See CORPORATION OF THE CITY OF
THUNDER BAY, THE*
TBC CONSTRUCTIONS INC   *p* 1263
760 AV GODIN, QUEBEC, QC, G1M 2K4
(418) 681-0671   *SIC* 1711
TBG CONTRACTING LTD   *p* 124
12311 17 ST NE, EDMONTON, AB, T6S
1A7
SIC 1442
TBG ENVIRONMENTAL INC   *p* 1016
425 WHITEVALE RD UNIT 5, WHITEVALE,
ON, L0H 1M0
(905) 620-1222   *SIC* 0782
TBM HOLDCO LTD   *p* 25
1601 AIRPORT RD NE SUITE 705, CAL-
GARY, AB, T2E 6Z8
(800) 663-3342   *SIC* 5211
TBM SERVICE GROUP INC   *p* 718
2450 DUNWIN DR UNIT 6, MISSISSAUGA,
ON, L5L 1J9
(905) 608-8989   *SIC* 7349
TBQ'S OTHER PASTRY PLACE & CAFE *p*
1025
See TEE-BEE-QUE LIMITED
TBS CANADA INC   *p* 736
7090 EDWARDS BLVD, MISSISSAUGA,
ON, L5S 1Z1
(905) 362-5206   *SIC* 8748
TC   *p* 1074
See TERMINAL & CABLE TC INC
TC BIZZ.COM CORP   *p* 932
449 CHURCH ST, TORONTO, ON, M4Y 2C5
(416) 323-0772   *SIC* 5947
TC ENERGY CORPORATION   *p* 61
450 1 ST SW, CALGARY, AB, T2P 5H1
(403) 920-2000   *SIC* 4922
TC INDUSTRIES OF CANADA COMPANY *p*
604
249 SPEEDVALE AVE W, GUELPH, ON,
N1H 1C5
(519) 836-7100   *SIC* 3531
TCA CANADA LOCAL 728   *p* 1364
*See SYNDICAT NATIONAL DES TRA-
VAILLEURS ET TRAVAILLEUSES DE
L'AUTOMOBILE DU CANADA INC*
TCB TRI-CITIES BUILDERS SUPPLY LTD *p*
223
1650 SPRINGFIELD RD, KELOWNA, BC,
V1Y 5V4
(250) 763-5040   *SIC* 5251
TCBC HOLDINGS INC   *p* 229
26712 BLOUCESTER WAY SUITE 203,
LANGLEY, BC, V3W 3V6
(604) 626-4412   *SIC* 5531
TCCI   *p* 947
*See TATA CONSULTANCY SERVICES
CANADA INC*
TCDSB   *p* 773
*See TORONTO CATHOLIC DISTRICT
SCHOOL BOARD*
TCED INTL INC   *p* 1315
700 CH DU GRAND-BERNIER N, SAINT-
JEAN-SUR-RICHELIEU, QC, J2W 2H1
(450) 348-8720   *SIC* 5013
TCG INTERNATIONAL INC   *p* 183
8658 COMMERCE CRT, BURNABY, BC,
V5A 4N6
(604) 438-1000   *SIC* 7536
TCG TOYS   *p* 792
See CANADIAN GROUP, THE
TCP   *p* 977
*See CENTRE FOR PHENOGENOMICS
INC, THE*
TCS   *p* 226
*See CRESTWOOD ENGINEERING COM-
PANY LTD*

TCS   *p* 689
See STATE GROUP INC, THE
TCS CONSTRUCTION   *p* 756
*See TECHNICAL CONCRETE SOLUTIONS
LTD*
TCS GROUP   *p* 999
See TRENTON COLD STORAGE INC
TCT   *p* 3
See TRANSCANADA TURBINES LTD
TCU FINANCIAL GROUP   *p* 1435
307 LUDLOW ST, SASKATOON, SK, S7S
1N6
(306) 651-6700   *SIC* 6062
TCU PLACE   *p* 1429
*See SASKATOON CENTENNIAL AUDITO-
RIUM FOUNDATION*
TD ASSET FINANCE CORP   *p* 970
55 KING ST W, TORONTO, ON, M5K 1A2
(416) 982-2322   *SIC* 6159
TD ASSET MANAGEMENT INC   *p* 967
161 BAY ST SUITE 3200, TORONTO, ON,
M5J 2T2
(416) 361-5400   *SIC* 6722
TD BANK   *p* 91
See TORONTO-DOMINION BANK, THE
TD BANK   *p* 733
See TORONTO-DOMINION BANK, THE
TD BANK   *p* 970
See TORONTO-DOMINION BANK, THE
TD CANADA TRUST   *p* 701
See TORONTO-DOMINION BANK, THE
TD CANADA TRUST   *p* 970
See TORONTO-DOMINION BANK, THE
TD CAPITAL GROUP LIMITED   *p* 970
100 WELLINGTON ST W, TORONTO, ON,
M5K 1A2
(800) 430-6095   *SIC* 6211
TD ENERGY TRADING INC   *p* 61
421 7 AVE SW SUITE 36, CALGARY, AB,
T2P 4K9
(403) 299-8572   *SIC* 4924
TD FINANCING SERVICES HOME INC *p*
921
25 BOOTH AVE SUITE 101, TORONTO,
ON, M4M 2M3
(416) 463-4422   *SIC* 6141
TD INSURANCE   *p* 970
See TD LIFE INSURANCE COMPANY
TD INVESTMENT SERVICES INC   *p* 970
55 KING ST W, TORONTO, ON, M5K 1A2
(416) 944-5728   *SIC* 6282
TD LIFE INSURANCE COMPANY   *p* 970
55 KING ST W, TORONTO, ON, M5K 1A2
SIC 6311
TD MELOCHE MONNEX   *p* 672
*See MELOCHE MONNEX FINANCIAL
SERVICES INC*
TD PLACE   *p* 818
*See LANSDOWNE STADIUM LIMITED
PARTNERSHIP*
TD SECURITIES INC   *p* 970
66 WELLINGTON ST W, TORONTO, ON,
M5K 1A2
(416) 307-8500   *SIC* 6211
TD WATERHOUSE CANADA INC   *p* 970
79 WELLINGTON ST W 10TH FL,
TORONTO, ON, M5K 1A1
(416) 307-6672   *SIC* 6211
TD WATERHOUSE CANADA INC   *p* 976
77 BLOOR ST W SUITE 3, TORONTO, ON,
M5S 1M2
(416) 982-7686   *SIC* 6211
**TD WATERHOUSE PRIVATE INVESTMENT
COUNSEL INC**   *p* 970
66 WELLINGTON ST W, TORONTO, ON,
M5K 1A2
(416) 308-1933   *SIC* 6722
TD WEALTH   *p* 970
See TD WATERHOUSE CANADA INC
TDAM USA INC   *p* 967
161 BAY ST SUITE 3200, TORONTO, ON,
M5J 2T2
(416) 982-6681   *SIC* 6722
TDB   *p* 393

See THOMAS DESIGN BUILDERS LTD

TDC CONTRACTING LTD *p 435*
1 BREYNAT ST, FORT SMITH, NT, X0E 0P0
(867) 872-2458 *SIC 5171*

TDG FURNITURE INC *p 389*
116 NATURE PARK WAY, WINNIPEG, MB,
R3P 0X8
(204) 989-9898 *SIC 5712*

TDI-DYNAMIC CANADA ULC *p 872*
1870 BIRCHMOUNT RD, SCARBOROUGH,
ON, M1P 2J7
(877) 722-2003 *SIC 2321*

TDL CANADA *p 999*
See TRENTON DISTRIBUTORS LIMITED

TDL GROUP CORP, THE *p 19*
7460 51 ST SE, CALGARY, AB, T2C 4B4
(403) 203-7400 *SIC 5812*

TDL GROUP CORP, THE *p 79*
120 JOHN MORRIS WAY SUITE 300,
CHESTERMERE, AB, T1X 1V3
(403) 248-0000 *SIC 5812*

TDL GROUP CORP, THE *p 607*
950 SOUTHGATE DR, GUELPH, ON, N1L
1S7
(519) 824-1304 *SIC 5812*

TDL GROUP CORP, THE *p 987*
130 KING ST SUITE 300, TORONTO, ON,
M5X 1E1
(905) 845-6511 *SIC 6794*

TDS LAVAL *p 1362*
See SYNCREON CANADA INC

TEACH AWAY INC *p 300*
896 CAMBIE ST SUITE 301, VANCOUVER,
BC, V6B 2P6
(604) 628-1822 *SIC 8741*

TEACHERS CREDIT UNION LIMITED *p 613*
75 JAMES ST S, HAMILTON, ON, L8P 2Y9
(905) 525-8131 *SIC 6062*

TEACHERS LIFE *p 578*
See TEACHERS LIFE INSURANCE SOCI-
ETY (FRATERNAL)

TEACHERS LIFE INSURANCE SOCIETY
(FRATERNAL) *p 578*
916 THE EAST MALL SUITE C, ETOBI-
COKE, ON, M9B 6K1
(416) 620-1140 *SIC 6311*

TEACHERS RETIREMENT ALLOWANCES
FUND BOARD *p 379*
25 FORKS MARKET RD SUITE 330, WIN-
NIPEG, MB, R3C 4S8
(204) 949-0048 *SIC 6371*

TEAHEN & TEAHEN BUILDING SUPPLIES
LTD *p 651*
1780 DUNDAS ST, LONDON, ON, N5W 3E5
(519) 455-0660 *SIC 5211*

TEAHEN HOME HARDWARE BUILDING
CENTRE *p 859*
See TEAHEN, R & R BUILDING SUPPLIES
LTD

TEAHEN, R & R BUILDING SUPPLIES LTD
p 859
1272 LONDON RD SUITE 1707, SARNIA,
ON, N7S 1P5
(519) 337-3783 *SIC 5251*

TEAL CEDAR PRODUCTS LTD *p 282*
17897 TRIGGS RD, SURREY, BC, V4N 4M8
(604) 587-8700 *SIC 2429*

TEAM CHRYSLER JEEP DODGE *p 744*
See TEAM CHRYSLER JEEP DODGE INC

TEAM CHRYSLER JEEP DODGE INC*p 744*
777 BANCROFT DR, MISSISSAUGA, ON,
L5V 2Y6
(905) 819-0001 *SIC 5511*

TEAM CID INC *p 500*
175 SUN PAC BLVD SUITE 2A, BRAMP-
TON, ON, L6S 5Z6
(905) 595-0411 *SIC 5072*

TEAM EAGLE LTD *p 540*
10 TRENT DR, CAMPBELLFORD, ON, K0L
1L0
(705) 653-2956 *SIC 5084*

TEAM FORD SALES LIMITED *p 121*
3304 91 ST NW, EDMONTON, AB, T6N 1C1
(780) 462-8300 *SIC 5511*

TEAM FUTURES SCHOOL OF GYMNAS-
TICS INC *p*
727
6991 MILLCREEK DR, MISSISSAUGA, ON,
L5N 6B9
SIC 8699

TEAM HONDA POWERHOUSE OF MILTON
p 682
See 2095008 ONTARIO INC

TEAM INDUSTRIAL SERVICES *p 680*
See CGRIFF21 HOLDINGS INC

TEAM INDUSTRIAL SERVICES (CANADA)
INC *p 680*
25 BODRINGTON CRT, MARKHAM, ON,
L6G 1B6
(905) 940-9334 *SIC 1799*

TEAM TRUCK CENTRES LIMITED *p 662*
1040 WILTON GROVE RD, LONDON, ON,
N6N 1C7
(519) 453-2970 *SIC 5511*

TEAM TRUCK CENTRES LIMITED *p 662*
795 WILTON GROVE RD, LONDON, ON,
N6N 1N7
(519) 681-6868 *SIC 5511*

TEAMRECRUITER.COM INC *p 675*
15 ALLSTATE PKY SUITE 600, MARKHAM,
ON, L3R 5B4
(905) 889-8326 *SIC 7361*

TEAMSTERS CANADA *p 1087*
2540 BOUL DANIEL-JOHNSON, COTE
SAINT-LUC, QC, H7T 2S3
(450) 682-5521 *SIC 8631*

TEAMSTERS LOCAL UNION 938 *p 707*
275 MATHESON BLVD E, MISSISSAUGA,
ON, L4Z 1X8
(905) 502-0062 *SIC 8631*

TEAMSTERS UNION LOCAL NO. 213*p 289*
490 BROADWAY E SUITE 464, VANCOU-
VER, BC, V5T 1X3
(604) 874-3654 *SIC 8631*

TEC BUSINESS SOLUTIONS LTD *p 700*
1048 RONSA CRT, MISSISSAUGA, ON,
L4W 3Y4
(905) 828-8132 *SIC 5112*

TEC THE EDUCATION COMPANY INC *p*
223
1632 DICKSON AVE SUITE 100,
KELOWNA, BC, V1Y 7T2
(250) 860-2787 *SIC 8222*

TECFAB INTERNATIONAL INC *p 1305*
11535 1RE AV BUREAU 500, SAINT-
GEORGES, QC, G5Y 7H5
(418) 228-8031 *SIC 3312*

TECFAB INTERNATIONAL INC *p 1367*
5190 RANG SAINT-MATHIEU, SHAWINI-
GAN, QC, G0X 1L0
(819) 536-4445 *SIC 3312*

TECFAB METAL EXPERT *p 1305*
See TECFAB INTERNATIONAL INC

TECH DATA CANADA CORPORATION *p*
727
6911 CREDITVIEW RD, MISSISSAUGA,
ON, L5N 8G1
(905) 286-6800 *SIC 5045*

TECH DIGITAL MANUFACTURING LTD *p*
675
350 STEELCASE RD W, MARKHAM, ON,
L3R 1B3
(905) 513-8094 *SIC 3679*

TECH INCENTIVES INC *p 41*
1816 CROWCHILD TRAIL NW UNIT 700,
CALGARY, AB, T2M 3Y7
(403) 713-1050 *SIC 8748*

TECH-CON AUTOMATION ULC *p 525*
1219 CORPORATE DR, BURLINGTON,
ON, L7L 5V5
(905) 639-4989 *SIC 3599*

TECH-TREK LTD *p 700*
1015 MATHESON BLVD E SUITE 6, MIS-
SISSAUGA, ON, L4W 3A4
(905) 238-0319 *SIC 5065*

TECHALLOY WELDING PRODUCTS *p 839*
See CENTRAL WIRE INDUSTRIES LTD

TECHFORM *p 838*

See MAGNA CLOSURES INC

TECHINSIGHTS INC *p 832*
1891 ROBERTSON RD SUITE 500, OT-
TAWA, ON, K2H 5B7
(613) 599-6500 *SIC 8711*

TECHMATION ELECTRIC & CONTROLS
LTD *p 3*
117 KINGSVIEW RD SE, AIRDRIE, AB, T4A
0A8
(403) 243-0990 *SIC 5084*

TECHNAKORD CHEMICAL INDUSTRIES
INC *p 588*
5 MCLACHLAN DR, ETOBICOKE, ON,
M9W 1E3
(416) 798-9898 *SIC 2819*

TECHNI-AIR 2000 INC *p 1252*
97 BOUL HYMUS, POINTE-CLAIRE, QC,
H9R 1E2
(514) 918-0299 *SIC 8711*

TECHNI-DATA PERFORMANCE INC *p 1248*
12305 BOUL METROPOLITAIN E, POINTE-
AUX-TREMBLES, QC, H1B 5R3
(514) 640-1666 *SIC 8742*

TECHNICA GROUP INC *p 647*
225 FIELDING RD, LIVELY, ON, P3Y 1L8
(705) 692-2204 *SIC 1499*

TECHNICA MINING *p 647*
See TECHNICA GROUP INC

TECHNICAL ADHESIVES LIMITED *p 703*
3035 JARROW AVE, MISSISSAUGA, ON,
L4X 2C6
(905) 625-1284 *SIC 2891*

TECHNICAL CONCRETE SOLUTIONS LTD
p 756
1341 KERRISDALE BLVD, NEWMARKET,
ON, L3Y 8W8
(905) 761-9330 *SIC 7353*

TECHNICAL STANDARDS AND SAFETY
AUTHORITY *p 588*
345 CARLINGVIEW DR, ETOBICOKE, ON,
M9W 6N9
(416) 734-3300 *SIC 8733*

TECHNICAL VOCATIONAL HIGH SCHOOL
p 381
See WINNIPEG SCHOOL DIVISION

TECHNICARE *p 86*
See TECHNICARE IMAGING LTD

TECHNICARE IMAGING LTD *p 86*
10924 119 ST NW, EDMONTON, AB, T5H
3P5
(780) 424-7161 *SIC 7384*

TECHNICO INC *p 413*
299 MCILVEEN DR, SAINT JOHN, NB, E2J
4Y6
(506) 633-1300 *SIC 7389*

TECHNICORE UNDERGROUND INC *p 880*
102 BALES DRIVE E, SHARON, ON, L0G
1V0
(905) 898-4889 *SIC 1622*

TECHNIGLOBE INC *p 1200*
666 RUE SHERBROOKE O UNITE 800,
MONTREAL, QC, H3A 1E7
(514) 987-1815 *SIC 7322*

TECHNILAB PHARMA INC *p 1153*
17800 RUE LAPOINTE, MIRABEL, QC, J7J
0W8
(450) 433-7673 *SIC 6712*

TECHNIPFMC CANADA LTD *p 431*
131 KELSEY DR, ST. JOHN'S, NL, A1B 0L2
(709) 724-1851 *SIC 1382*

TECHNIPFMC PLC *p 6*
253 TOWNSHIP RD 394 SUITE 27312,
BLACKFALDS, AB, T0M 0J0
(780) 926-2108 *SIC 1389*

TECHNIPFMC PLC *p 7*
380 WELL ST, BROOKS, AB, T1R 1C2
(403) 363-0028 *SIC 1381*

TECHNIPRODEC LTEE *p 1162*
11865 AV ADOLPHE-CARON, MONTREAL,
QC, H1E 6J8
(514) 648-5423 *SIC 3728*

TECHNISEAL *p 1072*
See 9343-8919 QUEBEC INC

TECHNO MOTOSPORT *p 1051*

See TECHNO SPORT INTERNATIONAL
LTEE

TECHNO SPORT INTERNATIONAL LTEE *p*
1051
7850 RUE BOMBARDIER BUREAU 263,
ANJOU, QC, H1J 2G3
(514) 356-2151 *SIC 5136*

TECHNOCELL INC *p 1099*
3075 RUE KUNZ, DRUMMONDVILLE, QC,
J2C 6Y4
(819) 475-0066 *SIC 2621*

TECHNODIESEL INC *p 1115*
1260 CH DES PRAIRIES, JOLIETTE, QC,
J6E 0L4
(450) 759-3709 *SIC 7538*

TECHNOLOGIE AVID CANADA *p 1185*
See AVID TECHNOLOGY CANADA CORP

TECHNOLOGIE DE PENSEE LTEE *p 1228*
5250 RUE FERRIER BUREAU 812, MON-
TREAL, QC, H4P 1L4
(514) 489-8251 *SIC 3841*

TECHNOLOGIE S-ONE CANADA *p 1207*
See ONEPOINT CANADA INC

TECHNOLOGIES 20-20 INC *p 1241*
400 BOUL ARMAND-FRAPPIER BUREAU
2020, MONTREAL-OUEST, QC, H7V 4B4
(514) 332-4110 *SIC 7372*

TECHNOLOGIES BIONEST INC *p 1369*
55 12E RUE, SHAWINIGAN, QC, G9T 5K7
(819) 538-5662 *SIC 5039*

TECHNOLOGIES DE MOULAGE *p 1074*
See PABER ALUMINIUM INC

TECHNOLOGIES DE TRANSFERT DE
CHALEUR MAYA LTEE *p 1402*
4999 RUE SAINTE-CATHERINE O BU-
REAU 400, WESTMOUNT, QC, H3Z 1T3
(514) 369-5706 *SIC 7373*

TECHNOLOGIES DUAL-ADE INC *p 1374*
4025 RUE LETELLIER, SHERBROOKE,
QC, J1L 1Z3
(819) 829-2100 *SIC 3613*

TECHNOLOGIES ELEMENT PSW INC *p*
1391
1117 RUE DES MANUFACTURIERS, VAL-
D'OR, QC, J9P 6Y7
(819) 825-1117 *SIC 5082*

TECHNOLOGIES GLOBALSTEP INC *p*
1167
2030 BOUL PIE-IX BUREAU 307, MON-
TREAL, QC, H1V 2C8
(514) 496-0093 *SIC 8742*

TECHNOLOGIES GREAT NORTH INC *p*
1118
3551 BOUL SAINT-CHARLES BUREAU
363, KIRKLAND, QC, H9H 3C4
(514) 620-3724 *SIC 3844*

TECHNOLOGIES GSC INC *p 1318*
160 RUE VANIER, SAINT-JEAN-SUR-
RICHELIEU, QC, J3B 3R4
(450) 245-0373 *SIC 2821*

TECHNOLOGIES HOPPER, LES *p 1182*
See HOPPER INC

TECHNOLOGIES HUMANWARE INC*p 1099*
1800 RUE JEAN-BERCHMANS-MICHAUD,
DRUMMONDVILLE, QC, J2C 7G7
(819) 471-4818 *SIC 3669*

TECHNOLOGIES INOCYBE *p 1062*
See KONTRON CANADA INC

TECHNOLOGIES INTERACTIVES MEDIA-
GRIF INC *p*
1145
1111 RUE SAINT-CHARLES O BUREAU
255, LONGUEUIL, QC, J4K 5G4
(450) 449-0102 *SIC 7372*

TECHNOLOGIES ITF INC *p 1327*
400 BOUL MONTPELLIER, SAINT-
LAURENT, QC, H4N 2G7
(514) 748-4848 *SIC 3545*

TECHNOLOGIES IWEB INC *p 1396*
20 PLACE DU COMMERCE, VERDUN, QC,
H3E 1Z6
(514) 286-4242 *SIC 4813*

TECHNOLOGIES K.K. INC, LES *p 1243*
64 RUE HUOT, NOTRE-DAME-DE-L'ILE-

PERROT, QC, J7V 7Z8

(514) 453-6732   *SIC* 3599

TECHNOLOGIES METAFORE INC *p* 1051
9393 BOUL LOUIS-H.-LAFONTAINE, AN-
JOU, QC, H1J 1Z1

(514) 354-3810   *SIC* 7371

TECHNOLOGIES MOHAWK D'INTERNET *p*
1206

*See MOHAWK INTERNET TECHNOLO-
GIES*

TECHNOLOGIES MPB INC, LES *p* 1252
151 BOUL HYMUS, POINTE-CLAIRE, QC,
H9R 1E9

(514) 694-8751   *SIC* 8734

TECHNOLOGIES ORBITE INC *p* 1242
500 BOUL CARTIER O BUREAU 249,
MONTREAL-OUEST, QC, H7V 5B7

(450) 680-3341   *SIC* 1081

TECHNOLOGIES RECYCLAGE RE-NEWYT
p 1134

See FCM RECYCLING INC

TECHNOLOGIES SANGOMA *p* 674
*See SANGOMA TECHNOLOGIES CORPO-
RATION*

TECHNOLOGIES SERESCO *p* 1228
*See SOLUTIONS D'AIR DESHUMIDIFIE
INC*

**TECHNOLOGIES SURFACE PRAXAIR
MONTREAL S.E.C.** *p* 1095
10300 AV RYAN, DORVAL, QC, H9P 2T7

(514) 631-2240   *SIC* 3479

**TECHNOLOGIES SURFACE PRAXAIR
MONTREAL S.E.C.** *p* 1331
2300 RUE COHEN, SAINT-LAURENT, QC,
H4R 2N8

(514) 333-0030   *SIC* 1721

TECHNOLOGIES SYNERGX INC *p* 1342
2912 RUE JOSEPH-A.-BOMBARDIER,
SAINT-LAURENT, QC, H7P 6E3

(450) 978-1240   *SIC* 7389

TECHNOLOGIES VICONICS *p* 1181
See VICONICS TECHNOLOGIES INC

TECHNOLOGIES VIGILANT *p* 1213
See DRW CANADA CO

**TECHNOLOGY EVALUATION CENTERS
INC** *p* 1145
1000 RUE DE SERIGNY BUREAU 300,
LONGUEUIL, QC, J4K 5B1

(514) 954-3665   *SIC* 7371

TECHNOMEDIA FORMATION INC *p* 1200
1001 BOUL DE MAISONNEUVE O, MON-
TREAL, QC, H3A 3C8

(514) 287-1561   *SIC* 7371

TECHNOPARC MONTREAL *p* 1336
7150 RUE ALBERT-EINSTEIN BUREAU
200, SAINT-LAURENT, QC, H4S 2C1

(514) 956-2525   *SIC* 6531

TECHNOR DEVELOPMENTS LIMITED *p*
777
85 SCARSDALE RD, NORTH YORK, ON,
M3B 2R2

(905) 889-4653   *SIC* 7997

TECHNOSUB *p* 1288
See 121352 CANADA INC

TECHO-BLOC INC *p* 1309
5255 RUE ALBERT-MILLICHAMP, SAINT-
HUBERT, QC, J3Y 8Z8

(877) 832-4625   *SIC* 3272

TECHSOL MARINE INC *p* 1268
4800 RUE RIDEAU, QUEBEC, QC, G1P 4P4

(418) 688-2230   *SIC* 3625

TECHSPAN AUTOMOTIVE *p* 718
See TECHSPAN INDUSTRIES INC

TECHSPAN INDUSTRIES INC *p* 718
3131 PEPPER MILL CRT UNIT 1, MISSIS-
SAUGA, ON, L5L 4X6

(905) 820-6150   *SIC* 3643

TECHSTAR PLASTICS INC *p* 848
15400 OLD SIMCOE RD, PORT PERRY,
ON, L9L 1L8

(905) 985-8479   *SIC* 3089

TECHTRONIC INDUSTRIES CANADA INC *p*
675
7303 WARDEN AVE SUITE 202,

MARKHAM, ON, L3R 5Y6

(905) 479-4355   *SIC* 5072

TECK COAL LIMITED *p* 32
205 9 AVE SE SUITE 1000, CALGARY, AB,
T2G 0R3

(403) 767-8500   *SIC* 1221

TECK COAL LIMITED *p* 136
GD STN MAIN, HINTON, AB, T7V 1T9

(780) 692-5100   *SIC* 1221

TECK COAL LIMITED *p* 212
GD, ELKFORD, BC, V0B 1H0

(250) 865-2271   *SIC* 1221

TECK COAL LIMITED *p* 269
GD, SPARWOOD, BC, V0B 2G0

(250) 425-8325   *SIC* 1221

TECK COAL LIMITED *p* 269
GD, SPARWOOD, BC, V0B 2G0

(250) 425-2555   *SIC* 1221

TECK COAL LIMITED *p* 269
2261 CORBIN RD, SPARWOOD, BC, V0B
2G0

(250) 425-6305   *SIC* 1221

TECK CONSTRUCTION LTD *p* 228
5197 216 ST, LANGLEY, BC, V3A 2N4

(604) 534-7917   *SIC* 1542

**TECK HIGHLAND VALLEY COPPER PART-
NERSHIP** *p*
230
HWY 97C HIGHLAND VALLEY COPPER
MINESITE, LOGAN LAKE, BC, V0K 1W0

(250) 523-2443   *SIC* 1021

TECK METALS LTD *p* 284
25 ALDRIDGE AVE, TRAIL, BC, V1R 4L8

(250) 364-4222   *SIC* 1081

TECK METALS LTD *p* 957
11 KING ST W SUITE 1700, TORONTO,
ON, M5H 4C7

(647) 788-3000   *SIC* 1081

TECK NEWS AGENCY (1977) LIMITED *p*
634
5 KIRKLAND ST E, KIRKLAND LAKE, ON,
P2N 1N9

SIC 5192

TECK RESOURCES LIMITED *p* 264
12380 HORSESHOE WAY, RICHMOND,
BC, V7A 4Z1

(778) 296-4900   *SIC* 8731

TECK RESOURCES LIMITED *p* 310
550 BURRARD ST SUITE 3300, VANCOU-
VER, BC, V6C 0B3

(604) 699-4000   *SIC* 1021

TECK RESOURCES LIMITED *p* 425
32 RTE 370, MILLERTOWN, NL, A0H 1V0

(709) 852-2195   *SIC* 1081

TECK-BULLMOOSE COAL INC *p* 310
550 BURRARD ST SUITE 3300, VANCOU-
VER, BC, V6C 0B3

(604) 699-4000   *SIC* 1221

TECMOTIV CORPORATION *p* 559
131 SARAMIA CRES 2ND FL, CONCORD,
ON, L4K 4P7

(905) 669-5911   *SIC* 3795

TECNICKROME AERONAUTIQUE INC *p*
1248
12264 RUE APRIL BUREAU 1, POINTE-
AUX-TREMBLES, QC, H1B 5N5

(514) 640-0333   *SIC* 3471

**TECO-WESTINGHOUSE MOTORS
(CANADA) INC** *p* 103
18060 109 AVE NW, EDMONTON, AB, T5S
2K2

(780) 444-8933   *SIC* 5063

TECSULT INTERNATIONAL *p* 1185
See CONSULTANTS AECOM INC

TECSYS INC *p* 1221
1 PLACE ALEXIS NIHON BUREAU 800,
MONTREAL, QC, H3Z 3B8

(514) 866-0001   *SIC* 6712

TECTONIC INFRASTRUCTURE INC *p* 664
120 RODINEA RD UNIT 1, MAPLE, ON,
L6A 1R5

(416) 637-6073   *SIC* 1629

TECUMSEH HOME HARDWARE *p* 1017
See 734046 ONTARIO LIMITED

**TECUMSEH PRODUCTS OF CANADA, LIM-
ITED** *p*
482
200 ELM ST, AYLMER, ON, N5H 2M8

(519) 765-1556   *SIC* 5084

**TEDI TRANSLOGIC EXPRESS DEDICATED
INC** *p* 510
241 CLARENCE ST UNIT 21-24, BRAMP-
TON, ON, L6W 4P2

(905) 451-3033   *SIC* 4212

TEE, FRANK PHARMACIES LTD *p* 826
702 BANK ST SUITE 700, OTTAWA, ON,
K1S 3V2

(613) 233-3202   *SIC* 5912

TEE-BEE-QUE LIMITED *p* 1025
1855 HURON CHURCH RD, WINDSOR,
ON, N9C 2L6

SIC 5812

TEEKAY *p* 434
*See TEEKAY (ATLANTIC) MANAGEMENT
ULC*

TEEKAY (ATLANTIC) MANAGEMENT ULC
p 434
5 SPRINGDALE ST SUITE 105, ST.
JOHN'S, NL, A1E 0E4

(855) 485-9351   *SIC* 4412

TEEKAY SHIPPING (CANADA) LTD *p* 310
550 BURRARD ST SUITE 2000, VANCOU-
VER, BC, V6C 2K2

(604) 683-3529   *SIC* 4412

**TEEN CHALLENGE OF CENTRAL
CANADA INC** *p* 376
414 EDMONTON ST, WINNIPEG, MB, R3B
2M2

(204) 949-9484   *SIC* 8699

TEH - TFS *p* 778
*See TOUR EAST HOLIDAYS (CANADA)
INC*

TEHSAKOTITSEN-THA *p* 1117
*See KATERI MEMORIAL HOSPITAL CEN-
TRE*

TEJAZZ MANAGEMENT SERVICES INC *p*
241
4238 ST. PAULS AVE, NORTH VANCOU-
VER, BC, V7N 1T5

(604) 986-9475   *SIC* 5812

TEK STAFF IT SOLUTIONS INC *p* 857
30 VIA RENZO DR SUITE 200, RICHMOND
HILL, ON, L4S 0B8

(416).438-1099   *SIC* 7361

TEK-MOR INCORPORATED *p* 495
20 SIMPSON RD, BOLTON, ON, L7E 1G9

(905) 857-6415   *SIC* 1761

TEKALIA AERONAUTIK (2010) INC *p* 1160
3900 BOUL DU TRICENTENAIRE, MON-
TREAL, QC, H1B 5L6

(514) 640-2411   *SIC* 7629

TEKLASER *p* 1109
See LABELIX INC

TEKNA PLASMA *p* 1374
See TEKNA SYSTEMES PLASMA INC

TEKNA SYSTEMES PLASMA INC *p* 1374
2935 BOUL INDUSTRIEL, SHERBROOKE,
QC, J1L 2T9

(819) 820-2204   *SIC* 3569

TEKNICA OVERSEAS LTD *p* 61
350 7 AVE SW SUITE 2700, CALGARY, AB,
T2P 3N9

SIC 8999

TEKNION (ALBERTA) LTD *p* 19
6403 48 ST SE SUITE 60, CALGARY, AB,
T2C 3J7

(403) 264-4210   *SIC* 2521

TEKNION CONCEPT *p* 1139
See TEKNION LIMITED

TEKNION CORPORATION *p* 784
1150 FLINT RD, NORTH YORK, ON, M3J
2J5

(416) 661-1577   *SIC* 2522

TEKNION FORM *p* 559
See TEKNION LIMITED

TEKNION FURNITURE SYSTEMS *p* 784
See TEKNION HOLDINGS (CANADA) INC

**TEKNION FURNITURE SYSTEMS CO. LIM-
ITED** *p*
784
1150 FLINT RD, NORTH YORK, ON, M3J
2J5

(416) 661-3370   *SIC* 5021

TEKNION HOLDINGS (CANADA) INC *p* 784
1150 FLINT RD, NORTH YORK, ON, M3J
2J5

(416) 661-1577   *SIC* 6712

TEKNION LIMITED *p* 559
1400 ALNESS ST UNIT 12, CONCORD,
ON, L4K 2W6

(905) 669-2035   *SIC* 2522

TEKNION LIMITED *p* 784
1150 FLINT RD, NORTH YORK, ON, M3J
2J5

(416) 661-1577   *SIC* 2522

TEKNION LIMITED *p* 1139
975 RUE DES CALFATS BUREAU 45,
LEVIS, QC, G6Y 9E8

(418) 833-0047   *SIC* 2522

TEKNION LIMITED *p* 1160
45 CH DES CASCADES, MONTMAGNY,
QC, G5V 3M6

(418) 248-5711   *SIC* 2522

TEKNION LS INC *p* 1133
359 RUE SAINT-JOSETH, LAURIER-
STATION, QC, G0S 1N0

(418) 830-0855   *SIC* 2211

TEKNION QUEBEC *p* 1160
See TEKNION LIMITED

TEKNION ROY & BRETON INC *p* 1139
975 RUE DES CALFATS, LEVIS, QC, G6Y
9E8

(418) 884-4041   *SIC* 5021

TEKNION SOLUTIONS WOODWORK *p* 19
See TEKNION (ALBERTA) LTD

TEKRAN INSTRUMENTS CORPORATION *p*
872
330 NANTUCKET BLVD, SCARBOROUGH,
ON, M1P 2P4

(416) 449-3084   *SIC* 3821

TEKROLL FORMS, DIV OF *p* 784
See TEKNION LIMITED

TEKSAVVY SOLUTIONS INC *p* 543
800 RICHMOND ST, CHATHAM, ON, N7M
5J5

(519) 360-1575   *SIC* 4813

TEKSIGN INC *p* 516
86 PLANT FARM BLVD, BRANTFORD, ON,
N3S 7W3

(519) 756-1089   *SIC* 3993

TEKSMED SERVICES INC *p* 197
8635 YOUNG RD SUITE 7, CHILLIWACK,
BC, V2P 4P3

(604) 702-3380   *SIC* 6411

TEKSYSTEMS *p* 711
See TEKSYSTEMS CANADA CORP

TEKSYSTEMS CANADA CORP *p* 711
350 BURNHAMTHORPE RD W, MISSIS-
SAUGA, ON, L5B 3J1

(905) 283-1300   *SIC* 7361

TEKTELIC COMMUNICATIONS INC *p* 26
7657 10 ST NE, CALGARY, AB, T2E 8X2

(403) 338-6900   *SIC* 4899

TEL-E CONNECT SYSTEMS LTD *p* 784
7 KODIAK CRES, NORTH YORK, ON, M3J
3E5

(416) 635-1234   *SIC* 1731

TEL-PAL COMM INC *p* 228
20316 56 AVE SUITE 225, LANGLEY, BC,
V3A 3Y7

(250) 202-8770   *SIC* 4813

**TEL-STAR MARKETING GROUP (1993)
LTD** *p* 1034
64 TROWERS RD UNIT 2, WOODBRIDGE,
ON, L4L 7K5

SIC 5194

TELDON MEDIA GROUP INC *p* 256
12751 VULCAN WAY SUITE 100, RICH-
MOND, BC, V6V 3C8

(604) 231-3454   *SIC* 2752

TELDON PRINT MEDIA, DIV OF *p* 256
See TELDON MEDIA GROUP INC

TELE 4 *p 1262*
See GROUPE TVA INC
TELE-MOBILE COMPANY *p 867*
200 CONSILIUM PL SUITE 1600, SCAR-
BOROUGH, ON, M1H 3J3
(800) 308-5992 *SIC 4899*
TELE-MOBILE COMPANY *p 1336*
8851 RTE TRANSCANADIENNE BUREAU
1, SAINT-LAURENT, QC, H4S 1Z6
(514) 832-2000 *SIC 4899*
TELE-QUEBEC *p 1174*
*See GOUVERNEMENT DE LA PROVINCE
DE QUEBEC*
TELE-SONDAGES PLUS INC *p 1192*
505 BOUL RENE-LEVESQUE O BUREAU
1400, MONTREAL, QC, H2Z 1Y7
(514) 392-4702 *SIC 8732*
TELE-SURVEYS PLUS *p 1192*
See TELE-SONDAGES PLUS INC
TELEBEC *p 1056*
*See TELEBEC, SOCIETE EN COMMAN-
DITE*
TELEBEC INTERNET *p 1186*
*See TELEBEC, SOCIETE EN COMMAN-
DITE*
TELEBEC, SOCIETE EN COMMANDITE *p
1056*
625 AV GODEFROY, BECANCOUR, QC,
G9H 1S3
SIC 4813
TELEBEC, SOCIETE EN COMMANDITE *p
1186*
87 RUE ONTARIO O 200, MONTREAL, QC,
H2X 0A7
(514) 493-5300 *SIC 4813*
TELEBEC, SOCIETE EN COMMANDITE *p
1391*
100 RUE DES DISTRIBUTEURS, VAL-
D'OR, QC, J9P 6Y1
(819) 824-7451 *SIC 4813*
TELECOM COMPUTER INC *p 525*
5245 HARVESTER RD, BURLINGTON, ON,
L7L 5L4
(905) 333-9621 *SIC 5045*
TELECOM SDP *p 1095*
See SDP TELECOM ULC
**TELECOMMUNICATION WORKERS PEN-
SION PLAN** *p
191*
4603 KINGSWAY SUITE 303, BURNABY,
BC, V5H 4M4
(604) 430-1317 *SIC 6371*
TELECOMMUNICATIONS DE L'EST *p 1151*
*See TELECOMMUNICATIONS DENIS
GIGNAC INC*
**TELECOMMUNICATIONS DENIS GIGNAC
INC** *p 1151*
143 BOUL DION, MATANE, QC, G4W 3L8
(418) 562-9000 *SIC 4899*
**TELECOMMUNICATIONS GLOBAL
CROSSING-CANADA LTEE** *p 1200*
1140 BOUL DE MAISONNEUVE O, MON-
TREAL, QC, H3A 1M8
(800) 668-4210 *SIC 4899*
TELECON DESIGN INC *p 1181*
7450 RUE DU MILE END, MONTREAL, QC,
H2R 2Z6
(514) 644-2333 *SIC 8711*
TELECON INC *p 1181*
7450 RUE DU MILE END, MONTREAL, QC,
H2R 2Z6
(514) 644-2333 *SIC 6712*
TELECON INC *p 1240*
6789 BOUL LEGER, MONTREAL-NORD,
QC, H1G 6H8
SIC 4899
TELECON INC *p 1293*
104 RUE D'ANVERS, SAINT-AUGUSTIN-
DE-DESMAURES, QC, G3A 1S4
(418) 878-9595 *SIC 4899*
**TELECONFERENCE GLOBAL CROSSING-
CANADA LTEE** *p
1200*
1140 BOUL DE MAISONNEUVE O, MON-

TREAL, QC, H3A 1M8
SIC 4899
TELECOR INC *p 743*
6205 KESTREL RD, MISSISSAUGA, ON,
L5T 2A1
(905) 564-0801 *SIC 8712*
TELEDYNE CARIS, INC. *p 401*
115 WAGGONERS LANE, FREDERICTON,
NB, E3B 2L4
(506) 458-8533 *SIC 7371*
**TELEDYNE DALSA SEMICONDUCTEUR
INC** *p 1068*
18 BOUL DE L'AEROPORT, BROMONT,
QC, J2L 1S7
(450) 534-2321 *SIC 3674*
TELEDYNE DALSA, INC *p 1011*
605 MCMURRAY RD, WATERLOO, ON,
N2V 2E9
(519) 886-6000 *SIC 3827*
**TELEDYNE QUANTITATIVE IMAGING COR-
PORATION** *p
273*
19535 56 AVE SUITE 101, SURREY, BC,
V3S 6K3
(604) 530-5800 *SIC 3861*
TELEFLEX MEDICAL CANADA INC *p 676*
500 HOOD RD SUITE 310, MARKHAM, ON,
L3R 9Z3
(800) 387-9699 *SIC 5047*
TELEFLEX MEDICAL L.P *p 676*
165 GIBSON DR SUITE 1, MARKHAM, ON,
L3R 3K7
(905) 943-9000 *SIC 5047*
TELEGRAM, THE *p 433*
See MEDIAS TRANSCONTINENTAL INC
TELELINK CALL CENTRE *p 429*
See CALL CENTRE INC, THE
**TELEMETRIX DOWNHOLE TECHNOLO-
GIES INC** *p
76*
85 FREEPORT BLVD BE BAY 102, CAL-
GARY, AB, T3J 4X8
(403) 243-2331 *SIC 1381*
TELEPARTNERS *p 996*
5407 EGLINTON AVE W SUITE 103,
TORONTO, ON, M9C 5K6
(416) 621-7600 *SIC 7389*
TELEPARTNERS CALL CENTRE INC *p 578*
5429 DUNDAS ST W, ETOBICOKE, ON,
M9B 1B5
(416) 231-0520 *SIC 7389*
TELEPERFORMANCE CANADA *p 922*
*See MMCC SOLUTIONS CANADA COM-
PANY*
TELEPERFORMANCE CANADA *p 1166*
*See MMCC SOLUTIONS CANADA COM-
PANY*
TELEPIN SOFTWARE CORPORATION *p
625*
411 LEGGET DR SUITE 100, KANATA, ON,
K2K 3C9
(613) 366-1910 *SIC 7371*
TELESAT CANADA *p 618*
GD, HANOVER, ON, N4N 3C2
(519) 364-1221 *SIC 4899*
TELESAT CANADA *p 834*
160 ELGIN ST SUITE 2100, OTTAWA, ON,
K2P 2P7
(613) 748-0123 *SIC 4841*
TELESTA THERAPEUTICS INC *p 1336*
2600 BOUL ALFRED-NOBEL BUREAU 301,
SAINT-LAURENT, QC, H4S 0A9
(514) 697-6636 *SIC 2834*
TELEXPRESS COURIER INC *p 500*
5 EDVAC DR UNIT 10, BRAMPTON, ON,
L6S 5P3
(905) 792-2222 *SIC 7389*
TELFER, S & T MERCHANDISING LTD *p
746*
525 QUEEN ST W, MOUNT FOREST, ON,
N0G 2L1
(519) 323-1080 *SIC 5014*
TELFORD INVESTMENTS LTD *p 103*
17551 108 AVE NW, EDMONTON, AB, T5S

1G2
(780) 489-9562 *SIC 5947*
TELIGENCE (CANADA) LTD *p 300*
303 PENDER ST W UNIT 300, VANCOU-
VER, BC, V6B 1T3
(604) 629-6055 *SIC 8741*
TELIO *p 1327*
See TELIO & CIE INC
TELIO & CIE INC *p 1327*
625 RUE DESLAURIERS, SAINT-
LAURENT, QC, H4N 1W8
(514) 271-4607 *SIC 5131*
TELIPHONE CORP *p 318*
1550 ALBERNI ST 3RD FL, VANCOUVER,
BC, V6G 1A5
(604) 990-2000 *SIC 4899*
TELIPHONE NAVAIGATA WESTEL *p 318*
See TELIPHONE CORP
TELLZA INC *p 914*
190 BOROUGH DR SUITE 3302,
TORONTO, ON, M1P 0B6
SIC 4899
TELMAR NETWORK TECHNOLOGY *p 793*
*See PRECISION COMMUNICATION SER-
VICES CORP*
TELSCO ALARM *p 94*
See TELSCO SECURITY SYSTEMS INC
TELSCO SECURITY SYSTEMS INC *p 94*
12750 127 ST NW, EDMONTON, AB, T5L
1A5
(780) 424-6971 *SIC 5065*
TELSON MINING CORPORATION *p 316*
1111 MELVILLE ST SUITE 1000, VANCOU-
VER, BC, V6E 3V6
(604) 684-8071 *SIC 1041*
TELUQ *p 1260*
See UNIVERSITE DU QUEBEC
TELUS *p 456*
See G.B.S. COMMUNICATIONS INC
TELUS BUSINESS SOLUTIONS *p 300*
See TELUS COMMUNICATIONS INC
TELUS COMMUNICATIONS (QUEBEC) INC
p 1209
630 BOUL RENE-LEVESQUE O BUREAU
2200, MONTREAL, QC, H3B 1S6
(514) 242-8870 *SIC 4899*
TELUS COMMUNICATIONS (QUEBEC) INC
p 1285
6 RUE JULES-A.-BRILLANT BUREAU
20602, RIMOUSKI, QC, G5L 1W8
(418) 723-2271 *SIC 6712*
TELUS COMMUNICATIONS COMPANY *p
191*
3777 KINGSWAY SUITE 501, BURNABY,
BC, V5H 3Z7
(604) 432-2151 *SIC 4899*
TELUS COMMUNICATIONS INC *p 191*
3777 KINGSWAY, BURNABY, BC, V5H 3Z7
(604) 432-5010 *SIC 4899*
TELUS COMMUNICATIONS INC *p 300*
510 WEST GEORGIA ST 7TH FL, VAN-
COUVER, BC, V6B 0M3
(888) 493-2007 *SIC 4899*
TELUS COMMUNICATIONS INC *p 1212*
111 BOUL ROBERT-BOURASSA UNITE
4200, MONTREAL, QC, H3C 2M1
(514) 392-0373 *SIC 4899*
TELUS COMMUNICATIONS INC *p 1285*
See TELUS COMMUNICATIONS INC
TELUS COMMUNICATIONS INC *p 1285*
6 RUE JULES-A.-BRILLANT BUREAU
20602, RIMOUSKI, QC, G5L 1W8
(418) 310-1212 *SIC 4899*
TELUS CORPORATION *p 300*
510 WEST GEORGIA ST FL 8, VANCOU-
VER, BC, V6B 0M3
(604) 697-8044 *SIC 4899*
TELUS HEALTH WOLF EMR *p 1209*
See TELUS SOLUTIONS EN SANTE INC
TELUS MOBILITY *p 867*
See TELE-MOBILE COMPANY
TELUS MOBILITY *p 1336*
See TELE-MOBILE COMPANY
TELUS SOLUTIONS D'AFFAIRES *p 1212*

See TELUS COMMUNICATIONS INC
TELUS SOLUTIONS EN SANTE INC *p 1209*
22E ETAGE 630, BOUL RENE-LEVESQUE
O, MONTREAL, QC, H3B 1S6
(514) 665-3050 *SIC 7372*
TELUS SPARK *p 21*
*See CALGARY SCIENCE CENTRE SOCI-
ETY*
TELUS TV *p 191*
See TELUS COMMUNICATIONS INC
TELUS WORLD OF SCIENCE-EDMONTON
p 95
*See EDMONTON SPACE & SCIENCE
FOUNDATION*
TEMA CONTER MEMORIAL TRUST, THE *p
629*
175 PATRICIA DR, KING CITY, ON, L7B 1H3
SIC 6732
TEMBEC *p 546*
See RAYONIER A.M. CANADA G.P.
TEMBEC *p 1054*
See RAYONIER A.M. CANADA G.P.
TEMBEC *p 1151*
See RAYONIER A.M. CANADA G.P.
TEMBEC *p 1207*
See RAYONIER A.M. CANADA G.P.
TEMBEC INC *p 542*
175 PLANER RD, CHAPLEAU, ON, P0M
1K0
(705) 864-3014 *SIC 2421*
TEMBEC INC *p 627*
1 GOVERNMENT RD W, KAPUSKASING,
ON, P5N 2X8
(705) 337-9784 *SIC 2621*
TEMBEC INC *p 913*
5310 HWY 101 W, TIMMINS, ON, P4N 7J3
(705) 268-1462 *SIC 2611*
TEMBEC INDUSTRIES *p 1207*
*See RAYONIER A.M. CANADA INDUS-
TRIES INC*
TEMISKAMING LODGE *p 607*
See JARLETTE LTD
TEMISKO *p 1243*
See TEMISKO (1983) INC
TEMISKO (1983) INC *p 1243*
91 RUE ONTARIO, NOTRE-DAME-DU-
NORD, QC, J0Z 3B0
(819) 723-2416 *SIC 3715*
**TEML SASKATCHEWAN PIPELINES LIM-
ITED** *p
1406*
402 KENSINGTON AVE, ESTEVAN, SK,
S4A 2K9
(306) 634-2681 *SIC 4612*
TEMPCO DRILLING COMPANY INC *p 11*
720 28 ST NE SUITE 114, CALGARY, AB,
T2A 6R3
(403) 259-5533 *SIC 1381*
TEMPCO HEATING & SHEET METAL INC *p
588*
180 BELFIELD RD, ETOBICOKE, ON, M9W
1H1
(416) 766-1237 *SIC 5051*
TEMPEL CANADA COMPANY *p 525*
5045 NORTH SERVICE RD, BURLINGTON,
ON, L7L 5H6
(905) 335-2530 *SIC 3469*
TEMPERENCECO INC *p 957*
10 TEMPERANCE ST SUITE 202,
TORONTO, ON, M5H 1Y4
(647) 348-7000 *SIC 5812*
TEMPLE AND TEMPLE TOURS INC *p 930*
819 YONGE ST 2ND FL, TORONTO, ON,
M4W 2G9
(416) 928-3227 *SIC 4725*
TEMPLE GARDENS MINERAL SPA INC *p
1411*
24 FAIRFORD ST E, MOOSE JAW, SK, S6H
0C7
(306) 694-5055 *SIC 7011*
TEMPLE HOTELS INC *p 711*
55 CITY CENTRE DR SUITE 1000, MISSIS-
SAUGA, ON, L5B 1M3
(905) 281-4800 *SIC 6798*

TEMPLE LIFESTYLE INCORPORATED *p* 1179
9600 RUE MEILLEUR BUREAU 932, MONTREAL, QC, H2N 2E3
(514) 382-3805 *SIC* 5149

TEMPLE, LE *p* 1387
See 9065-1837 QUEBEC INC

TEMPLETON INTERNATIONAL STOCK FUND *p* 915
5000 YONGE ST SUITE 900, TORONTO, ON, M2N 0A7
(416) 364-4672 *SIC* 6722

TEMPO CANADA ULC *p* 806
1175 NORTH SERVICE RD W SUITE 200, OAKVILLE, ON, L6M 2W1
(905) 339-3309 *SIC* 5169

TEMPO DRAFTING SERVICES INC *p* 676
260 TOWN CENTRE BLVD SUITE 300, MARKHAM, ON, L3R 8H8
(905) 470-7000 *SIC* 7389

TEMPO FLEXO LTD *p* 622
2237 INDUSTRIAL PARK RD, INNISFIL, ON, L9S 3V9
(705) 436-4442 *SIC* 2671

TEN BUSS LIMITED *p* 497
430 HOLLAND ST W SUITE 446, BRADFORD, ON, L3Z 0G1
(905) 778-4330 *SIC* 5999

TEN TEN SINCLAIR HOUSING INC *p* 370
1010 SINCLAIR ST, WINNIPEG, MB, R2V 3H7
(204) 339-9268 *SIC* 8361

TEN THOUSAND VILLAGES *p* 391
See MENNONITE CENTRAL COMMITTEE CANADA

TENAQUIP LIMITEE *p* 1367
22555 AUT TRANSCANADIENNE, SENNEVILLE, QC, H9X 3L7
(514) 457-7801 *SIC* 5085

TENARIS GLOBAL SERVICES (CANADA) INC *p* 61
530 8 AVE SW SUITE 400, CALGARY, AB, T2P 3S8
(403) 767-0100 *SIC* 3312

TENCO INC *p* 1377
1318 RUE PRINCIPALE, ST-VALERIEN, QC, J0H 2B0
(800) 318-3626 *SIC* 3711

TENCORR PACKAGING INC *p* 507
6 SHAFTSBURY LANE, BRAMPTON, ON, L6T 3X7
(905) 799-9955 *SIC* 2679

TENDER CHOICE FOODS *p* 520
See 864773 ONTARIO INC

TENDER POULTRY *p* 792
See 2308061 ONTARIO LIMITED

TENDERCARE NURSING HOME *p* 877
See EXTENDICARE INC

TENDERCARE NURSING HOMES LIMITED *p* 878
1020 MCNICOLL AVE SUITE 436, SCARBOROUGH, ON, M1W 2J6
(416) 497-3639 *SIC* 8051

TENNIS CANADA *p* 786
See CANADIAN TENNIS ASSOCIATION

TENOVA GOODFELLOW INC *p* 727
6711 MISSISSAUGA RD SUITE 200, MISSISSAUGA, ON, L5N 2W3
(905) 567-3030 *SIC* 3823

TENROX ENTREPRISES, LES *p* 1343
See UPLAND SOFTWARE INC

TENTNOLOGY CO *p* 272
See INTERNATIONAL TENTNOLOGY CORP

TEPPERMAN'S *p* 661
See TEPPERMAN, N. LIMITED

TEPPERMAN'S *p* 1021
See TEPPERMAN, N. LIMITED

TEPPERMAN, N. LIMITED *p* 661
1150 WHARNCLIFFE RD S, LONDON, ON, N6L 1K3
(519) 433-5353 *SIC* 5712

TEPPERMAN, N. LIMITED *p* 1021
2595 OUELLETTE AVE, WINDSOR, ON,

N8X 4V8
(519) 969-9700 *SIC* 5712

TERADICI CORPORATION *p* 189
4601 CANADA WAY SUITE 300, BURNABY, BC, V5G 4X8
(604) 451-5800 *SIC* 3674

TERAGO *p* 905
See TERAGO NETWORKS INC

TERAGO INC *p* 905
55 COMMERCE VALLEY DR W SUITE 800, THORNHILL, ON, L3T 7V9
(866) 837-2465 *SIC* 4813

TERAGO NETWORKS INC *p* 905
55 COMMERCE VALLEY DR W SUITE 800, THORNHILL, ON, L3T 7V9
(866) 837-2461 *SIC* 4813

TERANET ENTERPRISES INC *p* 967
123 FRONT ST W SUITE 700, TORONTO, ON, M5J 2M2
(416) 360-5263 *SIC* 7371

TERANET INC *p* 941
1 ADELAIDE ST E SUITE 600, TORONTO, ON, M5C 2V9
(416) 360-5263 *SIC* 7371

TERANET INC *p* 967
123 FRONT ST W SUITE 700, TORONTO, ON, M5J 2M2
(416) 360-5263 *SIC* 7371

TERANGA GOLD CORPORATION *p* 970
77 KING ST W SUITE 2110, TORONTO, ON, M5K 2A1
(416) 594-0000 *SIC* 1041

TERANORTH CONSTRUCTION & ENGINEERING LIMITED *p* 901
799 LUOMA RD, SUDBURY, ON, P3G 1J4
(705) 523-1540 *SIC* 1611

TERASEN GAS LTD *p* 281
2310 KING GEORGE BOULEVARD, SURREY, BC, V4A 5A5
(604) 536-2956 *SIC* 4923

TERASEN PIPELINES PETROLEUM *p* 61
300 5 AVE SW SUITE 2700, CALGARY, AB, T2P 5J2
(403) 514-6400 *SIC* 4923

TERASEN WESTERN REGION *p* 183
7815 SHELLMONT ST, BURNABY, BC, V5A 4S9
SIC 4923

TERAXION INC *p* 1268
2716 RUE EINSTEIN, QUEBEC, QC, G1P 4S8
(418) 658-9500 *SIC* 3661

TERCIER MOTORS LTD *p* 6
6413 50 AVE, BONNYVILLE, AB, T9N 2L9
(780) 826-3301 *SIC* 5511

TERCON CONSTRUCTION LTD *p* 269
610 DOUGLAS FIR, SPARWOOD, BC, V0B 2G0
SIC 1611

TERDUN MATERIAL MANAGEMENT INC *p* 701
5130 CREEKBANK RD, MISSISSAUGA, ON, L4W 2G2
(905) 602-4567 *SIC* 2675

TERGEL INC *p* 1382
895 RUE ITALIA, TERREBONNE, QC, J6Y 2C8
(450) 621-2345 *SIC* 2899

TERIS SERVICES D'APPROVISIONNEMENT INC *p* 1362
3180 MONTEE SAINT-AUBIN, SAINTEROSE, QC, H7L 3H8
(450) 622-2710 *SIC* 5191

TERLIN CONSTRUCTION LTD *p* 833
1240 TERON ROAD, OTTAWA, ON, K2K 2B5
(613) 821-0768 *SIC* 1542

TERMACO LTEE *p* 1318
325 BOUL INDUSTRIEL, SAINT-JEANSUR-RICHELIEU, QC, J3B 7M3
(450) 346-6871 *SIC* 3444

TERMEL INDUSTRIES LTD *p* 239
1667 RAILWAY ST, NORTH VANCOUVER,

BC, V7J 1B5
(604) 984-9652 *SIC* 3499

TERMINAL & CABLE TC INC *p* 1074
1930 CH BELLERIVE, CARIGNAN, QC, J3L 4Z4
(450) 658-1742 *SIC* 3714

TERMINAL 3 *p* 1386
See SOMAVRAC INC

TERMINAL BRIGHAM INC *p* 1110
280 RUE SAINT-CHARLES S, GRANBY, QC, J2G 7A9
(450) 378-4108 *SIC* 4923

TERMINAL CITY CLUB INC *p* 310
837 HASTINGS ST W SUITE 100, VANCOUVER, BC, V6C 1B6
(604) 488-8970 *SIC* 8699

TERMINAL FOREST PRODUCTS LTD *p* 256
12180 MITCHELL RD, RICHMOND, BC, V6V 1M8
(604) 717-1200 *SIC* 2421

TERMINAL FOREST PRODUCTS LTD *p* 291
8708 YUKON ST, VANCOUVER, BC, V5X 2Y9
(604) 327-6344 *SIC* 2421

TERMINAL FRUIT & PRODUCE LTD *p* 296
788 MALKIN AVE, VANCOUVER, BC, V6A 2K2
(604) 251-3383 *SIC* 5148

TERRA BEATA FARMS LTD *p* 462
161 MONK POINT RD, LUNENBURG, NS, B0J 2C0
(902) 634-4435 *SIC* 5149

TERRA COTTA FOODS LTD *p* 594
36 ARMSTRONG AVE UNIT 9, GEORGETOWN, ON, L7G 4R9
(905) 877-4216 *SIC* 2052

TERRA ENVIRONMENTAL TECHNOLOGIES *p*
564
See TERRA INTERNATIONAL (CANADA) INC

TERRA FIRMA CAPITAL CORPORATION *p* 926
22 ST CLAIR AVE E SUITE 200, TORONTO, ON, M4T 2S3
(416) 792-4700 *SIC* 6159

TERRA FOOTWEAR *p* 536
See KODIAK GROUP HOLDINGS CO

TERRA GRAIN FUELS INC *p* 1404
5 KM N KALIUM RD, BELLE PLAINE, SK, S0G 0G0
(306) 345-2280 *SIC* 1541

TERRA INTERNATIONAL (CANADA) INC *p* 564
161 BICKFORD LINE, COURTRIGHT, ON, N0N 1H0
(519) 867-2739 *SIC* 2819

TERRA NOVA *p* 431
See TERRA NOVA MOTORS LIMITED

TERRA NOVA FOODS INC *p* 434
49 JAMES LANE, ST. JOHN'S, NL, A1E 3H3
(709) 579-2121 *SIC* 5142

TERRA NOVA MOTORS LIMITED *p* 431
595 KENMOUNT RD, ST. JOHN'S, NL, A1B 3P9
(709) 364-4130 *SIC* 5511

TERRA NOVA STEEL & IRON (ONTARIO) INC *p* 712
3595 HAWKESTONE RD, MISSISSAUGA, ON, L5C 2V1
(905) 273-3872 *SIC* 5051

TERRA NOVA STEEL INC *p* 210
7812 PROGRESS WAY, DELTA, BC, V4G 1A4
(604) 946-5383 *SIC* 5051

TERRA RESTORATION STEAMATIC HAMILTON *p* 615
115 HEMPSTEAD DR SUITE 5, HAMILTON, ON, L8W 2Y6
(905) 387-0662 *SIC* 6331

TERRACE BAY ENTERPRISES LIMITED *p* 903
HWY 17 3 SIMCOE PLAZA, TERRACE BAY, ON, P0T 2W0

(807) 825-3226 *SIC* 5541

TERRACE BAY PULP INC *p* 903
21 MILL RD, TERRACE BAY, ON, P0T 2W0
SIC 2611

TERRACE FORD LINCOLN SALES INC *p* 528
900 WALKER'S LINE, BURLINGTON, ON, L7N 2G2
(905) 632-6252 *SIC* 5511

TERRACE LODGE HOME FOR THE AGED *p* 482
See CORPORATION OF THE COUNTY OF ELGIN

TERRACE TOTEM FORD SALES LTD *p* 283
4631 KEITH AVE, TERRACE, BC, V8G 1K3
(250) 635-4978 *SIC* 5511

TERRACO *p* 351
See 68235 MANITOBA LTD

TERRACO GOLD CORP *p* 316
1055 HASTINGS ST W SUITE 2390, VANCOUVER, BC, V6E 2E9
(604) 443-3830 *SIC* 1041

TERRACON GEOTECHNIQUE LTD *p* 61
800-734 7 AVE SW, CALGARY, AB, T2P 3P8
(403) 266-1150 *SIC* 1389

TERRACON GEOTECHNIQUE LTD *p* 129
8212 MANNING AVE, FORT MCMURRAY, AB, T9H 1V9
(780) 743-9343 *SIC* 8711

TERRAEX HOLDINGS INC *p* 416
1942 MANAWAGONISH RD, SAINT JOHN, NB, E2M 5H5
(506) 672-4422 *SIC* 6712

TERRALINK TECHNOLOGIES CANADA INC *p* 923
181 EGLINTON AVE E SUITE 206, TORONTO, ON, M4P 1J4
(416) 593-0700 *SIC* 7371

TERRAN NETWORKS CORP. *p* 451
5503 ATLANTIC ST, HALIFAX, NS, B3H 1G5
(902) 497-1191 *SIC* 3825

TERRAPAVE CONSTRUCTION LTD *p* 498
12 CADETTA RD UNIT 1, BRAMPTON, ON, L6P 0X4
(905) 761-2865 *SIC* 1521

TERRAPEX *p* 1071
See TERRAPEX ENVIRONNEMENT LTEE

TERRAPEX ENVIRONMENTAL LTD *p* 777
90 SCARSDALE RD, NORTH YORK, ON, M3B 2R7
(416) 245-0011 *SIC* 8748

TERRAPEX ENVIRONNEMENT LTEE *p* 1071
3615 RUE ISABELLE BUREAU A, BROSSARD, QC, J4Y 2R2
(450) 444-3255 *SIC* 8748

TERRAPRO INC *p* 161
53345 RANGE ROAD 232, SHERWOOD PARK, AB, T8A 4V2
(780) 449-2091 *SIC* 1389

TERRAPROBE INC *p* 507
11 INDELL LANE, BRAMPTON, ON, L6T 3Y3
(905) 796-2650 *SIC* 8711

TERRAPROBE LIMITED *p* 510
10 BRAM CRT, BRAMPTON, ON, L6W 3R6
(905) 796-2650 *SIC* 8748

TERRAPURE ENVIRONMENTAL *p* 524
See REVOLUTION ENVIRONMENTAL SOLUTIONS ACQUISITION GP INC

TERRAPURE ENVIRONMENTAL *p* 524
See REVOLUTION ENVIRONMENTAL SOLUTIONS LP

TERRAPURE ENVIRONMENTAL LTD *p* 525
1100 BURLOAK DR SUITE 500, BURLINGTON, ON, L7L 6B2
(800) 263-8602 *SIC* 4959

TERRASSES DE LA CHAUDIERE INC, LES *p* 1105
25 RUE EDDY BUREAU 203, GATINEAU, QC, J8X 4B5
(819) 997-7129 *SIC* 6719

TERRATEAM EQUIPMENT RENTALS INC *p* 164

110 MANITOBA CRT, SPRUCE GROVE, AB, T7X 0V5
(780) 962-9598   *SIC* 7353
TERRATEC ENVIRONMENTAL LTD *p* 610
200 EASTPORT BLVD, HAMILTON, ON, L8H 7S4
(905) 544-0444   *SIC* 4953
TERRAVEST INCOME FUND *p* 170
4901 BRUCE RD, VEGREVILLE, AB, T9C 1C3
(780) 632-7774   *SIC* 6722
TERRAVEST INDUSTRIES INC *p* 170
4901 BRUCE RD, VEGREVILLE, AB, T9C 1C3
(780) 632-2040   *SIC* 3714
TERRAVEST INDUSTRIES LIMITED PARTNERSHIP *p* 170
4901 BRUCE RD, VEGREVILLE, AB, T9C 1C3
(780) 632-2040   *SIC* 3533
TERRAZZO MOSAIC & TILE COMPANY LIMITED *p* 994
900 KEELE ST, TORONTO, ON, M6N 3E7
(416) 653-6111   *SIC* 1743
TERREAU BIOGAS, LIMITED PARTNERSHIP *p* 1271
1327 AV MAGUIRE BUREAU 100, QUEBEC, QC, G1T 1Z2
(418) 476-1686   *SIC* 4922
TERREBONNE FORD INC *p* 1381
2730 CH GASCON, TERREBONNE, QC, J6X 4H6
(450) 968-9000   *SIC* 5511
TERREQUITY REALTY INC *p* 768
211 CONSUMERS RD UNIT 105, NORTH YORK, ON, M2J 4G8
(416) 496-9220   *SIC* 6531
TERRINGTON CONSUMERS CO-OPERATIVE SOCIETY LIMITED *p* 424
1 ABBOTT DR, HAPPY VALLEY-GOOSE BAY, NL, A0P 1E0
(709) 896-5737   *SIC* 5411
TERRITORIAL ELECTRIC LTD *p* 117
8303 ROPER RD NW, EDMONTON, AB, T6E 6S4
(780) 465-7591   *SIC* 1731
TERROCO INDUSTRIES LTD *p* 154
GD, RED DEER, AB, T4N 5E1
(403) 346-1171   *SIC* 1389
TERROCO OILFIELD SERVICES *p* 154
See TERROCO INDUSTRIES LTD
TERRW INCONNUE *p* 1186
See PROPERTIES TERRA INCOGNITA INC
TERRY FOX FOUNDATION, THE *p* 183
8960 UNIVERSITY HIGH ST SUITE 150, BURNABY, BC, V5A 4Y6
(604) 200-0541   *SIC* 6732
TERRY FOX SECONDARY SCHOOL *p* 246
See SCHOOL DISTRICT NO. 43 (COQUITLAM)
TERRY'S INDEPENDENT GROCERY *p* 598
See 1127919 ONTARIO LIMITED
TERTAC *p* 1239
See 119678 CANADA INC
TERUS CONSTRUCTION LTD *p* 273
15288 54A AVE UNIT 300, SURREY, BC, V3S 6T4
(604) 575-3689   *SIC* 1611
TERVITA CORPORATION *p* 32
140 10 AVE SE SUITE 1600, CALGARY, AB, T2G 0R1
(855) 837-8482   *SIC* 8748
TERVITA DRILLING AND CORING SERVICES LTD *p* 19
9919 SHEPARD RD SE, CALGARY, AB, T2C 3C5
(855) 837-8482   *SIC* 1081
TESC CONTRACTING COMPANY LTD *p* 899

874 LAPOINTE ST, SUDBURY, ON, P3A 5N8
(705) 566-5702   *SIC* 1541
TESHMONT *p* 392
See TESHMONT CONSULTANTS INC
TESHMONT CONSULTANTS INC *p* 392
1190 WAVERLEY ST, WINNIPEG, MB, R3T 0P4
(204) 284-8100   *SIC* 6712
TESHMONT CONSULTANTS LP *p* 392
1190 WAVERLEY ST, WINNIPEG, MB, R3T 0P4
(204) 284-8100   *SIC* 8711
TESKEY CONCRETE COMPANY CORP *p* 786
20 MURRAY RD, NORTH YORK, ON, M3K 1T2
(416) 638-0340   *SIC* 3273
TESKEY CONSTRUCTION COMPANY LTD *p* 786
20 MURRAY RD, NORTH YORK, ON, M3K 1T2
(416) 638-0340   *SIC* 1794
TESSIER LTEE *p* 1260
21 RUE DU MARCHE-CHAMPLAIN, QUEBEC, QC, G1K 8Z8
(418) 569-3739   *SIC* 7353
TESSIER TRANSLATIONS CORPORATION *p* 1107
188 RUE MONTCALM BUREAU 100, GATINEAU, QC, J8Y 3B5
(819) 776-6687   *SIC* 7389
TESTFORCE *p* 1336
See SYSTEMES TESTFORCE INC
TESTON PIPELINES LIMITED *p* 559
379 BOWES RD, CONCORD, ON, L4K 1J1
(905) 761-6955   *SIC* 1623
TETI BAKERY INC *p* 588
27 SIGNAL HILL AVE SUITE 3, ETOBICOKE, ON, M9W 6V8
(416) 798-8777   *SIC* 5461
TETRA PAK CANADA INC *p* 784
20 DE BOERS DR SUITE 420, NORTH YORK, ON, M3J 0H1
(647) 775-1837   *SIC* 5084
TETRA TECH CANADA INC *p* 19
200 RIVERCREST DR SE SUITE 115, CALGARY, AB, T2C 2X5
(403) 203-3355   *SIC* 8711
TETRA TECH CANADA INC *p* 106
14940 123 AVE NW, EDMONTON, AB, T5V 1B4
(780) 451-2121   *SIC* 8711
TETRA TECH CANADA INC *p* 376
161 PORTAGE AVE E SUITE 400, WINNIPEG, MB, R3B 0Y4
(204) 954-6800   *SIC* 8711
TETRA TECH CANADA INC *p* 727
6835 CENTURY AVE UNIT A, MISSISSAUGA, ON, L5N 7K2
(905) 369-3000   *SIC* 8711
TETRA TECH CANADA INC *p* 909
725 HEWITSON ST, THUNDER BAY, ON, P7B 6B5
(807) 345-5453   *SIC* 8711
TETRA TECH CANADA INC *p* 957
330 BAY ST SUITE 900, TORONTO, ON, M5H 2S8
(416) 368-9080   *SIC* 8711
TETRA TECH CANADA INC *p* 1430
410 22ND ST E SUITE 1400, SASKATOON, SK, S7K 5T6
(306) 244-4888   *SIC* 8711
TETRA TECH INDUSTRIES INC *p* 1167
5100 RUE SHERBROOKE E, MONTREAL, QC, H1V 3R9
(514) 257-1112   *SIC* 8711
TETRA TECH INDUSTRIES INC *p* 1167
5100 RUE SHERBROOKE E BUREAU 400, MONTREAL, QC, H1V 3R9
(514) 257-0707   *SIC* 8711
TETRA TECH OGD INC *p* 262
10851 SHELLBRIDGE WAY SUITE 100, RICHMOND, BC, V6X 2W8

(604) 270-7728   *SIC* 8711
TETRA TECH QE INC *p* 1167
5100 RUE SHERBROOKE E BUREAU 900, MONTREAL, QC, H1V 3R9
(514) 257-0707   *SIC* 8711
TETREM CAPITAL MANAGEMENT LTD *p* 376
201 PORTAGE AVE SUITE 1910, WINNIPEG, MB, R3B 3K6
(204) 975-2865   *SIC* 6722
TEULON HUNTER MEMORIAL HOSPITAL *p* 359
See INTERLAKE REGIONAL HEALTH AUTHORITY INC
TEVA CANADA INNOVATION G.P. -S.E.N.C. *p* 1192
1080 COTE DU BEAVER HALL, MONTREAL, QC, H2Z 1S8
(514) 878-0095   *SIC* 5122
TEVA CANADA LIMITED *p* 676
575 HOOD RD, MARKHAM, ON, L3R 4E1
(905) 475-3370   *SIC* 2834
TEVA CANADA LIMITED *p* 865
30 NOVOPHARM CRT, SCARBOROUGH, ON, M1B 2K9
(416) 291-8876   *SIC* 2834
TEVA CANADA LIMITED *p* 895
5691 MAIN ST, STOUFFVILLE, ON, L4A 1H5
(416) 291-8888   *SIC* 2834
TEVA CANADA LIMITED *p* 1153
17800 RUE LAPOINTE BUREAU 123, MIRABEL, QC, J7J 0W8
(450) 433-7673   *SIC* 2834
TEVA NOVOPHARM *p* 865
See TEVA CANADA LIMITED
TEVELEC LIMITED *p* 701
5350 TIMBERLEA BLVD SUITE 1, MISSISSAUGA, ON, L4W 2S6
(905) 624-5241   *SIC* 5051
TEX-DON LTD *p* 751
2135 ROBERTSON RD, NEPEAN, ON, K2H 5Z2
(613) 829-9580   *SIC* 5531
TEXADA QUARRYING LTD *p* 284
2 AIRPORT RD, VAN ANDA, BC, V0N 3K0
(604) 486-7627   *SIC* 1422
TEXAS INSTRUMENTS CANADA LIMITED *p* 625
505 MARCH RD SUITE 200, KANATA, ON, K2K 3A4
(613) 271-8649   *SIC* 5065
TEXCAN, DIV OF *p* 103
See SONEPAR CANADA INC
TEXCAN, DIV OF *p* 275
See SONEPAR CANADA INC
TEXEL MATERIAUX TECHNIQUES *p* 1360
See TEXEL MATERIAUX TECHNIQUES INC
TEXEL MATERIAUX TECHNIQUES INC *p* 1299
485 RUE DES ERABLES, SAINT-ELZEAR, QC, G0S 2J0
(418) 387-5910   *SIC* 2297
TEXEL MATERIAUX TECHNIQUES INC *p* 1360
1300 2E RUE DU PARC-INDUSTRIEL, SAINTE-MARIE, QC, G6E 1G8
(418) 658-0200   *SIC* 2297
TEXLIMA *p* 1308
See DISTRIBUTION CLUB TISSUS (1994) INC
TEXPRESS *p* 903
See 1456661 ONTARIO INCORPORATED
TEXTBOOKRENTAL CA, INC *p* 916
34 ASHWARRREN RD, TORONTO, ON, M3J 1Z7
SIC 5961
TEXTILE PRODUCTS LTD *p* 701
1581 MATHESON BLVD, MISSISSAUGA, ON, L4W 1H9
(905) 361-1831   *SIC* 5131
TEXTILES BAKER INC, LES *p* 1129
1812 RUE ONESIME-GAGNON, LACHINE,

QC, H8T 3M6
(514) 931-0831   *SIC* 5131
TEXTILES CAMELOT *p* 1333
See EUGENE TEXTILES (2003) INC
TEXTILES D. ZINMAN LTEE *p* 1226
459 RUE DESLAURIERS, MONTREAL, QC, H4N 1W2
(514) 276-2597   *SIC* 5131
TEXTILES ELITE FABRICS *p* 1051
See TEXTILES ELITE INC
TEXTILES ELITE INC *p* 1051
9200 RUE CLAVEAU, ANJOU, QC, H1J 1Z4
(514) 352-2291   *SIC* 5131
TEXTILES J.P. DOUMAK INC *p* 1341
855 RUE MCCAFFREY, SAINT-LAURENT, QC, H4T 1N3
(514) 342-9397   *SIC* 5131
TEXTILES LINCOLN, LES *p* 1097
See TEXTILES MONTEREY (1996) INC
TEXTILES MONTEREY (1996) INC *p* 1097
2575 BOUL SAINT-JOSEPH, DRUMMONDVILLE, QC, J2B 7V4
(819) 475-4333   *SIC* 2221
TEXTILES ROBLIN INC *p* 1051
9151 BOUL LOUIS-H.-LAFONTAINE, ANJOU, QC, H1J 1Z1
(514) 353-8100   *SIC* 5131
TEXTILES WIN-SIR INC, LES *p* 1076
295 BOUL INDUSTRIEL BUREAU A, CHATEAUGUAY, QC, J6J 4Z2
(450) 691-2747   *SIC* 2322
TEXTURES FINE CRAFTS *p* 613
236 LOCKE ST S, HAMILTON, ON, L8P 4B7
(905) 523-0636   *SIC* 8621
TFB & ASSOCIATES LIMITED *p* 676
7300 WARDEN AVE SUITE 210, MARKHAM, ON, L3R 9Z6
(905) 940-0889   *SIC* 5122
TFI FOODS *p* 879
See TAI FOONG INVESTMENTS LTD
TFI FOODS LTD *p* 875
44 MILNER AVE, SCARBOROUGH, ON, M1S 3P8
(416) 299-7575   *SIC* 5146
TFI HOLDINGS LIMITED PARTNERSHIP *p* 1138
See GESTION TFI, SOCIETE EN COMMANDITE
TFI INTERNATIONAL INC *p* 1336
8801 RTE TRANSCANADIENNE BUREAU 500, SAINT-LAURENT, QC, H4S 1Z6
(514) 331-4113   *SIC* 4213
TFI TRANSPORT 12 L.P. / TRANSPORT TFI 12, S.E.C. *p* 1336
8801 RTE TRANSCANADIENNE UNIT? 500, SAINT-LAURENT, QC, H4S 1Z6
(514) 331-4000   *SIC* 4213
TFI TRANSPORT 17 LP *p* 588
96 DISCO RD, ETOBICOKE, ON, M9W 0A3
(416) 679-7979   *SIC* 4731
TFORCE FINAL MILE CANADA INC *p* 507
107 ALFRED KUEHNE BLVD, BRAMPTON, ON, L6T 4K3
(905) 494-7600   *SIC* 7389
TFORCE FINAL MILE CANADA INC *p* 650
2515 BLAIR BLVD SUITE B, LONDON, ON, N5V 3Z9
(519) 659-8224   *SIC* 7389
TFORCE FINAL MILE CANADA INC *p* 1430
3275 MINERS AVE, SASKATOON, SK, S7K 7Z1
(306) 975-1010   *SIC* 7389
TFORCE HOLDINGS INC *p* 1336
8801 RTE TRANSCANADIENNE BUREAU 500, SAINT-LAURENT, QC, H4S 1Z6
(514) 331-4000   *SIC* 6719
TFORCE INTEGRATED SOLUTIONS *p* 588
See TFI TRANSPORT 17 LP
TFT GLOBAL INC *p* 912
25 TOWNLINE RD SUITE 200, TILLSONBURG, ON, N4G 2R5
(519) 842-4540   *SIC* 4225
TG INDUSTRIES INC *p* 289
107 3RD AVE E, VANCOUVER, BC, V5T

1C7
(604) 872-6676   *SIC* 7389
TG MINTO   *p 836*
See TG MINTO CORPORATION
TG MINTO CORPORATION   *p 836*
300 TORONTO ST, PALMERSTON, ON,
N0G 2P0
(519) 343-2800   *SIC* 3089
TGAA   *p 224*
*See GERMAN ADVERTISING ADVANTAGE
INC, THE*
TGM HOLDINGS LTD   *p 67*
115 17 AVE SW, CALGARY, AB, T2S 0A1
(403) 228-5120   *SIC* 8072
TGP   *p 105*
*See FEDERATED CO-OPERATIVES LIM-
ITED*
**TGS HARVARD PROPERTY MANAGE-
MENT INC**   *p*
1430
135 21ST ST E SUITE 21, SASKATOON,
SK, S7K 0B4
(306) 668-8350   *SIC* 6531
TGST   *p 997*
*See   TRIUMPH   GEAR   SYSTEMS-
TORONTO ULC*
THAI INDOCHINE TRADING INC   *p 678*
50 TRAVAIL RD, MARKHAM, ON, L3S 3J1
(416) 292-2228   *SIC* 5141
THAI OCCIDENTAL LTD   *p 773*
5334 YONGE ST SUITE 907, NORTH
YORK, ON, M2N 6V1
SIC 2258
THAI UNION CANADA INC   *p 419*
78 RUE DU QUAI, VAL-COMEAU, NB, E1X
4L1
(506) 395-3292   *SIC* 2092
THAI UNITED FOOD TRADING LTD *p 194*
7978 NORTH FRASER WAY SUITE 2,
BURNABY, BC, V5J 0C7
(604) 437-4933   *SIC* 5149
THALES CANADA INC   *p 778*
105 MOATFIELD DR SUITE 100, NORTH
YORK, ON, M3B 0A4
(416) 742-3900   *SIC* 8711
**THALES CANADA, DIVISION AERONAU-
TIQUE**   *p*
778
See THALES CANADA INC
THALES OPTRONIQUE CANADA INC   *p*
1331
4868   RUE   LEVY,   SAINT-LAURENT,   QC,
H4R 2P1
(514) 337-7878   *SIC* 3827
**THAMES EMERGENCY MEDICAL SER-
VICES INC**   *p*
656
340 WATERLOO ST, LONDON, ON, N6B
2N6
(519) 679-5466   *SIC* 4119
THAMES RIVER CHEMICAL CORP   *p 525*
5230 HARVESTER RD, BURLINGTON, ON,
L7L 4X4
(905) 681-5353   *SIC* 5169
THAMES TOWER'S APARTMENTS   *p 542*
See FALOM INC
THAMES VALLEY CHILDREN'S CENTRE *p*
656
779 BASE LINE RD E, LONDON, ON, N6C
5Y6
(519) 685-8680   *SIC* 8093
**THAMES   VALLEY   DISTRICT   SCHOOL
BOARD**   *p 479*
14405 MEDWAY RD, ARVA, ON, N0M 1C0
(519) 660-8418   *SIC* 8211
**THAMES   VALLEY   DISTRICT   SCHOOL
BOARD**   *p 482*
362 TALBOT ST W, AYLMER, ON, N5H 1K6
(519) 773-3174   *SIC* 8211
**THAMES   VALLEY   DISTRICT   SCHOOL
BOARD**   *p 622*
37 ALMA ST, INGERSOLL, ON, N5C 1N1
(519) 485-1200   *SIC* 8211
THAMES   VALLEY   DISTRICT   SCHOOL

BOARD   *p 651*
1250 DUNDAS ST, LONDON, ON, N5W 5P2
(519) 452-2000   *SIC* 8211
**THAMES   VALLEY   DISTRICT   SCHOOL
BOARD**   *p 651*
656 TENNENT AVE, LONDON, ON, N5X
1L8
(519) 452-2600   *SIC* 8211
**THAMES   VALLEY   DISTRICT   SCHOOL
BOARD**   *p 652*
1350 HIGHBURY AVE N, LONDON, ON,
N5Y 1B5
(519) 452-2730   *SIC* 8211
**THAMES   VALLEY   DISTRICT   SCHOOL
BOARD**   *p 652*
951 LEATHORNE ST SUITE 1, LONDON,
ON, N5Z 3M7
(519) 452-2444   *SIC* 8211
**THAMES   VALLEY   DISTRICT   SCHOOL
BOARD**   *p 656*
371 TECUMSEH AVE E, LONDON, ON,
N6C 1T4
(519) 452-2860   *SIC* 8211
**THAMES   VALLEY   DISTRICT   SCHOOL
BOARD**   *p 656*
450 MILLBANK DR, LONDON, ON, N6C
4W7
(519) 452-2840   *SIC* 8211
**THAMES   VALLEY   DISTRICT   SCHOOL
BOARD**   *p 656*
509 WATERLOO ST, LONDON, ON, N6B
2P8
(519) 452-2620   *SIC* 8211
**THAMES   VALLEY   DISTRICT   SCHOOL
BOARD**   *p 657*
565 BRADLEY AVE, LONDON, ON, N6E
3Z8
(519) 452-8680   *SIC* 8211
**THAMES   VALLEY   DISTRICT   SCHOOL
BOARD**   *p 658*
950 LAWSON RD, LONDON, ON, N6G 3M2
(519) 452-8690   *SIC* 8211
**THAMES   VALLEY   DISTRICT   SCHOOL
BOARD**   *p 659*
1040 OXFORD ST W, LONDON, ON, N6H
1V4
(519) 452-2750   *SIC* 8211
**THAMES   VALLEY   DISTRICT   SCHOOL
BOARD**   *p 659*
230 BASE LINE RD W, LONDON, ON, N6J
1W1
(519) 452-2900   *SIC* 8211
**THAMES   VALLEY   DISTRICT   SCHOOL
BOARD**   *p 660*
941 VISCOUNT RD, LONDON, ON, N6K
1H5
(519) 452-2770   *SIC* 8211
**THAMES   VALLEY   DISTRICT   SCHOOL
BOARD**   *p 890*
241 SUNSET DR, ST THOMAS, ON, N5R
3C2
(519) 633-0090   *SIC* 8211
**THAMES   VALLEY   DISTRICT   SCHOOL
BOARD**   *p 890*
41 FLORA ST, ST THOMAS, ON, N5P 2X5
(519) 631-3770   *SIC* 8211
**THAMES   VALLEY   DISTRICT   SCHOOL
BOARD**   *p 912*
37 GLENDALE DR SUITE 16, TILLSON-
BURG, ON, N4G 1J6
(519) 842-4207   *SIC* 8211
**THAMES   VALLEY   DISTRICT   SCHOOL
BOARD**   *p 1035*
700 COLLEGE AVE, WOODSTOCK, ON,
N4S 2C8
(519) 539-0020   *SIC* 8211
**THAMES   VALLEY   DISTRICT   SCHOOL
BOARD**   *p 1035*
900 CROMWELL ST, WOODSTOCK, ON,
N4S 5B5
(519) 537-2347   *SIC* 8211
THAMES VALLEY PROCESSORS LTD *p*
634
15 LINE 155390, KINTORE, ON, N0M 2C0

SIC 2015
THANE DIRECT CANADA INC   *p 701*
5255 ORBITOR DR SUITE 501, MISSIS-
SAUGA, ON, L4W 5M6
(905) 625-3800   *SIC* 5023
THANE DIRECT COMPANY   *p 701*
5255 ORBITOR DR SUITE 501, MISSIS-
SAUGA, ON, L4W 5M6
(905) 625-3800   *SIC* 5023
THE AIIM GROUP   *p 480*
*See AVANT IMAGING & INTEGRATED ME-
DIA INC*
THE BAY   *p 198*
See HUDSON'S BAY COMPANY
THE BAY   *p 270*
See HUDSON'S BAY COMPANY
THE BAY   *p 332*
See HUDSON'S BAY COMPANY
THE BAY   *p 579*
See HUDSON'S BAY COMPANY
THE BAY   *p 767*
See HUDSON'S BAY COMPANY
THE BAY   *p 820*
See HUDSON'S BAY COMPANY
THE BAY   *p 929*
See HUDSON'S BAY COMPANY
THE BAY   *p 1021*
See HUDSON'S BAY COMPANY
THE BAY LIMERIDGE   *p 616*
See HUDSON'S BAY COMPANY
THE BAY MAYFAIR   *p 338*
See HUDSON'S BAY COMPANY
THE BAY SOUTH CENTRE   *p 39*
See HUDSON'S BAY COMPANY
**THE BOARD OF EDUCATION OF SCHOOL
DISTRICT #82 (COAST MOUNTAIN)** *p 223*
*See BOARD OF EDUCATION OF SCHOOL
DISTRICT #82 (COAST M*
THE BOUNDLESS SCHOOL   *p 836*
See BOUNDLESS ADVENTURES INC
THE BRICK   *p 702*
See BRICK WAREHOUSE LP, THE
THE BRICK   *p 912*
See 1562246 ONTARIO INC
THE BRITON HOUSE   *p 925*
See WELLS GORDON LIMITED
THE BUCKLEY'S COMPANY   *p 722*
*See   GLAXOSMITHKLINE   CONSUMER
HEALTHCARE INC*
THE CANADIAN WAR MUSEUM   *p 1108*
See MUSEE CANADIEN DE L'HISTOIRE
THE CAPE BRETON POST   *p 467*
*See   MEDIAS   TRANSCONTINENTAL
S.E.N.C.*
THE CHINESE ACADEMY   *p 40*
*See CHINESE ACADEMY FOUNDATION,
THE*
THE CHRONICLE HERALD   *p 440*
See HALIFAX HERALD LIMITED, THE
**THE COUNCIL OF ONTARIO UNIVERSI-
TIES**   *p*
944
See COU HOLDING ASSOCIATION INC
THE CREDIT VALLEY HOSPITAL   *p 719*
See TRILLIUM HEALTH PARTNERS
THE DIVERSICARE CANADA   *p 72*
See LODGE AT VALLEY RIDGE, THE
**THE DOMINION OF CANADA GENERAL
INSURANCE COMPANY**   *p 958*
*See TRAVELERS INSURANCE COMPANY
OF CANADA*
THE DORSEY GROUP   *p 514*
*See DORSEY GROUP INSURANCE PLAN-
NERS INC, THE*
THE DRAKE HOTEL   *p 990*
*See DRAKE HOTEL PROPERTIES (DHP)
INC*
THE EAGLE 94.1 FM SWIFT CURRENT SK
p 345
See GOLDEN WEST BROADCASTING
THE ELECTRONIC AUCTION MARKET *p 34*
See CALGARY STOCKYARDS LTD
THE ELITE MEAT COMPANY   *p 473*
See D & S MEAT PRODUCTS LTD

THE ELMS, THE DIV OF   *p 471*
*See WOLFVILLE NURSING HOMES LIM-
ITED*
THE EQUIPMENT SOLUTION   *p 681*
See ARNOTT CONSTRUCTION LIMITED
THE FSA GROUP   *p 738*
*See DATA COMMUNICATIONS MANAGE-
MENT CORP*
THE GLOBAL GROUP   *p 783*
See GLOBAL UPHOLSTERY CO. INC
THE GRANDMOTHER'S TOUCH   *p 695*
See GRANDMOTHER'S TOUCH INC
**THE GREATER NIAGARA GENERAL HOS-
PITAL**   *p*
759
See NIAGARA HEALTH SYSTEM
THE GREEN SPOT   *p 346*
See 5517509 MANITOBA LTD
THE GUARANTEE   *p 1035*
*See GUARANTEE COMPANY OF NORTH
AMERICA, THE*
THE HARMAN TRANSPORT   *p 531*
See 3394603 CANADA INC
THE HIDI GROUP   *p 915*
See THE HIDI GROUP INC
THE HIDI GROUP INC   *p 915*
155 GORDON BAKER RD SUITE 200,
TORONTO, ON, M2H 3N5
(416) 364-2100   *SIC* 8711
THE HUDSON GROUP   *p 450*
See HUDSON GROUP CANADA, INC
THE HULL GROUP   *p 967*
*See THOMAS I. HULL INSURANCE LIM-
ITED*
**THE   INSURANCE   SERVICES   DEPART-
MENT**   *p*
260
*See LONDON DRUGS INSURANCE SER-
VICES LTD*
THE KITCHING GROUP (CANADA) INC. *p*
388
747 CORYDON AVE SUITE B, WINNIPEG,
MB, R3M 0W5
SIC 6712
THE KOPERNIK LODGE   *p 288*
*See M. KOPERNIK (NICOLAUS COPERNI-
CUS) FOUNDATION*
**THE LABORS INTERNATIONAL UNION OF
NORTH AMERICA**   *p 85*
*See CONSTRUCTION & GENERAL WORK-
ERS UNION LOCAL NO. 92*
**THE   LAW   SOCIETY   OF   BRITISH
COLUMBIA**   *p 299*
*See LSBC CAPTIVE INSURANCE COM-
PANY LTD*
**THE MANUFACTURING & TECHNOLOGY
CENTRE**   *p 1013*
See 1378045 ONTARIO INC
THE MARKET ON MACLEOD   *p 38*
*See WALKERS OWN PRODUCE INTER-
NATIONAL INC*
THE MILLER TAVERN   *p 787*
See 2389807 ONTARIO INC
THE MOVER   *p 124*
See HIGHLAND MOVING & STORAGE LTD
THE OLD COUNTRY MARKET   *p 198*
See BILLY GRUFF MARKETING LTD
THE ORIGINAL CAKERIE   *p 661*
See 0429746 B.C. LTD
THE ORIGINAL RISTORANTE   *p 343*
See PANZEX VANCOUVER INC
THE PACIFICA   *p 283*
*See PACIFICA RESORT LIVING RETIRE-
MENT, THE*
THE PADDOCK   *p 331*
See BIG D PRODUCTS LTD
THE PERSONNEL DEPARTMENT LTD *p*
327
980 HOWE ST UNIT 201, VANCOUVER,
BC, V6Z 0C8
(604) 685-3530   *SIC* 8741
THE Q GROUP   *p 779*
*See JMC MARKETING COMMUNICA-
TIONS CORPORATION*

THE REC ROOM *p* 120
See CINEPLEX ENTERTAINMENT LIMITED PARTNERSHIP

THE RIDE TO CONQUER CANCER *p* 947
See PRINCESS MARGARET CANCER FOUNDATION, THE

THE ROSEDALE GROUP *p* 742
See ROSEDALE TRANSPORT LIMITED

THE SHOE CLUB *p* 581
See 2076631 ONTARIO LIMITED

THE TORONTO ATHLETIC CLUB *p* 969
See FITNESS INSTITUTE LIMITED, THE

THE TORONTO SUN *p* 932
See 1032451 B.C. LTD

THE UPS STORE (FRANCHISOR) *p* 806
See MBEC COMMUNICATIONS INC

THE VILLAGE GROCER *p* 665
See 892316 ONTARIO LIMITED

THE VILLAGE OF RIVERSIDE GLEN *p* 604
See SCHLEGEL VILLAGES INC

THE VILLAGE OF WENTWORTH HEIGHTS *p* 616
See SCHLEGEL VILLAGES INC

THE WHALESBONE OYSTER HOUSE *p* 833
See 1750769 ONTARIO INC

THE WILDS *p* 432
See WILDS AT SALMONIER RIVER INC, THE

THE WINDSOR ARMS HOTEL *p* 976
See WINDSOR ARMS DEVELOPMENT CORPORATION

THE&PARTNERSHIP INC *p* 984
99 SPADINA AVE UNIT 100, TORONTO, ON, M5V 3P8
(647) 252-6801 *SIC* 8741

THEA PHARMA INC *p* 799
2150 WINSTON PARK DR UNIT 4, OAKVILLE, ON, L6H 5V1
(905) 829-5283 *SIC* 5048

THEATRE DENISE PELLETIER INC *p* 1167
4353 RUE SAINTE-CATHERINE E, MONTREAL, QC, H1V 1Y2
(514) 253-8974 *SIC* 7922

THEATRE SAINT-DENIS *p* 1175
See COMPAGNIE FRANCE FILM INC

THEATRIXX TECHNOLOGIES INC *p* 1216
1655 RUE RICHARDSON, MONTREAL, QC, H3K 3J7
(514) 939-3077 *SIC* 3613

THEMIS SOLUTIONS INC *p* 189
4611 CANADA WAY SUITE 300, BURNABY, BC, V5G 4X3
(604) 210-2944 *SIC* 7371

THEO MINEAULT INC *p* 1103
2135 CH DE MONTREAL O, GATINEAU, QC, J8M 1P3
(819) 986-3190 *SIC* 2431

THERADIOMAN *p* 488
See ROYAL IRAQI HEAVY EQUIPMENT CORPORATION, THE

THERAPEUTIQUE KNIGHT INC *p* 1221
3400 BOUL DE MAISONNEUVE O BUREAU 1055, MONTREAL, QC, H3Z 3B8
(514) 484-4483 *SIC* 2834

THERAPURE BIOPHARMA INC *p* 727
2585 MEADOWPINE BLVD, MISSISSAUGA, ON, L5N 8H9
(905) 286-6200 *SIC* 2834

THERATECHNOLOGIES INC *p* 1200
2015 RUE PEEL SUITE 1100, MONTREAL, QC, H3A 1T8
(514) 336-7800 *SIC* 8731

THEREDPIN.COM REALTY INC., BROKERAGE *p* 943
5 CHURCH ST, TORONTO, ON, M5E 1M2
(416) 800-0812 *SIC* 6531

THERIAULT, A. F. & SON LTD *p* 462
9027 MAIN HWY, METEGHAN RIVER, NS, B0W 2L0
(902) 645-2327 *SIC* 3731

THERMAFIX A. J. INC *p* 1377
1396 RTE DU RONDIN, ST-NAZAIRE-DU-LAC-ST-JEAN, QC, G0W 2V0
(418) 668-6131 *SIC* 3211

THERMAL PRODUCTS - LONG MANUFACTURING *p* 803
See DANA CANADA CORPORATION

THERMAL SYSTEMS KWC LTD *p* 160
261185 WAGON WHEEL WAY, ROCKY VIEW COUNTY, AB, T4A 0E2
(403) 250-5507 *SIC* 1761

THERMALITE PRODUCTS INC *p* 396
2598 CH ACADIE, CAP-PELE, NB, E4N 1E3
(506) 577-4351 *SIC* 3086

THERMI GROUP *p* 727
6745 FINANCIAL DR, MISSISSAUGA, ON, L5N 7J7
(905) 813-9600 *SIC* 7389

THERMO CRS LTD *p* 525
5250 MAINWAY, BURLINGTON, ON, L7L 5Z1
(905) 332-2000 *SIC* 8742

THERMO DESIGN ENGINEERING LTD *p* 123
1424 70 AVE NW, EDMONTON, AB, T6P 1P5
(780) 440-6064 *SIC* 3569

THERMO DESIGN INSULATION LTD *p* 111
3520 56 AVE NW, EDMONTON, AB, T6B 3S7
(780) 468-2077 *SIC* 1742

THERMO FISHER SCIENTIFIC *p* 525
See THERMO CRS LTD

THERMO FISHER SCIENTIFIC (MISSISSAUGA) INC *p* 728
2845 ARGENTIA RD UNIT 4, MISSISSAUGA, ON, L5N 8G6
(905) 890-1034 *SIC* 5049

THERMO KING OF BRITISH COLUMBIA INC *p* 202
68 FAWCETT RD, COQUITLAM, BC, V3K 6V5
(604) 526-4414 *SIC* 7623

THERMO KING OF TORONTO *p* 736
See 1008648 ONTARIO INC

THERMO KING WESTERN INC *p* 106
15825 118 AVE NW, EDMONTON, AB, T5V 1B7
(780) 447-1578 *SIC* 3713

THERMO-KINETICS COMPANY LIMITED *p* 743
6740 INVADER CRES, MISSISSAUGA, ON, L5T 2B6
(905) 670-2266 *SIC* 3829

THERMO-PROTEC *p* 1262
See ISOLATION AIR-PLUS INC

THERMOFIN *p* 1072
See 3075109 CANADA INC

THERMOFORM OF AMERICA *p* 1242
See THERMOFORME D'AMERIQUE INC

THERMOFORME D'AMERIQUE INC *p* 1242
970 RUE THEOPHILE-SAINT-LAURENT, NICOLET, QC, J3T 1B4
(819) 293-8899 *SIC* 3089

THERMOGENICS INC *p* 482
6 SCANLON CRT, AURORA, ON, L4G 7B2
(905) 727-1901 *SIC* 1711

THERMON CANADA INC *p* 26
1806 CENTRE AVE NE, CALGARY, AB, T2E 0A6
(403) 273-5558 *SIC* 5063

THERMON CANADA INC *p* 111
5607 67 ST NW, EDMONTON, AB, T6B 3H5
(780) 437-6326 *SIC* 5075

THERMON HEAT TRACING *p* 26
See THERMON CANADA INC

THERMON HEAT TRACING SERVICES *p* 111
See THERMON CANADA INC

THERMON HEATING SYSTEMS, INC *p* 111
5918 ROPER RD NW, EDMONTON, AB, T6B 3E1
(780) 466-3178 *SIC* 3443

THERMON HEATING SYSTEMS, INC *p* 810

1 HUNTER VALLEY RD, ORILLIA, ON, L3V 0Y7
(705) 325-3473 *SIC* 3443

THERMOPLAST INC *p* 1101
3035 BOUL LE CORBUSIER BUREAU 7, FABREVILLE, QC, H7L 4C3
(450) 687-5115 *SIC* 3544

THERMOPOMPES N & R SOL INC *p* 1076
2325 BOUL FORD, CHATEAUGUAY, QC, J6J 4Z2
(450) 699-3232 *SIC* 1731

THERMOR LTD *p* 756
16975 LESLIE ST, NEWMARKET, ON, L3Y 9A1
(905) 952-3737 *SIC* 5047

THERMOSHELL *p* 850
See 2714159 CANADA INC

THERRIEN COUTURE AVOCATS S.E.N.C.R.L. *p* 1313
1200 RUE DANIEL-JOHNSON O # 7000, SAINT-HYACINTHE, QC, J2S 7K7
(450) 773-6326 *SIC* 8111

THERRIEN ENTREPRENEUR GENERAL *p* 1242
See CONSTRUCTION G. THERRIEN 2010 INC

THES DAVIDSTEA, LES *p* 1156
See DAVIDSTEA INC

THESCORE INC *p* 984
500 KING ST W 4TH FL, TORONTO, ON, M5V 1L9
(416) 479-8812 *SIC* 7372

THETA INDUSTRIES LIMITED *p* 488
8 TRUMAN RD, BARRIE, ON, L4N 8Y8
(705) 726-2620 *SIC* 3469

THETA TTS INC *p* 488
8 TRUMAN RD, BARRIE, ON, L4N 8Y8
(705) 726-2620 *SIC* 3469

THEVCO ELECTRONIQUE INC *p* 1309
5200 RUE ARMAND-FRAPPIER, SAINT-HUBERT, QC, J3Z 1G5
(450) 926-2777 *SIC* 3822

THI CANADA INC *p* 525
5230 HARVESTER RD UNIT 3, BURLINGTON, ON, L7L 4X4
(905) 849-3633 *SIC* 3465

THIARA SUPERMARKET LTD. *p* 728
3899 TRELAWNY CIR SUITE 1, MISSISSAUGA, ON, L5N 6S3
(905) 824-8960 *SIC* 5411

THIBAULT CHEVROLET CADILLAC BUICK GMC DE ROUYN-NORANDA LTEE *p* 1290
375 BOUL RIDEAU, ROUYN-NORANDA, QC, J9X 5Y7
(819) 762-1751 *SIC* 5511

THIBAULT, JACQUES ENTREPRISES INC *p* 1076
97 BOUL D'ANJOU, CHATEAUGUAY, QC, J6J 2R1
(450) 691-2622 *SIC* 5912

THIBAULT, RONALD CHEVROLET CADILLAC BUICK GMC LTEE *p* 1374
3839 RUE KING O, SHERBROOKE, QC, J1L 1W7
(819) 563-7878 *SIC* 5511

THIBEAULT MASONRY LTD *p* 26
1815 27 AVE NE SUITE 7, CALGARY, AB, T2E 7E1
SIC 1741

THICKWOOD GARDEN MARKET I G A *p* 129
See SOBEYS CAPITAL INCORPORATED

THICKWOOD SAFEWAY *p* 129
See SOBEYS WEST INC

THIESSEN EQUIPMENT LTD *p* 228
20131 LOGAN AVE, LANGLEY, BC, V3A 4L5
(604) 532-8611 *SIC* 5082

THIINC LOGISTICS INC *p* 957
120 ADELAIDE ST W SUITE 2150, TORONTO, ON, M5H 1T1
(416) 862-5552 *SIC* 8742

THINADDICTIVES INC *p* 1327

258 BOUL LEBEAU, SAINT-LAURENT, QC, H4N 1R4
(514) 484-4321 *SIC* 2052

THINGS ENGRAVED *p* 642
See THINGS ENGRAVED INC

THINGS ENGRAVED INC *p* 642
61 MCBRINE PL, KITCHENER, ON, N2R 1H5
(519) 748-2211 *SIC* 5947

THINK RESEARCH CORPORATION *p* 934
351 KING ST E SUITE 500, TORONTO, ON, M5A 0L6
(416) 977-1955 *SIC* 7371

THINK4D INC *p* 345
511 INDUSTRIAL DR, ALTONA, MB, R0G 0B0
(204) 324-6401 *SIC* 7389

THINKING IN PICTURES EDUCATIONAL SERVICE *p* 626
160 TERENCE MATTHEWS CRES SUITE B2, KANATA, ON, K2M 0B2
(613) 592-8800 *SIC* 8699

THINKMAX CONSULTING INC *p* 1324
1111 BOUL DR.-FREDERIK-PHILIPS BUREAU 500, SAINT-LAURENT, QC, H4M 2X6
(514) 316-8959 *SIC* 8741

THINKUNSURE LTD *p* 676
11 ALLSTATE PKY UNIT 206, MARKHAM, ON, L3R 9T8
(905) 415-8800 *SIC* 6331

THINKWRAP SOLUTIONS INC *p* 625
450 MARCH RD SUITE 500, KANATA, ON, K2K 3K2
(613) 751-4441 *SIC* 7371

THINQ TECHNOLOGIES LTD *p* 655
572 WELLINGTON ST, LONDON, ON, N6A 3R3
(519) 659-4900 *SIC* 5045

THIRAU INC *p* 1399
489 BOUL PIERRE-ROUX E BUREAU 200, VICTORIAVILLE, QC, G6T 1S9
(819) 752-9741 *SIC* 1731

THIRAU LTEE *p* 1399
489 BOUL PIERRE-ROUX E, VICTORIAVILLE, QC, G6T 1S9
(819) 752-9741 *SIC* 1623

THIRD ACADEMY , THE *p* 74
See THIRD ACADEMY INTERNATIONAL LTD, THE

THIRD ACADEMY INTERNATIONAL LTD, THE *p* 74
2452 BATTLEFORD AVE SW, CALGARY, AB, T3E 7K9
(403) 288-5335 *SIC* 8211

THIRD PLANET FOODS, DIV OF *p* 266
See WESTERN RICE MILLS LTD

THISTLE PRINTING LIMITED *p* 916
35 MOBILE DR, TORONTO, ON, M4A 2P6
(416) 288-1288 *SIC* 2752

THK RHYTHM AUTOMOTIVE CANADA LIMITED *p* 912
1417 BELL MILL SIDEROAD, TILLSONBURG, ON, N4G 4G9
(519) 688-4200 *SIC* 3089

THOMAS A. BLAKELOCK HIGH SCHOOL *p* 803
See HALTON DISTRICT SCHOOL BOARD

THOMAS ALLEN & SON LIMITED *p* 676
195 ALLSTATE PKWY, MARKHAM, ON, L3R 4T8
(905) 475-9126 *SIC* 5192

THOMAS BELLEMARE LTEE *p* 1388
8750 BOUL INDUSTRIEL, TROIS-RIVIERES, QC, G9A 5E1
(819) 379-2535 *SIC* 1794

THOMAS CAVANAGH CONSTRUCTION LIMITED *p* 479
9094A CAVANAGH RD, ASHTON, ON, K0A 1B0
(613) 257-2918 *SIC* 1611

THOMAS DESIGN BUILDERS LTD *p* 393
2395 MCGILLIVRAY BLVD UNIT C, WINNIPEG, MB, R3Y 1G6

(204) 989-5400   *SIC* 1542
THOMAS FRESH INC   *p* 19
5470 76 AVE SE, CALGARY, AB, T2C 4S3
(403) 236-8234   *SIC* 5148
THOMAS FRUITS ET LEGUMES   *p* 1224
See 2944715 CANADA INC
THOMAS GROUP INC   *p* 26
1115 55 AVE NE, CALGARY, AB, T2E 6W1
(403) 275-3666   *SIC* 1742
**THOMAS HEALTH CARE CORPORATION,
THE**   *p* 894
490 HIGHWAY 8, STONEY CREEK, ON,
L8G 1G6
(905) 573-4900   *SIC* 6513
THOMAS I. HULL INSURANCE LIMITED *p*
967
220 BAY ST SUITE 600, TORONTO, ON,
M5J 2W4
(416) 865-0131   *SIC* 6411
THOMAS MOTORS LTD   *p* 1410
1955 HWY 6TH S, MELFORT, SK, S0E 1A0
(306) 752-5663   *SIC* 5511
THOMAS PONTIAC BUICK GMC LTD *p* 545
100 UNIVERSITY AVE E, COBOURG, ON,
K9A 1C8
(905) 372-5447   *SIC* 5511
THOMAS SKINNER & SON LIMITED *p* 256
13880 VULCAN WAY, RICHMOND, BC, V6V
1K6
(604) 276-2131   *SIC* 5084
THOMAS, J.O. & ASSOCIATES LTD *p* 285
1370 KOOTENAY ST, VANCOUVER, BC,
V5K 4R1
(604) 291-6340   *SIC* 8748
THOMAS, LARGE & SINGER INC   *p* 676
15 ALLSTATE PKY SUITE 500, MARKHAM,
ON, L3R 5B4
(800) 268-5542   *SIC* 5141
THOMAS, RENE & FILS INC   *p* 1393
10 RUE BEAUREGARD, VARENNES, QC,
J3X 1R1
(450) 652-2927   *SIC* 5211
THOMPSON AHERN INTERNATIONAL   *p*
690
See THOMPSON, AHERN & CO. LIMITED
THOMPSON BROS. (CONSTR.) LTD *p* 164
411 SOUTH AVE, SPRUCE GROVE, AB,
T7X 3B4
(780) 962-1030   *SIC* 1629
**THOMPSON COMMUNITY ASSOCIATION,
THE**   *p* 266
5151 GRANVILLE AVE, RICHMOND, BC,
V7C 1E6
(604) 238-8422   *SIC* 8322
THOMPSON COMMUNITY CENTRE   *p* 266
*See THOMPSON COMMUNITY ASSOCIA-
TION, THE*
THOMPSON FORD SALES LTD   *p* 360
15 STATION RD, THOMPSON, MB, R8N
0N6
(204) 778-6386   *SIC* 5511
THOMPSON INFRASTRUCTURE LTD *p* 164
411 SOUTH AVE, SPRUCE GROVE, AB,
T7X 3B4
(780) 962-1030   *SIC* 1623
THOMPSON PLYMOUTH CHRYSLER *p* 632
See MCKEOWN MOTORS LIMITED
**THOMPSON RIVER VENEER PRODUCTS
LIMITED**   *p* 218
8405 DALLAS DR, KAMLOOPS, BC, V2C
6X2
(250) 573-6002   *SIC* 2436
THOMPSON RIVERS UNIVERSITY   *p* 218
805 TRU WAY, KAMLOOPS, BC, V2C 0C8
(250) 828-5000   *SIC* 8221
THOMPSON TORONTO   *p* 981
See HOTEL 550 WELLINGTON GP LTD
THOMPSON, AHERN & CO. LIMITED *p* 690
6299 AIRPORT RD SUITE 506, MISSIS-
SAUGA, ON, L4V 1N3
(905) 677-3471   *SIC* 4731
**THOMPSON, J. WALTER COMPANY LIM-
ITED**   *p*
930

160 BLOOR ST E SUITE 1100, TORONTO,
ON, M4W 3P7
(416) 926-7300   *SIC* 7311
**THOMPSON, ROACH & HUGHES CON-
SULTING INC**   *p*
559
261 MILLWAY AVE UNIT 1, CONCORD, ON,
L4K 4K9
(905) 669-9517   *SIC* 8741
THOMPSONS LIMITED   *p* 493
2 HYLAND DR, BLENHEIM, ON, N0P 1A0
(519) 676-5411   *SIC* 5153
THOMSON ASSOCIATES   *p* 958
*See THOMSON, WILLIAM E ASSOCIATES
INC*
THOMSON COMPANY INC, THE   *p* 957
65 QUEEN ST W SUITE 2400, TORONTO,
ON, M5H 2M8
(416) 364-8700   *SIC* 2731
THOMSON METALS AND DISPOSAL LP *p*
525
961 ZELCO DR, BURLINGTON, ON, L7L
4Y2
(905) 681-8832   *SIC* 4953
THOMSON POWER SYSTEMS   *p* 229
See REGAL BELOIT CANADA ULC
**THOMSON REUTERS (FINANCIAL & RISK)
CANADA, A DIV OF**   *p* 957
*See THOMSON REUTERS CANADA LIM-
ITED*
THOMSON REUTERS CANADA LIMITED *p*
957
333 BAY ST SUITE 400, TORONTO, ON,
M5H 2R2
(416) 687-7500   *SIC* 8999
THOMSON REUTERS CORPORATION   *p*
957
333 BAY ST, TORONTO, ON, M5H 2R2
(416) 687-7500   *SIC* 7299
**THOMSON REUTERS DT IMPOT ET
COMPTABILITE INC**   *p* 1155
3333 BOUL GRAHAM BUREAU 222,
MONT-ROYAL, QC, H3R 3L5
(514) 733-8355   *SIC* 7372
THOMSON ROGERS   *p* 957
390 BAY ST SUITE 3100, TORONTO, ON,
M5H 1W2
(416) 868-3100   *SIC* 8111
**THOMSON SCHINDLE GREEN INSUR-
ANCE & FINANCIAL SERVICES LTD**   *p*
146
623 4 ST SE SUITE 100, MEDICINE HAT,
AB, T1A 0L1
(403) 526-3283   *SIC* 6411
THOMSON TERMINALS LIMITED   *p* 588
102 IRON ST, ETOBICOKE, ON, M9W 5L9
(416) 240-0897   *SIC* 4213
THOMSON TERMINALS LIMITED   *p* 588
55 CITY VIEW DR, ETOBICOKE, ON, M9W
5A5
(416) 240-0897   *SIC* 4225
THOMSON, A R LTD   *p* 121
10030 31 AVE NW, EDMONTON, AB, T6N
1G4
(780) 450-8080   *SIC* 6712
THOMSON, G. CAPITAL LIMITED   *p* 525
961 ZELCO DR, BURLINGTON, ON, L7L
4Y2
(905) 681-8832   *SIC* 6712
THOMSON, JEMMETT, VOGELZANG *p* 630
See INSURANCE CENTRE INC, THE
THOMSON, PETER & SONS INC   *p* 476
256 VICTORIA ST W, ALLISTON, ON, L9R
1L9
SIC 5031
THOMSON, WILLIAM E ASSOCIATES INC *p*
958
390 BAY ST SUITE 1102, TORONTO, ON,
M5H 2Y2
(416) 947-1300   *SIC* 6211
THOMSON-GORDON GROUP INC   *p* 526
3225 MAINWAY, BURLINGTON, ON, L7M
1A6
(905) 335-1440   *SIC* 6712

THORBURN FLEX INC   *p* 1252
173 AV ONEIDA, POINTE-CLAIRE, QC,
H9R 1A9
(514) 695-8710   *SIC* 5251
THORBURN INTERNATIONAL INC *p* 1252
173 AV ONEIDA, POINTE-CLAIRE, QC,
H9R 1A9
(514) 695-8710   *SIC* 6712
THORDON BEARINGS INC   *p* 526
3225 MAINWAY, BURLINGTON, ON, L7M
1A6
(905) 335-1440   *SIC* 5085
THORFLEX   *p* 526
See THORDON BEARINGS INC
THORLAKSON FEEDYARDS INC   *p* 3
GD STN MAIN, AIRDRIE, AB, T4A 0H4
(403) 948-5434   *SIC* 5191
THORNBURY FINANCIAL LTD   *p* 780
23 PRINCE ANDREW PL, NORTH YORK,
ON, M3C 2H2
(416) 444-3050   *SIC* 8743
THORNCLIFFE PARK PUBLIC SCHOOL *p*
919
*See TORONTO DISTRICT SCHOOL
BOARD*
THORNCLIFFE SAFEWAY   *p* 40
See SOBEYS WEST INC
THORNCREST SHERWAY INC   *p* 576
1575 THE QUEENSWAY, ETOBICOKE, ON,
M8Z 1T9
(416) 521-7000   *SIC* 5511
THORNCRETE CONSTRUCTION LIMITED *p*
559
381 SPINNAKER WAY, CONCORD, ON,
L4K 4N4
(905) 669-6510   *SIC* 1771
THORNES   *p* 414
See SOURCE ATLANTIC LIMITED
THORNHILL GOLF & COUNTRY CLUB   *p*
906
7994 YONGE ST, THORNHILL, ON, L4J
1W3
(905) 881-3000   *SIC* 7997
THORNHILL RESEARCH INC   *p* 947
210 DUNDAS ST W SUITE 200, TORONTO,
ON, M5G 2E8
(416) 597-1325   *SIC* 8733
**THORNHILL VOLUNTEER FIREFIGHTERS
ASSOCIATION**   *p* 283
3128 16 HWY E, THORNHILL, BC, V8G 4N8
(250) 638-1466   *SIC* 8699
THORNLEA SECONDARY SCHOOL *p* 905
*See YORK REGION DISTRICT SCHOOL
BOARD*
THORNTON GROUT FINNIGAN LLP *p* 968
See 1367313 ONTARIO INC
THORNTON STEAD ENTERPRISES INC *p*
207
1223 DERWENT WAY, DELTA, BC, V3M
5V9
(604) 524-8000   *SIC* 6712
**THORNTONVIEW LONG TERM CARE RES-
IDENCE**   *p*
814
See REVERA LONG TERM CARE INC
THORNVALE HOLDINGS LIMITED   *p* 439
441 CAPE AUGET RD, ARICHAT, NS, B0E
1A0
(902) 226-3510   *SIC* 4222
THORNVALE HOLDINGS LIMITED   *p* 440
757 BEDFORD HWY, BEDFORD, NS, B4A
3Z7
(902) 443-0550   *SIC* 6712
THORNVALE HOLDINGS LIMITED   *p* 461
68 WATER ST, LOCKEPORT, NS, B0T 1L0
(902) 656-2413   *SIC* 2092
THORNVALE HOLDINGS LIMITED   *p* 462
240 MONTAGUE ST, LUNENBURG, NS,
B0J 2C0
(902) 634-8049   *SIC* 2092
THOROLD AUTO PARTS & RECYCLERS *p*
906
See 581917 ONTARIO INC
THORPE BROTHERS LIMITED   *p* 1414

HWY 2 S 44TH ST, PRINCE ALBERT, SK,
S6V 5R4
(306) 763-8454   *SIC* 1711
THORSTEINSSONS   *p* 329
595 BURRARD ST SUITE 49123, VANCOU-
VER, BC, V7X 1J2
(604) 689-1261   *SIC* 7291
THOUGHTCORP SYSTEMS INC   *p* 773
4950 YONGE ST SUITE 1700, NORTH
YORK, ON, M2N 6K1
(416) 591-4004   *SIC* 7379
THOUSAND ISLANDS BRIDGE AUTHOITY
p 643
See THOUSAND ISLANDS BRIDGE CO
THOUSAND ISLANDS BRIDGE CO *p* 643
379 HWY 137, LANSDOWNE, ON, K0E 1L0
(613) 659-2308   *SIC* 4785
**THOUSAND ISLANDS INSURANCE & FI-
NANCIAL GROUP LIMITED**   *p*
631
1996 HIGHWAY 15, KINGSTON, ON, K7L
4V3
(613) 542-4440   *SIC* 6411
**THOUSAND ISLANDS SECONDARY
SCHOOL**   *p* 520
*See UPPER CANADA DISTRICT SCHOOL
BOARD, THE*
THQ CANADA   *p* 300
See RELIC ENTERTAINMENT, INC
THRASHER SALES & LEASING LTD *p* 477
251 SIMCOE ST, AMHERSTBURG, ON,
N9V 1M5
(519) 736-6481   *SIC* 5511
THREAD COLLECTIVE INC   *p* 1341
850 RUE MCCAFFREY, SAINT-LAURENT,
QC, H4T 1N1
(514) 345-1777   *SIC* 5136
**THREE AMIGO'S BEAUTY SUPPLY CO
LTD**   *p* 339
555 ARDERSIER RD UNIT A8, VICTORIA,
BC, V8Z 1C8
(250) 475-3099   *SIC* 5087
THREE H   *p* 753
*See THREE H FURNITURE SYSTEMS LIM-
ITED*
THREE H FURNITURE SYSTEMS LIMITED
p 753
156462 CLOVER VALLEY RD, NEW
LISKEARD, ON, P0J 1P0
(705) 647-4323   *SIC* 2521
THREE HILLS FOOD STORES LTD *p* 169
119 4TH AVE N, THREE HILLS, AB, T0M
2A0
(403) 443-5022   *SIC* 5411
THREE HILLS IGA   *p* 169
See THREE HILLS FOOD STORES LTD
THREE POINT MOTORS   *p* 334
See 1712318 ONTARIO LIMITED
THREE STAR INDUSTRIES   *p* 787
See T.J. TRADING CO. INC
THREE-H MANUFACTURING LTD   *p* 753
156462 CLOVER VALLEY RD, NEW
LISKEARD, ON, P0J 1P0
(705) 647-4323   *SIC* 5712
THRIFT LODGE   *p* 1429
See REMAI INVESTMENT CORPORATION
THRIFTY CAR RENTAL   *p* 489
See WILLIAMS, JIM LEASING LIMITED
THRIFTY FOODS   *p* 203
See CAMCOURT HOLDINGS LTD
THRIFTY FOODS   *p* 211
See JACE HOLDINGS LTD
THRIFTY FOODS   *p* 238
See JACE HOLDINGS LTD
THRIFTY FOODS   *p* 267
See JACE HOLDINGS LTD
THRIFTY FOODS   *p* 337
See JACE HOLDINGS LTD
THRIFTY FOODS NANAIMO   *p* 233
See JACE HOLDINGS LTD
THRIFTY KITCHENS   *p* 267
See JACE HOLDINGS LTD
THUNDER AIRLINES LIMITED   *p* 910
310 HECTOR DOUGALL WAY, THUNDER

BAY, ON, P7E 6M6
(807) 475-4211   SIC 4522
THUNDER BAY CATHOLIC DISTRICT SCHOOL BOARD   p 907
285 GIBSON ST, THUNDER BAY, ON, P7A 2J6
(807) 344-8433   SIC 8211
THUNDER BAY CATHOLIC DISTRICT SCHOOL BOARD   p 909
459 VICTORIA AVE W, THUNDER BAY, ON, P7C 0A4
(807) 625-1555   SIC 8211
THUNDER BAY CATHOLIC DISTRICT SCHOOL BOARD   p 910
621 SELKIRK ST S, THUNDER BAY, ON, P7E 1T9
(807) 623-5218   SIC 8211
THUNDER BAY DISTRICT HEALTH UNIT p 909
999 BALMORAL ST, THUNDER BAY, ON, P7B 6E7
(807) 625-5900   SIC 8621
THUNDER BAY ELECTRONICS LIMITED p 907
87 HILL ST N, THUNDER BAY, ON, P7A 5V6
(807) 346-2600   SIC 4833
THUNDER BAY FLIGHT REFUELING LIMITED   p 910
304 HECTOR DOUGALL WAY, THUNDER BAY, ON, P7E 6M6
(807) 577-1178   SIC 5172
THUNDER BAY HYDRAULICS LTD p 910
701 MONTREAL ST, THUNDER BAY, ON, P7E 3P2
(807) 623-3151   SIC 5084
THUNDER BAY HYDRO ELECTRICITY DISTRIBUTION INC   p 907
34 CUMBERLAND ST N SUITE 101, THUNDER BAY, ON, P7A 4L4
(807) 343-1111   SIC 4911
THUNDER BAY MARINE SERVICES (1998) LTD   p 909
100 MAIN ST SUITE 600, THUNDER BAY, ON, P7B 6R9
(807) 344-9221   SIC 6712
THUNDER BAY REGIONAL HEALTH SCIENCES CENTRE   p 909
980 OLIVER RD RM 1480, THUNDER BAY, ON, P7B 6V4
(807) 684-6500   SIC 8062
THUNDER BAY TRUCK CENTRE INC p 910
1145 COMMERCE ST, THUNDER BAY, ON, P7E 6E8
(807) 577-5793   SIC 5012
THUNDER TOOL & MANUFACTURING LTD p 588
975 MARTIN GROVE RD, ETOBICOKE, ON, M9W 4V6
(416) 742-1936   SIC 3469
THURBER ENGINEERING LTD   p 38
7330 FISHER ST SE SUITE 180, CALGARY, AB, T2H 2H8
(403) 253-9217   SIC 8711
THURBER ENGINEERING LTD   p 117
9636 51 AVE NW SUITE 200, EDMONTON, AB, T6E 6A5
(780) 438-1460   SIC 8711
THURBER MANAGEMENT LTD   p 339
4396 WEST SAANICH RD SUITE 100, VICTORIA, BC, V8Z 3E9
(250) 727-2201   SIC 8741
THURSTON MACHINE COMPANY LIMITED p 847
45 INVERTOSE DR, PORT COLBORNE, ON, L3K 5V8
(905) 834-3606   SIC 3547
THWAITES FARMS LTD   p 761
1984 TOWNLINE RD SUITE 3, NIAGARA ON THE LAKE, ON, L0S 1J0
(905) 934-3880   SIC 0179

THYSSEN MINING CONSTRUCTION OF CANADA LTD   p 1419
2409 ALBERT ST N, REGINA, SK, S4P 3E1
(306) 949-6606   SIC 1629
THYSSENKRUPP ELEVATOR   p 877
See   THYSSENKRUPP   ELEVATOR (CANADA) LIMITED
THYSSENKRUPP ELEVATOR (CANADA) LIMITED   p 19
2419 52 AVE SE UNIT 5, CALGARY, AB, T2C 4X7
(403) 259-4183   SIC 7699
THYSSENKRUPP ELEVATOR (CANADA) LIMITED   p 877
410 PASSMORE AVE UNIT 1, SCARBOROUGH, ON, M1V 5C3
(416) 291-2000   SIC 1796
THYSSENKRUPP ELEVATORS   p 19
See   THYSSENKRUPP   ELEVATOR (CANADA) LIMITED
THYSSENKRUPP INDUSTRIAL SERVICES CANADA   p 1021
See THYSSENKRUPP SUPPLY CHAIN SERVICES CA, INC
THYSSENKRUPP INDUSTRIAL SOLUTIONS (CANADA) INC   p 74
4838 RICHARD RD SW SUITE 400, CALGARY, AB, T3E 6L1
(403) 245-2866   SIC 8711
THYSSENKRUPP MATERIALS CA, LTD p 559
2821 LANGSTAFF RD, CONCORD, ON, L4K 5C6
(905) 669-0247   SIC 6221
THYSSENKRUPP MATERIALS CA, LTD p 1336
4700 CH DU BOIS-FRANC, SAINT-LAURENT, QC, H4S 1A7
(514) 337-0161   SIC 5093
THYSSENKRUPP MATERIALS NA   p 559
See THYSSENKRUPP MATERIALS CA, LTD
THYSSENKRUPP NORTHERN ELEVATOR CORPORATION   p 877
410 PASSMORE AVE UNIT 1, SCARBOROUGH, ON, M1V 5C3
(416) 291-2000   SIC 3534
THYSSENKRUPP SUPPLY CHAIN SERVICES CA, INC   p 1021
2491 OUELLETTE AVE, WINDSOR, ON, N8X 1L5
(519) 977-8420   SIC 4225
TI AUTOMOTIVE CANADA INC   p 507
316 ORENDA RD, BRAMPTON, ON, L6T 1G3
(905) 793-7100   SIC 3465
TI FOODS   p 678
See THAI INDOCHINE TRADING INC
TI GROUP AUTOMOTIVE OF CANADA p 500
See 1939243 ONTARIO INC
TI GROUP INC   p 919
115 THORNCLIFFE PARK DR, TORONTO, ON, M4H 1M1
(416) 696-2853   SIC 2752
TI HOLDINGS INC   p 919
115 THORNCLIFFE PARK DR, TORONTO, ON, M4H 1M1
(416) 696-2853   SIC 6712
TI TITANIUM LTEE   p 1331
5055 RUE LEVY, SAINT-LAURENT, QC, H4R 2N9
(514) 334-5781   SIC 3443
TIAN BAO TRAVEL CO INC   p 875
4002 SHEPPARD AVE E UNIT 106A, SCARBOROUGH, ON, M1S 4R5
(416) 292-9990   SIC 4724
TIAN BAO TRAVEL LTD   p 854
60 WEST WILMOT ST UNIT 1, RICHMOND HILL, ON, L4B 1M6
(905) 695-2229   SIC 4724
TIANJIN AUTO PARTS INC   p 754

431 WOODSPRING AVE, NEWMARKET, ON, L3X 3H5
(647) 999-9612   SIC 4731
TIBO   p 1299
See I. THIBAULT INC
TICKETMASTER   p 984
See TICKETMASTER CANADA LP
TICKETMASTER CANADA HOLDINGS ULC   p 984
1 BLUE JAYS WAY SUITE 3900, TORONTO, ON, M5V 1J3
(416) 345-9200   SIC 6712
TICKETMASTER CANADA LP   p 984
1 BLUE JAYS WAY SUITE 3900, TORONTO, ON, M5V 1J3
(416) 345-9200   SIC 7999
TICKETMASTER CANADA LP   p 1274
2505 BOUL LAURIER BUREAU 300, QUEBEC, QC, G1V 2L2
(418) 694-2300   SIC 7922
TICKETPRO INC   p 1200
1981 AV MCGILL COLLEGE BUREAU 1600, MONTREAL, QC, H3A 2Y1
(514) 849-0237   SIC 7922
TIDAL ENERGY MARKETING INC   p 61
237 4 AVE SW SUITE 2000, CALGARY, AB, T2P 4K3
(403) 205-7770   SIC 5172
TIDAL ORGANICS INCORPORATED p 465
2433 HIGHWAY UNIT 3, PUBNICO, NS, B0W 2W0
(902) 762-3525   SIC 5191
TIDAL VIEW MANOR   p 471
64 VANCOUVER ST, YARMOUTH, NS, B5A 2P5
   SIC 8051
TIDAN INC   p 1200
666 RUE SHERBROOKE O BUREAU 2300, MONTREAL, QC, H3A 1E7
(514) 845-6393   SIC 6513
TIDES CANADA INITIATIVES SOCIETY p 300
163 HASTINGS ST W SUITE 400, VANCOUVER, BC, V6B 1H5
(604) 647-6611   SIC 8699
TIDEVIEW TERRACE   p 449
See DIGBY TOWN AND MUNICIPAL HOUSING CORPORATION, THE
TIDEWATER MIDSTREAM AND INFRASTRUCTURE LTD   p 61
222 3 AVE SW SUITE 900, CALGARY, AB, T2P 0B4
(587) 475-0210   SIC 4922
TIER 1 ENERGY SOLUTIONS INC   p 117
453-97 ST EDMONTON AB, EDMONTON, AB, T6E 5Y7
(780) 476-0099   SIC 1382
TIERCON CORP   p 893
352 ARVIN AVE, STONEY CREEK, ON, L8E 2M4
(905) 662-1097   SIC 3714
TIERCON CORP   p 893
591 ARVIN AVE, STONEY CREEK, ON, L8E 5N7
(905) 643-4176   SIC 3714
TIERRA SOL CERAMIC TILE LTD   p 183
4084 MCCONNELL CRT UNIT 100, BURNABY, BC, V5A 3L8
(604) 435-5400   SIC 5032
TIFFANY & CO. CANADA   p 976
150 BLOOR ST W SUITE M108, TORONTO, ON, M5S 2X9
(416) 921-3900   SIC 5944
TIFFANY GATE FOODS INC   p 588
195 STEINWAY BLVD, ETOBICOKE, ON, M9W 6H6
(416) 213-9720   SIC 5149
TIFFANY METAL CASTING LTD   p 864
286075 COUNTY RD 10, SCARBOROUGH, ON, L9W 6P5
(519) 941-7026   SIC 3321
TIGER AUTO PARTS INC   p 869
117 SINNOTT RD, SCARBOROUGH, ON,

M1L 4S6
(888) 664-6618   SIC 5531
TIGER AUTOMOTIVE DIV OF   p 1427
See GRANDWEST ENTERPRISES INC
TIGER CALCIUM SERVICES INC   p 150
603 15 AVE, NISKU, AB, T9E 7M6
(403) 955-5004   SIC 1499
TIGER COURIER INC   p 1430
705 47TH ST E, SASKATOON, SK, S7K 5G5
(306) 242-7499   SIC 7389
TIGER DRYLAC CANADA INC   p 602
110 SOUTHGATE DR, GUELPH, ON, N1G 4P5
(519) 766-4781   SIC 2851
TIGER JEET SINGH PUBLIC SCHOOL p 683
See HALTON DISTRICT SCHOOL BOARD
TIGER MACHINING INC.   p 163
15 TURBO DR, SHERWOOD PARK, AB, T8H 2J6
   SIC 7538
TIGER NORTH AMERICA INC   p 872
1170 BIRCHMOUNT RD, SCARBOROUGH, ON, M1P 5E3
(416) 752-8100   SIC 7331
TIGER-VAC   p 1134
See TIGER-VAC INTERNATIONAL INC
TIGER-VAC INTERNATIONAL INC   p 1134
2020 BOUL DAGENAIS O, LAVAL-OUEST, QC, H7L 5W2
(450) 622-0100   SIC 5087
TIGERCAT INDUSTRIES INC   p 515
54 MORTON AVE E, BRANTFORD, ON, N3R 7J7
(519) 753-2000   SIC 3531
TIGERCAT INDUSTRIES INC   p 1035
1403 DUNDAS ST, WOODSTOCK, ON, N4S 7V9
(519) 537-3000   SIC 3531
TIGERCAT INTERNATIONAL INC   p 535
200 AVENUE RD, CAMBRIDGE, ON, N1R 8H5
(519) 620-0500   SIC 6712
TIGERTEL COMMUNICATIONS INC p 1200
550 RUE SHERBROOKE O BUREAU 1650, MONTREAL, QC, H3A 1B9
(514) 843-4313   SIC 7389
TIGES QUATRE SAISONS (2009) INC, LES p 1352
192 6E RANG, SAINT-ROSAIRE, QC, G0Z 1K0
(819) 758-1155   SIC 5051
TIGH-NA-MARA RESORT HOTEL   p 243
See TIGH-NA-MARA RESORTS LTD
TIGH-NA-MARA RESORTS LTD   p 243
1155 RESORT DR, PARKSVILLE, BC, V9P 2E3
(250) 248-2072   SIC 7011
TIGRE GEANT   p 1148
See TORA MAGOG LIMITEE
TIGRE GEANT   p 1297
See TORA SAINT-CHARLES-BORROMEE LIMITEE
TIGRE GEANT   p 1385
See TORA CAP-DE-LA-MADELEINE LIMITEE
TIGRE GEANT   p 1391
See TIGRE VAL D'OR LIMITEE
TIGRE VAL D'OR LIMITEE   p 1391
825 3E AV, VAL-D'OR, QC, J9P 1T2
(819) 825-8106   SIC 5311
TIKINAGAN CHILD & FAMILY SERVICES p 881
63 KING ST, SIOUX LOOKOUT, ON, P8T 1B1
(807) 737-3466   SIC 8322
TILBURY AUTO SALES AND RV INC. p 911
20600 COUNTY ROAD 42, TILBURY, ON, N0P 2L0
(866) 980-2512   SIC 5511
TILBURY CHRYSLER   p 911
See RALY AUTOMOTIVE GROUP LTD
TILBURY FOOD MARKET   p 911

See *K-TILBURY FOOD MARKET LTD*

TILBURY FOODLAND *p* 911
See *KNECHTEL'S FOOD MARKET*

TILBURY MANOR NURSING HOME *p* 721
See *DIVERSICARE CANADA MANAGE-MENT SERVICES CO., INC*

TILBURY MANOR NURSING HOME *p* 911
See *DIVERSICARE CANADA MANAGE-MENT SERVICES CO., INC*

TILLEY ENDURABLES, INC *p* 780
60 GERVAIS DR, NORTH YORK, ON, M3C 1Z3
(416) 441-6141 *SIC* 5699

TILLICUM HAUS SOCIETY *p* 233
602 HALIBURTON ST, NANAIMO, BC, V9R 4W5
(250) 753-6578 *SIC* 8699

TILLSONBURG & DISTRICT MULTI-SERVICE CENTRE INC *p* 912
96 TILLSON AVE, TILLSONBURG, ON, N4G 3A1
(519) 842-9000 *SIC* 8399

TILLSONBURG DISTRICT MEMORIAL HOSPITAL TRUST *p* 912
167 ROLPH ST SUITE 3100, TILLSON-BURG, ON, N4G 3Y9
(519) 842-3611 *SIC* 8062

TILLSONBURG NEWS *p* 911
See *1032451 B.C. LTD*

TILRAY *p* 235
See *TILRAY CANADA LTD*

TILRAY CANADA LTD *p* 235
1100 MAUGHAN RD, NANAIMO, BC, V9X 1J2
(250) 722-3991 *SIC* 2833

TILT-TECH CONSTRUCTION LTD *p* 175
34077 GLADYS AVE UNIT 320, ABBOTS-FORD, BC, V2S 2E8
(604) 746-5456 *SIC* 1542

TILWOOD DIRECT MARKETING INC *p* 507
300 ORENDA RD, BRAMPTON, ON, L6T 1G2
(905) 793-8225 *SIC* 5192

TILWOOD PUBLISHING SERVICES *p* 507
See *TILWOOD DIRECT MARKETING INC*

TILWOOD PUBLISHING SERVICES INC *p* 507
300 ORENDA RD, BRAMPTON, ON, L6T 1G2
(905) 793-8225 *SIC* 5192

TIM CURRY SALES LIMITED *p* 340
855 LANGFORD PKY, VICTORIA, BC, V9B 4V5
(250) 474-2291 *SIC* 5311

TIM DEALER SERVICES INCORPORATED *p* 448
250 BROWNLOW AVE SUITE 7, DART-MOUTH, NS, B3B 1W9
(902) 468-7177 *SIC* 7371

TIM HORTON CHILDREN'S FOUNDATION, INC *p* 137
GD, KANANASKIS, AB, T0L 2H0
(403) 673-2494 *SIC* 7032

TIM HORTON CHILDREN'S FOUNDATION, INC *p* 681
550 LORIMER LAKE RD, MCDOUGALL, ON, P2A 2W7
(705) 389-2773 *SIC* 7032

TIM HORTON CHILDREN'S FOUNDATION, INC *p* 888
264 GLEN MORRIS RD, ST GEORGE BRANT, ON, N0E 1N0
(519) 448-1264 *SIC* 7032

TIM HORTON CHILDREN'S FOUNDATION, INC *p* 888
264 GLEN MORRIS RD SUITE 2, ST GEORGE BRANT, ON, N0E 1N0
(519) 448-1248 *SIC* 7032

TIM HORTON CHILDREN'S RANCH *p* 137
See *TIM HORTON CHILDREN'S FOUNDA-TION, INC*

TIM HORTON MEMORIAL CAMP *p* 681
See *TIM HORTON CHILDREN'S FOUNDA-*

TION, INC

TIM HORTON ONONDAGA FARMS *p* 888
See *TIM HORTON CHILDREN'S FOUNDA-TION, INC*

TIM HORTON REGIONAL OFFICE *p* 19
See *TDL GROUP CORP, THE*

TIM HORTON REGIONAL OFFICE *p* 607
See *TDL GROUP CORP, THE*

TIM HORTONS *p* 10
See *YIKES ENTERPRISES LTD*

TIM HORTONS *p* 26
1185 49 AVE NE, CALGARY, AB, T2E 8V2
(403) 730-0556 *SIC* 5461

TIM HORTONS *p* 38
5A HERITAGE GATE SE, CALGARY, AB, T2H 3A7
(403) 692-6629 *SIC* 5461

TIM HORTONS *p* 71
11488 24 ST SE SUITE 400, CALGARY, AB, T2Z 4C9
(403) 236-3749 *SIC* 5461

TIM HORTONS *p* 75
See *ELIZABETHS BAKERY LTD*

TIM HORTONS *p* 79
See *TDL GROUP CORP, THE*

TIM HORTONS *p* 83
See *NORTH-ED (1994) LTD*

TIM HORTONS *p* 92
See *293967 ALBERTA LTD*

TIM HORTONS *p* 107
9902 153 AVE NW, EDMONTON, AB, T5X 6A4
(780) 448-9722 *SIC* 5461

TIM HORTONS *p* 133
See *S & T ALLARD FOOD LTD*

TIM HORTONS *p* 144
4301 75 AVE, LLOYDMINSTER, AB, T9V 2X4
(780) 808-2600 *SIC* 5461

TIM HORTONS *p* 178
See *I & G BISMARKATING LTD*

TIM HORTONS *p* 211
See *ADAMS 22 HOLDINGS LTD*

TIM HORTONS *p* 213
See *CHEBUCTO VENTURES CORP*

TIM HORTONS *p* 231
See *EPIC FOOD SERVICES INC*

TIM HORTONS *p* 320
See *4TH & BURRARD ESSO SERVICE*

TIM HORTONS *p* 365
See *J & S HOLDINGS INC*

TIM HORTONS *p* 370
2500 MAIN ST, WINNIPEG, MB, R2V 4Y1
(204) 334-3126 *SIC* 5461

TIM HORTONS *p* 388
570 PEMBINA HWY, WINNIPEG, MB, R3M 2M5
(204) 452-2531 *SIC* 5461

TIM HORTONS *p* 406
See *COREY CRAIG LTD*

TIM HORTONS *p* 411
280 RESTIGOUCHE RD, OROMOCTO, NB, E2V 2G9
(506) 446-9343 *SIC* 5461

TIM HORTONS *p* 413
See *SPRINGER INVESTMENTS LTD*

TIM HORTONS *p* 421
8 TRANS CANADA HWY, BISHOPS FALLS, NL, A0H 1C0
(709) 258-2156 *SIC* 5461

TIM HORTONS *p* 443
See *MAJA HOLDINGS LTD*

TIM HORTONS *p* 443
See *DOWN EAST HOSPITALITY INCOR-PORATED*

TIM HORTONS *p* 456
See *ROBIE & KEMPT SERVICES LIMITED*

TIM HORTONS *p* 458
See *ALYRIN OPERATIONS LTD*

TIM HORTONS *p* 464
See *MACDONALD, R & G ENTERPRISES LIMITED*

TIM HORTONS *p* 467
See *WILSON'S INVESTMENTS LIMITED*

TIM HORTONS *p* 474
See *R.A.F. HOLDINGS LTD*

TIM HORTONS *p* 477
See *PIONEER FOOD SERVICES LIMITED*

TIM HORTONS *p* 484
See *EAGLE'S NEST COFFEE AND BAKED GOODS INC*

TIM HORTONS *p* 492
165 COLLEGE ST W, BELLEVILLE, ON, K8P 2G7
(613) 967-2197 *SIC* 5461

TIM HORTONS *p* 496
See *MATTCO SERVICES LIMITED*

TIM HORTONS *p* 497
See *HKH OPPORTUNITIES INC*

TIM HORTONS *p* 508
15 BOVAIRD DR E, BRAMPTON, ON, L6V 0A2
(905) 456-0263 *SIC* 5963

TIM HORTONS *p* 526
See *BRULE FOODS LTD*

TIM HORTONS *p* 531
See *849432 ONTARIO LIMITED*

TIM HORTONS *p* 534
See *MCGLINCHEY ENTERPRISES LIM-ITED*

TIM HORTONS *p* 535
See *1148290 ONTARIO INC*

TIM HORTONS *p* 568
See *1459564 ONTARIO LTD*

TIM HORTONS *p* 591
See *NORMA DONUTS LIMITED*

TIM HORTONS *p* 610
136 KENILWORTH AVE N SUITE 130, HAMILTON, ON, L8H 4R8
(905) 543-1811 *SIC* 5461

TIM HORTONS *p* 615
See *1555965 ONTARIO INC*

TIM HORTONS *p* 617
See *DR. DONUT INC*

TIM HORTONS *p* 618
See *1129822 ONTARIO INC*

TIM HORTONS *p* 623
20945 DALTON RD, JACKSONS POINT, ON, L0E 1R0
(905) 722-7762 *SIC* 5461

TIM HORTONS *p* 631
See *AGNEW, J. E. FOOD SERVICES LTD*

TIM HORTONS *p* 634
See *GRAHAM, L.G. HOLDINGS INC*

TIM HORTONS *p* 636
See *940734 ONTARIO LIMITED*

TIM HORTONS *p* 652
See *1212551 ONTARIO INC*

TIM HORTONS *p* 679
See *RYASH COFFEE CORPORATION*

TIM HORTONS *p* 703
See *BURGESS, JOHN WILLIAM ENTER-PRISES INC*

TIM HORTONS *p* 751
See *JONATHAN'S DONUTS LTD*

TIM HORTONS *p* 811
See *1574942 ONTARIO LIMITED*

TIM HORTONS *p* 848
925 EDWARD ST, PRESCOTT, ON, K0E 1T0
(613) 925-1465 *SIC* 5461

TIM HORTONS *p* 857
See *ENTERPRISE PARIS INC*

TIM HORTONS *p* 860
See *ELYOD INVESTMENTS LIMITED*

TIM HORTONS *p* 870
See *2549204 ONTARIO INC*

TIM HORTONS *p* 881
See *NELSON, NELSON FOODS INC*

TIM HORTONS *p* 884
See *MORZOC INVESTMENT INC*

TIM HORTONS *p* 886
See *OJEKA GALLERY INC*

TIM HORTONS *p* 890
See *TISDELLE ENTERPRISES (EX-PRESS) LIMITED*

TIM HORTONS *p* 895
See *COFFEE COOP, THE*

TIM HORTONS *p* 897
166 ONTARIO ST, STRATFORD, ON, N5A 3H4
(519) 273-2421 *SIC* 5461

TIM HORTONS *p* 909
1127 OLIVER RD, THUNDER BAY, ON, P7B 7A4
(807) 344-0880 *SIC* 5461

TIM HORTONS *p* 923
See *YORKDALE CAFE LTD*

TIM HORTONS *p* 987
See *TDL GROUP CORP, THE*

TIM HORTONS *p* 998
See *BIG SHO FOODS LTD*

TIM HORTONS *p* 999
221 R.C.A.F. RD, TRENTON, ON, K8V 5P8
(613) 965-0555 *SIC* 7389

TIM HORTONS *p* 1004
See *1087299 ONTARIO LTD*

TIM HORTONS *p* 1006
See *828590 ONTARIO INC*

TIM HORTONS *p* 1014
See *LAARK ENTERPRISES LIMITED*

TIM HORTONS *p* 1020
See *WATSON, T.J. ENTERPRISES INC*

TIM HORTONS *p* 1029
See *770976 ONTARIO LIMITED*

TIM HORTONS *p* 1044
See *9124-4269 QUEBEC INC*

TIM HORTONS *p* 1118
See *TRANSPORT DIANE PICHE INC*

TIM HORTONS *p* 1131
See *GESTIONS PARKER-SCOTT INC*

TIM HORTONS *p* 1144
See *BEIGNES M.W.M. INC., LES*

TIM HORTONS *p* 1171
See *DAMSAR INC*

TIM HORTONS *p* 1300
See *9038-7200 QUEBEC INC*

TIM HORTONS *p* 1319
See *9098-2067 QUEBEC INC*

TIM HORTONS *p* 1369
See *GESTION DENISON TH INC*

TIM HORTONS *p* 1370
See *9317-3649 QUEBEC INC*

TIM HORTONS LTD *p* 604
1 NICHOLAS BEAVER RD, GUELPH, ON, N1H 6H9
(519) 822-4748 *SIC* 5461

TIM HORTONS RESTAURANTS *p* 1119
1225 AUT DUPLESSIS, L'ANCIENNE-LORETTE, QC, G2G 2B4
(418) 877-0989 *SIC* 5461

TIM HORTONS,DIVISION OF *p* 491
See *HANLEY CORPORATION*

TIM-BR MARTS LTD *p* 26
1601 AIRPORT RD NE SUITE 705, CAL-GARY, AB, T2E 6Z8
(403) 717-1990 *SIC* 7389

TIMBER INVESTMENT HOLDINGS INC *p* 4
262029 BALZAC BLVD, BALZAC, AB, T4B 2T3
(403) 226-8617 *SIC* 2439

TIMBER REALIZATION COMPANY LIM-ITED *p* 26
3420 12 ST NE UNIT 108, CALGARY, AB, T2E 6N1
(403) 219-3303 *SIC* 5023

TIMBER RIDGE OUTFITTERS *p* 469
See *MARGOLIANS MARITIMES LIMITED*

TIMBER-TECH TRUSS INC *p* 141
1405 31 ST N, LETHBRIDGE, AB, T1H 5G8
(403) 328-5499 *SIC* 2439

TIMBERCREEK ASSET MANAGEMENT INC *p* 930
25 PRICE ST, TORONTO, ON, M4W 1Z1
(416) 306-9967 *SIC* 6282

TIMBERCREEK FINANCIAL CORP *p* 930
25 PRICE ST, TORONTO, ON, M4W 1Z1
(416) 923-9967 *SIC* 6162

TIMBERCREEK INVESTMENT MANAGE-MENT INC *p* 931

25 PRICE ST, TORONTO, ON, M4W 1Z1
(416) 306-9967   SIC 6282

TIMBERCREEK INVESTMENTS INC p 931
25 PRICE ST, TORONTO, ON, M4W 1Z1
(416) 923-9967   SIC 6553

TIMBERFIELD ROOF TRUSS p 648
See 1312983 ONTARIO INC

TIMBERLAND EQUIPMENT LIMITED p 1036
459 INDUSTRIAL AVE, WOODSTOCK, ON, N4S 7L1
(519) 537-6262   SIC 3531

TIMBERLAND FORD INC p 913
445 ALGONQUIN BLVD W, TIMMINS, ON, P4N 2S4
(705) 268-3673   SIC 5511

TIMBERLAND HOTEL CORPORATION p 136
114 PARK ST, HINTON, AB, T7V 2B1
(780) 865-2231   SIC 5921

TIMBERLEA PUBLIC SCHOOL p 129
See FORT MCMURRAY PUBLIC SCHOOL DISTRICT #2833

TIMBERTOWN BUILDING CENTRE LTD p 26
3440 12 ST NE SUITE G, CALGARY, AB, T2E 6N1
(403) 291-1317   SIC 5211

TIMBERWEST p 316
See TIMBERWEST FOREST COMPANY

TIMBERWEST FOREST COMPANY p 316
1055 GEORGIA ST W SUITE 2300, VANCOUVER, BC, V6E 0B6
(604) 654-4600   SIC 0831

TIMBERWEST FOREST CORP p 316
2000-1055 HASTINGS ST W, VANCOUVER, BC, V6E 2E9
(604) 654-4600   SIC 5099

TIMBERWOLF FOREST PRODUCTS INC p 477
7781 HOWARD AVE, AMHERSTBURG, ON, N0R 1J0
(519) 726-9653   SIC 5085

TIMBERWOLF FOREST PRODUCTS INC p 1024
2015 NORTH TALBOT RD, WINDSOR, ON, N9A 6J3
SIC 5085

TIMBRO p 1012
See TIMMS, R CONSTRUCTION AND ENGINEERING LIMITED, THE

TIMCAL GRAPHITE & CARBONE p 1381
See IMERYS GRAPHITE & CARBON CANADA INC

TIMCON CONSTRUCTION (1988) LTD p 156
7445 45 AVE CLOSE SUITE 100, RED DEER, AB, T4P 4C2
(403) 347-1953   SIC 1542

TIME BOMB TRADING INC p 194
8067 NORTH FRASER WAY, BURNABY, BC, V5J 5M8
(604) 251-1097   SIC 5139

TIME BOUTIQUE p 288
See ANN-LOUISE JEWELLERS LTD

TIME BUSINESS MACHINES LTD p 103
17620 107 AVE NW, EDMONTON, AB, T5S 1G8
(780) 483-3040   SIC 5999

TIME CHECK PLUS p 855
See FAR EAST WATCHCASES LTD

TIMECO WATCH & CLOCK REPAIRS LTD p 189
4459 CANADA WAY, BURNABY, BC, V5G 1J3
(604) 435-6383   SIC 7631

TIMES & TRANSCRIPT p 406
See BRUNSWICK NEWS INC

TIMES COLONIST p 334
See GLACIER MEDIA INC

TIMES FIBER CANADA LIMITED p 850
580 O'BRIEN RD, RENFREW, ON, K7V 3Z2
(613) 432-8566   SIC 3669

TIMEX GROUP CANADA, INC p 676
7300 WARDEN AVE 115, MARKHAM, ON,

L3R 9Z6
(905) 477-8463   SIC 5094

TIMISKAMING CHILD AND FAMILY SERVICES p
753
25 PAGET ST, NEW LISKEARD, ON, P0J 1P0
(705) 647-1200   SIC 8322

TIMISKAMING DISTRICT SECONDARY SCHOOL p 753
See DISTRICT SCHOOL BOARD ONTARIO NORTH EAST

TIMISKAMING HEALTH UNIT p 753
See BOARD OF HEALTH FOR THE TIMISKAMING HEALTH UNIT

TIMKEN CANADA LP p 690
5955 AIRPORT RD SUITE 100, MISSISSAUGA, ON, L4V 1R9
(905) 826-9520   SIC 3562

TIMKEN CANADA LP p 1430
868 60TH ST E, SASKATOON, SK, S7K 8G8
(306) 931-3343   SIC 3599

TIMMINCO LIMITED p 958
150 KING ST W SUITE 2401, TORONTO, ON, M5H 1J9
(416) 364-5171   SIC 3339

TIMMINCO METALS, DIV OF p 958
See TIMMINCO LIMITED

TIMMINCO SOLAR p 1056
See SILICIUM BECANCOUR INC

TIMMINS AND DISTRICT HOSPITAL p 913
700 ROSS AVE E SUITE 1559, TIMMINS, ON, P4N 8P2
(705) 267-2131   SIC 8062

TIMMINS GARAGE p 619
See EXPERT GARAGE LIMITED

TIMMINS GARAGE INCORPORATED p 913
1395 RIVERSIDE DR, TIMMINS, ON, P4R 1A6
(705) 268-4122   SIC 5511

TIMMINS KENWORTH LTD p 913
4041 HWY 101 W, TIMMINS, ON, P4R 0E8
(705) 268-7800   SIC 5511

TIMMINS NISSAN p 913
See BUPONT MOTORS INC

TIMMS, R CONSTRUCTION AND ENGINEERING LIMITED, THE p 1012
34 EAST MAIN ST SUITE B, WELLAND, ON, L3B 3W3
(905) 734-4513   SIC 1542

TINK PROFITABILITE NUMERIQUE INC p 1212
87 RUE PRINCE BUREAU 140, MONTREAL, QC, H3C 2M7
(514) 866-0995   SIC 7371

TINKA RESOURCES LIMITED p 317
1090 GEORGIA ST W SUITE 1305, VANCOUVER, BC, V6E 3V7
(604) 685-9316   SIC 1031

TIO NETWORKS CORP p 310
250 HOWE ST UNIT 1550, VANCOUVER, BC, V6C 3R8
(604) 298-4636   SIC 6211

TIP TOP BINDERY LTD p 877
335 PASSMORE AVE, SCARBOROUGH, ON, M1V 4B5
(416) 609-3281   SIC 2789

TIP TOP PARTS p 280
See SHAIR SALES LTD

TIPCO INC p 507
1 COVENTRY RD, BRAMPTON, ON, L6T 4B1
(905) 791-9811   SIC 3544

TIPPET-RICHARDSON LIMITED p 596
See SHEFFIELD MOVING AND STORAGE INC

TIRCONNELL PHARMACY LIMITED p 718
3163 WINSTON CHURCHILL BLVD SUITE 1098, MISSISSAUGA, ON, L5L 2W1
(905) 607-7871   SIC 5912

TIRE DISCOUNTER GROUP INC p 864
65379 COUNTY RD 3, SCARBOROUGH,

ON, L9W 7J8
(519) 941-4136   SIC 5014

TIRE RECYCLING ATLANTIC CANADA CORPORATION p
149 INDUSTRIAL PARK RD, MINTO, NB, E4B 3A6
(506) 327-4355   SIC 5531

TIRE TERMINAL, THE p 690
See 1371500 ONTARIO INC

TIRE WAREHOUSE, THE p 117
See WAYNE'S TIRE WAREHOUSE LTD

TIRECRAFT p 103
See TIRECRAFT EDMONTON TRUCK CENTRE INC

TIRECRAFT AUTO CENTER p 229
See TCBC HOLDINGS INC

TIRECRAFT EDMONTON TRUCK CENTRE INC p 103
17803 118 AVE NW, EDMONTON, AB, T5S 1L6
(780) 452-4481   SIC 5531

TIRECRAFT WESTERN CANADA LTD p 94
14404 128 AVE NW, EDMONTON, AB, T5L 3H6
(780) 509-1664   SIC 5531

TIREKICKER INSPECTIONS INC p 622
3230 THOMAS ST, INNISFIL, ON, L9S 3W5
(705) 436-4111   SIC 5012

TIREMASTER LIMITED p 510
145 ORENDA RD, BRAMPTON, ON, L6W 1W3
(905) 453-4300   SIC 5014

TIRU (CANADA) INC p 1257
1210 BOUL MONTMORENCY, QUEBEC, QC, G1J 3V9
(418) 648-8818   SIC 4953

TISDALE HOSPITAL p 1437
See KELSEY TRAIL REGIONAL HEALTH AUTHORITY

TISDALE SALES & SERVICES LTD p 1408
105 11 AVE E, KINDERSLEY, SK, S0L 1S0
(306) 463-2686   SIC 5511

TISDELLE ENTERPRISES (EXPRESS) LIMITED p
890
6 PRINCESS AVE SUITE 5, ST THOMAS, ON, N5R 3V2
(519) 631-0116   SIC 5812

TISI CANADA INC p 805
781 WESTGATE RD, OAKVILLE, ON, L6L 6R7
(905) 845-9542   SIC 3398

TISI INSPECTION SERVICES p 805
See TISI CANADA INC

TISSUS MASTER LTEE, LES p 1051
7963 RUE ALFRED, ANJOU, QC, H1J 1J3
(514) 351-9715   SIC 5131

TISSUS RENTEX INC., LES p 1158
8650 CH DELMEADE, MONT-ROYAL, QC, H4T 1L6
(514) 735-2641   SIC 2258

TITAN ACADIE BATHURST p 395
See TITAN ACADIE BATHURST (2013) INC, LE

TITAN ACADIE BATHURST (2013) INC, LE p 395
14 SEAN COUTURIER AVE, BATHURST, NB, E2A 6X2
(506) 549-3300   SIC 7941

TITAN AUTOMOTIVE GROUP LTD p 1421
755 BROAD ST, REGINA, SK, S4R 8G3
(306) 775-3388   SIC 5511

TITAN ENVIRONMENTAL CONTAINMENT LTD p 351
777 QUEST BLVD, ILE DES CHENES, MB, R0A 0T1
(204) 878-3955   SIC 1629

TITAN FOUNDRY p 19
See TROJAN INDUSTRIES INC

TITAN LUMBER CORP p 78
4615 39 ST, CAMROSE, AB, T4V 0Z4
(780) 608-1236   SIC 5211

TITAN METALS LTD p 998
5982 6TH LINE, TOTTENHAM, ON, L0G

1W0
(905) 729-4347   SIC 1761

TITAN MINING CORPORATION p 310
999 CANADA PL UNIT 555, VANCOUVER, BC, V6C 3C1
(604) 687-1717   SIC 1031

TITAN SECURITE p 1171
See 9270-6258 QUEBEC INC

TITAN SUPPLY p 111
See TS LP

TITAN TOOL & DIE LIMITED p 1021
2801 HOWARD AVE, WINDSOR, ON, N8X 3Y1
(519) 966-1234   SIC 3469

TITAN TRAILERS INC p 564
1129 HIGHWAY 3, DELHI, ON, N4B 2W6
(519) 688-4826   SIC 3715

TITAN TUBULAR SOLUTIONS LTD p 150
606 22 AVE, NISKU, AB, T9E 7X6
(780) 955-7002   SIC 5051

TITAN WORLDWIDE MATERIALS HANDLING SOLUTIONS, DIV OF p
910
See THUNDER BAY HYDRAULICS LTD

TITANIUM LOGISTICS INC p 495
32 SIMPSON RD, BOLTON, ON, L7E 1G9
(905) 851-1688   SIC 4731

TITANIUM TRANSPORTATION GROUP INC p 495
32 SIMPSON RD, BOLTON, ON, L7E 1G9
(905) 851-1688   SIC 4231

TITANIUM TRUCKING SERVICES INC p 495
32 SIMPSON RD, BOLTON, ON, L7E 1G9
(905) 851-1688   SIC 4213

TITLE & JONES INVESTMENTS LTD p 707
4230 SHERWOODTOWNE BLVD, MISSISSAUGA, ON, L4Z 2G6
(905) 281-3463   SIC 6798

TITLEIST FOOTJOY p 754
See ACUSHNET CANADA INC

TITUS INC p 826
343 PRESTON ST SUITE 800, OTTAWA, ON, K1S 1N4
(613) 820-5111   SIC 7372

TIVERON FARMS p 708
See 783312 ONTARIO LIMITED

TIW STEEL PLATEWORK INC p 885
23 SMITH ST, ST CATHARINES, ON, L2P 3J7
(905) 684-9421   SIC 3441

TIW WESTERN INC p 19
7770 44 ST SE, CALGARY, AB, T2C 2L5
(403) 279-8310   SIC 3433

TJ AUTO PARTS p 754
See TIANJIN AUTO PARTS INC

TKS CONTROLS LTD p 167
4605 41 ST, STETTLER, AB, T0C 2L0
(403) 740-4071   SIC 5084

TLABC p 317
See TRIAL LAWYERS ASSOCIATION OF BRITISH COLUMBIA

TLC p 431
See TLC NURSING AND HOME CARE SERVICES LIMITED

TLC NURSING AND HOME CARE SERVICES LIMITED p
431
25 ANDERSON AVE, ST. JOHN'S, NL, A1B 3E4
(709) 726-3473   SIC 8741

TLD (CANADA) INC p 1372
800 RUE CABANA, SHERBROOKE, QC, J1K 3C3
(819) 566-8118   SIC 3531

TLI CHO CONSTRUCTION LTD p 435
GD, BEHCHOKO, NT, X0E 0Y0
(867) 766-4909   SIC 1542

TLI CHO LOGISTICS INC p 436
25 STANTON PLAZA, YELLOWKNIFE, NT, X1A 2N6
(867) 920-7288   SIC 8742

TLS p 1024
See TRANSIT LOGISTICS SOLUTIONS INC

TLTC HOLDINGS INC *p 227*
6270 205 ST, LANGLEY, BC, V2Y 1N7
(604) 533-3294 *SIC 2759*

TM CANADA ACQUISITION CORP *p 256*
3831 NO. 6 RD, RICHMOND, BC, V6V 1P6
(604) 270-6899 *SIC 6712*

TM4 INC *p 1067*
135 RUE J.-A.-BOMBARDIER BUREAU 25, BOUCHERVILLE, QC, J4B 8P1
(450) 645-1444 *SIC 3621*

TMAC RESOURCES INC *p 967*
95 WELLINGTON ST W SUITE 1010, TORONTO, ON, M5J 2N7
(416) 628-0216 *SIC 1041*

TMCC *p 1419*
See THYSSEN MINING CONSTRUCTION OF CANADA LTD

TME *p 743*
See TORONTO MICROELECTRONICS INC

TMF FOODS *p 892*
See MEAT FACTORY LIMITED, THE

TMG LOGISTICS INC *p 273*
14722 64 AVE UNIT 9, SURREY, BC, V3S 1X7
(604) 598-3680 *SIC 4213*

TMG NORTH AMERICA INC *p 589*
155 REXDALE BLVD SUITE 207, ETOBICOKE, ON, M9W 5Z8
(416) 303-3504 *SIC 5084*

TML SUPPLY COMPANY *p 842*
See TRENT METALS (2012) LIMITED

TMMC *p 539*
See TOYOTA MOTOR MANUFACTURING CANADA INC

TMS *p 225*
See TMS TRANSPORTATION MANAGEMENT SERVICES LTD

TMS *p 332*
See TOLKO MARKETING AND SALES LTD

TMS FULFILMENT INC *p 707*
5641 MCADAM RD, MISSISSAUGA, ON, L4Z 1N9
(416) 706-9658 *SIC 7389*

TMS INTERNATIONAL CANADA LIMITED *p 971*
199 BAY ST SUITE 5300, TORONTO, ON, M5L 1B9
SIC 5093

TMS TRANSPORTATION *p 224*
See 425480 B.C. LTD

TMS TRANSPORTATION MANAGEMENT SERVICES LTD *p 225*
9975 199B ST, LANGLEY, BC, V1M 3G4
(604) 882-2550 *SIC 6712*

TMT *p 994*
See TERRAZZO MOSAIC & TILE COMPANY LIMITED

TMX GROUP LIMITED *p 958*
100 ADELAIDE ST W SUITE 300, TORONTO, ON, M5H 1S3
(416) 947-4670 *SIC 6231*

TN ARENA LIMITED PARTNERSHIP *p 379*
345 GRAHAM AVE, WINNIPEG, MB, R3C 5S6
(204) 987-7825 *SIC 7941*

TN ICEPLEX LIMITED PARTNERSHIP *p 387*
3969 PORTAGE AVE, WINNIPEG, MB, R3K 1W4
SIC 7999

TNG CANADA *p 527*
See 1087338 ONTARIO LIMITED

TNR INDUSTRIAL DOORS INC *p 488*
200 FAIRVIEW RD UNIT 2, BARRIE, ON, L4N 8X8
(705) 792-9968 *SIC 3442*

TNR INDUSTRIES *p 488*
See TNR INDUSTRIAL DOORS INC

TNT CRANE & RIGGING CANADA INC *p 177*
2190 CARPENTER ST, ABBOTSFORD, BC, V2T 6B4
(800) 667-2215 *SIC 7353*

TNT FOODS INTERNATIONAL INC *p 507*
20 WESTWYN CRT, BRAMPTON, ON, L6T 4T5
(905) 672-1787 *SIC 2015*

TNT FOODS INTERNATIONAL INC *p 507*
20 WESTWYN CRT, BRAMPTON, ON, L6T 4T5
(905) 672-1787 *SIC 5144*

TNT TOURS *p 930*
See TEMPLE AND TEMPLE TOURS INC

TO-LE-DO FOODSERVICE *p 393*
See TO-LE-DO FOODSERVICE REALTY HOLDINGS LTD

TO-LE-DO FOODSERVICE REALTY HOLDINGS LTD *p 393*
2430 MCGILLIVRAY BLVD, WINNIPEG, MB, R3Y 1G6
(204) 487-3340 *SIC 5147*

TOASTY PISTACHIOS ROASTING & COATING *p 738*
See CENTRAL ROAST INC

TOBIQUE FARMS OPERATING (2012) LIMITED *p 398*
2424 ROUTE 108, DSL DE DRUMMOND, NB, E3Y 2K7
(506) 553-9913 *SIC 5148*

TOCAN HOLDING CORP *p 704*
1333 TONOLLI RD, MISSISSAUGA, ON, L4Y 4C2
(905) 279-9555 *SIC 3341*

TODAY'S COLONIAL FURNITURE *p 811*
See TODAY'S COLONIAL FURNITURE 2000 INC

TODAY'S COLONIAL FURNITURE 2000 INC *p 811*
1680 VIMONT CRT SUITE 100, ORLEANS, ON, K4A 3M3
(613) 837-5900 *SIC 5712*

TODAY'S TRUCKING MAGAZINE *p 996*
See NEWCOM MEDIA INC

TODD'S YIG 803 LTD *p 607*
5121 COUNTY RD 21 RR 3, HALIBURTON, ON, K0M 1S0
(705) 455-9775 *SIC 5411*

TODDGLEN MANAGEMENT LIMITED *p 768*
2225 SHEPPARD AVE E SUITE 1100, NORTH YORK, ON, M2J 5C2
(416) 492-2450 *SIC 8741*

TODDGLEN WINDERMERE LIMITED *p 768*
2225 SHEPPARD AVE E SUITE 1100, NORTH YORK, ON, M2J 5C2
(416) 492-2450 *SIC 8742*

TOFIELD HEALTH CENTER *p 170*
5543 44 ST, TOFIELD, AB, T0B 4J0
(780) 662-3263 *SIC 8062*

TOFIELD I G A *p 170*
See HARE FOODS LTD

TOFINO RESORT + MARINA INC *p 283*
634 CAMPBELL ST, TOFINO, BC, V0R 2Z0
(250) 725-3277 *SIC 7011*

TOITURES COUTURE & ASSOCIES INC *p 1309*
6565 BOUL MARICOURT, SAINT-HUBERT, QC, J3Y 1S8
(450) 678-2562 *SIC 1761*

TOITURES FECTEAU INC *p 1294*
320 RTE 271, SAINT-BENOIT-LABRE, QC, G0M 1P0
(418) 228-9651 *SIC 2439*

TOITURES HOGUE INC, LES *p 1060*
745 BOUL INDUSTRIEL, BLAINVILLE, QC, J7C 3V3
(450) 435-6336 *SIC 1761*

TOITURES P.L.C. INC, LES *p 1133*
235 RUE DE LA STATION, LAURIER-STATION, QC, G0S 1N0
(418) 682-2033 *SIC 2439*

TOITURES VICK & ASSOCIES INC, LES *p 1376*
71 CH GODIN, SHERBROOKE, QC, J1R 0S6
(450) 658-4300 *SIC 1761*

TOKMAKJIAN INC *p 559*
221 CALDARI RD, CONCORD, ON, L4K 3Z9
(905) 669-2850 *SIC 4142*

TOKYU CANADA CORPORATION *p 310*
999 CANADA PL SUITE 515, VANCOUVER, BC, V6C 3E1
SIC 7011

TOLIN ENTERPRISES LTD *p 559*
400 CREDITSTONE RD, CONCORD, ON, L4K 3Z3
(905) 669-2711 *SIC 1522*

TOLKO FOREST PRODUCTS LTD *p 332*
3000 28 ST, VERNON, BC, V1T 9W9
(250) 545-4411 *SIC 2421*

TOLKO INDUSTRIES LTD *p 135*
11401 92 ST SS 1 SUITE 1, HIGH LEVEL, AB, T0H 1Z0
(780) 926-3781 *SIC 2421*

TOLKO INDUSTRIES LTD *p 135*
HWY 2 W, HIGH PRAIRIE, AB, T0G 1E0
(780) 523-2101 *SIC 2631*

TOLKO INDUSTRIES LTD *p 180*
844 OTTER LAKE CROSS RD, ARMSTRONG, BC, V0E 1B6
(250) 546-3171 *SIC 2421*

TOLKO INDUSTRIES LTD *p 198*
6200 JEFFERS DR, COLDSTREAM, BC, V1B 3G4
(250) 545-4992 *SIC 2421*

TOLKO INDUSTRIES LTD *p 218*
6275 OLD HWY 5, KAMLOOPS, BC, V2H 1T8
(250) 578-7212 *SIC 2435*

TOLKO INDUSTRIES LTD *p 232*
1750 LINDLEY CREEK RD, MERRITT, BC, V1K 0A2
(250) 378-2224 *SIC 2421*

TOLKO INDUSTRIES LTD *p 252*
1879 BROWNMILLER RD, QUESNEL, BC, V2J 6R9
(250) 992-1700 *SIC 2421*

TOLKO INDUSTRIES LTD *p 332*
3000 28 ST, VERNON, BC, V1T 1W1
(250) 545-4411 *SIC 2421*

TOLKO INDUSTRIES LTD *p 344*
5000 SODA CREEK RD, WILLIAMS LAKE, BC, V2G 5E4
(250) 398-3600 *SIC 2421*

TOLKO INDUSTRIES LTD *p 360*
HWY 10 N, THE PAS, MB, R9A 1L4
(204) 623-7411 *SIC 2674*

TOLKO INDUSTRIES LTD *p 360*
HWY 10 N, THE PAS, MB, R9A 1S1
(204) 623-7411 *SIC 2499*

TOLKO MANITOBA KRAFT PAPERS, DIV OF *p 360*
See TOLKO INDUSTRIES LTD

TOLKO MANITOBA SOLID WOOD DIVISION *p 360*
See TOLKO INDUSTRIES LTD

TOLKO MARKETING AND SALES LTD *p 332*
3000 28 ST, VERNON, BC, V1T 9W9
(250) 545-4411 *SIC 5031*

TOLKO, DIV OF *p 1410*
See MEADOW LAKE OSB LIMITED PARTNERSHIP

TOLL PLAZA COBEQUID PASS *p 450*
See ATLANTIC HIGHWAYS MANAGEMENT CORPORATION LIMITED

TOLLESTRUP HOLDINGS LTD *p 143*
806 2 AVE S, LETHBRIDGE, AB, T1J 0C6
(403) 328-8196 *SIC 1611*

TOLLOS *p 485*
See 1073849 ONTARIO LIMITED

TOLLOS MANUFACTURING *p 485*
See 2437090 ONTARIO LTD

TOLMIE, M. B. DRUGS LTD *p 682*
9226 93 HWY, MIDLAND, ON, L4R 4K4
(705) 526-7855 *SIC 5912*

TOM HARRIS CELLULAR LTD *p 339*
3680 UPTOWN BLVD UNIT 209, VICTORIA, BC, V8Z 0B9
(250) 360-0606 *SIC 5999*

TOM LEE MUSIC CO. LTD *p 300*
650 GEORGIA ST W SUITE 310, VANCOUVER, BC, V6B 4N7
(604) 685-2521 *SIC 5736*

TOM MARA ENTERPRISE LIMITED *p 463*
699 WESTVILLE RD, NEW GLASGOW, NS, B2H 2J6
(902) 755-5581 *SIC 5531*

TOM'S INDEPENDENT GROCER *p 1421*
336 N MCCARTHY BLVD SUITE A, REGINA, SK, S4R 7M2
(306) 949-1255 *SIC 5411*

TOMANICK GROUP, THE *p 151*
10 SOUTHRIDGE DR, OKOTOKS, AB, T1S 1N1
(403) 995-0224 *SIC 5812*

TOMASSO'S ITALIAN GRILLE *p 999*
See KOTSOVOS RESTAURANTS LIMITED

TOMATES BONBON *p 1262*
See QUEBEC MULTIPLANTS

TOMATO KING 2010 INC *p 996*
165 THE QUEENSWAY SUITE 232, TORONTO, ON, M8Y 1H8
(416) 259-5410 *SIC 5148*

TOMCO PRODUCTION SERVICES LTD *p 159*
4227 46TH AVE, ROCKY MOUNTAIN HOUSE, AB, T4T 1A8
(403) 844-2141 *SIC 1389*

TOMKINSON, D.N. INVESTMENTS LTD *p 65*
340 12 AVE SW SUITE 900, CALGARY, AB, T2R 1L5
(403) 269-8887 *SIC 8713*

TOMLINSON ENVIRONMENTAL SERVICES LTD *p 752*
970 MOODIE DR, NEPEAN, ON, K2R 1H3
(613) 820-2332 *SIC 3559*

TOMLINSON, R. W. LIMITED *p 832*
100 CITIGATE DR, OTTAWA, ON, K2J 6K7
(613) 822-1867 *SIC 1411*

TOMLINSON, R. W. LIMITED *p 1002*
8125 RUSSELL RD, VARS, ON, K0A 3H0
(613) 835-3395 *SIC 5211*

TOMMY HILFIGER *p 744*
See PVH CANADA, INC

TOMMY'S TRANSPORT, DIV OF *p 123*
See RED CARPET TRANSPORT LTD

TOMRA CANADA INC *p 1054*
20500 AV CLARK-GRAHAM, BAIE-D'URFE, QC, H9X 4B6
(514) 457-4177 *SIC 5084*

TONA LOGISTICS *p 726*
See PIONEER HI-BRED LIMITED

TONA, ALAN PHARMACY LIMITED *p 545*
270 SPRING ST, COBOURG, ON, K9A 3K2
(905) 372-3333 *SIC 5912*

TONDA CONSTRUCTION LIMITED *p 662*
1085 WILTON GROVE RD, LONDON, ON, N6N 1C9
(519) 686-5200 *SIC 1542*

TONE TAI SUPERMARKET *p 766*
See 2100050 ONTARIO INC

TONER CHEVROLET BUICK GMC LTD *p 403*
877 BOUL EVERARD H DAIGLE, GRAND-SAULT/GRAND FALLS, NB, E3Z 3C7
(506) 473-2727 *SIC 5511*

TONER EXPRESS *p 742*
See PHILIP BUSINESS DEVELOPMENT & INVESTMENT LTD.

TONIK-GROUPIMAGE *p 1052*
See SAJY COMMUNICATIONS INC

TONOLLI CANADA *p 524*
See REVOLUTION VSC LP

TONY GRAHAM KANATA LIMITED *p 627*
2500 PALLADIUM DR SUITE 600, KANATA, ON, K2V 1E2
(613) 271-8200 *SIC 5511*

TONY GRAHAM NISSAN *p 751*
See GRAHAM AUTOMOTIVE SALES LTD

TONY ROMA'S *p 37*
See SOUTH ALBERTA RIBS (2002) LTD

TONY ROMA'S *p 104*

See ALBERTS RESTAURANTS LTD
TONY ROMA'S *p 943*
See ONTARIO RIBS INC
TONY'S NO FRILLS LTD *p 617*
770 UPPER JAMES ST SUITE 723, HAMILTON, ON, L9C 3A2
(905) 574-2069 *SIC 5411*
TOOLBOX SOLUTIONS INC *p 507*
126 DEVON RD SUITE 2, BRAMPTON, ON, L6T 5B3
(905) 458-9262 *SIC 7379*
TOOLBOXSOLUTIONS.COM *p 507*
See TOOLBOX SOLUTIONS INC
TOOLE PEET & CO LIMITED *p 67*
1135 17 AVE SW, CALGARY, AB, T2T 0B6
(403) 245-4366 *SIC 6531*
TOOLE PEET INSURANCE *p 67*
See TOOLE PEET & CO LIMITED
TOOLPLAS SYSTEMS INC *p 807*
1905 BLACKACRE DR, OLDCASTLE, ON, N0R 1L0
(519) 737-9948 *SIC 3089*
TOOLQUIP AGENCY LTD *p 571*
270 BROWNS LINE, ETOBICOKE, ON, M8W 3T5
SIC 5013
TOOLWAY INDUSTRIES LTD *p 1028*
31 CONAIR PKY, WOODBRIDGE, ON, L4H 0S4
(905) 326-5450 *SIC 5084*
TOON BOOM ANIMATION INC *p 1184*
4200 BOUL SAINT-LAURENT BUREAU 1020, MONTREAL, QC, H2W 2R2
(514) 278-8666 *SIC 5734*
TOONBOX ENTERTAINMENT LTD *p 921*
100 BROADVIEW AVE UNIT 400, TORONTO, ON, M4M 3H3
(416) 362-8783 *SIC 7812*
TOOR & ASSOCIATES INC *p 806*
270 NORTH SERVICE RD W, OAKVILLE, ON, L6M 2R8
(905) 849-8100 *SIC 5812*
TOOTSI IMPEX INC *p 1336*
8800 BOUL HENRI-BOURASSA O, SAINT-LAURENT, QC, H4S 1P4
(514) 381-9790 *SIC 5145*
TOOTSIE ROLL OF CANADA ULC *p 559*
345 COURTLAND AVE, CONCORD, ON, L4K 5A6
(905) 660-8989 *SIC 5145*
TOOTSIE ROLL OF CANADA ULC *p 559*
519 NORTH RIVERMEDE RD, CONCORD, ON, L4K 3N1
(905) 738-9108 *SIC 2064*
TOOTSIES FACTORY SHOE MARKET *p 514*
See 991909 ONTARIO INC
TOP ACES INC *p 1091*
79B BOUL BRUNSWICK, DOLLARD-DES-ORMEAUX, QC, H9B 2J5
(514) 694-5565 *SIC 8299*
TOP ACES INC *p 1095*
1675 RTE TRANSCANADIENNE BUREAU 201, DORVAL, QC, H9P 1J1
(514) 694-5565 *SIC 8299*
TOP BEDDING *p 1047*
See LAREAU, FRANK INC
TOP CROP GARDEN FARM & PET *p 204*
2101 CRANBROOK ST N, CRANBROOK, BC, V1C 5M6
(250) 489-4555 *SIC 0181*
TOP GRADE MOLDS LTD *p 701*
929 PANTERA DR, MISSISSAUGA, ON, L4W 2R9
(905) 625-9865 *SIC 3544*
TOP LIFT ENTERPRISES INC *p 893*
42 PINELANDS AVE, STONEY CREEK, ON, L8E 5X9
(905) 662-4137 *SIC 5084*
TOP NOTCH CONSTRUCTION LTD *p 19*
5415 56 AVE SE, CALGARY, AB, T2C 3X6
SIC 1794
TOP RANK BUSINESS ASSOCIATES GROUP OF COMPANY INC *p 917*
2863 ST CLAIR AVE E, TORONTO, ON,

M4B 1N4
SIC 8741
TOP SHOP INC, THE *p 650*
502 FIRST ST, LONDON, ON, N5V 1Z3
(519) 455-9400 *SIC 5211*
TOP-CO INC *p 123*
7720 17 ST NW, EDMONTON, AB, T6P 1S7
(780) 440-4440 *SIC 3559*
TOPAC ENTERPRISES INC *p 495*
9 SIMPSON RD, BOLTON, ON, L7E 1E4
(905) 857-2209 *SIC 4212*
TOPAC EXPRESS *p 495*
See TOPAC ENTERPRISES INC
TOPAX PROTEKTIVEPACKAGING *p 548*
See 473464 ONTARIO LIMITED
TOPCO MFG RECERTIFICATION CENTRE, DIV OF *p 121*
See TOPCO OILSITE PRODUCTS LTD
TOPCO OILSITE PRODUCTS LTD *p 121*
9519 28 AVE NW, EDMONTON, AB, T6N 0A3
(800) 222-6448 *SIC 1389*
TOPCROP *p 570*
See ESSEX TOPCROP SALES LIMITED
TOPLINE TRAILER & EQUIPMENT SALES, DIV OF *p 1016*
See WEAGANT FARM SUPPLIES LIMITED
TOPMADE ENTERPRISES LTD *p 19*
7177 40 ST SE, CALGARY, AB, T2C 2H7
(403) 236-7557 *SIC 5141*
TOPPITS *p 1034*
See TOPPITS FOODS LTD
TOPPITS FOODS LTD *p 1034*
301 CHRISLEA RD, WOODBRIDGE, ON, L4L 8N4
(905) 850-8900 *SIC 5146*
TOPRINGS LTEE *p 1111*
1020 BOUL INDUSTRIEL, GRANBY, QC, J2J 1A4
(450) 375-1828 *SIC 5085*
TOPS PRODUCTS CANADA *p 732*
See MOORE CANADA CORPORATION
TOPS PRODUCTS CANADA *p 1050*
See MOORE CANADA CORPORATION
TOPVIEW TECHNOLOGY CORP *p 257*
14488 KNOX WAY UNIT 123, RICHMOND, BC, V6V 2Z5
(604) 231-5858 *SIC 3634*
TOR BAY FISHERIES LIMITED *p 460*
472 TOR BAY BRANCH RD, LARRYS RIVER, NS, B0H 1T0
(902) 525-2423 *SIC 7389*
TORA *p 884*
See TORA INVESTMENTS INC
TORA CAP-DE-LA-MADELEINE LIMITEE *p 1385*
800 BOUL THIBEAU, TROIS-RIVIERES, QC, G8T 7A6
(819) 697-3833 *SIC 5311*
TORA INVESTMENTS INC *p 884*
15 CUSHMAN RD, ST CATHARINES, ON, L2M 6S7
(905) 227-5088 *SIC 7549*
TORA INVESTMENTS INC *p 884*
453 EASTCHESTER AVE E, ST CATHARINES, ON, L2M 6S2
(905) 685-5409 *SIC 7549*
TORA LONDON LIMITED *p 652*
1251 HURON ST, LONDON, ON, N5Y 4V1
(613) 521-8222 *SIC 5399*
TORA MAGOG LIMITEE *p 1148*
1730 RUE SHERBROOKE, MAGOG, QC, J1X 2T3
(819) 843-3043 *SIC 5399*
TORA SAINT-CHARLES-BORROMEE LIMITEE *p 1297*
197 RUE DE LA VISITATION BUREAU 109, SAINT-CHARLES-BORROMEE, QC, J6E 4N6
(450) 760-3568 *SIC 5311*
TORA STRATFORD LIMITED *p 897*
477 HURON ST, STRATFORD, ON, N5A 5T8
(519) 272-2029 *SIC 5399*

TORA WESTERN CANADA LTD *p 11*
4710 17 AVE SE SUITE G2, CALGARY, AB, T2A 0V1
(403) 207-5200 *SIC 5137*
TORBA RESTAURANTS INC *p 879*
6 FATHER COSTELLO DR, SCHUMACHER, ON, P0N 1G0
(705) 267-4150 *SIC 5812*
TORBAY AERO SERVICES *p 428*
See PAL AERO SERVICES LTD
TORBRAM ELECTRIC SUPPLY CORPORATION *p 227*
6360 202 ST SUITE 103, LANGLEY, BC, V2Y 1N2
(604) 539-9331 *SIC 5063*
TORBRIDGE CONSTRUCTION LTD *p 559*
3300 HIGHWAY 7 SUITE 803, CONCORD, ON, L4K 4M3
SIC 1611
TORBRIDGE CONSTRUCTION LTD *p 589*
61 STEINWAY BLVD, ETOBICOKE, ON, M9W 6H6
(905) 669-3909 *SIC 1622*
TORC OIL & GAS LTD *p 61*
525 8 AVE SW SUITE 1800, CALGARY, AB, T2P 1G1
(403) 930-4120 *SIC 1381*
TORCAD LIMITED *p 576*
275 NORSEMAN ST, ETOBICOKE, ON, M8Z 2R5
(416) 239-3928 *SIC 3471*
TORCAN LIFT EQUIPMENT LTD *p 559*
166 BOWES RD, CONCORD, ON, L4K 1J6
(905) 760-1582 *SIC 5084*
TORCAN LIFT EQUIPMENT LTD *p 795*
115 RIVALDA RD, NORTH YORK, ON, M9M 2M6
(416) 743-2500 *SIC 7353*
TORCE FINANCIAL GROUPE INC *p 1324*
575 RUE DORAIS, SAINT-LAURENT, QC, H4M 1Z7
SIC 8741
TOREX GOLD RESOURCES INC *p 987*
130 KING ST W SUITE 740, TORONTO, ON, M5X 2A2
(647) 260-1500 *SIC 1081*
TORKIN MANES LLP *p 941*
151 YONGE ST SUITE 1500, TORONTO, ON, M5C 2W7
(416) 863-1188 *SIC 8111*
TORLYS INC *p 736*
1900 DERRY RD E, MISSISSAUGA, ON, L5S 1Y6
(905) 612-8772 *SIC 5023*
TORNADO *p 208*
See TORNADO BUILDING MAINTENANCE CORPORATION
TORNADO BUILDING MAINTENANCE CORPORATION *p 208*
9453 120 ST SUITE 201, DELTA, BC, V4C 6S2
(604) 930-6030 *SIC 7349*
TORNADO COMBUSTION TECHNOLOGIES INC *p 160*
261200 WAGON WHEEL WAY SUITE 200, ROCKY VIEW COUNTY, AB, T4A 0E3
(403) 244-3333 *SIC 3533*
TORNADO GLOBAL HYDROVACS LTD *p 38*
7015 MACLEOD TRAIL SW SUITE 510, CALGARY, AB, T2H 2K6
(403) 204-6363 *SIC 3531*
TORNADO INSULATION LTD *p 661*
4231 BLAKIE RD, LONDON, ON, N6L 1B8
(519) 652-5183 *SIC 1711*
TORNATECH INC *p 1087*
4100 DESSTE SUD LAVAL (A-440) O, COTE SAINT-LUC, QC, H7T 0H3
(514) 334-2503 *SIC 3625*
TORNGAIT SERVICES INC *p 424*
215 HAMILTON RIVER RD, HAPPY VALLEY-GOOSE BAY, NL, A0P 1E0
(709) 896-5431 *SIC 1629*

TORNGAIT UJAGANNIAVINGIT CORPORATION *p 427*
2 MORHDT RD, NAIN, NL, A0P 1L0
(709) 922-2143 *SIC 3281*
TORNGAT REGIONAL HOUSING ASSOCIATION *p 424*
436 HAMILTON RD, HAPPY VALLEY-GOOSE BAY, NL, A0P 1C0
(709) 896-8126 *SIC 6531*
TORO ALUMINUM *p 559*
330 APPLEWOOD CRES, CONCORD, ON, L4K 4V2
(905) 738-5220 *SIC 3442*
TORODE RESIDENTIAL LTD *p 61*
209 8 AVE SW SUITE 301, CALGARY, AB, T2P 1B8
(403) 355-6000 *SIC 1522*
TOROMONT CAT *p 625*
See TOROMONT INDUSTRIES LTD
TOROMONT CAT *p 1073*
See TOROMONT INDUSTRIES LTD
TOROMONT CAT *p 1293*
See TOROMONT INDUSTRIES LTD
TOROMONT CAT *p 1391*
See TOROMONT INDUSTRIES LTD
TOROMONT CAT (MARITIMES) *p 448*
See TOROMONT INDUSTRIES LTD
TOROMONT CAT - MATERIAL HANDLING DIVISION *p 1252*
See TOROMONT INDUSTRIES LTD
TOROMONT CAT, DIV OF *p 559*
See TOROMONT INDUSTRIES LTD
TOROMONT ENERGY LTD *p 559*
3131 HIGHWAY 7 SUITE A, CONCORD, ON, L4K 5E1
(416) 667-5758 *SIC 4911*
TOROMONT INDUSTRIES LTD *p 370*
140 INKSBROOK DR, WINNIPEG, MB, R2R 2W3
(204) 453-4343 *SIC 7699*
TOROMONT INDUSTRIES LTD *p 401*
165 URQUHART CRES, FREDERICTON, NB, E3B 8K4
(506) 452-6651 *SIC 5082*
TOROMONT INDUSTRIES LTD *p 427*
24 THIRD ST, MOUNT PEARL, NL, A1N 2A5
(709) 282-5537 *SIC 5082*
TOROMONT INDUSTRIES LTD *p 448*
175 AKERLEY BLVD, DARTMOUTH, NS, B3B 3Z6
(902) 468-0581 *SIC 5082*
TOROMONT INDUSTRIES LTD *p 559*
3131 HIGHWAY 7 SUITE A, CONCORD, ON, L4K 5E1
(416) 667-5511 *SIC 5082*
TOROMONT INDUSTRIES LTD *p 559*
548 EDGELEY BLVD, CONCORD, ON, L4K 4G4
(416) 667-5900 *SIC 5082*
TOROMONT INDUSTRIES LTD *p 625*
5 EDGEWATER ST, KANATA, ON, K2L 1V7
(613) 836-5171 *SIC 5082*
TOROMONT INDUSTRIES LTD *p 647*
25 MUMFORD RD, LIVELY, ON, P3Y 1K9
(705) 692-4764 *SIC 5082*
TOROMONT INDUSTRIES LTD *p 893*
460 SOUTH SERVICE RD, STONEY CREEK, ON, L8E 2P8
(905) 561-5901 *SIC 7699*
TOROMONT INDUSTRIES LTD *p 893*
880 SOUTH SERVICE RD, STONEY CREEK, ON, L8E 5M7
(905) 643-9410 *SIC 7359*
TOROMONT INDUSTRIES LTD *p 934*
65 VILLIERS ST, TORONTO, ON, M5A 3S1
(416) 465-7581 *SIC 3585*
TOROMONT INDUSTRIES LTD *p 1073*
350 AV LIBERTE, CANDIAC, QC, J5R 6X1
(450) 638-6091 *SIC 5082*
TOROMONT INDUSTRIES LTD *p 1252*
4000 AUT TRANSCANADIENNE, POINTE-

CLAIRE, QC, H9R 1B2
(514) 426-6700 *SIC* 5082
TOROMONT INDUSTRIES LTD *p* 1293
100 RUE DE ROTTERDAM, SAINT-AUGUSTIN-DE-DESMAURES, QC, G3A 1T2
(418) 878-3000 *SIC* 5082
TOROMONT INDUSTRIES LTD *p* 1391
1200 3E AV E, VAL-D'OR, QC, J9P 0J6
(819) 825-5494 *SIC* 5082
TOROMONT REMAN *p* 559
See TOROMONT INDUSTRIES LTD
TORONTAIR *p* 676
See TORONTO AIRWAYS LIMITED
TORONTO AGED MEN'S AND WOMEN'S HOMES, THE *p* 974
55 BELMONT ST SUITE 403, TORONTO, ON, M5R 1R1
(416) 964-9231 *SIC* 8361
TORONTO AIRPORT CHRISTIAN FELLOWSHIP *p*
589
272 ATTWELL DR, ETOBICOKE, ON, M9W 6M3
(416) 674-8463 *SIC* 8661
TORONTO AIRPORT MARRIOTT LTD, THE *p* 589
901 DIXON RD, ETOBICOKE, ON, M9W 1J5
(416) 674-9400 *SIC* 7011
TORONTO AIRWAYS LIMITED *p* 676
2833 16TH AVE SUITE 100, MARKHAM, ON, L3R 0P8
(905) 477-8100 *SIC* 4581
TORONTO AND REGION CONSERVATION AUTHORITY *p* 784
1000 MURRAY ROSS PKY, NORTH YORK, ON, M3J 2P3
(416) 736-1740 *SIC* 8412
TORONTO AREA CONTROL CENTRE *p*
698
See NAV CANADA
TORONTO ARTSCAPE FOUNDATION *p* 992
See TORONTO ARTSCAPE INC
TORONTO ARTSCAPE INC *p* 992
171 EAST LIBERTY ST SUITE 224, TORONTO, ON, M6K 3P6
(416) 392-1038 *SIC* 8399
TORONTO AUTO GROUP, DIV OF *p* 870
See AUTOMOTIVE WHOLESALE INC
TORONTO BARBER & BEAUTY SUPPLY LIMITED *p* 790
112 ORFUS RD, NORTH YORK, ON, M6A 1L9
(416) 787-1211 *SIC* 5122
TORONTO BLUE JAYS BASEBALL CLUB *p* 983
See ROGERS BLUE JAYS BASEBALL PARTNERSHIP
TORONTO CATHOLIC DISTRICT SCHOOL BOARD *p* 573
721 ROYAL YORK RD, ETOBICOKE, ON, M8Y 2T3
(416) 393-5549 *SIC* 8211
TORONTO CATHOLIC DISTRICT SCHOOL BOARD *p* 770
211 STEELES AVE E, NORTH YORK, ON, M2M 3Y6
(416) 393-5508 *SIC* 8211
TORONTO CATHOLIC DISTRICT SCHOOL BOARD *p* 770
3379 BAYVIEW AVE, NORTH YORK, ON, M2M 3S4
(416) 393-5516 *SIC* 8211
TORONTO CATHOLIC DISTRICT SCHOOL BOARD *p* 773
80 SHEPPARD AVE E, NORTH YORK, ON, M2N 6E8
(416) 222-8282 *SIC* 8211
TORONTO CATHOLIC DISTRICT SCHOOL BOARD *p* 773
80 SHEPPARD AVE E SUITE 222, NORTH YORK, ON, M2N 6E8
(416) 222-8282 *SIC* 8211

TORONTO CATHOLIC DISTRICT SCHOOL BOARD *p* 785
1440 FINCH AVE W, NORTH YORK, ON, M3J 3G3
(416) 393-5527 *SIC* 8211
TORONTO CATHOLIC DISTRICT SCHOOL BOARD *p* 788
101 MASON BLVD, NORTH YORK, ON, M5M 3E2
(416) 393-5510 *SIC* 8211
TORONTO CATHOLIC DISTRICT SCHOOL BOARD *p* 866
685 MILITARY TRAIL, SCARBOROUGH, ON, M1E 4P6
(416) 393-5531 *SIC* 8211
TORONTO CATHOLIC DISTRICT SCHOOL BOARD *p* 869
100 BRIMLEY RD S, SCARBOROUGH, ON, M1M 3X4
(416) 393-5519 *SIC* 8211
TORONTO CATHOLIC DISTRICT SCHOOL BOARD *p* 877
3200 KENNEDY RD, SCARBOROUGH, ON, M1V 3S8
(416) 393-5544 *SIC* 8211
TORONTO CATHOLIC DISTRICT SCHOOL BOARD *p* 919
49 FELSTEAD AVE, TORONTO, ON, M4J 1G3
(416) 393-5546 *SIC* 8211
TORONTO CATHOLIC DISTRICT SCHOOL BOARD *p* 990
270 BARTON AVE, TORONTO, ON, M6G 1R4
(416) 393-5293 *SIC* 8211
TORONTO CATHOLIC DISTRICT SCHOOL BOARD *p* 994
99 HUMBER BLVD, TORONTO, ON, M6N 2H4
(416) 393-5555 *SIC* 8211
TORONTO CATHOLIC DISTRICT SCHOOL BOARD *p* 994
70 GUESTVILLE AVE, TORONTO, ON, M6N 4N3
(416) 393-5247 *SIC* 8211
TORONTO CENTRAL CCAC *p* 978
See TORONTO CENTRAL COMMUNITY CARE ACCESS CENTRE
TORONTO CENTRAL COMMUNITY CARE ACCESS CENTRE *p* 978
250 DUNDAS ST W SUITE 305, TORONTO, ON, M5T 2Z5
(416) 506-9888 *SIC* 8699
TORONTO CENTRAL COUNCIL *p* 936
See ST VINCENT DE PAUL SOCIETY
TORONTO CHRYSLER DODGE JEEP RAM *p* 933
See FORT YORK C MOTORS LP
TORONTO COMMUNITY HOUSING CORPORATION *p* 931
931 YONGE ST SUITE 400, TORONTO, ON, M4W 2H2
(416) 981-5500 *SIC* 6531
TORONTO CONGRESS CENTRE LTD *p* 589
650 DIXON RD, ETOBICOKE, ON, M9W 1J1
(416) 245-5000 *SIC* 7389
TORONTO CONVENTION & VISITORS ASSOCIATION *p* 967
207 QUEENS QUAY W SUITE 405, TORONTO, ON, M5J 1A7
(416) 203-2600 *SIC* 8611
TORONTO CRICKET SKATING AND CURLING CLUB *p* 788
141 WILSON AVE, NORTH YORK, ON, M5M 3A3
(416) 487-4581 *SIC* 7997
TORONTO DELTA MEADOWVALE RESORT & CONFERENCE CENTRE, THE *p* 721
See DELTA HOTELS LIMITED
TORONTO DISTRICT SCHOOL BOARD *p*

573
675 ROYAL YORK RD, ETOBICOKE, ON, M8Y 2T1
(416) 394-6910 *SIC* 8211
TORONTO DISTRICT SCHOOL BOARD *p* 577
86 MONTGOMERY RD, ETOBICOKE, ON, M9A 3N5
(416) 394-7840 *SIC* 8211
TORONTO DISTRICT SCHOOL BOARD *p* 578
50 WINTERTON DR, ETOBICOKE, ON, M9B 3G7
(416) 394-7110 *SIC* 8211
TORONTO DISTRICT SCHOOL BOARD *p* 581
1675 MARTIN GROVE RD, ETOBICOKE, ON, M9V 3S3
(416) 394-7570 *SIC* 8211
TORONTO DISTRICT SCHOOL BOARD *p* 581
2580 KIPLING AVE, ETOBICOKE, ON, M9V 3B2
(416) 394-7550 *SIC* 8211
TORONTO DISTRICT SCHOOL BOARD *p* 766
50 FRANCINE DR, NORTH YORK, ON, M2H 2G6
(416) 395-3140 *SIC* 8211
TORONTO DISTRICT SCHOOL BOARD *p* 770
155 HILDA AVE, NORTH YORK, ON, M2M 1V6
(416) 395-3280 *SIC* 8211
TORONTO DISTRICT SCHOOL BOARD *p* 773
5050 YONGE ST 5TH FL, NORTH YORK, ON, M2N 5N8
(416) 397-3000 *SIC* 8211
TORONTO DISTRICT SCHOOL BOARD *p* 773
100 PRINCESS AVE, NORTH YORK, ON, M2N 3R7
(416) 395-3210 *SIC* 8211
TORONTO DISTRICT SCHOOL BOARD *p* 775
15 WALLINGFORD RD, NORTH YORK, ON, M3A 2V1
(416) 395-3310 *SIC* 8211
TORONTO DISTRICT SCHOOL BOARD *p* 778
490 YORK MILLS RD, NORTH YORK, ON, M3B 1W6
(416) 395-3340 *SIC* 8211
TORONTO DISTRICT SCHOOL BOARD *p* 780
9 GRENOBLE DR, NORTH YORK, ON, M3C 1C3
(416) 397-2900 *SIC* 8211
TORONTO DISTRICT SCHOOL BOARD *p* 780
55 OVERLAND DR, NORTH YORK, ON, M3C 2C3
(416) 395-5080 *SIC* 8211
TORONTO DISTRICT SCHOOL BOARD *p* 780
130 OVERLEA BLVD, NORTH YORK, ON, M3C 1B2
(416) 396-2465 *SIC* 8211
TORONTO DISTRICT SCHOOL BOARD *p* 786
7 HAWKSDALE RD, NORTH YORK, ON, M3K 1W3
(416) 395-3200 *SIC* 8211
TORONTO DISTRICT SCHOOL BOARD *p* 787
450 BLYTHWOOD RD, NORTH YORK, ON, M4N 1A9
(416) 393-9275 *SIC* 8211
TORONTO DISTRICT SCHOOL BOARD *p* 790
38 ORFUS RD, NORTH YORK, ON, M6A 1L6
(416) 395-3350 *SIC* 8211

TORONTO DISTRICT SCHOOL BOARD *p* 790
640 LAWRENCE AVE W, NORTH YORK, ON, M6A 1B1
(416) 395-3303 *SIC* 8211
TORONTO DISTRICT SCHOOL BOARD *p* 865
150 TAPSCOTT RD, SCARBOROUGH, ON, M1B 2L2
(416) 396-5892 *SIC* 8211
TORONTO DISTRICT SCHOOL BOARD *p* 865
5400 LAWRENCE AVE E, SCARBOROUGH, ON, M1C 2C6
(416) 396-6802 *SIC* 8211
TORONTO DISTRICT SCHOOL BOARD *p* 866
2222 ELLESMERE RD, SCARBOROUGH, ON, M1G 3M3
(416) 396-4575 *SIC* 8211
TORONTO DISTRICT SCHOOL BOARD *p* 866
350 MORNINGSIDE AVE, SCARBOROUGH, ON, M1E 3G3
(416) 396-6864 *SIC* 8211
TORONTO DISTRICT SCHOOL BOARD *p* 866
145 GUILDWOOD PKY, SCARBOROUGH, ON, M1E 1P5
(416) 396-6820 *SIC* 8211
TORONTO DISTRICT SCHOOL BOARD *p* 866
120 GALLOWAY RD, SCARBOROUGH, ON, M1E 1W7
(416) 396-6765 *SIC* 8211
TORONTO DISTRICT SCHOOL BOARD *p* 867
550 MARKHAM RD, SCARBOROUGH, ON, M1H 2A2
(416) 396-4400 *SIC* 8211
TORONTO DISTRICT SCHOOL BOARD *p* 867
21 GATESVIEW AVE, SCARBOROUGH, ON, M1J 3G4
(416) 396-6120 *SIC* 8211
TORONTO DISTRICT SCHOOL BOARD *p* 869
3800 ST CLAIR AVE E, SCARBOROUGH, ON, M1M 1V3
(416) 396-5550 *SIC* 8211
TORONTO DISTRICT SCHOOL BOARD *p* 872
1555 MIDLAND AVE, SCARBOROUGH, ON, M1P 3C1
(416) 396-6695 *SIC* 8211
TORONTO DISTRICT SCHOOL BOARD *p* 872
2740 LAWRENCE AVE E, SCARBOROUGH, ON, M1P 2S7
(416) 396-5525 *SIC* 8221
TORONTO DISTRICT SCHOOL BOARD *p* 875
2621 MIDLAND AVE, SCARBOROUGH, ON, M1S 1R6
(416) 396-6675 *SIC* 8211
TORONTO DISTRICT SCHOOL BOARD *p* 875
2450 BIRCHMOUNT RD, SCARBOROUGH, ON, M1T 2M5
(416) 396-8000 *SIC* 8211
TORONTO DISTRICT SCHOOL BOARD *p* 875
1050 HUNTINGWOOD DR, SCARBOROUGH, ON, M1S 3H5
(416) 396-6830 *SIC* 8211
TORONTO DISTRICT SCHOOL BOARD *p* 875
52 MCGRISKIN RD, SCARBOROUGH, ON, M1S 5C5
(416) 396-7610 *SIC* 8211
TORONTO DISTRICT SCHOOL BOARD *p* 877
1550 SANDHURST CIR, SCARBOROUGH, ON, M1V 1S6

(416) 396-6684   *SIC* 8211
TORONTO DISTRICT SCHOOL BOARD *p* 878
2501 BRIDLETOWNE CIR, SCARBOROUGH, ON, M1W 2K1
(416) 396-6745   *SIC* 8211
TORONTO DISTRICT SCHOOL BOARD *p* 917
650 COSBURN AVE, TORONTO, ON, M4C 2V2
(416) 396-2355   *SIC* 8211
TORONTO DISTRICT SCHOOL BOARD *p* 918
305 RUMSEY RD, TORONTO, ON, M4G 1R4
(416) 396-2395   *SIC* 8211
TORONTO DISTRICT SCHOOL BOARD *p* 919
80 THORNCLIFFE PARK DR, TORONTO, ON, M4H 1K3
(416) 396-2460   *SIC* 8211
TORONTO DISTRICT SCHOOL BOARD *p* 919
1 HANSON ST, TORONTO, ON, M4J 1G6
(416) 393-0190   *SIC* 8211
TORONTO DISTRICT SCHOOL BOARD *p* 920
1 DANFORTH AVE, TORONTO, ON, M4K 1M8
(416) 393-9740   *SIC* 8211
TORONTO DISTRICT SCHOOL BOARD *p* 921
1094 GERRARD ST E, TORONTO, ON, M4M 2A1
(416) 393-9820   *SIC* 8211
TORONTO DISTRICT SCHOOL BOARD *p* 923
17 BROADWAY AVE, TORONTO, ON, M4P 1T7
(416) 393-9180   *SIC* 8211
TORONTO DISTRICT SCHOOL BOARD *p* 923
851 MOUNT PLEASANT RD, TORONTO, ON, M4P 2L5
(416) 393-0270   *SIC* 8211
TORONTO DISTRICT SCHOOL BOARD *p* 931
711 BLOOR ST E, TORONTO, ON, M4W 1J4
(416) 393-1580   *SIC* 8211
TORONTO DISTRICT SCHOOL BOARD *p* 932
495 JARVIS ST, TORONTO, ON, M4Y 2G8
(416) 393-0140   *SIC* 8211
TORONTO DISTRICT SCHOOL BOARD *p* 976
725 BATHURST ST, TORONTO, ON, M5S 2R5
(416) 393-0060   *SIC* 8211
TORONTO DISTRICT SCHOOL BOARD *p* 989
991 ST CLAIR AVE W, TORONTO, ON, M6E 1A3
(416) 393-1780   *SIC* 8211
TORONTO DISTRICT SCHOOL BOARD *p* 990
286 HARBORD ST, TORONTO, ON, M6G 1G5
(416) 393-1650   *SIC* 8211
TORONTO DISTRICT SCHOOL BOARD *p* 990
570 SHAW ST, TORONTO, ON, M6G 3L6
(416) 393-0030   *SIC* 8211
TORONTO DISTRICT SCHOOL BOARD *p* 992
209 JAMESON AVE, TORONTO, ON, M6K 2Y3
(416) 393-9000   *SIC* 8211
TORONTO DISTRICT SCHOOL BOARD *p* 992
100 CLOSE AVE, TORONTO, ON, M6K 2V3
(416) 530-0683   *SIC* 8211
TORONTO DISTRICT SCHOOL BOARD *p* 993

100 EMMETT AVE, TORONTO, ON, M6M 2E6
(416) 394-3280   *SIC* 8211
TORONTO DISTRICT SCHOOL BOARD *p* 993
2690 EGLINTON AVE W, TORONTO, ON, M6M 1T9
(416) 394-3000   *SIC* 8211
TORONTO DISTRICT SCHOOL BOARD *p* 994
69 PRITCHARD AVE, TORONTO, ON, M6N 1T6
(416) 394-2340   *SIC* 8211
TORONTO DISTRICT SCHOOL BOARD *p* 997
100 PINE ST, TORONTO, ON, M9N 2Y9
(416) 394-3250   *SIC* 8211
TORONTO EAST GENERAL GIFT SHOP *p* 917
825 COXWELL AVE, TORONTO, ON, M4C 3E7
(416) 469-6050   *SIC* 5947
TORONTO EAST HEALTH NETWORK *p* 917
825 COXWELL AVE, TORONTO, ON, M4C 3E7
(416) 461-8272   *SIC* 8062
TORONTO EAST TAX SERVICES OFFICE *p* 870
See CANADA TAXES
TORONTO EATON CENTRE *p* 935
See CADILLAC FAIRVIEW CORPORATION LIMITED, THE
TORONTO FRENCH SCHOOL *p* 787
306 LAWRENCE AVE E, NORTH YORK, ON, M4N 1T7
(416) 484-6980   *SIC* 8211
TORONTO GENERAL & WESTERN HOSPITAL FOUNDATION *p* 947
190 ELIZABETH ST, TORONTO, ON, M5G 2C4
(416) 340-3935   *SIC* 7389
TORONTO GENERAL HOSPITAL *p* 947
See UNIVERSITY HEALTH NETWORK
TORONTO GOLF CLUB LINKS, THE *p* 712
1305 DIXIE RD, MISSISSAUGA, ON, L5E 2P5
(905) 278-5255   *SIC* 7997
TORONTO HONDA *p* 917
See ISON T.H. AUTO SALES INC
TORONTO HUMANE SOCIETY, THE *p* 934
11 RIVER ST, TORONTO, ON, M5A 4C2
(416) 392-2273   *SIC* 8699
TORONTO HYDRO *p* 770
See TORONTO HYDRO-ELECTRIC SYSTEM LIMITED
TORONTO HYDRO CORPORATION *p* 936
14 CARLTON ST SUITE 6, TORONTO, ON, M5B 1K5
(416) 542-8000   *SIC* 4911
TORONTO HYDRO-ELECTRIC SYSTEM LIMITED *p* 770
5800 YONGE ST, NORTH YORK, ON, M2M 3T3
(416) 542-3564   *SIC* 4911
TORONTO HYDRO-ELECTRIC SYSTEM LIMITED *p* 936
14 CARLTON ST, TORONTO, ON, M5B 1K5
(416) 542-3100   *SIC* 4911
TORONTO ICE HOCKEY LEAGUE *p* 772
See PEAK SPORTS MANAGEMENT INC
TORONTO IMAGE WORKS LIMITED *p* 984
80 SPADINA AVE SUITE 207, TORONTO, ON, M5V 2J4
(416) 703-1999   *SIC* 7384
TORONTO INTERNATIONAL FILM FESTIVAL INC *p* 984
350 KING ST W SUITE 477, TORONTO, ON, M5V 3X5
(416) 967-7371   *SIC* 8699
TORONTO KIA *p* 917
2222 DANFORTH AVE, TORONTO, ON, M4C 1K3

(416) 421-9000   *SIC* 5511
TORONTO LUBE SERVICE *p* 665
See 673927 ONTARIO INC
TORONTO MARRIOTT BLOOR YORKVILLE *p* 930
See PLAZA II CORPORATION, THE
TORONTO MICROELECTRONICS INC *p* 743
6185 DANVILLE RD, MISSISSAUGA, ON, L5T 2H7
(905) 362-8090   *SIC* 3861
TORONTO MONTESSORI SCHOOLS *p* 854
8569 BAYVIEW AVE, RICHMOND HILL, ON, L4B 3M7
(905) 889-6882   *SIC* 8211
TORONTO MOTORSPORTS PARK *p* 541
See 1233481 ONTARIO INC
TORONTO OFFICE (RESERVEAMERICA) *p* 719
See ACTIVE NETWORK
TORONTO PARKING AUTHORITY, THE *p* 941
33 QUEEN ST E, TORONTO, ON, M5C 1R5
(416) 393-7275   *SIC* 7521
TORONTO PEARSON INTERNATIONAL AIRPORT *p* 729
See GREATER TORONTO AIRPORTS AUTHORITY
TORONTO PORT AUTHORITY *p* 967
60 HARBOUR ST, TORONTO, ON, M5J 1B7
(416) 863-2000   *SIC* 4581
TORONTO PROFESSIONAL FIREFIGHTERS ASSOCIATION LOCAL 3888 *p* 872
14 COSENTINO DR, SCARBOROUGH, ON, M1P 3A2
(416) 466-1167   *SIC* 8631
TORONTO PUBLIC LIBRARY BOARD *p* 931
789 YONGE ST, TORONTO, ON, M4W 2G8
(416) 397-5946   *SIC* 8231
TORONTO REAL ESTATE BOARD, THE *p* 778
1400 DON MILLS RD SUITE 1, NORTH YORK, ON, M3B 3N1
(416) 443-8100   *SIC* 8611
TORONTO REDI MIX LIMITED *p* 559
401 BOWES RD, CONCORD, ON, L4K 1J4
(416) 798-7060   *SIC* 3273
TORONTO REHAB *p* 947
See TORONTO REHABILITATION INSTITUTE
TORONTO REHABILITATION INSTITUTE *p* 918
520 SUTHERLAND DR, TORONTO, ON, M4G 3V9
(416) 597-3422   *SIC* 8093
TORONTO REHABILITATION INSTITUTE *p* 947
550 UNIVERSITY AVE, TORONTO, ON, M5G 2A2
(416) 597-3422   *SIC* 8093
TORONTO RESEARCH CHEMICALS INC *p* 785
2 BRISBANE RD, NORTH YORK, ON, M3J 2J8
(416) 665-9696   *SIC* 2819
TORONTO ROCK LACROSSE INC *p* 799
1132 INVICTA DR, OAKVILLE, ON, L6H 6G1
(416) 596-3075   *SIC* 7941
TORONTO SKY AVIATION INC *p* 559
30 RAYETTE RD, CONCORD, ON, L4K 2G3
(905) 760-0731   *SIC* 4581
TORONTO SMART CARS LTD *p* 906
7200 YONGE ST SUITE 1, THORNHILL, ON, L4J 1V8
(905) 762-1020   *SIC* 5511
TORONTO STAR *p* 943
See TORONTO STAR NEWSPAPERS LIMITED
TORONTO STAR NEWSPAPERS LIMITED *p* 943
1 YONGE ST SUITE 400, TORONTO, ON, M5E 1E6

(416) 869-4000   *SIC* 2711
TORONTO STAR NEWSPAPERS LIMITED *p* 1034
1 CENTURY PL, WOODBRIDGE, ON, L4L 8R2
(416) 502-8273   *SIC* 2711
TORONTO STOCK EXCHANGE *p* 958
See TSX INC
TORONTO SUN WAH TRADING INC *p* 576
18 CANMOTOR AVE, ETOBICOKE, ON, M8Z 4E5
(416) 252-7757   *SIC* 5113
TORONTO TERMINALS RAILWAY COMPANY LIMITED, THE *p* 967
50 BAY ST SUITE 1400, TORONTO, ON, M5J 3A5
(416) 864-3440   *SIC* 1629
TORONTO TOURS LTD *p* 934
259 LAKE SHORE BLVD E, TORONTO, ON, M5A 3T7
(416) 868-0400   *SIC* 4725
TORONTO TRANSIT COMMISSION *p* 919
400 GREENWOOD AVE, TORONTO, ON, M4J 4Y5
(416) 393-3176   *SIC* 4111
TORONTO TRANSIT COMMISSION *p* 924
1900 YONGE ST SUITE 400, TORONTO, ON, M4S 1Z2
(416) 393-4000   *SIC* 4111
TORONTO WATERFRONT REVITALIZATION CORPORATION *p* 968
20 BAY ST SUITE 1310, TORONTO, ON, M5J 2N8
(416) 214-1344   *SIC* 8748
TORONTO ZENITH CONTRACTING LIMITED *p* 559
226 BRADWICK DR UNIT 1, CONCORD, ON, L4K 1K8
(905) 738-1500   *SIC* 1622
TORONTO ZOO *p* 864
See BOARD OF MANAGEMENT OF THE TORONTO ZOO
TORONTO-DOMINION BANK, THE *p* 91
10004 JASPER AVE NW SUITE 500, EDMONTON, AB, T5J 1R3
(780) 448-8251   *SIC* 6021
TORONTO-DOMINION BANK, THE *p* 701
4880 TAHOE BLVD 5TH FL, MISSISSAUGA, ON, L4W 5P3
(905) 293-5613   *SIC* 6021
TORONTO-DOMINION BANK, THE *p* 733
20 MILVERTON DR SUITE 10, MISSISSAUGA, ON, L5R 3G2
(905) 568-3600   *SIC* 6021
TORONTO-DOMINION BANK, THE *p* 970
55 KING ST W, TORONTO, ON, M5K 1A2
(416) 982-5722   *SIC* 6021
TORONTO-DOMINION BANK, THE *p* 970
66 WELLINGTON ST W, TORONTO, ON, M5K 1A2
(416) 982-7650   *SIC* 6021
TORQ INSTRUMENT SUPPLY INC *p* 133
11436 97 AVE, GRANDE PRAIRIE, AB, T8V 5Z5
(780) 532-1115   *SIC* 4911
TORQUE *p* 560
See TORQUE BUILDERS INC
TORQUE BUILDERS INC *p* 560
72 CORSTATE AVE, CONCORD, ON, L4K 4X2
(905) 660-3334   *SIC* 1542
TORQUE INDUSTRIAL LTD *p* 213
5100 46 AVE, FORT NELSON, BC, V0C 1R0
(250) 233-8675   *SIC* 1799
TORQUEST PARTNERS INC *p* 968
161 BAY ST SUITE 4240, TORONTO, ON, M5J 2S1
(416) 956-7022   *SIC* 6712
TORQUIN CORPORATION LIMITED *p* 757
200 PONY DR, NEWMARKET, ON, L3Y 7B6

(905) 836-0988   *SIC* 7359
TORRES AVIATION INCORPORATED *p* 676
95 ROYAL CREST CRT UNIT 5, MARKHAM, ON, L3R 9X5
(905) 470-7655   *SIC* 7383
TORSTAR   *p* 984
See TORSTAR CORPORATION
TORSTAR CORPORATION   *p* 639
160 KING ST E, KITCHENER, ON, N2G 4E5
(519) 821-2022   *SIC* 2711
TORSTAR CORPORATION   *p* 813
865 FAREWELL ST, OSHAWA, ON, L1H 6N8
(905) 579-4400   *SIC* 2711
TORSTAR CORPORATION   *p* 943
1 YONGE ST, TORONTO, ON, M5E 1E5
(416) 869-4010   *SIC* 2752
TORSTAR CORPORATION   *p* 984
590 KING ST W SUITE 400, TORONTO, ON, M5V 1M3
  SIC 2752
TORY TAPE LTD   *p* 1034
230 TROWERS RD UNIT 9-11, WOODBRIDGE, ON, L4L 7J1
(416) 410-1404   *SIC* 5085
TORYCO SERVICES   *p* 968
See 373813 ONTARIO LIMITED
TORYS LLP   *p* 970
79 WELLINGTON ST W SUITE 3000, TORONTO, ON, M5K 1N2
(416) 865-0040   *SIC* 8111
TOSCANA ENERGY INCOME CORPORATION   *p* 61
207 9 AVE SW SUITE 900, CALGARY, AB, T2P 1K3
(403) 410-6790   *SIC* 1311
TOSCANO   *p* 789
See P.Y.A. IMPORTER LTD
TOSHIBA   *p* 676
See TOSHIBA TEC CANADA BUSINESS SOLUTIONS INC
TOSHIBA BUSINESS SOLUTIONS   *p* 19
See TOSHIBA BUSINESS SYSTEMS
TOSHIBA BUSINESS SYSTEMS   *p* 19
5329 72 AVE SE UNIT 62, CALGARY, AB, T2C 4X6
(403) 273-5200   *SIC* 7389
TOSHIBA OF CANADA LIMITED   *p* 676
75 TIVERTON CRT, MARKHAM, ON, L3R 4M8
(905) 470-3500   *SIC* 5064
TOSHIBA TEC CANADA BUSINESS SOLUTIONS INC   *p* 676
75 TIVERTON CRT, MARKHAM, ON, L3R 4M8
(905) 470-3500   *SIC* 5044
TOSHIBA TEC CANADA INC   *p* 676
75 TIVERTON CRT, MARKHAM, ON, L3R 4M8
(905) 470-3500   *SIC* 5044
TOTAL CANADA INC   *p* 1132
220 AV LAFLEUR, LASALLE, QC, H8R 4C9
(514) 595-7579   *SIC* 2911
TOTAL CREDIT RECOVERY LIMITED *p* 768
225 YORKLAND BLVD, NORTH YORK, ON, M2J 4Y7
(416) 774-4000   *SIC* 7322
TOTAL DELIVERY SYSTEMS INC   *p* 339
450 BANGA PL, VICTORIA, BC, V8Z 6X5
(250) 382-9110   *SIC* 7389
TOTAL E&P CANADA LTD   *p* 61
240 4 AVE SW SUITE 2900, CALGARY, AB, T2P 4H4
(403) 571-7599   *SIC* 1311
TOTAL ENERFLEX   *p* 133
See ROSKA DBO INC
TOTAL ENERGY SERVICES INC   *p* 19
6900 112 AVE SE, CALGARY, AB, T2C 4Z1
(403) 235-5877   *SIC* 1382
TOTAL ENERGY SERVICES INC   *p* 61
311 6 AVE SW SUITE 800, CALGARY, AB, T2P 3H2

(403) 216-3939   *SIC* 1382
TOTAL EXPRESS, THE   *p* 687
See 979861 ONTARIO INC
TOTAL FIRE PROTECTION   *p* 816
See 1084999 ONTARIO INC
TOTAL HEALTH AND FAMILY CENTRE *p* 704
1090 DUNDAS ST E SUITE 1105, MISSISSAUGA, ON, L4Y 2B8
(905) 275-4993   *SIC* 6321
TOTAL LEASE & TRUCK SALES LTD *p* 220
2655 ENTERPRISE WAY, KELOWNA, BC, V1X 7Y6
(250) 712-0668   *SIC* 5511
TOTAL METAL RECUPERATION (TMR) INC *p* 1232
2000 RUE LEOPOLD-HAMELIN, MONTREAL, QC, H7E 4P2
(450) 720-1331   *SIC* 3341
TOTAL POWER LIMITED   *p* 743
6450 KESTREL RD UNIT 3, MISSISSAUGA, ON, L5T 1Z7
(905) 670-1535   *SIC* 3621
TOTAL RETURN SOLUTIONS CORP *p* 560
51 GRANITERIDGE RD, CONCORD, ON, L4K 5M9
(905) 761-6835   *SIC* 4731
TOTAL RM CANADA   *p* 1132
See TOTAL CANADA INC
TOTAL SAFETY SERVICES INC   *p* 239
1336 MAIN ST, NORTH VANCOUVER, BC, V7J 1C3
  SIC 8748
TOTAL SWINE GENETICS INC   *p* 912
223277 OSTRANDER RD SUITE 7, TILLSONBURG, ON, N4G 4H1
(519) 877-4350   *SIC* 5159
TOTAL TECH POOLS INC   *p* 805
1380 SPEERS RD SUITE 1, OAKVILLE, ON, L6L 5V3
(905) 825-1389   *SIC* 7389
TOTALE ALIMENTATION INC   *p* 1089
130 CH SAINT-MICHEL RR 3, CRABTREE, QC, J0K 1B0
(450) 754-3785   *SIC* 5143
TOTALLY ONE COMMUNICATIONS INC *p* 560
60 SARAMIA CRES SUITE 3, CONCORD, ON, L4K 4J7
(905) 761-1331   *SIC* 5999
TOTEM APPLIANCE & REFRIGERATION LTD *p* 194
5950 IMPERIAL ST, BURNABY, BC, V5J 4M2
(604) 437-5136   *SIC* 7629
TOTEM COVE HOLDINGS INC   *p* 342
5776 MARINE DR, WEST VANCOUVER, BC, V7W 2S2
(604) 921-7434   *SIC* 4493
TOTES   *p* 743
See TOTES ISOTONER CANADA LIMITED
TOTES ISOTONER CANADA LIMITED *p* 743
6335 SHAWSON DR, MISSISSAUGA, ON, L5T 1S7
(905) 564-4798   *SIC* 5139
TOTRAN TRANSPORTATION SERVICES LTD *p* 78
9350 VENTURE AVE SE, CALGARY, AB, T3S 0A2
(403) 723-0025   *SIC* 4213
TOTTEN INSURANCE GROUP INC *p* 947
20 DUNDAS ST W SUITE 910, TORONTO, ON, M5G 2C2
(416) 342-1159   *SIC* 6411
TOTTENHAM FOODLAND STORE   *p* 998
See SOBEYS CAPITAL INCORPORATED
TOUCH CANADA BROADCASTING INC *p* 119
5316 CALGARY TRAIL NW, EDMONTON, AB, T6H 4J8
(780) 469-5200   *SIC* 4832
TOUCHETTE PNEUS & MECANIQUE *p* 1397
4101 BOUL CHAMPLAIN, VERDUN, QC,

H4G 1A6
(514) 766-4291   *SIC* 5531
TOUCHIE ENGINEERING, DIV OF *p* 768
See R. V. ANDERSON ASSOCIATES LIMITED
TOUCHSTONE EXPLORATION INC *p* 61
350 7TH AVE SW UNIT 4100, CALGARY, AB, T2P 3N9
(403) 750-4400   *SIC* 1381
TOUCHTUNES DIGITAL JUKEBOX INC *p* 1181
7250 RUE DU MILE END BUREAU 202, MONTREAL, QC, H2R 3A4
(514) 762-6244   *SIC* 3931
TOULON   *p* 1402
See TOULON DEVELOPMENT CORPORATION
TOULON DEVELOPMENT CORPORATION *p* 471
76 STARRS RD, YARMOUTH, NS, B5A 2T5
(902) 742-9518   *SIC* 7299
TOULON DEVELOPMENT CORPORATION *p* 1402
4060 RUE SAINTE-CATHERINE O BUREAU 700, WESTMOUNT, QC, H3Z 2Z3
(514) 931-5811   *SIC* 6531
TOUR EAST HOLIDAYS (CANADA) INC *p* 778
15 KERN RD SUITE 9, NORTH YORK, ON, M3B 1S9
(416) 250-1098   *SIC* 4724
TOURAM LIMITED PARTNERSHIP *p* 690
5925 AIRPORT RD SUITE 700, MISSISSAUGA, ON, L4V 1W1
(905) 615-8020   *SIC* 4724
TOURAM LIMITED PARTNERSHIP *p* 1214
1440 RUE SAINTE-CATHERINE O BUREAU 600, MONTREAL, QC, H3G 1R8
(514) 876-0700   *SIC* 4724
TOURBES NIROM PEAT MOSS INC, LES *p* 1287
315 CH DES RAYMOND, RIVIERE-DU-LOUP, QC, G5R 5Y5
(418) 862-0075   *SIC* 5159
TOURBIERE MALPEC   *p* 1286
See PREMIER HORTICULTURE LTEE
TOURBIERES BERGER LTEE, LES *p* 394
4188 ROUTE 117, BAIE-SAINTE-ANNE, NB, E9A 1R7
  SIC 1499
TOURBIERES BERGER LTEE, LES *p* 1349
121 1ER RANG, SAINT-MODESTE, QC, G0L 3W0
(418) 862-4462   *SIC* 5159
TOURBIERES LAMBERT INC   *p* 1287
106 CH LAMBERT, RIVIERE-OUELLE, QC, G0L 2C0
(418) 852-2885   *SIC* 1499
TOURISM CALGARY-CALGARY CONVENTION & VISITORS BUREAU *p* 32
238 11 AVE SE SUITE 200, CALGARY, AB, T2G 0X8
(403) 263-8510   *SIC* 7389
TOURISM HR CANADA   *p* 822
See CANADIAN TOURISM HUMAN RESOURCE COUNCIL
TOURISM TORONTO   *p* 967
See TORONTO CONVENTION & VISITORS ASSOCIATION
TOURISM VANCOUVER   *p* 305
See GREATER VANCOUVER CONVENTION AND VISITORS BUREAU
TOURISM VICTORIA   *p* 336
See GREATER VICTORIA VISITORS & CONVENTION BUREAU
TOURISME LAVAL   *p* 1087
See OFFICE DU TOURISME DE LAVAL INC
TOURISME OUTAOUAIS   *p* 1105
See L'ASSOCIATION TOURISTIQUE DE L'OUTAOUAIS
TOURLAND TRAVEL LTD   *p* 262
8899 ODLIN CRES, RICHMOND, BC, V6X

3Z7
(604) 276-9592   *SIC* 4725
TOURMALINE OIL CORP   *p* 61
250 6 AVE SW UNIT 3700, CALGARY, AB, T2P 3H7
(403) 266-5992   *SIC* 1382
TOURNAMENT SPORTS MARKETING INC *p* 1007
185 WEBER ST S, WATERLOO, ON, N2J 2B1
(519) 888-6500   *SIC* 5091
TOURNEES CLUB SELECT INC, LES *p* 1137
874 RUE ARCHIMEDE, LEVIS, QC, G6V 7M5
(418) 835-3336   *SIC* 4725
TOURS CHANTECLERC INC   *p* 1191
152 RUE NOTRE-DAME E, MONTREAL, QC, H2Y 3P6
(514) 398-9535   *SIC* 4725
TOURS JUMPSTREET TOURS INC, LES *p* 1223
780 AV BREWSTER SUITE 02-300, MONTREAL, QC, H4C 2K1
(514) 843-3311   *SIC* 4724
TOURS NEW YORK INC   *p* 1200
1410 RUE STANLEY BUREAU 1015, MONTREAL, QC, H3A 1P8
(514) 287-1066   *SIC* 4725
TOUT-PRET INC   *p* 1275
2950 AV WATT BUREAU 12, QUEBEC, QC, G1X 4A8
(418) 527-5557   *SIC* 5149
TOWER ARCTIC LTD   *p* 1200
2055 RUE PEEL BUREAU 960, MONTREAL, QC, H3A 1V4
  SIC 1542
TOWER CHRYSLER DODGE JEEP RAM *p* 39
See TWR C MOTORS LP
TOWER CHRYSLER PLYMOUTH LTD *p* 39
10901 MACLEOD TRAIL SW, CALGARY, AB, T2J 4L3
(403) 278-2020   *SIC* 5511
TOWER CLEANERS   *p* 33
See 1768652 ALBERTA LTD
TOWER EVENTS & SEATING RENTALS INC *p* 589
365 ATTWELL DR, ETOBICOKE, ON, M9W 5C2
(416) 213-1666   *SIC* 7389
TOWER MILLWORKS, DIV OF   *p* 268
See PHILBROOK'S BOATYARD LTD
TOWERHILL SOBEYS   *p* 839
See 1441571 ONTARIO INC
TOWERS WATSON CANADA INC   *p* 61
111 5 AVE SW SUITE 1600, CALGARY, AB, T2P 3Y6
(403) 261-1400   *SIC* 8741
TOWERS WATSON CANADA INC   *p* 711
201 CITY CENTRE DR SUITE 1000, MISSISSAUGA, ON, L5B 4E4
(905) 272-6322   *SIC* 6411
TOWERS WATSON CANADA INC   *p* 931
175 BLOOR ST E SUITE 1701, TORONTO, ON, M4W 3T6
(416) 960-2700   *SIC* 8999
TOWERS WATSON CANADA INC   *p* 1200
1800 AV MCGILL COLLEGE BUREAU 2200, MONTREAL, QC, H3A 3J6
(514) 982-9411   *SIC* 8999
TOWERS WATSON ULC   *p* 958
20 QUEEN ST W SUITE 2800, TORONTO, ON, M5H 3R3
(416) 960-2700   *SIC* 8741
TOWERS WATSON ULC   *p* 1200
600 BOUL DE MAISONNEUVE O BUREAU 2400, MONTREAL, QC, H3A 3J2
  SIC 8741
TOWLE, RUSSELL L ENTERPRISES LTD *p* 931
25 YORKVILLE AVE, TORONTO, ON, M4W 1L1
(416) 923-0993   *SIC* 7231

TOWN & COUNTRY BMW p 1000
See TOWN & COUNTRY MOTORS (1989) LIMITED

TOWN & COUNTRY CHRYSLER LIMITED p 882
245 LOMBARD ST, SMITHS FALLS, ON, K7A 5B8
(613) 283-7555   SIC 5511

TOWN & COUNTRY MOTORS (1989) LIMITED p 1000
8111 KENNEDY RD, UNIONVILLE, ON, L3R 5M2
(905) 948-2948   SIC 5511

TOWN & COUNTRY MUTUAL INSURANCE COMPANY p 897
79 CARADOC ST N, STRATHROY, ON, N7G 2M5
(519) 246-1132   SIC 6331

TOWN & COUNTRY PLUMBING & HEATING (2004) LTD p 1419
1450 SOUTH RAILWAY ST, REGINA, SK, S4P 0A2
(306) 352-4328   SIC 1711

TOWN & COUNTRY PLUMBING AND HEATING p 1419
See TOWN & COUNTRY PLUMBING & HEATING (2004) LTD

TOWN OF COMOX, THE p 203
377 LERWICK RD, COURTENAY, BC, V9N 9G4
(250) 334-2527   SIC 7999

TOWNE MEADOW DEVELOPMENT CORPORATION INC p 676
80 TIVERTON CRT SUITE 300, MARKHAM, ON, L3R 0G4
(905) 477-7609   SIC 1521

TOWNE MILLWORK LTD p 177
2690 PROGRESSIVE WAY SUITE A, ABBOTSFORD, BC, V2T 6H9
(604) 850-7738   SIC 5031

TOWNE SALES AND SERVICE LIMITED p 405
2227 KING GEORGE HWY, MIRAMICHI, NB, E1V 6N1
(506) 622-9020   SIC 5511

TOWNSEND BUTCHERS INC p 881
419 CONCESSION 14 TOWNSEND, SIMCOE, ON, N3Y 4K3
(519) 426-6750   SIC 5147

TOWNSEND LUMBER INC p 912
1300 JACKSON SUITE 2, TILLSONBURG, ON, N4G 4G7
(519) 842-7381   SIC 5031

TOWNSHIP OF LANGLEY FIRE DEPARTMENT p 226
See LANGLEY, CORPORATION OF THE TOWNSHIP OF

TOWNSHIP OF LEEDS AND THE THOUSAND ISLANDS p 663
GD, LYNDHURST, ON, K0E 1N0
(613) 928-3303   SIC 1521

TOWNSHIP OF OSGOODE CARE CENTRE p 681
7650 SNAKE ISLAND RD RR 3, METCALFE, ON, K0A 2P0
SIC 8051

TOWNSVIEW LIFECARE CENTRE p 614
See MARTINO NURSING CENTRES LIMITED

TOY-SPORT AGENCIES LIMITED p 877
120 DYNAMIC DR SUITE 22, SCARBOROUGH, ON, M1V 5C8
(905) 640-6598   SIC 7389

TOYO ENGINEERING CANADA LTD p 61
727 7 AVE SW SUITE 1400, CALGARY, AB, T2P 0Z5
(403) 266-4400   SIC 8711

TOYO PUMPS NORTH AMERICA CORP p 202
1550 BRIGANTINE DR, COQUITLAM, BC, V3K 7C1
(604) 298-1213   SIC 3561

TOYO TIRE CANADA INC p 258
7791 NELSON RD UNIT 120, RICHMOND, BC, V6W 1G3
(604) 304-1941   SIC 5531

TOYO TIRES p 258
See TOYO TIRE CANADA INC

TOYOTA p 1079
See ROCOTO LTEE

TOYOTA p 1154
See CLAUDE AUTO (1984) INC

TOYOTA p 1316
See DERY AUTOMOBILE LTEE

TOYOTA A STE-AGATHE p 1354
See 1857-2123 QUEBEC INC

TOYOTA BOSHOKU CANADA, INC p 568
45 SOUTH FIELD DR SUITE 1, ELMIRA, ON, N3B 3L6
(519) 669-8883   SIC 3089

TOYOTA BOSHOKU CANADA, INC p 1036
230 UNIVERSAL RD, WOODSTOCK, ON, N4S 7W3
(519) 421-7556   SIC 3089

TOYOTA CANADA p 157
413 LANTERN ST, RED DEER COUNTY, AB, T4E 0A5
(403) 343-3444   SIC 5511

TOYOTA CANADA INC p 867
1 TOYOTA PL, SCARBOROUGH, ON, M1H 1H9
(416) 438-6320   SIC 5012

TOYOTA CITY (WETASKIWIN) p 172
See 1133571 ALBERTA LTD

TOYOTA CREDIT CANADA INC p 676
80 MICRO CRT SUITE 200, MARKHAM, ON, L3R 9Z5
(905) 513-8200   SIC 6141

TOYOTA DEALERS ADVERTISING ASSOCIATION p 32
411 11 AVE SE, CALGARY, AB, T2G 0Y5
(403) 237-2388   SIC 5521

TOYOTA DRUMMONDVILLE p 1097
See 9122-4568 QUEBEC INC

TOYOTA DUVAL p 1063
See 2945-9708 QUEBEC INC

TOYOTA GATINEAU p 1104
See 177786 CANADA INC

TOYOTA MAGOG p 1147
See 2709970 CANADA INC

TOYOTA MONTREAL NORD p 1240
See PIE IX TOYOTA INC

TOYOTA MOTOR MANUFACTURING p 1036
See TOYOTA MOTOR MANUFACTURING CANADA INC

TOYOTA MOTOR MANUFACTURING CANADA INC p 539
1055 FOUNTAIN ST N, CAMBRIDGE, ON, N3H 4R7
(519) 653-1111   SIC 3711

TOYOTA MOTOR MANUFACTURING CANADA INC p 1036
1717 DUNDAS ST, WOODSTOCK, ON, N4S 0A4
(519) 653-1111   SIC 3711

TOYOTA MOTOR MANUFACTURING CANADA INC p 1036
715106 OXFORD RD SUITE 4, WOODSTOCK, ON, N4S 7V9
SIC 3711

TOYOTA ON FRONT p 978
See 1390835 ONTARIO LIMITED

TOYOTA PLAZA p 429
See 11336 NEWFOUNDLAND INC

TOYOTA RICHMOND p 1081
See 9127-7509 QUEBEC INC

TOYOTA TSUSHO CANADA INC p 538
1080 FOUNTAIN ST N UNIT 2, CAMBRIDGE, ON, N3E 1A3
(519) 653-6600   SIC 5013

TOYOTA TSUSHO CANADA INC p 1036
270 BEARDS LANE, WOODSTOCK, ON, N4S 7W3
(519) 533-5577   SIC 5013

TOYOTA VICTORIAVILLE p 1397
See GARAGE REJEAN ROY INC

TOYOTATOWN p 660
See CANADIAN PREMIER AUTOMOTIVE LTD

TOYOTETSU CANADA, INC p 881
88 PARK RD, SIMCOE, ON, N3Y 4J9
(519) 428-6500   SIC 3465

TOYS 'R' US p 923
See TOYS 'R' US (CANADA) LTD

TOYS 'R' US (CANADA) LTD p 560
2777 LANGSTAFF RD, CONCORD, ON, L4K 4M5
(905) 660-2000   SIC 5945

TOYS 'R' US (CANADA) LTD p 923
2300 YONGE ST, TORONTO, ON, M4P 1E4
(416) 322-1599   SIC 5945

TOYS FOR BIG BOYS LTD p 409
633 SALISBURY RD, MONCTON, NB, E1E 1B9
(506) 858-8088   SIC 5571

TOYS, TOYS, TOYS INC p 915
1800 SHEPPARD AVE E, TORONTO, ON, M2J 5A7
(416) 773-1950   SIC 5945

TP-HOLIDAY GROUP LIMITED p 1165
4875 BOUL DES GRANDES-PRAIRIES, MONTREAL, QC, H1R 1X4
(514) 325-0660   SIC 5099

TPC TORONTO p 477
See OSPREY VALLEY RESORTS INC

TPD p 327
See THE PERSONNEL DEPARTMENT LTD

TPH p 973
See PRINTING HOUSE LIMITED, THE

TPI PERSONNEL p 704
See TREBOR PERSONNEL INC

TR WESTCAN INC p 194
8035 NORTH FRASER WAY, BURNABY, BC, V5J 5M8
(604) 324-5015   SIC 4214

TRA ATLANTIC p 431
63 GLENCOE DR, ST. JOHN'S, NL, A1B 4A5
(709) 364-7771   SIC 4213

TRA MARITIMES p 395
3917 MAIN ST, BELLEDUNE, NB, E8G 2K3
SIC 5411

TRA STELLARTON p 466
GD, STELLARTON, NS, B0K 1S0
(902) 752-1525   SIC 5141

TRAC RAIL INC p 662
955 GREEN VALLEY RD, LONDON, ON, N6N 1E4
(519) 452-1233   SIC 3625

TRACADIE FOOD WAREHOUSE p 419
See ATLANTIC WHOLESALERS LTD

TRACC p 405
See TIRE RECYCLING ATLANTIC CANADA CORPORATION

TRACER CANADA COMPANY p 103
11004 174 ST NW, EDMONTON, AB, T5S 2P3
(780) 455-8111   SIC 1389

TRACER INDUSTRIES CANADA LIMITED p 103
11004 174 ST NW, EDMONTON, AB, T5S 2P3
(780) 455-8111   SIC 1389

TRACKER CONTRACTING LTD p 214
7648 100 AVE, FORT ST. JOHN, BC, V1J 1V9
SIC 1623

TRACKLESS VEHICLES LIMITED p 564
55 THUNDERBIRD DR, COURTLAND, ON, N0J 1E0
(519) 688-0370   SIC 3711

TRACKS & WHEELS EQUIPMENT BROKERS INC p 899
400 HWY 69 N, SUDBURY, ON, P3A 4S9

(705) 566-5438   SIC 5082

TRACTEL LTD p 873
1615 WARDEN AVE, SCARBOROUGH, ON, M1R 2T3
(416) 298-8822   SIC 3446

TRACTEL NORTH AMERICA INC p 873
1615 WARDEN AVE, SCARBOROUGH, ON, M1R 2T3
(416) 298-8822   SIC 3446

TRACTION ON DEMAND p 183
See TRACTION SALES AND MARKETING INC

TRACTION SALES AND MARKETING INC p 183
2700 PRODUCTION WAY SUITE 500, BURNABY, BC, V5A 0C2
(604) 917-0274   SIC 8741

TRADE ALLIANCE & INVESTMENT CORP p 968
161 BAY ST, TORONTO, ON, M5J 2S1
SIC 6282

TRADE CENTRE LIMITED p 454
1800 ARGYLE ST SUITE 801, HALIFAX, NS, B3J 3N8
(902) 421-8686   SIC 6512

TRADE SECRET PRINTING INC p 576
40 HORNER AVE, ETOBICOKE, ON, M8Z 4X3
(416) 231-9660   SIC 2752

TRADE SECRETS p 1031
See HIGHFIELD HOLDINGS INC

TRADE-MARK INDUSTRIAL INC p 538
250 ROYAL OAK RD, CAMBRIDGE, ON, N3E 0A4
(519) 650-7444   SIC 1796

TRADEGECKO SOFTWARE CANADA LTD p 984
409 KING ST W SUITE 201, TORONTO, ON, M5V 1K1
(647) 621-5456   SIC 8742

TRADEMARK INDUSTRIES INC p 679
380 MARKLAND ST, MARKHAM, ON, L6C 1T6
(905) 532-0442   SIC 5072

TRADEMARK TOOLS INC p 560
21 STAFFERN DR, CONCORD, ON, L4K 2X2
(905) 532-0442   SIC 5072

TRADER CORPORATION p 189
3555 GILMORE WAY 1 WEST, BURNABY, BC, V5G 0B3
(604) 540-4455   SIC 2721

TRADER CORPORATION p 580
405 THE WEST MALL SUITE 110, ETOBICOKE, ON, M9C 5J1
(416) 784-5200   SIC 2721

TRADER CORPORATION p 1215
1600 BOUL RENE-LEVESQUE O BUREAU 140, MONTREAL, QC, H3H 1P9
(514) 764-4000   SIC 2721

TRADERS INTERNATIONAL FRANCHISE MANAGEMENT INC p 335
508 DISCOVERY ST, VICTORIA, BC, V8T 1G8
SIC 6794

TRADESPAN CARGO LTD p 743
6305 DANVILLE RD UNIT 2, MISSISSAUGA, ON, L5T 2H7
(416) 410-1009   SIC 4731

TRADEWOOD INDUSTRIES LIMITED p 885
7 WRIGHT ST, ST CATHARINES, ON, L2P 3J2
(905) 641-4949   SIC 2431

TRADEWOOD WINDOWS & DOORS p 885
See TRADEWOOD INDUSTRIES LIMITED

TRADEX p 680
See PLANTBEST, INC

TRADEX FOODS INC p 338
3960 QUADRA ST UNIT 410, VICTORIA, BC, V8X 4A3
(250) 479-1355   SIC 5146

TRADEX INTERNATIONAL CORP p 795
809 ARROW RD, NORTH YORK, ON, M9M 2L4

SIC 6799
TRADEX SUPPLY LTD
3505 EDMONTON TRAIL NE, CALGARY, AB, T2E 3N9
(403) 250-7842 *SIC 5099*
TRADITION p 1100
See MARCHE J P FONTAINE INC
TRADITION p 1163
See ALIMENTATION BLANCHETTE & CYRENNE INC
TRADITION FINE FOODS LTD p 869
663 WARDEN AVE, SCARBOROUGH, ON, M1L 3Z5
(416) 444-4777 *SIC 2053*
TRADITION FORD (VENTES) LTEE p 1099
1163 BOUL SAINT-JOSEPH, DRUMMONDVILLE, QC, J2C 2C8
(819) 477-3050 *SIC 5511*
TRADITOURS p 1237
See VOYAGES TRADITOURS INC
TRADUCTIONS HOULE INC p 1105
540 BOUL DE L'HOPITAL BUREAU 401, GATINEAU, QC, J8V 3T2
(819) 568-1022 *SIC 7389*
TRADUCTIONS SERGE BELAIR INC p 1191
276 RUE SAINT-JACQUES BUREAU 900, MONTREAL, QC, H2Y 1N3
(514) 844-4682 *SIC 7389*
TRAF p 379
See TEACHERS RETIREMENT ALLOWANCES FUND BOARD
TRAFALGAR INDUSTRIES OF CANADA LIMITED p 785
333 RIMROCK RD, NORTH YORK, ON, M3J 3J9
(416) 638-1111 *SIC 7389*
TRAFFIC TECH p 1118
See TRAFFIC TECH INC
TRAFFIC TECH INC p 1118
16711 RTE TRANSCANADIENNE, KIRKLAND, QC, H9H 3L1
(514) 343-0044 *SIC 4731*
TRAFFIC TECH INTERNATIONAL INC p 1118
16711 RTE TRANSCANADIENNE, KIRKLAND, QC, H9H 3L1
(514) 343-0044 *SIC 4731*
TRAFFIX p 682
See 673753 ONTARIO LIMITED
TRAFFIX p 800
See 673753 ONTARIO LIMITED
TRAFIGURA CANADA GENERAL PARTNERSHIP p 61
400 3 AVE SW SUITE 3450, CALGARY, AB, T2P 4H2
(403) 294-0400 *SIC 6211*
TRAIL APPLIANCES p 38
See TRAIL APPLIANCES HOLDINGS LTD
TRAIL APPLIANCES HOLDINGS LTD p 38
6880 11 ST SE, CALGARY, AB, T2H 2T9
(403) 253-5442 *SIC 5722*
TRAIL APPLIANCES LTD p 38
6880 11 ST SE, CALGARY, AB, T2H 2T9
(403) 253-5442 *SIC 5722*
TRAIL APPLIANCES LTD p 257
3388 SWEDEN WAY, RICHMOND, BC, V6V 0B2
(604) 233-2030 *SIC 5722*
TRAIL BAY DEVELOPMENTS LTD p 268
5755 COWRIE ST SUITE 1, SECHELT, BC, V0N 3A0
(604) 885-9812 *SIC 5411*
TRAIL BUILDING SUPPLIES LTD p 117
9450 45 AVE NW, EDMONTON, AB, T6E 5V3
(780) 463-1737 *SIC 5211*
TRAILBLAZER R.V. CENTRE LTD p 150
2302 SPARROW DR, NISKU, AB, T9E 8A2
(780) 955-0300 *SIC 5571*
TRAILCON LEASING INC p 500
15 SPAR DR, BRAMPTON, ON, L6S 6E1
(905) 670-9061 *SIC 7519*

TRAILER WIZARDS LTD p 187
4649 HASTINGS ST, BURNABY, BC, V5C 2K6
(604) 320-1666 *SIC 7519*
TRAILER WIZARDS LTD p 701
1880 BRITANNIA RD E, MISSISSAUGA, ON, L4W 1J3
(905) 670-7077 *SIC 7519*
TRAILERMASTER FREIGHT CARRIERS LTD p 576
34 CANMOTOR AVE, ETOBICOKE, ON, M8Z 4E5
(416) 252-7725 *SIC 4212*
TRAILTECH INC p 1407
GD, GRAVELBOURG, SK, S0H 1X0
(306) 648-3158 *SIC 3537*
TRAILWOOD TRANSPORT LTD p 476
4925 C.W. LEACH RD, ALLISTON, ON, L9R 2B1
(705) 435-4362 *SIC 4213*
TRAIN TRAILER RENTALS LIMITED p 743
400 ANNAGEM BLVD, MISSISSAUGA, ON, L5T 3A8
(905) 564-7247 *SIC 7519*
TRAITEMENT ROBERT p 1368
See ROBERT FER ET METEAUX S.E.C.
TRAITEMENTS DES EAUX POSEIDON, LES p 1095
See SUEZ CANADA INC
TRAITEURS J. D. INC, LES p 1110
635 RUE COWIE, GRANBY, QC, J2G 8J2
SIC 5962
TRAK SPORT INC p 1089
135 RUE DEAN BUREAU 4, COWANSVILLE, QC, J2K 3Y2
SIC 3949
TRANE CANADA ULC p 220
2260 HUNTER RD SUITE 3, KELOWNA, BC, V1X 7J8
(250) 491-4600 *SIC 5075*
TRANE CANADA ULC p 676
525 COCHRANE DR SUITE 101, MARKHAM, ON, L3R 8E3
(416) 499-3600 *SIC 3585*
TRANE NORTHWEST p 220
See TRANE CANADA ULC
TRANS 99 LOGISTICS p 602
See 7013990 CANADA INC
TRANS AM PIPING PRODUCTS LTD p 78
9335 ENDEAVOR DR SE, CALGARY, AB, T3S 0A1
(403) 236-0601 *SIC 5085*
TRANS BIOTECH p 1137
201 MGR BOURGET, LEVIS, QC, G6V 9V6
(418) 833-8876 *SIC 8731*
TRANS CANADA p 733
See WELLS FARGO FINANCIAL RETAIL SERVICES COMPANY OF CANADA
TRANS CANADA MOTORS (PETERBOROUGH) LIMITED p 842
1189 LANSDOWNE ST W, PETERBOROUGH, ON, K9J 7M2
(705) 743-4141 *SIC 5511*
TRANS CANADA TRAIL p 1191
321 RUE DE LA COMMUNE O BUREAU 300, MONTREAL, QC, H2Y 2E1
(514) 485-3959 *SIC 7389*
TRANS CANADERM, DIV OF p 1328
See 1506369 ALBERTA ULC
TRANS CONTINENTAL TEXTILE RECYCLING LTD p 278
13120 78A AVE, SURREY, BC, V3W 1P4
(604) 592-2845 *SIC 4953*
TRANS GLOBAL LIFE INSURANCE COMPANY p 97
16930 114 AVE NW SUITE 275, EDMONTON, AB, T5M 3S2
(780) 930-6000 *SIC 6311*
TRANS MIX CONCRETE DIV OF p 1417
See CINDERCRETE PRODUCTS LIMITED
TRANS MOUNTAIN CANADA INC p 61

300 5 AVE SW SUITE 2700, CALGARY, AB, T2P 5J2
(403) 514-6400 *SIC 4612*
TRANS PEACE CONSTRUCTION (1987) LTD p 80
9626 69 AVE, CLAIRMONT, AB, T8X 5A1
(780) 539-6855 *SIC 1629*
TRANS POWER p 560
See TRANS POWER UTILITY CONTRACTORS INC
TRANS POWER UTILITY CONTRACTORS INC p 560
585 APPLEWOOD CRES, CONCORD, ON, L4K 5V7
(905) 660-9764 *SIC 1623*
TRANS UNION OF CANADA, INC p 528
3115 HARVESTER RD SUITE 201, BURLINGTON, ON, L7N 3N8
(800) 663-9980 *SIC 7323*
TRANS-CANADA ENERGIE p 1315
See TCED INTL INC
TRANS-CONTINENTAL TEXTILE EXPORTERS INC p 869
16 UPTON RD, SCARBOROUGH, ON, M1L 2B8
(416) 285-8951 *SIC 5137*
TRANS-HERB E INC p 1296
1090 RUE PARENT, SAINT-BRUNO, QC, J3V 6L8
(450) 441-0779 *SIC 2099*
TRANS-NORTHERN PIPELINES INC p 854
45 VOGELL RD SUITE 310, RICHMOND HILL, ON, L4B 3P6
(905) 770-3353 *SIC 4613*
TRANS-OCEANIC HUMAN RESOURCES INC p 19
5515 40 ST SE, CALGARY, AB, T2C 2A8
SIC 7361
TRANS-ONTARIO CEILING & WALL SYSTEMS INC p 560
231 MILLWAY AVE UNIT 11, CONCORD, ON, L4K 3W7
(905) 669-0666 *SIC 1742*
TRANS-PACIFIC TRADING LTD p 257
13091 VANIER PL UNIT 368, RICHMOND, BC, V6V 2J1
(604) 232-5400 *SIC 5031*
TRANS-PLUS V.M. INC p 1336
2400 RUE HALPERN, SAINT-LAURENT, QC, H4S 1S8
(514) 332-5020 *SIC 4731*
TRANS-SOL AVIATION SERVICE INC p 1278
230 2E AV DE L'AEROPORT, QUEBEC, QC, G2G 2T2
(418) 877-6708 *SIC 2759*
TRANS-TECH NETWORK p 1137
See TRANS BIOTECH
TRANS4 LOGISTICS p 701
1575 SOUTH GATEWAY RD UNIT A&B, MISSISSAUGA, ON, L4W 5J1
(905) 212-9001 *SIC 4213*
TRANSALTA CORPORATION p 65
110 12 AVE SW, CALGARY, AB, T2R 0G7
(403) 267-7110 *SIC 4911*
TRANSALTA ENERGY MARKETING CORP p 66
110 12 AVE SW, CALGARY, AB, T2R 0G7
(403) 267-7987 *SIC 8732*
TRANSALTA GENERATION PARTNERSHIP p 66
110 12 AVE SW, CALGARY, AB, T2R 0G7
(403) 267-7110 *SIC 4931*
TRANSALTA RENEWABLES INC p 61
110 12TH AVE SW, CALGARY, AB, T2P 2M1
(403) 267-2520 *SIC 4911*
TRANSAM CARRIERS INC p 560
205 DONEY CRES, CONCORD, ON, L4K 1P6
(416) 907-8101 *SIC 4213*
TRANSAMERICAS BUSINESS GROUP p

389
See TRANSAMERICAS TRADING INC
TRANSAMERICAS TRADING INC p 389
1248 WILKES AVE, WINNIPEG, MB, R3P 1C2
(204) 831-3663 *SIC 5193*
TRANSASIAN FINE CARS LTD p 934
183 FRONT ST E, TORONTO, ON, M5A 1E7
(416) 867-1577 *SIC 5511*
TRANSASIAN FINE CARS LTD p 1000
5201 HIGHWAY 7 E, UNIONVILLE, ON, L3R 1N3
(905) 948-8866 *SIC 5511*
TRANSAT A.T. INC p 1186
300 RUE LEO-PARISEAU BUREAU 600, MONTREAL, QC, H2X 4C2
(514) 987-1616 *SIC 6712*
TRANSAT DISTRIBUTION CANADA INC p 580
191 THE WEST MALL SUITE 700, ETOBICOKE, ON, M9C 5K8
SIC 4724
TRANSAT DISTRIBUTION CANADA INC p 1186
300 RUE LEO-PARISEAU BUREAU 600, MONTREAL, QC, H2X 4C2
(514) 987-1616 *SIC 4725*
TRANSAT TOURS CANADA INC p 1186
300 RUE LEO-PARISEAU BUREAU 500, MONTREAL, QC, H2X 4B3
(514) 987-1616 *SIC 4725*
TRANSATLANTIC ANGELS TRADING CO LTD p 262
11482 RIVER RD, RICHMOND, BC, V6X 1Z7
(604) 231-1960 *SIC 5093*
TRANSAXLE PARTS HAMILTON INC p 893
730 SOUTH SERVICE RD UNIT 1, STONEY CREEK, ON, L8E 5S7
(905) 643-0700 *SIC 5013*
TRANSBOIS (CANADA) LTEE p 1349
631 RUE PRINCIPALE N, SAINT-PAMPHILE, QC, G0R 3X0
(418) 356-3371 *SIC 4212*
TRANSCANADA PIPELINE USA LTD p 62
450 1 ST SW, CALGARY, AB, T2P 5H1
(403) 920-2000 *SIC 5541*
TRANSCANADA PIPELINES LIMITED p 62
450 1 ST SW, CALGARY, AB, T2P 5H1
(403) 920-2000 *SIC 4922*
TRANSCANADA PIPELINES LIMITED p 676
675 COCHRANE DR SUITE 701, MARKHAM, ON, L3R 0B8
(905) 946-7800 *SIC 4922*
TRANSCANADA PIPELINES LTD p 163
2301 PREMIER WAY UNIT 112, SHERWOOD PARK, AB, T8H 2K8
SIC 4922
TRANSCANADA PIPELINES LTD p 623
11235 ZERON RD, IROQUOIS, ON, K0E 1K0
(613) 652-4287 *SIC 4922*
TRANSCANADA PIPELINES SERVICES LTD p 62
450 1 ST SW, CALGARY, AB, T2P 5H1
(403) 920-2000 *SIC 1389*
TRANSCANADA QUEBEC INC p 1056
7005 BOUL RAOUL-DUCHESNE, BECANCOUR, QC, G9H 4X6
(819) 294-1282 *SIC 4911*
TRANSCANADA TRUCK STOP LTD p 158
1900 HWY DR S UNIT 2, REDCLIFF, AB, T0J 2P0
(403) 548-7333 *SIC 5541*
TRANSCANADA TURBINES LTD p 3
998 HAMILTON BLVD NE, AIRDRIE, AB, T4A 0K8
(403) 420-4200 *SIC 7699*
TRANSCAT CANADA INC p 1091
90A BOUL BRUNSWICK BUREAU A, DOLLARD-DES-ORMEAUX, QC, H9B 2C5
(514) 685-9626 *SIC 5084*
TRANSCENDENT MINING & MOBILIZA-

TION INC   p
212
4A FRONT ST, ELKFORD, BC, V0B 1H0
(778) 521-5144   SIC 1629

TRANSCOBEC (1987) INC   p 1320
21 RUE JOHN-F.-KENNEDY, SAINT-JEROME, QC, J7Y 4B4
(450) 432-9748   SIC 4151

TRANSCOLD DISTRIBUTION LTD   p 207
1460 CLIVEDEN AVE, DELTA, BC, V3M 6L9
(604) 519-0600   SIC 5143

TRANSCOM WORLDWIDE (NORTH AMERICA) INC   p
884
300 BUNTING RD 4, ST CATHARINES, ON, L2M 3Y3
(905) 323-3939   SIC 4899

TRANSCONA ROOFING (2000) LTD   p 367
992 DUGALD RD, WINNIPEG, MB, R2J 0G9
(204) 233-3716   SIC 1761

TRANSCONA TRAILER SALES LTD   p 367
1330 DUGALD RD, WINNIPEG, MB, R2J 0H2
(204) 237-7272   SIC 5561

TRANSCONTINENTAL   p 679
See 8388059 CANADA INC

TRANSCONTINENTAL FINE CARS LTD   p
934
328 BAYVIEW AVE, TORONTO, ON, M5A 3R7
(416) 961-2834   SIC 5511

TRANSCONTINENTAL FLEXSTAR INC   p
257
13320 RIVER RD, RICHMOND, BC, V6V 1W7
(604) 273-9277   SIC 2671

TRANSCONTINENTAL GAGNE   p 1146
See IMPRIMERIES TRANSCONTINENTAL 2005 S.E.N.C

TRANSCONTINENTAL GOURMET FOODS   p 560
See VLR FOOD CORPORATION

TRANSCONTINENTAL INC   p 459
11 RAGGED LAKE BLVD, HALIFAX, NS, B3S 1R3
(902) 450-5611   SIC 2752

TRANSCONTINENTAL INC   p 464
9185 COMMERCIAL ST SUITE 2, NEW MINAS, NS, B4N 3G1
(902) 681-2121   SIC 2711

TRANSCONTINENTAL INC   p 1200
2001 BOUL ROBERT-BOURASSA UNITE 900, MONTREAL, QC, H3A 2A6
(514) 499-0491   SIC 2721

TRANSCONTINENTAL INC   p 1209
1 PLACE VILLE-MARIE BUREAU 3240, MONTREAL, QC, H3B 0G1
(514) 954-4000   SIC 6712

TRANSCONTINENTAL INTERACTIF INC   p
1209
1 PLACE VILLE-MARIE BUREAU 3240, MONTREAL, QC, H3B 0G1
(514) 954-4000   SIC 7311

TRANSCONTINENTAL O'KEEFE MONTREAL   p
1162
See IMPRIMERIES TRANSCONTINENTAL 2005 S.E.N.C

TRANSCONTINENTAL PACKAGING WHITBY ULC   p 1015
201 SOUTH BLAIR ST, WHITBY, ON, L1N 5S6
(905) 668-5811   SIC 2671

TRANSCONTINENTAL PRINTING INC   p 35
See IMPRIMERIES TRANSCONTINENTAL INC

TRANSCONTINENTAL PRINTING INC   p
206
See IMPRIMERIES TRANSCONTINENTAL INC

TRANSCONTINENTAL PRINTING INC   p
372
See IMPRIMERIES TRANSCONTINENTAL INC

TRANSCONTINENTAL PRINTING INC   p
481
See IMPRIMERIES TRANSCONTINENTAL INC

TRANSCONTINENTAL PRINTING INC   p
835
See IMPRIMERIES TRANSCONTINENTAL INC

TRANSCONTINENTAL PRINTING INC   p
1027
See IMPRIMERIES TRANSCONTINENTAL INC

TRANSCONTINENTAL PRINTING INC   p
1049
See IMPRIMERIES TRANSCONTINENTAL INC

TRANSCONTINENTAL PRINTING INC   p
1055
See IMPRIMERIES TRANSCONTINENTAL INC

TRANSCONTINENTAL PRINTING INC   p
1065
See IMPRIMERIES TRANSCONTINENTAL INC

TRANSCONTINENTAL PRINTING INC   p
1132
See IMPRIMERIES TRANSCONTINENTAL INC

TRANSCONTINENTAL PRINTING INC   p
1313
See IMPRIMERIES TRANSCONTINENTAL INC

TRANSCONTINENTAL PRINTING INC   p
1373
See IMPRIMERIES TRANSCONTINENTAL INC

TRANSCORE LINK LOGISTICS CORPORATION   p
707
2 ROBERT SPECK PKY SUITE 900, MISSISSAUGA, ON, L4Z 1H8
(905) 795-0580   SIC 4731

TRANSCRIPT HEROES TRANSCRIPTION SERVICES INC   p 943
1 YONGE ST SUITE 1801, TORONTO, ON, M5E 1W7
(647) 478-5188   SIC 7389

TRANSDEV CANADA INC   p 1209
1100 BOUL RENE-LEVESQUE O BUREAU 1305, MONTREAL, QC, H3B 4N4
(450) 970-8899   SIC 6712

TRANSDEV QUEBEC INC   p 1057
1500 RUE LOUIS-MARCHAND, BELOEIL, QC, J3G 6S3
(450) 446-8899   SIC 4131

TRANSDEV QUEBEC INC   p 1318
720 RUE TROTTER, SAINT-JEAN-SUR-RICHELIEU, QC, J3B 8T2
(514) 787-1998   SIC 4151

TRANSDIFF INC   p 1275
2901 AV WATT, QUEBEC, QC, G1X 3W1
(418) 653-3422   SIC 5511

TRANSDIFF PETERBILT DE QUEBEC   p
1275
See TRANSDIFF INC

TRANSELEC/COMMON INC   p 1085
2075 BOUL FORTIN, COTE SAINT-LUC, QC, H7S 1P4
(514) 382-1550   SIC 1623

TRANSENERGIE ET PRODUCTION, DIVISIONS DE   p
1053
See HYDRO-QUEBEC

TRANSFACTOR INDUSTRIES INC   p 560
65 BASALTIC RD, CONCORD, ON, L4K 1G4
(905) 695-8844   SIC 3612

TRANSFORCE   p 1336
See TFI INTERNATIONAL INC

TRANSFORM AUTOMOTIVE CANADA LIMITED   p
662
3745 COMMERCE RD, LONDON, ON, N6N 1R1

(519) 644-2434   SIC 3714

TRANSFORMATEUR CARTE INTERNATIONAL   p
1074
See CARTE INTERNATIONAL INC

TRANSFORMATEUR DELTA   p 1108
See 3680258 CANADA INC

TRANSFORMATEUR FEDERAL LTEE   p
1248
5059 BOUL SAINT-JEAN-BAPTISTE, POINTE-AUX-TREMBLES, QC, H1B 5V3
(514) 640-5059   SIC 5099

TRANSFORMATEURS DELTA STAR INC   p
1316
860 RUE LUCIEN-BEAUDIN, SAINT-JEAN-SUR-RICHELIEU, QC, J2X 5V5
(450) 346-6622   SIC 3612

TRANSFORMATION BFL   p 1403
See 9071-3975 QUEBEC INC

TRANSFORMIX ENGINEERING INC   p 633
1150 GARDINERS RD, KINGSTON, ON, K7P 1R7
(613) 544-5970   SIC 3569

TRANSFRT MCNAMARA INC   p 483
1126 INDUSTRIAL RD, AYR, ON, N0B 1E0
(519) 740-6500   SIC 4231

TRANSGAS LIMITED   p 1419
1777 VICTORIA AVE SUITE 500, REGINA, SK, S4P 4K5
(306) 777-9500   SIC 4923

TRANSGLOBAL FINE CARS LTD   p 906
480 STEELES AVE W, THORNHILL, ON, L4J 1A2
(905) 886-3380   SIC 5511

TRANSGLOBE ENERGY CORPORATION   p
62
250 5TH ST SW SUITE 2300, CALGARY, AB, T2P 0R4
(403) 264-9888   SIC 1382

TRANSGLOBE PROPERTY MANAGEMENT SERVICES LTD   p
690
5935 AIRPORT RD UNIT 600, MISSISSAUGA, ON, L4V 1W5
SIC 6531

TRANSIT DEPARTMENT   p 1420
See CITY OF REGINA, THE

TRANSIT LOGISTICS SOLUTIONS INC   p
1024
4455 COUNTY RD 42, WINDSOR, ON, N9A 6J3
(519) 967-0911   SIC 4213

TRANSIT MONTANK   p 1239
See VOPAK TERMINALS OF CANADA INC

TRANSIT PAVING INC   p 147
3047 GERSHAW DR SW, MEDICINE HAT, AB, T1B 3N1
(403) 526-0386   SIC 1611

TRANSIT PETROLEUM   p 604
516 IMPERIAL RD N, GUELPH, ON, N1H 1G4
(519) 571-1220   SIC 5172

TRANSIT POLICE   p 237
See SOUTH COAST BRITISH COLUMBIA TRANSPORTATION AUTHORITY

TRANSIT TRAILER LIMITED   p 543
22217 BLOOMFIELD RD SUITE 3, CHATHAM, ON, N7M 5J3
(519) 354-9944   SIC 5012

TRANSIT WAREHOUSE DISTRIBUTION   p
1139
See PIECES D'AUTO TRANSIT INC, LES

TRANSITAIRE HERCULES   p 236
See HERCULES FORWARDING ULC

TRANSITAIRES DAVID KIRSCH LTEE   p
1096
455 BOUL FENELON BUREAU 130, DORVAL, QC, H9S 5T8
(514) 636-0233   SIC 4731

TRANSITAIRES INTERNATIONAUX SKYWAY LTEE   p
1129
9262 CH DE LA COTE-DE-LIESSE, LACHINE, QC, H8T 1A1

(514) 636-0250   SIC 4731

TRANSLINK   p 237
See SOUTH COAST BRITISH COLUMBIA TRANSPORTATION AUTHORITY

TRANSMONTAIGNE MARKETING CANADA INC   p 844
1305 PICKERING PKY SUITE 101, PICKERING, ON, L1V 3P2
SIC 2911

TRANSMOUNT TRANSPORT   p 509
See FORBES HEWLETT TRANSPORT INC

TRANSNAT EXPRESS INC   p 1246
1397 RUE SAVOIE, PLESSISVILLE, QC, G6L 1J8
(819) 362-7333   SIC 4213

TRANSNAT LOGISTIQUE   p 1246
See TRANSNAT EXPRESS INC

TRANSNET FREIGHT LTD   p 507
247 SUMMERLEA RD, BRAMPTON, ON, L6T 4E1
(647) 868-2762   SIC 4731

TRANSOCEANIC FINE CARS LTD   p 906
220 STEELES AVE W, THORNHILL, ON, L4J 1A1
(905) 886-8800   SIC 5511

TRANSOURCE FREIGHTWAYS   p 19
See TRANSOURCE FREIGHTWAYS LTD

TRANSOURCE FREIGHTWAYS LTD   p 19
19-6991 48 ST SE, CALGARY, AB, T2C 5A4
(403) 726-4366   SIC 4213

TRANSOURCE FREIGHTWAYS LTD   p 207
1659 FOSTER'S WAY, DELTA, BC, V3M 6S7
(604) 525-0527   SIC 4213

TRANSPECT INVESTMENT INC   p 707
4 ROBERT SPECK PKY SUITE 1500, MISSISSAUGA, ON, L4Z 1S1
(905) 366-7320   SIC 4731

TRANSPERFECT TRANSLATION INC   p
1200
1010 RUE SHERBROOKE O BUREAU 811, MONTREAL, QC, H3A 2R7
(514) 861-5177   SIC 7389

TRANSPHARM INC   p 1395
585 AV SAINT-CHARLES BUREAU 180, VAUDREUIL-DORION, QC, J7V 8P9
(450) 455-5568   SIC 5912

TRANSPLACE CANADA LTD   p 854
45A WEST WILMOT ST UNIT 213, RICHMOND HILL, ON, L4B 2P2
(800) 463-3102   SIC 4731

TRANSPLANT QUEBEC   p 1169
4100 RUE MOLSON BUREAU 200, MONTREAL, QC, H1Y 3N1
(514) 286-1414   SIC 8742

TRANSPORT A. LABERGE ET FILS INC   p
1158
255 104 RTE, MONT-SAINT-GREGOIRE, QC, J0J 1K0
(450) 347-4336   SIC 4212

TRANSPORT ALFRED BOIVIN INC   p 1080
2205 RUE DE LA FONDERIE, CHICOUTIMI, QC, G7H 8B9
(418) 693-8681   SIC 4212

TRANSPORT BAIE-COMEAU INC   p 1052
62 AV WILLIAM-DOBELL, BAIE-COMEAU, QC, G4Z 1T7
(418) 296-5229   SIC 4213

TRANSPORT BELLEMARE INTERNATIONAL INC   p
1389
8750 BOUL INDUSTRIEL, TROIS-RIVIERES, QC, G9A 5E1
(819) 379-4546   SIC 4213

TRANSPORT BERNIERES INC   p 1265
1721 RUE A.-R.-DECARY, QUEBEC, QC, G1N 3Z7
(418) 684-2421   SIC 4213

TRANSPORT BOURASSA INC   p 1318
800 RUE DE DIJON, SAINT-JEAN-SUR-RICHELIEU, QC, J3B 8G3
(450) 346-5313   SIC 4212

TRANSPORT BOURRET INC   p 1099
375 BOUL LEMIRE, DRUMMONDVILLE, QC, J2C 0C6

(819) 477-2202   *SIC 4212*
TRANSPORT CANADA   p 1168
3400 RUE NOTRE-DAME E, MONTREAL, QC, H1W 2J2
(514) 283-7020   *SIC 4111*
TRANSPORT CARLANN   p 1293
See EQUIPEMENTS PLANNORD LTEE
TRANSPORT COUTURE & FILS LTEE   p 1300
99 RTE 271 S, SAINT-EPHREM-DE-BEAUCE, QC, G0M 1R0
(418) 484-2104   *SIC 4213*
TRANSPORT DE PRODUITS FORESTIERS C.D.L   p 1092
See TRANSPORT MATTE LTEE
TRANSPORT DEMARK INC   p 1132
9235 RUE BOIVIN, LASALLE, QC, H8R 2E8
(514) 365-5666   *SIC 4212*
TRANSPORT DIANE PICHE INC   p 1118
3862 BOUL SAINT-CHARLES, KIRKLAND, QC, H9H 3C3
(514) 693-9059   *SIC 5499*
TRANSPORT DIVISION   p 504
See MIDLAND TRANSPORT LIMITED
TRANSPORT DOUCET & FILS MISTASSINI INC   p 1090
124 RUE LAVOIE, DOLBEAU-MISTASSINI, QC, G8L 4M8
(418) 276-7395   *SIC 4213*
TRANSPORT DP INC   p 1154
1213 RUE INDUSTRIELLE, MONT-JOLI, QC, G5H 3T9
(418) 775-1311   *SIC 5143*
TRANSPORT EASE & MANAGEMENT SERVICES   p 366
See NATIONAL SHIPPERS & RECEIVERS INC
TRANSPORT ECOLE-BEC MONTREAL (EBM) INC   p 1336
8835 BOUL HENRI-BOURASSA O, SAINT-LAURENT, QC, H4S 1P7
(514) 595-5609   *SIC 4212*
TRANSPORT EN COMMUN LA QUEBE-COISE INC   p 1123
300 RUE DES CONSEILLERS, LA PRAIRIE, QC, J5R 2E6
(450) 659-8598   *SIC 4111*
TRANSPORT EN VRAC ST-DENIS ENR   p 1377
See 2171-0751 QUEBEC INC
TRANSPORT ES FOUCAULT   p 1320
See MAURICE FOUCAULT INC
TRANSPORT EXPRESS MINIMAX INC   p 562
605 EDUCATION RD, CORNWALL, ON, K6H 6C7
(613) 936-0660   *SIC 4212*
TRANSPORT F. GILBERT LTEE   p 1080
150 RUE DES ROUTIERS, CHICOUTIMI, QC, G7H 5B1
(418) 698-4848   *SIC 4731*
TRANSPORT FERROVIAIRE   p 1389
See TRANSPORT FERROVIAIRE TSHI-UETIN INC
TRANSPORT FERROVIAIRE TSHIUETIN INC   p 1389
148 BOUL DES MONTAGNAIS, UASHAT, QC, G4R 5R2
(418) 960-0982   *SIC 4011*
TRANSPORT FORTUNA   p 1101
See 9342-7490 QUEBEC INC
TRANSPORT GILMYR INC   p 1160
315 CH DU COTEAU, MONTMAGNY, QC, G5V 3R8
(418) 241-5747   *SIC 4213*
TRANSPORT GREGOIRE   p 1337
See TRANSPORT TFI 15 S.E.C.
TRANSPORT GUILBAULT CANADA INC   p 1265
435 RUE FARADAY, QUEBEC, QC, G1N 4G6
(418) 681-5272   *SIC 4213*
TRANSPORT GUILBAULT INC   p 1265

435 RUE FARADAY, QUEBEC, QC, G1N 4G6
(418) 681-0575   *SIC 4213*
TRANSPORT GUILBAULT INTERNA-TIONAL INC   p
1265
435 RUE FARADAY, QUEBEC, QC, G1N 4G6
(418) 681-0575   *SIC 4213*
TRANSPORT GUILBAULT LONGUE DIS-TANCE INC   p
1265
435 RUE FARADAY, QUEBEC, QC, G1N 4G6
(418) 681-0575   *SIC 4731*
TRANSPORT GUY BOURASSA   p 1318
See TRANSPORT BOURASSA INC
TRANSPORT GUY LEVASSEUR INC p 1246
876 RUE PRINCIPALE, POHENEGAMOOK, QC, G0L 1J0
(418) 859-2294   *SIC 4213*
TRANSPORT J.C. GERMAIN   p 1337
See TRANSPORT TFI 1, S.E.C.
TRANSPORT J.C. GERMAIN   p 1389
See TRANSPORT TFI 1, S.E.C.
TRANSPORT JACQUES AUGER INC   p 1137
860 RUE ARCHIMEDE, LEVIS, QC, G6V 7M5
(418) 835-9266   *SIC 4212*
TRANSPORT JACQUES AUGER INC   p 1248
12305 BOUL METROPOLITAIN E, POINTE-AUX-TREMBLES, QC, H1B 5R3
(514) 493-3835   *SIC 4212*
TRANSPORT JAGUAR INTERNATIONAL INC   p 1062
3777 RUE LA FAYETTE O, BOISBRIAND, QC, J7H 1N5
(450) 433-8000   *SIC 4213*
TRANSPORT L.F.L. INC   p 1392
431 CH DE L'ECORE N, VALLEE-JONCTION, QC, G0S 3J0
(418) 253-5423   *SIC 4213*
TRANSPORT LAURENTIEN LTEE   p 1060
926 RUE JACQUES PASCHINI BUREAU 300, BOIS-DE-FILION, QC, J6Z 4W4
(450) 628-2372   *SIC 4212*
TRANSPORT LEMIEUX, HERVE (1975) INC   p 1336
6500 CH SAINT-FRANCOIS, SAINT-LAURENT, QC, H4S 1B7
(514) 337-2203   *SIC 4212*
TRANSPORT LOGI-PRO INC.   p 1051
9001 RUE DU PARCOURS, ANJOU, QC, H1J 2Y1
(514) 493-1717   *SIC 5147*
TRANSPORT LYON INC   p 1239
9999 RUE NOTRE-DAME E, MONTREAL-EST, QC, H1L 3R5
(514) 322-4422   *SIC 4214*
TRANSPORT M. J. LAVOIE INC   p 1351
800 RUE NOTRE-DAME, SAINT-REMI, QC, J0L 2L0
(450) 454-5333   *SIC 4953*
TRANSPORT MATTE LTEE   p 1092
487 RUE PAGE, DONNACONA, QC, G3M 1W6
(418) 285-0777   *SIC 4213*
TRANSPORT MICHEL BLOUIN   p 1357
See SERVICES JAG INC, LES
TRANSPORT MICHEL GASSE ET FILS INC   p 1283
219 RUE DE CAPRI, REPENTIGNY, QC, J6A 5L1
(450) 657-4667   *SIC 1542*
TRANSPORT MORNEAU INC   p 1051
9601 BOUL DES SCIENCES, ANJOU, QC, H1J 0A6
(514) 325-2727   *SIC 4213*
TRANSPORT MORNEAU INC   p 1292
40 RUE PRINCIPALE, SAINT-ARSENE, QC, G0L 2K0
(418) 862-2727   *SIC 4213*

TRANSPORT N SERVICE INC   p 604
5075 WHITELAW RD, GUELPH, ON, N1H 6J4
(519) 821-0400   *SIC 4213*
TRANSPORT NORD-OUEST INC   p 1391
1355B CH SULLIVAN, VAL-D'OR, QC, J9P 1M2
(819) 874-2003   *SIC 4213*
TRANSPORT REMCO LIMITEE   p 1129
5203 RUE FAIRWAY, LACHINE, QC, H8T 3K8
(514) 737-1900   *SIC 4731*
TRANSPORT ROBERT   p 1065
See GROUPE ROBERT INC
TRANSPORT ROBERT (1973) LTEE p 1068
65 RUE DE VAUDREUIL, BOUCHERVILLE, QC, J4B 1K7
(514) 521-1416   *SIC 4213*
TRANSPORT ROBERT (1973) LTEE p 1125
4075 RUE VILLENEUVE, LAC-MEGANTIC, QC, G6B 2C2
(819) 583-2230   *SIC 4213*
TRANSPORT ROBERT (1973) LTEE p 1288
500 RTE 112, ROUGEMONT, QC, J0L 1M0
(450) 469-3153   *SIC 4213*
TRANSPORT ROBERT (1973) LTEE p 1360
1199 2E RUE DU PARC-INDUSTRIEL, SAINTE-MARIE, QC, G6E 1G7
(514) 521-1416   *SIC 4213*
TRANSPORT ROLLEX LTEE   p 1393
910 BOUL LIONEL-BOULET, VARENNES, QC, J3X 1P7
(450) 652-4282   *SIC 4953*
TRANSPORT S A S DRUMMONDVILLE INC   p 1099
850 RUE LABONTE, DRUMMONDVILLE, QC, J2C 5Y4
(819) 477-6599   *SIC 4213*
TRANSPORT S. & M. GASS   p 1283
See TRANSPORT MICHEL GASSE ET FILS INC
TRANSPORT S.A.F. 1994   p 1296
See TRANSPORT SAF (1994) INC
TRANSPORT SAF (1994) INC   p 1296
1227 RANG SAINT-JOSEPH, SAINT-CELESTIN, QC, J0C 1G0
(819) 229-3638   *SIC 4731*
TRANSPORT SALES & SERVICE   p 532
See 374872 ONTARIO LIMITED
TRANSPORT SCOLAIRE SOGESCO INC p 1099
1125 BOUL SAINT-JOSEPH BUREAU 320, DRUMMONDVILLE, QC, J2C 2C8
(819) 472-1991   *SIC 6712*
TRANSPORT SGH   p 1331
See 9162-7331 QUEBEC INC
TRANSPORT SN   p 1110
See 9055-5749 QUEBEC INC
TRANSPORT SOLUTIONS   p 407
883 MAIN ST, MONCTON, NB, E1C 1G5
(506) 857-1095   *SIC 7361*
TRANSPORT ST-LAMBERT   p 1139
See TRANSPORT TFI 11 S.E.C.
TRANSPORT SYLVESTER & FORGET INC p 1353
320 RTE 201, SAINT-STANISLAS-DE-KOSTKA, QC, J0S 1W0
(450) 377-2535   *SIC 4213*
TRANSPORT TFI 1, S.E.C.   p 1337
8801 RTE TRANSCANADIENNE BUREAU 500, SAINT-LAURENT, QC, H4S 1Z6
(514) 331-4000   *SIC 5122*
TRANSPORT TFI 1, S.E.C.   p 1389
1200 RUE DU PERE-DANIEL, TROIS-RIVIERES, QC, G9A 5R6
(819) 370-3422   *SIC 4213*
TRANSPORT TFI 11 S.E.C.   p 1139
1956B 3E RUE, LEVIS, QC, G6W 5M6
(418) 839-6655   *SIC 4213*
TRANSPORT TFI 14 S.E.C.   p 1337
8801 RTE TRANSCANADIENNE BUREAU 500, SAINT-LAURENT, QC, H4S 1Z6
(514) 331-4000   *SIC 4213*
TRANSPORT TFI 15 S.E.C.   p 1337

8801 RTE TRANSCANADIENNE BUREAU 500, SAINT-LAURENT, QC, H4S 1Z6
(514) 331-4000   *SIC 4213*
TRANSPORT TFI 16, S.E.C.   p 1060
801 BOUL INDUSTRIEL BUREAU 228, BOIS-DES-FILION, QC, J6Z 4T3
(450) 628-8000   *SIC 4214*
TRANSPORT TFI 19, S.E.C.   p 1303
1214 RTE 255, SAINT-FELIX-DE-KINGSEY, QC, J0B 2T0
(819) 848-2042   *SIC 4213*
TRANSPORT TFI 2, S.E.C.   p 1337
8801 RTE TRANSCANADIENNE BUREAU 500, SAINT-LAURENT, QC, H4S 1Z6
(514) 331-4000   *SIC 4213*
TRANSPORT TFI 21, S.E.C.   p 1337
8801 RTE TRANSCANADIENNE BUREAU 500, SAINT-LAURENT, QC, H4S 1Z6
(514) 856-7500   *SIC 5021*
TRANSPORT TFI 22 S.E.C.   p 1337
8801 RTE TRANSCANADIENNE BUREAU 500, SAINT-LAURENT, QC, H4S 1Z6
(514) 331-4000   *SIC 4212*
TRANSPORT TFI 23 S.E.C.   p 1046
200 RUE DES ROUTIERS, AMOS, QC, J9T 3A6
(819) 727-1304   *SIC 4212*
TRANSPORT TFI 3 L.P.   p 676
2815 14TH AVE, MARKHAM, ON, L3R 0H9
(800) 268-6231   *SIC 4213*
TRANSPORT TFI 4, S.E.C.   p 1293
140 RUE DES GRANDS-LACS, SAINT-AUGUSTIN-DE-DESMAURES, QC, G3A 2K1
(418) 870-5454   *SIC 4213*
TRANSPORT TFI 5, S.E.C.   p 701
1100 HAULTAIN CRT, MISSISSAUGA, ON, L4W 2T1
(905) 624-4050   *SIC 4213*
TRANSPORT TFI 5, S.E.C.   p 1337
6700 CH SAINT-FRANCOIS, SAINT-LAURENT, QC, H4S 1B7
(514) 856-5559   *SIC 4213*
TRANSPORT TFI 6 S.E.C.   p 1139
1950 3E RUE, LEVIS, QC, G6W 5M6
(418) 834-9891   *SIC 4213*
TRANSPORT TFI 6 S.E.C.   p 1359
100A RUE SAINT-ALPHONSE, SAINTE-LUCE, QC, G0K 1P0
(418) 731-2327   *SIC 4213*
TRANSPORT TFI 7 S.E.C   p 94
14520 130 AVE NW, EDMONTON, AB, T5L 3M6
(780) 482-9483   *SIC 4731*
TRANSPORT TFI 7 S.E.C   p 183
7867 EXPRESS ST, BURNABY, BC, V5A 1S7
(604) 420-2030   *SIC 4213*
TRANSPORT TFI 7 S.E.C   p 1337
8801 RTE TRANSCANADIENNE BUREAU 500, SAINT-LAURENT, QC, H4S 1Z6
(514) 331-4000   *SIC 4213*
TRANSPORT TRANS-ACTION   p 1336
See TRANSPORT LEMIEUX, HERVE (1975) INC
TRANSPORT TRANSBO   p 1300
See OLYMEL S.E.C.
TRANSPORT TRANSBO INC   p 1353
170 RUE SAINT-EDOUARD, SAINT-SIMON-DE-BAGOT, QC, J0H 1Y0
(450) 798-2155   *SIC 4212*
TRANSPORT WATSON MONTREAL p 1348
See 7853807 CANADA INC
TRANSPORT YN.-GONTHIER INC p 1139
2170 3E RUE, LEVIS, QC, G6W 6V4
(418) 839-7311   *SIC 4212*
TRANSPORTATION AND INDUSTRIAL FUNDING   p 722
See GENERAL ELECTRIC CAPITAL CANADA
TRANSPORTATION SCHOOL BUSSING p 465
See CAPE BRETON-VICTORIA REGIONAL SCHOOL BOARD
TRANSPORTATION SERVICES.CA p 547

See 2088847 ONTARIO INC
TRANSPORTEURS EN VRAC SHEFFORD INC, LES   p 1110
438 RUE DE LA PROVIDENCE, GRANBY, QC, J2H 1H1
(450) 375-2331   SIC 4731

TRANSPORTS DELSON LTEE, LES p 1089
121 RUE PRINCIPALE N, DELSON, QC, J5B 1Z2
(450) 632-2960   SIC 4212

TRANSPORTS DUCAMPRO INC   p 1298
229 RTE 204, SAINT-DAMASE-DES-AULNAIES, QC, G0R 2X0
(418) 598-9319   SIC 4213

TRANSPORTS DUCAMPRO INC   p 1316
1200 BOUL SAINT-LUC, SAINT-JEAN-SUR-RICHELIEU, QC, J2Y 1A5
(450) 348-4400   SIC 4213

TRANSPORTS ET LOGISTIQUES DES AMERIQUES CANADA   p 1084
See AMERICAN TRANSPORTATION & LOGISTICS (AT&L) CANADA INC

TRANSPORTS FUEL INC, LES   p 1131
2480 RUE SENKUS, LASALLE, QC, H8N 2X9
(514) 948-2225   SIC 4731

TRANSPORTS INTER-NORD INC, LES   p 1319
455 BOUL LAJEUNESSE O, SAINT-JEROME, QC, J5L 2P7
(450) 438-7133   SIC 4212

TRANSPORTS J.M. BERNIER INC   p 1151
75 RUE DES ERABLES, METABETCHOUAN-LAC-A-LA-CROIX, QC, G8G 1P9
(418) 349-3496   SIC 4213

TRANSPORTS LACOMBE INC, LES p 1165
5644 RUE HOCHELAGA, MONTREAL, QC, H1N 3L7
(514) 256-0050   SIC 4212

TRANSPORTS M. CHARETTE INC p 1115
635 RUE NAZAIRE-LAURIN, JOLIETTE, QC, J6E 0L6
(450) 760-9600   SIC 4212

TRANSPORTS R.M.T. INC   p 1283
400 BOUL RICHELIEU, RICHELIEU, QC, J3L 3R8
(450) 658-1795   SIC 4212

TRANSPORTS YVON TURCOTTE LTEE, LES   p 1097
675 BOUL LEMIRE O, DRUMMONDVILLE, QC, J2B 8A9
(819) 474-4884   SIC 4213

TRANSTAR SANITATION SUPPLY LTD. p 194
3975 NORTH FRASER WAY, BURNABY, BC, V5J 5H9
(604) 439-9585   SIC 5087

TRANSWEST AIR LIMITED PARTNERSHIP p 1414
GD, PRINCE ALBERT, SK, S6V 5R4
(306) 764-1404   SIC 4522

TRANSWORLD FINE CARS LTD   p 906
222 STEELES AVE W, THORNHILL, ON, L4J 1A1
(905) 886-6880   SIC 5511

TRANSWORLD IMPORTS INC   p 258
22071 FRASERWOOD WAY SUITE 100, RICHMOND, BC, V6W 1J5
(604) 272-3432   SIC 5099

TRANSX LOGISTICS   p 159
See TRANSX LTD

TRANSX LTD   p 159
285115 61 AVE SE, ROCKY VIEW COUNTY, AB, T1X 0K3
(403) 236-9300   SIC 4213

TRANSX LTD   p 379
2595 INKSTER BLVD, WINNIPEG, MB, R3C 2E6
(204) 632-6694   SIC 4213

TRANSX TRANSPORT INC   p 380
2595 INKSTER BLVD SUITE 2, WINNIPEG, MB, R3C 2E6
(204) 632-6694   SIC 4213

TRANSX TRANSPORT INC   p 1395
2351 RUE HENRY-FORD, VAUDREUIL-DORION, QC, J7V 0J1
(450) 424-0114   SIC 4731

TRAPA   p 257
See TRANS-PACIFIC TRADING LTD

TRAPEZE   p 702
See VOLARIS GROUP INC

TRAPEZE GROUP   p 701
See TRAPEZE SOFTWARE GROUP, INC

TRAPEZE SOFTWARE GROUP, INC p 701
5800 EXPLORER DR UNIT 500, MISSISSAUGA, ON, L4W 5K9
(905) 629-8727   SIC 7371

TRAPP AVE INDUSTRIES   p 181
6010 TRAPP AVE APP AVE, BURNABY, BC, V3N 2V4
(604) 526-2333   SIC 3441

TRAPPERS TRANSPORT LTD   p 363
1300 REDONDA ST, WINNIPEG, MB, R2C 2Z2
(204) 697-7647   SIC 4213

TRASK LOBSTERS   p 457
See FISHERMAN'S MARKET INTERNATIONAL INCORPORATED

TRAUGOTT BUILDING CONTRACTORS INC   p 537
95 THOMPSON DR, CAMBRIDGE, ON, N1T 2E4
(519) 740-9444   SIC 1542

TRAVAIL ADAPTE DE LANAUDIERE p 1281
3131 5E AV, RAWDON, QC, J0K 1S0
(450) 834-7678   SIC 3549

TRAVAILLEURS & TRAVAILLEUSES UNIS DE L'ALIMENTATION ET DU COMMERCE T U A C LOCAL 501   p 1346
4850 BOUL METROPOLITAIN E BUREAU 501, SAINT-LEONARD, QC, H1S 2Z7
(514) 725-9525   SIC 8631

TRAVAILLEURS ET TRAVAILLEUSES UNIS DE L'ALIMENTATION ET DU COMMERCE LOCAL-500   p 1181
1200 BOUL CREMAZIE E BUREAU 100, MONTREAL, QC, H2P 3A7
(514) 332-5825   SIC 8631

TRAVALE TIRE & SERVICE INC   p 611
340 WENTWORTH ST N, HAMILTON, ON, L8L 5W3
(905) 777-8473   SIC 5531

TRAVAUX MARITIMES OCEAN INC p 1260
105 RUE ABRAHAM-MARTIN BUREAU 500, QUEBEC, QC, G1K 8N1
(418) 694-1414   SIC 1629

TRAVAUX PUBLICS   p 1237
See VILLE DE LAVAL

TRAVAUX PUBLIQUES   p 1397
See VILLE DE MONTREAL

TRAVEL ALBERTA IN-PROVINCE   p 86
10949 120 ST NW, EDMONTON, AB, T5H 3R2
SIC 4724

TRAVEL BEST BETS   p 182
See JUBILEE TOURS & TRAVEL LTD

TRAVEL CENTRE CANADA INC, THE p 1036
535 MILL ST, WOODSTOCK, ON, N4S 7V6
(519) 421-3144   SIC 5172

TRAVEL CORPORATION (CANADA), THE p 778
33 KERN RD, NORTH YORK, ON, M3B 1S9
(416) 322-8468   SIC 4725

TRAVEL DISCOUNTERS   p 788
1927 AVENUE RD, NORTH YORK, ON, M5M 4A2
(416) 481-6701   SIC 7389

TRAVEL EDGE (CANADA) INC   p 941
2 QUEEN ST E SUITE 200, TORONTO, ON, M5C 3G7
(416) 649-9093   SIC 4724

TRAVEL GALLERY, THE   p 1422
1230 BLACKFOOT DR SUITE 110, REGINA, SK, S4S 7G4
SIC 4724

TRAVEL GROUP, THE   p 301

See 1987 THE TRAVEL GROUP LTD
TRAVEL HEALTHCARE INSURANCE SOLUTIONS INC   p 905
300 JOHN ST SUITE 405, THORNHILL, ON, L3T 5W4
(905) 731-8140   SIC 6321

TRAVEL INSURANCE OFFICE INC   p 665
190 BULLOCK DR SUITE 2, MARKHAM, ON, L3P 7N3
(905) 201-1571   SIC 6321

TRAVEL MASTERS INC   p 322
2678 BROADWAY W SUITE 200, VANCOUVER, BC, V6K 2G3
(604) 659-4150   SIC 4724

TRAVEL MASTERS PRINCE ALBERT p 322
See TRAVEL MASTERS INC

TRAVEL STORE, THE   p 728
See 1572900 ONTARIO INC

TRAVEL STORE, THE   p 1039
See RAYLINK LTD

TRAVEL SUPERSTORE INC   p 614
77 JAMES ST N SUITE 230, HAMILTON, ON, L8R 2K3
(905) 570-9999   SIC 4724

TRAVEL TRUST INTERNATIONAL   p 942
See DUFFERIN TRAVEL INC

TRAVELAND LEISURE CENTRE (REGINA) LTD   p 1419
GD LCD MAIN, REGINA, SK, S4P 2Z4
(306) 789-3311   SIC 5561

TRAVELAND LEISURE VEHICLES LTD p 228
20529 LANGLEY BYPASS, LANGLEY, BC, V3A 5E8
(604) 530-8141   SIC 5561

TRAVELAND R.V. RENTALS LTD   p 228
20257 LANGLEY BYPASS, LANGLEY, BC, V3A 6K9
(604) 532-8128   SIC 5571

TRAVELAND RV   p 1419
See TRAVELAND LEISURE CENTRE (REGINA) LTD

TRAVELAND RV SUPERCENTRE   p 228
See TRAVELAND LEISURE VEHICLES LTD

TRAVELBRANDS INC   p 701
5450 EXPLORER DR UNIT 300, MISSISSAUGA, ON, L4W 5M1
(416) 649-3939   SIC 4725

TRAVELBRANDS INC   p 943
26 WELLINGTON ST E, TORONTO, ON, M5E 1S2
(416) 364-5100   SIC 4725

TRAVELERS INSURANCE COMPANY OF CANADA   p 958
165 UNIVERSITY AVE SUITE 101, TORONTO, ON, M5H 3B9
(416) 362-7231   SIC 6351

TRAVELERS INSURANCE COMPANY OF CANADA   p 958
20 QUEEN ST W SUITE 300, TORONTO, ON, M5H 3R3
(416) 360-8183   SIC 6351

TRAVELERS TRANSPORTATION SERVICES INC   p 510
195 HEART LAKE RD, BRAMPTON, ON, L6W 3N6
(905) 457-8789   SIC 4213

TRAVELERS TRANSPORTATION SERVICES INC   p 1005
735 GILLARD ST, WALLACEBURG, ON, N8A 5G7
(519) 627-5848   SIC 4213

TRAVELEX CANADA LIMITED   p 941
100 YONGE ST, TORONTO, ON, M5C 2W1
(416) 359-3700   SIC 6099

TRAVELEX GLOBAL BUSINESS PAYMENTS   p 941
See TRAVELEX CANADA LIMITED

TRAVELLERS FINANCE LTD   p 274

800-9900 KING GEORGE BLVD, SURREY, BC, V3T 0K7
(604) 293-0202   SIC 6159

TRAVELODGE TORONTO AIRPORT p 587
See ROYAL HOST INC

TRAVELPLUS   p 580
See TRANSAT DISTRIBUTION CANADA INC

TRAVOIS HOLDINGS LTD   p 68
8240 COLLICUTT ST SW, CALGARY, AB, T2V 2X1
(403) 252-4445   SIC 8051

TRAXLE MANUFACTURING   p 603
See LINAMAR CORPORATION

TRAXOL CHEMICALS   p 168
See GUARDIAN CHEMICALS INC

TRAXPO   p 1099
See SOPREMA INC

TRAYNOR BAKERY WHOLESALE   p 611
See 386140 ONTARIO LIMITED

TRC DISTRIBUTION   p 26
See TIMBER REALIZATION COMPANY LIMITED

TRC HYDRAULICS INC   p 398
855 RUE CHAMPLAIN, DIEPPE, NB, E1A 1P6
(506) 853-1986   SIC 5084

TRC SMI   p 1178
See GROUPE S.M. INTERNATIONAL INC, LE

TRC TIMBER REALISATION COMPANY, A DIV OF   p 26
See TIMBERTOWN BUILDING CENTRE LTD

TREASURE COVE CASINO   p 251
See PRINCE GEORGE CASINO SUPPLY COMPANY INC

TREASURY BOARD OF CANADA   p 824
See TREASURY BOARD OF CANADA SECRETARIAT

TREASURY BOARD OF CANADA SECRETARIAT   p 824
90 ELGIN ST FL 8, OTTAWA, ON, K1P 0C6
(613) 369-3200   SIC 6712

TREATMENT CENTRE OF WATERLOO REGION, THE   p 1007
500 HALLMARK DR, WATERLOO, ON, N2K 3P5
(519) 886-8886   SIC 8361

TREATY ENTERPRISE INC   p 461
10 TREATY TRAIL, LOWER TRURO, NS, B6L 1V9
(902) 897-2650   SIC 5411

TREATY ENTERPRISES   p 442
600 CALDWELL RD, DARTMOUTH, NS, B2V 2S8
(902) 434-7777   SIC 5541

TREATY ENTERTAINMENT   p 461
See TREATY ENTERPRISE INC

TREATY GAS   p 442
See TREATY ENTERPRISES

TREB   p 778
See TORONTO REAL ESTATE BOARD, THE

TREBAS INSTITUTE ONTARIO INC p 994
2340 DUNDAS ST W SUITE 2, TORONTO, ON, M6P 4A9
(416) 966-3066   SIC 8221

TREBOR PERSONNEL INC   p 704
1090 DUNDAS ST E SUITE 203, MISSISSAUGA, ON, L4Y 2B8
(905) 566-0922   SIC 7361

TRECC ELECTRIC   p 25
See RESIDENTIAL ELECTRICAL CONTRACTOR CORPORATION, THE

TREDD INSURANCE BROKERS LTD p 958
141 ADELAIDE ST W SUITE 1410, TORONTO, ON, M5H 3L5
(416) 306-6000   SIC 6411

TREE ISLAND INDUSTRIES LTD   p 257
3933 BOUNDARY RD, RICHMOND, BC, V6V 1T8

(604) 524-3744   *SIC* 3496
TREE ISLAND STEEL LTD   *p* 257
3933 BOUNDARY RD, RICHMOND, BC,
V6V 1T8
(604) 524-3744   *SIC* 3496
TREE OF LIFE CANADA ULC   *p* 733
6185 MCLAUGHLIN RD, MISSISSAUGA,
ON, L5R 3W7
(905) 507-6161   *SIC* 5141
TREELAND REALTY LTD   *p* 227
6337 198 ST SUITE 101, LANGLEY, BC,
V2Y 2E3
(604) 533-3491   *SIC* 6531
TREELINE WELL SERVICES INC   *p* 66
333 11 AVE SW SUITE 750, CALGARY, AB,
T2R 1L9
(403) 266-2868   *SIC* 1381
TREEN PACKERS LTD   *p* 1437
GD, SWIFT CURRENT, SK, S9H 3V4
(306) 773-4473   *SIC* 5147
TREGUNNO FRUIT FARMS INC   *p* 761
15176 NIAGARA RIVER PKY, NIAGARA ON
THE LAKE, ON, L0S 1J0
(905) 262-4755   *SIC* 2037
TREIT HOLDINGS 21 INC   *p* 467
380 ESPLANADE ST, SYDNEY, NS, B1P
1B1
(902) 562-6500   *SIC* 7011
TREK ESCAPE   *p* 118
See *WESTCAN TRAVEL LTD*
TREL OF SARNIA LIMITED   *p* 859
1165 CONFEDERATION ST, SARNIA, ON,
N7S 3Y5
(519) 344-7025   *SIC* 3599
TREMBLAY ASSURANCE LTEE   *p* 1045
575 BOUL DE QUEN, ALMA, QC, G8B 5Z1
(418) 662-6413   *SIC* 6331
TREMBLAY ASSURANCE LTEE   *p* 1151
15   RUE   SAINT-ANTOINE,
METABETCHOUAN-LAC-A-LA-CROIX, QC,
G8G 1H2
(418) 349-2841   *SIC* 6411
**TREMBLAY BOIS MIGNAULT LEMAY & AS-
SOCIES INC**   *p*
1274
1195 AV LAVIGERIE BUREAU 200, QUE-
BEC, QC, G1V 4N3
(418) 658-9966   *SIC* 8111
TREMBLAY ET FRERES LTEE   *p* 1391
97 BOUL LAMAQUE, VAL-D'OR, QC, J9P
2H7
(819) 825-7470   *SIC* 5211
**TREMBLAY, ANDREE P. PHARMACIEN
ENR**   *p* 1057
350 BOUL SIR-WILFRID-LAURIER, BE-
LOEIL, QC, J3G 4G7
(450) 467-0296   *SIC* 5912
TREMBLAY, C.J. INVESTMENTS INC *p* 714
900 SOUTHDOWN RD, MISSISSAUGA,
ON, L5J 2Y4
(905) 822-6234   *SIC* 5531
TREMBLAY, FRANCOIS PHARMACIE   *p*
1105
640 BOUL MALONEY O, GATINEAU, QC,
J8T 8K7
(819) 246-9662   *SIC* 5912
**TREMBLAY, RODRIGUE (SHERBROOKE)
INC**   *p* 1372
2540 RUE ROY, SHERBROOKE, QC, J1K
1C1
(819) 346-4527   *SIC* 5033
TREMBLETTS VALU-MART   *p* 917
See *1437384 ONTARIO LIMITED*
TREMCAR DRUMMOND INC   *p* 1099
1450 RUE HEBERT, DRUMMONDVILLE,
QC, J2C 0C7
(450) 469-4840   *SIC* 3443
TREMCAR INC   *p* 1316
790 AV MONTRICHARD, SAINT-JEAN-
SUR-RICHELIEU, QC, J2X 5G4
(450) 347-7822   *SIC* 3443
TREMCO CANADA   *p* 919
See *RPM CANADA*
TRENCH CANADA COIL PRODUCTS *p* 877

See *TRENCH LIMITED*
TRENCH LIMITED   *p* 872
390 MIDWEST RD, SCARBOROUGH, ON,
M1P 3B5
(416) 751-8570   *SIC* 3612
TRENCH LIMITED   *p* 877
71 MAYBROOK DR, SCARBOROUGH, ON,
M1V 4B6
(416) 298-8108   *SIC* 3699
TREND AUTO GROUP INC   *p* 262
11631 BRIDGEPORT RD, RICHMOND, BC,
V6X 1T5
(604) 638-9899   *SIC* 5511
TREND COLOUR   *p* 790
See *TREND COLOUR LABS INC*
TREND COLOUR LABS INC   *p* 790
1194D CALEDONIA RD, NORTH YORK,
ON, M6A 2W5
SIC 7384
TREND MARKETING WHOLESALE INC   *p*
785
1500 LODESTAR RD, NORTH YORK, ON,
M3J 3C1
(416) 663-3939   *SIC* 5139
TREND-LINE FURNITURE LTD   *p* 787
166 NORFINCH DR, NORTH YORK, ON,
M3N 1Y4
(416) 650-0504   *SIC* 2512
TREND-TEX FABRICS INC   *p* 247
1317 KEBET WAY, PORT COQUITLAM, BC,
V3C 6G1
(604) 941-4620   *SIC* 5131
TRENDINNOVATIONS   *p* 1222
See *7818696 CANADA INC*
**TRENDS ELECTRONICS INTERNATIONAL
INC**   *p* 183
2999 UNDERHILL AVE SUITE 202, BURN-
ABY, BC, V5A 3C2
(604) 988-2966   *SIC* 5065
**TRENDS INTERNATIONAL PUBLISHING
CORPORATION**   *p* 718
3500 LAIRD RD UNIT 2, MISSISSAUGA,
ON, L5L 5Y4
(905) 569-8500   *SIC* 2741
TRENDWEST   *p* 228
20258 FRASER HWY SUITE 104, LANG-
LEY, BC, V3A 4E6
(604) 534-5044   *SIC* 5999
TRENDWOOD LIMITED   *p* 124
2431 121 AVE NE, EDMONTON, AB, T6S
1B2
(780) 472-6606   *SIC* 4731
TRENERGY INC   *p* 885
87 GRANTHAM AVE, ST CATHARINES,
ON, L2P 3K2
(905) 687-8736   *SIC* 3443
TRENT METALS (2012) LIMITED   *p* 842
2040 FISHER DR, PETERBOROUGH, ON,
K9J 6X6
(705) 745-4736   *SIC* 3567
TRENT VALLEY HONDA   *p* 815
See *970207 ONTARIO LIMITED*
TRENTON COLD STORAGE INC   *p* 999
17489 TELEPHONE RD, TRENTON, ON,
K8V 5P4
(613) 394-3317   *SIC* 4225
TRENTON COLD STORAGE INC   *p* 999
21 ALBERT ST, TRENTON, ON, K8V 4S4
(613) 394-3317   *SIC* 4222
TRENTON DISTRIBUTORS LIMITED *p* 999
75 HUFF AVE, TRENTON, ON, K8V 0H3
(613) 392-3875   *SIC* 5063
TRENTON HIGH SCHOOL   *p* 999
See *HASTINGS AND PRINCE EDWARD
DISTRICT SCHOOL BOARD*
TRENTON MEMORIAL HOSPITAL   *p* 999
See *QUINTE HEALTHCARE CORPORA-
TION*
TRENTON MEMORIAL HOSPITAL   *p* 999
242 KING ST, TRENTON, ON, K8V 3X1
(613) 392-2541   *SIC* 8062
TRENTWAY-WAGAR INC   *p* 492
75 BRIDGE ST E, BELLEVILLE, ON, K8N
1L9

(613) 962-2163   *SIC* 5963
TRENTWAY-WAGAR INC   *p* 690
6020 INDIAN LINE, MISSISSAUGA, ON,
L4V 1G5
(905) 677-3841   *SIC* 4142
TRENTWAY-WAGAR INC   *p* 758
4555 ERIE AVE, NIAGARA FALLS, ON, L2E
7G9
(905) 358-7230   *SIC* 4111
TRENTWAY-WAGAR INC   *p* 842
2015 FISHER DR UNIT 101, PETERBOR-
OUGH, ON, K9J 6X6
(705) 748-6411   *SIC* 4131
TREPANIER, PHILIPPE INC   *p* 1116
4573 CH SAINT-ISIDORE, JONQUIERE,
QC, G7X 7V5
(418) 547-4734   *SIC* 1791
TRESMAN STEEL INDUSTRIES LTD *p* 736
286 STATESMAN DR, MISSISSAUGA, ON,
L5S 1X7
(905) 795-8757   *SIC* 3441
TRESORS D'AGAPE, AUX   *p* 1255
See *ENTRAIDE AGAPE*
TREVALI MINING CORPORATION   *p* 317
1199 HASTINGS ST W UNIT 1400, VAN-
COUVER, BC, V6E 3T5
(604) 488-1661   *SIC* 1031
TREVI   *p* 1068
See *TREVI FABRICATION INC*
TREVI   *p* 1152
See *INVESTISSEMENTS TREVI INC*
TREVI FABRICATION INC   *p* 1068
1235 RUE AMPERE, BOUCHERVILLE, QC,
J4B 7M6
(514) 228-7384   *SIC* 5999
TREVI FABRICATION INC   *p* 1153
12775 RUE BRAULT, MIRABEL, QC, J7J
0C4
(514) 228-7384   *SIC* 3949
TREVLUC HOLDINGS LTD   *p* 357
2976 DAY ST, SPRINGFIELD, MB, R2C 2Z2
(204) 777-5345   *SIC* 3448
TREVOR J LOWE INC   *p* 596
2010 OGILVIE RD, GLOUCESTER, ON, K1J
8X3
(613) 748-0637   *SIC* 5251
TRI CITY CANADA INC   *p* 218
150 VICTORIA ST SUITE 102, KAMLOOPS,
BC, V2C 1Z7
(250) 372-5576   *SIC* 1542
TRI CITY HOME HEALTH   *p* 248
See *FRASER HEALTH AUTHORITY*
TRI CITY MITSUBISHI   *p* 246
See *1002495 B.C. LTD*
TRI PROVINCE ENTERPRISES (1984) LTD
p 406
158 TOOMBS ST, MONCTON, NB, E1A 3A5
(506) 858-8110   *SIC* 5051
TRI STAR GAS MART   *p* 332
See *TRI STAR GAS MART (1992) LTD*
TRI STAR GAS MART (1992) LTD   *p* 332
3308 48 AVE, VERNON, BC, V1T 3R6
(250) 558-7800   *SIC* 5541
**TRI-AD INTERNATIONAL FREIGHT FOR-
WARDING LTD**   *p*
743
375 ANNAGEM BLVD UNIT 100, MISSIS-
SAUGA, ON, L5T 3A7
(905) 624-8214   *SIC* 4731
TRI-B ACRES INC   *p* 645
132 MERSEA ROAD 5, LEAMINGTON, ON,
N8H 3V5
(519) 326-0042   *SIC* 5148
TRI-CITY HAULAGE   *p* 605
See *798826 ONTARIO INC*
TRI-CITY TRANSITIONS SOCIETY   *p* 247
2540 SHAUGHNESSY ST SUITE 200,
PORT COQUITLAM, BC, V3C 3W4
(604) 941-7111   *SIC* 8699
TRI-CO GROUP INC, THE   *p* 831
47-B ANTARES DR, OTTAWA, ON, K2E
7W6
(613) 736-7777   *SIC* 2752
TRI-CON CONCRETE FINISHING CO. LTD *p*

785
835 SUPERTEST RD SUITE 100, NORTH
YORK, ON, M3J 2M9
(416) 736-7700   *SIC* 1771
TRI-COR CONSTRUCTION INC   *p* 1028
310 VAUGHAN VALLEY BLVD UNIT 1,
WOODBRIDGE, ON, L4H 3C3
SIC 1542
TRI-CORP CANADA INVESTMENTS INC *p*
91
203 TRI-CORP CENTRE, EDMONTON, AB,
T5J 1V8
(780) 496-9607   *SIC* 6211
TRI-COUNTY BEHAVIOURAL SERVICES *p*
840
See *TRI-COUNTY COMMUNITY SUP-
PORT SERVICES*
**TRI-COUNTY COMMUNITY SUPPORT
SERVICES**   *p* 840
349A GEORGE ST N UNIT 303, PETER-
BOROUGH, ON, K9H 3P9
(705) 876-9245   *SIC* 8399
TRI-COUNTY INSURACE GROUP   *p* 881
See *MANN, R. E. BROKERS LTD*
**TRI-COUNTY MENNONITE HOMES ASSO-
CIATION**   *p*
897
90 GREENWOOD DR SUITE 117, STRAT-
FORD, ON, N5A 7W5
(519) 273-4662   *SIC* 8059
TRI-COUNTY REGIONAL SCHOOL BOARD
p 471
79 WATER ST, YARMOUTH, NS, B5A 1L4
(902) 749-5696   *SIC* 8211
TRI-ED DISTRIBUTION   *p* 690
See *TRI-ED LTD*
TRI-ED LTD   *p* 690
3688 NASHUA DR UNIT A-F, MISSIS-
SAUGA, ON, L4V 1M5
(905) 677-8664   *SIC* 5065
TRI-GEN CONSTRUCTION LTD   *p* 7
GD, BOYLE, AB, T0A 0M0
(780) 689-3831   *SIC* 1521
TRI-KRETE LIMITED   *p* 794
152 TORYORK DR, NORTH YORK, ON,
M9L 1X6
(416) 746-2479   *SIC* 3272
TRI-LAD FLANGE AND FITTINGS INC   *p*
837
30 WOODSLEE AVE, PARIS, ON, N3L 3N6
(519) 442-6520   *SIC* 3462
TRI-LAKE HEALTH CENTRE   *p* 351
See *PRAIRIE MOUNTAIN HEALTH*
**TRI-LEAF COLONY OF HUTTERIAN
BRETHREN**   *p* 345
GD, BALDUR, MB, R0K 0B0
(204) 535-2274   *SIC* 0191
TRI-LINE CARRIERS LP   *p* 160
235185 RYAN RD, ROCKY VIEW COUNTY,
AB, T1X 0K1
(403) 279-7070   *SIC* 4213
TRI-MACH GROUP INC   *p* 568
23 DONWAY CRT, ELMIRA, ON, N3B 0B1
(519) 744-6565   *SIC* 3541
**TRI-MEDIA INTEGRATED MARKETING
TECHNOLOGIES INC**   *p* 887
20 CORPORATE PARK DR SUITE 103, ST
CATHARINES, ON, L2S 3W2
SIC 7311
TRI-METAL FABRICATORS   *p* 280
19150 21 AVE, SURREY, BC, V3Z 3M3
(604) 531-5518   *SIC* 3499
TRI-STAR GRAPHICS   *p* 471
See *TRI-STAR INDUSTRIES LIMITED*
TRI-STAR INDUSTRIES LIMITED   *p* 471
88 FOREST ST, YARMOUTH, NS, B5A 4G6
(902) 742-2355   *SIC* 3711
TRI-STAR SEAFOOD SUPPLY LTD   *p* 262
11751 VOYAGEUR WAY, RICHMOND, BC,
V6X 3J4
(604) 273-3324   *SIC* 5146
TRI-TEXCO INC   *p* 1302
1001   BOUL   INDUSTRIEL,   SAINT-
EUSTACHE, QC, J7R 6C3

(450) 974-1001   *SIC* 2865
TRIAD INTERNATIONAL CORP   *p* 1034
690 ROWNTREE DAIRY RD SUITE 201, WOODBRIDGE, ON, L4L 5T7
(905) 264-9031   *SIC* 6289
TRIAL DESIGN INC   *p* 1366
570 BOUL DES ERABLES, SALABERRY-DE-VALLEYFIELD, QC, J6T 6G4
(450) 370-1377   *SIC* 5712
TRIAL LAWYERS ASSOCIATION OF BRITISH COLUMBIA   *p* 317
1100 MELVILLE ST SUITE 1111, VANCOUVER, BC, V6E 4A6
(604) 682-5343   *SIC* 8621
TRIALTO WINE GROUP LTD   *p* 300
1260 HAMILTON ST SUITE 300, VANCOUVER, BC, V6B 2S8
(778) 331-8999   *SIC* 5182
TRIANGLE FREIGHT SERVICES LTD *p* 701
5355 CREEKBANK RD, MISSISSAUGA, ON, L4W 5L5
(905) 624-1614   *SIC* 4212
TRIANGLE FREIGHT SERVICES LTD *p* 1432
3550 IDYLWYLD DR N, SASKATOON, SK, S7L 6G3
(306) 373-7744   *SIC* 4213
TRIANGLE KITCHEN LTD   *p* 398
679 RUE BABIN, DIEPPE, NB, E1A 5M7
(506) 858-5855   *SIC* 1751
TRIANGLE LOGISTICS SOLUTIONS INC *p* 905
8500 LESLIE ST SUITE 320, THORNHILL, ON, L3T 7M8
(416) 747-6474   *SIC* 4213
TRIANGLE STEEL LTD   *p* 19
2915 54 AVE SE, CALGARY, AB, T2C 0A9
(403) 279-2622   *SIC* 3312
TRIATHLON LTD   *p* 257
13800 COMMERCE PKWY, RICHMOND, BC, V6V 2J3
(604) 233-5000   *SIC* 7389
TRIAX DIVERSIFIED HIGH-YIELD TRUST *p* 968
95 WELLINGTON ST W SUITE 1400, TORONTO, ON, M5J 2N7
(416) 362-2929   *SIC* 6726
TRIBAL NOVA INC   *p* 1185
4200 BOUL SAINT-LAURENT BUREAU 1203, MONTREAL, QC, H2W 2R2
(514) 598-0444   *SIC* 5092
TRIBAL NOVA KIDS   *p* 1185
See TRIBAL NOVA INC
TRIBE MEDICAL GROUP   *p* 650
See TRIBE MEDICAL GROUP INC
TRIBE MEDICAL GROUP INC   *p* 650
580 SOVEREIGN RD, LONDON, ON, N5V 4K7
(519) 680-0707   *SIC* 5047
TRIBURY CONSTRUCTION (1995) INC *p* 899
1549 FAIRBURN ST, SUDBURY, ON, P3A 1N6
(705) 560-8743   *SIC* 1542
TRIBUTE COMMUNITIES   *p* 845
See WESTHALL INVESTMENTS LTD
TRICA INC   *p* 1321
800 RUE PASTEUR, SAINT-JEROME, QC, J7Z 7K9
(450) 431-4897   *SIC* 2519
TRICAN PACKAGING INC   *p* 541
1078 KOHLER RD, CAYUGA, ON, N0A 1E0
(905) 772-0711   *SIC* 5085
TRICAN PARTNERSHIP   *p* 80
See TRICAN WELL SERVICE LTD
TRICAN PRODUCTION SERVICES   *p* 150
See TRICAN WELL SERVICE LTD
TRICAN WELL SERVICE LTD   *p* 62
645 7 AVE SW SUITE 2900, CALGARY, AB, T2P 4G8
(403) 266-0202   *SIC* 6712
TRICAN WELL SERVICE LTD   *p* 71
11979 40 ST SE UNIT 418, CALGARY, AB, T2Z 4M3

(403) 723-3688   *SIC* 1389
TRICAN WELL SERVICE LTD   *p* 80
9701 99 ST, CLAIRMONT, AB, T8X 5A8
(780) 567-5200   *SIC* 1389
TRICAN WELL SERVICE LTD   *p* 150
2305 5A ST, NISKU, AB, T9E 8G6
(780) 955-5675   *SIC* 1389
TRICAN WELL SERVICE LTD   *p* 347
59 LIMESTONE RD, BRANDON, MB, R7A 7L5
    SIC 1389
TRICAR   *p* 662
See CARVEST PROPERTIES LIMITED
TRICAR DEVELOPMENTS INC   *p* 662
3800 COLONEL TALBOT RD, LONDON, ON, N6P 1H5
(519) 652-8900   *SIC* 1522
TRICENTRIS   *p* 1103
See TRICENTRIS - TRI, TRANSFORMATION, SENSIBILISATION
TRICENTRIS - TRI, TRANSFORMATION, SENSIBILISATION   *p* 1103
45 RUE PIERRE-MENARD, GATINEAU, QC, J8R 3X3
(819) 643-4448   *SIC* 5084
TRICIFIC ENTERPRISES INC   *p* 877
155 DYNAMIC DR, SCARBOROUGH, ON, M1V 5L8
(905) 470-8811   *SIC* 5023
TRICITY MITSUBISHI   *p* 246
See 1079259 B.C. LTD
TRICKLE CREEK MARRIOTT   *p* 67
See RESORTS OF THE CANADIAN ROCKIES INC
TRICLO INC   *p* 571
241 BIRMINGHAM ST, ETOBICOKE, ON, M8V 2C7
(416) 252-4777   *SIC* 5162
TRICO DEVELOPMENTS CORPORATION *p* 66
1005 11 AVE SW, CALGARY, AB, T2R 0G1
(403) 287-9300   *SIC* 1521
TRICO EVOLUTION   *p* 831
See TRI-CO GROUP INC, THE
TRICO HOMES   *p* 66
See TRICO DEVELOPMENTS CORPORATION
TRICO HOMES INC   *p* 66
1005 11 AVE SW, CALGARY, AB, T2R 0G1
(403) 287-9300   *SIC* 6553
TRICOM SECURITY SERVICES INC *p* 958
20 QUEEN ST W, TORONTO, ON, M5H 3R3
(416) 651-7890   *SIC* 5999
TRICON CAPITAL GROUP INC   *p* 976
7 ST THOMAS ST SUITE 801, TORONTO, ON, M5S 2B7
(416) 925-7228   *SIC* 6719
TRICORBRAUN   *p* 202
See TRICORBRAUN CANADA, INC
TRICORBRAUN CANADA, INC   *p* 202
1650 BRIGANTINE DR SUITE 500, COQUITLAM, BC, V3K 7B5
(604) 540-8166   *SIC* 5099
TRICOT IDEAL INC   *p* 1179
9494 BOUL SAINT-LAURENT BUREAU 400, MONTREAL, QC, H2N 1P4
(514) 381-4496   *SIC* 2253
TRICOT MONDIAL INC   *p* 1327
490 BOUL MONTPELLIER, SAINT-LAURENT, QC, H4N 2G7
(514) 279-9333   *SIC* 5091
TRICOTS DUVAL & RAYMOND LTEE, LES *p* 1254
11 RUE SAINT-JACQUES O, PRINCEVILLE, QC, G6L 5E6
(819) 364-2927   *SIC* 2252
TRICOTS LELA INC, LES   *p* 1183
5425 AV CASGRAIN BUREAU 601, MONTREAL, QC, H2T 1X6
(514) 271-3102   *SIC* 5137
TRICOTS LIESSE (1983) INC   *p* 1222
2125 RUE LILY-SIMON, MONTREAL, QC, H4B 3A1
(514) 342-0685   *SIC* 2257

TRICOTS MAXIME   *p* 1325
See 8756074 CANADA INC
TRICOTS MAXIME INC, LES   *p* 1054
19500 AV CLARK-GRAHAM, BAIE-D'URFE, QC, H9X 3R8
(514) 336-0445   *SIC* 2258
TRIDEL CORPORATION   *p* 781
4800 DUFFERIN ST SUITE 200, NORTH YORK, ON, M3H 5S9
(416) 661-9290   *SIC* 6553
TRIDEN DISTRIBUTORS LIMITED   *p* 845
922 DILLINGHAM RD, PICKERING, ON, L1W 1Z6
(416) 291-2955   *SIC* 5131
TRIDENT EXPLORATION CORP   *p* 62
3100-888 3 ST SW, CALGARY, AB, T2P 5C5
(403) 770-0333   *SIC* 1382
TRIDENT INDUSTRIES INC, LES   *p* 1163
8277 BOUL HENRI-BOURASSA E, MONTREAL, QC, H1E 1P4
(514) 648-0285   *SIC* 3728
TRIDENT MILLWORK AND DISPLAY INDUSTRIES LTD   *p* 262
11140 RIVER RD, RICHMOND, BC, V6X 1Z5
(604) 276-2855   *SIC* 5031
TRIDENT RESOURCES CORP   *p* 62
888 3 ST SW SUITE 3100, CALGARY, AB, T2P 5C5
(403) 770-0333   *SIC* 1382
TRIEAGLE MARKETING   *p* 646
See EAGLE, JAMES R. HOLDINGS LIMITED
TRIGO   *p* 843
See PIC GROUP LTD, THE
TRIGON CONSTRUCTION INC   *p* 1036
35 RIDGEWAY CIR, WOODSTOCK, ON, N4V 1C9
(519) 602-2222   *SIC* 1542
TRIJAN INDUSTRIES   *p* 859
See 612031-376964 ONTARIO LTD
TRILAND REALTY LTD   *p* 651
235 NORTH CENTRE RD SUITE 1, LONDON, ON, N5X 4E7
(519) 661-0380   *SIC* 6531
TRILAND REALTY LTD   *p* 656
240 WATERLOO ST UNIT 103, LONDON, ON, N6B 2N4
(519) 672-9880   *SIC* 6531
TRILLIANT ENERGY SERVICES INC *p* 560
20 FLORAL PKY, CONCORD, ON, L4K 4R1
(905) 669-6223   *SIC* 3825
TRILLIANT HOLDINGS (ONTARIO) INC *p* 560
20 FLORAL PKY, CONCORD, ON, L4K 4R1
(905) 669-6223   *SIC* 3825
TRILLIANT NETWORKS (CANADA) INC *p* 1111
610 RUE DU LUXEMBOURG, GRANBY, QC, J2J 2V2
(450) 375-0556   *SIC* 3825
TRILLIUM ARCHITECTURAL PRODUCTS LTD   *p* 780
52 PRINCE ANDREW PL, NORTH YORK, ON, M3C 2H4
(416) 391-5555   *SIC* 5072
TRILLIUM BEVERAGE INC   *p* 787
125 BERMONDSEY RD, NORTH YORK, ON, M4A 1X3
(416) 759-6565   *SIC* 2082
TRILLIUM CENTRE   *p* 632
See SPECIALTY CARE EAST INC
TRILLIUM COURT SENIORS COMMUNITY *p* 629
See REVERA LONG TERM CARE INC
TRILLIUM FORD LINCOLN LTD   *p* 476
1 ADDISON RD HWY 89 E, ALLISTON, ON, L9R 1W1
(705) 435-7609   *SIC* 5511
TRILLIUM GIFT OF LIFE NETWORK *p* 947
483 BAY ST SOUTH TOWER 4TH FLOOR, TORONTO, ON, M5G 2C9
(416) 363-4001   *SIC* 8099

TRILLIUM HEALTH CARE PRODUCTS INC *p* 520
2337 PARKDALE AVE E, BROCKVILLE, ON, K6V 5W5
(613) 342-4436   *SIC* 2834
TRILLIUM HEALTH PARTNERS   *p* 711
100 QUEENSWAY W, MISSISSAUGA, ON, L5B 1B8
(905) 848-7580   *SIC* 8062
TRILLIUM HEALTH PARTNERS   *p* 719
2200 EGLINTON AVE W SUITE 905, MISSISSAUGA, ON, L5M 2N1
(905) 813-2200   *SIC* 8062
TRILLIUM HEALTH PARTNERS   *p* 996
150 SHERWAY DR, TORONTO, ON, M9C 1A5
(416) 259-6671   *SIC* 8062
TRILLIUM HEALTH PARTNERS VOLUNTEERS   *p*
711
100 QUEENSWAY W, MISSISSAUGA, ON, L5B 1B8
(905) 848-7276   *SIC* 5947
TRILLIUM LAKELANDS DISTRICT SCHOOL BOARD   *p* 590
66 LINDSAY ST, FENELON FALLS, ON, K0M 1N0
(705) 887-2018   *SIC* 8211
TRILLIUM LAKELANDS DISTRICT SCHOOL BOARD   *p* 646
24 WELDON RD, LINDSAY, ON, K9V 4R4
(705) 324-3585   *SIC* 8211
TRILLIUM LAKELANDS DISTRICT SCHOOL BOARD   *p* 646
260 KENT ST W, LINDSAY, ON, K9V 2Z5
(705) 324-3556   *SIC* 8211
TRILLIUM LAKELANDS DISTRICT SCHOOL BOARD   *p* 646
300 COUNTY RD 36, LINDSAY, ON, K9V 4R4
(705) 324-6776   *SIC* 8211
TRILLIUM LODGE   *p* 243
See VANCOUVER ISLAND HEALTH AUTHORITY
TRILLIUM MANOR HOME FOR THE AGED *p* 809
See CORPORATION OF THE COUNTY OF SIMCOE
TRILLIUM MARKETING GROUP LTD. *p* 785
77 MARTIN ROSS AVE, NORTH YORK, ON, M3J 2L5
(416) 667-3030   *SIC* 5199
TRILLIUM METAL STAMPINGS   *p* 637
See 506165 ONTARIO LIMITED
TRILLIUM MUTUAL INSURANCE COMPANY   *p*
647
495 MITCHELL RD S, LISTOWEL, ON, N4W 0C8
(519) 291-9300   *SIC* 6411
TRILLIUM PRACTICE MANAGEMENT LTD *p* 856
9625 YONGE ST SUITE F, RICHMOND HILL, ON, L4C 5T2
(905) 918-9573   *SIC* 8741
TRILLIUM THERAPEUTICS INC   *p* 718
2488 DUNWIN DR, MISSISSAUGA, ON, L5L 1J9
(416) 595-0627   *SIC* 8071
TRILLIUM VILLA NURSING HOME   *p* 859
See STEEVES & ROZEMA ENTERPRISES LIMITED
TRILOGY BRAND MANAGEMENT, DIV OF *p* 528
See M.C.P. MCCAUGHEY CONSUMER PRODUCTS MANAGEMENT INC
TRILOGY INTERNATIONAL PARTNERS INC   *p* 987
100 KING ST W SUITE 7050, TORONTO, ON, M5X 1C7
(416) 360-6390   *SIC* 6722
TRILOGY METALS INC   *p* 330
609 GRANVILLE ST SUITE 1150, VANCOUVER, BC, V7Y 1G5

(604) 638-8088   *SIC* 1021
TRILOGY RETAIL ENTERPRISES L.P *p* 968
161 BAY ST SUITE 4900, TORONTO, ON, M5J 2S1
(416) 943-4110   *SIC* 6712
TRIM CARPENTERS SUPPLY   *p* 585
See LAMBTON LUMBER INC
TRIMAC   *p* 54
See MUNICIPAL TANK LINES LIMITED
TRIMAC TRANSPORTATION MANAGE-MENT LTD   *p* 62
800 5 AVE SW UNIT 2100, CALGARY, AB, T2P 3T6
(403) 298-5100   *SIC* 6712
TRIMAR STEEL   *p* 1005
3595 AMENT LINE RR 3, WALLENSTEIN, ON, N0B 2S0
(519) 699-5444   *SIC* 5051
TRIMARK HEALTHCARE SERVICES LTD *p* 318
1500 GEORGIA ST W SUITE 1300, VAN-COUVER, BC, V6G 2Z6
(604) 425-2208   *SIC* 8741
TRIMASTER MANUFACTURING INC *p* 606
95 CURTIS DR, GUELPH, ON, N1K 1E1
(519) 823-2661   *SIC* 3444
TRIMAX SECURITE INC   *p* 1237
1965 BOUL INDUSTRIEL BUREAU 200, MONTREAL, QC, H7S 1P6
(450) 934-5200   *SIC* 7389
TRIMEN PACIFIC   *p* 794
See TRUE ROCK FINANCIAL INC
TRIMETALS MINING INC   *p* 310
580 HORNBY ST SUITE 880, VANCOU-VER, BC, V6C 3B6
(604) 639-4523   *SIC* 1081
TRIMONT MFG. INC   *p* 875
115 MILNER AVE SUITE 2, SCARBOR-OUGH, ON, M1S 4L7
(416) 640-2045   *SIC* 2211
TRIMSEAL PLASTICS LTD   *p* 257
3511 JACOMBS RD, RICHMOND, BC, V6V 1Z8
(604) 278-3803   *SIC* 2782
TRINIDAD DRILLING LTD   *p* 62
400 5TH AVE SUITE 1000, CALGARY, AB, T2P 0L6
(403) 262-1361   *SIC* 1381
TRINITY CAPITAL GP LTD   *p* 62
205 5 AVE SW SUITE 3030, CALGARY, AB, T2P 2V7
(403) 266-1985   *SIC* 5172
TRINITY COMMUNICATION SERVICES LTD *p* 576
86 TORLAKE CRES, ETOBICOKE, ON, M8Z 1B8
(416) 503-9796   *SIC* 1731
TRINITY DEVELOPMENT GROUP INC   *p* 834
359 KENT ST SUITE 400, OTTAWA, ON, K2P 0R6
SIC 1542
TRINITY POWER CORPORATION   *p* 202
1301 KETCH CRT UNIT 8B, COQUITLAM, BC, V3K 6X7
(604) 529-1134   *SIC* 4911
TRINITY POWER RENTALS   *p* 202
See TRINITY POWER CORPORATION
TRINITY VILLAGE CARE CENTRE   *p* 636
See LUTHERAN HOMES KITCHENER-WATERLOO
TRINITY WESTERN UNIVERSITY   *p* 227
7600 GLOVER RD, LANGLEY, BC, V2Y 1Y1
(604) 888-7511   *SIC* 8221
TRIO-SELECTION INC   *p* 1341
8305 CH DE LA C?TE-DE-LIESSE, SAINT-LAURENT, QC, H4T 1G5
(514) 387-2591   *SIC* 5137
TRIODETIC LTD   *p* 479
10 DIDAK DR, ARNPRIOR, ON, K7S 0C3
(613) 623-3434   *SIC* 3441
TRIONEX INC   *p* 1046
121 RUE DES METIERS, AMOS, QC, J9T

4M4
(819) 732-5327   *SIC* 5084
TRIOS CORPORATION   *p* 728
6755 MISSISSAUGA RD SUITE 103, MIS-SISSAUGA, ON, L5N 7Y2
(905) 814-7212   *SIC* 8211
TRIOTECH AMUSEMENT INC   *p* 1115
780 RUE MARION, JOLIETTE, QC, J6E 8S2
(450) 760-9082   *SIC* 3999
TRIOVEST REALTY ADVISORS INC   *p* 968
40 UNIVERSITY AVE SUITE 1200, TORONTO, ON, M5J 1T1
(416) 362-0045   *SIC* 6531
TRIPAR ENOVA, DIV OF   *p* 1161
See TRIPAR INC
TRIPAR INC   *p* 1161
9750 BOUL MAURICE-DUPLESSIS, MON-TREAL, QC, H1C 1G1
(514) 648-7471   *SIC* 3469
TRIPAR TRANSPORTATION LP   *p* 799
2180 BUCKINGHAM RD, OAKVILLE, ON, L6H 6H1
(905) 829-8500   *SIC* 4731
TRIPCENTRAL.CA   *p* 614
See TRAVEL SUPERSTORE INC
TRIPEMCO BURLINGTON INSURANCE GROUP LIMITED   *p* 894
99 HIGHWAY 8, STONEY CREEK, ON, L8G 1C1
(905) 664-2266   *SIC* 6411
TRIPLE A ELECTRIC LTD   *p* 154
6209 46 AVE SUITE 1, RED DEER, AB, T4N 6Z1
(403) 346-6156   *SIC* 1731
TRIPLE A LIVING COMMUNITIES INC *p* 70
14911 5 ST SW SUITE 115, CALGARY, AB, T2Y 5B9
(403) 410-9155   *SIC* 8059
TRIPLE A PHARMACY INC   *p* 811
1675E TENTH LINE RD, ORLEANS, ON, K1E 3P6
(613) 837-6078   *SIC* 5912
TRIPLE CANON CORPORATION   *p* 786
1140 SHEPPARD AVE W UNIT 13, NORTH YORK, ON, M3K 2A2
SIC 1521
TRIPLE CROWN ENTERPRISES LTD *p* 610
665 PARKDALE AVE N, HAMILTON, ON, L8H 5Z1
(905) 540-1630   *SIC* 1541
TRIPLE CROWN FOODS LTD   *p* 340
2945 JACKLIN RD SUITE 200, VICTORIA, BC, V9B 5E3
(250) 478-8998   *SIC* 5411
TRIPLE DELTA HOLDINGS INC   *p* 690
6205 AIRPORT RD SUITE 500, MISSIS-SAUGA, ON, L4V 1E1
(905) 677-5480   *SIC* 6712
TRIPLE E CANADA LTD   *p* 361
301 ROBLIN BLVD, WINKLER, MB, R6W 4C4
(204) 325-4361   *SIC* 3711
TRIPLE E CANADA LTD   *p* 361
135 CANADA ST, WINKLER, MB, R6W 0J3
(204) 325-4345   *SIC* 3792
TRIPLE E RV, DIV OF   *p* 361
See TRIPLE E CANADA LTD
TRIPLE EIGHT TRANSPORT INC   *p* 177
2548 CLEARBROOK RD 1ST FL, ABBOTS-FORD, BC, V2T 2Y4
(604) 755-2285   *SIC* 4213
TRIPLE FIVE CORPORATION INC   *p* 104
8882 170 ST NW SUITE 3000, EDMON-TON, AB, T5T 4M2
(780) 444-8100   *SIC* 6712
TRIPLE FLIP INC   *p* 38
6120 11 ST SE UNIT 7, CALGARY, AB, T2H 2L7
(403) 769-3547   *SIC* 5621
TRIPLE J LIVESTOCK LTD   *p* 172
9004 110A ST, WESTLOCK, AB, T7P 2N4
(780) 349-3153   *SIC* 5154
TRIPLE J PHARMACY LTD   *p* 500
980 CENTRAL PARK DR, BRAMPTON, ON,

L6S 3L7
(905) 791-1797   *SIC* 5912
TRIPLE K TRANSPORT LTD   *p* 891
6640 HAZELDEAN RD, STITTSVILLE, ON, K2S 1B9
(613) 836-7333   *SIC* 4213
TRIPLE M HOUSING LTD   *p* 141
3501 GIFFEN RD N, LETHBRIDGE, AB, T1H 0E8
(403) 320-8588   *SIC* 2451
TRIPLE M METAL LP   *p* 507
471 INTERMODAL DR, BRAMPTON, ON, L6T 5G4
(905) 793-7083   *SIC* 3341
TRIPLE M METAL LP   *p* 610
1640 BRAMPTON ST, HAMILTON, ON, L8H 3S1
(905) 545-7083   *SIC* 5093
TRIPLE P POWER SERVICE LTD   *p* 145
GD, MA-ME-O BEACH, AB, T0C 1X0
(780) 586-2778   *SIC* 1623
TRIPLE SEVEN CHRYSLER   *p* 1419
See 583455 SASKATCHEWAN LTD
TRIPLE THREE TRADING LTD   *p* 32
908 34 AVE SE, CALGARY, AB, T2G 1V3
(403) 240-2540   *SIC* 2673
TRIPLEWELL ENTERPRISES LTD   *p* 878
3440 PHARMACY AVE UNIT 9, SCARBOR-OUGH, ON, M1W 2P8
(416) 498-5637   *SIC* 2399
TRIQUEST NDT   *p* 19
See TRIQUEST NONDESTRUCTIVE TEST-ING CORP
TRIQUEST NONDESTRUCTIVE TESTING CORP   *p* 19
7425 107 AVE SE, CALGARY, AB, T2C 5N6
(403) 263-2216   *SIC* 8734
TRISAN CONSTRUCTION   *p* 879
See 614128 ONTARIO LTD
TRISAN GENERAL CONTRACTORS INC *p* 743
6459 NETHERHART RD, MISSISSAUGA, ON, L5T 1C3
SIC 1542
TRISCAP CANADA, INC   *p* 475
501 CLEMENTS RD W SUITE 1, AJAX, ON, L1S 7H4
(905) 428-0982   *SIC* 1731
TRISTAN   *p* 1215
See BOUTIQUE TRISTAN & ISEUT INC
TRISTAR CAP & GARMENT LTD   *p* 257
12671 BATHGATE WAY UNIT 1, RICH-MOND, BC, V6V 1Y5
(604) 279-4287   *SIC* 5136
TRISTAR DAIRY CENTRE LTD   *p* 350
26147 WIENS RD, GRUNTHAL, MB, R0A 0R0
(204) 434-6801   *SIC* 5083
TRISTAR INDUSTRIES LTD   *p* 589
160 BETHRIDGE RD, ETOBICOKE, ON, M9W 1N3
(416) 747-5767   *SIC* 5093
TRITECH GROUP LTD   *p* 230
5413 271 ST, LANGLEY, BC, V4W 3Y7
(604) 607-8878   *SIC* 1629
TRITON DIGITAL CANADA INC   *p* 1214
1440 RUE SAINTE-CATHERINE O BU-REAU 1200, MONTREAL, QC, H3G 1R8
(514) 448-4037   *SIC* 4899
TRIUM MOBILIER DE BUREAU INC *p* 1216
3200 RUE SAINT-PATRICK, MONTREAL, QC, H3K 3H5
(514) 878-8000   *SIC* 5021
TRIUMF   *p* 325
4004 WESBROOK MALL, VANCOUVER, BC, V6T 2A3
(604) 222-1047   *SIC* 8733
TRIUMPH EXPRESS SERVICE CANADA INC   *p* 690
3030 ORLANDO DR SUITE 509, MISSIS-SAUGA, ON, L4V 1S8
(905) 673-9300   *SIC* 4731
TRIUMPH FASHIONS LTD   *p* 296
1275 VENABLES ST SUITE 300, VANCOU-

VER, BC, V6A 2E4
(604) 254-6969   *SIC* 5137
TRIUMPH FOODS   *p* 1059
See OLYMEL S.E.C.
TRIUMPH GEAR SYSTEMS-TORONTO ULC   *p* 794
11 FENMAR DR, NORTH YORK, ON, M9L 1L5
(416) 743-4417   *SIC* 3089
TRIUMPH GEAR SYSTEMS-TORONTO ULC   *p* 997
9 FENMAR DR, TORONTO, ON, M9L 1L5
(416) 743-4417   *SIC* 3728
TRIUMPH TOOL LTD   *p* 606
91 ARROW RD, GUELPH, ON, N1K 1S8
(519) 836-4811   *SIC* 5084
TRIUS AUTOMOBILE INC   *p* 530
629 BRANT ST, BURLINGTON, ON, L7R 2H1
(905) 333-4144   *SIC* 5511
TRIUS WINERY - HILLEBRAND   *p* 760
See ANDREW PELLER LIMITED
TRIWARE TECHNOLOGIES INC   *p* 434
76 BROOKFIELD RD, ST. JOHN'S, NL, A1E 3T9
(709) 579-5000   *SIC* 5045
TRIWASTE SERVICES (2002)   *p* 570
See 1416720 ONTARIO LIMITED
TRJ TELECOM INC   *p* 1115
1355 RUE LEPINE, JOLIETTE, QC, J6E 4B7
(450) 499-1017   *SIC* 4899
TROCHU MEAT PROCESSORS LTD *p* 170
233 NORTH RD, TROCHU, AB, T0M 2C0
(403) 442-4202   *SIC* 5142
TROCHU MOTORS LTD   *p* 170
102 ECKENFELDER ST, TROCHU, AB, T0M 2C0
(403) 442-3866   *SIC* 5999
TROIKA VENTURES INC   *p* 223
1856 AMBROSI RD SUITE 114, KELOWNA, BC, V1Y 4R9
(250) 869-4945   *SIC* 1522
TROIS DIAMANTS AUTOS (1987) LTEE *p* 1150
3035 CH GASCON, MASCOUCHE, QC, J7L 3X7
(450) 477-6348   *SIC* 5511
TROIS-PISTOLES SERVICE   *p* 1384
289 RUE NOTRE-DAME E, TROIS-PISTOLES, QC, G0L 4K0
(418) 851-2219   *SIC* 1542
TROIS-RIVIERES CHEVROLET BUICK GMC CADILLAC INC   *p* 1389
4201 BOUL GENE-H.-KRUGER, TROIS-RIVIERES, QC, G9A 4M9
(819) 376-3791   *SIC* 5511
TROIS-RIVIERES HONDA   *p* 1389
See 9027-9118 QUEBEC INC
TROIS-RIVIERES HYUNDAI   *p* 1386
See AUTOS YOMO INC, LES
TROIS-RIVIERES NISSAN INC   *p* 1389
4700 RUE REAL-PROULX, TROIS-RIVIERES, QC, G9A 6P9
(819) 379-2611   *SIC* 5511
TROISIEME DIVISION M.R. INC   *p* 1370
880 RUE LONGPRE, SHERBROOKE, QC, J1G 5B9
(819) 562-7772   *SIC* 7389
TROJAN CONSOLIDATED INVESTMENTS LIMITED   *p* 780
18 WYNFORD DR SUITE 516, NORTH YORK, ON, M3C 3S2
SIC 8742
TROJAN INDUSTRIES INC   *p* 19
4900 54 AVE SE, CALGARY, AB, T2C 2Y8
(403) 269-6525   *SIC* 5051
TROJAN SAFETY SERVICES LTD   *p* 214
11116 TAHLTAN RD, FORT ST. JOHN, BC, V1J 7C4
(250) 785-9557   *SIC* 1389
TROJAN SECURITY AND INVESTIGATION SERVICES   *p* 885
See 295823 ONTARIO INC

TROJAN TECHNOLOGIES GROUP ULC *p* 650
3020 GORE RD, LONDON, ON, N5V 4T7
(519) 457-3400 *SIC* 3589
TROPBON *p* 1292
See 6702601 CANADA INC
TROPHY FOODS INC *p* 19
6210 44 ST SE, CALGARY, AB, T2C 4L3
(403) 571-6887 *SIC* 5149
TROPHY FOODS INC *p* 743
71 ADMIRAL BLVD, MISSISSAUGA, ON, L5T 2T1
(905) 670-8050 *SIC* 5145
TROPICAL TREETS *p* 787
See CARIBBEAN ICE CREAM COMPANY LTD
TROTT TRANSIT LTD *p* 719
15 JAMES ST, MISSISSAUGA, ON, L5M 1R4
SIC 4142
TROTTER & MORTON FACILITY SERVICES INC *p* 38
5711 1 ST SE, CALGARY, AB, T2H 1H9
(403) 255-7535 *SIC* 1711
TROTTER AND MORTON BUILDING TECHNOLOGIES INC *p* 38
5711 1 ST SE, CALGARY, AB, T2H 1H9
(403) 255-7535 *SIC* 1711
TROTTER AND MORTON LIMITED *p* 38
5711 1 ST SE, CALGARY, AB, T2H 1H9
(403) 255-7535 *SIC* 8741
TROUNCY INC *p* 535
200 FRANKLIN BLVD SUITE 16A, CAMBRIDGE, ON, N1R 8N8
(519) 623-2361 *SIC* 5251
TROUSDALE'S I G A *p* 902
5 GEORGE ST, SYDENHAM, ON, K0H 2T0
(613) 376-6609 *SIC* 5411
TROUW NUTRITION *p* 150
See HI-PRO FEEDS LP
TROUW NUTRITION CANADA INC *p* 197
46255 CHILLIWACK CENTRAL RD, CHILLIWACK, BC, V2P 1J7
(604) 702-4500 *SIC* 2048
TROUW NUTRITION CANADA INC *p* 602
150 RESEARCH LANE SUITE 200, GUELPH, ON, N1G 4T2
(519) 823-7000 *SIC* 2048
TROUW NUTRITION CANADA INC *p* 1310
4780 RUE MARTINEAU, SAINT-HYACINTHE, QC, J2R 1V1
(450) 799-5011 *SIC* 2048
TROW ASSOCIES *p* 1366
See L B C D INGENIEURS CONSEILS INC
TROY LIFE & FIRE SAFETY LTD *p* 836
1042 2ND AVE E, OWEN SOUND, ON, N4K 2H7
(519) 371-4747 *SIC* 1711
TRQSS, INC *p* 902
255 PATILLO RD, TECUMSEH, ON, N8N 2L9
(519) 973-7400 *SIC* 2399
TRS HEATING & COOLING LTD *p* 568
3520 COON'S RD, ELIZABETHTOWN, ON, K6T 1A6
(613) 342-9733 *SIC* 1711
TRU LINE TRUSS *p* 198
See PACIFIC BUILDING SYSTEMS INC
TRU SIMULATION + FORMATION *p* 1341
See TRU SIMULATION + TRAINING CANADA INC
TRU SIMULATION + TRAINING CANADA INC *p* 1341
6767 CH DE LA COTE-DE-LIESSE, SAINT-LAURENT, QC, H4T 1E5
(514) 342-0800 *SIC* 3699
TRU TECH CORPORATION *p* 1028
20 VAUGHAN VALLEY BLVD, WOODBRIDGE, ON, L4H 0B1
(905) 856-0096 *SIC* 3442
TRU TECH DOORS *p* 1028
See TRU TECH CORPORATION
TRU-DIE LIMITED *p* 890

236 EDWARD ST, ST THOMAS, ON, N5P 1Z5
(519) 633-1040 *SIC* 3545
TRU-NOR TRUCK CENTRES *p* 898
See 862390 ONTARIO INC
TRU-NORTH RV, AUTO & MARINE SALES INC *p* 1414
4189 2ND AVE W, PRINCE ALBERT, SK, S6W 1A1
(306) 763-8100 *SIC* 5551
TRU-WAY ENTERPRISES LTD *p* 252
135 KEIS AVE, QUESNEL, BC, V2J 3S1
(250) 992-8512 *SIC* 5074
TRUCASH *p* 693
See DCR STRATEGIES INC
TRUCK OUTFITTERS INC, THE *p* 119
6525 GATEWAY BLVD NW, EDMONTON, AB, T6H 2J1
(780) 439-2360 *SIC* 5531
TRUCK TRANSFER INC *p* 701
5939 SHAWSON DR, MISSISSAUGA, ON, L4W 3Y2
(416) 717-1000 *SIC* 4731
TRUDEAU CORPORATION 1889 INC *p* 1068
1600 RUE EIFFEL, BOUCHERVILLE, QC, J4B 5Y1
(450) 655-7441 *SIC* 5023
TRUDELL MEDICAL INTERNATIONAL *p* 650
725 BARANSWAY DR, LONDON, ON, N5V 5G4
(519) 455-7060 *SIC* 3841
TRUDELL MEDICAL INTERNATIONAL EUROPE LIMITED *p* 650
725 BARANSWAY DR, LONDON, ON, N5V 5G4
(519) 455-7060 *SIC* 5047
TRUDELL MEDICAL MARKETING LIMITED *p* 650
758 BARANSWAY DR, LONDON, ON, N5V 5J7
(519) 685-8800 *SIC* 5047
TRUE HARDWARE *p* 501
See ATLAS BEARINGS CORPORATION
TRUE NORTH AUTOMATION INC *p* 38
7180 11 ST SE, CALGARY, AB, T2H 2S9
(403) 984-2000 *SIC* 8742
TRUE NORTH CHEVROLET CADILLAC LTD *p* 764
1370 SEYMOUR ST, NORTH BAY, ON, P1B 9V6
(705) 472-1210 *SIC* 5511
TRUE NORTH COMMERCIAL REIT *p* 996
3280 BLOOR ST W SUITE 1400, TORONTO, ON, M8X 2X3
(416) 234-8444 *SIC* 6722
TRUE NORTH IMAGING INC *p* 906
7330 YONGE ST SUITE 120, THORNHILL, ON, L4J 7Y7
(905) 889-5926 *SIC* 8071
TRUE NORTH SALMON CO. LTD *p* 395
669 MAIN ST, BLACKS HARBOUR, NB, E5H 1K1
(506) 456-6600 *SIC* 2092
TRUE NORTH SALMON LIMITED PARTNERSHIP *p* 395
669 MAIN ST, BLACKS HARBOUR, NB, E5H 1K1
(506) 456-6610 *SIC* 2092
TRUE NORTH SOLUTIONS *p* 38
See TRUE NORTH AUTOMATION INC
TRUE NORTH SPORTS & ENTERTAINMENT LIMITED *p* 380
345 GRAHAM AVE, WINNIPEG, MB, R3C 5S6
(204) 987-7825 *SIC* 7941
TRUE NORTH TIMBER *p* 541
See 1260261 ONTARIO INC
TRUE ROCK FINANCIAL INC *p* 794
1240 ORMONT DR, NORTH YORK, ON, M9L 2V4

(905) 669-8333 *SIC* 3589
TRUE STAR CONSULTING *p* 927
See TRUESTAR HEALTH INC
TRUE STEEL SECURITY *p* 900
See NORTHERN COMMUNICATION SERVICES INC
TRUE VALUE FOOD CENTRE LTD *p* 180
7108 WEST SAANICH RD, BRENTWOOD BAY, BC, V8M 1P8
(250) 544-8183 *SIC* 5411
TRUEFOAM LIMITED *p* 448
11 MOSHER DR, DARTMOUTH, NS, B3B 1L8
(902) 468-5440 *SIC* 5211
TRUEMAN DISTRIBUTION LTD *p* 19
6280 76 AVE SE UNIT 10, CALGARY, AB, T2C 5N5
(403) 236-3008 *SIC* 5149
TRUENORTH SPECIALTY PRODUCTS, DIV OF *p* 262
See UNIVAR CANADA LTD
TRUESTAR HEALTH INC *p* 927
55 ST CLAIR AVE W SUITE 600, TORONTO, ON, M4V 2Y7
SIC 8621
TRUGREEN *p* 695
See GREENLAWN, LTD
TRUK-KING, DIV OF *p* 890
See ZAVCOR TRUCKING LIMITED
TRUKKERS *p* 158
See TRANSCANADA TRUCK STOP LTD
TRULIFE LIMITED *p* 999
39 DAVIS ST E, TRENTON, ON, K8V 4K8
(613) 392-6528 *SIC* 3842
TRULITE GLASS & ALUMINUM SOLUTIONS CANADA, ULC *p* 1028
20 ROYAL GROUP CRES, WOODBRIDGE, ON, L4H 1X9
(905) 605-7040 *SIC* 3211
TRUMP'S *p* 296
See TRUMPS FOOD INTEREST LTD
TRUMPS FOOD INTEREST LTD *p* 296
646 POWELL ST, VANCOUVER, BC, V6A 1H4
(604) 732-8473 *SIC* 5142
TRUONG'S ENTERPRISES LTD *p* 179
40 264 ST, ALDERGROVE, BC, V4W 2L6
(604) 856-5674 *SIC* 0182
TRURO AND DISTRICT LIONS CLUB *p* 469
1100 PRINCE ST, TRURO, NS, B2N 1J1
(902) 893-4773 *SIC* 8699
TRURO SUPERSTORE *p* 469
See LOBLAW PROPERTIES LIMITED
TRUS(T)LIFT *p* 102
See RAM MANUFACTURING LTD
TRUSS DIVISION *p* 15
See DAVIDSON ENMAN LUMBER LIMITED
TRUSTING INVESTMENT & CONSULTING CO., LTD *p* 266
10891 HOGARTH DR, RICHMOND, BC, V7E 3Z9
(778) 321-7399 *SIC* 6719
TRUSTWAVE CANADA, INC *p* 537
231 SHEARSON CRES SUITE 205, CAMBRIDGE, ON, N1T 1J5
(519) 620-7227 *SIC* 7371
TRUTH HARDWARE *p* 501
See ATLAS HOLDINGS COMPANY LIMITED
TRW AUTOMOTIVE *p* 1017
See ZF AUTOMOTIVE CANADA LIMITED
TRW AUTOMOTIVE *p* 1036
See ZF AUTOMOTIVE CANADA LIMITED
TRY HARD INDUSTRIAL SUPPLY CO LTD *p* 743
1411 COURTNEYPARK DR E, MISSISSAUGA, ON, L5T 2E3
(905) 565-8700 *SIC* 5085
TRY RECYCLING INC *p* 564
11010 LONGWOODS RD, DELAWARE, ON, N0L 1E0
(519) 858-2199 *SIC* 4953
TRYDOR INDUSTRIES *p* 278

See 4499034 CANADA INC
TRYLON TSF INC *p* 568
21 SOUTH FIELD DR, ELMIRA, ON, N3B 0A6
(519) 669-5421 *SIC* 1731
TRYTON INVESTMENT COMPANY LIMITED *p* 385
590 BERRY ST, WINNIPEG, MB, R3H 0R9
(204) 772-7110 *SIC* 3821
TRYTON TOOL SERVICES LTD *p* 144
6702 56 ST, LLOYDMINSTER, AB, T9V 3T7
(780) 875-0800 *SIC* 3533
TS LP *p* 111
5135 67 AVE NW, EDMONTON, AB, T6B 2R8
(780) 481-1122 *SIC* 5084
TS MACHINES AND SERVICE CORP *p* 701
5940 SHAWSON DR, MISSISSAUGA, ON, L4W 3W5
(905) 670-5785 *SIC* 5072
TS TECH CANADA INC *p* 757
17855 LESLIE ST, NEWMARKET, ON, L3Y 3E3
(905) 953-0098 *SIC* 2531
TS TECH CO *p* 875
See TRIMONT MFG. INC
TSANG, A.J. PHARMACY LTD *p* 244
19150 LOUGHEED HWY SUITE 110, PITT MEADOWS, BC, V3Y 2H6
(604) 465-8122 *SIC* 5912
TSC NURSERY SALES LIMITED *p* 257
18071 WESTMINSTER HWY, RICHMOND, BC, V6V 1B1
(604) 214-4575 *SIC* 5193
TSC STORES L.P. *p* 650
1000 CLARKE RD, LONDON, ON, N5V 3A9
(519) 453-5270 *SIC* 5251
TSE STEEL LTD *p* 19
4436 90 AVE SE, CALGARY, AB, T2C 2S7
(403) 279-6060 *SIC* 3441
TSG INSURANCE *p* 146
See THOMSON SCHINDLE GREEN INSURANCE & FINANCIAL SERVICES LTD
TSI *p* 424
See TORNGAIT SERVICES INC
TSI INSULATION LTD *p* 2
27392 ELLIS RD, ACHESON, AB, T7X 6N3
(780) 484-1344 *SIC* 5211
TSN 1200 *p* 821
See CFGO
TSO3 INC *p* 1268
2505 AV DALTON, QUEBEC, QC, G1P 3S5
(418) 651-0003 *SIC* 3842
TSSA *p* 588
See TECHNICAL STANDARDS AND SAFETY AUTHORITY
TST AUTOMOTIVE SERVICES *p* 1015
See TST SOLUTIONS L.P.
TST AUTOMOTIVE SERVICES, DIV OF *p* 701
See TST SOLUTIONS L.P.
TST OVERLAND EXPRESS *p* 701
See TST SOLUTIONS L.P.
TST OVERLAND EXPRESS *p* 701
5200 MAINGATE DR, MISSISSAUGA, ON, L4W 1G5
(905) 625-7500 *SIC* 8742
TST PORTER, DIV OF *p* 370
See TST SOLUTIONS L.P.
TST SOLUTIONS L.P. *p* 370
1987 BROOKSIDE BLVD, WINNIPEG, MB, R2R 2Y3
(204) 697-5795 *SIC* 4231
TST SOLUTIONS L.P. *p* 701
5200 MAINGATE DR, MISSISSAUGA, ON, L4W 1G5
(905) 625-7601 *SIC* 4213
TST SOLUTIONS L.P. *p* 701
5200 MAINGATE DR, MISSISSAUGA, ON, L4W 1G5
SIC 4111
TST SOLUTIONS L.P. *p* 701
5200 MAINGATE DR, MISSISSAUGA, ON,

L4W 1G5
(905) 624-7058   *SIC* 4731
TST SOLUTIONS L.P.   *p* 1015
1601 TRICONT AVE, WHITBY, ON, L1N 7N5
    SIC 4225
TSUBAKI OF CANADA LIMITED   *p* 736
1630 DREW RD, MISSISSAUGA, ON, L5S 1J6
(905) 676-0400   *SIC* 5085
TSX   *p* 958
See TMX GROUP LIMITED
TSX INC   *p* 958
100 ADELAIDE ST W SUITE 300, TORONTO, ON, M5H 4H1
(888) 873-8392   *SIC* 6231
TSYCCO LTD   *p* 685
290 BRONTE ST S, MILTON, ON, L9T 1Y8
(905) 625-1234   *SIC* 6531
TT GROUP LIMITED   *p* 661
1806 WHARNCLIFFE RD S, LONDON, ON, N6L 1K1
(519) 652-0080   *SIC* 5139
TTA   *p* 1332
See BOLLORE LOGISTIQUES CANADA INC
TTC   *p* 924
See TORONTO TRANSIT COMMISSION
TTC TECHNOLOGY CORP   *p* 257
13151 VANIER PL SUITE 150, RICHMOND, BC, V6V 2J1
(604) 276-9884   *SIC* 3829
TTCI   *p* 538
See TOYOTA TSUSHO CANADA INC
TTI CANADA   *p* 675
See TECHTRONIC INDUSTRIES CANADA INC
TTM TECHNOLOGIES INC   *p* 914
8150 SHEPPARD AVE E SUITE 1, TORONTO, ON, M1B 5K2
(416) 208-2159   *SIC* 5013
TTR   *p* 967
See TORONTO TERMINALS RAILWAY COMPANY LIMITED, THE
TU-MEC INC   *p* 1163
11700 AV LUCIEN-GENDRON, MONTREAL, QC, H1E 7J7
(514) 881-1801   *SIC* 1711
TUBE TECHNOLOGIES   *p* 473
See 2072223 ONTARIO LIMITED
TUBE-FAB LTD   *p* 701
1020 BREVIK PL UNIT 11, MISSISSAUGA, ON, L4W 4N7
(905) 206-0311   *SIC* 3469
TUBE-LINE MANUFACTURING LTD   *p* 568
6455 REID WOODS DR SUITE 4, ELMIRA, ON, N3B 2Z3
(519) 669-9488   *SIC* 3523
TUBE-MAC PIPING TECHNOLOGIES LTD *p* 893
853 ARVIN AVE SUITE 1, STONEY CREEK, ON, L8E 5N8
(905) 643-8823   *SIC* 1799
TUBOQUIP   *p* 1390
See EQUIPMENTS INDUSTRIELS I.B.S. VAL D'OR INC, LES
TUBOSCOPE   *p* 150
See TUBOSCOPE VETCO CANADA ULC
TUBOSCOPE CANADA   *p* 149
See NOV ENERFLOW ULC
TUBOSCOPE VETCO CANADA ULC *p* 150
2201 9 ST, NISKU, AB, T9E 7Z7
(780) 955-7675   *SIC* 1389
TUBULAR STEEL INC   *p* 868
285 RALEIGH AVE, SCARBOROUGH, ON, M1K 1A5
(416) 261-2089   *SIC* 5051
TUC'S CONTRACTING LTD   *p* 129
283 MACALPINE CRES SUITE C, FORT MCMURRAY, AB, T9H 4Y4
(780) 743-8110   *SIC* 4212
TUCKER HI-RISE CONSTRUCTION INC *p* 878
3755 VICTORIA PARK AVE, SCARBOR-

OUGH, ON, M1W 3Z4
(416) 441-2730   *SIC* 1541
TUCKER WIRELINE SERVICES CANADA INC   *p* 62
444 5 AVE SW SUITE 900, CALGARY, AB, T2P 2T8
(403) 264-7040   *SIC* 1389
TUCKER WIRELINE SERVICES CANADA INC   *p* 140
7123 SPARROW DR, LEDUC, AB, T9E 7L1
    SIC 1389
TUCKER'S MARKETPLACE   *p* 586
See NEWGEN RESTAURANT SERVICES INC
TUCKER'S MARKETPLACE   *p* 732
See NEWGEN RESTAURANT SERVICES INC
TUCKER'S MARKETPLACE   *p* 780
See NEWGEN RESTAURANT SERVICES INC
TUCKER'S MARKETPLACE   *p* 821
See NEWGEN RESTAURANT SERVICES INC
TUCKER'S TRAFFIC CONTROL   *p* 174
5195 ODIAN ST, 108 MILE RANCH, BC, V0K 2Z0
(250) 791-5725   *SIC* 7359
TUCOWS INC   *p* 992
96 MOWAT AVE, TORONTO, ON, M6K 3M1
(416) 535-0123   *SIC* 4813
TUCOWS.COM CO   *p* 992
96 MOWAT AVE, TORONTO, ON, M6K 3M1
(416) 535-0123   *SIC* 4813
TUDHOPE CARTAGE LIMITED   *p* 448
4 VIDITO DR, DARTMOUTH, NS, B3B 1P9
(902) 468-4447   *SIC* 4213
TUDOR HOUSE LTD   *p* 356
800 MANITOBA AVE, SELKIRK, MB, R1A 2C9
(204) 482-6601   *SIC* 8051
TUFF CONTROL SYSTEMS LIMITED *p* 794
5145 STEELES AVE W SUITE 201, NORTH YORK, ON, M9L 1R5
    SIC 7381
TUFF-TOTE   *p* 474
See IDEAL INDUSTRIES (CANADA), CORP
TUFFORD NURSING HOME   *p* 885
See UNGER NURSING HOMES LIMITED
TUFFORD NURSING HOME LTD   *p* 885
312 QUEENSTON ST, ST CATHARINES, ON, L2P 2X4
(905) 682-0411   *SIC* 8051
TUFTRAK: MANTRAK   *p* 1394
See EUTECTIC CANADA INC
TUGO   *p* 262
See NORTH AMERICAN AIR TRAVEL INSURANCE AGENTS LTD
TUILES POLYCOR   *p* 1259
See POLYCOR INC
TULA FOUNDATION   *p* 215
1713 HYACINTHE BAY RD, HERIOT BAY, BC, V0P 1H0
(250) 285-2628   *SIC* 8699
TULIPE JUVENILE   *p* 1254
See NATART JUVENILE INC
TULLAMORE NURSING HOME   *p* 509
See DIVERSICARE CANADA MANAGEMENT SERVICES CO., INC
TULLETT PREBON CANADA LIMITED *p* 941
1 TORONTO ST SUITE 803, TORONTO, ON, M5C 2V6
(416) 941-0606   *SIC* 6099
TULMAR SAFETY SYSTEMS INC   *p* 619
1123 CAMERON ST, HAWKESBURY, ON, K6A 2B8
(613) 632-1282   *SIC* 3069
TULMAR TECHNICAL SERVICES   *p* 619
See TULMAR SAFETY SYSTEMS INC
TULSAR CANADA LTD   *p* 516
15 WORTHINGTON DR, BRANTFORD, ON, N3S 0H4
(519) 748-5055   *SIC* 3625

TULSAR CUSTOMS CONTROL   *p* 516
See TULSAR CANADA LTD
TUMBLERS GYMNASTIC CENTRE   *p* 811
330 VANTAGE DR, ORLEANS, ON, K4A 3W1
(613) 834-4334   *SIC* 8699
TUNCER TRADE INC   *p* 685
235 STEELES AVE E, MILTON, ON, L9T 1Y2
(905) 878-5829   *SIC* 5541
TUNDRA   *p* 890
See TUNDRA STRATEGIES, INC
TUNDRA INTERNATIONAL INC   *p* 890
1393 CENTRE LINE RD, STAYNER, ON, L0M 1S0
(705) 428-0544   *SIC* 8742
TUNDRA OIL & GAS LIMITED   *p* 376
1 LOMBARD PL SUITE 1700, WINNIPEG, MB, R3B 0X3
(204) 934-5850   *SIC* 1382
TUNDRA PROCESS SOLUTIONS LTD *p* 71
3200 118 AVE SE, CALGARY, AB, T2Z 3X1
(403) 255-5222   *SIC* 5085
TUNDRA RESCUE   *p* 890
See TUNDRA INTERNATIONAL INC
TUNDRA STRATEGIES, INC   *p* 890
1393 CENTRE LINE RD, STAYNER, ON, L0M 1S0
(705) 734-7700   *SIC* 8742
TURBOMECA CANADA   *p* 1153
See SAFRAN MOTEURS D'HELICOPTERES CANADA INC
TURBOTRONICS   *p* 1432
230 29TH ST E, SASKATOON, SK, S7L 6Y6
(306) 242-7644   *SIC* 5541
TURCON CONSTRUCTION GROUP   *p* 133
See TURCON UNITED BUILDING SYSTEMS INC
TURCON UNITED BUILDING SYSTEMS INC   *p* 133
99200 100 AVE SUITE B, GRANDE PRAIRIE, AB, T8V 0T9
(780) 532-5533   *SIC* 1542
TURF CARE PRODUCTS CANADA LIMITED   *p* 757
200 PONY DR, NEWMARKET, ON, L3Y 7B6
(905) 836-0988   *SIC* 3523
TURF OPERATIONS SCARBOROUGH INC *p* 865
80 AUTO MALL DR, SCARBOROUGH, ON, M1B 5N5
(416) 269-8333   *SIC* 0782
TURIN COLONY   *p* 170
See GOLDRIDGE FARMING CO. LTD
TURK, ROY INDUSTRIAL SALES LIMITED *p* 589
106 VULCAN ST, ETOBICOKE, ON, M9W 1L2
(416) 742-2777   *SIC* 5085
TURKEY HILL SUGARBUSH LIMITED *p* 1400
10 RUE DE WATERLOO, WATERLOO, QC, J0E 2N0
(450) 539-4822   *SIC* 5145
TURKSTRA INDUSTRIES INC   *p* 616
1050 UPPER WELLINGTON ST, HAMILTON, ON, L9A 3S6
(905) 388-8220   *SIC* 2431
TURKSTRA LUMBER COMPANY LIMITED *p* 616
1050 UPPER WELLINGTON ST, HAMILTON, ON, L9A 3S6
(905) 388-8220   *SIC* 5211
TURKSTRA MILL   *p* 616
See TURKSTRA INDUSTRIES INC
TURKSTRA WINDOWS   *p* 616
See TURKSTRA LUMBER COMPANY LIMITED
TURN KEY STAFFING SOLUTIONS INC *p* 757
200 DAVIS DR SUITE 7, NEWMARKET, ON, L3Y 2N4
(905) 953-9133   *SIC* 7363

TURN-KEY   *p* 801
See TURNKEY MODULAR SYSTEMS INC
TURNER & PORTER   *p* 995
See TURNER & PORTER FUNERAL DIRECTORS LIMITED
TURNER & PORTER FUNERAL DIRECTORS LIMITED   *p* 995
380 WINDERMERE AVE, TORONTO, ON, M6S 3L4
(416) 767-7452   *SIC* 7261
TURNER & TOWNSEND CM2R INC   *p* 927
2 ST CLAIR AVE W 12TH FL, TORONTO, ON, M4V 1L5
(416) 925-1424   *SIC* 8713
TURNER FENTON SECONDARY SCHOOL *p* 510
See PEEL DISTRICT SCHOOL BOARD
TURNER FLEISCHER ARCHITECTS INC *p* 778
67 LESMILL RD SUITE A, NORTH YORK, ON, M3B 2T8
(416) 425-2222   *SIC* 8712
TURNER VOLKSWAGON & AUDI   *p* 222
See MERVYN MOTORS LIMITED
TURNER, GRANT C. T. ENTERPRISES INC *p* 332
SUITE 345 4900 27 ST, VERNON, BC, V1T 7G7
(250) 549-2131   *SIC* 5251
TURNING POINT YOUTH SERVICES *p* 932
95 WELLESLEY ST E, TORONTO, ON, M4Y 2X9
(416) 925-9250   *SIC* 8322
TURNKEY MODULAR SYSTEMS INC *p* 801
2590 SHERIDAN GARDEN DR, OAKVILLE, ON, L6J 7R2
(905) 608-8006   *SIC* 3559
TURNKEY SOLUTIONS INC   *p* 9
4300 26 ST NE BAY SUITE 105, CALGARY, AB, T1Y 7H7
    SIC 3679
TURPIN GROUP LTD   *p* 627
2500 PALLADIUM DR UNIT 200, KANATA, ON, K2V 1E2
    SIC 5511
TURPIN PONTIAC BUICK GMC   *p* 627
See TURPIN GROUP LTD
TURPIN SATURN SAAB ISUZU LIMITED *p* 627
2500 PALLADIUM DR UNIT 400, KANATA, ON, K2V 1E2
    SIC 5511
TURPLE BROS LTD   *p* 157
175 LEVA AVE, RED DEER COUNTY, AB, T4E 0A5
(403) 346-5238   *SIC* 5571
TURPOL TECH INDUSTRIES INC   *p* 615
100 LANCING DR UNIT 3, HAMILTON, ON, L8W 3L6
(905) 512-9881   *SIC* 3325
TURQUOISE HILL RESOURCES LTD *p* 310
200 GRANVILLE ST SUITE 354, VANCOUVER, BC, V6C 1S4
(604) 688-5755   *SIC* 1081
TURQUOISE, CABINET EN ASSURANCE DE DOMMAGES INC, LA   *p* 1243
481 131 RTE, NOTRE-DAME-DES-PRAIRIES, QC, J6E 0M1
(450) 759-6265   *SIC* 6411
TURTLE JACK'S RESTAURANT INC *p* 528
3370 SOUTH SERVICE RD SUITE 102, BURLINGTON, ON, L7N 3M6
(905) 332-6833   *SIC* 5812
TURTLE MOUNTAIN SCHOOL DIVISION *p* 351
435 WILLIAMS AVE, KILLARNEY, MB, R0K 1G0
(204) 523-7531   *SIC* 8211
TURTLE RIVER SCHOOL DIVISION *p* 352
808 BURROWS RD, MCCREARY, MB, R0J 1B0
(204) 835-2067   *SIC* 8211
TURVEY FINANCIAL GROUP INC, THE *p*

264
11388 NO. 5 RD SUITE 110, RICHMOND, BC, V7A 4E7
(604) 279-8484   *SIC* 6712
TUSK ENERGY INC   *p* 62
700 4 AVE SW SUITE 1950, CALGARY, AB, T2P 3J4
SIC 1311
TUSKET FORD   *p* 469
See TUSKET SALES & SERVICE LIMITED
TUSKET SALES & SERVICE LIMITED*p* 469
4143 GAVEL RD, TUSKET, NS, B0W 3M0
(902) 648-2600   *SIC* 7532
TUXEDO ROYALE FORMAL WEAR   *p* 854
See TUXEDO ROYALE LIMITED
TUXEDO ROYALE LIMITED   *p* 854
9078 LESLIE ST UNIT 5&6, RICHMOND HILL, ON, L4B 3L8
(416) 798-7617   *SIC* 7299
TUXEDO SAFEWAY   *p* 389
See SOBEYS WEST INC
TUYAUX ET MATERIEL DE FONDATION LTEE   *p* 1309
5025 RUE RAMSAY, SAINT-HUBERT, QC, J3Y 2S3
(450) 445-0050   *SIC* 5051
TUZY-MUZY DRIED FLOWERS   *p* 668
See CELLAY CANADA INC
TV NEWS   *p* 979
See CANADIAN BROADCASTING CORPORATION
TVA INTERACTIF   *p* 1176
See TVA VENTES ET MARKETING INC
TVA PUBLICATIONS INC   *p* 1244
7 CH BATES, OUTREMONT, QC, H2V 4V7
(514) 848-7000   *SIC* 2759
TVA TELE 7   *p* 1373
See GROUPE TVA INC
TVA VENTES ET MARKETING INC *p* 1176
1600 BOUL DE MAISONNEUVE E, MONTREAL, QC, H2L 4P2
(514) 526-9251   *SIC* 7319
TVC HOLDINGS LIMITED   *p* 801
2740 SHERWOOD HEIGHTS DR, OAKVILLE, ON, L6J 7V5
(905) 829-0280   *SIC* 5031
TVCC   *p* 656
See THAMES VALLEY CHILDREN'S CENTRE
TVE INDUSTRIAL SERVICES LTD   *p* 218
60 VICARS RD, KAMLOOPS, BC, V2C 6A4
(250) 377-3533   *SIC* 1799
TVH   *p* 736
See TVH CANADA LTD
TVH CANADA LTD   *p* 736
1039 CARDIFF BLVD, MISSISSAUGA, ON, L5S 1P4
(905) 564-0003   *SIC* 5013
TVI PACIFIC INC   *p* 62
505 2 ST SW SUITE 806, CALGARY, AB, T2P 1N8
(403) 265-4356   *SIC* 1081
TVM   *p* 535
See 1625443 ONTARIO INC
TVONTARIO   *p* 924
See ONTARIO EDUCATIONAL COMMUNICATIONS AUTHORITY, THE
TVT   *p* 809
See MARINE PLAZA TVT
TWA PANEL SYSTEMS INC   *p* 150
1201 4 ST, NISKU, AB, T9E 7L3
(780) 955-8757   *SIC* 3634
TWC ENTERPRISES LIMITED   *p* 629
15675 DUFFERIN ST, KING CITY, ON, L7B 1K5
(905) 841-5372   *SIC* 7999
TWD ROADS MANAGEMENT INC   *p* 560
7077 KEELE ST SUITE 100, CONCORD, ON, L4K 0B6
(905) 532-5200   *SIC* 1611
TWD ROADS MANAGEMENT INC   *p* 631
1010 MIDDLE RD, KINGSTON, ON, K7L 4V3
SIC 5082

TWD TECHNOLOGIES LTD   *p* 525
905 CENTURY DR, BURLINGTON, ON, L7L 5J8
(905) 634-3324   *SIC* 8711
TWEED VALUE MART   *p* 999
See M & M MARKETS LTD
TWEEDIE BRUNSWICK & LAVESQUE   *p* 399
36 RUE DE L'EGLISE, EDMUNDSTON, NB, E3V 1J2
(506) 735-5515   *SIC* 6331
TWG CANADA CONSOLIDATED INC *p* 280
19350 22 AVE, SURREY, BC, V3Z 3S6
(604) 547-2100   *SIC* 3531
TWI FOODS INC   *p* 589
40 SHAFT RD SUITE 20, ETOBICOKE, ON, M9W 4M2
(647) 775-1400   *SIC* 2051
TWILIGHT COLONY   *p* 127
See TWILIGHT HUTTERIAN BRETHREN
TWILIGHT HUTTERIAN BRETHREN *p* 127
GD, FALHER, AB, T0H 1M0
SIC 7389
TWIN CITY ALARMS LIMITED   *p* 456
6371 LADY HAMMOND RD, HALIFAX, NS, B3K 2S2
(902) 455-0645   *SIC* 1731
TWIN CITY ELECTRIC   *p* 456
See TWIN CITY ALARMS LIMITED
TWIN CITY REFRESHMENTS LIMITED   *p* 909
637 SQUIER ST, THUNDER BAY, ON, P7B 4A7
(807) 344-8651   *SIC* 5963
TWIN CREEK COLONY   *p* 167
See TWIN CREEK HUTTERIAN BRETHREN
TWIN CREEK HUTTERIAN BRETHREN   *p* 167
GD, STANDARD, AB, T0J 3G0
(403) 644-2283   *SIC* 8811
TWIN EQUIPMENT LTD   *p* 827
3091 ALBION RD N, OTTAWA, ON, K1V 9V9
(613) 745-7095   *SIC* 5082
TWIN HILLS FORD LINCOLN LIMITED   *p* 856
10801 YONGE ST, RICHMOND HILL, ON, L4C 3E3
(905) 884-4441   *SIC* 5511
TWIN LAKES TERRACE   *p* 859
See STEEVES & ROZEMA ENTERPRISES LIMITED
TWIN MOTORS LTD   *p* 360
1637 GORDON AVE, THE PAS, MB, R9A 1L1
(204) 623-6402   *SIC* 5511
TWIN OAKS SENIOR CITIZENS ASSOCIATION   *p* 463
7702 # 7 HWY, MUSQUODOBOIT HARBOUR, NS, B0J 2L0
(902) 889-3474   *SIC* 8361
TWIN PEAKS HYDROPONICS INC   *p* 634
2237 COUNTY RD 31, KINGSVILLE, ON, N9Y 2E5
(519) 326-1000   *SIC* 0182
TWIN RIVERS PAPER COMPANY INC*p* 399
27 RUE RICE, EDMUNDSTON, NB, E3V 1S9
(506) 735-5551   *SIC* 2621
TWIN RIVERS PAPER COMPANY INC*p* 411
31 RENOUS RD SUITE 36, PLASTER ROCK, NB, E7G 4B5
(506) 356-4132   *SIC* 2421
TWIN SEAFOOD LIMITED   *p* 461
6689 WOOD HARBOUR RD, LOWER WOODS HARBOUR, NS, B0W 2E0
(902) 723-9003   *SIC* 5146
TWIN VALLEY CO-OP LTD   *p* 345
861 VINE ST, BIRTLE, MB, R0M 0C0
(204) 842-3387   *SIC* 5411
TWINCORP INC   *p* 1007
316 MARSLAND DR, WATERLOO, ON, N2J

3Z1
(519) 885-4600   *SIC* 5812
TWINKLE ENTERPRISES LTD   *p* 300
308 WATER ST, VANCOUVER, BC, V6B 1B6
SIC 5199
TWINPAK ATLANTIC INC   *p* 409
66 ENGLISH DR, MONCTON, NB, E1E 4G1
(506) 857-8116   *SIC* 3089
TWINS LAKES SECONDARY SCHOOL   *p* 810
See SIMCOE COUNTY DISTRICT SCHOOL BOARD, THE
TWO BLOOR RESIDENCES LIMITED *p* 786
3625 DUFFERIN ST SUITE 500, NORTH YORK, ON, M3K 1Z2
(416) 635-7520   *SIC* 1522
TWO RIVERS TRANSPORT   *p* 251
9408 PENN RD, PRINCE GEORGE, BC, V2N 5T6
SIC 7389
TWO SISTERS VINEYARD CORP   *p* 761
240 JOHN ST E, NIAGARA ON THE LAKE, ON, L0S 1J0
(905) 468-0592   *SIC* 2084
TWO SMALL MEN WITH BIG HEARTS MOVING (B.C.) CORPORATION   *p* 275
11180 SCOTT RD, SURREY, BC, V3V 8B8
(604) 581-1616   *SIC* 4214
TWO WHEEL MOTORSPORT   *p* 602
See 775757 ONTARIO INC
TWOMEY, DR HUGH HEALTH CARE CENTRE   *p* 421
See CENTRAL REGIONAL HEALTH AUTHORITY
TWR C MOTORS LP   *p* 39
10901 MACLEOD TRAIL SW, CALGARY, AB, T2J 4L3
(403) 225-6193   *SIC* 5511
TXT CARBON FASHIONS INC   *p* 1179
433 RUE CHABANEL O BUREAU 400, MONTREAL, QC, H2N 2J4
(514) 382-8271   *SIC* 5136
TY-CROP MANUFACTURING LTD   *p* 266
9880 MCGRATH RD, ROSEDALE, BC, V0X 1X0
(604) 794-7078   *SIC* 5013
TYAM EXCAVATION & SHORING LTD*p* 208
6955 120 ST SUITE 202, DELTA, BC, V4E 2A8
(778) 593-2900   *SIC* 1794
TYCO ELECTRONICS CANADA ULC *p* 676
20 ESNA PARK DR, MARKHAM, ON, L3R 1E1
(905) 475-6222   *SIC* 3643
TYCO INTEGRATED FIRE & SECURITY CANADA, INC   *p* 26
615 18 ST SE, CALGARY, AB, T2E 3L9
(403) 569-4606   *SIC* 1731
TYCO INTEGRATED FIRE & SECURITY CANADA, INC   *p* 32
431 MANITOU RD SE, CALGARY, AB, T2G 4C2
(403) 287-3202   *SIC* 7389
TYCO INTEGRATED FIRE & SECURITY CANADA, INC   *p* 38
401 FORGE RD SE, CALGARY, AB, T2H 0S9
SIC 8748
TYCO INTEGRATED FIRE & SECURITY CANADA, INC   *p* 103
17402 116 AVE NW, EDMONTON, AB, T5S 2X2
(780) 452-5280   *SIC* 7389
TYCO INTEGRATED FIRE & SECURITY CANADA, INC   *p* 207
1485 LINDSEY PL, DELTA, BC, V3M 6V1
(604) 515-8872   *SIC* 7389
TYCO INTEGRATED FIRE & SECURITY CANADA, INC   *p* 701
2400 SKYMARK AVE SUITE 1, MISSISSAUGA, ON, L4W 5K5
(905) 212-4400   *SIC* 1731

TYCO INTEGRATED FIRE & SECURITY CANADA, INC   *p* 781
5000 DUFFERIN ST, NORTH YORK, ON, M3H 5T5
SIC 7381
TYCO INTEGRATED FIRE & SECURITY CANADA, INC   *p* 1331
5700 BOUL HENRI-BOURASSA O, SAINT-LAURENT, QC, H4R 1V9
(514) 737-5505   *SIC* 7382
TYCO INTEGRATED FIRE & SECURITY CANADA, INC   *p* 1331
5800 BOUL HENRI-BOURASSA O, SAINT-LAURENT, QC, H4R 1V9
(514) 737-5505   *SIC* 7389
TYCO SAFETY PRODUCTS CANADA LTD*p* 560
3301 LANGSTAFF RD, CONCORD, ON, L4K 4L2
(905) 760-3000   *SIC* 3699
TYCO SAFETY PRODUCTS CANADA LTD*p* 790
95 BRIDGELAND AVE, NORTH YORK, ON, M6A 1Y7
(905) 760-3000   *SIC* 3699
TYCO SAFETY PRODUCTS CANADA LTD*p* 1071
9995 RUE DE CHATEAUNEUF UNITE L, BROSSARD, QC, J4Z 3V7
(450) 444-2040   *SIC* 3699
TYCORRA INVESTMENTS INC   *p* 635
10 FORWELL RD, KITCHENER, ON, N2B 3E7
(519) 576-9290   *SIC* 5012
TYCROP   *p* 266
See TY-CROP MANUFACTURING LTD
TYEE CHEVROLET BUICK GMC LTD *p* 195
570 13TH AVE, CAMPBELL RIVER, BC, V9W 4G8
(250) 287-9511   *SIC* 5511
TYNDALE UNIVERSITY COLLEGE & SEMINARY   *p* 915
3377 BAYVIEW AVE, TORONTO, ON, M2M 3S4
(416) 226-6380   *SIC* 8221
TYNDALL NURSING HOME LIMITED *p* 701
1060 EGLINTON AVE E SUITE 417, MISSISSAUGA, ON, L4W 1K3
(905) 624-1511   *SIC* 8051
TYSACH HIGGINS LTD   *p* 283
3059 152 ST SUITE 485, SURREY, BC, V4P 3K1
(604) 542-4326   *SIC* 5014
TYSON FOODS CANADA INC   *p* 707
226 BRITANNIA RD E, MISSISSAUGA, ON, L4Z 1S6
(905) 206-0443   *SIC* 5142
TYSON TOOL COMPANY LIMITED   *p* 794
75 ORMONT DR, NORTH YORK, ON, M9L 2S3
(416) 746-3688   *SIC* 5084
TYT   *p* 1097
See TRANSPORTS YVON TURCOTTE LTEE, LES

U

U B C TRAFFIC OFFICE   *p* 325
2075 WESBROOK MALL SUITE 204, VANCOUVER, BC, V6T 1Z1
(604) 822-6786   *SIC* 7521
U N D E LOCAL 641   *p* 630
See UNION OF NATIONAL DEFENCE EMPLOYEES
U OF A STUDENT UNION   *p* 117
See GOVERNORS OF THE UNIVERSITY OF ALBERTA, THE
U OF T INNIS RESIDENCE   *p* 976
111 ST. GEORGE ST, TORONTO, ON, M5S 2E8
(416) 978-2512   *SIC* 6531
U P A CENTRE DU QUEBEC   *p* 1243
1940 RUE DES PINS, NICOLET, QC, J3T 1Z9

(819) 293-5838 *SIC 8748*
U-BUY DISCOUNT FOODS LIMITED *p 560*
8811 KEELE ST, CONCORD, ON, L4K 2N1
(905) 669-8002 *SIC 5141*
U-HAUL CO. (CANADA) LTD *p 608*
526 GRAYS RD, HAMILTON, ON, L8E 2Z4
(905) 560-0014 *SIC 7519*
U-PAK DISPOSALS (1989) LTD *p 589*
15 TIDEMORE AVE, ETOBICOKE, ON, M9W 7E9
(416) 675-3700 *SIC 4953*
U-PARK ENTERPRISES *p 335*
See ROBINS PARKING SERVICES LTD
U-RENT-IT BANQUET & PARTY CENTRE *p 381*
See BRYJON ENTERPRISES LTD
U.A.P. NAPA AUTO PARTS *p 1437*
See T C ENTERPRISES LTD
U.B.P. SERVICES LIMITED *p 1011*
151 FROBISHER DR SUITE E220, WATERLOO, ON, N2V 2C9
(519) 725-8818 *SIC 6371*
U.G.C.C. HOLDINGS INC *p 325*
5185 UNIVERSITY BLVD, VANCOUVER, BC, V6T 1X5
(604) 224-1018 *SIC 7997*
U.P. INC *p 1381*
3745 RUE PASCAL-GAGNON, TERREBONNE, QC, J6X 4J3
(450) 477-1122 *SIC 5039*
U.S. TRAFFIC LIMITED *p 728*
6645 KITIMAT RD SUITE 18, MISSISSAUGA, ON, L5N 6J3
(905) 858-2222 *SIC 4731*
U.S.N.R. *p 1246*
See USNR/KOCKUMS CANCAR COMPANY
U.T.V. INTERNATIONAL *p 1157*
See 3645118 CANADA INC
U3O8 CORP *p 941*
36 TORONTO ST SUITE 1050, TORONTO, ON, M5C 2C5
(416) 868-1491 *SIC 1081*
UA LOCAL 663 *p 859*
See UNITED ASSOCIATION OF JOURNEYMEN AND APPRENTICES OF THE PLUMBING AND PIPEFITTING INDUSTRY
UAP *p 565*
See UNITED AGRI PRODUCTS CANADA INC
UAP INC *p 38*
5530 3 ST SE SUITE 489, CALGARY, AB, T2H 1J9
(403) 212-4600 *SIC 5013*
UAP INC *p 225*
9325 200 ST UNIT 100, LANGLEY, BC, V1M 3A7
(604) 513-9458 *SIC 5013*
UAP INC *p 538*
525 BOXWOOD DR, CAMBRIDGE, ON, N3E 1A5
(519) 650-4444 *SIC 5015*
UAP INC *p 1165*
2095 AV HAIG, MONTREAL, QC, H1N 3E2
(514) 251-7638 *SIC 5013*
UAP INC *p 1165*
7025 RUE ONTARIO E, MONTREAL, QC, H1N 2B3
(514) 251-6565 *SIC 5013*
UAP NAPA *p 1119*
See PIECES D'AUTO ALAIN COTE INC
UAP PIECES D'AUTO *p 1165*
See UAP INC
UAP/NAPA AUTO PARTS INC *p 409*
325 EDINBURGH DR, MONCTON, NB, E1E 4A6
(506) 857-1111 *SIC 5531*
UBA INC *p 1389*
3450 BOUL GENE-H.-KRUGER BUREAU 100, TROIS-RIVIERES, QC, G9A 4M3
(819) 379-3311 *SIC 5169*
UBC BOOKSTORE *p 325*
See UNIVERSITY OF BRITISH COLUMBIA, THE

UBC ENGINEERING *p 325*
See UNIVERSITY OF BRITISH COLUMBIA, THE
UBC PROPERTIES INVESTMENTS LTD *p 324*
3313 SHRUM LANE UNIT 200, VANCOUVER, BC, V6S 0C8
(604) 731-3103 *SIC 6553*
UBC PROPERTIES TRUST *p 324*
See UBC PROPERTIES INVESTMENTS LTD
UBCP/ACTRA *p 292*
See UNION OF BC PERFORMERS
UBERVU *p 289*
See HOOTSUITE INC
UBISOFT ARTS NUMERIQUES INC *p 1183*
5505 BOUL SAINT-LAURENT BUREAU 2000, MONTREAL, QC, H2T 1S6
(514) 490-2000 *SIC 7336*
UBISOFT DIVERTISSEMENTS *p 1260*
See UBISOFT DIVERTISSEMENTS INC
UBISOFT DIVERTISSEMENTS INC *p 1183*
5505 BOUL SAINT-LAURENT BUREAU 5000, MONTREAL, QC, H2T 1S6
(514) 490-2000 *SIC 7371*
UBISOFT DIVERTISSEMENTS INC *p 1191*
250 RUE SAINT-ANTOINE O BUREAU 700, MONTREAL, QC, H2Y 0A3
(514) 908-8100 *SIC 7371*
UBISOFT DIVERTISSEMENTS INC *p 1260*
390 BOUL CHAREST E BUREAU 600, QUEBEC, QC, G1K 3H4
(418) 524-1222 *SIC 3944*
UBS BANK (CANADA) *p 958*
154 UNIVERSITY AVE SUITE 700, TORONTO, ON, M5H 3Y9
(416) 343-1800 *SIC 6021*
UBS GLOBAL ASSET MANAGEMENT (CANADA) INC *p 968*
161 BAY ST SUITE 4000, TORONTO, ON, M5J 2S1
(416) 681-5200 *SIC 6282*
UCAN FASTENING PRODUCTS *p 782*
See BRITISH FASTENING SYSTEMS LIMITED
UCC GROUP INC *p 589*
262 GALAXY BLVD, ETOBICOKE, ON, M9W 5R8
(416) 675-7455 *SIC 1771*
UCC INDUSTRIES INTERNATIONAL INC *p 845*
895 SANDY BEACH RD UNIT 12, PICKERING, ON, L1W 3N7
(905) 831-7724 *SIC 5051*
UCFV *p 198*
See UNIVERSITY OF THE FRASER VALLEY
UCORE RARE METALS INC *p 440*
210 WATERFRONT DR SUITE 106, BEDFORD, NS, B4A 0H3
(902) 482-5214 *SIC 1481*
UCS FOREST GROUP *p 728*
See UPPER CANADA FOREST PRODUCTS LTD
UDISCO LTEE *p 1220*
4660 BOUL DECARIE, MONTREAL, QC, H3X 2H5
(514) 481-8107 *SIC 5092*
UE ENCLOSURES *p 643*
See 1443190 ONTARIO INC
UFA *p 74*
See UNITED FARMERS OF ALBERTA CO-OPERATIVE LIMITED
UFA *p 146*
See 976576 ALBERTA LTD
UFCW *p 728*
See UNITED FOOD & COMMERCIAL WORKER CANADA
UFCW CANADA *p 589*
See UNITED FOOD AND COMMERCIAL WORKERS CANADA UNION
UFG FLORAL SUPPLIES *p 194*
See UNITED FLORAL HOLDINGS INC
UFP CANADA INC *p 1294*

110 MONTEE GUAY, SAINT-BERNARD-DE-LACOLLE, QC, J0J 1V0
(450) 246-3829 *SIC 2499*
UFR URBAN FOREST RECYCLERS INC *p 1437*
201 INDUSTRIAL DR, SWIFT CURRENT, SK, S9H 5R4
(306) 777-0600 *SIC 2679*
UFV BOOKSTORE *p 175*
See UNIVERSITY OF THE FRASER VALLEY
UGE INTERNATIONAL LTD *p 958*
56 TEMPERANCE ST 7 FL, TORONTO, ON, M5H 3V5
(416) 789-4655 *SIC 1711*
UGO-SAC IMPORTS LTD *p 1179*
9500 RUE MEILLEUR BUREAU 600, MONTREAL, QC, H2N 2B7
(514) 382-4271 *SIC 5137*
UHAUL COMPANY OF EASTERN ONTARIO *p 998*
240 REXDALE BLVD, TORONTO, ON, M9W 1R2
(416) 335-1250 *SIC 7359*
UKE 2000 HOLDINGS LIMITED *p 267*
2200 KEATING CROSS RD UNIT E, SAANICHTON, BC, V8M 2A6
(250) 652-5266 *SIC 5049*
UKEN GAME *p 984*
See UKEN STUDIOS INC
UKEN STUDIOS INC *p 984*
266 KING ST W 2ND FL, TORONTO, ON, M5V 1H8
(416) 616-8901 *SIC 7372*
UKRAINIAN CANADIAN CARE CENTRE, THE *p 577*
See ST DEMETRIUS (UKRAINIAN CATHOLIC) DEVELOPMENT CORPORATION, THE
UKRAINIAN FARMERS CO-OPERATIVE LIMITED *p 350*
22 TACHE ST, FISHER BRANCH, MB, R0C 0Z0
(204) 372-6202 *SIC 5171*
UKRAINIAN FRATERNAL SOCIETY OF CANADA *p 371*
235 MCGREGOR ST, WINNIPEG, MB, R2W 4W5
(204) 586-4482 *SIC 6311*
UKRAINIAN HOME FOR THE AGED *p 718*
3058 WINSTON CHURCHILL BLVD SUITE 1, MISSISSAUGA, ON, L5L 3J1
(905) 820-0573 *SIC 8361*
UKRANIAN CATHOLIC ARCHEPARCHY OF WINNIPEG *p 370*
233 SCOTIA ST, WINNIPEG, MB, R2V 1V7
(204) 338-7801 *SIC 8661*
ULBRICH OF CANADA INC *p 1028*
150 NEW HUNTINGTON RD UNIT 1, WOODBRIDGE, ON, L4H 4N4
(416) 663-7130 *SIC 5051*
ULCH TRANSPORT LIMITED *p 889*
100 SOUTH SERVICE RD, ST MARYS, ON, N4X 1A9
(519) 349-2340 *SIC 4212*
ULINE CANADA CORPORATION *p 685*
3333 JAMES SNOW PKY N, MILTON, ON, L9T 8L1
(800) 295-5510 *SIC 5113*
ULINE SHIPPING SUPPLIES *p 685*
See ULINE CANADA CORPORATION
ULLINWOOD BUILDING SUPPLIES, DIV OF *p 159*
See ROCKY WOOD PRESERVERS LTD
ULLMAN, KEN ENTERPRISES INC *p 482*
92 KENNEDY ST W, AURORA, ON, L4G 2L7
(905) 727-5677 *SIC 2841*
ULMER CHEV (LLOYDMINSTER) *p 1409*
See ULMER, ROSS CHEVROLET CADILLAC LTD
ULMER, ROSS CHEVROLET CADILLAC LTD *p 1409*
2101 50 AVE, LLOYDMINSTER, SK, S9V

1Z7
(306) 825-8866 *SIC 5511*
ULS MAINTENANCE & LANDSCAPING INC *p 160*
240085 FRONTIER CRES, ROCKY VIEW COUNTY, AB, T1X 0W2
(403) 235-5353 *SIC 0781*
ULSAN HYUNDAI *p 1094*
See HYUNDAI AUTOMOBILES ULSAN LTEE
ULT POWERTRAIN *p 815*
See 1551121 ONTARIO INC
ULTAMIG *p 1284*
See AMH CANADA LTEE
ULTERRA LP *p 140*
7010 45 ST, LEDUC, AB, T9E 7E7
(780) 980-3500 *SIC 1381*
ULTIDENT *p 1331*
See 2946-5440 QUEBEC INC
ULTIMA *p 1056*
See CHAPDELAINE ASSURANCE ET SERVICES FINANCIERS INC
ULTIMATE CONSTRUCTION INC *p 488*
39 CHURCHILL DR SUITE 1, BARRIE, ON, L4N 8Z5
(705) 726-2300 *SIC 1521*
ULTIMATE DRIVING COMPANY INC, THE *p 431*
120 KENMOUNT RD, ST. JOHN'S, NL, A1B 3R2
(709) 754-3269 *SIC 5531*
ULTIMATE GOLF VACATIONS *p 799*
See ULTIMATE TRAVEL GROUP INC
ULTIMATE POWER SPORTS INC *p 492*
1037 WALLBRIDGE RD, BELLEVILLE, ON, K8N 4Z5
SIC 5571
ULTIMATE TRAVEL GROUP INC *p 799*
1660 NORTH SERVICE RD E SUITE 101, OAKVILLE, ON, L6H 7G3
(905) 755-0999 *SIC 4725*
ULTRA ELECTRONICS CANADA INC *p 444*
40 ATLANTIC ST, DARTMOUTH, NS, B2Y 4N2
(902) 466-7491 *SIC 3812*
ULTRA ELECTRONICS FORENSIC TECHNOLOGY INC *p 1083*
5757 BOUL CAVENDISH BUREAU 200, COTE SAINT-LUC, QC, H4W 2W8
(514) 489-4247 *SIC 3821*
ULTRA ELECTRONICS MARITIME SYSTEMS INC *p 444*
40 ATLANTIC ST, DARTMOUTH, NS, B2Y 4N2
(902) 466-7491 *SIC 3679*
ULTRA ELECTRONICS TCS INC *p 1158*
5990 CH DE LA COTE-DE-LIESSE, MONTROYAL, QC, H4T 1V7
(514) 855-6363 *SIC 3679*
ULTRA FRESH *p 644*
See HOWARD HUY FARMS LTD
ULTRA MANUFACTURING LIMITED *p 642*
60 WASHBURN DR, KITCHENER, ON, N2R 1S2
(519) 893-3831 *SIC 3089*
ULTRA-FIT MANUFACTURING INCORPORATED *p 743*
1840 COURTNEYPARK DR E, MISSISSAUGA, ON, L5T 1W1
(905) 795-0344 *SIC 3498*
ULTRA-FORM MFG. CO. LTD *p 581*
73 BAYWOOD RD, ETOBICOKE, ON, M9V 3Y8
(416) 749-9323 *SIC 3545*
ULTRA-LITE DOORS *p 19*
See ULTRA-LITE OVERHEAD DOORS LTD
ULTRA-LITE OVERHEAD DOORS LTD *p 19*
7307 40 ST SE, CALGARY, AB, T2C 2K4
(403) 280-2000 *SIC 5031*
ULTRA-TECH CLEANING SYSTEMS LTD *p 285*

1420 ADANAC ST SUITE 201, VANCOUVER, BC, V5L 2C3
(604) 253-4698   SIC 7349
ULTRACONFORT   p 1195
See ENERGIE VALERO INC
ULTRACUTS LTD   p 364
167 ST MARY'S RD, WINNIPEG, MB, R2H 1J1
(204) 231-0110   SIC 6794
ULTRAMAR   p 1195
See ENERGIE VALERO INC
ULTRAMAR BUSINESS & HOME ENERGY p 410
335 MACNAUGHTON AVE, MONCTON, NB, E1H 2J9
(506) 855-2424   SIC 4924
ULTRASOL INDUSTRIES   p 118
See 753146 ALBERTA LTD
ULTRASPEC FINISHING INC   p 1337
2600 RUE DE MINIAC, SAINT-LAURENT, QC, H4S 1L7
(514) 337-1782   SIC 3479
ULTRATEC RIVE-NORD   p 1133
See TOITURES P.L.C. INC, LES
ULTRAVAC   p 604
See WALINGA INC
UM CANADA   p 963
See INTERPUBLIC GROUP OF COMPANIES CANADA, INC, THE
UMA ACOM   p 691
See AECOM CANADA LTD
UMANO MEDICAL INC   p 1121
230 BOUL NILUS-LECLERC, L'ISLET, QC, G0R 2C0
(418) 247-3986   SIC 3841
UMBRA LTD   p 875
40 EMBLEM CRT, SCARBOROUGH, ON, M1S 1B1
(416) 299-0088   SIC 5023
UMBRELLA FAMILY AND CHILD CENTRES OF HAMILTON   p 617
310 LIMERIDGE RD W UNIT 9, HAMILTON, ON, L9C 2V2
(905) 312-9836   SIC 8351
UMICORE AUTOCAT CANADA CORPp 525
4261 MAINWAY, BURLINGTON, ON, L7L 5N9
(905) 336-3424   SIC 2819
UMICORE PRECIOUS METALS CANADA INC   p 676
451 DENISON ST, MARKHAM, ON, L3R 1B7
(905) 475-9566   SIC 3341
UMOE SOLAR NEW BRUNSWICK INC p 405
345 CURTIS RD, MIRAMICHI, NB, E1V 3R7
SIC 2621
UMSU   p 392
See UNIVERSITY OF MANITOBA STUDENTS UNION
UNALLOY-IWRC, DIV OF   p 522
See HERCULES SLR INC
UNATA INC   p 984
504 WELLINGTON ST W SUITE 200, TORONTO, ON, M5V 1E3
(416) 305-9977   SIC 5411
UNB   p 402
See UNIVERSITY OF NEW BRUNSWICK
UNCLE BEN'S   p 157
See GO RV & MARINE RED DEER LTD
UNCLE RAY'S RESTAURANT CO. LTD p 195
1361 16TH AVE, CAMPBELL RIVER, BC, V9W 2C9
(250) 287-2631   SIC 5812
UNDERCOVER WEAR FASHIONS & LINGERIE   p 227
4888 236 ST, LANGLEY, BC, V2Z 2S5
SIC 5632
UNDERGROUND CLOTHING   p 25
See STILES' CLOTHIERS INC
UNDERHILL FOOD SERVICES LTD p 140
6504 SPARROW DR, LEDUC, AB, T9E 6T9

(780) 986-5323   SIC 5812
UNDERWRITERS INSURANCE   p 218
See UNDERWRITERS INSURANCE BROKERS (B.C.) LTD
UNDERWRITERS INSURANCE BROKERS (B.C.) LTD   p 218
310 NICOLA ST UNIT 103, KAMLOOPS, BC, V2C 2P5
(250) 374-2139   SIC 6411
UNDERWRITING COMPLIANCE SERVICES p 676
25 VALLEYWOOD DR SUITE 7, MARKHAM, ON, L3R 5L9
(905) 754-6324   SIC 6411
UNFI CANADA GROCERY CENTRAL p 560
See UNFI CANADA, INC
UNFI CANADA, INC   p 187
4535 STILL CREEK AVE, BURNABY, BC, V5C 5W1
(604) 253-6549   SIC 5149
UNFI CANADA, INC   p 560
8755 KEELE ST, CONCORD, ON, L4K 2N1
(905) 738-4204   SIC 5149
UNGAVA HOSPITAL   p 1118
See CENTRE DE SANTE TULATTAVIK DE L'UNGAVA
UNGER FARM MARKET INC   p 659
1010 GAINSBOROUGH RD, LONDON, ON, N6H 5L4
(519) 472-8126   SIC 5461
UNGER NURSING HOMES LIMITED p 531
75 PLAINS RD W SUITE 214, BURLINGTON, ON, L7T 1E8
(905) 631-0700   SIC 8051
UNGER NURSING HOMES LIMITED p 885
312 QUEENSTON ST, ST CATHARINES, ON, L2P 2X4
(905) 682-0503   SIC 8051
UNI SELECT PRAIRIES DIV   p 103
See UNI-SELECT EASTERN INC
UNI-FAB   p 643
See 944743 ONTARIO INC
UNI-RAM CORPORATION   p 676
381 BENTLEY ST SUITE 117, MARKHAM, ON, L3R 9T2
(905) 477-5911   SIC 5084
UNI-SELECT   p 1359
See PIECES D'AUTOS O. FONTAINE INC
UNI-SELECT EASTERN INC   p 103
11754 170 ST NW, EDMONTON, AB, T5S 1J7
(780) 452-2440   SIC 5013
UNI-SELECT EASTERN INC   p 1068
170 BOUL INDUSTRIEL, BOUCHERVILLE, QC, J4B 2X3
(450) 641-2440   SIC 5013
UNI-SELECT INC   p 507
145 WALKER DR SUITE 1, BRAMPTON, ON, L6T 5P5
(905) 789-0115   SIC 5013
UNI-SELECT INC   p 1068
170 BOUL INDUSTRIEL, BOUCHERVILLE, QC, J4B 2X3
(450) 641-2440   SIC 5013
UNI-SELECT PACIFIC INC   p 202
91 GLACIER ST, COQUITLAM, BC, V3K 5Z1
(604) 472-4900   SIC 5013
UNI-SELECT QUEBEC INC   p 1068
170 BOUL INDUSTRIEL, BOUCHERVILLE, QC, J4B 2X3
(450) 641-2440   SIC 5531
UNIBEL COMPANY LTD   p 576
44 ATOMIC AVE, ETOBICOKE, ON, M8Z 5L1
(416) 533-3591   SIC 5141
UNIBETON   p 1123
See CIMENT QUEBEC INC
UNIBETON   p 1294
See CIMENT QUEBEC INC
UNIBOARD CANADA INC   p 1155
845 RUE JEAN-BAPTISTE-REID, MONT-LAURIER, QC, J9L 3W3
(819) 623-7133   SIC 2493

UNIBOARD CANADA INC   p 1232
5555 RUE ERNEST-CORMIER, MONTREAL, QC, H7C 2S9
(450) 661-7122   SIC 2426
UNIBOARD CANADA INC   p 1232
5555 RUE ERNEST-CORMIER, MONTREAL, QC, H7C 2S9
(450) 664-6000   SIC 2493
UNIBOARD CANADA INC   p 1366
152 RTE POULIOT, SAYABEC, QC, G0J 3K0
(418) 536-5465   SIC 2493
UNIBOARD CANADA INC   p 1391
2700 BOUL JEAN-JACQUES-COSSETTE, VAL-D'OR, QC, J9P 6Y5
(819) 825-6550   SIC 2493
UNIBOARD SURFACES   p 1232
See UNIBOARD CANADA INC
UNICA INSURANCE INC   p 745
7150 DERRYCREST DR SUITE 1, MISSISSAUGA, ON, L5W 0E5
(905) 677-9777   SIC 6331
UNICEF CANADA   p 924
See CANADIAN UNICEF COMMITTEE
UNICELL LIMITED   p 918
50 INDUSTRIAL ST, TORONTO, ON, M4G 1Y9
(416) 421-6845   SIC 3713
UNICER FOODS INC   p 994
370 ALLIANCE AVE, TORONTO, ON, M6N 2H8
(416) 766-9535   SIC 5141
UNICITY NETWORK CANADA, LTD p 278
7495 132 ST SUITE 1007, SURREY, BC, V3W 1J8
SIC 5122
UNICLEAN BUILDING MAINTENANCE p 748
See 1048536 ONTARIO LTD
UNICO INC   p 560
8000 KEELE ST, CONCORD, ON, L4K 2A4
(905) 669-9633   SIC 5141
UNICOM GRAPHICS LIMITED   p 32
4501 MANITOBA RD SE, CALGARY, AB, T2G 4B9
(403) 287-2020   SIC 2752
UNICON CONCRETE SPECIALTIES LTD p 97
11740 156 ST NW, EDMONTON, AB, T5M 3T5
(780) 455-3737   SIC 5211
UNICOOP, COOPERATIVE AGRICOLE p 1360
500 RTE CAMERON BUREAU 100, SAINTE-MARIE, QC, G6E 0L9
(418) 386-2667   SIC 5191
UNICORN SECURITY   p 237
624 SIXTH ST UNIT 201, NEW WESTMINSTER, BC, V3L 3C4
(604) 593-5454   SIC 6289
UNIDINDON   p 1314
See COOP FEDEREE, LA
UNIDINDON   p 1315
See OLYMEL S.E.C.
UNIFIED ALLOYS   p 117
See UNIFIED ALLOYS (EDMONTON) LTD
UNIFIED ALLOYS (BRITISH COLUMBIA) LTD   p 230
26835 GLOUCESTER WAY, LANGLEY, BC, V4W 3Y3
(604) 607-6750   SIC 5051
UNIFIED ALLOYS (EDMONTON) LTD p 117
8835 50 AVE NW, EDMONTON, AB, T6E 5H4
(780) 468-5656   SIC 5051
UNIFIED AUTO PARTS INC   p 1414
365 36TH ST W, PRINCE ALBERT, SK, S6V 7L4
(306) 764-4220   SIC 5013
UNIFIED HOLDINGS LTD   p 1414
99 RIVER ST E, PRINCE ALBERT, SK, S6V 0A1
(306) 922-2770   SIC 5171
UNIFIED SYSTEMS GROUP INC   p 38

1235 64 AVE SE UNIT 4A, CALGARY, AB, T2H 2J7
(403) 240-2280   SIC 1731
UNIFIED VALVE GROUP LTD   p 10
3815 32 ST NE, CALGARY, AB, T1Y 7C1
(403) 215-7800   SIC 7699
UNIFILLER SYSTEMS INC   p 210
7621 MACDONALD RD, DELTA, BC, V4G 1N3
(604) 940-2233   SIC 5461
UNIFIN INTERNATIONAL, DIV OF p 893
See WABTEC CANADA INC
UNIFIRST CANADA LTD   p 19
5728 35 ST SE, CALGARY, AB, T2C 2G3
(403) 279-2800   SIC 7213
UNIFIRST CANADA LTD   p 117
3691 98 ST NW, EDMONTON, AB, T6E 5N2
(780) 423-0384   SIC 7213
UNIFIRST CANADA LTD   p 225
9189 196A ST, LANGLEY, BC, V1M 3B5
(604) 888-8119   SIC 7213
UNIFIRST CANADA LTD   p 701
5250 ORBITOR DR, MISSISSAUGA, ON, L4W 5G7
(905) 624-8525   SIC 7213
UNIFIRST CANADA LTD   p 718
2290 DUNWIN DR, MISSISSAUGA, ON, L5L 1C7
(905) 828-9621   SIC 7213
UNIFIRST CANADA LTD   p 1132
8951 RUE SALLEY, LASALLE, QC, H8R 2C8
(514) 365-8301   SIC 7218
UNIFOR   p 215
1045 GIBSONS WAY, GIBSONS, BC, V0N 1V4
(604) 886-2722   SIC 8631
UNIFOR   p 477
110 ST. ARNAUD ST, AMHERSTBURG, ON, N9V 2N8
(519) 730-0099   SIC 8631
UNIFOR   p 492
160 CATHARINE ST, BELLEVILLE, ON, K8P 1M8
(613) 962-8122   SIC 8631
UNIFOR   p 507
15 WESTCREEK BLVD SUITE 1, BRAMPTON, ON, L6T 5T4
(905) 874-4026   SIC 8631
UNIFOR   p 565
34 QUEEN ST, DRYDEN, ON, P8N 1A3
(807) 223-8146   SIC 8631
UNIFOR   p 632
728 ARLINGTON PARK PL, KINGSTON, ON, K7M 8H9
(613) 542-7368   SIC 8631
UNIFOR   p 637
1111 HOMER WATSON BLVD, KITCHENER, ON, N2C 2P7
SIC 8631
UNIFOR   p 766
205 PLACER CRT, NORTH YORK, ON, M2H 3H9
(416) 497-4110   SIC 8631
UNIFOR   p 847
115 AV SHIPLEY, PORT ELGIN, ON, N0H 2C5
(519) 389-3200   SIC 8631
UNIFOR   p 887
20 WALNUT ST, ST CATHARINES, ON, L2T 1H5
(905) 227-7717   SIC 8631
UNIFOR FAMILY EDUCATION CENTER p 847
See UNIFOR
UNIFOR LEGAL SERVICES PLAN p 927
1 ST CLAIR AVE W SUITE 600, TORONTO, ON, M4V 3C3
(416) 960-2410   SIC 8111
UNIFORME PREMIER CHOIX   p 1132
See UNIFIRST CANADA LTD
UNIFORMES F.O.B. (1991) LTEE p 1122
645 14E AV, LA GUADELOUPE, QC, G0M 1G0

SIC 2311

UNIFORMS & LINGE D'HOTELERIE ALSCO *p 1130*
See ALSCO CANADA CORPORATION

UNIFUND ADJUSTING INC *p 431*
68 PORTUGAL COVE RD, ST. JOHN'S, NL, A1B 2L9
(709) 737-1680 *SIC 6411*

UNIFUND ASSURANCE COMPANY *p 432*
10 FACTORY LANE, ST. JOHN'S, NL, A1C 6H5
(709) 737-1500 *SIC 6331*

UNIFUND ASSURANCE COMPANY *p 432*
See JOHNSON INC

UNIGAZ *p 1161*
See 9180-2710 QUEBEC INC

UNIGLOBE BEACON TRAVEL LTD *p 42*
1400 KENSINGTON RD NW SUITE 200, CALGARY, AB, T2N 3P9
(877) 596-6860 *SIC 4724*

UNIGLOBE GEO TRAVEL LTD *p 91*
10237 109 ST NW, EDMONTON, AB, T5J 1N2
(780) 424-8310 *SIC 4899*

UNIGLOBE ONE TRAVEL INC *p 318*
1444 ALBERNI ST SUITE 300, VANCOUVER, BC, V6G 2Z4
(604) 688-3551 *SIC 4724*

UNIGLOBE PREMIERE TRAVEL PLANNERS INC *p 1001*
24 SELKIRK ST SUITE 100, VANIER, ON, K1L 0A4
(613) 230-7411 *SIC 4724*

UNIGLOBE TOUS TRAVEL GROUP *p 696*
See ISYARI CANADA INC

UNIGLOBE TRAVEL (WESTERN CANADA) INC *p 320*
2695 GRANVILLE ST SUITE 600, VANCOUVER, BC, V6H 3H4
(604) 602-3470 *SIC 6794*

UNIGLOBE TRAVEL INTERNATIONAL LIMITED *p 317*
1199 PENDER ST W SUITE 900, VANCOUVER, BC, V6E 2R1
(604) 718-2600 *SIC 4724*

UNIGLOBE VISION TRAVEL GROUP INC *p 319*
1444 ALBERNI ST SUITE 300, VANCOUVER, BC, V6G 2Z4
(604) 688-3551 *SIC 4724*

UNIGLOBE VOYAGE LEXUS *p 1197*
See LEXUS TRAVEL INC

UNIGLOBE WESTERN CANADA REGION *p 320*
See UNIGLOBE TRAVEL (WESTERN CANADA) INC

UNIGOLD INC *p 941*
44 VICTORIA ST SUITE 504, TORONTO, ON, M5C 1Y2
(416) 866-8157 *SIC 1081*

UNIGRAPHICS LIMITED *p 382*
488 BURNELL ST, WINNIPEG, MB, R3G 2B4
(204) 784-1030 *SIC 2732*

UNIKTOUR INC *p 1192*
555 BOUL RENE-LEVESQUE O BUREAU 3, MONTREAL, QC, H2Z 1B1
(514) 722-0909 *SIC 4724*

UNILEVER BEST FOODS *p 931*
See UNILEVER CANADA INC

UNILEVER BESTFOODS *p 1157*
See UNILEVER CANADA INC

UNILEVER CANADA INC *p 589*
195 BELFIELD RD, ETOBICOKE, ON, M9W 1G8
(416) 246-1650 *SIC 2099*

UNILEVER CANADA INC *p 881*
175 UNION ST, SIMCOE, ON, N3Y 2B1
(519) 426-1673 *SIC 2024*

UNILEVER CANADA INC *p 931*
160 BLOOR ST E SUITE 1400, TORONTO, ON, M4W 3R2

UNILEVER CANADA INC *p 1157*
5430 CH DE LA COTE-DE-LIESSE, MONT-ROYAL, QC, H4P 1A5
SIC 2086

UNILOCK LTD *p 580*
401 THE WEST MALL SUITE 610, ETOBICOKE, ON, M9C 5J5
(416) 646-5180 *SIC 3272*

UNIMOTION GEAR *p 481*
See MAGNA POWERTRAIN INC

UNIMOTOR, DIVISION OF *p 889*
See SMP MOTOR PRODUCTS LTD

UNION ADVERTISING CANADA LP *p 984*
479 WELLINGTON ST W, TORONTO, ON, M5V 1E7
(416) 598-4944 *SIC 7311*

UNION CLUB OF BRITISH COLUMBIA *p 337*
805 GORDON ST, VICTORIA, BC, V8W 1Z6
(250) 384-1151 *SIC 8621*

UNION CREATIVE *p 984*
See UNION ADVERTISING CANADA LP

UNION DES ARTISTES *p 1214*
1441 BOUL RENE-LEVESQUE O BUREAU 400, MONTREAL, QC, H3G 1T7
(514) 288-6682 *SIC 8621*

UNION DES EMPLOYES ET EMPLOYEES DE SERVICE, SECTION LOCALE 800 *p 1171*
920 RUE DE PORT-ROYAL E, MONTREAL, QC, H2C 2B3
(514) 385-1717 *SIC 8631*

UNION DES PRODUCTEURS AGRICOLE, L' *p 1143*
555 BOUL ROLAND-THERRIEN BUREAU 100, LONGUEUIL, QC, J4H 3Y9
(450) 679-0530 *SIC 8631*

UNION DRAWN STEEL II LIMITED *p 610*
1350 BURLINGTON ST E, HAMILTON, ON, L8H 3L3
(905) 547-4480 *SIC 3316*

UNION DRAWN STEEL II LIMITED PARTNERSHIP *p 610*
1350 BURLINGTON ST E, HAMILTON, ON, L8H 3L3
(905) 547-4480 *SIC 3316*

UNION ELECTRIC LIGHTING CO. LTD *p 993*
1491 CASTLEFIELD AVE, TORONTO, ON, M6M 1Y3
(416) 652-2200 *SIC 5719*

UNION GAS *p 482*
9924 SPRINGER HILL RD, AYLMER, ON, N5H 2R3
(519) 765-1487 *SIC 4923*

UNION GAS *p 565*
PO BOX 280 STN MAIN, DRYDEN, ON, P8N 2Y8
SIC 4923

UNION GAS *p 662*
1151 GREEN VALLEY RD, LONDON, ON, N6N 1E4
SIC 4923

UNION GAS LIMITED *p 660*
109 COMMISSIONERS RD W, LONDON, ON, N6J 1X7
(519) 667-4100 *SIC 4923*

UNION LIGHTING & FURNISHINGS *p 993*
See UNION ELECTRIC LIGHTING CO. LTD

UNION LUMINAIRE & DECOR *p 1227*
See CIE D'ECLAIRAGE UNION LTEE, LA

UNION MISSION FOR MEN, THE *p 822*
35 WALLER ST, OTTAWA, ON, K1N 7G4
(613) 234-1144 *SIC 8399*

UNION OF BC PERFORMERS *p 292*
380 2ND AVE W UNIT 300, VANCOUVER, BC, V5Y 1C8
(604) 689-0727 *SIC 8631*

UNION OF NATIONAL DEFENCE EMPLOYEES *p 630*
17 PRINCESS MARY, KINGSTON, ON, K7K 7B4
SIC 8631

UNION OF ONTARIO INDIANS *p 564*
1024 MISSISSAUGA RD, CURVE LAKE, ON, K0L 1R0
(705) 657-9383 *SIC 8399*

UNION POULTRY CANADA INC *p 676*
70 DENISON ST SUITE 2, MARKHAM, ON, L3R 1B6
(905) 305-1913 *SIC 5144*

UNION QUEBECOISE, COMPAGNIE D'ASSURANCES GENERALES *p 1388*
See OPTIMUM ASSURANCE AGRICOLE INC

UNION TRACTOR LTD *p 150*
3750 13 ST, NISKU, AB, T9E 1C6
(780) 979-8500 *SIC 7699*

UNION, THE *p 117*
6240 99 ST NW, EDMONTON, AB, T6E 6C7
(780) 702-2582 *SIC 6512*

UNION-VIE, COMPAGNIE MUTUELLE D'ASSURANCE, L' *p 1100*
142 RUE HERIOT, DRUMMONDVILLE, QC, J2C 1J8
(819) 478-1315 *SIC 6311*

UNIONVILLE HOME SOCIETY *p 676*
4300 HIGHWAY 7 E SUITE 1, MARKHAM, ON, L3R 1L8
(905) 477-2822 *SIC 8361*

UNIONVILLE HOME SOCIETY FOUNDATION *p 676*
4300 HIGHWAY 7 E SUITE 1, MARKHAM, ON, L3R 1L8
(905) 477-2822 *SIC 7389*

UNIONVILLE MOTORS (1973) LIMITED *p 1000*
4630 HIGHWAY 7 E, UNIONVILLE, ON, L3R 1M5
SIC 5511

UNIPAC PACKAGING PRODUCTS LTD *p 103*
11133 184 ST NW, EDMONTON, AB, T5S 2L6
(780) 466-3121 *SIC 5411*

UNIPECHE M.D.M. LTEE *p 1245*
66 AV DU QUAI, PASPEBIAC, QC, G0C 2K0
(418) 752-6700 *SIC 2092*

UNIPETRO DIXIE INC *p 733*
6035 MCLAUGHLIN RD, MISSISSAUGA, ON, L5R 1B9
(905) 712-8800 *SIC 5541*

UNIPHARM WHOLESALE DRUGS LTD *p 257*
2051 VAN DYKE PL SUITE 100, RICHMOND, BC, V6V 1X6
(604) 270-9745 *SIC 5122*

UNIPRIX *p 1097*
See GESTION G.G.V.M. INC

UNIPRIX *p 1154*
See AROMATHEQUE INC

UNIPRIX *p 1185*
See BISHARA PHARMA INC

UNIPRIX *p 1297*
See DESSUREAULT, JEAN-CLAUDE PHARMACIEN

UNIPRIX *p 1300*
See 2846-6589 QUEBEC INC

UNIPRIX *p 1345*
See GESTION PHARMASSO INC

UNIPRIX *p 1346*
See 2739-0988 QUEBEC INC

UNIPRIX *p 1384*
See ENTREPRISES DONTIGNY ET TREMBLAY INC, LES

UNIPRIX DANIEL GUAY & JULIE BEAUPRE (AFFILIATED PHARMACY) *p 1075*
1682 RUE PRINCIPALE, CHAMBORD, QC, G0W 1G0
(418) 342-6263 *SIC 5122*

UNIPRIX GUAY ET BEAUPRE *p 1287*
See 9206-5580 QUEBEC INC

UNIPRIX INC *p 1346*
5000 BOUL METROPOLITAIN E BUREAU 100, SAINT-LEONARD, QC, H1S 3G7
(514) 725-1212 *SIC 5912*

UNIPRIX ISABELLE DUPONT *p 1108*
See 9267-8010 QUEBEC INC

UNIPRIX LAURENT TETREAULT & ASSOCIATE (AFFILIATED PHARMACY) *p 1184*
5647 AV DU PARC, MONTREAL, QC, H2V 4H2
(514) 276-9353 *SIC 2834*

UNIPRIX PHARMACY *p 1116*
2095 RUE SAINTE-FAMILLE, JONQUIERE, QC, G7X 4W8
(418) 547-3689 *SIC 5912*

UNIPRIX PIERRE BERGERON ET MARISA SGRO (PHARMACIE AFFILIEE) *p 1118*
2963 BOUL SAINT-CHARLES, KIRKLAND, QC, H9H 3B5
(514) 694-3074 *SIC 5912*

UNIPRIX SANTE *p 1346*
See UNIPRIX INC

UNIPRIX ST PHANE SANSREGRET *p 1241*
See 3474534 CANADA INC

UNIQUE ASSURANCES GENERALES INC, L' *p 1260*
625 RUE SAINT AMABLE, QUEBEC, QC, G1K 0E1
(418) 683-2711 *SIC 6331*

UNIQUE BROADBAND SYSTEMS LTD *p 560*
400 SPINNAKER WAY SUITE 1, CONCORD, ON, L4K 5Y9
(905) 669-8533 *SIC 4813*

UNIQUE CHRYSLER *p 528*
See UNIQUE MOTORS LTD

UNIQUE CHRYSLER DODGE JEEP LTD *p 528*
915 WALKER'S LINE, BURLINGTON, ON, L7N 3V8
(905) 631-8100 *SIC 5511*

UNIQUE MOTORS LTD *p 528*
915 WALKER'S LINE, BURLINGTON, ON, L7N 3V8
(905) 631-8100 *SIC 5511*

UNIQUE RESTORATION LTD *p 701*
1220 MATHESON BLVD E, MISSISSAUGA, ON, L4W 1R2
(905) 629-9100 *SIC 1542*

UNIQUE SCAFFOLD INC *p 19*
4750 104 AVE SE, CALGARY, AB, T2C 2H3
(403) 203-3422 *SIC 1799*

UNIQUE STORE FIXTURES LTD *p 560*
554 MILLWAY AVE, CONCORD, ON, L4K 3V5
(905) 738-6588 *SIC 2541*

UNIQUE TOOL & GAUGE INC *p 1024*
1505 MORO DR, WINDSOR, ON, N9A 6J3
(519) 737-1159 *SIC 3544*

UNIRES, DIV DE *p 1391*
See UNIBOARD CANADA INC

UNIROC INC *p 1154*
5605 RTE ARTHUR-SAUVE, MIRABEL, QC, J7N 2W4
(450) 258-4242 *SIC 1611*

UNIROPE LIMITED *p 703*
3070 UNIVERSAL DR, MISSISSAUGA, ON, L4X 2C8
(905) 624-5131 *SIC 5251*

UNISELECT *p 404*
See BASQUE, GILLES SALES LTD

UNISON INSURANCE & FINANCIAL SERVICES INC. *p 703*
2077 DUNDAS ST E SUITE 103, MISSISSAUGA, ON, L4X 1M2
(905) 624-5300 *SIC 6311*

UNISYNC CORP *p 310*
885 WEST GEORGIA ST SUITE 1328, VANCOUVER, BC, V6C 3E8
(778) 370-1725 *SIC 2339*

UNISYNC GROUP LIMITED *p 743*
6375 DIXIE RD UNIT 6, MISSISSAUGA, ON, L5T 2E7
(905) 361-8989 *SIC 2337*

UNISYS CANADA INC *p* 454
1809 BARRINGTON ST SUITE 600, HALIFAX, NS, B3J 3K8
(902) 704-5340 *SIC* 7371
UNIT ELECTRICAL ENGINEERING LTD *p*
242
1406 MAPLE ST, OKANAGAN FALLS, BC,
V0H 1R2
(250) 497-5254 *SIC* 3613
UNIT PARK MANAGEMENT INC *p* 943
1 YONGE ST SUITE 1510, TORONTO, ON,
M5E 1E5
(416) 366-7275 *SIC* 7521
UNITE DE SANTE INTERNATIONALE *p*
1186
850 RUE SAINT-DENIS BUREAU S03,
MONTREAL, QC, H2X 0A9
(514) 890-8156 *SIC* 8742
UNITEC INC *p* 859
1271 LOUGAR AVE, SARNIA, ON, N7S 5N5
(519) 332-0430 *SIC* 6719
UNITEC WELDING ALLOYS *p* 560
61 VILLARBOIT CRES, CONCORD, ON,
L4K 4R2
(905) 669-4249 *SIC* 5084
**UNITECH ELECTRICAL CONTRACTING
INC** *p* 38
700 58 AVE SE SUITE 11, CALGARY, AB,
T2H 2E2
(403) 255-2277 *SIC* 1731
UNITECH LUBRICANTS AMERICA *p* 1011
155 FROBISHER DR UNIT 218, WATERLOO, ON, N2V 2E1
(519) 208-2900 *SIC* 5172
**UNITED ACOUSTIQUE & PARTITIONS CO
INC** *p* 1341
645 RUE MCCAFFREY, SAINT-LAURENT,
QC, H4T 1N3
(514) 737-8337 *SIC* 1742
UNITED AGRI PRODUCTS CANADA INC *p*
565
789 DONNYBROOK DR SUITE 2, DORCHESTER, ON, N0L 1G5
(519) 268-5900 *SIC* 5191
UNITED AIRLINES *p* 729
PO BOX 247 STN TORONTO AMF, MISSISSAUGA, ON, L5P 1B1
SIC 4729
UNITED ASSOCIATION LOCAL 46 *p* 869
*See PLUMBERS AND STEAMFITTERS
UNION LOCAL 46*
**UNITED ASSOCIATION OF JOURNEYMEN
AND APPRENTICES OF THE PLUMBING
AND PIPEFITTING INDUSTRY** *p* 859
1151 CONFEDERATION ST, SARNIA, ON,
N7S 3Y5
(519) 337-6261 *SIC* 8611
UNITED AUTO SALES & SERVICE LTD *p*
402
14 AVONLEA CRT, FREDERICTON, NB,
E3C 1N8
(506) 454-2886 *SIC* 5511
UNITED BROTHERHOOD OF CARPENTERS JOINERS AMERICA LOCAL 83 *p*
1034
222 ROWNTREE DAIRY RD SUITE 598,
WOODBRIDGE, ON, L4L 9T2
(416) 749-0675 *SIC* 8631
UNITED BROTHERHOOD OF CARPENTERS JOINERS AMERICA LOCAL 83 *p*
1041
22 ENMAN CRES, CHARLOTTETOWN, PE,
C1E 1E6
(902) 566-1414 *SIC* 8631
UNITED BROTHERHOOD OF CARPENTERS LOCAL 1338 *p*
1041
See UNITED BROTHERHOOD OF CARPENTERS JOINERS AMERICA LOCAL 83
UNITED BUNKERS INVESTORS CORPORATION *p*
958
180 UNIVERSITY AVE SUITE 04,
TORONTO, ON, M5H 0A2

(416) 567-0089 *SIC* 6111
UNITED CHURCH HOME FOR SENIOR CITIZENS INC, THE *p*
412
165 MAIN ST, SACKVILLE, NB, E4L 4S2
(506) 364-4900 *SIC* 8051
UNITED CHURCH OF CANADA, THE *p* 572
3250 BLOOR ST W SUITE 300, ETOBICOKE, ON, M8X 2Y4
(416) 231-5931 *SIC* 8661
UNITED CHURCH OF CANADA, THE *p*
1083
5790 AV PARKHAVEN, COTE SAINT-LUC,
QC, H4W 1X9
SIC 8051
UNITED CONCRETE & GRAVEL LTD *p* 252
1077 CARSON PIT RD, QUESNEL, BC, V2J
7H2
(250) 992-7281 *SIC* 5032
**UNITED COUNTIES OF LEEDS AND
GRENVILLE** *p* 479
746 COUNTY RD 42, ATHENS, ON, K0E
1B0
(613) 924-2696 *SIC* 8361
**UNITED COUNTIES OF LEEDS AND
GRENVILLE** *p* 520
25 CENTRAL AVE W SUITE 100,
BROCKVILLE, ON, K6V 4N6
(613) 342-3840 *SIC* 4119
**UNITED CYCLE & MOTOR COMPANY
(1975) LIMITED** *p* 117
7620 GATEWAY BLVD NW, EDMONTON,
AB, T6E 4Z8
(780) 433-1181 *SIC* 5941
UNITED CYCLE SOURCE FOR SPORTS *p*
117
*See UNITED CYCLE & MOTOR COMPANY
(1975) LIMITED*
UNITED ENTERPRISES LTD *p* 1413
992 101ST ST, NORTH BATTLEFORD, SK,
S9A 0Z3
(306) 445-9425 *SIC* 7011
UNITED EXPRESS *p* 1344
*See EMPAQUETEURS UNIS DE FRUITS
DE MER LTEE, LES*
UNITED FARMERS OF ALBERTA COOPERATIVE LIMITED *p*
74
4838 RICHARD RD SW SUITE 700, CALGARY, AB, T3E 6L1
(403) 570-4500 *SIC* 5172
UNITED FLORAL DISTRIBUTORS *p* 590
See 968502 ONTARIO INC
UNITED FLORAL HOLDINGS INC *p* 194
4085 MARINE WAY, BURNABY, BC, V5J
5E2
(604) 438-3535 *SIC* 7389
UNITED FLORAL INC *p* 194
4085 MARINE WAY, BURNABY, BC, V5J
5E2
(604) 438-3535 *SIC* 5193
**UNITED FOOD & COMMERCIAL WORKER
CANADA** *p* 728
2200 ARGENTIA RD SUITE 175, MISSISSAUGA, ON, L5N 2K7
(905) 821-8329 *SIC* 8631
UNITED FOOD & COMMERCIAL WORKERS LOCAL NO. 832 *p*
382
1412 PORTAGE AVE, WINNIPEG, MB, R3G
0V5
(204) 786-5055 *SIC* 8631
UNITED FOOD & COMMERCIAL WORKERS UNION LOCAL 1518 *p*
191
4021 KINGSWAY, BURNABY, BC, V5H 1Y9
(604) 434-3101 *SIC* 8631
UNITED FOOD AND COMMERCIAL WORKERS CANADA UNION *p*
589
61 INTERNATIONAL BLVD UNIT 300, ETOBICOKE, ON, M9W 6K4
(416) 675-1104 *SIC* 8631
UNITED HEALTH SERVICES CORPORA-

TION *p*
382
599 EMPRESS ST, WINNIPEG, MB, R3G
3P3
(204) 775-0151 *SIC* 6324
**UNITED JEWISH APPEAL OF GREATER
TORONTO** *p* 775
4600 BATHURST ST UNIT 5, NORTH
YORK, ON, M2R 3V3
(416) 631-5716 *SIC* 6732
UNITED LIBRARY SERVICES INC *p* 38
7140 FAIRMOUNT DR SE, CALGARY, AB,
T2H 0X4
(403) 252-4426 *SIC* 5192
UNITED LUMBER AND BUILDING SUPPLIES COMPANY LIMITED *p*
485
520 BAYFIELD ST, BARRIE, ON, L4M 5A2
(705) 726-8132 *SIC* 5211
UNITED MALWOOD MERCHANTS INC *p*
626
8181 CAMPEAU DR SUITE 457, KANATA,
ON, K2T 1B7
(613) 599-5105 *SIC* 5531
UNITED MARITIME SUPPLIERS INC *p* 285
1854 FRANKLIN ST, VANCOUVER, BC,
V5L 1P8
(604) 255-6525 *SIC* 5088
**UNITED MENNONITE HOME FOR THE
AGED** *p* 1003
4024 23RD ST, VINELAND, ON, L0R 2C0
(905) 562-7385 *SIC* 8361
UNITED NATURALS INC *p* 289
2416 MAIN ST UNIT 132, VANCOUVER,
BC, V5T 3E2
(604) 999-9999 *SIC* 2833
UNITED NURSES OF ALBERTA *p* 92
11150 JASPER AVE NW SUITE 700, EDMONTON, AB, T5K 0C7
(780) 425-1025 *SIC* 8621
UNITED OPTICAL *p* 190
See METROTOWN OPTICAL LTD
UNITED PARCEL SERVICE CANADA LTD *p*
26
3650 12 ST NE SUITE D, CALGARY, AB,
T2E 6N1
SIC 4731
UNITED PARCEL SERVICE CANADA LTD *p*
97
11204 151 ST NW, EDMONTON, AB, T5M
4A9
(800) 742-5877 *SIC* 7389
UNITED PARCEL SERVICE CANADA LTD *p*
207
790 BELGRAVE WAY, DELTA, BC, V3M 5R9
(800) 742-5877 *SIC* 7389
UNITED PARCEL SERVICE CANADA LTD *p*
401
900 HANWELL RD, FREDERICTON, NB,
E3B 6A2
(506) 447-3601 *SIC* 4513
UNITED PARCEL SERVICE CANADA LTD *p*
407
1 FACTORY LANE SUITE 200, MONCTON,
NB, E1C 9M3
(506) 877-4929 *SIC* 7389
UNITED PARCEL SERVICE CANADA LTD *p*
407
77 FOUNDRY ST, MONCTON, NB, E1C
5H7
(506) 877-6657 *SIC* 4212
UNITED PARCEL SERVICE CANADA LTD *p*
560
2900 STEELES AVE W, CONCORD, ON,
L4K 3S2
(800) 742-5877 *SIC* 4212
UNITED PARCEL SERVICE CANADA LTD *p*
608
456 GRAYS RD, HAMILTON, ON, L8E 2Z4
(905) 578-2699 *SIC* 7389
UNITED PARCEL SERVICE CANADA LTD *p*
638
65 TRILLIUM PARK PL, KITCHENER, ON,
N2E 1X1

(800) 742-5877 *SIC* 7389
UNITED PARCEL SERVICE CANADA LTD *p*
662
60 MIDPARK RD, LONDON, ON, N6N 1B3
(519) 686-8200 *SIC* 4513
UNITED PARCEL SERVICE CANADA LTD *p*
690
3195 AIRWAY DR, MISSISSAUGA, ON, L4V
1C2
(800) 742-5877 *SIC* 7389
UNITED PARCEL SERVICE CANADA LTD *p*
736
1930 DERRY RD E, MISSISSAUGA, ON,
L5S 1E2
(800) 742-5877 *SIC* 4212
UNITED PARCEL SERVICE CANADA LTD *p*
819
2281 STEVENAGE DR, OTTAWA, ON, K1G
3W1
(613) 670-6061 *SIC* 4215
UNITED PARCEL SERVICE CANADA LTD *p*
984
12 MERCER ST, TORONTO, ON, M5V 1H3
SIC 4513
UNITED PARCEL SERVICE CANADA LTD *p*
1017
5325 RHODES DR, WINDSOR, ON, N8N
2M1
(519) 251-7050 *SIC* 7389
UNITED PARCEL SERVICE CANADA LTD *p*
1060
71 RUE OMER-DESERRES, BLAINVILLE,
QC, J7C 5N3
(450) 979-9390 *SIC* 4212
UNITED PARCEL SERVICE CANADA LTD *p*
1071
3850 BOUL MATTE, BROSSARD, QC, J4Y
2Z2
(800) 742-5877 *SIC* 7389
UNITED PARCEL SERVICE CANADA LTD *p*
1129
1221 32E AV BUREAU 209, LACHINE, QC,
H8T 3H2
(514) 633-0010 *SIC* 7389
UNITED PARCEL SERVICE CANADA LTD *p*
1277
625 RUE DES CANETONS, QUEBEC, QC,
G2E 5X6
(418) 872-2686 *SIC* 7389
UNITED POULTRY CO LTD *p* 296
534 CORDOVA ST E, VANCOUVER, BC,
V6A 1L7
(604) 255-9308 *SIC* 5144
UNITED PROTECTION SERVICES *p* 1432
2366 AVENUE C N, SASKATOON, SK, S7L
5X5
(306) 382-0002 *SIC* 7381
UNITED PROTECTIONS *p* 116
See STEELE SECURITY & INVESTIGATION SERVICE DIVISION OF UNITED PROTECTIONS
**UNITED REFRIGERATION OF CANADA
LTD** *p* 676
130 RIVIERA DR, MARKHAM, ON, L3R
5M1
(905) 479-1212 *SIC* 5078
UNITED RENTALS OF CANADA, INC *p* 515
150 ROY BLVD, BRANTFORD, ON, N3R
7K2
(519) 756-0700 *SIC* 8741
UNITED SAFETY LTD *p* 3
104 EAST LAKE RD NE, AIRDRIE, AB, T4A
2J8
(403) 912-3690 *SIC* 1389
UNITED STEELWORKERS OF AMERICA *p*
438
10 TANTRAMAR PL, AMHERST, NS, B4H
2A1
(902) 667-0727 *SIC* 8631
UNITED STEELWORKERS OF AMERICA *p*
468
1 DIAMOND ST, TRENTON, NS, B0K 1X0
SIC 8631
UNITED STEELWORKERS OF AMERICA *p*

547
1000 26 HWY, COLLINGWOOD, ON, L9Y 4V8
SIC 8631

UNITED STEELWORKERS OF AMERICA p 923
234 EGLINTON AVE E SUITE 800, TORONTO, ON, M4P 1K7
(416) 487-1571   SIC 8631

UNITED THERMO GROUP LTD   p 1034
261 TROWERS RD, WOODBRIDGE, ON, L4L 5Z8
(905) 851-0500   SIC 1711

UNITED VAN LINES (CANADA) LTD p 743
7229 PACIFIC CIR, MISSISSAUGA, ON, L5T 1S9
(905) 564-6400   SIC 4212

UNITED WAY OF GREATER TORONTO p 943
26 WELLINGTON ST E FL 12, TORONTO, ON, M5E 1S2
(416) 777-2001   SIC 8699

UNITED WAY OF WINNIPEG   p 376
580 MAIN ST, WINNIPEG, MB, R3B 1C7
(204) 477-5360   SIC 8399

UNITED WAY TORONTO AND YORK REGION p 943
See UNITED WAY OF GREATER TORONTO

UNITED WAY/CENTRAIDE OTTAWA p 820
363 COVENTRY RD, OTTAWA, ON, K1K 2C5
(613) 228-6700   SIC 6732

UNITED WE CAN   p 296
See SAVE OUR LIVING ENVIRONMENT SOCIETY (S.O.L.E.)

UNITED WIRE & CABLE (CANADA) INC p 854
1 WEST PEARCE ST UNIT 303, RICHMOND HILL, ON, L4B 3K3
(905) 771-0099   SIC 5051

UNITES MOBILES DE COIFFURE DE MONTREAL INC, LES p 1224
6226 BOUL MONK, MONTREAL, QC, H4E 3H7
(514) 766-3553   SIC 7231

UNITOW SERVICES (1978) LTD   p 296
1717 VERNON DR, VANCOUVER, BC, V6A 3P8
(604) 659-1225   SIC 7549

UNITREND PLASTICS MANUFACTURING LTD p 210
7351 PROGRESS PL, DELTA, BC, V4G 1A1
(604) 940-8900   SIC 2673

UNITRON CONNECT   p 639
See UNITRON HEARING LTD

UNITRON HEARING DIVISION   p 637
See NATIONAL HEARING SERVICES INC

UNITRON HEARING LTD   p 639
20 BEASLEY DR, KITCHENER, ON, N2G 4X1
(519) 895-0100   SIC 3842

UNITY   p 757
See UNITY CONNECTED SOLUTIONS INC

UNITY & DISTRICT HEALTH CENTRE p 1437
100 1ST AVE W UNIT 1, UNITY, SK, S0K 4L0
(306) 228-2666   SIC 8062

UNITY APARTMENTS, DIV OF   p 988
See PHC PROPERTY MANAGEMENT CORP

UNITY CONNECTED SOLUTIONS INC p 757
450 HARRY WALKER PKY S, NEWMARKET, ON, L3Y 8E3
(905) 952-2475   SIC 5065

UNITY MANAGING UNDERWRITERS HOLDCO LIMITED p 770
5734 YONGE ST SUITE 605, NORTH YORK, ON, M2M 4E7
(416) 222-0676   SIC 6411

UNIVAR CANADA LTD   p 262
9800 VAN HORNE WAY, RICHMOND, BC, V6X 1W5
(604) 273-1441   SIC 5169

UNIVAR CANADA LTD   p 785
777 SUPERTEST RD, NORTH YORK, ON, M3J 2M9
(416) 740-5300   SIC 4225

UNIVAR CANADA LTD   p 795
64 ARROW RD, NORTH YORK, ON, M9M 2L9
(416) 740-5300   SIC 5169

UNIVAR CANADA LTD   p 1095
2200 CH SAINT-FRANCOIS, DORVAL, QC, H9P 1K2
(514) 421-0303   SIC 5169

UNIVAR SOLUTIONS CANADA   p 785
See UNIVAR CANADA LTD

UNIVAR SOLUTIONS CANADA   p 795
See UNIVAR CANADA LTD

UNIVAR SOLUTIONS CANADA   p 1095
See UNIVAR CANADA LTD

UNIVCO INVESTMENTS LTD   p 287
2835 12TH AVE E, VANCOUVER, BC, V5M 4P9
(604) 253-4000   SIC 5074

UNIVERIS CORPORATION   p 934
111 GEORGE ST 3RD FL, TORONTO, ON, M5A 2N4
(416) 979-3700   SIC 7371

UNIVERSAL AVIATION SERVICES CORPORATION p 129
GD LCD MAIN, FORT MCMURRAY, AB, T9H 3E2
(780) 791-9881   SIC 5172

UNIVERSAL CHINA LAMP & GLASS COMPANY LIMITED p 790
121 CARTWRIGHT AVE, NORTH YORK, ON, M6A 1V4
(416) 787-8900   SIC 5063

UNIVERSAL CONCEPTS   p 862
130 WELLINGTON ST E, SAULT STE. MARIE, ON, P6A 2L5
(705) 575-7521   SIC 1542

UNIVERSAL DENTAL & PACIFIC RIM p 186
See PACIFIC FIRST

UNIVERSAL DRUG STORE LTD   p 367
1329 NIAKWA RD E UNIT 9, WINNIPEG, MB, R2J 3T4
(204) 255-9911   SIC 5961

UNIVERSAL FABRICATING   p 633
See 1627198 ONTARIO INC

UNIVERSAL FILMS CANADA   p 768
See UNIVERSAL STUDIOS CANADA INC

UNIVERSAL FOOD & PAPER PRODUCTS LTD p 291
8595 FRASER ST, VANCOUVER, BC, V5X 3Y1
(604) 324-0331   SIC 5087

UNIVERSAL FORD LINCOLN SALES LTD p 10
2800 BARLOW TRAIL NE, CALGARY, AB, T1Y 1A2
(403) 291-2850   SIC 5511

UNIVERSAL GEOMATICS SOLUTIONS CORP. p 106
15111 123 AVE NW, EDMONTON, AB, T5V 1J7
(780) 454-3030   SIC 8713

UNIVERSAL GEOSYSTEMS   p 62
910 7 AVE SW SUITE 1015, CALGARY, AB, T2P 3N8
(403) 262-1336   SIC 1382

UNIVERSAL HEALTH PRODUCTS p 1021
635 TECUMSEH RD W, WINDSOR, ON, N8X 1H4
(519) 258-6717   SIC 5047

UNIVERSAL HELICOPTERS (NFLD) LIMITED p 424
82 WINNIPEG ST, HAPPY VALLEY-GOOSE BAY, NL, A0P 1C0

(709) 896-2444   SIC 4522
UNIVERSAL INDUSTRIAL SUPPLY GROUP INC p 633
505 O'CONNOR DR, KINGSTON, ON, K7P 1J9
(613) 634-6272   SIC 5013

UNIVERSAL INDUSTRIES (FOREMOST) CORP p 144
5014 65 ST, LLOYDMINSTER, AB, T9V 2K2
(780) 875-6161   SIC 3443

UNIVERSAL LAMP MFG   p 790
See UNIVERSAL CHINA LAMP & GLASS COMPANY LIMITED

UNIVERSAL LINENS   p 1340
See MARIMAC INC

UNIVERSAL LOGISTICS INC   p 905
125 COMMERCE VALLEY DR W SUITE 750, THORNHILL, ON, L3T 7W4
(905) 882-4880   SIC 4731

UNIVERSAL MACHINERY SERVICES, DIV OF p 289
See FINNING INTERNATIONAL INC

UNIVERSAL MUSIC CANADA INC p 768
2450 VICTORIA PARK AVE SUITE 1, NORTH YORK, ON, M2J 5H3
(416) 718-4000   SIC 5099

UNIVERSAL PACKAGING   p 332
See UPI GLASS INC

UNIVERSAL POWER CANADA, DIV OF p 504
See KLEEN-FLO TUMBLER INDUSTRIES LIMITED

UNIVERSAL PROPERTIES   p 451
See UNIVERSAL PROPERTY MANAGEMENT LIMITED

UNIVERSAL PROPERTY MANAGEMENT LIMITED p 451
1190 BARRINGTON ST 4TH FLOOR, HALIFAX, NS, B3H 2R4
(902) 425-8877   SIC 6513

UNIVERSAL PROTECTION SERVICE OF CANADA CO p 238
627 COLUMBIA ST SUITE 200A, NEW WESTMINSTER, BC, V3M 1A7
(604) 522-5550   SIC 7381

UNIVERSAL REHABILITATION SERVICE AGENCY p 26
808 MANNING RD NE, CALGARY, AB, T2E 7N8
(403) 272-7722   SIC 8361

UNIVERSAL RELOAD DIV   p 392
See SEARCY TRUCKING LTD

UNIVERSAL RESTORATION SYSTEMS LTD p 251
3675 OPIE CRES, PRINCE GEORGE, BC, V2N 1B9
(250) 612-5177   SIC 1521

UNIVERSAL STUDIOS CANADA INC p 768
2450 VICTORIA PARK AVE SUITE 4, NORTH YORK, ON, M2J 4A2
(416) 491-3000   SIC 7822

UNIVERSAL SYSTEMS LTD   p 401
829 WOODSTOCK RD, FREDERICTON, NB, E3B 7R7
(506) 458-8533   SIC 6712

UNIVERSAL TRUCK & TRUCK TRAILER p 398
925 RUE CHAMPLAIN, DIEPPE, NB, E1A 5T6
(506) 857-2222   SIC 5511

UNIVERSE MACHINE & WELDING, DIV p 117
See UNIVERSE MACHINE CORPORATION

UNIVERSE MACHINE CORPORATION p 117
5545 91 ST NW, EDMONTON, AB, T6E 6K4
(780) 468-5211   SIC 3494

UNIVERSITE BISHOP'S   p 1375
2600 RUE COLLEGE, SHERBROOKE, QC, J1M 1Z7
(819) 822-9600   SIC 8221

UNIVERSITE CONCORDIA   p 1214
1600 RUE SAINTE-CATHERINE O 1ER ETAGE FB-117, MONTREAL, QC, H3G 1M8

(514) 848-3600   SIC 8221
UNIVERSITE CONCORDIA   p 1214
1455 BOUL DE MAISONNEUVE O, MONTREAL, QC, H3G 1M8
(514) 848-2424   SIC 8221

UNIVERSITE DE MONCTON   p 406
18 AV ANTONINE-MAILLET, MONCTON, NB, E1A 3E9
(506) 858-4000   SIC 8221

UNIVERSITE DE MONTREAL   p 1219
2900 BOUL EDOUARD-MONTPETIT, MONTREAL, QC, H3T 1J4
(514) 343-6111   SIC 8221

UNIVERSITE DE MONTREAL   p 1219
3744 RUE JEAN-BRILLANT, MONTREAL, QC, H3T 1P1
(514) 343-6090   SIC 8221

UNIVERSITE DE MONTREAL, L'   p 1219
See UNIVERSITE DE MONTREAL

UNIVERSITE DE SHERBROOKE   p 1145
150 PLACE CHARLES-LE MOYNE BUREAU 200, LONGUEUIL, QC, J4K 0A8
(450) 463-1835   SIC 8221

UNIVERSITE DE SHERBROOKE   p 1372
2500 BOUL DE L'UNIVERSITE, SHERBROOKE, QC, J1K 2R1
(819) 821-7000   SIC 8221

UNIVERSITE DU QUEBEC   p 1087
531 BOUL DES PRAIRIES, COTE SAINT-LUC, QC, H7V 1B7
(450) 687-5010   SIC 8221

UNIVERSITE DU QUEBEC   p 1108
283 BOUL ALEXANDRE-TACHE, GATINEAU, QC, J9A 1L8
(819) 595-3900   SIC 8221

UNIVERSITE DU QUEBEC   p 1123
500 RUE PRINCIPALE BUREAU AR60, LA SARRE, QC, J9Z 2A2
(819) 333-2624   SIC 8221

UNIVERSITE DU QUEBEC   p 1137
1595 BOUL ALPHONSE-DESJARDINS, LEVIS, QC, G6V 0A6
(418) 833-8800   SIC 8221

UNIVERSITE DU QUEBEC   p 1175
See FONDATION UNIVERSITE DU QUEBEC

UNIVERSITE DU QUEBEC   p 1186
315 RUE SAINTE-CATHERINE E BUREAU 3570, MONTREAL, QC, H2X 3X2
(514) 987-3000   SIC 8221

UNIVERSITE DU QUEBEC   p 1212
1440 RUE SAINT-DENIS, MONTREAL, QC, H3C 3P8
(514) 987-3092   SIC 8221

UNIVERSITE DU QUEBEC   p 1260
490 RUE DE LA COURONNE, QUEBEC, QC, G1K 9A9
(418) 687-6400   SIC 8221

UNIVERSITE DU QUEBEC   p 1260
490 RUE DE LA COURONNE, QUEBEC, QC, G1K 9A9
(418) 654-2665   SIC 8732

UNIVERSITE DU QUEBEC   p 1260
455 RUE DU PARVIS BUREAU 2140, QUEBEC, QC, G1K 9H6
(418) 657-2262   SIC 8221

UNIVERSITE DU QUEBEC   p 1260
475 RUE DU PARVIS, QUEBEC, QC, G1K 9H7
(418) 657-3551   SIC 8221

UNIVERSITE DU QUEBEC   p 1285
300 ALLEE DES URSULINES, RIMOUSKI, QC, G5L 3A1
(418) 723-1986   SIC 8221

UNIVERSITE DU QUEBEC   p 1290
445 BOUL DE L'UNIVERSITE, ROUYN-NORANDA, QC, J9X 5E4
(819) 762-0971   SIC 8221

UNIVERSITE DU QUEBEC   p 1386
3351 BOUL DES FORGES, TROIS-RIVIERES, QC, G8Z 4M3
(819) 376-5011   SIC 8221

UNIVERSITE DU QUEBEC   p 1393
1650 BOUL LIONEL-BOULET, VARENNES,

QC, J3X 1P7
(450) 929-8100 *SIC* 8733
UNIVERSITE DU QUEBEC A MONTREAL *p* 1212
See UNIVERSITE DU QUEBEC
UNIVERSITE DU QUEBEC A MONTREAL (UQAM) *p* 1260
See UNIVERSITE DU QUEBEC
UNIVERSITE DU QUEBEC A RIMOUSKI *p* 1285
See UNIVERSITE DU QUEBEC
UNIVERSITE LAVAL *p* 1274
2375 RUE DE LA TERRASSE, QUEBEC, QC, G1V 0A6
(418) 656-2454 *SIC* 3851
UNIVERSITE LAVAL *p* 1274
1065 AV DE LA MEDECINE PAVILLON ADRIEN-POULIOT, QUEBEC, QC, G1V 0A6
(418) 656-3474 *SIC* 8221
UNIVERSITE LAVAL *p* 1274
1030 AV DES SCIENCES HUMAINES, QUEBEC, QC, G1V 0A6
(418) 656-2131 *SIC* 8221
UNIVERSITE LAVAL *p* 1274
2345 ALLEE DES BIBLIOTHEQUES, QUEBEC, QC, G1V 0A6
(418) 656-3530 *SIC* 8221
UNIVERSITE MCGILL *p* 1200
845 RUE SHERBROOKE O BUREAU 310, MONTREAL, QC, H3A 0G4
(514) 398-4455 *SIC* 8221
UNIVERSITE SAINTE-ANNE *p* 442
1695 RTE 1, CHURCH POINT, NS, B0W 1M0
(902) 769-2114 *SIC* 8221
UNIVERSITIES CANADA *p* 825
350 ALBERT ST SUITE 1710, OTTAWA, ON, K1R 1B1
(613) 563-1236 *SIC* 8621
UNIVERSITY COLLEGE OF THE NORTH *p* 360
436 7TH ST E, THE PAS, MB, R9A 1M7
(204) 627-8500 *SIC* 8221
UNIVERSITY GOLF CLUB *p* 325
See U.G.C.C. HOLDINGS INC
UNIVERSITY HEALTH NETWORK *p* 947
620 UNIVERSITY AVE SUITE 706, TORONTO, ON, M5G 2C1
(416) 946-2294 *SIC* 8733
UNIVERSITY HEALTH NETWORK *p* 947
200 ELIZABETH ST SUITE 224, TORONTO, ON, M5G 2C4
(416) 340-3111 *SIC* 8011
UNIVERSITY HEALTH NETWORK *p* 947
200 ELIZABETH ST, TORONTO, ON, M5G 2C4
(416) 340-3111 *SIC* 8062
UNIVERSITY OF BRITISH COLUMBIA, THE *p* 289
950 10TH AVE E RM 3350, VANCOUVER, BC, V5T 2B2
SIC 8221
UNIVERSITY OF BRITISH COLUMBIA, THE *p* 294
2775 LAUREL ST 11 FL, VANCOUVER, BC, V5Z 1M9
(604) 875-4192 *SIC* 8221
UNIVERSITY OF BRITISH COLUMBIA, THE *p* 325
2332 MAIN MALL SUITE 5000, VANCOUVER, BC, V6T 1Z4
(604) 822-0895 *SIC* 8221
UNIVERSITY OF BRITISH COLUMBIA, THE *p* 325
2366 MAIN MALL SUITE 201, VANCOUVER, BC, V6T 1Z4
(604) 822-3061 *SIC* 8221
UNIVERSITY OF BRITISH COLUMBIA, THE *p* 325
2366 MAIN MALL UNIT 289, VANCOUVER, BC, V6T 1Z4
(604) 822-6894 *SIC* 8221
UNIVERSITY OF BRITISH COLUMBIA, THE *p* 325

5959 STUDENT UNION BLVD, VANCOUVER, BC, V6T 1K2
(604) 822-1000 *SIC* 8221
UNIVERSITY OF BRITISH COLUMBIA, THE *p* 325
6081 UNIVERSITY BLVD RM 210, VANCOUVER, BC, V6T 1Z1
(604) 822-9192 *SIC* 8221
UNIVERSITY OF BRITISH COLUMBIA, THE *p* 325
6270 UNIVERSITY BLVD RM 3200, VANCOUVER, BC, V6T 1Z4
(604) 822-2133 *SIC* 8221
UNIVERSITY OF BRITISH COLUMBIA, THE *p* 325
1822 EAST MALL, VANCOUVER, BC, V6T 1Y1
(604) 822-2275 *SIC* 8221
UNIVERSITY OF BRITISH COLUMBIA, THE *p* 325
1871 WEST MALL UNIT 607, VANCOUVER, BC, V6T 1Z2
(604) 822-0019 *SIC* 8221
UNIVERSITY OF BRITISH COLUMBIA, THE *p* 325
1873 EAST MALL RM 1097, VANCOUVER, BC, V6T 1Z1
(604) 822-9171 *SIC* 8221
UNIVERSITY OF BRITISH COLUMBIA, THE *p* 325
1984 MATHEMATICS RD RM 121, VANCOUVER, BC, V6T 1Z2
(604) 822-2666 *SIC* 8221
UNIVERSITY OF BRITISH COLUMBIA, THE *p* 325
2053 MAIN MALL SUITE 247, VANCOUVER, BC, V6T 1Z2
(604) 822-8500 *SIC* 8221
UNIVERSITY OF BRITISH COLUMBIA, THE *p* 325
2121 WEST MALL, VANCOUVER, BC, V6T 1Z4
(604) 822-1555 *SIC* 8221
UNIVERSITY OF BRITISH COLUMBIA, THE *p* 325
2194 HEALTH SCIENCES MALL, VANCOUVER, BC, V6T 1Z6
(604) 822-5773 *SIC* 8221
UNIVERSITY OF BRITISH COLUMBIA, THE *p* 325
2194 HEALTH SCIENCES MALL UNIT 317, VANCOUVER, BC, V6T 1Z6
(604) 822-2421 *SIC* 8221
UNIVERSITY OF BRITISH COLUMBIA, THE *p* 325
2211 WESBROOK MALL RM T201, VANCOUVER, BC, V6T 2B5
(604) 822-7417 *SIC* 8221
UNIVERSITY OF BRITISH COLUMBIA, THE *p* 325
2215 WESBROOK MALL 3RD FL, VANCOUVER, BC, V6T 1Z3
(604) 822-1388 *SIC* 8221
UNIVERSITY OF BRITISH COLUMBIA, THE *p* 325
2329 WEST MALL, VANCOUVER, BC, V6T 1Z4
(604) 822-2211 *SIC* 8221
UNIVERSITY OF GUELPH *p* 602
50 STONE RD E, GUELPH, ON, N1G 2W1
(519) 824-4120 *SIC* 8221
UNIVERSITY OF GUELPH *p* 602
95 STONE RD W, GUELPH, ON, N1G 2Z4
(519) 767-6299 *SIC* 8221
UNIVERSITY OF GUELPH *p* 627
830 PRESCOTT ST, KEMPTVILLE, ON, K0G 1J0
(613) 258-8336 *SIC* 8221
UNIVERSITY OF GUELPH *p* 857
120 MAIN ST, RIDGETOWN, ON, N0P 2C0
(519) 674-1500 *SIC* 8221
UNIVERSITY OF KING'S COLLEGE *p* 451
6350 COBURG RD, HALIFAX, NS, B3H 2A1
(902) 422-1271 *SIC* 8221

UNIVERSITY OF LETHBRIDGE, THE *p* 91
10707 100 AVE NW SUITE 1100, EDMONTON, AB, T5J 3M1
SIC 8221
UNIVERSITY OF LETHBRIDGE, THE *p* 143
4401 UNIVERSITY DR W, LETHBRIDGE, AB, T1K 3M4
(403) 329-2244 *SIC* 8221
UNIVERSITY OF MANITOBA STUDENTS UNION *p* 392
81 UNIVERSITY CRES SUITE 101, WINNIPEG, MB, R3T 4W9
(204) 474-8678 *SIC* 8641
UNIVERSITY OF MANITOBA THE *p* 381
675 MCDERMOT AVE SUITE 5008, WINNIPEG, MB, R3E 0V9
(204) 787-2137 *SIC* 8221
UNIVERSITY OF MANITOBA THE *p* 392
181 FREEDMAN CRES SUITE 121, WINNIPEG, MB, R3T 5V4
(204) 474-6200 *SIC* 8221
UNIVERSITY OF MANITOBA,THE *p* 381
727 MCDERMOT AVE SUITE 408, WINNIPEG, MB, R3E 3P5
(204) 474-9668 *SIC* 8221
UNIVERSITY OF NEW BRUNSWICK *p* 401
767 KINGS COLLEGE RD, FREDERICTON, NB, E3B 5A3
(506) 453-4889 *SIC* 7382
UNIVERSITY OF NEW BRUNSWICK *p* 402
3 BAILEY DR, FREDERICTON, NB, E3B 5A3
(506) 453-4666 *SIC* 8221
UNIVERSITY OF NEW BRUNSWICK *p* 415
100 TUCKER PARK RD, SAINT JOHN, NB, E2L 4L5
(506) 648-5500 *SIC* 8221
UNIVERSITY OF NEW BRUNSWICK SAINT JOHN *p* 415
See UNIVERSITY OF NEW BRUNSWICK
UNIVERSITY OF ONTARIO INSTITUTE OF TECHNOLOGY *p* 812
2000 SIMCOE ST N, OSHAWA, ON, L1G 0C5
(905) 721-8668 *SIC* 8221
UNIVERSITY OF OTTAWA *p* 819
451 SMYTH RD SUITE RGN, OTTAWA, ON, K1H 8M5
(613) 562-5800 *SIC* 8221
UNIVERSITY OF OTTAWA *p* 822
120 UNIVERSITE PVT UNIT 3010, OTTAWA, ON, K1N 6N5
(613) 562-5800 *SIC* 8221
UNIVERSITY OF OTTAWA *p* 822
55 LAURIER AVE E SUITE 5105, OTTAWA, ON, K1N 6N5
(613) 562-5731 *SIC* 8221
UNIVERSITY OF OTTAWA *p* 822
800 KING EDWARD AVE SUITE 2002, OTTAWA, ON, K1N 6N5
(613) 562-5800 *SIC* 8221
UNIVERSITY OF OTTAWA *p* 822
75 LAURIER AVE E, OTTAWA, ON, K1N 6N5
(613) 562-5700 *SIC* 8221
UNIVERSITY OF OTTAWA HEART INSTITUTE *p* 828
40 RUSKIN ST, OTTAWA, ON, K1Y 4W7
(613) 696-7000 *SIC* 8731
UNIVERSITY OF PRINCE EDWARD ISLAND *p* 1040
550 UNIVERSITY AVE, CHARLOTTETOWN, PE, C1A 4P3
(902) 628-4353 *SIC* 8221
UNIVERSITY OF REGINA *p* 1422
3737 WASCANA PKY, REGINA, SK, S4S 0A2
(306) 584-1255 *SIC* 8221
UNIVERSITY OF REGINA *p* 1422
3737 WASCANA PKY SUITE 148, REGINA, SK, S4S 0A2
(306) 585-4111 *SIC* 8221

UNIVERSITY OF SASKATCHEWAN *p* 1434
107 WIGGINS RD 4TH FL SUITE B419, SASKATOON, SK, S7N 5E5
(306) 966-8641 *SIC* 8221
UNIVERSITY OF SASKATCHEWAN *p* 1434
107 ADMINISTRATION PL SUITE 201, SASKATOON, SK, S7N 5A2
(306) 966-8514 *SIC* 8221
UNIVERSITY OF SASKATCHEWAN *p* 1434
105 ADMINISTRATION PL SUITE E, SASKATOON, SK, S7N 5A2
(306) 966-4343 *SIC* 8221
UNIVERSITY OF SASKATCHEWAN *p* 1434
104 CLINIC PLACE, SASKATOON, SK, S7N 2Z4
(306) 966-6221 *SIC* 8221
UNIVERSITY OF SASKATCHEWAN *p* 1434
103 HOSPITAL DR, SASKATOON, SK, S7N 0W8
(306) 844-1132 *SIC* 8221
UNIVERSITY OF SASKATCHEWAN *p* 1434
103 HOSPITAL DR, SASKATOON, SK, S7N 0W8
(306) 844-1068 *SIC* 8221
UNIVERSITY OF SASKATCHEWAN *p* 1434
107 WIGGINS RD SUITE B103, SASKATOON, SK, S7N 5E5
(306) 966-6135 *SIC* 8221
UNIVERSITY OF SASKATCHEWAN *p* 1434
57 CAMPUS DR RM 3B48, SASKATOON, SK, S7N 5A9
(306) 966-5273 *SIC* 8221
UNIVERSITY OF SASKATCHEWAN *p* 1434
52 CAMPUS DR RM 3101, SASKATOON, SK, S7N 5B4
(306) 966-7477 *SIC* 8221
UNIVERSITY OF SASKATCHEWAN *p* 1434
51 CAMPUS DR RM 5D34, SASKATOON, SK, S7N 5A8
(306) 966-6829 *SIC* 8221
UNIVERSITY OF SASKATCHEWAN *p* 1434
28 CAMPUS DR SUITE 3079, SASKATOON, SK, S7N 0X1
(306) 966-7619 *SIC* 8221
UNIVERSITY OF SASKATCHEWAN *p* 1434
117 SCIENCE PL RM 323, SASKATOON, SK, S7N 5C8
(306) 966-1985 *SIC* 8221
UNIVERSITY OF SASKATCHEWAN STUDENTS' UNION *p* 1434
1 CAMPUS DR RM 65, SASKATOON, SK, S7N 5A3
(306) 966-6960 *SIC* 8611
UNIVERSITY OF ST MICHAEL'S COLLEGE, THE *p* 976
81 ST MARY ST, TORONTO, ON, M5S 1J4
(416) 926-1300 *SIC* 8221
UNIVERSITY OF THE FRASER VALLEY *p* 175
33844 KING RD, ABBOTSFORD, BC, V2S 7M8
(604) 504-7441 *SIC* 8221
UNIVERSITY OF THE FRASER VALLEY *p* 198
45190 CAEN AVE, CHILLIWACK, BC, V2R 0N3
(604) 792-0025 *SIC* 8221
UNIVERSITY OF TORONTO *p* 975
See GOVERNING COUNCIL OF THE UNIVERSITY OF TORONTO, THE
UNIVERSITY OF TORONTO - SCARBOROUGH CAMPUS (UTSC) *p* 865
See GOVERNING COUNCIL OF THE UNIVERSITY OF TORONTO, THE
UNIVERSITY OF TORONTO ENGINEERING SOCIETY, THE *p* 976
10 KING'S COLLEGE RD SUITE B740, TORONTO, ON, M5S 3G4
(416) 978-2917 *SIC* 8641
UNIVERSITY OF TORONTO PRESS *p* 781
5201 DUFFERIN ST, NORTH YORK, ON, M3H 5T8

(416) 667-7791 *SIC* 2731
UNIVERSITY OF TORONTO PRESS *p* 932
10 ST MARY ST SUITE 700, TORONTO, ON, M4Y 2W8
(416) 978-2239 *SIC* 2731
UNIVERSITY OF VICTORIA *p* 333
3800 FINNERTY RD, VICTORIA, BC, V8P 5C2
(250) 721-7211 *SIC* 8221
UNIVERSITY OF VICTORIA *p* 333
3800A FINNERTY RD SUITE 168, VICTORIA, BC, V8P 5C2
(250) 721-6673 *SIC* 8221
UNIVERSITY OF VICTORIA STUDENTS' SOCIETY *p* 333
3800 FINNERTY RD RM B128, VICTORIA, BC, V8P 5C2
(250) 472-4317 *SIC* 8399
UNIVERSITY OF WATERLOO *p* 1009
200 UNIVERSITY AVE W, WATERLOO, ON, N2L 3G1
(519) 888-4567 *SIC* 8221
UNIVERSITY OF WESTERN ONTARIO, THE *p* 655
1151 RICHMOND ST RM 4, LONDON, ON, N6A 5C1
(519) 661-2111 *SIC* 8062
UNIVERSITY OF WESTERN ONTARIO, THE *p* 655
1151 RICHMOND ST SUITE 2, LONDON, ON, N6A 5B8
(519) 661-2111 *SIC* 8221
UNIVERSITY OF WESTERN ONTARIO, THE *p* 655
1151 RICHMOND ST SUITE 3, LONDON, ON, N6A 5B9
(519) 661-2111 *SIC* 6531
UNIVERSITY OF WESTERN ONTARIO, THE *p* 655
1151 RICHMOND ST SUITE 3140, LONDON, ON, N6A 3K7
(519) 661-2111 *SIC* 8748
UNIVERSITY OF WESTERN ONTARIO, THE *p* 658
1137 WESTERN RD SUITE 1118, LONDON, ON, N6G 1G7
(519) 661-3182 *SIC* 8221
UNIVERSITY OF WINDSOR *p* 1024
401 SUNSET AVE SUITE G07, WINDSOR, ON, N9B 3P4
(519) 253-3000 *SIC* 8221
UNIVERSITY OF WINNIPEG, THE *p* 376
515 PORTAGE AVE, WINNIPEG, MB, R3B 2E9
(204) 786-7811 *SIC* 8221
UNIVERSITY PLUMBING & HEATING LTD *p* 785
3655 KEELE ST, NORTH YORK, ON, M3J 1M8
(416) 630-6010 *SIC* 1711
UNIVERSITY PRESS OF NEW BRUNSWICK *p* 402
984 PROSPECT ST, FREDERICTON, NB, E3B 2T8
(506) 452-6671 *SIC* 2711
UNIVERSITY SPRINKLER SYSTEMS INCORPORATED *p* 211
1777 56 ST UNIT 500, DELTA, BC, V4L 0A6
(604) 421-4555 *SIC* 1711
UNIVERSITY SPRINKLERS *p* 211
See UNIVERSITY SPRINKLER SYSTEMS INCORPORATED
UNIVESTA ASSURANCES & SERVICES FINANCIERS INC *p* 1168
3925 RUE RACHEL E BUREAU 100, MONTREAL, QC, H1X 3G8
(514) 899-5377 *SIC* 6411
UNIVEX MANAGEMENT LIMITED *p* 597
303 RIVER RD SUITE 3, GLOUCESTER, ON, K1V 1H2
(613) 526-1500 *SIC* 8741
UNIVINS ET SPIRITUEUX (CANADA) INC *p*

1226
1350 RUE MAZURETTE BUREAU 326, MONTREAL, QC, H4N 1H2
(514) 522-9339 *SIC* 5182
UNIWELL INTERNATIONAL ENTERPRISES CORP *p* 294
999 BROADWAY W SUITE 880, VANCOUVER, BC, V5Z 1K5
(604) 730-2877 *SIC* 5063
UNIWORLD APPAREL INDUSTRIES *p* 39
See KOOPMAN RESOURCES, INC
UNIWORLD TRAVEL & TOURS INC *p* 768
235 YORKLAND BLVD SUITE 300, NORTH YORK, ON, M2J 4Y8
(416) 493-3322 *SIC* 4724
UNLIMITED POTENTIAL COMMUNITY SERVICES SOCIETY *p* 103
10403 172 ST NW SUITE 145, EDMONTON, AB, T5S 1K9
(780) 440-0708 *SIC* 8322
UPA *p* 1143
See UNION DES PRODUCTEURS AGRICOLE, L'
UPA CONSTRUCTION GROUP LIMITED PARTNERSHIP *p* 69
10655 SOUTHPORT RD SW SUITE 700, CALGARY, AB, T2W 4Y1
(403) 262-4440 *SIC* 1522
UPA PIECES D'AUTO *p* 538
See UAP INC
UPEI *p* 1040
See UNIVERSITY OF PRINCE EDWARD ISLAND
UPFIELD CANADA INC *p* 947
480 UNIVERSITY AVE SUITE 803, TORONTO, ON, M5G 1V2
(416) 595-5300 *SIC* 2079
UPG PROPERTY GROUP INC *p* 237
555 SIXTH ST UNIT 330, NEW WESTMINSTER, BC, V3L 5H1
(604) 525-8292 *SIC* 6531
UPGI PHARMA INC *p* 1123
100 BOUL DE L'INDUSTRIE, LA PRAIRIE, QC, J5R 1J1
(514) 998-9059 *SIC* 2834
UPI ENERGY *p* 604
See UPI INC
UPI GLASS INC *p* 332
1810 KOSMINA RD, VERNON, BC, V1T 8T2
(250) 549-1323 *SIC* 7389
UPI INC *p* 604
105 SILVERCREEK PKY N SUITE 200, GUELPH, ON, N1H 8M1
(519) 821-2667 *SIC* 5541
UPI OIL LP *p* 658
3462 WHITE OAK RD, LONDON, ON, N6E 2Z9
(519) 681-3772 *SIC* 5172
UPLAND CONTRACTING LTD *p* 194
7295 GOLD RIVER HWY, CAMPBELL RIVER, BC, V9H 1P1
(250) 286-1148 *SIC* 1794
UPLAND EXCAVATING LTD *p* 194
7295 GOLD RIVER HWY, CAMPBELL RIVER, BC, V9H 1P1
(250) 286-1148 *SIC* 6712
UPLAND SOFTWARE INC *p* 1343
275 BOUL ARMAND-FRAPPIER BUREAU 531, SAINT-LAURENT, QC, H7V 4A7
(450) 688-3444 *SIC* 7371
UPLANDS MOTORING COMPANY LTD *p* 333
3095 SHELBOURNE ST, VICTORIA, BC, V8R 4M9
(250) 592-2444 *SIC* 5541
UPONOR INFRA LTD *p* 621
37 CENTRE ST N, HUNTSVILLE, ON, P1H 1X4
(705) 789-2396 *SIC* 3088
UPONOR INFRA LTD *p* 1425
348 EDSON ST, SASKATOON, SK, S7J 0P9
(306) 242-0755 *SIC* 3498
UPONOR LTD *p* 1416

662 E 1ST AVE SUITE 200, REGINA, SK, S4N 5T6
(306) 721-2449 *SIC* 5075
UPPAL BUILDING SUPPLIES LTD *p* 278
7846 128 ST, SURREY, BC, V3W 4E8
(604) 594-4142 *SIC* 5211
UPPER CANADA - SIERRA GROUP SERVICE *p* 728
7088 FINANCIAL DR, MISSISSAUGA, ON, L5N 7H5
(905) 814-8800 *SIC* 5031
UPPER CANADA COLLEGE *p* 927
200 LONSDALE RD, TORONTO, ON, M4V 1W6
(416) 488-1125 *SIC* 8211
UPPER CANADA CREATIVE CHILD CARE CENTRES OF ONTARIO *p* 854
30 FULTON WAY UNIT 4, RICHMOND HILL, ON, L4B 1E6
(289) 982-1113 *SIC* 8351
UPPER CANADA DISTRICT SCHOOL BOARD, THE *p* 520
225 CENTRAL AVE W, BROCKVILLE, ON, K6V 5X1
(613) 342-0371 *SIC* 8211
UPPER CANADA DISTRICT SCHOOL BOARD, THE *p* 520
2510 PARKEDALE AVE, BROCKVILLE, ON, K6V 3H1
(613) 342-1100 *SIC* 8211
UPPER CANADA FOREST PRODUCTS LTD *p* 728
7088 FINANCIAL DR, MISSISSAUGA, ON, L5N 7H5
(905) 814-8000 *SIC* 5031
UPPER CANADA FUELS (2001) LIMITED *p* 842
660 THE QUEENSWAY, PETERBOROUGH, ON, K9J 7H2
(705) 742-8815 *SIC* 5172
UPPER CANADA GROWERS LTD *p* 761
149 READ RD, NIAGARA ON THE LAKE, ON, L0S 1J0
(289) 646-0737 *SIC* 0191
UPPER CANADA MOTOR SALES LIMITED *p* 746
12375 COUNTY ROAD 28, MORRISBURG, ON, K0C 1X0
(613) 543-2925 *SIC* 5511
UPPER CANADA SOAP & CANDLE MAKERS CORPORATION *p* 733
5875 CHEDWORTH WAY, MISSISSAUGA, ON, L5R 3L9
(905) 897-1710 *SIC* 5199
UPPER CANADA SPECIALTY HARDWARE LIMITED *p* 676
7100 WARDEN AVE UNIT 1, MARKHAM, ON, L3R 8B5
(905) 940-8358 *SIC* 5072
UPPER CRUST *p* 781
See 2168587 ONTARIO LTD
UPPER CRUST *p* 794
See 2168587 ONTARIO LTD
UPPER CRUST CAFE *p* 118
See UPPER CRUST CATERERS LTD
UPPER CRUST CATERERS LTD *p* 118
10909 86 AVE NW, EDMONTON, AB, T6G 0W8
(780) 758-5599 *SIC* 5812
UPPER GRAND DISTRICT SCHOOL BOARD, THE *p* 600
500 VICTORIA RD N, GUELPH, ON, N1E 6K2
(519) 822-4420 *SIC* 8211
UPPER GRAND DISTRICT SCHOOL BOARD, THE *p* 604
155 PAISLEY ST SUITE UPPER, GUELPH, ON, N1H 2P3
(519) 824-9800 *SIC* 8211
UPPER GRAND DISTRICT SCHOOL BOARD, THE *p* 607
1428 GORDON ST, GUELPH, ON, N1L 1C8

(519) 836-7280 *SIC* 8211
UPPER GRAND DISTRICT SCHOOL BOARD, THE *p* 809
300 ALDER ST, ORANGEVILLE, ON, L9W 5A2
(519) 938-9355 *SIC* 8211
UPPER GRAND DISTRICT SCHOOL BOARD, THE *p* 836
GD, PALMERSTON, ON, N0G 2P0
(519) 343-3107 *SIC* 8211
UPPER GRAND DISTRICT SCHOOL BOARD, THE *p* 880
150 FOURTH AVE, SHELBURNE, ON, L9V 3R5
(519) 925-3834 *SIC* 8211
UPPER ISLAND GERIATRIC OUTREACH PROGRAM *p* 198
See ST JOSEPH'S GENERAL HOSPITAL
UPPER JAMES 2004 LTD *p* 616
1550 UPPER JAMES ST, HAMILTON, ON, L9B 2L6
(905) 383-9700 *SIC* 5411
UPPER ROOM HOME FURNISHINGS INC, THE *p* 751
545 WEST HUNT CLUB RD, NEPEAN, ON, K2G 5W5
(613) 721-5873 *SIC* 5712
UPS *p* 26
See UNITED PARCEL SERVICE CANADA LTD
UPS *p* 97
See UNITED PARCEL SERVICE CANADA LTD
UPS *p* 207
See UNITED PARCEL SERVICE CANADA LTD
UPS *p* 401
See UNITED PARCEL SERVICE CANADA LTD
UPS *p* 407
See UNITED PARCEL SERVICE CANADA LTD
UPS *p* 608
See UNITED PARCEL SERVICE CANADA LTD
UPS *p* 638
See UNITED PARCEL SERVICE CANADA LTD
UPS *p* 662
See UNITED PARCEL SERVICE CANADA LTD
UPS *p* 690
See UNITED PARCEL SERVICE CANADA LTD
UPS *p* 819
See UNITED PARCEL SERVICE CANADA LTD
UPS *p* 984
See UNITED PARCEL SERVICE CANADA LTD
UPS *p* 1017
See UNITED PARCEL SERVICE CANADA LTD
UPS *p* 1060
See UNITED PARCEL SERVICE CANADA LTD
UPS *p* 1071
See UNITED PARCEL SERVICE CANADA LTD
UPS *p* 1129
See UNITED PARCEL SERVICE CANADA LTD
UPS *p* 1277
See UNITED PARCEL SERVICE CANADA LTD
UPS CANADA *p* 560
See UNITED PARCEL SERVICE CANADA LTD
UPS CANADA *p* 736
See UNITED PARCEL SERVICE CANADA LTD
UPS CARTAGE SERVICES INC *p* 1092
750 BOUL STUART-GRAHAM S, DORVAL, QC, H4Y 1G2

(514) 636-1333   *SIC* 4731
UPS SCS INC   *p* 258
7451 NELSON RD, RICHMOND, BC, V6W 1L7
(604) 270-9449   *SIC* 4731
UPS SCS INC   *p* 525
4156 MAINWAY, BURLINGTON, ON, L7L 0A7
(905) 315-5500   *SIC* 4212
UPS SCS INC   *p* 525
4156 MAINWAY, BURLINGTON, ON, L7L 0A7
(905) 315-5500   *SIC* 4731
UPS SCS INC   *p* 560
777 CREDITSTONE RD, CONCORD, ON, L4K 5R5
(905) 660-6040   *SIC* 7389
UPS SCS INC   *p* 690
6655 AIRPORT RD, MISSISSAUGA, ON, L4V 1V8
(905) 677-6735   *SIC* 4731
UPS SCS INC   *p* 736
1930 DERRY RD E, MISSISSAUGA, ON, L5S 1E2
(800) 742-5877   *SIC* 4512
UPS SCS INC   *p* 1327
101 BOUL MARCEL-LAURIN, SAINT-LAURENT, QC, H4N 2M3
(514) 285-1500   *SIC* 4731
UPS SCS, INC   *p* 258
See UPS SCS INC
UPS SCS, INC   *p* 525
See UPS SCS INC
UPS SCS, INC   *p* 560
See UPS SCS INC
UPS SCS, INC   *p* 690
See UPS SCS INC
UPS SCS, INC   *p* 736
See UPS SCS INC
UPS SCS, INC   *p* 1092
800 BOUL STUART-GRAHAM S BUREAU 351, DORVAL, QC, H4Y 1J6
SIC 4731
UPS SCS, INC   *p* 1327
See UPS SCS INC
UPS SUPPLY CHAIN SOLUTION   *p* 525
See UPS SCS INC
UPS SUPPLY CHAIN SOLUTION   *p* 1092
See UPS SCS, INC
UPSIDE ENGINEERING LTD   *p* 32
409 10 AVE SE, CALGARY, AB, T2G 0W3
(403) 290-4650   *SIC* 8711
UPSOURCE CANADA CORP   *p* 464
116 KING ST UNIT 9A, NORTH SYDNEY, NS, B2A 3R7
SIC 4899
UPSTREAM WORKS SOFTWARE LTD   *p* 1034
777 WESTON RD SUITE 1000, WOOD-BRIDGE, ON, L4L 0G9
(905) 660-0969   *SIC* 7371
UPTOWN AUTOMOBILES INC   *p* 1157
8665 BOUL DECARIE, MONT-ROYAL, QC, H4P 2T9
(514) 737-6666   *SIC* 5511
UPTOWN COMMUNICATION HOUSE INC *p* 854
10 WEST PEARCE ST, RICHMOND HILL, ON, L4B 1B6
(905) 731-7318   *SIC* 5999
UPTOWN VOLVO   *p* 1157
See UPTOWN AUTOMOBILES INC
UR-ENERGY INC   *p* 824
55 METCALFE ST SUITE 1300, OTTAWA, ON, K1P 6L5
(613) 236-3882   *SIC* 1094
URANIUM ONE INC   *p* 958
333 BAY ST SUITE 1200, TORONTO, ON, M5H 2R2
(647) 788-8500   *SIC* 1094
URBACON   *p* 921
See URBACON BUILDINGS GROUP CORP
URBACON BUILDINGS GROUP CORP *p*

921
750 LAKE SHORE BLVD E, TORONTO, ON, M4M 3M3
(416) 865-9405   *SIC* 8741
URBACON LIMITED   *p* 921
750 LAKE SHORE BLVD E, TORONTO, ON, M4M 3M3
(416) 865-9405   *SIC* 1541
URBACON LIMITED/URBACON LIMITEE *p* 921
See URBACON LIMITED
URBAN BARN LTD   *p* 194
4085 MARINE WAY UNIT 1, BURNABY, BC, V5J 5E2
(604) 456-2200   *SIC* 5712
URBAN DINING GROUP INC   *p* 976
192 BLOOR ST W SUITE 201, TORONTO, ON, M5S 1T8
(416) 967-9671   *SIC* 5812
URBAN ENVIRONMENT CENTRE (TORONTO), THE   *p* 576
74 SIX POINT RD, ETOBICOKE, ON, M8Z 2X2
(416) 203-3106   *SIC* 8748
URBAN FARE   *p* 225
See SAVE-ON-FOODS LIMITED PARTNERSHIP
URBAN FARE   *p* 316
See SAVE-ON-FOODS LIMITED PARTNERSHIP
URBAN II RECYCLERS & TOOLS   *p* 291
See URBAN WOOD WASTE RECYCLERS LTD
URBAN IMPACT RECYCLING LTD   *p* 257
15360 KNOX WAY, RICHMOND, BC, V6V 3A6
(604) 273-0089   *SIC* 4953
URBAN MECHANICAL CONTRACTING LTD   *p* 589
254 ATTWELL DR, ETOBICOKE, ON, M9W 5B2
(416) 240-8830   *SIC* 1711
URBAN REALTY INC   *p* 920
840 PAPE AVE, TORONTO, ON, M4K 3T6
(416) 461-9900   *SIC* 6531
URBAN SHREDDING SYSTEMS   *p* 257
See URBAN IMPACT RECYCLING LTD
URBAN STRATEGIES INC   *p* 978
197 SPADINA AVE SUITE 600, TORONTO, ON, M5T 2C8
(416) 340-9004   *SIC* 8748
URBAN SYSTEMS LTD   *p* 218
286 ST PAUL ST SUITE 200, KAMLOOPS, BC, V2C 6G4
(250) 374-8311   *SIC* 8711
URBAN SYSTEMS LTD   *p* 223
1353 ELLIS ST UNIT 304, KELOWNA, BC, V1Y 1Z9
(250) 762-2517   *SIC* 8711
URBAN TACTICAL   *p* 384
See CORPORATE SECURITY SUPPLY LTD
URBAN TRAIL   *p* 393
See 2302659 MANITOBA LTD
URBAN WOOD WASTE RECYCLERS LTD *p* 291
110 69TH AVE E, VANCOUVER, BC, V5X 4K6
SIC 1629
URBANA CORPORATION   *p* 958
150 KING ST W SUITE 1702, TORONTO, ON, M5H 1J9
(416) 595-9106   *SIC* 6726
URBANDALE CONSTRUCTION LIMITED *p* 819
2193 ARCH ST, OTTAWA, ON, K1G 2H5
(613) 731-6331   *SIC* 1521
URBANDALE CORPORATION   *p* 819
2193 ARCH ST, OTTAWA, ON, K1G 2H5
(613) 731-6331   *SIC* 6513
URBANMINE INC   *p* 389
72 ROTHWELL RD, WINNIPEG, MB, R3P 2H7
(204) 774-0192   *SIC* 5093
URGEL CHARETTE TRANSPORT LIMITEE

p 1360
555 BOUL SAINT-JEAN-BAPTISTE E RR 3, SAINTE-MARTINE, QC, J0S 1V0
(450) 691-5151   *SIC* 4212
URGENCES-SANTE   *p* 1165
6700 RUE JARRY E, MONTREAL, QC, H1P 0A4
(514) 723-5600   *SIC* 4119
URS CANADA INC   *p* 854
30 LEEK CRES 4TH FL, RICHMOND HILL, ON, L4B 4N4
(905) 882-9190   *SIC* 8711
URS FLINT   *p* 33
See AECOM ENERGY SERVICES LTD
URSA   *p* 26
See UNIVERSAL REHABILITATION SERVICE AGENCY
URSULINE COLLEGE (THE PINES)   *p* 542
See ST. CLAIR CATHOLIC DISTRICT SCHOOL BOARD
URSULINE RELIGIOUS OF THE DIOCESE OF LONDON IN ONTARIO   *p* 658
1285 WESTERN RD, LONDON, ON, N6G 1H2
(519) 432-8353   *SIC* 8221
URSUS TRANSPORT INC   *p* 589
85 VULCAN ST, ETOBICOKE, ON, M9W 1L4
(416) 243-8780   *SIC* 4213
URTHECAST CORP   *p* 310
1055 CANADA PL UNIT 33, VANCOUVER, BC, V6C 0C3
(604) 265-6266   *SIC* 8713
US CUSTOMS & BORDER PROTECTION *p* 26
2016D AIRPORT ROAD NE UNIT 172A, CALGARY, AB, T2E 3B9
(403) 221-1641   *SIC* 4731
USACAN MEDIA DISTRIBUTION SERVICE INC   *p* 1331
1459 RUE BEGIN, SAINT-LAURENT, QC, H4R 1V8
SIC 5199
USASK SMALL ANIMAL CLINICAL STUD *p* 1434
52 CAMPUS DR, SASKATOON, SK, S7N 5B4
(306) 966-7126   *SIC* 8699
USC CONSULTING GROUP (CANADA), LP *p* 690
5925 AIRPORT RD SUITE 730, MISSISSAUGA, ON, L4V 1W1
(905) 673-2600   *SIC* 8741
USG CANADIAN MINING LTD   *p* 470
669 WENTWORTH RD, WINDSOR, NS, B0N 2T0
(902) 798-4676   *SIC* 1499
USIHOME INC   *p* 1148
1455 BOUL INDUSTRIEL, MAGOG, QC, J1X 4P2
(819) 847-0666   *SIC* 1752
USINAGE SBB   *p* 1058
See ACIER PROFILE S.B.B. INC
USINATECH CANADA   *p* 1151
See USINATECH INC
USINATECH INC   *p* 1151
1099 CH D'ELY, MELBOURNE, QC, J0B 2B0
(819) 826-3774   *SIC* 3599
USINE BEDFORD   *p* 1313
See PAVAGES MASKA INC
USINE CAUSAP   *p* 1074
See BOIS D'OEUVRE CEDRICO INC
USINE DE CANDIAC   *p* 1073
See OC CANADA HOLDINGS COMPANY
USINE DE CONGELATION   *p* 1296
See USINE DE CONGELATION DE ST-BRUNO INC
USINE DE CONGELATION DE ST-BRUNO INC   *p* 1296
698 RUE MELANCON, SAINT-BRUNO-LAC-SAINT-JEAN, QC, G0W 2L0
(418) 343-2206   *SIC* 4222
USINE DE PAPIERS WINDSOR   *p* 1392

See DOMTAR INC
USINE GAILURON   *p* 1256
See MULTI-MARQUES INC
USINE SARTIGAN INC   *p* 1307
888 RTE 269, SAINT-HONORE-DE-SHENLEY, QC, G0M 1V0
(418) 485-6797   *SIC* 2421
USINE TAC TIC INC, L'   *p* 1305
2030 127E RUE, SAINT-GEORGES, QC, G5Y 2W8
(418) 227-4279   *SIC* 2789
USINES D'AUTRAY LTEE, LES   *p* 1303
4581 RANG CASTLE-D'AUTRAY, SAINT-FELIX-DE-VALOIS, QC, J0K 2M0
(450) 889-5505   *SIC* 6712
USINES GIANT INC   *p* 1238
11021 RUE NOTRE-DAME E, MONTREAL-EST, QC, H1B 2V5
(514) 645-8893   *SIC* 3639
USNR/KOCKUMS CANCAR COMPANY *p* 1246
1600 RUE SAINT-PAUL, PLESSISVILLE, QC, G6L 1C1
(819) 362-7362   *SIC* 3553
USTRI CANADA INC   *p* 300
1122 MAINLAND ST SUITE 470, VANCOUVER, BC, V6B 5L1
SIC 7371
UTC FIRE & SECURITY CANADA INC *p* 701
5201 EXPLORER DR, MISSISSAUGA, ON, L4W 4H1
(905) 629-2600   *SIC* 3669
UTECH ELECTRONICS   *p* 1001
25 ANDERSON BLVD, UXBRIDGE, ON, L9P 0C7
(416) 609-2900   *SIC* 5065
UTHANE RESEARCH LTD   *p* 676
140 BENTLEY ST UNIT 2, MARKHAM, ON, L3R 3L2
(905) 940-2356   *SIC* 3081
UTI, CANADA, INC   *p* 507
70 DRIVER RD UNIT 4, BRAMPTON, ON, L6T 5V2
(905) 790-1616   *SIC* 4731
UTI, CANADA, INC   *p* 701
2540 MATHESON BLVD E, MISSISSAUGA, ON, L4W 4Z2
SIC 4731
UTIL CANADA LIMITED   *p* 560
270 SPINNAKER WAY SUITE 13, CONCORD, ON, L4K 4W1
(905) 760-8088   *SIC* 3469
UTIL GROUP   *p* 550
See CAPITAL TOOL & DESIGN LTD.
UTILITY INTERNATIONAL INC   *p* 475
610 FINLEY AVE SUITE 6, AJAX, ON, L1S 2E3
(905) 686-3512   *SIC* 4731
UTILITY SERVICES LTD.   *p* 816
1611 LIVERPOOL CRT, OTTAWA, ON, K1B 4L1
SIC 1521
UTMC CANADA INC   *p* 718
2390 DUNWIN DR, MISSISSAUGA, ON, L5L 1J9
(905) 828-9300   *SIC* 3827
UTOPIA DAY SPAS & SALONS LTD   *p* 227
20486 64 AVE UNIT 106, LANGLEY, BC, V2Y 2V5
(604) 539-8772   *SIC* 7991
UTOURS INC   *p* 984
345 ADELAIDE ST W SUITE 400, TORONTO, ON, M5V 1R5
(416) 479-3972   *SIC* 8742
UTP DISTRIBUTION, DIV OF   *p* 781
See UNIVERSITY OF TORONTO PRESS
UTP NORTH YORK, DIV OF   *p* 781
See UNIVERSITY OF TORONTO PRESS
UTRAMAR RAFFINERIE JEAN GAULIN *p* 1136
See ENERGIE VALERO INC
UTSTARCOM CANADA COMPANY   *p* 257
4600 JACOMBS RD SUITE 120, RICHMOND, BC, V6V 3B1

---

(604) 276-0055   *SIC* 3663
UTTER-MORRIS INSURANCE BROKERS LIMITED   *p* 527
3070 MAINWAY UNIT 5, BURLINGTON, ON, L7M 3X1
(905) 332-7877   *SIC* 6411
UVALUX INTERNATIONAL INC   *p* 1036
470 INDUSTRIAL AVE, WOODSTOCK, ON, N4S 7L1
(519) 421-1212   *SIC* 5064
UVIEW ULTRAVIOLET SYSTEMS INC*p* 704
1324 BLUNDELL RD, MISSISSAUGA, ON, L4Y 1M5
(905) 615-8620   *SIC* 3714
UXBRIDGE COTTAGE HOSPITAL   *p* 1001
See MARKHAM STOUFFVILLE HOSPITAL

V

V & L ASSOCIATES INC   *p* 743
6315 DANVILLE RD, MISSISSAUGA, ON, L5T 2H7
(905) 565-7535   *SIC* 5092
V I P GARMENTS   *p* 26
See V I P GARMENTS OF CANADA LTD
V I P GARMENTS OF CANADA LTD   *p* 26
1339 40 AVE NE SUITE 11, CALGARY, AB, T2E 8N6
      SIC 5137
V I P SOAP PRODUCTS LTD   *p* 233
32859 MISSION WAY, MISSION, BC, V2V 6E4
(604) 820-8665   *SIC* 2841
V INTERACTIONS INC   *p* 1209
355 RUE SAINTE-CATHERINE O, MONTREAL, QC, H3B 1A5
(514) 390-6100   *SIC* 4833
V J L R H LONDON INC   *p* 661
1035 WHARNCLIFFE RD S, LONDON, ON, N6L 1J9
(519) 681-9400   *SIC* 5511
V K DELIVERY & MOVING SERVICES LTD*p* 207
588 ANNANCE CRT UNIT 2, DELTA, BC, V3M 6Y8
(604) 540-0384   *SIC* 4731
V T L LOCATION INC   *p* 1347
CP 99, SAINT-LOUIS-DU-HA-HA, QC, G0L 3S0
(418) 854-7383   *SIC* 5012
V.A. HEALTH CARE INC   *p* 1007
50 WEBER ST N, WATERLOO, ON, N2J 3G7
(519) 880-8083   *SIC* 5912
V.C. RENOVATION   *p* 396
103 VANIER ST, CAMPBELLTON, NB, E3N 1T8
(506) 753-6273   *SIC* 1521
V.D.M. TRUCKING SERVICE LTD   *p* 123
2010 76 AVE NW, EDMONTON, AB, T6P 1J5
(780) 467-9897   *SIC* 4213
V.H. FUELS INC   *p* 869
1896 EGLINTON AVE E, SCARBOROUGH, ON, M1L 2L9
(416) 751-8896   *SIC* 5541
V.I.C. SAFETY INCORPORATED   *p* 1028
377 VAUGHAN VALLEY BLVD, WOODBRIDGE, ON, L4H 3B5
(905) 850-0838   *SIC* 5136
V.I.P. MAZDA   *p* 177
See V.I.P. SALES LTD
V.I.P. SALES LTD   *p* 177
30270 AUTOMALL DR, ABBOTSFORD, BC, V2T 5M1
(604) 857-1600   *SIC* 5511
V.R. SOULIERE INC   *p* 1130
179 RUE DU PARC-INDUSTRIEL, LANORAIE, QC, J0K 1E0
(450) 589-1110   *SIC* 5571
V.S.I. INC   *p* 513
18 REGAN RD UNIT 31, BRAMPTON, ON, L7A 1C2
      SIC 7381
VAC AERO INTERNATIONAL INC   *p* 525

5420 NORTH SERVICE RD SUITE 205, BURLINGTON, ON, L7L 6C7
(905) 827-4171   *SIC* 3567
VAC OXYGENE ULC   *p* 1145
1733 BOUL TASCHEREAU, LONGUEUIL, QC, J4K 2X9
(450) 679-3406   *SIC* 5169
VAC SERVICE OF CANADA INC   *p* 819
1001 THOMAS SPRATT PL, OTTAWA, ON, K1G 5L5
      SIC 6351
VACANCES COMPASS HOLIDAYS   *p* 854
See TIAN BAO TRAVEL LTD
VACANCES TOURBEC   *p* 579
See JONVIEW CANADA INC
VACHON, ENRIGHT & PETER INSURANCE LTD   *p* 578
5468 DUNDAS ST W UNIT 200, ETOBICOKE, ON, M9B 6E3
(416) 239-3373   *SIC* 6411
VACUUM TRUCKS OF CANADA ULC *p* 495
180 HEALEY RD, BOLTON, ON, L7E 5B1
(905) 857-7474   *SIC* 4212
VADERSTAD INDUSTRIES INC   *p* 1409
HWY 9, LANGBANK, SK, S0G 2X0
(306) 538-2221   *SIC* 3523
VAIL, MIKE TRUCKING LTD   *p* 13
4531 32 ST SE, CALGARY, AB, T2B 3P8
(403) 272-5487   *SIC* 4212
VAILLANCOURT INC   *p* 1306
252 BOUL INDUSTRIEL, SAINT-GERMAIN-DE-GRANTHAM, QC, J0C 1K0
(819) 395-4484   *SIC* 3089
VAILLANCOURT PORTES ET FENETRES*p* 1306
See VAILLANCOURT INC
VAL ALBERT MOTORS LIMITED   *p* 627
392 GOVERNMENT RD E RR 1, KAPUSKASING, ON, P5N 2X7
(705) 335-5000   *SIC* 5511
VAL EST PHARMACY   *p* 1001
See NICKEL CENTRE PHARMACY INC
VAL RITA TIRE SALES LTD   *p* 1001
96 GOVERNMENT RD, VAL RITA, ON, P0L 2G0
(705) 335-8496   *SIC* 5541
VALACTA, SOCIETE EN COMMANDITE   *p* 1355
555 BOUL DES ANCIENS-COMBATTANTS, SAINTE-ANNE-DE-BELLEVUE, QC, H9X 3R4
(514) 459-3030   *SIC* 8742
VALARD CONSTRUCTION LTD   *p* 117
4209 99 ST NW SUITE 308, EDMONTON, AB, T6E 5V7
(780) 436-9876   *SIC* 1623
VALARD CONSTRUCTION LTD   *p* 133
14310 97 ST, GRANDE PRAIRIE, AB, T8V 7B7
(780) 539-4750   *SIC* 1623
VALARD CONSTRUCTION LTD   *p* 283
3120 BRAUN ST, TERRACE, BC, V8G 5N9
      SIC 1623
VALBELLA MEATS   *p* 79
See PIONEER MEATS LTD
VALCO MANUFACTURING INC   *p* 1022
1235 ST LUKE RD, WINDSOR, ON, N8Y 4W7
(519) 971-9666   *SIC* 3541
VALCOM CONSULTING GROUP INC *p* 411
281 RESTIGOUCHE RD SUITE 204, OROMOCTO, NB, E2V 2H2
(506) 357-5835   *SIC* 8748
VALCOM CONSULTING GROUP INC *p* 824
85 ALBERT ST SUITE 300, OTTAWA, ON, K1P 6A4
(613) 594-5200   *SIC* 8711
VALE CANADA LIMITED   *p* 360
1 PLANT RD, THOMPSON, MB, R8N 1P3
(204) 778-2211   *SIC* 1061
VALE CANADA LIMITED   *p* 773
5 PARK HOME AVE SUITE 300, NORTH YORK, ON, M2N 6L4
      SIC 1629

VALE CANADA LIMITED   *p* 847
187 DAVIS ST, PORT COLBORNE, ON, L3K 5W2
(905) 835-6000   *SIC* 7389
VALE CANADA LIMITED   *p* 968
200 BAY ST SUITE 1500 ROYAL BANK PLZ, TORONTO, ON, M5J 2K2
(416) 361-7511   *SIC* 1629
VALE NEWFOUNDLAND & LABRADOR LIMITED   *p* 429
18 HEBRON WAY LEVEL 2 KMK PLACE, ST. JOHN'S, NL, A1A 0L9
(709) 758-8888   *SIC* 1629
VALEANT CANADA LIMITEE   *p* 1363
2150 BOUL SAINT-ELZEAR O, SAINTE-ROSE, QC, H7L 4A8
(514) 744-6792   *SIC* 2834
VALEANT CANADA S.E.C.   *p* 1363
2150 BOUL SAINT-ELZEAR O, SAINTE-ROSE, QC, H7L 4A8
(514) 744-6792   *SIC* 5122
VALENER INC   *p* 1174
1717 RUE DU HAVRE, MONTREAL, QC, H2K 2X3
(514) 598-6220   *SIC* 6712
VALENTE, REMO REAL ESTATE (1990) LIMITED   *p* 1025
2985 DOUGALL AVE, WINDSOR, ON, N9E 1S1
(519) 966-7777   *SIC* 6531
VALENTINE GROUP HOME   *p* 538
See COMMUNITY LIVING CAMBRIDGE
VALENTINE TRAVEL   *p* 658
See JUST VACATIONS INC
VALENTINE VOLVO   *p* 73
See HALFORD & VALENTINE (1991) LTD
VALERIO, TOMASELLI   *p* 1245
4930 BOUL SAINT-JEAN, PIERREFONDS, QC, H9H 4B2
(514) 620-7920   *SIC* 5912
VALEURA ENERGY INC   *p* 62
202 6 AVE SW SUITE 1200, CALGARY, AB, T2P 2R9
(403) 237-7102   *SIC* 1382
VALEURS MOBILIERES BANQUE LAURENTIENNE INC   *p* 1214
1360 BOUL RENE-LEVESQUE O BUREAU 620, MONTREAL, QC, H3G 0E8
(514) 350-2800   *SIC* 6211
VALEURS MOBILIERES DESJARDINS INC *p* 1209
1170 RUE PEEL BUREAU 300, MONTREAL, QC, H3B 0A9
(514) 987-1749   *SIC* 6211
VALEURS MOBILIERES DESJARDINS INC *p* 1230
2 COMPLEXE DESJARDINS TOUR E 15 +TAGE, MONTREAL, QC, H5B 1J2
(514) 286-3180   *SIC* 6211
VALHALLA INN TORONTO   *p* 578
See SANTEK INVESTMENTS (1991) INC
VALHALLA PURE OUTFITTERS INC *p* 332
2700 30 AVE, VERNON, BC, V1T 2B6
(250) 542-9800   *SIC* 5941
VALIA TRADING CORP   *p* 707
4 ROBERT SPECK PKWY 15 FL SUITE 1530, MISSISSAUGA, ON, L4Z 1S1
(647) 701-9656   *SIC* 5146
VALIANT AUTOMATION & ASSEMBLY, DIV OF   *p* 1019
See VALIANT MACHINE & TOOL INC
VALIANT CORPORATION   *p* 1019
6555 HAWTHORNE DR, WINDSOR, ON, N8T 3G6
(519) 974-5200   *SIC* 6712
VALIANT MACHINE & TOOL INC   *p* 1017
9355 ANCHOR DR, WINDSOR, ON, N8N 5A8
(519) 974-5200   *SIC* 3541
VALIANT MACHINE & TOOL INC   *p* 1019
6555 HAWTHORNE DR, WINDSOR, ON, N8T 3G6
(519) 974-5200   *SIC* 3548

VALIANT PROPERTY MANAGEMENT*p* 812
See VALIANT RENTAL PROPERTIES LIMITED
VALIANT RENTAL PROPERTIES LIMITED*p* 812
177 NONQUON RD, OSHAWA, ON, L1G 3S2
(905) 579-1626   *SIC* 6513
VALIANT TOOL & GAGE   *p* 1017
See VALIANT MACHINE & TOOL INC
VALIANT TOOL & MOLD INC   *p* 1019
6775 HAWTHORNE DR, WINDSOR, ON, N8T 3B8
(519) 251-4800   *SIC* 3089
VALID MANUFACTURING LTD   *p* 268
5320 48 AVE SE, SALMON ARM, BC, V1E 1X2
(250) 832-6477   *SIC* 3716
VALIDUS RESEARCH INC   *p* 1007
187 KING ST S SUITE 201, WATERLOO, ON, N2J 1R1
(519) 783-9100   *SIC* 6411
VALIFF SALES INC   *p* 830
1660 CARLING AVE SUITE 290, OTTAWA, ON, K2A 1C5
(613) 725-3111   *SIC* 5531
VALLEE DU PARC   *p* 1112
See VALLEE DU PARC DE SHAWINIGAN INC
VALLEE DU PARC DE SHAWINIGAN INC *p* 1112
10000 CH VALLEE-DU-PARC, GRANDMERE, QC, G9T 5K5
(819) 538-1639   *SIC* 7999
VALLEN   *p* 111
See VALLEN CANADA INC
VALLEN CANADA INC   *p* 111
4810 92 AVE NW, EDMONTON, AB, T6B 2X4
(780) 468-3366   *SIC* 5085
VALLEY AUCTION INC   *p* 180
903 HWY 97A, ARMSTRONG, BC, V0E 1B7
(250) 546-9420   *SIC* 5154
VALLEY BLADES LIMITED   *p* 1009
435 PHILLIP ST, WATERLOO, ON, N2L 3X2
(519) 885-5500   *SIC* 3531
VALLEY BUS LINES LTD   *p* 627
782 VAN BUREN ST, KEMPTVILLE, ON, K0G 1J0
(613) 258-4022   *SIC* 4111
VALLEY CARRIERS LTD   *p* 178
4491 GLADWIN RD, ABBOTSFORD, BC, V4X 1W6
(604) 853-1075   *SIC* 4213
VALLEY CATERERS   *p* 479
See ROXSON ENTERPRISES LIMITED
VALLEY COMFORT SYSTEMS INC   *p* 244
1290 COMMERCIAL WAY, PENTICTON, BC, V2A 3H5
(250) 493-7444   *SIC* 3433
VALLEY COUNTER TOPS LTD   *p* 177
30781 SIMPSON RD, ABBOTSFORD, BC, V2T 6X4
(604) 852-8125   *SIC* 6712
VALLEY CUT STEEL   *p* 282
See VCS VALLEY CUT STEEL CORP
VALLEY EAST LONG TERM CARE *p* 1001
See JARLETTE LTD
VALLEY EQUIPMENT LIMITED   *p* 403
289 MCLEAN AVE, HARTLAND, NB, E7P 2K7
(506) 375-4412   *SIC* 5511
VALLEY FIRST CREDIT UNION   *p* 244
184 MAIN ST, PENTICTON, BC, V2A 8G7
(250) 490-2720   *SIC* 6062
VALLEY FORD LIMITED   *p* 460
898 PARK ST, KENTVILLE, NS, B4N 3V7
(902) 678-1330   *SIC* 5511
VALLEY FORD SALES   *p* 1407
224 EAST SERVICE RD, HAGUE, SK, S0K 1X0
(306) 225-3673   *SIC* 5511
VALLEY FORD SALES   *p* 1413
See QUICK LANE TIRE AND AUTO CEN-

TRE

VALLEY GRAVEL SALES LTD *p 178*
700 LEFEUVRE RD, ABBOTSFORD, BC, V4X 1H7
(604) 856-4461 *SIC 5032*

VALLEY INDUSTRIES (2007) LTD *p 460*
110 LAWRENCETOWN LANE, LAWRENCETOWN., NS, B0S 1M0
(902) 584-2211 *SIC 5999*

VALLEY INTEGRATION TO ACTIVE LIVING SOCIETY *p 212*
80 STATION ST SUITE 217, DUNCAN, BC, V9L 1M4
(250) 748-5899 *SIC 8699*

VALLEY MANOR INC *p 489*
88 MINTHA ST, BARRYS BAY, ON, K0J 1B0
(613) 756-2643 *SIC 8051*

VALLEY PARK MANOR NURSING HOME *p 154*
5505 60 AVE, RED DEER, AB, T4N 4W2
SIC 8051

VALLEY PARK MIDDLE SCHOOL *p 780*
See TORONTO DISTRICT SCHOOL BOARD

VALLEY PERSONNEL LTD *p 247*
2509 KINGSWAY AVE, PORT COQUITLAM, BC, V3C 1T5
SIC 8741

VALLEY REFRIGERATION & AIR CONDITIONING LTD *p 404*
35 KINNEY RD, JACKSONVILLE, NB, E7M 3G1
(506) 325-2204 *SIC 1711*

VALLEY SEARCH & RESCUE *p 441*
5876 HWY 1 BLDG 2, CAMBRIDGE, NS, B0P 1G0
SIC 8999

VALLEY SELECT FOODS INC *p 178*
41212 NO. 3 RD, ABBOTSFORD, BC, V3G 2S1
(604) 823-2341 *SIC 0723*

VALLEY SHELL *p 165*
See BENEDICT HOLDINGS LTD

VALLEY TOYOTA *p 197*
See VT VENTURES INC

VALLEY TRAFFIC SYSTEMS INC *p 225*
19689 TELEGRAPH TRAIL, LANGLEY, BC, V1M 3E6
(604) 513-0210 *SIC 7389*

VALLEY TRANSFER *p 439*
See MERKS FARMS LIMITED

VALLEY TRUCK & SPRING SERVICE *p 838*
See CLOUTHIER, BILL & SONS LTD

VALLEY VIEW *p 775*
See ADVENT HEALTH CARE CORPORATION

VALLEY VOLKSWAGEN *p 442*
See 2463103 NOVA SCOTIA LTD

VALLEYFIELD CHEVROLET BUICK GMC *p 1365*
See AUTOMOBILES REGATE INC

VALLEYVIEW CARE CENTRE *p 348*
See REVERA INC

VALLEYVIEW COLONY *p 170*
See HUTTERIAN BRETHREN CHURCH OF VALLEYVIEW RANCH

VALLEYVIEW CONSUMERS CO-OP LTD *p 360*
250 PRINCESS ST W, VIRDEN, MB, R0M 2C0
(204) 748-2520 *SIC 5411*

VALLEYVIEW IGA *p 98*
See ADVANCE FOODS LTD

VALLEYVIEW MOHAWK *p 252*
See KTW HOLDINGS LTD

VALMET LTEE *p 1331*
4900 BOUL THIMENS, SAINT-LAURENT, QC, H4R 2B2
(514) 335-5426 *SIC 3554*

VALMETAL INC *p 1306*
230 BOUL INDUSTRIEL, SAINT-GERMAIN-DE-GRANTHAM, QC, J0C 1K0
(819) 395-4282 *SIC 3523*

VALMONT *p 1359*
See LAMPADAIRES FERALUX INC

VALMONT WC ENGINEERING GROUP LTD *p 210*
7984 RIVER RD, DELTA, BC, V4G 1E3
(604) 946-1256 *SIC 5211*

VALOR FIREPLACES *p 238*
See MILES INDUSTRIES LTD

VALORE METALS CORP *p 310*
800 PENDER ST W SUITE 1020, VANCOUVER, BC, V6C 2V6
(604) 646-4527 *SIC 1094*

VALOROSO FOODS (1996) LTD *p 223*
1467 SUTHERLAND AVE, KELOWNA, BC, V1Y 5Y4
(250) 860-3631 *SIC 5141*

VALOUR DECORATING (1988) LTD *p 382*
889 WALL ST, WINNIPEG, MB, R3G 2T9
(204) 786-5875 *SIC 1721*

VALSPAR INC *p 562*
1915 SECOND ST W, CORNWALL, ON, K6H 5R6
(613) 932-8960 *SIC 2821*

VALTECH DIGITAL CANADA INC *p 984*
49 SPADINA AVE SUITE 205, TORONTO, ON, M5V 2J1
(416) 203-2997 *SIC 7374*

VALTECH FABRICATION INC *p 1366*
730 BOUL DES ERABLES, SALABERRY-DE-VALLEYFIELD, QC, J6T 6G4
(450) 371-0033 *SIC 3443*

VALTROL EQUIPMENT LIMITED *p 805*
2305 WYECROFT RD, OAKVILLE, ON, L6L 6R2
(905) 828-9900 *SIC 5085*

VALU-MART INC *p 646*
42 RUSSELL ST W, LINDSAY, ON, K9V 2W9
(705) 328-0622 *SIC 5411*

VALU-MART ON BAYVIEW *p 769*
See 1265768 ONTARIO LTD

VALUE ADDED REMAN *p 196*
See WESTERN FOREST PRODUCTS INC

VALUE BUILDER SYSTEM *p 917*
See BUILT TO SELL INC

VALUE CREATION INC *p 62*
635 8 AVE SW UNIT 1100, CALGARY, AB, T2P 3M3
(403) 539-4500 *SIC 1382*

VALUE GRAPHICS *p 896*
See INTERNATIONAL GRAPHICS ULC

VALUE MART *p 680*
See MARMORA FOOD MARKET LIMITED

VALUE STEEL & PIPE *p 143*
See VARZARI TRADING LTD

VALUE STEEL & PIPE, DIV OF *p 143*
See VARSTEEL LTD

VALUE VILLAGE *p 1020*
See VALUE VILLAGE STORES, INC

VALUE VILLAGE STORES, INC *p 10*
3405 34 ST NE, CALGARY, AB, T1Y 6T6
(403) 291-3323 *SIC 5399*

VALUE VILLAGE STORES, INC *p 143*
1708 MAYOR MAGRATH DR S, LETHBRIDGE, AB, T1K 2R5
(403) 320-5358 *SIC 5399*

VALUE VILLAGE STORES, INC *p 181*
7350 EDMONDS ST, BURNABY, BC, V3N 0G7
(604) 540-4916 *SIC 5399*

VALUE VILLAGE STORES, INC *p 1020*
4322 WALKER RD, WINDSOR, ON, N8W 3T5
(519) 250-0199 *SIC 5399*

VALUMART *p 931*
See VALUMART LTD

VALUMART LTD *p 931*
55 BLOOR ST W, TORONTO, ON, M4W 1A5
(416) 923-8831 *SIC 5411*

VALVE *p 429*
See VALE NEWFOUNDLAND & LABRADOR LIMITED

VALVE MANUFACTURING, DIV OF *p 1027*

See CRANE CANADA CO.

VAN ACTION (2005) INC *p 1342*
4870 RUE COURVAL, SAINT-LAURENT, QC, H4T 1L1
(514) 342-5000 *SIC 3716*

VAN ACTION SAVARIA *p 1342*
See VAN ACTION (2005) INC

VAN BELLE NURSERY INC *p 178*
34825 HALLERT RD, ABBOTSFORD, BC, V3G 1R3
(604) 853-3415 *SIC 5193*

VAN DE WATER-RAYMOND 1960 LTEE *p 1084*
1600A BOUL SAINT-MARTIN E UNITE 680, COTE SAINT-LUC, QC, H7G 4R8
(888) 597-5538 *SIC 5084*

VAN DEN ELZEN DEVELOPMENTS LTD *p 223*
2949 PANDOSY ST SUITE 103, KELOWNA, BC, V1Y 1W1
(250) 769-5315 *SIC 5541*

VAN DER GRAAF INC *p 507*
2 VAN DER GRAAF CRT UNIT 1, BRAMPTON, ON, L6T 5R6
(905) 793-8100 *SIC 3568*

VAN DONGEN LANDSCAPING & NURSERIES LTD *p 620*
6750 TRAFALGAR RD SUITE 1, HORNBY, ON, L0P 1E0
(905) 878-1105 *SIC 5261*

VAN DONGEN TREE FARM *p 620*
See VAN DONGEN LANDSCAPING & NURSERIES LTD

VAN EEGHEN *p 1342*
See WORLEE INTERNATIONAL INC

VAN GOGH DESIGNS FURNITURE LTD *p 280*
19178 34A AVE, SURREY, BC, V3Z 1A7
(604) 372-3001 *SIC 2512*

VAN HORNE CONSTRUCTION LIMITED *p 1003*
51A CALDARI RD UNIT 1M, VAUGHAN, ON, L4K 4G3
(905) 677-5150 *SIC 1542*

VAN HOUTTE *p 1170*
See SERVICES DE CAFE VAN HOUTTE INC

VAN HOUTTE COFFEE SERVICE *p 650*
775 INDUSTRIAL RD UNIT 1, LONDON, ON, N5V 3N5
SIC 5149

VAN ISLE BRICKLOK SURFACING & LANDSCAPE SUPPLIES LTD *p 340*
2717 PEATT RD SUITE 101, VICTORIA, BC, V9B 3V2
(250) 382-5012 *SIC 1611*

VAN ISLE INSURANCE SERVICES (1983) INC *p 212*
471 TRANS CANADA HWY, DUNCAN, BC, V9L 3R7
SIC 6411

VAN LEEUWEN PIPE AND TUBE (CANADA) INC *p 123*
2875 64 AVE NW, EDMONTON, AB, T6P 1R1
(780) 469-7410 *SIC 5051*

VAN MEEKEREN FARMS LTD *p 460*
237 THORPE RD, KENTVILLE, NS, B4N 3V7
(902) 678-2366 *SIC 5148*

VAN NELLE CANADA LIMITED *p 420*
147 HELLER RD, WOODSTOCK, NB, E7M 1X4
(506) 325-1930 *SIC 2655*

VAN RAAY PASKAL FARMS LTD *p 152*
GD, PICTURE BUTTE, AB, T0K 1V0
(403) 732-5641 *SIC 0211*

VAN ZUTPHEN, J & T CONSTRUCTION INC *p 462*
10442 HWY 19 SW, MABOU, NS, B0E 1X0
(902) 945-2300 *SIC 1611*

VAN'ISLE WINDOWS LTD *p 335*
404 HILLSIDE AVE, VICTORIA, BC, V8T 1Y7
(250) 383-7128 *SIC 5211*

VAN-KAM FREIGHTWAYS *p 275*
See VAN-KAM FREIGHTWAYS LTD

VAN-KAM FREIGHTWAYS LTD *p 275*
10155 GRACE RD, SURREY, BC, V3V 3V7
(604) 582-7451 *SIC 4213*

VAN-WHOLE PRODUCE *p 296*
See VAN-WHOLE PRODUCE LTD

VAN-WHOLE PRODUCE LTD *p 296*
830 MALKIN AVE, VANCOUVER, BC, V6A 2K2
(604) 251-3330 *SIC 4225*

VANAN FOODS LIMITED *p 98*
9106 142 ST NW, EDMONTON, AB, T5R 0M7
(780) 483-1525 *SIC 5411*

VANBOTS *p 550*
See CARILLION CONSTRUCTION INC

VANBREE, J HOLDINGS LTD *p 628*
9644 TOWNSEND LINE, KERWOOD, ON, N0M 2B0
(519) 247-3752 *SIC 6712*

VANCITY COMMUNITY INVESTMENT BANK *p 300*
401 HASTINGS ST W SUITE 401, VANCOUVER, BC, V6B 1L5
(604) 708-7800 *SIC 6021*

VANCITY COMMUNITY INVESTMENT BANK *p 310*
815 HASTINGS ST W SUITE 401, VANCOUVER, BC, V6C 1B4
(604) 708-7800 *SIC 6021*

VANCITY CREDIT UNION *p 296*
See VANCOUVER CITY SAVINGS CREDIT UNION

VANCO FARMS LTD *p 1041*
280 CROOKED CREEK RD -RTE 251, MONCTON, PE, C1E 0M1
(902) 651-2970 *SIC 0191*

VANCO FARMS LTD *p 1042*
9311 TRANS CANADA HWY - RTE 1, MOUNT ALBION, PE, C1B 0R4
(902) 651-2005 *SIC 5148*

VANCOUVER ACCOUNTING *p 302*
See BDO CANADA LLP

VANCOUVER AIRPORT AUTHORITY *p 265*
3211 GRANT MCCONACHIE WAY, RICHMOND, BC, V7B 0A4
(604) 207-7077 *SIC 4581*

VANCOUVER AIRPORT CENTRE LIMITED *p 262*
5911 MINORU BLVD, RICHMOND, BC, V6X 4C7
(604) 273-6336 *SIC 7011*

VANCOUVER AIRPORT CENTRE LIMITED *p 262*
7571 WESTMINSTER HWY, RICHMOND, BC, V6X 1A3
(604) 276-2112 *SIC 7011*

VANCOUVER AIRPORT MARRIOTT HOTEL *p 262*
See VANCOUVER AIRPORT CENTRE LIMITED

VANCOUVER ALARMS *p 259*
See VANCOUVER FIRE PREVENTION SERVICE CO. LTD

VANCOUVER AQUARIUM GIFT SHOP *p 318*
See OCEAN WISE CONSERVATION ASSOCIATION

VANCOUVER ART GALLERY ASSOCIATION, THE *p 327*
750 HORNBY ST, VANCOUVER, BC, V6Z 2H7
(604) 662-4700 *SIC 8412*

VANCOUVER BAY CLUBS LTD *p 310*
610 GRANVILLE ST SUITE 201, VANCOUVER, BC, V6C 3T3
(604) 682-5213 *SIC 7999*

VANCOUVER BOARD OF EDUCATION *p 320*
See BOARD OF EDUCATION OF SCHOOL

DISTRICT NO. 39 (VANCOUVER), THE
VANCOUVER BULLION AND CURRENCY EXCHANGE LTD *p* 310
800 PENDER ST W SUITE 120, VANCOUVER, BC, V6C 2V6
(604) 685-1008   *SIC* 6099
VANCOUVER CAREER COLLEGE (BURNABY) INC *p*
310
400 BURRARD ST SUITE 1800, VANCOUVER, BC, V6C 3A6
(604) 915-7288   *SIC* 8211
VANCOUVER CITY SAVINGS CREDIT UNION *p* 296
183 TERMINAL AVE, VANCOUVER, BC, V6A 4G2
(604) 877-7013   *SIC* 6062
VANCOUVER CLUB, THE *p* 310
915 HASTINGS ST W, VANCOUVER, BC, V6C 1C6
(604) 685-9321   *SIC* 8641
VANCOUVER COASTAL HEALTH *p* 240
231 15TH ST E, NORTH VANCOUVER, BC, V7L 2L7
(604) 988-3131   *SIC* 8062
VANCOUVER COASTAL HEALTH AUTHORITY *p*
248
7105 KEMANO ST, POWELL RIVER, BC, V8A 1L8
(604) 485-9868   *SIC* 8361
VANCOUVER COASTAL HEALTH AUTHORITY *p*
262
See RICHMOND HOSPITAL, THE
VANCOUVER COASTAL HEALTH AUTHORITY *p*
288
3425 CROWLEY DR, VANCOUVER, BC, V5R 6G3
(604) 872-2511   *SIC* 8322
VANCOUVER COASTAL HEALTH AUTHORITY *p*
289
377 2ND AVE E, VANCOUVER, BC, V5T 1B9
(604) 658-1253   *SIC* 8062
VANCOUVER COASTAL HEALTH AUTHORITY *p*
294
855 12TH AVE W SUITE 101, VANCOUVER, BC, V5Z 1M9
(604) 875-4111   *SIC* 8062
VANCOUVER COASTAL HEALTH AUTHORITY *p*
294
4255 LAUREL ST, VANCOUVER, BC, V5Z 2G9
(604) 734-1313   *SIC* 8093
VANCOUVER COASTAL HEALTH AUTHORITY *p*
294
2647 WILLOW ST RM 100, VANCOUVER, BC, V5Z 1M9
(604) 875-4372   *SIC* 8733
VANCOUVER COASTAL HEALTH AUTHORITY *p*
294
2635 LAUREL ST, VANCOUVER, BC, V5Z 1M9
(604) 675-2575   *SIC* 8733
VANCOUVER COASTAL HEALTH AUTHORITY *p*
296
569 POWELL ST, VANCOUVER, BC, V6A 1G8
(604) 255-3151   *SIC* 8011
VANCOUVER COASTAL HEALTH AUTHORITY *p*
324
700 57TH AVE W SUITE 909, VANCOUVER, BC, V6P 1S1
(604) 321-3231   *SIC* 8331
VANCOUVER COASTAL HEALTH AUTHORITY *p*

THORITY *p*
325
2211 WESBROOK MALL, VANCOUVER, BC, V6T 2B5
(604) 822-7121   *SIC* 8062
VANCOUVER COLLEGE LIMITED *p* 323
5400 CARTIER ST, VANCOUVER, BC, V6M 3A5
(604) 261-4285   *SIC* 8211
VANCOUVER COMMUNITY COLLEGE *p*
289
1155 BROADWAY E SUITE 2713, VANCOUVER, BC, V5T 4V5
(604) 871-7000   *SIC* 8221
VANCOUVER COMMUNITY COLLEGE *p*
301
250 PENDER ST W SUITE 358, VANCOUVER, BC, V6B 1S9
(604) 443-8484   *SIC* 8221
VANCOUVER CONDOMINIUM SERVICES LTD *p* 317
1281 GEORGIA ST W SUITE 400, VANCOUVER, BC, V6E 3J7
(604) 684-6291   *SIC* 6519
VANCOUVER DETOX CENTRE *p* 289
See VANCOUVER COASTAL HEALTH AUTHORITY
VANCOUVER DODGEBALL LEAGUE SOCIETY *p*
288
5695 ABERDEEN ST, VANCOUVER, BC, V5R 4M5
(604) 353-7892   *SIC* 8699
VANCOUVER ENGLISH CENTRE INC *p* 301
250 SMITHE ST, VANCOUVER, BC, V6B 1E7
SIC 8299
VANCOUVER EXTENDED STAY LTD *p* 317
1288 GEORGIA ST W UNIT 101, VANCOUVER, BC, V6E 4R3
(604) 891-6100   *SIC* 7389
VANCOUVER FILM SCHOOL LIMITED *p*
301
198 HASTINGS ST W SUITE 200, VANCOUVER, BC, V6B 1H2
(604) 685-5808   *SIC* 8299
VANCOUVER FIRE PREVENTION SERVICE CO. LTD *p* 259
22131 FRASERWOOD WAY, RICHMOND, BC, V6W 1J5
(604) 232-3478   *SIC* 7382
VANCOUVER FRASER PORT AUTHORITY *p* 310
999 CANADA PL SUITE 100, VANCOUVER, BC, V6C 3T4
(604) 665-9000   *SIC* 4491
VANCOUVER GENERAL HOSPITAL *p* 294
See VANCOUVER COASTAL HEALTH AUTHORITY
VANCOUVER GOLF CLUB *p* 202
771 AUSTIN AVE, COQUITLAM, BC, V3K 3N2
(604) 936-3404   *SIC* 7997
VANCOUVER HOCKEY LIMITED PARTNERSHIP *p*
301
800 GRIFFITHS WAY, VANCOUVER, BC, V6B 6G1
(604) 899-4600   *SIC* 7941
VANCOUVER HONDA *p* 323
See MARINE DRIVE IMPORTED CARS LTD
VANCOUVER ISLAND AUTO SALES LTD *p*
235
2575 BOWEN RD, NANAIMO, BC, V9T 3L4
(250) 751-1168   *SIC* 5511
VANCOUVER ISLAND HEALTH AUTHORITY *p*
204
2696 WINDERMERE ST, CUMBERLAND, BC, V0R 1S0
(250) 331-8505   *SIC* 8011
VANCOUVER ISLAND HEALTH AUTHORITY *p*

212
3045 GIBBINS RD, DUNCAN, BC, V9L 1E5
(250) 737-2030   *SIC* 8011
VANCOUVER ISLAND HEALTH AUTHORITY *p*
243
180 MCCARTER ST SUITE 100, PARKSVILLE, BC, V9P 2H3
(250) 731-1315   *SIC* 8011
VANCOUVER ISLAND HEALTH AUTHORITY *p*
243
GD, PARKSVILLE, BC, V9P 2G2
(250) 947-8230   *SIC* 8011
VANCOUVER ISLAND HEALTH AUTHORITY *p*
252
777 JONES ST, QUALICUM BEACH, BC, V9K 2L1
(250) 947-8220   *SIC* 8011
VANCOUVER ISLAND HEALTH AUTHORITY *p*
333
1952 BAY ST, VICTORIA, BC, V8R 1J8
(250) 519-7700   *SIC* 8011
VANCOUVER ISLAND HEALTH AUTHORITY *p*
333
2400 ARBUTUS RD, VICTORIA, BC, V8N 1V7
(250) 519-5390   *SIC* 8011
VANCOUVER ISLAND HEALTH AUTHORITY *p*
339
1 HOSPITAL WAY, VICTORIA, BC, V8Z 6R5
(250) 370-8355   *SIC* 8011
VANCOUVER ISLAND HEALTH AUTHORITY *p*
340
567 GOLDSTREAM AVE, VICTORIA, BC, V9B 2W4
(250) 370-5790   *SIC* 8051
VANCOUVER ISLAND MOTORSPORT CIRCUIT *p*
211
See 1946328 ONTARIO LIMITED
VANCOUVER ISLAND REGIONAL LIBRARY *p*
235
6250 HAMMOND BAY RD, NANAIMO, BC, V9T 6M9
(250) 758-4697   *SIC* 8231
VANCOUVER ISLAND UNIVERSITY *p* 233
90 FIFTH ST, NANAIMO, BC, V9R 1N1
(250) 753-3245   *SIC* 8221
VANCOUVER LAWN TENNIS AND BADMINTON CLUB *p*
321
1630 15TH AVE W, VANCOUVER, BC, V6J 2K7
(604) 731-9411   *SIC* 7997
VANCOUVER LOGISTICS CENTER *p* 258
See HUDSON'S BAY COMPANY
VANCOUVER MARRIOTT PINNACLE DOWNTOWN *p* 299
See PINNACLE INTERNATIONAL MANAGEMENT INC
VANCOUVER MARRIOTT PINNACLE DOWNTOWN HOTEL *p* 317
1128 HASTINGS ST W, VANCOUVER, BC, V6E 4R5
(604) 684-1128   *SIC* 7389
VANCOUVER PARTYWORKS *p* 278
See VANCOUVER PARTYWORKS INTERACTIVE CO INC
VANCOUVER PARTYWORKS INTERACTIVE CO INC *p*
278
8473 124 ST UNIT 13, SURREY, BC, V3W 9G4
(604) 599-5541   *SIC* 7359
VANCOUVER PILE DRIVING LTD *p* 239
20 BROOKSBANK AVE, NORTH VANCOUVER, BC, V7J 2B8

(604) 986-5911   *SIC* 1629
VANCOUVER PUBLIC LIBRARY FOUNDATION *p*
301
350 GEORGIA ST W, VANCOUVER, BC, V6B 6B1
(604) 331-3603   *SIC* 8231
VANCOUVER QUILTING MANUFACTURING LTD *p*
285
188 VICTORIA DR, VANCOUVER, BC, V5L 4C3
(604) 253-7744   *SIC* 5131
VANCOUVER REAL ESTATE BOARD *p* 320
See REAL ESTATE BOARD OF GREATER VANCOUVER
VANCOUVER SHIPYARDS CO. LTD *p* 242
10 PEMBERTON AVENUE, NORTH VANCOUVER, BC, V7P 2R1
(604) 988-6361   *SIC* 3731
VANCOUVER SYMPHONY ORCHESTRA *p*
301
See VANCOUVER SYMPHONY SOCIETY
VANCOUVER SYMPHONY SOCIETY *p* 301
843 SEYMOUR ST SUITE 500, VANCOUVER, BC, V6B 3L4
(604) 684-9100   *SIC* 7929
VANCOUVER TAXI LTD *p* 286
790 CLARK DR, VANCOUVER, BC, V5L 3J2
(604) 871-1111   *SIC* 4121
VANCOUVER TECHNICAL SECONDARY SCHOOL *p* 286
See BOARD OF EDUCATION OF SCHOOL DISTRICT NO. 39 (VANCOUVER), THE
VANCOUVER TOURS AND TRANSIT LTD *p*
210
8730 RIVER RD, DELTA, BC, V4G 1B5
(604) 940-1707   *SIC* 4142
VANCOUVER WATER ENTERPRISES CANADA CO., LTD *p* 198
44488 SOUTH SUMAS RD SUITE 125, CHILLIWACK, BC, V2R 5M3
(604) 824-7455   *SIC* 5149
VANCOUVER WHITECAPS *p* 301
See VANCOUVER WHITECAPS FC L.P.
VANCOUVER WHITECAPS FC L.P. *p* 301
375 WATER ST SUITE 550, VANCOUVER, BC, V6B 5C6
(604) 669-9283   *SIC* 7941
VANCOUVER, CITY OF *p* 323
5251 OAK ST, VANCOUVER, BC, V6M 4H1
(604) 257-8666   *SIC* 8422
VANCOUVER, CITY OF *p* 342
1950 MARINE DR, WEST VANCOUVER, BC, V7V 1J8
(604) 925-7400   *SIC* 8231
VANDAELE SEEDS LTD *p* 352
GD, MEDORA, MB, R0M 1K0
(204) 665-2384   *SIC* 5191
VANDEGRIFT CANADA ULC *p* 589
63 GALAXY BLVD UNIT 1-2, ETOBICOKE, ON, M9W 5R7
(416) 213-9093   *SIC* 4731
VANDEN BUSSCHE IRRIGATION & EQUIPMENT LIMITED *p*
564
2515 PINEGROVE RD, DELHI, ON, N4B 2E5
(519) 582-2380   *SIC* 5083
VANDENBRINK FARM EQUIPMENT INC *p*
882
7565 QUAKER RD, SPARTA, ON, N0L 2H0
(519) 775-2601   *SIC* 5083
VANDENBURG, ROMEO DRUG COMPANY LTD *p* 917
3003 DANFORTH AVE, TORONTO, ON, M4C 1M9
(416) 694-2131   *SIC* 5912
VANDER ZAAG, H. J. FARM EQUIPMENT LTD *p* 476
5900 COUNTY RD 10 SUITE 2, ALLISTON, ON, L9R 1V2
(705) 435-3226   *SIC* 5083

VANDERGRIFT WHOLESALE FLORIST LTD *p* 600
353 ELIZABETH ST, GUELPH, ON, N1E 2W9
(519) 822-8097 *SIC* 5193
VANDERMAREL TRUCKING LIMITED *p* 590
655 DICKSON DR, FERGUS, ON, N1M 2W7
(519) 787-1563 *SIC* 4213
VANDERMEER GREENHOUSES LTD *p* 351
21065 DUMAINE RD, ILE DES CHENES, MB, R0A 0T0
(204) 878-3420 *SIC* 5193
VANDERMEER NURSERY LTD *p* 475
588 LAKE RIDGE RD S SUITE 1, AJAX, ON, L1Z 1X3
(905) 427-2525 *SIC* 5261
VANDERVAART SALES & SERVICE LTD *p* 565
409 GOVERNMENT ST, DRYDEN, ON, P8N 2P4
(807) 223-4026 *SIC* 5531
VANDERWELL CONTRACTORS (1971) LTD *p* 164
695 WEST MITSUE IND RD, SLAVE LAKE, AB, T0G 2A0
(780) 849-3824 *SIC* 2421
VANDERWESTEN & RUTHERFORD ASSOCIATES, INC *p* 661
7242 COLONEL TALBOT RD, LONDON, ON, N6L 1H8
(519) 652-5047 *SIC* 8711
VANDUSEN BOTANICAL GARDEN *p* 323
See VANCOUVER, CITY OF
VANEE FARM CENTRE INC *p* 141
510 36 ST N, LETHBRIDGE, AB, T1H 5H6
(403) 327-1100 *SIC* 5083
VANEE MOTORS *p* 142
See CENTRAL TRUCK EQUIPMENT INC
VANGA PRODUCTS (PLASTICS) INC *p* 280
2330 190 ST SUITE 102, SURREY, BC, V3Z 3W7
(604) 538-4088 *SIC* 3089
VANGENT CANADA *p* 750
See GENERAL DYNAMICS INFORMATION TECHNOLOGY CANADA, LIMITED
VANGUARD DELIVERS *p* 733
See 1519418 ONTARIO INC
VANGUARD FTSE CANADA INDEX ETF *p* 984
155 WELLINGTON ST W SUITE 3720, TORONTO, ON, M5V 3H1
(888) 293-6728 *SIC* 6722
VANGUARD FTSE DEVELOPED EX NORTH AMERICA INDEX ETF *p* 984
155 WELLINGTON ST W SUITE 3720, TORONTO, ON, M5V 3H1
(888) 293-6728 *SIC* 6726
VANGUARD INVESTMENTS CANADA INC. *p* 984
155 WELLINGTON ST W SUITE 3720, TORONTO, ON, M5V 3H1
(416) 263-7100 *SIC* 6282
VANGUARD NETWORKING INC *p* 890
1217 TALBOT ST, ST THOMAS, ON, N5P 1G8
SIC 5122
VANGUARD STEEL LTD *p* 728
2160 MEADOWPINE BLVD, MISSISSAUGA, ON, L5N 6H6
(905) 821-1100 *SIC* 5051
VANHOUTTE COFFEE SERVICES LTD *p* 202
9 BURBIDGE ST SUITE 120, COQUITLAM, BC, V3K 7B2
(604) 552-5452 *SIC* 7389
VANICO-MARONYX INC *p* 1382
1151 BOUL DE LA PINIERE, TERREBONNE, QC, J6Y 0P3
(450) 471-4447 *SIC* 2434
VANIER CHILDREN'S SERVICES *p* 652
See MADAME VANIER CHILDREN'S SERVICES

VANIER COLLEGE OF GENERAL AND VOCATIONAL EDUCATION *p* 1323
821 AV SAINTE-CROIX, SAINT-LAURENT, QC, H4L 3X9
(514) 744-7500 *SIC* 8222
VANILLA *p* 570
See CANADIAN TEST CASE 174
VANISLE MARINA CO. LTD *p* 268
2320 HARBOUR RD, SIDNEY, BC, V8L 2P6
(250) 656-1138 *SIC* 4493
VANITY FASHIONS LIMITED *p* 448
34 PAYZANT AVE, DARTMOUTH, NS, B3B 1Z6
(902) 468-6763 *SIC* 5094
VANKLEEK HILL LIVESTOCK EXCHANGE LIMITED *p* 1001
1239 RIDGE RD, VANKLEEK HILL, ON, K0B 1R0
(613) 678-3008 *SIC* 5154
VANN, GREG NISSAN INC *p* 539
2386 EAGLE ST N, CAMBRIDGE, ON, N3H 4R7
(519) 650-9200 *SIC* 5511
VANNES ET RACCORDS LAURENTIEN LTEE *p* 1337
2425 RUE HALPERN, SAINT-LAURENT, QC, H4S 1S3
(418) 872-3622 *SIC* 5085
VANRX PHARMASYSTEMS INC *p* 194
3811 NORTH FRASER WAY SUITE 200, BURNABY, BC, V5J 5J2
(604) 453-8660 *SIC* 3559
VANSHAW ENTERPRISES LTD *p* 147
1051 ROSS GLEN DR SE, MEDICINE HAT, AB, T1B 3T8
(403) 504-4584 *SIC* 7993
VANTAGE BUILDERS LTD *p* 170
4723 49 AVE, VEGREVILLE, AB, T9C 1L1
(780) 632-3422 *SIC* 1542
VANTAGE ENDOSCOPY INC *p* 638
20 STECKLE PL UNIT 16, KITCHENER, ON, N2E 2C3
(866) 677-4121 *SIC* 5047
VANTAGE FOODS (MB) INC *p* 367
41 PAQUIN RD, WINNIPEG, MB, R2J 3V9
(204) 667-9903 *SIC* 2011
VANTAGE FOODS INC *p* 32
4000 4 ST SE SUITE 225, CALGARY, AB, T2G 2W3
(403) 215-2820 *SIC* 2011
VANTAGE FOODS INC *p* 198
8200 BRANNICK PL, CHILLIWACK, BC, V2R 0E9
(604) 795-4774 *SIC* 2011
VANTAGE FOODS INC *p* 367
41 PAQUIN RD, WINNIPEG, MB, R2J 3V9
(204) 667-9903 *SIC* 2011
VANTAGE REALTY LTD *p* 604
214 SPEEDVALE AVE W SUITE 1, GUELPH, ON, N1H 1C4
(519) 822-7842 *SIC* 6531
VANTAGEONE FINANCIAL CORP *p* 332
3108 33 AVE, VERNON, BC, V1T 2N7
(250) 260-4513 *SIC* 6531
VANTREIGHT FARMS *p* 267
8277 CENTRAL SAANICH RD, SAANICHTON, BC, V8M 1T7
(250) 652-7777 *SIC* 5191
VANZUYLEN'S ALIGNMENT SERVICE LIMITED *p* 630
213 CONCESSION ST, KINGSTON, ON, K7K 2B6
(613) 548-7444 *SIC* 5531
VAP HOLDINGS L.P. *p* 32
4211 13A ST SE, CALGARY, AB, T2G 3J6
(403) 299-0844 *SIC* 2011
VAPAC *p* 1050
See SOLUTIONS D'AIR NORTEK QUEBEC, INC
VAPERMA INC *p* 1352
2111 4E RUE BUREAU 101, SAINT-ROMUALD, QC, G6W 5M6

VAPEUR EXPRESS, LE *p* 1225
See 8268533 CANADA INC
VAPOR RAIL *p* 1324
See WABTEC CANADA INC
VAPOR RAIL DIV OF *p* 1337
See WABTEC CANADA INC
VARALEX *p* 1286
See PRELCO INC
VARCO CANADA ULC *p* 111
7127 56 AVE NW, EDMONTON, AB, T6B 3L2
(780) 665-0200 *SIC* 7353
VARCO CANADA ULC *p* 140
6621 45 ST, LEDUC, AB, T9E 7E3
(780) 986-6063 *SIC* 7353
VARCO INDUSTRIAL SALES *p* 648
See 680061 ONTARIO LIMITED
VARD MARINE INC *p* 287
2930 VIRTUAL WAY SUITE 180, VANCOUVER, BC, V5M 0A5
(604) 216-3360 *SIC* 8711
VARI-FORM MANUFACTURING INC *p* 897
233 LOTHIAN AVE, STRATHROY, ON, N7G 4J1
(519) 245-5200 *SIC* 3469
VARIETES CHARRON & LECLERC, SENC *p* 1125
6240 RUE SALABERRY, LAC-MEGANTIC, QC, G6B 1H8
(819) 583-2123 *SIC* 5912
VARIETES LNJF INC *p* 1123
84 5E AV E BUREAU 73, LA SARRE, QC, J9Z 1K9
(819) 333-5458 *SIC* 6519
VARIETES PIERRE PRUD'HOMME INC, LES *p* 1320
801 RUE PRICE, SAINT-JEROME, QC, J7Y 4E2
(450) 438-2977 *SIC* 5099
VARIETY FOOD FAIR *p* 706
See RABBA, J. COMPANY LIMITED, THE
VARIPERM (CANADA) LIMITED *p* 10
3424 26 ST NE SUITE 10, CALGARY, AB, T1Y 4T7
(403) 250-7263 *SIC* 5082
VARISYSTEMS CORP *p* 13
5304 HUBALTA RD SE, CALGARY, AB, T2B 1T6
(403) 272-0318 *SIC* 3679
VARITRON *p* 1308
See GROUPE VARITRON INC
VARSHNEY CAPITAL CORPORATION *p* 310
925 GEORGIA ST W SUITE 1304, VANCOUVER, BC, V6C 3L2
(604) 684-2181 *SIC* 6282
VARSITY CHRYSLER JEEP DODGE *p* 40
See VARSITY CHRYSLER JEEP DODGE RAM LTD
VARSITY CHRYSLER JEEP DODGE RAM LTD *p* 40
665 GODDARD AVE NE, CALGARY, AB, T2K 6K1
(403) 730-4000 *SIC* 5511
VARSITY PLYMOUTH CHRYSLER (1994) LTD *p* 40
4914 6 ST NE, CALGARY, AB, T2K 4W5
(403) 250-5541 *SIC* 5521
VARSTEEL LTD *p* 141
2900 5 AVE N, LETHBRIDGE, AB, T1H 6K3
(403) 329-0233 *SIC* 5051
VARSTEEL LTD *p* 143
220 4 ST S SUITE 330, LETHBRIDGE, AB, T1J 4J7
(403) 320-1953 *SIC* 5051
VARTEGEZ SIMONIAN PHARMACY LTD *p* 728
6040 GLEN ERIN DR SUITE 1, MISSISSAUGA, ON, L5N 3M4
(905) 821-8020 *SIC* 5912
VARZARI TRADING LTD *p* 143
220 4 ST S UNIT 330, LETHBRIDGE, AB, T1J 4J7

(403) 320-1953 *SIC* 5051
VAS *p* 600
See 7093373 CANADA INC
VAST-AUTO DISTRIBUTION ATLANTIC LTD *p* 402
50 WHITING RD, FREDERICTON, NB, E3B 5V5
(506) 453-1600 *SIC* 5015
VAST-AUTO DISTRIBUTION LTEE *p* 1346
4840 BOUL DES GRANDES-PRAIRIES, SAINT-LEONARD, QC, H1R 1A1
(514) 955-3188 *SIC* 5013
VAST-AUTO DISTRIBUTION ONTARIO LTD *p* 507
10 DRIVER RD, BRAMPTON, ON, L6T 5V2
(905) 595-2886 *SIC* 5013
VASTLON INVESTMENTS INC *p* 560
291 EDGELEY BLVD, CONCORD, ON, L4K 3Z4
(905) 660-9900 *SIC* 6712
VAUDREUIL HONDA INC *p* 1395
9 BOUL DE LA CITE-DES-JEUNES, VAUDREUIL-DORION, QC, J7V 0N3
(450) 424-2500 *SIC* 5511
VAUDREUIL VOLKSWAGEN *p* 1394
See 9207-8922 QUEBEC INC
VAUGHAN AUTOMOTIVE SUPPLIES *p* 555
See MAR DEVELOPMENTS INC
VAUGHAN MASONRY INC *p* 560
111 ORTONA CRT, CONCORD, ON, L4K 3M3
(905) 669-6825 *SIC* 1741
VAUGHAN METAL POLISHING LIMITED *p* 794
206 MILVAN DR, NORTH YORK, ON, M9L 1Z9
(416) 743-7500 *SIC* 3471
VAUGHAN PAVING LTD *p* 560
220 BASALTIC RD, CONCORD, ON, L4K 1G6
(905) 669-9579 *SIC* 1611
VAUGHAN PRESS CENTRE *p* 1034
See TORONTO STAR NEWSPAPERS LIMITED
VAUGHAN PUBLIC LIBRARIES *p* 663
2191 MAJOR MACKENZIE DR, MAPLE, ON, L4A 4W2
(905) 653-7323 *SIC* 8231
VAUGHAN SECONDARY SCHOOL *p* 906
See YORK REGION DISTRICT SCHOOL BOARD
VAUGHN CUSTOM SPORTS CANADA LTD *p* 651
455 HIGHBURY AVE N, LONDON, ON, N5W 5K7
(519) 453-4229 *SIC* 3949
VAUGHN SPORTS *p* 651
See VAUGHN CUSTOM SPORTS CANADA LTD
VAUGHN YARD, THE *p* 642
See PARSEC INTERMODAL OF CANADA LIMITED
VAUGHNE ASSURANCE LIMITED *p* 471
379 MAIN ST, YARMOUTH, NS, B5A 1G1
(902) 742-2000 *SIC* 6411
VAULT CREDIT CORPORATION *p* 916
41 SCARSDALE RD SUITE 5, TORONTO, ON, M3B 2R2
(416) 499-8466 *SIC* 8741
VAULT PIPELINES LTD *p* 129
142 DICKINS DR BAY 4, FORT MCMURRAY, AB, T9K 1X4
(587) 537-5520 *SIC* 4922
VAUNTEK HOLDINGS INC. *p* 906
8707 DUFFERIN ST SUITE 10, THORNHILL, ON, L4J 0A6
SIC 6712
VAW SYSTEMS LTD *p* 373
1300 INKSTER BLVD, WINNIPEG, MB, R2X 1P5
(204) 697-7770 *SIC* 3625
VBALLS TARGET SYSTEMS INC *p* 387
51 ALLARD AVE, WINNIPEG, MB, R3K 0S8
SIC 3949

VBC *p 190*
See *CH2M HILL CANADA LIMITED*

VBCE *p 310*
See *VANCOUVER BULLION AND CURRENCY EXCHANGE LTD*

VCC CARGO SERVICE INC *p 729*
6500 SILVER DART DR, MISSISSAUGA, ON, L5P 1B1
(905) 676-4047   *SIC 4512*

VCC ENTREPRENEUR GENERAL INC *p 1401*
42 RTE MAQUATUA, WEMINDJI, QC, J0M 1L0
(819) 978-3335   *SIC 1521*

VCC GENERAL CONTRACTOR *p 1401*
See *VCC ENTREPRENEUR GENERAL INC*

VCL CONSTRUCTION *p 625*
See *1514505 ONTARIO INC*

VCS INVESTIGATION INC *p 1129*
10500 CH DE LA COTE-DE-LIESSE BUREAU 200, LACHINE, QC, H8T 1A4
(514) 737-1911   *SIC 7389*

VCS VALLEY CUT STEEL CORP *p 282*
9515 190 ST SUITE 4, SURREY, BC, V4N 3S1
(604) 513-8866   *SIC 5051*

VDI *p 854*
See *VISUAL DEFENCE INC*

VDI HEALTHCARE LOGISTICS *p 502*
See *DSV SOLUTIONS INC*

VEA GROUP INC, THE *p 75*
150 CROWFOOT CRES NW SUITE 105, CALGARY, AB, T3G 3T2
(403) 547-7727   *SIC 8741*

VECIMA NETWORKS INC *p 339*
771 VANALMAN AVE SUITE 201, VICTORIA, BC, V8Z 3B8
(250) 881-1982   *SIC 3663*

VECIMA NETWORKS INC *p 1432*
150 CARDINAL PL, SASKATOON, SK, S7L 6H7
(306) 955-7075   *SIC 8731*

VECO CANADA *p 14*
See *CH2M HILL ENERGY CANADA LTD*

VECTOR AEROSPACE ENGINE SERVICES-ATLANTIC INC *p 1043*
800 AEROSPACE BLVD, SUMMERSIDE, PE, C1N 4P6
(902) 436-1333   *SIC 4581*

VECTOR COMMUNICATIONS LTD *p 133*
11213 97 AVE, GRANDE PRAIRIE, AB, T8V 5N5
(780) 532-2555   *SIC 5999*

VECTOR CONSTRUCTION LTD *p 393*
474 DOVERCOURT DR, WINNIPEG, MB, R3Y 1G4
(204) 489-6300   *SIC 1771*

VECTOR ELECTRIC AND CONTROLS *p 111*
5344 36 ST NW, EDMONTON, AB, T6B 3P3
(780) 469-7900   *SIC 1731*

VECTOR ENERGY INC *p 62*
855 2 ST SW SUITE 1760, CALGARY, AB, T2P 4J7
(403) 265-9500   *SIC 4924*

VECTOR GROUP, THE *p 111*
See *VECTOR ELECTRIC AND CONTROLS*

VECTOR MANAGEMENT LTD *p 393*
474 DOVERCOURT DR, WINNIPEG, MB, R3Y 1G4
(204) 489-6300   *SIC 1611*

VEDDER STEEL LTD *p 225*
9663 199A ST UNIT 4, LANGLEY, BC, V1M 2X7
(604) 882-0035   *SIC 1542*

VEDDER TRANSPORT LTD *p 175*
400 RIVERSIDE RD, ABBOTSFORD, BC, V2S 7M4
(604) 853-3341   *SIC 4213*

VEG-PAK PRODUCE LIMITED *p 573*
165 THE QUEENSWAY RM 249, ETOBICOKE, ON, M8Y 1H8
(416) 259-4686   *SIC 5148*

VEGA *p 189*
See *SEQUEL NATURALS ULC*

VEGETARIEN TROIS RIVIERES INC *p 1385*
3960 BOUL DES FORGES, TROIS-RIVIERES, QC, G8Y 1V7
(819) 372-9730   *SIC 5431*

VEGEWAX CANDLEWORX LTD *p 560*
300 NORTH RIVERMEDE RD, CONCORD, ON, L4K 3N6
(905) 760-7944   *SIC 2844*

VEGFRESH INC *p 794*
1290 ORMONT DR, NORTH YORK, ON, M9L 2V4
(416) 667-0518   *SIC 5461*

VEGPRO INTERNATIONAL INC *p 1376*
147 RANG SAINT-PAUL, SHERRINGTON, QC, J0L 2N0
(450) 454-7712   *SIC 5148*

VEGREVILLE & DISTRICT CO-OP LTD *p 170*
4914 51 AVE GD, VEGREVILLE, AB, T9C 1V5
(780) 632-2884   *SIC 5411*

VEGREVILLE FORD SALES & SERVICE INC *p 170*
6106 50 AVE, VEGREVILLE, AB, T9C 1N6
(780) 632-2060   *SIC 5511*

VEHCOM MANUFACTURING *p 603*
See *LINAMAR CORPORATION*

VEHICULES ELECTRIQUES SIMON ANDRE *p 1384*
See *ANDRE SIMON INC*

VELAN INC *p 1111*
1010 RUE COWIE, GRANBY, QC, J2J 1E7
(450) 378-2305   *SIC 3494*

VELAN INC *p 1324*
2125 RUE WARD, SAINT-LAURENT, QC, H4M 1T6
(514) 748-7743   *SIC 3494*

VELAN INC *p 1342*
550 RUE MCARTHUR, SAINT-LAURENT, QC, H4T 1X8
(514) 748-7743   *SIC 3494*

VELAN INC *p 1342*
7007 CH DE LA COTE-DE-LIESSE, SAINT-LAURENT, QC, H4T 1G2
(514) 748-7743   *SIC 3494*

VELANOFF, JACK HOLDINGS LIMITED *p 560*
3200 RUTHERFORD RD SUITE 653, CONCORD, ON, L4K 5R3
(905) 303-9148   *SIC 5251*

VELCAN FOREST PRODUCTS INC *p 814*
1240 SKAE DR, OSHAWA, ON, L1J 7A1
(905) 571-2477   *SIC 5031*

VELCRO CANADA INC *p 507*
114 EAST DR, BRAMPTON, ON, L6T 1C1
(905) 791-1630   *SIC 3965*

VELLA, PAUL SHOES (MISSISSAUGA) LIMITED *p 785*
365 FLINT RD UNIT 1, NORTH YORK, ON, M3J 2J2
(416) 667-8929   *SIC 5661*

VELLNER LEISURE PRODUCTS (1980) LTD *p 157*
1890 49 AVE, RED DEER, AB, T4R 2N7
(403) 343-1464   *SIC 5561*

VELOCITY EXPRESS CANADA LTD *p 111*
4424 55 AVE NW, EDMONTON, AB, T6B 3S2
(780) 465-3777   *SIC 7389*

VELOCITY FOREIGN EXCHANGE SERVICES *p 941*
See *VELOCITY TRADE HOLDINGS LTD*

VELOCITY TRADE CANADA LTD. *p 941*
100 YONGE ST UNIT 1800, TORONTO, ON, M5C 2W1
(416) 855-2800   *SIC 6211*

VELOCITY TRADE HOLDINGS LTD *p 941*
100 YONGE ST SUITE 1800, TORONTO, ON, M5C 2W1
(416) 855-2800   *SIC 6099*

VELOCITYTRADE *p 941*
See *VELOCITY TRADE CANADA LTD.*

VELTRI HOWARD DIV *p 1022*
See *VENTRA GROUP CO*

VELUX CANADA INC *p 801*
2740 SHERWOOD HEIGHTS DR, OAKVILLE, ON, L6J 7V5
(905) 829-0280   *SIC 5031*

VEMCO *p 440*
See *INNOVASEA MARINE SYSTEMS CANADA INC*

VEMCO, DIV OF *p 440*
See *AMIRIX SYSTEMS INC*

VEN-REZ PRODUCTS LIMITED *p 466*
380 SANDY POINT RD, SHELBURNE, NS, B0T 1W0
(902) 875-3178   *SIC 2531*

VENABLES MACHINE WORKS LTD *p 1430*
502 50TH ST E, SASKATOON, SK, S7K 6L9
(306) 931-7100   *SIC 1791*

VENATOR ELECTRONICS SALES & SERVICE LTD *p 701*
4500 DIXIE RD UNIT 10, MISSISSAUGA, ON, L4W 1V7
SIC 5065

VENDASTA *p 1430*
See *VENDASTA TECHNOLOGIES INC*

VENDASTA TECHNOLOGIES INC *p 1430*
220 3RD AVE S SUITE 405, SASKATOON, SK, S7K 1M1
(306) 955-5512   *SIC 7372*

VENDEX REALTY INC *p 512*
4 MCLAUGHLIN RD S UNIT 10, BRAMPTON, ON, L6Y 3B2
(905) 452-7272   *SIC 6531*

VENDING PRODUCTS OF CANADA LIMITED *p 589*
108 WOODBINE DOWNS BLVD UNIT 1, ETOBICOKE, ON, M9W 5S6
(416) 213-8363   *SIC 5145*

VENDOME TELE *p 1216*
See *PRODUCTIONS VENDOME II INC, LES*

VENETOR CRANE LTD *p 893*
45 ORIOLE AVE, STONEY CREEK, ON, L8E 5C4
(905) 643-7943   *SIC 7353*

VENGROWTH ASSET MANAGEMENT INC *p 958*
105 ADELAIDE ST W SUITE 1000, TORONTO, ON, M5H 1P9
(416) 971-6656   *SIC 8741*

VENMAR VENTILATION ULC *p 1100*
550 BOUL LEMIRE, DRUMMONDVILLE, QC, J2C 7W9
(819) 477-6226   *SIC 3634*

VENOM ENERGY *p 173*
3749 30 ST, WHITECOURT, AB, T7S 0E4
(780) 778-2440   *SIC 1389*

VENSHORE MECHANICAL LTD *p 909*
1019 NORTHERN AVE, THUNDER BAY, ON, P7C 5L6
(807) 623-6414   *SIC 1711*

VENT DE L'EST INC *p 1149*
711 BOUL PERRON, MARIA, QC, G0C 1Y0
(418) 759-3054   *SIC 3621*

VENTA CARE CENTRE LTD *p 84*
13525 102 ST NW, EDMONTON, AB, T5E 4K3
(780) 476-6633   *SIC 8051*

VENTANA CONSTRUCTION CORPORATION *p 187*
3875 HENNING DR SUITE 100, BURNABY, BC, V5C 6N5
(604) 291-9000   *SIC 1542*

VENTE AU DETAIL BESTSELLER CANADA INC *p 1181*
225A RUE DE LIEGE O, MONTREAL, QC, H2P 1H4
(514) 381-4392   *SIC 5136*

VENTERRA REALTY (CANADA) INC *p 854*

VENTES ALLAJOY LTEE *p 1051*
8301 RUE J.-RENE-OUIMET, ANJOU, QC, H1J 2H7
(514) 374-9010   *SIC 2782*

VENTES ET SERVICE CUMMINS *p 1250*
See *CUMMINS EST DU CANADA SEC*

VENTES FORD BRUNELLE LTEE, LES *p 1301*
500 RUE DUBOIS, SAINT-EUSTACHE, QC, J7P 4W9
(450) 491-1110   *SIC 5511*

VENTES FORD ELITE (1978) INC *p 1320*
2171 BOUL DU CURE-LABELLE, SAINT-JEROME, QC, J7Y 1T1
(450) 436-3142   *SIC 5511*

VENTES INTERNATIONALES D'ANIMAUX - TRUDEAU INC *p 1359*
726 MONT?E SAINTE-JULIE, SAINTE-JULIE, QC, J3E 1W9
(450) 649-1122   *SIC 5154*

VENTES LIFE TIME, LES *p 1221*
See *BESCO BEAUTE (1980) LTEE*

VENTES RUDOLPH 2000 INC, LES *p 1173*
4625 RUE D'IBERVILLE, MONTREAL, QC, H2H 2L9
(514) 596-1998   *SIC 5149*

VENTILABEC DUNOR *p 1357*
See *VENTILABEC INC*

VENTILABEC INC *p 1357*
1955 BOUL SAINT-ELZEAR O, SAINTE-DOROTHEE, QC, H7L 3N7
(450) 686-7062   *SIC 1711*

VENTILABEC INC *p 1357*
1955 BOUL SAINT-ELZEAR O, SAINTE-DOROTHEE, QC, H7L 3N7
(514) 745-0230   *SIC 7623*

VENTILATION G.R. *p 1363*
See *VENTILATION G.R. INC*

VENTILATION G.R. INC *p 1363*
1645 BOUL SAINT-ELZEAR O, SAINTE-ROSE, QC, H7L 3N6
(450) 688-9832   *SIC 1711*

VENTILATION MAXIMUM LTEE *p 1163*
9229 RUE PIERRE-BONNE, MONTREAL, QC, H1E 7J6
(514) 648-8011   *SIC 3564*

VENTILEX INC *p 1302*
348 BOUL INDUSTRIEL, SAINT-EUSTACHE, QC, J7R 5R4
(450) 473-9843   *SIC 1711*

VENTRA GROUP CO *p 498*
75 REAGEN'S INDUSTRIAL PKY, BRADFORD, ON, L3Z 0Z9
(705) 778-7900   *SIC 3465*

VENTRA GROUP CO *p 642*
675 TRILLIUM DR, KITCHENER, ON, N2R 1G6
(519) 895-0290   *SIC 3714*

VENTRA GROUP CO *p 902*
538 BLANCHARD PK, TECUMSEH, ON, N8N 2L9
(519) 727-3931   *SIC 3714*

VENTRA GROUP CO *p 998*
65 INDUSTRIAL RD, TOTTENHAM, ON, L0G 1W0
(905) 936-4245   *SIC 3465*

VENTRA GROUP CO *p 1015*
200 MONTECORTE ST, WHITBY, ON, L1N 9V8
SIC 3714

VENTRA GROUP CO *p 1019*
2800 KEW DR, WINDSOR, ON, N8T 3C6
(519) 944-1102   *SIC 3089*

VENTRA GROUP CO *p 1022*
1425 HOWARD AVE, WINDSOR, ON, N8X 5C9
(519) 258-3509   *SIC 3465*

VENTRA OSHAWA SPD, DIV OF *p 1015*
See *VENTRA GROUP CO*

VENTRA PLASTIC KITCHENER *p 642*
See *VENTRA GROUP CO*

VENTRA PLASTICS DIVISIONS p 1019
See VENTRA GROUP CO
VENTRA PLASTICS MISSISSAUGA SPD p 902
See VENTRA GROUP CO
VENTRA PLASTICS PETERBOROUGH p 840
See FLEX-N-GATE CANADA COMPANY
VENTREX VENDING SERVICES INC p 816
1550 LIVERPOOL CRT UNIT 6, OTTAWA, ON, K1B 4L2
(613) 747-0455   SIC 5044
VENTURE COMMUNICATIONS LTD p 42
2540 KENSINGTON RD NW, CALGARY, AB, T2N 3S3
(403) 265-4659   SIC 7311
VENTURE STEEL INC p 589
60 DISCO RD, ETOBICOKE, ON, M9W 1L8
(416) 798-9396   SIC 5051
VENTUREKIDS TECH ORGANIZATION p 971
30 WELLINGTON ST W 5TH FL, TORONTO, ON, M5L 1E2
(416) 985-6839   SIC 8399
VENTURER ELECTRONICS INC p 676
725 DENISON ST, MARKHAM, ON, L3R 1B8
(905) 477-7878   SIC 5065
VENTURES ENTERPRISES LTD p 454
1525 BIRMINGHAM ST, HALIFAX, NS, B3J 2J6
(902) 429-5680   SIC 6512
VENTURES WEST MANAGEMENT INC p 310
999 HASTINGS ST W SUITE 400, VANCOUVER, BC, V6C 2W2
SIC 6799
VENTURES WEST TRANSPORT INC p 130
182 STURGEON WAY, FORT SASKATCHEWAN, AB, T8L 2N9
(780) 449-5542   SIC 4213
VENTURI-SCHULZE LTD p 198
4235 VINEYARD RD, COBBLE HILL, BC, V0R 1L5
(250) 743-5630   SIC 5182
VENTURI-SCHULZE VINEYARDS p 198
See VENTURI-SCHULZE LTD
VENTURIS CAPITAL CORPORATION p 282
19433 96 AVE UNIT 102, SURREY, BC, V4N 4C4
(604) 607-8000   SIC 7359
VENTYX, DIV p 259
See ABB INC
VEOLIA EAU TECHNOLOGIES CANADA INC p 1337
3901 RUE SARTELON, SAINT-LAURENT, QC, H4S 2A6
(514) 334-7230   SIC 1629
VEOLIA EAU TECHNOLOGIES CANADA INC p 1337
4105 RUE SARTELON, SAINT-LAURENT, QC, H4S 2B3
(514) 334-7230   SIC 1629
VEOLIA ES CANADA SERVICES INDUSTRIELS INC p 595
4140 BELGREEN DR, GLOUCESTER, ON, K1G 3N2
(613) 739-1150   SIC 7389
VEOLIA ES CANADA SERVICES INDUSTRIELS INC p 1248
1705 3E AV, POINTE-AUX-TREMBLES, QC, H1B 5M9
(514) 645-1621   SIC 4953
VEOLIA ES CANADA SERVICES INDUSTRIELS INC p 1310
7950 AV PION, SAINT-HYACINTHE, QC, J2R 1R9
(450) 796-6060   SIC 4953
VEOLIA SERVICE A L'ENVIRONNEMENT p 1139
See VEOLIA SERVICE A

L'ENVIRONNEMENT
VEOLIA SERVICE A L'ENVIRONNEMENT p 1139
2800 RUE DE L'ETCHEMIN, LEVIS, QC, G6W 7X6
(418) 833-6840   SIC 8748
VEOLIA TRANSDEV CANADA p 1209
See TRANSDEV CANADA INC
VEOLIA WATER CANADA, INC p 757
150 PONY DR UNIT 2, NEWMARKET, ON, L3Y 7B6
(905) 868-9683   SIC 4941
VEONEER CANADA, INC p 676
7455 BIRCHMOUNT RD, MARKHAM, ON, L3R 5C2
(905) 475-4150   SIC 3679
VERANOVA PROPERTIES LIMITED p 768
505 CONSUMERS RD SUITE 812, NORTH YORK, ON, M2J 4V8
(416) 701-9000   SIC 6531
VERAX SOLUTIONS CORPORATION p 958
120 ADELAIDE ST W SUITE 1501, TORONTO, ON, M5H 1T1
(416) 363-3030   SIC 8748
VERBOM INC p 1392
5066 RTE 222, VALCOURT, QC, J0E 2L0
(450) 532-3672   SIC 5051
VERBOM INC p 1392
5066 RTE 222, VALCOURT, QC, J0E 2L0
(819) 566-4200   SIC 3365
VERCHERES AUTO INC p 1145
3551 CH DE CHAMBLY, LONGUEUIL, QC, J4L 4E2
(450) 679-4710   SIC 5511
VERDANT VALLEY FARMING CO LTD p 82
GD, DRUMHELLER, AB, T0J 0Y0
(403) 823-4388   SIC 0191
VEREQUEST INCORPORATED p 984
370 QUEENS QUAY W SUITE 301, TORONTO, ON, M5V 3J3
(416) 362-6777   SIC 8742
VERESEN MIDSTREAM LIMITED PARTNERSHIP p 62
222 3 AVE SW SUITE 900, CALGARY, AB, T2P 0B4
(403) 296-0140   SIC 4922
VERGE INSURANCE BROKERS LIMITED p 886
131 ONTARIO ST, ST CATHARINES, ON, L2R 5J9
(905) 688-9170   SIC 6411
VERGER BELLIVEAU ORCHARD LTD p 405
1209 RUE PRINCIPALE, MEMRAMCOOK, NB, E4K 2S6
(506) 758-0295   SIC 5148
VERGER DU PERE DE LA FRAISE, LE p 1350
1740 RUE PRINCIPALE E, SAINT-PAUL-D'ABBOTSFORD, QC, J0E 1A0
(450) 379-5271   SIC 5148
VERGER LACROIX INC p 1322
649 CH PRINCIPAL, SAINT-JOSEPH-DU-LAC, QC, J0N 1M0
(450) 623-4888   SIC 5148
VERGERS ENDERLE p 1113
See POMMES ENDERLE INC, LES
VERGERS LEAHY INC p 1102
1772 RTE 209, FRANKLIN, QC, J0S 1E0
(450) 827-2544   SIC 0175
VERGERS LEAHY, LES p 1102
See VERGERS LEAHY INC
VERGERS PAUL JODOIN INC p 1315
3333 RANG DU CORDON, SAINT-JEAN-BAPTISTE, QC, J0L 2B0
(450) 467-4744   SIC 0175
VERI-CHEQUE LTD p 905
8500 LESLIE ST SUITE 500, THORNHILL, ON, L3T 7M8
(905) 709-0928   SIC 6351
VERI-CREDIT p 905
See VERI-CHEQUE LTD
VERICO CML CANADIAN MORTGAGE

LENDER INC p 26
2316 6 ST NE, CALGARY, AB, T2E 3Z1
(866) 265-7988   SIC 6211
VERICO ONE-LINK MORTGAGE AND FINANCIAL p 393
See 4549440 MANITOBA LTD
VERICO SELECT MORTGAGE p 339
See SELECT MORTGAGE CORP
VERIDAY INC p 701
5520 EXPLORER DR UNIT 400, MISSISSAUGA, ON, L4W 5L1
(905) 273-4399   SIC 8743
VERIDIAN CONNECTIONS INC p 475
55 TAUNTON RD E, AJAX, ON, L1T 3V3
(905) 427-9870   SIC 4911
VERIDIAN CORPORATION p 475
55 TAUNTON RD E, AJAX, ON, L1T 3V3
(905) 427-9870   SIC 4911
VERINT VIDEO SOLUTIONS p 1362
See SYSTEMES VERINT CANADA, INC
VERIS GOLD CORP p 301
688 HASTINGS ST W SUITE 900, VANCOUVER, BC, V6B 1P1
(604) 688-9427   SIC 1081
VERITAS COMMUNICATIONS INC p 984
370 KING ST W SUITE 800, TORONTO, ON, M5V 1J9
(416) 482-2248   SIC 8748
VERITAS TOOLS INC p 832
1090 MORRISON DR, OTTAWA, ON, K2H 1C2
(613) 596-1922   SIC 3423
VERITIV CANADA, INC p 26
6040 11 ST NE, CALGARY, AB, T2E 9B1
(403) 250-5416   SIC 5111
VERITIV CANADA, INC p 207
1425 DERWENT WAY, DELTA, BC, V3M 6N3
(604) 520-7500   SIC 5199
VERITIV CANADA, INC p 743
1475 COURTNEYPARK DR E, MISSISSAUGA, ON, L5T 2R1
(905) 795-7400   SIC 5113
VERITIV CANADA, INC p 1342
4300 RUE HICKMORE, SAINT-LAURENT, QC, H4T 1K2
(514) 367-3111   SIC 5111
VERIZON BUSINESS p 941
See VERIZON CANADA LTD
VERIZON CANADA LTD p 941
1 ADELAIDE ST E SUITE 2400, TORONTO, ON, M5C 2V9
(416) 933-6500   SIC 4899
VERLY CONSTRUCTION GROUP INC p 701
1650 SISMET RD, MISSISSAUGA, ON, L4W 1R4
(905) 212-9420   SIC 1542
VERMEER CANADA INC p 893
1100 SOUTH SERVICE RD SUITE 423, STONEY CREEK, ON, L8E 0C5
(289) 765-5260   SIC 5084
VERMEER GREENHOUSES (WELLAND) INC p 1012
684 SOUTH PELHAM RD, WELLAND, ON, L3C 3C8
(905) 735-5744   SIC 5992
VERMEER SALES & SERVICES p 893
See VERMEER CANADA INC
VERMEER'S GARDEN CENTRE & FLOWER SHOP p 1012
See VERMEER GREENHOUSES (WELLAND) INC
VERMILION ENERGY INC p 62
520 3RD AVE SW SUITE 3500, CALGARY, AB, T2P 0R3
(403) 269-4884   SIC 1382
VERMILION HEALTH CARE CENTRE p 170
See ALBERTA HEALTH SERVICES
VERMILLION FARMS LTD p 356
GD, SANFORD, MB, R0G 2J0
(204) 736-2787   SIC 0191
VERMONT SQUARE p 972
See 601092 ONTARIO LIMITED

VERNON CHRYSLER DODGE LTD p 332
4607 27 ST, VERNON, BC, V1T 4Y8
(250) 545-2261   SIC 5511
VERNON D'EON FISHING SUPPLIES LTD p 462
373 ROUTE 335, MIDDLE WEST PUBNICO, NS, B0W 2M0
(902) 762-2217   SIC 5941
VERNON DODGE JEEP p 332
See VERNON CHRYSLER DODGE LTD
VERNON HYUNDAI p 331
See 0127494 B.C. LTD
VERNON INSURANCE SERVICES INC p 332
3118 32 AVE, VERNON, BC, V1T 2L9
(250) 549-3074   SIC 6411
VERNON INTERIOR HEALTH p 331
See NORTH OKANAGAN REGIONAL HEALTH BOARD
VERNON NISSAN p 331
See 0809021 B.C. LTD
VERNON SECONDARY SCHOOL p 332
See SCHOOL DISTRICT NO 22 (VERNON)
VERO MODA p 1179
See 9292-1394 QUEBEC INC
VERRE SELECT INC p 1381
3816 RUE GEORGES-CORBEIL, TERREBONNE, QC, J6X 4J4
(450) 968-0112   SIC 3211
VERREAULT INC p 1192
1080 COTE DU BEAVER HALL BUREAU 800, MONTREAL, QC, H2Z 1S8
(514) 845-4104   SIC 1541
VERREAULT INC p 1237
1200 BOUL SAINT-MARTIN O BUREAU 300, MONTREAL, QC, H7S 2E4
(514) 845-4104   SIC 1542
VERREAULT NAVIGATION INC p 1135
108 RUE DU COLLEGE, LES MECHINS, QC, G0J 1T0
(418) 729-3733   SIC 3732
VERRERIE WALKER LTEE, LA p 1051
9551 BOUL RAY-LAWSON, ANJOU, QC, H1J 1L5
(514) 352-3030   SIC 3231
VERSA CARE p 917
See REVERA LONG TERM CARE INC
VERSA CARE CENTER p 884
See REVERA LONG TERM CARE INC
VERSA FITTINGS INC p 744
290 COURTNEYPARK DR E, MISSISSAUGA, ON, L5T 2S5
(905) 564-2600   SIC 5074
VERSA SYSTEMS LTD p 769
200 YORKLAND BLVD SUITE 200, NORTH YORK, ON, M2J 5C1
(416) 493-1833   SIC 7372
VERSA-CARE CENTRE HAMILTON p 612
See REVERA LONG TERM CARE INC
VERSA-CARE CENTRE OF BRANTFORD p 515
See REVERA LONG TERM CARE INC
VERSA-CARE HALLOWELL HOUSE p 845
See REVERA LONG TERM CARE INC
VERSABANK p 655
140 FULLARTON ST SUITE 2002, LONDON, ON, N6A 5P2
(519) 645-1919   SIC 6021
VERSACOLD CANADA CORPORATION p 286
2115 COMMISSIONER ST SUITE 1, VANCOUVER, BC, V5L 1A6
(604) 255-4656   SIC 4222
VERSACOLD GROUP LIMITED PARTNERSHIP p 19
5600 76 AVE SE, CALGARY, AB, T2C 4N4
(403) 216-5600   SIC 4222
VERSACOLD GROUP LIMITED PARTNERSHIP p 207
1188 DERWENT WAY, DELTA, BC, V3M 5R1
(604) 216-6238   SIC 4222

VERSACOLD GROUP LIMITED PARTNER-SHIP *p* 507
107 WALKER DR, BRAMPTON, ON, L6T 5K5
(905) 793-2653   *SIC* 4222

VERSACOLD INTERNATIONAL CORPO-RATION *p* 286
2115 COMMISSIONER ST SUITE 1, VANCOUVER, BC, V5L 1A6
(604) 255-4656   *SIC* 4222

VERSACOLD LOGISTICS SERVICES *p* 207
See *VERSACOLD GROUP LIMITED PARTNERSHIP*

VERSACOLD LOGISTICS SERVICES *p* 257
3371 NO. 6 RD, RICHMOND, BC, V6V 1P6
(604) 258-0350   *SIC* 4222

VERSACOLD LOGISTICS SERVICES *p* 507
See *VERSACOLD GROUP LIMITED PARTNERSHIP*

VERSACOM *p* 1199
See *SERVICES LINGUISTIQUES VERSACOM INC*

VERSAPAY *p* 317
See *WESTERN PACIFIC ACCEPTANCE CORPORATION*

VERSATECH INDUSTRIES INC *p* 385
500 MADISON ST, WINNIPEG, MB, R3H 0L4
(204) 956-9700   *SIC* 4953

VERSATECH MECHANICAL LTD *p* 869
50 SKAGWAY AVE SUITE A, SCARBOROUGH, ON, M1M 3V1
(416) 292-9220   *SIC* 1711

VERSATERM INC *p* 830
2300 CARLING AVE, OTTAWA, ON, K2B 7G1
(613) 820-0311   *SIC* 7371

VERSATILE LEASING *p* 235
3851 SHENTON RD SUITE 3, NANAIMO, BC, V9T 2H1
(250) 758-7311   *SIC* 5511

VERSATILE SPRAY PAINTING LTD *p* 495
102 HEALEY RD, BOLTON, ON, L7E 5A7
(905) 857-4915   *SIC* 3479

VERSENT CORPORATION ULC *p* 690
3415 AMERICAN DR, MISSISSAUGA, ON, L4V 1T4
(416) 613-4555   *SIC* 7929

VERSPEETEN CARTAGE LIMITED *p* 622
274129 WALLACE LINE RR 4, INGERSOLL, ON, N5C 3J7
(519) 425-7881   *SIC* 4213

VERTECH FENEXPERT *p* 1062
See *VITRERIE VERTECH (2000) INC*

VERTEX *p* 134
705079 RANGE ROAD 61, GRANDE PRAIRIE, AB, T8W 5A8
(780) 532-7707   *SIC* 8748

VERTEX CUSTOMER MANAGEMENT (CANADA) LIMITED *p* 680
185 CLEGG RD, MARKHAM, ON, L6G 1B7
(905) 944-3200   *SIC* 7389

VERTEX ONE ASSET MANAGEMENT INC *p* 317
1021 HASTINGS ST W SUITE 3200, VANCOUVER, BC, V6E 0C3
(604) 681-5787   *SIC* 6282

VERTEX RESOURCE GROUP LTD *p* 163
2055 PREMIER WAY SUITE 161, SHERWOOD PARK, AB, T8H 0G2
(780) 464-3295   *SIC* 1522

VERTEX RESOURCE SERVICES LTD *p* 163
2055 PREMIER WAY SUITE 161, SHERWOOD PARK, AB, T8H 0G2
(780) 464-3295   *SIC* 1542

VERTICA AU SERVICE DES RESIDENTS INC *p* 943
33 YONGE ST SUITE 1000, TORONTO, ON, M5E 1S9
(416) 507-2929   *SIC* 6531

VERTICAL BUILDING SOLUTIONS INC *p* 133

64071 HWY 43, GRANDE PRAIRIE, AB, T8V 3A5
(780) 532-0366   *SIC* 1791

VERTIV CANADA ULC *p* 718
3800B LAIRD RD UNIT 7, MISSISSAUGA, ON, L5L 0B2
(905) 569-8282   *SIC* 5063

VERY JAZZROO ENTERPRISES INCORPORATED *p* 264
11720 HORSESHOE WAY, RICHMOND, BC, V7A 4V5
(604) 248-1806   *SIC* 2599

VESEY'S HOLDINGS LTD *p* 1043
411 YORK RD HWY SUITE 25, YORK, PE, C0A 1P0
(902) 368-7333   *SIC* 6712

VESEY'S SEEDS LTD *p* 1043
411 YORK RD, YORK, PE, C0A 1P0
(902) 368-7333   *SIC* 5261

VESEYS *p* 1043
See *VESEY'S HOLDINGS LTD*

VESPA SCOOTERS *p* 650
See *SIMPLY MOBILE LTD*

VESPUCCI HOLDINGS INC *p* 68
8244 ELBOW DR SW, CALGARY, AB, T2V 1K4
(403) 252-9558   *SIC* 6712

VESTA SOLUTIONS COMMUNICATIONS CORP *p* 1107
200 BOUL DE LA TECHNOLOGIE BUREAU 300, GATINEAU, QC, J8Z 3H6
(819) 778-2053   *SIC* 3669

VESTACON LIMITED *p* 1003
3 BRADWICK DR, VAUGHAN, ON, L4K 2T4
(416) 440-7970   *SIC* 1542

VESTAS-CANADIAN WIND TECHNOLOGY, INC *p* 958
65 QUEEN ST W SUITE 2000, TORONTO, ON, M5H 2M5
(647) 837-6101   *SIC* 3443

VESTAS.COM *p* 958
See *VESTAS-CANADIAN WIND TECHNOLOGY, INC*

VESTATE (CANADA) LTD *p* 97
16602 114 AVE NW, EDMONTON, AB, T5M 3R8
(780) 433-1695   *SIC* 5023

VESTATE MOULDING *p* 97
See *VESTATE (CANADA) LTD*

VESTCOR INVESTMENT MANAGEMENT CORPORATION, THE *p* 402
440 KING ST SUITE 581, FREDERICTON, NB, E3B 5H8
(506) 444-5800   *SIC* 6733

VESTKEY GRAPHIC COMMUNICATIONS INC *p* 183
See *WESTKEY GRAPHICS LTD*

VESTSHELL INC *p* 1240
10378 AV PELLETIER, MONTREAL-NORD, QC, H1H 3R3
(514) 326-1280   *SIC* 3324

VESUVIUS CANADA INC *p* 1012
333 PRINCE CHARLES DR, WELLAND, ON, L3C 5A6
(905) 732-4441   *SIC* 3297

VET DIET *p* 1049
See *J. E. MONDOU LTEE*

VET'S SHEET METAL LTD *p* 111
6111 56 AVE NW, EDMONTON, AB, T6B 3E2
(780) 434-7476   *SIC* 1711

VETEMENT CLOTHESLINE *p* 1177
See *2810221 CANADA INC*

VETEMENTS B.D. *p* 1150
See *9029-2970 QUEBEC INC*

VETEMENTS COOKSHIRE ENR *p* 1082
See *VETEMENTS COOKSHIRE INC*

VETEMENTS COOKSHIRE INC *p* 1082
725 RUE POPE, COOKSHIRE-EATON, QC, J0B 1M0
(819) 875-5538   *SIC* 2337

VETEMENTS DE SPORT R.G.R. INC *p* 1305
4100 10E AV, SAINT-GEORGES, QC, G5Y 7S3
(418) 228-9458   *SIC* 5136

VETEMENTS EFG INC *p* 1337
3335 BOUL PITFIELD, SAINT-LAURENT, QC, H4S 1H3
(514) 333-9119   *SIC* 5621

VETEMENTS GOLDEN BRAND (CANADA) LTEE *p* 1051
9393 BOUL METROPOLITAIN E, ANJOU, QC, H1J 3C7
(514) 272-8841   *SIC* 5136

VETEMENTS MAJCO INC *p* 1327
1200 BOUL JULES-POITRAS BUREAU 100, SAINT-LAURENT, QC, H4N 1X7
(514) 956-0322   *SIC* 5137

VETEMENTS MARK-EDWARDS INC *p* 1181
8480 RUE JEANNE-MANCE BUREAU 201, MONTREAL, QC, H2P 2S3
(514) 388-2353   *SIC* 5137

VETEMENTS NORFIL, LES *p* 1053
See *GROUPE DE LA COTE INC*

VETEMENTS NTD INC, LES *p* 1342
700 RUE MCCAFFREY, SAINT-LAURENT, QC, H4T 1N1
(514) 341-8330   *SIC* 5136

VETEMENTS PEERLESS INC *p* 1171
8888 BOUL PIE-IX, MONTREAL, QC, H1Z 4J5
(514) 593-9300   *SIC* 2311

VETEMENTS PRESTIGIO INC, LES *p* 1345
6370 BOUL DES GRANDES-PRAIRIES, SAINT-LEONARD, QC, H1P 1A2
(514) 955-7131   *SIC* 7389

VETEMENTS ROADRUNNER, LES *p* 1128
See *ROADRUNNER APPAREL INC*

VETEMENTS S & F (CANADA) LTEE *p* 1062
3720 RUE LA VERENDRYE, BOISBRIAND, QC, J7H 1R5
SIC 2311

VETEMENTS S F CANADA, LES *p* 1062
See *VETEMENTS S & F (CANADA) LTEE*

VETEMENTS S P INC, LES *p* 1111
1237 BOUL INDUSTRIEL, GRANBY, QC, J2J 2B8
(450) 776-6111   *SIC* 2329

VETEMENTS URBAN RAGS INC *p* 1179
9130 AV DU PARC, MONTREAL, QC, H2N 1Z2
(514) 384-6922   *SIC* 5137

VETEMENTS VA-YOLA LTEE, LES *p* 1327
550 RUE DESLAURIERS, SAINT-LAURENT, QC, H4N 1V8
(514) 337-4175   *SIC* 5137

VETEMENTS WET DOG *p* 1156
See *9168-8820 QUEBEC INC*

VETERAN COLONY *p* 171
See *HUTTERIAN BRETHREN CHURCH OF VETERAN*

VETERINARY PURCHASING COMPANY LIMITED *p* 889
485 QUEEN ST W, ST MARYS, ON, N4X 1B7
(519) 284-1371   *SIC* 5047

VETERINARY REFERRAL CLINIC *p* 931
920 YONGE ST SUITE 117, TORONTO, ON, M4W 3C7
(416) 920-2002   *SIC* 8734

VETOQUINOL N.-A. INC *p* 1134
2000 CH GEORGES, LAVALTRIE, QC, J5T 3S5
(450) 586-2252   *SIC* 5122

VETOQUINOL PROLAB *p* 1134
See *VETOQUINOL N.-A. INC*

VETS GROUP *p* 111
See *VET'S SHEET METAL LTD*

VEXOS *p* 669
See *EPM GLOBAL SERVICES INC*

VEZINA ASSURANCES INC *p* 1167
4374 AV PIERRE-DE COUBERTIN BUREAU 220, MONTREAL, QC, H1V 1A6
(514) 253-5221   *SIC* 6411

VEZINA DUFAULT *p* 1167
See *VEZINA ASSURANCES INC*

VEZINA OPTICIANS *p* 810

5929 JEANNE D'ARC BLVD S SUITE AA, ORLEANS, ON, K1C 6V8
(613) 837-1119   *SIC* 5995

VF SERVICES (CANADA) INC *p* 834
280 METCALFE ST SUITE 200, OTTAWA, ON, K2P 1R7
(613) 686-9911   *SIC* 8748

VFA CANADA CORPORATION *p* 191
4211 KINGSWAY SUITE 400, BURNABY, BC, V5H 1Z6
(604) 685-3757   *SIC* 8748

VGI SOLUTIONS *p* 1169
See *EFFIGIS GEO SOLUTIONS INC*

VHA HOME HEALTHCARE *p* 924
30 SOUDAN AVE SUITE 500, TORONTO, ON, M4S 1V6
(416) 489-2500   *SIC* 8059

VI-LUX BUILDING PRODUCTS INC *p* 748
105 RICHMOND BLVD, NAPANEE, ON, K7R 3Z8
(613) 354-4830   *SIC* 5162

VIA CAPITALE DU MONT ROYAL *p* 1173
1152 AV DU MONT-ROYAL E, MONTREAL, QC, H2J 1X8
(514) 597-2121   *SIC* 6531

VIA PERSONNEL SERVICES LTD *p* 1009
105 BAUER PL, WATERLOO, ON, N2L 6B5
SIC 7361

VIA RAIL CANAADA, CENTRE DE MAINTENANCE DE MONTREAL BUREAU DE VENTES DE TELEPHONE *p* 1209
See *VIA RAIL CANADA INC*

VIA RAIL CANADA INC *p* 451
1161 HOLLIS ST, HALIFAX, NS, B3H 2P6
(902) 494-7900   *SIC* 4111

VIA RAIL CANADA INC *p* 531
1199 WATERDOWN RD, BURLINGTON, ON, L7T 4A8
SIC 4111

VIA RAIL CANADA INC *p* 968
65 FRONT ST W SUITE 222, TORONTO, ON, M5J 1E6
(888) 842-7245   *SIC* 4111

VIA RAIL CANADA INC *p* 1209
3 PLACE VILLE-MARIE BUREAU 500, MONTREAL, QC, H3B 2C9
(514) 871-6000   *SIC* 4111

VIA RAIL CANADA INC *p* 1209
895 RUE DE LA GAUCHETIERE O BUREAU 429, MONTREAL, QC, H3B 4G1
(514) 989-2626   *SIC* 4111

VIA RAIL CANADA INC *p* 1245
44 132 RTE O BUREAU LB1, PERCE, QC, G0C 2L0
(418) 782-2747   *SIC* 4111

VIA TRANS INTERNATIONAL *p* 1179
See *9108-1950 QUEBEC INC*

VIA-CON MASONRY INC *p* 794
87 IRONDALE DR UNIT 100, NORTH YORK, ON, M9L 2S6
(416) 745-0709   *SIC* 1741

VIADUCT SHEET METAL LTD *p* 273
18787 52 AVE, SURREY, BC, V3S 8E5
(604) 575-1600   *SIC* 1711

VIAMFILMS *p* 1130
See *INTEPLAST BAGS AND FILMS CORPORATION*

VIANDE DUBREUIL INC *p* 1358
172 RUE PRINCIPALE, SAINTE-HENEDINE, QC, G0S 2R0
(418) 935-3935   *SIC* 2011

VIANDE RICHELIEU INC *p* 1150
595 RUE ROYALE, MASSUEVILLE, QC, J0G 1K0
(450) 788-2667   *SIC* 2011

VIANDES AGRO INC *p* 1331
3100 BOUL DE LA COTE-VERTU BUREAU 210, SAINT-LAURENT, QC, H4R 2J8
(514) 335-6606   *SIC* 5147

VIANDES BERNARD CENTRALE INC, LES *p* 1129
2001 AV 32E, LACHINE, QC, H8T 3J1
(514) 780-8585   *SIC* 5144

VIANDES BOVITENDRES INC *p* 1235

95 RUE DE LA POINTE-LANGLOIS, MON-TREAL, QC, H7L 3J4

(450) 663-4375 *SIC* 5147

VIANDES C .D .S. INC, LES *p 1080*
598 BOUL DU SAGUENAY O, CHICOUTIMI, QC, G7J 1H4

(418) 549-9614 *SIC* 5147

VIANDES CONCORD, LES *p 1301*
See *CONCORD PREMIUM MEATS LTD*

VIANDES DU BRETON INC, LES *p 1287*
150 CH DES RAYMOND, RIVIERE-DU-LOUP, QC, G5R 5X8

(418) 863-6711 *SIC* 2011

VIANDES FORGET, LES *p 1380*
See *FORGET, JACQUES LTEE*

VIANDES FRANCOEUR INC, LES *p 1359*
1841 RUE LAVOISIER, SAINTE-JULIE, QC, J3E 1Y6

(450) 922-4538 *SIC* 5147

VIANDES LACROIX INC, LES *p 1313*
4120 BOUL CASAVANT O, SAINT-HYACINTHE, QC, J2S 8E3

(450) 778-0188 *SIC* 2011

VIANDES MONTCALM INC, LES *p 1051*
7755 RUE GRENACHE, ANJOU, QC, H1J 1C4

(514) 327-1310 *SIC* 5147

VIANDES OR-FIL INTERNATIONAL INC, LES *p 1235*
2080 RUE MONTEREY, MONTREAL, QC, H7L 3S3

(450) 687-5664 *SIC* 5147

VIANDES P.P. HALLE LTEE, LES *p 1268*
2610 BOUL WILFRID-HAMEL, QUEBEC, QC, G1P 2J1

(418) 687-4740 *SIC* 5147

VIANDES PERREAULT PELLERIN INC *p 1350*
11 RUE DU CURE-VALOIS, SAINT-PAUL, QC, J6E 7L8

(450) 759-8023 *SIC* 5147

VIANDES RIENDEAU LTEE *p 1282*
399 RUE DES INDUSTRIES, RE-PENTIGNY, QC, J5Z 4Y8

(450) 654-6262 *SIC* 5147

VIANDES SEFICLO INC *p 1056*
1660 AV LE NEUF, BECANCOUR, QC, G9H 2E4

(819) 233-2653 *SIC* 2015

VIANDEX INC *p 1261*
199 RUE JOLY, QUEBEC, QC, G1L 1N7

(418) 780-3211 *SIC* 5143

VIASYSTEMS TORONTO INC *p 914*
8150 SHEPPARD AVE E, TORONTO, ON, M1B 5K2

(416) 208-2100 *SIC* 3672

VIATEUR PAQUETTE & FILS INC *p 1113*
1026 133 RTE, HENRYVILLE, QC, J0J 1E0

SIC 5411

VIAU, ROGER & FILS INC *p 1181*
1100 BOUL CREMAZIE E BUREAU 500, MONTREAL, QC, H2P 2X2

(514) 374-9345 *SIC* 6411

VIBAC CANADA INC *p 1248*
12250 BOUL INDUSTRIEL, POINTE-AUX-TREMBLES, QC, H1B 5M5

(514) 640-0250 *SIC* 2672

VIBRA FINISH LIMITED *p 701*
5329 MAINGATE DR, MISSISSAUGA, ON, L4W 1G6

(905) 625-9955 *SIC* 3541

VIBRANT HEALTH PRODUCTS INC *p 175*
34494 MCLARY AVE, ABBOTSFORD, BC, V2S 4N8

(604) 850-5600 *SIC* 2051

VIBRANT PERFORMANCE *p 744*
See *VIBRANT POWER INC*

VIBRANT POWER INC *p 744*
310 COURTNEYPARK DR E, MISSIS-SAUGA, ON, L5T 2S5

(905) 564-8644 *SIC* 5072

VIBRO-ACOUSTICS *p 675*
See *SWEGON NORTH AMERICA INC*

VIBROSYSTM INC *p 1146*

2727 BOUL JACQUES-CARTIER E, LONGUEUIL, QC, J4N 1L7

(450) 646-2157 *SIC* 3823

VIC AUTORAMA INC *p 1399*
21 BOUL ARTHABASKA E, VICTORIAV-ILLE, QC, G6T 0S4

(819) 758-1588 *SIC* 5511

VIC MOBILIER DE MAGASINS INC *p 1398*
1440 RUE NOTRE-DAME O, VICTORIAV-ILLE, QC, G6P 7L7

(819) 758-0626 *SIC* 2542

VIC PROGRESSIVE DIAMOND DRILLING INC *p 411*
12992 ROUTE 114 HWY, PENOBSQUIS, NB, E4G 2Z9

(506) 433-6139 *SIC* 1799

VIC SOLUTIONS DETAIL *p 1398*
See *VIC MOBILIER DE MAGASINS INC*

VIC VAN ISLE CONSTRUCTION *p 253*
See *VVI CONSTRUCTION LTD*

VIC VAN ISLE CONSTRUCTION LTD *p 253*
96 CARTIER ST, REVELSTOKE, BC, V0E 2S0

(250) 837-2919 *SIC* 1542

VICEROY RUBBER AND PLASTICS *p 794*
See *ALLIED PLASTIC GROUP OF COMPA-NIES LTD*

VICKAR COMMUNITY CHEVROLET LTD *p 363*
964 REGENT AVE W, WINNIPEG, MB, R2C 3A8

(204) 661-8391 *SIC* 5511

VICKAR MITSUBISHI *p 362*
See *LAKESIDE AUTOMOTIVE GROUP LTD*

VICKROOS *p 856*
See *VICTOR'S SPECIALTY FOODS LTD*

VICONICS TECHNOLOGIES INC *p 1181*
7262 RUE MARCONI, MONTREAL, QC, H2R 2Z5

(514) 321-5660 *SIC* 3822

VICOR MECHANICAL LTD *p 589*
11 HAAS RD, ETOBICOKE, ON, M9W 3A1

SIC 1711

VICTAULIC COMPANY OF CANADA ULC *p 856*
123 NEWKIRK RD, RICHMOND HILL, ON, L4C 3G5

(905) 884-7444 *SIC* 3494

VICTOR CUSTOM QUALITY MEATS LTD *p 560*
101 CITATION DR UNIT 14, CONCORD, ON, L4K 2S4

SIC 5142

VICTOR GROUP *p 1305*
See *DUVALTEX (CANADA) INC*

VICTOR MEATS *p 560*
See *VICTOR CUSTOM QUALITY MEATS LTD*

VICTOR TRAVEL AGENCY *p 548*
See *375645 ONTARIO LIMITED*

VICTOR'S SPECIALTY FOODS LTD *p 856*
280 STOUFFVILLE RD, RICHMOND HILL, ON, L4E 3P4

SIC 5159

VICTORIA AIRPORT AUTHORITY *p 238*
1640 ELECTRA BLVD SUITE 201, NORTH SAANICH, BC, V8L 5V4

(250) 953-7500 *SIC* 4581

VICTORIA COLLEGE *p 976*
See *VICTORIA UNIVERSITY*

VICTORIA COOL AID SOCIETY, THE *p 337*
749 PANDORA AVE SUITE 102, VICTORIA, BC, V8W 1N9

(250) 380-2663 *SIC* 8399

VICTORIA FIREFIGHTERS SOCIETY *p 335*
1234 YATES ST, VICTORIA, BC, V8V 3M8

(250) 384-1122 *SIC* 8611

VICTORIA FIREMAN'S MUTUAL BENEFIT SOCIETY *p 335*
1234 YATES ST, VICTORIA, BC, V8V 3M8

SIC 6141

VICTORIA FORD ALLIANCE LTD *p 339*
3377 DOUGLAS ST, VICTORIA, BC, V8Z 3L4

(250) 475-2255 *SIC* 5511

VICTORIA FUJIYA FOODS LTD *p 333*
3624 SHELBOURNE ST, VICTORIA, BC, V8P 4H2

(250) 598-3711 *SIC* 5411

VICTORIA GENERAL HOSPITAL *p 339*
See *VANCOUVER ISLAND HEALTH AU-THORITY*

VICTORIA GENERAL HOSPITAL *p 392*
2340 PEMBINA HWY, WINNIPEG, MB, R3T 2E8

(204) 269-3570 *SIC* 8062

VICTORIA GLEN MANOR INC *p 404*
30 BEECH GLEN RD, LOWER KINTORE, NB, E7H 1J9

(506) 273-4885 *SIC* 8051

VICTORIA GOLF CLUB *p 334*
1110 BEACH DR, VICTORIA, BC, V8S 2M9

(250) 598-4224 *SIC* 7997

VICTORIA HIGH SCHOOL *p 334*
See *BOARD OF EDUCATION OF SCHOOL DISTRICT NO. 61 (GREATER VICTORIA)*

VICTORIA HOSPICE SOCIETY *p 333*
1952 BAY ST, VICTORIA, BC, V8R 1J8

(250) 370-8715 *SIC* 8051

VICTORIA INN *p 347*
See *GENESIS HOSPITALITY INC*

VICTORIA INN WINNIPEG INC *p 385*
1808 WELLINGTON AVE, WINNIPEG, MB, R3H 0G3

(204) 786-4801 *SIC* 7011

VICTORIA MANOR *p 645*
See *CORPORATION OF THE CITY OF KAWARTHA LAKES, THE*

VICTORIA MARRIOTT INNER HARBOUR, THE *p 336*
See *ATLIFIC INC*

VICTORIA PARK COLLEGIATE INSTITUTE *p 775*
See *TORONTO DISTRICT SCHOOL BOARD*

VICTORIA PARK COMMUNITY HOMES INC *p 614*
155 QUEEN ST N, HAMILTON, ON, L8R 2V6

(905) 527-0221 *SIC* 6514

VICTORIA REFRIGERATION *p 8*
See *CORAL CANADA WIDE LTD*

VICTORIA REGENT HOTEL *p 337*
See *STRATA CORPORATION # 962*

VICTORIA SHIPYARDS CO. LTD *p 340*
825 ADMIRALS RD, VICTORIA, BC, V9A 2P1

(250) 380-1602 *SIC* 3731

VICTORIA ST GAS BAR LTD *p 640*
593 VICTORIA ST N, KITCHENER, ON, N2H 5E9

(519) 741-0424 *SIC* 5541

VICTORIA STAR MOTORS INC *p 636*
125 CENTENNIAL RD, KITCHENER, ON, N2B 3E9

(519) 579-4460 *SIC* 5511

VICTORIA UNIVERSITY *p 976*
75 QUEEN'S PARK CRES E, TORONTO, ON, M5S 1K7

(416) 585-4467 *SIC* 8742

VICTORIA UNIVERSITY *p 976*
140 CHARLES ST W, TORONTO, ON, M5S 1K9

(416) 585-4524 *SIC* 8221

VICTORIA VILLAGE INC *p 488*
78 ROSS ST, BARRIE, ON, L4N 1G3

(705) 728-3456 *SIC* 8051

VICTORIA VILLAGE MANOR *p 488*
See *VICTORIA VILLAGE INC*

VICTORIA WOMEN IN NEED SOCIETY *p 337*
785 PANDORA AVE, VICTORIA, BC, V8W 1N9

(250) 480-4006 *SIC* 8399

VICTORIA'S SECRET *p 1095*
See *VICTORIA'S SECRET (CANADA) CORP.*

VICTORIA'S SECRET (CANADA) CORP. *p 1095*

1608 BOUL SAINT-REGIS, DORVAL, QC, H9P 1H6

(514) 684-7700 *SIC* 5632

VICTORIAN EPICURE INC *p 268*
10555 WEST SAANICH RD, SIDNEY, BC, V8L 6A8

(250) 656-5751 *SIC* 5149

VICTORIAN ORDER OF NURSES *p 909*
See *VON CANADA FOUNDATION*

VICTORIAN ORDER OF NURSES FOR CANADA *p 68*
9705 HORTON RD SW SUITE 100, CAL-GARY, AB, T2V 2X5

(403) 640-4765 *SIC* 8082

VICTORIAN ORDER OF NURSES FOR CANADA *p 438*
43 PRINCE ARTHUR ST, AMHERST, NS, B4H 1V8

(902) 667-8796 *SIC* 8082

VICTORIAN ORDER OF NURSES FOR CANADA *p 469*
30 DUKE ST SUITE 5, TRURO, NS, B2N 2A1

(902) 893-3803 *SIC* 8082

VICTORIAN ORDER OF NURSES FOR CANADA *p 611*
414 VICTORIA AVE N SUITE M2, HAMIL-TON, ON, L8L 5G8

(905) 529-0700 *SIC* 8082

VICTORIAN ORDER OF NURSES FOR CANADA *p 651*
1151 FLORENCE ST SUITE 100, LONDON, ON, N5W 2M7

(519) 659-2273 *SIC* 8082

VICTORIAN ORDER OF NURSES FOR CANADA *p 676*
7100 WOODBINE AVE SUITE 402, MARKHAM, ON, L3R 5J2

(905) 479-3201 *SIC* 8082

VICTORIAN ORDER OF NURSES FOR CANADA *p 819*
2315 ST. LAURENT BLVD SUITE 100, OT-TAWA, ON, K1G 4J8

(613) 233-5694 *SIC* 8082

VICTORIAN ORDER OF NURSES FOR CANADA *p 836*
1280 20TH ST E, OWEN SOUND, ON, N4K 6H6

(519) 376-5895 *SIC* 8611

VICTORIAN ORDER OF NURSES FOR CANADA *p 840*
360 GEORGE ST N SUITE 25, PETERBOR-OUGH, ON, K9H 7E7

(705) 745-9155 *SIC* 8082

VICTORIAN ORDER OF NURSES FOR CANADA *p 861*
1705 LONDON LINE, SARNIA, ON, N7W 1B2

(519) 542-2310 *SIC* 8082

VICTORIAN ORDER OF NURSES FOR CANADA *p 999*
80 DIVISION ST SUITE 14, TRENTON, ON, K8V 5S5

(613) 392-4181 *SIC* 8082

VICTORIAN ORDER OF NURSES NEW BRUNSWICK BRANCH INC *p 409*
1077 ST GEORGE BLVD SUITE 310, MONCTON, NB, E1E 4C9

SIC 8082

VICTORIAVILLE & CO INC *p 1399*
333 RUE DE LA JACQUES-CARTIER, VIC-TORIAVILLE, QC, G6T 1Y1

(819) 752-3388 *SIC* 3995

VICTORY FORD LINCOLN SALES LTD *p 543*
301 RICHMOND ST, CHATHAM, ON, N7M 1P5

(519) 436-1430 *SIC* 5013

VICTORY MEAT MARKET LTD *p 402*
334 KING ST, FREDERICTON, NB, E3B 1E3

(506) 458-8480 *SIC* 5147

VICWEST BUILDING PRODUCTS *p 525*

See VICWEST INC
VICWEST INC   p 525
200-5050 SOUTH SERVICE RD, BURLINGTON, ON, L7L 5Y7
(905) 825-2252   *SIC 3444*
VICWEST INC   p 897
362 LORNE AVE E, STRATFORD, ON, N5A 6S4
(519) 271-5553   *SIC 3444*
VICWEST INC   p 1399
707 BOUL PIERRE-ROUX E, VICTORIAVILLE, QC, G6T 1S7
(819) 758-0661   *SIC 3444*
VIDEO MAISON CMR   p 1248
See 163453 CANADA INC
VIDEOGLOBE 1 INC   p 1192
455 RUE SAINT-ANTOINE O BUREAU 300, MONTREAL, QC, H2Z 1J1
(514) 738-6665   *SIC 5065*
VIDEON CABLESYSTEMS INC   p 62
630 3 AVE SW SUITE 900, CALGARY, AB, T2P 4L4
(403) 750-4500   *SIC 4841*
VIDEOTRON LTEE   p 1212
612 RUE SAINT-JACQUES BUREAU 700, MONTREAL, QC, H3C 4M8
(514) 281-1232   *SIC 4841*
VIDEOTRON SERVICE INFORMATIQUE LTEE   p 1186
300 AV VIGER E BUREAU 6, MONTREAL, QC, H2X 3W4
(514) 281-1232   *SIC 7374*
VIDIR MACHINE INC   p 345
8126 RD 138 NORTH, ARBORG, MB, R0C 0A0
(204) 364-2442   *SIC 3399*
VIDYARD   p 639
See BUILDSCALE, INC
VIENNA MEAT PRODUCTS   p 875
See SOFINA FOODS INC
VIESSMANN MANUFACTURING COMPANY INC   p 1011
750 MCMURRAY RD, WATERLOO, ON, N2V 2G5
(519) 885-6300   *SIC 3433*
VIEWMARK HOMES LTD   p 676
80 TIVERTON CRT SUITE 300, MARKHAM, ON, L3R 0G4
(905) 477-7609   *SIC 1521*
VIEWORX GEOPHOTO INC   p 133
8716 108 ST UNIT 112, GRANDE PRAIRIE, AB, T8V 4C7
(780) 532-3353   *SIC 1541*
VIEWPOINTS RESEARCH LTD   p 376
115 BANNATYNE AVE SUITE 404, WINNIPEG, MB, R3B 0R3
(204) 988-9253   *SIC 8732*
VIGI SANTE LTEE   p 1071
5955 GRANDE-ALLEE, BROSSARD, QC, J4Z 3S3
(450) 656-8500   *SIC 8361*
VIGI SANTE LTEE   p 1150
2893 AV DES ANCETRES, MASCOUCHE, QC, J7K 1X6
(450) 474-6991   *SIC 8051*
VIGI SANTE LTEE   p 1155
275 AV BRITTANY, MONT-ROYAL, QC, H3P 3C2
(514) 739-5593   *SIC 8361*
VIGI SANTE LTEE   p 1221
2055 AV NORTHCLIFFE BUREAU 412, MONTREAL, QC, H4A 3K6
(514) 788-2085   *SIC 8361*
VIGI SANTE LTEE   p 1245
14775 BOUL DE PIERREFONDS BUREAU 229, PIERREFONDS, QC, H9H 4Y1
(514) 620-1220   *SIC 8361*
VIGI SANTE LTEE   p 1294
4954 RUE CLEMENT-LOCKQUELL, SAINT-AUGUSTIN-DE-DESMAURES, QC, G3A 1V5
(418) 871-1232   *SIC 8361*
VIGI SANTE LTEE   p 1310
2042 BOUL MARIE, SAINT-HUBERT, QC,

J4T 2B4
(450) 671-5596   *SIC 8051*
VIGI SANTE LTEE   p 1369
5000 AV ALBERT-TESSIER, SHAWINIGAN, QC, G9N 8P9
(819) 539-5408   *SIC 8361*
VIGI SANTE LTEE   p 1371
3220 12E AV N, SHERBROOKE, QC, J1H 5H3
(819) 820-8900   *SIC 8051*
VIH AEROSPACE INC   p 238
1962 CANSO RD, NORTH SAANICH, BC, V8L 5V5
(250) 656-3987   *SIC 4581*
VIH HELICOPTERS LTD   p 238
1962 CANSO RD, NORTH SAANICH, BC, V8L 5V5
(250) 656-3987   *SIC 4522*
VIIZ COMMUNICATIONS CANADA INC p 38
6420 6A ST SE UNIT 200, CALGARY, AB, T2H 2B7
(403) 476-9400   *SIC 4899*
VIKING AIR LIMITED   p 269
1959 DE HAVILLAND WAY, SIDNEY, BC, V8L 5V5
(250) 656-7227   *SIC 3728*
VIKING AUCTION MARKET LTD   p 171
GD, VIKING, AB, T0B 4N0
(780) 688-2020   *SIC 7389*
VIKING BAKERY   p 574
See DIMPFLMEIER BAKERY LIMITED
VIKING CHAINS INC   p 210
7392 PROGRESS PL, DELTA, BC, V4G 1A1
(604) 952-4146   *SIC 5072*
VIKING FUR INC   p 421
160 MAIN RD, CAVENDISH, NL, A0B 1J0
(709) 588-2820   *SIC 0271*
VIKING INSTALLATIONS (CALGARY) LTD p 32
4020 4 ST SE, CALGARY, AB, T2G 2W3
(403) 273-7716   *SIC 1711*
VIKING LIMITED PARTNERSHIP   p 958
333 BAY ST SUITE 2500, TORONTO, ON, M5H 2R2
(416) 408-3221   *SIC 8741*
VIKING PUMP OF CANADA INC   p 1024
661 GROVE AVE, WINDSOR, ON, N9A 6G7
(519) 256-5438   *SIC 5084*
VIKING SURPLUS OIL FIELD EQUIPMENT LTD   p 1406
36 HWY 39 E, ESTEVAN, SK, S4A 2L7
SIC 5084
VIKING TRUCK SALES INC   p 483
2943 CEDAR CREEK RD SUITE 1187, AYR, ON, N0B 1E0
(519) 740-1656   *SIC 5511*
VIKING-CIVES LTD   p 746
42626 GREY RD 109, MOUNT FOREST, ON, N0G 2L0
(519) 323-4433   *SIC 3711*
VILEDA PROFESSIONAL   p 674
See PRODUITS MENAGERS FREUDENBERG INC
VILLA ACADIENNE INC   p 462
8403 HWY 1, METEGHAN, NS, B0W 2J0
(902) 645-2065   *SIC 8051*
VILLA BEAUSEJOUR INC   p 396
253 BOUL ST-PIERRE O, CARAQUET, NB, E1W 1A4
(506) 726-2744   *SIC 8361*
VILLA CATHAY CARE HOME SOCIETY p 296
970 UNION ST, VANCOUVER, BC, V6A 3V1
(604) 254-5621   *SIC 8059*
VILLA CHARITIES INC   p 790
901 LAWRENCE AVE W, NORTH YORK, ON, M6A 1C3
(416) 789-7011   *SIC 6732*
VILLA COLOMBO HOMES FOR THE AGED INC   p 791
40 PLAYFAIR AVE, NORTH YORK, ON, M6B 2P9
(416) 789-2113   *SIC 8361*
VILLA COLOMBO VAUGHAN   p 642

10443 HWY 27, KLEINBURG, ON, L0J 1C0
(289) 202-2222   *SIC 6513*
VILLA DI MANNO BAKERY LTD   p 560
22 BUTTERMILL AVE, CONCORD, ON, L4K 3X4
(905) 761-9191   *SIC 2051*
VILLA DU DECOR 1999 CANADA   p 1108
See 3592898 CANADA INC
VILLA DU REPOS INC   p 406
125 MURPHY AVE, MONCTON, NB, E1A 8V2
(506) 857-3560   *SIC 8361*
VILLA FORUM   p 707
175 FORUM DR, MISSISSAUGA, ON, L4Z 4E5
(905) 501-1443   *SIC 8051*
VILLA GEORGES FOURNIER   p 1046
See AIDE-MAISON VALLEE DE LA MATAPEDIA
VILLA ITALIA RETIREMENT RESIDENCE p 617
See SON'S OF ITALY CHARITABLE CORPORATION
VILLA LEONARDO GAMBIN   p 1033
See SRIULLI LONG TERM CARE
VILLA MARCONI LONG TERM CARE CENTRE   p 831
1026 BASELINE RD, OTTAWA, ON, K2C 0A6
(613) 727-6201   *SIC 8051*
VILLA MARIA INC   p 417
19 RUE DU COLLEGE, SAINT-LOUIS-DE-KENT, NB, E4X 1C2
(506) 876-3488   *SIC 8051*
VILLA MEDICA INC   p 1186
225 RUE SHERBROOKE E, MONTREAL, QC, H2X 1C9
(514) 288-8201   *SIC 8069*
VILLA PROVIDENCE SHEDIAC INC   p 417
403 MAIN ST, SHEDIAC, NB, E4P 2B9
(506) 532-4484   *SIC 8051*
VILLA SAINTE MARCELLINE   p 1401
815 AV UPPER BELMONT, WESTMOUNT, QC, H3Y 1K5
(514) 488-2528   *SIC 8211*
VILLA ST-GEORGES INC   p 1398
185 RUE SAINT-GEORGES, VICTORIAVILLE, QC, G6P 9H6
(819) 758-6760   *SIC 8361*
VILLA TOYOTA   p 1107
See 2088941 CANADA INC
VILLA-MARIA   p 1221
4245 BOUL DECARIE, MONTREAL, QC, H4A 3K4
(514) 484-4950   *SIC 8222*
VILLAG HISTORIQUE ACADIEN   p 396
14311 ROUTE 11, CARAQUET, NB, E1W 1B7
(506) 726-2600   *SIC 8699*
VILLAGE 360   p 1189
See LEGER MARKETING INC
VILLAGE CHRYSLER DODGE JEEP LTD p 475
201 BAYLY ST W, AJAX, ON, L1S 3K3
(905) 683-5429   *SIC 5511*
VILLAGE DES MAGI-PRIX   p 1083
See MAGI-PRIX INC
VILLAGE FARMS   p 210
See VILLAGE FARMS INTERNATIONAL INC
VILLAGE FARMS INTERNATIONAL INC p 210
4700 80 ST, DELTA, BC, V4K 3N3
(604) 940-6012   *SIC 6712*
VILLAGE FOOD MARKETS   p 269
See LOGAN GROUP PARTNERSHIP
VILLAGE FORD LINCOLN SALES LTD p 1411
1708 MAIN ST N, MOOSE JAW, SK, S6J 1L4
(306) 693-3673   *SIC 5511*
VILLAGE GREEN   p 841
See OMNI HEALTH CARE LTD

VILLAGE MALL DELICATESSEN LTD   p 41
1921 20 AVE NW, CALGARY, AB, T2M 1H6
(403) 282-6600   *SIC 6712*
VILLAGE MANOR (TO) LTD   p 974
14 MADISON AVE, TORONTO, ON, M5R 2S1
(416) 927-1722   *SIC 5813*
VILLAGE MANOR LTD   p 974
14 MADISON AVE, TORONTO, ON, M5R 2S1
(416) 927-1722   *SIC 6712*
VILLAGE MOBILE HOMES LTD   p 1416
2901 POWERHOUSE DR, REGINA, SK, S4N 0A1
(306) 525-5666   *SIC 5561*
VILLAGE NISSAN   p 1000
See VILLAGE NISSAN LIMITED
VILLAGE NISSAN LIMITED   p 1000
25 SOUTH UNIONVILLE AVE, UNIONVILLE, ON, L3R 6B8
(905) 604-0147   *SIC 5511*
VILLAGE OF WINSTON PARK, THE   p 638
See WINSTON HALL NURSING HOME LTD
VILLAGE QUEBECOIS D'ANTAN INC   p 1100
1425 RUE MONTPLAISIR, DRUMMONDVILLE, QC, J2C 0M2
(819) 478-1441   *SIC 7999*
VILLAGE QUEBECOIS D'ANTAN, LE   p 1100
1425 RUE MONTPLAISIR, DRUMMONDVILLE, QC, J2C 0M2
(819) 478-1441   *SIC 8412*
VILLAGE RETIREMENT, THE   p 857
See REVERA INC
VILLAGE RV   p 1416
See VILLAGE MOBILE HOMES LTD
VILLAGE SENIORS COMMUNITY, THE   p 618
See REVERA INC
VILLAGE, THE   p 396
See CAMPBELLTON NURSING HOME INC
VILLAS PRIVEES DE LUXE   p 1224
See LUXURY RETREATS INTERNATIONAL ULC
VILLE DE LAVAL   p 1237
2550 BOUL INDUSTRIEL, MONTREAL, QC, H7S 2G7
(450) 662-4600   *SIC 4953*
VILLE DE MONTREAL   p 1161
12001 BOUL MAURICE-DUPLESSIS, MONTREAL, QC, H1C 1V3
(514) 280-4359   *SIC 7389*
VILLE DE MONTREAL   p 1161
12001 BOUL MAURICE-DUPLESSIS, MONTREAL, QC, H1C 1V3
(514) 280-4400   *SIC 4971*
VILLE DE MONTREAL   p 1167
2269 RUE VIAU, MONTREAL, QC, H1V 3H8
(514) 872-4303   *SIC 7538*
VILLE DE MONTREAL   p 1177
9335 RUE SAINT-HUBERT, MONTREAL, QC, H2M 1Y7
(514) 385-2893   *SIC 8322*
VILLE DE MONTREAL   p 1397
1177 RUE DUPUIS, VERDUN, QC, H4G 3L4
(514) 872-7680   *SIC 1611*
VILLE DE MONTREAL   p 1397
4110 BOUL LASALLE, VERDUN, QC, H4G 2A5
(514) 765-7130   *SIC 7999*
VILLE DE RIMOUSKI   p 1285
475 2E RUE E, RIMOUSKI, QC, G5M 0A1
(418) 724-3142   *SIC 8743*
VILLE DE SALABERRY DE VALLEYFIELD p 1365
275 RUE HEBERT, SALABERRY-DE-VALLEYFIELD, QC, J6S 5Y9
(450) 370-4820   *SIC 8743*
VILLE DE SHERBROOKE   p 1372
1800 RUE ROY, SHERBROOKE, QC, J1K 1B6
(819) 821-5727   *SIC 4911*

VILLE MARIE SUZUKI AUTOMOBILE INC *p* 1168
2995 RUE HOCHELAGA, MONTREAL, QC, H1W 1G1
(514) 598-8666   *SIC* 5511
VILLENEUVE HONDA   *p* 1243
See AUTOMOBILES VILLENEUVE JOLI-ETTE (1996) INC
VILLENEUVE TANK LINES   *p* 562
See DYER ROAD LEASING LTD
VILLENEUVE, C. CONSTRUCTION CO. LTD *p* 619
1533 HWY 11 W, HEARST, ON, P0L 1N0
(705) 372-1838   *SIC* 1611
VILLEROY & BOCH CANADA   *p* 757
See VILLEROY & BOCH TABLEWARE LTD
VILLEROY & BOCH TABLEWARE LTD   *p* 757
1100 GORHAM ST UNIT 22, NEWMARKET, ON, L3Y 8Y8
(705) 458-0435   *SIC* 5023
VIMC   *p* 402
See VESTCOR INVESTMENT MANAGE-MENT CORPORATION, THE
VIMETAL INC   *p* 1337
4700 CH DU BOIS-FRANC, SAINT-LAURENT, QC, H4S 1A7
(514) 336-6824   *SIC* 5051
VIMETAL, DIV OF   *p* 1336
See THYSSENKRUPP MATERIALS CA, LTD
VIMONT TOYOTA LAVAL   *p* 1235
See AUTO SENATEUR INC
VIMY RIDGE GROUP LTD, THE   *p* 867
2000 ELLESMERE RD UNIT 16, SCAR-BOROUGH, ON, M1H 2W4
(416) 438-6727   *SIC* 8731
VINCE'S COUNTRY MARKET   *p* 754
See 1340123 ONTARIO LTD
VINCE'S COUNTRY MARKET   *p* 880
See 677957 ONTARIO INC
VINCENT ASSOCIATES INC   *p* 778
38 LESMILL RD, NORTH YORK, ON, M3B 2T5
(416) 445-5443   *SIC* 8742
VINCENT FARM EQUIPMENT (SEAFORTH) INC   *p* 879
42787 HYDROLINE RD, SEAFORTH, ON, N0K 1W0
(519) 527-0120   *SIC* 5083
VINCENT MASSEY HIGH SCHOOL   *p* 347
See BRANDON SCHOOL DIVISION, THE
VINCENT MASSEY SECONDARY SCHOOL *p* 1025
See GREATER ESSEX COUNTY DISTRICT SCHOOL BOARD
VINCENT S. VARIETE LIMITEE   *p* 1282
433 RUE SAINT-PAUL, REPENTIGNY, QC, J5Z 0C9
(450) 585-1687   *SIC* 5149
VINCENT SELECTION 1971   *p* 1282
See VINCENT S. VARIETE LIMITEE
VINCOR QUEBEC   *p* 1288
See ARTERRA WINES CANADA, INC
VINELAND ESTATES WINERY   *p* 1003
See 984379 ONTARIO INC
VINELAND GROWERS CO-OPERATIVE LIMITED   *p* 623
4150 JORDAN RD SUITE 700, JORDAN STATION, ON, L0R 1S0
(905) 562-4133   *SIC* 5148
VINELAND MANUFACTURING LTD   *p* 1003
4937 VICTORIA AVE SUITE 1, VINELAND STATION, ON, L0R 2E0
(905) 562-7308   *SIC* 3714
VINEYARD ESTATE WINES   *p* 599
See ANDREW PELLER LIMITED
VINNIE ZUCCHINI'S CORPORATION *p* 560
9100 JANE ST BLDG G UNIT 48, CONCORD, ON, L4K 0A4
(905) 761-1361   *SIC* 5812
VINPAC LINES (TORONTO) INC   *p* 701
2601 MATHESON BLVD E UNIT 202, MISSISSAUGA, ON, L4W 5A8

SIC 4731
VINS ARTERRA CANADA, DIVISION QUEBEC, INC   *p* 1288
175 CH DE MARIEVILLE, ROUGEMONT, QC, J0L 1M0
(514) 861-2404   *SIC* 2084
VINS PHILLIPE DANDURAND WINES *p* 699
See PHILIPPE DANDURAND WINES LIMITED
VINS PLASTICS LTD   *p* 498
12 INDUSTRIAL CRT, BRADFORD, ON, L3Z 3G6
(905) 775-7901   *SIC* 3081
VINS VIP, LES   *p* 1396
See CHARTON-HOBBS INC
VINTAGE HARDWOOD FLOORING   *p* 573
See 8008655 CANADA INC.
VINTECH DRAFTING INC   *p* 181
7893 EDMONDS ST SUITE 203, BURNABY, BC, V3N 1B9
(604) 523-6439   *SIC* 7389
VINTEX INC   *p* 746
1 MOUNT FOREST DR SS 2, MOUNT FOREST, ON, N0G 2L2
(519) 323-0100   *SIC* 2399
VINTNERS CELLAR SASKATOON   *p* 1435
1824 MCORMOND DR SUITE 146, SASKATOON, SK, S7S 0A6
(306) 371-9463   *SIC* 5182
VINYL VVID   *p* 1337
See 9248-9202 QUEBEC INC
VINYL WINDOW DESIGNS LTD   *p* 787
550 OAKDALE RD, NORTH YORK, ON, M3N 1W6
(416) 741-7820   *SIC* 5039
VINYLBILT GROUP INC   *p* 560
3333 LANGSTAFF RD SUITE 1, CONCORD, ON, L4K 5A8
(905) 669-1200   *SIC* 2431
VINYLBILT WINDOWS   *p* 560
See VINYLBILT GROUP INC
VINYLTEK WINDOWS   *p* 205
See CANADIAN VINYLTEK WINDOWS CORPORATION
VIOLETTE LTEE   *p* 403
157 MADAWASKA RD, GRAND-SAULT/GRAND FALLS, NB, E3Z 3E8
(506) 473-1770   *SIC* 5511
VIOLETTE MOTORS LTD   *p* 399
70 CHIEF JOANNA BLVD MMFN, ED-MUNDSTON, NB, E7C 0C1
(506) 737-9520   *SIC* 5521
VIOLETTEFORD   *p* 403
See VIOLETTE LTEE
VIP SITTERS INC   *p* 943
22 LEADER LANE SUITE 540, TORONTO, ON, M5E 0B2
(416) 999-6666   *SIC* 4212
VIPOND INC   *p* 744
6380 VIPOND DR, MISSISSAUGA, ON, L5T 1A1
(905) 564-7060   *SIC* 3569
VIQ SOLUTIONS INC   *p* 690
5915 AIRPORT RD SUITE 700, MISSISSAUGA, ON, L4V 1T1
(905) 948-8266   *SIC* 3651
VIQUA HOLDINGS   *p* 607
425 CLAIR RD W, GUELPH, ON, N1L 1R1
(519) 763-1032   *SIC* 2899
VIRDEN HEALTH CENTRE   *p* 360
See PRAIRIE MOUNTAIN HEALTH
VIRDEN MAINLINE MOTOR PRODUCTS LIMITED   *p* 360
HWY 1 W, VIRDEN, MB, R0M 2C0
(204) 748-3811   *SIC* 5511
VIRGIN & ALL SAINTS CO. LTD, THE *p* 1015
1755 DUNDAS ST W, WHITBY, ON, L1P 1Y9
(905) 665-9270   *SIC* 5541
VIRGIN RADIO   *p* 1175
See BELL MEDIA INC
VIROX TECHNOLOGIES INC   *p* 799

2770 COVENTRY RD, OAKVILLE, ON, L6H 6R1
(905) 813-0110   *SIC* 2842
VIRTEK VISION INTERNATIONAL INC *p* 1011
785 BRIDGE ST W SUITE 8, WATERLOO, ON, N2V 2K1
(519) 746-7190   *SIC* 3699
VIRTU ITG CANADA CORP   *p* 988
130 KING ST W SUITE 1040, TORONTO, ON, M5X 2A2
(416) 874-0900   *SIC* 6211
VIRTUAL BROKERS   *p* 773
See BBS SECURITIES INC
VIRTUS GROUP CHARTERED ACCOUNTANTS & BUSINESS ADVISORS LLP *p* 1430
157 2ND AVE N SUITE 200, SASKATOON, SK, S7K 2A9
(306) 653-6100   *SIC* 8721
VISA CANADA INC   *p* 958
40 KING ST W SUITE 3710, TORONTO, ON, M5H 3Y2
(416) 367-8472   *SIC* 8741
VISCOFAN CANADA INC   *p* 1327
290 RUE BENJAMIN-HUDON BUREAU 2, SAINT-LAURENT, QC, H4N 1J4
(514) 333-1700   *SIC* 5149
VISCOR INC   *p* 795
35 OAK ST, NORTH YORK, ON, M9N 1A1
(416) 245-7991   *SIC* 3646
VISCOUNT GLASS & ALUMINUM   *p* 599
See 727849 ONTARIO LIMITED
VISCOUNT GORT HOTEL   *p* 386
See VISCOUNT GORT MOTOR HOTEL LTD
VISCOUNT GORT MOTOR HOTEL LTD *p* 386
1670 PORTAGE AVE, WINNIPEG, MB, R3J 0C9
(204) 775-0451   *SIC* 7011
VISHAY PRECISION GROUP CANADA ULC *p* 778
48 LESMILL RD, NORTH YORK, ON, M3B 2T5
(416) 445-5850   *SIC* 3823
VISIER SOLUTIONS INC   *p* 301
858 BEATTY ST SUITE 400, VANCOUVER, BC, V6B 1C1
(778) 331-6950   *SIC* 7371
VISION   *p* 507
See VISION TRANSPORTATION SYSTEMS INC
VISION '74 INC   *p* 861
229 WELLINGTON ST, SARNIA, ON, N7T 1G9
(519) 336-6551   *SIC* 8051
VISION (2000) TRAVEL GROUP-ALBERTA *p* 27
See 320114 ALBERTA INC
VISION 2000 TRAVEL GROUP   *p* 42
See 320114 ALBERTA INC
VISION 2000 TRAVEL MANAGEMENT INC *p* 769
1200 SHEPPARD AVE E SUITE 201, NORTH YORK, ON, M2K 2S5
(416) 487-5385   *SIC* 4724
VISION 7 COMMUNICATIONS INC   *p* 992
32 ATLANTIC AVE, TORONTO, ON, M6K 1X8
(647) 253-0570   *SIC* 4899
VISION 7 COMMUNICATIONS INC   *p* 1214
2100 RUE DRUMMOND, MONTREAL, QC, H3G 1X1
(514) 845-2727   *SIC* 8743
VISION 7 COMMUNICATIONS INC   *p* 1214
2100 RUE DRUMMOND, MONTREAL, QC, H3G 1X1
(514) 845-4040   *SIC* 8743
VISION 7 COMMUNICATIONS INC   *p* 1214
2100 RUE DRUMMOND, MONTREAL, QC, H3G 1X1
(514) 282-4709   *SIC* 4899
VISION 7 COMMUNICATIONS INC   *p* 1260

300 RUE SAINT-PAUL BUREAU 300, QUEBEC, QC, G1K 7R1
(418) 647-2727   *SIC* 6712
VISION 7 INTERNATIONAL INC   *p* 1260
300 RUE SAINT-PAUL BUREAU 300, QUEBEC, QC, G1K 7R1
(418) 647-2727   *SIC* 6712
VISION CENTER AT WALMART   *p* 143
See WAL-MART CANADA CORP
VISION CHEVROLET BUICK GMC INC *p* 1089
30 RTE 132, DELSON, QC, J5B 1H3
(450) 632-2220   *SIC* 5511
VISION COATERS CANADA LTD   *p* 794
73 PENN DR, NORTH YORK, ON, M9L 2A6
(416) 746-2988   *SIC* 1799
VISION EXTRUSIONS GROUP LIMITED *p* 1029
201 ZENWAY BLVD, WOODBRIDGE, ON, L4H 3H9
(905) 265-9970   *SIC* 3089
VISION FABRICS   *p* 114
See ENNIS, J. FABRICS LTD
VISION FORD INC   *p* 394
105 SISTER GREEN RD, ATHOLVILLE, NB, E3N 5C5
(506) 753-5001   *SIC* 5511
VISION GLOBAL   *p* 1212
See VISION GLOBALE A.R. LTEE
VISION GLOBALE A.R. LTEE   *p* 1212
80 RUE QUEEN BUREAU 201, MONTREAL, QC, H3C 2N5
(514) 879-0020   *SIC* 7812
VISION GROUP OF COMPANIES LTD, THE *p* 984
99 BLUE JAYS WAY SUITE 300, TORONTO, ON, M5V 9G9
(416) 341-2474   *SIC* 4725
VISION HARLEY DAVIDSON   *p* 1282
See 6535577 CANADA INC
VISION MED   *p* 89
See FAMILY VISION CARE LTD
VISION NEW WAVE TRAVEL INC   *p* 976
1075 BAY ST, TORONTO, ON, M5S 2B1
(416) 928-3113   *SIC* 4724
VISION NURSING HOME   *p* 861
See VISION '74 INC
VISION PACIFIC   *p* 343
See VISION WEST DEVELOPMENT LTD
VISION PLASTICS INC   *p* 228
5800 PRODUCTION WAY, LANGLEY, BC, V3A 4N4
(604) 530-1882   *SIC* 3089
VISION R.V. CORPORATION   *p* 2
26301A TWP RD 531A, ACHESON, AB, T7X 5A3
(780) 962-0012   *SIC* 5571
VISION RESEARCH INC   *p* 1041
94 WATTS AVE, CHARLOTTETOWN, PE, C1E 2C1
(902) 569-7300   *SIC* 8733
VISION TRANSPORTATION SYSTEMS INC *p* 507
7659 BRAMALEA RD, BRAMPTON, ON, L6T 5V3
(905) 858-7333   *SIC* 4731
VISION TRAVEL   *p* 1326
See LGV QUEBEC INC
VISION TRAVEL DT ONTARIO-WEST INC *p* 915
251 CONSUMERS RD SUITE 700, TORONTO, ON, M2J 4R3
(416) 487-5385   *SIC* 4724
VISION WEST DEVELOPMENT LTD   *p* 343
6717 CRABAPPLE DR, WHISTLER, BC, V0N 1B6
(604) 932-5275   *SIC* 1521
VISION33 CANADA INC   *p* 189
6400 ROBERTS ST SUITE 200, BURNABY, BC, V5G 4C9
(604) 473-2100   *SIC* 7372
VISIONCORP INTERNATIONAL INC   *p* 97
16715 113 AVE NW, EDMONTON, AB, T5M 2X2

(780) 489-2012　SIC 5099
VISIONMAX SOLUTIONS INC　p 701
2680 SKYMARK AVE SUITE 600, MISSISSAUGA, ON, L4W 5L6
(905) 282-0503　SIC 7371
VISIONS ELECTRONICS　p 33
See 668824 ALBERTA LTD
VISIONS OF INDEPENDENCE INC　p 380
190 SHERBROOK ST, WINNIPEG, MB, R3C 2B6
(204) 453-5982　SIC 6321
VISIONS OF INDEPENDENCE INC.　p 355
20 SASKATCHEWAN AVE W, PORTAGE LA PRAIRIE, MB, R1N 0L9
(204) 239-6698　SIC 8699
VISIONS ONE HOUR OPTICAL LTD　p 175
2030 SUMAS WAY UNIT 100, ABBOTSFORD, BC, V2S 2C7
(604) 854-3266　SIC 3851
VISIONS PERSONNEL SERVICES INC　p 795
2300 FINCH AVE W UNIT 30, NORTH YORK, ON, M9M 2Y3
(416) 740-3319　SIC 8741
VISIONWALL CORPORATION　p 103
17915 118 AVE NW, EDMONTON, AB, T5S 1L6
(780) 451-4000　SIC 5211
VISSCHER LUMBER INC　p 198
6545 LICKMAN RD, CHILLIWACK, BC, V2R 4A9
(604) 858-3375　SIC 5031
VISSCHER SPECIALTY PRODUCTS　p 198
See VISSCHER LUMBER INC
VISSER, GERRIT & SONS (1991) INC　p 1043
6346 TRANS CANADA HWY - RTE 1, VERNON BRIDGE, PE, C0A 2E0
(902) 651-2371　SIC 5148
VISTA CONTRACTING LTD.　p 539
1316 DICKIE SETTLEMENT RD, CAMBRIDGE, ON, N3H 4R8
(519) 650-3481　SIC 1611
VISTA MEDICAL LTD　p 393
55 HENLOW BAY UNIT 3, WINNIPEG, MB, R3Y 1G4
(204) 949-7678　SIC 3841
VISTA PARK LODGE　p 368
144 NOVAVISTA DR, WINNIPEG, MB, R2N 1P8
(204) 257-6688　SIC 8322
VISTA PROJECTS LIMITED　p 32
4000 4 ST SE SUITE 330, CALGARY, AB, T2G 2W3
(403) 255-3455　SIC 8711
VISTA PROPERTY MANAGEMENT INC　p 580
380 DIXON RD SUITE 100, ETOBICOKE, ON, M9R 1T3
(416) 241-9171　SIC 6531
VISTA RADIO LTD　p 203
910 FITZGERALD AVE UNIT 201, COURTENAY, BC, V9N 2R5
(250) 334-2421　SIC 4832
VISTA RAILING SYSTEMS INC　p 231
23282 RIVER RD, MAPLE RIDGE, BC, V2W 1B6
(604) 467-5147　SIC 2431
VISTA SECURITY AND INVESTIGATIONS　p 513
See V.S.I. INC
VISTA SUDBURY HOTEL INC　p 901
85 STE ANNE RD, SUDBURY, ON, P3E 4S4
(705) 675-1123　SIC 7011
VISTACARE COMMUNICATIONS SERVICES OF CANADA INC　p 440
200 BLUEWATER RD UNIT 201, BEDFORD, NS, B4B 1G9
(902) 444-7404　SIC 4899
VISTEK LTD　p 934
496 QUEEN ST E, TORONTO, ON, M5A 4G8
(416) 365-1777　SIC 5946

VISTEK WEST CALGARY INC　p 86
10569 109 ST NW, EDMONTON, AB, T5H 3B1
(780) 484-0333　SIC 5946
VISUAL DEFENCE INC　p 854
9225 LESLIE ST SUITE 7, RICHMOND HILL, ON, L4B 3H6
(905) 731-1254　SIC 7372
VISUAL ELEMENTS　p 1034
See VISUAL ELEMENTS MANUFACTURING INC
VISUAL ELEMENTS MANUFACTURING INC　p 1034
21 REGINA RD, WOODBRIDGE, ON, L4L 8L9
(905) 761-5222　SIC 2541
VISUAL PLANNING CORPORATION　p 703
3071 UNIVERSAL DR, MISSISSAUGA, ON, L4X 2E2
(905) 629-7397　SIC 5099
VISUALGATE SYSTEMS INC　p 785
64 BAKERSFIELD ST, NORTH YORK, ON, M3J 2W7
SIC 6211
VISUASCAN INC　p 1345
9066 RUE PASCAL-GAGNON, SAINT-LEONARD, QC, H1P 2X4
(514) 322-2725　SIC 5084
VITA　p 794
See VITA COMMUNITY LIVING SERVICES OF TORONTO
VITA AND DISTRICT HEALTH CENTRE　p 360
See SOUTHERN HEALTH-SANTE SUD
VITA COMMUNITY LIVING SERVICES OF TORONTO　p 794
4301 WESTON RD, NORTH YORK, ON, M9L 2Y3
(416) 783-6227　SIC 8699
VITA HEALTH NATURAL FOOD STORES OF MANITOBA　p 387
See HOLTMANN, J. HOLDINGS INC
VITA HEALTH PRODUCTS INC　p 367
150 BEGHIN AVE, WINNIPEG, MB, R2J 3W2
(204) 661-8386　SIC 2833
VITA-TECH　p 670
See GENTOX LABORATORIES INC
VITAL　p 212
See VALLEY INTEGRATION TO ACTIVE LIVING SOCIETY
VITAL BENEFITS INCORPORATED　p 66
224 11 AVE SW SUITE 301, CALGARY, AB, T2R 0C3
(403) 209-3817　SIC 6311
VITAL HEALTH PRODUCTS　p 914
See INTERPHARM LTD
VITAL PHARMACY INC　p 434
250 LEMARCHANT RD, ST. JOHN'S, NL, A1E 1P7
(709) 739-9751　SIC 5912
VITALAIRE CANADA INC　p 728
6990 CREDITVIEW RD UNIT 6, MISSISSAUGA, ON, L5N 8R9
(905) 855-0414　SIC 5169
VITALAIRE HEALTHCARE/SANTE　p 728
See VITALAIRE CANADA INC
VITALITE HEALTH NETWORK　p 395
275 MAIN ST SUITE 600, BATHURST, NB, E2A 1A9
(506) 544-2133　SIC 8062
VITALITE HEALTH NETWORK　p 403
625 BOUL EVERARD H DAIGLE, GRAND-SAULT/GRAND FALLS, NB, E3Z 2R9
(506) 473-7555　SIC 8062
VITALITE HEALTH NETWORK　p 407
330 AV UNIVERSITE, MONCTON, NB, E1C 2Z3
(506) 862-4000　SIC 8062
VITALUS NUTRITION INC　p 178
3911 MT LEHMAN RD, ABBOTSFORD, BC, V2T 5W5
(604) 857-9080　SIC 2023
VITERRA INC　p 1422

2625 VICTORIA AVE, REGINA, SK, S4T 1Z8
(306) 569-4411　SIC 4221
VITESSE TRUCK REPAIR SERVICES　p 1128
See SERVICES DE CAMIONNAGE VITESSE INC
VITO'S NO FRILLS　p 781
See 1791884 ONTARIO LIMITED
VITRAN EXPRESS CANADA INC　p 275
10077 GRACE RD, SURREY, BC, V3V 3V7
(604) 582-4500　SIC 4213
VITRAN EXPRESS CANADA INC　p 560
1201 CREDITSTONE RD, CONCORD, ON, L4K 0C2
(416) 798-4965　SIC 4213
VITRECO INC　p 1085
1860 RUE CUNARD, COTE SAINT-LUC, QC, H7S 2B2
(450) 681-0483　SIC 1793
VITRERIE BAIE ST-PAUL　p 1049
See INDUSTRIES COVER INC
VITRERIE LABERGE (1988) INC　p 1255
415 RUE DES ALLEGHANYS, QUEBEC, QC, G1C 4N4
(418) 663-6363　SIC 5231
VITRERIE LEVIS INC　p 1137
12 RUE DU TERROIR, LEVIS, QC, G6V 9J3
(418) 833-2161　SIC 5031
VITRERIE LONGUEUIL INC　p 1144
241 BOUL SAINTE-FOY, LONGUEUIL, QC, J4J 1X1
(450) 651-0900　SIC 5039
VITRERIE M.P.M.　p 1293
See PORTES ET FENETRES M.P.M. INC
VITRERIE NORCRISTAL (1982) INC　p 1367
360 AV PERREAULT, SEPT-ILES, QC, G4R 1K3
(418) 968-8796　SIC 5051
VITRERIE POMERLEAU　p 1046
See COMMUNICATIONS POMERLEAU INC
VITRERIE VERTECH (2000) INC　p 1062
4275 BOUL DE LA GRANDE-ALLEE, BOIS-BRIAND, QC, J7H 1M7
(450) 430-6161　SIC 1751
VITRUM HOLDINGS LTD　p 226
9739 201 ST, LANGLEY, BC, V1M 3E7
(604) 882-3513　SIC 6712
VITRUM INDUSTRIES LTD　p 226
9739 201 ST, LANGLEY, BC, V1M 3E7
(604) 882-3513　SIC 3231
VITRXPERT LEVIS　p 1138
See GARAGE CLEMENT FOURNIER INC
VITULLO BROS. PLUMBING CO. LTD　p 560
121 BRADWICK DR UNIT 3, CONCORD, ON, L4K 1K5
(905) 669-2843　SIC 1711
VIVA HEALTHCARE PACKAGING (CANADA) LTD　p 879
1663 NEILSON RD SUITE 13, SCARBOROUGH, ON, M1X 1T1
(416) 321-0622　SIC 3083
VIVA MEDIA PACKAGING (CANADA) LTD　p 879
1663 NEILSON RD SUITE 13, SCARBOROUGH, ON, M1X 1T1
(416) 321-0622　SIC 3089
VIVA PHARMACEUTICAL INC　p 257
13880 VIKING PL, RICHMOND, BC, V6V 1K8
(604) 718-0816　SIC 5912
VIVACO, GROUPE COOPERATIF　p 1398
5 AV PIE-X, VICTORIAVILLE, QC, G6P 4R8
(819) 758-4770　SIC 5191
VIVAH FASHION ACCESSORIES & JEWELRY　p 783
See DIRECTIONS EAST TRADING LIMITED
VIVANT GROUP INC, THE　p 26
1820 30 AVE NE SUITE 3, CALGARY, AB, T2E 7M5
(403) 974-0370　SIC 6712

VIVENDI VISUAL ENTERTAINMENT　p 768
See UNIVERSAL MUSIC CANADA INC
VIVIER PHARMA INC　p 1395
288 RUE ADRIEN-PATENAUDE, VAUDREUIL-DORION, QC, J7V 5V5
(450) 455-9779　SIC 2834
VIVIX　p 738
See CONXCORP LTD
VIXS SYSTEMS INC　p 769
1210 SHEPPARD AVE E SUITE 800, NORTH YORK, ON, M2K 1E3
(416) 646-2000　SIC 3674
VIZEUM　p 1223
See VIZEUM CANADA INC
VIZEUM CANADA INC　p 1223
3970 RUE SAINT-AMBROISE, MONTREAL, QC, H4C 2C7
(514) 270-1010　SIC 7311
VIZIMAX INC　p 1142
2284 RUE DE LA PROVINCE, LONGUEUIL, QC, J4G 1G1
(450) 679-0003　SIC 5065
VKI TECHNOLOGIES　p 1170
See KEURIG CANADA INC
VLR FOOD CORPORATION　p 560
575 OSTER LANE, CONCORD, ON, L4K 2B9
(905) 669-0700　SIC 2038
VMA TOTTENHAM　p 998
See VENTRA GROUP CO
VMAC (VEHICLE MOUNTED AIR COMPRESSORS)　p 235
See VMAC GLOBAL TECHNOLOGY INC
VMAC GLOBAL TECHNOLOGY INC　p 235
1333 KIPP RD, NANAIMO, BC, V9X 1R3
(250) 740-3200　SIC 3563
VMC GAME LABS　p 1209
See VOLT CANADA INC
VMC GAMES LABS　p 707
See VOLT CANADA INC
VMS　p 837
See PARIS SOUTHERN LIGHTS INC
VMS VENTURES INC　p 240
200 ESPLANADE W SUITE 500, NORTH VANCOUVER, BC, V7M 1A4
(604) 986-2020　SIC 1081
VO'S YIG　p 848
See VO'S YIG #00835
VO'S YIG #00835　p 848
1893 SCUGOG ST, PORT PERRY, ON, L9L 1H9
(905) 985-9772　SIC 5411
VOA CANADA INC　p 547
190 MACDONALD RD, COLLINGWOOD, ON, L9Y 4N6
(705) 444-2561　SIC 2241
VOCATION SERVICES　p 602
See COMMUNITY LIVING GUELPH WELLINGTON
VODDEN FOODLAND　p 500
456 VODDEN ST E, BRAMPTON, ON, L6S 5Y7
(905) 453-3100　SIC 5411
VOESTALPINE HIGH PERFORMANCE METALS LTD　p 728
2595 MEADOWVALE BLVD, MISSISSAUGA, ON, L5N 7Y3
(905) 812-9440　SIC 5051
VOESTALPINE NORTRAK LTD　p 257
5500 PARKWOOD WAY, RICHMOND, BC, V6V 2M4
(604) 273-3030　SIC 3312
VOESTALPINE ROTEC SUMMO CORP　p 525
1200 BURLOAK DR, BURLINGTON, ON, L7L 6B4
(905) 336-0014　SIC 5051
VOESTALPINE ROTEC SUMMO CORP　p 525
4041 NORTH SERVICE RD, BURLINGTON, ON, L7L 4X6
(905) 336-0014　SIC 3714
VOG　p 1357

See SERRES LEFORT INC, LES

VOGOGO INC p 974
5 HAZELTON AVE SUITE 300, TORONTO, ON, M5R 2E1
(647) 715-3707   SIC 6099

VOGUE OPTICAL p 1040
See VOGUE OPTICAL GROUP INC

VOGUE OPTICAL GROUP INC p 1040
5 BRACKLEY POINT RD, CHARLOTTE-TOWN, PE, C1A 6X8
(902) 566-3326   SIC 5995

VOICE CONSTRUCTION LTD p 111
7545 52 ST NW, EDMONTON, AB, T6B 2G2
(780) 469-1351   SIC 1629

VOICE CONSTRUCTION LTD p 129
200 MACDONALD CRES, FORT MCMUR-RAY, AB, T9H 4B2
(780) 790-0981   SIC 1794

VOIE RAPIDE DES LAURENTIDES p 1321
155 BOUL LACHAPELLE BUREAU 158, SAINT-JEROME, QC, J7Z 7L2
(450) 436-2264   SIC 5511

VOILA LEARNING p 932
See 7226438 CANADA INC

VOIS INC p 66
628 12 AVE SW UNIT 201, CALGARY, AB, T2R 0H6
(403) 775-2000   SIC 4899

VOITH CANADA INC p 619
925 TUPPER ST, HAWKESBURY, ON, K6A 3T5
(613) 632-4163   SIC 2221

VOITH HYDRO INC p 1071
9955 RUE DE CHATEAUNEUF BUREAU 160, BROSSARD, QC, J4Z 3V5
(450) 766-2100   SIC 1731

VOITH PAPER FABRIC & ROLL SYSTEMS p 619
See VOITH CANADA INC

VOL-HAM AUTOMOTIVE INC p 934
43 EASTERN AVE, TORONTO, ON, M5A 1H1
(416) 868-1880   SIC 5511

VOLAILLE GIANNONE INC p 1298
2320 RUE PRINCIPALE, SAINT-CUTHBERT, QC, J0K 2C0
(450) 836-3063   SIC 2011

VOLAILLES ET VIANDE AMGA LTEE p 1337
9555 RTE TRANSCANADIENNE, SAINT-LAURENT, QC, H4S 1V3
(514) 273-8848   SIC 5144

VOLAILLES MARTEL INC, LES p 1100
2350 BOUL FOUCAULT, DRUM-MONDVILLE, QC, J2E 0E8
(819) 478-7495   SIC 0251

VOLAILLES MIRABEL LTEE p 1154
9051 RTE SIR-WILFRID-LAURIER, MIRABEL, QC, J7N 1L6
(450) 258-0444   SIC 6799

VOLAILLES REGAL INC p 1363
955 RUE MICHELIN, SAINTE-ROSE, QC, H7L 5B6
(450) 667-7070   SIC 5144

VOLANT PRODUCTS INC p 111
4110 56 AVE NW, EDMONTON, AB, T6B 3R8
(780) 490-5185   SIC 3533

VOLANTE SOFTWARE INC p 778
49 COLDWATER RD, NORTH YORK, ON, M3B 1Y8
(416) 988-6333   SIC 7372

VOLANTE SYSTEMS p 778
See VOLANTE SOFTWARE INC

VOLARIS GROUP INC p 702
5060 SPECTRUM WAY SUITE 110, MIS-SISSAUGA, ON, L4W 5N5
(905) 267-5400   SIC 7371

VOLCO ENTERPRISES LTD p 257
12291 BRIDGEPORT RD, RICHMOND, BC, V6V 1J4
(604) 270-4727   SIC 5531

VOLCO TIRES & WHEELS p 257
See VOLCO ENTERPRISES LTD

VOLD, JONES & VOLD AUCTION CO LTD p 152
4410 HIGHWAY 2A, PONOKA, AB, T4J 1J8
(403) 783-5561   SIC 5154

VOLKER STEVIN CONTRACTING LTD p 38
7175 12 ST SE SUITE 7175, CALGARY, AB, T2H 2S6
(403) 571-5800   SIC 1611

VOLKER STEVIN CONTRACTING LTD p 141
4004 6 AVE N, LETHBRIDGE, AB, T1H 6W4
(403) 320-4920   SIC 1611

VOLKER STEVIN HIGHWAY p 141
See VOLKER STEVIN CONTRACTING LTD

VOLKSWAGEN p 234
See HARBOURVIEW AUTOHAUS LTD

VOLKSWAGEN p 475
See VOLKSWAGEN GROUP CANADA INC

VOLKSWAGEN p 1064
See DUVAL VOLKSWAGEN INC

VOLKSWAGEN p 1173
See AUTOMOBILES POPULAR INC, LES

VOLKSWAGEN AUDI LANDROVER JAGUAR p 254
See G.E. COWELL HOLDINGS LTD

VOLKSWAGEN CENTRE OF SASKATOON p 1425
See 101105464 SASKATCHEWAN LTD

VOLKSWAGEN DE L'ESTRIE p 1375
See SHERBROOKE AUTOMOBILE INC

VOLKSWAGEN FINANCE p 1328
See CREDIT VW CANADA, INC

VOLKSWAGEN GROUP CANADA INC p 475
777 BAYLY ST W, AJAX, ON, L1S 7G7
(905) 428-6700   SIC 5012

VOLKSWAGEN LAUZON SAINT-EUSTACHE p 1300
See 4486404 CANADA INC

VOLKSWAGEN MIDTOWN p 914
3450 SHEPPARD AVE E, TORONTO, ON, M1T 3K4
(416) 291-6456   SIC 5511

VOLKSWAGEN OF WINDSOR p 1017
See 1461616 ONTARIO INC

VOLKSWAGEN RIMOUSKI p 1285
See 4134320 CANADA INC

VOLKSWAGEN ST-HYACINTHE p 1311
See AUTOMOBILES F.M. INC

VOLKSWAGEN VILLA p 906
See TRANSWORLD FINE CARS LTD

VOLLMER INC p 1025
3822 SANDWICH ST, WINDSOR, ON, N9C 1C1
(519) 966-6100   SIC 1711

VOLT CANADA INC p 707
3 ROBERT SPECK PKY SUITE 260, MIS-SISSAUGA, ON, L4Z 2G5
(905) 306-1920   SIC 7361

VOLT CANADA INC p 1209
1155 RUE METCALFE BUREAU 2002, MONTREAL, QC, H3B 2V6
(514) 787-3175   SIC 8734

VOLTAGE POWER LTD p 385
1313 BORDER ST UNIT 26, WINNIPEG, MB, R3H 0X4
(204) 594-1140   SIC 1623

VOLTAM INC p 1116
3455 RUE DU TRANSPORT, JONQUIERE, QC, G7X 0B6
(418) 548-0002   SIC 5065

VOLTIGEURS, LES p 1098
See CLUB DE HOCKEY LES VOLTIGEURS

VOLUMAT INC p 1391
1716 CH SULLIVAN, VAL-D'OR, QC, J9P 1M5
(819) 825-3070   SIC 5251

VOLUME TANK TRANSPORT INC p 702
1230 SHAWSON DR, MISSISSAUGA, ON, L4W 1C3
(905) 670-7090   SIC 4212

VOLUNTEER ENTERPRISES OF THE HEALTH SCIENCES CENTRE INC p 373

820 SHERBROOK ST SUITE MS210, WIN-NIPEG, MB, R3A 1R9
(204) 787-7313   SIC 5499

VON & SUBARU SALES PARTS & SERVICES p 323
See DON DOCKSTEADER MOTORS LTD

VOLVO CARS OF CANADA CORP p 854
9130 LESLIE ST SUITE 101, RICHMOND HILL, ON, L4B 0B9
(905) 695-9626   SIC 5012

VOLVO DE BROSSARD p 1069
See 9039-7571 QUEBEC INC

VOLVO LAVAL p 1085
See 4093640 CANADA INC

VOLVO OF DURHAM p 844
920 KINGSTON RD, PICKERING, ON, L1V 1B3
(905) 421-9515   SIC 5511

VOLVO OF EDMONTON p 125
See 1412873 ALBERTA LTD

VOLVO OF HALIFAX p 454
See 3025052 NOVA SCOTIA LIMITED

VOLVO OF LONDON p 661
See V J L R H LONDON INC

VOLVO OF NORTH VANCOUVER p 242
809 AUTOMALL DR, NORTH VANCOU-VER, BC, V7P 3R8
(604) 986-9889   SIC 5511

VOLVO OF OAKVILLE p 805
770 PACIFIC RD, OAKVILLE, ON, L6L 6M5
(905) 825-8088   SIC 5511

VOLVO OF TORONTO p 934
See VOL-HAM AUTOMOTIVE INC

VOLVO POINTE-CLAIRE p 1249
See AUTOMOBILES FAIRVIEW INC

VOLVO TROIS-RIVIERES p 1384
See 9308-5934 QUEBEC INC

VOLVO TRUCK CENTRE-EDMONTON p 99
See CALMONT TRUCK CENTRE LTD

VOLVO VILLA p 906
See TRANSOCEANIC FINE CARS LTD

VOLVO WINNIPEG p 386
See JLV ENTERPRISES

VOMAR INDUSTRIES INC p 351
GD, LA SALLE, MB, R0G 1B0
(204) 736-4288   SIC 5984

VON p 409
See VICTORIAN ORDER OF NURSES NEW BRUNSWICK BRANCH INC

VON p 819
See VICTORIAN ORDER OF NURSES FOR CANADA

VON BATHURST DISTRICT p 861
See VICTORIAN ORDER OF NURSES FOR CANADA

VON CALGARY DISTRICT p 68
See VICTORIAN ORDER OF NURSES FOR CANADA

VON CANADA FOUNDATION p 460
46 CHIPMAN DR SUITE 1, KENTVILLE, NS, B4N 3V7
(902) 678-1733   SIC 8621

VON CANADA FOUNDATION p 611
414 VICTORIA AVE N SUITE 568, HAMIL-TON, ON, L8L 5G8
(905) 529-0700   SIC 8399

VON CANADA FOUNDATION p 909
214 RED RIVER RD SUITE 200, THUNDER BAY, ON, P7B 1A6
(807) 344-0012   SIC 8082

VON COLCHESTER EAST HANTS DISTRICT p 469
See VICTORIAN ORDER OF NURSES FOR CANADA

VON COMMITTEE SUPPORT p 460
See VON CANADA FOUNDATION

VON CONSTRUCTION p 795
See REA INVESTMENTS LIMITED

VON CUMBERLAND DISTRICT p 438
See VICTORIAN ORDER OF NURSES FOR CANADA

VON GREY BRUCE DISTRICT p 836

See VICTORIAN ORDER OF NURSES FOR CANADA

VON HAMILTON p 611
See VON CANADA FOUNDATION

VON HAMILTON DISTRICT p 611
See VICTORIAN ORDER OF NURSES FOR CANADA

VON HASTINGS-NORTHUMBERLAND-PE DISTRICT p 999
See VICTORIAN ORDER OF NURSES FOR CANADA

VON MIDDLESEX-ELGIN MAIN OFFICE p 651
See VICTORIAN ORDER OF NURSES FOR CANADA

VON PETERBOROUGH-VICTORIA-HALIBURTON DISTRICT p 840
See VICTORIAN ORDER OF NURSES FOR CANADA

VON TORONTO-YORK REGION p 676
See VICTORIAN ORDER OF NURSES FOR CANADA

VON WEISE OF CANADA COMPANY p 535
505 CONESTOGA BLVD, CAMBRIDGE, ON, N1R 7P4
SIC 3621

VONAGE CANADA CORP p 702
2660 MATHESON BLVD E SUITE 301, MIS-SISSAUGA, ON, L4W 5M2
(416) 907-6100   SIC 4899

VOORTMAN COOKIES LIMITED p 525
4475 NORTH SERVICE RD SUITE 600, BURLINGTON, ON, L7L 4X7
(905) 335-9500   SIC 2052

VOPAK TERMINAL MONTREAL-EST p 1239
See VOPAK TERMINAUX DE L'EST DU CANADA INC

VOPAK TERMINALS OF CANADA INC p 1239
2775 AV GEORGES-V, MONTREAL-EST, QC, H1L 6J7
(514) 687-3193   SIC 5169

VOPAK TERMINAUX DE L'EST DU CANADA INC p 1239
2775 AV GEORGES-V, MONTREAL-EST, QC, H1L 6J7
(514) 687-3193   SIC 5169

VORTEX FREIGHT SYSTEMS INC p 744
6615 ORDAN DR UNIT 14-15, MISSIS-SAUGA, ON, L5T 1X2
(905) 499-3000   SIC 4731

VORTEX STRUCTURES AQUATIQUES INTERNATIONALES INC p 1252
328 AV AVRO, POINTE-CLAIRE, QC, H9R 5W5
(514) 694-3868   SIC 3949

VOS VACATION p 1181
8060 RUE SAINT-HUBERT, MONTREAL, QC, H2R 2P3
(514) 270-3186   SIC 4724

VOSKAMP GREENHOUSES INC p 661
6867 WELLINGTON RD S, LONDON, ON, N6L 1M3
(519) 686-0303   SIC 1542

VOTI DETECTION p 1324
See VOTI INC

VOTI INC p 1324
790 RUE BEGIN, SAINT-LAURENT, QC, H4M 2N5
(514) 782-1566   SIC 3845

VOX INTEGRATED SOLUTIONS MODEL INC p 921
36 GLENGOWAN RD, TORONTO, ON, M4N 1E8
(905) 840-7477   SIC 7371

VOXDATA CALL CENTER p 774
See VOXDATA SOLUTIONS INC

VOXDATA SOLUTIONS INC p 774
20 YORK MILLS RD SUITE 201, NORTH YORK, ON, M2P 2C2
SIC 4899

VOXDATA SOLUTIONS INC   p 1209
1155 RUE METCALFE BUREAU 1860,
MONTREAL, QC, H3B 2V6
(514) 871-1920   SIC 4899
VOXDATA TELECOM   p 1209
See VOXDATA SOLUTIONS INC
VOYAGE 2040   p 1195
See DESTINATIONS ETC INC
VOYAGE GARTH ALLEN MARKSTED INCp
1157
8260 CH DEVONSHIRE BUREAU 210,
MONT-ROYAL, QC, H4P 2P7
(514) 344-8888   SIC 4724
VOYAGE WORLDVIEW (CANADA)   p 941
See TRAVEL EDGE (CANADA) INC
VOYAGER R.V. CENTRE LTD   p 224
9250 HIGHWAY 97, LAKE COUNTRY, BC,
V4V 1P9
(250) 766-4607   SIC 5561
VOYAGES A RABAIS   p 1385
See VOYAGESARABAIS INC
VOYAGES ARC-EN-CIEL   p 1385
See SERVICES DE VOYAGES YVES BOR-
DELEAU INC, LES
VOYAGES BERGERON INC   p 1181
7725 RUE SAINT-DENIS, MONTREAL, QC,
H2R 2E9
(514) 273-3301   SIC 4724
VOYAGES BERNARD GENDRON INC   p
1365
1465 BOUL MONSEIGNEUR-LANGLOIS,
SALABERRY-DE-VALLEYFIELD, QC, J6S
1C2
(450) 373-8747   SIC 4724
VOYAGES ENCORE TRAVEL INC   p 1327
1285 RUE HODGE BUREAU 101, SAINT-
LAURENT, QC, H4N 2B6
(514) 738-7171   SIC 4724
VOYAGES ESCAPADE INC   p 1374
2855 RUE KING O, SHERBROOKE, QC,
J1L 1C6
(819) 563-5344   SIC 4724
VOYAGES FUNTASTIQUE LONGUEUIL   p
1143
See 2759-9687 QUEBEC INC.
VOYAGES JET-SET   p 1171
See 3225518 CANADA INC
VOYAGES LA CLE DES CHAMPS   p 1137
See TOURNEES CLUB SELECT INC, LES
VOYAGES LAURIER DU VALLON INC, LES
p 1274
2450 BOUL LAURIER BUREAU 10, QUE-
BEC, QC, G1V 2L1
(418) 653-1882   SIC 4724
VOYAGES MALAVOY INC   p 1168
3425 RUE BEAUBIEN E, MONTREAL, QC,
H1X 1G8
(514) 286-7559   SIC 4724
VOYAGES TRADITOURS INC   p 1237
1575 BOUL DE L'AVENIR BUREAU 100,
MONTREAL, QC, H7S 2N5
(514) 907-7712   SIC 4724
VOYAGES VISION DT QUEBEC-EST INC p
1226
400 AV SAINTE-CROIX 100 O, MON-
TREAL, QC, H4N 3L4
(514) 748-2522   SIC 4724
VOYAGESARABAIS INC   p 1385
699 BOUL THIBEAU BUREAU 100, TROIS-
RIVIERES, QC, G8T 7A2
(819) 693-8937   SIC 4724
VOYAGEUR AEROTECH INC   p 764
1500 AIRPORT RD, NORTH BAY, ON, P1B
8G2
(705) 476-1750   SIC 4581
VOYAGEUR AIRWAYS LIMITED   p 764
1500 AIRPORT RD, NORTH BAY, ON, P1B
8G2
(705) 476-1750   SIC 4512
VOYAGEUR AVIATION CORP.   p 764
1500 AIRPORT RD, NORTH BAY, ON, P1B
8G2
(705) 476-1750   SIC 6712
VOYAGEUR PATIENT TRANSFER SER-

VICES INC   p
650
573 ADMIRAL CRT, LONDON, ON, N5V 4L3
(519) 455-4579   SIC 4111
**VOYAGEUR SOAP & CANDLE COMPANY
LTD**   p 273
19257 ENTERPRISE WAY SUITE 14, SUR-
REY, BC, V3S 6J8
(604) 530-8979   SIC 2841
VOYAGEUR TRANSPORTATION SERVICES
p 648
See 947465 ONTARIO LTD
VOYER & JOBIN LTEE   p 1351
268 RUE SAINT-JOSEPH, SAINT-
RAYMOND, QC, G3L 1J3
(418) 337-2278   SIC 5411
VOYSUS GROUP INC   p 914
5900 FINCH AVE EAST UNIT 200B,
TORONTO, ON, M1B 5P8
(416) 291-0224   SIC 7389
VOYZANT INC   p 677
7100 WOODBINE AVE UNIT 102,
MARKHAM, ON, L3R 5J2
(647) 783-3371   SIC 4724
VP PROTECTION INC   p 769
259 YORKLAND RD 3RD FL, NORTH
YORK, ON, M2J 5B2
(416) 218-3226   SIC 7381
VPC GROUP INC   p 785
150 TORO RD, NORTH YORK, ON, M3J
2A9
(416) 630-6633   SIC 2824
VPG REALTY INC   p 239
1233 LYNN VALLEY RD SUITE 159,
NORTH VANCOUVER, BC, V7J 0A1
(604) 770-4353   SIC 6531
VPS   p 795
See VISIONS PERSONNEL SERVICES
INC
VR MECHANICAL SOLUTIONS INC p 475
464 KINGSTON RD W, AJAX, ON, L1T 3A3
(905) 426-7551   SIC 1711
VR ST-CYR INC   p 1348
3465 CH DE L'INDUSTRIE, SAINT-
MATHIEU-DE-BELOEIL, QC, J3G 0R9
(450) 446-3660   SIC 5571
VR TRAVEL LTD   p 931
2 BLOOR ST W SUITE 2120, TORONTO,
ON, M4W 3E2
   SIC 4724
VRANCOR GROUP OF COMPANIES p 613
See VRANCOR PROPERTY MANAGE-
MENT INC
**VRANCOR PROPERTY MANAGEMENT
INC**   p 613
366 KING ST W, HAMILTON, ON, L8P 1B3
(905) 540-4800   SIC 6553
VRETTA INC   p 941
120 ADELAIDE ST E, TORONTO, ON, M5C
1K9
(866) 522-9228   SIC 7389
VRG CAPITAL   p 968
See XPV WATER PARTNERS INC
VSA HIGHWAY MAINTENANCE LTD p 180
1504 BLATTNER RD, ARMSTRONG, BC,
V0E 1B0
(250) 546-8844   SIC 1611
VSA HIGHWAY MAINTENANCE LTD p 232
2925 POOLEY AVE, MERRITT, BC, V1K
1C2
(250) 315-0166   SIC 1611
VT VENTURES INC   p 197
8750 YOUNG RD, CHILLIWACK, BC, V2P
4P4
(604) 792-1167   SIC 5511
VTECH ENGINEERING CANADA LTDp 262
7671 ALDERBRIDGE WAY SUITE 200,
RICHMOND, BC, V6X 1Z9
(604) 273-5131   SIC 8711
VTR   p 600
See VTR FEEDER SOLUTIONS INC
VTR FEEDER SOLUTIONS INC   p 600
623 SOUTH SERVICE RD UNIT 6,
GRIMSBY, ON, L3M 4E8

(905) 643-7300   SIC 3559
VTRAC CONSULTING CORPORATION   p
773
4950 YONGE ST SUITE 1005, NORTH
YORK, ON, M2N 6K1
(416) 366-2600   SIC 8748
VULCAN AUTOMOTIVE EQUIPMENT LTDp
207
788 CALDEW ST UNIT 121, DELTA, BC,
V3M 5S2
(604) 526-1167   SIC 5511
VULCAN ELECTRICAL LTD   p 103
18225 107 AVE NW, EDMONTON, AB, T5S
1K4
(780) 483-0036   SIC 1731
VULCRAFT CANADA, INC   p 478
1362 OSPREY DR, ANCASTER, ON, L9G
4V5
(289) 443-2000   SIC 3312
VULSAY INDUSTRIES LTD   p 513
35 REGAN RD, BRAMPTON, ON, L7A 1B2
(905) 846-2200   SIC 7389
VUPOINT SYSTEMS LTD   p 658
1025 HARGRIEVE RD UNIT 8, LONDON,
ON, N6E 1P7
(519) 690-0865   SIC 1521
VUTEQ CANADA INC   p 1036
885 KEYES DR, WOODSTOCK, ON, N4V
1C3
(519) 421-0011   SIC 3465
VUTEQ CANADA INC   p 1036
920 KEYES DR, WOODSTOCK, ON, N4V
1C3
(519) 421-0011   SIC 3089
VVI CONSTRUCTION LTD   p 253
96 CARTIER ST, REVELSTOKE, BC, V0E
2S0
(250) 837-2919   SIC 1521
VWR INTERNATIONAL CO.   p 728
2360 ARGENTIA RD, MISSISSAUGA, ON,
L5N 5Z7
(905) 813-7377   SIC 5049
VYEFIELD ENTERPRISES LTD   p 32
3815 16 ST SE, CALGARY, AB, T2G 4W5
(403) 290-1838   SIC 5144

W

W C KENNEDY COLLEGIATE INSTITUTE p
1021
See GREATER ESSEX COUNTY DISTRICT
SCHOOL BOARD
W D LIVESTOCK   p 355
See 65548 MANITOBA LTD
W INTERCONNECTIONS CANADA INC   p
677
10 SPY CRT, MARKHAM, ON, L3R 5H6
(905) 475-1507   SIC 5065
W L SEATON SECONDARY SCHOOL p 332
See SCHOOL DISTRICT NO 22 (VERNON)
W MODE INC   p 41
3553 31 ST NW SUITE 201, CALGARY, AB,
T2L 2K7
(403) 260-8690   SIC 7372
W O STINSON & SON LTD   p 628
2955 HWY 43, KEMPTVILLE, ON, K0G 1J0
(613) 258-1826   SIC 5172
WSCC   p 436
See WORKERS' SAFETY AND COMPEN-
SATION COMMISSION OF THE NORTH-
WEST TERRITORIES AND NUNAVUT
W S MACHINING & FABRICATION INC   p
359
49 LIFE SCIENCES PKY, STEINBACH, MB,
R5G 2G7
(204) 326-5444   SIC 3599
W T TOWNSHEND PUBLIC SCHOOL p 638
See WATERLOO REGION DISTRICT
SCHOOL BOARD
W-S FEED & SUPPLIES LIMITED   p 902
45 MARIA ST, TAVISTOCK, ON, N0B 2R0
(519) 664-2237   SIC 2048
W-S FEEDS   p 902
See W-S FEED & SUPPLIES LIMITED
W. B. WHITE INSURANCE LIMITED p 813

110 KING ST E, OSHAWA, ON, L1H 1B6
(905) 576-6400   SIC 6411
W. CHAN INVESTMENTS LTD   p 67
501 18 AVE SW SUITE 600, CALGARY, AB,
T2S 0C7
(403) 229-3838   SIC 6531
W. GORDON INC   p 1222
2125 BOUL CAVENDISH, MONTREAL, QC,
H4B 2Y2
(514) 481-7771   SIC 5531
W. H. ESCOTT COMPANY LIMITED   p 376
95 ALEXANDER AVE, WINNIPEG, MB, R3B
2Y8
(204) 942-5127   SIC 7389
W. H. SCRIVENS & SON LIMITED   p 834
270 MACLAREN ST, OTTAWA, ON, K2P
0M3
(613) 236-9101   SIC 6411
W. H. STUART & ASSOCIATES   p 1000
See STUART, W H MUTUALS LTD
W. I. WOODTONE INDUSTRIES INC p 198
8007 AITKEN RD, CHILLIWACK, BC, V2R
4H5
(604) 792-3680   SIC 5031
W. R. GRACE CANADA CORP   p 1365
42 RUE FABRE, SALABERRY-DE-
VALLEYFIELD, QC, J6S 4K7
(450) 373-4224   SIC 2819
W. RALSTON (CANADA) INC   p 82
1100 RAILWAY AVE S, DRUMHELLER, AB,
T0J 0Y0
(403) 823-3468   SIC 3089
W. RALSTON (CANADA) INC   p 1331
3300 BOUL DE LA COTE-VERTU BUREAU
200, SAINT-LAURENT, QC, H4R 2B7
(514) 334-5656   SIC 2673
W. S. TYLER CANADA LTD   p 886
225 ONTARIO ST, ST CATHARINES, ON,
L2R 7J2
(905) 688-2644   SIC 3496
W.A. GRAIN PULSE SOLUTIONS   p 136
See 1309497 ALBERTA LTD
W.B.C. CORPORATION   p 1209
1000 RUE DE LA GAUCHETIERE O, MON-
TREAL, QC, H3B 4W5
   SIC 8999
W.C.S. FINANCIAL SERVICES INC p 854
20 WERTHEIM CRT SUITE 40, RICHMOND
HILL, ON, L4B 3A8
(905) 731-1984   SIC 6282
W.D. COLLEDGE COMPANY LIMITEDp 690
3220 ORLANDO DR UNIT 3, MISSIS-
SAUGA, ON, L4V 1R5
(905) 677-4428   SIC 5046
W.D. PACKAGING INC   p 568
49 INDUSTRIAL DR, ELMIRA, ON, N3B
3B1
(519) 669-5486   SIC 7389
W.D.I. SERVICES LTD   p 324
1588 RAND AVE, VANCOUVER, BC, V6P
3G2
(604) 263-2739   SIC 4225
W.E. RENTALS 2K LTD   p 133
11489 95 AVE, GRANDE PRAIRIE, AB, T8V
5P7
(780) 539-1709   SIC 7353
W.E. TRAVEL   p 240
See WORKING ENTERPRISES TRAVEL
SERVICES LTD
W.F.M.H. ENGINEERING LIMITED   p 641
546 BELMONT AVE W, KITCHENER, ON,
N2M 5E3
   SIC 8711
W.H. LUBRICANTS LTD   p 1011
185 FROBISHER DR, WATERLOO, ON,
N2V 2E6
(519) 513-9805   SIC 5172
W.H.B. IDENTIFICATION SOLUTIONS INCp
677
7010 COCHRANE DR, MARKHAM, ON, L3R
5N7
(905) 764-1122   SIC 5099
W.J. DEANS TRANSPORTATION INC   p
1089

196 RUE SUTTON, DELSON, QC, J5B 1X3
(450) 638-5933   SIC 4213

W.J. MOUAT SECONDARY SCHOOL p 177
See SCHOOL DISTRICT NO 34 (ABBOTS-FORD)

W.J. PARISEAU SALES LTD p 436
328 OLD AIRPORT RD, YELLOWKNIFE, NT, X1A 3T3
(867) 873-2403   SIC 5531

W.J.B. MOTORS LIMITED p 805
1291 SPEERS RD, OAKVILLE, ON, L6L 2X5
(905) 827-4242   SIC 5511

W.O. STINSON & SON LIMITED p 597
4726 BANK ST, GLOUCESTER, ON, K1T 3W7
(613) 822-7400   SIC 5541

W.O.H.A HOLDINGS LIMITED p 71
11505 35 ST SE SUITE 111, CALGARY, AB, T2Z 4B1
(403) 250-5722   SIC 8748

W.O.W. HOSPITALITY CONCEPTS INC p 388
529 WELLINGTON CRES 3RD FL, WINNIPEG, MB, R3M 0A1
(204) 942-1090   SIC 8741

W.R.A. ENTERPRISES PORTAGE LA PRAIRIE LTD p 355
2100 SASKATCHEWAN AVE W, PORTAGE LA PRAIRIE, MB, R1N 0P3
(204) 857-4700   SIC 5411

W.S. NICHOLLS CONSTRUCTION INC p 535
48 COWANSVIEW RD, CAMBRIDGE, ON, N1R 7N3
(519) 740-3757   SIC 1731

W3 SOLUTIONS p 342
See WGI SERVICE PLAN DIVISION INC

WABASH CANADA p 635
See TYCORRA INVESTMENTS INC

WABASH MFG. INC p 172
9312 110A ST, WESTLOCK, AB, T7P 2M4
(780) 349-4282   SIC 3443

WABI IRON & STEEL CORP p 753
330 BROADWOOD AVE, NEW LISKEARD, ON, P0J 1P0
(705) 647-4383   SIC 3325

WABISA MUTUAL INSURANCE COMPANY p 623
35 TALBOT ST W, JARVIS, ON, N0A 1J0
(519) 587-4454   SIC 6331

WABTEC CANADA INC p 893
475 SEAMAN ST, STONEY CREEK, ON, L8E 2R2
(905) 561-8700   SIC 3743

WABTEC CANADA INC p 1005
40 MASON ST, WALLACEBURG, ON, N8A 4M1
(519) 627-1244   SIC 3321

WABTEC CANADA INC p 1324
10000 BOUL CAVENDISH, SAINT-LAURENT, QC, H4M 2V1
(514) 335-4200   SIC 5051

WABTEC CANADA INC p 1337
10655 BOUL HENRI-BOURASSA O, SAINT-LAURENT, QC, H4S 1A1
(514) 335-4200   SIC 3743

WABTEC FOUNDRY p 1005
See WABTEC CANADA INC

WACKY'S CARPET & FLOOR CENTRE p 444
See 98599 CANADA LTD

WADDEN F J FOOD SERVICE DIV OF p 427
See WADDEN, F.J. & SONS LIMITED

WADDEN, F.J. & SONS LIMITED p 427
51 GLENCOE DR, MOUNT PEARL, NL, A1N 4S6
(709) 364-1444   SIC 5145

WADDICK FUELS p 543
See KENT PETROLEUM LIMITED

WADDINGTON AUTIONEER p 935
See WADDINGTON MCLEAN & COMPANY LIMITED

WADDINGTON MCLEAN & COMPANY LIMITED p

935
275 KING ST E, TORONTO, ON, M5A 1K2
(416) 504-9100   SIC 7389

WADE ATLANTIC p 444
See 3102597 NOVA SCOTIA LIMITED

WADE GENERAL CONTRACTING LTD p 839
56 INDUSTRIAL AVE, PETAWAWA, ON, K8H 2W8
(613) 687-8585   SIC 1542

WADE, R.S. HEALTH CARE LTD p 398
18 RUE CHAMPLAIN UNIT 1, DIEPPE, NB, E1A 1N3
(506) 389-1680   SIC 5912

WADE-TECH CAD & GRAPHICS p 547
See 1509611 ONTARIO INC

WADLAND PHARMACY LIMITED p 512
1 PRESIDENTS CHOICE CIR, BRAMPTON, ON, L6Y 5S5
(905) 459-2500   SIC 5912

WAGGWARE p 527
See 1428427 ONTARIO LTD

WAGONMASTER ENTERPRISES (BC) INC p 257
12671 BATHGATE WAY SUITE 3, RICHMOND, BC, V6V 1Y5
(604) 270-2033   SIC 5013

WAGONMASTER ENTERPRISES B.C. INC p 856
561 EDWARD AVE UNIT 11, RICHMOND HILL, ON, L4C 9W6
(905) 737-4627   SIC 6399

WAGONMASTER ONTARIO p 856
See WAGONMASTER ENTERPRISES B.C. INC

WAH LOONG LTD p 257
5388 PARKWOOD PL, RICHMOND, BC, V6V 2N1
(604) 273-1688   SIC 5146

WAH LUNG LABELS p 677
See WAH LUNG LABELS (CANADA) INC

WAH LUNG LABELS (CANADA) INC p 677
150 TELSON RD, MARKHAM, ON, L3R 1E5
(905) 948-8877   SIC 2241

WAHA ENTERPRISES INC p 748
100 BAYSHORE DR, NEPEAN, ON, K2B 8C1
(613) 721-2918   SIC 5812

WAHKEHEKUN BUILDING SUPPLIES DIV p 366
See OLYMPIC BUILDING SYSTEMS LTD

WAHL CONSTRUCTION LTD p 146
830 15 ST SW, MEDICINE HAT, AB, T1A 4W7
(403) 526-6235   SIC 1521

WAI CANADA INC p 1003
535 MILLWAY AVE SUITE 1, VAUGHAN, ON, L4K 3V4
(905) 660-7274   SIC 5531

WAINALTA MOTORS (1988) LTD p 171
2110 15 AVE, WAINWRIGHT, AB, T9W 1L2
(780) 842-4255   SIC 5511

WAINBEE LIMITED p 707
5789 COOPERS AVE, MISSISSAUGA, ON, L4Z 3S6
(905) 568-1700   SIC 5084

WAINBEE S H C N INC p 1367
453 AV NOEL, SEPT-ILES, QC, G4R 1M1
(418) 962-4949   SIC 5084

WAIWARD CONSTRUCTION MANAGEMENT INC p 106
13015 163 ST NW, EDMONTON, AB, T5V 1M5
(780) 447-1308   SIC 1623

WAIWARD INDUSTRIAL LIMITED PARTNERSHIP p 111
10030 34 ST NW, EDMONTON, AB, T6B 2Y5
(780) 469-1258   SIC 3499

WAJAX CORPORATION p 703
3280 WHARTON WAY, MISSISSAUGA, ON, L4X 2C5

(905) 212-3300   SIC 5084

WAJAX EQUIPMENT p 1
See INTEGRATED DISTRIBUTION SYSTEMS LIMITED PARTNERSHIP

WAJAX EQUIPMENT p 101
See INTEGRATED DISTRIBUTION SYSTEMS LIMITED PARTNERSHIP

WAJAX EQUIPMENT p 703
See INTEGRATED DISTRIBUTION SYSTEMS LIMITED PARTNERSHIP

WAJAX EQUIPMENT p 1086
See INTEGRATED DISTRIBUTION SYSTEMS LIMITED PARTNERSHIP

WAJAX INDUSTRIAL COMPONENTS p 1129
See WAJAX INDUSTRIAL COMPONENTS LIMITED PARTNERSHIP

WAJAX INDUSTRIAL COMPONENTS LIMITED PARTNERSHIP p 1129
2200 52E AV, LACHINE, QC, H8T 2Y3
(514) 636-3333   SIC 5084

WAJAX INDUSTRIAL COMPONENTS LIMITED PARTNERSHIP p 1129
2202 52E AV, LACHINE, QC, H8T 2Y3
(514) 636-3333   SIC 5084

WAJAX LIMITED p 728
2250 ARGENTIA RD, MISSISSAUGA, ON, L5N 6A5
(905) 212-3300   SIC 5084

WAJAX POWER SYSTEMS p 1275
See INTEGRATED DISTRIBUTION SYSTEMS LIMITED PARTNERSHIP

WAJAX POWER SYSTEMS p 1306
See INTEGRATED DISTRIBUTION SYSTEMS LIMITED PARTNERSHIP

WAKEFIELD CANADA INC p 571
3620 LAKE SHORE BLVD W, ETOBICOKE, ON, M8W 1N6
(416) 252-5511   SIC 5172

WAKEFIELD-SPERLING AUTO PARTS LTD p 175
33406 SOUTH FRASER WAY, ABBOTSFORD, BC, V2S 2B5
(604) 853-8179   SIC 5013

WAKEHAM TAYLOR HOLDINGS INC p 578
5363 DUNDAS ST W, ETOBICOKE, ON, M9B 1B1
SIC 5531

WAL MART p 535
See WAL-MART CANADA CORP

WAL MART p 836
See WAL-MART CANADA CORP

WAL MART p 838
See WAL-MART CANADA CORP

WAL MART p 850
See WAL-MART CANADA CORP

WAL MART p 1283
See WAL-MART CANADA CORP

WAL MART 1025 p 1151
See WAL-MART CANADA CORP

WAL MART GRANBY STORE- #3035 p 1111
See WAL-MART CANADA CORP

WAL-MART p 168
See WAL-MART CANADA CORP

WAL-MART p 248
See WAL-MART CANADA CORP

WAL-MART p 269
See WAL-MART CANADA CORP

WAL-MART p 284
See WAL-MART CANADA CORP

WAL-MART p 468
See WAL-MART CANADA CORP

WAL-MART p 994
See WAL-MART CANADA CORP

WAL-MART p 1125
See WAL-MART CANADA CORP

WAL-MART p 1150
See WAL-MART CANADA CORP

WAL-MART CANADA CORP p 3
2881 MAIN ST SE SUITE 1050, AIRDRIE, AB, T4B 3G5
(403) 945-1295   SIC 5311

WAL-MART CANADA CORP p 7
917 3 ST W SUITE 3658, BROOKS, AB, T1R 1L5
(403) 793-2111   SIC 5199

WAL-MART CANADA CORP p 12
3800 MEMORIAL DR NE SUITE 1100, CALGARY, AB, T2A 2K2
(403) 235-2352   SIC 5311

WAL-MART CANADA CORP p 26
1110 57 AVE NE SUITE 3013, CALGARY, AB, T2E 9B7
(403) 730-0990   SIC 5311

WAL-MART CANADA CORP p 39
9650 MACLEOD TRAIL SE, CALGARY, AB, T2J 0P7
(403) 258-3988   SIC 5311

WAL-MART CANADA CORP p 41
5005 NORTHLAND DRIVE NW, CALGARY, AB, T2L 2K1
(403) 247-8585   SIC 5311

WAL-MART CANADA CORP p 70
310 SHAWVILLE BLVD SE SUITE 100, CALGARY, AB, T2Y 3S4
(403) 201-5415   SIC 5311

WAL-MART CANADA CORP p 73
1212 37 ST SW SUITE 3009, CALGARY, AB, T3C 1S3
(403) 242-2205   SIC 5311

WAL-MART CANADA CORP p 75
8888 COUNTRY HILLS BLVD NW SUITE 200, CALGARY, AB, T3G 5T4
(403) 567-1502   SIC 5311

WAL-MART CANADA CORP p 78
6800 48 AVE UNIT 400, CAMROSE, AB, T4V 4T1
(780) 608-1211   SIC 5311

WAL-MART CANADA CORP p 81
4702 43 AVE SUITE 3640, COLD LAKE, AB, T9M 1M9
(780) 840-2340   SIC 5311

WAL-MART CANADA CORP p 82
1801 SOUTH RAILWAY AVE, DRUMHELLER, AB, T0J 0Y2
(403) 820-7744   SIC 5311

WAL-MART CANADA CORP p 82
5217 POWER CENTRE BLVD, DRAYTON VALLEY, AB, T7A 0A5
(780) 514-3207   SIC 5311

WAL-MART CANADA CORP p 103
18521 STONY PLAIN RD NW SUITE 3027, EDMONTON, AB, T5S 2V9
(780) 487-8626   SIC 5311

WAL-MART CANADA CORP p 107
13703 40 ST NW SUITE 3028, EDMONTON, AB, T5Y 3B5
(780) 476-4460   SIC 5311

WAL-MART CANADA CORP p 107
5004 98 AVE NW SUITE 1, EDMONTON, AB, T6A 0A1
(780) 466-2002   SIC 5311

WAL-MART CANADA CORP p 121
1203 PARSONS RD NW SUITE 3029, EDMONTON, AB, T6N 0A9
(780) 468-1755   SIC 5311

WAL-MART CANADA CORP p 126
5750 2 AVE, EDSON, AB, T7E 0A1
(780) 723-6357   SIC 5311

WAL-MART CANADA CORP p 129
2 HOSPITAL ST, FORT MCMURRAY, AB, T9H 5E4
(780) 790-6012   SIC 5311

WAL-MART CANADA CORP p 130
9551 87 AVE, FORT SASKATCHEWAN, AB, T8L 4N3
(780) 998-3633   SIC 5311

WAL-MART CANADA CORP p 133
11050 103 AVE, GRANDE PRAIRIE, AB, T8V 7H1
(780) 513-3740   SIC 5311

WAL-MART CANADA CORP p 136
900 CARMICHAEL LANE SUITE 100, HINTON, AB, T7V 1Y6
(780) 865-1421   SIC 5311

WAL-MART CANADA CORP p 140

5302 DISCOVERY WAY, LEDUC, AB, T9E 8J7

(780) 986-7574   *SIC* 5311

WAL-MART CANADA CORP   *p* 141
3195 26 AVE N SUITE 1078, LETHBRIDGE, AB, T1H 5P3

(403) 380-6722   *SIC* 5311

WAL-MART CANADA CORP   *p* 143
3700 MAYOR MAGRATH DR S SUITE 3048, LETHBRIDGE, AB, T1K 7T6

(403) 328-6277   *SIC* 5311

WAL-MART CANADA CORP   *p* 144
4210 70 AVE SUITE 3168, LLOYDMINSTER, AB, T9V 2X3

(780) 875-4777   *SIC* 5311

WAL-MART CANADA CORP   *p* 147
2051 STRACHAN RD SE, MEDICINE HAT, AB, T1B 0G4

(403) 504-4410   *SIC* 5311

WAL-MART CANADA CORP   *p* 152
1100 TABLE MOUNTAIN RD, PINCHER CREEK, AB, T0K 1W0

(403) 627-1790   *SIC* 5311

WAL-MART CANADA CORP   *p* 155
6375 50 AVE, RED DEER, AB, T4N 4C7

(403) 346-6650   *SIC* 5311

WAL-MART CANADA CORP   *p* 157
2010 50 AVE SUITE 3194, RED DEER, AB, T4R 3A2

(403) 358-5842   *SIC* 5311

WAL-MART CANADA CORP   *p* 162
239 WYE RD, SHERWOOD PARK, AB, T8B 1N1

(780) 464-2105   *SIC* 5311

WAL-MART CANADA CORP   *p* 164
1500 MAIN ST SW, SLAVE LAKE, AB, T0G 2A4

(780) 849-9579   *SIC* 5311

WAL-MART CANADA CORP   *p* 166
700 ST ALBERT TRAIL SUITE 3087, ST. ALBERT, AB, T8N 7A5

(780) 458-1629   *SIC* 5311

WAL-MART CANADA CORP   *p* 167
4724 70TH ST, STETTLER, AB, T0C 2L1

(403) 742-4404   *SIC* 5311

WAL-MART CANADA CORP   *p* 168
200 RANCH MARKET, STRATHMORE, AB, T1P 0A8

(403) 934-9776   *SIC* 5311

WAL-MART CANADA CORP   *p* 169
3420 47 AVE, SYLVAN LAKE, AB, T4S 0B6

(403) 887-7590   *SIC* 5311

WAL-MART CANADA CORP   *p* 169
4500 64 ST SUITE 1, TABER, AB, T1G 0A4

(403) 223-3458   *SIC* 5311

WAL-MART CANADA CORP   *p* 170
6809 16A HWY W, VEGREVILLE, AB, T9C 0A2

(780) 632-6016   *SIC* 5311

WAL-MART CANADA CORP   *p* 171
2901 13 AVE SUITE 1062, WAINWRIGHT, AB, T9W 0A2

(780) 842-3144   *SIC* 5311

WAL-MART CANADA CORP   *p* 173
5005 DAHL DR, WHITECOURT, AB, T7S 1X6

(780) 706-3323   *SIC* 5311

WAL-MART CANADA CORP   *p* 176
1812 VEDDER WAY SUITE 3019, ABBOTSFORD, BC, V2S 8K1

(604) 854-3575   *SIC* 5311

WAL-MART CANADA CORP   *p* 180
9855 AUSTIN RD SUITE 300, BURNABY, BC, V3J 1N5

(604) 421-0661   *SIC* 5311

WAL-MART CANADA CORP   *p* 198
45610 LUCKAKUCK WAY UNIT 200, CHILLIWACK, BC, V2R 1A2

(604) 858-5100   *SIC* 5311

WAL-MART CANADA CORP   *p* 204
2100 WILLOWBROOK DR SUITE 3183, CRANBROOK, BC, V1C 7H2

(250) 489-3202   *SIC* 5311

WAL-MART CANADA CORP   *p* 205

600 HIGHWAY 2, DAWSON CREEK, BC, V1G 0A4

(250) 719-0128   *SIC* 5311

WAL-MART CANADA CORP   *p* 212
3020 DRINKWATER RD, DUNCAN, BC, V9L 6C6

(250) 748-2566   *SIC* 5311

WAL-MART CANADA CORP   *p* 214
9007 96A ST, FORT ST. JOHN, BC, V1J 7B6

(250) 261-5544   *SIC* 5311

WAL-MART CANADA CORP   *p* 218
1055 HILLSIDE DR UNIT 100, KAMLOOPS, BC, V2E 2S5

(250) 374-1591   *SIC* 5311

WAL-MART CANADA CORP   *p* 220
1555 BANKS RD, KELOWNA, BC, V1X 7Y8

(250) 860-8811   *SIC* 5311

WAL-MART CANADA CORP   *p* 227
20202 66 AVE, LANGLEY, BC, V2Y 1P3

(604) 539-5210   *SIC* 5531

WAL-MART CANADA CORP   *p* 232
3900 CRAWFORD AVE SUITE 100, MERRITT, BC, V1K 0A4

(250) 315-1366   *SIC* 5311

WAL-MART CANADA CORP   *p* 233
31956 LOUGHEED HWY SUITE 1119, MISSION, BC, V2V 0C6

(604) 820-0048   *SIC* 5311

WAL-MART CANADA CORP   *p* 235
6801 ISLAND HWY N SUITE 3059, NANAIMO, BC, V9T 6N8

(250) 758-0343   *SIC* 5311

WAL-MART CANADA CORP   *p* 236
1000 LAKESIDE DR, NELSON, BC, V1L 5Z4

(250) 352-3782   *SIC* 5311

WAL-MART CANADA CORP   *p* 242
925 MARINE DR SUITE 3057, NORTH VANCOUVER, BC, V7P 1S2

(604) 984-6830   *SIC* 5311

WAL-MART CANADA CORP   *p* 244
275 GREEN AVE W SUITE 135, PENTICTON, BC, V2A 7J2

(250) 493-6681   *SIC* 5311

WAL-MART CANADA CORP   *p* 245
3355 JOHNSTON RD, PORT ALBERNI, BC, V9Y 8K1

(250) 720-0912   *SIC* 5311

WAL-MART CANADA CORP   *p* 248
7100 ALBERNI ST SUITE 23, POWELL RIVER, BC, V8A 5K9

(604) 485-9811   *SIC* 5311

WAL-MART CANADA CORP   *p* 251
6565 SOUTHRIDGE AVE SUITE 3651, PRINCE GEORGE, BC, V2N 6Z4

(250) 906-3203   *SIC* 5311

WAL-MART CANADA CORP   *p* 252
890 RITA RD, QUESNEL, BC, V2J 7J3

(250) 747-4464   *SIC* 5311

WAL-MART CANADA CORP   *p* 269
39210 DISCOVERY WAY SUITE 1015, SQUAMISH, BC, V8B 0N1

(604) 815-4625   *SIC* 5311

WAL-MART CANADA CORP   *p* 271
1000 GUILDFORD TOWN CTR, SURREY, BC, V3R 7C3

(604) 581-1932   *SIC* 5311

WAL-MART CANADA CORP   *p* 278
12451 88 AVE, SURREY, BC, V3W 1P8

(604) 597-7117   *SIC* 5311

WAL-MART CANADA CORP   *p* 280
2355 160 ST, SURREY, BC, V3Z 9N6

(604) 541-9015   *SIC* 5311

WAL-MART CANADA CORP   *p* 283
4427 16 HWY W, TERRACE, BC, V8G 5L5

(250) 615-4728   *SIC* 5311

WAL-MART CANADA CORP   *p* 284
1601 MARCOLIN DR SUITE 1011, TRAIL, BC, V1R 4Y1

(250) 364-1802   *SIC* 5311

WAL-MART CANADA CORP   *p* 284
1601 MARCOLIN DR SUITE 1011, TRAIL, BC, V1R 4Y1

(250) 364-2688   *SIC* 5311

WAL-MART CANADA CORP   *p* 332
2200 58 AVE SUITE 3169, VERNON, BC, V1T 9T2

(250) 558-0425   *SIC* 5311

WAL-MART CANADA CORP   *p* 339
3460 SAANICH RD SUITE 3109, VICTORIA, BC, V8Z 0B9

(250) 475-3356   *SIC* 5311

WAL-MART CANADA CORP   *p* 347
903 18TH ST N, BRANDON, MB, R7A 7S1

(204) 726-5821   *SIC* 5311

WAL-MART CANADA CORP   *p* 349
1450 MAIN ST S UNIT A, DAUPHIN, MB, R7N 3H4

(204) 638-4808   *SIC* 5311

WAL-MART CANADA CORP   *p* 355
2348 SISSONS DR, PORTAGE LA PRAIRIE, MB, R1N 0G5

(204) 857-5011   *SIC* 5311

WAL-MART CANADA CORP   *p* 360
300 MYSTERY LAKE RD SUITE 3102, THOMPSON, MB, R8N 0M2

(204) 778-4669   *SIC* 5311

WAL-MART CANADA CORP   *p* 361
1000 NAVIGATOR RD, WINKLER, MB, R6W 0L8

(204) 325-4160   *SIC* 5311

WAL-MART CANADA CORP   *p* 368
1225 ST MARY'S RD SUITE 54, WINNIPEG, MB, R2M 5E6

(204) 256-7027   *SIC* 5311

WAL-MART CANADA CORP   *p* 370
2370 MCPHILLIPS ST SUITE 3118, WINNIPEG, MB, R2V 4J6

(204) 334-2273   *SIC* 5311

WAL-MART CANADA CORP   *p* 382
1001 EMPRESS ST, WINNIPEG, MB, R3G 3P8

(204) 284-6900   *SIC* 5311

WAL-MART CANADA CORP   *p* 387
3655 PORTAGE AVE, WINNIPEG, MB, R3K 2G6

(204) 897-3410   *SIC* 5311

WAL-MART CANADA CORP   *p* 389
1665 KENASTON BLVD, WINNIPEG, MB, R3P 2M4

(204) 488-2052   *SIC* 5311

WAL-MART CANADA CORP   *p* 394
4 RUE JAGOE, ATHOLVILLE, NB, E3N 5C3

(506) 753-7105   *SIC* 5311

WAL-MART CANADA CORP   *p* 395
900 ST. ANNE ST, BATHURST, NB, E2A 6X2

(506) 546-0500   *SIC* 5311

WAL-MART CANADA CORP   *p* 399
805 RUE VICTORIA SUITE 1033, EDMUNDSTON, NB, E3V 3T3

(506) 735-8412   *SIC* 5311

WAL-MART CANADA CORP   *p* 400
125 TWO NATIONS XG SUITE 1067, FREDERICTON, NB, E3A 0T3

SIC 5311

WAL-MART CANADA CORP   *p* 402
1399 REGENT ST, FREDERICTON, NB, E3C 1A3

(506) 452-1511   *SIC* 5311

WAL-MART CANADA CORP   *p* 405
200 DOUGLASTOWN BLVD, MIRAMICHI, NB, E1V 7T9

(506) 778-8224   *SIC* 5311

WAL-MART CANADA CORP   *p* 407
25 PLAZA BLVD SUITE 3659, MONCTON, NB, E1C 0G3

(506) 853-7394   *SIC* 5311

WAL-MART CANADA CORP   *p* 413
450 WESTMORLAND RD SUITE 3091, SAINT JOHN, NB, E2J 4Z2

(506) 634-6600   *SIC* 5311

WAL-MART CANADA CORP   *p* 418
80 MAIN ST, SUSSEX, NB, E4E 1Y6

(506) 432-9333   *SIC* 5311

WAL-MART CANADA CORP   *p* 420
430 CONNELL ST, WOODSTOCK, NB, E7M 5R5

(506) 324-8099   *SIC* 5311

WAL-MART CANADA CORP   *p* 421
120 COLUMBUS DR, CARBONEAR, NL, A1Y 1B3

(709) 596-5009   *SIC* 5311

WAL-MART CANADA CORP   *p* 422
16 MURPHY SQ, CORNER BROOK, NL, A2H 1R4

(709) 634-2310   *SIC* 5311

WAL-MART CANADA CORP   *p* 423
55 AV ROE, GANDER, NL, A1V 0H6

(709) 256-7581   *SIC* 5311

WAL-MART CANADA CORP   *p* 424
19 CROMER AVE, GRAND FALLS-WINDSOR, NL, A2A 2K5

(709) 489-5739   *SIC* 5311

WAL-MART CANADA CORP   *p* 425
500 VANIER AVE SUITE 1035, LABRADOR CITY, NL, A2V 2W7

(709) 944-3378   *SIC* 5311

WAL-MART CANADA CORP   *p* 427
60 MERCHANT DR, MOUNT PEARL, NL, A1N 5J5

(709) 364-4214   *SIC* 5311

WAL-MART CANADA CORP   *p* 431
75 KELSEY DR, ST. JOHN'S, NL, A1B 0C7

(709) 722-6707   *SIC* 5311

WAL-MART CANADA CORP   *p* 434
42 QUEEN ST, STEPHENVILLE, NL, A2N 3A7

(709) 643-5018   *SIC* 5311

WAL-MART CANADA CORP   *p* 436
313 OLD AIRPORT RD, YELLOWKNIFE, NT, X1A 3T3

(867) 873-4545   *SIC* 5311

WAL-MART CANADA CORP   *p* 438
46 ROBERT ANGUS DR, AMHERST, NS, B4H 4R7

(902) 661-3476   *SIC* 5311

WAL-MART CANADA CORP   *p* 438
50 MARKET ST, ANTIGONISH, NS, B2G 3B4

(902) 867-1279   *SIC* 5311

WAL-MART CANADA CORP   *p* 440
141 DAMASCUS RD, BEDFORD, NS, B4A 0C2

(902) 865-4000   *SIC* 5311

WAL-MART CANADA CORP   *p* 441
60 PINE GROVE RD, BRIDGEWATER, NS, B4V 4H2

(902) 543-8680   *SIC* 5311

WAL-MART CANADA CORP   *p* 448
90 LAMONT TERR, DARTMOUTH, NS, B3B 0B5

(902) 461-4474   *SIC* 5311

WAL-MART CANADA CORP   *p* 457
6990 MUMFORD RD SUITE 3636, HALIFAX, NS, B3L 4W4

(902) 454-7990   *SIC* 5311

WAL-MART CANADA CORP   *p* 459
220 CHAIN LAKE DR, HALIFAX, NS, B3S 1C5

(902) 450-5570   *SIC* 5311

WAL-MART CANADA CORP   *p* 463
713 WESTVILLE RD SUITE 3061, NEW GLASGOW, NS, B2H 2J6

(902) 928-0008   *SIC* 5311

WAL-MART CANADA CORP   *p* 464
9097 COMMERCIAL ST SUITE 3738, NEW MINAS, NS, B4N 3E6

(902) 681-4271   *SIC* 5311

WAL-MART CANADA CORP   *p* 465
47 PAINT ST UNIT 17, PORT HAWKESBURY, NS, B9A 3J9

(902) 625-0954   *SIC* 5311

WAL-MART CANADA CORP   *p* 467
800 GRAND LAKE RD, SYDNEY, NS, B1P 6S9

(902) 562-1110   *SIC* 5311

WAL-MART CANADA CORP   *p* 468
65 KELTIC DR, SYDNEY, NS, B1S 1P4

(902) 562-3353   *SIC* 5311

WAL-MART CANADA CORP   *p* 469
140 WADE RD, TRURO, NS, B2N 7H3

▲ Public Company   ■ Public Company Family Member   **HQ** Headquarters   **BR** Branch   **SL** Single Location

(902) 893-5582 *SIC* 5311
WAL-MART CANADA CORP *p* 471
108 STARRS RD, YARMOUTH, NS, B5A
2T5

(902) 749-2306 *SIC* 5311
WAL-MART CANADA CORP *p* 475
270 KINGSTON RD E, AJAX, ON, L1Z 1G1

(905) 426-6160 *SIC* 5311
WAL-MART CANADA CORP *p* 478
1051 GARNER RD W SUITE 3127, AN-
CASTER, ON, L9G 3K9

(905) 648-9980 *SIC* 5311
WAL-MART CANADA CORP *p* 482
135 FIRST COMMERCE DR, AURORA,
ON, L4G 0G2

(905) 841-0300 *SIC* 5311
WAL-MART CANADA CORP *p* 485
450 BAYFIELD ST, BARRIE, ON, L4M 5A2

(705) 728-2833 *SIC* 5311
WAL-MART CANADA CORP *p* 488
35 MAPLEVIEW DR W, BARRIE, ON, L4N
9H5

(705) 728-9122 *SIC* 5311
WAL-MART CANADA CORP *p* 492
274 MILLENNIUM PKY, BELLEVILLE, ON,
K8N 4Z5

(613) 966-9466 *SIC* 5311
WAL-MART CANADA CORP *p* 507
30 COVENTRY RD, BRAMPTON, ON, L6T
5P9

(905) 793-1983 *SIC* 5311
WAL-MART CANADA CORP *p* 508
50 QUARRY EDGE DR, BRAMPTON, ON,
L6V 4K2

(905) 874-0112 *SIC* 5311
WAL-MART CANADA CORP *p* 515
300 KING GEORGE RD SUITE 1, BRANT-
FORD, ON, N3R 5L7

(519) 759-3450 *SIC* 5311
WAL-MART CANADA CORP *p* 520
1942 PARKEDALE AVE SUITE 3006,
BROCKVILLE, ON, K6V 7N4

(613) 342-9293 *SIC* 5311
WAL-MART CANADA CORP *p* 527
4515 DUNDAS ST SUITE 1, BURLINGTON,
ON, L7M 5B4

(905) 331-0027 *SIC* 5311
WAL-MART CANADA CORP *p* 530
2065 FAIRVIEW ST, BURLINGTON, ON,
L7R 0B4

(905) 637-3100 *SIC* 5999
WAL-MART CANADA CORP *p* 535
22 PINEBUSH RD, CAMBRIDGE, ON, N1R
8K5

(519) 624-7467 *SIC* 5311
WAL-MART CANADA CORP *p* 542
881 ST CLAIR ST, CHATHAM, ON, N7L 0E9

(519) 352-1142 *SIC* 5311
WAL-MART CANADA CORP *p* 545
73 STRATHY RD, COBOURG, ON, K9A
5W8

(905) 373-1239 *SIC* 5311
WAL-MART CANADA CORP *p* 547
10 CAMBRIDGE, COLLINGWOOD, ON,
L9Y 0A1

(705) 445-9262 *SIC* 5311
WAL-MART CANADA CORP *p* 561
101 EDGELEY BLVD SUITE 3145, CON-
CORD, ON, L4K 4Z4

(905) 761-7945 *SIC* 5311
WAL-MART CANADA CORP *p* 562
6227 BOUNDARY RD, CORNWALL, ON,
K6H 5R5

(613) 932-7879 *SIC* 4212
WAL-MART CANADA CORP *p* 563
950 BROOKDALE AVE, CORNWALL, ON,
K6J 4P5

(613) 933-8366 *SIC* 5311
WAL-MART CANADA CORP *p* 565
HWY 17 E, DRYDEN, ON, P8N 2Y6

(807) 223-7190 *SIC* 5311
WAL-MART CANADA CORP *p* 580
165 NORTH QUEEN ST SUITE 3031, ETO-
BICOKE, ON, M9C 1A7

(416) 239-7090 *SIC* 5311
WAL-MART CANADA CORP *p* 589
2245 ISLINGTON AVE SUITE 3740, ETOBI-
COKE, ON, M9W 3W6

(416) 747-6499 *SIC* 5311
WAL-MART CANADA CORP *p* 592
1250 KING'S HWY, FORT FRANCES, ON,
P9A 2X6

(807) 274-1373 *SIC* 5311
WAL-MART CANADA CORP *p* 592
750 GARRISON RD, FORT ERIE, ON, L2A
1N7

(905) 991-9971 *SIC* 5311
WAL-MART CANADA CORP *p* 597
35400 HURON RD, GODERICH, ON, N7A
3X8

(519) 524-5060 *SIC* 5311
WAL-MART CANADA CORP *p* 604
11 WOODLAWN RD W, GUELPH, ON, N1H
1G8

(519) 767-1600 *SIC* 5311
WAL-MART CANADA CORP *p* 617
2190 RYMAL RD E SUITE 1042, HANNON,
ON, L0R 1P0

(905) 692-7000 *SIC* 5311
WAL-MART CANADA CORP *p* 617
675 UPPER JAMES ST, HAMILTON, ON,
L9C 2Z5

(905) 389-6333 *SIC* 5311
WAL-MART CANADA CORP *p* 618
1100 10TH ST, HANOVER, ON, N4N 3B8

(519) 364-0867 *SIC* 5311
WAL-MART CANADA CORP *p* 621
111 HOWLAND DR UNIT 10, HUNTSVILLE,
ON, P1H 2P4

(705) 787-1137 *SIC* 5311
WAL-MART CANADA CORP *p* 626
500 EARL GREY DR, KANATA, ON, K2T
1B6

(613) 599-6765 *SIC* 5311
WAL-MART CANADA CORP *p* 627
350 GOVERNMENT RD E, KAPUSKASING,
ON, P5N 2X7

(705) 335-6111 *SIC* 5311
WAL-MART CANADA CORP *p* 628
24 MIIKANA WAY UNIT 1, KENORA, ON,
P9N 4J1

(807) 468-6379 *SIC* 5311
WAL-MART CANADA CORP *p* 633
1130 MIDLAND AVE, KINGSTON, ON, K7P
2X9

(613) 384-9071 *SIC* 5311
WAL-MART CANADA CORP *p* 637
2960 KINGSWAY DR SUITE 3045, KITCH-
ENER, ON, N2C 1X1

(519) 894-6600 *SIC* 5311
WAL-MART CANADA CORP *p* 638
1400 OTTAWA ST S UNIT E, KITCHENER,
ON, N2E 4E2

(519) 576-0921 *SIC* 5311
WAL-MART CANADA CORP *p* 645
304 ERIE ST S, LEAMINGTON, ON, N8H
3C5

(519) 326-3900 *SIC* 5311
WAL-MART CANADA CORP *p* 651
330 CLARKE RD, LONDON, ON, N5W 6G4

(519) 455-8910 *SIC* 5311
WAL-MART CANADA CORP *p* 658
1105 WELLINGTON RD SUITE 3051, LON-
DON, ON, N6E 1V4

(519) 681-7500 *SIC* 5311
WAL-MART CANADA CORP *p* 677
5000 HIGHWAY 7 E UNIT Y006A,
MARKHAM, ON, L3R 4M9

(905) 477-6060 *SIC* 5311
WAL-MART CANADA CORP *p* 682
16845 12 HWY, MIDLAND, ON, L4R 0A9

(705) 526-4754 *SIC* 5311
WAL-MART CANADA CORP *p* 685
1280 STEELES AVE E SUITE 1000, MIL-
TON, ON, L9T 6R1

(905) 864-6027 *SIC* 5311
WAL-MART CANADA CORP *p* 711
100 CITY CENTRE DR SUITE 100, MISSIS-

SAUGA, ON, L5B 2G7
(905) 270-9300 *SIC* 5311
WAL-MART CANADA CORP *p* 718
2160 BURNHAMTHORPE RD W, MISSIS-
SAUGA, ON, L5L 5Z5

(905) 608-0922 *SIC* 5311
WAL-MART CANADA CORP *p* 728
3155 ARGENTIA RD, MISSISSAUGA, ON,
L5N 8E1

(905) 821-8150 *SIC* 5311
WAL-MART CANADA CORP *p* 728
1940 ARGENTIA RD, MISSISSAUGA, ON,
L5N 1P9

(905) 821-2111 *SIC* 5311
WAL-MART CANADA CORP *p* 728
1940 ARGENTIA RD, MISSISSAUGA, ON,
L5N 1P9

(800) 328-0402 *SIC* 5311
WAL-MART CANADA CORP *p* 728
6600 KITIMAT RD, MISSISSAUGA, ON, L5N
1L9

(905) 817-1824 *SIC* 5311
WAL-MART CANADA CORP *p* 752
3651 STRANDHERD DR, NEPEAN, ON,
K2J 4G8

(613) 823-8714 *SIC* 5311
WAL-MART CANADA CORP *p* 757
17940 YONGE ST, NEWMARKET, ON, L3Y
8S4

(905) 853-8811 *SIC* 5311
WAL-MART CANADA CORP *p* 759
7481 OAKWOOD DR, NIAGARA FALLS,
ON, L2G 0J5

(905) 371-3999 *SIC* 5311
WAL-MART CANADA CORP *p* 764
1500 FISHER ST SUITE 102, NORTH BAY,
ON, P1B 2H3

(705) 472-1704 *SIC* 5311
WAL-MART CANADA CORP *p* 799
234 HAYS BLVD, OAKVILLE, ON, L6H 6M4

(905) 257-5740 *SIC* 5311
WAL-MART CANADA CORP *p* 810
175 MURPHY RD, ORILLIA, ON, L3V 0B5

(705) 325-7403 *SIC* 5311
WAL-MART CANADA CORP *p* 811
3900 INNES RD, ORLEANS, ON, K1W 1K9

(613) 837-9399 *SIC* 5311
WAL-MART CANADA CORP *p* 814
1471 HARMONY RD N SUITE 3161, OS-
HAWA, ON, L1K 0Z6

(905) 404-6581 *SIC* 5311
WAL-MART CANADA CORP *p* 819
450 TERMINAL AVE SUITE 1031, OTTAWA,
ON, K1G 0Z3

(613) 562-0500 *SIC* 5311
WAL-MART CANADA CORP *p* 827
2210 BANK ST, OTTAWA, ON, K1V 1J5

(613) 247-1184 *SIC* 5311
WAL-MART CANADA CORP *p* 836
1555 18TH AVE E, OWEN SOUND, ON,
N4K 0E2

(519) 371-6900 *SIC* 5311
WAL-MART CANADA CORP *p* 837
1 PINE DR, PARRY SOUND, ON, P2A 3C3

(705) 746-1573 *SIC* 5311
WAL-MART CANADA CORP *p* 838
1108 PEMBROKE ST E, PEMBROKE, ON,
K8A 8P7

(613) 735-4997 *SIC* 5311
WAL-MART CANADA CORP *p* 840
1002 CHEMONG RD SUITE 3071, PETER-
BOROUGH, ON, K9H 7E2

(705) 742-1685 *SIC* 5311
WAL-MART CANADA CORP *p* 844
1899 BROCK RD UNIT B, PICKERING, ON,
L1V 4H7

(905) 619-9588 *SIC* 5311
WAL-MART CANADA CORP *p* 850
980 O'BRIEN RD SUITE 1, RENFREW, ON,
K7V 0B4

(613) 432-4676 *SIC* 5311
WAL-MART CANADA CORP *p* 857
3001 RICHELIEU ST, ROCKLAND, ON, K4K
0B5

(613) 446-5730 *SIC* 5399
WAL-MART CANADA CORP *p* 859
1444 QUINN DR, SARNIA, ON, N7S 6M8

(519) 542-4272 *SIC* 5311
WAL-MART CANADA CORP *p* 861
GD LCD MAIN, SARNIA, ON, N7T 7H7

(519) 542-1854 *SIC* 5311
WAL-MART CANADA CORP *p* 865
785 MILNER AVE, SCARBOROUGH, ON,
M1B 3C3

(416) 281-2929 *SIC* 5311
WAL-MART CANADA CORP *p* 869
800 WARDEN AVE, SCARBOROUGH, ON,
M1L 4T7

(416) 615-2697 *SIC* 5311
WAL-MART CANADA CORP *p* 872
300 BOROUGH DR SUITE 2, SCARBOR-
OUGH, ON, M1P 4P5

(416) 290-1916 *SIC* 5311
WAL-MART CANADA CORP *p* 875
3850 SHEPPARD AVE E SUITE 3000,
SCARBOROUGH, ON, M1T 3L4

(416) 291-4100 *SIC* 5311
WAL-MART CANADA CORP *p* 877
5995 STEELES AVE E SUITE SIDE, SCAR-
BOROUGH, ON, M1V 5P7

(416) 298-1210 *SIC* 5311
WAL-MART CANADA CORP *p* 882
114 LOMBARD ST, SMITHS FALLS, ON,
K7A 5B8

(613) 284-0838 *SIC* 5311
WAL-MART CANADA CORP *p* 884
525 WELLAND AVE, ST CATHARINES, ON,
L2M 6P3

(905) 685-4100 *SIC* 5311
WAL-MART CANADA CORP *p* 887
420 VANSICKLE RD SUITE 2, ST
CATHARINES, ON, L2S 0C7

(905) 687-9212 *SIC* 5311
WAL-MART CANADA CORP *p* 890
1063 TALBOT ST UNIT 60, ST THOMAS,
ON, N5P 1G4

(519) 631-1253 *SIC* 5311
WAL-MART CANADA CORP *p* 895
1050 HOOVER PARK DR, STOUFFVILLE,
ON, L4A 0K2

(905) 640-8848 *SIC* 5311
WAL-MART CANADA CORP *p* 897
150 CARROLL ST E, STRATHROY, ON,
N7G 4G2

(519) 245-7200 *SIC* 5311
WAL-MART CANADA CORP *p* 899
1349 LASALLE BLVD SUITE 3097, SUD-
BURY, ON, P3A 1Z2

(705) 566-3700 *SIC* 5311
WAL-MART CANADA CORP *p* 909
777 MEMORIAL AVE, THUNDER BAY, ON,
P7B 6S2

(807) 346-9441 *SIC* 5311
WAL-MART CANADA CORP *p* 912
400 SIMCOE ST, TILLSONBURG, ON, N4G
4X1

(519) 842-7770 *SIC* 5311
WAL-MART CANADA CORP *p* 990
900 DUFFERIN ST SUITE 3106,
TORONTO, ON, M6H 4B1

(416) 537-2561 *SIC* 5311
WAL-MART CANADA CORP *p* 992
1305 LAWRENCE AVE W, TORONTO, ON,
M6L 1A5

(416) 244-1171 *SIC* 5311
WAL-MART CANADA CORP *p* 994
2525 ST CLAIR AVE W, TORONTO, ON,
M6N 4Z5

(416) 763-7325 *SIC* 5311
WAL-MART CANADA CORP *p* 999
HWY 2 AT 2ND DUGHILL RD, TRENTON,
ON, K8V 5P7

(613) 394-2191 *SIC* 5311
WAL-MART CANADA CORP *p* 1001
6 WELWOOD DR, UXBRIDGE, ON, L9P
1Z7

(905) 862-0721 *SIC* 5311
WAL-MART CANADA CORP *p* 1005

▲ Public Company ■ Public Company Family Member **HQ** Headquarters **BR** Branch **SL** Single Location

60 MCNAUGHTON AVE UNIT 16, WAL-LACEBURG, ON, N8A 1R9
(519) 627-8840 SIC 5311

WAL-MART CANADA CORP p 1012
102 PRIMEWAY DR, WELLAND, ON, L3B 0A1
(905) 735-3500 SIC 5311

WAL-MART CANADA CORP p 1016
4100 BALDWIN ST S, WHITBY, ON, L1R 3H8
(905) 655-0206 SIC 5311

WAL-MART CANADA CORP p 1019
7100 TECUMSEH RD E SUITE 3115, WINDSOR, ON, N8T 1E6
(519) 945-3065 SIC 5311

WAL-MART CANADA CORP p 1025
3120 DOUGALL AVE, WINDSOR, ON, N9E 1S7
(519) 969-8121 SIC 5311

WAL-MART CANADA CORP p 1036
499 NORWICH AVE, WOODSTOCK, ON, N4S 9A2
(519) 539-5120 SIC 5311

WAL-MART CANADA CORP p 1041
80 BUCHANAN DR, CHARLOTTETOWN, PE, C1E 2E5
(902) 628-4600 SIC 5311

WAL-MART CANADA CORP p 1043
511 GRANVILLE ST, SUMMERSIDE, PE, C1N 5J4
(902) 432-3570 SIC 5311

WAL-MART CANADA CORP p 1045
1755 AV DU PONT S BUREAU 5795, ALMA, QC, G8B 7W7
(418) 480-3887 SIC 5311

WAL-MART CANADA CORP p 1053
630 BOUL LAFLECHE BUREAU 3002, BAIE-COMEAU, QC, G5C 2Y3
(418) 589-9971 SIC 5311

WAL-MART CANADA CORP p 1071
9000 BOUL LEDUC UNITE 102, BROSSARD, QC, J4Y 0E6
(450) 672-5000 SIC 5311

WAL-MART CANADA CORP p 1080
3017-1451 BOUL TALBOT, CHICOUTIMI, QC, G7H 5N8
(418) 693-1500 SIC 5311

WAL-MART CANADA CORP p 1085
1660 BOUL LE CORBUSIER, COTE SAINT-LUC, QC, H7S 1Z2
(450) 681-1126 SIC 5311

WAL-MART CANADA CORP p 1089
1770 RUE DU SUD, COWANSVILLE, QC, J2K 3G8
(450) 263-6006 SIC 5311

WAL-MART CANADA CORP p 1100
1205 BOUL RENE-LEVESQUE, DRUM-MONDVILLE, QC, J2C 7V4
(819) 472-7446 SIC 5311

WAL-MART CANADA CORP p 1105
640 BOUL MALONEY O, GATINEAU, QC, J8T 8K7
(819) 246-8808 SIC 5311

WAL-MART CANADA CORP p 1108
35 BOUL DU PLATEAU, GATINEAU, QC, J9A 3G1
(819) 772-1911 SIC 5311

WAL-MART CANADA CORP p 1111
75 RUE SIMONDS N, GRANBY, QC, J2J 2S3
(450) 777-8863 SIC 5311

WAL-MART CANADA CORP p 1115
1505 BOUL FIRESTONE BUREAU 521, JOLIETTE, QC, J6E 9E5
(450) 752-8210 SIC 5311

WAL-MART CANADA CORP p 1118
17000 RTE TRANSCANADIENNE, KIRK-LAND, QC, H9J 2M5
(514) 695-3040 SIC 5311

WAL-MART CANADA CORP p 1125
3130 RUE LAVAL, LAC-MEGANTIC, QC, G6B 1A4
(819) 583-2882 SIC 5311

WAL-MART CANADA CORP p 1129

480 AV BETHANY, LACHUTE, QC, J8H 4H5
(450) 562-0258 SIC 5311

WAL-MART CANADA CORP p 1131
6797 BOUL NEWMAN, LASALLE, QC, H8N 3E4
(514) 368-2248 SIC 5311

WAL-MART CANADA CORP p 1137
5303 RUE LOUIS-H.-LA FONTAINE, LEVIS, QC, G6V 8X4
(418) 833-8555 SIC 5311

WAL-MART CANADA CORP p 1139
700 RUE DE LA CONCORDE, LEVIS, QC, G6W 8A8
(418) 834-5115 SIC 5311

WAL-MART CANADA CORP p 1146
1999 BOUL ROLAND-THERRIEN, LONGUEUIL, QC, J4N 1A3
(450) 448-2688 SIC 5311

WAL-MART CANADA CORP p 1148
1935 RUE SHERBROOKE, MAGOG, QC, J1X 2T5
(819) 868-9775 SIC 5311

WAL-MART CANADA CORP p 1150
155 MONTEE MASSON BUREAU 3149, MASCOUCHE, QC, J7K 3B4
(450) 474-2679 SIC 5311

WAL-MART CANADA CORP p 1151
150 RUE PIUZE, MATANE, QC, G4W 4T2
(418) 566-4779 SIC 5311

WAL-MART CANADA CORP p 1228
5400 RUE JEAN-TALON O, MONTREAL, QC, H4P 2T5
(514) 735-0913 SIC 5311

WAL-MART CANADA CORP p 1240
6140 BOUL HENRI-BOURASSA E, MONTREAL-NORD, QC, H1G 5X3
(514) 324-7853 SIC 5311

WAL-MART CANADA CORP p 1278
1470 AV JULES-VERNE BUREAU 3146, QUEBEC, QC, G2G 2R5
(418) 874-6068 SIC 5311

WAL-MART CANADA CORP p 1283
100 BOUL BRIEN BUREAU 66, RE-PENTIGNY, QC, J6A 5N4
(450) 654-8886 SIC 5311

WAL-MART CANADA CORP p 1285
415 MONTEE INDUSTRIELLE-ET-COMMERCIALE BUREAU 3198, RIMOUSKI, QC, G5M 1Y1
(418) 722-1990 SIC 5311

WAL-MART CANADA CORP p 1287
100 RUE DES CERISIERS, RIVIERE-DU-LOUP, QC, G5R 6E8
(418) 862-3003 SIC 5311

WAL-MART CANADA CORP p 1288
401 BOUL LABELLE BUREAU 3080, ROSEMERE, QC, J7A 3T2
(450) 435-2982 SIC 5311

WAL-MART CANADA CORP p 1290
275 BOUL RIDEAU BUREAU 3136, ROUYN-NORANDA, QC, J9X 5Y6
(819) 762-0619 SIC 5311

WAL-MART CANADA CORP p 1296
1475 BOUL SAINT-BRUNO, SAINT-BRUNO, QC, J3V 6J1
(450) 653-9996 SIC 5311

WAL-MART CANADA CORP p 1298
500 VOIE DE LA DESSERTE UNITE 132, SAINT-CONSTANT, QC, J5A 2S5
(450) 632-2192 SIC 5311

WAL-MART CANADA CORP p 1302
764 BOUL ARTHUR-SAUVE BUREAU 3089, SAINT-EUSTACHE, QC, J7R 4K3
(450) 491-6922 SIC 5311

WAL-MART CANADA CORP p 1305
750 107E RUE, SAINT-GEORGES, QC, G5Y 0A1
(418) 220-0010 SIC 5311

WAL-MART CANADA CORP p 1311
5950 RUE MARTINEAU, SAINT-HYACINTHE, QC, J2R 2H6
(450) 796-4001 SIC 5311

WAL-MART CANADA CORP p 1315
100 BOUL OMER-MARCIL, SAINT-JEAN-

SUR-RICHELIEU, QC, J2W 2X2
(450) 349-0666 SIC 5311

WAL-MART CANADA CORP p 1320
1030 BOUL DU GRAND-HERON, SAINT-JEROME, QC, J7Y 5K8
(450) 438-6776 SIC 5311

WAL-MART CANADA CORP p 1346
7445 BOUL LANGELIER, SAINT-LEONARD, QC, H1S 1V6
(514) 899-1889 SIC 5311

WAL-MART CANADA CORP p 1354
400 RUE LAVERDURE, SAINTE-AGATHE-DES-MONTS, QC, J8C 0A2
(819) 326-9559 SIC 5311

WAL-MART CANADA CORP p 1361
5205 BOUL ROBERT-BOURASSA, SAINTE-ROSE, QC, H7E 0A3
(450) 661-7447 SIC 5311

WAL-MART CANADA CORP p 1363
700 CHOMEDEY (A-13) O, SAINTE-ROSE, QC, H7X 3S9
(450) 969-3226 SIC 5311

WAL-MART CANADA CORP p 1365
2050 BOUL MONSEIGNEUR-LANGLOIS, SALABERRY-DE-VALLEYFIELD, QC, J6S 5R1
(450) 371-9026 SIC 5311

WAL-MART CANADA CORP p 1367
1005 BOUL LAURE BUREAU 500, SEPT-ILES, QC, G4R 4S6
(418) 968-5151 SIC 5311

WAL-MART CANADA CORP p 1369
1600 BOUL ROYAL, SHAWINIGAN, QC, G9N 8S8
(819) 537-0113 SIC 5311

WAL-MART CANADA CORP p 1374
4050 BOUL JOSAPHAT-RANCOURT BU-REAU 3086, SHERBROOKE, QC, J1L 3C6
(819) 823-1661 SIC 5311

WAL-MART CANADA CORP p 1383
1025 BOUL FRONTENAC E, THETFORD MINES, QC, G6G 6S7
(418) 338-4884 SIC 5311

WAL-MART CANADA CORP p 1385
300 RUE BARKOFF, TROIS-RIVIERES, QC, G8T 2A3
(819) 379-2992 SIC 5311

WAL-MART CANADA CORP p 1389
4520 BOUL GENE-H.-KRUGER, TROIS-RIVIERES, QC, G9A 4N1
(819) 372-1181 SIC 5399

WAL-MART CANADA CORP p 1391
1855 3E AV BUREAU 3139, VAL-D'OR, QC, J9P 7A9
(819) 874-8411 SIC 5311

WAL-MART CANADA CORP p 1395
3050 BOUL DE LA GARE, VAUDREUIL-DORION, QC, J7V 0H1
(450) 510-3314 SIC 5311

WAL-MART CANADA CORP p 1398
110 BOUL ARTHABASKA O, VICTORIAV-ILLE, QC, G6S 0P2
(819) 758-5136 SIC 5311

WAL-MART CANADA CORP p 1407
413 KENSINGTON AVE, ESTEVAN, SK, S4A 2A5
(306) 634-2110 SIC 5311

WAL-MART CANADA CORP p 1408
710 11TH AVENUE E, KINDERSLEY, SK, S0L 1S2
(306) 463-1330 SIC 5311

WAL-MART CANADA CORP p 1411
551 THATCHER DR E SUITE 3173, MOOSE JAW, SK, S6J 1L8
(306) 693-3218 SIC 5311

WAL-MART CANADA CORP p 1413
601 CARLTON TRAIL SUITE 1, NORTH BATTLEFORD, SK, S9A 4A9
(306) 445-8105 SIC 5311

WAL-MART CANADA CORP p 1414
800 15TH ST E SUITE 100, PRINCE AL-BERT, SK, S6V 8E3
(306) 764-9770 SIC 5311

WAL-MART CANADA CORP p 1422

2150 PRINCE OF WALES DR, REGINA, SK, S4V 3A6
(306) 780-3700 SIC 5311

WAL-MART CANADA CORP p 1422
2715 GORDON RD, REGINA, SK, S4S 6H7
(306) 584-0061 SIC 5311

WAL-MART CANADA CORP p 1423
3939 ROCHDALE BLVD, REGINA, SK, S4X 4P7
(306) 543-3237 SIC 5311

WAL-MART CANADA CORP p 1433
225 BETTS AVE, SASKATOON, SK, S7M 1L2
(306) 382-5454 SIC 5311

WAL-MART CANADA CORP p 1434
1706 PRESTON AVE N SUITE 3084, SASKATOON, SK, S7N 4Y1
(306) 373-2300 SIC 5311

WAL-MART CANADA CORP p 1435
3035 CLARENCE AVE S, SASKATOON, SK, S7T 0B6
(306) 653-8200 SIC 5311

WAL-MART CANADA CORP p 1437
1800 22ND AVE NE, SWIFT CURRENT, SK, S9H 0E5
(306) 778-3489 SIC 5311

WAL-MART CANADA CORP p 1438
1000 SIMS AVE, WEYBURN, SK, S4H 3N9
(306) 842-6030 SIC 5311

WAL-MART CANADA CORP p 1439
240 HAMILTON RD, YORKTON, SK, S3N 4C6
(306) 782-9820 SIC 5311

WAL-MART CANADA CORP p 1440
9021 QUARTZ RD, WHITEHORSE, YT, Y1A 4P9
(867) 667-2652 SIC 5311

WAL-MART NORTHEAST p 107
See WAL-MART CANADA CORP

WAL-MART SPORTS CENTER-KITIMAT p 728
See WAL-MART CANADA CORP

WALCAN SEAFOOD LTD p 215
GD, HERIOT BAY, BC, V0P 1H0
(250) 285-3361 SIC 2091

WALCO p 245
See WALCO INDUSTRIES LTD

WALCO CANADA ANIMAL HEALTH p 101
See KANE VETERINARY SUPPLIES LTD

WALCO EQUIPMENT LTD p 568
20 ARTHUR ST N, ELMIRA, ON, N3B 1Z9
(519) 669-4025 SIC 5083

WALCO INDUSTRIES LTD p 245
6113 BEAVER CREEK RD, PORT AL-BERNI, BC, V9Y 8X4
(250) 723-6919 SIC 4959

WALDALE MANUFACTURING LIMITED p 438
17 TANTRAMAR CRES, AMHERST, NS, B4H 4J6
(902) 667-3307 SIC 3469

WALDHEIM COLONY FARMS LTD p 349
16025 RD 58 NW, ELIE, MB, R0H 0H0
(204) 353-2473 SIC 0291

WALDIE, D.S. HOLDINGS INCORPORATED p 278
8140 120 ST, SURREY, BC, V3W 3N3
SIC 5531

WALDORF EDUCATION SOCIETY OF ED-MONTON p 117
7114 98 ST NW, EDMONTON, AB, T6E 3M1
(780) 466-3312 SIC 8699

WALDUN FOREST PRODUCTS LTD p 231
9393 287 ST, MAPLE RIDGE, BC, V2W 1L1
(604) 462-8266 SIC 2429

WALES HOME, THE p 1081
506 RTE 243, CLEVELAND, QC, J0B 2H0
(819) 826-3266 SIC 8361

WALES MCLELLAND CONSTRUCTION COMPANY (1988) LIMITED p 259
6211 FRASERWOOD PL, RICHMOND, BC, V6W 1J2
(604) 638-1212 SIC 1542

WALINGA INC *p* 604
5656 HIGHWAY 6, GUELPH, ON, N1H 6J2
(519) 824-8520 *SIC* 3713

WALK WITH RONSON *p* 264
See RONSONS SHOE STORES LTD

WALKER COMMUNITY DEVELOPMENT CORP *p* 758
2800 THOROLD TOWN LINE, NIAGARA FALLS, ON, L2E 6S4
(905) 227-4142 *SIC* 1422

WALKER DAIRY INC *p* 482
50828 TALBOT ST E, AYLMER, ON, N5H 2R1
(519) 765-2406 *SIC* 5154

WALKER GROUP, THE *p* 341
See C. WALKER GROUP INC

WALKER INDUSTRIES HOLDINGS LIMITED *p* 758
2800 THOROLD TOWN LINE, NIAGARA FALLS, ON, L2E 6S4
(905) 227-4142 *SIC* 1411

WALKER INVESTIGATION BUREAU LTD *p* 409
1765 MAIN ST, MONCTON, NB, E1E 1H3
(506) 857-8343 *SIC* 7381

WALKER VILLE SECONDARY SCHOOL *p* 1022
See GREATER ESSEX COUNTY DISTRICT SCHOOL BOARD

WALKER'S GROCERY LTD *p* 5
1040 FIRST AVE, BEAVERLODGE, AB, T0H 0C0
(780) 354-2092 *SIC* 5411

WALKERS OWN PRODUCE INTERNATIONAL INC *p* 38
7711 MACLEOD TRAIL SW, CALGARY, AB, T2H 0M1
(587) 583-8050 *SIC* 5431

WALKERS POINT MARINA *p* 598
See DUNN HOLDINGS INC

WALKING ON A CLOUD *p* 784
See SANPAUL INVESTMENTS LIMITED

WALKING ON A CLOUD *p* 785
See VELLA, PAUL SHOES (MISSISSAUGA) LIMITED

WALKOM'S VALUE MART *p* 745
See 2026798 ONTARIO LIMITED

WALKWOOD SUPPLY *p* 841
See PETERBOROUGH AUTOMOTIVE & MACHINE LTD

WALL FINANCIAL CORPORATION *p* 327
1088 BURRARD ST, VANCOUVER, BC, V6Z 2R9
(604) 331-1000 *SIC* 7011

WALL GRAIN *p* 392
See WALL GRAIN HANDLING SYSTEMS LTD

WALL GRAIN HANDLING SYSTEMS LTD *p* 392
1460 CHEVRIER BLVD UNIT 202, WINNIPEG, MB, R3T 1Y6
(204) 269-7616 *SIC* 5084

WALLACE & CAREY (B.C.) LTD *p* 207
551 CHESTER RD, DELTA, BC, V3M 6G7
(604) 522-9930 *SIC* 5141

WALLACE & CAREY INC *p* 40
5445 8 ST NE, CALGARY, AB, T2K 5R9
(403) 275-7360 *SIC* 5194

WALLACE & CAREY INC *p* 207
551 CHESTER RD, DELTA, BC, V3M 6G7
(604) 522-9930 *SIC* 5148

WALLACE CONSTRUCTION SPECIALTIES LTD *p* 1430
1940 ONTARIO AVE, SASKATOON, SK, S7K 1T6
(306) 653-2020 *SIC* 5039

WALLACE EQUIPMENT LTD *p* 402
25 GILLIS RD, FREDERICTON, NB, E3C 2G3
(506) 458-8380 *SIC* 5084

WALLACE INTERNATIONAL LTD *p* 389
115 LOWSON CRES, WINNIPEG, MB, R3P 1A6
(204) 452-2700 *SIC* 3312

WALLACE PERIMETER SECURITY *p* 389
See WALLACE INTERNATIONAL LTD

WALLACE PERIMETER SECURITY *p* 389
115 LOWSON CRES, WINNIPEG, MB, R3P 1A6
(866) 300-1110 *SIC* 3446

WALLACEBURG AUTOMOTIVE INC *p* 1005
330 SELKIRK ST, WALLACEBURG, ON, N8A 3X7
(519) 627-2288 *SIC* 5511

WALLACEBURG DISTRICT SECONDARY SCHOOL *p* 1005
See LAMBTON KENT DISTRICT SCHOOL BOARD

WALLACEBURG PREFERRED PARTNERS CORP *p* 543
203 KEIL DR S, CHATHAM, ON, N7M 6J5
(519) 351-5558 *SIC* 3711

WALLCROWN LIMITED *p* 589
88 RONSON DR, ETOBICOKE, ON, M9W 1B9
(416) 245-2900 *SIC* 2679

WALLENSTEIN FEED & SUPPLY LTD *p* 1005
7307 WELLINGTON ROAD 86, WALLENSTEIN, ON, N0B 2S0
(519) 669-5143 *SIC* 5191

WALLMARC WOOD INDUSTRIES LIMITED *p* 905
59 GLEN CAMERON RD, THORNHILL, ON, L3T 1W2
(905) 889-1342 *SIC* 5084

WALLMART MCDONALDS *p* 463
See SWENSON, LARRY ENTERPRISES LTD

WALLS ALIVE LTD *p* 67
1328 17 AVE SW, CALGARY, AB, T2T 0C3
(403) 244-8931 *SIC* 5198

WALLSA HOLDINGS LTD *p* 210
8188 RIVER WAY, DELTA, BC, V4G 1K5
(604) 940-8891 *SIC* 4225

WALLWIN ELECTRIC *p* 488
See WALLWIN ELECTRIC SERVICES LIMITED

WALLWIN ELECTRIC SERVICES LIMITED *p* 488
50 INNISFIL ST, BARRIE, ON, L4N 4K5
(705) 726-1859 *SIC* 1731

WALMAR VENTILATION PRODUCTS *p* 750
See RANDEBAR ENTERPRISES INC

WALMART *p* 7
See WAL-MART CANADA CORP

WALMART *p* 12
See WAL-MART CANADA CORP

WALMART *p* 82
See WAL-MART CANADA CORP

WALMART *p* 107
See WAL-MART CANADA CORP

WALMART *p* 126
See WAL-MART CANADA CORP

WALMART *p* 133
See WAL-MART CANADA CORP

WALMART *p* 164
See WAL-MART CANADA CORP

WALMART *p* 167
See WAL-MART CANADA CORP

WALMART *p* 169
See WAL-MART CANADA CORP

WALMART *p* 204
See WAL-MART CANADA CORP

WALMART *p* 214
See WAL-MART CANADA CORP

WALMART *p* 232
See WAL-MART CANADA CORP

WALMART *p* 271
See WAL-MART CANADA CORP

WALMART *p* 280
See WAL-MART CANADA CORP

WALMART *p* 284
See WAL-MART CANADA CORP

WALMART *p* 332
See WAL-MART CANADA CORP

WALMART *p* 339
See WAL-MART CANADA CORP

WALMART *p* 394
See WAL-MART CANADA CORP

WALMART *p* 395
See WAL-MART CANADA CORP

WALMART *p* 400
See WAL-MART CANADA CORP

WALMART *p* 420
See WAL-MART CANADA CORP

WALMART *p* 422
See WAL-MART CANADA CORP

WALMART *p* 425
See WAL-MART CANADA CORP

WALMART *p* 436
See WAL-MART CANADA CORP

WALMART *p* 438
See WAL-MART CANADA CORP

WALMART *p* 457
See WAL-MART CANADA CORP

WALMART *p* 471
See WAL-MART CANADA CORP

WALMART *p* 520
See WAL-MART CANADA CORP

WALMART *p* 547
See WAL-MART CANADA CORP

WALMART *p* 592
See WAL-MART CANADA CORP

WALMART *p* 617
See WAL-MART CANADA CORP

WALMART *p* 621
See WAL-MART CANADA CORP

WALMART *p* 638
See WAL-MART CANADA CORP

WALMART *p* 837
See WAL-MART CANADA CORP

WALMART *p* 857
See WAL-MART CANADA CORP

WALMART *p* 875
See WAL-MART CANADA CORP

WALMART *p* 882
See WAL-MART CANADA CORP

WALMART *p* 897
See WAL-MART CANADA CORP

WALMART *p* 999
See WAL-MART CANADA CORP

WALMART *p* 1001
See WAL-MART CANADA CORP

WALMART *p* 1005
See WAL-MART CANADA CORP

WALMART *p* 1045
See WAL-MART CANADA CORP

WALMART *p* 1085
See WAL-MART CANADA CORP

WALMART *p* 1089
See WAL-MART CANADA CORP

WALMART *p* 1105
See WAL-MART CANADA CORP

WALMART *p* 1108
See WAL-MART CANADA CORP

WALMART *p* 1115
See WAL-MART CANADA CORP

WALMART *p* 1139
See WAL-MART CANADA CORP

WALMART *p* 1228
See WAL-MART CANADA CORP

WALMART *p* 1240
See WAL-MART CANADA CORP

WALMART *p* 1278
See WAL-MART CANADA CORP

WALMART *p* 1285
See WAL-MART CANADA CORP

WALMART *p* 1290
See WAL-MART CANADA CORP

WALMART *p* 1298
See WAL-MART CANADA CORP

WALMART *p* 1305
See WAL-MART CANADA CORP

WALMART *p* 1311
See WAL-MART CANADA CORP

WALMART *p* 1354
See WAL-MART CANADA CORP

WALMART *p* 1361
See WAL-MART CANADA CORP

WALMART *p* 1367
See WAL-MART CANADA CORP

WALMART *p* 1374
See WAL-MART CANADA CORP

WALMART *p* 1383
See WAL-MART CANADA CORP

WALMART *p* 1433
See WAL-MART CANADA CORP

WALMART *p* 1438
See WAL-MART CANADA CORP

WALMART #3069 *p* 355
See WAL-MART CANADA CORP

WALMART BAIE COMEAU *p* 1053
See WAL-MART CANADA CORP

WALMART CANADA *p* 759
See WAL-MART CANADA CORP

WALMART CANADA LOGISTICS ULC *p* 10
3400 39 AVE NE, CALGARY, AB, T1Y 7J4
(403) 250-3648 *SIC* 4225

WALMART CANADA LOGISTICS ULC *p* 160
261039 WAGON WHEEL CRES, ROCKY VIEW COUNTY, AB, T4A 0E2
(403) 295-8364 *SIC* 4225

WALMART CANADA LOGISTICS ULC *p* 745
200 COURTNEYPARK DR W, MISSISSAUGA, ON, L5W 1Y6
(905) 564-1484 *SIC* 4225

WALMART CANADA LOGISTICS ULC *p* 745
6800 MARITZ DR, MISSISSAUGA, ON, L5W 1W2
(905) 670-9966 *SIC* 4225

WALMART DE LEVIS *p* 1137
See WAL-MART CANADA CORP

WALMART MAGASIN *p* 1389
See WAL-MART CANADA CORP

WALMART PHARMACIES *p* 233
See WAL-MART CANADA CORP

WALMART QUESNEL *p* 252
See WAL-MART CANADA CORP

WALMART STORE 3126 *p* 597
See WAL-MART CANADA CORP

WALMART STORE 3645 *p* 682
See WAL-MART CANADA CORP

WALMART SUPERCENTRE *p* 478
See WAL-MART CANADA CORP

WALMART SUPERCENTRE *p* 530
See WAL-MART CANADA CORP

WALMART SUPERCENTRE *p* 718
See WAL-MART CANADA CORP

WALMART SUPERCENTRE *p* 1071
See WAL-MART CANADA CORP

WALMART SUPERCENTRE *p* 1131
See WAL-MART CANADA CORP

WALMART SUPERCENTRE *p* 1315
See WAL-MART CANADA CORP

WALMART SUPERCENTRE *p* 1346
See WAL-MART CANADA CORP

WALMART TIRE & LUBE EXPRESS *p* 227
See WAL-MART CANADA CORP

WALNUT GROVE SECONDARY SCHOOL *p* 225
See SCHOOL DISTRICT NO. 35 (LANGLEY)

WALPER TERRACE HOTEL INC *p* 639
1 KING ST W, KITCHENER, ON, N2G 1A1
(519) 745-4321 *SIC* 7011

WALRUS FOUNDATION, THE *p* 935
411 RICHMOND ST E SUITE B15, TORONTO, ON, M5A 3S5
(416) 971-5004 *SIC* 8699

WALSH CANADA *p* 775
See WCC CONSTRUCTION CANADA, ULC

WALT DISNEY COMPANY (CANADA) LTD, THE *p* 984
200 FRONT ST W SUITE 2900, TORONTO, ON, M5V 3L4
(416) 596-7000 *SIC* 6794

WALTER FEDY PARTNERSHIP, THE *p* 641
675 QUEEN ST S SUITE 111, KITCHENER, ON, N2M 1A1
(519) 576-2150 *SIC* 8711

▲ Public Company ■ Public Company Family Member **HQ** Headquarters **BR** Branch **SL** Single Location

WALTER H GAGE RESIDENCE *p* 325
See UNIVERSITY OF BRITISH COLUMBIA, THE

WALTER MURRAY COLLEGIATE *p* 1424
See BOARD OF EDUCATION OF SASKATOON SCHOOL DIVISION NO. 13 OF SASKATCHEWAN, THE

WALTER TECHNOLOGIES POUR SURFACES *p* 1248
See 190394 CANADA INC

WALTER'S GREENHOUSES & GARDEN CENTRE *p* 836
See BLYLEVEN ENTERPRISES INC

WALTER'S GROUP INC *p* 615
1318 RYMAL RD E, HAMILTON, ON, L8W 3N1
(905) 388-7111 *SIC* 3499

WALTER'S INC *p* 615
1318 RYMAL RD E, HAMILTON, ON, L8W 3N1
(905) 388-7111 *SIC* 3499

WALTER'S SHOE CARE INC *p* 795
180 BARTOR RD, NORTH YORK, ON, M9M 2W6
(416) 782-4492 *SIC* 3999

WALTER'S TRUCKING *p* 141
See WALTER, B & D TRUCKING LTD

WALTER, B & D TRUCKING LTD *p* 141
1435 31 ST N, LETHBRIDGE, AB, T1H 5G8
SIC 4213

WALTERS VALU-MART *p* 850
6179 PERTH ST, RICHMOND, ON, K0A 2Z0
(613) 838-8800 *SIC* 5411

WALTON ENTERPRISES LTD *p* 814
460 TAUNTON RD E, OSHAWA, ON, L1K 1A8
(905) 404-1413 *SIC* 7533

WALTON INTERNATIONAL GROUP INC *p* 62
215 2 ST SW SUITE 2500, CALGARY, AB, T2P 1M4
(403) 265-4255 *SIC* 6719

WAM INDUSTRIES LTD *p* 794
375 FENMAR DR, NORTH YORK, ON, M9L 2X4
(416) 741-0660 *SIC* 2541

WAM MOTORS GP INC *p* 389
485 STERLING LYON PKY, WINNIPEG, MB, R3P 2S8
(204) 284-2834 *SIC* 5511

WANDEROSA WOOD PRODUCTS LIMITED PARTNERSHIP *p* 496
150 PARR BLVD, BOLTON, ON, L7E 4E6
(905) 857-6227 *SIC* 5031

WANG, JOHN C *p* 324
7547 CAMBIE ST, VANCOUVER, BC, V6P 3H6
(604) 322-3000 *SIC* 6531

WANG, MAURICE DRUGS LTD *p* 931
20 BLOOR ST E, TORONTO, ON, M4W 3G7
(416) 967-7787 *SIC* 5912

WANSTEAD FARMERS CO-OPERATIVE CO., LIMITED *p* 1037
5495 ELEVATOR ST, WYOMING, ON, N0N 1T0
(519) 845-3301 *SIC* 5191

WAPITI GRAVEL SUPPLIERS, DIV OF *p* 132
See N.P.A. LTD

WAPITI REGIONAL LIBRARY *p* 1414
145 12TH ST E, PRINCE ALBERT, SK, S6V 1B7
(306) 764-0712 *SIC* 8231

WAPOSE MEDICAL SERVICES INC *p* 129
431 MACKENZIE BLVD SUITE 12, FORT MCMURRAY, AB, T9H 4C5
(780) 714-6654 *SIC* 7363

WAPPEL CONCRETE & CONSTRUCTION CO. LTD *p* 1416
230 E 10TH AVE, REGINA, SK, S4N 6G6
(306) 569-3000 *SIC* 6712

WAR AMPUTATIONS OF CANADA, THE *p* 828

2827 RIVERSIDE DR SUITE 101, OTTAWA, ON, K1V 0C4
(613) 731-3821 *SIC* 8641

WAR AMPUTATIONS OF CANADA, THE *p* 914
1 MAYBROOK DR, TORONTO, ON, M1V 5K9
(416) 412-0600 *SIC* 8699

WARCO EQUIPMENT LTD *p* 1342
364 RUE MCARTHUR, SAINT-LAURENT, QC, H4T 1X8
(514) 685-7878 *SIC* 6712

WARD BROS CONSTRUCTION LTD *p* 141
3604 18 AVE N, LETHBRIDGE, AB, T1H 5S7
(403) 328-6698 *SIC* 1542

WARD EMPIRE GROUP INC, THE *p* 941
2 LOMBARD ST SUITE 203, TORONTO, ON, M5C 1M1
(416) 366-7227 *SIC* 3441

WARD TIRES, INC *p* 13
3307 48 AVE SE, CALGARY, AB, T2B 2Y8
(403) 273-0202 *SIC* 5531

WARDALE EQUIPMENT (1998) LTD *p* 1439
230 BROADWAY ST E, YORKTON, SK, S3N 4C6
(306) 783-8508 *SIC* 5083

WARDELL, A & M SALES LTD *p* 167
6607 50 AVE, STETTLER, AB, T0C 2L2
(403) 742-8319 *SIC* 5531

WARDILL, J.A. ENTERPRISES INC *p* 340
2945 JACKLIN RD SUITE 300, VICTORIA, BC, V9B 5E3
(250) 474-1114 *SIC* 5912

WARE MALCOMB INC *p* 561
80 BASS PRO MILLS DR UNIT 1, CONCORD, ON, L4K 5W9
(905) 760-1221 *SIC* 7389

WAREHOUSE *p* 1026
See REJUDICARE SYNERGY LTD

WAREHOUSE DISTRIBUTION CENTRE *p* 23
See GRAND & TOY LIMITED

WAREHOUSE ONE - THE JEAN STORE *p* 392
See WAREHOUSE ONE CLOTHING LTD

WAREHOUSE ONE CLOTHING LTD *p* 392
1530 GAMBLE PL, WINNIPEG, MB, R3T 1N6
(204) 885-4200 *SIC* 5651

WAREHOUSE SERVICES INC *p* 117
9815 42 AVE NW, EDMONTON, AB, T6E 0A3
(780) 437-4917 *SIC* 5013

WARFIELD FIRE DEPARTMENT *p* 284
555 SCHOFIELD HWY, TRAIL, BC, V1R 2G7
(250) 368-9300 *SIC* 7389

WARM UP WINNIPEG *p* 371
See B.U.I.L.D. BUILDING URBAN INDUSTRIES FOR LOCAL DEVELOPMENT INC

WARM WITH CORN INC *p* 537
55 FLEMING DR UNIT 6, CAMBRIDGE, ON, N1T 2A9
(519) 624-5974 *SIC* 4925

WARMAN HOME CENTRE LP *p* 1437
601 SOUTH RAILWAY ST W, WARMAN, SK, S0K 4S0
(306) 933-4950 *SIC* 5211

WARMAN TRUSS *p* 1437
See WARMAN HOME CENTRE LP

WARNER BUS INDUSTRIES LTD *p* 1416
330 E 4TH AVE, REGINA, SK, S4N 4Z6
(306) 359-1930 *SIC* 5012

WARNER INDUSTRIES *p* 1416
See WARNER TRUCK INDUSTRIES LTD

WARNER MUSIC CANADA CO. *p* 766
155 GORDON BAKER RD UNIT 401, NORTH YORK, ON, M2H 3N5
(416) 491-5005 *SIC* 3652

WARNER TRUCK INDUSTRIES *p* 1416
See WARNER BUS INDUSTRIES LTD

WARNER TRUCK INDUSTRIES LTD *p* 1416
330 E 4TH AVE, REGINA, SK, S4N 4Z6

(306) 359-1930 *SIC* 5511

WARREN AUTOMOTIVE DE MEXICO *p* 561
401 SPINNAKER WAY, CONCORD, ON, L4K 4N4
SIC 5015

WARREN GIBSON LIMITED *p* 476
206 CHURCH ST S, ALLISTON, ON, L9R 2B7
(705) 435-4342 *SIC* 4213

WARREN INDUSTRIES LTD *p* 561
401 SPINNAKER WAY, CONCORD, ON, L4K 4N4
(905) 669-1260 *SIC* 3465

WARREN READY-MIX LTD *p* 411
58 CALIFORNIA RD, REXTON, NB, E4W 1W8
(506) 523-4240 *SIC* 3273

WARREN TRANSPORT LTD *p* 411
58 CALIFORNIA RD, REXTON, NB, E4W 1W8
SIC 4213

WARRIAN, KAREN PHARMACY *p* 573
125 THE QUEENSWAY, ETOBICOKE, ON, M8Y 1H6
(416) 766-6196 *SIC* 5912

WARRINGTON PCI MANAGEMENT *p* 317
See WARRINGTON PROPERTY GROUP INCORPORATED, THE

WARRINGTON PROPERTY GROUP INCORPORATED, THE *p* 317
1030 GEORGIA ST W SUITE 1700, VANCOUVER, BC, V6E 2Y3
(604) 602-1887 *SIC* 6531

WARRIOR RIG TECHNOLOGIES LIMITED *p* 12
1515 28 ST NE, CALGARY, AB, T2A 3T1
(403) 291-6444 *SIC* 3533

WARRIOR RIG TECHNOLOGIES LIMITED *p* 12
1515 28 ST NE, CALGARY, AB, T2A 3T1
(403) 291-6444 *SIC* 5084

WARTSILA CANADA, INCORPORATED *p* 257
1771 SAVAGE RD, RICHMOND, BC, V6V 1R1
(604) 244-8181 *SIC* 3731

WARWICK STRUCTURES GROUP LTD *p* 160
285188A FRONTIER RD, ROCKY VIEW COUNTY, AB, T1X 0V9
(403) 695-9999 *SIC* 1791

WASAGA 500 GO-KARTS LTD *p* 1005
152 RIVER RD W, WASAGA BEACH, ON, L9Z 2X2
(705) 322-2594 *SIC* 5599

WASAUKSING FIRST NATION *p* 764
1508 LANE G PARRY ISLAND, NORTH BAY, ON, P2A 2X4
(705) 746-2531 *SIC* 6519

WASAYA AIRWAYS LIMITED PARTNERSHIP *p* 592
300 ANEMKI PL UNIT B, FORT WILLIAM FIRST NATION, ON, P7J 1H9
(807) 473-1200 *SIC* 4512

WASCHUK PIPE LINE CONSTRUCTION LTD *p* 158
39015 HIGHWAY 2A SUITE 127, RED DEER COUNTY, AB, T4S 2A3
(403) 346-1114 *SIC* 1623

WASHINGTON MILLS ELECTRO MINERALS CORPORATION *p* 758
7780 STANLEY AVE, NIAGARA FALLS, ON, L2E 6X8
(905) 357-5500 *SIC* 3291

WASIP LTD *p* 878
3771 VICTORIA PARK AVE, SCARBOROUGH, ON, M1W 3Z5
(416) 297-5020 *SIC* 5099

WASSERMAN & PARTNERS ADVERTISING INC *p* 301

1020 MAINLAND ST UNIT 160, VANCOUVER, BC, V6B 2T5
(604) 684-1111 *SIC* 7311

WASTE CONNECTIONS OF CANADA INC *p* 160
285122 BLUEGRASS DR, ROCKY VIEW COUNTY, AB, T1X 0P5
(403) 236-3883 *SIC* 4953

WASTE CONNECTIONS OF CANADA INC *p* 176
34321 INDUSTRIAL WAY, ABBOTSFORD, BC, V2S 7M6
(604) 517-2617 *SIC* 4953

WASTE CONNECTIONS OF CANADA INC *p* 497
580 ECCLESTONE DR, BRACEBRIDGE, ON, P1L 1R2
(705) 645-4453 *SIC* 4953

WASTE CONNECTIONS OF CANADA INC *p* 561
610 APPLEWOOD CRES, CONCORD, ON, L4K 0E3
(905) 532-7510 *SIC* 4953

WASTE CONNECTIONS OF CANADA INC *p* 595
1152 KENASTON ST, GLOUCESTER, ON, K1B 3P5
(613) 749-8000 *SIC* 4953

WASTE CONNECTIONS OF CANADA INC *p* 1062
4141 BOUL DE LA GRANDE-ALLEE, BOISBRIAND, QC, J7H 1M7
(450) 435-2627 *SIC* 4953

WASTE CONNECTIONS, INC *p* 1003
610 APPLEWOOD CRES, VAUGHAN, ON, L4K 0C3
(905) 532-7510 *SIC* 4953

WASTE MANAGEMENT *p* 541
See WASTE MANAGEMENT OF CANADA CORPORATION

WASTE MANAGEMENT *p* 1011
See WASTE MANAGEMENT OF CANADA CORPORATION

WASTE MANAGEMENT OF CANADA CORPORATION *p* 13
4668 25 ST SE, CALGARY, AB, T2B 3M2
SIC 4953

WASTE MANAGEMENT OF CANADA CORPORATION *p* 223
350 BEAVER LAKE RD, KELOWNA, BC, V4V 1S5
(250) 766-9100 *SIC* 4953

WASTE MANAGEMENT OF CANADA CORPORATION *p* 507
117 WENTWORTH CRT, BRAMPTON, ON, L6T 5L4
(905) 595-3360 *SIC* 4953

WASTE MANAGEMENT OF CANADA CORPORATION *p* 541
254 WESTBROOK RD, CARP, ON, K0A 1L0
(613) 831-1281 *SIC* 4953

WASTE MANAGEMENT OF CANADA CORPORATION *p* 561
550 BOWES RD, CONCORD, ON, L4K 1K2
(905) 669-7196 *SIC* 4953

WASTE MANAGEMENT OF CANADA CORPORATION *p* 884
124 CUSHMAN RD, ST CATHARINES, ON, L2M 6T6
(905) 687-9605 *SIC* 4953

WASTE MANAGEMENT OF CANADA CORPORATION *p* 1008
219 LABRADOR DR SUITE 100, WATERLOO, ON, N2K 4M8
(519) 886-3974 *SIC* 4953

WASTE MANAGEMENT OF CANADA CORPORATION *p*

▲ Public Company ■ Public Company Family Member **HQ** Headquarters **BR** Branch **SL** Single Location

1011
645 CONRAD PL, WATERLOO, ON, N2V 1C4
(519) 886-6932   SIC 4953

WASTE MANAGEMENT OF CANADA CORPORATION p 1363
2535 1RE RUE, SAINTE-SOPHIE, QC, J5J 2R7
(450) 431-2313   SIC 4212

WASTE-NOT RECYCLING AND DISPOSAL INC p 264
12171 HORSESHOE WAY, RICHMOND, BC, V7A 4V4
(604) 273-0089   SIC 4953

WASTECO PEEL DIV p 790
See SOUTHERN SANITATION INC

WAT SUPPLY SANITATION & PAPER PRODUCTS p 901
See 1558775 ONTARIO LIMITED

WATCH TOWER BIBLE AND TRACT SOCIETY OF CANADA p 594
13893 HIGHWAY 7, GEORGETOWN, ON, L7G 4S4
(905) 873-4100   SIC 8661

WATCH TOWER BIBLE AND TRACT SOCIETY OF CANADA p 1012
390 CLARE AVE, WELLAND, ON, L3C 5R2
SIC 8661

WATCHFIRE CORPORATION p 625
1 HINES RD, KANATA, ON, K2K 3C7
SIC 7372

WATER BLAST MANUFACTURING LP p 106
16712 118 AVE NW, EDMONTON, AB, T5V 1P7
(780) 451-4521   SIC 5999

WATER PIK TECHNOLOGIES CANADA INC p 677
625 COCHRANE DR, MARKHAM, ON, L3R 9R9
SIC 5074

WATER SECURITY AGENCY p 1411
111 FAIRFORD ST E SUITE 400, MOOSE JAW, SK, S6H 7X9
(306) 694-3900   SIC 4941

WATER STREET (VANCOUVER) SPAGHETTI CORP p 337
703 DOUGLAS ST, VICTORIA, BC, V8W 2B4
(250) 381-8444   SIC 5812

WATER TREATMENT PLANT p 1433
See SASKATOON, CITY OF

WATERBORNE UNDERWRITING SERVICES LTD p 310
409 GRANVILLE ST SUITE 1157, VANCOUVER, BC, V6C 1T2
SIC 6331

WATERCO CANADA INC p 1068
1380 RUE NEWTON BUREAU 208, BOUCHERVILLE, QC, J4B 5H2
(450) 748-1421   SIC 3585

WATERDALE INC p 702
1303 AEROWOOD DR, MISSISSAUGA, ON, L4W 2P6
(905) 624-2600   SIC 5193

WATERDOWN DISTRICT HIGH SCHOOL p 1005
See HAMILTON-WENTWORTH DISTRICT SCHOOL BOARD, THE

WATERFLOOD SERVICE & SALES LTD p 1407
130 PERKINS ST, ESTEVAN, SK, S4A 2K1
(306) 634-7212   SIC 3533

WATERFORD LTC RESIDENCE, THE p 805
See CHARTWELL RETIREMENT RESIDENCES

WATERFORD SERVICES INC p 677
800 DENISON ST UNIT 7, MARKHAM, ON, L3R 5M9
(905) 470-7766   SIC 7349

WATERFRONT EMPLOYERS OF B.C. p 296
349 RAILWAY ST SUITE 400, VANCOUVER, BC, V6A 1A4
(604) 689-7184   SIC 7374

WATERFRONT HOTEL - DOWNTOWN WINDSOR p 1023
See INNVEST PROPERTIES CORP

WATERFRONT TORONTO p 968
See TORONTO WATERFRONT REVITALIZATION CORPORATION

WATERITE TECHNOLOGIES p 369
See 4131827 MANITOBA LTD

WATERITE, INC p 370
200 DISCOVERY PLACE UNIT 5, WINNIPEG, MB, R2R 0P7
(204) 786-1604   SIC 3589

WATERLOO BEDDING p 642
See WATERLOO BEDDING COMPANY, LIMITED

WATERLOO BEDDING COMPANY, LIMITED p 642
825 TRILLIUM DR, KITCHENER, ON, N2R 1J9
SIC 2515

WATERLOO BREWING LTD p 636
400 BINGEMANS CENTRE DR, KITCHENER, ON, N2B 3X9
(519) 742-2732   SIC 5921

WATERLOO CATHOLIC DISTRICT SCHOOL BOARD p 532
50 SAGINAW PKY, CAMBRIDGE, ON, N1P 1A1
(519) 621-4050   SIC 8211

WATERLOO CATHOLIC DISTRICT SCHOOL BOARD p 535
185 MYERS RD, CAMBRIDGE, ON, N1R 7H2
(519) 622-1290   SIC 8211

WATERLOO CATHOLIC DISTRICT SCHOOL BOARD p 637
1500 BLOCK LINE RD, KITCHENER, ON, N2C 2S2
(519) 745-6891   SIC 8211

WATERLOO CATHOLIC DISTRICT SCHOOL BOARD p 640
35A WEBER ST W, KITCHENER, ON, N2H 3Z1
(519) 578-3660   SIC 8211

WATERLOO CATHOLIC DISTRICT SCHOOL BOARD p 641
455 UNIVERSITY AVE W, KITCHENER, ON, N2N 3B9
(519) 741-1990   SIC 8211

WATERLOO CATHOLIC DISTRICT SCHOOL BOARD p 641
560 PIONEER DR, KITCHENER, ON, N2P 1P2
(519) 895-1716   SIC 8211

WATERLOO COLLEGIATE INSTITUTE p 1009
See WATERLOO REGION DISTRICT SCHOOL BOARD

WATERLOO CONSERVATIVE EDA p 1009
420 ERB ST W UNIT 5 STE 424, WATERLOO, ON, N2L 6K6
(519) 888-8300   SIC 8699

WATERLOO DODGE CHRYSLER LTD p 1007
150 WEBER ST S, WATERLOO, ON, N2J 2A8
(519) 743-0300   SIC 5511

WATERLOO FLOWERS LIMITED p 518
1001 KRAMP RD, BRESLAU, ON, N0B 1M0
SIC 5193

WATERLOO FORD p 86
See PURVIS HOLDINGS LTD

WATERLOO HONDA p 1008
See JAPAN AUTO LEASING INC

WATERLOO INN CONFERRANCE HOTEL p 1007
See WATERLOO MOTOR INN LIMITED

WATERLOO MANUFACTURING COMPANY LIMITED p 1009

.505 DOTZERT CRT UNIT 1, WATERLOO, ON, N2L 6A7
(519) 884-0600   SIC 5074

WATERLOO MAPLE INC p 1011
615 KUMPF DR, WATERLOO, ON, N2V 1K8
(519) 747-2373   SIC 7372

WATERLOO MEMORIAL RECREATION COMPLEX p 1008
See CORPORATION OF THE CITY OF WATERLOO, THE

WATERLOO MOTOR INN LIMITED p 1007
475 KING ST N, WATERLOO, ON, N2J 2Z5
(519) 885-0721   SIC 7011

WATERLOO NISSAN INC p 1009
141 NORTHFIELD DR W, WATERLOO, ON, N2L 5A6
(866) 978-9411   SIC 5511

WATERLOO NORTH HYDRO HOLDING CORPORATION p 1007
526 COUNTRY SQUIRE RD, WATERLOO, ON, N2J 4G8
(519) 886-5090   SIC 6712

WATERLOO NORTH HYDRO INC p 1007
526 COUNTRY SQUIRE RD, WATERLOO, ON, N2J 4G8
(519) 886-5090   SIC 4911

WATERLOO OXFORD DISTRICT SECONDARY SCHOOL p 484
See WATERLOO REGION DISTRICT SCHOOL BOARD

WATERLOO POTTERS' WORKSHOP p 1007
75 KING ST S, WATERLOO, ON, N2J 1P2
(519) 885-5570   SIC 8699

WATERLOO REGION DISTRICT SCHOOL BOARD p 484
1206 SNYDER'S RD W, BADEN, ON, N3A 1A4
(519) 634-5441   SIC 8211

WATERLOO REGION DISTRICT SCHOOL BOARD p 535
200 WATER ST N, CAMBRIDGE, ON, N1R 6V2
(519) 623-3600   SIC 8211

WATERLOO REGION DISTRICT SCHOOL BOARD p 535
30 SOUTHWOOD DR, CAMBRIDGE, ON, N1S 4K3
(519) 621-5920   SIC 8211

WATERLOO REGION DISTRICT SCHOOL BOARD p 535
55 MCKAY ST, CAMBRIDGE, ON, N1R 4G6
(519) 621-9510   SIC 8211

WATERLOO REGION DISTRICT SCHOOL BOARD p 537
355 HOLIDAY INN DR, CAMBRIDGE, ON, N3C 1Z2
(519) 658-4910   SIC 8211

WATERLOO REGION DISTRICT SCHOOL BOARD p 539
550 ROSE ST, CAMBRIDGE, ON, N3H 2E6
(519) 653-2367   SIC 8211

WATERLOO REGION DISTRICT SCHOOL BOARD p 568
4 UNIVERSITY AVE W, ELMIRA, ON, N3B 1K2
(519) 669-5414   SIC 8211

WATERLOO REGION DISTRICT SCHOOL BOARD p 637
51 ARDELT AVE, KITCHENER, ON, N2C 2R5
(519) 570-0300   SIC 8211

WATERLOO REGION DISTRICT SCHOOL BOARD p 638
245 ACTIVA AVE, KITCHENER, ON, N2E 4A3
(519) 579-1160   SIC 8211

WATERLOO REGION DISTRICT SCHOOL BOARD p 639
301 CHARLES ST E, KITCHENER, ON, N2G 2P8
(519) 578-8330   SIC 8211

WATERLOO REGION DISTRICT SCHOOL BOARD p 640
760 WEBER ST E, KITCHENER, ON, N2H 1H6
(519) 742-1848   SIC 8211

WATERLOO REGION DISTRICT SCHOOL BOARD p 641
255 FISCHER HALLMAN RD, KITCHENER, ON, N2M 4X8
(519) 744-6567   SIC 8211

WATERLOO REGION DISTRICT SCHOOL BOARD p 1007
80 BLUEVALE ST N, WATERLOO, ON, N2J 3R5
(519) 885-4620   SIC 8211

WATERLOO REGION DISTRICT SCHOOL BOARD p 1008
520 CHESAPEAKE DR, WATERLOO, ON, N2K 4G5
(519) 880-0300   SIC 8211

WATERLOO REGION DISTRICT SCHOOL BOARD p 1009
300 HAZEL ST, WATERLOO, ON, N2L 3P2
(519) 884-9590   SIC 8211

WATERLOO WELLINGTON CCAC p 604
See WATERLOO WELLINGTON LOCAL HEALTH INTEGRATION NETWORK

WATERLOO WELLINGTON LHIN p 1006
See HEALTH INTEGRATION NETWORK OF WATERLOO WELLINGTON

WATERLOO WELLINGTON LOCAL HEALTH INTEGRATION NETWORK p 604
450 SPEEDVALE AVE W SUITE 201, GUELPH, ON, N1H 7G7
(519) 823-2550   SIC 8082

WATERLOO WELLINGTON LOCAL HEALTH INTEGRATION NETWORK p 1007
141 WEBER ST S, WATERLOO, ON, N2J 2A9
(519) 748-2222   SIC 8399

WATERMANIA p 259
14300 ENTERTAINMENT BLVD, RICHMOND, BC, V6W 1K3
(604) 448-9616   SIC 7999

WATEROUS ENERGY FUND p 62
301 8 AVE SW SUITE 600, CALGARY, AB, T2P 1C5
(403) 930-6048   SIC 6722

WATERPLAY SOLUTIONS CORP p 223
1451 ELLIS ST UNIT B, KELOWNA, BC, V1Y 2A3
(250) 712-3393   SIC 4941

WATERS EDGE CARE COMMUNITY p 762
See 2063414 ONTARIO LIMITED

WATERS LIMITED p 690
6427 NORTHAM DR, MISSISSAUGA, ON, L4V 1J2
(905) 678-2162   SIC 5049

WATERS LTEE p 1072
9935 RUE DE CHATEAUNEUF UNITE 330, BROSSARD, QC, J4Z 3V4
(450) 656-0120   SIC 8734

WATERSIDE INN, THE p 712
See CENTRE CITY CAPITAL LIMITED

WATERVILLE TG INC p 843
4491 DISCOVERY LINE, PETROLIA, ON, N0N 1R0
(519) 882-4366   SIC 3069

WATERVILLE TG INC p 1082
500 RUE DIONNE, COATICOOK, QC, J1A 2E8
(819) 849-7031   SIC 3069

WATERVILLE TG INC p 1400
10 RUE DU DEPOT, WATERVILLE, QC, J0B 3H0
(819) 837-2421   SIC 2891

WATFORD ROOF TRUSS LIMITED p 1011
330 FRONT ST, WATFORD, ON, N0M 2S0
(519) 876-2612   SIC 2439

WATKIN MOTORS PARTNERSHIP p 332
4602 27 ST, VERNON, BC, V1T 4Y6
(250) 260-3411   SIC 5511

WATROUS MAINLINE MOTOR PRODUCTS LIMITED p 1437
208 1ST AVE E HWY SUITE 2, WATROUS,

SK, S0K 4T0
(306) 946-3336   SIC 5511
WATSON & ASH TRANSPORTATION COMPANY LTD   p
195
1050 9TH AVE, CAMPBELL RIVER, BC, V9W 4C2
(250) 287-7433   SIC 4731
WATSON BUILDING SUPPLIES INC p 1029
50 ROYAL GROUP CRES UNIT 2, WOODBRIDGE, ON, L4H 1X9
(905) 669-1898   SIC 5039
WATSON GLOVES   p 194
See WATSON, JOHN LIMITED
WATSON GROUP LTD, THE   p 854
95 WEST BEAVER CREEK RD UNIT 10, RICHMOND HILL, ON, L4B 1H2
(905) 889-9119   SIC 1711
WATSON HOLDINGS LTD   p 1411
468 LILLOOET ST W, MOOSE JAW, SK, S6H 7T1
(306) 692-1516   SIC 5411
WATSON, JOHN LIMITED   p 194
7955 NORTH FRASER WAY, BURNABY, BC, V5J 0A4
(604) 874-1105   SIC 5136
WATSON, T.J. ENTERPRISES INC   p 1020
4255 TECUMSEH RD E, WINDSOR, ON, N8W 1K2
(519) 250-0955   SIC 5812
WATSON, WAYNE CONSTRUCTION LTD   p
249
730 3RD AVE, PRINCE GEORGE, BC, V2L 3C5
(250) 562-8251   SIC 1542
WATT & STEWART COMMODITIES INC   p
80
4134 3 ST E, CLARESHOLM, AB, T0L 0T0
(403) 625-4436   SIC 4213
WATT CARMICHAEL INC   p 941
1 QUEEN ST E SUITE 1900, TORONTO, ON, M5C 2W6
(416) 864-1500   SIC 6211
WATT CONSULTING GROUP LTD   p 12
3016 5 AVE NE SUITE 310, CALGARY, AB, T2A 6K4
(403) 273-9001   SIC 8711
WATT INTERNATIONAL INC   p 984
590 KING ST W SUITE 300, TORONTO, ON, M5V 1M3
(416) 364-9384   SIC 7389
WATTS PROJECTS INC   p 156
82 QUEENS DR, RED DEER, AB, T4P 0R4
(403) 358-5555   SIC 4789
WATTS WATER TECHNOLOGIES (CANADA) INC   p 525
5435 NORTH SERVICE RD, BURLINGTON, ON, L7L 5H7
(905) 332-4090   SIC 5085
WATTS' GROUP LIMITED   p 968
156 FRONT ST W SUITE 610, TORONTO, ON, M5J 2L6
(416) 755-1374   SIC 5812
WAUKLEHEGAN MANOR INC   p 404
11 SAUNDERS RD, MCADAM, NB, E6J 1K9
(506) 784-6303   SIC 8322
WAV INSPECTION LTD   p 7
710 1 AVE E, BROOKS, AB, T1R 1E4
(403) 362-2008   SIC 7389
WAVEMAKER CANADA ULC   p 931
160 BLOOR ST E 5TH FL, TORONTO, ON, M4W 3S7
(416) 987-9100   SIC 7311
WAWA VALU-MART   p 1011
See HAMAN, B. & A. LIMITED
WAWANESA LIFE INSURANCE COMPANY, THE   p 66
708 11 AVE SW SUITE 600, CALGARY, AB, T2R 0E4
(403) 536-9258   SIC 6311
WAWANESA LIFE INSURANCE COMPANY, THE   p 380
200 MAIN ST SUITE 400, WINNIPEG, MB, R3C 1A8

(204) 985-3940   SIC 6311
WAWANESA LIFE INSURANCE COMPANY, THE   p 774
4110 YONGE ST SUITE 100, NORTH YORK, ON, M2P 2B7
(519) 886-4320   SIC 6311
WAWANESA MUTUAL INSURANCE COMPANY   p
66
See WAWANESA LIFE INSURANCE COMPANY, THE
WAWANESA MUTUAL INSURANCE COMPANY, THE   p
66
708 11 AVE SW SUITE 600, CALGARY, AB, T2R 0E4
(403) 266-8600   SIC 6331
WAWANESA MUTUAL INSURANCE COMPANY, THE   p
117
8657 51 AVE NW SUITE 100, EDMONTON, AB, T6E 6A8
(780) 469-5700   SIC 6331
WAWANESA MUTUAL INSURANCE COMPANY, THE   p
321
1985 BROADWAY W SUITE 400, VANCOUVER, BC, V6J 4Y3
(800) 665-2778   SIC 6331
WAWANESA MUTUAL INSURANCE COMPANY, THE   p
380
191 BROADWAY SUITE 900, WINNIPEG, MB, R3C 3P1
(204) 985-3923   SIC 6331
WAWANESA MUTUAL INSURANCE COMPANY, THE   p
409
1010 ST GEORGE BLVD, MONCTON, NB, E1E 4R5
(506) 853-1010   SIC 6331
WAWANESA MUTUAL INSURANCE COMPANY, THE   p
774
4110 YONGE ST SUITE 100, NORTH YORK, ON, M2P 2B7
(416) 250-9292   SIC 6331
WAWANESA MUTUAL INSURANCE COMPANY, THE   p
1157
8585 BOUL DECARIE, MONT-ROYAL, QC, H4P 2J4
(514) 342-2211   SIC 6331
WAWANOSH ENTERPRISES   p 860
See SARNIA AND DISTRICT ASSOCIATION FOR COMMUNITY LIVING
WAWASUM ENERGY INC   p 351
200 ALPINE WAY UNIT 135, HEADINGLEY, MB, R4H 0B7
(204) 299-9400   SIC 1623
WAWOTA MEMORIAL HEALTH CENTRE   p
1437
See SUN COUNTRY REGIONAL HEALTH AUTHORITY
WAX PARTNERSHIP INCORPORATED p 67
333 24 AVE SW SUITE 320, CALGARY, AB, T2S 3E6
(403) 262-9323   SIC 7389
WAXMAN INDUSTRIAL SERVICES CORP p
525
4350 HARVESTER RD, BURLINGTON, ON, L7L 5S4
(905) 639-1111   SIC 5093
WAY'S PHARMACY LIMITED   p 434
390 TOPSAIL RD, ST. JOHN'S, NL, A1E 2B8
(709) 368-6084   SIC 5912
WAY, G RESTAURANTS SERVICES LTD   p
515
299 WAYNE GRETZKY PKY, BRANTFORD, ON, N3R 8A5
(519) 751-2304   SIC 5812
WAYDEX SERVICES LP   p 133
11420 96 AVE, GRANDE PRAIRIE, AB, T8V 5M4

(780) 538-9101   SIC 1389
WAYFINDER CORP   p 26
4311 12 ST NE SUITE 305, CALGARY, AB, T2E 4P9
SIC 1389
WAYMARC INDUSTRIES LTD   p 97
16304 117 AVE NW, EDMONTON, AB, T5M 3W2
(780) 453-2358   SIC 5046
WAYNE BIRD FUELS   p 547
See WN BIRD FINANCIAL GROUP INC
WAYNE BUILDING PRODUCTS LTD   p 94
12603 123 ST NW, EDMONTON, AB, T5L 0H9
(780) 455-8929   SIC 5039
WAYNE SAFETY INC   p 786
1250 SHEPPARD AVE W, NORTH YORK, ON, M3K 2A6
(416) 661-1100   SIC 5099
WAYNE'S TIRE WAREHOUSE LTD   p 117
4717 99 ST NW, EDMONTON, AB, T6E 4Y1
(780) 437-4555   SIC 5531
WAYNE-DALTON COMMERCIAL DOORS p
706
See KINNEAR INDUSTRIES CORPORATION LIMITED
WAYPOINT CENTRE FOR MENTAL HEALTH CARE   p 838
500 CHURCH ST, PENETANGUISHENE, ON, L9M 1G3
(705) 549-3181   SIC 8063
WAYPOINT INSURANCE SERVICES INC   p
195
1400 DOGWOOD ST UNIT 700, CAMPBELL RIVER, BC, V9W 3A6
(250) 287-9184   SIC 6411
WAYS MENTAL HEALTH SUPPORT   p 651
714 YORK ST, LONDON, ON, N5W 2S8
(519) 432-2209   SIC 8361
WAYSIDE MANAGEMENT LTD   p 144
5411 44 ST, LLOYDMINSTER, AB, T9V 0A9
(780) 875-4404   SIC 7011
WB MELBACK CORPORATION   p 753
742252 DAWSON POINT RD, NEW LISKEARD, ON, P0J 1P0
(705) 647-5879   SIC 1711
WBLI CHARTERED ACCOUNTANTS p 440
See WHITE BURGESS LANGILLE INMAN
WBM TECHNOLOGIES INC   p 1435
3718 KINNEAR PL UNIT 104, SASKATOON, SK, S7P 0A6
(306) 664-2686   SIC 5045
WBS CONSTRUCTION   p 361
See WINKLER BUILDING SUPPLIES (1981) LTD
WCB ALBERTA   p 92
See WORKERS' COMPENSATION BOARD ALBERTA
WCC CONSTRUCTION CANADA, ULC   p
775
36 YORK MILLS RD SUITE 302, NORTH YORK, ON, M2P 2E9
(416) 849-9000   SIC 1522
WCEBP   p 376
See WINNIPEG CIVIC EMPLOYEES BENEFITS PROGRAM, THE
WCFS   p 785
See WHOLISTIC CHILD AND FAMILY SERVICES INC
WCG INTERNATIONAL CONSULTANTS LTD   p 335
915 FORT ST, VICTORIA, BC, V8V 3K3
(250) 389-0699   SIC 7361
WD-40 COMPANY (CANADA) LTD   p 996
5399 EGLINTON AVE W SUITE 214, TORONTO, ON, M9C 5K6
(416) 622-9881   SIC 5172
WDFG   p 265
See WDFG CANADA INC
WDFG CANADA INC   p 265
3211 GRANT MCCONACHIE WAY, RICHMOND, BC, V7B 0A4
(604) 273-1708   SIC 5399
WE CARE HEALTH SERVICES INC   p 386

1661 PORTAGE AVE SUITE 209, WINNIPEG, MB, R3J 3T7
(204) 987-3044   SIC 8051
WE CARE HEALTH SERVICES INC   p 407
236 ST GEORGE ST SUITE 110, MONCTON, NB, E1C 1W1
(506) 384-2273   SIC 8093
WE CARE HEALTH SERVICES INC   p 572
3300 BLOOR ST W SUITE 900, ETOBICOKE, ON, M8X 2X2
(416) 922-7601   SIC 6794
WE CARE HEALTH SERVICES INC   p 656
190 WORTLEY RD SUITE 100F, LONDON, ON, N6C 4Y7
(519) 642-1208   SIC 8322
WE CARE HEALTH SERVICES INC   p 708
160 TRADERS BLVD E SUITE 208, MISSISSAUGA, ON, L4Z 3K7
(905) 275-7250   SIC 8051
WE CARE HEALTH SERVICES INC   p 757
1124 STELLAR DR, NEWMARKET, ON, L3Y 7B7
(905) 715-7950   SIC 8082
WE CARE HOME HEALTH SERVICES   p 39
10325 BONAVENTURE DR SE SUITE 100, CALGARY, AB, T2J 7E4
(403) 225-1222   SIC 8059
WE CARE HOME HEALTH SERVICES p 174
See 446784 B.C. LTD
WE CARE HOME HEALTH SERVICES p 233
2349 EAST WELLINGTON RD, NANAIMO, BC, V9R 6V7
(250) 740-0035   SIC 8741
WE CARE HOME HEALTH SERVICES p 407
See WE CARE HEALTH SERVICES INC
WE CARE HOME HEALTH SERVICES p 572
See WE CARE HEALTH SERVICES INC
WE CARE HOME HEALTH SERVICES p 866
See CAREMED SERVICES INC
WE CARE HOME HEALTH SERVICES   p
1013
See CAREMED SERVICES INC
WE CHARITY   p 935
339 QUEEN ST E, TORONTO, ON, M5A 1S9
(416) 925-5894   SIC 8699
WE CHC   p 1022
See WINDSOR ESSEX COMMUNITY HEALTH CENTRE
WE-CAS   p 1022
See WINDSOR-ESSEX CHILDREN'S AID SOCIETY
WEAGANT FARM SUPPLIES LIMITED   p
1016
11250 COUNTY RD 43, WINCHESTER, ON, K0C 2K0
(613) 774-2887   SIC 5999
WEALTH MINERALS LTD   p 317
1177 HASTINGS ST W SUITE 2300, VANCOUVER, BC, V6E 2K3
(604) 331-0096   SIC 1041
WEALTHTERRA CAPITAL MANAGEMENT INC   p 80
105 1ST ST W SUITE 104, COCHRANE, AB, T4C 1A4
(403) 981-1156   SIC 6211
WEARWELL   p 466
See WEARWELL GARMENTS LIMITED
WEARWELL GARMENTS LIMITED   p 466
126 ACADIA AVE, STELLARTON, NS, B0K 1S0
(902) 752-4190   SIC 5136
WEATHER NETWORK   p 1174
See PELMOREX WEATHER NETWORKS (TELEVISION) INC
WEATHER NETWORK, THE   p 798
See PELMOREX WEATHER NETWORKS (TELEVISION) INC
WEATHER WIRELINE   p 80
See WEATHERFORD CANADA LTD
WEATHERCRAFT HOLDINGS LIMITED   p
794
230 BARMAC DR, NORTH YORK, ON, M9L 2Z3

(416) 740-8020   *SIC* 6712

WEATHERFORD ARTIFICIAL LIFT SYSTEMS CANADA LTD   *p* 144
4206 59 AVE, LLOYDMINSTER, AB, T9V 2V4
(780) 875-2730   *SIC* 1389

WEATHERFORD CANADA LTD   *p* 6
4816 56 AVE, BONNYVILLE, AB, T9N 2N8
(780) 826-7878   *SIC* 3533

WEATHERFORD CANADA LTD   *p* 80
8001 102 ST, CLAIRMONT, AB, T8X 5A7
(780) 539-6400   *SIC* 3533

WEATHERFORD CANADA LTD   *p* 123
2004 64 AVE NW, EDMONTON, AB, T6P 1Z3
(780) 465-9311   *SIC* 3533

WEATHERFORD CANADA LTD   *p* 123
1917A 84 AVE NW, EDMONTON, AB, T6P 1K1
(780) 449-3266   *SIC* 3533

WEATHERFORD CANADA LTD   *p* 133
9601 156 AVE, GRANDE PRAIRIE, AB, T8V 2P3
(780) 567-6250   *SIC* 3533

WEATHERFORD CANADA LTD   *p* 144
4604 62 AVE, LLOYDMINSTER, AB, T9V 2G2
(780) 875-6123   *SIC* 3533

WEATHERFORD CANADA LTD   *p* 150
2603 5 ST, NISKU, AB, T9E 0C2
(780) 979-4500   *SIC* 3533

WEATHERFORD CANADA LTD   *p* 1409
3915 52 STREET CLOSE, LLOYDMINSTER, SK, S9V 2G9
(306) 820-5530   *SIC* 7699

WEATHERFORD COMPLETION & PRODUCT SYSTEMS   *p* 1409
See WEATHERFORD CANADA LTD

WEATHERFORD LABORATORIES (CANADA) LTD   *p* 26
1620 27 AVE NE, CALGARY, AB, T2E 8W4
(403) 736-3500   *SIC* 8731

WEATHERHAVEN GLOBAL RESOURCES LTD   *p* 202
2120 HARTLEY AVE, COQUITLAM, BC, V3K 6W5
(604) 451-8900   *SIC* 5211

WEATHERTECH RESTORATION SERVICES INC   *p* 650
553 CLARKE RD, LONDON, ON, N5V 2E1
(519) 258-0535   *SIC* 1771

WEATHERWISE INDUSTRIES DIV OF   *p* 242
See AQUILA CEDAR PRODUCTS LTD

WEAVER WELDING LTD   *p* 152
7501 107 AVE, PEACE RIVER, AB, T8S 1M6
(780) 618-7522   *SIC* 4619

WEAVER, J & D HOLDINGS LTD   *p* 333
3993 CEDAR HILL RD, VICTORIA, BC, V8N 4M9
(250) 721-1125   *SIC* 5531

WEAVERCROFT INTERNATIONAL   *p* 565
3038 HAMILTON RD SUITE 119, DORCHESTER, ON, N0L 1G5
(519) 868-0330   *SIC* 5154

WEAVERS ART INC   *p* 988
1400 CASTLEFIELD AVE, TORONTO, ON, M6B 4N4
(416) 923-7929   *SIC* 7389

WEBB, J.N. & SONS LIMITED   *p* 592
930 FIFTH ST W, FORT FRANCES, ON, P9A 3C7
(807) 274-5613   *SIC* 5141

WEBB, JERVIS B. COMPANY OF CANADA, LTD   *p* 610
1647 BURLINGTON ST E, HAMILTON, ON, L8H 3L2
(905) 547-0411   *SIC* 3535

WEBBER ACADEMY FOUNDATION   *p* 75
1515 93 ST SW, CALGARY, AB, T3H 4A8
(403) 277-4700   *SIC* 8211

WEBBER NATURALS   *p* 202
See WN PHARMACEUTICALS LTD

WEBCO PRINTING   *p* 1020
See WINDSOR PENNYSAVER

WEBCOM INC   *p* 878
3480 PHARMACY AVE, SCARBOROUGH, ON, M1W 2S7
(416) 496-1000   *SIC* 2732

WEBCT EDUCATIONAL TECHNOLOGIES CORPORATION   *p* 325
2389 HEALTH SCIENCES MALL SUITE 2, VANCOUVER, BC, V6T 1Z3
(604) 221-0558   *SIC* 7371

WEBER INTERNATIONAL PACKAGING CORPORATION   *p* 1395
269 RUE ADRIEN-PATENAUDE, VAUDREUIL-DORION, QC, J7V 5V5
(450) 455-0169   *SIC* 3085

WEBER MANUFACTURING TECHNOLOGIES INC   *p* 682
16566 HWY 12, MIDLAND, ON, L4R 4L1
(705) 526-7896   *SIC* 3541

WEBER SHANDWICK WORLDWIDE (CANADA) INC   *p* 935
351 KING ST E SUITE 800, TORONTO, ON, M5A 0L6
(416) 964-6444   *SIC* 8743

WEBER SUPPLY COMPANY INC   *p* 642
1830 STRASBURG RD, KITCHENER, ON, N2R 1E9
(519) 888-4200   *SIC* 5085

WEBER TOOL & MOLD, DIV OF   *p* 682
See WEBER MANUFACTURING TECHNOLOGIES INC

WEBER-STEPHEN (CANADA) COMPANY   *p* 1029
1 ROYBRIDGE GATE, WOODBRIDGE, ON, L4H 4E6
(905) 850-8999   *SIC* 5023

WEBSTER & FILS LIMITEE   *p* 1327
2585 CH DE LA COTE-DE-LIESSE, SAINT-LAURENT, QC, H4N 2M8
(514) 332-4541   *SIC* 5032

WEBSTER & SONS   *p* 1327
See WEBSTER & FILS LIMITEE

WEC INTERNATIONAL   *p* 613
See WORLDWIDE EVANGELIZATION FOR CHRIST

WEC TOURS QUEBEC INC   *p* 1151
300 RUE DU PORT, MATANE, QC, G4W 3M6
(514) 363-7266   *SIC* 1771

WECAN- WINDSOR ETHICS CAPITAL ANGEL NETWORK   *p* 1024
720 OUELLETTE AVE, WINDSOR, ON, N9A 1C2
(519) 259-9836   *SIC* 6282

WECO   *p* 143
See WILBUR-ELLIS COMPANY OF CANADA LIMITED

WEDDINGSTAR INC   *p* 83
2032 BULLSHEAD RD, DUNMORE, AB, T1B 0K9
(403) 529-1110   *SIC* 5199

WEDGEWOOD HOTEL, THE   *p* 327
See WEDGEWOOD VILLAGE ESTATES LTD

WEDGEWOOD VILLAGE ESTATES LTD   *p* 327
845 HORNBY ST, VANCOUVER, BC, V6Z 1V1
(604) 689-7777   *SIC* 7011

WEDGWOOD INSURANCE LIMITED   *p* 431
85 THORBURN RD SUITE 102, ST. JOHN'S, NL, A1B 3M2
(709) 753-3210   *SIC* 6411

WEDLOCK PAPER CONVERTERS LIMITED   *p* 704
2327 STANFIELD RD, MISSISSAUGA, ON, L4Y 1R6
(905) 277-9461   *SIC* 2674

WEE-TOTE ENTERPRISES LTD   *p* 194
7011 RANDOLPH AVE, BURNABY, BC, V5J 4W5
(604) 430-1411   *SIC* 7389

WEECHI - IT - TE - WIN FAMILY SERVICES INC   *p* 592
1450 IDYLWYLD DR, FORT FRANCES, ON, P9A 3M3
(807) 274-3201   *SIC* 8399

WEED MAN   *p* 865
See TURF OPERATIONS SCARBOROUGH INC

WEED MAN   *p* 1233
See 156560 CANADA INC

WEEDON AUTOMOBILE (1977) INC   *p* 1401
326 2E AV, WEEDON, QC, J0B 3J0
(819) 877-2833   *SIC* 5511

WEEKS, S.W. CONSTRUCTION LIMITED   *p* 463
186 TERRA COTTA DR, NEW GLASGOW, NS, B2H 5W5
(902) 755-3777   *SIC* 1611

WEENEEBAYKO GENERAL HOSPITAL   *p* 746
See WEENEEBAYKO HEALTH AHTUSKAYWIN

WEENEEBAYKO HEALTH AHTUSKAYWIN   *p* 746
19 HOSPITAL DR, MOOSE FACTORY, ON, P0L 1W0
(705) 658-4544   *SIC* 8062

WEESAPOU GROUPE HOME   *p* 1081
See HOSPITAL CHISASIBI

WEETABIX OF CANADA LIMITED   *p* 545
751 D'ARCY ST, COBOURG, ON, K9A 4B1
(905) 372-5441   *SIC* 2043

WEFF HOLDINGS LTD   *p* 1424
1702 8TH ST E, SASKATOON, SK, S7H 0T5
(306) 952-4262   *SIC* 7549

WEG ELECTRIC MOTORS   *p* 988
64 SAMOR RD, TORONTO, ON, M6A 1J6
(416) 781-4617   *SIC* 5063

WEGU MANUFACTURING INC   *p* 1015
1707 HARBOUR ST, WHITBY, ON, L1N 9G6
(905) 668-2359   *SIC* 2821

WEICHERT WORKFORCE MOBILITY CANADA ULC   *p* 38
6700 MACLEOD TRAIL SE SUITE 210, CALGARY, AB, T2H 0L3
(888) 588-6664   *SIC* 7389

WEICKERT, C & R ENTERPRISES LTD   *p* 457
10 RADCLIFFE DR SUITE 465, HALIFAX, NS, B3M 4K7
(902) 823-2499   *SIC* 5531

WEIDMULLER CANADA   *p* 677
See W INTERCONNECTIONS CANADA INC

WEIDNER CHEVROLET   *p* 138
See WEIDNER MOTORS LIMITED

WEIDNER MOTORS LIMITED   *p* 138
5640 HIGHWAY 2A, LACOMBE, AB, T4L 1A3
(403) 782-3626   *SIC* 5511

WEIGH-TRONIX CANADA, ULC   *p* 1228
6429 RUE ABRAMS, MONTREAL, QC, H4S 1X9
(514) 695-0380   *SIC* 3596

WEINGARTEN, ALAN DRUGS LTD   *p* 571
2850 LAKE SHORE BLVD W, ETOBICOKE, ON, M8V 1H9
(416) 255-2397   *SIC* 5912

WEINRICH CONTRACTING LTD   *p* 123
7212 8 ST NW, EDMONTON, AB, T6P 1V1
(780) 487-6734   *SIC* 1611

WEINS CANADA INC   *p* 677
3120 STEELES AVE E, MARKHAM, ON, L3R 1G9
(905) 475-0308   *SIC* 5511

WEIR CANADA, INC   *p* 728
2360 MILLRACE CRT, MISSISSAUGA, ON, L5N 1W2
(905) 812-7100   *SIC* 3569

WEIR CANADA, INC   *p* 728

WEIR CANADA, INC   *p* 728
2360 MILLRACE CRT, MISSISSAUGA, ON, L5N 1W2
(905) 812-7100   *SIC* 5084

WEIR CANADA, INC   *p* 1133
9401 RUE WANKLYN, LASALLE, QC, H8R 1Z2
(514) 366-4310   *SIC* 5084

WEIR MINERALS   *p* 728
See WEIR CANADA, INC

WEIRFOULDS LLP   *p* 970
66 WELLINGTON ST W SUITE 4100, TORONTO, ON, M5K 1B7
(416) 365-1110   *SIC* 8111

WEISDORF GROUP OF COMPANIES INC, THE   *p* 677
2801 JOHN ST, MARKHAM, ON, L3R 2Y8
(905) 477-9901   *SIC* 5099

WEISDORF, IRVING HOLDINGS INC   *p* 677
2801 JOHN ST, MARKHAM, ON, L3R 2Y8
(905) 477-9901   *SIC* 5099

WEISHARDT INTERNATIONAL NA   *p* 1382
See TERGEL INC

WEISS-JOHNSON SHEET METAL LTD   *p* 111
5803 ROPER RD NW, EDMONTON, AB, T6B 3L6
(780) 463-3096   *SIC* 1731

WELCH LLP   *p* 815
123 SLATER ST, OTTAWA, ON, K1A 1B9
(613) 236-9191   *SIC* 8721

WELCO LUMBER CORP   *p* 187
4445 LOUGHEED HWY SUITE 1001, BURNABY, BC, V5C 0E4
(604) 732-1411   *SIC* 5031

WELCOME PHARMACY (QUEEN) LTD   *p* 992
1488 QUEEN ST W, TORONTO, ON, M6K 1M4
(416) 533-2391   *SIC* 5122

WELDCO COMPANIES   *p* 106
See WELDCO-BEALES MFG. ALBERTA LTD

WELDCO-BEALES MANUFACTURING   *p* 228
See WELDCO-BEALES MFG. ALBERTA LTD

WELDCO-BEALES MFG. ALBERTA LTD   *p* 106
12155 154 ST NW, EDMONTON, AB, T5V 1J3
(780) 454-5244   *SIC* 3531

WELDCO-BEALES MFG. ALBERTA LTD   *p* 228
5770 PRODUCTION WAY, LANGLEY, BC, V3A 4N4
(604) 533-8933   *SIC* 3531

WELDCO-BEALES MFG. ONTARIO LTD   *p* 488
515 WELHAM RD SUITE 1, BARRIE, ON, L4N 8Z6
(705) 733-2668   *SIC* 3531

WELDED TUBE OF CANADA CORP   *p* 561
541 BOWES RD, CONCORD, ON, L4K 1J5
(905) 669-1111   *SIC* 3317

WELDED TUBE OF CANADA CORP   *p* 561
111 RAYETTE RD, CONCORD, ON, L4K 2E9
(905) 669-1111   *SIC* 3312

WELL-TECH ENERGY SERVICES INC   *p* 169
6006 58 ST, TABER, AB, T1G 2B8
(403) 223-4244   *SIC* 1389

WELLA CANADA, INC   *p* 733
5800 AVEBURY RD UNIT 1, MISSISSAUGA, ON, L5R 3M3
(905) 568-2494   *SIC* 5131

WELLA MARKET   *p* 733
See WELLA CANADA, INC

WELLAND & DISTRICT SOCIETY FOR THE PREVENTION OF CRUELTY TO ANIMALS   *p* 1012
60 PROVINCIAL ST, WELLAND, ON, L3B 5W7
(905) 735-1552   *SIC* 8699

WELLAND ASSOCIATION FOR COMMU-NITY LIVING *p* 1012
535 SUTHERLAND AVE, WELLAND, ON, L3B 5A4
(905) 735-0081 *SIC* 8399

WELLAND HOSPITAL SITE *p* 887
See NIAGARA HEALTH SYSTEM

WELLAND HYDRO-ELECTRIC SYSTEMS CORP *p* 1012
950 EAST MAIN ST, WELLAND, ON, L3B 3Y9
SIC 4911

WELLBURN'S FINE FOODS *p* 335
See LUM & SON FINE FOODS LTD

WELLER, W.M. TREE SERVICE LTD *p* 628
18 CIRCLE RIDGE DR, KESWICK, ON, L4P 2G9
(905) 476-4593 *SIC* 0783

WELLESLEY CENTRAL PLACE *p* 932
160 WELLESLEY ST E SUITE 2044, TORONTO, ON, M4Y 1J2
(416) 929-9385 *SIC* 8051

WELLESLEY INSTITUTE *p* 927
10 ALCORN AVE SUITE 300, TORONTO, ON, M4V 3A9
(416) 972-1010 *SIC* 8699

WELLINGTON BREWERY *p* 606
See WELLINGTON COUNTY BREWERY INC

WELLINGTON CATHOLIC DISTRICT SCHOOL BOARD *p* 600
57 VICTORIA RD N, GUELPH, ON, N1E 5G9
(519) 822-4290 *SIC* 8211

WELLINGTON CATHOLIC DISTRICT SCHOOL BOARD *p* 605
54 WESTMOUNT RD, GUELPH, ON, N1H 5H7
(519) 836-2170 *SIC* 8211

WELLINGTON CATHOLIC DISTRICT SCHOOL BOARD *p* 607
200 CLAIR RD W, GUELPH, ON, N1L 1G1
(519) 822-8502 *SIC* 8211

WELLINGTON CENTRE FOR CONTINUING EDUCATION *p* 607
See UPPER GRAND DISTRICT SCHOOL BOARD, THE

WELLINGTON CONSTRUCTION CO LTD *p* 1043
1742 124 RTE, WELLINGTON STATION, PE, C0B 2E0
(902) 854-2650 *SIC* 1542

WELLINGTON COUNTY BREWERY INC *p* 606
950 WOODLAWN RD W, GUELPH, ON, N1K 1G2
(519) 837-2337 *SIC* 2082

WELLINGTON HOUSE *p* 848
See DEEM MANAGEMENT SERVICES LIMITED

WELLINGTON MOTOR FREIGHT *p* 535
See 2136284 ONTARIO INC

WELLINGTON MOTORS LIMITED *p* 606
935 WOODLAWN RD W, GUELPH, ON, N1K 1B7
(519) 651-2422 *SIC* 5511

WELLINGTON MUSHROOM FARM *p* 493
See HIGHLINE PRODUCE LIMITED

WELLINGTON MUSHROOM FARM *p* 644
See HIGHLINE PRODUCE LIMITED

WELLINGTON SECONDARY SCHOOL *p* 234
See SCHOOL DISTRICT NO. 68 (NANAIMO-LADYSMITH)

WELLINGTON WEST *p* 44
See BANQUE NATIONALE DU CANADA

WELLINGTON WINDSOR HOLDINGS LTD *p* 984
255 WELLINGTON ST W, TORONTO, ON, M5V 3P9
(416) 581-1800 *SIC* 7011

WELLINGTON, THE *p* 615
See BARTON RETIREMENT INC

WELLINGTON-ALTUS PRIVATE WEALTH INC *p* 376
201 PORTAGE AVEE 3RD FL, WINNIPEG, MB, R3B 3K6
(888) 315-8729 *SIC* 8742

WELLMASTER CARTS *p* 912
See WELLMASTER PIPE AND SUPPLY INC

WELLMASTER PIPE AND SUPPLY INC *p* 912
1494 BELL MILL SIDEROAD, TILLSON-BURG, ON, N4G 5Y1
(519) 688-0500 *SIC* 3533

WELLNESS LIVING SYSTEMS INC *p* 854
30 FULTON WAY BLDG 8 SUITE 203, RICHMOND HILL, ON, L4B 1E6
(888) 668-7728 *SIC* 7372

WELLONS CANADA CORP *p* 282
19087 96 AVE, SURREY, BC, V4N 3P2
(604) 888-0122 *SIC* 3567

WELLS FARGO CAPITAL FINANCE *p* 958
See WELLS FARGO FINANCIAL CORPO-RATION CANADA

WELLS FARGO FINANCIAL CORPORA-TION CANADA *p* 958
40 KING ST W SUITE 3200, TORONTO, ON, M5H 3Y2
(800) 626-2805 *SIC* 6159

WELLS FARGO FINANCIAL RETAIL SER-VICES COMPANY OF CANADA *p* 733
55 STANDISH CRT SUITE 300, MISSIS-SAUGA, ON, L5R 4B2
SIC 7322

WELLS FORD SALES LTD *p* 890
48 BELLEVILLE RD, STIRLING, ON, K0K 3E0
(613) 395-3375 *SIC* 5511

WELLS GORDON LIMITED *p* 925
720 MOUNT PLEASANT RD, TORONTO, ON, M4S 2N6
(416) 487-3392 *SIC* 8361

WELLSPRING PHARMACEUTICAL CANADA CORP *p* 799
400 IROQUOIS SHORE RD, OAKVILLE, ON, L6H 1M5
(905) 337-4500 *SIC* 2834

WELLWOOD COLONY FARMS LTD *p* 353
GD, NINETTE, MB, R0K 1R0
(204) 776-2130 *SIC* 0119

WELSH, FRED LTD *p* 202
94 GLACIER ST UNIT 201, COQUITLAM, BC, V3K 6B2
(604) 942-0012 *SIC* 1711

WEM HOLDINGS INC *p* 104
8882 170 ST NW SUITE 3000, EDMON-TON, AB, T5T 4M2
(780) 444-5200 *SIC* 6712

WENCO *p* 257
See WENCO INTERNATIONAL MINING SYSTEMS LTD

WENCO INTERNATIONAL MINING SYS-TEMS LTD *p* 257
13777 COMMERCE PKY SUITE 100, RICH-MOND, BC, V6V 2X3
(604) 270-8277 *SIC* 7371

WENDCORP HOLDINGS INC *p* 518
202 GRAND RIVER AVE SUITE 1, BRANT-FORD, ON, N3T 4X9
(519) 756-8431 *SIC* 5812

WENDELL MOTOR SALES LTD *p* 637
549 FAIRWAY RD S, KITCHENER, ON, N2C 1X4
(519) 893-1501 *SIC* 5511

WENDY'S *p* 401
See MOORE ENTERPRISES INC

WENDY'S *p* 455
See CHARLTOM RESTAURANTS LIMITED

WENDY'S OLD FASHION HAMBURGERS *p* 802
See WENDY'S RESTAURANTS OF CANADA INC

WENDY'S OLD FASHIONED HAMBURG-ERS *p* 518
See WENDCORP HOLDINGS INC

WENDY'S RESTAURANT *p* 661
See AFFINITY FOOD GROUP INC

WENDY'S RESTAURANT *p* 862
See 985907 ONTARIO LIMITED

WENDY'S RESTAURANTS *p* 879
See TORBA RESTAURANTS INC

WENDY'S RESTAURANTS OF CANADA INC *p* 802
240 WYECROFT RD, OAKVILLE, ON, L6K 2G7
(905) 337-8041 *SIC* 5812

WENGER LTEE *p* 1331
3521 BOUL THIMENS, SAINT-LAURENT, QC, H4R 1V5
(514) 337-4455 *SIC* 5094

WENTWORTH HOTELS LTD *p* 317
1177 MELVILLE ST, VANCOUVER, BC, V6E 0A3
(604) 669-5060 *SIC* 7011

WENTWORTH MOLD LTD *p* 516
156 ADAMS BLVD, BRANTFORD, ON, N3S 7V5
(519) 754-5400 *SIC* 2821

WENTWORTH MOLD, DIV OF *p* 891
See 1589711 ONTARIO INC

WENTWORTH TECH INC *p* 516
156 ADAMS BLVD, BRANTFORD, ON, N3S 7V5
(519) 754-5400 *SIC* 7389

WENTWORTH TEXTILES INC *p* 893
590 SOUTH SERVICE RD, STONEY CREEK, ON, L8E 2W1
(905) 643-6066 *SIC* 2241

WENTWORTH-HALTON X-RAY AND UL-TRASOUND INC *p* 612
1 YOUNG ST SUITE 218, HAMILTON, ON, L8N 1T8
(905) 522-2344 *SIC* 8071

WENZEL DOWNHOLE TOOLS LTD *p* 38
5920 MACLEOD TRAIL SW SUITE 504, CALGARY, AB, T2H 0K2
(403) 205-6696 *SIC* 3533

WENZEL DOWNHOLE TOOLS LTD *p* 121
3115 93 ST NW, EDMONTON, AB, T6N 1L7
(780) 440-4220 *SIC* 3533

WENZEL INTERNATIONAL INC *p* 1015
500 BEECH ST W, WHITBY, ON, L1N 7T8
(905) 668-3324 *SIC* 3679

WEPAWAUG CANADA CORP *p* 845
870 BROCK RD, PICKERING, ON, L1W 1Z8
(905) 839-1138 *SIC* 6712

WEREK ENTERPRISES INC *p* 677
164 TORBAY RD, MARKHAM, ON, L3R 1G6
(905) 479-3131 *SIC* 7349

WERKLUND CAPITAL CORPORATION *p* 62
400 3 AVE SW SUITE 4500, CALGARY, AB, T2P 4H2
(403) 231-6545 *SIC* 1389

WERTEX HOSIERY INCORPORATED *p* 974
1191 BATHURST ST, TORONTO, ON, M5R 3H4
(416) 537-2137 *SIC* 5137

WERTHER'S ORIGINAL *p* 707
See STORCK CANADA INC

WES-T-RANS COMPANY *p* 370
515 OAK POINT HWY, WINNIPEG, MB, R2R 1V2
(204) 633-9282 *SIC* 3714

WESA *p* 540
See BLUMETRIC ENVIRONMENTAL INC

WESBELL GROUP OF COMPANIES INC, THE *p* 744
6300 ORDAN DR, MISSISSAUGA, ON, L5T 1W6
(905) 595-8000 *SIC* 4899

WESBELL TECHNOLOGIES *p* 744
See WESBELL GROUP OF COMPANIES INC, THE

WESBILD HOLDINGS LTD *p* 199
3251 PLATEAU BLVD, COQUITLAM, BC, V3E 3B8
(604) 945-4007 *SIC* 7997

WESBILD HOLDINGS LTD *p* 317
1055 W GEORGIA ST SUITE 2600, VAN-COUVER, BC, V6E 3P3
(604) 694-8800 *SIC* 6512

WESBILD SHOPPING CENTRES *p* 317
See WESBILD HOLDINGS LTD

WESBRIDGE STEELWORKS LIMITED *p* 210
7480 WILSON AVE, DELTA, BC, V4G 1H3
(604) 946-8618 *SIC* 1791

WESBURN MANOR *p* 578
See CORPORATION OF THE CITY OF TORONTO

WESCAM INC. *p* 529
649 NORTH SERVICE RD, BURLINGTON, ON, L7P 5B9
(905) 633-4000 *SIC* 3663

WESCAN ELECTRICAL MECHANICAL SERVICES *p* 393
See T. & D. ENTERPRISES LTD

WESCAST INDUSTRIES INC *p* 518
150 SAVANNAH OAKS DR, BRANTFORD, ON, N3V 1E7
(519) 750-0000 *SIC* 3714

WESCAST INDUSTRIES INC *p* 1026
100 WATER ST, WINGHAM, ON, N0G 2W0
(519) 357-3450 *SIC* 3714

WESCAST INDUSTRIES INC *p* 1026
200 WATER ST, WINGHAM, ON, N0G 2W0
(519) 357-3450 *SIC* 3714

WESCAST INDUSTRIES MACHINING WINGHAM *p* 1026
See WESCAST INDUSTRIES INC

WESCLEAN EQUIPMENT & CLEANING SUPPLIES LTD *p* 97
11450 149 ST NW, EDMONTON, AB, T5M 1W7
(780) 451-1533 *SIC* 5087

WESCLEAN NORTHERN SALES LTD *p* 435
15 INDUSTRIAL DR, HAY RIVER, NT, X0E 0R6
(867) 875-5100 *SIC* 5087

WESCO AIRCRAFT EUROPE, LTD *p* 589
22 WORCESTER RD, ETOBICOKE, ON, M9W 5X2
(416) 674-0770 *SIC* 5085

WESCO DISTRIBUTION CANADA LP *p* 103
18207 111 AVE NW, EDMONTON, AB, T5S 2P2
(780) 452-7920 *SIC* 5063

WESCO DISTRIBUTION CANADA LP *p* 677
500 HOOD RD, MARKHAM, ON, L3R 9Z3
(905) 475-7400 *SIC* 5063

WESCO DISTRIBUTION CANADA LP *p* 733
6170 BELGRAVE RD, MISSISSAUGA, ON, L5R 4G8
(905) 890-3344 *SIC* 5063

WESCO INDUSTRIES LTD *p* 226
9663 199A ST UNIT 1, LANGLEY, BC, V1M 2X7
(604) 881-3000 *SIC* 5085

WESCOR CONTRACTING LTD *p* 339
3368 TENNYSON AVE, VICTORIA, BC, V8Z 3P6
(250) 475-8882 *SIC* 1542

WESDAN HOLDINGS INC *p* 215
1100 SUNSHINE COAST HWY, GIBSONS, BC, V0N 1V7
(604) 886-3487 *SIC* 5411

WESDOME GOLD MINES LTD *p* 968
220 BAY ST SUITE 1200, TORONTO, ON, M5J 2W4
(416) 360-3743 *SIC* 1041

WESGAR INC *p* 247
1634 KEBET WAY UNIT 1, PORT COQUIT-LAM, BC, V3C 5W9
(604) 942-9558 *SIC* 3444

WESGROUP PROPERTIES *p* 329
See WESGROUP PROPERTIES LIMITED PARTNERSHIP

WESGROUP PROPERTIES LIMITED PART-

NERSHIP   *p*
329
1055 DUNSMUIR ST SUITE 910, VANCOU-
VER, BC, V7X 1J1
(604) 632-1727   *SIC 6512*
WESKO LOCKS LTD   *p 702*
4570 EASTGATE PKY, MISSISSAUGA, ON,
L4W 3W6
(905) 629-3227   *SIC 3429*
WESLEY CLOVER CORPORATION *p 625*
390 MARCH RD SUITE 110, KANATA, ON,
K2K 0G7
(613) 271-6305   *SIC 6799*
WESLEYAN CHURCH OF CANADA *p 663*
3545 CENTENNIAL RD, LYN, ON, K0E 1M0
(613) 345-3424   *SIC 8661*
WESMAN SALVAGE   *p 346*
See *KAR-BASHER MANITOBA LTD*
WESONT LUMBER, DIV OF   *p 526*
See *NICHOLSON AND CATES LIMITED*
**WESPAC ELECTRICAL CONTRACTORS
LTD**   *p 202*
106 BLUE MOUNTAIN ST, COQUITLAM,
BC, V3K 4G8
(604) 522-1322   *SIC 1731*
WEST AIR SHEET METAL LTD   *p 26*
1238 45 AVE NE, CALGARY, AB, T2E 2P1
(403) 250-7518   *SIC 1761*
WEST ARM TRUCK LINES LTD   *p 195*
1077 COLUMBIA RD, CASTLEGAR, BC,
V1N 4K5
(250) 365-2127   *SIC 4213*
WEST AUTO SALES LTD   *p 202*
1881 UNITED BLVD SUITE D, COQUIT-
LAM, BC, V3K 0B6
(604) 777-1292   *SIC 5511*
WEST BAY MECHANICAL LTD   *p 341*
584 LEDSHAM RD, VICTORIA, BC, V9C
1J8
(250) 478-8532   *SIC 1711*
WEST BROS FURNITURE   *p 618*
See *WEST FURNITURE CO INC*
WEST CANADIAN DIGITAL IMAGING INC *p*
32
1601 9 AVE SE SUITE 200, CALGARY, AB,
T2G 0H4
(403) 245-2555   *SIC 2752*
**WEST CANADIAN INDUSTRIES GROUP
LTD**   *p 32*
1601 9 AVE SE SUITE 200, CALGARY, AB,
T2G 0H4
(403) 245-2555   *SIC 7336*
WEST CARLETON SAND & GRAVEL INC *p*
541
3232 CARP RD, CARP, ON, K0A 1L0
(613) 839-2816   *SIC 1771*
WEST CARLETON SECONDARY SCHOOL
p 567
See *OTTAWA-CARLETON DISTRICT
SCHOOL BOARD*
WEST CENTRAL PIPE DIV   *p 252*
See *TRU-WAY ENTERPRISES LTD*
**WEST CHILCOTIN FOREST PRODUCTS
LTD**   *p 179*
21841 CHILCOTIN HWY SUITE 20,
ANAHIM LAKE, BC, V0L 1C0
SIC 5031
WEST COAST AIR LTD   *p 265*
4760 INGLIS DR, RICHMOND, BC, V7B
1W4
(604) 278-3478   *SIC 4512*
WEST COAST AIR LTD   *p 265*
5220 AIRPORT RD S, RICHMOND, BC, V7B
1B4
SIC 4512
WEST COAST DUTY FREE STORE LTD *p*
280
111 176 ST SUITE 1, SURREY, BC, V3Z
9S4
(604) 538-3222   *SIC 5399*
**WEST COAST FISHCULTURE (LOIS LAKE)
LTD**   *p 248*
11060 MORTON RD, POWELL RIVER, BC,
V8A 0L9

(604) 487-9200   *SIC 0273*
WEST COAST FORD LINCOLN   *p 231*
See *WEST COAST MOTORS LTD*
WEST COAST GENERAL HOSPITAL *p 245*
3949 PORT ALBERNI HWY, PORT AL-
BERNI, BC, V9Y 4S1
(250) 731-1370   *SIC 8062*
WEST COAST HELICOPTERS   *p 248*
See *WEST COAST HELICOPTERS MAIN-
TENANCE AND CONTRACTING LTD*
**WEST COAST HELICOPTERS MAINTE-
NANCE AND CONTRACTING LTD**   *p*
248
1011 AIRPORT RD, PORT MCNEILL, BC,
V0N 2R0
(250) 956-2244   *SIC 4522*
WEST COAST IMPORT VEHICLES LTD *p*
245
19950 LOUGHEED HWY, PITT MEADOWS,
BC, V3Y 2S9
(604) 465-3209   *SIC 5511*
WEST COAST MACHINERY LTD   *p 230*
27050 GLOUCESTER WAY, LANGLEY, BC,
V4W 3Y5
(604) 855-5101   *SIC 5082*
WEST COAST MACHINERY, DIV OF *p 177*
See *SHEARFORCE EQUIPMENT*
WEST COAST MOTORS LTD   *p 231*
20370 LOUGHEED HWY, MAPLE RIDGE,
BC, V2X 2P8
(604) 465-5481   *SIC 5511*
WEST COAST PROCESS SERVING *p 237*
See *WEST COAST TITLE SEARCH LTD*
WEST COAST REALTY LTD   *p 242*
889 HARBOURSIDE DR SUITE 100,
NORTH VANCOUVER, BC, V7P 3S1
(604) 365-9120   *SIC 6531*
WEST COAST REDUCTION LTD   *p 19*
7030 OGDEN DALE PL SE, CALGARY, AB,
T2C 2A3
(403) 279-4441   *SIC 2077*
WEST COAST REDUCTION LTD   *p 296*
1292 VENABLES ST, VANCOUVER, BC,
V6A 4B4
(604) 255-9301   *SIC 2077*
WEST COAST SEEDS LTD   *p 211*
5344 34B AVE, DELTA, BC, V4L 2P1
(604) 952-8820   *SIC 5191*
WEST COAST SEEDS RETAIL STORE   *p*
211
See *WEST COAST SEEDS LTD*
WEST COAST SIGHT SEEING   *p 341*
See *492632 BC LTD*
WEST COAST SIGHTSEEING LTD   *p 301*
200-110 CAMBIE ST, VANCOUVER, BC,
V6B 2M8
(604) 451-1600   *SIC 4141*
WEST COAST TITLE SEARCH LTD   *p 237*
99 SIXTH ST, NEW WESTMINSTER, BC,
V3L 5H8
(604) 659-8600   *SIC 6541*
WEST COAST TOYOTA   *p 245*
See *WEST COAST IMPORT VEHICLES
LTD*
WEST COAST VIDEO   *p 825*
See *1039658 ONTARIO INC*
**WEST COUNTRY NURSERY & LAND-
SCAPE CENTRE**   *p*
67
See *ALBERTA BUILDING CONTRACTORS
LTD*
WEST CREDIT SECONDARY SCHOOL   *p*
725
See *PEEL DISTRICT SCHOOL BOARD*
WEST EDMONTON MALL   *p 104*
See *WEM HOLDINGS INC*
WEST EDMONTON MALL PROPERTY INC
p 104
8882 170 ST NW SUITE 3000, EDMON-
TON, AB, T5T 4M2
(780) 444-5200   *SIC 6512*
WEST EDMONTON TRUCKLAND LTD   *p*
106
16806 118 AVE NW, EDMONTON, AB, T5V

1M8
(780) 452-3532   *SIC 5541*
**WEST END MOTORS (FORT FRANCES) IN-
CORPORATED**   *p*
592
600 KING'S HWY, FORT FRANCES, ON,
P9A 2W9
(807) 274-7751   *SIC 5511*
WEST END NISSAN   *p 102*
See *PLUTO INVESTMENTS LTD*
WEST END PETRO PASS   *p 105*
See *DANDY OIL PRODUCTS LTD*
WEST END TIRE (1990) LTD   *p 367*
1991 DUGALD RD, WINNIPEG, MB, R2J
0H3
(204) 663-9037   *SIC 5531*
WEST FACE CAPITAL INC   *p 931*
2 BLOOR ST E SUITE 3000, TORONTO,
ON, M4W 1A8
(647) 724-8900   *SIC 6722*
WEST FOUR GROUP OF COMPANIES INC
p 1430
2505 WENTZ AVE, SASKATOON, SK, S7K
2K9
(306) 934-5147   *SIC 3442*
WEST FRASER   *p 253*
See *WEST FRASER TIMBER CO. LTD*
WEST FRASER LVL   *p 159*
See *WEST FRASER TIMBER CO. LTD*
WEST FRASER MILLS LTD   *p 6*
GD, BLUE RIDGE, AB, T0E 0B0
(780) 648-6333   *SIC 2421*
WEST FRASER MILLS LTD   *p 136*
99 WEST RIVER RD, HINTON, AB, T7V 1Y7
(780) 865-8900   *SIC 5211*
WEST FRASER MILLS LTD   *p 164*
GD, SLAVE LAKE, AB, T0G 2A0
(780) 849-4145   *SIC 2421*
WEST FRASER MILLS LTD   *p 173*
53115 HWY 47, YELLOWHEAD COUNTY,
AB, T7E 3E9
(780) 723-3977   *SIC 5031*
WEST FRASER MILLS LTD   *p 174*
1020 CHASM RD, 70 MILE HOUSE, BC,
V0K 2K0
(250) 459-2229   *SIC 2421*
WEST FRASER MILLS LTD   *p 196*
3598 FRASER ST W, CHETWYND, BC,
V0C 1J0
(250) 788-2686   *SIC 2421*
WEST FRASER MILLS LTD   *p 214*
6626 HIGHWAY 16 E, FRASER LAKE, BC,
V0J 1S0
(250) 699-6235   *SIC 2621*
WEST FRASER MILLS LTD   *p 252*
1250 BROWNMILLER RD, QUESNEL, BC,
V2J 6P5
(250) 992-9244   *SIC 5031*
WEST FRASER MILLS LTD   *p 252*
1000 PLYWOOD RD, QUESNEL, BC, V2J
3J5
(250) 991-7619   *SIC 2421*
WEST FRASER MILLS LTD   *p 252*
2000 PLYWOOD RD, QUESNEL, BC, V2J
5W1
(250) 992-5511   *SIC 2435*
WEST FRASER MILLS LTD   *p 269*
2375 TATLOW RD, SMITHERS, BC, V0J
2N5
(250) 847-2656   *SIC 2421*
WEST FRASER MILLS LTD   *p 301*
858 BEATTY ST SUITE 501, VANCOUVER,
BC, V6B 1C1
(604) 895-2700   *SIC 2421*
WEST FRASER MILLS LTD   *p 344*
4200 MACKENZIE AVE N, WILLIAMS
LAKE, BC, V2G 1N4
(250) 392-7731   *SIC 2421*
WEST FRASER MILLS LTD   *p 344*
4255 ROTTACKER RD, WILLIAMS LAKE,
BC, V2G 5E4
(250) 392-7784   *SIC 2421*
WEST FRASER TIMBER CO. LTD   *p 159*
GD STN MAIN, ROCKY MOUNTAIN

HOUSE, AB, T4T 1T1
(403) 845-5522   *SIC 5031*
WEST FRASER TIMBER CO. LTD   *p 173*
9 KM W OF WHITECOURT HWY SUITE 43,
WHITECOURT, AB, T7S 1P9
(780) 778-7000   *SIC 2621*
WEST FRASER TIMBER CO. LTD   *p 174*
910 EXETER RD, 100 MILE HOUSE, BC,
V0K 2E0
(250) 395-8200   *SIC 5031*
WEST FRASER TIMBER CO. LTD   *p 253*
1000 FINNING RD, QUESNEL, BC, V2J 6A1
(250) 992-8919   *SIC 2611*
WEST FRASER TIMBER CO. LTD   *p 253*
1250 BROWNMILLER RD, QUESNEL, BC,
V2J 6P5
(250) 992-9244   *SIC 5031*
WEST FRASER TIMBER CO. LTD   *p 301*
858 BEATTY ST SUITE 501, VANCOUVER,
BC, V6B 1C1
(604) 895-2700   *SIC 5031*
WEST FURNITURE CO INC   *p 618*
582 14TH ST, HANOVER, ON, N4N 2A1
(519) 364-7770   *SIC 2511*
WEST GUARD SECURITY   *p 234*
See *SECURIGUARD SERVICES LIMITED*
WEST HALDIMAND GENERAL HOSPITAL
p 607
75 PARKVIEW RD, HAGERSVILLE, ON,
N0A 1H0
(905) 768-3311   *SIC 8062*
WEST HILL COLLEGIATE INSTITUTE *p 866*
See *TORONTO DISTRICT SCHOOL
BOARD*
WEST HUMBER COLLEGIATE INSTITUTE
p 581
See *TORONTO DISTRICT SCHOOL
BOARD*
WEST ISLAND HOTELS INC   *p 1252*
6700 RTE TRANSCANADIENNE, POINTE-
CLAIRE, QC, H9R 1C2
(514) 697-7110   *SIC 7011*
WEST KINGS DISTRICT HIGH SCHOOL *p*
439
See *ANNAPOLIS VALLEY REGIONAL
SCHOOL BOARD*
WEST KIRKLAND MINING INC   *p 317*
1100 MELVILLE ST SUITE 838, VANCOU-
VER, BC, V6E 4A6
(604) 685-8311   *SIC 1041*
WEST KOOTENAY DISTRICT OFFICE *p 236*
310 WARD ST SUITE 400, NELSON, BC,
V1L 5S4
(250) 354-6521   *SIC 5082*
**WEST KOOTENAY MECHANICAL (2001)
LTD**   *p 284*
8131 OLD WANETA RD, TRAIL, BC, V1R
4X1
(250) 364-1541   *SIC 1711*
WEST LAKE ENERGY CORP   *p 62*
600 3 AVE SW SUITE 700, CALGARY, AB,
T2P 0G5
(403) 215-2045   *SIC 1382*
**WEST LORNE BIOOIL CO-GENERATION
LIMITED PARTNERSHIP**   *p 1013*
191 JANE ST, WEST LORNE, ON, N0L 2P0
SIC 2911
**WEST NIPISSING GENERAL HOSPITAL,
THE**   *p 898*
725 COURSOL RD SUITE 427, STUR-
GEON FALLS, ON, P2B 2Y6
(705) 753-3110   *SIC 8062*
WEST NOVA FUELS LIMITED   *p 462*
73 FALKLAND ST, LUNENBURG, NS, B0J
2C0
(902) 634-3835   *SIC 5172*
WEST OAK PUBLIC SCHOOL   *p 805*
See *HALTON DISTRICT SCHOOL BOARD*
WEST OAK VILLAGE   *p 806*
See *REVERA LONG TERM CARE INC*
WEST OILFIELD HOLDINGS LTD   *p 38*
5940 MACLEOD TRAIL SW UNIT 202, CAL-
GARY, AB, T2H 2G4
(403) 452-0844   *SIC 1389*

WEST PARK HEALTHCARE CENTRE *p* 993
82 BUTTONWOOD AVE SUITE 1121, TORONTO, ON, M6M 2J5
(416) 243-3600   *SIC* 8069

WEST PARK MANOR PERSONAL CARE HOME INC   *p* 389
3199 GRANT AVE, WINNIPEG, MB, R3R 1X2
(204) 889-3330   *SIC* 8051

WEST PARK MOTORS LTD   *p* 345
248 CENTRE AVE SE SS 3, ALTONA, MB, R0G 0B3
(204) 324-6494   *SIC* 5511

WEST PARRY SOUND HEALTH CENTRE *p* 837
6 ALBERT ST, PARRY SOUND, ON, P2A 3A4
(705) 746-9321   *SIC* 8062

WEST PENETONE INC   *p* 1051
10900 RUE SECANT, ANJOU, QC, H1J 1S5
(514) 355-4660   *SIC* 2842

WEST POINT GREY ACADEMY   *p* 324
See WEST POINT GREY INDEPENDENT SCHOOL SOCIETY

WEST POINT GREY INDEPENDENT SCHOOL SOCIETY   *p* 324
4125 8TH AVE W, VANCOUVER, BC, V6R 4P9
(604) 222-8750   *SIC* 8211

WEST REGION CHILD AND FAMILY SERVICES COMMITTEE INCORPORATED   *p* 349
GD, ERICKSON, MB, R0J 0P0
(204) 636-6100   *SIC* 8399

WEST RICHMOND COMMUNITY CENTRE *p* 266
See RICHMOND, CITY OF

WEST SAFETY SERVICES CANADA INC *p* 1337
7150 RUE ALEXANDER-FLEMING, SAINT-LAURENT, QC, H4S 2C8
(514) 340-3300   *SIC* 4899

WEST SHORE PARKS AND RECREATION SOCIETY   *p* 340
1767 ISLAND HWY, VICTORIA, BC, V9B 1J1
(250) 478-8384   *SIC* 7999

WEST SIDE ACURA   *p* 104
See ZACH & KAYLYN ENTERPRISES INC

WEST SIDE MITSUBISHI   *p* 98
See 965515 ALBERTA LTD

WEST SIDE PHARMACY INC   *p* 416
667 FAIRVILLE BLVD, SAINT JOHN, NB, E2M 3W2
(506) 636-7740   *SIC* 5912

WEST STAR PRINTING LIMITED   *p* 576
10 NORTH QUEEN ST, ETOBICOKE, ON, M8Z 2C4
(416) 201-0881   *SIC* 2752

WEST VAN FLORIST HOME AND GARDEN *p* 342
See WEST VAN FLORIST LTD

WEST VAN FLORIST LTD   *p* 342
1821 MARINE DR, WEST VANCOUVER, BC, V7V 1J7
(604) 922-4171   *SIC* 5992

WEST VANCOUVER CARE CENTRE *p* 342
See ARCAN DEVELOPMENTS LTD

WEST VANCOUVER MEMORIAL LIBRARY *p* 342
See VANCOUVER, CITY OF

WEST VANCOUVER SECONDARY SCHOOL   *p* 342
See SCHOOL DISTRICT NO. 45 (WEST VANCOUVER)

WEST WAWANOSH MUTUAL INSURANCE COMPANY, THE   *p* 567
81 SOUTHAMPTON ST SUITE 1, DUNGANNON, ON, N0M 1R0
(519) 529-7921   *SIC* 6331

WEST WIND AVIATION INC   *p* 1432
3A HANGAR RD, SASKATOON, SK, S7L 5X4
(306) 652-9121   *SIC* 7359

WEST WIND AVIATION LIMITED PARTNERSHIP   *p*
1432
3 HANGAR RD, SASKATOON, SK, S7L 5X4
(306) 652-9121   *SIC* 4522

WEST YORK CHEVROLET INC   *p* 994
1785 ST CLAIR AVE W, TORONTO, ON, M6N 1J6
(416) 656-1200   *SIC* 5511

WEST-CAN AUTO PARTS   *p* 252
See JHAJ HOLDINGS LTD

WEST-CAN SEAL COATING INC   *p* 7
55501 RR 203, BRUDERHEIM, AB, T0E 0S0
(780) 796-3437   *SIC* 1611

WEST-WOOD INDUSTRIES LTD   *p* 417
249 PARKER RD, SCOUDOUC, NB, E4P 3P8
(506) 532-0908   *SIC* 5039

WESTAIM CORPORATION, THE   *p* 968
70 YORK ST SUITE 1700, TORONTO, ON, M5J 1S9
(416) 969-3333   *SIC* 6211

WESTAQUA COMMODITY GROUP   *p* 241
See 0695602 BC LTD

WESTARIO POWER INC   *p* 1004
24 EASTRIDGE RD, WALKERTON, ON, N0G 2V0
(519) 507-6937   *SIC* 4911

WESTBANK FIRST NATION PINE ACRES HOME   *p* 342
1902 PHEASANT LANE, WESTBANK, BC, V4T 2H4
(250) 768-7676   *SIC* 8361

WESTBAY INSTRUMENTS DIV OF   *p* 308
See NOVA METRIX GROUND MONITORING (CANADA) LTD

WESTBERG HOLDINGS INC   *p* 327
1176 GRANVILLE ST, VANCOUVER, BC, V6Z 1L8
(604) 688-8701   *SIC* 7011

WESTBERRY FARMS LTD   *p* 176
34488 BATEMAN RD, ABBOTSFORD, BC, V2S 7Y8
(604) 850-0377   *SIC* 0171

WESTBORO AUTO IMPORTS LTD   *p* 829
225 RICHMOND RD, OTTAWA, ON, K1Z 6W7
(613) 728-5813   *SIC* 5511

WESTBORO FLOORING & DECOR INC   *p* 750
195 COLONNADE RD S, NEPEAN, ON, K2E 7K3
(613) 226-3830   *SIC* 1752

WESTBORO SUBARU   *p* 829
See WESTBORO AUTO IMPORTS LTD

WESTBRIDGE PET CONTAINERS LIMITED *p* 19
3838E 80 AVE SE, CALGARY, AB, T2C 2J7
(403) 248-1513   *SIC* 3089

WESTBROOK FLORAL LTD   *p* 490
4994 NORTH SERVICE RD, BEAMSVILLE, ON, L0R 1B3
(905) 945-9611   *SIC* 5193

WESTBROOK GREENHOUSES LIMITED *p* 490
4994 NORTH SERVICE RD, BEAMSVILLE, ON, L0R 1B3
(289) 432-1199   *SIC* 0181

WESTBURNE ELECTRIC   *p* 385
See REXEL CANADA ELECTRICAL INC

WESTBURNE ELECTRIC SUPPLY BC   *p* 184
See REXEL CANADA ELECTRICAL INC

WESTBURNE ONTARIO   *p* 742
See REXEL CANADA ELECTRICAL INC

WESTBURNE RUDDY ELECTRIC   *p* 742
See REXEL CANADA ELECTRICAL INC

WESTBURY NATIONAL SHOW SYSTEMS LTD   *p* 869
772 WARDEN AVE, SCARBOROUGH, ON, M1L 4T7
(416) 752-1371   *SIC* 7359

WESTCAL INSULATION LTD   *p* 38

7005 FAIRMOUNT DR SE UNIT 4165, CALGARY, AB, T2H 0J1
(403) 242-1357   *SIC* 1711

WESTCAN AUTO PARTS PLUS   *p* 217
See JASSUN HOLDINGS LTD

WESTCAN BULK TRANSPORT LTD   *p* 19
3780 76 AVE SE, CALGARY, AB, T2C 1J8
(403) 279-5505   *SIC* 4131

WESTCAN BULK TRANSPORT LTD   *p* 124
12110 17 ST NE, EDMONTON, AB, T6S 1A5
(780) 472-6951   *SIC* 4212

WESTCAN BULK TRANSPORT LTD *p* 1411
850 MANITOBA ST E, MOOSE JAW, SK, S6H 4P1
(306) 692-6478   *SIC* 4213

WESTCAN BULK TRANSPORT LTD *p* 1435
110 71ST ST W, SASKATOON, SK, S7R 1A1
(306) 242-5899   *SIC* 4213

WESTCAN FLOWERS   *p* 193
See MAKE SCENTS FLOWER DISTRIBUTORS INC

WESTCAN FREIGHT SYSTEMS   *p* 124
See WESTCAN BULK TRANSPORT LTD

WESTCAN RAIL LTD   *p* 178
31220 SOUTH FRASER WAY, ABBOTSFORD, BC, V2T 6L5
(604) 534-0124   *SIC* 5088

WESTCAN TRAVEL LTD   *p* 118
8412 109 ST NW, EDMONTON, AB, T6G 1E2
(780) 439-9118   *SIC* 4724

WESTCAN WIRELESS   *p* 93
See HELIX ADVANCED COMMUNICATIONS & INFRASTRUCTURE, INC

WESTCAN WIRELESS   *p* 94
12540 129 ST NW, EDMONTON, AB, T5L 4R4
(780) 451-2355   *SIC* 4899

WESTCANA ELECTRIC INC   *p* 251
1643 OGILVIE ST S, PRINCE GEORGE, BC, V2N 1W7
(250) 564-5800   *SIC* 1731

WESTCAP MGT. LTD   *p* 1430
410 22ND ST E SUITE 830, SASKATOON, SK, S7K 5T6
(306) 652-5557   *SIC* 6282

WESTCASTLE MOTORS LTD   *p* 152
1100 WATERTON AVE, PINCHER CREEK, AB, T0K 1W0
(403) 627-3223   *SIC* 5511

WESTCLIFF MANAGEMENT LTD   *p* 1200
600 BOUL DE MAISONNEUVE O BUREAU 2600, MONTREAL, QC, H3A 3J2
(514) 499-8300   *SIC* 6512

WESTCO   *p* 390
See CONGEBEC LOGISTIQUE INC

WESTCO INTERNATIONAL DEVELOPMENT CORP   *p* 38
7245 12 ST SE, CALGARY, AB, T2H 2S6
SIC 6712

WESTCOAST CELLUFIBRE, DIV OF *p* 290
See HOWE SOUND PULP & PAPER CORPORATION

WESTCOAST ENERGY INC   *p* 62
425 1 ST SW SUITE 2600, CALGARY, AB, T2P 3L8
(403) 699-1999   *SIC* 4924

WESTCOAST ENERGY VENTURES INC *p* 245
4529 MELROSE ST, PORT ALBERNI, BC, V9Y 1K7
SIC 4924

WESTCOAST ENGLISH LANGUAGE CENTER LIMITED   *p* 301
888 CAMBIE ST, VANCOUVER, BC, V6B 2P6
(604) 684-1010   *SIC* 8299

WESTCOAST GREEN ENERGY SYSTEMS LTD.   *p* 265
6880 MILLER RD, RICHMOND, BC, V7B

1L3
(604) 244-0421   *SIC* 4924

WESTCOAST MOULDING & MILLWORK LIMITED   *p* 282
18810 96 AVE, SURREY, BC, V4N 3R1
(604) 513-1138   *SIC* 5211

WESTCOAST VEGETABLES LTD   *p* 211
5369 49B AVE, DELTA, BC, V4K 4R7
(604) 940-4748   *SIC* 5431

WESTCON EQUIPMENT & RENTALS LTD *p* 1419
HWY 1 E, REGINA, SK, S4P 3B1
(306) 359-7273   *SIC* 1629

WESTCON PRECAST INC   *p* 166
19 RIEL DR, ST. ALBERT, AB, T8N 3Z2
(780) 459-6695   *SIC* 3272

WESTCON TERMINALS (ONTARIO) LIMITED   *p* 507
30 MIDAIR CRT, BRAMPTON, ON, L6T 5V1
(905) 494-0880   *SIC* 4731

WESTCOR CONSTRUCTION LTD   *p* 26
2420 39 AVE NE, CALGARY, AB, T2E 6X1
(403) 663-8677   *SIC* 1542

WESTCORP PROPERTIES INC   *p* 118
8215 112 ST NW SUITE 200, EDMONTON, AB, T6G 2C8
(780) 431-3300   *SIC* 6531

WESTDALE CONSTRUCTION CO. LIMITED *p* 778
35 LESMILL RD, NORTH YORK, ON, M3B 2T3
(416) 703-1877   *SIC* 6513

WESTDALE PROPERTIES   *p* 778
See WESTDALE CONSTRUCTION CO. LIMITED

WESTDALE SECONDARY SCHOOL   *p* 614
See HAMILTON-WENTWORTH DISTRICT SCHOOL BOARD, THE

WESTECH BUILDING PRODUCTS ULC *p* 19
5201 64 AVE SE, CALGARY, AB, T2C 4Z9
(403) 279-4497   *SIC* 3089

WESTECH INDUSTRIAL LTD   *p* 38
5636 BURBANK CRES SE, CALGARY, AB, T2H 1Z6
(403) 252-8803   *SIC* 5084

WESTECH INTERIORS LTD   *p* 81
21 PINEHURST RR 3, DE WINTON, AB, T0L 0X0
(403) 630-6768   *SIC* 7389

WESTECK WINDOWS & DOORS   *p* 198
See WESTECK WINDOWS MFG. INC

WESTECK WINDOWS MFG. INC   *p* 198
8104 EVANS RD, CHILLIWACK, BC, V2R 5R8
(604) 792-6700   *SIC* 5211

WESTEEL DIVISION   *p* 364
See AG GROWTH INTERNATIONAL INC

WESTERN ARCHRIB   *p* 107
See 316291 ALBERTA LTD

WESTERN ASPHALT PRODUCTS   *p* 7
See WEST-CAN SEAL COATING INC

WESTERN ASSURANCE COMPANY *p* 715
2225 ERIN MILLS PKY SUITE 1000, MISSISSAUGA, ON, L5K 2S9
(905) 403-2333   *SIC* 6331

WESTERN ASSURANCE COMPANY *p* 943
10 WELLINGTON ST E, TORONTO, ON, M5E 1C5
(416) 366-7511   *SIC* 6411

WESTERN AVIONICS   *p* 21
See AVMAX GROUP INC

WESTERN BELTING & HOSE (1986) LTD *p* 187
6468 BERESFORD ST, BURNABY, BC, V5E 1B6
(604) 451-4133   *SIC* 5084

WESTERN BUILDING LTD   *p* 423
25 POPLAR RD, CORNER BROOK, NL, A2H 4T6
(709) 634-3163   *SIC* 5211

WESTERN CANADA EXPRESS INC *p* 561
62 ADMINISTRATION RD, CONCORD, ON,

L4K 2R7
(905) 738-2106 *SIC* 4731
WESTERN CANADA HIGH SCHOOL *p* 66
See *CALGARY BOARD OF EDUCATION*
WESTERN CANADA LOTTERY CORPORATION *p*
380
125 GARRY ST SUITE 1000, WINNIPEG, MB, R3C 4J1
(204) 942-8217 *SIC* 7999
WESTERN CANADA LOTTERY CORPORATION *p*
1430
1935 1ST AVE N, SASKATOON, SK, S7K 6W1
(306) 933-6850 *SIC* 7999
WESTERN CANADA STEEL & TECHNOLOGIES INC *p*
262
5811 NO. 3 RD UNIT 1807, RICHMOND, BC, V6X 4L7
(604) 247-1442 *SIC* 5051
WESTERN CANADA WILDERNESS COMMITTEE *p*
301
341 WATER ST, VANCOUVER, BC, V6B 1B8
(604) 609-3752 *SIC* 8999
WESTERN CANADIAN TIMBER PRODUCTS LTD *p*
215
14250 MORRIS VALLEY RD, HARRISON MILLS, BC, V0M 1L0
(604) 796-0314 *SIC* 2411
WESTERN CHEVROLET PONTIAC BUICK GMC LTD *p* 83
906 HWY 9 S, DRUMHELLER, AB, T0J 0Y0
(403) 823-3371 *SIC* 5511
WESTERN COLLEGE OF VETERINARY MEDICINE *p* 1434
See *UNIVERSITY OF SASKATCHEWAN*
WESTERN CONCORD MANUFACTURING (NEW WEST) LTD *p* 207
880 CLIVEDEN AVE, DELTA, BC, V3M 5R5
(604) 525-1061 *SIC* 3086
WESTERN COPPER AND GOLD CORPORATION *p*
317
1040 GEORGIA ST W FL 15, VANCOUVER, BC, V6E 4H1
(604) 684-9497 *SIC* 1081
WESTERN DODGE CHRYSLER JEEP *p*
1411
See *598840 SASKATCHEWAN LTD*
WESTERN DRUG DISTRIBUTION CENTER LIMITED *p* 103
17611 109A AVE NW, EDMONTON, AB, T5S 2W4
(780) 413-2508 *SIC* 5047
WESTERN ENERGY SERVICES CORP *p* 62
215 9TH AVE SW SUITE 1700, CALGARY, AB, T2P 1K3
(403) 984-5916 *SIC* 1389
WESTERN EQUIPMENT LIMITED *p* 542
97 ST CLAIR ST, CHATHAM, ON, N7L 3J2
(519) 352-0530 *SIC* 5063
WESTERN EQUIPMENT LTD *p* 273
5219 192 ST UNIT 114, SURREY, BC, V3S 4P6
(604) 574-3311 *SIC* 5085
WESTERN EXPLOSIVES *p* 197
See *SARDIS EXPLOSIVES (2000) LTD*
WESTERN FACILITY *p* 215
See *ROXUL INC*
WESTERN FINANCIAL GROUP (NETWORK) INC *p*
136
1010 24 ST SE, HIGH RIVER, AB, T1V 2A7
(403) 652-2663 *SIC* 6411
WESTERN FINANCIAL GROUP INC *p* 136
1010 24 ST SE, HIGH RIVER, AB, T1V 2A7
(403) 652-2663 *SIC* 6311
WESTERN FINANCIAL GROUP INC *p* 382
777 PORTAGE AVE, WINNIPEG, MB, R3G

0N3
(204) 943-0331 *SIC* 6411
WESTERN FIRST NATIONS HOSPITALITY LIMITED PARTNERSHIP *p* 1414
914 CENTRAL AVE, PRINCE ALBERT, SK, S6V 4V3
(306) 922-0088 *SIC* 7011
WESTERN FOODS *p* 340
See *E88TLC90 HOLDINGS LTD*
WESTERN FOREST PRODUCTS INC *p* 196
2860 VICTORIA ST, CHEMAINUS, BC, V0R 1K0
(250) 246-3221 *SIC* 2611
WESTERN FOREST PRODUCTS INC *p* 196
9469 TRANS CANADA HWY, CHEMAINUS, BC, V0R 1K4
(250) 246-1566 *SIC* 2611
WESTERN FOREST PRODUCTS INC *p* 215
300 WESTERN DR, GOLD RIVER, BC, V0P 1G0
(250) 283-2961 *SIC* 2611
WESTERN FOREST PRODUCTS INC *p* 234
495 DUNSMUIR ST UNIT 201, NANAIMO, BC, V9R 6B9
(250) 734-4700 *SIC* 2611
WESTERN FOREST PRODUCTS INC *p* 234
31 PORT WAY, NANAIMO, BC, V9R 5L5
(250) 755-4600 *SIC* 2611
WESTERN FOREST PRODUCTS INC *p* 234
500 DUKE PT RD, NANAIMO, BC, V9R 1K1
(250) 722-2533 *SIC* 2611
WESTERN FOREST PRODUCTS INC *p* 245
2500 1ST AVE, PORT ALBERNI, BC, V9Y 8H7
(250) 724-7438 *SIC* 2611
WESTERN FOREST PRODUCTS INC *p* 317
800-1055 GEORGIA ST W, VANCOUVER, BC, V6E 0B6
(604) 648-4500 *SIC* 2611
WESTERN FOREST PRODUCTS INC *p* 330
700 GEORGIA ST W SUITE 510, VANCOUVER, BC, V7Y 1K8
SIC 2421
WESTERN GASCO CYLINDERS LTD *p* 282
18925 94 AVE UNIT 4, SURREY, BC, V4N 4X5
(604) 513-4429 *SIC* 5999
WESTERN GLOVE WORKS *p* 373
555 LOGAN AVE, WINNIPEG, MB, R3A 0S4
(204) 788-4249 *SIC* 5137
WESTERN GLOVE WORKS LTD *p* 373
555 LOGAN AVE, WINNIPEG, MB, R3A 0S4
(204) 788-4249 *SIC* 7363
WESTERN GROCERS *p* 17
See *LOBLAWS INC*
WESTERN HATCHERY LTD *p* 178
505 HAMM ST SUITE 1, ABBOTSFORD, BC, V2T 6B6
(604) 859-7168 *SIC* 0254
WESTERN HEALTH *p* 434
See *WESTERN REGIONAL INTERGREATED HEALTH AUTHORITY*
WESTERN HOG EXCHANGE *p* 85
10319 PRINCESS ELIZABETH AVE NW, EDMONTON, AB, T5G 0Y5
(780) 474-8292 *SIC* 5154
WESTERN HOSPITAL *p* 1038
148 POPULAR ST, ALBERTON, PE, C0B 1B0
(902) 853-8650 *SIC* 8062
WESTERN HOSPITAL & MAPPLEWOOD MANOR *p* 1038
See *WESTERN HOSPITAL*
WESTERN HYUNDAI *p* 1411
1774 MAIN ST N, MOOSE JAW, SK, S6J 1L4
(306) 691-5444 *SIC* 5511
WESTERN IMPACT SALES & MARKETING INC *p* 12
3223 5 AVE NE UNIT 309, CALGARY, AB, T2A 6E9
(403) 272-3065 *SIC* 5141
WESTERN INDUSTRIAL CONTRACTORS LTD *p* 249

4912 HART HWY, PRINCE GEORGE, BC, V2K 3A1
(250) 962-6011 *SIC* 1541
WESTERN INVENTORY SERVICE LTD *p* 12
720 28 ST NE SUITE 128, CALGARY, AB, T2A 6R3
(403) 272-3850 *SIC* 7389
WESTERN INVENTORY SERVICE LTD *p*
364
73 GOULET ST, WINNIPEG, MB, R2H 0R5
(204) 669-6505 *SIC* 7389
WESTERN INVENTORY SERVICE LTD *p*
690
3770 NASHUA DR SUITE 5, MISSISSAUGA, ON, L4V 1M5
(905) 677-1947 *SIC* 7389
WESTERN INVENTORY SERVICE LTD *p*
1402
4865 BOUL DE MAISONNEUVE O, WESTMOUNT, QC, H3Z 1M7
(514) 483-1337 *SIC* 7389
WESTERN INVESTMENT COMPANY OF CANADA LIMITED, THE *p* 136
1010 24 ST SE, HIGH RIVER, AB, T1V 2A7
(403) 701-7546 *SIC* 2021
WESTERN LIFE *p* 382
See *WESTERN LIFE ASSURANCE COMPANY*
WESTERN LIFE ASSURANCE COMPANY *p*
382
717 PORTAGE AVE 4TH FLOOR, WINNIPEG, MB, R3G 0M8
(204) 786-6431 *SIC* 6311
WESTERN LOGISTICS INC *p* 202
1555 BRIGANTINE DR, COQUITLAM, BC, V3K 7C2
(604) 525-7211 *SIC* 4731
WESTERN MACHINE WORKS, A DIV OF *p*
238
See *ALLIED SHIPBUILDERS LTD*
WESTERN MARINE COMPANY *p* 286
1494 POWELL ST, VANCOUVER, BC, V5L 5B5
(604) 253-7721 *SIC* 5088
WESTERN MATERIALS HANDLING & EQUIPMENT LTD *p* 19
7805 46 ST SE, CALGARY, AB, T2C 2Y5
(403) 236-0305 *SIC* 5084
WESTERN MECHANICAL ELECTRICAL MILLWRIGHT SERVICES LTD *p* 488
160 BROCK ST, BARRIE, ON, L4N 2M4
(705) 737-4135 *SIC* 1796
WESTERN MESSENGER & TRANSFER LIMITED *p* 383
839 ELLICE AVE, WINNIPEG, MB, R3G 0C3
(204) 987-7020 *SIC* 7389
WESTERN OIL SERVICES LTD *p* 228
19840 57A AVE, LANGLEY, BC, V3A 6G6
(604) 514-4787 *SIC* 5084
WESTERN PACIFIC ACCEPTANCE CORPORATION *p*
317
1199 PENDER ST W SUITE 510, VANCOUVER, BC, V6E 2R1
(604) 678-3230 *SIC* 7389
WESTERN PACIFIC ENTERPRISES GP *p*
202
1321 KETCH CRT, COQUITLAM, BC, V3K 6X7
(604) 540-1321 *SIC* 1731
WESTERN PACIFIC MARINE LTD *p* 319
501 DENMAN ST, VANCOUVER, BC, V6G 2W9
(604) 681-5199 *SIC* 4482
WESTERN PETROLEUM *p* 427
See *WESTERN PETROLEUM NEWFOUNDLAND LIMITED*
WESTERN PETROLEUM NEWFOUNDLAND LIMITED *p*
427
4 RIVERHEAD CENTER UNIT 2, RIVERHEAD HARBOUR GRACE, NL, A0A 3P0
(709) 596-4181 *SIC* 5541

WESTERN POLYMERS CORP *p* 26
1003 55 AVE NE SUITE A, CALGARY, AB, T2E 6W1
(403) 295-7194 *SIC* 5085
WESTERN PONTIAC BUICK GMC (1999) LTD *p* 103
18325 STONY PLAIN RD NW, EDMONTON, AB, T5S 1C6
(780) 486-3333 *SIC* 5511
WESTERN PONTIAC GMC 1999 LTD *p* 103
18325 STONY PLAIN RD, EDMONTON, AB, T5S 1C6
(780) 486-3333 *SIC* 5511
WESTERN PRODUCER PUBLICATIONS *p*
1427
See *GLACIER MEDIA INC*
WESTERN PROTECTION ALLIANCE INC *p*
264
11771 HORSESHOE WAY UNIT 1, RICHMOND, BC, V7A 4V4
(604) 271-7475 *SIC* 7381
WESTERN QUEBEC SCHOOL BOARD *p*
1108
15 RUE KATIMAVIK, GATINEAU, QC, J9J 0E9
(819) 684-1313 *SIC* 8211
WESTERN REGIONAL INTEGRATED HEALTH AUTHORITY, THE *p* 423
1 BROOKFIELD AVE, CORNER BROOK, NL, A2H 6J7
(709) 637-5000 *SIC* 8062
WESTERN REGIONAL INTEGRATED HEALTH AUTHORITY, THE *p* 427
GD, NORRIS POINT, NL, A0K 3V0
(709) 458-2211 *SIC* 8062
WESTERN REGIONAL INTEGRATED HEALTH AUTHORITY, THE *p* 434
142 MINNESOTA DR, STEPHENVILLE, NL, A2N 3X9
(709) 643-5111 *SIC* 8062
WESTERN REGIONAL INTERGREATED HEALTH AUTHORITY *p* 434
149 MONTANA DR, STEPHENVILLE, NL, A2N 2T4
(709) 643-8608 *SIC* 8621
WESTERN REPAIR & SALES INC *p* 374
500 HIGGINS AVE, WINNIPEG, MB, R3A 0B1
(204) 925-7900 *SIC* 7389
WESTERN RESOURCES CORP *p* 317
1111 GEORGIA ST W SUITE 1400, VANCOUVER, BC, V6E 4M3
(604) 689-9378 *SIC* 1081
WESTERN RICE MILLS LTD *p* 266
6231 WESTMINSTER HWY UNIT 120, RICHMOND, BC, V7C 4V4
(604) 321-0338 *SIC* 5149
WESTERN RV CENTRE LEDUC INC *p* 140
7503 SPARROW DR, LEDUC, AB, T9E 0H3
(780) 986-2880 *SIC* 5571
WESTERN RV COUNTRY *p* 140
See *WESTERN RV CENTRE LEDUC INC*
WESTERN RV COUNTRY LTD *p* 3
61 EAST LAKE RAMP NE, AIRDRIE, AB, T4A 2K4
(403) 912-2634 *SIC* 5561
WESTERN SALES (1986) LTD *p* 1423
405 HWY 7 W, ROSETOWN, SK, S0L 2V0
(306) 882-4291 *SIC* 5083
WESTERN SCALE CO LTD *p* 247
1670 KINGSWAY AVE, PORT COQUITLAM, BC, V3C 3Y9
(604) 941-3474 *SIC* 3596
WESTERN SCHOOL DIVISION *p* 352
75 THORNHILL ST UNIT 4, MORDEN, MB, R6M 1P2
(204) 822-4448 *SIC* 8211
WESTERN STAR FREIGHTLINER *p* 217
See *RJAMES MANAGEMENT GROUP LTD*
WESTERN STAR SALES THUNDER BAY LTD *p* 909
3150 ARTHUR ST W, THUNDER BAY, ON, P7C 4V1
(807) 939-2537 *SIC* 5511

▲ Public Company ■ Public Company Family Member **HQ** Headquarters **BR** Branch **SL** Single Location

WESTERN STAR TRUCKS (NORTH) LTD *p* 2
26229 TOWNSHIP ROAD 531A, ACHESON, AB, T7X 5A4
(780) 453-3452   *SIC* 5511
WESTERN STERLING TRUCKS LTD *p* 104
18353 118 AVE NW, EDMONTON, AB, T5S 1M8
(780) 481-7400   *SIC* 5511
WESTERN STEVEDORING COMPANY LIMITED *p* 239
15 MOUNTAIN HWY, NORTH VANCOUVER, BC, V7J 2J9
(604) 904-2800   *SIC* 4491
WESTERN SURETY COMPANY *p* 1419
1881 SCARTH ST UNIT 2100, REGINA, SK, S4P 4K9
(306) 791-3735   *SIC* 6351
WESTERN TOYOTA *p* 422
See JAGO AUTO LTD
WESTERN TRACTOR COMPANY INC *p* 141
3214 5 AVE N, LETHBRIDGE, AB, T1H 0P4
(403) 327-5512   *SIC* 5083
WESTERN UNION BUSINESS SOLUTIONS *p* 279
See CUSTOM HOUSE ULC
WESTERN UNIVERSITY *p* 655
See UNIVERSITY OF WESTERN ONTARIO, THE
WESTERN WAFFLES *p* 518
See WESTERN WAFFLES CORP
WESTERN WAFFLES CORP *p* 207
529 ANNANCE CRT, DELTA, BC, V3M 6Y7
(604) 524-2540   *SIC* 2038
WESTERN WAFFLES CORP *p* 518
175 SAVANNAH OAKS DR, BRANTFORD, ON, N3V 1E8
(519) 759-2025   *SIC* 2038
WESTERN WATER INDUSTRIES *p* 1434
301 CENTRAL AVE, SASKATOON, SK, S7N 2E9
(306) 374-8555   *SIC* 5149
WESTERN WHOLESALERS, DIV OF *p* 434
See FOCENCO LIMITED
WESTERNGECO CANADA *p* 32
See SCHLUMBERGER CANADA LIMITED
WESTERNONE INC *p* 310
925 GEORGIA ST W SUITE 910, VANCOUVER, BC, V6C 3L2
(604) 678-4042   *SIC* 6722
WESTERNZAGROS RESOURCES ULC *p* 63
255 5 AVE SW SUITE 1000, CALGARY, AB, T2P 3G6
(403) 693-7001   *SIC* 1382
WESTFAIR DRUGS LTD *p* 19
3916 72 AVE SE, CALGARY, AB, T2C 2E2
(403) 279-1600   *SIC* 5199
WESTFAIR FOODS *p* 24
See LOBLAW COMPANIES LIMITED
WESTFAIR FOODS LTD *p* 368
215 ST ANNE'S RD, WINNIPEG, MB, R2M 2Z9
(204) 258-2419   *SIC* 5411
WESTFIELD INDUSTRIES LTD *p* 355
74 HWY 205 E, ROSENORT, MB, R0G 1W0
(204) 746-2396   *SIC* 3523
WESTFORM METALS INC *p* 198
6435 LICKMAN RD, CHILLIWACK, BC, V2R 4A9
(604) 858-7134   *SIC* 3444
WESTFORT FOODS INC *p* 910
111 FREDERICA ST E, THUNDER BAY, ON, P7E 3V4
(807) 623-4220   *SIC* 5411
WESTGATE CHEVROLET LTD *p* 104
10145 178 ST NW, EDMONTON, AB, T5S 1E4
(780) 483-3320   *SIC* 5511
WESTGATE HONDA *p* 658
See 242747 ONTARIO LIMITED
WESTGATE LODGE *p* 492
See CROWN RIDGE HEALTH CARE SER-

VICES INC
WESTGEN, WESTERN CANADA'S GENETICS CENTRE *p* 232
6681 GLOVER RD, MILNER, BC, V0X 1T0
(604) 530-1141   *SIC* 5159
WESTHALL INVESTMENTS LTD *p* 845
1815 IRONSTONE MANOR UNIT 1, PICKERING, ON, L1W 3W9
(905) 839-3500   *SIC* 6712
WESTIN BAYSHORE VANCOUVER, THE *p* 318
See BLUE TREE HOTELS INVESTMENT (CANADA), LTD
WESTIN CALGARY, THE *p* 60
See STARWOOD CANADA ULC
WESTIN EDMONTON,THE *p* 87
See BLUE TREE HOTELS GP ULC
WESTIN HARBOUR CASTLE *p* 959
See BLUE TREE HOTELS INVESTMENT (CANADA), LTD
WESTIN NOVA SCOTIAN HOTEL, THE *p* 451
See HOTEL N.S. OWNERSHIP LIMITED PARTNERSHIP
WESTIN OTTAWA, THE *p* 822
See STARWOOD CANADA ULC
WESTIN RESORT & SPA *p* 342
See OHR WHISTLER MANAGEMENT LTD
WESTIN TRILLIUM HOUSE BLUE MOUNTAIN, THE *p* 493
See INTRAWEST ULC
WESTJET *p* 26
See WESTJET AIRLINES LTD
WESTJET AIRLINES LTD *p* 26
22 AERIAL PL NE, CALGARY, AB, T2E 3J1
(888) 937-8538   *SIC* 4512
WESTJET AIRLINES LTD *p* 265
3880 GRANT MCCONACHIE WAY SUITE 4130, RICHMOND, BC, V7B 0A5
(604) 249-1165   *SIC* 4512
WESTKEY GRAPHICS LTD *p* 181
8315 RIVERBEND CRT, BURNABY, BC, V3N 5E7
(604) 549-2350   *SIC* 5943
WESTKEY GRAPHICS LTD *p* 183
3212 LAKE CITY WAY, BURNABY, BC, V5A 3A4
(604) 421-7778   *SIC* 5734
WESTLAKE & ASSOCIATES HOLDINGS INC *p* 527
1149 NORTHSIDE RD, BURLINGTON, ON, L7M 1H5
(905) 336-5200   *SIC* 6712
WESTLAM INDUSTRIES LTD *p* 226
19755 98 AVE, LANGLEY, BC, V1M 2X5
(604) 888-2894   *SIC* 2435
WESTLAND CONSTRUCTION LTD *p* 393
475 DOVERCOURT DR UNIT 1, WINNIPEG, MB, R3Y 1G4
(204) 633-6272   *SIC* 1541
WESTLAND INSURANCE GROUP LTD *p* 280
2121 160 ST SUITE 200, SURREY, BC, V3Z 9N6
(604) 543-7788   *SIC* 6411
WESTLAND INSURANCE LIMITED PARTNERSHIP *p* 280
2121 160 ST UNIT 200, SURREY, BC, V3Z 9N6
(604) 543-7788   *SIC* 6411
WESTLAND PLASTICS LTD *p* 389
12 ROTHWELL RD, WINNIPEG, MB, R3P 2H7
(204) 488-6075   *SIC* 3089
WESTLANE SECONDARY SCHOOL *p* 760
See DISTRICT SCHOOL BOARD OF NIAGARA
WESTLOCK BUILDINGS SUPPLIES, A DIV OF *p* 95
See C.A. FISCHER LUMBER CO. LTD
WESTLOCK HEALTHCARE CENTRE *p* 171

See ALBERTA HEALTH SERVICES
WESTLOCK TERMINALS (NGC) LTD *p* 172
9921 108 ST, WESTLOCK, AB, T7P 2J1
(780) 349-7034   *SIC* 5153
WESTMAN COMMUNICATIONS GROUP *p* 348
See WESTMAN MEDIA COOPERATIVE LTD
WESTMAN LABORATORY *p* 347
See WESTMAN REGIONAL LABORATORY SERVICES INC
WESTMAN MEDIA COOPERATIVE LTD *p* 348
1906 PARK AVE, BRANDON, MB, R7B 0R9
(204) 725-4300   *SIC* 4841
WESTMAN REGIONAL LABORATORY SERVICES INC *p* 347
150 MCTAVISH AVE E SUITE 1, BRANDON, MB, R7A 7H8
(204) 578-4440   *SIC* 8071
WESTMAN STEEL INC *p* 357
2976 DAY ST, SPRINGFIELD, MB, R2C 2Z2
(204) 777-5345   *SIC* 3444
WESTMAN STEEL INDUSTRIES *p* 357
2976 DAY ST, SPRINGFIELD, MB, R2C 2Z2
(204) 777-5345   *SIC* 3312
WESTMAR REALTY LTD *p* 266
5188 WESTMINSTER HWY SUITE 203, RICHMOND, BC, V7C 5S7
(604) 506-5352   *SIC* 6531
WESTMARK HOTELS OF CANADA LTD *p* 1440
2288 2ND AVE, WHITEHORSE, YT, Y1A 1C8
(867) 668-4747   *SIC* 7011
WESTMARK HOTELS OF CANADA LTD *p* 1440
201 WOOD ST, WHITEHORSE, YT, Y1A 2E4
(867) 393-9700   *SIC* 7011
WESTMARK KLONDIKE INN *p* 1440
See WESTMARK HOTELS OF CANADA LTD
WESTMINSTER CENTRE *p* 237
See UPG PROPERTY GROUP INC
WESTMINSTER HOUSE SOCIETY *p* 238
228 SEVENTH ST, NEW WESTMINSTER, BC, V3M 3L3
(604) 524-5633   *SIC* 8699
WESTMINSTER MUTUAL INSURANCE COMPANY *p* 493
14122 BELMONT RD, BELMONT, ON, N0L 1B0
(519) 644-1663   *SIC* 6331
WESTMINSTER SAVINGS CREDIT UNION *p* 274
13450 102 AVE SUITE 1900, SURREY, BC, V3T 5Y1
(604) 517-0100   *SIC* 6062
WESTMINSTER SECONDARY SCHOOL *p* 659
See THAMES VALLEY DISTRICT SCHOOL BOARD
WESTMINSTER SELECT TRADING CORPORATION *p* 935
397 DUNDAS ST E, TORONTO, ON, M5A 2A7
(416) 363-2727   *SIC* 5094
WESTMINSTER VOLKSWAGEN LTD *p* 199
2555 BARNET HWY, COQUITLAM, BC, V3H 1W4
(604) 461-5000   *SIC* 5511
WESTMONT HOSPITALITY MANAGEMENT LIMITED *p* 589
600 DIXON RD, ETOBICOKE, ON, M9W 1J1
(416) 240-7511   *SIC* 7011
WESTMONT HOSPITALITY MANAGEMENT LIMITED *p* 602
601 SCOTTSDALE DR, GUELPH, ON, N1G 3E7
(519) 836-0231   *SIC* 7011
WESTMORLAND FISHERIES LTD *p* 396

64 GAUTREAU ST, CAP-PELE, NB, E4N 1V3
(506) 577-4325   *SIC* 2091
WESTMORLAND-ALBERT SOLID WASTE CORPORATION *p* 395
2024 ROUTE 128, BERRY MILLS, NB, E1G 4K6
(506) 877-1050   *SIC* 4953
WESTMOUNT CHARTER SCHOOL SOCIETY *p* 74
2519 RICHMOND RD SW, CALGARY, AB, T3E 4M2
(403) 217-0426   *SIC* 8211
WESTMOUNT GOLF & COUNTRY CLUB *p* 641
See WESTMOUNT GOLF AND COUNTRY CLUB LIMITED
WESTMOUNT GOLF AND COUNTRY CLUB LIMITED *p* 641
50 INVERNESS DR, KITCHENER, ON, N2M 4Z9
(519) 742-2323   *SIC* 7997
WESTMOUNT MORTGAGE CORPORATION *p* 63
605 5 AVE SW SUITE 2300, CALGARY, AB, T2P 3H5
(403) 269-1027   *SIC* 6162
WESTMOUNT SECONDARY SCHOOL *p* 616
See HAMILTON-WENTWORTH DISTRICT SCHOOL BOARD, THE
WESTMOUNT STOREFRONT SYSTEMS LTD *p* 636
20 RIVERVIEW PL, KITCHENER, ON, N2B 3X8
(519) 570-2850   *SIC* 1793
WESTON BAKERIES LIMITED *p* 629
See 2104225 ONTARIO LTD
WESTON BAKERIES LIMITED *p* 901
695 MARTINDALE RD, SUDBURY, ON, P3E 4H6
(705) 673-4185   *SIC* 2051
WESTON BAKERIES LIMITED *p* 1103
See 2104225 ONTARIO LTD
WESTON BAKERIES LIMITED *p* 1145
See 2104225 ONTARIO LTD
WESTON BAKERIES LIMITED *p* 1242
See 2104225 ONTARIO LTD
WESTON BAKERIES LIMITED *p* 1417
See 2104225 ONTARIO LTD
WESTON BAKERIES LIMITED *p* 1419
See 2104225 ONTARIO LTD
WESTON COLLEGIATE INSTITUTE *p* 997
See TORONTO DISTRICT SCHOOL BOARD
WESTON CONSULTING *p* 561
See WESTON CONSULTING GROUP INC
WESTON CONSULTING GROUP INC *p* 561
201 MILLWAY AVE UNIT 19, CONCORD, ON, L4K 5K8
(905) 738-8080   *SIC* 8742
WESTON FOODS (CANADA) INC *p* 576
1425 THE QUEENSWAY, ETOBICOKE, ON, M8Z 1T3
(416) 252-7323   *SIC* 2051
WESTON FOREST PRODUCTS INC *p* 686
7600 TORBRAM RD, MISSISSAUGA, ON, L4T 3L8
(905) 677-9364   *SIC* 5031
WESTON TERRACE CARE COMMUNITY *p* 997
See 2063414 ONTARIO LIMITED
WESTON WOOD SOLUTIONS INC *p* 507
300 ORENDA RD, BRAMPTON, ON, L6T 1G2
(905) 677-9120   *SIC* 5031
WESTON'S OUTLET STORE *p* 573
See 2104225 ONTARIO LTD
WESTOWER COMMUNICATIONS LTD *p* 169
4933 46TH ST, THORSBY, AB, T0C 2P0
(780) 789-2375   *SIC* 1623

WESTOWER COMMUNICATIONS LTD   *p* 273
17886 55 AVE, SURREY, BC, V3S 6C8
(604) 576-4755   *SIC* 1623
WESTOWNE MAZDA   *p* 578
See WESTOWNE MOTORS (1983) LIMITED
WESTOWNE MOTORS (1983) LIMITED   *p* 578
5511 DUNDAS ST W, ETOBICOKE, ON, M9B 1B8
(416) 232-2011   *SIC* 5511
WESTPARK   *p* 317
See WESTPARK PARKING SERVICES (2015) INC
WESTPARK PARKING SERVICES (2015) INC   *p* 317
1140 PENDER ST W SUITE 1310, VANCOUVER, BC, V6E 4G1
(604) 669-7275   *SIC* 7521
WESTPOINT MANAGEMENT INC   *p* 41
3604 52 AVE NW SUITE 114, CALGARY, AB, T2L 1V9
(403) 282-7770   *SIC* 6531
WESTPORT FUEL SYSTEMS INC   *p* 324
1750 75TH AVE W SUITE 101, VANCOUVER, BC, V6P 6G2
(604) 718-2000   *SIC* 3519
WESTPORT LIGHT DUTY INC   *p* 324
1750 75TH AVE W SUITE 101, VANCOUVER, BC, V6P 6G2
(604) 718-2000   *SIC* 3519
WESTPORT MANUFACTURING CO LTD   *p* 324
1122 MARINE DR SW, VANCOUVER, BC, V6P 5Z3
(604) 261-9326   *SIC* 2391
WESTPORT POWER INC   *p* 324
1750 75TH AVE W SUITE 101, VANCOUVER, BC, V6P 6G2
(604) 718-2000   *SIC* 8748
WESTPORT POWER INC   *p* 640
100 HOLLINGER CRES, KITCHENER, ON, N2K 2Z3
(519) 576-4270   *SIC* 3714
WESTPOWER EQUIPMENT LTD   *p* 19
4451 54 AVE SE, CALGARY, AB, T2C 2A2
(403) 720-3300   *SIC* 5084
WESTPRO INFRASTRUCTURE LTD   *p* 278
8241 129 ST, SURREY, BC, V3W 0A6
(604) 592-9767   *SIC* 1542
WESTQUIP DIESEL SALES (ALTA) LTD   *p* 2
11162 261 ST, ACHESON, AB, T7X 6C7
(780) 960-5560   *SIC* 5084
WESTRAN PORTSIDE TERMINAL LIMITED   *p* 259
16060 PORTSIDE RD, RICHMOND, BC, V6W 1M1
(604) 244-1975   *SIC* 4492
WESTRIDGE   *p* 1416
See WESTRIDGE CONSTRUCTION LTD
WESTRIDGE BUICK GMC   *p* 144
See WESTRIDGE PONTIAC BUICK GMC LTD
WESTRIDGE CABINETS (1993) LTD   *p* 157
412 LIBERTY AVE, RED DEER COUNTY, AB, T4E 1B9
(403) 342-6671   *SIC* 2434
WESTRIDGE CONSTRUCTION LTD   *p* 1416
435 HENDERSON DR, REGINA, SK, S4N 5W8
(306) 352-2434   *SIC* 1542
WESTRIDGE PONTIAC BUICK GMC LTD   *p* 144
2406 50 AVE, LLOYDMINSTER, AB, T9V 2W7
(780) 875-3366   *SIC* 5511
WESTROCK COMPANY OF CANADA CORP   *p* 33
1115 34 AVE SE, CALGARY, AB, T2G 1V5
(403) 214-5200   *SIC* 2653
WESTROCK COMPANY OF CANADA CORP   *p* 576
730 ISLINGTON AVE, ETOBICOKE, ON, M8Z 4N8
(416) 259-8421   *SIC* 2653
WESTROCK COMPANY OF CANADA CORP   *p* 605
390 WOODLAWN RD W, GUELPH, ON, N1H 7K3
(519) 821-4930   *SIC* 2653
WESTROCK COMPANY OF CANADA CORP   *p* 1124
1000 CH DE L'USINE BUREAU 2632, LA TUQUE, QC, G9X 3P8
(819) 676-8100   *SIC* 2657
WESTROCK COMPANY OF CANADA CORP   *p* 1157
5550 AV ROYALMOUNT, MONT-ROYAL, QC, H4P 1H7
(514) 736-6889   *SIC* 4225
WESTROCK COMPANY OF CANADA CORP   *p* 1247
15400 RUE SHERBROOKE E BUREAU A-15, POINTE-AUX-TREMBLES, QC, H1A 3S2
(514) 642-9251   *SIC* 2657
WESTROCK COMPANY OF CANADA CORP   *p* 1360
433 2E AV DU PARC-INDUSTRIEL, SAINTE-MARIE, QC, G6E 3H2
(418) 387-5438   *SIC* 2657
WESTROCK COMPANY OF CANADA CORP   *p* 1421
1400 1ST AVE, REGINA, SK, S4R 8G5
(306) 525-7700   *SIC* 2653
WESTROCK PACKAGING COMPANY   *p* 690
3270 AMERICAN DR, MISSISSAUGA, ON, L4V 1B5
(416) 683-1270   *SIC* 2679
WESTROCK PACKAGING COMPANY   *p* 690
3270 AMERICAN DR, MISSISSAUGA, ON, L4V 1B5
(905) 677-3592   *SIC* 2752
WESTROCK PACKAGING SYSTEMS LP   *p* 475
281 FAIRALL ST, AJAX, ON, L1S 1R7
(905) 683-2330   *SIC* 2657
WESTRON PUMPS & COMPRESSORS LTD   *p* 26
3600 21 ST NE UNIT 3, CALGARY, AB, T2E 6V6
(403) 291-6777   *SIC* 3561
WESTROW FOOD BROKERS INC   *p* 19
2880 GLENMORE TRAIL SE SUITE 115, CALGARY, AB, T2C 2E7
(403) 720-0703   *SIC* 5141
WESTROW FOOD GROUP   *p* 19
See WESTROW FOOD BROKERS INC
WESTRUM LUMBER LTD   *p* 1423
611 WECKMAN DR, ROULEAU, SK, S0G 4K0
(306) 776-2505   *SIC* 5211
WESTSHORE TERMINALS INVESTMENT CORPORATION   *p* 310
1067 CORDOVA ST W SUITE 1800, VANCOUVER, BC, V6C 1C7
(604) 946-4491   *SIC* 6722
WESTSHORE TERMINALS LTD   *p* 211
1 ROBERTS BANK RD, DELTA, BC, V4M 4G5
(604) 946-4491   *SIC* 4491
WESTSIDE NURSING SERVICES LTD   *p* 321
1892 BROADWAY W SUITE 200, VANCOUVER, BC, V6J 1Y9
(604) 261-9161   *SIC* 8741
WESTSIDE SECONDARY SCHOOL   *p* 809
See UPPER GRAND DISTRICT SCHOOL BOARD, THE
WESTVAC INDUSTRIAL LTD   *p* 2
26609 111 AVE, ACHESON, AB, T7X 6E1
(780) 962-1218   *SIC* 5084
WESTVIEW CO-OPERATIVE ASSOCIATION LIMITED   *p* 151
5330 46 ST, OLDS, AB, T4H 1P6
(403) 556-3335   *SIC* 5411
WESTVIEW FORD SALES LTD   *p* 203
4901 ISLAND HWY N, COURTENAY, BC, V9N 5Y9
(250) 334-3161   *SIC* 5511
WESTVIEW INN LTD   *p* 98
16625 STONY PLAIN RD NW, EDMONTON, AB, T5P 4A8
(780) 484-7751   *SIC* 7011
WESTVIEW SALES LTD   *p* 208
7251 120 ST, DELTA, BC, V4C 6P5
(604) 591-7747   *SIC* 5051
WESTVIEW SECONDARY SCHOOL   *p* 231
See SCHOOL DISTRICT NO 42 (MAPLE RIDGE-PITT MEADOWS)
WESTWARD ENTERPRISES LTD   *p* 196
5001 50TH AVE, CHETWYND, BC, V0C 1J0
(250) 788-2422   *SIC* 5411
WESTWARD PARTS SERVICES LTD   *p* 156
6517 67 ST, RED DEER, AB, T4P 1A3
(403) 347-2200   *SIC* 5083
WESTWARD TOOLS & EQUIPMENT, DIV OF   *p* 92
See ACKLANDS - GRAINGER INC
WESTWAY HOLDINGS CANADA INC   *p* 1069
6 RUE DE LA PLACE-DU-COMMERCE BUREAU 202, BROSSARD, QC, J4W 3J9
(450) 465-1715   *SIC* 5191
WESTWAY MACHINERY LTD   *p* 709
2370 CAWTHRA RD, MISSISSAUGA, ON, L5A 2X1
(905) 803-9999   *SIC* 5084
WESTWIND SCHOOL DIVISION #74   *p* 79
730 4TH AVE W, CARDSTON, AB, T0K 0K0
(403) 653-4955   *SIC* 8211
WESTWIND SCHOOL DIVISION #74   *p* 153
145 N 200 W, RAYMOND, AB, T0K 2S0
(403) 752-3004   *SIC* 8211
WESTWOOD CRUISESHIPCENTERS   *p* 246
2748 LOUGHEED HWY SUITE 304, PORT COQUITLAM, BC, V3B 6P2
(604) 464-7447   *SIC* 4724
WESTWOOD ELECTRIC LTD   *p* 332
887 FAIRWEATHER RD, VERNON, BC, V1T 8T8
(250) 542-5481   *SIC* 1623
WESTWOOD FIBRE PRODUCTS INC   *p* 341
2677 KYLE RD SUITE E, WEST KELOWNA, BC, V1Z 2M9
(250) 769-1427   *SIC* 5099
WESTWOOD FINE CABINETRY INC   *p* 223
2140 LECKIE PL, KELOWNA, BC, V1Y 7W7
(250) 860-3900   *SIC* 2434
WESTWOOD INDUSTRIAL ELECTRIC   *p* 332
See WESTWOOD ELECTRIC LTD
WESTWOOD PLATEAU GOLF & COUNTRY CLUB   *p* 199
See WESBILD HOLDINGS LTD
WESTWORLD ALBERTA   *p* 184
See CANADA WIDE MEDIA LIMITED
WESTWORLD COMPUTERS LTD   *p* 98
10333 170 ST NW, EDMONTON, AB, T5P 4V4
(780) 454-5190   *SIC* 4899
WET'SUWET'EN TREATY OFFICE   *p* 269
3873 1ST AVE, SMITHERS, BC, V0J 2N0
(250) 847-3630   *SIC* 8699
WETASKIWIN CHEVROLET OLDSMOBILE (2001) LTD   *p* 172
4710 56 ST, WETASKIWIN, AB, T9A 1V7
SIC 5511
WETASKIWIN CO-OPERATIVE ASSOCIATION LIMITED   *p* 172
4707 40 AVE, WETASKIWIN, AB, T9A 2B8
(780) 352-9121   *SIC* 2048
WETASKIWIN COMPOSITE HIGHSCHOOL   *p* 172
See WETASKIWIN REGIONAL PUBLIC SCHOOLS
WETASKIWIN READY MIX LTD   *p* 172
5410 50 ST, WETASKIWIN, AB, T9A 2G9
(780) 352-4301   *SIC* 3273
WETASKIWIN REGIONAL PUBLIC SCHOOLS   *p* 172
4619 50 AVE, WETASKIWIN, AB, T9A 0R6
(780) 352-2295   *SIC* 8211
WETASKIWIN REGIONAL PUBLIC SCHOOLS   *p* 172
5515 47A AVE, WETASKIWIN, AB, T9A 3S3
(780) 352-6018   *SIC* 8211
WEXFORD RESIDENCE INC, THE   *p* 873
1860 LAWRENCE AVE E, SCARBOROUGH, ON, M1R 5B1
(416) 752-8877   *SIC* 8361
WEXFORD, THE   *p* 873
See WEXFORD RESIDENCE INC, THE
WEXXAR BEL   *p* 257
See WEXXAR PACKAGING INC
WEXXAR PACKAGING INC   *p* 257
13471 VULCAN WAY, RICHMOND, BC, V6V 1K4
(604) 930-9300   *SIC* 3556
WEYBURN CREDIT UNION LIMITED   *p* 1438
205 COTEAU AVE, WEYBURN, SK, S4H 0G5
(306) 842-6641   *SIC* 6062
WEYBURN GENERAL HOSPITAL IN SCHR   *p* 1438
See SUN COUNTRY REGIONAL HEALTH AUTHORITY
WEYBURN LIVESTOCK EXCHANGE   *p* 1437
See 324007 ALBERTA LTD
WEYERHAEUSER AVIATION   *p* 317
See WEYERHAEUSER COMPANY LIMITED
WEYERHAEUSER COMPANY LIMITED   *p* 82
GD STN MAIN, DRAYTON VALLEY, AB, T7A 1T1
(780) 542-8000   *SIC* 2493
WEYERHAEUSER COMPANY LIMITED   *p* 131
GD, GRANDE CACHE, AB, T0E 0Y0
SIC 2421
WEYERHAEUSER COMPANY LIMITED   *p* 133
GD STN MAIN, GRANDE PRAIRIE, AB, T8V 3A9
(780) 539-8500   *SIC* 5031
WEYERHAEUSER COMPANY LIMITED   *p* 207
1272 DERWENT WAY, DELTA, BC, V3M 5R1
(604) 526-4665   *SIC* 2421
WEYERHAEUSER COMPANY LIMITED   *p* 245
GD LCD MAIN, PORT ALBERNI, BC, V9Y 7M3
(250) 724-6511   *SIC* 2421
WEYERHAEUSER COMPANY LIMITED   *p* 252
201 OLD HEDLEY RD, PRINCETON, BC, V0X 1W0
(250) 295-3281   *SIC* 2421
WEYERHAEUSER COMPANY LIMITED   *p* 288
3650 E KENT AVE S, VANCOUVER, BC, V5S 2J2
SIC 2421
WEYERHAEUSER COMPANY LIMITED   *p* 317
1140 PENDER ST W SUITE 440, VANCOUVER, BC, V6E 4G1
(604) 661-8000   *SIC* 2421
WEYERHAEUSER COMPANY LIMITED   *p* 592
40 DUNLOP ST, FORT ERIE, ON, L2A 4H8
SIC 5031
WEYERHAEUSER COMPANY LIMITED   *p* 628
1000 JONES RD, KENORA, ON, P9N 3X8
(807) 548-8000   *SIC* 2439
WEYERHAEUSER COMPANY LIMITED   *p* 1407
HIWAY 9 S, HUDSON BAY, SK, S0E 0Y0
(306) 865-1700   *SIC* 2421
WEYLAND, LAURA PHARMACY LTD   *p* 984

388 KING ST W SUITE 1320, TORONTO, ON, M5V 1K2

(416) 597-6550   SIC 5912

WF HERMAN SCHOOL   p 1020
See GREATER ESSEX COUNTY DISTRICT SCHOOL BOARD

WF STEEL & CRANE LTD   p 150
705 23 AVE, NISKU, AB, T9E 7Y5

(587) 410-0625   SIC 5084

WFCU   p 1022
See WINDSOR FAMILY CREDIT UNION LIMITED

WFG   p 773
See WORLD FINANCIAL GROUP INSURANCE AGENCY OF CANADA INC

WFS ENTERPRISES INC   p 1022
730 NORTH SERVICE RD E, WINDSOR, ON, N8X 3J3

(519) 966-2202   SIC 5085

WFS LTD   p 1022
730 NORTH SERVICE RD E, WINDSOR, ON, N8X 3J3

(519) 966-2202   SIC 5085

WG PRO-MANUFACTURING INC   p 500
2110 WILLIAMS PKY SUITE 6, BRAMPTON, ON, L6S 5X6

(905) 790-3377   SIC 7389

WGI MANUFACTURING INC   p 342
1455 BELLEVUE AVE SUITE 300, WEST VANCOUVER, BC, V7T 1C3

(604) 922-6563   SIC 2842

WGI SERVICE PLAN DIVISION INC   p 342
1455 BELLEVUE AVE SUITE 300, WEST VANCOUVER, BC, V7T 1C3

(604) 922-6563   SIC 6351

WGI WESTMAN GROUP INC   p 357
2976 DAY ST, SPRINGFIELD, MB, R2C 2Z2

(204) 777-5345   SIC 3441

WHALLEY & DISTRICT SENIOR CITIZEN HOUSING SOCIETY   p 274
13333 OLD YALE RD, SURREY, BC, V3T 5A2

(604) 588-0445   SIC 8059

WHAT A BLOOM CANADA   p 994
See 1882540 ONTARIO INC

WHD CANADA   p 642
See PACA INDUSTRIAL DISTRIBUTION LTD

WHEAT BELT EQUIPMENT LTD   p 347
10 CAMPBELL'S TRAILER CRT, BRANDON, MB, R7A 5Y5

(204) 725-2273   SIC 5083

WHEAT CITY CONCRETE PRODUCTS LTD   p 347
4801 VICTORIA AVE E, BRANDON, MB, R7A 7L2

(204) 725-5600   SIC 3273

WHEATHEART MANUFACTURING LTD   p 1432
3455 IDYLWYLD DR N, SASKATOON, SK, S7L 6B5

(306) 934-0611   SIC 3523

WHEATLAND HUTTERIAN BRETHREN OF CABRI INC   p 1405
GD, CABRI, SK, S0N 0J0

(306) 587-2458   SIC 2429

WHEATON CHEVROLET LTD   p 1421
260 N ALBERT ST, REGINA, SK, S4R 3C1

(306) 543-1555   SIC 5511

WHEATON GM   p 1430
See WHEATON GMC BUICK CADILLAC LTD

WHEATON GMC BUICK CADILLAC LTD   p 1430
2102 MILLAR AVE, SASKATOON, SK, S7K 6P4

(306) 244-8131   SIC 5511

WHEATON PONTIAC BUICK GMC (NANAIMO) LTD   p 235
2590 BOWEN RD, NANAIMO, BC, V9T 3L3

(250) 758-2438   SIC 5511

WHEATON PRECIOUS METALS CORP   p 317
1021 HASTINGS ST W SUITE 3500, VAN-

COUVER, BC, V6E 0C3

(604) 684-9648   SIC 1044

WHEATON, GARNET FARM LIMITED   p 441
518 SHAW RD RR 3, BERWICK, NS, B0P 1E0

(902) 538-9793   SIC 5712

WHEEL COVERS UNLIMITED   p 1021
See 944746 ONTARIO INC

WHEEL'S AUTOMOTIVE DEALER SUPPLIES INC   p 893
600 ARVIN AVE, STONEY CREEK, ON, L8E 5P1

(800) 465-8831   SIC 5511

WHEELS & DEALS LTD   p 400
402 SAINT MARYS ST, FREDERICTON, NB, E3A 8H5

(506) 459-6832   SIC 5521

WHEELS ADS   p 893
See WHEEL'S AUTOMOTIVE DEALER SUPPLIES INC

WHEELTRONIC   p 727
See SNAP-ON TOOLS OF CANADA LTD

WHIRLPOOL CANADA LP   p 728
6750 CENTURY AVE UNIT 200, MISSISSAUGA, ON, L5N 0B7

(905) 821-6400   SIC 3633

WHIRLPOOL JET BOAT TOURS   p 761
See NIAGARA GORGE JET BOATING LTD

WHISSELL CONTRACTING LTD   p 71
2500 107 AVE SE SUITE 200, CALGARY, AB, T2Z 3R7

(403) 236-2200   SIC 1623

WHISSELL ENGINEERING   p 71
See WHISSELL CONTRACTING LTD

WHISTLER & BLACKCOMB MOUNTAIN RESORTS LIMITED   p 343
4545 BLACKCOMB WAY RR 4, WHISTLER, BC, V0N 1B4

(604) 932-3141   SIC 7011

WHISTLER & BLACKCOMB MOUNTAINS   p 343
See WHISTLER MOUNTAIN RESORT LIMITED PARTNERSHIP

WHISTLER CONNECTION   p 343
See WHISTLER CONNECTION TOUR & TRAVEL SERVICES LTD

WHISTLER CONNECTION TOUR & TRAVEL SERVICES LTD   p 343
8056 NESTERS RD, WHISTLER, BC, V8E 0G4

(604) 938-9711   SIC 4725

WHISTLER GOLF CLUB   p 343
See WHISTLER RESORT ASSOCIATION

WHISTLER MOUNTAIN RESORT LIMITED PARTNERSHIP   p 343
4545 BLACKCOMB WAY, WHISTLER, BC, V8E 0X9

(604) 932-3141   SIC 7011

WHISTLER PLATINUM RESERVATIONS   p 343
204 4230 GATEWAY DR, WHISTLER, BC, V8E 0Z8

(604) 932-0100   SIC 4725

WHISTLER REAL ESTATE COMPANY LIMITED, THE   p 343
4308 MAIN ST SUITE 17, WHISTLER, BC, V8E 1A9

(604) 932-5538   SIC 6531

WHISTLER RESORT ASSOCIATION   p 343
4010 WHISTLER WAY, WHISTLER, BC, V8E 1J2

(604) 664-5625   SIC 8743

WHISTLER TAXI LTD   p 343
1080 MILLAR CREEK RD SUITE 201, WHISTLER, BC, V8E 0S7

(604) 932-4430   SIC 4121

WHITBY HYDRO ENERGY SERVICES CORPORATION   p 812
100 TAUNTON RD E, OSHAWA, ON, L1G 7N1

(905) 668-5878   SIC 4911

WHITBY MAZDA   p 1013

WHITBY TOYOTA COMPANY   p 1016
1025 DUNDAS ST W, WHITBY, ON, L1P 1Z1

(905) 668-4792   SIC 5511

WHITBY-OSHAWA HONDA   p 1015
See WHITBY-OSHAWA IMPORTS LTD

WHITBY-OSHAWA IMPORTS LTD   p 1015
300 THICKSON RD S, WHITBY, ON, L1N 9Z1

(905) 666-1772   SIC 7515

WHITE & PETERS LTD   p 202
1368 UNITED BLVD UNIT 101, COQUITLAM, BC, V3K 6Y2

(604) 540-6585   SIC 5013

WHITE BURGESS LANGILLE INMAN   p 440
26 UNION ST 2ND FLR, BEDFORD, NS, B4A 2B5

(902) 835-7333   SIC 8721

WHITE CLARKE NORTH AMERICA INC   p 985
901 KING ST W SUITE 202, TORONTO, ON, M5V 3H5

(416) 467-1900   SIC 8748

WHITE COURT IGA   p 172
See 2125341 ALBERTA LTD

WHITE GLOVE TRANSPORTATION SYSTEMS LTD   p 744
215 COURTNEYPARK DR E, MISSISSAUGA, ON, L5T 2T6

(905) 565-1053   SIC 4212

WHITE GLOVE TRANSPORTATION SYSTEMS LTD   p 744
6141 VIPOND DR, MISSISSAUGA, ON, L5T 2B2

(905) 565-1053   SIC 4212

WHITE GOLD CORP   p 941
82 RICHMOND ST E, TORONTO, ON, M5C 1P1

(416) 643-3880   SIC 1041

WHITE HILLS PROPERTY INC   p 429
251 EAST WHITE HILLS RD SUITE 100, ST. JOHN'S, NL, A1A 5X7

(709) 726-7596   SIC 6519

WHITE HORSE   p 1440
See YUKON HOUSING CORPORATION

WHITE HOUSE DESIGN COMPANY INC   p 183
3676 BAINBRIDGE AVE UNIT 100, BURNABY, BC, V5A 2T4

(604) 451-1539   SIC 8712

WHITE OAK CUSTOM WOODWORKING LTD   p 496
10 BROWNING CRT, BOLTON, ON, L7E 1G8

(905) 669-0919   SIC 5712

WHITE OAK TRANSPORT LIMITED   p 893
365 LEWIS RD, STONEY CREEK, ON, L8E 5N4

(905) 643-9500   SIC 4213

WHITE OAKS CONFERENCE RESORT & SPA   p 761
See WHITE OAKS TENNIS WORLD INC

WHITE OAKS PUBLIC SCHOOL   p 657
See THAMES VALLEY DISTRICT SCHOOL BOARD

WHITE OAKS SECONDARY SCHOOL   p 797
See HALTON DISTRICT SCHOOL BOARD

WHITE OAKS TENNIS WORLD INC   p 761
253 TAYLOR RD SS 4, NIAGARA ON THE LAKE, ON, L0S 1J0

(905) 688-2550   SIC 7389

WHITE PAPER COMPANY   p 210
See S.O.F. WHITE PAPER COMPANY LTD

WHITE POINT BEACH RESORT   p 459
See WHITE POINT HOLDINGS LIMITED

WHITE POINT HOLDINGS LIMITED   p 459
75 WHITE POINT RD SUITE 2, HUNTS POINT, NS, B0T 1G0

(902) 354-2711   SIC 6712

WHITE RIVER FOREST PRODUCTS GP INC   p 1016

315 HWY 17, WHITE RIVER, ON, P0M 3G0

(807) 822-1818   SIC 2421

WHITE RIVER FOREST PRODUCTS LTD   p 1016
315 HWY 17, WHITE RIVER, ON, P0M 3G0

(807) 822-1818   SIC 2426

WHITE ROCK CHRISTIAN ACADEMY SOCIETY   p 281
2265 152 ST, SURREY, BC, V4A 4P1

(604) 531-9186   SIC 8699

WHITE ROCK CHRYSLER LTD   p 283
3050 KING GEORGE BLVD UNIT 7, SURREY, BC, V4P 1A2

(604) 531-9156   SIC 5511

WHITE ROCK HONDA   p 283
See KING GEORGE CARRIAGE LTD

WHITE SPOT LIMITED   p 180
4075 NORTH RD, BURNABY, BC, V3J 1S3

(604) 421-4620   SIC 5812

WHITE SPOT LIMITED   p 199
3025 LOUGHEED HWY SUITE 500, COQUITLAM, BC, V3B 6S2

(604) 942-9224   SIC 5812

WHITE SPOT LIMITED   p 239
333 BROOKSBANK AVE SUITE 1100, NORTH VANCOUVER, BC, V7J 3S8

(604) 988-6717   SIC 5812

WHITE SPOT LIMITED   p 262
5880 NO. 3 RD, RICHMOND, BC, V6X 2E1

(604) 273-3699   SIC 5812

WHITE SPOT LIMITED   p 291
1126 MARINE DR SE, VANCOUVER, BC, V5X 2V7

(604) 321-6631   SIC 5812

WHITE SPOT LIMITED   p 294
650 41ST AVE W SUITE 613A, VANCOUVER, BC, V5Z 2M9

(604) 261-2820   SIC 5812

WHITE SPOT LIMITED   p 342
752 MARINE DR UNIT 1108, WEST VANCOUVER, BC, V7T 1A6

(604) 922-4520   SIC 5812

WHITE SPOT RESTAURANT   p 180
See WHITE SPOT LIMITED

WHITE SPOT RESTAURANT   p 239
See WHITE SPOT LIMITED

WHITE SPOT RESTAURANT   p 249
See DHILLON FOOD SERVICES LTD

WHITE SPOT RESTAURANT   p 262
See WHITE SPOT LIMITED

WHITE SPOT RESTAURANT   p 291
See WHITE SPOT LIMITED

WHITE SPOT RESTAURANT   p 294
See WHITE SPOT LIMITED

WHITE SPOT RESTAURANT   p 342
See WHITE SPOT LIMITED

WHITE STORE EQUIPMENT LTD   p 837
21 WOODSLEE AVE, PARIS, ON, N3L 3T6

(519) 442-4461   SIC 5199

WHITE VEAL MEAT PACKERS LTD   p 561
1536 9TH LINE, COOKSTOWN, ON, L0L 1L0

(416) 745-7448   SIC 5147

WHITE, BART SALES LTD   p 753
997431 HWY 11, NEW LISKEARD, ON, P0J 1P0

(705) 647-7331   SIC 5014

WHITE, GLEN INDUSTRIES LTD   p 482
7825 SPRINGWATER RD, AYLMER, ON, N5H 2R4

(519) 765-2244   SIC 3441

WHITE, GLEN INVESTMENTS LTD   p 482
7825 SPRINGWATER RD RR 5, AYLMER, ON, N5H 2R4

(519) 765-2244   SIC 6712

WHITE, WILLIAM F. INTERNATIONAL INC   p 576
800 ISLINGTON AVE, ETOBICOKE, ON, M8Z 6A1

(416) 239-5050   SIC 7819

WHITE-WOOD DISTRIBUTORS LTD   p 373
119 PLYMOUTH ST, WINNIPEG, MB, R2X 2T3

(204) 982-9450　*SIC* 5211
WHITE-WOOD FOREST PRODUCTS　*p* 373
See WHITE-WOOD DISTRIBUTORS LTD
WHITEBIRD　*p* 609
See HT PRODUCTIONS INC
WHITECAP MOTORS　*p* 164
804 MAIN ST SW, SLAVE LAKE, AB, T0G 2A0
(780) 849-2600　*SIC* 5511
WHITECAP RECREATION, DIV OF　*p* 164
See WHITECAP MOTORS
WHITECAP RESOURCES INC　*p* 63
525 8 AVE SW UNIT 3800, CALGARY, AB, T2P 1G1
(403) 817-2209　*SIC* 6719
WHITECAPS FOOTBALL CLUB LTD　*p* 301
375 WATER ST SUITE 550, VANCOUVER, BC, V6B 5C6
(604) 669-9283　*SIC* 7941
WHITECLIFF　*p* 280
See LIFESTYLE OPERATIONS LP
WHITECOURT FORD INC　*p* 173
4144 KEPLER ST, WHITECOURT, AB, T7S 0A3
(780) 778-4777　*SIC* 5511
WHITECOURT PULP DIVISION　*p* 173
See MILLAR WESTERN FOREST PRODUCTS LTD
WHITECOURT WOOD PRODUCT DIVISION　*p* 173
See MILLAR WESTERN INDUSTRIES LTD
WHITEHILL TECHNOLOGIES INC　*p* 410
260 MACNAUGHTON AVE, MONCTON, NB, E1H 2J8
SIC 7371
WHITEHILL TECHNOLOGIES INC　*p* 677
19 ALLSTATE PKY SUITE 400, MARKHAM, ON, L3R 5A4
(905) 475-2112　*SIC* 7371
WHITEHORSE GENERAL HOSPITAL　*p* 1440
See YUKON HOSPITAL CORPORATION
WHITEHORSE MOTORS LIMITED　*p* 1440
4178 4TH AVE, WHITEHORSE, YT, Y1A 1J6
(867) 667-7866　*SIC* 5511
WHITEHOTS INC　*p* 482
205 INDUSTRIAL PKY N UNIT 3, AURORA, ON, L4G 4C4
(905) 727-9188　*SIC* 5192
WHITELAW TWINING　*p* 311
See YEUNG, GAYNOR C. LAW CORPORATION
WHITEMUD GROUP LTD　*p* 111
8170 50 ST NW SUITE 300, EDMONTON, AB, T6B 1E6
(780) 701-3295　*SIC* 1791
WHITEMUD IRONWORKS GROUP INC　*p* 111
8170 50 ST NW SUITE 300, EDMONTON, AB, T6B 1E6
(780) 701-3295　*SIC* 1791
WHITEMUD IRONWORKS LIMITED　*p* 123
7727 18 ST NW, EDMONTON, AB, T6P 1N9
(780) 465-5888　*SIC* 1791
WHITEOAK FORD LINCOLN SALES LIMITED　*p* 712
3285 MAVIS RD, MISSISSAUGA, ON, L5C 1T7
(905) 270-8210　*SIC* 5511
WHITEROCK CHRYSLER JEEP LIMITED　*p* 283
3050 KING GEORGE BLVD, SURREY, BC, V4P 1A2
(604) 531-9156　*SIC* 5511
WHITEWATER COMPOSITES LTD　*p* 223
9505 HALDANE RD, KELOWNA, BC, V4V 2K5
(250) 766-5152　*SIC* 3299
WHITEWATER SKI RESORT LTD　*p* 236
602 LAKE ST, NELSON, BC, V1L 4C8
(250) 354-4944　*SIC* 7011
WHITEWATER WEST INDUSTRIES LTD　*p*

259
6700 MCMILLAN WAY, RICHMOND, BC, V6W 1J7
(604) 273-1068　*SIC* 5091
WHITEWOOD AUCTION SERVICE LTD　*p* 1438
HWY 1, WHITEWOOD, SK, S0G 5C0
(306) 735-2822　*SIC* 5154
WHITEWOOD LIVESTOCK SALES　*p* 1438
See WHITEWOOD AUCTION SERVICE LTD
WHITFIELD WELDING INC　*p* 807
5425 ROSCON INDUSTRIAL DR, OLD-CASTLE, ON, N0R 1L0
(519) 737-1814　*SIC* 7692
WHITING DOOR MANUFACTURING LIMITED　*p* 528
3435 SOUTH SERVICE RD, BURLINGTON, ON, L7N 3W6
(905) 333-6745　*SIC* 5211
WHITING EQUIPMENT CANADA INC　*p* 1012
350 ALEXANDER ST, WELLAND, ON, L3B 2R3
(905) 732-7585　*SIC* 3559
WHITING GROUP OF CANADA INC　*p* 528
3435 SOUTH SERVICE RD, BURLINGTON, ON, L7N 3W6
(905) 333-6745　*SIC* 3442
WHITSON CONTRACTING LTD　*p* 168
51-26004 TWP RD 544, STURGEON COUNTY, AB, T8T 0B6
(780) 421-4292　*SIC* 1542
WHITSON MANUFACTURING INC　*p* 1001
2725 BELISLE DR, VAL CARON, ON, P3N 1B3
(705) 897-4971　*SIC* 2892
WHOLE FOODS MARKET CANADA INC　*p* 342
925 MAIN ST, WEST VANCOUVER, BC, V7T 2Z3
(604) 678-0500　*SIC* 5411
WHOLE NEW HOME　*p* 299
See KABUNI TECHNOLOGIES INC
WHOLESALE CLUB　*p* 344
See LOBLAWS INC
WHOLESALE LETTERING AND CARVING LIMITED　*p* 744
6215 NETHERHART RD, MISSISSAUGA, ON, L5T 1G5
SIC 5099
WHOLESALE STONE INDUSTRIES INC　*p* 91
10180 101 ST NW SUITE 3400, EDMONTON, AB, T5J 3S4
(587) 523-1127　*SIC* 3281
WHOLESALE TIRE DISTRIBUTORS INC　*p* 561
35 CITRON CRT, CONCORD, ON, L4K 2S7
(905) 882-6797　*SIC* 5014
WHOLESOME HARVEST BAKING LTD　*p* 19
4320 80 AVE SE, CALGARY, AB, T2C 4N6
(403) 203-1675　*SIC* 2051
WHOLESOME HARVEST BAKING LTD　*p* 561
144 VICEROY RD, CONCORD, ON, L4K 2L8
(905) 738-1242　*SIC* 2051
WHOLISTIC CHILD AND FAMILY SERVICES INC　*p* 785
601 MAGNETIC DR UNIT 39, NORTH YORK, ON, M3J 3J2
(416) 531-5616　*SIC* 8748
WHSC　*p* 677
See WORKERS HEALTH AND SAFETY CENTRE FEDERATION OF ONTARIO
WHSCC　*p* 416
See WORKPLACE HEALTH, SAFETY & COMPENSATION COMMISSION OF NEW BRUNSWICK
WHYTE, J. G. & SON LIMITED　*p* 750
15 CAPELLA CRT SUITE 124, NEPEAN,

ON, K2E 7X1
SIC 5092
WIBERG CORPORATION　*p* 805
931 EQUESTRIAN CRT, OAKVILLE, ON, L6L 6L7
(905) 825-9900　*SIC* 2099
WICKANINNISH INN LIMITED　*p* 283
500 OSPREY LANE, TOFINO, BC, V0R 2Z0
(250) 725-3106　*SIC* 7011
WIDE LOYAL DEVELOPMENT LTD　*p* 257
13160 VANIER PL SUITE 160, RICHMOND, BC, V6V 2J2
(604) 303-0931　*SIC* 5063
WIDE RANGE TRANSPORTATION GROUP　*p* 600
See WIDE RANGE TRANSPORTATION SERVICES INC
WIDE RANGE TRANSPORTATION SERVICES INC　*p* 600
689 SOUTH SERVICE RD, GRIMSBY, ON, L3M 4E8
(905) 643-5100　*SIC* 4731
WIDEX CANADA LTD　*p* 525
5041 MAINWAY SUITE 1, BURLINGTON, ON, L7L 5H9
(905) 315-8303　*SIC* 3842
WIEBE, DR. C.W. MEDICAL CORPORATION　*p* 361
385 MAIN ST, WINKLER, MB, R6W 1J2
(204) 325-4312　*SIC* 8011
WIEBE, J. BUILDING MATERIALS LTD　*p* 645
241 OAK ST E, LEAMINGTON, ON, N8H 4W8
(519) 326-4474　*SIC* 5211
WIELAND ELECTRIC INC　*p* 799
2889 BRIGHTON RD, OAKVILLE, ON, L6H 6C9
(905) 829-8414　*SIC* 5063
WIELER ENTERPRISES LTD　*p* 359
88 MILLWORK DR, STEINBACH, MB, R5G 1V9
(204) 326-4313　*SIC* 6712
WIELER HUNT INVESTMENTS INC　*p* 822
60 BY WARD MARKET SQ, OTTAWA, ON, K1N 7A2
(613) 562-9111　*SIC* 5712
WIENS FAMILY FARM INC　*p* 761
1178 6 RD, NIAGARA ON THE LAKE, ON, L0S 1J0
SIC 0191
WIERSEMA, TRACY PHARMACY LTD　*p* 488
649 YONGE ST, BARRIE, ON, L4N 4E7
(705) 792-4388　*SIC* 5912
WIETZES MOTORS LIMITED　*p* 561
7080 DUFFERIN ST, CONCORD, ON, L4K 0A1
(905) 761-5133　*SIC* 5511
WIETZES TOYOTA　*p* 561
See WIETZES MOTORS LIMITED
WIFF　*p* 1024
See WINDSOR INTERNATIONAL FILM FESTIVAL
WIG'S PUMPS AND WATERWORKS LTD　*p* 1430
227B VENTURE CRES, SASKATOON, SK, S7K 6N8
(306) 652-4276　*SIC* 5082
WIGMORE CROP PRODUCTION PRODUCTS LTD　*p* 1404
140 NELSON INDUSTRIAL DR, AVONLEA, SK, S0H 0C0
(306) 868-2252　*SIC* 5159
WIKA INSTRUMENTS LTD　*p* 121
3103 PARSONS RD NW, EDMONTON, AB, T6N 1C8
(780) 438-6662　*SIC* 3823
WIKITOR　*p* 857
129 ROSE BRANCH DR, RICHMOND HILL, ON, L4S 1H6

(647) 498-8773　*SIC* 8748
WIKOFF COLOR CORPORATION - CANADA INC　*p* 561
475 BOWES RD, CONCORD, ON, L4K 1J5
(905) 669-1311　*SIC* 2893
WIKWEMIKONG TRIBAL POLICE　*p* 1016
2074 WIKWEMIKONG WAY, WIK-WEMIKONG, ON, P0P 2J0
(705) 859-3141　*SIC* 7381
WIL-TECH INDUSTRIES LTD　*p* 1407
69 ESCANA ST, ESTEVAN, SK, S4A 2H7
(306) 634-6743　*SIC* 1389
WILBUR, DAVID PRODUCTS LTD　*p* 1040
155 BELVEDERE AVE, CHARLOTTE-TOWN, PE, C1A 2Y9
SIC 5172
WILBUR-ELLIS COMPANY OF CANADA LIMITED　*p* 143
212084 TOWNSHIP ROAD 81A, LETH-BRIDGE, AB, T1K 8G6
(403) 328-3311　*SIC* 5191
WILBY COMMERCIAL LTD　*p* 677
110 TORBAY RD UNIT 3-4, MARKHAM, ON, L3R 1G6
(905) 513-7505　*SIC* 5141
WILCO CONTRACTORS NORTHWEST INC　*p* 124
14420 154 AVE NW SUITE 107, EDMONTON, AB, T6V 0K8
(780) 447-1199　*SIC* 8742
WILCOX BODIES LIMITED　*p* 685
550 MCGEACHIE DR, MILTON, ON, L9T 3Y5
(905) 203-9995　*SIC* 3713
WILCOX DOOR SERVICE INC　*p* 712
1045 RANGEVIEW RD, MISSISSAUGA, ON, L5E 1H2
(905) 274-5850　*SIC* 1751
WILCOX GROUND SERVICES　*p* 685
See WILCOX BODIES LIMITED
WILD BILL'S SALOON INC　*p* 79
737 MAIN ST, CANMORE, AB, T1W 2B2
(403) 762-0333　*SIC* 5812
WILD BILLS　*p* 79
See WILD BILL'S SALOON INC
WILD FLAVORS (CANADA) INC　*p* 744
7315 PACIFIC CIR, MISSISSAUGA, ON, L5T 1V1
(905) 670-1108　*SIC* 2087
WILD GOOSE STORAGE INC. & DESIGN　*p* 63
607 8 AVE SW SUITE 400, CALGARY, AB, T2P 0A7
(403) 513-8616　*SIC* 4922
WILD ROSE SCHOOL DIVISION NO. 66　*p* 159
4912 43 ST, ROCKY MOUNTAIN HOUSE, AB, T4T 1P4
(403) 845-3376　*SIC* 8211
WILD WATERWORKS　*p* 608
See HAMILTON REGION CONSERVATION AUTHORITY
WILD'S HOME HARDWARE BUILDING CENTRE　*p* 168
See WILD'S TIMBER CONTRACTORS LTD
WILD'S TIMBER CONTRACTORS LTD　*p* 168
HIGHWAY 584 W, SUNDRE, AB, T0M 1X0
(403) 638-3508　*SIC* 5251
WILDERNESS COMMITTEE　*p* 301
See WESTERN CANADA WILDERNESS COMMITTEE
WILDS AT SALMONIER RIVER INC, THE　*p* 432
299 SALMONIER LINE, ST. JOHN'S, NL, A1C 5L7
(709) 229-5444　*SIC* 7992
WILDWOOD　*p* 1424
See MCDONALDS RESTAURANT
WILDWOOD CABINETS LTD　*p* 407
400 COLLISHAW ST, MONCTON, NB, E1C 0B4
(506) 858-9219　*SIC* 2541
WILF BRANDT TRUCKING LTD　*p* 171

48176 HWY 770, WARBURG, AB, T0C 2T0

(780) 848-7668　*SIC* 4212

WILF'S DRUG STORE LTD　*p* 490

330 NOTRE DAME ST, BELLE RIVER, ON, N0R 1A0

(519) 728-1610　*SIC* 5912

WILF'S ELIE FORD SALES LTD　*p* 349

HWY 1, ELIE, MB, R0H 0H0

(204) 353-2481　*SIC* 5511

WILFRID JURY PUBLIC SCHOOL　*p* 658

See THAMES VALLEY DISTRICT SCHOOL BOARD

WILFRID LAURIER UNIVERSITY　*p* 1009

75 UNIVERSITY AVE W, WATERLOO, ON, N2L 3C5

(519) 884-1970　*SIC* 8221

WILKENING TRANSPORT　*p* 111

See WILKENING, HARV TRANSPORT LTD

WILKENING, HARV TRANSPORT LTD　*p* 111

4205 76 AVE NW, EDMONTON, AB, T6B 2H7

(780) 466-9155　*SIC* 4213

WILKIE & DISTRICT HEALTH CENTRE　*p* 1438

See SASKATCHEWAN HEALTH AUTHORITY

WILKINS LIMITED　*p* 443

36 BAKER DR, DARTMOUTH, NS, B2W 6K1

(902) 435-3330　*SIC* 5511

WILKINSON & COMPANY LLP　*p* 999

71 DUNDAS ST W, TRENTON, ON, K8V 3P4

(888) 713-7283　*SIC* 8721

WILL INSURANCE BROKERS LTD　*p* 645

148 ERIE ST N, LEAMINGTON, ON, N8H 3A2

(519) 326-5746　*SIC* 6411

WILLARD MANUFACTURING INC　*p* 525

5295 JOHN LUCAS DR SUITE 1, BURLINGTON, ON, L7L 6A8

(905) 633-6905　*SIC* 2844

WILLBROS CANADA　*p* 126

See WILLBROS MINE SERVICES, L.P.

WILLBROS CANADA　*p* 129

See WILLBROS MINE SERVICES, L.P.

WILLBROS MINE SERVICES, L.P.　*p* 126

1103 95 ST SW, EDMONTON, AB, T6X 0P8

(780) 400-4200　*SIC* 1623

WILLBROS MINE SERVICES, L.P.　*p* 129

1005 MEMORIAL DR, FORT MCMURRAY, AB, T9K 0K4

(780) 743-6247　*SIC* 1623

WILLBROS PSS MIDSTREAM (CANADA) L.P.　*p* 126

1103 95 ST SW, EDMONTON, AB, T6X 0P8

(780) 400-4200　*SIC* 1623

WILLE DODGE CHRYSLER LTD　*p* 339

3240 DOUGLAS ST, VICTORIA, BC, V8Z 3K7

(250) 475-3511　*SIC* 5511

WILLIAM A.(BILL) GEORGE EXTENDED CARE FACILITY　*p* 881

See SIOUX LOOKOUT MENO-YA-WIN HEALTH CENTRE PLANNING CORPORATION

WILLIAM ABERHART SCHOOL　*p* 41

See CALGARY BOARD OF EDUCATION

WILLIAM DAM SEEDS LIMITED　*p* 566

279 HWY 8, DUNDAS, ON, L9H 5E1

(905) 628-6641　*SIC* 5961

WILLIAM DYCK & SONS (1993)　*p* 353

See 3084761 MANITOBA LTD

WILLIAM E HAY CENTRE　*p* 819

See YOUTH SERVICES BUREAU OF OTTAWA

WILLIAM E. BURROWES INC　*p* 1068

1570B BOUL DE MONTARVILLE, BOUCHERVILLE, QC, J4B 5Y3

(450) 655-6023　*SIC* 6411

WILLIAM OSLER HEALTH SYSTEM　*p* 498

2100 BOVAIRD DR E, BRAMPTON, ON, L6R 3J7

(905) 494-2120　*SIC* 8062

WILLIAM OSLER HEALTH SYSTEM　*p* 581

101 HUMBER COLLEGE BLVD, ETOBICOKE, ON, M9V 1R8

(416) 494-2120　*SIC* 8062

WILLIAM R KIRK SCHOOL　*p* 492

See HASTINGS AND PRINCE EDWARD DISTRICT SCHOOL BOARD

WILLIAM ROPER HULL SCHOOL　*p* 68

See CALGARY BOARD OF EDUCATION

WILLIAMS BROTHERS CORPORATION, THE　*p* 879

777 TAPSCOTT RD, SCARBOROUGH, ON, M1X 1A2

(416) 299-7767　*SIC* 3442

WILLIAMS CHRYSLER JEEP & RV CENTRE　*p* 129

See WILLIAMS CHRYSLER LTD

WILLIAMS CHRYSLER LTD　*p* 129

324 GREGOIRE DR, FORT MCMURRAY, AB, T9H 3R2

(780) 790-9000　*SIC* 5511

WILLIAMS LAKE PLYWOOD　*p* 344

See WEST FRASER MILLS LTD

WILLIAMS MACHINERY LIMITED PARTNERSHIP　*p* 275

10240 GRACE RD, SURREY, BC, V3V 3V6

(604) 930-3300　*SIC* 5084

WILLIAMS MINE　*p* 664

See WILLIAMS OPERATING CORPORATION

WILLIAMS MOVING & STORAGE (B.C.) LTD　*p* 202

2401 UNITED BLVD, COQUITLAM, BC, V3K 5X9

SIC 4214

WILLIAMS MOVING INTERNATIONAL　*p* 202

See WILLIAMS MOVING & STORAGE (B.C.) LTD

WILLIAMS OPERATING CORPORATION　*p* 664

HWY 17, MARATHON, ON, P0T 2E0

(807) 238-1100　*SIC* 1041

WILLIAMS PHARMALOGISTICS INC　*p* 1129

2165 RUE ONESIME-GAGNON, LACHINE, QC, H8T 3M7

(514) 526-5901　*SIC* 4213

WILLIAMS SCOTSMAN OF CANADA INC　*p* 2

9529 266 ST, ACHESON, AB, T7X 6H9

(780) 638-9210　*SIC* 5271

WILLIAMS SCOTSMAN OF CANADA, INC　*p* 3

19 EAST LAKE AVE, AIRDRIE, AB, T4A 2G9

(403) 241-5357　*SIC* 7519

WILLIAMS TELECOMMUNICATIONS CORP　*p* 708

5610 KENNEDY RD, MISSISSAUGA, ON, L4Z 2A9

(905) 712-4242　*SIC* 5065

WILLIAMS, DAVE & PAT SALES LTD　*p* 274

13665 102 AVE SUITE 489, SURREY, BC, V3T 1N7

(604) 583-8473　*SIC* 5531

WILLIAMS, E. S. & ASSOCIATES INC　*p* 134

10514 67 AVE SUITE 306, GRANDE PRAIRIE, AB, T8W 0K8

(780) 539-4544　*SIC* 7379

WILLIAMS, JIM LEASING LIMITED　*p* 489

191 MAPLEVIEW DR W, BARRIE, ON, L4N 9E8

(705) 734-1200　*SIC* 5511

WILLIAMS, KELLER REALTY　*p* 728

7145 WEST CREDIT AVE BLDG 1 SUITE 201, MISSISSAUGA, ON, L5N 6J7

(905) 812-8123　*SIC* 6531

WILLIAMS, R. B. INDUSTRIAL SUPPLY LTD　*p* 150

3280 10 ST, NISKU, AB, T9E 1E7

(780) 955-9332　*SIC* 5085

WILLIAMS-SONOMA CANADA, INC　*p* 790

3401 DUFFERIN ST SUITE 215, NORTH YORK, ON, M6A 2T9

(416) 785-1233　*SIC* 5712

WILLIAMSON GROUP INC, THE　*p* 515

225 KING GEORGE RD, BRANTFORD, ON, N3R 7N7

(519) 756-9560　*SIC* 6411

WILLIAMSON LEASING　*p* 1001

See ALEX WILLIAMSON MOTOR SALES LIMITED

WILLIAMSON-DICKIE CANADA COMPANY　*p* 537

415 THOMPSON DR, CAMBRIDGE, ON, N1T 2K7

(888) 664-6636　*SIC* 2326

WILLINGDON CARE CENTRE　*p* 191

See WILLINGDON PARK HOSPITAL LTD

WILLINGDON PARK HOSPITAL LTD　*p* 191

4435 GRANGE ST, BURNABY, BC, V5H 1P4

(604) 433-2455　*SIC* 8051

WILLIS CANADA INC　*p* 988

100 KING ST W SUITE 4700, TORONTO, ON, M5X 1K7

(416) 368-9641　*SIC* 6411

WILLIS SUPPLY COMPANY LIMITED, THE　*p* 527

1149 PIONEER RD, BURLINGTON, ON, L7M 1K5

(905) 639-8584　*SIC* 5039

WILLIS TOWERS WATSON　*p* 988

See WILLIS CANADA INC

WILLIS TOWERS WATSON(MC)　*p* 1200

See TOWERS WATSON CANADA INC

WILLOW CREEK COLONY FARMS LTD　*p* 348

GD, CARTWRIGHT, MB, R0K 0L0

(204) 529-2178　*SIC* 3537

WILLOW CREEK LODGE　*p* 167

See COUNTY STETTLER HOUSING AUTHORITY, THE

WILLOW FUN WORLD LTD　*p* 227

19609 WILLOWBROOK DR UNIT 2, LANGLEY, BC, V2Y 1A5

(604) 530-5324　*SIC* 5092

WILLOW SPRING CONSTRUCTION (ALTA) LTD　*p* 117

8616 51 AVE UNIT 250, EDMONTON, AB, T6E 6E6

(780) 438-1990　*SIC* 1542

WILLOW VIDEO GAMES　*p* 227

See WILLOW FUN WORLD LTD

WILLOWBROOK CHRYSLER　*p* 228

See WILLOWBROOK MOTORS LTD

WILLOWBROOK MOTORS LTD　*p* 228

19611 LANGLEY BYPASS, LANGLEY, BC, V3A 4K8

(604) 530-7361　*SIC* 5511

WILLOWBROOK NURSERIES INC　*p* 590

935 VICTORIA AVE, FENWICK, ON, L0S 1C0

(905) 892-5350　*SIC* 0181

WILLOWDALE FARMS INCORPORATED　*p* 441

72 CHASE RD RR 1, BERWICK, NS, B0P 1E0

(902) 538-7324　*SIC* 0191

WILLOWDALE NISSAN LTD　*p* 906

7200 YONGE ST SUITE 881, THORNHILL, ON, L4J 1V8

(905) 881-3900　*SIC* 5511

WILLOWDALE SUBARU　*p* 905

See 1543738 ONTARIO LIMITED

WILLOWGROVE, THE　*p* 478

See 1457271 ONTARIO LIMITED

WILLOWRIDGE CONSTRUCTION LTD　*p* 130

11870 88 AVE UNIT 148, FORT SASKATCHEWAN, AB, T8L 0K1

(780) 998-9133　*SIC* 1541

WILLOWS CONSTRUCTION (2001) LTD　*p* 82

6305 54 AVE, DRAYTON VALLEY, AB, T7A 1R0

(780) 621-0447　*SIC* 1794

WILLOWS ESTATE NURSING HOME, THE　*p* 481

See OMNI HEALTH CARE LTD

WILLOWS NATURAL RESOURCE GROUP　*p* 82

See WILLOWS CONSTRUCTION (2001) LTD

WILLS CHEVROLET LTD　*p* 600

337 MAIN ST E, GRIMSBY, ON, L3M 5N9

(905) 309-3356　*SIC* 5511

WILLS TRANSFER LIMITED　*p* 882

146 HWY 15, SMITHS FALLS, ON, K7A 4S7

(613) 283-0225　*SIC* 4225

WILLSCOT　*p* 2

See WILLIAMS SCOTSMAN OF CANADA INC

WILLSON INTERNATIONAL LIMITED　*p* 728

2345 ARGENTIA RD SUITE 201, MISSISSAUGA, ON, L5N 8K4

(905) 363-1133　*SIC* 4731

WILLYS URBANE CULTURE　*p* 921

276 CARLAW AVE SUITE 218B, TORONTO, ON, M4M 3L1

(416) 462-2038　*SIC* 5136

WILMAR IMPLEMENT CO LTD　*p* 153

5803 47 AVE, PROVOST, AB, T0B 3S0

(780) 753-2278　*SIC* 5083

WILSON AUTO ELECTRIC　*p* 371

See 3225537 NOVA SCOTIA LIMITED

WILSON BANWELL INTERNATIONAL INC　*p* 311

355 BURRARD ST SUITE 1600, VANCOUVER, BC, V6C 2G8

(604) 689-1717　*SIC* 6712

WILSON CHEVROLET BUICK GMC　*p* 753

See WILSON CHEVROLET LIMITED

WILSON CHEVROLET LIMITED　*p* 753

100 WILSON ST, NEW LISKEARD, ON, P0J 1P0

(705) 647-2031　*SIC* 5511

WILSON CONTINGENT TALENT SOLUTIONS, INC　*p* 941

44 VICTORIA ST SUITE 2000, TORONTO, ON, M5C 1Y2

(416) 440-0097　*SIC* 8748

WILSON DISPLAY　*p* 702

See WILSON, J. A. DISPLAY LTD

WILSON EQUIPMENT LIMITED　*p* 449

66 ATLANTIC CENTRAL DR, EAST MOUNTAIN, NS, B6L 2A3

(902) 895-1611　*SIC* 5082

WILSON FOODS CENTRE LTD　*p* 753

1000 REGIONAL RD 17, NEWCASTLE, ON, L1B 0T7

(905) 987-0505　*SIC* 5812

WILSON FOODS KINGSWAY LTD　*p* 813

1300 KING ST E, OSHAWA, ON, L1H 8J4

(905) 442-3545　*SIC* 5812

WILSON FUEL CO. LIMITED　*p* 456

3617 BARRINGTON ST SUITE 289, HALIFAX, NS, B3K 2Y3

(902) 429-3835　*SIC* 5172

WILSON HOT TUB AND POOLS　*p* 650

See WILSON, J C CHEMICALS LTD

WILSON INDEPENDENT　*p* 826

See 1179132 ONTARIO LIMITED

WILSON INSURANCE LTD　*p* 402

404 QUEEN ST, FREDERICTON, NB, E3B 1B6

(506) 458-8505　*SIC* 6411

WILSON MEMORIAL GENERAL HOSPITAL　*p* 664

26 PENINSULA RD, MARATHON, ON, P0T 2E0

(807) 229-1740　*SIC* 8062

WILSON MIDDLE SCHOOL　*p* 141

See LETHBRIDGE SCHOOL DISTRICT NO. 51

WILSON RELOCATION　*p* 878

See ABBEYWOOD MOVING & STORAGE INC

WILSON TOOL CANADA   p 513
See EXACTA TOOL 2010 ULC
WILSON WINDINGS, DIV OF   p 792
See 1100378 ONTARIO LIMITED
WILSON WREATH CO LTD   p 412
11 SQUIRE ST, SACKVILLE, NB, E4L 4K8
SIC 3999
WILSON'S BUSINESS SOLUTIONS   p 565
See WILSON, ROY V (1984) LTD
WILSON'S GAS STOP   p 456
See WILSON FUEL CO. LIMITED
WILSON'S INVESTMENTS LIMITED   p 467
197 CHARLOTTE ST SUITE 203, SYDNEY,
NS, B1P 1C4
(902) 564-4399   SIC 5461
WILSON'S SHOPPING CENTRE LIMITED p
439
3536 HWY 3, BARRINGTON PASSAGE,
NS, B0W 1G0
(902) 637-2300   SIC 5712
WILSON'S TRANSPORTATION LTD   p 339
4196 GLANFORD AVE, VICTORIA, BC, V8Z
4B6
(250) 475-3235   SIC 4142
WILSON'S TRUCK LINES INC   p 580
111 THE WEST MALL, ETOBICOKE, ON,
M9C 1C1
(416) 621-9020   SIC 4212
WILSON'S TRUCK LINES LIMITED   p 580
111 THE WEST MALL, ETOBICOKE, ON,
M9C 1C1
(416) 621-9020   SIC 6712
**WILSON'S, MARK BETTER USED CAR
LIMITED**   p 601
700 YORK RD, GUELPH, ON, N1E 6A5
(519) 836-2900   SIC 5521
WILSON, DAVID W. MANUFACTURING LTD
p 541
193 HWY 53, CATHCART, ON, N0E 1B0
(519) 458-8911   SIC 3499
WILSON, J C CHEMICALS LTD   p 650
1900 HURON ST UNIT 2, LONDON, ON,
N5V 4A3
SIC 5169
WILSON, J. A. DISPLAY LTD   p 702
1610 SISMET RD, MISSISSAUGA, ON,
L4W 1R4
(905) 625-6778   SIC 2542
WILSON, J. A. DISPLAY LTD   p 702
1645 AIMCO BLVD, MISSISSAUGA, ON,
L4W 1H8
(905) 625-9200   SIC 2542
**WILSON, JIM PONTIAC CHEVROLET
BUICK GMC INC**   p 810
MULCAHY PO BOX 20 STN MAIN, ORIL-
LIA, ON, L3V 6H9
(705) 325-1322   SIC 5511
WILSON, ROY V (1984) LTD   p 565
32 KING ST, DRYDEN, ON, P8N 1B3
(807) 223-3316   SIC 5943
**WILSON-NIBLETT   CHEVROLET
CORVETTE**   p 856
See WILSON-NIBLETT MOTORS LIMITED
WILSON-NIBLETT MOTORS LIMITED p 856
10675 YONGE ST, RICHMOND HILL, ON,
L4C 3E1
(905) 884-0991   SIC 5511
WILSONART CANADA ULC   p 1133
385 AV LAFLEUR, LASALLE, QC, H8R 3H7
(514) 366-2710   SIC 2821
WILSONCTS   p 941
See WILSON CONTINGENT TALENT SO-
LUTIONS, INC
**WILTON GROVE TRUCK SALES & SER-
VICES LIMITED**   p
662
1445 SISE RD SUITE 1, LONDON, ON,
N6N 1E1
(519) 649-1771   SIC 5511
WILTON INDUSTRIES CANADA COMPANY
p 589
98 CARRIER DR, ETOBICOKE, ON, M9W
5R1
(416) 679-0790   SIC 5023

WIMCO NURSERIES LTD   p 246
1300 DOMINION AVE, PORT COQUITLAM,
BC, V3B 8G7
(604) 942-7518   SIC 5261
**WINACOTT SPRING TRACTOR TRAILER
REPAIR CENTRE LTD**   p 1430
3002 FAITHFULL AVE SUITE 1, SASKA-
TOON, SK, S7K 0B1
(306) 931-4448   SIC 5013
**WINACOTT SPRING WESTERN STAR
TRUCKS**   p 1430
See WINACOTT SPRING TRACTOR
TRAILER REPAIR CENTRE LTD
WINBOURNE PARK   p 475
See REVERA LONG TERM CARE INC
WINCHESTER AUBURN MILLS INC p 565
70 DUNDAS ST, DESERONTO, ON, K0K
1X0
(877) 224-2673   SIC 2298
**WINCHESTER DISTRICT MEMORIAL HOS-
PITAL**   p
1016
566 LOUISE ST RR 4, WINCHESTER, ON,
K0C 2K0
(613) 774-2420   SIC 8062
WIND POWER MEDIA INC   p 866
49 FEAGAN DR, SCARBOROUGH, ON,
M1C 3B6
(416) 471-4420   SIC 8748
WIND WORKS POWER CORP   p 518
14 LAKECREST CIR, BRIGHTON, ON, K0K
1H0
(613) 226-7883   SIC 3621
WINDERMERE CARE CENTRE INC p 294
900 12TH AVE W SUITE 811, VANCOU-
VER, BC, V5Z 1N3
(604) 736-8676   SIC 8059
WINDERMERE GARDEN CENTRE p 1000
See EMMONS GREENHOUSES INC
WINDIGO AVENTURE INC   p 1244
400 AV ATLANTIC BUREAU 802, OUT-
REMONT, QC, H2V 1A5
(514) 948-4145   SIC 8699
WINDJAMMER INVESTMENTS INC p 423
30 CONFEDERATION DR, CORNER
BROOK, NL, A2H 6T2
(709) 634-8881   SIC 5511
**WINDLEY ELY LEGAL SERVICES PRO-
FESSIONAL CORPORATION**   p
656
275 COLBORNE ST, LONDON, ON, N6B
2S7
(519) 657-4242   SIC 8742
WINDMILL CROSSING LIMITED   p 454
1475 LOWER WATER ST SUITE 100, HAL-
IFAX, NS, B3J 3Z2
(902) 422-6412   SIC 6531
WINDMILL DEVELOPMENT GROUP LTD p
825
6 BOOTH ST, OTTAWA, ON, K1R 6K8
(613) 820-5600   SIC 1522
WINDMILL DEVELOPMENTS   p 825
See WINDMILL DEVELOPMENT GROUP
LTD
WINDMULLER, MONICA & KLAUS p 496
1 WARBRICK LANE, BOLTON, ON, L7E
1G3
(905) 857-0882   SIC 5999
WINDOW CITY INDUSTRIES INC p 1034
5690 STEELES AVE W, WOODBRIDGE,
ON, L4L 9T4
(905) 265-9975   SIC 3231
WINDOWCITY MFRS. INC.   p 1034
5690 STEELES AVE W, WOODBRIDGE,
ON, L4L 9T4
(905) 265-9975   SIC 3231
WINDSET FARMS   p 210
See GREENHOUSE GROWN FOODS INC
WINDSET FARMS   p 211
See WINDSET HOLDINGS 2010 LTD
WINDSET FARMS   p 211
3660 41B ST, DELTA, BC, V4K 3N2
(604) 940-7700   SIC 0182
WINDSET FARMS (CANADA) LTD p 211

3660 41B ST, DELTA, BC, V4K 3N2
(604) 940-7700   SIC 0182
WINDSET HOLDINGS 2010 LTD   p 211
3660 41B ST, DELTA, BC, V4K 3N2
(604) 940-7700   SIC 0182
WINDSHIELD SURGEONS LTD   p 111
5203 82 AVE NW, EDMONTON, AB, T6B
2J6
(780) 466-9166   SIC 7536
**WINDSOR ARMS DEVELOPMENT CORPO-
RATION**   p
976
18 SAINT THOMAS ST, TORONTO, ON,
M5S 3E7
(416) 971-9666   SIC 7011
WINDSOR BUILDING SUPPLIES LTD p 226
20039 96 AVE, LANGLEY, BC, V1M 3C6
(604) 455-9663   SIC 5074
WINDSOR CANADA UTILITIES LTD p 1024
787 OUELLETTE AVE, WINDSOR, ON,
N9A 4J4
(519) 255-2727   SIC 4911
WINDSOR CASINO LIMITED   p 1024
377 RIVERSIDE DR E, WINDSOR, ON,
N9A 7H7
(519) 258-7878   SIC 7011
WINDSOR CERAMICS, DIV OF   p 571
See FLEXTILE LTD
WINDSOR CHRYSLER   p 1018
See 1681230 ONTARIO INC
WINDSOR COURT   p 399
See ATLANTIC RETIREMENT CONCEPTS
INC
**WINDSOR COURT RETIREMENT RESI-
DENCE LIMITED PARTNERSHIP**   p
400
10 BARTON CRES SUITE 421, FREDERIC-
TON, NB, E3A 5S3
(506) 450-7088   SIC 6513
**WINDSOR ELMS VILLAGE FOR CONTINU-
ING CARE SOCIETY**   p
470
590 KING ST, WINDSOR, NS, B0N 2T0
(902) 798-2251   SIC 8051
**WINDSOR ESSEX COMMUNITY HEALTH
CENTRE**   p 1022
1361 OUELLETTE AVE UNIT 101, WIND-
SOR, ON, N8X 1J6
(519) 253-8481   SIC 8322
**WINDSOR ESSEX COUNTY HUMANE SO-
CIETY**   p
1020
1375 PROVINCIAL RD, WINDSOR, ON,
N8W 5V8
(519) 966-5751   SIC 8699
**WINDSOR ESSEX COUNTY RIGHT TO
LIFE**   p 1025
See RIGHT TO LIFE ASSOCIATION OF
WINDSOR AND AREA
**WINDSOR FAMILY CREDIT UNION LIM-
ITED**   p
1022
3000 MARENTETTE AVE, WINDSOR, ON,
N8X 4G2
(519) 974-1181   SIC 6062
WINDSOR FIRE & RESCUE SERVICES p
1023
See CORPORATION OF THE CITY OF
WINDSOR
WINDSOR FORD   p 133
See WINDSOR MOTORS (1975) LTD
WINDSOR HOME HARDWARE   p 442
See REDDEN, C. I. LTD
WINDSOR HONDA   p 1018
See 147766 CANADA INC
**WINDSOR INTERNATIONAL FILM FESTI-
VAL**   p
1024
101 UNIVERSITY AVE W, WINDSOR, ON,
N9A 5P4
(226) 826-9433   SIC 7999
**WINDSOR MACHINE & STAMPING (2009)
LTD**   p 1026
1555 TALBOT RD SUITE 401, WINDSOR,

ON, N9H 2N2
(519) 737-7155   SIC 3312
WINDSOR MACHINE GROUP   p 1026
See WINDSOR MACHINE & STAMPING
(2009) LTD
WINDSOR METAL TECHNOLOGIES INC p
807
3900 DELDUCA DR, OLDCASTLE, ON,
N0R 1L0
(519) 737-7611   SIC 3544
WINDSOR MOLD INC   p 477
95 VICTORIA ST N, AMHERSTBURG, ON,
N9V 3L1
(519) 736-5466   SIC 3089
WINDSOR MOLD INC   p 1020
1628 DURHAM PL, WINDSOR, ON, N8W
2Z8
(519) 258-7300   SIC 3544
WINDSOR MOLD INC   p 1022
310 ELLIS ST E, WINDSOR, ON, N8X 2H2
(519) 258-3211   SIC 3089
WINDSOR MOLD INC   p 1025
4035 MALDEN RD, WINDSOR, ON, N9C
2G4
(519) 972-9032   SIC 3544
WINDSOR MOLD TOOLING, DIV OF p 1025
See WINDSOR MOLD INC
WINDSOR MOTORS (1975) LTD   p 133
13105 100 ST, GRANDE PRAIRIE, AB, T8V
4H3
(780) 532-9153   SIC 5511
WINDSOR PALLET LIMITED   p 1017
2890 N TALBOT, WINDSOR, ON, N0R 1K0
(519) 737-1406   SIC 5085
WINDSOR PENNYSAVER   p 1020
4525 RHODES DR UNIT 400, WINDSOR,
ON, N8W 5R8
SIC 2741
WINDSOR PLYWOOD   p 226
See WINDSOR BUILDING SUPPLIES LTD
WINDSOR PLYWOOD   p 385
See SUNPLY CORPORATION
WINDSOR REGIONAL CHILDREN CENTRE
p 1025
See WINDSOR REGIONAL HOSPITAL
WINDSOR REGIONAL HOSPITAL   p 1020
1995 LENS AVE, WINDSOR, ON, N8W 1L9
(519) 254-5577   SIC 8062
WINDSOR REGIONAL HOSPITAL   p 1025
3901 CONNAUGHT AVE, WINDSOR, ON,
N9C 4H4
(519) 257-5215   SIC 8093
WINDSOR SALT   p 1251
See K+S SEL WINDSOR LTEE
WINDSOR SECONDARY SCHOOL   p 238
See SCHOOL DISTRICT NO. 44 (NORTH
VANCOUVER)
WINDSOR SECURITY LIMITED   p 283
10833 160 ST SUITE 626, SURREY, BC,
V4N 1P3
(604) 689-7588   SIC 7381
WINDSOR SPITFIRES INC   p 1018
8787 MCHUGH ST, WINDSOR, ON, N8S
0A1
(519) 254-9256   SIC 7941
WINDSOR STAR PRINT PLANT   p 1020
3000 STARWAY AVE, WINDSOR, ON, N8W
5P1
(519) 255-5730   SIC 2759
WINDSOR STAR, THE   p 1023
See POSTMEDIA NETWORK INC
WINDSOR TRANSMISSION PLANT p 1019
See GENERAL MOTORS OF CANADA
COMPANY
WINDSOR UTILITIES COMMISSION p 1024
787 OUELLETTE AVE, WINDSOR, ON,
N9A 4J4
(519) 255-2727   SIC 8611
WINDSOR WHOLESALE BAIT LTD p 1025
500 NORTHWOOD ST, WINDSOR, ON,
N9E 4Z2
(519) 966-8540   SIC 5199
**WINDSOR-ESSEX CATHOLIC DISTRICT
SCHOOL BOARD, THE**   p 643

2555 SANDWICH WEST PKY, LASALLE, ON, N9H 2P7
(519) 972-6050   SIC 8211
WINDSOR-ESSEX CATHOLIC DISTRICT SCHOOL BOARD, THE   p 1022
441 TECUMSEH RD E, WINDSOR, ON, N8X 2R7
(519) 256-3171   SIC 8211
WINDSOR-ESSEX CATHOLIC DISTRICT SCHOOL BOARD, THE   p 1024
1325 CALIFORNIA AVE, WINDSOR, ON, N9B 3Y6
(519) 253-2481   SIC 8211
WINDSOR-ESSEX CATHOLIC DISTRICT SCHOOL BOARD, THE   p 1024
2800 NORTH TOWN LINE RD, WINDSOR, ON, N9A 6Z6
(519) 734-6444   SIC 8211
WINDSOR-ESSEX CATHOLIC DISTRICT SCHOOL BOARD, THE   p 1025
1100 HURON CHURCH RD, WINDSOR, ON, N9C 2K7
(519) 256-7801   SIC 8211
WINDSOR-ESSEX CATHOLIC DISTRICT SCHOOL BOARD, THE   p 1025
1400 NORTHWOOD ST, WINDSOR, ON, N9E 1A4
(519) 966-2504   SIC 8211
WINDSOR-ESSEX CHILDREN'S AID SOCIETY   p 861
161 KENDALL ST, SARNIA, ON, N7V 4G6
(519) 336-0623   SIC 8399
WINDSOR-ESSEX CHILDREN'S AID SOCIETY   p 1022
1671 RIVERSIDE DR E, WINDSOR, ON, N8Y 5B5
(519) 252-1171   SIC 8322
WINDSOR-ESSEX COUNTY HOUSING CORPORATION   p 1024
945 MCDOUGALL ST, WINDSOR, ON, N9A 1L9
(519) 254-1681   SIC 6531
WINDSPEAR CENTRE   p 91
9720 102 AVE NW, EDMONTON, AB, T5J 4B2
(780) 401-2520   SIC 8699
WINDSPEC INC   p 561
1310 CREDITSTONE RD, CONCORD, ON, L4K 5T7
(905) 738-8311   SIC 3444
WINEGARD MOTORS LIMITED   p 532
140 ARGYLE ST S, CALEDONIA, ON, N3W 1E5
(905) 765-4444   SIC 5511
WING HING LUNG LIMITED   p 996
550 KIPLING AVE, TORONTO, ON, M8Z 5E9
(416) 531-5768   SIC 2098
WING ON CHEONG (CANADA) LIMITED   p 677
235 HOOD RD UNIT 2, MARKHAM, ON, L3R 4N3
SIC 5199
WING ON NEW GROUP CANADA INC p 677
351 FERRIER ST SUITE 6, MARKHAM, ON, L3R 5Z2
(905) 604-4677   SIC 5411
WING TAT GAME BIRD PACKERS INC   p 264
11951 FORGE PL, RICHMOND, BC, V7A 4V9
(604) 278-4450   SIC 4731
WINGBACK ENTERPRISES LIMITED p 921
1 FIRST AVE, TORONTO, ON, M4M 1W7
(416) 367-9957   SIC 7991
WINGENBACK INC   p 26
707 BARLOW TRAIL SE, CALGARY, AB, T2E 8C2
(403) 221-8120   SIC 3299
WINGHAM AND DISTRICT HOSPITAL   p 1026
270 CARLING TERR, WINGHAM, ON, N0G

2W0
(519) 357-3210   SIC 8062
WINGHAM CASTINGS   p 1026
See WESCAST INDUSTRIES INC
WINGS FOOD PRODUCTS   p 996
See WING HING LUNG LIMITED
WINGS OF CANADA   p 677
See WING ON CHEONG (CANADA) LIMITED
WINGSUM INTERNATIONAL TRADING INC   p 259
21331 GORDON WAY UNIT 3110, RICHMOND, BC, V6W 1J9
(604) 370-3610   SIC 6799
WINKLER BUILDING SUPPLIES (1981) LTD   p 361
570 CENTENNIAL ST UNIT 300, WINKLER, MB, R6W 1J4
(204) 325-4336   SIC 1542
WINKLER MEATS LTD   p 361
270 GEORGE AVE, WINKLER, MB, R6W 3M4
(204) 325-9593   SIC 5147
WINKLER WALMART   p 361
See WAL-MART CANADA CORP
WINKLES INDEPENDANT GROCER   p 569
See 1148956 ONTARIO LTD
WINMAGIC CORP   p 733
5600A CANCROSS CRT, MISSISSAUGA, ON, L5R 3E9
(905) 502-7000   SIC 7371
WINMAGIC INC   p 733
5600 CANCROSS CRT, MISSISSAUGA, ON, L5R 3E9
(905) 502-7000   SIC 7372
WINMAR WINNIPEG   p 380
See 6119701 MANITOBA LTD
WINNER SPORTSWEAR LTD   p 296
1223 FRANCES ST, VANCOUVER, BC, V6A 1Z4
(604) 253-0411   SIC 5651
WINNERS   p 41
See WINNERS MERCHANTS INTERNATIONAL L.P.
WINNERS   p 75
See WINNERS MERCHANTS INTERNATIONAL L.P.
WINNERS   p 327
See WINNERS MERCHANTS INTERNATIONAL L.P.
WINNERS   p 677
See WINNERS MERCHANTS INTERNATIONAL L.P.
WINNERS   p 690
See WINNERS MERCHANTS INTERNATIONAL L.P.
WINNERS   p 748
See WINNERS MERCHANTS INTERNATIONAL L.P.
WINNERS   p 790
See WINNERS MERCHANTS INTERNATIONAL L.P.
WINNERS   p 799
See WINNERS MERCHANTS INTERNATIONAL L.P.
WINNERS   p 936
See WINNERS MERCHANTS INTERNATIONAL L.P.
WINNERS   p 1082
See WINNERS MERCHANTS INTERNATIONAL L.P.
WINNERS   p 1165
See WINNERS MERCHANTS INTERNATIONAL L.P.
WINNERS   p 1200
See WINNERS MERCHANTS INTERNATIONAL L.P.
WINNERS   p 1389
See WINNERS MERCHANTS INTERNATIONAL L.P.
WINNERS DISTRIBUTON CENTRE   p 507
See WINNERS MERCHANTS INTERNATIONAL L.P.
WINNERS HOME CENTRAL INC   p 894

2105 RYMAL RD E, STONEY CREEK, ON, L8J 2R8
(905) 560-0800   SIC 6794
WINNERS MERCHANTS INTERNATIONAL L.P.   p 41
5111 NORTHLAND DR NW SUITE 200, CALGARY, AB, T2L 2J8
(403) 247-8100   SIC 5651
WINNERS MERCHANTS INTERNATIONAL L.P.   p 75
5498 SIGNAL HILL CTR SW, CALGARY, AB, T3H 3P8
(403) 246-4999   SIC 5651
WINNERS MERCHANTS INTERNATIONAL L.P.   p 245
19800 LOUGHEED HWY SUITE 160, PITT MEADOWS, BC, V3Y 2W1
(604) 465-4330   SIC 5651
WINNERS MERCHANTS INTERNATIONAL L.P.   p 327
798 GRANVILLE ST SUITE 300, VANCOUVER, BC, V6Z 3C3
(604) 683-1058   SIC 5651
WINNERS MERCHANTS INTERNATIONAL L.P.   p 507
55 WEST DR, BRAMPTON, ON, L6T 4A1
(905) 451-7200   SIC 5651
WINNERS MERCHANTS INTERNATIONAL L.P.   p 677
5000 HIGHWAY 7 E, MARKHAM, ON, L3R 4M9
(905) 415-1441   SIC 5651
WINNERS MERCHANTS INTERNATIONAL L.P.   p 690
3185 AMERICAN DR, MISSISSAUGA, ON, L4V 1B8
(905) 672-2228   SIC 5651
WINNERS MERCHANTS INTERNATIONAL L.P.   p 733
60 STANDISH CRT, MISSISSAUGA, ON, L5R 0G1
(905) 405-8000   SIC 5651
WINNERS MERCHANTS INTERNATIONAL L.P.   p 748
100 BAYSHORE DR, NEPEAN, ON, K2B 8C1
(613) 721-6451   SIC 5651
WINNERS MERCHANTS INTERNATIONAL L.P.   p 790
3090 BATHURST ST SUITE 1, NORTH YORK, ON, M6A 2A1
(416) 782-4469   SIC 5651
WINNERS MERCHANTS INTERNATIONAL L.P.   p 799
2460 WINSTON CHURCHILL BLVD SUITE 1, OAKVILLE, ON, L6H 6J5
(905) 829-9086   SIC 5651
WINNERS MERCHANTS INTERNATIONAL L.P.   p 936
444 YONGE ST UNIT G3, TORONTO, ON, M5B 2H4
(416) 598-8800   SIC 5651
WINNERS MERCHANTS INTERNATIONAL L.P.   p 1082
6900 BOUL DECARIE BUREAU 3550, COTE SAINT-LUC, QC, H3X 2T8
(514) 733-4200   SIC 5651
WINNERS MERCHANTS INTERNATIONAL L.P.   p 1165
7275 RUE SHERBROOKE E BUREAU 2000, MONTREAL, QC, H1N 1E9
(514) 798-1908   SIC 5651
WINNERS MERCHANTS INTERNATIONAL L.P.   p 1200
1500 AV MCGILL COLLEGE, MONTREAL, QC, H3A 3J5
(514) 788-4949   SIC 5651
WINNERS MERCHANTS INTERNATIONAL L.P.   p 1248
1050 CHOMEDEY (A-13) O, POINTE-CLAIRE, QC, H7X 4C9
(450) 969-2007   SIC 5651
WINNERS MERCHANTS INTERNATIONAL L.P.   p 1389

4125 BOUL DES RECOLLETS, TROIS-RIVIERES, QC, G9A 6M1
(819) 370-2001   SIC 5651
WINNIFRED COLONY   p 145
See HUTTERIAN BRETHREN OF WINNIFRED
WINNIFRED STEWART ASSOCIATION FOR THE MENTALLY HANDICAPPED   p 97
11130 131 ST NW, EDMONTON, AB, T5M 1C1
(780) 453-6707   SIC 8322
WINNIPEG ACCOUNTING   p 377
See BDO CANADA LLP
WINNIPEG AIRPORTS AUTHORITY INC   p 385
2000 WELLINGTON AVE RM 249, WINNIPEG, MB, R3H 1C2
(204) 987-9400   SIC 4581
WINNIPEG BUILDING & DECORATING LTD   p 381
1586 WALL ST, WINNIPEG, MB, R3E 2S4
(204) 942-6121   SIC 1521
WINNIPEG C MOTORS LP   p 370
1900 MAIN ST, WINNIPEG, MB, R2V 3S9
(204) 339-2011   SIC 5511
WINNIPEG CIVIC EMPLOYEES BENEFITS PROGRAM, THE   p 376
317 DONALD ST SUITE 5, WINNIPEG, MB, R3B 2H6
(204) 986-2522   SIC 6371
WINNIPEG CLINIC   p 380
425 ST MARY AVE, WINNIPEG, MB, R3C 0N2
(204) 957-1900   SIC 8011
WINNIPEG CONVENTION CENTRE   p 377
See CONVENTION CENTRE CORPORATION, THE
WINNIPEG DODGE CHRYSLER JEEP p 387
See WINNIPEG DODGE CHRYSLER LTD
WINNIPEG DODGE CHRYSLER LTD   p 387
3965 PORTAGE AVE UNIT 90, WINNIPEG, MB, R3K 2H3
(204) 774-4444   SIC 5511
WINNIPEG EQUIPMENT SALES LTD   p 370
33 OAK POINT HWY, WINNIPEG, MB, R2R 0T8
(204) 632-9100   SIC 5012
WINNIPEG FREE PRESS   p 372
See FP CANADIAN NEWSPAPERS LIMITED PARTNERSHIP
WINNIPEG HONDA   p 390
See 75040 MANITOBA LTD
WINNIPEG HUMANE SOCIETY FOR THE PREVENTION CRUELTY TO ANIMALS   p 392
45 HURST WAY, WINNIPEG, MB, R3T 0R3
(204) 982-2021   SIC 8699
WINNIPEG JETS HOCKEY CLUB   p 380
See WINNIPEG JETS HOCKEY CLUB LIMITED PARTNERSHIP
WINNIPEG JETS HOCKEY CLUB LIMITED PARTNERSHIP   p 380
345 GRAHAM AVE, WINNIPEG, MB, R3C 5S6
(204) 987-7825   SIC 7941
WINNIPEG LIVESTOCK SALES LTD   p 380
GD, WINNIPEG, MB, R3C 2E6
(204) 694-8328   SIC 5154
WINNIPEG MOTOR EXPRESS   p 371
See 7062001 CANADA LIMITED
WINNIPEG MOTOR EXPRESS INC   p 373
1180 FIFE ST, WINNIPEG, MB, R2X 2N6
SIC 4213
WINNIPEG OLD COUNTRY SAUSAGE LTD   p 371
691 DUFFERIN AVE, WINNIPEG, MB, R2W 2Z3
(204) 589-8331   SIC 2013
WINNIPEG PANTS & SPORTSWEAR MFG. LTD   p 374
85 ADELAIDE ST, WINNIPEG, MB, R3A 0V9
(204) 942-3494   SIC 2326
WINNIPEG REGIONAL HEALTH AUTHOR-

ITY *p*
381
See WINNIPEG REGIONAL HEALTH AUTHORITY, THE
WINNIPEG REGIONAL HEALTH AUTHORITY, THE *p*
367
345 DE BAETS ST, WINNIPEG, MB, R2J 3V6
(204) 654-5100   *SIC* 8099
WINNIPEG REGIONAL HEALTH AUTHORITY, THE *p*
367
975 HENDERSON HWY, WINNIPEG, MB, R2K 4L7
(204) 938-5000   *SIC* 8093
WINNIPEG REGIONAL HEALTH AUTHORITY, THE *p*
368
735 ST ANNE'S RD, WINNIPEG, MB, R2N 0C4
(204) 255-9073   *SIC* 8361
WINNIPEG REGIONAL HEALTH AUTHORITY, THE *p*
374
490 HARGRAVE ST, WINNIPEG, MB, R3A 0X7
(204) 940-2665   *SIC* 8093
WINNIPEG REGIONAL HEALTH AUTHORITY, THE *p*
374
820 SHERBROOK ST SUITE 543, WINNIPEG, MB, R3A 1R9
(204) 774-6511   *SIC* 8062
WINNIPEG REGIONAL HEALTH AUTHORITY, THE *p*
376
650 MAIN ST 4TH FL, WINNIPEG, MB, R3B 1E2
(204) 926-7000   *SIC* 8062
WINNIPEG REGIONAL HEALTH AUTHORITY, THE *p*
381
720 MCDERMOT AVE RM AD301, WINNIPEG, MB, R3E 0T3
(204) 787-1165   *SIC* 8062
WINNIPEG SCHOOL DIVISION *p* 370
2424 KING EDWARD ST, WINNIPEG, MB, R2R 2R2
(204) 694-0483   *SIC* 8211
WINNIPEG SCHOOL DIVISION *p* 371
401 CHURCH AVE, WINNIPEG, MB, R2W 1C4
(204) 589-4374   *SIC* 8211
WINNIPEG SCHOOL DIVISION *p* 373
1360 REDWOOD AVE, WINNIPEG, MB, R2X 0Z1
(204) 589-8321   *SIC* 8211
WINNIPEG SCHOOL DIVISION *p* 381
2 SARGENT PARK PL, WINNIPEG, MB, R3E 0V8
(204) 775-8985   *SIC* 8211
WINNIPEG SCHOOL DIVISION *p* 381
1577 WALL ST E, WINNIPEG, MB, R3E 2S5
(204) 775-0231   *SIC* 8211
WINNIPEG SCHOOL DIVISION *p* 381
1555 WALL ST, WINNIPEG, MB, R3E 2S2
(204) 786-1401   *SIC* 8211
WINNIPEG SCHOOL DIVISION *p* 381
1395 SPRUCE ST SUITE 1, WINNIPEG, MB, R3E 2V8
(204) 786-0344   *SIC* 8211
WINNIPEG SCHOOL DIVISION *p* 381
720 ALVERSTONE ST, WINNIPEG, MB, R3E 2H1
(204) 783-7131   *SIC* 8211
WINNIPEG SCHOOL DIVISION *p* 383
3 BORROWMAN PL, WINNIPEG, MB, R3G 1M6
(204) 774-5401   *SIC* 8211
WINNIPEG SCHOOL DIVISION *p* 387
510 HAY ST, WINNIPEG, MB, R3L 2L6
(204) 474-1301   *SIC* 8211
WINNIPEG SCHOOL DIVISION *p* 388

155 KINGSWAY, WINNIPEG, MB, R3M 0G3
(204) 474-1492   *SIC* 8211
WINNIPEG SCHOOL DIVISION *p* 388
450 NATHANIEL ST, WINNIPEG, MB, R3M 3E3
(204) 452-3112   *SIC* 8211
WINNIPEG SPORT & LEISURE *p* 364
See 2474761 MANITOBA LTD
WINNIPEG SYMPHONY ORCHESTRA INC *p* 376
555 MAIN ST RM 1020, WINNIPEG, MB, R3B 1C3
(204) 949-3950   *SIC* 7929
WINNIPEG TECHNICAL COLLEGE *p* 393
130 HENLOW BAY, WINNIPEG, MB, R3Y 1G4
(204) 989-6500   *SIC* 8222
WINOA CANADA INC *p* 1012
650 RUSHOLME RD, WELLAND, ON, L3B 5N7
(905) 735-4691   *SIC* 3291
WINPAK LTD *p* 386
100 SAULTEAUX CRES, WINNIPEG, MB, R3J 3T3
(204) 889-1015   *SIC* 3081
WINPAK PORTION PACKAGING LTD *p* 589
26 TIDEMORE AVE, ETOBICOKE, ON, M9W 7A7
(416) 741-6182   *SIC* 3089
WINSHAM FABRIK CANADA LTD *p* 905
25 MINTHORN BLVD, THORNHILL, ON, L3T 7N5
(905) 882-1827   *SIC* 5023
WINSLOW-GEROLAMY MOTORS LIMITED *p* 842
1018 LANSDOWNE ST W, PETERBOROUGH, ON, K9J 1Z9
(705) 742-3411   *SIC* 5511
WINSPEAR CENTRE FOR MUSIC *p* 88
See EDMONTON CONCERT HALL FOUNDATION
WINSPORT CANADA *p* 72
See CALGARY OLYMPIC DEVELOPMENT ASSOCIATION
WINSTON CHURCHILL HIGH SCHOOL *p* 141
See LETHBRIDGE SCHOOL DISTRICT NO. 51
WINSTON HALL NURSING HOME LTD *p* 638
695 BLOCK LINE RD, KITCHENER, ON, N2E 3K1
(519) 576-2430   *SIC* 8051
WINSTON KNOLL COLLEGIATE *p* 1423
See BOARD OF EDUCATION REGINA SCHOOL DIVISION NO. 4 OF SASKATCHEWAN
WINSTON STEEL INC *p* 736
7496 TRANMERE DR, MISSISSAUGA, ON, L5S 1K4
(905) 747-7579   *SIC* 5051
WINSUN DISTRIBUTING *p* 389
2025 CORYDON AVE SUITE 267, WINNIPEG, MB, R3P 0N5
(204) 888-1873   *SIC* 5963
WINTERGREEN LEARNING MATERIALS LIMITED *p* 498
3075 LINE 8, BRADFORD, ON, L3Z 3R5
(905) 778-8584   *SIC* 5049
WINTERMAR FARMS (1989) LTD *p* 1013
265 KATHERINE ST S SUITE 1, WEST MONTROSE, ON, N0B 2V0
(519) 664-3701   *SIC* 5191
WINTERS INSTRUMENTS LTD *p* 775
121 RAILSIDE RD, NORTH YORK, ON, M3A 1B2
(416) 444-2345   *SIC* 3824
WINVAN PAVING LTD *p* 237
220 EDWORTHY WAY, NEW WESTMINSTER, BC, V3L 5G5
(604) 522-3921   *SIC* 1611
WIP INTERNATIONAL *p* 1374
See WIPTEC INC
WIPECO *p* 1228

See WIPECO INDUSTRIES INC, LES
WIPECO INDUSTRIES INC, LES *p* 1228
3333 RUE DOUGLAS-B.-FLOREANI, MONTREAL, QC, H4S 1Y6
(514) 935-2551   *SIC* 5093
WIPRO SOLUTIONS CANADA LIMITED *p* 91
10040 104 ST NW SUITE 100, EDMONTON, AB, T5J 0Z2
(780) 420-7875   *SIC* 8742
WIPTEC INC *p* 1374
3160 BOUL INDUSTRIEL, SHERBROOKE, QC, J1L V8
(819) 564-7117   *SIC* 5031
WIRCO PRODUCTS LIMITED *p* 658
1011 ADELAIDE ST S, LONDON, ON, N6E 1R4
(519) 681-2100   *SIC* 3496
WIRE ROPE INDUSTRIES *p* 610
See SLING-CHOKER MFG. (HAMILTON) LTD
WIRECOMM SYSTEMS (2008), INC *p* 489
122 SAUNDERS RD SUITE 10, BARRIE, ON, L4N 9A8
(905) 405-8018   *SIC* 4899
WIRELESS EXPRESS *p* 665
See PRIME COMMUNICATIONS CANADA INC
WIRELESS PERSONAL COMMUNICATIONS INC *p*
790
166 BENTWORTH AVE, NORTH YORK, ON, M6A 1P7
(416) 667-4189   *SIC* 5999
WIRSBO *p* 1416
See UPONOR LTD
WIS INTERNATIONAL *p* 12
See WESTERN INVENTORY SERVICE LTD
WIS INTERNATIONAL *p* 364
See WESTERN INVENTORY SERVICE LTD
WIS INTERNATIONAL *p* 690
See WESTERN INVENTORY SERVICE LTD
WISE OWL FRAUD PREVENTION *p* 143
135 1 AVE S, LETHBRIDGE, AB, T1J 0A1
(403) 330-5020   *SIC* 7381
WISEMAN EXPORT *p* 792
See 576195 ONTARIO LIMITED
WISMER DEVELOPMENTS INC *p* 1008
443 WISMER ST, WATERLOO, ON, N2K 2K6
(519) 743-1412   *SIC* 2013
WISMETTAC ASIAN FOODS, INC *p* 264
11388 NO. 5 RD SUITE 130, RICHMOND, BC, V7A 4E7
(604) 303-8620   *SIC* 5141
WITHERS L.P. *p* 168
3602 93 ST, STURGEON COUNTY, AB, T8W 5A8
(780) 539-5347   *SIC* 4213
WITHERS TRUCKING *p* 168
See WITHERS L.P.
WITRON CANADA CORPORATION *p* 948
480 UNIVERSITY AVE SUITE 1500, TORONTO, ON, M5G 1V2
(416) 598-7096   *SIC* 8742
WITRON LOGISTIK+INFORMATIK *p* 948
See WITRON CANADA CORPORATION
WITTEN LLP *p* 91
10303 JASPER AVE NW SUITE 2500, EDMONTON, AB, T5J 3N6
(780) 428-0501   *SIC* 8111
WITTINGTON INVESTMENTS, LIMITED *p*
926
22 ST CLAIR AVE E SUITE 2001, TORONTO, ON, M4T 2S3
(416) 967-7990   *SIC* 6512
WJS CANADA *p* 231
See STELMASCHUK, W.J. AND ASSOCIATES LTD
WK MANUFACTURING, DIV OF *p* 223
See STOBER, AL CONSTRUCTION LTD

WL MOBILE APPS *p* 854
See WELLNESS LIVING SYSTEMS INC
WLB SERVICES LIMITED *p* 427
54 O'FLAHERTY CRES, MOUNT PEARL, NL, A1N 4M1
(709) 747-2340   *SIC* 7231
WLT HOLDINGS LTD *p* 387
3965 PORTAGE AVE SUITE 70, WINNIPEG, MB, R3K 2H8
(204) 889-3700   *SIC* 5511
WM QUEBEC INC *p* 1051
9501 BOUL RAY-LAWSON BUREAU 114, ANJOU, QC, H1J 1L4
(514) 352-1596   *SIC* 4953
WM QUEBEC INC *p* 1051
2457 CH DU LAC, LONGUEUIL, QC, J4N 1P1
(450) 646-7870   *SIC* 4953
WM.R.MURPHY FISHERIES LTD *p* 439
52 WHARF RD LITTLE RIVER HARBOUR, ARCADIA, NS, B0W 1B0
(902) 663-4301   *SIC* 2091
WMI MANUFACTURING CORP *p* 223
1451 ELLIS ST, KELOWNA, BC, V1Y 2A3
(250) 712-3393   *SIC* 3949
WN BIRD FINANCIAL GROUP INC *p* 547
387 RAGLAN ST, COLLINGWOOD, ON, L9Y 3Z1
(705) 445-4501   *SIC* 5172
WN PHARMACEUTICALS LTD *p* 202
2000 BRIGANTINE DR, COQUITLAM, BC, V3K 7B5
(778) 284-7400   *SIC* 2834
WOBURN COLLEGIATE INSTITUTE *p* 866
See TORONTO DISTRICT SCHOOL BOARD
WOLF CREEK BUILDING SUPPLIES LTD *p* 138
5645 WOLF CREEK DR SUITE 5808, LACOMBE, AB, T4L 2H8
(403) 782-1780   *SIC* 5031
WOLF CREEK PUBLIC SCHOOL *p* 153
See WOLF CREEK SCHOOL DIVISION NO.72
WOLF CREEK SCHOOL DIVISION NO.72 *p* 153
6000 HIGHWAY 2A, PONOKA, AB, T4J 1P6
(403) 783-5441   *SIC* 8211
WOLF STEEL LTD *p* 485
24 NAPOLEON RD, BARRIE, ON, L4M 0G8
(705) 721-1212   *SIC* 3433
WOLF STEEL LTD *p* 485
9 NAPOLEON RD, BARRIE, ON, L4M 0G8
(705) 721-1212   *SIC* 3433
WOLF, PAUL LIGHTING & ELECTRIC SUPPLY LIMITED *p*
994
425 ALLIANCE AVE, TORONTO, ON, M6N 2J1
(416) 504-8195   *SIC* 5063
WOLFE AUTOMOTIVE FAMILY *p* 285
See WOLFE MOTORS LTD
WOLFE MOTORS LTD *p* 285
1595 BOUNDARY RD, VANCOUVER, BC, V5K 5C4
(604) 293-1311   *SIC* 5511
WOLFE'S LANGLEY MAZDA *p* 271
See 328633 BC LTD
WOLFF, MARY ANN DRUGS LTD *p* 477
199 SANDWICH ST S, AMHERSTBURG, ON, N9V 1Z9
(519) 736-5435   *SIC* 5912
WOLFTEK INDUSTRIES INC *p* 251
4944 CONTINENTAL WAY, PRINCE GEORGE, BC, V2N 5S5
(250) 561-1556   *SIC* 5084
WOLFVILLE NURSING HOMES LIMITED *p* 471
601 MAIN ST SUITE 2, WOLFVILLE, NS, B4P 1E9
(902) 542-2429   *SIC* 8051
WOLFVILLE VOLUNTEER FIRE DEPARTMENT *p*
471

355 MAIN ST, WOLFVILLE, NS, B4P 1A1
(902) 542-5635   SIC 7389

WOLLE REALTY INC   p 636
842 VICTORIA ST N SUITE 15, KITCH-
ENER, ON, N2B 3C1
(519) 578-7300   SIC 6531

WOLSELEY CANADA INC   p 528
880 LAURENTIAN DR SUITE 1, BURLING-
TON, ON, L7N 3V6
(905) 335-7373   SIC 5074

WOLSELEY CANADA INC   p 1236
4200 RUE LOUIS-B.-MAYER, MONTREAL,
QC, H7P 0G1
(450) 680-4040   SIC 5075

WOLSELEY CANADA INC   p 1342
4200 RUE HICKMORE, SAINT-LAURENT,
QC, H4T 1K2
(514) 344-9378   SIC 5074

WOLSELEY HOLDINGS CANADA INC   p
528
880 LAURENTIAN DR SUITE 1, BURLING-
TON, ON, L7N 3V6
(905) 335-7373   SIC 6712

WOLTERS KLUWER CANADA LIMITED   p
773
90 SHEPPARD AVE E SUITE 300, NORTH
YORK, ON, M2N 6X1
(416) 224-2224   SIC 2721

WOLTERS KLUWER CANADA LIMITED   p
1372
1120 RUE DE CHERBOURG, SHER-
BROOKE, QC, J1K 2N8
(819) 566-2000   SIC 7291

WOLVERINE FORD SALES (2006) LTD   p
135
10102 97 ST SS 1, HIGH LEVEL, AB, T0H
1Z0
(780) 926-2291   SIC 5511

WOLVERINE FREIGHT SYSTEM   p 1019
See 591182 ONTARIO LIMITED

WOLVERINE WORLD WIDE CANADA ULC
p 728
6225 MILLCREEK DR, MISSISSAUGA, ON,
L5N 0G2
(905) 285-9560   SIC 5139

WOLVERTON SECURITIES LTD   p 330
777 DUNSMUIR ST SUITE 1700, VANCOU-
VER, BC, V7Y 1J5
(604) 622-1000   SIC 8742

**WOMEN'S CHRISTIAN ASSOCIATION OF
LONDON**   p 660
2022 KAINS RD SUITE 2105, LONDON,
ON, N6K 0A8
(519) 432-2648   SIC 8361

WOMEN'S COLLEGE HOSPITAL   p 976
76 GRENVILLE ST, TORONTO, ON, M5S
1B2
(416) 323-6400   SIC 8062

**WOMEN'S COLLEGE RESEARCH INSTI-
TUTE**   p
976
See WOMEN'S COLLEGE HOSPITAL

WONG, VICKY C.K. DRUGS LTD   p 679
9255 WOODBINE AVE SUITE 27,
MARKHAM, ON, L6C 1Y9
(905) 887-3000   SIC 5912

WOOD & ENERGY STORE   p 95
See DYAND MECHANICAL SYSTEMS INC

WOOD AUTOMOTIVE GROUP   p 71
11580 24 ST SE, CALGARY, AB, T2Z 3K1
(403) 640-8494   SIC 5531

WOOD BUFFALO HELICOPTERS   p 127
See AURORA HELICOPTERS LTD

**WOOD BUFFALO HOUSING & DEVELOP-
MENT CORPORATION**   p
129
9915 FRANKLIN AVE SUITE 9011, FORT
MCMURRAY, AB, T9H 2K4
(780) 799-4050   SIC 6531

WOOD CANADA LIMITED   p 63
801 6 AVE SW SUITE 900, CALGARY, AB,
T2P 3W3
(403) 298-4170   SIC 8711

WOOD CANADA LIMITED   p 111

5681 70 ST NW, EDMONTON, AB, T6B 3P6
(780) 436-2152   SIC 8711

WOOD CANADA LIMITED   p 187
4445 LOUGHEED HWY SUITE 600, BURN-
ABY, BC, V5C 0E4
(604) 294-3811   SIC 8711

WOOD CANADA LIMITED   p 284
1385 CEDAR AVE, TRAIL, BC, V1R 4C3
(250) 368-2400   SIC 8711

WOOD CANADA LIMITED   p 301
111 DUNSMUIR ST SUITE 400, VANCOU-
VER, BC, V6B 5W3
(604) 664-4315   SIC 8711

WOOD CANADA LIMITED   p 528
3215 NORTH SERVICE RD, BURLINGTON,
ON, L7N 3G2
(905) 335-2353   SIC 8711

WOOD CANADA LIMITED   p 799
2020 WINSTON PARK DR SUITE 700,
OAKVILLE, ON, L6H 6X7
(905) 829-5400   SIC 8741

WOOD CANADA LIMITED   p 873
104 CROCKFORD BLVD, SCARBOR-
OUGH, ON, M1R 3C3
(416) 751-6565   SIC 8711

WOOD CANADA LIMITED   p 1095
1425 RTE TRANSCANADIENNE BUREAU
400, DORVAL, QC, H9P 2W9
(514) 684-5555   SIC 8748

WOOD FIBER CANADA INC   p 1139
2341 AV DE LA ROTONDE, LEVIS, QC,
G6X 2M2
(418) 832-2918   SIC 3425

WOOD GROUP   p 796
See AMEC FOSTER WHEELER INC

**WOOD GROUP ASSET INTEGRITY SOLU-
TIONS, INC**   p
33
4242 7 ST SE SUITE 118, CALGARY, AB,
T2G 2Y8
(403) 245-5666   SIC 8711

WOOD GROUP PSN CANADA INC   p 432
277 WATER ST, ST. JOHN'S, NL, A1C 6L3
(709) 778-4000   SIC 8711

WOOD HOMES FOUNDATION   p 42
805 37 ST NW, CALGARY, AB, T2N 4N8
(403) 270-1718   SIC 8322

WOOD MOTORS (1972) LIMITED   p 402
880 PROSPECT ST, FREDERICTON, NB,
E3B 2T8
(506) 452-6611   SIC 5511

WOOD MOTORS FORD   p 402
See WOOD MOTORS (1972) LIMITED

WOOD SHOPPE, THE   p 762
See AFFIRMATIVE DYNAMIC INDUSTRY
INC

WOOD TAVERN AND GRILL   p 364
See NORWOOD HOTEL CO LTD

WOOD WYANT CANADA INC   p 1398
42 RUE DE L'ARTISAN, VICTORIAVILLE,
QC, G6P 7E3
(819) 758-1541   SIC 2842

WOOD'S HOMES BOWNESS TREATMENT
p 72
See WOOD'S HOMES SOCIETY

WOOD'S HOMES SOCIETY   p 42
805 37 ST NW, CALGARY, AB, T2N 4N8
(403) 220-0349   SIC 8641

WOOD'S HOMES SOCIETY   p 72
9400 48 AVE NW, CALGARY, AB, T3B 2B2
(403) 247-6751   SIC 8361

WOOD, BRENDAN INTERNATIONAL LTD p
974
17 PRINCE ARTHUR AVE, TORONTO, ON,
M5R 1B2
(416) 924-8110   SIC 8741

WOODALL CONSTRUCTION CO. LIMITED
p 1022
620 NORTH SERVICE RD E, WINDSOR,
ON, N8X 3J3
(519) 966-3381   SIC 1541

WOODBINE CHRYSLER   p 677
See WOODBINE CHRYSLER LTD

WOODBINE CHRYSLER LTD   p 677

8280 WOODBINE AVE, MARKHAM, ON,
L3R 2N8
(905) 415-2260   SIC 5511

WOODBINE ENTERTAINMENT GROUP   p
998
555 REXDALE BLVD, TORONTO, ON, M9W
5L2
(416) 675-7223   SIC 7948

WOODBINE RACETRACK   p 998
See   WOODBINE   ENTERTAINMENT
GROUP

**WOODBINE TOOL & DIE MANUFACTUR-
ING LTD**   p
677
190 ROYAL CREST CRT, MARKHAM, ON,
L3R 9X6
(905) 475-5223   SIC 3541

**WOODBINE TOOL & DIE MANUFACTUR-
ING LTD**   p
677
3300 14TH AVE, MARKHAM, ON, L3R 0H3
(905) 475-5223   SIC 3469

WOODBRIDGE COMPANY LIMITED, THE p
958
65 QUEEN ST W SUITE 2400, TORONTO,
ON, M5H 2M8
(416) 364-8700   SIC 6712

WOODBRIDGE FOAM CORPORATION   p
708
4240 SHERWOODTOWNE BLVD SUITE
300, MISSISSAUGA, ON, L4Z 2G6
(905) 896-3626   SIC 3086

WOODBRIDGE GROUP, THE   p 708
See WOODBRIDGE FOAM CORPORA-
TION

WOODBRIDGE LUMBER INC   p 1034
8100 KIPLING AVE, WOODBRIDGE, ON,
L4L 2A1
(905) 581-2804   SIC 5031

WOODBRIDGE PALLET LTD   p 1034
7200 MARTIN GROVE RD, WOODBRIDGE,
ON, L4L 9J3
(905) 856-3332   SIC 7699

WOODBRIDGE TOYOTA   p 1033
See SCHON, GEORGE MOTORS LIMITED

WOODBRIDGE VISTA CARE COMMUNITY
p 1029
See 2063414 ONTARIO LIMITED

WOODCHESTER I.D.A. PHARMACY p 714
See ANGELS PHARMACEUTICAL SER-
VICES LTD

WOODCHESTER IMPORTS INC   p 718
3089 WOODCHESTER DR, MISSIS-
SAUGA, ON, L5L 1J2
(905) 828-2289   SIC 5511

WOODCHESTER INFINITI NISSAN   p 718
See WOODCHESTER NISSAN INC

WOODCHESTER KIA   p 718
See WOODCHESTER IMPORTS INC

WOODCHESTER NISSAN INC   p 718
2560 MOTORWAY BLVD, MISSISSAUGA,
ON, L5L 1X3
(905) 828-7001   SIC 5511

WOODCOCK BROTHERS   p 879
See 410648 ONTARIO LIMITED

**WOODCOCK TRANSPORTATION SER-
VICES INC**   p
879
225 HERON RD, SEBRINGVILLE, ON, N0K
1X0
(519) 393-5353   SIC 4731

WOODGREEN COMMUNITY SERVICES   p
919
815   DANFORTH   AVE   SUITE   100,
TORONTO, ON, M4J 1L2
(416) 645-6000   SIC 8399

WOODHALL PARK HOLDING CORP p 512
10250 KENNEDY RD SUITE UNIT, BRAMP-
TON, ON, L6Z 4N7
(905) 846-1441   SIC 6513

WOODHAVEN CAPITAL CORP   p 141
3125 24 AVE N, LETHBRIDGE, AB, T1H
5G2
(403) 320-7070   SIC 6712

WOODHAVEN LEXUS TOYOTA   p 387
See WLT HOLDINGS LTD

WOODHAVEN, THE   p 678
See CHARTWELL RETIREMENT RESI-
DENCES

WOODHOUSE INVESTMENTS INC   p 639
207 MADISON AVE S SUITE 2, KITCH-
ENER, ON, N2G 3M7
(519) 749-3790   SIC 6712

WOODLAND EQUIPMENT INC   p 216
2015 TRANS CANADA HWY W, KAM-
LOOPS, BC, V1S 1A7
(250) 372-2855   SIC 5084

**WOODLAND HOME HARDWARE BUILD-
ING CENTRE**   p
132
See FISCHER, C.A. LIMBER, CO. LTD

WOODLAND IMPROVEMENTS CORPp 415
300 UNION ST, SAINT JOHN, NB, E2L 4Z2
(506) 632-7777   SIC 2421

WOODLAND SECONDARY SCHOOL p 234
See   SCHOOL   DISTRICT   NO.   68
(NANAIMO-LADYSMITH)

WOODLAND SUPPLY & MFG. CO.   p 364
867 MCLEOD AVE, WINNIPEG, MB, R2G
0Y4
(204) 668-0079   SIC 2431

WOODLAND TOYOTA   p 1397
See WOODLAND VERDUN LTEE

WOODLAND VERDUN LTEE   p 1397
1009 RUE WOODLAND, VERDUN, QC,
H4H 1V7
(514) 761-3444   SIC 5511

WOODLAND VILLA NURSING HOME p 662
See OMNI HEALTH CARE LTD

WOODLANDS SCHOOL   p 712
See PEEL DISTRICT SCHOOL BOARD

WOODLORE INTERNATIONAL INC   p 507
160 DELTA PARK BLVD, BRAMPTON, ON,
L6T 5T6
(905) 791-9555   SIC 2521

WOODRIDGE FORD LINCOLN LTD   p 71
11580 24 ST SE, CALGARY, AB, T2Z 3K1
(403) 253-2211   SIC 5511

WOODRILL LTD   p 605
7861 7 HWY, GUELPH, ON, N1H 6H8
(519) 821-1018   SIC 5153

**WOODROFFE   SECONDARY   HIGH
SCHOOL**   p 830
See   OTTAWA-CARLETON   DISTRICT
SCHOOL BOARD

WOODS HOMES   p 42
See WOOD HOMES FOUNDATION

WOODS, DON FUELS LIMITED   p 999
20 RIVER ST, TWEED, ON, K0K 3J0
(613) 478-3039   SIC 5172

WOODSTOCK 230 TRAVEL CENTRE   p
1036
See TRAVEL CENTRE CANADA INC, THE

WOODSTOCK FLYING CLUB   p 1036
GD LCD MAIN, WOODSTOCK, ON, N4S
7W4
(519) 539-3303   SIC 8699

WOODSTOCK FORD   p 1034
See 2079608 ONTARIO INC

**WOODSTOCK   GENERAL   HOSPITAL
TRUST**   p 1036
310 JULIANA DR, WOODSTOCK, ON, N4V
0A4
(519) 421-4211   SIC 8062

WOODSTOCK HYDRO SERVICES INC   p
1036
16 GRAHAM ST SUITE 1598, WOOD-
STOCK, ON, N4S 6J6
(519) 537-7172   SIC 4911

**WOODSTOCK INDEPENDENT GROCER
ASSOCIATE, INC.**   p 1036
645 DUNDAS ST SUITE 1, WOODSTOCK,
ON, N4S 1E4
(519) 421-3420   SIC 5411

WOODSTOCK SERVICE CENTRE   p 1036
See TOYOTA TSUSHO CANADA INC

WOODSTREAM CANADA CORPORATION
p 513

4 LOWRY DR, BRAMPTON, ON, L7A 1C4
(905) 840-2640   SIC 5191

WOODTIRE CRAFT   p 13
See WARD TIRES, INC

WOODTONE SPECIALTIES INC   p 180
4175 CROZIER RD, ARMSTRONG, BC,
V0E 1B6
(250) 546-6808   SIC 2431

WOODVIEW CHILDREN'S CENTRE   p 529
69 FLATT RD, BURLINGTON, ON, L7P 0T3
(905) 689-4727   SIC 8069

WOODWARD MEAT PURVEYORS INC   p 805
1346 SPEERS RD, OAKVILLE, ON, L6L 5V3
(905) 847-7200   SIC 5147

WOODWARD'S LIMITED   p 424
16 LORING DR, HAPPY VALLEY-GOOSE
BAY, NL, A0P 1C0
(709) 896-2421   SIC 4581

WOODWARD'S OIL LIMITED   p 424
16 LORING DR, HAPPY VALLEY-GOOSE
BAY, NL, A0P 1C0
(709) 896-2421   SIC 5983

WOODWOORK & PUB INTERIORS   p 92
See 1471899 ALBERTA LTD

WOODY'S ON BRUNETTE   p 202
935 BRUNETTE AVE, COQUITLAM, BC,
V3K 1C8
(604) 526-1718   SIC 5921

WOODY'S ON BRUNETTE PUB   p 202
See WOODY'S ON BRUNETTE

WOODY'S RV WORLD LTD   p 157
1702 49 AVE, RED DEER, AB, T4R 2N7
(403) 346-1130   SIC 5561

WOOLFITT'S ART ENTERPRISES INC   p 991
1153 QUEEN ST W, TORONTO, ON, M6J
1J4
(416) 536-7878   SIC 5092

WOOLWICH AGRICULTURAL SOCIETY   p 569
7445 WELLINGTON RD 21, ELORA, ON,
N0B 1S0
(519) 846-5455   SIC 7948

WOOLWICH DAIRY   p 808
See SAPUTO INC

WORK ABLE CENTRES INC   p 769
4 LANSING SQ SUITE 102, NORTH YORK,
ON, M2J 5A2
(416) 496-6166   SIC 6321

WORK CENTER, THE   p 247
See VALLEY PERSONNEL LTD

WORK COMP TECH LTD   p 33
1401 1 ST SE SUITE 200, CALGARY, AB,
T2G 2J3
(403) 294-0501   SIC 6331

WORK OPPORTUNITIES   p 97
See WINNIFRED STEWART ASSOCIA-
TION FOR THE MENTALLY HANDICAPPED

**WORKERS COMPENSATION BOARD OF
NOVA SCOTIA**   p 454
5668 SOUTH ST, HALIFAX, NS, B3J 1A6
(902) 491-8999   SIC 6331

**WORKERS COMPENSATION BOARD OF
PRINCE EDWARD ISLAND**   p 1040
14 WEYMOUTH ST, CHARLOTTETOWN,
PE, C1A 4Y1
(902) 368-5680   SIC 6331

**WORKERS HEALTH AND SAFETY CEN-
TRE FEDERATION OF ONTARIO**   p 677
710-675 COCHRANE DR, MARKHAM, ON,
L3R 0B8
(416) 441-1939   SIC 8733

WORKERS REHABILITATION CENTER   p 416
See WORKPLACE HEALTH, SAFETY &
COMPENSATION COMMISSION OF NEW
BRUNSWICK

WORKERS' COMPENSATION BOARD   p 250
See WORKERS' COMPENSATION BOARD
OF BRITISH COLUMBIA

WORKERS' COMPENSATION BOARD AL-

BERTA   p
26
4311 12 ST NE SUITE 150, CALGARY, AB,
T2E 4P9
(403) 517-6000   SIC 6331

**WORKERS' COMPENSATION BOARD AL-
BERTA**   p
92
9912 107 ST NW, EDMONTON, AB, T5K
1G5
(780) 498-3999   SIC 6331

**WORKERS' COMPENSATION BOARD OF
BRITISH COLUMBIA**   p 235
4980 WILLS RD, NANAIMO, BC, V9T 6C6
(604) 273-2266   SIC 6331

**WORKERS' COMPENSATION BOARD OF
BRITISH COLUMBIA**   p 250
1066 VANCOUVER ST, PRINCE GEORGE,
BC, V2L 5M4
(250) 561-3715   SIC 6331

**WORKERS' COMPENSATION BOARD OF
BRITISH COLUMBIA**   p 266
6951 WESTMINSTER HWY, RICHMOND,
BC, V7C 1C6
(604) 231-8888   SIC 6331

**WORKERS' SAFETY AND COMPENSA-
TION COMMISSION OF THE NORTHWEST
TERRITORIES AND NUNAVUT**   p 436
5022 49 ST, YELLOWKNIFE, NT, X1A 3R8
(867) 920-3888   SIC 6331

**WORKING ENTERPRISES TRAVEL SER-
VICES LTD**   p
240
233 1ST ST W SUITE 430, NORTH VAN-
COUVER, BC, V7M 1B3
(604) 969-5585   SIC 4724

**WORKING OPPORTUNITY FUND (EVCC)
LTD**   p 317
1055 GEORGIA ST W SUITE 260, VAN-
COUVER, BC, V6E 0B6
(604) 633-1418   SIC 6722

WORKOPOLIS INC   p 943
1 YONGE ST SUITE 402, TORONTO, ON,
M5E 1E6
(416) 957-8300   SIC 7361

WORKOPOLIS.COM   p 943
See WORKOPOLIS INC

WORKPLACE ESSENTIALS LTD   p 460
59 WEBSTER ST, KENTVILLE, NS, B4N
1H6
(902) 678-6106   SIC 5021

**WORKPLACE HEALTH SAFETY & COM-
PENSATION COMMISSION OF NEW-
FOUNDLAND AND LABRADOR**   p
429
148 FOREST RD UNIT 146, ST. JOHN'S,
NL, A1A 1E6
(709) 778-1000   SIC 6331

**WORKPLACE HEALTH, SAFETY & COM-
PENSATION COMMISSION OF NEW
BRUNSWICK**   p 416
1 PORTLAND ST, SAINT JOHN, NB, E2L
3X9
(506) 632-2200   SIC 6331

**WORKPLACE HEALTH, SAFETY & COM-
PENSATION COMMISSION OF NEW
BRUNSWICK**   p 416
3700 WESTFIELD RD, SAINT JOHN, NB,
E2M 5Z4
(506) 738-8411   SIC 8011

WORKPLACE RESOURCE   p 981
See HERMAN MILLER CANADA, INC

**WORKPLACE SAFETY & INSURANCE
BOARD, THE**   p 613
120 KING ST W, HAMILTON, ON, L8P 4V2
(800) 387-0750   SIC 6331

**WORKPLACE SAFETY & INSURANCE
BOARD, THE**   p 639
55 KING ST W SUITE 502, KITCHENER,
ON, N2G 4W1
(800) 387-0750   SIC 6331

**WORKPLACE SAFETY & INSURANCE
BOARD, THE**   p 655
148 FULLARTON ST SUITE 402, LONDON,

ON, N6A 5P3
(800) 387-0750   SIC 6331

**WORKPLACE SAFETY & INSURANCE
BOARD, THE**   p 824
180 KENT ST SUITE 400, OTTAWA, ON,
K1P 0B6
(416) 344-1000   SIC 6331

**WORKPLACE SAFETY & INSURANCE
BOARD, THE**   p 901
30 CEDAR ST, SUDBURY, ON, P3E 1A4
(705) 677-4260   SIC 6331

**WORKPLACE SAFETY & INSURANCE
BOARD, THE**   p 985
200 FRONT ST W SUITE 101, TORONTO,
ON, M5V 3J1
(416) 344-1000   SIC 6331

**WORKPLACE SAFETY & INSURANCE
BOARD, THE**   p 1022
2485 OUELLETTE AVE, WINDSOR, ON,
N8X 1L5
(800) 387-0750   SIC 6331

**WORKPLACE SAFETY & PREVENTION
SERVICES**   p 702
5110 CREEKBANK RD SUITE 300, MISSIS-
SAUGA, ON, L4W 0A1
(905) 614-1400   SIC 8748

WORKPLACE SAFETY NORTH   p 764
690 MCKEOWN AVE, NORTH BAY, ON,
P1B 7M2
(705) 474-7233   SIC 6331

WORKSAFE BC   p 235
See WORKERS' COMPENSATION BOARD
OF BRITISH COLUMBIA

WORKSAFE BC   p 266
See WORKERS' COMPENSATION BOARD
OF BRITISH COLUMBIA

WORKSAFE NOVA SCOTIA   p 454
See WORKERS COMPENSATION BOARD
OF NOVA SCOTIA

WORKSAFEBC   p 266
6951 WESTMINSTER HWY SUITE 600,
RICHMOND, BC, V7C 1C6
(604) 231-8888   SIC 6331

WORKSHOPX INC   p 828
6 HAMILTON AVE N SUITE 004, OTTAWA,
ON, K1Y 4R1
(613) 860-7000   SIC 8731

WORLD AUTO PARTS (CANADA) LTD   p 589
355 CARLINGVIEW DR UNIT 1, ETOBI-
COKE, ON, M9W 5G8
(416) 675-6750   SIC 5511

WORLD AUTOMOTIVE WAREHOUSE   p 589
See WORLD AUTO PARTS (CANADA) LTD

WORLD AVIATION CORP   p 561
45 CORSTATE AVE, CONCORD, ON, L4K
4Y2
(905) 660-4462   SIC 7694

WORLD FAMOUS SALES OF CANADA INC   p 561
333 CONFEDERATION PKY SUITE 1,
CONCORD, ON, L4K 4S1
(905) 738-4777   SIC 5091

**WORLD FINANCIAL GROUP INSURANCE
AGENCY OF CANADA INC**   p 773
5000 YONGE ST SUITE 800, NORTH
YORK, ON, M2N 7E9
SIC 6311

WORLD HEALTH CLUB   p 71
See INTERNATIONAL FITNESS HOLD-
INGS INC

WORLD INSURANCE SERVICES LTD   p 262
7100 RIVER RD UNIT 2, RICHMOND, BC,
V6X 1X5
SIC 6411

WORLD LINK FOOD DISTRIBUTORS INC   p 450
209 AEROTECH DR UNIT 10-12B, GOFFS,
NS, B2T 1K3
(902) 423-0787   SIC 5146

WORLD MEATS INC   p 718
2255 DUNWIN DR UNIT 1, MISSISSAUGA,
ON, L5L 1A3
(905) 569-0559   SIC 5147

WORLD OF WATER   p 372
See DEWPOINT BOTTLING COMPANY
LTD

**WORLD POND HOCKEY CHAMPIONSHIP
INC**   p 411
159 MAIN ST, PLASTER ROCK, NB, E7G
2H2
(506) 356-6070   SIC 7941

WORLD SOURCE FILTRATION INC   p 861
321 QUEEN ST SUITE 1, SARNIA, ON, N7T
2S3
(519) 383-7771   SIC 5085

WORLD TECHNOLOGY GROUP INC   p 702
1660 TECH AVE SUITE 2, MISSISSAUGA,
ON, L4W 5S7
(905) 678-7588   SIC 6712

WORLD TRADE GROUP   p 936
See WORLD TRADE GROUP (NORTH
AMERICA) INC

**WORLD TRADE GROUP (NORTH AMER-
ICA) INC**   p
936
211 YONGE ST, TORONTO, ON, M5B 1M4
(416) 214-3400   SIC 7389

WORLD TRAVEL PROTECTION   p 985
See WORLD TRAVEL PROTECTION
CANADA INC

**WORLD TRAVEL PROTECTION CANADA
INC**   p 985
901 KING ST W SUITE 300, TORONTO,
ON, M5V 3H5
(416) 205-4618   SIC 6411

WORLD VISION CANADA   p 744
1 WORLD DR SUITE 2500, MISSISSAUGA,
ON, L5T 2Y4
(905) 565-6100   SIC 8322

WORLD WIDE CARRIERS LTD   p 496
124 COMMERCIAL RD, BOLTON, ON, L7E
1K4
(416) 213-1334   SIC 4213

WORLD WIDE CUSTOMS BROKERS LTD   p 63
GD LCD 1, CALGARY, AB, T2P 2G8
(403) 538-3199   SIC 4731

WORLD WIDE CUSTOMS BROKERS LTD   p 77
10710 25 ST NE UNIT 133, CALGARY, AB,
T3N 0A1
(403) 291-2543   SIC 4731

WORLD WIDE ENTERPRISES LIMITED   p 325
10991 SHELLBRIDGE WAY STE 490, VAN-
COUVER, BC, V6X 3C6
SIC 5961

WORLD WIDE IOZZA LTD   p 589
240 HUMBERLINE DR SUITE D, ETOBI-
COKE, ON, M9W 5X1
(416) 675-1930   SIC 5131

WORLD WIDE LOGISTICS INC   p 1002
330 NEW HUNTINGTON RD SUITE 101,
VAUGHAN, ON, L4H 4C9
(416) 213-9522   SIC 4731

WORLD WIDE SHORE SERVICES   p 305
See HOLLAND AMERICA LINE

WORLD WIDE WARRANTY INC   p 342
1455 BELLEVUE AVE SUITE 300, WEST
VANCOUVER, BC, V7T 1C3
(604) 922-0305   SIC 6351

WORLD WILDLIFE FUND CANADA   p 985
410 ADELAIDE ST W SUITE 400,
TORONTO, ON, M5V 1S8
(416) 489-8800   SIC 8699

WORLD WONDERS   p 1010
See MCM GROUP LTD

**WORLD'S FINEST CHOCOLATE CANADA
COMPANY**   p 539
See 3059714 NOVA SCOTIA COMPANY

WORLDLINE;295.CA   p 538
See FIBERNETICS CORPORATION

WORLDMARK AT VICTORIA   p 336
120 KINGSTON ST, VICTORIA, BC, V8V
1V4
(250) 386-8555   SIC 7389

WORLDPAC CANADA INC   p 744

6956 COLUMBUS RD, MISSISSAUGA, ON, L5T 2G1
(905) 238-9390 *SIC* 5013
WORLDSOURCE FINANCIAL MANAGEMENT INC *p*
677
625 COCHRANE DR SUITE 700, MARKHAM, ON, L3R 9R9
(905) 940-0044 *SIC* 6282
WORLDSOURCE SECURITIES INC *p* 677
625 COCHRANE DR SUITE 700, MARKHAM, ON, L3R 9R9
(905) 940-0094 *SIC* 8748
WORLDSOURCE WEALTH MANAGEMENT INC *p* 677
625 COCHRANE DR SUITE 700, MARKHAM, ON, L3R 9R9
(905) 940-5500 *SIC* 8741
WORLDWIDE DISTRIBUTORS *p* 560
See U-BUY DISCOUNT FOODS LIMITED
WORLDWIDE EVANGELIZATION FOR CHRIST *p* 613
37 ABERDEEN AVE, HAMILTON, ON, L8P 2N6
(905) 529-0166 *SIC* 7389
WORLDWIDE FLIGHT SERVICES LTD *p* 1154
11955 RUE HENRY-GIFFARD SUITE 200, MIRABEL, QC, J7N 1G3
(450) 476-9248 *SIC* 4731
WORLDWIDE MATTRESS OUTLET *p* 1019
See WORLDWIDE SLEEP CENTRE LIMITED
WORLDWIDE SLEEP CENTRE LIMITED *p* 1019
2525 JEFFERSON BLVD, WINDSOR, ON, N8T 2W5
(519) 944-3552 *SIC* 5712
WORLEE INTERNATIONAL INC *p* 1342
750 RUE GOUGEON, SAINT-LAURENT, QC, H4T 4L5
(514) 332-6455 *SIC* 5149
WORLEY CANADA SERVICES LTD *p* 38
8500 MACLEOD TRAIL SE, CALGARY, AB, T2H 2N1
(403) 258-8000 *SIC* 8711
WORLEYCORD LP *p* 38
8500 MACLEOD TRAIL SE SUITE 400, CALGARY, AB, T2H 2N1
(780) 465-5516 *SIC* 1629
WORLEYCORD LP *p* 124
2455 130 AVE NE, EDMONTON, AB, T6S 0A4
(780) 440-6942 *SIC* 1623
WORLEYPARSONS EDMONTON *p* 117
See WORLEYPARSONSCORD LP
WORLEYPARSONSCORD LP *p* 66
540 12 AVE SW, CALGARY, AB, T2R 0H4
SIC 8711
WORLEYPARSONSCORD LP *p* 111
9405 50 ST NW SUITE 101, EDMONTON, AB, T6B 2T4
(780) 440-8100 *SIC* 8711
WORLEYPARSONSCORD LP *p* 117
5008 86 ST NW SUITE 120, EDMONTON, AB, T6E 5S2
(780) 440-5300 *SIC* 8711
WORLEYPARSONSCORD LP *p* 124
See WORLEYCORD LP
WORLEYPARSONSCORD LP *p* 187
4321 STILL CREEK DR SUITE 600, BURNABY, BC, V5C 6S7
(604) 298-1616 *SIC* 8711
WORLEYPARSONSCORD LP *p* 240
233 1ST ST W, NORTH VANCOUVER, BC, V7M 1B3
SIC 8711
WORLEYPARSONSCORD LP *p* 702
2645 SKYMARK AVE, MISSISSAUGA, ON, L4W 4H2
(905) 940-4774 *SIC* 8711
WORLEYPARSONSCORD LP *p* 859
1086 MODELAND RD BLDG 1050, SARNIA, ON, N7S 6L2

(519) 332-0160 *SIC* 8742
WORLEYPARSONSCORD LP *p* 1000
8133 WARDEN AVE, UNIONVILLE, ON, L6G 1B3
(905) 940-4774 *SIC* 8711
WORTH PERSONNEL LTD *p* 813
219 WENTWORTH ST E, OSHAWA, ON, L1H 3V7
(905) 725-5544 *SIC* 8741
WORX ENVIRONMENTAL PRODUCTS OF CANADA INC *p* 19
2305 52 AVE SE UNIT 10, CALGARY, AB, T2C 4X7
(403) 538-0203 *SIC* 5169
WOTHERSPOON, DON & ASSOCIATES LTD *p* 187
4634 HASTINGS ST SUITE 101, BURNABY, BC, V5C 2K5
(604) 294-3242 *SIC* 6411
WOW UNLIMITED MEDIA INC *p* 322
2025 BROADWAY W SUITE 200, VANCOUVER, BC, V6J 1Z6
(604) 714-2600 *SIC* 7812
WOWU FACTOR DESSERTS LTD *p* 161
152 CREE RD, SHERWOOD PARK, AB, T8A 3X8
(780) 464-0303 *SIC* 2053
WPK *p* 386
See WINPAK LTD
WPP *p* 543
See WALLACEBURG PREFERRED PARTNERS CORP
WPP GROUP CANADA COMMUNICATIONS LIMITED *p* 931
160 BLOOR ST E SUITE 800, TORONTO, ON, M4W 1B9
(416) 987-5121 *SIC* 8743
WPP GROUP CANADA COMMUNICATIONS LIMITED *p* 943
33 YONGE ST, TORONTO, ON, M5E 1X6
(416) 367-3573 *SIC* 7311
WPP GROUP CANADA COMMUNICATIONS LIMITED *p* 943
33 YONGE ST SUITE 1100, TORONTO, ON, M5E 1X6
(416) 367-3573 *SIC* 7311
WPSL SECURITY SOLUTIONS *p* 903
See 2521153 ONTARIO INC
WPT INDUSTRIAL REAL ESTATE INVESTMENT TRUST *p* 971
199 BAY ST SUITE 4000, TORONTO, ON, M5L 1A9
(800) 230-9505 *SIC* 6021
WPW INC *p* 140
GD, LESLIEVILLE, AB, T0M 1H0
(403) 729-3007 *SIC* 1623
WR DISPLAY & PACKAGING *p* 374
See WESTERN REPAIR & SALES INC
WRANGLER RENTALS LTD *p* 140
3911 ALLARD AVE, LEDUC, AB, T9E 0R8
(780) 980-1331 *SIC* 7359
WRANK ENTERPRISES LTD *p* 1026
3920 DOUGALL AVE, WINDSOR, ON, N9G 1X2
(519) 966-3650 *SIC* 5531
WRAP-IT-UP INC *p* 918
660 EGLINTON AVE E, TORONTO, ON, M4G 2K2
SIC 5947
WRD BORGER CONSTRUCTION LTD *p* 160
261046 HIGH PLAINS BLVD, ROCKY VIEW COUNTY, AB, T4A 3L3
(403) 279-7235 *SIC* 1623
WRIGHT AUTO SALES INC *p* 1007
35 WEBER ST N, WATERLOO, ON, N2J 3G5
(519) 742-5622 *SIC* 5521
WRIGHT CONSTRUCTION WESTERN INC *p* 1430
2919 CLEVELAND AVE, SASKATOON, SK,

S7K 8A9
(306) 934-0440 *SIC* 1542
WRIGHT INTERNATIONAL AIRCRAFT MAINTENANCE SERVICES INC *p* 690
3182 ORLANDO DR SUITE 14, MISSISSAUGA, ON, L4V 1R5
(905) 677-6393 *SIC* 4581
WRIGHT, GEORGE A. & SON (TORONTO) LIMITED *p* 877
21 STATE CROWN BLVD, SCARBOROUGH, ON, M1V 4B1
(416) 261-6499 *SIC* 3599
WRIGHT, HAL CHEVROLET CADILLAC *p* 836
See OWEN SOUND MOTORS LIMITED
WRIGLEY CANADA INC *p* 766
3389 STEELES AVE E, NORTH YORK, ON, M2H 3S8
(416) 449-8600 *SIC* 2067
WSB TITAN INC *p* 1029
50 ROYAL GROUP CRES UNIT 2, WOODBRIDGE, ON, L4H 1X9
(905) 669-1898 *SIC* 8741
WSB TITAN, DIV OF *p* 268
See SLEGG LIMITED PARTNERSHIP
WSI *p* 702
See WORLD TECHNOLOGY GROUP INC
WSI INTERNET CONSULTING & EDUCATION *p* 587
See RESEARCH AND MANAGEMENT CORPORATION
WSI MANUFACTURING *p* 91
See WHOLESALE STONE INDUSTRIES INC
WSI SIGN SYSTEMS LTD *p* 496
31 SIMPSON RD, BOLTON, ON, L7E 2R6
(905) 857-8044 *SIC* 3993
WSIB *p* 613
See WORKPLACE SAFETY & INSURANCE BOARD, THE
WSIB *p* 655
See WORKPLACE SAFETY & INSURANCE BOARD, THE
WSIB *p* 824
See WORKPLACE SAFETY & INSURANCE BOARD, THE
WSIB *p* 985
See WORKPLACE SAFETY & INSURANCE BOARD, THE
WSIB *p* 1022
See WORKPLACE SAFETY & INSURANCE BOARD, THE
WSP *p* 242
889 HARBOURSIDE DR SUITE 210, NORTH VANCOUVER, BC, V7P 3S1
(604) 990-4800 *SIC* 8748
WSP GLOBALE *p* 1389
See WSP CANADA INC
WSP CANADA GROUP LIMITED *p* 327
1000-840 HOWE ST, VANCOUVER, BC, V6Z 2M1
(604) 685-9381 *SIC* 8711
WSP CANADA GROUP LIMITED *p* 905
100 COMMERCE VALLEY DR W, THORNHILL, ON, L3T 0A1
(905) 882-1100 *SIC* 8711
WSP CANADA INC *p* 63
112 4 AVE SW SUITE 1000, CALGARY, AB, T2P 0H3
(403) 266-2800 *SIC* 1382
WSP CANADA INC *p* 63
717 7 AVE SW SUITE 1800, CALGARY, AB, T2P 0Z3
(403) 263-8200 *SIC* 8713
WSP CANADA INC *p* 92
9925 109 ST NW SUITE 1000, EDMONTON, AB, T5K 2J8
(780) 466-6555 *SIC* 8713
WSP CANADA INC *p* 163
2693 BROADMOOR BLVD SUITE 132, SHERWOOD PARK, AB, T8H 0G1
(780) 410-6740 *SIC* 8711
WSP CANADA INC *p* 214

10716 100 AVE, FORT ST. JOHN, BC, V1J 1Z3
(250) 787-0300 *SIC* 8713
WSP CANADA INC *p* 677
600 COCHRANE DR FLOOR 5, MARKHAM, ON, L3R 5K3
(905) 475-8727 *SIC* 7363
WSP CANADA INC *p* 677
600 COCHRANE DR SUITE 500, MARKHAM, ON, L3R 5K3
(905) 475-7270 *SIC* 8711
WSP CANADA INC *p* 830
2611 QUEENSVIEW DR SUITE 300, OTTAWA, ON, K2B 8K2
(613) 829-2800 *SIC* 8711
WSP CANADA INC *p* 909
1269 PREMIER WAY, THUNDER BAY, ON, P7B 0A3
(807) 625-6700 *SIC* 8711
WSP CANADA INC *p* 1087
2525 BOUL DANIEL-JOHNSON BUREAU 525, COTE SAINT-LUC, QC, H7T 1S9
(450) 686-0980 *SIC* 8711
WSP CANADA INC *p* 1215
1600 BOUL RENE-LEVESQUE O 16E ETAGE, MONTREAL, QC, H3H 1P9
(514) 340-0046 *SIC* 6712
WSP CANADA INC *p* 1389
3450 BOUL GENE-H.-KRUGER BUREAU 300, TROIS-RIVIERES, QC, G9A 4M3
(819) 375-1292 *SIC* 8711
WULFTEC INTERNATIONAL INC *p* 1052
209 RUE WULFTEC, AYER'S CLIFF, QC, J0B 1C0
(819) 838-4232 *SIC* 5084
WURTH CANADA LIMITED *p* 600
345 HANLON CREEK BLVD, GUELPH, ON, N1C 0A1
(905) 564-6225 *SIC* 5085
WW CANADA LTD *p* 799
1415 JOSHUAS CREEK DR UNIT 200, OAKVILLE, ON, L6H 7G4
(800) 387-8227 *SIC* 8099
WW HOTELS (WHISTLER) LIMITED PARTNERSHIP *p* 343
4050 WHISTLER WAY, WHISTLER, BC, V8E 1H9
(604) 932-1982 *SIC* 7011
WW HOTELS CORP *p* 702
5090 EXPLORER DR SUITE 700, MISSISSAUGA, ON, L4W 4T9
(905) 624-9720 *SIC* 8741
WW HOTELS CORP *p* 769
55 HALLCROWN PL, NORTH YORK, ON, M2J 4R1
(416) 493-7000 *SIC* 7011
WWF - CANADA *p* 985
See WORLD WILDLIFE FUND CANADA
WWG TOTALLINE *p* 734
See CARRIER ENTERPRISE CANADA, L.P.
WWL VEHICLE SERVICES CANADA LTD *p* 207
820 DOCK RD UNIT 100, DELTA, BC, V3M 6A3
(604) 521-6681 *SIC* 4013
WWW.PROCESSIA.COM *p* 1087
See SOLUTIONS PROCESSIA INC
WWW.RANGEMENTDOUTILS.COM *p* 1097
See SPG INTERNATIONAL LTEE
WYATT INSURANCE & FINANCIAL *p* 363
See WYATT NU TREND INSURANCE AGENCY LTD
WYATT NU TREND INSURANCE AGENCY LTD *p* 363
138 REGENT AVE W, WINNIPEG, MB, R2C 1P9
(204) 222-3221 *SIC* 6411
WYCLIFFE BIBLE TRANSLATORS OF CANADA INC *p* 26
4316 10 ST NE, CALGARY, AB, T2E 6K3
(403) 250-5411 *SIC* 7389
WYCLIFFE CANADA *p* 26
See WYCLIFFE BIBLE TRANSLATORS OF

CANADA INC

WYMAN, JASPER & SON CANADA INC *p* 1042
41 MCQUIN RD, MORELL, PE, C0A 1S0
(902) 961-3330   *SIC* 5142

WYNDHAM MANOR LONG-TERM CARE CENTRE *p* 800
See *EXTENDICARE INC*

WYNDHAM WORLDWIDE CANADA INC *p* 416
180 CROWN ST SUITE 200, SAINT JOHN, NB, E2L 2X7
(506) 646-2700   *SIC* 4899

WYNFORD GROUP INC, THE *p* 778
101 DUNCAN MILL RD SUITE 500, NORTH YORK, ON, M3B 1Z3
(416) 443-9696   *SIC* 4724

WYNFORD TRAVEL SERVICES *p* 778
See *WYNFORD GROUP INC, THE*

WYNN PARK VILLA LIMITED *p* 469
32 WINDSOR WAY, TRURO, NS, B2N 0B4
(902) 843-3939   *SIC* 8361

WYNNDEL BOX & LUMBER COMPANY LTD *p* 344
1140 WINLAW RD, WYNNDEL, BC, V0B 2N1
(250) 866-5231   *SIC* 2421

WYNWARD INSURANCE GROUP *p* 376
1 LOMBARD PL SUITE 1240, WINNIPEG, MB, R3B 0V9
(204) 943-0721   *SIC* 6331

WYNYARD HOSPITAL *p* 1438
300 10 ST E, WYNYARD, SK, S0A 4T0
(306) 554-2586   *SIC* 8062

WYNYARD INTEGRATED HOSPITAL *p* 1438
See *WYNYARD HOSPITAL*

WYSDOM.AI *p* 851
See *CROWDCARE CORPORATION*

WZMH ARCHITECTS *p* 927
95 ST CLAIR AVE W SUITE 1500, TORONTO, ON, M4V 1N6
(416) 961-4111   *SIC* 8712

X

X O TOURS CANADA LTD *p* 322
1788 BROADWAY W UNIT 600, VANCOUVER, BC, V6J 1Y1
(604) 738-6188   *SIC* 4725

X-ACT TECHNOLOGIES LTD *p* 13
4447 46 AVE SE SUITE 151, CALGARY, AB, T2B 3N6
(403) 291-9175   *SIC* 3496

X-CALIBUR GROUND DISTURBANCE SOLUTIONS *p* 159
See *X-CALIBUR PIPELINE AND UTILITY LOCATION INC*

X-CALIBUR PIPELINE AND UTILITY LOCATION INC *p* 159
4407 45A AVE, ROCKY MOUNTAIN HOUSE, AB, T4T 1T1
(403) 844-8662   *SIC* 1389

X-L-AIR ENERGY SERVICES LTD *p* 541
141 WESCAR LANE, CARP, ON, K0A 1L0
(613) 836-5002   *SIC* 1711

XACT DOWNHOLE TELEMETRY INC *p* 26
906 55 AVE NE, CALGARY, AB, T2E 6Y4
(403) 568-6010   *SIC* 1389

XANA INTERNATIONAL INC *p* 856
55 ADMINISTRATION RD UNITS 33 & 34, RICHMOND HILL, ON, L4K 4G9
(416) 477-4770   *SIC* 1542

XCEL FABRICATION & DESIGN LTD *p* 912
24 CLEARVIEW DR, TILLSONBURG, ON, N4G 4G8
(519) 688-3193   *SIC* 3441

XCG CONSULTING LIMITED *p* 800
2620 BRISTOL CIR SUITE 300, OAKVILLE, ON, L6H 6Z7
(905) 829-8880   *SIC* 8748

XDG CONSTRUCTION LIMITED *p* 518
250 WOOLWICH ST S, BRESLAU, ON, N0B 1M0
(519) 648-2121   *SIC* 1542

XE CORPORATION *p* 757
1145 NICHOLSON RD SUITE 200, NEWMARKET, ON, L3Y 9C3
(416) 214-5606   *SIC* 6712

XE.COM *p* 757
See *XE CORPORATION*

XEBEC *p* 1058
See *9183-7252 QUEBEC INC*

XEBEC ADSORPTION INC *p* 1060
730 BOUL INDUSTRIEL, BLAINVILLE, QC, J7C 3V4
(450) 979-8700   *SIC* 3567

XENALI CORPORATE FURNISHINGS *p* 104
See *XENALI INC*

XENALI INC *p* 104
11430 170 ST NW, EDMONTON, AB, T5S 1L7
(780) 487-6669   *SIC* 5021

XENON PHARMACEUTICALS INC *p* 189
3650 GILMORE WAY, BURNABY, BC, V5G 4W8
(604) 484-3300   *SIC* 8731

XENTEX TRADING INC *p* 702
5960 SHAWSON DR, MISSISSAUGA, ON, L4W 3W5
(905) 696-9329   *SIC* 5199

XERIUM CANADA INC *p* 460
650 PARK ST, KENTVILLE, NS, B4N 3W6
(902) 678-7311   *SIC* 2211

XEROX *p* 317
See *XEROX CANADA LTD*

XEROX CANADA INC *p* 91
10180 101 ST NW SUITE 1350, EDMONTON, AB, T5J 3S4
(780) 493-7800   *SIC* 5044

XEROX CANADA INC *p* 715
2660 SPEAKMAN DR, MISSISSAUGA, ON, L5K 2L1
(905) 823-7091   *SIC* 8731

XEROX CANADA INC *p* 775
20 YORK MILLS RD 5TH FLR, NORTH YORK, ON, M2P 2C2
(416) 229-3769   *SIC* 5044

XEROX CANADA LTD *p* 74
37 RICHARD WAY SW SUITE 200, CALGARY, AB, T3E 7M8
(403) 260-8800   *SIC* 5044

XEROX CANADA LTD *p* 317
1055 GEORGIA ST W, VANCOUVER, BC, V6E 0B6
(604) 668-2300   *SIC* 5044

XEROX CANADA LTD *p* 392
895 WAVERLEY ST, WINNIPEG, MB, R3T 5P4
(204) 488-5100   *SIC* 5044

XEROX CANADA LTD *p* 449
215-237 BROWNLOW AVE, DARTMOUTH, NS, B3B 2C6
(902) 470-3000   *SIC* 5044

XEROX CANADA LTD *p* 690
3060 CARAVELLE DR, MISSISSAUGA, ON, L4V 1L7
(905) 672-4700   *SIC* 7374

XEROX CANADA LTD *p* 690
5925 AIRPORT RD, MISSISSAUGA, ON, L4V 1W1
SIC 5044

XEROX CANADA LTD *p* 690
6800 NORTHWEST DR, MISSISSAUGA, ON, L4V 1Z1
(905) 672-4700   *SIC* 5044

XEROX CANADA LTD *p* 690
6800 NORTHWEST DR, MISSISSAUGA, ON, L4V 1Z1
(905) 672-4709   *SIC* 5044

XEROX CANADA LTD *p* 775
20 YORK MILLS RD SUITE 500, NORTH YORK, ON, M2P 2C2
(416) 733-6501   *SIC* 5999

XEROX CANADA LTD *p* 826
333 PRESTON ST SUITE 1000, OTTAWA, ON, K1S 5N4
(613) 230-1002   *SIC* 5044

XEROX CANADA LTD *p* 931
33 BLOOR ST E, TORONTO, ON, M4W 3H1
(416) 921-0210   *SIC* 5044

XEROX CANADA LTD *p* 1221
3400 BOUL DE MAISONNEUVE O BUREAU 900, MONTREAL, QC, H3Z 3G1
(514) 939-3769   *SIC* 5044

XEROX RESEARCH CENTRE OF CDA *p* 715
See *XEROX CANADA INC*

XEVA MORTGAGE *p* 342
1455 BELLEVUE AVE SUITE 213, WEST VANCOUVER, BC, V7T 1C3
SIC 6163

XIBITA *p* 256
See *PORTABLES EXHIBIT SYSTEMS LIMITED, THE*

XL ELECTRIC LIMITED *p* 449
118 CUTLER AVE, DARTMOUTH, NS, B3B 0J6
(902) 468-7708   *SIC* 1731

XL FOODS *p* 35
See *JBS CANADA INC*

XL IRONWORKS *p* 278
12720 82 AVE, SURREY, BC, V3W 3G1
(604) 596-1747   *SIC* 1791

XLR8 MEDIA INC *p* 1186
3575 BOUL SAINT-LAURENT BUREAU 400, MONTREAL, QC, H2X 2T7
(514) 286-9000   *SIC* 7311

XLTEK *p* 797
See *EXCEL-TECH LTD*

XMARK CORPORATION *p* 625
309 LEGGET DR SUITE 100, KANATA, ON, K2K 3A3
(613) 592-6997   *SIC* 3679

XMC *p* 980
See *EXPERIENTIAL MARKETING LIMITED PARTNERSHIP*

XMETAL *p* 1121
See *9091-4532 QUEBEC INC*

XN RISK *p* 1199
See *SERVICES FINANCIERS XN (CANADA) INC*

XPEDX CANADA, INC *p* 507
156 PARKSHORE DR, BRAMPTON, ON, L6T 5M1
(905) 595-4351   *SIC* 5111

XPEDX STORE *p* 507
See *XPEDX CANADA, INC*

XPERA RISK MITIGATION & INVESTIGATION LP *p* 766
155 GORDON BAKER RD SUITE 101, NORTH YORK, ON, M2H 3N5
(416) 449-8677   *SIC* 8741

XPLORNET *p* 420
See *XPLORNET COMMUNICATIONS INC*

XPLORNET COMMUNICATIONS INC *p* 347
5 GRANITE RD, BRANDON, MB, R7A 7V2
(204) 578-7840   *SIC* 4813

XPLORNET COMMUNICATIONS INC *p* 367
275 DE BAETS ST SUITE 4, WINNIPEG, MB, R2J 4A8
(204) 669-7007   *SIC* 4813

XPLORNET COMMUNICATIONS INC *p* 420
300 LOCKHART MILL RD, WOODSTOCK, NB, E7M 6B5
(506) 328-8853   *SIC* 4813

XPLORNET LIMITED *p* 404
300 LOCKHART MILL RD, JACKSONVILLE, NB, E7M 5C3
(506) 328-1274   *SIC* 4813

XPO LOGISTICS FREIGHT CANADA INC *p* 702
5425 DIXIE RD ROOM 202, MISSISSAUGA, ON, L4W 1E6
(905) 602-9477   *SIC* 4213

XPRESS FOOD AND GAS (MOOSE JAW) LTD *p* 1437
1510 SOUTH SERVICE RD W, SWIFT CURRENT, SK, S9H 3T1
(306) 773-6444   *SIC* 5541

XPV WATER PARTNERS INC *p* 968
40 UNIVERSITY AVE SUITE 801, TORONTO, ON, M5J 1T1
(416) 581-8850   *SIC* 6351

XSEALENT SEAFOOD COMPANY *p* 439
See *GERRET ENTERPRISES INCORPORATED*

XSTREAM SOFTWARE INC *p* 819
2280 ST. LAURENT BLVD SUITE 101, OTTAWA, ON, K1G 4K1
(613) 731-9443   *SIC* 7371

XTC-COM *p* 830
See *1043133 ONTARIO INC*

XTECH EXPLOSIVE DECONTAMINATION INC *p* 151
900 VILLAGE LANE SUITE 14, OKOTOKS, AB, T1S 1Z6
(403) 938-3883   *SIC* 5169

XTL TRANSPORT INC *p* 589
75 REXDALE BLVD, ETOBICOKE, ON, M9W 1P1
(416) 742-0610   *SIC* 4213

XTOWN MOTORS LP *p* 106
15520 123 AVE NW, EDMONTON, AB, T5V 1K8
(780) 488-4881   *SIC* 5511

XTREME DRILLING CORP *p* 63
333 7TH AVE SW SUITE 1000, CALGARY, AB, T2P 2Z1
(403) 292-7979   *SIC* 1381

XTREME OILFIELD TECHNOLOGY LTD *p* 165
4905 50 AVE, ST PAUL, AB, T0A 3A0
(780) 645-5979   *SIC* 1389

XTRUX INC *p* 744
6175 KENWAY DR, MISSISSAUGA, ON, L5T 2L3
(905) 362-1277   *SIC* 4731

XWAVE, DIV OF *p* 452
See *BELL ALIANT REGIONAL COMMUNICATIONS, LIMITED PARTNERSHIP*

XYLEM APPLIED WATER SYSTEMS *p* 604
See *SOCIETE XYLEM CANADA*

XYLEM APPLIED WATER SYSTEMS *p* 1252
See *SOCIETE XYLEM CANADA*

XYNYTH MANUFACTURING CORP *p* 187
3989 HENNING DR UNIT 122, BURNABY, BC, V5C 6P8
(604) 473-9343   *SIC* 2899

XYZ TECHNOLOGIE CULTURELLE INC *p* 1172
5700 RUE FULLUM, MONTREAL, QC, H2G 2H7
(514) 340-7717   *SIC* 8999

Y

Y DES FEMMES *p* 1212
See *ASSOCIATION CHRETIENNE DES JEUNES FEMMES DE MONTREAL*

Y FIRM MANAGEMENT INC *p* 997
2700-130 KING ST, TORONTO, ON, M9N 1L5
(416) 860-8370   *SIC* 8741

Y M C A *p* 126
See *CALGARY YOUNG MEN'S CHRISTIAN ASSOCIATION*

Y M C A CALGARY *p* 45
See *CALGARY YOUNG MEN'S CHRISTIAN ASSOCIATION, THE*

Y M C OF NIAGARA *p* 760
See *YOUNG MENS CHRISTIAN ASSOCIATION*

Y W C A *p* 311
See *YOUNG WOMEN'S CHRISTIAN ASSOCIATION*

Y.W.C.A QUEBEC *p* 1270
See *ASSOCIATION YWCA DE QUEBEC, L'*

YAK COMMUNICATIONS INC *p* 944
48 YONGE ST SUITE 1202, TORONTO, ON, M5E 1G6
(800) 490-7235   *SIC* 4899

YALE INDUSTRIAL TRUCKS INC *p* 1034
340 HANLAN RD, WOODBRIDGE, ON, L4L 3P6
(905) 851-6620   *SIC* 5084

YALE SECONDARY SCHOOL p 175
See SCHOOL DISTRICT NO 34 (ABBOTS-FORD)
YALETOWN HOUSE SOCIETY p 301
1099 CAMBIE ST, VANCOUVER, BC, V6B 5A8
(604) 689-0022 *SIC 8051*
YAMACO p 1403
See 9138-9494 QUEBEC INC
YAMAHA CANADA MUSIC LTD p 875
135 MILNER AVE, SCARBOROUGH, ON, M1S 3R1
(416) 298-1311 *SIC 5099*
YAMAHA MOTOR CANADA LTD p 766
480 GORDON BAKER RD, NORTH YORK, ON, M2H 3B4
(416) 498-1911 *SIC 5091*
YAMANA GOLD INC p 968
200 BAY ST ROYAL BANK PLAZA NORTH TOWER STE 2200, TORONTO, ON, M5J 2J3
(416) 815-0220 *SIC 1041*
YAMATECH SCIENTIFIC LTD p 1083
5568 AV KING-EDWARD, COTE SAINT-LUC, QC, H4V 2K4
(514) 737-5434 *SIC 5045*
YAMATECH Y C S p 1083
See YAMATECH SCIENTIFIC LTD
YANCH HEATING AND AIR CONDITIONING (BARRIE) LIMITED p 489
89 RAWSON AVE, BARRIE, ON, L4N 6E5
(705) 728-5406 *SIC 1711*
YANGARRA RESOURCES LTD p 63
715 5 AVE SW SUITE 1530, CALGARY, AB, T2P 2X6
(403) 262-9558 *SIC 1311*
YANJACO INC p 1395
435 BOUL HARWOOD, VAUDREUIL-DORION, QC, J7V 7W1
(450) 455-3336 *SIC 5812*
YANKE GROUP OF COMPANIES p 1432
See N. YANKE TRANSFER LTD
YAO SUN LOONG KONG CHICKEN LTD p 257
2391 VAUXHALL PL, RICHMOND, BC, V6V 1Z5
SIC 0259
YARA BELLE PLAINE INC p 1404
2 KALIUM RD, BELLE PLAINE, SK, S0G 0G0
(306) 345-4200 *SIC 2874*
YARA BELLE PLAINE INC p 1419
1874 SCARTH ST SUITE 1800, REGINA, SK, S4P 4B3
(306) 525-7600 *SIC 2874*
YARA CANADA INC p 1419
1874 SCARTH ST SUITE 1800, REGINA, SK, S4P 4B3
(306) 525-7600 *SIC 5191*
YARDI SYSTEMS p 690
5925 AIRPORT RD SUITE 605, MISSISSAUGA, ON, L4V 1W1
(905) 671-0315 *SIC 7372*
YARMOUTH ASSOCIATION FOR COMMUNITY RESIDENTIAL OPTIONS p 449
1 GLOSTER CRT, DARTMOUTH, NS, B3B 1X9
(902) 832-0433 *SIC 8322*
YARMOUTH CRANE SERVICE p 890
See YARMOUTH GROUP INC, THE
YARMOUTH GROUP INC, THE p 890
9462 TOWER RD, ST THOMAS, ON, N5P 3S7
(519) 631-2663 *SIC 3499*
YARMOUTH MALL ADMINISTRATION p 471
See TOULON DEVELOPMENT CORPORATION
YARMOUTH SEA PRODUCTS LTD p 462
GD, METEGHAN, NS, B0W 2J0
(902) 645-2417 *SIC 5091*
YASKAWA CANADA INC p 718
3530 LAIRD RD UNIT 3, MISSISSAUGA, ON, L5L 5Z7

(905) 569-6686 *SIC 5084*
YATSEN GROUP INC p 677
7650 BIRCHMOUNT RD, MARKHAM, ON, L3R 6B9
(905) 474-0710 *SIC 5812*
YAYAA BUILDING MATERIALS p 511
See 9306609 CANADA INC
YCO CORPORATE INVESTMENTS LTD p 317
1040 GEORGIA ST W SUITE 1900, VANCOUVER, BC, V6E 4H3
(604) 689-1811 *SIC 6719*
YEE HONG p 678
See YEE HONG CENTRE FOR GERIATRIC CARE
YEE HONG p 877
See YEE HONG CENTRE FOR GERIATRIC CARE
YEE HONG CENTRE FOR GERIATRIC CARE p 678
2780 BUR OAK AVE, MARKHAM, ON, L6B 1C9
(905) 471-3232 *SIC 8059*
YEE HONG CENTRE FOR GERIATRIC CARE p 875
60 SCOTTFIELD DR SUITE 428, SCARBOROUGH, ON, M1S 5T7
(416) 321-3000 *SIC 8059*
YEE HONG CENTRE FOR GERIATRIC CARE p 877
2311 MCNICOLL AVE, SCARBOROUGH, ON, M1V 5L3
SIC 8051
YEE HONG CENTRE SCARBOROUGH FINCH p 875
See YEE HONG CENTRE FOR GERIATRIC CARE
YELLOW MEDIA p 1216
See PAGES JAUNES LIMITEE
YELLOW PAGES p 1396
See GROUPE PAGES JAUNES CORP
YELLOWHEAD HELICOPTERS LTD p 284
3010 SELWYN RD, VALEMOUNT, BC, V0E 2Z0
(250) 566-4401 *SIC 4522*
YELLOWHEAD MOTOR INN p 106
See YELLOWHEAD MOTOR INN LTD
YELLOWHEAD MOTOR INN LTD p 106
15004 YELLOWHEAD TRAIL NW, EDMONTON, AB, T5V 1A1
(780) 447-2400 *SIC 7011*
YELLOWHEAD PETROLEUM PRODUCTS LTD p 123
8901 20 ST NW, EDMONTON, AB, T6P 1K8
(780) 449-1171 *SIC 5171*
YELLOWHEAD ROAD & BRIDGE (KOOTENAY) LTD p 236
110 CEDAR ST, NELSON, BC, V1L 6H2
(250) 352-3242 *SIC 1611*
YELLOWKNIFE CATHOLIC SCHOOLS p 436
See YELLOWKNIFE PUBLIC DENOMINATIONAL DISTRICT EDUCATION AUTHORITY
YELLOWKNIFE CHRYSLER LTD p 436
340 OLD AIRPORT RD, YELLOWKNIFE, NT, X1A 3T3
(867) 873-4222 *SIC 5511*
YELLOWKNIFE DIRECT CHARGE COOPERATIVE LIMITED p 436
321 OLD AIRPORT RD, YELLOWKNIFE, NT, X1A 3T3
(867) 873-5770 *SIC 5411*
YELLOWKNIFE INN LTD p 436
5010 49TH ST, YELLOWKNIFE, NT, X1A 2N4
(867) 873-2601 *SIC 5812*
YELLOWKNIFE PUBLIC DENOMINATIONAL DISTRICT EDUCATION AUTHORITY p 436
5124 49 ST, YELLOWKNIFE, NT, X1A 1P8

(867) 766-7400 *SIC 8211*
YELLOWKNIFER, THE p 436
See NORTHERN NEWS SERVICES LTD
YEN BROS. FOOD SERVICE LTD p 296
1988 VERNON DR, VANCOUVER, BC, V6A 3Y6
(604) 255-6522 *SIC 5148*
YES ADVERTISING p 915
See YESUP ECOMMERCE SOLUTIONS INC
YESHIVA YESODEI HATORAH p 788
77 GLEN RUSH BLVD, NORTH YORK, ON, M5N 2T8
(416) 787-1101 *SIC 8211*
YESNABY INVESTMENTS LTD p 253
105 NORTH STAR RD, QUESNEL, BC, V2J 5K2
(250) 992-6868 *SIC 5812*
YESUP ECOMMERCE SOLUTIONS INC p 915
200 CONSUMERS RD SUITE 308, TORONTO, ON, M2J 4R4
(416) 499-8009 *SIC 8731*
YETMAN'S LTD p 373
949 JARVIS AVE, WINNIPEG, MB, R2X 0A1
(204) 586-8046 *SIC 5083*
YEUNG, GAYNOR C. LAW CORPORATION p 311
200 GRANVILLE ST SUITE 2400, VANCOUVER, BC, V6C 1S4
(604) 682-5466 *SIC 8111*
YGGDRASIL HOLDINGS LTD. p 324
4550 LANGARA AVE, VANCOUVER, BC, V6R 1C8
SIC 6712
YI JIA INTERNATIONAL GROUP (CANADA) LTD p 191
4720 KINGSWAY UNIT 2335, BURNABY, BC, V5H 4N2
(778) 379-0118 *SIC 6211*
YIKES ENTERPRISES LTD p 10
3508 32 AVE NE UNIT 500, CALGARY, AB, T1Y 6J2
(403) 291-2925 *SIC 5461*
YKK CANADA INC p 1331
3939 BOUL THIMENS, SAINT-LAURENT, QC, H4R 1X3
(514) 332-3350 *SIC 3965*
YM INC. (SALES) p 790
50 DUFFLAW RD SUITE 364, NORTH YORK, ON, M6A 2W1
(416) 789-1071 *SIC 5621*
YMCA p 769
See YMCA OF GREATER TORONTO
YMCA p 834
See OTTAWA YOUNG MEN'S AND YOUNG WOMEN'S CHRISTIAN ASSOCIATION
YMCA p 925
See YMCA OF GREATER TORONTO
YMCA p 1005
See YMCA OF HAMILTON/BURLINGTON/BRANTFORD
YMCA p 1012
See YMCA OF NIAGARA
YMCA BRANDON p 347
See YOUNG MEN'S CHRISTIAN ASSOCIATION OF BRANDON, THE
YMCA CAMP PINE CREST p 998
See YMCA OF GREATER TORONTO
YMCA DU QUEBEC, LES p 1184
5550 AV DU PARC, MONTREAL, QC, H2V 4H1
(514) 271-3437 *SIC 7991*
YMCA DU QUEBEC, LES p 1214
1435 RUE DRUMMOND BUREAU 4E, MONTREAL, QC, H3G 1W4
(514) 849-5331 *SIC 8399*
YMCA DU QUEBEC, LES p 1253
230 BOUL BRUNSWICK, POINTE-CLAIRE, QC, H9R 5N5
(514) 630-9622 *SIC 8399*
YMCA HERITAGE p 68
See CALGARY YOUNG MEN'S CHRISTIAN ASSOCIATION

YMCA OF GREATER SAINT JOHN INC, THE p 414
191 CHURCHILL BLVD, SAINT JOHN, NB, E2K 3E2
(506) 693-9622 *SIC 7999*
YMCA OF GREATER TORONTO p 489
22 GROVE ST W, BARRIE, ON, L4N 1M7
(705) 726-6421 *SIC 8699*
YMCA OF GREATER TORONTO p 711
325 BURNHAMTHORPE RD W, MISSISSAUGA, ON, L5B 3R2
(905) 897-6801 *SIC 7991*
YMCA OF GREATER TORONTO p 769
567 SHEPPARD AVE E, NORTH YORK, ON, M2K 1B2
(416) 225-9622 *SIC 8351*
YMCA OF GREATER TORONTO p 925
2200 YONGE ST SUITE 300, TORONTO, ON, M4S 2C6
(416) 928-9622 *SIC 8699*
YMCA OF GREATER TORONTO p 998
1090 GULLWING LAKE RD RR 1, TORRANCE, ON, P0C 1M0
(705) 762-3377 *SIC 7032*
YMCA OF GREATER VANCOUVER, THE p 197
45844 HOCKING AVE, CHILLIWACK, BC, V2P 1B4
(604) 792-3371 *SIC 7999*
YMCA OF GREATER VANCOUVER, THE p 288
5055 JOYCE ST SUITE 300, VANCOUVER, BC, V5R 6B2
(604) 681-9622 *SIC 8399*
YMCA OF HAMILTON/BURLINGTON/BRANTFORD p 530
500 DRURY LANE, BURLINGTON, ON, L7R 2X2
(905) 632-5000 *SIC 7997*
YMCA OF HAMILTON/BURLINGTON/BRANTFORD p 607
1883 KOSHLONG LAKE RD, HALIBURTON, ON, K0M 1S0
(705) 457-2132 *SIC 7999*
YMCA OF HAMILTON/BURLINGTON/BRANTFORD p 613
79 JAMES ST S, HAMILTON, ON, L8P 2Z1
(905) 529-7102 *SIC 7997*
YMCA OF HAMILTON/BURLINGTON/BRANTFORD p 1005
207 PARKSIDE DR, WATERDOWN, ON, L8B 1B9
(905) 690-3555 *SIC 7997*
YMCA OF KITCHENER WATERLOO p 640
See KITCHENER WATERLOO YOUNG MENS CHRISTIAN ASSOCIATION, THE
YMCA OF LETHBRIDGE p 142
See LETHBRIDGE YOUNG MEN'S CHRISTIAN ASSOCIATION, THE
YMCA OF NIAGARA p 884
25 YMCA DR, ST CATHARINES, ON, L2N 7P9
(905) 646-9622 *SIC 8699*
YMCA OF NIAGARA p 1012
310 WOODLAND RD, WELLAND, ON, L3C 7N3
(905) 735-9622 *SIC 8641*
YMCA OF NORTH BAY p 764
See YOUNG MEN'S CHRISTIAN ASSOCIATION OF NORTH BAY AND DISTRICT
YMCA OF NORTHERN ALBERTA p 91
See YOUNG MEN'S CHRISTIAN ASSOCIATION OF EDMONTON, THE
YMCA OF NORTHERN ALBERTA p 91
10030 102A AVE NW SUITE 300, EDMONTON, AB, T5J 0G5
(780) 421-9622 *SIC 8699*
YMCA OF WINDSOR-ESSEX COUNTY p 1024
See YOUNG MEN'S CHRISTIAN ASSOCI-

ATION OF WINDSOR AND ESSEX COUNTY

YMCA OF WOOD BUFFALO *p* 91
10030 102A AVE NW SUITE 300, EDMONTON, AB, T5J 0G5
(780) 423-9609 *SIC* 8699

YMCA OF WOOD BUFFALO *p* 129
221 TUNDRA DR, FORT MCMURRAY, AB, T9H 4Z7
(780) 790-9622 *SIC* 8699

YMCA POINTE CLAIRE *p* 1253
See YMCA DU QUEBEC, LES

YMCA SASKATOON *p* 1429
See SASKATOON FAMILY YOUNG MEN'S CHRISTIAN ASSOCIATION

YMCA SUDBURY *p* 901
See YOUNG MENS CHRISTIAN ASSOCIATION

YMCA TRANSITIONAL HOUSING *p* 91
See YMCA OF NORTHERN ALBERTA

YMCA WANAKITA *p* 607
See YMCA OF HAMILTON/BURLINGTON/BRANTFORD

YMCA-YWCA OF BROCKVILLE AND AREA *p* 520
345 PARK ST, BROCKVILLE, ON, K6V 5Y7
(613) 342-7961 *SIC* 8641

YMCA-YWCA OF GREATER VICTORIA *p* 337
851 BROUGHTON ST, VICTORIA, BC, V8W 1E5
(250) 386-7511 *SIC* 8011

YMCA-YWCA OF THE CENTRAL OKANAGAN *p* 219
4075 GORDON DR, KELOWNA, BC, V1W 5J2
(250) 764-4040 *SIC* 7997

YMCA-YWCA WINNIPEG *p* 376
See YOUNG MEN'S AND YOUNG WOMEN'S CHRISTIAN ASSOCIATION OF WINNIPEG INCORPORATED, THE

YOGEN FRUZ *p* 677
See YOGEN FRUZ CANADA INC

YOGEN FRUZ CANADA INC *p* 677
210 SHIELDS CRT SUITE 1, MARKHAM, ON, L3R 8V2
(905) 479-8762 *SIC* 6794

YOGIBO LIFESTYLE *p* 199
See 9391134 CANADA LTD

YOKOGAWA CANADA INC *p* 20
11133 40 ST SE SUITE 4, CALGARY, AB, T2C 2Z4
(403) 258-2681 *SIC* 8742

YOKOHAMA TIRE (CANADA) INC *p* 226
9325 200 ST SUITE 500, LANGLEY, BC, V1M 3A7
(604) 546-9656 *SIC* 5531

YONGE EGLINTON CENTRE MANAGEMENT SERVICES IN TRUST *p* 923
20 EGLINTON AVE W SUITE 401, TORONTO, ON, M4R 1K8
(416) 489-2300 *SIC* 6512

YONGE NORTH MITSUBISHI *p* 856
See 2634912 ONTARIO INC

YONGE STREET HOTEL LTD *p* 932
475 YONGE ST, TORONTO, ON, M4Y 1X7
(416) 924-0611 *SIC* 7011

YONGE STREET MISSION, THE *p* 978
365 SPADINA AVE, TORONTO, ON, M5T 2G3
(416) 929-9614 *SIC* 8322

YONGE-ROSEDALE CHARITABLE FOUNDATION *p* 931
877 YONGE ST SUITE 1603, TORONTO, ON, M4W 3M2
(416) 923-8887 *SIC* 6513

YOPLAIT LIBERTE CANADA CIE *p* 1069
1423 BOUL PROVENCHER, BROSSARD, QC, J4W 1Z3
SIC 2026

YOPLAIT LIBERTE CANADA CIE *p* 1310
5000 RUE J.-A.-BOMBARDIER, SAINT-

HUBERT, QC, J3Z 1H1
(450) 926-5222 *SIC* 2022

YOR-SUP-NET SUPPORT SERVICE NETWORK *p* 757
102 MAIN ST S UNIT 3, NEWMARKET, ON, L3Y 3Y7
(905) 898-3721 *SIC* 8399

YORK BARBELL CO. LTD *p* 805
1450 SOUTH SERVICE RD W, OAKVILLE, ON, L6L 5T7
(905) 827-6362 *SIC* 3949

YORK CATHOLIC DISTRICT SCHOOL BOARD *p* 482
210 BLOOMINGTON RD SUITE SIDE, AURORA, ON, L4G 0P9
(905) 727-2455 *SIC* 8211

YORK CATHOLIC DISTRICT SCHOOL BOARD *p* 482
320 BLOOMINGTON RD, AURORA, ON, L4G 0M1
(905) 713-1211 *SIC* 8211

YORK CATHOLIC DISTRICT SCHOOL BOARD *p* 628
185 GLENWOODS AVE, KESWICK, ON, L4P 2W6
(905) 656-9140 *SIC* 8211

YORK CATHOLIC DISTRICT SCHOOL BOARD *p* 664
400 ST. JOAN OF ARC AVE, MAPLE, ON, L6A 2S8
(905) 303-6121 *SIC* 8211

YORK CATHOLIC DISTRICT SCHOOL BOARD *p* 678
5300 14TH AVE, MARKHAM, ON, L3S 3K8
(905) 472-4961 *SIC* 8211

YORK CATHOLIC DISTRICT SCHOOL BOARD *p* 679
2188 RODICK RD, MARKHAM, ON, L6C 1S3
(905) 887-6171 *SIC* 8211

YORK CATHOLIC DISTRICT SCHOOL BOARD *p* 757
1 CRUSADER WAY, NEWMARKET, ON, L3Y 6R2
(905) 895-3340 *SIC* 8211

YORK CATHOLIC DISTRICT SCHOOL BOARD *p* 905
8101 LESLIE ST, THORNHILL, ON, L3T 7P4
(905) 889-4982 *SIC* 8211

YORK CATHOLIC DISTRICT SCHOOL BOARD *p* 1029
120 LA ROCCA AVE, WOODBRIDGE, ON, L4H 2A9
(905) 303-4646 *SIC* 8211

YORK CATHOLIC DISTRICT SCHOOL BOARD *p* 1034
7501 MARTIN GROVE RD, WOODBRIDGE, ON, L4L 1A5
(905) 851-6699 *SIC* 8211

YORK CATHOLIC DISTRICT SCHOOL BOARD *p* 1034
250 ANSLEY GROVE RD, WOODBRIDGE, ON, L4L 3W4
(905) 851-6643 *SIC* 8211

YORK CENTRAL HOSPITAL *p* 855
See MACKENZIE HEALTH

YORK CONDOMINIUM CORPORATION NO 382 *p* 571
2045 LAKE SHORE BLVD W, ETOBICOKE, ON, M8V 2Z6
(416) 252-7701 *SIC* 6531

YORK CONDOMINIUM CORPORATION NO. 510 *p* 968
55 HARBOUR SQ SUITE 3212, TORONTO, ON, M5J 2L1
(416) 362-1174 *SIC* 6531

YORK CONSULTING INC *p* 770
19 HENDON AVE, NORTH YORK, ON, M2M 4G8
(416) 410-2222 *SIC* 7389

YORK COUNTY BOWMEN INC *p* 757
15887 MCCOWAN RD, NEWMARKET, ON,

L3Y 4W1
SIC 7999

YORK DISPOSAL SERVICE LIMITED *p* 561
650 CREDITSTONE RD, CONCORD, ON, L4K 5C8
(905) 669-1900 *SIC* 4953

YORK ELECTRONICS (2010) LTD *p* 12
1430 28 ST NE UNIT 8, CALGARY, AB, T2A 7W6
(403) 207-0202 *SIC* 5065

YORK FINANCIAL SERVICES INC. *p* 402
440 YORK ST, FREDERICTON, NB, E3B 3P7
(506) 443-7776 *SIC* 6411

YORK HUMBER HIGH SCHOOL *p* 993
See TORONTO DISTRICT SCHOOL BOARD

YORK MAJOR HOLDINGS INC *p* 664
10000 DUFFERIN ST, MAPLE, ON, L6A 1S3
(905) 417-2300 *SIC* 6552

YORK MANOR INC *p* 400
100 SUNSET DR SUITE 121, FREDERICTON, NB, E3A 1A3
(506) 444-3880 *SIC* 8051

YORK MANOR NURSING HOME *p* 400
See YORK MANOR INC

YORK MARBLE TILE & TERRAZZO INC *p* 792
2 SHEFFIELD ST, NORTH YORK, ON, M6M 3E6
(416) 235-0161 *SIC* 1743

YORK MEDICAL *p* 754
See 1246110 ONTARIO INC

YORK MEMORIAL COLLEGIATE INSTITUTE *p* 993
See TORONTO DISTRICT SCHOOL BOARD

YORK MILLS COLLEGIATE INSTITUTE *p* 778
See TORONTO DISTRICT SCHOOL BOARD

YORK REGION CHILDREN AID SOCIETY *p* 755
See CHILDREN AND FAMILY SERVICES FOR YORK REGION

YORK REGION DISTRICT SCHOOL BOARD *p* 482
60 WELLINGTON ST W, AURORA, ON, L4G 3H2
(905) 727-3141 *SIC* 8211

YORK REGION DISTRICT SCHOOL BOARD *p* 628
100 BISCAYNE BLVD, KESWICK, ON, L4P 3S2
(905) 476-0933 *SIC* 8211

YORK REGION DISTRICT SCHOOL BOARD *p* 629
2001 KING RD, KING CITY, ON, L7B 1K2
(905) 833-5332 *SIC* 8211

YORK REGION DISTRICT SCHOOL BOARD *p* 664
50 SPRINGSIDE RD, MAPLE, ON, L6A 2W5
(905) 417-9444 *SIC* 8211

YORK REGION DISTRICT SCHOOL BOARD *p* 665
89 CHURCH ST, MARKHAM, ON, L3P 2M3
(905) 294-1886 *SIC* 8211

YORK REGION DISTRICT SCHOOL BOARD *p* 678
525 HIGHGLEN AVE, MARKHAM, ON, L3S 3L5
(905) 472-8900 *SIC* 8211

YORK REGION DISTRICT SCHOOL BOARD *p* 679
90 BUR OAK AVE, MARKHAM, ON, L6C 2E6
(905) 887-2216 *SIC* 8211

YORK REGION DISTRICT SCHOOL BOARD *p* 754
705 COLUMBUS WAY, NEWMARKET, ON, L3X 2M7
(905) 967-1045 *SIC* 8211

YORK REGION DISTRICT SCHOOL BOARD *p* 757
135 BRISTOL RD, NEWMARKET, ON, L3Y 8J7
(905) 836-0021 *SIC* 8211

YORK REGION DISTRICT SCHOOL BOARD *p* 757
40 HURON HEIGHTS DR, NEWMARKET, ON, L3Y 3J9
(905) 895-2384 *SIC* 8211

YORK REGION DISTRICT SCHOOL BOARD *p* 757
505 PICKERING CRES, NEWMARKET, ON, L3Y 8H1
(905) 895-5159 *SIC* 8211

YORK REGION DISTRICT SCHOOL BOARD *p* 854
81 STRATHEARN AVE, RICHMOND HILL, ON, L4B 2J5
(905) 508-0806 *SIC* 8211

YORK REGION DISTRICT SCHOOL BOARD *p* 856
10077 BAYVIEW AVE, RICHMOND HILL, ON, L4C 2L4
(905) 884-4453 *SIC* 8211

YORK REGION DISTRICT SCHOOL BOARD *p* 856
106 GARDEN AVE, RICHMOND HILL, ON, L4C 6M1
(905) 889-6266 *SIC* 8211

YORK REGION DISTRICT SCHOOL BOARD *p* 856
300 MAJOR MACKENZIE DR W, RICHMOND HILL, ON, L4C 3S3
(905) 884-0554 *SIC* 8211

YORK REGION DISTRICT SCHOOL BOARD *p* 895
801 HOOVER PARK DR, STOUFFVILLE, ON, L4A 0A4
(905) 640-1433 *SIC* 8211

YORK REGION DISTRICT SCHOOL BOARD *p* 902
20798 DALTON RD, SUTTON WEST, ON, L0E 1R0
(905) 722-3281 *SIC* 8211

YORK REGION DISTRICT SCHOOL BOARD *p* 905
8075 BAYVIEW AVE, THORNHILL, ON, L3T 4N4
(905) 889-9696 *SIC* 8211

YORK REGION DISTRICT SCHOOL BOARD *p* 906
1401 CLARK AVE W, THORNHILL, ON, L4J 7R4
(905) 660-1397 *SIC* 8211

YORK REGION DISTRICT SCHOOL BOARD *p* 1000
1000 CARLTON RD, UNIONVILLE, ON, L3P 7P5
(905) 940-8840 *SIC* 8211

YORK REGION DISTRICT SCHOOL BOARD *p* 1029
4901 RUTHERFORD RD, WOODBRIDGE, ON, L4H 3C2
(905) 850-5012 *SIC* 8211

YORK REGION PSYCHOLOGICAL SERVICES *p* 905
See ROCKMAN PSYCHOLOGY PROFESSIONAL CORPORATION

YORK REGIONAL POLICE ASSOCIATION, THE *p* 754
600 STONEHAVEN AVE, NEWMARKET, ON, L3X 2M4
(905) 830-4947 *SIC* 8631

YORK SCHOOL, THE *p* 926
1320 YONGE ST, TORONTO, ON, M4T 1X2
(416) 926-1325 *SIC* 8211

YORK SHEET METAL LIMITED *p* 1034
227 WESTCREEK DR, WOODBRIDGE, ON, L4L 9T7
(416) 742-8242 *SIC* 3444

YORK STREET COURIER *p* 401
See JOBS UNLIMITED INC

YORK SUPPORT SERVICES NETWORK p
757
See YOR-SUP-NET SUPPORT SERVICE NETWORK
YORK UNIVERSITY   p 785
4700 KEELE ST, NORTH YORK, ON, M3J
1P3
(416) 736-2100   *SIC* 8221
YORK UNIVERSITY   p 785
4700 KEELE ST RM 428, NORTH YORK,
ON, M3J 1P3
(416) 736-5113   *SIC* 8221
**YORKDALE ADULT LEARNING CENTRE &
SECONDARY SCHOOL**   p 790
*See TORONTO DISTRICT SCHOOL
BOARD*
YORKDALE CAFE LTD   p 923
2377 YONGE ST SUITE 823, TORONTO,
ON, M4P 2C8
(416) 484-4231   *SIC* 5461
**YORKDALE FORD LINCOLN SALES LIM-
ITED**   p
790
3130 DUFFERIN ST, NORTH YORK, ON,
M6A 2S6
(416) 787-4534   *SIC* 5511
**YORKDALE SHOPPING CENTRE HOLD-
INGS INC**   p
790
1 YORKDALE RD SUITE 500, NORTH
YORK, ON, M6A 3A1
(416) 256-5066   *SIC* 6512
YORKDALE VOLKSWAGEN   p 785
See 2031113 ONTARIO LIMITED
YORKE TOWNE SUPPLIES LIMITED p 854
1235 REID ST, RICHMOND HILL, ON, L4B
1G4
(905) 762-1200   *SIC* 5198
YORKLAND CONTROLS LIMITED   p 785
2693 STEELES AVE W SUITE 661, NORTH
YORK, ON, M3J 2Z8
(416) 661-3306   *SIC* 5074
YORKTON CO-OP   p 1439
*See YORKTON CO-OPERATIVE ASSOCIA-
TION LIMITED, THE*
**YORKTON CO-OPERATIVE ASSOCIATION
LIMITED, THE**   p 1439
30 ARGYLE ST, YORKTON, SK, S3N 0P6
(306) 783-3601   *SIC* 5171
YORKTON DODGE   p 1439
270 HAMILTON RD, YORKTON, SK, S3N
4C6
(306) 783-9022   *SIC* 5511
YORKTON PLUMBING & HEATING LTD p
1439
HWY 9 N, YORKTON, SK, S3N 4A9
(306) 782-4588   *SIC* 1711
YORKTON REGIONAL HIGH SCHOOL   p
1438
*See BOARD OF EDUCATION OF THE
GOOD SPIRIT SCHOOL DIVISION NO. 204
OF SASKATCHEWAN*
**YORKTON ROMAN CATHOLIC SEPERATE
SCHOOL DIVISION NO. 86**   p 1439
259 CIRCLEBROOKE DR, YORKTON, SK,
S3N 2S8
SIC 8211
YORKVILLE SOUND   p 845
See LONG & MCQUADE LIMITED
YORKWEST PLUMBING SUPPLY INC   p
1034
201 AVIVA PARK DR, WOODBRIDGE, ON,
L4L 9C1
(905) 856-9466   *SIC* 5074
YOU I LABS INC   p 625
307 LEGGET DR, KANATA, ON, K2K 3C8
(613) 228-9107   *SIC* 7371
YOU.I TV   p 625
See YOU I LABS INC
**YOUNG & RUBICAM GROUP OF COMPA-
NIES ULC, THE**   p
931
160 BLOOR ST E SUITE 500, TORONTO,
ON, M4W 1B9

(416) 987-9100   *SIC* 7311
**YOUNG & RUBICAM GROUP OF COMPA-
NIES ULC, THE**   p
931
60 BLOOR ST W SUITE 8, TORONTO, ON,
M4W 3B8
SIC 7311
**YOUNG & RUBICAM GROUP OF COMPA-
NIES ULC, THE**   p
985
495 WELLINGTON ST W SUITE 102,
TORONTO, ON, M5V 1E9
SIC 7311
YOUNG & YOUNG TRADING CO. LIMITEDp
872
328 NANTUCKET BLVD UNIT 8, SCAR-
BOROUGH, ON, M1P 2P4
(416) 288-9298   *SIC* 5141
**YOUNG AUTOMOTIVE PROFESSIONALS,
THE**   p 846
See 638691 ONTARIO LIMITED
YOUNG BROTHERS   p 138
See LAC LA BICHE INN LTD
**YOUNG ENTREPRENEUR LEADERSHIP
LAUNCHPAD (YELL)**   p 319
1500 GEORGIA ST W UNIT 1250, VAN-
COUVER, BC, V6G 2Z6
(778) 808-4641   *SIC* 8699
**YOUNG MEN'S AND YOUNG WOMEN'S
CHRISTIAN ASSOCIATION OF WINNIPEG
INCORPORATED, THE**   p 376
301 VAUGHAN ST, WINNIPEG, MB, R3B
2N7
(204) 661-9474   *SIC* 8641
**YOUNG MEN'S AND YOUNG WOMEN'S
CHRISTIAN ASSOCIATION OF WINNIPEG
INCORPORATED, THE**   p 387
3550 PORTAGE AVE, WINNIPEG, MB, R3K
0Z8
(204) 889-8052   *SIC* 8641
**YOUNG MEN'S CHRISTIAN ASSOCIATION
OF BRANDON, THE**   p 347
231 8TH ST, BRANDON, MB, R7A 3X2
(204) 727-5456   *SIC* 8699
**YOUNG MEN'S CHRISTIAN ASSOCIATION
OF CAMBRIDGE**   p 535
250 HESPELER RD, CAMBRIDGE, ON,
N1R 3H3
(519) 623-9622   *SIC* 8641
**YOUNG MEN'S CHRISTIAN ASSOCIATION
OF EDMONTON, THE**   p 91
10211 105 ST NW, EDMONTON, AB, T5J
1E3
(780) 429-9622   *SIC* 8699
**YOUNG MEN'S CHRISTIAN ASSOCIATION
OF EDMONTON, THE**   p 104
7121 178 ST NW, EDMONTON, AB, T5T
5T9
(780) 930-2311   *SIC* 8699
**YOUNG MEN'S CHRISTIAN ASSOCIATION
OF GREATER VANCOUVER**   p 197
*See YMCA OF GREATER VANCOUVER,
THE*
**YOUNG MEN'S CHRISTIAN ASSOCIATION
OF NORTH BAY AND DISTRICT**   p 764
186 CHIPPEWA ST W, NORTH BAY, ON,
P1B 6G2
(705) 497-9622   *SIC* 8641
**YOUNG MEN'S CHRISTIAN ASSOCIATION
OF WINDSOR AND ESSEX COUNTY**p 1024
500 VICTORIA AVE, WINDSOR, ON, N9A
4M8
(519) 258-3881   *SIC* 8699
YOUNG MENS CHRISTIAN ASSOCIATION
p 760
7150 MONTROSE RD, NIAGARA FALLS,
ON, L2H 3N3
(905) 358-9622   *SIC* 8699
YOUNG MENS CHRISTIAN ASSOCIATION
p 901
140 DURHAM ST, SUDBURY, ON, P3E 3M7
(705) 673-9136   *SIC* 8641
**YOUNG MENS CHRISTIAN ASSOCIATION
OF REGINA**   p 1419

2400 13TH AVE, REGINA, SK, S4P 0V9
(306) 757-9622   *SIC* 8641
**YOUNG MENS' CHRISTIAN ASSOCIATION
FOUNDATION OF ED**   p 104
*See YOUNG MEN'S CHRISTIAN ASSOCI-
ATION OF EDMONTON, THE*
**YOUNG WOMEN'S CHRISTIAN ASSOCIA-
TION**   p
311
535 HORNBY ST, VANCOUVER, BC, V6C
2E8
(604) 895-5800   *SIC* 7011
**YOUNG WOMEN'S CHRISTIAN ASSOCIA-
TION**   p
311
535 HORNBY ST SUITE 100, VANCOU-
VER, BC, V6C 2E8
(604) 895-5777   *SIC* 8641
**YOUNG WOMEN'S CHRISTIAN ASSOCIA-
TION**   p
454
1239 BARRINGTON ST, HALIFAX, NS, B3J
1Y3
(902) 423-6162   *SIC* 8699
**YOUNG WOMEN'S CHRISTIAN ASSOCIA-
TION OF CANADA, THE**   p
33
2003 16 ST SE, CALGARY, AB, T2G 5B7
(403) 266-0707   *SIC* 8322
**YOUNG WOMEN'S CHRISTIAN ASSOCIA-
TION OF CANADA, THE**   p
91
10080 JASPER AVE NW SUITE 400, ED-
MONTON, AB, T5J 1V9
(780) 423-9922   *SIC* 8399
**YOUNG WOMEN'S CHRISTIAN ASSOCIA-
TION OF CANADA, THE**   p
436
5004 50TH AVE, YELLOWKNIFE, NT, X1A
2P3
(867) 920-2777   *SIC* 7011
**YOUNG WOMEN'S CHRISTIAN ASSOCIA-
TION OF GREATER TORONTO**   p
926
80 WOODLAWN AVE E, TORONTO, ON,
M4T 1C1
(416) 923-8454   *SIC* 8399
**YOUNG WOMEN'S CHRISTIAN ASSOCI-
ATION OF PETERBOROUGH, VICTORIA &
HALIBURTON**   p 840
216 SIMCOE ST, PETERBOROUGH, ON,
K9H 2H7
(705) 743-3526   *SIC* 8399
**YOUNG WOMEN'S CHRISTIAN ASSOCIA-
TION OF SASKATOON**   p
1430
510 25TH ST E, SASKATOON, SK, S7K 4A7
(306) 244-0944   *SIC* 8322
YOUNG, GARY AGENCIES LTD   p 251
1085 GREAT ST, PRINCE GEORGE, BC,
V2N 2K8
(250) 563-1725   *SIC* 5171
YOUNG, GEO H & CO LTD   p 376
167 LOMBARD AVE UNIT 809, WINNIPEG,
MB, R3B 3H8
(204) 947-6851   *SIC* 4731
YOUNG, J. & S. MERCHANTS LTD p 1009
656 ERB ST W, WATERLOO, ON, N2T 2Z7
(519) 884-1255   *SIC* 5531
YOUNG, PETER LIMITED   p 679
9693 KENNEDY RD, MARKHAM, ON, L6C
1A4
(905) 887-9122   *SIC* 4959
YOUNG, ROBERT E CONSTRUCTION LTD
p 842
1488 CHEMONG RD, PETERBOROUGH,
ON, K9J 6X2
(705) 745-1488   *SIC* 1442
YOUNG-DAVIDSON MINE   p 680
See ALAMOS GOLD INC
YOUNGHUSBAND RESOURCES LTD p 247
1628 KEBET WAY UNIT 100, PORT CO-
QUITLAM, BC, V3C 5W9
(604) 466-1220   *SIC* 8741

YOUNGS INSURANCE BROKERS INC   p
887
110B HANNOVER DR SUITE 106, ST
CATHARINES, ON, L2W 1A4
(905) 688-1100   *SIC* 6351
YOUNGS INSURANCE BROKERS INC   p
1012
55 EAST MAIN ST, WELLAND, ON, L3B
3W4
(905) 735-7212   *SIC* 6411
YOUNGS PHARMACY & HOMECAREp 594
See YOUNGS PHARMACY LIMITED
YOUNGS PHARMACY LIMITED   p 594
47 MAIN ST S, GEORGETOWN, ON, L7G
3G2
(905) 877-2711   *SIC* 5912
YOUR 50 PLUS INSURANCE BROKERS p
570
See IVES INSURANCE BROKERS LTD
YOUR COMMUNITY REALTY INC   p 856
9050 YONGE ST SUITE 100, RICHMOND
HILL, ON, L4C 9S6
(905) 884-8700   *SIC* 6531
YOUR CREDIT UNION LTD   p 826
14 CHAMBERLAIN AVE SUITE 200, OT-
TAWA, ON, K1S 1V9
(613) 238-8001   *SIC* 6062
YOUR DOLLAR STORE WITH MORE INC p
220
160 DOUGALL RD S UNIT 200, KELOWNA,
BC, V1X 3J4
(250) 860-4225   *SIC* 5399
**YOUR FATHER'S MOUSTACHE PUB &
EATERY**   p 452
See BRULE HOLDINGS LTD
**YOUR NEIGHBOURHOOD CREDIT UNION
LIMITED**   p 641
38 EXECUTIVE PL, KITCHENER, ON, N2P
2N4
(519) 804-9190   *SIC* 6062
YOUR PETSCHOICE ULC   p 677
7300 WARDEN AVE SUITE 106,
MARKHAM, ON, L3R 9Z6
(905) 946-1200   *SIC* 5149
YOUR TELEPHONE SECRETARY   p 517
See EXTEND COMMUNICATIONS INC
YOUTH FOR CHRIST CANADA   p 228
19705 FRASER HWY UNIT 135, LANGLEY,
BC, V3A 7E9
SIC 8699
YOUTH MENTAL HEALTH   p 932
See OOLAGEN COMMUNITY SERVICES
YOUTH PROTECTION   p 1391
700 BOUL FOREST, VAL-D'OR, QC, J9P
2L3
(819) 825-0002   *SIC* 8399
YOUTH SERVICES BUREAU OF OTTAWAp
819
3000 HAWTHORNE RD, OTTAWA, ON, K1G
5Y3
(613) 738-7776   *SIC* 8322
YOUTH SERVICES BUREAU OF OTTAWAp
830
2675 QUEENSVIEW DR, OTTAWA, ON,
K2B 8K2
(613) 729-1000   *SIC* 8322
YOUVILLE HOME   p 166
*See YOUVILLE HOME (GREY NUNS) OF
ST ALBERT*
**YOUVILLE HOME (GREY NUNS) OF ST AL-
BERT**   p
166
9 ST VITAL AVE, ST. ALBERT, AB, T8N 1K1
(780) 460-6900   *SIC* 8059
YOUVILLE RESIDENCE   p 293
*See PROVIDENCE HEALTH CARE SOCI-
ETY*
YPH MECHANICAL   p 1439
*See YORKTON PLUMBING & HEATING
LTD*
YQR REGINA INTERNATIONAL   p 1422
See REGINA AIRPORT AUTHORITY INC
YRB MANAGEMENT CORP   p 249
2424 HART HWY, PRINCE GEORGE, BC,

V2K 2X8
(250) 614-7604   *SIC* 1611

YRC FREIGHT CANADA COMPANY *p* 106
16060 128 AVE NW, EDMONTON, AB, T5V 1B6
(780) 447-2434   *SIC* 4213

YRC FREIGHT CANADA COMPANY *p* 187
3985 STILL CREEK AVE, BURNABY, BC, V5C 4E2
(604) 433-3321   *SIC* 4213

YRC FREIGHT CANADA COMPANY *p* 373
1400 INKSTER BLVD, WINNIPEG, MB, R2X 1R1
(204) 958-5000   *SIC* 4213

YRC FREIGHT CANADA COMPANY *p* 702
5919 SHAWSON DR, MISSISSAUGA, ON, L4W 3Y2
(905) 670-9366   *SIC* 4213

YRC FREIGHT CANADA COMPANY *p* 1096
1725 CH SAINT-FRANCOIS, DORVAL, QC, H9P 2S1
(514) 684-9970   *SIC* 4231

YRC REIMER *p* 106
See YRC FREIGHT CANADA COMPANY

YTV CANADA, INC *p* 935
25 DOCKSIDE DR, TORONTO, ON, M5A 0B5
(416) 479-7000   *SIC* 4833

YUILL'S VALU-MART *p* 489
19625 OPEONGO ST, BARRYS BAY, ON, K0J 1B0
(613) 756-2023   *SIC* 5141

YUKON COLLEGE *p* 1440
500 COLLEGE DR, WHITEHORSE, YT, Y1A 5K4
(867) 668-8800   *SIC* 8221

YUKON COR CORPORATION *p* 561
30 PENNSYLVANIA AVE UNIT 17A, CONCORD, ON, L4K 4A5
SIC 1771

YUKON ENERGY CORPORATION *p* 1440
2 MILES CANYON RD, WHITEHORSE, YT, Y1A 6S7
(867) 393-5300   *SIC* 4911

YUKON HOSPITAL CORPORATION *p* 1440
5 HOSPITAL RD, WHITEHORSE, YT, Y1A 3H7
(867) 393-8930   *SIC* 8062

YUKON HOUSING CORPORATION *p* 1440
410 JARVIS ST UNIT H, WHITEHORSE, YT, Y1A 2H5
(867) 667-5759   *SIC* 6531

YUKON INN, THE *p* 1440
See 13601 YUKON INC.

YUKON LIQUOR CORPORATION *p* 1440
9031 QUARTZ RD, WHITEHORSE, YT, Y1A 4P9
(867) 667-5245   *SIC* 5921

YUKON OCCUPATIONAL HEALTH *p* 1440
401 STRICKLAND ST, WHITEHORSE, YT, Y1A 5N8
(867) 667-5450   *SIC* 8742

YUKON TIRE CENTRE LTD *p* 1440
107 INDUSTRIAL RD, WHITEHORSE, YT, Y1A 2T7
(867) 667-6102   *SIC* 5541

YUMMY MARKET INC *p* 664
1390 MAJOR MACKENZIE DR, MAPLE, ON, L6A 4H6
(905) 417-4117   *SIC* 5411

YUMMY MARKET INC *p* 781
4400 DUFFERIN ST UNIT B-4, NORTH YORK, ON, M3H 6A8
(416) 665-0040   *SIC* 5411

YUSEN LOGISTICS (CANADA) INC *p* 507
261 PARKHURST SQ, BRAMPTON, ON, L6T 5H5
(905) 458-9622   *SIC* 4731

YVES PONROY CANADA *p* 1128
See INSTITUT DE RECHERCHE BIOLOGIQUE YVES PONROY (CANADA) INC

YVES ROCHER AMERIQUE DU NORD INC *p* 1142

2199 BOUL FERNAND-LAFONTAINE, LONGUEUIL, QC, J4G 2V7
(450) 442-9555   *SIC* 5999

YVR *p* 265
See VANCOUVER AIRPORT AUTHORITY

YWCA *p* 613
See HAMILTON YOUNG WOMEN'S CHRISTIAN ASSOCIATION, THE

YWCA CALGARY *p* 28
See CALGARY YOUNG WOMEN'S CHRISTIAN ASSOCIATION

YWCA DURHAM *p* 813
See OSHAWA YOUNG WOMEN CHRISTIAN ASSOCIATION, THE

YWCA OF CALGARY *p* 28
See CALGARY YOUNG WOMEN'S CHRISTIAN ASSOCIATION, THE

YWCA OF HALIFAX *p* 454
See YOUNG WOMEN'S CHRISTIAN ASSOCIATION

YWCA OF PETERBOROUGH VICTORIA & HALIBURTON *p* 840
See YOUNG WOMEN'S CHRISTIAN ASSOCIATION OF PETERBOROUGH, VICTORIA & HALIBURTON

YWCA OF SASKATOON *p* 1430
See YOUNG WOMEN'S CHRISTIAN ASSOCIATION OF SASKATOON

YWCA SHERIFF KING HOME *p* 33
See YOUNG WOMEN'S CHRISTIAN ASSOCIATION OF CANADA, THE

YWCA TORONTO *p* 926
See YOUNG WOMEN'S CHRISTIAN ASSOCIATION OF GREATER TORONTO

YWCA YELLOWKNIFE *p* 436
See YOUNG WOMEN'S CHRISTIAN ASSOCIATION OF CANADA, THE

YYJ AIRPORT SHUTTLE *p* 339
See WILSON'S TRANSPORTATION LTD

YYJ FBO SERVICES LTD *p* 238
1962 CANSO RD SUITE 101, NORTH SAANICH, BC, V8L 5V5
(250) 655-8833   *SIC* 5172

YYOGA *p* 293
See PURE FREEDOM YYOGA WELLNESS INC

YYZ TRAVEL SERVICES (INT'L) INC *p* 906
7851 DUFFERIN ST SUITE 100, THORNHILL, ON, L4J 3M4
(905) 660-7000   *SIC* 4725

Z

Z GROUP *p* 652
See Z REALTY COMPANY LIMITED

Z REALTY COMPANY LIMITED *p* 652
1135 ADELAIDE ST N SUITE 300, LONDON, ON, N5Y 5K7
(519) 673-1730   *SIC* 6513

Z-SC1 BIOMEDICAL *p* 1221
See Z-SC1 CORP

Z-SC1 CORP *p* 1221
4148A RUE SAINTE-CATHERINE O BUREAU 337, MONTREAL, QC, H3Z 0A2
(877) 381-5500   *SIC* 3821

Z. & R. HOLDINGS LTD *p* 229
5744 198 ST, LANGLEY, BC, V3A 7J2
(604) 530-2311   *SIC* 3231

Z.M.C. METAL COATING INC *p* 1034
40 GAUDAUR RD SUITE 3, WOODBRIDGE, ON, L4L 4S6
(905) 856-3838   *SIC* 3479

Z.M.C. WINDOW COVERINGS SUPPLIES *p* 1034
See Z.M.C. METAL COATING INC

Z69115 ALBERTA LTD *p* 74
37 RICHARD WAY SW SUITE 200, CALGARY, AB, T3E 7M8
SIC 6531

ZABE JEANS *p* 1285
See ENTREPRISES VAGABOND INC, LES

ZABER TECHNOLOGIES INC *p* 324
605 KENT AVE NORTH W UNIT 2, VANCOUVER, BC, V6P 6T7
(604) 569-3780   *SIC* 3625

ZABS PHARMACY LTD *p* 1419
2202 BROAD ST SUITE 422, REGINA, SK, S4P 4V6
(306) 777-8166   *SIC* 5912

ZACH & KAYLYN ENTERPRISES INC *p* 104
17707 111 AVE NW, EDMONTON, AB, T5S 0A1
(780) 484-5444   *SIC* 5511

ZACKS *p* 1177
See 6938001 CANADA INC

ZAD HOLDINGS LTD *p* 322
1903 BROADWAY W, VANCOUVER, BC, V6J 1Z3
(604) 739-4477   *SIC* 1752

ZADI FOODS LIMITED *p* 507
65 DEERHURST DR, BRAMPTON, ON, L6T 5R7
(905) 799-6666   *SIC* 2013

ZAHID, M. DRUGS LTD *p* 757
1111 DAVIS DR SUITE 46, NEWMARKET, ON, L3Y 8X2
(905) 898-7771   *SIC* 5912

ZAK'S BUILDING SUPPLIES & CONTRACTING *p* 1407
See H & S HOLDINGS INC

ZALEV BROTHERS CO *p* 1022
200 GRAND MARAIS RD E, WINDSOR, ON, N8X 3H2
(519) 966-0620   *SIC* 5093

ZANE HOLDINGS LTD *p* 84
9525 127 AVE NW, EDMONTON, AB, T5E 6M7
(780) 474-7921   *SIC* 7538

ZANEEN GROUP INC *p* 791
30 TYCOS DR, NORTH YORK, ON, M6B 1V9
(416) 247-9221   *SIC* 5063

ZANEEN LIGHTNING *p* 791
See ZANEEN GROUP INC

ZARA *p* 936
220 YONGE ST SUITE C-4A, TORONTO, ON, M5B 2H1
(647) 288-0333   *SIC* 5141

ZARA *p* 1209
See ZARA CANADA INC

ZARA CANADA *p* 936
See ZARA

ZARA CANADA INC *p* 1209
1200 AV MCGILL COLLEGE BUREAU 1550, MONTREAL, QC, H3B 4G7
(514) 868-1516   *SIC* 5651

ZARCONE BROTHERS LTD *p* 615
20 HEMPSTEAD DR, HAMILTON, ON, L8W 2E7
(905) 574-1500   *SIC* 5149

ZARKY'S FINE FOODS *p* 526
See 1540886 ONTARIO INC

ZARKY'S FINE FOODS *p* 615
See ZARCONE BROTHERS LTD

ZAROWNY MOTORS (ST PAUL) LTD *p* 165
5508 50 AVE, ST PAUL, AB, T0A 3A1
(780) 645-4468   *SIC* 5511

ZAVCOR LOGISTICS *p* 890
See ZAVCOR TRUCKING LIMITED

ZAVCOR TRUCKING LIMITED *p* 890
3650 EAGLE ST, STEVENSVILLE, ON, L0S 1S0
(905) 382-3444   *SIC* 4213

ZAVIDA COFFEE COMPANY INC *p* 561
70 CONNIE CRES UNIT 12, CONCORD, ON, L4K 1L6
(905) 738-0103   *SIC* 5149

ZAVITZ, G. LIMITED *p* 760
5795 THOROLD STONE RD, NIAGARA FALLS, ON, L2J 1A1
(905) 356-4945   *SIC* 4213

ZAYO CANADA INC *p* 824
45 O'CONNOR ST SUITE 1400, OTTAWA, ON, K1P 1A4
(613) 688-4688   *SIC* 4899

ZAYO CANADA INC *p* 985
200 WELLINGTON ST W SUITE 800, TORONTO, ON, M5V 3C7

(416) 363-4444   *SIC* 4899

ZAZULA PROCESS EQUIPMENT LTD *p* 33
4609 MANITOBA RD SE, CALGARY, AB, T2G 4B9
(403) 244-0751   *SIC* 5084

ZCL COMPOSITES INC *p* 126
1420 PARSONS RD SW, EDMONTON, AB, T6X 1M5
SIC 3299

ZE POWERGROUP INC *p* 266
5920 NO. 2 RD SUITE 130, RICHMOND, BC, V7C 4R9
(604) 244-1469   *SIC* 8741

ZEBRA PAPER CONVERTERS INC *p* 702
5130 CREEKBANK RD, MISSISSAUGA, ON, L4W 2G2
(905) 602-1100   *SIC* 5113

ZEBRA TECHNOLGIES CANADA, ULC *p* 728
2100 MEADOWVALE BLVD, MISSISSAUGA, ON, L5N 7J9
(905) 813-9900   *SIC* 3663

ZECHNER'S FOOD MARKET *p* 761
See ZECHNER'S LIMITED

ZECHNER'S LIMITED *p* 761
155 RAILWAY ST, NIPIGON, ON, P0T 2J0
(807) 887-2910   *SIC* 5411

ZEDCOR ENERGY INC *p* 63
330 5 AVE SW SUITE 2400, CALGARY, AB, T2P 0L4
(403) 930-5430   *SIC* 1389

ZEDCOR ENERGY SERVICES CORP *p* 63
500 4 AVE SW UNIT 3000, CALGARY, AB, T2P 2V6
(403) 930-5430   *SIC* 7353

ZEDD CUSTOMER SOLUTIONS L P INC *p* 764
180 SHIRREFF AVE SUITE 225, NORTH BAY, ON, P1B 7K9
(705) 495-1333   *SIC* 7389

ZEDD CUSTOMER SOLUTIONS LP *p* 865
325 MILNER AVE, SCARBOROUGH, ON, M1B 5N1
(416) 745-1333   *SIC* 7389

ZEDI CANADA INC *p* 66
902 11 AVE SW, CALGARY, AB, T2R 0E7
(403) 444-1100   *SIC* 5084

ZEDI INC *p* 66
902 11 AVE SW, CALGARY, AB, T2R 0E7
(403) 444-1100   *SIC* 1731

ZEHR INSURANCE BROKERS LIMITED *p* 753
59 HURON ST, NEW HAMBURG, ON, N3A 1K1
(519) 662-1710   *SIC* 6411

ZEHRMART INC *p* 489
620 YONGE ST, BARRIE, ON, L4N 4E6
(705) 735-2390   *SIC* 5411

ZEHRMART INC *p* 496
487 QUEEN ST S, BOLTON, ON, L7E 2B4
(905) 951-7505   *SIC* 5411

ZEHRMART INC *p* 512
1 PRESIDENTS CHOICE CIR, BRAMPTON, ON, L6Y 5S5
(905) 459-2500   *SIC* 5411

ZEHRMART INC *p* 515
410 FAIRVIEW DR SUITE 1, BRANTFORD, ON, N3R 7V7
(519) 754-4932   *SIC* 5411

ZEHRMART INC *p* 535
400 CONESTOGA BLVD, CAMBRIDGE, ON, N1R 7L7
(519) 620-1376   *SIC* 5411

ZEHRMART INC *p* 590
800 TOWER ST S, FERGUS, ON, N1M 2R3
(519) 843-5500   *SIC* 5411

ZEHRMART INC *p* 598
HWY 8 S, GODERICH, ON, N7A 4C6
(519) 524-2229   *SIC* 5411

ZEHRMART INC *p* 601
297 ERAMOSA RD, GUELPH, ON, N1E 2M7
(519) 763-4550   *SIC* 5411

ZEHRMART INC *p* 635

1375 WEBER ST E, KITCHENER, ON, N2A 3Y7
(519) 748-4570 *SIC 5411*
ZEHRMART INC *p 643*
5890 MALDEN RD, LASALLE, ON, N9H 1S4
(519) 966-6030 *SIC 5411*
ZEHRMART INC *p 881*
125 QUEENSWAY E, SIMCOE, ON, N3Y 5M7
(519) 426-7743 *SIC 5411*
ZEHRMART INC *p 1007*
315 LINCOLN RD SUITE 1, WATERLOO, ON, N2J 4H7
(519) 885-1360 *SIC 5411*
ZEHRMART INC *p 1009*
450 ERB ST W, WATERLOO, ON, N2T 1H4
(519) 886-4900 *SIC 5411*
ZEHRMART INC *p 1012*
821 NIAGARA ST, WELLAND, ON, L3C 1M4
(905) 732-9380 *SIC 5411*
ZEHRS FOOD PLUS *p 1012*
See LOBLAWS SUPERMARKETS LIMITED
ZEHRS MARKET *p 1009*
See ZEHRMART INC
ZEHRS MARKETS *p 489*
See ZEHRMART INC
ZEHRS MARKETS *p 512*
See ZEHRMART INC
ZEHRS MARKETS *p 515*
See ZEHRMART INC
ZEHRS MARKETS *p 535*
See ZEHRMART INC
ZEHRS MARKETS *p 590*
See ZEHRMART INC
ZEHRS MARKETS *p 598*
See ZEHRMART INC
ZEHRS MARKETS *p 601*
See ZEHRMART INC
ZEHRS MARKETS *p 635*
See ZEHRMART INC
ZEHRS MARKETS *p 643*
See ZEHRMART INC
ZEHRS MARKETS *p 1007*
See ZEHRMART INC
ZEHRS MARKETS *p 1012*
See ZEHRMART INC
ZEHRS MARKETS 58 *p 496*
See ZEHRMART INC
ZEIDCO INC *p 383*
905 PORTAGE AVE, WINNIPEG, MB, R3G 0P3
(204) 987-8840 *SIC 5411*
ZEIDLER PARTNERSHIP ARCHITECTS *p 985*
315 QUEEN ST W UNIT 200, TORONTO, ON, M5V 2X2
(416) 596-8300 *SIC 8712*
ZEIFMANS LLP *p 790*
201 BRIDGELAND AVE SUITE 1, NORTH YORK, ON, M6A 1Y7
(416) 256-4000 *SIC 8721*
ZEISS, CARL VISION CANADA INC *p 778*
45 VALLEYBROOK DR, NORTH YORK, ON, M3B 2S6
(416) 449-4523 *SIC 3851*
ZELLSTOFF CELGAR LIMITED PARTNERSHIP *p 195*
1921 ARROW LAKES DR, CASTLEGAR, BC, V1N 3H9
(250) 365-7211 *SIC 2611*
ZELUS MATERIAL HANDLING INC *p 893*
730 SOUTH SERVICE RD, STONEY CREEK, ON, L8E 5S7
(905) 643-4928 *SIC 7699*
ZENABIS GLOBAL INC *p 281*
1688 152 ST SUITE 205, SURREY, BC, V4A 4N2
(604) 888-0420 *SIC 8422*
ZENAR GROUP INC, THE *p 66*
1508 8 ST SW SUITE 203, CALGARY, AB, T2R 1R6
(403) 261-1566 *SIC 5141*
ZENCO ALBERTA LTD *p 166*

19 RIEL DR, ST. ALBERT, AB, T8N 3Z2
(780) 459-6695 *SIC 3272*
ZENCOR EQUITIES LIMITED *p 164*
HWY 16A GOLDEN SPIKE RD, SPRUCE GROVE, AB, T7X 2Y3
(780) 962-3000 *SIC 5511*
ZENDER FORD SALES LTD *p 164*
HWY 16A GOLDEN SPIKE RD, SPRUCE GROVE, AB, T7X 2Y3
(780) 962-3000 *SIC 5511*
ZENITH MEDIA *p 930*
See PUBLICIS MEDIA CANADA INC
ZENTIL, D. MECHANICAL INC *p 561*
633 EDGELEY BLVD, CONCORD, ON, L4K 4H6
(905) 738-0569 *SIC 1711*
ZEP MANUFACTURING COMPANY OF CANADA *p 99*
See ACUITY HOLDINGS, INC
ZEPHYR MINERALS LTD *p 454*
1959 UPPER WATER ST SUITE 1300, HALIFAX, NS, B3J 3N2
(902) 446-4189 *SIC 1081*
ZESTA ENGINEERING LIMITED *p 708*
212 WATLINE AVE, MISSISSAUGA, ON, L4Z 1P4
(905) 568-3112 *SIC 5075*
ZETEC *p 1263*
See 3089554 NOVA SCOTIA ULC
ZETON INC *p 525*
740 OVAL CRT, BURLINGTON, ON, L7L 6A9
(905) 632-3123 *SIC 3569*
ZETON INTERNATIONAL INC *p 525*
740 OVAL CRT, BURLINGTON, ON, L7L 6A9
(905) 632-3123 *SIC 6712*
ZEUGMA SYSTEMS INC *p 257*
13571 COMMERCE PKY SUITE 250, RICHMOND, BC, V6V 2R2
(604) 247-3250 *SIC 4813*
ZF AUTOMOTIVE CANADA LIMITED *p 682*
16643 HWY 12, MIDLAND, ON, L4R 4L5
(705) 526-8791 *SIC 3544*
ZF AUTOMOTIVE CANADA LIMITED *p 912*
101 SPRUCE ST, TILLSONBURG, ON, N4G 5C4
(519) 688-4200 *SIC 3714*
ZF AUTOMOTIVE CANADA LIMITED *p 1017*
3355 MUNICH CRT, WINDSOR, ON, N8N 5G2
(519) 739-9861 *SIC 5013*
ZF AUTOMOTIVE CANADA LIMITED *p 1036*
155 BEARDS LANE, WOODSTOCK, ON, N4S 7W3
(519) 537-2331 *SIC 3714*
ZGEMI INC *p 507*
100 WILKINSON RD UNIT 18, BRAMPTON, ON, L6T 4Y9
(905) 454-0111 *SIC 1521*
ZIEBARTH ELECTRICAL CONTRACTORS LIMITED *p 830*
890 BOYD AVE, OTTAWA, ON, K2A 2E3
(613) 798-8020 *SIC 1731*
ZIGGYS *p 749*
See LOBLAWS SUPERMARKETS LIMITED
ZIM CIE DE SERVICES DE NAVIGATION INTEGREE (CANADA) LTEE *p 1209*
1155 BOUL RENE-LEVESQUE O BUREAU 400, MONTREAL, QC, H3B 4R1
(844) 454-5072 *SIC 4491*
ZIM CONTAINER SERVICE *p 1209*
See ZIM CIE DE SERVICES DE NAVIGATION INTEGREE (CANADA) LTEE
ZIMMER BIOMET *p 728*
See ZIMMER OF CANADA LIMITED
ZIMMER OF CANADA LIMITED *p 728*
2323 ARGENTIA RD, MISSISSAUGA, ON, L5N 5N3
(905) 858-8588 *SIC 5047*
ZIMMER WHEATON BUICK GMC LTD *p 218*
685 NOTRE DAME DR, KAMLOOPS, BC, V2C 5N7

(250) 374-1148 *SIC 5511*
ZIN RESTAURANT & LOUNGE *p 311*
See AB PALISADES LIMITED PARTNERSHIP
ZINC ELECTROLYTIQUE DU CANADA LIMITEE *p 1366*
860 BOUL GERARD-CADIEUX, SALABERRY-DE-VALLEYFIELD, QC, J6T 6L4
(450) 373-9144 *SIC 1031*
ZINCORE METALS INC *p 323*
5626 LARCH ST SUITE 202, VANCOUVER, BC, V6M 4E1
(604) 669-6611 *SIC 1031*
ZINETTI FOOD PRODUCTS LTD *p 273*
17760 66 AVE, SURREY, BC, V3S 7X1
(604) 574-2028 *SIC 2038*
ZION PARK MANOR *p 272*
See LUTHERN SENIOR CITIZEN HOUSING SOCIETY
ZIP SIGNS LTD *p 526*
5040 NORTH SERVICE RD, BURLINGTON, ON, L7L 5R5
(905) 332-8332 *SIC 3993*
ZIPPO CANADA SALES *p 759*
See 2010162 ONTARIO LTD
ZLC FINANCIAL GROUP LTD *p 311*
666 BURRARD ST SUITE 1200, VANCOUVER, BC, V6C 2X8
(604) 684-3863 *SIC 6411*
ZOCHEM ULC *p 507*
1 TILBURY CRT, BRAMPTON, ON, L6T 3T4
(905) 453-4100 *SIC 2816*
ZODIAC HURRICANE TECHNOLOGIES INC *p 210*
7830 VANTAGE WAY, DELTA, BC, V4G 1A7
(604) 940-2999 *SIC 3732*
ZODIAC QUARTZ SURFACING *p 1383*
See PIONEER HI-BRED LIMITED
ZOHAR PLASTIQUE GROUP *p 1160*
See 6894658 CANADA INC
ZOMEL HOLDINGS LTD *p 335*
506 FINLAYSON ST, VICTORIA, BC, V8T 5C8
(250) 388-6921 *SIC 5511*
ZOMONGO.TV CORP *p 78*
229 AVRO LANE, CALGARY, AB, T3Z 3S5
(403) 870-4951 *SIC 7311*
ZONE *p 1173*
See CONCEPTS ZONE INC, LES
ZONE DIRECT MWD SERVICES LTD *p 12*
15-2916 5 AVE NE, CALGARY, AB, T2A 6K4
(403) 457-0133 *SIC 1381*
ZONE EN SECURITE *p 1186*
See 9310-8405 QUEBEC INC
ZONE3 INC *p 1176*
1055 BOUL RENE-LEVESQUE E BUREAU 300, MONTREAL, QC, H2L 4S5
(514) 284-5555 *SIC 7812*
ZONE3 SPECTACLES *p 1176*
See ZONE3 INC
ZOOK CANADA INC *p 526*
4400 SOUTH SERVICE RD, BURLINGTON, ON, L7L 5R8
(905) 681-2885 *SIC 2892*
ZOOLOGICAL SOCIETY OF MANITOBA *p 389*
54 ZOO DR, WINNIPEG, MB, R3P 2N8
(204) 982-0660 *SIC 6732*
ZOOM *p 1146*
See VIBROSYSTM INC
ZOOM MARKETING ACTIF *p 1197*
See GROUPE ZOOM MEDIA INC
ZOOMER MEDIA LIMITED *p 992*
70 JEFFERSON AVE, TORONTO, ON, M6K 1Y4
(416) 367-5353 *SIC 8732*
ZOOMERMEDIA LIMITED *p 992*
70 JEFFERSON AVE, TORONTO, ON, M6K 1Y4
(416) 607-7735 *SIC 7313*
ZORBA'S BAKERY & FOODS LTD *p 194*
7173 BULLER AVE, BURNABY, BC, V5J

4S1
(604) 439-7731 *SIC 5149*
ZOREN INDUSTRIES *p 547*
See 1719108 ONTARIO INC
ZP HOLDINGS INC *p 111*
7450 ROPER RD NW, EDMONTON, AB, T6B 3L9
(780) 490-5269 *SIC 5511*
ZTR CONTROL SYSTEMS CANADA *p 662*
See TRAC RAIL INC
ZUBAR HOLDINGS LTD *p 26*
919 DRURY AVE NE, CALGARY, AB, T2E 0M3
(403) 813-1914 *SIC 6712*
ZUBICK, JOHN LIMITED *p 651*
105 CLARKE RD, LONDON, ON, N5W 5C9
(519) 451-5470 *SIC 5093*
ZUCHTER BERK CREATIVE CATERERS INC *p 778*
1895 LESLIE ST, NORTH YORK, ON, M3B 2M3
(416) 386-1086 *SIC 5812*
ZUCKER, SIMON & ASSOCIATES *p 921*
3080 YONGE ST SUITE 5010, TORONTO, ON, M4N 3N1
(416) 489-8277 *SIC 5141*
ZULU ALPHA KILO INC *p 935*
260 KING ST E SUITE B 101, TORONTO, ON, M5A 4L5
(416) 777-9858 *SIC 7311*
ZUREIT HOLDINGS LIMITED *p 786*
620 WILSON AVE SUITE 401, NORTH YORK, ON, M3K 1Z3
(416) 630-6927 *SIC 6712*
ZURICH CANADIAN HOLDINGS LIMITED *p 988*
100 KING ST W SUITE 5500, TORONTO, ON, M5X 1C9
(416) 586-3000 *SIC 6712*
ZURICH INSURANCE COMPANY LTD *p 988*
100 KING ST W SUITE 5500, TORONTO, ON, M5X 2A1
(416) 586-3000 *SIC 6411*
ZUTPHEN CONTRACTORS *p 462*
See VAN ZUTPHEN, J & T CONSTRUCTION INC
ZUTPHEN CONTRACTORS INC *p 462*
10442 HIGHWAY 19, MABOU, NS, B0E 1X0
(902) 945-2300 *SIC 1794*
ZWILLING J.A. HENCKELS CANADA LTD *p 677*
435 COCHRANE DR SUITE 4, MARKHAM, ON, L3R 9R5
(905) 475-2555 *SIC 5023*
ZYCOM TECHNOLOGY INC *p 630*
271 CONCESSION ST, KINGSTON, ON, K7K 2B7
(613) 549-6558 *SIC 5045*
ZYMEWORKS INC *p 320*
1385 8TH AVE W SUITE 540, VANCOUVER, BC, V6H 3V9
(604) 678-1388 *SIC 8733*
ZYWOT, T. HOLDINGS LIMITED *p 748*
476 CENTRE ST N, NAPANEE, ON, K7R 1P8
(613) 354-2222 *SIC 5531*
ZZEN DESIGN BUILD LIMITED *p 1029*
100 ZENWAY BLVD, WOODBRIDGE, ON, L4H 2Y7
(905) 264-5962 *SIC 7372*

3325 Steel Foundries, Nec
3331 Primary Smelting and Refining of Copper
3332 Primary Smelting and Refining of Lead
3333 Primary Smelting and Refining of Zinc
3334 Primary Production of Aluminum
3339 Primary Smelting and Refining of Nonferrous Metals, Nec
3341 Secondary Smelting and Refining of Nonferrous Metals
3351 Rolling, Drawing, and Extruding of Copper
3353 Aluminum Sheet, Plate, Foil
3354 Aluminum Extruded Products
3355 Aluminum Rolling and Drawing
3356 Rolling, Drawing, and Extruding of Nonferrous Metals
3357 Drawing and Insulating of Nonferrous Wire
3361 Aluminum Foundries
3362 Brass, Bronze, Copper, Copper Base Alloy Foundries
3369 Nonferrous Foundries
3398 Metal Heat Treating
3399 Primary Metal Products

3 4   Fabricated Metal Products
3411 Metal Cans
3412 Metal Shipping Barrels, Drums, Kegs, Pails
3421 Cutlery
3423 Hand and Edge Tools
3425 Hand Saws and Saw Blades
3429 Hardware, Nec
3431 Enameled Iron and Metal Sanitary Ware
3432 Plumbing Fixture Fittings and Trim (Brass Goods)
3433 Heating Equipment
3441 Fabricated Structural Metal
3442 Metal Doors, Sash, Frames, Molding, Trim
3443 Fabricated Plate Work (Boiler Shops)
3444 Sheet Metal Work
3446 Architectural and Ornamental Metal Work
3448 Prefabricated Metal Buildings and Components
3449 Miscellaneous Metal Work
3451 Screw Machine Products
3452 Bolts, Nuts, Screws, Rivets, and Washers
3462 Iron and Steel Forgings
3463 Nonferrous Forgings
3465 Automotive Stampings
3466 Crowns and Closures
3469 Metal Stampings
3471 Electroplating, Plating, Polishing, Anodizing, Colourizing
3479 Metallic Coating, Engraving, and Allied Services
3482 Small Arms Ammunition
3483 Ammunition
3484 Small Arms
3493 Steel Springs
3494 Valves and Pipe Fittings
3495 Wire Springs
3496 Fabricated Wire Products
3497 Metal Foil and Leaf
3498 Fabricated Pipe and Pipe Fittings
3499 Fabricated Metal Products

3 5   Machinery Except Electrical
3511 Steam, Gas, Hydraulic Turbines, Turbine Generator Set Units
3519 Internal Combustion Engines, Nec
3523 Farm Machinery and Equipment
3524 Garden Tractors, Lawn and Garden Equipment
3531 Construction Machinery and Equipment
3532 Mining Machinery and Equipment
3533 Oil Field Machinery and Equipment
3534 Elevators and Moving Stairways
3535 Conveyors and Conveying Equipment
3536 Hoists, Industrial Cranes, Monorail Systems
3537 Industrial Trucks, Tractors, Trailers, Stackers
3541 Machine Tools, Metal Cutting Types
3542 Machine Tools, Metal Forming Types
3544 Special Dies and Tools, Die Sets, Jigs and Fixtures, Industrial Molds
3545 Machine Tool Accessories, Measuring Devices

3546 Power-Driven Hand Tools
3547 Rolling Mill Machinery and Equipment
3549 Metalworking Machinery
3551 Food Products Machinery
3552 Textile Machinery
3553 Woodworking Machinery
3554 Paper Industries Machinery
3555 Printing Trades Machinery and Equipment
3559 Special Industry Machinery
3561 Pumps and Pumping Equipment
3562 Ball and Roller Bearings
3563 Air and Gas Compressors
3564 Blowers, Exhaust and Ventilation Fans
3565 Industrial Patterns
3566 Speed Changers, Industrial High Speed Drives, and Gears
3567 Industrial Process Furnaces and Ovens
3568 Mechanical Power Transmission Equipment
3569 General Industrial Machinery and Equipment
3572 Typewriters
3573 Electronic Computing Equipment
3574 Calculating and Accounting Machines
3575 Personal Computers
3576 Scales and Balances
3579 Office Machines, Nec
3581 Automatic Merchandising Machines
3582 Commercial Laundry, Dry Cleaning, Pressing Machines
3585 Refrigerating and Heating Equipment
3586 Measuring and Dispensing Pumps
3589 Service Industry Machines, Nec
3592 Carburetors, Pistons, Piston Rings and Valves
3599 Machinery

3 6   Electrical Equipment
3612 Power, Distribution, Specialty Transformers
3613 Switchgear, Switchboard Apparatus
3621 Motors and Generators
3622 Industrial Controls
3623 Welding Apparatus, Electric
3624 Carbon and Graphite Products
3629 Electrical Industrial Apparatus, Nec
3631 Household Cooking Equipment
3632 Household Refrigerators, Home and Farm Freezers
3633 Household Laundry Equipment
3634 Electric Housewares and Fans
3635 Household Vacuum Cleaners
3636 Sewing Machines
3639 Household Appliances, Nec
3641 Electric Lamps
3643 Current-Carrying Wiring Devices
3644 Noncurrent-Carrying Wiring Devices
3645 Residential Electric Lighting Fixtures
3646 Commercial, Industrial, Institutional Electric Lighting Fixtures
3647 Vehicular Lighting Equipment
3648 Lighting Equipment
3651 Electronic Equipment for Home Entertainment
3652 Phonograph Records and Pre-Recorded Magnetic Tape
3661 Telephone and Telegraph Apparatus
3662 Radio and Television Communication Equipment
3671 Radio and Television Receiving Type Electron Tubes
3672 Cathode Ray Television Picture Tubes
3673 Transmitting, Industrial, and Special Purpose Electron Tubes
3674 Semiconductors and Related Devices
3675 Electronic Capacitors
3676 Electronic Resistors
3677 Electronic Coils, Transformers, Other Inductors
3678 Electronic Connectors
3679 Electronic Components
3691 Storage Batteries
3692 Primary Batteries, Dry and Wet
3693 X-Ray Apparatus, Nec
3694 Electrical Equipment for Internal

Combustion Engines
3699 Electrical Machinery, Equipment, and Supplies

3 7   Transportation Equipment
3711 Passenger Car Bodies
3713 Truck and Bus Bodies
3714 Motor Vehicle Parts and Accessories
3715 Truck Trailers
3716 Motor Homes
3721 Aircraft
3724 Aircraft Engines and Engine Parts
3728 Aircraft Parts and Auxiliary Equipment
3731 Ship Building and Repairing
3732 Boat Building and Repairing
3743 Railroad Equipment
3751 Motorcycles, Bicycles, Parts
3769 Guided Missile, Space Vehicle Parts, Auxiliary Equipment
3792 Travel Trailers and Campers
3795 Tanks and Components
3799 Transportation Equipment

3 8   Measuring, Analyzing & Controlling Instruments
3811 Engineering, Laboratory, Scientific Research Instruments, Associated Equip
3822 Automatic Controls for Regulating Residential, Commercial Environments and Appliances
3823 Process Control Instruments
3824 Fluid Meters and Counting Devices
3825 Instruments for Measuring, Testing of Electricity, Electrical Signals
3829 Measuring and Controlling Devices
3832 Optical Instruments, Lenses
3841 Surgical and Medical Instruments
3842 Orthopedic, Prosthetic, Surgical Appliances, Supplies
3843 Dental Equipment, Supplies
3851 Ophthalmic Goods
3861 Photographic Equipment, Supplies
3873 Watches, Clocks, Clockwork Devices, Parts

3 9   Miscellaneous Manufacturing
3911 Jewelry, Precious Metal
3914 Silverware, Plated Ware, Stainless Steel Ware
3915 Jewelers' Findings, Materials, Lapidary Work
3931 Musical Instruments and Parts
3942 Dolls
3944 Games, Toys, Children's Vehicles
3949 Sporting, Athletic Goods
3951 Pens, Mechanical Pencils, Parts
3952 Lead Pencils, Crayons, Artists' Materials
3953 Marking Devices
3955 Carbon Paper, Inked Ribbons
3961 Costume Jewelry and Costume Novelties
3962 Feathers, Plumes, Artificial Trees, Flowers
3963 Buttons
3964 Needles, Pins, Hooks and Eyes, Similar Notions
3991 Brooms and Brushes
3993 Signs and Advertising Displays
3995 Burial Caskets
3996 Hard Surface Floor Coverings
3999 Manufacturers, Nec

40 – 49
Transportation, Communication & Utilities

4 0   Railroad Transportation
4011 Railroads, Line-Haul Operating
4013 Railroads – Switching and Terminal Establishments

4 1   Local Passenger Transportation
4111 Passenger Transportation – Local and Suburban Transit
4119 Local Passenger Transportation
4121 Taxicabs
4131 Intercity and Rural Highway Passenger Transportation

4141 Local Passenger Transportation Charter Service
4142 Passenger Transportation Charter Service
4151 School Bus Service
4171 Transportation – Terminal and Joint Terminal Maintenance Facilities
4172 Transportation – Maintenance and Service Facilities

42 Trucking & Warehousing
4212 Local Trucking Without Storage
4213 Trucking, Long Distance
4214 Local Trucking With Storage
4221 Farm Product Warehousing and Storage
4222 Refrigerated Warehousing
4224 Household Goods Warehousing and Storage
4225 General Warehousing and Storage
4226 Special Warehousing and Storage, Nec
4231 Freight Terminal and Joint Terminal Maintenance

43 Canadian Postal Service

44 Water Transportation
4411 Deep Sea – Foreign Transportation
4421 Deep Sea Transportation to and Between Noncontiguous Territories
4422 Deep Sea – Coastwise Transportation
4423 Deep Sea – Intercoastal Transportation
4431 Great Lakes – St. Lawrence Seaway Transportation
4441 Transportation on Rivers and Canals
4452 Local Water – Ferries
4453 Local Water – Lighterage
4454 Local Water – Towing and Tugboat Service
4459 Local Water Transportation, Nec
4463 Marine Cargo Handling
4464 Canal Operation
4469 Water Transportation Services

45 Air Transportation
4511 Air Transportation, Certified Carriers
4521 Air Transportation, Noncertified Carriers
4582 Airports and Flying Fields
4583 Airport Terminal Services

46 Pipe Line Transportation
4612 Crude Petroleum Pipe Lines
4613 Refined Petroleum Pipe Lines
4619 Pipe Lines, Nec

47 Transportation Services
4712 Freight Forwarding
4722 Arrangement of Passenger Transportation
4723 Arrangement of Transportation of Freight and Cargo
4742 Rental of Railroad Cars With Care of Lading
4743 Rental of Railroad Car
4783 Packing and Crating for Transportation
4784 Fixed Facilities for Handling Motor Vehicle Transportation, Nec
4789 Transportation Services

48 Communications
4811 Telephone Communication (Wire or Radio)
4821 Telegraph Communication (Wire or Radio)
4832 Radio Broadcasting
4833 Television Broadcasting
4899 Communication Services, Nec

49 Electric, Gas & Sanitary Services
4911 Electric Services
4922 Natural Gas Transmission
4923 Natural Gas Transmission and Distribution
4924 Natural Gas Distribution
4925 Mixed, Manufactured or Liquified Petrol Gas Production and/or Distribution
4931 Electric and Other Services Combined
4932 Gas and Other Services Combined
4939 Combination Utilities
4941 Water Supply
4952 Sewage Systems
4953 Refuse Systems
4959 Sanitary Services, Nec

4961 Steam Supply
4971 Irrigation Systems

50 – 51
Wholesale Trade

50 Wholesale Durables
5012 Wholesales Automobiles and Other Motor Vehicles
5013 Automotive Parts and Supplies
5014 Tires and Tubes
5021 Furniture
5023 Wholesales Home Furnishings
5031 Lumber, Plywood, and Millwork
5039 Construction Materials
5041 Wholesales Sporting, Recreational Goods and Supplies
5042 Toys, Hobby Goods and Supplies
5043 Photographic Equipment and Supplies
5051 Ferrous and Nonferrous Metal Semi-Finished Products
5052 Coal, Other Minerals, Ores
5063 Wholesalers Electrical Apparatus, Equipment, Wiring Supplies, Construction Materials
5064 Wholesalers Household Appliances, Electrical
5065 Electronic Parts and Equipment
5072 Hardware
5074 Plumbing and Heating Equipment, and Supplies
5075 Warm Air Heating, Air Conditioning Equipment, Supplies
5078 Refrigeration Equipment and Supplies
5081 Commercial Machines and Equipment
5082 Construction, Mining Machinery, Equipment
5083 Farm and Garden Machinery, and Equipment
5084 Industrial Machinery and Equipment
5085 Industrial Supplies
5086 Professional Equipment and Supplies
5087 Service Establishment Equipment and Supplies
5088 Transportation Equipment and Supplies
5093 Scrap and Waste Materials
5094 Jewelry, Watches, Diamonds, Other Precious Metals
5099 Durable Goods, Nec

51 Wholesale Non-Durables
5111 Printing and Writing Paper
5112 Stationery Supplies
5113 Industrial and Personal Service Paper
5122 Drug Proprietaries
5133 Piece Goods (Woven Fabrics)
5134 Wholesale Notions, Other Dry Goods
5136 Men's, Boys' Clothing, Furnishings
5137 Women's, Children's, Infants' Clothing and Accessories
5139 Footwear
5141 Wholesales Groceries, General Line
5142 Wholesales Frozen Foods
5143 Dairy Products
5144 Poultry and Poultry Products
5145 Confectionery
5146 Fish and Seafood
5147 Meats and Meat Products
5148 Fresh Fruits and Vegetables
5149 Wholesales Groceries and Related Products
5152 Cotton
5153 Grain
5154 Livestock
5159 Farm Product Raw Materials
5161 Chemicals and Allied Products
5171 Petroleum Bulk Stations and Terminals
5172 Petroleum Products
5181 Beer and Ale
5182 Wines and Distilled Alcoholic Beverages
5191 Farm Supplies
5194 Tobacco and Tobacco Products
5198 Paints, Varnishes, and Supplies
5199 Nondurable Goods, Nec

52 – 59
Retail Trade

52 Building Materials, Hardware, Garden Supply & Mobile Home Dealers
5211 Lumber and Other Building Materials
5231 Paint, Glass, and Wallpaper
5251 Retails Hardware
5261 Nursery Stock, Lawn and Garden Supplies
5271 Mobile Homes

53 General Merchandise
5311 Department Stores
5331 Variety Stores
5399 General Merchandise

54 Food Stores
5411 Grocery Stores
5422 Freezer and Locker Meat Provisioners
5423 Meat and Fish (Seafood)
5431 Fruit and Vegetables
5441 Candy, Nuts, and Confectionery
5451 Dairy Products
5462 Retail Bakeries
5463 Retail Bakeries – Selling Only
5499 Miscellaneous Food Stores

55 Auto Dealers & Service Stations
5511 Motor Vehicles (New and Used)
5521 Motor Vehicles (Used Only)
5531 Auto and Home Supplies
5541 Gasoline Service Stations
5551 Boats and Marine Supplies
5561 Recreational and Utility Trailers
5571 Motorcycles
5599 Recreational Vehicles

56 Apparel & Accessory Stores
5611 Men's, Boys' Clothing, Furnishings
5621 Women's Ready-to-Wear
5631 Women's Accessories and Specialties
5641 Children's, Infants' Wear
5651 Family Clothing
5661 Shoes
5681 Furs and Accessories
5699 Miscellaneous Apparel and Accessories

57 Furniture & Home Furnishings
5712 Furniture
5713 Floor Coverings
5714 Drapery, Curtain and Upholstery
5719 Miscellaneous Home Furnishings
5722 Household Appliances
5731 Personal Computers
5732 Home Entertainment Appliance Stores
5733 Music Stores

58 Eating & Drinking Places
5812 Eating Places
5813 Drinking Places (Alcoholic Beverages)

59 Miscellaneous Retail Stores
5912 Drugs and Proprietaries
5921 Liquor
5931 Used Merchandise
5941 Retails Sporting Goods and Bicycles
5942 Books
5943 Stationery
5944 Jewelry
5945 Hobbies, Toys and Games
5946 Cameras and Photographic Supplies
5947 Gifts, Novelties, Souvenirs
5948 Luggage and Leather Goods
5949 Sewing, Needlework and Piece Goods
5961 Mail Order Houses
5962 Automatic Merchandising Machine Operators
5963 Direct Selling Establishments
5982 Fuel and Ice
5983 Fuel Oil
5984 Liquified Petroleum Gas (Bottled Gas)
5992 Flowers

5993 Cigar Stores and Stands
5994 News Dealers and Newsstands
5999 Miscellaneous Products

60 – 67
Finance, Insurance & Real Estate

60 Banking
6011 Central Bank
6022 Provincial Banks
6025 Federal Banks
6042 Trust Companies
6052 Foreign Exchange Establishments
6054 Safety Deposit Companies
6059 Related Banking Functions

61 Credit Agencies (Except Banks)
6112 Deposit Accepting Mortgage Companies
6113 Rediscounting and Financing Institutions for Agriculture
6122 Federal Savings and Loan Associations
6125 Provincial Savings and Loan Associations
6131 Agricultural Credit Institutions
6142 Federal Credit Unions
6143 Provincial Credit Unions
6144 Industrial Loan Companies
6145 Consumer Loan Companies
6146 Installment Sales Finance Companies
6149 Other Personal Credit Institutions
6153 Business Financing Companies
6159 Long Term or Other Business Financing Companies
6162 Mortgage Dealers and Loan Correspondents
6163 Loan Brokers

62 Security and Commercial Broker Services
6211 Security Brokers, Dealers, and Flotation Companies
6221 Commodity Contracts Brokers and Dealers
6231 Security and Commodity Exchanges
6281 Securities Services

63 Insurance Carriers
6311 Life Insurance
6321 Accident and Health Insurance
6324 Hospital and Medical Service Plans
6331 Fire, Marine, Property and Casualty Insurance
6351 Surety Insurance
6361 Title Insurance
6371 Pension, Health, and Welfare Funds
6399 Insurance Carriers

64 Insurance Agents

65 Real Estate
6512 Operators of Nonresidential Buildings
6513 Operators of Apartment Buildings
6514 Operators of Dwellings
6515 Operators of Residential Mobile Home Sites
6517 Lessors of Railroad Property
6519 Lessors of Real Property
6531 Agents and Managers
6541 Title Abstract Offices
6552 Subdividers and Developers
6553 Cemetery Subdividers and Developers

66 Combined Real Estate

67 Holding Companies, Re-Investment
6711 Holding Companies
6722 Management Investment Offices, Open-End
6723 Management Investment Offices, Closed-End
6724 Unit Investment Trusts
6725 Face Amount Certificate Offices
6732 Educational, Religious, and Charitable Trusts
6733 Trusts
6792 Oil Royalty Traders

6793 Commodity Traders
6794 Patent Owners and Lessors
6798 Real Estate Investment Trusts
6799 Investors, Nec

70 – 89
Services

70 Hotels, Rooming Houses, Camps & Other Lodging Places
7011 Hotels, Motels, Tourist Courts
7021 Rooming and Boarding Houses
7032 Sporting and Recreational Camps
7033 Trailer Parks and Camp Sites
7041 Hotels and Lodging Houses – Membership Basis

72 Personal Services
7211 Power Laundries, Family and Commercial
7212 Garment Pressing, and Agents for Laundries and Dry Cleaners
7213 Linen Supply Services
7214 Diaper Service
7215 Coin-Operated Laundries and Dry Cleaners
7216 Dry Cleaning Plant (Excluding Rug)
7217 Carpet and Upholstery Cleaners
7218 Industrial Launderers
7219 Laundry and Garment Services
7221 Photographic Studios, Portrait
7231 Beauty Shops
7241 Barber Shops
7251 Shoe Repair Shops, Shoe Shine Parlors, and Hat Cleaning Shops
7261 Funeral Service and Crematories
7299 Miscellaneous Personal Services

73 Business Services
7311 Advertising Agency
7312 Outdoor Advertising Services
7313 Radio, Television, and Publishers' Advertising Representatives
7319 Advertising
7321 Credit Reporting – Collection
7331 Direct Mail Advertising Services
7332 Blueprinting and Photocopying Services
7333 Commercial Photography, Art, Graphics
7339 Stenographic and Reproduction Services
7341 Window Cleaning
7342 Disinfecting and Exterminating Services
7349 Building Cleaning and Maintenance Services
7351 News Syndicates
7361 Employment Agencies
7362 Temporary Help Supply Services
7369 Personnel Supply Services
7372 Computer Programming and Other Software Services
7374 Data Processing Services
7379 Computer-Related Services
7391 Research and Development Laboratories
7392 Management, Consulting, and Public Relations Services
7393 Detective Agencies and Protective Services
7394 Equipment Rental and Leasing Services
7395 Photofinishing Laboratories
7396 Trading Stamp Services
7397 Commercial Testing Laboratories
7399 Business Services

75 Auto Repair Services & Garages
7512 Passenger Car Rental and Leasing
7513 Truck Rental and Leasing
7519 Utility Trailers and Recreational Vehicle Rental
7523 Parking Lots
7525 Parking Structures
7531 Top and Body Repair Shops
7534 Tire Retreading and Repair Shops
7535 Paint Shop
7538 General Automotive Repair Shops
7539 Automotive Repair Shops
7542 Car Wash
7549 Automotive Services, Nec

76 Miscellaneous Repair Services
7622 Radio and Television Repair Shops
7623 Refrigeration and Air Conditioning Service
7629 Electrical and Electronic Repair Shops
7631 Watch, Clock, and Jewelry Repair
7641 Reupholstery and Furniture Repair
7692 Welding Repair
7694 Armature Rewinding Shops
7699 Repair Shops and Related Services

78 Motion Pictures
7813 Motion Picture Production (Excluding TV)
7814 Motion Picture and Tape Production for Television
7819 Services Allied to Motion Picture Production
7823 Motion Picture Film Exchanges
7824 Film or Tape Distribution for Television
7829 Services Allied to Motion Picture Distribution
7832 Motion Picture Theatres
7833 Drive-In Motion Picture Theatres
7841 Pre-recorded Video Programs

79 Amusement & Recreation Services
7911 Dance Halls, Studios, and Schools
7922 Theatrical Producers and Related Services
7929 Bands, Orchestras, Actors, Other Entertainers, Entertainment Groups
7932 Billiard and Pool Establishments
7933 Bowling Alleys
7941 Professional Sports Clubs and Promoters
7948 Racing, Including Track Operation
7992 Public Golf Courses
7993 Coin-Operated Amusement Devices
7996 Amusement Parks
7997 Membership Sports and Recreation Clubs
7999 Amusement and Recreation Services

80 Health Services
8011 Physicians
8021 Dentists
8031 Osteopathic Physicians
8041 Chiropractors
8042 Optometrists
8049 Health Practitioners
8051 Skilled Nursing Care Facilities
8059 Nursing and Personal Care Facilities
8062 General Medical and Surgical Hospitals
8063 Psychiatric Hospitals
8069 Specialty Hospitals
8071 Medical Laboratories
8072 Dental Laboratories
8081 Outpatient Care Facilities
8091 Health and Allied Services

81 Legal Services

82 Educational Services
8211 Elementary and Secondary Schools
8221 Colleges, Universities, and Professional Schools
8222 Junior Colleges and Technical Institutes
8231 Libraries and Information Centers
8241 Correspondence Schools
8243 Data Processing Schools
8244 Business and Secretarial Schools
8249 Vocational Schools
8299 Schools and Educational Services

83 Social Services
8321 Individual and Family Social Services
8331 Job Training and Vocational Rehabilitation Services
8351 Child Day Care Services
8361 Social Service – Residential Care
8399 Social Services, Nec

84 Museums, Art Galleries, Botanical & Zoological Gardens
8411 Museums and Art Galleries
8421 Arboreta, Botanical, and Zoological Gardens

91 – 94
Public Administration